The Original

THOROUGHBRED TIMES RACING ALMANAC™ 2007

THOROUGHBRED TIMES BOOKS

The Original

THOROUGHBRED TIMES

RACING ALMANAC™

2007

A Thoroughbred Times Book™

Editor in Chief: Mark Simon
Editorial Director: Don Clippinger
Editors: Frank Angst, Tom Law, John P. Sparkman
Information Technology: Alan Johnson, Jonathan McKinney
Editorial Research: Jeff Apel, Steve Bailey, Liane Crossley, Mike Curry, Pete Denk, Ed DeRosa, Allison Fuchs, Myra Lewyn, Jeff Lowe, Tom Musgrave, Mary Simon, Denise Steffanus
Statistical Research: Gail Allensworth, Melissa Humphrey, Colleen Jonsson, Aylett Melton, Carlos Peña-Rivera, Patrick Reed
Editorial Assistants: Deanna Bowden, K. T. Donovan, Elaine Parker
Art Director: Jeanette Vance
Production Coordinator: Betty Gee
Production Staff: Gail Burge, Nicole Elliott, Tami Helmreich-Zigo, David Kaplan, Laura Lacy, Amy McLean, Sheena Sparks
Cover Photo: Enzina Mastrippolito

Thoroughbred Times Co. Inc.
Publisher: Norman Ridker
President: Mark Simon
Editorial Office: 2008 Mercer Rd., Lexington, KY 40511

THOROUGHBRED TIMES RACING ALMANAC welcomes comments and suggestions from readers. Every communication is read by the editors and receives consideration and attention. **THOROUGHBRED TIMES RACING ALMANAC** does not decide wagers.

International Standard Serial Number (ISSN) 1540-5486
ISBN Number 1-933958-00-6

THOROUGHBRED TIMES RACING ALMANAC ™
Thoroughbred Times Books™
An imprint of BowTie Press™
www.thoroughbredtimes.com
e-mail: letters@thoroughbredtimes.com

FOREWORD

An Industry That Cares

The Triple Crown is always a time of high drama in Thoroughbred racing, and the 2006 campaign was all the more dramatic because of the life-threatening injury to Barbaro, the runaway winner of the Kentucky Derby (G1), shortly after the start of the Preakness Stakes (G1). Barbaro's devastating fracture of his right hind leg touched off a series of events that revealed the heart of the sport and the heart of America. To be sure, Thoroughbred racing does not enjoy the same popularity as it did in the 1950s and '60s, when leisure time and spending expanded greatly and racing was the only legal gambling sport in town. But the horse still has the power to touch America's heart strings.

The outpouring of emotion as Barbaro's life hung in the balance was amazing, and the star-crossed colt was accorded notice on the front cover of *Newsweek* and other national magazines. In addition to the University of Pennsylvania's New Bolton Center and the National Thoroughbred Racing Association, THOROUGHBRED TIMES set up a link on its website, *www.thoroughbredtimes.com*, to send get-well wishes to Barbaro. Within the first hours of the TIMES link being in place, more than 300 visitors to the website had sent their hopes and best wishes to Barbaro, his owners, Roy and Gretchen Jackson, and trainer Michael Matz.

More than a month after his injury, Barbaro was still not out of the woods. His injury was so severe that his surgeon, Dean Richardson, D.V.M., said it will be several months before he would be able to say with any certainty that Barbaro would survive his horrific fractures, which required a stabilizing plate and 27 screws to repair. That he survived at all is a tribute to many people within the industry who genuinely care about the horses that provide their livelihoods. Among them were jockey Edgar Prado, who pulled him up quickly after the breakdown, and Rafael Orozco, one of Matz's grooms, who rushed to the colt's side to quiet him after the accident. No less heroic were the actions of Pimlico Race Course's veterinary personnel, whose professionalism assured that the badly fractured leg was quickly stabilized. After an 80-mile van trip, Barbaro was placed in the care of the renowned New Bolton Center in the heart of Pennsylvania's horse country. There, a day after the Preakness, Richardson and Penn's veterinary school staff successfully performed surgery that had never been attempted before. If he survives, Barbaro indeed will be a miracle horse.

Some members of the Thoroughbred community are still waiting for their miracle to occur. They are the 55 former jockeys who are in wheelchairs or permanently disabled because of riding accidents. For years, the sport believed that a Jockeys' Guild fund took care of these injured riders' needs. With the change in the Guild's administration, however, it was disclosed that the fund was empty. The industry did not walk away from the former riders who had given so much of their lives to racing. In May 2006, several industry leaders came together to form the Permanently Disabled Jockeys Fund, with the goal of providing each disabled jockey a monthly stipend of at least $1,000. Barbaro's injury elicited several significant contributions to equine research, and the Thoroughbred Racing Associations, the Jockeys' Guild, and other organizations are providing leadership to take care of the individuals who are seriously hurt while participating in the sport. Indeed, racing is a sport that cares. Both efforts—for the horse and for the individuals who were hurt while riding races—deserve support.

The mark of any successful organization is being able to adapt to change and exceeding expectations in the midst of change. The *Thoroughbred Times Racing Almanac* underwent considerable change this year when the almanac editor assumed several more duties at a crucial time during the annual production cycle. But the editorial staff of Thoroughbred Times Co. again exceeded expectations in producing this volume, complete, authoritative, and on time. As always, the Research Department pulled together many of the statistics that form the core of the *Thoroughbred Times Racing Almanac*. Gail Allensworth, Colleen Jonsson, Melissa Humphrey, and Aylett Melton were joined this year by Patrick Reed and Carlos Peña-Rivera. John P. Sparkman, the bloodstock/sales editor who directed the Research Department before his retirement, has made significant contributions to this volume over its history. Editorial intern Allison Fuchs waded through mounds of statistics to produce several tables and profiled individuals added to the People chapter.

Once the statistics are developed, it falls to the Art Department to put them all together in a layout that is pleasing to the eye and easy to use. Art Director Jeanette Vance and Production Coordinator Betty Gee worked diligently to bring together thousands of individual elements into this volume. In the best tradition of Thoroughbred Times Co., they exceeded expectations to produce a volume that is bigger and better than ever. We hope you find the *2007 Thoroughbred Times Racing Almanac* to be your essential reference guide to Thoroughbred racing.

Don Clippinger, Editorial Director
Lexington, Kentucky
June 23, 2006

TABLE OF CONTENTS

GENERAL INDEX

STATE OF THE INDUSTRY

Thoroughbred Economy in 2005

Of three industry statistics that define in the broadest terms the health of the Thoroughbred economy, only one—bloodstock sales—was positive in 2005. After ringing up a 23.3% increase in 2004, the commercial auction market moved ahead another 8% in 2005 to $1,138,739,345. If bloodstock sales are a measure of consumer sentiment—and they are—horse buyers were feeling good about their investment in 2005. In fact, the positive outlook continued into 2006, with record sales for two-year-olds in training, including a record $16-million juvenile, The Green Monkey. Barring any new economic disasters, higher juvenile sales should mean more money flowing into the huge yearling market, and the commercial breeding industry will be on the road to a fourth consecutive year of increased revenues in 2006.

The two other numbers—pari-mutuel wagering and racetrack purses—were not so good. In 2003, wagering on Thoroughbred racing had increased modestly while purses declined. That statistic was troubling because purses are supposed to move in lockstep with wagering handle. The next year, purses increased to a record $1,177,769,765, but wagering declined 0.7%. Clearly, the traditional relationship between handle and purses had been broken.

The industry took a double whammy in 2005 when both wagering and purses declined. The handle was off 3% to $15,129,000,000 while purse accounts slipped 2.4% to $1,149,003,138. In announcing the second straight year of declining handle, officials of the National Thoroughbred Racing Association and Equibase attributed the steep drop to Hurricanes Katrina and Rita, which obliterated New Orleans and closed Delta Downs for months. But the lost race cards do not tell the entire story.

Equibase and the NTRA reported that wagering on U.S. racing—excluding Canada—totaled $15,099,011,926 in 2004 over 6,423 programs. In 2005, the number of racing programs slipped 2.3% to 6,276, and wagering declined to $14,580,757,317, a 3.4% decline. The larger percentage of handle decline indicates quite clearly that something more than disastrously bad weather had occurred. On average, $2,350,773 was bet on each race card in the U.S. in 2004; that average slipped 1.2% to $2,323,256 in '05. In other words, the average race program lost $27,517 in wagers. Neither loss seems particularly large, but, calculated on a daily basis, the sport was losing $473,124 in wagers a day.

Those dollars did not blow away in the wind. First, it is painfully obvious that the full-card simulcasting revolution has run its course. The two declines in handle over the last three years are evidence that the industry can no longer depend on full-card wagering—as it is currently constituted—to pay for further enhancements to the sport.

Another factor that is not easily found in the numbers is that some big bettors referred to as "whales"—big-dollar bettors who populated the offshore rebate shops that offered healthy rebates on heavy play—have swum away. Based

North American Purses

Year	Total Purses	Average Purse
2005	$1,149,003,138	$20,051
2004	1,177,769,765	20,069
2003	1,154,238,845	19,626
2002	1,170,169,267	19,597
2001	1,146,337,367	18,936
2000	1,093,661,241	18,053
1999	1,008,162,608	6,770
1998	968,366,929	15,838
1997	888,667,752	13,997
1996	845,916,706	13,163

(Excluding Puerto Rico and Mexico)

North American Thoroughbred Pari-Mutuel Wagering
(Millions of Dollars)

	United States			Canada			Total	
Year	On-Track	Off-Track	Total	On-Track	Off-Track	Total	Total	Change
2005	$1,741	$12,819	$14,561	$144	$423	$568	$15,129	–3.0%
2004	1,860	13,239	15,099	137	364	502	15,601	–0.7%
2003	1,902	13,278	15,180	139	394	534	15,714	0.5%
2002	2,029	13,033	15,062	153	414	567	15,629	3.2%
2001	2,112	12,487	14,599	153	387	540	15,139	2.3%
2000	2,270	12,051	14,321	150	325	475	14,796	4.5%
1999	2,359	11,365	13,724	161	278	439	14,163	4.0%
1998	2,498	10,617	13,115	188	310	498	13,613	4.2%
1997	2,703	9,839	12,542	217	310	527	13,069	6.5%
1996	2,944	8,683	11,627	259	383	642	12,269	9.3%

on industry and regulator investigations, several tracks shut off wagers from certain offshore sites. It is unknown where these bettors have gone, but their money is missing from the pools.

For racing, the next big thing is alternative gaming, which usually means slot machines or video lottery terminals. Those dollars are found in the purse figures, and they also do not augur well for Thoroughbred racing as a sport that can stand on its own and support itself with its own revenues. The 2.4% decline in 2005 purses wiped out all of the 2% increase from 2004 and more. In current dollars, purses in 2005 were only slightly ahead of '01 when purses totaled $1,146,337,367.

Best estimates now are that slot machines and other forms of alternative gaming contributed $200-million to purses in 2005. In percentage terms, that $200-million represented 17.4% of all 2005 purses, and the percentage is likely to increase in coming years as more states—including New York and Pennsylvania—adopt purse subsidies from slots revenue. In 2005, one new racetrack opened in the United States, Zia Park in Hobbs, New Mexico, and its existence was made possible by slots. (For more on purses, see "All About Purses" in this chapter. For more on racetracks with slot machines or other forms of gaming, see "Racing Enters the Racino Age" at the end of this chapter.)

The lone bright spot in the Thoroughbred economy in 2005 was the commercial bloodstock business, and its fortunes are detailed in "Auction Review" in the Auctions chapter. Business was excellent in 2004 and very good in '05, with no portents of trouble in the '06 juvenile sales. Buyers were pursuing the top prospects with gusto, and the resurgence of the economy and stock market after the 2000-'02 mini-crash—off 40.1% as measured by the Standard & Poor's index of 500 large-capitalization stocks—almost certainly contributed to the run-up.

The auction markets and the securities markets approximate each other in a very rough fashion. The bloodstock dip after the September 11, 2001, terrorist attacks presaged a decline in the stock market the following year, and both the stock market and the bloodstock market have moved up together since—with bloodstock sales rising 48.5% since 2002 and the S&P 500 increasing 41.9% over the same period. Nearing midyear, it appeared that the bloodstock markets would outperform the securities markets in 2006.

While the stock market and business appreciation provide the dollars for bloodstock purchases, the economic rationale for investing in racing prospects or broodmares relies on the state of purses—how much a buyer potentially can earn on the racetrack. The buyer must have a reasonable expectation of profitability—even if he or she does not make a profit with an in-

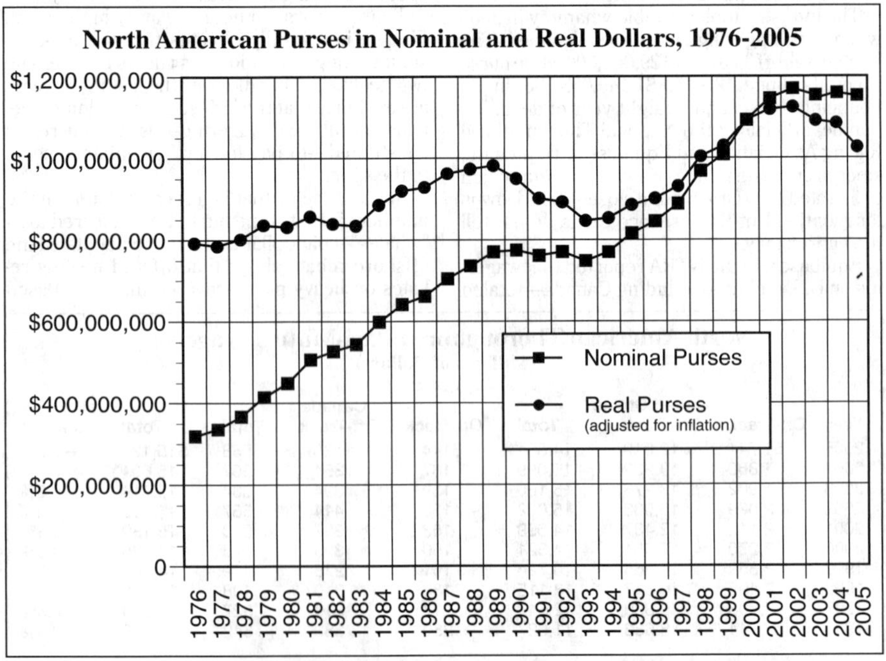

dividual horse or an entire stable.

One yardstick of potential profitability is the purse money available on the racetrack. (Another, of course, is residual value of the horses as breeding stock, which is a longshot but nonetheless a rational basis for investment.) When a billion dollars is out there for the taking, it makes sense to invest an amount less than $1-billion in horseflesh to chase those purse dollars. At a certain point, usually where purse dollars and bloodstock expenditures are roughly equal, horse buyers back off.

As full-card dollars flowed into purses in the mid-1990s, the ratio of bloodstock dollars to purse dollars began at 73.4% in '96 and gradually moved upward to 99.4% in '99 and 99.8% in 2000. The bloodstock market retreated in 2001 and '02 because of the twin blows of a stock-market decline and 9/11, and the bloodstock-purses ratio slipped to 65.6% in '02. Since then, the bloodstock market has advanced swiftly, to the point where auction sales were 99.1% of purses in 2005. How high the bloodstock market can go without a correction for lagging purses remains a question that will not be answered until later in the decade.—*Don Clippinger*

Racing Dates, Races, Runners, Starts, Purses by State and Province in 2005

	Racing Dates	Races	Runners	Starts	Purses
NORTH AMERICA	**6,837**	**57,481**	**72,784**	**469,580**	**$1,153,930,533**
Arizona	267	2,020	3,078	16,060	15,059,026
Arkansas	55	560	1,847	4,910	13,920,240
California	738	5,012	7,877	37,672	157,696,453
Colorado	37	253	665	2,107	1,994,800
Delaware	138	1,214	3,276	8,928	37,144,734
Florida	358	3,732	7,851	31,322	79,663,332
Georgia	2	10	68	68	357,350
Idaho	3	27	186	190	187,500
Illinois	321	2,970	4,665	23,405	57,679,139
Indiana	106	1,074	2,894	9,686	13,198,400
Iowa	95	707	1,277	5,345	13,106,685
Kansas	52	253	834	2,013	1,295,876
Kentucky	260	2,556	6,938	22,140	78,442,077
Louisiana	330	3,352	6,999	29,878	69,745,031
Maryland	208	1,834	4,541	14,598	41,610,385
Massachusetts	124	1,146	1,399	8,921	11,883,068
Michigan	129	964	1,287	7,048	10,485,982
Minnesota	68	585	1,275	4,787	9,000,620
Montana	34	182	351	1,184	421,295
Nebraska	106	932	1,480	8,012	6,159,743
Nevada	6	30	104	166	123,189
New Jersey	122	1,141	2,977	8,626	41,401,466
New Mexico	262	1,453	2,584	11,954	23,992,591
New York	415	3,745	6,566	29,161	152,425,752
North Carolina	4	18	95	115	284,600
North Dakota	21	103	301	741	306,031
Ohio	433	3,226	5,476	27,023	24,522,000
Oklahoma	150	905	2,421	8,295	8,707,420
Oregon	97	726	1,207	5,308	2,530,899
Pennsylvania	402	3,681	6,278	30,348	47,572,021
South Carolina	4	20	142	169	525,900
South Dakota	2	2	16	16	4,400
Tennessee	1	6	46	46	320,800
Texas	213	1,868	4,043	16,418	27,094,286
Virginia	50	421	1,917	3,644	9,547,194
Washington	116	1,006	1,758	7,782	11,040,320
West Virginia	459	4,472	9,156	39,630	73,178,910
Wyoming	14	37	127	268	67,496
UNITED STATES	**6,202**	**52,243**	**66,908**	**427,984**	**$1,042,697,011**
Alberta	166	1,151	1,692	8,740	12,489,605
British Columbia	91	798	1,049	5,877	12,092,925
Manitoba	75	590	883	4,607	4,603,020
Ontario	268	2,466	3,712	20,620	81,387,184
Saskatchewan	35	233	414	1,752	660,788
CANADA	**635**	**5,238**	**7,372**	**41,596**	**$111,233,522**

Revenues to Government From Horse Racing

Through much of the 20th century and into the 21st century, government has looked to gambling as a tax upon the willing, a way to ease the burden of most taxpayers by levying a heavy tax load on all gambling wagers. In the 1940s, the tax burden on racetracks exploded. In the 1970s and '80s, the states created lotteries, which had a heavy tax burden but nonetheless drew patrons through slick advertising and hefty jackpots. In the 1990s and beyond, the attention of state government shifted to slot machines and casino games. Some of the machine wagering was authorized for racetracks.

The following table, compiled by the Association of Racing Commissioners International, illustrates very clearly the rise of horse racing—principally Thoroughbred racing but also Quarter Horse and Standardbred racing—as a source of government income and its decline. In the depths of the Great Depression, the horse-racing industry was not taxed heavily, either in current dollars or inflation-adjusted dollars. That circumstance began to change in the late 1930s, as the nation began to emerge from the Depression and, with war on the horizon, to change to a military economy. For the first time in 1939, revenues to government passed the $10-million level. By 1942, the tax had more than doubled, and it doubled again by '44.

After World War II, demands on states and local governments for schools and other services grew exponentially, and so did the taxes on horse racing. By 1951, horse racing contributed more than $100-million in taxes; by '56, the tax had doubled again. Also in 1956, the tax on racing surpassed $1-billion in inflation-adjusted dollars for the first time. It peaked at more than $2-billion in deflated dollars in 1975.

At approximately that time, Thoroughbred racing began a slow, steady slide. As racing lost patrons to other sports—all of which had, unlike racing, embraced television as a way to enlarge their fan bases—racetracks were transformed from monopolist profit centers to marginally profitable or even losing operations. The tracks made compelling arguments to state governments that unless pari-mutuel taxes were reduced drastically, the racetracks would be unable to remain in business, and the state would lose both jobs and revenue on wagers placed at the track. The argument that a small tax was better than nothing carried the day, and subsequently some states eliminated the pari-mutuel tax altogether.

Revenue to States from Horse Racing

Year	Current Dollars	Deflated Dollars	Year	Current Dollars	Deflated Dollars
2004	$338,885,365	$313,144,858	1968	$426,856,448	$1,713,388,384
2003	343,588,382	325,152,249	1967	394,381,913	1,650,616,971
2002	346,799,090	333,637,106	1966	388,452,125	1,676,096,501
2001	351,511,182	343,363,174	1965	369,892,036	1,641,411,298
2000	367,786,590	367,786,590	1964	350,095,928	1,581,925,480
1999	392,201,085	400,744,968	1963	316,570,791	1,452,292,830
1998	431,722,361	447,510,533	1962	287,930,030	1,334,925,263
1997	441,768,972	463,002,255	1961	264,853,077	1,244,727,310
1996	443,882,538	472,960,127	1960	258,039,385	1,226,364,645
1995	455,764,292	494,825,844	1959	243,388,655	1,172,900,848
1994	451,546,549	500,278,697	1958	222,049,651	1,083,274,715
1993	471,735,474	533,752,135	1957	216,747,621	1,081,682,907
1992	491,259,606	568,686,237	1956	207,456,272	1,069,748,218
1991	523,249,392	619,640,699	1955	186,989,588	997,650,259
1990	623,839,806	764,603,268	1954	178,015,828	966,584,286
1989	584,888,183	744,549,344	1953	167,426,465	917,757,304
1988	596,202,319	787,648,055	1952	142,489,696	790,643,081
1987	608,351,461	831,126,648	1951	117,250,564	661,759,589
1986	587,357,677	824,361,652	1950	98,366,167	601,591,138
1985	625,159,697	896,762,006	1949	95,327,053	582,968,768
1984	650,262,852	961,145,299	1948	95,803,364	584,808,717
1983	641,387,176	983,617,060	1947	97,926,984	631,542,525
1982	652,888,463	1,040,857,799	1946	94,035,859	672,357,064
1981	680,199,584	1,150,560,030	1945	65,265,405	522,541,273
1980	712,727,523	1,318,815,615	1944	55,971,233	460,062,740
1979	680,919,798	1,374,262,933	1943	38,194,727	321,342,142
1978	673,063,831	1,470,952,709	1942	22,005,278	195,099,548
1977	700,239,986	1,637,911,644	1941	21,128,173	201,893,674
1976	714,629,120	1,777,861,280	1940	16,145,182	164,612,378
1975	780,081,431	2,052,737,832	1939	10,369,807	106,960,361
1974	645,980,984	1,860,276,412	1938	9,576,335	97,817,518
1973	585,201,524	1,837,425,112	1937	8,434,792	83,653,595
1972	531,404,550	1,761,600,975	1936	8,611,538	89,100,238
1971	512,838,417	1,773,852,226	1935	8,386,255	87,740,688
1970	486,403,097	1,766,554,431	1934	6,024,193	64,292,348
1969	461,498,886	1,764,881,586			

Revenues to States From Thoroughbred Racing and All Forms of Racing in 2004

State	Thoroughbred	Mixed	Total
Alabama	$ 1,111,643		$ 1,111,643
Arizona		$5,694,162	5,694,162
Arkansas	1,112,472	2,160,467	3,272,939
California	41,864,373	3,833,814	48,322,118
Colorado		549,420	549,420
Connecticut		9,177,162	9,177,162
Delaware	262,128	156,336	609,328
Florida	11,547,844	1,513,020	13,060,865
Idaho		539,130	539,130
Illinois	17,229,807	839,230	25,112,434
Indiana		1,957,278	5,932,737
Iowa		545,717	545,717
Kansas		1,717,426	1,717,426
Kentucky	3,440,621	2,689,567	6,408,714
Louisiana		6,109,390	6,109,390
Maine		1,617,731	1,836,302
Maryland	1,766,950	1,412,894	3,972,224
Massachusetts	1,835,576	242,451	2,679,372
Michigan	7,968,900	10,373	12,651,285
Minnesota	188,279	511,969	714,196
Montana	98,217		98,217
Nebraska	839,821		839,965
Nevada	$ 4,729,214	$ 99,880	$ 5,293,518
New Hampshire	2,767,248		3,341,912
New Jersey	574,260	29,473	1,086,758
New Mexico		1,096,304	1,096,304
New York	98,058,110	1,273,005	116,708,103
North Dakota		120,176	120,176
Ohio	1,035,159	8,849,773	11,342,797
Oklahoma		3,486,038	3,486,038
Oregon		3,015,130	3,015,130
Pennsylvania	20,852,127		23,720,741
Rhode Island		3,212,369	3,212,369
South Dakota		131,434	131,434
Texas		7,449,680	7,449,680
Virginia	3,085,616	10,755	3,962,233
Washington	1,796,407	79,908	1,898,992
West Virginia	842,958	696,354	1,539,312
Wisconsin		128,913	128,913
Wyoming		360,210	360,210
Totals	**$222,909,513**	**$69,938,496**	**$338,885,365**

*denotes tax revenue from mixed meets and in some cases full-card simulcasting

Source: Association of Racing Commissioners International

Pari-Mutuel Wagering by State in 2004

State	On-Track	Intertrack	Off-Track	Total
Alabama			$ 37,054,768	$ 37,054,768
Arizona	$ 18,931,755	$ 16,210,690	143,895,727	179,038,172
Arkansas	56,811,557		147,708,854	204,520,411
California	488,789,618	1,152,129,769	595,483,650	2,236,403,037
Colorado	2,059,365		65,304,384	67,363,749
Connecticut			246,378,814	246,378,814
Delaware	25,843,302		104,223,758	130,067,060
Florida	201,376,240	119,703,791	602,035,404	923,115,435
Idaho	1,726,462		19,692,455	21,418,917
Illinois	129,058,664	198,020,873	732,303,750	1,059,383,287
Indiana	10,670,948	6,992,650	169,490,415	187,154,013
Iowa	6,825,039		24,635,872	31,460,911
Kansas	2,287,909		45,363,133	47,651,042
Kentucky	158,459,276	71,968,703	298,363,224	528,791,203
Louisiana	55,210,635	60,572,974	248,587,875	364,371,484
Maine	6,541,929	1,371,954	57,376,746	65,290,629
Maryland	47,049,240	32,466,507	412,742,778	492,258,525
Massachusetts	23,726,005	3,293,124	183,726,808	210,745,937
Michigan	23,934,235	12,704,660	300,834,567	337,473,462
Minnesota	17,990,353		63,951,151	81,941,504
Montana	1,940,755		7,880,908	9,821,663
Nebraska	8,664,785	5,054,982	93,675,566	107,395,333
Nevada	310,572		505,329,100	505,639,672
New Hampshire	3,589,610		171,843,507	175,433,117
New Jersey	211,510,938	69,467,512	760,880,045	1,041,858,495
New Mexico	26,976,577	6,916,413	70,948,662	104,841,652
New York	378,536,148	886,715,589	1,452,913,832	2,718,165,569
North Dakota	426,259		5,243,019	5,669,278
Ohio	85,053,759	28,802,535	384,982,058	498,838,352
Oklahoma	12,196,358	2,870,471	112,130,519	127,197,358
Oregon	3,616,547	1,364,215	905,889,514	910,870,276
Pennsylvania	51,944,510		995,496,151	1,047,440,661
Rhode Island			62,315,617	62,315,617
South Dakota	279,255		9,709,690	9,988,945
Texas	83,062,587	19,761,947	346,438,428	449,262,962
Virginia	5,991,577	1,577,555	137,825,348	145,394,480
Washington	25,113,218	6,905,227	105,129,569	137,148,014
West Virginia	40,913,736	4,963,282	60,176,612	106,053,630
Wisconsin			44,401,964	44,401,964
Wyoming	1,192,475		17,479,892	18,672,367
Totals	**$2,215,022,588**	**$2,881,678,930**	**$10,753,433,744**	**$15,502,858,648**

*handle includes mixed meets. Source: Association of Racing Commissioners International

Pari-Mutuel Takeout by State

Pari-mutuel takeout is the amount deducted from wagers before odds are calculated and payments are made to winning bettors.

The money taken out from the wagers goes to state taxes, horsemen as purses, the racetrack operators, breed enhancement funds, and other funds.

Arizona—Up to 25% on win-place-show wagers; up to 30% on two-horse wagers; up to 35% on multiple-horse wagers.

Arkansas—17% on win-place-show wagers; 21% on multiple wagers.

California—15.43% on win-place-show wagers; 20.68% on exotic wagers.

Colorado—18.5% on win-place-show wagers; 28% on exotic wagers.

Delaware—17% on win-place-show wagers; 19% on daily doubles and exactas; 27% on all other exotic wagers.

Florida—Individual tracks determine takeout rate.

Idaho—23% on win-place-show wagers; 23.75% on exotic wagers.

Illinois—17% on total handle; 20.5% on two-horse wagers; 25% on wagers involving three or more horses.

Indiana—18% on win-place-show wagers; 21.5% on exotic wagers.

Iowa—Up to 18% on win-place-show wagers; up to 24% on two-horse wagers; up to 25% on all other wagers.

Kansas—18% on win-place-show wagers; up to 22% on multiple wagers.

Kentucky—At tracks above $1,200,000 daily average: 16% on win-place-show wagers; 19% on exotic wagers. At tracks below $1,200,000 daily average: 17.5% on win-place-show wagers; 19% on exotic wagers.

Louisiana—17% on win-place-show wagers; 20.5% on two-horse wagers; 25% on multiple-horse wagers.

Maryland—At mile tracks, 18% on win-place-show wagers; 21% on two-horse multiple wagers; 25.75% on three-horse multiple wagers.

Massachusetts—19% on win-place-show wagers; 26% on exotic wagers (24% at fairs).

Michigan—17% on win-place-show wagers; up to 28% on multiples; up to 35% on multiple wagers with permission of racing commissioner.

Minnesota—Up to 17% on win-place-show wagers; 23% on exotic wagers.

Missouri—18% on straight wagers, 20% on two-horse wagers, 25% on other wagers.

Montana—20% on win-place-show wagers; up to 25% on exotic wagers.

Nebraska—15% to 18% on win-place-show wagers; up to 24% on exotic wagers.

New Hampshire—19% on win-place-show wagers; 26% on multiple wagers.

New Jersey—17% on win-place-show wagers; 19% on two-horse wagers; 25% on all other wagers.

New Mexico—Class A tracks: 19% on win-place-show wagers; 21% to 25% on exotic wagers. Class B tracks: 18.75% to 25% on win-place-show wagers; 21% to 30% on exotic wagers.

New York—At NYRA racetracks, 14% on win-place-show wagers; 17.5% on multiple wagers; 25% on exotics and super exotics. At Finger Lakes, 18% on win-place-show wagers, 20% on multiple wagers, 25% on exotics and super exotics.

Ohio—18% on win-place-show wagers; 22.5% on exotic wagers.

Oklahoma—18% on win-place-show wagers; 20% on multiple-horse wagers; 20% on up to three-race wagers (such as Pick Three); 25% on multiple-race wagers (more than three races, such as Pick Six).

Oregon—19% on win-place-show wagers; 22% on multiple wagers. At fairs, up to 22% on all wagers.

Pennsylvania—17% on regular wagering pools; 19% if average daily handle is less than $300,000; 20% on exactas, daily doubles and quinellas; 26% to 35% on trifectas.

Texas—18% on win-place-show wagers; up to 21% on two-horse wagers; up to 25% on three-horse wagers.

Virginia—18% on win-place-show wagers; 22% on all other wagers.

Washington—16.1% on win-place-show wagers; 22.1% on all other wagers.

West Virginia—17.25% on win-place-show wagers; 19% on two-horse wagers; 25% on three horses or more.

Wyoming—20.9% on win-place-show wagers; 25.9% on exotic wagers.

2005 Aggregate Purse Earnings by State Where Bred

United States

State	Starters	Starts	Winners	Wins	Earnings
Alabama	88	479	22	32	$ 534,699
Arizona	571	3,701	245	429	3,834,417
Arkansas	663	4,326	281	441	5,332,695
California	6,421	39,162	2,958	5,007	91,642,871
Colorado	376	1,882	114	179	1,921,189
Connecticut	2	7	2	2	19,561
Florida	9,934	72,166	5,180	9,202	169,947,619
Georgia	77	420	32	49	609,213
Idaho	268	1,128	92	136	1,101,697
Illinois	2,020	14,594	1,000	1,688	28,670,451
Indiana	1,095	6,940	423	673	8,505,004
Iowa	858	6,066	413	650	9,460,440
Kansas	197	1,088	83	120	1,072,189
Kentucky	18,393	119,496	9,496	16,341	410,180,835
Louisiana	3,046	16,821	1,115	1,678	37,057,730
Maryland	2,388	15,889	1,175	2,018	39,470,318
Massachusetts	145	1,082	59	94	1,464,356
Michigan	690	4,872	344	570	8,567,162
Minnesota	432	2,375	160	239	4,087,923
Mississippi	32	162	9	13	188,080
Missouri	47	295	21	32	234,715
Montana	118	537	38	54	323,749
Nebraska	353	2,501	177	264	2,272,966
Nevada	4	20	2	4	20,614
New Hampshire	2	4	0	0	80
New Jersey	895	6,023	381	610	17,014,790
New Mexico	1,186	6,526	441	686	12,161,549
New York	3,581	24,478	1,713	2,853	70,336,412
North Carolina	24	132	9	10	135,551
North Dakota	80	349	19	26	231,321
Ohio	1,437	10,216	678	1,120	13,129,962
Oklahoma	1,673	9,515	650	1,010	10,604,546
Oregon	479	3,091	237	419	2,184,708
Pennsylvania	1,781	12,190	801	1,355	23,762,849
South Carolina	93	708	47	81	1,217,430
South Dakota	65	257	19	25	148,044
Tennessee	32	217	11	18	346,028
Texas	3,332	20,719	1,380	2,287	28,301,345
Utah	72	376	31	42	305,655
Virginia	744	4,679	330	556	12,409,405
Washington	1,820	11,286	887	1,526	15,006,514
West Virginia	763	4,536	253	354	8,075,485
Wisconsin	10	77	5	9	66,039
Wyoming	7	28	0	0	4,212

Canada

Province	Starters	Starts	Winners	Wins	Earnings
Alberta	1,041	6,015	460	712	$ 7,676,291
British Columbia	1,082	6,893	528	897	11,729,153
Manitoba	221	1,203	84	121	2,104,493
Ontario	2,535	16,262	1,206	1,940	53,286,295
Quebec	21	132	7	12	324,097
Saskatchewan	115	630	48	79	460,028

Claiming Activity by State and Claiming Category in 2005

	No. Claims	Value	Average
North America			
Maiden Claiming	**1,821**	**$34,049,775**	**$18,698**
$0-$4,999	**2,215**	**7,765,900**	**3,506**
$5,000-$9,999	**5,330**	**32,395,375**	**6,078**
$10,000-$19,999	**4,606**	**58,616,500**	**12,726**
$20,000 and up	**3,229**	**101,665,000**	**31,485**
Total	**15,380**	**200,442,775**	**13,033**
United States			
Maiden Claiming	**1,641**	**30,598,900**	**18,646**
$0-$4,999	**2,140**	**7,507,500**	**3,508**
$5,000-$9,999	**5,012**	**30,384,750**	**6,062**
$10,000-$19,999	**4,299**	**54,380,500**	**12,650**
$20,000 and up	**2,879**	**91,105,500**	**31,645**
Total	**14,330**	**183,378,250**	**12,797**
Arizona			
Maiden Claiming	59	368,500	6,246
$0-$4,999	307	1,004,900	3,273
$5,000-$9,999	187	1,153,250	6,167
$10,000-$19,999	68	838,000	12,324
$20,000 and up	8	160,000	20,000
Total	570	3,156,150	5,537
Arkansas			
Maiden Claiming	30	660,000	22,000
$0-$4,999	0	0	0
$5,000-$9,999	81	497,500	6,142
$10,000-$19,999	94	1,184,000	12,596
$20,000 and up	89	2,439,000	27,404
Total	264	4,120,500	15,608
California			
Maiden Claiming	439	11,261,500	25,653
$0-$4,999	387	1,257,900	3,250
$5,000-$9,999	518	3,393,000	6,550
$10,000-$19,999	747	9,713,000	13,003
$20,000 and up	1,000	33,736,000	33,736
Total	2,652	48,099,900	18,137
Colorado			
Maiden Claiming	2	15,000	7,500
$0-$4,999	7	24,000	3,429
$5,000-$9,999	11	59,250	5,386
$10,000-$19,999	3	30,000	10,000
$20,000 and up	0	0	0
Total	21	113,250	5,393
Delaware			
Maiden Claiming	46	923,500	20,076
$0-$4,999	0	0	0
$5,000-$9,999	329	$1,901,500	$ 5,780
$10,000-$19,999	232	2,977,000	12,832
$20,000 and up	85	2,382,500	28,029
Total	646	7,261,000	11,240
Florida			
Maiden Claiming	200	4,754,000	23,770
$0-$4,999	0	0	0
$5,000-$9,999	241	1,625,000	6,743
$10,000-$19,999	474	6,335,000	13,365
$20,000 and up	323	10,688,500	33,091
Total	1,038	18,648,500	17,966
Idaho			
Maiden Claiming	0	0	0
$0-$4,999	2	6,400	3,200
$5,000-$9,999	0	0	0
$10,000-$19,999	0	0	0
$20,000 and up	0	0	0
Total	2	6,400	3,200
Illinois			
Maiden Claiming	86	1,235,200	14,363
$0-$4,999	107	412,000	3,850
$5,000-$9,999	203	1,200,750	5,915
$10,000-$19,999	441	5,696,500	12,917
$20,000 and up	191	5,350,000	28,010
Total	942	12,659,250	13,439
Indiana			
Maiden Claiming	9	57,500	6,389
$0-$4,999	57	228,000	4,000
$5,000-$9,999	68	399,750	5,879
$10,000-$19,999	3	32,500	10,833
$20,000 and up	0	0	0
Total	128	660,250	5,158
Iowa			
Maiden Claiming	10	130,000	13,000
$0-$4,999	5	20,000	4,000
$5,000-$9,999	15	94,250	6,283
$10,000-$19,999	44	552,000	12,545
$20,000 and up	22	530,000	24,091
Total	86	1,196,250	13,910
Kansas			
Maiden Claiming	0	0	0
$0-$4,999	9	24,500	2,722
$5,000-$9,999	6	30,000	5,000
$10,000-$19,999	1	10,000	10,000
$20,000 and up	0	0	0
Total	16	64,500	4,031

	No. Claims	Value	Average
Kentucky			
Maiden Claiming	136	$ 2,815,000	$20,699
$0-$4,999	7	28,000	4,000
$5,000-$9,999	297	1,821,250	6,132
$10,000-$19,999	287	3,622,500	12,622
$20,000 and up	255	7,860,500	30,825
Total	846	13,332,250	15,759
Louisiana			
Maiden Claiming	98	1,570,000	16,020
$0-$4,999	115	438,000	3,809
$5,000-$9,999	365	2,143,500	5,873
$10,000-$19,999	332	4,161,500	12,535
$20,000 and up	146	4,390,000	30,068
Total	958	11,133,000	11,621
Maryland			
Maiden Claiming	66	1,085,500	16,447
$0-$4,999	7	28,000	4,000
$5,000-$9,999	201	1,330,500	6,619
$10,000-$19,999	225	3,102,000	13,787
$20,000 and up	129	3,271,500	25,360
Total	562	7,732,000	13,758
Massachusetts			
Maiden Claiming	2	17,500	8,750
$0-$4,999	33	134,500	4,076
$5,000-$9,999	70	419,000	5,986
$10,000-$19,999	23	286,000	12,435
$20,000 and up	1	20,000	20,000
Total	127	859,500	6,768
Michigan			
Maiden Claiming	5	40,000	8,000
$0-$4,999	7	28,000	4,000
$5,000-$9,999	18	132,500	7,361
$10,000-$19,999	4	48,500	12,125
$20,000 and up	0	0	0
Total	29	209,000	7,207
Minnesota			
Maiden Claiming	1	10,000	10,000
$0-$4,999	14	56,000	4,000
$5,000-$9,999	32	217,500	6,797
$10,000-$19,999	18	221,000	12,278
$20,000 and up	4	85,000	21,250
Total	68	579,500	8,522
Montana			
Maiden Claiming	0	0	0
$0-$4,999	3	6,500	2,167
$5,000-$9,999	0	0	0
$10,000-$19,999	0	0	0
$20,000 and up	0	0	0
Total	3	6,500	2,167

	No. Claims	Value	Average
Nebraska			
Maiden Claiming	1	$ 5,000	$ 5,000
$0-$4,999	84	243,000	2,893
$5,000-$9,999	26	144,500	5,558
$10,000-$19,999	4	45,000	11,250
$20,000 and up	0	0	0
Total	114	432,500	3,794
New Jersey			
Maiden Claiming	15	377,500	25,167
$0-$4,999	0	0	0
$5,000-$9,999	79	508,250	6,434
$10,000-$19,999	120	1,549,500	12,913
$20,000 and up	106	2,822,000	26,623
Total	305	4,879,750	15,999
New Mexico			
Maiden Claiming	13	133,000	10,231
$0-$4,999	13	51,200	3,938
$5,000-$9,999	192	1,195,000	6,224
$10,000-$19,999	74	837,500	11,318
$20,000 and up	12	275,000	22,917
Total	291	2,358,700	8,105
New York			
Maiden Claiming	59	1,682,000	28,508
$0-$4,999	84	336,000	4,000
$5,000-$9,999	33	222,750	6,750
$10,000-$19,999	128	1,763,500	13,777
$20,000 and up	360	13,372,500	37,146
Total	605	15,694,750	25,942
North Dakota			
Maiden Claiming	0	0	0
$0-$4,999	2	6,000	3,000
$5,000-$9,999	0	0	0
$10,000-$19,999	0	0	0
$20,000 and up	0	0	0
Total	2	6,000	3,000
Ohio			
Maiden Claiming	21	100,500	4,786
$0-$4,999	131	479,500	3,660
$5,000-$9,999	82	465,000	5,671
$10,000-$19,999	12	134,500	11,208
$20,000 and up	1	25,000	25,000
Total	226	1,104,000	4,885
Oklahoma			
Maiden Claiming	4	32,500	8,125
$0-$4,999	22	77,000	3,500
$5,000-$9,999	39	247,000	6,333
$10,000-$19,999	9	110,000	12,222
$20,000 and up	0	0	0
Total	70	434,000	6,200

	No. Claims	Value	Average
Oregon			
Maiden Claiming	3	$ 19,450	$ 6,483
$0-$4,999	60	173,100	2,885
$5,000-$9,999	16	88,000	5,500
$10,000-$19,999	1	10,000	10,000
$20,000 and up	0	0	0
Total	77	271,100	3,521

	No. Claims	Value	Average
Pennsylvania			
Maiden Claiming	98	1,171,000	11,949
$0-$4,999	217	825,500	3,804
$5,000-$9,999	427	2,658,500	6,226
$10,000-$19,999	325	3,994,000	12,289
$20,000 and up	60	1,418,000	23,633
Total	1,029	8,896,000	8,645

	No. Claims	Value	Average
South Carolina			
Maiden Claiming	0	0	0
$0-$4,999	0	0	0
$5,000-$9,999	0	0	0
$10,000-$19,999	1	10,000	10,000
$20,000 and up	0	0	0
Total	1	10,000	10,000

	No. Claims	Value	Average
Texas			
Maiden Claiming	19	320,000	16,842
$0-$4,999	22	87,000	3,955
$5,000-$9,999	104	645,000	6,202
$10,000-$19,999	97	1,107,500	11,418
$20,000 and up	49	1,320,000	26,939
Total	272	3,159,500	11,616

	No. Claims	Value	Average
Virginia			
Maiden Claiming	10	148,500	14,850
$0-$4,999	0	0	0
$5,000-$9,999	10	69,000	6,900
$10,000-$19,999	21	291,500	13,881
$20,000 and up	10	235,000	23,500
Total	41	595,500	14,524

	No. Claims	Value	Average
Washington			
Maiden Claiming	72	691,250	9,601
$0-$4,999	72	266,500	3,701
$5,000-$9,999	132	833,750	6,316
$10,000-$19,999	64	825,000	12,891
$20,000 and up	15	375,000	25,000
Total	283	2,300,250	8,128

	No. Claims	Value	Average
West Virginia			
Maiden Claiming	137	975,000	7,117
$0-$4,999	365	1,263,500	3,462
$5,000-$9,999	1,230	6,889,500	5,601
$10,000-$19,999	447	4,893,000	10,946
$20,000 and up	13	350,000	26,923
Total	2,055	13,396,000	6,519

	No. Claims	Value	Average
Wyoming			
Maiden Claiming	0	$ 0	$ 0
$0-$4,999	1	2,500	2,500
$5,000-$9,999	0	0	0
$10,000-$19,999	0	0	0
$20,000 and up	0	0	0
Total	1	2,500	2,500

	No. Claims	Value	Average
Canada			
Maiden Claiming	**180**	**3,450,875**	**19,172**
$0-$4,999	**75**	**258,400**	**3,445**
$5,000-$9,999	**318**	**2,010,625**	**6,323**
$10,000-$19,999	**307**	**4,236,000**	**13,798**
$20,000 and up	**350**	**10,559,500**	**30,170**
Total	**1,050**	**17,064,525**	**16,252**

	No. Claims	Value	Average
Alberta			
Maiden Claiming	20	251,500	12,575
$0-$4,999	10	25,500	2,550
$5,000-$9,999	78	514,000	6,590
$10,000-$19,999	134	1,919,500	14,325
$20,000 and up	52	1,326,000	25,500
Total	274	3,785,000	13,814

	No. Claims	Value	Average
British Columbia			
Maiden Claiming	39	404,000	10,359
$0-$4,999	8	36,000	4,500
$5,000-$9,999	108	678,000	6,278
$10,000-$19,999	51	671,000	13,157
$20,000 and up	48	1,267,000	26,396
Total	215	2,652,000	12,335

	No. Claims	Value	Average
Manitoba			
Maiden Claiming	2	14,375	7,188
$0-$4,999	38	134,000	3,526
$5,000-$9,999	26	165,625	6,370
$10,000-$19,999	3	32,500	10,833
$20,000 and up	0	0	0
Total	67	332,125	4,957

	No. Claims	Value	Average
Ontario			
Maiden Claiming	119	2,781,000	23,370
$0-$4,999	11	43,500	3,955
$5,000-$9,999	106	653,000	6,160
$10,000-$19,999	119	1,613,000	13,555
$20,000 and up	250	7,966,500	31,866
Total	486	10,276,000	21,144

	No. Claims	Value	Average
Saskatchewan			
Maiden Claiming	0	0	0
$0-$4,999	8	19,400	2,425
$5,000-$9,999	0	0	0
$10,000-$19,999	0	0	0
$20,000 and up	0	0	0
Total	8	19,400	2,425

Auction Sales by State and Province in 2005

	Yearling	Two-Year-Old	Weanling	Broodmare	Others	Total
North America	**$554,093,373**	**$190,882,771**	**$79,703,444**	**$308,602,769**	**$5,456,988**	**$1,138,739,345**
Arizona	788,700	8,300	14,300	12,600	1,500	825,400
California	7,638,400	23,649,600	441,300	3,120,300	564,300	35,413,900
Florida	22,336,700	123,240,000	5,795,100	11,813,800	140,500	163,326,100
Illinois	0	200,500	0	0	0	200,500
Indiana	25,800	4,800	1,000	21,700	0	53,300
Iowa	261,900	183,800	3,700	5,000	2,500	456,900
Kentucky	449,047,700	20,114,600	71,510,800	288,967,400	4,332,600	833,973,100
Louisiana	1,726,400	885,600	52,650	492,100	56,850	3,213,600
Maryland	14,835,700	19,746,000	1,442,900	2,342,800	160,600	38,528,000
Michigan	159,000	23,000	0	13,200	6,850	202,050
Minnesota	287,700	0	0	9,700	2,700	300,100
New Mexico	1,479,050	17,600	0	176,500	4,250	1,677,400
New York	39,748,900	0	194,200	387,900	16,800	40,347,800
Oklahoma	100,650	107,550	14,200	314,650	75,950	613,000
Oregon	109,900	0	20,250	44,450	2,100	176,700
Texas	3,419,100	2,651,500	72,700	405,100	21,300	6,569,700
Washington	3,151,750	0	33,200	135,750	2,200	3,322,900
West Virginia	38,100	35,350	0	35,950	9,600	119,000
United States	**$545,155,450**	**$190,868,200**	**$79,596,300**	**$308,298,900**	**$5,400,600**	**$1,129,319,450**
Alberta	1,025,356	595	3,742	52,471	1,956	1,084,120
British Columbia	1,517,826	10,531	1,953	59,702	0	1,590,012
Manitoba	90,435	0	0	0	0	90,435
Ontario	6,304,306	3,445	101,449	191,696	54,432	6,655,328
Canada	**$8,937,923**	**$14,571**	**$107,144**	**$303,869**	**$56,388**	**$9,419,895**

Auction Prices in Current and Deflated Dollars, 1990-2005

	All Horses			Yearlings		
Year	**No. Sold**	**Nominal Dollars**	**Deflated Dollars**	**No. Sold**	**Nominal Dollars**	**Deflated Dollars**
2005	20,737	$1,138,739,345	$1,015,706,782	10,128	$554,093,373	$494,227,586
2004	20,234	1,054,747,313	966,780,001	9,421	496,937,672	455,492,417
2003	19,110	855,725,521	804,972,034	8,840	424,884,038	399,683,964
2002	18,473	767,816,102	736,959,603	8,928	391,472,126	375,739,897
2001	19,191	846,478,571	826,857,248	9,081	473,487,556	462,512,143
2000	21,225	1,091,872,249	1,091,872,249	9,527	519,775,432	519,775,432
1999	20,184	1,002,587,575	1,024,428,388	8,705	439,800,627	449,381,439
1998	19,653	828,664,233	858,968,647	8,260	354,191,040	367,143,876
1997	18,444	687,534,250	720,580,051	8,057	307,689,262	322,478,108
1996	18,871	620,712,382	661,373,633	8,026	277,221,538	295,381,599
1995	18,518	526,647,938	571,784,616	7,882	243,392,908	264,253,043
1994	17,972	448,685,293	497,108,646	7,744	210,460,233	233,173,681
1993	16,605	364,519,425	412,440,938	7,460	187,232,894	211,847,449
1992	17,504	348,995,344	403,999,935	7,933	176,825,683	204,694,893
1991	18,977	401,102,091	474,991,818	8,179	213,940,466	253,351,885
1990	21,153	500,167,261	613,025,200	8,937	268,378,588	328,935,639

Average Auction Prices by State and Province in 2005

	Yearling	Two-Year-Old	Weanling	Broodmare	Others	Total
North America	**$54,709**	**$60,926**	**$43,793**	**$57,596**	**$18,312**	**$54,913**
Arizona	7,583	2,766	4,766	1,260	1,500	6,821
California	12,859	52,091	5,516	6,342	7,947	20,942
Florida	16,681	70,909	17,886	13,997	5,620	38,249
Illinois	0	14,321	0	0	0	14,321
Indiana	1,612	2,400	500	1,276	0	1,440
Iowa	5,036	10,211	925	1,250	2,500	5,783
Kentucky	87,465	164,873	62,618	100,896	48,140	89,175
Louisiana	5,793	7,837	4,387	2,167	2,105	4,746
Maryland	22,209	43,397	11,827	8,249	10,037	24,937
Michigan	3,878	1,916	0	942	1,370	2,806
Minnesota	7,571	0	0	970	675	5,771
New Mexico	9,860	3,520	0	3,096	1,416	7,801
New York	120,087	0	6,473	5,967	3,360	93,614
Oklahoma	3,050	3,841	2,840	2,600	2,812	2,864
Oregon	2,497	0	2,892	1,033	2,100	1,860
Texas	9,768	17,330	1,913	5,127	7,100	10,545
Washington	12,122	0	1,660	2,154	733	9,603
West Virginia	2,116	3,927	0	1,382	1,066	1,919
United States	**$57,566**	**$61,058**	**$44,492**	**$59,061**	**18,558**	**$56,761**

	Yearling	Two-Year-Old	Weanling	Broodmare	Others	Total
Alberta	$ 6,103	$ 297	$ 935	$1,140	$ 978	$ 4,883
British Columbia	11,675	2,632	1,953	2,595	0	10,063
Manitoba	3,118	0	0	0	0	3,118
Ontario	19,046	3,445	3,901	2,778	10,886	15,405
Canada	**$13,583**	**$2,081**	**$3,456**	**$2,201**	**$ 8,055**	**$11,200**

Median Auction Prices by State and Province in 2005

	Yearling	Two-Year-Old	Weanling	Broodmare	Others	Total
North America	**$13,186**	**$22,000**	**$15,000**	**$9,000**	**$3,700**	**$13,000**
Arizona	4,500	2,100	6,200	1,050	0	3,700
California	5,500	20,000	3,000	3,500	4,500	6,000
Florida	8,000	25,000	9,000	6,000	2,700	12,000
Illinois	0	10,000	0	0	0	10,000
Indiana	1,500	2,400	500	850	0	1,200
Iowa	2,500	8,350	850	1,000	0	2,500
Kentucky	30,000	110,000	30,000	25,500	15,750	30,000
Louisiana	3,500	5,000	4,000	1,400	1,500	2,500
Maryland	10,000	26,000	5,000	3,900	3,750	10,000
Michigan	2,500	2,100	0	625	500	1,800
Minnesota	4,000	0	0	900	650	2,100
New Mexico	5,500	3,500	0	1,600	650	4,000
New York	40,000	0	4,100	3,200	4,000	16,000
Oklahoma	2,500	2,800	2,200	1,700	1,700	2,000
Oregon	1,900	0	1,900	900	0	1,400
Texas	4,200	10,000	1,700	2,300	3,700	4,500
Washington	7,600	0	850	800	1,000	5,500
West Virginia	1,750	3,500	0	650	900	1,125
United States	**$15,000**	**$22,000**	**$16,000**	**$10,000**	**$3,700**	**$14,500**
Alberta	4,127	298	468	850	978	2,552
British Columbia	8,494	1,996	0	2,548	0	5,096
Manitoba	1,681	0	0	0	0	1,681
Ontario	9,666	0	3,014	2,153	14,642	6,459
Canada	**$6,724**	**$1,868**	**$2,583**	**$1,446**	**$6,459**	**$4,623**

Yearling Auction Prices in Nominal and Deflated Dollars, 1990-2005

Year	Average	Change	Deflated Average	Median	Change	Deflated Median	S&P 500	Change S&P
2005	$54,913	4%	$48,798	$13,186	1%	$11,761	$1,248	11%
2004	52,747	10%	48,348	13,000	8%	11,916	1,122	1%
2003	48,063	10%	45,212	12,000	9%	11,288	1,112	26%
2002	43,847	–16%	42,085	11,000	22%	10,558	880	–23%
2001	52,140	–4%	50,931	9,000	–22%	8,791	1,148	–13%
2000	54,558	8%	54,558	11,538	–4%	11,538	1,320	–10%
1999	50,522	18%	51,623	12,000	1%	12,261	1,469	20%
1998	42,880	12%	44,448	11,900	8%	12,335	1,229	27%
1997	38,189	11%	40,025	11,000	16%	11,529	971	31%
1996	34,540	12%	36,803	9,500	–5%	10,122	741	20%
1995	30,879	14%	33,526	10,000	11%	10,857	616	34%
1994	27,177	8%	30,110	9,000	13%	9,971	459	–2%
1993	25,098	13%	28,398	8,000	14%	9,052	466	7%
1992	22,289	–15%	25,802	7,000	17%	8,103	436	4%
1991	26,157	–13%	30,976	6,000	–14%	7,105	417	24%
1990	30,030	–7%	36,806	7,000	8%	8,579	336	–5%

North American Mares Bred, 2001-2005

	2005	2004	2003	2002	2001
North America	**62,794**	**62,400**	**60,992**	**61,978**	**61,889**
Alabama	122	136	112	93	90
Alaska	1	3	2	0	0
Arizona	535	485	513	503	402
Arkansas	551	593	546	634	550
California	5,150	5,747	5,725	5,716	5,720
Colorado	423	431	448	416	407
Connecticut	0	1	5	0	5
Delaware	0	0	0	5	0
District of Columbia	0	0	0	21	0
Florida	7,220	6,935	6,609	7,136	6,813
Georgia	82	116	87	114	92
Idaho	218	308	268	254	272
Illinois	928	1,067	1,106	1,172	1,211
Indiana	543	685	800	825	752
Iowa	470	505	595	632	708
Kansas	155	189	150	155	177
Kentucky	20,899	20,346	20,156	19,984	20,962
Louisiana	3,554	3,090	2,617	2,157	2,064
Maine	0	0	5	3	3
Maryland	1,727	1,603	1,646	1,835	1,851
Massachusetts	30	68	81	106	104
Michigan	432	544	482	429	526
Minnesota	407	341	324	299	240
Mississippi	48	72	66	72	68
Missouri	89	73	77	140	139
Montana	145	181	172	231	219

	2005	2004	2003	2002	2001
Nebraska	318	360	331	298	326
Nevada	16	15	9	10	15
New Hampshire	0	0	0	0	5
New Jersey	299	257	318	435	238
New Mexico	1,781	1,528	1,393	1,402	1,149
New York	2,405	2,591	2,683	2,554	2,206
North Carolina	53	61	58	55	55
North Dakota	102	110	67	71	80
Ohio	449	515	580	823	789
Oklahoma	1,484	1,488	1,449	1,613	1,858
Oregon	458	449	406	356	420
Pennsylvania	1,213	1,003	966	996	952
Puerto Rico	796	775	714	679	704
Rhode Island	4	1	2	0	0
South Carolina	130	140	146	165	229
South Dakota	126	111	104	138	166
Tennessee	103	56	78	93	83
Texas	2,827	2,882	3,044	3,323	3,297
Utah	195	216	88	107	197
Vermont	2	4	2	11	39
Virginia	227	387	415	484	505
Washington	1,175	1,160	1,090	1,090	1,263
West Virginia	1,220	1,048	981	878	587
Wisconsin	29	22	41	35	24
Wyoming	26	19	27	29	47
United States	**59,167**	**58,717**	**57,584**	**58,577**	**58,609**
Alberta	944	914	821	864	825
British Columbia	856	786	739	700	790
Manitoba	165	184	193	196	221
New Brunswick	2	3	1	1	7
Northwest Territories	0	0	0	5	0
Nova Scotia	0	1	1	5	5
Ontario	1,493	1,619	1,530	1,445	1,276
Prince Edward Island	0	0	0	14	0
Quebec	14	13	0	16	7
Saskatchewan	153	163	123	155	149
Canada	**3,627**	**3,683**	**3,408**	**3,401**	**3,280**

Source: Association of Racing Commissioners International

Mares Bred in North America, 1997-2005

Year	Mares Bred	Change
2005	62,794	0.6%
2004	62,400	2.3%
2003	60,992	–1.6%
2002	61,978	0.1%
2001	61,889	4.0%
2000	59,487	3.2%
1999	57,629	2.0%
1998	56,472	–0.6%
1997	56,791	

North American Stallons in Production, 2001-2005

	2005	2004	2003	2002	2001
North America	**3,659**	**3,739**	**3,719**	**3,828**	**4,007**
Alabama	19	25	19	20	16
Alaska	1	1	1	0	0
Arizona	50	53	51	60	58
Arkansas	57	68	60	71	61
California	319	376	363	355	385
Colorado	49	62	69	70	66
Connecticut	0	1	1	0	1
Delaware	0	0	0	1	0
District of Columbia	0	0	0	1	0

	2005	2004	2003	2002	2001
North America	**3,659**	**3,739**	**3,719**	**3,828**	**4,007**
Florida	235	228	238	260	268
Georgia	18	20	15	24	19
Idaho	34	45	42	45	52
Illinois	95	111	105	110	122
Indiana	80	86	89	99	87
Iowa	39	45	42	56	63
Kansas	20	25	25	23	27
Kentucky	349	352	364	368	429
Louisiana	270	228	194	176	172
Maine	0	0	2	2	3
Maryland	71	67	73	92	95
Massachusetts	10	17	19	24	21
Michigan	47	57	61	53	64
Minnesota	35	32	30	35	27
Mississippi	13	14	14	14	12
Missouri	17	17	17	28	25
Montana	34	42	33	38	38
Nebraska	37	36	38	28	32
Nevada	5	6	4	4	4
New Hampshire	0	0	0	0	1
New Jersey	24	25	33	37	43
New Mexico	166	148	141	135	133
New York	115	142	145	141	121
North Carolina	12	17	15	16	16
North Dakota	16	19	14	9	12
Ohio	78	83	89	92	95
Oklahoma	188	171	176	196	217
Oregon	52	46	44	32	44
Pennsylvania	118	109	104	100	106
Puerto Rico	57	53	58	62	62
Rhode Island	1	1	2	0	0
South Carolina	23	24	23	26	24
South Dakota	16	9	13	13	18
Tennessee	22	13	17	24	23
Texas	310	319	335	346	363
Utah	26	27	24	18	42
Vermont	1	3	2	5	3
Virginia	55	53	53	56	69
Washington	89	94	79	89	105
West Virginia	88	77	73	60	47
Wisconsin	10	7	12	13	12
Wyoming	7	6	11	10	14
United States	**3,378**	**3,460**	**3,432**	**3,537**	**3,717**
Alberta	83	71	80	81	74
British Columbia	57	58	54	61	74
Manitoba	21	21	20	22	22
New Brunswick	1	2	1	1	2
Northwest Territories	0	0	0	1	0
Nova Scotia	0	1	1	2	2
Ontario	96	102	111	92	91
Prince Edward Island	0	0	0	1	0
Quebec	3	4	0	7	4
Saskatchewan	20	20	20	23	21
Canada	**281**	**279**	**287**	**291**	**290**

North American Stallions in Production, 1997-2005

Year	Stallions Standing	Change
2005	3,659	–2.1%
2004	3,739	0.5%
2003	3,719	–2.8%
2002	3,828	–4.5%
2001	4,007	11.1%
2000	3,608	–3.9%
1999	3,754	–3.5%
1998	3,889	–6.9%
1997	4,178	

North American Live Foals, 1997-2005

Year	Live Foals	Change
2005	40,607	2.0%
2004	39,812	2.6%
2003	38,793	2.6%
2002	37,796	–6.2%
2001	40,309	10.2%
2000	36,567	5.7%
1999	34,594	1.7%
1998	34,030	1.8%
1997	33,443	

North American Live Foals, 2001-2005

	2005	2004	2003	2002	2001
NORTH AMERICA	**40,607**	**39,812**	**38,793**	**37,796**	**40,309**
Alabama	60	58	53	55	61
Alaska	1	1	1	0	0
Arizona	317	338	316	267	316
Arkansas	335	306	353	317	323
California	3,960	4,045	4,043	4,022	3,796
Colorado	253	264	225	217	205
Connecticut	0	0	0	4	5
Delaware	1	1	2	0	24
Florida	4,290	4,229	4,595	4,517	4,527
Georgia	51	55	68	58	51
Hawaii	1	0	0	1	0
Idaho	165	151	128	142	201
Illinois	621	600	593	658	630
Indiana	346	420	408	379	363
Iowa	285	342	314	403	384
Kansas	80	84	72	91	107
Kentucky	14,748	14,476	13,076	12,276	14,615
Louisiana	1,880	1,598	1,275	1,305	1,309
Maine	2	0	3	2	3
Maryland	1,076	1,081	1,231	1,189	1,213
Massachusetts	37	50	76	48	58
Michigan	330	318	284	317	236
Minnesota	169	194	168	138	90
Mississippi	35	33	33	37	26
Missouri	49	51	65	69	92
Montana	107	103	119	93	149
Nebraska	204	169	179	159	173
Nevada	7	11	9	18	5
New Hampshire	1	1	0	1	6
New Jersey	163	208	271	179	184
New Mexico	932	808	771	650	580
New York	1,656	1,703	1,587	1,423	1,411
North Carolina	31	33	37	35	54
North Dakota	43	42	43	56	46
Ohio	293	343	459	453	477
Oklahoma	845	814	897	1,016	1,069
Oregon	302	274	255	267	213
Pennsylvania	574	574	607	546	601
Puerto Rico	552	530	512	530	629
Rhode Island	1	1	0	0	0
South Carolina	67	51	76	117	89
South Dakota	54	40	46	63	64
Tennessee	35	44	54	31	38
Texas	1,710	1,835	1,881	1,979	2,009
Utah	112	58	55	121	124
Vermont	3	1	6	3	0
Virginia	240	285	311	323	373
Washington	738	603	706	823	987
West Virginia	542	548	468	350	295
Wisconsin	7	22	16	15	27
Wyoming	13	13	20	25	20
UNITED STATES	**38,324**	**37,809**	**36,767**	**35,788**	**38,258**
Alberta	524	449	456	446	485
British Columbia	502	452	441	473	511
Manitoba	95	82	91	95	106
New Brunswick	1	1	0	1	1
Nova Scotia	0	1	4	3	3
Ontario	1,067	958	941	896	832
Prince Edward Island	0	0	12	0	0
Quebec	3	0	8	4	5
Saskatchewan	91	60	73	90	108
CANADA	**2,283**	**2,003**	**2,026**	**2,008**	**2,051**

Aggregate Revenues From Stud Fees by Year, 2001-2005

Year	Aggregate	Change
2005	$525,557,450	6.0%
2004	495,898,625	–4.8%
2003	520,884,750	10.8%
2002	470,076,700	5.4%
2001	445,861,075	0.0%

Average North American Stud Fees by Year, 2001-2005

Year	Average	Change
2005	15,189	3.3%
2004	14,710	–9.6%
2003	16,269	8.3%
2002	15,028	11.1%
2001	13,531	0.0%

Aggregate Revenues From Stud Fees

Calculated by multiplying actual number of live foals by stallion times the stud fee.

	2005	2004	2003	2002	2001
NORTH AMERICA	**$525,555,950**	**$495,898,625**	**$520,884,750**	**$470,047,700**	**$445,861,075**
Alabama	20,100	27,500	34,200	20,250	18,800
Arizona	191,600	179,250	151,350	68,800	110,300
Arkansas	332,500	309,250	292,250	262,750	327,000
California	16,424,200	17,654,950	15,114,850	19,629,650	17,903,850
Colorado	193,250	191,000	181,300	85,600	69,250
Connecticut	0	0	0	2,250	3,750
Delaware	0	0	0	0	2,500
Florida	22,145,000	21,602,950	20,761,300	18,906,050	17,980,100
Georgia	18,100	28,450	27,400	31,050	7,950
Idaho	127,450	77,300	110,000	129,150	126,800
Illinois	815,750	698,950	668,950	722,200	673,150
Indiana	373,450	443,600	322,100	295,450	324,700
Iowa	472,650	499,450	349,300	354,750	328,750
Kansas	17,100	16,450	27,750	50,800	62,250

	2005	2004	2003	2002	2001
Kentucky	$448,619,300	$420,514,550	$448,111,500	$399,539,750	$379,143,300
Louisiana	2,720,950	1,933,700	1,348,350	1,348,050	1,276,250
Maine	0	0	1,000	0	0
Maryland	7,785,250	7,031,850	8,488,400	7,626,850	7,117,200
Massachusetts	21,500	31,000	41,500	38,500	50,450
Michigan	319,700	317,650	284,900	287,050	135,450
Minnesota	232,650	221,350	142,100	80,600	45,150
Mississippi	3,500	6,750	5,050	6,000	6,500
Missouri	22,000	9,500	13,700	34,100	23,500
Montana	51,050	32,600	45,700	48,450	45,300
Nebraska	143,750	112,000	132,500	88,450	174,750
Nevada	5,000	0	2,500	2,500	0
New Hampshire	0	0	0	0	750
New Jersey	411,000	505,250	658,500	167,750	194,000
New Mexico	1,557,000	917,000	645,350	434,650	402,100
New York	8,092,350	8,960,050	8,584,750	6,450,300	7,577,650
North Carolina	2,000	19,800	25,800	30,100	14,550
North Dakota	16,700	14,500	28,600	30,500	10,400
Ohio	203,900	210,450	312,100	377,200	419,200
Oklahoma	619,400	706,675	664,800	774,950	838,025
Oregon	327,500	294,800	264,000	378,350	335,900
Pennsylvania	1,173,250	998,750	960,250	793,550	942,050
Puerto Rico	152,000	331,000	117,500	204,000	208,500
South Carolina	30,500	17,850	22,500	113,000	116,000
South Dakota	41,600	27,900	20,100	20,200	5,700
Tennessee	7,550	9,800	13,000	2,800	2,000
Texas	3,565,850	3,916,550	4,238,000	3,136,000	2,443,150
Utah	34,500	8,800	10,100	74,500	129,000
Virginia	780,800	746,750	795,500	421,500	520,100
Washington	1,179,450	808,300	1,104,450	1,362,700	1,252,700
West Virginia	763,350	837,200	596,000	385,050	224,550
Wisconsin	600	2,800	0	1,200	4,000
Wyoming	5,000	2,950	0	1,000	400
UNITED STATES	**$520,020,100**	**$491,277,225**	**$515,719,250**	**$464,818,350**	**$441,597,725**
Alberta	690,000	637,000	701,250	603,200	596,750
British Columbia	1,034,850	1,032,000	940,350	1,026,100	612,550
Manitoba	76,400	45,800	55,800	78,350	66,250
Ontario	3,654,700	2,856,700	3,438,250	3,467,600	2,913,050
Quebec	0	0	0	400	0
Saskatchewan	79,900	49,900	29,850	53,700	74,750
CANADA	**$5,535,850**	**$4,621,400**	**$5,165,500**	**$5,229,350**	**$4,263,350**

Average North American Stud Fees, 2001-2005

	2005	2004	2003	2002	2001
NORTH AMERICA	**$15,190**	**$14,711**	**$16,270**	**$15,029**	**$13,531**
Alabama	1,182	1,196	1,315	920	940
Arizona	1,228	1,080	1,173	983	985
Arkansas	1,205	1,222	1,133	1,257	1,428
California	5,096	5,205	5,003	5,763	5,764
Colorado	1,271	1,273	1,648	1,259	899
Connecticut				750	750
Delaware					500
Florida	5,543	5,297	4,978	4,634	4,367
Georgia	1,207	1,355	1,442	1,194	795
Idaho	1,225	1,017	1,467	1,389	1,075
Illinois	1,728	1,652	1,604	1,550	1,562
Indiana	1,675	1,680	1,220	1,349	1,510
Iowa	1,921	1,777	1,397	1,186	1,162
Kansas	900	823	816	1,058	1,270
Kentucky	31,107	30,030	34,930	32,979	26,328
Louisiana	1,775	1,494	1,342	1,398	1,404
Maine			500		
Maryland	7,443	6,801	7,175	6,816	6,366
Massachusetts	1,433	1,409	1,297	1,833	1,682
Michigan	1,816	1,755	1,737	1,586	1,411
Minnesota	1,723	1,570	1,366	1,089	1,328
Mississippi	700	563	561	667	650
Missouri	1,158	950	913	1,795	904
Montana	865	776	879	1,242	1,105
Nebraska	1,188	1,287	1,366	1,638	1,165
Nevada	2,500		2,500	2,500	
New Hampshire					750
New Jersey	$2,834	$2,871	$2,953	$1,598	$1,528
New Mexico	2,608	2,304	1,871	1,659	1,535
New York	5,218	5,938	6,097	4,981	5,990
North Carolina	1,000	990	1,032	1,075	1,039
North Dakota	928	630	894	847	693
Ohio	1,324	1,291	1,284	1,387	1,310
Oklahoma	1,153	1,260	1,227	1,298	1,324
Oregon	1,300	1,254	1,195	1,674	1,836
Pennsylvania	2,210	2,094	2,017	1,816	1,892
Puerto Rico	1,854	2,399	1,780	2,400	2,044
South Carolina	1,220	939	833	1,527	1,657
South Dakota	904	900	874	721	633
Tennessee	755	700	929	700	667
Texas	2,848	2,916	3,273	2,306	2,017
Utah	1,190	800	481	1,433	1,654
Virginia	4,109	3,539	3,414	1,960	1,838
Washington	2,176	2,138	2,004	2,016	1,939
West Virginia	1,739	1,800	1,509	1,226	854
Wisconsin	300	933		600	500
Wyoming	1,000	738		500	400
UNITED STATES	**$15,835**	**$15,280**	**$16,961**	**$15,664**	**$13,982**
Alberta	1,971	1,954	2,021	1,764	2,072
British Columbia	2,835	2,723	2,718	2,890	2,211
Manitoba	1,124	935	858	1,018	989
Ontario	3,955	3,700	4,152	4,412	4,216
Quebec				400	
Saskatchewan	1,567	1,559	1,298	1,343	1,699
CANADA	**$3,149**	**$2,966**	**$3,210**	**$3,266**	**$3,119**

All About Purses 2005

by Mark Simon

In 2005, total purses, average purse per race, and average earnings per runner all declined, marking the first time since this study began in 1972 that all three of those key economic indicators took a downturn in the same year. On several occasions, two of those three indicators declined in the same year, but all three declining should be of concern to owners.

The good news is that total purses dropped only 2.4%, and the total remained well above $1-billion. But, when taking inflation into account, total purses took a rather serious 5.1% drop in real dollars. The average inflation-adjusted purse declined 2.8%. The declines in those two economic measures suggest that owners, on average, had a tougher year in 2005 than they were letting on at sales, where total receipts increased 8%.

The decline in total purses was presaged by the announcement by the National Thoroughbred Racing Association that 2005 total wagering in the United States on Thoroughbred races dipped 3.4%, to $14.6-billion, from '04. The declines in handle and concomitant revenue to purses were offset in part by an increasingly important contribution to purses from alternate forms of gaming, such as slot machines and video lottery terminals, which contributed about $200-million to purses in 2005.

In the meantime, the data on 2005 purses in North America suggest that it is still hard for the majority of horses to pay their way, and only a small percentage of runners earn significant sums for their owners. The average racehorse in North America in 2005 earned $15,851, a sum that does not pay the annual training bills for a runner training and racing on a major circuit.

On the other hand, those owners who campaigned a stakes winner or a horse that earned in the top 2% of all runners fared quite well. Stakes winners earned an average of $145,051 in 2005, and 1,284 horses earned $100,000 or more.

Highlights of the data in this comprehensive annual review of purses and runners in North America include:

- A total of $1,149,003,138 in purses was distributed in 57,305 races, the fewest races held in North America since 1971;
- Average purse was almost exactly the same as in 2004, although it did decline slightly from the record $20,069;
- The total number of runners, 72,487, decreased for the first time since 1998;
- Average earnings per runner decreased 0.5%, the second time in three years that measure has declined;
- Real average earnings per runner—when adjusted for inflation—declined 3.2%, the fifth straight year of decline;
- Nominal median earnings per runner—measured in current dollars—increased 4.4%, to an all-time record $6,135;
- A total of 5,665 runners—7.8% of all starters—failed to earn any part of a purse;
- More than half of all starters—52.9%—failed to win a race;
- Horses that were able to win at least one race earned an average of $29,740; horses that failed to win a race earned an average of $3,475;
- Horses that won a stakes race earned an average of $145,051;
- Horses that were able to win at least one race collectively earned 88.4% of all purse money;
- 17.3% of all runners earned more than $25,000 and collectively won 67.1% of all purse money;
- Stakes races constituted 4.6% of all races and offered 24.3% of all purses;

Table 1

Selected Racing Statistics, North American Thoroughbred Racing, 1996-2005

Year	No. of Runners	No. of Races	Total Purses	Average Purse	Earnings per Runner: Average	Earnings per Runner: Median	Percentage of Runners Earning Purses
2005	72,487	57,305	$1,149,003,138	$20,051	$15,851	$6,135	92.2%
2004	73,915	58,686	1,177,769,765	20,069	15,934	5,877	91.5%
2003	73,614	58,813	1,154,238,845	19,626	15,680	5,714	90.3%
2002	72,504	59,712	1,170,169,267	19,597	16,139	6,003	89.6%
2001	70,942	60,538	1,146,337,367	18,936	16,159	6,010	90.6%
2000	69,230	60,579	1,093,661,241	18,053	15,798	5,796	90.2%
1999	68,435	60,118	1,008,162,608	16,770	14,732	5,310	89.1%
1998	68,419	61,141	968,366,929	15,838	14,153	4,939	88.8%
1997	69,067	63,491	888,667,752	13,997	12,867	4,425	88.9%
1996	70,371	64,263	845,916,706	13,163	12,021	3,937	88.1%
Change:							
2004-2005	–1.9%	–2.4%	–2.4%	–0.1%	–0.5%	4.4%	0.8%
1996-2005	–3.0%	–10.8%	35.8%	52.3%	31.9%	55.8%	4.7%
Average change:							
1996-2005	–0.3%	–1.1%	3.6%	5.2%	3.2%	5.6%	0.5%

Table 2

Distribution of Earnings of Runners for 2005

Earnings range	No. of Runners	Percent of Runners	Earnings	Percent of Earnings	Average Earnings
$300,000 or more	162	0.2%	$ 97,525,444	8.5%	$602,009
$200,000 - 299,999	188	0.3%	45,190,681	3.9%	240,376
$100,000 - 199,999	934	1.3%	124,345,799	10.8%	133,133
$75,000 - 99,999	933	1.3%	80,131,587	7.0%	85,886
$50,000 - 74,999	2,470	3.4%	149,208,950	13.0%	60,408
$25,000 - 49,999	7,874	10.9%	274,964,275	23.9%	34,921
$20,000 - 24,999	3,472	4.8%	77,666,722	6.8%	22,369
$15,000 - 19,999	4,954	6.8%	85,924,401	7.5%	17,344
$10,000 - 14,999	7,316	10.1%	90,183,537	7.8%	12,327
$9,000 - 9,999	1,827	2.5%	17,333,919	1.5%	9,488
$8,000 - 8,999	2,004	2.8%	17,005,626	1.5%	8,486
$7,000 - 7,999	2,127	2.9%	15,935,096	1.4%	7,492
$6,000 - 6,999	2,322	3.2%	15,069,060	1.3%	6,490
$5,000 - 5,999	2,487	3.4%	13,641,633	1.2%	5,485
$4,000 - 4,999	2,764	3.8%	12,419,022	1.1%	4,493
$3,000 - 3,999	2,916	4.0%	10,146,975	0.9%	3,480
$2,000 - 2,999	3,741	5.2%	9,238,497	0.8%	2,470
$1,000 - 1,999	5,390	7.4%	7,821,622	0.7%	1,451
$1 - 999	12,941	17.9%	5,250,292	0.5%	406
None	5,665	7.8%	0	0.0%	0
Totals	**72,487**	**100.0%**	**$1,149,003,138**	**100.0%**	**$ 15,851**

- Claiming races—straight claiming and maiden claiming—accounted for 66% of all races but distributed just 37.1% of all purses;
- For runners age three and up, more than half of all races—50.1%—were contested at six furlongs or less;
- The average number of starts per horse dropped to 6.5, the fewest ever; and
- Average field size declined to 8.2 starters per race, just above the all-time low of 8.1 in 2000.

"All About Purses" was first published in *The Thoroughbred Record* in 1973, covering the '72 racing year, and has been published in THOROUGHBRED TIMES since '90. As in the past, the data reflect all Thoroughbred purses distributed to racehorses in North America in 2005, excluding Mexico and Puerto Rico, and were provided to THOROUGHBRED TIMES based on data obtained from the Jockey Club Information Systems Inc. Steeplechase races are excluded.

Purses Down in 2005

The biggest of the big pictures for racehorse owners—total purses distributed in North America—took a downturn in 2005. Total purses of $1,149,003,138 declined 2.4% from the record total paid in 2004. That marks the second downturn in total purses in three years, and the total has not made appreciable strides since 1999, when it surpassed $1-billion for the first time.

The big-picture statistics on racing in 2005, summarizing purses, runners, races, and earnings, are presented in **Table 1**. The table presents a ten-year snapshot of key statistics.

The total purses paid in 2005 were almost identical to the $1.146-billion paid four years earlier. Still, a billion dollars is a billion dollars, and the amount of money spent on racing prospects at auctions in 2005—for weanlings, yearlings, and two-year-olds—was $824.7-million (another $308.6-million was spent on broodmares). Those numbers suggest that owners and breeders see a fairly strong relationship between purses and how much they are willing to spend.

The big picture outlined in Table 1, though, points out several warning signs for owners because a number of key measures took downturns in 2005. Average purse and average earnings per runner both declined, even though the number of races and number of runners declined to help mitigate the damage.

Average purse of $20,051 was almost identical to the record $20,069 of 2004, but it nonetheless declined 0.1%. It was the first decline in average purse since 1991 and only the second decline in that measure since this study started. Average purse increased 52.3% in the ten years ended in 2005.

Average earnings per runner declined 0.5%, to $15,851, falling for the third time in four years. That measure peaked in 2001 at $16,159. In the ten-year period, average earnings per runner increased 31.9%. By contrast, in the ten-year period from 1991 to 2000, average earnings per runner increased 79.4% as the number of runners decelerated dramatically and purses blossomed with full-card simulcasting revenue.

The number of races in North America declined 2.4%, to 57,305, the fewest since 1971, when 57,219 races were held. The number of races peaked in 1989, at 82,726, and has declined 30.7% to 2005.

Also declining in 2005 was the number of runners, by 1.9%, to 72,487, the first decline in runners since 1998. That dip helped average earnings per runner because fewer horses were compet-

Table 3

Earnings as a Function of Number of Wins for 2005

Races Won	No. of Runners	Percent of Runners	Total Earnings	Percent of Earnings	Average Earnings
More than 9	0	0.0%	$ 0	0.0%	$ 0
9	5	0.0%	414,890	0.0%	82,978
8	18	0.0%	2,899,479	0.3%	161,082
7	36	0.0%	3,873,306	0.3%	107,592
6	136	0.2%	9,729,323	0.8%	71,539
5	457	0.6%	38,517,444	3.4%	84,283
4	1,400	1.9%	103,741,562	9.0%	74,101
3	3,647	5.0%	192,524,351	16.8%	52,790
2	8,887	12.3%	302,381,083	26.3%	34,025
1	19,571	27.0%	361,738,210	31.5%	18,483
0	38,330	52.9%	133,183,490	11.6%	3,475
Totals	**72,487**	**100.0%**	**$1,149,003,138**	**100.0%**	**$ 15,851**

ing for purses. Over a decade and a half, the decline in both runners and races—while total purses continued to increase—helped to fuel the sizable increase in average purse and average earnings per runner. The number of starters in North America peaked in 1989 at 91,436, three years after the foal crop peaked at 51,296.

The largest percentage gain for any key measure in Table 1 was median earnings per runner, which increased 4.4% to a record $6,135. On the other hand, that statistic also means that half of all runners earned less than that amount. Horses that earn the median and are in training for any period of time most likely are not paying their way. Median earnings have increased 55.8% the last ten years.

In 2005, the percentage of runners earning part of a purse increased once again, to an all-time high of 92.2% from 91.5% in '04. That number is not really significant because a small percentage of runners earned the lion's share of the purses.

Effects of Inflation

When the effects of inflation are squeezed from the 2005 purse totals, using the federal government's gross domestic product implicit price deflator, an even darker picture emerges. All key measures—except for median—showed large declines when adjusted for inflation. Total real purses declined 5.1% from 2004, and the total of $1,024,861,647 was 8.8% below the record $1,123,143,259 distributed in '02. In ten years, deflated total purses have increased just 13.7% despite the economic boost of full-card simulcasting.

Deflated average earnings per runner declined 3.2% to $14,140, the lowest figure since 1997. Deflated average earnings per runner have declined every year since peaking in 2000 at $15,798. In ten years, the adjusted earnings per runner increased just 1% per year on average.

Deflated average earnings per runner have shown little improvement in the past 35 years. In 1970, deflated average earnings were $13,862, a figure not surpassed until 1998. Since 1970, real average earnings per runner rose just 2%.

Real median earnings per runner have fared a bit better, increasing 1.6% in 2005 and 30.4% over the last ten years. But, in looking over a longer time horizon, that statistic is doing worse than real average earnings per runner. In 1970, real median earnings per runner came to $5,672, 3.5% higher than in 2005.

Real total purses in North America have been on a general increase through the duration of this study. In 1973, real total purses stood at $733,657,961 (when nominal purses totaled $233,662,724). In 32 years, real total purses have increased 39.7%, or 1.2% a year, in an era when other forms of gaming have proliferated, essentially taking market share from racing.

Table 2 breaks down earnings for all runners by dollar range. That table indicates that 5,665 horses, 7.8% of the total, earned nothing, which is an improvement over 2004, when 8.5% of all runners failed to earn any part of a purse. And 17.9% of all runners, or 12,941 starters, earned between $1 and $999. At the other end of the spectrum, 1.8% of all runners, 1,284 horses, earned $100,000 or more. Those runners took home 23.2% of all purse money, an average of $207,992 each.

Starting and Winning

An owner cannot win money unless his or her horse reaches the starting gate. Average earnings per runner rise for every start made from one through nine. Horses that started just once earned an average of $2,035. Horses that started twice earned roughly twice as much. Horses that made five starts earned an average of $15,101; horses that made nine starts earned an average of $24,953. A large percentage of horses failed to get into the starting gate anywhere near enough times to earn a meaningful amount of money for their owners. Almost one-third of all starters, 31.9%, made three or fewer starts. Those 23,174 runners collectively earned just 8.9% of all purses.

Horses that started the most times earned the most. The 18.9% of runners that made more than ten starts in 2005 earned 30.2% of all purse money, an average of $25,347, or 59.9% more than the average earnings per runner for the year. Average earnings per start in 2005 came to $2,454.

In looking at all the data related to purses and earnings, the most important factor to earning money on the racetrack is winning. **Table 3**, which reports earnings as a function of number of wins, graphically illustrates that winners take home the vast majority of the purse spoils.

Horses that were able to win just one race earned an average of $18,483, 16.6% more than the overall average earnings per runner for the year. Horses able to win two races earned an average of $34,025, $15,542 more than horses able to win just one race. Each additional win was increasingly more rewarding, with three wins being worth $18,765 more than two wins, and four wins being worth $21,311 more than three wins.

As horses move up the win ladder, the number of horses able to win one more race declines dramatically. Only 652 horses were able to win five or more races. Horses that won seven times earned an average of $107,592; those able to win eight races, just 18 horses, earned an average of $161,082, the most of any win category. Only five horses were able to win nine races in 2005.

Racing bestows the majority of each purse on the winner to ensure the integrity of racing, so that owners, trainers, and jockeys are trying their best to win and are compensated highly only when their horse wins. In 2005, winners collectively earned 88.4% of all purse money, as shown in **Figure 1**. That means nearly nine out of every ten dollars distributed in 2005 went only to winners. The 47.1% of runners that won a race collectively earned 100% of first-place money, 74.7% of all second-place money, 70.5% of all third-place money, 68.3% of all fourth-place money, 66.5% of all fifth-place money, and 59.9% of all sixth-place money or lower, for an overall average per runner of $29,740. The 14.4% of runners that could finish no better than second in any race earned 8.3% of all purse money, an average of $9,081.

Table 4

Distribution of Races and Purses by Age and Sex for 2005

Sex	No. of Races	Percent of Races	Purses	Percent of Purses	Average Purse per Race
			TWO-YEAR-OLDS		
Females	2,021	3.5%	$ 59,258,315	5.2%	$29,321
Males	53	0.1%	4,372,581	0.4%	82,502
Either Sex	2,288	4.0%	62,989,681	5.5%	27,530
Overall	4,362	7.6%	126,620,577	11.0%	29,028
			THREE-YEAR-OLDS		
Females	2,716	4.7%	80,109,726	7.0%	29,495
Males	51	0.1%	2,376,331	0.2%	46,595
Either Sex	2,991	5.2%	102,235,672	8.9%	34,181
Overall	5,758	10.0%	184,721,729	16.1%	32,081
			THREE-YEAR-OLDS AND UP		
Females	15,484	27.0%	278,359,198	24.2%	17,977
Males	40	0.1%	916,296	0.1%	22,907
Either Sex	23,045	40.2%	394,924,379	34.4%	17,137
Overall	38,569	67.3%	674,199,873	58.7%	17,480
			FOUR-YEAR-OLDS		
Females	70	0.1%	1,771,193	0.2%	25,303
Males	0	0.0%	0	0.0%	0
Either Sex	97	0.2%	2,518,766	0.2%	25,967
Overall	167	0.3%	4,289,959	0.4%	25,688
			FOUR-YEAR-OLDS AND UP		
Females	3,156	5.5%	61,449,195	5.3%	19,471
Males	5	0.0%	296,937	0.0%	59,387
Either Sex	5,288	9.2%	97,468,447	8.5%	18,432
Overall	8,449	14.7%	159,214,579	13.9%	18,844
			FIVE-YEAR-OLDS AND UP		
Females	0	0.0%	0	0.0%	0
Males	0	0.0%	0	0.0%	0
Either Sex	3	0.0%	9,421	0.0%	3,140
Overall	3	0.0%	9,421	0.0%	3,140
			TOTALS		
Females	**23,447**	**40.9%**	**$480,947,627**	**41.9%**	**$20,512**
Males	**149**	**0.3%**	**$7,962,145**	**0.7%**	**$53,437**
Either Sex	**33,712**	**58.8%**	**$660,146,366**	**57.5%**	**$19,582**
Overall	**57,308**	**100.0%**	**$1,149,056,138**	**100.0%**	**$20,051**

Horses that finished first and second collectively earned 96.7% of all purse money.

Figure 1

Distribution of Purses by Best Finish Position

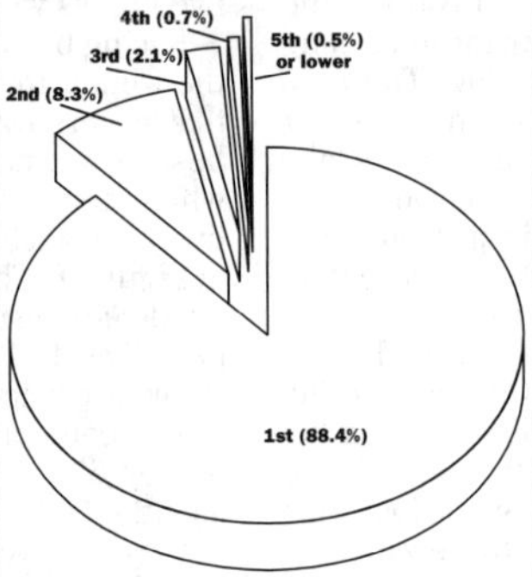

Age and Sex Differences

Horses' potential to earn purse money differs by age and sex, and **Table 4** illustrates those differences. Three-year-olds, which compete in the highest-profile division in racing, have the most lucrative opportunities. While just 10% of all races in 2005 were restricted to three-year-olds, those 5,758 races distributed 16.1% of all purses, an average purse of $32,081. The handful of races restricted to sophomore males offered an average of $46,595, and those open to either sex paid an average of $34,181. Races restricted to three-year-old fillies offered an average purse of $29,495.

Two-year-old racing offered the second-best average purse structure, with the 4,362 races—7.6% of the total—offering 11% of all purses, an average of $29,028. The most common races were carded for three-year-olds and older; the 38,569 races in that category amounted to 67.3% of all races and 58.7% of all purses, with an average purse of $17,480.

Disparities in earnings opportunities for males and females also are pronounced. Races open to either sex—which, for all practical purposes, are races for males—were far more abundant than races exclusively for females, with 58.8% of all races being open and 40.9% restricted to females. Just 0.3% of all races were restricted to males. The 23,447 races restricted to females had slightly higher purses on average than races open to all sexes, by a margin of $20,512 to $19,582. But, because females had fewer races, they earned an average of $15,234 in 2005 and males $16,336. **Table 5** shows that, while females accounted for 43.9% of all runners, they collectively earned 42.2% of all purses. In every age bracket, males earned more than females. Among three-year-olds, the highest earnings bracket by age, males earned an average of $19,508, while females averaged $17,737.

Claiming game

Claiming races are the most common event carded, and **Table 6** shows how prevalent claiming races are in North America. In 2005, claiming races constituted almost two out of every

Table 5

Distribution of Runners and Earnings by Age and Sex for 2005

Sex	No. of Runners	Percent of Runners	Earnings	Percent of Earnings	Avg. Earnings
			TWO-YEAR-OLDS		
Females	5,627	7.8%	$ 61,018,337	5.3%	$10,844
Males	5,568	7.7%	65,595,090	5.7%	11,781
Overall	11,196	15.4%	126,613,827	11.0%	11,309
			THREE-YEAR-OLDS		
Females	9,894	13.6%	175,493,667	15.3%	17,737
Males	10,233	14.1%	199,626,727	17.4%	19,508
Overall	20,130	27.8%	375,125,851	32.6%	18,635
			FOUR-YEAR-OLDS		
Females	8,254	11.4%	143,600,611	12.5%	17,398
Males	9,399	13.0%	177,925,182	15.5%	18,930
Overall	17,656	24.4%	321,579,092	28.0%	18,214
			FIVE-YEAR-OLDS		
Females	4,471	6.2%	67,981,354	5.9%	15,205
Males	6,336	8.7%	108,638,440	9.5%	17,146
Overall	10,808	14.9%	176,633,789	15.4%	16,343
			SIX-YEAR-OLDS AND UP		
Females	3,601	5.0%	37,074,523	3.2%	10,296
Males	9,096	12.5%	111,976,056	9.7%	12,310
Overall	12,697	17.5%	149,050,579	13.0%	11,739
			TOTALS		
Females	**31,847**	**43.9%**	**$485,168,492**	**42.2%**	**$15,234**
Males	**40,632**	**56.1%**	**$663,761,495**	**57.8%**	**$16,336**
Overall	**72,487**	**100.0%**	**$1,149,003,138**	**100.0%**	**$15,851**

Table 6
Distribution of Races by Class for 2005

	No. of Races	Percent of Races	No. of Starts	Average Starters	Purses	Percent of Purses	Avg. Purse per Race
MAIDEN CLAIMING	9,934	17.3%	86,442	8.7	$ 109,710,197	9.5%	$ 11,044
CLAIMING	27,859	48.6%	226,182	8.1	316,458,692	27.5%	11,359
$0 to 999	0	0.0%	0	0.0	0	0.0%	0
$1,000 to 1,999	131	0.2%	883	6.7	263,557	0.0%	2,012
$2,000 to 2,999	1,134	2.0%	8,885	7.8	4,444,993	0.4%	3,920
$3,000 to 3,999	3,010	5.3%	25,802	8.6	17,418,190	1.5%	5,787
$4,000 to 4,999	3,684	6.4%	30,928	8.4	25,883,572	2.3%	7,026
$5,000 to 5,999	5,885	10.3%	50,630	8.6	52,526,246	4.6%	8,925
$6,000 to 6,999	1,141	2.0%	8,968	7.9	11,513,037	1.0%	10,090
$7,000 to 7,999	1,999	3.5%	16,614	8.3	18,457,721	1.6%	9,233
$8,000 to 8,999	884	1.5%	6,744	7.6	8,774,877	0.8%	9,926
$9,000 to 9,999	27	0.0%	194	7.2	153,203	0.0%	5,674
$10,000 to 14,999	4,153	7.2%	32,522	7.8	54,121,659	4.7%	13,032
$15,000 to 19,999	2,191	3.8%	16,923	7.7	33,386,843	2.9%	15,238
$20,000 and up	3,620	6.3%	27,089	7.5	89,514,794	7.8%	24,728
TOTAL CLAIMING	**37,793**	**66.0%**	**312,624**	**8.3**	**$ 426,168,889**	**37.1%**	**$ 11,276**
Optional claiming	2,436	4.3%	17,412	7.1	77,897,201	6.8%	31,978
Starter allowance	1,289	2.2%	9,736	7.6	20,043,555	1.7%	15,550
Starter handicap	106	0.2%	783	7.4	2,068,513	0.2%	19,514
Maiden	6,365	11.1%	55,058	8.7	160,415,757	14.0%	25,203
Allowance	6,620	11.6%	51,651	7.8	181,771,563	15.8%	27,458
Handicap	68	0.1%	448	6.6	1,637,073	0.1%	24,075
Stakes	2,628	4.6%	20,453	7.8	279,000,587	24.3%	106,165
TOTAL NON-CLAIMING	**19,512**	**34.0%**	**155,541**	**8.0**	**$ 722,834,249**	**62.9%**	**$ 37,046**
TOTAL ALL RACES	**57,305**	**100.0%**	**468,165**	**8.2**	**$1,149,003,138**	**100.0%**	**$ 20,051**

three races. Of the 57,305 races, 37,793, or 66%, were for claimers, including maiden claiming, which alone accounted for 17.3% of all races. Straight claiming races accounted for almost half—48.6%—of all races. Claiming races, however, offer below-average purses.

The $37,046 average non-claiming purse in 2005 was almost 3.3 times larger than the $11,276 average claiming purse. Allowance races were the second-most common race type in 2005, with about one in every eight or nine races.

The third-most common race was straight maiden races, representing 11.1% of all races. In 2005, stakes races featured an average purse of $106,165, distributing 24.3% of all purses while accounting for just 4.6% of all races. The average stakes purse declined 2.8% from 2004, from $109,235.

Table 7 presents the distribution of purses in North America in 2005 by value. In 2005, just 79 races, 0.1% of the total, offered a purse of $500,000 or more. Another 819 races, 1.4% of the total, offered purses of $100,000 to $499,999. Those 898 races distributed $197,609,362, 17.2% of all money.

At the other end of the purse spectrum, 2,016 races, 3.5% of the total, offered a purse of less than $4,000, and just 0.5% of all purses. In 2005, 39.2% of all races had a purse under $10,000.

Table 8 reports the average number of starts

Table 7
Distribution of all North American Races by Purse for 2005

Range of Purses	No. of Races	Total Purses
$499 or less	3	$ 0
$500-999	0	0
$1,000-1,999	514	858,553
$2,000-2,999	722	1,813,203
$3,000-3,999	777	2,652,594
$4,000-4,999	3,218	14,345,180
$5,000-5,999	2,828	15,367,292
$6,000-6,999	3,783	24,104,847
$7,000-7,999	3,762	27,940,119
$8,000-8,999	3,574	29,950,391
$9,000-9,999	3,273	30,847,611
$10,000-12,499	6,691	73,730,701
$12,500-14,999	4,488	61,112,129
$15,000-19,999	6,923	118,037,772
$20,000-24,999	4,125	91,594,466
$25,000-29,999	3,517	94,229,596
$30,000-39,999	2,878	97,779,697
$40,000-49,999	3,264	143,240,944
$50,000-74,999	1,776	99,864,668
$75,000-99,999	291	23,924,013
$100,000-199,999	611	75,369,276
$200,000-299,999	138	32,168,339
$300,000-399,999	45	14,191,236
$400,000-499,999	25	10,656,176
$500,000-749,999	35	17,841,300
$750,000-999,999	25	19,750,475
$1,000,000 and up	19	27,632,560
Totals	**57,305**	**$1,149,003,138**

Table 8

Average Field Size and Number of Starts

Year	Avg Number of Starts	Avg Field Size	Year	Avg Number of Starts	Avg Field Size
2005	6.5	8.2	1995	7.7	8.2
2004	6.6	8.3	1994	7.8	8.3
2003	6.6	8.3	1993	7.9	8.6
2002	6.8	8.3	1992	7.9	8.6
2001	7.0	8.2	1991	7.9	8.7
2000	7.1	8.1	1990	7.9	8.9
1999	7.2	8.2	1989	8.0	8.8
1998	7.6	8.5	1988	8.0	9.1
1997	7.6	8.2	1987	8.1	9.0
1996	7.6	8.3	1986	8.2	9.1

per horse and average field size since 1987. In 1972, the first year of this study, horses started an average of 10.1 times.

As discussed earlier, earnings are related to the number of starts, and, with the average number of starts dropping, opportunities to win money decline. The decline in starts comes at the same time that average field size is declining. With fewer starters per race, it should be easier to get a horse into the starting gate, but average field size also has been in a slow decline for several decades. In 2005, average field size was 8.2, well below the 9.1 average number of starters per race in 1988.

Table 9 examines purses as a function of distance (excluding two-year-old races, which are primarily sprints for much of the year). As shown in the table, average purse rises as races are run at longer distances. The mile mark seems to be the dividing line. Average purse for races at distances of less than a mile—except for seven furlongs—are all less than the overall $19,311 average purse (excluding two-year-old racing) in 2005. Races at seven furlongs, 5.4% of all races run, offered higher-than-average purses of $23,068.

Races at a mile or longer generally featured above-average purses. Races at a flat mile offered an average purse of $19,445, almost exactly the overall average. At all other distance categories of more than a mile—except for the distances of one mile and 40 yards and one mile and 70 yards—the average purse was greater than the overall average. The 34,062 races at less than a mile offered an average purse of $15,498; the average purse for the 10,816 races at more than a mile was $31,218, a fraction more than twice as much. While 64.4% of all races were contested at less than a mile, those races distributed just 51.7% of all purses. Most common race was six furlongs, with 29.2% of all races being run at that distance. The 15,455 six-furlong races distributed 24.3% of all purses, with a below-average pot of $16,045.

In summary, making a lot of money owning racehorses is a tough proposition. Relatively few runners in any given year earn a substantial amount of money, and that was again the case in 2005. For those owners lucky enough to get horses in the top 2% or so of earners, the rewards were good. Owners that campaign average earners, however, very likely should be in racing for the fun of ownership and getting into the winner's circle while they continue their pursuit of the horse with substantial earnings potential. The data from 2005 indicate that purses today are not keeping up with inflation despite generous subsidies from alternative forms of gaming.

Mark Simon is president and editor of THOROUGHBRED TIMES.

Table 9

Distribution of Races and Purses by Distance for 2005

(All two-year-old races omitted)

Distance	Number of Races	Percent of Races	Purses	Percent of Purses	Avg. Purse per Race
Less than 5 furlongs	2,517	4.8%	$ 24,310,138	2.4%	$ 9,658
5 furlongs	2,669	5.0%	38,467,114	3.8%	14,413
Between 5 and 6 furlongs	5,887	11.1%	68,981,057	6.7%	11,718
6 furlongs	15,455	29.2%	247,971,047	24.3%	16,045
Between 6 and 7 furlongs	4,108	7.8%	72,120,154	7.1%	17,556
7 furlongs	2,844	5.4%	65,604,903	6.4%	23,068
Between 7 and 8 furlongs	582	1.1%	10,452,945	1.0%	17,960
1 mile	8,065	15.2%	156,826,578	15.3%	19,445
1 mile 40 yds.	55	0.1%	764,182	0.1%	13,894
1 mile 70 yds.	3,400	6.4%	45,680,297	4.5%	13,435
1$\frac{1}{16}$ miles	5,545	10.5%	152,852,408	15.0%	27,566
1$\frac{1}{8}$ miles	1,407	2.7%	83,646,924	8.2%	59,451
1$\frac{3}{16}$ miles	51	0.1%	6,008,222	0.6%	117,808
1$\frac{1}{4}$ miles	140	0.3%	29,432,305	2.9%	210,231
1$\frac{5}{16}$–1$\frac{3}{8}$ miles	87	0.2%	6,257,921	0.6%	71,930
1$\frac{7}{16}$ miles	1	0.0%	32,000	0.0%	32,000
1$\frac{1}{2}$ miles	87	0.2%	11,722,776	1.1%	134,745
More than 1$\frac{1}{2}$ miles	43	0.1%	1,251,590	0.1%	29,107
Totals	**52,943**	**100.0%**	**$1,022,382,561**	**100.0%**	**$ 19,311**

Purse Distribution by Track in 2005

Northeast

Track, State	Average Daily Racing Days	Average Purse Distribution (Change from Previous Year)		Average Purse	Average Stakes Purses (% Total Purse)	
Aqueduct, N.Y.	121	$365,708	(–1%)	$40,935	$116,196	(19%)
Atlantic City Race Course, N.J.	4	145,200	(–4%)	20,743	0	(0%)
Belmont Park, N.Y.	97	548,901	(0%)	60,162	198,033	(42%)
Finger Lakes, N.Y.	160	107,550	(2%)	12,067	79,568	(8%)
Meadowlands, N.J.	27	309,056	(–9%)	34,625	85,056	(30%)
Monmouth Park, N.J.	90	355,182	(2%)	36,955	105,079	(27%)
Northampton Fair, Ma.	7	24,793	(–1%)	3,275	14,950	(9%)
Saratoga Race Course, N.Y.	36	645,738	(2%)	67,774	211,107	(44%)
Suffolk Downs, Ma.	117	100,081	(–9%)	10,713	41,216	(6%)

Mid-Atlantic

Track, State	Average Daily Racing Days	Average Purse Distribution (Change from Previous Year)		Average Purse	Average Stakes Purses (% Total Purse)	
Charles Town Races, W.V.	243	$166,355	(–26%)	$16,921	$ 69,022	(5%)
Colonial Downs, Va.	41	212,661	(7%)	23,629	137,178	(28%)
Delaware Park, De.	138	269,165	(6%)	30,597	125,751	(17%)
Laurel Park, Md.	134	194,425	(17%)	21,949	89,964	(19%)
Mountaineer Race Track, W.V.	216	151,642	(–12%)	15,725	113,325	(8%)
Penn National Race Course, Pa.	189	78,818	(6%)	9,028	44,400	(2%)
Philadelphia Park, Pa.	210	154,195	(10%)	16,054	107,696	(8%)
Pimlico Race Course, Md.	61	233,069	(18%)	25,756	131,963	(28%)
Timonium, Md.	8	129,057	(–2%)	13,409	50,000	(10%)

Southeast

Track, State	Average Daily Racing Days	Average Purse Distribution (Change from Previous Year)		Average Purse	Average Stakes Purses (% Total Purse)	
Calder Race Course, Fl.	175	$226,638	(–1%)	$21,579	$ 87,299	(29%)
Gulfstream Park, Fl.	86	297,089	(–1%)	29,537	180,638	(33%)
Ocala Training Center, Fl.	1	377,000	(–1%)	62,833	62,833	(100%)
Tampa Bay Downs, Fl.	95	147,132	(9%)	13,730	71,195	(17%)

Midwest

Track, State	Average Daily Racing Days	Average Purse Distribution (Change from Previous Year)		Average Purse	Average Stakes Purses (% Total Purse)	
Anthony Downs, Ks.	6	$ 11,042	(–15%)	$ 3,487	$ 6,650	(60%)
Arlington Park, Il.	94	257,187	(–6%)	27,598	127,237	(27%)
Beulah Park, Oh.	130	47,787	(9%)	6,096	43,667	(11%)
Brown County Fair, S.D.	1	2,050		2,050	0	(0%)
Canterbury Park, Mn.	68	132,362	(7%)	15,386	53,192	(24%)
Chippewa Downs, N.D.	6	8,175	(–5%)	1,582	2,650	(11%)
Churchill Downs, Ky.	73	482,415	(–10%)	47,270	218,647	(35%)
Columbus Races, Ne.	24	49,486	(11%)	5,737	11,941	(11%)
Ellis Park, Ky.	41	142,864	(–13%)	14,356	78,700	(13%)
Eureka Downs, Ks.	20	5,639	(–1%)	2,088	0	(0%)
Fairmount Park, Il.	102	64,077	(0%)	6,880	41,259	(6%)
Fonner Park, Ne.	38	58,775	(–2%)	6,102	26,907	(18%)
Fort Pierre, S.D.	1	2,350		2,350	0	(0%)
Great Lakes Downs, Mi.	100	103,264	(28%)	11,224	69,063	(19%)
Hawthorne Race Course, Il.	125	215,742	(1%)	23,573	130,869	(17%)
Hoosier Park, In.	59	152,292	(10%)	13,802	100,033	(17%)
Horsemen's Atokad Downs, Ne.	3	70,264	(–2%)	11,711	0	(0%)
Horsemen's Park, Ne.	4	127,706	(–1%)	31,927	43,033	(51%)
Indiana Downs, In.	47	89,643	(5%)	9,960	40,514	(7%)
Keeneland Race Course, Ky.	33	626,178	(2%)	67,529	249,975	(46%)
Kentucky Downs, Ky.	5	225,000	(–1%)	32,143	98,000	(44%)
Lincoln State Fair, Ne.	37	54,514	(12%)	6,206	16,056	(10%)
Mt. Pleasant Meadows, Mi.	29	5,502	(35%)	3,626	0	(0%)
North Dakota Horse Park, N.D.	15	17,132	(–7%)	3,569	14,201	(33%)
Prairie Meadows Racetrack, Ia.	95	137,965	(2%)	18,538	78,554	(23%)
River Downs, Oh.	119	57,013	(5%)	7,683	58,167	(13%)
Thistledown, Oh.	184	62,637	(–6%)	8,705	61,750	(11%)
Turfway Park, Ky.	107	144,995	(–7%)	14,664	92,708	(18%)
Woodlands, Ks.	26	42,956	(–1%)	6,205	20,333	(22%)

Southwest

Track, State	Average Daily Racing Days	Average Purse Distribution (Change from Previous Year)		Average Purse	Average Stakes Purses (% Total Purse)	
Blue Ribbon Downs, Ok.	53	$ 12,487	(61%)	$ 4,270	$ 9,988	(9%)
Delta Downs, La.	53	172,616	(–13%)	17,262	73,106	(21%)
Downs at Albuquerque, N.M.	59	44,940	(–8%)	9,931	38,494	(33%)
Evangeline Downs, La.	100	179,298	(48%)	18,002	62,500	(7%)
Fair Grounds, La.	36	238,932	(–5%)	23,566	0	(0%)
Fair Meadows at Tulsa, Ok.	31	46,036	(–28%)	9,775	35,294	(10%)

Track, State	Average Daily Racing Days	Average Purse Distribution (Change from Previous Year)	Average Purse	Average Stakes Purses (% Total Purse)
Gillespie County Fairgrounds, Tx.	8	$ 15,412 (10%)	$ 5,138	$ 0 (0%)
Lone Star Park, Tx.	67	213,845 (8%)	21,808	107,051 (28%)
Louisiana Downs, La.	141	241,596 (31%)	23,316	32,472 (20%)
Manor Downs, Tx.	13	20,831 (29%)	5,887	19,000 (14%)
Oaklawn Park, Ar.	55	253,095 (6%)	24,858	155,093 (30%)
Remington Park, Ok.	66	100,280 (21%)	10,958	50,772 (20%)
Retama Park, Tx.	43	92,924 (2%)	10,799	61,828 (25%)
Ruidoso Downs, N.M.	56	45,480 (0%)	9,684	37,224 (31%)
Sam Houston Race Park, Tx.	82	102,157 (–3%)	10,865	60,033 (21%)
Sunland Park, N.M.	67	167,608 (8%)	22,459	113,467 (29%)
SunRay Park, N.M.	38	49,439 (–6%)	11,183	55,265 (26%)
Zia Park, N.M.	42	135,377	22,297	78,144 (34%)

West Coast

Track, State	Average Daily Racing Days	Average Purse Distribution (Change from Previous Year)	Average Purse	Average Stakes Purses (% Total Purse)
Apache County Fair, Az.	4	$ 10,211 (–2%)	$ 1,776	$ 0 (0%)
Arapahoe Park, Co.	37	53,914 (1%)	7,885	30,653 (26%)
Bay Meadows Fair, Ca.	12	129,505 (9%)	15,698	0 (0%)
Bay Meadows Race Course, Ca.	109	165,458 (2%)	19,582	84,131 (12%)
Cochise County Fair, Az.	4	8,078 (5%)	1,795	2,447 (15%)
Cow Capital Turf Club, Mt.	2	6,800 (6%)	2,720	4,600 (34%)
Crooked River Roundup, Or.	4	15,575 (–8%)	2,709	3,900 (6%)
Del Mar, Ca.	43	514,064 (5%)	59,582	185,039 (35%)
Eastern Oregon Livestock Show, Or.	3	13,217 (7%)	2,332	3,500 (9%)
Elko County Fair, Nv.	6	20,532 (18%)	4,106	19,575 (32%)
Emerald Downs, Wa.	101	107,941 (14%)	11,786	50,652 (21%)
Fairplex Park, Ca.	16	269,035 (7%)	26,247	72,102 (28%)
Ferndale, Ca.	10	24,182 (30%)	5,758	9,063 (19%)
Flagstaff, Az.	4	25,086 (–9%)	4,363	0 (0%)
Fresno, Ca.	11	58,632 (3%)	10,402	52,300 (16%)
Gila County Fair, Az.	4	10,142 (5%)	1,764	0 (0%)
Golden Gate Fields, Ca.	98	170,602 (7%)	20,265	77,468 (12%)
Graham County Fair, Az.	4	5,797 (–39%)	1,784	2,133 (37%)
Grants Pass, Or.	16	14,251 (–5%)	2,000	3,831 (8%)
Great Falls, Mt.	10	13,070 (–3%)	2,143	6,900 (16%)
Greenlee County Fair, Az.	4	10,098 (–7%)	1,923	2,931 (29%)
Hastings Race Course, B.C.	82	145,515 (–18%)	15,742	56,366 (24%)
Hollywood Park, Ca.	91	399,881 (3%)	46,713	166,329 (33%)
Kalispell, Mt.	5	11,290 (24%)	2,171	3,062 (22%)
Les Bois Park, Id.	3	62,500 (219%)	6,944	15,278 (73%)
Los Alamitos Race Course, Ca.	188	13,569 (3%)	6,591	0 (0%)
Mohave County Fair, Az.	4	8,339 (–1%)	1,962	2,414 (14%)
Oak Tree at Santa Anita, Ca.	31	405,436	47,073	153,008 (40%)
Pleasanton, Ca.	11	145,705 (1%)	16,871	51,220 (16%)
Portland Meadows, Or.	71	30,391 (3%)	3,909	11,852 (15%)
Rillito Park, Az.	13	11,609 (5%)	1,986	3,667 (2%)
Santa Anita Park, Ca.	85	436,057 (0%)	50,843	182,938 (36%)
Santa Cruz County Fair, Az.	4	9,171 (9%)	1,931	2,894 (32%)
Santa Rosa, Ca.	12	144,107 (4%)	17,293	69,250 (16%)
Solano County Fair, Ca.	11	123,761 (1%)	14,483	52,683 (12%)
Stockton, Ca.	10	82,552 (2%)	10,721	0 (0%)
Sun Downs, Wa.	10	9,922 (20%)	1,682	2,300 (2%)
Tillamook County Fair, Or.	3	14,382 (2%)	2,157	3,637 (8%)
Turf Paradise, Az.	167	76,227 (3%)	8,877	33,707 (27%)
Walla Walla, Wa.	5	7,805 (125%)	1,774	2,262 (12%)
Western Montana Fair and Races, Mt.	6	17,582 (–9%)	2,776	4,481 (30%)
Wyoming Downs, Wy.	14	4,821 (29%)	1,824	4,507 (47%)
Yavapai Downs, Az.	55	33,282 (10%)	5,186	16,612 (16%)
Yellowstone Downs, Mt.	11	10,459 (–14%)	2,212	3,600 (3%)

Canada

Track, Province	Average Daily Racing Days	Average Purse Distribution (Change from Previous Year)	Average Purse	Average Stakes Purses (% Total Purse)
Assiniboia Downs, Mb.	75	$ 61,374 (–20%)	$ 7,802	$ 34,390 (22%)
Fort Erie, On.	104	103,046 (–46%)	11,281	76,109 (11%)
Grand Prairie, Ab.	21	11,607 (0%)	3,125	4,915 (26%)
Kamloops, B.C.	6	13,786 (75%)	3,760	10,457 (13%)
Kin Park, B.C.	2	23,090 (61%)	4,198	8,170 (18%)
Lethbridge, Ab.	27	16,906 (–34%)	6,521	10,975 (67%)
Marquis Downs, Sk.	29	21,933 (0%)	3,014	7,124 (24%)
Millarville Race Society, Ab.	1	76,378 (601%)	10,911	20,126 (53%)
Northlands Park, Ab.	72	104,457 (–18%)	12,269	52,896 (25%)
Stampede Park, Ab.	45	93,157 (–19%)	10,945	44,545 (14%)
Sunflower Downs, B.C.	1	31,756	4,537	8,141 (26%)
Woodbine, On.	164	430,916 (–13%)	46,616	177,540 (28%)
Yorkton Exhibition, Sk.	6	4,122 (–3%)	1,124	2,042 (17%)

Racing Enters the Racino Era

Racino is a highly descriptive new word, created by combining a racetrack with a casino. The concept also is relatively new, dating from the 1990s. Initially, the racino concept—which essentially puts video lottery terminals or slot machines into racetracks or free-standing facilities at racetracks—rescued three racing operations, Mountaineer Race Track in West Virginia, Prairie Meadows Racetrack in Iowa, and historic Delaware Park. Gaming machines have spread from those three locations to Louisiana, New Mexico, New York, and Oklahoma. By the end of 2007, electronic gaming may be in operation in Pennsylvania and Florida. In some cases, the gaming machines have saved racetracks from possible closure. In other jurisdictions, the machines have transformed marginal tracks into highly profitable businesses paying race purses near or above the North American average.

Governmental bodies such as state legislatures have passed electronic-gaming legislation over the opposition of antigambling organizations, and politicians have been willing to risk the wrath of these groups because slots and VLTs represent a tax upon the willing—that is, those individuals who go to the track or some other site to play the slots. Like the state's cut from lotteries, casino taxes tend to be high. Until the 1980s, horse racing represented a tax on the willing horseplayer who went to the track despite takeouts that included a hefty state tax. As horse racing began to be marginalized as a major sport and wagering handle stagnated or declined in the 1980s and '90s, states were forced to cut taxes on horse-racing wagers sharply.

Like most revolutions in the horse-racing industry, the era of racinos began with little notice and far from the recognized centers of the sport. The racino revolution began on June 8, 1990, at Mountaineer in Chester, West Virginia. Mountaineer, which was known as Waterford Park from its founding in 1951 until '87, certainly needed help. It paid very low purses, and its horses occupied racing's bottom rung. The West Virginia lottery, which began operation in 1986, put 160 voucher-spitting video lottery terminals at Mountaineer to help the track and to help itself. A dispute over the machines went to the state Supreme Court, which ruled that the video lottery terminals had to be authorized by the Legislature or shut down. With no interruption in play, the Legislature approved video lottery terminals in 1994, local voters endorsed the machines, and the newly legitimate VLTs began operating on May 10, 1994. Mountaineer changed its name to Mountaineer Race Track and Gaming Resort in 2001.

The state's other Thoroughbred track, Charles Town Races, was purchased in 1996 by Penn National Gaming Inc. after voters in the county in which the track is located approved machine gaming. While successful from the start, Mountaineer and Charles Town received a significant boost when the state Legislature authorized the tracks to install coin-drop video lottery terminals in fall 1999. Like tracks elsewhere, purses have increased tremendously in the years since the machines were installed, but both tracks have experienced declines in later years.

The second significant launch of video lottery terminals occurred on April 1, 1995, when the first slot machines began operation at Prairie Meadows Racetrack in Altoona, Iowa. Prairie Meadows had struggled from its first days in 1989. Even full-card simulcasting could not save the track from a bankruptcy filing in 1991, and the facility closed its doors on September 2, 1991. Because Polk County, which includes the track, had underwritten the $40-million in bonds to build the track, the county ended up owning the track in 1993, and racing resumed that May. Acting on a positive recommendation of a gambling task force, the Legislature and local voters authorized slot machines at the state's horse and dog tracks in 1994, and the machines began spewing revenues. The total play for 1995 totaled nearly $1-billion.

From the start, however, the county and horsemen were locked in a battle over who should get the lion's share of the slots revenue. The horsemen thought that they should; the county and several prominent citizens argued for minimal contribution to purses and maximum contribution to local government and civic projects. The issue has never been completely resolved, although the balance of power has tilted toward the property owner, Polk County. While Prairie Meadows's purses climbed toward the North American per-race average for several years, a new contract between the county and the track's operator in 2002 resulted in a purse cut beginning in '03. Purses fell further in 2004. This pattern—an initial sharp increase in purses followed by, for a number of reasons, stagnant or declining purses—has been repeated elsewhere.

Delaware Park followed a pattern similar to Prairie Meadows. Built in the later years of the Great Depression by William duPont Jr. and associates, the track near Wilmington opened in June 1937 and for many years was a magnet for racing fans in the Philadelphia area. In the 1970s and '80s, new competitors arose, and the Maryland tracks—which had used Delaware as a summer base—began racing year-round. In 1982, the track closed and was dormant until William

Rickman Sr. bought it in late '83. The track reopened in 1984 and survived on creative management and fan loyalty for the next decade. Full-card simulcasting helped, but Delaware Park turned the corner with passage of the Horse Racing Redevelopment Act in June 1994. Delaware Park's slot machines began operation on December 29, 1995. To be sure, the racetrack and its purses received a generous portion of the slots revenue, but most money went to the state. In 2005, the state's share from Delaware Park and two Standardbred tracks was $199-million, or 7.1% of state revenue.

With the slots money, Delaware Park was able to rebuild its purse structure and its stakes program, and its purses are now well above the North American average. The track also has encountered changes in the purse payouts as events unrelated to the racetrack have affected slots play. For instance, after the state of Delaware banned smoking in public places in late 2002, slots play declined for a while, and as a result purses declined in '03, although they rose again in '04.

In the mid-1990s, New Mexico's racetracks were on the ropes. But the tracks and horsemen lobbied for slots, won approval for them, and entered the racino age in February 1999 at Sunland Park, which is just across the Texas border from El Paso. The state's other tracks followed suit, and all have experienced sizable increases in purses. The casino boom proved so alluring that a new track, Zia Park, was built in Hobbs. Its casino began operation in November 2004, and racing at the $54-million facility began in 2005.

Riverboat gambling began in Louisiana in 1993, video poker machines were added to the gambling mix in '98, and land-based casinos opened in '99. Slot machines arrived at the racetrack on February 13, 2002, in sleepy Vinton, not far from the Texas border at Delta Downs. By the time the first slot machines were played, gambling interests had readily identified the value of such a franchise. Las Vegas speculator Shawn Scott bought the track for $10-million in 1999; Boyd Gaming Corp. bought it for a reported $125-million two years later. Louisiana Gaming Control Board reports make clear why the price went through the roof. By the end of 2002, Delta's slots had generated $60-million in net win—after the 652,038 slots players had gotten their share—with the state receiving $9.1-million in taxes. Purses and breeders' funds received $10.8-million.

Louisiana Downs, purchased by Harrah's Inc., opened its slots operation on May 21, 2003, and Evangeline Downs, relocated to St. Landry Parish after local voters rejected slots at its former site, began casino operations on December 19, 2003. Fair Grounds most likely will trade its video-poker machines for slots in late 2006. Without question, Louisiana's purses have benefited greatly from slots. At Delta, purses increased from an average of $8,783 for its 2001-'02 meet to $19,675 per race for the 2003-'04 season. End-of-year figures indicate how profitable the machines are. In all, 3.2-million slots players went to Louisiana track facilities in 2004, and the net win was $142.9-million. After deductions for purses, breeders' funds, and community grants, the net taxable total was $117.1-million. Louisiana's tax was $21.7-million at 18.5%.

Slot machines also were installed in Ontario's two Thoroughbred tracks, at Fort Erie in 1999 and Woodbine in 2000, with positive results initially. However, reduced play on the machines resulted in lower purses at both tracks in 2004 and '05. Canada was not the only location with a mixed picture from the slot machines. Although New York approved video lottery terminals at racetracks in the wake of the September 11, 2001, terrorist attack on the World Trade Center's twin towers, the first slots operation did not open until January 2003 at Saratoga Raceway, a Standardbred track, and Finger Lakes became the first Thoroughbred track in New York with VLTs on February 18, 2004. A proposed VLT operation at Aqueduct, which was expected to do a sizable volume, was repeatedly delayed but finally appeared to be moving forward in 2006.

Video lottery terminals were authorized in both Pennsylvania and Oklahoma in 2004, and Oklahoma began operations in '05. In a 2005 referendum, voters in Broward County, Florida, authorized video lottery terminals at Gulfstream Park, but enabling legislation and tax issues delayed the debut of machines at Gulfstream.

—Don Clippinger

Racinos and Daily Purses, 1998-2005

Delaware

Delaware Park

Year	Types of Gaming	Racing Days	Avg. Daily Purse Distribution	Avg. Purse Change
2005	Pari-Mutuel, Slot Machines	138	$269,165	(6%)
2004	Pari-Mutuel, Slot Machines	134	253,345	(8%)
2003	Pari-Mutuel, Slot Machines	141	233,813	(–20%)
2002	Pari-Mutuel, Slot Machines	141	291,204	(14%)
2001	Pari-Mutuel, Slot Machines	139	255,018	(4%)
2000	Pari-Mutuel, Slot Machines	149	245,466	(5%)
1999	Pari-Mutuel, Slot Machines	143	234,071	(19%)
1998	Pari-Mutuel, Slot Machines	140	195,935	(11%)

Iowa

Prairie Meadows Racetrack

Year	Types of Gaming	Racing Days	Avg. Daily Purse Distribution	Avg. Purse Change
2005	Pari-Mutuel, Slot Machines	95	$137,965	(2%)
2004	Pari-Mutuel, Slot Machines	96	135,639	(–4%)
2003	Pari-Mutuel, Slot Machines	100	141,619	(–15%)
2002	Pari-Mutuel, Slot Machines	98	166,172	(4%)
2001	Pari-Mutuel, Slot Machines	97	160,447	(10%)
2000	Pari-Mutuel, Slot Machines	98	146,500	(17%)
1999	Pari-Mutuel, Slot Machines	98	125,414	(11%)
1998	Pari-Mutuel, Slot Machines	97	112,499	(19%)

Louisiana

Delta Downs

Year	Types of Gaming	Racing Days	Avg. Daily Purse Distribution	Avg. Purse Change
2005	Pari-Mutuel, Slot Machines	53	$172,616	(–13%)
2004	Pari-Mutuel, Slot Machines	99	197,760	(0%)
2003	Pari-Mutuel, Slot Machines	82	196,899	(85%)
2002	Pari-Mutuel, Slot Machines	88	106,421	(115%)
2001	Pari-Mutuel	85	49,404	(–4%)
2000	Pari-Mutuel	52	51,200	(32%)
1999	Pari-Mutuel	50	38,860	(16%)
1998	Pari-Mutuel	50	33,642	(–2%)

Evangeline Downs

Year	Types of Gaming	Racing Days	Avg. Daily Purse Distribution	Avg. Purse Change
2005	Pari-Mutuel, Slot Machines	100	$179,298	(48%)
2004	Pari-Mutuel, Slot Machines	92	121,317	(67%)
2003	Pari-Mutuel	87	72,805	(–8%)
2002	Pari-Mutuel	82	79,104	(4%)
2001	Pari-Mutuel	82	75,848	(–4%)
2000	Pari-Mutuel	82	78,779	(–1%)
1999	Pari-Mutuel	82	79,840	(3%)
1998	Pari-Mutuel	82	77,489	(23%)

Fair Grounds

Year	Types of Gaming	Racing Days	Avg. Daily Purse Distribution	Avg. Purse Change
2005	Pari-Mutuel, Video Poker	36	$238,932	(–5%)
2004	Pari-Mutuel, Video Poker	82	251,513	(–2%)
2003	Pari-Mutuel, Video Poker	83	256,249	(–4%)
2002	Pari-Mutuel, Video Poker	80	265,740	(–2%)
2001	Pari-Mutuel, Video Poker	89	271,595	(2%)
2000	Pari-Mutuel, Video Poker	90	266,958	(–2%)
1999	Pari-Mutuel, Video Poker	89	273,763	(15%)
1998	Pari-Mutuel, Video Poker	88	238,166	(14%)

Louisiana Downs

Year	Types of Gaming	Racing Days	Avg. Daily Purse Distribution	Avg. Purse Change
2005	Pari-Mutuel, Slot Machines	141	$241,596	(31%)
2004	Pari-Mutuel, Slot Machines	102	183,924	(2%)
2003	Pari-Mutuel, Slot Machines	80	180,934	(14%)
2002	Pari-Mutuel	80	158,176	(27%)
2001	Pari-Mutuel	89	124,801	(–15%)
2000	Pari-Mutuel	83	146,226	(2%)
1999	Pari-Mutuel	82	143,137	(5%)
1998	Pari-Mutuel	86	136,463	(–3%)

New Mexico

Ruidoso Downs

Year	Types of Gaming	Racing Days	Avg. Daily Purse Distribution	Avg. Purse Change
2005	Pari-Mutuel, Slot Machines	56	$45,480	(0%)
2004	Pari-Mutuel, Slot Machines	57	45,582	(–16%)
2003	Pari-Mutuel, Slot Machines	57	54,420	(25%)
2002	Pari-Mutuel, Slot Machines	57	43,458	(4%)
2001	Pari-Mutuel, Slot Machines	57	41,615	(7%)
2000	Pari-Mutuel, Slot Machines	57	38,890	(34%)
1999	Pari-Mutuel, Slot Machines	57	28,995	(27%)
1998	Pari-Mutuel	46	22,861	(41%)

Sunland Park

Year	Types of Gaming	Racing Days	Avg. Daily Purse Distribution	Avg. Purse Change
2005	Pari-Mutuel, Slot Machines	67	$167,608	(8%)
2004	Pari-Mutuel, Slot Machines	92	155,473	(–5%)
2003	Pari-Mutuel, Slot Machines	75	162,876	(59%)
2002	Pari-Mutuel, Slot Machines	78	102,135	(31%)
2001	Pari-Mutuel, Slot Machines	79	78,144	(28%)
2000	Pari-Mutuel, Slot Machines	86	60,852	(116%)
1999	Pari-Mutuel, Slot Machines	87	28,211	(37%)
1998	Pari-Mutuel	59	20,556	(16%)

SunRay Park

Year	Types of Gaming	Racing Days	Avg. Daily Purse Distribution	Avg. Purse Change
2005	Pari-Mutuel, Slot Machines	38	$49,439	(–6%)
2004	Pari-Mutuel, Slot Machines	44	52,611	(–28%)
2003	Pari-Mutuel, Slot Machines	40	73,074	(–5%)
2002	Pari-Mutuel, Slot Machines	35	76,840	(65%)
2001	Pari-Mutuel, Slot Machines	46	46,621	(14%)
2000	Pari-Mutuel, Slot Machines	41	41,063	(26%)
1999	Pari-Mutuel, Slot Machines	28	32,509	

The Downs at Albuquerque

Year	Types of Gaming	Racing Days	Avg. Daily Purse Distribution	Avg. Purse Change
2005	Pari-Mutuel, Slot Machines	59	$44,940	(–8%)
2004	Pari-Mutuel, Slot Machines	69	48,663	(–12%)
2003	Pari-Mutuel, Slot Machines	67	55,118	(–8%)
2002	Pari-Mutuel, Slot Machines	64	59,890	(13%)
2001	Pari-Mutuel, Slot Machines	63	52,892	(17%)
2000	Pari-Mutuel, Slot Machines	69	45,256	(30%)
1999	Pari-Mutuel	54	34,893	(–21%)
1998	Pari-Mutuel	52	44,115	(–9%)

Zia Park

Year	Types of Gaming	Racing Days	Avg. Daily Purse Distribution	Avg. Purse Change
2005	Pari-Mutuel, Slot Machines	42	$135,377	—

New York

Finger Lakes

Year	Types of Gaming	Racing Days	Avg. Daily Purse Distribution	Avg. Purse Change
2005	Pari-Mutuel, Slot Machines	160	$107,550	(2%)
2004	Pari-Mutuel, Slot Machines	157	105,755	(40%)
2003	Pari-Mutuel	154	75,282	(–4%)
2002	Pari-Mutuel	161	78,223	(0%)
2001	Pari-Mutuel	165	78,302	(–3%)
2000	Pari-Mutuel	167	80,655	(1%)
1999	Pari-Mutuel	176	80,048	(1%)
1998	Pari-Mutuel	170	79,128	(21%)

Ontario

Fort Erie

Year	Types of Gaming	Racing Days	Avg. Daily Purse Distribution	Avg. Purse Change
2005	Pari-Mutuel, Slot Machines	104	$103,046	(–46%)
2004	Pari-Mutuel, Slot Machines	81	191,755	(–4%)
2003	Pari-Mutuel, Slot Machines	114	200,504	(1%)
2002	Pari-Mutuel, Slot Machines	116	197,936	(16%)
2001	Pari-Mutuel, Slot Machines	116	170,310	(52%)
2000	Pari-Mutuel, Slot Machines	107	111,681	(32%)
1999	Pari-Mutuel, Slot Machines	107	84,554	(44%)
1998	Pari-Mutuel	75	58,823	(–8%)

Woodbine

Year	Types of Gaming	Racing Days	Avg. Daily Purse Distribution	Avg. Purse Change
2005	Pari-Mutuel, Slot Machines	164	$430,916	(–13%)
2004	Pari-Mutuel, Slot Machines	167	498,136	(–13%)
2003	Pari-Mutuel, Slot Machines	162	571,514	(2%)
2002	Pari-Mutuel, Slot Machines	166	558,598	(13%)
2001	Pari-Mutuel, Slot Machines	165	494,595	(2%)
2000	Pari-Mutuel, Slot Machines	160	483,979	(53%)
1999	Pari-Mutuel	165	316,586	(27%)
1998	Pari-Mutuel	171	249,594	(17%)

West Virginia

Charles Town Races

Year	Types of Gaming	Racing Days	Avg. Daily Purse Distribution	Avg. Purse Change
2005	Pari-Mutuel, Video Lottery	243	$166,355	(–26%)
2004	Pari-Mutuel, Video Lottery	231	224,692	(52%)
2003	Pari-Mutuel, Video Lottery	235	148,243	(13%)
2002	Pari-Mutuel, Video Lottery	254	131,273	(–8%)
2001	Pari-Mutuel, Video Lottery	233	142,154	(48%)
2000	Pari-Mutuel, Video Lottery	208	96,022	(25%)
1999	Pari-Mutuel, Video Lottery	213	76,933	(81%)
1998	Pari-Mutuel, Video Lottery	206	42,563	(23%)

Mountaineer Race Track

Year	Types of Gaming	Racing Days	Avg. Daily Purse Distribution	Avg. Purse Change
2005	Pari-Mutuel, Video Lottery	216	$151,642	(–12%)
2004	Pari-Mutuel, Video Lottery	219	171,818	(–2%)
2003	Pari-Mutuel, Video Lottery	222	175,244	(5%)
2002	Pari-Mutuel, Video Lottery	230	166,383	(14%)
2001	Pari-Mutuel, Video Lottery	228	145,463	(30%)
2000	Pari-Mutuel, Video Lottery	221	111,797	(32%)
1999	Pari-Mutuel, Video Lottery	211	84,760	(28%)
1998	Pari-Mutuel, Video Lottery	212	66,381	(43%)

YEAR IN REVIEW

2005 in Review: *Jockeys' Guild Turmoil*

Organization Ousts Controversial President Gertmenian after Congressional Hearings into Insurance

Thoroughbred racing has spent millions of dollars attempting to have its voice heard in Washington, D.C., to preserve its gaming and tax advantages. In 2005, the Jockeys' Guild put the industry squarely in front of the United States Congress for an entirely different reason. The focus fell on the management of the Jockeys' Guild and the organization's failure to maintain catastrophic-injury insurance in a pair of congressional hearings with testimony from Guild leaders and industry executives.

At the center of the hearings and the media focus was Guild President Wayne Gertmenian, a Pepperdine University economics professor who, through his Matrix Capital Associates, took over management of the Guild in June 2001. For the next several years, the organization operated confrontationally and with minimal effectiveness within the industry. The Guild's leadership came into question when Gary Birzer was paralyzed in a riding accident in July 2004 at Mountaineer Race Track in West Virginia. The Guild's health insurance did not cover jockeys while they rode—a change Gertmenian had made in 2002 without telling the riders.

When jockeys questioned the lack of coverage, Gertmenian's answer was to blame the tracks. In November 2004, he orchestrated a walkout of jockeys at Churchill Downs in Louisville and Hoosier Park in Anderson, Indiana, to protest the tracks' policy of providing riders with no more than $100,000 in coverage.

The action sparked discussion and some change during the early part of 2005. The National Thoroughbred Racing Association convened a special task force to discuss jockey issues; Kentucky Governor Ernie Fletcher convened a panel to study jockey insurance; and 35 racetracks throughout the U.S. and Canada raised their insurance coverage to at least $500,000. Churchill Downs Inc. and all Kentucky tracks were among a majority that secured $1-million policies for race riders.

Gertmenian's actions would soon draw attention beyond the racing industry. On April 20, the U.S. House of Representatives Energy and Commerce Committee's Subcommittee on Oversight and Investigations sent a letter to the Guild requesting information pertaining to Gertmenian's management style and compensation package, as well as the Guild's financial records.

The congressional investigation lasted six months and culminated in hearings on October 18 and November 17. The first hearing featured testimony of Guild associates, including Gertmenian and Vice President Albert Fiss. A second hearing featured testimony by racetrack executives and representatives of horsemen's groups. Neither Congress nor many Guild members were happy with Gertmenian's answers at the October hearing, which led to a change in Guild management as anti-Gertmenian forces began to mobilize quickly with a petition circulated throughout jockeys' rooms the following week.

Guild Treasurer Jeff Johnston acknowledged on October 28 that such a petition existed but said he had not seen anyone sign it. A week later, however, the Guild Senate announced it would convene a special meeting on November 15 to consider Gertmenian's future with the organization. Gertmenian and Fiss were terminated, and former member representative Darrell Haire became the organization's interim national manager.

At the November congressional hearing, Haire outlined four goals for the new Guild:

- Amend the Interstate Horseracing Act to require that, as a condition of broadcasting a simulcast signal, workers' compensation coverage must be in place for jockeys;
- Amend the Interstate Horseracing Act of 1978 to include jockeys in the provisions that the racing signal cannot be broadcast unless the horsemen have in place agreements to compensate them for their media rights;
- Encourage national health and safety standards for jockeys; and
- Amend the National Labor Relations Act to give jockeys collective bargaining rights.

The subcommittee appeared receptive to mandating that jockeys receive a bigger stake in the overall industry, as Representative Bart Stupak (D-Michigan) told industry leaders that he expects the government to intervene in the business of racing, including amending the Interstate Horseracing Act to give jockeys a larger say in how tracks and horsemen conduct the business of racing.

Haire spent much of his first four weeks in office doing damage control, traveling the country to meet with jockeys and industry representatives in the hopes of saving the Guild, which then faced a $10-million lawsuit filed by Birzer, unpaid bills, and empty coffers.

As much as the Guild would like to put the Gertmenian era behind it, some lingering effects of his management remained as the Guild and its attorneys grappled with several legal issues, including Birzer's lawsuit against the Guild, Gertmenian, and Fiss.

While the Guild was busy with internal affairs throughout much of the year, it was called on twice to provide support for its members as they dealt with the on-track deaths of two riders for the second consecutive year. In 2004, Michael Rowland and Chris Quinn died, and Michel Lapensee and Josh Radosevich died in '05. Radosevich was a 16-year-old apprentice who had won 19 of 92 starts in just 1½ months of riding, and his death prompted the Ohio Racing Commission to consider raising the minimum age for jockeys to 18.

The new Guild administration worked diligently in its first month of management to learn the financial status of its organization, and on December 8 it revealed that Gertmenian inappropriately spent approximately $2.1-million during the final two years of his tenure.

The problem, however, was not only misspent money, but also money not spent. The Guild announced it had a large number of unpaid bills, no investments made since June, and no health claims transactions since July.

Also, on the day he was fired, Gertmenian authorized more than $217,000 in checks made to himself, Matrix Capital, and Fiss. The Guild said those payments were not authorized and was able to stop payment on $104,000 of that total. It also sought repayment of the balance.

The Guild also physically distanced itself from the Gertmenian administration. In early December, it moved its offices from a building controlled by Matrix Capital Associates in Monrovia, California, to a building in nearby Duarte. The move reduced the Guild's rent by more than half from $4,000 a month for the 1,800-square-foot space in Monrovia to $1,700 a month for 2,000 square feet of space in Duarte. When Gertmenian had taken over, he moved the Guild's offices from Kentucky.—*Ed DeRosa*

Other Top Stories of 2005

Turmoil is nothing new in Thoroughbred racing, but in 2005 the industry went through more than a few unusual twists and turns from coast to coast.

In New York, the stream of problems at the New York Racing Association was seemingly endless, with criminal charges filed in two separate cases, one for incorrectly recorded jockey weights and the other for alleged horse doping, while the franchise desperately tried to stay out of bankruptcy. In Florida, Louisiana, and Kentucky, natural disasters affected racetracks owned by Churchill Downs Inc. In California, Hollywood Park, a member of the Churchill conglomerate at the start of the year, faced an uncertain future after being sold to Bay Meadows Land Co.

These and other significant events that took place on the track and in the sales ring were among the leading vote-getters as the top news stories of 2005, according to the editors and staff writers of THOROUGHBRED TIMES. Leading the list as Newsmaker of the Year was the unrest within the Jockeys' Guild, and following are the year's second- through tenth-ranked most important stories.

2. NYRA's ongoing crisis. Even as the New York Racing Association escaped the cloud of its darkest days, uncertainty continued to envelop the beleaguered franchise that runs Aqueduct, Belmont Park, and Saratoga Race Course.

On September 13, a United States District Court Judge dismissed NYRA's deferred indictment, concluding a deferred prosecution deal from 2003 over the organization's role in a tax-evasion scheme by its pari-mutuel clerks. Less than a month later, NYRA President Charles Hayward told an oversight board that the association would attempt to sell famous racing artworks and property near Aqueduct in hopes of raising $20-million to avoid bankruptcy. The New York State Racing and Wagering Board halted the art sale, contending that the state, not NYRA, owned the paintings.

On the year's final business day, NYRA and New York state officials announced a memorandum of agreement that would give the racing association $30-million in short-term financial assistance to forestall a bankruptcy filing. Among the provisions was the sale of the Aqueduct land to the Port Authority of New York and New Jersey, which operates adjacent John F. Kennedy International Airport. NYRA received $1-million immediately and $4-million at closing.

The association also received a $5-million loan from the Empire State Development Corp., to be repaid from revenues generated by 4,500 video lottery terminals at a future Aqueduct racino. New York Governor George Pataki Jr. also proposed legislation that would provide NYRA with a $20-million loan to continue operation of the three tracks and to construct the racino, which was authorized in the weeks following the September 11, 2001, terrorist attacks on the World Trade Center in lower Manhattan.

During the year, NYRA endured a probe by state officials that led to an indictment of Clerk of Scales Mario Sclafani and Assistant Clerk of Scales Braulio Baeza for allegedly allowing jockeys to ride overweight without the public's knowledge. NYRA also cracked down on backstretch security, including mandated stints in detention for all horses on race day, in the wake of a federal indictment on January 13 that tied trainer Greg Martin to a horse-doping scheme as part of an alleged gambling ring. NYRA's franchise to operate the three tracks expires at the end of 2007.

3. Popular success of Afleet Alex. For the second year in a row, a Mid-Atlantic-based colt captured two legs of the Triple Crown and the attention of mainstream America.

A year after Pennsylvania-bred Smarty Jones won the Kentucky Derby (G1) and Preakness Stakes (G1), Florida-bred Afleet Alex scored in the 2005 Preakness and Belmont Stakes (G1) for a self-described small-time trainer, Tim Ritchey, and a fun-loving group of five owners who base their operation at Delaware Park.

The partners' Cash is King stable used Afleet Alex to promote Alex's Lemonade Stand, a charity that raises money for the fight against pediatric cancer. The much-publicized connection was enhanced by the magical journey Afleet Alex took in May and June, starting with a close third-place finish in the Kentucky Derby on May 7.

As the favorite in the Preakness two weeks later, Afleet Alex amazed the record crowd of 115,318 fans at Pimlico Race Course and millions of television viewers. After clipping heels and bumping leader Scrappy T at the top of the lane, Afleet Alex somehow recovered with athleticism and tenacity, and then spurted away to a 4¾-length victory under the guidance of young jockey Jeremy Rose.

The Belmont proved much less eventful on June 11, when Afleet Alex overpowered ten rivals for a seven-length victory at odds of 1.15-to-1. As with Smarty Jones in 2004, the Belmont would be the conclusion to Afleet Alex's racing career.

Sidelined in July with a condylar fracture, the Northern Afleet colt was retired on December 1 after his connections decided he could not return to full strength. Afleet Alex entered stud in 2006 at Gainesway in Lexington. Like Smarty Jones, he was voted an Eclipse Award as champion three-year-old male.

4. Hurricane halts racing at Fair Grounds. Fair Grounds emerged from bankruptcy in September 2004 with Churchill Downs Inc. as its new owner only to be engulfed a little less than a year later by the flooding that followed Hurricane Katrina.

Four-foot-deep waters covered most of the track property while Churchill officials hastily made arrangements for the 2005-'06 Fair Grounds meet to be conducted at Louisiana Downs. The immediate future of the historic racetrack remained uncertain while the Fair Grounds meet unfolded about 340 miles northwest of New Orleans in Bossier City.

Churchill President Tom Meeker stressed that the company remained committed to reestablishing Fair Grounds, possibly under an ambitious expansion plan that would include a hotel, and in 2006 Churchill committed to running in New Orleans. Meeker said the company would monitor the redevelopment of the New Orleans market and infrastructure before it makes definitive plans. Churchill's $200-million insurance policy covered losses from the flood damage, but the company's ability to maintain adequate insurance could be an issue in the future.

Churchill also dealt with extensive damage from natural disasters at Florida's Calder Race Course and Kentucky's Ellis Park. On October 24, Hurricane Wilma damaged Calder's clubhouse, stable area, and infield tote board. The track reopened for simulcasting five days later, and live racing resumed on October 30.

A tornado destroyed ten barns and severely damaged Ellis's grandstand terrace, paddock, jockeys' quarters, and infield tote board on November 6. Ellis officials said they would conduct live racing as scheduled in 2006.

5. Billion-dollar bloodstock boom. The North American Thoroughbred auction market exceeded the $1-billion mark for the second consecutive year with a record $1,138,751,345 in total receipts. The previous record was $1,091,345,649 in 2000.

Amid mixed results for sales of two-year-olds in training, Sheikh Mohammed bin Rashid al Maktoum's Darley provided a highlight with its purchase of a Tale of the Cat colt for a world-record $5.2-million at the Fasig Tipton Calder selected two-year-olds in training sale on March 1. The yearling market, though, continued to dictate the market's success, specifically through the results of the Keeneland September yearling sale. The 2005 edition, the largest September sale in history, was the ultimate pacesetter with a world-record $384,349,900 in total proceeds.

Sheikh Mohammed also accounted for record prices at Keeneland September and the Keeneland November breeding stock sale with his respective purchases of a Storm Cat colt for $9.7-million and 2004 champion three-year-old filly Ashado for $9-million. Keeneland November followed the September explosion with steady gains in gross and average, bolstered by spending sprees by Courtlandt Farm and Jess Jackson.

6. Hollywood Park's uncertain future. Bay Meadows Land Co. purchased Hollywood Park for $257.5-million in September and warned that the track property would be developed if California's gaming landscape remained unchanged over the following three years. The new owner committed to operating the track through 2008, but in the fall it began the legal process for developing the Inglewood, California, facility, which opened in 1938.

Churchill Downs Inc., which bought Hollywood in 1999 for $140-million from a group led by R. D. Hubbard, hoped to operate alternative gaming at the track, but state voters soundly defeated such a measure in November 2004.

The absence of Hollywood would create a large hole on the Southern California racing schedule. Hollywood traditionally operates a spring meet with approximately 65 dates and a fall meet with approximately 31 dates. If the track should close, a group of investors was committed to expanding Los Alamitos Race Course in Cypress into a major league venue for Thoroughbred and Quarter Horse racing, as long as others in the industry support the endeavor. Los Alamitos owner Ed Allred backed out of a partnership with prominent Thoroughbred owner-breeder Mike Pegram, who has invested more than $1-million and allied with the late Bob Lewis in preparing for the venture.

Meanwhile, Bay Meadows Land Co. was proceeding with plans to abandon racing at Bay Meadows Race Course and develop the property, which it has owned since 1997.

7. Turfway Park debuts Polytrack. After three years of planning, the Polytrack racing surface made its North American racing debut at Turfway's 22-day fall meet. Following that meet, the owners of Del Mar, Hollywood Park, and Woodbine all said they were considering an artificial surface at their facilities. Keeneland Race Course and Woodbine installed Polytrack surfaces in 2006, and Hollywood installed a Cushion Track surface.

Polytrack has been in use in England since the late 1980s but only arrived in North America in September 2004, when Keeneland Association installed the surface on its training track.

Keeneland and Harrah's Entertainment Inc. each own a 50% share in Turfway, which spent between $4-million and $5-million for its Polytrack surface. Keeneland manufactures Polytrack at its Lexington facility and was installing the surface on the Keeneland main track during the summer of 2006, to be ready for its fall meet.

Polytrack is praised for being kind to horses, and Turfway President Bob Elliston said the track's horse ambulance was not used during training hours or races in the fall meet. The number of horses that failed to finish their races during the fall meet, Elliston said, declined from 21 in 2004 to ten in '05.

8. Leading jockeys retire. Pat Day and Gary Stevens, who together collected more than 13,000 wins and $500-million in purse earnings, concluded their Racing Hall of Fame careers nearly four months apart at Churchill Downs. In the first weeks of 2006, fellow Racing Hall of Fame member Jerry Bailey announced he would retire following the Sunshine Millions races at Gulfstream Park on January 28.

Day retired on August 4 as Thoroughbred racing's all-time leading rider by purse earnings with $297,912,019, and fourth in races won, with 8,803. Day, 51, said he was heeding God's call to end his career without a serious injury or a decline in skill. "I want to do what God wants me to do," said Day,

Leaders of 2005

Category	Leader	Leading Statistic
Owner by Wins	Michael J. Gill	351
Owner by Earnings	Michael J. Gill	$6,397,180
Owner by Grade 1 Wins	(tie) Phipps Stable; Starlight Stable, Paul Saylor, and Johns Martin; Mr. and Mrs. William K. Warren Jr.	4
Owner by Grade 1 Earnings	Mr. and Mrs. William K. Warren Jr.	$3,696,960
Owner by Graded Stakes Winners	(tie) Live Oak Plantation, Phipps Stable	6
Breeder by Wins	John Franks	464
Breeder by Earnings	Adena Springs Farm	$11,613,323
Breeder by Grade 1 Wins	Edward P. Evans	4
Breeder by Grade 1 Earnings	Edward P. Evans	$3,844,460
Breeder by Graded Stakes Winners	Adena Springs Farm	6
Trainer by Wins	Steven M. Asmussen	474
Trainer by Earnings	Todd A. Pletcher	$20,867,842
Trainer by Grade 1 Wins	(tie) Robert J. Frankel, Todd A. Pletcher	10
Trainer by Grade 1 Earnings	Todd A. Pletcher	$5,826,793
Trainer by Graded Stakes Winners	Todd A. Pletcher	25
Jockey by Wins	Russell A. Baze	375
Jockey by Earnings	John R. Velazquez	$20,799,923
Jockey by Grade 1 Wins	Jerry D. Bailey	13
Jockey by Grade 1 Earnings	Jerry D. Bailey	$7,544,781
Jockey by Graded Stakes Winners	John R. Velazquez	29
Sire by Earnings	Saint Ballado	$9,211,300
Sire by Wins	Langfuhr	192
Sire by Winners	Langfuhr	104
Sire by Graded Stakes Winners	A.P. Indy	10
Sire by Grade 1 Wins	Saint Ballado	7
Sire by Grade 1 Earnings	Saint Ballado	$4,731,794
Horse by Wins	(tie) Don Cholo, Gold Gift, Triano	10
Horse by Earnings	Saint Liam	$3,696,960
Horse by Graded Stakes Wins	(tie) Intercontinental (GB), Lost in the Fog	5
Horse by Grade 1 Wins	Saint Liam	4
Horse by Starts	(tie) Beer Goggles, Trick Hunter	31
Oldest Stakes Winner	(tie) Lost Again, Proven Cure	11
Oldest Graded Stakes Winner	Rochester	9
Broodmare by Earnings	Quiet Dance	$3,788,933

who began devoting his attention to ministries, including the Race Track Chaplaincy of America. "But I love this game. I'm going to miss it a lot and [the Kentucky Derby] in particular. ... I've been blessed to participate as a jockey for 22 years. To not have that opportunity again is sad."

Stevens, 42, retired at the conclusion of the Churchill fall meet on November 26, ending a 27-year career that included eight classic wins. He earned his 5,000th career victory on October 30. Stevens became a racing analyst for Television Games Network and NBC in January.

Bailey, 48 at the time of his retirement, had won seven Eclipse Awards as outstanding jockey and 15 Breeders' Cup races, both records. He won the 2005 Breeders' Cup Classic (G1) aboard Saint Liam, 2005's Horse of the Year, and concluded his brilliant career with purse earnings of more than $295.8-million, second only to Day. He began a career as a race analyst for ABC and ESPN after his retirement.

9. Giacomo's stunning Kentucky Derby win. Giacomo entered the starting gate for this year's Kentucky Derby as a 50.30-to-1 longshot still eligible for an entry-level allowance race. With a sweeping burst from the back of the pack, he crossed the finish line as one of the most unlikely winners in the classic's 131-year history. Giacomo was the second-highest-priced Derby winner, following 91.45-to-1 longshot Donerail in 1913.

The gray or roan son of Holy Bull also lifted his reserved and patient trainer, John Shirreffs, into the spotlight and rewarded owners and breeders Jerry and Ann Moss, who had their first starter in America's signature race. The colt also vindicated jockey Mike Smith, who gained his first Derby win after three second-place finishes and one third-place finish, in addition to two off-the-board finishes on post-time favorites.

Giacomo followed his Derby shocker with a third-place finish in the Preakness and a seventh-place finish in the Belmont. After the Belmont, Giacomo underwent knee and ankle surgery.

10. More records for Pletcher and Velazquez. Jockey John Velazquez and trainer Todd Pletcher have operated as a potent combination in New York since the turn of the 21st century, and both earned Eclipse Awards as the best in their profession in 2004. Then they took their success to a new level in 2005, and again were rewarded with Eclipse Awards.

On November 25, Pletcher eclipsed the North American single-season record for stable earnings by passing the previous mark of $19,147,129 set by Bobby Frankel in 2003. Pletcher ended the year with earnings of $20,867,842.

Velazquez, Pletcher's first-call jockey, broke the record for purse earnings by a North American-based jockey on November 20 and concluded the year with total purses of $24,399,923, including $3.6-million from his Dubai World Cup (UAE-G1) victory aboard Roses in May. Jerry Bailey set the previous mark of $23,354,960 in 2003.

Velazquez garnered more than half of his purse earnings aboard horses trained by Pletcher. They combined for 30 graded stakes wins, including the Blue Grass Stakes (G1) with Bandini, Beldame Stakes (G1) with Ashado, E. P. Taylor Stakes (Can-G1) with Honey Ryder, and Travers Stakes (G1) with Flower Alley.—*Jeff Lowe*

Barbaro: Triumph and then disaster

Within two weeks in May 2006, the American racing community and much of America went from a moment of considerable hope—Barbaro's powerful 6½-length victory in the Kentucky Derby (G1)—to an excruciating period of helplessness when the undefeated Dynaformer colt sustained life-threatening fractures of his right hind leg in the first 200 yards of the Preakness Stakes (G1).

Repeatedly over the preceding decade, Thoroughbred racing had been teased with the prospect of a 12th Triple Crown winner to end the longest drought between winners in the American sport's history. Real Quiet almost had it won in 1998 before Victory Gallop nailed him on the money in the Belmont Stakes (G1), and Smarty Jones looked unbeatable in 2004 until his overeagerness beat him in the Belmont. Barbaro also assumed the mantle of likely Triple Crown winner.

Like Smarty Jones, Barbaro came into the Derby unbeaten, and won decisively at Churchill Downs. Smarty Jones also won the Preakness with authority, by a record 11½ lengths, and Barbaro was odds-on to win the Preakness. After breaking through the starting gate before the start, Barbaro sustained multiple fractures to his right hind leg, and jockey Edgar Prado quickly pulled him up.

After he was stabilized at Pimlico Race Course, Barbaro was shipped hours later to the New Bolton Center of the University of Pennsylvania's Veterinary School, located not far from the farms of owners-breeders Roy and Gretchen Jackson and trainer Michael Matz. The day after the Preakness, Barbaro underwent surgery to install a titanium plate and 27 screws in his mangled leg. He came through the surgery well and initially proved a tractable patient, but his surgeon, Dean Richardson, D.V.M., said the process of recovery would take months and was fraught with numerous perils that could end Barbaro's life.

Barbaro's injury and recovery became a front-page story around the country, and get-well wishes flooded in from around the world.

—*Don Clippinger*

Chronology of 2005 and 2006

2005

January 3, 2005—Gulfstream Park announces that it will test horses for milkshaking, an alkaline mixture given to a horse before it competes to reduce the buildup of lactic acid in muscles. Mr. Light (Arg) clocks a world-record mile of 1:31.41 in a turf race at Gulfstream Park.

January 4—Churchill Downs announces it has doubled the guaranteed purse for the 2005 Kentucky Derby (G1) to $2-million.

January 7—The California Horse Racing Board votes to accept a judge's recommendations that would clear the way for jockey Patrick Valenzuela to resume riding after a series of drug problems.

January 9—Santa Anita Park becomes the first Southern California racetrack in a decade to cancel racing due to heavy rain.

January 11—An audit by the New York comptroller's office charges that NYRA shortchanged the state by more than $500,000 in 2004 with improper travel and entertainment deductions.

January 12—Coolmore Stud's auction of stallion seasons raises $3.5-million for Red Cross tsunami relief in Southeast Asia. NYRA suspends Clerk of Scales Mario Sclafani and Assistant Clerk of Scales Braulio Baeza during an ongoing investigation into incorrectly reported weight assignments.

January 13—Jockey Rene Douglas boots home his 3,000th career winner, aboard Grey Misty, at Santa Anita Park. New York trainer Greg Martin is indicted on charges of wire fraud, conspiracy, and horse doping in attempting to fix the outcome of a December 18 race at Aqueduct.

January 15—Keeneland announces that for the third consecutive year it will not hold a July selected yearling sale. New York Comptroller Alan Hevesi accuses NYRA of violating state laws by awarding no-bid contracts in the purchasing of goods and services.

January 17—Owner Ken Ramsey, a 2004 Eclipse Award finalist, receives a $25,000 fine and seven-day suspension from the Kentucky Horse Racing Authority for asking another owner to scratch a horse out of a December 31 race at Turfway Park.

January 19—Racing Hall of Fame jockey Chris McCarron announces that he will leave his executive position with Magna Entertainment Corp. to open a jockey school in Kentucky.

January 20—Jockey Ramon Dominguez is honored with the 2004 Isaac Murphy Award for the jockey with the highest winning percentage, supplanting nine-time winner Russell Baze.

January 21—Jockey Jorge Chavez scores his 4,000th career victory, aboard A Rizzi Rueben at Gulfstream Park.

January 22—Racing Hall of Fame rider Russell Baze passes Bill Shoemaker and moves into second place among North America's all-time winning jockeys with a victory aboard Hollow Memories at Golden Gate Fields.

January 23—Australian-bred Silent Witness extends his undefeated record to 14 with a victory in the Bauhinia Sprint Trophy at Sha Tin racecourse in Hong Kong.

January 24—Ghostzapper outpolls Smarty Jones to claim 2004 Horse of the Year honors at the Eclipse Awards ceremony in Beverly Hills, California. Declan's Moon and Wilko top the 2004 Experimental Free Handicap for males at 126 pounds; Sweet Catomine tops fillies at 124.

January 30—Jockey Gary Boulanger, a winner of 3,104 races, is critically injured when thrown from his mount in the Mac Diarmida Handicap (G3) at Gulfstream Park.

February 4—Racing Services Inc. founder Susan Bala is convicted of operating an illegal gambling operation in North Dakota. Jockey Richard Migliore scores his 4,000th career win, aboard Benjamin Baby at Aqueduct.

February 9—Champions Declan's Moon and Sweet Catomine open as future book favorites for the Kentucky Derby (G1) and Kentucky Oaks (G1).

February 11—Industry innovator John R. Gaines, whose visionary ideas included the Breeders' Cup and Kentucky Horse Park, among others, dies at age 76.

February 16—NYRA begins pre- and post-race testing for milkshaking. Jockey Calvin Borel records his 4,000th career victory, aboard Jet Angel at Oaklawn Park.

February 17—Irish trainer Dermot Weld saddles his 3,000th career winner with King Jock, at Nad al Sheba Racecourse in Dubai.

February 20—Retired jockey Ray Sibille is named 2005 recipient of the George Woolf Memorial Jockey Award.

February 21—Maryland-based trainer Howard Wolfendale saddles career winner number 1,000, with Warison, at Laurel Park. Jockey Jose Amy, who was suspended in 1980 for holding back horses, rides his first winner in nearly 25 years, at Aqueduct.

March 1—A Tale of the Cat colt sets a world record for a two-year-old sold at public auction when he brings $5.2-million at Fasig-Tipton's Calder sale.

March 2—MI Developments Inc., parent company of Magna Entertainment Corp., reports an $8.5-million loss for 2004. Fasig-Tipton's select Florida sale ends after breaking all-time records for a juvenile auction in both gross receipts and average.

March 9—Five-time Eclipse Award winner John Henry celebrates his 30th birthday at the Kentucky Horse Park, with 200 fans and jockey Chris McCarron.

March 11—Undefeated juvenile champion and early Kentucky Derby favorite Declan's Moon is indefinitely sidelined with a knee injury. Jockey Tyler Baze posts his 1,000th career victory, aboard Mashiko at Santa Anita Park.

March 15—Churchill Downs quarantines two barns after a horse is diagnosed with the contagious bacterial respiratory disease known as strangles, and two days later 19 horses at Churchill Downs's Trackside Louisville training center test positive for strangles.

March 19—Highly regarded classic prospect Roman Ruler drops out of the Kentucky Derby picture with a quarter crack.

March 20—Jockey Joe Martinez scores his 2,000th career victory, aboard Roll On Retsina at Sunland Park.

March 21—An ESPN Sports poll indicates a 5.1% increase in fan interest for horse racing, the largest increase for any sport in 2004.

March 24—Seven horses test positive for strangles at Palm Meadows Training Center in Florida.

March 26—American-bred Roses in May captures the $6-million Dubai World Cup (UAE-G1).

March 29—Jockey Glen Murphy scores career win 2,000, aboard Red Lifesaver, at Sunland Park. Betcris.com, an on-line sports and race book, pays $15,000 on eBay to advertise for two months on jockey Pat Valenzuela's riding pants and collar.

April 3—Silent Witness notches his 16th consecutive victory, at Sha Tin in Hong Kong, equaling the 20th century American record of Citation and Cigar.

April 7—Jockey Jon Court wins his 3,000th lifetime victory, with Brite Lorelei, at Santa Anita Park.

April 9—Champion filly Sweet Catomine finishes fifth as favorite in the Santa Anita Derby (G1). Bellamy Road wins the Wood Memorial Stakes (G1) by 17½ lengths, equaling Aqueduct's record of 1:47.16 for 1⅛ miles. Procreate sets a five-furlong world record of :53.79 in the Yankee Affair Stakes at Gulfstream Park.

April 19—D. G. Van Clief Jr. is named NTRA commissioner and chief executive officer through 2007.

April 23—Hollywood Park stewards drop a complaint filed by the California Horse Racing Board against Sweet Catomine co-owner Martin Wygod following her poor Santa Anita Derby performance.

April 24—Hong Kong sensation Silent Witness scores his 17th consecutive victory, surpassing 20th century North American and European marks of 16 straight set by Citation, *Ribot, and Cigar. Brazilian jockey Jorge Ricardo joins Laffit Pincay Jr. as the only riders to reach the 9,000-win milestone.

April 27—Dear Birdie, dam of champion Bird Town and classic winner Birdstone, is named 2004 Broodmare of the Year.

May 2—Visa announces it will not renew its ten-year sponsorship of the Triple Crown series and will instead sponsor only the Kentucky Derby beginning in 2006.

May 5—Racing Hall of Fame rider Ted Atkinson dies at 88. The United States House of Representatives passes a resolution to honor Jimmy Winkfield, one of the last great African-American jockeys.

May 6—Churchill Downs sets a Kentucky Oaks (G1) day attendance record of 111,243.

May 7—Maiden winner Giacomo scores a 50.30-to-1 Kentucky Derby upset. The Derby becomes North America's first race to surpass $100-million in wagers. Total on- and off-track wagering on the 12-race Derby day program establishes an American record of $155,133,631.

May 10—Florida-based Farnsworth Farms, Eclipse Award-winning breeder of 1996, announces it will cease operations by the end of the year.

May 14—Silent Witness's historic 17-race win streak ends in the Champions Mile (HK-G1) at Sha Tin.

May 18—Tests confirm that several horses stabled at Churchill Downs are suffering from equine herpesvirus; three barns are quarantined.

May 21—Favored Afleet Alex wins the Preakness Stakes (G1) after recovering from a dramatic near-fall entering the stretch.

May 24—Jockey Eddie Zuniga scores his 1,000th career victory, aboard Shrewd Maria, at Indiana Downs.

May 26—Well-known owner Gary Tanaka is arrested for allegedly using millions of dollars of client money from his investment company to buy racehorses.

May 30—Reigning Horse of the Year Ghostzapper wins Belmont Park's Metropolitan Handicap (G1) by 6¼ lengths after a seven-month layoff.

June 2—Racing Hall of Fame jockey Russell Baze scores his 9,000th career victory, aboard Queen of the Hunt, at Golden Gate Fields.

June 3—NYRA and New York Thoroughbred Horsemen's Association launch the "Ferdinand fee," a voluntary $2 starting fee to be used to fight horse slaughter.

June 8—The U.S. House of Representatives passes an amendment to remove U.S. Agriculture Department funding for inspections of horse meat to be shipped abroad for consumption. Second all-time winning jockey Russell Baze is injured in a spill at Golden Gate Fields.

June 11—Favored Afleet Alex wins the Belmont Stakes (G1) by seven lengths. THOROUGHBRED TIMES is named Best Overall Publication at the American Horse Publications awards banquet in Seattle.

June 13—2004 Horse of the Year Ghostzapper is retired from racing after chipping a sesamoid in his left foreleg.

June 20—Twenty-four-year-old graded stakes-winning millionaire Taylor's Special becomes an Old Friends retiree at Hurstland Farm in Kentucky. In August, he is joined by Grade 1 winners Fraise, Ogygian, and Special Ring.

June 21—Central Kentucky's Bluegrass Region is listed as one of the world's 100 most endangered sites, according to conservation organization World Monuments Fund.

July 3—Jockey Jeremy Rose records his 1,000th career victory, with Margarita Maggie, at Delaware Park.

July 6—Churchill Downs Inc. announces the sale of Hollywood Park to Bay Meadows Land Co. for $260-million.

July 9—Calder Race Course postpones by one day its $1.9-million Summit of Speed card due to the effects of Hurricane Dennis.

July 10—Unbeaten Lost in the Fog goes eight-for-eight by winning Calder's $300,000 Carry Back Stakes (G2) by 7¼ lengths, at 1-to-20 odds, in stakes-record time.

July 24—Keep the Faith (Aus) establishes a world record for six furlongs on grass, running the distance in 1:06.82 at Belmont Park.

July 28—Dual 2005 classic winner Afleet Alex is sidelined with a condylar fracture of his left front ankle.

August 3—Racing Hall of Fame jockey Pat Day announces his retirement from the saddle, after 8,803 victories.

August 5—Trainer Steve Asmussen saddles career winner number 3,000, with Forest Music, in Saratoga's Honorable Miss Handicap (G2).

August 8—Trainer Nick Zito is inducted into the Racing Hall of Fame in Saratoga Springs. Also inducted are steeplechase great Lonesome Glory, trainer Sidney Watters Jr., and jump jockey Tommy Walsh.

August 17—Congress requests information on Jockeys' Guild President L. Wayne Gertmenian's management practices and the lapse of a catastrophic insurance policy covering jockeys.

August 20—Deceased Danehill becomes the first stallion to sire 300 stakes winners, when Nevis wins a listed stake in Australia.

August 23—NYRA announces $16-million in financial losses for 2004, after losing $22-million in 2003.

August 26—Calder Race Course cancels live card due to effects of Hurricane Katrina on South Florida.

August 27—Undefeated Lost in the Fog makes it nine in a row in Saratoga's King's Bishop Stakes (G1).

August 29—Fair Grounds racetrack in New Orleans sustains structural damage and flooding during Hurricane Katrina. Churchill Downs Inc. subsequently announces plans to shift some of the Fair Grounds 2005-'06 dates to Louisiana Downs.

September 11—Keeneland's September yearling sale kicks off with a record 5,110 hip numbers.

September 12—Horse of the Year Ghostzapper's 2006 stud fee is announced at $200,000.

September 13—A Storm Cat colt sets a September sales record of $9.7-million, third-highest price ever paid for an auction yearling. Jockey Harry Vega scores victory number 3,000, aboard Quies, at Philadelphia Park.

September 14—Federal prosecutors drop criminal case against NYRA, stating it had corrected practices that had led to tax evasion and other illegal activities.

September 20—The United States Senate joins the House of Representatives in passing an amendment barring federal funds for use in facilitating horse slaughter.

September 21—NYRA Clerk of Scales Mario Sclafani and Assistant Clerk of Scales Braulio Baeza are indicted for fraud, conspiracy, falsifying records, tampering with a sports contest, and grand larceny, for allegedly allowing jockeys to ride while overweight.

September 23—Zia Park racetrack opens in Hobbs, New Mexico.

September 26—Keeneland's September yearling auction ends with records for gross revenue, number sold, and average and median price. Storm Cat offspring average a sale record $1,766,731.

October 1—Jockey Eddie King earns his 2,000th career win, on Annies Fuse, at Meadowlands. Undefeated Lost in the Fog scores his tenth consecutive victory, in the Bay Meadows Speed Handicap.

October 6—Braulio Baeza, a Racing Hall of Fame jockey and former NYRA Assistant Clerk of Scales, pleads not guilty to charges that he allowed jockeys to ride overweight without informing the public.

October 8—Heavy rain forces postponement of the Maryland Million card at Laurel Park.

October 12—Trainer Neil Howard saddles his 1,000th career winner, with Soul Search, at Keeneland Race Course. Overbrook Farm announces that Storm Cat's fee for 2006 will remain at $500,000, the world's highest stud fee.

October 14—Jockey Rafael Bejarano scores his 1,000th career victory, with Northern Vacation, at Keeneland Race Course.

October 19—NYRA President Charles Hayward says he favors an end to live racing at Aqueduct so that the track could be used as a gaming facility. A congressional subcommittee sharply criticizes Jockeys' Guild management for allowing its catastrophic insurance policy to lapse.

October 24—Hurricane Wilma causes damage to Calder Race Course's clubhouse and delays construction of Gulfstream Park's new grandstand. Calder reopens for simulcast wagering on October 29 and resumes limited racing the following day.

October 29—The 22nd Breeders' Cup is contested at Belmont Park. Favored Saint Liam wins the Classic (G1) before a crowd of 54,289. Lost in the Fog finishes seventh in the Sprint (G1), his first loss in 11 starts. Breeders' Cup wagering reaches a record $122,106,154. Jockey Todd Kabel earns his 3,000th career victory, aboard Sprightly, at Woodbine. Trainer Scott Lake saddles his 3,000th winner, Unaccounted Gift, at Philadelphia Park.

October 30—Jockey Gary Stevens scores career win number 5,000, with Joint Aspiration (GB), at Belmont Park.

October 31—Makybe Diva wins her third consecutive Melbourne Cup (Aus-G1) and retires as the world's leading money-winning female, with $8,449,006.

November 1—Hollywood Park cancels all grass racing scheduled for its fall meeting due to dissatisfaction with the newly installed turf course. A barn fire at Fair Hill Training Center in Maryland kills 24 Thoroughbreds.

November 2—The U. S. Senate passes an amendment withdrawing federal funding for U.S. Agriculture meat inspectors at the three horse slaughterhouses in America.

November 6—A tornado rips through Ellis Park racetrack in Kentucky, killing three horses and causing major damage to the grandstand and stable areas.

November 7—At Keeneland's November sale, champion Ashado brings a $9-million world-record price for a broodmare.

November 12—San Mateo, California, city council votes unanimously to permit demolition of historic Bay Meadows Race Course to make way for retail and residential development.

November 13—Taylor Made Sales Agency breaks its own world record for gross generated by a consignor during a single public auction, when its Keeneland November sales top $61.9-million.

November 15—Jockeys' Guild fires President L. Wayne Gertmenian for mismanagement of more than $2-million in Guild funds.

November 16—Three-year-old Prix de l'Arc de Triomphe (Fr-G1) winner Hurricane Run is named Europe's 2005 Cartier Horse of the Year.

November 20—Jockey John Velazquez surpasses Jerry Bailey's single-season earnings record, with $23,356,456 in purse winnings.

November 27—Racing Hall of Fame jockey Gary Stevens announces his retirement from riding after more than 25 years and 5,005 victories. Trainer Todd Pletcher establishes a North American single-season record for stable earnings, with $19,150,856.

December 1—Preakness and Belmont Stakes winner Afleet Alex is retired due to an injury.

December 7—NYRA proposes a $4-million reduction in its 2006 stakes purses and plans to eliminate nine stakes.

December 8—Trainer Bruce Kravets saddles his 3,000th winner, Skip the Wedding, at Penn National Race Course.

December 10—Trainer Bruce Levine gets career victory number 1,000, with Preminger, at Aqueduct. The Port Authority of New York and New Jersey agrees to buy land near Aqueduct for $5-million, providing cash to financially troubled NYRA.

December 16—A Bit O' Gold is named Canada's 2005 Horse of the Year.

December 23—A three-year-old filly from Turfway Park is euthanized due to equine herpesvirus.

December 30—NYRA and the State of New York agree to a $30-million financial bailout package, avoiding a threatened bankruptcy filing by NYRA.

2006

January 2—A Thoroughbred at Pimlico Race Course is euthanized due to equine herpesvirus, and five other horses show signs of infection.

January 3—Three-time leading North American sire Danzig dies at Claiborne Farm.

January 4—Internationally renowned owner-breeder and Dubai ruler Sheikh Maktoum bin Rashid al Maktoum dies unexpectedly in Australia.

January 10—The first foal by dual classic winner Smarty Jones arrives at Stone Farm in Kentucky.

January 13—Keeneland's January mixed stock sale sets a new record gross after the fifth of seven sessions, surpassing the $66.7-million mark set in 1988.

January 17—Racing Hall of Fame rider Russell Baze wins his tenth Isaac Murphy Award, for the highest winning percentage of 2005.

January 18—Racing Hall of Fame jockey Jerry Bailey announces he will retire at the end of the month, to join ESPN and ABC Sports as a racing analyst.

January 19—Three barns at Pimlico Race Course are quarantined due to an outbreak of equine herpesvirus (EHV-1). A horse at Penn National Race Course is also diagnosed with the potentially fatal illness.

January 21—The Maryland Jockey Club places Pimlico under quarantine until further notice.

January 23—Saint Liam is named 2005 Horse of the Year at the Eclipse Award banquet in Beverly Hills, California.

January 25—Laurel Park-based General Strike becomes the third horse to be euthanized due to equine herpesvirus.

January 26—Champion juveniles Stevie Wonderboy and Folklore are the top-weighted male and filly on the 2005 Experimental Free Handicap.

January 28—Racing Hall of Fame jockey Jerry Bailey finishes second in his career finale, aboard Silver Tree, in the Sunshine Millions Turf at Gulfstream Park.

February 1—Yum! Brands Inc. signs with Churchill Downs to become the first-ever presenting sponsor of the Kentucky Derby.

February 4—Jockey Jose Santos records his 4,000th career win, on Melodeeman, at Aqueduct.

February 5—A barn fire at Eureka Downs in Kansas claims the lives of 43 racehorses.

February 6—Champion Stevie Wonderboy suffers a hairline fracture in a workout at Hollywood Park. Jockey Chance Rollins notches career win number 2,000, with Cherryonthebottom, at Bay Meadows Race Course.

February 9—Jockey Mark Guidry is announced as the 57th recipient of the 2006 George Woolf Memorial Jockey Award.

February 17—Eclipse Award-winning owner Robert Lewis dies at age 81.

February 20—Jockey Roberto Gonzalez earns his 4,000th career win, with Barbecue Bob, at Golden Gate Fields.

February 20—The Maryland Jockey Club cancels the 2006 Barbara Fritchie (G2) and General George (G2) Breeders' Cup Handicaps due to the EHV-1 outbreak.

February 25—Trainer Bernie Flint records his 3,000th career victory, with More Than Pretty, at Oaklawn Park.

February 28—A juvenile son of Forestry brings a world-record $16-million auction price for a Thoroughbred of any age, at the Fasig-Tipton Calder select sale of two-year-olds in training; he is subsequently named The Green Monkey.

March 3—Maryland's Department of Agriculture lifts quarantine on barns at Pimlico and Bowie Training Center after four horses test negative for equine herpesvirus.

March 19—Jockey Victor Espinoza posts his 2,000th career victory, aboard Fear No Darkness, at Santa Anita Park.

March 24—The New York Legislature backs a deal providing a $5-million loan to NYRA and $2-million for a breeding and development fund.

March 25—Godolphin Racing's Electrocutionist wins the 11th running of the $6-million Dubai World Cup (UAE-G1) at Nad al Sheba racecourse.

March 29—Racing Hall of Fame jockey Gary Stevens signs a long-term contract with NBC Sports to work as a broadcaster for horse racing programs.

April 7—Jockey Rob Williams records his 4,000th career victory, on Sweet Evil Hariet, at Fonner Park.

April 8—Mr. Sekiguchi, an $8-million yearling in 2004, earns his first career victory at Santa Anita Park.

April 13—Fair Grounds applies to conduct an 81-day meeting in 2006-2007, the first live racing there since Hurricane Katrina extensively damaged the facility.

April 19—Keeneland announces that it will join Turfway Park and Woodbine as the third North American racetrack to install a Polytrack synthetic racing surface.

April 27—Baby Zip, the dam of champion Ghostzapper and Grade 1 winner City Zip, is named 2006 Broodmare of the Year by the Kentucky Thoroughbred Owners and Breeders Association.

April 28—The Kentucky state budget includes $300,000 for the North American Racing Academy, the country's first school for jockeys, to be launched by Chris McCarron at the Kentucky Horse Park.

May 1—Jockey Tony Black becomes the 21st North American jockey to ride 5,000 winners, aboard Actcentric, at Philadelphia Park.

May 2—Breeders' Cup Ltd. announces that it will raise its championship-day purses from $14-million in 2005 to $20-million in 2006.

May 5—Lemons Forever posts the biggest upset in the 132-year history of the Kentucky Oaks (G1), at odds of 47.10-to-1.

May 6—Undefeated Barbaro streaks to a 6½-length victory in the Kentucky Derby before the second-largest crowd in race history.

May 11—The California Senate passes a bill requiring the state's major racetracks to install synthetic racing surfaces by 2008.

May 20—Bernardini wins the Preakness, as a record Pimlico crowd watches heavily favored Barbaro suffer a potentially fatal injury.

May 21—A five-hour surgery is successfully performed on Barbaro's badly fractured right hind leg at the University of Pennsylvania's New Bolton Center.

May 30—The Racing Hall of Fame announces that, for the first time since its inception 50 years ago, no contemporary individuals or horses will be inducted for 2006. Old-timer additions to the Hall are trainer Carl Hanford, jockey Bill Boland, and *Cougar II.

2005-2006 Obituaries

Joe Agrella, 93, longtime handicapper and Turf writer, winner of the Walter Haight Award, past president of the National Turf Writers Association; on March 11, 2006, in Chicago.

Mike Allen, 60, noted jazz musician who played at many major Central Kentucky horse parties and events; following an extended illness, on January 10, 2005, in Lexington.

Bert Altfillisch, 87, longtime California breeder and founder of Granja Vista del Rio farm, whose top homebreds included graded stakes winner Hombre Rapido; in early February 2006, in California.

Susan Jane Anstey, 59, Canadian owner and breeder, publisher of the magazines *Canadian Thoroughbred, Horse Sport*, and *Horse Canada*, and president of the International Alliance of Equestrian Journalists; of cancer, on November 9, 2005, in Nobleton, Ontario.

Bernard T. Applegarth, 95, longtime Midwest-based owner-breeder, member of the Nebraska Thoroughbred Association; on April 29, 2005, in Alliance, Nebraska.

John Appleton, 55, son of Arthur I. Appleton, owner of Bridlewood Farm in Florida; in a skydiving accident, on May 1, 2005, in Texas.

Jack Arnold, 94, longtime California-based owner, who with his wife, Florence, bred and raced major Southern California stakes winner Stormy Jack; on July 24, 2005, in California.

J. Fred Arnold Jr., 80, veterinarian, Kentucky's Veterinarian of the Year in 1987, past president of the American Association of Equine Practitioners, co-breeder of graded stakes winner Militron; on April 6, 2006, in Lexington.

Ron Ashdown, noted Queensland, Australia breeder, who owned and once stood Group 1 winner and successful sire General Nediym at his Glengarry Stud; in June 2005, while visiting Italy.

Ted Atkinson, 88, Racing Hall of Fame jockey and leading American rider of 1944 and 1946, whose 3,795 career winners included champions Tom Fool, Nashua, Devil Diver, Gallorette, and Capot; at his home, on May 5, 2005, in Beaver Dam, Virginia.

Aurelio Baez, 87, a backstretch employee for trainer Ron McAnally since the early 1960s and who helped manage McAnally's stable; of heart problems, in late October 2005, in California.

R. L. "Bobby" Baird, 85, retired jockey, trainer, and jockey's agent, who rode 3,749 winners in a career spanning six decades, with five mounts in the Kentucky Derby (G1), and a member of the Louisiana Hall of Fame; of an aneurysm, on December 16, 2005, near Chicago.

Ivor Balding, 96, longtime farm manager and trainer for leading breeder C. V. Whitney, who urged Whitney to import *Mahmoud, retired seven-goal professional polo player, uncle of top English trainers Ian and Toby Balding; on January 21, 2005, in Camden, South Carolina.

Arthur Baumohl, 78, noted bloodstock agent and handicapper, co-breeder of 15 stakes winners, uncle of Hopewell Farm owner Rick Trontz, adviser to prominent breeder Nelson Bunker Hunt; of congestive heart failure, on January 12, 2005, in Lexington.

Ian Baxter, 58, Australian Thoroughbred industry executive, past chairman and director of the Brisbane Turf Club and a founding director of the QBBS Thoroughbred sales company in Queensland; after a long illness, on February 5, 2005, in Australia.

Barbara Baze, 77, Northwestern horsewoman, who along with her husband, Earl, campaigned horses for many years in Washington, Oregon, and Canada, including stakes winner Pharsong, mother of trainer Lisa Baze; of congestive heart failure, on September 12, 2005, in Eatonville, Washington.

Earl Baze, 82, former jockey, owner, and trainer, member of Washington's famed Baze racing family, who with his wife, Barbara, campaigned runners for many years in Washington, Oregon, and Canada, father of trainer Lisa Baze; of surgery complications, on September 11, 2005, in Auburn, Washington.

Piers Bengough, 75, Queen Elizabeth II's longtime representative at Ascot, former amateur rider, owner, Jockey Club steward, and racetrack executive; after a short illness, on April 18, 2005, in England.

Bob Birch, 76, a leading breeder in South Africa, whose family-bred champions included *Colorado King, *Top Gallant, Bold Tropic (SAf), and Wolf Power (SAf); after a long illness, in March 2006, in South Africa.

Tony Blickenstaff, 33, exercise rider and former jockey at Mid-Atlantic racetracks; on February 17, 2005, at his home in Funkstown, Maryland.

James Bohanon, 59, longtime Thoroughbred owner and breeder, who was a partner for several years in Claim to Fame Stables; on May 11, 2005, in Louisville.

William Boniface, 89, founder of Bonita Farm in Maryland, retired longtime Turf writer for the Baltimore *Sun*, father of noted trainer Billy Boniface and grandfather of Maryland Horse Breeders Association President William K. Boniface; after a short illness, on August 31, 2005, in Maryland.

David Bourke, 74, well-known Australian racing executive for more than 50 years, former chairman of the Victoria Racing Club in May 2005 in Melbourne, Australia after a short illness.

Dan Bowmar, 76, author of the 1960 book *Giants of the Turf* and retired owner of Bowmar Thoroughbred Consultants; on August 6, 2005, in Lexington.

Merle Hunter Boyce, 78, owner, breeder, and member of the California Thoroughbred Breeders Association, whose stakes winner Confederate Yankee competed in the 1974 Kentucky Derby (G1); in January 2005, in California.

Ann Brede, longtime Thoroughbred owner, breeder, and show judge, 2006 Pennsylvania Horsewoman of the Year, co-owner of Audley End Farm in Kentucky; of ovarian cancer, on May 28, 2006, in Kentucky.

Jean Brennan, 79, trainer for nearly a half-century, whose top runners included stakes winners Hempen and Houdini; father of trainer Terry Brennan; of heart problems, on December 26, 2005, in Hot Springs, Arkansas.

Bruce Brinkley, 67, presiding steward at Sunland Park, former Thoroughbred and Quarter Horse jockey based in the Southwest; on April 4, 2005, in El Paso, Texas.

B. Giles Brophy, 69, managing partner of the group that raced 1991 Kentucky Derby (G1) winner Strike the Gold, and who also raced Grade 1 winner Thirty Six Red; after a long battle with cancer, on April 9, 2006, in South Carolina.

Colin Browell, 33, among the leading jockeys in Victoria during the late 1980s and 1990s; of leukemia, on February 22, 2005, in Bendigo, Australia.

James Brummit, blacksmith, who had worked for trainers Bill Mott, Shug McGaughey, and Christophe Clement; after an illness, on January 11, 2006, in Florida.

Kay Stammers Bullitt, 91, Wimbledon doubles champion, breeder of graded stakes winner Millie's Quest, and known for hosting prominent Kentucky Derby parties at Oxmoor Farm near Louisville; on December 23, 2005, in Louisville.

Lowell "Newt" Bunyard, 86, a trainer for more than a half-century, whose runners included stakes winners King's Marshall and Lichi Lichi; of complications from a stroke, on July 19, 2005, in Prescott, Arizona.

Charlie Campbell, 53, New York Racing Association blacksmith whose father and twin brother also were farriers; after a long battle with cancer, on July 4, 2005, in New York.

Graham Campbell, former professional golfer, prominent Australian owner and breeder, founder of Blue Gun Farm, general manager of Dalgety Bloodstock; on June 14, 2005, in Australia.

John Campo Sr., 67, noted trainer whose 1,431 winners included champion and dual classic winner Pleasant Colony and champion juveniles Protagonist and Talking Picture; on November 14, 2005, in New York.

Constantine "Costy" Caras, 81, longtime announcer at Charles Town Races; on January 7, 2006, in Charles Town, West Virginia.

Alice Carney, 78, wife of Rockingham Park owner and president Thomas Carney; on July 12, 2005, in Winston-Salem, North Carolina.

George "Buddy" Carter, 76, longtime Canadian-based trainer, who ranked six times among Ontario's leading conditioners and whose notable runners included Mister Jive and Top Call; of cancer, on July 18, 2005, in Toronto.

Snowden Carter, 83, longtime Maryland horse owner, award-winning journalist, former editor of *The Maryland Horse* magazine, general manager of the Maryland Horse Breeders Association; of heart failure, on February 3, 2005, in Owings Mills, Maryland.

Eleanor Casey, 73, co-founder of Taylor Mountain Farm, a leading West Virginia Thoroughbred breeding and racing operation; of a heart attack after being injured in an accident at Charles Town Races, on July 28, 2005, in West Virginia.

Roy Chapman, 79, co-owner and co-breeder of 2004 champion and dual classic winner Smarty Jones; after a long battle with emphysema and asthma, on February 17, 2006, in Doylestown, Pennsylvania.

Anthony "Tote" Cherry-Downes, 62, British bloodstock agent, a leading buyer at North American auctions during the 1980s, who in 1987 purchased the Keeneland September sale's first $1-million yearling; after a long illness, on April 30, 2005.

Gerald Chige, 88, owner-breeder who campaigned for 20 years on the East Coast under the name Chige Stable and raced stakes winner Wild Moment; of a brain tumor, on February 3, 2005, in Dunedin, Florida.

Peter Chiodo, 59, Canadian-based owner who campaigned 1996 Sovereign Award-winning three-year-old filly Silent Fleet; on May 8, 2005, in Toronto.

Al Christensen, 67, a Midwest-based trainer since 1978, whose top runner was multiple 2004 stakes winner Grayglen; of a heart attack, in his shedrow at Fonner Park, near Grand Island, Nebraska.

Alex Christian, 57, former trainer, jockey, and Washington-based exercise rider; of complications following a heart attack, on March 27, 2006, in Tacoma, Washington.

Sir Rupert Clark, 85, chairman of Australia's Victoria Amateur Turf Club between 1972 and 1988, chairman of the trustees of Caulfield Racecourse Reserve; after a long illness, on February 4, 2005, in Melbourne.

Dr. Theodore Classen, 88, owner and breeder of eight Ohio champions, including Horses of the Year Brent's Prince and Rhinflo, member of the Ohio Racing Hall of Fame, three-term president of the Ohio Thoroughbred Owners and Breeders Association; on October 20, 2005, near Cleveland.

Roy Colosia, 84, former trainer, who broke Kentucky Derby winners Whirlaway and Pensive for Calumet Farm and Shut Out for Greentree Stable; after a long illness, on December 20, 2005, in Arcadia, California.

Robert Congleton, 80, construction entrepreneur, co-owner of 1984 Broodmare of the Year Hasty Queen II, former owner of Oakland Farm near Versailles, Kentucky; of heart failure, on March 29, 2005, in Kentucky.

Nelson Crews, 46, a Mid-Atlantic-based trainer of 33 winners, including 1998 St. Brendan Stakes winner Kool Krafty; of injuries sustained in a propane explosion at his home, on January 6, 2005, in Elk Township, Pennsylvania.

Pat Daly, 43, Kentucky-based trainer of 69 winners, including 2003 Oklahoma Derby (G3) winner Comic Truth, former assistant trainer for Ken McPeek; of a ruptured brain aneurysm, on December 28, 2005, in Louisville.

Stanley Dancer, 78, legendary, record-setting Standardbred driver, who drove and trained three Standardbred Triple Crown winners and won 3,781 races; on September 8, 2005, in Pompano Beach, Florida.

Roger Danjean, 60, former jockey who rode more than 700 winners, including Timely Writer in the 1981 Hopeful Stakes (G1); in a car accident, on January 23, 2005, in Hollywood, Florida.

Michael Dargan, 86, past chairman of Goffs Bloodstock Sales and Aer Lingus airline, and a former senior steward of the Irish Turf Club; on January 11, 2005, at his home in Dublin.

Edwin L. Davis, 68, retired trainer; at his home, on March 29, 2006, in Louisville.

James de Pasquale, 74, former executive director of the New York State Thoroughbred Capital Investment Fund; of a heart attack, on June 18, 2005, at his home in Oceanside, New York.

Alphonse DeRossi, 84, lifelong Thoroughbred racing fan and owner of the popular Saratoga Springs, New York, restaurant DeRossi's; on February 2, 2005, in New York.

Richard W. Deyette, 86, former trainer on the Pennsylvania and New England circuits; in December 2005, in Grafton, Massachusetts.

Bernard "Buddy D" Diliberto, 73, longtime New Orleans sports commentator and racing fan, father of Fair Grounds oddsmaker Mike Diliberto; of an apparent heart attack, on January 7, 2005, at his home in Metairie, Louisiana.

Victor Doleski, 82, longtime Kentucky-based trainer, whose best runner was three-time Ben Ali Handicap (G3) winner Knight Counter; on January 19, 2005, in Louisville.

Margaret Donnelly, 90, first woman to train at Hazel Park and Detroit Race Course, saddled more than 100 winners. Former editor of the *Michigan Thoroughbred* magazine; on July 9, 2005, in Michigan.

Charlie Dougherty, 85, former Northern California-based steward, owner and breeder; of congestive heart failure, on March 25, 2005, in Burlingame, California.

Penny Hall Dumas, 48, assistant to trainer Henry Collazzo, who previously had worked for Racing Hall of Fame horsemen Nick Zito and Jonathan Sheppard; of an apparent aneurysm, on June 27, 2005, at Calder Race Course, in Florida.

Allaire duPont, 92, prominent Maryland horsewoman, breeder of more than 40 stakes winners, including the great Kelso, whom she campaigned to five Horse of the Year titles, member of the Jockey Club, and a founder of Thoroughbred Charities of America; on January 6, 2006, at Woodstock Farm, in Chesapeake City, Maryland.

Martin J. Durkan Sr., 81, former lobbyist for Longacres racetrack, who as a U.S. senator from Washington, wrote tax and regulatory legislation beneficial to the horse industry in his state; of a heart attack, on May 29, 2005, in Washington.

Jim Eckrosh, 94, well-known Midwest-based trainer for several decades before his retirement at age 92, whose top runners included 1970 Louisiana Derby winner Jim's Alibhi; on August 29, 2005, in Des Moines, Iowa.

Oliver "Buddy" Edwards, 48, longtime Florida-based horseman who was leading trainer at Calder Race Course in 1989 and at Gulfstream Park in 1990; of a heart attack, on July 29, 2005, in Florida.

Meggs Elkington, 77, former jockey who later trained Australian classic winners Begonia Belle, Venus And Mars, and several other Group 1 winners, father of trainer Bruce Elkington; on February 2, 2005, in Australia.

George Ennor, 65, award-winning English Turf writer, who worked 12 years at *Racing Post*, including several as chief reporter, and 26 years at *Sporting Life*; of cancer, on December 31, 2005, in England.

William Erminelli, 56, trainer who campaigned runners primarily at Rockingham Park and Tampa Bay Downs; of complications of Lou Gehrig's disease, on January 22, 2006, in Zephyrhills, Florida.

George Evans Jr., 86, former member of the Kentucky Racing Commission; after a long illness, on May 9, 2005, in Lexington.

Gomer Evans, 84, trainer, who owned and trained 1964 and '65 Oaklawn Handicap winner Gay Revoke; in his sleep, on February 9, 2006, in Tulsa, Oklahoma.

Sidney Factor, 89, former owner and breeder, cosmetics magnate who helped build Max Factor into an internationally renowned company, and whose top runners included multiple stakes winner Quita Dude; of natural causes, on December 15, in Beverly Hills, California.

Daniel "Skeeter" Figgins, 58, former broodmare manager at Sagamore Farm for Alfred G. Vanderbilt, and later at Stoneworth Farm; on August 7, 2005, in Maryland.

Tom Filipowich, 84, a longtime owner whose best runners included multiple stakes winner Countess Steffi; following a lengthy illness, on May 8, 2006, in Canada.

Jack L. Finley, 83, owner whose top runners included Grade 1 winner Lite Light and graded stakes winners Dancing Femme, Raja's Delight, and Sheesham; on September 4, 2005, in Paradise Valley, Arizona.

Elder Ayres "Bud" Fisher, 83, former sports writer for the Akron *Beacon-Journal* who covered horse racing in the Northeast Ohio area; after a lengthy illness, on December 9, 2005, in Indianapolis.

Thomas "Peaches" Fleming, 94, trainer for more than 60 years, former jockey and owner; on February 19, 2005, in Texas.

Leroy Foster, 77, one of the first African-American horsemen to campaign runners on the New York racing circuit, champion 1991 owner in Barbados; of cancer, on October 8, 2005.

Paul R. Fout, 78, trainer, whose winners on the flat and over jumps included 1975 steeplechase champion Life's Illusion and Grade 1-winning millionaire Colstar, father of trainer Doug Fout; after a brief illness, on August 16, 2005, in Middleburg, Virginia.

Mahmoud Fustok, 69, owner of the Buckram Oak breeding and racing operation, whose runners included 2005 Breeders' Cup Sprint (G1) winner Silver Train, champion Green Forest, and classic winners In Fijar and Siberian Express; of injuries sustained when struck by a car, on February 8, 2006, in Pompano Beach, Florida.

Frank Gabriel Sr., 86, former owner, trainer, jockey's agent, and racing secretary, father of Dubai Racing Club chief executive Frank Gabriel Jr.; following a long illness, on March 1, 2005, in Florida.

John R. Gaines, 76, a Thoroughbred industry pioneer who conceived the idea of the Breeders' Cup, established Gainesway Farm, was a leading force in creating the Kentucky Horse Park and the precursor to the National Thoroughbred Racing Association, winner of an Eclipse Award of Merit; of diabetes, on February 11, 2005, in Lexington.

Peter Gallagher, 54, owner of 1976 Irish champion two-year-old and English Group 1 winner Godswalk; in March 2006, in Ireland.

Louise Jones Gans, 102, longtime racing fan, who attended 85 runnings of the Kentucky Derby, beginning with Sir Barton's victory in 1919; at her home, on January 12, 2006, in Louisville.

Eduardo Gaviria, 65, South American businessman who bred 1997 Kentucky Derby (G1) and Preakness Stakes (G1) winner Real Quiet; in April 2006, in Colombia.

Joe Gerrity Jr., 89, chairman of Saratoga Raceway Standardbred track, owner and breeder of several Thoroughbred stakes winners, including homebreds

Dave, Vodka, and Ora; following a long illness, on October 10, 2005, in New York.

Louis Goodwin, 85, successful owner-breeder in Maryland for more than 30 years, who campaigned in the name of Mom's Delight Stable; on February 10, 2005, in Baltimore.

Akili Gray, 30, Texas-based jockey who won 16 Thoroughbred races, from head injuries sustained in a July spill at the Gillespie County Fair, on April 15, 2006, in Texas.

Art "Duke" Green, 69, head starter at Finger Lakes Race Track since 1987, former jockey who had led the standings at Waterford Park and Scarborough Downs; in January 2006.

Stanley Greene, 82, who trained horses for several prominent owners during the 1960s before establishing the Virginia Stallion Station in 1977, former state steward at Charles Town Races; on March 12, 2005, in Purcellville, Virginia.

Elsa Grether, 77, wife of owner Tom Grether, whose family campaigned graded stakes winners Crafty C. T. and Madame Pietra; on February 28, 2006, in California.

Mel Gross, 58, former Mid-Atlantic-based trainer, whose runners included 1977 Jockey Club Gold Cup (G1) winner On the Sly and Canadian champion Canadian Factor; of stroke complications, on June 5, 2005.

Michael Guarino, 80, New Jersey-based owner, part-owner of LOTSOC Stables; on October 26, 2005, in Wilmington, North Carolina.

Joseph Haller, 76, former co-owner of Wafare Farm in Midway, Kentucky, who raced several stakes winners, including Dancing Missile, Millee Van, and Sugar's Best; on September 8, 2005, in Omaha, Nebraska.

Tom Halliday, 20, apprentice steeplechase jockey, who had won four races in his brief career; of injuries sustained in a spill at Market Rasen racecourse, on July 3, 2005, in London, England.

Waddell Hancock, 90, widow of Claiborne Farm scion Arthur B. "Bull" Hancock Jr., mother of Claiborne President Seth Hancock, Stone Farm owner Arthur Hancock III, and equine photographer Dell Hancock; on June 17, 2005, at Claiborne, in Paris, Kentucky.

William Hanrahan, 89, circulation manager at the *Daily Racing Form* for more than 50 years, on March 18, 2006, in Westmont, Illinois.

Billy Hardcastle, 69, longtime breeder, owner, and trainer who raced at Oaklawn Park; of cancer, on January 2, 2006.

Kim Hart, president and chief executive of Horsepower Broadcasting Network International Ltd., past director and vice president of the HBPA of British Columbia, a leading owner at Hastings Park; of natural causes, on February 10, 2005, in British Columbia.

Alex Harthill, 80, famed veterinarian, who treated 18 Kentucky Derby winners from Citation in 1948 to Fusaichi Pegasus in 2000; of complications related to a stroke and pneumonia, on July 16, 2005, in Louisville.

James "Chris" Herrell, 31, Midwest-based jockey, who rode 353 winners, with purse earnings of nearly $3-million over 14 seasons; of sudden and unknown causes, on November 12, 2005, at his home in Louisville.

James Hines, Jr., 69, owner and breeder of 2005 graded stakes winner and classics prospect Lawyer Ron; of accidental drowning, on February 21, 2006, at his home near Owensboro, Kentucky.

Virgil Hisel, 91, owner of Twin Eagles Farm near Lexington, breeder of several stakes winners, member of the Thoroughbred Farm Managers Club; on March 8, 2006, in Nicholasville, Kentucky.

Bruce Hobbs, 84, trainer and former jockey, who in 1938 became the youngest rider to win England's Grand National Steeplechase, aboard Battleship, and who later trained English flat champions Tromos (GB), Take a Reef, and Jacinth; on November 21, 2005, in Newmarket, England.

Lou Hodges Sr., 88, longtime track photographer at Fair Grounds, member of the Fair Grounds Press Box Hall of Fame, father of current Fair Grounds photographer Lou Hodges Jr.; on November 29, 2005, in Baton Rouge, Louisiana.

Harry Hoffheimer, 93, prominent lawyer who served on the Ohio Racing Commission during the 1950s and 1960s, past president of the National Association of State Racing Commissioners; on February 13, 2006, in Ohio.

Pat Hogan, 83, successful bloodstock agent, whose clients included Robert Sangster, and who purchased such stars as Rheingold, French Horse of the Year Detroit (Fr), and classic winner Assert (Ire). Former five-time leading amateur rider in Ireland; in July 2005, in Kilmallock, Ireland.

Roger Howard, 45, former jockey and a longtime jockey's agent, brother of trainers Tom Howard and Sam Howard; of cancer, on March 17, 2005.

Ted Howarth, 80, longtime Australasian owner and breeder, past president of the New Zealand Thoroughbred Breeders' Association; in December 2005, in New Zealand.

Donald Hughes, 73, longtime Maryland-based Thoroughbred breeder and trainer, who purchased his first racehorse in 1968 and founded DWOH Farm near Westminster; of cancer, on November 21, 2005, in Baltimore.

Norman Hughes, 71, former jockey, co-founder of Silver Fox Stables, which specialized in quarantine services and repair of leg injuries; on April 29, 2005, in Florida.

Jose Luis Hugo, 75, former South American trainer, longtime hotwalker for trainer Mike Hushion; on November 30, 2005, of an apparent heart attack, at Aqueduct racetrack, in New York.

Barbara Smith Huguelet, 72, a co-owner of major stakes winner and 1967 Kentucky Derby runner-up Barbs Delight, member of the Keeneland Association; on June 9, 2005, in Lexington.

Jose Hurst, 29, Chicago-based exercise rider for his uncle, trainer Wayne Catalano; of injuries sustained when his bicycle was hit by a truck near Hawthorne Race Course, on October 17, 2005, in Chicago.

Bruce Hutchison, 63, Australian-born horseman who trained in Hong Kong for nearly a quarter-century and saddled more than 300 winners; of a probable heart attack, on July 23, 2005, in Macau.

Don Enrico Incisa, 70, well-known trainer in the north of England, noted for rejuvenating injured horses; on April 30, 2005, in England.

Tom Ivers, 61, equine exercise physiologist, who created a scientific approach to equine nutrition and training, owner of Equine Racing Systems, author of *The Fit Racehorse* and *The Fit Racehorse II*; of lymphoma cancer, on November 13, 2005, in Washington.

Jack Jackson, racetrack groom for nearly 50 years, who rubbed champions Genuine Risk and Honest Pleasure for trainer LeRoy Jolley; in 2005.

Robert W. Jeans, 82, who groomed Racing Hall of Fame champion Buckpasser and other notable runners for trainer Eddie Neloy; of natural causes, on April 15, 2005.

Nick Jemas, 86, former jockey and longtime Jockeys' Guild national manager, who successfully worked toward raising jockey mount fees, father of New Jersey Sports and Exposition Authority Vice President James Jemas; on April 14, 2005, in New Jersey.

Kay Eric Jensen, 86, a former leading jockey in Sweden, believed to be the only rider to win a flat race and a steeplechase on the same card, at Belmont Park, retired trainer of graded stakes winners Golden Don, Heron Cove, and He's Vivacious; after a brief illness, on May 13, 2005, in Warrenton, Virginia.

Norman "Bootie" Johnson, 64, veteran Maryland-based trainer whose runners included stakes-winning Ayeaspecialgirl; on January 11, 2005, in Maryland.

Harry Jones, 58, trainer, husband of Monmouth Park paddock judge Evelyn "Cookie" Jones; after falling from his mount, on July 23, 2005, at Philadelphia Park.

J. Bradley Jones, 67, co-owner of Regal Heir Farms; of injuries sustained in a helicopter crash on farm property on April 20, 2006, near Grantville, Pennsylvania.

Stanley Jones, 91, longtime trainer who saddled winners at tracks in Maryland, Pennsylvania, and West Virginia, member of the Charles Town HBPA; on February 10, 2006, in Ranson, West Virginia.

Attie Saffie Joseph Sr., 92, prominent Caribbean owner whose runners since the 1940s included winners of the Trinidad and United Barbados Derbys; on January 23, 2005, in Barbados.

Peter Karches, 53, former co-chairman of NYRA, Jockey Club member, TOBA trustee, and owner, whose graded stakes winners included Dynever and Statesmanship; of lymphocytic leukemia, on April 13, 2006, in Boston.

Marty Katz, 51, a *Daily Racing Form* clocker for more than 20 years before becoming a private New York-based clocker; on January 29, 2006, in New York.

Deb Kay, 50, who rehabilitated and retrained retired racehorses as proprietor of the Oaks of Kendall Woods; stabbed to death on January 30, 2005, at her home in Houston.

Harold E. Kelley, 84, former member of the Kentucky State Racing Commission; of injuries sustained in a car accident, on December 23, 2005, in Lexington.

Kevin Kerr, late 80s, European-based trainer whose runners included Irish classic winners *Sea Charger and *Green Banner; in April 2005, in Dublin.

Brent King, 44, longtime manager of his family's King's Way Farm in Paris, Kentucky, where he helped raise 1987 Breeders' Cup Sprint (G1) winner Very Subtle; after a long illness, on November 21, 2005, in Kentucky.

Art Krawitz, 53, former Western advertising representative for *Daily Racing Form* and advertising manager for the *Thoroughbred of California* magazine; after a long battle with cancer, on November 9, 2005, in Santa Monica, California.

Michel Lapensee, 58, jockey, who in a 38-year career rode 2,678 winners, for purse earnings of $12.4-million; of injuries sustained in an October 24 accident during a race at Suffolk Downs, on October 28, 2005, in Boston.

Russ Lawler, 84, longtime steward in Washington state, and former trainer, jockey's agent, and clerk of scales, for whom Racing Hall of Fame jockey Russell Baze was named; of injuries sustained in a car accident, in late March 2005.

Nina Leatherman, 60, longtime owner, breeder, and trainer, who saddled 84 winners, including stakes winner Milk Money, mother of Retama Park racing secretary James Leatherman; on December 13, 2005, in Temple, Texas.

Adrian Ledger, 25, Australian jockey who had ridden approximately 150 winners; from head injuries sustained in a fall on March 13, 2005, at Corowa racecourse, in Canberra, Australia.

Frederick M. Lege III, 87, Virginia farm owner and breeder, who bred 1984 Sunny Slope Stakes (G3) winner Matthew T. Parker and other stakes winners; on March 23, 2005, in Virginia.

Alain Lequeux, 59, a former leading French jockey, whose 33 Group or Grade 1 victories included the French One Thousand Guineas and the Hollywood Turf Cup; of a cerebral hemorrhage, on April 25, 2006, in Senlis, France.

Alice Lewis, 83, Thoroughbred owner, who with her husband, James, campaigned multiple Grade 1 winner Mecke and 1992 Kentucky Derby (G1) entrant Sir Pinder; of heart failure, on May 2, 2005, in Florida.

James Lewis, 83, Thoroughbred owner, who with his wife, Alice, campaigned multiple Grade 1 winner Mecke and 1992 Kentucky Derby (G1) entrant Sir Pinder; of heart and kidney failure, on May 10, 2005, in Florida.

Robert Lewis, 81, Eclipse Award-winning owner, who with wife Beverly campaigned champions Silver Charm, Charismatic, Serena's Song, Orientate, Folklore, and Timber Country. Member of the Jockey Club; on February 17, 2006, in Newport Beach, California.

Robert Levine, 86, New York-based owner and trainer who saddled 187 winners, including 2005 Bonnie Miss Stakes (G2) winner Jill Robin L, and as an owner campaigned multiple Grade 2 winner Koluctoo's Jill; father of trainer Bruce Levine; on March 17, 2005, in New York.

Brenda Linville, 41, stallion secretary at Lane's End; of pancreatic cancer, on January 5, 2005, in Lexington.

Gavin Lisk, 23, Australian apprentice jockey; from head and spinal injuries suffered in a fall at Moe racecourse, on March 15, 2005, in Melbourne.

Frank Lodato Jr., 52, former trainer, jockey's agent, and clocker at Fair Grounds in Louisiana; on April 8, 2005, in New Orleans.

James Logsdon, D.V.M., 69, longtime veterinarian at racetracks in Arkansas and Chicago, whose patients had included Secretariat, Buckpasser, and John Henry, on-call veterinarian for ESPN and ABC television; on May 27, 2006, in Little Rock, Arkansas.

Gillian Carol Luxton, 63, owner and breeder, director for the Ontario division of the Canadian Thoroughbred Horse Society; following an illness, on September 9, 2005, in Puslinch, Ontario.

Francisco Eduardo de Paula Machado, 90, former president of the Brazilian Jockey Club, prominent owner-breeder who campaigned North American Grade 1 winners Siphon (Brz) and Virginie (Brz); of a heart attack, on January 1, 2005, in Rio de Janeiro.

Dennis Madonna, 48, co-owner of Regal Heir Farms; of injuries sustained in a helicopter crash on farm property, on April 20, 2006, near Grantville, Pennsylvania.

Carl Maggio, 59, former California-based owner, whose top runners included graded stakes winners Marisma and Cat Girl; of brain cancer, on October 31, 2005, in California.

Sheikh Maktoum bin Rashid al Maktoum, 62, ruler of Dubai, renowned Thoroughbred industry leader, and owner of four international breeding farms under the banner of Gainsborough Stud Management; of a probable heart attack, on January 4, 2006, in Australia.

Foster Lee "Pete" Maloy, 71, prominent Florida owner and breeder who raised 2005 Santa Anita Derby (G1) winner Buzzards Bay on his Hidden Hills Farm in Ocala; of gunshot wounds, on August 12, 2005, near Umatilla, Florida.

Landon Manning, 88, retired Turf writer, racing editor for *The Saratogian* newspaper for nearly 40 years, author of two books, including *Extra Sugar for Kelso*; on February 22, 2006, in Saratoga Springs, New York.

William Marshall, 87, former jockey and successful National Hunt and flat trainer in England and Barbados, only trainer to saddle winners on four continents, 11-time champion trainer in Barbados, where he saddled 648 winners since 1981; on October 31, 2005, in Barbados.

Robert "R. J." Martin, 77, former jockey who ranked among the leading New England-based riders for 40 years and won the riding title at Narragansett Park in 1947 and 1987; following a lengthy illness, on March 10, 2005, in Aventura, Florida.

Roye McClain, 38, assistant starter at Tampa Bay Downs, former assistant starter for the Kentucky Derby (G1) and Dubai World Cup (UAE-G1); of unreported causes, on February 26, 2006, at his home in Tampa Bay, Florida.

Ronald "Chick" McClellan, 86, former jockey and trainer and longtime California-based jockey's agent, whose clients included Racing Hall of Fame rider Sandy Hawley, and whose son Scotty is also a well-known agent; on July 30, 2005, in Arcadia, California.

Seamus McGrath, 83, retired four-time champion trainer in Ireland, whose runners included French Horse of the Year Levmoss and six Irish classic winners, including *Panaslipper, Weavers' Hall, and Silken Glider; in July 2005.

Edward McKinsey, 74, former general manager of Atlantic City Race Course and Hialeah, Arlington, Monmouth, Delaware, and Gulfstream Parks; of surgical complications, on January 29, 2005, in North Miami Beach, Florida.

Bill McNerney Jr., 51, longtime valet at Michigan racetracks, former clocker and colors man in the Great Lakes Downs jockeys' room; on September 14, 2005, at his home in Muskegon, Michigan.

Sam McRae, 16, New Zealand-based apprentice jockey; as the result of a freak accident at Riverton racecourse, on March 26, 2005, near Invergargill, New Zealand.

Walter Medio, 77, retired horseman, 1991 trainer of the year at Atlantic City Race Course, whose runners included champion New Jersey-bred filly Plain all Over and stakes-winning Over Protected; on April 8, 2006, in Vineland, New Jersey.

Walter Merrick, 94, prominent Midwest-based owner-breeder, member of the Oklahoma Horse Racing Hall of Fame, bred at least a dozen Thoroughbred stakes winners and the Quarter Horse champion Easy Jet; on February 4, 2006, in Oklahoma.

Cathie Atkinson Metzler, 64, daughter of the late Racing Hall of Fame jockey Ted Atkinson, widow of trainer Ray Metzler, mother of television racing journalist Caton Bredar; of complications from heart surgery, on April 25, 2006, in Chicago.

Jerome Meyer, 78, two-time leading Canadian trainer, member of the Canadian Racing Hall of Fame, whose 2,500-plus winners included Canadian champions Good Old Mort and Northernette, and major stakes winner Verbatim; of cancer, on July 15, 2005, in Toronto.

Elmer Miller, 75, Midwest owner-breeder who raced 14 stakes winners, including 1984 Kentucky Derby (G1) runner-up Coax Me Chad and homebred graded stakes winner Coaxing Matt; of cancer, on September 19, 2005, in Cincinnati.

Paulie Miller, 86, racing fan, Thoroughbred owner, well-known Kentucky political figure and legendary high school football coach; of complications from a stomach perforation, on June 29, 2005, in Louisville.

Dick Mitchell, 66, noted handicapper, author of several books on handicapping, including the bestseller *Winning Thoroughbred Strategies*, and founder of Cynthia Publishing Co.; of non-Hodgkin's lymphoma, on November 27, 2005, in Yuma, Arizona.

Robert S. Mitchell, 83, longtime Midwest-based owner, who campaigned graded winners Well Noted and Testify, and whose Our Trade Winds was unplaced in the 1972 Kentucky Derby; of Parkinson's disease, on July 30, 2005, in Tulsa, Oklahoma.

Christine Moore, Thoroughbred owner and breeder in the Southwest for more than 30 years, mother of Texas Thoroughbred Association director Sherry Raska, owner of South 64 Ranch; on April 4, 2005, in Texas.

James J. Moran, 45, former owner and trainer in New York, Maryland, and Delaware; of complications following surgery, on June 13, 2005, in Ohio.

Veda Morris, successful New Zealand breeder, who with her husband, Jim, bred 1984 Australian Derby (Aus-G1) winner Importune and Group 1 winner Cariere; on July 31, 2005, in New Zealand.

Patrick F. Murphy, 81, retired steeplechase rider; at his home, on June 14, 2005, in Lexington.

William Murray, 78, well-known author of novels with horse racing settings, including *Tip on a Dead Crab* and *Dead Heat*; of a heart attack, on March 8, 2005, in New York City.

James Musto, 75, owner of Jimmy's Turf Clothes

and Accessories at Monmouth Park, father of New Jersey Thoroughbred Horsemen's Association Executive Director Mike Musto; after a long illness, on August 22, 2005, in New Jersey.

Rev. Herman Naber, 72, a Roman Catholic priest who conducted church services every Sunday during live Churchill Downs meetings; on October 31, 2005, in Louisville.

Marty Nadel, 71, longtime owner; of pneumonia after a long battle with pancreatic cancer, on April 17, 2006, in California.

John Nichols Sr., 71, well-known farrier and former trainer and jockey, father of clocker John Nichols Jr., brother of the late jockey Jimmy Nichols; on February 6, 2006, in Jeffersonville, Indiana.

Charles Nuckols Jr., 83, prominent Kentucky horseman, who in various partnerships bred dozens of stakes winners, including champion and dual classic winner War Emblem; Jockey Club member, Breeders' Cup director, past president of the Thoroughbred Club of America; of congestive heart failure, on September 2, 2005, at Nuckols Farm, in Midway, Kentucky.

George L. Ohrstrom Jr., 78, Thoroughbred owner and breeder whose runners included French champion *Comtesse de Loir and homebred Grade 1 winner Mossflower, publisher of *The Chronicle of the Horse* magazine for 50 years; after a long illness, on October 6, 2005, in The Plains, Virginia.

Joseph "Poppa Joe" Osborne Jr., 68, longtime Kentucky-based owner; on February 19, 2006, in Florida.

Michael Osborne, 71, veterinarian, former manager of North Ridge Farm and managing director of the Irish National Stud, who helped establish international racing in Dubai and launch the world's richest race, the Dubai World Cup (UAE-G1); after a short illness, on December 23, 2005.

Kerry Packer, 68, billionaire media mogul noted as Australia's wealthiest citizen, who campaigned 1987 Sydney Cup (Aus-G1) winner Major Drive; in his sleep, on December 26, 2005, in Australia.

Luis "Albert" Palacios, 73, leading Ohio trainer, who saddled 1,437 winners, including 61 stakes winners, and won five training titles at River Downs; of injuries sustained in a car accident, on September 22, 2005, in Wilmington, Ohio.

Judy Parsons, 53, member of the Hollywood Park clocking crew, former trainer and assistant to Ross Fenstermaker with 1985 Eclipse Award-winning sprinter Precisionist; of cancer, on February 10, 2005, in California.

Pat Pastore, 86, longtime Northern California trainer, whose runners included stakes-winning Little Duke, former semi-pro baseball player who once hit a home run off Satchel Paige in an exhibition game; on October 10, 2005, in California.

John H. Peace, 81, New York owner and breeder, who campaigned homebred graded stakes winners West by West and Top Secret, trustee emeritus of NYRA, member of the Jockey Club, past Breeders' Cup board member; on October 22, 2005, in Sleepy Hollow, New York.

Melvin Peterson, 83, retired jockey who rode *Olhaverry to victory in the 1947 Santa Anita Handicap, and who finished fourth aboard Billings in the 1948 Kentucky Derby; on January 3, 2005, in Phoenix.

James "Jack" Phillips, a leading trainer at La Mesa Park in the 1950s and '60s, who later trained at Santa Anita, Churchill Downs, and Del Mar, and whose top runners included stakes winners Earl of Milldale and Smokite; on April 11, 2006, in Raton, New Mexico.

Thomas Pollard, 54, longtime trainer in the West, son of the late, leading Northern California trainer Damon "Buster" Pollard; of a brain hemorrhage, on December 19, 2005, in El Paso, Texas.

Joseph Pons Sr., 83, patriarch of his family's Country Life Farm, a leading Thoroughbred breeding facility where Racing Hall of Fame champion Cigar was raised; at Country Life, on October 10, 2005, near Bel Air.

Josh Radosevich, 16, apprentice jockey who had ridden 19 winners since launching his career in October, ranked among the leading riders at Beulah Park; of injuries sustained in a spill during a race at Beulah Park, on November 16, 2005, in Grove City, Ohio.

Jim Randle, 66, Arizona-based owner and breeder, founder and co-owner of Pinnacle Vista Ranch near Phoenix; on February 9, 2005, in Arizona.

Sheilah Rathbun, 81, owner of a successful racing and breeding facility near Middleburg, Virginia, breeder of $543,432 stakes winner Shiny Sheet; of emphysema, on January 10, 2005, in Arlington, Virginia.

Leon Reed, 47, assistant starter at Finger Lakes racetrack; after being kicked while loading a horse into the starting gate, on November 19, 2005, in New York.

Richard Stone Reeves, 85, renowned equine painter, whose commissions included many of the world's greatest Thoroughbreds, and whose work was published in several books; on October 7, 2005, in Greenport, New York.

Bruce Reid, 84, prominent Australian owner, co-owner of 2004 Cox Plate (Aus-G1) winner Savabeel and 2004 Caulfield Guineas (Aus-G1) winner Econsul; of complications from heart surgery, on March 13, 2005, in Australia.

Arthur Renihan, Jr., 77, former trainer and owner, past member of the Thoroughbred Club of America; on February 24, 2005, in Indiana.

Lucy Reum, 91, the first woman to head a racing commission in this country when appointed chairwoman of the Illinois Racing Board in 1977, Chicago HBPA Horseman of the Year in 1975; on July 18, 2005, in Chicago.

Willys Rhodes Sr., 84, longtime Mississippi-based owner, breeder, and trainer, who saddled 71 winners, including stakes winner Burgled; on April 16, 2005, in Bay St. Louis, Mississippi.

Ray Richards, 76, a Thoroughbred owner since 1983, who campaigned 1986 Kentucky Derby (G1) runner-up and French champion Bold Arrangement (GB) with his brother Tony; in 2005, in England.

William M. Rickman Sr., 84, horse breeder who bought and revived Delaware Park racetrack during the mid-1980s, after it had been shut down due to financial difficulties; on September 30, 2005, in Rockville, Maryland.

Vittorio Riva, 66, a leading Italian owner-breeder,

who raced champion Red Arrow and bred Group 1 winner Mendez; owned Hanes du Thenney in Normandy. Former vice president of the Italian Jockey Club; on May 7, 2005, in Saroma, Italy.

Dr. Ben F. Roach, 86, founder of Parrish Hill Farm in Kentucky, breeder of 1999 Horse of the Year Charismatic and 1984 Breeders' Cup Distaff winner Princess Rooney; after hitting his head in a fall at his home, on September 16, 2005, in Lexington.

Roland "Roly" Roberts, 75, longtime racetrack executive, former chief financial officer of the Ontario Jockey Club, winner of a special Sovereign Award in 2002 for his commitment to Canadian racing; on March 4, 2006, in Toronto.

Kevin Robinson, 75, noted Australian trainer who saddled Kenbelle for a victory in the 1996 Australian Jockey Club Oaks (Aus-G1); on May 6, 2005, in Australia after a long illness.

Edmund B. Ross, 85, longtime Thoroughbred owner-breeder, raced stakes winner Royal Form, member of the Essex Hunt Club; following a brief illness, on January 17, 2005, in Morristown, New Jersey.

Sam Rubin, 91, Eclipse Award-winning co-owner with wife Dorothy, who campaigned two-time Horse of the Year and former all-time leading Thoroughbred earner John Henry in the name of their Dotsam Stable; on February 13, 2006, in Palm Beach, Florida.

Stuart "Beef" Rubin, 51, well-known horseplayer and racing fan, who frequented press boxes at New York and New Jersey racetracks, winner of the 2002 Sports Haven Handicapping Challenge; of a heart attack, on September 16, 2005, at the Fiddler's Elbow OTB, in the Bronx, New York.

Leslie Salminen, owner, noted mathematician; of breast cancer, on April 25, in Monongahela, Pennsylvania.

Abdussamed Samadi, 84, Maryland-based owner-breeder, who bred stakes-winning Kayacan in the name of his Turkeli Farms; of complications from a stroke, on February 5, 2005, at his home near Hollywood, Maryland.

Emanuel Jose Sanchez, 22, apprentice jockey, who had recorded his first career winner on June 19, 2005; after collapsing in the Colonial Downs' jockeys' room, on July 23, 2005, in Richmond, Virginia.

Robert Scanlon, 57, a perennial leading two-year-old sales consignor and operator of Scanlon Training Center in Florida, whose graduates included dual 2005 classic winner Afleet Alex, champion Artax, and Grade 1 winners Lion Heart and Unbridled's Song; of cancer, on October 13, 2005, in Florida.

Dorothy Scharbauer, 73, who raced dual classic winner and 1988 Horse of the Year Alysheba with her daughter, Pamela, co-owner of Valor Farm in Texas; of pancreatic cancer, on February 23, 2005, in Midland, Texas.

Harry L. Schmidt Jr., 81, who oversaw the early lives of Mr. Prospector and Majestic Prince as broodmare manager of Spendthrift Farm; on February 8, 2005, in Lexington.

Hubert "Whitey" Schweickhardt, 82, head of press box security at Churchill Downs for 20 years; on February 18, 2006, in Louisville.

Wilton Scott, 93, well-known Texas-based owner-breeder, owner of Scott Ranch near Huntsville, whose homebreds included $417,965-earner Boots on Sunday and 2005 stakes winner Goosey Moose; while undergoing heart surgery, on June 30, 2005, in Houston.

Hilde Shapiro, 73, Virginia-based owner and breeder for nearly 50 years, owner of Hiljo Farm near Goldvein; on October 11, 2005, in Fredericksburg, Virginia.

Leo Shirley, 93, past president of the National Association of State Racing Commissioners, Michigan racing commissioner from 1968 to 1975, longtime FBI agent; on October 13, 2005, in Traverse City, Michigan.

Wayne Shumate, 71, past president of the Association of Racing Commissioners International, member of the Kentucky Racing Commission; following an illness and a car accident, on November 14, 2005, in Lexington.

Sam Siciliano, 89, former award-winning publicity director at Pimlico Race Course, past president of Turf Publicists of America, New Jersey columnist for *Daily Racing Form*; of congestive heart failure, on January 31, 2006, in Shrewsbury, New Jersey.

Carol Sue Smalley, 59, member of the Thoroughbred Owners and Breeders Association and the Oklahoma Thoroughbred Association; on January 5, 2005, in Chelsea, Oklahoma.

R. Gene Smith, 70, Louisville-based owner, breeder, businessman, and philanthropist, campaigned graded stakes winner Inkatha; of a heart attack, on March 13, 2005, in Louisville.

Daniel M. "Mikey" Smithwick, 77, Racing Hall of Fame steeplechase trainer, whose top runners included Hall of Fame jumper Neji and champions Bon Nouvel, Ancestor, Top Bid, Mako, and Straight and True; of Parkinson's disease, on May 29, 2006, near Hydes, Maryland.

Brad Smythe, 48, Sovereign Award winner as Canada's outstanding apprentice jockey of 1977; of cancer, on February 4, 2005, in Alberta.

Mickey Solomon, 75, former longtime head clocker for *Daily Racing Form* at Churchill Downs and Keeneland; following a long illness, on April 17, 2006, in Louisville.

Norine Spadaro, 61, wife of New York Thoroughbred Breeding and Development Fund Deputy Executive Director Joe Spadaro; following a long illness, on July 11, 2005, in New York.

Fred Spohn, 79, British Columbia-based owner-breeder, who bred 1974 Canadian champion Rushton's Corsair in the name of his Clearbrook Stock Farm; on July 3, 2005, in Fort Langley, Canada.

Hassel Spraberry, 74, owner-breeder of 2004 WinStar Derby winner Hi Teck Man, campaigned 1997 New Mexico champion Missy Cherub, longtime member of the Texas Thoroughbred Association; owner Hi-Lo Farms, on February 21, 2005, in Texas.

Steve Stavro, 78, Canadian-based owner and breeder who campaigned more than 50 stakes winners and six Canadian champions under the name of Knob Hill Stable; of an apparent heart attack, on April 24, 2006, in Ontario.

Alyce Stevens, 77, New York-based owner whose Inniscarra Stable campaigned multiple stakes winner Chowder's First; of cancer, on January 23, 2006, at her home in Delray Dunes, Florida.

William Steward, 46, assistant starter at Penn National Race Course; of injuries sustained when he was run over by the starting gate, on June 8, 2005, in Pennsylvania.

George Stidham, 78, former jockey, trainer, and business manager-agent for Racing Hall of Fame rider Bill Hartack, father of trainer Mike Stidham; on April 1, 2005, in Glendora, California.

John Sullivan, 77, West Coast-based trainer, who saddled Grade 1 winners The Bart, Forzando (GB), and Yashgan (GB); of cancer, on March 20, 2006, in Arcadia, California.

Jack Taylor, 70, noted New Zealand-based trainer, vice president of Stratford Racing Club, whose runners included 1984 New Zealand Two Thousand Guineas (NZ-G1) winner Kingdom Bay; in May 2005, in New Zealand.

William K. Taylor, 87, general manager of Claiborne Farm from 1957 to 1975, former manager of Nelson Bunker Hunt's Bluegrass Farm, developer of Springland Farm in Paris, Kentucky; on February 8, 2005, in Lexington.

Alvin Toffel, 69, California-based owner and breeder, who co-bred and -raced stakes winners Riva Ranger, Only the Best, and Rexy Sexy; of a stroke, on March 5, 2005, in Las Vegas.

Ward Theisen, 84, owner-breeder who with his wife campaigned homebred multiple stakes winner Din's Dancer, an unplaced finisher in the 1988 Kentucky Derby; on October 17, 2005, in Ocala.

Kenny Thornton, 77, well-known van driver who drove more than 5-million miles over nearly a half-century, and who transported such champions as Native Dancer and Northern Dancer; on December 23, 2005, in West Chester, Pennsylvania.

Maude Thornton, 82, a longtime administrative assistant who was executive director of the Thoroughbred Club of America from 1977 to 1987 and a bookkeeper for several Central Kentucky farms; on July 16, 2005, in Versailles, Kentucky.

Gerald Turner, 58, five-time champion South African jockey who won several classic races in his native country, longtime chairman of the Transvaal Jockeys' Association; of a heart attack, on February 9, 2005, in South Africa.

Bob Umphrey, 53, racing secretary at Calder Race Course. Former racing secretary at Hollywood, Laurel, and Arlington Parks, served as racing secretary for the inaugural Breeders' Cup in 1984; from complications of a heart attack and stroke, on January 2, 2006, in Hollywood, Florida.

Jose Valenzuela, 72, former jockey, cousin of retired jockey Milo Valenzuela; on April 3, 2006, in Ceres, California.

John Valpredo, 96, California owner-breeder for 50 years, father of Jockey Club member Don Valpredo, bred graded stakes winners Dimaggio and Fifty Six Ina Row, imported and raced major 1970s stakes winners *Lucie Manet and *Star Ball; on January 12, 2005, in Bakersfield, California.

Theresa Vella, 50, wife of trainer Danny Vella; following a long battle with cancer, on December 16, 2005, in Toronto.

Philip Lee Walters, 64, owner-breeder, former trainer, owner of Afton Farm in Kentucky; of a heart attack on May 14, 2006, at his farm, near Midway, Kentucky.

Madeline Walton, 76, longtime Canadian-based trainer, who took out her first license in 1955 at Stampede Park; after being kicked by one of her horses, on July 4, 2005, at Marquis Downs, in Saskatchewan.

Paul Ward, 70, former jockey who consistently ranked among Ohio's leading riders during a 17-year riding career in the 1950s and '60s, lead outrider for more than 30 years at Beulah Park; on March 21, 2005, near Canal Winchester, Ohio.

Michael Watral, 87, New York-based owner and breeder, whose runners included Grade 1 winner Dixie Brass and stakes winner Packett's Landing; on September 17, 2005, on Long Island, New York.

James "Jamey" Weatherly, 27, jockey, who rode 494 winners of nearly $4.4-million in 11 seasons of competition; of injuries sustained in a car accident, on February 2, 2006, near Lafayette, Louisiana.

Randy Weinsier, 93, longtime Thoroughbred owner whose top runners included homebred 1977 champion two-year-old filly Lakeville Miss and homebred Grade 1 winner Golferette; on February 2, 2006, in Florida.

Michael Weissman, 82, trainer of multiple stakes winners Milwaukee Avenue and Powerless during the 1970s; after suffering a massive heart attack, on October 20, 2005, in Chicago.

Betsy Wells, 55, barn foreman and exercise rider for trainer Jonathan Sheppard during the 1980s, galloped Storm Cat and steeplechase champions Highland Bud and Flatterer; of ovarian cancer, on February 13, 2006.

Donald Lee West, 74, a farrier and former jockey in Kentucky and Louisiana; on September 4, 2005, in Apollo Beach, Florida.

Walter Wickes Jr., 90, longtime owner, breeder, and trainer, who with his wife, Helen, owned Carter's Thicket Farm in Pennsylvania, and who campaigned stakes winners Vendetta and Archie Beamish; on December 13, 2005, in Chester County, Pennsylvania.

Derrick Wiid, longtime South African-based owner, breeder, and bookmaker, who raced such noted runners as Kiaat, Artificer, and Salute Her; in a car accident, on May 10, 2006, in Johannesburg, South Africa.

Eddie Wingate, 86, well-known owner at Detroit Race Course; on May 5, 2006, in Las Vegas, Nevada.

Donna Dixon Woodall, 54, noted equine photographer, accomplished horsewoman, and animal rights advocate; after a 17-year battle with cancer, on September 29, 2005, in Lexington.

John C. Wyatt, 76, longtime Central Kentucky-based photographer who worked for Keeneland Race Course and for a local newspaper; on April 19, 2005, in Lexington.

Bill Wylie, prominent West Australian owner, who raced multiple 2001 Australian classic winner Magical Miss; in March 2006, in Australia.

John Zimmerman, 46, trainer, who saddled 1,469 winners, including graded stakes winner More Smoke and five-furlong world-record-setter Procreate, 2005 trainer of the year at Penn National; of a heart attack, on April 9, 2006, in Aventura, Florida.

Horse Deaths 2005 and 2006

AARON'S CONCORDE, 1984 dk. b. or br. h., Super Concorde—La Legende, by Reviewer. 40-6-8-9, $160,692. Won the 1988 Daniel Haines S. Sire of 1996 Gotham S. (G2) winner Romano Gucci and Maryland Million Distaff H. winner Flippy Diane; of colic, on June 20, 2005.

ACAROID, 1978 dk. b. or br. h., Big Spruce—Arachne, by Intentionally. 27-10-5-5, $452,907. Won the 1983 United Nations H. (G1). Iowa's leading sire of 1994 and '95. Sire of seven stakes winners, including Grade 1 winner Captive Miss; of a heart attack, in April 2006, at Timber Creek Farm, in Mitchellsville, Iowa.

ACATENANGO, 1982 ch. h., Surumu—Aggravate, by *Aggressor II. Two-time German Horse of the Year. Four-time leading sire in Germany. Sire of 69 stakes winners, including three champions; of injuries sustained in a paddock accident, on April 2, 2005, at Gestut Fahrhof, in Germany.

ADAM SMITH (GB), 1988 b. h., Sadler's Wells—Krakow, by Malinowski. 21-7-7-0, $367,186. Won the 1993 and '94 Fort Marcy H. (G3); of laminitis, in August 2005, at Fresh Start Thoroughbreds, near Lexington.

A HUEVO, 1996 b. g., Cool Joe—Verabald, by Baldski. 12-6-0-0, $389,750. Won the 2003 Frank J. De Francis Memorial Dash S. (G1); euthanized after breaking down in the West Virginia Breeders' Classic S., on October 8, 2005, at Charles Town Races, in West Virginia.

AL JADEED, 2000 b. h., Coronado's Quest—Aljawza, by Riverman. 10-3-1-2, $139,417. Won the 2004 Royal Lodge S. (Eng-G2); of a pulmonary hemorrhage, in early December 2005, at Berkley Stud, in New Zealand.

ALL ALONG (FR), 1979 b. m., Targowice—Agujita (FR), by Vieux Manoir. 21-9-4-2, $2,125,828. U.S. Horse of the Year, champion grass female of 1983, champion in France. Won the 1983 Prix de l'Arc de Triomphe (Fr-G1), Turf Classic (G1). Dam of French group winner Along All and stakes winner Arnaqueur; of old age, on February 23, 2005, at Three Chimneys Farm, in Midway, Kentucky.

All the Boys, 1997 b. g., Foreign Survivor—Dearness, by Affirmed. 33-9-2-3, $343,690. Second in the 2003 San Juan Capistrano Invitational H. (G1); after breaking down in a race at Hollywood Park, on May 29, 2005, in California.

ALVEAR, 1989 d. b. or br. m., Seattle Slew—Andover Way, by His Majesty. 9-2-0-1, $21,240. Dam of 2005 Suburban H. (G1) winner Offlee Wild; from surgery complications, on October 6, 2005, in Lexington.

American Day, 1992 b. h., Nureyev—Ubetshedid, by King Pellinore. 8-2-1-2, $94,312. Grade 3-placed. Half brother to Grade 1 winner Best Pal. Sire of winners and three stakes-placed runners; in 2005, in California.

ARGOSY, 1981 b. h., Affirmed—My Charmer, by Poker. 3-2-0-0, $22,279. Half brother to Seattle Slew sold for $1.5-million as yearling. Stakes winner in Ireland. Sire of at least ten stakes winners, including Group 1 winners Vistula and Lindberg; of laminitis, in January 2005, at Southford Stud, in South Africa.

AUENWEISE, 2002 dk. b. or br. f., Big Shuffle—Auenglocke, by Surumu. 2-1-1-0, $47,401. Stakes winner in Germany and a favorite for the 2005 Henkel-Rennen (Ger-G1) (German One Thousand Guineas); after breaking down, in April 2005, in Germany.

AU PRINTEMPS, 1979 b. m., Dancing Champ—*Lorgnette II, by High Hat. 30-7-5-4, $124,383. Stakes winner. Dam of Canadian champion Charlie Barley, 1987 Breeders' Cup Juvenile (G1) winner Success Express, and Grade 1 winner Greenwood Lake; after foaling, on May 10, 2005, at Pennbrook Farm, in Lexington.

AVE'S FLAG, 1992 b. g., Personal Flag—Ave Maria (Ger), by Experte. 60-11-9-3, $502,375. Champion New York-bred three-year-old male of 1995. Won the 1996 Gallant Fox H. (G3); of injuries sustained in a farm accident, on July 1, 2005, at Victory Lane Farm, in Millbrook, New York.

AYAM ZAMAN, 2002 b. f., Montjeu (Ire)—Kardashina (Fr), by Darshaan. 5-2-0-1, $47,019. Won the 2004 William Claridge Memorial Zetland S.; after breaking down in the Premio Oaks d'Italia (Ity-G1), on June 18, 2005, in Italy.

BALLET DE FRANCE, 1981 b. m., Northern Dancer—Fabulous Native, by *Le Fabuleux. 5-2-0-1, $20,299. Won the 1983 C. L. Weld Park S. (Ire-G3). Dam of Irish and Italian highweight Muhtarram and Grade 3 winner Profit Column; euthanized on August 5, 2005, at Dinwiddie Farm, in Middleburg, Virginia.

Bay Sweetie Babe, 2001 b. f., Archers Bay—Sweet Summit, by Bold Executive. 13-5-3-1, $300,027. Multiple stakes-placed in Canada; broke down during a workout, on October 2, 2005, at Woodbine racetrack, near Toronto.

BEACON SHINE, 2003 dk. b. or br. c., Montbrook—Unlimited Pleasure, by Valid Appeal. 5-2-0-1, $106,530. Won the 2005 Flash S. (G3); of colic, on April 8, 2006, at Churchill Downs.

Beckys Shirt, 1991 b. m., Cure the Blues—Thundertee, by Ye. 17-5-4-3, $174,856. Grade 2-placed. Dam of 2003 Breeders' Cup Sprint (G1) winner Cajun Beat; of colic after foaling, on April 3, 2005, at Ashford Stud, in Versailles, Kentucky.

Bedouin, 1981 ro. g., Al Hattab—Lady in Red, by Prince John. 67-14-6-4, $311,394. Stakes-placed. Finished 15th in the 1984 Kentucky Derby (G1); on April 12, 2006, at the California Equine Retirement Foundation ranch, in Winchester, California.

BEFORE DAWN, 1979 b. m., Raise a Cup—Moonbeam, by Tim Tam. 14-9-2-1, $432,855. Champion filly at two. Won the 1981 Spinaway S. (G1), Matron S. (G1). Dam of 11 winners from 11 starters, grandam of Australian Group 1 winner Prowl; in early 2006, in Kentucky.

BEST MATE, 1995 b. g., Un Desperado—Katday, by Miller's Mate. 22-14-7-0, $1,668,166. Three-time winner of the Cheltenham Gold Cup Steeplechase; of a heart attack, in the Haldon Gold Cup Steeplechase H., on November 1, 2005, at Exeter, in England.

BEST WALKING, 1999 gr. or ro. m., Big Shuffle—Bergwelt, by Solarstern. 13-3-1-2, $83,886. Won the 2003 Prix de Saint-Georges (Fr-G3); of colic, in spring 2005, at Coolmore, in Ireland.

BIG RUT, 1993 ch. g., Kokand—Miss Baltimore, by Gun Bow. 91-22-18-16, $570,488. Winner of seven stakes, including the 1996 Annapolis S.; in 2005.

BLUES AND ROYALS, 2002 b. c., Honour and Glory—Dixieland Blues, by Dixieland Band. 4-2-1-0, $1,216,980. Won the 2005 UAE Derby (UAE-G2); due to complications of colitis and laminitis, in mid-June 2005, at Belmont Park, in New York.

BLUSH WITH PRIDE, 1979 ch. m., Blushing Groom (Fr)—Best in Show, by Traffic Judge. 16-6-4-2, $536,807. Won the 1982 Kentucky Oaks (G1), Santa Susana S. (G1). Dam of graded or group winners Smolensk, Better Than Honour, and Turnberry Isle (Ire); grandam of 2006 Belmont Stakes (G1) winner Jazil; on August 16, 2005, in Ireland.

BRAVE RAJ, 1984 dk. b. or br. m., Rajab—Bravest Yet, by Bravo. 9-6-1-0, $933,650. Champion filly at two. Won the 1986 Breeders' Cup Juvenile Fillies (G1). Dam of stakes winners Russian Tango and Bravo Bull; of foaling difficulties, on January 28, 2006, at Patchen Wilkes Farm, in Lexington.

CARTWRIGHT, 1990 b. h., Forty Niner—Persuadable, by What a Pleasure. Unraced. Among the leading sires in Illinois. Sire of 13 stakes winners, including Wiggins and Crack the Vault; after suffering a broken femur, on August 10, 2005, at the University of Illinois, in Champaign, Illinois.

CATCOMINATCHA, 2003 ch. c., Tale of the Cat—Certainly a Star, by Red Ransom. 10-2-2-0, $215,706. Won the 2005 Iroquois S. (G3); euthanized after fracturing his right cannon bone during the Swale S. (G2), on March 4, 2006, at Gulfstream Park, in Florida.

CAT'S CAT, 2000 ch. m., Tabasco Cat—Catchofthecentury, by Carson City. 24-3-7-2, $168,513. Won the 2003 Hatoof S.; euthanized after breaking down in the San Felipe S., on January 8, 2005, at Sam Houston Race Park, in Texas.

CENT HOME, 1995 br. g., Lord Ballina—Centuria, by Centaine. 43-12-5-3, $329,619. New Zealand highweight in 2001. Multiple Group 1 winner; euthanized after breaking down in the Zabeel Classic (NZ-G1), on January 3, 2005, in New Zealand.

CHIMES BAND, 1991 dk. b. or br. h., Dixieland Band—Chimes, by Mr. Prospector. 19-7-2-2, $416,961. Group and graded winner in France and the U.S. Three-time leading New Mexico sire. Sire of 11 stakes winners, including Ceeband; in January 2005, following surgery for wobbler syndrome, in New Mexico.

CHUM SALMON, 1980 dk. b. or br. g., Gaelic Dancer—Saree, by The Dude. 29-13-4-5, $388,195. Won the 1985 Longacres Mile (G2) and eight other stakes; of old age, on December 19, 2005, in Washington.

CINDERELLA'S DREAM, 2003 b. f., Prime Timber—Broadway Hoofer, by Belong to Me. 4-2-2-0, $133,600. Won the 2005 Maid of the Mist S.; of a probable heart attack during a workout on January 8, 2006, at Palm Meadows Training Center, in Florida.

CIRCULATING, 1990 b. h., Bold Ruckus—Periphery, by Vice Regent. 14-5-0-2, $323,026. Won the 1992 Coronation Futurity. Three-time leading Manitoba sire. Sire of eight stakes winners, including Dawn Edition; on December 8, 2005, in Manitoba.

CITI STATE, 2000 ch. m., Citidancer—Bal Du Bois, by Balzac. 32-3-3-5, $104,170; of injuries suffered in a spill during the Conniver S., on March 12, 2005, at Laurel Park, in Maryland.

CLASSIFIED FACTS, 1993 b. h., Seattle Slew—Bald Facts, by In Reality. 15-2-3-0, $33,085. Among the leading 2005 sires in Illinois. Sire of 30 winners from 40 starters; in 2005, in Illinois.

CLASSY WOMEN, 1988 b. m., Relaunch—Aironlass, by Proud Clarion. 10-4-0-1, $154,708. Won the 1991 Hillsborough H. (G3). Dam of English Group 1 winner and Irish highweight Ad Valorem; euthanized due to chronic lameness, on March 15, 2006, at Calumet Farm, in Lexington.

COASTAL, 1976 ch. h., Majestic Prince—Alluvial, by Buckpasser. 14-8-1-3, $493,929. Won the 1979 Belmont S. (G1). Sire of 19 stakes winners, including Grade 1 winners Little Brianne and Danger's Hour. Broodmare sire of 53 stakes winners; of old age, in September 2005, at Summerhill Stud, in South Africa.

CODYS KEY, 1989 ro. h., Corridor Key—Go Thither, by Cabin. 56-14-4-10, $326,957. Won the 1993 Roseben H. (G3). Sire of stakes winner Foxy Scott; in 2006, in North Dakota.

COLORFUL VICES, 1993 ch. m., Regal Classic—Xoc, by Blade. 22-10-2-4, $417,150. Canadian champion grass female of 1998. Dam of graded stakes winner Colorful Judgement; in 2005.

COMMANCHE RUN, 1981 b. h., Run the Gantlet—Volley, by Ratification. 14-7-0-0, $607,912. Won the 1984 St. Leger (Eng-G1). Sire of 15 stakes winners, including Wavy Run (Ire) and Commanche Court; of heart failure, in March 2005, at Astley Grange Stud, in England.

CORONADO'S QUEST, 1995 ch. h., Forty Niner—Laughing Look, by Damascus. 17-10-2-0, $2,046,190. Won the 1998 Travers S. (G1). Sire of ten stakes winners, including multiple Grade 1 winner Society Selection; of a heart attack, on March 8, 2006, at JBBA Shizunai Stallion Station, in Hokkaido, Japan.

CORSLEW, 1990 b. h., Seattle Slew—Corsage, by Native Royalty. 31-8-5-2, $246,155. Multiple California stakes winner. Sire of four stakes winners, including Lethal Grande; euthanized after attacking a handler, on May 17, 2006, at Victory Rose Thoroughbreds, in Vacaville, California.

COUNTERFEIT GOLD, 2003 b. g., Twining—Counterfeit Bid, by Sheikh Albadou (GB). 5-2-1-1, $58,000. Won the 2005 Prairie Gold Juvenile S.; after breaking down in an allowance race, on May 6, 2006, at Canterbury Downs, in Minnesota.

COUNTESS DIANA, 1995 b. m., Deerhound—T. V. Countess, by T. V. Commercial. 14-7-2-0, $1,117,185. Champion filly at two. Won the 1997 Breeders' Cup Juvenile Fillies (G1). Dam of stakes winner Mama Nadine; of wobbler syndrome, in May 2006, at Rood & Riddle Equine Hospital, in Lexington.

COUPE AUX MARRONS, 2002 ch. f., Horse Chestnut (SAf)—Life Is Delicious, by Raft. 4-0-1-2, $14,090; euthanized due to equine herpesvirus, on December 23, 2005, at Hagyard Equine Medical Institute, in Lexington.

Cowboy Badgett, 2002 b. g., Bold Badgett—Gung Ho Ho, by Cartesian. 12-1-1-1, $22,870. Stakes-placed; after breaking down in a race at Golden Gate Fields, on June 8, 2005, in California.

CRAFTY EMBER, 1987 dk. b. or br. m., Crafty Prospector—Autumn Ember, by *Gallant Man. 39-10-7-6, $133,835. Won the 1992 Wintergreen S. Dam of 2005 Juddmonte Spinster S. (G1) winner Pampered Princess; from complications of foaling, on February 18, 2006, at Trackside Farm, in Versailles, Kentucky.

CRESTED WAVE (ran as Crest of the Wave in the U.S.), 1976 dk. b. or br. h., Crozier—Fading Wave, by *Quibu. 31-6-5-5, $284,965. Won the 1978 Futurity S. (G1). Leading New Zealand sire 1990-'91. Sire of 25 stakes winners, including champions Surfers Paradise (NZ) and Plume; euthanized in March 2006, at Cheval Stud, in New Zealand.

CRIMINAL TYPE, 1985 ch. h., Alydar—Klepto, by No Robbery. 24-10-5-3, $2,351,274. Horse of the

Year in 1990. Won the 1990 Hollywood Gold Cup H. (G1), Pimlico Special H. (G1). Sire of seven stakes winners. Broodmare sire of Ten Most Wanted; of a gastric rupture, on March 9, 2005, at Otsuka Bokujo, in Japan.

CRIMPLENE (IRE), 1997 ch. m., Lion Cavern—Crimson Conquest, by Diesis (GB). 16-6-1-4, $768,358. Highweighted filly at three on the English Free Handicap. Won the 2000 Coronation S. (Eng-G1). Dam of group-placed Crimson Sun; after foaling prematurely, in January 2005.

CRIMSON STAG, 2002 b. c., Glitterman—Alabama Anne, by D'Accord. 12-4-3-1, $265,410. Won the 2005 Louisiana Premier Night Prince S., '04 Louisiana Champions Day Juvenile S.; in a paddock accident, on December 6, 2005.

CROCROCK, 1997 b. g., North Prospect—Spice Wreath, by Summing. 42-16-6-3, $359,977. Winner of nine stakes, including the 2000 Minnesota Derby; after breaking down in a race, on April 26, 2005, at Prairie Meadows Racetrack, in Iowa.

CROWN JESTER, 1978 ch. h., Baguette—Anjudy, by Wilkes. Champion Australian two-year-old of 1980. Sire of at least 12 stakes winners, including Australian Group 1-winning millionaire Guineas; euthanized in November 2005, at Raheen Stud, in Queensland, Australia.

CRYPTO'S REDJET, 1992 b. m., Cryptoclearance—Doc's Lear Jet, by Lear Fan. 39-17-3-7, $364,640. Two-time Ohio horse of the year. Dam of stakes winner Crypto's Prospect; of complications from foaling, on April 14, 2005, at Willow Springs Farm, near Columbus, Ohio.

CULLEN, 1996 b. h., Danehill—Princess Tracy (Ire), by Ahonoora. 25-4-3-5, $203,279. Won the 1999 Blue Diamond Preview (Aus-G3), 2001 Rubiton S. (Aus-G3); due to complications of a high fever, in November 2005, at Westbury Stud, in New Zealand.

DANA NICOLE, 1983 b. m., Flying Paster—Carols Christmas, by Whitesburg. Unraced. Dam of Grade 2-winning millionaire Bien Nicole and stakes winner Sky Aly; of cancer, in November 2005, near Perkins, Oklahoma.

DANCE DAILY, 2003 ch. f., Five Star Day—Dance Alexa, by Southern Halo. 12-3-0-2, $184,426. Won the 2006 Santa Ynez S. (G2); after breaking down in the Stonerside Beaumont S. (G2), on April 13, 2006, at Keeneland Race Course.

DANCE QUIET, 2002 gr. or ro. c., Saint Ballado—Quiet Dance, by Quiet American. 12-2-4-0, $79,628. Full brother to 2005 Breeders' Cup Classic (G1) winner Saint Liam; after breaking down in an allowance race at Aqueduct, on November 16, 2005, in New York.

Danetime, 1994 b. h., Danehill—Allegheny River, by Lear Fan. 15-3-2-4, $193,190. Group 1-placed in England. Sire of six stakes winners, including English Group 2 winner The Kiddykid; of a ruptured artery, on September 8, 2005, in Australia.

DANOLI, 1988 b. g., The Parson—Blaze Gold, by Arizona Duke. 32-17-3-6, $520,945. Multiple stakes-winning hurdler in England and Ireland; of colic, in April 2006, at the Irish National Stud, in Kildare, Ireland.

DANZIG, 1977 b. h., Northern Dancer—Pas de Nom, by Admiral's Voyage. 3-3-0-0, $32,400. Three-time leading North American sire. Sire of at least 189 stakes winners, including Danehill and Dance Smartly. Broodmare sire of at least 132 stakes winners; euthanized due to infirmities of age, on January 3, 2006, at Claiborne Farm, in Paris, Kentucky.

DAWN'S CURTSEY, 1982 ch. m., Far North—Liberty Spirit, by Graustark. 28-5-3-7, $362,063. Won the 1985 Flower Bowl H. (G1). Dam of ten winners, including stakes winner Triumph At Dawn; of foaling complications, on March 15, 2006, in Kentucky.

DEEP GOLD, 1996 ch. h., Olympio—Distinctive Review, by Distinctive Pro. 33-7-6-3, $364,938. Won the 2000 Deputy Minister H. (G3). His first foals raced in 2006; from injuries sustained in a paddock accident, on May 15, 2005, at Cedar Creek Ranch, in New Mexico.

DEVIL'S BAG, 1981 b. h., Halo—Ballade, by *Herbager. 9-8-0-0, $445,860. Undefeated champion at two. Sire of 43 stakes winners, including Grade 1 winners Devil His Due, Twilight Agenda, Buy the Sport, and Devil's Orchid; euthanized after suffering a stall injury, on February 3, 2005, at Claiborne Farm, in Paris, Kentucky.

DIAGHLYPHARD, 1982 b. h., Lyphard—Jump Seat, by Hasty Road. 13-4-4-0, $47,123. Twice leading sire in Scandinavia. Sire of champions Songline and Kokomo; in early 2005, at Ravdansen Stuteri, near Stockholm, Sweden.

DIAMOND OMI, 2003 ch. f., Giant's Causeway—Hum Along, by Fappiano. 5-2-0-1, $160,740. Won the 2005 Oak Leaf S. (G2); of pneumonia, on November 17, 2005, in Chino, California.

DISMASTED, 1982 dk. b. or br. m., Restless Native—Nashima, by Nashua. 36-14-5-5, $629,803. Won the 1986 Flower Bowl H. (G1). Dam of graded or group-placed Gen Stormin'norman and Native Crown; due to infirmities of age, on September 10, 2005, at Spring Hill Farm, in Casanova, Virginia.

DISTINCTIVE PRO, 1979 dk. b. or br. h., Mr. Prospector—Well Done, by Distinctive. 13-8-3-1, $179,187. Won the 1982 Hutcheson S. (G2). Sire of 44 stakes winners, including Grade 1 winner Quick Mischief; of laminitis, on February 22, 2005, at Sugar Maple Farm, in Poughquag, New York.

DIXIELAND GOLD, 1992 b. m., Dixieland Band—Easy 'n Gold, by Slew o' Gold. 9-6-2-0, $226,232. Won the 1995 Beaumont S. (G2), La Troienne S. Dam of three winners; in 2005.

Dixiewink (GB), 2003 dk. b. or br. c., Dixie Union—More Silver, by Silver Hawk. 4-1-1-2, $77,400. Grade 2-placed at two; euthanized after breaking his shoulder in a workout on January 15, 2006, at Oaklawn Park, in Arkansas.

DON JAUN CON, 2003 b. g., Suggest—Nifty Slew, by Slewdledo. 7-2-2-1, $79,075. Won the 2005 Alameda County Futurity; of hemorrhaging, after breaking down in the Mill Valley S., on November 26, 2005, at Golden Gate Fields, in California.

EAGLE RISE (IRE), 2000 b. h., Danehill—Evening Breeze, by Surumu. 21-8-1-2, $370,493. Highweighted male at two and four in Germany; after breaking down in a race, on September 24, 2005, in Germany.

EGG HEAD, 2002 dk. b. or br. c., Honor Grades—Redding Ridge, by Screen King. 7-4-2-0, $145,420. Won the 2005 Francis "Jock" LaBelle Memorial S., Grade 2-placed; of colitis and laminitis, on July 11, 2005, in New York.

EL DUCE (PER), 1985 gr. or ro. h., Niobrara—Fleetness, by Flamigero. 41-14-10-5, $604,652. Four-time champion in Peru. Won the 1988 Derby Nacional (Per-G1). Sire of four known stakes winners, including three group winners; of unspecified causes, late in 2005, in Peru.

EL ELOGIADO (ARG), 2000 gr. or ro. h., Acceptable—Ellerstina, by Equalize. 11-3-1-3, $49,386. Won the 2003 Colonel Miguel F. Martinez S. (Arg-G2); after breaking down in an optional claiming race at Hollywood Park, on December 19, 2005, in California.

ELLE SEULE, 1983 ch. m., Exclusive Native—Fall Aspen, by Pretense. 16-3-4-2, $101,478. French Group 2 winner. Dam of four stakes winners, including 1994 Irish One Thousand Guineas (Ire-G1) winner Mehthaaf and Group 1 winner Elnadim; of a ruptured aneurysm, on February 21, 2005, at Shadwell Farm, in Lexington.

EPITRE, 1997 b. h., Common Grounds—Epistolienne, by Law Society. 29-5-6-2, $183,990. Highweighted at three on the French Free Handicap, 14 furlongs and up. Multiple group winner; of injuries sustained in a hurdle race, at Fontwell Park, in England.

ESCAPE THE STORM, 1994 ch. m., Storm Cat—Great Escape, by Relaunch. Unraced. Dam of 2005 Grade 1 winner Unfurl the Flag; euthanized due to foaling complications, on February 1, 2006, at Mill Ridge Farm, in Lexington.

ESTRAPADE, 1980 ch. m., *Vaguely Noble—Klepto, by No Robbery. 30-12-5-5, $1,937,142. Champion turf female of 1986. Won five Grade 1 stakes, including the 1986 Arlington Million S. Dam of stakes winner Rice; of a heart attack, on February 25, 2005, at Hill 'n' Dale Farms, in Lexington.

EXACTLY SO (IRE), 1977 ch. m., Caro (Ire)—Exactitude, by Exbury. 20-3-5-1, $137,468. Won the 1981 Gallorette H. (G3). Dam of German highweight and French Group 1 winner Exactly Sharp; on July 26, 2005, at Our Mims Retirement Haven at Ahwenasa Farm, in Paris, Kentucky.

FAIR TO ALL, 1986 b. m., Al Nasr (Fr)—Gonfalon, by Francis S. Unraced. Half sister to Grade 1 winner Ogygian. Dam of Grade 1-winning millionaire and leading juvenile sire Honour and Glory; in February 2006, at Coolmore Stud, in Ireland.

FAMILY TRADITION (IRE), 1994 b. m., Sadler's Wells—Sequel, by Law Society. 11-3-0-3, $88,657. Multiple stakes winner in Ireland, Group 1-placed in France; in 2005.

FANTASTIC FIND, 1986 dk. b. or br. m., Mr. Prospector—Blitey, by Riva Ridge. 14-6-3-2, $335,410. Won the 1990 Hempstead H. (G1). Dam of multiple Grade 1 winner Finder's Fee; of foaling complications, on March 7, 2006, at Claiborne Farm, in Paris, Kentucky.

FANTASTIC GIRL, 1976 b. m., Riva Ridge—Lady of Elegance, by Tom Fool. 18-7-2-4, $109,300. Won the 1979 Rancho Bernardo H. Dam of Grade 1 winner Fantastic Look and stakes winners Fantastic Ways, Bravo Fox, and Majestic Style; due to infirmities of age, in November 2005, at Golden Eagle Farm, in Ramona, California.

FARMER JACK, 1996 b. g., Alflora—Cheryls Pet, by General Ironside. 27-10-3-1, $419,744. Multiple English stakes winner; of a probable heart attack after morning training on March 16, 2005, in England.

FIGHTING FIT, 1979 ch. h., Full Pocket—Napalm, by *Nilo. 49-14-7-8, $1,004,174. Won the 1985 Paterson H. (G2). Sire of 13 stakes winners, including graded winners Fighting Fantasy and Lady Sonata; due to infirmities of age, on August 10, 2005, at Ballena Vista Farm, in Ramona, California.

Fine and Dandy, 1999 b. h., Danzig—Chosen Lady, by Secretariat. 24-2-3-3, $89,430. Stakes-placed half brother to two graded stakes winners; after breaking down in a race at Mountaineer Race Track, on July 24, 2005, in West Virginia.

FIRST CHARTER, 1999 b. h., Polish Precedent—By Charter, by Shirley Heights. 21-6-4-3, $323,685. Won the Lonsdale Cup (Eng-G2); while undergoing surgery to remove bone chips from his knees, in October 2005, in England.

FLAME MCGOON, 1986 ch. m., Staff Writer—Wicca, by Noble Table. 20-5-1-4, $139,264. Won the 1988 Longacres Lassie S. Dam of stakes winner Infernal McGoon; while foaling, in early 2006, in Washington.

FLAME OF TARA (IRE), 1980 b. m., Artaius—Welsh Flame, by Welsh Pageant. 21-8-3-1, $165,970. Won the 1983 Coronation S. (Eng-G2). Dam of four graded stakes winners, including European highweight and triple classic winner Salsabil (Ire) and Group 1 winner Marju; of old age, in August 2005, at Kilcarn Stud, in Ireland.

FOLLOW THE RAINBOW, 2002 b. c., Event of the Year—Star of the River (GB), by Soviet Star. 11-3-3-3, $177,100. Won the 2005 El Cajon S.; after breaking down in an optional claiming race, on March 2, 2006, at Santa Anita Park, in California.

FOREVER SILVER, 1985 gr. h., Silver Buck—Disabled Maid, by Correlation. 47-8-9-9, $1,001,974. Won the 1989 Brooklyn H. (G1). Sire of stakes winners Carlow and Nu Rival; euthanized due to a leg injury, on December 8, 2005, at the Cornell University Equine Research Park, in Ithaca, New York.

FOURSTARS ALLSTAR, 1988 b. h., Compliance—Broadway Joan, by Bold Arian. Won the 1991 Irish Two Thousand Guineas (Ire-G1). Sire of six stakes winners; euthanized after breaking his neck in an accident, in February 2005, at Newmarket.

FRAISE, 1988 b. h., Strawberry Road (Aus)—Zalataia (Fr), by Dictus. 34-10-5-6, $2,613,105. Won the 1992 Breeders' Cup Turf (G1), Sword Dancer H. (G1). Sire of winners in Japan; of a ruptured abdominal blood vessel, on November 6, 2005, at Old Friends equine retirement home, in Midway, Kentucky.

FRENCH COTTON, 1982 ch. g., Estaminet—Cotton Blossom, by Attalus. Won the 1986 South Australia Derby (Aus-G1). Died in late 2005, in Australia.

FUNFAIR (GB), 1999 b. g., Singspiel (Ire)—Red Carnival, by Mr. Prospector. 17-6-2-2, $432,459. Won the 2005 Kelso Breeders' Cup H. (G2); euthanized after fracturing a hind leg in the Breeders' Cup Mile (G1); on October 29, 2005, at Belmont Park, in New York.

GANA FACIL, 1981, ch. m., *Le Fabuleux—Charedi, by In Reality. 19-6-1-2, $85,100. Dam of champion and leading sire Unbridled and Grade 1 winner Cahill Road; in February 2006, at Coolmore Stud, in Ireland.

GARRISON SAVANNAH, 1983 b. g., Random Shot—Merry Coin, by Current Coin. 48-9-9-9, $400,947. Won the 1991 Cheltenham Gold Cup Steeplechase, second in the '91 Grand National Steeplechase; after being kicked by another horse in a farm accident, on August 17, 2005, in England.

GENERAL ASSEMBLY, 1976 ch. h., Secretariat—Exclusive Dancer, by Native Dancer. 17-7-6-1, $463,245.

Won the 1979 Travers S. (G1). Sire of 31 stakes winners, including champions Steady Flame and Irie. Broodmare sire of 53 stakes winners and six champions; of heart and circulatory problems, in March 2005, at Gestut Olympia, in Germany.

GHADEER, 1978 b. h., Lyphard—Swanilda, by Habitat. 17-3-3-2, $68,935. Italian group winner. Leading sire and six-time leading broodmare sire in Brazil. Sire of 81 stakes winners. Broodmare sire of at least 82 stakes winners and 13 champions, including Riboletta (Brz); of heart failure, on February 10, 2005, at Haras Fazenda Mondesir, in Brazil.

GILD, 1986 ch. m., Mr. Prospector—Veroushka, by Nijinsky II. 6-3-0-2, $177,264. Won the 1988 Gardenia S. (G2). Dam of stakes winner Poker Brad. Grandam of Dominican Republic champion Top Lightning; in 2005.

GLITTER WOMAN, 1994 b. m., Glitterman—Carols Folly, by Taylor's Falls. 23-10-9-3, $1,256,805. Won the 1997 Ashland S. (G1). Dam of 2005 Grade 3-placed Political Force; of colic, on January 12, 2006, after delivering a filly by Fusaichi Pegasus, which also died, at Claiborne Farm, in Paris, Kentucky.

GOLDEN VOYAGER, 1987 b. h., Mr. Prospector—La Voyageuse, by Tentam. 14-3-3-3, $96,875. Sire of at least 16 stakes winners and seven champions, including 1999 Chilean Horse of the Year Crystal House (Chi); following colic surgery, on April 8, 2005, at Haras Old Friends, in Brazil.

Gold Shadow, 1984 dk. b. or br. m., Mr. Prospector—Vific (Fr), by Rheffic. 9-4-0-1, $31,050. Stakes-placed. Dam of graded stakes winner Keys to the Heart and stakes winners Avie's Shadow and Nastassja; in 2005.

GOLD TOKEN, 1993, b. h., Mr. Prospector—Connie's Gift, by Nijinsky II. 26-7-6-2, $320,368. Won the 1998 Polynesian S. Sire of five stakes winners, including Gold and Roses; in a farm accident, on April 30, 2006, at Sugar Maple Farm, in Poughquag, New York.

GRAND ESPOIR BLANC, 1984 w. g., One for All—Erasure, by What a Pleasure. 16-3-2-1, $35,530. One of the first white Thoroughbreds registered by the Jockey Club; euthanized due to loss of coordination, in December 2005, in Shreveport, Louisiana.

GRATIAEN, 1997 b. h., Cure the Blues—Adorable Minister, by Deputy Minister. 32-7-2-1, $288,164. Won the 2000 Albany H. at Saratoga Race Couse; after breaking down in a race at Aqueduct on February 5, 2005, in New York.

GREEN TEAM, 1999 b. g., Huddle Up—Scare Tactics, by Moscow Ballet. 39-10-10-5, $620,827. Won the 2003 California Cup Sprint H; euthanized after breaking down in the Padua Stables Sprint S. at Santa Anita Park, on January 29, 2005, in California.

GROOVY, 1983 ch. h., Norcliffe—Tinnitus, by Restless Wind. 26-12-4-1, $1,346,956. Champion sprinter of 1987. Won the 1987 Vosburgh S. (G1). Sire of 18 stakes winners, including Grade 1 winner Brutally Frank; due to infirmities of old age, on January 26, 2006, at WinStar Farm, near Versailles, Kentucky.

GRUB'S DANCER, 1993 gr. m., Grub—Rattling Fool, by Rattle Dancer. 16-2-5-1, $33,505. Dam of 2005 Dubai Golden Shaheen (UAE-G1) winner Saratoga County; of a respiratory ailment, on April 27, 2006, at Hagyard Equine Medical Institute, in Lexington.

GYPSY KING, 2002 b. c., Sadler's Wells—Love for Ever, by Darshaan. 4-2-0-0, $145,160. Won the 2005 Dee S. (Eng-G3); euthanized after fracturing a shoulder in the Irish Derby (Ire-G1) at the Curragh on June 26, 2005, in Ireland.

HALF A YEAR, 1984 ch. h., Riverman—Six Months Long, by Northern Dancer. 8-3-2-1, $141,220. Highweighted at three in England. Sire of 12 stakes winners, including Grade 2 winner Yearly Tour and millionaire Full Moon Madness; of colic, in summer 2005, at Paddockhurst Stables, in Alberta.

HALO CAT, 1998 b. g., Southern Halo—Carson Kitty, by Carson City. 38-14-10-5, $493,480. Track record-setting winner of six sprint stakes; Grade 3-placed; of colic, on April 9, 2006, in California.

HEROICITY (AUS), 1988 gr. or ro. h., Cheraw (Ire)—Fleeting World, by Wolverton. 9-6-2-1, $757,845. Multiple Group 1 winner in Australia. Sire of three known stakes winners; of an acute gastric rupture, on November 16, 2005, at Hilltop Farm, in Colora, Maryland.

HOLY ORDERS, 1997 b. g., Unblest—Shadowglow, by Shaadi. 62-12-4-5, $493,536. Won the 2004 Ballycullen S. in Ireland; after breaking down in the Ladbrokes World Hurdle, on March 16, 2006, at Cheltenham Race Course, in England.

HOMEBUILDER, 1984 ch. h., Mr. Prospector—Smart Heiress, by *Vaguely Noble. 60-11-11-17, $1,172,153. Won the Fayette H. (G2). Sire of 11 stakes winners, including graded winners Built for Pleasure and Built Up; of a heart condition, in December 2005, at Red River Farms, in Coushatta, Louisiana.

HOPELESSLY DEVOTED, 2001 b. f., Storm Creek—Silver Treego, by Silver Buck. 16-6-4-0, $499,385. Won the 2004 Calder Oaks; collapsed during the Marshua's River S. at Gulfstream Park on January 9, 2005, in Florida.

HORATIO NELSON, 2003 b. c., Danehill—Imagine (Ire), by Sadler's Wells. 7-4-1-0, $488,433. Won the 2005 Prix Jean-Luc Lagardere-Grand Criterium (Fr-G1); euthanized after breaking down in the Epsom Derby (Eng-G1), on June 3, 2006, at Epsom Downs, in England.

HORATIUS, 1975 ch. h., Proudest Roman—True Charm, by Cohoes. 54-18-13-4, $383,899. Won the 1979 Riggs H. (G3). Maryland's leading sire of 1989 and '90. Sire of 25 stakes winners, including 1989 champion sprinter Safely Kept; of natural causes, on February 3, 2006, at Thornmar, in Chestertown, Maryland.

HOUSEBUSTER, 1987 dk. b. or br. h., Mt. Livermore—Big Dreams, by Great Above. 22-15-3-1, $1,229,696. Two-time champion sprinter. Leading sire in Virginia and West Virginia. Sire of at least 34 stakes winners, including 2002 Hong Kong Horse of the Year Electronic Unicorn; of unknown causes, on May 15, 2005, in West Virginia.

Huckster, 1980 dk. b. or br. h., Mr. Prospector—Land Girl, by Sir Ivor. 60-8-6-14, $234,508. Stakes-placed. Sire of five stakes winners; euthanized due to infirmities of age, on April 17, 2005, at Sue Hubbard and Associates Farm, in Creston, California.

HUM ALONG, 1989 dk. b. or br. m., Fappiano—Minstress, by The Minstrel. 2-0-0-1, $4,680. Dam of champion Storm Song, graded stakes winner Diamond Omi, and $6.8-million record Keeneland September yearling Tasmanian Tiger; after foaling, on February 23, 2005, at Ashford Stud, in Versailles, Kentucky.

ICANTGOFORTHAT, 1999 b. m., In Excess (Ire)—Texinadress, by Copelan. 35-7-3-6, $472,484. Won the

2003 Monrovia H. (G3), Survive S.; of laminitis, in August 2005, in California.

IGNITE THE PASSION, 1995 ch. m., Country Light—Dubinnet, by Gummo. 34-6-4-6, $151,778. Won the 1999 Emerald Breeders' Cup Distaff H.; from complications of foaling, in early March 2006, in Washington.

Imperial Jade, 1982 b. m., Lochnager—Songs Jest, by Song. 25-4-0-0, $52,302. Group-placed in England. Dam of English group winner Averti and German stakes winner Indian Lake; due to infirmities of age, in November 2005, at Oakgrove Stud, in England.

IN HAND, 2000 dk. b. or br. g., Belong to Me—Summer Fantasy, by Summer Squall. 19-5-1-2, $222,199. Won the 2004 Greenwood Cup H. Euthanized after breaking down in the Mac Diarmida H. (G3), at Gulfstream Park, on January 30, 2005, in Florida.

INTERSTELLAR, 1986 ch. h., Star Way—Gelu, by Agricola. Won the 1990 Canterbury Guineas (Aus-G1). Sire of millionaire and multiple Australian Group 1 winner Yippyio; in May 2005, at Copenhagen Stud, in Victoria, Australia.

IS BIG, 1996 dk. b. or br. g., Big Shuffle—Isande, by Gift Card. 68-9-7-10, $102,711. Won the 2004 Preis des Murgtals; of complications from injuries suffered in a race, on May 25, 2005, in Germany.

IS IT TRUE MEX, 1996 b. g., Is It True—Celesa, by Bailjumper. 71-17-14-11, $386,895. Popular West Coast turf sprinter; after breaking down in a race at Hollywood Park, on June 11, 2005, in California.

I TWO STEP TOO, 1993 dk. b. or br. g., Spook Dance—Augustar, by Star Envoy. 53-7-13-13, $24,538. One of the horses who played Seabiscuit in the movie of that name; euthanized due to a rare nasal tumor, on March 7, 2005, at the Kentucky Horse Park.

IWOODIFICOULD, 1998 dk. b. or br. h., Peaks and Valleys—Wood So, by Baederwood. 34-12-4-2, $212,245. Two-time winner of the Free Press S. at Assiniboia Downs; after breaking down in a race at Assiniboia Downs, on July 8, 2005, in Manitoba.

JADESCENT, 2002 b. f., Green Perfume—China Girl, by Danehill. 6-3-3-0, $180,689. Won the 2005 William Crockett S.; of injuries sustained in a paddock accident, in early December 2005, at Gilgai Farm, in Australia.

JAMBALAYA JAZZ, 1992 ch. h., Dixieland Band—Glorious Morning, by Graustark. 28-9-5-6, $503,201. Won the 1994 Kentucky Jockey Club S. (G3). Sire of three stakes winners; when struck by lightning, on June 27, 2005, at Nuckols Farm, in Midway, Kentucky.

JEUNE, 1989 ch. h., Kalaglow—Youthful, by Green Dancer. 42-10-10-7, $2,136,858. Australian Horse of the Year in 1995. Won the 1994 Melbourne Cup (Aus-G1). Sire of 14 stakes winners, including Group 1 winners Mummify and True Steel; of heart failure, on January 3, 2006, at Collingrove Stud, in Australia.

JIVA COOLIT, 1972 b. g., Jussive—Hope Against Hope, by Mt. Hope. 113-36-32-26, $218,292. Won the 1977 Valley Sprint Championship H. Set four track records from four to six furlongs; in May 2005, in Virginia.

J. J.'s Cowboy, 1991 dk. b. or br. g., Jerimi Johnson—Santa Moon, by Moonsplash. 53-7-10-6, $64,021. Stakes-placed. Ridden from Texas to New York City to raise money for September 11, 2001, terrorism victims; of heat stroke and colic, on September 6, 2005, at Les Nichols Farm, in Celeste, Texas.

JOANIES BELLA, 1999 dk. b. or br. m., Mercer Mill—Bello Senorita, by Northrup. 11-6-2-1, $274,265. Ohio-bred champion juvenile filly of 2001. Won the 2001 Arlington-Washington Lassie S. (G3); of colic, on February 15, 2006, at Rood & Riddle Equine Clinic, in Lexington.

JOLIE'S HALO, 1987 dk. b. or br. h., Halo—Jolie Jolie, by Sir Ivor. 20-8-0-2, $1,218,120. Won the 1992 Philip H. Iselin H. (G1). Sire of 18 stakes winners, including Grade 1-winning millionaire Hal's Hope; of injuries sustained in a paddock accident, in spring 2005, at East Stud, on Hokkaido, Japan.

JOLYPHA, 1989 dk. b. or br. m., Lyphard—Navajo Princess, by Drone. 10-4-2-1, $988,691. European highweight at three. Won the 1992 Prix de Diane (Fr-G1) (French Oaks). Dam of two winners; of complications from foaling, on March 26, 2005, at Juddmonte Farms, in Lexington.

JOYEUX DANSEUR, 1993 b. h., Nureyev—Fabuleux Jane, by *Le Fabuleux. 14-8-0-1, $645,228. Won the 1998 Early Times Turf Classic S. (G1). Sire of three stakes winners, including Panamanian champion Xirius; of acute appendicitis, in early November 2005, at Wattle Brae Stud, in Queensland, Australia.

JOYFUL BALLAD, 2000 dk. b. or br. m., Saint Ballado—Bring Me Joy, by Deputy Minister. 20-6-1-4, $164,925. Won the 2005 Wayward Lass S.; euthanized after suffering head injuries in a paddock accident, on August 26, 2005, at Del Mar, in California.

J. R.'S HORIZON, 1987 dk. b. or br. g., Caveat—Metrica, by Holy War. 51-7-10-5, $282,570. Won the 1991 John B. Campbell H. (G3); after being hit by lightning, on May 14, 2005, at a farm near Middleburg, Virginia.

JULIE'S PRIZE, 2000 dk. b. or br. m., El Prado (Ire)—Julie Mis, by Miswaki. 26-7-5-5, $441,491. Illinois champion filly at three. Won the 2002 Illinois Breeders Debutante S.; of an apparent heart attack, on March 4, 2006, after finishing fifth in the Wayward Lass S. at Tampa Bay Downs, in Florida.

KAAPSTAD, 1984 dk. b. or br. h., *Sir Tristram—Eight Carat, by *Pieces of Eight II. 13-5-5-2. Won the 1987 Sires' Produce S. (Aus-G1). Sire of 43 stakes winners; euthanized due to failing health, on May 8, 2006, at Windsor Park Stud, in New Zealand.

KATEB, 1989 ch. h., Pennine Walk (Ire)—Ridge the Times, by Riva Ridge. 34-12-4-1, $181,545. Highweighted at four on the Scandanavian Free H. Sire of 2004 champion Scandanavian miler Hovman; in February 2006, at Blesbjerg Stud, in Denmark.

KAYUDEE, 1980 ch. g., Nebbiolo—Wet Powder, by Above Suspicion. 28-4-6-1, $63,841. Won the 1985 Tote Cesarewitch H.; of old age, in 2005, in England.

KEEN, 1981 ch. h., Sharpen Up (GB)—Doubly Sure (GB), by Reliance II. 5-2-0-0, $37,350. Won the 1984 Bonusprint Easter S., group-placed. Sire of seven stakes winners, including millionaire Grade 1 winner River Keen (Ire); of a heart attack, on August 10, 2005, at Beechwood Grange Stud, in England.

Kentucky Jazz, 1987 ch. h., Dixieland Band—Tinnitus, by Restless Wind. 11-3-2-2, $124,700. Graded stakes-placed. Half brother to champion Groovy. Sire of seven stakes winners, including Kentucky Bay and Dramatic Jazz; on May 31, 2005, in Texas.

KING'S SWAN, 1980 b. g., King's Bishop—Royal Cygnet, by *Sea-Bird. 107-31-19-18, $1,924,845. Won 12 stakes, including the 1986 Vosburgh S. (G1); of complications associated with a leg injury suffered in late 2005, on February 7, 2006, at Mid-Atlantic Equine Center, in New Jersey.

KITTEN'S FIRST, 1991 b. m., Lear Fan—That's My Hon, by L'Enjoleur. 2-1-0-0, $14,412. Dam of 2004 champion turf male Kitten's Joy and stakes winner Justenuffheart; of laminitis, on January 14, 2006, in Kentucky.

KNIGHT, 1985 b. h., Mr. Prospector—Issues n' Answers, by Jacinto. Unraced. Sire of stakes winners Knight Villain, Whitewater Rush, and Profitable Knight. Broodmare sire of graded stakes winner Pass Rush; in 2005, in Ohio.

Kohut, 2002 dk. b. or br. g., Fortunate Prospect—Amavalidhope, by Valid Appeal. 20-6-3-2, $173,839. Multiple stakes-placed in Florida; after breaking down in an allowance race, on April 22, 2006, at Aqueduct, in New York.

LANCE CORPORAL, 1996 b. g., Military Plume—Beading, by Lyphard. 39-8-5-4, $182,212. Won the 2003 Australian Grand National Steeplechase; euthanized after fracturing his pelvis in a race at Cheltenham, on March 5, 2005, in Australia.

LASER LIGHT, 1979 b. h., Majestic Light—Peaceful Union, by Royal Union. 13-2-3-2, $291,624. Won the 1981 Remsen S. (G1), second in the '82 Kentucky Derby (G1). Sire of two winners from six foals; due to infirmities of age, on February 10, 2005, at Live Oak Stud, in Ocala.

Late Carson, 1996 b. g., Carson City—Can't Be Late, by Seattle Slew. 53-13-10-4, $502,398. Graded stakes-placed; euthanized due to injuries suffered in a racetrack accident, in June 2005.

LEAFY, 1986 b. h., Tanthem—Sally's Orbit, by Lt. Stevens. 33-8-1-0, $50,006. Won the 1990 Leon Valley H. Sire of winners; in 2005, in Texas.

LEVIRAT, 1999 ch. h., Lomitas (GB)—Laurier d'Or, by Sassafras (Fr). 23-2-5-2, $106,664. Stakes-winning, group-placed hurdler; after breaking down in a race, in early November 2005, at Munich, Germany.

LILANDE, 1993 ch. m., Marscay—Ladyeri, by Salieri. 3-0-0-0, $0. Dam of multiple Australian Group 1 winner Defier; euthanized as a result of injuries sustained in a paddock accident, in February 2005, at Arrowfield Stud, in Australia.

LINGO, 1999 b. g., Poliglote (GB)—Sea Ring, by Bering (GB). 18-8-2-1, $225,718. Won the 2005 Greatwood Hurdle H., 2004 Tolworth Hurdle; euthanized after breaking down during a workout, on February 4, 2006, in England.

LITTLE IRISH NUT, 1989 b. m., Irish Tower—Such a Nut, by Naskra. 72-9-14-12, $148,792. Won the 1991 Cimarron S. Dam of graded stakes winner Sister Star; euthanized after delivering a premature foal, on April 8, 2006, at Calumet Farm, in Lexington.

LOCAL TALENT, 1986 b. h., Northern Dancer—Home Love, by *Vaguely Noble. 7-3-1-0, $175,318. Won the 1989 Prix Jean Prat (Fr-G1). Sire of 16 stakes winners, including Grade 1 winner Larry the Legend and Peruvian champion Sol Del Norte; in March 2006, in Punjab, India.

Logiciel (GB), 1983, dk. b. or br. m., Known Fact—*Femina, by Le Haar. 11-4-2-1, $21,569. Stakes-placed in France. Dam of graded stakes-winning millionaire Talloires; of foaling complications, on May 13, 2006, at Machmer Hall, in Paris, Kentucky.

LORD CARSON, 1992 b. h., Carson City—Bedgay's Lady, by Lord Gaylord. 27-12-5-0, $654,742. Won the 1996 Boojum H. (G2). Sire of at least 12 stakes winners, including Puerto Rican champion Andiroba; of injuries suffered in a breeding shed accident, on March 16, 2005, at Tommy Town Thoroughbreds, in Santa Ynez, California.

LOVE FROM MOM, 1981 b. m., Mr. Prospector—Hoso, by Solo Landing. Unraced. Dam of graded stakes winners Love That Jazz, Fight for Love, Dancing Jon, and Sea of Secrets; of colic, on February 16, 2006, at Hagyard Equine Medical Institute, in Lexington.

LUCAYAN PRINCE, 1993 dk. b. or br. h., Fast Play—Now That's Funny, by Saratoga Six. 38-6-8-8, $400,457. English highweighted sprinter at three. Irish highweighted sprinter at four. Sire of stakes winner Beezer; of a ruptured aorta, on May 4, 2006, at Rancho San Roberto, in Bakersfield, California.

LUCKY LUCKY LUCKY, 1981 b. m., Chieftain—Just One More Time, by Raise a Native. 22-6-5-5, $847,126. Won the 1984 Kentucky Oaks (G1). Brought a Keeneland January broodmare record of $3-million in 1986. Dam of five winners; due to infirmities of age, on August 25, 2005, at Shadwell Farm, in Lexington.

LUCKY SPELL, 1971 b. m., Lucky Mel—Incantation, by Prince Blessed. 69-12-8-11, $253,655. Won the 1974 Las Palmas H. (G3). Dam of three stakes winners; grandam of Grade 1 winner and sire Unbridled's Song; of heart failure, on October 4, 2005, at Magali Farms, in Santa Ynez, California.

LUCKY TEC, 1998 b. g., Technology—Lucky Minister, by Bold Ruckus. 52-12-6-10, $428,797. Won the 2004 Niagara Falls S.; collapsed and died of a heart attack in the winner's circle at Fort Erie, on May 23, 2006, in Canada.

LYPHARD, 1969 b. h., Northern Dancer—Goofed, by *Court Martial. 12-6-1-0, $195,427. Stakes winner. Leading North American sire of 1986. Twice leading sire in France. Sire of 115 stakes winners and eight champions. Broodmare sire of at least 207 stakes winners; of old age, on June 10, 2005, at Gainesway, in Lexington.

MAC DIARMIDA, 1975 dk. b. or br. h., Minnesota Mac—Flying Tammie, by Tim Tam. 16-12-0-2, $503,184. Champion turf horse of 1978. Won the 1978 Washington, D.C., International (G1), Canadian International Championship S. (G1). Sire of four stakes winners; of old age, on September 8, 2005, at Cashel Stud, in Ocala.

MADE OF GOLD, 1989 ch. h., Green Forest—Vindaria, by *Roi Dagobert. 17-5-4-0, $292,370. Won the 1991 William Hill S. (Eng-G2). Former leading freshman sire in Australia. Sire of 14 stakes winners, including nine group winners; of a ruptured intestine, on May 5, 2006, at Eldon Park Stud, in Australia.

MAJESTERIAN, 1988 dk. b. or br. h., Pleasant Colony—Linda North, by Northern Dancer. 20-4-4-4, $262,294. Won the 1991 Col. R. S. McLaughlin H. Sire of six stakes winners, including Love All the Way; of a heart attack, on March 22, 2006, at Marble Hill Stables, in Yakima, Washington.

MANCHURIAN, 2000 ch. h., Deputy Minister—Ajina, by Strawberry Road (Aus). 9-3-2-0, $125,575. Won the 2006 Stymie H.; euthanized after breaking down in an optional claiming race, on March 24, 2006, at Aqueduct, in New York.

MARACAIBO, 1994 b. h., Skip Trial—Traki Traki, by Mo Power. 33-12-1-5, $222,924. Won the 1998 Charles Staats Memorial S. Half brother to 2006 Ashland S.

(G1) winner Bushfire; from a breeding shed injury, in April 2006, in New York.

MARKET GARDEN, 2000 b. m., Bold Badgett—Margaret's Native, by He's Our Native. 35-6-5-8, $363,958. Won the 2004 Pio Pico S.; collapsed and died after finishing unplaced in the B. Thoughtful S., at Hollywood Park, on April 24, 2005, in California.

MATADOR MARSHAL, 2000 ch. h., Parade Marshal—Mat Music, by Mat-Boy (Arg). Multiple 2005 Group 1 winner in Argentina; euthanized after breaking down in a workout, at Palermo racecourse, on December 5, 2005, in Argentina.

MAYBE JACK, 1993 b. g., Classic Account—Hester Lou, by Summing. 122-35-17-17, $534,715. Won the 1997 Bruce G. Smith Memorial S. at Suffolk Downs; after finishing fourth in an $8,000 claiming race at Gulfstream Park on January 22, 2005, in Florida.

MEADOWLAKE, 1983 ch. h., Hold Your Peace—Suspicious Native, by Raise a Native. 3-3-0-0, $308,580. Won the 1985 Arlington-Washington Futurity (G1). Sire of 54 stakes winners, including champion Meadow Star. Broodmare sire of at least 32 stakes winners, including Henny Hughes; of ruptured intestinal tract, at Darby Dan Farm, on November 6, 2005, near Lexington.

MIA'S HOPE, 1992 dk. b. or br. m., Rexson's Hope—Pia Mia, by Pia Star. 20-7-3-1, $327,740. Won the 1995 Bonnie Miss S. (G2). Dam of three stakes winners, including Grade 1-winning millionaire Hal's Hope; of a farm injury, in April 2006, in Florida.

MILLENAIRE (BRZ), 1999 b. c., Jules—Eternita, by Ghadeer. 21-5-1-2, $32,780. Group 2 winner in Brazil; in the United States, in 2005.

MIMBET, 1983 b. m., Raise a Native—Our Mims, by *Herbager. 6-0-0-0, $1,380. Dam of 1997 Breeders' Cup Sprint (G1) winner Elmhurst; euthanized due to infirmities of age, on March 9, 2006, at Three Chimneys Farm, in Midway, Kentucky.

MISWAKI GOLD, 1985 b. h., Miswaki—Star Formation, by Lt. Stevens. Unraced. Sire of four stakes winners, including J W Jet and Waki Decision; of a heart attack, on June 8, 2005, at Robeson Road Farms, in Beeville, Texas.

M K BECK, 2002 dk. b. or br. f., Moon Up T. C.—Well Played, by Well Decorated. 14-2-3-2, $48,720. Won the 2004 Diane Kem S.; after breaking down in the Washington Breeders' Cup Oaks, on August 20, 2005, at Emerald Downs, in Washington.

MODEL MAN, 1982 br. h., Elliodor—Top Model, by Filipepi. South Africa's first equine millionaire and its 1986 Horse of the Year. Sire of at least 26 stakes winners, including champions Special Preview and Private Reserve; following a farm accident, in October 2005, at Odessa Stud, in South Africa.

Monarchoftheglen, 1999 dk. b. or br. g., A.P. Indy—Milliardaire, by Alydar. 36-7-9-4, $141,204. $1.5-million Keeneland July yearling. Half brother to Grade 1 winner Lakeway. Stakes-placed in England; of a heart attack after a $5,000 claiming race on March 11, 2006, at Mountaineer Race Track, in West Virginia.

MONDRIAN, 1986 ch. h., Surumu—Mole, by *Espresso. 26-12-5-1, $754,014. Two-time German Horse of the Year. Winner of seven Group 1 races. Sire of five stakes winners, including Group 1 winner Well Made; in 2005, in Germany.

MOON CACTUS, 1987 b. m., Kris—Lady Moon, by Mill Reef. 7-3-3-1, $274,512. Won the 1989 Prestige S. (Eng-G3). Dam of four stakes winners, including Group 1-winning highweights Moonshell (Ire) and Doyen; of foaling complications, on February 5, 2006, at Dalham Hall Stud, in England.

MOONSHELL (IRE), 1992 b. m., Sadler's Wells—Moon Cactus, by Kris. 5-2-0-2, $277,282. Highweighted filly at three on the European Free H. (11 to 13½ furlongs). Won the 1995 Epsom Oaks (Eng-G1); of hemorrhaging after foaling, on January 21, 2006, at Woodpark Stud, in Ireland.

MUMMIFY, 1999 b. g., Jeune—Cleopatra's Girl, by At Talaq. 48-9-8-9, $3,689,295. Won five Group 1 races, including the 2003 Caulfield Cup (Aus-G1); after breaking down at the finish of the 2005 Caulfield Cup, on October 15, 2005, in Australia.

MY PRINCE CHARMING, 1983 ch. h., Sir Wimborne—Maid in Waiting, by Stage Door Johnny. 43-7-7-5, $363,583. Won a division of the 1986 Fountain of Youth S. (G2). Leading New Jersey sire of 1999. Sire of stakes winner Mr. Denim; in February 2005, in New Jersey.

MY TURBULENT MISS, 1976 b. m., My Dad George—Turbulent Miss, by *Petare. Unraced. Dam of six stakes winners, including 1989 Breeders' Cup Turf (G1) winner Prized and Grade 2 winner Exploit; on May 13, 2005, at Our Mims Retirement Haven at Ahwenasa Farm, in Paris, Kentucky.

NASTY AFFAIR, 1984 b. m., Nasty and Bold—L'Affaire, by Seventh Landing. 25-13-7-2, $260,383. Won the 1987 Princess Rooney S. Dam of graded stakes winner Mountain Affair and stakes winner Donna Doo; euthanized on March 9, 2006, at Indian Creek Farm, in Paris, Kentucky.

Naevus, 1980 ch. h., Mr. Prospector—Mudville, by Bold Lad. 8-2-3-2, $111,250. Grade 1-placed. Leading 2001 sire in Texas. Sire of 31 stakes winners, including Grade 1-winning millionaire King Glorious and German highweight Green Perfume; euthanized due to complications of laminitis, on August 12, 2005, at Stoneview Farm, in Hempstead, Texas.

NATIONAL TREASURE, 1993 dk. b. or br. m., Recusant—Ivory Treasure, by Sir Ivor. 36-9-3-3, $280,440. Won the 1998 Beaugay H. (G3); of foaling complications, on May 2, 2005, at Windfields Farm, in Canada.

NATIVE SCOUT, 1996 b. g., Be My Native—Carmels Castle, by Deep Run. 38-10-9-2, $231,320. Won the 2004 Tied Cottage Steeplechase; after breaking a shoulder in the Normans Grove Steeplechase, at Fairyhouse racecourse, on January 16, 2005, in Ireland.

NEW DREAMS (BRZ), 1999 b. m., Blush Rambler—Dream of Sinless, by White Clover. 19-5-1-3, $103,693. Won the 2003 Grande Premio Marciano de Aguiar Moreira (Brz-G1); from a training injury, while carrying a foal by Mineshaft, on July 17, 2005.

NICOSIA, 1972 dk. b. or br. m., Gallant Romeo—Nicoma, by Nashua. 19-8-2-0, $254,495. Won the 1975 Hollywood Oaks (G2), '76 Matron H. (G2). Dam of stakes winner Soli; of old age, in mid-January 2006, at Mill Ridge Farm, in Lexington.

NIJINSKY'S TABLE, 1985 b. h., Nijinsky II—Tableaux, by Round Table. 2-0-0-0, $675. Sire of Santa Ynez S. (G3) winner Nijinsky's Passion; in 2005, at Los Amigos Thoroughbreds, in Temecula, California.

NIMBLE FEET, 1985 b. m., Danzig—Nimble Folly, by Cyane. 8-1-0-3, $11,106. Dam of four stakes winners, including graded or group winners Forest Gazelle and

Eltish; of complications from foaling, on March 19, 2005, at Juddmonte Farms, in Lexington.

NIX OF TIME, 1996 dk. b. or br. g., Bold Nix—Pickett Star, by Aferd. 79-12-5-10, $162,892. Won the 1999 Minnesota Derby; broke down after finishing second in a claiming race at Canterbury Park, on May 20, 2006, in Minnesota.

NOM D'UNE PIPE, 1997 gr. g., Linamix—Newness, by Simply Great. 22-5-5-14, $377,846. Won the 2003 Prix Carmarthen; euthanized after breaking down in a race at Cagnes-Sur-Mer, on January 5, 2006, in France.

NORTHERN QUEST (FR), 1995 dk. b. or br. h., Rainbow Quest—Northern Goddess, by Night Shift. 25-7-2-4, $664,003. Won the 2000 Del Mar H. (G2); after shattering a hock in a paddock accident, on September 16, 2005, at Dormello II Stud, in Decatur, Texas.

NUREYEV DANCER, 1984 b. h., Nureyev—La Ristonica (Fr), by Tombeur. 16-2-2-1, $12,338. Sire of at least six stakes winners, including 2001 champion steeplechaser Pompeyo (Chi); of injuries sustained in a farm accident, on January 22, 2006, at Haras Santa Amelia, in Chile.

ON THIN ICE, 2001 gr. or ro. g., Tactical Cat—Frigid Zone, by Procida. 16-6-3-2, $206,390. Won the 2006 Hal's Hope H. (G3) in track-record time; following a training accident, on May 27, 2006, at Monmouth Park, in New Jersey.

OSCEOLA, 2001 ch. f., American Gipsy—Speed Daughter, by Rahy. 10-4-0-0, $35,013. Won the 2005 Grande Premio Diana (Brz-G1); of a heart attack during training, in March 2005, in Rio de Janiero.

OUR COUNTRY PLACE, 1992 dk. b. or br. m., Pleasant Colony—Maplejinsky, by Nijinsky II. Unraced. Dam of Grade 1-winning millionaire Pleasant Home and Grade 2 winner Country Hideaway; of laminitis, on February 27, 2006, at Rood & Riddle Equine Hospital, in Lexington.

OUTTA HERE, 2000 ch. h., Dehere—Just Out, by Forty Niner. 28-3-5-6, $657,167. Won the 2002 Delta Jackpot S.; euthanized due to complications following surgery for a sesamoid injury, on February 18, 2006, at Alamo Pintado Equine Medical Center, in Los Olivos, California.

PALMEIRO, 1998 dk. b. or br. g., Pleasant Tap—Fortune Pending, by Fortunate Prospect. 39-9-9-3, $475,338. Won the 2002 All American H. (G3); after breaking down in a $12,500 claiming race, on March 10, 2006, at Golden Gate Fields, in California.

PANCHO VILLA, 1982 ch. h., Secretariat—Crimson Saint, by Crimson Satan. Full brother to Terlingua, half brother to Royal Academy. 18-7-5-0, $596,734. Won the 1985 Bay Shore S. (G2). Sire of 22 stakes winners; of a heart attack, on February 20, 2006, at Cedarcrest Farm and Equine Clinic, in Palestine, Texas.

PEBBLES (GB), 1981 ch. m., Sharpen Up (GB)—La Dolce (GB), by Connaught. 15-8-4-0, $1,419,632. Champion English miler and champion American turf female of 1985. Won the 1985 Breeders' Cup Turf (G1); from infirmities of age, in 2005, at Darley's Fukumitsu Farm, in Japan.

PEGASO (PER), 1999 dk. b. or br. h., Play the Gold—Mainz, by Privato. 22-12-2-2, $70,349. Champion Peruvian miler of 2003. Won the 2002 Polla de Potrillos (Per-G1) (Peruvian Two Thousand Guineas); after breaking down in a race at Gulfstream Park, on February 28, 2005, in Florida.

PEIGNOIR, 1987 b. m., Tights—Dark Heavens, by Lord Dudley. Multiple stakes winner in Australia. Dam of South African group winner Full Press; in 2005, in Australia.

PERSONAL FLAG, 1983 dk. b. or br. h., Private Account—Grecian Banner, by Hoist the Flag. 24-8-4-4, $1,258,924. Won the 1988 Suburban H. (G1). Sire of 37 stakes winners, including graded winner Say Florida Sandy; from infirmities of age, on July 17, 2005, at McMahon of Saratoga Thoroughbreds, in Saratoga Springs, New York.

PHIZAM, 1979 ch. h., Zamazaan—Phius, by Oncidium. Won the 1985 Winfield-Perth Cup (Aus-G1). Sire of seven stakes winners, including Group 1 winners Mr. Prudent and Zamination; in June 2005, at Benalla Park Stud, in Victoria, Australia.

PHONE TRICK, 1982 b. h., Clever Trick—Over the Phone, by Finnegan. 10-9-1-0, $395,112. Grade 2 winner. Sire of at least 54 stakes winners, including 1997 Horse of the Year Favorite Trick and champion Phone Chatter. New York's leading sire of 2001; of natural causes, on October 12, 2005, at Milfer Farm, in Unadilla, New York.

POHAVE, 1998 gr. or ro. g., Holy Bull—Trail Robbery, by Alydar. 27-5-9-4, $576,240. Won the 2004 Triple Bend Breeders' Cup Invitational H. (G1); euthanized due to laminitis following liver surgery, on April 28, 2005, in Dubai.

POLISH PRECEDENT, 1986 b. h., Danzig—Past Example, by Buckpasser. 9-7-1-0, $579,058. Highweighted at three in France. Sire of 24 stakes winners, including champion and 1996 Breeders' Cup Turf (G1) winner Pilsudski (Ire); following colic surgery, on June 21, 2005, in England.

PRIMARILY, 1988 b. m., Lord At War (Arg)—Mostly, by *Grey Dawn II. 4-2-1-0, $63,036. Stakes winner. Canadian Broodmare of the Year in 2000. Dam of Canadian champions Primaly and Poetically, and noted sire Whiskey Wisdom; from injuries sustained in a fall, on March 30, 2005, at Adena Springs, in Versailles, Kentucky.

PROUD TRUTH, 1982 ch. h., Graustark—Wake Robin, by Summer Tan. 21-10-4-0, $2,198,895. Won the 1985 Breeders' Cup Classic (G1). Panama's leading sire of 2003, '04, and '05. Sire of 38 stakes winners and nine champions, including Canadian champion Truth of It All; on August 15, 2005, at Haras Cerro Punta, in Panama.

QUADRATIC, 1975 b. h., Quadrangle—Smartaire, by *Quibu. 19-6-4-4, $233,941. Won the 1977 Cowdin S. (G2). Leading sire in Virginia in 1990. Sire of 25 stakes winners, including Grade 1 winner Home At Last; on October 20, 2005, at Deer Haven Farm in Virginia.

QUI BID, 1985 gr. m., Spectacular Bid—Qui Royalty, by Native Royalty. Unraced. Dam of three stakes winners, including German group winner and highweight Que Belle; of laminitis, on March 25, 2006, at Hedgestone Management, in Ontario.

Quiet Mike, 1997 b. g., Quiet American—Northern Fable, by Northern Dancer. 40-10-9-6, $295,433. Stakes-placed; after breaking down in a race on June 20, 2005, at Philadelphia Park, in Pennsylvania.

QUINTONS GOLD RUSH, 2001 ch. c., Wild Rush—Hollywood Gold, by Mr. Prospector. 10-3-1-0, $329,835. Won the 2004 Coolmore Lexington S. (G2); died while undergoing a biopsy, in January 2005, at San Luis Rey Equine Hospital, in Bonsall, California.

RABIYA, 2001 b. g., Jallad—Mystic Spring, by Royal Academy. Won the 2005 Cape Argus Guineas (SAf-G1), Graham Beck Cape Derby (SAf-G1); euthanized after breaking down in the Durban July (SAf-G1), on July 2, 2005, at Greyville racecourse, in South Africa.

RADICAL RATE, 1996 b. g., Basic Rate—Radical Gal, by Radar Ahead. 16-5-1-2, $84,658. Won the 1999 Arizona Breeders' Derby, Arizona Stallion S.; after breaking down in a race at Arapahoe Park, on July 10, 2005, in Colorado.

RAFT, 1981 dk. b. or br. h., Nodouble—Gangster of Love, by Round Table. 10-5-0-2, $87,109. Won the 1984 Prix de la Cote Normande (Fr-G2); sire of stakes winners Life Is Delicious, The Frog Man, and Zattare; in 2005, in West Virginia.

REALLY GOLDEN, 1989 ch. h., In Reality—Gold Mine, by Raise a Native. 2-0-0-0, $530. Sire of stakes winners Milady's Golden and Golden Aztec; in 2005, in Oregon.

RED BORDEAUX, 2003 ch. c., Gulch—Elissa Beethoven (GB), by Royal Academy. 3-1-0-0, $23,400; euthanized after fracturing a foreleg during the Risen Star S. (G3), on January 14, 2006, at Louisiana Downs, in Louisiana.

REGAL REMARK, 1982 ch. h., Vice Regent—Male Strike, by Speak John. 19-7-5-2, $279,879. Won the 1985 Tampa Bay Derby (G3). Six-time leading sire in Alberta. Sire of 38 stakes winners; due to infirmities of age, on January 2, 2005, at Horizon Farm, in Alberta.

RELKEEL, 1989 gr. g., Relkino—Secret Keel, by Balinger. 21-12-3-2, $228,486. Six-time stakes-winning hurdler in England; euthanized due to arthritis and infirmities of age, in March 2006, in England.

Rich Man's Gold, 1992 ch. h., Forty Niner—Honest Joy, by Honest Pleasure. 7-2-2-1, $58,990. Grade 3-placed. Sire of at least 11 stakes winners, including champions Lido Palace (Chi), Isola Piu Bella (Chi), and St. Jacques; of a heart attack, in early November 2005, at Wilgerbosdrift Stud, in South Africa.

Ride and Shine, 1997 ch. g., High Brite—Shining Ryder, by Red Ryder. 71-8-12-11, $526,476. Stakes-placed in Southern California; after breaking down in a race at Santa Anita Park, on April 17, 2005, in Arcadia, California.

ROOSTER BOOSTER, 1994 gr. g., Riverwise—Came Cottage, by Nearly a Hand. 46-10-14-6, $1,147,195. Top English hurdler; of an apparent heart attack during training, on December 20, 2005, in England.

ROSSARD (DEN), 1980 dk. b. or br. m., Glacial—Peas-Blossom, by Midsummer Night. Champion in Sweden and Denmark. Won the 1984 Flower Bowl H. (G1). Dam of stakes winner Unusual Heat; due to infirmities of age, on March 18, 2005, at Hunterton Farm, in Paris, Kentucky.

Roy, 1983 b. h., Fappiano—Adlibber, by Never Bend. 17-3-2-3, $91,567. Grade 2-placed. Twice leading sire in Argentina. Leading 1994 sire in Chile. Sire of 115 stakes winners and 15 champions. Broodmare sire of seven champions; of a respiratory ailment, on January 7, 2005, at Haras La Esperanza, in Argentina.

Royal Affirmed, 1998 b. h., Affirmed—Royal Herat, by Herat. 39-7-6-6, $291,684. Graded stakes-placed; after breaking down in summer 2005.

ROYAL MERLOT, 1993 ch. h., Forty Niner—Gana Facil, by *Le Fabuleux. 7-1-2-1, $27,760. Half brother to champion Unbridled. Leading sire in Puerto Rico. Sire of five stakes winners, including champions Hispanica and El Truckero; of a leg injury, on March 27, 2006, at Haras Santa Isabel, in Puerto Rico.

ROYAL SAINT, 2002 ch. c., Saint Ballado—Deputy Royal, by Deputy Minister. 6-4-0-0, $75,300. Won the 2005 Prelude S.; collapsed and died in midstretch of the Super Derby (G2), on October 1, 2005, at Louisiana Downs, in Bossier City, Louisiana.

RUBITON, 1983 br. h., Century—Ruby, by Seventh Hussar. Multiple Group 1 winner. Sire of at least 28 stakes winners, including champion Ruby Clipper (NZ) and Group 1 winner Fields Of Omagh; of an infection, on November 20, 2005, in Australia.

RULES OF WAR, 2001 b. g., Cromwell—Nannetta, by Falstaff. 9-3-1-1, $64,730. Won the 2004 Richmond Derby Trial H.; of a virus that caused him to founder, on May 5, 2005, in British Columbia.

RUN KUSH RUN, 1998 ch. g., Concorde's Tune—Swingin Low, by Steve's Friend. 41-11-9-7, $409,094. Won the 2001 Skip Trial S.; after breaking down in a race, on August 20, 2005, at Suffolk Downs, in Massachusetts.

SAINT CYRIEN, 1980 b. h., Luthier—Sevres (Fr), by Riverman. 6-3-1-0, $133,622. Champion at two in France. Among the leading French sires. Sire of 32 stakes winners, including European highweight Epervier Bleu; on December 14, 2005, in France.

Saint Etienne (Ire), 2001 b. f., Robellino—Stop Out, by Rudimentary. 14-4-1-1, $114,023. Group-placed in Canada; after breaking down in an allowance race, on October 2, 2005, at Woodbine, near Toronto.

SAN SEBASTIAN, 1994 ch. g., Niniski—Top of The League, by High Top. 52-11-9-4, $383,060. Won the 2000 Prix du Cadran (Fr-G1); of a probable brain hemorrhage, in December 2005, in New Zealand.

SAPPHIRE BEADS, 1991 ch. m., Unreal Zeal—Petite Jolie, by Jig Time. 29-11-4-5, $241,339. Won the 1996 Frances Slocum S., '97 Mill Race H. Dam of three winners, including Grade 3-placed Ashmore; died in 2005.

SARATOGA COUNTY, 2001 b. c., Valid Expectations—Grub's Dancer, by Grub. 17-6-4-1, $1,646,590. Won the 2005 Dubai Golden Shaheen (UAE-G1), General George H. (G2); of laminitis, on July 29, 2005, in Saratoga Springs, New York.

SARATOGA VIEW, 2002 ch. g., Distant View—Prologue, by Theatrical (Ire). 1-1-0-0, $27,000. Winner of his only start by 8½ lengths; euthanized after breaking down in a workout on August 22, 2005, at Saratoga Race Course, in New York.

SAVEDBYTHELIGHT, 2000 dk. b. or br. m., Saint Ballado—Wild Royal, by Wild Again. 20-3-4-5, $388,944. Won the 2003 Ladies H. (G3), Grade 1-placed; in 2006.

SCENIC (IRE), 1986 dk. b. or br. h., Sadler's Wells—Idyllic, by Foolish Pleasure. 12-4-2-1, $245,011. Won the 1988 Three Chimneys Dewhurst S. (Eng-G1). Sire of 54 stakes winners and three champions, including Australian champion Universal Prince; of a heart attack, on March 6, 2005, at Durham Lodge Stud, in Australia.

SCOOP THE GOLD, 1990 ch. m., Forty Niner—Leap Lively, by Nijinsky II. 21-4-2-2, $114,527. Won the 1995 Likely Exchange S. Dam of millionaire Grade 1 winner High Yield; of a ruptured aorta, on April 17, 2005, at Fares Farm, in Lexington.

SEABREEZE BLVD., 2003 b. c., Mt. Livermore—Surprise K, by Great Above. 3-2-0-0, $59,400. Won the

2006 Inaugural S.; after breaking down in a workout, on April 19, 2006, at Lone Star Park, in Texas.

SEA CHAMPAGNE, 1989 ch. m., Sea Aglo—Gilt Complex, by Canadian Gil. 70-18-13-8, $81,085. Winner of five stakes at Portland Meadows; of colic, on March 24, 2006.

SEATTLE PATTERN, 1995 dk. b. or br. h., Seattle Slew—Pattern Step, by Nureyev. 18-5-3-5, $206,994. Won the 1999 Awesome Again S. Sire of winners; after suffering a seizure in late 2005, at Q6 Ranch, near Belton, Texas.

SEATTLES BEST JOE, 2002 b. g., Personable Joe—First Class Action, by Chisos. 10-4-2-1, $150,515. Champion Washington-bred juvenile male of 2004. Won the 2004 Sunny Slope S., Emerald Express S.; euthanized after breaking down in a workout, on February 24, 2006, at Golden Gate Fields, in California.

Secret 'n Classy, 1987 ch. h., Secretariat—Classy 'n Smart, by Smarten. Half brother to 1991 Canadian Horse of the Year Dance Smartly. 16-4-5-4, $183,104. Classic-placed in Canada. Sire of German group winner Dictum; after breaking a leg, in May 2006, at Vitezslav Vanda Stud, in Czechoslovakia.

SECRETTAME, 1978 ch. m., Secretariat—Tamerett, by Tim Tam. 10-6-1-0, $101,598. Won the 1983 Shirley Jones H. Dam of Grade 1 winner and leading sire Gone West and Grade 2 winner Lion Cavern; of colic, on March 17, 2006, at Rood & Riddle Equine Hospital, in Lexington.

SEEKING THE PEARL, 1994 b. m., Seeking the Gold—Page Proof, by Seattle Slew. 21-8-2-3, $4,021,716. European highweight at four. Group 1 winner in France. Dam of Group 2 winner Seeking the Dia; when struck by lightning, on June 10, 2005, at Lane's End, in Versailles, Kentucky.

SEMIPALATINSK, 1978 b. h., Nodouble—School Board, by Reverse. 8-3-3-0, $41,559. Won the 1980 Premio Bimbi. Sire of 22 stakes winners, including Australian champion Tennessee Blue and Australia highweight Palatious; of old age, in January 2006, at Eureka Stud, in Queensland, Australia.

SERRA LAKE, 1997 b. m., Seattle Slew—Tara Roma, by Lyphard. 15-7-1-1, $486,760. Won the 2001 Go for Wand H. (G1); euthanized after fracturing her right hind leg in a paddock accident, on November 16, 2005, at Middlebrook Farm, in Lexington.

SHADEED, 1982 b. h., Nijinsky II—Continual, by Damascus. 7-4-0-2, $278,652. Won the 1985 Two Thousand Guineas (Eng-G1). Sire of 15 stakes winners, including champions or classic winners Shadayid and Sayyedati (GB), and leading Canadian sire Alydeed; due to an illness, on November 13, 2005, at Gainsborough Farm, in Versailles, Kentucky.

SHARED INTEREST, 1988 b. m., Pleasant Colony—Surgery, by Dr. Fager. 23-10-5-3, $667,610. Won the 1993 Ruffian H. (G1). Dam of Grade 1 winners Cash Run and Forestry; of complications from foaling, on March 10, 2005, at Taylor Made Farm, in Nicholasville, Kentucky.

SHOWER OF ROSES, 1999 br. m., Zabeel—Our Marquise, by Gold and Ivory. 15-5-1-1, $395,683. Won the 2003 Storm Queen S. (Aus-G1); due to colic complications after foaling, in mid-August 2005, at Gooree Stud, in New South Wales, Australia.

SHUAILAAN, 1989 ch. h., Roberto—Lassie's Lady, by Alydar. 15-5-3-2, $134,910. Won the 1992 Winter Hill S. in England. Sire of seven stakes winners, including champions La Tizona and I Will Dance; of colic, on January 31, 2006, at Equine Transitional Training Alliance, in Midway, Kentucky.

SILVER WIZARD, 1990 b. h., Silver Hawk—Cherie's Hope, by Flying Paster. 33-8-3-7, $493,563. Stakes winner in England and the U.S. Won the 1995 American H. (G2). Grade 1-placed. Sire of winners; died early in 2005, in Italy.

SISTER ACT, 1995 gr. or ro. m., Saint Ballado—La Ice Queen, by Icecapade. 13-7-4-0, $579,394. Won the 1999 Hempstead H. (G1), '98 La Troienne S. (G3); of laminitis, on August 24, 2005, at WinStar Farm, in Versailles, Kentucky.

SLEWDLEDO, 1981 dk. b. or br. h., Seattle Slew—M'lle. Cyanne, by Cyane. Unraced. Leading Washington sire in 2003, '04, and '05. Sire of 36 stakes winners, including Grade 3 winners Snipledo and Slewsbox; of bladder cancer, on May 1, 2006, at Lucky Acres Farm, in Yakima, Washington.

Slewsbag, 2002 dk. b. or br. g., Devil's Bag—Slew's M. D., by Slew o' Gold. 14-1-1-2, $82,176. Graded stakes-placed at two; after breaking down in the Snow Chief S. on April 24, 2005, at Hollywood Park, in California.

Slew the Coup, 1981 b. h., Seattle Slew—Evasive, by Buckpasser. 10-3-2-1, $90,734. Grade 1-placed. Sire of four stakes winners, including Lemon Grass and Coup Verville; of colic, on December 5, 2005, in Oklahoma.

SMILE N CARSON, 2001 ch. c., Carson City—Smile n Molly, by Dixieland Band. 13-2-2-1, $28,286. Full brother to 1999 Sapling S. (G3) winner Dont Tell the Kids; after breaking down in a race at Tampa Bay Downs, on January 26, 2005, in Florida.

SMOKESTER, 1998 dk. b. or br. h., Never Tabled—Small World, by Transworld. 4-2-0-1, $35,600. Among California's leading sires. Sire of ten stakes winners, including Grade 1 winner Free House; of an apparent heart attack, on February 21, 2005, at Cardiff Stud Farms, in Creston, California.

SNACK, 2002 ch. c., Afternoon Deelites—Miss Riverton, by Fred Astaire. 9-4-2-2, $97,400. Won the 2005 Turfway Prevue S., '04 Indiana Futurity; euthanized after breaking down in the Santa Catalina S., on March 5, 2005, at Santa Anita Park, in California.

SOLDIER'S KISS, 2002 gr. or ro. f., One Man Army—Butterfly Kiss, by Corwyn Bay (Ire). 9-4-0-2, $188,878. Won the 2005 Fleet Treat and NTRA S.; euthanized after breaking down in a workout, in January 2006, at Santa Anita Park, in California.

Sophisticated Girl, 1980 dk. b. or br. m., Stop the Music—Close Control, by Dunce. 12-2-3-0, $122,066. Grade 1-placed. Dam of Grade 2 winner Doneraile Court; due to infirmities of age, in November 2005, at Golden Eagle Farm, in Ramona, California.

SOUND ACTION, 1999 ch. m., Vettori—Dance With Royalty, by Palace Music. 15-8-1-1, $522,356. Won the 2003 Australian Oaks (Aus-G1); euthanized after emergency surgery for a pedal bone injury, on June 18, 2005, in Australia.

South Sea Dancer, 1981 b. m., Northern Dancer—South Ocean, by New Providence. 14-2-4-3, $62,200. Stakes-placed. Sold for a yearling filly record of $1.8-million. Dam of Grade 3 winner Signal Tap; on February 2, 2006, at Knockgriffin Farm, in Paris, Kentucky.

SPORTSWORLD, 1988 b. h., Alleged—Gallanta (Fr), by Nureyev. 5-3-1-0, $104,736. Won the 1991 Gallinule S. (Ire-G2). Sire of at least 17 stakes winners, including 2005 South African champion Jamaica and

Group 1 winners Kournikova and Sport's Chestnut; euthanized due to a hock injury, in January 2005, at Daytona Stud in South Africa.

STAR OVER THE BAY, 1998 gr. or ro. g., Cozzene—Lituya Bay, by Empery. 43-10-4-3, $917,353. Won the 2004 Clement L. Hirsch Memorial Turf Championship (G1), Del Mar H. (G2); euthanized after breaking down in the International Cup (Sin-G1), on May 15, 2005, in Singapore.

STELLA GRANDE, 2001 b. g., Marquetry—Currastar, by Curravilla (Ire). 16-4-4-4, $466,816. Won the 2005 Tulloch S. (Aus-G2); of an infection, in early November 2005, in Australia.

STOP THE MUSIC, 1970 b. h., Hail to Reason—Bebopper, by Tom Fool. 30-11-10-4, $448,922. Grade 2 winner. Sired 46 stakes winners, including champion Temperence Hill and Grade 1 winner Cure the Blues. Broodmare sire of at least 89 stakes winners, including 2005 Kentucky Derby (G1) winner Giacomo; of old age, on July 8, 2005, at Gainesway, in Lexington.

Stormy Afternoon, 2002 ch. c., Afternoon Deelites—Temporada, by Summer Squall. 6-1-3-0, $49,965. Stakes-placed at two; of a heart attack, on April 15, 2005, while training at Churchill Downs, in Louisville.

STRIKE GOLD, 1980 dk. b. or br. h., Mr. Prospector—Newchance Lady, by *Roi Dagobert. 6-4-1-0, $71,760. Won the 1983 Bay Shore S. (G3). Sire of 25 stakes winners, including three Grade 3 winners; of old age, on October 7, 2005, JZ Stock Farm, in Temecula, California.

STRIKE THE BRASS, 1997 b. g., Dixie Brass—Strike It Easy, by Easy Goer. 66-11-12-9, $314,719. Won the 2002 Wine Country H.; after breaking down in a race on April 28, 2005, at Charles Town Races, in West Virginia.

SUPERIORITY, 1996 ch. g., Arazi—Outstandingly, by Exclusive Native. 37-11-1-4, $210,337. Won the National Day Cup in the United Arab Emirates; after breaking down in a race on September 13, 2005, at Suffolk Downs, in Massachusetts.

TABA (Arg), 1973 b. m., Table Play—Filipina, by Fomento. Argentine champion and classic winner. Dam of 1986 champion older male Turkoman and stakes winner Slow Fuse; of natural causes, on February 11, 2005, at Our Mims Retirement Haven at Ahwenasa Farm, in Paris, Kentucky.

TEMPERATURE, 2002 ch. g., Bering (GB)—Thermal Spring, by Zafonic. 3-2-0-0, $27,022. Winner of his first two starts impressively; after breaking down in the Prix Greffulhe (Fr-G2), on May 16, 2005, at St. Cloud racecourse, in France.

Tequila Sheila, 1978 dk. b. or br. m., Hagley—Well Bold, by Boldnesian. 28-5-6-4, $77,312. Stakes-placed. Dam of Canadian Grade 3 winner Sheila's Prospect and stakes winner Lite Twilight; of an aneurysm, on April 15, 2005.

TERESA MC, 1988 b. m., Moscow Ballet—Shayne McGuire, by Mickey McGuire. 24-8-4-3, $302,945. Won the 1991 La Brea S. (G3). Dam of three winners; after rupturing an artery, in mid-2005, at Harris Farms, in Coalinga, California.

THATSUSINTHEOLBEAN, 1994 ch. h., El Prado (Ire)—Belfast Becky, by Overskate. 77-18-9-16, $452,082. Won 12 stakes, including the 1997 Alysheba Breeders' Cup S.; following a breeding shed accident, on February 13, 2006, at A&A Ranch, in Anthony, New Mexico.

The Bink, 1991 b. m., Seeking the Gold—Toll Fee, by Topsider. 19-3-5-5, $135,889. Graded stakes-placed. Dam of Grade 1-winning millionaire Riskaverse and graded stakes winner Cozzy Corner; of foaling complications, on February 24, 2006, at Valkyre Stud, in Georgetown, Kentucky.

THESIS, 1998 ch. g., Definite Article (GB)—Chouette, by Try My Best. 28-6-6-6, $176,412. Won the 2003 Ladbroke Hurdle; of injuries sustained in a racing accident, at Kempton Park, on January 31, 2005, in England.

THE THOUGHT OCCURS, 2003 dk. b. or br. c., Souvenir Copy—Mysteryachievement, by Regal Classic. 4-1-0-2, $43,964. Won the 2005 Beau Brummel S.; after breaking down past the finish of the Sunny Slope S., on October 22, 2005, at Santa Anita Park, in Arcadia, California.

TIC N TIN, 1995 dk. b. or br. g., Lac Ouimet—Catching a Buzz, by Distinctive. 97-29-19-6, $771,570. Winner of nine stakes in the Midwest; after breaking down in a race on June 12, 2005, at Arlington Park, in Illinois.

TIMBERA, 1994 dk. b. or br. g., Commanche Run—Morry's Lady, by The Parson. 27-7-4-1, $211,526. Won the 2003 Irish Grand National Steeplechase; after breaking down in a race, on March 17, 2005, in Ireland.

TIME CHARTER, 1979 b. m., Saritamer—Centrocon (GB), by High Line. 20-9-0-0, $918,320. England's champion older female of 1983. Won the 1982 Epsom Oaks (Eng-G1). Dam of two group winners, including English highweight Time Allowed; of old age, in July 2005, at Fair Winter Farm, in Buckinghamshire, England.

TORTELLINI ROMA, 1985 b. m., Darby Creek Road—Miss Eight Eighty, by Dr. Fager. 11-4-1-0, $128,428. Won the 1987 Longacres Lassie S.; dam of five winners, including stakes-placed Mynexthorse; on September 25, 2005.

TOTAL ENJOYMENT, 1999 b. m., Flemensfirth—Oak Court, by Bustineto. 7-4-0-1, $93,485. Multiple stakes-winning hurdler in England and Ireland; of laminitis, in 2005.

TOUR D' OR, 1982 ch. h., Medaille d' Or—Debby's Turn, by Turn to Mars. 47-19-6-4, $479,153. Won the 1989 Walter Haight H. Sire of 23 stakes winners, including graded Express Tour, Tour of the Cat, and Phantom On Tour; of laminitis, in late July 2005, at the University of Florida Veterinary Medical Center.

TRIOCALA, 1978 dk. b. or br. h., Tri Jet—Hail Proudly, by Francis S. 63-14-14-7, $465,660. Won the 1981 Count Fleet S. Sire of two stakes winners, including Grade 3 winner Tri for the Gold; of congestive heart failure, on August 5, 2005, at High Cliff Farm, in Delanson, New York.

TRISCAY, 1987 ch. m., Marscay—Tristram Lady, by *Sir Tristram. 29-19-5-5, $2,180,112. Australian champion at three. Won the 1991 Australian Oaks (Aus-G1). Dam of Group 1 winner La Baraka and Group 2 winner Tsuimai; of colic, in March 2006, in Australia.

TRISHYDE, 1989 ch. m., Nureyev—Rose Du Boele (Fr), by Rheffic. 16-6-3-1, $467,153. 16-6-3-1, $467,153. Group 2 winner in France. Won the 1994 Fleur de Lis H. (G3); due to foaling complications, on March 2, 2005, at Spendthrift Farm, in Lexington.

TUCKED AWAY, 2000 dk. b. or br. m., Unusual Heat—Chemolo, by Be a Native. 29-5-7-5, $582,956. Won the 2005 Clement L. Hirsch H. (G2); euthanized on September 4, 2005, following surgical complications after breaking down in a workout at Del Mar, in California.

TURKO WITZ, 1979 b. m., Stop the Music—Chateaucreek, by Chateaugay. 9-2-0-0, $4,245. Dam of four stakes winners, including Grade 1 winners Mr Purple and Queens Court Queen; of old age, on June 14, 2005, at Darby Dan Farm, in Lexington.

TWO MILE HILL, 2000 b. m., A.P. Indy—Flat Fleet Feet, by Afleet. 12-4-2-1, $165,747. Won the 2004 Golden Sylvia H.; after breaking down in the Banshee Breeze S., on January 23, 2005, at Gulfstream Park, in Florida.

Tycoon (GB), 2001 b. c., Sadler's Wells—Fleeting Glimpse, by Rainbow Quest. 13-1-2-5, $430,645. Classic-placed in England and Ireland; after breaking down in the Abu Dhabi Championship, on April 10, 2005, in the United Arab Emirates.

ULAAN BAATAR, 1997 dk. b. or br. g., Jackson's Drift—Leinster Lady, by Lord Chancellor. 11-4-3-0, $131,374. Won the 2005 Arkle Perpetual Challenge Cup Steeplechase; after breaking down in a workout, on April 22, 2005, in Ireland.

UNNAMED, 2004 b. c., In Excess (Ire)—Fabulous Ballet, by Moscow Ballet. Half brother to 2005 Test S. (G1) winner Leave Me Alone and to 1998 California Sprint Championship H. winner Stoney; of gunshot wounds sustained in a drive-by shooting, in his pasture, in March 2005, in Fresno, California.

UNNAMED, 2005 b. c., Empire Maker—Bird Town, by Cape Town. First foal out of 2003 champion three-year-old filly Bird Town, from the first crop of '03 Belmont Stakes (G1) winner Empire Maker; following surgery for a shoulder injury, on December 21, 2005, in Kentucky.

UP AN OCTAVE, 2003 dk. b. or br. c., Brahms—Afleet Change, by Time for a Change. 7-3-1-1, $184,672. Won the 2006 Forerunner S.; euthanized after breaking down following his victory in the Forerunner, on April 20, 2006, at Keeneland Race Course.

Valor Within, 2002 dk. b. or br. f., Souvenir Copy—Double Link, by Private Thoughts. 21-2-5-4, $45,806. Multiple stakes-placed; euthanized after breaking down in an allowance race, on May 5, 2006, at Churchill Downs.

Verbasle, 1988 dk. b. or br. m., Slewpy—Verbality, by Verbatim. 26-4-4-8, $250,801. Grade 1-placed. Dam of three stakes winners, including 2005 Florida Derby (G1) winner High Fly; of laminitis, on August 16, 2005, at Hagyard Equine Medical Institute, in Lexington.

WAKRIA, 1990 b. m., Sadler's Wells—Spirits Dancing, by Melyno (Ire). 16-3-3-1, $69,380. Won the 1993 Prix de Saint-Cyr. Dam of six winners, including four stakes-placed runners; in 2005.

WAY WEST (FR), 1990 b. h., Gone West—Greenway (Fr), by Targowice. 18-3-2-5, $125,574. Won the 1994 Prix Servanne. Sire of four stakes winners, including millionaire graded winner Western Pride; of laminitis, on March 26, 2006, in West Virginia.

WESTERN SYMPHONY, 1981 b. h., Nijinsky II—Millicent, by Cornish Prince. 8-3-2-2, $40,131. Won the 1983 Larkspur S. (Ire-G3). Sire of 28 stakes winners. Broodmare sire of 21 stakes winners, including three-time Australian Horse of the Year Sunline; in April 2005, at Emerald Park Stud, in New Zealand.

WESTWARD LINDA, 1998 b. m., West by West—Linda Vi, by Vigors. 5-1-0-0, $4,410. Dam of one winner; found dead of gunshot wounds, in early February 2006, in her paddock at Bangtail Farm, in Mad River, California.

WHAT A NUISANCE, 1978 b. g., St Puckle—Fashion Bell, by Belmura. Won ten races, including the 1985 Melbourne Cup (Aus-G1); of natural causes in his paddock at trainer Pat Hyland's farm, on April 20, 2005, near Cranbourne, Australia.

WHAT A SONG, 2003 dk. b. or br. c., Songandaprayer—What a Knight, by Tough Knight. 3-3-0-0, $179,700. Won the 2005 Best Pal S. (G2), Hollywood Juvenile Championship S. (G3); after breaking down in a morning gallop, on August 19, 2005, at Del Mar, in California.

WHIFFLING, 1985 b. m., Wavering Monarch—Queen's Gambit, by Bold Ruler. 9-1-0-3, $27,900. Dam of champion Prairie Bayou and Grade 2 winner Flitch; euthanized due to infirmities of age, on December 5, 2005, at Calumet Farm, in Lexington.

WHY ME LORD, 1974, dk. b. or br. m., Bold Reasoning—Tomorrowland, by *Pappa Fourway. 11-1-1-0, $3,613. Dam of ten winners, including German champion and North American Grade 1 winner Allez Milord; of old age, on April 21, 2006, at Gallagher's Stud, in Ghent, New York.

WILD WONDER, 1994 gr. or ro. h., Wild Again—Carol's Wonder, by Pass the Tab. 20-9-5-4, $639,036. Won the 1998 Mervyn Leroy H. (G2). Sire of 2005 graded stakes winners Wild Fit and Fusaichi Rock Star; of a ruptured aorta, on January 25, 2006, at Buck Pond Farm, in Versailles, Kentucky.

WINGS OF JONES, 1996 ch. g., Seneca Jones—Dapple Dawn, by Timeless Moment. 102-19-8-18, $361,682. Champion two-year-old in Texas. Won the 1998 Middleground S.; after breaking down in a race, on November 15, 2005, at Suffolk Downs, in Massachusetts.

WINNING MINISTER, 2003 dk. b. or br. c., Deputy Minister—Biding Time, by Seeking the Gold. 4-1-0-1, $38,800; after breaking down in the Cowdin S. (G2), on October 2, 2005, at Belmont Park, in New York.

WITH A CITY, 2003 ch. c., City Zip—With a Princess, by With Approval. 13-4-0-2, $359,680. Won the 2006 Lane's End S. (G2); euthanized due to an unknown illness, on April 23, 2006, at Hagyard Equine Medical Institute, in Lexington.

WOODMAN'S GIRL, 1990 b. m., Woodman—Becky Be Good, by Naskra. 28-3-3-5, $69,195. Dam of millionaire Grade 1 winner More Than Ready; of colic, following surgery to deliver her Mineshaft foal, on February 21, 2005, in Kentucky.

YANKEE FAN, 1984 ch. h., Our Native—Cee Lyn Zee, by Cimmarron. 18-5-4-2, $90,596. Sire of ten stakes winners, including 12-time black-type winner Nomistakethistime; of laminitis, on September 29, 2005, at Kansas State University's College of Veterinary Medicine.

ZADRACARTA, 1985 dk. b. or br. m., Bold Ruckus—Montmorency, by Selari. 27-8-7-3, $385,363. Won the 1987 Fanfreluche S. Dam of stakes winner Major Zee; on April 2, 2005, of foaling complications, in Florida.

ZINAAD, 1989 b. h., Shirley Heights—Time Charter, by Saritamer. 12-3-1-4, $130,501. Won the 1993 Jockey Club S. (Eng-G2). Sire of at least four stakes winners, including European champion and 2002 Epsom Oaks (Eng-G1) winner Kazzia (Ger); of a heart attack, on August 27, 2005, at Hauptgestut Graditz, in Germany.

ZINGAM, 1999 b. g., Zabeel—Danendri, by Danehill. 27-7-4-1, $203,976. Winner of three stakes, including the 2005 Sky Channel Chairman's H. (Aus-G3); of a probable heart attack after a workout, in May 2006, at Warwick Farm, in Australia.

HISTORY OF RACING

by Mary Simon

Horse racing officially appeared in the annals of history in approximately 1000 B.C. when Greeks started racing horses with chariots drawn behind them, a dangerous game that subsequently was adopted by the Romans and Egyptians. For the 33rd Olympiad in 644 B.C., formal competition began with riders astride the horses. The Romans, who conquered England in 43 A.D. under Emperor Claudius and ruled it until 410 A.D., carried their horses and their sport to the island nation, where a millennium later it would blossom into the sport known as Thoroughbred racing.

By the late 1500s, racing had become a favorite pastime of English noblemen. King Henry VIII and his daughter Queen Elizabeth I both maintained racing stables, and Elizabeth's cousin King James I established Newmarket racecourse early in the 17th century. His son Charles I also was a racing enthusiast, but he was overthrown and beheaded in 1649, and Lord Protector Oliver Cromwell banned horse racing. After the restoration of the monarchy in 1660, racing flourished under its ardent devotee King Charles II.

Because of Charles II's love for the sport, racing became known as the sport of kings, and during his rule the first of three imported Arabian stallions began the genetic progression toward the Thoroughbred of today. In 1688, Capt. Robert Byerly purportedly returned from Hungary with a captured stallion who became known as the Byerly Turk. Sixteen years later, British consul Thomas Darley smuggled an Arabian stallion out of Syria and transplanted him to Yorkshire; he became known as the Darley Arabian. In approximately 1730, an Arabian stallion of unknown lineage appeared in the stable of the Earl of Godolphin and became known as the Godolphin Arabian. These three stallions would become the foundation sires of the Thoroughbred. The Darley Arabian sired Flying Childers, generally regarded as the first great Thoroughbred, in 1714. (For more on the development of the Thoroughbred, see Evolution of the Breed.)

In the late 18th century, racing began to assume a formal structure. Racecourses were established, and the first of the English classics, the St. Leger Stakes, was run in 1776. The Epsom Derby followed four years later, and the Two Thousand Guineas had its first running in 1809. As racing developed in England, it found its way to the American colonies. In 1665, New York Governor Richard Nicholls gave the name Newmarket to America's first racetrack. Although the first track was located in New York, horse racing tended to be frowned upon by religious leaders and communities in the North, but the sport flourished in the South. The first known Thoroughbred sire imported to North America from England was *Bulle Rock, an aged son of the Darley Arabian. Although *Bulle Rock had no lasting influence, pre-Revolution imports such as *Fearnought, pint-sized *Janus, and the *Cub mare influenced the breed's development.

19th Century

Early American presidents, particularly those from the South, were racing fans. Thomas Jefferson approved the Senate's practice of adjourning early to attend local meets. Senators of the day might have marveled at the fabled 28-foot stride of the great colt Florizel or witnessed the unbeatable brilliance of First Consul during his 21-race winning streak.

It was an era of often unrecorded and disputed genealogies, and races were crudely timed, if at all. The 1823 victory of American Eclipse over Henry in the North-South match at Long Island's Union Course proved a milestone in post-Colonial racing. The $20,000-a-side event drew a significant portion of the New York populace and helped American Eclipse stake his claim as the first American earnings champion, with $56,700. At the same time, *Leviathan was standing for America's highest known fee—$75—but he was not the most notable stallion of the period. That honor went to *Diomed, a British castoff after the Revolutionary War. The inaugural Epsom Derby winner in 1780, he arrived on American shores in Virginia in '98, acquired for a meager $250. *Diomed proceeded over 11 seasons to reshape the American Thoroughbred in his own remarkable image, getting runners that were uniformly taller, heavier of bone, stouter, stronger, and faster than their contemporaries.

Unlike England, where the Epsom Derby and St. Leger heralded a trend toward shorter races, America maintained its long heat races for the first half of the century. While the style of racing evolved over time, change of another kind arrived on March 17, 1850, when *Diomed's great-great grandson Lexington was born on a Central Kentucky farm. Brilliant on the racecourse and even more accomplished at stud, Lexington would reign 16 times—including 14 in succession—as the country's leading sire.

As the century progressed, races became shorter, purses rose, and racing began to become organized. Saratoga Race Course, Pimlico Race Course, Churchill Downs, and Fair Grounds opened for business. The Travers Stakes had its first running in 1864, and the Belmont Stakes was run for the first time in 1867. The Preakness Stakes followed in 1873, and the Kentucky Derby was staged for the first time in '75. Late in the century, the Jockey Club was established to oversee the growing sport, and it soon assumed control of the *American Stud Book*. In 1889, Miss Woodford became the first American Thoroughbred to top $100,000 in career earnings. Two-year-old racing gained popularity with the inaugural 1888 Futurity, worth $40,000 to the winner; five years later, a juvenile named Domino set a single-season earnings record of $170,790 that would stand for decades. Kingston—last of the great iron horses of a dying era—retired in 1894 with 89 victories, a record to this day. By the end of the 19th century, Kentucky had become the heart of America's Thoroughbred business, with more professional horsemen than any other region. America and its Thoroughbred industry were thus poised to enter a modern era of even greater change.

1901-'10

The American century's first decade was one of promise and turmoil for the Thoroughbred racing industry. Trouble brewed even as financier James R. Keene's great Commando blistered the track at the dawn of the century and as Commando's unbeatable son Colin carried the Keene colors to victory after brilliant victory a few years later. Even as Keene's stable racked up unprecedented earnings, as record purses were dispensed, and as Belmont Park opened its glorious gates, a dark cloud was settling ominously on racing's horizon.

Racing may have been the sport of kings, but it was also part of a larger gambling industry. Increasingly, the taint of corruption eroded public confidence in the sport as high-profile incidents were exposed. Keene's Sysonby, one of the sport's all-time greats, suffered his only loss in the 1904 Futurity after being drugged by a groom. Delhi, the 1904 Belmont Stakes winner, later ran sluggishly and was found to have sponges inserted far up into his nostrils. Electric prods, dopings, ringers, crooked jockeys, and diverse gambling scams involving track bookmakers were daily journalistic fodder.

By 1907, anti-racetrack wagering laws had been simmering for some time on legislative back burners across America. In June 1908, New York passed the Agnew-Hart bill with the ardent blessing of Governor Charles Evans Hughes, who used the legislation as a weapon against the Tammany Hall political machine, a major beneficiary of racing in the New York metropolitan area. Without revenues from legalized gambling, racing soon found it impossible to support itself. In 1910, historic Saratoga was among the racetracks that ceased operation, and E. J. "Lucky" Baldwin's original Santa Anita Park was forced to close.

A domino effect occurred as other states rushed to pass similar legislation. The national purse structure collapsed, declining from a 1907 average of $949 per race to $643 in '09. Top stables, including Keene's, shipped overseas in a European invasion so successful that it would pave the way for the next great blow to the American Thoroughbred industry—the English Jockey Club's 1913 passage of the "Jersey Act" banning most American-breds from their Stud Book. In 1908, Churchill Downs's energetic general manager, Col. Matt Winn, pulled some old pari-mutuel machines out of storage, dusted them off, and put them back into use. When racing resumed in the next decade, the pari-mutuel wagering system quickly would become dominant.

Despite all, several great competitors appeared on racing's stage to illuminate the era. Colin was one of nine future Racing Hall of Fame members who campaigned during the decade. Man o' War's fiery sire, Fair Play, was another, along with Commando, Sysonby, Artful, Beldame, Roseben, Broomstick, and Peter Pan.

1911-'20

As indignation among the American populace swelled over the puritan campaigners' assault on gambling and alcohol consumption, a group of wealthy horsemen began to stockpile a fund with which to hold future race meets. The future came quickly. Although the Agnew-Hart legislation moldered on the books until 1934, the penalties associated with it were stripped away by May 30, 1913, when Belmont Park opened for the first time since 1910. Between 1908 and '13, however, American breeders had sent overseas more than 1,500 horses, among them at least 24 champions. Some eventually came back, but many did not. Leading sires *Rock Sand and *Meddler, also part of the exodus, were lost forever to American breeding.

The British responded with the Jersey Act in 1913, which effectively barred many old American lines from England's *General Stud Book,* but the first shots of World War I one year later quickly changed the United States from an exporter of bloodstock into an aggressive importer. Between 1916-'20, numerous English-breds and French-breds became American champions, including *Short Grass, *Sun Briar, *Hourless, *Omar Khayyam, *Johren, *Sunbonnet, *Enfilade, and *Constancy.

Even in the shadow of war, the decade was memorable for its outstanding runners, including future Racing Hall of Fame geldings Roamer, Old Rosebud, and Exterminator. Together, they won 129 races and set or equaled 29 records from five furlongs to 2¼ miles at 14 different racetracks. Iron Mask set a North American record for 5½ furlongs that would stand for 30 years, and the mare Pan Zareta took a back seat to no male in the realm of blazing speed. H. P. Whitney's Regret routinely whipped the boys and in 1915 became the first filly to win the Kentucky Derby. The Triple Crown was won for the first time in 1919 by Sir Barton, although the sweep did not take on its popular name until the '30s.

Sir Barton won the Belmont on June 11, five days after the decade's finest specimen made his first career start at Belmont Park. Man o' War, considered the greatest American horse of all time, was ineligible for admission to the *General Stud Book*, but in 16 months of competition redefined greatness. He lost one race at two that he should have won, failing to overcome a bad start in the Sanford Stakes at Saratoga Race Course and losing to Upset, but he never lost again. In 1920, "Big Red" established five American and two track records in 11 starts and won his races by a combined 164 lengths. Man o' War capped his extraordinary career on October 12, 1920, by galloping away from Sir Barton in a winner-take-all race at Kenilworth Park in Canada. The $80,000 purse sent him to stud as the richest American Thoroughbred in history with $249,465.

1921-'30

On the surface at least, the Roaring Twenties were a time of outrageous fun—flappers and the fox trot are indelible images of the era—and horse racing rode the crest of this postwar celebration. Elaborate new racetracks were the overt symbol of this prosperity—at least 15 of note were constructed in the United States during the 1920s, including Arlington and Washington Parks in Chicago and Hialeah Park in Florida. Purses went through the roof. In 1923, Zev became the first American racehorse to bank $200,000 in a season and, by '30, Gallant Fox—the second Triple Crown winner and the first to be recognized for sweeping the three American classics—had raised that bar to $300,000. Jockey Earle Sande, trainer James Fitzsimmons, breeder Harry Payne Whitney, and owner Harry Sinclair each established earnings records that would stand for years. Bloodstock prices also went into orbit, with a yearling commanding a record $75,000 in 1928.

Because the Jersey Act remained in force, horses mostly migrated to the west. Future leading sires *St. Germans, *Sickle, and *Challenger II were among the importees, as was the great matron *La Troienne. In late 1925, *Sir Gallahad III arrived at Claiborne Farm, where he would reign four times as America's premier sire and 12 times as its leading broodmare sire. *Sir Gallahad III's American-bred counterpart was Man o' War, a private stallion who had seven of his eight champions in his first four crops and in 1926—with only three crops racing—set a progeny earnings record of $409,927.

No single racehorse towered above all others in the 1920s as Man o' War and Colin had before, but the decade nonetheless yielded 15 Racing Hall of Fame members. Foremost among them was Exterminator, the wonderful gelding who scored a 20th-century record 34 stakes victories and retired as America's richest Thoroughbred. Grey Lag flirted with greatness, as did champions Sarazen, Blue Larkspur, Reigh Count, and Gallant Fox. Zev, Crusader, and Sun Beau were big money winners. Princess Doreen won 34 races and broke Miss Woodford's 40-year female earnings record with $174,745. Other notable fillies included 1924 Preakness winner Nellie Morse; multiple champions Black Maria and Bateau; and Rose of Sharon, considered best of either sex at three in 1929. For a time, it appeared the good times would go on forever, but the stock market crashed in October 1929, which led to events that caused the Great Depression.

1931-'40

As the Depression shrunk race purses 40%, the average yearling price slumped to $570 in 1932. But, as the Depression eased, the Thoroughbred industry entered one of its healthiest eras. Purses rose by decade's end to record heights, and yearling sales gained strength. Racing also had some wealthy, influential leaders. Joseph E. Widener, vice chairman of the New York Jockey Club, crusaded tirelessly to return the sport in the Empire State to its former glory. Jockey Club Chairman William Woodward campaigned 1935 Triple Crown winner Omaha, but more importantly that year he fired some of the angriest, most articulate words at England's discriminatory Jersey Act. During the decade, increasingly sophisticated stall starting gates were developed, photo-finish cameras were installed, and saliva testing for drugs gained widespread use. Keeneland Race Course, Del Mar Thoroughbred Club, Santa Anita Park, and Hollywood Park opened for business.

Although the 1930s featured many standout racehorses, including 17 future Racing Hall of Fame members and two Triple Crown winners, three in particular captured the hearts of America—C. V. Whitney's Equipoise, Australasian wonder *Phar Lap, and claimer-turned-champion Seabiscuit. Although bred in the purple and owned by one of America's wealthiest bluebloods, there was nothing pretentious about Equipoise, a son of Pennant who was a champion at two in 1930, a three-time handicap champion, and a world-record miler. Seabiscuit, an undersized Wheatley Stable reject, developed into a megastar, reigning as '38 Horse of the Year and twice as America's handicap champion. In one of the decade's greatest moments, Seabiscuit defeated 1937 Triple Crown winner War Admiral in the two-horse '38 Pimlico Special Stakes. *Phar Lap illuminated the Depression's darkest hour by winning the 1932 Agua Caliente Handicap in record time, but the huge New Zealander died just 17 days later under suspicious circumstances.

The 1930s launched a feminine revolution of sorts. Top Flight defeated males in the 1931 Futurity to become the first $200,000 juvenile earner and richest American female. Mrs. Payne Whitney's Twenty Grand won that year's Kentucky Derby, and Isabel Dodge Sloane became America's leading owner in 1934. As war in Europe approached, America imported several top stallions. In 1936, Hancock organized a syndicate to purchase *Blenheim II, for $250,000; four years later, C. V. Whitney acquired the stallion's classic-winning son, *Mahmoud.

1941-'50

Despite a world at war for half the decade, the 1940s very well may have been racing's finest hour, with four Triple Crown winners crowning the decade. The war years were grim for the sport, however. Southern California's tracks were shut down—Santa Anita was an internment camp for Japanese-Americans, Hollywood was an army storage unit, and Del Mar was used for assembling aircraft wings. Travel restrictions crippled the Saratoga yearling sale and led to the creation of the Breeders' Sales Co., precursor of Keeneland Sales. In late 1944, the government banned racing, and only victory in Europe saved the '45 Triple Crown.

Leavening the somber news from overseas were the exploits of Whirlaway, Calumet's "Mr. Longtail," winner of the 1941 Triple Crown. Then there was Alsab, a $700 yearling of peasant lineage who outgamed Whirlaway by a nose in a famous 1942 match race at Narragansett Park. Mrs. John D. Hertz's 1943 Triple Crown winner, Count Fleet, habitually crushed his opposition and romped to a 25-length Belmont Stakes victory, despite a career-ending injury. High-headed, flame-coated Stymie was not the best, but he was nevertheless beloved by fans who made him the people's horse. Claimed for $1,500 from King Ranch by trainer Hirsch Jacobs, Stymie became the first Thoroughbred to surpass $900,000 in career earnings. King Ranch had Assault, who overcame a deformed right fore foot to win the 1946 Triple Crown. The 1940s also produced several top fillies, including Racing Hall of Fame members Twilight Tear, Busher, Gallorette, Bewitch, Two Lea, and Bed o' Roses. Argentine-bred *Miss Grillo set a 2½-mile world record in the 1948 Pimlico Cup Handicap.

The decade virtually belonged to Warren Wright's magnificent Calumet Stable, whose champions were trained by Ben and Jimmy Jones and in many cases ridden by Eddie Arcaro—all Racing Hall of Fame members. Calumet reigned as America's top owner seven times during the decade, edged only by a trio of prominent women—Mrs. Payne Whitney (1942), Elizabeth Graham ('45), and Isabel Dodge Sloane ('50). Runners who carried the feared devil's red and blue silks during the 1940s included Racing Hall of Fame members Whirlaway, Twilight Tear, Armed, Citation, Bewitch, Coaltown, and Two Lea, and father-son Kentucky Derby winners Pensive and Ponder. Citation was not only Calumet's best but also one of the century's most talented runners. Champion at two and three, American Triple Crown hero, and winner of 16 consecutive races, Citation would become the sport's first millionaire in 1951.

Late in the decade, Claiborne Farm acquired *Nasrullah, a rogue stallion who would transform the American bloodstock industry. Also in 1949, England's Jockey Club backed down after 36 years and rescinded the despised Jersey Act, by now long outdated and hindering rather than helping the British breeding industry. America thus regained its former stature as a respected source of international bloodstock.

1951-'60

As it entered the second half of the 20th century, the U.S. confronted a rapidly changing world. It was at war in Korea, the threat of Nazism had been replaced by the peril of nuclear cataclysm, television was helping to create a truly national society, and polio had been conquered. America's appetite for racing seemed utterly insatiable; attendance and handle records were established almost annually. Perhaps it was too successful. In this decade, racing failed to build a lasting partnership with television—an arrogant decision that the industry would regret into the 21st century.

The 1950s were a time of rising incomes and rising expectations. In 1956, Nashua became the first million-dollar stallion syndication. Also that year, jockey Bill Hartack became the first to ride winners of $2-million in a single season; he topped $3-million the following year. The 1950s witnessed a growing interest in early competition—particularly after the spectacular 1953 debut of the world's richest race, the $270,000 Garden State Stakes for two-year-olds at Garden State Park in New Jersey. Soundness became an issue in the 1950s, with the high-profile breakdowns of such stars as Hail to Reason and Swaps. In the late 1950s, phenylbutazone—an anti-inflammatory drug popularly known as Bute—came into wide use to ease the aches and pains of thoroughbreds, though not legal for racing.

Racing in the 1950s had several stars but no Triple Crown winner. (Jockey Eddie Arcaro blamed himself for Nashua's loss to Swaps in the 1955 Derby. Nashua subsequently won the Preakness and Belmont.) The first equine superhero of the TV age was Native Dancer—the "Gray Ghost of Sagamore," whose only loss in 22 starts was by a head in the 1953 Kentucky Derby. Also racing at that time was Tom Fool, who carried heavy imposts to ten straight victories. As Native Dancer and Tom Fool exited the stage, the prodigiously talented pair of Nashua and Swaps took their place. They met twice, with Swaps winning the 1955 Derby and Nashua the '55 $100,000 Washington Park match race. The foal crop of 1954 contained Bold Ruler, Round Table, and *Gallant Man, all Racing Hall of Fame members. Round Table lasted the longest, 66 races, and was America's first great grass horse. Talent was so widespread that no one noticed an ordinary-looking bay gelding who won only a maiden race in 1959. But Kelso went on to become one of the major heroes of the 1960s.

1961-'70

The 1960s were a watershed for America and American racing. Inaugurated in January 1961 was John F. Kennedy, the first president born in the 20th century. Racial segregation was overthrown in the South, but lives were lost in the battle. Kennedy's assassination in 1963 shook America to its core, and soon the collective conformism of the '50s crumbled. As men walked on the moon, young soldiers were dying in an unpopular Vietnam war.

Racing increasingly became a game of haves and have-nots. In 1967, Damascus banked a single-season record $817,941. That same year, North America's earnings per runner averaged $3,359, or about half of training costs for a year. Medication also became an issue, especially when Dancer's Image was disqualified from his 1968 Kentucky Derby victory over a Bute positive.

State legislators looked to racing to plug budget gaps; at the end of the decade, proposed federal tax changes led to the creation of the American Horse Council to help lobby on behalf of horse racing and breeding interests. Simultaneously, racing was losing some of its audience as other professional sports and entertainment forms gained popularity. National attendance declined in 1967 for the first time since World War II, despite nearly 100 added racing days. During the 1960s, total racing days increased 35%, while average daily attendance declined 3%. At decade's end, off-track betting was approved in New York, which would lead to even larger attendance declines.

Against this chaotic and disquieting backdrop, Kelso—and others like him—redeemed this troubled era and made it one of the most remarkable in 200 years. Allaire duPont's Kelso tore through the handicap ranks, ruling as Horse of the Year from 1960 through '64. Carry Back emerged from Florida to win the 1961 Kentucky Derby and Preakness Stakes. Other outstanding performers of the era were Arts and Letters, Majestic Prince, Nodouble, Northern Dancer, and Fort Marcy, but the second half of the decade belonged to Buckpasser, Damascus, and Dr. Fager. Together, they started 85 times and compiled a 64-13-5 record.

Fillies of the 1960s deserve special mention. Cicada, Old Hat, Affectionately, Straight Deal, Tosmah, Politely, Gamely, and Shuvee averaged 56 career starts. Cicada set an earnings record; Moccasin became the first juvenile filly to take Horse of the Year honors in the 1965 Thoroughbred Racing Associations poll; Dark Mirage was first to sweep New York's filly triple crown in 1968; Dr. Fager's younger half sister, Ta Wee, toted an average of 136 pounds in 1970. Women gained the right to ride in races in 1969, and trailblazer Diane Crump rode in the '70 Derby. Bloodstock prices were heating up, and Nijinsky II was syndicated for a record $5.44-million in 1970.

1971-'80

In some respects, the decade between 1971 and '80 was one of the century's most satisfying periods for American Thoroughbred racing. Great runners and big money energized the era, but they also disguised some troubling problems, such as race fixing, increasingly lenient medication rules, and a declining audience. The 1970s were racing's best years since the '40s, with three Triple Crown winners within five years. The bloodstock markets were supercharged as well, with the beginning of the Northern Dancer era and the speculative buying that eventually damaged the markets in the 1980s.

Secretariat, Seattle Slew, and Affirmed, the three Triple Crown winners, attracted most of the attention, and they shared the limelight with Forego, Ruffian, and Spectacular Bid, among others. It has been said that Secretariat appeared at the precise moment when America and racing needed him most. A transcendent, larger-than-life figure bursting with almost supernatural vitality, he streaked across racing's stage in 1972 and '73, leaving behind an impression of pure greatness unrivaled since Man o' War. After he won the 1973 Kentucky Derby (G1) in record time (1:59⅖, a mark that still stands) and the Preakness Stakes (G1) with consummate ease (also probably a record even though the timing was botched), Secretariat quieted every skeptic with his 31-length triumph in the Belmont Stakes (G1) in 2:24, 2⅕ seconds—11 lengths—faster than the existing world record. Seattle Slew blazed through the Triple Crown, becoming the first to complete the sweep with an unbeaten record, and one year later Affirmed won the Triple Crown over his nemesis Alydar, who was second in all three races.

The Triple Crown winners did not stand alone in the spotlight. Twenty-two future Racing Hall of Fame members campaigned during this decade, including six from a remarkable 1970 foal crop. Among them were the first distaff millionaire, Dahlia, 12-for-12 juvenile La Prevoyante, and Forego, who was Horse of the Year three times. Ruffian cruised unbeaten through ten starts until the ill-fated 1975 match race with Kentucky Derby winner Foolish Pleasure that took her life. The era closed with yet another performer for the ages. The Triple Crown eluded Spectacular Bid, but not much else did between 1978 and '80. The compact gray colt set nine track, American, and world standards. In 1980, Genuine Risk became only the second filly in 106 years to win the Kentucky Derby.

The 1970s signaled the dramatic rise of top Hispanic jockeys, with none more prominent than Laffit Pincay Jr. Among trainers, the torch passed to Charlie Whittingham and Laz Barrera, whose West Coast-based stables also hailed the arrival of California as a centerpiece of American racing. The industry was changing in other ways, due in part to the 1971 introduction of off-track betting in New York. By 1977, OTB wagers finally exceeded money wagered on track in New York, and the gap would widen thereafter.

1981-'90

The breeding industry follows the fortunes of the racetrack, but for a few years in the 1980s that relationship became temporarily detached, or so it seemed, as rich foreign buyers pursued yearlings by Northern Dancer and his sons. In 1985, a Nijinsky II colt was sold for a record $13.1-million at the Keeneland July sale of selected yearlings, but by then the bloodstock markets had entered a slide that would last into the 1990s. Stud fees climbed to unsupportable levels on the fantasy, and everything came crashing down. On the track, attendance was falling while wagering and purses stagnated.

In 1982, at the peak of the bloodstock boom, horseman John Gaines worried over the industry's fundamentals and came up with an idea to market it. One year earlier, the Arlington Million had been inaugurated at Arlington Park as the world's first $1-million Thoroughbred race. Enthusiastically received, it had drawn a field of international grass stars and was won by John Henry. Gaines envisioned a single championship day of racing, offering millions of dollars in purse money, paid for by stallion and foal nomination fees. In November 1984 at Hollywood Park, his dream became reality at the first Breeders' Cup championship day, arguably the sport's greatest innovation since the Triple Crown.

Although he missed the first Breeders' Cup and never raced again, Dotsam Stable's John Henry proved once again that the American Dream was alive and well. He was a gelded son of an obscure sire, and he earned more than $6.5-million. In the 1980s, fillies shined brightest. Eight of the decade's 13 Racing Hall of Fame performers thus far have been members of the distaff set, including Horses of the Year All Along (Fr) and Lady's Secret, 1988 Kentucky Derby winner Winning Colors, undefeated champions Personal Ensign (13-for-13) and Landaluce (5-for-5 before her death), and two-time champion Go for Wand, who died on the track in the 1990 Breeders' Cup Distaff (G1). Also notable were two-time champions Bayakoa (Arg) and Miesque.

Although males of the 1980s lacked the brilliance of their female counterparts, they did provide memorable moments. Ferdinand gave Whittingham his first Kentucky Derby victory at age 73 in 1986, and in '87 he fought to the bitter end under Racing Hall of Fame member Bill Shoemaker to edge Derby winner Alysheba in the Breeders' Cup Classic (G1). The fierce 1989 rivalry between Sunday Silence and Easy Goer ranks among the sport's best, and also memorable was Conquistador Cielo's 14-length triumph in the 1982 Belmont Stakes, the first of trainer Woody Stephens's historic five straight wins in that classic. One of the decade's most poignant moments was trainer Carl Nafzger's spontaneous televised description of Unbridled's 1990 Kentucky Derby stretch run for 92-year-old owner Frances Genter. Trainer D. Wayne Lukas rewrote the record books repeatedly during these years, setting and breaking his own earnings standards.

1991-2000

The century's final decade was a breakthrough for America's racetracks, which built a solid foundation first on intrastate intertrack wagering and then on the true bonanza, interstate full-card wagering. The full-card explosion forever altered the sport. By mid-decade, off-site wagering accounted for 74% of racing's handle, a figure that jumped to 82% by 1999. Some tracks added slot machines to boost both purses and profits without putting any new patrons in the stands. The bloodstock markets recovered from a prolonged recession and rose to new heights as the decade ended.

Lexington ad executive Fred Pope, with counsel from John Gaines, in 1996 proposed an industry alliance to revitalize the sport and create a "major league of racing." Their National Thoroughbred Association, an owner-driven organization, soon was swallowed up by the National Thoroughbred Racing Association (NTRA), which was launched in April 1998 and reached into every corner of the sport. Racing series added hours of television coverage, and in 1999 Television Games Network (TVG) debuted on satellite and a few cable systems.

In the bloodstock market, stallion owners began breeding their stars to large books of mares and sent them to the Southern Hemisphere for double duty. A record for a stallion syndication was set in 2000 when Fusaichi Pegasus commanded a record $60-million to $70-million price tag.

A trio of sensational grays—Holy Bull, Silver Charm, and Skip Away—and Allen Paulson's marvelous bay Cigar captured the imagination of the racing public in the 1990s. Together they won classics, championships, and $30-million, but they were sired by stallions with average stud fees of just $7,800. Among females, Serena's Song and Dance Smartly were the decade's standouts.

It was an exciting classics decade, with the Triple Crown on the line each year between 1997 and '99, with Silver Charm, Real Quiet, and Charismatic winning the Derby and Preakness before coming up short in the Belmont. Silver Charm and Real Quiet were trained by Bob Baffert, but the classics of the 1990s virtually belonged to Lukas, who won six consecutive classic races with five different horses and also trained Charismatic for Robert and Beverly Lewis, Californians who owned Silver Charm and Serena's Song. Cigar, a two-time Horse of the Year, won 16 consecutive races but proved sterile.

Class I racing returned to Texas, but the first two tracks to open, Sam Houston Race Park and Retama Park, struggled initially. Lone Star Park in the populous Dallas-Fort Worth area was a success from its opening in April 1997. An important trend that began toward the end of the decade was the consolidation of racetrack ownership under Magna Entertainment Corp. and Churchill Downs Inc. That consolidation would continue into the 21st century.

2001-'05

The beginning of the new century was indelibly scarred by an act of unspeakable horror, a terrorist attack with commercial jetliners that killed approximately 3,000 innocent people in New York's World Trade Center towers, at the Pentagon, and in a rural Pennsylvania field, where passengers sacrificed their lives to protect American institutions from Islamist terrorists who had hijacked their plane. September 11, 2001, forever will be seared on the American psyche, along with December 7, 1941, and November 22, 1963. On each of those dates, America lost some of its innocence and confronted a changing and frightening world. In 2001, a racing event, the Breeders' Cup World Thoroughbred Championships, marked the first international sporting event in the New York region following the terrorist attacks.

In the first half of the 21st century's first decade, Thoroughbred racing experienced triumphs and it engaged in self-evaluation as the gambling element of the sport began to change. It also had to deal with an attempt to fix the outcome of a bet on the 2002 Breeders' Cup. Meanwhile, the consolidation of American racing into the hands of a few publicly traded companies continued. On the track, the dominant news events were three rags-to-riches horses who stepped out of obscurity and stood on the brink of the sport's ultimate prize, the Triple Crown. War Emblem was the first Derby-Preakness winner of the 21st century in 2002, and he was followed by Funny Cide, a crowd-pleasing gelding owned by a group of fun-loving friends. But without question the horse who captured America's heart was Smarty Jones, who won the 2004 Derby as the favorite and scored in the Preakness by a record margin. He finished second in the Belmont, however, and was whisked off to stud.

In the new century's first five years, the sport began to come to grips with a new phenomenon, offshore betting operations known as rebaters (because they rebated part of every bet to their high-dollar players). Some rebaters paid money to purses and others did not. As a result, total North American wagering rose in 2003 while purses declined. The following year, purses rose while wagering declined, a sign of the emergence of racinos—racetracks with slot-machine casinos attached to them.

The sport began an evaluation of its wagering systems in 2002 when three former fraternity brothers fixed the Breeders' Cup Ultra Pick Six wager. It was an inside job, by a programmer for tote provider Autotote, and the fix was quickly uncovered when 43.50-to-1 Volponi won the Breeders' Cup Classic (G1). Industry officials came together with the tote companies to strengthen safeguards and protect the integrity of horse-race wagering. In another stroke for the sport's integrity, the Racing Medication and Testing Consortium developed model rules on racing drugs and lobbied successfully for their adoption in most racing states. Also, the industry mobilized against alkalizing agents, known as milkshakes, which reputedly delayed the onset of muscle fatigue.

The Kentucky commercial breeding industry, plunged into recession after the 2001 terrorist attacks, sustained a significant blow in '01 and beyond from mare reproductive loss syndrome (MRLS), which caused the loss of more than 500 late-term fetuses and almost 3,000 early-term fetuses in Central Kentucky. Attributed to Eastern tent caterpillars, MRLS cost the Kentucky Thoroughbred industry an estimated $300-million and contributed to the demise of the Keeneland July sale of selected yearlings. The bloodstock markets recovered in 2003 and '04.

The consolidation of the American racetrack industry continued when Magna Entertainment Corp. bought Lone Star Park in Texas and controlling interest in Maryland's major tracks, Pimlico Race Course and Laurel Park, in 2002. In 2004, Churchill Downs Inc. bought Fair Grounds in New Orleans for $47-million but sold Hollywood Park the following year.

Condensed from "Racing Through the Century," for which Mary Simon was awarded the 2000 Eclipse Award for outstanding features-enterprise writing and which was later published as a book with additional material.

History of Racing Silks

Worn by each jockey to represent a horse's owner, racing silks have been associated with horse racing for nearly two millennia. *Kennets Roman Antiquities* (1696) cites colors worn at chariot races: "At these races, the Romans rode in different colours, particularly the companies of Charioteers, to distinguish themselves." Nero was so fond of his green colors that he often wore a green toga when he attended the races during the first century.

The records of England's King Henry VIII mention jockeys' attire in the first half of the 16th century. His 1530 purse accounts show payments for "doublets [shirts] of Bruges Satin for the boys that runne the gueldings" and for "ryding cappes of Black Satin lyned with black vellute [velvet]." Silk, though expensive, was used for jockeys' jackets and caps because of its light weight and soft, smooth texture. Velvet also was used through the first half of the 19th century.

On October 4, 1762, 19 members of the English Jockey Club registered their colors at Newmarket "for the greater convenience of distinguishing the horses in running." Across the Atlantic Ocean just four years later, Philadelphia horsemen registered their silks with the Philadelphia Jockey Club. Registering yellow silks was Lewis Morris Jr., a signer of the Declaration of Independence.

One of the longest-used silks in America belonged to Howell E. Jackson, a relative of President Andrew Jackson who chose all-maroon colors first used in the early 1820s. The all-scarlet silks of Francis Morris (no relation to Lewis) were first worn in 1862 at the Union Course on Long Island. The Morris family used those colors for four generations through John A. Morris.

Rules published for the October 17-19, 1826, race meeting in Lexington required jockeys to wear a silk jacket and cap. The American Jockey Club, founded in 1894, registered silks for $1 annually or $25 lifetime. The most famous silks in American racing have been those of prominent, private stables—the devil's red and blue of Calumet Farm, the plain black jacket with cherry cap of the late Ogden Phipps, and the all-orange silks of Claiborne Farm.

Sporadically, racetracks have experimented with color-coded silks and jockeys' caps. In 1947, Portland Meadows assigned silks colors by post positions, an idea that was copied at Sportsman's Park and Prescott Downs. Narragansett Park matched the colors of jockeys' caps with post positions. Neither experiment caught on nationally.

In the evolution of Thoroughbred racing in the United States, silk has mostly yielded to nylon or Lycra as the preferred fabric of jockeys' colors. Aerodynamic silks have become commonplace in American racing. First unveiled in 1988 when trainer D. Wayne Lukas used them on all 12 of his horses in the Breeders' Cup, aerodynamic silks, though more costly, are widely available today.

Approximately 28,000 sets of silks are registered with the Jockey Club. Owners pay an annual fee of $15 or $60 every five years. The Jockey Club ceased registering lifetime silks in 1964 while perpetually reserving 3,500 designs.

The Jockey Club has registered silks with various punctuation marks, geometric figures, riding equipment, racetracks, vegetables, musical notes, instruments, birds, dogs, horses, foxes, and even an elephant. Though silks can vary from state to state, roughly 95% of all silks designs are registered with the Jockey Club.

—*Bill Heller*

Key Dates in American Racing History

1665 New York Governor Richard Nicolls establishes America's first formal racecourse on Long Island, names it "New Market."

1730 The Darley Arabian's son *Bulle Rock becomes the first recognized Thoroughbred imported to America, into the Virginia colony.

1752 The great racemare *Selima wins an intercolonial race in Virginia worth $10,000 **(December)**.

1764 Undefeated racehorse and foundation sire Eclipse is born in England during a solar eclipse. Future influential sire *Fearnought is imported to America.

1780 The inaugural Epsom Derby is won by Sir Charles Bunbury's *Diomed **(May 4)**.

1798 *Diomed is imported to Virginia at age 21 for the equivalent of $250; he becomes America's most important early sire. *Spread Eagle, 1795 Epsom Derby winner, is imported into Virginia.

1801 *Spread Eagle reportedly covers 234 mares. Leviathan, American racing's first great gelding, concludes a 23-race win streak, which remains an American record for more than two centuries.

1802 Leviathan wins a five-mile race carrying 180 pounds.

1804 *Sir Harry, 1798 Epsom Derby winner, is imported into Virginia.

1805 American foundation sire Sir Archy is foaled.

1806 Northern champion First Consul runs his undefeated streak to 21.

1808 *Diomed dies in Virginia at age 31 **(March 10)**.

1810 Maria runs five four-mile heats to win a $500 purse at Fairfield, Virginia **(October 3)**.

1820 American Eclipse covers 87 mares for a $12.50 fee.

1821 Union Course opens on Long Island, becomes America's first famous racetrack **(October 15)**.

1823 American Eclipse defeats Henry in North-South match over the Union Course; he becomes America's leading earner, with $56,700 **(May 27)**.

1833 Leading sires Sir Archy and his best son, Sir Charles, die on same day **(June 7)**.

1836 *Glencoe, winner of the 1834 Two Thousand Guineas, is imported into Alabama.

1842 Fashion defeats Boston in a Union Course match race before a crowd of more than 50,000 **(May 10)**.

1845 Peytona defeats Fashion in a $20,000 match race over two four-mile heats at the Union Course and surpasses American Eclipse as the leading American money winner, with $62,400 **(May 13)**. Fashion defeats Peytona in two four-mile heats at Camden, New Jersey **(May 28)**.

1850 Lexington is born **(March 17)**.

1852 Black Swan defeats Governor Pio Pico's non-Thoroughbred stallion Sarco in a nine-mile match race at Los Angeles for a $2,000 purse and 1,000 head of cattle **(March)**.

1855 Lexington sets a four-mile world record of 7:19¾ **(April 2)**. Lexington defeats Lecomte in a match race at New Orleans **(April 14)**.

1856 Lexington sells for an American record $15,000 to Robert A. Alexander.

1857 American-bred Prioress wins England's Cesarewitch Handicap at Newmarket **(October 13)**. Lexington retires to Woodburn Stud in Kentucky.

1860 Don Juan wins the first running of Canada's Queen's Plate **(June 27)**. Revenue becomes America's first leading sire based on progeny earnings instead of winners.

1861 Lexington leads the American sire list for the first of a record 16 times. Planet surpasses Peytona as America's leading money winner, with $69,700.

1864 Lexington's unbeaten son Norfolk wins America's first Derby—the $1,000 Jersey Derby at Paterson **(June 7)**. Saratoga Race Course opens; the inaugural Travers Stakes is won by Lexington's son Kentucky **(August 2)**. Asteroid, another undefeated son of Lexington, is stolen from Woodburn Stud by Confederate guerillas **(October 22)**, recovered a week later. Norfolk is sold for an American record $15,001.

1866 Jerome Park opens in New York **(September 25)**.

1867 The inaugural Belmont Stakes is won by the filly Ruthless at Jerome Park **(June 19)**. Robert A. Alexander dies at Woodburn at age 48 **(December)**.

1868 The Ladies Handicap is inaugurated at Jerome Park, becoming the first major American race to be carded annually for fillies and mares **(June 16)**.

1870 Monmouth Park opens in New Jersey **(July 30)**. Pimlico Race Course opens in Maryland **(October 25)**.

1872 Fair Grounds racetrack opens in New Orleans **(April 13)**.

1873 The inaugural Preakness Stakes at Pimlico is won by Survivor **(May 27)**. Volume I of the *American Stud Book* is published.

1874 Pari-mutuel wagering is introduced at Jerome Park.

1875 *Kentucky Livestock Record* begins publication **(February 5)**, with a subscription cost of $3 per year. Churchill Downs opens; the inaugural Kentucky Derby is won by Aristides **(May 17)**. Lexington dies **(July 1)**.

1877 Congress adjourns to watch Parole defeat Tom Ochiltree and Ten Broeck at Pimlico **(October 24)**.

1878 Ten Broeck defeats Mollie McCarthy in East-West match at Louisville **(July 4)**.

1880 America's first recorded post parade is held before the Belmont Stakes **(June 14)**. Sheepshead Bay racecourse opens in New York **(June 19)**. Blue Gown, the 1868 Epsom Derby winner, dies en route to America.

1881 Pierre Lorillard's Iroquois becomes the first American-owned and -bred Epsom Derby winner **(June 1)**. Hindoo wins his 18th consecutive race **(September 1)**. Parole retires as the leading American money winner, with $82,816.

1882 Fair Grounds racetrack installs electric lights in its grandstand.

1883 The Louisville Jockey Club racetrack is renamed Churchill Downs.

1884 Buchanan becomes the first maiden Kentucky Derby winner **(May 16)**.

1886 Miss Woodford becomes the first American Thoroughbred to top $100,000 in earnings **(June 2)**. Two-year-old Tremont wins each of his 13 career starts in a ten-week span that ends on **August 7**.

1887 Hanover wins 17 consecutive races.

1888 Trainer R. Wyndham Walden saddles a record seventh Preakness Stakes winner, Refund **(May 11)**. King Thomas brings an American yearling auction record of $40,000 **(June 26)**. The inaugural Futurity Stakes at Sheepshead Bay is worth $40,900 to winner Proctor Knott **(September 3)**.

1889 Hanover ends Miss Woodford's reign as the leading American money winner **(August 29)**, retiring with earnings of $118,887. U.S. purse distribution is $2.4-million; 4,820 races are run.

1890 The Preakness Stakes is run at Morris Park in New York **(June 10)**. Salvator runs a world-record 1:35½ mile down the straightaway at Monmouth Park **(August 28)**.

1891 Hawthorne Race Course opens near Chicago **(May 20)**. *St. Blaise sells for a world auction record $100,000 at the August Belmont I estate dispersal **(October 16)**.

1892 Kingston surpasses Hanover as America's top earner, with $138,917, on his way to $140,195.

1893 Boundless wins the American Derby at Washington Park, after an hour and 40-minute delay at the starting post **(June 24)**. *Ormonde, regarded as Europe's best horse of the 19th century, arrives for stud duty in California **(September 8)**. Two-year-old Domino sets a single-season earnings record of $170,890 and becomes America's leading money winner **(September 29)**. Himyar sets a single-season progeny earnings record of $249,502.

1894 The Jockey Club is incorporated **(February 9)**. Kingston scores a record 89th career victory **(August 21)**. Aqueduct racetrack opens in New York **(September 27)**. *Daily Racing Form* begins publication **(November 17)**. *Sir Modred becomes the only California-based stallion to lead the American year-end sire list.

1895 *Livestock Record* changes its name to *The Thoroughbred Record* **(February 2)**. August Belmont II heads the new Westchester Racing Association, the controlling body of New York racing **(August 14)**. Domino retires with record American earnings of $193,550 **(September 17)**.

1896 Domino arrives in Lexington and makes his last public appearance before entering stud **(February 3)**.

1897 Jockey Club buys the *American Stud Book* from H. Sanders Bruce for $35,000 **(May 17)**. Lucretia Borgia races against time at Oakland, California, setting a world four-mile record of 7:11 that remains on the books today. Domino dies of meningitis at age six **(July 29)**.

1898 Fasig-Tipton auction company is incorporated. American-born jockey Tod Sloan introduces his high-stirrup, crouched ("monkey-on-a-stick") riding style to England.

1899 Fasig-Tipton Co. conducts its first Thoroughbred auction, under electric lights at Madison Square Garden, New York **(June 19)**. Champion and four-time leading sire Hanover dies **(March 23)**.

1900 Pari-mutuel wagering is introduced at Fair Grounds. The Jockey Club registers 3,476 foals. Johnny Reiff becomes the first American to top the English jockey standings, with 143 victories.

1901 William Collins Whitney becomes the second American owner to win the Epsom Derby, with Volodyovski **(June 5)**. James R. Keene's American-bred Cap and Bells, by Domino, wins the Epsom Oaks **(June 7)**. Racing Hall of Fame racehorse and leading sire Hindoo dies at age 23 **(July 4)**. Champion Hamburg sells for $60,000 at the Marcus Daly estate dispersal **(October 1)**. Future five-time leading sire *Star Shoot is imported.

1902 Savable earns the decade's largest winner's purse, $44,500, in the Futurity Stakes **(August 30)**.

1903 Flocarline is the first filly to win the Preakness Stakes **(May 30)**. Africander is the first three-year-old Suburban Handicap winner **(June 18)**.

1904 Oaklawn Park opens in Arkansas **(February 24)**. Leading owner W. C. Whitney dies **(March 7)**. Elwood becomes the first Kentucky Derby winner owned and bred by women **(May 2)**. Hamburg sells for $70,000 at the W. C. Whitney estate dispersal **(October 10)**.

1905 Champion Commando dies of tetanus at age seven **(March 13)**. Belmont Park opens **(May 4)**. Tanya becomes the second filly to win the Belmont Stakes **(May 24)**. Artful hands Sysonby his only defeat, in the Futurity Stakes **(August 27)**. Roseben sets an American six-furlong record of 1:11⅗ under 147 pounds in the Manhattan Handicap **(October 6)**.

1906 An earthquake destroys San Francisco's Ingleside racetrack **(April 18)**. Sysonby dies of septic poisoning at age four **(June 17)**. Roseben wins the Manhattan Handicap for a second time under 147 pounds **(October 12)**. Kentucky appoints the first state racing commission.

1907 Colin launches his perfect 15-for-15 career with a maiden victory at Belmont Park **(May 29)**. The original Santa Anita Park opens in California **(December 7)**. Commando posthumously breaks his grandsire Himyar's single-season progeny earnings record, with $270,345.

1908 California-bred Rubio wins England's Grand National Steeplechase **(March 26)**. Bookmakers are barred from Churchill Downs and 15 pari-mutuel machines are installed **(March)**. Agnew-Hart legislation outlaws public betting in New York, though racing continues without wagering **(June 13)**. Colin ends his career in the Tidal Stakes, a betless exhibition at Sheepshead Bay **(June 20)**. The Locke Law ends racing in New Orleans.

1909 The Walker-Otis Anti-Racetrack Gambling Bill is passed in California, effectively blacking out racing there for a quarter-century **(February 19)**. The Preakness winner's silks are painted on the Pimlico Clubhouse's weathervane for the first time **(May 12)**.

1910 New York passes the Director's Criminal Liability Act, making racetrack operators and executives subject to imprisonment if gambling is found to occur on track premises. All New York tracks cease operation. A mass exodus of American breeding stock and racehorses to Europe begins.

1911 Laurel Race Course opens in Maryland **(October 2)**. Three-hundred ninety yearlings average $230 at U.S. auctions. The average U.S. purse reaches a 20th-century low $371.

1912 Wishing Ring wins at Latonia, paying a record $1,885.50 for a $2 wager **(June 17)**. James R. Keene sells Castleton Stud in Kentucky for $225 an acre. Star Charter is the season's leading money winner, with $14,655. Influential sire *Rock Sand and champion Tanya are included in the mass exportation of bloodstock to Europe.

1913 The English Jockey Club passes the Jersey Act, excluding most American pedigrees from admission to the *General Stud Book* **(April)**. Donerail wins the Kentucky Derby at record odds of 91.45-to-1 **(May 10)**. Belmont Park reopens without legal wagering **(May 30)**. Whisk Broom II becomes the first to sweep New York's handicap triple crown—the Metropolitan, Brooklyn, and Suburban Handicaps **(June 28)**. James R. Keene's estate dispersal is conducted at Madison Square Garden, and future Racing Hall of Fame member Peter Pan tops the sale at $38,000 **(September 2)**.

1914 Iron Mask carries 150 pounds to victory at Juarez, Mexico, setting a 5½-furlong world record of 1:03⅗ that stands for 30 years **(March 8)**. Old Rosebud sets a Kentucky Derby record of 2:03⅖ that stands for 17 years **(May 9)**.

1915 Pan Zareta gives ten pounds to Joe Blair and beats him in a match race at Juarez, setting a five-furlong world record of :57⅕ that stands for 36 years **(February 10)**. Pan Zareta carries 146 pounds to victory at Juarez, giving rivals from 31 to 54 pounds **(March 26)**. Regret becomes the first filly to win the Kentucky Derby **(May 8)**. The Preakness Stakes is run in two divisions for the only time **(May 15)**.

1916 *Star Shoot sires a record 27 juvenile winners.

1917 The New York State Racing Commission recommends to the Legislature that pari-mutuel wagering be legalized **(January)**. Man o' War is born **(March 29)**. *Omar Khayyam becomes the first foreign-bred Kentucky Derby winner **(May 12)**. Borrow wins the Brooklyn Handicap over Kentucky Derby winners Regret, Old Rosebud, and *Omar Khayyam **(June 25)**.

1918 Exterminator wins the Kentucky Derby at 29.60-to-1 odds **(May 11)**. Man o' War is sold to Samuel D. Riddle for $5,000 at the Saratoga yearling sale **(August 17)**. Roamer is the first to crack a 1:35 mile, running in 1:34⅘ at Saratoga **(August 21)**.

1919 Sir Barton, a maiden, wins the Kentucky Derby **(May 10)**; he becomes the first American Triple Crown winner in winning the Belmont Stakes **(June 18)**. Man o' War wins his first start, at Belmont Park **(June 6)**; he suffers his only career defeat, to Upset, in Saratoga's Sanford Memorial **(August 13)**. Purchase walks over in the inaugural Jockey Club Gold Cup **(September 13)**. The American Jockey Club registers a century-low 1,665 foals.

1920 Man o' War smashes the world record for 1⅜ miles in winning the Belmont Stakes by 20 lengths **(June 12)**; wins the Lawrence Realization Stakes by approximately 100 lengths **(September 4)**; carries 138 pounds to win the Potomac Handicap at Havre de Grace while setting a 1$\frac{1}{16}$-mile track record **(September 18)**; defeats Sir Barton in an $80,000 match race at Kenilworth Park in Canada **(October 12)**; retires as America's leading earner, with $249,465.

1921 Man o' War makes a farewell public gallop around the Kentucky Association racetrack in Lexington **(January 28)**. Counterclockwise racing begins at Belmont Park.

1922 Morvich scores his 11th victory in 11 starts in the Kentucky Derby **(May 13)**, joining Regret as the only undefeated Derby winners to that time. Kentucky Derby winner and future Racing Hall of Fame member Old Rosebud breaks down in a race at Jamaica racetrack and dies at age 11 **(May 23)**.

1923 Exterminator scores a record 34th stakes victory **(April 21)**. Kentucky Derby winner Zev defeats Epsom Derby winner *Papyrus in a Belmont Park match **(October 20)**. Zev becomes the first American racehorse to top $200,000 in single-season earnings ($272,008). Earl Sande rides the winners of $569,394, a record that stands for 20 years.

1924 Nellie Morse is the fourth and final filly Preakness winner **(May 12)**. Nine-year-old Exterminator finishes third in his 100th and final career start **(June 21)**. Three "international specials" are staged in the U.S. and are won by American-breds Wise Counsellor at Belmont Park **(September 1)**, Ladkin at Aqueduct **(September 27)**, and Sarazen at Latonia **(October 11)**. French star *Epinard finishes second in all three. Man o' War is represented by his first stakes winner when By Hisself wins the Autumn Days Stakes at Empire City **(October 20)**.

1925 Hialeah Park opens in Florida, ushering in an era of big-time winter racing **(January 15)**. Network radio's first broadcast of a Kentucky Derby is aired from Louisville's WHAS **(May 16)**. River Downs opens near Cincinnati **(July 6)**. War Feathers, a Man o' War–*Tuscan Red filly, sells at Saratoga for $50,500, an American yearling auction record **(August 10)**. *Sir Gallahad III arrives at Claiborne Farm from France, becoming the first major American stallion syndication **(December 15)**.

1926 Boot to Boot wins Washington Park's American Derby, the first U.S. race to offer a $100,000-added purse **(July 31)**. Man o' War sets a single-season progeny earnings record of $408,137 with just two crops racing. North American yearling sales average is $2,640.

1927 John Longden scores the first of his 6,032 career victories aboard Hugo K. Asher at Salt Lake City **(October 4)**. Arlington Park racetrack opens near Chicago **(October 13)**.

1928 New Broom, a yearling son of Whisk Broom II, sells for $75,000, an auction record that stands for 26 years **(August 7)**. Wirt G. Bowman becomes America's first flying Thoroughbred, traveling by airplane from San Diego to San Francisco **(October)**.

1929 The $100,000 Coffroth Handicap at Tijuana, Mexico, is won by Golden Prince **(March 17)**. Clyde Van Dusen becomes the eighth gelding to win the Kentucky Derby **(May 18)**. Whichone wins the Futurity Stakes, earning America's first six-figure winner's purse, $105,730 **(September 14)**.

1930 The Preakness Stakes is the first American classic to be started from a gate **(May 9)**. Gallant Fox sweeps the Triple Crown **(June 7)**. Jim Dandy defeats Gallant Fox at 100-to-1 odds in the Travers Stakes **(August 16)**. Gallant Fox becomes the first racehorse to surpass $300,000 in single-season earnings **(September 17)**.

1931 Hawthorne Park is the first track in the U.S. to use an electronic timer **(August 3)**. Top Flight becomes the leading distaff money winner and the first juvenile to top $200,000 in earnings **(November 7)**. Tropical Park racetrack opens in Florida **(December 26)**. Influential broodmare *La Troienne is imported.

1932 Eddie Arcaro rides his first winner, at Agua Caliente **(January 14)**. Australian wonder horse *Phar Lap wins the $50,000 Agua Caliente Handicap **(March 20)**; dies in California under mysterious circumstances **(April 5)**. Sportsman's Park opens near Chicago **(May 2)**. The North American yearling sales average declines to $570.

1933 The Woolwine-Maloney Bill legalizes pari-mutuel wagering in California **(February 19)**. Brokers Tip, a maiden, wins the Kentucky Derby in a "fighting finish" involving jockeys Don Meade and Herb Fisher, aboard Head Play **(May 6)**. Longacres racetrack opens in Washington state **(August 3)**. Saliva drug testing instituted at Hialeah Park. Legal bookmaking returns to New York. Walter Vosburgh compiles weights for the first Experimental Free Handicap.

1934 Bay Meadows Race Course opens in Northern California and is the first in America to use a photo-finish camera **(November 3)**. Santa Anita Park opens in Southern California **(December 25)**. The Kentucky Derby purse is reduced from $50,000 to $30,000. Hialeah Park builds the first modern American grass course.

1935 The inaugural $100,000 Santa Anita Handicap is won by *Azucar, with Twenty Grand and Equipoise in the beaten field **(February 23)**. Mary Hirsch is the first woman awarded a trainer's license from the Jockey Club **(April)**. Omaha becomes the third Triple Crown winner **(June 8)**. Suffolk Downs opens in Massachusetts **(July 10)**.

1936 Jockey Ralph Neves pronounced "dead" after a racing accident at Bay Meadows; he returns to the track that day **(May 12)**. Keeneland Race Course opens in Kentucky **(October 15)**. *Daily Racing Form* begins formal recognition of annual divisional champions, names Granville the first Horse of the Year. Black Toney stands for an American-high $2,000 fee.

1937 Stagehand receives 30 pounds from Seabiscuit and beats him by a nose in the Santa Anita Handicap **(March 5)**. War Admiral becomes the fourth Triple Crown winner **(June 5)**. Delaware Park opens **(June 26)**. Bing Crosby and Pat O'Brien open Del Mar racetrack in California **(July 3)**. Sir Barton, America's first Triple Crown winner, dies in Wyoming **(October 30)**.

1938 Hollywood Park opens in California **(June 10)**. Equipoise dies at age ten **(August 10)**. Seabiscuit defeats *Ligaroti in a Del Mar match race **(August 12)**; Seabiscuit defeats War Admiral in a two-horse Pimlico Special **(November 1)**.

1939 Gulfstream Park opens in Florida **(February 1)**. Ben A. Jones becomes Calumet Farm's trainer **(July)**. The Grayson Foundation is established to finance equine research **(August 12)**. Bay Meadows Race Course installs America's first electric, enclosed starting gate, developed by Clay Puett.

1940 In his third try, Seabiscuit wins the Santa Anita Handicap and retires as the world's leading money winner, with $437,730 **(March 2)**. Pari-mutuel wagering is legalized in New York **(April 1)**; Jamaica racetrack opens in New York with pari-mutuel wagering **(April 15)**.

1941 Golden Gate Fields opens in California **(February 1)**. Merrick dies at age 38, as the oldest known Thoroughbred **(March 13)**. Whirlaway becomes the fifth American Triple Crown winner **(June 7)**.

1942 Thoroughbred Racing Associations is formed **(March 19)**. Garden State Park opens in New Jersey **(July 18)**. Future leading American sire and broodmare sire *Princequillo is claimed for $2,500 **(August 20)**. Alsab defeats Whirlaway in a $25,000 match at Narragansett Park **(September 19)**. Jockey Eddie Arcaro is suspended by Jockey Club stewards for one year for dangerous riding in the Cowdin Stakes **(September 26)**. Whirlaway becomes the first $500,000 earner **(October 3)**. Santa Anita is used as an internment center for Japanese-Americans. Co. North American yearlings average $638, about half the 1941 average.

1943 Man o' War is pensioned from stud duty at age 26 **(March)**. Stymie is claimed by trainer Hirsch Jacobs for $1,500 **(June 2)**. Tanforan racetrack in California is utilized as a naval training base **(June 3)**. Count Fleet wins the Belmont Stakes by 25 lengths to become the sixth Triple Crown winner **(June 5)**. The Breeders' Sales Co. is organized in Kentucky **(September)**. A wartime ban on "pleasure driving" causes the cancellation or relocation of several race meetings.

1944 The only triple dead-heat in a North American stakes race occurs in Aqueduct's Carter Handicap, between Bossuet, Wait a Bit, and Brownie **(June 10)**. The Breeders' Sales Co. conducts its first yearling auction, at Keeneland **(July 31-August 3)**.

1945 Horse racing in the United States is called off by order of the War Mobilization Board **(January 3)**. American racing resumes four days after Nazi Germany surrenders **(May 12)**. Owner Fred Hooper wins the Kentucky Derby with his first horse, Hoop, Jr. **(June 9)**. North American yearling average soars to $5,146.

1946 Jockey George "The Iceman" Woolf dies following a spill at Santa Anita **(January 4)**. The first transcontinental flight with a Thoroughbred passenger is recorded when Historian flies from Chicago to Los Angeles **(May 29)**. Assault becomes the seventh Triple Crown winner **(June 1)**. Atlantic City Race Course opens **(July 22)**. *Fair Truckle is first to break 1:09 for six furlongs, running 1:08⅘ at Golden Gate Fields **(October 4)**. Assault becomes the first $400,000 single-season earner **(November 9)**. The first transatlantic flight with racehorses on board takes place, from Ireland to New Jersey **(November 26-27)**. Lip tattoos are adopted as a method of identifying racehorses.

1947 Stepfather brings a world auction record of $200,000 at the Louis B. Mayer dispersal **(February 27)**. Seabiscuit dies at age 14 **(May 17)**. Armed defeats Assault at Belmont Park in the first $100,000 winner-take-all match race **(September 27)**. Man o' War dies at age 30 **(November 1)**. Stymie retires with record earnings of $918,485. Calumet is the first stable to top $1-million in a season. Automatic hotwalking machines are introduced.

1948 *Alibhai is syndicated for a record $500,000. Citation becomes the eighth Triple Crown winner **(June 12)**. Gallorette is the first racemare to top $400,000 in career earnings **(July 17)**. Citation ends his campaign with a new single-season earnings record of $709,470 **(December 11)**. *Shannon II becomes the first to crack 2:00 for 1¼ miles, running the distance in 1:59⅘ at Golden Gate Fields **(October 23)**.

1949 Apprentice Bill Shoemaker rides his first winner, at Golden Gate Fields **(April 20)**. Hollywood Park's grandstand and clubhouse are destroyed by fire **(May 6)**. England's Jockey Club rescinds the Jersey Act after 36 years **(June)**. *Nasrullah is purchased by an American syndicate for $340,000. Keeneland installs America's first aluminum rail.

1950 Detroit Race Course opens **(May 25)**. Future five-time leading American sire *Nasrullah arrives at Claiborne Farm in Kentucky **(July)**. The National Museum of Racing is chartered at Saratoga Springs, New York **(October)**. Gordon Glisson wins the first George Woolf Memorial Jockey Award.

1951 The Santa Anita Maturity offers a record $205,700 purse, with a record winner's share of $144,325 going to Great Circle **(February 3)**. Citation becomes racing's first equine millionaire, winning the Hollywood Gold Cup in his final start **(July 14)**. Bewitch passes Gallorette as leading distaff earner with $462,605. **(July 14)**. The Pimlico Special, won by Bryan G., becomes the first nationally televised race **(November 16)**. Lloyd's of London pays off a $250,000 insurance claim on gravely injured Your Host, who survives to sire Kelso.

1952 The Kentucky Derby is broadcast for the first time on national television, by CBS, and is won by Hill Gail, Ben Jones's record sixth winner **(May 3)**. English representative *Wilwyn wins the inaugural Washington, D.C., International at Laurel Park **(October 18)**. Apprentice jockey Tony DeSpirito scores a single-season record 390 victories **(December 31)**.

1953 Dark Star, 24.90-to-1, hands Native Dancer his only defeat, in the Kentucky Derby **(May 2)**. Charlie Whittingham saddles his first career stakes winner, Porterhouse **(June 10)**. Tom Fool is the second New York handicap triple crown winner, taking the Brooklyn Handicap under 136 pounds **(July 11)**. The Garden State Stakes is inaugurated as the world's richest race, worth $239,000 **(October 31)**. R. H. "Red" McDaniel becomes the first trainer to saddle 200 winners in a season **(December 1)**. Santa Anita opens its Camino Real grass course **(December 26)**. Bill Shoemaker smashes the single-season win record, with 485 victories **(December)**. *Royal Charger is advertised at an American record $10,000 stud fee.

1954 The San Juan Capistrano Handicap is America's first $100,000 grass race **(March 6)**. Bold Ruler and Round Table are foaled at Claiborne Farm in Kentucky **(April 6)**. Determine becomes the first gray Kentucky Derby winner **(May 1)**. Never Say Die is the second American-bred Epsom Derby winner, 73 years after Iroquois **(June 2)**.

1955 The National Museum of Racing opens at Saratoga Springs; the Racing Hall of Fame is instituted **(August 6)**. Camarero's undefeated streak concludes after a world-record 56 consecutive victories, in Puerto Rico **(August)**. Nashua defeats Swaps in a $100,000 match race at Washington Park **(August 31)**. Nashua becomes the first $1-million stallion syndication, for $1,251,000. **(December 15)**. New York Racing Association Inc. is established. *Sir Gallahad III leads the American broodmare sire list for a record 12th time.

1956 Turf Paradise opens in Arizona **(January 7)**. Nashua becomes racing's second equine millionaire **(February 18)**. Woodbine opens in Canada **(June 12)**. John Longden becomes the world's winningest jockey, with 4,871 victories **(September 3)**. Bill Shoemaker and Bill Hartack become the first to ride winners of $2-million in a season. Swaps carries 130 pounds to a 1:39 clocking for 1¹⁄₁₆ miles, a mark that stands as a dirt record for 27 years **(June 23)**. The original Aqueduct racetrack is torn down.

1957 Florida Breeders' Sales Co. conducts the first two-year-olds in training sale, at Hialeah **(January 28)**. Bold Ruler defeats Round Table and *Gallant Man in the three-horse Trenton Handicap, described as the race of the year **(November 9)**. Bill Hartack is the first jockey to top $3-million in single-season earnings. The American foal crop tops 10,000 for the first time.

1958 Round Table becomes racing's third equine millionaire **(May 11)**. Future Hall of Fame jockey Jack Westrope is killed in a spill during the Hollywood Oaks **(June 19)**. Round Table supplants Nashua as the world's all-time leading money winner **(October 11)**.

1959 *Tomy Lee is the second foreign-bred winner of the Kentucky Derby **(May 2)**. Jamaica racetrack in New York is torn down to make way for a housing development **(August)**. Modern $32-million Aqueduct racetrack opens in New York **(September 14)**.

1960 Undefeated *Ribot arrives in the U.S. for stud duty **(June 23)**. Kelso wins the first of five Horse of the Year titles. The Animal Insurance Co. of America pays off a $1-million policy on Bally Ache, who died on October 28 **(December)**.

1961 Northern Dancer is born **(May 27)**. Ben A. Jones, Racing Hall of Fame trainer, dies **(June 13)**. A son of Swaps, Swapson, becomes the first six-figure American auction yearling, selling for $130,000 at Keeneland July **(July 24)**. National Association of State Racing Commissioners recommends a general ban on all drugs, narcotics, anesthetics, and analgesics. Kelso becomes the third winner of New York's handicap triple crown **(July 22)**. Racing Hall of Fame jockey Eddie Arcaro retires **(November 18)**.

1962 Champion Crimson Satan is the first high-profile positive finding for phenylbutazone after winning the Leonard Richards Handicap at Delaware Park **(July 23)**. Angel Cordero Jr. rides his first North American winner **(July 26)**. Crazy Kid is first to break 1:08 for six furlongs, clocking 1:07⅘ at Del Mar **(August 18)**. Never Say Die becomes the first American-bred to lead the English sire list.

1963 Bold Ruler leads the American sire list for the first of eight times.

1964 Northern Dancer wins the Kentucky Derby in track-record time of 2:00 **(May 2)**. Laffit Pincay Jr. scores his first career victory, in Panama **(May 19)**. Seven-year-old Kelso wins a fifth Jockey Club Gold Cup **(October 31)** and earns a record fifth Horse of the Year title. Wagering in the United States tops $3-billion.

1965 Affectionately wins the Vagrancy Handicap under 137 pounds, the most weight successfully carried by a filly in 49 years **(July 26)**. Buckpasser breaks the juvenile earnings record, with $568,096 **(October 16)**. Northern Dancer stands his first season for a $10,000 stud fee. Moccasin becomes the first juvenile filly to be named Horse of the Year, in the Thoroughbred Racing Associations poll.

1966 Graustark is syndicated for a record $2.4-million **(June)**. Kelso retires as the world's leading money winner, with $1,977,165 **(March 2)**. John Longden wins the San Juan Capistrano aboard George Royal in his final career ride and retires with a world record 6,032 victories **(March 12)**. Three-year-old Buckpasser becomes the youngest equine millionaire **(August 20)**. American foal registrations top 20,000 for the first time.

1967 Buckpasser concludes a 15-race win streak in the Metropolitan Handicap at Aqueduct **(May 30)**. Damascus defeats Buckpasser and Dr. Fager by ten lengths in the Woodward Stakes **(September 30)**; banks record single-season earnings of $817,941. Future double classic winner Majestic Prince brings a yearling auction record of $250,000 at Keeneland July **(July 24)**. National racetrack attendance declines for the first time since World War II. Buckpasser is syndicated for a record $4.8-million. Bold Ruler becomes the first to sire juvenile winners of more than $1-million in a season.

1968 Dancer's Image becomes the only disqualified Kentucky Derby winner, after the then-illegal phenylbutazone shows up in his post-race test **(May 4)**. American-bred Sir Ivor wins the Epsom Derby **(May 29)**. Dark Mirage is the first New York filly triple crown winner **(June 22)**. A *Sea-Bird filly sets a world auction record of $405,000 at Keeneland July **(July 23)**. Native Diver becomes the first California-bred millionaire **(July 15)**. Dr. Fager wins the Washington Park Handicap with 134 pounds, in a world-record 1:32⅕ mile **(August 24)**. Dr. Fager carries 139 pounds to victory in the Vosburgh Handicap, his final career start **(November 2)**. *Vaguely Noble is syndicated for $5-million.

1969 Male riders boycott a race at Tropical Park in which Barbara Jo Rubin was scheduled to ride **(January 15)**. Diane Crump becomes the first female to compete in an American Thoroughbred pari-mutuel race, finishing tenth at Hialeah **(February 7)**. Rubin becomes the first of her sex to a win a pari-mutuel Thoroughbred race in America, at Charles Town Races **(February 22)**; Diane Crump is the first female rider to win a stakes, on Easy Lime in Fair Grounds's Spring Fiesta Cup **(March 29)**. Richard Nixon is the first sitting 20th-century president to attend the Kentucky Derby **(May 3)**. Not-for-profit Oak Tree Racing Association launches its first meeting, at Santa Anita **(October 7)**.

1970 Secretariat is foaled in Virginia **(March 30)**. The New York Legislature votes to legalize city-operated off-track betting parlors **(April 8)**. New York Governor Nelson Rockefeller signs a bill legalizing OTB in the Empire State **(April 22)**. Diane Crump finishes 15th as the first female to ride in the Kentucky Derby **(May 2)**. Exacta wagering is introduced in New York and New Jersey **(June)**. Crowned Prince sets a $510,000 world yearling record at Keeneland July **(July 20)**. Citation dies at age 25 **(August 8)**. Bill Shoemaker passes John Longden as the all-time winning jockey, with victory number 6,033 **(September 7)**. Canadian-bred Nijinsky II sweeps undefeated through the English Triple Crown **(September 12)**. Nijinsky II is syndicated for a record $5.44-million.

1971 Eclipse Awards are instituted by Thoroughbred Racing Associations, *Daily Racing Form*, and National Turf Writers Association. Off-track betting begins in New York **(April 8)**. Canonero II, a $1,200 auction yearling, wins the Kentucky Derby **(May 1)** and Preakness Stakes **(May 15)**. Eight-time leading sire Bold Ruler dies at age 17 **(July 12)**. Former Illinois Governor Otto Kerner is indicted on federal charges that included bribery to influence racing matters **(December)**. National purse distribution tops $200-million.

1972 European racing authorities institute pattern system to rate best races. Jockey Bill Shoemaker sets an all-time stakes record with win number 555 **(March 2)**. What a Treat brings a $450,000 auction record for a female Thoroughbred **(March 6)**. *Morning Telegraph* daily racing newspaper suspends publication after 139 years **(April 10)**. Kentucky's Court of Appeals awards Forward Pass the winner's purse from the 1968 Kentucky Derby, making him Calumet Farm's eighth Derby winner **(April 28)**. American-owned and -bred Roberto wins the Epsom Derby (Eng-G1) **(June 7)**. Convenience defeats Typecast in a $250,000 Hollywood match race **(June 17)**. Secretariat finishes fourth in his debut **(July 4)** but goes on to win seven of nine starts and is voted Horse of the Year at the conclusion of his two-year-old season. Roberto ends Brigadier Gerard's 15-race win streak, in the Benson and Hedges Gold Cup (Eng-G1) **(August 15)**. Four-time leading breeder Arthur B. "Bull" Hancock Jr. dies **(September 14)**.

1973 At urging of European racing authorities, North American Graded Stakes Committee is formed and begins grading of North American races. Champion mare Typecast brings a world auction record of $725,000 **(January 28)**. Secretariat's record $6.08-million syndication is announced **(February 26)**. Sunday racing begins in California at Hollywood Park **(April 15)**. Secretariat sets a Kentucky Derby (G1) record of 1:59$\frac{2}{5}$ **(May 5)**. *Cougar II becomes the first foreign-bred millionaire **(May 5)**. Secretariat wins the Belmont Stakes (G1) by 31 lengths in a world record 2:24 for 1$\frac{1}{2}$ miles, becoming the ninth Triple Crown winner **(June 9)**. Secretariat is featured simultaneously on the covers of *Time, Newsweek*, and *Sports Illustrated* **(June 11)**. Wajima, from the last crop of Bold Ruler, brings a world record yearling price of $600,000 at Keeneland July **(July)**. Secretariat defeats stablemate Riva Ridge in the inaugural Marlboro Cup, setting a world record of 1:45$\frac{2}{5}$ for 1$\frac{1}{8}$ miles **(September 15)**. Secretariat ends his career triumphantly in the Canadian International Championship (G2) **(October 28)**. Count Fleet dies at age 33 **(December 3)**. Sandy Hawley is the first jockey to ride 500 winners in a season **(December 15)**.

1974 The centennial Kentucky Derby (G1) is won by Cannonade before a record crowd of 163,628 **(May 4)**. Chris Evert defeats Miss Musket by approximately 50 lengths in a $350,000 match race at Hollywood **(July 20)**. Dahlia is the first distaff millionaire **(August 20)**. D. Wayne Lukas saddles his first Thoroughbred stakes winner, Harbor Hauler, in a division of the Foothill Stakes at Pomona **(September 13)**. Dahlia becomes a stakes winner in five countries **(October 27)**. Louisiana Downs opens **(October 30)**. Apprentice jockey Chris McCarron sets a single-season win record of 546. Dan Lasater nearly doubles the previous single-season earnings record for an owner, with $3,020,521.

1975 Ruffian breaks down in Belmont Park's "battle of the sexes" match race against Foolish Pleasure **(July 6)**; dies following surgery and is buried in the Belmont infield **(July 7)**. Seattle Slew sells as a yearling for $17,500 at the Fasig-Tipton Kentucky July sale **(July 19)**. Two yearling colts are stolen from their stalls at the Keeneland fall sale **(September 7)** and are never recovered. On-track betting in the United States tops $5-billion for the first time. On-track attendance tops 50-million for the first time. Champion Wajima is syndicated for a world-record $7.2-million.

1976 Secretariat's son Canadian Bound is the world's first seven-figure auction yearling, bringing $1.5-million at Keeneland July **(July 20)**. Connecticut opens its Teletrack satellite wagering site. Forego wins his third straight Horse of the Year title. What a Pleasure is syndicated for a world-record $8-million.

1977 Washington Park is destroyed by fire **(February 5)**. Garden State Park's grandstand and clubhouse are destroyed by fire **(April 14)**. Seattle Slew becomes the first undefeated American Triple Crown winner **(June 11)**. Champion Fanfreluche is stolen from a pasture at Claiborne Farm **(June 24)**; recovered unharmed six months later. Seattle Slew suffers his first career loss in the Swaps Stakes at Hollywood Park **(July 3)**. Maryland Governor Marvin Mandel is convicted on racing-related racketeering and mail fraud charges **(August 23)**. The Meadowlands in New Jersey opens its first Thoroughbred meet **(September 6)**. American foal registrations top 30,000 for the first time. Lebon-*Cinzano ringer scandal breaks in New York **(September 23)**. Steve Cauthen becomes the first to ride winners of $6-million in a single season **(December 10)** and is later named *Sports Illustrated*'s Sportsman of the Year and Professional Athlete of the Year by the Associated Press. The Minstrel is syndicated for a world-record $9-million.

1978 John Henry wins a $25,000 claiming race **(May 21)**; switches to turf and wins for $35,000 claiming tag at Belmont Park **(June 1)**. Affirmed becomes the 11th Triple Crown winner **(June 10)**. Triple Crown winners meet for the first time, with Seattle Slew defeating Affirmed in the Marlboro Cup Handicap (G1) **(September 16)**. Affirmed is syndicated for a world-record $14.4-million.

1979 Affirmed becomes the first career $2-million earner **(June 24)**. Affirmed defeats Kentucky Derby (G1) and Preakness Stakes (G1) victor Spectacular Bid in the Jockey Club Gold Cup (G1); becomes the first to earn $1-million in a single season **(October 6)**. Hollywood Park introduces pick-six wagering **(April 23)**. Turf female division added to annual North American championships.

1980 Genuine Risk becomes the second filly Kentucky Derby winner **(May 3)**. Ex-jockey Con Errico is convicted of race fixing in New York **(May 19)**, is sentenced to ten years in prison. Spectacular Bid walks over in Woodward Stakes (G1) **(September 20)**. Prerace drug testing of horses begins at Aqueduct **(October 14)**. Spectacular Bid is syndicated for a record $22-million.

1981 Julie Krone rides her first winner, at Tampa Bay Downs **(February 12)**. The Arlington Million is inaugurated at Arlington Park as the world's first $1-million Thoroughbred race, with John Henry defeating The Bart by a nose. **(August 30)**. Storm Bird is syndicated for a record $30-million.

1982 Mary Russ becomes the first female jockey to win a North American Grade 1 race, with Lord Darnley in the Widener Handicap **(February 27)**. Trainer Woody Stephens saddles the first of five consecutive Belmont Stakes (G1) winners, Conquistador Cielo **(June 5)**. A son of Nijinsky II—Spearfish brings a record $4.25-million at Keeneland July. Simulcasting begins at Woodbine and Fort Erie in Canada. John Gaines conceives the idea for the Breeders' Cup. Conquistador Cielo is syndicated for a record $36.4-million.

1983 European champion Shergar is stolen from Ballymany Stud in Ireland **(February 8)**; he was never recovered. Genuine Risk produces a stillborn colt by Secretariat, the first offspring of two Kentucky Derby (G1) winners **(April 4)**. Shareef Dancer is syndicated for a record $40-million. Jockey Angel Cordero Jr. rides to a record $10-million season. All Along (Fr) becomes America's first foreign-bred Horse of the Year. Simulcasting begins from the Meadowlands to Atlantic City Race Course **(September 28)**. John Henry becomes the first $4-million earner **(December 11)**. Fourteen Northern Dancer sales yearlings average $3,320,357. The Hollywood Futurity (G1) is carded as racing's first $1-million event for two-year-olds **(December 18)**.

1984 A share in Seattle Slew sells for $3-million **(May)**. Swale collapses and dies eight days after winning the Belmont Stakes **(June 17)**. Equine viral arteritis (EVA) halts Kentucky breeding season two weeks early **(June)**. Fit to Fight becomes the fourth horse to sweep New York's handicap triple crown **(July 21)**. The inaugural Breeders' Cup is run at Hollywood Park before 64,625 on-track fans and 50-million television viewers; Wild Again wins the $3-million Breeders' Cup Classic (G1) **(November 10)**. Nine-year-old John Henry retires with record earnings of $6,597,947.

1985 Bill Shoemaker is the first jockey to reach $100-million in purse winnings **(March 3)**. Garden State Park, rebuilt at a cost of approximately $200-million, reopens **(April 1)**. Spend a Buck earns $2.6-million in purse and bonus money following his Jersey Derby (G3) victory **(May 27)**. Steve Cauthen becomes the first American jockey to win both a Kentucky Derby (G1) and Epsom Derby (Eng-G1) **(June 5)**. Creme Fraiche becomes the first gelding to win the Belmont Stakes **(June 8)**. Seattle Dancer sells for a world auction record of $13.1-million at Keeneland July **(July 23)**. Arlington Park's grandstand is destroyed by fire **(July 31)**. Teleprompter (GB) wins the Arlington Million (G1) in front of a razed grandstand and an on-track crowd of 35,651 **(August 25)**. THOROUGHBRED TIMES weekly news magazine publishes its inaugural edition **(September 20)**. Miss Oceana brings a world-record broodmare price of $7-million at the Newstead Farm dispersal **(November 10)**. American foal registrations top 50,000 for the first time.

1986 A season to 25-year-old Northern Dancer sells at auction for $710,000 **(January)**. The Santa Anita Handicap (G1) becomes the first $1-million-guaranteed handicap, won by Greinton (GB) **(March 2)**. Jan Ciochetti is the first woman to call a race at a major track (Hialeah) **(March 21)**. Woody Stephens saddles his fifth straight Belmont Stakes (G1) winner, Danzig Connection **(June 7)**. Laurel Park inaugurates the Maryland Million **(October 18)**. Lawmaker breaks *Star Shoot's 70-year-old record by siring his 28th juvenile winner **(December 12)**; ends the year with 30 two-year-old winners. Jockey Club foal registrations reach an all-time annual high of 51,293. The Jockey Club launches a mandatory blood-typing program. Joint nomination to Triple Crown races begins.

1987 Jockey Chris Antley wins a record nine races in a single day, at Aqueduct and Meadowlands **(October 31)**. Tejano becomes the first juvenile millionaire **(December 12)**. Northern Dancer retires from breeding. Chrysler Corp. becomes first sponsor of the $5-million Triple Crown Challenge.

1988 Winning Colors is the third filly Kentucky Derby (G1) winner **(May 7)**. Personal Ensign ends her 13-for-13 career with a thrilling victory over Winning Colors in the Breeders' Cup Distaff (G1) **(November 5)**. Alysheba wins the Breeders' Cup Classic (G1) and retires as the leading American money earner, with $6,679,242 **(November 5)**.

1989 E. P. Taylor, breeder of Northern Dancer and Nijinsky II, dies at age 88 **(May 14)**. Belmont Park is the first American racetrack to time races in hundredths of a second. Arlington International Racecourse opens **(June 28)**. Northern Park, the last Northern Dancer yearling sold at auction, brings $2.8-million at Keeneland **(July 18)**. Secretariat dies at age 19 **(October 4)**. Pari-mutuel wagering on horse racing returns to Texas for the first time since 1937 **(October 6)**. Jockey Kent Desormeaux establishes a single-season win record of 547 **(November 30)**; ends the year with 598 winners.

1990 Bill Shoemaker retires as the world's winningest jockey, with 8,833 victories **(February 3)**. D. Wayne Lukas becomes the first trainer to saddle career winners of $100-million **(May 12)**. Champion Go for Wand breaks down fatally in the Breeders' Cup Distaff (G1) **(October 27)**. Northern Dancer dies at age 29 **(November 16)**. Alydar dies at Calumet Farm under suspicious circumstances **(November 17)**.

1991 The American Championship Racing Series is launched as a designed-for-television event. Bill Shoemaker is paralyzed in a California car accident **(April 8)**. Equibase, a joint venture of the Jockey Club and Thoroughbred Racing Associations, is formed and begins gathering past-performance data in competition with *Daily Racing Form*.

1992 Henryk de Kwiatkowski buys Calumet Farm for $17-million at a bankruptcy auction **(March 26)**. Gilded Time runs the fastest six furlongs ever recorded by a two-year-old, 1:07.84, in the Sapling Stakes at Monmouth Park **(August 8)**.

1993 At age 16, Kentucky Derby (G1) winner Genuine Risk produces her first live foal, a colt by Rahy **(May 15)**. Julie Krone becomes the first female jockey to win an American classic, with Colonial Affair in the Belmont Stakes **(June 5)**. Claude R. "Shug" McGaughey III saddles five graded stakes winners at Belmont Park in single day **(October 16)**. Arcangues wins the Breeders' Cup Classic at record 133.60-to-1 odds **(November 6)**. Fair Grounds's grandstand is destroyed by fire **(December 17)**.

1994 Thoroughbred Racing Associations appoints Brian McGrath as its first and only commissioner **(January 17)**. The American Championship Racing Series is canceled. Class 1 racing begins in Texas at Sam Houston Race Park **(April 29)**. Thoroughbred Owners of California is launched.

1995 New York becomes the last North American racing jurisdiction to legalize race-day use of the antibleeder medication furosemide **(September 1)**. Hoosier Park opens **(September 1)**. Visa International begins sponsorship of the American Triple Crown races. Jockey Jerry Bailey wins a single-season record $16-million in purse money. Delaware Park and Prairie Meadows Racetrack install slot machines.

1996 Cigar scores his 16th consecutive victory, tying Citation's modern record **(July 13)**. Cigar retires as the world's leading money winner, with $9,999,815 **(October 26)**. Serena's Song becomes the top North American distaff earner, with $3,283,388.

1997 A $25-million infertility insurance claim is paid off on Cigar **(March 24)**. Racing Hall of Fame member Exceller is killed in a Swedish slaughterhouse at age 24 **(April 7)**. Keeneland utilizes a public address system for the first time, at its spring meeting. Colonial Downs opens as Virginia's first pari-mutuel racetrack **(September 1)**. Arlington International announces that it will suspend racing because of financial losses, political climate in Illinois **(September 8)**. Racing Hall of Fame jockey Eddie Arcaro dies at age 81 **(November 14)**.

1998 The National Thoroughbred Racing Association (NTRA) is launched **(April 1)**. Tim Smith is named NTRA commissioner **(April 21)**. Real Quiet fails by a nose in his quest for the Triple Crown **(June 6)**. Elusive Quality clocks a world-record 1:31.63 mile on Belmont Park's grass **(July 4)**. Company controlled by Frank Stronach buys Santa Anita Park. Equibase becomes the sport's sole provider of past-performance data and acquires *Daily Racing Form* database.

1999 Julie Krone retires as the all-time winningest female jockey, with 3,546 victories **(April 18)**. ESPN honors Secretariat as one of the top 50 athletes of the 20th century **(May 19)**. Mr. Prospector dies at age 29 **(June 1)**. Television Games Network (TVG) debuts **(July 14)**. Dale Baird becomes the first trainer to saddle 8,000 winners **(July 22)**. Churchill Downs Inc. purchases Hollywood Park for $140-million **(September 10)**. Laffit Pincay Jr. passes Bill Shoemaker as the world's winningest jockey **(December 10)**, with 8,834 victories. Frank Stronach-controlled Magna Entertainment Corp. buys Gulfstream Park, Golden Gate Fields, Thistledown, and Remington Park. Churchill Downs Inc. acquires Calder Race Course.

2000 Julie Krone becomes the first female elected to the Racing Hall of Fame **(May 2)**. Arlington Park reopens after a two-year hiatus **(May 14)**. NTRA and Breeders' Cup Ltd. consolidate **(May 18)**. Fusaichi Pegasus becomes the first favorite to win the Kentucky Derby in 21 years **(May 6)**; syndicated for a reported record $60-million to $70-million **(June 25)**. Leading breeder Allen Paulson dies at 78 **(July 19)**. Breeder Fred Hooper dies at 102 **(August 3)**. Churchill Downs Inc. buys Arlington Park **(September)**.

2001 Triple Crown winner Affirmed dies at 26 **(January 12)**. The Breeders' Cup becomes formally known as the Breeders' Cup World Thoroughbred Championships **(June 26)**. Jerry Bailey becomes the first jockey to ride winners of $20-million in a season **(October 7)**. Tiznow becomes the first two-time winner of the Breeders' Cup Classic **(October 27)**. Laura Hillenbrand's *Seabiscuit: An American Legend* tops the New York *Times* bestseller list for nonfiction.

2002 Japan-based T.M.Opera O, the world's richest Thoroughbred, retires with earnings of $16,200,337 **(January 25)**. Seattle Slew, the last living American Triple Crown winner, dies at age 28 **(May 7)**. Racing Hall of Fame jockey Chris McCarron retires after career victory number 7,139 **(June 23)**. Volponi scores the second-biggest upset in Breeders' Cup Classic (G1) history, with an $89 payoff **(October 26)**. Ultra Pick Six wager on Breeders' Cup races is found to have been fixed, and three former Drexel University fraternity brothers plead guilty to $3-million scam. Julie Krone wins at Santa Anita in comeback after 3½ years in retirement **(November 7)**. Magna International buys Lone Star Park **(October 30)** and the controlling interest in Maryland tracks **(November 13)**.

2003 Johnny Longden dies on his 96th birthday **(February 14)**. Laffit Pincay Jr. retires as all-time leading jockey by wins, with 9,530 **(April 29)**. Funny Cide becomes first gelding to win Kentucky Derby since Clyde Van Dusen in 1929 **(May 3)**. *Seabiscuit*, the film, opens to good reviews **(July 25)**. Bill Shoemaker dies at age 72 **(October 12)**. Richard Mandella wins a record four Breeders' cup races **(October 25)**. Trainer Bobby Frankel set records for single-season earnings and Grade 1 victories.

2004 Owner-breeder William T. Young dies at age 85 **(January 12)**. Smarty Jones wins the Kentucky Derby **(May 1)** and the Preakness by a record 11½ lengths **(May 15)**, but finishes second in the Belmont **(June 5)**. Churchill Downs buys Fair Grounds **(October 15)**.

2005 John R. Gaines, creator of the Breeders' Cup, dies at age 76 **(February 11)**. Churchill Downs Inc. sells Hollywood Park **(July 6)**. Hurricane Katrina damages Fair Grounds, and shortened 2005-'06 meet is moved Louisiana Downs **(August 29)**. Ashado sells for record $9-million as broodmare prospect **(November 7)**. Jockeys' Guild ousts President L. Wayne Gertmenian **(November 15)**. Single year earnings records are set by trainer Todd Pletcher ($20,867,842) and jockey John Velasquez ($20,799,923).

2006 Breeders' Cup Ltd. increases World Championships purses to $20-million **(May 2)**. Barbaro wins Kentucky Derby **(May 6)** but breaks down in Preakness **(May 20)**.

Notable Horses in Racing

Racing Hall of Fame members are listed in italics

The name of each horse is followed by year of birth and year of death, if known. Color and sex (colt, filly, or gelding) are followed by sire, dam, and broodmare sire. The horse's race record is detailed by number of starts, wins, seconds, thirds, and earnings, followed by championship honors and most important wins. Records from the 18th and 19th centuries may be incomplete, and earnings may be impossible to determine. If the horse sired or produced significant stakes winners, that information follows the race record. A sire's or dam's place in important male or female lines is also noted.

ACKACK, 1966-1990. B. c., Battle Joined—Fast Turn, by *Turn-to. 27-19-6-0, $636,641, Horse of the Year in 1971, champion sprinter, champion older male, Santa Anita H., Hollywood Gold Cup H., etc. Sire of 54 stakes winners, including Youth, Broad Brush, Ack's Secret, Rascal Lass, Caline. Broodmare sire of Sharp Cat, Royal Anthem, Benny the Dip, North Sider, Lost Code.

AFFECTIONATELY, 1960-1979. Dk. b. or br. f., Swaps—Searching, by War Admiral. 52-28-8-6, $546,659, champion two-year-old filly, champion sprinter, champion older mare, Top Flight H., Spinaway S., etc. Dam of Personality.

AFFIRMED, 1975-2001. Ch. c., Exclusive Native—Won't Tell You, by Crafty Admiral. 29-22-5-1, $2,393,818, Horse of the Year in 1978-'79, champion two- and three-year-old male, champion older male, Triple Crown, Jockey Club Gold Cup (G1), etc. Sire of more than 80 stakes winners, including Flawlessly, Quiet Resolve, Affirmed Success, Peteski, Zoman, Charlie Barley, Bint Pasha. Broodmare sire of Chelsey Flower, Harlan's Holiday, Stinger, Balanchine.

AFLEET ALEX, 2002-. B. c., Northern Afleet—Maggy Hawk, by Hawkster. 12-8-2-1, $2,765,800, champion three-year-old male, Preakness S. (G1), Belmont S. (G1), Hopeful S. (G1), etc. Best known for recovering from a near fall in 2005 Preakness Stakes before 4¾-length victory.

AFRICANDER, 1900-unknown. B. c. *Star Ruby—Afric Queen, by *Darebin. 60-19-15-8, $102,325, champion three-year-old, Belmont S., Suburban H., etc.

ALARM, 1869-1895. B. c., *Eclipse—*Maud, by Stockwell. 9-6-2-1, $12,500, match race with Inverary. Sire of Himyar, Panique, Danger, Ann Fief, Fidele. First American male-line ancestor of Domino, Plaudit lines.

ALCIBIADES, 1927-1957. Ch. f., Supremus—*Regal Roman, by Roi Herode. 23-7-2-4, $47,860, champion two-year-old filly, Kentucky Oaks, etc. Dam of Menow, Lithe, Salaminia. Foundation mare of family that includes Sir Ivor, Firm Policy, Rash Statement, Twice the Vice, Shine Again, Halo America.

ALL ALONG (FR), 1979-2005. B. f., Targowice—Agujita (Fr), by Vieux Manoir. 21-9-4-2, $2,125,809, Horse of the Year in 1983, champion older female, champion older horse in France, Prix de l'Arc de Triomphe (Fr-G1), Turf Classic S. (G1), etc. Dam of Along All, Arnaqueur.

ALLEGED, 1974-2000. B. c., Hoist the Flag—Princess Pout, by Prince John. 10-9-1-0, $623,187, champion three-year-old in England and France, champion older horse in Europe, Prix de l'Arc de Triomphe (Fr-G1) twice, etc. One of only five horses to win consecutive runnings of the Prix de l'Arc de Triomphe. Sire of 100 stakes winners, including Miss Alleged, Law Society, Midway Lady, Shantou, Muhtarram, Romanette. Broodmare sire of Suave Dancer, Dr Devious (Ire), Dream Well (Fr), Go and Go (Ire), Sulamani (Ire).

ALLEZ FRANCE, 1970-1989, B. f., *Sea-Bird—Priceless Gem, by Hail to Reason. 21-13-3-1, $1,262,801, Horse of the Year in France in 1974, champion two- and three-year-old filly, champion older mare twice, Prix de l'Arc de Triomphe (Fr-G1), etc. Dam of Action Francaise. Considered greatest filly ever trained in France.

ALMAHMOUD, 1947-1971. Ch. f., *Mahmoud—Arbitrator, by Peace Chance. 11-4-0-1, $32,760, Vineland H., etc. Dam of Cosmah, Natalma. Foundation mare of family that includes Northern Dancer, Halo, Danehill, Tosmah, Flawlessly, Arctic Tern, Machiavellian, Bago, L'Emigrant, Cannonade, La Prevoyante.

ALSAB, 1939-1963. B. c., Good Goods—Winds Chant, by Wildair. 51-25-11-5, $350,015, champion two- and three-year-old colt, Preakness S., American Derby, etc. Sire of 17 stakes winners, including Myrtle Charm, Armageddon, Sabette. Defeated Triple Crown winner Whirlaway in match race. Tail-male ancestor of line that leads to Broad Brush.

ALYDAR, 1975-1990. Ch. c., Raise a Native—Sweet Tooth, by On-and-On. 26-14-9-1, $957,195, Travers S. (G1), Florida Derby (G1), etc. Leading sire in 1990. Sire of 77 stakes winners, including Alysheba, Easy Goer, Criminal Type, Turkoman, Althea, Alydaress, Strike the Gold, Miss Oceana, Endear, Peinture Bleue, Winglet. Broodmare sire of Ajina, Amilynx, Anees, Cat Thief, General Meeting, Lakeway, Lure, Peintre Celebre.

ALYSHEBA, 1984- . B. c., Alydar—Bel Sheba, by Lt. Stevens. 26-11-8-2, $6,679,242, Horse of the Year in 1988, champion three-year-old male, champion older male, Kentucky Derby (G1), Preakness S. (G1), Breeders' Cup Classic (G1), etc. Sire of more than 15 stakes winners, including Alywow, Bright Moon, Moonlight Dance.

AMERICAN ECLIPSE, 1814-1847. Ch. c., Duroc—Millers Damsel, by *Messenger. 8-8-0-0, $56,700, North-South Match Race with (Sir) Henry. Sire of Black Maria, Ariel, Medoc, Fanny, Lance. First great American champion.

AMERICAN FLAG, 1922-1942. Ch. c., Man o' War—*Lady Comfey, by Roi Herode. 17-8-1-1, $82,725, champion three-year-old colt, Belmont S., Withers S., etc. Sire of 16 stakes winners including Nellie Flag, Gusto. Broodmare sire of Raise You, Mar-Kell.

ANCIENT TITLE, 1970-1981. Dk. b. or br. g., Gummo—Hi Little Gal, by Bar Le Duc. 57-24-11-9, $1,252,791, Hollywood Gold Cup Invitational H. (G1), Charles H. Strub S. (G1), etc. Won 20 stakes; leading California-bred money earner at the time of his death.

ANITA PEABODY, 1925-1934. B. or br. f., Luke McLuke—*La Dauphine, by The Tetrarch. 8-7-0-1, $113,105, champion two-year-old filly, Futurity S., Debutante S., etc. Dam of Our Count.

A.P. INDY, 1989- . Dk. b. or br. c., Seattle Slew—Weekend Surprise, by Secretariat. 11-8-0-1, $2,979,815, Horse of the Year in 1992, champion three-year-old male, Belmont S. (G1), Breeders' Cup Classic (G1), etc. Sire of more than 75 stakes winners, including Mineshaft, Tempera, Golden Missile, Aptitude, Lu Ravi, Secret Status, A P Valentine, Old Trieste.

ARAZI, 1989-. Ch. c., Blushing Groom (Fr)—Danseur Fabuleux, by Northern Dancer. 14-9-1-1, $1,212,351, champion two-year-old male, Horse of the Year in Europe, Breeders' Cup Juvenile (G1), Grand Criterium (Fr-G1), etc. Sire of 15 stakes winners, including Congaree, First Magnitude (Ire), America (Ire).

ARISTIDES, 1872-1893. Ch. c., *Leamington—Sarong, by Lexington. 21-9-5-1, $18,325, Kentucky Derby, Withers S., Jerome S., etc. First winner of Kentucky Derby in 1875.

ARMED, 1941-1964. Br. g., Bull Lea—Armful, by Chance Shot. 81-41-20-10, $817,475, Horse of the Year in 1947, champion handicap horse twice, Suburban H., Widener H. twice, Gulfstream Park H., etc.

ARTFUL, 1902-1927. B. f., Hamburg—Martha II, by Dandie Dinmont. 8-6-2-0, $81,125, Futurity S., etc. Only horse to defeat Sysonby. Tail-female ancestor of family that includes Runaway Groom.

ARTS AND LETTERS, 1966-1998. Ch. c., *Ribot—All Beautiful, by Battlefield. 23-11-6-1, $632,404, Horse of the Year in 1969, champion three-year-old colt, champion handicap horse, Belmont S., Jockey Club Gold Cup, etc. Sire of 30 stakes winners, including Codex, Winter's Tale, Illiterate.

ASSAULT, 1943-1971. Ch. c., Bold Venture—Igual, by Equipoise. 42-18-6-7, $675,470, Horse of the Year in 1946, champion three-year-old colt, Triple Crown, Suburban H., Brooklyn H. twice, etc. Sterile at stud.

ASTEROID, 1861-1886. B. c., Lexington—Nebula, by *Glencoe. 12-12-0-0, $12,800, Woodlawn Vase, etc. One of three sons of Lexington, along with Kentucky and Norfolk, to be considered the best racehorses of the 1860s, called the "great triumvirate." Sire of Creedmoor, Ballankeel.

***AUSTRALIAN**, 1858-1879. Ch. c. West Australian—*Emilia, by Young Emilius. 10-3-3-3, $12,150, Doswell S., Galt House S. Sire of Spendthrift, Wildidle, Baden Baden, Fellowcraft, Joe Daniels, Springbok. American founder of male line that includes Man o' War, War Admiral, In Reality, Tiznow.

AZERI, 1998- . Ch. f., Jade Hunter—Zodiac Miss (Aus), by Ahonoora. 24-17-4-0, $4,079,820, Horse of the Year in 2002, champion older female 2002, '03, '04, Breeders' Cup Distaff (G1), Apple Blossom H. (G1) 2002-'04, etc. Leading North American distaff earner.

BALD EAGLE, 1955-1977. B. c., *Nasrullah—Siama, by Tiger. 29-12-5-4, $692,946, champion older horse, Metropolitan H., Suburban H., etc. Sire of 12 stakes winners, including Too Bald, San San. Broodmare sire of 33 stakes winners, including Exceller, Capote.

BALLOT, 1904-1937. Ch. c., *Voter—*Cerito, by Lowland Chief. 38-20-6-6, $154,545, Suburban H., etc. Sire of Midway, Chilhowee, Star Voter. Broodmare sire of Bull Lea.

BATTLEFIELD, 1948-1964. Ch. c., War Relic—Dark Display, by Display. 44-22-14-2, $474,727, champion two-year-old colt, Futurity S., Hopeful S., Travers S., etc. Sire of Yorktown. Broodmare sire of Arts and Letters, Steeple Jill.

BATTLESHIP, 1927-1958. Ch. c., Man o' War—*Quarantaine, by Sea Sick. 55-24-6-4, $71,641, Grand National Steeplechase in England and U.S., etc. Sire of Shipboard, War Battle.

BAYAKOA (Arg), 1984-1997. B. f., Consultant's Bid—Arlucea (Arg), by Good Manners. 39-21-9-0, $2,861,701, champion older female twice, Breeders' Cup Distaff (G1) twice, Spinster S. (G1) twice, etc.

BED O' ROSES, 1947-1953. B. f., Rosemont—Good Thing, by Discovery. 46-18-8-6, $383,925, champion two-year-old filly, champion handicap mare, Santa Margarita H., Matron S., etc.

BELDAME, 1901-1923. Ch. f., Octagon—*Bella Donna, by Hermit. 31-17-6-4, $102,135, Suburban H., Alabama S., Ladies H., etc. Dam of Belvale. Tail-female ancestor of family that includes Revoked, Lion Heart.

BEN ALI, 1883-unknown. Br. c., Virgil—Ulrica, by Lexington. 40-12-3-5, $25,090, Kentucky Derby, Hopeful S., etc.

BEN BRUSH, 1893-1918. B. c., Bramble—Roseville, by Reform. 40-25-5-5, $65,208, Kentucky Derby, Suburban H., etc. Leading sire in 1909. Sire of Broomstick, Sweep, Delhi, Meridian, Pebbles, Theo Cook, Von Tromp.

BEND OR, 1877-1903. Ch. c., Doncaster—Rouge Rose, by Thormanby. 14-10-2-0, $90,304, Epsom Derby, Champion S., etc. Sire of *Ormonde, Bona Vista, Kendal, Orvieto. Tail-male ancestor of Phalaris, *Teddy lines.

BEST PAL, 1988-1998. B. g., *Habitony—Ubetshedid, by King Pellinore. 47-18-11-4, $5,668,245, Santa Anita H. (G1), Hollywood Gold Cup H. (G1), etc. Leading California-bred money earner at retirement.

BEWITCH, 1945-1959. Br. f., Bull Lea—Potheen, by Wildair. 55-20-10-11, $462,605, champion two-year-old filly, champion handicap mare, Arlington Lassie S., Vanity H., etc. Defeated stablemate Citation in 1947 Washington Park Futurity.

BIMELECH, 1937-1966. B. c., Black Toney—*La Troienne, by *Teddy. 15-11-2-1, $248,745, champion two- and three-year-old colt, Preakness S., Belmont S., etc. Sire of 30 stakes winners, including Better Self, Be Faithful, Guillotine, Hilarious, Brookfield. Broodmare sire of Lalun, No Robbery. Full brother to Black Helen.

BIRDCATCHER, 1833-1860. Ch. c., Sir Hercules—Guiccioli, by Bob Booty. 18-6-4-4, $6,666 in Ireland, Madrid Plate, Peel Cup, etc. Sire of *Alfred, The Baron, Bird on the Wing, Chanticleer, Daniel O'Rourke, Kingfisher. Tail-male ancestor of Phalaris, *Teddy, Blandford male lines. Famous for passing on dark spots in his chestnut coat, known as "Birdcatcher spots."

BLACK GOLD, 1921-1928. Bl. c., Black Toney—Useeit, by Bonnie Joe. 35-18-5-4, $110,553, champion three-year-old colt, Kentucky Derby, Ohio Derby, etc. Broke down fatally at seven and buried in the infield at Fair Grounds.

BLACK HELEN, 1932-1957. B. f., Black Toney—*La Troienne, by *Teddy. 22-15-0-2, $61,800, champion three-year-old filly, Coaching Club American Oaks, Florida Derby, etc. Tail-female ancestor of family that includes Pleasant Tap, Go for Gin, But Why Not, Princess Rooney. Full sister to Bimelech.

BLACK MARIA, 1826-unknown. Bl. f., American Eclipse—Lady Lightfoot, by Sir Archy. 26-13-(placings unknown), $14,900, Jockey Club Purse, etc. Ran 17 times in four-mile heats. Won a five-heat, four-mile heat race that caused death of one opponent from exhaustion.

BLACK MARIA, 1923-1932. Bl. f., Black Toney—*Bird Loose, by Sardanapale. 52-18-14-6, $110,350, champion three-year-old filly, champion older mare twice, Kentucky Oaks, Metropolitan H., Ladies H. twice, etc. Tail-female ancestor of family that includes Polynesian, Air Forbes Won.

BLACK TIE AFFAIR (Ire), 1986-. Gr. or ro. c., Miswaki—Hat Tab Girl, by Al Hattab. 45-18-9-6, $3,370,694, Horse of the Year in 1991, champion older male, Breeders' Cup Classic (G1), Philip H. Iselin H. (G1), etc. Sire of more than 30 stakes winners, including Formal Gold, Evening Attire. Exported from the United States to Japan in 1997; returned in 2003.

BLACK TONEY, 1911-1938. Br. c., Peter Pan—Belgravia, by Ben Brush. 37-12-10-7, $12,815, Independence H., Valuation S., etc. Sire of more than 35 stakes winners, including Balladier, Big Hurry, Bimelech, Black Gold, Black Helen, Black Maria, Black Servant, Brokers Tip, Miss Jemima. Broodmare sire of more than 25 stakes winners, including Bridal Flower, Elkridge, Relic, Searching. Foundation sire of Col. E. R. Bradley's Idle Hour Farm.

BLANDFORD, 1919-1935. Br. c., Swynford—Blanche, by White Eagle. 4-3-1-0, $16,041, Princess of Wales's S., etc. Leading sire three times in England. Sire of *Blenheim II, *Bahram, Brantome, Windsor Lad, Campanula, Trigo, Dalmary, Mistress Ford, Pasch, Udaipur, Umidwar. Tail-male ancestor of line leading to The Axe II, Quadrangle, Crepello, Mtoto.

***BLENHEIM II**, 1927-1958. Br. c., Blandford—Malva, by Charles O'Malley. 10-5-3-0, $73,060, Epsom Derby, etc. Leading sire in 1941. Sire of more than 45 stakes winners, including Whirlaway, *Mahmoud, Donatello II, Mar-Kell, Fervent, A Gleam, Jet Pilot. Broodmare sire of A Glitter, Coaltown, Hill Gail, Kauai King, Le Paillon, *Nasrullah, Wistful. Tail-male ancestor of line leading to The Axe II, Quadrangle, Crepello, Mtoto.

BLUE LARKSPUR, 1926-1947. B. c., Black Servant—Blossom Time, by *North Star III. 16-10-3-1, $272,070, regarded as Horse of the Year in 1929, champion three-year-old colt, champion handicap horse, Belmont S., Classic S., etc. Sire of 44 stakes winners, including But Why Not, Myrtlewood, Painted Veil, Blue Swords, Alablue, Revoked, Blue Delight, Bee Ann Mac. Broodmare sire of Alanesian, Be Faithful, Busanda, By Jimminy, Cohoes, Durazna, Real Delight, Twilight Tear.

BLUSHING GROOM (Fr), 1974-1992. Ch. c., Red God—Runaway Bride (GB), by Wild Risk. 10-7-1-2, $407,153, champion two-year-old in France, champion miler in France, Grand Criterium (Fr-G1), Poule d'Essai des Poulains (French Two Thousand Guineas) (Fr-G1), etc. Leading sire in England in 1989. Sire of 92 stakes winners, including Nashwan, Rainbow Quest, Arazi, Sky Beauty, Rahy, Blushing John, Runaway Groom, Al Bahathri, Blush With Pride, Mt. Livermore. Broodmare sire of Awesome Again, Flute, Kahyasi, Lammtarra, Macho Uno, Stravinsky, T.M.Opera O.

BOLD FORBES, 1973-2000. Dk. b. or br. c., Irish Castle—Comely Nell, by Commodore M. 18-13-1-4, $546,536, champion three-year-old male, champion two-year-old in Puerto Rico, Kentucky Derby (G1), Belmont S. (G1), etc. Sire of 29 stakes winners, including Tiffany Lass, Air Forbes Won.

BOLD LAD, 1962-1986. Ch. c., Bold Ruler—Misty Morn, by *Princequillo. 19-14-2-1, $516,465, champion two-year-old, Metropolitan H., Futurity S., Hopeful S., etc. Sire of 29 stakes winners, including Sirlad (Ire), Bold Fascinator, Gentle Thoughts, Rube the Great.

BOLD 'NDETERMINED, 1977-1997. B. f., Bold and Brave—Pidi, by Determine. 20-16-2-0, $949,599, Coaching Club American Oaks (G1), Kentucky Oaks (G1), etc. Winner of six Grade 1 races at three in 1980, she had the misfortune of being in the same crop as Kentucky Derby (G1) winner and champion three-year-old filly Genuine Risk. Defeated Genuine Risk in the 1980 Maskette Stakes (G2).

BOLD RULER, 1954-1971. Dk. b. c., *Nasrullah—Miss Disco, by Discovery. 33-23-4-2, $764,204, Horse of the Year in 1957, champion three-year-old colt, champion sprinter, Preakness S., Futurity S., Suburban H., etc. Leading sire eight times, seven in succession (1963-'69). Sire of 82 stakes winners, including Secretariat, Gamely, Lamb Chop, Bold Lad (out of Misty Morn), Bold Lad (out of *Barn Pride), Bold Bidder, Wajima, Queen Empress, Queen of the Stage, Boldnesian, Chieftain, Dewan, Reviewer. Broodmare sire of Autobiography, Christmas Past, Private Terms, Sensational. Tail-male ancestor of Seattle Slew line.

BOLD VENTURE, 1933-1958. Ch. c., *St. Germans—Possible, by Ultimus. 11-6-2-0, $68,300, champion three-year-old colt, Kentucky Derby, Preakness S. Sire of 12 stakes winners, including Assault, Middleground. Broodmare sire of Miss Cavandish, Prove Out.

BON NOUVEL, 1960-unknown. B. g., Duc de Fer—Good News, by *Happy Argo. 51-16-11-7, $176,148, champion steeplechaser three times, Temple Gwathmey Stp. H., Brook Stp. H. twice, etc.

BORROW, 1908-unknown. Ch. g., Hamburg—Forget, by Exile. 91-24-20-12. $87,275, Middle Park Plate (in England), Brooklyn H., etc. Defeated three Kentucky Derby winners in 1917 Brooklyn H.

BOSTON, 1833-1850. Ch. c., Timoleon—Sister to Tuckahoe, by Ball's Florizel. 45-40-2-1, $51,700, champion of his era. Leading sire three times. Sire of Lexington, Lecomte, Commodore, Madeline, Nina, Ringgold, Red Eye. Won 70 of 81 heats, 47 at 4 miles. Lost famous match race with Fashion.

BOURTAI, 1942-1970. B. f., Stimulus—Escutcheon, by *Sir Gallahad III. 12-2-1-2, $3,850, 3rd Pimlico Nursery S. Dam of Bayou, Levee, Delta, Banta, Ambassador. Tail-female ancestor of Aptitude, Big Spruce, Coastal, Dike, Sacahuista, Shuvee, Sleepytime, Slew o' Gold, Talking Picture.

BOWL OF FLOWERS, 1958-unknown. Ch. f., Sailor—Flower Bowl, by *Alibhai. 16-10-3-3, $398,504, champion two- and three-year-old filly, Coaching Club American Oaks, Spinster S., etc. Dam of sires Whiskey Road, Big Burn.

BRIGADIER GERARD, 1968-'89. B. c., Queen's Hussar—La Paiva, by Prince Chevalier. 18-17-1-0, $631,199, Horse of the Year in England, champion miler twice, champion older horse, Two Thousand Guineas, King George VI and Queen Elizabeth II S., etc. Sire of 28 stakes winners, including Light Cavalry, Vayrann, Comrade in Arms, General (Fr). One of the greatest English horses of the 20th century and grandsire of Lord At War (Arg), one of the last representatives of the Fairway male line.

BROAD BRUSH, 1983- . B. c., Ack Ack—Hay Patcher, by Hoist the Flag. 27-14-5-5, $2,656,793, Santa Anita H. (G1), Suburban H. (G1), etc. Leading sire in 1994. Sire of more than 85 stakes winners, including Farda Amiga, Concern, Include, Broad Appeal, Pompeii.

BROOMSTICK, 1901-1931. B. c., Ben Brush—*Elf, by Galliard. 39-14-11-5, $74,730, Travers S., Brighton H., etc. Leading sire 1913-'15; leading broodmare sire 1932-'33. Sire of 69 stakes winners, including Regret, Whisk Broom II, Bostonian, Broomspun, Cudgel, Halcyon, Sweeper, Traffic; Transmute, Wildair, Escoba, Flying Witch, Remembrance. Broodmare sire of Equipoise, Mother Goose, Whichone.

BROWN BESS, 1982- . Dk. b. or br. f., *Petrone—Chickadee, by Windy Sands. 36-16-8-6, $1,300,920, champion grass female, Santa Barbara H. (G1), Ramona H. (G1), Yellow Ribbon Inv. S. (G1), etc.

BUCKPASSER, 1963-1978. B. c., Tom Fool—Busanda, by War Admiral. 31-25-4-1, $1,462,014, Horse of the Year in 1966, champion two- and three-year-old colt, champion handicap horse twice, Jockey Club Gold Cup, Metropolitan H., etc. Leading broodmare sire 1983-'84, '88-'89. Sire of 35 stakes winners, including Numbered Account, Relaxing, La Prevoyante, L'Enjoleur, Norcliffe, State Dinner, Silver Buck, Buckaroo, Quick as Lightning, Lassie Dear, Passing Mood. Broodmare sire of Slew o' Gold, Seeking the Gold, Coastal, Woodman, Private Account, Easy Goer, El Gran Senor, Miswaki, Touch Gold.

***BULL DOG**, 1927-1954. Dk. b. or br. c., *Teddy—Plucky Liege, by Spearmint. 8-2-1-0, $7,802 Prix Daphnis, etc. Leading sire in 1943; leading broodmare sire in 1953, '54, '56. Sire of 52 stakes winners, including Bull Lea, Occupy, Our Boots, Occupation, Johns Joy, The

Doge, Canina, Miss Dogwood, Miss Mommy, Tiger. Broodmare sire of Tom Fool, Decathlon, Dark Star, Rough'n Tumble. Full brother to *Sir Gallahad III; half brother to Bois Roussel, Admiral Drake.

***BULLE ROCK**, 1709-unknown. B. c., Darley Arabian—Byerley Turk mare, by Byerley Turk. Earliest Thoroughbred recorded as imported (in 1730) to the United States in the *American Stud Book*. No horse matching his description and pedigree appears in the *General Stud Book*, but he is generally accepted as America's first Thoroughbred.

BULL LEA, 1935-1964. Br. c., *Bull Dog—Rose Leaves, by Ballot. 27-10-7-3, $94,825, Widener H., Blue Grass S., etc. Leading sire in 1947, '48, '49, '52, '53; leading broodmare sire 1958-'61. Sire of 57 stakes winners, ten champions, including Citation, Coaltown, Hill Gail, Two Lea, Twilight Tear, Bewitch, Real Delight, Iron Liege, Armed, Durazna, Next Move. Broodmare sire of Barbizon, Bramalea, Gate Dancer, Idun, Leallah, Pucker Up, Quadrangle, Tim Tam.

BUSHER, 1942-1955. Ch. f., War Admiral—Baby League, by Bubbling Over. 21-15-3-1, $334,035, Horse of the Year in 1945, champion two- and three-year-old filly, champion handicap mare, Hollywood Derby, Santa Margarita H., etc. Dam of Jet Action. Tail-female ancestor of family that includes Beau's Eagle, Play On.

BUSHRANGER, 1930-1937. Ch. g., *Stefan the Great—War Path, by Man o' War. 21-11-3-1, $20,635, champion steeplechaser, Grand National Stp. H., Broad Hollow Stp. H. twice, etc.

BYERLEY TURK, ca. 1680. Bl. c. of unknown parentage. Sire of Jigg, Basto, Black Hearty. One of three Thoroughbred male-line foundation sires. Tail-male ancestor of the Herod line leading to *Ambiorix, The Tetrarch, Dr Devious (Ire), Indian Ridge.

CAFE PRINCE, 1970-unknown. B. g., Creme dela Creme—Princess Blair, by Blue Prince. 52-18-5-4, $228,238, champion steeplechaser twice, Colonial Cup International Stp. twice, etc.

CANONERO II, 1968-1981. B. c., *Pretendre—Dixieland II, by Nantallah. 23-9-3-4, $360,933, champion three-year-old male, Kentucky Derby, Preakness S.-ntr, etc. Sire of five stakes winners, including Cannon Boy. First foreign-trained horse to win Kentucky Derby.

CAPOT, 1946-1974. Br. c., Menow—Piquet, by *St. Germans. 28-12-4-7, $347,260, Horse of the Year in 1949, champion three-year-old colt, Preakness S., Belmont S., etc. Sired 13 foals, no stakes winners.

CARBINE, 1885-1913. B. c., Musket—Mersey, by Knowsley. 43-33-6-3, $143,982, Melbourne Cup twice, Sydney Cup twice, etc.. Sire of Amberite, *Bomba, Fowling-Piece, Greatorex, Miss Gunning, Ramrod, Spearmint, Wallace. Won 1890 Melbourne Cup under 145 pounds. Still widely considered best New Zealand-bred of all time.

CARRY BACK, 1958-1983. Br. c., Saggy—Joppy, by Star Blen. 62-21-11-11, $1,241,165, champion three-year-old colt, Kentucky Derby, Preakness S., etc. Sire of ten stakes winners, including Taken Aback, Sharp Gary, Back in Paris.

CAVALCADE, 1931-1940. Br. c., *Lancegaye—*Hastily, by Hurry On. 22-8-5-3, $127,165, Horse of the Year in 1934, champion two- and three-year-old colt, Kentucky Derby, American Derby, etc. Sire of three stakes winners.

CHALLEDON, 1936-1958. B. c., *Challenger II—Laura Gal, by *Sir Gallahad III. 44-20-7-6, $334,660, Horse of the Year in 1939 and '40, champion three-year-old colt, champion handicap horse, Preakness S., Whitney S., etc. Sire of 13 stakes winners, including Ancestor, Tenacious, Donor.

CHARISMATIC, 1996- . Ch. c., Summer Squall—Bali Babe, by Drone. 17-5-2-4, $2,038,064, Horse of the Year in 1999, champion three-year-old male, Kentucky Derby (G1), Preakness S. (G1), etc. Exported to Japan in 2002.

CHIEF'S CROWN, 1982-1997. B. c., Danzig—Six Crowns, by Secretariat. 21-12-3-3, $2,191,168, champion two-year-old male, Breeders' Cup Juvenile (G1), Travers S. (G1), etc. Sire of more than 50 stakes winners, including Erhaab, Grand Lodge, Chief Bearhart, Concerto, Chief Honcho.

CHRIS EVERT, 1971-2001. Ch. f., Swoon's Son—Miss Carmie, by T. V. Lark. 15-10-2-2, $679,475, champion three-year-old filly, filly triple crown, Coaching Club American Oaks (G1), Hollywood Special S. (match race with Miss Musket), etc. Dam of Six Crowns, Wimbledon Star. Second dam of Chief's Crown.

CICADA, 1959-1981. B. f., Bryan G.—Satsuma, by Bossuet. 42-23-8-6, $783,674, champion two- and three-year-old filly, champion older mare, Kentucky Oaks, Beldame S., etc. Dam of Cicada's Pride. Retired as world's leading money-winning female.

CIGAR, 1990- . B. c., Palace Music—Solar Slew, by Seattle Slew. 33-19-4-5, $9,999,815, Horse of the Year in 1995 and '96, champion older male twice, Breeders' Cup Classic (G1), Dubai World Cup, etc. Leading earner of all-time in North America. Sterile at stud. Resides at Kentucky Horse Park.

CITATION, 1945-1970. B. c., Bull Lea—*Hydroplane II, by Hyperion. 45-32-10-2, $1,085,760, Horse of the Year in 1948, champion two- and three-year-old colt, champion handicap horse, Triple Crown, Jockey Club Gold Cup, Hollywood Gold Cup, etc. First $1-million earner. Sire of 12 stakes winners, including Silver Spoon, Fabius.

CLEOPATRA, 1917-unknown. Ch. f., Corcyra—*Gallice, by Gallinule. 26-8-10-4, $55,937, champion three-year-old filly, Coaching Club American Oaks, Alabama S., etc. Dam of Pompey, Laughing Queen; third dam of Tom Fool. Tail-female ancestor of family that includes Ambiopoise, Dust Commander.

COALTOWN, 1945-1965. B. c., Bull Lea—Easy Lass, by *Blenheim II. 39-23-6-3, $415,675, Horse of the Year in 1949, champion sprinter, champion handicap horse, Jerome H., Blue Grass S., etc. Never sired a stakes winner. Exported to France in 1955.

COLIN, 1905-1932. Br. c., Commando—*Pastorella, by Springfield. 15-15-0-0, $178,110, champion two- and three-year-old colt, Belmont S., Futurity S., etc. Sire of Jock, Neddie, On Watch. Shy breeder. Tail-male ancestor of line that leads to Broad Brush.

COMMANDO, 1898-1905. B. c., Domino—Emma C., by *Darebin. 9-7-2-0, $58,196, champion two- and three-year-old colt, Belmont S., Junior Champion S., etc. Leading sire in 1907. Sire of ten stakes winners from 27 foals, including Colin, Peter Pan, Celt, Hippodrome, Superman, Transvaal, and of Ultimus.

CONQUISTADOR CIELO, 1979-2002. B. c., Mr. Prospector—K D Princess, by Bold Commander. 13-9-0-2, $474,328, Horse of the Year in 1982, champion three-year-old male, Belmont S. (G1), Metropolitan H. (G1), etc. Sire of more than 65 stakes winners, including Marquetry, Forty Niner Days, Wagon Limit. Broodmare sire of more than 80 stakes winners, including Apelia, Dixie Dot Com, Thornfield.

CORRECTION, 1888-unknown. B. f., Himyar—Mannie Gray, by Enquirer. 122-38-35-22, $45,600, Toboggan Slide H., etc. Dam of Yankee, Miss Malaprop, Nature. Tail-female ancestor of family that includes Affirmed, Lil E. Tee, Ghostzapper. Full sister to Domino.

COSMAH, 1953-1979. B. f., Cosmic Bomb—Almahmoud, by *Mahmoud. 30-9-5-2, $86,525, Astarita S., etc. Broodmare of the Year in 1974. Dam of Tosmah, Halo, Fathers Image, Maribeau. Foundation mare of family that includes Flawlessly, L'Emigrant, Cannonade, Stephan's Odyssey.

***COUGAR II**, 1966-1989. Dk b. or br. c., Tale of Two Cities—*Cindy Lou II, by Madara. 50-20-7-17, $1,172,625, champion grass horse, Santa Anita H. (G1), Sunset H. (G1), etc. Sire of 24 stakes winners, including Gato Del Sol, Exploded.

COUNTERPOINT, 1948-1970. Ch. c., Count Fleet—Jabot, by *Sickle. 21-10-3-1, $284,575, Horse of the Year in 1951, champion three-year-old colt, Belmont S., Jockey Club Gold Cup, etc. Sire of 11 stakes winners, including Dotted Swiss, Harmonizing, Honey Dear, Snow White.

COUNT FLEET, 1940-1973. Br. c., Reigh Count—Quickly, by Haste. 21-16-4-1, $250,300, Horse of the Year in 1943, champion two- and three-year-old colt, Triple Crown, Champagne S., Withers S., etc. Leading sire in 1951; leading broodmare sire in 1963. Sire of 39 stakes winners, including Counterpoint, One Count, Kiss Me Kate, Count Turf, Straight Face, Count of Honor, Countess Fleet, County Delight, Juliets Nurse. Broodmare sire of Kelso, Prince John, Quill, Fleet Nasrullah, Gallant Romeo, Lamb Chop.

CREME FRAICHE, 1982-2003. B. g., Rich Cream—Likely Exchange, by Terrible Tiger. 64-17-12-13, $4,024,727, Belmont S. (G1), Jockey Club Gold Cup (G1) twice, Super Derby (G1), etc.

CRIMINAL TYPE, 1985-2005. Ch. c., Alydar—Klepto, by No Robbery. 24-10-5-3, $2,351,274, Horse of the Year in 1990, champion older male, Hollywood Gold Cup (G1), Pimlico Special H. (G1), Metropolitan H. (G1), etc. Sire of seven stakes winners, including Hoolie. Exported to Japan in 1992.

CRIMSON SATAN, 1959-1982. Ch. c., Spy Song—*Papila, by Requiebro. 58-18-9-9, $796,077, champion two-year-old colt, Garden State S., Charles H. Strub S., etc. Sire of 33 stakes winners, including Crimson Saint, Krislin, Whitesburg.

CRUSADER, 1923-1940. Ch. c., Man o' War—Star Fancy, by *Star Shoot. 42-18-8-4, $203,261, consensus Horse of the Year in 1926, champion three-year-old colt, Belmont S., Jockey Club Gold Cup, Suburban H. twice, etc. Sire of six stakes winners, including *Crossbow II.

DAHLIA, 1970-2001. Ch. f., *Vaguely Noble—Charming Alibi, by Honeys Alibi. 48-15-3-7, $1,489,105, Horse of the Year in England in 1974 and '75, champion three-year-old in Ireland, champion three-year-old in England, champion grass horse in U.S., champion older mare twice in England, King George VI and Queen Elizabeth S. (Eng-G1) twice, Washington, D.C., International (G1), etc. Dam of Dahar, Rivlia, Delegant, Dahlia's Dreamer, Wajd, Llandaff. First distaff millionaire.

DALAKHANI, 2000- . Gr. c., Darshaan—Daltawa, by Miswaki. 9-8-1-0, $2,496,059, European Horse of the Year and champion three-year-old in 2003, Prix de l'Arc de Triomphe (Fr-G1), Prix du Jockey-Club (Fr-G1) (French Derby), etc.

DAMASCUS, 1964-1995. B. c., Sword Dancer—Kerala, by *My Babu. 32-21-7-3, $1,176,781, Horse of the Year in 1967, champion three-year-old colt, champion handicap horse, Preakness S., Belmont S., Jockey Club Gold Cup S., etc. Sire of 71 stakes winners, including Private Account, Desert Wine, Highland Blade, Ogygian, Honorable Miss, Time for a Change, Judger, Bailjumper, Timeless Moment, Cutlass. Broodmare sire of more than 155 stakes winners, including Boundary, Chilukki, Coronado's Quest, Shadeed.

DANCE SMARTLY, 1988- . Dk. b. or br. f., Danzig—Classy 'n Smart, by Smarten. 17-12-2-3, $3,263,835, champion three-year-old filly in U.S., Canadian Horse of the Year, champion two- and three-year-old filly in Canada, Canadian Triple Crown, Breeders' Cup Distaff (G1), Queen's Plate S., etc. Dam of Queen's Plate winners Scatter the Gold, Dancethruthedawn.

DANEHILL, 1986-2003. B. c., Danzig—Razyana, by His Majesty. 9-4-1-2, $321,064, Ladbroke Sprint S. (Eng-G1), etc. Brother to Eagle Eyed, Harpia, Shibboleth, half brother to Euphonic. Leading sire in Australia eight times, leading sire in France twice, leading sire in U.S. Sire of more than 280 stakes winners, including Rock of Gibraltar (Ire), Flying Spur, Danewin, Fairy King Prawn, Dane Ripper, Banks Hill (GB).

DANZIG, 1977-2006. B. c., Northern Dancer—Pas de Nom, by Admiral's Voyage. 3-3-0-0, $32,400. Leading sire 1991-'93. Sire of more than 185 stakes winners, including Chief's Crown, Polish Precedent, Dayjur, Danehill, Dance Smartly, Langfuhr, Anabaa, Green Desert, Pine Bluff. Broodmare sire of more than 125 stakes winners, including Caller One, Fusaichi Pegasus.

DARK MIRAGE, 1965-1969. Dk. b. or br. f., *Persian Road II—Home by Dark, by Hill Prince. 27-12-3-2, $362,788, champion three-year-old filly, first winner of the filly triple crown in New York, Kentucky Oaks, Delaware Oaks, etc. Won nine consecutive stakes and broke down trying for tenth. Died at four.

DARK STAR, 1950-1972. Br. c., *Royal Gem II—Isolde, by *Bull Dog. 13-6-2-2, $131,337, Kentucky Derby, Derby Trial, etc. Only horse to defeat Native Dancer. Sire of 26 stakes winners, including *Gazala II, My Dad George, Hidden Treasure. Broodmare sire of Youth, Mississipian, Too Bald.

DARLEY ARABIAN, 1700. B. c. of unknown parentage. Sire of Flying Childers, Aleppo, Almanzor, Bartlett's Childers. One of three male-line foundation sires of the Thoroughbred breed. Tail-male ancestor of the Eclipse male line leading to Phalaris, Blandford, Hyperion, *Teddy, Domino lines.

DARSHAAN, 1981-2001. Br. c., Shirley Heights—Delsy, by Abdos. 8-5-0-1, $226,979, champion three-year-old in France, Prix du Jockey-Club (Fr-G1) (French Derby), etc. Leading sire in France in 2003, leading broodmare sire in England twice, leading broodmare sire in France. Sire of more than 90 stakes winners, including Dalakhani, Kotashaan (Fr), Aliysa (Ire), Mark of Esteem (Ire). Broodmare sire of High Chaparral (Ire), Ebadiyla, Islington (Ire), Yesterday (Ire).

DAVONA DALE, 1976-unknown. B. f., Best Turn—Royal Entrance, by Tim Tam. 18-11-2-1, $641,612, champion three-year-old filly, filly triple crown, Kentucky Oaks (G1), etc.

DECATHLON, 1953-1972. B. c., Olympia—Dog Blessed, by *Bull Dog. 42-25-8-1, $269,530, champion sprinter twice, Oceanport H. twice, Hutcheson S., etc. Sire of 12 stakes winners, including Juanita.

***DELANCEY'S CUB MARE**, 1762. F., Cub—Second mare (dam of Amaranthus), by Second. One of the first great imported American foundation mares. Dam of (Maria) Slamerkin. Tail-female ancestor of family that includes Nearco, Neckar, Golden Trail, Parole, Imp, Black Gold, Mad Hatter, Sun Beau, Flirtilla, Sumpter, Artful, Delhi, Falsetto, Halma.

DEPUTY MINISTER, 1979-2004. Dk. b. or br. c., Vice Regent—Mint Copy, by Bunty's Flight. 22-12-2-2, $696,964, champion two-year-old male in U.S., Horse of the Year in Canada in 1981, champion two-year-old male in Canada, Laurel Futurity (G1), Donn H. (G2), etc.

er. 15-12-1-0, $194,685, champion three-year-
gland, St. Leger S., Champion S. twice, etc.
re in England four times; leading broodmare
gland in 1946 and '47. Sire of Blue Peter, Fair
Trial, Full Sail, Garden Path, Honeyway, Rib-
Way, *Watling Street. Founder of sire line that
hergar, Troy, Ela-Mana-Mou, Brigadier Ger-
At War (Arg).

ASPEN, 1976-1998. Ch. f., Pretense—Change
Swaps. 20-8-3-0, $198,037, Matron S. (G1), Pri-
etc. Broodmare of the Year in 1994. Dam of
s winners, including Timber Country, North-
ı, Hamas (Ire), Elle Seule, Colorado Dancer
t Wood. Tail-female ancestor of family that in-
bai Millennium, Charnwood Forest (Ire), El-
ehthaaf, Occupandiste.

ION, 1837-1860. Ch. f., *Trustee—Bonnets o'
ir Charles. 36-32-0-0, $41,500, won match race
on, etc. Dam of A la Mode. Greatest of four-
fillies.

RITE TRICK, 1995-2006. Dk. b. or br. c., Phone
Evil Elaine, by Medieval Man. 16-12-0-1,
3, Horse of the Year in 1997, champion two-
nale, Breeders' Cup Juvenile (G1), Hopeful S.
First two-year-old since Secretariat in 1972 to
Horse of the Year.

RNOUGHT, 1755-1776. B. c., Regulus—Sil-
Heneage's Whitenose. Five wins in England,
King's Plates. Early American foundation sire.
nme's Wildair, Fitzhugh's Regulus, Spotswood's
len's Whynot, Gallant, Othello, Harris's Eclipse,
er.

INAND, 1983-2002. Ch. c., Nijinsky II—Banja
Double Jay. 29-8-9-6, $3,777,978, Horse of the
987, champion older male, Kentucky Derby
eeders' Cup Classic (G1), etc. Sire of eight
nners, including Bull Inthe Heather. Exported
in 1995 and slaughtered there.

NZE (FIRENZI), 1884-1902. B. f., Glenelg—
by Virgil. 82-47-21-9, $112,471, Gazelle S., Mon-
., Jerome S. (beating Hanover), etc. Tail-female
of family that includes Carry Back, Paul Jones.

T FLIGHT, 1944-1975. B. f., *Mahmoud—Fly
by *Dis Donc. 24-11-3-3, $197,965, champion
-old filly, Matron S., Monmouth Oaks, etc. De-
t Pilot in Futurity S.

T LANDING, 1956-1987. B. c., *Turn-to—
by Bubbling Over. 37-19-9-2, $779,577, cham-
-year-old colt, Champagne S., Hopeful S., etc.
7 stakes winners, including Riva Ridge, First
Gladwin.

TTERER, 1979-. Dk. b. or br. g., Mo Bay—Hor-
by Nade. 51-24-7-5, $534,854, four-time cham-
plechaser 1983-'86, Marion duPont Scott Colonial
rnational Stp. three times, Temple Gwathmey
hase H. twice, etc.

WLESSLY, 1988-2002. B. f., Affirmed—La Con-
by Nijinsky II. 28-16-4-3, $2,572,536, champion
male twice, Beverly D. S. (G1), Matriarch S.
ee times, etc.

WER BOWL, 1952-1968. B. f., *Alibhai—Flower
*Beau Pere. 32-7-4-3, $174,625, Ladies H.,
e H., etc. Dam of Bowl of Flowers, Graustark,
esty.

LISH PLEASURE, 1972-1994. B. c., What a
e—Fool-Me-Not, by Tom Fool. 26-16-4-3,
05, champion two-year-old male, Kentucky Derby
burban H. (G1), Great Match S. (with Ruffian),
of 43 stakes winners, including Baiser Vole,
Kiri's Clown, Maudlin, Prayers'n Promises.

FOREGO, 1970-1997. B. g., *Forli—Lady Golconda, by Hasty Road. 57-34-9-7, $1,938,957, three-time Horse of the Year 1974-'76, champion older male 1974-'77, champion sprinter, Marlboro Cup H. (G1), Metropolitan H. (G1) twice, Woodward H. (G1) three times, etc. Last of the great weight carriers.

***FORLI**, 1963-1988. Ch. c., Aristophanes—Trevisa, by Advocate. 10-9-1-0, $156,648, Horse of the Year in Argentina, Quadruple Crown, Gran Premio Carlos Pellegrini, Gran Premio Nacional (Argentine Derby), Coronado S.-ncr, etc. Brother to *Tirreno, Tibur. Sire of 60 stakes winners, including Forego, Thatch, Intrepid Hero, Sadeem, Formidable. Broodmare sire of Swale, Nureyev, Precisionist.

FORT MARCY, 1964-1991. B. g., *Amerigo—Key Bridge, by *Princequillo. 75-21-18-14, $1,109,791, Horse of the Year in 1970, champion grass horse twice, champion handicap horse, Washington, D.C., International S. twice, Man o' War S., etc. Half-brother to Key to the Mint.

FORWARD GAL, 1968-1984. Ch. f., Native Charger—Forward Thrust, by Jet Action. 26-12-4-6, $438,933, champion two-year-old filly, Frizette S., Monmouth Oaks, etc. Third dam of Freedom Cry (GB).

FOURSTARDAVE, 1985-2002. Ch. g., Compliance—Broadway Joan, by Bold Arian. 100-21-18-16, $1,636,737, St. Paul Derby (G2), Daryl's Joy S. (G3) twice, etc. Won a race at Saratoga Race Course for eight consecutive years. Full brother to Irish classic winner Fourstars Allstar.

FREE FOR ALL, 1942-1964. Br. c., Questionnaire—Panay, by *Chicle. 7-6-0-0, $111,225, Arlington Futurity, Washington Park Futurity, etc. Sire of Rough'n Tumble. Tail-male ancestor of Dr. Fager, Holy Bull.

FRIAR ROCK, 1913-1928. Ch. c., *Rock Sand—*Fairy Gold, by Bend Or. 21-9-1-3, $20,365, champion three-year-old, Belmont S., Suburban H., Brooklyn H., etc. Sire of Pilate, Friar's Carse, Apprehension, Inchcape, Black Curl, Emotion, Heloise, Tenez.

FRIZETTE, 1905-unknown. B. f., Hamburg—*Ondulee, by St. Simon. 36-12-8-7, $16,135, Rosedale S., Laureate S., etc. Dam of Banshee, Durzetta, *Lespedeza II. Foundation mare of family that includes Myrtlewood, Seattle Slew, Mr. Prospector, Tourbillon, Sinndar, Cordova, Darshaan, Corejada, *Apollonia, Akiyda, Acamas, Akarad, *Priam II, *Djeddah, Sing Sing, Jet Pilot, Shecky Greene, Typecast, Bahri, Forestry, Chief Bearhart, Escena, Dahlia, Vitriolic, Vagrancy, Anees, Truly Bound, Baldric, Honorable Miss.

FUSAICHI PEGASUS, 1997- . B. c., Mr. Prospector—Angel Fever, by Danzig. 9-6-2-0, $1,994,400, Kentucky Derby (G1), Wood Memorial S. (G2), etc. Syndicated for a world-record $60-million to $70-million in 2000. Sire of Bandini.

GALLANT BLOOM, 1966-1991. B. f., *Gallant Man—Multiflora, by Beau Max. 22-16-1-1, $535,739, champion two- and three-year-old filly, champion handicap mare, Santa Margarita Invitational H., Spinster S., Monmouth Oaks, etc.

GALLANT FOX, 1927-1954. B. c., *Sir Gallahad III—Marguerite, by Celt. 17-11-3-2, $328,165, consensus Horse of the Year in 1930, champion three-year-old colt, Triple Crown, Jockey Club Gold Cup, etc. Sire of 18 stakes winners, including Omaha, Granville, Flares.

****GALLANT MAN***, 1954-1988. B. c., *Migoli—*Majideh, by *Mahmoud. 26-14-4-1, $510,355, Belmont S.-ntr, Jockey Club Gold Cup, etc. Sire of 51 stakes winners, including Gallant Bloom, Gallant Romeo, War Censor, Spicy Living, Ring Twice. Broodmare sire of Genuine Risk, *Habitony, Lord Avie.

Leading sire in 1997 and '98. Sire of more than 80 stakes winners, including Go for Wand, Open Mind, Awesome Again, Dehere, Touch Gold. Broodmare sire of more than 105 stakes winners, including Halfbridled.

DESERT VIXEN, 1970-1982. Dk. b. or br. f., In Reality—Desert Trial, by Moslem Chief. 28-13-6-3, $421,538, champion three-year-old filly, champion older female, Alabama S. (G1), Beldame S. (G1) twice, etc. Dam of Real Shadai; full sister to Valid Appeal.

DETERMINE, 1951-1972. Gr. c., *Alibhai—Koubis, by *Mahmoud. 44-18-7-9, $573,360, Kentucky Derby, Santa Anita Derby, etc. First gray winner of the Kentucky Derby. Sire of 21 stakes winners, including Decidedly, Warfare, Donut King. Broodmare sire of Bold 'n Determined, Gummo, Princess Pout.

DEVIL DIVER, 1939-1961. B. c., *St. Germans—Dabchick, by *Royal Minstrel. 47-22-12-3, $261,064, champion handicap horse twice, Metropolitan H. twice, Suburban H., Whitney S., etc. Sire of 17 stakes winners, including Beau Diable, Call Over, Ruddy.

***DIOMED**, 1777-1808. Ch. c., Florizel—Spectator mare (sister to Juno), by Spectator. 20-11-5-3, $38,200, champion three-year-old in England. First winner of the Epsom Derby. Sire of Sir Archy, Haynie's Maria, Ball's Florizel, Duroc, Fanny, Young Giantess, Potomac, Virginius. Imported to U.S. in 1798. Tail-male ancestor of Boston, Lexington.

DISCOVERY, 1931-1958. Ch. c., Display—Ariadne, by *Light Brigade. 63-27-10-10, $195,287, Horse of the Year in 1935, champion handicap horse twice, Whitney S. three times, Brooklyn H. three times, etc. Sire of 25 stakes winners, including Conniver, Miss Disco, Find, Loser Weeper, Traffic Court. Broodmare sire of Bold Ruler, Native Dancer, Intentionally, Hasty Road, Traffic Judge, Bed o' Roses. Famed as a weight carrier.

DISGUISE, 1897-1927. B. c., Domino—*Bonnie Gal, by Galopin. 8-3-0-4, $40,275, Jockey Club S., 3rd Epsom Derby, etc. Sire of Maskette, Court Dress, Harmonicon, Helmet, Miss Puzzle, Wonder, Comely.

DISPLAY, 1923-1944. B. c., Fair Play—*Cicuta, by *Nassovian. 103-23-25-27, $256,326, Preakness S., Hawthorne Gold Cup, etc. Sire of 11 stakes winners, including Discovery, Parade Girl.

DOMINO, 1891-1897. Br. c., Himyar—Mannie Gray, by Enquirer. 25-19-2-1, $193,550, Champion two-year-old, Futurity S., Withers S., etc. Sire of Commando, Cap and Bells, Disguise, Noonday, Running Stream, Pink Domino. Sired only 20 foals in two crops, eight stakes winners, two classic winners.

DR. FAGER, 1964-1976. B. c., Rough'n Tumble—Aspidistra, by Better Self. 22-18-2-1, $1,002,642, Horse of the Year in 1968, champion older horse, champion sprinter twice, champion grass horse, Whitney S., Vosburgh H. twice, etc. Leading sire in 1977. Sire of 35 stakes winners, including Dr. Patches, Dearly Precious, L'Alezane, Dr. Blum, Tree of Knowledge, Lie Low, Lady Love. Broodmare sire of Cure the Blues, Equalize, Fappiano, Quiet American, Sewickley. Won every championship for which he was eligible in 1968.

DUKE OF MAGENTA, 1875-1899. B. c., Lexington—Magenta, by *Yorkshire. 19-15-3-1, $45,913, Belmont S., Preakness S., Travers S., etc. Sire of Duke, Eric, Ballyhoo. Sent to England with Parole after three-year-old season, but became a roarer and never raced again.

EASY GOER, 1986-1994. Ch. c., Alydar—Relaxing, by Buckpasser. 20-14-5-1, $4,873,770, champion two-year-old male, Belmont S. (G1), Jockey Club Gold Cup (G1), etc. Sire of nine stakes winners, including Will's Way, My Flag, Furlough. Broodmare sire of champion Storm Flag Flying.

ECLIPSE, 1764-1789. Ch. c
Regulus. 18-18-0-0, undefeated
won 11 King's Plates. Never lea
11 times. Sire of Pot8O's, King
gannon, Alexander, Joe Andre
Saltram, Volunteer. Tail-male lin
95% of modern Thoroughbreds,
perion, Blandford lines.

***ECLIPSE**, 1855-1878. B. c.,
Middleton. 9-4-0-1, $9,015, New
Sire of Alarm, Ruthless. Tail-male
Plaudit, Dr. Fager, Holy Bull, B

EIGHT THIRTY, 1936-1965.
Time, by High Time. 27-16-3-5,
Whitney S., Metropolitan H., etc
ners, including Sailor, Bolero, R
fume, Sunday Evening, Make
Broodmare sire of Cornish Prin
Your Peace, Jaipur, Rare Treat.

ELKRIDGE, 1938-1961. B. g.
by Black Toney. 123-31-18-15, $230
chaser twice, North American St
River Stp. H. four times, etc.

EMPEROR OF NORFOLK,
folk—Marian, by Malcolm. 29-2
can Derby, Brooklyn Derby, etc.
del Carreras), Cruzados. Buried

ENDURANCE BY RIGHT, 1
tor B.—*Early Morn, by Silvest
champion two-year-old filly, Cham
etc. Dam of Stamina. Tail-female
includes Plucky Play, Windjamm

***EPINARD**, 1920-unknown. C
Blanche, by *Rock Sand. 20-12-6-
two-year-old in France, Grand C
han, etc. Great French champio
each of three international races i
Rodosto, Marica, Epithet.

EQUIPOISE, 1928-1938. Ch.
ing, by Broomstick. 51-29-10-4, $
Year in 1932 and '33, champion h
times, champion two-year-old colt,
Whitney S., etc. Leading sire in 19
winners, including Shut Out, Leve
Attention, Swing and Sway. Brood
Myrtle Charm.

EXCELLER, 1973-1997. B. c., *
Bald, by Bald Eagle. 33-15-5-6, $1,
Gold Cup (G1), Grand Prix de Pa
of 19 stakes winners, including Sl
Song. Died in a slaughterhouse in

EXTERMINATOR, 1915-1945.
Fair Empress, by Jim Gore. 100-50-
tucky Derby, Saratoga Cup twice,
stakes races. Won 19 times carrying

FAIRMOUNT, 1921-unknown.
Sunflower, by *Rock Sand. 22-12-5
Gwathmey Memorial Steeplechase
ley Memorial Steeplechase H., etc.

FAIR PLAY, 1905-1929. Ch. c.
Gold, by Bend Or. 32-10-11-3, $86,9
Island Jockey Club S., etc. Leading
leading broodmare sire in 1931, '34
War, Chance Play, Mad Hatter, Dis
Mad Play, Ladkin, Chatterton, Ol
Masda, Native Wit, Oval. Broodmare
Jamestown, Stagehand, Sun Beau.
of line leading to In Reality, Valid A

FAIRWAY, 1925-1948. B. c., Pha

by Chau
old in E
Leading
sire in E
Copy, Fa
bon, Tid
leads to
ard, Lor
FAL
Water, b
oress S.
nine sta
ern Asp
(Ire), Fo
cludes I
nadim,
FAS
Blue, by
with Bo
mile he
FAV
Trick—
$1,726,
year-old
(G1), et
be vote
*FE
vertail,
won thr
Sire of S
Apollo,
Goldfin
FER
Luka, b
Year in
(G1), F
stakes
to Japa
FIR
Florida
mouth
ancest
FIR
Swatte
two-ye
feated
FIR
Hilden
pion tw
Sire of
Family
FL
izontal
pion st
Cup In
Steepl
FL
fidenc
grass
(G1) t
FL
Bed,
Delaw
His M
FO
Pleas
$1,216
(G1),
etc. Si
Marfa

GALLORETTE, 1942-1959. Ch. f., *Challenger II—Gallette, by *Sir Gallahad III. 72-21-20-13, $445,535, champion handicap mare, Metropolitan H., Whitney S., Beldame H., etc. World's leading money-earning female at retirement. Dam of Mlle. Lorette, Courbette. Foundation mare of family that includes Minstrella, Misty Gallore, Silver Ghost, White Gloves, Greenwood Lake, Dancing Moss.

GAMELY, 1964-1975. B. f., Bold Ruler—Gambetta, by *My Babu. 41-16-9-6, $574,961, champion three-year-old filly, champion older mare twice, Alabama S., Beldame S. twice, etc. Dam of Cellini.

GENUINE RISK, 1977- . Ch. f., Exclusive Native—Virtuous, by *Gallant Man. 15-10-3-2, $646,587, champion three-year-old filly, Kentucky Derby (G1), Ruffian H. (G1), etc. Second filly to win Kentucky Derby.

GHOSTZAPPER, 2000-. B. h., Awesome Again—Baby Zip, by Relaunch. 11-9-0-1, $3,446,120, 2004 Horse of the Year and champion older male, Breeders' Cup Classic (G1) in track and stakes record, Metropolitan H. (G1), Vosburgh H. (G1), Woodward S. (G1), etc.

***GLENCOE**, 1831-1858. Ch. c., Sultan—Trampoline, by Tramp. 10-8-1-1, $33,459, Two Thousand Guineas, Ascot Gold Cup, etc. Sire of Pocahontas, Peytona, Reel, Pryor, Star Davis, Vandal. Male-line ancestor of Hanover, Hamburg.

GODOLPHIN ARABIAN, 1724-1753. Br. c. of unknown parentage. Leading sire in England three times. Sire of Cade, Lath, Dismal, Regulus, Babraham, Blank. One of three male-line foundation sires of the Thoroughbred breed. Tail-male ancestor of Matchem line leading to Man o' War, In Reality, Tiznow.

GO FOR WAND, 1987-1990. B. f., Deputy Minister—Obeah, by Cyane. 13-10-2-0, $1,373,338, champion two- and three-year-old filly, Alabama S. (G1), Breeders' Cup Juvenile Fillies (G1), etc. Died at three in Breeders' Cup Distaff (G1). Buried in infield at Saratoga Race Course.

GOOD AND PLENTY, 1900-1907. B. g., Rossington—Famine, by Jils Johnson. 21-14-4-1, $45,815, Grand National Steeplechase H., Westbury Steeplechase H., etc.

GRANVILLE, 1933-1951. B. c., Gallant Fox—Gravita, by *Sarmatian. 18-8-4-3, $111,820, Horse of the Year in 1936, champion three-year-old colt, Belmont S., Travers S., etc. Sired only two stakes winners.

GREY LAG, 1918-1942. Ch. c., *Star Shoot—Miss Minnie, by *Meddler. 47-25-9-3, $136,715, Horse of the Year in 1921, champion three-year-old colt, champion handicap horse twice, Belmont S., Metropolitan H., Suburban H., etc. Shy breeder, sired only one stakes winner from 17 foals.

GUN BOW, 1960-unknown. B. c., Gun Shot—Ribbons and Bows, by War Admiral. 42-17-8-4, $798,722, Metropolitan H., Whitney S., etc. Sire of six stakes winners, including Pistol Packer. Exported to Japan in 1973.

HAIL TO REASON, 1958-1976. Br. c., *Turn-to—Nothirdchance, by Blue Swords. 18-9-2-2, $328,434, champion two-year-old colt, Hopeful S., Sanford S., etc. Broke down and retired at end of two-year-old season. Leading sire in 1970. Sire of 43 stakes winners, including Roberto, Halo, Stop the Music, Mr. Leader, Bold Reason, Trillion, Priceless Gem, Straight Deal, Hail to All, Regal Gleam, Personality, Proud Clarion, Admiring. Broodmare sire of Allez France, Escaline (Fr), Royal Glint, Silver Buck, Triptych. Tail-male ancestor of line that includes Saint Ballado, Sunday Silence, Red Ransom, Brian's Time.

HALO, 1969-2000. Dk. b. or br. c., Hail to Reason—Cosmah, by Cosmic Bomb. 31-9-8-5, $259,553, United Nations H. (G1), Tidal H. (G2), etc. Leading sire in 1983 and '89. Sire of 63 stakes winners, including Sunday Silence, Sunny's Halo, Glorious Song, Devil's Bag, Saint Ballado, Rainbow Connection, Goodbye Halo, Lively One, Jolie's Halo, Coup de Folie. Broodmare sire of Halo America, Machiavellian, Pine Bluff, Rahy, Singspiel (Ire).

HAMBURG, 1895-1915. B. c., Hanover—Lady Reel, by Fellowcraft. 21-16-3-2, $60,380, consensus champion three-year-old colt, Lawrence Realization, Brighton Cup, etc. Leading sire in 1905. Sire of Artful, Borrow, Burgomaster, Frizette, Prince Eugene, Lady Hamburg II, Biturica, Jersey Lightning, Rosie O'Grady.

HANOVER, 1884-1899. Ch. c., Hindoo—Bourbon Belle, by *Bonnie Scotland. 50-32-14-2, $118,887, consensus champion three-year-old colt, Belmont S., Lawrence Realization, etc. Won 17 consecutive races. Leading sire 1895-'98. Sire of Hamburg, Abe Frank, Blackstock, David Garrick, Halma, Handspun, Rhoda B., Tea's Over, The Commoner, Urania, Yankee.

HARRY BASSETT, 1868-1878. Ch. c., Lexington—Canary Bird, by *Albion. 36-23-6-3 $59,450, consensus champion three-year-old colt, Belmont S., Travers S., etc.

HASTINGS, 1893-1917. Br. c., Spendthrift—*Cinderella, by Tomahawk or Blue Ruin. 21-10-8-0, $16,340, Belmont S., Toboggan H., etc. Leading sire 1902, '08. Sire of Fair Play, Gunfire, Don Enrique, Flittergold, Masterman. Notorious for his savage temperament.

HAYNIE'S MARIA, 1808-unknown. Ch. f., *Diomed—Bellair mare, by Bellair. 9-8-1-0. Won at distances from four furlongs to four-mile heats. Famed as the nemesis of the stable of Andrew Jackson who said, "I could not beat her."

***HELIOPOLIS**, 1936-1959. B. c., Hyperion—Drift, by Swynford. 15-5-2-1, $71,216, Prince of Wales's S., Imperial Produce S., etc. Leading sire in 1950, '54. Sire of 53 stakes winners, including High Gun, Olympia, Helioscope, Grecian Queen, Parlo, Berlo, Aunt Jinny, Summer Tan, Princess Turia, Camargo. Broodmare sire of Riva Ridge, Summer Guest.

HENRY (SIR HENRY), 1819-1837. Ch. c., Sir Archy—Diomed mare, by *Diomed. Southern representative in first great North-South four-mile heat match race against American Eclipse at the Union Course, New York, in 1823. Won first heat, but beaten in second and third. Won four-mile and three-mile heat races, including 1823 Jockey Club Purse at Petersburg, Virginia. Sire of Post Boy, Decatur, Alice Grey.

HENRY OF NAVARRE, 1891-1917. Ch. c., Knight of Ellerslie—Moss Rose, by *The Ill-Used. 42-29-8-3, $68,985, champion three-year-old colt, Belmont S., Travers S., etc. Sire of Grave and Gay, Orienta.

HEROD, 1758-1780. B. c., Tartar—Cypron, by Blaze. 10-6-3-0, Match against Antinous, etc. Leading sire in England eight times. Sire of Highflyer, Florizel, Woodpecker, Bridget, Bagot, Maid Of The Oaks, Phenomenom. Tail-male line ancestor of The Tetrarch, Tourbillon, *Ambiorix, Ahonoora, Dr Devious (Ire), Indian Ridge.

HIGHFLYER, 1774-1793. B. c., Herod—Rachel, by Blank. 12-12-0-0, Grosvenor S., Great Subscription Race, etc. Leading sire in England a record 13 times, record 12 in succession. Sire of Sir Peter Teazle, Delpini, Huncamunca, Noble, Rockingham, Skyscraper, Maid Of All Work, Prunella.

HIGH GUN, 1951-1962. Br. c., *Heliopolis—Rocket Gun, by Brazado. 24-11-5-4, $486,025, champion three-year-old colt, champion handicap horse, Belmont S., Jockey Club Gold Cup, etc. Virtually sterile; sired only four foals.

HILL PRINCE, 1947-1970. B. c., *Princequillo—Hildene, by Bubbling Over. 30-17-5-4, $422,140, Horse of the Year in 1950, champion two- and three-year-old colt, champion handicap horse, Preakness S., Jockey Club Gold Cup, etc. Sire of 23 stakes winners, including Bayou, Levee, Royal Living, Middle Brother. Broodmare sire of Dark Mirage, Shuvee.

HILLSDALE, 1955-1972. B. c., Take Away—Johann, by Johnstown. 41-23-6-4, $646,935, Hollywood Gold Cup H., Californian S., etc. Sire of nine stakes winners, including Bravery II and Hi Q.

HINDOO, 1878-1901. B. c., Virgil—Florence, by Lexington. 35-30-3-2, $71,875, champion two- and three-year-old colt, Kentucky Derby, Travers S., etc. Won 18 consecutive races at two and three. Sire of Hanover, Buddhist, Hindoo Rose, Jim Gore, Sallie McClelland.

HIS MAJESTY, 1968-'95. B. c., *Ribot—Flower Bowl, by *Alibhai. 22-5-6-3, $99,430, Everglades S., Leading sire in 1982. Sire of 59 stakes winners, including Pleasant Colony, Tight Spot, Majesty's Prince, Cetewayo, Mehmet. Broodmare sire of Danehill, Dynaformer, Midway Lady, Risen Star. Brother to Graustark, half brother to Bowl of Flowers.

HOLY BULL, 1991- . Gr. c., Great Above—Sharon Brown, by Al Hattab. 16-13-0-0, $2,481,760, Horse of the Year in 1994, champion three-year-old male, Travers S. (G1), Metropolitan H. (G1), etc. Sire of more than 20 stakes winners, including Macho Uno, Giacomo.

HYPERION, 1930-1960. Ch. c., Gainsborough—Selene, by Chaucer. 13-9-1-2, $124,386, champion three-year-old in England, Epsom Derby, St. Leger S., etc. Leading sire in England six times; leading broodmare sire in England four times. Sire of *Alibhai, Aristophanes, Aureole, Godiva, Gulf Stream, *Heliopolis, High Hat, *Khaled, Owen Tudor, Pensive, Sun Chariot. Broodmare sire of Alycidon, *Aunt Edith II, *Carrozza, Citation, Nearctic, Pretense. Foundation sire of line that leads to *Forli, Star Kingdom, *Vaguely Noble, Marscay, Nodouble, Efisio.

IMP, 1894-1909. Br. f., Wagner—Fondling, by Fonso. 171-62-35-29, $70,069, champion older mare twice, Suburban H., etc. Immortalized in verse as "My Coal Black Lady."

INSIDE INFORMATION, 1991-. B. m., Private Account—Pure Profit, by Key to the Mint. 17-14-1-2, $1,641,806. Champion older female in 1995 and winner of that year's Breeders' Cup Distaff (G1) by a Breeders' Cup record 13½ lengths. Also won Spinster S. (G1), Ashland S. (G1), Ruffian H. (G1), Acorn S. (G1), etc. Dam of 2005 champion three-year-old filly Smuggler.

IROQUOIS, 1878-1899. B. c., *Leamington—Maggie B.B., by *Australian. 26-12-4-3, $99,707, champion three-year-old in England, Epsom Derby, St. Leger S., etc. First American-bred winner of the Epsom Derby in 1881. Leading sire in 1892. Sire of Tammany, Huron.

JAIPUR, 1959-1987. Dk. b. c., *Nasrullah—Rare Perfume, by Eight Thirty. 19-10-6-0, $618,926, champion three-year-old colt, Belmont S., Travers S., etc. Sire of Amber Rama, Mansingh, Pontifex.

***JANUS (LITTLE JANUS)**, 1746-1780. Ch. c., Janus—Fox mare, by Fox. Won twice in England and once in the U.S. at four-mile heats. Sire of Meade's Celer, Clodius, Goode's Old Twigg. Early Colonial Thoroughbred foundation sire and foundation sire of the original Virginia Quarter Horse.

JAY TRUMP, 1957-1988. Dk. b. or br. g., Tonga Prince—Be Trump, by *Bernborough. 29-13-5-2, Grand National Steeplechase H. in England, etc. Also won three Maryland Hunt Cups.

JIM DANDY, 1927-unknown. Ch. g., Jim Gaffney—Thunderbird, by *Star Shoot. 141-7-6-8, $49,570, Travers S., Grand Union Hotel S., etc. Upset Gallant Fox and Whichone in 1930 Travers S. at 100-to-1.

JOHN HENRY, 1975- . B. g., Ole Bob Bowers—Once Double, by Double Jay. 83-39-15-9, $6,591,860, Horse of the Year 1981, '84, champion grass male four times, Santa Anita H. (G1) twice, Jockey Club Gold Cup (G1), Oak Tree Invitational (G1) three times, Hollywood Invitational H. (G1) three times, etc.

JOHN P. GRIER, 1917-1943. Ch. c., Whisk Broom II—Wonder, by Disguise. 17-10-4-2, $37,006, Queens County H., Aqueduct H., etc. Sire of more than 25 stakes winners, including Boojum, El Chico, Jack High, White Lies. Pressed Man o' War to narrowest victory in 1920 Dwyer H.

JOHNSTOWN, 1936-1950. B. c., Jamestown—La France, by *Sir Gallahad III. 21-14-0-3, $169,315, Kentucky Derby, Belmont S., etc. Sire of Flood Town, Acoma. Broodmare sire of Nashua.

JOLLY ROGER, 1922-1948. Ch. g., Pennant—Lethe, by *All Gold. 49-18-9-9, $143,240, Grand National Steeplechase H. twice, Brook Stp. H., etc.

***KAYAK II**, 1935-1946. Dk. br. c., Congreve—Mosquita, by Your Majesty. 26-14-8-1, $213,205, champion handicap horse, Santa Anita H., Hollywood Gold Cup, etc. Shy breeder.

KELSO, 1957-1983. Dk. b. or br. g., Your Host—Maid of Flight, by Count Fleet. 63-39-12-2, $1,977,896, Horse of the Year 1960-'64, champion three-year-old male, champion older horse four times, handicap triple crown, Jockey Club Gold Cup five times, Woodward S. three times, etc. Only five-time Horse of the Year.

KENTUCKY, 1861-1875. B. c., Lexington—Magnolia, by *Glencoe. 23-21-0-0, $33,700, Travers S., Saratoga Cup twice, etc. Won 20 consecutive races; first winner of the Travers S. Sire of Nina, Woodbine. Along with Norfolk and Asteroid, one of three dominant sons of Lexington, called the "great triumvirate."

***KHALED**, 1943-1968. Br. c., Hyperion—Eclair, by Ethnarch. 12-6-1-1, $38,860, Middle Park S., Coventry S., etc. Sire of 61 stakes winners, including Swaps, Terrang, Going Abroad, New Policy, Correspondent, A Glitter, Bushel-n-Peck. Broodmare sire of Candy Spots, Outing Class, Prove It.

KINCSEM, 1874-unknown. B. f., Cambuscan—Waternymph, by Cotswold. 54-54-0-0, Goodwood Cup, etc. All-time leader by number of wins among unbeaten horses. Greatest horse ever bred in Hungary. Raced all over Europe and in England.

KING'S BISHOP, 1969-1981. B. c., Round Table—Spearfish, by Fleet Nasrullah. 28-11-4-3, $308,079, Carter H. (G2), Fall Highweight H. (G3), etc. Sire of 30 stakes winners, including King's Swan, Possible Mate, Queen to Conquer, Queen Lib, Bishop's Ring.

KINGSTON, 1884-1912. Br. c., Spendthrift—*Kapanga, by Victorious. 138-89-33-12, $140,195, First Special S., etc. Leading sire in 1900, '10. Sire of Novelty, Wild Mint, Lida B. Holds American record for most races won at 89.

KINGSTON TOWN, 1976-'91. Dk. b. or br. g., Bletchingly—Ada Hunter (Ger), by Andrea Mantegna. 42-32-6-2, $1,565,015, Horse of the Year in Australia, champion miler, champion older horse, W. S. Cox Plate (Aus-G1) three times, AJC Derby (Aus-G1), Sydney Cup (Aus-G1), etc. Greatest Australian racehorse of second half of 20th century.

KOTASHAAN (FR), 1988- . Dk. b. or br. c., Darshaan—Haute Autorite, by Elocutionist. 22-10-5-2, Horse of the Year in 1993, champion grass male, Breeders' Cup Turf (G1), Eddie Read H. (G1), etc. Exported to Japan in 1994.

LADY LIGHTFOOT, 1812-1834. Br. f., Sir Archy—

Black Maria, by *Shark. Won at least 23 races, 15 at four-mile heats. Dam of Black Maria, Terror.

LADY'S SECRET, 1982-2003. Gr. f., Secretariat—Great Lady M., by Icecapade. 45-25-9-3, $3,021,325, Horse of the Year in 1986, champion older female, Breeders' Cup Distaff (G1), Whitney H. (G1), etc. All-time distaff leading earner at time of retirement.

LANDALUCE, 1980-1982. Dk. b. or br. f., Seattle Slew—Strip Poker, by Bold Bidder. 5-5-0-0, $372,365, champion two-year-old filly, Oak Leaf S. (G1), Del Mar Debutante S. (G2), etc. Died at two.

LA PREVOYANTE, 1970-1974. B. f., Buckpasser—Arctic Dancer, by Nearctic. 39-25-5-3, $572,417, champion two-year-old filly in U.S., Horse of the Year in Canada in 1972, champion two-year-old filly in Canada, champion older female in Canada, Frizette S., Spinaway S., etc. Won all 12 of her starts at two. Died at four.

***LA TROIENNE**, 1926-1954. B. f., *Teddy—Helene de Troie, by Helicon. 7-0-1-1, $146. Greatest American foundation mare of the 20th century. Dam of Bimelech, Black Helen. Foundation mare of family that includes Buckpasser, Easy Goer, Allez France, Affectionately, Busher, Glamour, Numbered Account, Private Account, Woodman, Bee Ann Mac, Autobiography, Cohoes, The Axe II, Big Hurry, Searching, Relaxing, Bridal Flower, Caerleon, Straight Deal, Glowing Tribute, Sea Hero, Lite Light, Go for Gin, Pleasant Tap, Princess Rooney, Prairie Bayou.

LECOMTE, 1850-1856. Ch. c., Boston—Reel, by *Glencoe. 16-11-5-0, $12,630, Jockey Club Purse, etc. Only horse to defeat Lexington. Sire of Umpire, Sherrod.

****L'ESCARGOT***, 1963-1984. Ch. g., Escart III—What a Daisy, by Grand Inquisitor. 63-14-15-8, $237,572, champion steeplechaser, Cheltenham Gold Cup Steeplechase H. twice, Meadow Brook Steeplechase H., etc.

LEXINGTON, 1850-1875. B. c., Boston—Alice Carneal, by *Sarpedon. 7-6-1-0, $56,600, Great State Post S., etc. Leading sire 1861-'74, '76, '78. Sire of Asteroid, Norfolk, Kentucky, Tom Ochiltree, Duke of Magenta, Tom Bowling, Harry Bassett, Sultana, Maiden, Florence, General Duke, Hira, Idlewild, Lida, Preakness, Salina, Ulrica, War Dance. Leading sire record 16 times, 14 in succession.

LONESOME GLORY, 1988-2002. Ch. g., Transworld—Stronghold (Fr), by Green Dancer. 44-24-5-6, $1,325,868, champion steeplechaser five times, Carolina Cup Hurdle S. twice, Colonial Cup Steeplechase S. twice, etc. First steeplechase millionaire.

LONGFELLOW, 1867-1893. Br. c., *Leamington—Nantura, by Brawner's Eclipse. 16-13-2-0, $11,200, Monmouth Cup twice, Saratoga Cup, etc. Leading sire in 1891. Sire of Freeland, The Bard, Thora, Longstreet, Leonatus, Riley.

LUKE BLACKBURN, 1877-1904. B. c., *Bonnie Scotland—Nevada, by Lexington. 39-25-6-2, $49,460, Champion S., Kenner S., etc. Won 22 of 24 races at three. Sire of Proctor Knott.

LYPHARD, 1969-2005. B. c., Northern Dancer—Goofed, by *Court Martial. 12-6-1-0, $195,427, Prix Jacques le Marois, Prix de la Foret, etc. Leading sire in U.S. in 1986, leading sire in France 1978 and '79; leading broodmare sire in France in 1985 and '86. Sire of 115 stakes winners, including Dancing Brave, Manila, Three Troikas (Fr), Reine de Saba (Fr), Jolypha, Dancing Maid (Fr), Pharly, Bellypha (Ire), Sangue (Ire), Sabin, Al Nasr (Fr), Elliodor, Featherhill (Fr), Lypheor (GB), Skimble. Broodmare sire of Bering (GB), Groom Dancer, Hatoof.

MAD HATTER, 1916-1935. B. or br. c., Fair Play—Madcap, by *Rock Sand. 98-32-22-15, $194,525, consensus champion handicap horse, Jockey Club Gold Cup twice, Toboggan H., etc. Sire of 22 stakes winners, including Snowflake, The Nut.

MAGGIE B.B., 1867-1889. B. f., *Australian—Madeline, by Boston. 7-3-4-0, $2,950, Sequel S. Greatest American broodmare of 19th century. Dam of Iroquois, Harold, Jaconet, Pera, Panique, Red and Blue. Tail-female ancestor of family that includes Alanesian, Boldnesian, Lawrin, Idun, Top Flight, Whisk Broom II, Life's Magic, Bald Eagle, Dubai Millennium.

***MAHMOUD**, 1933-1962. Gr. c., *Blenheim II—Mah Mahal, by Gainsborough. 11-4-2-3, $85,413, champion three-year-old in England, Epsom Derby, Champagne S., etc. Leading sire in 1946; leading broodmare sire in 1957. Sire of 66 stakes winners, including The Axe II, Oil Capitol, Cohoes, First Flight, Vulcan's Forge, Mount Marcy, Adile, Snow Goose, Almahmoud, Happy Mood, Mahmoudess. Broodmare sire of Cosmah, Determine, *Gallant Man, *Grey Dawn II, Misty Morn, Silver Spoon, Your Host. Made the gray coat color popular in America.

MAIDEN, 1862-1880. B. f., Lexington—Kitty Clark, by *Glencoe. 15-5-8-3, $5,500, Travers S., Produce S., etc. Second Travers S. winner. Dam of Parole, sixth dam of Nearco.

MAJESTIC PRINCE, 1966-1981. Ch. c., Raise a Native—Gay Hostess, by *Royal Charger. 10-9-1-0, $414,200, Kentucky Derby, Preakness S., etc. Sire of 33 stakes winners, including Majestic Light, Coastal, Sensitive Prince, Eternal Prince.

MAN O'WAR, 1917-1947. Ch. c., Fair Play—Mahubah, by *Rock Sand. 21-20-1-0, $249,465, consensus champion two- and three-year-old colt, Belmont S., Travers S., etc. Leading sire in 1926. Sire of 62 stakes winners, including War Admiral, Crusader, American Flag, War Relic, Bateau, Scapa Flow, Edith Cavell, Maid at Arms, Florence Nightingale, Battleship, Clyde Van Dusen, Hard Tack. Broodmare sire of Blue Swords, Helioscope, Mata Hari, Pavot, Vagrancy. Tail-male ancestor of line that leads to In Reality, Tiznow. Still considered by many to be the greatest racehorse of all time.

MASKETTE, 1906-c.1930. B. f., Disguise—Biturica, by Hamburg. 17-12-3-0, $77,090, consensus champion two- and three-year-old filly, Futurity S., Alabama S., Matron S., Spinaway S., etc.

MAKYBE DIVA, 1999-. B. m., Desert King—Tugela, by Riverman. 36-15-4-3, $10,767,186. 2005 Horse of the Year in Australia, Melbourne Cup (Aus-G1) three times, W. S. Cox Plate (Aus-G1), etc. Retired as world's leading female earner after winning record third Melbourne Cup.

MANILA, 1983-. B. h., Lyphard—Dona Ysidra, by *Le Fabuleux. 18-12-5-0, $2,692,799. Champion grass male in 1986, when he won the Breeders' Cup Turf (G1). Also won Arlington Million (G1), Turf Classic (G1), United Nations H. (G1) (twice), etc. Sire of Bien Bien; leading broodmare sire in Turkey in 2003.

MATA HARI, 1931-1957. Br. f., Peter Hastings—War Woman, by Man o' War. 16-7-0-2, $66,699, consensus champion two- and three-year-old filly, Breeders' Futurity, Kentucky Jockey Club S., Illinois Derby, etc. Dam of Spy Song, Mr. Music.

MATCHEM, 1748-1781. B. c., Cade—Partner mare, by Partner. 8 wins, The Whip, etc. Leading sire three times in England. Sire of Conductor, Pantaloon, Alfred, Hollandaise, Tetotum. Male-line ancestor of Man o' War, In Reality, Tiznow, Hurry On, Sassafras (Fr).

MATE, 1928-1953. Ch. c., Prince Pal—Killashandra, by *Ambassador IV. 75-20-14-19, $301,810, Preakness S., American Derby, etc. Great rival of Equipoise, Twenty

Grand. Sire of five stakes winners, including two-time champion steeplechaser Elkridge.

***MEDLEY**, 1776-1792. Gr. c., Gimcrack—Arminda, by Snap. 13 wins. Sire of Bellair, Calypso, Grey Diomed, Grey Medley, Lamplighter. Early American foundation sire.

***MESSENGER**, 1780-1808. Gr. c., Mambrino—Turf mare, by Turf. 10 wins, $7,365. Sire of Miller's Damsel, Tippoo Saib, Potomac, Bright Phoebus, Mambrino. Early American foundation sire; also foundation sire of the American Standardbred breed.

MIDDLEGROUND, 1947-1972. Ch. c., Bold Venture—Verguenza, by Chicaro. 15-6-6-2, $237,725, Kentucky Derby, Belmont S., Hopeful S., etc. Sire of seven stakes winners, including Resaca. Shy breeder.

MIESQUE, 1984- . B. f., Nureyev—Pasadoble, by Prove Out. 16-12-3-1, $2,070,163, champion grass female twice in U.S., champion two-year-old in France, champion miler in England, champion older mare in France, Breeders' Cup Mile (G1) twice, One Thousand Guineas (Eng-G1), etc. Dam of Kingmambo, East of the Moon, Miesque's Son, Moon Is Up.

MILL REEF, 1968-1986. B. c., Never Bend—Milan Mill, by *Princequillo. 14-12-2-0, $450,533, Horse of the Year in Europe, champion three-year-old in England and France, champion older horse in France, Epsom Derby, Prix de l'Arc de Triomphe, etc. Leading sire in England twice. Sire of 62 stakes winners, including Reference Point, Shirley Heights, Acamas, Glint of Gold, Ibn Bey (GB). Broodmare sire of Last Tycoon (Ire), Pentire. Tail-male ancestor of line that includes Darshaan, Dalakhani, Daylami (Ire).

MINESHAFT, 1999-. Dk.b. or br. c., A. P. Indy–Propectors Delite, by Mr. Prospector. 18-10-3-1, $2,283,402. Horse of the Year in 2003, champion older male, Jockey Club Gold Cup (G1), etc.

MISS WOODFORD, 1880-1899. Br. f., *Billet—Fancy Jane, by Neil Robinson. 48-37-7-2, $118,270, Alabama S., Spinaway S., Pimlico S., etc. First American horse to earn $100,000.

MOCCASIN, 1963-1986. Ch. f., Nantallah—*Rough Shod II, by Gold Bridge. 21-11-2-4, $388,075, Horse of the Year in 1965 Thoroughbred Racing Associations poll, champion two-year-old filly, Gardenia S., Test S., etc. Dam of Apalachee, Scuff, Flippers.

MODESTY, 1881-unknown. Ch. f., War Dance—Ballet, by Planet. 82-35-8-11, $49,135, Kentucky Oaks, American Derby, etc. First filly winner of the American Derby. Tail-female ancestor of family that includes Regret, Thunderer, First Fiddle.

MOLLIE MCCARTHY, 1873-unknown. B. f., Monday—Hennie Farrow, by Shamrock. 17-15-0-0, $18,750, Winter S., Garden City Cup, etc. One of the last great four-mile heat fillies.

MONSIEUR TONSON, 1822-unknown. B. c., Pacolet—Madame Tonson, by Top Gallant. 12-11-0-0. Leading sire in 1834. Sire of Argyle. First horse bred west of the Appalachians to win in the East.

MORVICH, 1919-unknown. Bl. c., Runnymede—Hymir, by Dr. Leggo. 16-12-2-1, $172,909, Kentucky Derby, Hopeful S., etc. First California-bred winner of the Kentucky Derby in 1922, won first 12 starts. Sire of 12 stakes winners.

MOTHER GOOSE, 1922-unknown. Br. f., *Chicle—Flying Witch, by Broomstick. 10-3-1-3, $72,755, consensus champion two-year-old filly, Futurity S. (defeated 28 others in a record field), Fashion S., etc. Dam of Arbitrator. Full sister to Whichone. Tail-female ancestor of family that includes Northern Dancer, Halo, Arctic Tern, Machiavellian, La Prevoyante, Tosmah, Danehill.

MR. PROSPECTOR, 1970-1999. B. c., Raise a Native—Gold Digger, by Nashua. 14-7-4-2, $112,171, Gravesend H., Whirlaway S., etc. Leading sire in 1987-'88; leading broodmare sire in 1997-2004. Sire of 180 stakes winners, including Forty Niner, Fusaichi Pegasus, Seeking the Gold, It's in the Air, Fappiano, Woodman, Gulch, Carson City, Conquistador Cielo, Gone West, Gold Beauty, Kingmambo, Machiavellian, Miswaki. Broodmare sire of Dayjur, Fasliyev, Hollywood Wildcat, Pulpit, Mineshaft.

MUMTAZ MAHAL, 1921-1945. Gr. f., The Tetrarch—Lady Josephine, by Sundridge. 10-7-2-0, $67,421, champion two-year-old, champion sprinter, Champagne S., Nunthorpe S., etc. Dam of Mirza II, Badruddin. Tail-female ancestor of *Nasrullah, *Royal Charger, Abernant, Petite Etoile, Shergar, Octagonal, Oh So Sharp (GB), *Migoli, Aliya, Risen Star, Left Bank, Kalamoun. Known as "the Flying Filly." Still considered by many the fastest filly ever to race in England.

MY CHARMER, 1969-1993. B. f., Poker—Fair Charmer, by Jet Action. 32-6-4-2, $34,133, Fair Grounds Oaks. Dam of Seattle Slew, Lomond, Seattle Dancer (record $13.1-million yearling).

MYRTLEWOOD, 1932-1950. B. f., Blue Larkspur—*Frizeur, by *Sweeper. 22-15-4-2, $40,620, champion sprinter, champion handicap mare, Ashland S., Hawthorne Sprint H., etc. Set five track records and equaled three. Dam of Durazna, Miss Dogwood. Foundation mare of family that includes Seattle Slew, Mr. Prospector, Myrtle Charm, Lomond, Typecast, Siberian Express, Highest Trump, Bahri, Ajina, Escena, Sewickley, Forestry, Chief Bearhart.

NASHUA, 1952-1982. B. c., *Nasrullah—Segula, by Johnstown. 30-22-4-1, $1,288,565, Horse of the Year in 1955, champion two- and three-year-old colt, Preakness S., Belmont S., Jockey Club Gold Cup twice, etc. Sire of 77 stakes winners, including Shuvee, Noble Nashua, Diplomat Way, Producer, Marshua, Bramalea, Bombay Duck, Good Manners, Nalee. Broodmare sire of Mr. Prospector, Roberto. First $1-million syndicated stallion.

***NASRULLAH**, 1940-1959. B. c., Nearco—Mumtaz Begum, by *Blenheim II. 10-5-1-2, $15,259, champion two-year-old colt in England, Champion S., Coventry S., etc. Leading sire in 1955-'56, '59-'60, '62 in U.S.; leading sire in England. Sire of 93 stakes winners, including Bold Ruler, Nashua, Never Bend, Nearula, *Musidora, Never Say Die, Jaipur, Bald Eagle, Red God, Delta, Grey Sovereign. Broodmare sire of Drumtop, Natashka, *Sovereign II, Talking Picture, Turkish Trousers. Tail-male ancestor of Bold Ruler, Never Bend, Blushing Groom (Fr), Caro (Ire) lines.

NATIVE DANCER, 1950-1967. Gr. c., Polynesian—Geisha, by Discovery. 22-21-1-0, $785,240, Horse of the Year in 1952, '54, champion two- and three-year-old colt, champion handicap horse, Belmont S., Preakness S., Travers S., Futurity S., etc. Sire of 43 stakes winners, including Raise a Native, Hula Dancer, Dan Cupid, Secret Step, Kauai King, Dancer's Image, Native Charger, Native Street, Exclusive Dancer. Broodmare sire of Northern Dancer, General Assembly, Icecapade, Ruffian. Founder of male line that includes Mr. Prospector, Alydar, *Sea-Bird, Forty Niner, Seeking the Gold, Woodman, Thunder Gulch.

NATIVE DIVER, 1959-1967. Br. g., Imbros—Fleet Diver, by Devil Diver. 81-37-7-12, $1,026,500, Hollywood Gold Cup three times, San Carlos H. twice, etc. Won 33 stakes. Became the first California-bred millionaire.

NEARCO, 1935-1957. B. c., Pharos—Nogara, by Havresac II. 14-14-0-0, $85,974, champion two- and three-year-old in Italy, Grand Prix de Paris, Derby Italiano, etc. Leading sire three times in England; leading broodmare sire three times in England. Sire of *Nasrullah, Dante, *Masaka, *Amerigo, Mossborough, Narrator, Nimbus, *Royal Charger, Sayajirao, Infatuation, *Malindi, Neasham Belle, Netherton Maid, *Rivaz. Broodmare sire of *Arctic Prince, Charlottesville, Saint Crespin III, Sheshoon, *Tulyar, *Vaguely Noble. Tail-male ancestor of Northern Dancer, Bold Ruler, Blushing Groom (Fr), Never Bend, Caro (Ire) male lines.

NEARCTIC, 1954-1973. Br. c., Nearco—*Lady Angela, by Hyperion. 47-21-5-3, $152,384, Horse of the Year in Canada in 1958, Michigan Mile, Saratoga Special S., Canadian Maturity, etc. Sire of 49 stakes winners, including Northern Dancer, Icecapade, Nonoalco, Briartic, Cool Reception, Cold Comfort, Cool Moon, Arctic Dancer, Christmas Wind. Broodmare sire of Kennedy Road, La Prevoyante.

NEEDLES, 1953-1984. B. c., Ponder—Noodle Soup, by Jack High. 21-11-3-3, $600,355, champion two- and three-year-old colt, Kentucky Derby, Belmont S., etc. Sire of 21 stakes winners, including Irish Rebellion. First Florida-bred winner of the Kentucky Derby.

NEJI, 1950-1982. Ch. g., *Hunters Moon IV—Accra, by Annapolis. 46-17-11-8, $270,694, champion steeplechaser three times, Temple Gwathmey Steeplechase H. twice, Grand National Steeplechase H. twice, etc.

NELLIE FLAG, 1932-1953. Ch. f., American Flag—Nellie Morse, by Luke McLuke. 22-6-5-1, $59,665, champion two-year-old filly, Kentucky Jockey Club S., Matron S., etc. Dam of Mar-Kell, Sunshine Nell, Nellie L. Foundation mare of family that includes Forego, Bold Forbes, Bet Twice, Lakeway, Mark-Ye-Well, Saratoga Six.

NELLIE MORSE, 1921-1941. B. f., Luke McLuke—La Venganza, by Abercorn. 34-7-9-3, $73,565, consensus champion three-year-old filly, Preakness S., Fashion S., etc. Dam of Nellie Flag, Count Morse.

NEVER SAY DIE, 1951-1975. Ch. c., *Nasrullah—Singing Grass, by War Admiral. 12-3-1-3, $89,200, champion three-year-old in England, Epsom Derby, St. Leger S., etc. Leading sire in England in 1962. Sire of 41 stakes winners, including Never Too Late, Saidam, Die Hard. Broodmare sire of 95 stakes winners. Second American-bred to win the Epsom Derby. First American-bred to lead English sire list.

NEXT MOVE, 1947-1968. Br. f., Bull Lea—Now What, by Chance Play. 46-17-11-3, $398,550, champion three-year-old filly, champion older mare, Coaching Club American Oaks, Beldame H. twice, etc. Dam of Good Move, Restless Native. Fourth dam of Peteski.

NIJINSKY II, 1967-1992. B. c., Northern Dancer—Flaming Page, by Bull Page. 13-11-2-0, $667,220, Horse of the Year in Europe in 1970, champion two- and three-year-old in England and Ireland, English Triple Crown, King George VI and Queen Elizabeth S., etc. Last winner of the English Triple Crown. Leading sire in England in 1986; leading broodmare sire in U.S. in 1993-'94. Sire of 155 stakes winners, including Caerleon, Lammtarra, Ferdinand, Ile de Bourbon, Sky Classic, Golden Fleece, Royal Academy, Green Dancer, Number, Javamine, Maplejinsky. Broodmare sire of more than 245 stakes winners, including Fantastic Light, Flawlessly, Forest Flower, Heavenly Prize, Java Gold, Rubiano, Sky Beauty.

NODOUBLE, 1965-1990. Ch. c., *Noholme II—Abla-Jay, by Double Jay. 42-13-11-5, $846,749, champion handicap horse twice, Santa Anita H., Metropolitan H., etc. Leading sire in 1981. Sire of 91 stakes winners, including Overskate, Mairzy Doates, Coolawin, Chain Store. Broodmare sire of 89 stakes winners, including Sky Classic, Regal Classic.

****NOOR***, 1945-1974. Br. c., *Nasrullah—Queen of Baghdad, by *Bahram. 31-12-5-3, $356,940, champion handicap horse, Santa Anita H., Hollywood Gold Cup H., etc. Sire of Yours, Flutterby, Noureddin. Broodmare sire of Dancer's Image, Delta Judge. Defeated Citation four times at five.

NORFOLK, 1861-1890. B. c., Lexington—Novice, by *Glencoe. 5-5-0-0, $10,550, Jersey Derby, etc. Sire of Emperor of Norfolk, El Rio Rey, Flood, Ralston. Member of sire Lexington's "great triumvirate" with Asteroid and Kentucky.

NORTHERN DANCER, 1961-1990. B. c. Nearctic—Natalma, by Native Dancer. 18-14-2-2, $580,647, champion three-year-old colt, Horse of the Year in 1964 in Canada, champion two-year-old colt in Canada, Kentucky Derby, Preakness S., etc. Leading sire in U.S. in 1971, leading broodmare sire in U.S. in 1991; leading sire in England four times. Sire of 146 stakes winners, including Nijinsky II, Sadler's Wells, Nureyev, The Minstrel, El Gran Senor, Storm Bird, Lyphard, Northern Taste, Northfields, Unfuwain, Northernette, Fanfreluche, Shareef Dancer, Try My Best, Be My Guest, Cool Mood, Dixieland Band. Broodmare sire of more than 240 stakes winners, including Arazi, Eillo, L'Alezane, L'Enjoleur, Narita Brian, Noverre, Rhythm, Ryafan, Southern Halo.

NUREYEV, 1977-2001. B. c., Northern Dancer—Special, by *Forli. 3-2-0-0, $42,522, champion miler in France, Prix Thomas Bryon (Fr-G3), Prix Djebel. Disqualified from victory in 1980 Two Thousand Guineas (Eng-G1). Leading sire twice in France. Sire of more than 135 stakes winners, including Miesque, Peintre Celebre, Theatrical (Ire), Soviet Star, Sonic Lady, Fasliyev. Broodmare sire of more than 135 stakes winners, including Desert King, East of the Moon, Kingmambo, Peteski, Zabeel.

OEDIPUS, 1946-1978. Br. g., Blue Larkspur—Be Like Mom, by *Sickle. 58-14-12-9, $132,405, champion steeplechaser three times, Grand National Steeplechase H., Brook Steeplechase H. twice, etc.

OLD ROSEBUD, 1911-1922. B. g., Uncle—Ivory Bells, by Himyar. 80-40-13-8, $74,729, Kentucky Derby, Carter H., Flash S., etc. Set Kentucky Derby record that stood for 17 years.

OMAHA, 1932-1959. Ch. c., Gallant Fox—Flambino, by *Wrack. 22-9-7-2, $154,705, champion three-year-old colt, Triple Crown, Dwyer S., Classic S., etc. Sire of seven stakes winners, including Prevaricator. Broodmare sire of Summer Tan.

ONE COUNT, 1949-1966. Dk. br. c., Count Fleet—Ace Card, by Case Ace. 23-9-3-3, $245,625, Horse of the Year in 1952, champion three-year-old colt, Belmont S., Travers S., etc. Sire of 12 stakes winners, including Airmans Guide. Broodmare sire of Fit to Fight, Obeah.

***ORMONDE**, 1883-1904. B. c., Bend Or—Lily Agnes, by Macaroni. 16-16-0-0, $138,340, Champion at two, three, and four in England, English Triple Crown. Sire of Orme, Ormondale, *Gold Finch, Ossary. Progressively sterile. Tail-male ancestor of *Teddy line. Widely considered the greatest English racehorse of 19th century; he was a roarer.

PAN ZARETA, 1910-1918. Ch. f., Abe Frank—Caddie Griffith, by Rancocas. 151-76-31-21, $39,082, Juarez H., Rio Grande H., etc. Won carrying 140 pounds or more five times. Died at eight and is buried in infield at Fair Grounds. Holds record for most wins by American distaffer.

***PAPYRUS**, 1920-1941. Br. c., Tracery—Miss Matty, by Marcovil. 18-9-5-1, $110,068, Epsom Derby, Chester Vase, etc. First Epsom Derby winner to race in the U.S.

in international match race against Zev in 1923. Sire of Barbara Burrini, *Cosquilla, *Osiris II, Honey Buzzard.

PARLO, 1951-1978. Ch. f., *Heliopolis—Fairy Palace, by Pilate. 34-8-6-3, $309,240, champion three-year-old filly, champion handicap mare twice, Alabama S., Beldame H., etc. Tail-female ancestor of Arts and Letters, Silverbulletday, Saudi Poetry, Zaccio, Waquoit.

PAROLE, 1873-1903. Br. g., *Leamington—Maiden, by Lexington. 127-59-22-16, $82,111, Saratoga Cup, Epsom Gold Cup (in England), etc. Leading American money winner 1881-1885.

PASEANA (Arg), 1987-. B. f., Ahmad—Pasiflin (Arg), by Flintham. 36-19-10-2, $3,317,427, champion older female twice, Breeders' Cup Distaff (G1), Milady H. (G1) twice, Apple Blossom H. (G1) twice, etc.

PAVOT, 1942-1975. Br. c., Case Ace—Coquelicot, by Man o' War. 32-14-6-2, $373,365, undefeated champion two-year-old colt, Belmont S., Futurity S., etc. Sire of 14 stakes winners, including Andre, Cigar Maid.

PERSONAL ENSIGN, 1984-. B. f., Private Account—Grecian Banner, by Hoist the Flag. 13-13-0-0, $1,679,880, champion older female, Breeders' Cup Distaff (G1), Beldame S. (G1) twice, etc. Broodmare of the Year in 1996. Dam of My Flag, Miner's Mark, Traditionally; grandam of Storm Flag Flying.

PETER PAN, 1904-1933. B. c., Commando—*Cinderella, by Hermit. 17-10-3-1, $115,450, Belmont S., Hopeful S., etc. Sire of Black Toney, Pennant, Peter Hastings, Tryster, Prudery, Vexatious, Panoply, Wendy.

PEYTONA, 1839-1858. Ch. f., *Glencoe—Giantess, by *Leviathan. 8-6-1-0, $62,400, Peyton S., North-South Match, etc. One-time leading American money earner; defeated Fashion in last great North-South match race.

PHALARIS, 1913-1931. B. c., Polymelus—Bromus, by Sainfoin. 24-16-2-1, $26,376, Challenge S. twice, Stud Produce S., etc. Leading sire twice in England. Sire of 65 stakes winners, including Pharos, Fairway, Colorado, Manna, Fair Isle, *Sickle, *Pharamond II, Chatelaine. Broodmare sire of *Easton, Godiva, Mid-day Sun, Picture Play. Tail-male ancestor of *Nasrullah, Northern Dancer, Native Dancer, Buckpasser sire lines.

PHARIS, 1936-1957. Br. c., Pharos—Carissima, by Clarissimus. 3-3-0 0, $47,531, champion three-year-old in France, Prix du Jockey-Club (French Derby), Grand Prix de Paris, etc. Leading sire in France four times. Sire of *Ardan, Auriban, Philius, Dynamiter, *Priam II, Asterblute. Greatest horse bred in France in first half of 20th century. Racing career cut short by World War II; confiscated by the Nazis during the war and spent five years in Germany.

***PHAR LAP**, 1926-1932. Ch. g., Night Raid—Entreaty, by Winkie. 51-37-3-2, $305,921, AJC Derby, Victoria Derby, W. S. Cox Plate twice; won Agua Caliente H. in only start in North America; died shortly after under mysterious circumstances. Considered Australia's greatest racehorse.

PLANET, 1855-1875. Ch. c., Revenue—Nina, by Boston. 31-27-4-0, $69,700, Great Post S. twice, etc. Sire of Katy Pease, Hubbard, Ballet. Replaced Peytona as America's leading money earner.

PLAUDIT, 1895-1919 B. c., Himyar—*Cinderella, by Tomahawk or Blue Ruin. 20-8-5-0, $32,715, Kentucky Derby, Champagne S., etc. Sire of King James, Casuarina, Rosa Mundi, Spoonful. Tail-male ancestor of Dr. Fager, Holy Bull, Giacomo.

POCAHONTAS, 1837-1870. B. f., *Glencoe—Marpessa, by Muley. 9-0-3-0, $0. Greatest English broodmare of 19th century, dam of Stockwell, King Tom, Rataplan. Ancestress of modern families that include foundation mares Rosy Legend, Kizil-Kourgan, Traverse, Traffic Court, Segula as well as racehorses and sires Dante, Sayajirao, *Ksar, *Kantar, Traffic Judge, Hasty Road, Nashua, Louis Quatorze.

POINT GIVEN, 1998- . Ch. c., Thunder Gulch—Turko's Turn, by Turkoman. 13-9-3-0, $3,968,500, Horse of the Year in 2001, champion three-year-old male, Belmont S. (G1), Preakness S. (G1), etc.

POT8O'S, 1773-unknown. Ch. c., Eclipse—Sportsmistress, by Sportsman. 30 wins in England, Craven S., Jockey Club Plate three times, etc. Sire of Champion, Coriander, Mandane, Waxy. Tail-male line ancestor of Phalaris, Hyperion, Blandford, Domino lines.

PREAKNESS, 1867-1881. B. c., Lexington—Bayleaf, by *Yorkshire. 39-18-11-5, $43,679, Dinner Party S., Saratoga Cup, etc. Sire in England of Fiddler, Piccadilly.

PRECISIONIST, 1981- . Ch. c., Crozier—Excellently, by *Forli. 46-20-10-4, $3,485,398, champion sprinter, Breeders' Cup Sprint (G1), Woodward S. (G1), etc. Virtually sterile. Sired only four foals.

PRETTY POLLY, 1901-1931. Ch. f., Gallinule—Admiration, by Saraband. 24-22-2-0, $187,780, champion two- and three-year-old in England, Epsom Oaks, St. Leger S., Coronation Cup twice, etc. Dam of Molly Desmond, Polly Flinders. Tail-female ancestor of Abadan, Arabella, Brigadier Gerard, Carroll House, *Daumier, Donatello II, Flute Enchantee, Flying Water, Luthier, Marwell, Nearctic, Northern Taste, Premonition, Psidium, St. Paddy, Supreme Court, Swain (Ire). Widely regarded as the greatest English racemare of all time; known as "the peerless Pretty Polly."

PRIMONETTA, 1958-1993. Ch. f., Swaps—Banquet Bell, by Polynesian. 25-17-2-2, $306,690, champion older mare, Alabama S., Spinster S. twice, etc. Broodmare of the Year in 1978; dam of Prince Thou Art, Maud Muller, Cum Laude Laurie, Grenfall. Sister to Chateaugay.

***PRINCEQUILLO**, 1940-1964. B. c., Prince Rose—*Cosquilla, by *Papyrus. 33-12-5-7, $96,550, Jockey Club Gold Cup, Saratoga Cup, etc. Leading sire 1957-'58; leading broodmare sire 1966-'70, '72, '73, '76. Sire of 65 stakes winners, including Round Table, Dedicate, Prince John, How, Quill, Hill Prince, Misty Morn, Princessnesian, Discipline. Broodmare sire of Bold Lad, *Comtesse de Loir, Fort Marcy, Key to the Mint, Kris S., Mill Reef, Secretariat, Sham, Sir Gaylord.

PRINCESS DOREEN, 1921-1952. B. f., *Spanish Prince II—Lady Doreen, by Ogden. 94-34-15-17, $174,754, Coaching Club American Oaks, Saratoga H., etc. Dam of Miss Doreen. Tail-female ancestor of Brown Bess, Caller I. D.

PRINCESS ROONEY, 1980- . Gr. f., Verbatim—Parrish Princess, by Drone. 21-17-2-1, $1,343,339, champion older female, Breeders' Cup Distaff (G1), Spinster S. (G1), etc.

PRIORESS, 1853-1868. B. f., *Sovereign—Reel, by *Glencoe. 24-10-1-3, $22,637, Cesarewitch H., two Queen's Plates, etc. First American-bred to win in England, victorious in a runoff after a dead heat in the 1857 Cesarewitch H.

PROCTOR KNOTT, 1886-unknown. Ch. g., Luke Blackburn—Tallapoosa, by *Great Tom. 26-11-6-4, $80,040, Futurity S., Junior Champion S., 2nd Kentucky Derby, etc. First winner of the Futurity Stakes (now at Belmont Park) in 1888, the race that swung the pendulum of American racing toward two-year-old speed because of its large purse.

PRUDERY, 1918-1930. B. f., Peter Pan—Polly Flinders, by Burgomaster. 22-7-6-5, $47,625, consensus champion two-year-old filly, Alabama S., Spinaway S., etc. Dam of Whiskery, Victorian, Halcyon. Tail-female ancestor of Taylor's Special.

QUESTIONNAIRE, 1927-1950. B. c., Sting—Miss Puzzle, by Disguise. 45-19-8-4, $89,611, Metropolitan H., Brooklyn H., etc. Sire of 24 stakes winners, including Requested, Free For All, Carolyn A., Hash, Stefanita, Third Degree. Tail-male line ancestor of Dr. Fager, Holy Bull, Giacomo.

RAISE A NATIVE, 1961-1988. Ch. c., Native Dancer—Raise You, by Case Ace. 4-4-0-0, $45,955, champion two-year-old colt, Juvenile S., Great American S. Sire of 78 stakes winners, including Alydar, Mr. Prospector, Exclusive Native, Majestic Prince, Laomedonte, Crowned Prince, Native Royalty, Marshua's Dancer, Native Partner, Where You Lead. Broodmare sire of Ajdal, Meadowlake, Slightly Dangerous.

REAL DELIGHT, 1949-1969. B. f., Bull Lea—Blue Delight, by Blue Larkspur. 15-12-1-0, $261,822, champion three-year-old filly, champion handicap mare, Coaching Club American Oaks, Kentucky Oaks, etc. Dam of Plum Cake, No Fooling, Spring Sunshine. Foundation mare of family that includes Alydar, Our Mims, Codex, Rich Cream, Christmas Bonus, Grand Slam, Sugar and Spice, Christmas Past.

REAL QUIET, 1995- . B. c., Quiet American—Really Blue, by Believe It. 20-6-5-6, $3,271,802, champion three-year-old male, Kentucky Derby (G1), Preakness S. (G1), Hollywood Gold Cup S. (G1), etc. Came within a nose of winning Triple Crown in 1998 Belmont S. (G1). Sire of No Place Like It.

REEL, 1838-unknown. Gr. f., *Glencoe—*Gallopade, by Catton. 8-7-1-0. Dam of Lecomte, Prioress, Starke, War Dance. Tail-female ancestor of modern family that includes Two Lea, Tim Tam, Miz Clementine, Best Turn, Chris Evert, Chief's Crown, Winning Colors.

REGRET, 1912-1934. Ch. f., Broomstick—Jersey Lightning, by Hamburg. 11-9-1-0, $35,093, Kentucky Derby, Hopeful S., etc. First filly to win the Kentucky Derby. Tail-female ancestor of family that includes First Fiddle, Divine Comedy.

REIGH COUNT, 1925-1948. Ch. c., *Sunreigh—*Contessina, by Count Schomberg. 27-12-4-0, $178,170, champion two- and three-year-old colt, Kentucky Derby, Jockey Club Gold Cup S., Coronation Cup (in England), etc. Sire of 22 stakes winners, including Count Fleet, Triplicate, Count Arthur. Broodmare sire of Gallahadion.

REVENUE, 1843-unknown. B. c., *Trustee—Rosalie Somers, by Sir Charles. 21-16-5-0. Jockey Club Purse, Proprietor's Purse, etc. Leading sire in 1860. Sire of Planet, Fanny Washington, Revolver.

***RIBOT**, 1952-1972. B. c., Tenerani—Romanella, by El Greco. 16-16-0-0, $288,648, champion at two, three, and four in Italy, champion at four in England and France, Prix de l'Arc de Triomphe twice, King George VI and Queen Elizabeth S., etc. Leading sire three times in England. Sire of 65 stakes winners, including Arts and Letters, Tom Rolfe, Graustark, His Majesty, Ragusa, Molvedo, *Prince Royal II. Broodmare sire of more than 100 stakes winners, including Cannonade, Cascapedia, Majestic Light, Grandsire of Pleasant Colony.

RIVA RIDGE, 1969-1985. B. c., First Landing—Iberia, by *Heliopolis. 30-17-3-1, $1,111,497, champion two-year-old male, champion handicap male, Kentucky Derby, Belmont S., etc. Sire of 29 stakes winners, including Tap Shoes, Rivalero, Blitey. Broodmare sire of more than 45 stakes winners, including Life At the Top.

RIVERMAN, 1969-1999. B. c., Never Bend—River Lady, by Prince John. 8-5-2-1, $223,960, Poule d'Essai des Poulains (French Two Thousand Guineas), etc. Leading sire in France in 1980-'81. Sire of 128 stakes winners, including Irish River (Fr), Triptych, Bahri, Gold River (Fr), Detroit (Fr), Imperfect Circle, Korveya. Broodmare sire of Bosra Sham, Carnegie (Ire), Erhaab, Hector Protector, Highest Honor (Fr), Saint Cyrien, Spinning World.

ROAMER, 1911-1919. B. g., *Knight Errant—*Rose Tree II, by Bona Vista. 98-39-26-9, $98,828, Travers S., Carter H., Saratoga H. three times, etc.

ROBERTO, 1969-1988. B. c., Hail to Reason—Bramalea, by Nashua. 14-7-4-0, $332,272, champion three-year-old in England in 1972, champion two-year-old in Ireland in 1971, Epsom Derby, etc. Sire of 85 stakes winners, including Sunshine Forever, Brian's Time, Plenty of Grace, Dynaformer, and Red Ransom. Broodmare sire of more than 145 stakes winners, including Blushing K. D., Commander in Chief, Warning (GB).

ROCK OF GIBRALTAR (Ire), 1999- . B. c., Danehill—Offshore Boom, by Be My Guest. 13-10-2-0, $1,888,048, Horse of the Year in Europe, champion three-year-old colt, highweighted colt at three on International Classification at 7-9½ furlongs, Two Thousand Guineas (Eng-G1), Sussex S. (Eng-G1), Prix du Moulin de Longchamp (Fr-G1), etc. Won record seven Group 1 races in succession in 2001-'02.

ROSEBEN, 1901-1918. B. g., *Ben Strome—Rose Leaf, by Duke of Montrose. 111-52-25-12, $75,110, Carter H., Manhattan H. twice, etc. Great sprinter who won 14 races under 140 pounds or more, known as "the big train."

ROUGH'N TUMBLE, 1948-1968. B. c., Free For All—Roused, by *Bull Dog. 16-4-5-4, $126,980, Santa Anita Derby, Primer S., etc. Sire of 24 stakes winners, including Dr. Fager, My Dear Girl, Flag Raiser, Ruffled Feathers, Minnesota Mac, Treasure Chest. Florida foundation sire.

***ROUGH SHOD II**, 1944-1965. B. f., Gold Bridge—Dalmary, by Blandford. 7-1-1-1, $1,306. Dam of Moccasin, Ridan, Lt. Stevens, Gambetta, Thong. Foundation mare of family that includes Sadler's Wells, Nureyev, Thatch, Gamely, Drumtop, Fairy King, King Pellinore, El Condor Pasa, Number, Bienamado.

ROUND TABLE, 1954-1987. B. c., *Princequillo—*Knight's Daughter, by Sir Cosmo. 66-43-8-5, $1,749,869, Horse of the Year in 1958, champion grass horse three times, champion handicap horse twice, Santa Anita H., Hollywood Gold Cup H., etc. Leading sire in 1972. Sire of 83 stakes winners, including Baldric, Apalachee, Flirting Around, Targowice, Royal Glint, King Pellinore, Drumtop, Knightly Manner, Advocator, King's Bishop, Artaius, Dancealot, Foreseer, Poker, Tell. Broodmare sire of 125 stakes winners, including Bowl Game, Caerleon, Hidden Lake, Outstandingly, Topsider.

***ROYAL CHARGER**, 1942-1961. Ch. c., Nearco—Sun Princess by Solario. 20-6-7-2, $20,291, Queen Anne S., Ayr Gold Cup, etc. Sire of 54 stakes winners, including *Turn-to, Mongo, *Royal Serenade, Royal Native, Idun, Royal Orbit, Gilles de Retz, Happy Laughter, Royal Palm, *Banri an Oir. Broodmare sire of Majestic Prince, Tudor Queen. Tail-male ancestor of Roberto, Halo lines.

RUFFIAN, 1972-1975. Dk. b. or br. f., Reviewer—Shenanigans, by Native Dancer. 11-10-0-0, $313,428, champion two- and three-year-old filly, filly triple crown, Spinaway S. (G1), etc. Broke down in match race with Foolish Pleasure and euthanized when she reinjured leg after surgery. Buried in infield at Belmont Park.

RUTHLESS, 1864-1876. B. f., *Eclipse—Barbarity, by *Simoom. 11-7-4-0, $11,000, Belmont S., Travers S., etc. Won first Belmont S. Best of five high-class sisters out of Barbarity nicknamed "the barbarous battalion."

SABIN, 1980- . Ch. f., Lyphard—Beaconaire, by *Vaguely Noble. 25-18-0-2, $1,098,341, Yellow Ribbon

Invitational S. (G1), etc. Dam of Sabina, Al Sabin.

SADLER'S WELLS, 1981-. B. c., Northern Dancer—Fairy Bridge, by Bold Reason. 11-6-3-0, $713,690, Irish Two Thousand Guineas (Ire-G1), Eclipse S. (Eng-G1), etc. Leading sire in England 14 times. Sire of more than 255 stakes winners, including Galileo (Ire), High Chaparral (Ire), In the Wings (GB), Salsabil (Ire), Old Vic, Northern Spur (Ire), El Prado (Ire), Montjeu (Ire), Carnegie (Ire), Barathea (Ire), Imagine, King of Kings (Ire), Fort Wood. Broodmare sire of more than 120 stakes winners.

SAFELY KEPT, 1986-. B. f., Horatius—Safely Home, by Winning Hit. 31-24-2-3, $2,194,206, champion sprinter, Breeders' Cup Sprint (G1), Test S. (G1), etc.

SALVATOR, 1886-1909. Ch. c., *Prince Charlie—Salina, by Lexington. 19-16-1-1, $113,240, consensus champion three-year-old, Suburban H., Lawrence Realization, etc. Sire of Salvation. Subject of the Ella Wheeler Wilcox poem "How Salvator Won."

SARAZEN, 1921-1940. Ch. g., High Time—Rush Box, by Box. 55-27-2-6, $225,000, Champagne S., Carter H., Dixie H. twice, etc. Defeated *Epinard in third race of the International Series of 1924.

SAINT LIAM, 2000-. B. h., Saint Ballado—Quiet Dance, by Quiet American. 20-9-6-1, 2005 Horse of the Year and champion older male, Breeders' Cup Classic (G1), Stephen Foster H. (G1), Donn H. (G1), Woodward S. (G1), etc.

SCEPTRE, 1899-1927. Br. f., Persimmon—Ornament, by Bend Or. 25-13-4-4, $192,544, champion three-year-old, champion older horse, Epsom Oaks, Two Thousand Guineas, One Thousand Guineas, St. Leger S., etc. Dam of Curia, Grosvenor. Tail-female ancestor of Buchan, Commanche Run, Craig an Eran, Relko, Reliance, *Match II, *Noor, *St. Germans, Sunny Jane, Torbido. One of two fillies to win four of the five English classics.

***SEA-BIRD**, 1962-1973. Ch. c., Dan Cupid—Sicalade, by Sicambre. 8-7-1-0, $645,283, Horse of the Year in France and England, Epsom Derby, Prix de l'Arc de Triomphe, etc. Sire of 33 stakes winners, including Allez France, Little Current, Gyr, Arctic Tern. Broodmare sire of Alydar's Best, Assert (Ire), Bikala, Miss Oceana. Considered France's greatest racehorse.

SEABISCUIT, 1933-1947. B. c., Hard Tack—Swing On, by Whisk Broom II. 89-33-15-13, $437,730, Horse of the Year in 1938, champion handicap male twice, Pimlico Special, Santa Anita H., etc. Sire of four stakes winners, including Sea Swallow.

SEARCHING, 1952-1973. B. f., War Admiral—Big Hurry, by Black Toney. 89-25-14-16, $327,381, Maskette H., Diana H. twice, etc. Dam of Affectionately, Priceless Gem, Admiring. Foundation mare of family that includes Allez France, Sea Hero, Lite Light, Personality, Al Mamoon.

SEATTLE SLEW, 1974-2002. Dk. b. or br. c., Bold Reasoning—My Charmer, by Poker. 17-14-2-0, $1,208,726, Horse of the Year in 1977, champion two- and three-year-old colt, champion older horse, Triple Crown, Woodward S. (G1), etc. Leading sire in 1984; leading broodmare sire 1995-'96. Sire of more than 110 stakes winners, including A.P. Indy, Swale, Slew o' Gold, Surfside, Capote, Landaluce, Vindication, Slew City Slew, Taiki Blizzard, Lakeway, Honest Lady, General Meeting, Avenue of Flags, Slewvescent, Slewacide. Broodmare sire of more than 135 stakes winners, including Cigar, Agnes World, Escena, Lemon Drop Kid, Golden Attraction, Seeking the Pearl. Only horse to win Triple Crown while undefeated.

SECRETARIAT, 1970-1989. Ch. c., Bold Ruler—Somethingroyal, by *Princequillo. 21-16-3-1, $1,316,808, Horse of the Year in 1972-'73, champion two- and three-year-old male, champion grass horse, Triple Crown, Marlboro Cup H., etc. Leading broodmare sire in 1992. Sire of 56 stakes winners, including Lady's Secret, Risen Star, Medaille d'Or, Terlingua, General Assembly, Tinners Way, Weekend Surprise, Secrettame, Six Crowns. Broodmare sire of more than 160 stakes winners, including A.P. Indy, Chief's Crown, Dehere, Gone West, Secreto, Storm Cat, Summer Squall.

***SELIMA**, 1745-1766. B. f., Godolphin Arabian—Shireborn mare, by Hobgoblin. 2-2-0-0, $10,200, Great Intercolonial Match Race with Tryal. Dam of Ariel, Selim, Ebony, Bellair, Lightfoot's Partner. Tail-female ancestor of family that includes Hanover, Inspector B., Peytona, Foxhall, The Vid, Pirate's Revenge, Cherokee Run.

SENSATION, 1877-1899. Br. c., *Leamington—Susan Beane, by Lexington. 8-8-0-0, $20,250, champion two-year-old colt, Flash S., Nursery S., etc. Sire of Democrat.

SERENA'S SONG, 1992- . B. f., Rahy—Imagining, by Northfields. 38-18-11-3, $3,283,388, champion three-year-old filly, Mother Goose S. (G1), Beldame S. (G1), etc. Leading North American money-earning female at time of retirement. Dam of Serena's Tune, Sophisticat, Grand Reward.

SHIRLEY JONES, 1956-1978. B. f., Double Jay—L'Omelette, by *Alibhai. 49-18-9-5, $282,313, Test S., Maskette H., etc.

SHUVEE, 1966-1986. Ch. f., Nashua—Levee, by Hill Prince. 44-16-10-6, $890,445, champion handicap mare, champion older female, filly triple crown, Jockey Club Gold Cup twice, etc. Dam of Tom Swift, Shukey, Benefice.

***SICKLE**, 1924-1943. Br. c., Phalaris—Selene, by Chaucer. 10-3-4-2, $23,629, Prince of Wales's S., etc. Leading sire in 1936, '38. Sire of 41 stakes winners, including Stagehand, Brevity, Unbreakable, Star Pilot, Cravat, Reaping Reward, Misty Isle, Jabot. Broodmare sire of Bornastar, Counterpoint, Dan Cupid, How, Social Outcast. Tail-male ancestor of Native Dancer sire line.

SILENT WITNESS, 1999-. B. g., El Moxie—Jade Tiara, by Bureaucracy. 20-18-1-1, $5,885,654, Hong Kong Horse of the Year and champion sprinter in 2004-'05, Sprinters S., Hong Kong Sprint (HK-G1) twice, etc. Australian-bred won first 17 races, 2002-'05, and never defeated in 18 starts at 1,400 meters (6.96 furlongs) or shorter through 2005.

SILVERBULLETDAY, 1996- . B. f., Silver Deputy—Rokeby Rose, by Tom Rolfe. 23-15-3-1, $3,093,207, champion two- and three-year-old filly, Breeders' Cup Juvenile Fillies (G1), Kentucky Oaks (G1), etc.

SILVER CHARM, 1994- . Gr. or ro. c., Silver Buck—Bonnie's Poker, by Poker. 24-12-7-2, $6,944,369, champion three-year-old male, Kentucky Derby (G1), Preakness S. (G1), Dubai World Cup (UAE-G1), etc.

SILVER SPOON, 1956-1978. Ch. f., Citation—Silver Fog, by *Mahmoud. 27-13-3-4, $313,930, champion three-year-old filly, Santa Anita Derby, Milady H., etc. Dam of Inca Queen. Tail-female ancestor of family that includes Catinca, Metfield.

SIR ARCHY, 1805-1833. Ch. c., *Diomed—*Castianira, by Rockingham. 7-4-1-0, Post S. Leading Colonial sire. Sire of Sir Charles, Timoleon, Flirtilla, Bertrand, Henry, Kosciusko, Lady Lightfoot, Sumpter, Reality. Oldest member of the Racing Hall of Fame.

SIR BARTON, 1916-1937. Ch. c., *Star Shoot—Lady Sterling, by Hanover. 31-13-6-5, $116,857, consensus champion three-year-old colt, Triple Crown, Saratoga H., etc. First winner of the American Triple Crown. Sire of seven stakes winners, including Easter Stockings.

***SIR GALLAHAD III**, 1920-1949. B. c., *Teddy—Plucky Liege, by Spearmint. 24-11-3-3, $17,009, Poule d'Essai des Poulains (French Two Thousand Guineas), Prix Jacques le Marois, match race with *Epinard, etc. Leading sire 1930, '33-'34, '40; leading broodmare sire '39, '43-'52, '55. Sire of 56 stakes winners, including Gallant Fox, Gallahadion, High Quest, Vagrancy, Foxbrough, Fighting Fox, Hoop, Jr., Roman. Broodmare sire of 180 stakes winners, including Beaugay, Challedon, *Galatea II, Gallorette, Johnstown, Royal Native. Greatest American broodmare sire of the 20th century. First major American stallion syndication.

SKIP AWAY, 1993- . Gr. or ro. c., Skip Trial—Ingot Way, by Diplomat Way. 38-18-10-6, $9,616,360, Horse of the Year in 1998, champion three-year-old male, champion older male twice, Breeders' Cup Classic (G1), Jockey Club Gold Cup (G1) twice, etc. Sire of 11 stakes winners.

SKY BEAUTY, 1990- 2004. B. f., Blushing Groom (Fr)—Maplejinsky, by Nijinsky II. 21-15-2-2, $1,336,000, champion older female, filly triple crown, Alabama S. (G1), Ruffian H. (G1), etc.

SLEW O' GOLD, 1980- . B. c., Seattle Slew—Alluvial, by Buckpasser. 21-12-5-1, $3,533,534, champion three-year-old male, champion older male, Jockey Club Gold Cup (G1) twice, Woodward S. (G1) twice, etc. Sire of 29 stakes winners, including Golden Opinion, Gorgeous, Dramatic Gold, Thirty Six Red, Awe Inspiring. Broodmare sire of Kona Gold.

SMARTY JONES, 2001-. Ch. h., Elusive Quality—I'll Get Along, by Smile. 9-8-1-0, $7,613,155, champion three-year-old male, Kentucky Derby (G1), Preakness S. (G1), Arkansas Derby (G2), etc. First undefeated horse since Seattle Slew to win the Kentucky Derby; received $5-million bonus for winning Derby and two Oaklawn Park races.

SOMETHINGROYAL, 1952-1983. B. f., *Princequillo—Imperatrice, by Caruso. 1-0-0-0, $0. Broodmare of the Year in 1973. Dam of Secretariat, Sir Gaylord, First Family, Syrian Sea, Somethingfabulous. Foundation mare of family that includes Saratoga Dew, Alada, John Cherry, Personal Business.

SPECTACULAR BID, 1976-2003 . Gr. or ro. c., Bold Bidder—Spectacular, by Promised Land. 30-26-2-1, $2,781,608, Horse of the Year in 1980, champion two- and three-year-old male, champion older male, Kentucky Derby (G1), Preakness S. (G1), etc. Sire of more than 40 stakes winners, including Lotus Pool, Double Feint, Spectacular Love. Broodmare sire of more than 85 stakes winners.

SPEND A BUCK, 1982-2002. B. c., Buckaroo—Belle de Jour, by Speak John. 15-10-3-2, $4,220,689, Horse of the Year in 1985, champion three-year-old male, Kentucky Derby (G1), Monmouth H. (G1), etc. Sire of more than 30 stakes winners, including Antespend, Hard Buck (Brz). Exported to Brazil in 1997.

SPENDTHRIFT, 1876-1900. Ch. c., *Australian—Aerolite, by Lexington. 13-10-5-0, $27,250, Belmont S., Jersey Derby, etc. Sire of Kingston, Hastings, Lamplighter. Tail-male ancestor of line that leads to Fair Play, Man o' War, War Admiral, In Reality, Tiznow.

SPINAWAY, 1878-unknown. Ch. f., *Leamington—Megara, by *Eclipse. 9-7-2-0, $16,225, champion two-year-old filly, Hopeful S., Juvenile S., etc. Dam of Lazzarone. Tail-female ancestor of family that includes Giant's Causeway, Tanya, Floradora, Star Pilot, By Land By Sea, Gummo, Spearfish, Gaily, King's Bishop.

SPY SONG, 1943-1973. Br. c., Balladier—Mata Hari, by Peter Hastings. 36-15-9-4, $206,325, Arlington Futurity, Clang H., etc. Sire of 28 stakes winners, including Crimson Satan, Sly Pola, Sari's Song. Broodmare sire of 91 stakes winners, including Blue Tom, Faraway Son, Liloy (Fr), Singh.

***STAR SHOOT**, 1898-1919. B. c., Isinglass—Astrology, by Hermit. 10-3-1-1, $34,747 in England, National Breeders' Produce S., etc. Leading sire 1911-'12, '16-'17, '19; leading broodmare sire 1924-'26, '28-'29. Sire of Sir Barton, Grey Lag, Uncle, Wistful, Daylight Saving, Mindful, Priscilla. Broodmare sire of Blazes, Crusader, Gusto, Jack High. Sired a record 27 juvenile winners in 1916 that stood for 70 years.

STOCKWELL, 1849-1870. Ch. c., The Baron—Pocahontas, by *Glencoe. 16-11-3-0, $48,457, champion three-year-old in England, Two Thousand Guineas, St. Leger S., etc. Leading sire in England seven times. Sire of Doncaster, Achievement, Caller Ou, Cantiniere, Chevisaunce, Lord Lyon, Regalia, St. Albans, The Marquis. Known as the "Emperor of Stallions." Tail-male ancestor of Phalaris, *Teddy male lines.

STRAIGHT DEAL, 1962-1982. B. f., Hail to Reason—No Fiddling, by King Cole. 99-21-21-9, $733,020, champion handicap mare, Delaware H., Santa Margarita H., etc. Dam of Desiree, Reminiscing.

ST. SIMON, 1881-1908. Br. c., Galopin—St. Angela, by King Tom. 9-9-0-0, $23,121, Ascot Gold Cup, Epsom Gold Cup, Goodwood Cup, etc. Leading sire in England nine times. Sire of Persimmon, Diamond Jubilee, St. Frusquin, Rabelais, Chaucer, Memoir, La Fleche. Tail-male ancestor of *Ribot, *Princequillo male lines.

STYMIE, 1941-1962. Ch. c., Equestrian—Stop Watch, by On Watch. 131-35-33-28, $918,485, champion handicap horse, Metropolitan H. twice, Whitney S., etc. Sire of 12 stakes winners, including Rare Treat, Joe Jones, Paper Tiger. Broodmare sire of Regal Gleam, What a Treat. Retired as world's leading money earner in 1950.

SUN BEAU, 1925-1944. B. c., *Sun Briar—Beautiful Lady, by Fair Play. 74-33-12-10, $376,744, consensus champion handicap horse three times, Hawthorne Gold Cup three times, Aqueduct H., etc. Sire of six stakes winners, including Sun Lover. Leading money earner at his retirement in 1931.

***SUN BRIAR**, 1915-1943. B. c., Sundridge—*Sweet Briar II, by St. Frusquin. 22-8-4-5, $74,355, consensus champion two-year-old colt, Travers S., Hopeful S., etc. Sire of more than 30 stakes winners, including Sun Beau, Pompey, Firethorn.

SUNDAY SILENCE, 1986-2002. Dk. b. or br. c., Halo—Wishing Well, by Understanding. 14-9-5-0, $4,968,554, Horse of the Year in 1989, champion three-year-old male, Kentucky Derby (G1), Preakness S. (G1), Breeders' Cup Classic (G1), etc. Leading sire in Japan 1995-2004. Sire of more than 135 stakes winners, including Air Shakur, Dance Partner, Marvelous Sunday, Dance in the Dark, Bubble Gum Fellow, Fuji Kiseki, Special Week, Stay Gold, Genuine, Tayasu Tsuyoshi. All-time leading sire by earnings, exceeding $530-million.

SUNLINE, 1995. B. f., Desert Sun (GB)—Songline, by Western Symphony. 48-32-9-3, $6,625,105, Horse of the Year three times in Australia, Cox Plate (Aus-G1) twice, Flight S. (Aus-G1), Doncaster H. (Aus-G1) twice, etc. All-time leading money winner in Australia and New Zealand.

SUSAN'S GIRL, 1969-1988. B. f., Quadrangle—Quaze, by *Quibu. 63-29-14-11, $1,251,668, champion three-year-old filly, champion older female twice, Spinster S. (G1) twice, Delaware H. (G1) twice, etc. Dam of Copelan, Paramount Jet.

SWALE, 1981-1984. Dk. b. or br. c., Seattle Slew—Tuerta, by *Forli. 14-9-2-2, $1,583,660, champion three-year-old male, Kentucky Derby (G1), Belmont S. (G1), etc. Died eight days after winning Belmont Stakes.

SWAPS, 1952-1972. Ch. c., *Khaled—Iron Reward, by *Beau Pere. 25-19-2-2, $848,900, Horse of the Year in 1956, champion handicap horse, Kentucky Derby, Hollywood Gold Cup H., etc. Sire of 35 stakes winners, including Affectionately, Chateaugay, Primonetta, No Robbery. Broodmare sire of Best Turn, Fall Aspen, Numbered Account, Personality.

SWOON'S SON, 1953-1977. B. c., The Doge—Swoon, by Sweep Like. 51-30-10-3, $970,605, American Derby, Arlington Classic, etc. Sire of 22 stakes winners, including Chris Evert, Loom, Mr. Washington. Won 22 stakes.

SWORD DANCER, 1956-1984. Ch. c., Sunglow—Highland Fling, by By Jimminy. 39-15-7-4, $829,610, Horse of the Year in 1959, champion three-year-old colt, champion handicap horse, Belmont S., Jockey Club Gold Cup, etc. Sire of 15 stakes winners, including Damascus, Lady Pitt.

SYSONBY, 1902-1906. B. c., *Melton—*Optime, by Orme. 15-14-0-1, $184,438, champion two- and three-year-old colt, Metropolitan H., Saratoga Special, etc. Died at four.

TANYA, 1902-1929. Ch. f., *Meddler—Handspun, by Hanover. 10-6-1-1, $73,127, Belmont S., Hopeful S., Spinaway S., etc. Second filly to win the Belmont S.

TA WEE, 1966-1980. Dk. b. or br. f., Intentionally—Aspidistra, by Better Self. 21-15-2-1, $284,941, champion sprinter twice, Vosburgh H., Fall Highweight H. twice, etc. Dam of Great Above, Tax Holiday, Entropy, Tweak.

***TEDDY**, 1913-1936. B. c., Ajax—Rondeau, by Bay Ronald. 8-5-1-2, Gran Premio de San Sebastian, Prix des Trois Ans, etc. Leading sire in France twice. Sire of *Sir Gallahad III, *Bull Dog, *La Troienne, *Ortello, Aethelstan, Asterus, Rose of England, Brumeux, Case Ace, Sun Teddy, Anne de Bretagne, Anna Bolena, Assignation, Boxeuse, Coeur a Coeur, La Moqueuse. Tail-male ancestor of line leading to Damascus, Private Account, Captain Steve.

TEMPTED, 1955-unknown. Ch. f., *Half Crown—Enchanted Eve, by Lovely Night. 45-18-4-9, $330,760, champion handicap mare, Alabama S., Ladies H., etc. Dam of Lead Me On.

TEN BROECK, 1872-1887. B. c., *Phaeton—Fanny Holton, by Lexington. 30-23-3-1, $27,550, Phoenix Hotel S., Louisville Cup, etc. Sire of Jim Gray. Once held every major American record from one to four miles.

TENNY, 1886-1909. B. c., *Rayon d'Or—Belle of Maywood, by Hunter's Lexington. 65-25-15-12, $88,442, Brooklyn H., First Special S., etc. Defeated Racing Hall of Fame members Firenze, Hanover, and Kingston, but consistently beaten by Racing Hall of Famer Salvator.

THE TETRARCH, 1911-1935. Gr. c., Roi Herode—Vahren, by Bona Vista. 7-7-0-0, $55,206, Champagne S., Coventry S., etc. Leading sire in England in 1924. Sire of Mumtaz Mahal, Tetratema, Salmon Trout, *Stefan the Great, Caligula, Polemarch, Paola, Snow Maiden, *The Satrap. Called "the Spotted Wonder"; revived the Herod male line in England and popularized the gray coat color.

THE VERY ONE, 1975-1992. B. f., One for All—*Veruschka, by Venture. 71-22-12-9, $1,104,623, Santa Barbara H. (G1), Black Helen H. (G2), etc.

THUNDER GULCH, 1992- . Ch. c., Gulch—Line of Thunder, by Storm Bird. 16-9-2-2, $2,915,086, champion three-year-old male, Kentucky Derby (G1), Belmont S. (G1), etc. Sire of more than 35 stakes winners, including Point Given, Spain, Tweedside.

TIMOLEON, 1813-1836. Ch. c., Sir Archy—Saltram mare, by *Saltram. 16-14-0-0. Sire of Boston, Hotspur, Sally Walker, Saluda, Omega, Washington.

TIM TAM, 1955-1982. Dk. b. c., Tom Fool—Two Lea, by Bull Lea. 14-10-1-2, $467,475, champion three-year-old colt, Kentucky Derby, Preakness S., etc. Sire of 14 stakes winners, including Tosmah, Timmy Lad, Nancy Jr. Broodmare sire of Before Dawn, Davona Dale, Known Fact, Mac Diarmida, Tentam.

TIPPITY WITCHET, 1915-unknown. B. g., Broomstick—*Lady Frivoles, by St. Simon. 266-78-52-42, $88,241. Raced to age 14, beginning his career in stakes but descending to the claiming ranks.

TIZNOW, 1997- . B. c., Cee's Tizzy—Cee's Song, by Seattle Song. 15-8-4-2, $6,427,830, Horse of the Year in 2000, champion three-year-old male, champion older male, Breeders' Cup Classic (G1) twice, Santa Anita H. (G1), etc. Only dual winner of the Breeders' Cup Classic. Sire of champion Folklore.

T.M.OPERA O, 1996-. Ch. c., Opera House (GB)—Once Wed, by Blushing Groom (Fr). 26-14-6-3, $16,200,337, Horse of the Year in Japan, champion three-year-old in Japan, Japan Cup (Jpn-G1), etc. World's leading money-winning Thoroughbred.

TOM BOWLING, 1870-unknown. B. c., Lexington—Lucy Fowler, by *Albion. 17-14-3-0, $35,000, champion three-year-old colt, Travers S., Jersey Derby, Jerome S., Monmouth Cup, etc. Sire of General Monroe.

TOM FOOL, 1949-1976. B. c., Menow—Gaga, by *Bull Dog. 30-21-7-1, $570,165, Horse of the Year in 1953, champion two-year-old colt, champion handicap horse, champion sprinter, handicap triple crown, Futurity S., etc. Leading broodmare sire in England in 1965. Sire of 36 stakes winners, including Buckpasser, Tim Tam, Silly Season, Tompion, Dunce, Jester, Funloving, Sweet Folly, Dinner Partner, Dunce Cap II. Broodmare sire of 90 stakes winners, including Foolish Pleasure, Hatchet Man, Late Bloomer, *Meadow Court, Stop the Music, Majesty's Prince.

TOM ROLFE, 1962-1989. B. c., *Ribot—Pocahontas, by Roman. 32-16-5-5, $671,297, champion three-year-old colt, Preakness S., American Derby-ntr, etc. Sire of 49 stakes winners, including Hoist the Flag, Run the Gantlet, Droll Role, Bowl Game. Broodmare sire of more than 105 stakes winners, including Diminuendo, Environment Friend, Forty Niner, Life's Magic, Niniski, Notebook, Silverbulletday.

TOP FLIGHT, 1929-1949. Dk. br. f., *Dis Donc—Flyatit, by Peter Pan. 16-12-0-0, $275,900, champion two-and three-year-old filly, Coaching Club American Oaks, Futurity S., etc. Dam of Flight Command. Tail-female ancestor of family that includes Watch Fob, Sikeston. World's leading money-winning female at time of retirement.

TOSMAH, 1961-1992. B. f., Tim Tam—Cosmah, by Cosmic Bomb. 39-23-6-2, $612,588, champion two- and three-year-old filly, champion handicap mare, Frizette S., Beldame S., etc. Dam of La Guidecca.

TREMONT, 1884-1901. Bl. c., Virgil—Ann Fief, by Alarm. 13-13-0-0, $39,135, champion two-year-old colt, Great American S., etc.

***TURN-TO**, 1951-1973. B. c., *Royal Charger—*Source Sucree, by Admiral Drake. 8-6-1-1, $280,032, Garden State S., Flamingo S., etc. Sire of 25 stakes winners, including First Landing, Hail to Reason, Sir Gaylord, Best Turn, Cyane. Broodmare sire of 63 stakes winners, including Ack Ack, Bessarabian, Chinook Pass. Male line ancestor of Halo, Roberto lines.

T. V. LARK, 1957-1975. B. c., *Indian Hemp—Miss Larksfly, by Heelfly. 72-19-13-6, $902,194, champion grass horse, Washington, D.C., International S., United Nations H., etc. Leading sire in 1974. Sire of 53 stakes winners, including Quack, T. V. Commercial, Pink Pigeon, Buffalo Lark, Golden Don, T. V. Vixen, Romeo. Broodmare sire of 85 stakes winners, including Bates Motel, Chris Evert.

TWENTY GRAND, 1928-1948. B. c., *St. Germans—Bonus, by *All Gold. 23-14-4-3, $261,790, Horse of the Year in 1931, champion three-year-old colt, Kentucky Derby, Belmont S., etc. Sterile at stud.

TWILIGHT TEAR, 1941-1954. B. f., Bull Lea—Lady Lark, by Blue Larkspur. 24-18-2-2, $202,165, Horse of the Year in 1944, champion two- and three-year-old filly, champion handicap mare, Coaching Club American Oaks, Pimlico Special, etc. Dam of A Gleam, Bardstown, Coiner. Tail-female ancestor of family that includes Before Dawn, Gleaming, A Glitter.

TWO LEA, 1946-1973. B. f., Bull Lea—Two Bob, by The Porter. 26-15-6-3, $309,250, champion three-year-old filly, champion handicap mare, Hollywood Gold Cup H., Santa Margarita H., etc. Dam of Tim Tam, On-and-On, Pied d'Or.

ULTIMUS, 1906-1921. Ch c., Commando—Running Stream, by Domino. Unraced. Sire of Luke McLuke, High Time, High Cloud, Infinite, Stimulus, Supremus. Broodmare sire of Bold Venture, Case Ace, Flying Heels. One of the very few unraced successful sires; inbred 2x2 to Domino.

UNBRIDLED, 1987-2001. B. c., Fappiano—Gana Facil, by *Le Fabuleux. 24-8-6-6, $4,489,475, champion three-year-old male, Kentucky Derby (G1), Breeders' Cup Classic (G1), etc. Sire of more than 40 stakes winners, including Banshee Breeze, Anees, Unbridled's Song, Halfbridled, Empire Maker, Red Bullet.

UPSET, 1917-1941. Ch. c., Whisk Broom II—Pankhurst, by *Voter. 17-5-7-1, $37,504, Sanford S., etc. Only horse to defeat Man o' War. Sire of 11 stakes winners, including Misstep.

VAGRANCY, 1939-1964. Dk. b. f., *Sir Gallahad III—Valkyr, by Man o' War. 42-15-8-8, $102,480, champion three-year-old filly, champion handicap mare, Coaching Club American Oaks, Alabama S., etc. Dam of Black Tarquin, Vulcania. Tail-female ancestor of family that includes Ferdinand, Fiddle Isle, Natashka, Tallahto, Hidden Light, Truly Bound, Anees.

VANDAL, 1850-unknown. B. c., *Glencoe—Tranby mare, by *Tranby. 6-4-1-1. Sire of Vandalite, Survivor, Virgil, Capitola, Vicksburg, Mollie Jackson, Ella D.

VERTEX, 1954-1981. Ch. c., The Rhymer—Kanace, by Case Ace. 25-17-3-1, $453,424, Pimlico Special, Gulfstream Park H., etc. Sire of 25 stakes winners, including Lucky Debonair, Top Knight, Vertee. Broodmare sire of 50 stakes winners.

VICTORIA PARK, 1957-1985. B. c., Chop Chop—Victoriana, by Windfields. 19-10-4-2, $250,076, Horse of the Year in Canada, Queen's Plate, Remsen S., etc. Sire of 25 stakes winners, including Kennedy Road, Solometeor, Victorian Era, Floral Victory. Broodmare sire of Northern Taste, The Minstrel.

***VOTER**, 1894-unknown. Ch. c., Friar's Balsam—*Mavourneen, by Barcaldine. 49-26-6-7, $34,217, Metropolitan H., Toboggan H., etc. Sire of Ballot, Runnymede, Curiosity, Inaugural, Pankhurst.

WAGNER, 1834-1862. Ch. c., Sir Charles—Maria West, by Marion. 18-12-6-0, $34,150, Jockey Club Purse, etc. Sire of Starke, Lavender, Rhynodyne, Neil Robinson, Endorser.

WANDA, 1882-1905. Ch. f., *Mortemer—Minnie Minor, by Lexington. 24-12-8-0, $58,160, Monmouth Oaks, Champion Stallion S., etc. Tail-female ancestor of family that includes Swaps, Iron Liege, Flying Ebony, Creme dela Creme, Cascapedia, Althea, Green Desert, *Durbar II, Kauai King.

WAR ADMIRAL, 1934-1959. Br. c., Man o' War—Brushup, by Sweep. 26-21-3-1, $273,240, Horse of the Year in 1937, champion three-year-old colt, Triple Crown, Jockey Club Gold Cup, Whitney S., etc. Leading sire in 1945; leading broodmare sire '62, '64. Sire of 40 stakes winners, including Busher, Blue Peter, Searching, Admiral Vee, Busanda, War Date, Blue Banner, Mr. Busher, Bee Mac, Striking. Broodmare sire of 112 stakes winners, including Affectionately, Better Self, Buckpasser, Crafty Admiral, Gun Bow, Hoist the Flag, Iron Liege, Never Say Die, Priceless Gem.

WAR RELIC, 1938-1963. Ch. c., Man o' War—Friar's Carse, by Friar Rock. 20-9-4-2, $89,495, Massachusetts H., Kenner S., etc. Sire of Battlefield, Intent, Relic, Missile. Broodmare sire of Hail to All, My Dear Girl. Tail-male ancestor of male line that includes Tiznow, In Reality, Relaunch.

WEEKEND SURPRISE, 1980-2001. B. f., Secretariat—Lassie Dear, by Buckpasser. 31-7-5-10, $402,892, Golden Rod S. (G3), Schuylerville S. (G3), etc. Broodmare of the Year in 1992. Dam of A.P. Indy, Summer Squall, Welcome Surprise, Honor Grades.

WHICHONE, 1927-1944. Br. c., *Chicle—Flying Witch, by Broomstick. 14-10-2-1, $192,705, consensus champion two-year-old colt, Futurity S., Champagne S., etc. Sire of ten stakes winners, including Handcuff, Today. Rival of Gallant Fox; first winner of $100,000 first-prize purse in 1929 Futurity. Broodmare sire of Lord Boswell, Vulcan's Forge. Full brother to Mother Goose.

WHIRLAWAY, 1938-1953. Ch. c., *Blenheim II—Dustwhirl, by Sweep. 60-32-15-9, $561,161, Horse of the Year in 1941-'42, champion two- and three-year-old colt, champion handicap horse, Triple Crown, Jockey Club Gold Cup, Travers S., etc. Sire of 18 stakes winners, including Scattered, Kurun, Whirl Some. Broodmare sire of Lady Pitt, Beau Prince. Exported to France in 1950.

WHISK BROOM II, 1907-1928. Ch. c., Broomstick—Audience, by Sir Dixon. 26-10-8-0, $38,776, first winner of America's handicap triple crown, Victoria Cup (in England), etc. Sire of Whiskery, Diavolo, Victorian, Whiskaway, John P. Grier, Broomshot, Swing On, Upset, Weno. Broodmare sire of Seabiscuit, Double Jay.

WINNING COLORS, 1985- . Ro. f., Caro (Ire)—All Rainbows, by Bold Hour. 19-8-3-1, $1,526,837, champion three-year-old filly, Kentucky Derby (G1), Santa Anita Derby (G1), etc. Third filly to win Kentucky Derby.

YO TAMBIEN, 1889-1896. Ch. f., Joe Hooker—Marian, by Malcolm. 73-44-11-9, $89,480, Garfield Park Derby, etc. Half sister to Emperor of Norfolk, El Rio Rey.

YOUR HOST, 1947-1961. Ch. c., *Alibhai—*Boudoir II, by *Mahmoud. 23-13-5-2, $384,795, Santa Anita Derby, Del Mar Futurity, etc. Sire of 16 stakes winners, including Kelso, Social Climber, Windy Sands. Broodmare sire of Tosho Boy, Terry's Secret, Ruken.

ZACCIO, 1976- . Ch. g., *Lorenzaccio—Delray Dancer, by Chateaugay. 42-22-7-3, $288,124, champion steeplechaser three times, Colonial Cup International Steeplechase twice, Temple Gwathmey Steeplechase H., etc.

ZEV, 1920-1943. Br. c., The Finn—Miss Kearney, by *Planudes. 43-23-8-5, $313,639, champion two- and three-year-old colt, Kentucky Derby, Belmont S., International Race S., etc. Sire of two stakes winners. Defeated *Papyrus in first international race in U.S. Retired as world's leading money earner.

Profiles of Oldest Notable Horses

Listed alphabetically by age

MERRICK (38), 1903-1941. Ch. g., *Golden Garter—Bianca, by Wildidle. 205-61-40-24, $26,785. Won Pontchartrain Selling S. Died on March 13, 1941, at Merrick Place in Lexington, where he was buried.

BARGAIN DAY (37), 1965-2002. B. h., Prove It—Special Price, by *Toulouse Lautrec. 43-13-3-7, $146,575. Won 1970 Bing Crosby H. at Del Mar in course record 1:27.60 for 7½ furlongs on grass. Sire of 24 stakes winners, including 1⅛-mile course-record-setter Hoedown's Day (1:38.40). Died of natural causes on June 24, 2002, at Van Mar Farm, in Galt, California.

LYPHARD (36), 1969-2005. See Notable Horses in Racing in this chapter.

PRIMONETTA (35), 1958-1993. See Notable Horses in Racing in this chapter.

STOP THE MUSIC (35), 1970-2005. B. h., Hail to Reason—Bebopper, by Tom Fool. 30-11-10-4, $448,922. Won 1972 Champagne S. (on disqualification of Secretariat), 1973 Dwyer S. (G2). Sire of 46 stakes winners, including champion and classic winner Temperence Hill and Grade 1 winners Music Merci, Dontstop Themusic, Cure the Blues, etc. Broodmare sire of at least 86 stakes winners including Giacomo. Pensioned at Gainesway, in Lexington.

***GALLANT MAN (34)**, 1954-1988. See Notable Horses in Racing in this chapter.

*GREEN VALLEY II **(34),** 1967-2001. Dk. b. or br. m., *Val de Loir—Sly Pola, by Spy Song. Unraced. Dam of six stakes winners, including French classic winner and leading sire Green Dancer and graded/group winners Val Danseur and Ercolano. Died on July 22, 2001, at Haras de Saint-Leonard, in France.

IMPERATRICE (34), 1938-1972. Dk. b. or br. m., Caruso—Cinquepace, by Brown Bud. 31-11-7-2, $37,255. Won the 1941 Test S., 1942 Fall Highweight H. Dam of six stakes winners, including Scattered, Squared Away, and Imperium. Grandam of Secretariat. Euthanized in October 1972 at The Meadow, in Doswell, Virginia, where she was buried.

***JANUS (34)**, 1746-1780. See Notable Horses in Racing in this chapter.

KENILWORTH (34), 1898-1932. Br. h., *Sir Modred—*Queen Bess, by Gilroy or St. Martin. 168-61-18-22, $31,270. Sire. Died of a ruptured artery, on December 16, 1932, at the ranch of owner L. M. Bugeia, in Marin County, California.

LUCKY SPELL (34), 1971- . B. m., Lucky Mel—Incantation, by Prince Blessed. 69-12-8-11, $253,655. Won 1974 Princess S. (G3) and Las Palmas H. (G3). Dam of three stakes winners, including English Group 3 winner Merlins Charm. Grandam of 1995 Breeders' Cup Juvenile (G1) winner Unbridled's Song. Pensioned in California.

MISS DEBBIE LEE (34), 1966-2000. B. m., Accomplish—Lucky Gay, by Blue Gay. 14-1-5-1, $6,152. Dam of four stakes winners, including Strate Sunshine and Strate Miss. Died in December 2000 at Dash Goff's ranch in Arkansas.

RAJA BABA (34), 1968-2002. B. h., Bold Ruler—Missy Baba, by *My Babu. 41-7-12-9, $123,287. Stakes winner. Leading American sire, juvenile sire of 1980. Leading 1976 freshman sire. Sire of 62 stakes winners, including champion Sacahuista and Grade 1 winners Is It True, Junius, Well Decorated, etc. Broodmare sire of more than 75 stakes winners. Euthanized on October 9, 2002, at Hermitage Farm, in Goshen, Kentucky, where he stood his entire career. Buried on the farm.

VIEUX MANOIR (34), 1947-1981. B. h., Brantome—Vieille Canaille, by Finglas. Champion at three in France. Leading French sire of 1958. Among the leading French broodmare sires. Sire of 26 stakes winners, including French champion and leading sire *Val de Loir. Died November 19, 1981, at Haras de Meautry in Normandy, France.

AMERICAN ECLIPSE (33), 1814-1847. See Notable Horses in Racing in this chapter.

BALLOT (33), 1904-1937. See Notable Horses in Racing in this chapter.

BILLY BARTON (33), 1918-1951. Br. g., *Huon—Mary Le Bus, by *St. Savin. Great American steeplechaser. Second to Tipperary Tim in the 1928 Grand National at Aintree, England—the only two horses to finish that year. Died March 11, 1951, at Belmont Farm, in Elkridge, Maryland.

BROWN BERRY (33), 1960-1993. B. m., Mount Marcy—Brown Baby, by Phalanx. 29-6-3-3, $53,625. Won 1962 Del Mar Debutante. Dam of 1975 Belmont Stakes (G1) winner Avatar, 1988 French Derby (Fr-G1) winner Hours After, and 1972 Charles H. Strub S. winner Unconscious. Died May 18, 1993, at Brookdale Farm, in Versailles, Kentucky. Buried on the farm.

CHATEAUCREEK (33), 1970-2003. Ch. m., Chateaugay—Mooncreek, by Sailor. 29-6-1-2, $24,203. Stakes winner. Dam of 1980 champion and Epsom Derby (Eng-G1) winner Henbit. Grandam of Grade 1 winners Mr Purple and Queens Court Queen. Euthanized due to infirmities of age on August 7, 2003, at Mineola Farm, in Lexington. Buried on the farm.

COUNT FLEET (33), 1940-1973. See Notable Horses in Racing in this chapter.

GA HAI (33), 1971-2004. Gr. h., Determine—Goyala, by Goyamo. 43-13-2-5, $257,548. Won 1975 and 1976 Arcadia H. (G3). Sire of seven stakes winners. Pensioned in 1995. Died on March 17, 2004, at Reigle Heir Farms, in Grantville, Pennsylvania. Buried on the farm.

GREEN FINGER (33), 1958-1991. Dk. b. or br. m., Better Self—Flower Bed, by *Beau Pere. 18-1-3-1, $5,935. Dam of two stakes winners, including Grade 2 winner Free Hand. Died in 1991 and buried at Old Frankfort Stud (formerly King Ranch), near Lexington.

LUCKY MEL (33), 1954-1987. Ch. h., Olympia—*Royal Mink, by *Royal Charger. 12-7-0-1, $106,450. Stakes winner at two. Set five-furlong world record of :56.60, at Hollywood Park. Sire of 23 stakes winners, including graded winners Copper Mel and Lucky Spell. Broodmare sire of 44 stakes winners. Died at Old English Rancho, in Fresno, California.

MATCHEM (33), 1748-1781. See Notable Horses in Racing in this chapter.

MR. LEADER (33), 1966-1999. B. h., Hail to Reason—Jolie Deja, by *Djeddah. 25-10-3-3, $219,803. Won 1970 Tidal H., Stars and Stripes H. Sire of 83 stakes winners, including Grade 1 winners Ruhlmann, Hurry Up Blue, Wise Times, Quiet Little Table, Martial Law. Broodmare sire of more than 110 stakes winners, including champion Epitome. Euthanized on April 20, 1999, at Nuckols Farm in Midway, Kentucky, and buried at the farm.

NAPALM (33), 1963-1996. Ch. m., *Nilo—Fire Falls, by *Bull Dog. 17-2-2-5, $9,575. Dam of millionaire Grade

2 winner Fighting Fit and stakes winner Hot Words. Euthanized on February 9, 1996, at Nuckols Farm in Midway, Kentucky.

NORTHERN TASTE (33), 1971-2004. Ch. h., Northern Dancer—Lady Victoria, by Victoria Park. 23-5-3-4, $154,177. Won 1974 Prix de la Foret (Fr-G1). Nine-time leading sire in Japan, four-time leading Japanese broodmare sire. Sire of 48 stakes winners and six champions. Died in December 2004 at Shadai Stallion Station, on Hokkaido, Japan. Cremated and buried at the farm.

POCAHONTAS (33), 1837-1870. See Notable Horses in Racing in this chapter.

ROUND TABLE (33), 1954-1987. See Notable Horses in Racing in this chapter.

SWEEPIDA (33), 1937-1970. Br. g., Sweepster—Rapida, by *Hand Grenade. 65-18-12-10, $111,640. Won 1940 Santa Anita Derby, Bay Meadows H., etc. Died May 8, 1970, at the San Joaquin County Fair in Stock-

Oldest Notable Horses of All Time

Age	Horse, YOB, Sex, Sire	Record (Starts-Wins-2nd-3rd)	Earnings
38	Merrick, 1903 g., by *Golden Garter	205-61-40-24	$26,785
37	Bargain Day, 1965 h., by Prove It	43-13-3-7	146,575
36	Lyphard, 1969 h., by Northern Dancer	12-6-1-0	195,427
35	Busted, 1963 h., by Crepello	11-5-0-0	140,308
	Primonetta, 1958 m., by Swaps	25-17-2-2	306,690
	Stop the Music, 1970 h., by Hail to Reason	30-11-10-4	448,922
	Young Langford, 1840 h., by *Langford	No record	
34	*Gallant Man, 1954 h., by *Migoli	26-14-4-1	510,355
	*Green Valley II, 1967 m., by *Val de Loir	Unraced	
	Imperatrice, 1938 m., by Caruso	31-11-7-2	37,255
	*Janus, 1746 h., by Janus	3 wins	
	Kenilworth, 1898 h., by *Sir Modred	163, 61 wins	31,270
	Lucky Spell, 1971 m., by Lucky Mel	69-12-8-11	253,655
	Nicosia, 1972 m., by Gallant Romeo	19-8-2-0	254,495
	Raja Baba, 1968 h., by Bold Ruler	41-7-12-9	123,287
33	American Eclipse, 1814 h., by Duroc	8-8-0-0	56,700
	Ballot, 1904 h., by *Voter	38-20-6-6	154,545
	Billy Barton, 1918 g., by *Huon	No record	43,040
	Brown Berry, 1960 m., by Mount Marcy	29-6-3-3	53,625
	Chateaucreek, 1970 m., by Chateaugay	29-6-1-2	24,203
	Count Fleet, 1940 h., by Reigh Count	21-16-4-1	250,300
	Ga Hai, 1971 h., by Determine	43-13-2-5	257,548
	Green Finger, 1958 m., by Better Self	18-1-3-1	5,935
	*Inspirado, 1964 h., by Souepi	37-4-10-5	9,932
	Lucky Mel, 1954 h., by Olympia	12-7-0-1	106,450
	Mary's Fantasy, 1973 m., by Olympian King	***36-8-5-4***	***82,093***
	Matchem, 1748 h., by Cade	8 wins	
	Miss Debbie Lee, 1966 m., by Accomplish	14-1-5-1	6,152
	Mr. Leader, 1966 h., by Hail to Reason	25-10-3-3	219,803
	Napalm, 1963 m., by *Nilo	17-2-2-5	9,575
	Northern Taste, 1971 h., by Northern Dancer	23-5-3-4	154,177
	Old Friendship, 1783 h., by Apollo	No record	
	Pocahontas, 1837 m., by *Glencoe	9-0-3-0	0
	Round Table, 1954 h., by *Princequillo	66-43-8-5	1,749,869
	Sweepida, 1937 g., by Sweepster	65-18-12-10	111,640
	Tamerett, 1962 m., by Tim Tam	35-4-6-10	25,415
	Tripping, 1908 m., by Delhi	No record	
	Twosy, 1942 m., by Bull Lea	52-21-17-3	101,375
32	Arts and Letters, 1966 h., by *Ribot	23-11-6-1	632,404
	Big Spruce, 1969 h., by *Herbager	40-9-9-7	673,117
	Come My Prince, 1972 m., by Prince John	Unraced	
	Cormorant, 1974 h., by His Majesty	***12-8-2-0***	***243,174***
	Crimson Saint, 1969 m., by Crimson Satan	11-7-0-2	91,770
	Exclusive Ribot, 1972 h., by *Ribot	32-6-4-3	43,974
	Fanfreluche, 1967 m., by Northern Dancer	21-11-6-2	238,688
	Honey Jay, 1968 h., by Double Jay	63-24-10-11	223,853
	Hope of Glory, 1972 m., by Mr. Leader	35-9-3-5	168,421
	Introductivo, 1969 h., by *Sensitivo	54-6-10-15	107,128
	Kittiwake, 1968 m., by *Sea-Bird	54-18-12-9	338,086
	Knightly Manner, 1961 h., by Round Table	67-16-13-10	436,676
	Legendra, 1944 m., by *Challenger II	32-6-2-5	23,220
	Little Current, 1971 h., by *Sea-Bird	16-4-3-1	354,704
	Little Hut, 1952 m., by Occupy	55-5-7-14	22,220
	Minnesota Mac, 1964 h., by Rough'n Tumble	11-4-2-2	63,275
	Miss Justice (GB), 1961 m., by King's Bench	2-1-0-0	970
	*Monade, 1959 m., by *Klairon	35-10-5-4	252,016
	Oracle II, 1910 g., by Oxford	No record	
	*Philomela, 1954 m., by *Tudor Minstrel	23-1-2-2	560
	Queen Sucree, 1966 m., by *Ribot	4-1-0-0	3,925
	Sampson, 1745 h., by Blaze	No record	
	*Slady Castle, 1969 h., by *Tudor Melody	19-4-3-3	20,835
	S. S. Bellstar, 1966 h., by Eagle Admiral	36-10-10-5	40,637
	Taba (Arg), 1973 m., by Table Play	8-3-0-1	20,609
	The Ghizeh, 1948 m., by Questionnaire	47-4-8-7	13,610
	*Tobin Bronze, 1962 h., by Arctic Explorer	60-28-10-5	391,447

ton, California, where he had lived as a pensioner. Buried in front of the racetrack grandstand.

TAMERETT (33), 1962-1995. Dk. b. or br. m., Tim Tam—*Mixed Marriage, by *Tudor Minstrel. 35-4-6-10, $25,415. Dam of five stakes winners, including English champion miler Known Fact and Grade 1 winner Tentam. Grandam of noted sire Gone West. Died September 15, 1995, at Mare Haven Farm, in Lexington and buried on the farm.

TRIPPING (33), 1908-1941. B. m., Delhi—*Fairy Slipper, by St. Serf. 20-2-0-4, $950. Dam of two stakes winners, including 1920 Futurity S. winner Step Lightly. Died September 21, 1941, at Haylands Farm, in Lexington.

TWOSY (33), 1942-1975. B. m., Bull Lea—Two Bob, by The Porter. 52-21-17-3, $101,375. Multiple stakes winner. Sister to Racing Hall of Fame member Two Lea and to major stakes winner Miz Clementine. Dam of four winners and one stakes-placed runner. Died and was buried at Calumet Farm in Lexington.

VICTORIAN HEIRESS (33), 1968-2001. B. m, Northern Dancer—Victoriana, by Windfields. 12-3-0-1, $20,590. Dam of Canadian champion Northern Blossom. Half sister to 1960 Canadian Horse of the Year Victoria Park. Died in fall 2001 at Tranquility Farm in Tehachapi, California.

ARTS AND LETTERS (32), 1966-1998. See Notable Horses in Racing in this chapter.

BIG SPRUCE (32), 1969-2001. Dk. b. or br. h., *Herbager—Silver Sari, by Prince John. 40-9-9-7, $673,117. Won 1974 Governors S. (G1). Sire of 43 stakes winners, including Grade 1 winners Super Moment, Acaroid, Catatonic, Splendid Spruce, Sweet Diane, Back Bay Barrister, and Spruce Needles. Euthanized due to infirmities of age on December 28, 2001, at Gainesway, in Lexington.

COME MY PRINCE (32), 1972-2004. Ro. m., Prince John—Come Hither Look, by *Turn-to. Unraced. Dam of Grade/Group 1 winner and 1995 leading North American sire Palace Music. Euthanized due to infirmities of age on March 7, 2004, at Warfield Stud, in Butler, Missouri.

CRIMSON SAINT (32), 1969-2001. Ch. m., Crimson Satan—Bolero Rose, by Bolero. 11-7-0-2, $91,770. Won 1973 Hollywood Express (G3). Equaled the four-furlong world record. Dam of four stakes winners, including Breeders' Cup Mile (G1) winner Royal Academy and Grade 2 winners Terlingua and Pancho Villa. Grandam of leading sire Storm Cat. Euthanized due to infirmities of age on May 12, 2001, at Offutt-Cole Farm, in Midway, Kentucky.

Exclusive Ribot (32), 1972-2004. B. h., *Ribot—Exclusive, by Shut Out. 32-6-4-3, $43,974. Stakes-placed. Half brother to two-time leading North American sire Exclusive Native. Sire of six stakes winners, including millionaire Grade 2 winner Men's Exclusive and Grade 2 winner Exclusive Partner. Died of heart failure on August 8, 2004, at Dormello II Stud in Decatur, Texas.

FANFRELUCHE (32), 1967-1999. B. m., Northern Dancer—Ciboulette, by Chop Chop. 21-11-6-2, $238,688. Canadian Horse of the Year in 1970. Canadian Broodmare of the Year in 1978. Dam of five stakes winners, including Canadian Horse of the Year L'Enjoleur and Canadian champions La Voyageuse and Medaille d' Or. Stolen from her Claiborne Farm paddock in 1977; later recovered. Euthanized in July 1999 at Big Sink Farm in Midway, Kentucky, and buried at the farm.

HONEY JAY (32), 1968-2000. B. h., Double Jay—Roman Honey, by Roman. 63-24-10-11, $223,853. Won 1972 and '73 Phoenix H. Sire of 44 stakes winners, including Grade 1 winner Sweet Missus. Broodmare sire of 40 stakes winners. Euthanized February 22, 2000, at Fair Winds Farm in Waynesville, Ohio, and buried on the farm.

HOPE OF GLORY (32), 1972-2004. B. m., Mr. Leader—Daizel, by Manteau. 35-9-3-5, $168,421. Multiple graded stakes winner. Dam of nine winners from nine starters, including stakes-placed Grab the Glory. Euthanized after suffering a stroke on October 13, 2004, at Our Mims Retirement Haven in Paris, Kentucky.

KITTIWAKE (32), 1968-2000. B. m., *Sea-Bird—Ole Liz, by Double Jay. 54-18-12-9, $338,086. Won 1973 Columbiana H. (G2). Dam of four stakes winners, including Grade 1 winners Miss Oceana and Kitwood, and Grade 2 winner Larida. Euthanized due to infirmities of age on May 19, 2000, at Lazy Lane Farms in Upperville, Virginia.

KNIGHTLY MANNER (32), 1961-1993. B. h., Round Table—Courtesy, by *Nasrullah. 67-16-13-10, $436,676. Won or placed in 27 stakes. Sire of 14 stakes winners, including Italian classic winner Azzurrina (GB), Ohio Derby (G2) winner Stonewalk, and Grade 2 winner Cycylya Zee. Died in August 1993 in Australia.

Legendra (32), 1944-1976. B. m., *Challenger II—Lady Legend, by Dark Legend. 32-6-2-5, $23,220. Stakes-placed. Dam of four stakes winners, including Sky Clipper and Rich Tradition. Great-grandam of champion Shareef Dancer. Died February 6, 1976, at Newstead Farm, in Upperville, Virginia.

LITTLE CURRENT (32), 1971-2003. Ch. h., *Sea-Bird—Luiana, by *My Babu. 16-4-3-1, $354,704. Champion at three. Won 1974 Preakness S. (G1) and Belmont S. (G1). Sire of 35 stakes winners, including Grade 1 winners Current Hope and Prize Spot. Broodmare sire of 46 stakes winners. Euthanized January 20, 2003, due to strangulation of the small intestine, at Pacific Equine Clinic in Monroe, Washington.

MINNESOTA MAC (32), 1964-1996. B. h., Rough 'n Tumble—*Cow Girl II, by Mustang. 11-4-2-2, $63,275. Stakes winner. Sire of 18 stakes winners, including 1978 grass champion Mac Diarmida. Paternal grandsire of Holy Bull. Pensioned in 1984 at Tartan Farms in Florida, where he died on April 25, 1996. Buried at the farm.

***MONADE (32)**, 1959-1991. Br. m., *Klairon—Mormyre, by Atys. 35-10-5-4, $252,016. Champion at three in England and France. Won 1962 Epsom Oaks. Dam of stakes winner Pressing Date.

*PHILOMELA (32), 1954-1986. Ch. m., Tudor Minstrel—Petrovna II, by Blue Peter. 23-1-2-2, $560. Dam of California champion and G2 winner Messenger of Song and stakes-winning Procne. Grandam of California champion and leading sire Flying Paster. Died September 14, 1986, at Murrieta Stud in Murrieta, California.

QUEEN SUCREE (32), 1966-1998. B. m., *Ribot—Cosmah, by Cosmic Bomb. 4-1-0-0, $3,925. Dam of four stakes winners, including 1974 Kentucky Derby (G1) winner Cannonade and graded stakes winner Circle Home. Grandam of Grade 1 winners Stephan's Odyssey and Lotka. Pensioned in 1994. Euthanized on June 27, 1998, at Windward Oaks Farm in Harrodsburg, Kentucky. Buried at the farm.

TABA (Arg) (32), 1973-2005. B. m., Table Play—Filipina, by Fomento. Champion at two in Argentina. Dam of champion Grade 1 winner Turkoman and stakes winner Slow Fuse.

***TOBIN BRONZE (32)**, 1962-1994. Ch. h., Arctic Explorer—Amarco, by Masthead. 60-28-10-5, $391,447. Champion older horse in Australia. Sire of 15 stakes winners, including Canadian champion Proud Tobin and Grade 1 winner Trojan Bronze. Euthanized due to infirmities of old age in 1994. Buried at Rancho de Esperanza, in Hemet, California.

ECLIPSE AWARDS

History of the Eclipse Awards

Thoroughbred racing's first official champions were recognized for the 1936 racing season by *Daily Racing Form*, which named Granville as Horse of the Year and selected champions in six divisions. Beginning in the 1950 racing season, Thoroughbred Racing Associations, formed eight years earlier, announced its own set of champions. Usually the *Form*'s and TRA's separate lists of champions coincided, but sometimes they did not. For example, Horse of the Year titles went separately to One Count and Native Dancer in 1952, Bold Ruler and Dedicate in '57, Roman Brother and Moccasin in '65, and Fort Marcy and Personality in '70.

In 1971, J. B. Faulconer, then president of the Turf Publicists of America, an organization of marketing and public-relations representatives from racetrack and industry organizations, was asked by Monmouth Park executive Philip H. Iselin to head a special committee to consolidate the year-end championship honors. Faulconer helped to bring together the *Form*, TRA, and the National Turf Writers Association to select one set of champions.

Faulconer is credited with naming the Eclipse Award, which honors the great 18th-century English racehorse and sire from whom most modern-day Thoroughbreds descend in male line. He selected Lexington artist Adalin Wichman to design the award statuette of a lone Thoroughbred tacked in preparation for a race, and he served as master of ceremonies at the inaugural awards dinner on January 26, 1972, at New York's Waldorf Astoria. Faulconer was the host through 1976.

Today, the National Thoroughbred Racing Association has replaced the TRA in the three voting groups. Members of the three eligible organizations vote on winners of the ten divisional categories and then select the Horse of the Year. In addition, the groups vote on the outstanding breeder, owner, trainer, jockey, and apprentice jockey. For the first time in 2003, Eclipse Award winners were determined on a one-person, one-vote basis. Formerly, the Eclipse Award winners were determined by bloc voting, with each organization having equal weight.

Eclipse Awards generally are presented shortly after the conclusion of the previous year's racing season. Since the awards were founded, a few notable events have occurred. In 1978, a tie in the voting for outstanding two-year-old filly resulted in It's in the Air and Candy Eclair being named co-champions, while Dr. Patches and J. O. Tobin were voted co-champion sprinters. Voting procedures were changed to eliminate ties. In 1979, the champion turf horse division was divided into male and female categories. In Eclipse Award history, two-year-olds have been voted Horse of the Year just twice: Secretariat (1972) and Favorite Trick ('97).

Eclipse Award-Winning Horses

Horse of the Year

2005 Saint Liam
2004 Ghostzapper
2003 Mineshaft
2002 Azeri (female)
2001 Point Given
2000 Tiznow
1999 Charismatic
1998 Skip Away
1997 Favorite Trick
1996 Cigar
1995 Cigar
1994 Holy Bull
1993 Kotashaan (Fr)
1992 A.P. Indy
1991 Black Tie Affair (Ire)
1990 Criminal Type
1989 Sunday Silence
1988 Alysheba
1987 Ferdinand
1986 Lady's Secret (female)
1985 Spend a Buck
1984 John Henry
1983 All Along (Fr) (female)
1982 Conquistador Cielo
1981 John Henry
1980 Spectacular Bid
1979 Affirmed
1978 Affirmed
1977 Seattle Slew
1976 Forego
1975 Forego
1974 Forego
1973 Secretariat
1972 Secretariat
1971 Ack Ack

Two-Year-Old Male

2005 Stevie Wonderboy
2004 Declan's Moon
2003 Action This Day
2002 Vindication
2001 Johannesburg
2000 Macho Uno
1999 Anees
1998 Answer Lively
1997 Favorite Trick
1996 Boston Harbor
1995 Maria's Mon
1994 Timber Country
1993 Dehere
1992 Gilded Time
1991 Arazi
1990 Fly So Free
1989 Rhythm
1988 Easy Goer
1987 Forty Niner
1986 Capote
1985 Tasso
1984 Chief's Crown
1983 Devil's Bag
1982 Roving Boy
1981 Deputy Minister
1980 Lord Avie
1979 Rockhill Native
1978 Spectacular Bid
1977 Affirmed
1976 Seattle Slew
1975 Honest Pleasure
1974 Foolish Pleasure
1973 Protagonist
1972 Secretariat
1971 Riva Ridge

Two-Year-Old Filly

2005 Folklore
2004 Sweet Catomine
2003 Halfbridled
2002 Storm Flag Flying
2001 Tempera
2000 Caressing
1999 Chilukki
1998 Silverbulletday
1997 Countess Diana
1996 Storm Song
1995 Golden Attraction
1994 Flanders
1993 Phone Chatter
1992 Eliza
1991 Pleasant Stage
1990 Meadow Star
1989 Go for Wand
1988 Open Mind
1987 Epitome
1986 Brave Raj
1985 Family Style
1984 Outstandingly
1983 Althea
1982 Landaluce
1981 Before Dawn
1980 Heavenly Cause
1979 Smart Angle
1978 †It's in the Air
†Candy Eclair
1977 Lakeville Miss
1976 Sensational
1975 Dearly Precious
1974 Ruffian
1973 Talking Picture
1972 La Prevoyante
1971 Numbered Account

†Tied in voting, named co-champions

Three-Year-Old Male

2005 Afleet Alex
2004 Smarty Jones
2003 Funny Cide
2002 War Emblem
2001 Point Given
2000 Tiznow
1999 Charismatic
1998 Real Quiet
1997 Silver Charm
1996 Skip Away
1995 Thunder Gulch
1994 Holy Bull
1993 Prairie Bayou
1992 A.P. Indy
1991 Hansel
1990 Unbridled
1989 Sunday Silence
1988 Risen Star
1987 Alysheba
1986 Snow Chief
1985 Spend a Buck

1984 Swale
1983 Slew o' Gold
1982 Conquistador Cielo
1981 Pleasant Colony
1980 Temperence Hill
1979 Spectacular Bid
1978 Affirmed
1977 Seattle Slew
1976 Bold Forbes
1975 Wajima
1974 Little Current
1973 Secretariat
1972 Key to the Mint
1971 Canonero II

Three-Year-Old Filly

2005 Smuggler
2004 Ashado
2003 Bird Town
2002 Farda Amiga
2001 Xtra Heat
2000 Surfside
1999 Silverbulletday
1998 Banshee Breeze
1997 Ajina
1996 Yanks Music
1995 Serena's Song
1994 Heavenly Prize
1993 Hollywood Wildcat
1992 Saratoga Dew
1991 Dance Smartly
1990 Go for Wand
1989 Open Mind
1988 Winning Colors
1987 Sacahuista
1986 Tiffany Lass
1985 Mom's Command
1984 Life's Magic
1983 Heartlight No. One
1982 Christmas Past
1981 Wayward Lass
1980 Genuine Risk
1979 Davona Dale
1978 Tempest Queen
1977 Our Mims
1976 Revidere
1975 Ruffian
1974 Chris Evert
1973 Desert Vixen
1972 Susan's Girl
1971 Turkish Trousers

Older Male

2005 Saint Liam
2004 Ghostzapper
2003 Mineshaft
2002 Left Bank
2001 Tiznow
2000 Lemon Drop Kid
1999 Victory Gallop
1998 Skip Away
1997 Skip Away
1996 Cigar
1995 Cigar
1994 The Wicked North
1993 Bertrando
1992 Pleasant Tap
1991 Black Tie Affair (Ire)
1990 Criminal Type
1989 Blushing John
1988 Alysheba
1987 Ferdinand
1986 Turkoman
1985 Vanlandingham
1984 Slew o' Gold
1983 Bates Motel
1982 Lemhi Gold
1981 John Henry
1980 Spectacular Bid
1979 Affirmed
1978 Seattle Slew
1977 Forego
1976 Forego
1975 Forego
1974 Forego
1973 Riva Ridge
1972 Autobiography
1971 Ack Ack

Older Female

2005 Ashado
2004 Azeri
2003 Azeri
2002 Azeri
2001 Gourmet Girl
2000 Riboletta (Brz)
1999 Beautiful Pleasure
1998 Escena
1997 Hidden Lake
1996 Jewel Princess
1995 Inside Information
1994 Sky Beauty
1993 Paseana (Arg)
1992 Paseana (Arg)
1991 Queena
1990 Bayakoa (Arg)
1989 Bayakoa (Arg)
1988 Personal Ensign
1987 North Sider
1986 Lady's Secret
1985 Life's Magic
1984 Princess Rooney
1983 Ambassador of Luck
1982 Track Robbery
1981 Relaxing
1980 Glorious Song
1979 Waya (Fr)
1978 Late Bloomer
1977 Cascapedia
1976 Proud Delta
1975 Susan's Girl
1974 Desert Vixen
1973 Susan's Girl
1972 Typecast
1971 Shuvee

Turf Male[1]

2005 Leroidesanimaux (Brz)
2004 Kitten's Joy
2003 High Chaparral (Ire)
2002 High Chaparral (Ire)
2001 Fantastic Light
2000 Kalanisi (Ire)
1999 Daylami (Ire)
1998 Buck's Boy
1997 Chief Bearhart
1996 Singspiel (Ire)
1995 Northern Spur (Ire)
1994 Paradise Creek
1993 Kotashaan (Fr)
1992 Sky Classic
1991 Tight Spot
1990 Itsallgreektome
1989 Steinlen (GB)
1988 Sunshine Forever
1987 Theatrical (Ire)
1986 Manila
1985 Cozzene
1984 John Henry
1983 John Henry
1982 Perrault (GB)
1981 John Henry
1980 John Henry
1979 Bowl Game

Turf Female[1]

2005 Intercontinental (GB)
2004 Ouija Board (GB)
2003 Islington (Ire)
2002 Golden Apples (Ire)
2001 Banks Hill (GB)
2000 Perfect Sting
1999 Soaring Softly
1998 Fiji (GB)
1997 Ryafan
1996 Wandesta (GB)
1995 Possibly Perfect
1994 Hatoof
1993 Flawlessly
1992 Flawlessly
1991 Miss Alleged
1990 Laugh and Be Merry
1989 Brown Bess
1988 Miesque
1987 Miesque
1986 Estrapade
1985 Pebbles (GB)
1984 Royal Heroine (Ire)
1983 All Along (Fr)
1982 April Run (Ire)
1981 De La Rose
1980 Just a Game (Ire)
1979 Trillion

Turf Horse[1]

1978 Mac Diarmida
1977 Johnny D.
1976 Youth
1975 *Snow Knight
1974 Dahlia (female)
1973 Secretariat
1972 *Cougar II
1971 Run the Gantlet

[1]One turf category prior to 1979

Sprinter

2005 Lost in the Fog
2004 Speightstown
2003 Aldebaran
2002 Orientate
2001 Squirtle Squirt
2000 Kona Gold
1999 Artax
1998 Reraise
1997 Smoke Glacken
1996 Lit de Justice
1995 Not Surprising
1994 Cherokee Run
1993 Cardmania
1992 Rubiano
1991 Housebuster
1990 Housebuster
1989 Safely Kept (female)
1988 Gulch
1987 Groovy
1986 Smile
1985 Precisionist
1984 Eillo
1983 Chinook Pass
1982 Gold Beauty (female)
1981 Guilty Conscience
1980 Plugged Nickle
1979 Star de Naskra
1978 †Dr. Patches
†J. O. Tobin
1977 What a Summer (female)
1976 My Juliet (female)
1975 Gallant Bob
1974 Forego
1973 Shecky Greene
1972 Chou Croute (female)
1971 Ack Ack

†Tied in voting, named co-champions

Steeplechaser

2005 McDynamo
2004 Hirapour (Ire)
2003 McDynamo
2002 Flat Top
2001 Pompeyo (Chi)
2000 All Gong (GB)
1999 Lonesome Glory
1998 Flat Top
1997 Lonesome Glory
1996 Correggio (Ire)
1995 Lonesome Glory
1994 Warm Spell
1993 Lonesome Glory
1992 Lonesome Glory
1991 Morley Street (Ire)
1990 Morley Street (Ire)
1989 Highland Bud
1988 Jimmy Lorenzo (GB)
1987 Inlander (GB)
1986 Flatterer
1985 Flatterer
1984 Flatterer
1983 Flatterer
1982 Zaccio
1981 Zaccio
1980 Zaccio
1979 Martie's Anger
1978 Cafe Prince
1977 Cafe Prince
1976 Straight and True
1975 Life's Illusion
1974 *Gran Kan
1973 Athenian Idol
1972 Soothsayer
1971 Shadow Brook

Eclipse Award-Winning Individuals

Owner

2005 Michael Gill
2004 Kenneth and Sarah Ramsey
2003 Juddmonte Farms
2002 Richard Englander
2001 Richard Englander
2000 Frank Stronach
1999 Frank Stronach
1998 Frank Stronach
1997 Carolyn Hine
1996 Allen E. Paulson
1995 Allen E. Paulson
1994 John Franks
1993 John Franks
1992 Juddmonte Farms
1991 Sam-Son Farm
1990 Mrs. Frances Genter
1989 Ogden Phipps
1988 Ogden Phipps
1987 Mr. and Mrs. Eugene Klein
1986 Mr. and Mrs. Eugene Klein
1985 Mr. and Mrs. Eugene Klein
1984 John Franks
1983 John Franks
1982 Viola Sommer
1981 Dotsam Stable
1980 Mr. and Mrs. Bertram Firestone
1979 Harbor View Farm
1978 Harbor View Farm
1977 Maxwell Gluck
1976 Dan Lasater
1975 Dan Lasater
1974 Dan Lasater
1973 Not awarded
1972 Not awarded
1971 Mr. and Mrs. E. E. Fogelson

Breeder

2005 Adena Springs (Frank Stronach)
2004 Adena Springs (Frank Stronach)
2003 Juddmonte Farms
2002 Juddmonte Farms
2001 Juddmonte Farms
2000 Frank Stronach
1999 William S. Farish & Partners
1998 John and Betty Mabee
1997 John and Betty Mabee
1996 Farnsworth Farms
1995 Juddmonte Farms
1994 William T. Young
1993 Allen E. Paulson
1992 William S. Farish
1991 John and Betty Mabee
1990 Calumet Farm
1989 North Ridge Farm
1988 Ogden Phipps
1987 Nelson Bunker Hunt
1986 Paul Mellon
1985 Nelson Bunker Hunt
1984 Claiborne Farm
1983 E. P. Taylor
1982 Fred W. Hooper
1981 Golden Chance Farm
1980 Adele Paxson
1979 Claiborne Farm
1978 Harbor View Farm
1977 E. P. Taylor
1976 Nelson Bunker Hunt
1975 Fred W. Hooper
1974 John W. Galbreath
1973 Not awarded
1972 Not awarded
1971 Not awarded

Owner-Breeder

1973 Meadow Stable-Meadow Stud (C. T. Chenery)
1972 Meadow Stable-Meadow Stud (C. T. Chenery)
1971 Paul Mellon

Trainer

2005 Todd Pletcher
2004 Todd Pletcher
2003 Bobby Frankel
2002 Bobby Frankel
2001 Bobby Frankel
2000 Bobby Frankel
1999 Bob Baffert
1998 Bob Baffert
1997 Bob Baffert
1996 Bill Mott
1995 Bill Mott
1994 D. Wayne Lukas
1993 Bobby Frankel
1992 Ron McAnally
1991 Ron McAnally
1990 Carl Nafzger
1989 Charles Whittingham
1988 C. R. McGaughey
1987 D. Wayne Lukas
1986 D. Wayne Lukas
1985 D. Wayne Lukas
1984 Jack Van Berg
1983 Woody Stephens
1982 Charles Whittingham
1981 Ron McAnally
1980 Grover G. "Buddy" Delp
1979 Lazaro Barrera
1978 Lazaro Barrera
1977 Lazaro Barrera
1976 Lazaro Barrera
1975 Steve DiMauro
1974 Sherrill Ward
1973 H. Allen Jerkens
1972 Lucien Laurin
1971 Charles Whittingham

Jockey

2005 John Velazquez
2004 John Velazquez
2003 Jerry Bailey
2002 Jerry Bailey
2001 Jerry Bailey
2000 Jerry Bailey
1999 Jorge Chavez
1998 Gary Stevens
1997 Jerry Bailey
1996 Jerry Bailey
1995 Jerry Bailey
1994 Mike Smith
1993 Mike Smith
1992 Kent Desormeaux
1991 Pat Day
1990 Craig Perret
1989 Kent Desormeaux
1988 Jose Santos
1987 Pat Day
1986 Pat Day
1985 Laffit Pincay Jr.
1984 Pat Day
1983 Angel Cordero Jr.
1982 Angel Cordero Jr.
1981 William Shoemaker
1980 Chris McCarron
1979 Laffit Pincay Jr.
1978 Darrel McHargue
1977 Steve Cauthen
1976 Sandy Hawley
1975 Braulio Baeza
1974 Laffit Pincay Jr.
1973 Laffit Pincay Jr.
1972 Braulio Baeza
1971 Laffit Pincay Jr.

Apprentice Jockey

2005 Emma-Jayne Wilson
2004 Brian Hernandez Jr.
2003 Eddie Castro
2002 Ryan Fogelsonger
2001 Jeremy Rose
2000 Tyler Baze
1999 Ariel Smith
1998 Shaun Bridgmohan
1997 Roberto Rosado, Philip Teator (tie)
1996 Neil Poznansky
1995 Ramon Perez
1994 Dale Beckner
1993 Juan L. Umana
1992 †Rosemary Homeister Jr.
1991 Mickey Walls
1990 Mark Johnston
1989 Michael Luzzi
1988 Steve Capanas
1987 Kent Desormeaux
1986 Allen Stacy
1985 Art Madrid Jr.
1984 Wesley Ward
1983 Declan Murphy
1982 Alberto Delgado
1981 Richard Migliore
1980 Frank Lovato Jr.
1979 Cash Asmussen
1978 Ron Franklin
1977 Steve Cauthen
1976 George Martens
1975 Jimmy Edwards
1974 Chris McCarron
1973 Steve Valdez
1972 Thomas Wallis
1971 Gene St. Leon

†Jesus Bracho was originally awarded the title but relinquished it in 1994.

Eclipse Award of Merit

2005 Helen "Penny" Chenery
2004 Oaklawn Park and Cella Family
2003 Richard L. Duchossois
2002 Ogden Phipps and Howard Battle
2001 Harry T. Mangurian Jr.
Pete Pedersen
2000 Jim McKay
1999 Not awarded
1998 D. G. Van Clief Jr.
1997 Bob and Beverly Lewis
1996 Allen E. Paulson
1995 James E. "Ted" Bassett III
1994 Alfred G. Vanderbilt
1993 Paul Mellon
1992 Robert P. Strub, Joe Hirsch
1991 Fred W. Hooper

1990 Warner L. Jones
1989 Michael Sandler
1988 John Forsythe
1987 J. B. Faulconer
1986 Herman Cohen
1985 Keene Daingerfield
1984 John Gaines
1983 Not awarded
1982 Not awarded
1981 William Shoemaker
1980 John D. Schapiro
1979 Frank E. "Jimmy" Kilroe
1978 Ogden Mills "Dinny" Phipps
1977 Steve Cauthen
1976 Jack J. Dreyfus Jr.

Special Award

2005 Cash is King Stable
2004 Dale Baird
2003 Not awarded
2002 Keeneland Library
2001 Sheikh Mohammed bin Rashid al Maktoum
2000 John Hettinger
1999 Laffit Pincay Jr.
1998 Oak Tree Racing Association
1997 Not awarded
1996 Not awarded
1995 Russell Baze
1994 Eddie Arcaro, John Longden
1993 Not awarded
1992 Not awarded
1991 Not awarded
1990 Not awarded
1989 Richard L. Duchossois
1988 Edward J. DeBartolo Sr.
1987 Anheuser-Busch
1986 Not awarded
1985 Arlington Park
1984 C. V. Whitney
1983 Not awarded
1982 Not awarded
1981 Not awarded
1980 John T. Landry, Pierre E. Bellocq
1979 Not awarded
1978 Not awarded
1977 Not awarded
1976 William Shoemaker
1975 Not awarded
1974 Charles Hatton
1973 Not awarded
1972 Not awarded
1971 Robert J. Kleberg

Man of the Year

1975 John A. Morris
1974 William L. McKnight
1973 Edward P. Taylor
1972 John W. Galbreath

Outstanding Achievement

1972 Arthur B. Hancock Jr. (posthumously)
1971 Charles Engelhard (posthumously)

Eclipse Award Media Winners

Outstanding Newspaper Writing

1999 Maryjean Wall, Lexington *Herald-Leader*
1998 Tom Keyser, Baltimore *Sun*
1997 Maryjean Wall, Lexington *Herald-Leader*
1996 Tom Keyser, Baltimore *Sun*
1995 Stephanie Diaz, Riverside *Press-Enterprise*
1994 Mike Downey, Los Angeles *Times*
1993 Jennie Rees, Louisville *Courier-Journal*
1992 James Wallace, Seattle *Post Intelligencer*
1990 Paul Moran, *Newsday*
1989 Ronnie Virgets, *Gambit*
1988 Billy Reed, Lexington *Herald-Leader*
1987 Tim Layden, Capital Newspapers
1986 Edwin Pope, Miami *Herald*
1985 Paul Moran, *Newsday*
1984 Bill Christine, Los Angeles *Times*
Eddie Donnally, Dallas *Morning News*
1983 Dave Koemer, Louisville *Times*
1982 Edwin Pope, Miami *Herald*
1981 Dave Kindred, Washington *Post*
1980 Maryjean Wall, Lexington *Herald*
1979 Billy Reed, Louisville *Courier-Journal*
1978 Joe Hirsch, *Daily Racing Form*
1977 Skip Bayless, Los Angeles *Times*
1976 Edwin Pope, Miami *Herald*
1975 Bob Harding, Newark *Star-Ledger*
1974 William H. Rudy, New York *Post*
1973 Red Smith, New York *Times*
1972 Phil Ranallo, Buffalo *Courier Express*
1971 Scott Young, Toronto *Telegram*

Outstanding Magazine Writing

1999 Tom Keyser, Baltimore *Sun*
1998 Laura Hillenbrand, *American Heritage*
1997 Bill Heller, *The Backstretch*
1996 Don Clippinger, *Mid-Atlantic Thoroughbred*
1995 Not awarded
1994 Jay Hovdey, *The Blood-Horse*
1993 Stephanie Diaz, *The Backstretch*
1992 Joseph P. Pons Jr., *The Blood-Horse*
1990 Bill Nack, *Sports Illustrated*
1989 Bill Nack, *Sports Illustrated*
1988 Jennie Rees, Louisville *Courier-Journal* (Sunday Magazine)
1987 Jack Mann, *Spur*
1986 Bill Nack, *Sports Illustrated*
1985 Bill Mooney, *The Thoroughbred Record*
1984 Frank Deford, *Sports Illustrated*
1983 Arnold Kirkpatrick, *Keeneland*
1982 Jay Hovdey, *Horsemen's Journal*
1981 Joseph P. Pons Jr., *The Blood-Horse*
1980 Clive Gammon, *Sports Illustrated*
1979 William Leggett, *Sports Illustrated*
1978 Bill Nack, *Sports Illustrated*
1977 Whitney Tower, *Classic*
1976 Whitney Tower, *Classic*
1975 Frank Deford, *Sports Illustrated*
1974 Chet Hagan, *Spur*
1973 Pete Axthelm, *Newsweek*
1972 Edward L. Bowen, *The Blood-Horse*
1971 Bill Surface, *Reader's Digest*

Outstanding Feature and Enterprise Writing

2005 Janet Patton, Lexington *Herald-Leader*
2004 Mike Jensen, Philadelphia *Inquirer*
2003 Bill Nack, *GQ*
2002 John Jeremiah Sullivan, *Harper's*
2001 Laura Hillenbrand, *EQUUS*
2000 Mary Simon, THOROUGHBRED TIMES

Outstanding Feature Writing

1991 Bill Nack, *Sports Illustrated*

Outstanding News Writing

1991 Bill Nack, *Sports Illustrated*

Outstanding News and Commentary Writing

2005 Bob Ford, Philadelphia *Inquirer*
2004 Bill Christine, Los Angeles *Times*
2003 Jay Hovdey, *Daily Racing Form*
2002 Joe Drape, New York *Times*
2001 Janet Patton, Lexington *Herald-Leader*
2000 Jay Hovdey, *Daily Racing Form*

Local Television Achievement

2005 WAVE-TV, Louisville
2004 WAVE-TV, Louisville
2003 WKYT, Lexington
2002 Fox Sports Net Southwest
2001 WTVI, Charlotte, NC
2000 WMAR-TV, Baltimore
1999 Amy Zimmerman & Michael Ewing, Fox-TV Sports West
1998 Jeff Lifson, WHAS-TV, Louisville
1997 Brian Blessing, Ontario Jockey Club
1996 Kenny Rice, WTVQ-TV, Lexington
1995 JCM Productions, New York
1994 Ronnie Virgets, WNXO, New Orleans
1993 Stephen Sadis, KBTC, Tacoma
1992 Rick Cushing, WKPC-TV, Louisville
1991 WABC-TV, New York

1990 Philip Von Borries, WKPC-TV, Louisville
1989 Chris Thomas, WFLA-TV, Tampa
1988 Joseph Kwong, KCET-TV, Los Angeles
1987 Arlington Park
1986 Louisiana Downs
1985 Oak Tree Racing Association
1984 NYRA/Cinema Mistral
1983 Cawood Ledford Productions
1982 ON-TV, Los Angeles
1981 WHAS, Louisville
1980 WCAU, Philadelphia
1979 Dave Johnson, ON-TV
1978 Cawood Ledford, WHAS, Louisville
1977 Jane Chastain, KABC, Los Angeles
1976 NYRA-OTB Race of the Week
1975 Cawood Ledford, WHAS, Louisville

National Television Achievement

1999 Mark Shapiro and William Rapaport, ESPN
1998 E. S. Lamoreaux III, *CBS News Sunday Morning*
1997 E. S. Lamoreaux III, *CBS News Sunday Morning*
1996 NBC Sports
1995 ABC's Wide World of Sports
1994 ABC's Wide World of Sports
1993 E. S. Lamoreaux III, CBS News, *Sunday Morning with Charles Kuralt*
1992 ABC Sports
1991 CBS News, *Sunday Morning with Charles Kuralt*
1990 ABC Sports
1989 ABC Sports
1988 Thoroughbred Sports, *Racing Across America*
1987 ABC
1986 ABC
1985 CBS
1984 NBC
1983 CBS
1982 ESPN
1981 Canadian Broadcasting Corp.
1980 ABC
1979 Don Ohlmeyer, NBC
1978 Roger Murphy, Public Broadcasting System
1977 Jack Whitaker, CBS
1976 CBS
1975 CBS
1974 Pen Densham, John Watson, Insight Productions
1973 Chuck Milton, Tony Verna, CBS
1972 Chuck Milton, Tony Verna, CBS
1971 Burt Bacharach, CBS

National Television—Live Racing Programming

2005 NBC Sports
2004 NBC Sports
2003 NBC Sports
2002 NBC Sports
2001 NBC
2000 ABC Sports
1999 Curt Gowdy Jr., Craig Janoff, Howard Katz, and John Filippelli, ABC Sports

National Television—Features

2005 NBC Sports
2004 ESPN
2003 MSNBC and ESPN Classic
2002 NBC Sports
2001 ESPN Classic

Audio–Multimedia–Internet

2005 Sirius Satellite Radio
2004 Premiere Radio Networks
2003 KSPN/ESPN Radio, Los Angeles; WBAL, Baltimore
2002 Shelby Whitfield, Premiere Radio

Radio Achievement

2001 WBAL, Baltimore
2000 Shelby Whitfield, Premiere Radio
1999 Tom Leach, WVLK-AM, Lexington
1998 Not awarded
1997 John Patti, WBAL, Baltimore
1996 Robin Dawson, CJCL, Toronto
1995 Vic Stauffer, KKAR, Omaha
1994 John Asher, WHAS, Louisville
1993 Tom Leach, WVLK, Lexington
1992 John Asher, WHAS, Louisville
1991 Julia McEvoy, National Public Radio
1990 John Asher, WHAS, Louisville
1989 John Asher, WAVG, Louisville
1988 John Asher, WAVG, Louisville
1987 Bob Lauder, WHAS, Louisville
1986 ABC Radio Network
1985 Bob Lauder, WHAS, Louisville
1984 WBAL, Baltimore
1983 Tom Davis, WCBM, Baltimore
1982 ABC Radio Network
1981 WBAL, Baltimore
1980 Not awarded
1979 Dick Woolley, WITH, Baltimore
1978 Ted Patterson, WBAL, Baltimore
1977 Not awarded
1976 Win Elliot, CBS
1975 Not awarded
1974 Not awarded
1973 Not awarded
1972 Not awarded
1971 Win Elliot, CBS

Film Achievement

1972 Joseph Burnham

Photography Achievement

2005 Lynn Roberts, Fair Grounds
2004 Cindy Pierson Dulay, *Mid-Atlantic Thoroughbred*
2003 Frank Anderson, THOROUGHBRED TIMES
2002 Michael Clevenger, Louisville *Courier-Journal*
2001 Barbara Livingston, *The Thoroughbred Chronicle*
2000 Dave Landry, *Canadian Thoroughbred*
1999 Michael J. Marten, *Daily Racing Form*
1998 Ryan Haynes, Northlands Park
1997 Jean Raftery, Calder Race Course
1996 Skip Dickstein, *The Blood-Horse*
1995 Michael J. Marten, *Daily Racing Form*
1994 Tony Leonard, THOROUGHBRED TIMES
1993 Michael Burns, Ontario Jockey Club
1992 Barbara Livingston, *The Blood-Horse*
1991 Rayetta Burr, Benoit and Associates
1990 Michael Cartee, *Thoroughbred of California*
1989 Ron Cortes, Philadelphia *Inquirer*
1988 Ben Van Hook, Louisville *Courier-Journal*
1987 Dan Farrell, New York *Daily News*
1986 Janice Wilkman, Los Angeles *Times*
1985 Kim Pratt, Garden State Park
1984 Bill Straus, *The Thoroughbred Record*
1983 Rayetta Burr, *Paddock*
1982 Kay Coyte, *Horsemen's Journal*
1981 Tom Baker, River Downs
1980 Bob Coglianese, New York Racing Association
1979 Skip Ball, *Maryland Horse*
1978 Douglas Lees, Fauquier *Democrat*
1977 John Walther, Miami *Herald*
1976 John J. Vasile, Covina (California) *Sentinel*
1975 John Pineda, Miami *Herald*
1974 Michael Burns, Ontario Jockey Club
1973 Harry Leder, United Press International
1972 Bob Coglianese, New York Racing Association
1971 Art Rogers, Los Angeles *Times*

Owners of Eclipse Award Winners

Aga Khan—Kalanisi (Ire).
Alexander, Helen, David Aykroyd, and Helen Groves—Althea.
Aleo, Harry—Lost in the Fog.
Allbritton, Joseph—Hansel.
Anderson, Frank, Verne H. Winchell, and Rick Carradini—Tight Spot.
Augustin Stables—Cafe Prince (1977, '78), Pompeyo (Chi).
Bacharach, Burt C.—Heartlight No. One.
Bailey, Richard E.—Dearly Precious.
Beal, Barry and L. R. French—Landaluce, Sacahuista.
Beal, Barry, L. R. French, and Eugene Klein—Capote.
Bell III, John A.—Epitome.
Blue Vista—Possibly Perfect.
Brant, Peter M.—Gulch, Just a Game (Ire), Waya (Fr).
Bray Jr., Dana S.—Johnny D.
Buckland Farm—Pleasant Colony, Pleasant Stage, Pleasant Tap.
Caibett, Edgar—Canonero II.
Calbourne Farm—Brown Bess.
Calumet Farm—Before Dawn, Davona Dale, Our Mims.
Calumet Farm and Jurgen Arnemann—Criminal Type.
Cash is King Stable—Afleet Alex.
Cee's Stable—Tiznow (2001).
Cella, Charles—Northern Spur (Ire).
Centennial Farms—Rubiano.
Christiana Stables—Go for Wand (1989, '90).
Claiborne Farm—Forty Niner, Swale.
Clark Jr., Mrs. F. Ambrose—*Gran Kan.
Clark Jr., Stephen C.—Shadow Brook.
Clay, Robert and Tracy Farmer—Hidden Lake.
Cooper, Audrey H. and Michael Fennessy—Yanks Music.
Couvercelle, Jean—Cardmania.
Cowan, Irving and Marjorie—Hollywood Wildcat.
Craig, Sidney and Jenny—Paseana (Arg) (1992, '93).
Croll Jr., Warren A.—Holy Bull.
Crown Stable—Eillo.
Darby Dan Farm—Little Current, Sunshine Forever, Tempest Queen.
Davison, Mrs. Richard—Guilty Conscience.
De Camargo, Jose, Winner Silk Inc., and Old Friends Inc.—Farda Amiga.
De Kwiatkowski, Henryk—Conquistador Cielo, De La Rose.
Lord Derby—Ouija Board (GB).
Dogwood Stable—Inlander (GB), Storm Song.
Dotsam Stable—John Henry (1980, '81, '83, '84).
Due Process Stables—Dehere.
East-West Stable—Wajima.
Eldon Farm—Hirapour (Ire).
Elmendorf Farm—Protagonist, Talking Picture.
Engel, Charles F.—Saratoga Dew.
Envoy Stable—Ambassador of Luck.
Equusequity Stable—Slew o' Gold (1983, '84).
Evergreen Farm—Lit de Justice.
Fares, Issam M.—Miss Alleged.
Farish, William S., James Elkins, and Temple Webber Jr.—Mineshaft.
Farish, Will, William Kilroy, Harold Goodman, and Tomonori Tsurumaki—A.P. Indy.
Fey, Barry, Moon Han, Class Racing Stable, Larry Opas, Frank Sinatra, and Craig Dollase—Reraise.
Firestone, Mr. and Mrs. Bertram R.—April Run (Ire), Genuine Risk, Honest Pleasure, Jimmy Lorenzo (GB), What a Summer.
505 Farms and Ed Nahem—Bertrando.
Flaxman Holdings—Aldebaran.
Flying Zee Stables—Wayward Lass.
Folsom Farm and J. Merrick Jones Jr.—Chou Croute.
Forked Lightning Ranch—Ack Ack.
Fradkoff, Serge and Baron Thierry Van Zuylen de Nyevelt—Perrault (GB).
Franks, John—Answer Lively.
Fuller, Peter—Mom's Command.
Genter, Frances A. Stable—Smile, Unbridled.
Gerry, Nancy—Flat Top (1998, 2002).
Godolphin Racing—Daylami (Ire), Fantastic Light, Tempera.
Green, Dolly—Brave Raj.
Greentree Stable—Bowl Game, Late Bloomer.
Greer, John L.—Foolish Pleasure.
Griffin, Merv Ranch Co.—Stevie Wonderboy.
Griggs, John K.—Warm Spell.
Grinstead, Carl and Ben Rochelle—Snow Chief.
Guest, Virginia—Life's Illusion.
Hamilton, Emory Alexander—Queena.
Hancock III, Arthur, Charlie Whittingham, and Dr. Ernest Gaillard—Sunday Silence.
Harbor View Farm—Affirmed (1977, '78, '79), Flawlessly (1992, '93), It's in the Air, Outstandingly.
Hatley, Melvin E. and Eugene V. Klein—Life's Magic.
Hawksworth Farm—Spectacular Bid (1978, '79, '80).
Henley Jr., Mrs. Jesse M.—Highland Bud.
Hersh, Trust of Philip and Sophie—The Wicked North.
Hibbert, Robert E.—Roving Boy.
Hickory Tree Stable—Devil's Bag.
Hine, Carolyn H.—Skip Away (1996, '97, '98).
Hi Yu Stable—Chinook Pass.

Leading Owners

Wholly or in partnership, by number of titles won, including Horse of the Year

12—Allen E. Paulson
9—Harbor View Farm
8—Eugene V. Klein
7—Lazy F Ranch
7—Robert and Beverly Lewis
6—Dotsam Stable
6—Mr. and Mrs. Bertram Firestone
6—William L. Pape
5—Calumet Farm
5—Mrs. Walter M. Jeffords Jr.
5—Meadow Stable
5—Overbrook Farm
5—Ogden Phipps
5—Michael Tabor
5—The Thoroughbred Corp.
4—George Harris
4—Hawksworth Farm
4—Carolyn Hine
4—Fred W. Hooper
4—Nelson Bunker Hunt
4—Juddmonte Farms
4—Allen E. Paulson Living Trust
4—Ogden Mills Phipps
4—Jonathan Sheppard
4—Stronach Stable

By Individual Winners

9—Allen E. Paulson
5—Mr. and Mrs. Bertram Firestone
5—Eugene V. Klein
5—Bob and Beverly Lewis
5—Overbrook Farm
5—Ogden Phipps
4—Calumet Farm
4—Harbor View Farm
4—Juddmonte Farms
4—Ogden Mills Phipps
4—The Thoroughbred Corp.
3—Peter M. Brant
3—Buckland Farm
3—Darby Dan Farm
3—Godolphin Racing
3—Nelson Bunker Hunt
3—Loblolly Stable
3—Sheikh Mohammed bin Rashid al Maktoum
3—Sam-Son Farm
3—Stronach Stable

Hofmann, Mrs. Philip B.—Gold Beauty, Sky Beauty.
Hooper Sr., Fred W.—Precisionist, Susan's Girl (1972, '73, 1975).
Horton, Robert P.—Gallant Bob.
Houghland, Calvin—All Gong (GB).
Hughes, B. Wayne—Action This Day.
Hunt, Nelson Bunker—Dahlia, Youth.
Hunt, Nelson Bunker and Edward L. Stephenson—Trillion.
Hunter Farm—Spend a Buck.
Icahn, Carl—Meadow Star.
Jackson, Michael—Morley Street (Ire)

(1990, '91).
Jay Em Ess Stable—Declan's Moon.
Jayeff B Stables and Barry Weisbord—Safely Kept.
Jeffords Jr., Mrs. Walter M.—Lonesome Glory (1992, '93, '95, '97, '99).
Jhayare Stables—Itsallgreektome.
Jones, Aaron U.—Lemhi Gold, Tiffany Lass.
Jones, Aaron and Marie—Riboletta (Brz).
Jones Jr., J. Merrick and Folsom Farm—Chou Croute.
Jones, Mrs. Mary F.—*Cougar II.
Juddmonte Farms—Banks Hill (GB), Intercontinental (GB), Ryafan, Wandesta (GB).
Kaster, Mr. and Mrs. Richard and Mr. and Mrs. Donald Propson—Countess Diana.
Keck, Mrs. Howard B.—Ferdinand, Turkish Trousers.
Kellman, Joseph—Shecky Greene.
Klein, Eugene V.—Family Style, Open Mind (1988, '89), Winning Colors.
Klein, Mr. and Mrs. Eugene V.—Lady's Secret.
Klein, Eugene, L. R. French, and Barry Beal—Capote.
Klein, Eugene V. and Melvin E. Hatley—Life's Magic.
LaCombe, Joseph—Favorite Trick.
Lamarque Racing Stable and Louis J. Roussel III—Risen Star.
Lancaster Jr., Carlyle, et al.—Star de Naskra.
Lanzman, David—Squirtle Squirt.
La Presle Farm—Kotashaan (Fr).
Lazy F Ranch—Forego (1974, '75, '76, '77).
Levesque, Jean-Louis—La Prevoyante.
Levy, Morton and Marjoh, and Donald and David Willmot—Deputy Minister.
Levy, Robert P.—Housebuster (1990, '91).
Levy, Robert, William Roberts, and Alex Karkenny—Smoke Glacken.
Lewis, Robert and Beverly—Charismatic, Folklore, Orientate, Serena's Song, Silver Charm.
Lewis, Robert and Beverly, Gainesway Farm, and Overbrook Farm—Timber Country.
Lickle, William C.—Correggio (Ire).
Loblolly Stable—Prairie Bayou, Temperence Hill, Vanlandingham.
Locust Hill Farm—Ruffian (1974, '75).
Maktoum, Sheikh Maktoum bin Rashid al—Hatoof.
Maktoum, Sheikh Mohammed bin Rashid al—Pebbles (GB), Singspiel (Ire).
Maktoum, Sheikh Mohammed bin Rashid al and Allen E. Paulson—Arazi.
Mangurian Jr., Harry T.—Desert Vixen.
Meadow Stable—Riva Ridge, Secretariat (1972, '73).
Melnyk, Eugene and Laura—Speightstown.
Milch, David, Marc Silverman, and Jack Silverman—Gilded Time.
Mill House—Sensational.
Molasky, Irwin and Andrew, Bruce Headley, and High Tech Stable (Michael Singh)—Kona Gold.
Montpelier—Proud Delta, Soothsayer.
Moran, Michael—McDynamo (2003, '05).
Murdock, Mrs. Lewis C.—Zaccio (1980, '81, '82).
Nerud, John A.—Cozzene.
Niarchos, Stavros—Miesque (1987, '88).
Nishiyama, Masayuki—Paradise Creek.
Oak, Harry A.—Rockhill Native.
Overbrook Farm—Boston Harbor, Flanders, Golden Attraction, Surfside.
Oxley, John C.—Beautiful Pleasure.
Padua Stables—Vindication.
Pape, William L.—Athenian Idol, Martie's Anger.
Pape, William L., George Harris, and Jonathan Sheppard—Flatterer (1983, '84, '85, '86).
Paraneck Stable—Artax.
Paternostro, Paul, and D. Wayne Lukas—North Sider.
Paulson, Allen E.—Ajina, Blushing John, Cigar (1995, '96), Eliza, Escena, Estrapade.
Paulson, Allen E. Living Trust—Azeri (2002, '03, '04).
Paulson, Allen E. and Bertram R. Firestone—Theatrical (Ire).
Paulson, Allen E. and Sheikh Mohammed bin Rashid al Maktoum—Arazi.
Paxson, Adele—Candy Eclair.
Pegram, Mike—Real Quiet, Silverbulletday (1998, '99).
Perry, William H.—Revidere.
Phillips Racing Partnership—Soaring Softly.
Phipps, Cynthia—Christmas Past.
Phipps, Mrs. Ogden—Straight and True.
Phipps, Ogden—Easy Goer, Heavenly Prize, Numbered Account, Personal Ensign, Relaxing.
Phipps, Ogden Mills—Inside Information, Rhythm, Smuggler, Storm Flag Flying.
Pin Oak Stable—Laugh and Be Merry.
Pollard, Carl F.—Caressing.
Pope Jr., George A.—J. O. Tobin.
Prestonwood Farm—Groovy, Victory Gallop.
Quarter B. Farm—Buck's Boy.
Ramsey, Kenneth and Sarah—Kitten's Joy.
Ridder, Bernard R.—Cascapedia.
Riordan, Michael D.—Bates Motel.
Robins, Gerald W. and Timothy Sams—Tasso.
Robinson, Jill E.—Cherokee Run.
Rokeby Stable—Key to the Mint, Run the Gantlet.
Rosen, Carl—Chris Evert.
Rosenthal, Mrs. Morton—Maria's Mon.
Ryehill Farm—Heavenly Cause, Smart Angle.
Salman, Prince Fahd bin—Fiji (GB).
Sams, Timothy and Gerald W. Robins—Tasso.
Sam-Son Farm—Chief Bearhart, Dance Smartly, Sky Classic.
Sangster, Robert E.—Royal Heroine (Ire).
Sackatoga Stable—Funny Cide.
Sarkowsky, Herman—Phone Chatter.
Saron Stable—Turkoman.
Scharbauer, Dorothy and Pamela—Alysheba (1987, '88).
Schiff, John M.—Plugged Nickle.
Shannon, Bradley M.—Manila.
SKS Stable—Lord Avie.
Someday Farm—Smarty Jones.
Sommer, Sigmund—Autobiography.
Star Crown Stable—Chief's Crown.
Starlight Stables, Paul Saylor, and Johns Martin—Ashado (2004, '05).
Stephen, Martha and Richard and The Thoroughbred Corp.—Jewel Princess.
Stone, Mrs. Whitney—Shuvee.
Stonerside Stable—Chilukki.
Straub-Rubens, Cecilia, and Michael Cooper—Tiznow (2000).
Stronach, Frank and Nelson Bunker Hunt—Glorious Song.
Stronach Stable—Ghostzapper, Macho Uno, Perfect Sting.
Stud TNT and Stonewall Farm Stallions—Leroidesanimaux (Brz).
Sullivan, Jeffrey—Black Tie Affair (Ire).
Summa Stable—Track Robbery.
Tabor, Michael—Left Bank, Thunder Gulch.
Tabor, Michael and Susan Magnier—High Chaparral (Ire) (2002, '03), Johannesburg.
Tafel, James, Richard Santulli, and Jayeff B Stables—Banshee Breeze.
Tanaka, Gary—Golden Apples (Ire), Gourmet Girl.
Tartan Stable—Dr. Patches.
Tayhill Stable—Seattle Slew (1978).
Taylor, Mrs. Karen L.—Seattle Slew (1976, '77).
The Thoroughbred Corp.—Anees, Point Given.
The Thoroughbred Corp. and Russell Reineman—War Emblem.
Tizol, E. Rodriguez—Bold Forbes.
Torsney, Dr. Jerome M.—Mac Diarmida.
Tucker, Paula—Princess Rooney.
Valando, Thomas—Fly So Free.
Vance, Jeanne—Lemon Drop Kid.
Van Worp, Robert—Not Surprising.

Warren, Mr. and Mrs. William Jr.—Saint Liam.
Weasel Jr., George—My Juliet.
Weinsier, Randolph—Lakeville Miss.
Lord Weinstock, Executors of the late—Islington (Ire).
Wertheimer Farm—Halfbridled.
Westerly Stud—Typecast.
Whitham, Mr. and Mrs. Frank E.—Bayakoa (Arg) (1989, '90).
Whitney, Marylou—Bird Town.
Wildenstein, Daniel—All Along (Fr).
Wildenstein Stable—Steinlen (GB).
Windfields Farm and Neil Phillips—*Snow Knight.
Wygod, Martin and Pamela—Sweet Catomine.

Breeders of Eclipse Award Winners

Adams, Mrs. Vanderbilt—Desert Vixen.
Adena Springs—Ghostzapper, Macho Uno, Perfect Sting.
Aga Khan—Daylami (Ire), Hirapour (Ire), Kalanisi (Ire).
Alexander, Emory—Queena.
Allez France Stables—Steinlen (GB).
Augustus, Peggy—Johnny D.
Baker, Dr. Howard—Serena's Song.
Ballydoyle Stud—Correggio (Ire).
Ballymacoll Stud Farm—Islington (Ire).
Barnhart, Anna Marie—Skip Away (1996, '97, '98).
Bell, H. Bennett, and Jessica Bell Nicholson—Epitome.
Benjamin, Edward Bernard—Canonero II (Ire).
Benjamin, E. V. III, and William G. Clark—Chou Croute.
Bettersworth, J. R.—My Juliet.
Blue Bear Stud—Zaccio (1980, '81, '82).
Blue Diamond Ranch—Snow Chief.
Blue Seas Music Inc.—Heartlight No. One.
Brant, Peter M.—Gulch, Thunder Gulch.
Calbourne Farm—Brown Bess.
Calumet Farm—Before Dawn, Criminal Type, Davona Dale, Our Mims.
Cannata, Carl and Olivia—Gourmet Girl.
Carrion, Jaime S.—Action This Day, Meadow Star.
Castleman, Ben S.—Seattle Slew (1976, '77, '78).
Centurion Farms—Deputy Minister.
Chenery, Helen B.—Saratoga Dew.
Christiana Stables—Go for Wand (1989, '90).
Claiborne Farm—Forty Niner, Revidere, Slew o' Gold (1983, '84), Swale, Wajima.
Cleaboy Farms Co.—Inlander (GB).
Cohen, Ollie A.—Eillo.
Cojuangco, Edwardo M. Jr.—Manila.
Coughlan, Sean—High Chaparral (Ire) (2002, '03).
Cowan, Irving and Marjorie—Hollywood Wildcat.
Danada Farm—Proud Delta.
Darley Stud Management—Tempera.
Davison, Mrs. Richard—Guilty Conscience.
Dayton Ltd.—All Along (Fr), Waya (Fr).
Delta Thoroughbreds Inc.—Cardmania.
De Mestre, J.W.—Jimmy Lorenzo (GB).
Due Process Stables—Dehere, Open Mind (1988, '89).
Eaton Farms Inc. and Red Bull Stable—Bold Forbes.
Echo Valley Horse Farm Inc.—Chris Evert, Winning Colors.
Egan, James and David Hanley—Golden Apples (Ire).
Elmendorf Farm—Protagonist, Shadow Brook, Talking Picture.
Evans, Edward P.—Saint Liam.
Evans, Thomas Mellon—Pleasant Colony, Pleasant Tap.
Evans, Mrs. Thomas Mellon—Pleasant Stage.
Farfellow Farms Ltd.—Anees.
Farish, William S., James Elkins, and Temple Webber Jr.—Mineshaft.
Farish, William S., and W. S. Kilroy—A.P. Indy, Lemon Drop Kid.
Farish, William S., and Ogden Mills Phipps—Storm Song.
Farnsworth Farms—Beautiful Pleasure, Jewel Princess.
Feeney, F.—April Run (Ire).
Firestone, Mr. and Mrs. Bertram R.—Paradise Creek, Theatrical (Ire).
Flaxman Holdings Ltd.—Aldebaran, Miesque (1987, '88).
Floyd, William—Highland Bud.
Fox, Richard and Nathan, and Richard Kaster—McDynamo (2003, '05).
Franks, John—Answer Lively.
Freeman, Carl M.—Miss Alleged.
Fuller, C. T.—Ambassador of Luck.
Fuller, Peter—Mom's Command.
Gainesway Thoroughbreds Ltd.—Orientate.
Gainsborough Farm—Fantastic Light, Hatoof.
Galbreath, John W.—Little Current, Sunshine Forever.
Galbreath, Mrs. John W.—Tempest Queen.
Galbreath/Phillips Racing Partnership—Soaring Softly.
Genter Stable, Frances A.—Smile.
Golden Chance Farm Inc.—John Henry (1980, '81, '83, '84).
Greentree Stud—Bowl Game, Late Bloomer.
Groves, Helen, Helen Alexander, and David Aykroyd—Althea.
Guest, Raymond R.—Cascapedia.
Guest, Virginia D.—Life's Illusion.
Gunther, John, Tony Holmes, Walter Zent—Stevie Wonderboy.
Guggenheim, Harry F.—Ack Ack.
Hancock, Arthur B. III, and Leone J. Peters—Risen Star.
Happy Valley Farm—It's in the Air.
Haras Bage do Sul—Leroidesanimaux (Brz).

Leading Breeders

Wholly or in partnership, by number of titles won, including Horse of the Year

11—Allen E. Paulson
9—Harbor View Farm
7—William S. Farish and Partners
7—Lazy F Ranch
6—Claiborne Farm
6—Golden Chance Farm
6—Ogden Phipps
5—Calumet Farm
5—Walter M. Jeffords Jr.
5—Aaron U. Jones
5—Meadow Stud
5—William L. Pape and Jonathan Sheppard

By Individual Winners

6—Ogden Phipps
5—Claiborne Farm
5—Allen E. Paulson
4—Calumet Farm
4—Overbrook Farm
4—William Farish and Partners
4—Harbor View Farm
4—Juddmonte Farms
4—Nelson Bunker Hunt

Haras El Huerton—*Gran Kan.
Haras General Cruz—*Cougar II.
Haras Principal—Bayakoa (Arg) (1989, '90).
Haras Santa Ana do Rio Grande—Riboletta (Brz).
Haras Santa Amelia—Pompeyo (Chi).
Haras Vacacion—Paseana (Arg) (1992, '93).
Harbor View Farm—Affirmed (1977-'79), Athenian Idol, Outstandingly, Flawlessly (1992, '93).
Hartigan, John H.—Mac Diarmida.
Hayden, Mr. and Mrs. David—Safely Kept.
Hibbert, Robert E.—Roving Boy.
Hickey, P. Noel—Buck's Boy.
Highclere Inc. and Clear Creek—Silverbulletday (1998, '99).
Hi Yu Stables—Chinook Pass.
Hofmann, Mr. and Mrs. Philip B.—Gold Beauty.
Homan, J. L.—Gallant Bob.
Hooper, Fred W.—Susan's Girl (1972, '73, '75).
Hooper, Fred W.—Precisionist.
Humphrey, G. Watts Jr., and William S. Farish III—Sacahuista.
Humphrey, Mrs. G. Watts Jr.—Genuine Risk.

Hundley, Bruce, and Wayne Garrison—Fly So Free.
Hunt, Nelson Bunker—Dahlia, Estrapade, Trillion, Youth.
Iandoli, Lewis E.—Conquistador Cielo.
Irish American Bloodstock Agency Ltd.—Yanks Music.
Irish Hill Farm and Rowe W. Harper—Spend a Buck.
Janney, Mr. and Mrs. Stuart S. Jr.—Ruffian (1974, '75).
Jason, Mrs. William M., and Mrs. William Gilmore—Spectacular Bid (1978, '79, '80).
Jeffords, Walter M. Jr.—Lonesome Glory (1992, '93, '95, '97, '99).
Jones, Aaron U.—Lemhi Gold, Tiffany Lass.
Jones, Aaron U. and Marie D.—Ashado (2004, '05), Speightstown.
Jones, Brereton C.—Caressing.
Juddmonte Farms—Banks Hill (GB), Intercontinental (GB), Ryafan, Wandesta (GB).
Karutz, Dr. Wallace—Brave Raj.
Kaster, Richard S.—Countess Diana.
Keck, Howard B.—Ferdinand, Turkish Trousers.
Kellman, Joseph—Shecky Greene.
Kitchen, Edgar—Track Robbery.
Kluener, Robert G.—Warm Spell.
Knight, Landon—Flat Top (1998, 2002).
Kris Syndicate, and Kirtlington Stud Ltd.—All Gong (GB).
Lancaster, Carlyle J.—Star de Naskra.
Lazy F Ranch—Forego (1974, '75, '76, '77).
Levesque, Jean-Louis—La Prevoyante.
Levy, Blanche P., and Murphy Stable—Housebuster (1990, '91).
Levy, Robert P., and Cisley Stable—North Sider.
Lewis, Robert and Beverly—Folklore.
Lilley, J. A. C.—*Snow Knight.
Little Hill Farm—Real Quiet.
Little, Marvin A. Jr.—Hansel.
Loblolly Stable—Prairie Bayou, Vanlandingham.
Lowquest Ltd.—Timber Country.
Luro, Horatio A.—Wayward Lass.
Lyster III, W. G. and Jayeff B Stables—Johannesburg.
Madden, Preston—Alysheba (1987, '88).
Maktoum, Sheikh Mohammed bin Rashid al—Singspiel (Ire).
Mangurian, Mr. and Mrs. Harry T. Jr.—Gilded Time.
Maynard, Richard D.—Chief Bearhart.
Meadow Stud—Riva Ridge, Secretariat (1972, '73).
Mellon, Paul—Key to the Mint, Run the Gantlet.
Mill House—Sensational.
Nahem, Ed—Bertrando.
Narducci, M.D., Audrey—Squirtle Squirt.
Nerud, John A.—Cozzene.
Newgate Stud Company—Fiji (GB).
North Ridge Farm—Blushing John, Capote.
Nuckols Brothers—Typecast.
Nuckols, Charles Jr. and Sons—Hidden Lake, War Emblem.
Oak Cliff Thoroughbreds Ltd.—Sunday Silence.
Onett, George C.—Cherokee Run.
Overbrook Farm—Boston Harbor, Flanders, Golden Attraction, Surfside.
Pancoast, Mrs. Jean R.—Dearly Precious.
Pape, William L., and Jonathan Sheppard—Flatterer (1983, '84, '85, '86), Martie's Anger.
Parkhill, Marshall—Morley Street (Ire) (1990, '91).
Parrish, Douglas, Estate of Emma Haggin Parrish, and Dr. David C. Parrish III—Life's Magic.
Parrish Hill Farm and William S. Farish—Charismatic.
Paulson, Allen E.—Ajina, Azeri (2002, '03, '04), Cigar (1995, '96), Eliza, Escena.
Payson Stud—Farda Amiga, Vindication.
Paxson, Adele—Candy Eclair.
Pelican Stable—Holy Bull.
Perez, Carlos—Kona Gold.
Peskoff, Stephen D.—Black Tie Affair (Ire).
Phillips, Mrs. Jacqueline Getty—Bates Motel.
Phillips Racing Partnership/Galbreath—Soaring Softly.
Phipps, Cynthia—Christmas Past.
Phipps, Mrs. Ogden—Straight and True.
Phipps, Ogden—Easy Goer, Heavenly Prize, Numbered Account, Personal Ensign, Relaxing, Storm Flag Flying.
Phipps, Ogden Mills—Inside Information, Rhythm, Smuggler.
Pin Oak Farm—Laugh and Be Merry.
Polinger, Milton—What a Summer.
Polk, Dr. Albert F. Jr.—Temperence Hill.
Pope, George A. Jr.—J. O. Tobin.
Ramsey, Kenneth and Sarah—Kitten's Joy.
Rathvale Stud—Just a Game (Ire).
Ravenbrook Farm Inc.—Not Surprising.
Ridgely, Brice—Declan's Moon.
Roach, Dr. Ben, and Tom Roach—Princess Rooney.
Robertson, Corbin—Turkoman.
Robins, Gerald W. and Timothy H. Sams—Tasso.
Robinson, Marshall T.—Groovy.
Rosebrock, Perry M.—Smoke Glacken.
Rosen, Carl—Chief's Crown.
Rosenthal, Morton—Maria's Mon.
Ryan, B. L.—Royal Heroine (Ire).
Ryehill Farm—Heavenly Cause, Smart Angle.
Sam-Son Farm—Dance Smartly, Sky Classic.
Sarkowsky, Herman—Phone Chatter.
Schiff, John M.—Plugged Nickle.
Scott, Mrs. Marion duPont—Soothsayer.
Selective Seasons—Family Style.
Seper, Susan—Lost in the Fog.
Sergent, Willard—Reraise.
Shead, A. D. and F. H. Sasse—Perrault (GB).
Silvertand, John Martin—Afleet Alex.
Someday Farm—Smarty Jones.
Spendthrift Farm and Francis Kernan—Landaluce.
Spreen, Robert H.—Lady's Secret.
Stanley Estate and Stud Co.—Ouija Board (GB).
Stone, Whitney—Shuvee.
Straub-Rubens, Cecilia—Tiznow (2000, '01).
Sugar Maple Farm—Itsallgreektome, Sky Beauty.
Swettenham Stud—Lit de Justice.
Swettenham Stud and Partners—Northern Spur (Ire).
Tafel, James B.—Banshee Breeze.
Tall Oaks Farm—Victory Gallop.
Tartan Farms Corp.—Dr. Patches, Unbridled.
Taylor, E. P.—Devil's Bag, Glorious Song.
The Thoroughbred Corp.—Point Given.
Third Kirsmith Racing Associates—Rubiano.
Thomas, Dr. E. W., and Carolaine Farm—Rockhill Native.
Viking Farms Ltd.—Lord Avie.
Vinery and Carondelet Farm—Artax.
Waldemar Farms Inc.—Foolish Pleasure, Honest Pleasure.
Warren Hill Stud and Mimika Financiera—Pebbles (GB).
Weinsier, Randolph—Lakeville Miss.
Wertheimer and Brother—Halfbridled, Kotashaan (Fr).
West, Dr. and Mrs. R. Smiser, and MacKenzie Miller—De La Rose.
West, Dr. and Mrs. R. Smiser, and Mr. and Mrs. MacKenzie Miller—Chilukki.
Wheatley Stable—Autobiography.
Whitney, Marylou—Bird Town.
WinStar Farm—Funny Cide.
Wilson, Ralph C. Jr.—Arazi.
Winchell, Verne H.—Cafe Prince (1977-'78), Tight Spot.
Witt, Mr. and Mrs. Robert—Possibly Perfect.
Wood, Mr. and Mrs. M. L.—Favorite Trick.
Wootton, Mary Lou—Silver Charm.
Wygod, Martin and Pamela—Sweet Catomine.
Youngblood, John, and Fletcher Gray—Left Bank.
Zurek, Edward N.—The Wicked North.

Trainers of Eclipse Award Winners

Albertrani, Louis—Artax.
Alexander, Frank—Cherokee Run.
Allard, Edward T.—Mom's Command.
Anderson, Laurie—Chinook Pass.
Arias, Juan—Canonero II.
Badgett Jr., William—Go for Wand (1989, '90).
Baffert, Robert—Chilukki, Point Given, Real Quiet, Silverbulletday (1998, '99), Silver Charm, Vindication, War Emblem.
Balding, Gerald B. "Toby"—Morley Street (Ire) (1990, '91).
Barnett, Robert—Answer Lively.
Barrera, Lazaro S.—Affirmed (1977, '78, '79), Bold Forbes, It's in the Air, J. O. Tobin, Lemhi Gold, Tiffany Lass.
Bary, Pascal—Miss Alleged (with Charles Whittingham).
Belanger Jr., Gerald W.—Glorious Song.
Bernstein, David—The Wicked North.
Biancone, Patrick L.—All Along (Fr).
Bin Suroor, Saeed—Daylami (Ire), Fantastic Light.
Bohannan, Thomas—Prairie Bayou.
Boutin, Francois—April Run (Ire), Arazi, Miesque (1987, '88).
Brittain, Clive E.—Pebbles (GB).
Brothers, Frank—Hansel.
Burch, J. Elliot—Key to the Mint, Run the Gantlet.
Byrne, Patrick—Countess Diana, Favorite Trick.
Campbell, Gordon C.—Cascapedia.
Campo, John P.—Pleasant Colony, Protagonist, Talking Picture.
Canani, Julio—Sweet Catomine.
Cantey, Joseph B.—Temperence Hill.
Carroll, Henry—Smoke Glacken.
Cecil, Ben—Golden Apples (Ire).
Cocks, W. Burling—Zaccio (1980, '81, '82).
Croll Jr., Warren A.—Holy Bull, Housebuster (1990, '91).
Curtis Jr., William—Gold Beauty.
Day, Jim—Dance Smartly, Sky Classic.
Delp, Grover G.—Spectacular Bid (1978, '79, '80).
de Seroux, Laura—Azeri (2002, '03).
DiMauro, Steve—Dearly Precious, Wajima.
Dollase, Craig—Reraise.
Dollase, Wallace—Itsallgreektome, Jewel Princess.
Doyle, A. T.—Typecast.
Drysdale, Neil—A.P. Indy, Fiji (GB), Hollywood Wildcat, Princess Rooney, Tasso.
Dunham, Robert G.—Chou Croute.
Dunlop, Edward—Ouija Board (GB).
Dutrow, Richard Jr.—Saint Liam.
Elliot, Janet E.—Correggio (Ire), Flat Top (1998, 2002).
Ellis, Ron—Declan's Moon.
Euster, Eugene—My Juliet.
Fabre, Andre—Banks Hill (GB).
Fenstermaker, L. Ross—Precisionist, Susan's Girl (1975).
Fenwick, Charles—Inlander (GB).
Ferris, Richard D.—Star de Naskra.
Fout, Douglas—Hirapour (Ire).
Fout, Paul R.—Life's Illusion.
Frankel, Robert—Aldebaran, Bertrando, Ghostzapper, Intercontinental (GB), Leroidesanimaux (Brz), Possibly Perfect, Ryafan, Squirtle Squirt, Wandesta (GB).
Freeman, W. C.—Shuvee.
Furr, C.—*Gran Kan.
Frostad, Mark—Chief Bearhart.
Gambolati, Cam—Spend a Buck.
Gaver, John M.—Late Bloomer.
Gaver Jr., John M.—Bowl Game.
Gilchrist, Greg—Lost in the Fog.
Goldberg, Alan E.—Safely Kept.
Goldfine, Lou M.—Shecky Greene.
Gosden, John H. M.—Bates Motel, Royal Heroine (Ire).
Griggs, John K.—Warm Spell.
Harty, Eoin—Tempera.
Hassinger Jr., Alex—Anees, Eliza.
Hauswald, Phil—Epitome.
Head, Christiane—Hatoof.
Headley, Bruce—Kona Gold.
Hendriks, Sanna Neilson—McDynamo (2003, '05), Pomeyo (Chi).
Hertler, John O.—Slew o' Gold (1983, '84).
Hickey, P. Noel—Buck's Boy.
Hine, Hubert—Guilty Conscience, Skip Away (1996, '97, '98).
Howard, Neil—Mineshaft.
Howe, Peter M.—Proud Delta, Soothsayer.
Inda, Eduardo—Riboletta (Brz).
Jenda, Charles J.—Brown Bess.
Jerkens, H. Allen—Sky Beauty.
Jolley, LeRoy—Foolish Pleasure, Genuine Risk, Honest Pleasure, Manila, Meadow Star, What a Summer.
Jones, Gary—Turkoman.
Kay, Michael—Johnny D.
Kelly, Thomas J.—Plugged Nickle.
Kimmel, John—Hidden Lake.
King Jr., S. Allen—Candy Eclair.
Laurin, Lucien—Riva Ridge, Secretariat (1972, '73).
Laurin, Roger—Chief's Crown, Numbered Account.
Lepman, Budd—Eillo.
Lobo, Paulo—Farda Amiga.
Lukas, D. Wayne—Althea, Azeri (2004), Boston Harbor, Capote, Charismatic, Criminal Type, Family Style, Flanders, Folklore, Golden Attraction, Gulch, Lady's Secret, Landaluce, Life's Magic (1984, '85), North Sider, Open Mind (1988, '89), Orientate, Sacahuista, Serena's Song, Steinlen (GB), Surfside, Thunder Gulch, Timber Country, Winning Colors.
Lundy, Richard J.—Blushing John.
Mandella, Richard—Action This Day, Halfbridled, Kotashaan (Fr), Phone Chatter.
Manzi, Joseph—Roving Boy.
Marquette, Joseph D.—Gallant Bob.
Marti, Pedro—Heartlight No. One.
Martin, Frank—Autobiography, Outstandingly.
Martin, Jose—Groovy, Lakeville Miss, Wayward Lass.
McAnally, Ronald—Bayakoa (Arg) (1989, '90), John Henry (1980, '81, '83, '84), Northern Spur (Ire), Paseana (Arg) (1992, '93), Tight Spot.
McGaughey III, Claude R.—Easy Goer, Heavenly Prize, Inside Information, Personal Ensign, Queena, Rhythm, Smuggler, Storm Flag Flying, Vanlandingham.
Meredith, Derek—Cardmania.
Miller, F. Bruce—All Gong (GB), Lonesome Glory (1992, '93, '95, '97, '99).
Miller, MacKenzie—*Snow Knight.
Mott, Bill—Ajina, Cigar (1995, '96), Escena, Paradise Creek, Theatrical (Ire).
Nafzger, Carl A.—Banshee Breeze, Unbridled.
Nerud, Jan H.—Cozzene.
Nerud, John A.—Dr. Patches.
Nickerson, Victor J.—John Henry

Leading Trainers

Wholly or in partnership, by number of titles won, including Horse of the Year

29—D. Wayne Lukas
13—Charlie Whittingham
12—Ron McAnally
10—Lazaro Barrera
10—Robert Frankel
10—Jonathan Sheppard
9—Bob Baffert
9—Claude McGaughey III
9—Woody Stephens
8—Bill Mott
7—Frank Y. Whiteley Jr.
6—LeRoy Jolley
6—F. Bruce Miller
5—Neil Drysdale
5—Hubert Hine
5—Lucien Laurin
5—Richard Mandella
5—Flint S. Schulhofer

By Individual Winners

24—D. Wayne Lukas
9—Robert Frankel
9—Claude McGaughey III
9—Charles Whittingham
8—Woody Stephens
7—Bob Baffert
6—Laz Barrera
6—LeRoy Jolley
6—Jonathan Sheppard
5—Ron McAnally
5—Bill Mott
5—Flint S. Schulhofer

(1981).
Nobles, Reynaldo—Dehere.
O'Brien, Aidan—High Chaparral (Ire) (2002, '03), Johannesburg.
O'Brien, Leo—Yanks Music.
O'Neill, Doug—Stevie Wonderboy.
Orseno, Joseph F.—Macho Uno, Perfect Sting.
Penna, Angel—Relaxing.
Penna Jr., Angel—Christmas Past, Laugh and Be Merry.
Perlsweig, Daniel—Lord Avie.
Perdomo, Pico—Gourmet Girl.
Peterson, Douglas—Seattle Slew (1978).
Pletcher, Todd—Ashado (2004, '05), Left Bank, Speightstown.
Poulos, Ernie—Black Tie Affair (Ire).
Preger, Mitchell C.—Ambassador of Luck.
Ritchey, Tim—Afleet Alex.
Robbins, Jay—Tiznow (2000, '01).
Romans Dale L.—Kitten's Joy.
Rondinello, Thomas L.—Little Current, Tempest Queen.
Root Sr., T. F.—Desert Vixen.
Roussel III, Louis J.—Risen Star.
Russell, John W.—Susan's Girl (1972, '73).
Sahadi, Jenine—Lit de Justice.
Schosberg, Richard—Maria's Mon.
Schulhofer, Flint S.—Fly So Free, Lemon Drop Kid, Mac Diarmida, Rubiano, Smile.
Sciacca, Gary—Saratoga Dew.
Servis, John—Smarty Jones.
Sheppard, Jonathan E.—Athenian Idol, Cafe Prince (1977, '78), Flatterer (1983, '84, '85, '86), Highland Bud, Jimmy Lorenzo (GB), Martie's Anger.
Smithwick, D. Michael—Straight and True.
Speckert, Chris—Pleasant Stage, Pleasant Tap.
Starr, John—La Prevoyante.
Stephens, Woodford C.—Conquistador Cielo, De La Rose, Devil's Bag, Forty Niner, Heavenly Cause, Sensational, Smart Angle, Swale.
Stevens, Herbert—Rockhill Native.
Stoute, Sir Michael—Islington (Ire), Kalanisi (Ire), Singspiel (Ire).
Stute, Mel—Brave Raj, Snow Chief.
Tagg, Barclay—Funny Cide.
Tammaro, John—Deputy Minister.
Toner, James J.—Soaring Softly.
Trovato, Joseph A.—Chris Evert.
Turner Jr., William H.—Seattle Slew (1976-'77).
Van Berg, Jack—Alysheba (1987-'88).
Vance, David R.—Caressing.
Van Worp, Judson—Not Surprising.
Veitch, John M.—Before Dawn, Davona Dale, Our Mims, Sunshine Forever.
Vienna, Darrell—Gilded Time.
Walden, W. Elliott—Victory Gallop.
Ward, John T.—Beautiful Pleasure.
Ward, Sherrill W.—Forego (1974, '75).
Watters Jr., Sidney—Shadow Brook, Slew o' Gold (1983, '84).
Wheeler, Robert L. and John W. Russell—Track Robbery.
Whiteley, David A.—Just a Game (Ire), Revidere, Waya (Fr).
Whiteley Jr., Frank Y.—Forego (1976, '77), Ruffian (1974, '75).
Whittingham, Charles—Ack Ack, *Cougar II, Estrapade, Ferdinand, Flawlessly (1992, '93), Miss Alleged (with Pascal Bary), Perrault (GB), Sunday Silence, Turkish Trousers.
Zilber, Maurice—Youth, Dahlia, Trillion.
Zito, Nicholas P.—Bird Town, Storm Song.

Sires of Eclipse Award Winners

Ack Ack—Youth.
Affirmed—Flawlessly (1992, '93).
Ahmad—Paseana (Arg) (1992, '93).
Air Forbes Won—Yanks Music.
***Alcibiades II**—Athenian Idol.
Alleged—Flat Top (1998, 2002), Miss Alleged.
Alydar—Althea, Alysheba (1987, '88), Criminal Type, Easy Goer, Turkoman.
A.P. Indy—Mineshaft, Tempera.
Awesome Again—Ghostzapper.
Bagdad—Turkish Trousers.
Battle Joined—Ack Ack.
Best Turn—Davona Dale.
Blushing Groom (Fr)—Arazi, Blushing John, Sky Beauty.
Bold Bidder—Spectacular Bid (1978, '79, '80).
Bold Forbes—Tiffany Lass.
Bold Reasoning—Seattle Slew (1976, '77, '78).
Bold Ruler—Secretariat (1972, '73), Wajima.
Broad Brush—Farda Amiga.
Buckaroo—Spend a Buck.
Buckpasser—La Prevoyante, Numbered Account, Relaxing.
Bucksplasher—Buck's Boy.
Candy Stripes—Leroidesanimaux (Brz).
Cape Cross (Ire)—Ouija Board (GB).
Cape Town—Bird Town.
Capote—Boston Harbor.
Caro (Ire)—Cozzene, Winning Colors.
Cee's Tizzy—Gourmet Girl, Tiznow (2000, '01).
Cherokee Run—Chilukki.
Chief's Crown—Chief Bearhart.
Chieftain—Cascapedia.
Cohoes—Shadow Brook.
Consultant's Bid—Bayakoa (Arg) (1989, '90).
Cormorant—Saratoga Dew.
Court Ruling—Guilty Conscience.
Cox's Ridge—Cardmania, Life's Magic 1984, '85), Vanlandingham.
Creme dela Creme—Cafe Prince (1977, '78).
Crozier—Precisionist.
Cryptoclearance—Victory Gallop.
Danehill—Banks Hill (GB), Intercontinental (GB).
Danzatore—Reraise.
Danzig—Chief's Crown, Dance Smartly.
Darshaan—Kotashaan (Fr).
Deep Run—Morley Street (Ire) (1990, '91).
Deerhound—Countess Diana.
Delta Judge—Proud Delta.
Deputy Minister—Dehere, Go for Wand (1989, '90), Open Mind (1988, '89).
Distorted Humor—Funny Cide.
Djakao—Perrault (GB).
Doyoun—Daylami (Ire), Kalanisi (Ire).
Dr. Fager—Dearly Precious, Dr. Patches.
Dynaformer—McDynamo (2003, '05).
El Gran Senor—Lit de Justice.
El Prado (Ire)—Kitten's Joy.
Elusive Quality—Smarty Jones.
Erins Isle (Ire)—Laugh and Be Merry.
Exclusive Native—Affirmed (1977, '78, '79), Genuine Risk, Outstandingly.
Fappiano—Tasso, Unbridled, Rubiano.
Faraway Son—Waya (Fr).
Far North—The Wicked North.

Leading Sires

By number of titles won, including Horse of the Year

11—Mr. Prospector
9—Seattle Slew
8—Alydar
7—Exclusive Native
7—*Forli
6—Bold Ruler
6—Ole Bob Bowers
5—Deputy Minister
5—Sadler's Wells
5—Transworld

By Individual Winners

10—Mr. Prospector
6—Seattle Slew
5—Alydar
4—Sadler's Wells
4—Unbridled

Firestreak—*Snow Knight.
First Landing—Riva Ridge.
***Forli**—Forego (1974, '75, '76, '77).
French Deputy—Left Bank.
Gallant Romeo—Gallant Bob, My Juliet.
Gone West—Speightstown.
Graustark—Key to the Mint, Tempest Queen.
Great Above—Holy Bull.
***Grey Dawn II**—Christmas Past, Heavenly Cause.
Gulch—Thunder Gulch.
Habitat—Steinlen (GB).
Hail the Pirates—Wayward Lass.
Hail to Reason—Trillion.

Halo—Devil's Bag, Glorious Song, Sunday Silence.
Hennessy—Johannesburg.
***Herbager**—Our Mims.
His Majesty—Pleasant Colony, Tight Spot.
Hoist the Flag—Sensational.
Holy Bull—Macho Uno.
Honour and Glory—Caressing.
Horatius—Safely Kept.
Ile de Bourbon—Inlander (GB).
In Reality—Desert Vixen, Smile.
In the Wings (GB)—Singspiel (Ire).
Irish Castle—Bold Forbes.
Irish River (Fr)—Hatoof, Paradise Creek.
Jade Hunter—Azeri (2002, '03, '04).
Java Gold—Kona Gold.
Kahyasi—Hirapour (Ire).
Key to the Mint—Jewel Princess, Plugged Nickle.
Kingmambo—Lemon Drop Kid.
Kris—All Gong (GB).
Kris S.—Action This Day, Hollywood Wildcat, Soaring Softly.
Lear Fan—Ryafan.
Licencioso—*Gran Kan.
Little Missouri—Prairie Bayou.
Lively One—Answer Lively.
Lord Gaylord—Lord Avie.
***Lorenzaccio**—Zaccio (1980, '81, '82).
Lost Soldier—Lost in the Fog.
Lt. Stevens—Chou Croute.
Lyphard—Manila.
Lypheor (GB)—Royal Heroine (Ire).
Malibu Moon—Declan's Moon.
Marquetry—Artax, Squirtle Squirt.
Maudlin—Beautiful Pleasure.
Meadowlake—Meadow Star.
Medieval Man—Not Surprising.
Minnesota Mac—Mac Diarmida.
Miswaki—Black Tie Affair (Ire).
Mo Bay—Flatterer (1983, '84, '85, '86).
Mr. Prospector—Aldebaran, Conquistador Cielo, Eillo, Forty Niner, Gold Beauty, Golden Attraction, Gulch, It's in the Air, Queena, Rhythm.
Mt. Livermore—Housebuster (1990, '91), Eliza, Orientate.
***Mystic II**—Life's Illusion, Soothsayer.
Nashua—Shuvee.
Nashwan—Wandesta (GB).
Naskra—Star de Naskra.
Native Born—Chinook Pass.
Never Bend—J. O. Tobin, Straight and True.
Nijinsky II—De La Rose, Ferdinand, Sky Classic.
***Noholme II**—Shecky Greene.
Norcliffe—Groovy.
No Robbery—Track Robbery.
Northern Afleet—Afleet Alex.
Northern Baby—Highland Bud, Possibly Perfect, Warm Spell.
Northern Jove—Candy Eclair.
Nureyev—Miesque (1987, '88), Theatrical (Ire).
Nureyev Dancer—Pompeyo (Chi).
Olden Times—Roving Boy.
Ole Bob Bowers—John Henry (1980, '81, '83, '84).
Our Emblem—War Emblem.
Our Jimmy—Jimmy Lorenzo (GB).
Our Native—Rockhill Native.
Palace Music—Cigar (1995, '96).
***Petrone**—Brown Bess.
Phone Trick—Favorite Trick, Phone Chatter.
Pivotal—Golden Apples (Ire).
Pleasant Colony—Pleasant Stage, Pleasant Tap.
***Pretendre**—Canonero II.
Prince John—Protagonist, Typecast.
Private Account—Inside Information, Personal Ensign.
Quadrangle—Smart Angle, Susan's Girl (1972, '73, '75).
Quiet American—Hidden Lake, Real Quiet.
Rahy—Fantastic Light, Serena's Song.
Rainbow Quest—Fiji (GB).
Rainy Lake—Lakeville Miss.
Raise a Cup—Before Dawn.
Rajab—Brave Raj.
Raja Baba—Sacahuista.
Red Ransom—Perfect Sting.
Reflected Glory—Snow Chief.
Reviewer—Revidere, Ruffian (1974, '75).
Roberto—Sunshine Forever.
Rock Talk—Heartlight No. One.
Roi Normand—Riboletta (Brz).
Runaway Groom—Cherokee Run.
Run the Gantlet—April Run (Ire).
Sadler's Wells—Correggio (Ire), High Chaparral (Ire) (2002, '03), Islington (Ire), Northern Spur (Ire).
Saint Ballado—Ashado (2004, '05), Saint Liam.
***Sea-Bird**—Little Current.
Seattle Slew—A.P. Indy, Capote, Landaluce, Slew o' Gold (1983, '84), Surfside, Swale, Vindication.
Secretariat—Lady's Secret, Risen Star.
Seeking the Gold—Flanders, Heavenly Prize.
Sharpen Up (GB)—Pebbles (GB).
Silver Buck—Silver Charm.
Silver Deputy—Silverbulletday (1998, '99).
Sir Ivor—Bates Motel.
Skip Trial—Skip Away (1996, '97, '98).
***Sky High II**—Autobiography.
Skywalker—Bertrando.
Sovereign Dancer—Itsallgreektome.
Speak John—Talking Picture.
Spring Double—Martie's Anger.
Stage Door Johnny—Johnny D., Late Bloomer.
State Dinner—Family Style.
Stephen Got Even—Stevie Wonderboy.
Stop the Music—Temperence Hill.
Storm Cat—Storm Flag Flying, Sweet Catomine.
Strawberry Road (Aus)—Ajina, Escena.
Summer Squall—Charismatic, Storm Song.
Summing—Epitome.
Swoon's Son—Chris Evert.
Tale of Two Cities—*Cougar II.
Tarboosh—Just a Game (Ire).
Targowice—All Along (Fr).
Thunder Gulch—Point Given.
Time for a Change—Fly So Free.
Timeless Moment—Gilded Time.
Tiznow—Folklore.
Tom Rolfe—Bowl Game, Run the Gantlet.
Top Command—Mom's Command.
Topsider—North Sider.
Transworld—Lonesome Glory (1992, '93, '95, '97, '99).
Two Punch—Smoke Glacken.
Unbridled—Anees, Banshee Breeze, Halfbridled, Smuggler.
***Vaguely Noble**—Dahlia, Estrapade, Lemhi Gold.
Verbatim—Princess Rooney.
Vice Regent—Deputy Minister.
Wavering Monarch—Maria's Mon.
What a Pleasure—Foolish Pleasure, Honest Pleasure.
What Luck—Ambassador of Luck, What a Summer.
Woodman—Hansel, Timber Country.

Daily Racing Form/NTRA National Handicapping Championship

Year	Winner	Residence	Winning Total
2006	Ron Rippey	Wayne, N.J.	237.20
2005	Jamie Michelson Jr.	West Bloomfield, Mi.	240.40
2004	Kent Meyer	Sioux City, Ia.	238.40
2003	Steve Wolfson Jr.	Port Orange, Fl.	279.60
2002	Herman Miller	Oakland, Ca.	205.30
2001	Judy Wagner	New Orleans, La.	237.70
2000	Steve Walker	Lincoln, Ne.	305.40

2005 Eclipse Award Winners

SAINT LIAM

Horse of the Year

Older Male

2000 b. h., Saint Ballado—Quiet Dance, by Quiet American

Breeder: Edward P. Evans (Ky.)
Owners: Mr. and Mrs. William K. Warren Jr.
Trainer: Richard E. Dutrow Jr.
2005 Record: 6-4-1-0, $3,696,960
Lifetime Record Through 2005: 20-9-6-1, $4,456,995
2005 Stakes Victories: Breeders' Cup Classic (G1), Woodward S. (G1), Stephen Foster H. (G1), Donn H. (G1)

At the finish of the Breeders' Cup Classic (G1) on October 29, Saint Liam was undeniably the continent's leading older horse and a very strong candidate for Horse of the Year after finishing a length ahead of three-year-old Flower Alley. The Saint Ballado horse started his championship season with a 3¾-length victory in Gulfstream Park's Donn Handicap (G1) over Roses in May. The only true disappointment in his 2005 season was a sluggish sixth in the Santa Anita Handicap (G1). At Churchill Downs in June, Saint Liam won the Stephen Foster Handicap (G1) by 2¾ lengths. He prepared for the Breeders' Cup Classic with a two-length score in the Woodward Stakes (G1) in September at Belmont.

STEVIE WONDERBOY

Two-Year-Old Male

2003 ch. c., Stephen Got Even—Heat Lightning, by Summer Squall

Breeders: John Gunther, Tony Holmes, and Walter Zent (Ky.)
Owner: The Merv Griffin Ranch Co.
Trainer: Doug F. O'Neill
2005 Record: 5-3-1-1, $1,028,940
2005 Stakes Victories: Breeders' Cup Juvenile (G1), Del Mar Futurity (G2)

Stevie Wonderboy was named for the musical star Stevie Wonder, who had dazzled entertainment entrepreneur Merv Griffin many years earlier. After his maiden win in early August, he won the Del Mar Futurity (G2) by five lengths as the 5-to-2 favorite, and trainer Doug O'Neill counseled going nearly eight weeks without a race and training Stevie Wonderboy up to the Breeders' Cup Juvenile (G1). The strategy worked, and Stevie Wonderboy won by 1¼ lengths over Henny Hughes.

FOLKLORE

Two-Year-Old Filly

2003 b. f., Tiznow—Contrive, by Storm Cat

Breeders: Robert and Beverly Lewis (Ky.)
Owners: Estate of Robert B. Lewis
Trainer: D. Wayne Lukas
2005 Record: 7-4-3-0, $927,500
2005 Stakes Victories: Breeders' Cup Juvenile Fillies (G1), Matron S. (G1), Adirondack S. (G2)

Robert and Beverly Lewis bred Folklore, who is by two-time Breeders' Cup Classic (G1) winner Tiznow, and retained her on the recommendation of trainer D. Wayne Lukas. She scored her maiden victory in her second career start at Belmont and then finished second to rival Adieu in the 5½-furlong Astoria Stakes. When the action moved to Saratoga Race Course, Folklore scored her first stakes victory in the six-furlong Adirondack Stakes (G2), but fell again to Adieu in the subsequent Spinaway Stakes (G2) at seven furlongs. Lukas then switched jockeys, replacing Cornelio Velasquez with Edgar Prado, and the filly responded with a crushing, 14-length victory in the Matron Stakes (G1) at Belmont. Held just off the pace of Knights Templar in the Breeders' Cup Juvenile Fillies (G1), 2.35-to-1 favorite Folklore kicked clear of her nine opponents in the stretch and won by 1¼ lengths.

AFLEET ALEX

Three-Year-Old Male

2002 b. c., Northern Afleet—Maggy Hawk, by Hawkster

Breeder: John Martin Silvertand (Fl.)
Owner: Cash is King stable
Trainer: Timothy F. Ritchey
2005 Record: 6-4-0-1, $2,085,000
Lifetime Record Through 2005: 12-8-2-1, $2,765,800
2005 Stakes Victories: Preakness S. (G1), Belmont S. (G1), Arkansas Derby (G2), Mountain Valley S.

With his acrobatic athleticism in the Preakness Stakes (G1), Afleet Alex caught the attention and affection of American racing fans. Trainer Tim Ritchey followed the path of 2004 champion three-year-old male Smarty Jones and took Afleet Alex to Oaklawn Park, where he won the Mountain Valley Stakes in early March. Two weeks later in Oaklawn's Rebel Stakes (G3), he finished a poor sixth, apparently the result of a bronchial infection. Four weeks later, Afleet Alex scored an overwhelming, eight-length victory in the Arkansas Derby (G2). He finished a good third in the Kentucky Derby (G1), a length behind upset winner Giacomo, and then found his feet after clipping heels at the top of Pimlico Race Course's stretch. Jockey Jeremy Rose somehow managed to stay aboard the Northern Afleet colt, and they swept to a 4¾-length victory. Afleet Alex's seven-length win in the Belmont Stakes (G1) cemented his dominance of the division.

SMUGGLER

Three-Year-Old Filly

2002 b. f., Unbridled—Inside Information, by Private Account

Breeder: Ogden Mills Phipps (Ky.)
Owner: Phipps Stable
Trainer: Claude R. "Shug" McGaughey III
2005 Record: 4-3-1-0, $558,800
Lifetime Record Through 2005: 7-5-2-0, $634,600
2005 Stakes Victories: Coaching Club American Oaks (G1), Mother Goose S. (G1)

In a highly competitive season for three-year-old fillies, Smuggler stole away with the Eclipse Award on the strength of two Grade 1 victories at Belmont Park. Second in the Acorn Stakes (G1), in which she was unable to turn back the late challenge of Round Pond, Smuggler scored her first stakes victory in the Mother Goose Stakes (G1), winning by a neck. The Coaching Club American Oaks (G1) at 1¼ miles proved to be an ideal distance, and she won by 3½ lengths over Summerly.

ASHADO

Older Female

2001 dk. b. or br. f., Saint Ballado—Goulash, by Mari's Book

Breeders: Aaron U. and Marie D. Jones (Ky)
Owners: Starlight Stable, Paul Saylor, and Johns Martin

Trainer: Todd Pletcher
2005 Record: 7-3-1-1, $1,061,000
Lifetime Record Through 2005: 21-12-4-3, $3,931,440
2005 Stakes Victories: Beldame S. (G1), Ogden Phipps H. (G1), Go for Wand H. (G1)

Although not as dominant as she had been as a three-year-old, Ashado nonetheless stood head and shoulders above the other members of an inconsistent older female division and secured her second consecutive Eclipse Award. After defeats in Oaklawn Park's Apple Blossom Handicap (G1) and the Pimlico Breeders' Cup Distaff Handicap (G3), Ashado secured her first stakes win of 2005 with a pacesetting, three-length victory over Society Selection in the Ogden Phipps Handicap (G1). In Saratoga Race Course's Go for Wand Handicap (G1), Ashado scored her most dramatic victory of the year, pulling away through the stretch to a 9½-length score. A distant fourth in Saratoga's Personal Ensign Stakes (G1), she rebounded to win Belmont's Beldame Stakes (G1) in early October, but her bid for the North American female earnings title fell short when she finished a well-beaten third behind Pleasant Home in the Breeders' Cup Distaff (G1).

LEROIDESANIMAUX (BRZ)

Turf Male

2000 ch. h., Candy Stripes—Dissemble (GB), by Ahonoora (GB)
Breeder: Haras Bage Do Sul (Brz.)
Owners: Stud T N T and Stonewall Farm Stallions
Trainer: Robert Frankel
2005 Record: 4-3-1-0, $1,214,040
Lifetime Record Through 2005: 13-9-2-0, $1,658,377
2005 Stakes Victories: Atto Mile S. (Can-G1), Frank E. Kilroe Mile H. (G1), Fourstardave H. (G2)

With a limited racing schedule and only one defeat on the year, Leroidesanimaux (Brz) proved to be the king of the horses who raced on turf in North America in 2005. Trainer Bobby Frankel carefully structured the horse's season leading up to the Breeders' Cup Mile (G1), in which he was defeated by less than a length by Artie Schiller. Leroidesanimaux won his final five starts in 2004 and made it six in a row with a front-running, one-length victory in the Frank E. Kilroe Mile Handicap (G1), his March 2005 debut, on Santa Anita Park's turf course. In August, the Candy Stripes horse set a Saratoga Race Course mark for 1⅟₁₆ miles on the inner turf course, 1:39.92, with a 1¼-length score in the Fourstardave Handicap (G2). Frankel sent him to Woodbine for a 7¾-length victory in the Atto Mile Stakes (Can-G1).

INTERCONTINENTAL (GB)

Turf Female

2000 b. m., Danehill—Hasili (Ire), by Kahyasi
Breeder: Juddmonte Farms (Eng.)
Owner: Juddmonte Farms
Trainer: Robert Frankel
2005 Record: 7-5-1-1, $1,271,200
Lifetime Record Through 2005: 22-13-3-4, $2,052,463
2005 Stakes Victories: Breeders' Cup Filly and Mare Turf (G1), WinStar Galaxy S. (G2), Palomar Breeders' Cup H. (G2), Jenny Wiley S. (G3), Royal Heroine Invitational S. (G3)

Emulating older sister Banks Hill (GB), Intercontinental (GB) swept to a Breeders' Cup Filly and Mare Turf (G1) victory and a championship as North America's leading turf female in 2005. With trainer Bobby Frankel managing her cross-country campaign, Intercontinental won five of her seven 2005 starts and finished in the money in the other two. The Danehill mare won the Royal Heroine Invitational Stakes (G3) at Hollywood Park before finishing third in John C. Mabee Handicap (G1) at Del Mar. Frankel brought Intercontinental back to win Del Mar's Palomar Breeders' Cup Handicap (G2), and then shipped her again to Keeneland, where she won the WinStar Galaxy Stakes (G2).

LOST IN THE FOG

Sprinter

2002 dk. b. or br. c., Lost Soldier—Cloud Break, by Dr. Carter
Breeder: Susan Seper (Fl.)
Owner: Harry J. Aleo
Trainer: Greg Gilchrist
2005 Record: 9-8-0-0, $844,500
Lifetime Record Through 2005: 11-10-0-0, $889,075
2005 Stakes Victories: King's Bishop S. (G1), Carry Back S. (G2), Riva Ridge Breeders' Cup S. (G2), Swale S. (G2), Bay Shore S. (G3), Bay Meadows Speed H., Golden Bear Breeders' Cup S., Ocala Stud Dash S.

Although his unbeaten streak ended when he finished seventh in the Breeders' Cup Sprint (G1), Lost in the Fog established sufficient dominance at shorter distances to claim the sprinter title. After opening the season with a Sunshine Millions victory in the Ocala Stud Dash Stakes at Gulfstream Park in late January, Lost in the Fog briefly went on the Triple Crown trail by winning the Swale (G2) and Bay Shore (G3) Stakes, both at seven furlongs. The Lost Soldier colt won the Riva Ridge Breeders' Cup Stakes (G2) and rolled to a 7¼-length triumph in Calder Race Course's Carry Back Stakes (G2). At Saratoga Race Course, he collected his only Grade 1 victory in the King's Bishop Stakes.

MCDYNAMO

Steeplechaser

1997 b. g., Dynaformer—Rondonia, by Monteverdi (Ire)
Breeders: Richard Fox, Nathan Fox, and Richard Kaster (Ky.)
Owner: Michael Moran
Trainer: Sanna Neilson Hendriks
2005 Record: 6-2-3-1, $265,425
Lifetime Record Through 2005: 27-13-6-1, $877,994
2005 Stakes Victories: Breeders' Cup Steeplechase, Colonial Cup Hurdle S.

As autumn's days began to grow shorter, McDynamo's odds for a second Eclipse Award in three years seemed to grow longer. His losing streak extended all the way back to his second consecutive Breeders' Cup Steeplechase victory in mid-October 2004. But another visit to Far Hills, New Jersey, annual scene of the Breeders' Cup Steeplechase, proved to be a tonic for McDynamo's 2005 season. He had never been beaten there in four prior starts. Always on the pace, McDynamo steadily widened his advantage, jumped the final fence with an eight-length lead and won the Breeders' Cup Steeplechase by nine lengths. Five weeks later in the Colonial Cup Hurdle Stakes, McDynamo set all the pace again and withstood a challenge by 2004 champion Hirapour (Ire) in the stretch to win by 1¾ lengths.

Champions Before Eclipse Awards

Daily Racing Form (DRF) began naming champions in 1936. Beginning in 1950, the Thoroughbred Racing Associations (TRA) began naming its own champions. The following tables reflect the horses named champions by those two organizations. Where neither the letter (D) nor (T) follows the name of the horse, both the DRF and the TRA named that horse champion. When there were different champions named in any category, the DRF champion is noted with the letter (D) and the TRA with the letter (T). *Daily Racing Form*, the TRA, and the National Turf Writers Association joined forces in 1971 to create the Eclipse Awards, which now recognize the champions of racing in North America.

†-filly, *-imported horse; (D) *Daily Racing Form*; (T) Thoroughbred Racing Associations

Horse of the Year

1970	Fort Marcy (D)
	Personality (T)
1969	Arts and Letters
1968	Dr. Fager
1967	Damascus
1966	Buckpasser
1965	Roman Brother (D)
	†Moccasin (T)
1964	Kelso
1963	Kelso
1962	Kelso
1961	Kelso
1960	Kelso
1959	Sword Dancer
1958	Round Table
1957	Bold Ruler (D)
	Dedicate (T)
1956	Swaps
1955	Nashua
1954	Native Dancer
1953	Tom Fool
1952	One Count (D)
	Native Dancer (T)
1951	Counterpoint
1950	Hill Prince
1949	Capot
1948	Citation
1947	Armed
1946	Assault
1945	†Busher
1944	†Twilight Tear
1943	Count Fleet
1942	Whirlaway
1941	Whirlaway
1940	Challedon
1939	Challedon
1938	Seabiscuit
1937	War Admiral
1936	Granville

Two-Year-Old Male

1970	Hoist the Flag
1969	Silent Screen
1968	Top Knight
1967	Vitriolic
1966	Successor
1965	Buckpasser
1964	Bold Lad
1963	Hurry to Market
1962	Never Bend
1961	Crimson Satan
1960	Hail to Reason
1959	Warfare
1958	First Landing
1957	Nadir (D)
	Jewel's Reward (T)
1956	Barbizon
1955	Needles
1954	Nashua
1953	Porterhouse
1952	Native Dancer
1951	Tom Fool
1950	Battlefield
1949	Hill Prince
1948	Blue Peter
1947	Citation
1946	Double Jay
1945	Star Pilot
1944	Pavot
1943	Platter
1942	Count Fleet
1941	Alsab
1940	Our Boots
1939	Bimelech
1938	El Chico
1937	Menow
1936	Pompoon

Two-Year-Old Filly

1970	Forward Gal
1969	Fast Attack (D)
	Tudor Queen (T)
1968	Gallant Bloom (D)
	Process Shot (T)
1967	Queen of the Stage
1966	Regal Gleam
1965	Moccasin
1964	Queen Empress
1963	Tosmah (D)
	Castle Forbes (T)
1962	Smart Deb
1961	Cicada
1960	Bowl of Flowers
1959	My Dear Girl
1958	Quill
1957	Idun
1956	Leallah (D)
	Romanita (T)
1955	Doubledogdare (D)
	Nasrina (T)
1954	High Voltage
1953	Evening Out
1952	Sweet Patootie
1951	Rose Jet
1950	Aunt Jinny
1949	Bed o' Roses
1948	Myrtle Charm
1947	Bewitch
1946	First Flight
1945	Beaugay
1944	Busher
1943	Durazna
1942	Askmenow
1941	Petrify
1940	Level Best
1939	Now What
1938	Incoselda
1937	Jacola
1936	Apogee

Three-Year-Old Male

1970	Personality
1969	Arts and Letters
1968	Stage Door Johnny
1967	Damascus
1966	Buckpasser
1965	Tom Rolfe
1964	Northern Dancer
1963	Chateaugay
1962	Jaipur
1961	Carry Back
1960	Kelso
1959	Sword Dancer
1958	Tim Tam
1957	Bold Ruler
1956	Needles
1955	Nashua
1954	High Gun
1953	Native Dancer
1952	One Count
1951	Counterpoint
1950	Hill Prince
1949	Capot
1948	Citation
1947	Phalanx
1946	Assault
1945	Fighting Step
1944	By Jimminy
1943	Count Fleet
1942	Alsab
1941	Whirlaway
1940	Bimelech
1939	Challedon
1938	Stagehand
1937	War Admiral
1936	Granville

Three-Year-Old Filly

1970	Office Queen (D)
	Fanfreluche (T)
1969	Gallant Bloom
1968	Dark Mirage
1967	Furl Sail (D)
	Gamely (T)
1966	Lady Pitt
1965	What a Treat
1964	Tosmah
1963	Lamb Chop
1962	Cicada
1961	Bowl of Flowers

1960	Berlo
1959	Royal Native (D)
	Silver Spoon (T)
1958	Idun
1957	Bayou
1956	Doubledogdare
1955	Misty Morn
1954	Parlo
1953	Grecian Queen
1952	Real Delight
1951	Kiss Me Kate
1950	Next Move
1949	‡Two Lea
	‡Wistful
1948	Miss Request
1947	But Why Not
1946	Bridal Flower
1945	Busher
1944	Twilight Tear
1943	Stefanita
1942	Vagrancy
1941	Painted Veil
1940	Not awarded
1939	Unerring
1938	Not awarded
1937	Not awarded
1936	Not awarded

‡ (D) co-champions

Handicap Male

1970	Fort Marcy (D)
	Nodouble (T)
1969	Arts and Letters (D)
	Nodouble (T)
1968	Dr. Fager
1967	Damascus (D)
	Buckpasser (T)
1966	Buckpasser (D)
	Bold Bidder (T)
1965	Roman Brother
1964	Kelso
1963	Kelso
1962	Kelso
1961	Kelso
1960	Bald Eagle
1959	Sword Dancer (D)
	Round Table (T)
1958	Round Table
1957	Dedicate
1956	Swaps
1955	High Gun
1954	Native Dancer
1953	Tom Fool
1952	Crafty Admiral
1951	Hill Prince
1950	*Noor
1949	Coaltown
1948	Citation
1947	Armed
1946	Armed
1945	Stymie
1944	Devil Diver
1943	Market Wise
	Devil Diver
1942	Whirlaway
1941	Mioland
1940	Challedon
1939	*Kayak II
1938	Seabiscuit
1937	Seabiscuit
1936	Discovery

Handicap Female

1970	Shuvee
1969	Gallant Bloom (D)
	Gamely (T)
1968	Gamely
1967	Straight Deal
1966	Open Fire (D)
	Summer Scandal (T)
1965	Old Hat
1964	Tosmah (D)
	Old Hat (T)
1963	Cicada
1962	Primonetta
1961	Airmans Guide
1960	Royal Native
1959	Tempted
1958	Bornastar
1957	Pucker Up
1956	Blue Sparkler
1955	Misty Morn (D)
	Parlo (T)
1954	Parlo (D)
	Lavender Hill (T)
1953	Sickle's Image
1952	Real Delight (D)
	Next Move (T)
1951	Bed o' Roses
1950	Two Lea
1949	Bewitch
1948	Conniver
1947	But Why Not
1946	Gallorette
1945	Busher
1944	Twilight Tear
1943	Mar-Kell
1942	Vagrancy
1941	Fairy Chant
1940	War Plumage
1939	Lady Maryland
1938	Marica
1937	Not awarded
1936	Myrtlewood

Sprinter

1970	†Ta Wee
1969	†Ta Wee
1968	Dr. Fager
1967	Dr. Fager
1966	Impressive
1965	†Affectionately
1964	Ahoy
1963	Not awarded
1962	Not awarded
1961	Not awarded
1960	Not awarded
1959	Intentionally
1958	Bold Ruler
1957	Decathlon
1956	Decathlon
1955	Berseem
1954	White Skies
1953	Tom Fool
1952	Tea-Maker
1951	Sheilas Reward
1950	Sheilas Reward
1949	Delegate
	Royal Governor
1948	Coaltown
1947	Polynesian

1947: first year category included

Turf Horse

1970	Fort Marcy
1969	*Hawaii
1968	Dr. Fager (D)
	Fort Marcy (T)
1967	Fort Marcy
1966	Assagai
1965	Parka
1964	*Turbo Jet II
1963	Mongo
1962	Not awarded
1961	T. V. Lark
1960	Not awarded
1959	Round Table
1958	Round Table
1957	Round Table
1956	Career Boy
1955	*St. Vincent
1954	*Stan
1953	*Iceberg II

1953: first year category included

Steeplechase

1970	Top Bid
1969	*L'Escargot
1968	Bon Nouvel
1967	Quick Pitch
1966	Mako (D)
	Tuscalee (T)
1965	Bon Nouvel
1964	Bon Nouvel
1963	Amber Diver
1962	Barnabys Bluff
1961	Peal
1960	Benguala
1959	Ancestor
1958	Neji
1957	Neji
1956	Shipboard
1955	Neji
1954	King Commander
1953	The Mast
1952	Jam (D)
	Oedipus (T)
1951	Oedipus
1950	Oedipus
1949	Trough Hill
1948	American Way
1947	War Battle
1946	Elkridge
1945	Mercator
1944	Rouge Dragon
1943	Brother Jones
1942	Elkridge
1941	Speculate
1940	Not awarded
1939	Not awarded
1938	Not awarded
1937	Jungle King
1936	Bushranger

RACING HALL OF FAME

History of Racing Hall of Fame

The Racing Hall of Fame was founded in 1955 to honor the all-time greats of the sport, though it is largely limited to horses, jockeys, and trainers. Housed in the National Museum of Racing in Saratoga Springs, New York, the Racing Hall of Fame contains plaques that summarize the accomplishments of each inductee.

Each spring, a panel votes on the horses and people nominated for induction into the Hall of Fame. The results are announced in May, and the induction ceremony takes place the second Monday of August in Saratoga Springs. Categories under consideration each year are contemporary male, contemporary female, jockey, and trainer.

Nominees for induction into the Hall of Fame are first obtained from the 125 members of the Hall of Fame voting panel. Unsuccessful candidates who appeared on the final ballot in the previous three years automatically are added to the initial list of candidates. The suggestions then go before a nomination committee, which narrows the names down to three for each category for that year's ballots.

Names of the three finalists in each division then go before the entire voting panel. Beginning in 2006, members of the voting panel cast yes-or-no votes on the three candidates. A candidate must receive at least 75% of the votes cast to be eligible for induction. If more than one candidate receives more than 75% of the votes cast, the one with the most votes will be inducted. In case of ties for the top position, all candidates will be inducted. Before 2005, the top vote-getter in each category was selected as that year's inductee.

From time to time, the Historical Review Committee and the Steeplechase Committee make additional selections to the Hall of Fame.

Hall of Fame Eligibility Criteria:

1. Thoroughbreds become eligible when five calendar years have elapsed between their final racing year and their year of nomination.
2. Eligible Thoroughbreds are classified as contemporary male or female if they have been retired between five and 25 years. Horses that have been retired for more than 25 years are classified as horses of yesteryear and are considered by the Historical Review Committee.
3. Beginning in 2006, active jockeys become eligible after riding Thoroughbreds for 20 years (any interruptions in their careers for injury are not counted against them). Before 2006, the requirement was 15 years.
4. Active trainers become eligible after 25 years as licensed Thoroughbred trainers.
5. The 20- and 25-year requirements may be waived for retired jockeys and trainers, but a five-year waiting period is then observed before they become eligible. In cases of fragile health, the Hall of Fame Committee may request that the five-year waiting period be waived at the discretion of the Executive Committee.

Members of the National Museum of Racing Hall of Fame

Exemplars of Racing (Year Inducted)

John W. Hanes (1982)
C. V. Whitney (1991)
Walter M. Jeffords (1973)
Paul Mellon (1989)
George D. Widener (1971)

Jockeys (Year Inducted)

Frank D. "Dooley" Adams (1970)
John Adams (1965)
Joe Aitcheson Jr. (1978)
Edward Arcaro (1958)
Ted Atkinson (1957)
Braulio Baeza (1976)
Jerry Bailey (1995)
George Barbee (1996)
Carroll K. Bassett (1972)
Russell Baze (1999)
Walter Blum (1987)
Bill Boland (2006)
George "Pete" Bostwick (1968)
Sam Boulmetis Sr. (1973)
Steve Brooks (1963)
Don Brumfield (1996)
Thomas H. Burns (1983)
James H. Butwell (1984)
J. Dallett "Dolly" Byers (1967)
Steve Cauthen (1994)
Frank Coltiletti (1970)
Angel Cordero Jr. (1988)
Robert H. "Specs" Crawford (1973)
Pat Day (1991)
Eddie Delahoussaye (1993)
Kent Desormeaux (2004)
Lavelle "Buddy" Ensor (1962)
Laverne Fator (1955)
Earlie Fires (2001)
Jerry Fishback (1992)
Andrew "Mack" Garner (1969)
Edward "Snapper" Garrison (1955)
Avelino Gomez (1982)
Henry F. Griffin (1956)
Eric Guerin (1972)
William J. Hartack (1959)
Sandy Hawley (1992)
Albert Johnson (1971)
William J. Knapp (1969)
Julie Krone (2000)
Clarence Kummer (1972)
Charles Kurtsinger (1967)
John P. Loftus (1959)
John Longden (1958)
Daniel A. Maher (1955)
J. Linus McAtee (1956)
Chris McCarron (1989)
Conn McCreary (1975)
Rigan McKinney (1968)
James McLaughlin (1955)
Walter Miller (1955)
Isaac B. Murphy (1955)
Ralph Neves (1960)
Joe Notter (1963)
George M. Odom (1955)
Winfield "Winnie" O'Connor (1956)
Frank O'Neill (1956)
Ivan H. Parke (1978)
Gilbert W. Patrick (1970)
Laffit Pincay Jr. (1975)
Samuel Purdy (1970)
John Reiff (1956)
Alfred Robertson (1971)
John L. Rotz (1983)
Earl Sande (1955)
Carroll H. Schilling (1970)
William Shoemaker (1958)
Willie Simms (1977)
James "Tod" Sloan (1955)
Mike Smith (2003)
Alfred P. "Paddy" Smithwick (1973)
Gary Stevens (1997)
James Stout (1968)
Fred Taral (1955)
Bayard Tuckerman Jr. (1973)
Ron Turcotte (1979)
Nash Turner (1955)
Robert N. Ussery (1980)
Jacinto Vasquez (1998)
Jorge Velasquez (1990)
Thomas Walsh (2005)
Jack Westrope (2002)
George M. Woolf (1955)
Raymond Workman (1956)
Manuel Ycaza (1977)

Trainers (Year Inducted)

Lazaro S. Barrera (1979)
H. Guy Bedwell (1971)
Edward D. Brown (1984)
J. Elliott Burch (1980)
Preston M. Burch (1963)
William P. Burch (1955)
Fred Burlew (1973)
Frank E. Childs (1968)
Henry S. Clark (1982)
W. Burling Cocks (1985)
James P. Conway (1996)
Warren A. "Jimmy" Croll Jr. (1994)
Grover G. "Buddy" Delp (2002)
Neil Drysdale (2000)
William Duke (1956)
Louis Feustel (1964)
James Fitzsimmons (1958)
Robert Frankel (1995)
John M. Gaver Sr. (1966)
Carl Hanford (2006)
Thomas J. Healey (1955)
Sam C. Hildreth (1955)
Hubert "Sonny" Hine (2003)
Max Hirsch (1959)
William J. "Buddy" Hirsch (1982)
Thomas Hitchcock Sr. (1973)
Hollie Hughes (1973)
John J. Hyland (1956)
Hirsch Jacobs (1958)
H. Allen Jerkens (1975)
Philip G. Johnson (1997)
William R. Johnson (1986)
LeRoy Jolley (1987)
Ben A. Jones (1958)
Horace A. "Jimmy" Jones (1959)
Andrew Jackson Joyner (1955)
Thomas J. Kelly (1993)
Lucien Laurin (1977)
J. Howard Lewis (1969)
D. Wayne Lukas (1999)
Horatio Luro (1980)
John E. Madden (1983)
James W. Maloney (1989)
Richard Mandella (2001)
Frank "Pancho" Martin (1981)
Ron McAnally (1990)
Henry McDaniel (1956)
Claude R. "Shug" McGaughey III (2004)
MacKenzie "Mack" Miller (1987)
William Molter Jr. (1960)
William I. Mott (1998)
Winbert Mulholland (1967)
Edward A. Neloy (1983)
John A. Nerud (1972)
Burley Parke (1986)
Angel Penna Sr. (1988)
Jacob Pincus (1988)
John W. Rogers (1955)
James G. Rowe Sr. (1955)
Flint S. "Scotty" Schulhofer (1992)
Jonathan Sheppard (1990)
Robert A. Smith (1976)
Tom Smith (2001)
D. M. "Mike" Smithwick (1971)
Woodford C. "Woody" Stephens (1976)
Meshach "Mesh" Tenney (1991)
Henry J. Thompson (1969)
Harry Trotsek (1984)
Jack C. Van Berg (1985)
Marion H. Van Berg (1970)
Sylvester Veitch (1977)
Robert W. Walden (1970)
Michael Walsh (1997)
Sherrill Ward (1978)
Sidney Watters Jr. (2005)
Frank Whiteley Jr. (1978)
Charles Whittingham (1974)
Ansel Williamson (1998)
G. Carey Winfrey (1975)
William C. Winfrey (1971)
Nicholas P. Zito (2005)

Horses (Year Inducted, Year Foaled)

Ack Ack (1986, 1966)
Affectionately (1989, 1960)
Affirmed (1980, 1975)
All Along (Fr) (1990, 1979)
Alsab (1976, 1939)
Alydar (1989, 1975)
Alysheba (1993, 1984)
American Eclipse (1970, 1814)
A.P. Indy (2000, 1989)
Armed (1963, 1941)
Artful (1956, 1902)
Arts and Letters (1994, 1966)
Assault (1964, 1943)
Battleship (1969, 1927)
Bayakoa (Arg) (1998, 1984)
Bed o' Roses (1976, 1947)
Beldame (1956, 1901)
Ben Brush (1955, 1893)
Bewitch (1977, 1945)
Bimelech (1990, 1937)
Black Gold (1989, 1921)
Black Helen (1991, 1932)
Blue Larkspur (1957, 1926)
Bold 'n Determined (1997, 1977)
Bold Ruler (1973, 1954)
Bon Nouvel (1976, 1960)
Boston (1955, 1833)
Broomstick (1956, 1901)
Buckpasser (1970, 1963)
Busher (1964, 1942)
Bushranger (1967, 1930)
Cafe Prince (1985, 1970)
Carry Back (1975, 1958)
Cavalcade (1993, 1931)
Challedon (1977, 1936)
Chris Evert (1988, 1971)
Cicada (1967, 1959)
Cigar (2002, 1990)
Citation (1959, 1945)
Coaltown (1983, 1945)
Colin (1956, 1905)
Commando (1956, 1898)
*Cougar II (2006, 1966)
Count Fleet (1961, 1940)
Crusader (1995, 1923)
Dahlia (1981, 1970)
Damascus (1974, 1964)
Dance Smartly (2003, 1988)
Dark Mirage (1974, 1965)
Davona Dale (1985, 1976)
Desert Vixen (1979, 1970)
Devil Diver (1980, 1939)
Discovery (1969, 1931)
Domino (1955, 1891)
Dr. Fager (1971, 1964)
Easy Goer (1997, 1986)
Eight Thirty (1994, 1936)
Elkridge (1966, 1938)
Emperor of Norfolk (1988, 1885)
Equipoise (1957, 1928)
Exceller (1999, 1973)
Exterminator (1957, 1915)
Fairmount (1985, 1921)
Fair Play (1956, 1905)
Fashion (1980, 1837)
Firenze (1981, 1884)
Flatterer (1994, 1979)
Flawlessly (2004, 1988)
Foolish Pleasure (1995, 1972)
Forego (1979, 1970)
Fort Marcy (1998, 1964)
Gallant Bloom (1977, 1966)
Gallant Fox (1957, 1927)
*Gallant Man (1987, 1954)
Gallorette (1962, 1942)
Gamely (1980, 1964)
Genuine Risk (1986, 1977)
Go for Wand (1996, 1987)
Good and Plenty (1956, 1900)
Granville (1997, 1933)
Grey Lag (1957, 1918)
Gun Bow (1999, 1960)
Hamburg (1986, 1895)
Hanover (1955, 1884)
Henry of Navarre (1985, 1891)
Hill Prince (1991, 1947)
Hindoo (1955, 1878)
Holy Bull (2001, 1991)
Imp (1965, 1894)
Jay Trump (1971, 1957)
John Henry (1990, 1975)
Johnstown (1992, 1936)
Jolly Roger (1965, 1922)
Kelso (1967, 1957)
Kentucky (1983, 1861)
Kingston (1955, 1884)
Lady's Secret (1992, 1982)
La Prevoyante (1995, 1970)
*L'Escargot (1977, 1963)
Lexington (1955, 1850)
Lonesome Glory (2005, 1988)
Longfellow (1971, 1867)
Luke Blackburn (1955, 1877)
Majestic Prince (1988, 1966)
Man o' War (1957, 1917)
Maskette (2001, 1906)
Miesque (1999, 1984)
Miss Woodford (1967, 1880)
Myrtlewood (1979, 1932)
Nashua (1965, 1952)
Native Dancer (1963, 1950)
Native Diver (1978, 1959)
Needles (2000, 1953)
Neji (1966, 1950)
*Noor (2002, 1945)
Northern Dancer (1976, 1961)
Oedipus (1978, 1946)
Old Rosebud (1968, 1911)
Omaha (1965, 1932)
Pan Zareta (1972, 1910)
Parole (1984, 1873)
Paseana (Arg) (2001, 1987)
Personal Ensign (1993, 1984)
Peter Pan (1956, 1904)
Precisionist (2003,1981)
Princess Doreen (1982, 1921)
Princess Rooney (1991, 1980)
Real Delight (1987, 1949)
Regret (1957, 1912)
Reigh Count (1978, 1925)
Riva Ridge (1998, 1969)
Roamer (1981, 1911)
Roseben (1956, 1901)
Round Table (1972, 1954)
Ruffian (1976, 1972)
Ruthless (1975, 1864)
Salvator (1955, 1886)
Sarazen (1957, 1921)
Seabiscuit (1958, 1933)
Searching (1978, 1952)
Seattle Slew (1981, 1974)
Secretariat (1974, 1970)
Serena's Song (2002, 1992)
Shuvee (1975, 1966)
Silver Spoon (1978, 1956)
Sir Archy (1955, 1805)
Sir Barton (1957, 1916)
Skip Away (2004, 1993)
Slew o' Gold (1992, 1980)
Spectacular Bid (1982, 1976)
Stymie (1975, 1941)
Sun Beau (1996, 1925)
Sunday Silence (1996, 1986)
Susan's Girl (1976, 1969)
Swaps (1966, 1952)
Sword Dancer (1977, 1956)
Sysonby (1956, 1902)
Ta Wee (1994, 1966)
Ten Broeck (1982, 1872)
Tim Tam (1985, 1955)
Tom Fool (1960, 1949)
Top Flight (1966, 1929)
Tosmah (1984, 1961)
Twenty Grand (1957, 1928)
Twilight Tear (1963, 1941)
Two Lea (1982, 1946)
War Admiral (1958, 1934)
Whirlaway (1959, 1938)
Whisk Broom II (1979, 1907)
Winning Colors (2000, 1985)
Zaccio (1990, 1976)
Zev (1983, 1920)

Owners of Racing Hall of Fame Members

H. C. Applegate—Old Rosebud
Augustin Stables—Cafe Prince
E. J. "Lucky" Baldwin—Emperor of Norfolk
Edith W. Bancroft—Damascus
Belair Stud—Gallant Fox, Granville, Johnstown, Nashua, Omaha
August Belmont II—Beldame, Fair Play, Henry of Navarre
Col. E. R. Bradley—Bimelech, Black Helen, Blue Larkspur, Busher
William Brann—Challedon, Gallorette
Briardale Farm—Tosmah
Brookmeade Stable—Bowl of Flowers, Cavalcade, Sword Dancer
S. S. Brown—Broomstick
Calumet Farm—Alydar, Armed, Bewitch, Citation, Coaltown, Davona Dale, Real Delight, Tim Tam, Twilight Tear, Two Lea, Whirlaway
Christopher T. Chenery (Meadow Stable)—Hill Prince
Christiana Stable—Go for Wand
Claiborne Farm—Round Table
Gen. Nathaniel Coles—American Eclipse
E. T. Colton—Pan Zareta
Brownell Combs—Myrtlewood
Sidney H. Craig—Paseana (Arg)
Warren A. "Jimmy" Croll Jr.—Holy Bull
J. F. Cushman and E. V. Snedeker—Kingston
D & H Stable—Needles
Marcus Daly—Hamburg
Dotsam Stable—John Henry
Allaire duPont—Kelso
Mike Dwyer—Ben Brush
Phil and Mike Dwyer—Hanover, Hindoo, Kingston, Luke Blackburn, Miss Woodford
Rex Ellsworth—Swaps
Equusequity Stable—Slew o' Gold
Diana Firestone—Genuine Risk
Mr. and Mrs. E. E. Fogelson—Ack Ack
Dr. Ernest Gaillard, Arthur B. Hancock III, and Charles Whittingham—Sunday Silence
Gedney Farm—Gun Bow
Martha F. Gerry—Forego
William Gibbons—Fashion
Greentree Stable—Devil Diver, Tom Fool, Twenty Grand
John L. Greer—Foolish Pleasure
Harry Guggenheim—Ack Ack
James Ben Ali Haggin—Firenze, Salvator
Harbor View Farm—Affirmed, Flawlessly
Dan Harness—Imp
Frank Harper—Ten Broeck
John Harper—Longfellow
Hawksworth Farm—Spectacular Bid
Mrs. John D. Hertz—Count Fleet, Reigh Count
Carolyn Hine—Skip Away

Leading Owners of Racing Hall of Fame Horses

11— Calumet Farm
6— James R. Keene*
5— Belair Stud
Dwyer Brothers
4— Col. Edward R. Bradley
Meadow Stable
3— August Belmont II
Glen Riddle Farm
Brookmeade Stable
Ethel D. Jacobs
Greentree Stable
Ogden Phipps
Alfred G. Vanderbilt
C. V. Whitney
Harry Payne Whitney

*Includes partnerships

Max Hirsch—Grey Lag
Thomas Hitchcock—Elkridge, Good and Plenty
Fred Hooper—Precisionist, Susan's Girl
Rosa M. Hoots—Black Gold
Charles S. Howard—*Noor, Seabiscuit
Nelson Bunker Hunt—Dahlia, Exceller
John Hunter, George Osgood, and William Travers—Kentucky
Ethel Jacobs—Affectionately, Searching, Stymie
Kay Jeffords—Lonesome Glory
Col. William R. Johnson—Boston, Sir Archy
Davy C. Johnson—Roseben
B. B. and Monfort Jones—Princess Doreen
Mary Jones—*Cougar II
James R. Keene—Colin, Commando, Maskette, Peter Pan, Sysonby
James R. and Foxhall Keene—Domino
Kerr Stable—Round Table
Willis Sharpe Kilmer—Exterminator, Sun Beau
King Ranch—Assault, Gallant Bloom
Eugene Klein—Winning Colors
Mr. and Mrs. Eugene Klein—Lady's Secret
Eugene Leigh and Ed Brown—Ben Brush
Jean-Louis Levesque—La Prevoyante
Robert and Beverly Lewis—Serena's Song
Locust Hill Farm—Ruffian
Pierre Lorillard—Parole
Ralph Lowe—*Gallant Man
John E. Madden—Hamburg
Harry Mangurian Jr.—Desert Vixen
Louis B. Mayer—Busher
Bryon McClelland—Henry of Navarre
Frank McMahon—Majestic Prince
Meadow Stable (Christopher T. Chenery)—Cicada, Riva Ridge, Secretariat
Paul Mellon (Rokeby Stable)—Arts and Letters
J. Cal Milam—Exterminator
Andrew Miller—Roamer
Kent Miller—Elkridge
Lloyd Miller—Dark Mirage
Francis Morris—Ruthless
Mrs. Lewis C. Murdock—Zaccio
J. F. Newman—Pan Zareta
Stavros Niarchos—Miesque
Jonathan Sheppard, William Pape, and George Harris—Flatterer
Allen E. Paulson—Cigar
William Haggin Perry—Gamely
Lillian Bostwick Phipps—Neji, Oedipus
Ogden Phipps—Buckpasser, Easy Goer, Personal Ensign
Powhatan—*L'Escargot
Jack Price—Carry Back
Rancocas Stable—Zev
Mrs. Theodore Randolph—Bon Nouvel
Glen Riddle Farm—Crusader, Man o' War, War Admiral
Nathaniel Rives—Boston
Rokeby Stable (Paul Mellon)—Fort Marcy
Carl Rosen—Chris Evert
Commander J. K. L. Ross—Sir Barton
Albert Sabath—Alsab
Walter J. Salmon Jr.—Battleship
Sam-Son Farm—Dance Smartly
Saron Stable—Bold 'n Determined
Dorothy and Pamela Scharbauer—Alysheba
Marion duPont Scott—Battleship
Mr. and Mrs. L. K. Shapiro—Native Diver
Harry Sinclair—Grey Lag
Mrs. Mary Stephenson—Jay Trump
Mrs. Whitney Stone—Shuvee
Tartan Farms—Dr. Fager, Ta Wee
Tayhill Stable—Seattle Slew
E. P. Taylor—Northern Dancer
Richard Ten Broeck—Lexington
Tomonori Tsurumaki and Farish-Goodman-Kilroy—A.P. Indy
Paula Tucker—Princess Rooney
Cornelius W. Van Ranst—American Eclipse
Alfred G. Vanderbilt—Bed o' Roses, Discovery, Native Dancer
Mrs. W. K. Vanderbilt III—Sarazen
Wheatley Stable—Bold Ruler
Frank and Janis Whitham—Bayakoa (Arg)
C. V. Whitney—Equipoise, Silver Spoon, Top Flight
Harry Payne Whitney—Artful, Regret, Whisk Broom II
Mrs. Payne Whitney—Jolly Roger
George D. Widener—Eight Thirty
Joseph E. Widener—Bushranger, Fairmount
Daniel Wildenstein—All Along (Fr)
Capt. Jim Williams—Luke Blackburn

Breeders of Racing Hall of Fame Members

Muriel Vanderbilt Adams—Desert Vixen
H. H. Aga Khan—*Noor
H. H. Aga Khan and Prince Aly Khan—*Gallant Man
Lucien O. Appleby—Henry of Navarre
F. Wallis Armstrong—Cavalcade
Dr. Howard Baker—Serena's Song
Mrs. Thomas Bancroft—Damascus
Anna Marie Barnhart—Skip Away
Belair Stud—Gallant Fox, Granville, Nashua, Omaha
August Belmont II—Beldame, Fair Play, Man o' War
Bieber-Jacobs Stables—Affectionately
Blue Bear Stud—Zaccio

E. R. Bradley/Idle Hour Stock Farm—Bimelech, Black Helen, Blue Larkspur, Busher, Oedipus
William L. Brann—Challedon
Brookmeade Stable—Bowl of Flowers, Sword Dancer
S. S. Brown—Whisk Broom II
Preston Burch—Gallorette
Calumet Farm—Alydar, Armed, Bewitch, Citation, Coaltown, Davona Dale, Real Delight, Tim Tam, Twilight Tear, Two Lea, Whirlaway
Mrs. Thomas J. Carson—Roseben
Ben Castleman—Seattle Slew
Christopher T. Chenery—Hill Prince
Christiana Stables—Go for Wand
Claiborne Farm—Gamely, Round Table, Slew o' Gold
John Clay—Kentucky
Clay Brothers—Roamer
Gen. Nathaniel Coles—American Eclipse
Brownell Combs—Myrtlewood
Leslie Combs II—Majestic Prince
Dayton Ltd.—All Along (Fr)
Allaire duPont—Kelso
Echo Valley Farm—Chris Evert, Winning Colors
Rex Ellsworth—Swaps
Mrs. Charles W. Engelhard—Exceller
Con Enright—Hamburg
William S. Farish and W. S. Kilroy—A.P. Indy
Joseph F. Flanagan—Elkridge
Flaxman Holdings Ltd.—Miesque
Capt. James and A. C. Franklin—Luke Blackburn
William Gibbons—Fashion
Mrs. William Gilmore and Mrs. William Jason—Spectacular Bid
Golden Chance Farm—John Henry
Greentree Stable—Devil Diver, Jolly Roger, Twenty Grand
Harry Guggenheim—Ack Ack
Arthur B. Hancock Sr.—Johnstown
Haras General Cruz—*Cougar II
Haras Principal—Bayakoa (Arg)
Haras Vacacion—Paseana (Arg)
Harbor View Farm—Affirmed, Flawlessly
Dan Harness—Imp
Frank B. Harper—Good and Plenty

Leading Breeders of Racing Hall of Fame Horses

11—	Calumet Farm
6—	James R. Keene
5—	Idle Hour Stock Farm
	John Madden*
4—	Belair Stud
	Ogden Phipps
3—	August Belmont II
	Claiborne Farm
	Greentree Stable
	Meadow Stud
	Daniel Swigert
	Harry Payne Whitney

*Includes partnerships

John Harper—Ten Broeck, Longfellow
Duval Headley—Dark Mirage, Tom Fool
Mrs. John D. Hertz—Count Fleet
Max Hirsch and King Ranch—Stymie
Fred Hooper—Precisionist, Susan's Girl
Rosa M. Hoots—Black Gold
Mrs. G. Watts Humphrey Jr.—Genuine Risk
Nelson Bunker Hunt—Dahlia
Mr. and Mrs. Stuart S. Janney Jr.—Ruffian
Mrs. William Jason and Mrs. William Gilmore—Spectacular Bid
Walter Jeffords Jr.—Lonesome Glory
Marius E. Johnston—Sarazen
James R. Keene—Colin, Commando, Maskette, Peter Pan, Kingston, Sysonby
Willis Sharpe Kilmer—Reigh Count, Sun Beau
King Ranch—Assault, Gallant Bloom, Stymie
Dixie Knight—Exterminator
Gordon E. Layton—Bold 'n Determined
Lazy F Ranch—Forego
W. E. Leach—Needles
Jean-Louis Levesque—La Prevoyante
John E. Madden—Grey Lag, Old Rosebud, Princess Doreen, Zev
John E. Madden and Vivian A. Gooch—Sir Barton
Preston Madden—Alysheba
Maine Chance Farm—Gun Bow
Meadow Stud—Cicada, Riva Ridge, Secretariat
Paul Mellon—Arts and Letters, Fort Marcy

Mereworth Farm—Discovery
Eugene Mori—Tosmah
Francis Morris—Ruthless
J. F. Newman—Pan Zareta
Oak Cliff Thoroughbreds—Sunday Silence
Mrs. B. O'Neill—L'Escargot
William Pape and Jonathan Sheppard—Flatterer
Allen E. Paulson—Cigar
Pelican Stable—Holy Bull
Ogden Phipps—Buckpasser, Easy Goer, Personal Ensign, Searching
Thomas Piatt—Alsab
Jack Price—Carry Back
Dr. A. C. Randolph—Bon Nouvel
Capt. Archibald Randolph and Col. John Tayloe III—Sir Archy
Samuel D. Riddle—Crusader, War Admiral
Ben Roach and Tom Roach—Princess Rooney
Runnymede Farm—Ben Brush, Hanover
Walter J. Salmon—Discovery, Battleship
Sam-Son Farm—Dance Smartly
Marion duPont Scott—Neji
Jan Sensenich—Jay Trump
Mr. and Mrs. L. K. Shapiro—Native Diver
Robert H. Spreen—Lady's Secret
Whitney Stone—Shuvee
Daniel Swigert—Firenze, Hindoo, Salvator
Tartan Farms—Dr. Fager, Ta Wee
E. P. Taylor—Northern Dancer
Maj. Barak Thomas—Domino
Alfred G. Vanderbilt—Bed o' Roses, Native Dancer
Waldemar Farms—Foolish Pleasure
Elisha Warfield—Lexington
Aristides Welch—Parole
Wheatley Stable—Bold Ruler, Seabiscuit
C. V. Whitney—Silver Spoon
Harry Payne Whitney—Equipoise, Regret, Top Flight
William C. Whitney—Artful
John Wickham—Boston
George D. Widener—Eight Thirty
Joseph E. Widener—Bushranger, Fairmount
Verne H. Winchell—Cafe Prince
Theodore Winters—Emperor of Norfolk
Woodford and Clay—Miss Woodford
Col. Milton Young—Broomstick

Trainers of Racing Hall of Fame Members

Note: In instances when more than one trainer had a Hall of Fame horse during the horse's career, all are credited.

William Badgett—Go for Wand
Lazaro Barrera—Affirmed
Guy Bedwell—Sir Barton
John Belcher—Boston
Patrick Biancone—All Along (Fr)
Frank A. Bonsal—Ack Ack
George H. "Pete" Bostwick—Oedipus, Neji
Francois Boutin—Miesque
William Brennan—Twenty Grand
Charles Brossman—Imp
Ed Brown—Ben Brush
Henry Brown—Lexington
William Brown—Parole
J. Elliott Burch—Arts and Letters, Bowl of Flowers, Fort Marcy, Sword Dancer
Fred Burlew—Beldame
Matt Byrnes—Firenze, Salvator
Don Cameron—Count Fleet
Hardy Campbell—Kingston
Edward A. Christmas—Gallorette
W. Burling Cocks—Zaccio
Harry Colston—Ten Broeck
E. T. Colton—Pan Zareta
George Conway—Crusader, War Admiral
Warren A. "Jimmy" Croll—Holy Bull
James E. Day—Dance Smartly
Grover G. "Bud" Delp—Spectacular Bid
Neil Drysdale—A.P. Indy, Bold 'n Determined, Princess Rooney
Richard Dutrow Sr.—Flawlessly
Ross Fenstermaker—Precisionist, Susan's Girl
Louis Feustel—Man o' War
James "Sunny Jim" Fitzsimmons—Bold Ruler, Gallant Fox, Granville, Johnstown, Nashua, Omaha
Hugh Fontaine—Needles
E. Foucon—Pan Zareta
Willard C. Freeman—Shuvee
John M. Gaver Sr.—Devil Diver, Tom Fool
Jack Goldsborough—Roamer
Carl Hanford—Kelso
John Harper—Longfellow
J. H. "Casey" Hayes—Cicada, Hill Prince
Thomas J. Healey—Equipoise, Top Flight
S. M. Henderson—Princess Doreen
John Hertler—Slew o' Gold
Sam Hildreth—Grey Lag, Zev
Hubert "Sonny" Hine—Skip Away
Max Hirsch—Assault, Gallant Bloom, Sarazen
William Hirsch—Gallant Bloom
Reg Hobbs—Battleship

Freddy Hopkins—Equipoise
Will Hurley—Bimelech, Black Helen
John Hyland—Beldame, Henry of Navarre
Hirsch Jacobs—Affectionately, Searching, Stymie
William R. Johnson—Boston, Sir Archy
LeRoy Jolley—Foolish Pleasure, Genuine Risk
Ben A. Jones—Armed, Bewitch, Citation, Coaltown, Real Delight, Twilight Tear, Two Lea, Whirlaway
Horace A. "Jimmy" Jones—Bewitch, Citation, Coaltown, Tim Tam, Two Lea
Andrew J. Joyner—Fair Play, Whisk Broom II
Charles Kiernan—Good and Plenty
Ray Kindred—Myrtlewood
Everett King—Dark Mirage
Billy Lakeland—Domino, Hamburg
Thomas Larkin—Sir Archy
Lucien Laurin—Riva Ridge, Secretariat
John Lee—Kelso
J. Howard Lewis—Bushranger, Fairmount
John Longden—Majestic Prince
D. Wayne Lukas—Lady's Secret, Serena's Song, Winning Colors
Horatio Luro—Northern Dancer
John E. Madden—Hamburg
James W. Maloney—Gamely
Francois Mathet—Exceller
Ron McAnally—Bayakoa (Arg), John Henry, Paseana (Arg)
Frank McCabe—Hanover
Byron McClelland—Henry of Navarre
John McClelland—Emperor of Norfolk
Henry McDaniel—Exterminator, Reigh Count
Claude R. "Shug" McGaughey III—Easy Goer, Personal Ensign
Joe Mergler—Tosmah
B. S. Michell—Reigh Count
Bruce Miller—Lonesome Glory
Kent Miller—Elkridge
Buster Millerick—Native Diver

Leading Trainers of Racing Hall of Fame Horses

10— James Rowe Sr.
8— Ben A. Jones
6— James "Sunny Jim" Fitzsimmons
Charlie Whittingham
5— Horace A. "Jimmy" Jones
4— J. Elliott Burch
3— Neil Drysdale
Max Hirsch
Hirsch Jacobs
D. Wayne Lukas
Ron McAnally
John Nerud
Frank Whiteley Jr.
William C. Winfrey

A. J. Minor—Ruthless
William Molter—Round Table
D. L. Moore—Neji, *L'Escargot
William I. Mott—Cigar
W. F. "Bert" Mulholland—Eight Thirty
Tom Murphy—Twenty Grand
Edward Neloy—Buckpasser, Gun Bow
John Nerud—Dr. Fager, *Gallant Man, Ta Wee
H. S. Newman—Pan Zareta
J. L. Newman—Susan's Girl
Victor J. "Lefty" Nickerson—John Henry
George Odom—Busher
Burley Parke—*Noor
Chuck Parke—Susan's Girl
Douglas R. Peterson—Seattle Slew
Vincent Powers—Jolly Roger
Jack Price—Carry Back
John B. Pryor—Lexington
John W. Rogers—Artful
Tommy Root Sr.—Desert Vixen
James Rowe Jr.—Twenty Grand
James Rowe Sr.—Colin, Commando, Hindoo, Luke Blackburn, Maskette, Miss Woodford, Peter Pan, Regret, Sysonby, Whisk Broom II
John Russell—Precisionist, Susan's Girl
Louis J. Schaefer—Challedon
Flint S. "Scotty" Schulhofer—Ta Wee
Jonathan Sheppard—Cafe Prince, Flatterer
A. Shuttinger—Sun Beau
Robert A. Smith—Cavalcade
Thomas Smith—Seabiscuit
Crompton "Tommy" Smith Jr.—Jay Trump
D. Michael Smithwick—Bon Nouvel, Neji
E. V. Snedeker—Kingston
John Starr—La Prevoyante
J. H. Stotler—Discovery
August "Sarge" Swenke—Alsab
Arthur Taylor—Boston, Sir Archy
M. A. "Mesh" Tenney—Swaps
Bob Thomas—Emperor of Norfolk
H. J. Thompson—Blue Larkspur
G. R. Tompkins—Crusader
Joseph Trovato—Chris Evert
Bob Tucker—Broomstick
William H. Turner Jr.—Seattle Slew
Jack Van Berg—Alysheba
John Veitch—Alydar, Davona Dale
Sherrill Ward—Forego
Sidney Watters Jr.—Slew o' Gold
Hanley Webb—Black Gold
Frank D. Weir—Old Rosebud, Roseben
R. L. Wheeler—Silver Spoon
Frank Whiteley Jr.—Damascus, Forego, Ruffian
Charles Whittingham—Ack Ack, *Cougar II, Dahlia, Exceller, Flawlessly, Sunday Silence
J. Whyte—Sun Beau
Capt. Jim Williams—Luke Blackburn
Peter Wimmer—Broomstick, Imp
William C. Winfrey—Bed o' Roses, Buckpasser, Native Dancer
Maurice Zilber—Dahlia, Exceller
Unknown—American Eclipse, Fashion, Kentucky

Sires of Racing Hall of Fame Members

Abe Frank—Pan Zareta
Affirmed—Flawlessly
Ahmad—Paseana (Arg)
Alydar—Alysheba, Easy Goer
***Amerigo**—Fort Marcy
Battle Joined—Ack Ack
Ben Brush—Broomstick
***Ben Strome**—Roseben
Best Turn—Davona Dale
***Billet**—Miss Woodford
Black Servant—Blue Larkspur
Black Toney—Bimelech, Black Gold, Black Helen
***Blenheim II**—Whirlaway
Blue Larkspur—Myrtlewood, Oedipus
Bold and Brave—Bold 'n Determined
Bold Bidder—Spectacular Bid
Bold Reasoning—Seattle Slew
Bold Ruler—Gamely, Secretariat
Bold Venture—Assault
***Bonnie Scotland**—Luke Blackburn
Boston—Lexington
Bramble—Ben Brush
Broomstick—Regret, Whisk Broom II
Bryan G.—Cicada
Buckpasser—La Prevoyante
Bull Lea—Armed, Bewitch, Citation, Coaltown, Real Delight, Twilight Tear, Two Lea
Caro (Ire)—Winning Colors
***Challenger II**—Challedon, Gallorette
Citation—Silver Spoon
Commando—Colin, Peter Pan
Consultant's Bid—Bayakoa (Arg)
Creme dela Creme—Cafe Prince
Crozier—Precisionist
Danzig—Dance Smartly
Deputy Minister—Go for Wand
***Diomed**—Sir Archy
***Dis Donc**—Top Flight
Disguise—Maskette
Display—Discovery
Domino—Commando
Duc de Fer—Bon Nouvel
Duroc—American Eclipse
***Eclipse**—Ruthless
Equestrian—Stymie
Escart III—*L'Escargot
Exclusive Native—Affirmed, Genuine Risk
Fair Play—Fairmount, Man o' War
First Landing—Riva Ridge
***Forli**—Forego
Gallant Fox—Granville, Omaha
***Gallant Man**—Gallant Bloom
Glenelg—Firenze
Good Goods—Alsab
Great Above—Holy Bull
Gun Shot—Gun Bow
Halo—Sunday Silence
Hamburg—Artful
Hanover—Hamburg
Hard Tack—Seabiscuit
Hastings—Fair Play
High Time—Sarazen
Himyar—Domino
Hindoo—Hanover
***Hunters Moon IV**—Neji
Imbros—Native Diver
In Reality—Desert Vixen
Intentionally—Ta Wee

Jamestown—Johnstown
***Khaled**—Swaps
***Knight Errant**—Roamer
Knight of Ellerslie—Henry of Navarre
***Lancegaye**—Cavalcade
***Leamington**—Longfellow, Parole
Lexington—Kentucky
***Lorenzaccio**—Zaccio
Man o' War—Battleship, Crusader, War Admiral
Mate—Elkridge
***McGee**—Exterminator
***Melton**—Sysonby
Menow—Tom Fool
***Migoli**—*Gallant Man
Mo Bay—Flatterer
***Nasrullah**—Bold Ruler, Nashua, *Noor
Nearctic—Northern Dancer
Norfolk—Emperor of Norfolk
Nureyev—Miesque
Octagon—Beldame
Ole Bob Bowers—John Henry
Palace Music—Cigar
Pennant—Equipoise, Jolly Roger
***Persian Road II**—Dark Mirage
***Phaeton**—Ten Broeck
Pilate—Eight Thirty
Polynesian—Native Dancer
Ponder—Needles
***Prince Charlie**—Salvator
***Princequillo**—Hill Prince, Round Table
Private Account—Personal Ensign
Quadrangle—Susan's Girl
Rahy—Serena's Song
Raise a Native—Alydar, Majestic Prince

Leading Sires of Racing Hall of Fame Horses

7— Bull Lea
3— Black Toney
Man o' War
*Nasrullah
2— Alydar
Blue Larkspur
Bold Ruler
Broomstick
*Challenger II
Commando
Exclusive Native
Fair Play
Gallant Fox
*Leamington
Pennant
*Princequillo
Raise a Native
Seattle Slew
*St. Germans
*Star Shoot
Tom Fool
*Vaguely Noble
War Admiral

Reigh Count—Count Fleet
Reviewer—Ruffian
***Ribot**—Arts and Letters
Rosemont—Bed o' Roses
Rossington—Good and Plenty
Rough'n Tumble—Dr. Fager
Saggy—Carry Back
Sailor—Bowl of Flowers
Seattle Slew—A.P. Indy, Slew o' Gold
Secretariat—Lady's Secret
***Sir Gallahad III**—Gallant Fox
Skip Trial—Skip Away
***Spanish Prince II**—Princess Doreen
Spendthrift—Kingston
***St. Germans**—Devil Diver, Twenty Grand
***Star Shoot**—Grey Lag, Sir Barton
***Stefan the Great**—Bushranger
***Sun Briar**—Sun Beau
Sunglow—Sword Dancer
***Sunreigh**—Reigh Count
Swaps—Affectionately
Swoon's Son—Chris Evert
Sword Dancer—Damascus
Tale of Two Cities—*Cougar II
Targowice—All Along (Fr)
The Finn—Zev
Tim Tam—Tosmah
Timoleon—Boston
Tom Fool—Buckpasser, Tim Tam
Tonga Prince—Jay Trump
Transworld—Lonesome Glory
***Trustee**—Fashion
Uncle—Old Rosebud
***Vaguely Noble**—Dahlia, Exceller
Verbatim—Princess Rooney
Virgil—Hindoo
Wagner—Imp
War Admiral—Busher, Searching
What a Pleasure—Foolish Pleasure
Your Host—Kelso

Regional Halls of Fame

Arlington Park

No new members have been inducted since 1989.

Horses
Armed
Buckpasser
Candy Spots
Citation
Coaltown
Dr. Fager
Equipoise
Nashua
Native Dancer
Round Table
Secretariat
Tom Rolfe
T. V. Lark
Twilight Tear
Jockeys
Eddie Arcaro
Braulio Baeza
Steve Brooks
Doug Dodson
Bill Hartack
Johnny Sellers
Bill Shoemaker
Trainers
William Hal Bishop
Ben Jones
H. A. "Jimmy" Jones
Harry Trotsek
Arnold Winick
Stables
Calumet Farm
Hasty House Farm
William Hal Bishop Stable

Calder Race Course

Calder Race Course created its Hall of Fame in 1995 and annually inducts at least one new member in each of four categories.

Horses (Year Inducted)
Boots 'n Jackie (2005)
Brave Raj (1995)
Carterista (2004)
Chaposa Springs (2003)
Cherokee Run (1998)
Flying Pidgeon (2000)
Hollywood Wildcat (2002)
Judy's Red Shoes (1996)
Mecke (1999)
Princess Rooney (1995)
Shocker T. (2006)
Smile (1995)
Spend a Buck (1995)
Spirit of Fighter (1997)
The Vid (2001)
Jockeys (Year Inducted)
Eibar Coa (2004)
Mike Gonzalez (2001)
Walter Guerra (1998)
Rosemary Homeister Jr. (2006)
Michael Lee (1996)
Gene St. Leon (1995)
Miguel Rivera (2000)
Pedro Rodriguez (2005)
Mary Russ (2003)
Alex Solis (2002)
Jacinto Vasquez (1999)
Jose Velez Jr. (1997)
Owners-Breeders (Year Inducted)
Arthur Appleton (1999)
Bee Bee Stable (2005)
Gilbert Campbell (2004)
Cobble View Stable (2001)
Herb and Ione Elkins (2006)
Farnsworth Farms (1997)
John Franks (2003)
Frances Genter Stable (1998)
Fred Hooper (1995)
James Lewis Jr. (2000)
Harry T. Mangurian Jr. (1995)
Ocala Stud Farm (2002)
Tartan Farms (1996)
Trainers (Year Inducted)
James Bracken (2000)
Frank Gomez (1995)
Stanley Hough (1996)
Jose "Pepe" Mendez (2004)
Luis Olivares (2002)
Edward Plesa Jr. (2006)
Harold Rose (1997)
John Tammaro (1999)
Emanuel Tortora (1998)
Bill White (2005)
Martin D. Wolfson (2003)
Ralph Ziade (2001)

Canterbury Park

Created to honor those who contributed to the track and Minnesota racing, the Canterbury Park Hall of Fame inducts from one to three new members each year.

Horses
Blair's Cove
Come Summer
Hoist Her Flag
Honor the Hero
John Bullit (NZ)
K Z Bay
Northbound Pride
Princess Elaine
Timeless Prince
Valid Leader
Who Doctor Who
Jockeys
Sandy Hawley
Dean Kutz
Luis Quinonez
Mike Smith
Scott Stevens
Trainers
Carl Nafzger
Doug Oliver
Bernell Rhone
Owners
Chuck Bellingham
Frances Genter
Bobbi Knapper
Paul Knapper
Dan Mjolsness
Breeders
Almar Farms
Art and Gretchen Eaton
Robert Morehouse

Others
Brooks Fields
Tom Ryther Sr.
Curtis, Randy, Russ, and Paul Sampson
Dark Star
Jim Wells

Fair Grounds

Fair Grounds established its Hall of Fame in 1971 to honor those who made lasting contributions to racing on both the local and national levels.

Horses
A Letter to Harry
Black Gold
Blushing K. D.
Cabildo
Chou Croute
Colonel Power
Concern
Davona Dale
Diplomat Way
Dixie Poker Ace
Furl Sail
Grindstone
Lecomte
Lexington
Marriage
Master Derby
Mike's Red
Mineshaft
Monarchist
Monique Rene
No Le Hace
Pan Zareta
*Princequillo
Quatrain
Reel
Risen Star
Scott's Scoundrel
Silverbulletday
Spanish Play
Taylor's Special
Tenacious
Tiffany Lass
Tippety Witchet
Whirlaway
Yorktown
Jockeys
Eddie Arcaro
Robby Albarado
Ron Ardoin
Robert L. Baird
Raymond Broussard
Pat Day
Eddie Delahoussaye
Andrew "Uncle Mack" Garner
Edward "Snapper" Garrison
Eric Guerin
Abe Hawkins
Johnny Heckmann
John Longden
J. D. Mooney
Jimmy Nichols
Winnie O'Connor
Craig Perret
Randy Romero
Earle Sande
Bill Shoemaker
James Forman "Tod" Sloan
Larry Snyder
David Whited
Owners-Breeders
Col. Edward R. Bradley
Dorothy Brown
Jack DeFee
Joseph P. Dorignac Jr.
John Franks
T. A. Grissom
William G. Helis Sr.
Samuel Clay Hildreth
Duncan Farrar Kenner
Lane's End
Harvey Peltier
J. R. Strauss Sr.
Thomas Jefferson Wells
Roger W. Wilson
Anthony Zuppardo
Trainers
Tom Amoss
Bobby Barnett
Angel Barrera
W. Hal Bishop
Frank Brothers
Joseph "Spanky" Broussard
Grover "Bud" Delp
Joey Dorignac III
Henry Forrest
Norman "Butsy" Hernandez
Neil Howard
Ben Jones
Jack Lohman
J. O. Meaux
Bill Mott
Homer Pardue
Anthony Pelleteri
Louie Roussel III
Clifford Scott
Dewey Smith
Harry Trotsek
Jack Van Berg
Marion H. Van Berg
C. W. "Cracker" Walker
Vester R. "Tennessee" Wright
Others
Frank "Buddy" Abadie
Eric Wolfson Blind
Richard Ten Broeck
John Blanks Campbell
John F. Clark Jr.
Capt. William Cottrill
Francis Dunne
Marie Krantz
Sylvester W. Labrot Jr.
Allen "Black Cat" LaCombe
John S. Letellier
John G. Masoni
Claude Mauberret Jr.
Gardere "Gar" Moore
Mervin H. Muniz Jr.
Joseph A. Murphy
John Kenneth "Jack" O'Hara
Thomas P. Scott
Albert Stall Sr.

Gulfstream Park

Gulfstream Park's Garden of Champions inductees must be retired, have competed at Gulfstream at least once, and have been named divisional champions or have competed against the highest caliber of competition. The garden no longer exists because of massive renovations in 2002.

Horses
A.P. Indy
Ajina
Alydar
Armed
Artax
Arts and Letters
Bald Eagle
Banshee Breeze
Battlefield
Bayakoa (Arg)
Beautiful Pleasure
Black Tie Affair (Ire)
Blushing John
Bold Ruler
Bowl Game
Buck's Boy
Candy Eclair
Carry Back
Cherokee Run
Chief's Crown
Christmas Past
Cicada
Cigar
Coaltown
Counterpoint
Crafty Admiral
Cryptoclearance
Dark Star
Davona Dale
Daylami (Ire)
Decathlon
Dehere
De La Rose
Deputy Minister
Easy Goer
Eillo
Eliza
Escena
Favorite Trick
Fly So Free
Foolish Pleasure
Forego
Fort Marcy
Forty Niner
Forward Gal
Fraise
Funny Cide
Genuine Risk
Gilded Time
Go for Wand
Groovy
Hansel
Heavenly Prize
Hollywood Wildcat
Holy Bull
Honest Pleasure
Housebuster
Inside Information
Izvestia
Kelso
Lady's Secret
La Prevoyante
Late Bloomer
Left Bank
Lemon Drop Kid
Little Current
Lord Avie
Mac Diarmida
Nashua
Needles
Nodouble
Northern Dancer
Office Queen
Old Hat
Open Mind
Paradise Creek
Parka
Paseana (Arg)
Perfect Sting
Pleasant Colony
Pleasant Tap
Plugged Nickle
Princess Rooney
Roman Brother
Round Table
Rubiano
Sabin
Safely Kept
Sailor
Shecky Greene
Silverbulletday
Silver Charm
Skip Away
Sky Beauty
Sky Classic
Smile
Snow Chief
Soaring Softly
Spectacular Bid
Steinlen (GB)
Sunday Silence
Sunshine Forever
Swale
Swaps
Swoon's Son
Sword Dancer
Thunder Gulch
Tim Tam
Unbridled
Vanlandingham
Victory Gallop
Winning Colors
White Skies
With Approval

Hawthorne Race Course

Hawthorne Race Course launched its Hall of Fame on November 10, 1996, with a tribute to 21 jockey inductees. No new members have been inducted since trainers were honored for the first time in 1998.

Jockeys (Year Inducted)
Johnny Adams (1996)
Eddie Arcaro (1996)
Ted Atkinson (1996)
Braulio Baeza (1996)
Jerry Bailey (1996)
Robert L. Baird (1997)
Steve Brooks (1996)
Steve Cauthen (1996)
Angel Cordero Jr. (1996)
Pat Day (1996)
Eddie Delahoussaye (1996)
Juvenal Diaz (1998)
Earlie Fires (1997)
Gerland Gallitano (1997)
Chris McCarron (1996)
Randall Meier (1997)
Isaac Murphy (1996)
Laffit Pincay Jr. (1996)
Earle Sande (1996)
Shane Sellers (1997)
Bill Shoemaker (1996)
Ray Sibille (1998)
Carlos Silva (1998)
Ron Turcotte (1996)
Jorge Velasquez (1996)
George Woolf (1996)
Trainers (Year Inducted)
Ernie Poulos (1998)
Jere Smith Sr. (1998)
Other (Year Inducted)
Phil Georgeff (1996)

Monmouth Park

The Hall of Champions was established in 1986 to honor Monmouth-raced horses that achieved success on the national level.

Affectionately
Alydar
Alysheba
Bet Twice
Black Tie Affair (Ire)
Blue Sparkler
Bold Ruler
Buckpasser
Carry Back
Damascus
Dan Horn
Dearly Precious
Decathlon
Dehere
Desert Vixen
First Flight
Forego
Formal Gold
Forty Niner
Friendly Lover
Frisk Me Now
Hansel
Helioscope
Holy Bull
Inside Information
John Henry
Kelso
Lady's Secret
Lord Avie
Lost Code
Majestic Light
Misty Morn
Mongo
Nashua
Needles
Open Mind
Personal Ensign
Point Given
Politely
Polynesian
Riva Ridge
Ruffian
Safely Kept
Serena's Song
Silverbulletday
Skip Away
Smoke Glacken
Spectacular Bid
Spend a Buck
Stymie
Sword Dancer
Ta Wee
Teddy Drone
Touch Gold
With Anticipation

Nebraska Racing Hall of Fame

The Nebraska Racing Hall of Fame was established in 1966. No inductions have been made since 1993.

Horses (Year Inducted)
Gate Dancer (1991)
Omaha (1969)
Rose's Gem (1971)
Who Doctor Who (1993)
Jockeys (Year Inducted)
Irving Anderson (1976)
Steve Brooks (1971)
Earl Dew (1978)
Fred Ecoffey (1981)
Dave Erb (1972)
Ira Hanford (1968)
John Lively (1979)
Charley Thorpe (1978)
Trainers (Year Inducted)
Earl Beezley (1972)
Carl Hanford (1968)
Hoss Inman (1992)
C. B. Irwin (1979)
Robert Irwin (1973)
John Nerud (1970)
Lyman Rollins (1992)
Jack Van Berg (1976)
Marion H. Van Berg (1966)
Don Von Hemel (1991)
Robert L. Wheeler (1972)
Owners-Breeders (Year Inducted)
Mr. and Mrs. Al Cascio (1993)
Omer "Pete" Hall (1970)
Jack Fickler (1985)
Barton Ford (1978)
Mike Ford (1967)
William Fudge (1973)
Orville Kemling (1981)
Paul Kemling (1981)
Ken Opstein (1985)
Others (Year Inducted)
Warren Albert (1978)
Dale Becker (1985)
James E. "Tom" Bock (1973)
Ralph Boomer (1971)
Don Fair (1979)
Harry Farnham (1971)
J. J. "Jake" Isaacson (1969)
Don Lee (1992)
Earl Moyer (1967)
Murdock Platner (1979)
Grover Porter (1969)
Al Swihart (1992)
Howard Wolff (1969)

Prairie Meadows Racetrack

Iowa's first horse-racing facility established its Hall of Fame in 1998.

Horses (Year Inducted)
Dontforgethisname (1999)
Lady Tamworth (2003)
Nut N Better (2003)
Railroad Red (1998)
Prince Ariba (1999)
Sharky's Review (2005)
Sure Shot Biscuit (2004)
Vaguely Who (2001)
Owners-Breeders (Year Inducted)
Jim Bader (1998)
Jack Bishop (2002)
Bob and Marlene Bryant (2002)
Jim and Sandra Rasmussen (2000)
Others (Year Inducted)
Dick Clark (2004)
Ken Grandquist (2005)
Keith Hopkins (2001)
Gary Lucas (2005)
Berl Priebe (2005)
Ed Skinner (1999)
Jim Woodward (1999)

Remington Park

The Remington Hall of Fame was established in 1999. No others have been inducted since the original group.

Jockey
Pat Steinberg
Trainer
Donnie K. Von Hemel
Owner-Breeder
Ran Ricks Jr.
Horse
Clever Trevor

Texas Horse Racing Hall of Fame

The Texas Horse Racing Hall of Fame was created in 1999 at Retama Park to pay tribute to the people and horses who have influenced the state's racing industry.

Horses (Year Inducted)
Assault (1999)
Groovy (2001)
Middleground (2000)
Pan Zareta (1999)
Staunch Avenger (2002)
Stymie (2000)
Two Altazano (2003)
Jockeys (Year Inducted)
Cash Asmussen (2003)
Jerry Bailey (2000)
Bill Shoemaker (1999)
Trainer (Year Inducted)
Max Hirsch (2000)
Willard Proctor (2003)
Owners-Breeders (Year Inducted)
Williams S. Farish (2004)
Nelson Bunker Hunt (2004)
Robert Kleberg Jr. (1999)
Walter Merrick (2000)
Clarence Scharbauer Jr. (2001)
Joe R. Straus Sr. (2001)
Emerson Woodward (2001)
Others (Year Inducted)
Allen Bogan (2003)
Charles "Doc" Graham (2002)
Patricia Link (2004)
B. F. Phillips (1999)
W. T. Waggoner (2001)

Virginia Thoroughbred Hall of Fame

The Virginia Thoroughbred Hall of Fame began inducting members in 1978.

Horses
Cicada
Cyane
First Landing
Fort Marcy
Genuine Risk
Hansel
Hildene
Legendra
Lexington
Majesty's Prince
Mill Reef
Mongo
Norfolk
Paradise Creek
Pilate
Pleasant Colony
Quadrangle
Reigh Count
Saluter
Sea Hero
Secretariat
Seeking the Pearl
Sir Archy
Somethingroyal
Sword Dancer
Sun Beau
People
Ted Atkinson
Christopher Chenery
Melville Church II
Thomas Mellon Evans
Bertram and Diana Firestone
J. Jorth Fletcher
Kenneth Gilpin
Tyson Gilpin
Gordon Grayson
Richard Hancock
Taylor Hardin
Abraham S. Hewitt
Dr. Fritz Howard
Howell E. Jackson
Mrs. J. P. Jones
Keswick Stables
Dorothy N. Lee
Paul Mellon
James P. Mills
Dr. Frank O'Keefe
George L. Ohrstrom Jr.
William Haggin Perry
Mrs. A. C. Randolph
Marion duPont Scott
Isabell Dodge Sloan
Whitney Stone
Orme Wilson Jr.

Washington Thoroughbred Racing Hall of Fame

The first Washington Thoroughbred Racing Hall of Fame members were inducted in 2004.

Special Lifetime Achievement (Year Inducted)
Joe Gottstein (2003)
Breeders (Year Inducted)
Herb Armstrong (2003)
George Drumheller (2004)
Jerre Paxton (2003)
Guy and Barbara Roberts (2005)
Jockeys (Year Inducted)
Gary Baze (2003)
Russell Baze (2004)
Basil James (2005)
Ralph Neves (2003)
Gary Stevens (2003)
Trainers (Year Inducted)
Allen Drumheller Sr. (2003)
Bud Klokstad (2005)
Jim Penney (2003)
Tom Smith (2003)
Charlie Whittingham (2004)
Horses (Year Inducted)
Captain Condo (2003)
Chinook Pass (2003)
Saratoga Passage (2004)
Smogy Dew (2005)
Trooper Seven (2003)
Turbulator (2004)

TRIPLE CROWN

History of the Triple Crown

As with other great sporting events such as the Olympics and the World Series, the Triple Crown has a rich tradition and history. While modern memory places the Triple Crown in a fixed format—the Kentucky Derby (G1) on the first Saturday in May, the Preakness Stakes (G1) two weeks later, and the Belmont Stakes (G1) three weeks after the Preakness—the series has undergone changes ranging from subtle to seismic in its history.

Origins

The Triple Crown did not start with the inauguration of the three races—the Belmont in 1867, the Preakness six years later, and the Derby in '75. Of the three races, only the Derby has been run continuously, with gaps in the history of the Preakness (1891-'93) and the Belmont (1911 and '12, when antigambling legislation shut down New York racing). In some years, the Derby and Preakness were run within days of each other, and in two years (1917 and '22) they were run on the same day. In some years, the Preakness was run before the Derby.

Far from its current summit as the most prestigious race for American three-year-olds, the Derby in the early 20th century was a struggling regional race. The marketing and showmanship genius of Churchill Downs track executive Col. Matt J. Winn elevated the race to national and international prominence during the first quarter of the century.

When Sir Barton became the first Triple Crown winner in 1919, he was not recognized as a Triple Crown winner, only as a fast-developing three-year-old who went from maiden to multiple major stakes winner within two months.

In fact, the origin of the term "Triple Crown" (which had been in use in England for decades) has been disputed for many years. For decades, credit for coining the expression generally was accorded to legendary *Daily Racing Form* columnist Charlie Hatton. While Hatton's stature and repeated use of the term closely associated him with the Triple Crown, the phrase arguably was first put in print by New York *Times* writer Bryan Field, who used the expression in 1930 after Gallant Fox won the Belmont.

The Triple Crown has been characterized by clusters of winners, especially in the 1930s, '40s, and '70s, and long droughts in between. After Gallant Fox won the 1930 Triple Crown for owner-breeder Belair Stud, only five years passed before Gallant Fox's son Omaha won for Belair. Two years later in 1937, Man o' War's son War Admiral took the Triple Crown for Glen Riddle Farm.

The Triple Crown sweep was achieved four times in the 1940s. First, Calumet Farm and jockey Eddie Arcaro won in 1941 with Whirlaway, and Mrs. John D. Hertz's Count Fleet rolled to victory two years later with Johnny Longden in the saddle. In 1946, King Ranch's homebred Assault scored the triple, and two years later Arcaro and Calumet collected their second Triple Crown sweep with Citation.

In 1950, the Thoroughbred Racing Associations formally recognized the three-race series as the Triple Crown and commissioned Cartier to craft a three-sided trophy, one side for each race. The trophy was in storage many years before Secretariat breezed to a Triple Crown victory in 1973, the first sweep in a quarter-century. Four years later, the brilliant Seattle Slew became the first to win the series without a defeat on his record. In 1978, the first back-to-back Triple Crown sweep occurred when Affirmed defeated Alydar in three classic battles. Harbor View Farm's Affirmed would be

Triple Crown Television Ratings and Share

Year	Kentucky Derby Rating	Kentucky Derby Share	Preakness Stakes Rating	Preakness Stakes Share	Belmont Stakes Rating	Belmont Stakes Share
2006	7.0	18	5.4	14	3.5	9
2005	7.3	18	5.1	13	4.5	11
2004	7.4	18	6.1	15	11.3	26
2003	6.4	17	5.6	13	9.5	23
2002	7.1	18	5.7	14	7.6	21
2001	8.1	21	5.6	16	4.5	13
2000	5.8	17	3.6	10	2.8	9
1999	6.3	19	3.4	10	6.0	17
1998	6.1	18	3.6	11	5.9	18
1997	7.1	19	4.8	14	5.3	16
1996	7.4	21	3.7	11	2.9	9
1995	6.0	17	3.2	10	3.5	11
1994	7.5	21	4.4	14	3.9	12
1993	7.3	22	4.7	15	4.2	11

Each rating point represents 1,102,000 viewers as of May 2006.
Share is the percentage of televisions tuned to that program.

Birthplaces of Triple Crown Race Winners

Place of Birth	Winners	Place of Birth	Winners
Kentucky	275	New York	7
Virginia	21	Canada	4
Florida	19	Texas	4
New Jersey	13	Ireland	2
Maryland	11	Montana	2
Pennsylvania	11	Ohio	2
California	9	Illinois	1
United Kingdom	9	Kansas	1
Tennessee	8	Missouri	1

the last Triple Crown winner of the 20th century as another long drought took hold.

Modern Triple Crown

The perception that the Triple Crown's prestige made it an irresistible goal for the connections of leading three-year-olds was shaken twice in the 1980s. Gato Del Sol won the 1982 Derby, but trainer Eddie Gregson, speaking for owners-breeders Arthur Hancock III and Leone J. Peters, declined to run the colt in the Preakness. Well aware that Gato Del Sol was unsuited to a speed-favoring Pimlico Race Course for the Preakness, Gregson and his owners awaited the Belmont, in which Gato Del Sol finished a distant second to Conquistador Cielo.

Dennis Diaz's speedy Spend a Buck crushed his competition in the 1985 Derby, but Diaz turned his back on the Preakness and Belmont, opting for the $1-million Jersey Derby (G3) at the newly rebuilt Garden State Park and a $2-million bonus.

Through the remainder of the 20th century, five horses came within one race of winning the Triple Crown, but none collected the $5-million—first offered as a purse and bonus and exclusively as a bonus beginning in 1998. Alysheba won the first two races in 1987 but was a distant fourth to Bet Twice in the Belmont. Sunday Silence won two spirited battles with Easy Goer in 1989 and finished a well-beaten second to his nemesis in the Belmont. The Triple Crown bids of the 1990s occurred in three consecutive years, 1997-'99. In 1997, Derby and Preakness winner Silver Charm could not repel the late charge of Touch Gold in the Belmont. The following year, Real Quiet appeared to have the Belmont won but lost by a nose in the last stride to Victory Gallop. Charismatic, the 1999 Derby and Preakness winner, finished third by less than two lengths despite sustaining a leg fracture in the Belmont's late stages. At the start of the 21st century, War Emblem won the first two legs in 2002, only to finish eighth in the Belmont. In 2003, Funny Cide won the Derby and Preakness but finished third in the Belmont; in '04, Smarty Jones came within one length of becoming the 12th Triple Crown winner. Afleet Alex won the 2005 Preakess and Belmont after finishing third in the Derby

—John Harrell

Triple Crown Productions

Charged with marketing the Kentucky Derby (G1), Preakness Stakes (G1), and Belmont Stakes (G1), Triple Crown Productions was created at a time of turmoil within the industry and especially at the three tracks that stage the races. Threatened with a hostile takeover, Churchill Downs Inc. reorganized in 1984 and hired Thomas Meeker, a lawyer, as its president. The following year, Garden State Park reopened and lured the Derby winner, Spend a Buck, off the Triple Crown trail to the Jersey Derby (G3) with a $2-million bonus. Robert E. Brennan, then Garden State's chairman, spoke of the Jersey Derby taking the place of the Preakness at Pimlico Race Course in the Triple Crown. The New York Racing Association also was mired in internal turmoil.

Incorporated in September 1985, Triple Crown Productions opened its office at Churchill Downs in January '86, with Audrey R. Korotkin as its first executive director. In addition to its marketing function, Triple Crown Productions inaugurated a common nomination form and fees for the races, with early nominations of $600 each closing in mid-January and late nominations, originally $3,000 and now $6,000, closing six weeks before the Derby. Previously, each track obtained nominations for its own races. Supplemental entries (initially $150,000 for the Derby and $100,000 each for the Preakness and Belmont) were permitted beginning in 1990. The Derby supplemary fee was increased to $200,000 in 2005, and Greeley's Galaxy became the first supplemental nominee.

In 1987, the company offered the first Triple Crown Challenge—$5-million in purse money and bonuses to a Triple Crown winner and a $1-million bonus to the horse with the best overall performances in all three races. Triple Crown

Nominations Since Unified Under Triple Crown Productions

Year	Early	Late	Total	Total Fees	Each Track's Share
2006	426	14	440	$339,600	$113,200
2005	358	13	371	292,800	97,600
2004	434	14	448	344,400	114,800
2003	446	8	454	315,600	105,200
2002	405	12	417	315,000	105,000
2001	440	7	447	306,000	102,000
2000	387	13	400	310,200	103,400
1999	396	11	407	303,600	101,200
1998	384	6	390	266,800	88,933
1997	375	13	388	303,000	101,000
1996	354	7	361	254,800	84,800
1995	317	7	324	232,400	77,400
1994	354	9	363	266,400	88,800
1993	342	25	367	317,700	105,900
1992	389	18	407	314,400	104,800
1991	369	8	377	257,400	85,800
1990	315	33	348	282,000	94,000
1989	381	13	394	267,600	89,200
1988	381	20	401	288,600	96,200
1987	398	24	422	310,800	103,600
1986	422	30	452	343,200	144,400

Early nomination fee has been $600 since 1986; late nomination fee: 1986-'90, $3,000; 1991-'93, $4,500; 1994-present, $6,000.

Productions financed the first bonus year (Bet Twice collected $1-million after he finished second to Alysheba in the Derby and Preakness and won the Belmont). Chrysler Corp. became the sponsor of the bonus in '88.

Meeker, chairman of Triple Crown Productions, eliminated the executive director position in August 1989, but media attention the following winter led to hiring Edward Seigenfeld, a former NYRA marketing vice president, as the organization's executive director. In 1993, the $1-million bonus for the best overall finish was eliminated.

Chrysler bowed out as the Triple Crown Challenge sponsor after 1995 and was replaced by Visa USA, the credit-card marketing company. Beginning in 1998, a Triple Crown sweep would earn a $5-million bonus in addition to purse earnings from the three races. Visa ended its sponsorship in 2005. In 2004, NYRA abandoned the Triple Crown's joint television contract with NBC in a dispute over revenue splits. NYRA signed up with ABC beginning in 2006.

For the first time since the inception of Triple Crown Productions, no bonus of any kind was offered in 2006. Visa ended its Triple Crown sponsorship in 2005 as well as its sponsorship of a $5-million bonus to any horse that wins the Triple Crown. Visa reduced its sponsorship in 2006 to the Kentucky Derby. Triple Crown Productions officials said they would pursue a new bonus sponsorship, but none was found for 2006. Following are the conditions for the 2006 races.

Triple Crown 2006 Conditions

1. General.

Entries to the Races are received only upon the condition that the Applicant will comply with the rules and regulations governing Thoroughbred horse races adopted by the state where each Race is run and the rules and regulations of each Association and will comply with and abide by any decision of the state racing officials and/or the officers of the Association regarding the interpretation and application of such rules and regulations. To the extent of any inconsistency between these conditions and the rules and regulations of the state regulatory agency in the state in which a Race is run, such rules and regulations shall control in that state for the Race. The Applicant consents and agrees to all provisions of each Association's current application, entry form, condition book, conditions, and/or other application or agreement regarding the use of stall space (collectively, the "Stall Agreement"), the terms of which are specifically incorporated herein by reference, and upon request shall execute all such applications and/or agreements before bringing any horse upon the respective Association's grounds. In the event of a conflict between these conditions and an Association's Stall Agreement, the provisions of the Association's Stall Agreement shall govern. Without limiting the generality of this paragraph, the Applicant consents and agrees to abide by all provisions of the Rules for Advertising (including, without limiting, Rules for Jockey Advertising) for each Race as promulgated by the Association hosting that Race.

In making this application to participate in Thoroughbred racing, it is understood that an investigative report may be requested whereby information is obtained through personal interviews with third parties. The request may include information as to the Applicant's character, general reputation, personal characteristics, mode of living, or such other information as may be relevant to the Applicant's integrity as a racing participant. The Applicant shall have the right to make a written request to an Association within a reasonable period of time for a complete and accurate disclosure of additional information concerning the nature and scope of the investigation.

Each Association reserves the right to start all Races with or without a stall gate starting machine. Each Association reserves the right to cancel any Race, without notice, at any time prior to the actual running thereof, without liability, except for the return by the canceling Association of fees as described herein. In the event of cancellation of a Race or the revocation of, or refusal to accept an Applicant's nomination, entry or stall application, or denial of the right to start a Race, the Association taking such action shall return to the Applicant all entry, starting, and supplemental fees received by the Association and one-third (⅓) of the nomination fee paid by the Applicant and shall have no further liability to the Applicant as a result of such action.

Each Association reserves the right to make all decisions regarding preferences and conditions with regard to its respective Race and its decision shall be final. Each Association reserves the right, in its sole and absolute discretion, to refuse, cancel, or revoke any nomination or entry, stall application, or Stall Agreement or the transfer thereof and reserves the right to deny the right to start in a Race, without notice to the Applicant and for any reason, including but not limited to, the Applicant's failure to fully perform or abide by all provisions and conditions hereof. The Applicant hereby consents to and agrees that in the event any litigation is instituted which involves Churchill Downs Inc. or Triple Crown Productions LLC, the Applicant is subject to jurisdiction and venue in the courts of Jefferson County, Kentucky, and in the Federal Courts of the Western District of Kentucky. In the event any litigation is instituted which involves the Maryland Jockey Club of Baltimore City Inc., the Applicant hereby consents to and agrees that the Applicant is subject to jurisdiction and venue in the Circuit Court for Baltimore City, and in the Federal Courts for the District of Maryland. In the event litigation is instituted which involves the New York Racing Association Inc., the Applicant hereby consents to and agrees that the Applicant is subject to jurisdiction and venue in the Supreme Court of New York, County of Nassau, and the Federal Courts for the Eastern District of New York.

Triple Crown Productions reserves the right, in its sole and absolute discretion, to accept nominations without timely payment of required nomination fees or receipt of an executed nomination form. Facsimile nomination forms must be followed by timely payment of all nomination fees and subsequent delivery of an originally executed nomination form. The inclusion by Triple Crown Productions of a horse's name in the publicly released list of nominees to the Races shall constitute prima-facie evidence of the Applicant's nomination and liability for nomination fees. The Applicant shall be responsible for payment of all fees including, without limitation, the nomination fee. The Applicant is liable to and shall reimburse Triple Crown Productions for any costs, damages, or expenses incurred by it, including reasonable attorneys' fees, in collecting any unpaid nomination or other fees.

In the Kentucky Derby, post position shall be determined as follows: A nontransferable lot number shall be drawn for each horse named as a starter at the Closing. The lot number drawn for each starter shall determine the numerical order for selection of post position. Selection of post position shall be made by each owner of a horse (or, if more than one, the owners collectively) or the authorized agent of the horse's owner(s). Horses having common ties through ownership or training shall each be treated separately for purposes of selecting post position. Detailed rules governing the post-position draw process are available from the Racing Secretary's office and will be distributed prior to the Closing. These rules shall control.

2. Release and Indemnification.

In consideration of the Applicant's admission to each Association's facility, the Applicant hereby releases the Association from all claims for loss or damage of, or injury to, or death of any persons or property (including horses as well as loss of use of property) sustained by the Applicant and/or its invitees and/or the property owned or under the control of the Applicant located at the Association's facilities. The Applicant recognizes the risks of its activities to be undertaken at the Association's facilities, and it has inspected and is familiar with each Association's facilities and does voluntarily and fully assume all risk of loss, injury, damage, death, or destruction to any person or property. This release and assumption of risk provision shall not be effective as to any cause of loss attributable to any intentional, willful, gross, or reckless conduct of the Association.

The Applicant further agrees to protect, indemnify, and hold harmless the Association (or if indemnification is not available, to contribute to the Association's losses) from and against any loss, damage, claims, or expenses (including reasonable attorneys' and other fees), arising directly or indirectly from any acts or omissions of the Applicant, or any of the Applicant's horses, or any agent, employee, or invitee of the Applicant, arising out of or in connection with the Applicant's activities at the Association's facilities.

The foregoing release and indemnification provisions shall be construed in a manner consistent with the limitations set forth herein to be as broad and inclusive as permitted by and in a manner consistent with the laws and regulations of the Association's jurisdiction and shall be binding upon the Applicant, its successors, and/or assignees. The maintenance by the Association of insurance relating to the claims, released and/or indemnified hereby shall not affect the terms or interpretation of this Agreement, and the Applicant agrees that any and all insurers of the Applicant, whether insurers of property, personal injury, or any other loss, if their insurance policies do not already so provide, agree that they waive and will not exercise any rights of subrogation in the event of loss of or damage to the subject property, as well as the loss of use thereof, except that any waiver of subrogation will not be effective where such waiver will result in such liability policy becoming null and void. For purposes of this Agreement, the Association shall mean and include the Association and its officers, directors, trustees, agents, employees, contractors, servants, and licensees.

Responsibility for the maintenance of general liability and horse mortality insurance to cover the risks outlined above rests with the Applicant. Consultation with a competent insurance adviser is strongly recommended. Failure to maintain adequate insurance may subject the Applicant to the risks outlined above.

3. Reservation of Rights.

As the organizer, host, and sponsor of Thoroughbred horse races, each Association hereby reserves unto itself, its agents, assigns, and licensees, and the Applicant hereby assigns to the Association all interest it may have in the Host Rights, as herein defined. The Host Rights shall mean the sole and exclusive right to: (a) produce, exhibit, sell, license, transfer, or transmit in any manner still or motion pictures, radio and television broadcasts, interactive computer including Internet, or any other media transmission, now known or hereafter developed, of all events which occur on the Association's property, including without limitation, all activities occurring before, during, and after Thoroughbred horse races; (b) utilize the race and the results thereof, all for any purpose or use as the Association shall determine; (c) limit, prohibit, or regulate the display of any commercial advertising symbols, or other identification, other than an Applicant's registered silks, in connection with any race or related activities; and (d) develop, produce, and sell, by or through any licensee, goods using the Applicant's name or likeness, the name or likeness of any horse owned by the Applicant brought onto the Association's grounds, or any other identifying feature, silks, trademark or copyrighted material which is used in connection with the race. The submission of a nomination or making of an entry in any race shall mean that the Applicant consents to the above reservation of the Host Rights and consents to be photographed or to otherwise be a subject of still or moving pictures, radio, or television programs, without remuneration except for contributions to horsemen's purses from wagering on the races as established by contract or legislation. The Applicant agrees that he has not and will not execute any documents or take any other action, which purports to assign or otherwise transfer any interest in the Host Rights or assert any claim, demand or cause of action against the Association which is inconsistent with the full and exclusive exercise by the Association of its Host Rights.

4. Definition of Applicant.

As used herein, "Applicant" shall mean and include the nominating owner(s) and the owner's agents, trainers, and jockeys and their agents, heirs, representatives, successors, next of kin, and assigns; provided, however, that the rights and benefits of the Applicant under this Agreement are personal and no such right or benefit shall be subject to voluntary or involuntary alienation, assignment, or transfer. The Applicant covenants that all of the above persons have agreed to the foregoing conditions and further agrees that it will deliver their written consent and agreement to such conditions upon request of the Association. The Applicant shall indemnify and hold the Association harmless from and against any claim or cause of action (including any expense incurred in connection therewith, including reasonable attorneys' and other fees) that may be asserted by or on behalf of any person which is inconsistent with the release and indemnification provisions set forth in the foregoing paragraph.

The Triple Crown

First Closing, January 21, 2006 — $600
Second Closing, March 25, 2006 — $6,000

Nominations to each and all of the Triple Crown races, the Kentucky Derby, the Preakness Stakes, and the Belmont Stakes (the "Races") may be made by payment of a single nomination fee to Triple Crown Productions LLC as agent for Churchill Downs Inc., the Maryland Jockey Club of Baltimore City Inc., and the New York Racing Association Inc. (the "Association" or "Associations" as the case may be). The nomination fee for nominations postmarked or hand delivered by January 21, 2006, is $600 and for nominations postmarked or hand delivered from January 22 through March 25, 2006, is $6,000. Horses nominated on or before March 25, 2006, shall be considered original nominees ("Original Nominees").

At any time, prior to the Closing for the Kentucky Derby, as defined below, additional nominations to all three Races may be made upon payment of a supplementary fee of $200,000 to Churchill Downs Inc. Following the running of the Kentucky Derby, horses may be nominated at any time prior to Closing for the Preakness Stakes or the Belmont Stakes (time of Closing being defined below).

The supplementary fee payable for such nomination shall be $100,000 payable to the Maryland Jockey Club of Baltimore City Inc. for supplemental nomination to the Preakness Stakes and the Belmont Stakes or $100,000 payable to the New York Racing Association Inc. for supplemental nomination to the Belmont Stakes only. All supplemental fees will be included in the purse distribution for the Race run by the Association to which the supplemental nomination is paid, unless otherwise specified in the specific Race rules below. The ability of horses nominated by payment of the foregoing supplementary fees ("Supplemental Nominees") to enter any Race will be determined in accordance with the conditions of that Race. All nominees, original, supplemental, or otherwise, will be required to pay entry and starting fees for the Race or Races in which they participate before they may start.

132nd running of Kentucky Derby
$2,000,000 guaranteed
minimum gross (Grade 1)
To be run Saturday, May 6, 2006
One Mile and a Quarter

For three-year olds, with an entry fee of $25,000 each and a starting fee of $25,000 each. Supplemental nominations may be made upon payment of $200,000 and in accordance with the rules set forth herein. All fees, including supplemental nominations, in excess of $900,000 in the aggregate shall be paid to the winner. Churchill Downs Inc. shall guarantee a minimum gross purse of $2,000,000 (the "Guaranteed Purse"). The winner shall receive $1,240,000, second place shall receive $400,000, third place shall receive $200,000, fourth place shall receive $100,000, and fifth place shall receive $60,000 from the Guaranteed Purse (the Guaranteed Purse to each place to be divided equally in the event of a dead heat). Starters shall be named through the entry box on Wednesday, May 3, 2006, at 10 a.m. Eastern Daylight Time (the "Closing"). The maximum number of starters shall be limited to twenty (20). Colts and Geldings shall each carry a weight of one hundred twenty-six (126) pounds; Fillies shall each carry one hundred twenty-one (121) pounds. Supplemental Nominees will be allowed to enter but will not have preference over any Original Nominee and will not be allowed to start the Race if the maximum number of starters has otherwise been reached by Original Nominees prior to the Closing. If the number of nominees exceeds the number of available starting positions at the Closing, these conditions shall be applied to determine which nominees will be allowed to start. In the event that more than twenty (20) entries pass through the entry box at the Closing, the starters shall be determined at the Closing from Original Nominees first, then Supplemental Nominees if starting positions are still available with preference given to those horses that have accumulated the highest earnings in the Graded Stakes races, including all monies actually paid for performance in such Graded Stakes races. For purposes of this preference, the graded status of each race shall be the graded status assigned to the race by the International Cataloguing Standards Committee in Part I of the International Cataloguing Standards as published by the Jockey Club Information Systems Inc. each year. Should additional starters be needed to bring the field to twenty (20) the remaining starters shall be determined at the Closing with preference given to those horses that have accumulated the highest earnings in Nonrestricted Sweepstakes. For purposes of this preference, a "Nonrestricted Sweepstakes" shall mean those Sweepstakes whose conditions contain no restrictions other that that of age or sex. In the case of ties resulting from preferences or otherwise, the additional starter(s) shall be determined by lot. Any horse excluded from running because of the aforementioned preference(s) shall be refunded the $25,000 entry fee and the $200,000 supplemental fee, if applicable. An "also-eligible" list will not be maintained and in no event will starters be added or allowed to run in the Race which are not determined to be starters at the Closing. Post position shall be determined as follows: A nontransferable lot number shall be drawn for each horse named as a starter at the Closing. The lot number drawn for each starter shall determine the numerical order for selection of post position. Selection of post position shall be made by each owner of a horse (or, if more than one, the owners collectively) or the authorized agent of the horse's owner(s). Horses having common ties through ownership or training shall each be treated separately for purposes of selecting post position. In the event of one or more scratches after the selection of post position, then starters with the post position higher than the post position of the scratched starter will be moved to the lowest empty post position (i.e., toward the inside rail of the racetrack) so that there are no empty post positions at the start of the Kentucky Derby. Detailed rules governing the post-position draw process are available from the Racing Secretary's office and will be distributed prior to the Closing. These rules shall control. The owner of the winner of the Race shall receive a gold trophy.

131st running of Preakness Stakes
$1,000,000 guaranteed (Grade 1)
To be run Saturday, May 20, 2006
One mile and three-sixteenths

For three-year-olds, $10,000 to pass the entry box, starters to pay $10,000 additional. Supplemental nominations may be made in accordance with the rules, upon payment of $100,000, 60% of the purse to the winner, 20% to second, 11% to third, 6% to fourth, and 3% to fifth. Weight 126 pounds for Colts and Geldings, 121 pounds for Fillies. Starters to be named through the entry box on Wednesday, May 17, 2006, three days before the race by the usual time of closing (the "Closing"). The Preakness field will be limited to fourteen (14) entries and shall be determined on the Wednesday immediately preceding the day of the race. In the event that more than fourteen (14) horses are properly nominated and pass through the entry box by the usual time of Closing, the starters will be determined at the Closing with the first seven (7) horses given preference by accumulating the highest earnings in Graded Stakes (lifetime), for purposes of this preference, the graded status of each race shall be the graded status assigned to the race by the International Cataloguing Standards Committee in Part 1 of the International Cataloguing Standards as published by the Jockey Club Information Systems, Inc. each year. The next four (4) starters will be determined by accumulating the highest earnings (lifetime) in all nonrestricted stakes. "Nonrestricted Sweepstakes" shall mean those sweepstakes whose conditions contain no restrictions other than that of age or sex. The remaining three (3) starters shall be determined by accumulating the highest earnings (lifetime) in all races. Should this preference produce any ties, the additional starter(s) shall be determined by lot. In application of the above described rule, each horse will be separately considered without regard to identity of its owner. If the rules described in this paragraph result in the exclusion of any horse, the $10,000 entry fee previously paid will be refunded to the owner of said horse. The above conditions notwithstanding, no horse which earns purse money in the Kentucky Derby shall be denied the opportunity to enter and start in the Preakness Stakes. A replica of the Woodlawn Vase will be presented to the winning owner to remain his or her personal property.

138th running of Belmont Stakes
$1,000,000 (Grade 1)
To be run Saturday, June 10, 2006
One mile and a half

For three-year olds, by subscription of $600 each, to accompany the nomination, if made on or before January 21, 2006, or $6,000, if made on or before March 25, 2006, $10,000 to pass the entry box and $10,000 additional to start. At any time prior to the closing time of entries, horses may be nominated to the Belmont Stakes upon payment of a supplementary fee of $100,000 to the New York Racing Association Inc. All entrants, supplemental or otherwise, will be required to pay entry and starting fees. The Purse to be divided 60% to the winner, 20% to second, 11% to third, 6% to fourth, and 3% to fifth. Colts and Geldings, 126 pounds, Fillies, 121 pounds. Starters to be named at the closing time of entries. The Belmont field will be limited to sixteen (16) starters. In the event more than 16 entries pass through the entry box at the closing, the starters will be determined at the closing with the first eight (8) starters given preference by accumulating the highest earning in Graded Sweepstakes at a mile or over. For purposes of this preference, the graded status of each race shall be the Grade assigned by the International Cataloguing Standards Committee in Part I of the International Cataloguing Standards as published annually by the Jockey Club Information Systems Inc. The next five (5) starters will be determined by accumulating the highest earnings in all nonrestricted sweepstakes. "Nonrestricted sweepstakes" shall mean those sweepstakes whose conditions contain no restrictions other than age or sex. The remaining three (3) starters shall be determined by accumulating the highest earnings in all races. Should this preference produce any ties, the additional starter(s) shall be determined by lot. If the rules described result in the exclusion of any horse, the $10,000 entry fee will be refunded to the owner of said horse. The above conditions notwithstanding, any horse which earns purse money in either the Kentucky Derby or the Preakness Stakes shall be included in the initial eight (8) starters of the Belmont Stakes. The winning owner will be presented with the August Belmont Memorial Cup, to be retained for one year, as well as a trophy for permanent possession and trophies to the winning trainer and jockey.

Road to the Triple Crown

The following races are traditionally used as preps for the Triple Crown races. The table includes the dates and winners of the races in 2006.

Date	Race	Trk	Dist.	Time	First three finishers
1/1	Tropical Park Derby (G3)	Crc	1⅛mT	1:46.65	**BARBARO,** Wise River, **Lewis Michael**
1/7	Aventura S.	GP	1m	1:37.75	**DOCTOR DECHERD, Itsallaboutthechase, My Golden Song**
1/7	Count Fleet S.	Aqu	1m70yd	1:39.61	**ACHILLES OF TROY,** Extra Bend, **Platinum Couple**
1/8	San Miguel S.	SA	6f	1:08.59	**TOO MUCH BLING, Cause to Believe, Bound to Be M V P**
1/14	San Rafael S. (G2)	SA	1m	1:36.11	**BROTHER DEREK, Stevie Wonderboy, Wanna Runner**
1/14	Risen Star S. (G3)	LaD	1 1/16m	1:43.13	**LAWYER RON, Mark of Success, Hyte Regency**
1/22	Black Gold S.	LaD	1m70yd	1:45.64	**KINGSFIELD, Warwick Wonder, Lemonbuster**
1/28	Sunshine Millions Dash S.	GP	6f	1:08.94	**DA STOOPS,** Changing Weather, Brite Maneuvers
1/29	El Camino Real Derby (G3)	BM	1 1/16m	1:41.81	**CAUSE TO BELIEVE, Objective, Bold Chieftain**
2/4	Holy Bull S. (G3)	GP	1⅛m	1:49.31	**BARBARO, Great Point, My Golden Song**
2/4	Hutcheson S. (G2)	GP	7½f	1:27.12	**KEYED ENTRY, First Samurai, Express News**
2/4	Sham S. (G3)	SA	1⅛m	1:49.15	**BOB AND JOHN, Hawkinsville, Sacred Light**
2/11	Turf Paradise Derby	TuP	1 1/16m	1:43.90	KEAGAN, **Sky Diving,** Soft Seventeen
2/11	Whirlaway S.	Aqu	1 1/16m	1:43.28	**ACHILLES OF TROY, One Way Flight, Rob'em Blind**
2/12	San Vicente S. (G2)	SA	7f	1:22.50	**TOO MUCH BLING, Peace Chant, New Joysey Jeff**
2/18	Sam F. Davis S.	Tam	1 1/16m	1:44.17	**BLUEGRASS CAT, Deputy Glitters, R Loyal Man**
2/25	Southwest S.	OP	1m	1:40.00	**LAWYER RON, Steppenwolfer, Red Raymond**
2/26	Borderland Derby	Sun	1 1/16m	1:44.82	**INDY WILDCAT,** Wait in Line, Disappearing Trick
3/4	Fountain of Youth S. (G2)	GP	1⅛m	1:49.00	**FIRST SAMURAI, Flashy Bull, Corinthian (DQ from 1st)**
3/4	Santa Catalina S. (G2)	SA	1 1/16m	1:41.96	**BROTHER DEREK, Sacred Light, Latent Heat**
3/4	Swale S. (G2)	GP	7f	1:22.14	**SHARP HUMOR, Noonmark, Court Folly**
3/4	Baldwin S.	SA	6½f	1:15.11	**FAST PARADE,** The Pharaoh, **Da Stoops**
3/4	John Battaglia Memorial S.	TP	1 1/16m	1:46.88	LAITY, Pair of Kings, New Awakening
3/11	California Derby	GG	1 1/16m	1:41.07	**CAUSE TO BELIEVE, Sinister Minister, The Five J's**
3/12	Palm Beach S. (G3)	GP	1⅛mT	1:45.94	GO BETWEEN, **Up an Octave, Devil's Preacher**
3/18	San Felipe S. (G2)	SA	1 1/16m	1:42.40	**A. P. WARRIOR, Point Determined, Bob and John**
3/18	Gotham S. (G3)	Aqu	1 1/16m	1:43.17	**LIKE NOW, Keyed Entry, Sweetnorthernsaint**
3/18	Rebel S. (G3)	OP	1 1/16m	1:44.09	**LAWYER RON, Red Raymond, Steppenwolfer**
3/18	Tampa Bay Derby (G3)	Tam	1 1/16m	1:44.26	**DEPUTY GLITTERS, Bluegrass Cat,** Winnies Tigger Too
3/25	Lane's End S. (G2)	TP	1⅛m	1:51.11	**WITH A CITY, Seaside Retreat, Malameeze**
3/25	UAE Derby (UAE-G2)	Nad	1,800m	1:48.59	**DISCREET CAT, Testimony,** =Flamme de Passion (Jpn)
3/25	Rushaway S.	TP	1 1/16m	1:45.19	**HIGH COTTON, Special Interest, Bear Character**
4/1	Florida Derby (G1)	GP	1⅛m	1:49.01	**BARBARO, Sharp Humor, Sunriver**
4/1	WinStar Derby	Sun	1⅛m	1:48.88	**WANNA RUNNER,** Sky Diving, Belligerence
4/7	Transylvania S. (G3)	Kee	1mT	1:37.87	CHIN HIGH, Le Plaix (Fr), Wherethewestbegins
4/8	Santa Anita Derby (G1)	SA	1⅛m	1:48.00	**BROTHER DEREK, Point Determined, A. P. Warrior**
4/8	Wood Memorial S. (G1)	Aqu	1⅛m	1:51.54	**BOB AND JOHN, Jazil, Keyed Entry**
4/8	Illinois Derby (G2)	Haw	1⅛m	1:49.82	**SWEETNORTHERNSAINT, Mister Triester, Cause to Believe**
4/8	Bay Shore S. (G3)	Aqu	7f	1:22.40	**TOO MUCH BLING, Songster, One Way Flight**
4/9	Lafayette S.	Kee	6f	1:09.32	LIKELY, **Laptop Computer**, Skeleton Crew
4/9	San Pedro S.	SA	6½f	1:15.81	ARSON SQUAD, **Da Stoops**, The Pharaoh
4/15	Blue Grass S. (G1)	Kee	1⅛m	1:48.85	**SINISTER MINISTER, Storm Treasure, Strong Contender**
4/15	Arkansas Derby (G2)	OP	1⅛m	1:51.38	**LAWYER RON, Steppenwolfer, Private Vow**
4/20	Forerunner S.	Kee	1⅛mT	1:49.78	**UP AN OCTAVE**, Yate's Black Cat, **Tahoe Warrior**
4/22	Coolmore Lexington S. (G2)	Kee	1 1/16m	1:46.42	**SHOWING UP, Like Now, Bear Character**
4/29	Withers S. (G3)	Aqu	1m	1:35.07	**BERNARDINI, Doc Cheney**, Luxembourg
4/29	Derby Trial S.	CD	1m	1:36.32	**RECORD, Spotsgone, Mister Triester**
5/6	Kentucky Derby (G1)	CD	1¼m	2:01.36	**BARBARO, Bluegrass Cat, Steppenwolfer**
5/20	Preakness S. (G1)	Pim	1 3/16m	1:54.65	**BERNARDINI, Sweetnorthernsaint, Hemingway's Key**
5/20	Peter Pan S. (G2)	Bel	1⅛m	1:49.39	**SUNRIVER, Lewis Michael, Strong Contender**
6/10	Belmont S. (G1)	Bel	1½m	2:27.86	**JAZIL, Bluegrass Cat, Sunriver**

Triple Crown nominees are listed in bold.

Triple Crown Winners

America's Triple Crown Winners

Year	Horse	Owner	Trainer	Jockey
1978	**Affirmed**	Harbor View Farm	Lazaro Barrera	Steve Cauthen
1977	**Seattle Slew**	Karen L. Taylor	William Turner Jr.	Jean Cruguet
1973	**Secretariat**	Meadow Stable	Lucien Laurin	Ron Turcotte
1948	**Citation**	Calumet Farm	H. A. "Jimmy" Jones	Eddie Arcaro
1946	**Assault**	King Ranch	Max Hirsch	Warren Mehrtens
1943	**Count Fleet**	Mrs. John D. Hertz	Don Cameron	John Longden
1941	**Whirlaway**	Calumet Farm	Ben A. Jones	Eddie Arcaro
1937	**War Admiral**	Samuel D. Riddle	George Conway	Charles Kurtsinger
1935	**Omaha**	Belair Stud	James Fitzsimmons	William Saunders
1930	**Gallant Fox**	Belair Stud	James Fitzsimmons	Earle Sande
1919	**Sir Barton**	J. K. L. Ross	H. Guy Bedwell	John Loftus

Triple Crown Trophy

The Triple Crown trophy was commissioned in 1950 by the Thoroughbred Racing Associations, which copyrighted the term Triple Crown, and has three sides to symbolize the three races in the series. The trophy was presented retroactively to the eight previous winners of the three races.

The first three-year-old with a chance to claim the silver Triple Crown trophy was Tim Tam, who won the 1958 Kentucky Derby and Preakness Stakes but finished second to *Cavan in the Belmont Stakes. Secretariat in 1973 was the first horse to be presented the trophy after sweeping the three races.

Sir Barton

At the start of 1919, Sir Barton was far down the pecking order in trainer H. Guy Bedwell's stable. Commander J.K.L. Ross had purchased the *Star Shoot colt at Saratoga for $10,000 in 1918, but Sir Barton was winless in his six starts as a two-year-old and made his three-year-old debut in the '19 Kentucky Derby. His role in the Derby on May 10, 1919, was to serve as a pacemaker for his highly fancied stablemate, Billy Kelly. They went off at 2.60-to-1, second choice behind the 2.10-to-1 entry of Sailor and Eternal. Ridden by Johnny Loftus, Sir Barton bucked the odds, leading all the way and winning the Derby by five lengths over his stablemate. He was immediately shipped to Baltimore and won the Preakness Stakes on May 14 (a Wednesday) by four lengths over Eternal as the 7-to-5 favorite. In the Belmont Stakes on June 11, Sir Barton was 2-to-5 against the entry of Sweep On, third in the Preakness, and Natural Bridge. Sir Barton allowed Natural Bridge to set the pace for three-quarters of a mile before taking the lead and winning by five lengths. Between his Preakness and Belmont victories, Sir Barton won the Withers Stakes.

Sir Barton's achievement was unprecedented, but he was overshadowed by the appearance of Man o' War, who sustained the only defeat of his career in that year's Sanford Memorial Stakes at Saratoga Race Course.

As a four-year-old in 1920, Sir Barton alternated between brilliant and ordinary, winning five of 12 starts but finishing off the board twice. Because of his chronically sore feet and difficult temperament, he lost several races that he should have won against less talented opponents.

After losing a match race to Man o' War, Sir Barton faded from view. Retired to stud at the end of the 1920 season, he enjoyed only moderate success, was sold to the United States Cavalry Remount Station, and lived on a Wyoming ranch until his death in 1937.

Ch. c., 1916, by *Star Shoot—Lady Sterling, by Hanover

Owner: Commander J. K. L. Ross
Breeders: Madden and Gooch (Ky.)
Trainer: H. Guy Bedwell
Jockey: Johnny Loftus

Race Record

Year	Starts	1st	2nd	3rd	Earnings
1918	6	0	1 (1)	0	$ 4,113
1919	13	8 (8)	3 (2)	2 (1)	88,250
1920	12	5 (5)	2 (2)	3 (3)	24,494
	31	**13 (13)**	**6 (5)**	**5 (4)**	**$116,857**

1919—1st Kentucky Derby, Preakness S., Belmont S., Withers S., Potomac H., Maryland H., Pimlico Fall Series No. 2, Pimlico Fall Series No. 3
1920—1st Saratoga H., Merchants' and Citizens' H., Dominion H., Climax H., Rennert H.

Gallant Fox

B. c., 1927, by *Sir Gallahad III—Marguerite, by Celt					
Owner-Breeder: Belair Stud (Ky.)					
Trainer: James Fitzsimmons					
Jockey: Earl Sande					
		Race Record			
Year	**Starts**	**1st**	**2nd**	**3rd**	**Earnings**
1929	7	2 (2)	2 (1)	2 (2)	$ 19,890
1930	10	9 (9)	1 (1)	0	308,275
	17	**11 (11)**	**3 (2)**	**2 (2)**	**$328,165**

1929—1st Flash S., Junior Champion S.
1930—1st Kentucky Derby, Preakness S., Belmont S., Wood Memorial S., Dwyer S., Classic S., Saratoga Cup, Lawrence Realization S., Jockey Cup Gold Cup

Bred and owned by the Belair Stud of William Woodward, Gallant Fox marked a shift in the standards of American breeding. The introduction of *Sir Gallahad III to the United States from France in the late 1920s represented an important step forward for the American breeding industry. For the next several decades, American breeders went to Europe for proven stallions or prospects, particularly in England. The result was a significant increase in the quality of American racehorses. Woodward was one of the syndicate members involved in the purchase of *Sir Gallahad III, who stood at Claiborne Farm in Kentucky.

Gallant Fox was a good but not outstanding two-year-old, winning the Flash and Junior Champion Stakes and placing in three other stakes in his seven starts in 1929. In the care of trainer James "Sunny Jim" Fitzsimmons, Gallant Fox developed into an imposing physical specimen at three.

A four-length winner in Aqueduct's 1930 Wood Memorial Stakes, Gallant Fox hurtled through the Triple Crown, winning the Preakness on May 9 by three-quarters of a length, the Kentucky Derby eight days later by two lengths, and the Belmont on June 7 by three lengths over Whichone, his leading rival. Three weeks later, Gallant Fox added the Dwyer Stakes to his list of triumphs.

His only loss of the year occurred in the Travers Stakes at Saratoga Race Course, where he ran second to 100-to-1 longshot Jim Dandy.

At the end of the year, Gallant Fox was retired to stud at Claiborne, where he sired 1935 Triple Crown winner Omaha and '36 Belmont Stakes winner Granville. Gallant Fox died on November 13, 1954, and was buried at Claiborne alongside his sire and dam.

Omaha

Ch. c., 1932, by Gallant Fox—Flambino, by *Wrack					
Owner-Breeder: Belair Stud (Ky.)					
Trainer: James Fitzsimmons					
Jockey: Willie Saunders					
		Race Record			
Year	**Starts**	**1st**	**2nd**	**3rd**	**Earnings**
1934 (U.S.)	9	1	4 (3)	0	$ 3,850
1935 (U.S.)	9	6 (5)	1 (1)	2 (2)	142,255
1936 (Eng.)	4	2 (2)	2 (2)	0	8,650
	22	**9 (7)**	**7 (6)**	**2 (2)**	**$154,705**

1935—1st Kentucky Derby, Preakness S., Belmont S., Dwyer S., Classic S.
1936—(In England) 1st Victor Wild S., Queen's Plate

Five years after his Gallant Fox became the second Triple Crown winner, William Woodward saw his decision to participate in the syndication of French runner *Sir Gallahad III for stud duty in the United States pay off with a second Triple Crown winner. Omaha, a son of Gallant Fox and grandson of *Sir Gallahad III, won nine of 22 starts, but his career did not measure up to that of his sire. At two, Omaha won only once in nine starts, although he finished second in the Sanford and Champagne Stakes.

Once again, trainer James "Sunny Jim" Fitzsimmons's patient hand allowed the chestnut colt to fill out nicely over the winter between his two- and three-year-old years. On May 4, 1935, Omaha stepped onto an off track at Churchill Downs as the 4-to-1 second choice for the Kentucky Derby (favored at 3.80-to-1 was the filly Nellie Flag). Omaha made his move for the lead on the far turn, led by two lengths at the top of the stretch, and won by a relatively easy 1½ lengths over Roman Soldier.

One week later, Omaha was a runaway, six-length winner of the Preakness Stakes over Firethorn, who had skipped the Derby. Despite losing two weeks later in the Withers Stakes, Omaha won the Belmont Stakes by 1½ lengths on June 8. Omaha finished third in the Brooklyn Handicap in his next start but won his next two starts, the Dwyer Stakes and the Arlington Classic, before an injury ended his season.

As a four-year-old, Omaha was shipped to England and finished second in the Ascot Gold Cup. Omaha failed at stud, and Claiborne in 1943 sent him to a New York farm. Moved to a farm in Nebraska in 1950, Omaha died in '59 and was buried at Ak-Sar-Ben racetrack in Omaha.

War Admiral

Glen Riddle Farms owner Samuel Riddle owned War Admiral's famous sire, Man o' War, but chose to skip the Kentucky Derby with him in 1920. In Riddle's estimation, Churchill Downs was too far west, and the Derby was too early in the year for his comfort.

War Admiral, a striking brown colt out of the Sweep mare Brushup, had won three of six starts as a two-year-old, and his one stakes victory was in the minor Eastern Shore Handicap at Havre de Grace in Maryland. He returned to Havre de Grace for his first start of 1937 and won the Chesapeake Stakes. Riddle then decided to give War Admiral a shot at the Kentucky Derby.

Sent off as the 8-to-5 favorite in a Derby field of 20, War Admiral led at every point of call and easily held off champion two-year-old Pompoon in the final furlong to win by 1¾ lengths.

One week later, War Admiral was put to a much sterner test in the Preakness Stakes by Pompoon, who battled the Derby winner from the top of Pimlico Race Course's stretch. War Admiral won by a head. In the Belmont Stakes on June 5, War Admiral stumbled at the start, injuring his right foreleg, but the diminutive colt cruised to an easy, three-length victory over Sceneshifter.

Br. c., 1934, by Man o' War—Brushup, by Sweep

Owner: Glen Riddle Farms
Breeder: Samuel Riddle (Ky.)
Trainer: George Conway
Jockey: Charles Kurtsinger

Race Record

Year	Starts	1st	2nd	3rd	Earnings
1936	6	3 (1)	2 (2)	1 (1)	$ 14,800
1937	8	8 (6)	0	0	166,500
1938	11	9 (8)	1 (1)	0	90,840
1939	1	1	0	0	1,100
	26	**21 (15)**	**3 (3)**	**1 (1)**	**$273,240**

1936—1st Eastern Shore H.
1937—1st Kentucky Derby, Preakness S., Belmont S., Chesapeake S., Pimlico Special, Washington H.
1938—1st Whitney S., Jockey Club Gold Cup, Saratoga Cup, Saratoga H., Wilson S., Queens County H., Rhode Island H., Widener H.

Voted Horse of the Year and champion three-year-old, War Admiral lost a 1938 match race to Seabiscuit in the Pimlico Special.

At stud, War Admiral sired 40 stakes winners and two champions from 320 starters, 12.5% of starters, in his 20-year stud career. He died in 1959.

Whirlaway

Prone to wild trips around the racetrack, Whirlaway could be a danger to himself and those around him, but he was worth the risk to train and run. In his three- and four-year-old seasons, he made 42 starts, won 25 times, finished second 13 times, and was third in his other four starts. Handled patiently by Racing Hall of Fame trainer Ben Jones, Whirlaway became the first of eight Kentucky Derby winners and two Triple Crown winners for Calumet Farm.

For the Derby on May 3, 1941, Jones fashioned new blinkers for Whirlaway, cutting away the left cup but leaving the right cup intact. He also made a rider change, with Eddie Arcaro replacing Wendall Eads. On Derby day, Whirlaway displayed his customary tendency to run near the back of the pack early. With a quarter-mile left, Whirlaway had moved up to fourth place and was flying. He exploded through a final quarter-mile, running it in :24, and won by eight lengths.

Despite walking out of the gate and trailing by more than nine lengths after a half-mile of the Preakness on May 10, Whirlaway again came on late and won by 5½ lengths. Nearly one month later in the Belmont Stakes, Whirlaway stunned his three rivals by taking off after a half-mile and opening up a seven-length lead after six furlongs. Despite entering the stretch a bit wide, he won by 2½ lengths to become the fifth Triple Crown winner.

The colt maintained his brilliance through 1942, when he was named Horse of the Year a second time.

Sold to French interests, Whirlaway died in southern Normandy on April 6, 1953.

Ch. c., 1938, by *Blenheim II—Dustwhirl, by Sweep

Owner-Breeder: Calumet Farm (Ky.)
Trainer: Ben A. Jones
Jockey: Eddie Arcaro

Race Record

Year	Starts	1st	2nd	3rd	Earnings
1940	16	7 (4)	2 (2)	4 (3)	$77,275
1941	20	13 (8)	5 (5)	2	272,386
1942	22	12 (10)	8 (6)	2 (2)	211,250
1943	2	0	0	1	250
	60	**32 (22)**	**15 (13)**	**9 (5)**	**$561,161**

1940—1st Saratoga Special, Hopeful S., Breeders' Futurity, Walden S.
1941—1st Kentucky Derby, Preakness S., Belmont S., Travers S., Lawrence Realization S., Saranac H., Dwyer S., American Derby
1942—1st Brooklyn H., Jockey Club Gold Cup, Massachusetts H., Narragansett Special, Dixie H., Washington H., Louisiana H., Trenton H., Governor Bowie H., Clark H.

Count Fleet

Br. c., 1940, by Reigh Count—Quickly, by Haste

Owner-Breeder: Mrs. John D. Hertz (Ky.)
Trainer: Don Cameron
Jockey: John Longden

Race Record

Year	Starts	1st	2nd	3rd	Earnings
1942	15	10 (4)	4 (2)	1 (1)	$ 76,245
1943	6	6 (5)	0	0	174,055
	21	**16 (9)**	**4 (2)**	**1 (1)**	**$250,300**

1942—1st Champagne S., Pimlico Futurity, Walden S., Wakefield S.
1943—1st Kentucky Derby, Preakness S., Belmont S., Wood Memorial S., Withers S.

In 1927, Yellow Cab founder John D. Hertz watched a two-year-old race in which one of the runners reached out and bit another horse dueling with him for the lead. It was a remarkable display of aggression and a single-minded will to win. Hertz was sufficiently impressed to buy the colt, Reigh Count, who won the 1928 Kentucky Derby. Hertz never had much faith in Reigh Count as a stallion and bred him to only a few mares each year, including Quickly, who on March 24, 1940, gave birth to a gangly brown package named Count Fleet. The youngster was so clumsy and awkward that Hertz considered selling him as a yearling and again early in his two-year-old campaign. At two, Count Fleet won ten of 15 starts, was voted champion two-year-old colt, and on the Experimental Free Handicap was accorded highweight of 132 pounds, still the highest weight ever assigned.

As a three-year-old, Count Fleet had no equal. He usually went to the lead early, discouraged his competition by the stretch, and won as he pleased.

In the Kentucky Derby on May 1, Count Fleet went off as the 2-to-5 favorite in the field of ten. He broke sharply under John Longden, went immediately to the lead, opened two lengths after six furlongs, and won by an easy three lengths over Blue Swords. One week later, Count Fleet won the Preakness by eight lengths. In the Belmont Stakes on June 5, Count Fleet, at odds of 1-to-20, won by 25 lengths in 2:28⅕.

A seemingly minor injury to Count Fleet's left front ankle did not respond to treatment and ended his career. At stud, he sired champions Counterpoint and Kiss Me Kate as well as Count Turf, upset winner of the 1951 Kentucky Derby. Count Fleet died on December 3, 1973.

Assault

Ch. c., 1943, by Bold Venture—Igual, by Equipoise

Owner-Breeder: King Ranch (Tx.)
Trainer: Max Hirsch
Jockey: Warren Mehrtens

Race Record

Year	Starts	1st	2nd	3rd	Earnings
1945	9	2 (1)	2	1 (1)	$ 17,250
1946	15	8 (8)	2 (2)	3 (3)	424,195
1947	7	5 (5)	1	1 (1)	181,925
1948	2	1	0	0	3,250
1949	6	1 (1)	1	1 (1)	45,900
1950	3	1	0	1	2,950
	42	**18 (15)**	**6 (2)**	**7 (6)**	**$675,470**

1945—1st Flash S.
1946—1st Kentucky Derby, Preakness S., Belmont S., Wood Memorial S., Dwyer S., Westchester H., Pimlico Special, Experimental Free H. No. 1
1947—1st Suburban H., Brooklyn H., Butler H., Grey Lag H., Dixie H.
1949—1st Brooklyn H.

As a foal, Assault stepped on a surveyor's stake at King Ranch, which left him with a malformed right front hoof. As a result, he was called the club-footed comet.

Trainer Max Hirsch initially was unsure that Assault could withstand training because of the injury, but the Bold Venture colt won two of nine starts at two in 1945. He went off at 8.20-to-1 in the Kentucky Derby on May 4, 1946. Assault, with jockey Warren Mehrtens up, blew past Spy Song and Knockdown early in the stretch and won by eight lengths.

One week later in the Preakness Stakes, Assault's Triple Crown dreams nearly ended. Mehrtens decided to go for the knockout punch and sent Assault after the leaders going into the far turn. Assault tired and staggered home, winning by a fast-diminishing neck over Lord Boswell.

When the Belmont Stakes came around on June 1, many racing fans believed the 1½ miles would expose Assault. Lord Boswell was sent off as the 1.35-to-1 favorite, with Assault the second choice at 7-to-5. Mehrtens allowed Assault to reach contention gradually. Trailing Natchez by two lengths in midstretch, Assault exploded past him in the final 200 yards and won by three lengths.

Horse of the Year in 1946, Assault won five of seven starts in '47 and spent much of the year battling fellow handicappers Stymie and Armed for the all-time earnings crown.

Assault was retired to stud in early 1948 but proved to be sterile. Returned to the racetrack, he ran until he was seven. Pensioned at King Ranch, he was euthanized in 1971 after fracturing a leg.

Citation

B. c., 1945, by Bull Lea—*Hydroplane II, by Hyperion

Owner-Breeder: Calumet Farm (Ky.)
Trainers: Ben A. Jones and H. A. "Jimmy" Jones
Jockey: Eddie Arcaro

Race Record

Year	Starts	1st	2nd	3rd	Earnings
1947	9	8 (3)	1 (1)	0	$ 155,680
1948	20	19 (16)	1 (1)	0	709,470
1949	—	—	—	—	—
1950	9	2 (1)	7 (5)	0	73,480
1951	7	3 (2)	1 (1)	2	147,130
	45	**32 (22)**	**10 (8)**	**2**	**$1,085,760**

1947—1st Futurity S., Pimlico Futurity, Elementary S.
1948—1st Kentucky Derby, Preakness S., Belmont S., Jockey Club Gold Cup, Pimlico Special, Belmont Gold Cup, American Derby, Flamingo S., Jersey S., Stars and Stripes H., Tanforan H., Sysonby Mile, Chesapeake S., Seminole H., Derby Trial, Everglades H.
1950—1st Golden Gate Mile H.
1951—1st American H., Hollywood Gold Cup

Citation resulted from a mating of Calumet Farm's premier sire, Bull Lea, with *Hydroplane II, whom Warren Wright purchased from Lord Derby in the spring of 1941. Citation was foaled on April 11, 1945, and joined trainer H. A. "Jimmy" Jones's Maryland division in the spring of '47 to begin his racing career.

At two, his only loss was in the Washington Park Futurity to stablemate Bewitch.

Citation began his three-year-old season with two victories over older horses at Hialeah Park before winning the Everglades and Flamingo Stakes. His jockey, Al Snider, died in a boating accident after the Flamingo, and Jones induced Eddie Arcaro to take the mount.

In the Kentucky Derby against only five opponents on May 1, Citation spotted stablemate Coaltown six lengths in the opening half-mile and ran him down to win by 3½ lengths.

In the Preakness Stakes two weeks later, Citation set the pace and won by 5½ lengths as the 1-to-10 favorite. With four weeks between the Preakness and Belmont Stakes, Jones sent out Citation for an 11-length victory in the Jersey Stakes. On June 12 in the Belmont, Citation, at 1-to-5 odds, scored an eight-length triumph over Better Self.

Citation won 19 times in 1948, including a walkover in the Pimlico Special. At the end of his three-year-old season, Citation had 27 victories and two seconds in 29 starts, with earnings of $865,150.

In 1951, Citation won the Hollywood Gold Cup, becoming racing's first $1-million earner. Immediately retired to Calumet, he was an undistinguished sire. He died on August 8, 1970.

Secretariat

Ch. c., 1970, by Bold Ruler—Somethingroyal, by *Princequillo

Owner: Meadow Stable
Breeder: Meadow Stud (Va.)
Trainer: Lucien Laurin
Jockey: Ron Turcotte

Race Record

Year	Starts	1st	2nd	3rd	Earnings
1972	9	7 (5)	1 (1)	0	$ 456,404
1973	12	9 (9)	2 (2)	1 (1)	860,404
	21	**16 (14)**	**3 (3)**	**1 (1)**	**$1,316,808**

1972—1st Hopeful S., Futurity S., Garden State S., Laurel Futurity, Sanford S.,
1973—1st Kentucky Derby (G1), Preakness S. (G1), Belmont S. (G1), Man o' War S. (G1), Canadian International Championship S. (G2), Marlboro Cup H., Arlington Invitational S., Gotham S. (G2), Bay Shore S. (G3)

Like Man o' War, Secretariat was known as Big Red, and both were big in accomplishments. Secretariat, by leading sire Bold Ruler out of the *Princequillo mare Somethingroyal, made his career debut on July 4, 1972, in a 5½-furlong maiden race at Aqueduct and finished fourth with a late surge. Secretariat subsequently won five stakes impressively and was voted Horse of the Year.

In February 1973, as Secretariat was being prepared for the Triple Crown campaign, he was syndicated by Claiborne Farm for a record $6.08-million. Secretariat easily won his first two starts of the year, the Bay Shore (G3) and the Gotham (G2) Stakes, but the colt ran third in the Wood Memorial Stakes (G1) on April 20, most likely due to a lip abscess. His Kentucky Derby (G1) was one that will forever be remembered. After breaking near the back of the pack, Secretariat began picking up horses on the first turn, collared Sham at the top of the lane, and drew away to a 2½-length victory in a Derby record 1:59⅖ for 1¼ miles.

In the Preakness Stakes (G1), jockey Ron Turcotte sensed a slow early pace and allowed Secretariat to surge to the lead as the six-horse field entered the backstretch. Secretariat dominated the rest of the race and again won by 2½ lengths over Sham. A timer malfunction effectively nullified what should have been a track record.

Only Sham and three others showed up to oppose Secretariat in the Belmont Stakes (G1) on June 9. Secretariat and Sham dueled through the first six furlongs in 1:09⅘ before Sham surrendered. Secretariat steadily pulled away to win by 31 lengths while running 1½ miles in 2:24, an American record.

Retired to Claiborne, Secretariat was a good but not great sire. He died of complications from laminitis on October 4, 1989.

Seattle Slew

Dk. b. or br. c., 1974, by Bold Reasoning—My Charmer, by Poker					

Owners: Mickey and Karen L. Taylor, Dr. Jim and Sally Hill
Breeder: Ben S. Castleman (Ky.)
Trainers: William H. Turner Jr. (1976-'77); Doug Peterson (1978)
Jockey: Jean Cruguet

Race Record

Year	Starts	1st	2nd	3rd	Earnings
1976	3	3 (1)	0	0	$ 94,350
1977	7	6 (5)	0	0	641,370
1978	7	5 (3)	2 (2)	0	473,006
	17	**14 (9)**	**2 (2)**	**0**	**$1,208,726**

1976—1st Champagne S. (G1)
1977—1st Kentucky Derby (G1), Preakness S. (G1), Belmont S. (G1), Wood Memorial S. (G1), Flamingo S. (G1)
1978—1st Marlboro Cup Invitational H. (G1), Woodward S. (G1), Stuyvesant S. (G3)

A son of Bold Reasoning out of My Charmer, by Poker, Seattle Slew was brought along patiently by his young trainer, Billy Turner Jr. He was voted champion two-year-old male after a stunning Champagne Stakes (G1) win in just his third start.

At three, Seattle Slew won Hialeah Park's Flamingo Stakes (G1) by four lengths on March 26 and took Aqueduct's Wood Memorial Stakes (G1) by 3¼ lengths on April 23.

For the Derby on May 7, Seattle Slew went off as the 1-to-2 favorite. Disaster nearly struck at the start when he swerved out and was sharply taken up by jockey Jean Cruguet. At the top of the stretch, Seattle Slew put away For The Moment and then cruised home by 1¾ lengths over Run Dusty Run.

Two weeks later in the Preakness Stakes (G1), 2-to-5 Seattle Slew took command leaving the backstretch and won by 1½ lengths over Iron Constitution. Seattle Slew then dominated the Belmont Stakes (G1), winning by four lengths over Run Dusty Run. Seattle Slew was the first to complete the series without a defeat. Turner suggested a rest, but owners Karen and Mickey Taylor and Sally and Jim Hill insisted on running in Hollywood Park's Swaps Stakes (G1). Slew finished fourth and did not race again in 1977.

Seattle Slew made seven starts as a four-year-old for trainer Doug Peterson, and his five victories included an epic win over Affirmed in the Marlboro Cup Invitational Handicap (G1), the first meeting of Triple Crown winners. Standing first at Spendthrift Farm and then at Three Chimneys Farm, he sired A.P. Indy, 1992 Horse of the Year, and more than 100 stakes winners. He died on May 7, 2002, at Hill 'n' Dale Farm, where he was moved shortly before his death.

Affirmed

Ch. c., 1975, by Exclusive Native—Won't Tell You, by Crafty Admiral					

Owner-Breeder: Harbor View Farm (Fl.)
Trainer: Lazaro Barrera
Jockey: Steve Cauthen

Race Record

Year	Starts	1st	2nd	3rd	Earnings
1977	9	7 (6)	2 (2)	0	$ 343,477
1978	11	8 (7)	2 (2)	0	901,541
1979	9	7 (6)	1 (1)	1 (1)	1,148,800
	29	**22 (19)**	**5 (5)**	**1 (1)**	**$2,393,818**

1977—1st Hopeful S. (G1), Futurity S. (G1), Laurel Futurity (G1), Sanford S. (G2), Hollywood Juvenile Championship S. (G2), Youthful S.
1978—1st Kentucky Derby (G1), Preakness S. (G1), Belmont S. (G1), Santa Anita Derby (G1), Hollywood Derby (G1), San Felipe H. (G2), Jim Dandy S. (G3)
1979—1st Jockey Club Gold Cup (G1), Hollywood Gold Cup (G1), Santa Anita H. (G1), Woodward S. (G1), Californian S. (G1), Charles H. Strub S. (G1)

The 1978 Triple Crown, the first won in back-to-back years, belonged to Affirmed, but his name will forever be linked with Alydar, the first horse to finish second in all three races to a Triple Crown winner.

Both colts dominated their arenas at three, and the Kentucky Derby (G1), in which Alydar went off as the 6-to-5 favorite with Affirmed at 9-to-5, was a clash of titans. Third early under jockey Steve Cauthen, Affirmed surged past Believe It early in the stretch and opened a two-length lead in midstretch. Alydar made a late charge but finished second, beaten 1½ lengths.

Two weeks later on May 20, the two would stage an epic duel in the Preakness Stakes (G1). Affirmed, 1-to-2, once again stalked the early pace and inherited the lead after a quarter-mile. Jorge Velasquez asked Alydar for speed on the backstretch, and the Raise a Native colt reached Affirmed's side leaving the turn. They fought to the wire, with Affirmed winning by a neck.

In the Belmont Stakes (G1) three weeks later, 3-to-5 Affirmed was the only speed in a field of five, and 11-to-10 Alydar shadowed him practically from the start. After a half-mile, Affirmed led by one length, and by the top of Belmont Park's stretch they were a head apart. Alydar appeared to take a narrow lead inside the furlong pole, but Affirmed fought back and won by a head. He was voted Horse of the Year and repeated in 1979 with six consecutive Grade 1 victories. The sport's first $2-million earner, he sired more than 80 stakes winners. He died on January 12, 2001, at Jonabell Farm.

Near Triple Crown Winners

While the Triple Crown has been swept on 11 occasions, in 49 other years three-year-olds have won two legs of the Triple Crown. Among the 49 near successes were 20 horses who won the Kentucky Derby and Preakness Stakes but not the Belmont Stakes.

Of those 20, injury felled several in the Belmont (including Tim Tam and Charismatic), several have come agonizingly close (Silver Charm, Real Quiet, Smarty Jones), and two did not run in the Belmont (Burgoo King, Bold Venture) because of injuries before the race.

Following are the 49 horses who won two of the three races. Winner of the race the Triple Crown hopeful lost is in parentheses.

Year	Horse	Kentucky Derby	Preakness	Belmont
2005	Afleet Alex	3rd (Giacomo)	Won	Won
2004	Smarty Jones	Won	Won	2nd (Birdstone)
2003	Funny Cide	Won	Won	3rd (Empire Maker)
2002	War Emblem	Won	Won	8th (Sarava)
2001	Point Given	5th (Monarchos)	Won	Won
1999	Charismatic	Won	Won	3rd (Lemon Drop Kid)
1998	Real Quiet	Won	Won	2nd (Victory Gallop)
1997	Silver Charm	Won	Won	2nd (Touch Gold)
1995	Thunder Gulch	Won	3rd (Timber Country)	Won
1994	Tabasco Cat	6th (Go for Gin)	Won	Won
1991	Hansel	10th (Strike the Gold)	Won	Won
1989	Sunday Silence	Won	Won	2nd (Easy Goer)
1988	Risen Star	3rd (Winning Colors)	Won	Won
1987	Alysheba	Won	Won	4th (Bet Twice)
1984	Swale	Won	7th (Gate Dancer)	Won
1981	Pleasant Colony	Won	Won	3rd (Summing)
1979	Spectacular Bid	Won	Won	3rd (Coastal)
1976	Bold Forbes	Won	3rd (Elocutionist)	Won
1974	Little Current	5th (Cannonade)	Won	Won
1972	Riva Ridge	Won	4th (Bee Bee Bee)	Won
1971	Canonero II	Won	Won	4th (Pass Catcher)
1969	Majestic Prince	Won	Won	2nd (Arts and Letters)
1968	Forward Pass	Won†	Won	2nd (Stage Door Johnny)
1967	Damascus	3rd (Proud Clarion)	Won	Won
1966	Kauai King	Won	Won	4th (Amberoid)
1964	Northern Dancer	Won	Won	3rd (Quadrangle)
1963	Chateaugay	Won	2nd (Candy Spots)	Won
1961	Carry Back	Won	Won	7th (Sherluck)
1958	Tim Tam	Won	Won	2nd (*Cavan)
1956	Needles	Won	2nd (Fabius)	Won
1955	Nashua	2nd (Swaps)	Won	Won
1953	Native Dancer	2nd (Dark Star)	Won	Won
1950	Middleground	Won	2nd (Hill Prince)	Won
1949	Capot	2nd (Ponder)	Won	Won
1944	Pensive	Won	Won	2nd (Bounding Home)
1942	Shut Out	Won	5th (Alsab)	Won
1940	Bimelech	2nd (Gallahadion)	Won	Won
1939	Johnstown	Won	5th (Challedon)	Won
1936	Bold Venture	Won	Won	Did not start
1932	Burgoo King	Won	Won	Did not start
1931	Twenty Grand	Won	2nd (Mate)	Won
1923	Zev	Won	12th (Vigil)	Won
1922	Pillory	Did not start	Won	Won
1920	Man o' War	Did not start	Won	Won
1895	Belmar	Did not start	Won	Won
1881	Saunterer	Did not start	Won	Won
1880	Grenada	Did not start	Won	Won
1878	Duke of Magenta	Did not start	Won	Won
1877	Cloverbrook	Did not start	Won	Won

†Won on disqualification of Dancer's Image. Winner of race is in parentheses.

Leading Owners of Triple Crown Race Winners

17 **Calumet Farm:** Kentucky Derby: Whirlaway (1941), Pensive ('44), Citation ('48), Ponder ('49), Hill Gail ('52), Iron Liege ('57), Tim Tam ('58), Forward Pass ('68); Preakness: Whirlaway ('41), Pensive ('44), Faultless ('47), Citation ('48), Fabius ('56), Tim Tam ('58), Forward Pass ('68); Belmont: Whirlaway ('41), Citation ('48)

12 **Belair Stud:** Kentucky Derby: Gallant Fox (1930), Omaha ('35), Johnstown ('39); Preakness: Gallant Fox ('30), Omaha ('35), Nashua ('55); Belmont: Gallant Fox ('30), Faireno ('32), Omaha ('35), Granville ('36), Johnstown ('39), Nashua ('55)

10 **Harry P. Whitney:** Kentucky Derby: Regret (1915), Whiskery ('27); Preakness: Royal Tourist ('08), Broomspun ('21), Bostonian ('27), Victorian ('28); Belmont: Tanya ('05), Burgomaster ('06), Prince Eugene ('13), *Johren ('18)

9 **E. R. Bradley (Idle Hour Stock Farm):** Kentucky Derby: Behave Yourself (1921), Bubbling Over ('26), Burgoo King ('32), Brokers Tip ('33); Preakness: Kalitan ('17), Burgoo King ('32), Bimelech ('40); Belmont: Blue Larkspur ('29), Bimelech ('40)

8 **Dwyer Brothers:**
6—Dwyer Brothers (M. F. and Phil J.): Kentucky Derby: Hindoo (1881); Belmont: George Kinney ('83), Panique ('84), Inspector B. ('86), Hanover ('87), Sir Dixon ('88)
1—M. F. Dwyer: Kentucky Derby: Ben Brush (1896)
1—Phil J. Dwyer: Preakness: Half Time (1899)

George L. Lorillard: Preakness: Duke of Magenta (1878), Harold ('79), Grenada ('80), Saunterer ('81), Vanguard ('82); Belmont: Duke of Magenta ('78), Grenada ('80), Saunterer ('81)

7 **August Belmont II:** Preakness: Margrave (1896), Don Enrique (1907), Watervale ('11); Belmont: Hastings (1896), Masterman (1902), Friar Rock ('16), *Hourless ('17)

Glen Riddle Farms: Kentucky Derby: War Admiral (1937); Preakness: Man o' War ('20), War Admiral ('37); Belmont: Man o' War ('20), American Flag ('25), Crusader (1926), War Admiral ('37)

Greentree Stable: Kentucky Derby: Twenty Grand (1931), Shut Out ('42); Preakness: Capot ('49); Belmont: Twenty Grand ('31), Shut Out ('42), Capot ('49), Stage Door Johnny ('68)

James R. Keene:
6—James R. Keene: Belmont: Spendthrift (1879), Commando (1901), Delhi ('04), Peter Pan ('07), Colin ('08), Sweep ('10)
1—James R. Keene and Foxhall P. Keene: Preakness: Assignee (1894)

6 **Robert and Beverly Lewis:**
5—Robert and Beverly Lewis: Kentucky Derby: Silver Charm (1997), Charismatic ('99); Preakness: Silver Charm ('97), Charismatic ('99); Belmont: Commendable (2000)
1—Gainesway Farm, Robert and Beverly Lewis, and Overbrook Farm: Preakness: Timber Country (1995)

Meadow Stable (C. T. and Penny Chenery): Kentucky Derby: Riva Ridge (1972), Secretariat ('73); Preakness: Hill Prince ('50), Secretariat ('73); Belmont: Riva Ridge ('72), Secretariat ('73)

5 **Overbrook Farm (W. T. Young):**
2—Overbrook Farm: Kentucky Derby: Grindstone (1996); Belmont: Editor's Note ('96)
2—Overbrook Farm and David Reynolds: Preakness: Tabasco Cat (1994); Belmont: Tabasco Cat ('94)
1—Gainesway Farm, Robert and Beverly Lewis, and Overbrook Farm: Preakness: Timber Country (1995)

King Ranch: Kentucky Derby: Assault (1946), Middleground ('50); Preakness: Assault ('46); Belmont: Assault ('46), Middleground ('50), High Gun ('54)

Darby Dan Farm: Kentucky Derby: Chateaugay (1963), Proud Clarion ('67); Preakness: Little Current ('74); Belmont: Chateaugay ('63), Little Current ('74)

4 **Brookmeade Stable:** Kentucky Derby: Cavalcade (1934); Preakness: High Quest ('34), Bold ('51); Belmont: Sword Dancer ('59)

Mrs. John D. Hertz: Kentucky Derby: Reigh Count (1928), Count Fleet ('43); Preakness: Count Fleet ('43); Belmont: Count Fleet ('43)

J.K.L. Ross: Kentucky Derby: Sir Barton (1919); Preakness: Damrosch ('16), Sir Barton ('19); Belmont: Sir Barton ('19)

4 **The Thoroughbred Corp:** Kentucky Derby: War Emblem (2002); Preakness: Point Given ('01), War Emblem ('02); Belmont: Point Given ('01)

3 **William Condren:**
1—B. Giles Brophy, William Condren, and Joseph Cornacchia: Kentucky Derby: Strike the Gold (1991)
1—William Condren and Joseph Cornacchia: Kentucky Derby: Go for Gin (1994)
1—William Condren, Georgia Hofmann, and Joseph Cornacchia: Preakness: Louis Quatorze (1996)

Joseph Cornacchia:
1—B. Giles Brophy, William Condren, and Joseph Cornacchia: Kentucky Derby: Strike the Gold (1991)
1—William Condren and Joseph Cornacchia: Kentucky Derby: Go for Gin (1994)
1—William Condren, Georgia Hofmann, and Joseph Cornacchia: Preakness: Louis Quatorze (1996)

Arthur B. Hancock III:
1—Arthur B. Hancock III and Leone J. Peters: Kentucky Derby: Gato Del Sol (1982)
2—Arthur B. Hancock III, Ernest Gaillard, and Charlie Whittingham: Kentucky Derby: Sunday Silence (1989); Preakness: Sunday Silence ('89)

Harbor View Farm: Kentucky Derby: Affirmed (1978); Preakness: Affirmed ('78); Belmont: Affirmed ('78)

Loblolly Stable: Preakness: Pine Bluff (1992), Prairie Bayou ('93); Belmont: Temperence Hill ('80)

David McDaniel: Belmont: Harry Bassett (1871), Joe Daniels ('72), Springbok ('73)

Preakness Stable (James Galway): Preakness: Montague (1890), Belmar ('95); Belmont: Belmar ('95)

3 **Rokeby Stable:** Kentucky Derby: Sea Hero (1993); Belmont: Quadrangle ('64), Arts and Letters ('69)

Walter J. Salmon: Preakness: Vigil (1923), Display ('26), Dr. Freeland ('29)

H. F. Sinclair: Belmont: Grey Lag (1921), Zev ('23), Mad Play ('24)

3 **Karen and Mickey Taylor and Sally and James Hill:** Kentucky Derby: Seattle Slew (1977); Preakness: Seattle Slew ('77); Belmont: Seattle Slew ('77)

Joseph E. Widener: Belmont: Chance Shot (1927), Hurryoff ('33), Peace Chance ('34)

Richard T. Wilson Jr.: Preakness: The Parader (1901), Pillory ('22); Belmont: Pillory ('22)

Leading Breeders of Triple Crown Race Winners

18 **Calumet Farm:** Kentucky Derby: Whirlaway (1941), Pensive ('44), Citation ('48), Ponder ('49), Hill Gail ('52), Iron Liege ('57), Tim Tam ('58), Forward Pass ('68), Strike the Gold ('91); Preakness: Whirlaway ('41), Pensive ('44), Faultless ('47), Citation ('48), Fabius ('56), Tim Tam ('58), Forward Pass ('68); Belmont: Whirlaway ('41), Citation ('48)

15 **A. J. Alexander:** Kentucky Derby: Baden-Baden (1877), Fonso ('80), Joe Cotton ('85), Chant ('94); Preakness: Tom Ochiltree ('75), Shirley ('76), Grenada ('80), Duke of Magenta ('90); Belmont: Harry Bassett ('71), Joe Daniels ('72), Springbok ('73), Duke of Magenta ('78), Spendthrift ('79), Grenada ('80), Burlington ('90)

12 **Harry P. Whitney:** Kentucky Derby: Regret (1915), Whiskery ('27); Preakness: Royal Tourist ('08), Buskin ('13), Holiday ('14), Broomspun ('21), Bostonian ('27), Victorian ('28); Belmont: Tanya ('05), Burgomaster ('06), Prince Eugene ('13), *Johren ('18)

11 **John E. Madden**

8—John E. Madden: Kentucky Derby: Old Rosebud (1914), Paul Jones ('20), Zev ('23), Flying Ebony ('25); Belmont: Joe Madden ('09), The Finn ('15), Grey Lag ('21), Zev ('23)

3—John E. Madden and Vivian A. Gooch: Kentucky Derby: Sir Barton (1919); Preakness: Sir Barton ('19); Belmont: Sir Barton ('19)

10 **Belair Stud:** Kentucky Derby: Gallant Fox (1930), Omaha ('35); Preakness: Gallant Fox ('30), Omaha ('35), Nashua ('55); Belmont: Gallant Fox ('30), Faireno ('32), Omaha ('35), Granville ('36), Nashua ('55)

August Belmont II: Preakness: Margrave (1896), Don Enrique (1907), Watervale ('11), Damrosch ('16), Man o' War ('20); Belmont: Masterman ('02), Friar Rock ('16), *Hourless ('17), Man o' War ('20), Chance Shot ('27)

8 **E. R. Bradley (Idle Hour Stock Farm):** Kentucky Derby: Behave Yourself (1921), Bubbling Over ('26), Burgoo King ('32), Brokers Tip ('33); Preakness: Burgoo King ('32), Bimelech ('40); Belmont: Blue Larkspur ('29), Bimelech ('40)

7 **Greentree Stud:** Kentucky Derby: Twenty Grand (1931), Shut Out ('42); Preakness: Capot ('49); Belmont: Twenty Grand ('31), Shut Out ('42), Capot ('49), Stage Door Johnny ('68)

6 **William S. Farish**

3—William S. Farish and William S. Kilroy: Preakness: Summer Squall (1990); Belmont: A.P. Indy ('90), Lemon Drop Kid ('99)

2—Parrish Hill Farm and William S. Farish: Kentucky Derby: Charismatic (1999); Preakness: Charismatic ('99)

1—William S. Farish and E. J. Hudson: Belmont: Bet Twice (1987)

6 **James Ben Ali Haggin:** Kentucky Derby: Stone Street (1908); Preakness: Old England ('02), Cairngorm ('05), Rhine Maiden ('15); Belmont: Commanche (1893), Africander (1903)

Meadow Stud (C. T. Chenery): Kentucky Derby: Riva Ridge (1972), Secretariat ('73); Preakness: Hill Prince ('50), Secretariat ('73); Belmont: Riva Ridge ('72), Secretariat ('73)

5 **Ezekiel F. Clay**

4—Clay and Woodford: Kentucky Derby: Ben Brush (1896); Preakness: Buddhist ('89); Belmont: Hanover ('87), Sir Dixon ('88)

1—Ezekiel F. Clay: Kentucky Derby: Agile (1905)

John W. Galbreath: Kentucky Derby: Chateaugay (1963), Proud Clarion ('67); Preakness: Little Current ('74); Belmont: Chateaugay ('63), Little Current ('74)

James R. Keene: Belmont: Commando (1901), Delhi ('04), Peter Pan ('07), Colin ('08), Sweep ('10)

King Ranch: Kentucky Derby: Assault (1946), Middleground ('50); Preakness: Assault ('46); Belmont: Assault ('46), Middleground ('50)

Samuel D. Riddle: Kentucky Derby: War Admiral (1937); Preakness: War Admiral ('37); Belmont: American Flag ('25), Crusader ('26), War Admiral ('37)

4 **Arthur B. Hancock III**

3—Arthur B. Hancock III and Leone J. Peters: Kentucky Derby: Gato Del Sol (1982); Preakness: Risen Star ('88); Belmont: Risen Star ('88)

1—Arthur B. Hancock III and Stonerside Ltd.: Kentucky Derby: Fusaichi Pegasus (2000)

Arthur B. Hancock Sr.

3—Arthur B. Hancock: Kentucky Derby: Johnstown (1939); Preakness: Vigil ('23); Belmont: Johnstown ('39)

1—Arthur B. Hancock and Mrs. R. A. Van Clief: Kentucky Derby: Jet Pilot (1947)

Aristides Welch: Preakness: Harold (1879), Saunterer ('81); Belmont: Saunterer ('81), Panique ('84)

3 **August Belmont I:** Preakness: Jacobus (1883); Belmont: Fenian ('69), Forester ('82)

A. J. Cassatt: Preakness: Montague (1890); Belmont: Foxford ('91), Patron ('92)

Ben S. Castleman: Kentucky Derby: Seattle Slew (1977), Preakness: Seattle Slew ('77), Belmont: Seattle Slew ('77)

Claiborne Farm: Kentucky Derby: Swale (1984); Belmont: Coastal ('79), Swale ('84)

Harbor View Farm: Kentucky Derby: Affirmed (1978); Preakness: Affirmed ('78); Belmont: Affirmed ('78)

3 **Mrs. John D. Hertz:** Kentucky Derby: Count Fleet (1943); Preakness: Count Fleet ('43); Belmont: Count Fleet ('43)

George J. Long: Kentucky Derby: Azra (1892), Manuel (1899), Sir Huon (1906)

H. Price McGrath (McGrathiana Stud): Kentucky Derby: Aristides (1875); Preakness: Paul Kauvar ('97); Belmont: Calvin ('75)

Paul Mellon: Kentucky Derby: Sea Hero (1993); Belmont: Quadrangle ('64), Arts and Letters ('69)

3 **Overbrook Farm**

2—Overbrook Farm and David Reynolds: Preakness: Tabasco Cat (1994); Belmont: Tabasco Cat ('94)

1—Overbrook Farm: Kentucky Derby: Grindstone (1996)

Daniel Swigert: Kentucky Derby: Hindoo (1881), Apollo ('82), Ben Ali ('86)

Leading Trainers of Triple Crown Race Winners

13 **James "Sunny Jim" Fitzsimmons:** Kentucky Derby: Gallant Fox (1930), Omaha ('35), Johnstown ('39); Preakness: Gallant Fox ('30), Omaha ('35), Nashua ('55), Bold Ruler ('57); Belmont: Gallant Fox ('30), Faireno ('32), Omaha ('35), Granville ('36), Johnstown ('39), Nashua ('55)

D. Wayne Lukas: Kentucky Derby: Winning Colors (1988), Thunder Gulch ('95), Grindstone ('96), Charismatic ('99); Preakness: Codex ('80), Tank's Prospect ('85), Tabasco Cat ('94), Timber Country ('95), Charismatic ('99); Belmont: Tabasco Cat ('94), Thunder Gulch ('95), Editor's Note ('96), Commendable (2000)

11 **James Rowe Sr.:** Kentucky Derby: Hindoo (1881), Regret (1915); Preakness: Broomspun (1921); Belmont: George Kinney (1883), Panique (1884), Commando (1901), Delhi ('04), Peter Pan ('07), Colin ('08), Sweep ('10), Prince Eugene ('13)

R. Wyndham Walden: Preakness: Tom Ochiltree (1875), Duke of Magenta ('78), Harold ('79), Grenada ('80), Saunterer ('81), Vanguard ('82), Refund ('88); Belmont: Duke of Magenta ('78), Grenada ('80), Saunterer ('81), *Bowling Brook ('98)

9 **Max Hirsch:** Kentucky Derby: Bold Venture (1936), Assault ('46), Middleground ('50); Preakness: Bold Venture ('36), Assault ('46); Belmont: Vito ('28), Assault ('46), Middleground ('50), High Gun ('54)

B. A. "Ben" Jones: Kentucky Derby: Lawrin (1938), Whirlaway ('41), Pensive ('44), Citation ('48), Ponder ('49), Hill Gail ('52); Preakness: Whirlaway ('41), Pensive ('44); Belmont: Whirlaway ('41)

8 **Bob Baffert:** Kentucky Derby: Silver Charm (1997), Real Quiet ('98), War Emblem (2002); Preakness: Silver Charm ('97), Real Quiet ('98), Point Given (2001), War Emblem ('02); Belmont: Point Given ('01)

Woodford C. "Woody" Stephens: Kentucky Derby: Cannonade (1974), Swale ('84); Preakness: Blue Man ('52); Belmont: Conquistador Cielo ('82), Caveat ('83), Swale ('84), Creme Fraiche ('85), Danzig Connection ('86)

7 **H. A. "Jimmy" Jones:** Kentucky Derby: Iron Liege (1957), Tim Tam ('58); Preakness: Faultless ('47), Citation ('48), Fabius ('56), Tim Tam ('58); Belmont: Citation ('48)

Sam Hildreth: Belmont: Jean Bereaud (1899), Joe Madden (1909), Friar Rock ('16), *Hourless ('17), Grey Lag ('21), Zev ('23), Mad Play ('24)

6 **Thomas J. Healy:** Preakness: The Parader (1901), Pillory ('22), Vigil ('23), Display ('26), Dr. Freeland ('29); Belmont: Pillory ('22)

6 **Lucien Laurin:** Kentucky Derby: Riva Ridge (1972), Secretariat ('73); Preakness: Secretariat ('73); Belmont: Amberoid ('66), Riva Ridge ('72), Secretariat ('73)

5 **John M. Gaver:** Kentucky Derby: Shut Out (1942); Preakness: Capot ('49); Belmont: Shut Out ('42), Capot ('49), Stage Door Johnny ('68)

Lazaro Barrera: Kentucky Derby: Bold Forbes (1976), Affirmed ('78); Preakness: Affirmed ('78); Belmont: Bold Forbes ('76), Affirmed ('78)

H. J. "Dick" Thompson: Kentucky Derby: Behave Yourself (1921), Bubbling Over ('26), Burgoo King ('32), Brokers Tip ('33); Preakness: Burgoo King ('32)

4 **Henry Forrest:** Kentucky Derby: Kauai King (1966), Forward Pass ('68); Preakness: Kauai King ('66), Forward Pass ('68)

George Conway: Kentucky Derby: War Admiral (1937); Preakness: War Admiral ('37); Belmont: Crusader ('26), War Admiral ('37)

Frank McCabe: Preakness: Half Time (1899); Belmont: Inspector B. ('86), Hanover ('87), Sir Dixon ('88)

Nicholas P. Zito: Kentucky Derby: Strike the Gold (1991), Go for Gin ('94); Preakness: Louis Quatorze ('96); Belmont: Birdstone (2004)

3 **H. Guy Bedwell:** Kentucky Derby: Sir Barton (1919); Preakness: Sir Barton ('19); Belmont: Sir Barton ('19)

J. Elliott Burch: Belmont: Sword Dancer (1959), Quadrangle ('64), Arts and Letters ('69)

G. D. Cameron: Kentucky Derby: Count Fleet (1943); Preakness: Count Fleet ('43); Belmont: Count Fleet ('43)

Peter Coyne: Kentucky Derby: Sir Huon (1906); Belmont: Chance Shot ('27), Peace Chance ('34)

Edward Feakes: Preakness: Montague (1890), Belmar ('95); Belmont: Belmar ('95)

Thomas P. Hayes: Kentucky Derby: Donerail (1913); Preakness: Paul Kauvar (1897), Head Play (1933)

William Hurley: Preakness: Kalitan (1917), Bimelech ('40); Belmont: Bimelech ('40)

Horatio Luro: Kentucky Derby: Decidedly (1962), Northern Dancer ('64); Preakness: Northern Dancer ('64)

David McDaniel: Belmont: Harry Bassett (1871), Joe Daniels ('72), Springbok ('73)

James Rowe Jr.: Kentucky Derby: Twenty Grand (1931); Preakness: Victorian ('28), Belmont: Twenty Grand ('31)

William H. Turner Jr.: Kentucky Derby: Seattle Slew (1977); Preakness: Seattle Slew ('77); Belmont: ('77)

3 **James Whalen:** Preakness: Don Enrique (1907), Watervale ('11), Buskin ('13)
Frank Y. Whiteley Jr.: Preakness: Tom Rolfe (1965), Damascus ('67); Belmont: Damascus ('67)

3 **Charles Whittingham:** Kentucky Derby: Ferdinand (1986), Sunday Silence ('89); Preakness: Sunday Silence ('89)

Leading Jockeys of Triple Crown Race Winners

17 **Eddie Arcaro:** Kentucky Derby: Lawrin (1938), Whirlaway ('41), Hoop, Jr. ('45), Citation ('48), Hill Gail ('52); Preakness: Whirlaway ('41), Citation ('48), Hill Prince ('50), Bold ('51), Nashua ('55), Bold Ruler ('57); Belmont: Whirlaway ('41), Shut Out ('42), Pavot ('45), Citation ('48), One Count ('52), Nashua ('55)

11 **William Shoemaker:** Kentucky Derby: Swaps (1955), *Tomy Lee ('59), Lucky Debonair ('65), Ferdinand ('86); Preakness: Candy Spots ('63), Damascus ('67); Belmont: *Gallant Man ('57), Sword Dancer ('59), Jaipur ('62), Damascus ('67), Avatar ('75)

9 **Pat Day:** Kentucky Derby: Lil E. Tee (1992); Preakness: Tank's Prospect ('85), Summer Squall ('90), Tabasco Cat ('94), Timber Country ('95), Louis Quatorze ('96); Belmont: Easy Goer ('89), Tabasco Cat ('94), Commendable (2000)

9 **William J. Hartack:** Kentucky Derby: Iron Liege (1957), Venetian Way ('60), Decidedly ('62), Northern Dancer ('64), Majestic Prince ('69); Preakness: Fabius ('56), Northern Dancer ('64), Majestic Prince ('69); Belmont: *Celtic Ash ('60)
Earl Sande: Kentucky Derby: Zev (1923), Flying Ebony ('25), Gallant Fox ('30); Preakness: Gallant Fox ('30); Belmont: Grey Lag ('21), Zev ('23), Mad Play ('24), Chance Shot ('27), Gallant Fox ('30)

8 **James McLaughlin:** Kentucky Derby: Hindoo (1881); Preakness: Tecumseh ('85); Belmont: Forester ('82), George Kinney ('83), Panique ('84), Inspector B. ('86), Hanover ('87), Sir Dixon ('88)
Gary Stevens: Kentucky Derby: Winning Colors (1988), Thunder Gulch ('95), Silver Charm ('97); Preakness: Silver Charm ('97), Point Given (2001); Belmont: Thunder Gulch (1995), Victory Gallop ('98), Point Given (2001)

6 **Jerry Bailey:** Kentucky Derby: Sea Hero (1993), Grindstone ('96); Preakness: Hansel ('91), Red Bullet (2000); Belmont: Hansel (1991), Empire Maker (2003)
Angel Cordero Jr.: Kentucky Derby: Cannonade (1974), Bold Forbes ('76), Spend a Buck ('85); Preakness: Codex ('80), Gate Dancer ('84); Belmont: Bold Forbes ('76)
Charles Kurtsinger: Kentucky Derby: Twenty Grand (1931), War Admiral ('37); Preakness: Head Play ('33), War Admiral ('37); Belmont: Twenty Grand ('31), War Admiral ('37)
Chris McCarron: Kentucky Derby: Alysheba (1987), Go for Gin ('94); Preakness: Alysheba ('87), Pine Bluff ('92), Belmont: Danzig Connection ('86), Touch Gold ('97)
Ron Turcotte: Kentucky Derby: Riva Ridge (1972), Secretariat ('73); Preakness: Tom Rolfe ('65), Secretariat ('73); Belmont: Riva Ridge ('72), Secretariat ('73)

5 **Eddie Delahoussaye:** Kentucky Derby: Gato Del Sol (1982), Sunny's Halo ('83); Preakness: Risen Star ('88); Belmont: Risen Star ('88), A.P. Indy ('92)

5 **Lloyd Hughes:** Preakness: Tom Ochiltree (1875), Harold ('79), Grenada ('80); Belmont: Duke of Magenta ('78), Grenada ('80)
John Loftus: Kentucky Derby: George Smith (1916), Sir Barton ('19); Preakness: *War Cloud ('18), Sir Barton ('19); Belmont: Sir Barton ('19)
Willie Simms: Kentucky Derby: Ben Brush (1898), Plaudit ('98); Preakness: Sly Fox ('98); Belmont: Comanche ('93), Henry Of Navarre ('94)

4 **Braulio Baeza:** Kentucky Derby: Chateaugay (1963); Belmont: Sherluck ('61), Chateaugay ('63), Arts and Letters ('69)
George Barbee: Preakness: Survivor (1873), Shirley ('76), Jacobus ('83); Belmont: Saxon ('74)
William "Billy" Donohue: Kentucky Derby: Leonatus (1883); Preakness: Culpepper ('74), Dunboyne ('87); Belmont: Algerine ('76)
Eric Guerin: Kentucky Derby: Jet Pilot (1947); Preakness: Native Dancer ('53); Belmont: Native Dancer ('53), High Gun ('54)
Albert Johnson: Kentucky Derby: Morvich (1922), Bubbling Over ('26); Belmont: American Flag ('25), Crusader ('26)
Clarence Kummer: Preakness: Man o' War (1920), Coventry ('25); Belmont: Man o' War ('20), Vito ('28)
Conn McCreary: Kentucky Derby: Pensive (1944), Count Turf ('51); Preakness: Pensive ('44), Blue Man ('52)
Laffit Pincay Jr.: Kentucky Derby: Swale (1984); Belmont: Conquistador Cielo ('82), Caveat ('83), Swale ('84)
James Stout: Kentucky Derby: Johnstown (1939); Belmont: Granville ('36), Pasteurized ('38), Johnstown ('39)
Fred Taral: Kentucky Derby: Manuel (1899); Preakness: Assignee ('94), Belmar ('95); Belmont: Belmar ('95)
Ismael "Milo" Valenzuela: Kentucky Derby: Tim Tam (1958), Forward Pass ('68); Preakness: Tim Tam ('58), Forward Pass ('68)

3 **Chris Antley:** Kentucky Derby: Strike the Gold (1991), Charismatic ('99); Preakness: Charismatic ('99)
William Boland: Kentucky Derby: Middleground (1950); Belmont: Middleground ('50), Amberoid ('66)
James H. "Jimmy" Butwell: Preakness: Buskin (1913); Belmont: Sweep ('10), *Hourless ('17)
Steve Cauthen: Kentucky Derby: Affirmed (1978); Preakness: Affirmed ('78); Belmont: Affirmed ('78)
T. Costello: Preakness: Saunterer (1881), Vanguard ('82); Belmont: Saunterer ('81)
Jean Cruguet: Kentucky Derby: Seattle Slew (1977), Preakness: Seattle Slew ('77); Belmont: Seattle Slew ('77)
Kent Desormeaux: Kentucky Derby: Real Quiet (1998), Fusaichi Pegasus (2000); Preakness: Real Quiet (1998)

3 **Eddie Dugan:** Preakness: Royal Tourist (1908), Watervale ('11); Belmont: Joe Madden ('09)

Mack Garner: Kentucky Derby: Cavalcade (1934); Belmont: Blue Larkspur ('29), Hurryoff ('33)

C. Holloway: Preakness: Cloverbrook (1877), Duke of Magenta ('78); Belmont: Cloverbrook ('77)

John Longden: Kentucky Derby: Count Fleet (1943); Preakness: Count Fleet ('43); Belmont: Count Fleet ('43)

J. Linus "Pony" McAtee: Kentucky Derby: Whiskery (1927), Clyde Van Dusen ('29); Preakness: Damrosch ('16)

Warren Mehrtens: Kentucky Derby: Assault (1946); Preakness: Assault ('46), Belmont: Assault ('46)

Isaac Murphy: Kentucky Derby: Buchanan (1884), Riley ('90), Kingman ('91)

3 **Edgar Prado:** Kentucky Derby: Barbaro (2006); Belmont: Sarava (2002), Birdstone ('04)

Jose Santos: Kentucky Derby: Funny Cide (2003); Preakness: Funny Cide (2003); Belmont: Lemon Drop Kid (1999)

William "Smokey" Saunders: Kentucky Derby: Omaha (1935); Preakness: Omaha ('35); Belmont: Omaha ('35)

John Sellers: Kentucky Derby: Carry Back (1961); Preakness: Carry Back ('61); Belmont: Hail to All ('65)

Bobby Swim: Kentucky Derby: Vagrant (1876); Belmont: General Duke ('68), Calvin ('75)

Wayne D. Wright: Kentucky Derby: Shut Out (1942); Preakness: Polynesian ('45); Belmont: Peace Chance ('34)

Leading Sires of Triple Crown Race Winners

7 **Lexington:** Preakness Stakes: Tom Ochiltree (1875), Shirley (1876), Duke of Magenta (1878); Belmont: General Duke (1868), Kingfisher (1870), Harry Bassett (1871), Duke of Magenta (1878)

6 **Bull Lea:** Kentucky Derby: Citation (1948), Hill Gail (1952), Iron Liege (1957); Preakness: Faultless (1947), Citation (1948); Belmont: Citation (1948)

Man o' War: Kentucky Derby: Clyde Van Dusen (1929); War Admiral (1937); Preakness: War Admiral (1937); Belmont: American Flag (1925), Crusader (1926), War Admiral (1937)

***Sir Gallahad III:** Kentucky Derby: Gallant Fox (1930), Gallahadion (1940), Hoop, Jr. (1945); Preakness: Gallant Fox (1930), High Quest, (1934); Belmont: Gallant Fox (1930)

5 **Bold Venture:** Kentucky Derby: Assault (1946), Middleground (1950); Preakness: Assault (1946); Belmont: Assault (1946), Middleground (1950)

Broomstick: Kentucky Derby: Meridian (1911), Regret (1915); Preakness: Holiday (1914), Broomspun (1921), Bostonian (1927)

Fair Play: Preakness: Man o'War (1920), Display (1926); Belmont: Man o' War (1920), Mad Play (1924), Chance Shot (1927)

4 ***Australian:** Kentucky Derby: Baden-Baden (1877); Belmont: Joe Daniels (1872), Springbok (1873), Spendthrift (1879)

Alydar: Kentucky Derby: Alysheba (1987), Strike the Gold (1991); Preakness: Alysheba (1987); Belmont: Easy Goer (1989)

Black Toney: Kentucky Derby: Black Gold (1924), Brokers Tip (1933); Preakness: Bimelech (1940); Belmont: Bimelech (1940)

***Blenheim II:** Kentucky Derby: Whirlaway (1941), Jet Pilot (1947); Preakness: Whirlaway (1941); Belmont: Whirlaway (1941)

Exclusive Native: Kentucky Derby: Affirmed (1978); Genuine Risk (1980); Preakness: Affirmed (1978); Belmont: Affirmed (1978)

Falsetto: Kentucky Derby: Chant (1894), His Eminence (1901); Sir Huon (1906); Belmont: Patron (1892)

Gallant Fox: Kentucky Derby: Omaha (1935); Preakness: Omaha (1935); Belmont: Omaha (1935), Granville (1936)

4 **King Alfonso:** Kentucky Derby: Fonso (1880); Joe Cotton (1885); Preakness: Grenada (1880); Belmont: Grenada (1880)

***Leamington:** Kentucky Derby: Aristides (1875); Preakness: Harold (1879), Saunterer (1881); Belmont: Saunterer (1881)

***Nasrullah:** Preakness: Nashua (1955), Bold Ruler (1957); Belmont: Nashua (1955), Jaipur (1962)

***Star Shoot:** Kentucky Derby: Sir Barton (1919); Preakness: Sir Barton (1919); Belmont: Sir Barton (1919), Grey Lag (1921)

***St. Germans:** Kentucky Derby: Twenty Grand (1931); Bold Venture (1936); Preakness: Bold Venture (1936); Belmont: Twenty Grand (1931)

3 **Bold Bidder:** Kentucky Derby: Cannonade (1974), Spectacular Bid (1979); Preakness: Spectacular Bid (1979)

Bold Reasoning: Kentucky Derby: Seattle Slew (1977); Preakness: Seattle Slew (1977); Belmont: Seattle Slew (1977)

Bold Ruler: Kentucky Derby: Secretariat (1973); Preakness: Secretariat (1973); Belmont: Secretariat (1973)

Halo: Kentucky Derby: Sunny's Halo (1983); Sunday Silence (1989); Preakness: Sunday Silence (1989)

Hamburg: Preakness: Buskin (1913); Belmont: Burgomeister (1906), Prince Eugene (1913)

Longfellow: Kentucky Derby: Leonatus (1883); Riley (1890); Preakness: The Bard (1886)

Mr. Prospector: Kentucky Derby: Fusaichi Pegasus (2000); Preakness: Tank's Prospect (1985); Belmont: Conquistador Cielo (1982)

Reigh Count: Kentucky Derby: Count Fleet (1943); Preakness: Count Fleet (1943); Belmont: Count Fleet (1943)

Seattle Slew: Kentucky Derby: Swale (1984); Belmont: Swale (1984), A.P. Indy (1992)

The Finn: Kentucky Derby: Zev (1923), Flying Ebony (1925); Belmont: Zev (1923)

Unbridled: Kentucky Derby: Grindstone (1996); Preakness: Red Bullet (2000); Belmont: Empire Maker (2003)

Virgil: Kentucky Derby: Vagrant (1886), Hindoo (1881), Ben Ali (1886)

Woodman: Preakness: Hansel (1991), Timber Country (1995); Belmont: Hansel (1991)

Kentucky Derby History

The Kentucky Derby was the dream of Col. Meriwether Lewis Clark Jr., grandson of William Clark of Lewis and Clark Expedition fame. Just 29 when the first Derby was run in 1875, Meriwether Clark had the family's sense of adventure and ambition but devoted his energies to equine pursuits.

Racing in Louisville was essentially dead in the early 1870s following the closure in '70 of Woodlawn Course, located east of the city. In 1872, Clark traveled to England to observe its racing scene.

He returned with grand ambitions of creating a racing palace in Louisville with races modeled on such leading events in England as the Epsom Derby, Epsom Oaks, and St. Leger Stakes. With $32,000 in investment capital, Clark set about building Louisville's new racetrack in 1874. The facility, built on 80 acres of land leased from Clark's uncles, John and Henry Churchill, was called the Louisville Jockey Club.

The Louisville Jockey Club opened on Monday, May 17, 1875, with four races. It was a sunny day with a crisp breeze, according to an account in the *Live Stock Record* (precursor of *The Thoroughbred Record* and THOROUGHBRED TIMES), and the "course was in splendid order, and all the appurtenances requisite for the comfort and convenience of racing was ready to hand."

All 42 nominees for the inaugural Derby were listed in the program and 15 started, with H. P. McGrath's nobly named Aristides becoming the first Derby winner.

One week after the first meet ended, the *Live Stock Record*'s editor, Benjamin G. Bruce, noted that, while he had attended the inaugural meet at Jerome Park and had visited Saratoga Race Course and Long Branch, "never have we seen such a grand success, taking it from its beginning to its close, as the late inaugural meeting of the Louisville Jockey Club."

While the first race meet was an artistic success, at least in Bruce's view, the financial situation of the Louisville Jockey Club was perilous almost from its start. For most of its first 40 years, the Derby would be regarded as a strong regional race at best and an embarrassing farce at worst. There were many reasons for the race's decline. Louisville was still considered western territory to many leading Eastern stables, and the situation grew worse when a track official insulted leading owner James Ben Ali Haggin in 1886. The race's initial 1½-mile distance was considered too taxing for three-year-olds in the spring.

The revival of the track and its signature race began in 1902. Col. Matt Winn, a Louisville tailor with no racetrack management experience but an undying love for the track—he attended every Kentucky Derby from 1875 to 1949—recruited a group of Louisvillians to purchase the track for $40,000. Winn spent a decade straightening out the financial mess at the track, which by then was known as Churchill Downs. Then, he set out to revive the Kentucky Derby.

Kentucky Derby Attendance

Year	Attendance	Year	Attendance
2006	157,536	1987	130,532
2005	156,435	1986	123,819
2004	140,054	1985	108,573
2003	148,530	1984	126,453
2002	145,033	1983	134,444
2001	154,210	1982	141,009
2000	153,204	1981	139,195
1999	151,051	1980	131,859
1998	143,215	1979	128,488
1997	141,981	1978	131,004
1996	142,668	1977	124,038
1995	144,110	1976	115,387
1994	130,594	1975	113,324
1993	136,817	1974	163,628
1992	132,543	1973	134,476
1991	135,554	1972	130,564
1990	128,257	1971	123,284
1989	122,653	1970	105,087
1988	137,694		

The years 1913-'15 would establish the race's credentials from both a romantic and qualitative standpoint. The 1913 running was won by 91.45-to-1 longshot Donerail, who remains the race's longest-priced winner. The race also picked up an unofficial ambassador in winning rider Roscoe Goose, who lived for a half-century mere blocks from the track, dispensing wisdom and schooling such prospective jockeys as two-time Derby winner Charlie Kurtsinger.

The next year, the gallant gelding Old Rosebud won, enhancing the race's reputation. And, in 1915, New York owner Harry Payne Whitney shipped his marvelous, unbeaten filly Regret to Louisville, where she became the first filly to win the Derby. While some Eastern stables still shied away from shipping west for the Derby—most notably Samuel Riddle's decision not to run Man o' War in 1920—the Derby's reputation was set after 1915.

Winn was a showman who combined a promoter's instincts with a passion for the Derby. The Kentucky Derby benefited from Winn's skill until he died on October 6, 1949. By the time of his death, the Derby had become a national racing institution, traditionally run on the first Saturday in May and part of the Triple Crown, a three-race series for three-year-olds considered as the ultimate test for young horses. The track's twin spires, constructed in 1895 when the physical plant was rebuilt on what had been the backstretch side of the original track, were transformed from a unique architectural feature to an iconic symbol.

Before he died, however, Winn witnessed some

amazing Derbys. Longshot Exterminator won the 1918 Derby in his three-year-old debut after he was purchased to help train another horse who did not make the race. There were two famous victories by maidens: Sir Barton's 1919 victory launched the first successful Triple Crown campaign, while Brokers Tip won in '33 after his jockey, Don Meade, fought with Head Play's rider, Herb Fisher, down the stretch.

Winn also had to adjust to the circumstances of World War II. Travel restrictions in 1943 gave that Derby a distinctly local flavor, and it became known as the "Street Car Derby." Further war restrictions shut down the sport in early 1945; when the restrictions were lifted after V-E Day, the Derby was scheduled for June 9, the only time the race has been run in June. Three years later, Citation won the Triple Crown—the eighth during Winn's tenure at Churchill.

History flows easily through the Kentucky Derby. Each year seems to bring an amazing, astounding, or simply amusing story. From the sublime (Bill Shoemaker standing up at the sixteenth pole and possibly costing *Gallant Man the 1957 Derby) to the ridiculous (the antics of unraced Nevada gelding One Eyed Tom, who failed to make it to the starting gate in 1972), the Derby has something to offer every racing fan.

Over the past 30 years, the Derby's story has been about the growth of the event as a local and international event. Attendance rose from the 120,000-to-130,000 level in the late 1980s to more than 150,000 starting in 1999. (Security restrictions following the September 11, 2001, terrorist attacks and Churchill's rebuilding program held attendance below 150,000 from 2002 through '04.) Unsuccessful Triple Crown bids by Silver Charm, Real Quiet, and Charismatic from 1997-'99 and by War Emblem, Funny Cide, and Smarty Jones from 2002-'04 created a heightened level of awareness in the Triple Crown races. The efforts of Godolphin Racing (Dubai), The Thoroughbred Corp. (Saudi Arabia and owner of War Emblem), and Michael Tabor and John Magnier (Monaco and Ireland, respectively) to win the race in the late 1990s and early 2000s have given the race an international flavor.—*John Harrell*

Presidents at the Derby

Since World War II, attending the Kentucky Derby has become a pastime of United States presidents. Getting them to attend while they are actually in office, however, has proved to be a challenge.

Eight U.S. presidents have been seen under the twin spires on the first Saturday in May, but Richard Nixon is the only one to attend the race while in office. He attended the event in 1968 while he was running for his first term and then fulfilled a promise when he returned the next year, his first in the Oval Office.

Also attending the Derby in 1969 were two future presidents, Gerald Ford and Ronald Reagan. Ford returned in 1983, along with Jimmy Carter, who defeated him in the 1976 presidential race, and future President George H. W. Bush. Bush returned in 2000, along with his son and future President George W. Bush.

Other presidents who attended the race—though they were not in the Oval Office at the time—were Harry Truman and Lyndon B. Johnson.

Kentucky Derby Trophy

The Kentucky Derby trophy, featuring a simple but classic design with a horse and garland of roses on top, was first presented in 1924, when Black Gold won the 50th running of the Derby.

The trophy had been commissioned for the golden anniversary Derby by Churchill Downs President Col. Matt Winn, who wanted a standard trophy for the connections of each Derby winner. The original design remains to this day, except for one change, when the horseshoe on the trophy was inverted upward starting with the 1999 Derby. The horseshoe had been pointed down for 75 years, according to ancient belief that an upside-down shoe afforded protection. But, since racing superstition maintains that luck runs out of horseshoes that are pointed down, the shoe was inverted.

The only other changes made to the Derby trophy were for the 75th (1949), 100th ('74), and 125th ('99) runnings, when additional jewels were added. Several Derby trophies are on display at the Kentucky Derby Museum; the oldest is Flying Ebony's trophy from the 1925 Derby.

Glasses and Mint Julep Cups

The popularity of the mint julep as the official Kentucky Derby drink grew in proportion with the introduction of Derby glasses and sterling silver julep cups as Derby souvenirs in the middle years of the 20th century.

The Derby glass made its introduction in 1938 after Churchill officials noted that patrons took water glasses from their tables on Derby day as souvenirs. In 1939, glass manufacturers were encouraged to add color to the glasses, making them as attractive as mint julep glasses. Sales of mint juleps increased threefold, according to track officials, and the glasses have gone on to become the most popular Derby souvenirs.

The sterling silver cups were introduced in 1951 as part of the legacy of Col. Matt Winn, who had died two years earlier. Winn wished to make the cups an official Derby souvenir, and they have been part of Derby lore now for more than a half-century. The cups, which hold 12 fluid ounces, were unchanged in design until 1984, when noted owner-breeder Leslie Combs II pointed out that the horseshoe on the glass pointed down, a superstitious sign of bad luck in racing, although an upside-down shoe was regarded in folklore as affording protection. The horseshoe was turned upright and remains so to this day.

Although some relatively minor errors have occurred in the printing on the glasses, two significant mistakes occurred on approximately 100,400 of the half-million Derby glasses manufactured for the 2002 Derby. The erroneous glasses had Burgoo King winning the Triple Crown in 1932 (he won the Derby and Preakness but did not compete in the Belmont Stakes) and War Admiral failing to win the 1937 Triple Crown (he did). These erroneous glasses immediately became collectors' items.

Enduring Twin Spires

The twin spires atop Churchill Downs's grandstand are arguably the best-known architectural feature of any racetrack in the world. They date from the reconstruction of the Louisville track in 1894-'95. Designed by 24-year-old Louisville architect Joseph D. Baldez, the twin spires were intended only as an ornamental feature of the new grandstand, which was constructed at a cost of $100,000. Col. Matt Winn, Churchill's longtime president, once told Baldez, "Joe, when you die there's one monument that will never be taken down, the twin spires."

The spires are checked periodically for structural soundness, and they underwent a renovation in 2002 as part of the $27-million first phase of Churchill's $121-million renewal project. Workmen inspecting the spires found a copy of the Louisville *Courier-Journal* from 1907 and a flag wrapped around a '08 copy of the *Courier-Journal*.

Kentucky Derby Wagering

Each year, the Kentucky Derby attracts the largest crowd in North American racing, usually in excess of 140,000. The Derby also is the sport's biggest day for wagering in North America. In 2005, the Derby set a North American record for most money bet on a single race. Wagering on the Derby totaled $103,325,510, which was 4% above the 2003 record total of $99,364,088 from all sources. On-track wagering on the Derby was $10,055,508, also a record, and all-sources wagering on the Derby day program was $155,133,631, a North American mark.

Kentucky Derby Festival

Conducted annually since 1956, the Kentucky Derby Festival has grown into a weeks-long celebration of Louisville's premier attraction. A not-for-profit community organization, the Kentucky Derby Festival recruits 4,000 volunteers for 70 special events that annually attract approximately 1.5-million people to venues in and around Louisville. Financed by 325 corporate sponsors and the sale of Pegasus Pins, the festival contributes an estimated $93-million to the local economy.

Three of the best-known events of the Kentucky Derby Festival are the Pegasus Parade, the Great Balloon Race, and the Great Steamboat Race. In 1990, the Kentucky Derby Festival added a new attraction, Thunder Over Louisville. Held three weeks before the Derby, it is billed as the nation's largest fireworks display and attracts thousands to the banks of the Ohio River each April.

The schedule of events for the 2006 Kentucky Derby Festival included:

Basketball Classic	April 15
They're Off! Luncheon	April 21
Fillies' Derby Ball	April 21
Thunder Over Louisville	April 22
Great Balloon Race	April 28-29
Great Bed Races	May 1
Knights of Columbus Charity Dinner	May 1
Run for the Rosé	May 2
Derby Trainers Dinner	May 2
Great Steamboat Race	May 3
Pegasus Parade	May 4

"My Old Kentucky Home"

As the Kentucky Derby field parades onto the racetrack from the paddock, the University of Louisville Marching Band plays "My Old Kentucky Home," a song whose meaning and involvement with the Derby are shrouded in some mystery. Stephen Collins Foster (1826-'64) wrote the song in 1853, while visiting cousins at Federal Hill in Bardstown, Kentucky, a short distance from Louisville.

According to contemporary accounts, the song was first played at the Derby in 1921, and Damon Runyon reported in '29 that the song was played several times on Derby day. The following year, according to the Philadelphia *Public Ledger*, the song was played as the field came onto the track for the Derby.

The sentimental melody and its lyrics may well have foreshadowed the sadness that would fall upon the nation in the Civil War. A Pittsburgh native who lived many years of his brief life there, Foster began writing minstrel songs and had a national hit with "Oh, Susanna" in 1848. His view of slaves and slavery apparently changed in the next few years. According to some accounts, Foster may have been inspired to write "My Old Kentucky Home" after reading Harriet Beecher Stowe's *Uncle Tom's Cabin*, published in 1851. Foster's first draft in his song workbook was entitled "Poor Uncle Tome, Good Night."

"My Old Kentucky Home" came in the midst of Foster's most productive period. He wrote "Old Folks at Home" in 1851 and "Jeannie With the

Light Brown Hair" in '54. Foster died in January 1864 after sustaining a cut, probably alcohol-related, at a New York boarding house. One of his best-known songs, "Beautiful Dreamer," was published posthumously.

"My Old Kentucky Home, Good-Night!" was adopted by Kentucky as its state song in 1928. The official lyrics were subsequently changed to remove references to "darkies" in the original version. The song had three verses, but only the first is now sung. Here are the modern lyrics:

The sun shines bright in the old Kentucky home
'Tis summer, the people are gay;
The corn top's ripe and the meadow's in the bloom,
While the birds make music all the day;
The young folks roll on the little cabin floor,
All merry, all happy, and bright,
By'n by hard times comes a-knocking at the door,
Then my old Kentucky home, good night!
Chorus
Weep no more, my lady,
Oh weep no more today!
We will sing one song for the old Kentucky home,
For the old Kentucky home far away.

Kentucky Derby Future Wager

For years, future-book wagers on the Kentucky Derby have enriched Las Vegas casinos, and Churchill Downs tapped into that bet in 1999 with the Kentucky Derby Future Wager. The bet is offered three times each year, with four days in each wagering period.

Bettors choose the horse they believe will win, with the final pool being offered approximately four weeks before the Derby. From modest beginnings, the wager gained popularity and achieved a record mark of $1,655,034 in 2005.

Here are the amounts wagered by year:

Year	Pool 1	Pool 2	Pool 3	Total
2006	$552,627	$464,236	$454,743	$1,471,606
2005	620,535	511,655	522,844	1,655,034
2004	536,958	358,966	386,244	1,282,168
2003	516,906	391,002	222,261	1,130,169
2002	577,889	401,070	524,847	1,503,806
2001	510,815	372,961	425,871	1,309,647
2000	465,454	306,259	387,206	1,158,919
1999	267,748	178,811	229,674	676,233

Future Pool Payoffs

Year	Winner	Pool 1 Win Price	Pool 2 Win Price	Pool 3 Win Price	Derby Day Win Price
2006	Barbaro	$ 40.20	$ 32.20	$ 20.80	$ 14.20
2005	Giacomo	52.00	54.20	103.60	102.60
2004	Smarty Jones	5.60†	10.80†	23.60	10.20
2003	Funny Cide	188.00	120.80	107.40	27.60
2002	War Emblem	7.60†	16.00†	24.00†	43.00
2001	Monarchos	36.60	13.00	15.80	23.00
2000	Fusaichi Pegasus	27.80	26.40	8.00	6.60
1999	Charismatic	10.20†	30.20†	26.60†	64.60

† Part of mutuel field

Derby Winner's Garland of Roses

Run for the roses, the popular nickname of the Kentucky Derby, derives from the garland of roses that is laid over the winner's withers. By 1925, the rose garland was so much a part of the race's pageantry that New York sports columnist Bill Corum coined the "run for the roses" phrase. Corum would serve as Churchill Downs's president from 1950 to '58.

According to Derby lore, the rose was designated as the Derby's official flower in 1884 by Col. M. Lewis Clark, the race's founder. News articles reported that Ben Brush was presented with a collar of pink and white roses after his 1896 Derby win.

In 1931, Churchill commissioned Mrs. Kingsley Walker to create a rose garland for the Derby winner. Her design placed 500 dark-red roses and greenery on a cloth-backed blanket. Burgoo King wore the first Walker-designed garland in 1932, and she continued to craft the garlands until '74. Her daughter, Betty Korfhage, continued the tradition into the 1980s. Beginning in 1987, Kroger Co., a Cincinnati-based grocery chain, took over the task of creating the Derby winner's garland of roses.

Leading Derby Owners by Wins

8 **Calumet Farm:** Whirlaway, 1941; Pensive, 1944; Citation, 1948; Ponder, 1949; Hill Gail, 1952; Iron Liege, 1957; Tim Tam, 1958; Forward Pass, 1968.

4 **Col. E. R. Bradley:** Behave Yourself, 1921; Bubbling Over, 1926; Burgoo King, 1932; Brokers Tip, 1933.

3 **Belair Stud:** Gallant Fox, 1930; Omaha, 1935; Johnstown, 1939.

2 **Bashford Manor Stable:** Azra, 1892; Sir Huon, 1906.

Harry Payne Whitney: Regret, 1915; Whiskery, 1927.

Mrs. John D. Hertz: Reigh Count, 1928; Count Fleet, 1943.

Greentree Stable: Twenty Grand, 1931; Shut Out, 1942.

King Ranch: Assault, 1946; Middleground, 1950.

Darby Dan Farm: Chateaugay, 1963; Proud Clarion, 1967.

Meadow Stable: Riva Ridge, 1972; Secretariat, 1973.

William Condren and Joseph Cornacchia: Strike the Gold, 1991; Go for Gin, 1994.

Robert and Beverly Lewis: Silver Charm, 1997; Charismatic, 1999.

Owners With Most Derby Starters

Name	Strs.	Wins	2nd	3rd	Unplaced
Col. E. R. Bradley/ Idle Hour Stock Farm	28	4	4	1	19
Calumet Farm	20	8	4	1	7
Greentree Stable	19	2	2	1	14
Harry Payne Whitney	19	2	1	1	15
C. V. Whitney	15	0	1	1	13
Bashford Manor	11	2	2	1	6
† Overbrook Farm	11	1	0	2	8
† Michael Tabor	11	1	1	0	9
Milky Way Farm	10	1	0	2	7
Dixiana Farm	9	0	3	0	6
Belair Stud	8	3	1	0	4
Elmendorf Farm	8	0	0	0	8
Hal Price Headley	8	0	0	0	8
†Robert and Beverly Lewis	9	2	0	1	6
Three D's Stock Farm	8	0	0	1	7

†Includes partnerships

Leading Breeders of Derby Winners

9 **Calumet Farm:** Whirlaway, 1941; Pensive, 1944; Citation, 1948; Ponder, 1949; Hill Gail, 1952; Iron Liege, 1957; Tim Tam, 1958; Forward Pass, 1968; Strike the Gold, 1991.

5 **John Madden:** Old Rosebud, 1914; Sir Barton, 1919; Paul Jones, 1920; Zev, 1923; Flying Ebony, 1925.

4 **A. J. Alexander:** Baden-Baden, 1877; Fonso, 1880; Joe Cotton, 1885; Chant, 1894.

E. R. Bradley (Idle Hour Stock Farm):
1 E. R. Bradley: Behave Yourself, 1921.
2 Idle Hour Stock Farm: Bubbling Over, 1926; Brokers Tip, 1933.
1 H. N. Davis and Idle Hour Stock Farm: Burgoo King, 1932.

3 **Bashford Manor Stable (George J. Long):** Azra, 1892, Manuel, 1899; Sir Huon, 1906.

Daniel Swigert: Hindoo, 1881; Apollo, 1882; Ben Ali, 1886.

2 **Belair Stud:** Gallant Fox, 1930; Omaha, 1935.

Claiborne Farm: Johnstown, 1939; Swale, 1984.

R. A. Fairbairn: Gallahadion, 1940; Hoop, Jr., 1945.

2 **John W. Galbreath:** Chateaugay, 1963; Proud Clarion, 1967.

Greentree Stable: Twenty Grand, 1931; Shut Out, 1942.

Arthur B. Hancock III:
1 A. B. Hancock III and Leone J. Peters: Gato Del Sol, 1982.
1 A. B. Hancock III and Stonerside Ltd.: Fusaichi Pegasus, 2000.

King Ranch: Assault, 1946; Middleground, 1950.

Meadow Stud: Riva Ridge, 1972; Secretariat, 1973.

Harry Payne Whitney: Regret, 1915; Whiskey, 1927.

Milton Young: Montrose, 1887; Donau, 1910.

Leading Derby Trainers by Wins

6 **Ben A. Jones:** Lawrin, 1938; Whirlaway, 1941; Pensive, 1944; Citation, 1948; Ponder, 1949; Hill Gail, 1952.

4 **H. J. "Dick" Thompson:** Behave Yourself, 1921; Bubbling Over, 1926; Burgoo King, 1932; Brokers Tip, 1933.

D. Wayne Lukas: Winning Colors, 1988; Thunder Gulch, 1995; Grindstone, 1996; Charismatic, 1999.

3 **Bob Baffert:** Silver Charm, 1997; Real Quiet, 1998; War Emblem, 2002.

James "Sunny Jim" Fitzsimmons: Gallant Fox, 1930; Omaha, 1935; Johnstown, 1939.

Max Hirsch: Bold Venture, 1936; Assault, 1946; Middleground, 1950.

2 **John McGinty:** Leonatus, 1883; Montrose, 1887.

James Rowe Sr.: Hindoo, 1881; Regret, 1915.

H. A. "Jimmy" Jones: Iron Liege, 1957; Tim Tam, 1958.

Horatio Luro: Decidedly, 1962; Northern Dancer, 1964.

Henry Forrest: Kauai King, 1966; Forward Pass, 1968.

Lucien Laurin: Riva Ridge, 1972; Secretariat, 1973.

W. C. "Woody" Stephens: Cannonade, 1974; Swale, 1984.

LeRoy Jolley: Foolish Pleasure, 1975; Genuine Risk, 1980.

Lazaro Barrera: Bold Forbes, 1976; Affirmed, 1978.

Charlie Whittingham: Ferdinand, 1986; Sunday Silence, 1989.

Nicholas P. Zito: Strike the Gold, 1991; Go for Gin, 1994.

Female Trainers in the Derby

A woman has yet to win the Kentucky Derby as either a jockey or a trainer, but several female trainers have come close to landing one of racing's biggest prizes.

Northern California-based trainer Shelley Riley came closest to notching a Kentucky Derby victory when her 29.90-to-1 longshot, Casual Lies, finished second to Lil E. Tee in 1992.

Mary Hirsch, daughter of Racing Hall of Fame trainer Max Hirsch, was the first female trainer to saddle a Derby starter. No Sir, also owned by Mary Hirsch, finished 13th in 1937.

The women who have trained Derby starters:

Trainer	Horse	Year	Finish
Kristin Mulhall	Imperialism	2004	3rd
Jennifer Pederson	Song of the Sword	2004	11th
Jenine Sahadi	The Deputy (Ire)	2000	14th
Akiko Gothard	K One King	1999	8th
Kathy Walsh	Hanuman Highway	1998	7th
Cynthia Reese	In Contention	1996	15th
Shelly Riley	Casual Lies	1992	2nd
Patti Johnson	Fast Account	1985	4th
Dianne Carpenter	Kingpost	1988	14th
	Biloxi Indian	1984	12th
Mary Keim	Mr. Pak	1965	6th
Mrs. Albert Roth	Senecas Coin	1949	DNF
Mary Hirsch	No Sir	1937	13th

Trainers With Most Derby Starters

Trainer	Strs.	Wins	2nd	3rd	Unplaced
D. Wayne Lukas	42	4	1	5	32
H. J. Thompson	24	4	2	1	17
James Rowe Sr.*	18	2	1	1	14
Max Hirsch	14	3	0	2	9
W. C. Stephens	14	2	3	3	6
Nicholas P. Zito	19	2	0	0	17
LeRoy Jolley	13	2	2	1	8
Bob Baffert	17	3	1	2	11
Todd Pletcher	13	0	2	1	10
James Fitzsimmons	11	3	1	0	7
Ben A. Jones	11	6	2	1	2

*Information on James Rowe Sr. is incomplete

Leading Derby Jockeys by Wins

5 **Eddie Arcaro:** Lawrin, 1938; Whirlaway, 1941; Hoop, Jr., 1945; Citation, 1948; Hill Gail, 1952.

Bill Hartack: Iron Liege, 1957; Venetian Way, 1960; Decidedly, 1962; Northern Dancer, 1964; Majestic Prince, 1969.

4 **Bill Shoemaker:** Swaps, 1955; *Tomy Lee, 1959; Lucky Debonair, 1965; Ferdinand, 1986.

3 **Isaac Murphy:** Buchanan, 1884; Riley, 1890; Kingman, 1891.

Earl Sande: Zev, 1923; Flying Ebony, 1925; Gallant Fox, 1930.

Angel Cordero Jr.: Cannonade, 1974; Bold Forbes, 1976; Spend a Buck, 1985.

Gary Stevens: Winning Colors, 1988; Thunder Gulch, 1995; Silver Charm, 1997.

Jockeys With Most Derby Mounts

Jockey	Strs.	Wins	2nd	3rd	Unplaced
Bill Shoemaker	26	4	3	4	15
Pat Day	22	1	4	2	15
Eddie Arcaro	21	5	3	2	11
Laffit Pincay Jr.	21	1	4	2	14

Jockey	Strs.	Wins	2nd	3rd	Unplaced
Angel Cordero Jr.	17	3	1	0	13
Chris McCarron	18	2	3	0	13
Gary Stevens	18	3	2	1	12
Jerry Bailey	17	2	2	1	12
Jorge Velasquez	14	1	1	2	10
Mack Garner	14	1	0	1	12
Don Brumfield	13	1	0	1	11
Johnny Adams	13	0	2	0	11

African-American Jockeys in the Derby

African-American jockeys dominated the Kentucky Derby during the race's first quarter-century. Between 1875 and 1902, 11 African-American riders won 15 runnings of the Derby. The most famous were Isaac Murphy, the first jockey to win the Derby three times, and Jimmy Winkfield, who won the Derby in 1901 and '02.

Marlon St. Julien became the first African-American rider in the Derby in 79 years when he finished seventh aboard Curule in the 2000 renewal.

African-American riders who have won the Derby:

Jockey	Year	Mount
Jimmy Winkfield	1902	Alan-a-Dale
	1901	His Eminence
Willie Simms	1898	Plaudit
	1896	Ben Brush
James "Soup" Perkins	1895	Halma
Alonzo "Lonnie" Clayton	1892	Azra
Isaac Murphy	1891	Kingman
	1890	Riley
	1884	Buchanan
Isaac Lewis	1887	Montrose
Erskine Henderson	1885	Joe Cotton
Babe Hurd	1882	Apollo
George Garret Lewis	1880	Fonso
William Walker	1877	Baden-Baden
Oliver Lewis	1875	Aristides

Female Jockeys in the Derby

Jockey	Mount	Year	Finish
Rosemary Homeister	Supah Blitz	2003	13th
Julie Krone	Suave Prospect	1995	11th
	Ecstatic Ride	1992	14th
Andrea Seefeldt	Forty Something	1991	16th
Patricia Cooksey	So Vague	1984	11th
Diane Crump	Fathom	1970	15th

Leading Sires of Derby Winners

3 **Virgil:** Vagrant, 1876; Hindoo, 1881; Ben Ali, 1886.
Falsetto: Chant, 1894; His Eminence, 1901; Sir Huon, 1906.
***Sir Gallahad III:** Gallant Fox, 1930; Gallahadion, 1940; Hoop, Jr., 1945.
Bull Lea: Citation, 1948; Hill Gail, 1952; Iron Liege, 1957.

2 **King Alfonso:** Fonso, 1880; Joe Cotton, 1885.
Longfellow: Leonatus, 1883; Riley, 1890.
Broomstick: Meridian, 1911; Regret, 1915.
***McGee:** Donerail, 1913; Exterminator, 1918.
The Finn: Zev, 1923; Flying Ebony, 1925.
Black Toney: Black Gold, 1924; Brokers Tip, 1933.
Man o' War: Clyde Van Dusen, 1929; War Admiral, 1937.
***St. Germans:** Twenty Grand, 1931; Bold Venture, 1936.
***Blenheim II:** Whirlaway, 1941; Jet Pilot, 1947.
Bold Venture: Assault, 1946; Middleground, 1950.
Bold Bidder: Cannonade, 1974; Spectacular Bid, 1979.
Exclusive Native: Affirmed, 1978; Genuine Risk, 1980.
Halo: Sunny's Halo, 1983; Sunday Silence, 1989.
Alydar: Alysheba, 1987; Strike the Gold, 1991.

Derby Winners Who Sired Winners

2 **Bold Venture (1936):** Assault, 1946; Middleground, 1950.

1 **Halma (1895):** Alan-a-Dale, 1902.
Bubbling Over (1926): Burgoo King (1932)
Reigh Count (1928): Count Fleet, 1943.
Gallant Fox (1930): Omaha, 1935.
Count Fleet (1943): Count Turf (1951)
Pensive (1944): Ponder, 1949.
Ponder (1949): Needles, 1956.
Determine (1954): Decidedly, 1962.
Swaps (1955): Chateaugay, 1963.
Seattle Slew (1977): Swale, 1984.
Unbridled (1990): Grindstone, 1996.

Fastest Derby Winning Times

$1\frac{1}{4}$ miles

Year	Winner	Time	Cond.
1973	Secretariat	1:59$\frac{2}{5}$	Fast
2001	Monarchos	1:59.97	Fast
1964	Northern Dancer	2:00	Fast
1985	Spend a Buck	2:00$\frac{1}{5}$	Fast
1962	Decidedly	2:00$\frac{2}{5}$	Fast
1967	Proud Clarion	2:00$\frac{3}{5}$	Fast
1996	Grindstone	2:01.06	Fast
2000	Fusaichi Pegasus	2:01.12	Fast
2002	War Emblem	2:01.13	Fast
1978	Affirmed	2:01$\frac{1}{5}$	Fast
1965	Lucky Debonair	2:01$\frac{1}{5}$	Fast
1995	Thunder Gulch	2:01.27	Fast

Time recorded in hundredths of a second beginning in 1991

$1\frac{1}{2}$ miles

Year	Winner	Time	Cond.
1889	Spokane	2:34$\frac{1}{2}$	Fast
1886	Ben Ali	2:36$\frac{1}{2}$	Fast
1879	Lord Murphy	2:37	Fast
1878	Day Star	2:37$\frac{1}{4}$	Dusty
1885	Joe Cotton	2:37$\frac{1}{4}$	Good

Slowest Derby Winning Times

$1\frac{1}{4}$ miles

Year	Winner	Time	Cond.
1908	Stone Street	2:15$\frac{1}{5}$	Heavy
1907	Pink Star	2:12$\frac{3}{5}$	Heavy
1897	Typhoon II	2:12$\frac{1}{2}$	Heavy
1899	Manuel	2:12	Fast
1918	Exterminator	2:10$\frac{4}{5}$	Muddy
1929	Clyde Van Dusen	2:10$\frac{4}{5}$	Muddy
1905	Agile	2:10$\frac{3}{4}$	Heavy
1928	Reigh Count	2:10$\frac{2}{5}$	Heavy
1919	Sir Barton	2:09$\frac{4}{5}$	Heavy
1912	Worth	2:09$\frac{2}{5}$	Muddy

$1\frac{1}{2}$ miles

Year	Winner	Time	Cond.
1891	Kingman	2:52$\frac{1}{4}$	Slow
1890	Riley	2:45	Muddy
1883	Leonatus	2:43	Heavy
1892	Azra	2:41$\frac{1}{2}$	Heavy
1894	Chant	2:41	Fast

Fastest Derby Fractions

Quarter-Mile: :21⅘, Top Avenger (1981)
Half-Mile: :44.86, Songandaprayer (2001)
Six Furlongs: 1:09.25, Songandaprayer (2001)
One Mile: 1:34⅘, Spend a Buck (1985)

Evolution of Derby Stakes Record at 1¼ miles

Year	Winner	Time
1896	Ben Brush	2:07¾
1900	Lieut. Gibson	2:06¼
1911	Meridian	2:05
1913	Donerail	2:04⅘
1914	Old Rosebud	2:03⅖
1931	Twenty Grand	2:01⅘
1941	Whirlaway	2:01⅖
1962	Decidedly	2:00⅖
1964	Northern Dancer	2:00
1973	Secretariat	1:59⅖

Shortest-Priced Derby Beaten Favorites

Year	Horse	Odds	Finish
1976	Honest Pleasure	0.40-to-1	2nd
1940	Bimelech	0.40-to-1	2nd
1953	Native Dancer	0.70-to-1	2nd
1989	Easy Goer	0.80-to-1	2nd
1949	Olympia	0.80-to-1	6th
1936	Brevity	0.80-to-1	2nd
1992	Arazi	0.90-to-1	8th
1911	Governor Gray	1-to-1	2nd
1916	Thunderer	1.05-to-1	5th
1960	Tompion	1.10-to-1	4th
1962	Ridan	1.10-to-1	3rd
1946	Lord Boswell	1.10-to-1	4th
1921	Prudery	1.10-to-1	3rd

Shortest-Priced Winning Favorites

Year	Winner	Odds
1948	Citation	0.40-to-1
1943	Count Fleet	0.40-to-1
1977	Seattle Slew	0.50-to-1
1979	Spectacular Bid	0.60-to-1
1939	Johnstown	0.60-to-1
1912	Worth	0.80-to-1
1914	Old Rosebud	0.85-to-1
1931	Twenty Grand	0.88-to-1
1952	Hill Gail	1.10-to-1
1906	Sir Huon	1.10-to-1
1930	Gallant Fox	1.19-to-1

How Derby Favorites Fared Since 1979

Year	Favorite	Odds (to $1)	Finish
2006	Sweetnorthernsaint	5.50	7
2005	Bellamy Road	2.60	7
2004	**Smarty Jones**	**4.10**	**1**
2003	Empire Maker	2.50	2
2002	Harlan's Holiday	6.00	7
2001	Point Given	1.80	5
2000	**Fusaichi Pegasus**	**2.30**	**1**
1999	Excellent Meeting	e4.80	5
	General Challenge		11
1998	Indian Charlie	2.70	3
1997	Captain Bodgit	3.10	2
1996	Unbridled's Song	3.50	5
1995	Timber Country	e3.40	3
	Serena's Song		16
1994	Holy Bull	2.20	12
1993	Prairie Bayou	4.40	2
1992	Arazi	0.90	8
1991	Hansel	2.50	10
1990	Mister Frisky	1.90	8
1989	Easy Goer	e0.80	2
	Awe Inspiring		3
1988	Private Terms	3.40	9
1987	Demons Begone	2.20	Eased
1986	Snow Chief	2.10	11
1985	Chief's Crown	1.20	3
1984	Life's Magic	e2.80	8
	Althea		19
1983	Marfa	e2.40	5
	Balboa Native		9
	Total Departure		20
1982	Air Forbes Won	2.70	7
1981	Proud Appeal	e2.30	18
	Golden Derby		21
1980	Rockhill Native	2.10	5
1979	**Spectacular Bid**	**0.60**	**1**

e—entry

Longest Winning Odds

Year	Horse	Odds
1913	Donerail	91.45-to-1
2005	Giacomo	50.30-to-1
1940	Gallahadion	35.20-to-1
1999	Charismatic	31.30-to-1
1967	Proud Clarion	30.10-to-1
1918	Exterminator	29.60-to-1
1953	Dark Star	24.90-to-1
1995	Thunder Gulch	24.50-to-1
1908	Stone Street	23.72-to-1
1982	Gato Del Sol	21.20-to-1
2002	War Emblem	20.50-to-1
1936	Bold Venture	20.50-to-1
1923	Zev	19.20-to-1
1986	Ferdinand	17.70-to-1

Largest Winning Margins

Year	Winner	Lengths
1946	Assault	8
1941	Whirlaway	8
1939	Johnstown	8
1914	Old Rosebud	8
2006	Barbaro	6½
1945	Hoop, Jr.	6
1894	Chant	6
1985	Spend a Buck	5¼
1970	Dust Commander	5
1932	Burgoo King	5
1926	Bubbling Over	5
1919	Sir Barton	5
1895	Halma	5

Smallest Winning Margins

Year	Winner	Lengths
1996	Grindstone	nose
1959	*Tomy Lee	nose
1957	Iron Liege	nose
1933	Brokers Tip	nose
1902	Alan-a-Dale	nose
1898	Plaudit	nose
1896	Ben Brush	nose
1892	Azra	nose
1889	Spokane	nose
1997	Silver Charm	head
1953	Dark Star	head
1947	Jet Pilot	head

Year	Winner	Lengths
1936	Bold Venture	head
1927	Whiskery	head
1921	Behave Yourself	head
1920	Paul Jones	head

Birthplaces of Derby Winners

State	Winners
Kentucky	99
Florida	6
Virginia	4
California	3
Tennessee	3
New Jersey	2
Pennsylvania	2
Texas	2
Canada	2
Great Britain	2
Illinois	1
Kansas	1
Maryland	1
Missouri	1
Montana	1
New York	1
Ohio	1

Fillies in the Derby

In the long history of the Kentucky Derby, only three fillies have won the 1¼-mile classic: Regret in 1915, Genuine Risk in 1980, and Winning Colors in 1988.

Fillies to start in the Derby:

Year	Filly	Finish
1999	Excellent Meeting	5th
	Three Ring	19th
1995	Serena's Song	16th
1988	**Winning Colors**	1st
1984	Life's Magic	8th
	Althea	19th
1982	Cupecoy's Joy	10th
1980	**Genuine Risk**	1st
1959	Silver Spoon	5th
1945	Misweet	12th
1936	Gold Seeker	9th
1935	Nellie Flag	4th
1934	Mata Hari	4th
	Bazaar	9th
1932	Oscillation	13th
1930	Alcibiades	10th
1929	Ben Machree	18th
1922	Startle	8th
1921	Prudery	3rd
	Careful	5th
1920	Cleopatra	15th
1919	Regalo	9th
1918	Viva America	3rd
1915	**Regret**	1st
1914	Bronzewing	3rd
	Watermelon	7th
1913	Gowell	3rd
1912	Flamma	3rd
1911	Round the World	6th
1906	Lady Navarre	2nd
1883	Pike's Pride	6th
1879	Ada Glenn	7th
	Wissahickon	9th
1877	Early Light	8th
1876	Lizzie Stone	6th
	Marie Michon	7th
1875	Ascension	10th
	Gold Mine	15th

Maiden Winners of the Derby

Year	Winner
Brokers Tip	1933
Sir Barton	1919
Buchanan	1884

Maiden Starters Since 1950

Maidens in the Derby were a common occurrence until the mid-1930s. Since 1950, only seven maidens have run in the Derby, and none came close to winning. The connections of several runners, most notably Great Redeemer in 1979, were harshly criticized for running.

Year	Horse	Finish
1998	Nationalore	9th
1990	Pendleton Ridge	13
1979	Great Redeemer	10th
1971	Fourulla	19th
1959	The Chosen One	14
1958	Flamingo	13th
1950	On the Mark	8th

Geldings in the Derby

In all, 106 geldings have started in the Derby since 1908. Before then, records of starters were incomplete. The geldings that have started in the Kentucky Derby since 1980:

Year	Gelding	Finish
2006	Sweetnorthernsaint	7th
2003	**Funny Cide**	1st
	Buddy Gil	6th
2002	Perfect Drift	3rd
	Easy Grades	13th
2001	Balto Star	14th
1999	General Challenge	11th
1998	Hanuman Highway (Ire)	7th
1997	Celtic Warrior	10th
1996	Cavonnier	2nd
	Alyrob	8th
	Zarb's Magic	13th
1993	Prairie Bayou	2nd
	Truth of It All	10th
1991	Best Pal	2nd
1989	Wind Splitter	11th
	Clever Trevor	13th
1988	Kingpost	14th
1986	Bachelor Beau	14th
1984	Raja's Shark	14th
1983	My Mac	14th
1982	Real Dare	19th
1981	Television Studio	5th
	Beau Rit	13th
1980	Rockhill Native	5th
	Execution's Reason	11th

Gelding Winners of the Derby

With Funny Cide's victory in the 2003 Derby, the losing streak for geldings ended after 74 years, dating to Clyde Van Dusen in 1929. In the 1990s, three geldings finished second: Best Pal (1991), Prairie Bayou ('93), and Cavonnier ('96). The winning geldings:

Year	Gelding
2003	Funny Cide
1929	Clyde Van Dusen

Year	Gelding
1920	Paul Jones
1918	Exterminator
1914	Old Rosebud
1888	Macbeth II
1882	Apollo
1876	Vagrant

Front-Running Derby Winners

The following Kentucky Derby winners were on the lead at all points of call.

Year	Winner	Winning Margin
2002	War Emblem	4
1988	Winning Colors	neck
1985	Spend a Buck	5¼
1976	Bold Forbes	1
1972	Riva Ridge	3¼
1966	Kauai King	½
1955	Swaps	1½
1953	Dark Star	head
1947	Jet Pilot	head
1945	Hoop, Jr.	6
1943	Count Fleet	3
1939	Johnstown	8
1937	War Admiral	1¾
1929	Clyde Van Dusen	2
1926	Bubbling Over	5
1923	Zev	1½
1922	Morvich	1½
1920	Paul Jones	head
1919	Sir Barton	5
1915	Regret	2
1914	Old Rosebud	8
1912	Worth	neck
1911	Meridian	¾
1910	Donau	½
1909	Wintergreen	4
1905	Agile	3
1902	Alan-a-Dale	nose
1901	His Eminence	1½
1900	Lieut. Gibson	3
1897	Typhoon II	neck
1895	Halma	5
1894	Chant	6
1893	Lookout	4
1887	Montrose	2
1883	Leonatus	3
1881	Hindoo	4
1880	Fonso	1
1878	Day Star	1
1875	Aristides	2

Winning Derby Post Positions

Winning Derby post positions since 1900:

Post	Winners	Post	Winners
1	12	11	3
2	9	12	3
3	8	13	4
4	10	14	2
5	12	15	3
6	6	16	3
7	7	17	0
8	9	18	1
9	4	19	0
10	10	20	1

Undefeated Starters

Barbaro, the 2006 Kentucky Derby winner, was only the sixth undefeated horse to win the Derby. The other five were Regret in 1915, Morvich in '22, Majestic Prince in '69, Triple Crown winner Seattle Slew in '77, and Smarty Jones in 2004.

The undefeated Derby starters since Regret in 1915:

Year	Horse	Pre-Derby Starts	Derby Finish
2006	**Barbaro**	5	**1st**
2004	**Smarty Jones**	6	**1st**
2000	China Visit	2	6th
	Trippi	4	11th
1998	Indian Charlie	4	3rd
1990	Mister Frisky	16	8th
1988	Private Terms	7	9th
1982	Air Forbes Won	4	7th
1978	Sensitive Prince	6	6th
1977	**Seattle Slew**	6	**1st**
1969	**Majestic Prince**	7	**1st**
1963	Candy Spots	6	3rd
	No Robbery	5	5th
1953	Native Dancer	11	2nd
1948	Coaltown	4	2nd
1940	Bimelech	8	2nd
1922	**Morvich**	11	**1st**
1916	Thunderer	3	5th
1915	**Regret**	3	**1st**

Derby Winners Sold at Public Auction and Privately

Derby	Winner	Year	Sale	Price
2003	Funny Cide	2001	FT Saratoga	$22,000
		2002	Private	75,000
2002	War Emblem	2000	Kee Sept	20,000
		2002	Private	900,000
2001	Monarchos	1999	FT Saratoga	90,000 (RNA)
		2000	FT Calder	170,000
2000	Fusaichi Pegasus	1998	Kee July	4,000,000
1999	Charismatic	1996	Private	200,000
1998	Real Quiet	1996	Kee Sept	17,000
1997	Silver Charm	1995	OBSC Aug	16,500
		1996	OBSC April	100,000
1995	Thunder Gulch	1993	Kee July	40,000
		1994	Kee April	120,000 (RNA)
1994	Go for Gin	1991	FT Ky	32,000
		1992	FT Saratoga	150,000
1992	Lil E. Tee	1991	OBSC April	25,000
1990	Unbridled	1987	Tartan dispersal	90,000
1989	Sunday Silence	1987	Kee July	17,000 (RNA)
		1988	CTS March	32,000
1988	Winning Colors	1986	Kee July	575,000
1987	Alysheba	1985	Kee July	500,000
1985	Spend a Buck	1983	Private	12,500
1980	Genuine Risk	1978	FT Ky	32,000
1979	Spectacular Bid	1977	Kee Sept.	37,000
1977	Seattle Slew	1975	FT Ky	17,500
1976	Bold Forbes	1974	FT Ky	15,200
1975	Foolish Pleasure	1973	FT Saratoga	20,000
1971	Canonero II	1969	Kee Sept	1,200
1970	Dust Commander	1968	Kee Sept	6,500
1969	Majestic Prince	1967	Kee July	250,000
1966	Kauai King	1968	FT Saratoga	42,000
1960	Venetian Way	1958	Kee July	10,500
1959	*Tomy Lee	1956	Tatt Dec	6,762
1954	Determine	1952	Kee July	12,500
1953	Dark Star	1951	Kee July	6,500
1951	Count Turf	1949	FT Saratoga	3,700
1947	Jet Pilot	1945	Kee July	41,000
1945	Hoop, Jr.	1943	Kee July	10,200
1940	Gallahadion	1938	FT Saratoga	5,000
1934	Cavalcade	1932	FT Saratoga	1,200

FT Fasig-Tipton; CTS California Thoroughbred Sale; RNA Reserve Not Attained

Derby Winners Unraced at Two

A juvenile campaign of some sort is virtually a prerequisite for winning the Kentucky Derby. Only one horse, Apollo, has won the Derby without racing as a two-year-old, and he accomplished that feat in 1882, in the eighth running.

In recent years, only three horses have won the Derby after making only one start as a two-year-old. Tim Tam, trained by H. A. "Jimmy" Jones, won in 1958 after finishing unplaced in his only start at two. Also unplaced in his only juvenile start was Lucky Debonair, who won the 1965 Derby. Fusaichi Pegasus finished second in his only start as a two-year-old and won the Derby as the 2.30-to-1 favorite in 2000.

Derby Weather, Track Condition, and Temperature Since 1940

Year	Winner	Weather	Track Condition	Temp
2006	Barbaro	Clear	Fast	68
2005	Giacomo	Clear	Fast	79
2004	Smarty Jones	Thunderstorm	Sloppy	68
2003	Funny Cide	Partly cloudy	Fast	67
2002	War Emblem	Clear	Fast	71
2001	Monarchos	Clear	Fast	83
2000	Fusaichi Pegasus	Clear	Fast	82
1999	Charismatic	Clear	Fast	72
1998	Real Quiet	Clear	Fast	70
1997	Silver Charm	Overcast	Fast	51
1996	Grindstone	Thunderstorm	Fast	75
1995	Thunder Gulch	Partly cloudy	Fast	72
1994	Go for Gin	Thunderstorm	Sloppy	57
1993	Sea Hero	Overcast	Fast	69
1992	Lil E. Tee	Overcast	Fast	78
1991	Strike the Gold	Overcast	Fast	80
1990	Unbridled	Mostly cloudy	Good	63
1989	Sunday Silence	Overcast	Muddy	51
1988	Winning Colors	Clear	Fast	72
1987	Alysheba	Mostly cloudy	Fast	79
1986	Ferdinand	Partly cloudy	Fast	63
1985	Spend a Buck	Partly cloudy	Fast	72
1984	Swale	Overcast	Fast	71
1983	Sunny's Halo	Thunderstorm	Fast	81
1982	Gato Del Sol	Partly cloudy	Fast	75
1981	Pleasant Colony	Clear	Fast	55
1980	Genuine Risk	Clear	Fast	72
1979	Spectacular Bid	Clear	Fast	55
1978	Affirmed	Clear	Fast	67
1977	Seattle Slew	Partly cloudy	Fast	69
1976	Bold Forbes	Overcast	Fast	62
1975	Foolish Pleasure	Overcast	Fast	63
1974	Cannonade	Partly cloudy	Fast	68
1973	Secretariat	Partly cloudy	Fast	69
1972	Riva Ridge	Partly cloudy	Fast	75
1971	Canonero II	Partly cloudy	Fast	73
1970	Dust Commander	Partly cloudy	Good	64
1969	Majestic Prince	Partly cloudy	Fast	87
1968	Forward Pass	Partly cloudy	Fast	71
1967	Proud Clarion	Overcast	Fast	61
1966	Kauai King	Partly cloudy	Fast	67
1965	Lucky Debonair	Clear	Fast	84
1964	Northern Dancer	Overcast	Fast	76
1963	Chateaugay	Partly cloudy	Fast	80
1962	Decidedly	Partly cloudy	Fast	81
1961	Carry Back	Overcast	Good	81
1960	Venetian Way	Partly cloudy	Good	64
1959	*Tomy Lee	Partly cloudy	Fast	94
1958	Tim Tam	Partly cloudy	Muddy	86
1957	Iron Liege	Overcast	Fast	47
1956	Needles	Clear	Fast	82
1955	Swaps	Overcast	Fast	85
1954	Determine	Overcast	Fast	84
1953	Dark Star	Clear	Fast	76
1952	Hill Gail	Clear	Fast	79
1951	Count Turf	Partly cloudy	Fast	67
1950	Middleground	Overcast	Fast	70
1949	Ponder	Partly cloudy	Fast	57
1948	Citation	Overcast	Sloppy	72
1947	Jet Pilot	Overcast	Fast	57
1946	Assault	Overcast	Slow	68
1945	Hoop, Jr.	Partly cloudy	Muddy	77
1944	Pensive	Partly cloudy	Good	54
1943	Count Fleet	Clear	Fast	54
1942	Shut Out	Partly cloudy	Fast	87
1941	Whirlaway	Partly cloudy	Fast	76
1940	Gallahadion	Clear	Fast	62

Derby Trivia

Largest Field: 23 in 1974.

Smallest Field: Three in 1892 and 1905.

Longest-Priced Runner Since 1908: A Dragon Killer, seventh in 1958 at 294.40-to-1.

Most Maidens in One Race: Six in 1882 (Highflyer, seventh; Pat Malloy colt, ninth; Wallensee, tenth; Newsboy, 11th; Mistral, 12th; Robert Bruce, 14th).

Most Lifetime Starts Going into Derby: 66, Florizar, 1900 (second).

Fewest Lifetime Starts Going into Derby: Zero, 11 times, most recently by Col. Hogan, 1911 (seventh).

Mutuel Field Horses Who Won the Derby: Canonero II, 1971; Count Turf, 1951; Flying Ebony, 1925.

Derby Winners Who Never Started Again: Grindstone, 1996; Bubbling Over, 1926.

Derby Winner as Both Jockey and Trainer: Johnny Longden, rider of Count Fleet in 1943 and trainer of Majestic Prince in '69.

Longest-Priced Derby Favorite: Harlan's Holiday, 6-to-1, in 2002.

Status of Kentucky Derby Winners Since 1970

Year	Winner	Birthdate	Status	Where Stands/Stood	Location	Death Date
2006	Barbaro	4/29/2003	Retired			
2005	Giacomo	2/16/2002	In training			
2004	Smarty Jones	2/28/2001	Stallion	Three Chimneys Farm	Midway, Ky.	
2003	Funny Cide	4/20/2000	In training			
2002	War Emblem	2/20/1999	Stallion	Shadai Stallion Station	Hokkaido, Japan	
2001	Monarchos	2/9/1998	Stallion	Claiborne Farm	Paris, Ky.	
2000	Fusaichi Pegasus	4/12/1997	Stallion	Ashford Stud	Versailles, Ky.	
1999	Charismatic	3/13/1996	Stallion	JBBA Shizunai Stallion Station	Hokkaido, Japan	
1998	Real Quiet	3/7/1995	Stallion	Regal Heir Farms	Grantville, Pa.	
1997	Silver Charm	2/22/1994	Stallion	JBBA Shizunai Stallion Station	Hokkaido, Japan	
1996	Grindstone	1/23/1993	Stallion	Overbrook Farm	Lexington, Ky.	
1995	Thunder Gulch	5/23/1992	Stallion	Ashford Stud	Versailles, Ky.	

Year	Winner	Birthdate	Status	Where Stands/Stood	Location	Death Date
1994	Go for Gin	4/18/1991	Stallion	Bonita Farm	Darlington, Md.	
1993	Sea Hero	3/4/1990	Stallion	Karacabey Pension Stud	Izmit, Turkey	
1992	Lil E. Tee	3/29/1989	Stallion	Old Frankfort Stud	Lexington, Ky.	
1991	Strike the Gold	3/21/1988	Stallion	Karacabey Pension Stud	Izmit, Turkey	
1990	Unbridled	3/5/1987	Deceased	Claiborne Farm	Paris, Ky.	10/18/2001
1989	Sunday Silence	3/25/1986	Deceased	Shadai Stallion Station	Hokkaido, Japan	8/19/2002
1988	Winning Colors	3/14/1985	Broodmare	Gainesway	Lexington, Ky.	
1987	Alysheba	3/3/1984	Stallion	Janadriyah Stud Farm	Riyadh, Saudi Arabia	
1986	Ferdinand	3/12/1983	Deceased	Arrow Stud	Hokkaido, Japan	2002
1985	Spend a Buck	5/15/1982	Deceased	Haras Bage do Sul	Sao Paulo, Brazil	11/24/2002
1984	Swale	4/21/1981	Deceased			6/17/1984
1983	Sunny's Halo	2/11/1980	Deceased	Double S Thoroughbred Farm	Tyler, Tx.	6/3/2003
1982	Gato Del Sol	2/23/1979	Pensioned	Stone Farm	Paris, Ky.	
1981	Pleasant Colony	5/4/1978	Deceased	Lane's End	Versailles, Ky.	12/31/2002
1980	Genuine Risk	2/15/1977	Pensioned	Newstead Farm	Upperville, Va.	
1979	Spectacular Bid	2/17/1976	Deceased	Milfer Farm	Unadilla, N.Y.	6/9/2003
1978	Affirmed	2/21/1975	Deceased	Jonabell Farm	Lexington, Ky.	1/12/2001
1977	Seattle Slew	2/15/1974	Deceased	Three Chimneys Farm	Midway, Ky.	5/7/2002
1976	Bold Forbes	3/31/1973	Deceased	Stone Farm	Paris, Ky.	8/9/2000
1975	Foolish Pleasure	3/23/1972	Deceased	Horseshoe Ranch	Dayton, Wy.	11/17/1994
1974	Cannonade	5/12/1971	Deceased	Gainesway	Lexington, Ky.	8/3/1993
1973	Secretariat	3/30/1970	Deceased	Claiborne Farm	Paris, Ky.	10/4/1989
1972	Riva Ridge	4/13/1969	Deceased	Claiborne Farm	Paris, Ky.	4/21/1985
1971	Canonero II	4/24/1968	Deceased	Gainesway	Lexington, Ky.	11/11/1981
1970	Dust Commander	2/8/1967	Deceased	Springland Farm	Paris, Ky.	10/7/1991

Starts by Kentucky Derby Winners at Two and Three

Year	Winner	Starts at 2	Starts Before Derby at 3	Total Pre-Derby Starts	Total Starts at 3	Total Starts at 2-3	Derby Prep	Finish
2006	Barbaro	2	3	5	5	7	Florida Derby (G1)	1
2005	Giacomo	4	3	7	6	10	Santa Anita Derby (G1)	4
2004	Smarty Jones	2	4	6	7	9	Arkansas Derby (G2)	1
2003	Funny Cide	3	3	6	8	11	Wood Memorial S. (G1)	2
2002	War Emblem	3	4	7	10	13	Illinois Derby (G2)	1
2001	Monarchos	2	4	6	7	9	Wood Memorial S. (G2)	2
2000	Fusaichi Pegasus	1	4	5	8	9	Wood Memorial S. (G2)	1
1999	Charismatic	7	7	14	10	17	Lexington S. (G2)	1
1998	Real Quiet	9	3	12	6	15	Santa Anita Derby (G1)	2
1997	Silver Charm	3	3	6	7	10	Santa Anita Derby (G1)	2
1996	Grindstone	2	3	5	4	6	Arkansas Derby (G2)	2
1995	Thunder Gulch	6	3	9	10	16	Blue Grass S. (G2)	4
1994	Go for Gin	5	4	9	11	16	Wood Memorial S. (G1)	2
1993	Sea Hero	7	3	10	9	16	Blue Grass S. (G2)	4
1992	Lil E. Tee	4	4	8	6	10	Arkansas Derby (G2)	2
1991	Strike the Gold	3	4	7	12	15	Blue Grass S. (G2)	1
1990	Unbridled	6	4	10	11	17	Blue Grass S. (G2)	3
1989	Sunday Silence	3	3	6	9	12	Santa Anita Derby (G1)	1
1988	Winning Colors	2	4	6	10	12	Santa Anita Derby (G1)	1
1987	Alysheba	7	3	10	10	17	Blue Grass S. (G1)	1, pl 3
1986	Ferdinand	5	4	9	8	13	Santa Anita Derby (G1)	3
1985	Spend a Buck	8	3	3	7	15	Garden State S.	1
1984	Swale	7	4	11	7	14	Lexington S.	2
1983	Sunny's Halo	11	2	13	9	20	Arkansas Derby (G1)	1
1982	Gato Del Sol	8	4	12	9	17	Blue Grass S. (G1)	2
1981	Pleasant Colony	5	8	8	9	14	Wood Memorial S. (G1)	1
1980	Genuine Risk	4	3	7	8	12	Wood Memorial S. (G1)	3
1979	Spectacular Bid	9	5	14	12	21	Blue Grass S. (G1)	1
1978	Affirmed	9	4	13	11	20	Hollywood Derby (G1)	1
1977	Seattle Slew	3	3	6	7	10	Wood Memorial S. (G1)	1
1976	Bold Forbes	8	5	13	10	18	Wood Memorial S. (G1)	1
1975	Foolish Pleasure	7	4	11	11	18	Wood Memorial S. (G1)	1
1974	Cannonade	17	4	21	8	25	Churchill allowance	1
1973	Secretariat	9	3	12	12	21	Wood Memorial S. (G1)	3
1972	Riva Ridge	9	3	12	12	21	Blue Grass S.	1
1971	Canonero II	4	8	12	11	15	Series 4A-5A H.	3
1970	Dust Commander	14	8	22	23	37	Blue Grass S.	1
1969	Majestic Prince	2	5	7	8	10	Churchill allowance	1
1968	Forward Pass	10	7	17	13	23	Blue Grass S.	1
1967	Proud Clarion	3	5	8	13	16	Blue Grass S.	2
1966	Kauai King	4	8	12	12	16	Governor's Gold Cup	1
1965	Lucky Debonair	1	8	9	10	11	Blue Grass S.	1
1964	Northern Dancer	9	5	14	9	18	Blue Grass S.	1

Year	Winner	Starts at 2	Starts Before Derby at 3	Total Pre-Derby Starts	Total Starts at 3	Total Starts at 2-3	Derby Prep	Finish
1963	Chateaugay	5	3	8	12	17	Blue Grass S.	1
1962	Decidedly	8	4	12	12	20	Blue Grass S.	2
1961	Carry Back	21	7	28	16	37	Wood Memorial S.	2
1960	Venetian Way	9	5	14	11	20	Churchill allowance	2
1959	*Tomy Lee	8	4	12	7	15	Blue Grass S.	1
1958	Tim Tam	1	10	11	13	14	Derby Trial S.	1
1957	Iron Liege	8	9	17	17	25	Derby Trial S.	5
1956	Needles	10	3	13	8	18	Florida Derby	1
1955	Swaps	6	3	9	9	15	Churchill allowance	1
1954	Determine	14	8	22	15	29	Derby Trial S.	2
1953	Dark Star	6	5	11	7	13	Derby Trial S.	1
1952	Hill Gail	7	7	14	8	15	Derby Trial S.	1
1951	Count Turf	10	10	20	14	24	Wood Memorial S.	5
1950	Middleground	5	4	9	10	15	Derby Trial S.	2
1949	Ponder	4	8	12	21	25	Derby Trial S.	2
1948	Citation	9	7	16	20	29	Derby Trial S.	1
1947	Jet Pilot	12	2	14	5	17	Jamaica H.	1
1946	Assault	9	3	12	15	24	Derby Trial S.	4
1945	Hoop, Jr.	5	2	7	4	9	Cedar Manor Purse	2
1944	Pensive	5	7	12	17	22	Chesapeake S.	2
1943	Count Fleet	15	2	17	6	21	Wood Memorial S.	1
1942	Shut Out	9	2	11	12	21	Blue Grass S.	1
1941	Whirlaway	16	7	23	20	36	Derby Trial S.	2
1940	Gallahadion	5	9	14	17	22	Derby Trial S.	2
1939	Johnstown	12	3	15	9	21	Wood Memorial S.	1
1938	Lawrin	15	8	23	11	26	Derby Trial S.	2
1937	War Admiral	6	2	8	8	14	Chesapeake S.	1
1936	Bold Venture	8	1	9	3	11	South Shore Purse	1
1935	Omaha	9	2	11	9	18	Wood Memorial S.	3
1934	Cavalcade	11	2	13	7	18	Chesapeake S.	1
1933	Brokers Tip	4	1	5	5	9	Lexington allowance	2
1932	Burgoo King	12	1	13	4	16	Lexington allowance	2
1931	Twenty Grand	8	2	10	10	18	Preakness S.	2
1930	Gallant Fox	7	2	9	10	17	Preakness S.	1

Foreign-Based Runners in the Kentucky Derby

Following are horses that were trained primarily outside the U.S. prior to their start in the Kentucky Derby. Horses that made more than one U.S. start at three prior to their start in the Derby are not included.

Derby	Starter	Derby Finish	Country Where Based or Last Started
2002	Johannesburg	8	Ireland
	Essence of Dubai	9	United Arab Emirates
	Castle Gandolfo	12	Ireland
2001	Express Tour	8	United Arab Emirates
2000	China Visit	6	United Arab Emirates
	Curule	7	United Arab Emirates
1999	Worldly Manner	7	United Arab Emirates
1995	Eltish	6	England
	Citadeed	9	England
	Ski Captain	14	Japan
1994	Ulises[1]	14	Panama
1993	El Bakan[2]	18	Panama
1992	Dr Devious (Ire)	7	England
	Arazi	8	France
	Thyer	13	England
1986	Bold Arrangement (GB)[3]	2	England
1974	*Sir Tristram[4]	11	France
	Set n' Go[5]	15	Venezuela
	Lexico	22	Venezuela
1972	Pacallo[6]	16	Puerto Rico
1971	**Canonero II**	**1**	Venezuela

[1] Ulises started in the Lexington Stakes (G2) at Keeneland 13 days prior to the Derby.
[2] El Bakan started in the Lexington Stakes (G2) at Keeneland 13 days prior to the Derby.
[3] Bold Arrangement started in the Blue Grass Stakes (G1) at Keeneland nine days prior to the Derby.
[4] *Sir Tristram started in the Stepping Stone Purse at Churchill seven days prior to the Derby.
[5] Set n' Go started in the Carl G. Rose Memorial Handicap at Hialeah 24 days prior to the Derby.
[6] Pacallo started in the Stepping Stone Purse at Churchill seven days prior to the Derby.

Winners' Total Starts Before Derby

Decade	Total Starts Before Derby	Average No. Starts
2000-'06	42	6.0
1990-'99	90	9.0
1980-'89	93	9.3
1970-'79	136	13.6
1960-'69	129	12.9
1950-'59	137	13.7
1940-'49	138	13.8

Derby Winners' Starts at Two

Decade	Total Starts at Two	Average No. Starts
2000-'06	17	2.4
1990-'99	52	5.2
1980-'89	60	6.0
1970-'79	89	8.9
1960-'69	72	7.2
1950-'59	75	7.5
1940-'49	89	8.9

Winners' Starts at Three Before Derby

Decade	Total Starts at Three Before Derby	Average No. Starts
2000-'06	25	3.6
1990-'99	38	3.8
1980-'89	33	3.3
1970-'79	47	4.7
1960-'69	57	5.7
1950-'59	62	6.2
1940-'49	49	4.9

Total Pre-Derby Starts

Decade	Starters	Starts	Avg. No. Starts
2000-'06	128	898	7.02
1990-'99	167	1,387	8.31
1980-'89	171	1,720	10.06
1970-'79	149	1,945	13.05
1960-'69	126	2,151	17.07
1950-'59	145	2,316	15.97
1940-'49	126	1,805	14.33

Derby Starters' Starts at Two

Decade	Starters	Starts at 2	Avg. No. Starts
2000-'06	128	463	3.62
1990-'99	167	749	4.49
1980-'89	171	954	5.58
1970-'79	149	1,016	6.82
1960-'69	126	1,272	10.1
1950-'59	145	1,405	9.69
1940-'49	126	1,241	9.85

Pre-Derby Starts at Three

Decade	Starters	Starts at 3 Before Derby	Average No. Starts
2000-'06	128	435	3.40
1990-'99	167	638	3.82
1980-'89	171	766	4.48
1970-'79	149	929	6.23
1960-'69	126	879	6.98
1950-'59	145	911	6.28
1940-'49	126	564	4.48

Most Total Starts by Winner Before Derby

Total Starts	Horse	Year	Starts at Two	At Three Before Derby
28	Carry Back	1961	21	7
23	Whirlaway	1941	16	7
22	Determine	1954	14	8
	Dust Commander	1970	14	8
21	Cannonade	1974	17	4
20	Count Turf	1951	10	10
17	Count Fleet	1943	15	2
	Iron Liege	1957	8	9
	Forward Pass	1968	10	7
16	Citation	1948	9	7
14	Gallahadion	1940	5	9
	Jet Pilot	1947	12	2
	Hill Gail	1952	7	7
	Venetian Way	1960	9	5
	Northern Dancer	1964	9	5
	Spectacular Bid	1979	9	5
	Charismatic	1999	7	7

Fewest Total Starts by Winner Before Derby

Total Starts	Horse	Year	Starts at Two	At Three Before Derby
5	Barbaro	2006	2	3
	Fusaichi Pegasus	2000	1	4
	Grindstone	1996	2	3
6	Smarty Jones	2004	2	4
	Funny Cide	2003	3	3
	Monarchos	2001	2	4
	Silver Charm	1997	3	3
	Sunday Silence	1989	3	3
	Winning Colors	1988	2	4
	Seattle Slew	1977	3	3
7	Giacomo	2005	4	3
	War Emblem	2002	3	4
	Strike the Gold	1991	3	4
	Genuine Risk	1980	4	3
	Majestic Prince	1969	2	5
	Hoop, Jr.	1945	5	2

Kentucky Derby Handle

Year	On-Track	Off-Track	Total
2006	$12,075,504	$106,351,370	$118,426,874
2005	10,706,881	93,278,493	103,985,374
2004	9,488,539	89,875,549	99,364,088
2003	9,135,919	78,832,118	87,968,037
2002	8,630,408	70,464,398	79,094,806
2001	8,360,273	59,192,483	67,552,756
2000	8,737,659	53,059,793	61,797,452
1999	8,025,318	46,171,266	54,196,586
1998	7,890,907	44,586,385	52,477,292
1997	7,401,141	41,891,506	49,292,647
1996	7,488,725	37,734,438	45,223,163
1995	7,297,050	37,518,438	44,815,488
1994	7,449,744	37,289,274	44,739,018
1993	6,811,130	33,458,735	40,269,865
1992	6,690,746	28,250,209	34,940,955
1991	6,744,979	27,499,222	34,244,201
1990	6,948,762	27,452,177	34,400,939
1989	6,751,067	23,089,515	29,840,582
1988	7,346,411	25,525,312	32,871,723
1987	6,362,673	20,829,236	27,191,909
1986	6,165,119	19,932,231	26,097,350
1985	5,770,074	14,474,555	20,244,629
1984	5,420,787	13,521,146	18,941,933
1983	5,546,977	—	5,546,977
1982	5,011,575	—	5,011,575
1981	4,566,179	455,163	5,021,342

Kentucky Derby simulcast wagering began in 1981, when three tracks (Longacres, Yakima Meadows, and Centennial) wagered a total of $455,163. Simulcast wagering was shelved for two years and resumed in 1984. Off-track wagering includes interstate and intrastate wagering.

Kentucky Derby

Grade 1, Churchill Downs, three-year-olds, 1¼ miles, dirt. Held on May 6, 2006, with gross value of $2,213,200. First run in 1875. Weights: colts and geldings, 126 pounds; fillies, 121 pounds.

Year	Winner	Jockey	Second	Third	Strs	Time	Track	1st Purse
2006	**Barbaro**	E. Prado	Bluegrass Cat	Steppenwolfer	20	2:01.36	ft	$1,143,200
2005	**Giacomo**	M. Smith	Closing Argument	Afleet Alex	20	2:02.75	ft	1,639,600
2004	**Smarty Jones**	S. Elliott	Lion Heart	Imperialism	18	2:04.06	sy	**6,184,800**
2003	**‡Funny Cide**	J. Santos	Empire Maker	Peace Rules	16	2:01.19	ft	800,200
2002	**War Emblem**	V. Espinoza	Proud Citizen	Perfect Drift	18	2:01.13	ft	1,875,000
2001	**Monarchos**	J. Chavez	Invisible Ink	Congaree	17	1:59.97	ft	812,000
2000	**Fusaichi Pegasus**	K. Desormeaux	Aptitude	Impeachment	19	2:01.12	ft	888,400
1999	**Charismatic**	C. Antley	Menifee	Cat Thief	19	2:03.29	ft	886,200
1998	**Real Quiet**	K. Desormeaux	Victory Gallop	Indian Charlie	15	2:02.38	ft	738,800
1997	**Silver Charm**	G. Stevens	Captain Bodgit	Free House	13	2:02.44	ft	700,000
1996	**Grindstone**	J. Bailey	‡Cavonnier	Prince of Thieves	19	2:01.06	ft	869,800
1995	**Thunder Gulch**	G. Stevens	Tejano Run	Timber Country	19	2:01.27	ft	707,400
1994	**Go for Gin**	C. McCarron	Strodes Creek	Blumin Affair	14	2:03.72	sy	628,800
1993	**Sea Hero**	J. Bailey	‡Prairie Bayou	Wild Gale	19	2:02.42	ft	735,900
1992	**Lil E. Tee**	P. Day	Casual Lies	Dance Floor	18	2:03.04	ft	724,800
1991	**Strike the Gold**	C. Antley	‡Best Pal	Mane Minister	16	2:03.08	ft	655,800
1990	**Unbridled**	C. Perret	Summer Squall	Pleasant Tap	15	2:02	gd	581,000
1989	**Sunday Silence**	P. Valenzuela	Easy Goer	Awe Inspiring	15	2:05	my	574,200
1988	**†Winning Colors**	G. Stevens	Forty Niner	Risen Star	17	2:02⅕	ft	611,200
1987	**Alysheba**	C. McCarron	Bet Twice	Avies Copy	17	2:03⅖	ft	618,600
1986	**Ferdinand**	W. Shoemaker	Bold Arrangement (GB)	Broad Brush	16	2:02⅘	ft	609,400
1985	**Spend a Buck**	A. Cordero Jr.	Stephan's Odyssey	Chief's Crown	13	2:00⅕	ft	406,800
1984	**Swale**	L. Pincay Jr.	Coax Me Chad	At the Threshold	20	2:02⅖	ft	537,400
1983	**Sunny's Halo**	E. Delahoussaye	Desert Wine	Caveat	20	2:02⅕	ft	426,000
1982	**Gato Del Sol**	E. Delahoussaye	Laser Light	Reinvested	19	2:02⅖	ft	428,850
1981	**Pleasant Colony**	J. Velasquez	Woodchopper	Partez	21	2:02	ft	317,200
1980	**†Genuine Risk**	J. Vasquez	Rumbo	Jaklin Klugman	13	2:02	ft	250,550
1979	**Spectacular Bid**	R. Franklin	General Assembly	Golden Act	10	2:02⅖	ft	228,650
1978	**AFFIRMED**	S. Cauthen	Alydar	Believe It	11	2:01⅕	ft	186,900
1977	**SEATTLE SLEW**	J. Cruguet	Run Dusty Run	Sanhedrin	15	2:02⅕	ft	214,700
1976	**Bold Forbes**	A. Cordero Jr.	Honest Pleasure	Elocutionist	9	2:01⅗	ft	165,200
1975	**Foolish Pleasure**	J. Vasquez	Avatar	Diabolo	15	2:02	ft	209,600
1974	**Cannonade**	A. Cordero Jr.	Hudson County	Agitate	**23**	2:04	ft	274,000
1973	**SECRETARIAT**	R. Turcotte	Sham	Our Native	13	**1:59⅖**	ft	155,050
1972	**Riva Ridge**	R. Turcotte	No Le Hace	Hold Your Peace	16	2:01⅘	ft	140,300
1971	**Canonero II**	G. Avila	Jim French	Bold Reason	20	2:03⅕	ft	145,500
1970	**Dust Commander**	M. Manganello	My Dad George	High Echelon	17	2:03⅖	gd	127,800
1969	**Majestic Prince**	W. Hartack	Arts and Letters	Dike	8	2:01⅘	ft	113,200
1968	**Forward Pass**	I. Valenzuela	Francie's Hat	T. V. Commercial	14	2:02⅕	ft	122,600
1967	**Proud Clarion**	R. Ussery	Barbs Delight	Damascus	14	2:00⅗	ft	119,700
1966	**Kauai King**	D. Brumfield	Advocator	Blue Skyer	15	2:02	ft	120,500
1965	**Lucky Debonair**	W. Shoemaker	Dapper Dan	Tom Rolfe	11	2:01⅕	ft	112,000
1964	**Northern Dancer**	W. Hartack	Hill Rise	The Scoundrel	12	2:00	ft	114,300
1963	**Chateaugay**	B. Baeza	Never Bend	Candy Spots	9	2:01⅘	ft	108,900
1962	**Decidedly**	W. Hartack	Roman Line	Ridan	15	2:00⅖	ft	119,650
1961	**Carry Back**	J. Sellers	Crozier	Bass Clef	15	2:04	gd	120,500
1960	**Venetian Way**	W. Hartack	Bally Ache	Victoria Park	13	2:02⅖	gd	114,850
1959	***Tomy Lee**	W. Shoemaker	Sword Dancer	First Landing	17	2:02⅕	ft	119,650
1958	**Tim Tam**	I. Valenzuela	Lincoln Road	Noureddin	14	2:05	my	116,400
1957	**Iron Liege**	W. Hartack	*Gallant Man	Round Table	9	2:02⅕	ft	107,950
1956	**Needles**	D. Erb	Fabius	Come On Red	17	2:03⅖	ft	123,450
1955	**Swaps**	W. Shoemaker	Nashua	Summer Tan	10	2:01⅘	ft	108,400
1954	**Determine**	R. York	Hasty Road	Hasseyampa	17	2:03	ft	102,050
1953	**Dark Star**	H. Moreno	Native Dancer	Invigorator	11	2:02	ft	90,050
1952	**Hill Gail**	E. Arcaro	Sub Fleet	Blue Man	16	2:01⅗	ft	96,300
1951	**Count Turf**	C. McCreary	Royal Mustang	‡Ruhe	20	2:02⅗	ft	98,050
1950	**Middleground**	W. Boland	Hill Prince	Mr. Trouble	14	2:01⅗	ft	92,650
1949	**Ponder**	S. Brooks	Capot	Palestinian	14	2:04⅕	ft	91,600
1948	**CITATION**	E. Arcaro	Coaltown	My Request	6	2:05⅖	sy	83,400
1947	**Jet Pilot**	E. Guerin	Phalanx	Faultless	13	2:06⅘	sl	92,160
1946	**ASSAULT**	W. Mehrtens	Spy Song	Hampden	17	2:06⅗	sl	96,400
1945	**Hoop, Jr.**	E. Arcaro	Pot o'Luck	‡Darby Dieppe	16	2:07	my	64,850
1944	**Pensive**	C. McCreary	Broadcloth	‡Stir Up	16	2:04⅕	gd	64,675
1943	**COUNT FLEET**	J. Longden	Blue Swords	Slide Rule	10	2:04	ft	60,725
1942	**Shut Out**	W. Wright	Alsab	Valdina Orphan	15	2:04⅖	ft	64,225
1941	**WHIRLAWAY**	E. Arcaro	Staretor	Market Wise	11	2:01⅖	ft	61,275
1940	**Gallahadion**	C. Bierman	Bimelech	‡Dit	8	2:05	ft	60,150

Year	Winner	Jockey	Second	Third	Strs	Time	Track	1st Purse
1939	**Johnstown**	J. Stout	Challedon	Heather Broom	8	2:03⅖	ft	46,350
1938	**Lawrin**	E. Arcaro	Dauber	Can't Wait	10	2:04⅘	ft	47,050
1937	**WAR ADMIRAL**	C. Kurtsinger	Pompoon	Reaping Reward	20	2:03⅕	ft	52,050
1936	**Bold Venture**	I. Hanford	Brevity	Indian Broom	14	2:03⅗	ft	37,725
1935	**OMAHA**	W. Saunders	Roman Soldier	Whiskolo	18	2:05	gd	39,525
1934	**Cavalcade**	M. Garner	Discovery	Agrarian	13	2:04	ft	28,175
1933	**Brokers Tip**	D. Meade	Head Play	Charley O.	13	2:06⅘	gd	48,925
1932	**Burgoo King**	E. James	Economic	Stepenfetchit	20	2:05⅕	ft	52,350
1931	**Twenty Grand**	C. Kurtsinger	Sweep All	Mate	12	2:01⅘	ft	48,725
1930	**GALLANT FOX**	E. Sande	Gallant Knight	Ned O.	15	2:07⅗	gd	50,725
1929	**‡Clyde Van Dusen**	L. McAtee	Naishapur	Panchio	21	2:10⅘	my	53,950
1928	**Reigh Count**	C. Lang	Misstep	Toro	22	2:10⅖	hy	55,375
1927	**Whiskery**	L. McAtee	‡Osmand	Jock	15	2:06	sl	51,000
1926	**Bubbling Over**	A. Johnson	Bagenbaggage	Rock Man	13	2:03⅘	ft	50,075
1925	**Flying Ebony**	E. Sande	Captain Hal	Son of John	20	2:07⅗	sy	52,950
1924	**Black Gold**	J. Mooney	Chilhowee	Beau Butler	19	2:05⅕	ft	52,775
1923	**Zev**	E. Sande	Martingale	Vigil	21	2:05⅖	ft	53,600
1922	**Morvich**	A. Johnson	Bet Mosie	John Finn	10	2:04⅗	ft	53,775
1921	**Behave Yourself**	C. Thompson	Black Servant	†Prudery	12	2:04⅕	ft	38,450
1920	**‡Paul Jones**	T. Rice	Upset	On Watch	17	2:09	sl	30,375
1919	**SIR BARTON**	J. Loftus	‡Billy Kelly	*Under Fire	12	2:09⅘	hy	20,825
1918	**‡Exterminator**	W. Knapp	Escoba	†Viva America	8	2:10⅘	my	14,700
1917	***Omar Khayyam**	C. Borel	Ticket	Midway	15	2:04⅗	ft	16,600
1916	**George Smith**	J. Loftus	Star Hawk	Franklin	9	2:04	ft	9,750
1915	**†Regret**	J. Notter	Pebbles	‡Sharpshooter	16	2:05⅖	ft	11,450
1914	**‡Old Rosebud**	J. McCabe	‡Hodge	†Bronzewing	7	2:03⅖	ft	9,125
1913	**Donerail**	R. Goose	Ten Point	†Gowell	8	2:04⅘	ft	5,475
1912	**Worth**	C. Schilling	Duval	†Flamma	7	2:09⅖	my	4,850
1911	**Meridian**	G. Archibald	‡Governor Gray	Colston	7	2:05	ft	4,850
1910	**Donau**	F. Herbert	Joe Morris	Fighting Bob	7	2:06⅖	ft	4,850
1909	**Wintergreen**	V. Powers	‡Miami	Dr. Barkley	10	2:08⅕	sl	4,850
1908	**Stone Street**	A. Pickens	‡Sir Cleges	Dunvegan	8	2:15⅕	hy	4,850
1907	**Pink Star**	A. Minder	Zal	Ovelando	6	2:12⅗	hy	4,850
1906	**Sir Huon**	R. Troxler	†Lady Navarre	James Reddick	6	2:08⅘	ft	4,850
1905	**Agile**	J. Martin	Ram's Horn	Layson	3	2:10¾	hy	4,850
1904	**Elwood**	F. Prior	Ed Tierney	Brancas	5	2:08½	ft	4,850
1903	**Judge Himes**	H. Booker	Early	Bourbon	6	2:09	ft	4,850
1902	**Alan-a-Dale**	J. Winkfield	Inventor	The Rival	4	2:08¾	ft	4,850
1901	**His Eminence**	J. Winkfield	Sannazarro	Driscoll	5	2:07¾	ft	4,850
1900	**Lieut. Gibson**	J. Boland	Florizar	Thrive	7	2:06¼	ft	4,850
1899	**Manuel**	F. Taral	‡Corsine	Mazo	5	2:12	ft	4,850
1898	**Plaudit**	W. Simms	Lieber Karl	Isabey	4	2:09	gd	4,850
1897	**Typhoon II**	F. Garner	Ornament	Dr. Catlett	6	2:12½	hy	4,850
1896	**Ben Brush**	W. Simms	Ben Eder	Semper Ego	8	2:07¾	dy	4,850
1895	**Halma**	J. Perkins	Basso	Laureate	4	2:37½	ft	2,970
1894	**Chant**	F. Goodale	Pearl Song	Sigurd	5	2:41	ft	4,020
1893	**Lookout**	E. Kunze	Plutus	Boundless	6	2:39¼	ft	3,840
1892	**Azra**	A. Clayton	Huron	Phil Dwyer	3	2:41½	hy	4,230
1891	**Kingman**	I. Murphy	Balgowan	High Tariff	4	2:52¼	sl	4,550
1890	**Riley**	I. Murphy	Bill Letcher	Robespierre	6	2:45	my	5,460
1889	**Spokane**	T. Kiley	‡Proctor Knott	Once Again	8	2:34½	ft	4,880
1888	**‡Macbeth II**	G. Covington	Gallifet	White	7	2:38¼	ft	4,740
1887	**Montrose**	I. Lewis	Jim Gore	‡Jacobin	7	2:39¼	ft	4,200
1886	**Ben Ali**	P. Duffy	Blue Wing	Free Knight	10	2:36½	ft	4,890
1885	**Joe Cotton**	E. Henderson	Bersan	‡Ten Booker	10	2:37¼	gd	4,630
1884	**Buchanan**	I. Murphy	Loftin	Audrain	9	2:40¼	gd	3,990
1883	**Leonatus**	W. Donohue	‡Drake Carter	Lord Raglan	7	2:43	hy	3,760
1882	**‡Apollo**	B. Hurd	Runnymede	Bengal	14	2:40¼	gd	4,560
1881	**Hindoo**	J. McLaughlin	‡Lelex	Alfambra	6	2:40	ft	4,410
1880	**Fonso**	G. Lewis	Kimball	‡Bancroft	5	2:37½	dy	3,800
1879	**Lord Murphy**	C. Shauer	Falsetto	Strathmore	9	2:37	ft	3,550
1878	**Day Star**	J. Carter	Himyar	Leveller	9	2:37¼	dy	4,050
1877	**Baden-Baden**	W. Walker	Leonard	King William	11	2:38	ft	3,300
1876	**‡Vagrant**	B. Swim	Creedmore	Harry Hill	11	2:38¼	ft	2,950
1875	**Aristides**	O. Lewis	Volcano	Verdigris	15	2:37¾	ft	2,850

†—filly, ‡—gelding, *—imported horse

1875-'95: 1½ miles; 1973-present: Grade 1; 1968: Dancer's Image finished first but was disqualified from purse money; bold indicates records set in number of starters, time, and winning purse; War Emblem's record winning purse includes a $1-million bonus awarded by Sportman's Park for winning the Illinois Derby (G2) and a Triple Crown race. Smarty Jones's 2004 purse includes $5-million bonus from Oaklawn Park. Triple Crown winners are in all capitalized letters.

History of the Preakness Stakes

Born out of a party boast and named for a horse who met an unfortunate end, the Preakness Stakes (G1) is the second jewel of the American Triple Crown and the second-oldest American classic.

Both the Preakness Stakes and Pimlico Race Course, the track where the classic race is staged annually on the third Saturday of May, trace their roots to a party hosted by Milton H. Sanford in Saratoga Springs, New York, in 1868. At the party, Maryland Governor Oden Bowie promised that a new racetrack would open in Baltimore to play host to the Dinner Party Stakes, to which he pledged a hefty purse.

A 70-acre track site, which had been known as Pimlico since the 1850s and had been used for racing since then, was purchased by the Maryland Agricultural Society from Robert Wylie in 1866. The organization held a fair meet at the site in 1869 but failed to raise enough money to complete the track.

Bowie, a horse owner and sportsman, helped another group, the Maryland Jockey Club, to negotiate a lease of the property—$1,000 annual rent for ten years. Gen. John Elliott designed the track, and Pimlico opened on October 25, 1870. Among the amenities was the Pimlico Clubhouse, a Baltimore landmark until it was destroyed by fire in 1966.

Sanford, a New York horseman who made a portion of his fortune by selling blankets to the army in the Civil War, sent his three-year-old colt Preakness to make his only start of that year in the new Dinner Party Stakes. Bred in Kentucky by A. J. Alexander, Sanford bought the colt by Lexington out of Bay Leaf, by *Yorkshire, as a yearling for $2,000. He named the colt after his farms in New Jersey and Kentucky, which also bore the name Preakness. The name is derived from the language of the Minisi Indians in northern New Jersey; in their language, "pra-qua-les" meant "quail woods."

Under English jockey Billy Hayward, Preakness won the first Dinner Party Stakes, which today is known as the Dixie Stakes (G2) and is run on grass. Three years later, in 1873, the Maryland Jockey Club staged its first spring meeting and honored the winner of the first Dinner Party Stakes by naming the 1½-mile race for three-year-olds the Preakness Stakes.

Second race on a three-race program on Tuesday, May 23, 1873, the first Preakness Stakes attracted a field of seven to compete for the $2,050 total purse. A crowd estimated at 12,000 made Bowie's Catesby the favorite, but John Chamberlin's Survivor won by ten lengths, which until 2004 was the race's largest winning margin. In 2004, Roy and Patricia Chapman's Smarty Jones won by 11½ lengths.

Preakness Attendance

Year	On-Track	Total	Year	On-Track	Total
2006	118,402	128,643	1987		87,945
2005	115,318	125,687	1986		87,652
2004	112,668	124,351	1985		81,235
2003	100,268	109,931	1984		80,566
2002	101,138	117,055	1983		71,768
2001	104,454	118,926	1982		80,724
2000	98,304	111,821	1981		84,133
1999	100,311	116,526	1980		83,455
1998	91,122	103,269	1979		72,607
1997	88,594	102,118	1978		81,261
1996	85,122	97,751	1977		77,346
1995	87,707	100,818	1976		62,256
1994	86,343	99,834	1975		75,216
1993	85,495	97,641	1974		54,911
1992	85,294	96,865	1973		61,657
1991	87,245	96,695	1972		48,721
1990	86,531	96,106	1971		47,221
1989	90,145	98,896	1970		42,474
1988	81,282	88,654			

Attendance figures from 1988 to 2003 include combined intertrack sites (Laurel, Rosecroft, Delmarva Downs) and exclude Maryland off-track betting sites. Pimlico and Laurel Park in, 2004-'05.

Preakness, the horse for whom the race was named, continued to race until age eight, winning the 1875 Baltimore Cup and finishing in a dead heat with Springbok in that year's Saratoga Cup. Sold to England for stud, Preakness became difficult to handle in his later years and was shot to death by his owner, the Duke of Hamilton.

Pimlico staged the first 17 runnings of the Preakness, but the Maryland Jockey Club encountered financial difficulties in 1889, and the race was run the following year at Morris Park in New York. It was not run in 1891, '92, and '93—thus, though two years older than the Kentucky Derby, the Preakness has had one fewer running—and reappeared in 1894 at Gravesend Race Course in Brooklyn, where it would be renewed for 15 years.

Pimlico regained its financial health early in the new century, but the Preakness did not return to Baltimore until May 12, 1909, when Effendi set the pace and won by one length over Fashion Plate while running a mile in 1:39⅘. Unlike the Belmont Stakes, which was not run in 1911 and '12 because of New York antigambling legislation, the Preakness was run with betting through those years.

The race proved so popular that in 1918 the Preakness—then at 1⅛ miles—was run in two divisions, the only American classic race to be split. On May 14 of the following year, J.K.L. Ross's Sir Barton won the Preakness only four days after scoring his maiden victory in the Kentucky Derby. On June 11, 1919, the *Star Shoot colt defeated two opponents in the Belmont Stakes to become the first Triple Crown winner. The feat was noted after the fact when *Daily Racing Form* columnist Charles Hatton popularized the designation for the three races beginning in 1930.

The Preakness's reputation was sealed in 1920 when the great Man o' War opened his three-year-old season with a 1½-length victory over Upset, the only horse ever to defeat him. The Preakness remained at 1⅛ miles until 1925, when it was changed to its present 1³⁄₁₆ miles.

In 1930, the Preakness was the first race of Gallant Fox's Triple Crown, but after '31 the race took its place as second in the series. In 1945, after victory in Europe led to the lifting of a voluntary ban on racing, the Preakness was run one week after the Derby and one week before the Belmont.

Pimlico was the scene of three memorable Triple Crown efforts in the 1970s: Secretariat's sweeping move to the lead on the clubhouse turn in 1973, Seattle Slew's brilliance in '77, and the stretch-long battle of Affirmed and Alydar in '78.

The race has had its share of controversy as well. In 1962, Greek Money won by a nose over Ridan, whose rider, Manuel Ycaza, claimed foul. A head-on photo, however, disclosed that Ycaza was in fact using his hands and elbows to restrain Greek Money. In 1980, Kentucky Derby winner Genuine Risk was herded wide at the top of the stretch by winner Codex, ridden by Angel Cordero Jr. An objection by Genuine Risk's jockey, Jacinto Vasquez, was disallowed, and Bertram Firestone, the filly's co-owner, forced a long Maryland Racing Commission hearing into the result. The original order of finish was upheld.

The Preakness in the 1980s and '90s was notable for two close finishes: Sunday Silence's 1989 nose victory over Easy Goer and the '97 race, in which Silver Charm won by a head over Free House, with third-place finisher Captain Bodgit another head farther back.

In 2002, '03, and '04, the Derby winners scored victories in the Preakness. War Emblem won in 2002, and Funny Cide romped by 9¾ lengths, then the second-largest margin, in '03. Funny Cide was only the seventh gelding to win the Preakness. Smarty Jones won in 2004 by a record 11½ lengths. In 2005, Afleet Alex overcame a near fall and won by 4¾ lengths.—*Don Clippinger*

Woodlawn Vase

The Woodlawn Vase, said to be the most valuable trophy in sports, is presented annually to the owner of the Preakness Stakes winner. The trophy, 34 inches tall and weighing almost 30 pounds, was created in 1860 by Tiffany and Co. for the Woodlawn Racing Association in Louisville.

After being buried during the Civil War to prevent it from being melted down, the trophy was unearthed and remained in Louisville until 1878, when the Dwyer brothers won it. They presented it to the Coney Island Jockey Club, and it was subsequently presented at two other New York tracks, Jerome Park and Morris Park.

Thomas C. Clyde won the trophy in 1904 and gave it to the Maryland Jockey Club, of which he was a director, in '17. That year, E. R. Bradley's Kalitan was the first horse to win the Woodlawn Vase at Pimlico.

A Preakness Tradition

A Preakness Stakes tradition observed each year is the painting of the winner's silks on a weather vane atop the Preakness presentation stand. The practice dates to 1909, when lightning destroyed a weather vane atop the Members' Clubhouse, which dated to 1870. The track's directors commissioned a new weather vane depicting a horse and rider, and the weather vane was adorned with the colors of Effendi that year.

The clubhouse structure, an ornate Victorian building that contained dining rooms, sleeping rooms, and a library, burned to the ground in June 1966. Since then, winner's colors have been painted on a weather vane atop an infield replica of the old clubhouse's cupola.

Black-Eyed Susans in the Spring

The black-eyed Susan, Maryland's state flower since 1918, blooms each summer and fall in Maryland and other states, but not in the spring. Thus, the black-eyed Susans that adorn the Preakness Stakes (G1) winner's garland are not black-eyed Susans. Actually, they are Viking daisies in disguise.

The ersatz black-eyed Susans were first draped across Bimelech's withers after the 1940 Preakness. Today, the garland is 18" wide and 90" long, and assembling it requires two days. First, greenery is attached to a spongy rubber base, and then more than 80 bunches of daisies are secured to the base. Heavy felt is then attached to the back to protect the horse. After that, black lacquer is daubed on the center of the daisies to simulate black-eyed Susans.

Origins of the Alibi Breakfast

The Alibi Breakfast, a Preakness-week tradition, is a direct descendant of the informal gatherings on the porch of the historic Old Clubhouse in the 1930s, when trainers, journalists, racing officials, and others would gather during training hours to watch the horses and swap stories.

David Woods, Pimlico Race Course's publicity director in the 1940s, formalized the get-togethers as a Preakness event at which owners and trainers could explain why they believed their horses would win, or take the opportunity to propose an alibi or two in case they did not win.

The track's principal awards—the Old Hilltop Award, Special Award of Merit, and the David F. Woods Memorial Award—are presented during the breakfast.

"Maryland, My Maryland"

While the roots of "My Old Kentucky Home" most likely were opposition to slavery, "Maryland, My Maryland" was originally a nine-stanza poem written in support of the Confederacy.

The author was James Ryder Randall, who wrote it in April 1861 to protest Union troops marching through Baltimore. A Maryland native, Randall was then teaching in Louisiana.

His poem was set to the tune of "Lauriger Horatius" ("O, Tannenbaum"), and the song achieved wide popularity in Maryland and throughout the South before becoming the official state song in 1939.

The two stanzas that are sung:

The despot's heel is on thy shore,
Maryland!
His torch is at thy temple door,
Maryland!
Avenge the patriotic gore
That flecked the streets of Baltimore,
And be the battle queen of yore,
Maryland! My Maryland!

Thou wilt not cower in the dust,
Maryland!
Thy beaming sword shall never rust,
Maryland!
Remember Carroll's sacred trust,
Remember Howard's warlike thrust,
And all thy slumberers with the just,
Maryland! My Maryland!

Preakness Trivia

• Derby winners in recent years were not necessarily favored in the Preakness. Since 1986, the following Derby winners did not go off as the Preakness favorites: Ferdinand, 1986, second; Sunday Silence, 1989, won; Lil E. Tee, 1992, fifth; Sea Hero, 1993, fifth; Silver Charm, 1997, won; Real Quiet, 1998, won; Charismatic, 1999, won; Giacomo, 2005, third.

• Two individuals have won the Preakness both as jockeys and trainers. Louis Schaefer rode Dr. Freeland to victory in 1929 and one decade later trained Challedon to a Preakness win. Johnny Longden rode Count Fleet in 1943 and trained Majestic Prince in '69.

• A starting gate was first used for the Preakness in 1930.

• The Preakness has been run at seven different distances since 1873. The race was as short as one mile in 1909 and '10, as long as 1¾ miles in 1889, and 1³⁄₁₆ miles since 1925.

• Two African-American jockeys have won the Preakness: George B. "Spider" Anderson aboard Buddhist in 1889 and Willie Simms on Sly Fox in '98. The only black jockey to ride in the Preakness in modern times was Wayne Barnett, who finished eighth aboard Sparrowvon in 1985.

• The Preakness preceded the Kentucky Derby on the racing calendar 11 times between 1888 and 1931.

• In 1890, the Preakness and the Belmont Stakes were run on the same card at Morris Park.

• From 1910 through '16, the Preakness was run as a handicap. From 1895 through 1907, the race was under allowance conditions, limiting it to horses that had not won a race worth a certain amount.

• The Preakness was run in divisions in 1918, when *War Cloud and Jack Hare Jr. won.

Leading Preakness Owners by Wins

7 **Calumet Farm:** Whirlaway, 1941; Pensive, 1944; Faultless, 1947; Citation, 1948; Fabius, 1956; Tim Tam, 1958; Forward Pass, 1968.

5 **George L. Lorillard:** Duke of Magenta, 1878; Harold, 1879; Grenada, 1880; Saunterer, 1881; Vanguard, 1882.

4 **Harry Payne Whitney:** Royal Tourist, 1908; Broomspun, 1921; Bostonian, 1927; Victorian, 1928.

Added Value of the Preakness

The purse value of the Preakness Stakes has increased from $1,000 in 1873 to $1-million guaranteed, with the winner currently collecting a check for $650,000. The increase is significant; $1,000 in 1873 would equal only $14,210 today, which is the purse level of a good-quality claiming race.

The Preakness purse has been decreased on occasion, including once during the Great Depression (1933) and in consecutive years, 1949 and 1950. Following is the progression of the Preakness purse:

Year	Added Value	Year	Added Value
1998	*$1,000,000	1918	**$15,000
1989	500,000	1917	5,000
1985	350,000	1912	1,500
1979	200,000	1909	2,000
1959	150,000	1907	2,500
1953	100,000	1904	2,000
1951	75,000	1902	1,500
1950	50,000	1899	1,000
1949	75,000	1895	2,000
1946	100,000	1983	250,000
1937	50,000	1894	1,000
1933	25,000	1890	1,500
1922	50,000	1873	1,000
1921	40,000		
1919	25,000		

* guaranteed purse
** each division

Supplemental Nominations to the Preakness

When Triple Crown Productions launched a common nomination in 1986, no supplemental entries were permitted. The rules were changed in 1991 to allow supplemental entries, although no horse owner has yet to put up $100,000 to gain a place in the Preakness Stakes starting gate.

Supplemental entries to the Preakness were first permitted in 1938, and the first supplemental entrant to win was Citation, who won the '48 Triple Crown. Calumet Farm owner Warren Wright supplemented both Citation and Coaltown for $3,000 each, but only Citation started. Hill Prince (1950) and Master Derby ('75) were supplemental winners.

Here are the supplemented Preakness starters since 1959:

Year	Horse	Supplement	Finish	Purse Winnings
1985	Tajawa	$20,000	6th	$ 0
	Sport Jet	20,000	10th	0
	Hajji's Treasure	20,000	11th	0
1984	Fight Over	15,000	3rd	30,000
1982	Reinvested	10,000	6th	0
1981	Paristo	10,000	3rd	20,000
1980	Lucky Pluck	10,000	8th	0
1975	**Master Derby**	10,000	1st	158,100
	Native Guest	10,000	7th	0
1974	Super Florin	10,000	10th	0
1970	Dust Commander	10,000	9th	0
1968	Nodouble	10,000	3rd*	15,000
1967	Barb's Delight	10,000	6th	0
1959	Manassah Mauler	10,000	8th	0

* moved up from fourth via disqualification

3 **Belair Stud:** Gallant Fox, 1930; Omaha, 1935; Nashua, 1955.
E. R. Bradley: Kalitan, 1917; Burgoo King, 1932; Bimelech, 1940.
Robert and Beverly Lewis: Timber Country (co-owners), 1995; Silver Charm, 1997; Charismatic, 1999.
Walter J. Salmon: Vigil, 1923; Display, 1926; Dr. Freeland, 1929.

2 **August Belmont II:** Don Enrique, 1907; Watervale, 1911.
Brookmeade Stable: High Quest, 1934; Bold, 1951.
J. F. Chamberlin: Survivor, 1873; Tom Ochiltree, 1875.
Glen Riddle Farm: Man o'War, 1920; War Admiral, 1937.
Loblolly Stable: Pine Bluff, 1992; Prairie Bayou, 1993.
Overbrook Farm: Tabasco Cat (co-owner), 1994; Timber Country (co-owner), 1995.
Preakness Stable: Montague, 1890; Belmar, 1895.
J. K. L. Ross: Damrosch, 1916; Sir Barton, 1919.
The Thoroughbred Corp.: Point Given, 2001; War Emblem 2002.

Owners with Most Starters

Owner	Starters	Wins
Greentree Stable	20	1
Harry Payne Whitney	15	4
Calumet Farm	14	7
August Belmont II	11	2
George L. Lorillard	11	5
Overbrook Farm	11	2
Brookmeade Stable	9	2
King Ranch	8	1
Robert and Beverly Lewis	8	3
Pierre Lorillard	8	1
Wheatley Stable	7	1
Rancocas Stable	6	0
Mrs. Ethel D. Jacobs	6	1

Leading Preakness Breeders by Wins

7 **Calumet Farm:** Whirlaway, 1941; Pensive, 1944; Faultless, 1947; Citation, 1948; Fabius, 1956; Tim Tam, 1958; Forward Pass, 1968.

6 **Harry Payne Whitney:** Royal Tourist, 1908; Buskin, 1913; Holiday, 1914; Broomspun, 1921; Bostonian, 1927; Victorian, 1928.
August Belmont II: Jacobus, 1883; Margrave, 1896; Don Enrique, 1907; Watervale, 1911; Damrosch, 1916; Man o' War, 1920.

4 **A. J. Alexander:** Tom Ochiltree, 1875; Shirley, 1876; Duke of Magenta, 1878; Grenada, 1880.

3 **Belair Stud:** Gallant Fox, 1930; Omaha, 1935; Nashua, 1955.
James Ben Ali Haggin: Old England, 1902; Cairngorm, 1905; Rhine Maiden, 1915.

2 **William S. Farish:** Summer Squall (co-breeder), 1990; Charismatic (co-breeder), 1999.
Idle Hour Stock Farm: Burgoo King (co-breeder), 1932; Bimelech, 1940.
Loblolly Stable: Pine Bluff, 1992; Prairie Bayou, 1993.
Raceland Stud: Whimsical, 1906; Colonel Holloway, 1912.
Walter J. Salmon: Display, 1926; Dr. Freeland, 1929.
R. W. Walden: Vanguard, 1882; Refund, 1882.
Aristides Welch: Harold, 1879; Saunterer, 1881.

Leading Preakness Trainers by Wins

7 **R. Wyndham Walden:** Tom Ochiltree, 1875; Duke of Magenta, 1878; Harold, 1879; Grenada, 1880; Saunterer, 1881; Vanguard, 1882; Refund, 1888.

5 **Thomas J. Healey:** The Parader, 1901; Pillory, 1922; Vigil, 1923; Display, 1926; Dr. Freeland, 1929.
D. Wayne Lukas: Codex, 1980; Tank's Prospect, 1985; Tabasco Cat, 1994; Timber Country, 1995; Charismatic, 1999.

4 **Bob Baffert:** Silver Charm, 1997; Real Quiet, 1998; Point Given, 2001; War Emblem, 2002.

4 **James E. "Sunny Jim" Fitzsimmons:** Gallant Fox, 1930; Omaha, 1935; Nashua, 1955; Bold Ruler, 1957.
H. A. "Jimmy" Jones: Faultless, 1947; Citation, 1948; Fabius, 1956; Tim Tam, 1958.
3 **James Whalen:** Don Enrique, 1907; Watervale, 1911; Buskin, 1913.
2 **Thomas Bohannan:** Pine Bluff, 1992; Prairie Bayou, 1993.
Edward Feakes: Montague, 1890; Belmar, 1895.
Henry Forrest: Kauai King, 1966; Forward Pass, 1968.
T. P. Hayes: Paul Kauvar, 1897; Head Play, 1933.
J. S. Healey: Layminster, 1910; Holiday, 1914.
Max Hirsch: Bold Venture, 1936; Assault, 1946.
William Hurley: Kalitan, 1917; Bimelech, 1940.
B. A. "Ben" Jones: Whirlaway, 1941; Pensive, 1944.
Andrew W. Joyner: Cairngorm, 1905; Royal Tourist, 1908.
2 **Jack Van Berg:** Gate Dancer, 1984; Alysheba, 1987.
Frank Y. Whiteley Jr.: Tom Rolfe, 1965; Damascus, 1967.

Trainers with Most Starters

Trainer	Starters	Wins
D. Wayne Lukas	31	5
Max Hirsch	19	2
James E. Fitzsimmons	18	4
James Rowe Sr.	14	1
Nicholas Zito	17	1
Bob Baffert	9	4
Woody Stephens	9	1
Preston Burch	8	1
John P. Campo	8	1

Female Trainers in the Preakness

Here are the female trainers with Preakness starters:

Year	Horse	Trainer	Finish
2004	Imperialism	Kristin Mulhall	5th
	Water Cannon	Linda Albert	10th
2003	New York Hero	Jennifer Pedersen	6th
	Kissin Saint	Lisa Lewis	10th
2002	Magic Weisner	Nancy H. Alberts	2nd
2001	Griffinite	Jennifer Leigh-Peterson	5th
1998	Silver's Prospect	Jean Rolfe	10th
1996	In Contention	Cynthia Reese	6th
1993	Hegar	Penny Lewis	9th
1992	Casual Lies	Shelley Riley	3rd
	Speakerphone	Dean Gaudet	14th
1990	Fighting Notion	Nancy Heil	5th
1980	Samoyed	Judith Zouck	6th
1968	Sir Beau	Judy Johnson	7th

Leading Preakness Jockeys by Wins

Eddie Arcaro, known as "The Master," held sway over the Preakness Stakes in his storied career, winning the race six times in 15 starts. His closest challenger is Pat Day, who has won the race three consecutive times, 1994-'96, and has five victories with 17 Preakness starters.

The leading Preakness jockeys with two or more victories:

6 **Eddie Arcaro:** Whirlaway, 1941; Citation, 1948; Hill Prince, 1950; Bold, 1951; Nashua, 1955; Bold Ruler, 1957.
5 **Pat Day:** Tank's Prospect, 1985; Summer Squall, 1990; Tabasco Cat, 1994; Timber Country, 1995; Louis Quatorze, 1996.
3 **George Barbee:** Survivor, 1873; Shirley, 1876; Jacobus, 1883.
William Hartack: Fabius, 1956; Northern Dancer, 1964; Majestic Prince, 1969.
L. Hughes: Tom Ochiltree, 1875; Harold, 1879; Grenada, 1880.
2 **Jerry Bailey:** Hansel, 1991; Red Bullet, 2000.
Angel Cordero Jr.: Codex, 1980; Gate Dancer, 1984.
Costello: Saunterer, 1881; Vanguard, 1882.
Fisher: Knight of Ellersie, 1884; The Bard, 1886.
C. Holloway: Cloverbrook, 1877; Duke of Magenta, 1878.
Clarence Kummer: Man o'War, 1920; Coventry, 1925.
Charles Kurtsinger: Head Play, 1933; War Admiral, 1937.
John Loftus: War Cloud, 1918; Sir Barton, 1919.
Chris McCarron: Alysheba, 1987; Pine Bluff, 1992.
Conn McCreary: Pensive, 1944; Blue Man, 1952.
Bill Shoemaker: Candy Spots, 1963; Damascus, 1967.
Gary Stevens: Silver Charm, 1997; Point Given, 2001.
Fred Taral: Assignee, 1894; Belmar, 1895.
Ismael Valenzuela: Tim Tam, 1958; Forward Pass, 1968.

Most Preakness Mounts

Jockey	Starts	Wins
Pat Day	17	5
Eddie Arcaro	15	6
Gary Stevens	16	2
Jerry Bailey	15	2
Angel Cordero Jr.	13	2
Chris McCarron	13	2
Bill Shoemaker	12	2
William Hartack	11	3
Jorge Velasquez	11	1
Braulio Baeza	10	0
Linus McAtee	10	1

Female Jockeys in the Preakness

Only two female jockeys have ridden in the Preakness, and the best finish was by Patricia Cooksey, who was sixth aboard Tajawa in 1985. Andrea Seefeldt, a Maryland-based rider, finished seventh in 1994 aboard Looming.

Jockey	Year	Horse	Finish
Andrea Seefeldt	1994	Looming	7th
Patricia Cooksey	1985	Tajawa	6th

Leading Preakness Sires by Wins

3 **Lexington:** Tom Ochiltree, 1875; Shirley, 1876; Duck of Magenta, 1878.

Preakness Wagering, 1980-2005

Year	Preakness Winner	Preakness In-State Handle	Preakness Simulcasting	Preakness Total Handle
2006	Bernardini	$3,710,548	$52,684,102	$56,394,560
2005	Afleet Alex	4,079,858	56,781,232	60,861,090
2004	Smarty Jones	3,808,863	54,982,543	58,791,406
2003	Funny Cide	3,151,864	38,008,281	41,620,145
2002	War Emblem	3,440,321	44,254,871	47,695,192
2001	Point Given	3,342,237	37,352,557	40,694,884
2000	Red Bullet	2,482,262	26,550,064	29,032,326
1999	Charismatic	3,056,891	26,438,761	34,435,703
1998	Real Quiet	2,103,027	17,624,933	23,640,365
1997	Silver Charm	2,667,000	18,087,214	26,602,245
1996	Louis Quatorze	2,352,900	20,545,618	22,898,518
1995	Timber Country	2,519,388	20,869,915	23,389,303
1994	Tabasco Cat	2,548,282	21,461,540	24,009,822
1993	Prairie Bayou	2,269,946	19,293,287	21,563,233
1992	Pine Bluff	2,365,023	19,338,393	21,703,416
1991	Hansel	2,504,693	18,289,622	20,794,315
1990	Summer Squall	2,257,916	16,625,833	18,883,749
1989	Sunday Silence	2,519,893	17,306,821	19,826,714
1988	Risen Star	2,392,384	18,519,289	20,911,673
1987	Alysheba	1,846,768		
1986	Snow Chief	1,680,923		
1985	Tank's Prospect	1,461,997		
1884	Gate Dancer	1,358,444		
1983	Deputed Testamony	1,251,931		
1982	Aloma's Ruler	1,257,244		
1981	Pleasant Colony	1,387,797		
1980	Codex	1,215,664		

3 **Broomstick:** Holiday, 1914; Broomspun, 1921; Bostonian, 1927.

2 ***Leamington:** Harold, 1879; Saunterer, 1881.

***Watercress:** Watervale, 1911; Rhine Maiden, 1915.

Fair Play: Man o' War, 1920; Display, 1926.

***Sir Gallahad III:** Gallant Fox, 1930; High Quest, 1934.

Bull Lea: Faultless, 1947; Citation, 1948.

***Nasrullah:** Nashua, 1955; Bold Ruler, 1957.

Sovereign Dancer: Gate Dancer, 1984; Louis Quatorze, 1996.

Woodman: Hansel, 1991; Timber Country, 1995.

Preakness in the Pedigree

Preakness winners who have sired other Preakness winners:

Man o' War (1920): War Admiral (1937)
Gallant Fox (1930): Omaha (1935)
Bold Venture (1936): Assault (1946)
Polynesian (1945): Native Dancer (1953)
Citation (1948): Fabius (1956)
Native Dancer (1953): Kauai King (1966)
Bold Ruler (1957): Secretariat (1973)
Secretariat (1973): Risen Star (1988)
Summer Squall (1990): Charismatic (1999)

Fastest Runnings of the Preakness

Tank's Prospect and Louis Quatorze share the record for the fastest running of the Preakness Stakes, 1:53⅖. Louis Quatorze, the 1996 winner, was timed in 1:53.43, but Tank's Prospect in 1985 was timed in one-fifths of a second, the standard at that time.

Unofficially, Secretariat ran the Preakness's $1\frac{3}{16}$ miles in the same time. He was caught in 1:53⅖ by *Daily Racing Form* clockers who were hand-timing the race. A malfunctioning official timer recorded a time of 1:55, but that was subsequently adjusted to 1:54⅖.

Year	Winner	Time	Cond.
1996	Louis Quatorze	1:53.43	Fast
1985	Tank's Prospect	1:53⅖	Fast
1984	Gate Dancer	1:53⅗	Fast
1990	Summer Squall	1:53⅗	Fast
1971	Canonero II	1:54	Fast
1991	Hansel	1:54.05	Fast
1989	Sunday Silence	1:53⅘	
1979	Spectacular Bid	1:54⅕	Good
1995	Timber Country	1:54.45	Fast
1980	Codex	1:54⅕	Fast
1973	Secretariat	1:54⅖*	Fast
1977	Seattle Slew	1:54⅖	Fast
1978	Affirmed	1:54⅖	Fast
1981	Pleasant Colony	1:54⅗	Fast
1974	Little Current	1:54⅗	Good
1955	Nashua	1:54⅗	Fast
2006	Bernardini	1:54.65	Fast

* Hand-timed in 1:53⅖

Evolution of Preakness Stakes Record

Year	Winner	Time
1925	Coventry	1:59
1934	High Quest	1:58⅕
1942	Alsab	1:57
1949	Capot	1:56
1955	Nashua	1:54⅗
1971	Canonero II	1:54
1984	Gate Dancer	1:53⅗
1985	Tank's Prospect	1:53⅖
1996	Louis Quatorze	1:53⅖ (1:53.43)

Fastest Preakness Fractions

First Quarter-Mile: :22⅖ Flag Raiser (1965), Fight Over (1984), Eternal Prince (1985), Vicar (1999).
First Half-Mile: :45, Bold Forbes (1976).
First Six Furlongs: 1:09, Bold Forbes (1976).
Fastest First Mile: 1:34⅕, Chief's Crown (1985), Sunday Silence (1989).
Fastest Final Three-Sixteenths: :18, Summer Squall, 1990.

Slowest Preakness Times

Citation, a Triple Crown winner and regarded as one of the greatest Thoroughbreds of the 20th century, ran the slowest Preakness Stakes ever, 2:02⅖. But the *Daily Racing Form* chart characterized the track as heavy, which would have been considerably slower than today's speed-tuned racing surfaces.

Following are the slowest Preakness runnings since 1925, when the race's distance became 1$\frac{3}{16}$ miles.

Year	Winner	Time	Cond.
1948	Citation	2:02⅖	Heavy
1933	Head Play	2:02	Slow
1927	Bostonian	2:01⅗	Good
1929	Dr. Freeland	2:01⅗	Fast
1946	Assault	2:01⅖	Fast
1930	Gallant Fox	2:00⅗	Fast
1928	Victorian	2:00⅕	Fast
1932	Burgoo King	1:59⅘	Fast
1938	Dauber	1:59⅘	Sloppy
1939	Challedon	1:59⅘	Muddy
1926	Display	1:59⅘	Fast
1950	Hill Prince	1:59⅕	Slow
1944	Pensive	1:59⅕	Fast

Largest Winning Margins

Year	Winner	Lengths
2004	Smarty Jones	11½
1873	Survivor	10
2003	Funny Cide	9¾
1943	Count Fleet	8
1889	Buddhist	8
1991	Hansel	7
1974	Little Current	7
1951	Bold	7
1938	Dauber	7
1968	Forward Pass	6
1935	Omaha	6
1878	Duke of Magenta	6
1979	Spectacular Bid	5½
1948	Citation	5½
1941	Whirlaway	5½
2006	Bernardini	5¼
1950	Hill Prince	5
1912	Colonel Holloway	5

Smallest Winning Margins

Year	Winner	Margin
1989	Sunday Silence	nose
1962	Greek Money	nose
1936	Bold Venture	nose
1934	High Quest	nose
1928	Victorian	nose
1902	Old England	nose
1997	Silver Charm	head
1985	Tank's Prospect	head
1969	Majestic Prince	head
1949	Capot	head
1937	War Admiral	head
1932	Burgoo King	head
1926	Display	head
1922	Pillory	head
1905	Cairngorm	head
1900	Hindus	head

Preakness Odds-On Beaten Favorites

The shortest-priced beaten favorites in the Preakness Stakes were Riva Ridge in 1972 and Fusaichi Pegasus in 2000. Both entered the Preakness off Derby victories and both went off at 3-to-10. Riva Ridge fell to Bee Bee Bee on a sloppy track, and Fusaichi Pegasus finished second to Red Bullet.

Here are the odds-on beaten favorites in the Preakness:

Year	Horse	Odds	Finish
2006	Barbaro	0.50-to-1	DNF
2000	Fusaichi Pegasus	0.30-to-1	2nd
1972	Riva Ridge	0.30-to-1	4th
1939	Gilded Knight- Johnstown entry	0.45-to-1	2nd 5th
1982	Linkage	0.50-to-1	2nd
1989	Easy Goer	0.60-to-1	2nd
1956	Needles	0.60-to-1	2nd
1984	Swale	0.80-to-1	7th
1964	Hill Rise	0.80-to-1	3rd
1976	Honest Pleasure	0.90-to-1	5th
1954	Correlation	0.90-to-1	2nd

Shortest-Priced Preakness Winners

Year	Winner	Odds
1979	Spectacular Bid	0.10-to-1
1948	Citation	0.10-to-1
1943	Count Fleet	0.15-to-1
1953	Native Dancer	0.20-to-1
1973	Secretariat	0.30-to-1
1955	Nashua	0.30-to-1
1937	War Admiral	0.35-to-1
1977	Seattle Slew	0.40-to-1
1934	High Quest	0.45-to-1
1978	Affirmed	0.50-to-1

Longest-Priced Preakness Winners

Year	Winner	Odds
1975	Master Derby	23.40-to-1
1925	Coventry	21.80-to-1
1926	Display	19.35-to-1
1972	Bee Bee Bee	18.70-to-1
1983	Deputed Testamony	14.50-to-1
1974	Little Current	13.10-to-1
2006	Bernardini	12.90-to-1
1924	Nellie Morse	12.10-to-1
1945	Polynesian	12-to-1
1922	Pillory	11.15-to-1
1962	Greek Money	10.90-to-1
1976	Elocutionist	10.10-to-1

Winning Preakness Favorites Since 1979

Year	Winner	Odds
2005	Afleet Alex	3.30-to-1
2004	Smarty Jones	0.70-to-1

Year	Winner	Odds
2003	Funny Cide	1.90-to-1
2002	War Emblem	2.80-to-1
2001	Point Given	2.30-to-1
1995	Timber Country	1.90-to-1
1993	Prairie Bayou	2.20-to-1
1992	Pine Bluff	7-to-2
1987	Alysheba	2-to-1
1981	Pleasant Colony	3-to-2
1979	Spectacular Bid	1-to-10

Preakness Front-Running Winners

The following Preakness winners were on the lead at all points of call, beginning at a quarter-mile (approaching the clubhouse turn). Regarded as speed horses, neither Seattle Slew nor Affirmed led the opening quarter-mile in the Preakness.

Year	Winner	Winning Margin
1996	Louis Quatorze	3¼
1982	Aloma's Ruler	½
1972	Bee Bee Bee	1½
1960	Bally Ache	4
1957	Bold Ruler	2
1954	Hasty Road	neck
1951	Bold	7
1948	Citation	5½
1945	Polynesian	2½
1943	Count Fleet	8
1940	Bimelech	3
1937	War Admiral	head
1934	High Quest	nose
1933	Head Play	4
1920	Man o' War	1½
1919	Sir Barton	4
1918	Jack Hare Jr.	2
1915	Rhine Maiden	1½
1914	Holiday	¾
1911	Watervale	1
1909	Effendi	1
1902	Old England	nose
1899	Half Time	1
1896	Margrave	1
1889	Buddhist	8
1882	Vanguard	neck

Winning Preakness Post Positions

Since 1909, Preakness Stakes winners have come out of the sixth post position 15 times. Only two Preakness winners, Display in 1926 and Point Given in 2001, have come out of the 11th starting position.

Twelve winners have come out of the fourth hole, and 11 each have broken from the second, third, and seventh slots.

Here are the winning post positions since 1909:

Post	Winners	Post	Winners
1	9	4	12
2	11	5	10
3	11	6	15
7	11	10	2
8	10	11	2
9	3	12	3

Preakness Wins by Geldings

Year	Winner
2003	Funny Cide
1993	Prairie Bayou
1914	Holiday
1913	Buskin
1910	Layminster
1907	Don Enrique
1876	Shirley

Geldings were barred from 1920-'34.

Fillies in the Preakness

Since Genuine Risk finished second behind Codex in the controversial 1980 Preakness Stakes, only two other fillies have run in the race. Winning Colors finished a valiant third behind Risen Star after Forty Niner pressed her early, and Excellent Meeting did not finish in the 1999 Preakness.

Four fillies have won the Preakness: Flocarline in 1903, Whimsical in '06, Rhine Maiden in '15, and Nellie Morse in '24.

Here are the 52 fillies to compete in the Preakness:

Year	Horse	Owner	Finish
1999	Excellent Meeting	Golden Eagle Farm	DNF
1988	Winning Colors	Mr. & Mrs. Eugene V. Klein	3rd
1980	Genuine Risk	Diana Firestone	2nd
1939	Ciencia	King Ranch	6th
1937	Jewell Dorsett	J. W. Brown	8th
1935	Nellie Flag	Calumet Farm	7th
1930	Snowflake	W J. Salmon	3rd
1928	Bateau	W. M. Jeffords	8th
1927	Fair Star	Foxcatcher Farm	6th
1925	Maid At Arms	Glen Riddle Farm	11th
1924	**Nellie Morse**	H. C. Fisher	1st
1923	Sally's Alley	W. S. Kilmer	11th
1922	Miss Joy	Montford Jones	10th
1921	Polly Ann	S. L. Jenkins	2nd
	Careful	W. J. Salmon	12th
	Lough Storm	E. B. McLean	13th
1919	Milkmaid	J.K.L. Ross	8th
1918	Mary Maud	C. E. Clements	6th
	Quietude	A. H. Morris	9th
	Kate Bright	A. Neal	3rd
1917	Fruit Cake	E. T. Zollicoffer	4th
	Fox Trot	J. E. Griffith	14th
1915	**Rhine Maiden**	E. F. Whitney	1st
1913	Cadeau	J. G. Oxnard	5th
1912	Jeannette B.	C. C. Smithson	5th
1911	Heatherbroom	E. B. Cassatt	6th
1909	Hill Top	R. Angarola	3rd
	Arondack	Mrs. J. McLaughlin	6th
	Sans Souci II	G. J. Kraus	7th
	Grania	A. Garson	8th

Year	Horse	Owner	Finish
1906	**Whimsical**	T. J. Gaynor	1st
	Content	W. Clay	2nd
	Flip Flap	J. A. Bennet	7th
	Fatinitza	Palestine Stable	8th
1905	Kiamesha	Oneck Stable	2nd
	Coy Maid	Kenilworth Stable	3rd
	Bohemia	Albemarle Stable	5th
	Iota	H. B. Duryea	9th
1904	Possession	C. Oxx	7th
	Flammula	W. H. Kraft	8th
1903	**Flocarline**	M. H. Tichenor & Co.	1st
1902	Barouche	W. H. McCorkle	6th
	Sun Shower	Jere Dunn	7th
1901	Sadie S.	P. H. Sullivan	2nd
1896	Intermission	J. E. McDonald	3rd
	Cassette	A. Clason	4th
1895	Sue Kittie	O. A. Jones	3rd
	Bombazette	C. Littlefield Jr.	7th
1894	Flirt	Manhattan Stable	13th
1881	Aella	George L. Lorillard	6th
1880	Emily F.	J. J. Bevins	3rd
1875	Australind	Harbeck & Johnson	7th

Where Preakness Winners Were Foaled

State	Winners
Kentucky	88
Maryland	8
Florida	7
Pennsylvania	6
Virginia	6
California	4
New Jersey	4
New York	3
Tennessee	2
Ohio	1
Texas	1
Canada	1
England	1

Status of Preakness Winners Since 1970

Year	Winner	Birthdate	Status	Where Stands or Stood	Location	Death Date
2006	Bernardini	3/23/2003	In training			
2005	Afleet Alex	5/9/2002	Stallion	Gainesway	Lexington, Ky.	
2004	Smarty Jones	2/28/2001	Stallion	Three Chimneys Farm	Midway, Ky.	
2003	Funny Cide	4/20/2000	In training			
2002	War Emblem	2/20/1999	Stallion	Shadai Stallion Station	Hokkaido, Japan	
2001	Point Given	3/27/1998	Stallion	Three Chimneys Farm	Midway, Ky.	
2000	Red Bullet	4/13/1997	Stallion	Adena Springs South	Ocala, Fl.	
1999	Charismatic	3/13/1996	Stallion	JBBA Shizunai Stallion Station	Hokkaido, Japan	
1998	Real Quiet	3/7/1995	Stallion	Regal Heir Farms	Grantsville, Pa.	
1997	Silver Charm	2/22/1994	Stallion	JBBA Shizunai Stallion Station	Hokkaido, Japan	
1996	Louis Quatorze	3/13/1993	Stallion	Murmur Farm	Darlington, Md.	
1995	Timber Country	4/12/1992	Stallion	Shadai Stallion Station	Hokkaido, Japan	
1994	Tabasco Cat	4/15/1991	Deceased	JBBA Shizunai Stallion Station	Hokkaido, Japan	3/6/2004
1993	Prairie Bayou	3/14/1990	Deceased			6/5/1993
1992	Pine Bluff	5/10/1989	Stallion	Lane's End	Versailles, Ky.	
1991	Hansel	3/12/1988	Stallion	Lazy Lane Farms	Upperville, Va.	
1990	Summer Squall	3/12/1987	Pensioned	Lane's End	Versailles, Kyy.	
1989	Sunday Silence	3/25/1986	Deceased	Shadai Stallion Station	Hokkaido, Japan	8/19/2002
1988	Risen Star	3/25/1985	Deceased	Walmac International	Lexington, Ky.	3/13/1998
1987	Alysheba	3/3/1984	Stallion	Janadriyah Stud Farm	Aljanadriya, Saudi Arabia	
1986	Snow Chief	3/17/1983	Pensioned	Eagle Oak Ranch	Paso Robles, Ca.	
1985	Tank's Prospect	5/2/1982	Deceased	Venture Farms	Pilot Point, Tx.	3/2/1995
1884	Gate Dancer	3/31/1981	Deceased	Silverleaf Farm	Orange Lake, Fl.	3/6/1998
1983	Deputed Testamony	5/7/1980	Pensioned	Bonita Farm	Darlington, Md.	
1982	Aloma's Ruler	4/21/1979	Deceased	B & B Farm	Monee, Il.	6/21/2003
1981	Pleasant Colony	5/4/1978	Deceased	Lane's End	Versailles, Ky.	12/31/2002
1980	Codex	2/28/1977	Deceased	Tartan Farms	Ocala, Fl.	8/20/1984
1979	Spectacular Bid	2/17/1976	Deceased	Milfer Farm	Unadilla, Ny.	6/9/2003
1978	Affirmed	2/21/1975	Deceased	Jonabell Farm	Lexington, Ky.	1/12/2001
1977	Seattle Slew	2/15/1974	Deceased	Three Chimneys Farm	Midway, Ky.	5/7/2002
1976	Elocutionist	3/4/1973	Deceased	Airdrie Stud	Midway, Ky.	3/30/1995
1975	Master Derby	4/24/1972	Deceased	Not Just Another Horse Farm	Chino, Ca.	1/22/1999
1974	Little Current	4/5/1971	Deceased	Pacific Equine Clinic	Monroe, Wa.	1/19/2003
1973	Secretariat	3/30/1970	Deceased	Claiborne Farm	Paris, Ky.	10/4/1989
1972	Bee Bee Bee	4/3/1969	Deceased	JBBA Stallion Station	Hokkaido, Japan	
1971	Canonero II	4/24/1968	Deceased	Gainesway	Lexington, Ky.	11/11/1981
1970	Personality	5/27/1967	Deceased		Japan	1990

Preakness Stakes

Grade 1, Pimlico Race Course, three-year-olds, 1 3/16 miles, dirt. Held on May 15, 2004, with gross value of $1,000,000. First run in 1873. Weights: colts and geldings, 126 pounds; fillies, 121 pounds.

Year	Winner	Jockey	Second	Third	Strs	Time	Track	1st Purse
2006	**Bernardini**	J. Castellano	Sweetnorthernsaint	Hemingway's Key	9	1:54.65	ft	$600,000
2005	**Afleet Alex**	J. Rose	Scrappy T	Giacomo	14	1:55.04	ft	650,000
2004	**Smarty Jones**	S. Elliott	Rock Hard Ten	Eddington	10	1:55.59	ft	650,000
2003	**‡Funny Cide**	J. Santos	Midway Road	Scrimshaw	10	1:55.61	gd	650,000
2002	**War Emblem**	V. Espinoza	Magic Weisner	Proud Citizen	13	1:56.36	ft	650,000
2001	**Point Given**	G. Stevens	A P Valentine	Congaree	11	1:55.51	ft	650,000
2000	**Red Bullet**	J. Bailey	Fusaichi Pegasus	Impeachment	8	1:56.04	gd	650,000
1999	**Charismatic**	C. Antley	Menifee	Badge	13	1:55.32	ft	650,000
1998	**Real Quiet**	K. Desormeaux	Victory Gallop	Classic Cat	10	1:54.75	ft	**650,000**
1997	**Silver Charm**	G. Stevens	Free House	Captain Bodgit	10	1:54.84	ft	488,150
1996	**Louis Quatorze**	P. Day	Skip Away	Editor's Note	12	**1:53.43**	ft	458,120
1995	**Timber Country**	P. Day	Oliver's Twist	Thunder Gulch	11	1:54.45	ft	446,810
1994	**Tabasco Cat**	P. Day	Go for Gin	Concern	10	1:56.47	ft	447,720
1993	**‡Prairie Bayou**	M. Smith	Cherokee Run	‡El Bakan	12	1:56.61	ft	471,835
1992	**Pine Bluff**	C. McCarron	Alydeed	Casual Lies	14	1:55.60	gd	484,120
1991	**Hansel**	J. Bailey	Corporate Report	Mane Minister	8	1:54	ft	432,770
1990	**Summer Squall**	P. Day	Unbridled	Mister Frisky	9	1:53 3/5	ft	445,900
1989	**Sunday Silence**	P. Valenzuela	Easy Goer	Rock Point	8	1:53 4/5	ft	438,230
1988	**Risen Star**	E. Delahoussaye	Brian's Time	†Winning Colors	9	1:56 1/5	gd	413,700
1987	**Alysheba**	C. McCarron	Bet Twice	Cryptoclearance	9	1:55 4/5	ft	421,100
1986	**Snow Chief**	A. Solis	Ferdinand	Broad Brush	7	1:54 4/5	ft	411,900
1985	**Tank's Prospect**	P. Day	Chief's Crown	Eternal Prince	11	**1:53 2/5**	ft	423,200
1984	**Gate Dancer**	A. Cordero Jr.	Play On	Fight Over	10	1:53 3/5	ft	243,600
1983	**Deputed Testamony**	D. A. Miller Jr.	Desert Wine	High Honors	12	1:55 2/5	sy	251,200
1982	**Aloma's Ruler**	J. Kaenel	Linkage	Cut Away	7	1:55 2/5	ft	209,900
1981	**Pleasant Colony**	J. Velasquez	Bold Ego	Paristo	13	1:54 3/5	ft	200,800
1980	**Codex**	A. Cordero Jr.	†Genuine Risk	Colonel Moran	8	1:54 1/5	ft	180,600
1979	**Spectacular Bid**	R. Franklin	Golden Act	Screen King	5	1:54 1/5	gd	165,300
1978	**AFFIRMED**	S. Cauthen	Alydar	Believe It	7	1:54 2/5	ft	136,200
1977	**SEATTLE SLEW**	J. Cruguet	Iron Constitution	Run Dusty Run	9	1:54 2/5	ft	138,600
1976	**Elocutionist**	J. Lively	Play the Red	Bold Forbes	6	1:55	ft	129,700
1975	**Master Derby**	D. G. McHargue	Foolish Pleasure	Diabolo	10	1:56 2/5	ft	158,100
1974	**Little Current**	M. A. Rivera	‡Neapolitan Way	Cannonade	13	1:54 3/5	gd	156,500
1973	**SECRETARIAT**	R. Turcotte	Sham	Our Native	6	1:54 2/5	ft	129,900
1972	**Bee Bee Bee**	E. Nelson	No Le Hace	Key to the Mint	7	1:55 3/5	sy	135,300
1971	**Canonero II**	G. Avila	Eastern Fleet	Jim French	11	1:54	ft	137,400
1970	**Personality**	E. Belmonte	My Dad George	Silent Screen	14	1:56 1/5	ft	151,300
1969	**Majestic Prince**	W. Hartack	Arts and Letters	Jay Ray	8	1:55 3/5	ft	129,500
1968	**Forward Pass**	I. Valenzuela	Out of the Way	Nodouble	10	1:56 4/5	ft	142,700
1967	**Damascus**	W. Shoemaker	In Reality	Proud Clarion	10	1:55 1/5	ft	151,500
1966	**Kauai King**	D. Brumfield	Stupendous	Amberoid	9	1:55 2/5	ft	129,000
1965	**Tom Rolfe**	R. Turcotte	Dapper Dan	Hail to All	9	1:56 1/5	ft	128,100
1964	**Northern Dancer**	W. Hartack	The Scoundrel	Hill Rise	6	1:56 4/5	ft	124,200
1963	**Candy Spots**	W. Shoemaker	Chateaugay	Never Bend	8	1:56 1/5	ft	127,500
1962	**Greek Money**	J. L. Rotz	Ridan	Roman Line	11	1:56 1/5	ft	135,800
1961	**Carry Back**	J. Sellers	Globemaster	Crozier	9	1:57 3/5	ft	126,200
1960	**Bally Ache**	R. Ussery	Victoria Park	*Celtic Ash	6	1:57 3/5	ft	121,000
1959	**Royal Orbit**	W. Harmatz	Sword Dancer	Dunce	11	1:57	ft	136,200
1958	**Tim Tam**	I. Valenzuela	Lincoln Road	Gone Fishin'	12	1:57 1/5	ft	97,900
1957	**Bold Ruler**	E. Arcaro	Iron Liege	Inside Tract	7	1:56 1/5	ft	66,300
1956	**Fabius**	W. Hartack	Needles	No Regrets	9	1:58 2/5	ft	84,250
1955	**Nashua**	E. Arcaro	Saratoga	Traffic Judge	8	1:54 3/5	ft	67,550
1954	**Hasty Road**	J. Adams	Correlation	Hasseyampa	11	1:57 2/5	ft	91,600
1953	**Native Dancer**	E. Guerin	Jamie K.	Royal Bay Gem	7	1:57 4/5	ft	65,200
1952	**Blue Man**	C. McCreary	‡Jampol	One Count	10	1:57 2/5	ft	86,135
1951	**Bold**	E. Arcaro	Counterpoint	Alerted	8	1:56 2/5	ft	83,110
1950	**Hill Prince**	E. Arcaro	Middleground	Dooly	6	1:59 1/5	sl	56,115
1949	**Capot**	T. Atkinson	Palestinian	Noble Impulse	9	1:56	ft	79,985
1948	**CITATION**	E. Arcaro	Vulcan's Forge	Bovard	4	2:02 2/5	hy	91,870
1947	**Faultless**	D. Dodson	On Trust	Phalanx	11	1:59	ft	98,005
1946	**ASSAULT**	W. Mehrtens	Lord Boswell	Hampden	10	2:01 2/5	ft	96,620
1945	**Polynesian**	W. D. Wright	Hoop, Jr.	‡Darby Dieppe	9	1:58 4/5	ft	66,170
1944	**Pensive**	C. McCreary	Platter	‡Stir Up	7	1:59 1/5	ft	60,075
1943	**COUNT FLEET**	J. Longden	Blue Swords	Vincentive	4	1:57 2/5	gd	43,190
1942	**Alsab**	B. James	dh-Requested	dh-Sun Again	10	1:57	ft	58,175
1941	**WHIRLAWAY**	E. Arcaro	King Cole	Our Boots	8	1:58 4/5	gd	49,365
1940	**Bimelech**	F. A. Smith	Mioland	Gallahadion	9	1:58 3/5	ft	53,230

Year	Winner	Jockey	Second	Third	Strs	Time	Track	1st Purse
1939	**Challedon**	G. Seabo	Gilded Knight	Volitant	6	1:59⅘	my	53,710
1938	**Dauber**	M. Peters	Cravat	Menow	9	1:59⅘	sy	51,875
1937	**WAR ADMIRAL**	C. Kurtsinger	Pompoon	Flying Scot	8	1:58⅖	gd	45,600
1936	**Bold Venture**	G. Woolf	Granville	Jean Bart	11	1:59	ft	27,325
1935	**OMAHA**	W. Saunders	Firethorn	Psychic Bid	8	1:58⅖	ft	25,325
1934	**High Quest**	R. Jones	Cavalcade	Discovery	7	1:58⅕	ft	25,175
1933	**Head Play**	C. Kurtsinger	Ladysman	Utopian	10	2:02	sl	26,850
1932	**Burgoo King**	E. James	Tick On	Boatswain	9	1:59⅘	ft	50,375
1931	**Mate**	G. Ellis	Twenty Grand	Ladder	7	1:59	ft	48,225
1930	**GALLANT FOX**	E. Sande	Crack Brigade	†Snowflake	11	2:00⅗	ft	51,925
1929	**Dr. Freeland**	L. Schaefer	Minotaur	African	11	2:01⅗	ft	52,325
1928	**Victorian**	R. Workman	Toro	Solace	**18**	2:00⅕	ft	60,000
1927	**Bostonian**	A. Abel	Sir Harry	Whiskery	12	2:01⅗	gd	53,100
1926	**Display**	J. Malben	Blondin	Mars	13	1:59⅘	ft	53,625
1925	**Coventry**	C. Kummer	‡Backbone	Almadel	12	1:59	ft	52,700
1924	**†Nellie Morse**	J. Merimee	Transmute	Mad Play	15	1:57⅕	sy	54,000
1923	**Vigil**	B. Marinelli	Gen. Thatcher	‡Rialto	13	1:53⅗	ft	52,000
1922	**Pillory**	L. Morris	Hea	June Grass	12	1:51⅗	ft	51,000
1921	**Broomspun**	F. Coltiletti	†Polly Ann	Jeg	14	1:54⅕	sl	43,000
1920	**Man o' War**	C. Kummer	Upset	Wildair	9	1:51⅗	ft	23,000
1919	**SIR BARTON**	J. Loftus	Eternal	Sweep On	12	1:53	ft	24,500
1918	***War Cloud**	J. Loftus	Sunny Slope	*Lanius	10	1:53⅗	gd	12,250
	Jack Hare, Jr.	C. Peak	The Porter	†Kate Bright	6	1:53⅖	gd	11,250
1917	**Kalitan**	E. Haynes	Al. M. Dick	‡Kentucky Boy	14	1:54⅖	ft	4,800
1916	**Damrosch**	L. McAtee	Greenwood	Achievement	9	1:54⅘	ft	1,380
1915	**†Rhine Maiden**	D. Hoffman	Half Rock	Runes	6	1:58	my	1,275
1914	**‡Holiday**	A. Schuttinger	Brave Cunarder	Defendum	6	1:53⅘	ft	1,355
1913	**‡Buskin**	J. Butwell	Kleburne	‡Barnegat	8	1:53⅖	ft	1,670
1912	**Col. Holloway**	C. Turner	Bwana Tumbo	Tipsand	7	1:56⅗	sl	1,450
1911	**Watervale**	E. Dugan	Zeus	‡The Nigger	7	1:51	ft	2,700
1910	**‡Layminster**	R. Estep	Dalhousie	Sager	12	1:40⅕	ft	2,800
1909	**Effendi**	W. Doyle	Fashion Plate	†Hill Top	10	1:39⅘	ft	2,725
1908	**Royal Tourist**	E. Dugan	Live Wire	‡Robert Cooper	4	1:46⅖	ft	2,455
1907	**‡Don Enrique**	G. Mountain	Ethon	Zambesi	7	1:45⅖	hy	2,260
1906	**†Whimsical**	W. Miller	†Content	Larabie	10	1:45	ft	2,355
1905	**Cairngorm**	W. Davis	†Kiamesha	†Coy Maid	10	1:45⅘	ft	2,145
1904	**Bryn Mawr**	E. Hildebrand	Wotan	‡Dolly Spanker	10	1:44⅕	ft	2,355
1903	**†Flocarline**	W. Gannon	Mackey Dwyer	Rightful	6	1:44⅘	ft	1,875
1902	**Old England**	L. Jackson	Major Daingerfield	Namtor	7	1:45⅘	hy	2,240
1901	**The Parader**	F. Landry	†Sadie S.	Dr. Barlow	5	1:47⅕	hy	1,605
1900	**Hindus**	H. Spencer	*Sarmatian	Ten Candles	10	1:48⅖	ft	1,900
1899	**Half Time**	R. Clawson	Filigrane	Lackland	3	1:47	ft	1,580
1898	**Sly Fox**	W. Simms	The Huguenot	Nuto	4	1:49¾	gd	1,450
1897	**Paul Kauvar**	C. Thorpe	Elkin	On Deck	7	1:51¼	sy	1,420
1896	**Margrave**	H. Griffin	Hamilton II	*Intermission	4	1:51	ft	1,350
1895	**Belmar**	F. Taral	‡April Fool	†Sue Kittie	7	1:50½	ft	1,350
1894	**Assignee**	F. Taral	Potentate	‡Ed Kearney	14	1:49¼	ft	1,830
1890	**Montague**	J. Martin	Philosophy	Barrister	4	2:36¾	ft	1,215
1889	**Buddhist**	G. Anderson	Japhet	———	2	2:17½	ft	1,130
1888	**Refund**	F. Littlefield	Judge Murray	Glendale	4	2:49	hy	1,185
1887	**Dunboyne**	W. Donohue	Mahony	Raymond	4	2:39½	ft	1,675
1886	**The Bard**	S. Fisher	Eurus	Elkwood	5	2:45	gd	2,050
1885	**Tecumseh**	J. McLaughlin	Wickham	‡John C.	4	2:49	hy	2,160
1884	**Knight of Ellerslie**	S. Fisher	Welcher	———	2	2:39½	ft	1,905
1883	**Jacobus**	G. Barbee	Parnell	———	2	2:42½	gd	1,635
1882	**Vanguard**	T. Costello	Heck	‡Col. Watson	3	2:44½	gd	1,250
1881	**Saunterer**	T. Costello	‡Compensation	Baltic	6	2:40½	gd	1,950
1880	**Grenada**	L. Hughes	Oden	†Emily F.	5	2:40½	ft	2,000
1879	**Harold**	L. Hughes	Jerico	‡Rochester	6	2:40½	ft	2,550
1878	**Duke of Magenta**	C. Holloway	Bayard	‡Albert	3	2:41¾	gd	2,100
1877	**Cloverbrook**	C. Holloway	Bombast	Lucifer	4	2:45½	sl	1,600
1876	**‡Shirley**	G. Barbee	Rappahannock	Compliments	8	2:44¾	gd	1,950
1875	**Tom Ochiltree**	L. Hughes	Viator	†Bay Final	9	2:43½	sl	1,900
1874	**Culpepper**	W. Donohue	*King Amadeus	Scratch	6	2:56½	my	1,900
1873	**Survivor**	G. Barbee	John Boulger	Artist	7	2:43	sl	1,800

†—filly; ‡—gelding; *—imported horse; dh-dead heat; bold indicates records set in starters, time, and 1st purse; Triple Crown winners are in all capitalized letters.

1894, 1½ miles; 1889, 1¼ miles; 1894-1900,1908, 1 1/16 miles; 1901-'07, 1 mile and 70 yards; 1909,1910, 1 mile; 1911-'24, 1⅛ miles. 1891-'93, not run. 1890 held at Morris Park, New York; 1894-1908 Gravesend, New York. Run in two divisions in 1918. 1973-present, Grade 1. Dancer's Image disqualified from third to eighth in 1968. Secretariat's time in 1973 originally reported as 1:55; hand-timed by *Daily Racing Form* clockers in 1:53⅖

Belmont Stakes History

Unforgettable horses, jockeys, and trainers punctuate the glorious history of the Belmont Stakes, a compelling race if only because two three-year-olds carrying equal weights of 126 pounds can battle its testing 1½-mile distance and be separated at the finish line by inches. It has happened more than once in the final race of the Triple Crown.

First run in 1867, the Belmont Stakes is named for August Belmont I, a prominent investment banker and Thoroughbred owner who was president of the American Jockey Club. The Belmont Stakes preceded the Preakness by six years and the Kentucky Derby by eight. Francis Morris's filly Ruthless won the first Belmont Stakes, which was contested at Jerome Park in the Bronx on a Thursday afternoon at 1⅝ miles, "cleverly by a head" over De Coursey. The purse was $2,500.

The first 23 runnings of the Belmont Stakes were held on a ribbon-like course at Jerome Park. In 1890, the Belmont Stakes moved to Morris Park, a 1⅜-mile track a few miles east of what is now Van Cortland Park in the Bronx.

Fifteen years later, in 1905, the Belmont Stakes had a new home, Belmont Park, but the race was not run in 1911 and '12 because antigambling legislation shut down racing in New York in those years. Unlike the Belmont's current counterclockwise path, the race was run clockwise—like many English and European races—until 1921. By then, two great champions with a unique link had won the race known as the Test of Champions in strikingly different styles.

Colin is one of only two undefeated American champions with more than five starts in the past 96 years (the other is Personal Ensign). Colin nearly lost his unbeaten record because of a mistake by Joe Notter, his jockey in the 1908 Belmont Stakes. In a driving rainstorm so intense that no final time was taken, Notter misjudged the finish line on Colin, and his five-length lead was shaved to a head by a fast-closing Fair Play.

Colin continued to a perfect 15-for-15 record. Fair Play sired Man o' War, the once-beaten champion who won the Belmont by 20 lengths over his only challenger, Donnacona, at odds of 0.04-to-1.

Gallant Fox is one of only two Triple Crown winners who was not the favorite in the Belmont Stakes. The previous year, Whichone had beaten Gallant Fox in the 1929 Futurity and also had won the Champagne and Saratoga Special Stakes. Whichone missed the Kentucky Derby and Preakness Stakes the following spring because of knee problems, but he returned to win the Withers Stakes and went off the 7-to-10 favorite in the 1930 Belmont Stakes.

Belmont Attendance

Year	Attendance	Year	Attendance
2006	61,168	1987	64,772
2005	62,274	1986	42,555
2004	120,139	1985	43,446
2003	101,864	1984	46,430
2002	103,222	1983	56,677
2001	73,857	1982	46,050
2000	67,810	1981	61,200
1999	85,818	1980	58,883
1998	80,162	1979	59,073
1997	70,682	1978	65,417
1996	40,797	1977	71,026
1995	37,171	1976	58,788
1994	42,695	1975	60,611
1993	45,037	1974	52,153
1992	50,204	1973	67,605
1991	51,766	1972	54,635
1990	50,123	1971	82,694
1989	64,959	1970	54,299
1988	56,223		

Gallant Fox had won the Wood Memorial Stakes, Preakness, and Kentucky Derby (in that order), but he went off at odds of 8-to-5 in the field of just four in the Belmont. Gallant Fox uncharacteristically took the lead immediately and scampered to a surprisingly easy three-length victory in a stakes record of 2:31⅗ for 1½ miles.

Gallant Fox's winning Belmont Stakes margin paled next to the 25-length romp of Count Fleet, who completed his 1943 Triple Crown at odds of 1-to-20 "galloping," according to the Belmont chart. Three years later, Assault went off as the 7-to-5 second choice in the Belmont but, like Gallant Fox, he completed his Triple Crown with a three-length victory. Favored Lord Boswell finished fifth in the field of seven at 1.35-to-1.

In 1948, Citation cruised to an eight-length win in the Belmont to become the fourth Triple Crown winner in eight years. There would not be another for a quarter-century.

Plenty of upsets occurred in those 25 years from Citation to Secretariat, but none was more shocking than Sherluck's 1961 victory over 2-to-5 favorite Carry Back at odds of 65.05-to-1, which resulted in a then-record Belmont Stakes win payout of $132.10.

Carry Back, who finished seventh, joined Pensive (1944) and Tim Tam ('58) as Kentucky Derby and Preakness winners who lost in the Belmont Stakes. Five more followed Carry Back in the next ten years: Northern Dancer (1964), Kauai King ('66), Forward Pass ('68), Majestic Prince ('69), and Canonero II, who attracted 82,694, then the largest crowd in

Belmont Park history, on June 5, 1971, in his fourth-place finish to Pass Catcher, a 34.50-to-1 longshot.

Just when everybody thought there might not ever be another Triple Crown winner—the tremendous growth in the number of foals was frequently cited as a reason—along came Secretariat. To provide a perspective on his 31-length 1973 Belmont Stakes victory in a world record 2:24, consider that the next-fastest winners, Easy Goer in '89 and A.P. Indy in '92, went in 2:26, the equivalent of ten lengths slower.

Secretariat's 1973 Triple Crown was followed by two more in the ensuing five years: Seattle Slew, who in '77 became the first undefeated Triple Crown winner, and Affirmed one year later.

The Triple Crowns of 1977 and '78 were starkly different. Seattle Slew dominated his generation, while Affirmed was pushed to the limit by his nemesis, Alydar. The final sixteenth of a mile of the 1978 Belmont Stakes, with Affirmed on the inside under Steve Cauthen and Alydar at his throat under Jorge Velasquez, was a dramatic test of will in which Affirmed prevailed by a head. That was not the closest Belmont Stakes finish. Colin had won by the same margin, and Granville in 1936, Jaipur in '62, and Victory Gallop in '98 prevailed by a nose.

Spectacular Bid had a shot at becoming the third consecutive Triple Crown winner in 1979 but checked in third at 3-to-10 to Coastal in the Belmont after reportedly stepping on a safety pin that morning. Two years later, Derby and Preakness winner Pleasant Colony failed to sweep the series, finishing third to Summing.

Then, Woody Stephens took over. People questioned the Racing Hall of Fame trainer's judgment when he announced that Conquistador Cielo, who had just routed older horses by 7¼ lengths in the one-mile Metropolitan Handicap (G1) five days earlier, would start in the Belmont Stakes. Stephens knew his horse, and the colt won the Belmont by 14 lengths under Laffit Pincay Jr. Stephens-trained Caveat won the 1983 Belmont, and ill-fated Swale won in '84. Then Stephens ran first and second with Creme Fraiche and Stephan's Odyssey in 1985. In 1986, Stephens won his fifth consecutive Belmont Stakes with Danzig Connection, at odds of 8-to-1.

Three consecutive blowouts occurred in the late 1980s, with Bet Twice winning by 14 lengths over Derby and Preakness winner Alysheba (who finished fourth) in '87, Risen Star adding to his Preakness triumph with a 14¾-length Belmont romp, and Easy Goer avenging his Derby and Preakness losses to Sunday Silence by winning the '89 Belmont Stakes by eight lengths.

The middle years of the 1990s were dominated by Racing Hall of Fame trainer D. Wayne Lukas, who secured consecutive victories with Tabasco Cat (1994), Thunder Gulch ('95), and Editor's Note ('96).

Julie Krone became the first female rider to win a Triple Crown race when she guided Colonial Affair to a 2¼-length win in the 1993 Belmont for trainer Flint S. "Scotty" Schulhofer. The Racing Hall of Fame trainer collected his second Belmont victory in 1999 when Lemon Drop Kid denied Lukas-trained Charismatic a Triple Crown before a then-record crowd of 85,818.

Charismatic's loss marked the third straight year that a Triple Crown was on the line. In 1997, Silver Charm, trained by Bob Baffert, led 100 yards before the finish but was passed by Touch Gold, who won by three-quarters of a length. One year later, Baffert-trained Real Quiet looked home free in the Belmont before weakening late and losing by a nose in the final stride to Victory Gallop. Two years later, Baffert recorded his first Belmont win with Point Given's 2001 victory before 73,857, the largest Belmont Stakes crowd without a Triple Crown on the line. A Triple Crown was at stake in each of the next three years, but War Emblem, Funny Cide, and Smarty Jones were defeated. A record crowd of 120,139 turned out in 2004 for Smarty Jones's bid.—*Bill Heller*

Belmont Trophy and Tray

The Belmont Stakes trophy is a solid silver bowl originally crafted by Tiffany's, and it was the trophy that August Belmont I's Fenian won in 1869 after taking the third running of the race. The Belmont family presented it as a perpetual trophy for the Belmont Stakes in 1926, and each winning owner is given the option of keeping the trophy for the year his horse wins. Atop the cover of the trophy is a silver figure of Fenian. The bowl is supported by three horses representing influential sires Eclipse, Herod, and Matchem. The winning owner also receives a permanent large silver tray with the names of previous Belmont Stakes winners engraved on it. Trays also are presented to the winning trainer, jockey, exercise rider, and groom.

Carnation Blanket

The Kentucky Derby (G1) has its roses, the Preakness Stakes (G1) has ersatz black-eyed Susans, and the carnation is the official flower of the Belmont Stakes (G1). Imported from either California or Colombia, between 300 and 400 carnations are glued onto a green velveteen backing to create the blanket that adorns the Belmont winner.

From "Sidewalks" to "New York, New York"

Until 1997, the song that escorted the Belmont Stakes field onto the track was "Sidewalks of New York," written in 1894 by Charles Lawlor, a vaudevillian, and James W. Blake, a hat salesman and lyricist. More than one version of the lyrics exist, but the best-known stanza is:

East Side, West Side, all around the town
The kids sang "ring around rosie," "London Bridge is falling down"
Boys and girls together, me and Mamie O'Rourke
We tripped the light fantastic on the sidewalks of New York.

"New York, New York" is of much more recent vintage, written by John Kander and Fred Ebb in 1977 for the movie of the same name. Composer Kander and lyricist Ebb were one of Broadway's most successful teams; their credits included *Cabaret, Funny Lady, Woman of the Year,* and *Zorba. New York, New York,* not regarded as one of director Martin Scorsese's better films, starred Liza Minelli, who performed the song in the movie, and Robert de Niro. The song subsequently was recorded by Frank Sinatra and rose to number 32 on the hits chart in 1980.

Its lyrics:

Start spreading the news
I'm leaving today
I want to be a part of it, New York, New York
These vagabond shoes
Are longing to stray
And make a brand new start of it
New York, New York
I want to wake up in the city that never sleeps
To find I'm king of the hill, top of the heap
These little town blues
Are melting away
I'll make a brand new start of it
In old New York
If I can make it there
I'll make it anywhere
It's up to you, New York, New York.

Belmont Trivia

- The Belmont Stakes has not always been contested at 1½ miles. Prior to 1874, the race was run at 1⅝ miles. The Belmont was held at 1¼ miles from 1890 through '92, and in '95, 1904, and 1905. It was 1⅛ miles in 1893 and '94; at 1⅜ miles 1896 through 1903 and from 1906 through '25. The Belmont was run at 1½ miles from 1874 through '89 and from 1926 to the present.
- The Belmont Stakes was run at Aqueduct from 1963 through '67 while Belmont Park was being rebuilt.
- The smallest Belmont Stakes field was two. It happened in 1887, '88, '92, 1910, and '20. The largest Belmont Stakes field was 15 in 1983.
- Jazil was the 53rd bay to win the Belmont. Fifty winners have been chestnut, 29 dark bay or brown, three black, two gray, and one roan.

Belmont Wagering, 1980-2006

Year	Winner	On-Track Handle	OTB Handle	Simulcasting	Total Handle
2006	Jazil	$2,324,567		$42,781,075	$45,105,642
2005	Afleet Alex	2,736,948		45,312,800	48,049,748
2004	Birdstone	4,331,463		59,340,243	63,671,706
2003	Empire Maker	3,440,151		44,642,048	48,082,199
2002	Sarava	3,753,983		54,503,406	58,257,389
2001	Point Given	2,707,574		34,959,635	37,667,209
2000	Commendable	2,046,835		28,354,418	30,401,253
1999	Lemon Drop Kid	3,143,508		40,839,558	43,983,066
1998	Victory Gallop	2,521,457		25,864,228	28,385,685
1997	Touch Gold	2,229,860		22,546,860	24,776,720
1996	Editor's Note	1,639,134		18,714,712	20,353,846
1995	Thunder Gulch	1,571,891	$3,672,079	15,310,597	20,554,567
1994	Tabasco Cat	1,717,684	3,299,616	13,848,321	18,865,621
1993	Colonial Affair	2,793,320	4,567,493	17,472,438	24,833,251
1992	A.P. Indy	2,058,039	4,365,205	12,581,848	19,005,092
1991	Hansel	2,222,049	5,206,757	12,877,258	20,306,064
1990	Go and Go (Ire)	1,588,767	3,832,777	8,985,594	14,407,138
1989	Easy Goer	2,565,156	4,062,020	12,269,211	18,896,387
1988	Risen Star	1,439,045	4,135,493	8,685,408	14,259,946
1987	Bet Twice	2,703,924	6,794,377	8,242,290	17,740,591
1986	Danzig Connection	2,038,445	4,469,831	5,869,281	12,377,557
1985	Creme Fraiche	1,840,198	4,982,800	4,518,679	11,341,677
1884	Swale	2,063,135	5,540,202	4,080,482	11,683,819
1983	Caveat	1,530,010	3,724,455	2,961,256	8,215,721
1982	Conquistador Cielo	1,201,491	2,248,366	2,488,107	5,937,964
1981	Smarten	1,420,517	3,204,415	465,950	5,090,882
1980	Temperence Hill	1,603,057	3,769,868		5,372,925

Beginning in 1996, figures for OTB and simulcasting handle were combined.

- Thirty-six of the 137 runnings of the Belmont have been run on off tracks, the most recent in 2003 when Empire Maker won.
- The 2001 Belmont drew a crowd of 73,857, the largest for the race without a horse going for the Triple Crown and seventh highest behind 120,139 in 2004, 103,222 in '02, 101,864 in 2003, 85,818 in 1999, 82,694 in '71, and 80,162 in '98.
- Sarava was the 17th Belmont winner whose name began with the letter 'S'. Twenty Belmont winners had names beginning with 'C'.

Leading Belmont Owners by Wins

6 **James R. Keene:** Spendthrift, 1879; Commando, 1901; Delhi, 1904; Peter Pan, 1907; Colin 1908; Sweep, 1910.
Belair Stud: Gallant Fox, 1930; Faireno, 1932; Omaha, 1935; Granville, 1936; Johnstown, 1939; Nashua, 1955.
5 **Mike and Phil Dwyer:** George Kinney, 1883; Panique, 1884; Inspector B., 1886; Hanover, 1887; Sir Dixon, 1888.
4 **Glen Riddle Farms:** Man o' War, 1920; American Flag, 1925; Crusader, 1926; War Admiral, 1937.
Greentree Stable: Twenty Grand, 1931; Shut Out, 1942; Capot, 1949; Stage Door Johnny, 1968.
3 **August Belmont II:** Masterman, 1902; Friar Rock, 1916; *Hourless, 1917.
King Ranch: Assault, 1946; Middleground, 1950; High Gun, 1954.

Owners with Most Belmont Starters

Name	Starts	Wins	2nd	3rd	Unplaced
C. V. Whitney	20	2	2	4	12
August Belmont I	19	2	4	4	9
Greentree Stable	15	4	1	2	8
Belair Stud	14	6	0	1	7
King Ranch	14	3	2	1	8
James R. Keene	12	6	2	1	3
Calumet Farm	11	2	5	2	2
Brookmeade Stable	11	2	1	1	7
Wheatley Stable	11	0	0	3	8
George D. Widener	10	1	3	2	4
George Lorillard	8	3	3	0	2
Marcus Daly	8	1	1	2	4
Pierre Lorillard	8	1	0	3	4
Ogden Phipps	8	1	0	1	6
Dwyer Brothers	7	5	1	0	1
August Belmont II	7	3	2	0	2
D. McDaniel	7	3	0	0	4
Darby Dan Farm	7	2	0	1	4
Meadow Stable	7	2	0	1	4
Walter M. Jeffords	7	1	1	0	5
Buckland Stable	7	0	0	1	6

Leading Belmont Breeders by Wins

7 **A. J. Alexander:** Harry Bassett, 1871; Joe Daniels, 1872; Springbok, 1873; Duke of Magenta, 1878; Spendthrift, 1879; Grenada, 1880; Burlington, 1890.
5 **Belair Stud:** Gallant Fox, 1930; Faireno, 1932; Omaha, 1935; Granville, 1936; Nashua, 1955.
J. R. Keene: Commando, 1901; Delhi, 1904; Peter Pan, 1907; Colin, 1908; Sweep, 1910.
John E. Madden: Joe Madden, 1909; The Finn, 1915; Sir Barton, 1919; Grey Lag, 1921; Zev, 1923.
4 **August Belmont II:** Masterman, 1902; Friar Rock, 1916; *Hourless, 1917; Man o' War, 1920.
Greentree: Twenty Grand, 1931; Shut Out, 1942; Capot, 1949; Stage Door Johnny, 1968.
H. P. Whitney: Tanya, 1905; Burgomaster, 1906; Prince Eugene, 1913; *Johren, 1918.
3 **W. S. Farish:** Bet Twice, 1987; A.P. Indy, 1991; Lemon Drop Kid, 1999.
Sam Riddle: American Flag, 1925; Crusader, 1926; War Admiral, 1937.

Leading Belmont Trainers by Wins

8 **James Rowe:** George Kinney, 1883; Panique, 1884; Commando, 1901; Delhi, 1904; Peter Pan, 1907; Colin, 1908; Sweep, 1910; Prince Eugene, 1913.
7 **Sam Hildreth:** Jean Bereaud, 1899; Joe Madden, 1909; Friar Rock, 1916; Hourless, 1917; Grey Lag, 1921; Zev, 1923; Mad Play, 1924.
6 **James "Sunny Jim" Fitzsimmons:** Gallant Fox, 1930; Faireno, 1932; Omaha, 1935; Granville, 1936; Johnstown, 1939; Nashua, 1955.
5 **W. C. "Woody" Stephens:** Conquistador Cielo, 1982; Caveat, 1983; Swale, 1984; Creme Fraiche, 1985; Danzig Connection, 1986.
4 **Max Hirsch:** Vito, 1928; Assault, 1946; Middleground, 1950; High Gun, 1954.
D. Wayne Lukas: Tabasco Cat, 1994; Thunder Gulch, 1995; Editor's Note, 1996; Commendable, 2000.
R. W. Walden: Duke of Magenta, 1878; Grenada, 1880; Saunterer, 1881; *Bowling Brook, 1898.
3 **Elliott Burch:** Sword Dancer, 1959; Quadrangle, 1964; Arts and Letters, 1969.
John M. Gaver: Shut Out, 1942; Capot, 1949; Stage Door Johnny, 1968.
Lucien Laurin: Amberoid, 1966; Riva Ridge, 1972; Secretariat, 1973.
Frank McCabe: Inspector B., 1886; Hanover, 1887; Sir Dixon, 1888.
David McDaniel: Harry Bassett, 1871; Joe Daniels, 1872; Springbok, 1873.
2 **Tom Barry:** *Cavan, 1958; *Celtic Ash, 1960.
Flint S. "Scotty" Schulhofer: Colonial Affair, 1993; Lemon Drop Kid, 1999.
Sylvester Veitch: Phalanx, 1947; Counterpoint, 1951.
Oscar White: Pavot, 1945; One Count, 1952.

Trainers with Most Belmont Starters Since 1972

Name	Starts	Wins	2nd	3rd	Unplaced
D. Wayne Lukas	19	4	0	1	14
Nicholas P. Zito	17	1	6	2	8
LeRoy Jolley	10	0	2	1	7
John P. Campo	10	0	0	1	9
Woodford C. Stephens	9	5	1	1	2
Flint S. Schulhofer	7	2	1	9	4
Bob Baffert	7	1	2	0	4
Lou Rondinello	6	1	0	2	3
C. R. McGaughey III	5	1	1	1	2
Alfredo Callejas	5	0	0	0	5

Female Trainers in the Belmont

Seven women have trained Belmont Stakes starters, and the best finish was that by Dianne Carpenter-trained Kingpost, who finished a distant second behind Risen Star in 1988. In 2002, owner-breeder-trainer Nancy Alberts saddled Magic Weisner for a fourth-place finish behind upset winner Sarava.

Women who have trained Belmont starters:

Year	Trainer	Horse	Finish
2003	Linda Rice	Supervisor	5th
2002	Nancy Alberts	Magic Weisner	4th
1996	Cynthia Reese	In Contention	9th
1992	Shelley Riley	Casual Lies	5th
1988	Dianne Carpenter	Kingpost	2nd
1985	Patricia Johnson	Fast Account	4th
1984	Sarah Lundy	Minstrel Star	11th

Leading Belmont Jockeys by Wins

6 **Eddie Arcaro:** Whirlaway, 1941; Shut Out, 1942; Pavot, 1945; Citation, 1948; One Count, 1952; Nashua, 1955.

James McLaughlin: Forester, 1882; George Kinney, 1883; Panique, 1884; Inspector B., 1886; Hanover, 1887; Sir Dixon, 1888.

5 **Earle Sande:** Grey Lag, 1921; Zev, 1923; Mad Play, 1924; Chance Shot, 1927; Gallant Fox, 1930.

Bill Shoemaker: Gallant Man, 1957; Sword Dancer, 1959; Jaipur, 1962; Damascus, 1967; Avatar, 1975.

3 **Braulio Baeza:** Sherluck, 1961; Chateaugay, 1963; Arts and Letters, 1969.

Pat Day: Easy Goer, 1989; Tabasco Cat, 1994; Commendable, 2000.

Laffit Pincay Jr.: Conquistador Cielo, 1982; Caveat, 1983; Swale, 1984.

James Stout: Granville, 1936; Pasteurized, 1938; Johnstown, 1939.

Jockeys with Most Belmont Mounts Since 1938

Name	Starts	Wins	2nd	3rd	Unplaced
Eddie Arcaro	22	6	3	2	11
Angel Cordero Jr.	21	1	2	4	14
Jerry Bailey	20	2	1	1	16
Pat Day	17	3	2	2	10
Braulio Baeza	14	3	2	0	9
Laffit Pincay Jr.	13	3	3	0	7
Jorge Velasquez	13	0	1	5	7
Bill Shoemaker	11	5	1	1	4
Eric Guerin	11	2	2	1	6
Chris McCarron	11	2	1	2	6
Eddie Maple	11	2	0	1	8
Jose Santos	14	1	2	1	10
Jacinto Vasquez	10	0	3	1	6
Mike Smith	10	0	1	1	8
Gary Stevens	9	3	1	1	4
Ron Turcotte	9	2	1	9	6
Jorge Chavez	9	0	0	1	8
Ruben Hernandez	8	1	0	0	7
Bobby Ussery	8	0	1	0	7
John Sellers	7	1	1	1	4

Only One Female Jockey in Belmont

Julie Krone, the only female jockey in the Racing Hall of Fame, is the only female rider to have had a mount in the Belmont. Krone won the 1993 Belmont Stakes aboard Colonial Affair. She retired in 1999 but resumed her career in 2002 and retired in 2004.

Krone's Belmont Stakes mounts:

Year	Mount	Finish
1996	South Salem	DNF
1995	Star Standard	2nd
1993	**Colonial Affair**	1st
1992	Colony Light	6th
1991	Subordinated Debt	9th

Leading Sires of Belmont Winners

5 **Lexington:** General Duke, 1868; Kingfisher, 1870; Harry Bassett, 1871; Duke of Magenta, 1878; Saunterer, 1881.

3 ***Australian:** Joe Daniels, 1872; Springbok, 1873; Spendthrift, 1879.

Fair Play: Man o' War, 1920; Mad Play, 1924; Chance Shot, 1927.

Man o' War: American Flag, 1925; Crusader, 1926; War Admiral, 1937.

2 **Commando:** Peter Pan, 1907; Colin, 1908.

Count Fleet: Counterpoint, 1951; One Count, 1952.

Gallant Fox: Omaha, 1935; Granville, 1936.

Hamburg: Burgomaster, 1906; Prince Eugene, 1913.

***Nasrullah:** Nashua, 1955; Jaipur, 1962.

***Negofol:** *Hourless, 1917; Vito, 1928.

Seattle Slew: Swale, 1984; A.P. Indy, 1992.

***Star Shoot:** Sir Barton, 1919; Grey Lag, 1921.

Belmont Winners Who Sired Belmont Winners

3 **Man o' War (1920):** American Flag, 1925; Crusader, 1926; War Admiral, 1937.

2 **Commando (1901):** Peter Pan, 1907; Colin, 1908.

Gallant Fox (1930): Omaha, 1935; Granville, 1936.

Count Fleet (1943): Counterpoint, 1951; One Count, 1952.

Seattle Slew (1977): Swale, 1984; A.P. Indy, 1992.

1 **Duke of Magenta (1878):** Eric, 1889.

Spendthrift (1879): Hastings, 1896.

Hastings (1896): Masterman, 1902.

The Finn (1915): Zev, 1923.

Sword Dancer (1959): Damascus, 1967.

Secretariat (1973): Risen Star, 1988.

Derby-Preakness Winners Not Favored in the Belmont

Thirty-one three-year-olds swept the Kentucky Derby and Preakness to earn a chance at the Triple Crown. Ironically, the only two who were not the betting favorites in the Belmont Stakes became Triple Crown champions.

Gallant Fox in 1930 was the 8-to-5 second choice to 4-to-5 Whichone, who finished second. Assault in 1946 was the 7-to-5 second choice to 1.35-to-1 Lord Boswell, who finished fifth.

Fastest Belmont Times

Year	Winner	Time	Cond.
1973	Secretariat	2:24	Fast
1989	Easy Goer	2:26	Fast
1992	A.P. Indy	2:26	Good
1988	Risen Star	2:26⅖	Fast
2001	Point Given	2:26.56	Fast
1957	Gallant Man	2:26⅗	Fast
1978	Affirmed	2:26⅘	Fast
1994	Tabasco Cat	2:26.82	Fast

Fastest Fractions

Quarter-Mile	:23	Another Review, 1991
Half-Mile	:46⅕	Secretariat, 1973
Six Furlongs	1:09⅘	Secretariat, 1973
One Mile	1:34⅕	Secretariat, 1973
1¼ Miles	1:59	Secretariat, 1973

Slowest Winning Times

Year	Winner	Time	Cond.
1970	High Echelon	2:34	Sloppy
1928	Vito	2:33⅕	Fast
1932	Faireno	2:32⅘	Fast
1929	Blue Larkspur	2:32⅘	Sloppy
1933	Hurryoff	2:32⅗	Fast
1927	Chance Shot	2:32⅖	Fast
1944	Bounding Home	2:32⅕	Fast
1926	Crusader	2:32⅕	Fast
1995	Thunder Gulch	2:32.02	Good
1930	Gallant Fox	2:31⅗	Fast
2000	Commendable	2:31.19	Fast
1941	Whirlaway	2:31	Fast

Evolution of Belmont Stakes Record at 1½ Miles

Year	Winner	Time	Cond.
1874	Saxon	2:39½	Fast
1926	Crusader	2:32⅕	Sloppy
1930	Gallant Fox	2:31⅗	Good
1931	Twenty Grand	2:29⅗	Fast
1934	Peace Chance	2:29⅕	Fast
1937	War Admiral	2:28⅗	Fast
1943	Count Fleet	2:28⅕	Fast
1957	Gallant Man	2:26⅗	Fast
1973	Secretariat	2:24	Fast

Shortest-Priced Winning Favorites

Winner	Year	Odds
Man o' War	1920	0.04-to-1
Count Fleet	1943	0.05-to-1
Hanover	1887	0.05-to-1
George Kinney	1883	0.08-to-1
Secretariat	1973	0.10-to-1
Johnstown	1939	0.12-to-1
Sweep	1910	0.12-to-1
Nashua	1955	0.15-to-1
Citation	1948	0.20-to-1
Forester	1882	0.20-to-1
Whirlaway	1941	0.25-to-1
Chance Shot	1927	0.25-to-1
*Hourless	1917	0.25-to-1
Sir Dixon	1888	0.36-to-1
Burgomaster	1906	0.40-to-1
Sir Barton	1919	0.40-to-1
Seattle Slew	1977	0.40-to-1
Native Dancer	1953	0.45-to-1
Colin	1908	0.50-to-1
Jean Bereaud	1899	0.50-to-1
Grenada	1880	0.50-to-1

Longest Winning Odds

Year	Horse	Odds
2002	Sarava	70.25-to-1
1961	Sherluck	65.05-to-1
1980	Temperence Hill	53.40-to-1
2004	Birdstone	36.00-to-1
1971	Pass Catcher	34.50-to-1
1999	Lemon Drop Kid	29.75-to-1
2000	Commendable	18.80-to-1
1944	Bounding Home	16.35-to-1

Odds-On Beaten Favorites

Year	Horse	Odds	Finish
1958	Tim Tam	0.15-to-1	2nd
1979	Spectacular Bid	0.30-to-1	3rd
1938	Dauber	0.33-to-1	2nd
1922	*Snob II	0.33-to-1	2nd
2004	Smarty Jones	0.35-to-1	2nd
1942	Alsab	0.40-to-1	2nd
1928	Victorian	0.40-to-1	5th
1961	Carry Back	0.45-to-1	7th
1963	Candy Spots	0.50-to-1	2nd
1952	Blue Man	0.50-to-1	2nd
1944	Pensive	0.50-to-1	2nd
1900	Missionary	0.50-to-1	3rd
1966	Kauai King	0.60-to-1	4th
1915	Pebbles	0.60-to-1	3rd
1971	Canonero II	0.70-to-1	4th
1913	Rock View	0.70-to-1	2nd
1947	Faultless	0.75-to-1	5th
1998	Real Quiet	0.80-to-1	2nd
1987	Alysheba	0.80-to-1	4th
1981	Pleasant Colony	0.80-to-1	3rd
1964	Northern Dancer	0.80-to-1	3rd
1949	Ponder	0.80-to-1	2nd
1930	Whichone	0.80-to-1	2nd
1895	Counter Tenor	0.80-to-1	2nd
1891	Montana	0.80-to-1	2nd
1889	Diablo	0.80-to-1	2nd
1960	Tompion	0.85-to-1	4th
1957	Bold Ruler	0.85-to-1	3rd
1950	Hill Prince	0.85-to-1	7th
1989	Sunday Silence	0.90-to-1	2nd

Belmont Front-Runners

Since Capot in 1949, only six horses have won the Belmont while leading at every point of call, and none since Swale in '84. The following Belmont Stakes winners were on the lead at all points of call.

Year	Winner	Winning Margin
1898	*Bowling Brook	8
1901	Commando	½
1902	Masterman	2
1904	Delhi	3½
1905	Tanya	½
1906	Burgomaster	4
1907	Peter Pan	1
1908	Colin	Head
1910	Sweep	6
1915	The Finn	4
1916	Friar Rock	3
1917	*Hourless	10
1920	Man o' War	20
1923	Zev	1½
1927	Chance Shot	1½
1930	Gallant Fox	3
1932	Faireno	1½
1937	War Admiral	3
1939	Johnstown	5
1943	Count Fleet	25
1948	Citation	8
1949	Capot	½
1972	Riva Ridge	7
1973	Secretariat	31
1976	Bold Forbes	Neck
1977	Seattle Slew	4
1978	Affirmed	Head
1984	Swale	4

Winning Belmont Post Positions

Post	Winners	Post	Winners
1	23	7	11
2	11	8	6
3	13	9	4
4	9	10	2
5	13	11	2
6	7		

Largest Winning Margins

Year	Horse	Margin in Lengths
1973	Secretariat	31
1943	Count Fleet	25
1920	Man o' War	20
1988	Risen Star	14¾
1987	Bet Twice	14
1982	Conquistador Cielo	14
2001	Point Given	12¼
1888	Sir Dixon	12
1931	Twenty Grand	10
1917	*Hourless	10

Smallest Winning Margins

Year	Horse	Margin
1998	Victory Gallop	nose
1962	Jaipur	nose
1936	Granville	nose
1999	Lemon Drop Kid	head
1991	Hansel	head
1978	Affirmed	head
1908	Colin	head
1900	Ildrim	head
1899	Jean Bereaud	head
1895	Belmar	head
1893	Commanche	head
1889	Eric	head
1876	Algerine	head
1867	Ruthless	head
1981	Summing	neck
1976	Bold Forbes	neck
1975	Avatar	neck
1965	Hail to All	neck
1956	Needles	neck
1954	High Gun	neck
1953	Native Dancer	neck
1938	Pasteurized	neck
1936	Granville	neck
1896	Hastings	neck
1891	Foxford	neck
1881	Saunterer	neck
1874	Saxon	neck

Fillies in the Belmont

Ruthless left a tough act to follow when she won the inaugural Belmont Stakes in 1867. Only 20 other fillies have raced in the Belmont Stakes, and just one other, Tanya, in 1905, has won. Kentucky Derby winner and Preakness runner-up Genuine Risk was second to Temperence Hill in 1980, and six other fillies have finished third, most recently My Flag in '96.

Year	Filly	Finish
1999	Silverbulletday	7th
1996	My Flag	3rd
1988	Winning Colors	6th
1980	Genuine Risk	2nd
1954	Riverina	7th
1932	Laughing Queen	10th
1927	Flambino	3rd
1923	Miss Smith	8th
1913	Flying Fairy	3rd
1905	**Tanya**	1st
	Funders	7th
1885	Miss Palmer	9th
1871	Nellie Gray	4th
	Mary Clark	9th
1870	Midday	3rd
	Nellie James	4th
	Stamps	6th
1869	Invercauld	3rd
	Viola	7th
1868	Fanny Ludlow	3rd
1867	**Ruthless**	1st

Geldings in the Belmont

Creme Fraiche, owned by Elizabeth Moran's Brushwood Stable, remains the only gelding ever to have won the Belmont Stakes. In its early years, the Belmont conditions allowed geldings to run in the classic race, but America subsequently bowed to European practice, which barred geldings from major races. Lanius, a gelding, ran in the 1918 Belmont, but it was not until '57 that geldings again were permitted in the race. Creme Fraiche was the first gelding to compete in the Belmont since 1979 champion juvenile male Rockhill Native finished third in '80.

Geldings who have started in the Belmont since 1985:

Year	Gelding	Finish
2004	Tap Dancer	6th
2003	Funny Cide	3rd
2002	Magic Weisner	4th
	Perfect Drift	10th
2001	Balto Star	8th
2000	Unshaded	3rd
1998	Thomas Jo	3rd
1997	Irish Silence	5th
1996	Jamies First Punch	8th
1996	Cavonnier	DNF
1993	Prairie Bayou	DNF
1991	Subordinated Debt	9th
1988	Kingpost	2nd
1985	**Creme Fraiche**	1st

Birthplaces of Belmont Winners

Place of Birth	Winners
Kentucky	89
Virginia	11
New Jersey	7
England	6
Florida	6
New York	3
Pennsylvania	3
Tennessee	3
California	2
Ireland	2
Maryland	2
Texas	2
Canada	1
Montana	1

Status of Belmont Stakes Winners Since 1970

Year	Winner	Birthdate	Status	Where Stands/Stood	Location	Death Date
2006	Jazil	2/11/2003	In Training			
2005	Afleet Alex	3/9/2002	Stallion	Gainesway	Lexington, Ky.	
2004	Birdstone	5/16/2001	Stallion	Gainesway	Lexington, Ky.	
2003	Empire Maker	4/27/2000	Stallion	Juddmonte Farms	Lexington, Ky.	
2002	Sarava	3/2/1999	Stallion	CloverLeaf Farms II	Reddick, Fl.	
2001	Point Given	3/27/1998	Stallion	Three Chimneys Farm	Midway, Ky.	
2000	Commendable	4/13/1997	Stallion	KRA Jeju Stud Farm	South Korea	
1999	Lemon Drop Kid	5/26/1996	Stallion	Lane's End	Versailles, Ky.	
1998	Victory Gallop	5/30/1995	Stallion	WinStar Farm	Versailles, Ky.	
1997	Touch Gold	5/26/1994	Stallion	Adena Springs Kentucky	Versailles, Ky.	
1996	Editor's Note	4/26/1993	Stallion		Argentina	
1995	Thunder Gulch	5/23/1992	Stallion	Ashford Stud	Versailles, Ky.	
1994	Tabasco Cat	4/15/1991	Deceased	JBBA Shizunai Stallion Station	Hokkaido, Japan	3/6/2004
1993	Colonial Affair	4/19/1990	Stallion	Haras El Paraiso	Capitan Sarmiento, Argentina	
1992	A.P. Indy	3/31/1989	Stallion	Lane's End	Versailles, Ky.	
1991	Hansel	3/12/1988	Pensioned	Lazy Lane Farms	Upperville, Va.	
1990	Go and Go (Ire)	3/21/1987	Deceased	Waldorf Farm	North Chatham, N.Y.	3/2000
1989	Easy Goer	3/21/1986	Deceased	Claiborne Farm	Paris, Ky.	5/1/1994
1988	Risen Star	3/25/1985	Deceased	Walmac International	Lexington, Ky.	3/13/1998
1987	Bet Twice	4/20/1984	Deceased	Muirfield East	Chesapeake City, Md.	3/5/1999
1986	Danzig Connection	4/6/1983	Stallion	Allevamento Al-Ca Torre	Comiso, Italy	
1985	Creme Fraiche	4/7/1982	Deceased	Brushwood Farm	Malvern, Pa.	10/9/2003
1984	Swale	4/21/1981	Deceased			6/17/1984
1983	Caveat	3/16/1980	Deceased	Northview Stallion Station	Chesapeake City, Md.	2/1/1995
1982	Conquistador Cielo	3/20/1979	Deceased	Claiborne Farm	Paris, Ky.	12/17/2002
1981	Summing	4/16/1978	Pensioned	Getaway Thoroughbred Farms	Romoland, Ca.	
1980	Temperence Hill	3/6/1977	Deceased	Swang Jei Farm	Nontaburi, Thailand	6/03/2003
1979	Coastal	4/6/1976	Deceased	Summerhill Stud	Mooi River, South Africa	9/28/2005
1978	Affirmed	2/21/1975	Deceased	Jonabell Farm	Lexington, Ky.	1/12/2001
1977	Seattle Slew	2/15/1974	Deceased	Three Chimneys Farm	Midway, Ky.	5/7/2002
1976	Bold Forbes	3/31/1973	Deceased	Stone Farm	Paris, Ky.	8/9/2000
1975	Avatar	3/10/1972	Deceased	Frisch's Farm	Morrow, Oh.	12/3/1992
1974	Little Current	4/5/1971	Deceased	Pacific Equine Clinic	Monroe, Wa.	1/19/2003
1973	Secretariat	3/30/1970	Deceased	Claiborne Farm	Paris, Ky.	10/4/1989
1972	Riva Ridge	4/13/1969	Deceased	Claiborne Farm	Paris, Ky.	4/21/1985
1971	Pass Catcher	4/6/1968	Deceased	Ocala Stud Farm	Ocala, Fl.	1993
1970	High Echelon	3/22/1967	Deceased	Franks Farms	Ocala, Fl.	5/15/1991

Belmont Stakes

Grade 1, Belmont Park, three-year-olds, 1½ miles, dirt. Held on June 10, 2006, with gross value of $1,000,000. First run in 1867. Weights: colts and geldings, 126 pounds; fillies, 121 pounds.

Year	Winner	Jockey	Second	Third	Strs	Time	Track	1st Purse
2006	**Jazil**	F. Jara	Bluegrass Cat	Sunriver	12	2:27.86	ft	$600,000
2005	**Afleet Alex**	J. Rose	Andromeda's Hero	Nolan's Cat	11	2:28.75	ft	600,000
2004	**Birdstone**	E. Prado	Smarty Jones	Royal Assault	9	2:27.50	ft	600,000
2003	**Empire Maker**	J. Bailey	Ten Most Wanted	Funny Cide	6	2:28.26	sy	600,000
2002	**Sarava**	E. Prado	Medaglia d'Oro	Sunday Break (Jpn)	11	2:29.71	ft	600,000
2001	**Point Given**	G. Stevens	A P Valentine	Monarchos	9	2:26.56	ft	600,000
2000	**Commendable**	P. Day	Aptitude	‡Unshaded	11	2:31.19	ft	600,000
1999	**Lemon Drop Kid**	J. Santos	Vision and Verse	Charismatic	12	2:27.88	ft	600,000
1998	**Victory Gallop**	G. Stevens	Real Quiet	‡Thomas Jo	11	2:29.16	ft	**600,000**
1997	**Touch Gold**	C. McCarron	Silver Charm	Free House	7	2:28.82	ft	432,600
1996	**Editor's Note**	R. Douglas	Skip Away	†My Flag	14	2:28.96	ft	437,880
1995	**Thunder Gulch**	G. Stevens	Star Standard	‡Citadeed	11	2:32.02	ft	415,440
1994	**Tabasco Cat**	P. Day	Go for Gin	Strodes Creek	6	2:26.82	ft	392,280
1993	**Colonial Affair**	J. Krone	Kissin Kris	Wild Gale	13	2:29.97	gd	444,540
1992	**A.P. Indy**	E. Delahoussaye	My Memoirs (GB)	Pine Bluff	11	2:26.13	gd	458,880
1991	**Hansel**	J. Bailey	Strike the Gold	Mane Minister	11	2:28.10	ft	417,480
1990	**Go and Go (Ire)**	M. Kinane	Thirty Six Red	Baron de Vaux	9	2:27⅕	gd	411,600
1989	**Easy Goer**	P. Day	Sunday Silence	Le Voyageur	10	2:26	ft	413,520
1988	**Risen Star**	E. Delahoussaye	‡Kingpost	Brian's Time	6	2:26⅖	ft	303,720
1987	**Bet Twice**	C. Perret	Cryptoclearance	Gulch	9	2:28⅕	ft	329,160
1986	**Danzig Connection**	C. McCarron	Johns Treasure	Ferdinand	10	2:29⅘	sy	338,640
1985	**‡Creme Fraiche**	E. Maple	Stephan's Odyssey	Chief's Crown	11	2:27	my	307,740
1984	**Swale**	L. Pincay Jr.	Pine Circle	Morning Bob	11	2:27⅕	ft	310,020
1983	**Caveat**	L. Pincay Jr.	Slew o' Gold	Barberstown	**15**	2:27⅘	ft	215,100
1982	**Conquistador Cielo**	L. Pincay Jr.	Gato Del Sol	Illuminate	11	2:28⅕	sy	159,720
1981	**Summing**	G. Martens	Highland Blade	Pleasant Colony	11	2:29	ft	170,580
1980	**Temperence Hill**	E. Maple	†Genuine Risk	Rockhill Native	10	2:29⅘	my	176,228
1979	**Coastal**	R. Hernandez	Golden Act	Spectacular Bid	8	2:29⅗	ft	161,400
1978	**AFFIRMED**	S. Cauthen	Alydar	Darby Creek Road	5	2:26⅘	ft	110,580
1977	**SEATTLE SLEW**	J. Cruguet	Run Dusty Run	Sanhedrin	8	2:29⅗	my	109,080
1976	**Bold Forbes**	A. Cordero Jr.	McKenzie Bridge	Great Contractor	10	2:29	ft	117,000
1975	**Avatar**	W. Shoemaker	Foolish Pleasure	Master Derby	9	2:28⅕	ft	116,160
1974	**Little Current**	M. Rivera	Jolly Johu	Cannonade	9	2:29⅕	ft	101,970
1973	**SECRETARIAT**	R. Turcotte	Twice a Prince	My Gallant	5	**2:24**	ft	90,120
1972	**Riva Ridge**	R. Turcotte	Ruritania	Cloudy Dawn	10	2:28	ft	83,540
1971	**Pass Catcher**	W. Blum	Jim French	Bold Reason	13	2:30⅗	ft	97,710
1970	**High Echelon**	J. Rotz	Needles n Pens	Naskra	10	2:34	sy	115,000
1969	**Arts and Letters**	B. Baeza	Majestic Prince	Dike	6	2:28⅘	ft	104,050
1968	**Stage Door Johnny**	H. Gustines	Forward Pass	Call Me Prince	9	2:27⅕	ft	117,700
1967	**Damascus**	W. Shoemaker	Cool Reception	Gentleman James	9	2:28⅘	ft	104,950
1966	**Amberoid**	W. Boland	Buffle	Advocator	11	2:29⅗	ft	117,700
1965	**Hail to All**	J. Sellers	Tom Rolfe	First Family	8	2:28⅖	ft	104,150
1964	**Quadrangle**	M. Ycaza	Roman Brother	Northern Dancer	8	2:28⅖	ft	110,850
1963	**Chateaugay**	B. Baeza	Candy Spots	Choker	7	2:30⅕	gd	101,700
1962	**Jaipur**	W. Shoemaker	Admiral's Voyage	Crimson Satan	8	2:28⅘	ft	109,550
1961	**Sherluck**	B. Baeza	Globemaster	Guadalcanal	9	2:29⅕	ft	104,900
1960	***Celtic Ash**	W. Hartack	Venetian Way	Disperse	7	2:29⅗	ft	96,785
1959	**Sword Dancer**	W. Shoemaker	Bagdad	Royal Orbit	9	2:28⅗	sy	93,525
1958	***Cavan**	P. Anderson	Tim Tam	‡Flamingo	8	2:30⅕	ft	73,440
1957	***Gallant Man**	W. Shoemaker	Inside Tract	Bold Ruler	6	2:26⅗	ft	78,350
1956	**Needles**	D. Erb	Career Boy	Fabius	8	2:29⅘	ft	83,600
1955	**Nashua**	E. Arcaro	Blazing Count	Portersville	8	2:29	ft	83,700
1954	**High Gun**	E. Guerin	Fisherman	*Limelight	13	2:30⅘	ft	89,000
1953	**Native Dancer**	E. Guerin	Jamie K.	Royal Bay Gem	6	2:28⅗	ft	82,500
1952	**One Count**	E. Arcaro	Blue Man	Armageddon	6	2:30⅕	ft	82,400
1951	**Counterpoint**	D. Gorman	Battlefield	Battle Morn	9	2:29	ft	82,000
1950	**Middleground**	W. Boland	Lights Up	Mr. Trouble	9	2:28⅗	ft	61,350
1949	**Capot**	T. Atkinson	Ponder	Palestinian	8	2:30⅕	ft	60,900
1948	**CITATION**	E. Arcaro	Better Self	Escadru	8	2:28⅕	ft	77,700
1947	**Phalanx**	R. Donoso	Tide Rips	Tailspin	9	2:29⅗	ft	78,900
1946	**ASSAULT**	W. Mehrtens	Natchez	Cable	7	2:30⅘	ft	75,400
1945	**Pavot**	E. Arcaro	Wildlife	Jeep	8	2:30⅕	ft	52,675
1944	**Bounding Home**	G. L. Smith	Pensive	Bull Dandy	7	2:32⅕	ft	55,000
1943	**COUNT FLEET**	J. Longden	Fairy Manhurst	‡Deseronto	3	2:28⅕	ft	35,340
1942	**Shut Out**	E. Arcaro	Alsab	Lochinvar	7	2:29⅕	ft	44,520
1941	**WHIRLAWAY**	E. Arcaro	Robert Morris	‡Yankee Chance	4	2:31	ft	39,770
1940	**Bimelech**	F. Smith	Your Chance	Andy K.	6	2:29⅗	ft	35,030
1939	**Johnstown**	J. Stout	Belay	Gilded Knight	6	2:29⅗	ft	37,020
1938	**Pasteurized**	J. Stout	Dauber	Cravat	6	2:29⅖	ft	34,530
1937	**WAR ADMIRAL**	C. Kurtsinger	Sceneshifter	Vamoose	7	2:28⅗	ft	38,020

Year	Winner	Jockey	Second	Third	Strs	Time	Track	1st Purse
1936	**Granville**	J. Stout	Mr. Bones	Hollyrood	10	2:30	ft	29,800
1935	**OMAHA**	W. Saunders	Firethorn	Rosemont	5	2:30⅗	sy	35,480
1934	**Peace Chance**	W. Wright	High Quest	Good Goods	8	2:29⅕	ft	43,410
1933	**Hurryoff**	M. Garner	Nimbus	Union	9	2:32⅗	ft	49,490
1932	**Faireno**	T. Malley	Osculator	Flag Pole	11	2:32⅘	ft	55,120
1931	**Twenty Grand**	C. Kurtsinger	Sun Meadow	Jamestown	3	2:29⅗	ft	58,770
1930	**GALLANT FOX**	E. Sande	Whichone	Questionnaire	4	2:31⅗	gd	66,040
1929	**Blue Larkspur**	M. Garner	African	Jack High	8	2:32⅘	sy	59,650
1928	**Vito**	C. Kummer	Genie	Diavolo	6	2:33⅕	ft	63,430
1927	**Chance Shot**	E. Sande	Bois de Rose	†Flambino	6	2:32⅖	ft	60,910
1926	**Crusader**	A. Johnson	Espino	Haste	9	2:32⅕	sy	48,550
1925	**American Flag**	A. Johnson	Dangerous	Swope	7	2:16⅘	ft	38,500
1924	**Mad Play**	E. Sande	Mr. Mutt	Modest	11	2:18⅘	gd	42,880
1923	**Zev**	E. Sande	Chickvale	‡Rialto	8	2:19	gd	38,000
1922	**Pillory**	C. H. Miller	*Snob II	Hea	4	2:18⅘	ft	39,200
1921	**Grey Lag**	E. Sande	Sporting Blood	Leonardo II	4	2:16⅘	ft	8,650
1920	**Man o' War**	C. Kummer	*Donnacona	———	2	2:14⅕	ft	7,950
1919	**SIR BARTON**	J. Loftus	Sweep On	Natural Bridge	3	2:17⅖	ft	11,950
1918	***Johren**	F. Robinson	*War Cloud	‡Cum Sah	4	2:20⅖	ft	8,950
1917	***Hourless**	J. Butwell	Skeptic	Wonderful	3	2:17⅘	gd	5,800
1916	**Friar Rock**	E. Haynes	Spur	Churchill	4	2:22	my	4,100
1915	**The Finn**	G. Byrne	Half Rock	Pebbles	3	2:18⅖	ft	1,825
1914	**Luke McLuke**	M. Buxton	‡Gainer	‡Charlestonian	3	2:20	ft	3,275
1913	**Prince Eugene**	R. Troxler	Rock View	†Flying Fairy	4	2:18	ft	3,075
1910	**Sweep**	J. Butwell	Duke of Ormonde	———	2	2:22	ft	9,700
1909	**Joe Madden**	E. Dugan	Wise Mason	‡Donald Macdonald	5	2:21⅗	ft	24,550
1908	**Colin**	J. Notter	Fair Play	King James	4	n/a	sy	22,765
1907	**Peter Pan**	G. Mountain	Superman	Frank Gill	5	n/a	ft	22,765
1906	**Burgomaster**	L. Lyne	The Quail	Accountant	6	2:20	gd	22,700
1905	**†Tanya**	E. Hildebrand	Blandy	Hot Shot	7	2:08	ft	17,240
1904	**Delhi**	G. Odom	Graziallo	Rapid Water	8	2:06⅗	ft	14,685
1903	**Africander**	J. Bullman	Whorler	Red Knight	4	2:21¾	ft	12,285
1902	**Masterman**	J. Bullman	Ranald	King Hanover	6	2:22⅗	ft	12,020
1901	**Commando**	H. Spencer	The Parader	All Green	3	2:21	ft	11,595
1900	**Ildrim**	N. Turner	‡Petruchio	Missionary	7	2:21¼	ft	14,790
1899	**Jean Bereaud**	R. Clawson	Half Time	Glengar	4	2:23	ft	10,680
1898	***Bowling Brook**	F. Littlefield	Previous	Hamburg	4	2:32	hy	7,810
1897	**Scottish Chieftain**	J. Scherrer	On Deck	Octagon	6	2:23¼	ft	3,350
1896	**Hastings**	H. Griffin	Handspring	Hamilton II	4	2:24½	gd	3,025
1895	**Belmar**	F. Taral	Counter Tenor	Nanki Pooh	5	2:11½	hy	2,700
1894	**Henry of Navarre**	W. Simms	Prig	Assignee	3	1:56½	ft	6,680
1893	**Comanche**	W. Simms	Dr. Rice	Rainbow	5	1:53¼	ft	5,310
1892	**Patron**	W. Hayward	Shellbark	———	2	2:12	my	6,610
1891	**Foxford**	E. Garrison	Montana	Laurestan	6	2:08¾	gd	5,070
1890	**Burlington**	S. Barnes	Devotee	Padishah	9	2:07¾	ft	8,560
1889	**Eric**	W. Hayward	Diablo	Zephyrus	3	2:47¼	gd	4,960
1888	**Sir Dixon**	J. McLaughlin	Prince Royal	———	2	2:40¼	ft	3,440
1887	**Hanover**	J. McLaughlin	Oneko	———	2	2:43½	hy	2,900
1886	**Inspector B.**	J. McLaughlin	The Bard	Linden	5	2:41	ft	2,720
1885	**Tyrant**	P. Duffy	‡St. Augustine	Tecumseh	6	2:43	gd	2,710
1884	**Panique**	J. McLaughlin	Knight of Ellerslie	Himalaya	4	2:42	gd	3,150
1883	**George Kinney**	J. McLaughlin	‡Trombone	Renegade	4	2:42½	ft	3,070
1882	**Forester**	J. McLaughlin	Babcock	‡Wyoming	3	2:43	ft	2,600
1881	**Saunterer**	T. Costello	Eole	Baltic	6	2:47	hy	3,000
1880	**Grenada**	W. Hughes	Ferncliffe	Turenne	4	2:47	gd	2,800
1879	**Spendthrift**	G. Evans	‡Monitor	Jericho	6	2:24¾	sy	4,250
1878	**Duke of Magenta**	W. Hughes	Bramble	Sparta	6	2:43½	my	3,850
1877	**Cloverbrook**	C. Holloway	‡Loiterer	Baden-Baden	13	2:46	hy	5,200
1876	**Algerine**	W. Donohue	Fiddlesticks	Barricade	5	2:40½	ft	3,700
1875	**Calvin**	R. Swim	Aristides	Milner	14	2:42¼	ft	4,450
1874	**Saxon**	G. Barbee	Grinstead	Aaron Pennington	9	2:39½	ft	4,200
1873	**Springbok**	J. Rowe	Count d'Orsay	Strachino	10	3:01¾	fr	5,200
1872	**Joe Daniels**	J. Rowe	‡Meteor	Shylock	9	2:58¼	fr	4,500
1871	**Harry Bassett**	W. Miller	Stockwood	By the Sea	11	2:56	ft	5,450
1870	**Kingfisher**	Dick	Foster	†Midday	7	2:59½	ft	3,750
1869	**Fenian**	C. Miller	Glenelg	†Invercauld	8	3:04¼	hy	3,350
1868	**General Duke**	R. Swim	Northumberland	†Fanny Ludlow	6	3:02	ft	2,800
1867	**†Ruthless**	J. Gilpatrick	DeCourcey	Rivoli	4	3:05	hy	1,850

†—filly, ‡—gelding, *—imported horse

1867-'73, 1⅝ miles; 1890-'92, 1895, 1904-'05, 1¼ miles; 1893-'94, 1⅛ miles; 1896-1903, 1906-'25, 1⅜ miles. 1867-'89, held at Jerome Park; 1890-1904, Morris Park; 1963-'67, Aqueduct. Not run 1911 and '12. 1973-present, Grade 1. Hansel (1991), Risen Star (1988), and Bet Twice (1987) earned $1-million bonus from Triple Crown Productions. 1907-'08 no official time recorded; bold-faced type shows records in starters, time, and purse earnings.

2006 Kentucky Derby: Barbaro's Blowout

The 2006 edition of the Kentucky Derby (G1) may very well be remembered as an event jam-packed with enough heart-tugging storylines to fill a book: Accounts of men who overcame physical disabilities, stories about colts whose owners died in the midst of their Triple Crown bids, and even the tale of a man who was a real-life hero and shined on the Olympic stage for the United States converged on May 6 at Churchill Downs for America's most famous race.

The real story of the 132nd edition of the Derby is a yarn that has every right to be one of legend, about a colt who continued to prove his skeptics wrong with a thorough thrashing of one of the deepest and most talented fields assembled for the Kentucky Derby in recent years.

The main character in this story is Barbaro and on racing's grandest stage, in front of the second-largest Derby crowd ever (157,536) and a worldwide audience, he delivered a performance so brilliant that it stunned not only his opposition but also his own connections.

Barbaro, a Kentucky-bred colt by Dynaformer bred and owned by Roy and Gretchen Jackson's Lael Stables, rolled to a 6½-length victory over 30-to-1 longshot Bluegrass Cat in the $2,213,200 Kentucky Derby to stay undefeated in six career starts. Jockey Edgar Prado picked up his first Derby win and third career classic victory as Barbaro completed the 1¼-mile trip on a fast track in 2:01.36 to become just the sixth undefeated winner of the Derby, joining such notables as 1977 Triple Crown winner Seattle Slew and 2004 Derby hero Smarty Jones.

The story of Barbaro's Derby win is as unconventional as it was dominant.

The Kentucky Derby was Barbaro's second race in 13 weeks and his first since a game victory in the Florida Derby (G1) on April 1 at Gulfstream Park. The win was also a perfect postscript to a plan drawn up and executed to perfection by trainer Michael Matz, who carried the American flag at the 1996 Summer Olympics in Atlanta and won a silver medal in show-jumping.

The plan to get Barbaro to the Derby as fresh as possible started like so many others for scores of talented colts with Triple Crown aspirations, during his two-year-old campaign, albeit with a bit of a twist. The twist was that Barbaro not only came into his three-year-old campaign having never faced top-flight juvenile competition in places like New York, Kentucky, and California, but he also had never competed on dirt.

Matz and assistant Peter Brette outlined a plan heading into Barbaro's three-year-old campaign that would utilize the Tropical Park Derby (G3) on turf at Calder Race Course and two other judiciously spaced prep races on dirt at Gulfstream Park to get to the Kentucky Derby.

> **Owners-Breeders**
>
> **Roy Jackson** is the co-founder of Convest Inc., a firm representing Major League Baseball players that was sold in 2001. He met wife **Gretchen** in the 11th grade before they both attended the University of Pennsylvania. They bought the farm they later named Lael Stables in 1978. In addition to Barbaro, they bred 2006 English classic winner George Washington, who was sold as a yearling.

After a win in the Tropical Park Derby on January 1, Matz planned to use Gulfstream's Holy Bull Stakes (G3) on February 4 and the Florida Derby two months later as the final steppingstones to the Triple Crown.

The fact that Barbaro would not race for five weeks after the Florida Derby was a hot-button issue in the weeks and days leading up to the Kentucky Derby, almost to the point where reporters asked about that break more than Matz's heroism when he saved several children in a 1989 commercial airplane crash in Sioux City, Iowa, that killed 111 of the 296 passengers.

Brother Derek, the winner of the Santa Anita Derby (G1) who was seeking to provide a storybook ending for paralyzed trainer Dan Hendricks, led a strong contingent from California.

Santa Anita Derby runner-up Point Determined and Arkansas Derby (G2) winner Lawyer Ron would race in the colors of an owner who died in the midst of the Triple Crown prep season. Racing for the estate of James T. Hines Jr., who died in a swimming pool accident in his Owensboro, Kentucky, home shortly before the Southwest Stakes, Lawyer Ron came into the Derby riding a six-race win streak. Point Determined was co-owned by Bob Lewis. Maryland-based Illinois Derby (G2) winner Sweetnorthernsaint was favored at 5.50-to-1.

Keyed Entry seized the early initiative from Blue Grass Stakes (G1) winner Sinister Minister, who set quick but honest fractions of :22.63 and :46.07 for the first half-mile. Barbaro stumbled slightly from the eighth starting position when the gate opened, but he righted himself immediately, and Prado settled him nicely behind the early pace. Meanwhile, Brother Derek was shuffled back to ninth after breaking from the 18th post position and was wide after a half-mile. Lawyer Ron, Point Determined, and Bob and John were not in the race at that point and would not factor in the outcome.

Prado remained in the third path off the rail entering the far turn and past Keyed Entry's six-furlong split of 1:10.88. Just as Sinister Minister overtook a tiring Keyed Entry, Barbaro pounced to the lead approaching the quarter pole and poured it on late, leaving the field in tatters.

—*Tom Law*

TENTH RACE
Churchill
May 6, 2006

1¼ MILES (1:59⅖) on dirt. 132nd running of the Kentucky Derby. Grade 1. 3-year-olds. Purse $2,000,000 guaranteed.

Value of race $2,213,200; Winner $1,453,200; second $400,000; third $200,000; fourth $80,000 (DH).
Mutuel WPS Pool $49,682,267. Exacta Pool $23,071,712. Trifecta Pool $27,062,557. Superfecta Pool $8,776,694.

Horse	M/Eqt.	Wt.	PP	¼	½	¾	1 mi.	Str.	Fin.	Jockey	Odds $1
Barbaro, 3, c	L	126	8	$5^{\frac{1}{2}}$	$4^{1\frac{1}{2}}$	$4^{\frac{1}{2}}$	1^{3}	1^{4}	$1^{6\frac{1}{2}}$	Edgar Prado	6.10
Bluegrass Cat, 3, c	L	126	13	$8^{\frac{1}{2}}$	$5^{\frac{1}{2}}$	$6^{\frac{1}{2}}$	5^{5}	$2^{\frac{1}{2}}$	2^{2}	Ramon Dominguez	30.00
Steppenwolfer, 3, c	L	126	2	$18^{\frac{1}{2}}$	13^{hd}	$11^{\frac{1}{2}}$	7^{hd}	5^{1}	3^{1}	Robby Albarado	16.30
(DH) Jazil, 3, c	Lc	126	1	20	20	$19^{\frac{1}{2}}$	17^{2}	6^{1}	$4^{\frac{1}{2}}$	Fernando Jara	24.20
(DH) Brother Derek, 3, c	L	126	18	$9^{1\frac{1}{2}}$	$9^{\frac{1}{2}}$	$14^{\frac{1}{2}}$	10^{hd}	$7^{\frac{1}{2}}$	$4^{\frac{1}{2}}$	Alex Solis	7.70
Showing Up, 3, c	L	126	6	4^{hd}	3^{hd}	3^{hd}	$4^{\frac{1}{2}}$	$3^{1\frac{1}{2}}$	6^{3}	Cornelio Velasquez	26.20
Sweetnorthernsaint, 3, g	Lb	126	11	12^{1}	11^{1}	$5^{\frac{1}{2}}$	3^{hd}	4^{hd}	7^{1}	Kent Desormeaux	5.50*
Deputy Glitters, 3, c	L	126	14	13^{1}	$15^{\frac{1}{2}}$	$16^{\frac{1}{2}}$	9^{1}	10^{1}	$8^{1\frac{1}{4}}$	Jose Lezcano	60.60
Point Determined, 3, c	Lb	126	5	$11^{\frac{1}{2}}$	10^{hd}	7^{1}	$6^{\frac{1}{2}}$	$8^{\frac{1}{2}}$	9^{hd}	Rafael Bejarano	9.40
Seaside Retreat, 3, c	L	126	15	7^{hd}	$7^{1\frac{1}{2}}$	$10^{\frac{1}{2}}$	15^{hd}	9^{hd}	$10^{4\frac{1}{2}}$	Patrick Husbands	52.50
Storm Treasure, 3, c	L	126	19	$19^{2\frac{1}{2}}$	18^{2}	13^{hd}	12^{hd}	$11^{\frac{1}{2}}$	$11^{1\frac{3}{4}}$	David Flores	51.90
Lawyer Ron, 3, c	L	126	17	$6^{\frac{1}{2}}$	$8^{\frac{1}{2}}$	9^{hd}	$8^{\frac{1}{2}}$	$12^{1\frac{1}{2}}$	12no	John McKee	10.20
Cause to Believe, 3, c	L	126	16	$15^{\frac{1}{2}}$	19^{2}	20	18^{4}	17^{2}	13^{3}	Russell Baze	25.90
Flashy Bull, 3, c	Lc	126	20	16^{1}	17^{hd}	17^{1}	$14^{\frac{1}{2}}$	15^{1}	$14^{2\frac{1}{2}}$	Mike Smith	43.00
Private Vow, 3, c	L	126	12	$17^{\frac{1}{2}}$	$16^{\frac{1}{2}}$	$12^{\frac{1}{2}}$	$11^{\frac{1}{2}}$	$14^{1\frac{1}{2}}$	$15^{2\frac{3}{4}}$	Shaun Bridgmohan	40.50
Sinister Minister, 3, c	Lb	126	4	$2^{1\frac{1}{2}}$	2^{2}	$2^{1\frac{1}{2}}$	2^{hd}	$13^{1\frac{1}{2}}$	$16^{1\frac{1}{2}}$	Victor Espinoza	9.70
Bob and John, 3, c	Lb	126	7	$14^{\frac{1}{2}}$	12^{1}	8^{hd}	$16^{\frac{1}{2}}$	$16^{\frac{1}{2}}$	17^{nk}	Garrett Gomez	12.90
A. P. Warrior, 3, c	L	126	10	$10^{\frac{1}{2}}$	14^{1}	$18^{\frac{1}{2}}$	19^{5}	19^{5}	$18^{1\frac{1}{2}}$	Corey Nakatani	14.10
Sharp Humor, 3, c	L	126	9	$3^{1\frac{1}{2}}$	6^{hd}	$15^{1\frac{1}{2}}$	20	20	$19^{7\frac{1}{2}}$	Mark Guidry	30.10
Keyed Entry, 3, c	L	126	3	1^{hd}	1^{2}	$11^{\frac{1}{2}}$	13^{hd}	$18^{2\frac{1}{2}}$	20	Patrick Valenzuela	28.80

L=Salix b=blinkers c=mud calks

OFF AT 6:15. Times: :22.63, :46.07, 1:10.88, 1:37.02, 2:01.36.
Start: Good for all except #8. Track: Fast. Weather: Clear. Winner: Stumbled at start, five wide, driving.

$2 Mutuel Prices:				
	8—BARBARO	14.20	8.00	6.00
	13—BLUEGRASS CAT		28.40	15.40
	2—STEPPENWOLFER			7.80

$2 EXACTA 8-13 PAID $587.00 $2 TRIFECTA 8-13-2 PAID $11,418.40
$2 SUPERFECTA 8-13-2-1 PAID $84,860.40 $2 SUPERFECTA 8-13-2-18 PAID $59,839.00
$2 PICK THREE 8-9-8 (3 CORRECT) PAID $266.80 $2 PICK FOUR 8-8-9-8 (4 CORRECT) PAID $1,534.80
$2 PICK SIX 10-4-8-8-9-8 (5 CORRECT) PAID $877.80 $2 PICK SIX 10-4-8-8-9-8 (6 CORRECT) PAID $114,516.80
$2 DAILY DOUBLE 9-8 PAID $60.40 $2 DAILY DOUBLE OAKS/DERBY 14-8 PAID $890.20
$2 FUTURE WAGER POOL 1 - 3 PAID $40.20 $2 FUTURE WAGER POOL 2 - 2 PAID $32.20
$2 FUTURE WAGER POOL 3 - 3 PAID $20.80

Dk. b. or br. c., by Dynaformer out of La Ville Rouge, by Carson City. Trainer: Michael Matz. Breeder: Roy and Gretchen Jackson (Ky.). Owner: Lael Stables.

BARBARO stumbled at the start, bumped with BOB AND JOHN, raced under light restraint between horses, went to the leaders under his own power midway on the far turn, reached the front at the five-sixteenths pole, accelerated quickly to a clear advantage approaching the stretch, and drew off under strong hand urging as much the best. BLUEGRASS CAT, never far back, angled outside the winner nearing the final quarter, then could not menace at the end while clearly second best. STEPPENWOLFER, bumped after the start by KEYED ENTRY and forced in, worked his way out six wide when straightened into the stretch to make his run, loomed a threat through the upper stretch, then failed to sustain his bid. JAZIL swerved in at the start, rallied along the rail on the far turn, then angled out between foes four wide when entering the upper stretch but failed to sustain his effort. BROTHER DEREK worked his way in six wide by the first turn, moved out wider when the field bunched nearing the end of the backstretch where he was steadied twice, fanned out nine abreast when making a run into the upper stretch, but came up empty while finishing evenly with JAZIL for fourth. SHOWING UP bobbled at the break and bumped BOB AND JOHN, was just off the winner briefly when entering the stretch, and flattened out in the drive. SWEETNORTHERNSAINT, steadied when bumped at the start by A. P. WARRIOR and forced out on PRIVATE VOW, was steadied again under the wire the first time, boldly came through close quarters along the rail at the five-sixteenths pole, but faltered when straightened for the drive. DEPUTY GLITTERS, outrun early, came out 11 wide for the drive, leaned in and bumped SEASIDE RETREAT at the furlong grounds, then lacked a further response. POINT DETERMINED, well placed, moved between horses five wide into the lane, came out and bumped with SEASIDE RETREAT at the eighth pole, and was finished. SEASIDE RETREAT was bumped from both sides at the eighth pole and had no further account. STORM TREASURE made a mild move between rivals approaching the final quarter but failed to continue. LAWYER RON was steadied entering the backstretch, continued within striking distance until the stretch but tired. CAUSE TO BELIEVE never reached contention. FLASHY BULL broke awkwardly and raced wide most of the way. PRIVATE VOW was bumped soon after the start by SWEETNORTHERNSAINT and steadied, then never was a factor. SINISTER MINISTER vied for the lead, briefly gained the lead between calls approaching the stretch, and faded. BOB AND JOHN, bumped at the start by SHOWING UP and then BARBARO, was finished after seven furlongs. A. P. WARRIOR was finished early. SHARP HUMOR faded after a half. KEYED ENTRY led to the far turn and gave way readily after seven furlongs.

2006 Preakness: Heartbreak and Triumph

One year removed from being the scene of a great triumph in the face of tremendous adversity, Pimlico Race Course found itself as the scene of enormous heartbreak and devastation, a worldwide stage where the breakdown of a hugely talented and popular colt overshadowed a brilliant performance by another. The 2006 edition of the $1-million Preakness Stakes (G1), staged at aging Pimlico on a picture-perfect afternoon on May 20 and in front of a record crowd of 118,402, was not supposed to turn out this way. The Preakness was supposed to be all about Barbaro, the undefeated winner of the Kentucky Derby (G1). The 1³⁄₁₆-mile Preakness was another step on his way toward the Triple Crown, or at the very least a shot at a sweep three weeks later in the Belmont Stakes (G1). A cruel twist of fate changed all that.

Instead of being toasted, celebrated, and draped with a blanket of black-eyed Susans like Afleet Alex enjoyed in 2005 when he averted disaster after clipping the heels of another horse to win the Preakness, Barbaro was fighting for his life in the initial moments after the American classic was contested for the 131st time at Baltimore's Old Hilltop. Barbaro broke down shortly after the start of the Preakness with fractures to his right hind cannon bone, sesamoid, and long pastern bone and a dislocated fetlock, injuries that required surgery at the University of Pennsylvania's New Bolton Center in Kennett Square and threatened his life.

The horrific scene cast a pall on the entire event, and nothing provided more evidence of that fact than the shocked and almost ashen look on the face of trainer Tom Albertrani as he made his way through the crowd to greet Darley Stable's Bernardini, a lightly raced colt who turned in a truly professional effort to win the Preakness that was supposed to belong to Barbaro. Bernardini officially won the Preakness by 5¼ lengths over beaten Derby favorite Sweetnorthernsaint, with longshot Hemingway's Key another six lengths back in third, and hard-luck Brother Derek four lengths farther back in fourth. Bernardini, who ran the 1³⁄₁₆ miles on the fast track in one of the race's fastest times, 1:54.65, under Javier Castellano, pulled off his Preakness victory in just his fourth career start and a little more than two months after a maiden victory at Gulfstream Park.

The victory was the first American classic success for Sheikh Mohammed bin Rashid al Maktoum's Darley Stable and the initial classic scores for both Albertrani and Castellano, who had never competed in the Preakness. Such victories typically set off celebrations, and one indeed did occur at the stakes barn shortly after Barbaro was transported through the exiting Pimlico crowd with police escort to the veterinary hospital nearly 80 miles away, but the connections of Bernardini still kept things in perspective.

Owner-Breeder

Darley Stable is owned by Sheikh Mohammed bin Rashid al Maktoum, ruler of Dubai in the United Arab Emirates. Sheikh Mohammed has won 23 European classic races in 13 seasons with horses such as Shamardal and Dubawi, and numerous Grade 1 races. Bernardini was his first American classic starter to race in the name of Darley Stable rather than the Maktoum family's well-known Godolphin Racing.

Barbaro's injury occurred on a day that started festive as scores of casual fans and serious industry participants all but conceded victory to Barbaro, who was hammered down to 1-to-2, the shortest odds since Fusaichi Pegasus was sent off at 3-to-10 prior to his runner-up finish to Red Bullet in 2000.

Barbaro was so eager that he broke through the starting gate just as the outside horse, Diabolical, was loaded. Jockey Edgar Prado quickly snatched Barbaro up as a relative hush fell over the Pimlico crowd, a hush that would become an eerie silence just a few moments later. The roar of the crowd as the field was sent on its way was not enough to mute the sound the jockeys in the race heard as the group approached the finish line the first time. Alex Solis, who planned to follow Barbaro in the early stages and turn the tables after a failed Derby run aboard his mount, Brother Derek, heard the crack. Prado heard it, too, and quickly pulled up Barbaro before coming to a stop just past the wire.

With Barbaro pulled up and out of the race, Gotham Stakes (G3) winner Like Now went as expected to the lead and set a strong early pace of :23.21 for the opening quarter-mile and :46.69 for the half. In close pursuit were Brother Derek, who had to swerve slightly to avoid Barbaro; Sweetnorthernsaint; and Bernardini. Like Now clicked past six furlongs in 1:10.24 before Sweetnorthernsaint pounced on him to take the lead midway on the far turn.

Castellano angled Bernardini out into the four path around the far turn, took dead aim at Sweetnorthernsaint and Like Now approaching the quarter pole, and had little problem surging past the leader and away from the rest of the field in upper stretch. In almost the blink of an eye, Bernardini was well clear and 3½ lengths in front past the furlong marker.

"I had so much horse ... it was incredible," Castellano said. "I knew at the three-eighths pole. I had plenty of horse, and the two horses in front of me started tiring. At the quarter pole when I asked him, he took off."

Bernardini, a homebred by A.P. Indy out of the Grade 1-winning Quiet American mare Cara Rafaela, was on cruise control in deep stretch ahead of the strung-out field that avoided the stricken Barbaro. "[Castellano] gave me a beautiful ride; I mean it was picture perfect," said Albertrani. "He stayed close enough to the lead where he didn't have anything in his way. He just sat patiently, and my only concern was at the half-mile pole when I thought maybe he wasn't going forward at that time. He was very patient with him, and when he asked him he just pushed the button."

Castellano also rode the bay colt in the one-mile Withers Stakes (G3), an Aqueduct race that showed he was talented but also a race that he nearly did not contest. Albertrani entered Bernardini in an allowance race two days before the Withers but opted instead to send him in the stakes after New York Racing Association officials urged him to run with a short field looming for the April 29 race. Bernardini was as professional in the Withers as he was in the Preakness, stalking the early pace before drawing off to a 3¾-length win in 1:35.07.

The Withers came nearly two months after Bernardini posted his maiden victory going a mile at Gulfstream in 1:35.57, an effort that also came nearly two months after he finished fourth to eventual stakes winner Exclusive Quality in his career debut on January 7 at Gulfstream.

Bernardini, the first American classic winner unraced at two since 2000 Preakness winner Red Bullet, got his late start to the races due to a series of minor physical ailments and mental problems. Broken and trained early in his two-year-old season by the late Bob Scanlon and later by Scanlon's son, David, Bernardini arrived at Albertrani's Belmont Park barn in September.

—Tom Law

12th RACE
Pimlico
May 20, 2006

1 3/16 MILES (1:53 2/5) on dirt. 131st running of the Preakness Stakes. Grade 1. 3-year-olds. Purse $1,000,000 guaranteed.

Value of race $1,000,000; Winner $600,000; second $200,000; third $110,000; fourth $60,000, fifth $30,000.
Mutuel WPS Pool $21,156,656. Exacta Pool $12,186,518. Trifecta Pool $15,631,720. Superfecta Pool $6,488,237.

Horse	M/Eqt.	Wt.	PP	¼	½	¾	1 mi.	Str.	Fin.	Jockey	Odds $1
Bernardini, 3, c	L	126	8	5	3^{1}	4^{2}	4^{4}	$1^{3\frac{1}{2}}$	$1^{5\frac{1}{4}}$	Javier Castellano	12.90
Sweetnorthernsaint, 3, g	LAb	126	7	2	$2^{1\frac{1}{2}}$	$3^{\frac{1}{2}}$	$2^{1\frac{1}{2}}$	2^{6}	2^{6}	Kent Desormeaux	8.40
Hemingway's Key, 3, c	LAc	126	3	7	$7^{1\frac{1}{2}}$	$7^{\frac{1}{2}}$	$7^{\frac{1}{2}}$	4^{4}	3^{4}	Jeremy Rose	29.40
Brother Derek, 3, c	L	126	5	9	5^{4}	2^{hd}	3^{2}	$3^{1\frac{1}{2}}$	4^{7}	Alex Solis	3.20
Greeley's Legacy, 3, c	Lbf	126	4	3	8	8	6^{1}	6^{1}	5^{nk}	Richard Migliore	34.90
Platinum Couple, 3, c	Lf	126	2	4	6^{3}	$6^{2\frac{1}{2}}$	8	8	$6^{3\frac{1}{2}}$	Jose Espinoza	33.20
Like Now, 3, g	LA	126	1	1	$1^{\frac{1}{2}}$	1^{1}	$1^{\frac{1}{2}}$	5^{2}	$7^{2\frac{1}{4}}$	Garrett Gomez	17.40
Diabolical, 3, c	LA	126	9	6	$4^{1\frac{1}{2}}$	5^{5}	5^{4}	7^{1}	8	Ramon Dominguez	26.00
Barbaro, 3, c	LA	126	6	8	—	—	—	—	—	Edgar Prado	0.50*

L=Salix A=adjunct medication b=blinkers c=mud calks f=front bandages

OFF AT 6:19. Times: :23.21, :46.69, 1:10.24, 1:35.73, 1:54.65.
Start: Good for all. Track: Fast. Weather: Clear. Winner: Lug in, steady urging.

$2 Mutuel Prices:				
	8—BERNARDINI	27.80	9.40	5.80
	7—SWEETNORTHERNSAINT		7.80	5.00
	3—HEMINGWAY'S KEY			8.00

$2 PICK THREE 1-1/4-8 (3 CORRECT) PAID $446.20 $2 PICK FOUR 4-1-1/4-8 (FOUR CORRECT) PAID $1,620.80
$2 DAILY DOUBLE 1-8 PAID $66.20 $2 DAILY DOUBLE PIMLICO SPECIAL/PREAKNESS 4-8 PAID $121.00
$2 EXACTA 8-7 PAID $171.60 $2 TRIFECTA 8-7-3 PAID $3,912.80 $2 SUPERFECTA 8-7-3-5 PAID $22,302.40

B. c., by A.P. Indy out of Cara Rafaela, by Quiet American. Trainer: Tom Albertrani. Breeder: Darley (Ky.)

BERNARDINI was patiently rated three to four wide between rivals into the backstretch, took a firm hold when BROTHER DEREK made his move midway down the backstretch, angled in leaving the far turn, swung back out four wide approaching the quarter pole, surged to command in upper stretch, under strong left-handed urging opened a clear advantage in midstretch, and drew off through the final sixteenth while under a vigorous hand ride in the final 70 yards. SWEETNORTHERNSAINT prompted the pace two to three wide, opened a clear lead leaving the quarter pole, shied inward once headed at the three-sixteenths pole, and was clearly best of the rest. HEMINGWAY'S KEY was outrun early, angled out in upper stretch, drifted out briefly near the furlong marker, and finished willingly once straightened to gain a share. BROTHER DEREK broke a step slow and steadied, checked off the heels of BARBARO under the wire the first time, rushed up entering the backstretch, and then faded from the quarter pole. GREELEY'S LEGACY failed to menace. PLATINUM COUPLE flashed only brief speed and dropped back after six furlongs. LIKE NOW sprinted clear nearing the first turn, set a pressured pace leaving the backstretch, was headed leaving the five-sixteenths marker, and tired in upper stretch. DIABOLICAL chased the leaders for six furlongs then faltered. BARBARO broke through the gate before the start and then was pulled up after breaking down in his right hind when nearing the wire the first time.

2006 Belmont: Smooth Jazil

The conversation came at the rarest of opportunities, between two men from the Bluegrass of Kentucky and another from the deserts of Dubai on an infrequent trip to the United States, shortly after one of the world's most prestigious races. Their topic was race strategy, specifically how they could pull off a victory next time with a three-year-old colt who tended to run his best races when he settled well off the pace and made one burst in the stretch.

The three men—trainer Kiaran McLaughlin, Shadwell Stable's Vice President of U.S. Operations Rick Nichols, and Sheikh Hamdan bin Rashid al Maktoum—concluded that the colt, Jazil, needed to be closer to the pace than he had been when fourth in the Kentucky Derby (G1) if he was going to contend in the Belmont Stakes (G1), the final race of the 2006 Triple Crown.

Unlike so many other one-run closers who make their runs but always seem to come up short, Jazil did not make his connections wait for another day when he made a strong and sustained rally over the final half of a grueling 1½ miles to win the final American classic of 2006 in style before 61,168 fans on June 10. Jazil, campaigned by Sheikh Hamdan's Shadwell, won the 138th running of the Belmont under 18-year-old jockey Fernando Jara by 1¼ lengths over Derby runner-up and morning-line favorite Bluegrass Cat. Sunriver finished third, with 4.80-to-1 second choice Steppenwolfer fourth and 4.70-to-1 favorite Bob and John eighth in the field of 12. Jazil, the 6.20-to-1 fourth choice, won on a fast, drying-out Belmont track in 2:27.86.

The victory by Jazil, whose name means abundance in Arabic and is pronounced "Jazz-ul," became the first American classic win for Shadwell, and it surprisingly was just the second Grade 1 triumph in the U.S. for the powerful operation, which has numerous bases in Europe and another in Lexington. It also was the second win in the 2006 Triple Crown by a member of the Maktoum family. Bernardini, campaigned by Sheikh Mohammed bin Rashid al Maktoum's Darley Stable, won the family's first American classic three weeks earlier in the Preakness Stakes (G1).

Jazil, a Kentucky-bred colt by Seeking the Gold, was purchased for $725,000 at the 2004 Keeneland September yearling sale. Sheikh Hamdan traveled to Kentucky to attend his first Derby and watched Jazil turn in what had become a rather typical performance for him during his seven-race career. Jazil, who came into the Derby off a fast-closing second to Bob and John in the Wood Memorial Stakes (G1) on a sloppy track at Aqueduct, dropped back to last before weaving his way through traffic to eventually finish 9½ lengths behind Barbaro and in a dead heat with Brother Derek for fourth place.

The effort did enough to tempt his connections to briefly consider running Jazil back two weeks later in the Preakness, but they opted to join four other Derby starters and waited out the five-week gap for the Belmont. The plan to skip the Preakness and wait for the Belmont—a popular move that worked successfully with Commendable in 2000, Empire Maker in '03, and Birdstone in '04—came with a caveat issued by Sheikh Hamdan. Dubai's deputy ruler and minister of finance and industry of the United Arab Emirates, Sheikh Hamdan wanted to see Jazil a little closer to the pace without taking the colt completely out of his game. The Belmont figured to be the best place for Jazil to be closer to the early running, or at least nearer the leaders, due to its abnormally long distance and typically slower pace than the octane-driven nature of the Derby, Preakness, and so many other American races.

"We talked that evening, and [Sheikh Hamdan] didn't think we'd be able to win a Grade 1 race in America coming from that far off the pace, and he's right," said Nichols.

Despite that emphasis on being closer to the pace, McLaughlin was not tempted to put some speed into his charge at the expense of taking him out of his natural running style. He instead chose to take it relatively easy with Jazil in the time between the Derby and the Belmont and even scrapped his final scheduled workout for the colt less than a week before the race. Jazil, who turned in a sharp five-furlong breeze at Churchill Downs a week before the Derby, breezed a half-mile in :49.09 on May 21 and five furlongs in :59.65 on May 27. He was slated to breeze another half in the week leading up to the Belmont, but after rains soaked the New York metropolitan area and turned the Belmont main track into a sea of slop on a daily basis, McLaughlin chose to gallop the small bay colt up to the race.

Trainer Bob Baffert also put some speed into Stonerside Stable's Bob and John at his Santa Anita

Owner

Sheikh Hamdan bin Rashid al Maktoum's **Shadwell Stable** achieved its first North American classic win with Jazil's Belmont victory. Sheikh Hamdan, deputy ruler of Dubai and United Arab Emirates minister of finance and industry, first registered his racing colors in England in 1981. Some of his best horses have included dual English classic winner Nashwan, top sprinter Dayjur, and homebred Sakhee. Sheikh Hamdan also races horses as part of his family's Godolphin Racing.

Breeder

Skara Glen Stables' Stanley and Marcia Gumberg, whose family business is shopping-mall construction and development, founded their farm in 1962 on property in Greensburg, Pennsylvania, that since has been sold. Most of their horses are kept at Lane's End in Versailles, Kentucky, with European-based horses at Watership Down Stud in Newbury, Berkshire. The current operation also includes sons Andrew; Ira and his wife, Anita; and Lawrence.

Park home base with the intention of making sure that the Seeking the Gold colt would not be shuffled back in the early going of the Belmont, as he was when he finished 17th in the Derby. The complexion of the race changed significantly when Bob and John was hustled away from the gate at the start by Garrett Gomez and took the field through strong early fractions of :23.02 and :47.36. Jazil hit the side of the starting gate at the break, and Jara briefly lost his right stirrup, but the Panamanian showed coolness beyond his 18 years and quickly guided his foot back into the iron as the field headed into the first turn. Jazil was still relegated to his customary spot at the back and was last of 12 through the first six furlongs in 1:12.14, but he did not lose contact with the field and was never more than ten lengths back.

Bob and John still held a tenuous lead after a mile in 1:37.53, but the main competition was latched onto him around the far turn. That group included Bluegrass Cat, Sunriver, and Jazil, who had threaded his way deftly through traffic on the turn. Steppenwolfer and jockey Robby Albarado also started their typical late run as the field made its way around the far turn. Jazil and Bluegrass Cat moved as a team on the turn and blew past the tiring Bob and John nearing the three-eighths pole. Jazil took a clear advantage from Bluegrass Cat at the five-sixteenths pole while running six wide and drew clear in the final sixteenth-mile.—*Tom Law*

11TH RACE
Belmont
June 10, 2006

1½ MILES (2:24) on dirt. 138th running of the Belmont Stakes. Grade 1. 3-year-olds. Purse $1,000,000 guaranteed.

Value of race $1,000,000; Winner $600,000; second $200,000; third $110,000; fourth $60,000, fifth $30,000. Total WPS Pool $14,697,715. Exacta Pool $9,214,787. Trifecta Pool $12,198,978. Superfecta Pool $4,543,658.

Horse	M/Eqt.	Wt.	PP	¼	½	1 mi.	1¼	Str.	Fin.	Jockey	Odds $1
Jazil, 3, c	Lc	126	8	12	12	$7^{1/2}$	1^{hd}	$1^{1/2}$	$1^{1 1/4}$	Fernando Jara	6.20
Bluegrass Cat, 3, c	L	126	9	$5^{1/2}$	$5^{1 1/2}$	$3^{1/2}$	$2^{1 1/2}$	$2^{1 1/2}$	$2^{2 1/4}$	John Velazquez	4.90
Sunriver, 3, c	L	126	2	$6^{1 1/2}$	$6^{1/2}$	6^{hd}	$3^{1/2}$	$3^{1/2}$	$3^{1 1/4}$	Rafael Bejarano	6.00
Steppenwolfer, 3, c	Lc	126	11	$8^{1/2}$	$7^{1/2}$	$11^{1/2}$	4^{hd}	4^{6}	4^{5}	Robby Albarado	4.80
Oh So Awesome, 3, c	Lbc	126	6	$11^{1/2}$	$11^{1/2}$	12	$7^{1/2}$	5^{hd}	5^{2}	Mike Smith	12.00
Hemingway's Key, 3, c	Lc	126	3	$10^{4 1/2}$	10^{1}	$10^{1/2}$	8^{5}	$7^{1 1/2}$	$6^{4 1/2}$	Jeremy Rose	15.10
Platinum Couple, 3, c	Lbf	126	1	7^{hd}	$9^{4 1/2}$	$5^{1/2}$	6^{1}	8^{6}	$7^{2 1/2}$	Jose Espinoza	38.00
Bob and John, 3, c	Lb	126	4	$1^{1/2}$	$1^{1/2}$	1^{hd}	5^{1}	6^{hd}	$8^{4 1/4}$	Garrett Gomez	4.70 *
Sacred Light, 3, c	Lb	126	12	$9^{2 1/2}$	8^{hd}	$8^{1/2}$	$9^{1/2}$	$9^{3 1/2}$	$9^{6 1/2}$	Victor Espinoza	26.50
High Finance, 3, c	L	126	5	2^{hd}	$3^{1/2}$	$2^{1/2}$	10^{4}	10^{6}	$10^{11 1/4}$	Eibar Coa	10.40
Deputy Glitters, 3, c	L	126	7	3^{1}	$2^{1/2}$	$4^{1/2}$	11^{8}	11	11	Edgar Prado	12.20
Double Galore, 3, c	Lb	126	10	4^{hd}	$4^{1/2}$	9^{hd}	12	—	—	Michael Luzzi	45.75

L=Salix b=blinkers c=mud calks f=front bandages

OFF AT 6:35. Times: :23.02, :47.36, 1:12.14, 1:37.53, 2:02.69, 2:27.86.
Start: Good for all. Track: Fast. Weather: Clear.

$2 Mutuel Prices:				
	8—JAZIL	**14.40**	**6.70**	**4.70**
	9—BLUEGRASS CAT		**6.40**	**4.70**
	2—SUNRIVER			**6.10**

$2 EXACTA 8-9 PAID $92.00 $2 TRIFECTA 8-9-2 PAID $436.00 $2 SUPERFECTA 8-9-2-11 PAID $1,085.00
$2 PICK THREE 3-4-8 (3 CORRECT) PAID $390.50 $2 PICK FOUR 9-3-4-8 (4 CORRECT) PAID $1,869.00
$2 PICK SIX 7-2-9-3-4-8 (5 CORRECT) PAID $200.00 $2 PICK SIX 7-2-9-3-4-8 (6 CORRECT) PAID $17,541.00
$2 DAILY DOUBLE 4-8 PAID $67.50

B. c., by Seeking the Gold out of Better Than Honour, by Deputy Minister. Trainer: Kiaran McLaughlin. Breeder: Skara Glen Stables (Ky.).

JAZIL hit the side of the gate at the start, the rider quickly regained his iron and angled to the inside, began to move out midway down the backstretch, split horses to launch his rally on the far turn, surged to the front leaving the five-sixteenths pole, battled outside BLUEGRASS CAT entering the stretch, opened a clear advantage leaving the furlong marker, and then edged away under strong left-handed urging. BLUEGRASS CAT was strung out five wide while contesting the pace on the first turn, stalked the leaders while continuing very wide along the backstretch, launched his bid on the far turn, drew on even terms with the leaders while six wide on the turn, and dug in gamely in midstretch. SUNRIVER, in hand early, moved between horses on the far turn, raced just outside the winner into upper stretch, and finished willingly. STEPPENWOLFER raced well back for six furlongs, checked in traffic on the far turn, followed the winner while gaining at the top of the stretch, and rallied mildly through the final eighth. OH SO AWESOME lunged in the air after hesitating at the start, was outrun for a mile, gained a bit to reach contention entering the stretch, and then flattened out late. HEMINGWAY'S KEY saved ground while racing far back for most of the trip and then passed only tiring horses. PLATINUM COUPLE lodged a mild bid on the far turn but then lacked a further response. BOB AND JOHN set the pace while well off the rail for six furlongs, relinquished the lead midway on the turn, and steadily tired thereafter. SACRED LIGHT failed to mount a serious rally when asked for run on the turn. HIGH FINANCE pressed the issue inside BOB AND JOHN for a mile and then gave way on the turn. DEPUTY GLITTERS pressed the pace six wide to the far turn and then gave way abruptly on the turn. DOUBLE GALORE raced in good position to the far turn, steadily tired thereafter, and was eased through the final furlong.

BREEDERS' CUP

Breeders' Cup History

John R. Gaines, one of the central figures in the North American commercial breeding industry in the last quarter of the 20th century, was renowned for his creativity and his powers of persuasion. In the early 1980s, Gaines needed all his considerable talents to get a fractious industry lined up behind his concept, which he believed would help to define the Thoroughbred industry and give it a centerpiece.

Gaines's creation was the Breeders' Cup. From the perspective of the 21st century, the Breeders' Cup stands as the most successful initiative of the Thoroughbred industry in the last half of the 20th century. Creation of the Breeders' Cup allowed the sport to hold a championship day of racing in late fall for the majority of age and sex divisions, an important element missing from a sport that had its major fall championship races scattered across the nation at several tracks.

Gaines conceived the idea in part out of anger and frustration. He was angered by a television program in the early 1980s that had depicted Thoroughbred racing as a haven of drug abuse. Indeed, permissive medication policies at racetracks had eroded confidence in the sport's integrity, and racing had continued its long, slow slide in popularity—a decline that began shortly after World War II. Even as the commercial bloodstock markets boomed in the early 1980s, race purses in inflation-adjusted dollars were shrinking.

The highly successful owner of Gainesway in Lexington and an innovator in the stallion-station concept, Gaines developed the idea for a championship day of racing with multimillion-dollar purses to attract the world's best runners, with the races being broadcast nationally on a major television network. The day of racing, as important as it was, would not be an end unto itself. The event would be used to build racing's popularity, with the organization in charge of the event becoming a leader in marketing the sport.

Given the sport's propensity for infighting, it is surprising the Breeders' Cup came into being in very much the form that Gaines first envisioned Thoroughbred racing's championship day. But it was not easy.

Where Championship Days Were Held

Churchill Downs (5): 1988, 1991, 1994, 1998, 2000
Belmont Park (4): 1990, 1995, 2001, 2005
Hollywood Park (3): 1984, 1987, 1997
Gulfstream Park (3): 1989, 1992, 1999
Santa Anita Park (3): 1986, 1993, 2003
Arlington Park (1): 2002
Aqueduct (1): 1985
Lone Star Park (1): 2004
Woodbine (1) 1996

Gaines had to sell the concept to a skeptical industry in 1982, and he had to do it one person at a time. His first target was John W. Galbreath, owner of Darby Dan Farm and an influential sportsman in the United States and England. (At the time, Galbreath was the only person to have raced both a Kentucky Derby winner [Chateaugay] and an Epsom Derby victor [Roberto].)

Gaines went to Columbus, Ohio, to meet with Galbreath, who initially thought little of the idea. But, as Gaines sketched out his idea in detail, Galbreath came on board. Moving quickly, Gaines lined up other supporters, including Spendthrift Farm's Leslie Combs II, Nelson Bunker Hunt, Windfields Farms' Charles Taylor, Will Farish, Racing Hall of Fame trainer John Nerud, Brereton C. Jones, John T. L. Jones Jr., and Seth Hancock, who a decade earlier had taken over management of his family's Claiborne Farm.

All great ideas have their moments, and Gaines's idea came at just the right time for the Thoroughbred industry. Commercial breeders, who would pay a big part of the program's cost by nominating their stallions and foals, were enjoying unprecedented prosperity as bloodstock prices rose to record levels and stallion fees climbed.

At the same time, racing was perceived as a sport in trouble, and relatively low purse levels dissuaded some prospective owners from buying horses. Although overseas interests sent the bloodstock markets skyrocketing, many breeders re-

Breeders' Cup Attendance and Wagering by Year

Year	Site	On-Track Attendance	On-Track Wagering*	Total Wagering*
2005	Belmont	54,289	$13,385,593	**$116,465,923**
2004	Lone Star	53,717	**11,274,066**	109,838,668
2003	Santa Anita	51,486	13,678,118	107,535,731
2002	Arlington	46,118	12,143,114	108,885,673
2001	Belmont	52,987	12,067,995	98,008,747
2000	Churchill	76,043	13,579,798	101,283,427
1999	Gulfstream	45,124	11,065,973	96,485,255
1998	Churchill	**80,452**	13,544,859	91,338,477
1997	Hollywood	51,161	8,191,459	71,639,333
1996	Woodbine	42,243	5,925,469	67,738,890
1995	Belmont	37,246	7,590,332	64,075,207
1994	Churchill	71,671	10,146,524	78,224,530
1993	Santa Anita	55,130	12,142,750	79,744,742
1992	Gulfstream	45,415	9,915,542	76,876,726
1991	Churchill	66,204	11,945,562	67,588,113
1990	Belmont	51,236	9,107,270	55,328,195
1989	Gulfstream	51,342	10,216,258	55,345,677
1988	Churchill	71,237	9,219,083	42,932,379
1987	Hollywood	57,734	10,202,252	31,864,457
1986	Santa Anita	69,155	12,510,109	31,984,490
1985	Aqueduct	42,568	7,200,175	26,941,288
1984	Hollywood	64,254	8,443,070	16,452,179

*Breeders' Cup races only

alized the prices they received for their sale offerings and the stallion fees they charged were directly related to purses, which determined how much a sale purchase potentially could earn.

Gaines chose the sport's most prestigious event, the Kentucky Derby (G1), to announce his idea. He was honored at the Kentucky Derby Festival's "They're Off" luncheon on April 23, 1982, and there he outlined his idea, a $13-million afternoon featuring the world's best racehorses. Gaines named it the Breeders' Cup.

He moved quickly to name a board of directors and girded for the inevitable naysayers. New York racing interests were opposed because Gaines's proposal would diminish the importance of the New York Racing Association's fall races, which frequently decided year-end titles.

Smaller-scale breeders also voiced their opposition. Gaines said breeders could breed one more mare to a stallion to cover the cost of the stallion nomination fee each year. Such a strategy certainly would work for a breeder with barns filled with desirable stallions whose books were filled, and Gaines was one of those breeders. But, for a small-scale breeder trying to fill the book of a less-commercial stallion, the stallion nomination most likely would be paid out of the stallion owner's pocket.

Other breeders raised concerns that Gaines was putting all the money into one event, arguing that the money should be spread throughout the year to supplement purses of existing stakes races. On that point, a compromise was reached, with $10-million earmarked for the championship day and an equal portion going into Breeders' Cup-sponsored races around the country.

By the fall of 1982, the Breeders' Cup was beset with infighting, and Hancock delivered an unexpected blow when he did not nominate Claiborne's stallions on grounds that the organization had not developed a clear game plan. Gaines realized he had become a lightning rod for opponents and resigned the presidency on October 22, becoming chairman. C. Gibson Downing Jr., a Lexington lawyer with a modest-sized stud farm and a reputation for consensus building, became Breeders' Cup president. Hancock signed up after a rules book was written on how the money would be spent, and smaller breeders followed his lead. D. G. Van Clief Jr. came on board that fall as executive director.

For several months, Gaines and Nerud traveled around the country, selling breeders and racetrack operators on the concept. By April 15, 1983, 1,083 stallions had been nominated to the program, and the Breeders' Cup was up and running. Nerud said in 1985 that a decision was made early to hold the first Breeders' Cup in a warm climate so television viewers would see racing in a pleasant setting. Marjorie Everett, chief executive of Hollywood Park, lobbied heavily for the first event, and on February 24, 1983, the Inglewood, California, track was named as host of the first Breeders' Cup, to be held on November 10, 1984. In a bow to New York interests, Aqueduct was host of the second Breeders' Cup in 1985.

Television Ratings for Breeders' Cup

Date	Host Track	Rating/Share
2005	Belmont Park	1.5/4
2004	Lone Star Park	1.4/4
2003	Santa Anita Park	1.8/5
2002	Arlington Park	2.0/5
2001	Belmont Park	1.7/5
2000	Churchill Downs	1.8/5
1999	Gulfstream Park	1.9/5
1998	Churchill Downs	2.2/6
1997	Hollywood Park	2.2/6
1996	Woodbine	2.5/8
1995	Belmont Park	2.8/9
1994	Churchill Downs	2.7/8
1993	Santa Anita Park	3.4/9
1992	Gulfstream Park	3.0/8
1991	Churchill Downs	3.0/9
1990	Belmont Park	2.7/9
1989	Gulfstream Park	3.7/11
1988	Churchill Downs	4.0/11
1987	Hollywood Park	2.9/7
1986	Santa Anita Park	4.4/12
1985	Aqueduct	4.0/11
1984	Hollywood Park	5.1/13

At Nerud's suggestion, marketers Mike Letis and Mike Trager of Sports Marketing and Television International were brought in to negotiate a television deal, and a contract with NBC was signed on September 13, 1983. The show would run for four hours on a Saturday afternoon and would include live coverage of all seven Breeders' Cup championship races. In January 1984, all seven races were granted Grade 1 status.

From the first race, won by Chief's Crown in the $1-million Breeders' Cup Juvenile (G1), the Breeders' Cup was an unprecedented success. That afternoon's races attracted a crowd of 64,254, and the day concluded with a breathtaking $3-million Breeders' Cup Classic (G1), in which supplemental entry Wild Again edged Gate Dancer and Slew o' Gold for the biggest race purse ever offered to that time.

An even larger crowd, 69,155, attended the third Breeders' Cup at Santa Anita Park in suburban Los Angeles, but that record lasted only two years until Churchill Downs hosted the fifth Breeders' Cup in 1988 before a crowd of 71,237. On a dreary, rainy, chilly day in Louisville, they were treated to one of the event's most exciting races when undefeated Personal Ensign closed relentlessly in the final yards and caught that year's Kentucky Derby winner, Winning Colors, at the finish line to win the Breeders' Cup Distaff (G1) by a nose. With that victory, Personal Ensign was retired unbeaten in 13 starts.

The Breeders' Cup traveled to Florida for the first time in 1989, and Gulfstream Park was the scene for another monumental struggle in which Sunday Silence fought off the challenge of Easy Goer to win the Breeders' Cup Classic. The event reached its nadir the following year at Belmont Park, when Go for Wand sustained a fatal breakdown near the finish line of the Breeders' Cup Distaff and was humanely destroyed. Subsequently, Breeders' Cup Ltd. instituted prerace examinations in an effort to limit breakdowns.

As rich races became more common, especially internationally, Breeders' Cup Ltd. increased its championship day purses, raising the Classic to $4-million in 1996 and the Distaff to $2-million in '98. In 1999, a new race, the $1-million Filly and Mare Turf (G1), was added, raising the afternoon's total purses to $13-million. In 2001, the championship day was renamed the Breeders' Cup World Thoroughbred Championships, and in 2003 total purses increased to $14-million. In 2006, the championship day was renamed again, to the Breeders' Cup World Championships, and total purse money was increased to $20-million, with the Classic carrying a $5-million purse and the Turf raised to $3-million. All other races were allotted a $2-million purse.

By 2005, the Breeders' Cup Stakes program had grown to 125 stakes races, with purses exceeding $22.5-million. In 2003, Breeders' Cup increased total entry fees 50% to 3% of the race purse. Stallion nomination fees were adjusted beginning in 2006. Stallions with 50 to 99 live foals were assessed 1½ times the advertised stud fee, and stallions with more than 100 foals were assessed twice the stud fee.—*Don Clippinger*

Breeders' Cup Trophy

The Breeders' Cup trophy is an authentic reproduction of the Torrie horse, created by Giovanni da Bologna in Florence, Italy, mostly likely in the late 1580s. The sculpture is known as an ecorche or flayed horse and shows the horse's muscles in great detail.

Although its original commission is not known, the sculpture may have been a study made for an equestrian statue of Duke Cosimo I, which was completed in 1591 and stands today in the Piazza della Signoria in Florence.

The sculptor's original ecorche in bronze was acquired by Sir James Erskine of Torrie in the early 1800s. It was bequeathed to the University of Edinburgh in 1836 and today is housed in the university's Museum of Fine Arts in Scotland.

The Breeders' Cup trophy was cast from the original under supervision of University of Edinburgh curators, and the replica is owned by Breeders' Cup Ltd. Smaller replicas are presented to winners of each Breeders' Cup race, and winning breeders, trainers, and jockeys also are presented with replicas.

Breeders' Cup Purses

When John Gaines first proposed the Breeders' Cup

Breeders' Cup Supplemental Entries

From its beginning, the Breeders' Cup program has allowed supplemental entries for its championship races, but the supplemental fee has been expensive to encourage stallion and foal owners to nominate their horses to the program. The supplemental fee was originally 12% for horses whose sires were nominated to the Breeders' Cup, the European Breeders' Fund, or a common fund of the two organizations. If a stallion was not nominated to the program at the time of the foal's conception, the supplementary fee was 20%.

For the foal to be nominated, the stallion must first be nominated to the program. Thus, when John Henry was pre-entered for the first $2-million Breeders' Cup Turf (G1) in 1984, owners Sam and Dorothy Rubin had to pay a $400,000 fee to start the gelding because his sire, Ole Bob Bowers, was not nominated to the program. The Rubins paid a $133,000 pre-entry fee, which was nonrefundable, and John Henry did not start because of a minor injury.

The hefty fees for horses whose sires were not nominated to the program worked against Southern Hemisphere horses in particular. Frank and Janis Whitham paid $200,000 to start Bayakoa (Arg) in the 1989 Breeders' Cup Distaff (G1) and again put up a $200,000 supplemental fee to start her the following year. Bayakoa won both times, earning a first-place purse of $450,000 each year. At that time, the supplemental fees did not go into the race purses but were retained by Breeders' Cup Ltd.

The rules were changed for the 1998 Breeders' Cup championship. Beginning with foals of 1996, the supplemental fee for offspring of nominated stallions was reduced to 9%, while the fee remained at 12% for older horses and 20% for horses whose sires were not nominated to the program.

Another change allowed supplemented horses to receive a credit for the net supplementary fees, after pre-entry, entry, and starting fees were taken out. High Chaparral (Ire) started in the 2002 Breeders' Cup Turf with payment of a $180,000 supplemental fee. When he started the following year, he had a $120,000 credit for the supplemental fee—the original $180,000 payment less starting fees of 3% of the total purse, or $60,000. High Chaparral won in 2002 and finished in a dead heat for the win with Johar in '03.

A further change added the net supplemental fees to the race purse, also in 1998. As a result of this change, the Breeders' Cup Classic (G1) in 1998 had a record purse of $4,689,920.

in 1982, he envisioned a purse structure of $13-million for the championship day. As the concept was put into final form for the first championship day in 1984, purses and nominator fees totaled $10-million. Five of seven races had $1-million purses (Juvenile, Juvenile Fillies, Sprint, Distaff, Mile); the Turf had a $2-million purse, and the Classic was $3-million.

In 1996, the Classic was increased to $4-million, and the Distaff was raised to $2-million two years later. The $1-million Filly and Mare Turf was added in 1999, and the Juvenile and Mile were increased to $1.5-million each in 2003, raising total purses to $14-million.

A 1997 change in the rules for supplemental nominations has resulted in higher purses. Beginning in 1998, supplemental-nomination money is added to the total purse. Thus, the 1998 Breeders' Cup Classic, which contained supplemental nominees Gentlemen (Arg), Silver Charm, and Skip Away, raised the total purse ($4,689,920) and nominator fees above $5-million, then the biggest race purse ever.

In addition to purse money paid to the horse's owner or owners, the Breeders' Cup purse structure contains 5% awards for both the stallion nominator and the foal nominator. Here is the 2005 distribution for a $2-million race:

Distribution of $2-Million Purse

Finish	Purse	Owner	Stallion Nominator	Foal Nominator
1st	57.2%	$1,040,000	$52,000	$52,000
2nd	22.0%	400,000	20,000	20,000
3rd	12.1%	220,000	11,000	11,000
4th	5.7%	114,000		
5th	3.0%	60,000		
Total	**100.0%**	**$1,834,000**	**$83,000**	**$83,000**

Largest Breeders' Cup Purses

(Not including stallion and foal nominator fees)

Year	Race	Purse	Winner	Value to Winner
1998	Classic	$4,689,920	Awesome Again	$2,662,400
2000	Classic	4,369,320	Tiznow	2,480,400
2005	Classic	4,291,560	Saint Liam	2,433,600
1997	Classic	4,030,400	Skip Away	2,288,000
2004	Classic	3,668,000	Ghostzapper	2,080,000
2003	Classic	3,668,000	Pleasantly Perfect	2,080,000
2002	Classic	3,664,000	Volponi	2,080,000
2001	Classic	3,664,000	Tiznow	2,080,000
1999	Classic	3,664,000	Cat Thief	2,080,000
1996	Classic	3,664,000	Alphabet Soup	2,080,000
1995	Classic	2,798,000	Cigar	1,560,000
1994	Classic	2,748,000	Concern	1,560,000
1993	Classic	2,748,000	Arcangues	1,560,000
1992	Classic	2,748,000	A.P. Indy	1,560,000
1991	Classic	2,748,000	Black Tie Affair (Ire)	1,560,000

From 1984 through '90, the Breeders' Cup Classic had a race purse of $2,739,000 and a winner's share of $1.35-million. The next highest purse was $2,271,680 in the 2000 Breeders' Cup Turf, won by Kalanisi (Ire).

Breeders' Cup Leaders

Leading Owners by Wins

6 **Allen E. Paulson** (Escena, 1998 Distaff; Ajina, 1997 Distaff; Cigar, 1995 Classic; Eliza, 1992 Juvenile Fillies; Opening Verse, 1991 Mile; Theatrical [Ire], 1987 Turf)

5 **Flaxman Holdings/Stavros Niarchos** (Six Perfections [Fr], 2003 Mile; Domedriver [Ire], 2002 Mile; Spinning World, 1997 Mile; Miesque [twice], 1987, '88 Mile)

Eugene V. Klein (Is It True, 1988 Juvenile; Open Mind, 1988 Juvenile Fillies; Success Express, 1987 Juvenile; Twilight Ridge, 1985 Juvenile Fillies; Life's Magic, 1985 Distaff)

4 **Ogden Mills Phipps** (Pleasant Home, 2005 Distaff; Storm Flag Flying, 2002 Juvenile Fillies; Inside Information, 1995 Distaff; Rhythm, 1989 Juvenile)

Stronach Stables (Ghostzapper, 2004 Classic; Macho Uno, 2000 Juvenile; Perfect Sting, 2000 Filly and Mare Turf; Awesome Again, 1998 Classic)

3 **Godolphin Racing** (Fantastic Light, 2001 Turf; Tempera, 2001 Juvenile Fillies; Daylami [Ire], 1999 Turf)

Overbrook Farm (Cat Thief, 1999 Classic; Boston Harbor, 1996 Juvenile; Flanders, 1994 Juvenile Fillies)

Ogden Phipps (My Flag, 1995 Juvenile Fillies; Dancing Spree, 1989 Sprint; Personal Ensign, 1988 Distaff)

The Thoroughbred Corp. (Johar, 2003 Turf; Spain, 2000 Distaff; Anees, 1999 Juvenile)

Leading Breeders by Wins

6 **Allen E. Paulson** (Azeri, 2002 Distaff; Escena, 1998 Distaff; Ajina, 1997 Distaff; Cigar, 1995 Classic; Fraise, 1992 Turf; Eliza, 1992 Juvenile Fillies)

5 **Flaxman Holdings/Niarchos Family** (Six Perfections [Fr], 2003 Mile; Domedriver [Ire], 2002 Mile; Spinning World, 1997 Mile; Miesque [twice], 1987, '88 Mile)

4 **Ogden Phipps** (Storm Flag Flying, 2002 Juvenile Fillies; My Flag, 1995 Juvenile Fillies; Dancing Spree, 1989 Sprint; Personal Ensign, 1988 Distaff)

Frank Stronach (Ghostzapper, 2004 Classic; Macho Uno, 2000 Juvenile; Perfect Sting, 2000 Filly and Mare Turf; Awesome Again, 1998 Classic)

3 **Aga Khan** (Kalanisi [Ire], 2000 Turf; Daylami [Ire], 1999 Turf; Lashkari [GB], 1984 Turf)

Sean Coughlan (High Chaparral [Ire] [twice], 2002, '03 Turf; Ridgewood Pearl [GB], 1995 Mile)

Overbrook Farm (Cat Thief, 1999 Classic; Boston Harbor, 1996 Juvenile; Flanders, 1994 Juvenile Fillies)

Ogden Mills Phipps (Pleasant Home, 2005 Distaff; Inside Information, 1995 Distaff; Rhythm, 1989 Juvenile)

Leading Trainers by Wins

18 **D. Wayne Lukas** (Folklore, 2005 Juvenile Fillies; Orientate, 2002 Sprint; Spain, 2000 Distaff; Cat Thief, 1999 Classic; Cash Run, 1999 Juvenile Fillies; Boston Harbor, 1996 Juvenile; Timber Country, 1994 Juvenile; Flanders, 1994 Juvenile Fillies; Steinlen [GB], 1989 Mile; Is It True, 1988 Juvenile; Gulch, 1988 Sprint; Open Mind, 1988 Juvenile Fillies; Success Express, 1987 Juvenile; Sacahuista, 1987 Distaff; Capote, 1986 Juvenile; Lady's Secret, 1986 Distaff; Life's Magic, 1985 Distaff; Twilight Ridge, 1985 Juvenile Fillies)

9 **Claude R. "Shug" McGaughey III** (Pleasant Home, 2005 Distaff; Storm Flag Flying, 2002 Juvenile Fillies; Inside Information, 1995 Distaff; My Flag, 1995 Juvenile Fillies; Lure [twice], 1992, '93 Mile; Rhythm, 1989 Juvenile; Dancing Spree, 1989 Sprint; Personal Ensign, 1988 Distaff)

6 **Neil Drysdale** (War Chant, 2000 Mile; Hollywood Wildcat, 1993 Distaff; A.P. Indy, 1992 Classic; Prized, 1989 Turf; Tasso, 1985 Juvenile; Princess Rooney, 1984 Distaff)

Richard Mandella (Pleasantly Perfect, 2003 Classic; Johar, 2003 Turf; Action This Day, 2003 Juvenile; Halfbridled, 2003 Juvenile Fillies; Kotashaan [Fr], 1993 Turf;

Phone Chatter, 1993 Juvenile Fillies)

5 **William I. Mott** (Escena, 1998 Distaff; Ajina, 1997 Distaff; Cigar, 1995 Classic; Fraise, 1992 Turf; Theatrical [Ire], 1987 Turf)

4 **Andre Fabre** (Shirocco [Ger], 2005 Turf; Banks Hill [GB], 2001 Filly and Mare Turf; In the Wings [GB], 1990 Turf; Arcangues, 1993 Classic)

Robert Frankel (Intercontinental [GB], 2005 Filly and Mare Turf; Ghostzapper, 2004 Classic; Starine [Fr], 2002 Filly and Mare Turf; Squirtle Squirt, 2001 Sprint)

Ron McAnally (Northern Spur [Ire], 1995 Turf; Paseana [Arg], 1992 Distaff; Bayakoa [Arg] [twice], 1989, '90 Distaff)

3 **Bob Baffert** (Vindication, 2002 Juvenile; Silverbulletday, 1998 Juvenile Fillies; Thirty Slews, 1992 Sprint)

Pascal Bary (Six Perfections [Fr], 2003 Mile; Domedriver [Ire], 2002 Mile; Miss Alleged, 1991 Turf)

Francois Boutin (Arazi, 1991 Juvenile; Miesque [twice], 1987, '88 Mile)

Patrick Byrne (Awesome Again, 1998 Classic; Favorite Trick, 1997 Juvenile; Countess Diana, 1997 Juvenile Fillies)

Julio Canani (Sweet Catomine, 2004 Juvenile Fillies; Val Royal (Fr), 2001 Mile; Silic (Fr), 1999 Mile)

Aidan P. O'Brien (High Chaparral [Ire] [twice], 2002, '03 Turf; Johannesburg, 2001 Juvenile)

Sir Michael Stoute (Islington [Ire], 2003 Filly and Mare Turf; Kalanisi [Ire], 2000 Turf; Pilsudski [Ire], 1996 Turf)

Leading Jockeys by Wins

15 **Jerry Bailey** (Saint Liam, 2005 Classic; Six Perfections [Fr], 2003 Mile; Orientate, 2002 Sprint; Squirtle Squirt, 2001 Sprint; Macho Uno, 2000 Juvenile; Perfect Sting, 2000 Filly and Mare Turf; Soaring Softly, 1999 Filly and Mare Turf; Cash Run, 1999 Juvenile Fillies; Answer Lively, 1998 Juvenile; Boston Harbor, 1996 Juvenile; Cigar, 1995 Classic; My Flag, 1995 Juvenile Fillies; Concern, 1994 Classic; Arcangues, 1993 Classic; Black Tie Affair [Ire], 1991 Classic)

12 **Pat Day** (Unbridled Elaine, 2001 Distaff; Cat Thief, 1999 Classic; Awesome Again, 1998 Classic; Favorite Trick, 1997 Juvenile; Timber Country, 1994 Juvenile; Flanders, 1994 Juvenile Fillies; Dance Smartly, 1991 Distaff; Unbridled, 1990 Classic; Theatrical (Ire), 1987 Turf; Epitome, 1987 Juvenile Fillies; Lady's Secret, 1986 Distaff; Wild Again, 1984 Classic)

10 **Mike Smith** (Azeri, 2002 Distaff; Vindication, 2002 Juvenile; Skip Away, 1997 Classic; Ajina, 1997 Distaff; Unbridled's Song, 1995 Juvenile; Inside Information, 1995 Distaff; Tikkanen, 1994 Turf; Cherokee Run, 1994 Sprint; Lure [twice], 1992, '93 Mile)

9 **Chris McCarron** (Tiznow [twice], 2000, '01 Classic; Alphabet Soup, 1996 Classic; Northern Spur [Ire], 1995 Turf; Paseana [Arg], 1992 Distaff; Gilded Time, 1992 Juvenile; Sunday Silence, 1989 Classic; Alysheba, 1988 Classic; Precisionist, 1985 Sprint)

8 **Gary Stevens** (War Chant, 2000 Mile; Anees, 1999 Juvenile; Escena, 1998 Distaff; Silverbulletday, 1998 Juvenile Fillies; Da Hoss, 1996 Mile; One Dreamer, 1994 Distaff; Brocco, 1993 Juvenile; In the Wings [GB], 1990 Turf)

7 **Eddie Delahoussaye** (Hollywood Wildcat, 1993 Distaff; Cardmania, 1993 Sprint; A.P. Indy, 1992 Classic; Thirty Slews, 1992 Sprint; Pleasant Stage, 1991 Juvenile Fillies; Prized, 1989 Turf; Princess Rooney, 1984 Distaff)

Laffit Pincay Jr. (Phone Chatter, 1993 Juvenile Fillies; Bayakoa [Arg], [twice], 1989, '90 Distaff; Is It True, 1988 Juvenile; Skywalker, 1986 Classic; Capote, 1986 Juvenile; Tasso, 1985 Juvenile)

Jose Santos (Volponi, 2002 Classic; Chief Bearhart, 1997 Turf; Fly So Free, 1990 Juvenile; Meadow Star, 1990 Juvenile Fillies; Steinlen [GB], 1989 Mile; Success Express, 1987 Juvenile; Manila, 1986 Turf)

Patrick Valenzuela (Adoration, 2003 Distaff; Fraise, 1992 Turf; Eliza, 1992 Juvenile Fillies; Arazi, 1991 Juvenile; Opening Verse, 1991 Mile; Very Subtle, 1987 Sprint; Brave Raj, 1986 Juvenile Fillies)

6 **Corey Nakatani** (Sweet Catomine, 2004 Juvenile Fillies; Silic [Fr], 1999 Mile; Reraise, 1998 Sprint; Elmhurst, 1997 Sprint; Jewel Princess, 1996 Distaff; Lit de Justice, 1996 Sprint)

John Velazquez (Ashado, 2004 Distaff; Speightstown, 2004 Sprint; Storm Flag Flying, 2002 Juvenile Fillies; Starine (Fr), 2002 Filly and Mare Turf; Caressing, 2000 Juvenile Fillies; Da Hoss, 1998 Mile)

Leading Sires by Wins

6 **Sadler's Wells** (High Chaparral [Ire] [twice], 2002, '03 Turf; Islington [Ire], 2003 Filly and Mare Turf; Northern Spur [Ire], 1995 Turf; Barathea [Ire], 1994 Mile; In the Wings [GB], 1990 Turf)

5 **Danzig** (War Chant, 2000 Mile; Lure [twice], 1992, '93 Mile; Dance Smartly, 1991 Distaff; Chief's Crown, 1984 Juvenile)

Kris S. (Action This Day, 2003 Juvenile; Soaring Softly, 1999 Filly and Mare Turf; Brocco, 1993 Juvenile; Hollywood Wildcat, 1993 Distaff; Prized, 1989 Turf)

4 **Gone West** (Da Hoss 1996 and '98 Mile; Johar, 2003 Turf; Speightstown, 2004 Sprint)

Nureyev (Spinning World, 1997 Mile; Miesque [twice], 1987, '88 Mile; Theatrical [Ire], 1987 Turf)

Storm Cat (Storm Flag Flying, 2002 Juvenile Fillies; Cat Thief, 1999 Classic; Desert Stormer, 1995 Sprint; Sweet Catomine, 2004 Juvenile Fillies)

3 **Cox's Ridge** (Cardmania, 1993 Sprint; Twilight Ridge, 1985 Juvenile Fillies; Life's Magic, 1985 Distaff)

Deputy Minister (Awesome Again, 1999 Classic; Go for Wand, 1989 Juvenile Fillies; Open Mind, 1988 Juvenile Fillies)

Mr. Prospector (Rhythm, 1989 Juvenile; Gulch, 1988 Sprint; Eillo, 1984 Sprint)

Nijinsky II (Royal Academy, 1990 Mile; Dancing Spree, 1989 Sprint; Ferdinand, 1987 Classic)

Seattle Slew (Vindication, 2002 Juvenile; A.P. Indy, 1992 Classic; Capote, 1986 Juvenile)

Seeking the Gold (Pleasant Home, 2005 Distaff; Cash Run, 1999 Juvenile Fillies; Flanders, 1994 Juvenile Fillies)

Strawberry Road (Aus) (Escena, 1998 Distaff; Ajina, 1997 Distaff; Fraise, 1992 Turf)

Unbridled (Halfbridled, 2003 Juvenile Fillies; Anees, 1999 Juvenile; Unbridled's Song, 1995 Juvenile)

Leading Owners by Purses Won

Owner	Starts	Wins	Earnings
Allen E. Paulson	32	6	$7,570,000
Frank Stronach/Stronach Stables	22	4	7,538,000
Godolphin Racing	33	3	5,118,200
Susan Magnier and Michael Tabor	24	3	4,463,920
Overbrook Farm	28	3	4,387,000
The Thoroughbred Corp.	22	3	4,164,200
Juddmonte Farms	43	2	3,994,820
Wildenstein Stable	19	2	3,917,000
Flaxman Holdings/S. Niarchos	26	5	3,891,960
Ogden Phipps	19	3	3,611,000
Sheikh Mohammed bin Rashid al Maktoum	22	2	3,576,800
Robert and Beverly Lewis	12	2	3,108,000

Owner	Starts	Wins	Earnings
Sam-Son Farm	19	2	$3,018,760
Frances A. Genter	8	2	2,835,000
H. H. Aga Khan	8	2	2,790,400
Eugene V. Klein	18	4	2,701,000

Owners With Most Starts

Owner	Starts	Wins	Earnings
Juddmonte Farms	43	2	$3,994,820
Godolphin Racing	33	3	5,118,200
Allen E. Paulson	32	6	7,570,000
Overbrook Farm	28	3	4,387,000
Flaxman Holdings/S. Niarchos	26	5	3,891,960
Susan Magnier and Michael Tabor	24	3	4,463,920
Sheikh Mohammed bin Rashid al Maktoum	22	2	3,576,800
Frank Stronach/Stronach Stables	22	4	7,538,000
The Thoroughbred Corp.	22	3	4,164,200
Ogden Phipps	19	3	3,611,000
Sam-Son Farm	19	2	3,018,760
Wildenstein Stable	19	2	3,917,000

Owners With Most Starters on a Program

Starters	Owner	Year
8	Godolphin Racing	2001
7	Eugene V. Klein	1987

Leading Breeders by Purses Won

Breeder	Starts	Wins	Earnings
Allen E. Paulson	28	6	$7,854,800
Frank Stronach/Adena Springs	10	4	6,232,000
Cecilia Straub-Rubens	3	2	5,360,400
Overbrook Farm	26	3	4,618,000
Ogden Phipps	18	4	4,131,000
Juddmonte Farms	44	2	3,932,820
Flaxman Holdings/S. Niarchos	27	5	3,891,960
H. H. Aga Khan	11	3	3,780,400
Sheikh Mohammed bin Rashid al Maktoum	12	2	3,461,000
Oak Cliff Thoroughbreds	3	2	2,700,000

Breeders With Most Starts

Breeder	Starts	Wins	Earnings
Juddmonte Farms	44	2	$3,932,820
Allen E. Paulson	28	6	7,854,800
Flaxman Holdings/S. Niarchos	27	5	3,891,960
Overbrook Farm	26	3	4,618,000
John C. Mabee	20	0	1,555,800
Ogden Phipps	18	4	4,131,000
Sam-Son Farm	15	1	2,051,760
Bertram R. Firestone	13	1	2,240,000
Ogden Mills Phipps	14	3	2,448,000
Sheikh Mohammed bin Rashid al Maktoum	12	2	3,461,600
H. H. Aga Khan	11	3	3,780,400
John Franks	11	1	1,480,000
Harry T. Mangurian	11	1	720,000

Leading Trainers by Purses Won

Trainer	Starts	Wins	Earnings
D. Wayne Lukas	145	18	$19,645,520
Bobby Frankel	66	4	10,636,020
William I. Mott	46	5	8,542,960
Claude R. McGaughey III	48	8	8,153,560
Andre Fabre	38	4	7,621,000
Richard Mandella	28	6	7,116,960
Neil Drysdale	32	6	6,095,840
Aidan O'Brien	35	3	6,007,020
Bob Baffert	42	3	5,349,800
Jay Robbins	6	2	4,938,400
Charles Whittingham	24	2	4,298,000
Saeed bin Suroor	24	2	4,213,800

Trainers With Most Starts

Trainer	Starts	Wins	Earnings
D. Wayne Lukas	145	18	$19,645,520
Bobby Frankel	66	4	10,636,020
Claude R. McGaughey III	48	8	8,153,560
William I. Mott	46	5	8,542,960
Bob Baffert	42	3	5,349,800
Andre Fabre	38	4	7,621,000
Aidan O'Brien	35	3	6,007,020
Neil Drysdale	32	6	6,095,840
Richard Mandella	28	6	7,116,960
Ron McAnally	27	4	3,518,000
Nick Zito	27	1	3,443,820
Flint S. Schulhofer	26	2	2,841,400

Trainers With Multiple Victories on Breeders' Cup Program

4 **Richard Mandella** (2003 Classic, Turf, Juvenile, Juvenile Fillies)

3 **D.Wayne Lukas** (1988 Juvenile, Juvenile Fillies, Sprint)

2 **Patrick Byrne** (1998 Juvenile, Juvenile Fillies); **Richard Dutrow Jr.** (2005 Classic, Sprint); **D.Wayne Lukas** (five times) (1985 Distaff, Juvenile Fillies; 1986 Distaff, Juvenile; 1987 Distaff, Juvenile; 1994 Juvenile, Juvenile Fillies; 1999 Classic, Juvenile Fillies); **Richard Mandella** (1993 Turf, Juvenile Fillies); **C. R. "Shug" McGaughey III** (1989 Juvenile, Sprint); **Todd Pletcher** (2004 Distaff, Sprint)

Trainers With Most Starters on a Program

Starters	Trainer	Year
14	D. Wayne Lukas	1987
12	D. Wayne Lukas	1988
11	D. Wayne Lukas	1989
10	D. Wayne Lukas	1996
	D. Wayne Lukas	1985

Leading Jockeys by Purses Won

Jockey	Mounts	Wins	Earnings
Pat Day	117	12	$23,033,360
Jerry Bailey	102	15	22,006,440
Chris McCarron	101	9	17,669,600
Gary Stevens	99	8	13,723,910
Mike Smith	52	10	10,505,760
John Velazquez	55	6	8,107,800
Jose Santos	62	7	8,008,800
Corey Nakatani	58	6	7,905,280
Eddie Delahoussaye	68	7	7,775,000
Alex Solis	52	3	7,130,290

Jockeys With Multiple Victories on Breeders' Cup Program

2 **Jerry Bailey** (four times) (1995 Classic, Juvenile Fillies; 1996 Juvenile, Mile; 1999 Filly and Mare Turf, Juvenile Fillies; 2000 Juvenile, Filly and Mare Turf); **Jorge Chavez** (1999 Distaff, Sprint); **Angel Cordero Jr.** (1988 Juvenile Fillies, Sprint); **Pat Day** (twice) (1987 Turf, Juvenile Fillies; 1994 Juvenile, Juvenile Fillies); **Eddie Delahoussaye** (twice) (1992 Classic, Sprint; 1993 Distaff, Sprint); **Garrett Gomez** (2005 Juvenile, Mile); **Chris McCarron** (1992 Distaff, Juvenile); **Corey Nakatani** (1996 Distaff,

Sprint); **Laffit Pincay Jr.** (1986 Classic, Juvenile); **Edgar Prado** (2005 Juvenile Fillies, Sprint); **Jose Santos** (1990 Juvenile, Juvenile Fillies); **Mike Smith** (four times) (1994 Turf, Sprint; 1995 Distaff, Juvenile; 1997 Classic, Distaff; 2002 Distaff, Juvenile); **Alex Solis** (2003 Classic, Turf); **Gary Stevens** (1998 Distaff, Juvenile Fillies); **Patrick Valenzuela** (twice) (1991 Juvenile, Mile; 1992 Turf, Juvenile Fillies); **Jorge Velasquez** (1985 Classic, Juvenile Fillies); **John Velazquez** (twice) (2002 Filly and Mare Turf, Juvenile Fillies; 2004 Distaff, Sprint)

Jockeys With Most Mounts in Breeders' Cup

Jockey	Mounts	Wins	Earnings
Pat Day	117	12	$23,033,360
Jerry Bailey	102	15	22,006,440
Chris McCarron	101	9	17,669,600
Gary Stevens	99	8	13,723,910
Eddie Delahoussaye	68	7	7,775,000
Jose Santos	62	7	8,008,800
Laffit Pincay Jr.	61	7	6,811,000
Corey Nakatani	58	6	7,905,280
John Velazquez	55	6	8,107,800
Mike Smith	52	10	10,505,760
Alex Solis	52	3	7,130,290
Kent Desormeaux	50	2	4,773,200
Patrick Valenzuela	50	7	6,451,300

Jockeys with Most Mounts on a Program

Mounts	Jockey	Year
8	John Velazquez	2005
	Corey Nakatani	2004
	Edgar Prado	2004
	John Velazquez	2004
	John Velazquez	2003
	John Velazquez	2002
	Jerry Bailey	2001
	Jerry Bailey	2000
	Jerry Bailey	1999

Leading Sires by Purses Won

Sire	Starts	Wins	Earnings
Storm Cat	37	4	$7,136,300
Sadler's Wells	38	6	6,982,900
Deputy Minister	25	3	5,370,560
Cee's Tizzy	3	2	5,360,400
Danzig	43	5	4,657,320
Seattle Slew	26	3	4,655,400
Pleasant Colony	20	2	4,541,320
Alydar	19	1	4,495,000
Saint Ballado	5	2	3,893,600
Kris S.	13	5	3,721,900
Cozzene	9	2	3,468,000
Mr. Prospector	42	3	3,421,680
Nureyev	23	4	3,408,400
Fappiano	15	2	3,386,000
Nijinsky II	12	3	3,283,000

Leading Sires by Most Breeders' Cup Starts

Sire	Starts	Wins	Earnings
Danzig	**43**	5	$4,657,320
Mr. Prospector	**42**	3	3,421,680
Sadler's Wells	**38**	6	6,982,900
Storm Cat	**37**	4	7,136,300
Seattle Slew	**26**	3	4,655,400
Deputy Minister	**25**	3	5,370,560
Nureyev	**23**	4	$3,408,400
Dynaformer	**20**	0	2,060,440
Pleasant Colony	**20**	2	4,541,320
Alydar	**19**	1	4,495,000
Affirmed	**17**	0	817,880
A.P. Indy	**16**	1	1,341,600
Cox's Ridge	**16**	3	2,529,000
Gone West	**16**	4	2,856,000
Fappiano	**15**	2	3,386,000
Irish River (Fr)	**15**	0	1,700,140
Rahy	**15**	1	1,868,480
Relaunch	**15**	2	3,004,000

Leading Sires by Most Breeders' Cup Placings

Sire	1st	2nd	3rd	Placings
Storm Cat	4	6	4	**14**
Danzig	5	5	3	**13**
Sadler's Wells	6	2	5	**13**
Seattle Slew	3	4	3	**10**
Alydar	1	5	3	**9**
Cox's Ridge	3	2	4	**9**
Mr. Prospector	3	3	2	**8**
Nureyev	4	2	2	**8**
Sovereign Dancer	0	5	3	**8**
Deputy Minister	3	1	3	**7**
Nijinsky II	3	2	2	**7**
Pleasant Colony	2	4	1	**7**
Danehill	2	3	1	**6**
Fappiano	2	2	2	**6**
Gone West	4	2	0	**6**
Kris S.	5	0	1	**6**
Seeking the Gold	3	2	1	**6**
Unbridled	3	2	1	**6**

Winners by Country and State Bred

Country	Starts	Wins
Ireland	137	13
Great Britain	117	9
France	47	5
Argentina	12	3
Canada	69	3
Germany	7	1
State	**Starts**	**Wins**
Kentucky	1,087	99
Florida	193	18
Maryland	25	3
Pennsylvania	19	3
California	58	2
Illinois	9	1
New Jersey	10	1
Oklahoma	3	1

Breeders' Cup Race Winners by Total Earnings

Horse	Breeders' Cup Victory	Total Earnings
Cigar	1995 Classic	$9,999,815
Skip Away	1997 Classic	9,616,360
Fantastic Light	2001 Turf	8,486,957
Pleasantly Perfect	2003 Classic	7,789,880
Alysheba	1988 Classic	6,679,242
Tiznow	2000, '01 Classic	6,427,830
High Chaparral (Ire)	2002, '03 Turf	5,331,231
Sunday Silence	1989 Classic	4,968,554
Daylami (Ire)	1999 Turf	4,614,762
Unbridled	1990 Classic	4,489,475
Saint Liam	2005 Classic	4,456,995

Horse	Breeders' Cup Victory	Total Earnings
Awesome Again	1998 Classic	4,374,590
Pilsudski (Ire)	1996 Turf	4,080,297

Horses With Highest Earnings in Breeders' Cup Races

Horse	Year(s) Started	Earnings
Tiznow	2000, '01	$4,560,400
Awesome Again	1998	2,662,400
Pleasantly Perfect	2003, '04	2,520,000
Saint Liam	2005	2,433,600
Skip Away	1997, '98	2,288,000
Cat Thief	1998, '99, 2000	2,200,000
Alysheba	1986, '87, '88	2,080,000
Alphabet Soup	1996	2,080,000
Volponi	2002, '03	2,080,000
Cigar	1995, '96	2,080,000
High Chaparral (Ire)	2002, '03	2,021,600
Spain	1999, 2000, '01	1,755,200
Unbridled	1990, '91	1,710,000

Winning Favorites by Race

Race	Winning Favorites	Race	Winning Favorites
Distaff	45.5%	Filly and Mare Turf	42.9%
Juvenile Fillies	54.5%	Juvenile	36.4%
Mile	27.3%	Turf	31.8%
Sprint	22.7%	Classic	31.8%

Favored Winners and Average Odds by Year

Year	Site	Winning Favorites	Average Winning Odds
2005	Belmont Park	25%	10.18-to-1
2004	Lone Star Park	50%	10.51-to-1
2003	Santa Anita Park	25%	14.90-to-1
2002	Arlington Park	50%	11.62-to-1
2001	Belmont Park	12.5%	8.63-to-1
2000	Churchill Downs	25%	16.65-to-1
1999	Gulfstream Park	25%	12.69-to-1
1998	Churchill Downs	28.6%	4.31-to-1
1997	Hollywood Park	71.4%	4.34-to-1
1996	Woodbine	28.6%	7.48-to-1
1995	Belmont Park	42.9%	4.46-to-1
1994	Churchill Downs	42.9%	12.06-to-1
1993	Santa Anita Park	42.9%	21.19-to-1
1992	Gulfstream Park	42.9%	6.59-to-1
1991	Churchill Downs	28.6%	15.36-to-1
1990	Belmont Park	57.1%	3.74-to-1
1989	Gulfstream Park	28.6%	5.00-to-1
1988	Churchill Downs	42.9%	4.59-to-1
1987	Hollywood Park	28.6%	12.74-to-1
1986	Santa Anita Park	28.6%	10.36-to-1
1985	Aqueduct	42.9%	3.31-to-1
1984	Hollywood Park	57.1%	15.98-to-1

Largest Winning Margins

Year	Winner	Race	Margin
1995	Inside Information	Distaff	13½
2005	Pleasant Home	Distaff	9¼
1997	Countess Diana	Juvenile Fillies	8½
1984	Princess Rooney	Distaff	7
1990	Bayakoa (Arg)	Distaff	6¾
2002	Volponi	Classic	6½
1985	Life's Magic	Distaff	6¼
1997	Skip Away	Classic	6

Smallest Winning Margins

Year	Winner	Race	Margin
2003	High Chaparral (Ire), Johar	Turf	DH
2001	Tiznow	Classic	nose
2000	Macho Uno	Juvenile	nose
1998	Escena	Distaff	nose
1996	Alphabet Soup	Classic	nose
1993	Hollywood Wildcat	Distaff	nose
1992	Fraise	Turf	nose
1988	Personal Ensign	Distaff	nose
1987	Ferdinand	Classic	nose
1987	Epitome	Juvenile Fillies	nose
1985	Tasso	Juvenile	nose
1984	Eillo	Sprint	nose

Nominations, Pre-Entries, Entries, and Starters by Year

Year	Foal Nominations	Pre-Entries	Entries	Starters
2005	16,183	117	100	99
2004	15,947	101	93	91
2003	14,927	101	91	90
2002	13,846	104	92	90
2001	15,020	109	98	94

Breeders' Cup Winners Who Sired Breeders' Cup Winners

Breeders' Cup Winner/Sire	Offspring (Breeders' Cup Victory)
A.P. Indy (1992 Classic)	Tempera (2001 Juvenile Fillies)
Awesome Again (1998 Classic)	Wilko (2004 Juvenile), Ghostzapper (2004 Classic)
Capote (1986 Juvenile)	Boston Harbor (1996 Juvenile)
Chief's Crown (1984 Juvenile)	Chief Bearhart (1997 Turf)
Cozzene (1995 Mile)	Tikkanen (1994 Turf), Alphabet Soup (1996 Classic)
Royal Academy (1990 Mile)	Val Royal (Fr) (2001 Mile)
Tiznow (2000 and '01 Classic)	Folklore (2005 Juvenile Fillies)
Unbridled (1990 Classic)	Unbridled's Song (1995 Juvenile), Anees (1999 Juvenile), Halfbridled (2003 Juvenile Fillies)
Unbridled's Song (1995 Juvenile)	Unbridled Elaine (2001 Distaff)
Wild Again (1984 Classic)	Elmhurst (1997 Sprint)

Breeders' Cup Winners Who Produced Breeders' Cup Winners

Breeders' Cup Winner/Broodmare	Offspring (Breeders' Cup Victory)
Hollywood Wildcat (1993 Distaff)	War Chant (2000 Mile)
My Flag (1995 Juvenile Fillies)	Storm Flag Flying (2002 Juvenile Fillies)
Personal Ensign (1988 Distaff)	My Flag (1995 Juvenile Fillies)

Year	Foal Nominations	Pre-Entries	Entries	Starters
2000	15,760	135	105	103
1999	15,191	128	102	101
1998	14,081	117	85	82
1997	12,751	94	77	76
1996	11,971	90	85	82
1995	10,543	101	84	81
1994	9,738	126	94	91
1993	9,564	103	82	81
1992	9,392	112	92	91
1991	10,056	116	91	90
1990	11,003	110	91	83
1989	11,734	101	89	81
1988	11,276	87	79	75
1987	12,183	106	91	84
1986	11,494	90	79	76
1985	10,907	110	90	82
1984	10,034	77	69	68
1983	7,839			
1982	9,260			

Pre-entries are number of individual horses made eligible. Owners may pre-enter a horse in up to two races.

Average Field Sizes by Race

Race	Average Field	Most Starters	Fewest Starters
Distaff	8.95	14	6
Juvenile Fillies	11.4	14	8
Mile	13.1	14	10
Sprint	13.0	14	9
Filly and Mare Turf	12.9	14	12
Juvenile	12.0	14	8
Turf	11.9	14	8
Classic	11.5	14	8

Average Field Sizes by Year

Year	Site	Starters	Avg. Field
2005	Belmont Park	99	12.38
2004	Lone Star Park	91	11.38
2003	Santa Anita Park	90	11.25
2002	Arlington Park	90	11.25
2001	Belmont Park	94	11.75
2000	Churchill Downs	103	12.88
1999	Gulfstream Park	101	12.63
1998	Churchill Downs	82	11.71
1997	Hollywood Park	76	10.86
1996	Woodbine	82	11.71
1995	Belmont Park	81	11.57
1994	Churchill Downs	91	13.00
1993	Santa Anita Park	81	11.57
1992	Gulfstream Park	91	13.00
1991	Churchill Downs	90	12.86
1990	Belmont Park	83	11.86
1989	Gulfstream Park	81	11.57
1988	Churchill Downs	75	10.71
1987	Hollywood Park	84	12.00
1986	Santa Anita Park	76	10.86
1985	Aqueduct	82	11.71
1984	Hollywood Park	68	9.71

Most Pre-Entries for a Breeders' Cup Race

Year	Race	Pre-Entries
2000	Mile	29
1998	Mile	27
1999	Mile	25
1994	Sprint	25
1994	Turf	24
2002	Mile	24
1995	Mile	24
1998	Sprint	24

Largest Breeders' Cup On-Track Attendance

Year	Site	On-Track Attendance
1998	Churchill Downs	80,452
2000	Churchill Downs	76,043
1994	Churchill Downs	71,671
1988	Churchill Downs	71,237
1986	Santa Anita Park	69,155
1991	Churchill Downs	66,204

Smallest Breeders' Cup On-Track Attendance

Year	Site	On-Track Attendance
1995	Belmont Park	37,246
1996	Woodbine	42,243
1985	Aqueduct	42,568
1999	Gulfstream Park	45,124
1992	Gulfstream Park	45,415
2002	Arlington Park	46,118

Largest Breeders' Cup On-Track Wagering

Year	Site	On-Track Wagering
2003	Santa Anita Park	$13,678,118
2000	Churchill Downs	13,579,798
1998	Churchill Downs	13,544,859
2005	Belmont Park	13,385,593
1986	Santa Anita Park	12,510,109
2002	Arlington Park	12,143,114
1993	Santa Anita Park	12,142,750

Smallest Breeders' Cup On-Track Betting

Year	Site	On-Track Wagering
1996	Woodbine	$5,925,469
1985	Aqueduct	7,200,175
1995	Belmont Park	7,590,332
1997	Hollywood Park	8,191,459
1984	Hollywood Park	8,443,070
1990	Belmont Park	9,107,270

Shortest-Priced Winners

Year	Horse	Race	Odds
1990	Meadow Star	Juvenile Fillies	0.20-to-1
1994	Flanders	Juvenile Fillies	0.40-to-1*
1985	Life's Magic	Distaff	0.40-to-1*
1988	Personal Ensign	Distaff	0.50-to-1
1986	Lady's Secret	Distaff	0.50-to-1*
1991	Dance Smartly	Distaff	0.50-to-1*

* Part of entry

Longest-Priced Winners

Year	Horse	Race	Odds
1993	Arcangues	Classic	133.60-to-1
2000	Spain	Distaff	55.90-to-1
1984	Lashkari (GB)	Turf	53.40-to-1
1994	One Dreamer	Distaff	47.10-to-1
2000	Caressing	Juvenile Fillies	47.00-to-1
2002	Volponi	Classic	43.50-to-1
1991	Miss Alleged	Turf	42.10-to-1
2003	Adoration	Distaff	40.70-to-1
1986	Last Tycoon (Ire)	Mile	35.90-to-1
1999	Cash Run	Juvenile Fillies	32.50-to-1

History of Breeders' Cup Races

Breeders' Cup Classic

America's classic distance is 1¼ miles on dirt, and the Breeders' Cup Classic (G1) has offered some classic, spine-tingling contests. The race has been the kingmaker among the eight Breeders' Cup races, producing 11 Horses of the Year in its first 22 runnings. The respective winners in 2004 and '05, Ghostzapper and Saint Liam, were both voted Horse of the Year.

Although the year's best horse does not always win the Breeders' Cup Classic, the race has been extremely competitive, with eight of the races decided by less than one length. The only two runaway victories were Volponi's 6½-length upset in the 2002 Classic at Arlington Park and Skip Trial's six-length triumph at Hollywood Park in 1997.

The series began with a classic finish in the 1984 Breeders' Cup at Hollywood Park, with three horses charging together through the final furlong. Longshot supplemental entry Wild Again set the pace and prevailed by a neck on the inside. Gate Dancer bore in on favorite Slew o' Gold nearing the wire, and jockey Angel Cordero Jr. restrained Slew o' Gold through the final yards to protect the eventual champion older male. Gate Dancer finished second, but Hollywood's steward disqualified him to third, moving up Slew o' Gold to second.

The race did not yield its first Horse of the Year until 1987, when the Breeders' Cup returned to Hollywood and '86 Kentucky Derby (G1) winner Ferdinand met '87 Derby victor Alysheba. They hooked up inside the sixteenth pole and fought to the wire, with even-money favorite Ferdinand prevailing by a nose under jockey Bill Shoemaker. Ferdinand was voted Horse of the Year and champion older male, while Alysheba was honored as champion three-year-old male. The following year, Alysheba won the Classic in near darkness at Churchill Downs's first Breeders' Cup and was voted Horse of the Year.

The 1989 Breeders' Cup Classic reunited Triple Crown rivals Sunday Silence and Easy Goer, and they battled through deep stretch as they had in the Derby and Preakness Stakes (G1) that year. Sunday Silence, who had won both the Derby and Preakness, proved best and won by a neck over Belmont Stakes (G1) victor Easy Goer. Sunday Silence was voted champion three-year-old male and Horse of the Year. After a truncated four-year-old campaign, Sunday Silence was sold for stud duty in Japan, where he became that country's all-time leading sire.

Tiznow, the race's only two-time winner, provided two scintillating finishes, holding off Giant's Causeway in 2000 by a neck at Churchill and then coming back courageously to best Sakhee by a nose in '01 at Belmont Park.

Breeders' Cup Classic

Grade 1, $4-million, three-year-olds and up, 1¼ miles, dirt. Run October 29, 2005, at Belmont Park with gross value of $4,291,560. First run in 1984. Weights: Northern Hemisphere three-year-olds, 122 pounds; older, 126 pounds. Southern Hemisphere three-year-olds, 117 pounds; older, 126 pounds. Fillies and mares allowed three pounds.

Year	Winner	Jockey	Second	Third	Site	Time	Cond.	1st Purse
2005	**Saint Liam**, 5	J. Bailey	Flower Alley	Perfect Drift	Bel	2:01.49	ft	$2,433,600
2004	**Ghostzapper**, 4	J. Castellano	Roses in May	Pleasantly Perfect	LS	**1:59.02**	ft	2,080,000
2003	**Pleasantly Perfect**, 5	A. Solis	Medaglia d'Oro	Dynever	SA	1:59.88	ft	2,080,000
2002	**Volponi**, 4	J. Santos	Medaglia d'Oro	Milwaukee Brew	AP	2:01.39	ft	2,080,000
2001	**Tiznow**, 4	C. McCarron	Sakhee	Albert the Great	Bel	2:00.62	ft	2,080,000
2000	**Tiznow**, 3	C. McCarron	Giant's Causeway	Captain Steve	CD	2:00.75	ft	2,480,400
1999	**Cat Thief**, 3	P. Day	Budroyale	Golden Missile	GP	1:59.52	ft	2,080,000
1998	**Awesome Again**, 4	P. Day	Silver Charm	Swain (Ire)	CD	2:02.16	ft	**2,662,400**
1997	**Skip Away**, 4	M. Smith	Deputy Commander	Dowty	Hol	1:59.16	ft	2,288,000
1996	**Alphabet Soup**, 5	C. McCarron	Louis Quatorze	Cigar	WO	2:01.00	ft	2,080,000
1995	**Cigar**, 5	J. Bailey	L'Carriere	Unaccounted For	Bel	1:59.58	my	1,560,000
1994	**Concern**, 3	J. Bailey	Tabasco Cat	Dramatic Gold	CD	2:02.41	ft	1,560,000
1993	**Arcangues**, 5	J. Bailey	Bertrando	Kissin Kris	SA	2:00.83	ft	1,560,000
1992	**A.P. Indy**, 3	E. Delahoussaye	Pleasant Tap	Jolypha	GP	2:00.20	ft	1,560,000
1991	**Black Tie Affair (Ire)**, 5	J. Bailey	Twilight Agenda	Unbridled	CD	2:02.95	ft	1,560,000
1990	**Unbridled**, 3	P. Day	Ibn Bey (GB)	Thirty Six Red	Bel	2:02⅕	ft	1,350,000
1989	**Sunday Silence**, 3	C. McCarron	Easy Goer	Blushing John	GP	2:00⅕	ft	1,350,000
1988	**Alysheba**, 4	C. McCarron	Seeking the Gold	Waquoit	CD	2:04⅘	my	1,350,000
1987	**Ferdinand**, 4	W. Shoemaker	Alysheba	Judge Angelucci	Hol	2:01⅖	ft	1,350,000
1986	**Skywalker**, 4	L. Pincay Jr.	Turkoman	Precisionist	SA	2:00⅖	ft	1,350,000
1985	**Proud Truth**, 3	J. Velasquez	Gate Dancer	Turkoman	Aqu	2:00⅘	ft	1,350,000
1984	**Wild Again**, 4	P. Day	Slew o' Gold	Gate Dancer	Hol	2:03⅖	ft	1,350,000

1997: Skip Away supplemental entry, Whiskey Wisdom disqualified from third to fourth; 1984: Gate Dancer disqualified from second to third

Three-year-olds have done well in the Classic, winning seven of the first 22 runnings, and two three-year-old winners have become successful sires. The 1990 Classic winner, Derby victor Unbridled, sired winners of the Kentucky Derby and Preakness, as well as two Breeders' Cup Juvenile (G1) victors and a Juvenile Fillies (G1) winner. A.P. Indy, the 1992 winner and Horse of the Year, regularly ranks among North America's leading sires and sired 2001 Juvenile Fillies (G1) winner Tempera. Tiznow was a three-year-old when he won in 2000 and was voted Horse of the Year.

While the Classic has yielded some classic contests, it also has produced its share of puzzles and one especially bizarre finish. Arcangues won in 1993 at 133.60-to-1, the longest price for any Breeders' Cup winner, and Volponi won at 43.50-to-1 in 2002. The unusual finish came in the 1998 Classic, which featured the best field ever assembled for a Breeders' Cup race. Silver Charm took the lead in the stretch but began to bear out in the final furlong. Swain (Ire), a leading European contender, followed Silver Charm to the far outside under left-handed whipping by his jockey, Frankie Dettori. Awesome Again dashed through the hole they created and won by three-quarters of a length over Silver Charm. Skip Away, the 1.90-to-1 favorite who finished sixth, was voted champion older male and Horse of the Year.

Owners by Wins

2 **Stronach Stables** (Awesome Again, Ghostzapper)

1 **Amherst Stable and Spruce Pond Stable** (Volponi), **Black Chip Stable** (Wild Again), **Cee's Stable** (Tiznow), **Michael Cooper and Cecilia Straub-Rubens** (Tiznow), **Darby Dan Farm** (Proud Truth), **Diamond A Racing** (Pleasantly Perfect), **William S. Farish, Harold Goodman, William S. Kilroy, and Tomonori Tsurumaki** (A.P. Indy), **Frances Genter** (Unbridled), **Arthur Hancock III, Ernest Gaillard, and Charlie Whittingham** (Sunday Silence), **Carolyn Hine** (Skip Away), **Elizabeth Keck** (Ferdinand), **Robert Meyerhoff** (Concern), **Oak Cliff Stable** (Skywalker), **Overbrook Farm** (Cat Thief), **Allen E. Paulson** (Cigar), **Ridder Thoroughbred Stable** (Alphabet Soup), **Dorothy and Pamela Scharbauer** (Alysheba), **Jeffrey Sullivan** (Black Tie Affair [Ire]), **Mr. and Mrs. William K. Warren Jr.** (Saint Liam), **Daniel Wildenstein** (Arcangues)

Breeders by Wins

2 **Oak Cliff Thoroughbreds** (Skywalker, Sunday Silence), **Cecilia Straub-Rubens** (Tiznow [twice]), **Frank Stronach/Adena Springs** (Awesome Again, Ghostzapper)

1 **Allez France Stables** (Arcangues), **Amherst Stable** (Volponi), **Anna Marie Barnhart** (Skip Away), **Clovelly Farms** (Pleasantly Perfect), **Edward P. Evans** (Saint Liam), **William S. Farish and William S. Kilroy** (A.P. Indy), **Mrs. John W. Galbreath** (Proud Truth), **Howard B. Keck** (Ferdinand), **W. Paul Little** (Wild Again), **Preston Madden** (Alysheba), **Robert Meyerhoff** (Concern), **Overbrook Farm** (Cat Thief), **Allen E. Paulson** (Cigar), **Stephen Peskoff** (Black Tie Affair [Ire]), **Southeast Associates** (Alphabet Soup), **Tartan Farms** (Unbridled)

Trainers by Wins

2 **Jay Robbins** (Tiznow [twice]), **Charlie Whittingham** (Ferdinand, Sunday Silence)

1 **Patrick Byrne** (Awesome Again), **Neil Drysdale** (A.P. Indy), **Richard E. Dutrow Jr.** (Saint Liam), **Andre Fabre** (Arcangues), **Bobby Frankel** (Ghostzapper), **Hubert "Sonny" Hine** (Skip Away), **P. G. Johnson** (Volponi), **David Hofmans** (Alphabet Soup), **D. Wayne Lukas** (Cat Thief), **Richard Mandella** (Pleasantly Perfect), **Bill Mott** (Cigar), **Carl Nafzger** (Unbridled), **Ernie Poulos** (Black Tie Affair [Ire]), **Richard Small** (Concern), **Vincent Timphony** (Wild Again), **Jack Van Berg** (Alysheba), **John Veitch** (Proud Truth), **Mike Whittingham** (Skywalker)

Jockeys by Wins

5 **Jerry Bailey** (Arcangues, Black Tie Affair [Ire], Cigar, Concern, Saint Liam), **Chris McCarron** (Alphabet Soup, Alysheba, Sunday Silence, Tiznow [twice])

4 **Pat Day** (Awesome Again, Cat Thief, Unbridled, Wild Again)

1 **Javier Castellano** (Ghostzapper), **Eddie Delahoussaye** (A.P. Indy), **Laffit Pincay Jr.** (Skywalker), **Jose Santos** (Volponi), **Bill Shoemaker** (Ferdinand), **Mike Smith** (Skip Away), **Alex Solis** (Pleasantly Perfect), **Jorge Velasquez** (Proud Truth)

Sires by Wins

2 **Cee's Tizzy** (Tiznow [twice])

1 **Alydar** (Alysheba), **Awesome Again** (Ghostzapper), **Broad Brush** (Concern), **Cozzene** (Alphabet Soup), **Cryptoclearance** (Volponi), **Deputy Minister** (Awesome Again), **Fappiano** (Unbridled), **Graustark** (Proud Truth), **Halo** (Sunday Silence), **Icecapade** (Wild Again), **Miswaki** (Black Tie Affair [Ire]), **Nijinsky II** (Ferdinand), **Palace Music** (Cigar), **Pleasant Colony** (Pleasantly Perfect), **Relaunch** (Skywalker), **Sagace** (Arcangues), **Saint Ballado** (Saint Liam), **Seattle Slew** (A.P. Indy), **Skip Trial** (Skip Away), **Storm Cat** (Cat Thief)

Winners by Place Where Bred

Locality	Winners	Locality	Winners
Kentucky	13	Pennsylvania	1
Maryland	2	Canada	1
California	2	Ireland	1
Florida	2		

Supplemental Entries

Year	Runner	Fee	Finish	Earnings
2005	Starcraft (NZ)	$800,000	7	$0
2001	**Tiznow**	(credit)	1	2,080,000
	Gander	(credit)	9	0

Year	Runner	Fee	Finish	Earnings
2000	**Tiznow**	360,000	1	2,480,400
	Captain Steve	270,000†	3	562,800
	Gander	360,000	9	0
1998	Silver Charm	480,000	2	1,024,000
	Skip Away	(credit)	6	0
	Gentlemen (Arg)	800,000	10	0
1997	**Skip Away**	480,000	1	2,288,000
1994	Best Pal	360,000	5	60,000
	Bertrando	360,000	6	0
1993	Bertrando	360,000	2	600,000
	Best Pal	360,000	10	0
1988	Waquoit	360,000	3	324,000
	Cutlass Reality	360,000	7	0
1985	Vanlandingham	360,000	7	0
1984	**Wild Again**	360,000	1	1,350,000

† incl. credit from 1999

Eclipse Award Winners from Race

Year	Runner	Finish	Title
2005	**Saint Liam**	1	HOY, older male
2004	**Ghostzapper**	1	HOY, older male
2003	Funny Cide	9	3yo male
2002	War Emblem	8	3yo male
2001	**Tiznow**	1	Older male
2000	**Tiznow**	1	HOY, 3yo male
	Lemon Drop Kid	5	Older male
1998	Skip Away	6	HOY, older male
1997	**Skip Away**	1	Older male
1996	Cigar	3	HOY, older male
1995	**Cigar**	1	HOY, older male
1993	Bertrando	2	Older male
1992	**A.P. Indy**	1	HOY, 3yo male
1991	**Black Tie Affair (Ire)**	1	HOY, older male
1990	**Unbridled**	1	3yo male
1989	**Sunday Silence**	1	HOY, 3yo male
1988	**Alysheba**	1	HOY, older male
1987	**Ferdinand**	1	HOY, older male
	Alysheba	2	3yo male
1986	Turkoman	2	Older male
1985	Vanlandingham	7	Older male
1984	Slew o' Gold	2	Older male

HOY = Horse of the Year

Largest Winning Margins

Year	Winner	Margin
2002	Volponi	6½
1997	Skip Away	6
2004	Ghostzapper	3
1995	Cigar	2½
1993	Arcangues	2
1992	A.P. Indy	2

Smallest Winning Margins

Year	Winner	Margin
2001	Tiznow	nose
1996	Alphabet Soup	nose
1987	Ferdinand	nose
1985	Proud Truth	head
1984	Wild Again	head
2000	Tiznow	neck
1994	Concern	neck
1989	Sunday Silence	neck

Shortest-Priced Winners

Year	Winner	Odds
1995	Cigar	0.70-to-1
1987	Ferdinand	1.00-to-1
1988	Alysheba	1.50-to-1
1997	Skip Away	1.80-to-1

Longest-Priced Winners

Year	Winner	Odds
1993	Arcangues	133.60-to-1
2002	Volponi	43.50-to-1
1984	Wild Again	31.30-to-1
1996	Alphabet Soup	19.85-to-1
1999	Cat Thief	19.60-to-1

Fastest Winners

Year	Winner	Track	Time	Cond.
2004	Ghostzapper	LS	1:59.02	fast
1997	Skip Away	Hol	1:59.16	fast
1999	Cat Thief	GP	1:59.52	fast
1995	Cigar	Bel	1:59.58	muddy
2003	Pleasantly Perfect	SA	1:59.88	fast
1992	A.P. Indy	GP	2:00.20	fast
1989	Sunday Silence	GP	2:00⅕	fast

Slowest Winners

Year	Winner	Track	Time	Cond.
1988	Alysheba	CD	2:04⅘	muddy
1984	Wild Again	Hol	2:03⅗	fast
1991	Black Tie Affair (Ire)	CD	2:02.95	fast
1994	Concern	CD	2:02.41	fast

Most Starters

Year	Track	Starters
1999	Gulfstream Park	14
1994	Churchill Downs	14
1992	Gulfstream Park	14
1990	Belmont Park	14

Fewest Starters

Year	Track	Starters
1989	Gulfstream Park	8
1985	Aqueduct	8
1984	Hollywood Park	8
1997	Hollywood Park	9
1988	Churchill Downs	9

Winning Post Positions

Post	Starters	Winners	Percent
1	22	2	9.1%
2	22	3	13.7%
3	22	2	9.1%
4	22	1	4.5%
5	22	1	4.5%
6	22	3	13.7%
7	22	0	0.0%
8	22	2	9.1%
9	19	0	0.0%
10	17	2	11.8%
11	15	1	6.7%
12	12	4	33.3%
13	10	0	0.0%
14	4	1	25.0%

Changes in Classic

The only changes in the Breeders' Cup Classic were increases in the purse from $3-million to $4-million in 1996 and to $5-million in 2006.

Breeders' Cup Turf

The race conditions of the Breeders' Cup Turf (G1), 1½ miles on grass at weight for age, constitute the classic standard of European racing, and as a result, overseas runners have won a majority of the contests. But they have not been dominant, probably because running in late October or early November—sometimes in tropical conditions—is not part of the European schedule, which traditionally culminates for top horses in early October with the running of the Prix de l'Arc de Triomphe (Fr-G1).

In fact, American owners and trainers have fielded some outstanding grass runners, and they have defeated top-level European competitors over the years. At times, lesser American runners have prevailed because the Europeans were past their best form or did not adapt well to warm weather at Breeders' Cup sites.

Because of its importance on the world racing calendar, the Breeders' Cup Turf has become the definitive North American championship race. In every year except 1984 (John Henry's last championship season), '89 (when the male title went to Breeders' Cup Mile [G1] winner Steinlen [GB]), and 2005, when Europeans swept the top spots, a North American turf champion has come out of the Turf.

The 2003 edition featured the first dead heat in any Breeders' Cup race when High Chaparral (Ire) and Johar reached the finish line together. High Chaparral was the first dual Turf winner.

A decade earlier, American-trained Kotashaan (Fr) dominated grass racing in Southern California and scored a half-length victory over fellow Californian Bien Bien in the Turf. With a weak handicap division that year and no dominant three-year-old coming out of the Triple Crown series, Kotashaan was voted both champion turf male and Horse of the Year. He remains the only Turf winner to earn the top North American honor.

Early in the Turf's history, European runners gave indications they would dominate the race. Unheralded Lashkari (GB) won the inaugural running at Hollywood Park in 1984 at 53.40-to-1, the longest winning odds in the race's history. Lashkari, who never duplicated that effort, was bred and owned by the Aga Khan, who also bred back-to-back Turf winners Daylami (Ire), who was leased to Godolphin Racing, and Kalanisi (Ire), also owned by the Aga Khan. In 2001, Godolphin's Fantastic Light won at 7-to-5.

Pebbles (GB) was supplemented to the race in 1985 and scored a hard-fought victory over Strawberry Road (Aus). The Turf in the following year at Santa Anita Park was expected to showcase Dancing Brave, the Arc winner whose only career defeat was a second-place finish in the Epsom Derby (Eng-G1). But Dancing Brave was clearly

Breeders' Cup Turf

Grade 1, $2-million, three-year-olds and up, 1½ miles, turf. Run October 29, 2005, at Lone Star Park with gross value $2,090,760. First run in 1984. Weights: Northern Hemisphere three-year-olds, 121 pounds; older, 126 pounds; Southern Hemisphere three-year-olds, 116 pounds; older, 125 pounds. Fillies and mares allowed three pounds.

Year	Winner	Jockey	Second	Third	Site	Time	Cond.	1st Purse
2005	**Shirocco (Ger)**, 4	C. Soumillon	Ace (Ire)	Azamour (Ire)	Bel	2:29.30	gd	$1,185,600
2004	**Better Talk Now**, 5	R. Dominguez	Kitten's Joy	Powerscourt (GB)	LS	2:29.70	yl	1,040,000
2003	**(DH) High Chaparral**, 4	M. Kinane		Falbrav (Ire)	SA	2:24.24	fm	763,200
	(DH) Johar, 4	A. Solis						763,200
2002	**High Chaparral (Ire)**, 3	M. Kinane	With Anticipation	Falcon Flight (Fr)	AP	2:30.14	yl	1,258,400
2001	**Fantastic Light**, 5	L. Dettori	Milan (GB)	Timboroa (GB)	Bel	2:24.36	fm	1,112,800
2000	**Kalinisi (Ire)**, 4	J. Murtagh	Quiet Resolve	John's Call	CD	2:26.96	fm	**1,289,600**
1999	**Daylami (Ire)**, 5	L. Dettori	Royal Anthem	Buck's Boy	GP	2:24.73	gd	1,040,000
1998	**Buck's Boy**, 5	S. Sellers	Yagli	Dushyantor	CD	2:28.74	fm	1,040,000
1997	**Chief Bearhart**, 4	J. Santos	Borgia (Ger)	Flag Down	Hol	**2:23.92**	fm	1,040,000
1996	**Pilsudski (Ire)**, 4	W. Swinburn	Singspiel (Ire)	Swain (Ire)	WO	2:30.20	gd	1,040,000
1995	**Northern Spur (Ire)**, 4	C. McCarron	Freedom Cry (GB)	Carnegie (Ire)	Bel	2:42.07	sf	1,040,000
1994	**Tikkanen**, 3	M. Smith	Hatoof	Paradise Creek	CD	2:26.50	fm	1,040,000
1993	**Kotashaan (Fr)**, 5	K. Desormeaux	Bien Bien	Luazur (Fr)	SA	2:25.16	fm	1,040,000
1992	**Fraise**, 4	P. Valenzuela	Sky Classic	Quest for Fame (GB)	GP	2:24.08	fm	1,040,000
1991	**Miss Alleged**, f, 4	E. Legrix	Itsallgreektome	Quest for Fame (GB)	CD	2:30.95	fm	1,040,000
1990	**In the Wings (GB)**, 4	G. Stevens	With Approval	El Senor	Bel	2:29$\frac{3}{5}$	gd	900,000
1989	**Prized**, 3	E. Delahoussaye	Sierra Roberta (Fr)	Star Lift (GB)	GP	2:28	gd	900,000
1988	**Great Communicator**, 5	R. Sibille	Sunshine Forever	Indian Skimmer	CD	2:35$\frac{1}{5}$	gd	900,000
1987	**Theatrical (Ire)**, 5	P. Day	Trempolino	Village Star (Fr)	Hol	2:24$\frac{2}{5}$	fm	900,000
1986	**Manila**, 3	J. Santos	Theatrical (Ire)	Estrapade	SA	2:25$\frac{2}{5}$	fm	900,000
1985	**Pebbles (GB)**, f, 4	P. Eddery	Strawberry Road (Aus)	Mourjane (Ire)	Aqu	2:27	fm	900,000
1984	**Lashkari (GB)**, 3	Y. Saint-Martin	All Along (Fr)	Raami (GB)	Hol	2:25$\frac{1}{5}$	fm	900,000

2003: Dead heat. 2002, '03: High Chaparral (Ire), supplemental entry. 1985: Pebbles (GB), supplemental entry.

over the top and tired to finish fourth as Manila stormed to a neck victory over Theatrical (Ire), who would win the Turf the following year.

California-based runners Great Communicator and Prized won in 1988 and '89, respectively, and the American home-court advantage appeared to be an important factor in the Turf. But European runners won the following two years and subsequently have performed well. In 1996, overseas interests swept the top four spots as Pilsudski (Ire) finished ahead of Singspiel (Ire), Swain (Ire), and Shantou. Shirocco (Ger) led a similar rout in 2005.

Canadian-bred Chief Bearhart scored a popular 1.90-to-1 victory in 1997, and Illinois-bred Buck's Boy led a North American sweep of the top spots at Churchill Downs in '98. The European contingent then asserted itself through 2002, with California-based Johar sharing the winner's circle with High Chaparral in '03. In 2004, Maryland-based Better Talk Now won at 27.90-to-1 over 7-to-10 favorite Kitten's Joy at Lone Star Park.

Owners by Wins

2 **Aga Khan** (Kalanisi [Ire], Lashkari [GB]), **Godolphin Racing** (Daylami [Ire], Fantastic Light), **Susan Magnier and Michael Tabor** (High Chaparral [Ire] [twice]), **Sheikh Mohammed bin Rashid al Maktoum** (In the Wings [GB], Pebbles [GB])

1 **Augustin Stables** (Tikkanen), **Bushwood Racing Partners** (Better Talk Now), **Charles Cella** (Northern Spur [Ire]), **Class Act Stable** (Great Communicator), **Clover Racing Stable and Meadowbrook Farm** (Prized), **Fares Farm** (Miss Alleged), **La Presle Farm** (Kotashaan [Fr]), **Allen Paulson** (Theatrical [Ire]), **Madeleine Paulson** (Fraise), **Quarter B Farm** (Buck's Boy), **Sam-Son Farm** (Chief Bearhart), **Bradley M. "Mike" Shannon** (Manila), **The Thoroughbred Corp.** (Johar), **Baron Georg von Ullmann** (Shirocco [Ger]), **Lord Arnold Weinstock and executors of Simon Weinstock** (Pilsudski [Ire])

Breeders by Wins

3 **Aga Khan** (Daylami [Ire], Kalanisi [Ire], Lashkari [GB])

2 **Sean Coughlan** (High Chaparral [Ire] [twice])

1 **Ballymacoll Stud** (Pilsudski [Ire]), **Eduardo Cojuangco Jr.** (Manila), **Bertram and Diana Firestone** (Theatrical [Ire]), **Carl M. Freeman** (Miss Alleged), **Gainsborough Farm** (Fantastic Light), **Irish Acres Farm** (Buck's Boy), **Sheikh Mohammed bin Rashid al Maktoum** (In the Wings [GB]), **Richard Maynard** (Chief Bearhart), **Meadowbrook Farm** (Prized), **Allen E. Paulson** (Fraise), **George M. Strawbridge Jr.** (Tikkanen), **Swettenham Stud & Partners** (Northern Spur [Ire]), **The Thoroughbred Corp.** (Johar), **Baron Georg von Ullmann** (Shirocco [Ger]), **Warren Hill Stud** (Pebbles [GB]), **James B. Watriss** (Great Communicator), **Wertheimer & Frere** (Kotashaan [Fr]), **Wimborne Farm** (Better Talk Now)

Trainers by Wins

2 **Andre Fabre** (In the Wings [GB], Shirocco [Ger]), **Richard Mandella** (Kotashaan [Fr], Johar), **William Mott** (Fraise, Theatrical [Ire]), **Aidan O'Brien** (High Chaparral [Ire] [twice]), **Sir Michael Stoute** (Kalanisi [Ire], Pilsudski [Ire]), **Saeed bin Suroor** (Daylami [Ire], Fantastic Light)

1 **Thad Ackel** (Great Communicator), **Pascal Bary** (Miss Alleged), **Clive Brittain** (Pebbles [GB]), **Neil Drysdale** (Prized), **Mark Frostad** (Chief Bearhart), **P. Noel Hickey** (Buck's Boy), **LeRoy Jolley** (Manila), **Ron McAnally** (Northern Spur [Ire]), **H. Graham Motion** (Better Talk Now), **Jonathan Pease** (Tikkanen), **Alain de Royer-Dupre** (Lashkari [GB])

Jockeys by Wins

2 **Lanfranco Dettori** (Daylami [Ire], Fantastic Light), **Michael Kinane** (High Chaparral [Ire] [twice]), **Jose Santos** (Chief Bearhart, Manila)

1 **Pat Day** (Theatrical [Ire]), **Eddie Delahoussaye** (Prized), **Kent Desormeaux** (Kotashaan [Fr]), **Ramon Dominguez** (Better Talk Now), **Pat Eddery** (Pebbles [GB]), **Eric Legrix** (Miss Alleged), **Chris McCarron** (Northern Spur [Ire]), **John Murtagh** (Kalanisi [Ire]), **Yves Saint-Martin** (Lashkari [GB]), **Shane Sellers** (Buck's Boy), **Ray Sibille** (Great Communicator), **Mike Smith** (Tikkanen), **Alex Solis** (Johar), **Christophe Soumillon** (Shirocco [Ger]), **Gary Stevens** (In the Wings [GB]), **Walter Swinburn** (Pilsudski [Ire]), **Patrick Valenzuela** (Fraise)

Sires by Wins

4 **Sadler's Wells** (High Chaparral [Ire] [twice], In the Wings [GB], Northern Spur [Ire])

2 **Doyoun** (Daylami [Ire], Kalanisi [Ire])

1 **Alleged** (Miss Alleged), **Bucksplasher** (Buck's Boy), **Chief's Crown** (Chief Bearhart), **Cozzene** (Tikkanen), **Darshaan** (Kotashaan [Fr]), **Gone West** (Johar), **Key to the Kingdom** (Great Communicator), **Kris S.** (Prized), **Lyphard** (Manila), **Mill Reef** (Lashkari [GB]), **Monsun** (Shirocco [Ger]), **Nureyev** (Theatrical [Ire]), **Polish Precedent** (Pilsudski [Ire]), **Rahy** (Fantastic Light), **Sharpen Up (GB)** (Pebbles [GB]), **Strawberry Road (Aus)** (Fraise), **Talkin Man** (Better Talk Now)

Winners by Place Where Bred

Locality	Winners	Locality	Winners
Ireland	7	Florida	1
Kentucky	7	France	1
Great Britain	3	Germany	1
Illinois	1	Canada	1
Pennsylvania	1		

Supplemental Entries

Year	Runner	Fee	Finish	Earnings
2005	Shirocco (Ger)	$180,000	1	$1,185,600
	Azamour (Ire)	180,000	3	250,800
2003	**High Chaparral (Ire)**	(credit)	1	$762,200
2003	**High Chaparral (Ire)**	(credit)	1	762,200
	Falbrav (Ire)	180,000	3	233,200
2002	**High Chaparral (Ire)**	180,000	1	1,258,400
	Falcon Flight (Fr)	180,000	3	290,400
	Golan (Ire)	180,000	6	0

Year	Runner	Fee	Finish	Earnings
2001	Timboroa (GB)	180,000	3	256,800
2000	John's Call	240,000	3	297,600
	Montjeu (Ire)	180,000	7	0
	Subtle Power (Ire)	180,000	10	0
1986	Estrapade	240,000	3	216,000
1985	**Pebbles (GB)**	240,000	1	900,000
	Greinton (GB)	240,000	7	0

Eclipse Award Winners from Race

Year	Runner	Finish	Title
2004	**Kitten's Joy**	2	Turf male
2003	**High Chaparral (Ire)**	1 (dh)	Turf male
2002	**High Chaparral (Ire)**	1	Turf male
2001	**Fantastic Light**	1	Turf male
2000	**Kalanisi (Ire)**	1	Turf male
1999	**Daylami (Ire)**	1	Turf male
1998	**Buck's Boy**	1	Turf male
1997	**Chief Bearhart**	1	Turf male
1996	Singspiel (Ire)	2	Turf male
1995	**Northern Spur (Ire)**	1	Turf male
1994	Paradise Creek	3	Turf male
1993	**Kotashaan (Fr)**	1	Horse of the Year, Turf male
1992	Sky Classic	2	Turf male
1991	**Miss Alleged**	1	Turf female
1988	Sunshine Forever	2	Turf male
1987	**Theatrical (Ire)**	1	Turf male
1986	**Manila**	1	Turf male
1985	**Pebbles (GB)**	1	Turf female

Largest Winning Margins

Year	Winner	Margin
1999	Daylami (Ire)	2½
2004	Better Talk Now	1¾
1994	Tikkanen	1½
2002	High Chaparral (Ire)	1¼
1999	Buck's Boy	1¼
1996	Pilsudski (Ire)	1¼

Smallest Winning Margins

Year	Winner	Margin
2003	High Chaparral (Ire) Johar	Dead heat
1992	Fraise	nose
1989	Prized	head
1995	Northern Spur (Ire)	neck
1986	Manila	neck
1985	Pebbles (GB)	neck
1984	Lashkari (GB)	neck

Shortest-Priced Winners

Year	Winner	Odds
2002	High Chaparral (Ire)	0.90-to-1
2001	Fantastic Light	1.40-to-1
1993	Kotashaan (Fr)	1.50-to-1
1999	Daylami (Ire)	1.60-to-1
1987	Theatrical (Ire)	1.80-to-1

Longest-Priced Winners

Year	Winner	Odds
1984	Lashkari (GB)	53.40-to-1
1991	Miss Alleged	42.10-to-1
2004	Better Talk Now	27.90-to-1
1994	Tikkanen	16.60-to-1
2003	Johar	14.20-to-1
1992	Fraise	14.00-to-1

Odds-On Beaten Favorites

Year	Favorite	Odds	Finish
2004	Kitten's Joy	7-to-10	2
1994	Paradise Creek	4-to-5	3
1992	Sky Classic	9-to-10	2
1986	Dancing Brave	1-to-2	4

Fastest Winners

Year	Winner	Track	Time	Cond.
1997	Chief Bearhart	Hol	2:23.92	firm
1992	Fraise	GP	2:24.08	firm
2003	(DH) High Chaparral (Ire) (DH) Johar	SA	2:24.24	firm
2001	Fantastic Light	Bel	2:24.36	firm

Slowest Winners

Year	Winner	Track	Time	Cond.
1995	Northern Spur (Ire)	Bel	2:42.07	soft
1988	Great Communicator	CD	2:35⅕	good
1991	Miss Alleged	CD	2:30.95	firm
1996	Pilsudski (Ire)	WO	2:30.20	good
2002	High Chaparral (Ire)	AP	2:30.14	yielding

Most Starters

Year	Track	Starters
1999	Gulfstream Park	14
1996	Woodbine	14
1994	Churchill Downs	14
1993	Santa Anita Park	14
1989	Gulfstream Park	14
1987	Hollywood Park	14
1985	Aqueduct	14

Fewest Starters

Year	Track	Starters
2004	Lone Star Park	8
2002	Arlington Park	8
2003	Santa Anita Park	9
1986	Santa Anita Park	9
1992	Gulfstream Park	10
1988	Churchill Downs	10

Winning Post Positions

Post	Starters	Winners	Percent
1	22	2	9.1%
2	22	6	27.3%
3	22	2	9.1%
4	22	0	0.0%
5	22	3	13.7%
6	22	0	0.0%
7	22	1	4.5%
8	22	1	4.5%
9	20	3	15%
10	18	0	0.0%
11	16	0	0.0%
12	12	3	25%
13	12	2	16.7%
14	7	0	0.0%

Changes in Turf

For 2006, the purse of the Breeders' Cup Turf was increased to $3-million from $2-million.

Breeders' Cup Juvenile

Until a winner of the Breeders' Cup Juvenile (G1) delivers a Kentucky Derby (G1) victory, the 1⅟₁₆-mile race (run at 1⅛ miles in 2002, and at one mile in 1984, '85, and '87) will be regarded as a measure of two-year-old form—which it obviously is—rather than a reliable yardstick of classic potential.

The race has yet to yield a Derby or Belmont Stakes (G1) winner, and only one classic winner, 1995 Preakness Stakes (G1) victor Timber Country, has won the Juvenile.

With regularity, however, the Derby winner and other classic winners have been in the beaten Juvenile field, implying that classic winners were either not sufficiently precocious to win the Juvenile or found its distance to be too short for their best efforts.

The first Breeders' Cup Juvenile was won by Chief's Crown, who finished second or third in all of the following year's classics, won the Travers Stakes (G1) against three-year-olds, and took the Marlboro Cup Handicap (G1) against older horses. He had the three-year-old title and Horse of the Year honors in his sights until finishing fourth as the favorite in the 1985 Breeders' Cup Classic (G1).

Second to Chief's Crown in the 1984 Juvenile was Tank's Prospect, who won the following year's Preakness. Tiring to finish third, beaten only 1½ lengths, was Spend a Buck, the 1985 Derby winner who was voted champion three-year-old male and Horse of the Year.

The pattern would be repeated in subsequent editions of the Juvenile. Alysheba, third in 1986, won the following year's Derby and Preakness and was voted three-year-old male champion. Bet Twice, who conquered him in the Belmont Stakes (G1), finished fourth in the '86 Juvenile. Pine Bluff was seventh in the 1991 Juvenile but won the Preakness the following year. Sea Hero, seventh in the 1992 Juvenile, won the following year's Derby. Finishing third to Brocco in the 1993 Juvenile was Tabasco Cat, who would become a dual classic winner in '94 for D. Wayne Lukas, the leading trainer of Juvenile winners. Seven years later, Point Given came off a close second-place finish in the Juvenile to win the 2001 Preakness, Belmont, and Travers. Retired with an injury after the Travers, he was voted 2001 Horse of the Year and champion three-year-old male. Afleet Alex, second in the 2004 Juvenile, won the following year's Preakness and Belmont.

Losing a close decision was the best sire of the late 1990s and early 2000s, Storm Cat, who just failed to last the one-mile distance of the Juvenile at Aqueduct in '85. Capote, winner of the '86 Juvenile, never won again but became a successful sire, getting '96 Juvenile winner Boston Harbor.

Perhaps the most memorable running of the Juvenile occurred at Churchill Downs in 1991, when French-trained Arazi broke from the outside post position, blew by the field on the final turn, and romped to a five-length victory. Voted two-year-old male champion off that one North American start, Arazi was hampered by knee problems early in his three-year-old season. He finished eighth as the favorite in the '92 Derby.

Another disappointment was Favorite Trick, who was voted '97 Horse of the Year after an

Breeders' Cup Juvenile

Grade 1, $1.5-million, two-year-old colts and geldings, 1⅟₁₆ miles, dirt. Run on October 29, 2005, at Belmont Park with gross value of $1,458,030. First run in 1984. Weights: 122 pounds.

Year	Winner	Jockey	Second	Third	Site	Time	Cond.	1st Purse
2005	**Stevie Wonderboy**	G. Gomez	Henny Hughes	First Samurai	Bel	1:41.64	ft	**$826,800**
2004	**Wilko**	L. Dettori	Afleet Alex	Sun King	LS	1:42.09	ft	780,000
2003	**Action This Day**	D. Flores	Minister Eric	Chapel Royal	SA	1:43.62	ft	780,000
2002	**Vindication**	M. Smith	Kafwain	Hold That Tiger	AP	1:49.61	ft	556,400
2001	**Johannesburg**	M. Kinane	Repent	Siphonic	Bel	1:42.27	ft	520,000
2000	**Macho Uno**	J. Bailey	Point Given	Street Cry (Ire)	CD	1:42.05	ft	556,400
1999	**Anees**	G. Stevens	Chief Seattle	High Yield	GP	1:42.29	ft	556,400
1998	**Answer Lively**	J. Bailey	Aly's Alley	Cat Thief	CD	1:44	ft	520,000
1997	**Favorite Trick**	P. Day	Dawson's Legacy	Nationalore	Hol	**1:41.47**	ft	520,000
1996	**Boston Harbor**	J. Bailey	Acceptable	Ordway	WO	1:43.40	ft	520,000
1995	**Unbridled's Song**	M. Smith	Hennessy	Editor's Note	Bel	1:41.60	my	520,000
1994	**Timber Country**	P. Day	Eltish	Tejano Run	CD	1:44.55	ft	520,000
1993	**Brocco**	G. Stevens	Blumin Affair	Tabasco Cat	SA	1:42.99	ft	520,000
1992	**Gilded Time**	C. McCarron	It'sali'lknownfact	River Special	GP	1:43.43	ft	520,000
1991	**Arazi**	P. Valenzuela	Bertrando	Snappy Landing	CD	1:44.78	ft	520,000
1990	**Fly So Free**	J. Santos	Take Me Out	Lost Mountain	Bel	1:43⅖	ft	450,000
1989	**Rhythm**	C. Perret	Grand Canyon	Slavic	GP	1:43⅗	ft	450,000
1988	**Is It True**	L. Pincay Jr.	Easy Goer	Tagel	CD	1:46⅗	my	450,000
1987	**Success Express**	J. Santos	Regal Classic	Tejano	Hol	**1:35⅕**	ft	450,000
1986	**Capote**	L. Pincay Jr.	Qualify	Alysheba	SA	1:43⅘	ft	450,000
1985	**Tasso**	L. Pincay Jr.	Storm Cat	Scat Dancer	Aqu	1:36⅕	ft	450,000
1984	**Chief's Crown**	D. MacBeth	Tank's Prospect	Spend a Buck	Hol	1:36⅕	ft	450,000

2002: Run at 1⅛ miles. 1984-'85, 1987: run at one mile. 1985: Tasso supplementary entry.

overwhelming victory in the Juvenile. He finished eighth in the Derby.

The following year's Juvenile winner, Answer Lively, ran tenth in the 1999 Derby, and that year's Juvenile victor, Anees, was 13th at Churchill Downs the following May. Macho Uno, the 2000 Juvenile winner, did not make it to the following year's Derby, and '01 Juvenile winner Johannesburg ran eighth in the '02 Derby. Vindication, an easy winner at Arlington Park in 2002, did not start in the Derby. Action This Day, the 2003 Juvenile victor, finished sixth behind Smarty Jones in '04, and Wilko, the '04 Juvenile winner at Lone Star Park, came home sixth behind Giacomo in the '05 Derby.

Owners by Wins

1 **Barry A. Beal, Lloyd R. "Bob" French Jr., Eugene V. Klein** (Capote), **Mr. and Mrs. Albert Broccoli** (Brocco), **John Franks** (Answer Lively), **Gainesway Stable, Overbrook Farm, Robert and Beverly Lewis** (Timber Country), **Merv Griffin Ranch Co.** (Stevie Wonderboy), **B. Wayne Hughes** (Action This Day), **Joseph LaCombe** (Favorite Trick), **David Milch, Jack and Mark Silverman** (Gilded Time), **Overbrook Farm** (Boston Harbor), **Padua Stables** (Vindication), **Paraneck Stable** (Unbridled's Song), **Allen E. Paulson, Sheikh Mohammed bin Rashid al Maktoum** (Arazi), **Ogden Mills Phipps** (Rhythm), **J. Paul Reddam and Susan Roy** (Wilko), **Gerald Robins** (Tasso), **Stronach Stables** (Macho Uno), **Star Crown Stable** (Chief's Crown), **Michael Tabor and Susan Magnier** (Johannesburg), **The Thoroughbred Corp.** (Anees), **Thomas Valando** (Fly So Free)

Breeders by Wins

2 **Eugene V. Klein** (Is It True, Success Express)

1 **Adena Springs** (Macho Uno), **Jaime Carrion (trustee)** (Action This Day), **Farfellow Farms** (Anees), **John Franks** (Answer Lively), **John Gunther, Tony Holmes, and Walter Zent** (Stevie Wonderboy), **Bruce Hundley and Wayne Garrison** (Fly So Free), **Warner L. Jones** (Is It True), **Lowquest Ltd.** (Timber Country), **Wayne G. Lyster III and Jayeff B Stables** (Johannesburg), **Mandysland Farm** (Unbridled's Song), **Mr. and Mrs. Harry T. Mangurian Jr.** (Gilded Time), **Meadowbrook Farms** (Brocco), **North Ridge Farm** (Capote), **Overbrook Farm** (Boston Harbor), **Rosenda Parra** (Wilko), **Payson Stud** (Vindication), **Ogden Mills Phipps** (Rhythm), **Rosenda Parra** (Wilko), **Gerald L. Robins and Timothy H. Sams** (Tasso), **Carl Rosen** (Chief's Crown), **Tri Star Stable** (Success Express), **Ralph Wilson Jr.** (Arazi), **Mr. and Mrs. M. L. Wood** (Favorite Trick)

Trainers by Wins

5 **D. Wayne Lukas** (Boston Harbor, Timber Country, Is It True, Success Express, Capote)

1 **Bob Baffert** (Vindication), **Bobby Barnett** (Answer Lively), **Francois Boutin** (Arazi), **Patrick Byrne** (Favorite Trick), **Neil Drysdale** (Tasso), **Alex Hassinger Jr.** (Anees), **Roger Laurin** (Chief's Crown), **Richard Mandella** (Action This Day), **Claude R. "Shug" McGaughey III** (Rhythm), **Jeremy Noseda** (Wilko), **Aidan O'Brien** (Johannesburg), **Doug F. O'Neill** (Stevie Wonderboy), **Joseph Orseno** (Macho Uno), **James Ryerson** (Unbridled's Song), **Flint S. "Scotty" Schulhofer** (Fly So Free), **Darrell Vienna** (Gilded Time), **Randy Winick** (Brocco)

Jockeys by Wins

3 **Jerry Bailey** (Macho Uno, Answer Lively, Boston Harbor), **Laffit Pincay Jr.** (Is It True, Capote, Tasso)

2 **Pat Day** (Favorite Trick, Timber Country), **Jose Santos** (Fly So Free, Success Express), **Mike Smith** (Vindication, Unbridled's Song), **Gary Stevens** (Anees, Brocco)

1 **Lanfranco Dettori** (Wilko), **David Flores** (Action This Day), **Garrett Gomez** (Stevie Wonderboy), **Michael Kinane** (Johannesburg), **Don MacBeth** (Chief's Crown), **Chris McCarron** (Gilded Time), **Craig Perret** (Rhythm), **Patrick Valenzuela** (Arazi)

Sires by Wins

2 **Kris S.** (Brocco, Action This Day), **Seattle Slew** (Capote, Vindication), **Unbridled** (Anees, Unbridled's Song)

1 **Awesome Again** (Wilko), **Blushing Groom (Fr)** (Arazi), **Capote** (Boston Harbor), **Danzig** (Chief's Crown), **Fappiano** (Tasso), **Hennessy** (Johannesburg), **Hold Your Peace** (Success Express), **Holy Bull** (Macho Uno), **Lively One** (Answer Lively), **Mr. Prospector** (Rhythm), **Phone Trick** (Favorite Trick), **Raja Baba** (Is It True), **Stephen Got Even** (Stevie Wonderboy), **Time for a Change** (Fly So Free), **Timeless Moment** (Gilded Time), **Woodman** (Timber Country)

Winners by Place Where Bred

Locality	Winners
Kentucky	19
Florida	3

Supplemental Entries

Year	Runner	Fee	Finish	Earnings
2005	Jealous Profit	$135,000	10	$0
2002	Whywhywhy	90,000	10	0
2000	Arabian Light	90,000	5	21,400
1999	Captain Steve	90,000	11	0
1992	Caponostro	120,000	6	0
1991	Bertrando	120,000	2	200,000
	Agincourt	120,000	5	20,000
1990	Best Pal	120,000	6	10,000
1985	**Tasso**	120,000	1	450,000
1984	Spend a Buck	120,000	3	108,000

Eclipse Award Winners from Race

Year	Runner	Finish	Title
2005	**Stevie Wonderboy**	1	Juvenile male
2003	**Action This Day**	1	Juvenile male
2002	**Vindication**	1	Juvenile male
2001	**Johannesburg**	1	Juvenile male
2000	**Macho Uno**	1	Juvenile male
1999	**Anees**	1	Juvenile male
1998	**Answer Lively**	1	Juvenile male
1997	**Favorite Trick**	1	Horse of the Year, Juvenile male
1996	**Boston Harbor**	1	Juvenile male
1994	**Timber Country**	1	Juvenile male
1993	Dehere	8	Juvenile male
1992	**Gilded Time**	1	Juvenile male
1991	**Arazi**	1	Juvenile male
1990	**Fly So Free**	1	Juvenile male
1989	**Rhythm**	1	Juvenile male
1988	Easy Goer	2	Juvenile male
1986	**Capote**	1	Juvenile male
1985	**Tasso**	1	Juvenile male
1984	**Chief's Crown**	1	Juvenile male

Largest Winning Margins

Year	Winner	Margin
1997	Favorite Trick	5½
1993	Brocco	5
1991	Arazi	5

Smallest Winning Margins

Year	Winner	Margin
2000	Macho Uno	nose
1985	Tasso	nose
1998	Answer Lively	head

Shortest-Priced Winners

Year	Winner	Odds
1984	Chief's Crown	0.70-to-1
1997	Favorite Trick	1.20-to-1
1990	Fly So Free	1.40-to-1
1992	Gilded Time	2.00-to-1

Longest-Priced Winners

Year	Winner	Odds
1999	Anees	30.30-to-1
2004	Wilko	28.30-to-1
2003	Action This Day	26.80-to-1
1988	Is It True	9.20-to-1
2001	Johannesburg	7.20-to-1
2000	Macho Uno	6.30-to-1

Odds-On Beaten Favorites

Year	Favorite	Odds	Finish
2001	Officer	0.75-to-1	5
1993	Dehere	7-to-10	8
1988	Easy Goer	3-to-10	2

Fastest Winners

Year	Winner	Track	Time	Cond.
1997	Favorite Trick	Hol	1:41.47	fast
1995	Unbridled's Song	Bel	1:41.60	muddy
2005	Stevie Wonderboy	Bel	1:41.64	fast
2000	Macho Uno	CD	1:42.05	fast
2004	Wilko	LS	1:42.09	fast
2001	Johannesburg	Bel	1:42:27	fast

Slowest Winners

Year	Winner	Track	Time	Cond.
1988	Is It True	CD	1:46⅗	muddy
1991	Arazi	CD	1:44.78	fast
1994	Timber Country	CD	1:44.55	fast
1998	Answer Lively	CD	1:44.00	fast

Most Starters

Year	Track	Starters
2000	Churchill Downs	14
1999	Gulfstream Park	14
1991	Churchill Downs	14

Fewest Starters

Year	Track	Starters
2004	Lone Star Park	8
1997	Hollywood Park	8
1996	Woodbine	10
1988	Churchill Downs	10
1984	Hollywood Park	10

Winning Post Positions

Post	Starters	Winners	Percent
1	22	1	4.5%
2	22	2	9.1%
3	22	6	27.3%
4	22	2	9.1%
5	22	2	9.1%
6	22	1	4.5%
7	22	2	9.1%
8	22	2	9.1%
9	20	1	5.0%
10	20	0	0.0%
11	17	1	5.9%
12	15	1	0.0%
13	12	0	0.0%
14	3	1	33.3%

Changes in Juvenile

The Juvenile purse was increased to $1.5-million in 2003 and $2-million in 2006. Originally contested at one mile, the distance was changed to 1$\frac{1}{16}$ miles in 1988. It was contested at 1$\frac{1}{16}$ miles in 1986 and at 1⅛ miles in 2002.

Breeders' Cup Filly and Mare Turf

In July 1998, the Breeders' Cup board of directors voted to fill an obvious gap in its championship lineup by creating the $1-million Breeders' Cup Filly and Mare Turf (G1) at 1¼ miles. Until the first Filly and Mare Turf at Gulfstream Park in 1999, the female turf division had no definitive championship race, and distaffers were forced to race in open company.

The new race for fillies and mares, first run at 1⅜ miles because of Gulfstream's grass course configuration, fulfilled its intended function. Phillips Racing Partnership's Soaring Softly locked up an

Breeders' Cup Filly and Mare Turf

Grade 1, $1-million, fillies and mares, three-year-olds and up, 1⅜ miles, turf. Run October 29, 2005, at Belmont Park with gross value of $972,020. First run in 1999. Weights: Northern Hemisphere three-year-olds, 119 pounds; older, 123 pounds; Southern Hemisphere three-year-olds, 113 pounds; older, 123 pounds.

Year	Winner	Jockey	Second	Third	Site	Time	Cond.	1st purse
2005	**Intercontinental (GB)**, 5	R. Bejarano	Ouija Board (GB)	Film Maker	Bel	2:02.34	gd	$551,200
2004	**Ouija Board (GB)**, 3	K. Fallon	Film Maker	Wonder Again	LS	2:18.25	yl	**733,200**
2003	**Islington (Ire)**, 4	K. Fallon	L'Ancresse (Ire)	Yesterday (Ire)	SA	**1:59.15**	fm	551,200
2002	**Starine (Fr)**	J. Velazquez	Banks Hill (GB	Islington (GB)	AP	2:03.57	yl	665,600
2001	**Banks Hill (GB)**, 3	O. Peslier	Spook Express (SAf)	Spring Oak (GB)	Bel	2:00.36	fm	722,800
2000	**Perfect Sting**, 4	J. Bailey	Tout Charmant	Catella (Ger)	CD	2:13.07	fm	629,200
1999	**Soaring Softly**, 4	J. Bailey	Coretta (Ire)	Zomaradah (GB)	GP	2:13.89	gd	556,400

1999-2000, 2004, 1⅜ miles; 2001-'03, 1¼ miles

Eclipse Award as champion turf female with a three-quarter-length victory in 1999. The following year, Stronach Stable's Perfect Sting won by the same margin over Tout Charmant at Churchill Downs. Perfect Sting was subsequently voted champion turf female. European interests broke through in 2001 when Juddmonte Farms' French-based Banks Hill (GB) won by 5½ lengths at Belmont Park. For the first time in 2001, the Filly and Mare Turf was run at 1¼ miles, its prescribed distance when course configurations permit.

Beginning with Banks Hill, horses bred overseas dominated the Filly and Mare Turf. Horses bred outside North America took the first three finish positions in 2001, the top six spots the following year, the top five positions in '03, and the winning spot in '04, when few European-trained horses made the trip to Lone Star Park.

Banks Hill, a Danehill filly trained by Andre Fabre for her 2001 triumph, returned in '02 to seek a second victory, this time in the care of Bobby Frankel. She could manage no better than second, beaten 1½ lengths by Starine (Fr), who was owned and trained by Frankel. Islington (Ire) finished third in the 2002 Filly and Mare Turf, and she returned the following year to score a neck victory over L'Ancresse (Ire) in the Filly and Mare Turf at Santa Anita Park. In an unusual pattern to that race, all North American-bred horses finished behind the five top finishers. Irish-breds took the top three spots, followed by two fillies bred in Great Britain.

Britain's honor would be upheld in 2004 when Lord Derby's homebred Ouija Board (GB) invaded and scored a 1½-length victory over Film Maker. Europe's Horse of the Year after her victories in the Epsom Oaks (Eng-G1) and Darley Irish Oaks (Ire-G1), the Cape Cross (Ire) filly also was voted an Eclipse Award as North America's outstanding turf female. She returned in 2005 and finished second to eventual champion Intercontinental (GB), Banks Hill's sister.

Owners by Wins

2 **Juddmonte Farms** (Banks Hill [GB], Intercontinental [GB])

1 **Lord Derby** (Ouija Board [GB]), **Estate of Lord Weinstock** (Islington [Ire]), **Robert Frankel** (Starine [Fr]), **Phillips Racing Partnership** (Soaring Softly), **Stronach Stables** (Perfect Sting)

Breeders by Wins

2 **Juddmonte Farms** (Banks Hill [GB], Intercontinental [GB])

1 **Ballymacoll Stud Farm** (Islington [Ire]), **Catherine Dubois** (Starine [Fr]), **Galbreath-Phillips Racing Partnership** (Soaring Softly), **Stanley Estate and Stud Co.** (Ouija Board [GB]), **Frank Stronach** (Perfect Sting)

Trainers by Wins

2 **Robert Frankel** (Intercontinental [GB], Starine [Fr])

1 **Edward Dunlop** (Ouija Board [GB]), **Andre Fabre** (Banks Hill [GB]), **Joseph Orseno** (Perfect Sting), **Sir Michael Stoute** (Islington [Ire]), **James J. Toner** (Soaring Softly)

Jockeys by Wins

2 **Jerry Bailey** (Soaring Softly, Perfect Sting), **Kieren Fallon** (Ouija Board [GB], Islington [Ire])

1 **Rafael Bejarano** (Intercontinental [GB]), **Olivier Peslier** (Banks Hill [GB]), **John Velazquez** (Starine [Fr])

Sires by Wins

2 **Danehill** (Banks Hill [GB], Intercontinental [GB])

1 **Cape Cross (Ire)** (Ouija Board [GB]), **Kris S.** (Soaring Softly), **Mendocino** (Starine [Fr]), **Red Ransom** (Perfect Sting), **Sadler's Wells** (Islington [Ire])

Winners by Place Where Bred

Locality	Winners
Great Britain	3
Kentucky	2
France	1
Ireland	1

Supplemental Entries

Year	Runner	Fee	Finish	Earnings
2005	Ouija Board (GB)	(credit)	2	$212,000
	Megahertz (GB)	(credit)	8	0
	Flip Flop (Fr)	$90,000	12	0
2004	**Ouija Board (GB)**	$90,000	1	$733,200
	Moscow Burning	90,000	4	80,370
	Super Brand (SAf)	200,000	9	0
	Katdogwan (GB)	90,000	10	0
	Megahertz (GB)	(credit)	11	0
	Aubonne (Ger)	90,000	12	0
2003	**Islington (Ire)**	(credit)	1	551,200
	Megahertz (GB)	90,000	5	31,800
2002	**Starine (Fr)**	(credit)	1	665,600
	Islington (Ire)	90,000	3	153,600
	Golden Apples (Ire)	90,000	4	71,680
	Kazzia (Ger)	90,000	6	0
	Turtle Bow (Fr)	90,000	9	0
2001	Spook Express (SAf)	200,000	2	278,000
	Kalypso Katie (Ire)	200,000	6	0
	Starine (Fr)	90,000	10	0
	England's Legend (Fr)	90,000	11	0
2000	Caffe Latte (Ire)	(credit)	9	0
	Catella (Ger)	90,000	3	145,200
	Colstar	90,000	7	0
	Petrushka (Ire)	90,000	5	24,200
1999	Caffe Latte (Ire)	90,000	4	59,920

Eclipse Award Winners from Race

Year	Runner	Finish	Title
2004	**Ouija Board (GB)**	1	Turf female
2003	**Islington (Ire)**	1	Turf female
2002	Golden Apples (Ire)	4	Turf female
2001	**Banks Hill (GB)**	1	Turf female
2000	**Perfect Sting**	1	Turf female
1999	**Soaring Softly**	1	Turf female

Winning Margins

Year	Winner	Margin
2001	Banks Hill (GB)	5½
2004	Ouija Board (GB)	1½
2002	Starine (Fr)	1½
2005	Intercontinental (GB)	1¼
2000	Perfect Sting	¾

Year	Winner	Margin
1999	Soaring Softly	¾
2003	Islington (Ire)	neck

Beaten Favorites

Year	Favorite	Odds	Finish
2005	Ouija Board (GB)	2.30-to-1	2
2002	Golden Apples (Ire)	2.80-to-1	4
2001	Lailani (GB)	2.75-to-1	8
2000	Petrushka (Ire)	7-to-5	5

Odds of Winners

Year	Winner	Odds
2005	Intercontinental (GB)	15.10-to-1
2004	Ouija Board (GB)	0.90-to-1
2003	Islington (Ire)	2.90-to-1
2002	Starine (Fr)	13.20-to-1
2001	Banks Hill (GB)	6.00-to-1
2000	Perfect Sting	5.00-to-1
1999	Soaring Softly	3.60-to-1

Number of Starters

Year	Track	Starters
2005	Belmont Park	14
2004	Lone Star Park	12
2003	Santa Anita Park	12
2002	Arlington Park	12
2001	Belmont Park	12
2000	Churchill Downs	14
1999	Gulfstream Park	14

Winning Post Positions

Post	Starters	Winners	Percent
1	7	0	0.0%
2	7	0	0.0%
3	7	0	0.0%
4	7	1	14.3%
5	7	2	28.6%
6	7	0	0.0%
7	7	0	0.0%
8	7	1	14.3%
9	7	0	0.0%
10	7	1	14.3%
11	7	1	14.3%
12	7	1	14.3%
13	3	0	0.0%
14	3	0	0.0%

Changes in Filly and Mare Turf

The Filly and Mare Turf, inaugurated in 1999, has been held at 1⅜ miles three times rather than its prescribed 1¼ miles due to course configurations. Its purse was increased to $2-million in 2006.

Breeders' Cup Sprint

Roughly half of all North American races are run at six furlongs, and thus the $1-million Breeders' Cup Sprint (G1) is the prototypical American race. The six-furlong dash has proved to be a competitive contest, principally among North American runners, and in many years it has been a nightmare for handicappers.

As a championship event, the Breeders' Cup Sprint has been especially decisive in years when no horse clearly dominated the division. In 13 of the 22 runnings of the Sprint, the Eclipse Award for champion sprinter has gone to the winner.

The first Breeders' Cup Sprint in 1984 set the tone for the series, with Eillo desperately holding off Commemorate to win by a nose. Seven runnings of the Breeders' Cup Sprint have been decided by a neck or less. Eillo was favored at 1.30-to-1, and no favorite would again win the Sprint for ten years, until Cherokee Run (2.80-to-1) in 1994. Lit de Justice was a lukewarm 4-to-1 favorite in 1996, Kona Gold won at 1.70-to-1 in 2000, and Orientate prevailed at 2.70-to-1 in '02.

Breeders' Cup Sprint

Grade 1, $1-million, three-year-olds and up, 6 furlongs. Held on October 29, 2005, at Belmont Park with gross value of $972,020. First run in 1984. Weights: Northern Hemisphere three-year-olds, 123 pounds; older, 126 pounds; Southern Hemisphere three-year-olds, 122 pounds; older, 126 pounds; fillies and mares allowed three pounds.

Year	Winner	Jockey	Second	Third	Site	Time	Cond.	1st Purse
2005	**Silver Train**, 3	E. Prado	Taste of Paradise	Lion Tamer	Bel	1:08.86	ft	$551,200
2004	**Speightstown**, 6	J. Velazquez	Kela	My Cousin Matt	LS	1:08.11	ft	551,200
2003	**Cajun Beat**, 3	C. Velasquez	Bluesthestandard	Shake You Down	SA	1:07.95	ft	613,600
2002	**Orientate**	J. Bailey	Thunderello	Crafty C. T.	AP	1:08.89	ft	592,800
2001	**Squirtle Squirt**, 3	J. Bailey	Xtra Heat	Caller One	Bel	1:08.41	ft	520,000
2000	**Kona Gold**, 6	A. Solis	Honest Lady	Bet On Sunshine	CD	**1:07.77**	ft	520,000
1999	**Artax**, 4	J. Chavez	Kona Gold	Big Jag	GP	1:07.89	ft	**624,000**
1998	**Reraise**, 3	C. Nakatani	Grand Slam	Kona Gold	CD	1:09.07	ft	572,000
1997	**Elmhurst**, 7	C. Nakatani	Hesabull	Bet On Sunshine	Hol	1:08.01	ft	613,600
1996	**Lit de Justice**, 6	C. Nakatani	Paying Dues	Honour and Glory	WO	1:08.60	ft	520,000
1995	**Desert Stormer**, f, 5	K. Desormeaux	Mr. Greeley	Lit de Justice	Bel	1:09.14	my	520,000
1994	**Cherokee Run**, 4	M. Smith	Soviet Problem	Cardmania	CD	1:09.54	ft	520,000
1993	**Cardmania**, 7	E. Delahoussaye	Meafara	Gilded Time	SA	1:08.76	ft	520,000
1992	**Thirty Slews**, 5	E. Delahoussaye	Meafara	Rubiano	GP	1:08.21	ft	520,000
1991	**Sheikh Albadou (GB)**, 3	P. Eddery	Pleasant Tap	Robyn Dancer	CD	1:09.36	ft	520,000
1990	**Safely Kept**, f, 4	C. Perret	Dayjur	Black Tie Affair (Ire)	Bel	1:09 3/5	ft	450,000
1989	**Dancing Spree**, 4	A. Cordero Jr.	Safely Kept	Dispersal	GP	1:09	ft	450,000
1988	**Gulch**, 4	A. Cordero Jr.	Play the King	Afleet	CD	1:10 2/5	sy	450,000
1987	**Very Subtle**, f, 3	P. Valenzuela	Groovy	Exclusive Enough	Hol	1:08 4/5	ft	450,000
1986	**Smile**, 4	J. Vasquez	Pine Tree Lane	Beside Promise	SA	1:08 2/5	ft	450,000
1985	**Precisionist**, 4	C. McCarron	Smile	Mt. Livermore	Aqu	1:08 2/5	ft	450,000
1984	**Eillo**, 4	C. Perret	Commemorate	Fighting Fit	Hol	1:10 1/5	ft	450,000

Between Eillo and Cherokee Run, the Sprint was won by two other champions, Precisionist (1985) and Gulch ('88), who could not be characterized as pure sprinters. Fred Hooper's homebred Precisionist won the 1¼-mile Charles H. Strub Stakes (G1) the same year he was sprint champion, and Gulch was really best at one mile, winning the Metropolitan Handicap (G1) twice, 1987 and '88, the latter his championship year.

The Sprint in 1990 remains one of the most memorable in Breeders' Cup history. Safely Kept, the prior year's champion sprinter, fought a spirited, head-to-head battle with English invader Dayjur, the 2.40-to-1 favorite. Inside the furlong pole, Dayjur appeared to take command, but 40 yards from the wire he jumped the shadow of Belmont Park's grandstand and briefly lost his action. Those missteps proved sufficient for 12.20-to-1 Safely Kept to regain the lead and hold on for a neck victory.

Although Dayjur failed to become the first overseas horse to win the Sprint, the European contingent broke through the following year when Sheikh Albadou (GB) won at Churchill Downs. At 26.30-to-1, Sheikh Albadou remains the longest-priced winner of the Sprint. Average odds of Sprint winners were a healthy 9.76-to-1.

Kona Gold, the 2000 winner, proved that top-quality sprinters could be durable as well as fast. Carefully managed by co-owner and trainer Bruce Headley, the Java Gold gelding ran third in 1998, second in '99, and finally won at age six. In winning at Churchill Downs, Kona Gold set a track record, 1:07.77, the fastest time ever for the Sprint. Kona Gold was the 7-to-2 favorite when seeking a second straight win in 2001 but finished seventh behind winner Squirtle Squirt. In 2002, his record fifth start in the race, he finished fourth.

Racing Hall of Fame trainer D. Wayne Lukas may be best known for his classic horses, but he collected his second Sprint victory with favored Orientate in 2002 at Arlington Park. The following year, Cajun Beat stormed to a 22.80-to-1 victory over a talented field at Santa Anita Park, and the Eclipse Award went to race favorite Aldebaran, who finished sixth at 2.10-to-1. In 2004, Speightstown secured an Eclipse Award with a 1¼-length victory over Kela. The 2005 race was marked by unbeaten Lost in the Fog's bid for the three-year-old championship (Xtra Heat had gotten her divisional title with a second to Squirtle Squirt in 1999) but he finished seventh behind another three-year-old, Silver Train.

In the 1980s, the Sprint was a graveyard for one of the era's most talented sprinters, Groovy. He went off at 2-to-5 in the 1986 Sprint and finished fourth, 4¼ lengths behind front-running winner Smile. At Hollywood Park the following year, Groovy went off at 4-to-5 and ran second to another front-runner, Ben Rochelle's filly Very Subtle. Groovy was voted an Eclipse Award as outstanding sprinter in 1987. The only other Sprint starter to lose at odds-on was two-time champion Housebuster, who finished ninth at 2-to-5 odds in 1991.

Owners by Wins

1 **Peter M. Brant** (Gulch), **Buckram Oak Farm** (Silver Train), **Jean Couvercelle** (Cardmania), **Crown Stable** (Eillo), **Mitch Degroot, Dutch Masters III, and Mike Pegram** (Thirty Slews), **Craig Dollase, Barry Fey, Moon Han, and Frank Sinatra** (Reraise), **Evergreen Farm** (Lit de Justice), **Evergreen Farm and Jenine Sahadi** (Elmhurst), **Frances Genter Stable** (Smile), **Fred Hooper** (Precisionist), **Bruce Headley, Irwin and Andrew Molasky, and High Tech Stable** (Kona Gold), **Jayeff B Stables and Barry Weisbord** (Safely Kept), **David J. Lanzman** (Squirtle Squirt), **Robert and Beverly Lewis** (Orientate), **Eugene and Laura Melnyk** (Speightstown), **Joanne Nor** (Desert Stormer), **Padua Stable and John and Joseph Iracane** (Cajun Beat), **Paraneck Stable** (Artax), **Ogden Phipps** (Dancing Spree), **Jill Robinson** (Cherokee Run), **Ben Rochelle** (Very Subtle), **Hilal Salem** (Sheikh Albadou [GB])

Breeders by Wins

1 **Peter M. Brant** (Gulch), **Calumet Farm** (Elmhurst), **Carondelet Farm and Vinery** (Artax), **Ollie A. Cohen** (Eillo), **Delta Thoroughbreds** (Cardmania), **Gainesway Thoroughbreds Ltd.** (Orientate), **Frances Genter Stable** (Smile), **Grousemont Farm** (Thirty Slews), **Mr. and Mrs. David Hayden** (Safely Kept), **Highclere Stud** (Sheikh Albadou [GB]), **Fred Hooper** (Precisionist), **Aaron and Marie Jones** (Speightstown), **John T. L. Jones Jr. and H. Smoot Fahlgren** (Cajun Beat), **John Howard King** (Very Subtle), **Joe Mulholland Sr., Joe Mulholland Jr., et al.** (Silver Train), **Audrey Narducci, M.D.** (Squirtle Squirt), **Joanne Nor** (Desert Stormer), **George Onett** (Cherokee Run), **Carlos Perez** (Kona Gold), **Ogden Phipps** (Dancing Spree), **Swettenham Stud and Julian G. Rogers** (Lit de Justice), **Willard Sergent** (Reraise)

Trainers by Wins

2 **D. Wayne Lukas** (Gulch, Orientate), **Jenine Sahadi** (Elmhurst, Lit de Justice)

1 **Louis Albertrani** (Artax), **Frank Alexander** (Cherokee Run), **Bob Baffert** (Thirty Slews), **Craig Dollase** (Reraise), **Richard Dutrow Jr.** (Silver Train), **Ross Fenstermaker** (Precisionist), **Robert Frankel** (Squirtle Squirt), **Alan Goldberg** (Safely Kept), **Bruce Headley** (Kona Gold), **Budd Lepman** (Eillo), **Frank Lyons** (Desert Stormer), **Steve Margolis** (Cajun Beat), **Claude R. "Shug" McGaughey III** (Dancing Spree), **Derek Meredith** (Cardmania), **Todd Pletcher** (Speightstown), **Flint S. "Scotty" Schulhofer** (Smile), **Alexander Scott** (Sheikh Albadou [GB]), **Mel Stute** (Very Subtle)

Jockeys by Wins

3 **Corey Nakatani** (Reraise, Elmhurst, Lit de Justice)

2 **Jerry Bailey** (Squirtle Squirt, Orientate), **Angel Cordero Jr.** (Dancing Spree, Gulch), **Eddie Delahoussaye** (Cardmania, Thirty Slews), **Craig Perret** (Safely Kept, Eillo)

1 **Jorge Chavez** (Artax), **Kent Desormeaux** (Desert Stormer), **Pat Eddery** (Sheikh Albadou [GB]), **Chris McCarron** (Precisionist), **Edgar Prado** (Silver Train), **Mike Smith** (Cherokee Run), **Alex Solis** (Kona Gold), **Patrick Valenzuela** (Very Subtle), **Cornelio Velasquez** (Cajun Beat), **John Velazquez** (Speightstown), **Jacinto Vasquez** (Smile)

Sires of Winners

2 **Marquetry** (Artax, Squirtle Squirt), **Mr. Prospector** (Eillo, Gulch)

1 **Cox's Ridge** (Cardmania), **Crozier** (Precisionist), **Danzatore** (Reraise), **El Gran Senor** (Lit de Justice), **Gone West** (Speightstown), **Grand Slam** (Cajun Beat), **Green Desert** (Sheikh Albadou [GB]), **Hoist the Silver** (Very Subtle), **Horatius** (Safely Kept), **In Reality** (Smile), **Java Gold** (Kona Gold), **Mt. Livermore** (Orientate), **Nijinsky II** (Dancing Spree), **Old Trieste** (Silver Train), **Runaway Groom** (Cherokee Run), **Slewpy** (Thirty Slews), **Storm Cat** (Desert Stormer), **Wild Again** (Elmhurst)

Winners by Place Where Bred

Locality	Winners
Kentucky	16
Florida	4
Maryland	1
Great Britain	1

Supplemental Entries

Year	Runner	Fee	Finish	Earnings
2005	Lost in the Fog	$90,000	7	$0
2004	Pt's Grey Eagle	90,000	8	0
2003	Bluesthestandard	90,000	2	236,000
	Shake You Down	90,000	3	129,800
	Private Horde	90,000	9	0
2002	Disturbingthepeace	90,000	7	0
	Bonapaw	90,000	10	0
1999	Son of a Pistol	120,000	13	0
	Enjoy the Moment	120,000	14	0
1998	**Reraise**	120,000	1	572,000
1997	Men's Exclusive	200,000	6	0
1996	Criollito (Arg)	200,000	12	0
1994	**Cherokee Run**	120,000	1	520,000
	Soviet Problem	120,000	2	200,000
	Exclusive Praline	120,000	9	0
1989	Sewickley	120,000	5	50,000
1987	Zabaleta	120,000	4	70,000
	Zany Tactics	120,000	9	0
1985	Committed	200,000	7	0
1984	Pac Mania	200,000	9	0

Eclipse Award Winners from Race

Year	Runner	Finish	Title
2005	Lost in the Fog	7	Sprinter
2004	**Speightstown**	1	Sprinter
2003	Aldebaran	6	Sprinter
2002	**Orientate**	1	Sprinter
2001	**Squirtle Squirt**	1	Sprinter
	Xtra Heat	2	3yo filly
2000	**Kona Gold**	1	Sprinter
1999	**Artax**	1	Sprinter
1998	**Reraise**	1	Sprinter
1996	**Lit de Justice**	1	Sprinter
1995	Not Surprising	4	Sprinter
1994	**Cherokee Run**	1	Sprinter
1993	**Cardmania**	1	Sprinter
1992	Rubiano	3	Sprinter
1991	Housebuster	9	Sprinter
1989	Safely Kept	2	Sprinter
1988	**Gulch**	1	Sprinter
1987	Groovy	2	Sprinter
1986	**Smile**	1	Sprinter
1985	**Precisionist**	1	Sprinter
1984	**Eillo**	1	Sprinter

Largest Winning Margins

Year	Winner	Margin
1987	Very Subtle	4
1991	Sheikh Albadou (GB)	3
2003	Cajun Beat	2¼
1998	Reraise	2
2004	Speightstown	1¼
1996	Lit de Justice	1¼
1986	Smile	1¼

Smallest Winning Margins

Year	Winner	Margin
1984	Eillo	nose
2005	Silver Train	head
1994	Cherokee Run	head
1995	Desert Stormer	neck
1993	Cardmania	neck
1992	Thirty Slews	neck
1990	Safely Kept	neck
1989	Dancing Spree	neck

Shortest-Priced Winners

Year	Winner	Odds
1984	Eillo	1.30-to-1
2000	Kona Gold	1.70-to-1
2002	Orientate	2.70-to-1
1994	Cherokee Run	2.80-to-1
1985	Precisionist	3.40-to-1

Longest-Priced Winners

Year	Winner	Odds
1991	Sheikh Albadou (GB)	26.30-to-1
2003	Cajun Beat	22.80-to-1
1992	Thirty Slews	18.70-to-1
1997	Elmhurst	16.60-to-1
1989	Dancing Spree	16.60-to-1
1987	Very Subtle	16.40-to-1

Odds-On Beaten Favorites

Year	Favorite	Odds	Finish
1991	Housebuster	2-to-5	9
2005	Lost in the Fog	7-to-10	7
1987	Groovy	4-to-5	2
1986	Groovy	2-to-5	4

Fastest Winners

Year	Winner	Track	Time	Cond.
2000	Kona Gold	CD	1:07.77	fast
1999	Artax	GP	1:07.89	fast
2003	Cajun Beat	SA	1:07.95	fast
1997	Elmhurst	Hol	1:08.01	fast

Slowest Winners

Year	Winner	Track	Time	Cond.
1988	Gulch	CD	1:10⅖	sloppy
1984	Eillo	Hol	1:10⅕	fast
1990	Safely Kept	Bel	1:09⅗	fast
1994	Cherokee Run	CD	1:09.54	fast

Most Starters

Year	Track	Starters
2001	Belmont Park	14
2000	Churchill	14
1999	Gulfstream Park	14
1998	Churchill Downs	14
1997	Hollywood Park	14
1994	Churchill Downs	14
1993	Santa Anita Park	14
1992	Gulfstream Park	14
1990	Belmont Park	14
1985	Aqueduct	14

Fewest Starters

Year	Track	Starters
1986	Santa Anita Park	9
2005	Belmont Park	11
1991	Churchill Downs	11
1984	Hollywood Park	11

Winning Post Positions

Post	Starters	Winners	Percent
1	22	1	4.5%
2	22	3	13.6%
3	22	3	13.6%
4	22	2	9.1%
5	22	5	22.7%
6	22	0	0.0%
7	22	0	0.0%
8	22	1	4.5%
9	22	1	4.5%
10	21	3	14.3%
11	21	3	14.3%
12	18	0	0.0%
13	18	0	0.0%
14	10	0	0.0%

Changes in Sprint

The purse for the Sprint was doubled to $2-million in 2006.

Breeders' Cup Mile

In the Breeders' Cup Mile (G1), good things have come in twos. Four Breeders' Cup races have had repeat winners, and the Breeders' Cup Mile has had three horses who have posted two victories each.

Miesque, bred by owner Stavros Niarchos's Flaxman Holdings Ltd., sparkled in the Mile on turf at Hollywood Park in 1987 and conquered a significantly slower surface at Churchill Downs the following year. The remarkable Francois Boutin-trained filly won by 3½ lengths in California and by four lengths in Kentucky—the largest winning margins in the race's history. On the strength of her single North American victories, Miesque was voted champion grass female in 1987 and '88. The Niarchos family also campaigned Mile winners Spinning World (1997), Domedriver (Ire) (2002), and Six Perfections (Fr) ('03) in the name of Flaxman Holdings.

Claiborne Farm's homebred Lure, arguably one of the most accomplished horses never to win an end-of-year championship, also scored two daylight victories, winning by three lengths at Gulfstream Park in 1992 and by 2¼ lengths the following year at Santa Anita Park for trainer Claude R. "Shug" McGaughey III.

Although not necessarily possessing talent to equal Miesque or Lure, Da Hoss became a two-time Mile winner by virtue of his courage and the innovative training regimen of Michael Dickinson. In 1996, Dickinson had his assistant, Joan Wakefield, test the Woodbine turf course in high heels to determine the best path for the Gone West gelding, who won by 1½ lengths. Da Hoss missed the entire following season due to injury and came back to run in the 1998 Mile with only one start in two years. He rallied on a firm Churchill turf course to overtake Hawksley Hill (Ire) and win by a head.

European-based horses have had consistent

Breeders' Cup Mile

Grade 1, $1.5-million, three-year-olds and up, 1 mile, turf. Run October 29, 2005, at Belmont Park with gross value of $1,856,925. First run in 1984. Weights: Northern Hemisphere three-year-olds, 123 pounds; older, 126 pounds. Southern Hemisphere three-year-olds, 120 pounds; older, 126 pounds. Fillies and mares allowed three pounds.

Year	Winner	Jockey	Second	Third	Site	Time	Cond.	1st Purse
2005	**Artie Schiller**, 4	G. Gomez	Leroidesanimaux (Brz)	Gorella (Fr)	Bel	1:36.10	gd	**$1,053,000**
2004	**Singletary**, 4	D. Flores	Antonius Pius	Six Perfections (Fr)	LS	1:36.90	yl	873,600
2003	**Six Perfections (Fr)**, 3	J. Bailey	Touch of the Blues (Fr)	Century City (Ire)	SA	1:33.86	ft	780,000
2002	**Domedriver (Ire)**	T. Thulliez	Rock of Gibraltar (Ire)	Good Journey	AP	1:36.92	yl	556,400
2001	**Val Royal (Fr)**, 5	J. Valdivia Jr.	Forbidden Apple	Bach (Ire)	Bel	**1:32.05**	fm	592,800
2000	**War Chant**, 3	G. Stevens	North East Bound	Dansili (GB)	CD	1:34.67	fm	608,400
1999	**Silic (Fr)**, 4	C. Nakatani	Tuzla (Fr)	Docksider	GP	1:34.26	gd	520,000
1998	**Da Hoss**, 6	J. Velazquez	Hawksley Hill (Ire)	Labeeb (GB)	CD	1:35.27	fm	520,000
1997	**Spinning World**, 4	C. Asmussen	Geri	Decorated Hero (GB)	Hol	1:32.77	fm	572,000
1996	**Da Hoss**, 4	G. Stevens	Spinning World	Same Old Wish	WO	1:35.80	gd	520,000
1995	**Ridgewood Pearl (GB)**, f, 3	J. Murtagh	Fastness (Ire)	Sayyedati (GB)	Bel	1:43.65	sf	520,000
1994	**Barathea (Ire)**, 4	L. Dettori	Johann Quatz (Fr)	Unfinished Symph	CD	1:34.50	fm	520,000
1993	**Lure**, 4	M. Smith	Ski Paradise	Fourstars Allstar	SA	1:33.58	fm	520,000
1992	**Lure**, 3	M. Smith	Paradise Creek	Brief Truce	GP	1:32.90	fm	520,000
1991	**Opening Verse**, 5	P. Valenzuela	Val des Bois (Fr)	Star of Cozzene	CD	1:37.59	fm	520,000
1990	**Royal Academy**, 3	L. Piggott	Itsallgreektome	Priolo	Bel	1:35⅕	gd	450,000
1989	**Steinlen (GB)**, 6	J. Santos	Sabona	Most Welcome (GB)	GP	1:37⅕	gd	450,000
1988	**Miesque**, f, 4	F. Head	Steinlen (GB)	Simply Majestic	CD	1:38⅗	gd	450,000
1987	**Miesque**, f, 3	F. Head	Show Dancer	Sonic Lady	Hol	1:32⅘	fm	450,000
1986	**Last Tycoon (Ire)**, 3	Y. Saint-Martin	Palace Music	Fred Astaire	SA	1:35⅕	fm	450,000
1985	**Cozzene**, 5	W. Guerra	Al Mamoon	Shadeed	Aqu	1:35	fm	450,000
1984	**Royal Heroine (Ire)**, f, 4	F. Toro	Star Choice	Cozzene	Hol	1:32⅗	fm	450,000

1985—Palace Music disqualified from second to ninth.

success in the Mile. Nine of the first 22 winners were based with European trainers prior to their wins.

Most remarkable about the Mile has been the domination of the Northern Dancer sire line. Although the great Windfields Farm stallion did not sire a winner himself, six of his sons and three of his grandsons have sired winners, accounting for 13 victories in the first 22 years. His sons Danzig and Nureyev have each sired three winners.

The interests of the late Niarchos have had unprecedented success in the Mile. Following the victories of Miesque, the Niarchos family's Spinning World won in 1997, and the family recorded back-to-back victories in 2002 and '03, with Domedriver (Ire) and Six Perfections (Fr), respectively.

Owners by Wins

5 **Flaxman Holdings Ltd./Stavros Niarchos** (Domedriver [Ire], Miesque [twice], Six Perfections [Fr], Spinning World)

2 **Claiborne Farm** (Lure [twice]), **Prestonwood Farm and Wall Street Stable** (Da Hoss, [twice])

1 **Classic Thoroughbreds PLC** (Royal Academy), **Anne Coughlan** (Ridgewood Pearl [GB]), **Marjorie and Irving Cowan** (War Chant), **J. Terrence Lanni, Bernard Schiappa, Kenneth Poslosky, et al.** (Silic [Fr]), **Little Red Feather Racing** (Singletary), **David S. Milch** (Val Royal [Fr]), **Sheikh Mohammed bin Rashid al Maktoum and Gerald Leigh** (Barathea [Ire]), **John Nerud** (Cozzene), **Allen E. Paulson** (Opening Verse), **Richard C. Strauss** (Last Tycoon [Ire]), **Robert Sangster** (Royal Heroine [Ire]), **Mrs. Thomas J. Walsh and Timber Bay Farm** (Artie Schiller), **Wildenstein Stable** (Steinlen [GB])

Breeders by Wins

5 **Flaxman Holdings Ltd./Niarchos Family** (Domedriver [Ire], Miesque [twice], Six Perfections [Fr], Spinning World)

2 **Claiborne Farm and Gamely Corp.** (Lure [twice]), **Fares Farm** (Da Hoss [twice])

1 **Allez France Stables Ltd.** (Steinlen [GB]), **Tom Gentry** (Royal Academy), **Sean Coughlan** (Ridgewood Pearl [GB]), **Marjorie and Irving Cowan** (War Chant), **M. Armenio Simoes de Almeida** (Silic [Fr]), **Disler Farms Ltd.** (Singletary), **Kilfrush Stud Ltd.** (Last Tycoon [Ire]), **Jean-Luc Lagardere** (Val Royal [Fr]), **Gerald Leigh** (Barathea [Ire]), **Haras du Mezeray S.A.** (Artie Schiller), **John Nerud** (Cozzene), **B. L. Ryan** (Royal Heroine [Ire]), **Jacques D. Wimpfheimer** (Opening Verse)

Trainers by Wins

2 **Pascal Bary** (Domedriver [Ire], Six Perfections [Fr]), **Francois Boutin** (Miesque [twice]), **Julio Canani** (Silic [Fr], Val Royal [Fr]), **Michael Dickinson** (Da Hoss [twice]), **Claude R. "Shug" McGaughey III** (Lure [twice])

1 **Don Chatlos** (Singletary), **Robert Collet** (Last Tycoon [Ire]), **Luca Cumani** (Barathea [Ire]), **Neil Drysdale** (War Chant), **John Gosden** (Royal Heroine [Ire]), **James A. Jerkens** (Artie Schiller), **D. Wayne Lukas** (Steinlen [GB]), **Richard Lundy** (Opening Verse), **Jan Nerud** (Cozzene), **Michael O'Brien** (Royal Academy), **John Oxx** (Ridgewood Pearl [GB]), **Jonathan Pease** (Spinning World)

Jockeys by Wins

2 **Freddie Head** (Miesque [twice]), **Mike Smith** (Lure [twice]), **Gary Stevens** (Da Hoss, War Chant)

1 **Cash Asmussen** (Spinning World), **Jerry Bailey** (Six Perfections [Fr]), **Lanfranco Dettori** (Barathea [Ire]), **David Flores** (Singletary), **Garrett Gomez** (Artie Schiller), **Walter Guerra** (Cozzene), **John Murtagh** (Ridgewood Pearl [GB]), **Corey Nakatani** (Silic [Fr]), **Lester Piggott** (Royal Academy), **Yves Saint-Martin** (Last Tycoon [Ire]), **Jose Santos** (Steinlen [GB]), **Thierry Thulliez** (Domedriver [Ire]), **Fernando Toro** (Royal Heroine [Ire]), **Jose Valdivia Jr.** (Val Royal [Fr]), **John Velazquez** (Da Hoss), **Patrick Valenzuela** (Opening Verse)

Sires by Wins

3 **Danzig** (Lure [twice], War Chant), **Nureyev** (Miesque [twice], Spinning World)

2 **Gone West** (Da Hoss [twice]), **Indian Ridge** (Domedriver [Ire], Ridgewood Pearl [GB])

1 **Caro (Ire)** (Cozzene), **Celtic Swing** (Six Perfections [Fr]), **El Prado (Ire)** (Artie Schiller), **Habitat** (Steinlen [GB]), **Lypheor (GB)** (Royal Heroine [Ire]), **Nijinsky II** (Royal Academy), **Royal Academy** (Val Royal [Fr]), **Sadler's Wells** (Barathea [Ire]), **Sillery** (Silic [Fr]), **Sultry Song** (Singletary), **The Minstrel** (Opening Verse), **Try My Best** (Last Tycoon [Ire])

Winners by Place Where Bred

Locality	Winners
Kentucky	12
Ireland	4
France	3
Great Britain	2
Florida	1

Supplemental Entries

Year	Runner	Fee	Finish	Earnings
2005	Leroidesanimaux (Brz)	$135,000	2	$405,000
	Gorella (Fr)	135,000	3	222,750
	Majors Cast (Ire)	135,000	5	60,750
	Host (Chi)	300,000	7	0
2004	Blackdoun (Fr)	135,000	7	0
	Mr. O'Brien (Ire)	135,000	9	0
2002	Landseer (GB)	90,000	DNF	0
2001	**Val Royal (Fr)**	90,000	1	592,800
	Express Tour	90,000	10	0
2000	Ladies Din	120,000	8	0
	Indian Lodge (Ire)	90,000	13	0
1997	Lucky Coin	120,000	4	61,600
1992	Bistro Garden	120,000	14	0
1991	Star of Cozzene	120,000	3	120,000
1986	Hatim	120,000	13	0
	Truce Maker	120,000	14	0
1985	Rousillon	120,000	9	0
1984	Night Mover	120,000	8	0

DNF Did not finish

Eclipse Award Winners from Race

Year	Runner	Finish	Title
2005	Leroidesanimaux (Brz)	2	Turf male
1993	Flawlessly	9	Turf female
1991	Tight Spot	9	Turf male
1990	Itsallgreektome	2	Turf male
1989	**Steinlen (GB)**	1	Turf male
1988	**Miesque**	1	Turf female
1987	**Miesque**	1	Turf female
1985	**Cozzene**	1	Turf male
1984	**Royal Heroine (Ire)**	1	Turf female

Largest Winning Margins

Year	Winner	Margin
1988	Miesque	4
1987	Miesque	3½
1994	Barathea (Ire)	3
1992	Lure	3

Smallest Winning Margins

Year	Winner	Margin
1998	Da Hoss	head
1986	Last Tycoon (Ire)	head
2000	War Chant	neck
1999	Silic (Fr)	neck
1990	Royal Academy	neck

Shortest-Priced Winners

Year	Winner	Odds
1993	Lure	1.30-to-1
1984	Royal Heroine (Ire)	1.70-to-1*
1989	Steinlen (GB)	1.80-to-1
1988	Miesque	2.00-to-1*

*Part of entry

Longest-Priced Winners

Year	Winner	Odds
1986	Last Tycoon (Ire)	35.90-to-1
1991	Opening Verse	26.70-to-1
2002	Domedriver (Ire)	26.00-to-1
2004	Singletary	16.50-to-1
1998	Da Hoss	11.60-to-1
1994	Barathea (Ire)	10.40-to-1

Odds-On Beaten Favorites

Year	Favorite	Odds	Finish
2002	Rock of Gibraltar (Ire)	4-to-5	2
1994	Lure	9-to-10	9

Fastest Winners

Year	Winner	Track	Time	Cond.
2001	Val Royal (Fr)	Bel	1:32.05	firm
1984	Royal Heroine (Ire)	Hol	1:32⅗	firm
1997	Spinning World	Hol	1:32.77	firm
1987	Miesque	Hol	1:32⅘	firm
1992	Lure	GP	1:32.90	firm

Slowest Winners

Year	Winner	Track	Time	Cond.
1995	Ridgewood Pearl (GB)	Bel	1:43.65	soft
1988	Miesque	CD	1:38⅗	good
1991	Opening Verse	CD	1:37.59	firm
1989	Steinlen (GB)	GP	1:37⅕	good

Most Starters

Year	Track	Starters
2004	Lone Star Park	14
2002	Arlington Park	14
2000	Churchill Downs`	14
1999	Gulfstream Park	14
1998	Churchill Downs	14
1996	Woodbine	14
1994	Churchill Downs	14
1992	Gulfstream Park	14
1991	Churchill Downs	14
1987	Hollywood Park	14
1986	Santa Anita	14
1985	Aqueduct	14

Fewest Starters

Year	Track	Starters
1984	Hollywood Park	10
1989	Gulfstream Park	11
2005	Belmont Park	12
2001	Belmont Park	12
1997	Hollywood Park	12
1988	Churchill Downs	12

Winning Post Positions

Post	Starters	Winners	Percent
1	22	3	13.6%
2	22	4	18.2%
3	22	1	4.5%
4	22	2	9.1%
5	22	1	4.5%
6	22	2	9.1%
7	22	1	4.5%
8	22	1	4.5%
9	22	0	0.0%
10	22	2	9.1%
11	21	2	9.5%
12	20	3	15.0%
13	16	0	0.0%
14	12	0	0.0%

Changes in Mile

The purse of the Breeders' Cup Mile was increased to $1.5-million from $1-million in 2003 and to $2-million in 2006.

Breeders' Cup Juvenile Fillies

One of the most all-American of the Breeders' Cup races, the Breeders' Cup Juvenile Fillies (G1) has produced the most champions in year-end Eclipse Award balloting among Breeders' Cup races. Nineteen of the 22 winners were subsequently voted year-end champions.

The first Breeders' Cup Juvenile Fillies, the second race on the inaugural card in 1984, produced the afternoon's first bit of controversy. In making a winning move at the top of the stretch, Fran's Valentine knocked Pirate's Glow off stride and pushed her into Canadian star Bessarabian. Fran's Valentine held off Outstandingly to reach the finish line first, but stewards disqualified Fran's Valentine to tenth for causing interference. After Outstandingly followed with a win in the Hollywood Starlet Stakes (G1), she was voted an Eclipse Award as champion two-year-old filly, a title that would be earned by all but three of the succeeding Juvenile Fillies winners.

The Juvenile Fillies at Aqueduct in 1985 launched a dominating run by D. Wayne Lukas, who took the first two spots that year with Twilight Ridge and Family Style. Lukas saddled the top three finishers in 1988, with Open Mind the winner. In 1994, he sent out Flanders and Serena's Song to finish one-two. Flanders pulled up lame after the race and subsequently was retired. Serena's Song, second by a head, was champion three-year-old filly the following year and retired as North America's then-leading female earner with $3,283,388. Lukas also won in 1999 with longshot Cash Run and in 2005 with Folklore, the 11th favorite to win the race.

In addition to Open Mind, who was voted champion at two and three, Juvenile Fillies winners who earned two championship titles were Go for Wand and Silverbulletday. Go for Wand took the two-year-old title with a triumph at Gulfstream Park in 1989 and won an Eclipse Award as champion three-year-old filly posthumously after a fatal breakdown in the 1990 Breeders' Cup Distaff (G1). Silverbulletday scored a half-length victory over stablemate Excellent Meeting in the 1998 Juvenile Fillies and won four Grade 1 races the following year to wrap up the three-year-old filly title.

Ashado, second to Halfbridled in 2003, went on to win the Breeders' Cup Distaff (G1) in '04 and collect an Eclipse Award as champion three-year-old filly. She was voted champion older female after another stellar campaign that ended with a third-place finish in the Distaff. She subsequently was sold for a record $9-million as broodmare prospect.

Even more than the Breeders' Cup Juvenile (G1), the Juvenile Fillies in recent years has been noteworthy for the inability of its winners to maintain their form at age three. Storm Flag Flying, a daughter of 1995 Juvenile Fillies winner My Flag and unbeaten in 2002, failed to win at three, although she was a Grade 1 winner at four in '04 and finished second to Ashado in the '04 Distaff. Halfbridled, also unbeaten at two, failed to win her two starts at three in 2004 and was retired. Sweet Catomine, also an impressive Juvenile Fillies winner and a near-unanimous Eclipse Award champion, won twice at three, including an easy victory in the Santa Anita Oaks (G1), but was retired after running fifth in the Santa Anita Derby (G1).

The Juvenile Fillies also is notable for its number of odds-on winners. Lukas's three-horse entry was 3-to-5 in 1985, and in '88 his five-horse coupling was 7-to-10. Two years later at Belmont Park, LeRoy Jolley-trained Meadow Star went off at 1-to-5 and breezed home by five lengths. Lukas struck again at Churchill in 1994, when Flanders won at 2-to-5 in an entry with Cat Appeal. Silverbulletday, trained by Bob Baffert, won at 4-to-5 in 1998, and Ogden Mills Phipps's Storm Flag Flying won at 4-to-5 in 2002. The only filly beaten at odds-on was 0.95-to-1 You, who finished fourth in 2001.

Through 2005, only 12 overseas-based fillies have competed in the Juvenile Fillies, with their best finishes a pair of fourths in 1993 and '94. Godolphin Racing won in 2001 with Tempera, who was trained in the United States by Eoin Harty.

Owners by Wins

2 **Eugene V. Klein** (Twilight Ridge, Open Mind)

1 **John A. Bell III** (Epitome), **Buckland Farm** (Pleasant Stage), **Christiana Stable** (Go for Wand), **Dogwood Stable** (Storm Song), **Dolly Green** (Brave Raj), **Godolphin Racing** (Tempera), **Harbor View Farm** (Outstandingly), **Carl Icahn** (Meadow Star), **Richard A. Kaster, Nancy R. Kaster, Nancy A. Kaster, and Donald Prop-**

Breeders' Cup Juvenile Fillies

Grade 1, $1-million, two-year-old fillies, 1 1/16 miles, dirt. Run on October 29, 2005, at Belmont Park with gross value of $972,020. First run in 1984. Weights: 119 pounds

Year	Winner	Jockey	Second	Third	Site	Time	Cond.	1st Purse
2005	**Folklore**	E. Prado	Wild Fit	Original Sin	Bel	1:43.85	ft	$551,200
2004	**Sweet Catomine**	C. Nakatani	Balletto (UAE)	Runway Model	LS	1:41.65	ft	520,000
2003	**Halfbridled**	J. Krone	Ashado	Victory U. S. A.	SA	1:42.75	ft	520,000
2002	**Storm Flag Flying**	J. Velazquez	Composure	Santa Catarina	AP	1:49.60	gd	520,000
2001	**Tempera**	D. Flores	Imperial Gesture	Bella Bellucci	Bel	1:41.49	ft	520,000
2000	**Caressing**	J. Velazquez	Platinum Tiara	She's a Devil Due	CD	1:42.77	ft	**592,800**
1999	**Cash Run**	J. Bailey	Chilukki	Surfside	GP	1:43.31	ft	520,000
1998	**Silverbulletday**	G. Stevens	Excellent Meeting	Three Ring	CD	1:43.68	ft	520,000
1997	**Countess Diana**	S. Sellers	Career Collection	Primaly	Hol	**1:42.11**	ft	535,600
1996	**Storm Song**	C. Perret	Love That Jazz	Critical Factor	WO	1:43.60	ft	520,000
1995	**My Flag**	J. Bailey	Cara Rafaela	Golden Attraction	Bel	1:42.55	my	520,000
1994	**Flanders**	P. Day	Serena's Song	Stormy Blues	CD	1:45.28	ft	520,000
1993	**Phone Chatter**	L. Pincay	Sardula	Heavenly Prize	SA	1:43.08	ft	520,000
1992	**Eliza**	P. Valenzuela	Educated Risk	Boots 'n Jackie	GP	1:42.93	ft	520,000
1991	**Pleasant Stage**	E. Delahoussaye	La Spia	Cadillac Women	CD	1:46.48	ft	520,000
1990	**Meadow Star**	J. Santos	Private Treasure	Dance Smartly	Bel	1:44	ft	450,000
1989	**Go for Wand**	R. Romero	Sweet Roberta	Stella Madrid	GP	1:44 1/5	ft	450,000
1988	**Open Mind**	A. Cordero Jr.	Darby Shuffle	Lea Lucinda	CD	1:46 3/5	my	450,000
1987	**Epitome**	P. Day	Jeanne Jones	Dream Team	Hol	1:36 2/5	ft	450,000
1986	**Brave Raj**	P. Valenzuela	Tappiano	Saros Brig	SA	1:43 1/5	ft	450,000
1985	**Twilight Ridge**	J. Velasquez	Family Style	Steal a Kiss	Aqu	1:35 4/5	ft	450,000
1984	**Outstandingly**	W. Guerra	Dusty Heart	Fine Spirit	Hol	1:37 4/5	ft	450,000

1984-'85, '87—run at one mile; 2002—run at 1 1/8 miles; 1984—Fran's Valentine disqualified from first to tenth.

son (Countess Diana), **Robert and Beverly Lewis** (Folklore), **Overbrook Farm** (Flanders), **Padua Stables** (Cash Run), **Allen E. Paulson** (Eliza), **Mike Pegram** (Silverbulletday), **Ogden Phipps** (My Flag), **Ogden Mills Phipps** (Storm Flag Flying), **Carl F. Pollard** (Caressing), **Herman Sarkowsky** (Phone Chatter), **Wertheimer Farm** (Halfbridled), **Martin and Pamela Wygod** (Sweet Catomine)

Breeders by Wins

2 **Ogden Phipps** (My Flag, Storm Flag Flying)

1 **Thomas E. Burrow** (Twilight Ridge), **Jaime S. Carrion** (Meadow Star), **Christiana Stable** (Go for Wand), **Darley Stud Management** (Tempera), **Due Process Stable** (Open Mind), **Robert S. Evans** (Cash Run), **Mrs. Thomas M. Evans** (Pleasant Stage), **William S. Farish and Ogden Mills Phipps** (Storm Song), **Harbor View Farm** (Outstandingly), **Highclere Inc. and Clear Creek** (Silverbulletday), **Brereton C. Jones** (Caressing), **Richard A. and Nancy R. Kaster** (Countess Diana), **Wallace S. Karutz** (Brave Raj), **Robert and Beverly Lewis** (Folklore), **Jessica Bell Nicholson and H. Bennett Bell** (Epitome), **Overbrook Farm** (Flanders), **Allen E. Paulson** (Eliza), **Herman Sarkowsky** (Phone Chatter), **Wertheimer Farm et Frere** (Halfbridled), **Martin and Pamela Wygod** (Sweet Catomine)

Trainers by Wins

5 **D. Wayne Lukas** (Cash Run, Flanders, Folklore, Open Mind, Twilight Ridge)

2 **Richard Mandella** (Halfbridled, Phone Chatter), **Claude R. "Shug" McGaughey III** (My Flag, Storm Flag Flying)

1 **William Badgett** (Go for Wand), **Bob Baffert** (Silverbulletday), **Patrick Byrne** (Countess Diana), **Julio Canani** (Sweet Catomine), **Eoin Harty** (Tempera), **Alex Hassinger Jr.** (Eliza), **Philip Hauswald** (Epitome), **LeRoy Jolley** (Meadow Star), **Frank Martin** (Outstandingly), **Christopher Speckert** (Pleasant Stage), **Mel Stute** (Brave Raj), **David Vance** (Caressing), **Nick P. Zito** (Storm Song)

Jockeys by Wins

2 **Jerry Bailey** (My Flag, Cash Run), **Pat Day** (Epitome, Flanders), **John Velazquez** (Caressing, Storm Flag Flying), **Patrick Valenzuela** (Brave Raj, Eliza)

1 **Angel Cordero Jr.** (Open Mind), **Eddie Delahoussaye** (Pleasant Stage), **David Flores** (Tempera), **Walter Guerra** (Outstandingly), **Julie Krone** (Halfbridled), **Corey Nakatani** (Sweet Catomine), **Craig Perret** (Storm Song), **Laffit Pincay Jr.** (Phone Chatter), **Edgar Prado** (Folklore), **Randy Romero** (Go for Wand), **Jose Santos** (Meadow Star), **Shane Sellers** (Countess Diana), **Gary Stevens** (Silverbulletday), **Jorge Velasquez** (Twilight Ridge)

Sires by Wins

2 **Deputy Minister** (Open Mind, Go for Wand), **Seeking the Gold** (Flanders, Cash Run), **Storm Cat** (Sweet Catomine, Storm Flag Flying)

1 **A.P. Indy** (Tempera), **Cox's Ridge** (Twilight Ridge), **Deerhound** (Countess Diana), **Easy Goer** (My Flag), **Exclusive Native** (Outstandingly), **Honour and Glory** (Caressing), **Meadowlake** (Meadow Star), **Mt. Livermore** (Eliza), **Phone Trick** (Phone Chatter), **Pleasant Colony** (Pleasant Stage), **Rajab** (Brave Raj), **Silver Deputy** (Silverbulletday), **Summer Squall** (Storm Song), **Summing** (Epitome), **Tiznow** (Folklore), **Unbridled** (Halfbridled)

Winners by Place Where Bred

Locality	Winners
Kentucky	17
Florida	3
New Jersey	1
Pennsylvania	1

Supplemental Entries

Year	Runner	Fee	Finish	Earnings
2005	Wild Fit	$90,000	2	$212,000
2000	Cindy's Hero	90,000	4	63,840
	Out of Sync	90,000	9	0
1995	Tipically Irish	120,000	6	0
1994	Post It	120,000	6	0

Eclipse Award Winners from Race

Year	Runner	Finish	Title
2005	**Folklore**	1	Juvenile filly
2004	**Sweet Catomine**	1	Juvenile filly
2003	**Halfbridled**	1	Juvenile filly
2002	**Storm Flag Flying**	1	Juvenile filly
2001	**Tempera**	1	Juvenile filly
2000	**Caressing**	1	Juvenile filly
1999	Chilukki	2	Juvenile filly
1998	**Silverbulletday**	1	Juvenile filly
1997	**Countess Diana**	1	Juvenile filly
1996	**Storm Song**	1	Juvenile filly
1995	Golden Attraction	3	Juvenile filly
1994	**Flanders**	1	Juvenile filly
1993	**Phone Chatter**	1	Juvenile filly
1992	**Eliza**	1	Juvenile filly
1991	**Pleasant Stage**	1	Juvenile filly
1990	**Meadow Star**	1	Juvenile filly
1989	**Go for Wand**	1	Juvenile filly
1988	**Open Mind**	1	Juvenile filly
1987	**Epitome**	1	Juvenile filly
1986	**Brave Raj**	1	Juvenile filly
1985	Family Style	2	Juvenile filly
1984	**Outstandingly**	1	Juvenile filly

Largest Winning Margins

Year	Winner	Margin
1997	Countess Diana	8½
1986	Brave Raj	5½
1990	Meadow Star	5
1996	Storm Song	4½

Smallest Winning Margins

Year	Winner	Margin
1987	Epitome	nose
1994	Flanders	head
1993	Phone Chatter	head
1991	Pleasant Stage	head

Shortest-Priced Winners

Year	Winner	Odds
1990	Meadow Star	0.20-to-1
1994	Flanders	0.40-to-1*
1985	Twilight Ridge	0.60-to-1*
1988	Open Mind	0.70-to-1*
2002	Storm Flag Flying	0.80-to-1
1998	Silverbulletday	0.80-to-1

*Part of entry

Longest-Priced Winners

Year	Winner	Odds
2000	Caressing	47.00-to-1

Year	Winner	Odds
1999	Cash Run	32.50-to-1
1987	Epitome	30.40-to-1
1984	Outstandingly	22.80-to-1

Odds-On Beaten Favorites

Year	Favorite	Odds
2001	You	0.95-to-1

Fastest Winners at 1⅙ Miles

Year	Winner	Track	Time	Cond.
2001	Tempera	Bel	1:41.49	fast
2004	Sweet Catomine	LS	1:41.65	fast
1997	Countess Diana	Hol	1:42.11	fast
1995	My Flag	Bel	1:42.55	muddy
2003	Halfbridled	SA	1:42.75	fast
2000	Caressing	CD	1:42.77	fast
1992	Eliza	GP	1:42.93	fast

Slowest Winners at 1⅙ Miles

Year	Winner	Track	Time	Cond.
1988	Open Mind	CD	1:46⅗	muddy
1991	Pleasant Stage	CD	1:46.48	fast
1994	Flanders	CD	1:45.28	fast
1989	Go for Wand	GP	1:44⅕	fast

Most Starters

Year	Track	Starters
2003	Santa Anita Park	14
1997	Hollywood Park	14
1991	Churchill Downs	14
1994	Churchill Downs	13
1990	Belmont Park	13

Fewest Starters

Year	Track	Starters
1995	Belmont Park	8
1993	Santa Anita Park	8
2001	Belmont Park	9
1999	Gulfstream Park	9

Winning Post Positions

Post	Starters	Winners	Percent
1	22	2	9.1%
2	22	1	4.5%
3	22	1	4.5%
4	22	3	13.6%
5	22	1	4.5%
6	22	3	13.6%
7	22	0	0.0%
8	22	4	18.1%
9	20	4	20.0%
10	18	0	0.0%
11	15	1	6.7%
12	13	0	0.0%
13	5	0	0.0%
14	3	2	66.7%

Changes in Juvenile Fillies

Originally at one mile, the distance was changed to 1⅙ miles in 1988. It was contested at 1⅙ miles in 1986 and at 1⅛ miles in 2002. The purse was doubled to $2-million in 2006.

Breeders' Cup Distaff

Although the Breeders' Cup Distaff (G1) has produced three of the eight highest-priced winners in the event's history, the race for fillies and mares has in fact been one of the most consistent of the original seven races.

That record of consistency began with the inaugural Breeders' Cup Distaff at Hollywood Park in 1984. Princess Rooney, winner of the Vanity Handicap (G1) and Spinster Stakes (G1) in prior starts, went off as the 7-to-10 favorite and rolled

Breeders' Cup Distaff

Grade 1, $2-million, fillies and mares, three-year-olds and up, 1⅛ miles. Run October 29, 2005, at Belmont Park with gross value of $1,834,000. First run in 1984. Weights: Northern Hemisphere three-year-olds, 120 pounds; older, 123 pounds. Southern Hemisphere three-year-olds, 115 pounds; older, 123 pounds.

Year	Winner	Jockey	Second	Third	Site	Time	Cond.	1st Purse
2005	**Pleasant Home**, 4	C. Velazquez	Society Selection	Ashado	Bel	1:48.34	ft	$1,040,000
2004	**Ashado**, 4	J. Velazquez	Storm Flag Flying	Stellar Jayne	LS	1:48.26	ft	1,080,000
2003	**Adoration**, 4	P. Valenzuela	Elloluv	Got Koko	SA	1:49.17	ft	1,040,000
2002	**Azeri**	M. Smith	Farda Amiga	Imperial Gesture	AP	1:48.64	gd	1,040,000
2001	**Unbridled Elaine**, 3	P. Day	Spain	Two Item Limit	Bel	1:49.21	ft	1,227,200
2000	**Spain**, 3	V. Espinoza	Surfside	Heritage of Gold	CD	1:47.66	ft	**1,227,200**
1999	**Beautiful Pleasure**, 4	J. Chavez	Banshee Breeze	Heritage of Gold	GP	1:47.56	ft	1,040,000
1998	**Escena**, 5	G. Stevens	Banshee Breeze	Keeper Hill	CD	1:49.89	ft	1,040,000
1997	**Ajina**, 3	M. Smith	Sharp Cat	Escena	Hol	1:47.30	ft	520,000
1996	**Jewel Princess**, 4	C. Nakatani	Serena's Song	Different (Arg)	WO	1:48.40	ft	520,000
1995	**Inside Information**, 4	M. Smith	Heavenly Prize	Lakeway	Bel	**1:46.15**	my	520,000
1994	**One Dreamer**, 6	G. Stevens	Heavenly Prize	Miss Dominique	CD	1:50.70	ft	520,000
1993	**Hollywood Wildcat**, 3	E. Delahoussaye	Paseana (Arg)	Re Toss (Arg)	SA	1:48.35	ft	520,000
1992	**Paseana (Arg)**, 5	C. McCarron	Versailles Treaty	Magical Maiden	GP	1:48.17	ft	520,000
1991	**Dance Smartly**, 3	P. Day	Versailles Treaty	Brought to Mind	CD	1:50.95	ft	520,000
1990	**Bayakoa (Arg)**, 6	L. Pincay Jr.	Colonial Waters	Valay Maid	Bel	1:49⅕	ft	450,000
1989	**Bayakoa (Arg)**, 5	L. Pincay Jr.	Gorgeous	Open Mind	GP	1:47⅖	ft	450,000
1988	**Personal Ensign**, 4	R. Romero	Winning Colors	Goodbye Halo	CD	1:52	my	450,000
1987	**Sacahuista**, 3	R. Romero	Clabber Girl	Oueee Bebe	Hol	2:02⅘	ft	450,000
1986	**Lady's Secret**, 4	P. Day	Fran's Valentine	Outstandingly	SA	**2:01⅕**	ft	450,000
1985	**Life's Magic**, 4	A. Cordero Jr.	Lady's Secret	Dontstop Themusic	Aqu	2:02	ft	450,000
1984	**Princess Rooney**, 4	E. Delahoussaye	Life's Magic	Adored	Hol	2:02⅖	ft	450,000

1984-'87—run at 1¼ miles; 1989 and '90—Bayakoa (Arg) supplementary entry; 1992—Paseana (Arg) supplemental entry.

to a seven-length victory.

In subsequent editions, the Distaff generally was characterized by dominant winners scoring by open lengths. In fact, Inside Information's 13½-length win in 1995 remains the series' largest winning margin. Azeri waltzed away to a five-length victory in 2002 to lock up a Horse of the Year title, and Lady's Secret won by 2½ lengths in 1986, her Horse of the Year season. Odds-on favorites have won the race seven times.

The 1988 running remains one of the most memorable of all Breeders' Cup races. Undefeated Personal Ensign, seemingly beaten at the sixteenth pole, closed relentlessly on Winning Colors, that year's Kentucky Derby (G1) winner, and put her nose in front at the wire to close out her career undefeated in 13 starts.

In 14 of 22 years, both the champion three-year-old filly and older female have competed in the Distaff.

Supplemental entries, principally top-quality mares from South America, have had excellent success in the Distaff. Bayakoa (Arg), supplemented for $200,000 in 1989 and '90, won both years. Paseana (Arg), supplemented in 1992 and '93, won in her first try and finished second by a nose to Hollywood Wildcat in '93.

The biggest upset in Distaff history occurred in 2000, when dominant West Coast mare Riboletta (Brz) ran seventh as the 2-to-5 favorite.

Racing Hall of Fame members who have contested the race are Princess Rooney, Lady's Secret, Personal Ensign, Winning Colors, Bayakoa, Go for Wand, Dance Smartly, Paseana, and Serena's Song.

Owners by Wins

2 **Allen E. Paulson** (Ajina, Escena), **Ogden Mills Phipps** (Inside Information, Pleasant Home), **Frank and Janis Whitham** (Bayakoa [Arg] [twice])

1 **Amerman Racing Stable** (Adoration), **Barry A. Beal and L. R. French Jr.** (Sacahuista), **Irving and Marjorie Cowan** (Hollywood Wildcat), **Sidney Craig** (Paseana [Arg]), **Roger J. Devenport** (Unbridled Elaine), **Glen Hill Farm** (One Dreamer), **Mel Hatley and Eugene V. Klein** (Life's Magic), **Mr. and Mrs. Eugene V. Klein** (Lady's Secret), **John Oxley** (Beautiful Pleasure), **Allen E. Paulson Living Trust** (Azeri), **Ogden Phipps** (Personal Ensign), **Sam-Son Farm** (Dance Smartly), **Starlight Stables, Paul Saylor, and Johns Martin** (Ashado), **The Thoroughbred Corp. and Martha and Richard Stephen** (Jewel Princess), **The Thoroughbred Corp.** (Spain), **Paula Tucker** (Princess Rooney)

Breeders by Wins

3 **Allen E. Paulson** (Ajina, Azeri, Escena)

2 **Farnsworth Farms** (Beautiful Pleasure, Jewel Princess), **Haras Principal** (Bayakoa [Arg], twice), **Ogden Mills Phipps** (Inside Information, Pleasant Home)

1 **Lucy G. Bassett** (Adoration), **Irving and Marjorie Cowan** (Hollywood Wildcat), **Glen Hill Farm** (One Dreamer), **Golden Orb Farm and K. David Schwartz** (Unbridled Elaine), **Haras Vacacion** (Paseana [Arg]), **G. Watts Humphrey and William S. Farish** (Sacahuista), **Aaron and Marie Jones** (Ashado), **Mr. and Mrs. Douglas Parrish and David Parrish III** (Life's Magic), **Ogden Phipps** (Personal Ensign), **Ben and Tom Roach** (Princess Rooney), **Sam-Son Farm** (Dance Smartly), **Robert H. Spreen** (Lady's Secret), **The Thoroughbred Corp.** (Spain)

Trainers by Wins

4 **D. Wayne Lukas** (Lady's Secret, Life's Magic, Sacahuista, Spain)

3 **Ron McAnally** (Bayakoa [Arg] [twice], Paseana [Arg]), **Claude R. "Shug" McGaughey III** (Inside Information, Personal Ensign, Pleasant Home)

2 **Neil Drysdale** (Hollywood Wildcat, Princess Rooney), **William I. Mott** (Ajina, Escena)

1 **James Day** (Dance Smartly), **Laura de Seroux** (Azeri), **Wallace Dollase** (Jewel Princess), **David Hofmans** (Adoration), **Todd Pletcher** (Ashado), **Tom Proctor** (One Dreamer), **Dallas Stewart** (Unbridled Elaine), **John T. Ward Jr.** (Beautiful Pleasure)

Jockeys by Wins

3 **Pat Day** (Dance Smartly, Lady's Secret, Unbridled Elaine), **Mike Smith** (Azeri, Ajina, Inside Information)

2 **Eddie Delahoussaye** (Hollywood Wildcat, Princess Rooney), **Laffit Pincay Jr.** (Bayakoa [Arg] [twice]), **Randy Romero** (Personal Ensign, Sacahuista), **Gary Stevens** (Escena, One Dreamer)

1 **Jorge Chavez** (Beautiful Pleasure), **Angel Cordero** (Life's Magic), **Victor Espinoza** (Spain), **Chris McCarron** (Paseana [Arg]), **Corey Nakatani** (Jewel Princess), **Patrick Valenzuela** (Adoration), **Cornelio Velasquez** (Pleasant Home), **John Velazquez** (Ashado)

Sires by Wins

2 **Consultant's Bid** (Bayakoa [Arg], twice), **Private Account** (Inside Information, Personal Ensign), **Strawberry Road (Aus)** (Ajina, Escena)

1 **Ahmad** (Paseana [Arg]), **Cox's Ridge** (Life's Magic), **Danzig** (Dance Smartly), **Honor Grades** (Adoration), **Jade Hunter** (Azeri), **Key to the Mint** (Jewel Princess), **Kris S.** (Hollywood Wildcat), **Maudlin** (Beautiful Pleasure), **Raja Baba** (Sacahuista), **Relaunch** (One Dreamer), **Saint Ballado** (Ashado), **Secretariat** (Lady's Secret), **Seeking the Gold** (Pleasant Home), **Thunder Gulch** (Spain), **Unbridled's Song** (Unbridled Elaine), **Verbatim** (Princess Rooney)

Winners by Place Where Bred

Locality	Winners
Kentucky	13
Florida	4
Argentina	3
Oklahoma	1
Ontario	1

Supplemental Entries

Year	Runner	Fee	Finish	Earnings
2001	Miss Linda (Arg)	$400,000	6	$0
2000	Riboletta (Brz)	400,000	7	0
1996	Different (Arg)	200,000	3	120,000
1993	Paseana (Arg)	200,000	2	200,000
1992	**Paseana (Arg)**	200,000	1	520,000
1990	**Bayakoa (Arg)**	200,000	1	450,000
1989	**Bayakoa (Arg)**	200,000	1	450,000
1986	Classy Cathy	120,000	4	70,000
1985	Dontstop Themusic	120,000	3	108,000
	Isayso	120,000	6	10,000

Eclipse Award Winners from Race

Year	Runner	Finish	Title
2005	Ashado	3	Older female
2004	**Ashado**	1	3yo filly
2002	**Azeri**	1	Horse of the Year, Older female
	Farda Amiga	2	3yo filly
2000	Surfside	2	3yo filly
	Riboletta (Brz)	7	Older female
1999	**Beautiful Pleasure**	1	Older female
	Silverbulletday	6	3yo filly
1998	**Escena**	1	Older female
	Banshee Breeze	2	3yo filly
1997	**Ajina**	1	3yo filly
	Hidden Lake	7	Older female
1996	**Jewel Princess**	1	Older female
1995	**Inside Information**	1	Older female
	Serena's Song	5	3yo filly
1994	Heavenly Prize	2	3yo filly
	Sky Beauty	9	Older female
1993	**Hollywood Wildcat**	1	3yo filly
	Paseana (Arg)	2	Older female
1992	**Paseana (Arg)**	1	Older female
	Saratoga Dew	12	3yo filly
1991	**Dance Smartly**	1	3yo filly
	Queena	5	Older female
1990	**Bayakoa (Arg)**	1	Older female
	Go for Wand	DNF	3yo filly
1989	**Bayakoa (Arg)**	1	Older female
	Open Mind	3	3yo female
1988	**Personal Ensign**	1	Older female
	Winning Colors	2	3yo filly
1987	**Sacahuista**	1	3yo filly
	North Sider	6	Older female
1986	**Lady's Secret**	1	Horse of the Year, Older female
1985	**Life's Magic**	1	Older female
1984	**Princess Rooney**	1	Older female
	Life's Magic	2	3yo filly

Largest Winning Margins

Year	Winner	Margin
1995	Inside Information	13½
2005	Pleasant Home	9¼
1984	Princess Rooney	7
1990	Bayakoa (Arg)	6¾
1985	Life's Magic	6¼
2002	Azeri	5

Smallest Winning Margins

Year	Winner	Margin
1998	Escena	nose
1993	Hollywood Wildcat	nose
1988	Personal Ensign	nose
1994	One Dreamer	neck

Shortest-Priced Winners

Year	Winner	Odds
1985	Life's Magic	0.40-to-1*
1991	Dance Smartly	0.50-to-1*
1988	Personal Ensign	0.50-to-1
1986	Lady's Secret	0.50-to-1*
1989	Bayakoa (Arg)	0.70-to-1
1984	Princess Rooney	0.70-to-1

*Part of entry

Longest-Priced Winners

Year	Winner	Odds
2000	Spain	55.90-to-1
1994	One Dreamer	47.10-to-1
2003	Adoration	40.70-to-1
2005	Pleasant Home	30.75-to-1
2001	Unbridled Elaine	12.30-to-1
1997	Ajina	4.80-to-1*
1999	Beautiful Pleasure	3.00-to-1

*Part of entry

Odds-On Beaten Favorites

Year	Winner	Odds	Finish
2003	Sightseek	0.60-to-1	4
2000	Riboletta (Brz)	0.40-to-1	7
1998	Banshee Breeze	0.80-to-1	2
1990	Go for Wand	0.70-to-1	DNF
1987	Infinidad (Chi)	0.70-to-1	4

Fastest Winners at 1⅛ Miles

Year	Winner	Track	Time	Cond.
1995	Inside Information	Bel	1:46.15	muddy
1997	Ajina	Hol	1:47.30	fast
1989	Bayakoa (Arg)	GP	1:47⅘	fast
1999	Beautiful Pleasure	GP	1:47.56	fast
2000	Spain	CD	1:47.66	fast

Slowest Winners at 1⅛ Miles

Year	Winner	Track	Time	Cond.
1988	Personal Ensign	CD	1:52	muddy
1991	Dance Smartly	CD	1:50.95	fast
1994	One Dreamer	CD	1:50.70	fast
1998	Escena	CD	1:49.89	fast
2001	Unbridled Elaine	Bel	1:49.21	fast

Most Starters

Year	Track	Starters
1992	Gulfstream Park	14
2005	Belmont Park	13
1991	Churchill Downs	13
2004	Lone Star Park	11
2001	Belmont Park	11
1995	Belmont Park	10
1989	Gulfstream Park	10

Fewest Starters

Year	Track	Starters
1996	Woodbine	6
1987	Hollywood Park	6
2003	Santa Anita Park	7
1990	Belmont Park	7
1985	Aqueduct	7
1984	Hollywood Park	7

Winning Post Positions

Post	Starters	Winners	Percent
1	22	5	22.7%
2	22	1	4.5%
3	22	0	0.0%
4	22	5	22.7%
5	22	4	18.1%
6	22	3	13.6%
7	20	1	5.0%
8	16	0	0.0%
9	10	0	0.0%
10	7	1	14.3%
11	5	1	0.0%
12	3	0	0.0%
13	3	0	0.0%
14	1	1	100.0%

Changes in Distaff

Two significant changes have occurred in the conditions of the Breeders' Cup Distaff. For the 1988 running, the distance was shortened to 1⅛ miles from 1¼ miles, and in 1998 the purse was increased to $2–million from $1-million.

2005 Classic: A Saintly Victory

In the glow of a Breeders' Cup Classic (G1) victory that assured Saint Liam a Horse of the Year honor, co-owner William Warren looked back through the years. "I want to tell you what this race meant to me," he said. "I named Saint Liam after my father. My father had to drop out of school in the eighth grade to take care of his mother and his two sisters. And he raised himself up from his bootstraps. So I idolized my father."

Saint Liam proved he was North America's best older male with a powerful one-length victory over a courageous Flower Alley in the $4,291,560 Breeders' Cup Classic (G1) on October 29. Named for the late William Kelly Warren with a Gaelic Irish twist, Saint Liam also capped a tumultuous year for New York-based trainer Rick Dutrow Jr. and gave Racing Hall of Fame jockey Jerry Bailey his fifth Classic win.

"We have the best horse around," said Dutrow, who earlier in the day had upset Lost in the Fog in the Breeders' Cup Sprint (G1) with Silver Train. "Anybody left standing, they were in here, and we beat them [in the Classic] and throughout the year. Saint Liam, he's won everywhere. We didn't duck any kind of horse in any race. We went after them. That's because I've always felt he was the best horse."

Saint Liam, a Saint Ballado horse who stood at Lane's End in Versailles, Kentucky, in 2006 after racing in the fuchsia and green colors of William and Suzanne Warren one last time, overcame a disadvantageous outside post position to win the 1¼-mile Classic on a fast track in 2:01.49. Perfect Drift, making his fourth appearance in the Classic after finishing fourth a year ago, was third, 1½ lengths behind Flower Alley and just a neck ahead of 69.25-to-1 longshot Super Frolic, with Suave running fifth by another neck.

The Classic field lacked two notable runners in Santa Anita Handicap (G1) winner Rock Hard Ten, scratched by Hall of Fame trainer Richard Mandella the day before the race with a bruised left front foot, and Preakness (G1) and Belmont (G1) Stakes winner Afleet Alex, who missed the race after suffering a condylar fracture to his left front cannon bone in July.

The Breeders' Cup Classic was only Saint Liam's second career start at the 1¼-mile trip, but the distance was of no concern to either Dutrow or Bailey, and Saint Liam turned in the type of performance that fans had come to expect.

Saint Liam, who came to Dutrow late in his three-year-old campaign after starting his career with Kentucky-based conditioner Anthony Reinstedler, drew the unenviable 13 post in the full field of 14 that was entered for the Classic. The news was even worse for Australian champion Starcraft (NZ), who was supplemented to the race at a fee of $800,000 but would have to begin his quest for a Group or Grade 1 victory on his third continent from post 14. Belmont's configuration requires that 1¼-mile races start at an angle on the clubhouse turn, leaving those on the outside at a slight disadvantage and with a choice of either hustling toward the front to avoid losing ground or taking back from the start.

Saint Liam, sent off as the 2.40-to-1 favorite in a field devoid of any natural front-runners, was a few strides slower than normal from the gate as Pennsylvania Derby (G2) winner Sun King and Saratoga Breeders' Cup Handicap (G2) winner Suave took the early initiative just ahead of Flower Alley around the first turn. Jockey Club Gold Cup (G1) winner and 2.60-to-1 second choice Borrego also was off somewhat slowly under Garrett Gomez and raced toward the back of the field as Sun King carved out splits of :23.98 and :47.68 up the backstretch.

Bailey liked what he felt as he headed into the fading sunlight on the backstretch and kept Saint Liam 4½ lengths off the lead and in the clear on the outside while racing fourth behind Sun King, Suave, and Flower Alley after the opening half-mile. Approaching the far turn, Super Frolic, Oratorio (Ire), and Perfect Drift all passed Saint Liam, but those bids would be short-lived.

"I really felt confident the moment I turned up the backside," said Bailey, who won the Classic in 1991 with Black Tie Affair (Ire), in '93 with Arcangues, in '94 with Concern, and in '95 with Cigar. "I knew I had the horses in front of me. I felt pretty strongly. I know Borrego comes with a strong run, but I was actually pretty confident all around."

The tightly bunched field passed the quarter pole in 1:36.87, with Sun King, Suave, and Flower Alley across the track from the rail out, Saint Liam four wide, and Starcraft, Perfect Drift, Super Frolic, and Choctaw Nation right behind.

Saint Liam and Flower Alley raced side by side past the three-sixteenths pole and overtook Suave

Owners

William and **Suzanne Warren** are the respective chairman and executive vice president of Warren American Oil Co., based in Tulsa, Oklahoma. They have been Thoroughbred owners since 1983. Their charitable William K. Warren Foundation has made substantial donations to his alma mater, Notre Dame University, including the Warren Golf Course and the Warren Health Center.

Breeder

Edward P. Evans owns 3,000-acre Spring Hill Farm in Casanova, Virginia. Son of the late owner-breeder Thomas Mellon Evans, he is the former chairman of the publishing house Macmillan Inc. Among the horses he has bred or owned are Summer Colony, Raging Fever, Prenup, With Ability, and Gygistar.

almost simultaneously with a furlong to the finish. Those two were left to settle the issue in the stretch, and Flower Alley stuck a head in front in deep stretch before the Travers Stakes (G1) winner and jockey John Velazquez were overtaken in the shadow of the wire.

The effort turned in by Eugene Melnyk's Flower Alley was a bit of redemption for trainer Todd Pletcher, who saddled the three-year-old son of Distorted Humor to a distant fourth-place finish in the Jockey Club Gold Cup after back-to-back scores in the Jim Dandy Stakes (G2) and Travers at Saratoga Race Course. Flower Alley is one of 23 three-year-olds to either win or place in the Classic since its inception in 1984.

Saint Liam, who previously had won the Donn Handicap (G1) on February 5, Stephen Foster Handicap (G1) on June 18, and Woodward Stakes (G1) on September 10, not only completed a successful season, but also served as a comeback for his fun-loving, Maryland-born trainer who has ridden through a series of life's peaks and valleys but never gave up on his ultimate goal. After starting out as an assistant to his late father, Dick Dutrow Sr., at age 16, Dutrow went out on his own in the early 1990s. He readily admits he struggled personally and professionally, and the personal trials intensified when his father died of cancer. With plenty of help from longtime client Sanford Goldfarb, Dutrow eventually built one of New York's most successful stables. In Saint Liam's championship season, he also served a 60-day suspension for two medication positives.—*Tom Law*

TENTH RACE
Belmont Park
October 29, 2005

1¼ miles, dirt. 22nd running of the Breeders' Cup Classic (G1). Purse $4,000,000. 3-year-olds and up. Weights (Northern Hemisphere): 3-year-olds, 122 lbs. Older, 126 lbs. (Southern Hemisphere): 3-year-olds, 117 lbs. Older, 126 lbs. Fillies and mares allowed 3 lbs.

Value of race: $4,291,560. Value to winner: $2,433,600; second: $936,000; third: $514,800; fourth: $266,760; fifth: $140,400. Mutuel Pool $8,033,441.

Horse	Wgt.	M/Eqt	PP	St.	¼	½	¾	Str.	Fin.	Jockey	Odds $1
Saint Liam, 5, h.	126	Lb	12	4^{2}	4^{2}	$5^{1/2}$	$4^{1/2}$	$1^{1/2}$	1^{1}	J. Bailey	*2.40
Flower Alley, 3, c.	122	Lbc	8	$3^{2\frac{1}{2}}$	3^{2}	$4^{1/2}$	$3^{1/2}$	$2^{1/2}$	$2^{1\frac{1}{2}}$	J. Velazquez	10.00
Perfect Drift, 6, g.	126	L	4	5^{1}	$6^{1/2}$	$6^{1/2}$	$6^{1\frac{1}{2}}$	$5^{1/2}$	3^{nk}	M. Guidry	14.50
Super Frolic, 5, h.	126	L	6	10^{1}	$7^{1/2}$	3^{hd}	5^{2}	4^{hd}	4^{nk}	E. Coa	69.25
Suave, 4, c.	126	Lb	7	$2^{1\frac{1}{2}}$	2^{2}	2^{1}	$2^{1/2}$	$3^{1\frac{1}{2}}$	$5^{3/4}$	E. Prado	16.40
Choctaw Nation, 5, g.	126	Lbf	2	13	$12^{1/2}$	9^{hd}	8^{2}	8^{2}	$6^{1\frac{1}{4}}$	V. Espinoza	13.00
Starcraft (NZ), 5, h.	126	Lf	13	$11^{1\frac{1}{2}}$	$9^{1/2}$	8^{2}	7^{2}	$7^{1/2}$	$7^{1/2}$	P. Valenzuela	8.50
Sir Shackleton, 4, c.	126	Lc	5	$6^{1/2}$	$10^{1/2}$	13	$12^{1/2}$	11^{3}	8^{nk}	J. Castellano	36.50
Sun King, 3, c.	122	Lbc	1	1^{hd}	$1^{1/2}$	$1^{1/2}$	1^{hd}	$6^{1\frac{1}{2}}$	9^{2}	R. Bejarano	30.50
Borrego, 4, c.	126	L	10	8^{hd}	$11^{1/2}$	$12^{1/2}$	10^{2}	10^{1}	$10^{1\frac{1}{2}}$	G. Gomez	2.60
Oratorio (Ire), 3, c.	122	L	3	$7^{1/2}$	$5^{1/2}$	$7^{1/2}$	$9^{1\frac{1}{2}}$	$9^{1\frac{1}{2}}$	$11^{6\frac{1}{4}}$	K. Fallon	9.40
Jack Sullivan, 4, g.	126	L	9	$12^{1/2}$	13	$10^{1/2}$	13	12^{1}	12^{nk}	L. Dettori	51.25
A Bit O'Gold, 4, g.	126	L	11	$9^{1/2}$	8^{hd}	11^{2}	$11^{1/2}$	13	13	J. Jones	51.75

OFF AT 5:42. Start: 7. Winner: Wide Move, Clear.
Time: :23.98, :47.68, 1:12.23, 1:36.87, 2:01.49. Weather: Cloudy. Track: Fast.

$2 Mutuel Prices:				
	13—SAINT LIAM	6.80	5.10	4.20
	9—FLOWER ALLEY		8.70	7.10
	5—PERFECT DRIFT			7.80

$2 PICK THREE 11-2-13 PAID $2,045.00 $2 PICK FOUR 2-11-2-13 PAID $17,303.00
$2 PICK SIX 10-3-2-11-2-13 PAID $90,325.00 $2 DAILY DOUBLE 2-13 PAID $76.00
$2 EXACTA 13-9 PAID $62.00 $2 SUPERFECTA 13-9-5-7 PAID $12,636.00
$2 TRIFECTA 13-9-5 PAID $501.00

b. h., by Saint Ballado—Quiet Dance, by Quiet American. Trainer: Richard Dutrow Jr. Owner: Mr. and Mrs. William K. Warren Jr. Bred by Edward P. Evans (Ky.).

SAINT LIAM settled just off the early pace, was unhurried leaving the far turn, took up chase after the leaders entering the stretch, drew alongside FLOWER ALLEY to challenge in upper stretch, surged to the front leaving the furlong marker, and edged clear under steady right-hand urging. FLOWER ALLEY, close up on the outside, made a strong run to threaten in upper stretch, fought heads apart into deep stretch, and yielded grudgingly. PERFECT DRIFT, unhurried early, launched a bid leaving the turn, and closed late to gain a share. SUPER FROLIC stumbled badly at the start, closed ground steadily to reach contention on the turn, and closed willingly along the inside. SUAVE pressed the pace for a mile, battled heads apart for the lead in upper stretch, and tired from his early efforts. CHOCTAW NATION was outrun early and finished evenly. STARCRAFT (NZ) failed to mount a serious rally while racing wide. SIR SHACKLETON never reached contention. SUN KING dueled along the rail for a mile and gave way. BORREGO, outrun early, lodged a mild move between horses on the turn and flattened out. ORATORIO (IRE) saved ground to no avail. JACK SULLIVAN never reached contention. A BIT O'GOLD raced wide throughout.

2005 Turf: European Sweep

Standing on the sandy main track at Belmont Park moments after Shirocco (Ger) won the 22nd Breeders' Cup Turf (G1) on October 29 at Belmont Park, trainer Andre Fabre and his wife and assistant, Elisabeth, exuded the quiet dignity that comes from being the top French stable for nearly two decades. "It was a perfect race," Elisabeth Fabre said succinctly as they waited for Shirocco to return to the winner's circle.

The owner and breeder of the first German-bred horse to win a Breeders' Cup race, Baron Georg von Ullmann was not quite so regally calm. "Our first horse with you, and you win the Breeders' Cup," von Ullmann exulted as he grabbed the diminutive Andre Fabre in a bear hug big enough and exuberant enough to embrace all of New York City.

It was indeed a perfect race over perfect ground and at the perfect distance for a perfect representative of a German breeding and racing industry that has enjoyed a striking renaissance over the past two decades. That revival really began in the 1980s with Acatenango, a two-time German Horse of the Year who defeated France's best in the '86 Grand Prix de Saint-Cloud (Fr-G1). Acatenango also led the German sire list four times and sired major international winners Lando (Ger), Sabiango (Ger), Fraulein (GB), Blue Canari, a number of German highweights and classic winners, as well as English and French highweight Borgia (Ger). Borgia recorded the previous high-water mark for German breeding at the Breeders' Cup by running a game, closing second by three-quarters of a length to Chief Bearhart in the 1997 Turf at Hollywood Park.

Acatenango, bred and owned by Gestut Fahrhof, was building on more than a century of success in Germany by Gestut Schlenderhan, leading German breeder more than 30 times. Schlenderhan was founded by the Oppenheim family in the 19th century and is now owned by Georg von Ullmann and his mother, Baroness Karin von Ullmann. The von Ullmanns are major shareholders in Bankhaus Salomon Oppenheim Jr. and Cie., the largest private bank in Europe. Schlenderhan has bred 16 Deutsches Derby (Ger-G1) (German Derby) winners, and Shirocco added a personal victory in that classic for Georg von Ullmann in 2004.

Shirocco, who is by the Schlenderhan stallion Monsun (Ger), concluded his three-year-old season with a victory in the Gran Premio del Jockey Club Italiano (Ity-G1), inflicting the first defeat on Italian champion Electrocutionist. But a slight injury early in 2005 delayed his transfer from Andreas Schutz's stable to Fabre's until August.

Shirocco's late arrival left Fabre little time to prepare Shirocco for his major European objective of the year, the Prix de l'Arc de Triomphe (Fr-G1) on October 2. Fabre got one race into him before the Arc, a promising third to Pride and Alkaased in the Prix Foy (Fr-G2) on September 11, but he was inevitably a little short of his best in Europe's biggest race. Still, he ran a very good race in the Arc, staying on strongly up the straight for fourth, beaten 4¼ lengths by the brilliant Fabre-trained three-year-old Hurricane Run.

Belmont's rain-softened turf course was the cause of considerable consternation among both American and European trainers throughout the week, but it suited a strong galloper such as Shirocco, who tracked Shake the Bank, pacemaker for the 2004 Turf winner, Better Talk Now. Shake the Bank got as far as seven lengths in front down the backstretch, setting steady fractions of :23.95, :47.89, 1:13.20, and 1:39.53 before fading to last, but he could not draw Shirocco into a speed duel.

"Normally in Europe we try to follow the lead horse [more closely]," said Shirocco's rider, Christophe Soumillon. "Today, I didn't want to kill my horse. His pace [sitting second] was fast enough." Shirocco inhaled Shake the Bank heading into the far turn, pursued by English Channel and Ace (Ire), with last year's Arc winner, Bago (Fr), trapped down on the inside and slight favorite Azamour (Ire) trying to pull his feet out of the sticky ground just behind. Shirocco kept up his powerful gallop all the way to the finish line, gradually drawing away to a 1¾-length win at 8.80-to-1 odds. The colt completed the 1½-mile distance in 2:29.30 on a course rated as good. Ace kept on for second, while Azamour rallied late to pass Bago for third. The four Europeans finished 5¾ lengths ahead of the best American, English Channel. Better Talk Now made a run on the turn but then backed up to seventh.

John Magnier, whose wife, Susan, co-owns Ace with Michael Tabor and Mrs. Harry McCalmont, said: "That's as good as he is. He just always finds one in front of him. Other than that, he'd be good."

"He couldn't really quicken on the ground," trainer John Oxx said of the Aga Khan's Azamour. "He just lost a bit of momentum coming out of the back straight [as Shake the Bank backed

Owner-Breeder

Baron Georg von Ullmann is a major shareholder in Bankhaus Salomon Oppenheim Jr. and Cie., Europe's largest private bank. He owns Gestut Schlenderhan, Germany's oldest and most famous stud farm, with his mother, Baroness Karin von Ullmann. She is a member of the Oppenheim family, which founded Schlenderhan in the 19th century. The stud farm has bred 16 Deutsches Derby (Ger-G1) (German Derby) winners, and von Ullmann added the 17th with Shirocco.

up], and it might have cost him the race. He ran his usual good race; he always tries hard, but he couldn't really quicken on the ground."

"Just in the last ten strides he managed to quicken a bit," said Azamour's rider, Michael Kinane. Azamour went to a stud career at the Aga Khan's Gilltown Stud in Ireland.

Although the turf course was officially rated as good, to Europeans that means a nice, uniform surface with just a little give in it. Belmont's turf was far softer than that on October 29. The horses' hooves were going into the ground several inches and occasionally kicking up big divots. "The rider [Thierry Gillet] said he didn't like the soft ground," said Jonathan Pease, trainer of Bago. "The soft ground blunted his usual acceleration," said Alan Cooper, racing manager for Bago's owner, the Niarchos family's Flaxman Stable. "The track didn't dry out enough for him." Bago's racing career ended on a slightly disappointing note at four after earning French highweight honors at both two and three while winning seven of nine races. He added only one victory in 2005, a first-out win in the Prix Ganay (Fr-G1), in a season troubled by injury. Bago went to Shizunai Stallion Station in Japan.

The soft going held no such terrors for Shirocco. Given typical German weather conditions for much of the year, German-bred horses have long been well adapted to racing on soft ground. "He's a very typical representative of German breeding," Fabre said, "staying horses who act on any ground and a big heart."

—John P. Sparkman

NINTH RACE
Belmont Park
October 29, 2005

1½ miles on turf. 22nd running of the Breeders' Cup Turf (G1). Purse $2-million. 3-year-olds and up. Weights (Northern Hemisphere): 3-year-olds, 121 lbs. Older, 126 lbs. (Southern Hemisphere): 3-year-olds, 116 lbs. Older, 125 lbs. Fillies and mares allowed 3 lbs.

Value of race: $2,090,760. Value to winner: $1,185,600; second: $456,000; third: $250,800; fourth: $129,960; fifth: $68,400. Mutuel Pool $5,411,517.

Horse	Wt.	M/Eqt	PP	¼	½	1m	1¼	Str.	Fin.	Jockey	Odds $1
Shirocco (Ger), 4, c.	126		2	$2^{½}$	$2^{1½}$	$2^{½}$	$1^{½}$	$1^{½}$	$1^{1¾}$	C. Soumillon	8.80
Ace (Ire), 4, c.	126	Lb	6	$9^{1½}$	8^{1}	4^{hd}	$3^{½}$	$2^{1½}$	2^{nk}	K. Fallon	16.40
Azamour (Ire), 4, c.	126	L	5	8^{hd}	11^{3}	8^{hd}	$7^{½}$	$4^{2½}$	$3^{¾}$	M. Kinane	3.65*
Bago (Fr), 4, c.	126		3	$6^{½}$	5^{hd}	7^{hd}	6^{hd}	3^{2}	$4^{5¾}$	T. Gillet	4.50
English Channel, 3, c.	121	L	10	4^{hd}	4^{1}	3^{1}	$2^{½}$	5^{2}	$5^{¾}$	J. Velazquez	11.40
Silverfoot, 5, g.	126	L	8	13	13	$11^{½}$	$8^{½}$	7^{2}	6^{1}	R. Bejarano	31.00
Better Talk Now, 6, g.	126	Lbf	4	$10^{½}$	$9^{½}$	$6^{½}$	$5^{½}$	6^{1}	$7^{2½}$	R. Dominguez	8.70
Gun Salute, 3, c.	121	Lb	13	$7^{½}$	$7^{½}$	$10^{1½}$	9^{7}	8^{5}	8^{12}	C. Velasquez	21.40
Fourty Niners Son, 4, c.	126	L	9	$11^{2½}$	$10^{1½}$	9^{hd}	4^{hd}	9^{10}	$9^{11¼}$	C. Nakatani	10.80
Leprechaun Kid, 6, g.	126	L	12	$5^{½}$	$6^{½}$	13	$12^{2½}$	11^{3}	$10^{¾}$	G. Gomez	39.75
Laura's Lucky Boy, 4, c.	126	L	11	12^{2}	$12^{½}$	$12^{½}$	$10^{½}$	$10^{½}$	$11^{8¾}$	G. Stevens	36.50
Shakespeare, 4, c.	126	L	7	3^{hd}	3^{hd}	5^{hd}	11^{hd}	12^{7}	12^{8}	J. Bailey	3.90
Shake the Bank, 5, g.	126	Lb	1	$1^{3½}$	1^{7}	1^{2}	13	13	13	T. Turner	81.25

OFF AT 5:02. Start: Good. Winner: Drew clear when roused.
Time: :23.95, :47.89, 1:13.20, 1:39.53, 2:05.05, 2:29.30. Weather: Cloudy. Turf: Good.

$2 Mutuel Prices:	**2—SHIROCCO (GER)**	**19.60**	**11.80**	**4.70**
	6—ACE (IRE)		**15.40**	**10.00**
	5—AZAMOUR (IRE)			**4.70**

$2 PICK THREE 2-11-2 PAID $4,280.00 **$2 EXACTA 2-6 PAID $296.50**
$2 HEAD2HEAD 3 vs. 4 vs. 7 (WINNER 3) PAID $4.80
$2 SUPERFECTA 2-6-5-3 PAID $4,694.00 **$2 TRIFECTA 2--6-5 PAID $1,560.00**

B. c., by Monsun (Ger)—So Sedulous, by The Minstrel. Trainer: Andre Fabre. Owner: Baron Georg von Ullmann. Bred by Baron Georg von Ullmann (Ger).

SHIROCCO (GER) was well placed behind the early pacesetter, took charge at the quarter pole, dug in when threatened in midstretch, and edged away in the final sixteenth. ACE (IRE) raced in hand for a mile, steadily worked his way forward along the rail, made a move to threaten the winner in upper stretch, but was no match for the winner while holding well for the place. AZAMOUR (IRE), well back to the far turn, closed late to gain a share. BAGO (FR) rallied along the rail entering the stretch, checked in upper stretch, and then rallied belatedly. ENGLISH CHANNEL, up close while four wide, lodged a move from the outside to threaten entering the stretch but could not sustain his bid. SILVERFOOT steadied in traffic nearing the stretch and passed tiring horses. BETTER TALK NOW, rated early, lodged a brief move midway on the far turn and flattened out. GUN SALUTE was never a factor. FOURTY NINERS SON, in hand early, reached contention on the far turn and faded in the drive. LEPRECHAUN KID raced wide throughout. LAURA'S LUCKY BOY never reached contention. SHAKESPEARE raced up close for a mile, steadied on the turn, and faltered. SHAKE THE BANK drew clear quickly and was used up setting the pace.

2005 Juvenile: He's a Wonderboy

In 1967, Merv Griffin watched a 17-year-old prodigy named Little Stevie Wonder deliver a brilliant performance on his show, the youngster's elastic voice announcing the arrival of a new talent. In the decades that followed, Wonder would prove to be one of the most important singer-songwriters in American pop music history.

Flash forward to October 29, 2005, when Griffin watched his brilliant two-year-old colt Stevie Wonderboy, named after the singer, surge past First Samurai and Henny Hughes in deep stretch to secure a 1¼-length victory in the $1,458,030 Breeders' Cup Juvenile (G1) at Belmont Park. The victory assured an Eclipse Award as champion two-year-old male for Stevie Wonderboy and his owner, a 15-time Emmy Award winner who hosted his talk show from 1962 to '86 while along the way producing game-show stalwarts "Wheel of Fortune" and "Jeopardy!"

Stevie Wonderboy, named for a breakthrough performer, scored breakthroughs of his own. He gave Griffin his biggest victory. He gave trainer Doug O'Neill his first Breeders' Cup win and his first million-dollar race victory. He gave jockey Garrett Gomez his first Breeders' Cup victory, and he gave sire Stephen Got Even his first Grade 1 winner.

Tony Holmes, co-breeder of Stevie Wonderboy with friends John Gunther and Walter Zent, said the trio expected the colt to go for six figures when he was offered in the 2004 Keeneland September yearling sale as part of a Lane's End consignment. He failed to reach his $75,000 reserve.

Consignor Bobby Scanlon, who died only days before the Breeders' Cup, then offered Stevie Wonderboy at the Fasig-Tipton Calder selected two-year-olds in training sale, where Doug's brother Dennis O'Neill purchased him for $100,000 on behalf of Griffin.

Owner

Merv Griffin is a 15-time Emmy Award-winning television producer who hosted a popular talk show from 1962-'86. He also is the creator of the long-running game shows "Wheel of Fortune" and "Jeopardy!" He owns Griffin Ranch in La Quinta, California, where he maintains approximately 50 Thoroughbreds. He owns Teleview Racing Patrol, which provides closed-circuit coverage of horse races throughout the country.

Breeders

From varied backgrounds, **Tony Holmes**, **John Gunther**, and **Walter Zent** all have become Kentucky farm operators. Gunther, vice president of a stock brokerage and investment banking company in Vancouver, British Columbia, owns Glennwood Farm in Versailles. Holmes, formerly a dairy farmer in his native New Zealand, owns Marula Park Stud in Lexington with his wife, Susan. Zent, a veterinarian at Hagyard Equine Medical Institute in Lexington, operates a farm with his wife, June.

Stevie Wonderboy was officially clocked in 11 seconds for his furlong workout at the Calder sale, although Dennis O'Neill said he had him between 10.6 and 10.8 seconds. Holmes suspects that buyers doubted Stevie Wonderboy's ability for immediate success. "He just didn't go out there and wow anybody with his time," Holmes said.

Impressed by one of her previous colts, winner Our Imperial Bay, the trio of breeders purchased Heat Lightning while she was carrying Stevie Wonderboy for $62,000 at the 2002 Keeneland November breeding stock sale. He was born on March 27, 2003, at Gunther's Glennwood Farm in Versailles, Kentucky, and raised at Holmes's Marula Park Stud in Lexington.

Holmes said Stevie Wonderboy showed poise and maturity from a young age, a quality that Dennis O'Neill spotted. He purchases colts at sales and then younger brother Doug trains those horses. The team approach paid off in big ways at the Calder sale.

While commercial breeder Holmes thought Stevie Wonderboy deserved more interest at the sale, he complimented O'Neill's eye and looked forward to the Keeneland November breeding stock sale, where Heat Lightning sold for $1.1-million in foal to Birdstone.

Stevie Wonderboy wasted little time erasing doubts about his brilliance. After finishing second to ill-fated What a Song in his maiden debut, Stevie Wonderboy was third in the Hollywood Juvenile Championship Stakes (G3) before reeling off back-to-back wins at Del Mar, including a five-length score over ten rivals in the Del Mar Futurity (G2) that caught the eye of Gomez's wife, Pam.

"This horse has given my wife chills ever since she saw him run at Del Mar," said Gomez, who has ridden Stevie Wonderboy in all his career starts. "Ever since I sat on his back, I've had very high hopes for him, and he really came through."

He also had to overcome some difficulties in the 14-horse field. He was checked at the start, clipped heels of another horse, and stumbled. Those incidents left him 12th after a quarter-mile and 11th after a half, with longshot Dawn of War setting a moderate pace. Saratoga Special Stakes (G2) winner Henny Hughes, who had stalked the pacesetter, seized the lead before going six furlongs in 1:10.61 and carried that speed into deep stretch in his first start for trainer Kiaran McLaughlin. He could not resist Stevie Wonderboy's flash to the front inside the sixteenth pole, but he saved the place spot from 1.30-to-1 favorite First Samurai, who had defeated Henny Hughes in the Hopeful (G1) and Champagne (G1) Stakes to enter the Juvenile undefeated in four career starts.

Gomez also acknowledged the strength of his competitors. "Those other horses actually gave me more of a fight than I expected because my horse has a heck of a turn of foot when I asked him," Gomez said. "When my horse did find his best stride near the sixteenth pole, he went ahead and wore them down and ran a huge race."

Dennis O'Neill said he has served as brother Doug's buyer for the past three or four years. The team approach has helped O'Neill become one of the hottest trainers in Southern California. "We like the same things in horses, and he's gotten to the point that he's very trusting in me now," Dennis O'Neill said. "So I have pretty much free rein of putting horses in the barn."

Doug O'Neill said with year-round racing, it is difficult for a trainer to also buy horses at sales. "I think that's why you see so many family-run outfits. We're kind of first-generation horsemen jumping into it," Doug O'Neill said. "He's kind of our scout, and he has helped tremendously. I wouldn't be here without him."

Griffin said during a television interview that Doug O'Neill impressed him as someone who really cared about horses. Griffin, a longtime owner of Arabians and Thoroughbreds at his Griffin Ranch in La Quinta, California, contacted O'Neill about training his Thoroughbreds, and they have enjoyed success with multiple stakes winner Cee's Irish and Grade 3 winner Skipaslew.—*Frank Angst*

FOURTH RACE
Belmont Park
October 29, 2005

1$\frac{1}{16}$ miles on dirt. 22nd running of the Breeders' Cup Juvenile (G1). Purse $1,500,000. Colts and geldings, 2-year-olds. Weight: 122 lbs.

Value of race: $1,458,030. Value to winner: $826,800; second: $318,000; third: $174,900; fourth: $90,630; fifth: $47,700. Mutuel Pool $4,157,292.

Horse	Wt.	M/Eqt	PP	St.	¼	½	¾	Str.	Fin.	Jockey	Odds $1
Stevie Wonderboy, 2, c.	122	L	12	9	$12^{2\frac{1}{2}}$	11^{hd}	$5^{\frac{1}{2}}$	3^{3}	$1^{1\frac{1}{4}}$	G. Gomez	4.50
Henny Hughes, 2, c.	122	Lc	10	3	$2^{\frac{1}{2}}$	2^{hd}	1^{1}	1^{1}	2^{2}	E. Prado	9.30
First Samurai, 2, c.	122	L	9	10	9^{1}	8^{hd}	$3^{\frac{1}{2}}$	$2^{1\frac{1}{2}}$	$3^{5\frac{1}{4}}$	J. Bailey	1.30 *
Brother Derek, 2, c.	122	L	13	2	4^{hd}	4^{hd}	2^{hd}	$4^{\frac{1}{2}}$	4no	A. Solis	56.75
Superfly, 2, c.	122	Lc	1	13	13^{2}	10^{hd}	$8^{\frac{1}{2}}$	$5^{1\frac{1}{2}}$	$5^{3\frac{1}{4}}$	E. Coa	48.50
Sorcerer's Stone, 2, c.	122	Lb	8	6	5^{hd}	9^{2}	6^{hd}	$6^{2\frac{1}{2}}$	$6^{1\frac{1}{4}}$	M. Guidry	7.70
Dr. Pleasure, 2, c.	122	L	14	1	$8^{\frac{1}{2}}$	$13^{2\frac{1}{2}}$	13^{2}	10^{1}	$7^{2\frac{1}{2}}$	J. Santos	44.50
Stream Cat, 2, c.	122		7	14	14	14	$12^{1\frac{1}{2}}$	9^{hd}	$8^{1\frac{1}{2}}$	G. Stevens	22.60
Leo (GB), 2, c.	122		3	11	10^{hd}	6^{hd}	10^{hd}	7^{hd}	$9^{2\frac{1}{4}}$	L. Dettori	36.00
Jealous Profit, 2, c.	122	Lb	5	8	7^{hd}	7^{hd}	$9^{1\frac{1}{2}}$	8^{1}	$10^{17\frac{1}{4}}$	C. Nakatani	62.25
Dawn of War, 2, c.	122	L	6	4	$1^{\frac{1}{2}}$	$1^{\frac{1}{2}}$	4^{1}	11^{6}	$11^{1\frac{1}{2}}$	J. Castellano	32.50
Ivan Denisovich (Ire), 2, c.	122	L	2	12	$11^{\frac{1}{2}}$	12^{hd}	14	14	12^{1}	K. Fallon	16.40
Set Alight, 2, c.	122		4	7	$6^{\frac{1}{2}}$	$5^{1\frac{1}{2}}$	$11^{1\frac{1}{2}}$	$13^{\frac{1}{2}}$	13^{3}	R. Bejarano	41.00
Private Vow, 2, c.	122	L	11	5	3^{1}	3^{1}	7^{hd}	$12^{1\frac{1}{2}}$	14	J. Velazquez	10.30

OFF AT 2:01. Start: Good for all. Winner: Four wide, fast finish.
Time: :23.14, :45.75, 1:10.61, 1:35.34, 1:41.64. Weather: Cloudy. Track: Fast.

$2 Mutuel Prices:				
	12—STEVIE WONDERBOY	11.00	5.90	3.80
	10—HENNY HUGHES		8.80	4.90
	9—FIRST SAMURAI			2.50

$2 PICK THREE 6-1-12 PAID $252.00 $2 DAILY DOUBLE 1-12 PAID $45.60
$2 EXACTA 12-10 PAID $105.50
$2 HEAD2HEAD 7 vs. 8 vs. 12 (WINNER 12) PAID $4.00
$2 SUPERFECTA 12-10-9-13 PAID $7,051.00 $2 TRIFECTA 12-10-9 PAID $229.00

Ch. c., by Stephen Got Even—Heat Lightning, by Summer Squall. Trainer: Doug O'Neill. Owner: The Merv Griffin Ranch Co. Bred by John Gunther, Tony Holmes, and Walter Zent (Ky.).

STEVIE WONDERBOY clipped heels and stumbled along the backstretch, moved rapidly into contention on the far turn, charged to the front inside the sixteenth pole, and edged clear through the final 50 yards. HENNY HUGHES bobbled at the start, pressed the pace from the outside, accelerated to the front leaving the turn, maintained a clear lead in midstretch, and yielded to the winner inside the sixteenth pole. FIRST SAMURAI, rank at the gate, made a run to challenge from the outside in upper stretch, and weakened under pressure in the final eighth. BROTHER DEREK stalked the leaders, made a bid approaching the quarter pole, and tired from his early efforts. SUPERFLY moved into contention in early stretch and flattened out. SORCERER'S STONE raced in the middle of the pack and finished evenly. DR. PLEASURE outrun early, lacked a strong closing response. STREAM CAT was never a factor. LEO (GB) saved ground in traffic to the turn and steadily tired. JEALOUS PROFIT faded leaving the turn. DAWN OF WAR set pace to the turn and faltered. IVAN DENISOVICH (IRE) broke awkwardly and never reached contention. SET ALIGHT chased the pace, steadied sharply on the turn, and was never close thereafter. PRIVATE VOW bore out after his left rein broke on the backstretch and failed to menace thereafter.

2005 Filly and Mare Turf: Sister Act

Intercontinental (GB) entered the Breeders' Cup Filly and Mare Turf (G1) on October 29 with 12 wins in 21 starts in the United States and France; seven graded stakes victories in California, Kentucky, and New York; and earnings exceeding $1.5-million. The daughter of Danehill has a family with enough stars to fill the sky, including full sister Banks Hill (GB), who won the 2001 Filly and Mare Turf at Belmont Park in her North American debut and earned the Eclipse Award as champion turf female.

And, if that were not enough selling points on her résumé, Intercontinental headed into the Filly and Mare Turf following consecutive victories in the Palomar Breeders' Cup Handicap (G2) at Del Mar and the WinStar Galaxy Stakes (G2) at Keeneland Race Course. For the season, she had four wins, one second, and one third in six starts and earnings of $720,000. Alas, Intercontinental was the 15.10-to-1 sixth betting choice in the full field of 14 for the Filly and Mare Turf.

There were some reasons for the long odds, however, starting with the race distance. Intercontinental, a homebred racing for Khalid Abdullah's Juddmonte Farms, had never raced at 1¼ miles, the distance of the $972,020 Filly and Mare Turf, and she was winless in two starts at 1⅛ miles, the longest distance she had attempted. A third reason might have been that Jerry Bailey, who rode Intercontinental in her two previous races, was instead riding champion and defending race winner Ouija Board (GB).

In the days leading up to the race, trainer Bobby Frankel called Intercontinental "my sleeper" when compared with his other Breeders' Cup starters: Megahertz (GB), who would make her third consecutive start in the Filly and Mare Turf, and Leroidesanimaux (Brz), the heavy favorite for the Breeders' Cup Mile (G1). Learning that Banks Hill had never won beyond a mile before she captured the Filly and Mare Turf for trainer Andre Fabre gave Frankel an extra shot of confidence in her little sister.

"I've been inundated the last ten days with one question: Will the mare get the mile and a quarter?" said Dr. John Chandler, Juddmonte's president. "And I finally got an answer: She definitely will get a mile and a quarter."

Chandler made his statement after Rafael Bejarano skillfully rode Intercontinental to a front-running, 1¼-length victory over Ouija Board. The 2.30-to-1 favorite, Ouija Board steadily advanced to mount a challenge in the stretch but could not catch the winner. Grade 1 winner Film Maker, who was second in the race last year behind Ouija Board, crossed the finish line a neck farther back in third. Intercontinental's time on a Belmont inner turf course labeled as good was 2:02.34.

Intercontinental gave Frankel his second victory in the Filly and Mare Turf, following a triumph as an owner and trainer with Starine (Fr), who won in 2002 at Arlington Park over defending race winner Banks Hill. Intercontinental also topped Starine's longshot odds of 13.20-to-1.

Frankel began training Intercontinental after she was successful for Fabre in France, where she won two of three races at two and was third in the Grand Criterium (Fr-G1) in 2002. At three, she captured two of six races and was third behind Russian Rhythm and eventual Breeders' Cup Mile (G1) winner Six Perfections (Fr) in the One Thousand Guineas (Eng-G1).

Intercontinental was scheduled to make her North American debut in the mile Matriarch Stakes (G1) at Hollywood Park in November 2003 but missed the race due to a virus. Her year-older half sister, Heat Haze (GB), won the mile race for Frankel and Juddmonte in the final start of her career. Heat Haze was fourth behind Islington (Ire) in that year's Filly and Mare Turf at Santa Anita Park.

Intercontinental made her first start in this country in March 2004 at Santa Anita and rolled to three consecutive wins, including the 1$\frac{1}{16}$-mile Jenny Wiley Stakes (G3) at Keeneland Race Course and the one-mile Just a Game Breeders' Cup Handicap (G2) at Belmont. She was fifth behind Wonder Again and Riskaverse in the 1⅛-mile Diana Handicap (G1) at Saratoga Race Course and ended the season with a win in the Matriarch.

By the end of 2004, Ouija Board had earned the title as Europe's Horse of the Year with a rare sweep of the Epsom Oaks (Eng-G1) and Darley Irish Oaks (Ire-G1) and a third against males in the Prix de l'Arc de Triomphe (Fr-G1). With the shortest odds of any horse competing in 2004 World Thoroughbred Championships at Lone Star Park, Ouija Board at 9-to-10 won the race by 1½ lengths under Kieren Fallon. After some setbacks in 2005, Lord Derby's homebred won the Princess Royal Stakes (Eng-G3) on September 24 under Frankie Dettori and set up her return to the U.S.

With Fallon, now the stable jockey for trainer Aidan O'Brien, riding Mona Lisa (GB) in the Filly and Mare Turf and Dettori riding first call

Owner-Breeder

Khalid Abdullah's **Juddmonte Farms** is one of the world's most successful breeding and racing operations, with farms in England, Ireland, and Kentucky. Born in 1938 in Saudi Arabia, Abdullah has numerous business interests that operate under the banner of Mawared. He purchased his first racehorse in 1977 and had nearly 120 horses in training in England and France and another 40 in the United States with trainer Bobby Frankel. Juddmonte won Eclipse Awards as outstanding owner in 1992 and 2003 and as outstanding breeder in 1995 and 2001, '02, and '03.

for Godolphin and piloting Sundrop (Jpn) in the race, Bailey seized the opportunity to ride Ouija Board. Frankel said he did not decide until after Intercontinental's WinStar Galaxy win on October 9 that he would start Intercontinental in the Filly and Mare Turf. By then Bailey had made other plans, so Frankel turned to Bejarano, 23. "He's been so hot, Rafael, that he was the first person I thought of to ride her," Frankel said.

Bejarano topped all North American jockeys in 2004 with 455 wins and was the leading rider of Churchill Downs's spring season and Keeneland's fall meeting, during which he scored his 1,000th North American victory. "He's an aggressive rider, and he gets run out of horses," Frankel said of Bejarano. "I thought he'd put [Intercontinental] on the lead ... and then get that little extra out of her that we needed."

Bejarano carried out Frankel's instructions to perfection. Intercontinental broke well from the tenth post position and took the lead as the field headed into the first turn. She covered the first quarter-mile in :24.10 and the half-mile in :48.92 while Ouija Board was racing in midpack.

Ouija Board began to move up through the field entering the far turn, took over second from Wend, and was 3½ lengths behind Intercontinental in midstretch. Ouija Board closed the gap in the final furlong, but could not catch Intercontinental.

"She was traveling well, handled the ground well," Bailey said in describing Ouija Board's race. "I really thought I had a chance to run [Intercontinental] down on the lead, but she just never came back."—*Amy Owens*

FIFTH RACE
Belmont Park
October 29, 2005

1¼ miles on turf. 7th running of the Breeders' Cup Filly and Mare Turf (G1). Purse $1,000,000. Fillies and mares 3-year-olds and up. Weights (Northern Hemisphere): 3-year-olds, 119 lbs. Older, 123 lbs. (Southern Hemisphere): 3-year-olds, 114 lbs. Older, 123 lbs.

Value of race: $972,020. Value to winner: $551,200; second: $212,000; third: $116,600; fourth: $60,420; fifth: $31,800. Mutuel Pool $4,306,394.

Horse	Wt	M/Eqt	PP	¼	½	¾	1m	Str.	Fin.	Jockey	Odds $1
Intercontinental (GB), 5, m.	123	L	10	1½	1^{2}	1½	1^{3}	$1^{3\frac{1}{2}}$	$1^{1\frac{1}{4}}$	R. Bejarano	15.10
Ouija Board (GB), 4, f.	123	L	13	8^{hd}	7^{hd}	6½	2^{hd}	2½	2^{nk}	J. Bailey	*2.30
Film Maker, 5, m.	123	Lb	2	$11^{2\frac{1}{2}}$	11^{1}	8½	4^{2}	3^{5}	3^{4}	P. Valenzuela	9.10
Wonder Again, 6, m.	123	L	7	9^{1}	10½	10^{hd}	5^{hd}	4½	4^{2}	E. Prado	5.00
Favourable Terms (GB), 5, m.	123		9	$12^{2\frac{1}{2}}$	$12^{2\frac{1}{2}}$	12^{2}	8½	6^{hd}	5^{1}	M. Kinane	28.75
Wend, 4, f.	123	L	5	2^{1}	2^{1}	2½	3½	5^{1}	6^{nk}	J. Velazquez	12.70
Angara (GB), 4, f.	123	L	14	13^{6}	13^{8}	13^{6}	13^{5}	$7^{5\frac{1}{2}}$	$7^{4\frac{3}{4}}$	G. Stevens	29.50
Megahertz (GB), 6, m.	123	L	8	14	14	14	14	14	$8^{1\frac{1}{2}}$	A. Solis	5.00
Karen's Caper, 3, f.	119	L	12	6½	6½	3½	6^{1}	8^{1}	$9^{2\frac{3}{4}}$	R. Albarado	17.50
Mona Lisa (GB), 3, f.	119	L	11	4½	3½	4^{hd}	10½	10^{2}	10¾	K. Fallon	19.10
Luas Line (Ire), 3, f.	119	L	1	10^{hd}	9^{hd}	7^{hd}	12½	12½	$11^{5\frac{1}{2}}$	C. Soumillon	31.00
Flip Flop (Fr), 4, f.	123	L	6	5½	5^{hd}	5^{1}	9½	13^{hd}	$12^{7\frac{1}{4}}$	G. Gomez	34.00
Riskaverse, 6 m.	123	L	4	3^{hd}	4½	9^{hd}	11½	11½	$13^{6\frac{1}{4}}$	J. Santos	20.20
Sundrop (Jpn), 4 f	123	Lf	3	7^{hd}	8^{hd}	$11^{2\frac{1}{2}}$	7½	9^{1}	14	L. Dettori	38.25

OFF AT 2:40. Start: Good. Winner: Soon clear, driving.
Time: :24.10, :48.92, 1:13.62, 1:38.17, 2:02.34. Weather: Cloudy. Turf: Good.

$2 Mutuel Prices:				
	10—INTERCONTINENTAL (GB).....	**32.20**	**13.00**	**8.40**
	13—OUIJA BOARD (GB)...............		**5.90**	**4.30**
	2—FILM MAKER...........................			**6.40**

$2 PICK THREE 1-12-10 PAID $682.00 $2 EXACTA 10-13 PAID $131.50
$2 HEAD2HEAD 2 vs. 7 vs. 13 (WINNER 13) PAID $4.60
$2 SUPERFECTA 10-13-2-7 PAID $5,004.00 $2 TRIFECTA 10-13-2 PAID $1,167.00

B. m., by Danehill—Hasili, by Kahyasi. Trainer: Bobby Frankel. Owner: Juddmonte Farms. Bred by Juddmonte Farms (GB).

INTERCONTINENTAL (GB) took the lead soon after the start, opened a clear advantage on the backstretch, shook off a mild challenge from WEND leaving the far turn, maintained a comfortable advantage into midstretch, and held sway under steady right-hand urging. OUIJA BOARD (GB), unhurried early, launched a rally from outside entering the stretch and then closed steadily in the middle of the track while unable to overtake the winner. FILM MAKER clipped heels and stumbled early, raced far back for seven furlongs, and closed late to gain a share. WONDER AGAIN made a run to reach contention on the far turn, steadied in traffic, and lacked a closing bid. FAVOURABLE TERMS (GB) leapt in air at the start, advanced on the far turn, and failed to threaten with a mild rally. WEND chased the pace, challenged briefly on the far turn, and tired thereafter. ANGARA (GB) outrun early, made a mild rally on the inside. MEGAHERTZ (GB), outrun early, had no response when roused. KAREN'S CAPER chased the pace to the far turn and tired. MONA LISA (GB) chased the pace from the outside and was finished after three-quarters. LUAS LINE (IRE) faded after a mile. FLIP FLOP (FR), close up between rivals, steadied near the quarter pole and tired soon thereafter. RISKAVERSE raced just off the early pace and gave way midway on the final turn. SUNDROP (JPN) tired badly and was vanned off.

2005 Sprint: Speeding Train

Most handicappers expected a three-year old colt to win the $972,020 Breeders' Cup Sprint (G1) at Belmont Park on October 29. One did, but he came from nearby Queens borough, not Northern California. In the most exciting finish of the eight Breeders' Cup races on a cloudy, blustery afternoon, Buckram Oak Farm's Silver Train held off fast-finishing Taste of Paradise by a desperate head as previously unbeaten Lost in the Fog surrendered a clear lead in the stretch and finished seventh in the 11-horse field.

A claim of foul by Taste of Paradise's rider, Garrett Gomez, against the winner was dismissed by the stewards, giving Silver Train's respective jockey and trainer, Edgar Prado and Richard Dutrow Jr., their first of two Breeders' Cup victories on the day. Neither had ever won a Breeders' Cup race previously.

Lost in the Fog, trained by Northern California-based Greg Gilchrist, had won all of his ten career starts and went off as the 7-to-10 favorite. Gilchrist handled Lost in the Fog's first defeat with aplomb. "I'm not big on excuses," Gilchrist said. "We just got outrun."

Silver Train's fourth victory in 11 career starts was not a complete shock. He was the third choice in the wagering at 11.90-to-1 off two sensational victories and a third-place finish in his previous three starts. On July 2, he came within one one-hundredth of a second of matching Belmont's six-furlong track record of 1:07.66 in an allowance race. In the Amsterdam Stakes (G2) at Saratoga Race Course on August 7, he finished third by 1¼ lengths to Santana Strings as the 6-to-5 favorite after he apparently did not handle the track well.

Dutrow treated Silver Train for soreness behind, and the colt returned to win Belmont's one-mile Jerome Handicap (G2) by five lengths on September 11, thus giving Buckram Oak and the trainer two potential starters in the Breeders' Cup Sprint. Buckram Oak's four-year-old colt Tiger Heart proved he belonged with the country's best sprinters when he finished second by two lengths to Taste of Paradise in the Vosburgh Stakes (G1) at Belmont on October 1. On the morning of the Vosburgh, Silver Train registered the first of four consecutive five-furlong bullet workouts at Aqueduct.

But Silver Train came out of his final Breeders' Cup workout, five furlongs in :58.46 five days before the Sprint, sore behind again, and Dutrow considered scratching him. After consulting with veterinarian Stephen Allday, D.V.M., he decided to jog Silver Train up to the Sprint "to take some of the soreness out," Dutrow said. "It worked. Since this was run at Belmont, and he just loves this track, we decided to take a chance and run him in this race. We had nothing to lose by trying and everything to gain. I don't know if I would have done it if this race would have been at Monmouth [Park] or someplace else." Silver Train's defection would have further diminished a Sprint field that had lost High Fly, Roman Ruler, and Pomeroy following pre-entries.

The same day Taste of Paradise won the Vosburgh, Lost in the Fog extended his career record to a perfect ten in his first start against older horses, beating four overmatched rivals by 7¾ lengths in 1:08.05 at odds of 1-to-20 in the Bay Meadows Speed Handicap. The three-year-old son of Lost Soldier was undefeated in eight starts in 2005 and a legitimate contender for Horse of the Year honors.

To make Lost in the Fog the lone supplemental entry in the Sprint, 85-year-old owner Harry Aleo had to pony up $90,000, a decision he seemed completely at peace with the day before the Sprint. "This horse is like a dream you have all the time but never comes true," Aleo said as he watched Lost in the Fog outside his barn on the Belmont backstretch. "To think this horse is ten for ten. Instead of me being home watching this on the TV, I'm here with the favorite for the Sprint. I can't believe it. I can't imagine it at all. It's like winning the lottery. This horse is once in a lifetime."

Only one of Lost in the Fog's ten opponents in the Sprint went off at single-digit odds—Wildcat Heir was 6.40-to-1 off a 5¾-length romp in the Teddy Drone Stakes at Monmouth on August 7, his only start of the year.

Breaking a step slow from the seventh post position under Russell Baze, Lost in the Fog was fourth early before rushing up four wide to join three dueling leaders—45.50-to-1 longshot Attila's Storm, Battle Won, and Wildcat Heir—through a first quarter-mile in :22.01.

Around the turn while still four wide, Lost in the Fog surged to the lead after running a half-mile in :44.56.

But instead of spurting away after opening a one-length lead, Lost in the Fog began to labor as a game Attila's Storm rallied along his inside

Owner

Buckram Oak Farm is the racing operation of Mahmoud Fustok, who died on February 9, 2006. A Lebanese-born building contractor, he made his fortune in Saudi Arabia, where he had construction, real estate, and oil interests in addition to an auto dealership. He owned an Ocala farm and had sold his Lexington property in 2005.

Breeders

Joe Mulholland Sr. owns Mulholland Farm in Georgetown, Kentucky. His son **Joe Mulholland Jr.** manages the farm's yearling division, and another son, **John**, manages the farm.

and Silver Train and Taste of Paradise closed in. Prado, who had ended a zero for 41 Breeders' Cup drought by winning the Breeders' Cup Juvenile Fillies (G1) on Folklore earlier in the day, had settled Silver Train in fifth as he watched the four-way, front-end battle develop. Taste of Paradise had settled in seventh after breaking from the rail. Prado swung Silver Train to the outside for a clear run on the tiring leaders as Gomez moved Taste of Paradise closer on the inside.

When Silver Train surged to get past Lost in the Fog and Attila's Storm at the sixteenth pole, Gomez attempted to angle Taste of Paradise between a tiring Lost in the Fog, who was drifting out slightly, and Silver Train.

Gomez was hoping for a hole that never materialized, and he swung his horse to the outside of Silver Train, losing momentum as he did so. Then Taste of Paradise surged again, finishing a head behind Silver Train while three lengths clear of Lion Tamer, who edged Attila's Storm by a neck for third. Elusive Jazz was fifth, Lifestyle sixth, and Lost in the Fog seventh, six lengths behind the winner.

Gilchrist, who had notched a second-place finish with his only previous Breeders' Cup starter, Soviet Problem, in the 1994 Sprint, refused to look for an excuse. "What were the fractions?" Gilchrist asked. "He's certainly capable of that. He was wide, but he wasn't that wide. When he dug down, he didn't have it in him today. Maybe we took one trip too many."

Baze was unsure why Lost in the Fog sputtered in the stretch. "He just didn't have it the last quarter-mile, plain and simple," the Racing Hall of Fame jockey said. —*Bill Heller*

SIXTH RACE
Belmont Park
October 29, 2005

6 furlongs on dirt. 22nd running of the Breeders' Cup Sprint (G1). Purse $1,000,000. 3-year-olds and up. Weights (Northern Hemisphere): 3-year-olds, 124 lbs. Older, 126 lbs. (Southern Hemisphere): 3-year-olds, 122 lbs. Older, 126 lbs. Fillies and mares allowed 3 lbs.

Value of race: $972,020. Value to winner: $551,200; second: $212,000; third: $116,600; fourth: $60,420; fifth: $31,800. Mutuel Pool $4,302,323.

Horse	Wt.	M/Eqt	PP	St.	¼	½	Str.	Fin.	Jockey	Odds $1
Silver Train, 3, c.	124	L	3	2	5^{1}	$5^{1\frac{1}{2}}$	2^{hd}	1^{hd}	E. Prado	11.90
Taste of Paradise, 6, h.	126	Lb	1	6	$8^{1\frac{1}{2}}$	$7^{\frac{1}{2}}$	4^{1}	2^{3}	G. Gomez	12.50
Lion Tamer, 5, h.	126	Lc	5	10	$9^{\frac{1}{2}}$	8^{2}	$5^{\frac{1}{2}}$	3^{nk}	J. Velazquez	12.40
Attila's Storm, 3, c.	124	Lb	2	1	$1^{\frac{1}{2}}$	2^{1}	$3^{1\frac{1}{2}}$	4^{2}	P. Valenzuela	45.50
Elusive Jazz, 4, c.	126	Lf	8	7	6^{3}	$6^{\frac{1}{2}}$	6^{2}	5^{hd}	R. Albarado	53.50
Lifestyle, 5, h.	126	Lbf	9	9	10^{2}	$9^{1\frac{1}{2}}$	7^{hd}	$6^{\frac{1}{2}}$	A. Solis	55.25
Lost in the Fog, 3, c.	124	L	7	3	$4^{2\frac{1}{2}}$	$1^{\frac{1}{2}}$	1^{hd}	$7^{\frac{1}{2}}$	R. Baze	0.70*
Imperialism, 4, c.	126	Lb	10	11	11	11	9^{hd}	$8^{3\frac{1}{4}}$	V. Espinoza	19.50
Gygistar, 6, g.	126	L	11	8	$7^{\frac{1}{2}}$	10^{2}	10^{1}	$9^{5\frac{3}{4}}$	J. Castellano	14.20
Wildcat Heir, 5, h.	126	Lf	6	4	3^{hd}	$3^{\frac{1}{2}}$	8^{2}	$10^{2\frac{3}{4}}$	S. Elliott	6.40
Battle Won, 5, g.	126	L	4	5	2^{hd}	4^{hd}	11	11	R. Dominguez	16.30

OFF AT 3:15. Start: Good. Winner: Wide move, prevailed.
Time: :22:01, :44:56, :56.65, 1:08.86. Weather: Cloudy. Track: Fast.

$2 Mutuel Prices:

3—SILVER TRAIN	**25.80**	**10.40**	**8.10**
1—TASTE OF PARADISE		**10.60**	**7.20**
5—LION TAMER			**7.60**

$2 PICK THREE 12-10-3 PAID $2,371.00
$2 PICK FOUR 1-12-10-3 PAID $13,162.00 **$2 EXACTA 3-1 PAID $215.50**
$2 HEAD2HEAD 3 vs. 5 (WINNER 3) PAID $3.90
$2 SUPERFECTA 3-1-5-2 PAID $35,358.00 **$2 TRIFECTA 3-1-5 PAID $1,593.00**

Dkbbr. c., by Old Trieste—Ridden in Thestars, by Cormorant. Trainer: Richard Dutrow Jr. Owner: Buckram Oak Farm. Bred by Joe Mulholland Sr., Joe Mulholland Jr., et al. (Ky.).

SILVER TRAIN settled on the inside early, angled out to launch his bid on the turn, closed the gap to challenge in midstretch, surged to the front inside the furlong marker, and was all out to prevail at the finish. TASTE OF PARADISE, unhurried for a half, steadied while lacking room inside the furlong pole, swung out for running room, and was running fastest at the end. A claim of foul against the winner was disallowed. LION TAMER stumbled after the start, was far back for a half, and rallied belatedly to gain a share. ATTILA'S STORM rushed up along the rail, dueled into the early stretch, and tired. ELUSIVE JAZZ, bumped soundly at the start, raced in the middle of the pack and finished evenly. LIFESTYLE, bumped and steadied at the start, never reached contention. LOST IN THE FOG, bounced around between horses at the start, stalked for nearly a half, took the lead at the quarter pole, and faltered in the final eighth. IMPERIALISM never reached contention. GYGISTAR moved up briefly on the far turn and faded. WILDCAT HEIR, bumped at the start, dueled between horses for a half, faltered on the turn, fell after the finish, and was vanned off. BATTLE WON pressed the pace to the turn and gave way.

2005 Mile: Work of Artie

Jimmy Jerkens's father, Racing Hall of Fame trainer H. Allen Jerkens, has earned a reputation as the giant killer for his many upsets through the years, and the younger Jerkens pulled a modest but notable upset on October 29 when he saddled Artie Schiller to a three-quarter-length victory over favored Leroidesanimaux (Brz) in the $1,856,925 Breeders' Cup Mile (G1).

Leroidesanimaux—French for king of the animals—entered the Breeders' Cup as one of the day's shortest-priced favorites, 1.35-to-1, on the strength of an eight-race win streak that included a 7¾-length score in the Atto Mile Stakes (Can-G1) on September 18 at Woodbine, but he was no match at Belmont Park when confronted on the outside by 5.60-to-1 second choice Artie Schiller in deep stretch.

Jimmy Jerkens always was around horses growing up, and he worked as an assistant to his father for 20 years before opening a public stable in the fall of 1997, so it was only fitting that he earned the biggest win of his eight-year career with a horse he considers a member of the family. "I didn't think I'd be the first one [in my family to win a Breeders' Cup race], that's for sure," Jerkens said after winning the Mile. "[My dad] means the world to me. I started working for him when I was very young; it's the only thing I've ever known. It was something I've always been proud of."

Even before his Breeders' Cup Mile win, Artie Schiller was the type of horse that any trainer could be proud of. He came into the race with nine wins in 18 starts, including six stakes victories, and earnings of $950,853, but somehow a Grade 1 victory had eluded him.

"A lot of people can't believe he hasn't won one," Jerkens said. "He certainly is a Grade1-caliber horse. If he retired without winning one, I would have taken that as a personal disaster because he certainly is one great horse." The Breeders' Cup Mile raised Artie Schiller's career earnings to $2,003,853.

Fans expected that first Grade 1 victory on two occasions in the past year. Artie Schiller was the 3.80-to-1 favorite in last year's Breeders' Cup Mile and the 1.85-to-1 favorite in the Manhattan Handicap (G1) on June 11 at Belmont. Artie Schiller finished 12th of 14 in the Mile at Lone Star Park and third of 11 in the Manhattan, but both races provided valuable insights for Artie Schiller's connections.

The previous year's Breeders' Cup provided an experience both trainer and horse needed. It was the first such event for Jimmy Jerkens, as well as Artie Schiller's first try against older horses. Artie Schiller never contended and was steadied in both turns on a yielding Lone Star course.

The Belmont trip was much different, a one-turn mile on turf rated as good. The course also is right outside Artie Schiller's stall on the Belmont backstretch—a decided advantage, admitted Jerkens. It all added up to a great run for Artie Schiller and jockey Garrett Gomez, who won his second race of the day.

"He's become like a pet around here; he knows the place well," Jerkens said of Artie Schiller's familiarity with Belmont. "When he ships out of town, he does get a little upset, doesn't eat as well, a little studdish—all that takes something out of him. When you're at home, you just lead them right over from their stall."

As for the Manhattan, in which Artie Schiller finished a half-length behind Good Reward, Jerkens identified it as the turning point in the colt's season. Artie Schiller was coming off a nose loss to Cool Conductor in the Dixie Stakes (G2) and looked like a winner in the 1¼-mile Manhattan at the sixteenth pole before flattening out. It was at that point that Jerkens decided to target the Mile rather than the 1½-mile Breeders' Cup Turf (G1).

After breaking from the second post position, Gomez settled Artie Schiller into fifth position on the rail, about 3½ lengths behind pacesetter Sand Springs through opening quarter-miles of :23.47 and :23.21 (:46.68). Sand Springs gave way to Ad Valorem, who completed three-quarters in 1:11.15. Gomez then moved outside and began Artie Schiller's rally. Leroidesanimaux reached the front at the top of the stretch, but Artie Schiller surged past on his outside in the final sixteenth to win in 1:36.10 on a course rated as good.

"All the way up the backside he had himself in a good spot," Gomez said. "We were saving ground, got to the turn, and had a good trip. I just had to wait. I finally got out a little bit, and when he went, he really went and did what he had to do." Gomez acquired the mount on Artie Schiller after the El Prado (Ire) colt's regular

Owners

William Entenmann, under his stable name Timber Bay Farm, and his daughter Denise Walsh, own Artie Schiller, whom Entenmann purchased for $67,000 at the 2002 Keeneland September yearling sale and named for his friend Artie Schiller. Entenmann's grandfather founded Entenmann's Bakery in 1898, and William Entenmann served as the company's president until its sale. Denise Walsh lives in Southern Pines, North Carolina, where she trains her own horses.

Breeder

Haras du Mezeray is operated by Charles-Henri de Moussac, whose late father, Paul de Moussac, founded the 500-acre stud in Vimoutiers, France, in 1962. The Normandy farm stands Prix de l'Arc de Triomphe (Fr-G1) winner Trempolino and four other stallions.

jockey, Richard Migliore, suffered a fractured leg in a paddock accident on October 20, and he rode exactly as Jerkens had hoped he would when speaking about the probable trip two days before the race.

Leroidesanimaux held off Gorella (Fr) by a nose in a photo for second. Sand Springs faded to 11th and Ad Valorem to ninth, while last year's winner, Singletary, finished eighth after moving to within 1¼ lengths of the lead on the far turn. Whipper encountered the most trouble during the race but still ran on well at the end to finish fourth by less than a length.

The Mile received a jolt of news Breeders' Cup morning when trainer Bobby Frankel decided to outfit Leroidesanimaux with aluminum-padded horseshoes, a situation the Racing Hall of Fame trainer felt cost T N T Stud's son of Candy Stripes victory in the race. "I was disappointed at the barn this morning," Frankel said after the race. "I thought we'd take the bar shoes off, come out here, and win. He was lame without them, though. He's a better horse than what we saw today, but the shoes got him beat."

Leroidesanimaux was an imposing force on paper, and Jerkens certainly was aware of the toughness of his adversary. The two had never raced against each other, but a clash seemed possible in the Atto Mile until Jerkens declared Artie Schiller from that race to prep instead in the Kelso Breeders' Cup Handicap (G2) on October 2 at Belmont Park. Artie Schiller finished second to Funfair (GB) in that race.

"I thought I wanted to race a little closer to the Breeders' Cup to try to get him ready," Jerkens said. "Leroidesanimaux is something special. You hope you don't catch a horse like that on a good day." —*Ed DeRosa*

SEVENTH RACE
Belmont Park
October 29, 2005

1 mile on turf. 22nd running of the Breeders' Cup Mile (G1). Purse $1,500,000. 3-year-olds and up. Weights (Northern Hemisphere): 3-year-olds, 123 lbs. Older, 126 lbs. (Southern Hemisphere): 3-year-olds, 120 lbs. Older, 126 lbs. Fillies and mares allowed 3 lbs.

Value of race: $1,856,925. Value to winner: $1,053,000; second: $405,000; third: $222,750; fourth: $115,425; fifth: $60,750. Mutuel Pool $4,539,066.

Horse	Wt.	M/Eqt	PP	St.	¼	½	¾	Str.	Fin.	Jockey	Odds $1
Artie Schiller, 4, c.	126	L	2	10	5^{1}	$5^{1/2}$	4^{1}	2^{hd}	$1^{3/4}$	G. Gomez	5.60
Leroidesanimaux (Brz), 5, h.	126	L	11	2	$3^{2 1/2}$	$3^{2 1/2}$	2^{1}	$1^{1/2}$	2no	J. Velazquez	1.35*
Gorella (Fr), 3, f.	120	L	8	8	$10^{4 1/2}$	9^{1}	7^{1}	$5^{1/2}$	3^{hd}	G. Stevens	13.70
Whipper, 4, c.	126		3	9	7^{3}	7^{1}	5^{hd}	9^{7}	4^{1}	J. Murtagh	17.50
Majors Cast (Ire), 4, c.	126	L	7	7	$8^{1/2}$	$8^{1/2}$	$8^{1/2}$	$7^{1/2}$	$5^{1/2}$	L. Dettori	20.20
Limehouse, 4, c.	126	L	12	3	$6^{1/2}$	$6^{1/2}$	$6^{1/2}$	4^{hd}	$6^{1/2}$	J. Santos	36.25
Host (Chi), 5, h.	126	L	1	12	11	11	$10^{1/2}$	8^{hd}	$7^{2 1/4}$	R. Bejarano	15.60
Singletary, 5, h.	126	L	9	1	4^{hd}	$4^{1/2}$	$3^{1/2}$	6^{hd}	$8^{1 1/4}$	D. Flores	8.70
Ad Valorem, 3, c.	123	L	5	5	2^{hd}	$2^{1/2}$	1^{hd}	3^{hd}	$9^{9 1/2}$	K. Fallon	37.25
Valixir (Ire), 4, c.	126		10	11	$9^{1/2}$	$10^{2 1/2}$	11	$10^{3 1/2}$	$10^{3/4}$	C. Soumillon	10.40
Sand Springs, 5, m.	123	L	4	4	$1^{1/2}$	1^{hd}	9^{hd}	11	11	J. Bailey	18.80
Funfair (GB), 6, g.	126	L	6	6					DNF	E. Prado	12.80

OFF AT 3:51. Start: Good. Winner: Split rivals, resolute.
Time: :23.47, :46.68, 1:11.15, 1:36.10. Weather: Cloudy. Turf: Good.

$2 Mutuel Prices:				
	2—ARTIE SCHILLER	**13.20**	**5.00**	**3.90**
	11—LEROIDESANIMAUX (Brz)		**3.80**	**3.00**
	8—GORELLA (Fr)			**6.00**

$2 PICK THREE 10-3-2 PAID $2,974.00
$2 EXACTA 2-11 PAID $38.80 $2 HEAD2HEAD 2 vs. 8 vs. 9 (WINNER 2) PAID $3.70
$2 SUPERFECTA 2-11-8-3 PAID $7,021.00 $2 TRIFECTA 2-11-8 PAID $504.00

B. c., by El Prado (Ire)—Hidden Light, by Majestic Light. Trainer: Jimmy Jerkens. Owners: Timber Bay Farm and Mrs. Thomas J. Walsh. Bred by Haras du Mezeray S.A. (Ky.).

ARTIE SCHILLER, steadied along the inside in the early stages, launched a rally in traffic on the turn, surged to the front inside the furlong marker, and then edged clear through the final sixteenth. LEROIDESANIMAUX (BRZ) stalked the early pace from the outside, gained a narrow lead in upper stretch, battled inside the winner leaving the furlong marker, and held well for the place. GORELLA (FR) angled to the outside in midstretch and rallied belatedly. WHIPPER, unhurried for a half, launched his bid on the turn and rallied belatedly in the middle of the track. MAJORS CAST (IRE), steadied in traffic along the backstretch, improved his position with a mild rally. LIMEHOUSE, in the middle of the pack early, lacked a strong closing response. HOST (CHI) broke awkwardly, steadied in upper stretch, and failed to threaten thereafter. SINGLETARY, up close early, lodged a mild bid on the turn and faded in the stretch. AD VALOREM set or forced the pace for six furlongs and faltered. VALIXIR (IRE) never was a factor. SAND SPRINGS dueled for the lead early and gave way on the turn. FUNFAIR (GB) broke down on the backstretch and was vanned off.

2005 Juvenile Fillies: Folk Tale

There is an old saying in baseball that the best trades are often the ones you don't make. That sports adage could well apply to the 2005 Breeders' Cup Juvenile Fillies (G1). In 2003, Bob and Beverly Lewis owned a handful of homebred yearlings that they had consigned to the Keeneland September yearling sale. Four months before the sale, trainer D. Wayne Lukas, who has one of the best eyes in the business for yearlings, went to Taylor Made Farm in Nicholasville, Kentucky, where the Lewises' horses were raised and boarded, to inspect them.

"I saw a group of yearlings that they were going to sell," said Lukas, who trained for the Lewises for 15 years. "It was in May, because I was already at Churchill [Downs]. There were two or three that I liked, but I told Bob that there was one I really liked, by Tiznow. She was not big, but she reminded me of her sire. She was rangey and scopey."

Cataloged as hip number 2460 in book four of the Keeneland sale and to be offered on the seventh day, the Tiznow filly was out of the unraced Storm Cat mare Contrive. After Lukas saw the filly and made his recommendations, the Lewises decided not to trade their filly for cash and took her out of the sale. "He looked at seven or eight yearlings," recalled Frank Taylor, who co-owns Taylor Made with brothers Duncan, Mark, and Ben, and who helped syndicate and take a substantial ownership in two-time Breeders' Cup Classic (G1) winner Tiznow to stand at WinStar Farm. "There were some nice horses in there, and she was a standout."

The Lewises named the Tiznow filly Folklore, sent her to Florida to be broken, and later sent her to Lukas as a two-year-old to train. On October 29 at Belmont Park, Folklore went into the starting gate for the Juvenile Fillies as the favorite and confirmed all the promise Lukas saw in her 18 months earlier when she scored an impressive victory over nine rivals. She ran on or near the lead while setting fast fractions but was able to draw away in the stretch to score a comfortable, 1¼-length win over Wild Fit.

It capped a four-win campaign for Folklore that earned her an Eclipse Award as best of her division. It marked a record fifth Juvenile Fillies victory for Lukas and a record 18th Breeders' Cup win overall for the trainer. Lukas has won the Juvenile Fillies with Cash Run (1999), Flanders ('94), Open Mind ('88), and Twilight Ridge ('85). For the Lewises, it was their second Breeders' Cup win, having won the 2002 Breeders' Cup Sprint (G1) with Orientate. Bob Lewis died February 17, 2006, at age 81.

Folklore made her debut in a maiden race at Belmont on May 18 and finished second. By Breeders' Cup day, she had already made six starts, winning three times and finishing second three times. Folklore had defeated Adieu, regarded at times as the leader of the division, in the six-furlong Adirondack Stakes (G2) on July 27 at Saratoga Race Course, but two of her losses had come against Adieu. Trained by former Lukas assistant Todd Pletcher, Adieu defeated Folklore in the 5½-furlong Astoria Stakes on July 3 at Belmont and in the seven-furlong Spinaway Stakes (G2) on August 26 at Saratoga.

After the Spinaway, Lukas took Folklore back to Belmont, and the Tiznow filly scored a resounding, 14-length triumph in the seven-furlong Matron Stakes (G1) on September 17. Adieu skipped that race, prepping instead for the Juvenile Fillies with a two-length win in the mile Frizette Stakes (G1) on a sloppy track on October 8. Lukas kept Folklore in the barn for the Frizette, preferring to give his filly more time between races.

The Juvenile Fillies featured a field of ten, with Folklore earning 2.35-to-1 favoritism based on her rout of the Matron and a pedigree indicating that she would improve with distance. Adieu was the 4.20-to-1 second choice, with Arlington-Washington Breeders' Cup Lassie Stakes (G3) winner Original Spin a close 4.30-to-1 third choice. Supplemental nominee Wild Fit, winner of the Del Mar Debutante Stakes (G1) and second in the Oak Leaf Stakes (G2), was the fourth choice, and Canadian invader Knights Templar, 13¼-length winner of the Mazarine Breeders' Cup Stakes (Can-G3), the fifth choice.

The extra time between races made Folklore a bit sharper than usual and, as the gates sprung open, she took the lead from her one post when the field came out of the chute for the 1$\frac{1}{16}$-mile race. Ridden by Edgar Prado, who rode her for the first time in the Matron, Folklore ran the opening quarter-mile in :22.65 and the half-mile in a quick :45.34 while racing in tandem with

Owners-Breeders

Bob and Beverly Lewis, of Newport Beach, California, have been major players in racing since 1990. Bob Lewis, who died on February 17, 2006, owned Foothill Beverage Co. in Pomona, California. The Lewises campaigned 1999 Horse of the Year Charismatic, winner of the Kentucky Derby (G1) and Preakness Stakes (G1); dual classic winner and champion Silver Charm; champion filly Serena's Song, who retired as the leading female money earner in North America; champion sprinter and Breeders' Cup Sprint (G1) winner Orientate; and, in partnership, champion and classic winner Timber Country.

Knights Templar against a strong headwind.

Prado allowed Knights Templar to take a short head lead through the opening half-mile, tracking her while racing along the inside, well off the rail. Around the turn, Knights Templar, ridden by Gary Stevens, maintained her short lead, but approaching the stretch Prado asked his filly to reassert her claim and she did, quickly opening up a daylight lead in a matter of strides as she came out of the turn. Original Spin, ridden by Jerry Bailey, was observing the battle from a catbird seat in third, while Adieu was chasing about four lengths back in seventh and appearing to have little response. Lukas's other starter in the race, Ex Caelis, was mounting a charge from ninth and moving toward the leaders in the stretch.

Folklore sprinted to a dominant, three-length lead in midstretch with the wind at her back, and it did not appear that she would relinquish her sizable lead as a handful of fillies tried to rally in the stretch. After Knights Templar began her retreat, Ex Caelis, Original Spin, and, from last place, Wild Fit battled for the minor placings. Wild Fit, ridden by Alex Solis, was moving best of all, but she had to steady in traffic behind Sensation in midstretch. She was able to get up for second, finishing 4¾ lengths in front of Original Spin, with Ex Caelis another head back in fourth. Adieu never mounted a challenge and finished a dull seventh.

Folklore completed the 1$\frac{1}{16}$ miles on a fast track in 1:43.85, sixth slowest in the race's history in the 18 times the race has been contested at that distance. The victory earned Folklore $551,200, increasing her earnings to $927,500, and assured Tiznow leading freshman sire honors of 2005.—*Mark Simon*

THIRD RACE
Belmont Park
October 29, 2005

1$\frac{1}{16}$ miles on dirt. 22nd running of the Breeders' Cup Juvenile Fillies (G1). Purse $1-million. Fillies, 2-year-olds. Weight: 119 lbs.

Value of race: $972,020. Value to winner: $551,200; second: $212,000; third: $116,600; fourth: $60,420; fifth: $31,800. Mutuel Pool $3,329,694.

Horse	Wgt.	M/Eqt	PP	St.	¼	½	¾	Str.	Fin.	Jockey	Odds $1
Folklore, 2, f.	119	L	1	4	1½	$2^{1\frac{1}{2}}$	$2^{1\frac{1}{2}}$	1^{3}	$1^{1\frac{1}{4}}$	E. Prado	2.35*
Wild Fit, 2, f.	119	L	10	10	10	10	9^{2}	4^{hd}	$2^{4\frac{3}{4}}$	A. Solis	7.00
Original Spin, 2, f.	119	Lb	2	8	7½	4^{hd}	$3^{1\frac{1}{2}}$	3^{1}	3^{hd}	J. Bailey	4.30
Ex Caelis, 2, f.	119	L	9	3	9^{6}	9^{4}	5^{1}	2^{hd}	4^{3}	R. Bejarano	16.70
Sensation, 2, f.	119	Lc	7	2	8^{hd}	8^{hd}	6½	6^{2}	$5^{3\frac{1}{4}}$	E. Coa	11.40
Knights Templar, 2, f.	119	L	5	5	2½	1^{hd}	1^{hd}	$5^{1\frac{1}{2}}$	$6^{3\frac{1}{4}}$	G. Stevens	8.90
Adieu, 2, f.	119	L	6	1	3^{hd}	5^{1}	7^{1}	8^{1}	$7^{6\frac{1}{4}}$	J. Velazquez	4.20
Along the Sea, 2, f.	119	Lb	3	6	4½	3^{hd}	4½	$7^{2\frac{1}{2}}$	$8^{2\frac{1}{4}}$	J. Castellano	22.90
She Says It Best, 2, f.	119	L	8	7	5^{1}	6^{1}	8½	10	9^{2}	E. Martin Jr.	27.25
Diamond Omi, 2, f.	119	L	4	9	6^{hd}	7½	10	9½	10	V. Espinoza	19.60

OFF AT 1:22. Start: Good for all. Winner: Took over when asked.
Time: :22.65, :45.34, 1:10.39, 1:36.81, 1:43.85. Weather: Cloudy. Track: Fast.

$2 Mutuel Prices:	**1—FOLKLORE**	**6.70**	**4.20**	**2.70**
	10—WILD FIT		**6.40**	**4.30**
	2—ORIGINAL SPIN			**3.70**

$2 PICK THREE 6-6-1 PAID $267.50 $2 EXACTA 1-10 PAID $54.50
$2 HEAD2HEAD 4 vs. 9 (WINNER 9) PAID $3.40
$2 SUPERFECTA 1-10-2-9 PAID $1,762.00 $2 TRIFECTA 1-10-2 PAID $181.50

B. f., by Tiznow—Contrive, by Storm Cat. Trainer: D. Wayne Lukas. Owners: Robert and Beverly Lewis (Ky.). Bred by Robert and Beverly Lewis (Ky.).

FOLKLORE took the lead after the start, alternated for the lead on the backstretch, stalked KNIGHTS TEMPLAR entering the far turn, regained command approaching the quarter pole, extended her margin in upper stretch, and held off WILD FIT under steady right-hand encouragement. WILD FIT raced well back for five furlongs, launched her bid on the far turn, steadied behind Sensation at the five-sixteenths pole, and finished well in the middle of the track. ORIGINAL SPIN, bumped at the start, moved into contention at the top of the stretch but lacked a strong closing bid. EX CAELIS, bumped after the start, made a run to threaten in upper stretch but could not sustain her bid. SENSATION checked in traffic on the turn and finished evenly. KNIGHTS TEMPLAR showed the way to the turn, yielded to the winner at the five-sixteenths pole, and steadily tired thereafter. ADIEU chased the leaders for five furlongs and gave way abruptly. ALONG THE SEA raced up close for six furlongs and gave way. SHE SAYS IT BEST stumbled at the start and never threatened. DIAMOND OMI steadied while bounced around in the early stages and failed to threaten thereafter.

2005 Distaff: Pleasant Surprise

In the days leading up to the $1,834,000 Breeders' Cup Distaff (G1) on October 29 at Belmont Park, trainer Shug McGaughey had a little inside information for anyone visiting his barn. With such powerhouse females as Ashado, Stellar Jayne, Society Selection, and Happy Ticket scheduled to take on his Grade 3-winning filly Pleasant Home, McGaughey was content to lay low and let other trainers shine in the spotlight.

The Racing Hall of Fame trainer did not hesitate to tout Pleasant Home, who had finished a fast-closing second in the Juddmonte Spinster Stakes (G1) at a traditionally speed-favoring Keeneland Race Course. "She's been under the radar," McGaughey said two days before the Distaff. "She's going to be a big price. But she's coming back here to a one-turn race, and she made up a lot of ground at Keeneland. She made one of the best come-from-behind runs of anybody there this year. I think she's going to run much better than her price."

Sent off at a gaudy 30.75-to-1, the Phipps Stable homebred charged to the front in the upper stretch, took command with long, powerful strides midway through the lane, and drew away to an improbable 9¼-length romp in the 1⅛-mile race for fillies and mares. The victory came almost ten years to the day that McGaughey saddled Ogden Mills "Dinny" Phipps's Inside Information to a Breeders' Cup-record 13½-length victory in the Distaff on the same Belmont track.

Pleasant Home's victory was the first Grade 1 triumph for the four-year-old daughter of 1988 Breeders' Cup Classic (G1) runner-up Seeking the Gold, who also was trained by McGaughey, out of Phipps's Pleasant Colony mare Our Country Place.

The impressive performance on racing's grandest stage also prevented seven-time Grade 1 winner Ashado from capturing her second consecutive Distaff and vaulting past Azeri to become North America's all-time leading money-earning female. The darling of the 13-horse field, Ashado was trying to win her final start before being offered in the Keeneland November breeding stock sale, where she sold for a record $9-million. In the days leading up to the race, trainer Todd Pletcher acknowledged how much it would mean to him and to Ashado's connections if she were to win the Distaff.

The four-year-old daughter of the late Saint Ballado, who won the 2004 Distaff en route to champion three-year-old filly honors, won four of six starts as a juvenile, five of eight starts in '04, and three of her seven starts in '05, earning $3,931,440 to fall just shy of Azeri's $4,079,820 in career earnings for owners Starlight Stable, Paul Saylor, and Johns Martin. She was voted champion older female.

Andy Leggio Jr., the trainer of Grade 1 winner Happy Ticket, was attempting to will his filly to a victory that he hoped would give a measure of joy and hope to an area of the country ripped apart by hurricanes. Leggio, a resident of the New Orleans suburb of Metairie, Louisiana, and his wife were in Saratoga Springs, New York, saddling four-year-old Louisiana-bred Happy Ticket to a 5½-length victory in the Ballerina Stakes (G1) when Hurricane Katrina slammed into the Gulf Coast on August 29. His three children and 11 grandchildren evacuated to Shreveport and successfully rode out the storm. "Those people down there need a lift any way they can get one. Happy Ticket has a lot of fans down there who have been behind her from the beginning. ... Louisiana needs a champion right now," he said.

By post time of the Distaff, Ashado was the 2.25-to-1 favorite, followed by Happy Ticket and Godolphin Racing's multiple Grade 1 winner Stellar Jayne at 9-to-2, and Alabama Stakes (G1) winner Sweet Symphony at 7.70-to-1.

Pleasant Home turned out to be the fourth-longest shot on the board. The dark bay or brown filly had not reached the winner's circle since April, although she entered off a third-place effort behind Smokey Glacken in a six-furlong optional claiming race on August 14 at Saratoga Race Course and back-to-back runner-up finishes in the seven-furlong Ballerina on August 28 and the 1⅛-mile Spinster on October 9.

The ground-saving trip in the Spinster convinced McGaughey that Pleasant Home deserved a shot in the Distaff. "She had the one post that day when she broke, and I thought she was fighting the track at first," he said. "Going around the first turn, she got back farther than I thought she would, and I was afraid she wasn't going to run over the track. Then suddenly she came running, a little bit wide but not bad. But I thought that mile and an eighth over the track at Keeneland could set her up good for this one."

Owner-Breeder

Phipps Stable is the family racing and breeding operation co-managed by Ogden Mills "Dinny" Phipps, who was born on September 18, 1940, and resides in Palm Beach, Florida. Former chairman of the New York Racing Association, he is chairman of the Jockey Club, a position also held by his late father, Ogden Phipps. Beginning in the early 1990s, the horses bred by the elder Phipps were raced not in his name but in the name of Phipps Stable, which is overseen by Dinny Phipps and his sister, Cynthia. The family has won seven Breeders' Cup races from 38 starts since 1986. In his own name, Dinny Phipps raced winners Storm Flag Flying (2002 Juvenile Fillies), Inside Information (1995 Distaff) and Rhythm ('89 Juvenile).

Pleasant Home settled at the back of the field while saving ground under Cornelio Velasquez through the first three-quarters of a mile, with 57-to-1 Capeside Lady setting a 1:10.74 pace. The Phipps filly made a rapid move on the turn and angled out nearing the quarter pole. Velasquez then moved her between rivals while four wide at the quarter pole.

From there, she roared through traffic and charged to the lead, blowing by Society Selection, Ashado, and Stellar Jayne as she drew off with authority under steady right-hand urging from Velasquez. She covered the 1⅛-mile distance in 1:48.34 on a fast track and won by the second-largest margin in Breeders' Cup history, behind only Inside Information's Distaff romp a decade earlier. Grade 1 winner Society Selection, ridden by Edgar Prado, finished second, a neck in front of Ashado and jockey John Velazquez in third.

"The last time [in the Spinster Stakes], we had a problem because there was a soft pace and we couldn't get there in time," said Velasquez. "This time was better because of a fast pace. It gave us something to run at. When I entered the turn, I knew I had so much horse."

For Pletcher, Ashado's disappointing third-place finish put a period instead of an exclamation point on a stellar career. "It's bittersweet," Pletcher admitted. "We would have liked to finish up with a win, but it's been a tremendous run for three years with a first, a second, and a third in three Breeders' Cup races [she was second to Halfbridled in the 2003 Breeders' Cup Juvenile Fillies (G1)]. We're not going to hang our heads because she's had a fabulous career."—*Steve Bailey*

EIGHTH RACE
BELMONT Park
October 29, 2005

1⅛ miles, dirt. 22nd running of the Breeders' Cup Distaff (G1). Purse $2-million. Fillies and mares 3-year-olds and upward. Weights (Northern Hemisphere): 3-year-olds, 120 lbs. Older, 123 lbs. (Southern Hemisphere): 3-year-olds, 115 lbs. Older, 123 lbs.

Value of race: $1,834,000. Value to winner: $1,040,000; second: $400,000; third: $220,000; fourth: $114,000; fifth, $60,000. Mutuel Pool $4,683,655.

Horse	Wt.	M/Eqt	PP	St.	¼	½	¾	Str.	Fin.	Jockey	Odds $1
Pleasant Home, 4, f.	123	L	11	1	13	$12^{1\frac{1}{2}}$	11^{2}	1^{3}	$1^{9\frac{1}{4}}$	C. Velazquez	30.75
Society Selection, 4, f.	123	L	1	11	$10^{\frac{1}{2}}$	$9^{\frac{1}{2}}$	6^{hd}	$3^{1\frac{1}{2}}$	2^{nk}	E. Prado	11.80
Ashado, 4, f.	123	L	3	7	6^{hd}	5^{hd}	$5^{\frac{1}{2}}$	$2^{\frac{1}{2}}$	$3^{2\frac{1}{4}}$	J. Velazquez	2.25*
Stellar Jayne, 4, f.	123	L	2	8	2^{hd}	4^{hd}	2^{hd}	$5^{1\frac{1}{2}}$	$4^{2\frac{1}{4}}$	L. Dettori	4.50
In The Gold, 3, f.	120	L	10	13	11^{hd}	$11^{\frac{1}{2}}$	10^{hd}	6^{2}	5^{1}	G. Stevens	9.20
Capeside Lady, 4, f.	123	L	13	2	1^{1}	$1^{\frac{1}{2}}$	$1^{1\frac{1}{2}}$	4^{2}	$6^{\frac{3}{4}}$	C. DeCarlo	57.00
Nothing But Fun, 3, f.	120	L	4	12	12^{2}	$10^{2\frac{1}{2}}$	$8^{1\frac{1}{2}}$	$7^{2/}$	$7^{6\frac{1}{4}}$	A. Solis	32.00
Hollywood Story, 4, f.	123	L	9	9	$7^{\frac{1}{2}}$	$7^{\frac{1}{2}}$	$12^{1\frac{1}{2}}$	10^{3}	$8^{3\frac{1}{4}}$	P. Valenzuela	30.25
Sweet Symphony, 3, f.	120	L	12	10	9^{hd}	13	13	$9^{\frac{1}{2}}$	9^{4}	J. Bailey	7.70
Island Fashion, 5, m.	123	L	8	3	5^{1}	6^{hd}	$4^{\frac{1}{2}}$	$11^{2\frac{1}{2}}$	$10^{1\frac{1}{4}}$	R. Bejarano	27.75
Happy Ticket, 4, f.	123	L	7	5	$8^{1\frac{1}{2}}$	8^{1}	$3^{\frac{1}{2}}$	8^{1}	$11^{2\frac{1}{2}}$	V. Espinoza	4.50
Yolanda B. Too, 3, f.	120	L	5	6	$3^{\frac{1}{2}}$	$2^{\frac{1}{2}}$	7^{hd}	12^{10}	$12^{24\frac{1}{4}}$	E. Coa	64.25
Healthy Addiction, 4, f.	123	L	6	4	4^{hd}	3^{1}	9^{hd}	13	13	G. Gomez	18.40

OFF AT 4:32. Start: Good. Winner: Swung wide, drew off.
Time: :23.33, :46.31, 1:10.74, 1:35.82, 1:48.34. Weather: Cloudy. Track: Fast.

$2 Mutuel Prices:

11—PLEASANT HOME	**63.50**	**25.60**	**13.40**
1—SOCIETY SELECTION		**12.80**	**7.90**
3—ASHADO			**3.30**

$2 PICK THREE 3-2-11 PAID $8,668.00 **$2 EXACTA 11-1 PAID $692.00**
$2 HEAD2HEAD 6 vs. 12 (WINNER 12) PAID $2.90
$2 SUPERFECTA 11-1-3-2 PAID $20,363.00 **$2 TRIFECTA 11-1-3 PAID $3,453.00**

Dkbbr. f., by Seeking the Gold—Our Country Place by Pleasant Colony. Trainer: Shug McGaughey. Owner: Phipps Stable (Ky.). Bred by Phipps Stable (Ky.).

PLEASANT HOME trailed for a half, saved ground while rapidly making her move midway on the turn, quickly charged to the front in the upper stretch, and drew away with authority under steady right-hand encouragement. SOCIETY SELECTION, unhurried for a half, angled out for room at the quarter pole, exchanged bumps with ASHADO in upper stretch, and outfinished the favorite for the place. ASHADO steadied in traffic on the backstretch, launched a rally entering the stretch, bumped with SOCIETY SELECTION, and yielded second late. STELLAR JAYNE saved ground for seven furlongs, dropped back on the turn, and weakened in the drive. IN THE GOLD, outrun for a mile, passed tiring horses. CAPESIDE LADY was hustled to the front, set the pace to the top of the stretch, and gave way. NOTHING BUT FUN, outrun early, had no rally. HOLLYWOOD STORY was steadied on the turn and had no response when roused. SWEET SYMPHONY was never a factor. ISLAND FASHION showed speed for six furlongs and faltered. HAPPY TICKET made a middle move to threaten briefly on the turn and flattened out. YOLANDA B. TOO pressed the pace from the outside and gave way. HEALTHY ADDICTION was finished early.

RACING

Review of 2005 Racing Season

The racing season of 2005 bore an interesting and delightful resemblance to the year that had preceded it. It featured a three-year-old who won two-thirds of the Triple Crown but was denied a Horse of the Year trophy by an older male who simply was a better horse. Ghostzapper's consistency and Breeders' Cup Classic (G1) triumph trumped Smarty Jones's Kentucky Derby (G1) and Preakness Stakes (G1) victories in 2004. In 2005, Saint Liam's marvelous season, capped by a Breeders' Cup Classic win, overshadowed Afleet Alex's acrobatic Preakness triumph and his subsequent commanding victory in the Belmont Stakes (G1).

The 2005 racing year, like three others before it, boasted a top two-year-old filly, but the two-year-old males were much superior to the '03 and '04 groups. No three-year-old filly emerged to match the brilliance of Ashado as a three-year-old, and the title went by default to Smuggler, who completed her season with a victory in the Coaching Club American Oaks (G1). The sprinting was terrific, with Lost in the Fog leaving everyone in the dust until the final race of his season.

Following are reviews of the major runners and races in each division in 2005.

Two-Year-Old Males

After two mediocre two-year-old male divisions in 2003 and '04, several promising youngsters emerged in '05, and the Breeders' Cup Juvenile (G1) settled the championship in an interesting and competitive year.

Two of the first juvenile colts to emerge were Darley Stable's Henny Hughes, who scored a runaway maiden victory at Monmouth Park in mid-June and then ran off to a 15-length victory in Belmont Park's Tremont Stakes on July 4. A few days later, trainer Frank Brothers sent out First Samurai for a daylight victory in a Churchill Downs maiden special weight race. At Saratoga Race Course, Henny Hughes, trained by Patrick Biancone, scored a 3¾-length victory in the Saratoga Special Stakes (G2) on July 28. Ten days later, First Samurai triumphed by six lengths in an allowance race.

Henny Hughes, a Hennessy colt, and First Samurai, by Giant's Causeway, met for the first time in the Hopeful Stakes (G1) on August 27, and First Samurai bounded away to a 4¼-length victory after pressing the early pace. Henny Hughes, never far back, finished second.

First Samurai also would prevail in their meeting at Belmont Park in the one-mile Champagne Stakes (G1) on October 8. Racing over a sloppy, sealed track, First Samurai took over in the stretch and won by 2¾ lengths over Henny Hughes in each colt's final prep race for the Breeders' Cup Juvenile on the same Belmont track. Private Vow advanced steadily through the allowance ranks and won the Futurity Stakes (G2) in his first stakes win on September 17.

On the West Coast, Bob and Beverly Lewis's What a Song showed early promise. On June 18, the $1.9-million purchase at the Barretts Equine Ltd. March selected two-year-olds in training sale won his first career start, a 3¼-length victory over another first-time starter, Stevie Wonderboy, in a Hollywood Park maiden special weight race. They met again four weeks later in the Hollywood Juvenile Championship Stakes (G3), which What a Song won by a neck over Bashert, with Stevie Wonderboy third, beaten 1¼ lengths.

While Merv Griffin's Stevie Wonderboy dropped down to a Del Mar maiden special weight race to break his maiden by four lengths, What a Song scored a 2¾-length victory in Del Mar's Best Pal Stakes (G2) on August 14. Five days later, however, the Songandaprayer colt fractured sesamoids while galloping and was euthanized. Stevie Wonderboy continued to improve for trainer Doug O'Neill and won the seven-furlong Del Mar Futurity (G2), which would be his final race before the Breeders' Cup Juvenile. Brother Derek won the West Coast's traditional Breeders' Cup prep, the Norfolk Stakes (G2), at the Oak Tree meet at Santa Anita Park.

For the Breeders' Cup Juvenile, Henny Hughes was moved to the barn of trainer Kiaran McLaughlin, and the Hennessy colt pressed or set the pace into midstretch, but Stevie Wonderboy closed strongest to win by 1¼ lengths. First Samurai, the 1.30-to-1 favorite, finished well for third, with Brother Derek tiring to finish fourth. Private Vow, whose left rein broke early in the Juvenile in his last-place finish, came back to win the Kentucky Jockey Club Stakes (G2) at Churchill Downs. Bluegrass Cat notched a win in the Nashua Stakes (G3) a day before the Breeders' Cup and then won Aqueduct's Remsen Stakes (G2). Brother Derek closed the season with a Hollywood Futurity (G1) victory, but the title went to Stevie Wonderboy, who also was rated atop the Experimental Free Handicap.

Two-Year-Old Fillies

The preceding three seasons had featured dominant fillies who had won the Breeders' Cup Juvenile Fillies (G1) and been voted the top performers in their division. Although Folklore did not dominate in the same way as Storm Flag Flying (2002), Halfbridled ('03), and Sweet Catomine ('04), she nonetheless put together a quality season that carried her to the top of her division.

Making an early debut was Todd Pletcher-trained Adieu, who won a Keeneland Race Course maiden special weight race at 4½ furlongs on April 22. D. Wayne Lukas, who trained Folklore for Robert and Beverly Lewis, sent their homebred Tiznow filly out for her first start on May 18 at Belmont Park, and she collected second money. In her next start, on June 3, she scored a four-length maiden victory at Belmont. Adieu and Folklore met for the first time in Belmont's 5½-furlong Astoria Stakes, and Adieu went past pacesetter Folklore for a 1¼-length win. They next met in Saratoga Race Course's Adirondack Stakes (G2) at six furlongs, and Folklore prevailed by three-quarters of a length over Fifth Avenue, with Adieu checking in fourth as the 6-to-5 favorite.

Their rivalry continued in Saratoga's Spinaway Stakes (G2), and Adieu, never far off the early pace, won by a length over a closing Folklore. They then took different routes to the Breeders' Cup, with Adieu scoring a two-length win in the Frizette Stakes (G1) and Folklore attaining her initial Grade 1 victory with a 14-length score in the Matron Stakes.

While both Halfbridled and Sweet Catomine had emerged from the West Coast, California's two-year-old filly races offered few major contenders in 2005. Wild Fit jumped from a first-race maiden victory to a Del Mar Debutante Stakes (G1) win. In her next start, however, she finished second to Diamond Omi in the Oak Leaf Stakes (G2).

In the Breeders' Cup Juvenile Fillies, jockey Edgar Prado kept Folklore close to the pace, and they rolled to a 1¼-length victory over late-running Wild Fit, while Adieu finished a well-beaten seventh. Among late-blooming fillies, French Park won Churchill's Pocahontas (G3) and Golden Rod (G2) Stakes in November for trainer Helen Pitts.

Three-Year-Old Males

In the spring, the three-year-old male division looked to be highly competitive and of high quality. But, with a few exceptions, the competitiveness was limited to the spring, and the championship was all but determined at the finish line of the Belmont Stakes (G1). Trainer Nick Zito, inducted in August 2005 into the Racing Hall of Fame, held the year's hot hand, and his early leader was Live Oak Plantation's High Fly, winner of the Fountain of Youth Stakes (G2) and Florida Derby (G1). His hand grew even hotter when Kinsman Stable's Bellamy Road crushed his Wood Memorial Stakes (G1) opponents by 17½ lengths and ultimately would go off as the 2.60-to-1 Kentucky Derby favorite.

Although Zito filled one-quarter of the Derby gate with his five starters, he by no means had a lock on the race. Buzzards Bay won the Santa Anita Derby (G1) by a half-length, Bandini took the Blue Grass Stakes (G1) by a commanding six lengths, and Afleet Alex won the Arkansas Derby (G2) by eight lengths. Form often goes out the window when the gates open for the Derby, and Giacomo, ignored at 50.30-to-1 after his fourth-place finish in the Santa Anita Derby, scored by a half-length over Closing Argument. Among the favorites, the only one to run a respectable race was 9-to-2 Afleet Alex, who finished third.

In one of the most dramatic runnings of the Preakness, Afleet Alex, favored at 3.30-to-1, was making a winning move when pacesetter Scrappy T swerved into his path. Afleet Alex clipped his heels but managed to stay on his feet, and jockey Jeremy Rose somehow stayed in the irons. The Northern Afleet colt quickly gathered himself and ran on to a popular 4¾-length victory over Scrappy T, while Giacomo closed ground for third. The Belmont Stakes belonged entirely to Afleet Alex, who ran away to a seven-length victory.

In a sense, that was the end of the three-year-old male season. Afleet Alex sustained a condylar fracture of his left fore cannon bone and was subsequently retired to Gainesway. Giacomo never raced again in 2005. Bob Baffert-trained Roman Ruler won the Dwyer Stakes (G2) and Haskell Invitational Handicap (G1) in succession, but he was no match for Flower Alley in Saratoga's Travers Stakes (G1), in which Bellamy Road finished second in his first and only start in 2005 after the Derby. Flower Alley finished second in the Breeders' Cup Classic, but between those two races the Lane's End Stakes (G2) winner ran a poor fourth in the Jockey Club Gold Cup (G1) and lost all chance for a title. Late in the season, Elisabeth Alexander's Magna Graduate scored three consecutive stakes victories, in the Meadowlands's Pegasus Stakes (G3), Belmont's Discovery Handicap (G3) on the Breeders' Cup card, and Churchill's Clark Handicap (G2) against older horses.

Three-Year-Old Fillies

If the three-year-old male championship was predictable, the three-year-old filly division was inscrutable. At the beginning of the season, however, it appeared that Sweet Catomine would continue to dominate the division. The 2004 juvenile champion swept to victories in the Santa Ysabel Stakes (G3) and Santa Anita Oaks (G1) before going off as the even-money favorite in the Santa Anita Derby. But it was clear early that she was not herself in that race and finished fifth. A controversy ensued over an unreported trip off the racetrack grounds for treatment before the race, and owner-breeder Martin Wygod subsequently retired her and bred her to A.P. Indy.

Without a star performer, the division lost much of its continuity. Round Pond established early credentials, reeling off victories in the Fantasy (G2) and Acorn Stakes (G1) for trainer John Servis, but she finished second in the Delaware Oaks (G2) and was done for the year. Phipps Stable's Smuggler, trained by Shug McGaughey, finished second in the Acorn and then won the Mother Goose Stakes (G1) over Spun Sugar and the Coaching Club American Oaks over Kentucky Oaks (G1) winner Summerly. Neither Smuggler nor Summerly raced again in 2005, however.

For the remainder of the year, fillies would win major victories and then fail to reproduce that form. Sweet Symphony, owned by George Steinbrenner's Kinsman Stable, won Saratoga's Alabama Stakes (G1) by 6¼ lengths, but then ran without distinction against older females in the Beldame Stakes (G1) and the Breeders' Cup Distaff (G1). Peter Vegso's Splendid Blended was splendid in Hollywood Park's Vanity Handicap (G1), but that July 3 race ended her two-start season. Sis City won Keeneland's Ashland Stakes (G1) as the 8-to-5 favorite but did not hit the board again in three subsequent starts, including the Kentucky Oaks as the 3-to-5 favorite. Sharp Lisa won the Santa Ynez (G2) and Las Virgenes (G1) Stakes, but wrapped up 2005 with fourth-place finishes in the Fantasy and La Brea Stakes (G1). The Eclipse Award was bestowed on Smuggler in a year that just barely warranted a divisional champion.

Older Males

The 2005 handicap male season appeared at first to be a matchup of reigning Horse of the Year Ghostzapper and Saint Liam, the developing horse who had almost beaten the champion in the 2004 Woodward Stakes (G1). But Ghostzapper's 2005 season was limited to one marvelous race, a 6¼-length trouncing of Silver Wagon in the Metropolitan Handicap (G1), and the remainder of the campaign belonged almost exclusively to Saint Liam, who ultimately would be voted 2005 Horse of the Year.

Early in the year, Saint Liam served notice that he would be the horse to beat. At Gulfstream Park in early February, he scored a 3¾-length victory over Roses in May in the Donn Handicap (G1). After that race, Roses in May shipped to the Persian Gulf for a three-length victory in the Dubai World Cup (UAE-G1). The $6-million race would the be last of Roses in May's career, and he was sold for stud duty in Japan.

On the West Coast, Rock Hard Ten won the Strub Stakes (G2) in preparation for the Santa Anita Handicap (G1), which attracted Saint Liam from his East Coast base. The five-year-old Saint Ballado horse ran fourth, however, and Rock Hard Ten won by 1¾ lengths over Congrats.

Trainer Richard Dutrow Jr. returned Saint Liam to the East Coast and handed him over to his stable staff and trainer-of-record Bobby Frankel while he served a 60-day suspension for medications violations. Saint Liam won Churchill's Stephen Foster Handicap (G1) and, with Dutrow back on the job, finished second to a game Commentator in Saratoga's Whitney Handicap (G1).

On the West Coast, two new contenders emerged. Lava Man, a former claimer, won the Californian Stakes (G2) and Hollywood Gold Cup Handicap (G1) in succession. Borrego, a distant second in the Gold Cup, came back to win the Pacific Classic (G1) by a half-length over ageless Perfect Drift. Trained by Beau Greely, Borrego shipped east and won the Jockey Club Gold Cup (G1). Saint Liam skipped the Jockey Club Gold Cup after winning the Woodward, and Rock Hard Ten returned from a long layoff to win the Goodwood Breeders' Cup Handicap (G2). Thus, the stage was set for a highly competitive Breeders' Cup Classic, which was run without Rock Hard Ten when he scratched the day before the event because of a foot bruise. Saint Liam, never far back under Jerry Bailey, sailed to a one-length victory while Borrego finished a dull tenth. Voted Horse of the Year and champion older male, Saint Liam retired to Lane's End, where he was joined by Rock Hard Ten for the 2006 breeding season.

Older Females

Ashado was a good two-year-old and a dominant three-year-old. At four in 2005, she was easily the most accomplished member of her division, but her road to a second consecutive Eclipse

Award had a few bumps, and she fell short of the all-time North American female earnings mark when she finished third in the Breeders' Cup Distaff.

The season for handicap females begins each year in warm climates, and Miss Loren (Arg) broke out of the gate first with victories in Santa Anita's listed Paseana Handicap and the Santa Maria Handicap (G1). She won the Santa Maria by a nose over Good Student (Arg), with Hollywood Story picking up third money. Meanwhile, four-year-old Tarlow finished third in the El Encino Stakes (G2) and then notched a two-length victory in the La Canada Stakes (G2).

Purchased by Mercedes Stable after her Santa Maria victory and turned over to Richard Mandella, Miss Loren went off as the 5-to-2 favorite in the Santa Margarita Invitational Handicap (G1) in mid-March. But Tarlow set all the pace and barely held off Dream of Summer for a nose victory. Miss Loren finished third, three-quarters of a length behind the winner. Miss Loren, then seven, was retired shortly after the race; Tarlow never raced after the Santa Margarita and was retired in early 2006 by her owners, Jerry and Ann Moss.

Florida's races for older females offered no major contenders, and Ashado was shipped to Arkansas for her 2005 debut in Oaklawn Park's Apple Blossom Handicap (G1) at 1⅟₁₆ miles. Ashado, who had beaten older females in the Breeders' Cup Distaff in her prior start, went off as the 1-to-2 favorite, but she faltered in Oaklawn's stretch and finished fifth. Dream of Summer set all the pace and held off a determined late charge by Star Parade (Arg) to win by a neck. Shadow Cast finished third.

In her next start, the Pimlico Breeders' Cup Distaff Handicap (G3), Ashado appeared on paper to be a sure winner and went off at 3-to-10 odds. She set the pace but tired in deep stretch to finish second by three-quarters of a length to Silmaril. A filly of Ashado's quality could not be denied forever, however, and she finally broke through with a three-length win in the Ogden Phipps Handicap (G1) on June 18. At Saratoga in late July, she ran away to a 9½-length victory in the Go for Wand Handicap (G1), but she again took bettors into the drink when she finished fourth in the subsequent Personal Ensign Handicap (G1), beaten nearly 15 lengths by Shadow Cast, at 0.45-to-1 odds.

No other filly or mare made an especially strong impression over the summer, however, and Ashado headed into the fall championship period as the division leader. She confirmed her ascendancy with a half-length victory over Ballerina Stakes (G1) winner Happy Ticket in the Beldame Stakes (G1), her final start before the Breeders' Cup Distaff. Godolphin Racing's Stellar Jayne won the Ruffian Handicap (G1) at Belmont, and trainer Marty Wolfson shipped Pampered Princess to Keeneland Race Course for a modest upset in the Juddmonte Spinster Stakes (G1).

Rounding into top condition was Phipps Stable's Pleasant Home, a Seeking the Gold four-year-old who had been second in both the Ballerina and Spinster. She certainly was in top shape for the Breeders' Cup Distaff, in which she blew past Ashado in early stretch and won by 9¼ lengths. Society Selection finished second, a neck ahead of Ashado. A few days later at the Keeneland November sale, Ashado sold for a record $9-million as a broodmare prospect.

Sprinters

In some regards, 2005 would not be considered a vintage year for sprinters if the sole criterion were the number of top runners competing against each other regularly. But sometimes it takes only one horse to create a memorable year, and Lost in the Fog certainly provided some rich memories. Until he finished off the board in the Breeders' Cup Sprint (G1) and Saint Liam won the Breeders' Cup Classic, Harry Aleo's three-year-old Lost Soldier colt was creating some chatter as a Horse of the Year candidate.

Lost in the Fog's poor performance at Belmont Park in late October was perhaps understandable in light of the length of his campaign. He started his season in late January and made nine more starts over the ensuing nine months. Based in Northern California with trainer Greg Gilchrist, the Florida-bred began his season with a 4½-length frolic in the Sunshine Millions Dash Stakes at Gulfstream Park. He continued his unbeaten run with victories in the Swale (G2) and Bay Shore (G3) Stakes, both by more than four lengths.

While Lost in the Fog had an early start to the season, Saratoga County got the sprint campaign rolling with a 2½-length victory in Gulfstream's Mr. Prospector Stakes (G3) on January 8. After taking Laurel Park's General George Stakes (G2) by a nose on February 21, he shipped to the Middle East for a one-length victory in the $2-million Dubai Golden Shaheen (UAE-G1). Saratoga County never started again. The son of Valid Expectations developed laminitis in midsummer and was euthanized.

New York's sprint season begins with the Carter Handicap (G1) in April, and 0.85-to-1 favorite Forest Danger won by 1¾ lengths over

Medallist. The Forestry four-year-old was the 2-to-1 second choice behind Ghostzapper in the Metropolitan Handicap (G1) but finished fifth. He also finished a poor fifth to Mass Media in the Forego Handicap (G1) at Saratoga and was done for the season.

A Grade 1 victory would be Lost in the Fog's summertime goal. After a listed victory at home in Northern California, he shipped to Belmont Park for a 1¼-length victory in the Riva Ridge Breeders' Cup Stakes (G2) on Belmont Stakes day. Even a day's delay for Hurricane Dennis did not deter him in Florida, where he won Calder Race Course's Carry Back Stakes (G2) by 7¼ lengths on July 10. He finally picked up his first and only Grade 1 victory, an easy score in Saratoga's King's Bishop Stakes. Gilchrist then took Lost in the Fog home for his only other start before the Breeders' Cup, a paid workout in the Bay Meadows Speed Handicap on October 1.

In the interim, other sprinters were finding their best strides. Taste of Paradise, third to Imperialism in Del Mar's Pat O'Brien Breeders' Cup Handicap (G2), shipped to New York and pulled a 26.50-to-1 surprise in the Vosburgh Stakes (G1). Buckram Oak Farm's Silver Train, a three-year-old, improved from a third-place finish in Saratoga's Amsterdam Stakes (G2) to win the mile Jerome Handicap (G2) by five lengths over High Fly. The Old Trieste colt then gave trainer Richard Dutrow his first of two Breeders' Cup victories when he ran Lost in the Fog into the ground and won the Sprint by a head over Taste of Paradise. Though beaten once, Lost in the Fog still had sufficient support to win the Eclipse Award as champion sprinter.

Turf Males

When the first four finishers in the Breeders' Cup Turf (G1) are all based overseas, it is time to look for turf milers as potential champions. The mile category had two highly regarded contenders, and the nod went to Leroidesanimaux (Brz), whose only 2005 loss was to Artie Schiller in the Breeders' Cup Mile (G1) at Belmont Park. Among the top turf contenders, Leroidesanimaux had one of the earliest starts, winning the Frank E. Kilroe Memorial Handicap (G1) on March 5 at Santa Anita. Artie Schiller also began his 2005 campaign with a win, taking the Maker's Mark Mile Stakes (G2) as the 3-to-2 favorite on April 15.

Eight days later, Better Talk Now, upset winner of the 2004 Breeders' Cup Turf, notched a victory in Aqueduct's Fort Marcy Handicap (G3). He and Artie Schiller met at Pimlico Race Course in the Dixie Stakes (G2), but Cool Conductor nosed out Artie Schiller, with Good Reward third and Better Talk Now fourth. Good Reward came back three weeks later to win the Manhattan Handicap (G1), with Artie Schiller finishing third. With the help of rabbit Shake the Bank, Better Talk Now won Monmouth Park's United Nations Handicap (G1), and 2004 champion Kitten's Joy opened his season with a one-length victory in Churchill's Firecracker Breeders' Cup Handicap (G2) on July 4.

The Churchill race was intended to set up Kitten's Joy for the Arlington Million Stakes (G1), but the unpredictable Powerscourt (GB) maintained a straight course and won the 1¼-mile race by three lengths over Kitten's Joy. Neither would start again in 2005. On the Million card, Gun Salute scored a 1¾-length victory over English Channel in the Secretariat Stakes (G1).

Leroidesanimaux and Artie Schiller prepared for their fall campaigns at Saratoga, with Artie Schiller winning the Bernard Baruch Handicap (G2) and Leroidesanimaux prevailing in the Fourstardave Handicap (G2). The Candy Stripes horse came back to win the Atto Mile Stakes (Can-G1) at Woodbine, and Artie Schiller finished second to Funfair in the Kelso Breeders' Cup Handicap (G2). Better Talk Now prepared for his Breeders' Cup Turf defense with a win in the Man o' War Stakes (G1). In the Breeders' Cup Mile, Leroidesanimaux took the lead in mid-stretch, but Artie Schiller ran him down to win by three-quarters of a length, with Better Talk Now a distant seventh. Based on his overall 2005 record, Leroidesanimaux was voted the Eclipse Award.

Turf Females

From spring through fall, Intercontinental (GB) was the toast of her division, and she concluded her racing career for owner-breeder Juddmonte Farms with a victory in the Breeders' Cup Filly and Mare Turf (G1) at surprisingly long odds. Racing Hall of Fame trainer Bobby Frankel started the year with a two-barreled threat, Intercontinental and Megahertz (GB), a Pivotal mare owned by Michael Bello. Megahertz opened the season with consecutive victories at Santa Anita, where she won the Santa Ana Handicap (G2) in March and the Santa Barbara Handicap (G2) on April 17. On the same day, Frankel sent out Intercontinental for a one-length victory in Keeneland's Jenny Wiley Stakes (G3) in her 2005 debut. In her next start, Intercontinental finished second to Honey Fox Handicap (G3) winner Sands Springs in the Just a Game Breeders' Cup Handicap (G2) on the Belmont Stakes undercard. Two weeks later, Megahertz returned to action and won Hollywood's Beverly Hills Handicap (G2).

On the July 4 weekend, Claiborne Farm's fast-developing Pulpit filly Wend won the New York Handicap (G2). Perhaps the weekend's most fascinating winner, though, was Cesario (Jpn), winner of the Yushun Himba, the Japanese Oaks. She arrived at Hollywood and promptly drilled the American Invitational Oaks (G1), scoring by four lengths over Melhor Ainda. Cesario, the first Japanese horse to win an American Grade 1 race, did not start again in 2005 and was retired because of a ligament injury in her right front leg in April 2006.

Also that weekend, Intercontinental returned to the winner's circle after a 1¼-length victory in the Royal Heroine Stakes (G3). In the John C. Mabee Handicap (G1) at Del Mar, Intercontinental ran evenly and finished third to Amorama (Fr), who posted her only win of the year. Megahertz and Wend set their sights on Arlington Park and the Beverly D. Stakes (G1), but Angara (GB) outfinished Megahertz to win by a neck, with Wend checking in sixth. Angara also did not win again for the remainder of the year.

Frankel kept his two turf stars apart for much of the fall, with Intercontinental going into shorter races and Megahertz going a distance. Intercontinental took Del Mar's Palomar Handicap (G2) in early September and then won Keeneland's one-mile WinStar Galaxy Stakes (G2) by three-quarters of a length over Wend. Megahertz prepared for the Filly and Mare Turf with a one-length victory in Oak Tree's Yellow Ribbon Stakes (G1), and Frankel made a last-minute decision to start Intercontinental in the Breeders' Cup race despite its 1¼-mile distance. Under Rafael Bejarano, Intercontinental set all the pace and won by 1¼ lengths over fast-closing Ouija Board (GB), the 2004 winner and champion female turf. Megahertz finished eighth, thus assuring Intercontinental the female turf title.

Steeplechasers

By virtue of how they run (at a moderate pace for much of a race) and how they are trained (in the country, generally away from hard racetracks), steeplechase horses can stick around for a long, long time. Racing Hall of Fame member Lonesome Glory won the first of his five Eclipse Awards in 1992 and the final one in '99. Thus, it is not unheard of that champions of past years will return to slug it out over fences in a new season. For 2005, reigning champion Hirapour (Ire) returned for another engagement, and also back in form was McDynamo, who had won the title in 2003 and challenged for it again in '04 with his second consecutive Breeders' Cup Steeplechase win.

As the March-to-November season opened, Doug Fout-trained Hirapour looked to be the horse to beat. The nine-year-old Kahyasi (Ire) gelding, bred by the Aga Khan, opened the season in early April with a narrow second to Sur La Tete in the Carolina Cup Hurdle Stakes, and then took Keeneland's rich Royal Chase for the Sport of Kings Hurdle Stakes later that month by 1¼ lengths over Sur La Tete. McDynamo, making his first start of the year, finished third, another 3½ lengths farther back.

Hirapour sat out the longest major race of the year, the three-mile Iroquois Hurdle Stakes near Nashville. In his absence, Sur La Tete won by 2½ lengths over McDynamo. The Iroquois would be Sur La Tete's final race of the year. McDynamo, owned by Michael Moran and trained by Sanna Neilson Hendriks, looked to shorter races but could not find the winner's circle in Colonial Downs's David L. "Zeke" Ferguson Memorial Hurdle Stakes, finishing second at 1-to-2 to Paradise's Boss, a fast-developing five-year-old who won by 5¼ lengths.

Trained by Jack Fisher, Paradise's Boss proved that his Colonial win was no fluke when he won Saratoga's A. P. Smithwick Memorial Hurdle Stakes, with Hirapour finishing third. In Saratoga's major jumps event, the New York Turf Writers Steeplechase Handicap, Hirapour handled 158 pounds and won by 3¾ lengths as the 1.25-to-1 favorite. Paradise's Loss finished fifth, beaten 15 lengths, and did not start again in 2005.

Hendriks kept McDynamo away from Saratoga and looked for an easy spot at the Meadowlands, but the eight-year-old Dynaformer gelding could not run down pacesetter Preemptive Strike, who won by five lengths over the 2003 champion. When the racing moved to Far Hills, New Jersey, for the Breeders' Cup Steeplechase on October 22, McDynamo was in his element. Never beaten on the course, McDynamo surged to the early lead, set all the pace, and won his third straight Breeders' Cup Steeplechase by nine lengths. Three Carat finished second, 5¼ lengths ahead of Hirapour.

McDynamo still had only one win on the season to Hirapour's two, and they would decide the title at Camden, South Carolina, in the Marion duPont Scott Colonial Cup Hurdle Stakes, the year's final major race. McDynamo again set the pace, but Hirapour challenged him after the last fence and gradually reduced McDynamo's lead. But it was not enough. McDynamo won by 1½ lengths and secured his second championship in three years.—*Don Clippinger*

Richest North American Stakes Races of 2005

Race (Grade)	Purse	Track	Distance (Miles)	Winner	Value to Winner
Breeders' Cup Classic (G1)	$4,291,560	Belmont Park	1¼	Saint Liam	$2,433,600
Kentucky Derby (G1)	2,399,600	Churchill Downs	1¼	Giacomo	1,639,600
Breeders' Cup Turf (G1)	2,090,760	Belmont Park	1½T	Shirocco (Ger)	1,185,600
Breeders' Cup Mile (G1)	1,856,925	Belmont Park	1T	Artie Schiller	1,053,000
Breeders' Cup Distaff (G1)	1,834,000	Belmont Park	1⅛	Pleasant Home	1,040,000
Canadian International S. (G1)	1,684,885	Woodbine	1½T	Relaxed Gesture (Ire)	1,009,920
Breeders' Cup Juvenile (G1)	1,458,030	Belmont Park	1$\frac{1}{16}$	Stevie Wonderboy	826,800
Haskell Invitational H. (G1)	1,015,000	Monmouth Park	1⅛	Roman Ruler	600,000
Delaware H. (G2)	1,001,800	Delaware Park	1¼	Island Sand	600,000
Arkansas Derby (G2)	1,000,000	Oaklawn Park	1⅛	Afleet Alex	600,000
Arlington Million S. (G1)	1,000,000	Arlington Park	1¼T	Powerscourt (GB)	600,000
Belmont S. (G1)	1,000,000	Belmont Park	1½	Afleet Alex	600,000
Florida Derby (G1)	1,000,000	Gulfstream Park	1⅛	High Fly	600,000
Jockey Club Gold Cup S. (G1)	1,000,000	Belmont Park	1¼	Borrego	600,000
Pacific Classic S. (G1)	1,000,000	Del Mar	1¼	Borrego	600,000
Preakness S. (G1)	1,000,000	Pimlico	1$\frac{3}{16}$	Afleet Alex	650,000
Santa Anita H. (G1)	1,000,000	Santa Anita Park	1¼	Rock Hard Ten	600,000
Sunshine Millions Classic S.	1,000,000	Gulfstream Park	1⅛	Musique Toujours	550,000
Travers S. (G1)	1,000,000	Saratoga	1¼	Flower Alley	600,000
Breeders' Cup Filly & Mare Turf (G1)	972,020	Belmont Park	1¼T	Intercontinental (GB)	551,200
Breeders' Cup Juvenile Fillies (G1)	972,020	Belmont Park	1$\frac{1}{16}$	Folklore	551,200
Breeders' Cup Sprint (G1)	972,020	Belmont Park	6	Silver Train	551,200
Atto Mile S. (G1)	849,756	Woodbine	1T	Leroidesanimaux (Brz)	509,040
E. P. Taylor S. (G1)	843,959	Woodbine	1¼T	Honey Ryder	504,960
Stephen Foster H. (G1)	828,000	Churchill Downs	1⅛	Saint Liam	513,360
Queen's Plate S.	812,700	Woodbine	1¼	Wild Desert	486,840
Alabama S. (G1)	750,000	Saratoga	1¼	Sweet Symphony	450,000
American Invitational Oaks (G1)	750,000	Hollywood Park	1¼T	Cesario (Jpn)	450,000
Beldame S. (G1)	750,000	Belmont Park	1⅛	Ashado	450,000
Beverly D. S. (G1)	750,000	Arlington Park	1$\frac{3}{16}$T	Angara (GB)	450,000
Blue Grass S. (G1)	750,000	Keeneland	1⅛	Bandini	465,000
Flower Bowl Invitational S. (G1)	750,000	Belmont Park	1¼T	Riskaverse	450,000
Hawthorne Gold Cup S. (G2)	750,000	Hawthorne	1¼	Super Frolic	450,000
Hollywood Gold Cup H. (G1)	750,000	Hollywood Park	1¼	Lava Man	450,000
Joe Hirsch Turf Classic Invitational S. (G1)	750,000	Belmont Park	1½T	Shakespeare	450,000
Metropolitan H. (G1)	750,000	Belmont Park	1	Ghostzapper	450,000
Pennsylvania Derby (G2)	750,000	Philadelphia Park	1⅛	Sun King	397,500
Santa Anita Derby (G1)	750,000	Santa Anita Park	1⅛	Buzzards Bay	450,000
Super Derby (G2)	750,000	Louisiana Downs	1¼	The Daddy	450,000
United Nations S. (G1)	750,000	Monmouth Park	1⅜T	Better Talk Now	450,000
Virginia Derby (G3)	750,000	Colonial Downs	1¼T	English Channel	450,000
West Virginia Derby (G3)	750,000	Mountaineer Race Track	1⅛	Real Dandy	450,000
Whitney H. (G1)	750,000	Saratoga	1⅛	Commentator	450,000
Wood Memorial S. (G1)	750,000	Aqueduct	1⅛	Bellamy Road	450,000
Louisiana Derby (G2)	600,000	Fair Grounds	1$\frac{1}{16}$	High Limit	360,000
Shadwell Turf Mile S. (G1)	600,000	Keeneland	1T	Host (Chi)	372,000
Clark H. (G2)	573,500	Churchill Downs	1⅛	Magna Graduate	355,570
Kentucky Oaks (G1)	554,400	Churchill Downs	1⅛	Summerly	343,728
Indiana Derby (G2)	511,300	Hoosier Park	1$\frac{1}{16}$	Don't Get Mad	306,780
Kent Breeders' Cup S. (G3)	501,800	Delaware Park	1⅛T	Seeking Slew	300,000
Delaware Oaks (G2)	500,300	Delaware Park	1$\frac{1}{16}$	R Lady Joy	300,000
Apple Blossom H. (G1)	500,000	Oaklawn Park	1$\frac{1}{16}$	Dream of Summer	300,000
Ashland S. (G1)	500,000	Keeneland	1$\frac{1}{16}$	Sis City	310,000
Champagne S. (G1)	500,000	Belmont Park	1	First Samurai	300,000
Coaching Club American Oaks (G1)	500,000	Belmont Park	1¼	Smuggler	300,000
Colonial Turf Cup S.	500,000	Colonial Downs	1$\frac{3}{16}$T	English Channel	300,000
Diana S. (G1)	500,000	Saratoga	1⅛T	Sand Springs	300,000
Donn H. (G1)	500,000	Gulfstream Park	1⅛	Saint Liam	300,000
Frizette S. (G1)	500,000	Belmont Park	1	Adieu	300,000

Race (Grade)	Purse	Track	Distance (Miles)	Winner	Value to Winner
Illinois Derby (G2)	500,000	Hawthorne	1⅛	Greeley's Galaxy	300,000
Juddmonte Spinster S. (G1)	500,000	Keeneland	1⅛	Pampered Princess	310,000
Lane's End Breeders' Futurity (G1)	500,000	Keeneland	1 1/16	Dawn of War	310,000
Lane's End S. (G2)	500,000	Turfway Park	1⅛	Flower Alley	300,000
Man o' War S. (G1)	500,000	Belmont Park	1⅜T	Better Talk Now	300,000
Meadowlands Breeders' Cup S. (G2)	500,000	Meadowlands	1⅛	Tap Day	300,000
Mervin H. Muniz Jr. Memorial H. (G2)	500,000	Fair Grounds	1⅛T	A to the Z	300,000
New Orleans H. (G2)	500,000	Fair Grounds	1⅛	Badge of Silver	300,000
Pimlico Special H. (G1)	500,000	Pimlico	1 3/16	Eddington	300,000
Princess Rooney H. (G2)	500,000	Calder	6	Madcap Escapade	294,000
Queen Elizabeth II Challenge Cup S. (G1)	500,000	Keeneland	1⅛T	Sweet Talker	310,000
Smile Sprint H. (G2)	500,000	Calder	6	Woke Up Dreamin	294,000
Suburban H. (G1)	500,000	Belmont Park	1¼	Offlee Wild	300,000
Sunshine Millions Distaff S.	500,000	Santa Anita Park	1 1/16	Sweet Lips	275,000
Sunshine Millions Filly and Mare Turf S.	500,000	Gulfstream Park	1⅛T	Valentine Dancer	275,000
Sunshine Millions Turf S.	500,000	Santa Anita Park	1⅛T	Star Over the Bay	275,000
Sword Dancer Invitational S. (G1)	500,000	Saratoga	1½T	King's Drama (Ire)	300,000
Vosburgh S. (G1)	500,000	Belmont Park	6	Taste of Paradise	300,000
WinStar Derby	500,000	Sunland Park	1⅛	Thor's Echo	270,000
Yellow Ribbon S. (G1)	500,000	Oak Tree	1¼T	Megahertz (GB)	300,000
Jim Dandy S. (G2)	490,000	Saratoga	1⅛	Flower Alley	300,000
Oaklawn H. (G2)	490,000	Oaklawn Park	1⅛	Grand Reward	300,000
Woodward S. (G1)	490,000	Belmont Park	1⅛	Saint Liam	300,000
Goodwood Breeders' Cup H. (G2)	484,000	Oak Tree	1⅛	Rock Hard Ten	300,000
Woodford Reserve Turf Classic S. (G1)	470,400	Churchill Downs	1⅛T	America Alive	291,648
Hollywood Starlet S. (G1)	456,000	Hollywood Park	1 1/16	Diplomat Lady	273,600
West Virginia Breeders' Classic S.	450,000	Charles Town Races	1⅛	Speed Whiz	225,000
Gamely Breeders' Cup H. (G1)	441,500	Hollywood Park	1⅛T	Mea Domina	276,900
Commonwealth Breeders' Cup S. (G2)	424,900	Keeneland	7	Clock Stopper	263,438
Nearctic H. (G2)	423,159	Woodbine	6T	Steel Light	252,480
Breeders' S.	412,467	Woodbine	1½T	Jambalaya	246,690
Prince of Wales S.	409,600	Fort Erie	1 3/16	Ablo	245,760
Hollywood Futurity (G1)	407,250	Hollywood Park	1 1/16	Brother Derek	244,350
Indiana Breeders' Cup Oaks (G3)	405,100	Hoosier Park	1 1/16	Flying Glitter	243,060
Woodbine Oaks	401,800	Woodbine	1⅛	Gold Strike	240,120
Darley Alcibiades S. (G2)	400,000	Keeneland	1 1/16	She Says It Best	248,000
Del Mar Derby (G2)	400,000	Del Mar	1⅛T	Willow O Wisp	240,000
Eddie Read H. (G1)	400,000	Del Mar	1⅛T	Sweet Return (GB)	240,000
In Reality S.	400,000	Calder	1 1/16	Blazing Rate	240,000
John C. Mabee H. (G1)	400,000	Del Mar	1⅛T	Amorama (Fr)	240,000

Chronology of Richest North American Race

Purse	Race	Track	Year	Winner	Value to Winner
$4,689,920	Breeders' Cup Classic (G1)	Churchill Downs	1998	Awesome Again	$2,662,400
4,030,400	Breeders' Cup Classic (G1)	Hollywood Park	1997	Skip Away	2,288,000
3,664,000	Breeders' Cup Classic (G1)	Woodbine	1996	Alphabet Soup	2,080,000
2,798,000	Breeders' Cup Classic (G1)	Belmont Park	1995	Cigar	1,560,000
2,748,000	Breeders' Cup Classic (G1)	Churchill Downs	1991	Black Tie Affair (Ire)	1,560,000
2,739,000	Breeders' Cup Classic (G1)	Hollywood Park	1984	Wild Again	1,350,000
1,049,725	Hollywood Futurity (G1)	Hollywood Park	1983	Fali Time	549,849
1,000,000	Arlington Million S. (G1)	Arlington Park	1981	John Henry	600,000
549,000	Jockey Club Gold Cup S. (G1)	Belmont Park	1980	Temperence Hill	329,400
500,000	Hollywood Gold Cup H. (G1)	Hollywood Park	1979	Affirmed	275,000
385,350	Arlington-Washington Futurity	Arlington Park	1968	Strong Strong	212,850
367,700	Arlington-Washington Futurity	Arlington Park	1966	Diplomat Way	195,200
357,250	Arlington-Washington Futurity	Arlington Park	1962	Candy Spots	142,250
319,210	Garden State S.	Garden State Park	1956	Barbizon	168,430
282,370	Garden State S.	Garden State Park	1955	Prince John	157,918
269,965	Garden State S.	Garden State Park	1954	Summer Tan	151,096
269,395	Garden State S.	Garden State Park	1953	*Turn-to	151,282
205,700	Santa Anita Maturity	Santa Anita Park	1951	Great Circle	144,325

How American Races Are Graded

At the urging of European racing officials who in 1972 had created the pattern race system to identify and grade the best-quality races in Europe, the Thoroughbred Owners and Breeders Association created the North American Graded Stakes Committee and implemented a similar grading system for the '73 racing season. The gradings were principally designed to assist bloodstock buyers by identifying the North American races that in the recent past had consistently attracted the highest levels of competition. Grade 1 would be the highest level, followed by Grade 2 and Grade 3, the latter being the lowest level of stakes race accorded a grade.

2006 Graded Stakes by Racetrack

Track	G1	G2	G3	Total
Belmont Park	22	21	16	59
Santa Anita Park	14	30	15	59
Hollywood Park	13	14	18	45
Churchill Downs	14	10	19	43
Gulfstream Park	3	10	18	31
Saratoga Race Course	13	13	5	31
Aqueduct	3	8	15	26
Keeneland Race Course	6	9	11	26
Del Mar	6	11	2	19
Calder Race Course	1	4	12	17
Arlington Park	3	2	11	16
Monmouth Park	2	1	11	14
Pimlico Race Course	3	2	6	11
Oaklawn Park	1	3	6	10
Fair Grounds	0	4	6	10
Turfway Park	0	2	5	7
Hawthorne Race Course	0	2	4	6
Delaware Park	0	2	3	5
Golden Gate Fields	0	1	4	5
Lone Star Park	0	0	5	5
Bay Meadows Race Course	0	0	4	4
Meadowlands	0	1	3	4
Laurel Park	0	2	1	3
Colonial Downs	0	1	1	2
Hoosier Park	0	1	1	2
Philadelphia Park	0	2	0	2
Prairie Meadows	0	1	1	2
Tampa Bay Downs	0	0	2	2
Delta Downs	0	0	1	1
Ellis Park	0	0	1	1
Emerald Downs	0	0	1	1
Kentucky Downs	0	0	1	1
Louisiana Downs	0	1	0	1
Mountaineer Park	0	0	1	1
Sam Houston Race Park	0	0	1	1
Suffolk Downs	0	1	0	1
Thistledown	0	1	0	1
Totals	**104**	**160**	**211**	**475**

The first North American gradings, totaling 330 races, were announced in January 1973, and the English Jockey Club immediately accepted them. Fasig-Tipton Co. began to publish the gradings in its catalogs in 1975, and Keeneland Association followed in '76. In 1998, Canadian racing authorities began to grade that nation's races, and the name of the TOBA-led organization was changed to the American Graded Stakes Committee and dealt only with United States stakes races.

Grades of all America's best races are reviewed annually by the American Graded Stakes Committee because stakes programs are dynamic and ever-changing products of conditions. The quality of any race's contestants may differ markedly from one year to the next. When a trend in the quality of the field of a race is established, be it improving or deteriorating, the race is reevaluated for grading. Members have said they take a five-year view of each race when considering the gradings.

Committee

The committee has ten voting members: five TOBA members serving five-year terms and five racing official members elected by the TOBA committee members and serving three-year terms. In addition, the committee's grading sessions have guest observers and invited guests. To be considered for membership on the committee, a candidate must have served as a guest observer for at least one grading session.

Members of the committee for the December 1, 2005, sessions at which '06 gradings were determined:

TOBA: C. Steven Duncker (chairman), John Amerman, Rollin W. Baugh, Dell Hancock, and Peter Willmott.

Racing official members: Rogers Beasley, Michael Dempsey, Michael Harlow, Thomas S. Robbins, and Robert D. Umphrey.

Guest observers: Sam Abbey, P. J. Campo, Sean Greely, Rick Hammerle, and Eric Johnston.

Invited guests: Bob Bork, Bill Casner, Carl Hamilton, Junichi Hasegawa, and Iain Woolnough.

Criteria

To be eligible for grading, a race must meet several criteria for being graded and for retaining the status. Among the criteria are:

Purse: The race must have a minimum purse, excluding state-bred supplements, of: $250,000 for Grade 1, $150,000 for Grade 2, and $100,000 for Grade 3.

Continuity: In general, a race must have two prior runnings under essentially the same conditions to be graded, although in rare circumstances Grade 1 status has been accorded immediately to races of special note, such as the Breeders' Cup races. Races with restrictions other than sex or age are not eligible.

Drug testing: Post-race tests must meet or exceed guidelines in the committee's drug testing protocol.

In addition, if track management changes a graded race from dirt to grass, or vice versa, or changes the race's distance by more than one-quarter mile or from less than one mile to more than one mile, or vice versa, the race will be considered a new race and ineligible for grading until it has been run twice under the same conditions. If a race's place on the calendar is changed substantially, such as from July to January, the race's grading may be reviewed.

Seven votes are required to raise any grading, and six votes are needed to downgrade a race.

In determining a grading, the committee considers the quality of its field over the prior five years as measured by several statistical yardsticks. Among the considerations are:

Summary of Grade Changes

	No.	% Graded Stakes	Change from 2005
Grade 1	104	21.9%	4%
Grade 2	160	33.7%	0.6%
Grade 3	211	44.4%	1.4%

- Points based on number of in-the-money finishes in unrestricted black-type races;
- Percentage of graded stakes winners in the field;
- Quality points assigned to the race based on the number of graded stakes winners in the field; and
- Ratings of the North American Rating Committee, a panel composed of racing secretaries that each week assigns a hypothetical weight to every horse running in American black-type races.

Beginning in 1999, graded turf races moved to the main track because of course conditions were automatically downgraded one grade, although the American Graded Stakes Committee reviews each such race within five days of the running and can restore the original grading. The change in grading affects only that year's running and is not considered in the grading process.

The American Graded Stakes Committee no-

Purse Comparison of Graded and Group Races by Country

	Grade 1		Grade 2		Grade 3		Total	
Country	Races	Average First Money	Races	Average First Money	Races	Average First Money	Races	Average First Money
2004 Racing Season								
Canada	3	$650,000	10	$178,296	25	$114,418	38	$173,511
Ireland	12	378,076	8	107,627	26	65,516	46	154,376
Great Britain	31	326,886	40	104,883	62	53,718	133	133,476
France	27	254,844	27	78,387	54	45,786	108	106,197
Italy	8	225,094	5	101,293	13	52,081	27	106,197
Germany	7	244,733	13	80,378	28	47,892	48	85,396
United States	100	402,694	154	153,891	219	86,285	473	175,190
2003 Racing Season								
Canada*	4	$529,163	11	$181,931	25	$99,728	40	$165,277
Ireland	10	364,350	9	94,640	23	55,865	42	136,785
Great Britain	29	349,753	35	103,734	59	53,072	123	137,437
France	26	245,185	27	72,904	54	41,366	107	98,851
Italy	8	158,769	6	73,777	11	40,239	25	86,261
Germany	7	206,529	14	64,929	24	39,167	45	73,216
United States	101	344,786	148	150,868	213	88,597	462	164,552
2002 Racing Season								
Canada*	5	$456,000	10	$153,000	26	$86,538	41	$147,805
Ireland	10	322,186	5	83,002	23	50,275	38	126,136
Great Britain	28	300,829	29	91,728	54	46,879	111	122,656
France	26	186,720	27	55,834	54	31,680	107	75,456
Italy	8	160,793	6	71,087	11	42,502	25	87,21
Germany	7	187,475	13	63,804	25	38,246	45	68,843
United States	100	343,832	150	152,295	217	87,469	467	$163,187

*Canada listed in Canadian dollars; all others United States dollars or equivalents

tifies racetracks with races in the lowest echelons of their respective gradings that the races may be downgraded, but the race will not be considered for downgrading until it has been run another time.

More graded stakes are offered in the U.S. than all group races throughout Europe, which has evoked criticism among some Europeans who contend that American black type is cheapened by the plentiful graded races. However, less than 1% of all American races are graded, a smaller percentage than Ireland, Great Britain, or France.

2006 Grade Stakes Changes

Upgrades

Grade 2 to Grade 1: Clark Handicap (Churchill Downs), Oak Leaf Stakes (Oak Tree at Santa Anita), Princess Rooney Handicap (Calder Race Course), Spinaway Stakes (Saratoga Race Course).

Grade 3 to Grade 2: Ballston Spa Breeders' Cup Handicap (Saratoga), Bed o' Roses Breeders' Cup Handicap (Aqueduct), Jefferson Cup Stakes (Churchill), Jenny Wiley Stakes (Keeneland Race Course), Jim Murray Memorial Handicap (Hollywood Park), Vinery Madison Stakes (Keeneland), Virginia Derby (Colonial Downs).

Ungraded to Grade 3: Ack Ack Handicap (Hollywood), Arlington Oaks (Arlington Park), Bourbonette Breeders' Cup Stakes (Turfway Park), Dallas Turf Cup Handicap (Lone Star Park), Fair Grounds Breeders' Cup Handicap (Fair Grounds), John B. Connally Handicap (Sam Houston Race Park), Kenny Noe Jr. Handicap (Calder), Santa Paula Stakes (Santa Anita Park), Sham Stakes (Santa Anita), Sir Beaufort Stakes (Santa Anita), Stage Door Betty Handicap (Calder), Victory Ride Stakes (Saratoga).

Downgrades

Grade 2 to Grade 3: Orchid Handicap (Gulfstream Park), Pan American Handicap (Gulfstream).

Grade 3 to Ungraded: Desert Stormer Handicap (Hollywood), Flash Stakes (Belmont Park), Lafayette Stakes (Keeneland).

2006 Graded Stakes by State

State	G1	G2	G3	Total
California	33	56	43	132
New York	38	42	36	116
Kentucky	20	21	37	78
Florida	4	14	32	50
Illinois	3	4	15	22
New Jersey	2	2	14	18
Maryland	3	4	7	14
Louisiana	0	5	7	12
Arkansas	1	3	6	10
Texas	0	0	6	6
Delaware	0	2	3	5
Indiana	0	1	1	2
Iowa	0	1	1	2
Pennsylvania	0	2	0	2
Virginia	0	1	1	2
Ohio	0	1	0	1
Massachusetts	0	1	0	1
Washington	0	0	1	1
West Virginia	0	0	1	1
Totals	**104**	**160**	**211**	**475**

Percentages of Best Races by Country

	Total Races	Stakes	Graded Stakes	G1 Stakes
2004 Racing Season				
Canada	5,263	249 (4.7%)	38 (0.7%)	3 (0.1%)
Ireland	845	97 (11.5%)	46 (5.4%)	12 (1.4%)
Great Britain	5,241	279 (5.3%)	133 (2.5%)	31 (0.6%)
France	4,026	232 (5.7%)	108 (2.6%)	27 (0.6%)
Italy	4,898	78 (1.6%)	27 (0.5%)	9 (0.2%)
Germany	1,891	110 (5.8%)	48 (2.5%)	7 (0.2%)
United States	53,403	1,879 (2.5%)	473 (0.9%)	100 (0.2%)
2003 Racing Season				
Canada	5,498	259 (4.7%)	40 (0.7%)	4 (0.1%)
Ireland	850	94 (11.1%)	42 (4.9%)	10 (1.2%)
Great Britain	4,761	281 (5.9%)	1.3 (2.5%)	29 (0.6%)
France	3,981	231 (5.8%)	107 (2.6%)	26 (0.6%)
Italy	4,772	76 (1.6%)	25 (0.5%)	8 (0.2%)
Germany	2,060	108 (5.2%)	45 (2.2%)	7 (0.3%)
United States	53,309	1,923 (3.6%)	462 (0.9%)	101 (0.2%)
2002 Racing Season				
Canada	5,592	267 (4.8%)	41 (0.7%)	5 (0.1%)
Ireland	788	81 (10.3%)	38 (4.8%)	10 (1.2%)
Great Britain	4,572	250 (5.5%)	111 (2.4%)	28 (0.6%)
France	3,901	230 (5.9%)	107 (2.7%)	26 (0.7%)
Italy	4,752	73 (1.5%)	25 (0.5%)	8 (0.2%)
Germany	2,382	103 (4.3%)	45 (1.9%)	7 (0.3%)
United States	54,117	1,970 (3.6%)	467 (0.9%)	100 (0.2%)

American Graded Stakes

Ack Ack Handicap

Grade 3 in 2006. Churchill Downs, three-year-olds and up, 7½ furlongs, dirt. Held October 30, 2005, with a gross value of $112,200. First held in 1991. First graded in 1997. Stakes record 1:28.34 (2005 Straight Line).

Year	Winner	Jockey	Second	Third	Strs	Time	1st Purse
2005	**Straight Line**, 3, 114	S. Bridgmohan	Vicarage, 3, 117	Level Playingfield, 4, 115	9	**1:28.34**	$69,564
2004	**Sir Cherokee**, 4, 114	C. H. Borel	Fire Slam, 3, 117	Slate Run, 4, 106	6	1:29.48	102,486
2003	**Cappuchino**, 4, 117	J. K. Court	Pass Rush, 4, 116	Twilight Road, 6, 116	7	1:31.66	102,579
2002	**Twilight Road**, 5, 113	P. Day	Mountain General, 4, 116	Binthebest, 5, 113	9	1:29.39	69,874
2001	**Illusioned**, 3, 118	P. Day	Strawberry Affair, 3, 112	Fappie's Notebook, 4, 116	11	1:28.63	70,866
2000	**Chindi**, 6, 113	T. T. Doocy	Smolderin Heart, 5, 113	Millencolin, 3, 113	10	1:29.30	70,494
1999	**Littlebitlively**, 5, 119	C. H. Borel	Run Johnny, 7, 117	Tactical Cat, 3, 117	11	1:28.97	71,672
1998	**Distorted Humor**, 5, 120	C. H. Borel	Crafty Friend, 5, 113	Chindi, 4, 113	6	1:29.61	68,262
1997	**Cat's Career**, 4, 108	W. Martinez	Rare Rock, 4, 112	Victor Cooley, 4, 122	6	1:34.64	69,130
1996	**Western Trader**, 5, 113	C. H. Borel	Top Account, 4, 117	Strategic Intent, 4, 113	8	1:29.84	70,308
1995	**Mystery Storm**, 3, 112	C. Gonzalez	I'm Very Irish, 4, 113	Tarzans Blade, 4, 116	10	1:29.10	75,660
1994	**Lost Pan**, 4, 114	D. M. Barton	Sir Vixen, 6, 112	Groovy Jett, 3, 112	8	1:30.27	54,795
1991	**Seven Spades**, 4, 108	D. W. Cox	Discover, 3, 114	Senator to Be, 4, 115	12	1:37.62	38,513

Named for Forked Lightning Ranch's 1971 Horse of the Year and '69 Derby Trial winner Ack Ack (1966 c. by Battle Joined). Not held 1992-'93. Equaled track record 1995. Track record 2001.

Ack Ack Handicap

Grade 3 in 2006. Hollywood Park, three-year-olds and up, 7½ furlongs, dirt. Held June 10, 2006, with a gross value of $100,000. First held in 2001. First graded in 2006. Stakes record 1:27.15 (2003 Joey Franco).

Year	Winner	Jockey	Second	Third	Strs	Time	1st Purse
2006	**Lucky J. H.**, 4, 119	P. A. Valenzuela	Captain Squire, 7, 119	Primerica, 8, 115	7	1:29.66	$60,000
2005	**McCann's Mojave**, 5, 116	J. Valdivia Jr.	Congrats, 5, 121	St Averil, 4, 115	8	1:27.23	60,210
2004	**Taste of Paradise**, 5, 116	J. K. Court	Buddy Gil, 4, 122	Black Bart, 5, 116	8	1:28.02	46,845
2003	**Joey Franco**, 4, 118	P. A. Valenzuela	Kela, 5, 117	Publication, 4, 116	7	**1:27.15**	60,275
2001	**Grey Memo**, 4, 122	G. K. Gomez	National Saint, 5, 116	Elaborate, 6, 122	8	1:28.19	59,460

Named for Forked Lightning Ranch's 1971 Horse of the Year and '71 Hollywood Gold Cup winner Ack Ack (1966 c. by Battle Joined). Not held 2002. Ack Ack S. 2001. Four-year-olds and up 2001.

Acorn Stakes

Grade 1 in 2006. Belmont Park, three-year-olds, fillies, 1 mile, dirt. Held June 10, 2006, with a gross value of $250,000. First held in 1931. First graded in 1973. Stakes record 1:34.05 (2002 You).

Year	Winner	Jockey	Second	Third	Strs	Time	1st Purse
2006	**Bushfire**, 3, 121	A. O. Solis	Hello Liberty, 3, 121	Last Romance, 3, 121	7	1:35.89	$150,000
2005	**Round Pond**, 3, 121	S. Elliott	Smuggler, 3, 121	In the Gold, 3, 121	6	1:35.33	150,000
2004	**Island Sand**, 3, 121	T. J. Thompson	Society Selection, 3, 121	Friendly Michelle, 3, 121	8	1:34.89	150,000
2003	**Bird Town**, 3, 121	E. S. Prado	Lady Tak, 3, 121	Final Round, 3, 121	7	1:35.29	150,000
2002	**You**, 3, 121	J. D. Bailey	Willa On the Move, 3, 121	Bella Bellucci, 3, 121	5	**1:34.05**	150,000
2001	**Forest Secrets**, 3, 121	C. J. McCarron	Victory Ride, 3, 121	Real Cozzy, 3, 121	8	1:34.92	120,000
2000	**Finder's Fee**, 3, 121	J. R. Velazquez	C'Est L'Amour, 3, 121	Roxelana, 3, 121	10	1:37.38	120,000
1999	**Three Ring**, 3, 121	J. D. Bailey	Better Than Honour, 3, 121	Madison's Charm, 3, 121	8	1:36.16	120,000
1998	**Jersey Girl**, 3, 121	M. E. Smith	Santaria, 3, 121	Brave Deed, 3, 121	10	1:36.32	90,000
1997	**Sharp Cat**, 3, 121	G. L. Stevens	Dixie Flag, 3, 121	Ajina, 3, 121	7	1:34.41	90,000
1996	**Star de Lady Ann**, 3, 121	M. E. Smith	Yanks Music, 3, 121	Stop Traffic, 3, 121	12	1:34.62	90,000
1995	**Cat's Cradle**, 3, 121	C. W. Antley	Country Cat, 3, 121	Lucky Lavender Gal, 3, 121	7	1:37.53	90,000
1994	**Inside Information**, 3, 121	M. E. Smith	Cinnamon Sugar (Ire), 3, 121	Sovereign Kitty, 3, 121	5	1:34.26	90,000
1993	**Sky Beauty**, 3, 121	M. E. Smith	Educated Risk, 3, 121	In Her Glory, 3, 121	6	1:35.50	90,000
1992	**Prospectors Delite**, 3, 121	P. Day	Pleasant Stage, 3, 121	Turnback the Alarm, 3, 121	12	1:35.10	113,400
1991	**Meadow Star**, 3, 121	J. D. Bailey	Versailles Treaty, 3, 121	Dazzle Me Jolie, 3, 121	6	1:37.42	103,680
1990	**Stella Madrid**, 3, 121	A. T. Cordero Jr.	Danzig's Beauty, 3, 121	Seaside Attraction, 3, 121	7	1:36.00	104,580
1989	**Open Mind**, 3, 121	A. T. Cordero Jr.	Hot Novel, 3, 121	Triple Strike, 3, 121	11	1:35.40	111,960
1988	**Aptostar**, 3, 121	R. G. Davis	Topicount, 3, 121	Avie's Gal, 3, 121	9	1:34.80	109,980
1987	**Grecian Flight**, 3, 121	C. Perret	Fiesta Gal, 3, 121	Bound, 3, 121	13	1:35.20	113,580
1986	**Lotka**, 3, 121	J. D. Bailey	Dynamic Star, 3, 121	Life At the Top, 3, 121	8	1:35.20	136,080
1985	**Mom's Command**, 3, 121	A. Fuller	Le l'Argent, 3, 121	Diplomette, 3, 121	8	1:35.80	113,040
1984	**Miss Oceana**, 3, 121	E. Maple	Life's Magic, 3, 121	Proud Clarioness, 3, 121	9	1:35.80	135,720
1983	**Ski Goggle**, 3, 121	C. J. McCarron	Princess Rooney, 3, 121	Thirty Flags, 3, 121	9	1:35.00	69,360
1982	**Cupecoy's Joy**, 3, 121	A. Santiago	Nancy Huang, 3, 121	Vestris, 3, 121	9	1:34.20	51,750
1981	**Heavenly Cause**, 3, 121	L. A. Pincay Jr.	Dame Mysterieuse, 3, 121	Autumn Glory, 3, 121	7	1:35.20	50,850
1980	**Bold 'n Determined**, 3, 121	E. Delahoussaye	Mitey Lively, 3, 121	Sugar and Spice, 3, 121	8	1:36.80	50,400
1979	**Davona Dale**, 3, 121	J. Velasquez	Eloquent, 3, 121	Plankton, 3, 121	8	1:36.00	50,130
1978	**Tempest Queen**, 3, 121	J. Velasquez	Lakeville Miss, 3, 121	White Star Line, 3, 121	6	1:35.40	31,920
1977	**Bring Out the Band**, 3, 121	D. Brumfield	Your Place Or Mine, 3, 121	Mrs. Warren, 3, 121	11	1:36.80	33,690
1976	**Dearly Precious**, 3, 121	J. Velasquez	Optimistic Gal, 3, 121	Tell Me All, 3, 121	8	1:35.80	33,390
1975	**Ruffian**, 3, 121	J. Vasquez	Somethingregal, 3, 121	Gallant Trial, 3, 121	7	1:34.80	33,660

1974	**Special Team**, 3, 121	M. A. Rivera	Stage Door Betty, 3, 121	Raisela, 3, 121	9	1:35.40	$33,960
	Chris Evert, 3, 121	J. Velasquez	Clear Copy, 3, 121	Fiesta Libre, 3, 121	9	1:36.00	33,960
1973	**Windy's Daughter**, 3, 121	B. Baeza	Poker Night, 3, 121	Voler, 3, 121	11	1:35.40	36,540

Named for the phrase, "Great oaks from little acorns grow"; in the past the Acorn immediately preceded the Coaching Club American Oaks. Held at Aqueduct 1960-'67, 1969-'75. Two divisions 1951, 1970, 1974. Dead heat for first 1954, 1956.

Adena Stallions' Miss Preakness Stakes

Grade 3 in 2006. Pimlico Race Course, three-year-olds, fillies, 6 furlongs, dirt. Held May 19, 2006, with a gross value of $125,000. First held in 1986. First graded in 2002. Stakes record 1:10 (2000 Lucky Livi).

Year	Winner	Jockey	Second	Third	Strs	Time	1st Purse
2006	**Wildcat Bettie B**, 3, 118	R. A. Dominguez	Press Camp, 3, 116	G City Gal, 3, 118	7	1:10.05	$75,000
2005	**Burnish**, 3, 118	R. Bejarano	Partners Due, 3, 116	Hot Storm, 3, 122	7	1:12.40	60,000
2004	**Forest Music**, 3, 115	R. A. Dominguez	Stephan's Angel, 3, 119	Fall Fashion, 3, 119	11	1:10.97	60,000
2003	**Belong to Sea**, 3, 117	J. Castellano	Chimichurri, 3, 122	Forever Partners, 3, 119	5	1:11.10	60,000
2002	**Vesta**, 3, 117	M. G. Pino	Willa On the Move, 3, 117	Shameful, 3, 119	6	1:10.25	60,000
2001	**Kimbralata**, 3, 117	T. Dunkelberger	Carafe, 3, 117	Stormy Pick, 3, 122	5	1:11.20	60,000
2000	**Lucky Livi**, 3, 119	R. Wilson	Big Bambu, 3, 117	Swept Away, 3, 119	5	**1:10.00**	60,000
1999	**Hookedonthefeelin**, 3, 122	G. L. Stevens	Silent Valay, 3, 122	Paula's Girl, 3, 122	4	1:11.26	60,000
1998	**Storm Beauty**, 3, 119	C. R. Woods Jr.	Brac Drifter, 3, 115	Hair Spray, 3, 122	5	1:10.81	45,000
1997	**Weather Vane**, 3, 122	M. G. Pino	Move, 3, 122	Cayman Sunset, 3, 122	8	1:11.94	64,740
1996	**Nic's Halo**, 3, 117	R. Wilson	Palette Knife, 3, 115	Crafty But Sweet, 3, 122	4	1:11.75	32,655
1995	**Lilly Capote**, 3, 122	G. L. Stevens	Broad Smile, 3, 122	Norstep, 3, 122	7	1:10.90	32,640
1994	**Foolish Kisses**, 3, 113	E. S. Prado	Aly's Conquest, 3, 114	Platinum Punch, 3, 113	8	1:12.45	32,730
1993	**My Rosa**, 3, 113	E. S. Prado	Fighting Jet, 3, 121	Code Blum, 3, 121	5	1:11.33	32,175
1992	**Toots La Mae**, 3, 113	J. Bravo	Missy White Oak, 3, 118	Jazzy One, 3, 121	6	1:11.97	26,505
1991	**Missy's Music**, 3, 114	M. G. Pino	Dixie Rouge, 3, 113	Accent Knightly, 3, 113	6	1:11.48	15,975
1990	**Love Me a Lot**, 3, 115	C. J. McCarron	Dixie Landera, 3, 113	Tabs, 3, 116	6	1:11.40	19,170
1989	**Montoya**, 3, 118	L. A. Pincay Jr.	dh-Another Boom, 3, 121 dh-Cojinx, 3, 121		7	1:10.60	22,470
1988	**Caromine**, 3, 115	C. J. McCarron	Light Beat, 3, 118	Saved by Grace, 3, 118	9	1:13.00	24,911
1987	**Cutlasee**, 3, 116	C. J. McCarron	I'm Out, 3, 114	Pelican Bay, 3, 115	8	1:12.60	21,158
1986	**Marion's Madel**, 3, 115	C. J. McCarron	Zigbelle, 3, 115	Babbling Brook, 3, 116	8	1:12.80	21,060

Held day before the Preakness S. (G1). Sponsored by Adena Springs, which is owned by Magna Entertainment Corp. Chairman Frank Stronach 2004-'06. Miss Preakness S. 1986-2003. Dead heat for second 1989.

Adirondack Stakes

Grade 2 in 2006. Saratoga Race Course, two-year-olds, fillies, 6 furlongs, dirt. Held July 27, 2005, with a gross value of $150,000. First held in 1901. First graded in 1973. Stakes record 1:09.60 (1985 Nervous Baba).

Year	Winner	Jockey	Second	Third	Strs	Time	1st Purse
2005	**Folklore**, 2, 117	C. H. Velasquez	Fifth Avenue, 2, 121	Truart, 2, 117	7	1:13.66	$90,000
2003	**Whoopi Cat**, 2, 116	E. S. Prado	Unbridled Beauty, 2, 116	Eye Dazzler, 2, 116	7	1:17.51	90,000
2002	**Awesome Humor**, 2, 122	P. Day	Stellar, 2, 116	Holiday Runner, 2, 122	6	1:17.75	90,000
2001	**You**, 2, 115	E. S. Prado	Cashier's Dream, 2, 122	Magic Storm, 2, 115	7	1:15.16	90,000
2000	**Raging Fever**, 2, 122	J. D. Bailey	Two Item Limit, 2, 117	Secret Lover, 2, 117	6	1:17.47	90,000
1999	**Regally Appealing**, 2, 114	E. S. Prado	Miss Wineshine, 2, 122	Trump My Heart, 2, 114	6	1:16.86	90,000
1998	**Things Change**, 2, 114	J. A. Santos	Extended Applause, 2, 117	Brittons Hill, 2, 114	9	1:18.14	90,000
1997	**Salty Perfume**, 2, 114	S. J. Sellers	Brac Drifter, 2, 114	Joustabout, 2, 114	6	1:17.94	90,000
1996	**Storm Song**, 2, 113	P. Day	Last Two States, 2, 113	dh-Exclusive Hold, 2, 113 dh-Larkwhistle, 2, 116	9	1:17.60	84,075
1995	**Flat Fleet Feet**, 2, 113	M. E. Smith	Steady Cat, 2, 112	Western Dreamer, 2, 120	7	1:16.74	65,760
1994	**Seeking Regina**, 2, 114	J. D. Bailey	Changing Ways, 2, 119	Phone Bird, 2, 114	7	1:18.51	66,600
1993	**Astas Foxy Lady**, 2, 119	R. P. Romero	Footing, 2, 114	Casa Eire, 2, 119	6	1:10.11	68,520
1992	**Sky Beauty**, 2, 116	E. Maple	Missed the Storm, 2, 114	Distinct Habit, 2, 121	7	1:10.16	70,560
1991	**American Royale**, 2, 119	A. T. Gryder	Bless Our Home, 2, 114	Turnback the Alarm, 2, 119	8	1:10.72	71,640
1990	**Really Quick**, 2, 114	A. T. Cordero Jr.	Devilish Touch, 2, 119	Ferber's Follies, 2, 114	9	1:11.40	54,270
1989	**Dance Colony**, 2, 116	J. A. Santos	In Full Cry, 2, 114	Saratoga Sizzle, 2, 114	6	1:11.80	52,200
1988	**Pat Copelan**, 2, 114	P. Day	Channel Three, 2, 116	Premier Playmate, 2, 116	6	1:10.80	66,780
1987	**Over All**, 2, 121	A. T. Cordero Jr.	Flashy Runner, 2, 114	Careless Flirt, 2, 114	5	1:10.60	64,890
1986	**Sacahuista**, 2, 119	C. J. McCarron	Collins, 2, 114	Release the Lyd, 2, 116	7	1:11.00	53,280
1985	**Nervous Baba**, 2, 114	J. Velasquez	Family Style, 2, 114	Steal a Kiss, 2, 114	8	**1:09.60**	54,450
1984	**Contredance**, 2, 114	E. Maple	Outstandingly, 2, 114	Oriental, 2, 114	7	1:10.40	53,100
1983	**Buzz My Bell**, 2, 114	J. Velasquez	Upturning, 2, 116	Mrs. Flagler, 2, 116	6	1:12.40	33,720
1982	**Jelly Bean Holiday**, 2, 116	J. Fell	Midnight Rapture, 2, 114	Flying Lassie, 2, 114	7	1:10.80	34,920
1981	**Thrilld n Delightd**, 2, 114	J. Velasquez	Apalachee Honey, 2, 119	Trove, 2, 116	9	1:10.80	35,160
1980	**Sweet Revenge**, 2, 119	J. Velasquez	Companionship, 2, 114	Honey's Appeal, 2, 114	7	1:10.40	34,080
1979	**Smart Angle**, 2, 119	S. Maple	Lucky My Way, 2, 114	Andrea F., 2, 114	9	1:11.00	26,835
1978	**Whisper Fleet**, 2, 119	J. Cruguet	Island Kitty, 2, 114	Golferette, 2, 114	8	1:10.00	22,410
1977	**L'Alezane**, 2, 121	R. Turcotte	Sunny Bay, 2, 121	Misgivings, 2, 114	7	1:10.60	22,335
1976	**Harvest Girl**, 2, 114	J. Cruguet	Bonnie Empress, 2, 114	Drama Critic, 2, 119	7	1:11.00	22,545
1975	**Optimistic Gal**, 2, 120	B. Baeza	Glory Glory, 2, 120	Against all Flags, 2, 120	5	1:11.20	22,515

1974	**Laughing Bridge**, 2, 120	L. A. Pincay Jr.	Stulcer, 2, 120	Some Swinger, 2, 120	6	1:10.80	$16,950
1973	**Talking Picture**, 2, 120	B. Baeza	In Hot Pursuit, 2, 120	Bedknob, 2, 120	10	1:11.00	17,625

Named for the Adirondack mountain region of New York. Grade 3 1975-'83. Adirondack H. 1901-'45. Held at Belmont Park 1943-'45. Held at Jamaica 1953-'54. Not held 1911-'12, 1946-'52, 1956-'61, 2004. $5\frac{1}{2}$ furlongs 1953-'55. $6\frac{1}{2}$ furlongs 1994-2003. Both sexes 1901-'29. Dead heat for third 1996.

Aegon Turf Sprint Stakes

Grade 3 in 2006. Churchill Downs, three-year-olds and up, 5 furlongs, turf. Held May 5, 2006, with a gross value of $116,000. First held in 1995. First graded in 2001. Stakes record :56.01 (2003 Fiscally Speaking).

Year	Winner	Jockey	Second	Third	Strs	Time	1st Purse
2006	**Man Of Illusion (Aus)**, 5, 118	J. R. Leparoux	Justice for Auston, 7, 118	Atticus Kristy, 5, 124	12	:56.28	$66,886
2005	**Mighty Beau**, 6, 121	P. A. Valenzuela	Chosen Chief, 6, 119	Sgt. Bert, 4, 119	10	:56.18	70,370
2004	**Lydgate**, 4, 114	P. Day	Mighty Beau, 5, 117	Banned in Boston, 4, 114	11	:56.56	71,114
2003	**Fiscally Speaking**, 4, 114	J. K. Court	Morluc, 7, 122	Testify, 6, 122	11	**:56.01**	71,486
2002	**Testify**, 5, 119	E. Delahoussaye	Texas Glitter, 6, 122	Gone Fishin, 6, 116	10	:57.39	75,206
2001	**Morluc**, 5, 122	R. Albarado	Testify, 4, 119	Texas Glitter, 5, 122	9	:56.60	70,494
2000	**Bold Fact**, 5, 120	R. Migliore	Howbaddouwantit, 5, 123	Fantastic Finish, 4, 114	12	:56.37	75,330
1999	**Howbaddouwantit**, 4, 123	M. E. Smith	Mr Festus, 4, 114	Three Card Willie, 4, 118	11	:56.90	71,486
1998	**Indian Rocket (GB)**, 4, 116	G. L. Stevens	G H's Pleasure, 6, 120	Claire's Honor, 4, 114	12	:57.32	75,950
1997	**Sandtrap**, 4, 123	A. O. Solis	Appealing Skier, 4, 114	G H's Pleasure, 5, 120	11	:56.51	71,734
1996	**Danjur**, 4, 114	J. D. Bailey	Hello Paradise, 5, 114	Linear, 6, 123	10	:56.09	57,281
1995	**Long Suit**, 4, 114	W. Martinez	Bold n' Flashy, 6, 120	†Scottish Fantasy, 7, 111	11	:56.90	57,086

Sponsored by the AEGON Group N.V. of The Hague, the Netherlands 1999-2006. Churchill Downs Turf Sprint S. 1995-'98. Established course record 1995. Course record 1996, 2003. †Denotes female.

Affirmed Handicap

Grade 3 in 2006. Hollywood Park, three-year-olds, $1\frac{1}{16}$ miles, dirt. Held June 18, 2005, with a gross value of $102,998. First held in 1940. First graded in 1973. Stakes record 1:40.83 (1999 General Challenge).

Year	Winner	Jockey	Second	Third	Strs	Time	1st Purse
2005	**Indian Ocean**, 3, 115	J. K. Court	Surf Cat, 3, 116	Dover Dere, 3, 118	4	1:42.53	$63,060
2004	**Boomzeeboom**, 3, 115	V. Espinoza	Twice as Bad, 3, 121	Wimplestiltskin, 3, 116	9	1:42.11	66,120
2003	**Eye of the Tiger**, 3, 119	A. O. Solis	Ministers Wild Cat, 3, 118	Bullistic, 3, 115	4	1:42.30	63,120
2002	**Came Home**, 3, 124	C. J. McCarron	Tracemark, 3, 120	Calkins Road, 3, 117	6	1:41.99	64,500
2001	**Until Sundown**, 3, 117	G. L. Stevens	Top Hit, 3, 114	Bayou the Moon, 3, 118	5	1:43.10	60,000
2000	**Tiznow**, 3, 111	V. Espinoza	Dixie Union, 3, 122	Millencolin, 3, 117	6	1:42.35	80,550
1999	**General Challenge**, 3, 124	D. R. Flores	Desert Hero, 3, 120	Crowning Storm, 3, 116	5	**1:40.83**	75,000
1998	**Old Trieste**, 3, 118	C. J. McCarron	Old Topper, 3, 117	Kraal, 3, 116	4	1:41.84	62,340
1997	**Deputy Commander**, 3, 117	C. S. Nakatani	Hello (Ire), 3, 121	Holzmeister, 3, 121	6	1:42.80	61,500
1996	**Hesabull**, 3, 117	E. Delahoussaye	Benton Creek, 3, 116	Semoran, 3, 118	7	1:43.25	61,050
1995	**Mr Purple**, 3, 120	C. S. Nakatani	Pumpkin House, 3, 115	Oncefortheroad, 3, 114	6	1:42.37	77,050
1994	**R Friar Tuck**, 3, 113	J. D. Bailey	Pollock's Luck, 3, 114	Wild Invader, 3, 115	8	1:49.08	96,100
1993	**Codified**, 3, 117	G. L. Stevens	Roman Image, 3, 117	Future Storm, 3, 118	7	1:48.85	94,100
1992	**Natural Nine**, 3, 117	L. A. Pincay Jr.	Prospect for Four, 3, 114	Never Round, 3, 117	8	1:49.42	95,500
1991	**Compelling Sound**, 3, 118	G. L. Stevens	Best Pal, 3, 123	Caliche's Secret, 3, 117	5	1:47.90	91,300
1990	**Stalwart Charger**, 3, 120	L. A. Pincay Jr.	Toby Jug, 3, 112	Kentucky Jazz, 3, 120	5	1:48.40	91,100
1989	**Raise a Stanza**, 3, 115	C. A. Black	Broke the Mold, 3, 112	Prized, 3, 116	12	1:48.40	102,200
1988	**Iz a Saros**, 3, 113	A. T. Gryder	Stalwars, 3, 119	Bel Air Dancer, 3, 117	8	1:49.00	95,900
1987	**Candi's Gold**, 3, 116	G. L. Stevens	On the Line, 3, 116	The Medic, 3, 116	6	1:47.60	93,000
1986	**†Melair**, 3, 115	P. A. Valenzuela	Southern Halo, 3, 113	Snow Chief, 3, 127	12	1:32.80	220,000
1985	**Pancho Villa**, 3, 118	L. A. Pincay Jr.	Proudest Doon, 3, 118	Nostalgia's Star, 3, 118	9	1:33.80	64,050
1984	**Tights**, 3, 119	L. A. Pincay Jr.	M. Double M., 3, 116	Precisionist, 3, 121	6	1:48.60	46,850
1983	**My Habitony**, 3, 115	D. Pierce	Tanks Brigade, 3, 119	Hyperborean, 3, 115	6	1:48.60	47,250
1982	**Journey At Sea**, 3, 122	C. J. McCarron	Cassaleria, 3, 120	Guachan, 3, 112	9	1:46.80	49,600
1981	**Stancharry**, 3, 117	P. A. Valenzuela	Dusty Hula, 3, 116	Seafood, 3, 117	6	1:51.00	47,150
1980	**Score Twenty Four**, 3, 114	D. G. McHargue	dh-First Albert, 3, 116 dh-Loto Canada, 3, 119		6	1:48.20	37,200
1979	**Valdez**, 3, 119	L. A. Pincay Jr.	Pole Position, 3, 118	Beau's Eagle, 3, 123	5	1:47.40	37,500
1978	**Radar Ahead**, 3, 123	D. G. McHargue	Double Win, 3, 114	Think Snow, 3, 122	6	1:48.40	38,200
1977	**Text**, 3, 119	D. G. McHargue	Bad 'n Big, 3, 122	Sonny Collins, 3, 118	5	1:47.20	37,000
1976	**L'Heureux**, 3, 119	D. Pierce	Romeo, 3, 115	Crystal Water, 3, 125	7	1:47.40	38,600
1975	**Forceten**, 3, 119	D. Pierce	Sibirri, 3, 114	Larrikin, 3, 121	5	1:48.80	37,300
1974	**Battery E.**, 3, 117	L. A. Pincay Jr.	Stardust Mel, 3, 120	Agitate, 3, 124	5	1:47.80	36,800
1973	**Carry the Banner**, 3, 115	A. Pineda	Rod, 3, 119	Out of the East, 3, 120	8	1:41.20	39,200

Named for Harbor View Farm's 1978, '79 Horse of the Year, '78 Triple Crown winner, and '79 Hollywood Gold Cup H. (G1) winner Affirmed (1975 c. by Exclusive Native). Formerly named in honor of Hollywood's film industry. Formerly named in honor of the Forty-niners ("argonauts") who went west to California in search of gold. Grade 2 1973-'89. Argonaut H. 1940-'60, 1973-'78. Argonaut S. 1961-'72. Silver Screen H. 1979-'92. Held at Santa Anita Park 1949. Not held 1942-'43. $1\frac{1}{16}$ miles 1940, 1944, 1946-'53, 1960-'73. 1 mile 1941, 1945, 1954-'59, 1985-'86. $1\frac{1}{8}$ miles 1979-'84, 1987-'94. Turf 1968-'72. Four-year-olds and up 1940-'41. Three-year-olds and up 1944-'59, 1986. Two divisions 1963, 1967, 1970. Dead heat for second 1980. †Denotes female.

A Gleam Invitational Handicap

Grade 2 in 2006. Hollywood Park, three-year-olds and up, fillies and mares, 7 furlongs, dirt. Held July 9, 2005, with a gross value of $150,000. First held in 1941. First graded in 1973. Stakes record 1:20.53 (1998 A. P. Assay).

Year	Winner	Jockey	Second	Third	Strs	Time	1st Purse
2005	**Alphabet Kisses**, 4, 119	G. L. Stevens	Valentine Dancer, 5, 118	Muir Beach, 4, 114	9	1:21.67	$90,000
2004	**Dream of Summer**, 5, 114	M. E. Smith	Tucked Away, 4, 116	Elusive Diva, 3, 112	9	1:21.16	90,000
2003	**Cee's Elegance**, 6, 116	V. Espinoza	You, 4, 121	Affluent, 5, 119	5	1:21.47	150,000
2002	**Irguns Angel**, 4, 116	E. Delahoussaye	Secret Liaison, 4, 116	Kalookan Queen, 6, 122	10	1:22.50	120,000
2001	**Go Go**, 4, 124	E. Delahoussaye	Kitty On the Track, 4, 115	Nany's Sweep, 5, 117	5	1:22.19	120,000
2000	**Honest Lady**, 4, 121	K. Desormeaux	Seth's Choice, 4, 115	Hookedonthefeelin, 4, 116	5	1:21.47	120,000
1999	**Enjoy the Moment**, 4, 117	D. R. Flores	Snowberg, 4, 115	Woodman's Dancer, 5, 117	6	1:21.35	120,000
1998	**A. P. Assay**, 4, 116	E. Delahoussaye	Exotic Wood, 6, 124	Closed Escrow, 5, 114	7	**1:20.53**	150,000
1997	**Toga Toga Toga**, 5, 119	G. L. Stevens	Our Summer Bid, 5, 115	Radu Cool, 5, 116	7	1:22.75	65,040
1996	**Igotrhythm**, 4, 116	E. Delahoussaye	Klassy Kim, 5, 116	Cat's Cradle, 4, 118	5	1:21.54	63,840
1995	**Angi Go**, 5, 117	G. L. Stevens	Desert Stormer, 5, 118	Dancing Mirage, 4, 115	6	1:21.45	62,700
1994	**Golden Klair (GB)**, 4, 117	C. J. McCarron	Cargo, 5, 117	Minidar, 4, 117	4	1:22.00	60,400
1993	**Bold Windy**, 4, 115	G. L. Stevens	La Spia, 4, 115	Bountiful Native, 5, 122	9	1:21.62	65,700
1992	**Forest Fealty**, 5, 116	M. A. Pedroza	Brought to Mind, 5, 120	Devil's Orchid, 5, 120	8	1:22.13	64,800
1991	**Survive**, 7, 119	R. A. Baze	Stormy But Valid, 5, 121	Brought to Mind, 4, 117	6	1:22.10	62,400
1990	**Stormy But Valid**, 4, 120	G. L. Stevens	Hot Novel, 4, 118	Tis Juliet, 4, 114	5	1:21.20	61,300
1989	**Daloma (Fr)**, 5, 115	C. J. McCarron	Survive, 5, 116	Behind the Scenes, 5, 116	7	1:21.60	47,900
1988	**Integra**, 4, 118	G. L. Stevens	Behind the Scenes, 4, 116	Carol's Wonder, 4, 117	5	1:23.00	46,100
1987	**Le l'Argent**, 5, 118	D. G. McHargue	Sari's Heroine, 4, 117	Rare Starlet, 4, 115	8	1:23.00	48,650
1986	**Outstandingly**, 4, 120	G. L. Stevens	Eloquack, 4, 110	Shywing, 4, 120	5	1:21.80	46,100
1985	**Dontstop Themusic**, 5, 121	L. A. Pincay Jr.	Lovlier Linda, 5, 122	Mimi Baker, 4, 110	4	1:21.40	36,500
1984	**Lass Trump**, 4, 116	C. J. McCarron	Pleasure Cay, 4, 116	Angel Savage (Mex), 4, 112	9	1:21.20	39,400
1983	**Matching**, 5, 121	R. Sibille	Sierva (Arg), 5, 116	Bara Lass, 4, 117	7	1:22.40	31,800
1982	**Happy Bride (Ire)**, 4, 113	W. A. Guerra	Lucky Lady Ellen, 3, 117	Jones Time Machine, 3, 112	5	1:08.40	30,700
1981	**She Can't Miss**, 4, 117	P. A. Valenzuela	Cherokee Frolic, 3, 114	Shine High, 5, 122	8	1:09.00	32,050
1980	**Great Lady M.**, 5, 115	P. A. Valenzuela	Double Deceit, 4, 114	Splendid Girl, 4, 122	6	1:08.40	30,550
1979	**Delice**, 4, 116	E. Delahoussaye	Great Lady M., 4, 117	Sateen, 3, 111	6	1:08.80	25,100
1978	**Reminiscing**, 4, 124	L. A. Pincay Jr.	Sing Back, 5, 122	Thirteenth Hope, 5, 113	7	1:09.60	25,450
1977	**Just a Kick**, 5, 121	S. Hawley	Cornish Colleen, 4, 113	Winter Solstice, 5, 122	5	1:09.40	18,450
1976	**Winter Solstice**, 4, 119	J. Lambert	Vol Au Vent, 4, 120	Powerful Lady, 4, 118	8	1:09.00	19,700
1975	**Viva La Vivi**, 5, 125	L. A. Pincay Jr.	Modus Vivendi, 4, 122	Fleet Gazelle, 4, 112	6	1:08.40	18,800
1974	**Lt.'s Joy**, 4, 117	L. A. Pincay Jr.	Viva La Vivi, 4, 123	Shadycroft Gal, 5, 115	7	1:09.00	16,000
1973	**Wingo Belle**, 5, 118	R. Nono	Convenience, 5, 126	Veneke, 6, 116	8	1:08.60	19,150

Named for Calumet Farm's 1952, '53 Milady H. winner A Gleam (1949 f. by *Blenheim II). Formerly named for California's redwood, the sequoia. Grade 3 1986-'89. A Gleam H. 1997-2003. Sequoia H. 1959-'78. Not held 1942-'43, 1947-'58. 6 furlongs 1944, 1959-'82. Two-year-olds 1944. Equaled track record 1998.

Alabama Stakes

Grade 1 in 2006. Saratoga Race Course, three-year-olds, fillies, 1¼ miles, dirt. Held August 20, 2005, with a gross value of $750,000. First held in 1872. First graded in 1973. Stakes record 2:00.80 (1990 Go for Wand).

Year	Winner	Jockey	Second	Third	Strs	Time	1st Purse
2005	**Sweet Symphony**, 3, 121	J. D. Bailey	Spun Sugar, 3, 121	R Lady Joy, 3, 121	7	2:04.45	$450,000
2004	**Society Selection**, 3, 121	C. H. Velasquez	Stellar Jayne, 3, 121	Ashado, 3, 121	8	2:02.70	450,000
2003	**Island Fashion**, 3, 121	J. R. Velazquez	Awesome Humor, 3, 121	Spoken Fur, 3, 121	6	2:05.08	450,000
2002	**Farda Amiga**, 3, 121	P. Day	Allamerican Bertie, 3, 121	You, 3, 121	6	2:04.68	450,000
2001	**Flute**, 3, 121	E. S. Prado	Exogenous, 3, 121	Two Item Limit, 3, 121	7	2:01.88	450,000
2000	**Jostle**, 3, 121	M. E. Smith	Secret Status, 3, 121	Spain, 3, 121	8	2:04.72	450,000
1999	**Silverbulletday**, 3, 121	J. D. Bailey	Strolling Belle, 3, 121	Gandria, 3, 121	7	2:02.71	240,000
1998	**Banshee Breeze**, 3, 121	J. D. Bailey	Lu Ravi, 3, 121	Manistique, 3, 121	6	2:03.41	150,000
1997	**Runup the Colors**, 3, 121	J. D. Bailey	Ajina, 3, 121	Tomisue's Delight, 3, 121	6	2:02.28	150,000
1996	**Yanks Music**, 3, 121	J. R. Velazquez	Escena, 3, 121	My Flag, 3, 121	7	2:03.06	150,000
1995	**Pretty Discreet**, 3, 121	M. E. Smith	Friendly Beauty, 3, 121	Rogues Walk, 3, 121	9	2:02.14	120,000
1994	**Heavenly Prize**, 3, 121	M. E. Smith	Lakeway, 3, 121	Sovereign Kitty, 3, 121	7	2:03.25	120,000
1993	**Sky Beauty**, 3, 121	M. E. Smith	Future Pretense, 3, 121	Silky Feather, 3, 121	8	2:03.49	120,000
1992	**November Snow**, 3, 121	C. W. Antley	Saratoga Dew, 3, 121	Pacific Squall, 3, 121	7	2:02.75	120,000
1991	**Versailles Treaty**, 3, 121	A. T. Cordero Jr.	Til Forbid, 3, 121	Designated Dancer, 3, 121	6	2:02.57	120,000
1990	**Go for Wand**, 3, 121	R. P. Romero	Charon, 3, 121	Pampered Star, 3, 121	3	**2:00.80**	130,560
1989	**Open Mind**, 3, 121	A. T. Cordero Jr.	Dearly Loved, 3, 121	Dream Deal, 3, 121	7	2:04.20	139,440
1988	**Maplejinsky**, 3, 121	A. T. Cordero Jr.	Make Change, 3, 121	Willa On the Move, 3, 121	5	2:01.80	136,320
1987	**Up the Apalachee**, 3, 121	J. Velasquez	Without Feathers, 3, 121	Fiesta Gal, 3, 121	7	2:04.00	138,240
1986	**Classy Cathy**, 3, 121	E. Fires	Valley Victory (Ire), 3, 121	Life At the Top, 3, 121	7	2:04.20	138,720
1985	**Mom's Command**, 3, 121	A. Fuller	Fran's Valentine, 3, 121	Foxy Deen, 3, 121	5	2:03.20	84,000
1984	**Life's Magic**, 3, 121	J. Velasquez	Lucky Lucky Lucky, 3, 121	Class Play, 3, 121	5	2:02.60	98,100
1983	**Spit Curl**, 3, 121	J. Cruguet	Lady Norcliffe, 3, 121	Sabin, 3, 121	5	2:02.40	65,880
1982	**Broom Dance**, 3, 121	G. McCarron	Too Chic, 3, 121	Mademoiselle Forli, 3, 121	7	2:02.20	67,680
1981	**Prismatical**, 3, 121	E. Maple	Banner Gala, 3, 121	Discorama, 3, 121	6	2:02.40	66,000
1980	**Love Sign**, 3, 121	R. Hernandez	Weber City Miss, 3, 121	Sugar and Spice, 3, 121	6	2:01.00	65,880
1979	**It's in the Air**, 3, 121	J. Fell	Davona Dale, 3, 121	Mairzy Doates, 3, 121	5	2:01.40	64,980
1978	**White Star Line**, 3, 121	M. Venezia	Summer Fling, 3, 121	Tempest Queen, 3, 121	6	2:04.00	64,920

1977 **Our Mims**, 3, 121	J. Velasquez	Sensational, 3, 121	Cum Laude Laurie, 3, 121	11	2:03.00	$66,060
1976 **Optimistic Gal**, 3, 121	E. Maple	‡Javamine, 3, 121	Moontee, 3, 121	7	2:01.60	48,555
1975 **Spout**, 3, 121	J. Cruguet	Aunt Jin, 3, 121	Funalon, 3, 121	10	2:04.00	49,170
1974 **Quaze Quilt**, 3, 121	H. Gustines	Chris Evert, 3, 121	Fiesta Libre, 3, 115	8	2:02.60	33,660
1973 **Desert Vixen**, 3, 119	J. Velasquez	Bag of Tunes, 3, 119	Summer Festival, 3, 116	9	2:04.20	34,620

Named for the home state of Confederate Capt. Cottrill of Mobile, Alabama, the race's originator. Held at Belmont Park 1943-'45. Not held 1893-'96, 1898-1900, 1911-'12. 1⅛ miles 1872-'97, 1904, 1906-'16. 1¹⁄₁₆ miles 1901-'03, 1905. ‡Dona Maya finished second, DQ to fourth, 1976.

Alfred G. Vanderbilt Handicap

Grade 2 in 2006. Saratoga Race Course, three-year-olds and up, 6 furlongs, dirt. Held August 13, 2005, with a gross value of $200,000. First held in 1985. First graded in 1990. Stakes record 1:08.04 (2004 Speightstown).

Year	Winner	Jockey	Second	Third	Strs	Time	1st Purse
2005	**Pomeroy**, 4, 117	E. Coa	I'm the Tiger, 5, 114	Voodoo, 7, 112	7	1:08.69	$120,000
2004	**Speightstown**, 6, 120	J. R. Velazquez	Clock Stopper, 4, 115	Gators N Bears, 4, 118	6	**1:08.04**	120,000
2003	**Private Horde**, 4, 115	J. P. Lumpkins	Mountain General, 5, 118	Mike's Classic, 4, 114	5	1:09.18	120,000
2002	**Orientate**, 4, 121	J. D. Bailey	Say Florida Sandy, 8, 115	Multiple Choice, 4, 112	6	1:09.72	120,000
2001	**Five Star Day**, 5, 117	G. K. Gomez	Delaware Township, 5, 116	Bonapaw, 5, 117	7	1:08.57	120,000
2000	**‡Successful Appeal**, 4, 118	E. S. Prado	Intidab, 7, 117	Chasin' Wimmin, 5, 112	8	1:09.21	120,000
1999	**Intidab**, 6, 113	R. G. Davis	Artax, 4, 117	Yes It's True, 3, 117	7	1:09.03	90,000
1998	**Kelly Kip**, 4, 122	J. Samyn	Trafalger, 4, 114	Receiver, 5, 113	7	1:09.60	82,545
1997	**Royal Haven**, 5, 116	R. Migliore	Cold Execution, 6, 116	Punch Line, 7, 120	7	1:09.65	65,220
1996	**Prospect Bay**, 4, 113	J. D. Bailey	Honour and Glory, 3, 119	Lite the Fuse, 5, 123	7	1:08.29	65,760
1995	**Not Surprising**, 5, 115	R. G. Davis	Chimes Band, 4, 119	Mining Burrah, 5, 116	10	1:09.60	67,140
1994	**Boundary**, 4, 117	J. R. Velazquez	Cherokee Run, 4, 120	I Can't Believe, 6, 113	7	1:08.61	65,880
1993	**Gold Spring (Arg)**, 5, 119	P. Day	Friendly Lover, 5, 122	Detox, 4, 115	7	1:09.31	70,680
1992	**For Really**, 5, 115	P. Day	Burn Fair, 5, 115	Drummond Lane, 5, 122	9	1:08.68	71,520
1991	**Kid Russell**, 5, 115	R. Mojica Jr.	Mr. Nasty, 4, 122	To Freedom, 3, 117	8	1:09.52	71,400
1990	**Prospectors Gamble**, 5, 122	J. A. Garcia	Sewickley, 5, 115	Mr. Nickerson, 4, 122	4	1:09.20	50,400
1989	**Mr. Nickerson**, 3, 112	J. A. Santos	Quick Call, 5, 115	Miami Slick, 4, 119	6	1:08.80	52,650
1988	**High Brite**, 4, 122	A. T. Cordero Jr.	Abject, 4, 115	Uncle Ho, 5, 115	4	1:10.20	50,400
1987	**Banker's Jet**, 5, 115	J. L. Vargas	Royal Pennant, 4, 115	Sun Master, 6, 122	6	1:09.20	49,230
1986	**Cognizant**, 5, 117	P. Day	Royal Pennant, 3, 112	Cullendale, 4, 115	7	1:09.20	33,060
1985	**Cognizant**, 4, 117	P. Day	Mayanesian, 6, 117	Spender, 4, 117	7	1:09.60	33,360

Named for Alfred Gwynne Vanderbilt (1912-'99), chairman of NYRA, and president of Belmont and Pimlico. Formerly named for Brownell Combs II's 1983 Jim Dandy S. (G3) winner A Phenomenon (1980 c. by Tentam), who broke down while leading in the 1984 Forego H. (G2); A Phenomenon is one of four horses buried on the Saratoga grounds. Grade 3 1992-'94. A Phenomenon S. 1985-'93, 1996-'97. A Phenomenon H. 1994-'95, 1998-'99. A. G. Vanderbilt H. 2000-'02. ‡Intidab finished first, DQ to second, 2000.

Allaire duPont Breeders' Cup Distaff Handicap

Grade 3 in 2006. Pimlico Race Course, three-year-olds and up, fillies and mares, 1¹⁄₁₆ miles, dirt. Held May 19, 2006, with a gross value of $200,000. First held in 1992. First graded in 1994. Stakes record 1:42.71 (2006 Pool Land).

Year	Winner	Jockey	Second	Third	Strs	Time	1st Purse
2006	**Pool Land**, 4, 120	G. K. Gomez	Josh's Madelyn, 5, 118	In the Gold, 4, 124	9	**1:42.71**	$120,000
2005	**Silmaril**, 4, 115	R. Fogelsonger	Ashado, 4, 123	Friel's for Real, 5, 114	4	1:44.87	60,000
2004	**Friel's for Real**, 4, 115	A. Castellano Jr.	Saintly Action, 5, 114	Nonsuch Bay, 5, 116	8	1:45.03	90,000
2003	**Mandy's Gold**, 5, 117	J. D. Bailey	Summer Colony, 5, 121	Stormy Frolic, 4, 114	4	1:46.32	90,000
2002	**Summer Colony**, 4, 119	J. R. Velazquez	Dancethruthedawn, 4, 119	Happily Unbridled, 4, 115	7	1:42.90	90,000
2001	**Serra Lake**, 4, 112	P. Day	Jostle, 4, 119	Prized Stamp, 4, 114	6	1:50.22	120,000
2000	**Roza Robata**, 5, 114	P. Day	Bella Chiarra, 5, 118	On a Soapbox, 4, 116	8	1:49.82	120,000
1999	**Mil Kilates**, 6, 113	S. J. Sellers	Merengue, 4, 121	Unbridled Hope, 5, 116	8	1:49.05	120,000
1998	**Ajina**, 4, 120	J. D. Bailey	Naskra Colors, 6, 112	Pocho's Dream Girl, 4, 113	8	1:48.70	120,000
1997	**Rare Blend**, 4, 114	J. D. Bailey	Scenic Point, 4, 114	Aileen's Countess, 5, 114	5	1:51.51	120,000
1996	**Serena's Song**, 4, 123	G. L. Stevens	Shoop, 5, 116	Churchbell Chimes, 5, 114	4	1:49.75	120,000
1995	**Pennyhill Park**, 5, 115	M. E. Smith	Halo America, 5, 117	Calipha, 4, 121	6	1:49.32	120,000
1994	**Double Sixes**, 4, 112	E. S. Prado	Broad Gains, 4, 118	Mz. Zill Bear, 5, 118	6	1:51.19	120,000
1993	**Deputation**, 4, 114	C. W. Antley	D. Theatrical Gal, 4, 112	Low Tolerance, 4, 115	6	1:49.12	120,000
1992	**Wilderness Song**, 4, 121	C. Perret	Harbour Club, 5, 110	Brilliant Brass, 5, 117	7	1:49.06	150,000

Named for prominent Maryland owner and breeder Allaire C. duPont (1913-2006); duPont bred and raced five-time Horse of the Year Kelso. Races for females are typically referred to as distaff races. Pimlico Distaff H. 1992-2001. Pimlico Breeders' Cup Distaff H. 2002-'05. 1⅛ miles 1992-2001.

All American Handicap

Grade 3 in 2006. Golden Gate Fields, four-year-olds and up, 1⅛ miles, dirt. Held February 20, 2006, with a gross value of $150,000. First held in 1968. First graded in 1985. Stakes record 1:47.11 (2006 Buzzards Bay).

Year	Winner	Jockey	Second	Third	Strs	Time	1st Purse
2006	**Buzzards Bay**, 4, 117	J. Valdivia Jr.	Melanyhasthepapers, 5, 113	Ace Blue (Brz), 6, 116	6	**1:47.11**	$82,500
2005	**Yougottawanna**, 6, 118	J. P. Lumpkins	Jake Skate, 5, 119	Adreamisborn, 6, 119	7	1:41.42	41,250
2004	**Yougottawanna**, 5, 116	R. A. Baze	Gold Ruckus, 6, 115	Snorter, 4, 118	5	1:40.08	41,250
2003	**Reba's Gold**, 6, 118	C. J. Rollins	Free Corona, 5, 116	Truly a Judge, 5, 117	6	1:41.63	55,000
2002	**Palmeiro**, 4, 115	J. P. Lumpkins	Moonlight Meeting, 7, 116	Prodigious, 5, 116	9	1:42.31	82,500

2001	**Euchre**, 5, 118	J. P. Lumpkins	Irisheyesareflying, 5, 118	Moonlight Charger, 6, 115	8	1:41.69	$82,500
2000	**Peach Flat**, 6, 114	J. Valdivia Jr.	Boss Ego, 4, 115	Casey Griffin, 4, 115	5	1:42.48	75,000
1999	**Worldly Ways (GB)**, 5, 116	R. A. Baze	Barter Town, 4, 112	dh-Highland Gold, 4, 115 dh-Scooter Brown, 4, 114	8	1:40.62	60,000
1998	**Wild Wonder**, 4, 121	R. A. Baze	Crypto Star, 4, 118	General Royal, 4, 115	6	1:41.33	60,000
1997	**Mister Fire Eyes (Ire)**, 5, 115	R. J. Warren Jr.	Region, 8, 115	Tolemeo, 4, 113	6	1:41.28	60,000
1996	**Tzar Rodney (Fr)**, 4, 114	T. M. Chapman	Joy of Glory, 7, 115	Opera Score, 5, 115	6	1:49.74	60,000
1995	**Bluegrass Prince (Ire)**, 4, 114	T. M. Chapman	Lord Shirldor (SAf), 6, 116	Kinema Red, 5, 113	7	1:49.01	68,750
1994	**Slew of Damascus**, 6, 122	T. M. Chapman	Fast Cure, 5, 114	The Tender Track, 7, 116	6	1:43.75	55,000
1993	**Never Black**, 6, 115	C. S. Nakatani	Stark South, 5, 115	Daros (GB), 4, 114	6	1:42.53	55,000
1992	**Gum**, 6, 112	G. Boulanger	Forty Niner Days, 5, 116	Prudent Manner (Ire), 5, 115	7	1:41.73	55,000
1991	**Forty Niner Days**, 4, 115	T. T. Doocy	Neptuno (Arg), 5, 116	Trebizond, 5, 115	6	1:42.70	55,000
1990	**River Master**, 4, 116	R. G. Davis	Miswaki Tern, 5, 116	Exclusive Partner, 8, 117	8	1:43.20	55,000
1989	**Simply Majestic**, 5, 121	R. D. Hansen	Ongoing Mister, 4, 113	Astronaut Prince, 5, 115	6	1:42.40	55,000
1988	**Ifrad**, 6, 117	T. M. Chapman	Stop the Fighting (Ire), 5, 115	Nickle Band, 4, 113	7	1:43.40	55,000
1987	**Mangaki**, 6, 115	T. T. Doocy	Barbery, 6, 116	Santella Mac (Ire), 4, 115	12	1:34.40	84,410
1986	**Clever Song**, 4, 122	F. Toro	Truce Maker, 8, 114	Ocean View, 5, 117	7	1:28.00	63,000
1985	**Hegemony (Ire)**, 4, 121	D. G. McHargue	Champion Pilot, 4, 121	Nak Ack, 4, 117	5	1:28.40	71,740
1984	**Ancestral (Ire)**, 4, 115	R. Sibille	Otter Slide, 5, 116	dh-Famous Star (GB), 5, 115 dh-Silveyville, 6, 124	10	1:29.20	49,750
1983	**Major Sport**, 6, 115	T. M. Chapman	Aristocratical, 6, 114	Take the Floor, 4, 115	11	1:29.40	50,300
1982	**Crews Hill (GB)**, 6, 118	R. A. Baze	Shagbark, 7, 122	Hallowed Envoy, 5, 116	7	1:29.40	64,800
1981	**Borrego Sun**, 4, 114	R. A. Baze	Prenotion, 6, 116	Kane County, 4, 113	7	1:29.60	25,550
1980	**California Express**, 5, 110	J. Aragon	Kamehameha, 5, 121	Miami Sun, 6, 120	7	1:29.60	19,000
1979	**Struttin' George**, 5, 122	T. M. Chapman	Don Alberto, 4, 119	Charley Sutton, 5, 114	8	1:28.00	13,100
1978	**Maheras**, 5, 132	W. Mahorney	Charley Sutton, 4, 115	Oriental Magic, 6, 113	5	:56.20	15,550
1977	**L'Natural**, 4, 114	R. Caballero	Maheras, 4, 126	Sporting Goods, 7, 122	7	:56.00	15,800
1976	**Shirley's Champion**, 5, 114	F. Olivares	King Charly, 6, 113	Oriental Magic, 4, 114	7	:56.80	15,800
1975	**Cherry River**, 5, 126	W. Mahorney	El Potrero, 4, 115	Black Tornado, 5, 116	9	:56.80	16,200
1974	**Tragic Isle**, 5, 124	F. Mena	Prince Rameses, 5, 113	Times Rush, 6, 113	6	1:08.80	15,000
1973	**Selecting**, 4, 112	R. Yaka	I'm Ed, 4, 111	Goalie, 4, 120	7	1:09.00	15,150

In the past was a traditional Memorial Day weekend race. Formerly named for Charles S. Howard's 1938 Horse of the Year and '37, '38 Bay Meadows H. winner Seabiscuit (1933 c. by Hard Tack). Renamed in 2003 to coincide with the release of the movie *Seabiscuit*. Seabiscuit H. 2003. Seabiscuit Breeders' Cup H. 2004-'05. Held at Bay Meadows 2001-'05. 6 furlongs 1968-'74. 5 furlongs 1975-'78. 7½ furlongs 1979-'86. 1 mile 1987. 1$^{1}/_{16}$ miles 1988-'94, 1997-2005. Turf 1975-'96. Dead heat for third 1984, 1999.

American Derby

Grade 2 in 2006. Arlington Park, three-year-olds, 1$^{3}/_{16}$ miles, turf. Held July 23, 2005, with a gross value of $250,000. First held in 1884. First graded in 1973. Stakes record 1:54.60 (1955 Swaps).

Year	Winner	Jockey	Second	Third	Strs	Time	1st Purse
2005	**Gun Salute**, 3, 121	C. H. Velasquez	Purim, 3, 121	Exceptional Ride, 3, 119	8	1:55.31	$150,000
2004	**Simple Exchange (Ire)**, 3, 119	P. Smullen	Cool Conductor, 3, 119	Toasted, 3, 123	8	1:54.93	150,000
2003	**Evolving Tactics (Ire)**, 3, 117	P. Smullen	Californian (GB), 3, 121	Scottago, 3, 116	5	1:59.04	150,000
2002	**Mananan McLir**, 3, 116	R. R. Douglas	Jazz Beat (Ire), 3, 117	Extra Check, 3, 116	8	1:57.11	135,000
2001	**Fan Club's Mister**, 3, 121	R. A. Meier	Monsieur Cat, 3, 116	Royal Spy, 3, 123	7	2:03.27	150,000
2000	**Pine Dance**, 3, 114	E. Ahern	Hymn (Ire), 3, 114	Del Mar Show, 3, 114	4	1:55.46	120,000
1997	**Honor Glide**, 3, 120	G. K. Gomez	Worldly Ways (GB), 3, 120	Daylight Savings, 3, 114	8	1:55.94	120,000
1996	**‡Jaunatxo**, 3, 114	J. L. Diaz	Trail City, 3, 120	Marlin, 3, 114	12	1:55.82	180,000
1995	**Gold and Steel (Fr)**, 3, 114	A. T. Gryder	Torrential, 3, 120	Unanimous Vote (Ire), 3, 120	7	1:55.02	180,000
1994	**dh-Overbury (Ire)**, 3, 114 **dh-Vaudeville**, 3, 114	S. J. Sellers A. D. Lopez		Star Campaigner, 3, 114	10	1:55.29	120,000
1993	**Explosive Red**, 3, 120	S. J. Sellers	Earl of Barking (Ire), 3, 120	Newton's Law (Ire), 3, 114	9	1:59.92	180,000
1992	**The Name's Jimmy**, 3, 120	P. Day	Standiford, 3, 114	May I Inquire, 3, 114	14	1:59.41	180,000
1991	**Olympio**, 3, 126	E. Delahoussaye	Discover, 3, 114	Jackie Wackie, 3, 123	8	2:00.99	180,000
1990	**Real Cash**, 3, 123	P. A. Valenzuela	Home At Last, 3, 123	Adjudicating, 3, 117	6	2:02.00	180,000
1989	**Awe Inspiring**, 3, 126	C. Perret	Dispersal, 3, 123	Caesar, 3, 114	8	2:02.40	124,500
1987	**Fortunate Moment**, 3, 118	E. Fires	Fast Forward, 3, 118	Gem Master, 3, 118	9	2:03.80	100,350
1985	**Creme Fraiche**, 3, 123	E. Maple	Red Attack, 3, 114	Smile, 3, 123	5	2:01.60	96,000
1984	**dh-At the Threshold**, 3, 126 **dh-High Alexander**, 3, 120	P. Day G. Gallitano		Par Flite, 3, 114	7	2:04.00	46,800
1983	**Play Fellow**, 3, 123	P. Day	Le Cou Cou, 3, 114	Brother, 3, 114	8	2:04.40	65,100
1982	**Wolfie's Rascal**, 3, 123	R. Hernandez	Dew Line, 3, 114	Northern Majesty, 3, 120	8	2:05.60	65,100
1981	**Pocket Zipper**, 3, 120	R. Sibille	Fairway Phantom, 3, 123	Double Sonic, 3, 123	11	2:03.80	84,000
1980	**Hurry Up Blue**, 3, 114	G. Gallitano	Tizon, 3, 114	Spruce Needles, 3, 123	6	2:04.40	83,400
1979	**Smarten**, 3, 126	S. Maple	Super Hit, 3, 114	Weather Tamer, 3, 114	6	2:05.20	63,600
1978	**Nasty and Bold**, 3, 114	J. Samyn	Star de Naskra, 3, 114	Beau Sham, 3, 114	13	2:03.40	68,100
1977	**Silver Series**, 3, 126	L. Snyder	Run Dusty Run, 3, 126	Brach's Hilarious, 3, 112	6	2:02.40	68,880
1976	**Fifth Marine**, 3, 121	R. Turcotte	Majestic Light, 3, 121	Play the Red, 3, 121	11	1:49.20	93,400
1975	**Honey Mark**, 3, 116	G. Patterson	High Steel, 3, 112	Go to the Bank, 3, 111	14	1:44.40	93,400
1974	**Determined King**, 3, 112	D. Montoya	Orders, 3, 114	Sr. Diplomat, 3, 111	13	1:47.80	92,000
1973	**Bemo**, 3, 117	W. J. Passmore	Golden Don, 3, 115	Buffalo Lark, 3, 109	12	1:49.60	69,400

Formerly sponsored by PrimeCo Communications 1997. Grade 1 1973-'74, 1981-'89. PrimeCo American Derby 1997. Held at Washington Park 1884-1904, 1926-'27, 1929-'57. Held at Hawthorne Race Course 1916. Not held 1895-'97,

1899, 1905-'15, 1917-'25, 1936, 1938-'39, 1986, 1988, 1998-'99. 1½ miles 1884-1904, 1926-'27. 1¼ miles 1916, 1928-'51, 1962-'65, 1977-'91. 1⅛ miles 1952-'54, 1958-'61, 1966-'74, 1976. 1¹⁄₁₆ miles 1975. Dirt 1884-1954, 1958-'69, 1977-'91. Dead heat for first 1984, 1994. ‡Trail City finished first, DQ to second, 1996.

American Invitational Handicap

Grade 2 in 2006. Hollywood Park, three-year-olds and up, 1⅛ miles, turf. Held July 3, 2005, with a gross value of $250,000. First held in 1938. First graded in 1973. Stakes record 1:45.60 (1987 Clever Song).

Year	Winner	Jockey	Second	Third	Strs	Time	1st Purse
2005	**Whilly (Ire)**, 4, 117	F. F. Martinez	King of Happiness, 6, 120	Fourty Niners Son, 4, 115	8	1:46.30	$150,000
2004	**Bayamo (Ire)**, 5, 117	D. R. Flores	Sarafan, 7, 119	Night Patrol, 8, 114	5	1:46.60	90,000
2003	**Candy Ride (Arg)**, 4, 120	G. L. Stevens	Special Ring, 6, 118	Irish Warrior, 5, 116	5	1:46.20	90,000
2002	**The Tin Man**, 4, 115	M. E. Smith	Devine Wind, 6, 115	Kappa King, 5, 116	7	1:46.82	90,000
2001	**Takarian (Ire)**, 6, 114	G. K. Gomez	Fighting Falcon, 5, 114	Fateful Dream, 4, 116	7	1:48.19	90,000
2000	**Dark Moondancer (GB)**, 5, 122	C. J. McCarron	Sardaukar (GB), 4, 113	Sunshine Street, 5, 119	6	1:46.74	90,000
1999	**Takarian (Ire)**, 4, 114	G. K. Gomez	Montemiro (Fr), 5, 112	Special Quest (Fr), 4, 115	6	1:47.37	90,000
1998	**Magellan**, 5, 116	G. L. Stevens	Bonapartiste (Fr), 4, 116	Sharekann (Ire), 6, 112	8	1:47.05	90,000
1997	**El Angelo**, 5, 118	A. O. Solis	Naninja, 4, 114	Wavy Run (Ire), 6, 117	6	1:46.99	96,360
1996	**Labeeb (GB)**, 4, 119	E. Delahoussaye	Gold and Steel (Fr), 4, 118	Earl of Barking (Ire), 6, 116	8	1:45.78	66,120
1995	**Silver Wizard**, 5, 118	G. L. Stevens	Romarin (Brz), 5, 120	Savinio, 5, 118	5	1:46.02	91,900
1994	**Blues Traveller (Ire)**, 4, 115	C. W. Antley	Gothland (Fr), 5, 119	Johann Quatz (Fr), 5, 116	7	1:46.50	128,000
1993	**†Toussaud**, 4, 114	K. Desormeaux	Man From Eldorado, 5, 115	Journalism, 5, 117	6	1:46.87	126,000
1992	**Man From Eldorado**, 4, 114	K. Desormeaux	Bold Russian (GB), 5, 116	Golden Pheasant, 6, 123	4	1:47.11	122,000
1991	**Tight Spot**, 4, 123	L. A. Pincay Jr.	Exbourne, 5, 122	Super May, 5, 118	8	1:46.00	129,400
1990	**Classic Fame**, 4, 117	E. Delahoussaye	Steinlen (GB), 7, 125	Pleasant Variety, 6, 116	7	1:47.80	126,800
1989	**Mister Wonderful (GB)**, 6, 115	F. Toro	Steinlen (GB), 6, 121	Pranke (Arg), 5, 117	8	1:47.20	183,600
1988	**Skip Out Front**, 6, 115	C. J. McCarron	Steinlen (GB), 5, 121	World Court, 5, 113	4	1:46.40	120,800
1987	**Clever Song**, 5, 118	L. A. Pincay Jr.	Skip Out Front, 5, 114	Barbery, 6, 115	7	**1:45.60**	127,800
1986	**Al Mamoon**, 5, 119	P. A. Valenzuela	Truce Maker, 8, 111	Will Dancer (Fr), 4, 114	6	1:39.20	107,000
1985	**Tsunami Slew**, 4, 117	G. L. Stevens	Al Mamoon, 4, 117	Dahar, 4, 123	7	1:46.20	122,300
1984	**Bel Bolide**, 6, 121	T. Lipham	Silveyville, 6, 118	Vin St Benet (GB), 5, 118	8	1:46.80	123,600
1983	**John Henry**, 8, 127	C. J. McCarron	Prince Florimund (SAf), 5, 120	Tonzarun, 5, 114	8	1:48.40	97,100
1982	**Spence Bay (Ire)**, 7, 122	F. Toro	The Bart, 6, 124	Peter Jones, 4, 113	10	1:47.20	100,300
1981	**Bold Tropic (SAf)**, 6, 126	W. Shoemaker	The Bart, 5, 117	Don Roberto, 4, 112	9	1:46.80	98,100
1980	**Bold Tropic (SAf)**, 5, 122	W. Shoemaker	Inkerman, 5, 115	Borzoi, 4, 117	8	1:46.40	65,700
1979	**Smoggy (GB)**, 5, 114	D. G. McHargue	Dom Alaric (Fr), 5, 120	Inkerman, 4, 119	8	1:47.40	65,500
1978	**Effervescing**, 5, 119	L. A. Pincay Jr.	Diagramatic, 5, 123	April Axe, 3, 113	8	1:47.20	65,500
1977	**Hunza Dancer**, 5, 120	J. Cruguet	Anne's Pretender, 5, 121	Legendaire, 4, 115	11	1:47.20	68,900
1976	**King Pellinore**, 4, 121	W. Shoemaker	Riot in Paris, 5, 123	Caucasus, 4, 120	7	1:48.00	48,200
1975	**Pass the Glass**, 4, 115	F. Toro	Big Band, 5, 116	Against the Snow, 5, 114	11	1:48.20	53,800
	Montmartre, 5, 115	F. Toro	Top Crowd, 4, 115	Ancient Title, 5, 128	9	1:49.60	51,800
1974	**Plunk**, 4, 117	L. A. Pincay Jr.	Scantling, 4, 115	Mr. Cockatoo, 5, 114	11	1:48.20	51,900
1973	**Kentuckian**, 4, 114	R. Campas	Life Cycle, 4, 121	Wing Out, 5, 118	9	1:48.00	50,400

Traditionally held during the July 4 holiday. American H. 1938-2004. Held at Santa Anita Park 1949. Not held 1942-'43. 1¹⁄₁₆ miles 1945-'46, 1986. 1¼ miles 1950. Dirt 1938-'67. Four-year-olds and up 1945. Two divisions 1975. †Denotes female.

American Invitational Oaks

Grade 1 in 2006. Hollywood Park, three-year-olds, fillies, 1¼ miles, turf. Held July 3, 2005, with a gross value of $750,000. First held in 2002. First graded in 2004. Stakes record 1:59.03 (2005 Cesario [Jpn]).

Year	Winner	Jockey	Second	Third	Strs	Time	1st Purse
2005	**Cesario (Jpn)**, 3, 121	Y. Fukunaga	Melhor Ainda, 3, 121	Singhalese (GB), 3, 121	12	**1:59.03**	$450,000
2004	**Ticker Tape (GB)**, 3, 121	K. Desormeaux	Dance in the Mood (Jpn), 3, 121	Hollywood Story, 3, 121	13	2:01.54	450,000
2003	**Dimitrova**, 3, 121	D. R. Flores	Sand Springs, 3, 121	Atlantic Ocean, 3, 121	14	1:59.98	450,000
2002	**‡Megahertz (GB)**, 3, 121	A. O. Solis	Dublino, 3, 121	Alozaina (Ire), 3, 121	14	2:00.46	300,000

Held during the July 4 holiday. ‡Dublino finished first, DQ to second, 2002.

American Turf Stakes

Grade 3 in 2006. Churchill Downs, three-year-olds, 1¹⁄₁₆ miles, turf. Held May 5, 2006, with a gross value of $114,300. First held in 1992. First graded in 1998. Stakes record 1:40.93 (1997 Royal Strand [Ire]).

Year	Winner	Jockey	Second	Third	Strs	Time	1st Purse
2006	**Stream Cat**, 3, 122	J. R. Leparoux	Go Between, 3, 122	Gaelic Storm, 3, 117	6	1:42.27	$70,158
2005	**Rey de Cafe**, 3, 122	J. Castellano	Rush Bay, 3, 116	Guillaume Tell (Ire), 3, 116	9	1:42.00	71,114
2004	**Kitten's Joy**, 3, 123	J. D. Bailey	Prince Arch, 3, 123	Capo, 3, 117	9	1:43.31	70,556
2003	**Senor Swinger**, 3, 117	P. Day	Remind, 3, 117	Foufa's Warrior, 3, 117	10	1:41.38	75,268
2002	**Legislator**, 3, 116	E. S. Prado	Stage Call (Ire), 3, 123	Orchard Park, 3, 123	10	1:44.43	72,106
2001	**Strategic Partner**, 3, 116	J. R. Velazquez	Baptize, 3, 123	Dynameaux, 3, 120	6	1:42.89	73,098
2000	**King Cugat**, 3, 123	J. D. Bailey	Lendell Ray, 3, 116	Go Lib Go, 3, 123	11	1:41.25	73,222
1999	**Air Rocket**, 3, 120	J. D. Bailey	Haus of Dehere, 3, 116	Conserve, 3, 118	10	1:42.65	71,548
1998	**Dernier Croise (Fr)**, 3, 116	G. L. Stevens	Tenbyssimo (Ire), 3, 123	Silver Lord, 3, 114	10	1:44.28	78,120
1997	**Royal Strand (Ire)**, 3, 116	P. Day	Rob 'n Gin, 3, 118	Deputy Commander, 3, 115	10	**1:40.93**	71,796
1996	**Broadway Beau**, 3, 114	C. J. McCarron	Trail City, 3, 123	Gotcha, 3, 114	10	1:41.87	76,375

1995	**Unanimous Vote (Ire)**, 3, 120	G. L. Stevens	Nostra, 3, 116	Native Regent, 3, 123	12	1:42.07	$76,700
1994	**Jaggery John**, 3, 123	M. E. Smith	Milt's Overture, 3, 116	Zuno Star, 3, 116	10	1:45.05	56,453
1993	**‡Desert Waves**, 3, 118	S. J. Sellers	Compadre, 3, 116	Super Snazzie, 3, 116	5	1:42.64	36,628
1992	**Senor Tomas**, 3, 118	M. E. Smith	Coaxing Matt, 3, 114	Black Question, 3, 123	8	1:43.10	37,440

Sponsored by the Crown Royal Co. of Stamford, Connecticut 1995-2006. American Turf S. 1992-'94. ‡Compadre finished first, DQ to second, 1993. Course record 1997.

Amsterdam Stakes

Grade 2 in 2006. Saratoga Race Course, three-year-olds, 6 furlongs, dirt. Held August 7, 2005, with a gross value of $150,000. First held in 1901. First graded in 1998. Stakes record 1:08.64 (2003 Zavata).

Year	Winner	Jockey	Second	Third	Strs	Time	1st Purse
2005	**Santana Strings**, 3, 121	E. Coa	Social Probation, 3, 116	Silver Train, 3, 115	9	1:10.18	$90,000
2004	**Bwana Charlie**, 3, 123	S. J. Sellers	Pomeroy, 3, 123	Weigelia, 3, 123	7	1:09.40	90,000
2003	**Zavata**, 3, 119	J. D. Bailey	Great Notion, 3, 121	Trust N Luck, 3, 123	7	**1:08.64**	90,000
2002	**Listen Here**, 3, 121	P. Day	Boston Common, 3, 123	Bold Truth, 3, 115	8	1:09.58	90,000
2001	**City Zip**, 3, 123	J. F. Chavez	Speightstown, 3, 118	Smile My Lord, 3, 118	6	1:11.03	81,420
2000	**Personal First**, 3, 120	P. Day	Disco Rico, 3, 123	Trippi, 3, 123	6	1:09.33	66,000
1999	**Successful Appeal**, 3, 122	E. S. Prado	Lion Hearted, 3, 114	Silver Season, 3, 119	9	1:10.25	50,340
1998	**dh-Mint**, 3, 119	E. Coa		Southern Bostonion, 3, 119	8	1:10.28	33,060
	dh-Secret Firm, 3, 117	E. S. Prado					
1997	**Oro de Mexico**, 3, 117	C. W. Antley	Trafalger, 3, 122	Kelly Kip, 3, 122	7	1:10.58	16,425
1996	**Distorted Humor**, 3, 115	P. Day	Gold Fever, 3, 121	Stu's Choice, 3, 115	7	1:09.13	32,820
1995	**Kings Fiction**, 3, 112	P. Day	Lord Carson, 3, 115	Ft. Stockton, 3, 115	5	1:09.75	32,250
1994	**Chimes Band**, 3, 117	J. D. Bailey	Ledford, 3, 115	Halo's Image, 3, 115	6	1:09.90	32,325
	Mr. Shawklit, 3, 115	W. H. McCauley	Scarlet Rage, 3, 115	Groovy Jett, 3, 117	5	1:10.89	32,325
1993	**Evil Bear**, 3, 117	J. A. Santos	Punch Line, 3, 122	Digging In, 3, 119	5	1:22.09	28,800

Named for Amsterdam, New York, located in Montgomery County. Formerly named for Flying Zee Stable's G2 SW Screen King (1976 c. by Silent Screen); Screen King broke his maiden at Belmont Park and ended his career at Saratoga in the Travers S. (G1). Grade 3 1998-2000. Screen King S. 1993-'97. Held at Belmont Park 1993. Not held 1911-'12, 1924-'92. 1 mile 1901-'23. 7 furlongs 1993. Three-year-olds and up 1901-'23. Two divisions 1994. Dead heat for first 1998.

Ancient Title Breeders' Cup Handicap

Grade 1 in 2006. Oak Tree at Santa Anita, three-year-olds and up, 6 furlongs, dirt. Held October 8, 2005, with a gross value of $236,000. First held in 1985. First graded in 1990. Stakes record 1:07.67 (2001 Swept Overboard).

Year	Winner	Jockey	Second	Third	Strs	Time	1st Purse
2005	**Captain Squire**, 6, 124	A. O. Solis	Zanzibar (Arg), 4, 124	Indian Country, 4, 124	7	1:08.85	$150,000
2004	**Pt's Grey Eagle**, 3, 109	A. Bisono	Pohave, 6, 118	Hombre Rapido, 7, 114	8	1:08.84	120,000
2003	**Avanzado (Arg)**, 6, 116	T. Baze	Captain Squire, 4, 117	Bluesthestandard, 6, 115	6	1:08.12	81,375
2002	**†Kalookan Queen**, 6, 119	A. O. Solis	Crafty C. T., 4, 116	Mellow Fellow, 7, 117	6	1:08.26	125,625
2001	**Swept Overboard**, 4, 116	E. Delahoussaye	Kona Gold, 7, 127	I Love Silver, 3, 116	6	**1:07.67**	124,260
2000	**Kona Gold**, 6, 124	A. O. Solis	Regal Thunder, 6, 117	Elaborate, 5, 116	4	1:08.11	123,060
1999	**Lexicon**, 4, 116	K. Desormeaux	Kona Gold, 5, 120	Regal Thunder, 5, 117	8	1:07.84	125,400
1998	**Gold Land**, 7, 117	K. Desormeaux	†A. P. Assay, 4, 116	Swiss Yodeler, 4, 114	8	1:08.50	94,020
1997	**Elmhurst**, 7, 114	C. S. Nakatani	Swiss Yodeler, 3, 113	Larry the Legend, 5, 115	7	1:08.82	95,000
1996	**Lakota Brave**, 7, 117	E. Delahoussaye	Letthebighossroll, 8, 119	‡Paying Dues, 4, 118	5	1:08.16	93,700
1995	**†Track Gal**, 4, 116	G. L. Stevens	Siphon (Brz), 4, 117	Forest Gazelle, 4, 116	6	1:08.32	59,150
1994	**Saratoga Gambler**, 6, 113	M. A. Pedroza	Uncaged Fury, 3, 114	Concept Win, 4, 117	8	1:08.87	62,500
1993	**Cardmania**, 7, 116	E. Delahoussaye	Music Merci, 7, 117	Bahatur, 4, 114	8	1:08.04	61,975
1992	**Gray Slewpy**, 4, 118	K. Desormeaux	Trick Me, 4, 114	Light of Morn, 6, 117	9	1:08.48	59,372
1991	**Frost Free**, 6, 118	C. J. McCarron	Answer Do, 5, 118	Sir Beaufort, 4, 113	7	1:08.66	61,525
1990	**Corwyn Bay (Ire)**, 4, 118	E. Delahoussaye	Sensational Star, 6, 119	Yes I'm Blue, 4, 117	7	1:08.40	61,375
1989	**Sam Who**, 4, 120	L. A. Pincay Jr.	Sunny Blossom, 4, 116	Don's Irish Melody, 6, 114	5	1:08.00	46,050
1988	**Olympic Prospect**, 4, 123	L. A. Pincay Jr.	Sebrof, 4, 118	Reconnoitering, 4, 114	6	1:09.00	55,630
1987	**Zany Tactics**, 6, 123	J. L. Kaenel	On the Line, 3, 116	Carload, 5, 117	3	1:09.00	35,500
1986	**Groovy**, 3, 123	J. A. Santos	Rosie's K. T., 5, 117	Sun Master, 5, 114	8	1:08.20	49,450
1985	**Temerity Prince**, 5, 120	W. A. Ward	Debonaire Junior, 4, 124	Bid Us, 5, 115	6	1:09.20	37,150

Named for Kirkland Stable's 1975, '76 Californian S. (G1) winner Ancient Title (1970 g. by Gummo). Grade 3 1990-'98. Grade 2 1999-2000. Ancient Title H. 1985-'89. ‡Criollito (Arg) finished third, DQ to fourth, 1996. Track record 2001. †Denotes female.

Apple Blossom Handicap

Grade 1 in 2006. Oaklawn Park, four-year-olds and up, fillies and mares, 1$^1/_{16}$ miles, dirt. Held April 8, 2006, with a gross value of $500,000. First held in 1973. First graded in 1977. Stakes record 1:40.20 (1984 Heatherten).

Year	Winner	Jockey	Second	Third	Strs	Time	1st Purse
2006	**Spun Sugar**, 4, 116	M. J. Luzzi	Happy Ticket, 5, 119	La Reason, 6, 114	6	1:42.59	$300,000
2005	**Dream of Summer**, 6, 117	P. A. Valenzuela	Star Parade (Arg), 6, 116	Shadow Cast, 4, 116	7	1:43.86	300,000
2004	**Azeri**, 6, 123	M. E. Smith	‡Star Parade (Arg), 5, 114	Wild Spirit (Chi), 5, 119	6	1:41.24	300,000
2003	**Azeri**, 5, 123	M. E. Smith	Take Charge Lady, 4, 118	Mandy's Gold, 5, 116	7	1:43.00	300,000
2002	**Azeri**, 4, 117	M. E. Smith	Affluent, 4, 118	Miss Linda (Arg), 5, 118	5	1:42.75	300,000
2001	**Gourmet Girl**, 6, 113	C. H. Borel	Lu Ravi, 6, 114	Lazy Slusan, 6, 116	11	1:42.15	300,000

2000	**Heritage of Gold**, 5, 118	S. J. Sellers	Lu Ravi, 5, 114	Bordelaise (Arg), 5, 113	7	1:42.22	$300,000
1999	**Banshee Breeze**, 4, 122	J. D. Bailey	Sister Act, 4, 114	Silent Eskimo, 4, 112	6	1:41.64	300,000
1998	**Escena**, 5, 117	J. D. Bailey	Glitter Woman, 4, 119	Toda Una Dama (Arg), 5, 115	7	1:40.95	300,000
1997	**Halo America**, 7, 117	C. H. Borel	Jewel Princess, 5, 124	Different (Arg), 5, 121	8	1:41.65	300,000
1996	**Twice the Vice**, 5, 117	C. J. McCarron	Halo America, 6, 115	Serena's Song, 4, 124	7	1:41.71	300,000
1995	**Heavenly Prize**, 4, 120	P. Day	Halo America, 5, 116	Paseana (Arg), 8, 122	6	1:42.76	300,000
1994	**Nine Keys**, 4, 116	M. E. Smith	Mamselle Bebette, 4, 116	Re Toss (Arg), 7, 117	10	1:42.15	300,000
1993	**Paseana (Arg)**, 6, 124	C. J. McCarron	Looie Capote, 4, 115	Luv Me Luv Me Not, 4, 114	9	1:41.80	300,000
1992	**Paseana (Arg)**, 5, 124	C. J. McCarron	Fit for a Queen, 6, 121	Slide Out Front, 4, 109	8	1:42.13	300,000
1991	**Degenerate Gal**, 6, 115	P. Day	Charon, 4, 121	Fit to Scout, 4, 116	6	1:41.25	300,000
1990	**Gorgeous**, 4, 122	E. Delahoussaye	Bayakoa (Arg), 6, 126	Affirmed Classic, 4, 112	4	1:40.40	210,000
1989	**Bayakoa (Arg)**, 5, 120	L. A. Pincay Jr.	Goodbye Halo, 4, 125	Invited Guest (Ire), 5, 116	6	1:41.60	150,000
1988	**By Land by Sea**, 4, 121	F. Toro	Invited Guest (Ire), 4, 116	Hail a Cab, 5, 113	10	1:41.20	150,000
1987	**North Sider**, 5, 122	A. T. Cordero Jr.	Family Style, 4, 120	Queen Alexandra, 5, 119	7	1:41.20	162,300
1986	**Love Smitten**, 5, 119	C. J. McCarron	Lady's Secret, 4, 127	Sefa's Beauty, 7, 122	7	1:40.40	162,180
1985	**Sefa's Beauty**, 6, 120	P. Day	Heatherten, 6, 127	Life's Magic, 4, 123	7	1:42.20	161,700
1984	**Heatherten**, 5, 116	S. Maple	Try Something New, 5, 121	Holiday Dancer, 4, 115	10	**1:40.20**	167,400
1983	**Miss Huntington**, 6, 118	J. Velasquez	‡Sefa's Beauty, 4, 117	Queen of Song, 4, 114	13	1:44.80	172,620
1982	**Track Robbery**, 6, 124	E. Delahoussaye	Andover Way, 4, 120	Jameela, 6, 123	6	1:45.20	161,040
1981	**Bold 'n Determined**, 4, 124	E. Delahoussaye	La Bonzo, 5, 111	Karla's Enough, 4, 119	7	1:44.20	131,820
1980	**Billy Jane**, 4, 113	J. Lively	Jameela, 4, 118	Miss Baja, 5, 121	11	1:43.60	106,290
1979	**Miss Baja**, 4, 113	E. Maple	Kit's Double, 6, 114	Navajo Princess, 5, 121	10	1:43.00	106,800
1978	**Northernette**, 4, 119	D. Brumfield	Taisez Vous, 4, 124	Cum Laude Laurie, 4, 121	9	1:42.00	74,130
1977	**Hail Hilarious**, 4, 121	D. Pierce	Kittyluck, 4, 112	Summertime Promise, 5, 119	15	1:41.40	82,290
1976	**Summertime Promise**, 4, 119	D. G. McHargue	Baygo, 7, 114	Costly Dream, 5, 113	9	1:40.60	35,760
1975	**Susan's Girl**, 6, 124	J. Nichols	Truchas, 6, 116	Matuta, 4, 114	12	1:42.40	36,720
1974	**Big Dare**, 4, 116	R. N. Ussery	Gallant Davelle, 4, 122	Sixty Sails, 4, 115	13	1:11.80	19,050

Named for the apple trees typically in bloom during the Oaklawn Park meet. Grade 3 1977. Grade 2 1978-'81, 1990-'91. 6 furlongs 1974. 1 mile 70 yards 1975-'79. Three-year-olds and up 1974. ‡Number finished second, DQ to fourth, 1983. ‡Wild Spirit (Chi) finished second, DQ to third on an Arkansas Racing Commission decision, 2004. Held as an overnight handicap 1973.

Appleton Handicap

Grade 3 in 2006. Gulfstream Park, three-year-olds and up, 1 mile, turf. Held February 11, 2006, with a gross value of $100,000. First held in 1952. First graded in 1973. Stakes record 1:32.80 (2006 Gulch Approval).

Year	Winner	Jockey	Second	Third	Strs	Time	1st Purse
2006	**Gulch Approval**, 6, 115	R. E. Alvarado Jr.	Old Dodge (Brz), 5, 115	Drum Major, 4, 115	9	**1:32.80**	$60,000
2005	**Mr. Light (Arg)**, 6, 114	C. H. Velasquez	Host (Chi), 5, 119	Millennium Dragon (GB), 6, 120	8	1:32.98	60,000
2004	**Millennium Dragon (GB)**, 5, 116	R. Migliore	Political Attack, 5, 118	Proud Man, 6, 116	12	1:34.40	90,000
2003	**Point Prince**, 4, 115	M. R. Cruz	Krieger, 5, 115	Red Sea (GB), 7, 114	9	1:37.84	90,000
2002	**Pisces**, 5, 113	R. I. Velez	North East Bound, 6, 117	Capsized, 6, 114	10	1:39.41	90,000
2001	**Associate**, 6, 114	J. F. Chavez	Band Is Passing, 5, 119	El Mirasol, 6, 115	12	1:33.69	90,000
2000	**Band Is Passing**, 4, 115	E. Coa	Hibernian Rhapsody (Ire), 5, 115	Shamrock City, 5, 114	11	1:40.11	60,000
1999	**Behaviour (GB)**, 7, 113	S. J. Sellers	Notoriety, 6, 112	Legs Galore, 4, 113	6	1:45.77	60,000
1998	**Sir Cat**, 5, 119	J. D. Bailey	Wild Event, 5, 114	Kingcanrunallday, 5, 116	5	1:42.69	60,000
1997	**Montjoy**, 5, 116	M. E. Smith	Mighty Forum (GB), 6, 114	Elite Jeblar, 7, 114	12	1:39.88	60,000
1996	**The Vid**, 6, 122	W. H. McCauley	Dove Hunt, 5, 120	Montreal Red, 4, 114	11	1:41.79	60,000
1995	**Dusty Screen**, 7, 116	W. H. McCauley	The Vid, 5, 114	Dove Hunt, 4, 114	7	1:42.72	60,000
1994	**Paradise Creek**, 5, 121	M. E. Smith	Fourstars Allstar, 6, 117	Elite Jeblar, 4, 111	8	1:40.57	60,000
1993	**Cigar Toss (Arg)**, 6, 112	B. G. Moore	Bidding Proud, 4, 113	Archies Laughter, 5, 114	9	1:43.55	60,000
1992	**Royal Ninja**, 6, 112	J. D. Bailey	Archies Laughter, 4, 114	Native Boundary, 4, 116	12	1:42.49	60,000
1991	**Jolie's Halo**, 4, 110	R. Platts	Rowdy Regal, 4, 110	Shot Gun Scott, 4, 118	11	1:40.50	60,000
1990	**Highland Springs**, 6, 118	C. Perret	Prince Randi, 4, 115	Wanderkin, 7, 116	9	1:35.20	60,000
1989	**Fabulous Indian**, 4, 109	E. O. Nunez	Equalize, 7, 125	Simply Majestic, 5, 121	11	1:35.00	60,000
1988	**Yankee Affair**, 6, 116	R. P. Romero	Performing Pappy, 4, 114	Kings River (Ire), 6, 114	14	1:35.00	60,000
1987	**Regal Flier**, 6, 113	J. Vasquez	Wollaston, 5, 112	Hi Ideal, 5, 113	9	1:35.60	27,375
	Racing Star, 5, 111	S. B. Soto	Trubulare, 4, 111	Onyxly, 6, 116	10	1:35.60	27,975
1986	**Cool**, 5, 116	J. Vasquez	Dr. Schwartzman, 5, 120	Smart and Sharp, 7, 115	11	1:39.60	39,690
1985	**Smart and Sharp**, 6, 117	M. Russ	Amerilad, 4, 112	Dr. Schwartzman, 4, 117	11	1:34.60	31,740
	Star Choice, 6, 118	J. McKnight	Late Act, 6, 121	Solidified, 4, 114	10	1:34.40	31,440
1984	**Super Sunrise (GB)**, 5, 118	C. Perret	Smart and Sharp, 5, 110	Guston (Arg), 6, 115	11	1:34.40	23,628
	Great Substence, 6, 113	G. St. Leon	Dr. Schwartzman, 3, 109	Rising Raja, 4, 113	10	1:35.00	23,418
1983	**Northrop**, 4, 116	J. Velasquez	Forkali, 5, 114	North Course, 8, 113	6	1:22.00	26,754
1982	**Gleaming Channel**, 4, 116	C. Perret	Double Cadet, 4, 111	Victorian Double, 4, 112	9	1:36.00	18,375
	King of Mardi Gras, 6, 113	A. Smith Jr.	Some One Frisky, 6, 114	Explosive Bid, 4, 115	9	1:36.40	18,225
1981	**North Course**, 6, 115	B. Thornburg	Proctor, 4, 120	Royal Centurion, 4, 113	11	1:34.80	23,292
	Drum's Captain (Ire), 6, 114	A. Gilbert	Foretake, 5, 116	Poverty Boy, 6, 114	10	1:35.00	23,082
1980	**Morning Frolic**, 5, 117	A. T. Cordero Jr.	Match the Hatch, 4, 111	Nar, 5, 113	12	1:35.40	19,365
	Pipedreamer (GB), 5, 113	J. Cruguet	Houdini, 5, 119	Once Over Lightly, 7, 114	10	1:34.40	18,915
1979	**Fleet Gar**, 4, 114	J. Fell	Romeo, 6, 118	Vic's Magic, 6, 121	11	1:36.40	19,005
	Regal and Royal, 4, 120	J. Fell	North Course, 4, 114	Bob's Dusty, 5, 121	11	1:37.00	19,155
1978	**Qui Native**, 4, 117	D. MacBeth	All Friends (Ire), 6, 115	Tablao (Chi), 5, 114	10	1:36.40	19,350
	Do Lishus, 4, 110	J. D. Bailey	Haverty, 4, 113	Leader of the Band, 6, 113	11	1:37.20	19,500

1977	**Gay Jitterbug**, 4, 118	L. Saumell	What a Threat, 5, 110	Riverside Sam, 4, 109	9	1:36.40	$16,185
	Cinteelo, 4, 115	B. Thornburg	Commanding Lead, 6, 110	*El Guindo, 6, 111	10	1:36.20	16,335
1976	**Step Forward**, 4, 114	M. Solomone	Faithful Diplomat, 4, 111	Passionate Pirate, 5, 111	9	1:34.00	20,775
	Improviser, 4, 113	J. Cruguet	Odd Man, 5, 112	Peppy Addy, 4, 113	11	1:35.60	21,195
1975	**Duke Tom**, 5, 113	P. I. Grimm	Dartsum, 6, 116	Return to Reality, 6, 110	14	1:36.20	17,460
	Beau Bugle, 5, 116	M. Hole	The Grok, 4, 114	Mr. Door, 4, 115	13	1:36.20	16,860
1974	**Right On**, 5, 112	E. Maple	*Rey Maya, 7, 112	Rapid Sage, 4, 114	13	1:37.80	21,930
1973	**Windtex**, 4, 113	J. L. Rotz	Getajetholme, 4, 112	Prince of Truth, 5, 114	9	1:35.20	16,140
	Life Cycle, 4, 112	F. Iannelli	Roundhouse, 5, 108	Hope Eternal, 5, 112	10	1:35.40	16,290

Named in honor of Arthur I. Appleton, owner of Bridlewood Farm in Florida. Not graded 1975-'84. Grade 2 1998, 2000-'03. $1\frac{1}{16}$ miles 1952, 1992-2000. $1\frac{1}{8}$ miles 1953-'64. 7 furlongs 1965-'66, 1972, 1983. 1 mile 70 yards 1991. Dirt 1952-'66, 1972, 1983, 1991, 1993, 1995, 1998-'99. Two divisions 1973, 1975-'82, 1984-'85, 1987.

Aqueduct Handicap

Grade 3 in 2006. Aqueduct, three-year-olds and up, $1\frac{1}{16}$ miles. Held January 21, 2006, with a gross value of $110,000. First held in 1902. First graded in 1985. Stakes record 1:41.13 (1995 Danzig's Dance).

Year	Winner	Jockey	Second	Third	Strs	Time	1st Purse
2006	**Happy Hunting**, 5, 114	N. Arroyo Jr.	Evening Attire, 8, 118	Mr. Whitestone, 6, 114	8	1:44.56	$66,000
2005	**Country Be Gold**, 8, 114	J. L. Espinoza	Aggadan, 6, 123	Mahzouz, 4, 112	8	1:44.80	66,180
2004	**Seattle Fitz (Arg)**, 5, 114	A. T. Gryder	Evening Attire, 6, 122	Rogue Agent, 5, 112	8	1:42.13	66,060
2003	**Snake Mountain**, 5, 120	M. J. Luzzi	Ground Storm, 7, 117	Cat's At Home, 6, 114	5	1:44.17	64,440
2002	**Evening Attire**, 4, 116	S. Bridgmohan	Ground Storm, 6, 115	Tempest Fugit, 5, 114	7	1:42.69	65,520
2001	**Liberty Gold**, 7, 115	J. Bravo	Coyote Lakes, 7, 116	Talk's Cheap, 5, 116	7	1:42.20	66,300
2000	**Sky Approval**, 6, 115	C. H. Velasquez	Parental Pressure, 9, 115	Phone the King, 5, 114	8	1:44.45	49,770
1999	**Mr. Sinatra**, 5, 118	A. T. Gryder	Brushing Up, 6, 112	Wouldn't We All, 5, 117	5	1:43.11	49,335
1998	**Star of Valor**, 5, 113	A. T. Gryder	Christian Soldier, 4, 113	Mr. Sinatra, 4, 117	8	1:42.48	49,725
1997	**Pacific Fleet**, 5, 112	J. Chavez	More to Tell, 6, 116	Admiralty, 5, 116	8	1:43.45	39,924
1996	**Mighty Magee**, 4, 118	M. J. Luzzi	May I Inquire, 7, 113	More to Tell, 5, 115	8	1:43.89	39,780
1995	**Danzig's Dance**, 6, 111	J. F. Chavez	Key Contender, 7, 115	Golden Larch, 4, 112	8	**1:41.13**	50,010
1994	**As Indicated**, 4, 121	R. G. Davis	Primitive Hall, 5, 113	Jacksonport, 5, 112	6	1:45.77	48,690
1993	**Shots Are Ringing**, 6, 118	J. R. Velazquez	A Call to Rise, 5, 111	Federal Funds, 4, 109	6	1:44.44	52,650
1992	**‡Formal Dinner**, 4, 112	A. T. Cordero Jr.	Shots Are Ringing, 5, 113	Island Edition, 5, 110	6	1:43.60	51,750
1991	**Sports View**, 4, 115	J. D. Bailey	I'm Sky High, 5, 115	Lost Opportunity, 5, 112	6	1:43.41	51,750
1990	**Congeleur**, 5, 116	A. T. Cordero Jr.	Silver Survivor, 4, 118	King's Swan, 10, 116	7	1:44.80	52,020
1989	**Lord of the Night**, 6, 114	W. H. McCauley	Its Acedemic, 5, 110	True and Blue, 4, 113	6	1:42.80	52,110
1988	**‡Clever Secret**, 4, 112	E. T. Baird	Proud Debonair, 6, 114	Native Wizard, 5, 112	9	1:45.20	54,810
1987	**King's Swan**, 7, 118	J. A. Santos	Raja's Revenge, 4, 111	Cost Conscious, 5, 112	8	1:41.80	54,990
1986	**Aggressive Bid**, 5, 109	M. Venezia	Badwagon Harry, 7, 120	Carjack, 5, 114	6	1:43.80	50,850
1985	**Fight Over**, 4, 118	A. T. Cordero Jr.	Imp Society, 4, 113	Verbarctic, 5, 112	9	1:42.60	55,260
1984	**Moro**, 5, 120	J. Samyn	Jacksboro, 5, 120	Ask Muhammad, 5, 117	9	1:43.40	45,120
1983	**Fort Monroe**, 4, 108	V. H. Molina	Lark Oscillation (Fr), 8, 113	Fabulous Find, 5, 116	8	1:42.40	33,420
1982	**Reef Searcher**, 5, 114	A. T. Cordero Jr.	Deedee's Deal, 5, 107	Alla Breva, 5, 114	13	1:48.40	35,760
1981	**Irish Tower**, 4, 114	J. Fell	Dr. Blum, 4, 116	Lark Oscillation (Fr), 6, 108	5	1:44.60	32,760
1980	**Charlie Coast**, 5, 112	J. J. Miranda	Pole Position, 4, 126	Pirate's Bounty, 5, 112	12	1:44.80	35,400
1978	**Wise Philip**, 5, 117	J. Vasquez	Gallivantor, 6, 119	*Vanistorio, 6, 112	10	1:43.80	33,060
1977	**Magnetizer**, 4, 112	A. Santiago	Turn and Count, 4, 126	Due Diligence, 5, 112	6	1:45.40	32,580
1976	**Right Mind**, 5, 114	R. Turcotte	General Beauregard, 4, 119	Our Hero, 4, 115	5	1:38.80	32,670
1973	**Cannonade**, 2, 126	P. Anderson	Roger's Dandy, 2, 112	Flip Sal, 2, 116	7	1:51.60	34,080

Aqueduct S. 1962-'65, 1967-'68. Held at Belmont Park 1961. Not held 1910-'16, 1924, 1956-'58, 1969-'72, 1974-'75, 1979. $1\frac{1}{8}$ miles 1917-'19, 1926-'32, 1961-'73. $1\frac{5}{16}$ miles 1920-'23. 1 mile 1959-'60, 1976. Two-year-olds and up 1904. Two-year-olds 1973. ‡King's Swan finished first, DQ to fourth, 1988. ‡Shots Are Ringing finished first, DQ to second, 1992. Equaled track record 1995.

Arcadia Handicap

Grade 2 in 2006. Santa Anita Park, four-year-olds and up, 1 mile, turf. Held April 8, 2006, with a gross value of $150,000. First held in 1988. First graded in 1990. Stakes record 1:33.17 (2006 Silent Name [Jpn]).

Year	Winner	Jockey	Second	Third	Strs	Time	1st Purse
2006	**Silent Name (Jpn)**, 4, 116	R. Bejarano	Chinese Dragon, 4, 119	Milk It Mick (GB), 5, 117	10	**1:33.17**	$90,000
2005	**Singletary**, 5, 120	A. O. Solis	Sweet Return (GB), 5, 117	Buckland Manor, 5, 117	5	1:33.52	90,000
2004	**Diplomatic Bag**, 4, 116	D. R. Flores	Statement, 6, 114	Seinne (Chi), 7, 115	7	1:47.90	90,000
2003	**Century City (Ire)**, 4, 114	J. Valdivia Jr.	Gondolieri (Chi), 4, 116	Sunday Break (Jpn), 4, 117	9	1:47.84	90,000
2002	**Seinne (Chi)**, 5, 115	C. J. McCarron	Irish Prize, 6, 122	Kerrygold (Fr), 6, 116	9	1:47.16	90,000
2001	**Lazy Lode (Arg)**, 7, 121	L. A. Pincay Jr.	Night Patrol, 5, 116	Wake the Tiger, 5, 114	5	1:49.74	90,000
2000	**Falcon Flight (Fr)**, 4, 114	B. Blanc	Bonapartiste (Fr), 6, 118	Otavalo (Ire), 5, 114	7	1:47.88	97,950
1999	**Commitisize**, 4, 117	D. R. Flores	Majorien (GB), 5, 117	Ladies Din, 4, 119	7	1:48.25	90,000
1998	**Hawksley Hill (Ire)**, 5, 117	G. L. Stevens	Precious Ring, 5, 114	Kirkwall (GB), 4, 117	8	1:49.96	167,350
1997	**Labeeb (GB)**, 5, 120	E. Delahoussaye	Talloires, 7, 118	Pinfloron (Fr), 5, 115	5	1:35.80	80,100
1996	**Tychonic (GB)**, 6, 118	G. L. Stevens	Debutant Trick, 6, 117	Savinio, 6, 117	6	1:35.84	80,300
1995	**Savinio**, 5, 116	C. J. McCarron	River Flyer, 4, 121	Romarin (Brz), 5, 120	7	1:34.74	91,800
1994	**Norwich (GB)**, 7, 117	P. A. Valenzuela	Megan's Interco, 5, 119	Gothland (Fr), 5, 118	5	1:34.14	75,850
1993	**Val des Bois (Fr)**, 7, 118	P. A. Valenzuela	Star of Cozzene, 5, 122	C. Sam Maggio, 7, 113	7	1:35.07	77,750
1992	**Exbourne**, 6, 122	G. L. Stevens	Repriced, 4, 113	Madjaristan, 6, 115	6	1:33.21	95,000
1991	**Pharisien (Fr)**, 4, 113	C. S. Nakatani	Exbourne, 5, 118	Tartas (Fr), 5, 112	11	1:33.30	102,500

1990 **Steinlen (GB)**, 7, 125	J. A. Santos	Bruho, 4, 117	Wonder Dancer, 4, 111	6	1:33.40	$63,200
1989 **Political Ambition**, 5, 121	E. Delahoussaye	Patchy Groundfog, 6, 118	Steinlen (GB), 6, 122	5	1:35.60	62,600
1988 **Steinlen (GB)**, 5, 117	G. L. Stevens	Political Ambition, 4, 120	Neshad, 4, 117	9	1:34.80	88,760

Named for Arcadia, California, city in which Santa Anita Park is located. Formerly named for two California land grants called Rancho El Rincon. Grade 3 1990-'94. El Rincon H. 1988-2000. 1⅛ miles 1998-2004.

Aristides Breeders' Cup Handicap

Grade 3 in 2006. Churchill Downs, three-year-olds and up, 6 furlongs, dirt. Held June 3, 2006, with a gross value of $131,450. First held in 1989. First graded in 1999. Stakes record 1:07.59 (2005 Kelly's Landing).

Year	Winner	Jockey	Second	Third	Strs	Time	1st Purse
2006	**Lost in the Fog**, 4, 124	R. A. Baze	Kelly's Landing, 5, 117	Level Playingfield, 5, 114	6	1:08.52	$69,024
2005	**Kelly's Landing**, 4, 116	G. L. Stevens	Battle Won, 5, 117	Jet Prospector, 4, 116	6	**1:07.59**	100,719
2004	**Champali**, 4, 116	R. Bejarano	Beau's Town, 6, 121	Battle Won, 4, 114	6	1:09.04	100,533
2003	**Mountain General**, 5, 116	C. J. Lanerie	Beau's Town, 5, 123	Pass Rush, 4, 118	7	1:16.01	67,580
2002	**Orientate**, 4, 118	R. Albarado	Binthebest, 5, 114	No Armistice, 5, 116	5	1:14.41	66,650
2001	**Bet On Sunshine**, 9, 120	C. H. Borel	Alannan, 5, 119	Dash for Daylight, 4, 110	6	1:14.79	67,208
2000	**Bet On Sunshine**, 8, 119	F. C. Torres	Proven Cure, 6, 111	Sun Bull, 4, 111	7	1:15.11	68,014
1999	**Run Johnny**, 7, 116	P. Day	Squall Valley, 4, 112	Neon Shadow, 5, 114	8	1:16.27	68,572
1998	**Thisnearlywasmine**, 4, 115	S. J. Sellers	Partner's Hero, 4, 115	El Amante, 5, 118	7	1:15.72	67,518
1997	**High Stakes Player**, 5, 119	S. J. Sellers	Trafalger, 3, 106	Bet On Sunshine, 5, 112	7	1:15.85	21,800
1996	**Lord Carson**, 4, 115	D. M. Barton	Criollito (Arg), 5, 117	Bet On Sunshine, 4, 110	5	1:15.94	70,525
1995	**Boone's Mill**, 3, 106	D. M. Barton	Ojai, 6, 113	Hot Jaws, 5, 118	7	1:15.90	69,924
1994	**Never Wavering**, 5, 116	S. J. Sellers	Demaloot Demashoot, 4, 119	American Chance, 5, 117	8	1:16.55	53,479
1993	**Gold Spring (Arg)**, 5, 115	F. A. Arguello Jr.	Take Me Out, 5, 119	In the Zone, 4, 113	6	1:16.43	35,718
1992	**Tricky Fun**, 4, 113	P. Day	Guns of Cielo, 5, 112	Richman, 4, 118	6	1:16.35	44,720
1991	**Bio**, 5, 117	B. E. Bartram	Bratt's Choice, 4, 117	Guns of Cielo, 4, 112	6	1:16.62	44,668
1990	**Beau Genius**, 5, 122	R. D. Lopez	Bio, 4, 113	Launch a Dream, 5, 111	9	1:16.20	45,240
1989	**Bet the Pot**, 4, 115	C. R. Woods Jr.	Temptation Time, 5, 115	Good Roar, 5, 113	5	1:16.00	33,703

Named for the first winner of the Kentucky Derby, H. P. McGrath's Aristides (1872 c. by *Leamington). Aristides H. 1996-2003. 6½ furlongs 1989-2003. Track record 2000, 2005.

Arkansas Derby

Grade 2 in 2006. Oaklawn Park, three-year-olds, 1⅛ miles, dirt. Held April 15, 2006, with a gross value of $1,000,000. First held in 1936. First graded in 1973. Stakes record 1:46.80 (1984 Althea).

Year	Winner	Jockey	Second	Third	Strs	Time	1st Purse
2006	**Lawyer Ron**, 3, 122	J. McKee	Steppenwolfer, 3, 118	Private Vow, 3, 122	13	1:51.38	$600,000
2005	**Afleet Alex**, 3, 122	J. Rose	Flower Alley, 3, 122	Andromeda's Hero, 3, 122	10	1:48.80	600,000
2004	**Smarty Jones**, 3, 122	S. Elliott	Borrego, 3, 118	Pro Prado, 3, 122	11	1:49.41	600,000
2003	**Sir Cherokee**, 3, 118	T. J. Thompson	Eugene's Third Son, 3, 118	Christine's Outlaw, 3, 118	12	1:48.39	300,000
2002	**Private Emblem**, 3, 122	D. J. Meche	Wild Horses, 3, 118	dh-Bay Monster, 3, 118 dh-Windward Passage, 3, 122	11	1:52.20	300,000
2001	**Balto Star**, 3, 122	M. Guidry	Jamaican Rum, 3, 122	Son of Rocket, 3, 122	11	1:49.04	300,000
2000	**Graeme Hall**, 3, 118	R. Albarado	Snuck In, 3, 122	Impeachment, 3, 118	14	1:49.08	300,000
1999	**‡Certain**, 3, 122	K. Desormeaux	Torrid Sand, 3, 118	Ecton Park, 3, 122	7	1:49.30	300,000
1998	**Victory Gallop**, 3, 122	A. O. Solis	Hanuman Highway (Ire), 3, 118	Favorite Trick, 3, 122	9	1:49.86	300,000
1997	**Crypto Star**, 3, 122	P. Day	Phantom On Tour, 3, 122	Pacificbounty, 3, 122	11	1:49.20	300,000
1996	**Zarb's Magic**, 3, 122	R. D. Ardoin	Grindstone, 3, 122	Halo Sunshine, 3, 122	12	1:49.21	300,000
1995	**Dazzling Falls**, 3, 122	G. K. Gomez	Flitch, 3, 118	On Target, 3, 122	8	1:50.60	300,000
1994	**Concern**, 3, 118	G. K. Gomez	Blumin Affair, 3, 118	Silver Goblin, 3, 122	9	1:48.16	300,000
1993	**Rockamundo**, 3, 118	C. H. Borel	Kissin Kris, 3, 122	Foxtrail, 3, 122	10	1:48.17	300,000
1992	**Pine Bluff**, 3, 122	J. D. Bailey	Lil E. Tee, 3, 122	Desert Force, 3, 122	6	1:49.49	300,000
1991	**Olympio**, 3, 122	E. Delahoussaye	Corporate Report, 3, 118	Richman, 3, 122	11	1:47.67	300,000
1990	**Silver Ending**, 3, 122	G. L. Stevens	Real Cash, 3, 122	Power Lunch, 3, 118	13	1:48.00	300,000
1989	**Dansil**, 3, 121	L. Snyder	Clever Trevor, 3, 126	Advocate Training, 3, 115	11	1:49.20	240,000
1988	**Proper Reality**, 3, 118	J. D. Bailey	Primal, 3, 115	Sea Trek, 3, 123	8	1:48.40	300,000
1987	**Demons Begone**, 3, 123	P. Day	Lookinforthebigone, 3, 118	You're No Bargain, 3, 115	6	1:47.60	300,000
1986	**Rampage**, 3, 118	P. Day	Wheatly Hall, 3, 115	†Family Style, 3, 121	14	1:48.20	300,000
1985	**Tank's Prospect**, 3, 123	G. L. Stevens	Encolure, 3, 126	Irish Fighter, 3, 115	9	1:48.40	349,650
1984	**†Althea**, 3, 121	P. A. Valenzuela	Pine Circle, 3, 118	Gate Dancer, 3, 118	11	**1:46.80**	360,150
1983	**Sunny's Halo**, 3, 126	E. Delahoussaye	Caveat, 3, 120	Exile King, 3, 117	14	1:49.40	176,340
1982	**Hostage**, 3, 117	J. Fell	El Baba, 3, 126	Bold Style, 3, 123	10	1:51.60	170,580
1981	**Bold Ego**, 3, 123	J. Lively	Top Avenger, 3, 120	Woodchopper, 3, 123	9	1:50.40	137,160
1980	**Temperence Hill**, 3, 123	D. Haire	Bold 'n Rulling, 3, 117	Sun Catcher, 3, 120	10	1:50.60	107,160
1979	**Golden Act**, 3, 126	S. Hawley	Smarten, 3, 120	Strike the Main, 3, 115	10	1:50.00	107,280
1978	**Esops Foibles**, 3, 126	C. J. McCarron	Chief of Dixieland, 3, 117	Special Honor, 3, 120	13	1:52.20	82,470
1977	**Clev Er Tell**, 3, 126	R. Broussard	Kodiack, 3, 117	Best Person, 3, 117	12	1:50.60	80,520
1976	**Elocutionist**, 3, 126	J. Lively	New Collection, 3, 117	Klen Klitso, 3, 120	12	1:49.20	81,480
1975	**Promised City**, 3, 126	D. E. Whited	Bold Chapeau, 3, 117	My Friend Gus, 3, 120	14	1:51.80	82,140
1974	**J. R.'s Pet**, 3, 123	D. G. McHargue	Silver Florin, 3, 120	Nick's Folly, 3, 120	17	1:50.60	86,910
1973	**Impecunious**, 3, 126	J. Velasquez	Vodika, 3, 123	Warbucks, 3, 123	10	1:49.60	74,130

Formerly named Arkansas Centennial Derby in honor of the 100th anniversary of the founding of the state of Arkansas in 1936. Grade 1 1981-'88. Not held 1945. Dead heat for third 2002. ‡Valhol finished first, DQ to seventh for jockey's use of an illegal electrical stimulation device 1999. †Denotes female.

Arlington Classic Stakes

Grade 3 in 2006. Arlington Park, three-year-olds, 1¹/₁₆ miles, turf. Held July 2, 2005, with a gross value of $150,000. First held in 1929. First graded in 1973. Stakes record 1:41.95 (2002 Mr. Mellon).

Year	Winner	Jockey	Second	Third	Strs	Time	1st Purse
2005	**Purim**, 3, 119	M. Guidry	United, 3, 119	Cosmic Kris, 3, 119	9	1:42.65	$90,000
2004	**Toasted**, 3, 121	R. R. Douglas	Street Theatre, 3, 119	Cool Conductor, 3, 119	8	1:50.91	120,000
2003	**Lismore Knight**, 3, 119	R. R. Douglas	Remind, 3, 116	Good Day Too (Ire), 3, 116	10	1:42.73	105,000
2002	**Mr. Mellon**, 3, 121	R. R. Douglas	Doc Holiday (Ire), 3, 121	Seainsky, 3, 116	9	**1:41.95**	105,000
2001	**Baptize**, 3, 121	M. Guidry	Indygo Shiner, 3, 121	Cherokee Kim, 3, 116	6	1:48.80	120,000
2000	**King Cugat**, 3, 123	R. Albarado	Boyum, 3, 114	El Ballezano, 3, 114	5	1:48.16	90,000
1997	**Honor Glide**, 3, 114	G. K. Gomez	Brave Act (GB), 3, 120	Daylight Savings, 3, 114	8	1:47.59	75,000
1996	**Trail City**, 3, 114	P. Day	More Royal, 3, 120	Winter Quarters, 3, 114	5	1:48.61	120,000
1995	**Hawk Attack**, 3, 114	P. Day	Via Lombardia (Ire), 3, 120	Bryntirion, 3, 114	10	1:48.04	120,000
1994	**Eagle Eyed**, 3, 120	C. S. Nakatani	Mr. Angel, 3, 120	Star Campaigner, 3, 114	11	1:48.46	180,000
1993	**Boundlessly**, 3, 120	P. Day	Hegar, 3, 114	Williamstown, 3, 123	13	1:49.89	180,000
1992	**Saint Ballado**, 3, 120	J. A. Krone	Desert Force, 3, 114	Star Recruit, 3, 117	6	1:46.82	180,000
1991	**Whadjathink**, 3, 120	J. Velasquez	Freezing Dock, 3, 114	Character (GB), 3, 120	8	1:49.18	180,000
1990	**Sound of Cannons**, 3, 114	P. Day	Adjudicating, 3, 117	Home At Last, 3, 123	7	1:47.40	150,000
1989	**Clever Trevor**, 3, 126	D. R. Pettinger	Bio, 3, 114	Western Playboy, 3, 126	8	1:49.40	124,500
1987	**Lost Code**, 3, 123	G. St. Leon	Gem Master, 3, 120	Avies Copy, 3, 120	7	1:49.60	99,090
1986	**Sumptious**, 3, 115	R. P. Romero	Glow, 3, 120	Cheapskate, 3, 123	13	1:49.40	96,720
1985	**Smile**, 3, 117	J. Vasquez	Red Attack, 3, 114	Clever Allemont, 3, 123	6	1:51.20	114,000
1984	**At the Threshold**, 3, 126	P. Day	Par Flite, 3, 114	Dugan Knight, 3, 114	8	1:50.20	71,400
1983	**Play Fellow**, 3, 123	P. Day	Bet Big, 3, 114	Passing Base, 3, 114	9	1:49.00	65,400
1982	**Wolfie's Rascal**, 3, 114	A. T. Cordero Jr.	Drop Your Drawers, 3, 114	Dew Line, 3, 114	13	1:49.00	72,600
1981	**Fairway Phantom**, 3, 114	J. Lively	Golden Derby, 3, 114	Television Studio, 3, 117	11	1:53.40	84,000
1980	**Spruce Needles**, 3, 114	M. R. Morgan	I'ma Hell Raiser, 3, 114	Stone Manor, 3, 126	6	1:49.20	81,000
1979	**Steady Growth**, 3, 123	B. Swatuk	Private Account, 3, 114	Third and Lex, 3, 114	5	2:00.60	65,400
1978	**Alydar**, 3, 126	J. Fell	Chief of Dixieland, 3, 114	Gordie H., 3, 114	5	2:00.40	63,000
1977	**Private Thoughts**, 4, 117	R. R. Perez	Pay Tribute, 5, 118	Dragset, 6, 114	9	1:59.40	90,000
1973	**Linda's Chief**, 3, 123	B. Baeza	Blue Chip Dan, 3, 114	Golden Don, 3, 114	8	1:44.60	72,200

Formerly sponsored by General Motors Corp. of Detroit, Michigan 1971-'73. Not graded 1977. Grade 1 1981-'89. Grade 2 1990-2004. Classic S. 1929-'45. Pontiac Grand Prix S. 1971-'73. Held at Washington Park 1943-'45. Not held 1974-'76, 1988, 1998-'99. 1¹/₄ miles 1929-'51, 1977-'79. 1 mile 1952-'72. 1¹/₈ miles 1980-2001. Dirt 1929-'93. Three-year-olds and up 1977. Equaled course record 1997.

Arlington Handicap

Grade 3 in 2006. Arlington Park, three-year-olds and up, 1¹/₄ miles, turf. Held July 23, 2005, with a gross value of $200,000. First held in 1929. First graded in 1973. Stakes record 2:00.40 (1985 Pass the Line).

Year	Winner	Jockey	Second	Third	Strs	Time	1st Purse
2005	**Cool Conductor**, 4, 120	C. H. Velasquez	Vangelis, 6, 119	Major Rhythm, 6, 116	7	2:02.26	$120,000
2004	**Senor Swinger**, 4, 118	B. Blanc	Mystery Giver, 6, 120	Ballingarry (Ire), 5, 121	7	2:03.38	150,000
2003	**Honor in War**, 4, 120	D. R. Flores	Better Talk Now, 4, 115	Mystery Giver, 5, 118	10	2:02.71	150,000
2002	**Falcon Flight (Fr)**, 6, 115	R. R. Douglas	Kappa King, 5, 117	Gretchen's Star, 7, 115	10	2:03.13	135,000
2001	**Make No Mistake (Ire)**, 6, 116	R. Albarado	Takarian (Ire), 6, 116	El Gran Papa, 4, 115	7	2:02.53	150,000
2000	**Northern Quest (Fr)**, 5, 113	R. Albarado	Profit Option, 5, 112	Where's Taylor, 4, 114	11	2:02.13	90,000
1997	**Wild Event**, 4, 114	M. Guidry	Storm Trooper, 4, 114	Chorwon, 4, 113	8	2:01.52	90,000
1996	**Torch Rouge (GB)**, 5, 116	M. Guidry	Sentimental Moi, 6, 113	Volochine (Ire), 5, 115	6	2:03.32	120,000
1995	**Manilaman**, 4, 114	R. P. Romero	Snake Eyes, 5, 117	Bluegrass Prince (Ire), 4, 117	7	2:02.82	120,000
1994	**Fanmore**, 6, 119	P. Day	Marastani, 4, 114	Split Run, 6, 114	7	2:01.72	150,000
1993	**Evanescent**, 6, 114	A. T. Gryder	Split Run, 5, 113	Magesterial Cheer, 5, 112	9	2:00.93	150,000
1992	**Sky Classic**, 5, 125	P. Day	‡Duckaroo, 6, 111	Glity, 4, 116	9	2:00.62	150,000
1991	**Filago**, 4, 116	P. A. Valenzuela	Super Abound, 4, 113	Izvestia, 4, 120	12	2:01.40	150,000
1990	**Pleasant Variety**, 6, 115	E. Fires	Double Booked, 5, 114	Ten Keys, 6, 121	7	2:04.00	180,000
1989	**Unknown Quantity (GB)**, 4, 112	J. Velasquez	Frosty the Snowman, 4, 122	Delegant, 5, 113	5	2:11.20	120,000
1987	**Ifrad**, 5, 114	G. Baze	Storm On the Loose, 4, 115	Grey Classic, 4, 114	8	2:12.20	90,360
1986	**Mourjane (Ire)**, 6, 117	J. A. Santos	Will Dancer (Fr), 4, 115	Clever Song, 4, 118	9	2:01.40	112,350
1985	**Pass the Line**, 4, 113	J. L. Diaz	The Noble Player, 5, 118	Executive Pride (Ire), 4, 113	7	**2:00.40**	82,050
1984	**Who's for Dinner**, 5, 109	M. Venezia	Nijinsky's Secret, 6, 127	Star Choice, 5, 112	7	2:04.00	70,800
1983	**Palikaraki (Fr)**, 5, 116	W. Shoemaker	Rossi Gold, 7, 122	Late Act, 4, 113	11	2:35.80	76,200
1982	**Flying Target**, 5, 115	R. W. Cox	Rossi Gold, 6, 125	Don Roberto, 5, 118	8	2:32.40	71,640
1981	**Spruce Needles**, 4, 115	J. C. Espinoza	Summer Advocate, 4, 117	Sea Chimes (Ire), 5, 116	8	2:35.00	72,060
1980	**Yvonand (Fr)**, 4, 111	E. Beitia	Rossi Gold, 4, 120	Lyphard's Wish (Fr), 4, 121	8	2:31.40	71,700
1979	**Bowl Game**, 5, 124	J. Velasquez	Young Bob, 4, 110	†Liveinthesunshine, 4, 105	14	2:32.20	79,260
1978	**Romeo**, 5, 116	E. Fires	Fluorescent Light, 4, 118	Improviser, 6, 118	9	2:32.00	73,080
1977	**Cunning Trick**, 4, 110	B. Fann	‡*Vadim, 7, 118	No Turning, 4, 118	8	2:33.80	72,480
1976	**Victorian Prince**, 6, 118	R. Platts	Improviser, 4, 118	Bold Roll, 4, 112	12	1:58.20	90,000
1975	**Royal Glint**, 5, 125	J. E. Tejeira	*Zografos, 7, 113	Buffalo Lark, 5, 122	9	1:55.80	87,400
1974	**Buffalo Lark**, 4, 118	L. Snyder	Royal Glint, 4, 112	Spot T V, 7, 111	13	1:54.40	91,800
1973	**Dubassoff**, 4, 117	J. Vasquez	Jogging, 6, 114	Red Reality, 7, 118	14	1:58.60	72,750

Grade 2 1973-'80, 1990-'97. Grade 1 1981-'89. Arlington Park H. 1963, 1972, 1974. Held at Washington Park 1943-'45. Held at Hawthorne 1985. Not held 1940, 1969-'71, 1988, 1998-'99. 1¹/₈ miles 1929, 1952, 1965. 1³/₁₆ miles 1941,

1953-'62, 1964, 1973-'76. 1 mile 1963, 1966-'67. 7 furlongs 1968. 1½ miles 1972, 1977-'83. Dirt 1929-'39, 1942-'53, 1963, 1965-'72. Originally scheduled on turf 1975. ‡No Turning finished second, DQ to third, 1977. ‡Plate Dancer finished second, DQ to fifth, 1992. Track record 1975. †Denotes female.

Arlington Matron Handicap

Grade 3 in 2006. Arlington Park, three-year-olds and up, fillies and mares, 1⅛ miles, dirt. Held September 3, 2005, with a gross value of $150,000. First held in 1930. First graded in 1973. Stakes record 1:48.40 (1986 Queen Alexandra; 1989 Between the Hedges).

Year	Winner	Jockey	Second	Third	Strs	Time	1st Purse
2005	**‡Quick Temper**, 4, 114	S. Bridgmohan	Diavla, 4, 116	For Gillian, 4, 116	7	1:49.87	$90,000
2004	**Adoration**, 5, 123	V. Espinoza	Tamweel, 4, 116	Indy Groove, 4, 116	7	1:49.75	90,000
2003	**Take Charge Lady**, 4, 123	S. J. Sellers	Lakenheath, 5, 116	To the Queen, 4, 117	6	1:50.19	90,000
2002	**Lakenheath**, 4, 115	C. A. Emigh	With Ability, 4, 116	Your Out, 4, 115	5	1:50.78	90,000
2001	**Humble Clerk**, 4, 114	L. J. Melancon	Maltese Superb, 4, 115	Lakenheath, 3, 115	7	1:51.53	90,000
2000	**Megans Bluff**, 3, 111	C. R. Woods Jr.	On a Soapbox, 4, 115	Tutorial, 4, 113	8	1:51.41	90,000
1997	**Omi**, 4, 114	M. Guidry	Gold Memory, 4, 115	Trick Attack, 6, 114	6	1:51.93	60,000
1996	**Belle of Cozzene**, 4, 115	D. R. Pettinger	War Thief, 4, 113	Your Ladyship, 6, 116	9	1:49.34	75,000
1995	**Mariah's Storm**, 4, 117	R. N. Lester	Mysteriously, 4, 117	Minority Dater, 4, 114	9	1:50.98	60,000
1994	**Hey Hazel**, 4, 115	M. G. Pino	Passing Vice, 4, 114	Pennyhill Park, 4, 116	8	1:49.58	60,000
1993	**Erica's Dream**, 5, 115	W. Martinez	Pleasant Jolie, 5, 114	Meafara, 4, 123	6	1:50.09	60,000
1992	**Lemhi Go**, 4, 114	E. Fires	Beth Believes, 6, 112	Diamond City, 4, 113	8	1:49.67	45,000
1991	**Lucky Lady Lauren**, 4, 112	J. Velasquez	Beth Believes, 5, 113	Bungalow, 4, 112	6	1:49.21	45,000
1990	**Degenerate Gal**, 5, 117	R. P. Romero	Evangelical, 4, 115	Confirmed Dancer, 4, 113	6	1:49.20	48,555
1989	**Between the Hedges**, 5, 112	P. A. Johnson	Topicount, 4, 116	Stoneleigh's Hope, 4, 114	10	**1:48.40**	65,010
1987	**Family Style**, 4, 123	S. Hawley	Royal Cielo, 3, 113	Tide, 5, 114	7	1:52.20	49,320
1986	**Queen Alexandra**, 4, 122	D. Brumfield	Mr. T.'s Tune, 5, 113	Bessarabian, 4, 121	6	**1:48.40**	92,220
1985	**Heatherten**, 6, 126	R. P. Romero	Solo Skater, 5, 112	Mr. T.'s Tune, 4, 114	8	2:04.00	49,410
1984	**Choose a Partner**, 4, 116	D. Brumfield	First Flurry, 5, 113	Silvered Silk, 4, 117	7	2:04.00	62,595
1983	**May Day Eighty**, 4, 115	J. Vasquez	Sefa's Beauty, 4, 125	Stay a Leader, 4, 113	10	2:04.40	50,355
1982	**Sweetest Chant**, 4, 115	E. Fires	Miss Huntington, 5, 119	Turnablade, 5, 115	7	2:02.60	48,960
1981	**La Bonzo**, 5, 110	J. Lively	Wistful, 4, 123	Weber City Miss, 4, 123	8	2:02.60	66,360
1980	**Impetuous Gal**, 5, 115	E. Fires	Salzburg, 5, 112	Liveinthesunshine, 5, 108	10	2:01.40	67,200
1979	**Amerigirl**, 4, 115	B. Swatuk	Frosty Skater, 4, 118	Calderina (Ity), 4, 122	10	1:51.20	52,800
1978	**Rich Soil**, 4, 117	C. H. Silva	Satan's Cheer, 6, 112	Sans Arc, 4, 113	11	1:51.20	38,340
1977	**Javamine**, 4, 119	J. Velasquez	*Star Ball, 5, 119	Ivory Castle, 3, 110	9	1:53.20	52,620
1976	**Nicosia**, 4, 118	W. Gavidia	B. J. King, 4, 111	Hope of Glory, 4, 109	9	1:49.40	45,450
	Cycylya Zee, 3, 110	H. Arroyo	Sugar Plum Time, 4, 115	True Reality, 3, 109	9	1:49.60	46,200
1975	***Polynesienne**, 4, 110	L. Snyder	Princesse Grey, 4, 110	Pass a Glance, 4, 116	9	1:51.80	45,050
	Sixty Sails, 5, 114	L. Snyder	Victorian Queen, 4, 118	Princess Ormea, 3, 110	8	1:52.80	45,050
1974	**Sixty Sails**, 4, 121	D. E. Whited	*Protectora, 5, 113	What Will Be, 4, 118	14	1:50.60	46,300
1973	***Last Home**, 4, 112	F. Alvarez	North Broadway, 3, 115	Ziba Blue, 6, 114	12	1:50.00	35,800

Matron races are traditionally held for older fillies and mares. Grade 2 1973-'89. Matron H. 1964-'83. Held at Washington Park 1943-'45. Held at Hawthorne Race Course 1985. Not held 1933-'36, 1988, 1998-'99. 1 mile 1930-'57. 1¼ miles 1980-'85. Turf 1966-'79. Three-year-olds 1952. Fillies 1952. Two divisions 1975-'76. ‡Indy Groove finished first, DQ to seventh for a positive drug test, 2005.

Arlington Million Stakes

Grade 1 in 2006. Arlington Park, three-year-olds and up, 1¼ miles, turf. Held August 13, 2005, with a gross value of $1,000,000. First held in 1981. First graded in 1983. Stakes record 1:58.69 (1995 Awad).

Year	Winner	Jockey	Second	Third	Strs	Time	1st Purse
2005	**Powerscourt (GB)**, 5, 126	K. Fallon	Kitten's Joy, 4, 126	Fourty Niners Son, 4, 126	10	2:03.38	$600,000
2004	**‡Kicken Kris**, 4, 126	K. Desormeaux	Magistretti, 4, 126	Epalo (Ger), 5, 126	13	2:00.08	600,000
2003	**‡Sulamani (Ire)**, 4, 126	D. R. Flores	dh-Kaieteur, 4, 126 dh-Paolini (Ger), 6, 126		13	2:02.29	600,000
2002	**Beat Hollow (GB)**, 5, 126	J. D. Bailey	Sarafan, 5, 126	Forbidden Apple, 7, 126	9	2:02.94	600,000
2001	**Silvano (Ger)**, 5, 126	A. Suborics	Hap, 5, 126	Redattore (Brz), 6, 126	12	2:02.64	600,000
2000	**Chester House**, 5, 126	J. D. Bailey	Manndar (Ire), 4, 126	Mula Gula, 4, 126	7	2:01.37	1,200,000
1997	**Marlin**, 4, 126	G. L. Stevens	Sandpit (Brz), 8, 126	Percutant (GB), 6, 126	8	2:02.54	600,000
1996	**Mecke**, 4, 126	R. G. Davis	Awad, 6, 126	Sandpit (Brz), 7, 126	9	2:00.49	600,000
1995	**Awad**, 5, 126	E. Maple	Sandpit (Brz), 6, 126	The Vid, 5, 126	11	**1:58.69**	600,000
1994	**Paradise Creek**, 5, 126	P. Day	Fanmore, 6, 126	Muhtarram, 5, 126	14	1:59.78	600,000
1993	**Star of Cozzene**, 5, 126	J. A. Santos	Evanescent, 6, 126	Johann Quatz (Fr), 4, 126	8	2:07.50	600,000
1992	**Dear Doctor (Fr)**, 5, 126	C. B. Asmussen	Sky Classic, 5, 126	Golden Pheasant, 6, 126	12	1:59.84	600,000
1991	**Tight Spot**, 4, 126	L. A. Pincay Jr.	Algenib (Arg), 4, 122	†Kartajana (Ire), 4, 123	10	1:59.55	600,000
1990	**Golden Pheasant**, 4, 126	G. L. Stevens	With Approval, 4, 126	Steinlen (GB), 7, 126	11	1:59.60	600,000
1989	**Steinlen (GB)**, 6, 126	J. A. Santos	†Lady in Silver, 3, 117	Yankee Affair, 7, 126	13	2:03.60	600,000
1988	**Mill Native**, 4, 126	C. B. Asmussen	Equalize, 6, 126	Sunshine Forever, 3, 118	14	2:00.00	600,000
1987	**Manila**, 4, 126	A. T. Cordero Jr.	Sharrood, 4, 126	Theatrical (Ire), 5, 126	8	2:02.40	600,000
1986	**†Estrapade**, 6, 122	F. Toro	Divulge, 4, 126	Pennine Walk (Ire), 4, 126	14	2:00.80	600,000
1985	**Teleprompter (GB)**, 5, 126	T. A. Ives	Greinton (GB), 4, 126	Flying Pidgeon, 4, 126	13	2:03.40	600,000
1984	**John Henry**, 9, 126	C. J. McCarron	†Royal Heroine (Ire), 4, 122	Gato Del Sol, 5, 126	12	2:01.40	600,000
1983	**Tolomeo (Ire)**, 3, 118	P. Eddery	John Henry, 8, 126	Nijinsky's Secret, 5, 126	14	2:04.40	600,000

1982	**Perrault (GB)**, 5, 126	L. A. Pincay Jr.	Be My Native, 3, 118	Motavato, 4, 126	14	1:58.80	$600,000
1981	**John Henry**, 6, 126	W. Shoemaker	The Bart, 5, 126	†Madam Gay (GB), 3, 117	12	2:07.60	600,000

First million-dollar Thoroughbred race in North America. Formerly sponsored by the Anheuser-Busch Co. of St. Louis, Missouri 1982-'87. Arlington Million Invitational S. 1981. Budweiser Million S. 1982-'84. Budweiser-Arlington Million 1985-'87. Held at Woodbine Race Course 1989. Not held 1998-'99. Dead heat for second 2003. ‡Storming Home (GB) finished first, DQ to fourth, 2003. ‡Powerscourt (GB) finished first, DQ to fourth, 2004. Course record 1995. †Denotes female.

Arlington-Washington Breeders' Cup Futurity

Grade 3 in 2006. Arlington Park, two-year-olds, 1 mile, dirt. Held September 18, 2005, with a gross value of $198,500. First held in 1927. First graded in 1973. Stakes record 1:35.16 (2005 Sorceror's Stone).

Year	Winner	Jockey	Second	Third	Strs	Time	1st Purse
2005	**Sorcerer's Stone**, 2, 119	M. Guidry	Charley Tango, 2, 119	Red Raymond, 2, 119	9	**1:35.16**	$120,000
2004	**Three Hour Nap**, 2, 119	E. Razo Jr.	dh-Elusive Chris, 2, 122 dh-Straight Line, 2, 119		6	1:38.56	120,000
2003	**Cactus Ridge**, 2, 122	E. M. Martin Jr.	Glittergem, 2, 117	Texas Deputy, 2, 119	6	1:35.44	90,000
2002	**Most Feared**, 2, 122	M. Guidry	Anasheed, 2, 122	Unleash the Power, 2, 122	10	1:37.52	90,000
2001	**Publication**, 2, 122	R. A. Meier	It'sallinthechase, 2, 122	Dubai Squire, 2, 122	7	1:38.78	90,000
2000	**Trailthefox**, 2, 121	S. J. Sellers	Starbury, 2, 121	Blame It On Ruby, 2, 121	11	1:37.25	90,000
1997	**Cowboy Dan**, 2, 121	D. Kutz	Captain Maestri, 2, 121	Fiamma, 2, 121	9	1:37.68	90,000
1996	**Night in Reno**, 2, 121	M. Guidry	Flying With Eagles, 2, 121	Thisnearlywasmine, 2, 121	8	1:36.67	120,000
1994	**Evansville Slew**, 2, 121	P. Compton	Valid Wager, 2, 121	Mr Purple, 2, 121	9	1:37.84	120,000
1993	**Polar Expedition**, 2, 121	C. C. Bourque	Gimme Glory, 2, 121	Delicate Cure, 2, 121	6	1:39.28	120,000
1992	**Gilded Time**, 2, 121	C. J. McCarron	Boundlessly, 2, 121	Rockamundo, 2, 121	6	1:37.84	200,580
1991	**Caller I. D.**, 2, 121	J. D. Bailey	Count the Time, 2, 121	West by West, 2, 121	7	1:36.01	188,880
1990	**Hansel**, 2, 122	P. Day	Walesa, 2, 122	Discover, 2, 122	7	1:36.40	220,440
1989	**Secret Hello**, 2, 122	A. T. Gryder	Richard R., 2, 122	Bite the Bullet, 2, 122	6	1:35.80	220,860
1987	**Tejano**, 2, 122	J. Vasquez	Jim's Orbit, 2, 122	Native Stalwart, 2, 122	7	1:36.20	247,080
1986	**Bet Twice**, 2, 122	C. Perret	Conquistarose, 2, 122	Jazzing Around, 2, 122	11	1:37.20	300,420
1985	**Meadowlake**, 2, 122	J. L. Diaz	Bar Tender, 2, 122	Papal Power, 2, 122	6	1:16.80	286,320
1984	**Spend a Buck**, 2, 122	C. Hussey	Dusty's Darby, 2, 122	Viva Maxi, 2, 122	7	1:38.00	355,320
1983	**All Fired Up**, 2, 122	R. D. Evans	Holme On Top, 2, 122	Smart n Slick, 2, 122	17	1:27.00	330,135
1982	**Total Departure**, 2, 122	E. Fires	Coax Me Matt, 2, 122	Highland Park, 2, 122	8	1:23.60	271,515
1981	**Lets Dont Fight**, 2, 122	J. Lively	Tropic Ruler, 2, 122	Music Leader, 2, 122	15	1:29.20	305,385
1980	**Well Decorated**, 2, 122	L. A. Pincay Jr.	Lord Avie, 2, 122	Fairway Phantom, 2, 122	15	1:23.80	240,885
1979	**Execution's Reason**, 2, 122	E. Delahoussaye	Preemptive, 2, 122	Brent's Trans Am, 2, 122	9	1:22.40	89,790
1978	**Jose Binn**, 2, 122	A. T. Cordero Jr.	Exuberant, 2, 122	Strike Your Colors, 2, 122	12	1:17.40	120,660
1977	**Sauce Boat**, 2, 122	S. Cauthen	Gonquin, 2, 122	Forever Casting, 2, 122	14	1:16.60	130,665
1976	**Run Dusty Run**, 2, 122	D. G. McHargue	Royal Ski, 2, 122	Eagletar, 2, 122	11	1:16.40	120,465
1975	**Honest Pleasure**, 2, 122	D. G. McHargue	Khyber King, 2, 122	Rule the Ridge, 2, 122	19	1:18.40	140,610
1974	**Greek Answer**, 2, 122	M. A. Castaneda	Colonel Power, 2, 122	The Bagel Prince, 2, 122	7	1:17.80	122,505
1973	**Lover John**, 2, 122	R. N. Ussery	Beau Groton, 2, 122	Hula Chief, 2, 122	9	1:11.60	97,470

Merged with old Washington Park Futurity, renamed after closure of Washington Park. Grade 1 1973-'89. Grade 2 1990-2001. American National Futurity 1927-'28. Arlington Futurity 1932-'61. Held at Washington Park 1943-'45. Held at Hawthorne Race Course 1985. Not held 1929-'31, 1970, 1988, 1995, 1998-'99. 6 furlongs 1927-'61, 1971-'73. 7 furlongs 1962-'69, 1979-'83. 6½ furlongs 1974-'78, 1985. Colts and geldings 1973-'83. Dead heat for second 2004.

Arlington-Washington Breeders' Cup Lassie Stakes

Grade 3 in 2006. Arlington Park, two-year-olds, fillies, 1 mile, dirt. Held September 18, 2005, with a gross value of $147,000. First held in 1929. First graded in 1973. Stakes record 1:35.93 (2005 Original Spin).

Year	Winner	Jockey	Second	Third	Strs	Time	1st Purse
2005	**Original Spin**, 2, 116	J. M. Campbell	Ex Caelis, 2, 116	Coolwind, 2, 116	9	**1:35.93**	$90,000
2004	**Culinary**, 2, 116	C. H. Marquez Jr.	Runway Model, 2, 118	Kota, 2, 118	8	1:36.98	60,000
2003	**Zosima**, 2, 118	P. Day	Everyday Angel, 2, 116	Cryptos' Best, 2, 118	10	1:36.02	60,000
2002	**Moonlight Sonata**, 2, 121	S. Laviolette	Parting, 2, 121	Souris, 2, 121	13	1:37.82	60,000
2001	**Joanies Bella**, 2, 121	M. St. Julien	Brief Bliss, 2, 121	First Again, 2, 121	9	1:39.34	60,000
2000	**Thunder Bertie**, 2, 119	J. Beasley	Caressing, 2, 119	Zahwah, 2, 119	10	1:36.91	60,000
1997	**Silver Maiden**, 2, 119	B. S. Laviolette	Arctic Lady, 2, 119	So Generous, 2, 119	6	1:37.54	60,000
1996	**Southern Playgirl**, 2, 119	R. P. Romero	Leo's Gypsy Dancer, 2, 119	Broad Dynamite, 2, 119	7	1:38.27	90,000
1994	**Shining Light**, 2, 119	J. L. Diaz	She's a Lively One, 2, 119	Alltheway Bertie, 2, 119	5	1:41.70	90,000
1993	**Mariah's Storm**, 2, 119	R. N. Lester	Shapely Scrapper, 2, 119	Minority Dater, 2, 119	14	1:38.95	90,000
1992	**Eliza**, 2, 119	P. A. Valenzuela	Banshee Winds, 2, 119	Tourney, 2, 119	6	1:39.58	134,850
1991	**Speed Dialer**, 2, 119	P. Day	Cadillac Women, 2, 119	Mystic Hawk, 2, 119	7	1:36.58	141,390
1990	**Through Flight**, 2, 120	J. M. Johnson	Good Potential, 2, 120	Wild for Traci, 2, 120	6	1:39.00	138,870
1989	**Trumpet's Blare**, 2, 122	L. A. Pincay Jr.	Special Happening, 2, 122	Puffy Doodle, 2, 122	6	1:38.60	128,040
1987	**Joe's Tammie**, 2, 122	C. Perret	Tomorrow's Child, 2, 122	Pearlie Gold, 2, 122	6	1:25.00	186,840
1986	**Delicate Vine**, 2, 122	G. L. Stevens	Sacahuista, 2, 122	Ruling Angel, 2, 122	6	1:23.40	165,660
1985	**Family Style**, 2, 119	L. A. Pincay Jr.	Deep Silver, 2, 119	Pamela Kay, 2, 119	8	1:18.00	250,200
1984	**Contredance**, 2, 119	P. Day	Tiltalating, 2, 119	Miss Delice, 2, 119	5	1:26.00	211,560
1983	**Miss Oceana**, 2, 119	E. Maple	Life's Magic, 2, 119	Bottle Top, 2, 119	11	1:23.40	112,146
1982	**For Once'n My Life**, 2, 119	E. Maple	Some Kinda Flirt, 2, 119	How Clever, 2, 119	8	1:23.40	106,461
1981	**Milingo**, 2, 119	R. Sibille	Maniches, 2, 119	Justa Little One, 2, 119	15	1:25.20	129,798

1980	**Truly Bound**, 2, 119	W. Shoemaker	Safe Play, 2, 119	Masters Dream, 2, 119	11	1:25.20	$83,022
1979	**Sissy's Time**, 2, 119	E. Fires	Ellie Milove, 2, 119	Vogue Folks, 2, 119	6	1:11.00	63,399
1978	**It's in the Air**, 2, 119	E. Delahoussaye	Angel Island, 2, 119	Bequa, 2, 119	8	1:09.60	71,394
1977	**Stub**, 2, 119	R. Turcotte	Rainy Princess, 2, 119	Go Line, 2, 119	13	1:10.40	70,329
1976	**Special Warmth**, 2, 119	S. Maple	Wavy Waves, 2, 119	Drama Critic, 2, 119	10	1:10.40	68,700
1975	**Dearly Precious**, 2, 119	M. Hole	Free Journey, 2, 119	Head Spy, 2, 119	12	1:11.20	67,938
1974	**Hot n Nasty**, 2, 119	D. G. McHargue	Sharm a Sheikh, 2, 119	Mystery Mood, 2, 119	10	1:11.40	64,386
1973	**Special Team**, 2, 119	A. Pineda	Thirty One Jewels, 2, 119	Two Timing Lass, 2, 119	9	1:11.00	59,574

Merged with old Washington Park Lassie S., renamed after closure of Washington Park. Grade 2 1976-'80, 1990-'97. Grade 1 1981-'89. Lassie S. 1929-'31. Arlington Lassie S. 1932-'62. Arlington-Washington Lassie S. 1963-'69, 1972-'87, 1989-'94, 1996-'97, 2000-'04. Held at Washington Park 1943-'45. Not held 1970-'71, 1988, 1995, 1998-'99. $5\frac{1}{2}$ furlongs 1929-'31. 7 furlongs 1932, 1980-'84, 1986-'87. 6 furlongs 1933-'61, 1972-'79. $6\frac{1}{2}$ furlongs 1962-'69, 1985.

Ashland Stakes

Grade 1 in 2006. Keeneland Race Course, three-year-olds, fillies, $1\frac{1}{16}$ miles, dirt. Held April 8, 2006, with a gross value of $500,000. First held in 1879. First graded in 1973. Stakes record 1:41.72 (1999 Silverbulletday).

Year	Winner	Jockey	Second	Third	Strs	Time	1st Purse
2006	**Bushfire**, 3, 121	C. H. Velasquez	Wait a While, 3, 121	Balance, 3, 121	8	1:45.16	$310,000
2005	**Sis City**, 3, 121	E. S. Prado	Runway Model, 3, 121	Memorette, 3, 121	6	1:46.35	310,000
2004	**Madcap Escapade**, 3, 118	R. R. Douglas	Ashado, 3, 123	Last Song, 3, 120	4	1:44.55	310,000
2003	**Elloluv**, 3, 120	R. Albarado	Lady Tak, 3, 123	Holiday Lady, 3, 116	7	1:43.58	342,085
2002	**Take Charge Lady**, 3, 123	A. J. D'Amico	Take the Cake, 3, 118	Belterra, 3, 120	8	1:43.29	345,805
2001	**Fleet Renee**, 3, 116	J. R. Velazquez	Golden Ballet, 3, 123	Latour, 3, 120	11	1:43.77	357,275
2000	**Rings a Chime**, 3, 116	S. J. Sellers	Zoftig, 3, 116	Circle of Life, 3, 116	6	1:44.43	341,155
1999	**Silverbulletday**, 3, 123	J. D. Bailey	Marley Vale, 3, 115	Gold From the West, 3, 115	6	**1:41.72**	337,280
1998	**Well Chosen**, 3, 115	C. R. Woods Jr.	Let, 3, 115	Banshee Breeze, 3, 120	7	1:43.00	344,410
1997	**Glitter Woman**, 3, 121	M. E. Smith	Anklet, 3, 121	Storm Song, 3, 121	6	1:43.80	337,125
1996	**My Flag**, 3, 121	J. D. Bailey	Cara Rafaela, 3, 121	Mackie, 3, 118	5	1:42.69	335,265
1995	**Urbane**, 3, 115	E. Delahoussaye	Conquistadoress, 3, 115	Post It, 3, 121	6	1:43.41	207,483
1994	**Inside Information**, 3, 121	M. E. Smith	Bunting, 3, 115	Private Status, 3, 118	6	1:46.99	171,198
1993	**Lunar Spook**, 3, 121	S. J. Sellers	Avie's Shadow, 3, 115	Roamin Rachel, 3, 115	7	1:43.43	171,973
1992	**Prospectors Delite**, 3, 121	C. Perret	Spinning Round, 3, 121	Luv Me Luv Me Not, 3, 121	10	1:42.65	186,063
1991	**Do It With Style**, 3, 115	S. J. Sellers	Private Treasure, 3, 121	Til Forbid, 3, 112	7	1:43.67	182,894
1990	**Go for Wand**, 3, 121	R. P. Romero	Charon, 3, 121	Piper Piper, 3, 112	5	1:43.60	145,665
1989	**Gorgeous**, 3, 118	E. Delahoussaye	Blondeinamotel, 3, 115	Some Romance, 3, 121	13	1:43.20	157,430
1988	**Willa On the Move**, 3, 118	C. J. McCarron	On to Royalty, 3, 121	Colonial Waters, 3, 121	11	1:45.80	151,125
1987	**Chic Shirine**, 3, 118	S. Hawley	Buryyourbelief, 3, 112	Our Little Margie, 3, 113	12	1:44.60	117,683
1986	**Classy Cathy**, 3, 116	E. Fires	She's a Mystery, 3, 116	Patricia J. K., 3, 121	11	1:44.00	116,513
1985	**Koluctoo's Jill**, 3, 118	R. P. Romero	Lucy Manette, 3, 121	Foxy Deen, 3, 121	7	1:44.40	74,718
1984	**Enumerating**, 3, 114	D. Brumfield	Miss Oceana, 3, 121	Rose of Ashes, 3, 113	4	1:49.20	88,707
1983	**Princess Rooney**, 3, 121	J. Vasquez	Shamivor, 3, 114	Decision, 3, 116	6	1:45.40	74,133
1982	**Blush With Pride**, 3, 118	W. Shoemaker	Exclusive Love, 3, 116	Delicate Ice, 3, 113	10	1:45.00	83,070
1981	**Truly Bound**, 3, 121	W. Shoemaker	Wayward Lass, 3, 121	Dame Mysterieuse, 3, 121	5	1:44.00	56,778
1980	**Flos Florum**, 3, 112	R. P. Romero	Cerada Ridge, 3, 114	Lady Taurian Peace, 3, 116	8	1:26.40	41,210
	Sugar and Spice, 3, 113	J. Fell	Nice and Sharp, 3, 114	Satin Ribera, 3, 116	9	1:27.20	41,210
1979	**Candy Eclair**, 3, 121	A. S. Black	Himalayan, 3, 114	Countess North, 3, 115	7	1:27.00	39,618
1978	**Mucchina**, 3, 113	J. Amy	Grenzen, 3, 121	Bold Rendezvous, 3, 118	10	1:27.20	40,527
1977	**Sound of Summer**, 3, 118	F. Toro	Mrs. Warren, 3, 121	Our Mims, 3, 118	9	1:26.80	40,333
1976	**Optimistic Gal**, 3, 121	B. Baeza	Alvarada, 3, 116	Confort Zone, 3, 113	6	1:26.80	37,895
1975	**Sun and Snow**, 3, 116	G. Patterson	My Juliet, 3, 116	Red Cross, 3, 114	8	1:26.60	39,488
1974	**Maud Muller**, 3, 114	D. Brumfield	Clemanna, 3, 113	Irish Sonnet, 3, 119	9	1:27.00	29,834
	Winged Wishes, 3, 116	D. Brumfield	Cherished Moment, 3, 117	Jay Bar Pet, 3, 113	8	1:28.80	29,786
1973	**Raging Whirl**, 3, 113	W. Soirez	Protest, 3, 116	A Little Lovin, 3, 110	12	1:10.80	23,611

Named for Henry Clay's home, Ashland, located in Lexington. Sponsored by Ashland Inc. of Covington, Kentucky 1996-2006. Grade 3 1973-'78. Grade 2 1979-'85. Ashland Oaks 1879-1932. Held at Kentucky Association 1932. Held at Churchill Downs 1943-'45. Not held 1897-1911, 1933-'35, 1938-'39. $1\frac{1}{2}$ miles 1879-'82. $1\frac{1}{4}$ miles 1883-'89. 1 mile 1890-1926. 1 mile 70 yards 1932. 6 furlongs 1940-'73. About 7 furlongs 1974-'80. Three-year-olds and up 1936-'37. Fillies and mares 1936-'37. Two divisions 1974, 1980.

Astarita Stakes

Grade 3 in 2006. Belmont Park, two-year-olds, fillies, $6\frac{1}{2}$ furlongs, dirt. Held October 2, 2005, with a gross value of $108,400. First held in 1946. First graded in 1973. Stakes record 1:16.40 (1974 Stulcer).

Year	Winner	Jockey	Second	Third	Strs	Time	1st Purse
2005	**Sensation**, 2, 117	E. Coa	Swap Fliparoo, 2, 117	Unobstructed View, 2, 117	6	1:16.90	$65,040
2004	**Toll Taker**, 2, 117	E. Coa	Im a Dixie Girl, 2, 120	Summer Raven, 2, 117	6	1:18.16	64,800
2003	**Spectacular Moon**, 2, 117	J. F. Chavez	Feline Story, 2, 120	Smokey Glacken, 2, 117	9	1:17.16	90,000
2002	**Humorous Lady**, 2, 117	J. D. Bailey	Fast Cookie, 2, 117	Chimichurri, 2, 117	7	1:17.76	90,000
2001	**Bella Bellucci**, 2, 117	G. L. Stevens	Forest Heiress, 2, 120	Speed to Burn, 2, 117	4	1:16.67	63,955
2000	**Xtra Heat**, 2, 117	M. T. Johnston	Gold Mover, 2, 120	Major Wager, 2, 117	8	1:16.71	66,060
1999	**Silentlea**, 2, 119	R. G. Davis	Valerie's Dream, 2, 119	Lucky Livi, 2, 119	10	1:17.44	67,620
1998	**Paved in Gold**, 2, 119	J. F. Chavez	Blushing Deed, 2, 119	Paula's Girl, 2, 119	5	1:18.86	63,780
1997	**Ninth Inning**, 2, 119	R. G. Davis	Salty Perfume, 2, 119	Madam Fireplace, 2, 119	5	1:17.44	64,680
1996	**Broad Dynamite**, 2, 119	D. W. Cordova	Glitter Woman, 2, 119	Biding Time, 2, 119	4	1:24.02	63,960

1995	**Top Secret**, 2, 119	M. E. Smith	Plum Country, 2, 119	Mesabi Maiden, 2, 119	8	1:36.79	$69,480
1994	**Miss Golden Circle**, 2, 119	J. A. Krone	Golden Bri, 2, 119	Mistress S., 2, 119	6	1:23.67	64,740
1993	**Shapely Scrapper**, 2, 119	J. Bravo	Brighter Course, 2, 119	Fashion Maven, 2, 119	4	1:24.02	67,560
1992	**Missed the Storm**, 2, 119	M. E. Smith	Dispute, 2, 119	Statuette, 2, 119	6	1:24.90	67,920
1991	**Easy Now**, 2, 112	M. E. Smith	Stolen Beauty, 2, 113	Celeste Cielo, 2, 112	6	1:22.84	69,240
1990	**Devilish Touch**, 2, 116	C. Perret	Makin Faces, 2, 112	Missy's Mirage, 2, 112	8	1:18.00	71,760
1989	**Dance Colony**, 2, 119	J. A. Santos	Charging Fire, 2, 114	Trumpet's Blare, 2, 114	6	1:17.80	68,640
1988	**Channel Three**, 2, 116	C. Barrera	Pat Copelan, 2, 119	Mistaurian, 2, 112	7	1:17.00	83,460
1987	**Flashy Runner**, 2, 112	J. Vasquez	Tap Your Toes, 2, 112	Galway Song, 2, 112	8	1:16.60	70,560
1986	**Cagey Exuberance**, 2, 116	J. Nied Jr.	Sea Basque, 2, 112	Maxi Ruler, 2, 112	6	1:18.20	51,300
1985	**Guadery**, 2, 112	A. T. Cordero Jr.	Musical Lark (Ire), 2, 112	I'm Sweets, 2, 112	6	1:17.00	64,800
1984	**Mom's Command**, 2, 116	A. Fuller	Self Image, 2, 112	Winters' Love, 2, 112	10	1:17.80	54,900
1983	**Tina's Ten**, 2, 112	R. Migliore	Masked Barb, 2, 116	Upturning, 2, 114	9	1:19.20	34,740
1982	**Wings of Jove**, 2, 112	W. H. McCauley	On the Bench, 2, 112	Bammer, 2, 112	5	1:16.80	32,220
1981	**Before Dawn**, 2, 119	J. Velasquez	Betty Money, 2, 112	Take Lady Anne, 2, 112	5	1:16.60	33,540
1980	**Sweet Revenge**, 2, 116	J. Velasquez	Expressive Dance, 2, 113	Hagley's Point, 2, 112	9	1:17.20	33,360
1979	**Royal Suite**, 2, 114	J. Fell	Andrea F., 2, 112	Smart Angle, 2, 116	6	1:17.20	25,815
1978	**Fall Aspen**, 2, 112	R. I. Velez	Whisper Fleet, 2, 112	Island Kitty, 2, 112	6	1:17.00	25,755
1977	**Lakeville Miss**, 2, 112	R. Hernandez	Sherry Peppers, 2, 116	Tempermental Pet, 2, 112	6	1:17.80	21,990
1976	**Sensational**, 2, 112	A. T. Cordero Jr.	Tickle My Toes, 2, 112	Spy Flag, 2, 112	7	1:17.40	22,185
1975	**Picture Tube**, 2, 113	E. Maple	La Tamborera, 2, 115	Dottie's Doll, 2, 113	11	1:18.40	23,340
1974	**Stulcer**, 2, 113	A. T. Cordero Jr.	Copernica, 2, 113	But Exclusive, 2, 116	8	**1:16.40**	17,040
1973	**Raisela**, 2, 113	R. Turcotte	Nancy G., 2, 113	Quick Cure, 2, 115	10	1:16.80	17,610

Named for Astarita (1900 f. by *Bathampton), first winner of the Astoria S. at Gravesend Park in 1902. Grade 2 1981-2003. New York City Astarita S. 1995. Held at Aqueduct 1946-'55, 1962-'67, 1991-'94, 1996-'97. Not held 1958-'60. 6 furlongs 1946-'56. 7 furlongs 1957-'71, 1991-'94, 1996. 1 mile 1995.

Athenia Handicap

Grade 3 in 2006. Belmont Park, three-year-olds and up, fillies and mares, 1$^{1}/_{16}$ miles, dirt (originally scheduled as a Grade 3 on the turf). Held October 15, 2005, with a gross value of $111,300. First held in 1978. First graded in 1980. Stakes record 1:40.53 (2001 Babae [Chi] [2nd Div.]).

Year	Winner	Jockey	Second	Third	Strs	Time	1st Purse
2005	**Asti (Ire)**, 4, 114	J. F. Chavez	Bohemian Lady, 4, 120	Zosima, 4, 117	6	1:42.57	$66,780
2004	**Finery**, 4, 113	P. Fragoso	Madeira Mist (Ire), 5, 118	With Patience, 5, 114	11	1:43.73	69,420
2003	**Caught in the Rain**, 4, 115	R. Migliore	Lojo, 4, 114	Coney Kitty (Ire), 5, 113	8	1:47.05	67,800
2002	**Babae (Chi)**, 6, 120	J. F. Chavez	Strawberry Blonde (Ire), 4, 116	Silver Rail, 5, 112	12	1:44.90	70,020
2001	**Verruma (Brz)**, 5, 114	J. R. Velazquez	Siringas (Ire), 3, 112	Freefourracing, 3, 113	8	1:42.09	82,725
	Babae (Chi), 5, 116	J. F. Chavez	Batique, 5, 114	Sweet Prospect (GB), 3, 110	8	**1:40.53**	82,725
2000	**Wild Heart Dancing**, 4, 115	J. F. Chavez	Fickle Friends, 4, 114	Silken (GB), 4, 114	8	1:43.40	67,500
1999	**Antoniette**, 4, 119	J. F. Chavez	Dominique's Joy, 4, 113	Prospectress, 4, 115	8	1:41.89	66,840
1998	**Tampico**, 5, 114	J. Bravo	Irish Daisy, 5, 113	Rumpipumpy (GB), 5, 115	10	1:42.90	51,210
1997	**Rapid Selection**, 4, 113	J. Bravo	Dynasty, 4, 114	Preachersnightmare, 4, 111	6	1:47.11	65,940
1996	**Sixieme Sens**, 4, 116	J. D. Bailey	Rapunzel Runz, 5, 115	Fashion Star, 4, 113	7	1:37.92	66,660
1995	**Caress**, 4, 114	R. G. Davis	Manila Lila, 5, 115	Vinista, 5, 119	6	1:54.18	68,340
1994	**Lady Affirmed**, 3, 111	J. F. Chavez	Irving's Girl, 4, 110	Cox Orange, 4, 116	11	1:48.66	52,245
1993	**Trampoli**, 4, 117	M. E. Smith	Kirov Premiere (GB), 3, 110	Dahlia's Dreamer, 4, 110	8	2:17.16	54,000
1992	**Fairy Garden**, 4, 112	J. A. Krone	Passagere du Soir (GB), 5, 117	Seewillo, 4, 113	5	2:13.62	52,020
1991	**Flaming Torch (Ire)**, 4, 117	P. A. Valenzuela	Plenty of Grace, 4, 114	Highland Penny, 6, 116	9	2:13.99	55,800
1990	**Buy the Firm**, 4, 111	J. D. Bailey	Rigamajig, 4, 111	Igmaar (Fr), 4, 111	4	2:18.20	52,650
1989	**Capades**, 3, 115	A. T. Cordero Jr.	Miss Unnameable, 5, 114	Key Flyer, 3, 110	8	2:13.20	54,360
1988	**High Browser**, 3, 108	P. Day	Miss Unnameable, 4, 109	Gaily Gaily (Ire), 5, 110	10	2:18.60	57,780
1987	**Lead Kindly Light**, 4, 110	J. M. Pezua	Barbara's Moment, 3, 111	Spectacular Bev, 3, 114	7	2:23.80	70,920
1986	**Dawn's Curtsey**, 4, 111	E. Maple	Festivity, 3, 113	Perfect Point, 4, 115	10	2:16.00	55,440
1985	**Videogenic**, 3, 114	J. Cruguet	Persian Tiara (Ire), 5, 119	Key Witness, 3, 108	13	2:15.40	61,020
1984	**Key Dancer**, 3, 111	A. T. Cordero Jr.	Surely Georgie's, 3, 107	Rossard (Den), 4, 123	11	2:14.80	56,700
1983	**Rose Crescent**, 4, 108	R. G. Davis	Lady Norcliffe, 3, 111	Infinite, 3, 112	9	2:22.00	34,380
1982	**Mintage (Fr)**, 3, 114	J. Samyn	Doodle, 3, 119	Street Dance, 3, 112	8	2:17.80	32,790
	Middle Stage, 3, 112	J. J. Miranda	Realms Reason (Ire), 3, 114	Vocal, 3, 115	6	2:17.40	32,790
1981	**De La Rose**, 3, 125	E. Maple	Noble Damsel, 3, 111	Andover Way, 3, 113	8	2:00.40	51,120
1980	**Love Sign**, 3, 121	R. Hernandez	Rokeby Rose, 3, 111	Classic Curves, 3, 111	10	2:00.40	50,490
1979	**Poppycock**, 3, 114	J. Velasquez	Fourdrinier, 3, 114	Six Crowns, 3, 114	10	2:05.60	52,470
1978	**Terpsichorist**, 3, 114	M. Venezia	Consort, 3, 110	Bonnie Blue Flag, 3, 110	12	2:03.20	33,300

Named for Hal Price Headley's 1946 Ladies H. winner Athenia (1943 f. by *Pharamond II). Not graded 2005. Held at Aqueduct 1982, 1994-'95, 1998-2000, 2002-'04. 1$^{1}/_{4}$ miles 1978-'81. 1$^{3}/_{8}$ miles 1982-'93. 1$^{1}/_{8}$ miles 1994-'95, 1997. 1 mile 1996. Dirt 1979, 1990, 1995, 2005. Originally scheduled on turf 2005. Three-year-olds 1978-'83. Fillies 1978-'83. Two divisions 1982, 2001.

Azalea Breeders' Cup Stakes

Grade 3 in 2006. Calder Race Course, three-year-olds, fillies, 6 furlongs, dirt. Held July 10, 2005, with a gross value of $248,250. First held in 1972. First graded in 1996. Stakes record 1:10.32 (2005 Leave Me Alone).

Year	Winner	Jockey	Second	Third	Strs	Time	1st Purse
2005	**Leave Me Alone**, 3, 118	K. Desormeaux	Hide and Chic, 3, 114	Midtown Miss, 3, 114	6	**1:10.32**	$132,000
2004	**Dazzle Me**, 3, 115	S. J. Sellers	Reforest, 3, 114	Boston Express, 3, 114	7	1:11.40	177,000

2003	**Ebony Breeze**, 3, 118	C. H. Velasquez	Storm Flag, 3, 116	Crafty Brat, 3, 116	13	1:10.82	$176,025
2002	**Bold World**, 3, 118	C. H. Borel	Willa On the Move, 3, 114	Tchula Miss, 3, 114	10	1:10.86	105,000
2001	**Hattiesburg**, 3, 116	M. Guidry	Southern Tour, 3, 114	Spanish Glitter, 3, 116	11	1:11.81	150,000
2000	**Swept Away**, 3, 116	P. Day	Precious Feather, 3, 112	Watchfull, 3, 116	8	1:11.53	120,000
1999	**Show Me the Stage**, 3, 116	R. J. Courville	Could Be, 3, 116	Exact, 3, 116	9	1:11.91	75,000
1998	**Cassidy**, 3, 114	J. A. Rivera II	Holy Capote, 3, 114	Fantasy Angel, 3, 118	8	1:11.93	75,000
1997	**Little Sister**, 3, 116	F. Lovato Jr.	Princess Pietrina, 3, 112	Maggie Auxier, 3, 114	7	1:13.08	120,000
1996	**J J'sdream**, 3, 118	H. Castillo Jr.	Supah Avalanche, 3, 112	Race Artist, 3, 114	7	1:23.87	65,100
1995	**Lucky Lavender Gal**, 3, 116	R. R. Douglas	Chaposa Springs, 3, 117	Dancin Renee, 3, 116	6	1:23.50	60,000
1994	**Cut the Charm**, 3, 121	H. Castillo Jr.	Just a Little Kiss, 3, 114	Tasso Bee, 3, 112	11	1:25.51	60,000
1993	**Kimscountrydiamond**, 3, 115	J. Vasquez	Nijivision, 3, 113	Hollywood Wildcat, 3, 117	10	1:23.44	60,000
1992	**C. C.'s Return**, 3, 113	R. J. Thibeau Jr.	Fortune Forty Four, 3, 114	Subtle Dancer, 3, 113	7	1:25.33	30,000
1991	**Ranch Ragout**, 3, 113	E. O. Nunez	Parisian Flight, 3, 115	Foolishly Wild, 3, 110	8	1:18.53	33,120
1990	**Sweet Proud Polly**, 3, 115	P. A. Rodriguez	Highway Lady, 3, 115	Bald Cat, 3, 112	7	1:26.20	32,790
1989	**Princess Mora**, 3, 112	S. Gaffalione	Georgies Doctor, 3, 118	Silk Stocks, 3, 117	7	1:25.60	32,790
1988	**Grand Splash**, 3, 114	R. N. Lester	Myfavorite Charity, 3, 114	Hi Maudie, 3, 116	8	1:25.60	46,500
1987	**My Sweet Replica**, 3, 115	S. B. Soto	Shot Gun Bonnie, 3, 114	Ches Pie, 3, 116	10	1:25.20	33,990
1986	**Classy Tricks**, 3, 112	M. C. Suckie	Janjac, 3, 112	Thirty Zip, 3, 119	13	1:25.40	30,410
1985	**Jackie McCleaf**, 3, 120	C. Hussey	Nahema, 3, 118	Nyama, 3, 118	10	1:25.80	33,840
1984	**Birdie Belle**, 3, 120	H. A. Valdivieso	Sugar's Image, 3, 120	Scorched Panties, 3, 120	10	1:25.80	33,990
1983	**Current Gal**, 3, 112	E. Cardone	Silvered Silk, 3, 115	Paris Roulette, 3, 115	12	1:25.60	17,295
1982	**Here's to Peg**, 3, 116	J. A. Velez Jr.	Cut, 3, 114	Bad Dancin Rita, 3, 116	10	1:26.00	16,905
1981	**Ange Gal**, 3, 113	G. Cohen	Float Upstream, 3, 115	Whoop It, 3, 114	8	1:26.00	16,515
	Kaylem Ho, 3, 115	A. Smith Jr.	Toga Toga, 3, 119	Secret Kingdom, 3, 115	8	1:25.80	16,515
1980	**She Can't Miss**, 3, 122	W. A. Guerra	Nice and Sharp, 3, 115	Karla's Enough, 3, 119	7	1:11.20	16,515
1979	**Burn's Return**, 3, 115	M. A. Rivera	Solo Haina, 3, 120	Speier's Hope, 3, 115	9	1:24.00	16,860
1978	**Lucy Belle**, 3, 113	A. Smith Jr.	We Believe in You, 3, 113	Wings of Destiny, 3, 122	8	1:25.20	14,040
1977	**Countess Pruner**, 3, 116	J. S. Rodriguez	Delphic Oracle, 3, 113	White Goddess, 3, 119	5	1:11.20	13,440
1976	**Forty Nine Sunsets**, 3, 122	G. St. Leon	Head Spy, 3, 113	Noble Royalty, 3, 113	6	1:11.80	13,560
1975	**Solo Royal**, 3, 113	G. St. Leon	My Mom Nullah, 3, 119	Finery, 3, 119	11	1:12.40	14,640

Named for the azalea of the rhododendron family common to South Florida. Azalea H. 1972, 1992-'93. Azalea S. 1975-'95. Not held 1973-'74. 1$^1/_{16}$ miles 1972. 7 furlongs 1978-'79, 1981-'90, 1992-'96. Three-year-olds and up 1972. Fillies and mares 1972. Two divisions 1981.

Azeri Breeders' Cup Stakes

Grade 3 in 2006. Oaklawn Park, four-year-olds and up, fillies and mares, 1$^1/_{16}$ miles, dirt. Held March 11, 2006, with a gross value of $173,500. First held in 1987. First graded in 1990. Stakes record 1:42.01 (1999 Sister Act).

Year	Winner	Jockey	Second	Third	Strs	Time	1st Purse
2006	**Round Pond**, 4, 113	S. Elliott	Happy Ticket, 5, 119	Platinum Ballet, 5, 115	6	1:43.93	$105,000
2005	**Injustice**, 4, 115	L. S. Quinonez	Colony Band, 4, 113	Island Sand, 4, 113	6	1:43.40	105,000
2004	**Golden Sonata**, 5, 117	C. H. Marquez Jr.	Keys to the Heart, 5, 117	Mayo On the Side, 5, 113	10	1:44.32	120,000
2003	**Bien Nicole**, 5, 122	D. R. Pettinger	Red n'Gold, 5, 117	Mandy's Gold, 5, 117	9	1:44.19	120,000
2002	**Ask Me No Secrets**, 4, 116	M. E. Smith	Red n'Gold, 4, 116	Descapate, 4, 118	5	1:44.56	120,000
2001	**Heritage of Gold**, 6, 116	R. Albarado	Lu Ravi, 6, 118	Ive Gota Bad Liver, 4, 114	8	1:44.30	120,000
2000	**Heritage of Gold**, 5, 112	S. J. Sellers	Lu Ravi, 5, 112	Light Line, 5, 112	4	1:44.15	120,000
1999	**Sister Act**, 4, 113	C. H. Borel	Glitter Woman, 5, 114	Mil Kilates, 6, 114	6	**1:42.01**	60,000
1998	**Turn to the Queen**, 5, 112	T. T. Doocy	Danzalert, 4, 112	Leo's Gypsy Dancer, 4, 118	7	1:44.76	90,000
1997	**Halo America**, 7, 118	C. H. Borel	Gold n Delicious, 4, 112	Capote Belle, 4, 117	6	1:42.18	90,000
1996	**Belle of Cozzene**, 4, 113	D. R. Pettinger	Halo America, 6, 120	Little May, 6, 115	5	1:43.32	94,350
1995	**Halo America**, 5, 115	W. T. Cloninger Jr.	Heavenly Prize, 4, 121	Biolage, 6, 111	6	1:42.59	92,700
1994	**Morning Meadow**, 4, 116	S. P. Romero	Gravette, 4, 113	Her Valentine, 4, 113	10	1:44.60	94,650
1993	**Guiza**, 6, 118	C. S. Nakatani	Teddy's Top Ten, 4, 113	Fappies Cosy Miss, 5, 112	8	1:44.79	93,600
1992	**Cuddles**, 4, 118	D. Guillory	Rare Guest, 5, 112	Dixie Splash, 4, 113	10	1:43.82	94,500
1991	**A Wild Ride**, 4, 120	P. Day	Timber Ribbon, 4, 114	Topsa, 4, 107	9	1:42.31	94,770
1990	**A Penny Is a Penny**, 5, 116	A. T. Gryder	Affirmed Classic, 4, 114	Fit for a Queen, 4, 113	8	1:43.60	95,340
1989	**Savannah's Honor**, 4, 117	J. D. Bailey	Invited Guest (Ire), 5, 120	Barbara Sue, 5, 114	7	1:45.00	94,920
1988	**Ms. Margi**, 4, 116	J. D. Bailey	Queen Alexandra, 6, 121	Hail a Cab, 5, 116	7	1:42.20	94,890
1987	**North Sider**, 5, 121	A. T. Cordero Jr.	Queen Alexandra, 5, 122	Ann's Bid, 4, 123	8	1:42.20	79,872

Named for the Allen E. Paulson Living Trust's 2002 Horse of the Year and 2002, '03, '04 Apple Blossom H. (G1) winner Azeri (1998 f. by Jade Hunter). Not graded 1995, 1997-'99. Oaklawn Budweiser Breeders' Cup H. 1987-'91, 1993-'95. Oaklawn Breeders' Cup H. 1992, 1996-'97. Oaklawn Breeders' Cup S. 1998-2004. Three-year-olds and up 1987-'94, 1996-2005.

Baldwin Stakes

Not graded in 2006. Santa Anita Park, three-year-olds, 6½ furlongs, dirt (originally scheduled as a Grade 3 at about 6½ furlongs on the turf). Held March 4, 2006, with a gross value of $110,500. First held in 1968. First graded in 1973. Stakes record 1:12.56 (2003 Buddy Gil).

Year	Winner	Jockey	Second	Third	Strs	Time	1st Purse
2006	**Fast Parade**, 3, 115	G. K. Gomez	The Pharaoh, 3, 114	Da Stoops, 3, 122	7	1:15.11	$66,300
2005	**High Standards**, 3, 117	E. S. Prado	Talking to John, 3, 117	Run Thruthe Sun, 3, 117	7	1:16.16	66,270
2004	**Seattle Borders**, 3, 114	A. O. Solis	Stalking Tiger, 3, 117	Jungle Prince, 3, 114	10	1:14.09	68,010
2003	**Buddy Gil**, 3, 117	G. L. Stevens	King Robyn, 3, 116	Flirt With Fortune, 3, 116	11	**1:12.56**	68,730

2002	**Shuffling Kid (GB)**, 3, 117	P. A. Valenzuela	Red Briar (Ire), 3, 116	Dark Sorcerer (GB), 3, 114	12	1:13.30	$68,640
2001	**Skip to the Stone**, 3, 117	C. S. Nakatani	Trailthefox, 3, 122	Bills Paid, 3, 114	6	1:16.29	66,000
2000	**Fortifier**, 3, 114	B. Blanc	Performing Magic, 3, 116	Joopy Doopy, 3, 117	8	1:16.79	66,870
1999	**American Spirit**, 3, 114	E. Ramsammy	Chomper (Ire), 3, 115	Impressive Grades, 3, 119	13	1:13.93	69,300
1998	**Wrekin Pilot (GB)**, 3, 116	E. Delahoussaye	Commitisize, 3, 122	Tenbyssimo (Ire), 3, 117	8	1:13.32	66,240
1997	**Latin Dancer**, 3, 116	C. A. Black	King of Swing, 3, 116	Swiss Yodeler, 3, 122	11	1:14.48	67,850
1996	**Sandtrap**, 3, 114	C. S. Nakatani	Strangelove, 3, 115	Benton Creek, 3, 117	6	1:15.03	64,300
1995	**Sierra Diablo**, 3, 116	E. Delahoussaye	Raji, 3, 117	Huge Gator, 3, 116	6	1:15.36	47,300
1994	**Silver Music**, 3, 114	C. W. Antley	Eagle Eyed, 3, 117	Makinanhonestbuck, 3, 117	8	1:13.76	48,375
1993	**Future Storm**, 3, 117	K. Desormeaux	Concept Win, 3, 119	Siebe, 3, 117	11	1:15.02	51,550
1992	**Reckless Ruckus**, 3, 116	P. A. Valenzuela	Fabulous Champ, 3, 114	Slerp, 3, 115	8	1:17.28	49,850
1991	**What a Spell**, 3, 117	D. R. Flores	Broadway's Top Gun, 3, 122	Shining Prince, 3, 114	7	1:16.30	49,875
1990	**Farma Way**, 3, 115	R. Sibille	Iam the Iceman, 3, 117	Robyn Dancer, 3, 117	12	1:13.80	52,975
1989	**Tenacious Tom**, 3, 119	E. Delahoussaye	Mountain Ghost, 3, 122	Gum, 3, 119	11	1:14.80	51,900
1988	**Exclusive Nureyev**, 3, 116	E. Delahoussaye	Prospectors Gamble, 3, 117	Mehmetski, 3, 114	9	1:14.40	39,162
	Dr. Brent, 3, 117	A. O. Solis	Accomplish Ridge, 3, 117	Glad Music, 3, 114	9	1:15.00	39,262
1987	**Chime Time (GB)**, 3, 116	P. A. Valenzuela	Sweetwater Springs, 3, 117	McKenzie Prince, 3, 114	11	1:15.00	40,750
1986	**Jetting Home**, 3, 116	D. G. McHargue	Royal Treasure, 3, 114	El Corazon, 3, 114	6	1:17.40	38,350
1985	**Knighthood (Fr)**, 3, 114	G. L. Stevens	Full Honor, 3, 117	Infantryman, 3, 114	8	1:14.80	39,900
1984	**Debonaire Junior**, 3, 117	C. J. McCarron	Fortunate Prospect, 3, 119	Distant Ryder, 3, 117	11	1:14.40	41,700
1983	**Total Departure**, 3, 117	L. A. Pincay Jr.	Paris Prince, 3, 117	Morry's Champ, 3, 114	9	1:15.20	40,950
1982	**Remember John**, 3, 117	E. Delahoussaye	Time to Explode, 3, 120	Crystal Star, 3, 114	7	1:15.20	39,200
1981	**Descaro**, 3, 115	D. G. McHargue	Motivity, 3, 120	Steelinctive (GB), 3, 114	13	1:14.60	36,700
1980	**Corvette Chris**, 3, 115	F. Toro	Executive Counsel, 3, 114	Moorish Star, 3, 114	10	1:13.60	28,550
1979	**To B. Or Not**, 3, 114	C. Baltazar	Debonair Roger, 3, 116	Young Driver, 3, 114	7	1:15.60	27,000
1978	**B. W. Turner**, 3, 117	D. Pierce	O Big Al, 3, 120	Princely Lark, 3, 114	9	1:14.00	27,550
1977	**Current Concept**, 3, 120	S. Hawley	Bad 'n Big, 3, 114	Text, 3, 120	10	1:13.20	24,900
1976	**Gaelic Christian**, 3, 114	R. Rosales	El Portugues, 3, 117	Grandaries, 3, 114	9	1:13.60	20,750
1975	**Uniformity**, 3, 114	S. Hawley	Crumbs, 3, 114	Wine Nipper, 3, 114	7	1:13.20	20,050
1974	**Battery E.**, 3, 116	L. A. Pincay Jr.	Wedge Shot, 3, 117	Ride Off, 3, 117	5	1:14.00	19,150
1973	**Bensadream**, 3, 115	D. Pierce	Princely Axe, 3, 114	Gold Bag, 3, 115	9	1:14.00	21,350

Named for Elias J. "Lucky" Baldwin (1828-1909), builder of the original Santa Anita Park. Not graded 1975-'94, 2000, 2006. 6½ furlongs 1979, 1982-'83, 1986, 1991-'92, 1995, 2000-'01, 2005-'06. Dirt 1979, 1982-'83, 1986, 1991-'92, 1995, 2000-'01, 2005-'06. Originally scheduled on turf 2005-'06. Colts and geldings 1978-'87. Two divisions 1988.

Ballerina Stakes

Grade 1 in 2006. Saratoga Race Course, three-year-olds and up, fillies and mares, 7 furlongs, dirt. Held August 28, 2005, with a gross value of $250,000. First held in 1979. First graded in 1981. Stakes record 1:21.09 (2004 Lady Tak).

Year	Winner	Jockey	Second	Third	Strs	Time	1st Purse
2005	**Happy Ticket**, 4, 117	J. R. Velazquez	Pleasant Home, 4, 117	Molto Vita, 5, 117	7	1:24.53	$150,000
2004	**Lady Tak**, 4, 119	J. D. Bailey	My Trusty Cat, 4, 116	Harmony Lodge, 6, 119	7	**1:21.09**	150,000
2003	**Harmony Lodge**, 5, 115	R. Migliore	Shine Again, 6, 120	Gold Mover, 5, 118	8	1:22.23	150,000
2002	**Shine Again**, 5, 116	J. Samyn	Raging Fever, 4, 121	Mandy's Gold, 4, 118	7	1:22.26	150,000
2001	**Shine Again**, 4, 113	J. Samyn	Country Hideaway, 5, 118	Dream Supreme, 4, 122	5	1:22.33	150,000
2000	**Dream Supreme**, 3, 113	P. Day	Country Hideaway, 4, 117	Bourbon Belle, 5, 118	9	1:22.97	150,000
1999	**Furlough**, 5, 114	M. E. Smith	Bourbon Belle, 4, 117	dh-Catinca, 4, 121 dh-Hurricane Bertie, 4, 117	10	1:23.04	120,000
1998	**Stop Traffic**, 5, 118	S. J. Sellers	Runup the Colors, 4, 116	U Can Do It, 5, 115	6	1:22.23	120,000
1997	**Pearl City**, 3, 110	J. Bravo	Ashboro, 4, 115	Flashy n Smart, 4, 112	5	1:22.39	90,000
1996	**Chaposa Springs**, 4, 120	S. J. Sellers	Capote Belle, 3, 117	Broad Smile, 4, 114	6	1:21.88	90,000
1995	**Classy Mirage**, 5, 119	J. A. Krone	Inside Information, 4, 126	Laura's Pistolette, 4, 112	6	1:22.55	90,000
1994	**Roamin Rachel**, 4, 118	P. Day	Classy Mirage, 4, 123	Twist Afleet, 3, 113	6	1:21.85	65,040
1993	**Spinning Round**, 4, 119	J. F. Chavez	November Snow, 4, 119	Apelia, 4, 122	7	1:21.49	69,120
1992	**Serape**, 4, 116	C. W. Antley	Harbour Club, 5, 116	Nannerl, 5, 122	9	1:21.22	71,160
1991	**Queena**, 5, 119	M. E. Smith	Missy's Mirage, 3, 111	Dream Touch, 4, 110	9	1:22.00	72,240
1990	**Feel the Beat**, 5, 119	J. A. Santos	Fantastic Find, 4, 116	Proper Evidence, 5, 119	8	1:22.00	71,880
1989	**Proper Evidence**, 4, 116	C. W. Antley	Aptostar, 4, 119	Lake Valley, 4, 114	11	1:23.20	73,080
1988	**Cadillacing**, 4, 116	A. T. Cordero Jr.	Thirty Zip, 5, 116	Ready Jet Go, 3, 111	6	1:21.60	69,000
1987	**I'm Sweets**, 4, 119	E. Maple	Storm and Sunshine, 4, 116	Pine Tree Lane, 5, 122	5	1:22.60	82,260
1986	**Gene's Lady**, 5, 119	R. P. Romero	Le Slew, 5, 116	Tea Room, 4, 110	4	1:22.40	81,420
1985	**Lady's Secret**, 3, 117	D. MacBeth	Mrs. Revere, 4, 116	Solar Halo, 4, 116	9	1:22.60	67,680
1984	**Lass Trump**, 4, 122	P. Day	Adored, 4, 122	Sultry Sun, 4, 116	5	1:21.80	51,840
1983	**Ambassador of Luck**, 4, 124	A. Graell	Number, 4, 119	Broom Dance, 4, 122	4	1:22.20	32,640
1982	**Expressive Dance**, 4, 122	D. MacBeth	Tell a Secret, 5, 113	Sprouted Rye, 5, 113	8	1:22.80	35,160
1981	**Love Sign**, 4, 119	R. Hernandez	Jameela, 5, 122	Tell a Secret, 4, 113	4	1:22.60	32,400
1980	**Davona Dale**, 4, 119	J. Velasquez	Misty Gallore, 4, 124	It's in the Air, 4, 119	4	1:22.20	33,780
1979	**Blitey**, 3, 111	A. T. Cordero Jr.	Shukey, 4, 116	Bold Rendezvous, 4, 116	5	1:23.20	25,770

Named for Howell E. Jackson's Ballerina (1950 f. by Rosemont), first winner of the Maskette S. Grade 3 1981-'83. Grade 2 1984-'87. Ballerina H. 1994-2004. Dead heat for third 1999.

Ballston Spa Breeders' Cup Handicap

Grade 2 in 2006. Saratoga Race Course, three-year-olds and up, fillies and mares, 1 1/16 miles, turf. Held August 29, 2005, with a gross value of $135,966. First held in 1983. First graded in 1994. Stakes record 1:39.47 (1997 Valor Lady).

Year	Winner	Jockey	Second	Third	Strs	Time	1st Purse
2005	**Alinghi (Aus)**, 4, 119	E. S. Prado	Que Puntual (Arg), 5, 118	Delta Princess, 6, 118	11	1:40.30	$69,780
2004	**Ocean Drive**, 4, 119	J. R. Velazquez	Personal Legend, 4, 115	High Court (Brz), 4, 114	10	1:43.92	128,400
2003	**Stylish**, 5, 116	J. R. Velazquez	Snow Dance, 5, 117	Cozzy Corner, 5, 112	9	1:41.03	120,000
2002	**Surya**, 4, 114	J. D. Bailey	Shooting Party, 4, 118	Solvig, 5, 114	3	1:52.29	126,409
2001	**Penny's Gold**, 4, 118	J. D. Bailey	Babae (Chi), 5, 114	Chaste, 5, 113	6	1:40.69	126,120
2000	**License Fee**, 5, 116	P. Day	Pico Teneriffe, 4, 116	Hello Soso (Ire), 4, 114	7	1:43.53	125,700
1999	**Pleasant Temper**, 5, 118	J. D. Bailey	Cuanto Es, 4, 113	Lets Get Cozzy, 5, 114	5	1:41.84	124,680
1998	**Memories of Silver**, 5, 122	J. D. Bailey	Witchful Thinking, 4, 118	Ashford Castle, 4, 114	7	1:40.93	126,600
1997	**Valor Lady**, 5, 112	J. R. Velazquez	Antespend, 4, 116	Rumpipumpy (GB), 4, 114	6	**1:39.47**	130,200
1996	**Danish (Ire)**, 5, 115	J. A. Santos	Apolda, 5, 121	dh-Caress, 5, 113 dh-Upper Noosh, 4, 111	8	1:41.50	126,360
1995	**Weekend Madness (Ire)**, 5, 117	S. J. Sellers	Irish Linnet, 7, 120	Allez Les Trois, 4, 115	7	1:40.34	93,300
1994	**Weekend Madness (Ire)**, 4, 115	S. J. Sellers	You'd Be Surprised, 5, 120	Heed, 5, 110	8	1:43.77	93,510
1993	**One Dreamer**, 5, 116	E. Fires	Eenie Meenie Miney, 4, 111	Irish Linnet, 5, 116	10	1:39.38	94,440
1992	**Aurora**, 4, 114	C. Perret	Olden Rijn, 4, 112	Irish Linnet, 4, 113	7	1:36.94	93,870
1991	**Paris Opera**, 5, 116	G. L. Stevens	Daring Doone (GB), 8, 114	Le Famo, 5, 114	10	1:37.41	94,470
1990	**Fire the Groom**, 3, 114	L. Dettori	Sally Rous (Ire), 3, 114	Christiecat, 3, 115	12	1:35.20	95,820
1989	**Wakonda**, 5, 116	A. T. Cordero Jr.	Foresta, 3, 108	Toll Fee, 4, 111	5	1:33.80	93,900
1983	**Subversive Chick**, 3, 114	D. J. Murphy	Soft Morning, 4, 119	It Takes Only One, 3, 114	11	1:24.20	22,380

Named for Ballston Spa, New York, located south of Saratoga Springs. Grade 3 1994-2001, 2003-'05. Not graded 2002. Aqueduct Breeders' Cup H. 1989-'92. Aqueduct Budweiser Breeders' Cup H. 1993. Saratoga Budweiser Breeders' Cup H. 1994-'95. Saratoga Breeders' Cup H. 1996. Held at Aqueduct 1992-'93. Not held 1984-'88. 1 mile 1989-'93. 1 1/8 miles 2002. Dirt 1989, 2002. Originally scheduled on turf 2002. Dead heat for third 1996.

Barbara Fritchie Breeders' Cup Handicap

Grade 2 in 2006. Laurel Park, three-year-olds and up, fillies and mares, 7 furlongs, dirt. Held February 19, 2005, with a gross value of $200,000. First held in 1952. First graded in 1973. Stakes record 1:21.40 (1989 Tappiano).

Year	Winner	Jockey	Second	Third	Strs	Time	1st Purse
2005	**Cativa**, 5, 114	E. S. Prado	Sensibly Chic, 5, 115	Silmaril, 4, 114	10	1:23.64	$120,000
2004	**Bear Fan**, 5, 116	R. Fogelsonger	Gazillion, 5, 116	Bronze Abe, 5, 117	9	1:23.55	120,000
2003	**Xtra Heat**, 5, 125	R. Wilson	Carson Hollow, 4, 119	Spelling, 4, 113	7	1:24.76	120,000
2002	**Xtra Heat**, 4, 128	H. Vega	Prized Stamp, 5, 114	Kimbralata, 4, 114	8	1:22.70	120,000
2001	**Prized Stamp**, 4, 113	T. Dunkelberger	Superduper Miss, 5, 114	Tax Affair, 4, 113	6	1:23.74	120,000
2000	**Tap to Music**, 5, 115	J. Bravo	Her She Kisses, 4, 114	Di's Time, 5, 114	13	1:24.75	120,000
1999	**Passeggiata (Arg)**, 6, 113	M. G. Pino	Catinca, 4, 121	Nothing Special, 5, 108	8	1:23.55	150,000
1998	**J J'sdream**, 5, 115	L. C. Reynolds	Palette Knife, 5, 113	Stylish Encore, 5, 114	10	1:24.21	150,000
1997	**Miss Golden Circle**, 5, 118	R. Migliore	Lottsa Talc, 7, 119	Whaleneck, 4, 113	12	1:23.05	120,000
1996	**Lottsa Talc**, 6, 117	F. T. Alvarado	Up an Eighth, 5, 114	Evil's Pic, 4, 116	14	1:22.61	120,000
1995	**Smart 'N Noble**, 4, 117	M. G. Pino	Dust Bucket, 4, 114	Gooni Goo Hoo, 5, 110	10	1:24.13	120,000
1994	**Mixed Appeal**, 6, 111	A. C. Salazar	Known as Nancy, 4, 111	Winka, 4, 115	12	1:23.31	120,000
1993	**Moon Mist**, 4, 112	T. G. Turner	Ritchie Trail, 5, 113	Femma, 5, 114	9	1:23.50	120,000
1992	**Wood So**, 5, 113	M. G. Pino	Wide Country, 4, 120	Wait for the Lady, 5, 111	7	1:24.56	120,000
1991	**Fappaburst**, 4, 114	A. T. Cordero Jr.	Devil's Orchid, 4, 118	Diva's Debut, 5, 116	10	1:23.30	120,000
1990	**Amy Be Good**, 4, 112	M. E. Smith	Channel Three, 4, 111	Banbury Fair, 5, 110	10	1:23.40	120,000
1989	**Tappiano**, 5, 123	K. Desormeaux	Very Subtle, 5, 124	Tops in Taps, 6, 114	12	**1:21.40**	120,000
1988	**Psyched**, 5, 113	K. Desormeaux	Spring Beauty, 5, 116	Kerygma, 4, 115	10	1:22.60	81,250
1987	**Spring Beauty**, 4, 115	J. A. Santos	Notches Trace, 4, 110	Pine Tree Lane, 5, 126	12	1:25.40	88,770
1986	**Willowy Mood**, 4, 115	B. Thornburg	Aerturas (Fr), 5, 116	Alabama Nana (Ire), 5, 119	10	1:25.40	73,840
1985	**Dumdedumdedum**, 4, 115	D. A. Miller Jr.	Kattegat's Pride, 6, 119	Sharp Little Girl, 4, 110	8	1:25.00	87,993
	Flip's Pleasure, 5, 115	J. Samyn	Applause, 5, 120	Gene's Lady, 4, 109	8	1:24.00	71,793
1984	**Pleasure Cay**, 4, 115	D. A. Miller Jr.	Kattegat's Pride, 5, 117	Amanti, 5, 117	9	1:22.80	56,325
	Bara Lass, 5, 125	D. A. Miller Jr.	Owned by All, 4, 109	Willamae, 4, 113	7	1:24.00	55,025
1983	**Stellarette**, 5, 114	A. Delgado	Hoist Emy's Flag, 4, 116	Cheap Seats, 4, 122	10	1:24.40	74,100
1982	**Lady Dean**, 4, 119	D. A. Miller Jr.	Sweet Revenge, 4, 114	Sinister Queen, 6, 114	10	1:24.20	46,768
	The Wheel Turns, 5, 121	G. McCarron	Island Charm, 5, 122	Up the Flagpole, 4, 119	9	1:23.60	46,118
1981	**Skipat**, 7, 124	C. B. Asmussen	Whispy's Lass, 6, 114	Secret Emotion, 4, 113	8	1:23.00	72,865
1980	**Misty Gallore**, 4, 121	D. MacBeth	Gladiolus, 6, 122	Silver Ice, 5, 116	10	1:23.60	55,770
1979	**Skipat**, 5, 125	J. W. Edwards	Pearl Necklace, 5, 122	The Very One, 4, 113	8	1:22.40	53,755
1978	**Bold Brat**, 5, 115	J. W. Moseley	Spot Two, 4, 116	Satin Dancer, 5, 114	7	1:23.40	37,375
1977	**Mt. Airy Queen**, 4, 114	D. R. Wright	Avum, 4, 109	Forty Nine Sunsets, 4, 118	6	1:23.80	36,270
1976	**Donetta**, 5, 119	J. W. Moseley	Pinch Pie, 5, 117	Heydairya, 5, 108	11	1:24.60	37,765
1975	**Twixt**, 6, 126	W. J. Passmore	Crackerfax, 4, 109	Donetta, 4, 112	11	1:25.40	38,350
1974	**Twixt**, 5, 124	W. J. Passmore	Groton Miss, 5, 112	In the Mattress, 4, 109	10	1:24.40	38,350
1973	**First Bloom**, 5, 117	A. Gomez	Pas de Nom, 5, 116	Winged Affair, 5, 111	12	1:23.40	38,025

Named for Barbara Fritchie, a 95-year-old woman who, according to legend, waved her Union flag as Confederate General Thomas "Stonewall" Jackson passed through Frederick, Maryland. Grade 3 1973-'91. Held at Bowie 1952-'84. Not held 1960, 1972, 2006. 1 1/16 miles 1952-'54. 6 furlongs 1957-'59, 1963. 1 mile 1961. Two divisions 1982, 1984-'85.

Bashford Manor Stakes

Grade 3 in 2006. Churchill Downs, two-year-olds, 6 furlongs, dirt. Held July 10, 2005, with a gross value of $176,250. First held in 1902. First graded in 1991. Stakes record 1:09.68 (2002 Lone Star Sky).

Year	Winner	Jockey	Second	Third	Strs	Time	1st Purse
2005	**Deputy G**, 2, 117	G. L. Stevens	R Loyal Man, 2, 117	Honor Due, 2, 117	10	1:11.38	$109,275
2004	**Lunarpal**, 2, 121	S. J. Sellers	Storm Surge, 2, 117	Maximus C, 2, 117	7	1:11.54	101,184
2003	**Limehouse**, 2, 121	R. Albarado	First Money, 2, 117	Cuvee, 2, 121	6	1:10.62	100,905
2002	**Lone Star Sky**, 2, 115	M. Guidry	Posse, 2, 121	Cooper Crossing, 2, 115	7	**1:09.68**	84,475
2001	**Lunar Bounty**, 2, 115	F. Lovato Jr.	Binyamin, 2, 115	Storm Passage, 2, 115	5	1:09.90	82,925
2000	**Duality**, 2, 115	C. H. Borel	Strait Cat, 2, 114	Take Arms, 2, 115	9	1:10.09	86,258
1999	**Dance Master**, 2, 115	B. Peck	Sky Dweller, 2, 115	Snuck In, 2, 115	8	1:10.38	89,280
1998	**Time Bandit**, 2, 115	C. R. Woods Jr.	Yes It's True, 2, 121	Haus of Dehere, 2, 115	8	1:10.78	68,262
1997	**Favorite Trick**, 2, 121	P. Day	Double Honor, 2, 115	Cowboy Dan, 2, 118	8	1:09.92	68,696
1996	**Boston Harbor**, 2, 115	M. J. Luzzi	Prairie Junction, 2, 115	Nobel Talent, 2, 115	8	1:09.96	72,150
1995	**A. V. Eight**, 2, 115	A. J. Trosclair	Aggie Southpaw, 2, 115	Seeker's Reward, 2, 115	8	1:11.40	71,630
1994	**Hyroglyphic**, 2, 116	G. K. Gomez	Boone's Mill, 2, 116	Hobgoblin, 2, 116	13	1:10.25	75,660
1993	**†Miss Ra He Ra**, 2, 113	W. Martinez	Ramblin Guy, 2, 116	Riverinn, 2, 112	13	1:12.98	76,180
1992	**Mountain Cat**, 2, 116	C. R. Woods Jr.	Tempered Halo, 2, 121	Storm Flight, 2, 116	7	1:10.62	53,869
1991	**Pick Up the Phone**, 2, 116	J. C. Espinoza	Sprintmaster, 2, 116	Thanatopsis, 2, 112	7	1:12.08	35,815
1990	**To Freedom**, 2, 121	J. C. Espinoza	Richman, 2, 121	Discover, 2, 116	7	1:10.20	35,555
1989	**Summer Squall**, 2, 121	P. Day	Table Limit, 2, 118	Appealing Breeze, 2, 121	6	1:12.20	35,068
1988	**Bio**, 2, 118	P. A. Johnson	Revive, 2, 112	Curtis John, 2, 114	11	1:11.80	37,148
1987	**Blair's Cove**, 2, 114	S. J. Sellers	Endurance, 2, 118	Mr. Igloo, 2, 116	11	1:11.80	37,310
1986	**Faster Than Sound**, 2, 118	C. Perret	Renumeration, 2, 115	Arunti, 2, 121	7	1:11.20	46,648
1985	**Tile**, 2, 115	L. J. Melancon	Tug, 2, 115	Sir Grandeur, 2, 115	12	1:04.40	30,896
1984	**Jerry F.**, 2, 112	P. Day	Storm Scope, 2, 115	Wet My Whistle, 2, 115	3	1:05.80	17,241
1983	**Betwixt n' Between**, 2, 115	P. Day	Real Sharp Dancer, 2, 121	Biloxi Indian, 2, 118	13	1:05.00	22,896
1982	**Willow Drive**, 2, 115	J. Neagle	Stepping E. J., 2, 118	Mindboggling, 2, 115	11	1:05.00	20,264
1981	**T. V. Mark**, 2, 122	P. Nicolo	Shilling, 2, 122	Good Ole Master, 2, 122	10	:59.60	18,103
1980	**Golden Derby**, 2, 117	J. C. Espinoza	Wrong Impression, 2, 122	Stubilem, 2, 117	9	:59.00	19,338
1979	**Rajohn Greco**, 2, 122	J. C. Espinoza	Egg's Dynamite, 2, 122	Native Amber, 2, 122	6	1:00.20	19,451
1978	**Spy Charger**, 2, 127	G. Mahon	Uncle Fudge, 2, 122	Vennie Redberry, 2, 122	6	:58.40	14,089
1977	**Going Investor**, 2, 122	B. Sayler	Old Jake, 2, 117	Chwesboken, 2, 122	7	:58.40	14,235
1976	**Judge John Boone**, 2, 122	E. Delahoussaye	Wishem Well, 2, 122	Golden Trade, 2, 117	8	:58.60	14,625
1975	**Khyber King**, 2, 122	E. Delahoussaye	Bold Laddie, 2, 122	Right On Mike, 2, 122	5	:58.60	15,633
1974	**Pac Quick**, 2, 125	G. Patterson	Paris Dust, 2, 127	Kaanapali, 2, 122	9	:59.60	16,608
1973	**Tisab**, 2, 122	M. Manganello	No Advance, 2, 122	To the Rescue, 2, 122	9	:58.80	16,965

Named for an old Louisville-area plantation and neighborhood, Bashford Manor. Grade 2 1999-2001. 4½ furlongs 1902-'25. 5 furlongs 1926-'81. 5½ furlongs 1982-'85. Colts and geldings 1940-'81. †Denotes female.

Bayakoa Handicap

Grade 2 in 2006. Hollywood Park, three-year-olds and up, fillies and mares, 1 1/16 miles, dirt. Held December 11, 2005, with a gross value of $150,000. First held in 1981. First graded in 1983. Stakes record 1:41.02 (2003 Star Parade [Arg]).

Year	Winner	Jockey	Second	Third	Strs	Time	1st Purse
2005	**Star Parade (Arg)**, 6, 116	M. A. Pedroza	Dream of Summer, 6, 122	Island Fashion, 5, 119	9	1:41.96	$90,000
2004	**Hollywood Story**, 3, 115	V. Espinoza	Royally Chosen, 6, 116	A. P. Adventure, 3, 117	7	1:41.11	90,000
2003	**Star Parade (Arg)**, 4, 112	V. Espinoza	Adoration, 4, 121	Bare Necessities, 4, 119	6	**1:41.02**	90,000
2002	**Starrer**, 4, 118	P. A. Valenzuela	Cee's Elegance, 5, 113	Angel Gift, 4, 115	6	1:41.74	90,000
2001	**Starrer**, 3, 118	J. D. Bailey	Queenie Belle, 4, 118	Tropical Lady (Brz), 4, 115	7	1:42.52	90,000
2000	**Feverish**, 5, 119	E. Delahoussaye	Gourmet Girl, 5, 118	Lazy Slusan, 5, 117	9	1:42.26	90,000
1999	**Manistique**, 4, 124	C. S. Nakatani	Snowberg, 4, 115	Riboletta (Brz), 4, 116	7	1:43.16	90,000
1998	**Manistique**, 3, 119	G. L. Stevens	India Divina (Chi), 4, 114	Numero Uno, 4, 115	4	1:42.51	60,000
1997	**Sharp Cat**, 3, 121	A. O. Solis			1	1:42.68	60,000
1996	**Listening**, 3, 120	C. J. McCarron	Cat's Cradle, 4, 120	Belle's Flag, 3, 117	7	1:42.66	64,920
1995	**Pirate's Revenge**, 4, 119	C. W. Antley	Urbane, 3, 120	Ashtabula, 4, 116	5	1:41.80	61,900
1994	**Thirst for Peace**, 5, 115	A. O. Solis	Glass Ceiling, 4, 117	Dancing Mirage, 3, 119	7	1:42.28	63,500
1993	**Golden Klair (GB)**, 3, 115	C. J. McCarron	Pacific Squall, 4, 118	Cargo, 4, 116	7	1:41.20	63,500
1992	**Brought to Mind**, 5, 120	P. A. Valenzuela	Re Toss (Arg), 5, 115	Interactive, 3, 112	8	1:42.62	65,200
1991	**Paseana (Arg)**, 4, 117	C. J. McCarron	Damewood, 3, 116	Luna Elegante (Arg), 5, 117	6	1:42.70	62,700
1990	**Fantastic Look**, 4, 118	C. J. McCarron	Spanish Dior, 3, 112	Tis Juliet, 4, 115	6	1:42.40	62,200
1989	**Approved to Fly**, 3, 115	A. O. Solis	Saros Brig, 5, 115	Lucky Song, 3, 114	7	1:48.20	63,400
1988	**Nastique**, 4, 119	W. Shoemaker	Miss Brio (Chi), 4, 116	T. V. of Crystal, 3, 117	9	1:48.00	76,800
1986	**Family Style**, 3, 115	G. L. Stevens	Infinidad (Chi), 4, 114	Waterside, 4, 113	7	1:50.00	82,700
1985	**Love Smitten**, 4, 116	C. J. McCarron	Mimi Baker, 4, 111	Dontstop Themusic, 5, 125	5	1:47.80	61,600
1984	**Dontstop Themusic**, 4, 118	T. Lipham	Paradies (Arg), 4, 114	Fancy Wings, 4, 116	8	1:50.20	64,500
1983	**Sweet Diane**, 3, 115	R. Sibille	Miss Huntington, 6, 117	Bersid, 5, 118	11	1:48.00	67,900
1982	**Sierva (Arg)**, 4, 117	L. A. Pincay Jr.	Miss Huntington, 5, 117	Plenty O'Toole, 5, 115	11	1:48.20	68,900
1981	**Happy Guess (Arg)**, 5, 117	W. Shoemaker	Track Robbery, 5, 123	Targa, 4, 112	6	1:49.60	62,100

Named for Mr. and Mrs. Frank E. Whitham's 1989, '90 champion older female and '89 Vanity H. (G1) winner Bayakoa (Arg) (1984 f. by Consultant's Bid). Grade 3 1983-'85. Silver Belles H. 1981-'93. Not held 1987. 1⅛ miles 1981-'89. Won in a walkover 1997.

Bay Meadows Breeders' Cup Sprint Handicap

Grade 3 in 2006. Bay Meadows Race Course, three-year-olds and up, 6 furlongs, dirt. Held June 4, 2006, with a gross value of $108,125. First held in 1986. First graded in 2000. Stakes record 1:07.94 (2001 Lexicon).

Year	Winner	Jockey	Second	Third	Strs	Time	1st Purse
2006	**Carthage**, 6, 120	D. Carr	Trickey Trevor, 7, 120	Areyoutalkintome, 5, 116	4	1:09.33	$68,750
2004	**Court's in Session**, 5, 115	R. M. Gonzalez	Debonair Joe, 5, 117	Hombre Rapido, 7, 118	9	1:08.91	41,250
2003	**El Dorado Shooter**, 6, 120	C. P. Schvaneveldt	Halo Cat, 5, 118	Radar Contact, 7, 116	6	1:08.61	82,500
2002	**Mellow Fellow**, 7, 119	R. A. Baze	Explicit, 5, 120	Swept Overboard, 5, 122	6	1:08.35	110,000
2001	**Lexicon**, 6, 117	R. A. Baze	Swept Overboard, 4, 117	You and You Alone, 4, 115	4	**1:07.94**	82,500
2000	**Lexicon**, 5, 115	R. A. Baze	Men's Exclusive, 7, 115	Dixie Dot Com, 5, 116	5	1:09.19	110,000
1999	**Big Jag**, 6, 118	J. Valdivia Jr.	Men's Exclusive, 6, 115	Lexicon, 4, 116	6	1:08.87	110,000
1998	**Musafi**, 4, 116	D. R. Flores	dh-The Barking Shark, 5, 116 dh-Mr. Doubledown, 4, 116		7	1:08.59	110,000
1997	**Tres Paraiso**, 5, 116	C. S. Nakatani	Mashaka's Pride, 4, 112	Boundless Moment, 5, 117	5	1:07.98	110,000
1996	**Boundless Moment**, 4, 116	K. Desormeaux	Concept Win, 6, 115	Paying Dues, 4, 119	11	1:08.81	110,000
1995	**Lucky Forever**, 6, 116	G. F. Almeida	Wild Gold, 5, 115	Uncaged Fury, 4, 116	6	1:08.71	117,700
1994	**†Soviet Problem**, 4, 120	R. A. Baze	Wild Gold, 4, 115	Concept Win, 4, 119	6	1:08.58	31,200
1993	**Lucky Forever**, 4, 114	A. L. Castanon	Cardmania, 7, 116	Scherando, 4, 115	9	1:08.98	87,750
1992	**Superstrike (GB)**, 3, 114	D. Sorenson	Anjiz, 4, 114	Naevus Star, 6, 111	7	1:08.83	86,950
1991	**Robyn Dancer**, 4, 119	L. A. Pincay Jr.	Blue Eyed Danny, 5, 115	Letthebighossroll, 3, 116	7	1:09.30	84,728
1990	**Earn Your Stripes**, 6, 117	P. A. Valenzuela	Frost Free, 5, 116	Just Deeds, 4, 113	6	1:08.40	84,700
1989	**Happy Toss (Arg)**, 4, 115	F. Toro	No Marker, 5, 111	Hot Operator, 4, 113	6	1:39.80	86,250
1988	**Good Command**, 5, 117	R. A. Baze	Slyly Gifted, 5, 113	Miracle Horse (Fr), 4, 117	5	1:42.00	85,950
1987	**Judge Angelucci**, 4, 122	G. Baze	He's a Saros, 4, 115	Show Dancer, 5, 117	4	1:48.20	85,350
1986	**Hopeful Word**, 5, 120	F. Toro	Armin, 5, 114	Bozina, 5, 115	8	1:40.40	87,350

Bay Meadows Budweiser Breeders' Cup H. 1986-'95. Not held 2005. $1^1/_{16}$ miles 1986, 1988-'89. $1^1/_8$ miles 1987. Dead heat for second 1998. †Denotes female.

Bayou Breeders' Cup Handicap

Grade 3 in 2006. Fair Grounds at Louisiana Downs, four-year-olds and up, fillies and mares, $1^1/_{16}$ miles, turf. Held January 14, 2006, with a gross value of $269,600. First held in 1969. First graded in 2004. Stakes record 1:43.23 (2006 Snowdrops [GB]).

Year	Winner	Jockey	Second	Third	Strs	Time	1st Purse
2006	**Snowdrops (GB)**, 6, 119	B. Blanc	La Reason, 6, 115	Lenatareese, 5, 115	7	**1:43.23**	$161,760
2005	**Shadow Cast**, 4, 119	R. Albarado	Bijou, 6, 115	Sister Swank, 4, 120	8	1:53.75	75,000
2004	**Bedanken**, 5, 121	D. R. Pettinger	Due to Win Again, 6, 118	Lady Linda, 6, 115	10	1:52.74	75,000
2003	**Quick Tip**, 5, 116	R. Albarado	Histoire Sainte (Fr), 7, 118	Snow Dance, 5, 119	10	1:54.61	90,000
2002	**Katy Kat**, 4, 116	R. Albarado	Pretty Gale, 4, 113	Temis (Chi), 6, 109	6	1:50.67	90,000
2001	**On a Soapbox**, 5, 113	M. St. Julien	Always Sure, 5, 115	Lady Tamworth, 6, 111	6	1:53.82	94,770
2000	**Histoire Sainte (Fr)**, 4, 111	S. J. Sellers	Snow Polina, 5, 115	Neptune's Bride, 4, 115	9	1:49.32	65,850
1999	**Red Cat**, 4, 113	R. D. Ardoin	Swearingen, 5, 117	Justenuffheart, 4, 115	7	1:51.31	95,280
1998	**Cuando**, 4, 114	W. Martinez	Water Street, 4, 111	B. A. Valentine, 5, 118	8	1:53.60	52,620
1997	**Maxzene**, 4, 116	J. A. Krone	Flame Valley, 4, 112	Tough Broad, 5, 114	10	1:53.00	91,875
1996	**Tough Broad**, 4, 110	S. P. LeJeune Jr.	Brushing Gloom, 4, 112	Stellarina, 5, 114	11	1:51.38	91,875
1995	**Lismore Lass**, 6, 113	J. E. Broussard III	Onceinabluemamoon, 4, 115	Bendel Bonnet, 4, 110	10	1:53.97	36,000
1994	**Prominent Feather**, 5, 113	R. D. Ardoin	Mystical Path, 5, 112	Forever North, 6, 116	13	1:52.68	47,070
1993	**Liz Cee**, 5, 114	L. J. Martinez	To Be Dazzling, 5, 115	Trim Cut, 5, 112	14	1:52.20	32,130
1992	**Bishops Idea**, 4, 113	B. E. Poyadou	Palace Chill, 5, 120	Hero's Love, 4, 110	10	1:53.80	31,545
1991	**Phoenix Sunshine**, 6, 117	V. L. Smith	Leering, 4, 114	Chore Girl, 5, 113	12	1:52.30	19,755
1990	**Phoenix Sunshine**, 5, 115	C. J. Woodley	Regal Wonder, 6, 118	Lyphover, 5, 122	11	1:53.00	16,725
1989	**How I Wish**, 5, 120	C. H. Borel	Factually, 5, 112	Profit Island, 5, 113	12	1:52.00	16,815
1988	**How I Wish**, 4, 116	E. J. Perrodin	Robertina, 4, 117	Vigorous Market, 4, 112	9	1:48.00	16,575
1987	**Sastarda (Chi)**, 6, 120	K. Bourque	Anadia, 4, 110	Costa Del Sol, 6, 113	10	2:22.40	21,540
1986	**Dancing Slippers**, 5, 113	J. Samyn	Costa Del Sol, 5, 118	Lock's Dream, 4, 114	11	2:21.40	53,145
1985	**Over Your Shoulder**, 4, 114	G. St. Leon	Costa Del Sol, 4, 116	Erudite (Fr), 5, 113	12	2:19.00	40,325
1984	**Freeway Folly**, 5, 122	R. P. Romero	Gabfest, 5, 113	Erudite (Fr), 4, 116	10	2:33.00	39,025
1983	**Countess Tully (Ire)**, 5, 114	D. Brumfield	Full of Reason, 5, 114	Valid Bess, 5, 115	13	2:19.20	42,825
1982	**Vibro Vibes**, 5, 114	E. J. Perrodin	Lady Offshore, 5, 120	Sweetest Sound, 4, 113	14	2:17.60	40,100
1981	**Royal Saint**, 4, 118	J. McKnight	La Bonzo, 5, 122	Vibro Vibes, 4, 114	6	2:06.00	32,075
1980	**Holy Mount**, 4, 117	E. Fires	Salzburg, 5, 118	Fun Worthy, 4, 115	12	2:04.00	35,975
1979	**Lily S.**, 4, 112	D. Montoya	Flaunter, 4, 110	Jevalin, 4, 114	9	2:07.20	28,875
1978	**Quid Kit**, 4, 115	D. Copling	Famed Princess, 5, 118	La Doree (Arg), 4, 112	12	1:45.40	30,800
1977	**Forlana**, 4, 118	A. J. Trosclair	Hail to El, 5, 114	Critical Miss, 4, 117	10	1:44.60	20,550
1976	**Point in Time**, 4, 117	A. J. Trosclair	Hope She Does, 4, 116	Flama Ardiente, 4, 124	14	1:45.00	22,150
1975	**Truchas**, 6, 115	O. Sanchez	Big Dare, 5, 119	Stylish Genie, 4, 115	9	1:44.60	19,775
1974	**Sixty Sails**, 4, 120	P. Rubbicco	Sassy Bee, 4, 116	Knitted Gloves, 4, 117	7	1:44.40	12,050
1973	**Neigh Neigh**, 4, 112	D. Meade Jr.	Lyrs Poker, 4, 115	Daring Jester, 5, 114	10	1:46.60	11,225

Named for the swampy marshes found throughout Louisiana. Bayou H. 1969-'95. Held at Louisiana Downs 2006. 1 mile 70 yards 1969-'72. $1^1/_4$ miles 1979-'81. $1^3/_8$ miles 1982-'83, 1985-'87. $1^1/_2$ miles 1984. $1^1/_8$ miles 1989-'90, 1998, 2001-'02. About $1^1/_8$ miles 2005. Dirt 1969-'81, 1998, 2001-'02. Three-year-olds and up 1969-'78.

Bay Shore Stakes

Grade 3 in 2006. Aqueduct, three-year-olds, 7 furlongs, dirt. Held April 8, 2006, with a gross value of $147,000. First held in 1894. First graded in 1973. Stakes record 1:20.54 (1998 Limit Out).

Year	Winner	Jockey	Second	Third	Strs	Time	1st Purse
2006	**Too Much Bling**, 3, 120	G. K. Gomez	Songster, 3, 116	One Way Flight, 3, 120	5	1:22.40	$90,000
2005	**Lost in the Fog**, 3, 123	R. A. Baze	White Socks, 3, 116	Big Top Cat, 3, 116	6	1:21.33	90,000
2004	**Forest Danger**, 3, 116	J. R. Velazquez	Abbondanza, 3, 116	Indian War Dance, 3, 116	8	1:20.67	90,000
2003	**Halo Homewrecker**, 3, 116	J. R. Velazquez	Don Six, 3, 116	Stanislavsky, 3, 116	11	1:23.19	90,000
2002	**Roman Dancer**, 3, 120	K. Desormeaux	Warners, 3, 116	Monthir, 3, 116	10	1:22.21	90,000
2001	**Skip to the Stone**, 3, 120	V. Espinoza	Multiple Choice, 3, 116	Friday's a Comin', 3, 120	8	1:22.46	90,000
2000	**Precise End**, 3, 116	J. F. Chavez	Turnofthecentury, 3, 114	Port Herman, 3, 114	7	1:22.27	66,000
1999	**Perfect Score**, 3, 118	E. S. Prado	Royal Ruby, 3, 114	Prince Monty, 3, 116	8	1:22.98	66,120
1998	**Limit Out**, 3, 115	J. Samyn	Good and Tough, 3, 113	Diamond Studs, 3, 113	6	**1:20.54**	65,460
1997	**Hawks Landing**, 3, 114	R. Migliore	Adverse, 3, 113	Standing On Edge, 3, 113	7	1:22.00	66,480
1996	**Jamies First Punch**, 3, 115	J. R. Velazquez	Gold Fever, 3, 115	Firey Jennifer, 3, 115	9	1:22.13	67,200
1995	**Blissful State**, 3, 118	M. J. Luzzi	Northern Ensign, 3, 114	Pat n Jac, 3, 115	6	1:23.92	64,680
1994	**Prank Call**, 3, 113	J. R. Velazquez	Mr. Shawklit, 3, 117	Popol's Gold, 3, 122	7	1:09.84	65,940
1992	**Three Peat**, 3, 114	C. W. Antley	Goldwater, 3, 117	Best Decorated, 3, 114	10	1:21.68	75,600
1991	**Stately Wager**, 3, 119	J. F. Chavez	Mineral Ice, 3, 119	Vouch for Me, 3, 117	7	1:23.95	71,040
1990	**Richard R.**, 3, 117	J. A. Santos	For Really, 3, 114	Cielo, 3, 114	7	1:22.80	70,080
1989	**Houston**, 3, 116	L. A. Pincay Jr.	Mr. Nickerson, 3, 114	Wee Stark, 3, 119	6	1:22.40	69,000
1988	**Perfect Spy**, 3, 119	R. G. Davis	Success Express, 3, 123	Proud and Valid, 3, 117	5	1:22.60	98,460
1987	**Gulch**, 3, 123	J. A. Santos	High Brite, 3, 119	Shawklit Won, 3, 114	9	1:23.20	124,800
1986	**Zabaleta**, 3, 114	D. G. McHargue	Groovy, 3, 117	Belocolus, 3, 114	8	1:22.00	95,250
	Buck Aly, 3, 117	N. Santagata	Landing Plot, 3, 119	Raja's Revenge, 3, 119	8	1:23.80	95,250
1985	**Pancho Villa**, 3, 114	F. Lovato Jr.	El Basco, 3, 114	Spend a Buck, 3, 123	9	1:22.20	97,020
1984	**Secret Prince**, 3, 114	C. Perret	The Wedding Guest, 3, 126	I'm a Rounder, 3, 114	9	1:11.20	95,580
1983	**Strike Gold**, 3, 114	E. Maple	Assault Landing, 3, 114	Chas Conerly, 3, 114	9	1:22.60	34,620
1982	**Shimatoree**, 3, 114	A. T. Cordero Jr.	Big Brave Rock, 3, 114	John's Gold, 3, 114	7	1:23.20	33,000
1981	**Proud Appeal**, 3, 121	J. Fell	Willow Hour, 3, 114	Royal Pavilion, 3, 114	4	1:22.20	32,940
1980	**Colonel Moran**, 3, 121	J. Velasquez	Son of a Dodo, 3, 115	Dunham's Gift, 3, 114	7	1:23.80	34,260
1979	**Belle's Gold**, 3, 114	G. Martens	Screen King, 3, 121	General Assembly, 3, 123	4	1:21.80	32,040
1978	**Piece of Heaven**, 3, 119	R. Hernandez	Just Right Classi, 3, 114	Slap Jack, 3, 114	8	1:11.00	32,460
1977	**Cormorant**, 3, 121	D. R. Wright	Medieval Man, 3, 119	Hey Hey J. P., 3, 114	6	1:10.80	32,460
1976	**Bold Forbes**, 3, 119	A. T. Cordero Jr.	Eustace, 3, 121	Full Out, 3, 124	8	1:20.80	33,780
1975	**Laramie Trail**, 3, 113	M. Venezia	T. V. Charger, 3, 113	Ascetic, 3, 121	5	1:23.60	26,910
	Lefty, 3, 113	R. Turcotte	Tass, 3, 113	Gallant Bob, 3, 119	8	1:23.80	27,360
1974	**Hudson County**, 3, 113	M. Miceli	Frankie Adams, 3, 119	Instead of Roses, 3, 116	11	1:22.60	34,680
1973	**Secretariat**, 3, 126	R. Turcotte	Champagne Charlie, 3, 118	Impecunious, 3, 126	6	1:23.20	16,650

Named for Bay Shore, a resort community located on Long Island, New York. Grade 2 1985-'92. Bayshore S. 1894-1909. Bay Shore H. 1925-'62, 1979-'80. Held at Gravesend 1894-1909. Not held 1910-'24, 1956-'59, 1993. $1\frac{1}{16}$ miles 1894. 1 mile 1895, 1933, 1960-'63. 6 furlongs 1896-'98, 1934-'35, 1977-'78, 1984, 1994. About 6 furlongs 1899-1909. $6\frac{1}{2}$ furlongs 1936-'39. Three-year-olds and up 1894-1960. Two divisions 1975, 1986.

Beaugay Handicap

Grade 3 in 2006. Aqueduct, three-year-olds and up, fillies and mares, $1\frac{1}{16}$ miles, turf. Held April 29, 2006, with a gross value of $112,300. First held in 1978. First graded in 1986. Stakes record 1:40.16 (1991 Summer Secretary).

Year	Winner	Jockey	Second	Third	Strs	Time	1st Purse
2006	**Pommes Frites**, 4, 115	C. H. Velasquez	Naissance Royale (Ire), 4, 117	Brunilda (Arg), 6, 115	8	1:43.15	$67,380
2005	**Finery**, 5, 116	P. Fragoso	Changing World, 5, 118	Asti (Ire), 4, 117	9	1:44.56	67,680
2004	**Dedication (Fr)**, 5, 118	J. Castellano	Aud, 4, 117	Caught in the Rain, 5, 114	7	1:46.38	66,000
2003	**Delta Princess**, 4, 113	M. J. Luzzi	Wonder Again, 4, 118	Voodoo Dancer, 5, 120	9	1:42.36	67,440
2002	**Voodoo Dancer**, 4, 119	J. D. Bailey	Golden Corona, 4, 115	Babae (Chi), 6, 116	10	1:43.10	67,920
2001	**Gaviola**, 4, 120	J. D. Bailey	Truebreadpudding, 6, 113	Efficient Frontier, 4, 114	6	1:41.74	65,940
2000	**Perfect Sting**, 4, 119	J. D. Bailey	License Fee, 5, 114	Fictitious (GB), 4, 114	7	1:42.30	65,820
1999	**Tampico**, 6, 114	J. R. Velazquez	U R Unforgetable, 5, 115	Shashobegon, 4, 114	7	1:44.32	67,020
1998	**National Treasure**, 5, 117	R. Migliore	Aspiring, 5, 113	Dixie Ghost, 4, 111	7	1:37.94	67,740
1997	**Careless Heiress**, 4, 116	J. Bravo	Song of Africa, 4, 113	Gastronomical, 4, 115	6	1:46.28	65,760
1996	**Christmas Gift**, 4, 118	J. D. Bailey	Caress, 5, 119	Aucilla, 5, 113	9	1:42.89	50,805
1995	**Caress**, 4, 113	R. G. Davis	Shir Dar (Fr), 5, 113	Statuette, 5, 116	8	1:42.06	49,905
1994	**Cox Orange**, 4, 112	J. D. Bailey	Irish Linnet, 6, 116	Statuette, 4, 116	5	1:43.32	49,395
1993	**McKaymackenna**, 4, 113	J. Velasquez	Aurora, 5, 115	Chinese Empress, 4, 114	10	1:44.80	57,240
1992	**Christiecat**, 5, 116	J. Samyn	Metamorphose, 4, 113	Navarra, 4, 109	10	1:46.84	56,520
1991	**Summer Secretary**, 6, 116	J. Velasquez	Virgin Michael, 4, 113	Christiecat, 4, 115	7	**1:40.16**	54,270
1990	**Fieldy (Ire)**, 7, 119	C. Perret	Summer Secretary, 5, 114	Lady Talc, 6, 110	5	1:45.80	52,740
1989	**Summer Secretary**, 4, 109	J. Samyn	Far East, 6, 110	Fieldy (Ire), 6, 116	9	1:43.40	56,880
1988	**Key to the Bridge**, 4, 112	E. Maple	Marimascus, 4, 112	Just Class (Ire), 4, 115	5	1:51.80	65,160
1987	**Give a Toast**, 4, 111	R. G. Davis	Videogenic, 5, 117	Small Virtue, 4, 113	8	1:44.20	68,940
1986	**Duty Dance**, 4, 115	J. Cruguet	Possible Mate, 5, 124	Lucky Touch, 4, 109	10	1:40.20	55,800
1985	**Possible Mate**, 4, 119	J. Vasquez	Make the Magic, 4, 109	Annie Edge (Ire), 5, 114	8	1:40.60	42,600
1984	**Thirty Flags**, 4, 113	A. T. Cordero Jr.	Jubilous, 4, 114	Nany, 4, 111	12	1:42.00	45,840
1983	**Trevita (Ire)**, 6, 119	J. Velasquez	Beech Island, 5, 108	Top of the Barrel, 5, 105	12	1:47.80	37,020

1982	**Cheap Seats**, 3, 113	A. T. Cordero Jr.	Tina Tina Too, 4, 115	Fancy Naskra, 4, 112	7	1:45.20	$33,780
1981	**Andover Way**, 3, 120	A. T. Cordero Jr.	Water Dance, 4, 117	Tournament Star, 3, 109	10	1:44.00	34,440
1980	**Samarta Dancer**, 4, 114	L. Saumell	Plankton, 4, 121	Bien Fait, 4, 109	8	1:43.60	33,540
1979	**Plankton**, 3, 113	R. Hernandez	Miss Baja, 4, 114	Reflection Pool, 5, 112	6	1:46.00	25,612
	Heavenly Ade, 3, 114	M. Solomone	Propitiate, 4, 112	Gladiolus, 5, 122	5	1:45.60	25,613
1978	**Shukey**, 3, 113	J. Velasquez	Sans Critique, 4, 118	Whodatorsay, 4, 109	6	1:45.20	25,755

Named for Maine Chance Farm's 1945 champion two-year-old filly Beaugay (1943 f. by Stimulus). Held at Belmont Park 1983-'92. 1 mile 1998. Dirt 1978-'82, 1998. Two divisions 1979.

Bed o' Roses Breeders' Cup Handicap

Grade 2 in 2006. Aqueduct, three-year-olds and up, fillies and mares, 7 furlongs, dirt. Held April 22, 2006, with a gross value of $155,400. First held in 1957. First graded in 1973. Stakes record 1:23.87 (2006 Magnolia Jackson).

Year	Winner	Jockey	Second	Third	Strs	Time	1st Purse
2006	**Magnolia Jackson**, 4, 115	N. Arroyo Jr.	Grecian Lover, 4, 115	Annika Lass, 5, 114	5	**1:23.87**	$95,040
2005	**Pleasant Home**, 4, 114	C. H. Velasquez	Traci Girl, 6, 114	Cativa, 5, 117	7	1:36.72	95,220
2004	**Passing Shot**, 5, 115	J. A. Santos	Smok'n Frolic, 5, 119	Nonsuch Bay, 5, 116	6	1:35.50	95,040
2003	**Raging Fever**, 5, 119	A. T. Gryder	Smok'n Frolic, 4, 120	Nonsuch Bay, 4, 117	5	1:34.86	93,960
2002	**Raging Fever**, 4, 121	J. R. Velazquez	Atelier, 5, 119	Shiny Band, 4, 112	6	1:34.96	94,980
2001	**Country Hideaway**, 5, 117	J. R. Velazquez	Critical Eye, 4, 115	Jostle, 4, 117	7	1:34.98	95,520
2000	**Ruby Rubles**, 5, 113	C. C. Lopez	Up We Go, 4, 114	Go to the Ink, 4, 111	7	1:36.96	65,580
1999	**Catinca**, 4, 120	R. Migliore	Foil, 4, 113	License Fee, 4, 113	6	1:34.95	94,620
1998	**Dixie Flag**, 4, 117	M. J. Luzzi	Hidden Reserve, 4, 113	U Can Do It, 5, 118	9	1:33.60	96,780
1997	**Flat Fleet Feet**, 4, 121	M. E. Smith	Mama Dean, 4, 113	Ashboro, 4, 116	6	1:34.00	95,940
1996	**Punkin Pie**, 6, 110	J. C. Trejo	Incinerate, 6, 115	Lottsa Talc, 6, 121	6	1:35.13	65,220
1995	**Incinerate**, 5, 113	F. Leon	Imah, 5, 114	Beckys Shirt, 4, 113	5	1:35.86	63,960
1994	**Classy Mirage**, 4, 117	R. G. Davis	For all Seasons, 4, 115	Dispute, 4, 122	6	1:34.00	64,680
1993	**Lady d'Accord**, 6, 111	J. F. Chavez	Missy's Mirage, 5, 123	Buck Some Belle, 4, 106	5	1:36.76	67,320
1992	**Nannerl**, 5, 115	J. A. Krone	English Charm, 6, 111	Spy Leader Lady, 4, 115	7	1:37.27	68,100
	Lady d'Accord, 5, 114	J. F. Chavez	My Treasure, 5, 112	Crystal Vous, 4, 112	7	1:37.86	68,580
1991	**Devil's Orchid**, 4, 120	R. A. Baze	Colonial Waters, 6, 119	Sharp Dance, 5, 114	6	1:35.93	68,520
1990	**Survive**, 6, 117	J. A. Santos	Amy Be Good, 4, 114	Warfie, 4, 111	6	1:34.20	68,640
1989	**Banker's Lady**, 4, 118	A. T. Cordero Jr.	Aptostar, 4, 118	Avie's Gal, 4, 114	5	1:35.40	68,400
1988	**Aptostar**, 3, 103	J. A. Krone	Clabber Girl, 5, 117	Psyched, 5, 114	8	1:35.40	70,680
1987	**Ms. Eloise**, 4, 115	R. G. Davis	Spring Beauty, 4, 116	Tricky Squaw, 4, 115	9	1:36.60	84,660
1986	**Chaldea**, 6, 110	J. Samyn	Add Mint, 4, 111	Lady On the Run, 4, 120	9	1:36.00	75,120
1985	**Nany**, 5, 120	J. Vasquez	Flip's Pleasure, 5, 118	Sintrillium, 7, 120	6	1:36.00	50,850
1984	**Pleasure Cay**, 4, 115	R. G. Davis	Sweet Missus, 4, 103	Sintrillium, 6, 113	8	1:42.00	54,090
1983	**Broom Dance**, 4, 118	G. McCarron	Adept, 4, 109	Viva Sec, 5, 112	7	1:35.40	33,420
1982	**Who's to Answer**, 4, 108	E. Beitia	Real Prize, 4, 114	Faisana (Arg), 5, 110	9	1:36.60	33,180
1981	**Chain Bracelet**, 4, 114	F. Lovato Jr.	Lady Oakley (Ire), 4, 116	Contrary Rose, 5, 115	7	1:35.40	33,960
1980	**Misty Gallore**, 4, 125	D. MacBeth	Propitiate, 5, 115	Gueniviere, 4, 111	6	1:36.40	33,600
1979	**Lady Lonsdale**, 4, 111	C. B. Asmussen	Hagany, 5, 113	Back to Stay, 4, 107	7	1:36.80	31,980
	One Sum, 5, 118	J. Fell	Reflection Pool, 5, 113	Pearl Necklace, 5, 121	7	1:37.80	31,980
1978	**Fearless Queen**, 5, 108	M. Venezia	Notably, 5, 110	One Sum, 4, 123	7	1:46.20	25,785
1977	**Shawi**, 4, 109	M. Venezia	Proud Delta, 5, 125	Secret Lanvin, 4, 111	8	1:45.80	25,770
1976	**Imminence**, 4, 115	E. Maple	Spring Is Here, 4, 108	Land Girl, 4, 114	9	1:35.40	23,040
1975	**Shy Dawn**, 4, 121	D. Montoya	Something Super, 5, 118	Flo's Pleasure, 5, 115	7	1:36.20	16,860
1974	**Klepto**, 4, 123	D. Montoya	Ladies Agreement, 4, 112	Summer Guest, 5, 122	6	1:35.40	16,410
1973	**Poker Night**, 3, 108	R. Woodhouse	Numbered Account, 4, 123	Ferly, 5, 114	6	1:35.40	16,605

Named for Alfred G. Vanderbilt's 1949 champion two-year-old filly, '51 champion older female, and '49 Demoiselle S. winner Bed o' Roses (1947 f. by Rosemont). Grade 3 1975-'87, 1997-2005. Bed o' Roses H. 1957-'95. Held at Jamaica 1957-'59. 1$^1/_{16}$ miles 1957-'59, 1977-'78. 1 mile 70 yards 1984. 1 mile 1960-'76, 1979-'83, 1985-2005. Two divisions 1979, 1992.

Beldame Stakes

Grade 1 in 2006. Belmont Park, three-year-olds and up, fillies and mares, 1$^1/_8$ miles, dirt. Held October 1, 2005, with a gross value of $750,000. First held in 1905. First graded in 1973. Stakes record 1:45.80 (1990 Go for Wand).

Year	Winner	Jockey	Second	Third	Strs	Time	1st Purse
2005	**Ashado**, 4, 123	J. R. Velazquez	Happy Ticket, 4, 123	Society Selection, 4, 123	7	1:48.88	$450,000
2004	**Sightseek**, 5, 123	J. Castellano	Society Selection, 3, 120	Storm Flag Flying, 4, 123	5	1:49.60	450,000
2003	**Sightseek**, 4, 123	J. D. Bailey	Bird Town, 3, 120	Buy the Sport, 3, 120	7	1:49.27	450,000
2002	**Imperial Gesture**, 3, 120	J. D. Bailey	Mandy's Gold, 4, 123	Summer Colony, 4, 123	7	1:50.63	450,000
2001	**Exogenous**, 3, 120	J. Castellano	Flute, 3, 120	Spain, 4, 123	8	1:49.20	450,000
2000	**Riboletta (Brz)**, 5, 123	C. J. McCarron	Beautiful Pleasure, 5, 123	Pentatonic, 5, 123	5	1:46.14	450,000
1999	**Beautiful Pleasure**, 4, 123	J. F. Chavez	Silverbulletday, 3, 119	Catinca, 4, 123	5	1:47.74	300,000
1998	**Sharp Cat**, 4, 123	C. S. Nakatani	Tomisue's Delight, 4, 123	Pocho's Dream Girl, 4, 123	7	1:46.20	240,000
1997	**Hidden Lake**, 4, 123	R. Migliore	Ajina, 3, 119	Jewel Princess, 5, 123	8	1:48.26	240,000
1996	**Yanks Music**, 3, 119	J. R. Velazquez	Serena's Song, 4, 123	Clear Mandate, 4, 123	6	1:47.02	240,000
1995	**Serena's Song**, 3, 119	G. L. Stevens	Heavenly Prize, 4, 123	Lakeway, 4, 123	5	1:48.75	150,000
1994	**Heavenly Prize**, 3, 119	P. Day	Educated Risk, 4, 123	Classy Mirage, 4, 123	4	1:48.86	150,000
1993	**Dispute**, 3, 119	J. D. Bailey	Shared Interest, 5, 123	Vivano, 4, 123	6	1:47.22	150,000
1992	**Saratoga Dew**, 3, 119	W. H. McCauley	Versailles Treaty, 4, 123	Coxwold, 4, 123	5	1:46.99	150,000
1991	**Sharp Dance**, 5, 123	M. E. Smith	Versailles Treaty, 3, 119	Lady d'Accord, 4, 123	6	1:48.01	150,000
1990	**Go for Wand**, 3, 119	R. P. Romero	Colonial Waters, 5, 123	Buy the Firm, 4, 123	5	**1:45.80**	167,700

1989	**Tactile**, 3, 118	R. Migliore	Colonial Waters, 4, 123	Rose's Cantina, 5, 123	6	2:05.20	$170,100
1988	**Personal Ensign**, 4, 123	R. P. Romero	Classic Crown, 3, 118	Sham Say, 3, 118	5	2:01.20	199,440
1987	**Personal Ensign**, 3, 118	R. P. Romero	Coup de Fusil, 5, 123	Silent Turn, 3, 118	10	2:04.40	182,100
1986	**Lady's Secret**, 4, 123	P. Day	Coup de Fusil, 4, 123	Classy Cathy, 3, 118	4	2:01.60	189,600
1985	**Lady's Secret**, 3, 118	J. Velasquez	Isayso, 6, 123	Kamikaze Rick, 3, 118	5	2:03.60	160,920
1984	**Life's Magic**, 3, 118	J. Velasquez	Miss Oceana, 3, 118	Key Dancer, 3, 118	4	2:03.20	158,280
1983	**Dance Number**, 4, 123	A. T. Cordero Jr.	Heartlight No. One, 3, 118	Mochila, 4, 123	7	2:00.60	133,200
1982	**Weber City Miss**, 5, 123	A. T. Cordero Jr.	Mademoiselle Forli, 3, 118	Love Sign, 5, 123	9	2:04.20	134,100
1981	**Love Sign**, 4, 123	W. Shoemaker	dh-Glorious Song, 5, 123 dh-Jameela, 5, 123		7	2:01.80	131,100
1980	**Love Sign**, 3, 118	R. Hernandez	Misty Gallore, 4, 123	It's in the Air, 4, 123	4	2:02.80	96,300
1979	**Waya (Fr)**, 5, 123	C. B. Asmussen	Fourdrinier, 3, 118	Kit's Double, 6, 123	7	2:06.20	97,050
1978	**Late Bloomer**, 4, 123	J. Velasquez	Pearl Necklace, 4, 123	Cum Laude Laurie, 4, 123	4	2:02.20	78,150
1977	**Cum Laude Laurie**, 3, 118	A. T. Cordero Jr.	What a Summer, 4, 123	Charming Story, 3, 118	7	2:01.80	80,025
1976	**Proud Delta**, 4, 123	J. Velasquez	Revidere, 3, 118	*Bastonera II, 5, 120	8	1:46.80	64,920
1975	**Susan's Girl**, 6, 123	B. Baeza	*Tizna, 6, 123	Pass a Glance, 4, 123	9	1:48.40	67,980
1974	**Desert Vixen**, 4, 123	L. A. Pincay Jr.	Poker Night, 4, 123	*Tizna, 5, 123	9	1:46.60	68,760
1973	**Desert Vixen**, 3, 118	J. Velasquez	Poker Night, 3, 118	Susan's Girl, 4, 123	7	1:46.20	65,880

Named for August Belmont II's consensus champion racemare and 1904 Carter H. winner Beldame (1901 f. by Octagon). Beldame H. 1905-'59. Held at Aqueduct 1905-'56, 1959, 1962-'68. Not held 1908, 1910-'16, 1933-'38. 5 furlongs 1905-'32. $1\frac{1}{16}$ miles 1939. $1\frac{1}{4}$ miles 1977-'89. Two-year-olds 1905-'32. Fillies 1905-'32. Dead heat for second 1981. Equaled world record 1973. Equaled track record 1973.

Belmont Breeders' Cup Handicap

Grade 2 in 2006. Belmont Park, three-year-olds and up, $1\frac{1}{8}$ miles, turf. Held September 11, 2005, with a gross value of $197,200. First held in 1986. First graded in 1988. Stakes record 1:45.06 (2005 Shakespeare).

Year	Winner	Jockey	Second	Third	Strs	Time	1st Purse
2005	**Shakespeare**, 4, 114	J. D. Bailey	Meteor Storm (GB), 6, 118	Muqbil, 5, 115	4	**1:45.06**	$124,320
2004	**Senor Swinger**, 4, 117	E. S. Prado	Stroll, 4, 120	B. A. Way, 4, 113	4	1:52.72	124,680
2003	**Della Francesca**, 4, 114	J. F. Chavez	Rouvres (Fr), 4, 116	Volponi, 5, 119	7	1:47.48	125,760
2002	**Startac**, 4, 116	J. D. Bailey	Volponi, 4, 117	Dr. Kashnikow, 5, 115	6	1:46.60	125,160
2000	**Forbidden Apple**, 5, 114	J. A. Santos	Val's Prince, 8, 118	Altibr, 5, 115	6	1:51.73	126,000
1999	**With the Flow**, 4, 114	J. A. Santos	Comic Strip, 4, 118	Wised Up, 4, 112	9	1:49.39	127,620
1998	**Subordination**, 4, 121	D. R. Flores	Yagli, 5, 122	Bomfim, 5, 114	9	1:45.90	127,020
1997	**Fortitude**, 4, 112	R. G. Davis	Green Means Go, 5, 113	Boyce, 6, 118	8	1:38.53	126,600
1996	**‡Gentleman Beau**, 4, 114	J. A. Santos	Volochine (Ire), 5, 116	Kiri's Clown, 7, 114	7	1:41.18	127,140
1995	**Dove Hunt**, 4, 121	P. Day	Fly Cry, 4, 116	Unfinished Symph, 4, 122	6	1:40.18	92,970
1994	**A in Sociology**, 4, 116	J. Samyn	Fourstars Allstar, 6, 119	Home of the Free, 6, 114	10	1:40.19	34,290
1993	**Fourstars Allstar**, 5, 116	J. A. Santos	Lech, 5, 115	Cleone, 4, 113	6	1:39.88	92,880
1992	**Roman Envoy**, 4, 113	C. Perret	Lotus Pool, 5, 114	Daarik (Ire), 5, 114	10	1:41.50	34,800
1991	**Solar Splendor**, 4, 113	W. H. McCauley	Who's to Pay, 5, 118	Jalaajel, 7, 114	7	1:41.16	93,210
1990	**Who's to Pay**, 4, 113	J. D. Bailey	Jalaajel, 6, 115	Caltech, 4, 120	8	1:46.00	93,570
1989	**Highland Springs**, 5, 117	K. Desormeaux	Maceo, 5, 113	Slew City Slew, 5, 118	6	1:39.20	93,180
1988	**Steinlen (GB)**, 5, 120	P. Day	Iron Courage, 4, 113	Barood, 5, 110	6	1:43.40	93,540
1987	**Talakeno**, 7, 117	A. T. Cordero Jr.	Lightning Leap, 5, 110	Glaros (Fr), 5, 111	4	1:49.40	93,090
1986	**Danger's Hour**, 4, 116	J. D. Bailey	‡Salem Drive, 4, 115	Silver Voice, 3, 112	10	1:40.80	95,280

Grade 3 1988-'97. Saratoga Budweiser Breeders' Cup H. 1986-'93. Belmont Budweiser Breeders' Cup H. 1994-'95. Held at Saratoga Race Course 1986-'93. Not held due to World Trade Center attack 2001. $1\frac{1}{16}$ miles 1986-'97. ‡Silver Voice finished second, DQ to third, 1986. ‡Kiri's Clown finished first, DQ to third, 1996. Course record 1997, 2005.

Belmont Stakes

Grade 1 in 2006. Belmont Park, three-year-olds, $1\frac{1}{2}$ miles, dirt. Held June 10, 2006, with a gross value of $1,000,000. First held in 1867. First graded in 1973. Stakes record 2:24 (1973 Secretariat [current world and track record]).

(See Triple Crown section for complete history of the Belmont Stakes)

Year	Winner	Jockey	Second	Third	Strs	Time	1st Purse
2006	**Jazil**, 3, 126	F. Jara	Bluegrass Cat, 3, 126	Sunriver, 3, 126	12	2:27.86	$600,000
2005	**Afleet Alex**, 3, 126	J. Rose	Andromeda's Hero, 3, 126	Nolan's Cat, 3, 126	11	2:28.75	600,000
2004	**Birdstone**, 3, 126	E. S. Prado	Smarty Jones, 3, 126	Royal Assault, 3, 126	9	2:27.50	600,000
2003	**Empire Maker**, 3, 126	J. D. Bailey	Ten Most Wanted, 3, 126	Funny Cide, 3, 126	6	2:28.26	600,000
2002	**Sarava**, 3, 126	E. S. Prado	Medaglia d'Oro, 3, 126	Sunday Break (Jpn), 3, 126	11	2:29.71	600,000
2001	**Point Given**, 3, 126	G. L. Stevens	A P Valentine, 3, 126	Monarchos, 3, 126	9	2:26.56	600,000
2000	**Commendable**, 3, 126	P. Day	Aptitude, 3, 126	Unshaded, 3, 126	11	2:31.19	600,000
1999	**Lemon Drop Kid**, 3, 126	J. A. Santos	Vision and Verse, 3, 126	Charismatic, 3, 126	12	2:27.88	600,000
1998	**Victory Gallop**, 3, 126	G. L. Stevens	Real Quiet, 3, 126	Thomas Jo, 3, 126	11	2:29.16	600,000
1997	**Touch Gold**, 3, 126	C. J. McCarron	Silver Charm, 3, 126	Free House, 3, 126	7	2:28.82	432,600
1996	**Editor's Note**, 3, 126	R. R. Douglas	Skip Away, 3, 126	†My Flag, 3, 121	14	2:28.96	437,880
1995	**Thunder Gulch**, 3, 126	G. L. Stevens	Star Standard, 3, 126	Citadeed, 3, 126	11	2:32.02	415,440
1994	**Tabasco Cat**, 3, 126	P. Day	Go for Gin, 3, 126	Strodes Creek, 3, 126	6	2:26.82	392,280
1993	**Colonial Affair**, 3, 126	J. A. Krone	Kissin Kris, 3, 126	Wild Gale, 3, 126	13	2:29.97	444,540
1992	**A.P. Indy**, 3, 126	E. Delahoussaye	My Memoirs (GB), 3, 126	Pine Bluff, 3, 126	11	2:26.13	458,880
1991	**Hansel**, 3, 126	J. D. Bailey	Strike the Gold, 3, 126	Mane Minister, 3, 126	11	2:28.10	1,417,480
1990	**Go and Go (Ire)**, 3, 126	M. J. Kinane	Thirty Six Red, 3, 126	Baron de Vaux, 3, 126	9	2:27.20	411,600
1989	**Easy Goer**, 3, 126	P. Day	Sunday Silence, 3, 126	Le Voyageur, 3, 126	10	2:26.00	413,520

1988	**Risen Star**, 3, 126	E. Delahoussaye	Kingpost, 3, 126	Brian's Time, 3, 126	6	2:26.40	$1,303,720
1987	**Bet Twice**, 3, 126	C. Perret	Cryptoclearance, 3, 126	Gulch, 3, 126	9	2:28.20	1,329,160
1986	**Danzig Connection**, 3, 126	C. J. McCarron	Johns Treasure, 3, 126	Ferdinand, 3, 126	10	2:29.80	338,640
1985	**Creme Fraiche**, 3, 126	E. Maple	Stephan's Odyssey, 3, 126	Chief's Crown, 3, 126	11	2:27.00	307,740
1984	**Swale**, 3, 126	L. A. Pincay Jr.	Pine Circle, 3, 126	Morning Bob, 3, 126	11	2:27.20	310,020
1983	**Caveat**, 3, 126	L. A. Pincay Jr.	Slew o' Gold, 3, 126	Barberstown, 3, 126	15	2:27.80	215,100
1982	**Conquistador Cielo**, 3, 126	L. A. Pincay Jr.	Gato Del Sol, 3, 126	Illuminate, 3, 126	11	2:28.20	159,720
1981	**Summing**, 3, 126	G. Martens	Highland Blade, 3, 126	Pleasant Colony, 3, 126	11	2:29.00	170,580
1980	**Temperence Hill**, 3, 126	E. Maple	†Genuine Risk, 3, 121	Rockhill Native, 3, 126	10	2:29.80	176,220
1979	**Coastal**, 3, 126	R. Hernandez	Golden Act, 3, 126	Spectacular Bid, 3, 126	8	2:28.60	161,400
1978	**Affirmed**, 3, 126	S. Cauthen	Alydar, 3, 126	Darby Creek Road, 3, 126	5	2:26.80	110,580
1977	**Seattle Slew**, 3, 126	J. Cruguet	Run Dusty Run, 3, 126	Sanhedrin, 3, 126	8	2:29.60	109,080
1976	**Bold Forbes**, 3, 126	A. T. Cordero Jr.	McKenzie Bridge, 3, 126	Great Contractor, 3, 126	10	2:29.00	117,000
1975	**Avatar**, 3, 126	W. Shoemaker	Foolish Pleasure, 3, 126	Master Derby, 3, 126	9	2:28.20	116,160
1974	**Little Current**, 3, 126	M. A. Rivera	Jolly Johu, 3, 126	Cannonade, 3, 126	9	2:29.20	101,970
1973	**Secretariat**, 3, 126	R. Turcotte	Twice a Prince, 3, 126	My Gallant, 3, 126	5	**2:24.00**	90,120

Named for August Belmont I (1816-'90), president of Jerome Park. Belmont H. 1895, 1913. Held at Jerome Park 1867-'89. Held at Morris Park 1890-1904. Held at Aqueduct 1963-'67. Not held 1911-'12. $1\frac{5}{8}$ miles 1867-'73. $1\frac{1}{4}$ miles 1890-'92, 1895, 1904-'05. $1\frac{1}{8}$ miles 1893-'94. $1\frac{3}{8}$ miles 1896-1903, 1906-'25. Colts and fillies 1919-'56. World record 1973. Track record 1973. †Denotes female. $1,000,000 Triple Crown bonus awarded on a points basis 1987-'88, 1991.

Ben Ali Stakes

Grade 3 in 2006. Keeneland Race Course, four-year-olds and up, $1\frac{1}{8}$ miles, dirt. Held April 27, 2006, with a gross value of $150,000. First held in 1917. First graded in 1973. Stakes record 1:46.78 (2004 Midway Road).

Year	Winner	Jockey	Second	Third	Strs	Time	1st Purse
2006	**Wanderin Boy**, 5, 117	J. Castellano	Alumni Hall, 7, 117	Noble Causeway, 4, 117	6	1:49.18	$93,000
2005	**Alumni Hall**, 6, 121	R. Albarado	Pies Prospect, 4, 123	Go Now, 4, 117	8	1:51.29	93,000
2004	**Midway Road**, 4, 116	R. Albarado	Evening Attire, 6, 116	Sir Cherokee, 4, 120	5	**1:46.78**	93,000
2003	**Mineshaft**, 4, 120	R. Albarado	American Style, 4, 116	Metatron, 4, 116	4	1:48.52	68,386
2002	**Duckhorn**, 5, 116	J. F. Chavez	Parade Leader, 5, 120	Connected, 5, 118	4	1:50.18	66,464
2001	**Broken Vow**, 4, 116	E. S. Prado	Perfect Cat, 4, 116	Jadada, 6, 116	5	1:48.47	66,216
2000	**Midway Magistrate**, 6, 116	S. J. Sellers	Liberty Gold, 6, 116	Early Warning, 5, 118	7	1:49.15	67,518
1999	**Jazz Club**, 4, 115	P. Day	Smile Again, 4, 115	Early Warning, 4, 115	6	1:48.16	67,456
1998	**Storm Broker**, 4, 114	R. Albarado	Delay of Game, 5, 119	Gator Dancer, 5, 114	6	1:48.23	67,208
1997	**Louis Quatorze**, 4, 119	P. Day	Knockadoon, 5, 113	King James, 5, 113	5	1:49.60	66,526
1996	**Knockadoon**, 4, 112	J. D. Bailey	Halo's Image, 5, 117	Thorny Crown, 5, 113	4	1:48.92	66,216
1995	**Wildly Joyous**, 4, 114	M. Walls	Danville, 4, 117	Powerful Punch, 6, 113	7	1:49.68	50,406
1994	**Pistols and Roses**, 5, 123	M. E. Smith	Sunny Sunrise, 7, 119	Compadre, 4, 113	6	1:51.77	50,251
1993	**Sunny Sunrise**, 6, 119	R. Wilson	Conte Di Savoya, 4, 113	Prize Fight, 4, 112	8	1:48.90	50,933
1992	**dh-Loach**, 4, 117	P. A. Valenzuela		Out of Place, 5, 119	6	1:49.95	34,212
	dh-Profit Key, 5, 113	S. J. Sellers					
1991	**Sports View**, 4, 119	C. Perret	Bright Again, 4, 113	Exemplary Leader, 5, 112	6	1:49.67	53,495
1990	**Master Speaker**, 5, 121	J. D. Bailey	Lac Ouimet, 7, 114	Silver Survivor, 4, 119	7	1:49.00	54,893
1989	**Classic Account**, 4, 114	P. Day	Regal Classic, 4, 117	Brian's Time, 4, 121	5	1:50.60	53,885
1988	**Homebuilder**, 4, 119	D. Brumfield	Bet Twice, 4, 126	Blue Buckaroo, 5, 117	4	1:51.40	52,293
1987	**Intrusion**, 5, 111	S. Hawley	Coaxing Mark, 4, 114	Blue Buckaroo, 4, 117	5	1:49.60	34,678
1986	**Czar Nijinsky**, 4, 119	W. H. McCauley	Little Missouri, 4, 114	Minneapple, 4, 117	8	1:50.20	43,542
1985	**Bello**, 4, 116	G. Gallitano	Silent King, 4, 117	Hi Pi, 6, 113	7	1:48.80	35,295
1984	**Aspro**, 6, 116	D. Brumfield	Play Fellow, 4, 123	Jack Slade, 4, 115	5	1:50.80	34,564
1983	**Aspro**, 5, 115	V. A. Bracciale Jr.	Thirty Eight Paces, 5, 115	Rivalero, 7, 121	8	1:49.60	35,588
1982	**Withholding**, 5, 121	L. J. Melancon	Aspro, 4, 122	Swinging Light, 4, 113	8	1:49.60	35,880
1981	**Withholding**, 4, 113	B. Sayler	Summer Advocate, 4, 113	Two's a Plenty, 4, 115	6	1:50.20	34,986
1980	**Architect**, 4, 120	S. A. Spencer	Revivalist, 6, 116	All the More, 7, 116	6	1:48.80	27,999
1979	**Kodiack**, 5, 114	G. Gallitano	Hot Words, 4, 113	Morning Frolic, 4, 115	8	1:49.60	31,054
1978	**Prince Majestic**, 4, 118	E. Delahoussaye	Inca Roca, 5, 114	All the More, 5, 122	9	1:41.80	21,824
1977	**Honest Pleasure**, 4, 124	C. Perret	Inca Roca, 4, 118	Packer Captain, 5, 113	9	1:42.40	18,623
1976	**My Friend Gus**, 4, 114	D. G. McHargue	Packer Captain, 4, 116	Dragset, 5, 113	8	1:42.40	18,119
1975	**Navajo**, 5, 122	J. Nichols	L. Grant Jr., 5, 118	Hasty Flyer, 4, 115	12	1:43.80	19,419
1974	**Knight Counter**, 6, 119	E. Fires	Model Husband, 5, 117	Jim's Alibhi, 7, 113	6	1:41.80	17,648
1973	**Knight Counter**, 5, 120	D. Brumfield	‡Guitar Player, 5, 118	Introductivo, 4, 114	12	1:43.00	18,785

Named for James Ben Ali Haggin (1821-1914), native Kentuckian and owner of Elmendorf Farm, and his 1886 Kentucky Derby winner Ben Ali (1883 c. by Virgil). Ben Ali H. 1917-'89. Held at Kentucky Association 1917-'31. Held at Churchill Downs 1943-'45. Not held 1923-'27, 1932-'36. $1\frac{1}{16}$ miles 1917-'30, 1937-'53, 1963-'78. About 6 furlongs 1931. About 7 furlongs 1954-'62. Three-year-olds and up 1917-'85. Dead heat for first 1992. ‡Hustlin Greek finished second, DQ to twelfth for a positive drug test, 1973. Track record 2004.

Berkeley Handicap

Grade 3 in 2006. Golden Gate Fields, three-year-olds and up, $1\frac{1}{16}$ miles, dirt. Held June 11, 2005, with a gross value of $100,000. First held in 1933. First graded in 2000. Stakes record 1:40.94 (2005 Desert Boom).

Year	Winner	Jockey	Second	Third	Strs	Time	1st Purse
2005	**Desert Boom**, 5, 113	R. M. Gonzalez	Easy Million, 5, 116	Yougottawanna, 6, 118	7	**1:40.94**	$55,000
2004	**Snorter**, 4, 116	R. A. Baze	Yougottawanna, 5, 116	Taste of Paradise, 5, 116	5	1:33.92	55,000
2003	**I'madrifter**, 5, 115	R. M. Gonzalez	Palmeiro, 5, 117	Skip to the Stone, 5, 116	6	1:35.13	55,000

2002	**Irisheyesareflying**, 6, 120	J. Valdivia Jr.	Boss Ego, 6, 116	Palmeiro, 4, 116	11	1:35.41	$55,000
2001	**Blade Prospector (Brz)**, 6, 116	O. A. Berrio	Dixie Dot Com, 6, 119	Milk Wood (GB), 6, 115	6	1:34.18	55,000
2000	**Voice of Destiny**, 4, 113	R. Q. Meza	Mr. Doubledown, 6, 115	Twilight Affair, 6, 115	8	1:35.67	75,000
1999	**Hal's Pal (GB)**, 6, 117	B. Blanc	Wild Wonder, 5, 122	Worldly Ways (GB), 5, 115	7	1:34.96	75,000
1998	**Wild Wonder**, 4, 115	R. A. Baze	General Royal, 4, 115	March of Kings, 5, 116	7	1:35.19	47,700
1996	**Houston Fleet M D**, 2, 118	D. Carr	Slewp'a Doop, 2, 116	Big Find, 2, 116	5	1:36.67	26,600
1995	**Double Jab**, 4, 115	R. A. Baze	Corslew, 5, 116	Cleante (Arg), 6, 115	8	1:35.18	49,725
1994	**River Special**, 4, 115	T. M. Chapman	He's Illustrious, 7, 116	Misty Wind (Ire), 6, 114	8	1:34.33	32,600
1993	**Infamous Deed**, 5, 115	R. J. Warren Jr.	Misty Wind (Ire), 5, 116	J. F. Williams, 4, 115	7	1:35.67	25,960
1992	**Music Prospector**, 5, 118	R. D. Hansen	Michael's Flyer, 6, 115	Flying Continental, 6, 124	5	1:35.29	31,450
1991	**High Energy**, 4, 115	R. J. Warren Jr.	Bold Current, 4, 114	Beau's Alliance, 5, 115	8	1:35.70	32,800
1990	**On the Menu**, 4, 112	C. L. Davenport	Crackedbell, 5, 116	Ongoing Mister, 5, 117	6	1:34.80	31,600
1989	**Ongoing Mister**, 4, 114	T. T. Doocy	Present Value, 5, 113	Lucky Harold H., 5, 110	8	1:34.20	33,600
1988	**Sanger Chief**, 5, 114	T. T. Doocy	Lucky Harold H., 4, 114	Power Forward, 5, 119	7	1:35.60	31,900
1987	**Rocky Marriage**, 7, 116	R. A. Baze	Dormello (Arg), 6, 115	Bagdad Dawn, 5, 112	7	1:36.80	32,250
1986	**Sun Master**, 5, 117	M. Castaneda	Beldale Lear, 5, 123	Prairie Breaker, 6, 114	6	1:34.60	25,400
1985	**Nak Ack**, 4, 114	J. C. Judice	Holmbury, 5, 113	Chum Salmon, 5, 116	9	1:36.20	26,600
1984	**Songhay**, 5, 114	J. C. Judice	Grand Balcony, 5, 113	The Jandy Man, 4, 113	11	1:35.40	27,300
1983	**Pleasant Power**, 5, 115	J. R. Anderson	Lord Advocate, 4, 117	Red Crescent, 7, 119	13	1:40.60	27,800
1982	**Foyt's Ack**, 7, 115	R. M. Gonzalez	Borrego Sun, 5, 118	Pleasant Power, 4, 112	8	1:38.00	25,650
1981	**Head Hawk**, 5, 111	D. Sorenson	His Honor, 6, 115	Beau Moro, 6, 117	7	1:45.60	25,750
1979	**Gustoso**, 4, 120	R. Campas	Rassendyll, 5, 113	Rescator, 5, 117	7	1:34.40	20,500
1978	**Boy Tike**, 5, 114	A. L. Diaz	Dr. Krohn, 5, 120	Miami Sun, 4, 120	7	1:36.20	19,250
1977	**Lino**, 5, 112	R. Caballero	Crafty Native, 4, 114	Classy Surgeon, 4, 116	7	1:37.40	16,050
1976	**Branford Court**, 6, 113	A. L. Diaz	Austin Mittler, 4, 117	Carry the Banner, 6, 113	7	1:35.00	15,700
1975	**Star of Kuwait**, 7, 118	W. Mahorney	Willie Pleasant, 4, 116	Mac's L., 4, 111	10	1:44.80	16,450
1974	***Yvetot**, 6, 120	F. Olivares	Sensitive Music, 5, 114	*Larkal II, 6, 113	8	1:43.80	17,800
1973	***Yvetot**, 5, 112	V. Tejada	Cabin, 5, 121	Masked, 4, 120	10	1:44.20	18,050

Named for Berkeley, California, located near San Francisco. Berkeley S. 1948. Berkeley H. 1933, 1938, 1949-2003. Held at Tanforan 1933. Held at Bay Meadows 1938. Not held 1934-'37, 1939-'47, 1961-'62, 1980, 1997. About 6 furlongs 1933. 6 furlongs 1938-'50, 1952-'55, 1957-'59. 1 mile 1951, 1956, 1964, 1976-'80, 1982-2004. 1¼ miles 1966-'70. 1⅛ miles 1971. Turf 1972-'74, 1976. Originally scheduled on turf 1975. Two-year-olds and up 1933. Two-year-olds 1948, 1957, 1996. Three-year-olds 1949-'56, 1958-'65. Four-year-olds and up 1968. Colts and geldings 1948. Fillies 1956-'58, 1964. Non-winners of a race worth $12,500 to the winner 1973. Non-winners of a race worth $35,000 to the winner at one mile or over 1990, 1992.

Bernard Baruch Handicap

Grade 2 in 2006. Saratoga Race Course, three-year-olds and up, 1⅛ miles, turf. Held August 1, 2005, with a gross value of $147,000. First held in 1959. First graded in 1973. Stakes record 1:45.40 (1973 Tentam [1st Div.]).

Year	Winner	Jockey	Second	Third	Strs	Time	1st Purse
2005	**Artie Schiller**, 4, 122	R. Migliore	Silver Tree, 5, 117	America Alive, 4, 119	5	1:47.65	$90,000
2004	**Silver Tree**, 4, 116	J. D. Bailey	Nothing to Lose, 4, 117	Irish Colonial, 5, 113	7	1:49.66	90,000
2003	**Trademark (SAf)**, 7, 114	R. Migliore	Rouvres (Fr), 4, 116	Slew Valley, 6, 113	7	1:49.06	90,000
2002	**Del Mar Show**, 5, 120	J. D. Bailey	Volponi, 4, 116	Forbidden Apple, 7, 121	7	1:48.51	90,000
2001	**Hap**, 5, 121	J. D. Bailey	Royal Strand (Ire), 7, 115	Dr. Kashnikow, 4, 114	7	1:47.06	90,000
2000	**Hap**, 4, 115	J. D. Bailey	Inexplicable, 5, 115	Draw Shot, 7, 114	13	1:45.82	90,000
1999	**Middlesex Drive**, 4, 117	S. J. Sellers	Tangazi, 4, 114	Comic Strip, 4, 116	8	1:46.55	90,000
1998	**Yagli**, 5, 121	J. D. Bailey	Tamhid, 5, 113	Jambalaya Jazz, 6, 115	9	1:46.22	85,380
1997	**Sentimental Moi**, 7, 112	C. P. DeCarlo	Jambalaya Jazz, 5, 115	Boyce, 6, 120	8	1:46.11	66,480
1996	**Volochine (Ire)**, 5, 113	P. Day	Green Means Go, 4, 116	Compadre, 6, 108	10	1:47.58	68,700
1995	**Fourstars Allstar**, 7, 120	J. A. Santos	Turk Passer, 5, 114	Compadre, 5, 112	7	1:47.67	66,240
1994	**Lure**, 5, 125	M. E. Smith	Paradise Creek, 5, 126	Fourstardave, 9, 114	5	1:46.10	64,920
1993	**Furiously**, 4, 119	J. D. Bailey	Star of Cozzene, 5, 123	Royal Mountain Inn, 4, 114	5	1:45.46	70,320
1992	**Fourstars Allstar**, 4, 113	M. E. Smith	Lotus Pool, 5, 113	Maxigroom, 4, 114	6	1:46.06	70,680
1991	**Double Booked**, 6, 122	A. Madrid Jr.	Who's to Pay, 5, 118	Solar Splendor, 4, 113	8	1:49.14	71,400
1990	**Who's to Pay**, 4, 110	J. Samyn	Steinlen (GB), 7, 126	River of Sin, 6, 115	5	1:48.40	52,920
1989	**Steinlen (GB)**, 6, 121	J. A. Santos	Soviet Lad, 4, 111	Brian's Time, 4, 112	8	1:51.00	73,920
1988	**My Big Boy**, 5, 113	R. P. Romero	Steinlen (GB), 5, 120	Wanderkin, 5, 115	9	1:46.80	72,600
1987	**Talakeno**, 7, 115	A. T. Cordero Jr.	Manila, 4, 127	Duluth, 5, 114	4	1:47.40	85,380
1986	**Exclusive Partner**, 4, 112	J. Velasquez	I'm a Banker, 4, 111	Creme Fraiche, 4, 117	12	1:50.80	82,200
1985	**Win**, 5, 124	R. Migliore	Cozzene, 5, 120	Sitzmark, 5, 112	9	1:47.00	59,400
1984	**Win**, 4, 112	A. Graell	Intensify, 4, 113	Cozzene, 4, 114	9	1:47.40	57,510
1983	**Tantalizing**, 4, 115	J. D. Bailey	Ten Below, 4, 114	Acaroid, 5, 115	9	1:48.80	34,140
	Fray Star (Arg), 5, 114	O. Vergara	Fortnightly, 3, 113	Who's for Dinner, 4, 109	9	1:48.40	34,380
1982	**Pair of Deuces**, 4, 115	R. Hernandez	Native Courier, 7, 117	McCann, 4, 112	11	1:47.80	36,540
1981	**Native Courier**, 6, 114	E. Maple	Manguin, 5, 105	Proctor, 4, 118	7	1:47.40	33,450
	Great Neck, 5, 119	A. T. Cordero Jr.	War of Words, 4, 111	Match the Hatch, 5, 114	5	1:47.60	33,690
1980	**Premier Ministre**, 4, 116	R. I. Encinas	Great Neck, 4, 112	Tiller, 6, 126	11	2:13.60	35,700
1979	**Overskate**, 4, 128	R. Platts	Timbo, 3, 108	Native Courier, 4, 115	7	1:51.80	35,610
1978	**Dominion (GB)**, 6, 115	J. Samyn	Bill Brill, 4, 111	Upper Nile, 4, 119	11	1:49.00	24,480
1977	**Majestic Light**, 4, 126	S. Hawley	Alias Smith, 4, 112	Clout, 5, 114	11	1:46.20	23,175
1976	**Intrepid Hero**, 4, 123	E. Maple	Modred, 3, 118	Erwin Boy, 5, 126	8	1:50.40	22,530
1975	**dh-Salt Marsh**, 5, 116	E. Maple		Drollery, 5, 112	8	1:49.80	18,061
	dh-Ward McAllister, 4, 110	D. Montoya					

1974	**Golden Don**, 4, 113	V. A. Bracciale Jr.	Halo, 5, 119	Scantling, 4, 117	10	1:46.00	$23,580
1973	**Tentam**, 4, 118	J. Velasquez	Scrimshaw, 5, 111	Astray, 4, 114	10	**1:45.40**	14,265
	Red Reality, 7, 120	J. Velasquez	Tri Jet, 4, 121	Ruritania, 4, 113	9	1:46.60	14,190

Named for Bernard Baruch (1870-1965), avid racing fan and adviser to presidents. Grade 3 1973-'82. Grade 1 1988-'89. Bernard Baruch S. 1959-'60. 1$^{1}/_{16}$ miles 1962-'71. 1$^{3}/_{8}$ miles 1980. Dirt 1959-'60, 1979. Three-year-olds 1959-'60. Two divisions 1973, 1981, 1983. Dead heat for first 1975. Equaled course record 1993.

Best Pal Stakes

Grade 2 in 2006. Del Mar, two-year-olds, 6$^{1}/_{2}$ furlongs, dirt. Held August 14, 2005, with a gross value of $147,000. First held in 1967. First graded in 1983. Stakes record 1:15.08 (2001 Officer).

Year	Winner	Jockey	Second	Third	Strs	Time	1st Purse
2005	**What a Song**, 2, 123	V. Espinoza	Bashert, 2, 119	Plug Me In, 2, 117	4	1:15.64	$90,000
2004	**Roman Ruler**, 2, 118	C. S. Nakatani	Actxecutive, 2, 118	Slewsbag, 2, 116	5	1:15.93	90,000
2003	**Perfect Moon**, 2, 122	P. A. Valenzuela	Capitano, 2, 118	Military Mandate, 2, 118	10	1:16.90	90,000
2002	**Kafwain**, 2, 117	V. Espinoza	Chief Planner, 2, 117	Outta Here, 2, 117	7	1:17.00	90,000
2001	**Officer**, 2, 121	V. Espinoza	Metatron, 2, 117	Essence of Dubai, 2, 117	3	**1:15.08**	90,000
2000	**Flame Thrower**, 2, 117	C. S. Nakatani	Trailthefox, 2, 121	Legendary Weave, 2, 117	7	1:16.51	90,000
1999	**Dixie Union**, 2, 121	A. O. Solis	Exchange Rate, 2, 117	Captain Steve, 2, 117	5	1:16.40	90,000
1998	**Worldly Manner**, 2, 117	G. L. Stevens	Domination, 2, 117	Waki American, 2, 115	8	1:16.78	65,580
1997	**Old Topper**, 2, 117	A. O. Solis	King of the Wild, 2, 117	Souvenir Copy, 2, 117	8	1:16.57	68,825
1996	**Swiss Yodeler**, 2, 121	A. O. Solis	Golden Bronze, 2, 117	Deeds Not Words, 2, 117	8	1:16.12	65,550
1995	**Cobra King**, 2, 117	R. A. Baze	Northern Afleet, 2, 117	Desert Native, 2, 117	8	1:15.89	60,350
1994	**Timber Country**, 2, 117	A. O. Solis	Desert Mirage, 2, 115	Supremo, 2, 117	7	1:16.60	46,575
1993	**Creston**, 2, 117	C. A. Black	Troyalty, 2, 121	Flying Sensation, 2, 115	6	1:16.35	45,900
1992	**Devil Diamond**, 2, 117	K. Desormeaux	Wheeler Oil, 2, 119	Crafty, 2, 117	6	1:22.60	45,900
1991	**Scherando**, 2, 121	F. Mena	Star Recruit, 2, 117	Prince Wild, 2, 119	9	1:22.47	47,625
1990	**Best Pal**, 2, 119	P. A. Valenzuela	Xray, 2, 117	Sunshine Machine, 2, 117	7	1:22.20	46,575
1989	**A. Sir Dancer**, 2, 117	E. Delahoussaye	Drag Race, 2, 115	†Patches, 2, 113	7	1:23.00	47,550
1988	**Rob an Plunder**, 2, 119	C. J. McCarron	Mountain Ghost, 2, 117	Pokarito, 2, 117	8	1:23.00	48,050
1987	**Purdue King**, 2, 121	C. J. McCarron	Accomplish Ridge, 2, 117	Mixed Pleasure, 2, 119	8	1:23.20	38,500
1986	**Temperate Sil**, 2, 117	W. Shoemaker	Polar Jet, 2, 117	Gold On Green, 2, 115	8	1:23.00	32,250
1985	**Swear**, 2, 116	E. Delahoussaye	Bright Tom, 2, 116	Smokey Orbit, 2, 114	9	1:36.60	32,750
1984	**Saratoga Six**, 2, 120	A. T. Cordero Jr.	Private Jungle, 2, 117	Indigenous, 2, 116	7	1:36.80	31,650
1983	**Party Leader**, 2, 116	R. Sibille	Juliet's Pride, 2, 115	Gumboy, 2, 116	7	1:37.20	31,550
1982	**Roving Boy**, 2, 115	E. Delahoussaye	Encourager, 2, 115	Full Choke, 2, 117	5	1:35.40	30,650
1981	**The Captain**, 2, 117	L. A. Pincay Jr.	Distant Heart, 2, 115	Gato Del Sol, 2, 115	9	1:36.80	26,400
1980	**Bold and Gold**, 2, 113	D. C. Hall	Splendid Spruce, 2, 115	Sir Dancer, 2, 113	7	1:37.40	22,550
1979	**Doonesbury**, 2, 113	S. Hawley	Executive Counsel, 2, 115	Defiance, 2, 117	7	1:35.40	19,300
1978	**Flying Paster**, 2, 117	D. Pierce	Roman Oblisk, 2, 117	Runaway Hit, 2, 114	9	1:35.60	19,500
1977	**Spanish Way**, 2, 117	L. A. Pincay Jr.	Tampoy, 2, 114	Misrepresentation, 2, 114	10	1:36.00	16,700
1976	**Visible**, 2, 117	L. A. Pincay Jr.	*Habitony, 2, 114	Replant, 2, 115	8	1:35.80	16,200
1975	**Crazy Channon**, 2, 115	D. Pierce	Classy Surgeon, 2, 114	Lexington Laugh, 2, 117	9	1:37.20	13,700
1974	**Diabolo**, 2, 120	W. Shoemaker	Trond Sang, 2, 114	Neat Claim, 2, 114	7	1:35.60	13,050
1973	**Battery E.**, 2, 115	W. Harris	Jenny's Boy, 2, 120	Marchen McTavish, 2, 115	5	1:30.60	12,750

Named for Golden Eagle Farm's multiple Grade 1 SW and 1990 Balboa S. (G3) winner Best Pal (1988 g. by *Habitony); Best Pal retired as the leading California-bred earner. Formerly named for Vasco Nunez de Balboa, first European to see the Pacific Ocean. Grade 3 1983-2002. Balboa H. 1967. Balboa S. 1972-'95. Not held 1968-'71. About 7$^{1}/_{2}$ furlongs 1972-'73. 1 mile 1974-'85. 7 furlongs 1986-'92. Turf 1972-'73. †Denotes female. Non-winners of a race worth $10,000 to the winner 1974-'75.

Beverly D. Stakes

Grade 1 in 2006. Arlington Park, three-year-olds and up, fillies and mares, 1$^{3}/_{16}$ miles, turf. Held August 13, 2005, with a gross value of $750,000. First held in 1987. First graded in 1991. Stakes record 1:53.20 (1990 Reluctant Guest).

Year	Winner	Jockey	Second	Third	Strs	Time	1st Purse
2005	**Angara (GB)**, 4, 123	G. L. Stevens	Megahertz (GB), 6, 123	Melhor Ainda, 3, 117	9	1:58.30	$450,000
2004	**Crimson Palace (SAf)**, 5, 123	L. Dettori	Riskaverse, 5, 123	Necklace (GB), 3, 117	11	1:56.58	450,000
2003	**Heat Haze (GB)**, 4, 123	J. Valdivia Jr.	Bien Nicole, 5, 123	Riskaverse, 4, 123	7	1:55.94	420,000
2002	**Golden Apples (Ire)**, 4, 123	P. A. Valenzuela	Astra, 6, 123	England's Legend (Fr), 5, 123	6	1:54.86	420,000
2001	**England's Legend (Fr)**, 4, 123	C. S. Nakatani	The Seven Seas, 5, 123	Spook Express (SAf), 7, 123	9	1:56.75	420,000
2000	**Snow Polina**, 5, 123	J. D. Bailey	Happyanunoit (NZ), 5, 123	Country Garden (GB), 5, 123	10	1:55.87	300,000
1997	**Memories of Silver**, 4, 123	J. D. Bailey	Maxzene, 4, 123	Dance Design (Ire), 4, 123	6	1:54.38	300,000
1996	**Timarida (Ire)**, 4, 123	J. P. Murtagh	Perfect Arc, 4, 123	Alpride (Ire), 5, 123	11	1:54.06	300,000
1995	**Possibly Perfect**, 5, 123	C. S. Nakatani	Alice Springs, 5, 123	Alpride (Ire), 4, 123	7	1:54.95	300,000
1994	**Hatoof**, 5, 123	W. R. Swinburn	Flawlessly, 6, 123	Potridee (Arg), 5, 123	8	1:55.59	300,000
1993	**‡Flawlessly**, 5, 123	C. J. McCarron	Via Borghese, 4, 123	Let's Elope (NZ), 6, 123	7	1:55.61	300,000
1992	**Kostroma (Ire)**, 6, 123	K. Desormeaux	Ruby Tiger (Ire), 5, 123	Dance Smartly, 4, 123	13	1:54.10	300,000
1991	**Fire the Groom**, 4, 123	G. L. Stevens	Colour Chart, 4, 123	Miss Josh, 5, 123	7	1:53.58	300,000
1990	**Reluctant Guest**, 4, 123	R. G. Davis	Lady Winner (Fr), 4, 123	Royal Touch (Ire), 5, 123	12	**1:53.20**	300,000
1989	**Claire Marine (Ire)**, 4, 123	C. J. McCarron	Capades, 3, 117	Gaily Gaily (Ire), 6, 123	8	2:01.80	300,000
1987	**Dancing On a Cloud**, 4, 114	J. M. Lauzon	Spruce Luck, 6, 114	Caitie Kisses, 4, 112	10	1:55.00	34,650

Named for the late wife of Arlington Park Chairman Richard Duchossois, Beverly Duchossois. Not held 1988, 1998-'99. 1$^{1}/_{16}$ miles 1987. ‡Let's Elope (NZ) finished first, DQ to third, 1993.

Beverly Hills Handicap

Grade 2 in 2006. Hollywood Park, three-year-olds and up, fillies and mares, 1¼ miles, turf. Held June 25, 2005, with a gross value of $200,000. First held in 1938. First graded in 1973. Stakes record 1:58.56 (2002 Astra).

Year	Winner	Jockey	Second	Third	Strs	Time	1st Purse
2005	**Megahertz (GB)**, 6, 124	A. O. Solis	Winendynme, 4, 117	Halo Ola (Arg), 5, 115	6	2:01.78	$120,000
2004	**Light Jig (GB)**, 4, 114	A. O. Solis	Moscow Burning, 4, 117	Noches De Rosa (Chi), 6, 118	6	2:01.52	120,000
2003	**Voodoo Dancer**, 5, 120	C. S. Nakatani	Dublino, 4, 122	Megahertz (GB), 4, 117	5	2:00.80	120,000
2002	**Astra**, 6, 124	K. Desormeaux	Peu a Peu (Ger), 4, 116	Crazy Ensign (Arg), 6, 117	8	**1:58.56**	150,000
2001	**Astra**, 5, 121	K. Desormeaux	Happyanunoit (NZ), 6, 122	Kalypso Katie (Ire), 4, 116	5	1:59.61	120,000
2000	**Happyanunoit (NZ)**, 5, 121	B. Blanc	Sweet Life, 4, 115	Polaire (Ire), 4, 116	5	1:59.32	150,000
1999	**Virginie (Brz)**, 5, 118	L. A. Pincay Jr.	Tranquility Lake, 4, 122	Keeper Hill, 4, 118	6	2:00.21	150,000
1998	**Squeak (GB)**, 4, 115	G. L. Stevens	Sixy Saint, 4, 115	Freeport Flight, 4, 114	7	2:01.56	180,000
1997	**Windsharp**, 6, 122	C. S. Nakatani	Different (Arg), 5, 121	Donna Viola (GB), 5, 122	6	2:00.60	180,000
1996	**Different (Arg)**, 4, 117	C. J. McCarron	Bail Out Becky, 4, 118	Flagbird, 5, 118	8	2:00.74	163,800
1995	**Alpride (Ire)**, 4, 115	C. J. McCarron	Possibly Perfect, 5, 124	Wandesta (GB), 4, 119	6	1:46.67	185,000
1994	**Corrazona**, 4, 119	G. L. Stevens	Hollywood Wildcat, 4, 124	Flawlessly, 6, 124	7	1:47.40	188,400
1993	**Flawlessly**, 5, 123	C. J. McCarron	Jolypha, 4, 121	Party Cited, 4, 117	4	1:47.00	180,200
1992	**Flawlessly**, 4, 122	C. J. McCarron	Kostroma (Ire), 6, 124	Alcando (Ire), 6, 113	5	1:47.13	184,000
1991	**Alcando (Ire)**, 5, 113	J. A. Garcia	Fire the Groom, 4, 120	Countus In, 6, 117	8	1:46.50	130,200
1990	**dh-Beautiful Melody**, 4, 115	K. Desormeaux		Stylish Star, 4, 116	6	1:47.00	82,300
	dh-Reluctant Guest, 4, 116	R. G. Davis					
1989	**Claire Marine (Ire)**, 4, 120	C. J. McCarron	Fitzwilliam Place (Ire), 5, 121	No Review, 4, 116	6	1:47.20	93,100
1988	**Fitzwilliam Place (Ire)**, 4, 119	A. T. Gryder	Ladanum, 4, 114	Chapel of Dreams, 4, 117	9	1:47.20	98,200
1987	**Auspiciante (Arg)**, 6, 117	P. A. Valenzuela	Reloy, 4, 120	Festivity, 4, 114	8	1:46.20	64,600
1986	**Estrapade**, 6, 122	F. Toro	Treizieme, 5, 115	Sauna (Aus), 5, 117	7	1:59.00	63,800
1985	**Johnica**, 4, 115	G. L. Stevens	Estrapade, 5, 125	L'Attrayante (Fr), 5, 118	5	1:48.20	61,900
1984	**Royal Heroine (Ire)**, 4, 123	F. Toro	Adored, 4, 121	Comedy Act, 5, 118	9	1:47.20	93,200
1983	**Absentia**, 4, 115	F. Toro	Latrone, 6, 110	Triple Tipple, 4, 118	11	1:49.00	68,500
1982	**Sangue (Ire)**, 4, 119	W. Shoemaker	Ack's Secret, 6, 123	Miss Huntington, 5, 117	6	1:47.40	63,300
1981	**Track Robbery**, 5, 120	P. A. Valenzuela	Princess Karenda, 4, 121	Save Wild Life, 4, 115	5	1:46.80	61,800
1980	**Country Queen**, 5, 122	L. A. Pincay Jr.	Wishing Well, 5, 122	The Very One, 5, 117	10	1:47.40	50,550
1979	**Giggling Girl**, 5, 117	C. J. McCarron	Country Queen, 4, 123	More So (Ire), 4, 116	9	1:47.60	50,100
1978	**Swingtime**, 6, 119	F. Toro	Grande Brisa, 4, 115	Drama Critic, 4, 118	7	1:48.40	48,000
1977	**Swingtime**, 5, 120	F. Toro	Fortunate Betty, 4, 115	*Bastonera II, 6, 126	6	1:48.40	25,200
1976	***Bastonera II**, 5, 121	L. A. Pincay Jr.	Miss Toshiba, 4, 124	Miss Tokyo, 4, 115	7	1:50.20	38,800
1975	***La Zanzara**, 5, 122	D. Pierce	*Dulcia, 6, 123	Mercy Dee, 4, 110	5	2:14.80	46,500
1974	***La Zanzara**, 4, 120	D. Pierce	Mon Miel, 4, 114	Dogtooth Violet, 4, 116	6	2:14.20	38,000
1973	**Le Cle**, 4, 119	W. Shoemaker	Pallisima, 4, 115	Convenience, 5, 124	9	2:14.80	49,900

Named for Beverly Hills, California. Grade 1 1973-2002. Not held 1940-'67. 1$^1/_{16}$ miles 1938. 1 mile 1939. 1⅜ miles 1968-'75. 1⅛ miles 1976-'85, 1987-'95. Dirt 1938-'39. Three-year-olds 1939. Both sexes 1939. Dead heat for first 1990. California-breds 1938-'39.

Bewitch Stakes

Grade 3 in 2006. Keeneland Race Course, four-year-olds and up, fillies and mares, 1½ miles, turf. Held April 26, 2006, with a gross value of $107,400. First held in 1962. First graded in 1982. Stakes record 2:27.54 (1999 Bursting Forth).

Year	Winner	Jockey	Second	Third	Strs	Time	1st Purse
2006	**Noble Stella (Ger)**, 5, 118	E. S. Prado	Louve Royale (Ire), 5, 118	Sweet Science, 5, 118	5	2:33.15	$66,588
2005	**Angara (GB)**, 4, 118	G. L. Stevens	Cape Town Lass, 4, 118	Strike Me Lucky, 4, 118	7	2:36.24	67,766
2004	**Meridiana (Ger)**, 4, 118	E. S. Prado	Alternate, 5, 116	Binya (Ger), 5, 118	10	2:31.05	70,308
2003	**Lilac Queen (Ger)**, 5, 116	J. D. Bailey	Beyond the Waves, 6, 116	San Dare, 5, 118	10	2:29.70	69,503
2002	**Sweetest Thing**, 4, 120	M. Guidry	Lapuma, 5, 116	Lady Upstage (Ire), 5, 116	9	2:31.97	68,634
2001	**Keemoon (Fr)**, 5, 120	J. D. Bailey	Playact (Ire), 4, 116	Krisada, 5, 116	8	2:30.28	124,000
2000	**The Seven Seas**, 4, 116	A. O. Solis	Innuendo (Ire), 5, 116	Hollywood Baldcat, 4, 116	10	2:29.31	70,122
1999	**Bursting Forth**, 5, 114	J. F. Chavez	Moments of Magic, 4, 114	Pinafore Park, 4, 114	9	**2:27.54**	68,758
1998	**Maxzene**, 5, 113	J. A. Santos	Cuando, 4, 113	Gastronomical, 5, 113	8	2:30.50	69,626
1997	**Cymbala (Fr)**, 4, 113	P. Day	Noble Cause, 4, 113	Last Approach, 5, 113	10	2:28.87	69,130
1996	**Memories (Ire)**, 5, 117	S. J. Sellers	Future Act, 4, 117	Curtain Raiser, 4, 114	5	2:30.14	66,030
1995	**Market Booster**, 6, 119	P. Day	Memories (Ire), 4, 113	Abigailthewife, 6, 114	7	2:29.33	50,732
1994	**Freewheel**, 5, 114	P. Day	Key Chance, 5, 114	Amal Hayati, 4, 119	6	1:50.24	50,871
1993	**Miss Lenora**, 4, 112	J. A. Krone	Hero's Love, 5, 117	Radiant Ring, 5, 119	8	1:50.60	51,367
1992	**La Gueriere**, 4, 114	B. D. Peck	Indian Fashion, 5, 117	Plenty of Grace, 5, 112	10	1:48.37	54,438
1991	**Miss Unnameable**, 7, 112	P. Day	Cheerful Spree, 4, 117	The Caretaker (Ire), 4, 114	10	1:50.02	56,225
1990	**Coolawin**, 4, 122	J. D. Bailey	To the Lighthouse, 4, 114	Ann Alleged, 5, 112	7	1:49.20	54,048
1989	**Gaily Gaily (Ire)**, 6, 122	J. A. Krone	Chez Chez Chez, 5, 114	Blossoming Beauty, 4, 113	6	1:50.00	53,853
1988	**Beauty Cream**, 5, 121	P. Day	Native Mommy, 5, 121	Fraulein Lieber, 4, 113	9	1:51.60	55,933
1987	**Gerrie Singer**, 6, 113	R. L. Frazier	Innsbruck (GB), 4, 110	Debutant Dancer, 5, 110	10	1:52.60	36,221
1986	**Devalois (Fr)**, 4, 118	E. Maple	Debutant Dancer, 4, 113	Natural Approach, 5, 113	8	1:54.00	35,685
1985	**Sintra**, 4, 119	K. K. Allen	Electric Fanny, 4, 110	Switching Trick, 5, 110	7	1:43.60	43,964
1984	**Heatherten**, 5, 119	S. Maple	Any Spray, 4, 110	Marisma (Chi), 6, 119	10	1:45.80	36,628
1983	**Try Something New**, 4, 110	P. Day	Kattegat's Pride, 4, 119	Number, 4, 119	10	1:44.20	37,001
1982	**Expressive Dance**, 4, 116	D. Brumfield	Mean Martha, 4, 115	Really Royal, 4, 116	10	1:43.40	36,416
1981	**Bold 'n Determined**, 4, 121	E. Delahoussaye	Likely Exchange, 7, 113	Save Wild Life, 4, 110	5	1:43.80	38,236
1980	**Jolie Dutch**, 4, 113	R. P. Romero	Miss Baja, 5, 112	Mi Muchacha, 5, 113	9	1:43.00	29,039
1979	**Miss Baja**, 4, 119	E. Maple	Likely Exchange, 5, 110	Plains and Simple, 4, 113	7	1:43.00	23,286

1978	**Twenty One Inch**, 2, 119	E. Delahoussaye	All's Well, 2, 119	Satan's Pride, 2, 116	10	:52.60	$11,846
1977	**Crystalan**, 2, 119	G. Patterson	No No-Nos, 2, 119	Surprise Trip, 2, 119	11	:53.00	11,947
1976	**Olden**, 2, 116	R. Breen	Bagiorix, 2, 116	Foreverness, 2, 119	6	:51.40	11,030
	Fun and Tears, 2, 119	L. J. Melancon	Miss Cigarette, 2, 119	Every Move, 2, 116	9	:51.40	11,291
1975	**Pink Jade**, 2, 119	E. Delahoussaye	Old Goat, 2, 119	T. V. Vixen, 2, 119	12	:51.60	12,139
1974	**Secret's Out**, 2, 119	D. Brumfield	Floral Princess, 2, 116	Ain't Easy, 2, 119	8	:53.20	11,727
	Dancing Home, 2, 116	A. Patterson	Semi Princess, 2, 119	Spark, 2, 116	9	:53.60	11,793
1973	**Me and Connie**, 2, 121	J. Nichols	Lady Bahia, 2, 115	Bundler, 2, 115	8	:52.40	12,604

Named for Calumet Farm's 1947 champion two-year-old filly, '49 champion older female, and '48 Ashland S. winner Bewitch (1945 f. by Bull Lea). About 4 furlongs 1962-'64. 4½ furlongs 1965-'78. 1 1/16 miles 1979-'85. 1 1/8 miles 1986-'94. Dirt 1962-'85. Two-year-olds 1962-'78. Three-year-olds 1980-'85. Fillies 1962-'78. Two divisions 1974, 1976.

Bing Crosby Handicap

Grade 1 in 2006. Del Mar, three-year-olds and up, 6 furlongs, dirt. Held July 31, 2005, with a gross value of $300,000. First held in 1946. First graded in 1985. Stakes record 1:07.80 (1962 Crazy Kid; 1968 Pretense; 1969 Kissin' George; 1978 Bad 'n Big).

Year	Winner	Jockey	Second	Third	Strs	Time	1st Purse
2005	**Greg's Gold**, 4, 115	D. R. Flores	Battle Won, 5, 117	Taste of Paradise, 6, 115	9	1:08.04	$180,000
2004	**Kela**, 6, 113	T. Baze	Pohave, 6, 118	Hombre Rapido, 7, 115	10	1:08.51	150,000
2003	**Beau's Town**, 5, 119	P. A. Valenzuela	Captain Squire, 4, 117	Bluesthestandard, 6, 117	9	1:07.96	120,000
2002	**Disturbingthepeace**, 4, 116	V. Espinoza	Freespool, 6, 115	Mellow Fellow, 7, 118	9	1:09.21	90,000
2001	**Kona Gold**, 7, 126	A. O. Solis	Caller One, 4, 124	Swept Overboard, 4, 115	4	1:08.22	120,000
2000	**Kona Gold**, 6, 123	A. O. Solis	Love That Red, 4, 118	Lexicon, 5, 117	6	1:08.50	124,200
1999	**Christmas Boy**, 6, 114	C. S. Nakatani	Son of a Pistol, 7, 123	Expressionist, 4, 116	6	1:08.11	96,360
1998	**Son of a Pistol**, 6, 120	A. O. Solis	Gold Land, 7, 117	Boundless Moment, 6, 116	7	1:08.10	97,200
1997	**First Intent**, 8, 115	R. R. Douglas	Boundless Moment, 5, 118	High Stakes Player, 5, 120	7	1:08.80	102,000
1996	**Lit de Justice**, 6, 121	C. S. Nakatani	Concept Win, 6, 116	Gold Land, 5, 116	6	1:08.19	126,750
1995	**Gold Land**, 4, 116	E. Delahoussaye	Lucky Forever, 6, 118	G Malleah, 4, 116	6	1:08.07	89,300
1994	**King's Blade**, 3, 112	C. S. Nakatani	Memo (Chi), 7, 121	Gundaghia, 7, 118	8	1:08.64	62,400
1993	**The Wicked North**, 4, 116	C. A. Black	Thirty Slews, 6, 121	Black Jack Road, 9, 115	6	1:08.52	61,200
1992	**Thirty Slews**, 5, 116	E. Delahoussaye	Slerp, 3, 115	Anjiz, 4, 114	10	1:08.20	64,900
1991	**Bruho**, 5, 116	C. S. Nakatani	Thirty Slews, 4, 115	Due to the King, 4, 116	8	1:08.25	62,900
1990	**Sensational Star**, 6, 113	R. Q. Meza	Frost Free, 5, 116	Timeless Answer, 4, 116	5	1:08.00	60,150
1989	**On the Line**, 5, 124	G. L. Stevens	Speedratic, 4, 117	Cresting Water, 4, 115	7	1:08.00	63,800
1988	**Olympic Prospect**, 4, 121	A. O. Solis	Faro, 6, 118	Sebrof, 4, 119	6	1:08.80	59,410
1987	**Zany Tactics**, 6, 120	J. L. Kaenel	Bolder Than Bold, 5, 118	My Favorite Moment, 6, 115	8	1:09.00	38,600
1986	**American Legion**, 6, 119	E. Delahoussaye	Bold Brawley, 3, 113	‡Ondarty, 4, 112	7	1:08.20	38,000
1985	**My Favorite Moment**, 4, 116	E. Delahoussaye	Rosie's K. T., 4, 116	Fifty Six Ina Row, 4, 119	10	1:09.80	33,350
1984	**Night Mover**, 4, 120	L. E. Ortega	Premiership, 4, 119	Pac Mania, 4, 115	7	1:08.60	31,800
1983	**Chinook Pass**, 4, 125	L. A. Pincay Jr.	Vagabond Song, 4, 116	Haughty But Nice, 5, 115	7	1:08.60	32,000
1982	**Pencil Point (Ire)**, 4, 114	C. J. McCarron	Terresto's Singer, 5, 114	Shanekite, 4, 115	8	1:09.00	32,650
1981	**Syncopate**, 6, 120	E. Delahoussaye	Reb's Golden Ale, 6, 119	To B. Or Not, 5, 122	6	1:08.60	31,100
1980	**Reb's Golden Ale**, 5, 117	S. Hawley	Bolger, 4, 114	Bad 'n Big, 6, 118	4	1:08.80	24,400
1979	**Syncopate**, 4, 116	S. Hawley	White Rammer, 5, 122	Fleet Twist, 5, 116	7	1:08.40	22,750
1978	**Bad 'n Big**, 4, 124	W. Shoemaker	Amadevil, 4, 121	Decoded, 4, 115	8	**1:07.80**	19,400
1977	**Cherry River**, 7, 120	L. A. Pincay Jr.	*Leinster House, 4, 111	Mark's Place, 5, 124	7	1:08.40	15,800
1976	**Cherry River**, 6, 120	L. A. Pincay Jr.	Sawtooth, 5, 111	Fast Spot, 6, 115	7	1:09.40	15,900
1975	**Messenger of Song**, 3, 119	J. Lambert	‡Stake Driver, 5, 114	Century's Envoy, 4, 122	5	1:08.80	12,450
1974	**Rise High**, 4, 113	J. E. Tejeira	Tragic Isle, 5, 121	Against the Snow, 4, 115	8	1:09.00	13,250
1973	**Pataha Prince**, 8, 114	W. Shoemaker	King of Cricket, 6, 114	Rough Night, 5, 120	9	1:08.00	13,700

Named for movie star and singer H. L. "Bing" Crosby (1903-'77), first president of Del Mar Turf Club. Grade 3 1985-'98. Grade 2 1999-2003. Bing Crosby Breeders' Cup H. 1996-2004. About 7½ furlongs 1970. Turf 1970. ‡Beira finished second, DQ to fifth, 1975. ‡Triple Sec finished third, DQ to fourth, 1986.

Black-Eyed Susan Stakes

Grade 2 in 2006. Pimlico Race Course, three-year-olds, fillies, 1 1/8 miles, dirt. Held May 19, 2006, with a gross value of $250,000. First held in 1919. First graded in 1973. Stakes record 1:47.83 (1999 Silverbulletday).

Year	Winner	Jockey	Second	Third	Strs	Time	1st Purse
2006	**‡Regal Engagement**, 3, 116	R. A. Dominguez	Smart N Pretty, 3, 116	Baghdaria, 3, 122	7	1:50.11	$150,000
2005	**Spun Sugar**, 3, 116	J. R. Velazquez	R Lady Joy, 3, 122	Pleasant Chimes, 3, 116	6	1:53.27	120,000
2004	**Yearly Report**, 3, 122	J. D. Bailey	Pawyne Princess, 3, 115	Rare Gift, 3, 115	7	1:52.65	120,000
2003	**Roar Emotion**, 3, 122	J. R. Velazquez	Fircroft, 3, 119	Santa Catarina, 3, 117	8	1:52.33	120,000
2002	**Chamrousse**, 3, 115	J. D. Bailey	Shop Till You Drop, 3, 117	Autumn Creek, 3, 115	6	1:51.61	120,000
2001	**Two Item Limit**, 3, 122	R. Migliore	Indy Glory, 3, 117	Tap Dance, 3, 122	5	1:50.84	120,000
2000	**Jostle**, 3, 122	K. Desormeaux	March Magic, 3, 122	Impending Bear, 3, 122	7	1:52.56	120,000
1999	**Silverbulletday**, 3, 122	G. L. Stevens	Dreams Gallore, 3, 117	Vee Vee Star, 3, 115	7	**1:47.83**	120,000
1998	**Added Gold**, 3, 115	J. R. Velazquez	Tappin' Ginger, 3, 115	Hansel's Girl, 3, 117	8	1:49.75	120,000
1997	**Salt It**, 3, 117	C. H. Marquez Jr.	Buckeye Search, 3, 122	Holiday Ball, 3, 115	7	1:50.52	120,000
1996	**Mesabi Maiden**, 3, 115	M. E. Smith	Cara Rafaela, 3, 122	Ginny Lynn, 3, 122	8	1:51.00	120,000
1995	**Serena's Song**, 3, 122	G. L. Stevens	Conquistadoress, 3, 115	Rare Opportunity, 3, 115	7	1:48.45	120,000
1994	**Calipha**, 3, 114	R. Wilson	Bunting, 3, 114	Golden Braids, 3, 114	13	1:51.12	120,000
1993	**Aztec Hill**, 3, 122	M. E. Smith	Traverse City, 3, 114	Jacody, 3, 117	10	1:49.78	120,000
1992	**Miss Legality**, 3, 122	C. J. McCarron	Known Feminist, 3, 114	Diamond Duo, 3, 114	8	1:51.11	150,000

1991	**Wide Country**, 3, 122	S. N. Chavez	John's Decision, 3, 117	Nalees Pin, 3, 117	9	1:51.26	$150,000
1990	**Charon**, 3, 122	C. Perret	Valay Maid, 3, 122	Bright Candles, 3, 122	9	1:48.40	150,000
1989	**Imaginary Lady**, 3, 122	G. L. Stevens	Some Romance, 3, 122	Moonlight Martini, 3, 117	9	1:48.20	150,000
1988	**Costly Shoes**, 3, 121	P. Day	Thirty Eight Go Go, 3, 121	Lost Kitty, 3, 121	6	1:44.80	97,915
1987	**Grecian Flight**, 3, 121	C. Perret	Bal Du Bois, 3, 121	Arctic Cloud, 3, 121	10	1:44.20	101,750
1986	**Family Style**, 3, 121	C. J. McCarron	Steel Maiden, 3, 121	Firgie's Jule, 3, 121	8	1:44.60	100,385
1985	**Koluctoo's Jill**, 3, 121	C. J. McCarron	Denver Express, 3, 116	A Joyful Spray, 3, 121	7	1:43.00	74,295
1984	**Lucky Lucky Lucky**, 3, 121	A. T. Cordero Jr.	Sintra, 3, 116	Duo Disco, 3, 121	7	1:41.20	100,060
1983	**Batna**, 3, 121	L. D. Ruch	Lovin Touch, 3, 116	Weekend Surprise, 3, 121	10	1:42.40	75,400
1982	**Delicate Ice**, 3, 114	D. Brumfield	Trove, 3, 121	Milingo, 3, 121	10	1:44.60	74,945
1981	**Dame Mysterieuse**, 3, 121	E. Maple	Wayward Lass, 3, 121	Real Prize, 3, 121	7	1:44.20	72,800
1980	**Weber City Miss**, 3, 118	V. A. Bracciale Jr.	Bishop's Ring, 3, 111	Champagne Star, 3, 114	8	1:44.40	74,620
1979	**Davona Dale**, 3, 121	J. Velasquez	Phoebe's Donkey, 3, 118	Plankton, 3, 121	6	1:42.60	72,670
1978	**Caesar's Wish**, 3, 121	D. R. Wright	Jevalin, 3, 116	Miss Baja, 3, 121	8	1:44.20	55,120
1977	**Small Raja**, 3, 114	A. T. Cordero Jr.	Northern Sea, 3, 121	Enthused, 3, 116	5	1:42.80	54,503
1976	**What a Summer**, 3, 111	C. J. McCarron	Dearly Precious, 3, 121	Artfully, 3, 114	10	1:42.40	37,895
1975	**My Juliet**, 3, 116	A. Hill	Gala Lil, 3, 114	Funalon, 3, 121	6	1:44.00	37,635
1974	**Blowing Rock**, 3, 111	A. Agnello	Heydairya, 3, 111	Shantung Silk, 3, 116	8	1:43.00	22,425
1973	**Fish Wife**, 3, 111	D. Gargan	Guided Missle, 3, 112	Out Cold, 3, 116	6	1:44.00	22,685

Named for the Maryland state flower. Grade 3 1973-'75. Pimlico Oaks 1937-'49. Black-Eyed Susan H. 1951. Not held 1932-'36, 1950. $1^{1}/_{16}$ miles 1919-'29, 1931, 1937-'49, 1953-'88. 1 mile 70 yards 1930. $1^{3}/_{16}$ miles 1951. ‡Smart N Pretty finished first, DQ to second, 2006.

Blue Grass Stakes

Grade 1 in 2006. Keeneland Race Course, three-year-olds, $1^{1}/_{8}$ miles, dirt. Held April 15, 2006, with a gross value of $750,000. First held in 1911. First graded in 1973. Stakes record 1:47.29 (1996 Skip Away).

Year	Winner	Jockey	Second	Third	Strs	Time	1st Purse
2006	**Sinister Minister**, 3, 123	G. K. Gomez	Storm Treasure, 3, 123	Strong Contender, 3, 123	9	1:48.85	$465,000
2005	**Bandini**, 3, 123	J. R. Velazquez	High Limit, 3, 123	Closing Argument, 3, 123	7	1:50.16	465,000
2004	**The Cliff's Edge**, 3, 123	S. J. Sellers	Lion Heart, 3, 123	Limehouse, 3, 123	8	1:49.42	465,000
2003	**Peace Rules**, 3, 123	E. S. Prado	Brancusi, 3, 123	Offlee Wild, 3, 123	9	1:51.73	465,000
2002	**Harlan's Holiday**, 3, 123	E. S. Prado	Booklet, 3, 123	Ocean Sound (Ire), 3, 123	6	1:51.51	465,000
2001	**Millennium Wind**, 3, 123	L. A. Pincay Jr.	Songandaprayer, 3, 123	Dollar Bill, 3, 123	7	1:48.32	465,000
2000	**High Yield**, 3, 123	P. Day	More Than Ready, 3, 123	Wheelaway, 3, 123	8	1:48.79	465,000
1999	**Menifee**, 3, 123	P. Day	Cat Thief, 3, 123	Vicar, 3, 123	8	1:48.66	465,000
1998	**Halory Hunter**, 3, 123	G. L. Stevens	Lil's Lad, 3, 123	Cape Town, 3, 123	5	1:47.98	434,000
1997	**Pulpit**, 3, 121	S. J. Sellers	Acceptable, 3, 121	Stolen Gold, 3, 121	7	1:49.91	434,000
1996	**Skip Away**, 3, 121	S. J. Sellers	Louis Quatorze, 3, 121	Editor's Note, 3, 121	7	**1:47.29**	434,000
1995	**Wild Syn**, 3, 121	R. P. Romero	Suave Prospect, 3, 121	Tejano Run, 3, 121	6	1:49.31	310,000
1994	**Holy Bull**, 3, 121	M. E. Smith	Valiant Nature, 3, 121	Mahogany Hall, 3, 121	7	1:50.02	310,000
1993	**Prairie Bayou**, 3, 121	M. E. Smith	Wallenda, 3, 121	Dixieland Heat, 3, 121	9	1:49.62	310,000
1992	**Pistols and Roses**, 3, 121	J. Vasquez	Conte Di Savoya, 3, 121	Ecstatic Ride, 3, 121	11	1:49.19	325,000
1991	**Strike the Gold**, 3, 121	C. W. Antley	Fly So Free, 3, 121	Nowork all Play, 3, 121	6	1:48.44	260,520
1990	**Summer Squall**, 3, 121	P. Day	Land Rush, 3, 121	Unbridled, 3, 121	5	1:48.60	185,006
1989	**Western Playboy**, 3, 121	R. P. Romero	Dispersal, 3, 121	Tricky Creek, 3, 121	6	1:51.20	185,900
1988	**Granacus**, 3, 121	J. Vasquez	Intensive Command, 3, 121	Regal Classic, 3, 121	9	1:52.20	190,856
1987	**‡War**, 3, 121	W. H. McCauley	Leo Castelli, 3, 121	Alysheba, 3, 121	5	1:48.40	148,135
1986	**Bachelor Beau**, 3, 121	L. J. Melancon	Bolshoi Boy, 3, 121	Bold Arrangement (GB), 3, 121	11	1:51.20	171,290
1985	**Chief's Crown**, 3, 121	D. MacBeth	Floating Reserve, 3, 121	Banner Bob, 3, 121	4	1:47.60	127,740
1984	**Taylor's Special**, 3, 121	P. Day	Silent King, 3, 121	Charmed Rook, 3, 121	9	1:52.20	133,883
1983	**Play Fellow**, 3, 121	J. Cruguet	‡Desert Wine, 3, 121	Copelan, 3, 121	12	1:49.40	121,924
1982	**Linkage**, 3, 121	W. Shoemaker	Gato Del Sol, 3, 121	Wavering Monarch, 3, 121	9	1:48.00	127,774
1981	**Proud Appeal**, 3, 121	J. Fell	Law Me, 3, 121	Golden Derby, 3, 121	11	1:51.40	120,559
1980	**Rockhill Native**, 3, 121	J. Oldham	Super Moment, 3, 121	Gold Stage, 3, 121	11	1:50.00	84,208
1979	**Spectacular Bid**, 3, 121	R. J. Franklin	Lot o' Gold, 3, 121	Bishop's Choice, 3, 121	4	1:50.00	79,658
1978	**Alydar**, 3, 121	J. Velasquez	Raymond Earl, 3, 121	Go Forth, 3, 121	9	1:49.60	77,350
1977	**For The Moment**, 3, 121	A. T. Cordero Jr.	Run Dusty Run, 3, 121	Western Wind, 3, 121	11	1:50.20	77,578
1976	**Honest Pleasure**, 3, 121	B. Baeza	Certain Roman, 3, 121	Inca Roca, 3, 121	7	1:49.40	73,028
1975	**Master Derby**, 3, 123	D. G. McHargue	Honey Mark, 3, 117	Prince Thou Art, 3, 123	9	1:49.00	39,878
1974	**Judger**, 3, 123	L. A. Pincay Jr.	Big Latch, 3, 117	Gold and Myrrh, 3, 114	14	1:49.20	42,608
1973	**My Gallant**, 3, 117	A. T. Cordero Jr.	Our Native, 3, 123	dh-Impecunious, 3, 126 dh-Warbucks, 3, 117	9	1:49.60	37,765

Named for the Bluegrass region of Kentucky. Sponsored by Toyota Motor Manufacturing Co. of Georgetown, Kentucky 1996-2006. Grade 2 1990-'98. Held at Kentucky Association 1911-'36. Held at Churchill Downs 1943-'45. Not held 1915-'18, 1927-'36. 6 furlongs 1964. Dead heat for third 1973. ‡Marfa finished second, DQ to fourth, 1983. ‡Alysheba finished first, DQ to third, 1987.

Boiling Springs Stakes

Grade 3 in 2006. Monmouth Park, three-year-olds, fillies, $1^{1}/_{16}$ miles, dirt (originally scheduled as a Grade 3 on the turf). Held May 29, 2005, with a gross value of $136,500. First held in 1977. First graded in 1980. Stakes record 1:40.09 (1998 Mysterious Moll).

Year	Winner	Jockey	Second	Third	Strs	Time	1st Purse
2005	**Toll Taker**, 3, 118	A. T. Gryder	Pleasant Lyrics, 3, 116	Ruby Martini, 3, 116	3	1:44.36	$90,000

2004 **Seducer's Song**, 3, 119	J. Bravo	Go Robin, 3, 117	River Belle (GB), 3, 117	9	1:45.66	$90,000
2002 **Showlady**, 3, 114	R. Migliore	Dreamers Glory, 3, 116	With Patience, 3, 117	9	1:42.27	120,000
2001 **Mystic Lady**, 3, 120	E. Coa	Shooting Party, 3, 114	Plunderthepeasants, 3, 115	4	1:42.63	120,000
2000 **Storm Dream (Ire)**, 3, 116	J. Samyn	Watch, 3, 117	Lady Dora, 3, 114	11	1:47.09	60,000
1999 **Wild Heart Dancing**, 3, 116	J. F. Chavez	Confessional, 3, 118	Petunia, 3, 114	8	1:43.08	120,000
1998 **Mysterious Moll**, 3, 116	J. L. Espinoza	Who Did It and Run, 3, 120	Thunder Kitten, 3, 116	12	**1:40.09**	120,000
1997 **Stoneleigh**, 3, 114	J. A. Santos	Majestic Sunlight, 3, 114	Dancing Water, 3, 115	6	1:41.13	60,000
Victory Chime, 3, 114	M. E. Smith	Miss Pop Carn, 3, 111	Colonial Play, 3, 113	9	1:41.99	60,000
1996 **Careless Heiress**, 3, 118	C. Perret	Briarcliff, 3, 114	Dathuil (Ire), 3, 115	9	1:50.54	60,000
1995 **Christmas Gift**, 3, 116	W. H. McCauley	Ring by Spring, 3, 114	Transient Trend, 3, 114	7	1:43.49	48,000
Class Kris, 3, 118	R. Wilson	Twilight Encounter, 3, 112	Appointed One, 3, 114	7	1:43.27	48,000
1994 **Avie's Fancy**, 3, 119	J. C. Ferrer	Teasing Charm, 3, 114	Knocknock, 3, 115	7	1:41.41	45,000
1993 **Tribulation**, 3, 110	J. Samyn	Exotic Sea, 3, 114	Bright Penny, 3, 115	11	1:42.70	45,000
1992 **Captive Miss**, 3, 120	J. Bravo	Logan's Mist, 3, 116	Aquilegia, 3, 113	9	1:40.78	45,000
1991 **Dance O'My Life**, 3, 114	C. W. Antley	Monica Faye, 3, 110	Verbasle, 3, 115	11	1:41.44	45,000
1990 **Memories of Pam**, 3, 112	J. D. Bailey	Hot Marshmellow, 3, 114	Baltic Chill, 3, 118	8	1:41.00	41,550
Plenty of Grace, 3, 112	J. D. Bailey	Southern Tradition, 3, 120	Sabina, 3, 114	6	1:42.20	40,950
1989 **Darby Shuffle**, 3, 116	J. A. Krone	To the Lighthouse, 3, 116	Warranty Applied, 3, 115	9	1:40.60	53,730
1988 **Siggebo**, 3, 119	R. Wilson	Flashy Runner, 3, 115	Lusty Lady, 3, 113	7	1:43.20	51,930
1987 **Rullah Runner**, 3, 109	W. A. Guerra	Tappiano, 3, 119	Key Bid, 3, 120	12	1:41.40	35,460
1986 **Small Virtue**, 3, 114	J. A. Santos	Sweet Velocity, 3, 115	Country Recital, 3, 121	11	1:41.60	47,985
Spruce Fir, 3, 119	D. B. Thomas	Ala Mahlik (Ire), 3, 116	Spring Innocence, 3, 113	11	1:41.60	47,985
1985 **Jolly Saint (Ire)**, 3, 114	J. A. Santos	Miss Hardwick, 3, 115	Dawn's Curtsey, 3, 115	13	1:41.00	49,620
1984 **Possible Mate**, 3, 116	D. MacBeth	Distaff Magic, 3, 113	Miss Audimar, 3, 112	13	1:41.80	33,930
1983 **Sabin**, 3, 124	E. Maple	Aspen Rose, 3, 114	Propositioning, 3, 117	11	1:47.80	33,480
1982 **Sunny Sparkler**, 3, 113	J. Samyn	Fact Finder, 3, 113	Milingo, 3, 117	10	1:41.40	26,895
Larida, 3, 119	E. Maple	Doodle, 3, 115	Distinctive Moon, 3, 114	11	1:41.40	27,075
1981 **Irish Joy**, 3, 114	C. C. Lopez	First Approach, 3, 113	Dance Forth, 3, 114	11	1:42.40	26,925
Wings of Grace, 3, 112	J. Velasquez	Andover Way, 3, 114	Pukka Princess, 3, 120	8	1:41.40	26,385
1980 **Champagne Ginny**, 3, 114	J. Velasquez	Qui Royalty, 3, 112	Classic Curves, 3, 111	9	1:42.00	26,505
Refinish, 3, 113	C. J. McCarron	Keep Off (Ire), 3, 111	Cannon Boy, 3, 113	9	1:41.60	26,505
1979 **Jameela**, 3, 118	V. A. Bracciale Jr.	Fanny Saperstein, 3, 119	Whydidju, 3, 119	6	1:41.60	27,934
Gala Regatta, 3, 122	E. Maple	dh-Record Acclaim, 3, 114 dh-Tweak, 3, 113		6	1:41.00	27,934
1978 **Key to the Saga**, 3, 118	J. Samyn	Terpsichorist, 3, 117	Amerigirl, 3, 112	9	1:41.40	28,519
Sisterhood, 3, 112	B. Gonzalez	Island Kiss, 3, 108	White Star Line, 3, 122	9	1:41.40	28,519
1977 **Council House**, 3, 116	C. Perret	Rich Soil, 3, 119	Pressing Date, 3, 115	10	1:42.40	28,633
Critical Cousin, 3, 119	A. T. Cordero Jr.	Sans Arc, 3, 116	Small Raja, 3, 123	8	1:42.40	28,243

Named for former name of East Rutherford, New Jersey, home of the Meadowlands, the race's original location. Not graded 2001, 2005. Boiling Springs H. 1977-'78, 1981-'97. Boiling Springs Breeders' Cup H. 1998-2002. Held at the Meadowlands 1977-2002. Not held 2003. Dirt 1998, 2001, 2005. Originally scheduled on turf 2001, 2005. Two divisions 1977-'82, 1986, 1990, 1995, 1997. Dead heat for second 1979 (2nd Div.).

Bold Ruler Handicap

Grade 3 in 2006. Belmont Park, three-year-olds and up, 6 furlongs, dirt. Held May 13, 2006, with a gross value of $104,700. First held in 1976. First graded in 1982. Stakes record 1:07.54 (1999 Kelly Kip).

Year Winner	Jockey	Second	Third	Strs	Time	1st Purse
2006 **Tiger**, 5, 114	E. Coa	Dark Cheetah, 4, 115	Bishop Court Hill, 6, 119	5	1:08.49	$64,020
2005 **Uncle Camie**, 5, 115	R. Migliore	Don Six, 5, 120	Thunder Touch, 4, 114	5	1:08.67	63,960
2004 **Canadian Frontier**, 5, 111	J. Castellano	Key Deputy, 4, 114	First Blush, 4, 113	6	1:08.97	64,620
2003 **Shake You Down**, 5, 115	M. J. Luzzi	Here's Zealous, 6, 114	Peeping Tom, 6, 117	7	1:08.47	65,040
2002 **Left Bank**, 5, 121	J. R. Velazquez	Silky Sweep, 6, 114	Say Florida Sandy, 8, 116	4	1:09.30	63,646
2001 **Say Florida Sandy**, 7, 117	J. Bravo	Delaware Township, 5, 117	Lake Pontchartrain, 6, 113	7	1:08.67	65,520
2000 **Brutally Frank**, 6, 115	S. Bridgmohan	Kelly Kip, 6, 121	Kashatreya, 6, 115	7	1:08.64	65,880
1999 **Kelly Kip**, 5, 123	J. Samyn	Artax, 4, 115	Brushed On, 4, 115	5	**1:07.54**	64,440
1998 **Kelly Kip**, 4, 117	J. Samyn	Say Florida Sandy, 4, 111	Johnny Legit, 4, 114	8	1:07.61	66,120
1997 **Punch Line**, 7, 122	R. G. Davis	Golden Tent, 8, 111	Blissful State, 5, 116	6	1:08.80	64,980
1996 **Lite the Fuse**, 5, 119	J. A. Krone	Cold Execution, 5, 115	Splendid Sprinter, 4, 115	5	1:09.51	64,500
1995 **Rizzi**, 4, 112	D. V. Beckner	Lite the Fuse, 4, 111	Evil Bear, 5, 116	6	1:08.91	64,560
1994 **Chief Desire**, 4, 117	J. R. Velazquez	Boom Towner, 6, 120	Won Song, 4, 112	8	1:08.76	66,300
1993 **Slerp**, 4, 119	J. A. Santos	Argyle Lake, 7, 121	Big Jewel, 5, 121	8	1:09.17	70,200
1992 **Jolies Appeal**, 4, 119	W. H. McCauley	Reappeal, 6, 119	Fiercely, 4, 119	5	1:09.29	67,560
1991 **Rousing Past**, 4, 119	N. Santagata	True and Blue, 6, 121	Sunshine Jimmy, 4, 119	6	1:09.96	67,200
1990 **Mr. Nickerson**, 4, 119	C. W. Antley	Dancing Pretense, 5, 119	Diamond Donnie, 4, 119	5	1:09.20	66,240
1989 **Pok Ta Pok**, 4, 121	R. Migliore	Teddy Drone, 4, 119	Claim, 4, 119	6	1:09.80	67,560
1988 **King's Swan**, 8, 123	C. W. Antley	Seattle Knight, 4, 119	Faster Than Sound, 4, 123	7	1:10.20	103,680
1987 **†Pine Tree Lane**, 5, 118	A. T. Cordero Jr.	Love That Mac, 5, 123	Play the King, 4, 121	7	1:09.00	103,680
1986 **Phone Trick**, 4, 123	J. Velasquez	Love That Mac, 4, 119	Rexson's Bishop, 4, 121	7	1:08.80	70,680
1985 **Rocky Marriage**, 5, 119	A. T. Cordero Jr.	Entropy, 5, 121	Majestic Venture, 4, 119	6	1:08.80	51,390
1984 **Top Avenger**, 6, 121	A. Graell	Believe the Queen, 4, 119	Au Point, 4, 123	10	1:09.80	55,350
1983 **Maudlin**, 5, 119	J. D. Bailey	Top Avenger, 5, 123	Singh Tu, 4, 121	4	1:11.60	49,500

1982	**Always Run Lucky**, 4, 123	J. J. Miranda	King's Fashion, 7, 119	Band Practice, 4, 119	4	1:09.40	$49,050
1981	**Dave's Friend**, 6, 123	A. S. Black	Naughty Jimmy, 4, 119	Fappiano, 4, 119	6	1:09.60	48,510
1980	**Dave's Friend**, 5, 123	V. A. Bracciale Jr.	Tilt Up, 5, 121	Double Zeus, 5, 121	6	1:09.80	48,690
1979	**Star de Naskra**, 4, 119	J. Fell	Vencedor, 5, 126	Big John Taylor, 5, 119	8	1:09.20	48,420
1978	**Half High**, 5, 115	A. Santiago	Great Above, 6, 121	Cruise On In, 4, 110	6	1:09.40	25,665
1977	**Jaipur's Gem**, 4, 113	J. Samyn	Expletive Deleted, 4, 107	Cojak, 4, 126	6	1:09.60	22,050
1976	**Chief Tamanaco**, 3, 114	A. T. Cordero Jr.	Relent, 5, 114	Jackson Square, 4, 116	4	1:09.80	21,750

Named for Wheatley Stable's 1957 Horse of the Year and eight-time leading North American sire Bold Ruler (1954 c. by *Nasrullah). Grade 2 1985-'89. Bold Ruler S. 1979-'93. Held at Aqueduct 1976-2001. Track record 1998, 1999. †Denotes female.

Bonnie Miss Stakes

Grade 2 in 2006. Gulfstream Park, three-year-olds, fillies, 1⅛ miles, dirt. Held March 5, 2006, with a gross value of $150,000. First held in 1971. First graded in 1982. Stakes record 1:48.25 (2006 Teammate).

Year	Winner	Jockey	Second	Third	Strs	Time	1st Purse
2006	**Teammate**, 3, 116	C. H. Velasquez	Wonder Lady Anne L, 3, 120	Wait a While, 3, 120	7	**1:48.25**	$90,000
2005	**Jill Robin L**, 3, 116	J. D. Bailey	In the Gold, 3, 118	Holy Trinity, 3, 116	7	1:53.12	90,000
2004	**Last Song**, 3, 118	E. S. Prado	Society Selection, 3, 120	Rare Gift, 3, 116	5	1:50.60	120,000
2003	**Ivanavinalot**, 3, 122	J. R. Velazquez	My Boston Gal, 3, 120	Holiday Lady, 3, 118	7	1:50.72	120,000
2002	**Dust Me Off**, 3, 116	M. Guidry	Nonsuch Bay, 3, 116	Belterra, 3, 120	6	1:49.67	150,000
2001	**Tap Dance**, 3, 114	J. D. Bailey	Halo Reality, 3, 117	Unbridled Lassie, 3, 114	7	1:52.05	150,000
2000	**Cash Run**, 3, 119	J. D. Bailey	Deed I Do, 3, 114	Bejoyfulandrejoyce, 3, 114	6	1:44.11	120,000
1999	**Three Ring**, 3, 122	J. R. Velazquez	Olympic Charmer, 3, 117	Marley Vale, 3, 117	5	1:43.75	120,000
1998	**Banshee Breeze**, 3, 114	R. P. Romero	Santaria, 3, 114	Cotton House Bay, 3, 114	8	1:46.57	120,000
1997	**Glitter Woman**, 3, 117	M. E. Smith	Southern Playgirl, 3, 119	Dixie Flag, 3, 114	5	1:43.20	120,000
1996	**My Flag**, 3, 117	J. D. Bailey	Escena, 3, 114	La Rosa, 3, 117	5	1:45.77	120,000
1995	**Mia's Hope**, 3, 117	K. L. Chapman	Minister Wife, 3, 119	Incredible Blues, 3, 117	9	1:44.85	120,000
1994	**Inside Information**, 3, 114	M. E. Smith	Cinnamon Sugar (Ire), 3, 113	Jade Flush, 3, 114	10	1:42.94	120,000
1993	**Dispute**, 3, 114	J. D. Bailey	Sky Beauty, 3, 114	Lunar Spook, 3, 117	6	1:43.67	120,000
1992	**Spectacular Sue**, 3, 114	W. S. Ramos	Spinning Round, 3, 117	Tricky Cinderella, 3, 112	6	1:44.14	120,000
1991	**Withallprobability**, 3, 117	C. Perret	Fancy Ribbons, 3, 117	Outlasting, 3, 114	6	1:43.30	120,000
1990	**Charon**, 3, 121	E. Fires	Trumpet's Blare, 3, 121	De La Devil, 3, 121	7	1:44.60	120,000
1989	**Open Mind**, 3, 121	A. T. Cordero Jr.	Seattle Meteor, 3, 121	Surging, 3, 114	6	1:43.80	120,000
1988	**On to Royalty**, 3, 121	C. Perret	Tomorrow's Child, 3, 121	Make Change, 3, 112	12	1:45.60	120,000
1987	**Mar Mar**, 3, 121	W. A. Guerra	Super Cook, 3, 121	Without Feathers, 3, 118	12	1:44.60	90,000
1986	**Patricia J. K.**, 3, 121	J. A. Santos	Noranc, 3, 121	Family Style, 3, 121	11	1:45.20	135,570
1985	**Lucy Manette**, 3, 121	C. Perret	Outstandingly, 3, 121	Micki Bracken, 3, 121	9	1:44.80	72,240
1984	**Miss Oceana**, 3, 121	E. Maple	Enumerating, 3, 114	Katrinka, 3, 112	9	1:42.40	70,605
1983	**Unaccompanied**, 3, 116	R. Woodhouse	‡Bright Crocus, 3, 114	Dewl Reason, 3, 112	12	1:45.40	58,320
1982	**Christmas Past**, 3, 121	J. Vasquez	Norsan, 3, 113	Our Darling, 3, 112	6	1:44.20	34,830
1981	**Dame Mysterieuse**, 3, 118	J. Samyn	Banner Gala, 3, 113	Heavenly Cause, 3, 121	7	1:44.40	52,335
1980	**Lien**, 3, 112	E. Maple	Wistful, 3, 115	Champagne Ginny, 3, 114	9	1:22.00	18,510
1979	**Davona Dale**, 3, 122	J. Velasquez	Candy Eclair, 3, 122	Prove Me Special, 3, 114	4	1:21.00	17,545
1978	**Jevalin**, 3, 114	M. Solomone	‡Raise a Companion, 3, 110	Sharp Belle, 3, 114	10	1:23.80	18,600
1977	**Herecomesthebride**, 3, 114	L. Saumell	Grand Luxe, 3, 112	Rich Soil, 3, 112	9	1:21.80	20,970
1976	**Get Swinging**, 5, 111	A. Ramos	Twenty Six Girl, 4, 112	North of Boston, 4, 114	8	1:45.80	17,400
1975	**Cheers Marion**, 4, 113	M. Castaneda	Hinterland, 5, 116	Summer Sprite, 5, 114	8	1:42.20	10,207
	Diomedia, 4, 116	M. Castaneda	Gems and Roses, 5, 122	Exclusive Lady, 5, 113	8	1:42.00	10,207
1974	**City Girl**, 3, 112	E. Maple	Maud Muller, 3, 112	Double Bend, 3, 112	12	1:22.60	21,540
1973	**Fun Palace**, 4, 111	E. Fires	Hasty Jude, 4, 119	Viewpoise, 5, 113	12	1:44.40	14,145

Named for Bonnie Donn, daughter of James Donn Jr., president of Gulfstream Park from 1972-'78. Grade 3 1982-'87. Bonnie Miss H. 1976. About 1¹⁄₁₆ miles 1971. 7 furlongs 1972, 1974, 1977-'80. 1¹⁄₁₆ miles 1973, 1975-'76, 1981-2000. Turf 1971, 1975-'76. Originally scheduled on turf 1973. Three-year-olds and up 1971, 1973, 1975-'76. Fillies and mares 1971, 1973, 1975-'76. Two divisions 1975. ‡Cornish Queen finished second, DQ to fourth, 1978. ‡Miss Molly finished second, DQ to twelfth, 1983.

Bourbonette Breeders' Cup Stakes

Grade 3 in 2006. Turfway Park, three-year-olds, fillies, 1 mile, all weather. Held March 25, 2006, with a gross value of $150,000. First held in 1983. First graded in 2006. Stakes record 1:35.03 (1997 Buckeye Search).

Year	Winner	Jockey	Second	Third	Strs	Time	1st Purse
2006	**Top Notch Lady**, 3, 115	R. Albarado	Coronado's Vision, 3, 117	Lemons Forever, 3, 117	9	1:39.26	$93,000
2005	**Dance Away Capote**, 3, 121	R. Bejarano	Gallant Secret, 3, 114	Amazing Buy, 3, 121	11	1:37.52	93,000
2004	**Class Above**, 3, 121	J. D. Bailey	Susan's Angel, 3, 114	Native Annie, 3, 121	6	1:37.98	93,000
2003	**‡Adopted Daughter**, 3, 114	D. P. Butler	Golden Marlin, 3, 114	Unbridled Femme, 3, 121	11	1:37.41	93,000
2002	**Colonial Glitter**, 3, 112	P. Day	Southey, 3, 112	Madame X Ski, 3, 114	9	1:37.06	93,000
2001	**Sweet Nanette**, 3, 112	P. Day	Upside, 3, 115	Heathers Promise, 3, 114	7	1:37.55	62,600
2000	**Trip**, 3, 112	W. Martinez	Lorie Darlin, 3, 112	Upon a Thron, 3, 112	9	1:36.25	93,600
1999	**Sweeping Story**, 3, 112	J. F. Chavez	Elaines Reason, 3, 112	Bag Lady Jane, 3, 112	7	1:37.72	99,634
1998	**Nurse Goodbody**, 3, 112	W. Martinez	Victorica, 3, 112	Swoop City, 3, 112	7	1:36.05	62,600
1997	**Buckeye Search**, 3, 112	B. Peck	City Band, 3, 112	Fountain Square, 3, 112	7	**1:35.03**	62,600
1996	**Clamorosa**, 3, 113	J. D. Bailey	Ginny Lynn, 3, 112	Pledged, 3, 115	12	1:37.17	65,000
1995	**Sherzarcat**, 3, 115	K. Desormeaux	Minister Wife, 3, 118	Grand Charmer, 3, 115	9	1:38.98	65,000

1994	**Private Status**, 3, 112	P. Day	Princess Nana, 3, 112	Simply Nijinsky, 3, 112	10	1:38.09	$39,000
1993	**Sentimentaldiamond**, 3, 121	M. T. Johnston	Ruggles, 3, 112	Clarwithaflare, 3, 121	7	1:38.23	32,500
1992	**Preach**, 3, 121	J. A. Krone	Pleasureconnection, 3, 121	Pleasant Baby, 3, 114	9	1:40.95	39,000
1991	**Saratoga Dame**, 3, 121	M. McDowell	Promising Preppy, 3, 118	Flashing Eyes, 3, 121	11	1:37.10	35,149
1990	**Appella**, 3, 112	W. D. Troilo	Arm the Natives, 3, 112	Will Never Tell, 3, 115	9	1:41.00	34,580
	Joannie Banannie, 3, 121	P. Day	Coax Me Linn, 3, 110	Ioya, 3, 114	9	1:40.00	34,515
1989	**Gorgeous**, 3, 121	P. Day	Up, 3, 118	Blondeinamotel, 3, 121	9	1:36.20	28,681
1988	**Stolie**, 3, 112	M. McDowell	International Gal, 3, 114	Fun Ticket, 3, 111	8	1:40.80	28,048
	Darien Miss, 3, 121	R. P. Romero	Jump With Joy, 3, 112	Angry Angel, 3, 112	8	1:39.00	34,977
1987	**Combative**, 3, 112	P. Day	After the Show, 3, 118	Queen's Highness, 3, 112	10	1:38.60	27,630
1986	**Hail a Cab**, 3, 112	L. J. Melancon	Close Tolerance, 3, 110	Silver Saucer, 3, 112	12	1:40.40	25,680
	Pretty Sham, 3, 121	F. Lovato Jr.	Prime Union, 3, 121	Hagley's Relic, 3, 121	9	1:40.20	19,841
	Classy Carlotta, 3, 115	R. D. Fielding	Penalty Declared, 3, 113	Bold Princesa, 3, 112	11	1:40.00	20,004
1985	**Wealthy and Wise**, 3, 113	E. J. Sipus Jr.	Box of Birds, 3, 112	Delta Star, 3, 113	8	1:37.40	13,341
	Mahalia, 3, 113	C. Schwing	Sally Shark, 3, 114	Trops Gal, 3, 110	10	1:40.40	13,471
1984	**Dusty Gloves**, 3, 112	A. T. Cordero Jr.	Sean's Sommer, 3, 112	Rose of Ashes, 3, 115	12	1:38.80	12,450
1983	**Push On**, 3, 112	J. McKnight	Keep On Dancing, 3, 122	Shecky's Song, 3, 116	9	1:40.80	7,719
	Fiesty Belle, 3, 111	J. Velasquez	Talk About Home, 3, 122	Country Dust, 3, 111	9	1:39.00	9,376

The Bourbonette S. is traditionally run the same day as the Lane's End S., formerly the Jim Beam S., and was named as a comparable distaff race. Bourbonette S. 1983-'98. Host track known as Latonia Race Course 1983-'86. Dirt 1983-2005. Two divisions 1983, 1985, 1988, 1990. Three divisions 1986. ‡Golden Marlin finished first, DQ to second, 2003.

Bowling Green Handicap

Grade 2 in 2006. Belmont Park, three-year-olds and up, $1\frac{3}{8}$ miles, turf. Held July 16, 2005, with a gross value of $150,000. First held in 1958. First graded in 1973. Stakes record 2:10.20 (1990 With Approval).

Year	Winner	Jockey	Second	Third	Strs	Time	1st Purse
2005	**Cacht Wells (Arg)**, 5, 114	E. Coa	Relaxed Gesture (Ire), 4, 117	Dreadnaught, 5, 117	7	**2:15.49**	$90,000
2004	**Kicken Kris**, 4, 117	E. S. Prado	Better Talk Now, 5, 115	Gigli (Brz), 6, 113	10	2:12.19	90,000
2003	**Whitmore's Conn**, 5, 116	J. Samyn	Quest Star, 4, 117	Macaw (Ire), 4, 116	9	2:15.92	90,000
2002	**Whitmore's Conn**, 4, 112	S. Bridgmohan	Staging Post, 4, 115	Moon Solitaire (Ire), 5, 116	9	2:13.43	90,000
2001	**King Cugat**, 4, 119	J. D. Bailey	Slew Valley, 4, 112	Man From Wicklow, 4, 112	7	2:10.62	90,000
2000	**Elhayq (Ire)**, 5, 113	S. Bridgmohan	Yankee Dollar, 4, 110	Carpenter's Halo, 4, 115	9	2:13.81	90,000
1999	**Honor Glide**, 5, 114	J. A. Santos	Parade Ground, 4, 118	‡Fahris (Ire), 5, 114	6	2:11.07	90,000
1998	**Cetewayo**, 4, 112	J. R. Velazquez	Officious, 5, 113	Chief Bearhart, 5, 124	6	2:13.45	90,000
1997	**Influent**, 6, 120	J. Samyn	Flag Down, 7, 118	Notoriety, 4, 108	8	2:11.00	90,000
1996	**Flag Down**, 6, 118	J. A. Santos	Broadway Flyer, 5, 118	Diplomatic Jet, 4, 119	9	2:13.29	90,000
1995	**Sentimental Moi**, 5, 111	R. B. Perez	Awad, 5, 121	Proceeded, 4, 108	8	2:15.48	90,000
1994	**Turk Passer**, 4, 110	J. R. Velazquez	Sea Hero, 4, 117	Fraise, 6, 124	6	2:13.25	90,000
1993	**Dr. Kiernan**, 4, 114	C. W. Antley	Spectacular Tide, 4, 111	Lomitas (GB), 5, 117	9	2:17.70	90,000
1992	**Wall Street Dancer**, 4, 114	P. Day	Fraise, 4, 113	Libor, 5, 109	7	2:12.92	120,000
1991	**Three Coins Up**, 3, 111	J. D. Bailey	Phantom Breeze (Ire), 5, 117	Beyond the Lake (Ire), 5, 115	12	2:10.86	120,000
1990	**With Approval**, 4, 118	C. Perret	Chenin Blanc, 4, 113	El Senor, 6, 121	9	**2:10.20**	113,280
1989	**El Senor**, 5, 117	W. H. McCauley	Coeur de Lion (Fr), 5, 121	Pay the Butler, 5, 116	10	2:18.60	144,960
1988	**Coeur de Lion (Fr)**, 4, 117	C. Perret	Pay the Butler, 4, 112	Milesius, 4, 115	13	2:13.40	151,680
1987	**Theatrical (Ire)**, 5, 123	P. Day	Akabir, 6, 116	Dance of Life, 4, 121	10	2:14.00	144,960
1986	**Uptown Swell**, 4, 114	E. Maple	Palace Panther (Ire), 5, 116	Equalize, 4, 116	13	2:14.80	147,690
1985	**Sharannpour (Ire)**, 5, 114	A. T. Cordero Jr.	Flying Pidgeon, 4, 117	Long Mick (Fr), 4, 121	14	2:18.20	156,300
1984	**Hero's Honor**, 4, 120	J. D. Bailey	Nassipour, 4, 110	Super Sunrise (GB), 5, 123	11	2:14.00	144,120
1983	**Tantalizing**, 4, 113	J. Vasquez	Sprink, 5, 113	Majesty's Prince, 4, 122	7	2:14.80	105,120
1982	**Open Call**, 4, 124	J. Velasquez	Johnny Dance, 4, 114	Baltimore Canyon, 4, 116	10	2:24.80	89,850
1981	**Great Neck**, 5, 114	A. T. Cordero Jr.	Key to Content, 4, 119	Match the Hatch, 5, 115	8	2:12.00	84,450
1980	**Sten**, 5, 117	J. Fell	John Henry, 5, 128	Lyphard's Wish (Fr), 4, 120	9	2:13.20	86,550
1979	**Overskate**, 4, 117	R. Platts	†Waya (Fr), 5, 125	Bowl Game, 5, 123	7	2:11.40	84,525
1978	**Tiller**, 4, 117	J. Fell	Proud Arion, 4, 111	Bowl Game, 4, 124	10	2:12.40	70,260
1977	**Hunza Dancer**, 5, 117	J. Cruguet	Improviser, 5, 122	Noble Dancer (GB), 5, 117	13	1:58.80	68,580
1976	**Erwin Boy**, 5, 120	R. Turcotte	Drollery, 6, 111	Trumpeter Swan, 5, 111	9	2:26.00	34,740
1975	**Barcas**, 4, 113	M. Castaneda	Drollery, 5, 113	*Telefonico, 4, 124	6	2:32.20	33,240
1974	**Take Off**, 5, 120	R. Turcotte	†Garland of Roses, 5, 109	Astray, 5, 126	9	2:26.40	34,260
1973	**†Summer Guest**, 4, 119	J. Vasquez	Red Reality, 7, 124	Astray, 4, 113	9	2:29.20	34,200

Named for the lower tip of Manhattan Island, New York, where there was once a green for lawn bowling. Grade 1 1983-'89. Held at Aqueduct 1963-'67. $1\frac{1}{2}$ miles 1960-'62, 1968-'76. $1\frac{5}{8}$ miles 1963-'67. $1\frac{1}{4}$ miles 1977. Course record 1977. ‡Federal Trial finished third, DQ to fourth, 1999. †Denotes female.

Breeders' Cup Classic

Grade 1 in 2006. Belmont Park, three-year-olds and up, $1\frac{1}{4}$ miles, dirt. Held October 29, 2005, with a gross value of $4,680,000. First held in 1984. First graded in 1984. Stakes record 1:59.02 (2004 Ghostzapper).

Year	Winner	Jockey	Second	Third	Strs	Time	1st Purse
2005	**Saint Liam**, 5, 126	J. D. Bailey	Flower Alley, 3, 122	Perfect Drift, 6, 126	13	2:01.49	$2,433,600
2004	**Ghostzapper**, 4, 126	J. Castellano	Roses in May, 4, 126	Pleasantly Perfect, 6, 126	13	**1:59.02**	2,080,000
2003	**Pleasantly Perfect**, 5, 126	A. O. Solis	Medaglia d'Oro, 4, 126	Dynever, 3, 121	10	1:59.88	2,080,000

2002	**Volponi**, 4, 126	J. A. Santos	Medaglia d'Oro, 3, 121	Milwaukee Brew, 5, 126	12	2:01.39	$2,080,000
2001	**Tiznow**, 4, 126	C. J. McCarron	Sakhee, 4, 126	Albert the Great, 4, 126	13	2:00.62	2,080,000
2000	**Tiznow**, 3, 122	C. J. McCarron	Giant's Causeway, 3, 122	Captain Steve, 3, 122	13	2:00.75	2,480,400
1999	**Cat Thief**, 3, 122	P. Day	Budroyale, 6, 126	Golden Missile, 4, 126	14	1:59.52	2,080,000
1998	**Awesome Again**, 4, 126	P. Day	Silver Charm, 4, 126	Swain (Ire), 6, 126	10	2:02.16	2,662,400
1997	**Skip Away**, 4, 126	M. E. Smith	Deputy Commander, 3, 122	‡Dowty, 5, 126	9	1:59.16	2,288,000
1996	**Alphabet Soup**, 5, 126	C. J. McCarron	Louis Quatorze, 3, 121	Cigar, 6, 126	13	2:01.00	2,080,000
1995	**Cigar**, 5, 126	J. D. Bailey	L'Carriere, 4, 126	Unaccounted For, 4, 126	11	1:59.58	1,560,000
1994	**Concern**, 3, 122	J. D. Bailey	Tabasco Cat, 3, 122	Dramatic Gold, 3, 122	14	2:02.41	1,560,000
1993	**Arcangues**, 5, 126	J. D. Bailey	Bertrando, 4, 126	Kissin Kris, 3, 122	13	2:00.83	1,560,000
1992	**A.P. Indy**, 3, 121	E. Delahoussaye	Pleasant Tap, 5, 126	†Jolypha, 3, 118	14	2:00.20	1,560,000
1991	**Black Tie Affair (Ire)**, 5, 126	J. D. Bailey	Twilight Agenda, 5, 126	Unbridled, 4, 126	11	2:02.80	1,560,000
1990	**Unbridled**, 3, 121	P. Day	Ibn Bey (GB), 6, 126	Thirty Six Red, 3, 121	14	2:02.20	1,350,000
1989	**Sunday Silence**, 3, 122	C. J. McCarron	Easy Goer, 3, 122	Blushing John, 4, 126	8	2:00.20	1,350,000
1988	**Alysheba**, 4, 126	C. J. McCarron	Seeking the Gold, 3, 122	Waquoit, 5, 126	9	2:04.80	1,350,000
1987	**Ferdinand**, 4, 126	W. Shoemaker	Alysheba, 3, 122	Judge Angelucci, 4, 126	12	2:01.40	1,350,000
1986	**Skywalker**, 4, 126	L. A. Pincay Jr.	Turkoman, 4, 126	Precisionist, 5, 126	11	2:00.40	1,350,000
1985	**Proud Truth**, 3, 122	J. Velasquez	Gate Dancer, 4, 126	Turkoman, 3, 122	8	2:00.80	1,350,000
1984	**Wild Again**, 4, 126	P. Day	‡Slew o' Gold, 4, 126	Gate Dancer, 3, 122	8	2:03.40	1,350,000

Sponsored by the Dodge division of DaimlerChrysler of Detroit, Michigan 2003-'05. Held at Hollywood Park 1984, 1987, 1997. Held at Aqueduct 1985. Held at Santa Anita Park 1986, 1993, 2003. Held at Churchill Downs 1988, 1991, 1994, 1998, 2000. Held at Gulfstream Park 1989, 1992, 1999. Held at Woodbine 1996. Held at Arlington Park 2002. Held at Lone Star Park 2004. Track record 1996. ‡Gate Dancer finished second, DQ to third, 1984. ‡Whiskey Wisdom finished third, DQ to fourth, 1997. †Denotes female.

Breeders' Cup Distaff

Grade 1 in 2006. Belmont Park, three-year-olds and up, fillies and mares, 1$\frac{1}{8}$ miles, dirt. Held October 29, 2005, with a gross value of $2,000,000. First held in 1984. First graded in 1984. Stakes record 1:46.15 (1995 Inside Information).

Year	Winner	Jockey	Second	Third	Strs	Time	1st Purse
2005	**Pleasant Home**, 4, 123	C. H. Velasquez	Society Selection, 4, 123	Ashado, 4, 123	13	1:48.34	$1,040,000
2004	**Ashado**, 3, 119	J. R. Velazquez	Storm Flag Flying, 4, 123	Stellar Jayne, 3, 119	11	1:48.26	1,040,000
2003	**Adoration**, 4, 123	P. A. Valenzuela	Elloluv, 3, 119	Got Koko, 4, 123	7	1:49.17	1,040,000
2002	**Azeri**, 4, 123	M. E. Smith	Farda Amiga, 3, 119	Imperial Gesture, 3, 119	8	1:48.64	1,040,000
2001	**Unbridled Elaine**, 3, 120	P. Day	Spain, 4, 123	Two Item Limit, 3, 120	11	1:49.21	1,227,200
2000	**Spain**, 3, 120	V. Espinoza	Surfside, 3, 120	Heritage of Gold, 5, 123	9	1:47.66	1,227,200
1999	**Beautiful Pleasure**, 4, 123	J. F. Chavez	Banshee Breeze, 4, 123	Heritage of Gold, 4, 123	8	1:47.56	1,040,000
1998	**Escena**, 5, 123	G. L. Stevens	Banshee Breeze, 3, 120	Keeper Hill, 3, 120	8	1:49.89	1,040,000
1997	**Ajina**, 3, 120	M. E. Smith	Sharp Cat, 3, 120	Escena, 4, 123	8	1:47.30	520,000
1996	**Jewel Princess**, 4, 123	C. S. Nakatani	Serena's Song, 4, 123	Different (Arg), 4, 123	6	1:48.40	520,000
1995	**Inside Information**, 4, 123	M. E. Smith	Heavenly Prize, 4, 123	Lakeway, 4, 123	10	**1:46.15**	520,000
1994	**One Dreamer**, 6, 123	G. L. Stevens	Heavenly Prize, 3, 120	Miss Dominique, 5, 123	9	1:50.70	520,000
1993	**Hollywood Wildcat**, 3, 120	E. Delahoussaye	Paseana (Arg), 6, 123	Re Toss (Arg), 6, 123	8	1:48.35	520,000
1992	**Paseana (Arg)**, 5, 123	C. J. McCarron	Versailles Treaty, 4, 123	Magical Maiden, 3, 119	14	1:48.17	520,000
1991	**Dance Smartly**, 3, 120	P. Day	Versailles Treaty, 3, 120	Brought to Mind, 4, 123	13	1:50.95	520,000
1990	**Bayakoa (Arg)**, 6, 123	L. A. Pincay Jr.	Colonial Waters, 5, 123	Valay Maid, 3, 119	7	1:49.20	450,000
1989	**Bayakoa (Arg)**, 5, 123	L. A. Pincay Jr.	Gorgeous, 3, 119	Open Mind, 3, 119	10	1:47.40	450,000
1988	**Personal Ensign**, 4, 123	R. P. Romero	Winning Colors, 3, 119	Goodbye Halo, 3, 119	9	1:52.00	450,000
1987	**Sacahuista**, 3, 119	R. P. Romero	Clabber Girl, 4, 123	Oueee Bebe, 3, 119	6	2:02.80	450,000
1986	**Lady's Secret**, 4, 123	P. Day	Fran's Valentine, 4, 123	Outstandingly, 4, 123	8	2:01.20	450,000
1985	**Life's Magic**, 4, 123	A. T. Cordero Jr.	Lady's Secret, 3, 119	Dontstop Themusic, 5, 123	7	2:02.00	450,000
1984	**Princess Rooney**, 4, 123	E. Delahoussaye	Life's Magic, 3, 119	Adored, 4, 123	7	2:02.40	450,000

Sponsored by Emirates airline of Dubai, United Arab Emirates 2005. Formerly sponsored by Nextel Communications of Reston, Virginia 2004. Held at Hollywood Park 1984, 1987, 1997. Held at Aqueduct 1985. Held at Santa Anita Park 1986, 1993, 2003. Held at Churchill Downs, 1988, 1991, 1994, 1998, 2000. Held at Gulfstream Park 1989, 1992, 1999. Held at Woodbine 1996. Held at Arlington Park 2002. Held at Lone Star Park 2004. 1$\frac{1}{4}$ miles 1984-'87.

Breeders' Cup Filly and Mare Turf

Grade 1 in 2006. Belmont Park, three-year-olds and up, fillies and mares, 1$\frac{1}{4}$ miles, turf. Held October 29, 2005, with a gross value of $1,060,000. First held in 1999. First graded in 1999. Stakes record 2:00.36 (2001 Banks Hill [GB]).

Year	Winner	Jockey	Second	Third	Strs	Time	1st Purse
2005	**Intercontinental (GB)**, 5, 123	R. Bejarano	Ouija Board (GB), 4, 123	Film Maker, 5, 123	14	2:02.34	$551,200
2004	**Ouija Board (GB)**, 3, 118	K. Fallon	Film Maker, 4, 123	Wonder Again, 5, 123	12	2:18.25	733,200
2003	**Islington (Ire)**, 4, 123	K. Fallon	L'Ancresse (Ire), 3, 118	Yesterday (Ire), 3, 118	12	1:59.13	551,200
2002	**Starine (Fr)**, 5, 123	J. R. Velazquez	Banks Hill (GB), 4, 123	Islington (Ire), 3, 118	12	2:03.57	665,600
2001	**Banks Hill (GB)**, 3, 119	O. Peslier	Spook Express (SAf), 7, 123	Spring Oak (GB), 3, 119	12	**2:00.36**	722,800
2000	**Perfect Sting**, 4, 123	J. D. Bailey	Tout Charmant, 4, 123	Catella (Ger), 4, 123	14	2:13.07	629,200
1999	**Soaring Softly**, 4, 123	J. D. Bailey	Coretta (Ire), 5, 123	Zomaradah (GB), 4, 123	14	2:13.89	556,400

Sponsored by Emirates airline of Dubai, United Arab Emirates 2005. Formerly sponsored by the Alberto-Culver Co. of Chicago, Illinois 2004. Held at Gulfstream Park 1999. Held at Churchill Downs 2000. Held at Santa Anita Park 2003. Held at Lone Star Park 2004. 1$\frac{3}{8}$ miles 1999-2000, 2004.

Breeders' Cup Juvenile

Grade 1 in 2006. Belmont Park, two-year-olds, colts and geldings, 1 1/16 miles, dirt. Held October 29, 2005, with a gross value of $1,590,000. First held in 1984. First graded in 1984. Stakes record 1:41.47 (1997 Favorite Trick).

Year	Winner	Jockey	Second	Third	Strs	Time	1st Purse
2005	**Stevie Wonderboy**, 2, 122	G. K. Gomez	Henny Hughes, 2, 122	First Samurai, 2, 122	14	1:41.64	$826,800
2004	**Wilko**, 2, 122	L. Dettori	Afleet Alex, 2, 122	Sun King, 2, 122	8	1:42.09	780,000
2003	**Action This Day**, 2, 122	D. R. Flores	Minister Eric, 2, 122	Chapel Royal, 2, 122	12	1:43.62	780,000
2002	**Vindication**, 2, 122	M. E. Smith	Kafwain, 2, 122	Hold That Tiger, 2, 122	13	1:49.61	556,400
2001	**Johannesburg**, 2, 122	M. J. Kinane	Repent, 2, 122	Siphonic, 2, 122	12	1:42.27	520,000
2000	**Macho Uno**, 2, 122	J. D. Bailey	Point Given, 2, 122	Street Cry (Ire), 2, 122	14	1:42.05	556,400
1999	**Anees**, 2, 122	G. L. Stevens	Chief Seattle, 2, 122	High Yield, 2, 122	14	1:42.29	556,400
1998	**Answer Lively**, 2, 122	J. D. Bailey	Aly's Alley, 2, 122	Cat Thief, 2, 122	13	1:44.00	520,000
1997	**Favorite Trick**, 2, 122	P. Day	Dawson's Legacy, 2, 122	Nationalore, 2, 122	8	**1:41.47**	520,000
1996	**Boston Harbor**, 2, 122	J. D. Bailey	Acceptable, 2, 122	Ordway, 2, 122	10	1:43.40	520,000
1995	**Unbridled's Song**, 2, 122	M. E. Smith	Hennessy, 2, 122	Editor's Note, 2, 122	13	1:41.60	520,000
1994	**Timber Country**, 2, 122	P. Day	Eltish, 2, 122	Tejano Run, 2, 122	13	1:44.55	520,000
1993	**Brocco**, 2, 122	G. L. Stevens	Blumin Affair, 2, 122	Tabasco Cat, 2, 122	11	1:42.99	520,000
1992	**Gilded Time**, 2, 122	C. J. McCarron	It'sali'lknownfact, 2, 122	River Special, 2, 122	13	1:43.43	520,000
1991	**Arazi**, 2, 122	P. A. Valenzuela	Bertrando, 2, 122	Snappy Landing, 2, 122	14	1:44.78	520,000
1990	**Fly So Free**, 2, 122	J. A. Santos	Take Me Out, 2, 122	Lost Mountain, 2, 122	11	1:43.40	450,000
1989	**Rhythm**, 2, 122	C. Perret	Grand Canyon, 2, 122	Slavic, 2, 122	12	1:43.60	450,000
1988	**Is It True**, 2, 122	L. A. Pincay Jr.	Easy Goer, 2, 122	Tagel, 2, 122	10	1:46.60	450,000
1987	**Success Express**, 2, 122	J. A. Santos	Regal Classic, 2, 122	Tejano, 2, 122	13	1:35.20	450,000
1986	**Capote**, 2, 122	L. A. Pincay Jr.	Qualify, 2, 122	Alysheba, 2, 122	13	1:43.80	450,000
1985	**Tasso**, 2, 122	L. A. Pincay Jr.	Storm Cat, 2, 122	Scat Dancer, 2, 122	13	1:36.20	450,000
1984	**Chief's Crown**, 2, 122	D. MacBeth	Tank's Prospect, 2, 122	Spend a Buck, 2, 122	10	1:36.20	450,000

Sponsored by Bessemer Trust of New York City 2001-'05. Held at Hollywood Park 1984, 1987, 1997. Held at Aqueduct 1985. Held at Santa Anita Park 1986, 1993, 2003. Held at Churchill Downs 1988, 1991, 1994, 1998, 2000. Held at Gulfstream Park 1989, 1992, 1999. Held at Woodbine 1996. Held at Arlington Park 2002. Held at Lone Star Park 2004. 1 mile 1984-'85, 1987. 1 1/8 miles 2002.

Breeders' Cup Juvenile Fillies

Grade 1 in 2006. Belmont Park, two-year-olds, fillies, 1 1/16 miles, dirt. Held October 29, 2005, with a gross value of $972,020. First held in 1984. First graded in 1984. Stakes record 1:41.49 (2001 Tempera).

Year	Winner	Jockey	Second	Third	Strs	Time	1st Purse
2005	**Folklore**, 2, 119	E. S. Prado	Wild Fit, 2, 119	Original Spin, 2, 119	10	1:43.85	$551,200
2004	**Sweet Catomine**, 2, 119	C. S. Nakatani	Balletto (UAE), 2, 119	Runway Model, 2, 119	12	1:41.65	520,000
2003	**Halfbridled**, 2, 119	J. A. Krone	Ashado, 2, 119	Victory U. S. A., 2, 119	14	1:42.75	520,000
2002	**Storm Flag Flying**, 2, 119	J. R. Velazquez	Composure, 2, 119	Santa Catarina, 2, 119	10	1:49.60	520,000
2001	**Tempera**, 2, 119	D. R. Flores	Imperial Gesture, 2, 119	Bella Bellucci, 2, 119	9	**1:41.49**	520,000
2000	**Caressing**, 2, 119	J. R. Velazquez	Platinum Tiara, 2, 119	She's a Devil Due, 2, 119	12	1:42.77	592,800
1999	**Cash Run**, 2, 119	J. D. Bailey	Chilukki, 2, 119	Surfside, 2, 119	9	1:43.31	520,000
1998	**Silverbulletday**, 2, 119	G. L. Stevens	Excellent Meeting, 2, 119	Three Ring, 2, 119	10	1:43.68	520,000
1997	**Countess Diana**, 2, 119	S. J. Sellers	Career Collection, 2, 119	Primaly, 2, 119	14	1:42.11	535,600
1996	**Storm Song**, 2, 119	C. Perret	Love That Jazz, 2, 119	Critical Factor, 2, 119	12	1:43.60	520,000
1995	**My Flag**, 2, 119	J. D. Bailey	Cara Rafaela, 2, 119	Golden Attraction, 2, 119	8	1:42.55	520,000
1994	**Flanders**, 2, 119	P. Day	Serena's Song, 2, 119	Stormy Blues, 2, 119	13	1:45.28	520,000
1993	**Phone Chatter**, 2, 119	L. A. Pincay Jr.	Sardula, 2, 119	Heavenly Prize, 2, 119	8	1:43.08	520,000
1992	**Eliza**, 2, 119	P. A. Valenzuela	Educated Risk, 2, 119	Boots 'n Jackie, 2, 119	12	1:42.93	520,000
1991	**Pleasant Stage**, 2, 119	E. Delahoussaye	La Spia, 2, 119	Cadillac Women, 2, 119	14	1:46.48	520,000
1990	**Meadow Star**, 2, 119	J. A. Santos	Private Treasure, 2, 119	Dance Smartly, 2, 119	13	1:44.00	450,000
1989	**Go for Wand**, 2, 119	R. P. Romero	Sweet Roberta, 2, 119	Stella Madrid, 2, 119	12	1:44.20	450,000
1988	**Open Mind**, 2, 119	A. T. Cordero Jr.	Darby Shuffle, 2, 119	Lea Lucinda, 2, 119	12	1:46.60	450,000
1987	**Epitome**, 2, 119	P. Day	Jeanne Jones, 2, 119	Dream Team, 2, 119	12	1:36.40	450,000
1986	**Brave Raj**, 2, 119	P. A. Valenzuela	Tappiano, 2, 119	Saros Brig, 2, 119	12	1:43.20	450,000
1985	**Twilight Ridge**, 2, 119	J. Velasquez	Family Style, 2, 119	Steal a Kiss, 2, 119	12	1:35.80	450,000
1984	**‡Outstandingly**, 2, 119	W. A. Guerra	Dusty Heart, 2, 119	Fine Spirit, 2, 119	11	1:37.80	450,000

Sponsored by the Alberto-Culver Co. of Chicago, Illinois 2005. Formerly sponsored by Long John Silver's of Louisville, Kentucky 2002. Held at Hollywood Park 1984, 1987, 1997. Held at Aqueduct 1985. Held at Santa Anita Park 1986, 1993, 2003. Held at Churchill Downs 1988, 1991, 1994, 1998, 2000. Held at Gulfstream Park 1989, 1992, 1999. Held at Woodbine 1996. Held at Arlington Park 2002. Held at Lone Star Park 2004. 1 mile 1984-'85, 1987. 1 1/8 miles 2002. ‡Fran's Valentine finished first, DQ to tenth, 1984.

Breeders' Cup Mile

Grade 1 in 2006. Belmont Park, three-year-olds and up, 1 mile, turf. Held October 29, 2005, with a gross value of $2,025,000. First held in 1984. First graded in 1984. Stakes record 1:32.05 (2001 Val Royal [Fr]).

Year	Winner	Jockey	Second	Third	Strs	Time	1st Purse
2005	**Artie Schiller**, 4, 126	G. K. Gomez	Leroidesanimaux (Brz), 5, 126	†Gorella (Fr), 3, 120	12	1:36.10	$1,053,000
2004	**Singletary**, 4, 126	D. R. Flores	Antonius Pius, 3, 122	†Six Perfections (Fr), 4, 123	14	1:36.90	873,600
2003	**†Six Perfections (Fr)**, 3, 119	J. D. Bailey	Touch of the Blues (Fr), 6, 126	Century City (Ire), 4, 126	13	1:33.86	780,000
2002	**Domedriver (Ire)**, 4, 126	T. Thulliez	Rock of Gibraltar (Ire), 3, 122	Good Journey, 6, 126	14	1:36.92	556,400
2001	**Val Royal (Fr)**, 5, 126	J. Valdivia Jr.	Forbidden Apple, 6, 126	Bach (Ire), 4, 126	12	**1:32.05**	592,800

2000	**War Chant**, 3, 123	G. L. Stevens	North East Bound, 4, 126	Dansili (GB), 4, 126	14	1:34.67	$608,400
1999	**Silic (Fr)**, 4, 126	C. S. Nakatani	†Tuzla (Fr), 5, 123	Docksider, 4, 126	14	1:34.26	520,000
1998	**Da Hoss**, 6, 126	J. R. Velazquez	Hawksley Hill (Ire), 5, 126	Labeeb (GB), 6, 126	14	1:35.27	520,000
1997	**Spinning World**, 4, 126	C. B. Asmussen	Geri, 5, 126	Decorated Hero (GB), 5, 126	12	1:32.77	572,000
1996	**Da Hoss**, 4, 126	G. L. Stevens	Spinning World, 3, 122	Same Old Wish, 6, 126	14	1:35.80	520,000
1995	**†Ridgewood Pearl (GB)**, 3, 119	J. P. Murtagh	Fastness (Ire), 5, 126	†Sayyedati (GB), 5, 123	13	1:43.65	520,000
1994	**Barathea (Ire)**, 4, 126	L. Dettori	Johann Quatz (Fr), 5, 126	Unfinished Symph, 3, 123	14	1:34.50	520,000
1993	**Lure**, 4, 126	M. E. Smith	†Ski Paradise, 3, 120	Fourstars Allstar, 5, 126	13	1:33.58	520,000
1992	**Lure**, 3, 122	M. E. Smith	Paradise Creek, 3, 122	Brief Truce, 3, 122	14	1:32.90	520,000
1991	**Opening Verse**, 5, 126	P. A. Valenzuela	Val des Bois (Fr), 5, 126	Star of Cozzene, 3, 123	14	1:37.59	520,000
1990	**Royal Academy**, 3, 122	L. Piggott	Itsallgreektome, 3, 122	Priolo, 3, 122	13	1:35.20	450,000
1989	**Steinlen (GB)**, 6, 126	J. A. Santos	Sabona, 7, 126	Most Welcome (GB), 5, 126	11	1:37.20	450,000
1988	**†Miesque**, 4, 123	F. Head	Steinlen (GB), 5, 126	Simply Majestic, 4, 126	12	1:38.60	450,000
1987	**†Miesque**, 3, 120	F. Head	Show Dancer, 5, 126	†Sonic Lady, 4, 123	14	1:32.80	450,000
1986	**Last Tycoon (Ire)**, 3, 123	Y. Saint-Martin	Palace Music, 5, 126	Fred Astaire, 3, 123	14	1:35.20	450,000
1985	**Cozzene**, 5, 126	W. A. Guerra	‡Al Mamoon, 4, 126	Shadeed, 3, 123	14	1:35.00	450,000
1984	**†Royal Heroine (Ire)**, 4, 123	F. Toro	Star Choice, 5, 126	Cozzene, 4, 126	10	1:32.60	450,000

Sponsored by NetJets Inc. of Woodbridge, New Jersey 2002-'05. Held at Hollywood Park 1984, 1987, 1997. Held at Aqueduct 1985. Held at Santa Anita Park 1986, 1993, 2003. Held at Churchill Downs 1988, 1991, 1994, 1998, 2000. Held at Gulfstream Park 1989, 1992, 1999. Held at Woodbine 1996. Held at Arlington Park 2002. Held at Lone Star Park 2004. ‡Palace Music finished second, DQ to ninth, 1985. Course record 1992, 1994. †Denotes female.

Breeders' Cup Sprint

Grade 1 in 2006. Belmont Park, three-year-olds and up, 6 furlongs, dirt. Held October 29, 2005, with a gross value of $1,060,000. First held in 1984. First graded in 1984. Stakes record 1:07.77 (2000 Kona Gold).

Year	Winner	Jockey	Second	Third	Strs	Time	1st Purse
2005	**Silver Train**, 3, 124	E. S. Prado	Taste of Paradise, 6, 126	Lion Tamer, 5, 126	11	1:08.86	$551,200
2004	**Speightstown**, 6, 126	J. R. Velazquez	Kela, 6, 126	My Cousin Matt, 5, 126	13	1:08.11	551,200
2003	**Cajun Beat**, 3, 123	C. H. Velasquez	Bluesthestandard, 6, 126	Shake You Down, 5, 126	13	1:07.95	613,600
2002	**Orientate**, 4, 126	J. D. Bailey	Thunderello, 3, 123	Crafty C. T., 4, 126	13	1:08.89	592,800
2001	**Squirtle Squirt**, 3, 124	J. D. Bailey	†Xtra Heat, 3, 121	Caller One, 4, 126	14	1:08.41	520,000
2000	**Kona Gold**, 6, 126	A. O. Solis	†Honest Lady, 4, 123	Bet On Sunshine, 8, 126	14	**1:07.77**	520,000
1999	**Artax**, 4, 126	J. F. Chavez	Kona Gold, 5, 126	Big Jag, 6, 126	14	1:07.89	624,000
1998	**Reraise**, 3, 124	C. S. Nakatani	Grand Slam, 3, 124	Kona Gold, 4, 126	14	1:09.07	572,000
1997	**Elmhurst**, 7, 126	C. S. Nakatani	Hesabull, 4, 126	Bet On Sunshine, 5, 126	14	1:08.01	613,600
1996	**Lit de Justice**, 6, 126	C. S. Nakatani	Paying Dues, 4, 126	Honour and Glory, 3, 123	13	1:08.60	520,000
1995	**†Desert Stormer**, 5, 123	K. Desormeaux	Mr. Greeley, 3, 123	Lit de Justice, 5, 126	13	1:09.14	520,000
1994	**Cherokee Run**, 4, 126	M. E. Smith	†Soviet Problem, 4, 123	Cardmania, 8, 126	14	1:09.54	520,000
1993	**Cardmania**, 7, 126	E. Delahoussaye	†Meafara, 4, 123	Gilded Time, 3, 124	14	1:08.76	520,000
1992	**Thirty Slews**, 5, 126	E. Delahoussaye	†Meafara, 3, 120	Rubiano, 5, 126	14	1:08.21	520,000
1991	**Sheikh Albadou (GB)**, 3, 124	P. Eddery	Pleasant Tap, 4, 126	Robyn Dancer, 4, 126	11	1:09.36	520,000
1990	**†Safely Kept**, 4, 123	C. Perret	Dayjur, 3, 123	Black Tie Affair (Ire), 4, 126	14	1:09.60	450,000
1989	**Dancing Spree**, 4, 126	A. T. Cordero Jr.	†Safely Kept, 3, 121	Dispersal, 3, 124	13	1:09.00	450,000
1988	**Gulch**, 4, 126	A. T. Cordero Jr.	Play the King, 5, 126	Afleet, 4, 126	13	1:10.40	450,000
1987	**†Very Subtle**, 3, 121	P. A. Valenzuela	Groovy, 4, 126	Exclusive Enough, 3, 124	13	1:08.80	450,000
1986	**Smile**, 4, 126	J. Vasquez	†Pine Tree Lane, 4, 123	Bedside Promise, 4, 126	9	1:08.40	450,000
1985	**Precisionist**, 4, 126	C. J. McCarron	Smile, 3, 124	Mt. Livermore, 4, 126	14	1:08.40	450,000
1984	**Eillo**, 4, 126	C. Perret	Commemorate, 3, 124	Fighting Fit, 5, 126	11	1:10.20	450,000

Sponsored by TVG Network, a subsidiary of Gemstar-TV Guide International of Pasadena, California 2005. Formerly sponsored by NAPA Auto Parts of Atlanta, Georgia 2002. Formerly sponsored by Penske Auto Center 2001. Held at Hollywood Park 1984, 1987, 1997. Held at Aqueduct 1985. Held at Gulfstream Park 1989, 1992, 1999. Held at Santa Anita Park 1986, 1993, 2003. Held at Churchill Downs 1988, 1991, 1994, 1998, 2000. Held at Woodbine 1996. Held at Arlington Park 2002. Held at Lone Star Park 2004. Equaled track record 1996, 1999. Track record 2000. †Denotes female.

Breeders' Cup Turf

Grade 1 in 2006. Belmont Park, three-year-olds and up, 1½ miles, turf. Held October 29, 2005, with a gross value of $2,280,000. First held in 1984. First graded in 1984. Stakes record 2:23.92 (1997 Chief Bearhart).

Year	Winner	Jockey	Second	Third	Strs	Time	1st Purse
2005	**Shirocco (Ger)**, 4, 126	C. Soumillon	Ace (Ire), 4, 126	Azamour (Ire), 4, 126	13	2:29.30	$1,185,600
2004	**Better Talk Now**, 5, 126	R. A. Dominguez	Kitten's Joy, 3, 121	Powerscourt (GB), 4, 126	8	2:29.70	1,040,000
2003	**dh-High Chaparral (Ire)**, 4, 126	M. J. Kinane		Falbrav (Ire), 5, 126	9	2:24.24	763,200
	dh-Johar, 4, 126	A. O. Solis					
2002	**High Chaparral (Ire)**, 3, 121	M. J. Kinane	With Anticipation, 7, 126	Falcon Flight (Fr), 6, 126	8	2:30.14	1,258,400
2001	**Fantastic Light**, 5, 126	L. Dettori	Milan (GB), 3, 121	Timboroa (GB), 5, 126	11	2:24.36	1,112,800
2000	**Kalanisi (Ire)**, 4, 126	J. P. Murtagh	Quiet Resolve, 5, 126	John's Call, 9, 126	13	2:26.96	1,289,600
1999	**Daylami (Ire)**, 5, 126	L. Dettori	Royal Anthem, 4, 126	Buck's Boy, 6, 126	14	2:24.73	1,040,000
1998	**Buck's Boy**, 5, 126	S. J. Sellers	Yagli, 5, 126	Dushyantor, 5, 126	13	2:28.74	1,040,000
1997	**Chief Bearhart**, 4, 126	J. A. Santos	†Borgia (Ger), 3, 119	Flag Down, 7, 126	11	**2:23.92**	1,040,000
1996	**Pilsudski (Ire)**, 4, 126	W. R. Swinburn	Singspiel (Ire), 4, 126	Swain (Ire), 4, 126	14	2:30.20	1,040,000
1995	**Northern Spur (Ire)**, 4, 126	C. J. McCarron	Freedom Cry (GB), 4, 126	Carnegie (Ire), 4, 126	13	2:42.07	1,040,000

1994	**Tikkanen**, 3, 122	M. E. Smith	†Hatoof, 5, 123	Paradise Creek, 5, 126	14	2:26.50	$1,040,000
1993	**Kotashaan (Fr)**, 5, 126	K. Desormeaux	Bien Bien, 4, 126	Luazur (Fr), 4, 126	14	2:25.16	1,040,000
1992	**Fraise**, 4, 126	P. A. Valenzuela	Sky Classic, 5, 126	Quest for Fame (GB), 5, 126	10	2:24.08	1,040,000
1991	**†Miss Alleged**, 4, 123	E. Legrix	Itsallgreektome, 4, 126	Quest for Fame (GB), 4, 126	13	2:30.95	1,040,000
1990	**In the Wings (GB)**, 4, 126	G. L. Stevens	With Approval, 4, 126	El Senor, 6, 126	11	2:29.60	900,000
1989	**Prized**, 3, 122	E. Delahoussaye	†Sierra Roberta (Fr), 3, 119	Star Lift (GB), 5, 126	14	2:28.00	900,000
1988	**Great Communicator**, 5, 126	R. Sibille	Sunshine Forever, 3, 122	†Indian Skimmer, 4, 123	10	2:35.20	900,000
1987	**Theatrical (Ire)**, 5, 126	P. Day	Trempolino, 3, 122	Village Star (Fr), 4, 126	14	2:24.40	900,000
1986	**Manila**, 3, 122	J. A. Santos	Theatrical (Ire), 4, 126	†Estrapade, 6, 123	9	2:25.40	900,000
1985	**†Pebbles (GB)**, 4, 123	P. Eddery	Strawberry Road (Aus), 6, 126	Mourjane (Ire), 5, 126	14	2:27.00	900,000
1984	**Lashkari (GB)**, 3, 122	Y. Saint-Martin	†All Along (Fr), 5, 123	Raami (GB), 3, 122	11	2:25.20	900,000

Sponsored by John Deere & Co. of Moline, Illinois 2002-'05. Held at Hollywood Park 1984, 1987, 1997. Held at Aqueduct 1985. Held at Santa Anita Park 1986, 1993, 2003. Held at Churchill Downs 1988, 1991, 1994, 1998, 2000. Held at Gulfstream Park 1989, 1992, 1999. Held at Woodbine 1996. Held at Arlington Park 2002. Held at Lone Star Park 2004. Dead heat for first 2003. Course record 1992. †Denotes female.

Brooklyn Handicap

Grade 2 in 2006. Belmont Park, three-year-olds and up, 1 1/8 miles, dirt. Held June 11, 2005, with a gross value of $250,000. First held in 1887. First graded in 1973. Stakes record 1:46.21 (1997 Formal Gold).

Year	Winner	Jockey	Second	Third	Strs	Time	1st Purse
2005	**Limehouse**, 4, 115	J. R. Velazquez	Gygistar, 6, 117	‡Royal Assault, 4, 112	9	1:46.69	$150,000
2004	**Seattle Fitz (Arg)**, 5, 116	R. Migliore	Dynever, 4, 117	Newfoundland, 4, 115	6	1:46.30	150,000
2003	**Iron Deputy**, 4, 114	R. Migliore	Volponi, 5, 122	Saarland, 4, 115	5	1:47.84	150,000
2002	**Seeking Daylight**, 4, 113	E. S. Prado	Country Be Gold, 5, 113	Griffinite, 4, 114	8	1:46.35	150,000
2001	**Albert the Great**, 4, 122	J. F. Chavez	Perfect Cat, 4, 115	Top Official, 6, 113	7	1:47.41	150,000
2000	**Lemon Drop Kid**, 4, 120	E. S. Prado	Lager, 6, 114	Down the Aisle, 7, 112	7	1:49.93	150,000
1999	**Running Stag**, 5, 117	S. J. Sellers	Deputy Diamond, 4, 113	Sir Bear, 6, 119	8	1:46.39	210,000
1998	**Subordination**, 4, 114	E. Coa	Sir Bear, 5, 118	Mr. Sinatra, 4, 114	11	1:46.64	180,000
1997	**Formal Gold**, 4, 119	J. D. Bailey	Stephanotis, 4, 116	Circle of Light, 4, 111	8	**1:46.21**	180,000
1996	**Wekiva Springs**, 5, 120	M. E. Smith	Mahogany Hall, 5, 114	Admiralty, 4, 111	7	1:46.78	180,000
1995	**You and I**, 4, 115	J. F. Chavez	Key Contender, 7, 112	Slick Horn, 5, 113	9	1:49.02	150,000
1994	**Devil His Due**, 5, 120	M. E. Smith	Wallenda, 4, 118	Sea Hero, 4, 119	7	1:46.71	150,000
1993	**Living Vicariously**, 3, 111	R. G. Davis	Michelle Can Pass, 5, 116	Jacksonport, 4, 111	8	2:17.80	150,000
1992	**Chief Honcho**, 5, 117	R. P. Romero	‡Valley Crossing, 4, 113	Lost Mountain, 4, 114	11	2:16.91	210,000
1991	**Timely Warning**, 6, 112	M. J. Luzzi	Chief Honcho, 4, 121	De Roche, 5, 115	8	2:14.03	210,000
1990	**‡Montubio (Arg)**, 5, 113	J. Vasquez	Mi Selecto, 5, 114	De Roche, 4, 113	7	2:28.60	241,920
1989	**Forever Silver**, 4, 116	J. Vasquez	Drapeau Tricolore, 4, 112	Jack of Clubs, 6, 112	6	2:28.60	238,560
1988	**Waquoit**, 5, 121	J. A. Santos	Personal Flag, 5, 120	Creme Fraiche, 6, 118	4	2:28.80	229,740
1987	**Waquoit**, 4, 123	C. J. McCarron	Bordeaux Bob, 4, 112	Full Courage, 4, 108	9	2:28.40	249,480
1986	**Little Missouri**, 4, 109	J. Samyn	Roo Art, 4, 118	Creme Fraiche, 4, 118	6	2:26.40	195,900
1985	**Bounding Basque**, 5, 111	A. Graell	†Life's Magic, 4, 114	Pine Circle, 4, 115	10	2:28.40	207,300
1984	**Fit to Fight**, 5, 129	J. D. Bailey	Vision, 3, 109	Dew Line, 5, 116	8	2:27.40	201,600
1983	**Highland Blade**, 5, 117	J. Vasquez	Sing Sing, 5, 118	Silver Supreme, 5, 113	13	2:31.00	172,800
1982	**Silver Supreme**, 4, 111	A. T. Cordero Jr.	Princelet, 4, 112	Baltimore Canyon, 4, 113	6	2:29.40	131,700
1981	**Hechizado (Arg)**, 5, 116	R. Hernandez	The Liberal Member, 6, 113	Peat Moss, 6, 111	10	2:26.00	138,300
1980	**Winter's Tale**, 4, 120	J. Fell	State Dinner, 5, 121	Ring of Light, 5, 114	5	2:28.60	130,200
1979	**The Liberal Member**, 4, 114	R. I. Encinas	Bowl Game, 5, 119	State Dinner, 4, 123	5	2:28.80	99,000
1978	**Nasty and Bold**, 3, 112	J. Samyn	Father Hogan, 5, 116	Great Contractor, 5, 122	7	2:26.00	63,900
1977	**Great Contractor**, 4, 112	A. T. Cordero Jr.	Forego, 7, 137	American History, 5, 112	13	2:26.20	66,660
1976	**Forego**, 6, 134	H. Gustines	Lord Rebeau, 5, 114	Foolish Pleasure, 4, 126	8	2:01.20	67,860
1975	**Forego**, 5, 132	H. Gustines	Monetary Principle, 5, 109	Stop the Music, 5, 121	8	1:59.80	66,780
1974	**Forego**, 4, 129	H. Gustines	Billy Come Lately, 4, 114	Arbees Boy, 4, 116	7	1:54.80	66,600
1973	**Riva Ridge**, 4, 127	R. Turcotte	True Knight, 4, 117	Tentam, 4, 119	7	1:52.40	67,200

Named for the Brooklyn borough of New York City. Grade 1 1973-'92. Held at Gravesend Park 1887-1910. Held at Aqueduct 1914-'44, 1946-'55, 1960-'74, 1991-'93. Held at Jamaica 1956-'59. Not held 1911-'12. 1 1/4 miles 1887-1914, 1940-'55, 1960-'71, 1975-'76. 1 3/16 miles 1956-'59, 1972-'74. 1 3/8 miles 1991-'93. 1 1/2 miles 1977-'90. ‡Mi Selecto finished first, DQ to second, 1990. ‡Lost Mountain finished second, DQ to third, 1992. ‡Cuba finished third, DQ to fifth, 2005. World record 1973. Track record 1973, 1975. †Denotes female.

Buena Vista Handicap

Grade 2 in 2006. Santa Anita Park, four-year-olds and up, fillies and mares, 1 mile, turf. Held February 20, 2006, with a gross value of $150,000. First held in 1988. First graded in 1990. Stakes record 1:33.48 (1992 Gold Fleece [1st Div.]; 1997 Media Nox [GB]).

Year	Winner	Jockey	Second	Third	Strs	Time	1st Purse
2006	**Silver Cup (Ire)**, 4, 116	V. Espinoza	Elusive Diva, 5, 118	Mirabilis, 4, 118	11	1:34.92	$90,000
2005	**Uraib (Ire)**, 5, 115	J. K. Court	Resplendency, 4, 117	Elusive Diva, 4, 116	5	1:33.72	90,000
2004	**Fun House**, 5, 116	G. L. Stevens	Katdogawn (GB), 4, 117	Fudge Fatale, 4, 116	7	1:36.13	90,000
2003	**Final Destination (NZ)**, 5, 115	V. Espinoza	Garden in the Rain (Fr), 6, 115	Embassy Belle (Ire), 5, 116	6	1:35.99	90,000
2002	**Blue Moon (Fr)**, 5, 113	B. Blanc	Queen of Wilshire, 6, 116	Old Money (Aus), 5, 118	7	1:35.54	90,000
2001	**Rare Charmer**, 6, 115	L. A. Pincay Jr.	Elegant Ridge (Ire), 6, 117	Uncharted Haven (GB), 4, 116	11	1:36.67	90,000
2000	**Lexa (Fr)**, 6, 115	B. Blanc	Here's to You, 4, 114	Sierra Virgen, 5, 114	6	1:36.17	97,290
1999	**Tuzla (Fr)**, 5, 120	C. S. Nakatani	Supercilious, 6, 117	Green Jewel (GB), 5, 116	5	1:35.79	90,000

1998	**Dance Parade**, 4, 116	K. Desormeaux	Shake the Yoke (GB), 5, 116	Donna Viola (GB), 6, 121	10	1:36.03	$101,520
1997	**Media Nox (GB)**, 4, 115	C. S. Nakatani	Traces of Gold, 5, 115	Grafin, 6, 116	12	**1:33.48**	85,250
1996	**Matiara**, 4, 119	G. L. Stevens	Real Connection, 5, 114	Dirca (Ire), 4, 116	8	1:35.74	81,800
1995	**Lyin to the Moon**, 6, 116	K. Desormeaux	Jacodra's Devil, 4, 115	Exchange, 7, 122	5	1:36.77	61,700
1994	**‡Skimble**, 5, 118	C. S. Nakatani	Hero's Love, 6, 121	Possibly Perfect, 4, 120	9	1:34.85	66,300
1993	**Marble Maiden (GB)**, 4, 118	K. Desormeaux	Suivi, 4, 117	Party Cited, 4, 116	7	1:36.23	65,000
1992	**Gold Fleece**, 4, 114	A. O. Solis	Elegance, 5, 115	Danzante, 4, 114	9	**1:33.48**	52,100
	Appealing Missy, 5, 117	C. J. McCarron	Exchange, 4, 120	Re Toss (Arg), 5, 117	9	1:34.25	52,100
1991	**Taffeta and Tulle**, 5, 120	C. J. McCarron	Bequest, 5, 117	Somethingmerry, 4, 114	9	1:34.30	67,200
1990	**Saros Brig**, 6, 116	P. A. Valenzuela	Royal Touch (Ire), 5, 123	Nikishka, 5, 118	10	1:34.20	68,100
1989	**Annoconnor**, 5, 121	C. A. Black	Daring Doone (GB), 6, 112	Daloma (Fr), 5, 116	8	1:36.40	65,800
1988	**Davie's Lamb**, 4, 117	F. Toro	Sly Charmer, 4, 114	Pen Bal Lady (GB), 4, 119	9	1:39.00	63,050

Named for two 19th-century California ranchos named Buena Vista Rancho; buena vista means "good view." Grade 3 1990-'94, 2005. Dirt 2005. Originally scheduled on turf 2005. Two divisions 1992. ‡Lady Blessington (Fr) finished first, DQ to ninth, 1994.

Calder Derby

Grade 3 in 2006. Calder Race Course, three-year-olds, $1\frac{1}{8}$ miles, dirt (originally scheduled as a Grade 3 on the turf). Held October 15, 2005, with a gross value of $200,000. First held in 1972. First graded in 1996. Stakes record 1:47.70 (1998 Crowd Pleaser).

Year	Winner	Jockey	Second	Third	Strs	Time	1st Purse
2005	**Dazzling Dr. Cevin**, 3, 115	J. A. Garcia	Dream On Dream On, 3, 117	Talented Prince, 3, 115	7	1:52.44	$120,000
2004	**Eddington**, 3, 114	E. Coa	Bob's Proud Moment, 3, 116	‡Caballero Negro, 3, 114	12	1:51.25	120,000
2003	**Stroll**, 3, 122	J. D. Bailey	Certifiably Crazy, 3, 115	Super Frolic, 3, 119	9	1:48.39	120,000
2002	**Union Place**, 3, 115	E. Coa	Miesque's Approval, 3, 122	The Judge Sez Who, 3, 122	11	1:47.76	120,000
2001	**Western Pride**, 3, 122	D. G. Whitney	Tour of the Cat, 3, 113	Built Up, 3, 117	10	1:51.12	120,000
2000	**Whata Brainstorm**, 3, 122	R. Homeister Jr.	Muntej (GB), 3, 122	Womble, 3, 117	12	1:47.80	120,000
1999	**Isaypete**, 3, 122	J. C. Ferrer	Rhythmean, 3, 117	Phi Beta Doc, 3, 122	12	1:50.01	120,000
1998	**Crowd Pleaser**, 3, 122	J. Samyn	Stay Sound, 3, 122	The Kaiser, 3, 117	10	**1:47.70**	120,000
1997	**Blazing Sword**, 3, 117	G. Boulanger	dh-Royal Tuneup, 3, 117 dh-Topaz Runner, 3, 117		10	1:53.15	90,000
1996	**Laughing Dan**, 3, 117	P. A. Rodriguez	Sea Horse, 3, 117	†Flying Concert, 3, 114	11	1:50.75	66,300
1995	**Pineing Patty**, 3, 122	L. J. Melancon	Sea Emperor, 3, 122	Mucha Mosca, 3, 117	7	1:51.40	60,000
1994	**Halo's Image**, 3, 117	G. Boulanger	Honest Colors, 3, 117	Rocky's Halo, 3, 117	10	1:52.38	90,000
1993	**Medieval Mac**, 3, 113	M. Russ	Raise an Alarm, 3, 113	Fight for Love, 3, 116	9	1:41.79	30,000
1992	**Birdonthewire**, 3, 112	M. T. Hunter	Shahpour, 3, 113	Ponche, 3, 111	7	1:44.36	30,000
1991	**Scottish Ice**, 3, 113	R. N. Lester	Chihuahua, 3, 120	Jackie Wackie, 3, 121	9	1:46.10	33,450
1990	**Zalipour**, 3, 118	D. A. Acevedo	Country Isle, 3, 115	Rowdy Regal, 3, 114	7	1:46.60	32,580
1989	**‡Silver Sunsets**, 3, 114	M. A. Gonzalez	Compuquine, 3, 114	Run for Your Honey, 3, 111	6	1:45.80	32,190
1988	**Frosty the Snowman**, 3, 116	D. Valiente	In the Slammer, 3, 116	Distinctintentions, 3, 112	7	1:44.40	30,750
1987	**Schism**, 3, 117	R. N. Lester	Slewdonza, 3, 112	Fabulous Devotion, 3, 114	6	1:47.20	32,640
1986	**Annapolis John**, 3, 120	J. A. Velez Jr.	Kid Colin, 3, 115	Real Forest, 3, 118	7	1:46.20	28,160
1985	**Gray Haze**, 3, 115	F. A. Pennisi	Alfred, 3, 115	Jeblar, 3, 115	11	1:46.00	33,780
1984	**Opening Lead**, 4, 114	J. A. Santos	Ward Off Trouble, 4, 114	Darn That Alarm, 3, 112	14	1:47.60	34,860
1983	**Opening Lead**, 3, 117	B. Gonzalez	The Cerfer, 3, 112	Neutral Player, 3, 112	12	1:48.20	20,640
1982	**Glorious Past**, 3, 115	A. Smith Jr.	Count Rebeau, 3, 115	Ell's New Canaan, 3, 112	9	1:45.80	19,905
1981	**Poking**, 5, 122	G. Cohen	Yosi Boy, 5, 114	Pair of Deuces, 3, 112	10	1:53.40	23,415
1980	**J. Rodney G.**, 5, 113	F. Verardi	Two's a Plenty, 3, 109	Cherry Pop, 4, 125	8	1:53.20	23,040
1979	**Breezy Fire**, 4, 118	M. A. Rivera	Abba Cap, 5, 115	Selma's Boy, 4, 117	9	1:52.00	16,665
1978	**Ole Wilk**, 4, 114	I. J. Jimenez	America Behave, 4, 110	Classy State, 5, 115	10	1:42.60	18,600
1977	**What a Threat**, 5, 117	R. Gaffalione	†Noble Royalty, 4, 116	Lightning Thrust, 4, 122	8	1:42.60	17,400
1976	**Chilean Chief**, 5, 118	J. Imparato	El Rosillo, 3, 112	L. Grant Jr., 6, 116	9	1:45.80	17,700
1975	**dh-*Rimsky II**, 4, 116 **dh-Strand of Gold**, 5, 112	A. Haldar P. Nicolo		Plagiarize, 4, 121	12	1:42.20	12,400
1974	**‡Amberbee**, 6, 117	J. Garrido	Enchanted Ruler, 3, 112	Seminole Joe, 6, 113	9	1:46.60	14,280
1973	**Willmar**, 5, 122	G. St. Leon	Sea Phantom, 5, 118	†Hickory Gray, 4, 115	8	1:25.20	7,020

Formerly named for Hollywood, Florida, hometown of real-estate developer Stephen Calder, who built Calder Race Course. Not graded 1998-'99, 2001, 2005. Hollywood H. 1972-'81, 1984, 1987-'93. Hollywood S. 1982-'83, 1985-'86. Calder Breeders' Cup Derby 1996. 7 furlongs 1972-'73. $1\frac{1}{16}$ miles 1974-'78, 1982-'92. 1 mile 70 yards 1993. Dirt 1972-'74, 1976, 1979-'97, 2001, 2005. Originally scheduled on turf 2001, 2005. Three-year-olds and up 1972-'81, 1984. Dead heat for first 1975. Dead heat for second 1997. ‡Snurb finished first, DQ to seventh, 1974. ‡Big Stanley finished first, DQ to sixth, 1989. ‡Capias finished third, DQ to 12th, 2004. Track record 1993. †Denotes female.

Californian Stakes

Grade 2 in 2006. Hollywood Park, three-year-olds and up, $1\frac{1}{8}$ miles, dirt. Held June 18, 2005, with a gross value of $250,000. First held in 1954. First graded in 1973. Stakes record 1:45.80 (1980 Spectacular Bid).

Year	Winner	Jockey	Second	Third	Strs	Time	1st Purse
2005	**Lava Man**, 4, 118	P. A. Valenzuela	Anziyan Royalty, 5, 117	Skukuza, 5, 116	7	1:47.83	$150,000
2004	**Even the Score**, 6, 118	D. R. Flores	Total Impact (Chi), 6, 116	Nose The Trade (GB), 6, 116	8	1:47.64	150,000
2003	**Kudos**, 6, 116	A. O. Solis	Piensa Sonando (Chi), 5, 118	Reba's Gold, 6, 118	7	1:47.91	240,000
2002	**Milwaukee Brew**, 5, 122	K. Desormeaux	Bosque Redondo, 5, 118	Momentum, 4, 118	8	1:48.06	300,000
2001	**Skimming**, 5, 116	G. K. Gomez	Futural, 5, 120	Aptitude, 4, 116	8	1:48.12	300,000
2000	**Big Ten (Chi)**, 5, 116	A. O. Solis	Early Pioneer, 5, 118	Mojave Moon, 4, 116	5	1:49.22	150,000

1999	**Old Trieste**, 4, 116	C. J. McCarron	Budroyale, 6, 120	Puerto Madero (Chi), 5, 122	7	1:46.55	$180,000
1998	**Mud Route**, 4, 116	C. J. McCarron	Deputy Commander, 4, 122	Worldly Ways (GB), 4, 117	6	1:48.00	150,000
1997	**River Keen (Ire)**, 5, 117	K. Desormeaux	Hesabull, 4, 118	Benchmark, 6, 118	6	1:47.38	150,000
1996	**Tinners Way**, 6, 116	E. Delahoussaye	Helmsman, 4, 122	Mr Purple, 4, 122	4	1:46.60	151,980
1995	**Concern**, 4, 122	M. E. Smith	Tossofthecoin, 5, 118	Tinners Way, 5, 116	8	1:47.74	160,900
1994	**The Wicked North**, 5, 120	K. Desormeaux	Kingdom Found, 4, 116	Slew of Damascus, 6, 116	7	1:46.68	165,000
1993	**Latin American**, 5, 116	G. L. Stevens	Missionary Ridge (GB), 6, 116	Memo (Chi), 6, 118	7	1:46.92	220,000
1992	**Another Review**, 4, 119	K. Desormeaux	Defensive Play, 5, 120	Ibero (Arg), 5, 119	7	1:48.11	119,400
1991	**Roanoke**, 4, 116	E. Delahoussaye	Anshan (GB), 4, 118	Marquetry, 4, 113	10	1:48.30	175,600
1990	**Sunday Silence**, 4, 126	P. A. Valenzuela	Stylish Winner, 6, 115	Charlatan (Chi), 5, 111	3	1:48.00	168,400
1989	**Sabona**, 7, 115	C. J. McCarron	Blushing John, 4, 124	Lively One, 4, 118	6	1:46.80	185,800
1988	**Cutlass Reality**, 6, 115	C. J. McCarron	Gulch, 4, 126	Judge Angelucci, 5, 126	4	1:47.60	180,200
1987	**Judge Angelucci**, 4, 118	G. Baze	Iron Eyes, 4, 115	Snow Chief, 4, 126	8	1:48.20	193,200
1986	**Precisionist**, 5, 126	C. J. McCarron	Super Diamond, 6, 117	Skywalker, 4, 121	7	1:33.60	188,400
1985	**Greinton (GB)**, 4, 119	L. A. Pincay Jr.	Precisionist, 4, 126	Lord At War (Arg), 5, 126	4	1:32.60	179,600
1984	**Desert Wine**, 4, 121	E. Delahoussaye	Interco, 4, 126	Sari's Dreamer, 5, 116	8	1:47.60	193,600
1983	**The Wonder (Fr)**, 5, 119	W. Shoemaker	Prince Spellbound, 4, 122	Poley, 4, 117	8	1:48.40	192,000
1982	**Erins Isle (Ire)**, 4, 117	L. A. Pincay Jr.	It's the One, 4, 128	Major Sport, 5, 118	10	1:48.00	200,200
1981	**Eleven Stitches**, 4, 122	S. Hawley	Temperence Hill, 4, 130	†Kilijaro (Ire), 5, 123	12	1:48.40	207,600
1980	**Spectacular Bid**, 4, 130	W. Shoemaker	Paint King, 4, 115	Caro Bambino (Ire), 5, 118	7	**1:45.80**	184,450
1979	**Affirmed**, 4, 130	L. A. Pincay Jr.	Syncopate, 4, 114	Harry's Love, 4, 117	8	1:41.20	159,900
1978	**J. O. Tobin**, 4, 126	S. Cauthen	Replant, 4, 120	Cox's Ridge, 4, 127	6	1:41.00	124,550
1977	**Crystal Water**, 4, 128	L. A. Pincay Jr.	Mark's Place, 5, 121	Ancient Title, 7, 123	6	1:41.00	65,300
1976	**Ancient Title**, 6, 127	S. Hawley	Pay Tribute, 4, 117	Austin Mittler, 4, 116	6	1:41.20	65,300
1975	**Ancient Title**, 5, 126	L. A. Pincay Jr.	Big Band, 5, 117	Century's Envoy, 4, 117	10	1:40.20	73,100
1974	**Quack**, 5, 126	D. Pierce	Ancient Title, 4, 126	Woodland Pines, 5, 120	9	1:40.20	70,900
1973	**Quack**, 4, 126	D. Pierce	Royal Owl, 4, 125	Tri Jet, 4, 118	6	1:41.40	65,300

Named in honor of the residents of the state of California. Grade 1 1973-'96. $1\frac{1}{16}$ miles 1954-'79. Track record 1980. †Denotes female.

Cardinal Handicap

Grade 3 in 2006. Churchill Downs, three-year-olds and up, fillies and mares, $1\frac{1}{8}$ miles, turf. Held November 19, 2005, with a gross value of $175,050. First held in 1974. First graded in 1995. Stakes record 1:47.81 (1996 Bail Out Becky [DQ to second]).

Year	Winner	Jockey	Second	Third	Strs	Time	1st Purse
2005	**Sundrop (Jpn)**, 4, 117	M. Guidry	Delta Princess, 6, 118	Finery, 5, 116	12	1:50.10	$108,531
2004	**Aud**, 4, 115	B. Blanc	May Gator, 5, 117	Angela's Love, 4, 114	11	1:53.94	107,601
2003	**Riskaverse**, 4, 118	C. H. Velasquez	Bien Nicole, 5, 120	Firth of Lorne (Ire), 4, 116	12	1:50.53	108,624
2002	**Quick Tip**, 4, 114	R. Albarado	San Dare, 4, 114	Bien Nicole, 4, 118	10	1:51.08	107,322
2001	**Watch**, 4, 114	C. Perret	Sitka, 4, 111	Gino's Spirits (GB), 5, 118	9	1:49.12	104,997
2000	**Illiquidity**, 4, 115	J. K. Court	License Fee, 5, 118	Miss of Wales (Chi), 5, 114	12	1:49.72	109,182
1999	**Pratella**, 4, 114	B. Peck	Mingling Glances, 5, 116	Uanme, 4, 112	9	1:48.88	106,299
1998	**B. A. Valentine**, 5, 115	J. F. Chavez	Mingling Glances, 4, 112	Cuando, 4, 116	13	1:48.62	111,693
1997	**Colcon**, 4, 114	J. D. Bailey	Dance Clear (Ire), 4, 112	Sagar Pride (Ire), 4, 113	12	1:51.89	108,903
1996	**‡Miss Caerleona (Fr)**, 4, 114	L. J. Melancon	Bail Out Becky, 4, 121	Striesen, 4, 113	12	**1:47.81**	72,850
1995	**Apolda**, 4, 114	P. Day	Alive With Hope, 4, 114	Lady Reiko (Ire), 4, 115	11	1:49.59	75,530
1994	**Bold Ruritana**, 4, 116	P. Day	Eternal Reve, 3, 117	Monaassabaat, 3, 113	11	1:48.25	76,375
1993	**River Ball (Arg)**, 7, 109	J. Parsley	Marshua's River, 6, 112	Logan's Mist, 4, 118	9	1:55.79	74,945
1992	**Auto Dial**, 4, 113	S. J. Sellers	Radiant Ring, 4, 119	Red Journey, 4, 114	5	1:52.04	71,500
1991	**Christiecat**, 4, 118	A. T. Cordero Jr.	Super Fan, 4, 115	Screen Prospect, 4, 113	9	1:51.10	75,010
1990	**Dance for Lucy**, 4, 113	D. Penna	Betty Lobelia, 5, 114	Phoenix Sunshine, 5, 113	10	1:51.80	39,033
	Lady in Silver, 4, 122	P. Day	Coolawin, 4, 121	Splendid Try, 4, 112	8	1:51.40	38,789
1989	**Townsend Lass**, 4, 114	K. K. Allen	Bangkok Lady, 3, 112	Bearly Cooking, 6, 114	8	1:52.00	57,233
1988	**Top Corsage**, 5, 118	P. A. Valenzuela	Savannah's Honor, 3, 116	Graceful Darby, 4, 119	8	1:52.40	36,823
1987	**Lake Champlain (Ire)**, 4, 119	P. Day	Marianna's Girl, 4, 113	Shot Gun Bonnie, 3, 119	10	1:46.20	37,440
1986	**Oriental**, 4, 123	K. K. Allen	Kapalua Butterfly, 5, 112	Glorious View, 4, 120	13	1:45.80	31,281
1985	**Mrs. Revere**, 4, 112	L. J. Melancon	Wealthy and Wise, 3, 113	My Inheritance, 3, 112	8	1:48.20	22,219
	Mr. T.'s Tune, 4, 118	K. K. Allen	Gerrie Singer, 4, 115	Adaptable, 4, 112	8	1:47.40	22,219
1984	**Electric Fanny**, 3, 112	J. C. Espinoza	Straight Edition, 4, 115	Mickey's Echo, 5, 120	8	1:48.00	21,271
1983	**Charge My Account**, 4, 112	P. Day	Heatherten, 4, 123	Etoile Du Matin, 4, 115	10	1:47.20	18,801
1982	**Betty Money**, 3, 116	B. Sayler	Raja's Delight, 4, 112	Mezimica, 4, 112	15	1:38.80	20,792
	Promising Native, 3, 114	S. Maple	What Glitter, 4, 112	Sweetest Chant, 4, 123	13	1:39.60	20,629
1981	**Knights Beauty**, 4, 115	T. W. Hightower	Deuces Over Seven, 4, 117	Roger's Turn, 3, 115	15	1:24.80	20,768
	Safe Play, 3, 122	S. A. Spencer	Lillian Russell, 4, 122	La Vue, 4, 119	10	1:24.20	18,330
1980	**Vite View**, 4, 120	D. Brumfield	Doing It My Way, 4, 120	Jeanie's Fancy, 4, 117	8	1:24.80	19,581
	Champagne Ginny, 3, 119	D. Brumfield	Impetuous Gal, 5, 122	Red Chiffon, 3, 114	9	1:24.60	18,119
1979	**Impetuous Gal**, 4, 116	E. Fires	Billy Jane, 3, 114	Cookie Puddin, 3, 113	9	1:24.60	18,021
	Gap Axe, 4, 115	D. Brumfield	Unreality, 5, 120	Honey Blonde, 4, 112	8	1:24.80	19,484
1978	**Love to Tell**, 3, 116	E. Delahoussaye	Selari's Choice, 4, 112	Bit of Sunshine, 4, 112	8	1:24.40	17,883
	Unreality, 4, 123	L. P. Suire	Navajo Princess, 4, 123	Irish Agate, 3, 111	9	1:24.20	18,046
1977	**Likely Exchange**, 3, 114	J. McKnight	My Compliments, 5, 113	My Bold Beauty, 3, 114	8	1:24.80	14,675
	Famed Princess, 4, 113	C. Ledezma	Chatta, 3, 114	Leigh Simms, 4, 113	9	1:24.80	14,836
1976	**Hope of Glory**, 4, 114	D. Brumfield	Bronze Point, 3, 115	Straight, 4, 116	8	1:25.00	14,666
	Vivacious Meg, 4, 114	R. Breen	Regal Gal, 3, 115	Regal Rumor, 4, 119	8	1:25.40	14,666

1975	**Visier**, 3, 116	R. Riera Jr.	Slade's Prospect, 3, 116	Ski Run, 3, 116	6	1:45.80	$17,225
1974	**Cut the Talk**, 3, 116	D. Brown	Holding Pattern, 3, 126	Sturdy Steel, 3, 116	7	1:45.20	14,349

Named for Kentucky's state bird. Kentucky Cardinal S. 1974-'75, 1983-'85. Kentucky Cardinal H. 1976-'82. Cardinal S. 1986. 1$^{1}/_{16}$ miles 1974-'75, 1983-'87. 7 furlongs 1976-'81. 1 mile 1982. Dirt 1974-'86, 1988, 1992. Three-year-olds 1974-'75. Both sexes 1974-'75. Two divisions 1976-'82, 1985, 1990. ‡Bail Out Becky finished first, DQ to second, 1996.

Carleton F. Burke Handicap

Grade 3 in 2006. Oak Tree at Santa Anita, three-year-olds and up, 1$^{1}/_{2}$ miles, turf. Held October 30, 2005, with a gross value of $100,000. First held in 1969. First graded in 1973. Stakes record 2:24.24 (1996 Dernier Empereur).

Year	Winner	Jockey	Second	Third	Strs	Time	1st Purse
2005	**Golden Rahy**, 6, 115	A. O. Solis	Wild Buddy, 6, 114	†Stage Shy, 5, 118	6	2:27.02	$60,000
2004	**Habaneros**, 5, 116	D. R. Flores	Pellegrino (Brz), 5, 116	Gallant (GB), 7, 113	8	2:26.91	60,000
2003	**Runaway Dancer**, 4, 112	M. E. Smith	Labirinto, 5, 116	Senor Swinger, 3, 114	9	2:28.38	83,550
2002	**Special Matter**, 4, 110	T. Baze	Alyzig, 5, 113	Dance Dreamer, 4, 117	5	2:28.47	90,000
2001	**Cagney (Brz)**, 4, 116	M. E. Smith	Kerrygold (Fr), 5, 116	Northern Quest (Fr), 6, 118	9	2:26.10	90,000
2000	**Timboroa (GB)**, 4, 114	D. R. Flores	dh-Kerrygold (Fr), 4, 116 dh-Res Judicata (GB), 5, 115		9	2:27.91	84,990
1999	**Public Purse**, 5, 119	A. O. Solis	Star Performance, 6, 115	Achilles (GB), 4, 115	8	2:25.83	90,000
1998	**Perim (Fr)**, 5, 113	B. Blanc	Single Empire (Ire), 4, 116	Rate Cut, 4, 114	9	2:29.29	75,000
1997	**Prussian Blue**, 5, 117	K. Desormeaux	Embraceable You (Fr), 4, 116	Kessem Power (NZ), 5, 114	7	2:31.37	75,000
1996	**Dernier Empereur**, 6, 118	C. J. McCarron	Bon Point (GB), 6, 118	Party Season (GB), 5, 116	8	**2:24.24**	98,750
1995	**Varadavour (Ire)**, 6, 115	A. O. Solis	Patio de Naranjos (Chi), 4, 117	Raintrap (GB), 5, 116	7	2:30.27	90,350
1994	**Savinio**, 4, 114	C. J. McCarron	Square Cut, 5, 114	Sir Mark Sykes (Ire), 5, 117	8	2:02.69	95,700
1993	**Know Heights (Ire)**, 4, 117	K. Desormeaux	Fanmore, 5, 116	Myrakalu (Fr), 5, 114	7	2:00.07	96,000
1992	**Missionary Ridge (GB)**, 5, 117	K. Desormeaux	Carnival Baby, 4, 112	Myrakalu (Fr), 4, 113	9	2:00.89	98,000
1991	**Super May**, 5, 117	C. S. Nakatani	Algenib (Arg), 4, 121	Pride of Araby, 5, 112	9	1:58.58	103,700
1990	**‡Ultrasonido (Arg)**, 5, 114	C. J. McCarron	Rial (Arg), 5, 118	Eradicate (GB), 5, 117	8	1:59.80	129,400
1989	**Alwuhush**, 4, 120	J. A. Santos	Frankly Perfect, 4, 122	Speedratic, 4, 115	10	1:58.00	134,400
1988	**Nasr El Arab**, 3, 121	G. L. Stevens	Northern Provider, 6, 112	Trokhos, 5, 115	9	2:01.00	133,000
1987	**Rivlia**, 5, 121	L. A. Pincay Jr.	Captain Vigors, 5, 116	Circus Prince, 4, 115	10	2:03.20	102,500
1986	**Louis Le Grand**, 4, 115	W. Shoemaker	Schiller, 4, 114	Silveyville, 8, 120	10	2:01.20	133,700
1985	**Tsunami Slew**, 4, 121	G. L. Stevens	Yashgan (GB), 4, 121	Best of Both, 5, 115	7	1:59.60	78,500
1984	**Silveyville**, 6, 117	C. J. McCarron	Gordian (GB), 4, 115	Gato Del Sol, 5, 121	7	1:59.60	64,100
1983	**Bel Bolide**, 5, 122	T. Lipham	Travelling Victor, 4, 118	Bold Run (Fr), 4, 118	7	2:01.20	64,200
1982	**Mehmet**, 4, 117	E. Delahoussaye	Craelius, 3, 114	It's the One, 4, 124	7	1:58.60	63,600
1981	**Spence Bay (Ire)**, 6, 120	F. Toro	Providential (Ire), 4, 121	Super Moment, 4, 121	10	2:00.60	67,200
1980	**Bold Tropic (SAf)**, 5, 125	W. Shoemaker	Balzac, 5, 121	Shagbark, 5, 116	7	1:58.20	49,300
1979	**Silver Eagle (Ire)**, 5, 115	F. Toro	John Henry, 4, 118	Shagbark, 4, 118	9	1:59.20	50,200
1978	**Star of Erin (Ire)**, 4, 113	W. Shoemaker	Improviser, 6, 115	Mr. Redoy, 4, 118	9	1:59.00	38,400
	Palton (Chi), 5, 122	H. E. Moreno	Star Spangled, 4, 118	Lunar Probe (NZ), 4, 114	9	1:59.00	38,400
1977	**Double Discount**, 4, 116	F. Mena	No Turning, 4, 118	Vigors, 4, 120	8	1:57.40	33,000
1976	**King Pellinore**, 4, 124	W. Shoemaker	*Royal Derby II, 7, 116	George Navonod, 4, 115	8	1:57.60	33,300
1975	**Top Command**, 4, 113	W. Shoemaker	Against the Snow, 5, 116	Top Crowd, 4, 116	6	2:01.20	24,875
	Kirrary, 5, 114	F. Mena	Buffalo Lark, 5, 121	†*Dulcia, 6, 117	6	2:00.40	24,875
1974	**†Tallahto**, 4, 120	L. A. Pincay Jr.	High Protein, 4, 117	Scantling, 4, 117	6	1:59.00	32,300
1973	**‡Kentuckian**, 4, 117	D. Pierce	Wing Out, 5, 119	†Le Cle, 4, 116	8	1:59.00	33,400

Named for Carleton F. Burke (1882-1962), first chairman of the California Horse Racing Board. Grade 2 1973-'84, 1990-'97. Grade 1 1985-'89. Carleton F. Burke Invitational H. 1969-'70. 1$^{1}/_{4}$ miles 1969-'94. About 1$^{1}/_{2}$ miles 2000. Two divisions 1975, 1978. Dead heat for second 2000. ‡Groshawk finished first, DQ to fifth, 1973. ‡Rial (Arg) finished first, DQ to second, 1990. †Denotes female.

Carry Back Stakes

Grade 2 in 2006. Calder Race Course, three-year-olds, 6 furlongs, dirt. Held July 10, 2005, with a gross value of $300,000. First held in 1970. First graded in 2003. Stakes record 1:09.30 (2005 Lost in the Fog).

Year	Winner	Jockey	Second	Third	Strs	Time	1st Purse
2005	**Lost in the Fog**, 3, 122	R. A. Baze	Qureall, 3, 115	Hot Space, 3, 115	6	**1:09.30**	$177,000
2004	**Weigelia**, 3, 117	A. Toribio Jr.	Classy Migration, 3, 112	Bwana Charlie, 3, 119	11	1:10.50	177,000
2003	**Valid Video**, 3, 122	J. Bravo	Cajun Beat, 3, 117	Super Fuse, 3, 117	10	1:10.15	177,000
2002	**Royal Lad**, 3, 117	J. D. Bailey	Captain Squire, 3, 122	Friendly Frolic, 3, 114	9	1:10.73	150,000
2001	**Illusioned**, 3, 117	J. F. Chavez	Beyond Brilliant, 3, 117	Gallant Frolic, 3, 115	10	1:11.08	150,000
2000	**Caller One**, 3, 122	C. S. Nakatani	Fappie's Notebook, 3, 115	Malagot, 3, 115	9	1:10.35	120,000
1999	**Silver Season**, 3, 112	E. Coa	Deep Gold, 3, 117	Night Patrol, 3, 117	9	1:11.32	120,000
1998	**Mint**, 3, 115	E. Coa	Diamond Studs, 3, 115	Mt. Laurel, 3, 112	8	1:11.38	120,000
1997	**Renteria**, 3, 115	E. Coa	Red, 3, 122	Willow Skips Trial, 3, 115	11	1:11.28	120,000
1996	**Fortunate Review**, 3, 117	A. Toribio	Betweenhereorthere, 3, 115	Night Runner, 3, 113	12	1:23.27	60,000
1995	**Sonic Signal**, 3, 115	R. R. Douglas	Leave'm Inthedark, 3, 117	Too Great, 3, 113	10	1:24.79	60,000
1994	**Score a Birdie**, 3, 115	H. Castillo Jr.	Fortunate Joe, 3, 112	Ali'Ibito'reality, 3, 114	7	1:24.09	60,000
1993	**Humbugaboo**, 3, 112	M. Russ	Signoir Valery, 3, 112	Kassec, 3, 113	8	1:22.74	60,000
1992	**Always Silver**, 3, 116	M. A. Lee	Appealtothechief, 3, 114	Dr Arne, 3, 114	7	1:25.00	30,000
1991	**Ocala Flame**, 3, 113	R. N. Lester	Sunny and Pleasant, 3, 113	Jacquelyn's Groom, 3, 113	9	1:19.02	33,180
1990	**Country Isle**, 3, 114	H. Castillo Jr.	Run Turn, 3, 120	Ultimate Swale, 3, 112	10	1:24.80	33,840
1989	**Big Stanley**, 3, 120	D. Valiente	Valid Space, 3, 114	Jabotinsky, 3, 117	6	1:23.60	32,490

1988	**In the Slammer**, 3, 114	M. A. Gonzalez	Lover's Trust, 3, 122	Ashmint, 3, 115	6	1:23.80	$32,220
1987	**You're No Bargain**, 3, 117	O. J. Londono	Right Rudder, 3, 112	Jilsie's Gigalo, 3, 118	9	1:25.60	44,010
1986	**Kid Colin**, 3, 116	G. St. Leon	Big Jolt, 3, 116	Lucky Rebeau, 3, 116	13	1:25.80	38,610
1985	**Smile**, 3, 123	J. Vasquez	Paravon, 3, 112	Hickory Hill Flyer, 3, 114	7	1:23.80	46,260
1984	**Bowmans Express**, 3, 117	O. J. Londono	Mo Exception, 3, 114	No Room, 3, 119	12	1:25.40	19,305
1983	**Opening Lead**, 3, 112	B. Gonzalez	El Perico, 3, 117	Neutral Player, 3, 112	9	1:25.80	16,785
1982	**Rex's Profile**, 3, 115	E. Cardone	Libra Moon, 3, 118	Center Cut, 3, 123	7	1:11.40	16,395
1981	**Face the Moment**, 3, 115	E. Cardone	†Toga Toga, 3, 113	Incredible John, 3, 118	8	1:11.00	16,530
1980	**Diplomatic Note**, 3, 112	J. D. Bailey	Buckn' Shoe, 3, 115	Fast Fast Freddie, 3, 113	9	1:12.00	16,785
1979	**Breezy Fire**, 4, 120	M. A. Rivera	Cherry Pop, 3, 113	Noble Heart, 3, 111	9	1:24.60	16,770
1978	**Admiral Rix**, 2, 116	T. Barrow	Tartan Tam, 2, 116	Cherry Pop, 2, 116	9	1:07.40	14,160
1977	**Chwesboken**, 2, 119	D. Hidalgo	Noon Time Spender, 2, 122	Ski's Never Bend, 2, 116	5	1:05.40	13,320
1976	**Winners Hit**, 2, 119	R. Broussard	My Budget, 2, 119	Time for Fun, 2, 116	11	1:07.00	14,640
1975	**†Precipitory**, 2, 116	J. Salinas	Chic Ruler, 2, 116	Upper Current, 2, 119	10	1:06.80	14,400

Named for Dorchester Farm Stable's 1961 champion three-year-old male Carry Back (1958 c. by Saggy); Carry Back was the all-time leading Florida-bred earner at his retirement. Grade 3 2003-'04. Carry Back H. 1981-'93. Held at Tropical Park 1970. Not held 1972-'74. $5\frac{1}{2}$ furlongs 1975-'78. 7 furlongs 1979, 1984-'90, 1992-'96. $6\frac{1}{2}$ furlongs 1991. Two-year-olds 1975-'78. Three-year-olds and up 1979. †Denotes female.

Carter Handicap

Grade 1 in 2006. Aqueduct, three-year-olds and up, 7 furlongs, dirt. Held April 8, 2006, with a gross value of $300,000. First held in 1895. First graded in 1973. Stakes record 1:20.04 (1999 Artax).

Year	Winner	Jockey	Second	Third	Strs	Time	1st Purse
2006	**Bishop Court Hill**, 6, 115	J. A. Santos	Sir Greeley, 4, 116	Big Apple Daddy, 4, 114	6	1:23.27	$180,000
2005	**Forest Danger**, 4, 117	R. Bejarano	Medallist, 4, 117	Don Six, 5, 116	6	1:20.46	210,000
2004	**Pico Central (Brz)**, 5, 117	A. O. Solis	Strong Hope, 4, 119	Eye of the Tiger, 4, 114	9	1:20.22	210,000
2003	**Congaree**, 5, 122	G. L. Stevens	Aldebaran, 5, 118	Peeping Tom, 6, 114	5	1:21.48	210,000
2002	**Affirmed Success**, 8, 119	R. Migliore	Voodoo, 4, 113	Burning Roma, 4, 117	10	1:21.84	210,000
2001	**Peeping Tom**, 4, 118	S. Bridgmohan	Say Florida Sandy, 7, 116	Hook and Ladder, 4, 118	7	1:21.33	180,000
2000	**Brutally Frank**, 6, 116	S. Bridgmohan	Western Expression, 4, 113	Affirmed Success, 6, 122	7	1:21.66	120,000
1999	**Artax**, 4, 114	J. F. Chavez	Affirmed Success, 5, 119	Western Borders, 5, 113	9	**1:20.04**	120,000
1998	**Wild Rush**, 4, 117	K. Desormeaux	Banker's Gold, 4, 114	Western Borders, 4, 115	10	1:21.16	120,000
1997	**Langfuhr**, 5, 122	J. F. Chavez	Stalwart Member, 4, 113	Western Winter, 5, 112	9	1:22.99	90,000
1996	**Lite the Fuse**, 5, 121	J. A. Krone	Flying Chevron, 4, 115	Placid Fund, 4, 114	10	1:20.92	90,000
1995	**Lite the Fuse**, 4, 111	R. B. Perez	Our Emblem, 4, 114	You and I, 4, 113	9	1:21.48	90,000
1994	**Virginia Rapids**, 4, 118	J. Samyn	Punch Line, 4, 114	Cherokee Run, 4, 119	11	1:21.45	90,000
1993	**Alydeed**, 4, 122	C. Perret	Loach, 5, 112	Argyle Lake, 7, 113	10	1:22.70	90,000
1992	**Rubiano**, 5, 118	J. A. Santos	Kid Russell, 6, 112	In Excess (Ire), 5, 122	9	1:21.41	120,000
1991	**Housebuster**, 4, 122	C. Perret	Black Tie Affair (Ire), 5, 123	Gervazy, 4, 116	8	1:21.31	120,000
1990	**Dancing Spree**, 5, 123	C. W. Antley	Dancing Pretense, 5, 115	Sewickley, 5, 119	7	1:22.00	137,280
1989	**On the Line**, 5, 125	G. L. Stevens	True and Blue, 4, 114	Dr. Carrington, 4, 110	8	1:21.40	140,880
1988	**Gulch**, 4, 124	J. A. Santos	Afleet, 4, 124	Its Acedemic, 4, 108	8	1:20.40	174,300
1987	**†Pine Tree Lane**, 5, 119	R. P. Romero	King's Swan, 7, 123	Zany Tactics, 6, 119	6	1:21.20	170,400
1986	**Love That Mac**, 4, 117	E. Maple	Ziggy's Boy, 4, 118	King's Swan, 6, 120	7	1:21.60	116,460
1985	**Mt. Livermore**, 4, 117	J. D. Bailey	Rocky Marriage, 5, 122	Carr de Naskra, 4, 125	6	1:20.80	83,340
1984	**Bet Big**, 4, 115	J. Samyn	Cannon Shell, 5, 109	A Phenomenon, 4, 126	10	1:21.80	73,200
1983	**Vittorioso**, 4, 113	A. Smith Jr.	Sing Sing, 5, 122	Fit to Fight, 4, 116	9	1:22.80	67,800
1982	**Pass the Tab**, 4, 118	A. Graell	Royal Hierarchy, 5, 115	Maudlin, 4, 114	12	1:22.40	52,110
1981	**Amber Pass**, 4, 114	E. Maple	Guilty Conscience, 5, 111	Dunham's Gift, 4, 116	7	1:23.00	49,410
1980	**Czaravich**, 4, 126	L. Adams	Tanthem, 5, 122	Nice Catch, 6, 120	6	1:21.00	49,050
1979	**Star de Naskra**, 4, 122	J. Fell	Alydar, 4, 126	Sensitive Prince, 4, 126	6	1:21.80	48,690
1978	**Jaipur's Gem**, 5, 115	J. Samyn	Vencedor, 4, 111	Half High, 5, 118	7	1:21.60	32,070
	Pumpkin Moonshine, 4, 107	D. A. Borden	Prefontaine, 4, 112	Big John Taylor, 4, 113	6	1:22.20	31,920
1977	**dh-Gentle King**, 4, 110	D. Montoya		Full Out, 4, 117	8	1:22.00	21,914
	dh-Quiet Little Table, 4, 119	E. Maple					
	Soy Numero Uno, 4, 126	R. Broussard	Barrera, 4, 119	Gallant Bob, 5, 116	6	1:22.20	31,770
1976	**Due Diligence**, 4, 111	J. Amy	†Honorable Miss, 6, 122	Amerrico, 4, 112	8	1:22.40	33,810
1975	**Forego**, 5, 134	H. Gustines	Stop the Music, 5, 123	Orders, 4, 114	10	1:21.60	34,860
1974	**Forego**, 4, 129	H. Gustines	Mr. Prospector, 4, 124	Timeless Moment, 4, 113	8	1:22.20	33,900
1973	**King's Bishop**, 4, 114	E. Maple	Onion, 4, 114	Petrograd, 4, 118	10	1:20.40	35,220

Named for Capt. William Carter of Brooklyn, New York, who contributed $500 of the first $600 purse. Grade 2 1973-'87. Held at Belmont Park 1946, 1956-'59, 1968-'69, 1972-'74, 1986, 1994-'96. Not held 1909, 1911-'13. $1\frac{1}{4}$ miles 1895. $1\frac{1}{8}$ miles 1896. $1\frac{1}{16}$ miles 1897. About 7 furlongs 1898. $6\frac{1}{2}$ furlongs 1899-1902. Two divisions 1977-'78. Dead heat for first 1977 (1st Div.). Track record 1973, 1999. †Denotes female. Held as an allowance race 1933-'34.

CashCall Invitational Mile Stakes

Grade 3 in 2006. Hollywood Park, three-year-olds and up, fillies and mares, 1 mile, turf. Held July 3, 2005, with a gross value of $200,000. First held in 1998. First graded in 2001. Stakes record 1:33.98 (2000 Tranquility Lake).

Year	Winner	Jockey	Second	Third	Strs	Time	1st Purse
2005	**Intercontinental (GB)**, 5, 123	J. D. Bailey	Ticker Tape (GB), 4, 121	Navaja (NZ), 5, 117	5	1:34.33	$120,000
2004	**Janeian (NZ)**, 6, 121	K. Desormeaux	Katdogawn (GB), 4, 123	Makeup Artist, 4, 121	6	1:34.79	65,820
2003	**Magic Mission (GB)**, 5, 115	C. S. Nakatani	Little Treasure (Fr), 4, 121	Belleski, 4, 115	9	1:34.25	67,320

2002	**Surya**, 4, 117	K. Desormeaux	Angel Gift, 4, 117	Reine de Romance (Ire), 4, 121	12	1:34.73	$68,880
2001	**Kalatiara (Aus)**, 4, 114	C. J. McCarron	Dianehill (Ire), 5, 119	Al Desima (GB), 4, 116	7	1:34.41	65,940
2000	**Tranquility Lake**, 5, 121	E. Delahoussaye	Dianehill (Ire), 4, 119	Reciclada (Chi), 5, 119	6	**1:33.98**	46,590
1999	**Tuzla (Fr)**, 5, 123	C. S. Nakatani	Isle de France, 4, 119	Chime After Chime, 4, 113	5	1:34.32	42,240
1998	**Tuzla (Fr)**, 4, 115	C. S. Nakatani	Sonja's Faith (Ire), 4, 119	Plus (Chi), 5, 115	6	1:34.33	42,990

Formerly named for Robert E. Sangster's 1984 champion grass female and '84 Breeders' Cup Mile (at Hollywood Park) winner Royal Heroine (Ire) (1980 f. by Lypheor [GB]). Sponsored by CashCall Inc. of Fountain Valley, California 2006. Royal Heroine S. 1998-2004. Royal Heroine Invitational S. 2005.

Champagne Stakes

Grade 1 in 2006. Belmont Park, two-year-olds, 1 mile, dirt. Held October 8, 2005, with a gross value of $500,000. First held in 1867. First graded in 1973. Stakes record 1:34.20 (1983 Devil's Bag).

Year	Winner	Jockey	Second	Third	Strs	Time	1st Purse
2005	**First Samurai**, 2, 122	J. D. Bailey	Henny Hughes, 2, 122	Superfly, 2, 122	6	1:36.29	$300,000
2004	**Proud Accolade**, 2, 122	J. R. Velazquez	Afleet Alex, 2, 122	Sun King, 2, 122	8	1:42.30	300,000
2003	**Birdstone**, 2, 122	J. D. Bailey	Chapel Royal, 2, 122	Dashboard Drummer, 2, 122	7	1:44.05	300,000
2002	**Toccet**, 2, 122	J. F. Chavez	Icecoldbeeratreds, 2, 122	Erinsouthernman, 2, 122	9	1:44.45	300,000
2001	**Officer**, 2, 122	V. Espinoza	Jump Start, 2, 122	Heavyweight Champ, 2, 122	5	1:43.39	300,000
2000	**A P Valentine**, 2, 122	J. F. Chavez	Point Given, 2, 122	Yonaguska, 2, 122	10	1:41.45	300,000
1999	**Greenwood Lake**, 2, 122	J. Samyn	Chief Seattle, 2, 122	High Yield, 2, 122	7	1:43.70	240,000
1998	**The Groom Is Red**, 2, 122	C. S. Nakatani	Lemon Drop Kid, 2, 122	Weekend Money, 2, 122	7	1:42.91	240,000
1997	**Grand Slam**, 2, 122	G. L. Stevens	Lil's Lad, 2, 122	Halory Hunter, 2, 122	8	1:40.59	240,000
1996	**Ordway**, 2, 122	J. R. Velazquez	Traitor, 2, 122	Gold Tribute, 2, 122	12	1:42.09	240,000
1995	**Maria's Mon**, 2, 122	R. G. Davis	Diligence, 2, 122	Devil's Honor, 2, 122	8	1:42.39	300,000
1994	**Timber Country**, 2, 122	P. Day	Sierra Diablo, 2, 122	On Target, 2, 122	11	1:44.01	300,000
1993	**Dehere**, 2, 122	C. J. McCarron	Crary, 2, 122	Amathos, 2, 122	6	1:35.91	300,000
1992	**Sea Hero**, 2, 122	J. D. Bailey	Secret Odds, 2, 122	Press Card, 2, 122	10	1:34.87	300,000
1991	**Tri to Watch**, 2, 122	A. T. Cordero Jr.	Snappy Landing, 2, 122	Pine Bluff, 2, 122	15	1:36.61	300,000
1990	**Fly So Free**, 2, 122	J. A. Santos	Happy Jazz Band, 2, 122	Subordinated Debt, 2, 122	13	1:35.60	381,600
1989	**Adjudicating**, 2, 122	J. Vasquez	Rhythm, 2, 122	Senor Pete, 2, 122	6	1:37.60	343,200
1988	**Easy Goer**, 2, 122	P. Day	Is It True, 2, 122	Irish Actor, 2, 122	4	1:34.80	334,200
1987	**Forty Niner**, 2, 122	E. Maple	Parlay Me, 2, 122	Tejano, 2, 122	11	1:36.80	370,800
1986	**Polish Navy**, 2, 122	R. P. Romero	Demons Begone, 2, 122	Bet Twice, 2, 122	7	1:35.20	199,500
1985	**Mogambo**, 2, 122	A. T. Cordero Jr.	Groovy, 2, 122	Mr. Classic, 2, 122	5	1:37.20	194,700
1984	**For Certain Doc**, 2, 122	M. Zuniga	Mighty Appealing, 2, 122	Tank's Prospect, 2, 122	6	1:49.20	171,600
1983	**Devil's Bag**, 2, 122	E. Maple	Dr. Carter, 2, 122	Our Casey's Boy, 2, 122	12	**1:34.20**	142,200
1982	**Copelan**, 2, 122	J. D. Bailey	Pappa Riccio, 2, 122	El Cubanaso, 2, 122	13	1:37.80	144,000
1981	**Timely Writer**, 2, 122	J. Fell	†Before Dawn, 2, 119	New Discovery, 2, 122	13	1:36.40	90,150
1980	**Lord Avie**, 2, 122	J. Velasquez	Noble Nashua, 2, 122	Sezyou, 2, 122	9	1:37.20	85,350
1979	**Joanie's Chief**, 2, 122	R. Hernandez	Rockhill Native, 2, 122	Googolplex, 2, 122	8	1:38.20	81,750
1978	**Spectacular Bid**, 2, 122	J. Velasquez	General Assembly, 2, 122	Crested Wave, 2, 122	6	1:34.80	80,250
1977	**Alydar**, 2, 122	J. Velasquez	Affirmed, 2, 122	Darby Creek Road, 2, 122	6	1:36.60	80,400
1976	**Seattle Slew**, 2, 122	J. Cruguet	For The Moment, 2, 122	Sail to Rome, 2, 122	10	1:34.40	82,350
1975	**Honest Pleasure**, 2, 122	B. Baeza	Dance Spell, 2, 122	Whatsyourpleasure, 2, 122	14	1:36.40	89,625
1974	**Foolish Pleasure**, 2, 122	J. Vasquez	Harvard Man, 2, 122	Ramahorn, 2, 122	9	1:36.00	86,850
1973	**Holding Pattern**, 2, 122	M. Miceli	Green Gambados, 2, 122	Hosiery, 2, 122	10	1:36.00	55,425
	Protagonist, 2, 122	A. Santiago	Prince of Reason, 2, 122	Cannonade, 2, 122	10	1:36.00	55,425

Named after the Champagne S. (Eng-G2) in England, held at Doncaster. Sponsored by Moet & Chandon Champagne of Epernay, France 1994-'97. Held at Jerome Park 1867-'89. Held at Morris Park 1890-1904. Held at Aqueduct 1959, 1961, 1963-'67, 1984. Not held 1910-'13, 1956. 1 mile 1867-'70, 1890, 1940-'83, 1985-'93. 6 furlongs 1871-'89. 7 furlongs 1891-1904. About 7 furlongs 1905-'32. 6½ furlongs 1933-'39. 1⅛ miles 1984. 1¹⁄₁₆ miles 1994-2004. Two divisions 1973. †Denotes female.

Charles Whittingham Memorial Handicap

Grade 1 in 2006. Hollywood Park, three-year-olds and up, 1¼ miles, turf. Held June 10, 2006, with a gross value of $300,000. First held in 1969. First graded in 1973. Stakes record 1:57.75 (1993 Bien Bien).

Year	Winner	Jockey	Second	Third	Strs	Time	1st Purse
2006	**Lava Man**, 5, 122	C. S. Nakatani	King's Drama (Ire), 6, 122	Red Fort (Ire), 6, 118	9	2:00.29	$180,000
2005	**Sweet Return (GB)**, 5, 119	A. O. Solis	Red Fort (Ire), 5, 117	Vangelis, 6, 118	9	2:01.35	210,000
2004	**Sabiango (Ger)**, 6, 116	T. Baze	Bayamo (Ire), 5, 116	Just Wonder (GB), 4, 116	11	2:01.52	210,000
2003	**Storming Home (GB)**, 5, 124	G. L. Stevens	Mister Acpen (Chi), 5, 115	Cagney (Brz), 6, 114	6	2:00.66	210,000
2002	**Denon**, 4, 116	G. K. Gomez	Night Patrol, 6, 114	Skipping (GB), 5, 117	9	2:01.47	210,000
2001	**Bienamado**, 5, 124	C. J. McCarron	Senure, 5, 117	Timboroa (GB), 5, 116	9	1:59.34	210,000
2000	**White Heart (GB)**, 5, 117	K. Desormeaux	Self Feeder (Ire), 6, 116	Deploy Venture (GB), 4, 112	6	2:00.83	180,000
1999	**River Bay**, 6, 119	A. O. Solis	Majorien (GB), 5, 117	Alvo Certo (Brz), 6, 115	9	2:00.66	240,000
1998	**Storm Trooper**, 5, 117	K. Desormeaux	River Bay, 5, 121	Prize Giving (GB), 5, 116	7	2:03.05	240,000
1997	**Rainbow Dancer (Fr)**, 6, 116	A. O. Solis	Sunshack (GB), 6, 118	Marlin, 4, 120	6	2:00.00	240,000
1996	**Sandpit (Brz)**, 7, 120	C. S. Nakatani	Northern Spur (Ire), 5, 123	Awad, 6, 119	6	1:59.52	300,000
1995	**Earl of Barking (Ire)**, 5, 115	G. F. Almeida	Sandpit (Brz), 6, 122	Savinio, 5, 117	10	1:59.78	275,000
1994	**Grand Flotilla**, 7, 116	G. L. Stevens	Bien Bien, 5, 124	Blues Traveller (Ire), 4, 114	8	1:59.26	275,000
1993	**Bien Bien**, 4, 119	C. J. McCarron	Best Pal, 5, 122	Leger Cat (Arg), 7, 116	8	**1:57.75**	275,000

1992	**Quest for Fame (GB)**, 5, 122	G. L. Stevens	Classic Fame, 6, 120	River Traffic, 4, 114	9	1:58.99	$275,000
1991	**Exbourne**, 5, 119	G. L. Stevens	Itsallgreektome, 4, 123	Prized, 5, 123	6	2:00.10	275,000
1990	**Steinlen (GB)**, 7, 124	L. A. Pincay Jr.	Hawkster, 4, 122	Santangelo (Arg), 6, 110	6	2:03.00	275,000
1989	**Great Communicator**, 6, 123	R. Sibille	Nasr El Arab, 4, 124	Equalize, 7, 124	9	1:59.40	275,000
1988	**Political Ambition**, 4, 119	E. Delahoussaye	Baba Karam (Ire), 4, 116	dh-Great Communicator, 5, 120	7	1:58.60	165,000
				dh-Skip Out Front, 6, 115			
1987	**Rivlia**, 5, 117	C. J. McCarron	Great Communicator, 4, 112	Schiller, 5, 116	6	2:24.20	165,000
1986	**Flying Pidgeon**, 5, 120	S. B. Soto	Dahar, 5, 126	Both Ends Burning, 6, 122	6	2:27.00	165,000
1985	**Both Ends Burning**, 5, 121	E. Delahoussaye	Dahar, 4, 123	Swoon, 7, 114	5	2:25.00	165,000
1984	**John Henry**, 9, 126	C. J. McCarron	Galant Vert (Fr), 4, 116	Load the Cannons, 4, 120	9	2:25.00	165,000
1983	**Erins Isle (Ire)**, 5, 127	L. A. Pincay Jr.	Exploded, 6, 115	Prince Spellbound, 4, 120	12	2:25.80	165,000
1982	**Exploded**, 5, 117	L. A. Pincay Jr.	Lemhi Gold, 4, 123	The Bart, 6, 125	6	2:25.20	165,000
1981	**John Henry**, 6, 130	L. A. Pincay Jr.	Caterman (NZ), 5, 122	Galaxy Libra (Ire), 5, 118	7	2:27.80	110,000
1980	**John Henry**, 5, 128	D. G. McHargue	Balzac, 5, 120	Go West Young Man, 5, 117	10	2:25.40	137,500
1979	**Johnny's Image**, 4, 123	S. Hawley	Star Spangled, 5, 122	Dom Alaric (Fr), 5, 119	11	2:25.20	137,500
1978	**Exceller**, 5, 127	W. Shoemaker	Bowl Game, 4, 123	Noble Dancer (GB), 6, 126	12	2:25.80	110,000
1977	**Vigors**, 4, 117	J. Lambert	Caucasus, 5, 126	Anne's Pretender, 5, 122	12	2:26.80	120,000
1976	**†Dahlia**, 6, 117	W. Shoemaker	Caucasus, 4, 119	Pass the Glass, 5, 121	12	2:26.80	120,000
1975	***Barclay Joy**, 5, 113	A. L. Diaz	Captain Cee Jay, 5, 117	Chief Hawk Ear, 7, 119	10	2:27.00	75,000
1974	**Court Ruling**, 4, 117	W. Mahorney	Outdoors, 5, 113	London Company, 4, 123	10	2:27.60	75,000
1973	**Life Cycle**, 4, 115	L. A. Pincay Jr.	Wing Out, 5, 118	*Cougar II, 7, 130	10	2:25.60	75,000

Named for Racing Hall of Fame trainer Charles Whittingham (1913-'99). Formerly sponsored by Ford Motor Co. of Detroit, Michigan 1971. Hollywood Park Invitational Turf H. 1969-'70, 1972. Ford Pinto Invitational Turf H. 1971. Hollywood Invitational H. 1973-'88. Hollywood Turf H. 1989-'98. Charles Whittingham H. 1999-2002. 1½ miles 1969-'87. Dead heat for third 1988. Equaled course record 1973. Course record 1993. †Denotes female.

Chicago Breeders' Cup Handicap

Grade 3 in 2006. Arlington Park, three-year-olds and up, fillies and mares, 7 furlongs, dirt. Held June 18, 2005, with a gross value of $175,000. First held in 1986. First graded in 1992. Stakes record 1:21.24 (1992 Withallprobability).

Year	Winner	Jockey	Second	Third	Strs	Time	1st Purse
2005	**Happy Ticket**, 4, 116	E. Razo Jr.	Savorthetime, 6, 117	Injustice, 4, 116	7	1:22.54	$105,000
2004	**My Trusty Cat**, 4, 116	R. R. Douglas	Our Josephina, 4, 112	Smoke Chaser, 5, 116	5	1:23.54	105,000
2003	**For Rubies**, 4, 116	C. Perret	Raging Fever, 5, 120	Oglala Sue, 5, 113	8	1:24.21	69,450
2002	**Mandy's Gold**, 4, 116	R. R. Douglas	Cat and the Hat, 4, 116	Caressing, 4, 115	6	1:22.86	98,664
2001	**Trip**, 4, 114	C. Perret	Hidden Assets, 4, 115	Rose of Zollern (Ire), 5, 115	7	1:22.18	99,312
2000	**Saoirse**, 4, 118	D. Clark	The Happy Hopper, 4, 115	Dif a Dot, 5, 114	7	1:23.09	102,195
1997	**J J'sdream**, 4, 118	M. Guidry	Capote Belle, 4, 120	Eseni, 4, 117	7	1:22.20	101,625
1996	**Bunbeg**, 4, 114	M. Walls	Morris Code, 4, 118	Rhapsodic, 5, 114	8	1:23.86	102,990
1995	**Low Key Affair**, 4, 113	A. T. Gryder	Morning Meadow, 5, 115	Marina Park (GB), 5, 120	9	1:24.64	93,840
1994	**Minidar**, 4, 116	V. Belvoir	Spinning Round, 5, 118	Traverse City, 4, 113	10	1:22.49	93,960
1993	**Meafara**, 4, 121	J. L. Diaz	Shared Interest, 5, 115	Real Display, 4, 114	11	1:22.12	93,870
1992	**Withallprobability**, 4, 115	G. K. Gomez	Fit for a Queen, 6, 120	Madam Bear, 4, 114	9	**1:21.24**	93,450
1991	**Safely Kept**, 5, 126	C. Perret	Nurse Dopey, 4, 118	Token Dance, 4, 114	7	1:23.05	93,060
1990	**Fit for a Queen**, 4, 112	P. Day	Channel Three, 4, 113	Sexy Slew, 4, 113	12	1:23.00	94,650
1989	**Rose's Record**, 5, 114	J. Velasquez	Sunshine Always, 5, 114	‡Daloma (Fr), 5, 116	7	1:24.60	93,120
1987	**Lazer Show**, 4, 123	P. Day	Very Subtle, 3, 120	Moonbeam McQueen, 4, 111	6	1:22.80	46,275
1986	**Lazer Show**, 3, 115	P. Day	Balladry, 4, 115	Gene's Lady, 5, 122	8	1:21.40	93,360

Named for the city of Chicago, near suburban Arlington Heights, location of Arlington Park. Chicago Budweiser Breeders' Cup H. 1986-'95. Not held 1988, 1998-'99. ‡Josette finished third, DQ to fourth, 1989.

Chilukki Stakes

Grade 2 in 2006. Churchill Downs, three-year-olds and up, fillies and mares, 1 mile, dirt. Held November 6, 2005, with a gross value of $169,350. First held in 1986. First graded in 1988. Stakes record 1:33.57 (2000 Chilukki).

Year	Winner	Jockey	Second	Third	Strs	Time	1st Purse
2005	**Bending Strings**, 4, 117	R. Albarado	Prospective Saint, 4, 121	Miss Fortunate, 5, 121	11	1:35.19	$104,997
2004	**Halory Leigh**, 4, 115	C. Perret	Lady Tak, 4, 123	Susan's Angel, 3, 115	12	1:35.05	142,848
2003	**Lead Story**, 4, 114	C. H. Borel	Awesome Humor, 3, 118	Born to Dance, 4, 113	10	1:36.55	139,748
2002	**Softly**, 4, 114	J. K. Court	Bare Necessities, 3, 115	Victory Ride, 4, 118	9	1:35.07	138,632
2001	**Nasty Storm**, 3, 115	P. Day	Forest Secrets, 3, 113	Trip, 4, 117	8	1:35.30	137,764
2000	**Chilukki**, 3, 116	G. L. Stevens	Reciclada (Chi), 5, 113	Rose of Zollern (Ire), 4, 114	10	**1:33.57**	154,008
1999	**Let**, 4, 113	C. H. Borel	Roza Robata, 4, 114	Dif a Dot, 4, 115	9	1:34.41	138,880
1998	**Dream Scheme**, 5, 113	C. H. Borel	Sister Act, 3, 111	Beautiful Pleasure, 3, 110	9	1:34.41	139,624
1997	**Feasibility Study**, 5, 120	R. Albarado	J J'sdream, 4, 113	Mama's Pro, 4, 115	14	1:37.61	146,196
1996	**Fast Catch**, 4, 109	W. Martinez	Serena's Song, 4, 125	Bedroom Blues, 5, 112	9	1:36.55	139,624
1995	**Lakeway**, 4, 122	K. Desormeaux	Alcovy, 5, 113	Laura's Pistolette, 4, 116	8	1:35.94	137,280
1994	**Educated Risk**, 4, 118	P. Day	Pennyhill Park, 4, 117	Alcovy, 4, 116	8	1:35.74	138,125
1993	**Miss Indy Anna**, 3, 111	P. Day	One Dreamer, 5, 115	Deputation, 4, 119	13	1:37.72	141,960
1992	**Wilderness Song**, 4, 120	C. Perret	Miss Jealski, 3, 110	Dance Colony, 5, 113	11	1:36.22	102,440
1991	**Fit for a Queen**, 5, 121	R. D. Lopez	Wilderness Song, 3, 118	Summer Matinee, 4, 113	6	1:38.60	100,555
1990	**Oh My Jessica Pie**, 3, 114	M. A. Gonzalez	Seaside Attraction, 3, 115	Sweet Nostalgia, 3, 111	10	1:36.80	102,993
1989	**Classic Value**, 3, 114	P. Day	Coastal Connection, 4, 115	Rose's Record, 5, 117	12	1:35.40	102,960

1988	**Darien Miss**, 3, 116	P. A. Johnson	Sheena Native, 4, 117	Coastal Connection, 3, 112	13	1:36.80	$102,928
1987	**Bound**, 3, 113	E. Maple	Miss Bid, 4, 115	Intently, 4, 114	14	1:37.00	103,253
1986	**Lazer Show**, 3, 120	C. R. Woods Jr.	Balladry, 4, 116	Mrs. Revere, 5, 120	11	1:22.60	102,473

Named for Stonerside Stable's 1999 champion two-year-old filly and 2000 Churchill Downs Distaff H. (G2) winner Chilukki (f. by Cherokee Run). Grade 3 1988-'91. Churchill Downs Budweiser Breeders' Cup H. 1986-'91, 1993-'95. Churchill Downs Breeders' Cup H. 1992. Churchill Downs Distaff H. 1996-2004. 7 furlongs 1986. Track record 2000.

Churchill Distaff Turf Mile Stakes

Grade 3 in 2006. Churchill Downs, three-year-olds and up, fillies and mares, 1 mile, turf. Held May 6, 2006, with a gross value of $115,100. First held in 1983. First graded in 1997. Stakes record 1:33.96 (2003 Heat Haze [GB]).

Year	Winner	Jockey	Second	Third	Strs	Time	1st Purse
2006	**Mirabilis**, 4, 122	P. A. Valenzuela	Special Grayce, 4, 118	More Than Promised, 4, 122	10	1:35.93	$67,794
2005	**Miss Terrible (Arg)**, 6, 117	A. O. Solis	Sand Springs, 5, 123	Shaconage, 5, 121	7	1:35.89	69,564
2004	**Shaconage**, 4, 121	B. Blanc	Etoile Montante, 4, 123	Chance Dance, 4, 117	10	1:36.10	70,246
2003	**Heat Haze (GB)**, 4, 123	J. Valdivia Jr.	Quick Tip, 5, 123	Sentimental Value, 4, 121	11	**1:33.96**	72,540
2002	**Stylish**, 4, 116	J. D. Bailey	La Recherche, 4, 123	Dianehill (Ire), 6, 123	10	1:35.72	71,424
2001	**Iftiraas (GB)**, 4, 118	J. D. Bailey	Gino's Spirits (GB), 5, 118	Solvig, 4, 120	7	1:36.69	70,432
2000	**Don't Be Silly**, 5, 116	J. F. Chavez	Really Polish, 5, 114	Pricearose, 4, 116	8	1:34.78	71,548
1999	**Shires Ende**, 4, 118	J. R. Velazquez	Ashford Castle, 5, 120	Sophie My Love, 4, 123	9	1:35.43	74,152
1998	**Witchful Thinking**, 4, 120	S. J. Sellers	Colcon, 5, 123	Swearingen, 4, 123	10	1:37.23	74,896
1997	**B. A. Valentine**, 4, 114	S. J. Sellers	Striesen, 5, 116	Romy, 6, 123	10	1:36.98	71,796
1996	**Apolda**, 5, 123	J. D. Bailey	Country Cat, 4, 123	Bold Ruritana, 6, 123	8	1:36.50	55,283
1995	**Bold Ruritana**, 5, 123	P. Day	Icy Warning, 5, 116	Rapunzel Runz, 4, 114	10	1:34.64	56,111
1994	**Weekend Madness (Ire)**, 4, 123	C. R. Woods Jr.	Russian Bride, 4, 120	Suspect Terrain, 5, 114	9	1:38.58	55,770
1993	**Lady Blessington (Fr)**, 5, 120	P. Day	You'd Be Surprised, 4, 118	Wassifa (GB), 5, 116	9	1:34.96	37,570
1992	**Quilma (Chi)**, 5, 120	E. Delahoussaye	Behaving Dancer, 5, 123	Radiant Ring, 4, 123	10	1:35.36	38,285
1991	**Foresta**, 5, 123	A. T. Cordero Jr.	Coolawin, 5, 118	Primetime North, 4, 120	10	1:36.30	38,870
1990	**Foresta**, 4, 114	A. T. Cordero Jr.	Saros Brig, 6, 123	Bearly Cooking, 7, 114	5	1:37.20	36,205
1989	**Classic Account**, 4, 116	P. Day	Fast Forward, 5, 116	R. B. McCurry, 4, 112	4	1:51.20	35,132
1988	**Buoy**, 3, 123	P. Day	Frosty the Snowman, 3, 115	Cougarized, 3, 123	7	1:43.40	36,725
1987	**Fast Forward**, 3, 115	P. Day	Sooner Showers, 3, 115	Homebuilder, 3, 115	5	1:43.20	36,043
1983	**‡Le Cou Cou**, 3, 121	D. L. Howard	High Honors, 3, 121	Common Sense, 3, 121	10	1:49.60	34,125

Formerly named for Churchill Down's most recognized feature (and corporate logo), the twin spires atop its grandstand. Formerly sponsored by CompUSA Management Co. of Dallas 2005. Formerly sponsored by Argent Mortgage Co., of Orange, California 2004. Formerly sponsored by CITGO Petroleum Corp. of Tulsa, Oklahoma 2001-'03. Formerly sponsored by Ashland Inc. of Covington, Kentucky 1999. Formerly sponsored by AEGON Group N.V. of The Hague, the Netherlands 1998. Formerly sponsored by Providian Corp. of Louisville 1995-'97. Formerly sponsored by Capital Holding Corp. (predecessor of Providian Corp.) of Louisville 1988-'94. Twin Spires S. 1983-'87. Capital Holding Twin Spires S. 1988. Capital Holding Twin Spires H. 1989. Capital Holding Mile S. 1990-'91, 1993-'94. Capital Holding S. 1992. Providian Mile S. 1995-'97. Aegon Mile S. 1998. Ashland Mile S. 1999. Churchill Downs Distaff Turf Mile S. 2000. CITGO Distaff Turf Mile S. 2001-'03. Argent Mortgage Distaff Turf Mile S. 2004. CompUSA Turf Mile S. 2005. Not held 1984-'86. 1⅛ miles 1983, 1989. 1$^1/_{16}$ miles 1987-'88. Dirt 1983-'89. Three-year-olds 1983-'88. Both sexes 1983-'88. ‡High Honors finished first, DQ to second, 1983. Equaled course record 1992. Course record 1993.

Churchill Downs Handicap

Grade 2 in 2006. Churchill Downs, four-year-olds and up, 7 furlongs, dirt. Held May 6, 2006, with a gross value of $229,000. First held in 1911. First graded in 1992. Stakes record 1:20.50 (2001 Alannan).

Year	Winner	Jockey	Second	Third	Strs	Time	1st Purse
2006	**Trickey Trevor**, 7, 117	R. A. Baze	With Distinction, 5, 116	Level Playingfield, 5, 113	10	1:21.68	$134,881
2005	**Battle Won**, 5, 115	R. A. Dominguez	Level Playingfield, 4, 112	Pomeroy, 4, 118	11	1:20.56	143,220
2004	**Speightstown**, 6, 115	J. R. Velazquez	McCann's Mojave, 4, 117	Publication, 5, 116	7	1:21.38	137,516
2003	**Aldebaran**, 5, 120	J. D. Bailey	Pass Rush, 4, 117	Cappuchino, 4, 115	12	1:21.80	144,956
2002	**‡D'wildcat**, 4, 115	K. Desormeaux	Snow Ridge, 4, 119	Binthebest, 5, 113	10	1:22.37	106,299
2001	**Alannan**, 5, 116	E. S. Prado	Bonapaw, 5, 116	Exchange Rate, 4, 113	10	**1:20.50**	111,321
2000	**Straight Man**, 4, 112	J. F. Chavez	Mula Gula, 4, 114	Patience Game, 4, 114	7	1:21.53	104,904
1999	**Rock and Roll**, 4, 112	P. Day	Liberty Gold, 5, 114	Run Johnny, 7, 113	7	1:22.81	103,137
1998	**Distorted Humor**, 5, 119	G. L. Stevens	Gold Land, 7, 116	El Amante, 5, 113	7	1:21.18	103,509
1997	**Diligence**, 4, 114	M. E. Smith	Victor Cooley, 4, 115	Criollito (Arg), 6, 115	9	1:22.37	70,432
1996	**Criollito (Arg)**, 5, 115	C. J. McCarron	Forty Won, 5, 115	Powis Castle, 5, 114	9	1:22.01	74,620
1995	**Goldseeker Bud**, 4, 109	W. Martinez	Level Sands, 4, 112	Go for Gin, 4, 115	11	1:21.75	75,205
1994	**Honor the Hero**, 6, 116	G. K. Gomez	Memo (Chi), 7, 121	Saratoga Gambler, 6, 116	6	1:23.05	71,370
1993	**Callide Valley**, 5, 116	G. L. Stevens	Furiously, 4, 117	Ojai, 4, 110	11	1:22.01	56,063
1992	**Pleasant Tap**, 5, 120	E. Delahoussaye	Take Me Out, 4, 120	Cantrell Road, 6, 113	9	1:22.32	55,526
1991	**Thirty Six Red**, 4, 117	J. D. Bailey	Private School, 4, 113	Bratt's Choice, 4, 115	10	1:22.15	37,635
1990	**Beau Genius**, 5, 119	R. D. Lopez	Traskwood, 4, 113	Learn by Heart, 5, 115	12	1:23.20	37,830
1989	**Dancing Spree**, 4, 116	P. Day	Carborundum, 5, 117	Broadway Chief, 4, 115	13	1:24.00	38,253
1988	**Conquer**, 4, 117	G. L. Stevens	Homebuilder, 4, 121	Carborundum, 4, 115	9	1:23.20	36,823
1987	**Sovereign's Ace**, 5, 117	L. A. Pincay Jr.	Sun Master, 6, 123	Savings, 4, 114	5	1:22.00	21,236
1986	**Sovereign's Ace**, 4, 117	P. Rubbicco	Artichoke, 5, 120	Clever Wake, 4, 116	9	1:22.60	21,957
1985	**Rapid Gray**, 6, 120	P. Day	Roxbury Park, 4, 114	Steel Robbing, 5, 115	7	1:24.00	24,391
	Bayou Hebert, 4, 111	J. McKnight	Harry 'n Bill, 5, 117	Never Company, 5, 117	6	1:23.40	24,196
1984	**Habitonia**, 4, 118	P. Day	Roman Jamboree, 4, 114	Euathlos, 4, 113	5	1:23.00	20,914

1983 **Shot n' Missed**, 6, 118	L. Moyers	Vodika Collins, 5, 112	Gallant Gentleman, 4, 115	6	1:23.60	$21,239
1982 **Top Avenger**, 4, 114	R. P. Romero	It's a Rerun, 6, 110	Shot n' Missed, 5, 117	9	1:23.00	21,661
Bayou Black, 6, 119	R. D. Ardoin	Vodika Collins, 4, 118	Prince Crimson, 5, 116	6	1:22.80	23,433
1981 **Dreadnought**, 4, 112	J. C. Espinoza	Tiger Lure, 7, 113	Turbulence, 5, 119	12	1:23.60	19,874
1980 **Dr. Riddick**, 6, 114	D. Brumfield	Cregan's Cap, 5, 112	Silent Dignity, 4, 119	8	1:23.20	17,615
1979 **Trimlea**, 5, 113	J. Velasquez	Dr. Riddick, 5, 119	Cabrini Green, 4, 118	8	1:24.60	19,240
1978 **To the Quick**, 4, 116	J. Amy	It's Freezing, 6, 120	Prince Majestic, 4, 121	9	1:25.00	14,511
1977 **It's Freezing**, 5, 120	E. Delahoussaye	Buddy Larosa, 4, 112	Silver Hope, 6, 119	8	1:23.40	14,528
1976 **Yamanin**, 4, 115	G. Patterson	It's Freezing, 4, 117	Easter Island, 4, 115	9	1:23.80	14,495
1975 **Navajo**, 5, 123	J. Nichols	Silver Hope, 4, 116	Silver Badge, 4, 110	10	1:24.40	14,804
1974 **Barbizon Streak**, 6, 115	R. Wilson	Grocery List, 5, 117	Jim's Alibhi, 7, 114	11	1:25.40	15,015
1973 **Code of Honor**, 5, 115	E. Fires	Knight Counter, 5, 122	Hook It Up, 5, 115	10	1:23.00	15,096

Formerly sponsored by W. S. Farish's Lane's End, located in Versailles, Kentucky 2001. Formerly sponsored by Winner Communications, a telecommunications company involved in televised horse racing 2000. Grade 3 1992-'97. Winnercomm H. 2000. Lane's End Churchill Downs H. 2001. Not held 1914-'37. 1⅛ miles 1911-'13. Three-year-olds and up 1911-'13, 1938-'43, 1947-'88. Two divisions 1982, 1985. ‡Snow Ridge finished first, DQ to second, 2002. Track record 1998, 2001.

Cicada Stakes

Grade 3 in 2006. Aqueduct, three-year-olds, fillies, 6 furlongs. Held March 18, 2006, with a gross value of $110,600. First held in 1975. First graded in 1996. Stakes record 1:09.66 (2006 Wild Gams).

Year	Winner	Jockey	Second	Third	Strs	Time	1st Purse
2006	**Wild Gams**, 3, 118	E. Coa	Celestial Legend, 3, 122	Oprah Winney, 3, 116	7	**1:09.66**	$66,360
2005	**Dixie Talking**, 3, 116	A. Garcia	Acey Deucey, 3, 122	Alfonsina, 3, 116	8	1:23.04	65,880
2004	**Bohemian Lady**, 3, 116	E. S. Prado	Whoopi Cat, 3, 116	Baldomera, 3, 122	6	1:23.22	65,460
2003	**Cyber Secret**, 3, 122	S. Bridgmohan	Roar Emotion, 3, 116	Boxer Girl, 3, 118	6	1:22.55	64,980
2002	**Proper Gamble**, 3, 122	J. Castellano	Short Note, 3, 118	Forest Heiress, 3, 120	6	1:23.32	65,160
2001	**Xtra Heat**, 3, 122	R. Wilson	Erin Moor, 3, 116	Chasm, 3, 116	4	1:23.39	63,770
2000	**Finder's Fee**, 3, 118	J. D. Bailey	Apollo Cat, 3, 116	Southern Sandra, 3, 121	6	1:23.07	65,100
1999	**Potomac Bend**, 3, 118	M. T. Johnston	Carleaville, 3, 114	Jane, 3, 112	7	1:23.18	48,915
1998	**Jersey Girl**, 3, 116	R. Migliore	Vienna Blues, 3, 114	Babai Danzig, 3, 116	9	1:22.95	50,175
1997	**Vegas Prospector**, 3, 116	M. J. McCarthy	Ormsby County, 3, 112	Valid Affect, 3, 118	6	1:26.23	48,375
1996	**J J'sdream**, 3, 121	G. Boulanger	Dahl, 3, 114	Mystic Rhythms, 3, 118	9	1:23.44	50,310
1995	**Lucky Lavender Gal**, 3, 114	R. G. Davis	Stormy Blues, 3, 118	Dancin Renee, 3, 116	7	1:23.45	48,870
1994	**Our Royal Blue**, 3, 114	R. Wilson	Sovereign Kitty, 3, 118	Princess Joanne, 3, 113	5	1:22.38	48,375
1993	**Personal Bid**, 3, 118	J. A. Santos	Sheila's Revenge, 3, 118	In Excelcis Deo, 3, 116	4	1:23.52	31,800
1988	**Feel the Beat**, 3, 114	J. A. Santos	Bold Lady Anne, 3, 121	Dear Dusty, 3, 114	6	1:11.00	41,220
1983	**May Day Eighty**, 4, 117	J. Fell	Viva Sec, 5, 117	Clever Guest, 4, 117	9	1:42.80	26,430
1982	**Bold Ribbons**, 3, 116	A. T. Cordero Jr.	Cupecoy's Joy, 3, 121	Adept, 3, 114	11	1:11.00	34,980
1981	**In True Form**, 3, 114	A. Santiago	Wading Power, 3, 114	Hawkeye Express, 3, 114	12	1:12.80	34,800
1980	**The Wheel Turns**, 3, 114	M. Venezia	Darlin Momma, 3, 121	Remote Ruler, 3, 118	8	1:11.20	33,180
1979	**Spanish Fake**, 3, 114	J. Amy	Shirley the Queen, 3, 114	Quadrangles Plum, 3, 114	11	1:13.20	32,790
1978	**New Rinkle**, 3, 114	R. Hernandez	Star Gala, 3, 114	Idmon, 3, 114	6	1:13.00	25,440
1977	**Ring O'Bells**, 3, 118	A. T. Cordero Jr.	Shufleur, 3, 114	Maria's Baby, 3, 116	5	1:10.80	21,855
1976	**Tough Elsie**, 3, 116	J. Imparato	Light Frost, 3, 114	Quintas Vicki, 3, 118	13	1:10.20	23,610
1975	**Cast the Die**, 2, 116	R. Turcotte	Artfully, 2, 116	Veroom Maid, 2, 116	9	1:10.40	27,240

Named for Meadow Stable's 1961 champion two-year-old filly, '62 champion three-year-old filly, '62, '63 champion older female, and '62 Beldame H. winner Cicada (1959 f. by Bryan G.). Held at Belmont Park 1983, 1993. Not held 1984-'87, 1989-'92. 1$^1/_{16}$ miles 1983. 7 furlongs 1993-2005. Two-year-olds 1975. Three-year-olds and up 1983. Fillies and mares 1983.

Cinema Breeders' Cup Handicap

Grade 3 in 2006. Hollywood Park, three-year-olds, 1⅛ miles, turf. Held June 26, 2005, with a gross value of $153,450. First held in 1946. First graded in 1973. Stakes record 1:46.56 (1994 Unfinished Symph).

Year	Winner	Jockey	Second	Third	Strs	Time	1st Purse
2005	**Willow O Wisp**, 3, 119	G. K. Gomez	Osidy, 3, 119	Honorable Coach, 3, 113	5	1:48.59	$95,670
2004	**Greek Sun**, 3, 120	A. O. Solis	Laura's Lucky Boy, 3, 122	Whilly (Ire), 3, 117	7	1:48.40	97,470
2003	**Just Wonder (GB)**, 3, 117	K. Desormeaux	Bis Repetitas, 3, 115	Slew City Citadel, 3, 115	8	1:47.41	98,730
2002	**Inesperado (Fr)**, 3, 116	K. Desormeaux	Regiment, 3, 122	Johar, 3, 118	7	1:47.63	97,560
2001	**Sligo Bay (Ire)**, 3, 118	L. A. Pincay Jr.	Learing At Kathy, 3, 117	Marine (GB), 3, 119	7	1:48.40	65,160
2000	**David Copperfield**, 3, 116	V. Espinoza	Duke of Green (GB), 3, 117	Silver Axe, 3, 115	6	1:47.73	64,560
1999	**Fighting Falcon**, 3, 119	B. Blanc	Eagleton, 3, 120	Major Hero, 3, 113	8	1:48.06	66,000
1998	**Commitisize**, 3, 118	D. R. Flores	Killer Image, 3, 115	Lord Smith (GB), 3, 116	7	1:48.03	65,220
1997	**Worldly Ways (GB)**, 3, 115	C. S. Nakatani	P. T. Indy, 3, 118	Brave Act (GB), 3, 120	9	1:48.43	66,180
1996	**Let Bob Do It**, 3, 120	K. Desormeaux	Dr. Sardonica, 3, 115	Winter Quarters, 3, 115	8	1:47.58	81,660
1995	**Via Lombardia (Ire)**, 3, 119	E. Delahoussaye	Bryntirion, 3, 113	Oncefortheroad, 3, 115	9	1:47.22	65,400
1994	**Unfinished Symph**, 3, 118	G. Baze	Vaudeville, 3, 115	Fumo Di Londra (Ire), 3, 121	7	**1:46.56**	63,100
1993	**Earl of Barking (Ire)**, 3, 121	C. J. McCarron	Manny's Prospect, 3, 115	Minks Law, 3, 113	5	1:47.45	61,100
1992	**Bien Bien**, 3, 113	C. J. McCarron	Fax News, 3, 114	Prospect for Four, 3, 112	8	1:47.10	65,600
1991	**Character (GB)**, 3, 114	G. L. Stevens	River Traffic, 3, 117	Kalgrey (Fr), 3, 114	6	1:47.10	62,600
1990	**Jovial (GB)**, 3, 115	G. L. Stevens	Mehmetori, 3, 113	Itsallgreektome, 3, 117	10	1:47.80	67,400
1989	**‡Raise a Stanza**, 3, 114	G. L. Stevens	Exemplary Leader, 3, 116	Notorious Pleasure, 3, 120	6	1:47.80	62,100

1988 **Peace**, 3, 117	A. O. Solis	Blade of the Ball, 3, 113	Roberto's Dancer, 3, 115	8	1:46.80	$78,400
1987 **Something Lucky**, 3, 119	L. A. Pincay Jr.	The Medic, 3, 117	Savona Tower, 3, 115	6	1:46.80	62,400
1986 **Manila**, 3, 117	F. Toro	Vernon Castle, 3, 120	Full of Stars, 3, 115	10	1:47.00	80,400
1985 **Don't Say Halo**, 3, 116	D. G. McHargue	Derby Dawning, 3, 115	Emperdori, 3, 115	9	1:47.60	65,800
1984 **Prince True**, 3, 117	P. A. Valenzuela	M. Double M., 3, 116	Majestic Shore, 3, 115	7	1:40.20	63,700
1983 **Baron O'Dublin**, 3, 115	E. Delahoussaye	Tanks Brigade, 3, 119	Re Ack, 3, 116	9	1:43.00	66,300
1982 **Give Me Strength**, 3, 121	J. Samyn	Journey At Sea, 3, 122	Bargain Balcony, 3, 118	8	1:40.60	64,600
1981 **Minnesota Chief**, 3, 119	C. J. McCarron	Stancharry, 3, 117	Splendid Spruce, 3, 125	12	1:40.60	69,900
1980 **First Albert**, 3, 113	F. Mena	Big Doug, 3, 115	Kenderboun, 3, 117	12	1:48.00	68,800
1979 **Beau's Eagle**, 3, 121	S. Hawley	Ibacache (Chi), 3, 122	Paint King, 3, 113	8	1:47.00	64,500
1978 **Kamehameha**, 3, 120	T. M. Chapman	El Fantastico, 3, 114	Singular, 3, 118	12	1:47.40	102,800
1977 **Bad 'n Big**, 3, 121	L. A. Pincay Jr.	Iron Constitution, 3, 124	Minnesota Gus, 3, 112	8	1:48.00	96,450
1976 **Majestic Light**, 3, 121	S. Hawley	L'Heureux, 3, 120	*Bynoderm, 3, 116	10	1:48.20	67,200
1975 **Terete**, 3, 113	W. Shoemaker	Larrikin, 3, 125	Dusty County, 3, 117	6	1:48.60	46,400
1973 ***Amen II**, 3, 115	E. Belmonte	Kirrary, 3, 114	†Card Table, 3, 110	12	1:49.00	52,350

Named for Los Angeles's best-known industry. Grade 2 1973-'93. Cinema H. 1946-2001. Held at Santa Anita Park 1949. Not held 1974. 1$^1/_{16}$ miles 1946-'49, 1951-'55, 1981-'84. 1 mile 1950. Dirt 1946-'67. ‡Notorious Pleasure finished first, DQ to third, 1989. †Denotes female.

Citation Handicap

Grade 1 in 2006. Hollywood Park, three-year-olds and up, 1$^1/_{16}$ miles, turf. Held November 27, 2004, with a gross value of $400,000. First held in 1977. First graded in 1979. Stakes record 1:39.69 (1999 Brave Act [GB]).

Year	Winner	Jockey	Second	Third	Strs	Time	1st Purse
2004	**Leroidesanimaux (Brz)**, 4, 117	J. K. Court	A to the Z, 4, 115	Three Valleys, 3, 115	10	1:41.36	$240,000
2003	**Redattore (Brz)**, 8, 120	J. A. Krone	Irish Warrior, 5, 117	Mister Acpen (Chi), 5, 116	6	1:40.74	240,000
2002	**Good Journey**, 6, 123	P. Day	Seinne (Chi), 5, 115	White Heart (GB), 7, 115	10	1:41.45	300,000
2001	**Good Journey**, 5, 115	C. J. McCarron	Decarchy, 4, 117	Irish Prize, 5, 122	8	1:44.30	300,000
2000	**Charge d'Affaires (GB)**, 5, 116	J. A. Santos	Ladies Din, 5, 122	Native Desert, 7, 116	10	1:40.30	300,000
1999	**Brave Act (GB)**, 5, 119	A. O. Solis	Native Desert, 6, 116	Bouccaneer (Fr), 4, 119	11	**1:39.69**	300,000
1998	**Military**, 4, 118	G. K. Gomez	Mr Lightfoot (Ire), 4, 117	Worldly Ways (GB), 4, 114	8	1:50.58	180,000
1997	**Geri**, 5, 121	J. D. Bailey	Mufattish, 4, 116	Martiniquais (Ire), 4, 116	6	1:48.35	180,000
1996	**Gentlemen (Arg)**, 4, 119	G. L. Stevens	Smooth Runner, 5, 115	Via Lombardia (Ire), 4, 116	7	1:45.55	180,000
1995	**Fastness (Ire)**, 5, 120	G. L. Stevens	Earl of Barking (Ire), 5, 116	Silver Wizard, 5, 117	7	1:44.78	165,000
1994	**Southern Wish**, 5, 115	C. S. Nakatani	Square Cut, 5, 114	Jeune Homme, 4, 117	7	2:00.20	137,500
1993	**Jeune Homme**, 3, 114	T. Jarnet	Paradise Creek, 4, 120	Johann Quatz (Fr), 4, 120	8	1:45.84	137,500
1992	**Leger Cat (Arg)**, 6, 114	C. S. Nakatani	†Trishyde, 3, 111	Luthier Enchanteur, 5, 117	8	1:46.48	137,500
1991	**Notorious Pleasure**, 5, 118	L. A. Pincay Jr.	Somethingdifferent, 4, 114	Classic Fame, 5, 118	8	1:45.80	102,600
	Fly Till Dawn, 5, 119	L. A. Pincay Jr.	Best Pal, 3, 119	Wolf (Chi), 4, 119	8	1:45.86	102,600
1990	**Colway Rally (GB)**, 6, 114	C. A. Black	Exclusive Partner, 8, 117	The Medic, 6, 116	5	1:47.80	62,300
1989	**Fair Judgment**, 5, 117	E. Delahoussaye	Quiet Boy, 4, 113	Skip Out Front, 7, 117	6	1:50.00	63,300
1988	**Forlitano (Arg)**, 7, 118	P. A. Valenzuela	Precisionist, 7, 121	Skip Out Front, 6, 117	11	1:46.60	69,200
1987	**Forlitano (Arg)**, 6, 120	P. A. Valenzuela	Conquering Hero, 4, 115	Ifrad, 5, 115	12	1:47.40	71,500
1986	**Al Mamoon**, 5, 122	G. L. Stevens	Silveyville, 8, 118	Will Dancer (Fr), 4, 115	8	1:48.00	123,700
1985	**Zoffany**, 5, 116	E. Delahoussaye	Lord At War (Arg), 5, 125	Foscarini (Ire), 4, 115	9	1:44.80	69,100
1984	**Lord At War (Arg)**, 4, 117	W. Shoemaker	Executive Pride (Ire), 3, 116	Prairie Breaker, 4, 116	8	1:50.60	68,300
1983	**Beldale Lustre**, 4, 113	C. J. McCarron	The Hague, 4, 115	Sir Pele, 4, 114	10	1:49.40	53,000
	Pewter Grey, 4, 115	R. Sibille	Belmont Bay (Ire), 6, 119	Lucence, 4, 115	10	1:49.60	53,500
1982	**Caterman (NZ)**, 6, 121	C. J. McCarron	Cajun Prince, 5, 118	Island Whirl, 4, 123	5	1:41.00	46,700
1981	**Tahitian King (Ire)**, 5, 120	W. Shoemaker	King Go Go, 6, 115	Cajun Prince, 4, 113	11	1:48.80	136,000
1980	**Caro Bambino (Ire)**, 5, 118	P. A. Valenzuela	Life's Hope, 7, 116	Island Sultan, 5, 111	6	1:33.20	36,950
1979	**Text**, 5, 122	W. Shoemaker	Farnesio (Arg), 5, 117	Bad 'n Big, 5, 119	7	1:40.40	63,600
1978	**Effervescing**, 5, 120	L. A. Pincay Jr.	Dr. Patches, 4, 116	Text, 4, 122	6	1:40.20	62,700
1977	**Painted Wagon**, 4, 117	C. Baltazar	Legendaire, 4, 114	Pay Tribute, 5, 118	7	1:41.00	48,500

Named for Calumet Farm's 1948 Horse of the Year, '48 Triple Crown winner, and '51 Hollywood Gold Cup winner Citation (1945 c. by Bull Lea). Grade 3 1979-'80, 1984-'86. Not graded 1981-'83. Grade 2 1987-2003. Not held 2005. 1 mile 1980. 1$^1/_8$ miles 1981, 1983-'84, 1986-'93, 1995-'98. About 1$^1/_8$ miles 1985. 1$^1/_4$ miles 1994. Dirt 1977-'82, 1984. Two divisions 1983, 1991. Course record 1995. †Denotes female.

Clark Handicap

Grade 1 in 2006. Churchill Downs, three-year-olds and up, 1$^1/_8$ miles, dirt. Held November 25, 2005, with a gross value of $573,500. First held in 1875. First graded in 1973. Stakes record 1:48.26 (2001 Ubiquity).

Year	Winner	Jockey	Second	Third	Strs	Time	1st Purse
2005	**Magna Graduate**, 3, 116	J. R. Velazquez	Suave, 4, 118	Perfect Drift, 6, 122	12	1:50.89	$355,570
2004	**Saint Liam**, 4, 117	E. S. Prado	Seek Gold, 4, 111	Perfect Drift, 5, 118	9	1:50.81	345,960
2003	**‡Quest**, 4, 114	J. Castellano	Evening Attire, 5, 118	Aeneas, 4, 114	14	1:52.42	360,840
2002	**Lido Palace (Chi)**, 5, 121	J. F. Chavez	Crafty Shaw, 4, 115	Hero's Tribute, 4, 114	11	1:49.13	283,464
2001	**Ubiquity**, 4, 113	C. Perret	Include, 4, 120	Mr Ross, 6, 114	10	**1:48.26**	280,240
2000	**†Surfside**, 3, 113	P. Day	Guided Tour, 4, 114	Maysville Slew, 4, 113	9	1:48.75	276,272
1999	**Littlebitlively**, 5, 118	C. H. Borel	Pleasant Breeze, 4, 112	Nite Dreamer, 4, 114	12	1:50.88	284,456
1998	**Silver Charm**, 4, 124	G. L. Stevens	Littlebitlively, 4, 113	Wild Rush, 4, 117	8	1:49.07	275,776
1997	**Concerto**, 3, 113	J. D. Bailey	Terremoto, 6, 114	Rod and Staff, 4, 107	11	1:49.72	284,704
1996	**Isitingood**, 5, 120	D. R. Flores	Savinio, 6, 119	Coup D' Argent, 4, 110	9	1:48.99	174,220
1995	**Judge T C**, 4, 115	J. M. Johnson	Tyus, 5, 113	Alphabet Soup, 4, 117	14	1:49.82	153,140

1994	**Sir Vixen**, 6, 112	D. Kutz	Danville, 3, 113	Prize Fight, 5, 115	7	1:51.36	$143,130
1993	**Mi Cielo**, 3, 117	M. E. Smith	Take Me Out, 5, 115	Forry Cow How, 5, 115	13	1:51.43	150,540
1992	**Zeeruler**, 4, 113	G. K. Gomez	Flying Continental, 6, 118	Echelon's Ice Man, 4, 109	13	1:50.11	76,050
1991	**Out of Place**, 4, 119	W. H. McCauley	Echelon's Ice Man, 3, 110	British Banker, 3, 111	11	1:52.29	74,230
1990	**Secret Hello**, 3, 115	P. Day	Din's Dancer, 5, 119	De Roche, 4, 121	7	1:50.60	72,410
1989	**No Marker**, 5, 113	D. W. Cox	Set a Record, 5, 114	Stop the Stage, 4, 111	12	1:51.20	75,205
1988	**Balthazar B.**, 5, 112	K. Desormeaux	Clever Secret, 4, 115	Slew City Slew, 4, 123	9	1:51.20	80,835
1987	**Intrusion**, 5, 114	L. J. Melancon	Savings, 4, 116	Mister C., 4, 116	9	1:51.40	47,655
1986	**Come Summer**, 4, 112	P. A. Johnson	Taylor's Special, 5, 126	Sumptious, 3, 120	9	1:49.80	47,363
1985	**Hopeful Word**, 4, 118	P. Day	Dramatic Desire, 4, 113	Big Bobcat, 5, 111	9	1:51.00	49,510
1984	**Eminency**, 6, 121	P. Day	Jack Slade, 4, 122	Bayou Hebert, 3, 114	10	1:49.00	36,400
1983	**Jack Slade**, 3, 117	J. McKnight	Northern Majesty, 4, 122	Cad, 5, 118	8	1:49.80	35,912
1982	**Hechizado (Arg)**, 6, 117	R. P. Romero	Withholding, 5, 116	Pleasing Times, 3, 115	10	1:52.40	36,823
1981	**Withholding**, 4, 121	L. J. Melancon	Recusant, 3, 111	Hard Up, 5, 115	11	1:52.00	37,213
1980	**Sun Catcher**, 3, 117	D. Brumfield	Belle's Ruler, 5, 116	Withholding, 3, 116	10	1:53.40	35,636
1979	**Lot o' Gold**, 3, 123	J. C. Espinoza	Poverty Boy, 4, 114	Capital Idea, 6, 114	9	1:50.80	38,383
1978	**Bob's Dusty**, 4, 116	R. DePass	Kodiack, 4, 114	Raymond Earl, 3, 117	7	1:49.60	34,629
1977	**Bob's Dusty**, 3, 118	R. DePass	Packer Captain, 5, 116	Almost Grown, 5, 113	12	1:49.80	21,889
1976	**Yamanin**, 4, 120	G. Patterson	Warbucks, 6, 115	Play Boy, 3, 113	10	1:54.40	21,661
1975	**Warbucks**, 5, 124	L. J. Melancon	Silver Badge, 4, 118	†Shoo Dear, 4, 111	7	1:54.40	17,761
1974	**Mr. Door**, 3, 114	W. Gavidia	†Fairway Flyer, 5, 116	Cut the Talk, 3, 115	8	1:52.20	17,989
1973	**Golden Don**, 3, 122	M. Manganello	Amber Prey, 4, 115	Rastaferian, 4, 118	13	1:52.80	22,392

Named for Meriwether Lewis Clark (1846-'99), founder of the Kentucky Derby. Grade 3 1973-'97. Grade 2 1998-2005. Clark S. 1875-1901. 2 miles 1875-'80. $1\frac{1}{4}$ miles 1881-'95. $1\frac{1}{16}$ miles 1902-'21, 1925-'54. Three-year-olds 1875-1901. ‡Evening Attire finished first, DQ to second, 2003. †Denotes female.

Clement L. Hirsch Handicap

Grade 2 in 2006. Del Mar, three-year-olds and up, fillies and mares, $1\frac{1}{16}$ miles, dirt. Held August 7, 2005, with a gross value of $300,000. First held in 1937. First graded in 1983. Stakes record 1:40 (1982 Matching).

Year	Winner	Jockey	Second	Third	Strs	Time	1st Purse
2005	**Tucked Away**, 5, 115	A. O. Solis	Hollywood Story, 4, 119	Valentine Dancer, 5, 117	8	1:42.82	$180,000
2004	**Miss Loren (Arg)**, 6, 114	J. K. Court	House of Fortune, 3, 113	Royally Chosen, 6, 116	8	1:42.93	180,000
2003	**Azeri**, 5, 127	M. E. Smith	Got Koko, 4, 118	Tropical Blossom, 5, 108	5	1:42.12	180,000
2002	**Azeri**, 4, 126	M. E. Smith	Angel Gift, 4, 114	Se Me Acabo (Chi), 4, 114	5	1:42.66	180,000
2001	**Tranquility Lake**, 6, 120	E. Delahoussaye	Gourmet Girl, 6, 122	Nany's Sweep, 5, 116	4	1:41.78	180,000
2000	**Riboletta (Brz)**, 5, 125	C. J. McCarron	Bordelaise (Arg), 5, 115	Gourmet Girl, 5, 115	6	1:42.06	180,000
1999	**A Lady From Dixie**, 4, 116	C. W. Antley	Manistique, 4, 124	Yolo Lady, 4, 116	5	1:43.58	180,000
1998	**Sharp Cat**, 4, 124	C. S. Nakatani	Supercilious, 5, 115	Numero Uno, 4, 116	4	1:42.16	180,000
1997	**Radu Cool**, 5, 117	C. J. McCarron	Supercilious, 4, 113	Swoon River, 5, 110	6	1:42.66	180,000
1996	**Different (Arg)**, 4, 120	C. J. McCarron	Top Rung, 5, 115	Borodislew, 6, 117	4	1:42.48	189,200
1995	**Borodislew**, 5, 118	C. J. McCarron	Lakeway, 4, 121	Golden Klair (GB), 5, 118	6	1:41.87	178,100
1994	**Paseana (Arg)**, 7, 123	C. J. McCarron	Exchange, 6, 120	Magical Maiden, 5, 118	4	1:40.59	117,100
1993	**Magical Maiden**, 4, 120	G. L. Stevens	Vieille Vigne (Fr), 6, 111	Party Cited, 4, 117	8	1:42.68	123,600
1992	**Exchange**, 4, 120	L. A. Pincay Jr.	Fowda, 4, 120	Brought to Mind, 5, 119	8	1:42.00	123,100
1991	**Vieille Vigne (Fr)**, 4, 116	M. A. Pedroza	Formidable Lady, 5, 113	Lite Light, 3, 121	6	1:42.67	120,300
1990	**Bayakoa (Arg)**, 6, 127	L. A. Pincay Jr.	Fantastic Look, 4, 113	Formidable Lady, 4, 112	5	1:40.60	88,500
1989	**Goodbye Halo**, 4, 120	C. A. Black	Flying Julia, 6, 112	Kool Arrival, 3, 115	6	1:41.80	77,450
1988	**Clabber Girl**, 5, 120	C. J. McCarron	Annoconnor, 4, 118	Integra, 4, 119	5	1:41.60	75,100
1987	**Infinidad (Chi)**, 5, 118	C. A. Black	Margaret Booth, 4, 117	Le l'Argent, 5, 117	9	1:41.40	63,540
1986	**Fran's Valentine**, 4, 119	W. Shoemaker	Cenyak's Star, 4, 116	Dontstop Themusic, 6, 123	5	1:41.40	59,500
1985	**Dontstop Themusic**, 5, 122	D. G. McHargue	Golden Screen, 5, 112	Lovlier Linda, 5, 119	4	1:41.80	45,650
1984	**Princess Rooney**, 4, 123	P. A. Valenzuela	Flag de Lune, 4, 115	Moment to Buy, 3, 116	5	1:40.40	60,100
1983	**Sangue (Ire)**, 5, 121	W. Shoemaker	Avigaition, 4, 122	Skillful Joy, 4, 117	5	1:42.20	46,600
1982	**Matching**, 4, 116	R. Sibille	Miss Huntington, 5, 116	Cat Girl, 4, 117	4	**1:40.00**	45,850
1981	**Save Wild Life**, 4, 118	C. J. McCarron	Princess Karenda, 4, 120	Track Robbery, 5, 125	6	1:41.60	47,650
1980	**Wayside Station**, 5, 113	P. A. Valenzuela	Concussion, 6, 117	Mike Fogarty (Ire), 5, 115	6	1:28.80	19,775
	Galaxy Libra (Ire), 4, 118	W. Shoemaker	Wickerr, 5, 117	To B. Or Not, 4, 116	5	1:29.00	19,375
1979	**He's Dewan**, 4, 119	D. G. McHargue	Caro Bambino (Ire), 4, 119	No No, 4, 115	10	1:29.00	23,950
1978	**Nantequos**, 5, 120	D. G. McHargue	Lunar Probe (NZ), 4, 118	dh-Around We Go, 5, 117 dh-Crew of Ocala, 4, 114	10	1:29.40	20,250
1977	**Notably Different**, 4, 113	C. Baltazar	Key Account, 5, 114	Pikehall, 3, 109	8	1:29.40	13,375
	Authorization, 5, 113	D. G. McHargue	Cherry River, 7, 112	Mister Dan, 4, 114	7	1:29.20	13,175
1976	**Uniformity**, 4, 115	R. Campas	White Fir, 4, 118	*Royal Derby II, 7, 119	9	1:28.20	16,900
1975	**Bahia Key**, 5, 119	W. Harris	Fair Test, 7, 119	Top Command, 4, 117	5	1:34.00	12,750
1974	**Bahia Key**, 4, 120	A. Pineda	*Trotteur, 4, 117	Soft Victory, 6, 122	9	1:34.20	13,650
1973	**Grotonian**, 4, 117	W. Shoemaker	Expediter, 4, 115	China Silk, 4, 114	5	1:50.60	12,600

Named for Clement L. Hirsch (1914-2000), an original Del Mar director. Formerly named for the city of Chula Vista, California. Grade 3 1983-'85. Chula Vista H. 1937-'99. Not held 1938-'66, 1968-'72. $5\frac{1}{2}$ furlongs 1937. 1 mile 1967, 1974-'75. $1\frac{1}{8}$ miles 1973. $7\frac{1}{2}$ furlongs 1976-'80. Turf 1973, 1976-'80. Two-year-olds 1937. Both sexes 1973-'80. Two divisions 1977, 1980. Dead heat for third 1978. Nonwinners of a race worth $12,500 to the winner other than claiming 1974. California-breds 1937.

Clement L. Hirsch Memorial Turf Championship Stakes

Grade 1 in 2006. Oak Tree at Santa Anita, three-year-olds and up, 1¼ miles, turf. Held October 2, 2005, with a gross value of $250,000. First held in 1969. First graded in 1973. Stakes record 1:58.48 (1996 Bon Point [GB] [DQ to fifth]).

Year	Winner	Jockey	Second	Third	Strs	Time	1st Purse
2005	**Fourty Niners Son**, 4, 124	C. S. Nakatani	‡Leprechaun Kid, 6, 124	Laura's Lucky Boy, 4, 124	8	2:01.17	$150,000
2004	**Star Over the Bay**, 6, 124	T. Baze	Sarafan, 7, 124	Vangelis, 5, 124	7	1:58.70	150,000
2003	**Storming Home (GB)**, 5, 124	G. L. Stevens	Johar, 4, 124	Irish Warrior, 5, 124	4	2:01.64	150,000
2002	**The Tin Man**, 4, 124	M. E. Smith	Sarafan, 5, 124	Blue Steller (Ire), 4, 124	6	1:58.93	180,000
2001	**Senure**, 5, 124	A. O. Solis	White Heart (GB), 6, 124	Cagney (Brz), 4, 124	6	1:59.47	180,000
2000	**Mash One (Chi)**, 6, 124	D. R. Flores	Boatman, 4, 124	Asidero (Arg), 4, 124	6	2:00.67	180,000
1999	**Mash One (Chi)**, 5, 124	D. R. Flores	Lazy Lode (Arg), 5, 124	Bonapartiste (Fr), 5, 124	6	1:59.07	180,000
1998	**Military**, 4, 124	C. S. Nakatani	Bonapartiste (Fr), 4, 124	River Bay, 5, 124	5	2:02.04	180,000
1997	**Rainbow Dancer (Fr)**, 6, 124	A. O. Solis	‡Lord Jain (Arg), 5, 124	Sandpit (Brz), 8, 124	5	2:01.80	180,000
1996	**‡†Admise (Fr)**, 4, 121	K. Desormeaux	Khoraz, 6, 124	Golden Post, 6, 124	5	**1:58.48**	180,000
1995	**Northern Spur (Ire)**, 4, 124	C. J. McCarron	Sandpit (Brz), 6, 124	Royal Chariot, 5, 124	8	2:02.37	180,000
1994	**Sandpit (Brz)**, 5, 124	C. S. Nakatani	Grand Flotilla, 7, 124	Approach the Bench (Ire), 6, 124	5	2:25.12	180,000
1993	**Kotashaan (Fr)**, 5, 124	K. Desormeaux	Luazur (Fr), 4, 124	†Let's Elope (NZ), 6, 121	4	2:25.06	180,000
1992	**Navarone**, 4, 126	P. A. Valenzuela	Defensive Play, 5, 126	Daros (GB), 3, 121	6	2:24.29	240,000
1991	**Filago**, 4, 126	P. A. Valenzuela	Missionary Ridge (GB), 4, 126	†Kartajana (Ire), 4, 123	9	2:23.62	300,000
1990	**Rial (Arg)**, 5, 126	R. Q. Meza	Eradicate (GB), 5, 126	Saratoga Passage, 5, 126	11	2:23.80	300,000
1989	**Hawkster**, 3, 121	R. A. Baze	Pay the Butler, 5, 126	Saratoga Passage, 4, 126	9	2:22.80	300,000
1988	**Nasr El Arab**, 3, 121	G. L. Stevens	Great Communicator, 5, 126	Circus Prince, 5, 126	8	2:25.20	240,000
1987	**Allez Milord**, 4, 126	C. J. McCarron	Louis Le Grand, 5, 126	Rivlia, 5, 126	10	2:36.20	240,000
1986	**†Estrapade**, 6, 123	F. Toro	Theatrical (Ire), 4, 126	Uptown Swell, 4, 126	10	2:26.00	240,000
1985	**Yashgan (GB)**, 4, 126	C. J. McCarron	Both Ends Burning, 5, 126	Cariellor (Fr), 4, 126	10	2:27.20	240,000
1984	**Both Ends Burning**, 4, 126	R. A. Baze	Gato Del Sol, 5, 126	Raami (GB), 3, 121	12	2:25.40	240,000
1983	**†Zalataia (Fr)**, 4, 123	F. Head	John Henry, 8, 126	Load the Cannons, 3, 122	9	2:29.20	240,000
1982	**John Henry**, 7, 126	W. Shoemaker	Craelius, 3, 122	Regalberto, 4, 126	7	2:24.00	180,000
1981	**John Henry**, 6, 126	W. Shoemaker	Spence Bay (Ire), 6, 126	The Bart, 5, 126	7	2:23.40	180,000
1980	**John Henry**, 5, 126	L. A. Pincay Jr.	Balzac, 5, 126	Bold Tropic (SAf), 5, 126	10	2:23.40	120,000
1979	**Balzac**, 4, 126	C. J. McCarron	†Trillion, 5, 123	Silver Eagle (Ire), 5, 126	9	2:25.40	90,000
1978	**Exceller**, 5, 126	W. Shoemaker	Star of Erin (Ire), 4, 126	dh-As de Copas (Arg), 5, 126 dh-Good Lord (NZ), 7, 126	9	2:24.60	90,000
1977	**Crystal Water**, 4, 126	W. Shoemaker	Vigors, 4, 126	Ancient Title, 7, 126	10	2:26.40	60,000
1976	**King Pellinore**, 4, 126	W. Shoemaker	*Royal Derby II, 7, 126	L'Heureux, 3, 121	9	2:31.40	60,000
1975	**Top Command**, 4, 126	W. Shoemaker	Top Crowd, 4, 126	Buffalo Lark, 5, 126	8	2:26.00	60,000
1974	**†Tallahto**, 4, 123	L. A. Pincay Jr.	Within Hail, 3, 122	Montmartre, 4, 126	11	2:25.80	60,000
1973	**Portentous**, 3, 122	J. Ramirez	Groshawk, 3, 122	dh-Kentuckian, 4, 126 dh-Kirrary, 3, 122	8	2:25.60	60,000

Named for Clement L. Hirsch (1914-2000), co-founder and first president of Oak Tree Racing Association. The race is held during the Oak Tree meet at Santa Anita Park. Oak Tree S. 1969-'70. Oak Tree Invitational 1971-'95. Oak Tree Turf Championship 1996-'99. Clement L. Hirsch Turf Championship 2000. 1½ miles 1969-'94. Dead heat for third 1973, 1978. ‡Bon Point (GB) finished first, DQ to fifth, 1996. ‡Marlin finished second, DQ to fourth, 1997. ‡Whilly (Ire) finished second, DQ to fifth, 2005. †Denotes female.

Cliff Hanger Stakes

Grade 3 in 2006. The Meadowlands, three-year-olds and up, 1$^1/_{16}$ miles, turf. Held October 22, 2005, with a gross value of $150,000. First held in 1977. First graded in 1985. Stakes record 1:39.40 (1988 Wanderkin).

Year	Winner	Jockey	Second	Third	Strs	Time	1st Purse
2005	**Hotstufanthensome**, 5, 119	R. Maragh	Icy Atlantic, 4, 117	Stormy Ray, 6, 117	8	1:54.32	$90,000
2004	**Dr. Kashnikow**, 7, 116	R. Migliore	Tam's Terms, 6, 116	Host (Chi), 4, 117	8	1:42.41	120,000
2002	**Saint Verre**, 4, 113	J. Samyn	Pinky Pizwaanski, 4, 116	Spruce Run, 4, 115	4	1:42.40	90,000
2001	**Crash Course**, 5, 114	R. Wilson	Solitary Dancer, 5, 114	Union One, 4, 114	10	1:43.14	90,000
2000	**North East Bound**, 4, 118	J. A. Velez Jr.	Johnny Dollar, 4, 114	Swamp, 4, 120	11	1:41.78	90,000
1999	**Virginia Carnival**, 7, 114	J. Samyn	Star Connection, 5, 114	Grapeshot, 5, 116	12	1:42.44	90,000
1998	**Mi Narrow**, 4, 111	J. Bravo	Treat Me Doc, 4, 114	Boyce, 7, 114	6	1:43.58	60,000
1997	**Dixie Bayou**, 4, 114	J. R. Velazquez	Brave Note (Ire), 6, 115	Joker, 5, 116	10	1:39.45	60,000
1996	**Thorny Crown**, 5, 115	M. J. Luzzi	Ihtiraz (GB), 6, 114	Winnetou, 6, 112	5	1:44.71	60,000
1995	**‡Mighty Forum (GB)**, 4, 114	W. H. McCauley	Joker, 3, 106	Fourstars Allstar, 7, 120	7	1:41.09	60,000
1994	**Binary Light**, 5, 112	J. Samyn	Brazany, 4, 112	Burst of Applause, 5, 109	5	1:41.41	45,000
1993	**Excellent Tipper**, 5, 117	C. Perret	Rinka Das, 5, 115	First and Only, 6, 115	6	1:43.69	45,000
1992	**Roman Envoy**, 4, 116	C. Perret	Futurist, 4, 116	Royal Ninja, 6, 115	8	1:39.92	45,000
1991	**Finder's Choice**, 6, 114	R. Aviles	Royal Rue, 5, 113	Great Normand, 6, 117	8	1:40.31	45,000
1990	**Chas' Whim**, 3, 115	A. T. Stacy	Kali High, 6, 115	Royal Ninja, 4, 112	11	1:46.40	45,000
1989	**Ten Keys**, 5, 114	K. Desormeaux	Wanderkin, 6, 121	Soviet Lad, 4, 112	7	1:42.20	52,290
1988	**Wanderkin**, 5, 118	R. G. Davis	Salem Drive, 6, 117	San's the Shadow, 4, 117	9	**1:39.40**	53,730
1987	**Foligno**, 5, 115	J. A. Santos	Cost Conscious, 5, 116	Air Display, 4, 113	7	1:41.40	46,995
	Silver Comet, 4, 117	W. H. McCauley	Broadway Tommy, 5, 112	Prince Daniel, 4, 114	3	1:43.80	31,831
1986	**Explosive Darling**, 4, 118	R. P. Romero	Equalize, 4, 114	Lieutenant's Lark, 4, 120	7	1:40.00	48,360
1985	**Late Act**, 6, 117	J. D. Bailey	Silver Surfer, 4, 116	Pax Nobiscum, 5, 116	7	1:45.00	47,790
1984	**Late Act**, 5, 113	E. Maple	Sitzmark, 4, 111	Quick Dip, 4, 112	10	1:40.80	46,020
	Cozzene, 4, 115	W. A. Guerra	Ayman, 4, 112	Pin Puller, 5, 114	6	1:40.40	45,300
1983	**Erin's Tiger**, 5, 112	J. Velasquez	Who's for Dinner, 4, 113	Kentucky River, 5, 112	9	1:41.20	33,450

1982	**Erin's Tiger**, 4, 114	J. Velasquez	Santo's Joe, 5, 116	Dew Line, 3, 114	8	1:44.60	$26,295
	Acaroid, 4, 114	A. T. Cordero Jr.	North Course, 7, 114	Thirty Eight Paces, 4, 116	7	1:44.60	26,115
1981	**Bill Wheeler**, 4, 119	W. H. McCauley	Mannerism, 4, 113	Brahmin, 5, 115	15	1:43.60	33,510
1980	**Quality T. V.**, 3, 114	J. Velasquez	Conservatoire, 3, 109	Bill Wheeler, 3, 112	10	1:43.80	32,640
1979	**Exclusively Mine**, 3, 114	W. Nemeti	Telly Hill, 5, 126	Picturesque, 3, 116	7	1:44.20	34,678
1978	**Mr. Lincroft**, 4, 117	V. A. Bracciale Jr.	Telly Hill, 4, 119	†Forbidden Isle, 3, 109	15	1:44.20	36,270
1977	**Dan Horn**, 5, 125	D. MacBeth	Shore Patrol, 7, 113	Popular Victory, 5, 118	9	1:43.60	34,873

Named to honor the early movie industry in New Jersey, referring to suspenseful silent film serials. Grade 3 1985-2001. Not graded 2002. Cliff Hanger H. 1977-'81, 1983-2002, 2004. Not held 2003. Dirt 1978-'81, 1985, 1987, 1993, 1996, 1998, 2002. Originally scheduled on turf 2002. Two divisions 1982, 1984, 1987. Equaled course record 1997. ‡Joker finished first, DQ to second, 1995. †Denotes female.

Coaching Club American Oaks

Grade 1 in 2006. Belmont Park, three-year-olds, fillies, $1\frac{1}{4}$ miles, dirt. Held July 23, 2005, with a gross value of $500,000. First held in 1917. First graded in 1973. Stakes record 2:00.40 (1997 Ajina).

Year	Winner	Jockey	Second	Third	Strs	Time	1st Purse
2005	**Smuggler**, 3, 121	E. S. Prado	Summerly, 3, 121	Spun Sugar, 3, 121	7	2:04.39	$300,000
2004	**Ashado**, 3, 121	J. R. Velazquez	Stellar Jayne, 3, 121	Magical Illusion, 3, 121	6	2:02.43	300,000
2003	**Spoken Fur**, 3, 121	J. D. Bailey	Fircroft, 3, 121	Savedbythelight, 3, 121	7	2:31.02	300,000
2002	**Jilbab**, 3, 121	M. J. Luzzi	Tarnished Lady, 3, 121	Shop Till You Drop, 3, 121	7	2:31.48	210,000
2001	**Tweedside**, 3, 121	J. R. Velazquez	Exogenous, 3, 121	Unbridled Lassie, 3, 121	8	2:30.70	210,000
2000	**Jostle**, 3, 121	M. E. Smith	Resort, 3, 121	Secret Status, 3, 121	7	2:29.99	210,000
1999	**On a Soapbox**, 3, 121	J. D. Bailey	Dreams Gallore, 3, 121	Strolling Belle, 3, 121	8	2:29.31	210,000
1998	**Banshee Breeze**, 3, 121	J. D. Bailey	Keeper Hill, 3, 121	Best Friend Stro, 3, 121	6	2:31.56	180,000
1997	**Ajina**, 3, 121	M. E. Smith	Tomisue's Delight, 3, 121	Key Hunter, 3, 121	5	**2:00.40**	150,000
1996	**My Flag**, 3, 121	J. D. Bailey	Gold n Delicious, 3, 121	Weekend in Seattle, 3, 121	7	2:04.64	150,000
1995	**Golden Bri**, 3, 121	J. A. Santos	Serena's Song, 3, 121	Change Fora Dollar, 3, 121	6	2:03.86	150,000
1994	**Two Altazano**, 3, 121	J. A. Santos	Plenty of Sugar, 3, 121	Sovereign Kitty, 3, 121	7	2:02.88	150,000
1993	**Sky Beauty**, 3, 121	M. E. Smith	Future Pretense, 3, 121	Silky Feather, 3, 121	5	2:01.56	150,000
1992	**Turnback the Alarm**, 3, 121	C. W. Antley	Easy Now, 3, 121	Pleasant Stage, 3, 121	6	2:03.53	150,000
1991	**Lite Light**, 3, 121	C. S. Nakatani	Meadow Star, 3, 121	Car Gal, 3, 121	6	2:00.54	150,000
1990	**Charon**, 3, 121	C. Perret	Crowned, 3, 121	Paper Money, 3, 121	7	2:02.60	172,500
1989	**‡Open Mind**, 3, 121	A. T. Cordero Jr.	Nite of Fun, 3, 121	Rose Diamond, 3, 121	6	2:32.40	170,100
1988	**Goodbye Halo**, 3, 121	J. Velasquez	Aptostar, 3, 121	Make Change, 3, 121	6	2:32.80	170,400
1987	**Fiesta Gal**, 3, 121	A. T. Cordero Jr.	Mint Cooler, 3, 121	Run Come See, 3, 121	7	2:31.00	172,500
1986	**Valley Victory (Ire)**, 3, 121	R. P. Romero	Life At the Top, 3, 121	Lotka, 3, 121	8	2:28.00	166,680
1985	**Mom's Command**, 3, 121	A. Fuller	Bessarabian, 3, 121	Foxy Deen, 3, 121	9	2:32.00	142,560
1984	**Class Play**, 3, 121	J. Cruguet	Life's Magic, 3, 121	Miss Oceana, 3, 121	5	2:29.80	164,520
1983	**High Schemes**, 3, 121	J. Samyn	Spit Curl, 3, 121	Lady Norcliffe, 3, 121	16	2:30.20	107,460
1982	**Christmas Past**, 3, 121	J. Vasquez	Cupecoy's Joy, 3, 121	Flying Partner, 3, 121	10	2:28.60	84,900
1981	**‡Wayward Lass**, 3, 121	C. B. Asmussen	Real Prize, 3, 121	Banner Gala, 3, 121	6	2:28.20	81,750
1980	**Bold 'n Determined**, 3, 121	E. Delahoussaye	Erin's Word, 3, 121	Farewell Letter, 3, 121	7	2:31.80	84,000
1979	**Davona Dale**, 3, 121	J. Velasquez	Plankton, 3, 121	Croquis, 3, 121	5	2:30.00	79,575
1978	**Lakeville Miss**, 3, 121	R. Hernandez	Caesar's Wish, 3, 121	Tempest Queen, 3, 121	5	2:29.40	63,540
1977	**Our Mims**, 3, 121	J. Velasquez	Road Princess, 3, 121	Fia, 3, 121	12	2:29.40	65,880
1976	**Revidere**, 3, 121	J. Vasquez	Optimistic Gal, 3, 121	No Duplicate, 3, 121	10	2:28.40	68,640
1975	**Ruffian**, 3, 121	J. Vasquez	Equal Change, 3, 121	Let Me Linger, 3, 121	7	2:27.80	66,700
1974	**Chris Evert**, 3, 121	J. Velasquez	Fiesta Libre, 3, 121	Maud Muller, 3, 121	10	2:28.80	68,520
1973	**Magazine**, 3, 121	A. T. Cordero Jr.	Bag of Tunes, 3, 121	Lady Love, 3, 121	13	2:27.80	70,200

Named in honor of the Coaching Club of America, first sponsor of the race. The Coaching Club preserved the aristocratic traditions of driving four-in-hand coaches (a coach pulled by four horses with a single rein) socially and in competitions—the ability to drive one of these coaches was a condition of membership. Coaching Club American Oaks H. 1917-'27. Held at Aqueduct 1963-'67. $1\frac{1}{8}$ miles 1917. $1\frac{1}{2}$ miles 1942-'43, 1971-'89, 1998-2003. $1\frac{3}{8}$ miles 1919-'41, 1944-'58. ‡Real Prize finished first, DQ to second, 1981. ‡Nite of Fun finished first, DQ to second, 1989.

Comely Stakes

Grade 2 in 2006. Aqueduct, three-year-olds, fillies, 1 mile, dirt. Held April 15, 2006, with a gross value of $150,000. First held in 1945. First graded in 1973. Stakes record 1:35.50 (2002 Bella Bellucci).

Year	Winner	Jockey	Second	Third	Strs	Time	1st Purse
2006	**Miraculous Miss**, 3, 122	K. J. Desormeaux	Regal Engagement, 3, 120	Daytime Promise, 3, 120	6	1:36.67	$90,000
2005	**Acey Deucey**, 3, 118	D. Nelson	Seeking the Ante, 3, 116	Pleasant Chimes, 3, 116	8	1:35.95	90,000
2004	**Society Selection**, 3, 122	J. F. Chavez	Bending Strings, 3, 116	Daydreaming, 3, 116	8	1:35.89	67,200
2003	**Cyber Secret**, 3, 122	S. Bridgmohan	Storm Flag Flying, 3, 122	Bonay, 3, 116	5	1:35.97	64,740
2002	**Bella Bellucci**, 3, 122	G. L. Stevens	Short Note, 3, 116	Nonsuch Bay, 3, 116	5	**1:35.50**	64,920
2001	**‡Two Item Limit**, 3, 122	R. Migliore	Mandy's Gold, 3, 118	It All Adds Up, 3, 116	7	1:36.17	66,060
2000	**March Magic**, 3, 114	R. Migliore	Jostle, 3, 121	Finder's Fee, 3, 121	6	1:36.79	65,460
1999	**Madison's Charm**, 3, 112	J. Samyn	Better Than Honour, 3, 121	Oh What a Windfall, 3, 121	7	1:35.54	65,520
1998	**Fantasy Angel**, 3, 114	J. F. Chavez	Hansel's Girl, 3, 116	Best Friend Stro, 3, 118	12	1:37.44	69,300
1997	**Dixie Flag**, 3, 114	J. Samyn	Global Star, 3, 114	How About Now, 3, 114	7	1:36.96	66,120
1996	**Little Miss Fast**, 3, 118	J. F. Chavez	J J'sdream, 3, 118	Stop Traffic, 3, 112	7	1:36.58	65,940
1995	**Nappelon**, 3, 112	J. F. Chavez	Stormy Blues, 3, 121	Incredible Blues, 3, 114	6	1:36.26	64,440
1994	**Dixie Luck**, 3, 116	F. Leon	Penny's Reshoot, 3, 116	Our Royal Blue, 3, 112	7	1:37.02	66,240
1993	**Private Light**, 3, 112	R. G. Davis	Russian Bride, 3, 113	True Affair, 3, 118	6	1:44.19	68,280
1992	**Saratoga Dew**, 3, 114	W. H. McCauley	City Dance, 3, 113	Looking for a Win, 3, 114	7	1:37.22	69,480

1991 **Meadow Star**, 3, 121	C. W. Antley	Do It With Style, 3, 114	I'm a Thriller, 3, 118	5	1:38.02	$67,560
1990 **Fappaburst**, 3, 114	J. Vasquez	Miss Spentyouth, 3, 114	Bundle Bits, 3, 118	4	1:21.60	49,770
1989 **Surging**, 3, 118	A. T. Cordero Jr.	Nite of Fun, 3, 112	Luv That Native, 3, 112	6	1:23.00	52,290
1988 **Avie's Gal**, 3, 114	J. Velasquez	Topicount, 3, 116	Ready Jet Go, 3, 114	8	1:22.40	66,780
1987 **Devil's Bride**, 3, 116	R. Q. Meza	Oh So Precious, 3, 116	Valid Line, 3, 114	7	1:23.60	65,790
1986 **Misty Drone**, 3, 112	J. Vasquez	I'm Splendid, 3, 121	Storm and Sunshine, 3, 114	14	1:24.00	59,940
1985 **Mom's Command**, 3, 121	A. Fuller	Majestic Folly, 3, 113	Clocks Secret, 3, 121	9	1:22.20	55,170
1984 **Wild Applause**, 3, 113	P. Day	Suavite, 3, 113	Proud Clarioness, 3, 116	7	1:23.20	52,110
1983 **Able Money**, 3, 113	A. Graell	Stark Drama, 3, 113	Idle Gossip, 3, 113	10	1:23.80	35,580
1982 **Nancy Huang**, 3, 113	J. Velasquez	Broom Dance, 3, 113	Dance Number, 3, 113	10	1:24.40	34,860
1981 **Expressive Dance**, 3, 113	D. MacBeth	Tina Tina Too, 3, 118	Explosive Kingdom, 3, 114	11	1:23.40	35,220
1980 **Cybele**, 3, 113	C. B. Asmussen	Punta Punta, 3, 113	Kashan, 3, 113	7	1:22.60	27,225
1979 **Countess North**, 3, 113	A. T. Cordero Jr.	Palm Hut, 3, 116	Run Cosmic Run, 3, 113	5	1:23.40	25,725
1978 **Mashteen**, 3, 113	R. Hernandez	Tempest Queen, 3, 118	Mucchina, 3, 113	6	1:23.00	25,665
1977 **Bring Out the Band**, 3, 118	D. Brumfield	Cum Laude Laurie, 3, 113	Emmy, 3, 113	10	1:23.60	22,650
1976 **Tell Me All**, 3, 113	J. Ruane	Dearly Precious, 3, 121	Worthyana, 3, 113	5	1:23.20	22,080
1975 **Ruffian**, 3, 113	J. Vasquez	Aunt Jin, 3, 113	Point in Time, 3, 113	5	1:21.20	16,755
1974 **Clear Copy**, 3, 113	D. Montoya	Shy Dawn, 3, 118	Chris Evert, 3, 118	10	1:24.40	17,670
1973 **Java Moon**, 3, 116	A. T. Cordero Jr.	Windy's Daughter, 3, 121	Voler, 3, 116	11	1:22.80	17,610

Named for James Butler's Comely (1912 f. by Disguise); Butler was the owner of Empire City, where the race originated. Grade 3 1973-'87, 1996-2004. Comely H. 1945-'53. Held at Jamaica 1945-'51, 1959. Held at Empire City 1952-'53. Held at Belmont Park 1976, 1981, 1984-'85. Not held 1954-'58. 1$^1/_{16}$ miles 1945-'53, 1993. 5 furlongs 1959. 7 furlongs 1960-'90. Three-year-olds and up 1945-'53. Fillies and mares 1945-'53. Two-year-olds 1959. Both sexes 1959. ‡Mandy's Gold finished first, DQ to second, 2001.

Commonwealth Breeders' Cup Stakes

Grade 2 in 2006. Keeneland Race Course, three-year-olds and up, 7 furlongs, dirt. Held April 15, 2006, with a gross value of $443,200. First held in 1987. First graded in 1990. Stakes record 1:20.50 (1998 Distorted Humor).

Year Winner	Jockey	Second	Third	Strs	Time	1st Purse
2006 **Sun King**, 4, 120	C. S. Nakatani	Kazoo, 8, 118	Spanish Chestnut, 4, 118	12	1:23.30	$274,784
2005 **Clock Stopper**, 5, 118	J. D. Bailey	Gators N Bears, 5, 118	Silver Wagon, 4, 118	6	1:22.06	263,438
2004 **Lion Tamer**, 4, 122	M. E. Smith	Private Horde, 5, 120	Marino Marini, 4, 118	6	1:23.14	167,555
2003 **Smooth Jazz**, 4, 118	E. S. Prado	Crafty C. T., 5, 118	Multiple Choice, 5, 120	7	1:21.73	169,725
2002 **Orientate**, 4, 120	P. Day	Aldebaran, 4, 118	Twilight Road, 5, 118	7	1:21.54	168,640
2001 **Alannan**, 5, 118	E. S. Prado	Valiant Halory, 4, 118	Liberty Gold, 7, 118	8	1:22.39	170,965
2000 **Richter Scale**, 6, 121	R. Migliore	Son's Corona, 5, 117	Deep Gold, 4, 117	6	1:21.07	128,836
1999 **Good and Tough**, 4, 115	S. J. Sellers	Purple Passion, 5, 115	Crucible, 4, 115	5	1:22.09	127,906
1998 **Distorted Humor**, 5, 119	G. L. Stevens	El Amante, 5, 114	Partner's Hero, 4, 121	8	**1:20.50**	130,820
1997 **Victor Cooley**, 4, 114	E. M. Martin Jr.	Western Winter, 5, 112	Appealing Skier, 4, 121	7	1:22.40	129,332
1996 **Afternoon Deelites**, 4, 124	K. Desormeaux	Western Winter, 4, 113	Our Emblem, 5, 115	6	1:21.12	131,068
1995 **Golden Gear**, 4, 118	C. Perret	Turkomatic, 4, 112	Lit de Justice, 5, 121	8	1:22.06	130,758
1994 **Memo (Chi)**, 7, 118	P. Atkinson	American Chance, 5, 115	British Banker, 6, 115	10	1:22.32	69,378
1993 **Alydeed**, 4, 115	C. Perret	Binalong, 4, 118	Senor Speedy, 6, 115	6	1:21.43	113,057
1992 **Pleasant Tap**, 5, 116	E. Delahoussaye	To Freedom, 4, 115	Run On the Bank, 5, 118	6	1:22.40	118,138
1991 **Black Tie Affair (Ire)**, 5, 124	J. L. Diaz	Housebuster, 4, 124	Exemplary Leader, 5, 115	6	1:21.86	118,625
1990 **Black Tie Affair (Ire)**, 4, 121	M. Guidry	Shaker Knit, 5, 115	Momsfurrari, 6, 118	9	1:22.00	121,111
1989 **Sewickley**, 4, 115	R. P. Romero	Irish Open, 5, 118	Dancing Spree, 4, 115	9	1:22.40	36,368
1988 **Calestoga**, 6, 120	D. Brumfield	You're No Bargain, 4, 117	Carload, 6, 120	10	1:09.40	101,628
1987 **Exclusive Enough**, 3, 111	M. E. Smith	†Lazer Show, 4, 120	High Brite, 3, 120	8	1:08.40	101,010

Named for the Commonwealth of Kentucky. Grade 3 1990-'93. Commonwealth Breeders' Cup H. 1989. 6 furlongs 1987-'88. †Denotes female.

Coolmore Lexington Stakes

Grade 2 in 2006. Keeneland Race Course, three-year-olds, 1$^1/_{16}$ miles, dirt. Held April 22, 2006, with a gross value of $325,000. First held in 1936. First graded in 1986. Stakes record 1:41.06 (1999 Charismatic).

Year Winner	Jockey	Second	Third	Strs	Time	1st Purse
2006 **Showing Up**, 3, 117	C. H. Velasquez	Like Now, 3, 123	Bear Character, 3, 117	10	1:46.42	$201,500
2005 **Coin Silver**, 3, 117	J. Castellano	Sort It Out, 3, 117	Storm Surge, 3, 117	7	1:45.76	201,500
2004 **Quintons Gold Rush**, 3, 116	J. D. Bailey	Fire Slam, 3, 116	Song of the Sword, 3, 116	14	1:43.82	201,500
2003 **Scrimshaw**, 3, 116	E. S. Prado	Eye of the Tiger, 3, 116	Domestic Dispute, 3, 116	7	1:45.47	225,479
2002 **Proud Citizen**, 3, 116	M. E. Smith	Crimson Hero, 3, 116	Easyfromthegitgo, 3, 116	8	1:44.58	226,083
2001 **Keats**, 3, 116	L. J. Melancon	‡Griffinite, 3, 116	Bay Eagle, 3, 116	10	1:43.54	230,315
2000 **Unshaded**, 3, 116	S. J. Sellers	Globalize, 3, 120	Harlan Traveler, 3, 116	8	1:43.72	221,588
1999 **Charismatic**, 3, 115	J. D. Bailey	Yankee Victor, 3, 115	Finder's Gold, 3, 115	12	**1:41.06**	234,794
1998 **Classic Cat**, 3, 114	R. Albarado	Voyamerican, 3, 114	Grand Slam, 3, 123	8	1:42.85	228,300
1997 **Touch Gold**, 3, 115	G. L. Stevens	Smoke Glacken, 3, 118	Deeds Not Words, 3, 112	5	1:43.27	116,963
1996 **City by Night**, 3, 113	S. J. Sellers	Prince of Thieves, 3, 118	Roar, 3, 118	11	1:42.39	123,473
1995 **Star Standard**, 3, 115	P. Day	Royal Mitch, 3, 118	Guadalcanal, 3, 115	5	1:45.02	99,882
1994 **Southern Rhythm**, 3, 118	G. K. Gomez	Soul of the Matter, 3, 118	Ulises, 3, 113	8	1:45.72	85,095
1993 **Grand Jewel**, 3, 118	J. D. Bailey	El Bakan, 3, 113	Truth of It All, 3, 118	9	1:43.61	87,219
1992 **My Luck Runs North**, 3, 115	R. D. Lopez	Lure, 3, 118	Agincourt, 3, 115	5	1:44.06	89,083
1991 **Hansel**, 3, 121	J. D. Bailey	Shotgun Harry J., 3, 115	Speedy Cure, 3, 118	4	1:42.66	86,743

1990	**Home At Last**, 3, 118	J. D. Bailey	Pleasant Tap, 3, 115	Thirty Slews, 3, 116	9	1:43.40	$73,385
1989	**Notation**, 3, 115	P. Day	Bionic Prospect, 3, 114	Charlie Barley, 3, 118	8	1:44.40	71,663
1988	**Risen Star**, 3, 118	J. Vasquez	Forty Niner, 3, 121	Stalwars, 3, 118	5	1:42.80	68,673
1987	**War**, 3, 115	W. H. McCauley	Candi's Gold, 3, 115	Momentus, 3, 118	6	1:44.40	96,843
1986	**Wise Times**, 3, 112	K. K. Allen	Country Light, 3, 118	Blue Buckaroo, 3, 112	9	1:44.80	71,793
1985	**Stephan's Odyssey**, 3, 118	L. A. Pincay Jr.	Tajawa, 3, 112	Northern Bid, 3, 112	7	1:42.60	34,775
1984	**He Is a Great Deal**, 3, 111	J. C. Espinoza	Swale, 3, 123	Timely Advocate, 3, 112	5	1:45.40	34,450

Named for the city of Lexington, Kentucky. Sponsored by John and Susan Magnier's Coolmore Stud in County Tipperary, Ireland 1998-2006. Grade 3 1986-'87. Not held 1938-'83. 6 furlongs 1936-'37. Two-year-olds 1936-'37. ‡Mr. John finished second, DQ to eighth, 2001. Held as overnight handicap 1940.

Cotillion Handicap

Grade 2 in 2006. Philadelphia Park, three-year-olds, fillies, 1$^{1}/_{16}$ miles, dirt. Held October 1, 2005, with a gross value of $300,000. First held in 1969. First graded in 1973. Stakes record 1:41.68 (2004 Ashado).

Year	Winner	Jockey	Second	Third	Strs	Time	1st Purse
2005	**Nothing But Fun**, 3, 115	R. Migliore	Yolanda B. Too, 3, 117	Shebelongstoyou, 3, 117	6	1:46.64	$180,000
2004	**Ashado**, 3, 124	E. Coa	Ender's Sister, 3, 117	My Lordship, 3, 115	7	**1:41.68**	150,000
2003	**Fast Cookie**, 3, 116	N. Santagata	Ladyecho, 3, 116	Savedbythelight, 3, 117	5	1:45.83	150,000
2002	**Smok'n Frolic**, 3, 118	J. A. Velez Jr.	Pupil, 3, 114	Jilbab, 3, 120	9	1:44.27	150,000
2001	**Mystic Lady**, 3, 121	E. Coa	Zonk, 3, 117	Celtic Melody, 3, 115	8	1:43.86	150,000
2000	**Jostle**, 3, 124	M. E. Smith	Gold for My Gal, 3, 112	Prized Stamp, 3, 114	7	1:42.54	120,000
1999	**Skipping Around**, 3, 114	M. J. McCarthy	Strolling Belle, 3, 120	Waltz, 3, 114	10	1:43.45	120,000
1998	**Lu Ravi**, 3, 121	W. Martinez	Sister Act, 3, 115	Let, 3, 117	8	1:43.55	90,000
1997	**Snit**, 3, 114	R. E. Colton	Proud Run, 3, 116	Salt It, 3, 117	9	1:43.91	90,000
1996	**Double Dee's**, 3, 111	F. Leon	Ginny Lynn, 3, 121	Princess Eloise, 3, 113	5	1:44.69	90,000
1995	**Clear Mandate**, 3, 113	J. C. Ferrer	Blue Sky Princess, 3, 114	Country Cat, 3, 118	11	1:42.87	98,730
1994	**Sovereign Kitty**, 3, 118	W. H. McCauley	Cinnamon Sugar (Ire), 3, 120	Cavada, 3, 114	8	1:43.52	97,440
1993	**Jacody**, 3, 118	T. G. Turner	Aztec Hill, 3, 121	Cearas Dancer, 3, 109	6	1:43.22	95,520
1992	**Star Minister**, 3, 117	A. J. Seefeldt	Diamond Duo, 3, 121	Squirm, 3, 116	7	1:44.06	80,760
1990	**Valay Maid**, 3, 119	L. Saumell	Toffeefee, 3, 115	Trumpet's Blare, 3, 116	8	1:43.80	81,600
1989	**Sharp Dance**, 3, 115	K. Castaneda	Misty Ivor, 3, 113	Tactile, 3, 117	11	1:45.80	81,900
1988	**Aquaba**, 3, 115	J. Cruguet	Ice Tech, 3, 113	Mother of Eight, 3, 114	8	1:44.40	79,320
1987	**‡Silent Turn**, 3, 118	R. P. Romero	Sacahuista, 3, 119	Single Blade, 3, 117	8	1:42.80	65,280
1986	**Toes Knows**, 3, 119	D. Wright	Life At the Top, 3, 121	I'm Sweets, 3, 119	8	1:42.80	65,880
1985	**Koluctoo's Jill**, 3, 119	W. H. McCauley	Overwhelming, 3, 115	Tabayour, 3, 118	8	1:42.80	65,520
1984	**Squan Song**, 3, 122	R. Z. Hernandez	Given, 3, 122	You're Too Special, 3, 113	9	1:42.80	60,945
	Dowery, 3, 122	V. A. Bracciale Jr.	Duo Disco, 3, 122	Hot Milk, 3, 117	9	1:42.60	60,945
1983	**Quixotic Lady**, 3, 122	G. McCarron	Lady Hawthorn, 3, 117	Springtime Sharon, 3, 117	8	1:42.80	33,180
1982	**Lady Eleanor**, 3, 122	C. Perret	Smart Heiress, 3, 122	Glass House, 3, 117	12	1:45.00	34,800
1981	**Truly Bound**, 3, 121	R. J. Franklin	Pukka Princess, 3, 118	Debonair Dancer, 3, 118	8	1:42.80	33,810
1980	**Sugar and Spice**, 3, 116	G. Martens	Pepi Wiley, 3, 118	Nijit, 3, 116	8	1:45.00	34,800
1979	**Alada**, 3, 116	J. Fell	Too Many Sweets, 3, 116	Heavenly Ade, 3, 116	6	1:43.80	33,090
1978	**Queen Lib**, 3, 121	D. MacBeth	Silken Delight, 3, 116	Sharp Belle, 3, 116	11	1:43.20	28,620
1977	**Suede Shoe**, 3, 116	A. S. Black	Raise Old Glory, 3, 113	Bafflin Lil, 3, 116	11	1:42.60	27,930
1976	**Revidere**, 3, 118	J. Vasquez	Critical Miss, 3, 116	Hay Patcher, 3, 116	8	1:44.00	20,190
1975	**My Juliet**, 3, 116	D. Brumfield	Hot n Nasty, 3, 116	Gala Lil, 3, 118	7	1:43.60	20,160
1974	**Honky Star**, 3, 121	D. G. McHargue	Special Team, 3, 118	Kudara, 3, 121	7	1:44.00	32,910
1973	**Lilac Hill**, 3, 113	D. MacBeth	Ladies Agreement, 3, 114	Suzi Sunshine, 3, 114	10	1:43.60	34,590

A cotillion is a traditional dance where debutantes are formally presented to society. Grade 1 1973-'74. Grade 3 1981-'88. Cotillion S. 1975-'84. Held at Liberty Bell 1969-'74. Held at Keystone 1975-'84. Not held 1991. Two divisions 1984. ‡Sacahuista finished first, DQ to second, 1987.

Count Fleet Sprint Handicap

Grade 3 in 2006. Oaklawn Park, three-year-olds and up, 6 furlongs, dirt. Held April 13, 2006, with a gross value of $150,000. First held in 1974. First graded in 1986. Stakes record 1:08.18 (2001 Bonapaw).

Year	Winner	Jockey	Second	Third	Strs	Time	1st Purse
2006	**Bordonaro**, 5, 122	P. A. Valenzuela	Friendly Island, 5, 115	Semaphore Man, 4, 115	7	1:08.77	$90,000
2005	**Top Commander**, 5, 113	C. Gonzalez	Forest Grove, 4, 114	That Tat, 7, 119	8	1:08.74	90,000
2004	**Shake You Down**, 6, 121	R. A. Dominguez	Where's the Ring, 5, 115	Aloha Bold, 6, 114	6	1:09.27	90,000
2003	**Beau's Town**, 5, 122	J. Theriot	Honor Me, 5, 116	Sand Ridge, 8, 114	6	1:09.01	90,000
2002	**Explicit**, 5, 116	L. J. Meche	Entepreneur, 5, 115	Junior Deputy, 4, 113	5	1:08.60	90,000
2001	**Bonapaw**, 5, 118	G. Melancon	Chindi, 7, 114	Bidis, 4, 117	7	**1:08.18**	75,000
2000	**†Show Me the Stage**, 4, 116	D. R. Flores	Smolderin Heart, 5, 115	Vinnie's Boy, 4, 114	6	1:09.62	75,000
1999	**Reraise**, 4, 122	C. S. Nakatani	Run Johnny, 7, 114	E J Harley, 7, 115	6	1:08.59	75,000
1998	**Chindi**, 4, 113	D. R. Pettinger	E J Harley, 6, 113	Western Fame, 6, 115	8	1:09.77	75,000
1997	**High Stakes Player**, 5, 120	K. Desormeaux	†Capote Belle, 4, 116	Victor Avenue, 4, 116	7	1:08.86	90,000
1996	**Concept Win**, 6, 116	G. L. Stevens	Roythelittleone, 4, 114	Spiritbound, 4, 113	7	1:09.06	90,000
1995	**Hot Jaws**, 5, 113	C. H. Borel	Demaloot Demashoot, 5, 116	Mr. Cooperative, 4, 114	9	1:09.49	90,000
1994	**Demaloot Demashoot**, 4, 115	M. E. Smith	Honor the Hero, 6, 117	Sir Hutch, 4, 118	8	1:08.39	90,000
1993	**Approach**, 6, 116	P. Day	Ponche, 4, 113	Never Wavering, 4, 110	13	1:09.64	90,000
1992	**Gray Slewpy**, 4, 117	K. Desormeaux	Potentiality, 6, 116	Hidden Tomahawk, 4, 115	7	1:08.97	60,000
1991	**Overpeer**, 7, 122	P. Day	Silent Reflex, 5, 113	Peaked, 6, 118	7	1:08.37	60,000
1990	**Malagra**, 4, 117	V. L. Smith	Pentelicus, 6, 115	Sunny Blossom, 5, 120	10	1:08.80	60,000
1989	**Twice Around**, 4, 116	C. H. Borel	Be a Agent, 5, 117	Never Forgotten, 5, 114	10	1:09.20	60,000

1988	**Salt Dome**, 5, 116	L. Snyder	Pewter, 4, 113	Bold Pac Man, 4, 112	9	1:08.60	$60,000
1987	**Sun Master**, 6, 117	G. L. Stevens	Rocky Marriage, 7, 116	Chief Steward, 6, 118	8	1:09.40	69,540
1986	**Mister Gennaro**, 5, 115	F. Olivares	Beveled, 4, 114	Charging Falls, 5, 125	9	1:08.80	71,100
1985	**Taylor's Special**, 4, 123	R. P. Romero	Mt. Livermore, 4, 119	T. H. Bend, 4, 110	10	1:08.40	98,280
1984	**Dave's Friend**, 9, 122	E. Delahoussaye	†All Sold Out, 5, 114	Lucky Salvation, 4, 113	8	1:09.00	70,260
1983	**Dave's Friend**, 8, 124	L. Snyder	General Jimmy, 4, 117	Liberty Lane, 5, 113	9	1:10.00	70,320
1982	**Sandbagger**, 4, 114	D. Haire	Blue Water Line, 4, 117	Lockjaw, 4, 116	10	1:12.00	39,240
1981	**General Custer**, 5, 111	L. Snyder	Avenging Gossip, 4, 111	Be a Prospect, 4, 112	7	1:10.40	34,470
1980	**Silent Dignity**, 4, 114	S. Maple	Gustoso, 5, 111	J. Burns, 5, 115	7	1:11.00	34,680
1979	**Amadevil**, 5, 114	T. G. Greer	Little Reb, 4, 120	Sean's Song, 4, 114	7	1:11.20	34,890
1978	**Last Buzz**, 5, 126	A. Rini	Best Person, 4, 110	Sucha Pleasure, 4, 118	10	1:11.00	33,390
1977	**Silver Hope**, 6, 120	R. L. Turcotte	Dr's Enjoy Dollars, 5, 116	Brets Kicker, 6, 113	9	1:10.40	18,480
1976	**Brets Kicker**, 5, 111	J. D. Bailey	Silver Doctor, 6, 118	Mr. Barb, 4, 110	6	1:10.00	17,640
1975	**Prince Astro**, 6, 123	D. W. Whited	Silver Doctor, 5, 117	Faneuil Boy, 4, 112	7	1:10.00	18,030
1974	**Barbizon Streak**, 6, 114	R. Wilson	Pleasure Castle, 4, 120	Pesty Jay, 6, 122	7	1:11.00	17,370

Named for Mrs. John D. Hertz's 1943 Horse of the Year, '43 Triple Crown winner, and '51 leading North American sire Count Fleet (1940 c. by Reigh Count). Grade 2 1988-'89. Count Fleet H. 1974-'82. Four-year-olds and up 1976-1991, 1993-2005. †Denotes female.

Dahlia Handicap

Grade 2 in 2006. Hollywood Park, three-year-olds and up, fillies and mares, 1 1/16 miles, dirt. Held December 20, 2004, with a gross value of $150,000. First held in 1982. First graded in 1984. Stakes record 1:42.11 (2004 Festival [Jpn]).

Year	Winner	Jockey	Second	Third	Strs	Time	1st Purse
2004	**Festival (Jpn)**, 5, 111	D. Sorenson	Irgunette (Aus), 5, 113	Belle Ange (Fr), 3, 114	5	**1:42.11**	$90,000
2003	**Katdogawn (GB)**, 3, 116	M. E. Smith	Personal Legend, 3, 115	Betty's Wish, 3, 117	10	1:41.52	90,000
2002	**dh-Surya**, 4, 118	P. A. Valenzuela		Honestly Darling, 4, 114	9	1:44.55	60,000
	dh-Tout Charmant, 6, 119	A. O. Solis					
2001	**Verruma (Brz)**, 5, 115	G. K. Gomez	Vencera (Fr), 4, 115	Heads Will Roll (GB), 3, 117	8	1:43.24	90,000
2000	**Follow the Money**, 4, 115	V. Espinoza	Smooth Player, 4, 120	Beautiful Noise, 4, 117	7	1:40.71	90,000
1999	**Lady At Peace**, 3, 113	G. K. Gomez	Cyrillic, 4, 117	Country Garden (GB), 4, 115	5	1:41.50	90,000
1998	**Tuzla (Fr)**, 4, 119	C. S. Nakatani	Sonja's Faith (Ire), 4, 118	Curitiba, 4, 115	5	1:41.75	60,000
1997	**Golden Arches (Fr)**, 3, 117	C. J. McCarron	Sonja's Faith (Ire), 3, 113	Traces of Gold, 5, 116	8	1:41.09	60,000
1996	**Sixieme Sens**, 4, 116	C. S. Nakatani	Grafin, 5, 116	Admise (Fr), 4, 121	8	1:42.37	66,600
1995	**Didina (GB)**, 3, 115	E. Delahoussaye	Dirca (Ire), 3, 113	Rapunzel Runz, 4, 116	10	1:45.20	68,300
1994	**Skimble**, 5, 118	E. Delahoussaye	Queens Court Queen, 5, 118	Shir Dar (Fr), 4, 115	8	1:42.33	66,000
1993	**Kalita Melody (GB)**, 5, 115	C. A. Black	Vinista, 3, 116	Gumpher, 5, 116	7	1:44.73	64,500
1992	**Kostroma (Ire)**, 6, 124	G. L. Stevens	Vijaya, 5, 114	Guiza, 5, 116	8	1:41.40	66,500
1991	**Re Toss (Arg)**, 4, 115	C. S. Nakatani	Elegance, 4, 115	Gaelic Bird (Fr), 4, 114	11	1:40.77	70,400
1990	**Petalia**, 5, 113	K. Desormeaux	Bequest, 4, 117	Island Jamboree, 4, 113	6	1:41.40	48,900
	Little Brianne, 5, 119	J. A. Garcia	Stylish Star, 4, 119	Girl of France (GB), 4, 115	8	1:40.60	50,900
1989	**Stylish Star**, 3, 116	C. J. McCarron	Ariosa, 3, 113	Sugarplum Gal, 4, 114	9	1:40.40	51,600
	Saros Brig, 5, 114	G. L. Stevens	Nikishka, 4, 120	Beat, 4, 115	7	1:40.40	49,600
1988	**Balbonella (Fr)**, 4, 117	F. Toro	Goodbye Halo, 3, 120	Pen Bal Lady (GB), 4, 117	7	1:42.80	75,100
1987	**Invited Guest (Ire)**, 3, 114	W. Shoemaker	Secuencia (Chi), 5, 115	Smooch (GB), 4, 117	9	1:43.40	71,950
	Top Corsage, 4, 118	J. A. Santos	Any Song (Ire), 4, 116	Aberuschka (Ire), 5, 120	6	1:43.20	48,700
1986	**Aberuschka (Ire)**, 4, 122	P. A. Valenzuela	An Empress, 3, 117	Reloy, 3, 118	7	1:41.60	80,740
1985	**Capricorn Belle (GB)**, 4, 118	C. J. McCarron	Justicara (Ire), 4, 118	Solva (GB), 4, 115	9	1:41.60	66,200
1984	**Lina Cavalieri (GB)**, 4, 117	E. Delahoussaye	Pampas (Ire), 4, 115	Salt Spring (Arg), 5, 117	12	1:44.20	53,050
1983	**Geraldine's Store**, 4, 118	J. Samyn	Northerly Glow, 4, 111	Satin Ribera, 6, 115	8	1:42.40	32,500
	First Advance, 4, 114	T. Lipham	Absentia, 4, 116	Bersid, 5, 122	10	1:42.00	33,500
1982	**Sangue (Ire)**, 4, 122	L. A. Pincay Jr.	Star Pastures (GB), 4, 118	Pat's Joy, 4, 115	7	1:41.40	31,900
	Milingo, 3, 114	T. Lipham	Pink Safir (Fr), 6, 112	Berry Bush, 5, 119	10	1:42.60	33,400

Named for Nelson Bunker Hunt's 1973, '74 English Horse of the Year, '74 North American champion grass male, and '76 Hollywood Invitational H. (G1) winner Dahlia (1970 f. by *Vaguely Noble). Grade 3 1984-'89, 2004. Not held 2005. Dirt 2004. Originally scheduled on turf 2004. Two divisions 1982-'83, 1987, 1989-'90. Dead heat for first 2002.

Dallas Turf Cup Handicap

Grade 3 in 2006. Lone Star Park, three-year-olds and up, 1 1/8 miles, turf. Held June 18, 2005, with a gross value of $200,000. First held in 1997. First graded in 2006. Stakes record 1:45.54 (1998 Yaqthan [Ire]).

Year	Winner	Jockey	Second	Third	Strs	Time	1st Purse
2005	**Sea Dub**, 6, 115	L. Taylor	Fullbridled, 4, 114	Major Rhythm, 6, 116	11	1:48.82	$120,000
2004	**Maysville Slew**, 8, 115	M. C. Berry	Star Over the Bay, 6, 115	A to the Z, 4, 115	7	1:49.89	120,000
2003	**Patrol**, 4, 118	M. J. Luzzi	Slew the Red, 6, 114	Storybook Kid, 5, 113	10	1:48.75	150,000
2002	**Suances (GB)**, 5, 118	D. R. Flores	Our Main Man, 4, 113	Candid Glen, 5, 114	8	1:49.09	150,000
2001	**El Gran Papa**, 4, 113	G. K. Gomez	Dignitas Dancer, 5, 114	Nat's Big Party, 7, 114	8	1:49.30	180,000
2000	**Gold Nugget**, 5, 115	B. J. Walker Jr.	Majestic Jove, 6, 114	Northern Quest (Fr), 5, 112	10	1:53.17	150,000
1999	**Martiniquais (Ire)**, 6, 117	D. R. Flores	Special Moments, 6, 115	Burbank, 6, 115	9	1:49.39	90,000
1998	**Yaqthan (Ire)**, 8, 116	B. D. Peck	Burbank, 5, 116	Scott's Scoundrel, 6, 115	6	**1:45.54**	90,000
1997	**Burbank**, 4, 113	D. R. Pettinger	Lost Soldier, 7, 118	Hyderabad, 6, 114	8	1:47.55	90,000

Named for the city of Dallas; Lone Star Park is located in nearby Grand Prairie. Dallas Turf Cup S. 1999. Course record 1997, 1998.

Darley Alcibiades Stakes

Grade 2 in 2006. Keeneland Race Course, two-year-olds, fillies, 1¹/₁₆ miles, dirt. Held October 7, 2005, with a gross value of $400,000. First held in 1952. First graded in 1973. Stakes record 1:42.24 (1998 Silverbulletday).

Year	Winner	Jockey	Second	Third	Strs	Time	1st Purse
2005	**She Says It Best**, 2, 118	E. M. Martin Jr.	Ex Caelis, 2, 118	Performing Diva, 2, 118	11	1:49.07	$248,000
2004	**Runway Model**, 2, 118	R. Bejarano	Sharp Lisa, 2, 118	In the Gold, 2, 118	10	1:44.31	248,000
2003	**Be Gentle**, 2, 118	C. H. Velasquez	Galloping Gal, 2, 118	Deb's Charm, 2, 118	7	1:45.51	248,000
2002	**Westerly Breeze**, 2, 118	R. Albarado	Ruby's Reception, 2, 118	Final Round, 2, 118	9	1:46.90	276,024
2001	**Take Charge Lady**, 2, 118	A. J. D'Amico	Never Out, 2, 118	Cunning Play, 2, 118	11	1:46.23	280,736
2000	**She's a Devil Due**, 2, 118	M. Guidry	Nasty Storm, 2, 118	Cash Deal, 2, 118	7	1:44.86	270,320
1999	**Scratch Pad**, 2, 118	W. Martinez	Rare Beauty, 2, 118	Cash Run, 2, 118	8	1:44.16	274,288
1998	**Silverbulletday**, 2, 118	G. L. Stevens	Extended Applause, 2, 118	Grand Deed, 2, 118	11	**1:42.24**	281,976
1997	**Countess Diana**, 2, 118	S. J. Sellers	Lily O'Gold, 2, 118	Beautiful Pleasure, 2, 118	6	1:45.39	266,600
1996	**Southern Playgirl**, 2, 118	R. P. Romero	‡Screamer, 2, 118	Private Pursuit, 2, 118	7	1:46.94	168,330
1995	**Cara Rafaela**, 2, 118	P. Day	Birr, 2, 118	Gold Sunrise, 2, 118	10	1:44.43	139,252
1994	**Post It**, 2, 118	S. Maple	Morris Code, 2, 118	Cat Appeal, 2, 118	5	1:46.33	66,650
1993	**Stellar Cat**, 2, 118	S. J. Sellers	Slew Kitty Slew, 2, 118	Beau Blush, 2, 118	6	1:44.68	122,200
1992	**Eliza**, 2, 118	P. A. Valenzuela	Avie's Shadow, 2, 118	True Affair, 2, 118	6	1:43.30	122,200
1991	**Spinning Round**, 2, 118	J. M. Johnson	Queens Court Queen, 2, 118	Midnight Society, 2, 118	5	1:47.38	122,200
1990	**Private Treasure**, 2, 118	J. D. Bailey	Through Flight, 2, 118	Southern Bar Girl, 2, 118	8	1:43.80	173,420
1989	**Special Happening**, 2, 118	J. A. Santos	Talltalelady, 2, 118	Fashion Delight, 2, 118	7	1:44.60	141,375
1988	**Wonders Delight**, 2, 118	G. L. Stevens	Affirmed Classic, 2, 118	Seattle Meteor, 2, 118	7	1:46.40	130,000
1987	**Terra Incognita**, 2, 118	D. E. Foster	Epitome, 2, 118	Pearlie Gold, 2, 118	8	1:44.60	102,996
1986	**Zero Minus**, 2, 118	S. Hawley	Bound, 2, 118	Desirous, 2, 118	7	1:45.20	125,567
1985	**Silent Account**, 2, 118	K. K. Allen	Steal a Kiss, 2, 118	Python, 2, 118	10	1:46.20	132,321
1984	**Foxy Deen**, 2, 118	D. Montoya	Weekend Delight, 2, 118	Dusty Heart, 2, 118	12	1:45.60	117,224
1983	**Lucky Lucky Lucky**, 2, 118	J. Vasquez	Flippers, 2, 118	Geevilla, 2, 118	10	1:47.00	119,675
1982	**Jelly Bean Holiday**, 2, 118	D. Brumfield	Quarrel Over, 2, 118	Issues n' Answers, 2, 118	7	1:45.80	97,825
1981	**Apalachee Honey**, 2, 118	W. Shoemaker	Chilling Thought, 2, 118	Casual, 2, 118	10	1:45.20	102,034
1980	**Sweet Revenge**, 2, 118	J. Velasquez	Expressive Dance, 2, 118	Masters Dream, 2, 118	6	1:28.00	99,190
1979	**Salud**, 2, 118	J. C. Espinoza	Diorama, 2, 118	Sweetest Roman, 2, 118	6	1:28.20	93,503
1978	**Angel Island**, 2, 119	E. Delahoussaye	Terlingua, 2, 119	Too Many Sweets, 2, 119	7	1:26.40	89,619
1977	**L'Alezane**, 2, 119	R. Turcotte	Robalea, 2, 119	No No-Nos, 2, 119	5	1:27.20	80,990
1976	**Sans Supplement**, 2, 119	W. Gavidia	Avilion, 2, 119	Resolver, 2, 119	10	1:27.60	89,733
1975	**Optimistic Gal**, 2, 119	D. G. McHargue	Old Goat, 2, 119	Answer, 2, 119	9	1:28.00	79,593
1974	**Hope of Glory**, 2, 119	J. Nichols	Funny Cat, 2, 119	Snow Doll, 2, 119	9	1:27.20	54,197
1973	**City Girl**, 2, 119	E. Fires	Fairway Fable, 2, 119	Quick Cure, 2, 119	8	1:27.80	44,924

Named for Hal Price Headley's 1929 consensus champion two-year-old filly, '30 champion three-year-old filly, and '30 Kentucky Oaks winner Alcibiades (1927 f. by Supremus). Sponsored by Sheikh Mohammed bin Rashid al Maktoum's Darley 2003-'05. Formerly sponsored by Walmac Int'l. of Lexington 1997-2002. Grade 3 1973-'75. About 7 furlongs 1952-'80. ‡Private Pursuit finished second, DQ to third, 1996.

Davona Dale Stakes

Grade 2 in 2006. Gulfstream Park, three-year-olds, fillies, 1¹/₈ miles, dirt. Held February 4, 2006, with a gross value of $150,000. First held in 1988. First graded in 1993. Stakes record 1:50.20 (2005 Sis City).

Year	Winner	Jockey	Second	Third	Strs	Time	1st Purse
2006	**Wait a While**, 3, 119	J. R. Velazquez	Teammate, 3, 115	Wonder Lady Anne L, 3, 119	7	1:50.27	$90,000
2005	**Sis City**, 3, 121	J. R. Velazquez	In the Gold, 3, 117	Jill Robin L, 3, 117	6	**1:50.20**	90,000
2004	**Miss Coronado**, 3, 117	C. H. Velasquez	Eye Dazzler, 3, 115	Society Selection, 3, 121	7	1:44.62	90,000
2003	**Yell**, 3, 117	J. R. Velazquez	Ivanavinalot, 3, 121	Gold Player, 3, 115	5	1:44.96	90,000
2002	**Ms Brookski**, 3, 121	R. Homeister Jr.	Colonial Glitter, 3, 117	French Satin, 3, 115	9	1:45.14	60,000
2001	**Latour**, 3, 112	J. R. Velazquez	Gold Mover, 3, 116	Courageous Maiden, 3, 113	7	1:45.51	60,000
2000	**Cash Run**, 3, 118	J. D. Bailey	Regally Appealing, 3, 116	Secret Status, 3, 114	9	1:40.37	60,000
1999	**Three Ring**, 3, 118	J. R. Velazquez	Golden Temper, 3, 113	Gold From the West, 3, 116	5	1:41.53	60,000
1998	**Diamond On the Run**, 3, 112	P. Day	Uanme, 3, 114	Dixie Melody, 3, 113	10	1:42.65	60,000
1997	**Glitter Woman**, 3, 114	M. E. Smith	City Band, 3, 121	Southern Playgirl, 3, 121	6	1:39.31	60,000
1996	**Plum Country**, 3, 118	P. Day	‡My Flag, 3, 118	La Rosa, 3, 118	9	1:42.08	60,000
1995	**Mia's Hope**, 3, 114	K. L. Chapman	Minister Wife, 3, 121	Culver City, 3, 113	6	1:43.26	60,000
1994	**Cut the Charm**, 3, 118	J. D. Bailey	She Rides Tonite, 3, 114	Delightful Bet, 3, 113	8	1:41.44	60,000
1993	**Lunar Spook**, 3, 118	M. Guidry	Boots 'n Jackie, 3, 121	In Her Glory, 3, 112	7	1:42.09	30,000
1992	**Miss Legality**, 3, 116	J. A. Krone	November Snow, 3, 114	Spectacular Sue, 3, 114	8	1:42.00	30,000
1991	**Fancy Ribbons**, 3, 118	C. Perret	Hula Pride, 3, 114	Designated Dancer, 3, 116	9	1:41.10	45,420
1990	**Big Pride**, 3, 112	E. Fires	Crowned, 3, 121	Sonic Gray, 3, 112	6	1:26.00	21,000
1989	**Waggley**, 6, 122	J. Samyn	Plate Queen, 4, 113	Ataentsic, 5, 113	7	1:22.60	20,640
1988	**Charming Tigress**, 5, 115	P. Day	Polar Wind, 4, 117	No Doublet, 5, 115	8	1:24.60	21,069
	Cadillacing, 4, 122	R. P. Romero	Easter Mary, 4, 115	Saucey Missy, 5, 117	9	1:23.00	21,429

Named for Calumet Farm's 1979 champion three-year-old filly, '79 Filly Triple Crown winner, and '79 Bonnie Miss S. winner Davona Dale (1976 f. by Best Turn). Grade 3 1993-'97. Davona Dale H. 1988. Davona Dale Breeders' Cup S. 1989, 1991. 7 furlongs 1988-'90. 1 mile 70 yards 1991-2000. Four-year-olds and up 1988. Three-year-olds and up 1989. Fillies and mares 1988, 1989. Two divisions 1988. ‡Rare Blend finished second, DQ to sixth, 1996.

Debutante Stakes

Grade 3 in 2006. Churchill Downs, two-year-olds, fillies, 5½ furlongs, dirt. Held July 9, 2005, with a gross value of $112,600. First held in 1889. First graded in 1996. Stakes record 1:02.52 (2001 Cashier's Dream).

Year	Winner	Jockey	Second	Third	Strs	Time	1st Purse
2005	**Effectual**, 2, 117	R. Albarado	Joint Effort, 2, 117	Swept Gold, 2, 117	9	1:03.95	$69,812
2004	**Classic Elegance**, 2, 117	P. Day	Paragon Queen, 2, 117	Cool Spell, 2, 117	9	1:04.18	68,696
2003	**Be Gentle**, 2, 117	C. H. Velasquez	Renaissance Lady, 2, 117	Sweet Jo Jo, 2, 117	8	1:03.96	68,758
2002	**Awesome Humor**, 2, 115	C. H. Borel	Vibs, 2, 115	Attemptress, 2, 115	7	1:03.45	67,890
2001	**Cashier's Dream**, 2, 118	D. J. Meche	Lakeside Cup, 2, 115	Colonial Glitter, 2, 115	8	**1:02.52**	68,510
2000	**Gold Mover**, 2, 121	C. Perret	Princess Belle, 2, 115	Tricky Elaine, 2, 115	9	1:03.79	69,626
1999	**Chilukki**, 2, 121	W. Martinez	Miss Wineshine, 2, 112	Cecilia's Crown, 2, 115	9	1:03.66	69,998
1998	**Silverbulletday**, 2, 115	W. Martinez	The Happy Hopper, 2, 115	Mancari's Rose, 2, 115	9	1:04.70	69,502
1997	**Love Lock**, 2, 115	P. Day	Countess Diana, 2, 115	Quick Lap, 2, 115	13	1:03.84	72,478
1996	**Move**, 2, 121	P. Day	Sarah's Prospector, 2, 115	Live Your Best, 2, 115	10	1:05.66	73,840
1995	**Golden Attraction**, 2, 115	D. M. Barton	Western Dreamer, 2, 121	Tipically Irish, 2, 115	9	1:04.19	70,948
1994	**Chargedupsycamore**, 2, 121	P. Day	Phone Bird, 2, 116	Our Gem, 2, 116	9	1:05.24	54,405
1993	**Fly Love**, 2, 116	B. E. Bartram	Miss Ra He Ra, 2, 116	Astas Foxy Lady, 2, 121	11	1:05.23	37,635
1992	**Hollywood Wildcat**, 2, 116	F. A. Arguello Jr.	Cosmic Speed Queen, 2, 118	Dixie Band, 2, 115	14	1:06.02	38,480
1991	**Greenhaven Lane**, 2, 112	K. Tsuchiya	Moment of Grace, 2, 112	One for Smoke, 2, 116	11	1:06.23	36,953
1990	**Barbara's Nemesis**, 2, 116	J. Deegan	Gracielle, 2, 112	Cosmic Music, 2, 112	10	1:12.00	36,693
1989	**Icy Folly**, 2, 118	K. K. Allen	Hard Freeze, 2, 118	Lucy's Glory, 2, 118	14	1:11.20	37,993
1988	**Seaquay**, 2, 114	R. M. Ehrlinspiel	Weekend Spree, 2, 118	Coax Chelsie, 2, 112	8	1:11.20	35,718
1987	**Bold Lady Anne**, 2, 118	J. Davidson	Over All, 2, 118	Penny's Growl, 2, 114	7	1:11.60	25,773
	Dark Silver, 2, 116	M. McDowell	She's Freezing, 2, 116	Saved by Grace, 2, 116	9	1:12.60	26,260
1986	**Burnished Bright**, 2, 121	P. Day	Before Sundown, 2, 118	Shivering Gal, 2, 115	7	1:11.20	46,810
1985	**Tricky Fingers**, 2, 115	L. J. Melancon	Likker Is Quikker, 2, 118	Time for Honor, 2, 115	12	1:05.20	31,013
1984	**Knot**, 2, 115	K. K. Allen	Don't Joke, 2, 112	Off Shore Breeze, 2, 115	10	1:06.40	22,393
1983	**Arabizon**, 2, 115	L. Moyers	Ark, 2, 115	Starafar, 2, 113	9	1:05.80	22,181
1982	**Ice Fantasy**, 2, 115	P. A. Johnson	Wrong Answer, 2, 115	Fifth Affair, 2, 121	12	1:04.60	20,735
1981	**Pure Platinum**, 2, 119	P. Day	Miss Preakness, 2, 119	Cypress Bay, 2, 119	10	:58.80	19,939
1980	**Excitable Lady**, 2, 119	D. Brumfield	Masters Dream, 2, 119	Bend the Times, 2, 119	7	:58.60	19,484
1979	**Lissy**, 2, 114	M. S. Sellers	Barbizon's Flower, 2, 119	Happy Hollie, 2, 119	13	:59.80	20,426
1978	**Nervous John**, 2, 122	C. J. McCarron	Porpourie, 2, 114	Rainbow Streak, 2, 122	7	:58.40	14,658
1977	**Sweet Little Lady**, 2, 122	R. Turcotte	Sahsie, 2, 119	‡Crystalan, 2, 122	8	:58.00	14,706
1976	**Olden**, 2, 122	R. Breen	Jungle Angel, 2, 119	Every Move, 2, 114	9	:58.80	14,950
1975	**Answer**, 2, 119	M. Hole	Pink Jade, 2, 122	Turn Over, 2, 119	8	:58.20	16,283
1974	**Sun and Snow**, 2, 119	E. Guerin	Floral Princess, 2, 114	Classy Note, 2, 119	13	:59.40	17,794
1973	**Me and Connie**, 2, 124	J. Nichols	Bundler, 2, 119	Shanjar, 2, 114	7	:58.20	16,835

Young women making their first formal appearance in society are known as debutantes. Churchill Downs Debutante S. 1928. Not held 1932-'37. 4 furlongs 1895-1922. 4½ furlongs 1923-'25. 5 furlongs 1926-'81. 6 furlongs 1986-'90. Two divisions 1987. ‡Miss Poodle Pup finished third, DQ to fourth, 1977. Equaled track record 1997, 1999. Track record 2001.

Delaware Handicap

Grade 2 in 2006. Delaware Park, three-year-olds and up, fillies and mares, 1¼ miles, dirt. Held July 17, 2005, with a gross value of $1,001,800. First held in 1937. First graded in 1973. Stakes record 1:59.80 (1987 Coup de Fusil).

Year	Winner	Jockey	Second	Third	Strs	Time	1st Purse
2005	**Island Sand**, 4, 115	J. D. Bailey	Two Trail Sioux, 4, 117	Personal Legend, 5, 114	11	2:02.89	$600,000
2004	**Summer Wind Dancer**, 4, 116	V. Espinoza	Roar Emotion, 4, 117	Misty Sixes, 6, 116	8	2:03.63	450,000
2003	**Wild Spirit (Chi)**, 4, 117	J. D. Bailey	Take Charge Lady, 4, 120	Shiny Sheet, 5, 112	8	2:02.95	450,000
2002	**Summer Colony**, 4, 118	J. R. Velazquez	Your Out, 4, 113	Two Item Limit, 4, 115	9	2:04.52	360,000
2001	**Irving's Baby**, 4, 113	R. A. Dominguez	Under the Rug, 6, 115	Lazy Slusan, 6, 121	6	2:05.21	360,000
2000	**Lu Ravi**, 5, 117	P. Day	Tap to Music, 5, 116	Silverbulletday, 4, 119	8	2:02.21	360,000
1999	**Tap to Music**, 4, 116	P. Day	Keeper Hill, 4, 120	Unbridled Hope, 5, 114	13	2:02.15	300,000
1998	**Amarillo**, 4, 110	J. A. Krone	Tuxedo Junction, 5, 115	Timely Broad, 4, 110	9	2:04.37	300,000
1997	**Power Play**, 5, 114	L. C. Reynolds	Gold n Delicious, 4, 115	Effectiveness, 4, 113	11	2:03.40	210,000
1996	**Urbane**, 4, 117	A. O. Solis	Alcovy, 6, 117	Shoop, 5, 115	13	2:01.89	180,000
1995	**Night Fax**, 4, 108	J. D. Carle	Cavada, 4, 113	It's Personal, 5, 114	8	2:02.98	95,070
1994	**With a Wink**, 4, 114	R. Migliore	Passing Vice, 4, 115	Alphabulous, 5, 111	9	2:03.37	95,130
1993	**Green Darlin**, 4, 113	M. J. Luzzi	Girl On a Mission, 4, 116	Starry Val, 4, 112	11	2:03.76	96,300
1992	**Brilliant Brass**, 5, 117	E. S. Prado	Train Robbery, 5, 111	Risen Colony, 4, 113	6	2:03.11	93,780
1991	**Crowned**, 4, 117	R. Wilson	Maskra's Lady, 4, 114	Tia Juanita, 5, 113	8	2:04.01	69,420
1990	**Seattle Dawn**, 4, 115	R. E. Colton	Warfie, 4, 112	Thirty Eight Go Go, 5, 115	7	2:03.00	68,160
1989	**Nastique**, 5, 120	E. Maple	Colonial Waters, 4, 117	Thirty Eight Go Go, 4, 118	4	2:01.20	64,890
1988	**Nastique**, 4, 116	E. Maple	Ms. Eloise, 5, 117	Lawyer Talk, 4, 112	7	2:07.60	67,410
1987	**Coup de Fusil**, 5, 114	A. T. Cordero Jr.	Steal a Kiss, 4, 113	Catatonic, 5, 118	8	**1:59.80**	68,760
1986	**Shocker T.**, 4, 122	G. St. Leon	Endear, 4, 122	Leecoo, 5, 112	6	2:02.20	69,120
1985	**Basie**, 4, 110	J. Cruguet	Heatherten, 6, 126	Life's Magic, 4, 122	5	2:02.00	93,360
1984	**Adored**, 4, 120	L. A. Pincay Jr.	Mademoiselle Forli, 5, 114	Weekend Surprise, 4, 111	6	2:03.20	94,680
1983	**May Day Eighty**, 4, 115	J. Vasquez	Try Something New, 4, 116	Broom Dance, 4, 119	6	2:03.20	66,720
1982	**Jameela**, 6, 121	J. L. Kaenel	Zvetlana, 4, 111	Love Sign, 5, 125	9	2:02.60	74,523
1981	**Relaxing**, 5, 119	A. T. Cordero Jr.	Wistful, 4, 121	Lady of Promise, 4, 111	10	2:01.00	75,075
1980	**Heavenly Ade**, 4, 112	J. D. Bailey	Croquis, 4, 112	Blitey, 4, 113	9	2:00.00	93,893

1979	**Likely Exchange**, 5, 112	M. S. Sellers	Sans Critique, 5, 111	Plains and Simple, 4, 110	9	2:03.40	$73,938
1978	**Late Bloomer**, 4, 119	J. Velasquez	Dottie's Doll, 5, 117	Cum Laude Laurie, 4, 119	9	2:02.20	73,938
1977	**Our Mims**, 3, 117	J. Velasquez	Mississippi Mud, 4, 124	Dottie's Doll, 4, 118	5	2:01.00	70,785
1976	**Optimistic Gal**, 3, 119	E. Maple	T. V. Vixen, 3, 118	Vodka Time, 4, 115	6	2:01.00	65,040
1975	**Susan's Girl**, 6, 125	R. Broussard	Pass a Glance, 4, 116	Raisela, 4, 117	6	2:01.80	70,915
1974	**Krislin**, 5, 115	A. T. Cordero Jr.	Twixt, 5, 124	Summer Guest, 5, 114	9	2:01.60	74,555
1973	**Susan's Girl**, 4, 127	L. A. Pincay Jr.	Summer Guest, 4, 122	Light Hearted, 4, 125	6	2:00.60	71,305

Formerly named for the city of New Castle, Delaware. Grade 1 1973-'89. Grade 3 1996-2002. New Castle H. 1937-'54. Held at Saratoga 1983-'85. Not held 1943. 1$^1/_{16}$ miles 1937-'50.

Delaware Oaks

Grade 2 in 2006. Delaware Park, three-year-olds, fillies, 1$^1/_{16}$ miles, dirt. Held July 16, 2005, with a gross value of $500,300. First held in 1938. First graded in 1973. Stakes record 1:42.81 (1998 Nickel Classic).

Year	Winner	Jockey	Second	Third	Strs	Time	1st Purse
2005	**R Lady Joy**, 3, 119	J. Lezcano	Round Pond, 3, 122	Dance Away Capote, 3, 119	6	1:43.25	$300,000
2004	**Yearly Report**, 3, 122	J. D. Bailey	Ender's Sister, 3, 119	A Lulu Ofa Menifee, 3, 115	8	1:43.80	300,000
2003	**Island Fashion**, 3, 122	I. Puglisi	Awesome Humor, 3, 115	Ladyecho, 3, 115	9	1:44.95	300,000
2002	**Allamerican Bertie**, 3, 115	L. J. Melancon	Alternate, 3, 117	Pass the Virtue, 3, 119	6	1:43.81	150,000
2001	**Zonk**, 3, 115	M. J. McCarthy	Mystic Lady, 3, 122	Lady Andromeda, 3, 115	11	1:45.27	151,000
2000	**Sincerely**, 3, 117	M. J. McCarthy	Trip, 3, 119	Valleydar, 3, 117	5	1:43.83	150,000
1999	**Brushed Halory**, 3, 115	E. M. Martin Jr.	Gold From the West, 3, 115	Queen's Word, 3, 115	5	1:43.42	150,000
1998	**Nickel Classic**, 3, 119	C. H. Borel	Lu Ravi, 3, 122	Taffy Davenport, 3, 117	8	**1:42.81**	120,000
1997	**Runup the Colors**, 3, 116	P. Day	Timely Broad, 3, 113	City Band, 3, 113	10	1:44.20	90,000
1996	**Like a Hawk**, 3, 114	R. E. Colton	Mercedes Song, 3, 118	Winter Melody, 3, 118	10	1:37.01	30,000
1982	**Lady Eleanor**, 3, 115	R. Wilson	Sailing Hour, 3, 112	Milingo, 3, 115	10	1:50.20	38,480
1981	**Up the Flagpole**, 3, 112	K. D. Black	Stunning Native, 3, 112	Object d'Art, 3, 113	6	1:49.40	53,820
1980	**Bishop's Ring**, 3, 112	M. G. Pino	Diplomatic Role, 3, 122	Sugar and Spice, 3, 122	7	1:48.60	53,203
1979	**It's in the Air**, 3, 122	W. Shoemaker	Jameela, 3, 115	Himalayan, 3, 114	6	1:49.40	52,780
1978	**White Star Line**, 3, 122	J. Fell	Queen Lib, 3, 119	Silken Delight, 3, 114	6	1:52.60	35,230
1977	**Cum Laude Laurie**, 3, 112	J. Velasquez	Pressing Date, 3, 113	Sweet Alliance, 3, 122	7	1:48.20	35,490
1976	**‡Pacific Princess**, 3, 111	E. Maple	T. V. Vixen, 3, 125	All Rainbows, 3, 114	9	1:49.60	33,660
1975	**Let Me Linger**, 3, 117	C. Barrera	dh-Funalon, 3, 123 dh-M'lle. Cyanne, 3, 117		9	1:51.40	36,237
1974	**Plantain**, 3, 114	G. McCarron	Enchanted Native, 3, 111	Knightly Wooing, 3, 114	14	1:50.40	38,350
1973	**Desert Vixen**, 3, 121	J. Velasquez	Bag of Tunes, 3, 121	Ladies Agreement, 3, 112	10	1:49.20	37,083

Not held 1943, 1983-'95. 1$^1/_8$ miles 1938-'82. 1 mile 1996. Turf 1996. Dead heat for second 1975. ‡T. V. Vixen finished first, DQ to second, 1976.

Del Mar Breeders' Cup Handicap

Grade 2 in 2006. Del Mar, three-year-olds and up, 1 mile, turf. Held September 4, 2005, with a gross value of $338,000. First held in 1987. First graded in 1989. Stakes record 1:32.21 (2005 Three Valleys).

Year	Winner	Jockey	Second	Third	Strs	Time	1st Purse
2005	**Three Valleys**, 4, 119	P. A. Valenzuela	We All Love Aleyna, 4, 118	Wild Buddy, 6, 114	10	**1:32.21**	$210,000
2004	**Supah Blitz**, 4, 116	V. Espinoza	Domestic Dispute, 4, 117	During, 4, 117	6	1:35.14	150,000
2003	**Joey Franco**, 4, 116	P. A. Valenzuela	Reba's Gold, 6, 116	Grey Memo, 6, 117	7	1:35.70	90,000
2002	**Congaree**, 4, 119	M. E. Smith	Kela, 4, 117	Reba's Gold, 5, 116	6	1:36.34	150,000
2001	**El Corredor**, 4, 121	V. Espinoza	Figlio Mio, 4, 113	Performing Magic, 4, 116	6	1:35.24	150,000
2000	**El Corredor**, 3, 111	V. Espinoza	Cliquot, 4, 117	Literal Prowler, 6, 112	8	1:35.05	158,160
1999	**Hollycombe**, 5, 116	G. L. Stevens	Flying With Eagles, 5, 115	Old Trieste, 4, 122	8	1:35.46	126,060
1998	**Old Trieste**, 3, 116	C. J. McCarron	Grajagan (Arg), 4, 111	Stalwart Tsu, 4, 116	4	1:35.35	123,172
1997	**Benchmark**, 6, 117	E. Delahoussaye	Crafty Friend, 4, 118	Northern Afleet, 4, 120	5	1:35.57	126,700
1996	**Dramatic Gold**, 5, 118	K. Desormeaux	Alphabet Soup, 5, 120	Savinio, 6, 118	5	1:34.78	125,650
1995	**Alphabet Soup**, 4, 115	C. J. McCarron	Lykatill Hil, 5, 117	Luthier Fever, 4, 115	9	1:34.33	117,150
1994	**Lykatill Hil**, 4, 118	E. Delahoussaye	D'Hallevant, 4, 117	Stuka, 4, 116	6	1:34.01	62,200
1993	**Region**, 4, 115	C. S. Nakatani	Lottery Winner, 4, 115	L'Express (Chi), 4, 115	10	1:34.98	122,100
1992	**Reign Road**, 4, 114	D. R. Flores	Sir Beaufort, 5, 116	Charmonnier, 4, 115	10	1:35.29	122,000
1991	**Twilight Agenda**, 5, 122	K. Desormeaux	Opening Verse, 5, 117	Robyn Dancer, 4, 117	5	1:34.17	116,950
1990	**Stalwart Charger**, 3, 115	R. M. Gonzalez	Flying Continental, 4, 120	Ruhlmann, 5, 123	4	1:34.60	116,300
1989	**On the Line**, 5, 124	L. A. Pincay Jr.	Good Taste (Arg), 7, 117	Lively One, 4, 125	4	1:33.40	115,400
1988	**Precisionist**, 7, 125	C. J. McCarron	Lively One, 3, 114	He's a Saros, 5, 116	4	1:34.60	85,150
1987	**Good Command**, 4, 114	C. J. McCarron	Stop the Fighting (Ire), 4, 116	Candi's Gold, 3, 113	6	1:34.80	86,250

Grade 3 1989. Del Mar Budweiser Breeders' Cup H. 1987-'95. Dirt 1987-2004. Course record 2005.

Del Mar Debutante Stakes

Grade 1 in 2006. Del Mar, two-year-olds, fillies, 7 furlongs, dirt. Held August 27, 2005, with a gross value of $250,000. First held in 1951. First graded in 1973. Stakes record 1:21.45 (1994 Call Now).

Year	Winner	Jockey	Second	Third	Strs	Time	1st Purse
2005	**Wild Fit**, 2, 117	A. O. Solis	Mystery Girl, 2, 117	River's Prayer, 2, 121	11	1:23.20	$150,000
2004	**Sweet Catomine**, 2, 114	V. Espinoza	Souvenir Gift, 2, 120	Hello Lucky, 2, 116	9	1:24.18	150,000
2003	**Halfbridled**, 2, 116	J. A. Krone	Hollywood Story, 2, 115	Victory U. S. A., 2, 116	6	1:22.20	150,000
2002	**Miss Houdini**, 2, 116	G. L. Stevens	Santa Catarina, 2, 115	Indy Groove, 2, 115	8	1:23.43	150,000
2001	**Habibti**, 2, 115	V. Espinoza	Who Loves Aleyna, 2, 116	Tempera, 2, 119	5	1:22.22	150,000

2000	**Cindy's Hero**, 2, 114	G. K. Gomez	Notable Career, 2, 119	Euro Empire, 2, 119	5	1:22.61	$150,000
1999	**Chilukki**, 2, 121	D. R. Flores	Spain, 2, 115	She's Classy, 2, 116	7	1:23.54	150,000
1998	**Excellent Meeting**, 2, 115	K. Desormeaux	Antahkarana, 2, 115	Colorado Song, 2, 115	9	1:22.34	150,000
1997	**Vivid Angel**, 2, 115	K. Desormeaux	Griselle, 2, 115	Czarina, 2, 117	8	1:24.26	150,000
1996	**Sharp Cat**, 2, 115	R. R. Douglas	Desert Digger, 2, 119	Broad Dynamite, 2, 116	10	1:23.98	150,000
1995	**Batroyale**, 2, 119	M. A. Pedroza	Proud Dixie, 2, 117	General Idea, 2, 116	12	1:22.55	137,500
1994	**Call Now**, 2, 115	A. O. Solis	How So Oiseau, 2, 119	Ski Dancer, 2, 116	9	**1:21.45**	137,500
1993	**Sardula**, 2, 116	E. Delahoussaye	Phone Chatter, 2, 119	Ballerina Gal, 2, 114	8	1:21.61	137,500
1992	**Beal Street Blues**, 2, 116	G. L. Stevens	Fit n Fappy, 2, 114	Zoonaqua, 2, 120	10	1:37.17	137,500
1991	**La Spia**, 2, 114	A. O. Solis	Soviet Sojourn, 2, 120	Wicked Wit, 2, 118	7	1:37.09	161,000
1990	**Beyond Perfection**, 2, 114	A. O. Solis	Lite Light, 2, 120	Title Bought, 2, 116	7	1:34.80	191,400
1989	**Rue de Palm**, 2, 115	R. A. Baze	Dominant Dancer, 2, 118	Cheval Volant, 2, 118	9	1:35.00	202,050
1988	**‡Lea Lucinda**, 2, 114	G. L. Stevens	Approved to Fly, 2, 114	Beware of the Cat, 2, 115	8	1:36.40	193,850
1987	**Lost Kitty**, 2, 117	G. L. Stevens	Royal Weekend, 2, 113	Hasty Pasty, 2, 117	5	1:36.00	128,850
1986	**Brave Raj**, 2, 117	C. A. Black	Road to Happiness, 2, 113	Soft Copy, 2, 115	7	1:35.80	125,325
1985	**Arewehavingfunyet**, 2, 120	P. A. Valenzuela	Python, 2, 117	Wee Lavaliere, 2, 117	6	1:36.00	134,210
1984	**Fiesta Lady**, 2, 117	L. A. Pincay Jr.	Doon's Baby, 2, 119	Trunk, 2, 115	7	1:38.80	93,050
	Full O Wisdom, 2, 113	C. J. McCarron	Pirate's Glow, 2, 115	Wayward Pirate, 2, 119	5	1:37.40	91,050
1983	**Althea**, 2, 119	L. A. Pincay Jr.	Diachrony, 2, 113	Victorous Joy, 2, 113	6	1:36.00	126,190
1982	**Landaluce**, 2, 119	L. A. Pincay Jr.	Issues n' Answers, 2, 116	Granja Reina, 2, 113	6	1:35.60	124,655
1981	**Skillful Joy**, 2, 113	C. J. McCarron	Marl Lee Ann, 2, 113	A Kiss for Luck, 2, 116	12	1:37.40	138,310
1980	**Raja's Delight**, 2, 113	C. J. McCarron	Prestigious Lady, 2, 115	Native Fancy, 2, 119	10	1:37.40	110,225
1979	**Table Hands**, 2, 119	W. Shoemaker	Hazel R., 2, 116	Arcades Ambo, 2, 117	9	1:35.00	106,770
1978	**Terlingua**, 2, 119	D. G. McHargue	Beauty Hour, 2, 116	Blowin' Wild, 2, 113	8	1:36.20	79,140
1977	**Extravagant**, 2, 113	M. Castaneda	Foxy Juliana, 2, 115	Honey Jar, 2, 113	12	1:36.40	81,490
1976	**Telferner**, 2, 116	L. A. Pincay Jr.	Asterisca, 2, 113	Maxine N., 2, 113	7	1:37.20	65,175
1975	**Queen to Be**, 2, 116	D. G. McHargue	T. V. Terese, 2, 113	Awaken, 2, 113	6	1:36.80	57,805
1974	**Bubblewin**, 2, 113	W. Shoemaker	Spout, 2, 116	Cut Class, 2, 114	6	1:36.80	57,445
1973	**Fleet Peach**, 2, 116	D. Pierce	Fresno Star, 2, 113	Divine Grace, 2, 113	8	1:09.60	46,205

Young women making their first formal appearance in society are known as debutantes. Formerly sponsored by Vinery of Lexington, Kentucky 1999. Grade 2 1973-'98. 6 furlongs 1951-'73. 1 mile 1974-'92. Two divisions 1984. ‡Approved to Fly finished first, DQ to second, 1988.

Del Mar Derby

Grade 2 in 2006. Del Mar, three-year-olds, 1⅛ miles, turf. Held September 5, 2005, with a gross value of $400,000. First held in 1945. First graded in 1973. Stakes record 1:45.85 (2005 Willow O Wisp).

Year	Winner	Jockey	Second	Third	Strs	Time	1st Purse
2005	**Willow O Wisp**, 3, 122	G. K. Gomez	Tedo (Ger), 3, 122	Osidy, 3, 122	10	**1:45.85**	$240,000
2004	**Blackdoun (Fr)**, 3, 122	C. S. Nakatani	Toasted, 3, 122	Laura's Lucky Boy, 3, 122	10	1:46.75	240,000
2003	**Fairly Ransom**, 3, 122	A. O. Solis	Devious Boy (GB), 3, 122	Sweet Return (GB), 3, 122	9	1:46.45	180,000
2002	**Inesperado (Fr)**, 3, 121	C. S. Nakatani	Johar, 3, 121	Rock Opera, 3, 121	9	1:47.49	180,000
2001	**Romanceishope**, 3, 121	C. J. McCarron	Indygo Shiner, 3, 121	Blue Steller (Ire), 3, 121	10	1:47.93	180,000
2000	**Walkslikeaduck**, 3, 121	E. Delahoussaye	Purely Cozzene, 3, 121	†New Story, 3, 118	10	1:46.66	180,000
1999	**Val Royal (Fr)**, 3, 121	C. S. Nakatani	Fighting Falcon, 3, 121	In Frank's Honor, 3, 121	10	1:48.53	180,000
1998	**Ladies Din**, 3, 121	K. Desormeaux	Expressionist, 3, 121	Scooter Brown, 3, 121	9	1:48.59	180,000
1997	**Anet**, 3, 121	G. L. Stevens	Brave Act (GB), 3, 121	Worldly Ways (GB), 3, 121	7	1:48.42	180,000
1996	**Rainbow Blues (Ire)**, 3, 122	C. S. Nakatani	The Barking Shark, 3, 122	Mateo, 3, 122	9	1:50.01	180,000
1995	**Da Hoss**, 3, 122	R. R. Douglas	Lake George, 3, 122	Tabor, 3, 122	9	1:48.08	165,000
1994	**Ocean Crest**, 3, 122	L. A. Pincay Jr.	Unfinished Symph, 3, 122	‡Powis Castle, 3, 122	10	1:48.74	165,000
1993	**Guide (Fr)**, 3, 122	K. Desormeaux	Future Storm, 3, 122	The Real Vaslav, 3, 122	12	1:49.73	165,000
1992	**Daros (GB)**, 3, 122	E. Delahoussaye	Smiling and Dancin, 3, 122	Major Impact, 3, 122	12	1:48.80	165,000
1991	**Eternity Star**, 3, 122	F. T. Alvarado	Stark South, 3, 122	June's Reward, 3, 122	10	1:49.24	165,000
1990	**Tight Spot**, 3, 122	L. A. Pincay Jr.	Itsallgreektome, 3, 122	Predecessor, 3, 122	10	1:49.60	165,000
1989	**Hawkster**, 3, 121	P. A. Valenzuela	River Master, 3, 119	Lode, 3, 116	9	1:48.00	130,500
1988	**Silver Circus**, 3, 118	R. A. Baze	Perfecting, 3, 118	Roberto's Dancer, 3, 116	8	1:49.00	127,900
1987	**Deputy Governor**, 3, 119	E. Delahoussaye	Stately Don, 3, 120	The Medic, 3, 118	9	1:48.40	98,700
1986	**Vernon Castle**, 3, 123	E. Delahoussaye	Prince Bobby B., 3, 119	Mazaad (Ire), 3, 119	9	1:48.40	95,500
1985	**First Norman**, 3, 117	G. L. Stevens	Pretensor, 3, 116	Catane, 3, 112	9	1:48.00	82,300
1984	**Tsunami Slew**, 3, 119	E. Delahoussaye	Prince True, 3, 119	Majestic Shore, 3, 115	12	1:48.00	99,650
1983	**Tanks Brigade**, 3, 122	R. Q. Meza	Ansuan, 3, 115	Evening M'lord (Ire), 3, 117	11	1:49.00	85,350
1982	**Give Me Strength**, 3, 123	L. A. Pincay Jr.	Water Bank, 3, 117	Take the Floor, 3, 117	13	1:49.00	88,100
1981	**Juan Barrera**, 3, 115	F. Toro	Buen Chico, 3, 114	Rock Softly, 3, 113	10	1:49.00	83,950
1980	**Exploded**, 3, 117	L. A. Pincay Jr.	Aristocratical, 3, 120	Son of a Dodo, 3, 118	10	1:49.60	70,300
1979	**Relaunch**, 3, 121	L. A. Pincay Jr.	Kamalii King, 3, 111	Pole Position, 3, 120	8	1:48.80	51,450
1978	**Misrepresentation**, 3, 119	D. Pierce	Singular, 3, 119	Wayside Station, 3, 115	10	1:49.60	33,450
1977	**Text**, 3, 122	D. G. McHargue	Pay the Toll, 3, 119	Hill Fox, 3, 115	10	1:49.40	32,750
1976	**Montespan**, 3, 115	D. G. McHargue	Dr. Krohn, 3, 117	Today 'n Tomorrow, 3, 118	10	1:48.40	26,550
1975	**Larrikin**, 3, 116	D. Pierce	Messenger of Song, 3, 116	Wood Carver, 3, 115	9	1:48.80	28,900
1974	**Lightning Mandate**, 3, 116	A. Pineda	Within Hail, 3, 113	Prince Petrone, 3, 113	7	1:50.00	27,900
1973	**Right Honorable**, 3, 115	J. Lambert	Groshawk, 3, 119	Dancing Papa, 3, 113	10	1:49.20	28,650

Formerly named for William Quigley, a La Jolla, California, stockbroker and co-founder of the Del Mar Turf Club. Grade 3 1973-'80. Quigley Memorial H. 1945-'47. Del Mar Invitational Derby 1991-'96. 1$\frac{1}{16}$ miles 1945-'48. Dirt 1945-'69. Two divisions 1970. ‡Eagle Eyed finished third, DQ to seventh, 1994. Equaled course record 2000. Course record 2005. †Denotes female.

Del Mar Futurity

Grade 2 in 2006. Del Mar, two-year-olds, 7 furlongs, dirt. Held September 7, 2005, with a gross value of $250,000. First held in 1948. First graded in 1973. Stakes record 1:21.29 (2004 Declan's Moon).

Year	Winner	Jockey	Second	Third	Strs	Time	1st Purse
2005	**Stevie Wonderboy**, 2, 117	G. K. Gomez	The Pharaoh, 2, 117	Jealous Profit, 2, 117	11	1:22.43	$150,000
2004	**Declan's Moon**, 2, 116	V. Espinoza	Roman Ruler, 2, 120	Swiss Lad, 2, 116	4	**1:21.29**	150,000
2003	**Siphonizer**, 2, 116	J. A. Krone	Minister Eric, 2, 116	Perfect Moon, 2, 122	5	1:23.10	150,000
2002	**Icecoldbeeratreds**, 2, 119	D. R. Flores	Kafwain, 2, 119	Chief Planner, 2, 115	8	1:22.94	150,000
2001	**Officer**, 2, 121	V. Espinoza	Kamsack, 2, 115	Metatron, 2, 116	5	1:22.33	150,000
2000	**Flame Thrower**, 2, 119	J. D. Bailey	Street Cry (Ire), 2, 116	Arabian Light, 2, 119	8	1:22.00	150,000
1999	**Forest Camp**, 2, 116	D. R. Flores	Dixie Union, 2, 121	Captain Steve, 2, 115	5	1:21.67	150,000
1998	**Worldly Manner**, 2, 119	K. Desormeaux	Daring General, 2, 119	Waki American, 2, 114	7	1:23.05	150,000
1997	**Souvenir Copy**, 2, 115	C. J. McCarron	Old Topper, 2, 119	Commitisize, 2, 115	8	1:23.10	150,000
1996	**Silver Charm**, 2, 116	D. R. Flores	Gold Tribute, 2, 115	Swiss Yodeler, 2, 121	7	1:22.88	150,000
1995	**Future Quest**, 2, 115	K. Desormeaux	Othello, 2, 115	Cavonnier, 2, 117	8	1:21.81	137,500
1994	**On Target**, 2, 115	A. O. Solis	Supremo, 2, 115	Timber Country, 2, 119	9	1:22.37	137,500
1993	**Winning Pact**, 2, 115	C. S. Nakatani	Ramblin Guy, 2, 119	Ferrara, 2, 116	7	1:22.04	137,500
1992	**River Special**, 2, 115	C. J. McCarron	Sudden Hush, 2, 120	Seattle Sleet, 2, 114	7	1:36.64	137,500
1991	**Bertrando**, 2, 114	A. O. Solis	Zurich, 2, 114	Star Recruit, 2, 115	10	1:36.45	188,500
1990	**Best Pal**, 2, 120	P. A. Valenzuela	Pillaring, 2, 116	Got to Fly, 2, 117	11	1:35.40	231,600
1989	**Drag Race**, 2, 114	F. Olivares	†Rue de Palm, 2, 117	Single Dawn, 2, 114	12	1:35.40	241,600
1988	**Music Merci**, 2, 118	C. J. McCarron	Bruho, 2, 114	Texian, 2, 117	11	1:35.40	229,300
1987	**†Lost Kitty**, 2, 117	L. A. Pincay Jr.	Bold Second, 2, 118	Purdue King, 2, 118	9	1:36.20	174,800
1986	**Qualify**, 2, 114	G. L. Stevens	†Sacahuista, 2, 117	Brevito, 2, 116	9	1:35.60	158,535
1985	**Tasso**, 2, 117	L. A. Pincay Jr.	†Arewehavingfunyet, 2, 117	Snow Chief, 2, 117	6	1:36.00	155,760
1984	**Saratoga Six**, 2, 120	A. T. Cordero Jr.	Indigenous, 2, 114	Lomax, 2, 117	9	1:36.00	173,440
1983	**†Althea**, 2, 117	L. A. Pincay Jr.	Juliet's Pride, 2, 115	Gumboy, 2, 114	5	1:34.80	147,865
1982	**Roving Boy**, 2, 117	E. Delahoussaye	Desert Wine, 2, 120	Balboa Native, 2, 114	9	1:38.80	159,945
1981	**Gato Del Sol**, 2, 114	E. Delahoussaye	The Captain, 2, 120	Ring Proud, 2, 115	10	1:37.40	160,720
1980	**Bold and Gold**, 2, 114	D. C. Hall	Looks Like Rain, 2, 114	Sir Dancer, 2, 117	12	1:36.20	129,630
1979	**The Carpenter**, 2, 114	C. J. McCarron	Doonesbury, 2, 117	Executive Counsel, 2, 114	6	1:35.20	98,710
1978	**Flying Paster**, 2, 117	D. Pierce	Priority, 2, 117	Roman Oblisk, 2, 117	8	1:34.80	100,400
1977	**Go West Young Man**, 2, 114	F. Olivares	Tampoy, 2, 114	Spanish Way, 2, 117	10	1:35.60	85,845
1976	**Visible**, 2, 117	L. A. Pincay Jr.	*Habitony, 2, 114	Washoe County, 2, 115	10	1:35.60	74,535
1975	**Telly's Pop**, 2, 117	F. Mena	Lexington Laugh, 2, 114	Body Bend, 2, 114	8	1:36.00	66,275
1974	**Diabolo**, 2, 116	W. Shoemaker	George Navonod, 2, 119	Dimaggio, 2, 122	7	1:35.40	67,120
1973	**Such a Rush**, 2, 116	W. Shoemaker	Fast Pappa, 2, 116	The Gay Greek, 2, 115	11	1:29.80	65,740

Grade 1 1984-'89. 6 furlongs 1948-'70. 7½ furlongs 1971-'73. 1 mile 1974-'92. Turf 1971-'73. Two divisions 1971. †Denotes female.

Del Mar Handicap

Grade 2 in 2006. Del Mar, three-year-olds and up, 1⅜ miles, turf. Held August 28, 2005, with a gross value of $250,000. First held in 1937. First graded in 1973. Stakes record 2:12.15 (2002 Delta Form [Aus]).

Year	Winner	Jockey	Second	Third	Strs	Time	1st Purse
2005	**Leprechaun Kid**, 6, 113	T. Baze	Laura's Lucky Boy, 4, 118	Exterior, 4, 117	10	2:12.81	$150,000
2004	**Star Over the Bay**, 6, 116	T. Baze	Sarafan, 7, 121	†Moscow Burning, 4, 114	9	2:12.71	150,000
2003	**Irish Warrior**, 5, 116	A. O. Solis	Continental Red, 7, 117	Continuously, 4, 114	9	2:12.28	150,000
2002	**Delta Form (Aus)**, 6, 115	G. F. Almeida	The Tin Man, 4, 117	Blue Steller (Ire), 4, 117	10	**2:12.15**	150,000
2001	**Timboroa (GB)**, 5, 118	L. A. Pincay Jr.	Northern Quest (Fr), 6, 116	Super Quercus (Fr), 5, 117	7	2:12.59	150,000
2000	**Northern Quest (Fr)**, 5, 116	C. J. McCarron	‡Personnet (Chi), 5, 114	Alvo Certo (Brz), 7, 115	8	2:12.65	150,000
1999	**Sayarshan (Fr)**, 4, 115	B. Blanc	Dancing Place (Chi), 6, 116	Ladies Din, 4, 120	8	2:14.35	150,000
1998	**Bonapartiste (Fr)**, 4, 115	C. J. McCarron	River Bay, 5, 123	Military, 4, 116	6	2:14.18	150,000
1997	**Rainbow Dancer (Fr)**, 6, 118	A. O. Solis	Dowty, 5, 119	Lord Jain (Arg), 5, 114	8	2:13.68	150,000
1996	**Dernier Empereur**, 6, 116	P. A. Valenzuela	Talloires, 6, 119	Party Season (GB), 5, 117	7	2:13.89	150,000
1995	**Royal Chariot**, 5, 117	L. A. Pincay Jr.	River Rhythm, 8, 117	Party Season (GB), 4, 116	10	2:13.78	137,500
1994	**Navarone**, 6, 117	P. A. Valenzuela	Approach the Bench (Ire), 6, 116	Sir Mark Sykes (Ire), 5, 116	8	2:14.37	137,500
1993	**Luazur (Fr)**, 4, 116	P. Day	Kotashaan (Fr), 5, 123	Myrakalu (Fr), 5, 114	7	2:15.11	137,500
1992	**Navarone**, 4, 117	P. A. Valenzuela	Qathif, 5, 117	Stark South, 4, 117	8	2:15.17	137,500
1991	**My Style (Ire)**, 4, 115	K. Desormeaux	Forty Niner Days, 4, 118	Super May, 5, 117	9	2:13.38	165,000
1990	**Live the Dream**, 4, 118	A. O. Solis	Mehmetori, 3, 107	Soft Machine, 5, 113	12	2:13.00	165,000
1989	**Payant (Arg)**, 5, 118	R. G. Davis	Saratoga Passage, 4, 118	†No Review, 4, 112	9	2:15.20	165,000
1988	**Sword Dance (Ire)**, 4, 114	C. J. McCarron	Great Communicator, 5, 120	Baba Karam (Ire), 4, 115	11	2:15.80	165,000
1987	**Swink**, 4, 120	W. Shoemaker	Santella Mac (Ire), 4, 116	Skip Out Front, 5, 115	12	2:13.80	165,000
1986	**Raipillan (Chi)**, 4, 114	R. A. Baze	Schiller, 4, 113	Shulich (GB), 5, 113	12	2:14.40	165,000
1985	**Barberstown**, 5, 117	F. Toro	My Habitony, 5, 118	First Norman, 3, 114	10	1:58.00	137,000
1984	**Precisionist**, 3, 116	C. J. McCarron	Pair of Deuces, 6, 116	Super Diamond, 4, 117	10	1:56.80	137,000
1983	**Bel Bolide**, 5, 117	W. Shoemaker	Gato Del Sol, 4, 123	Egg Toss, 6, 117	9	1:58.20	82,500
1982	**Muttering**, 3, 117	W. Shoemaker	Regalberto, 4, 119	Exploded, 5, 121	9	1:57.00	82,500
1981	**Wickerr**, 6, 118	C. J. McCarron	Tahitian King (Ire), 5, 121	Galaxy Libra (Ire), 5, 121	8	1:57.40	82,500
1980	**Go West Young Man**, 5, 123	E. Delahoussaye	Relaunch, 4, 118	Balzac, 5, 121	9	1:58.20	75,000
1979	**Ardiente**, 4, 118	C. J. McCarron	Quick Turnover, 4, 122	Sudanes (Arg), 6, 111	10	1:56.80	75,000
1978	**Palton (Chi)**, 5, 114	H. E. Moreno	Farnesio (Arg), 4, 119	Vic's Magic, 5, 119	8	1:57.40	60,000
1977	**Ancient Title**, 7, 123	D. G. McHargue	Painted Wagon, 4, 118	†Cascapedia, 4, 117	9	1:55.40	60,000

1976 **Riot in Paris**, 5, 122	W. Shoemaker	Avatar, 4, 122	Good Report, 6, 115	8	1:57.40	$60,000
1975 ***Cruiser II**, 6, 117	F. Olivares	Top Crowd, 4, 115	Against the Snow, 5, 117	9	2:14.40	60,000
1974 ***Redtop III**, 5, 115	F. Toro	My Old Friend, 5, 118	Nantwice, 5, 111	10	2:16.00	60,000
1973 **Red Reality**, 7, 122	B. Baeza	Wing Out, 5, 119	Life Cycle, 4, 124	10	2:17.00	60,000

Del Mar Invitational H. 1973, 1975-'87, 1989-'96. Not held 1942-'44. 1$^1/_{16}$ miles 1937-'48. 1$^1/_8$ miles 1949-'69. 1$^3/_4$ miles 1971. About 1$^1/_4$ miles 1976-'85. Dirt 1937-'69, 1976-'85. Two divisions 1972. ‡Alvo Certo (Brz) finished second, DQ to third, 2000. Course record 1975. †Denotes female.

Del Mar Oaks

Grade 1 in 2006. Del Mar, three-year-olds, fillies, 1$^1/_8$ miles, turf. Held August 20, 2005, with a gross value of $300,000. First held in 1957. First graded in 1973. Stakes record 1:46.26 (2004 Amorama [Fr]).

Year	Winner	Jockey	Second	Third	Strs	Time	1st Purse
2005	**Singhalese (GB)**, 3, 122	M. E. Smith	Three Degrees (Ire), 3, 122	Dancing Edie, 3, 122	9	1:46.29	$180,000
2004	**Amorama (Fr)**, 3, 122	D. R. Flores	Ticker Tape (GB), 3, 122	Sweet Win, 3, 122	7	**1:46.26**	180,000
2003	**Dessert**, 3, 122	C. S. Nakatani	Solar Echo, 3, 122	Personal Legend, 3, 122	8	1:47.04	180,000
2002	**Dublino**, 3, 121	K. Desormeaux	Megahertz (GB), 3, 121	Alozaina (Ire), 3, 121	6	1:47.16	180,000
2001	**Golden Apples (Ire)**, 3, 121	G. K. Gomez	Affluent, 3, 121	Reine de Romance (Ire), 3, 121	8	1:47.98	180,000
2000	**No Matter What**, 3, 121	V. Espinoza	Theoretically, 3, 121	Premiere Creation (Fr), 3, 121	9	1:50.02	150,000
1999	**Tout Charmant**, 3, 121	D. R. Flores	Smooth Player, 3, 121	Sweet Ludy (Ire), 3, 121	10	1:48.64	150,000
1998	**Sicy d'Alsace (Fr)**, 3, 121	C. S. Nakatani	‡Adel, 3, 121	Tranquility Lake, 3, 121	10	1:48.26	150,000
1997	**Famous Digger**, 3, 121	B. Blanc	Golden Arches (Fr), 3, 121	See You Soon (Fr), 3, 121	10	1:49.14	150,000
1996	**Antespend**, 3, 120	C. W. Antley	Gastronomical, 3, 120	True Flare, 3, 120	8	1:48.93	150,000
1995	**Bail Out Becky**, 3, 120	S. J. Sellers	Sleep Easy, 3, 120	Top Ruhl, 3, 120	9	1:49.72	137,500
1994	**Twice the Vice**, 3, 120	G. L. Stevens	Malli Star, 3, 120	Pharma, 3, 120	6	1:47.73	96,250
1993	**Hollywood Wildcat**, 3, 120	E. Delahoussaye	Possibly Perfect, 3, 120	Miami Sands (Ire), 3, 120	10	1:48.31	96,250
1992	**Suivi**, 3, 120	A. O. Solis	Race the Wild Wind, 3, 120	Alysbelle, 3, 120	8	1:48.60	96,250
1991	**Flawlessly**, 3, 120	C. J. McCarron	Seattle Symphony, 3, 120	Fowda, 3, 120	6	1:49.50	96,250
1990	**Slew of Pearls**, 3, 117	C. A. Black	Adorable Emilie (Fr), 3, 115	Annual Reunion, 3, 117	12	1:49.80	97,900
1989	**Stylish Star**, 3, 115	C. J. McCarron	Darby's Daughter, 3, 119	General Charge (Ire), 3, 119	9	1:48.60	97,500
1988	**No Review**, 3, 115	R. Q. Meza	Do So, 3, 124	Jungle Gold, 3, 115	7	1:49.00	96,300
1987	**Lizzy Hare**, 3, 114	G. L. Stevens	Chapel of Dreams, 3, 114	Down Again, 3, 114	13	1:50.40	104,300
1986	**Hidden Light**, 3, 124	W. Shoemaker	Kraemer, 3, 114	Shotgun Wedding, 3, 119	7	1:47.80	92,700
1985	**Savannah Dancer**, 3, 119	W. Shoemaker	‡Magnificent Lindy, 3, 122	Queen of Bronze, 3, 115	8	1:48.80	94,250
1984	**Fashionably Late**, 3, 119	C. J. McCarron	Lucky Lucky Lucky, 3, 124	Auntie Betty, 3, 114	7	1:49.40	92,400
1983	**Heartlight No. One**, 3, 122	L. A. Pincay Jr.	Foggy Moon, 3, 115	Fabulous Notion, 3, 122	10	1:50.20	84,100
1982	**Castilla**, 3, 122	R. Sibille	Avigaition, 3, 119	Skillful Joy, 3, 119	8	1:50.20	81,050
1981	**French Charmer**, 3, 117	D. G. McHargue	Amber Ever, 3, 119	Shimmy, 3, 119	9	1:49.40	82,200
1980	**Movin' Money**, 3, 114	P. A. Valenzuela	Princess Karenda, 3, 122	Tobin's Rose, 3, 119	11	1:49.40	71,000
1979	**Our Suiti Pie**, 3, 113	C. J. McCarron	Caline, 3, 121	Ancient Art, 3, 116	9	1:49.80	52,300
1978	**Country Queen**, 3, 121	F. Toro	B. Thoughtful, 3, 124	Donna Inez, 3, 113	11	1:49.80	33,450
1977	**Taisez Vous**, 3, 121	D. Pierce	Drama Critic, 3, 114	Giggling Girl, 3, 113	9	1:48.80	31,550
1976	**Go March**, 3, 116	L. A. Pincay Jr.	Pennygown, 3, 113	Franmari, 3, 116	7	1:49.20	25,700
1975	**Snap Apple**, 3, 113	F. Mena	Mia Amore, 3, 115	Miss Francesca, 3, 116	8	1:50.00	21,450
1974	**Modus Vivendi**, 3, 113	D. Pierce	Move Abroad, 3, 116	Heather Road, 3, 115	9	1:50.20	21,850
1973	**Sandy Blue**, 3, 121	D. Pierce	Sphere, 3, 112	Meilleur, 3, 118	12	1:49.40	20,850

Grade 3 1973-'78, 1988-'91. Grade 2 1979-'87, 1992-'93. Del Mar Invitational Oaks 1992-'94, 1996. 1 mile 1957-'64. Dirt 1957-'64. Two divisions 1966, 1970. ‡Pirate's Glow finished second, DQ to fourth, 1985. ‡Tranquility Lake finished second, DQ to third, 1998.

Delta Jackpot Stakes

Grade 3 in 2006. Delta Downs, two-year-olds, 1$^1/_{16}$ miles, dirt. Held December 4, 2004, with a gross value of $1,000,000. First held in 2002. First graded in 2005. Stakes record 1:45.34 (2003 Mr. Jester).

Year	Winner	Jockey	Second	Third	Strs	Time	1st Purse
2004	**Texcess**, 2, 119	V. Espinoza	Closing Argument, 2, 119	Anthony J., 2, 117	10	1:48.20	$600,000
2003	**Mr. Jester**, 2, 115	R. Chapa	Fire Slam, 2, 115	Perfect Moon, 2, 115	10	**1:45.34**	600,000
2002	**Outta Here**, 2, 116	K. Desormeaux	Comic Truth, 2, 117	Cherokee's Boy, 2, 116	10	1:37.77	300,000

The Delta Jackpot S. (G3) is the second-richest race for juveniles in North America. Sponsored by Boyd Gaming Corp. of Las Vegas, Nevada, parent company of Delta Downs 2003-'04. Not held 2005.

Demoiselle Stakes

Grade 2 in 2006. Aqueduct, two-year-olds, fillies, 1$^1/_8$ miles, dirt. Held November 26, 2005, with a gross value of $196,000. First held in 1908. First graded in 1973. Stakes record 1:50 (1978 Plankton).

Year	Winner	Jockey	Second	Third	Strs	Time	1st Purse
2005	**Wonder Lady Anne L**, 2, 116	C. H. Velasquez	Cinderella's Dream, 2, 119	Wait a While, 2, 119	5	1:52.85	$120,000
2004	**Sis City**, 2, 119	J. R. Velazquez	Salute, 2, 115	Winning Season, 2, 115	7	1:50.39	120,000
2003	**Ashado**, 2, 117	J. D. Bailey	La Reina, 2, 121	Dr. Kathy, 2, 115	7	1:52.88	120,000
2002	**Roar Emotion**, 2, 115	J. R. Velazquez	Savedbythelight, 2, 115	Feisty Step, 2, 115	10	1:51.43	120,000
2001	**Smok'n Frolic**, 2, 121	J. R. Velazquez	Lady Shari, 2, 121	Proxy Statement, 2, 117	7	1:50.57	120,000
2000	**Two Item Limit**, 2, 122	R. Migliore	Sweep Dreams, 2, 116	Kingsland, 2, 116	8	1:52.25	120,000
1999	**Jostle**, 2, 121	S. Elliott	March Magic, 2, 112	Shawnee Country, 2, 121	8	1:51.51	120,000

1998	**‡Better Than Honour**, 2, 113	R. Migliore	Waltz On By, 2, 115	Oh What a Windfall, 2, 121	9	1:52.70	$120,000
1997	**Clark Street**, 2, 121	M. E. Smith	Soft Senorita, 2, 114	Mercy Me, 2, 121	8	1:53.98	120,000
1996	**Ajina**, 2, 121	P. Day	Hidden Reserve, 2, 114	Biding Time, 2, 114	9	1:53.74	120,000
1995	**La Rosa**, 2, 114	J. A. Krone	Quiet Dance, 2, 114	Escena, 2, 112	7	1:50.92	120,000
1994	**Minister Wife**, 2, 121	J. D. Bailey	Miss Golden Circle, 2, 118	Special Broad, 2, 121	9	1:53.48	120,000
1993	**Strategic Maneuver**, 2, 116	J. D. Bailey	Sovereign Kitty, 2, 112	‡Princess Tru, 2, 114	6	1:53.62	120,000
1992	**Fortunate Faith**, 2, 112	A. Madrid Jr.	True Affair, 2, 116	Our Tomboy, 2, 112	8	1:53.59	120,000
1991	**Stolen Beauty**, 2, 113	C. W. Antley	Turnback the Alarm, 2, 116	Easy Now, 2, 116	6	1:52.08	120,000
1990	**Debutant's Halo**, 2, 116	C. Perret	Private Treasure, 2, 121	Slept Thru It, 2, 112	7	1:53.80	69,960
1989	**Rootentootenwooten**, 2, 112	J. D. Bailey	Bookkeeper, 2, 113	Why Go On Dreaming, 2, 113	9	1:51.60	109,440
1988	**Open Mind**, 2, 121	A. T. Cordero Jr.	Darby's Daughter, 2, 119	Gild, 2, 121	10	1:52.00	147,120
1987	**Goodbye Halo**, 2, 113	A. T. Cordero Jr.	Tap Your Toes, 2, 112	Galway Song, 2, 119	9	1:53.00	142,080
1986	**Tappiano**, 2, 121	J. Cruguet	Soaring Princess, 2, 112	Graceful Darby, 2, 112	7	1:53.20	131,940
1985	**I'm Sweets**, 2, 121	E. Maple	Family Style, 2, 121	Steal a Kiss, 2, 112	8	1:50.20	98,280
1984	**Diplomette**, 2, 112	R. Hernandez	Golden Silence, 2, 114	Koluctoo's Jill, 2, 112	10	1:54.60	72,360
1983	**Qualique**, 2, 112	M. Venezia	Lucky Lucky Lucky, 2, 121	Buzz My Bell, 2, 121	6	1:51.20	65,160
1982	**Only Queens**, 2, 116	M. A. Rivera	Gold Spruce, 2, 113	National Banner, 2, 113	7	1:52.00	49,680
1981	**Snow Plow**, 2, 121	A. T. Cordero Jr.	Larida, 2, 113	Vain Gold, 2, 121	8	1:53.00	50,220
1980	**Rainbow Connection**, 2, 119	A. T. Cordero Jr.	De La Rose, 2, 116	Tina Tina Too, 2, 116	6	1:50.80	48,870
1979	**Genuine Risk**, 2, 116	L. A. Pincay Jr.	Smart Angle, 2, 121	Spruce Pine, 2, 112	7	1:51.20	49,185
1978	**Plankton**, 2, 112	R. Hernandez	Distinct Honor, 2, 113	Belladora, 2, 112	9	**1:50.00**	48,465
1977	**Caesar's Wish**, 2, 116	D. R. Wright	Lakeville Miss, 2, 121	Island Kiss, 2, 114	7	1:50.60	47,565
1976	**Bring Out the Band**, 2, 116	D. Brumfield	Our Mims, 2, 113	Road Princess, 2, 112	12	1:50.80	49,500
1975	**Free Journey**, 2, 117	L. A. Pincay Jr.	Artfully, 2, 112	Dottie's Doll, 2, 114	11	1:50.20	51,210
1974	**Land Girl**, 2, 116	J. Vasquez	Alpine Lass, 2, 121	Funalon, 2, 118	14	1:36.20	35,940
1973	**Chris Evert**, 2, 121	L. A. Pincay Jr.	Amberalero, 2, 116	Khaled's Kaper, 2, 116	11	1:36.40	17,370

Demoiselle in French means young female. Grade 3 1973-'75. Grade 1 1981-'89. Held at Empire City 1908-'14, 1917-'42. Held at Belmont Park 1915-'16, 1958. Held at Jamaica 1944-'53. Not held 1909, 1911-'13, 1933-'35, 1954-'57, 1960-'62. $5\frac{1}{2}$ furlongs 1908-'32. $5\frac{3}{4}$ furlongs 1936-'42. 6 furlongs 1943-'47. $1\frac{1}{16}$ miles 1948-'53. 7 furlongs 1958-'59. 1 mile 1963-'74. ‡Bunting finished third, DQ to fifth, 1993. ‡Tutorial finished first, DQ to fifth, 1998.

Deputy Minister Handicap

Grade 3 in 2006. Gulfstream Park, three-year-olds and up, $6\frac{1}{2}$ furlongs, dirt. Held February 5, 2006, with a gross value of $100,000. First held in 1990. First graded in 2000. Stakes record 1:15.17 (2003 Native Heir).

Year	Winner	Jockey	Second	Third	Strs	Time	1st Purse
2006	**Universal Form**, 5, 115	M. R. Cruz	War Front, 4, 115	Judiths Wild Rush, 5, 117	7	1:16.48	$60,000
2005	**Medallist**, 4, 115	J. A. Santos	Mister Fotis, 4, 113	Kela, 7, 119	6	1:15.62	60,000
2004	**Alke**, 4, 112	J. R. Velazquez	Cajun Beat, 4, 123	Coach Jimi Lee, 4, 115	7	1:15.80	60,000
2003	**Native Heir**, 5, 114	C. H. Velasquez	Binthebest, 6, 115	Fire and Glory, 4, 114	8	**1:15.17**	60,000
2002	**Fappie's Notebook**, 5, 116	J. F. Chavez	Twilight Road, 5, 113	Binthebest, 5, 114	7	1:16.19	60,000
2001	**Istintaj**, 5, 118	J. D. Bailey	Fappie's Notebook, 4, 113	Fantastic Finish, 5, 114	8	1:16.08	60,000
2000	**Deep Gold**, 4, 112	J. R. Velazquez	Forty One Carats, 4, 116	Klabin's Gold, 5, 114	8	1:15.89	60,000
1999	**Good and Tough**, 4, 115	S. J. Sellers	Western Borders, 5, 113	Mint, 4, 113	7	1:21.63	60,000
1998	**Irish Conquest**, 5, 113	E. Coa	Frisk Me Now, 4, 119	Oro de Mexico, 4, 114	10	1:22.54	60,000
1997	**Templado (Ven)**, 4, 113	J. D. Bailey	Sea Emperor, 5, 114	Punch Line, 7, 119	6	1:09.69	45,000
1996	**Jess C's Whirl**, 6, 115	J. A. Krone	Buffalo Dan, 5, 117	Patton, 5, 114	6	1:10.67	30,000
1995	**Chimes Band**, 4, 120	J. D. Bailey	Distinct Reality, 4, 112	Ponche, 6, 113	6	1:09.16	30,000
1994	**I Can't Believe**, 6, 113	E. Maple	Demaloot Demashoot, 4, 115	Devil On Ice, 5, 115	7	1:08.12	30,000
1993	**Loach**, 5, 114	J. A. Santos	Hidden Tomahawk, 5, 113	British Banker, 5, 114	6	1:22.51	30,000
1992	**Take Me Out**, 4, 118	J. D. Bailey	Drummond Lane, 5, 110	Frozen Runway, 5, 114	9	1:22.78	30,000
1991	**Unbridled**, 4, 119	P. Day	Housebuster, 4, 122	Shuttleman, 5, 114	9	1:21.92	30,000
1990	**Beau Genius**, 5, 118	C. Perret	The Red Rolls, 6, 112	Joel (Arg), 8, 112	7	1:23.00	30,000

Named for Centurion Farm's, Kinghaven Farm's, and Due Process Stable's 1981 Canadian Horse of the Year, '97, '98 leading North American sire, and '83 Donn H. (G2) winner Deputy Minister (1979 c. by Vice Regent). 7 furlongs 1990-'93, 1998-'99. 6 furlongs 1994-'97. Equaled track record 2003.

Diana Stakes

Grade 1 in 2006. Saratoga Race Course, three-year-olds and up, fillies and mares, $1\frac{1}{8}$ miles, turf. Held July 30, 2005, with a gross value of $500,000. First held in 1939. First graded in 1973. Stakes record 1:45.40 (1978 Waya [Fr]).

Year	Winner	Jockey	Second	Third	Strs	Time	1st Purse
2005	**Sand Springs**, 5, 120	J. R. Velazquez	Que Puntual (Arg), 5, 120	Angara (GB), 4, 118	7	1:46.91	$300,000
2004	**Wonder Again**, 5, 120	E. S. Prado	Riskaverse, 5, 118	Ocean Drive, 4, 118	7	1:48.99	300,000
2003	**Voodoo Dancer**, 5, 120	C. S. Nakatani	Heat Haze (GB), 4, 118	Pertuisane (GB), 4, 115	8	1:47.98	300,000
2002	**Tates Creek**, 4, 117	J. D. Bailey	Voodoo Dancer, 4, 120	Snow Dance, 4, 117	9	1:48.00	300,000
2001	**Starine (Fr)**, 4, 114	J. R. Velazquez	Babae (Chi), 5, 114	Penny's Gold, 4, 120	9	1:46.17	300,000
2000	**Perfect Sting**, 4, 123	J. D. Bailey	License Fee, 5, 116	Hello Soso (Ire), 4, 113	7	1:47.01	300,000
1999	**Heritage of Gold**, 4, 115	S. J. Sellers	Khumba Mela (Ire), 4, 114	Mossflower, 5, 114	9	1:45.93	180,000
1998	**Memories of Silver**, 5, 123	J. D. Bailey	B. A. Valentine, 5, 114	Auntie Mame, 4, 122	8	1:46.14	180,000
1997	**Rumpipumpy (GB)**, 4, 114	J. A. Santos	B. A. Valentine, 4, 116	Antespend, 4, 117	12	1:48.59	120,000
1996	**Electric Society (Ire)**, 5, 117	M. E. Smith	Powder Bowl, 4, 116	Upper Noosh, 4, 110	9	1:46.56	120,000

1995	**Perfect Arc**, 3, 113	J. R. Velazquez	Danish (Ire), 4, 118	Tiffany's Taylor, 6, 113	9	1:46.85	$85,125
1994	**Via Borghese**, 5, 115	J. A. Santos	Blazing Kadie, 4, 110	Coronation Cup, 3, 108	7	1:52.01	83,010
1993	**Ratings**, 5, 110	J. A. Krone	Lady Blessington (Fr), 5, 118	Garendare (GB), 4, 113	8	1:49.80	72,240
1992	**Plenty of Grace**, 5, 114	W. H. McCauley	Ratings, 4, 114	Highland Crystal, 4, 115	12	1:46.66	75,960
1991	**Christiecat**, 4, 117	J. Samyn	Virgin Michael, 4, 112	Senora Tippy, 5, 111	10	1:47.66	75,360
1990	**Foresta**, 4, 113	A. T. Cordero Jr.	To the Lighthouse, 4, 113	Songlines, 4, 111	11	1:48.40	56,790
1989	**‡Glowing Honor**, 4, 115	J. D. Bailey	Wooing, 4, 111	Laugh and Be Merry, 4, 114	9	1:50.20	76,200
1988	**Glowing Honor**, 3, 106	P. Day	Sunny Roberta, 3, 111	Graceful Darby, 4, 112	9	1:49.40	73,680
1987	**Bailrullah**, 5, 111	J. Cruguet	Perfect Point, 5, 114	Videogenic, 5, 116	13	1:46.20	91,860
1986	**Duty Dance**, 4, 118	J. Cruguet	Dismasted, 4, 115	Kapalua Butterfly, 5, 112	11	1:49.80	91,380
1985	**Lake Country**, 4, 117	J. Fell	Possible Mate, 4, 118	Key Dancer, 4, 120	11	1:48.40	58,230
1984	**Wild Applause**, 3, 109	W. A. Guerra	Pretty Perfect, 4, 109	Spit Curl, 4, 112	9	1:48.20	70,650
1983	**Geraldine's Store**, 4, 108	J. Samyn	Trevita (Ire), 6, 120	Infinite, 3, 111	8	1:47.20	33,840
	Hush Dear, 5, 123	J. Vasquez	If Winter Comes, 5, 112	First Approach, 5, 118	9	1:48.40	34,080
1982	**Hush Dear**, 4, 109	E. Beitia	Larida, 3, 114	So Pleasantly, 4, 113	11	1:47.40	34,170
	If Winter Comes, 4, 110	E. Beitia	Canaille (Ire), 4, 112	Noble Damsel, 4, 114	10	1:47.40	34,170
1981	**De La Rose**, 3, 114	E. Maple	Rokeby Rose, 4, 115	Euphrosyne, 5, 112	8	1:50.60	36,420
1980	**Just a Game (Ire)**, 4, 123	D. Brumfield	The Very One, 5, 117	Relaxing, 4, 113	9	1:49.00	35,520
1979	**Pearl Necklace**, 5, 124	J. Fell	Island Kiss, 4, 114	Terpsichorist, 4, 119	9	1:48.80	35,010
1978	**Waya (Fr)**, 4, 115	A. T. Cordero Jr.	Pearl Necklace, 4, 125	Fia, 4, 110	12	**1:45.40**	33,240
1977	**Javamine**, 4, 114	A. T. Cordero Jr.	Pearl Necklace, 3, 109	Rich Soil, 3, 114	8	1:48.40	32,640
1976	**Glowing Tribute**, 3, 116	R. Turcotte	Fleet Victress, 4, 117	Nijana, 3, 111	9	1:47.60	32,910
1975	**Heloise**, 4, 113	M. Venezia	Victorian Queen, 4, 118	Princesse Grey, 4, 112	12	1:47.40	35,250
1974	**Fairway Flyer**, 5, 118	J. Velasquez	North Broadway, 4, 117	Brindabella, 4, 113	9	1:47.20	35,070
1973	**Cathy Baby**, 4, 119	J. Velasquez	Something Super, 3, 113	Worldling, 4, 111	8	1:46.80	13,620
	Lightning Lucy, 3, 116	R. Turcotte	Flying Fur, 4, 114	Summer Guest, 4, 122	7	1:46.60	13,545

Named for the mythological Roman goddess of the hunt, Diana. Grade 2 1973-2002. Diana H. 1939-2004. Held at Belmont Park 1943-'45. Dirt 1939-'72. Two divisions 1973, 1982-'83. ‡Wooing finished first, DQ to second, 1989.

Discovery Handicap

Grade 3 in 2006. Belmont Park, three-year-olds, $1\frac{1}{16}$ miles, dirt. Held October 29, 2005, with a gross value of $287,250. First held in 1945. First graded in 1973. Stakes record 1:41.35 (2005 Magna Graduate).

Year	Winner	Jockey	Second	Third	Strs	Time	1st Purse
2005	**Magna Graduate**, 3, 117	J. R. Velazquez	Scrappy T, 3, 119	Buzzards Bay, 3, 121	11	**1:41.35**	$172,350
2004	**Zakocity**, 3, 116	J. Castellano	Stolen Time, 3, 116	Mahzouz, 3, 115	8	1:49.78	66,060
2003	**During**, 3, 120	J. A. Santos	Unforgettable Max, 3, 114	Inamorato, 3, 114	8	1:51.18	67,080
2002	**Saint Marden**, 3, 117	J. D. Bailey	Regency Park, 3, 115	No Parole, 3, 117	10	1:49.13	68,400
2001	**Evening Attire**, 3, 111	S. Bridgmohan	Street Cry (Ire), 3, 118	Free of Love, 3, 115	7	1:48.62	65,580
2000	**Left Bank**, 3, 119	J. R. Velazquez	Perfect Cat, 3, 114	Open Sesame, 3, 115	4	1:47.30	64,020
1999	**Adonis**, 3, 118	J. R. Velazquez	Best of Luck, 3, 118	Waddaan, 3, 113	6	1:50.11	64,980
1998	**Early Warning**, 3, 115	J. F. Chavez	Deputy Diamond, 3, 117	Gulliver, 3, 115	8	1:48.94	50,010
1997	**Mr. Sinatra**, 3, 116	M. E. Smith	Concerto, 3, 121	Twin Spires, 3, 116	5	1:49.55	64,626
1996	**Gold Fever**, 3, 121	M. E. Smith	Crafty Friend, 3, 115	Early Echoes, 3, 111	9	1:49.01	66,720
1995	**Michael's Star**, 3, 112	J. A. Krone	Hunting Hard, 3, 113	Reality Road, 3, 114	10	1:50.34	67,380
1994	**Serious Spender**, 3, 113	J. F. Chavez	Unaccounted For, 3, 121	Malmo, 3, 112	4	1:51.24	63,540
1993	**Prospector's Flag**, 3, 114	J. F. Chavez	Virginia Rapids, 3, 118	Living Vicariously, 3, 114	8	1:52.30	70,320
1992	**New Deal**, 3, 111	R. G. Davis	Offbeat, 3, 114	Dodsworth, 3, 113	11	1:48.08	74,880
1991	**Upon My Soul**, 3, 112	J. Samyn	Excellent Tipper, 3, 114	Honest Ensign, 3, 110	11	1:49.62	75,960
1990	**Sports View**, 3, 113	J. A. Santos	Chief Honcho, 3, 117	dh-Killer Diller, 3, 116 dh-Out of Place, 3, 112	7	1:48.60	52,830
1989	**Tricky Creek**, 3, 117	C. Perret	Traskwood, 3, 113	Farewell Wave, 3, 110	9	1:50.00	71,280
1988	**Dynaformer**, 3, 116	A. T. Cordero Jr.	Star Attitude, 3, 113	Congeleur, 3, 112	7	1:50.00	104,580
1987	**Parochial**, 3, 117	J. A. Krone	Homebuilder, 3, 112	Forest Fair, 3, 115	11	1:51.20	109,620
1986	**Moment of Hope**, 3, 108	M. Venezia	Gold Alert, 3, 109	Clear Choice, 3, 112	9	1:49.60	54,000
1985	**Proud Truth**, 3, 126	J. Velasquez	Important Business, 3, 113	Romancer, 3, 110	6	1:49.20	51,750
1984	**Key to the Moon**, 3, 120	D. Beckon	Silver Stark, 3, 110	Raja's Shark, 3, 124	6	1:50.00	42,300
1983	**Country Pine**, 3, 118	J. D. Bailey	Jacque's Tip, 3, 115	Father Don Juan, 3, 112	6	1:49.60	33,420
1982	**Trenchant**, 3, 113	J. Samyn	Dew Line, 3, 113	Exclusive Era, 3, 112	5	1:50.80	32,880
1981	**Princelet**, 3, 113	E. Maple	Accipiter's Hope, 3, 118	Pass the Tab, 3, 126	7	1:51.00	33,240
1980	**Fappiano**, 3, 114	A. T. Cordero Jr.	Reef Searcher, 3, 114	Royal Hierarchy, 3, 111	11	1:50.00	35,280
1979	**Belle's Gold**, 3, 121	A. T. Cordero Jr.	Smarten, 3, 122	Gallant Best, 3, 115	7	1:48.00	33,270
1978	**Sorry Lookin**, 3, 110	R. I. Velez	Silent Cal, 3, 115	Judge Advocate, 3, 114	6	1:49.60	31,740
1977	**Cox's Ridge**, 3, 126	E. Maple	Broadway Forli, 3, 123	Papelote, 3, 107	9	1:48.60	32,670
1976	**Wise Philip**, 3, 107	D. Montoya	Teddy's Courage, 3, 115	Patriot's Dream, 3, 112	8	1:48.60	32,460
1975	**Dr. Emil**, 3, 115	B. Baeza	Rushing Man, 3, 125	Syllabus, 3, 113	7	1:48.60	33,630
1974	**Rube the Great**, 3, 119	A. T. Cordero Jr.	Holding Pattern, 3, 126	Sharp Gary, 3, 118	8	1:48.20	33,270
	Green Gambados, 3, 120	A. T. Cordero Jr.	Best of It, 3, 116	Jolly Johu, 3, 121	9	1:48.20	33,570
1973	**Forego**, 3, 127	H. Gustines	My Gallant, 3, 122	‡Arbees Boy, 3, 114	7	1:47.20	33,300

Named for Alfred G. Vanderbilt's 1935 Horse of the Year and three-time Brooklyn H. winner Discovery (1931 c. by Display). Grade 2 1988-'89. Held at Aqueduct 1959, 1962-'67, 1971-2004. $1\frac{1}{8}$ miles 1945-2004. Two divisions 1974. Dead heat for third 1990. ‡Key to the Kingdom finished third, DQ to seventh, 1973.

Distaff Breeders' Cup Handicap

Grade 2 in 2006. Aqueduct, three-year-olds and up, fillies and mares, 6 furlongs, dirt. Held March 25, 2006, with a gross value of $154,500. First held in 1954. First graded in 1973. Stakes record 1:10.40 (1979 Skipat).

Year	Winner	Jockey	Second	Third	Strs	Time	1st Purse
2006	**Smokey Glacken**, 5, 120	J. Castellano	Magnolia Jackson, 4, 115	Annika Lass, 5, 114	6	1:10.49	$94,800
2005	**Bank Audit**, 4, 118	R. Migliore	Sensibly Chic, 5, 117	Travelator, 5, 116	7	1:22.07	95,040
2004	**Randaroo**, 4, 121	R. Migliore	Chirimoya, 5, 110	Storm Flag Flying, 4, 118	4	1:22.64	93,240
2003	**Carson Hollow**, 4, 120	M. J. Luzzi	Raging Fever, 5, 118	Bonefide Reason, 5, 112	6	1:22.42	94,740
2002	**Raging Fever**, 4, 120	J. R. Velazquez	Prized Stamp, 5, 114	La Galerie (Arg), 6, 115	6	1:21.78	94,680
2001	**Dream Supreme**, 4, 119	A. T. Gryder	Folly Dollar, 4, 113	Country Hideaway, 5, 118	5	1:23.66	108,960
2000	**Honest Lady**, 4, 117	B. Blanc	Her She Kisses, 4, 115	Tap to Music, 5, 118	8	1:22.10	111,300
1999	**Furlough**, 5, 115	H. Castillo Jr.	Catinca, 4, 121	Tomorrows Sunshine, 5, 113	9	1:23.23	112,260
1998	**Parlay**, 4, 114	R. Migliore	Lucky Marty, 5, 113	Green Light, 4, 114	9	1:24.10	67,260
1997	**Miss Golden Circle**, 5, 120	R. Migliore	Inquisitive Look, 4, 110	Punkin Pie, 7, 109	6	1:24.47	65,400
1996	**Lottsa Talc**, 6, 120	F. T. Alvarado	Traverse City, 6, 120	Dust Bucket, 5, 116	7	1:24.04	75,820
1995	**Recognizable**, 4, 120	M. E. Smith	Beckys Shirt, 4, 113	Kurofune Mystery, 5, 116	8	1:22.94	66,540
1994	**Classy Mirage**, 4, 114	R. G. Davis	Jill Miner, 4, 114	Air Port Won, 4, 109	8	1:11.37	66,480
1992	**Nannerl**, 5, 112	M. E. Smith	Missy's Mirage, 4, 119	Withallprobability, 4, 117	6	1:24.68	68,880
1991	**Devil's Orchid**, 4, 117	R. A. Baze	Your Hope, 6, 112	Fappaburst, 4, 114	5	1:21.18	67,080
1990	**Channel Three**, 4, 111	J. F. Chavez	Divine Answer, 4, 113	Hedgeabout, 6, 112	10	1:23.20	54,090
1989	**Avie's Gal**, 4, 112	N. Santagata	Haiati, 4, 111	Topicount, 4, 117	5	1:24.00	51,660
1988	**Cadillacing**, 4, 112	R. P. Romero	Cagey Exuberance, 4, 118	Bishop's Delight, 5, 111	5	1:22.60	50,670
1987	**Pine Tree Lane**, 5, 125	A. T. Cordero Jr.	Spring Beauty, 4, 117	Gene's Lady, 6, 117	7	1:22.40	52,650
1986	**Ride Sally**, 4, 118	W. A. Guerra	Willowy Mood, 4, 116	Clocks Secret, 4, 122	8	1:21.60	54,540
1985	**Give Me a Hint**, 5, 109	W. A. Ward	Nany, 5, 121	Descent, 5, 106	8	1:25.20	55,080
1984	**Am Capable**, 4, 125	A. T. Cordero Jr.	Sweet Missus, 4, 104	Fissure, 4, 107	7	1:11.00	52,290
1983	**Jones Time Machine**, 4, 122	A. T. Cordero Jr.	Fancy Naskra, 5, 113	Adept, 4, 111	6	1:23.20	32,880
1982	**Lady Dean**, 4, 120	D. A. Miller Jr.	Westport Native, 4, 114	Raise 'n Dance, 4, 107	8	1:23.80	33,000
1981	**Lady Oakley (Ire)**, 4, 114	J. Fell	It's in the Air, 5, 120	Lovin' Lass, 4, 110	8	1:25.40	33,900
1980	**Misty Gallore**, 4, 124	D. MacBeth	Lady Lonsdale, 5, 114	Spanish Fake, 4, 112	6	1:24.60	33,240
1979	**Skipat**, 5, 122	J. W. Edwards	Sweet Joyce, 4, 106	Unpossible, 4, 107	10	**1:10.40**	32,520
1978	**Vandy Sue**, 4, 112	A. M. Rodriguez	Sea Drone, 4, 108	Dalton Road, 5, 118	7	1:12.00	22,185
1977	**What a Summer**, 4, 118	E. Maple	Secret Lanvin, 4, 112	Shy Dawn, 6, 120	5	1:11.60	21,975
1976	**Shy Dawn**, 5, 118	A. T. Cordero Jr.	‡Land Girl, 4, 114	Ladies Agreement, 6, 114	8	1:24.20	22,590
1975	**Something Super**, 5, 115	J. Cruguet	Shy Dawn, 4, 121	Second Coming, 4, 108	8	1:22.20	16,996
1974	**Krislin**, 5, 113	V. A. Bracciale Jr.	Batucada, 5, 116	Ladies Agreement, 4, 112	8	1:22.00	16,770
1973	**Ferly**, 5, 113	R. Turcotte	Wakefield Miss, 5, 115	Twixt, 4, 112	8	1:24.00	16,920

Races for females are typically referred to as distaff races. Grade 3 1973-'88. Distaff H. 1954-'98. Held at Belmont Park 1956-'59. Not held 1993. 7 furlongs 1954-'76, 1980-'83, 1985-'92, 1995-2005. ‡Imminence finished second, DQ to fourth, 1976.

Dixie Stakes

Grade 2 in 2006. Pimlico Race Course, three-year-olds and up, 1⅛ miles, turf. Held May 20, 2006, with a gross value of $250,000. First held in 1870. First graded in 1973. Stakes record 1:46.34 (2004 Mr O'Brien [Ire]).

Year	Winner	Jockey	Second	Third	Strs	Time	1st Purse
2006	**Better Talk Now**, 7, 124	R. A. Dominguez	Dreadnaught, 6, 118	Artie Schiller, 5, 124	7	1:48.48	$150,000
2005	**Cool Conductor**, 4, 118	C. H. Velasquez	Artie Schiller, 4, 124	Good Reward, 4, 118	5	1:52.79	120,000
2004	**Mr O'Brien (Ire)**, 5, 119	R. A. Dominguez	Millennium Dragon (GB), 5, 121	Warleigh, 6, 124	11	**1:46.34**	120,000
2003	**Dr. Brendler**, 5, 117	R. A. Dominguez	Perfect Soul (Ire), 5, 117	Sardaukar (GB), 7, 117	6	1:57.78	120,000
2002	**Strut the Stage**, 4, 117	R. Albarado	Del Mar Show, 5, 119	Slew the Red, 5, 117	7	1:51.70	120,000
2001	**Hap**, 5, 119	J. D. Bailey	Make No Mistake (Ire), 6, 119	Cynics Beware, 7, 119	8	1:48.56	120,000
2000	**Quiet Resolve**, 5, 117	R. Albarado	Haami, 5, 117	Holditholditholdit, 4, 117	9	1:50.42	120,000
1999	**Middlesex Drive**, 4, 115	P. Day	Sky Colony, 6, 115	Divide and Conquer, 5, 115	10	1:48.64	120,000
1998	**Yagli**, 5, 121	J. D. Bailey	Sky Colony, 5, 115	Blazing Sword, 4, 115	12	1:51.01	120,000
1997	**Ops Smile**, 5, 115	E. S. Prado	Brave Note (Ire), 6, 115	Sharp Appeal, 4, 121	8	1:48.20	120,000
1996	**Gold and Steel (Fr)**, 4, 121	A. O. Solis	Same Old Wish, 6, 115	Comstock Lode, 4, 115	9	1:52.80	120,000
1995	**The Vid**, 5, 119	J. D. Bailey	Pennine Ridge, 4, 115	Blues Traveller (Ire), 5, 121	6	1:52.25	120,000
1994	**Paradise Creek**, 5, 124	P. Day	Lure, 5, 124	Astudillo (Ire), 4, 115	5	1:48.51	90,000
1993	**Lure**, 4, 124	M. E. Smith	Star of Cozzene, 5, 119	Binary Light, 4, 115	8	1:47.60	90,000
1992	**Sky Classic**, 5, 122	P. Day	Fourstars Allstar, 4, 116	Social Retiree, 5, 112	10	1:47.83	90,000
1991	**Double Booked**, 6, 118	P. Day	Chas' Whim, 4, 116	Opening Verse, 5, 118	9	1:47.04	90,000
1990	**Two Moccasins**, 4, 114	R. P. Romero	My Big Boy, 7, 115	Marksmanship, 5, 113	10	2:35.80	90,000
1989	**Coeur de Lion (Fr)**, 5, 121	J. Cruguet	Dance Card Filled, 6, 115	Dynaformer, 4, 118	10	2:38.40	90,000
1988	**Kadial (Ire)**, 5, 112	G. L. Stevens	Top Guest (Ire), 5, 118	Milesius, 4, 120	5	2:45.00	71,045
1987	**Akabir**, 6, 115	C. Perret	Little Bold John, 5, 117	Vilzak, 4, 113	9	2:28.60	74,360
1986	**Uptown Swell**, 4, 117	W. A. Guerra	Southern Sultan, 4, 112	†Carlypha (Ire), 5, 108	13	2:27.40	92,445
1985	**Nassipour**, 5, 115	V. A. Bracciale Jr.	†Persian Tiara (Ire), 5, 113	‡Computer's Choice, 5, 116	8	2:27.80	72,800
1984	**†Persian Tiara (Ire)**, 4, 109	R. L. Shelton	Crazy Moon, 4, 112	Canadian Factor, 4, 118	8	2:41.00	88,675
1983	**Khatango**, 4, 114	V. A. Bracciale Jr.	London Times, 5, 108	Super Sunrise (GB), 4, 114	10	2:28.60	75,075
1982	**Robsphere**, 5, 120	J. Velasquez	Present the Colors, 5, 113	Rich and Ready, 6, 115	13	2:30.20	76,960
1981	**El Barril (Chi)**, 5, 116	J. Vasquez	Buckpoint (Fr), 5, 119	Birthday List, 6, 108	9	2:29.80	73,255

1980	**Marquee Universal (Ire)**, 4, 118	H. Pilar	†The Very One, 5, 113	Match the Hatch, 4, 115	14	2:29.60	$77,155
1979	**†The Very One**, 4, 108	C. Cooke	That's a Nice, 5, 116	Fluorescent Light, 5, 124	8	2:28.60	72,995
1978	**Fluorescent Light**, 4, 114	V. A. Bracciale Jr.	That's a Nice, 4, 115	Improviser, 6, 118	7	2:33.20	37,343
	Bowl Game, 4, 120	J. Velasquez	Oilfield, 5, 110	Trumpeter Swan, 7, 110	9	2:33.40	37,993
1977	**Improviser**, 5, 120	M. A. Rivera	Grey Beret, 5, 114	Oilfield, 4, 118	12	2:29.40	56,875
1976	**Barcas**, 5, 112	V. A. Bracciale Jr.	One On the Aisle, 4, 122	Neapolitan Way, 5, 108	9	2:29.60	37,375
1975	**Bemo**, 5, 114	C. J. McCarron	Outdoors, 6, 115	Drollery, 5, 114	13	2:33.40	39,325
1974	**London Company**, 4, 122	A. T. Cordero Jr.	Scrimshaw, 6, 110	Mister Diz, 8, 110	9	2:28.80	38,025
1973	**Laplander**, 6, 111	V. A. Bracciale Jr.	Chrisaway, 5, 112	*Wustenchef, 8, 112	10	2:30.40	38,675

Named for Maj. Barak G. Thomas's mare Dixie (1859 f. by *Sovereign). Named the Reunion S. to signify a reunion of the original subscribers to the Dinner Party S. Originally named the Dinner Party S. The name originated with a Saratoga Springs dinner party attended by a group of men whose main topic of conversation was the revival of Baltimore racing after the Civil War; all present agreed to support the inaugural running of the race in 1870. Sponsored by CompUSA Management Co. of Dallas 2005-'06. Formerly sponsored by Argent Mortgage Co. of Orange, California 2004. Formerly sponsored by CITGO Petroleum Corp. of Tulsa, Oklahoma 2003. Formerly sponsored by Early Times Distillery Co. of Louisville 1991-'96. Grade 3 1990-'93. Dinner Party S. 1870. Dixie H. 1871, 1902-'04, 1925-'90, 1991-'94, 1996. Reunion S. 1872-'88. Held at Benning, Washington, D.C. 1902-'04. Not held 1889-1901, 1905-'23. 2 miles 1870-'88. $1\frac{3}{4}$ miles 1902-'04. $1\frac{3}{16}$ miles 1924. $1\frac{3}{8}$ miles 1955-'59. $1\frac{1}{2}$ miles 1960-'90. $1\frac{5}{8}$ miles 1988. Dirt 1870-1954, 1988. Three-year-olds 1870-1904. Two divisions 1965, 1978. ‡Pass the Line finished third, DQ to fourth, 1985. Course record 2004. †Denotes female.

Dogwood Breeders' Cup Stakes

Grade 3 in 2006. Churchill Downs, three-year-olds, fillies, 1 mile, dirt. Held June 3, 2006, with a gross value of $167,850. First held in 1975. First graded in 1998. Stakes record 1:35.49 (2006 Joint Effort).

Year	Winner	Jockey	Second	Third	Strs	Time	1st Purse
2006	**Joint Effort**, 3, 116	R. R. Douglas	Ready to Please, 3, 120	Victorina, 3, 116	9	**1:35.49**	$101,148
2005	**Miss Matched**, 3, 116	S. Bridgmohan	Culinary, 3, 120	Catta Pilosa, 3, 116	7	1:43.49	101,928
2004	**Stellar Jayne**, 3, 120	R. Albarado	Dynaville, 3, 114	Ender's Sister, 3, 122	5	1:43.14	100,068
2003	**Golden Marlin**, 3, 115	S. J. Sellers	Double Scoop, 3, 114	Throne, 3, 114	7	1:45.96	67,580
2002	**Take Charge Lady**, 3, 121	A. J. D'Amico	Charmed Gift, 3, 116	Allamerican Bertie, 3, 114	7	1:42.73	67,890
2001	**Nasty Storm**, 3, 114	L. J. Meche	Love At Noon, 3, 114	Golly Greeley, 3, 116	7	1:43.41	68,014
2000	**Welcome Surprise**, 3, 112	F. C. Torres	Lady Melesi, 3, 114	Vivid Sunset, 3, 114	7	1:46.80	68,014
1999	**Golden Temper**, 3, 116	S. J. Sellers	Boom Town Girl, 3, 121	Honey Hill Lil, 3, 116	8	1:43.73	69,068
1998	**Really Polish**, 3, 116	P. Day	‡Beat the Play, 3, 114	Victorica, 3, 121	5	1:44.78	67,642
1997	**Leo's Gypsy Dancer**, 3, 116	P. Day	Buckeye Search, 3, 121	Flying Lauren, 3, 118	7	1:44.95	69,006
1996	**Ginny Lynn**, 3, 121	L. J. Melancon	Everhope, 3, 121	Hidden Lake, 3, 114	7	1:43.22	53,576
1995	**Gal in a Ruckus**, 3, 121	W. H. McCauley	Country Cat, 3, 116	Naskra Colors, 3, 114	7	1:43.88	53,528
1994	**Briar Road**, 3, 114	L. J. Melancon	Stella Cielo, 3, 114	Shadow Miss, 3, 121	6	1:44.78	53,186
1993	**With a Wink**, 3, 114	C. R. Woods Jr.	Lovat's Lady, 3, 112	Unlaced, 3, 116	8	1:44.21	36,010
1992	**Hitch**, 3, 121	B. E. Bartram	Bionic Soul, 3, 121	Secretly, 3, 114	8	1:47.68	36,075
1991	**Be Cool**, 3, 121	A. T. Gryder	Barri Mac, 3, 114	Saratoga Dame, 3, 121	8	1:46.46	36,563
1990	**Patches**, 3, 118	K. K. Allen	Mrs. K., 3, 116	Mirth, 3, 114	4	1:46.60	34,873
1989	**Luthier's Launch**, 3, 118	P. Day	Motion in Limine, 3, 116	Dreamy Mimi, 3, 121	9	1:45.20	36,465
1988	**Darien Miss**, 3, 121	D. Brumfield	Stolie, 3, 118	Most Likely, 3, 116	8	1:43.80	35,848
1987	**Lady Gretchen**, 3, 112	M. McDowell	Super Cook, 3, 122	Jonowo, 3, 122	7	1:44.00	46,193
1986	**Hail a Cab**, 3, 119	P. A. Johnson	Tall Poppy, 3, 111	Marshesseaux, 3, 114	8	1:46.60	46,810
1985	**Foxy Deen**, 3, 118	D. Montoya	Weekend Delight, 3, 120	Clouhalo, 3, 112	8	1:50.00	35,945
1984	**Mrs. Revere**, 3, 121	L. J. Melancon	Rambling Rhythm, 3, 119	Robin's Rob, 3, 115	8	1:51.20	49,510
1983	**Bon Gout**, 3, 117	P. Day	Andthebeatgoeson, 3, 112	Workin Girl, 3, 112	8	1:53.00	36,368
1982	**Amazing Love**, 3, 117	L. J. Melancon	Sefa's Beauty, 3, 117	Bold Siren, 3, 113	8	1:46.60	23,546
1981	**Savage Love**, 3, 116	P. Nicolo	Westport Native, 3, 118	Brian's Babe, 3, 116	6	1:24.80	19,053
	Fancy Naskra, 3, 118	J. Lively	Contrefaire, 3, 121	Solo Disco, 3, 118	10	1:25.20	17,948
1980	**Quality Corner**, 3, 121	M. S. Sellers	Forever Cordial, 3, 121	No No Nona, 3, 121	8	1:24.00	19,403
1979	**Split the Tab**, 3, 121	D. Haire	Shawn's Gal, 3, 121	Safe, 3, 121	10	1:24.00	19,663
1978	**Bold Rendezvous**, 3, 121	A. Rini	Step in the Circle, 3, 118	Timeforaturn, 3, 118	8	1:23.40	14,446
1977	**Unreality**, 3, 121	M. Fromin	Shady Lou, 3, 121	Time for Pleasure, 3, 118	12	1:25.40	15,031
1976	**T. V. Vixen**, 3, 121	M. Manganello	Sunny Romance, 3, 116	Old Goat, 3, 121	6	1:23.40	14,154
1975	**My Juliet**, 3, 121	A. Hill	Snow Doll, 3, 118	Hope She Does, 3, 118	9	1:24.00	14,999

Named for the dogwood tree, plentiful in Kentucky. Dogwood S. 1975-2003. 7 furlongs 1975-'81. $1\frac{1}{16}$ 1982, 1986-2005. $1\frac{1}{8}$ miles 1983-'85. Two divisions 1981. ‡Nickel Classic finished second, DQ to fifth, 1998.

Donn Handicap

Grade 1 in 2006. Gulfstream Park, three-year-olds and up, $1\frac{1}{8}$ miles, dirt. Held February 4, 2006, with a gross value of $500,000. First held in 1959. First graded in 1973. Stakes record 1:46.40 (1979 Jumping Hill).

Year	Winner	Jockey	Second	Third	Strs	Time	1st Purse
2006	**Brass Hat**, 5, 118	W. Martinez	Pies Prospect, 5, 114	Andromeda's Hero, 4, 115	9	1:47.79	$300,000
2005	**Saint Liam**, 5, 119	E. S. Prado	Roses in May, 5, 121	Eddington, 4, 114	6	1:48.43	300,000
2004	**Medaglia d'Oro**, 5, 122	J. D. Bailey	Seattle Fitz (Arg), 5, 113	Funny Cide, 4, 119	8	1:47.68	300,000
2003	**Harlan's Holiday**, 4, 120	J. R. Velazquez	Hero's Tribute, 5, 114	Puzzlement, 4, 114	11	1:49.17	300,000
2002	**Mongoose**, 4, 114	E. S. Prado	‡Kiss a Native, 5, 114	Rize, 6, 114	14	1:49.63	300,000
2001	**Captain Steve**, 4, 120	J. D. Bailey	Albert the Great, 4, 119	Gander, 5, 115	7	1:48.95	300,000
2000	**Stephen Got Even**, 4, 115	S. J. Sellers	Golden Missile, 5, 114	Behrens, 6, 121	10	1:48.50	300,000

1999	**Puerto Madero (Chi)**, 5, 120	K. Desormeaux	Behrens, 5, 113	Silver Charm, 5, 126	12	1:48.34	$300,000
1998	**Skip Away**, 5, 126	J. D. Bailey	Unruled, 5, 112	Sir Bear, 5, 113	10	1:50.17	180,000
1997	**Formal Gold**, 4, 113	J. Bravo	Skip Away, 4, 123	Mecke, 5, 120	10	1:47.49	180,000
1996	**Cigar**, 6, 128	J. D. Bailey	Wekiva Springs, 5, 117	†Heavenly Prize, 5, 115	8	1:49.12	180,000
1995	**Cigar**, 5, 115	J. D. Bailey	Primitive Hall, 6, 112	Bonus Money (GB), 4, 112	9	1:49.68	180,000
1994	**Pistols and Roses**, 5, 113	H. Castillo Jr.	Eequalsmcsquared, 5, 113	Wallenda, 4, 118	11	1:50.67	180,000
1993	**Pistols and Roses**, 4, 112	H. Castillo Jr.	Irish Swap, 6, 118	Missionary Ridge (GB), 6, 118	9	1:50.10	240,000
1992	**Sea Cadet**, 4, 115	A. O. Solis	Out of Place, 5, 114	Sunny Sunrise, 5, 115	8	1:48.17	300,000
1991	**Jolie's Halo**, 4, 114	R. Platts	Sports View, 4, 116	Secret Hello, 4, 116	12	1:47.50	300,000
1990	**Primal**, 5, 120	E. Fires	Ole Atocha, 5, 111	Western Playboy, 4, 119	8	1:50.00	120,000
1989	**Cryptoclearance**, 5, 121	J. A. Santos	Slew City Slew, 5, 118	Primal, 4, 117	12	1:50.20	120,000
1988	**Jade Hunter**, 4, 112	J. D. Bailey	Cryptoclearance, 4, 123	Personal Flag, 5, 120	8	1:48.80	120,000
1987	**Little Bold John**, 5, 111	M. A. Gonzalez	Skip Trial, 5, 118	Wise Times, 4, 117	7	1:48.80	96,660
1986	**Creme Fraiche**, 4, 122	E. Maple	Skip Trial, 4, 122	Minneapple, 4, 113	13	1:51.20	77,280
1985	**Mo Exception**, 4, 115	R. Breen	Dr. Carter, 4, 120	Key to the Moon, 4, 122	10	1:48.60	74,280
1984	**Play Fellow**, 4, 122	P. Day	Courteous Majesty, 4, 111	Jack Slade, 4, 114	9	1:49.00	53,955
1983	**Deputy Minister**, 4, 122	D. MacBeth	Key Count, 4, 113	Rivalero, 7, 121	16	1:48.60	60,840
1982	**Joanie's Chief**, 5, 111	J. Samyn	Double Sonic, 4, 111	Lord Darnley, 4, 113	12	1:49.00	57,330
1981	**Hurry Up Blue**, 4, 116	C. C. Lopez	Tunerup, 5, 126	Joanie's Chief, 4, 107	5	1:49.00	51,345
1980	**Lot o' Gold**, 4, 119	D. Brumfield	Addison, 5, 111	Going Investor, 5, 112	9	1:48.80	54,600
1979	**Jumping Hill**, 7, 122	J. Fell	Bob's Dusty, 5, 120	Silent Cal, 4, 121	14	**1:46.40**	60,150
1978	**Man's Man**, 4, 115	R. Woodhouse	Intercontinent, 4, 116	Adriatico (Arg), 7, 110	11	1:42.20	39,000
1977	**Legion**, 7, 113	L. Saumell	Logical, 5, 114	Yamanin, 5, 124	7	1:48.80	37,440
1976	**Foolish Pleasure**, 4, 129	B. Baeza	Packer Captain, 4, 114	Home Jerome, 6, 112	10	1:21.40	37,980
1975	**Proud and Bold**, 5, 118	G. St. Leon	Holding Pattern, 4, 121	Arbees Boy, 5, 119	6	1:48.00	35,280
1974	**Forego**, 4, 125	H. Gustines	True Knight, 5, 123	Proud and Bold, 4, 122	5	1:48.60	36,000
1973	**Triumphant**, 4, 114	B. Baeza	Second Bar, 4, 121	Gentle Smoke, 4, 113	7	1:47.80	37,560

Named in honor of James Donn Sr. (1887-1972), founder of modern Gulfstream Park. Grade 3 1973-'74. Grade 2 1975-'87. 1½ miles 1959-'64. 7 furlongs 1976. 1¹⁄₁₆ miles 1978. Turf 1959-'64. ‡Red Bullet finished second, DQ to fourth, 2002. Track record 2006. †Denotes female.

Dwyer Stakes

Grade 2 in 2006. Belmont Park, three-year-olds, 1¹⁄₁₆ miles, dirt. Held July 4, 2005, with a gross value of $150,000. First held in 1887. First graded in 1973. Stakes record 1:40.02 (2004 Medallist).

Year	Winner	Jockey	Second	Third	Strs	Time	1st Purse
2005	**Roman Ruler**, 3, 119	J. D. Bailey	Flower Alley, 3, 123	Proud Accolade, 3, 119	6	1:40.83	$90,000
2004	**Medallist**, 3, 121	J. F. Chavez	The Cliff's Edge, 3, 123	Sir Shackleton, 3, 121	6	**1:40.02**	90,000
2003	**Strong Hope**, 3, 115	J. R. Velazquez	Nacheezmo, 3, 115	Sky Mesa, 3, 119	7	1:41.76	90,000
2002	**Gygistar**, 3, 121	J. R. Velazquez	Nothing Flat, 3, 117	American Style, 3, 115	6	1:42.59	90,000
2001	**E Dubai**, 3, 121	J. D. Bailey	Windsor Castle, 3, 119	Hero's Tribute, 3, 121	4	1:40.38	145,500
2000	**Albert the Great**, 3, 115	R. Migliore	More Than Ready, 3, 119	Red Bullet, 3, 123	4	1:42.62	90,000
1999	**Forestry**, 3, 122	J. D. Bailey	Doneraile Court, 3, 119	Successful Appeal, 3, 122	6	1:41.00	90,000
1998	**Coronado's Quest**, 3, 124	M. E. Smith	Ian's Thunder, 3, 112	Scatmandu, 3, 122	5	1:42.49	90,000
1997	**Behrens**, 3, 117	J. D. Bailey	Glitman, 3, 114	Banker's Gold, 3, 122	6	1:42.26	90,000
1996	**Victory Speech**, 3, 117	J. D. Bailey	Gold Fever, 3, 119	Robb, 3, 117	6	1:41.53	99,000
1995	**Hoolie**, 3, 117	R. G. Davis	Reality Road, 3, 112	Western Larla, 3, 119	6	1:42.74	90,000
1994	**Holy Bull**, 3, 124	M. E. Smith	Twining, 3, 122	Bay Street Star, 3, 119	4	1:41.15	90,000
1993	**Cherokee Run**, 3, 123	P. Day	Miner's Mark, 3, 123	Silver of Silver, 3, 123	6	1:47.62	120,000
1992	**‡Agincourt**, 3, 119	J. F. Chavez	Three Peat, 3, 119	Windundermywings, 3, 114	6	1:47.84	120,000
1991	**Lost Mountain**, 3, 123	C. Perret	Smooth Performance, 3, 114	Fly So Free, 3, 126	7	1:49.20	120,000
1990	**Profit Key**, 3, 123	J. A. Santos	Rhythm, 3, 123	Graf, 3, 114	4	1:47.40	102,960
1989	**Roi Danzig**, 3, 114	E. Maple	Contested Colors, 3, 114	Rampart Road, 3, 114	5	1:49.20	133,680
1988	**Seeking the Gold**, 3, 123	P. Day	Evening Kris, 3, 119	Gay Rights, 3, 123	7	1:48.00	137,040
1987	**Gone West**, 3, 123	E. Maple	Pledge Card, 3, 114	Polish Navy, 3, 123	6	1:48.40	138,240
1986	**Ogygian**, 3, 119	W. A. Guerra	Johns Treasure, 3, 114	Personal Flag, 3, 114	4	1:48.40	112,680
1985	**Stephan's Odyssey**, 3, 123	L. A. Pincay Jr.	Cutlass Reality, 3, 114	Important Business, 3, 126	8	1:49.20	88,500
1984	**Track Barron**, 3, 119	J. Cruguet	Darn That Alarm, 3, 123	Slew the Coup, 3, 114	7	1:47.80	99,600
1983	**Au Point**, 3, 114	J. D. Bailey	Potentiate, 3, 114	Intention, 3, 114	10	1:48.20	68,640
1982	**Conquistador Cielo**, 3, 126	E. Maple	John's Gold, 3, 114	Reinvested, 3, 119	6	1:45.80	67,560
1981	**Noble Nashua**, 3, 119	C. B. Asmussen	Tap Shoes, 3, 126	Silver Express, 3, 114	10	1:49.20	68,160
1980	**Amber Pass**, 3, 114	D. MacBeth	Temperence Hill, 3, 129	Comptroller, 3, 119	8	1:49.00	67,440
1979	**Coastal**, 3, 126	R. Hernandez	Private Account, 3, 114	Quiet Crossing, 3, 119	6	1:47.00	63,840
1978	**Junction**, 3, 120	J. Fell	Buckaroo, 3, 127	Darby Creek Road, 3, 121	3	1:48.80	47,025
1977	**Bailjumper**, 3, 116	A. T. Cordero Jr.	Lynn Davis, 3, 112	Iron Constitution, 3, 121	8	1:47.60	48,870
1976	**Quiet Little Table**, 3, 111	E. Maple	Sir Lister, 3, 116	Dance Spell, 3, 117	8	1:49.00	50,895
1975	**Valid Appeal**, 3, 110	J. S. Long	Wajima, 3, 118	Hunka Papa, 3, 116	8	1:48.40	50,400
1974	**Hatchet Man**, 3, 114	R. Turcotte	Rube the Great, 3, 124	Kin Run, 3, 112	9	2:01.20	51,120
1973	**Stop the Music**, 3, 120	H. Gustines	Arbees Boy, 3, 115	Duc de Flanagan, 3, 111	8	2:02.60	50,625

Named in honor of leading 19th-century owners Mike and Phil Dwyer. Formerly named in honor of the city of Brooklyn, New York. Grade 1 1983-'88. Brooklyn Derby 1887-1917. Dwyer H. 1956-'78. Held at Gravesend Park 1887-1910. Held at Aqueduct 1914-'55, 1960-'74, 1976. Held at Jamaica 1956, 1959. Not held 1911-'12. 1½ miles 1887, 1898-1909, 1926-'34. 1⅛ miles 1888-'97, 1915-'24, 1935-'39, 1975-'93. 1¼ miles 1910-'14, 1940-'55, 1960-'74. 1⁵⁄₁₆ miles 1925. 1³⁄₁₆ miles 1956-'59. ‡Three Peat finished first, DQ to second, 1992.

Eatontown Handicap

Grade 3 in 2006. Monmouth Park, three-year-olds and up, fillies and mares, 1$^1/_{16}$ miles, turf. Held July 3, 2005, with a gross value of $150,000. First held in 1971. First graded in 1996. Stakes record 1:40.40 (1996 Gail's Brush).

Year	Winner	Jockey	Second	Third	Strs	Time	1st Purse
2005	**Smart N Classy**, 5, 115	J. A. Velez Jr.	Lentil, 6, 116	Spotlight (GB), 4, 118	7	1:46.22	$90,000
2004	**Ocean Drive**, 4, 120	E. Coa	Honorable Cat, 5, 114	Fast Cookie, 4, 118	6	1:41.79	60,000
2003	**Stylish**, 5, 118	H. Castillo Jr.	Something Ventured, 4, 117	Sweet Deimos (GB), 4, 113	9	1:41.69	60,000
2002	**Clearly a Queen**, 5, 119	E. Coa	Laurica, 5, 114	Presumed Innocent, 5, 117	9	1:44.02	60,000
2001	**Cousin Gigi**, 4, 115	R. Wilson	Quidnaskra, 6, 116	Crystal Sea, 4, 113	8	1:47.50	60,000
2000	**Reciclada (Chi)**, 5, 115	A. O. Solis	Mumtaz (Fr), 4, 122	Dominique's Joy, 5, 117	8	1:44.34	60,000
1999	**Formal Tango**, 4, 113	J. D. Bailey	Proud Owner, 4, 115	Natalie Too, 5, 122	7	1:42.62	60,000
1998	**Gastronomical**, 5, 115	G. L. Stevens	Tampico, 5, 117	dh-Dance Clear (Ire), 5, 112 dh-Poopsie, 4, 114	10	1:43.39	41,400
1997	**B. A. Valentine**, 4, 122	C. J. McCarron	Everhope, 4, 112	Vashon, 4, 122	11	1:41.20	41,460
1996	**Gail's Brush**, 5, 116	G. Boulanger	Plenty of Sugar, 5, 117	Lady Affirmed, 5, 116	7	**1:40.40**	45,000
1995	**Symphony Lady**, 5, 119	J. Bravo	Cox Orange, 5, 122	Grafin, 4, 119	6	1:43.64	30,000
1994	**Verbal Volley**, 5, 119	R. E. Colton	Irving's Girl, 4, 114	Uptown Show, 5, 113	8	1:44.71	24,000
1993	**Topsa**, 6, 113	L. R. Rivera Jr.	Naked Royalty, 4, 115	Suspect Terrain, 4, 115	7	1:46.39	21,000
1992	**Red Journey**, 4, 115	N. Santagata	Hot Times Are Here, 4, 113	Flashing Eyes, 4, 113	7	1:45.06	21,000
1991	**Jacuzzi Boogie**, 4, 119	N. Santagata	Hear the Bells, 4, 113	Be Exclusive (Ire), 5, 113	5	1:41.67	21,000
1990	**Miss Unnameable**, 6, 113	L. Saumell	Lip Service, 5, 116	Perfect Coin, 4, 112	9	1:48.00	34,110
1989	**Highland Penny**, 4, 112	D. Carr	Starofanera, 4, 113	River Memories, 5, 114	9	1:50.00	34,770
1988	**Hear Music**, 5, 115	M. Castaneda	Fancy Pan, 5, 112	Antique Mystique, 4, 111	7	1:49.80	34,440
1987	**Bailrullah**, 5, 111	N. Santagata	Princely Proof, 4, 116	Krotz, 4, 118	10	1:44.00	28,590
	Cadabra Abra, 4, 118	W. H. McCauley	Treasure Map, 5, 115	Spruce Fir, 4, 121	6	1:43.80	28,110
1986	**Mazatleca (Mex)**, 6, 117	C. Perret	Cope of Flowers, 4, 114	Darbrielle, 4, 113	8	1:43.20	27,960
	Bharal, 5, 114	J. Velasquez	Thirteen Keys, 4, 114	Dawn's Curtsey, 4, 118	8	1:43.80	28,200
1985	**Agacerie**, 4, 118	A. T. Cordero Jr.	Meddlin Maggie, 4, 115	Natural Grace, 4, 114	8	1:44.20	34,830
1984	**Jubilous**, 4, 118	G. McCarron	Maidenhead, 5, 113	High Schemes, 4, 118	13	1:43.40	36,060
1983	**Doodle**, 4, 118	J. J. Miranda	Olamic, 4, 110	Bright Choice, 4, 112	12	1:44.00	28,410
1982	**Kuja Happa**, 4, 114	D. R. Wright	Qui Silent, 4, 113	Suave Princess, 4, 113	10	1:44.80	27,465
1981	**Wayward Lassie**, 4, 112	D. Montoya	Earlham, 5, 114	Paris Press, 4, 114	7	1:44.60	16,957
	Endicotta, 5, 116	D. Brumfield	Dance Troupe, 4, 115	Farewell Letter, 4, 113	5	1:44.80	16,717
1980	**Riddle's Reply**, 4, 113	E. Cardone	Sharp Zone, 4, 111	Newmarket Lady, 4, 112	8	1:44.20	20,078
	Nasty Jay, 5, 111	R. E. McKnight	T. V. Highlights, 6, 119	O'Connell Street, 4, 113	9	1:44.00	20,288
1979	**The Very One**, 4, 116	C. Cooke	Frosty Skater, 4, 120	Municipal Bond, 4, 113	8	1:46.20	25,236
1978	**Huggle Duggle**, 4, 113	B. Gonzalez	All Biz, 6, 118	Navajo Princess, 4, 114	9	1:42.60	22,116
1977	**Jolly Song**, 5, 112	J. Nied Jr.	T. V. Genie, 4, 112	All Biz, 5, 117	9	1:47.20	18,590
1976	**‡Collegiate**, 4, 113	J. W. Edwards	Copano, 4, 119	Double Ack, 3, 114	10	1:43.60	14,950
	Stage Luck, 4, 118	J. W. Edwards	Hinterland, 6, 114	*Deesse Du Val, 5, 121	9	1:43.80	14,788
1975	**Hinterland**, 5, 114	C. Perret	Ringmistress, 5, 114	Kudara, 4, 119	8	1:43.60	18,135
1974	**Bird Boots**, 5, 119	B. Thornburg	Belle Marie, 4, 117	Shaya, 4, 108	13	1:46.80	19,207
1973	**‡Telly**, 5, 110	V. A. Bracciale Jr.	Lightning Lucy, 3, 113	Wire Chief, 5, 111	8	1:43.60	14,763
	Cathy Baby, 4, 116	M. A. Rivera	Aglimmer, 4, 116	Bold Place, 4, 117	7	1:42.60	14,633

Named for Eatontown, New Jersey, located in Monmouth County. Eatontown S. 1991-'95, 1997-2000. 1$^1/_8$ miles 1988-'90, 2001. Dirt 1974, 1977. Two divisions 1972, 1973, 1976, 1980-'81, 1986-'87. Dead heat for third 1998. ‡Lightning Lucy finished first, DQ to second, 1973 (1st Div.). ‡Copano finished first, DQ to second, 1976 (1st Div.).

Eddie Read Handicap

Grade 1 in 2006. Del Mar, three-year-olds and up, 1$^1/_8$ miles, turf. Held July 24, 2005, with a gross value of $400,000. First held in 1974. First graded in 1980. Stakes record 1:45.87 (2003 Special Ring).

Year	Winner	Jockey	Second	Third	Strs	Time	1st Purse
2005	**Sweet Return (GB)**, 5, 120	A. O. Solis	Fourty Niners Son, 4, 117	Singletary, 5, 120	6	1:46.53	$240,000
2004	**Special Ring**, 7, 118	V. Espinoza	Bayamo (Ire), 5, 119	Sweet Return (GB), 4, 119	10	1:45.90	240,000
2003	**Special Ring**, 6, 117	D. R. Flores	Decarchy, 6, 117	Irish Warrior, 5, 114	6	**1:45.87**	240,000
2002	**Sarafan**, 5, 117	C. S. Nakatani	Beat Hollow (GB), 5, 122	Redattore (Brz), 7, 118	6	1:46.77	240,000
2001	**Redattore (Brz)**, 6, 115	A. O. Solis	Native Desert, 8, 116	Super Quercus (Fr), 5, 115	6	1:47.16	240,000
2000	**Ladies Din**, 5, 120	K. Desormeaux	Chester House, 5, 114	Gold Nugget, 5, 115	8	1:48.64	240,000
1999	**Joe Who (Brz)**, 6, 116	C. W. Antley	Ladies Din, 4, 119	Bouccaneer (Fr), 4, 115	10	1:48.75	240,000
1998	**Subordination**, 4, 117	D. R. Flores	Bonapartiste (Fr), 4, 115	Hawksley Hill (Ire), 5, 120	5	1:47.40	180,000
1997	**Expelled**, 5, 113	J. A. Garcia	El Angelo, 5, 119	Marlin, 4, 122	7	1:48.60	180,000
1996	**Fastness (Ire)**, 6, 124	C. S. Nakatani	Smooth Runner, 5, 114	Gold and Steel (Fr), 4, 118	6	1:47.05	193,000
1995	**Fastness (Ire)**, 5, 115	G. L. Stevens	Romarin (Brz), 5, 119	Northern Spur (Ire), 4, 118	8	1:48.42	182,600
1994	**Approach the Bench (Ire)**, 6, 113	C. S. Nakatani	Fastness (Ire), 4, 114	Johann Quatz (Fr), 5, 116	7	1:48.83	187,250
1993	**Kotashaan (Fr)**, 5, 122	K. Desormeaux	Leger Cat (Arg), 7, 116	Rainbow Corner (GB), 4, 114	6	1:48.45	183,750
1992	**Marquetry**, 5, 118	D. R. Flores	Luthier Enchanteur, 5, 116	Leger Cat (Arg), 6, 115	7	1:47.20	187,250
1991	**Tight Spot**, 4, 125	L. A. Pincay Jr.	Val des Bois (Fr), 5, 115	Madjaristan, 5, 116	7	1:47.32	188,500
1990	**Fly Till Dawn**, 4, 112	R. Q. Meza	Classic Fame, 4, 119	Golden Pheasant, 4, 122	8	1:48.20	157,750
1989	**Saratoga Passage**, 4, 116	E. Delahoussaye	Skip Out Front, 7, 116	Pasakos, 4, 116	8	1:49.00	162,750
1988	**Deputy Governor**, 4, 120	E. Delahoussaye	Santella Mac (Ire), 5, 114	Simply Majestic, 4, 115	12	1:48.80	176,500
1987	**Sharrood**, 4, 120	L. A. Pincay Jr.	Santella Mac (Ire), 4, 115	Skip Out Front, 5, 115	9	1:48.00	133,200
1986	**Al Mamoon**, 5, 121	P. A. Valenzuela	Zoffany, 6, 123	Truce Maker, 8, 115	7	1:46.60	113,400

1985	**Tsunami Slew**, 4, 119	G. L. Stevens	Al Mamoon, 4, 118	Both Ends Burning, 5, 123	7	1:46.80	$112,300
1984	**Ten Below**, 5, 117	L. A. Pincay Jr.	Silveyville, 6, 117	Desert Wine, 4, 124	6	1:48.20	96,200
1983	**Prince Spellbound**, 4, 121	C. Lamance	Bel Bolide, 5, 117	Ask Me, 4, 115	11	1:48.80	108,000
1982	**Wickerr**, 7, 119	E. Delahoussaye	Spence Bay (Ire), 7, 122	Perrault (GB), 5, 129	7	1:48.40	95,300
1981	**Wickerr**, 6, 115	C. J. McCarron	Super Moment, 4, 117	Mike Fogarty (Ire), 6, 114	7	1:49.80	80,750
1980	**Go West Young Man**, 5, 120	E. Delahoussaye	The Bart, 4, 118	Bold Tropic (SAf), 5, 124	6	1:47.60	64,250
1979	**Good Lord (NZ)**, 8, 115	W. Shoemaker	Shagbark, 4, 114	True Statement, 5, 115	11	1:49.20	42,450
1978	**Effervescing**, 5, 124	L. A. Pincay Jr.	Text, 4, 123	Bywayofchicago, 4, 117	9	1:48.60	33,050
1977	**No Turning**, 4, 115	F. Toro	Today 'n Tomorrow, 4, 119	†*Star Ball, 5, 111	9	1:48.80	32,400
1976	**Branford Court**, 6, 116	R. Campas	Diode, 4, 114	Austin Mittler, 4, 115	8	1:48.40	26,150
1975	**Blue Times**, 4, 115	J. Lambert	Portentous, 5, 112	Confederate Yankee, 4, 115	11	1:49.20	28,200
1974	**My Old Friend**, 5, 115	A. L. Diaz	Montmartre, 4, 116	War Heim, 7, 121	9	1:49.20	22,100

Named in honor of longtime Del Mar publicity director Eddie Read. Grade 3 1980-'81. Grade 2 1982-'87. Course record 2003. †Denotes female.

El Camino Real Derby

Grade 3 in 2006. Bay Meadows Race Course, three-year-olds, $1\frac{1}{16}$ miles, dirt. Held January 29, 2006, with a gross value of $250,000. First held in 1982. First graded in 1986. Stakes record 1:39.40 (1988 Ruhlmann).

Year	Winner	Jockey	Second	Third	Strs	Time	1st Purse
2006	**Cause to Believe**, 3, 117	R. A. Baze	Objective, 3, 115	Bold Chieftain, 3, 115	6	1:41.81	$137,500
2005	**Uncle Denny**, 3, 117	R. A. Baze	Wannawinemall, 3, 115	Buzzards Bay, 3, 117	10	1:42.22	110,000
2004	**Kilgowan**, 3, 116	C. J. Rollins	dh-Capitano, 3, 116 dh-Seattle Borders, 3, 117		10	1:43.87	110,000
2003	**Ocean Terrace**, 3, 115	M. E. Smith	Ministers Wild Cat, 3, 117	Ten Most Wanted, 3, 115	10	1:42.26	110,000
2002	**Yougottawanna**, 3, 120	J. P. Lumpkins	Danthebluegrassman, 3, 117	Lusty Latin, 3, 115	10	1:43.48	110,000
2001	**Hoovergetthekeys**, 3, 120	R. J. Warren Jr.	Startac, 3, 120	Mo Mon, 3, 115	8	1:40.85	110,000
2000	**Remember Sheikh**, 3, 117	F. T. Alvarado	True Confidence, 3, 116	Country Coast, 3, 115	14	1:43.47	110,000
1999	**Cliquot**, 3, 115	D. R. Flores	Charismatic, 3, 115	No Cal Bread, 3, 117	7	1:43.29	110,000
1998	**Event of the Year**, 3, 115	R. A. Baze	Post a Note, 3, 117	Clover Hunter, 3, 120	5	1:40.27	110,000
1997	**Pacificbounty**, 3, 120	K. Desormeaux	Wild Wonder, 3, 115	Carmen's Baby, 3, 117	6	1:41.85	110,000
1996	**Cavonnier**, 3, 115	M. A. Pedroza	Sergeant Stroh, 3, 113	E C's Dream, 3, 116	9	1:43.41	110,000
1995	**Jumron (GB)**, 3, 113	G. F. Almeida	Snow Kidd'n, 3, 113	American Day, 3, 113	8	1:43.73	110,000
1994	**Tabasco Cat**, 3, 113	P. Day	Flying Sensation, 3, 115	Robannier, 3, 115	7	1:42.78	110,000
1993	**El Atroz**, 3, 117	R. Q. Meza	Offshore Pirate, 3, 117	Lykatill Hil, 3, 119	9	1:43.77	110,000
1992	**Casual Lies**, 3, 117	A. Patterson	Seahawk Gold, 3, 115	Silver Ray, 3, 122	11	1:42.00	165,000
1991	**Sea Cadet**, 3, 117	T. M. Chapman	General Meeting, 3, 118	Mizter Interco, 3, 122	9	1:40.70	165,000
1990	**Silver Ending**, 3, 115	G. L. Stevens	Individualist, 3, 115	Single Dawn, 3, 122	8	1:43.00	165,000
1989	**Double Quick**, 3, 115	A. O. Solis	Rob an Plunder, 3, 119	Hawkster, 3, 122	6	1:43.60	165,000
1988	**Ruhlmann**, 3, 117	P. Day	Havanaffair, 3, 117	Chinese Gold, 3, 119	9	**1:39.40**	137,500
1987	**Masterful Advocate**, 3, 120	L. A. Pincay Jr.	Fast Delivery, 3, 120	Hot and Smoggy, 3, 120	11	1:42.40	137,500
1986	**Snow Chief**, 3, 120	A. O. Solis	Badger Land, 3, 120	Darby Fair, 3, 120	6	1:42.60	137,500
1985	**Tank's Prospect**, 3, 120	J. Velasquez	Right Con, 3, 120	‡Dan's Diablo, 3, 120	9	1:41.00	151,000
1984	**French Legionaire**, 3, 120	R. A. Baze	Gate Dancer, 3, 120	Heavenly Plain (Ire), 3, 120	11	1:42.40	126,200
1983	**Knightly Rapport**, 3, 120	F. Toro	Croeso, 3, 120	Twilight Career, 3, 120	9	1:44.80	96,700
1982	**Cassaleria**, 3, 120	D. G. McHargue	Crystal Star, 3, 120	Tropic Ruler, 3, 120	9	1:42.80	76,100

Named for the El Camino Real, "the Royal Road" through the California frontier. Held at Golden Gate Fields 2001-'04. Dead heat for second 2004. ‡Skywalker finished third, DQ to fourth, 1985.

El Conejo Handicap

Grade 3 in 2006. Santa Anita Park, four-year-olds and up, $5\frac{1}{2}$ furlongs, dirt. Held January 2, 2006, with a gross value of $112,100. First held in 1975. First graded in 2000. Stakes record 1:01.74 (1999 Kona Gold).

Year	Winner	Jockey	Second	Third	Strs	Time	1st Purse
2006	**With Distinction**, 5, 116	J. Santiago	Jungle Prince, 5, 116	Jet West, 5, 117	10	1:02.44	$67,260
2005	**Areyoutalkintome**, 4, 114	T. Baze	Hombre Rapido, 8, 116	Woke Up Dreamin, 5, 115	9	1:02.52	66,300
2004	**Boston Common**, 5, 117	G. L. Stevens	Summer Service, 4, 112	King Robyn, 4, 119	6	1:02.35	64,560
2003	**Kona Gold**, 9, 123	A. O. Solis	Radiata, 6, 115	No Armistice, 6, 116	7	1:02.63	65,280
2002	**Snow Ridge**, 4, 114	M. E. Smith	Explicit, 5, 117	Rio Oro, 7, 117	8	1:03.05	65,700
2000	**Freespool**, 4, 115	C. J. McCarron	Men's Exclusive, 7, 117	Lexicon, 5, 118	7	1:02.50	65,220
	Freespool, 4, 114	C. J. McCarron	Mellow Fellow, 5, 115	Old Topper, 5, 116	6	1:03.33	64,200
1999	**Kona Gold**, 5, 119	A. O. Solis	Big Jag, 6, 117	Mr. Doubledown, 5, 118	6	**1:01.74**	64,380
1998	**The Exeter Man**, 6, 114	G. K. Gomez	Tower Full, 6, 117	Red, 4, 114	5	1:02.23	64,020
1997	**High Stakes Player**, 5, 115	C. S. Nakatani	Kern Ridge, 6, 111	Subtle Trouble, 6, 114	5	1:02.89	63,850
1996	**Lit de Justice**, 6, 119	C. S. Nakatani	A. J. Jett, 4, 112	Fu Man Slew, 5, 116	6	1:01.85	64,250
1995	**Phone Roberto**, 6, 114	C. J. McCarron	‡Lost Pan, 5, 112	Rotsaluck, 4, 117	8	1:02.34	65,000
1994	**Gundaghia**, 7, 116	E. Delahoussaye	Sir Hutch, 4, 114	Davy Be Good, 6, 117	8	1:02.01	64,800
1993	**Fabulous Champ**, 4, 113	C. J. McCarron	Arrowtown, 5, 115	Slerp, 4, 117	7	1:02.66	63,800
1992	**Gray Slewpy**, 4, 114	K. Desormeaux	Frost Free, 7, 119	Cardmania, 6, 116	5	1:02.01	61,275
1991	**Black Jack Road**, 7, 115	G. L. Stevens	Laurens Quest, 6, 110	Lee's Tanthem, 4, 117	6	1:05.30	61,975
1990	**Frost Free**, 5, 115	C. J. McCarron	Sunny Blossom, 5, 119	Prospectors Gamble, 5, 114	5	1:03.00	45,900
1989	**Sunny Blossom**, 4, 114	F. H. Valenzuela	Sensational Star, 5, 115	Prospectors Gamble, 4, 116	7	1:04.60	47,100
1988	**Sylvan Express (Ire)**, 5, 119	E. Delahoussaye	Carload, 6, 117	High Brite, 4, 120	8	1:03.80	48,100
1986	**†Take My Picture**, 4, 119	G. L. Stevens	Rosie's K. T., 5, 119	Five North, 5, 114	5	1:03.00	37,300
1985	**Debonaire Junior**, 4, 126	C. J. McCarron	Much Fine Gold, 4, 112	Fifty Six Ina Row, 4, 119	7	1:02.60	38,950

1984	**Premiership**, 4, 115	R. Q. Meza	Haughty But Nice, 6, 116	Chip o' Lark, 5, 117	7	1:03.40	$30,425
	Night Mover, 4, 117	E. Delahoussaye	Dave's Friend, 9, 120	†Bara Lass, 5, 117	7	1:03.20	30,525
1983	**Pompeii Court**, 6, 123	L. A. Pincay Jr.	General Jimmy, 4, 115	Kangroo Court, 6, 120	8	1:02.80	39,350
1982	**To B. Or Not**, 6, 122	C. J. McCarron	Belfort (Fr), 5, 116	Terresto's Singer, 5, 115	8	1:02.20	39,350
1981	**To B. Or Not**, 5, 122	P. A. Valenzuela	Summer Time Guy, 5, 119	Cool Frenchy, 6, 115	11	1:02.40	35,500
1975	**Move Abroad**, 4, 113	S. Hawley	Reputation, 5, 115	Mercy Dee, 4, 121	5	1:49.20	11,375

Named for Rancho El Conejo, located in Ventura, California; conejo means rabbit. Not graded 2000 (January). Not held 1976-'80, 1987, 2001. Four-year-olds and up 1992-2000. Held in January and December 2000. Two divisions 1984. ‡Lit de Justice finished second, DQ to sixth, 1995. Track record 1992, 1996, 1999. †Denotes female.

El Encino Stakes

Grade 2 in 2006. Santa Anita Park, four-year-olds, fillies, 1 1/16 miles, dirt. Held January 15, 2006, with a gross value of $150,000. First held in 1954. First graded in 1980. Stakes record 1:41.20 (1980 It's in the Air; 1982 Edge; 1983 Beautiful Glass; 1990 Akinemod).

Year	Winner	Jockey	Second	Third	Strs	Time	1st Purse
2006	**Proposed**, 4, 118	P. A. Valenzuela	Play Ballado, 4, 117	Somethinaboutlaura, 4, 117	7	1:44.32	$90,000
2005	**Girl Warrior**, 4, 115	V. Espinoza	A. P. Adventure, 4, 119	Tarlow, 4, 116	7	1:42.76	90,000
2004	**Victory Encounter**, 4, 117	M. E. Smith	Personal Legend, 4, 115	Cat Fighter, 4, 115	7	1:42.52	90,000
2003	**Got Koko**, 4, 119	A. O. Solis	Bella Bellucci, 4, 117	Bare Necessities, 4, 119	8	1:42.25	90,000
2002	**Affluent**, 4, 119	E. Delahoussaye	Royally Chosen, 4, 117	Sea Reel, 4, 115	6	1:42.60	90,000
2001	**Chilukki**, 4, 119	G. L. Stevens	Spain, 4, 122	Queenie Belle, 4, 119	4	1:42.55	90,000
2000	**Olympic Charmer**, 4, 119	C. J. McCarron	Her She Kisses, 4, 115	Smooth Player, 4, 117	7	1:42.71	97,470
1999	**Manistique**, 4, 119	G. L. Stevens	Gourmet Girl, 4, 117	Magical Allure, 4, 119	3	1:43.10	90,000
1998	**‡Fleet Lady**, 4, 117	G. K. Gomez	Minister's Melody, 4, 117	I Ain't Bluffing, 4, 119	6	1:43.04	96,840
1997	**Belle's Flag**, 4, 119	C. S. Nakatani	Housa Dancer (Fr), 4, 115	Listening, 4, 119	9	1:41.61	82,650
1996	**Jewel Princess**, 4, 117	A. O. Solis	Sleep Easy, 4, 119	Urbane, 4, 119	4	1:41.94	78,800
1995	**Klassy Kim**, 4, 117	K. Desormeaux	Twice the Vice, 4, 119	Crissy Aya, 4, 115	5	1:42.43	61,400
1994	**Supah Gem**, 4, 117	C. S. Nakatani	Sensational Eyes, 4, 117	Stalcreek, 4, 119	8	1:41.33	64,500
1993	**Pacific Squall**, 4, 119	C. J. McCarron	Avian Assembly, 4, 117	Magical Maiden, 4, 119	7	1:45.67	63,900
1992	**Exchange**, 4, 117	L. A. Pincay Jr.	Grand Girlfriend, 4, 115	Damewood, 4, 115	10	1:43.32	67,000
1991	**A Wild Ride**, 4, 122	C. J. McCarron	Highland Tide, 4, 114	Somethingmerry, 4, 117	7	1:42.50	63,500
1990	**Akinemod**, 4, 119	G. L. Stevens	Luthier's Launch, 4, 117	Kelly, 4, 116	6	**1:41.20**	62,900
1989	**Goodbye Halo**, 4, 124	P. Day	T. V. of Crystal, 4, 117	Savannah's Honor, 4, 114	4	1:41.80	60,200
1988	**By Land by Sea**, 4, 115	F. Toro	Very Subtle, 4, 122	Annoconnor, 4, 114	8	1:41.60	64,300
1987	**Seldom Seen Sue**, 4, 114	W. Shoemaker	Miraculous, 4, 117	Top Corsage, 4, 122	6	1:43.00	61,850
1986	**Lady's Secret**, 4, 124	C. J. McCarron	Shywing, 4, 119	Sharp Ascent, 4, 119	10	1:41.80	65,850
1985	**Mitterand**, 4, 119	E. Delahoussaye	Percipient, 4, 117	Allusion, 4, 117	6	1:42.00	61,600
1984	**Lovlier Linda**, 4, 117	W. Shoemaker	Weekend Surprise, 4, 117	Angel Savage (Mex), 4, 114	8	1:42.00	51,250
1983	**Beautiful Glass**, 4, 119	C. J. McCarron	Header Card, 4, 119	Skillful Joy, 4, 122	11	**1:41.20**	50,550
1982	**Edge**, 4, 114	C. B. Asmussen	Safe Play, 4, 119	Northern Fable, 4, 117	12	**1:41.20**	68,000
1981	**Princess Karenda**, 4, 122	E. Delahoussaye	Swift Bird, 4, 117	Lisawan, 4, 114	10	1:42.00	49,650
1980	**It's in the Air**, 4, 124	L. A. Pincay Jr.	Prize Spot, 4, 121	‡Glorious Song, 4, 116	8	**1:41.20**	38,750
1979	**B. Thoughtful**, 4, 121	D. Pierce	Queen Yasna, 4, 116	Petron's Love, 4, 114	7	1:41.60	38,250
1978	**Taisez Vous**, 4, 121	D. Pierce	Little Happiness, 4, 116	Table the Rumor, 4, 121	4	1:41.80	30,200
1977	***Woodsome**, 4, 115	M. S. Sellers	*Lucie Manet, 4, 115	Granja Sueno, 4, 115	11	1:42.20	27,450
1976	**Fascinating Girl**, 4, 115	S. Hawley	Bold Baby, 4, 115	Just a Kick, 4, 121	6	1:42.40	18,850
1975	**Triggairo**, 6, 119	D. Pierce	*Benson, 6, 116	Lansquinet, 4, 119	7	1:49.40	19,700
1974	**Wild World**, 5, 118	W. Shoemaker	Class A, 6, 115	Proper Escort, 5, 112	10	1:49.80	18,150
1973	**Class A**, 5, 122	D. Tierney	Sitka D., 6, 119	Cabin, 5, 119	10	1:44.60	18,950

Named for Rancho El Encino, one of the original Spanish ranchos located in western Los Angeles County, California. Grade 3 1980-'89. El Encino H. 1954-'57, 1974-'75. El Encino Claiming S. 1968-'73. Not held 1958-'67, 1970. 1 1/4 miles 1955-'57. 1 1/8 miles 1974-'75. Turf 1955-'57. Four-year-olds and up 1954-'75. Both sexes 1954-'75. ‡Terlingua finished third, DQ to fourth, 1980. ‡I Ain't Bluffing finished first, DQ to third, 1998. Starters for a claiming price of $50,000 or less 1974.

Elkhorn Stakes

Grade 3 in 2006. Keeneland Race Course, four-year-olds and up, 1 1/2 miles, turf. Held April 28, 2006, with a gross value of $200,000. First held in 1986. First graded in 1988. Stakes record 2:27.84 (1999 African Dancer).

Year	Winner	Jockey	Second	Third	Strs	Time	1st Purse
2006	**Pellegrino (Brz)**, 7, 118	S. Bridgmohan	Go Deputy, 6, 118	Silverfoot, 6, 118	11	2:29.84	$124,000
2005	**Macaw (Ire)**, 6, 118	J. Castellano	European (Ire), 5, 118	Rochester, 9, 118	12	2:32.62	124,000
2004	**Epicentre**, 5, 116	J. D. Bailey	Rochester, 8, 116	Art Variety (Brz), 6, 116	10	2:31.96	93,000
2003	**Kim Loves Bucky**, 6, 117	K. Desormeaux	Man From Wicklow, 6, 123	Williams News, 8, 116	10	2:29.39	93,000
2002	**Kim Loves Bucky**, 5, 116	J. F. Chavez	Rochester, 6, 116	Cetewayo, 8, 118	10	2:32.49	93,000
2001	**Williams News**, 6, 116	R. Albarado	Gritty Sandie, 5, 116	Craigsteel (GB), 6, 116	9	2:29.13	70,308
2000	**Drama Critic**, 4, 116	J. D. Bailey	Craigsteel (GB), 5, 116	Dixie's Crown, 4, 116	10	2:28.03	69,750
1999	**African Dancer**, 7, 114	J. D. Bailey	Magest, 4, 114	Chorwon, 6, 113	8	**2:27.84**	68,138
1998	**African Dancer**, 6, 114	J. D. Bailey	Chief Bearhart, 5, 122	Chorwon, 5, 114	5	2:31.71	66,712
1997	**Chief Bearhart**, 4, 114	J. A. Santos	Snake Eyes, 7, 113	Lassigny, 6, 122	8	2:28.43	68,324
1996	**Vladivostok**, 6, 112	P. Day	Penn Fifty Three, 4, 114	Party Season (GB), 5, 119	7	2:30.83	68,262
1995	**Marvin's Faith (Ire)**, 4, 123	C. Perret	Hasten To Add, 5, 120	Opera Score, 4, 120	10	1:47.10	70,680
1994	**Lure**, 5, 123	M. E. Smith	Buckhar, 6, 120	Pride of Summer, 6, 120	5	1:53.76	66,526

1993	**Coaxing Matt**, 4, 118	P. Day	Cleone, 4, 113	Maxigroom, 5, 118	9 1:47.64	$68,603
1992	**Fourstars Allstar**, 4, 113	J. D. Bailey	Slew the Slewor, 5, 120	Rainbows for Life, 4, 120	10 1:47.66	72,995
1991	**Itsallgreektome**, 4, 123	R. A. Baze	Pirate Army, 5, 113	Spark O'Dan, 6, 113	7 1:51.28	71,143
1990	**Ten Keys**, 6, 123	R. P. Romero	Yankee Affair, 8, 123	Maceo, 6, 118	8 1:51.80	71,468
1989	**Exclusive Partner**, 7, 120	F. Toro	Yankee Affair, 7, 120	Pappas Swing, 4, 120	7 1:50.40	54,958
1988	**Yankee Affair**, 6, 123	P. Day	Storm On the Loose, 5, 118	Blazing Bart, 4, 123	10 1:49.60	56,485
1987	**Manila**, 4, 113	J. Vasquez	Lieutenant's Lark, 5, 112	Royal Treasurer, 4, 112	7 1:48.40	35,019
1986	**Lieutenant's Lark**, 4, 113	F. Lovato Jr.	Leprechauns Wish, 4, 115	Majestic Jabot, 5, 115	10 1:54.60	36,351

Named for a large local creek, the Elkhorn, long used as a water source by Bluegrass-area farms. Sponsored by Fifth Third Bancorp of Cincinnati 2005-'06. Grade 2 1990-'95. $1^1/_8$ miles 1986-'95. Course record 1995, 1999.

Endine Handicap

Grade 3 in 2006. Delaware Park, three-year-olds and up, fillies and mares, 6 furlongs, dirt. Held September 10, 2005, with a gross value of $200,900. First held in 1971. First graded in 2001. Stakes record 1:08.35 (2003 House Party).

Year	Winner	Jockey	Second	Third	Strs	Time	1st Purse
2005	**Umpateedle**, 6, 116	A. T. Gryder	Sensibly Chic, 5, 117	Ebony Breeze, 5, 118	8	1:10.18	$120,000
2004	**Ebony Breeze**, 4, 119	H. Castillo Jr.	Umpateedle, 5, 117	Bronze Abe, 5, 119	6	1:09.73	120,000
2003	**House Party**, 3, 117	J. A. Santos	Vision in Flight, 4, 114	Mooji Moo, 4, 115	8	**1:08.35**	120,000
2002	**Xtra Heat**, 4, 121	H. Vega	Outstanding Info, 4, 118	Urban Dancer, 4, 118	5	1:10.91	90,000
2001	**Xtra Heat**, 3, 118	R. Wilson	Ivy's Jewel, 4, 118	Big Bambu, 4, 121	5	1:09.64	90,000
2000	**Superduper Miss**, 4, 114	T. G. Turner	Debby d'Or, 5, 119	Cassidy, 5, 119	7	1:10.22	60,000
1999	**Hurricane Bertie**, 4, 117	P. Day	Little Sister, 5, 119	Bourbon Belle, 4, 119	4	1:08.75	60,000
1998	**Soverign Lady**, 4, 115	M. E. Smith	Weather Vane, 4, 122	Little Sister, 4, 117	8	1:09.43	45,000
1997	**Dancin Renee**, 5, 122	J. A. Velez Jr.	Two Punch Lil, 5, 122	Ana Belen (Chi), 4, 113	6	1:10.04	30,000
1996	**Hay Hanne**, 4, 114	J. A. Velez Jr.	Know B's, 4, 116	Ayrial Delight, 4, 122	8	1:10.30	22,770
1982	**Wading Power**, 4, 107	H. Pilar	Bravo Native, 4, 108	Lady Dean, 4, 123	9	1:10.80	14,723
1981	**Veiled Look**, 5, 120	W. J. Passmore	Rejuvavate, 5, 113	Tequila Sheila, 3, 109	7	1:08.80	17,875
1980	**Candy Eclair**, 4, 126	J. D. Bailey	‡Wondrous Me, 4, 108	Grecian Victory, 4, 112	9	1:09.80	29,803
1979	**Quatre Saisons**, 4, 115	V. A. Bracciale Jr.	Shanachie, 3, 112	Order in Court, 6, 115	6	1:12.00	21,580
1978	**Dainty Dotsie**, 4, 127	B. Phelps	Spot Two, 4, 123	Debby's Turn, 4, 113	5	1:09.60	21,450
1977	**My Juliet**, 5, 127	A. S. Black	Debby's Turn, 3, 115	Catabias, 5, 113	4	1:09.60	17,973
1976	**Donetta**, 5, 118	J. W. Moseley	Susie's Last, 4, 112	Crackerfax, 5, 115	10	1:12.00	17,145
1975	**Honky Star**, 4, 119	J. E. Tejeira	Laraka, 5, 117	Sailingon, 4, 114	7	1:11.00	18,655
1974	**Miss Rebound**, 6, 123	B. Baeza	Flo's Pleasure, 4, 116	Gallant Davelle, 4, 116	8	1:10.00	19,045
1973	**Light Hearted**, 4, 118	E. Nelson	Barely Even, 4, 125	Levee Night, 5, 113	7	1:10.00	18,525

Named for Christiana Stable's 1958, '59 Delaware H. winner Endine (1954 f. by *Rico Monte). Endine H. 1971-'82. Not held 1983-'95. ‡She Can't Miss finished second, DQ to fourth, 1980. Equaled track record 2003.

Essex Handicap

Grade 3 in 2006. Oaklawn Park, four-year-olds and up, $1^1/_{16}$ miles, dirt. Held February 11, 2006, with a gross value of $100,000. First held in 1976. First graded in 1985. Stakes record 1:41 (1976 Navajo; 1987 Sun Master).

Year	Winner	Jockey	Second	Third	Strs	Time	1st Purse
2006	**Rockport Harbor**, 4, 115	S. Elliott	Thunder Mission, 4, 116	Silver Axe, 9, 116	8	1:47.68	$60,000
2005	**Absent Friend**, 5, 112	R. Chapa	Mauk Four, 5, 112	Separato, 4, 113	10	1:43.66	60,000
2004	**Private Emblem**, 5, 113	T. T. Doocy	Pie N Burger, 6, 118	Crafty Shaw, 6, 118	8	1:43.66	60,000
2003	**Colorful Tour**, 4, 116	L. S. Quinonez	Ask the Lord, 6, 118	Premeditation, 4, 117	10	1:46.62	60,000
2002	**Crafty Shaw**, 4, 116	J. Lopez	Kiss of Lion (Arg), 7, 113	Remington Rock, 8, 116	6	1:43.14	45,000
2001	**Mr Ross**, 6, 117	D. R. Pettinger	Remington Rock, 7, 114	Maysville Slew, 5, 118	7	1:43.59	45,000
2000	**Maysville Slew**, 4, 115	L. S. Quinonez	Sand Ridge, 5, 112	Mr Ross, 5, 116	7	1:44.12	45,000
1999	**Brush With Pride**, 7, 116	T. T. Doocy	Littlebitlively, 5, 115	Treat Me Doc, 5, 114	7	1:43.26	45,000
1998	**Relic Reward**, 4, 113	C. H. Borel	Phantom On Tour, 4, 119	Brush With Pride, 6, 116	7	1:43.92	45,000
1997	**No Spend No Glow**, 5, 113	R. N. Lester	Illesam, 5, 113	Auggie My Dad, 6, 111	8	1:45.94	45,000
1996	**Classic Fit**, 6, 114	C. Gonzalez	Judge T C, 5, 122	Juliannus, 7, 113	4	1:42.98	47,700
1995	**Silver Goblin**, 4, 122	D. W. Cordova	Prince of the Mt., 4, 113	Golden Gear, 4, 113	7	1:42.10	33,150
1994	**Greatsilverfleet**, 4, 116	G. K. Gomez	Prize Fight, 5, 113	All Gone, 4, 111	5	1:42.08	32,250
1993	**Delafield**, 4, 113	P. Day	Famed Devil, 5, 117	Yukon Robbery, 4, 116	8	1:42.11	33,900
1992	**Allijeba**, 6, 118	P. Day	On the Edge, 5, 113	Bedeviled, 5, 116	10	1:43.95	34,500
1991	**Greydar**, 4, 117	P. Day	Silver Survivor, 5, 120	The Great Carl, 4, 112	8	1:42.08	34,770
1990	**Forli Light**, 4, 115	D. Guillory	Momsfurrari, 6, 115	Traskwood, 4, 115	9	1:42.80	36,930
1989	**Proper Reality**, 4, 120	J. D. Bailey	Contact Game, 5, 111	Lyphard's Ridge, 6, 112	6	1:44.00	34,530
1988	**Savings**, 5, 117	P. A. Johnson	Entitled To, 6, 117	Red Attack, 6, 115	8	1:42.60	43,680
1987	**Sun Master**, 6, 116	R. L. Frazier	Royal Troon, 5, 112	Lyphard's Ridge, 4, 111	9	**1:41.00**	36,750
1986	**Double Ready**, 6, 113	D. E. Whited	Red Attack, 4, 112	Khozaam, 4, 112	10	1:41.60	51,060
1985	**Star Choice**, 6, 121	J. McKnight	Plaza Star, 7, 115	Shamtastic, 5, 112	8	1:40.60	49,260
1984	**Le Cou Cou**, 4, 119	D. L. Howard	Hi Pi, 5, 120	Double Ready, 4, 114	8	1:41.80	36,480
1983	**Eminency**, 5, 121	W. Nemeti	Dance Pavilion, 4, 113	Majesty's Prince, 4, 125	12	1:42.40	38,670
1982	**Plaza Star**, 4, 113	R. P. Romero	Vodika Collins, 4, 118	Tally Ho the Fox, 7, 116	11	1:42.80	37,950
1981	**Prince Majestic**, 7, 118	G. Patterson	Blue Ensign, 4, 114	Uncool, 6, 117	9	1:42.40	34,650
1980	**J. Burns**, 5, 113	J. McKnight	Convenient, 4, 114	Daring Damascus, 4, 115	10	1:42.80	35,220
1979	**Cisk**, 5, 117	G. Patterson	Forever Casting, 4, 114	Oui Henry, 5, 117	10	1:42.40	35,850
1978	**Mark's Place**, 6, 122	R. Ramirez	Yallah Native, 5, 114	Dragset, 7, 118	11	1:41.60	36,570

1977	**Go to the Bank**, 5, 111	G. Patterson	Romeo, 4, 119	Limited Addition, 4, 114	13	1:42.40	$37,260
1976	**Navajo**, 6, 123	J. Nichols	My Friend Gus, 4, 121	Bold Trap, 4, 113	9	**1:41.00**	34,950

Named for old Essex Park in Hot Springs, Arkansas. 1 mile 70 yards 1976-'86.

Excelsior Breeders' Cup Handicap

Grade 3 in 2006. Aqueduct, three-year-olds and up, 1⅛ miles, dirt. Held April 1, 2006, with a gross value of $151,900. First held in 1903. First graded in 1973. Stakes record 1:47.69 (1997 Ormsby).

Year	Winner	Jockey	Second	Third	Strs	Time	1st Purse
2006	**West Virginia**, 5, 115	N. Arroyo Jr.	Funny Cide, 6, 115	Colita, 6, 114	9	1:48.28	$67,140
2005	**Offlee Wild**, 5, 121	R. Bejarano	Rogue Agent, 6, 115	Cuba, 4, 113	5	1:50.41	120,000
2004	**Funny Cide**, 4, 120	J. A. Santos	Evening Attire, 6, 119	Host (Chi), 4, 114	5	1:49.57	120,000
2003	**Classic Endeavor**, 5, 113	C. C. Lopez	Balto Star, 5, 119	Tempest Fugit, 6, 114	5	1:48.10	90,000
2002	**John Little**, 4, 111	N. Arroyo Jr.	Windsor Castle, 4, 113	Ground Storm, 6, 118	6	1:49.25	120,000
2001	**Cat's At Home**, 4, 115	F. Leon	Top Official, 6, 113	Boston Party, 5, 115	8	1:48.92	120,000
2000	**Lager**, 6, 113	H. Castillo Jr.	Best of Luck, 4, 114	Chester House, 5, 117	9	1:49.76	120,000
1999	**Smart Coupons**, 6, 114	R. R. Douglas	Archers Bay, 4, 118	Pasay, 4, 112	9	1:49.71	120,000
1998	**Sir Bear**, 5, 117	E. M. Jurado	K. J.'s Appeal, 4, 117	Accelerator, 4, 111	8	1:49.24	120,000
1997	**Ormsby**, 5, 116	C. C. Lopez	Greatsilverfleet, 7, 112	Circle of Light, 4, 111	9	**1:47.69**	120,000
1996	**May I Inquire**, 7, 111	J. Bravo	Personal Merit, 5, 114	Ormsby, 4, 115	8	1:50.67	120,000
1995	**Iron Gavel**, 5, 111	J. R. Martinez Jr.	Electrojet, 6, 114	Danzig's Dance, 6, 115	7	1:49.28	90,000
1994	**Colonial Affair**, 4, 121	J. A. Santos	Contract Court, 4, 109	West by West, 5, 116	6	1:49.82	90,000
1993	**Devil His Due**, 4, 117	M. E. Smith	Exotic Slew, 6, 109	Bill Of Rights, 4, 112	10	2:03.05	72,120
1992	**Defensive Play**, 5, 117	D. R. Flores	Alyten, 4, 111	Will to Reign, 4, 109	5	2:01.95	102,780
1991	**Chief Honcho**, 4, 117	M. E. Smith	I'm Sky High, 5, 115	Apple Current, 4, 115	6	2:02.69	102,060
1990	**Lay Down**, 6, 112	C. W. Antley	Lac Ouimet, 7, 113	Doc's Leader, 4, 112	5	2:02.20	100,980
1989	**Forever Silver**, 4, 111	J. A. Krone	Its Acedemic, 5, 113	Jack of Clubs, 6, 113	5	2:02.60	99,720
1988	**Lac Ouimet**, 5, 116	J. D. Bailey	Personal Flag, 5, 117	Talinum, 4, 116	9	2:00.20	140,880
1987	**Lac Ouimet**, 4, 114	E. Maple	Alioth, 4, 113	Proud Debonair, 5, 115	9	2:02.00	106,380
1986	**Garthorn**, 6, 124	R. Q. Meza	Nordance, 4, 110	Broadway Tommy, 4, 107	5	2:02.40	101,340
1985	**Morning Bob**, 4, 112	J. Vasquez	Lord of the Manor, 4, 112	Last Turn, 5, 110	8	2:04.20	87,750
1984	**Canadian Factor**, 4, 117	J. Velasquez	Luv a Libra, 4, 117	Canadian Calm, 4, 108	8	2:03.00	102,150
1983	**Fast Gold**, 4, 114	J. Samyn	Turn Bold, 4, 107	Sing Sing, 5, 124	7	2:04.00	67,200
1982	**Globe**, 5, 112	M. Venezia	Accipiter's Hope, 4, 116	Bar Dexter, 5, 118	9	2:03.40	66,480
1981	**Irish Tower**, 4, 127	J. Fell	Ring of Light, 6, 113	†Relaxing, 5, 125	6	2:00.80	64,680
1980	**Ring of Light**, 5, 114	C. B. Asmussen	Silent Cal, 5, 122	Rivalero, 4, 118	10	2:01.40	67,560
1979	**Special Tiger**, 4, 113	G. Martens	Mister Brea (Arg), 5, 125	Coverack, 6, 112	6	2:03.80	63,600
1978	**Cox's Ridge**, 4, 129	E. Maple	Pumpkin Moonshine, 4, 108	Nearly On Time, 4, 113	7	1:50.60	49,005
1977	**Turn and Count**, 4, 123	S. Cauthen	Festive Mood, 8, 115	Gabe Benzur, 4, 112	6	1:51.00	48,150
1976	**Double Edge Sword**, 6, 116	A. T. Cordero Jr.	Northerly, 4, 115	Sharp Gary, 5, 119	9	1:48.20	51,120
1975	**Step Nicely**, 5, 126	A. T. Cordero Jr.	Monetary Principle, 5, 113	Jolly Johu, 4, 119	8	1:48.40	33,990
1974	***Everton II**, 5, 117	M. A. Castaneda	Prince Dantan, 4, 123	Three Or Less, 4, 108	7	1:49.00	33,840
1973	**Key to the Mint**, 4, 126	R. Turcotte	King's Bishop, 4, 115	North Sea, 4, 120	5	1:47.80	32,640

Named for the state motto of New York, "Excelsior," meaning "upward, ever upward." Grade 2 1973-'97. Excelsior H. 1903-'95. Held at Jamaica 1903-'10, 1915-'59. Not held 1909, 1911-'12, 1914, 1933, 1967. 1$^1/_{16}$ miles 1903-'59. 1 mile 1960. 1¼ miles 1979-'93. †Denotes female.

Fair Grounds Breeders' Cup Handicap

Grade 3 in 2006. Fair Grounds at Louisiana Downs, four-year-olds and up, 1$^1/_{16}$ miles, turf. Held January 21, 2006, with a gross value of $189,800. First held in 1988. First graded in 2006. Stakes record 1:43.16 (2006 Fort Prado).

Year	Winner	Jockey	Second	Third	Strs	Time	1st Purse
2006	**Fort Prado**, 5, 121	R. Albarado	Onthedeanslist, 7, 118	Waupaca, 6, 116	8	**1:43.16**	$101,880
2005	**G P Fleet**, 5, 117	J. R. Martinez Jr.	Honor in War, 6, 119	Rapid Proof, 5, 116	9	1:53.79	75,000
2004	**Mystery Giver**, 6, 120	R. Albarado	Skate Away, 5, 118	Great Bloom, 6, 116	9	1:51.77	75,000
2003	**Mystery Giver**, 5, 117	R. Albarado	Dynameaux, 5, 115	Freefourinternet, 5, 115	9	1:50.41	90,000
2002	**Mystery Giver**, 4, 117	E. M. Martin Jr.	Even the Score, 4, 113	Candid Glen, 5, 115	13	1:50.13	90,000
2001	**Candid Glen**, 4, 113	E. J. Perrodin	Sunspot, 4, 113	Solitary Dancer, 5, 114	12	1:54.03	98,610
2000	**Profit Option**, 5, 111	L. J. Meche	Good Night, 4, 114	Garbu, 6, 115	8	1:52.52	95,460
1999	**Aboriginal Apex**, 6, 115	L. J. Melancon	Chorwon, 6, 117	Dernier Croise (Fr), 4, 113	11	1:51.71	67,770
1998	**Joyeux Danseur**, 5, 118	R. Albarado	Chorwon, 5, 114	Boy Stuff, 4, 112	7	1:50.60	77,640
1997	**Snake Eyes**, 7, 117	R. Albarado	Scott's Scoundrel, 5, 113	Da Bull, 5, 114	8	1:52.65	91,440
1996	**Born Wild**, 4, 116	M. Walls	Kazabaiyn, 6, 113	Bene Erit, 4, 113	8	1:52.97	61,395
1995	**Yukon Robbery**, 6, 113	R. J. Faul	Dynaguard, 4, 108	Milt's Overture, 4, 116	6	1:51.50	61,185
1994	**Yukon Robbery**, 5, 113	R. J. Faul	Grand Hooley, 5, 114	Empire Pool (GB), 4, 116	9	1:50.27	61,635
1993	**Yukon Robbery**, 4, 115	R. J. Faul	Spending Record, 6, 114	Seattle Bound, 5, 113	9	1:50.60	46,440
1992	**Rainbows for Life**, 4, 120	S. P. Romero	City Ballet, 5, 113	†Palace Chill, 5, 113	10	1:53.00	46,680
1991	**First Tea**, 4, 113	K. Bourque	Noble Savage (Ire), 5, 114	Take a Flight, 6, 116	9	1:53.30	46,500
1990	**Tower Above 'Em**, 6, 112	S. P. Romero	Jack's Kingdom, 7, 113	Majesty's Imp, 4, 114	10	1:55.80	46,080
1989	**Ingot's Ruler**, 7, 116	R. D. Ardoin	Vaguely Crafty, 6, 113	Top Guest (Ire), 6, 115	10	1:51.20	17,640
1988	**Top Guest (Ire)**, 5, 117	J. Samyn	Royal Treasurer, 5, 121	Grey Classic, 5, 119	9	1:54.20	40,125

Fair Grounds Budweiser Breeders' Cup H. 1988-'95. Held at Louisiana Downs 2006. 1⅛ miles 1988-2005. Dirt 1995. Three-year-olds and up 1988-'91, 1993, 1995-2000. †Denotes female.

Fair Grounds Oaks

Grade 2 in 2006. Fair Grounds, three-year-olds, fillies, 1$^1/_{16}$ miles, dirt. Held March 12, 2005, with a gross value of $300,000. First held in 1966. First graded in 1982. Stakes record 1:42.20 (1997 Blushing K. D.).

Year	Winner	Jockey	Second	Third	Strs	Time	1st Purse
2005	**Summerly**, 3, 121	J. D. Bailey	Carlea, 3, 121	Runway Model, 3, 121	6	1:43.79	$180,000
2004	**Ashado**, 3, 121	C. H. Velasquez	Victory U. S. A., 3, 121	Shadow Cast, 3, 121	6	1:43.07	180,000
2003	**Lady Tak**, 3, 121	D. J. Meche	Atlantic Ocean, 3, 121	Belle of Perintown, 3, 121	6	1:44.36	210,000
2002	**Take Charge Lady**, 3, 121	A. J. D'Amico	Lake Lady, 3, 121	Chamrousse, 3, 121	8	1:43.30	210,000
2001	**Real Cozzy**, 3, 121	E. M. Martin Jr.	Mystic Lady, 3, 121	She's a Devil Due, 3, 121	9	1:44.58	210,000
2000	**Shawnee Country**, 3, 121	D. J. Meche	Eden Lodge, 3, 121	Zoftig, 3, 121	9	1:44.81	210,000
1999	**Silverbulletday**, 3, 121	G. L. Stevens	Runaway Venus, 3, 112	Brushed Halory, 3, 114	7	1:44.99	223,740
1998	**Lu Ravi**, 3, 112	W. Martinez	Well Chosen, 3, 112	Silent Eskimo, 3, 112	6	1:43.70	180,000
1997	**Blushing K. D.**, 3, 121	L. J. Meche	Tomisue's Delight, 3, 114	Cozy Blues, 3, 112	5	**1:42.20**	105,000
1996	**Bright Time**, 3, 112	L. F. Diaz	Mackie, 3, 121	Proper Dance, 3, 114	6	1:45.98	94,530
1995	**Brushing Gloom**, 3, 112	J. Brown	Kuda, 3, 118	Legendary Priness, 3, 121	9	1:45.12	90,000
1994	**Two Altazano**, 3, 112	K. P. LeBlanc	Tricky Code, 3, 121	Minority Dater, 3, 112	6	1:42.50	93,840
1993	**Silky Feather**, 3, 112	E. J. Perrodin	She's a Little Shy, 3, 121	Sum Runner, 3, 121	7	1:44.60	64,080
1992	**Prospectors Delite**, 3, 118	P. Day	Glitzi Bj, 3, 118	Desert Radiance, 3, 118	7	1:44.20	63,990
1991	**Rare Pick**, 3, 112	P. A. Johnson	Nalees Pin, 3, 121	Lady Blockbuster, 3, 118	9	1:46.50	65,640
1990	**Pampered Star**, 3, 112	S. P. Romero	Windansea, 3, 118	Gayla's Pleasure, 3, 115	9	1:44.60	59,520
1989	**Mistaurian**, 3, 113	D. Valiente	Affirmed Classic, 3, 121	Exquisite Mistress, 3, 118	6	1:44.80	57,900
1988	**Quite a Gem**, 3, 115	E. J. Perrodin	False Glitter, 3, 118	Sable Decor, 3, 118	9	1:46.40	59,580
1987	**Up the Apalachee**, 3, 121	M. R. Torres	Cathy Quick, 3, 118	Out of the Bid, 3, 121	6	1:45.40	60,000
1986	**Tiffany Lass**, 3, 121	R. L. Frazier	Patricia J. K., 3, 121	Turn and Dance, 3, 112	6	1:45.00	97,400
1985	**Marshua's Echelon**, 3, 121	R. J. Franklin	Golden Silence, 3, 113	Little Biddy Comet, 3, 118	13	1:44.80	113,400
1984	**My Darling One**, 3, 112	C. J. McCarron	Texas Cowgirl Nite, 3, 118	Rays Joy, 3, 112	8	1:44.60	101,400
1983	**Bright Crocus**, 3, 121	S. Hawley	Miss Molly, 3, 118	Shamivor, 3, 115	6	1:45.80	66,100
1982	**Before Dawn**, 3, 121	J. Velasquez	Girlie, 3, 121	Linda North, 3, 118	7	1:45.40	66,400
1981	**Truly Bound**, 3, 121	W. Shoemaker	Lou's Dance, 3, 118	‡Sunwontshine, 3, 112	7	1:44.80	61,400
1980	**Honest and True**, 3, 118	A. Guajardo	Smart Angle, 3, 121	Lady Taurian Peace, 3, 118	8	1:44.40	33,875
1978	**La Doree (Arg)**, 4, 108	B. Fann	Royal Graustark, 4, 114	Burn the Money, 4, 107	10	1:52.40	25,738
	Shadycroft Lady, 3, 109	R. Martinez Jr.	Miss Baja, 3, 117	Belle of Dodge Me, 4, 114	9	1:52.60	25,737
1977	**Table the Rumor**, 3, 112	W. Shoemaker	La Doree (Arg), 3, 112	Ivory Castle, 3, 118	9	1:52.40	57,800
	Quid Kit, 3, 115	A. J. Trosclair	Royal Graustark, 3, 112	Pay Dust, 3, 112	11	1:45.60	21,025
1976	**Bronze Point**, 3, 118	H. Arroyo	Little Broadway, 3, 118	Confort Zone, 3, 118	9	1:44.40	20,075
1975	**Lucky Leslie**, 3, 118	D. Brumfield	Regal Rumor, 3, 121	Decanter, 3, 118	8	1:46.60	19,650
1974	**Bold Rosie**, 3, 118	P. Rubbicco	Trade Me Later, 3, 112	Kaye's Commander, 3, 118	12	1:46.60	20,625
1973	**Knitted Gloves**, 3, 118	J. C. Espinoza	Fussy Girl, 3, 121	Westward, 3, 118	11	1:46.00	14,825

Formerly sponsored by the Coca-Cola Co. of Atlanta 1989-'90. Grade 3 1982-2000. Coca-Cola Fair Grounds Oaks 1989-'90. Not held 1979. 1$^1/_8$ miles 1977-'78. Three- and four-year-olds 1978. Run in March and December 1977. Two divisions 1978. ‡Plain Speaking finished third, DQ to fourth, 1981. Equaled track record 1994.

Falls City Handicap

Grade 2 in 2006. Churchill Downs, three-year-olds and up, fillies and mares, 1$^1/_8$ miles, dirt. Held November 24, 2005, with a gross value of $338,700. First held in 1875. First graded in 1973. Stakes record 1:48.85 (1999 Silent Eskimo).

Year	Winner	Jockey	Second	Third	Strs	Time	1st Purse
2005	**Indian Vale**, 3, 115	J. R. Velazquez	Pampered Princess, 5, 123	Miss Fortunate, 5, 115	10	1:50.25	$209,994
2004	**Halory Leigh**, 4, 116	E. M. Martin Jr.	Susan's Angel, 3, 114	Miss Fortunate, 4, 113	7	1:51.81	201,624
2003	**Lead Story**, 4, 116	C. H. Borel	Mayo On the Side, 4, 114	Cloakof Vagueness, 3, 114	9	1:51.23	207,204
2002	**Allamerican Bertie**, 3, 117	P. Day	Take Charge Lady, 3, 122	Softly, 4, 116	6	1:49.60	167,400
2001	**Forest Secrets**, 3, 113	C. Perret	Printemps (Chi), 4, 117	Unbridled Elaine, 3, 121	7	1:49.49	169,570
2000	**Bordelaise (Arg)**, 5, 117	P. Day	Spain, 3, 122	On a Soapbox, 4, 116	5	1:50.01	168,020
1999	**Silent Eskimo**, 4, 117	C. H. Borel	Let, 4, 116	Pleasant Temper, 5, 115	8	**1:48.85**	171,585
1998	**Tomisue's Delight**, 4, 121	S. J. Sellers	Top Secret, 5, 115	Silent Eskimo, 3, 113	8	1:51.05	171,740
1997	**Feasibility Study**, 5, 122	M. E. Smith	Omi, 4, 114	Naskra Colors, 5, 112	7	1:50.65	170,345
1996	**Halo America**, 6, 118	C. H. Borel	Bedroom Blues, 5, 115	Debit My Account, 4, 113	8	1:49.08	171,120
1995	**Mariah's Storm**, 4, 120	R. N. Lester	Alcovy, 5, 112	Heavenliness, 5, 112	7	1:51.37	143,390
1994	**Alcovy**, 4, 114	S. E. Miller	Pennyhill Park, 4, 115	Hey Hazel, 4, 114	7	1:51.16	141,440
1993	**Gray Cashmere**, 4, 120	P. Day	Avie's Shadow, 3, 110	Princess Polonia, 3, 112	7	1:50.96	142,090
1992	**Bungalow**, 5, 118	P. Day	Wilderness Song, 4, 123	Auto Dial, 4, 115	7	1:52.03	70,915
1991	**Screen Prospect**, 4, 117	S. J. Sellers	Fit for a Queen, 5, 124	Bungalow, 4, 112	11	1:51.23	73,580
1990	**Screen Prospect**, 3, 114	P. Day	Sleek Feet, 3, 110	Degenerate Gal, 5, 119	13	1:51.40	75,920
1989	**Degenerate Gal**, 4, 116	L. J. Melancon	Luthier's Launch, 3, 113	Blackened, 3, 112	9	1:52.60	72,410
1988	**Top Corsage**, 5, 121	D. Brumfield	Epitome, 3, 116	Lawyer Talk, 4, 111	14	1:51.80	76,895
1987	**Royal Cielo**, 3, 114	K. K. Allen	Firgie's Jule, 4, 115	Fantasy Lover, 4, 113	8	1:53.00	47,330
1986	**Queen Alexandra**, 4, 124	D. Brumfield	Kapalua Butterfly, 5, 113	Gerrie Singer, 5, 116	13	1:51.40	49,248
1985	**Donut's Pride**, 3, 112	L. J. Melancon	Playful Queen, 4, 114	My Inheritance, 3, 111	8	1:53.20	35,743
	Electric Fanny, 4, 115	J. C. Espinoza	Mrs. Revere, 4, 121	Chattahoochee, 3, 113	10	1:52.60	26,780
1984	**Pretty Perfect**, 4, 121	G. Gallitano	Electric Fanny, 3, 116	Queen of Song, 5, 122	12	1:50.80	37,115
1983	**Narrate**, 3, 117	M. S. Sellers	Queen of Song, 4, 116	Promising Native, 4, 116	9	1:51.60	36,335
1982	**Mezimica**, 4, 112	D. E. Foster	Charge My Account, 3, 111	Shade Miss, 3, 112	10	1:51.40	39,910
	What Glitter, 4, 114	D. Brumfield	Sprite Flight, 4, 114	Betty Money, 3, 118	11	1:52.80	36,823

1981	**Safe Play**, 3, 123	S. A. Spencer	Sweetest Chant, 3, 118	Friendly Frolic, 4, 112	13	1:46.20	$37,993
1980	**Sweet Audrey**, 3, 113	C. R. Woods Jr.	Likely Exchange, 6, 123	Impetuous Gal, 5, 122	11	1:48.20	36,156
1979	**Holy Mount**, 3, 112	M. R. Morgan	Impetuous Gal, 4, 118	Cup of Honey, 3, 115	11	1:47.60	39,163
1978	**Navajo Princess**, 4, 123	C. Perret	Love to Tell, 3, 118	Likely Exchange, 4, 120	12	1:45.40	36,043
1977	**Time for Pleasure**, 3, 115	T. Barrow	Dear Irish, 3, 114	Famed Princess, 4, 115	13	1:46.20	22,084
1976	**Hope of Glory**, 4, 118	D. Brumfield	Hail to El, 4, 116	Flama Ardiente, 4, 117	12	1:48.20	21,938
1975	**Flama Ardiente**, 3, 119	B. Fann	Costly Dream, 4, 120	Go On Dreaming, 3, 116	11	1:38.20	18,623
1974	**Susan's Girl**, 5, 126	W. Gavidia	Crystal Stone, 4, 114	Enchanted Native, 3, 112	9	1:37.40	18,184
1973	**Delta Empress**, 3, 111	E. Fires	Pig Party, 4, 113	Fine Tuning, 3, 115	12	1:37.40	15,348
	Fairway Flyer, 4, 115	D. E. Whited	Nalees Folly, 4, 118	Knitted Gloves, 3, 113	11	1:37.20	15,185

Named for the early nickname of Louisville, "Falls City." Grade 3 1973-2001. Not held 1878-'81, 1885-'91, 1893-1909, 1928-'40. 1 mile 1875-'55, 1892, 1941-'75. 1½ miles 1882-'83. 1¹⁄₁₆ miles 1884, 1919, 1976-'81. 6 furlongs 1910, 1912-'18. Three-year-olds 1875-'77. Two-year-olds and up 1882-'92. Both sexes 1875-'77, 1882-'92, 1910-'26. Two divisions 1973, 1982, 1985.

Fantasy Stakes

Grade 2 in 2006. Oaklawn Park, three-year-olds, fillies, 1¹⁄₁₆ miles, dirt. Held April 14, 2006, with a gross value of $250,000. First held in 1973. First graded in 1975. Stakes record 1:41.20 (1984 My Darling One).

Year	Winner	Jockey	Second	Third	Strs	Time	1st Purse
2006	**Ready to Please**, 3, 117	S. Elliott	Miss Norman, 3, 117	Brownie Points, 3, 121	8	1:45.63	$150,000
2005	**Round Pond**, 3, 121	S. Elliott	Rugula, 3, 117	R Lady Joy, 3, 121	7	1:43.49	150,000
2004	**House of Fortune**, 3, 121	A. O. Solis	Island Sand, 3, 121	Stellar Jayne, 3, 121	11	1:42.62	120,000
2003	**Ruby's Reception**, 3, 121	T. J. Thompson	Harbor Blues, 3, 121	Go for Glamour, 3, 117	6	1:44.61	120,000
2002	**See How She Runs**, 3, 117	D. R. Pettinger	Lake Lady, 3, 121	Chamrousse, 3, 117	6	1:43.80	120,000
2001	**Mystic Lady**, 3, 121	E. Coa	Collect Call, 3, 121	Mysia Jo, 3, 117	10	1:43.32	120,000
2000	**Classy Cara**, 3, 121	I. Puglisi	Eden Lodge, 3, 117	Gold for My Gal, 3, 117	8	1:43.95	120,000
1999	**Excellent Meeting**, 3, 121	K. Desormeaux	The Happy Hopper, 3, 121	Dreams Gallore, 3, 121	6	1:42.73	150,000
1998	**Silent Eskimo**, 3, 117	C. Gonzalez	Misty Hour, 3, 121	Came Unwound, 3, 121	8	1:43.84	150,000
1997	**Blushing K. D.**, 3, 121	L. J. Meche	Valid Bonnet, 3, 121	Ajina, 3, 121	5	1:42.60	150,000
1996	**Escena**, 3, 117	P. Day	Antespend, 3, 121	Ski Trail, 3, 117	7	1:43.93	150,000
1995	**Cat's Cradle**, 3, 121	C. W. Antley	Forever Cherokee, 3, 117	Humble Eight, 3, 121	8	1:44.29	150,000
1994	**Two Altazano**, 3, 121	K. P. LeBlanc	Slide Show, 3, 121	Flying in the Lane, 3, 121	11	1:43.64	150,000
1993	**Aztec Hill**, 3, 121	M. E. Smith	Adorydar, 3, 117	Stalcreek, 3, 117	7	1:44.33	150,000
1992	**Race the Wild Wind**, 3, 117	C. J. McCarron	Golden Treat, 3, 121	Now Dance, 3, 117	8	1:43.74	150,000
1991	**Lite Light**, 3, 121	C. S. Nakatani	Withallprobability, 3, 121	Nalees Pin, 3, 121	8	1:41.93	150,000
1990	**Silvered**, 3, 112	D. L. Howard	Lonely Girl, 3, 114	Fit to Scout, 3, 118	8	1:44.20	150,000
1989	**Fantastic Look**, 3, 113	C. J. McCarron	Imaginary Lady, 3, 121	Affirmed Classic, 3, 114	7	1:43.20	150,000
1988	**Jeanne Jones**, 3, 118	W. Shoemaker	Fara's Team, 3, 112	Costly Shoes, 3, 114	7	1:42.20	150,000
1987	**‡Very Subtle**, 3, 121	C. J. McCarron	Up the Apalachee, 3, 121	Hometown Queen, 3, 116	7	1:42.40	162,780
1986	**Tiffany Lass**, 3, 121	G. L. Stevens	Lotka, 3, 116	Turn and Dance, 3, 112	8	1:42.00	164,640
1985	**Rascal Lass**, 3, 118	R. Sibille	Denver Express, 3, 113	Little Biddy Comet, 3, 114	11	1:43.20	169,620
1984	**My Darling One**, 3, 121	C. J. McCarron	Althea, 3, 121	Personable Lady, 3, 118	6	**1:41.20**	160,440
1983	**Brindy Brindy**, 3, 115	K. Jones Jr.	Fifth Question, 3, 115	Choose a Partner, 3, 112	11	1:44.60	169,080
1982	**Flying Partner**, 3, 118	R. Sibille	Skillful Joy, 3, 121	Before Dawn, 3, 121	7	1:47.00	163,020
1981	**Heavenly Cause**, 3, 121	L. A. Pincay Jr.	Nell's Briquette, 3, 121	Wayward Lass, 3, 121	9	1:43.80	133,890
1980	**Bold 'n Determined**, 3, 121	E. Delahoussaye	Satin Ribera, 3, 115	Honest and True, 3, 118	7	1:45.20	101,940
1979	**Davona Dale**, 3, 121	J. Velasquez	Caline, 3, 121	Very Special Lady, 3, 110	7	1:44.40	101,610
1978	**Equanimity**, 3, 110	H. E. Moreno	Ba Ba Bee, 3, 115	Miss Baja, 3, 121	11	1:44.60	77,850
1977	**Our Mims**, 3, 112	D. Brumfield	Sweet Alliance, 3, 118	Meteor Dancer, 3, 110	15	1:45.00	83,970
1976	**T. V. Vixen**, 3, 121	B. Walt	Answer, 3, 121	All Rainbows, 3, 112	8	1:43.40	73,170
1975	**Hoso**, 3, 121	M. Solomone	Luxury, 3, 114	Dancers Countess, 3, 118	6	1:46.00	70,830
1974	**Miss Musket**, 3, 121	W. Shoemaker	Out to Lunch, 3, 115	Fairway Fable, 3, 118	12	1:44.80	79,740
1973	**Knitted Gloves**, 3, 121	J. C. Espinoza	Fussy Girl, 3, 121	Westward, 3, 118	14	1:42.60	36,960

Grade 1 1978-'89. 1 mile 70 yards 1973. ‡Up the Apalachee finished first, DQ to second, 1987.

Fayette Stakes

Grade 3 in 2006. Keeneland Race Course, three-year-olds and up, 1⅛ miles, dirt. Held October 29, 2005, with a gross value of $150,000. First held in 1959. First graded in 1979. Stakes record 1:46.80 (1987 Good Command).

Year	Winner	Jockey	Second	Third	Strs	Time	1st Purse
2005	**Alumni Hall**, 6, 121	C. H. Borel	On Thin Ice, 4, 119	M B Sea, 6, 119	9	1:51.37	$93,000
2004	**Midway Road**, 4, 121	C. H. Borel	Total Impact (Chi), 6, 125	Alumni Hall, 5, 119	5	1:50.39	99,975
2003	**M B Sea**, 4, 119	C. Perret	Tenpins, 5, 121	dh-Changeintheweather, 4, 119 dh-Seattle Fitz (Arg), 4, 119	7	1:50.30	101,556
2002	**Tenpins**, 4, 123	C. Perret	X Country, 4, 119	Crafty Shaw, 4, 121	4	1:51.17	99,789
2001	**Connected**, 4, 119	M. St. Julien	Broken Vow, 4, 123	Outofthebox, 3, 122	9	1:50.05	103,509
2000	**Jadada**, 5, 118	S. J. Sellers	Mojave Moon, 4, 118	Get Away With It (Ire), 7, 118	5	1:54.92	133,176
1999	**Social Charter**, 4, 120	M. St. Julien	Master O Foxhounds, 4, 118	Early Warning, 4, 118	4	1:55.28	135,904
1998	**Arch**, 3, 123	S. J. Sellers	Touch Gold, 4, 115	Wild Tempest, 4, 115	4	1:53.87	98,394
1997	**Whiskey Wisdom**, 4, 115	W. Martinez	City by Night, 4, 123	Pyramid Peak, 5, 120	6	1:48.64	101,184
1996	**Isitingood**, 5, 120	D. R. Flores	Distorted Humor, 3, 114	Strawberry Wine, 4, 117	8	1:50.42	120,110
1995	**Judge T C**, 4, 114	J. M. Johnson	Powerful Punch, 6, 120	Sir Vixen, 7, 114	9	1:49.05	104,625
1994	**Sunny Sunrise**, 7, 120	J. D. Carle	Key Contender, 6, 117	Powerful Punch, 5, 117	7	1:50.18	67,766

1993	**Grand Jewel**, 3, 120	J. D. Bailey	Split Run, 5, 120	Secreto's Hideaway, 4, 114	8	1:46.87	$68,634
1992	**Barkerville**, 4, 114	S. J. Sellers	Medium Cool, 4, 117	Majesterian, 4, 114	11	1:48.43	70,680
1991	**Summer Squall**, 4, 122	P. Day	Unbridled, 4, 122	Secret Hello, 4, 115	5	1:48.84	69,810
1990	**Lac Ouimet**, 7, 119	R. P. Romero	Din's Dancer, 5, 121	Secret Hello, 3, 116	6	1:47.20	70,233
1989	**Drapeau Tricolore**, 4, 114	J. E. Bruin	Air Worthy, 4, 116	Blue Buckaroo, 6, 118	8	1:48.20	71,695
1988	**Homebuilder**, 4, 121	D. Brumfield	Blue Buckaroo, 5, 120	Ile de Jinsky, 4, 112	4	1:51.20	68,315
1987	**Good Command**, 4, 118	D. Brumfield	Minneapple, 5, 120	Savings, 4, 115	12	**1:46.80**	73,921
1986	**Harham's Sizzler**, 7, 120	R. A. Meier	Derby Wish, 4, 119	Pirate's Skiff, 3, 112	5	1:49.20	34,792
1985	**Wop Wop**, 3, 112	D. E. Foster	Banner Bob, 3, 117	Exclusive Greer, 4, 114	10	1:51.40	36,530
1984	**Star Choice**, 5, 112	J. McKnight	Explosive Wagon, 4, 117	Bright Baron, 4, 112	8	1:47.40	47,492
1983	**dh-Cad**, 5, 116	D. Brumfield		Bold Style, 4, 120	5	1:48.80	22,663
	dh-Frost King, 5, 123	R. Platts					
1982	**Rivalero**, 6, 115	R. P. Romero	Cad, 4, 114	Recusant, 4, 120	7	1:50.40	35,563
	El Baba, 3, 118	D. Brumfield	Vodika Collins, 4, 120	Hechizado (Arg), 6, 115	7	1:50.20	38,813
1981	**Ironworks**, 3, 117	P. Day	Two's a Plenty, 4, 116	Sun Catcher, 4, 118	11	1:49.20	39,861
1980	**Hurry Up Blue**, 3, 112	G. Gallitano	Marcy Road, 3, 111	All the More, 7, 116	10	1:49.00	39,423
1979	**Architect**, 3, 117	S. A. Spencer	Coverack, 6, 121	Trimlea, 5, 120	8	1:49.60	35,669
1978	**‡Silver Series**, 4, 121	D. Brumfield	Buckfinder, 4, 121	Romeo, 5, 118	6	1:41.20	20,768
1977	**Bob's Dusty**, 3, 117	R. DePass	Man's Man, 3, 115	Packer Captain, 5, 118	11	1:42.80	18,395
1976	**Silver Badge**, 5, 111	G. Patterson	Easy Gallop, 3, 117	Topinabee, 5, 112	9	1:44.60	17,981
	Yamanin, 4, 114	G. Patterson	Run for Clem, 3, 111	Faneuil Boy, 5, 118	8	1:43.20	17,899
1975	**Warbucks**, 5, 120	J. Nichols	Hasty Flyer, 4, 119	Mr. Door, 4, 114	11	1:44.40	18,460
1974	**Jesta Dream Away**, 4, 115	A. Rini	Super Sail, 6, 121	Joyous Jester, 4, 112	9	1:41.60	18,119
1973	**Chateauvira**, 5, 112	G. Gallitano	Grocery List, 4, 116	O So Big, 4, 115	13	1:42.80	19,093

Named for Fayette County, Kentucky, where Keeneland is located. Grade 2 1987-'96. Fayette H. 1959-'91. Fayette Breeders' Cup S. 1999-2000. $1\frac{1}{16}$ miles 1963-'78. $1\frac{3}{16}$ miles 1998-2000. Turf 1985. Two divisions 1976, 1982. Dead heat for first 1983. Dead heat for third 2003. ‡Buckfinder finished first, DQ to second, 1978. Equaled track record 1993. Track record 1998.

Fifth Season Stakes

Grade 3 in 2006. Oaklawn Park, four-year-olds and up, $1\frac{1}{16}$ miles, dirt. Held April 12, 2006, with a gross value of $100,000. First held in 1988. First graded in 1999. Stakes record 1:40.30 (1991 Hang On Slewpy).

Year	Winner	Jockey	Second	Third	Strs	Time	1st Purse
2006	**Kid Grindstone**, 4, 115	J. M. Campbell	Arch Hall, 5, 122	Greater Good, 4, 115	7	1:43.73	$60,000
2005	**Mauk Four**, 5, 113	J. Burningham	Clays Awesome, 5, 117	Absent Friend, 5, 122	8	1:42.89	60,000
2004	**Spanish Empire**, 4, 118	E. M. Martin Jr.	Crafty Shaw, 6, 122	No Comprende, 6, 122	8	1:42.50	60,000
2003	**Patton's Victory**, 5, 117	A. Birzer	Colorful Tour, 4, 122	Makors Mark, 6, 118	7	1:43.26	60,000
2001	**Remington Rock**, 7, 114	D. E. Simington	Kombat Kat, 4, 114	Da Devil, 6, 114	7	1:43.13	45,000
2000	**Mr Ross**, 5, 115	E. C. Perner	Relic Reward, 6, 114	Crimson Classic, 6, 114	7	1:42.93	60,000
1999	**Truluck**, 4, 114	L. J. Melancon	Slide to the Left, 4, 114	Rock and Roll, 4, 114	8	1:42.28	60,000
1998	**Acceptable**, 4, 117	A. O. Solis	Littlebitlively, 4, 117	Brush With Pride, 6, 124	8	1:42.50	60,000
1997	**Krigeorj's Gold**, 4, 119	J. Johnson	Bucks Nephew, 7, 117	Prince of the Mt., 6, 116	9	1:43.20	49,050
1996	**No Spend No Glow**, 4, 117	R. N. Lester	Bucks Nephew, 6, 117	Groovy Jett, 5, 117	7	1:42.96	47,880
1995	**Tyus**, 5, 114	C. H. Borel	Prince of the Mt., 4, 114	Joseph's Robe, 4, 114	7	1:42.98	26,760
1994	**Nelson**, 7, 117	S. P. Romero	Punch Line, 4, 117	Senor Tomas, 5, 114	6	1:43.16	41,640
1993	**Delafield**, 4, 117	J. A. Santos	Far Out Wadleigh, 5, 119	Lanyons Star, 5, 114	11	1:42.43	43,080
1992	**Medium Cool**, 4, 117	C. S. Nakatani	On the Edge, 5, 114	Hayes G., 5, 117	10	1:43.35	40,500
1991	**Hang On Slewpy**, 4, 119	D. L. Howard	Greydar, 4, 125	Traskwood, 5, 117	5	**1:40.30**	31,635
1990	**Idabel**, 4, 119	P. Day	Albert's First, 7, 117	Beirne Station, 4, 112	9	1:42.20	32,115
1989	**Smackover Creek**, 4, 114	D. L. Howard	Sir Bubby, 6, 114	Sarhilla, 5, 117	9	1:43.20	32,475
1988	**Contact Game**, 4, 113	J. D. Bailey	General Silver, 4, 113	Itsallinthegame, 5, 114	9	1:42.20	20,280

Named for Hot Springs, Arkansas's "fifth season," the Oaklawn Park race meet. Fifth Season Breeders' Cup S. 1989-2001. Not held 2002. Three-year-olds and up 1989-2001.

Firecracker Breeders' Cup Handicap

Grade 2 in 2006. Churchill Downs, three-year-olds and up, 1 mile, turf. Held July 4, 2005, with a gross value of $274,000. First held in 1983. First graded in 1995. Stakes record 1:33.78 (1995 Jaggery John).

Year	Winner	Jockey	Second	Third	Strs	Time	1st Purse
2005	**Kitten's Joy**, 4, 124	E. S. Prado	Old Forester, 4, 115	America Alive, 4, 119	6	1:35.25	$169,880
2004	**Quantum Merit**, 5, 117	S. J. Sellers	‡Perfect Soul (Ire), 6, 121	Senor Swinger, 4, 117	9	1:34.15	178,405
2003	**Tap the Admiral**, 5, 115	J. McKee	Freefourinternet, 5, 114	Package Store, 5, 114	9	1:35.48	178,870
2002	**Good Journey**, 6, 118	P. Day	Morluc, 6, 114	Even the Score, 4, 114	9	1:34.83	181,350
2001	**Irish Prize**, 5, 122	G. L. Stevens	‡Aly's Alley, 5, 117	Where's Taylor, 5, 114	7	1:34.68	175,770
2000	**Conserve**, 4, 116	S. J. Sellers	Riviera (Fr), 6, 115	King Slayer (GB), 5, 115	8	1:35.12	177,940
1999	**Joe Who (Brz)**, 6, 113	R. Albarado	Middlesex Drive, 4, 116	Wild Event, 6, 121	9	1:36.78	132,680
1998	**Claire's Honor**, 4, 109	A. J. D'Amico	Soviet Line (Ire), 8, 115	Optic Nerve, 5, 113	9	1:35.93	177,630
1997	**Soviet Line (Ire)**, 7, 114	P. Day	Volochine (Ire), 6, 115	Same Old Wish, 7, 118	10	1:37.60	126,077
1996	**Rare Reason**, 5, 115	P. A. Johnson	Artema (Ire), 5, 114	Wavy Run (Ire), 5, 116	9	1:33.81	131,950
1995	**Jaggery John**, 4, 113	D. Kutz	Rare Reason, 4, 115	Fly Cry, 4, 119	10	**1:33.78**	74,360
1994	**First and Only**, 7, 118	T. J. Hebert	†Weekend Madness (Ire), 4, 111	Avid Affection, 5, 112	8	1:35.33	73,580
1993	**Cleone**, 4, 115	C. Perret	Magesterial Cheer, 5, 113	Harlan, 4, 110	9	1:35.90	74,815

1985	**Rapid Gray**, 6, 122	L. J. Melancon	Silahis, 8, 116	Silver Wraith, 4, 110	5	1:21.20	$35,263
1984	**Turn and Cheer**, 4, 113	J. McKnight	Coax Me Matt, 4, 112	Keep At It, 3, 112	7	1:25.60	35,912
1983	**Shot n' Missed**, 6, 121	L. Moyers	Dave's Friend, 8, 124	Rackensack, 5, 118	4	1:23.20	28,145

Traditionally held during the July 4 holiday. Grade 3 1995-'99. Firecracker H. 1983-'95. Not held 1986-'92. 7 furlongs 1983-'85. Dirt 1983-'85. Course record 1995. ‡Where's Taylor finished second, DQ to third, 2001. ‡Senor Swinger finished second, DQ to third, 2004. †Denotes female.

First Flight Handicap

Grade 2 in 2006. Belmont Park, three-year-olds and up, fillies and mares, 7 furlongs, dirt. Held October 30, 2005, with a gross value of $150,000. First held in 1978. First graded in 1982. Stakes record 1:20.65 (1992 Shared Interest).

Year	Winner	Jockey	Second	Third	Strs	Time	1st Purse
2005	**Great Intentions**, 3, 114	E. S. Prado	Habiboo, 4, 113	Smokey Glacken, 4, 116	8	1:23.98	$90,000
2004	**Bending Strings**, 3, 116	S. Bridgmohan	Smokey Glacken, 3, 115	Passing Shot, 5, 118	6	1:22.13	90,000
2003	**Randaroo**, 3, 115	H. Castillo Jr.	Shine Again, 6, 121	Zawzooth, 4, 113	8	1:23.65	90,000
2002	**Shine Again**, 5, 117	J. Samyn	Redhead Riot, 3, 112	Raging Fever, 4, 119	5	1:23.75	90,000
2001	**Shine Again**, 4, 116	J. Samyn	Dream Supreme, 4, 121	Kalookan Queen, 5, 119	6	1:23.21	90,000
2000	**Country Hideaway**, 4, 117	J. L. Espinoza	Go to the Ink, 4, 113	Cat Cay, 3, 114	7	1:22.60	90,000
1999	**Country Hideaway**, 3, 114	H. Castillo Jr.	Harpia, 5, 117	Anklet, 5, 114	8	1:23.00	90,000
1998	**Catinca**, 3, 116	R. Migliore	Glitter Woman, 4, 121	Blue Begonia, 5, 115	7	1:22.14	82,260
1997	**Dixie Flag**, 3, 113	M. J. Luzzi	Silent City, 3, 113	Aldiza, 3, 116	4	1:22.84	64,800
1996	**Thunder Achiever**, 3, 112	R. G. Davis	Miss Golden Circle, 4, 117	Call Account, 4, 110	10	1:21.59	81,864
1995	**Twist Afleet**, 4, 121	G. L. Stevens	Igotrhythm, 3, 109	Lottsa Talc, 5, 116	5	1:22.95	66,780
1994	**Twist Afleet**, 3, 117	J. D. Bailey	Ann Dear, 4, 117	Incinerate, 4, 113	8	1:23.02	66,120
1993	**Raise Heck**, 5, 114	R. I. Velez	Regal Victress, 6, 113	Shared Interest, 5, 121	6	1:23.51	69,000
1992	**Shared Interest**, 4, 111	J. D. Bailey	Missy's Mirage, 4, 121	Nannerl, 5, 119	5	**1:20.65**	120,000
1991	**Missy's Mirage**, 3, 113	E. Maple	Makin Faces, 3, 112	Withallprobability, 3, 114	10	1:21.98	74,160
1990	**Queena**, 4, 113	J. D. Bailey	Quick Mischief, 4, 115	A Penny Is a Penny, 5, 122	5	1:22.40	51,480
1989	**Grecian Flight**, 5, 122	C. Perret	Feel the Beat, 4, 121	Dance Teacher, 4, 112	5	1:22.00	51,480
1988	**Cagey Exuberance**, 4, 119	J. Imparato	Nasty Affair, 4, 114	Intently, 5, 111	10	1:24.40	55,350
1987	**Al's Helen**, 4, 112	J. D. Bailey	Girl Powder, 4, 117	Willowy Mood, 5, 118	9	1:21.80	54,180
1986	**Chaldea**, 6, 115	J. Samyn	Le Slew, 5, 114	Gene's Lady, 5, 120	4	1:22.40	53,100
1985	**Alabama Nana (Ire)**, 4, 121	J. Velasquez	Gene's Lady, 4, 115	Paradies (Arg), 5, 119	5	1:22.20	50,040
1984	**Shortley**, 4, 114	M. G. Pino	Quixotic Lady, 4, 116	Rarely Layte, 4, 108	7	1:22.60	42,060
1983	**Pert**, 4, 112	F. Lovato Jr.	Pretty Sensible, 3, 112	Quixotic Lady, 3, 121	8	1:25.20	34,620
1982	**Number**, 3, 112	E. Maple	Lady Dean, 4, 123	Privacy, 4, 118	11	1:22.80	34,500
1981	**Island Charm**, 4, 120	R. Migliore	Tax Holiday, 4, 116	Chain Bracelet, 4, 123	8	1:23.60	33,720
1980	**Samarta Dancer**, 4, 112	C. B. Asmussen	Jedina, 4, 115	Damask Fan, 3, 112	9	1:25.60	33,780
1979	**Gladiolus**, 5, 120	L. A. Pincay Jr.	Imarebel, 4, 117	Plankton, 3, 114	5	1:22.40	25,740
1978	**What a Summer**, 5, 126	J. Fell	Flying Above, 4, 120	Mrs. Warren, 4, 113	5	1:22.20	25,410

Named for C. V. Whitney's 1946 champion two-year-old filly and '46 Futurity S. winner First Flight (1944 f. by *Mahmoud). Grade 3 1982-'89. I Love New York First Flight H. 1995. Held at Aqueduct 1978-'89, 1991, 1993-'94, 1996-2000, 2002, 2004.

First Lady Handicap

Grade 3 in 2006. Gulfstream Park, three-year-olds and up, fillies and mares, 6 furlongs, dirt. Held January 21, 2006, with a gross value of $100,000. First held in 1981. First graded in 1993. Stakes record 1:08.98 (2006 Smokey Glacken).

Year	Winner	Jockey	Second	Third	Strs	Time	1st Purse
2006	**Smokey Glacken**, 5, 117	J. Castellano	Kuanyan, 6, 116	So Much More, 7, 113	8	**1:08.98**	$60,000
2005	**Savorthetime**, 6, 116	J. R. Velazquez	Cologny, 5, 117	Ebony Breeze, 5, 116	7	1:09.21	60,000
2004	**Harmony Lodge**, 6, 119	R. Migliore	House Party, 4, 118	Mayo On the Side, 5, 115	9	1:09.64	60,000
2003	**Harmony Lodge**, 5, 113	J. R. Velazquez	Fly Me Crazy, 5, 114	Haunted Lass, 4, 114	7	1:10.31	60,000
2002	**Raging Fever**, 4, 118	J. R. Velazquez	Cat Cay, 5, 118	Mandy's Gold, 4, 116	7	1:10.36	60,000
2001	**Another**, 4, 113	E. S. Prado	Curious Treasures, 4, 114	Dynamite Diablo, 4, 115	11	1:10.41	60,000
2000	**Hurricane Bertie**, 5, 118	P. Day	Marley Vale, 4, 118	Cassidy, 5, 113	7	1:10.22	45,000
1999	**Scotzanna**, 7, 114	R. Migliore	U Can Do It, 6, 118	Foil, 4, 116	8	1:10.17	45,000
1998	**U Can Do It**, 5, 115	S. J. Sellers	Start At Once, 5, 113	Vivace, 5, 118	10	1:09.86	45,000
1997	**Chip**, 4, 113	J. Bravo	Phone the Doctor, 5, 116	Surprising Fact, 4, 113	10	1:09.76	45,000
1996	**Chaposa Springs**, 4, 122	J. D. Bailey	Phone the Doctor, 4, 117	Market Slide, 5, 113	9	1:10.23	45,000
1995	**Recognizable**, 4, 113	M. E. Smith	Insight to Cope, 5, 114	Maison de Reve, 5, 114	10	1:09.74	30,000
1994	**Santa Catalina**, 6, 114	J. D. Bailey	Insight to Cope, 4, 119	Capture the Crown, 5, 113	11	1:11.26	30,000
1993	**Si Si Sezyou**, 5, 112	R. Hernandez	Illeria, 6, 113	Jeano, 5, 114	11	1:10.06	30,000
1992	**Withallprobability**, 4, 118	C. Perret	Christina Czarina, 4, 114	Spirit of Fighter, 9, 114	14	1:11.14	30,000
1991	**Spirit of Fighter**, 8, 118	J. A. Velez Jr.	Mistaurian, 5, 115	Love's Exchange, 5, 128	9	1:11.70	30,000
1990	**Sez Fourty**, 4, 114	M. A. Gonzalez	Classic Value, 4, 118	Fit for a Queen, 4, 114	7	1:11.20	22,764
1989	**Waggley**, 6, 112	J. Samyn	Damality, 6, 113	My Peace, 4, 114	5	1:11.00	27,288
1988	**Funistrada**, 5, 120	W. A. Guerra	Easter Mary, 4, 114	Cadillacing, 4, 113	9	1:10.20	29,232
1987	**One Fine Lady**, 5, 114	R. Danjean	Fleur de Soleil, 4, 112	Sheer Ice, 5, 113	6	1:10.40	24,045
1986	**Sugar's Image**, 5, 115	J. A. Velez Jr.	Summer Mood, 5, 120	Mr. T.'s Tune, 5, 117	10	1:11.20	29,736
1985	**Nany**, 5, 120	G. St. Leon	Mickey's Echo, 6, 118	Birdie Belle, 4, 118	10	1:09.80	29,352
1983	**Prime Prospect**, 5, 118	D. MacBeth	Miss Hitch, 7, 114	Mrs. Roberts, 5, 113	16	1:10.80	24,282
1981	**Island Charm**, 4, 113	J. Velasquez	La Voyageuse, 6, 126	Lacey, 4, 114	11	1:10.60	22,536

Inaugurated in 1981 following a presidential election year and run in mid-January when presidential inaugurations are held, the race is named for the first lady of the United States. First Lady Breeders' Cup H. 1990. Not held 1982, 1984.

Fleur de Lis Handicap

Grade 2 in 2006. Churchill Downs, three-year-olds and up, fillies and mares, 1⅛ miles, dirt. Held June 18, 2005, with a gross value of $330,000. First held in 1975. First graded in 1988. Stakes record 1:48.26 (2000 Heritage of Gold).

Year	Winner	Jockey	Second	Third	Strs	Time	1st Purse
2005	**Two Trail Sioux**, 4, 114	P. Day	Storm's Darling, 4, 116	Rare Gift, 4, 115	7	1:48.53	$204,600
2004	**Adoration**, 5, 122	V. Espinoza	Bare Necessities, 5, 120	La Reason, 4, 110	6	1:52.15	272,304
2003	**You**, 4, 119	J. D. Bailey	Printemps (Chi), 6, 114	Nonsuch Bay, 4, 114	6	1:49.12	203,298
2002	**Spain**, 5, 121	J. F. Chavez	With Ability, 4, 117	Dancethruthedawn, 4, 119	6	1:49.64	204,228
2001	**Saudi Poetry**, 4, 114	V. Espinoza	Secret Status, 4, 119	Asher, 4, 112	8	1:49.27	206,460
2000	**Heritage of Gold**, 5, 121	S. J. Sellers	Silverbulletday, 4, 119	Roza Robata, 5, 115	5	**1:48.26**	201,252
1999	**Banshee Breeze**, 4, 124	R. Albarado	Silent Eskimo, 4, 114	Meadow Vista, 4, 109	4	1:50.02	197,718
1998	**Escena**, 5, 123	S. J. Sellers	One Rich Lady, 4, 113	Tomisue's Delight, 4, 118	5	1:50.19	199,020
1997	**Gold n Delicious**, 4, 113	C. H. Borel	Effectiveness, 4, 111	Everhope, 4, 111	10	1:52.87	104,718
1996	**Serena's Song**, 4, 124	G. L. Stevens	Halo America, 6, 117	Alcovy, 6, 117	9	1:50.30	109,493
1995	**Fit to Lead**, 5, 117	S. J. Sellers	Pennyhill Park, 5, 118	Low Key Affair, 4, 112	7	1:51.59	107,055
1994	**Trishyde**, 5, 117	C. J. McCarron	Eskimo's Angel, 5, 115	Ma Guerre, 4, 109	8	1:51.34	107,315
1993	**Quilma (Chi)**, 6, 117	R. P. Romero	Fappies Cosy Miss, 5, 110	Hitch, 4, 112	6	1:50.80	71,240
1992	**Bungalow**, 5, 114	F. C. Torres	Til Forbid, 4, 113	Beth Believes, 6, 112	12	1:50.87	74,815
1991	**Maskra's Lady**, 4, 111	J. M. Johnson	Fit for a Queen, 5, 116	Under Oath, 5, 113	10	1:50.46	73,515
1990	**A Penny Is a Penny**, 5, 120	A. T. Gryder	Stoneleigh's Hope, 5, 115	Lady Hoolihan, 4, 112	7	1:51.20	70,980
1989	**Stoneleigh's Hope**, 4, 112	J. Deegan	Way It Should Be, 5, 111	Lt. Lao, 5, 116	8	1:52.60	71,435
1988	**Lt. Lao**, 4, 116	D. Brumfield	Lawyer Talk, 4, 111	She's a Mystery, 5, 111	9	1:49.60	72,215
1987	**Infinidad (Chi)**, 5, 118	M. Solomone	Marianna's Girl, 4, 117	Queen Alexandra, 5, 126	8	1:50.60	64,815
1986	**Queen Alexandra**, 4, 117	D. Brumfield	Tide, 4, 111	Zenobia Empress, 5, 119	11	1:49.20	66,083
1985	**Straight Edition**, 5, 113	C. R. Woods Jr.	Dusty Gloves, 4, 110	Del Dun Gee, 5, 110	8	1:50.80	36,108
1984	**Heatherten**, 5, 124	S. Maple	Satiety, 5, 110	Hotsy Totsy, 4, 112	5	1:51.40	35,233
1983	**Try Something New**, 4, 121	P. Day	Naskra Magic, 4, 116	Header Card, 4, 114	5	1:51.60	35,328
1982	**Classic Ambition**, 4, 112	W. Gavidia	Beyond Reproof, 4, 113	Mean Martha, 4, 117	10	1:44.80	36,855
1981	**Forever Cordial**, 4, 114	D. Haire	Salud, 4, 114	Passolyn, 4, 118	10	1:45.40	23,205
1980	**Likely Exchange**, 6, 121	M. S. Sellers	Salzburg, 5, 116	Smooth Bore, 4, 115	9	1:45.00	23,026
1979	**Table the Rumor**, 5, 118	D. E. Whited	Likely Exchange, 5, 123	Pretty Delight, 4, 116	8	1:45.20	22,864
1978	**Likely Exchange**, 4, 113	J. McKnight	Time for Pleasure, 4, 123	Bold Rendezvous, 3, 114	5	1:45.40	13,894
1977	**Go On Dreaming**, 5, 115	P. Nicolo	B. J. King, 5, 114	Kittyluck, 4, 117	9	1:43.80	14,381
1976	**Pago Hop**, 4, 116	H. Arroyo	Flama Ardiente, 4, 122	Precious Proof, 5, 113	6	1:38.40	14,056
1975	**Bundler**, 4, 120	J. Nichols	Jay Bar Pet, 4, 112	Tappahannock, 4, 116	7	1:39.40	14,511

Named for the fleur de lis ("lily" in French), symbol of the city of Louisville. Grade 3 1998-2001. 1 mile 1975-'76. 1¹⁄₁₆ miles 1977-'82. Four-year-olds and up 1983-'85, 1987-'89.

Floral Park Handicap

Grade 3 in 2006. Belmont Park, three-year-olds and up, fillies and mares, 6 furlongs, dirt. Held September 17, 2005, with a gross value of $109,100. First held in 1995. First graded in 2002. Stakes record 1:09.20 (1995 Twist Afleet).

Year	Winner	Jockey	Second	Third	Strs	Time	1st Purse
2005	**Smokey Glacken**, 4, 114	J. R. Velazquez	Areek, 4, 116	Baldomera, 4, 113	6	1:10.26	$65,460
2004	**Feline Story**, 3, 114	E. S. Prado	Cologny, 4, 115	Travelator, 4, 116	5	1:10.69	63,840
2003	**Bauhauser (Arg)**, 5, 115	R. Migliore	Shine Again, 6, 120	Literary Light, 4, 113	6	1:10.84	65,100
2002	**Carson Hollow**, 3, 117	J. R. Velazquez	Gold Mover, 4, 117	Shiny Band, 4, 115	4	1:10.25	63,955
2001	**Gold Mover**, 3, 114	E. S. Prado	Dat You Miz Blue, 4, 119	Finder's Fee, 4, 115	6	1:10.03	65,040
2000	**Big Bambu**, 3, 114	R. G. Davis	Tropical Punch, 4, 114	Cash Run, 3, 114	5	1:09.81	64,620
1999	**Positive Gal**, 3, 113	J. D. Bailey	Final Proposal, 3, 113	Flamingo Way, 5, 113	7	1:09.23	49,125
1998	**Blue Begonia**, 5, 114	J. F. Chavez	Dixie Flag, 4, 117	Soverign Lady, 4, 116	5	1:10.30	48,570
1997	**Creamy Dreamy**, 4, 118	R. G. Davis	Silent City, 3, 113	Secret Prospect, 4, 118	5	1:10.56	47,835
1996	**Lottsa Talc**, 6, 119	F. T. Alvarado	Fresa, 4, 113	Culver City, 4, 113	5	1:09.81	38,736
1995	**Twist Afleet**, 4, 120	G. L. Stevens	For all Seasons, 5, 115	Regal Solution, 5, 113	6	**1:09.20**	32,490

Named for Floral Park, a community in Nassau County, New York, near Belmont Park.

Florida Derby

Grade 1 in 2006. Gulfstream Park, three-year-olds, 1⅛ miles, dirt. Held April 1, 2006, with a gross value of $1,000,000. First held in 1952. First graded in 1973. Stakes record 1:46.80 (1957 Gen. Duke).

Year	Winner	Jockey	Second	Third	Strs	Time	1st Purse
2006	**Barbaro**, 3, 122	E. S. Prado	Sharp Humor, 3, 122	Sunriver, 3, 122	11	1:49.01	$600,000
2005	**High Fly**, 3, 122	J. D. Bailey	Noble Causeway, 3, 122	B. B. Best, 3, 122	9	1:49.43	600,000
2004	**Friends Lake**, 3, 122	R. Migliore	Value Plus, 3, 122	The Cliff's Edge, 3, 122	10	1:51.38	600,000
2003	**Empire Maker**, 3, 122	J. D. Bailey	Trust N Luck, 3, 122	Indy Dancer, 3, 122	7	1:49.05	600,000
2002	**Harlan's Holiday**, 3, 122	E. S. Prado	Blue Burner, 3, 122	Peekskill, 3, 122	11	1:48.80	600,000
2001	**Monarchos**, 3, 122	J. F. Chavez	Outofthebox, 3, 122	Invisible Ink, 3, 122	13	1:49.95	600,000
2000	**Hal's Hope**, 3, 122	R. I. Velez	High Yield, 3, 122	Tahkodha Hills, 3, 122	10	1:51.49	450,000
1999	**Vicar**, 3, 122	S. J. Sellers	Wondertross, 3, 122	Cat Thief, 3, 122	10	1:50.83	450,000
1998	**‡Cape Town**, 3, 122	S. J. Sellers	Lil's Lad, 3, 122	Halory Hunter, 3, 122	6	1:49.21	450,000
1997	**Captain Bodgit**, 3, 122	A. O. Solis	Pulpit, 3, 122	Frisk Me Now, 3, 122	8	1:50.60	300,000
1996	**Unbridled's Song**, 3, 122	M. E. Smith	Editor's Note, 3, 122	Skip Away, 3, 122	9	1:47.85	300,000
1995	**Thunder Gulch**, 3, 122	M. E. Smith	Suave Prospect, 3, 122	Mecke, 3, 122	10	1:49.70	300,000

1994	**Holy Bull**, 3, 122	M. E. Smith	Ride the Rails, 3, 122	Halo's Image, 3, 122	14	1:47.66	$300,000
1993	**Bull Inthe Heather**, 3, 122	W. S. Ramos	Storm Tower, 3, 122	Wallenda, 3, 122	13	1:51.38	300,000
1992	**Technology**, 3, 122	J. D. Bailey	Dance Floor, 3, 122	Pistols and Roses, 3, 122	12	1:50.72	300,000
1991	**Fly So Free**, 3, 122	J. A. Santos	Strike the Gold, 3, 118	Hansel, 3, 122	8	1:50.44	300,000
1990	**Unbridled**, 3, 122	P. Day	Slavic, 3, 122	Run Turn, 3, 122	9	1:52.00	300,000
1989	**Mercedes Won**, 3, 122	E. Fires	Western Playboy, 3, 118	Big Stanley, 3, 122	11	1:49.60	300,000
1988	**Brian's Time**, 3, 118	R. P. Romero	Forty Niner, 3, 122	Notebook, 3, 122	10	1:49.80	300,000
1987	**Cryptoclearance**, 3, 122	J. A. Santos	No More Flowers, 3, 118	Talinum, 3, 122	9	1:49.60	300,000
1986	**Snow Chief**, 3, 122	A. O. Solis	Badger Land, 3, 122	Mogambo, 3, 122	16	1:51.80	300,000
1985	**Proud Truth**, 3, 122	J. Velasquez	Irish Sur, 3, 122	Do It Again Dan, 3, 122	11	1:50.00	180,000
1984	**Swale**, 3, 122	L. A. Pincay Jr.	Dr. Carter, 3, 122	Darn That Alarm, 3, 122	9	1:47.60	180,000
1983	**Croeso**, 3, 118	F. Olivares	Copelan, 3, 122	Law Talk, 3, 118	13	1:49.80	150,000
1982	**Timely Writer**, 3, 122	J. Fell	Star Gallant, 3, 122	Our Escapade, 3, 122	7	1:49.60	150,000
1981	**Lord Avie**, 3, 122	C. J. McCarron	Akureyri, 3, 122	Linnleur, 3, 118	11	1:50.40	147,388
1980	**Plugged Nickle**, 3, 122	B. Thornburg	Naked Sky, 3, 122	Lord Gallant, 3, 118	8	1:50.20	110,000
1979	**Spectacular Bid**, 3, 122	R. J. Franklin	Lot o' Gold, 3, 122	Fantasy 'n Reality, 3, 122	7	1:48.80	115,000
1978	**Alydar**, 3, 122	J. Velasquez	Believe It, 3, 122	Dr. Valeri, 3, 122	7	1:47.00	100,000
1977	**Coined Silver**, 3, 118	B. Thornburg	Nearly On Time, 3, 122	Fort Prevel, 3, 122	8	1:48.80	68,700
	Ruthie's Native, 3, 122	C. Perret	For The Moment, 3, 122	Sir Sir, 3, 122	10	1:50.20	69,900
1976	**Honest Pleasure**, 3, 122	B. Baeza	Great Contractor, 3, 122	Proud Birdie, 3, 122	6	1:47.80	91,440
1975	**Prince Thou Art**, 3, 118	B. Baeza	Sylvan Place, 3, 118	Foolish Pleasure, 3, 122	9	1:50.40	94,440
1974	**Judger**, 3, 118	L. A. Pincay Jr.	Cannonade, 3, 122	Buck's Bid, 3, 118	16	1:49.00	130,200
1973	**Royal and Regal**, 3, 122	W. Blum	Forego, 3, 118	Restless Jet, 3, 122	8	1:47.40	78,120

Honoring Gulfstream Park's home state, the race name first was used at Tampa in 1926. After a two-year hiatus, the race was run at Hialeah Park. In 1937, Hialeah's leading three-year-old race was renamed the Flamingo S. ‡Lil's Lad finished first, DQ to second, 1998. Two divisions 1977.

Flower Bowl Invitational Stakes

Grade 1 in 2006. Belmont Park, three-year-olds and up, fillies and mares, 1¼ miles, turf. Held October 1, 2005, with a gross value of $750,000. First held in 1978. First graded in 1980. Stakes record 2:00.27 (2005 Riskaverse).

Year	Winner	Jockey	Second	Third	Strs	Time	1st Purse
2005	**Riskaverse**, 6, 121	J. A. Santos	Wonder Again, 6, 121	Film Maker, 5, 119	9	**2:00.27**	$450,000
2004	**Riskaverse**, 5, 118	C. H. Velasquez	Commercante (Fr), 4, 118	Moscow Burning, 4, 120	8	2:04.65	450,000
2003	**Dimitrova**, 3, 114	J. D. Bailey	Walzerkoenigin, 4, 120	Heat Haze (GB), 4, 123	7	2:02.74	450,000
2002	**Kazzia (Ger)**, 3, 118	J. F. Chavez	Turtle Bow (Fr), 3, 115	Mot Juste (GB), 4, 118	7	2:05.22	450,000
2001	**Lailani (GB)**, 3, 118	J. D. Bailey	England's Legend (Fr), 4, 123	Starine (Fr), 4, 120	6	2:01.88	450,000
2000	**Colstar**, 4, 116	J. Samyn	Snow Polina, 5, 121	Pico Teneriffe, 4, 115	5	2:01.78	450,000
1999	**Soaring Softly**, 4, 118	J. D. Bailey	Coretta (Ire), 5, 118	Mossflower, 5, 115	7	2:01.41	300,000
1998	**Auntie Mame**, 4, 121	J. R. Velazquez	B. A. Valentine, 5, 114	Bahr (GB), 3, 118	5	1:59.33	240,000
1997	**Yashmak**, 3, 114	C. S. Nakatani	Maxzene, 4, 123	Memories of Silver, 4, 123	8	1:59.73	240,000
1996	**Chelsey Flower**, 5, 115	R. G. Davis	Powder Bowl, 4, 116	Electric Society (Ire), 5, 118	10	2:05.96	210,000
1995	**Northern Emerald**, 5, 113	R. B. Perez	Danish (Ire), 4, 116	Duda, 4, 113	10	2:06.68	120,000
1994	**Dahlia's Dreamer**, 5, 112	J. F. Chavez	Alywow, 3, 114	Danish (Ire), 3, 113	12	2:05.52	120,000
1993	**Far Out Beast**, 6, 111	J. Samyn	Dahlia's Dreamer, 4, 110	Lady Blessington (Fr), 5, 118	10	2:03.88	90,000
1992	**Christiecat**, 5, 116	J. Samyn	Ratings, 4, 114	Plenty of Grace, 5, 115	9	2:01.06	120,000
1991	**Lady Shirl**, 4, 117	R. Migliore	Franc Argument, 5, 111	Christiecat, 4, 120	12	2:02.43	120,000
1990	**Laugh and Be Merry**, 5, 115	W. H. McCauley	Foresta, 4, 115	Gaily Gaily (Ire), 7, 117	13	2:00.20	78,840
1989	**River Memories**, 5, 112	P. Day	Capades, 3, 116	Miss Unnameable, 5, 116	11	2:06.80	74,880
1988	**Gaily Gaily (Ire)**, 5, 109	J. A. Krone	Love You by Heart, 3, 113	Princely Proof, 5, 116	12	2:02.80	76,800
1987	**Slew's Exceller**, 5, 113	J. A. Santos	Videogenic, 5, 118	Fiesta Gal, 3, 114	8	2:02.20	91,020
1986	**dh-Dismasted**, 4, 115	J. Samyn		Cope of Flowers, 4, 112	12	2:00.00	52,152
	dh-Scoot, 3, 106	W. Shoemaker					
1985	**Dawn's Curtsey**, 3, 111	E. Maple	Vers La Caisse, 4, 116	Agacerie, 4, 117	9	2:02.20	87,540
1984	**Rossard (Den)**, 4, 117	L. A. Pincay Jr.	Aspen Rose, 4, 115	Persian Tiara (Ire), 4, 116	9	2:03.40	72,840
1983	**First Approach**, 5, 117	J. Velasquez	If Winter Comes, 5, 113	Mintage (Fr), 4, 111	8	2:00.20	68,160
1982	**Trevita (Ire)**, 5, 117	R. Hernandez	Hunston (GB), 4, 108	Hush Dear, 4, 112	12	2:01.40	71,880
1981	**Rokeby Rose**, 4, 114	J. Fell	De La Rose, 3, 116	Euphrosyne, 5, 110	6	2:01.60	67,200
1980	**Just a Game (Ire)**, 4, 124	D. Brumfield	Hey Babe, 4, 114	Euphrosyne, 4, 112	11	2:00.80	68,640
1979	**Pearl Necklace**, 5, 125	W. Shoemaker	The Very One, 4, 112	Terpsichorist, 4, 118	8	2:02.20	68,160
1978	**Waya (Fr)**, 4, 120	A. T. Cordero Jr.	Magnificence, 4, 108	Leave Me Alone, 5, 108	7	2:00.60	32,490

Named for Brookmeade Stable's 1956 Ladies H. winner Flower Bowl (1952 f. by *Alibhai), dam of champion Bowl of Flowers and leading sires Graustark and His Majesty. Grade 2 1980-'81. Flower Bowl H. 1978-'93. Flower Bowl Invitational H. 1994-2000. Dirt 1987. Dead heat for first 1986.

Forego Stakes

Grade 1 in 2006. Saratoga Race Course, three-year-olds and up, 7 furlongs, dirt. Held September 3, 2005, with a gross value of $250,000. First held in 1980. First graded in 1983. Stakes record 1:21 (1988 Quick Call).

Year	Winner	Jockey	Second	Third	Strs	Time	1st Purse
2005	**Mass Media**, 4, 117	J. Castellano	Battle Won, 5, 121	Silver Wagon, 4, 117	6	1:22.59	$150,000
2004	**Midas Eyes**, 4, 117	E. S. Prado	Clock Stopper, 4, 114	Gygistar, 5, 114	9	1:22.22	150,000

2003	**Aldebaran**, 5, 123	J. D. Bailey	Najran, 4, 114	Gygistar, 4, 119	7	1:21.26	$150,000
2002	**Orientate**, 4, 122	J. D. Bailey	Aldebaran, 4, 115	Multiple Choice, 4, 114	8	1:15.68	150,000
2001	**Delaware Township**, 5, 116	J. D. Bailey	Left Bank, 4, 115	Alannan, 5, 117	9	1:15.53	150,000
2000	**Shadow Caster**, 4, 113	J. F. Chavez	Intidab, 7, 118	Successful Appeal, 4, 119	10	1:15.00	150,000
1999	**Crafty Friend**, 6, 119	G. L. Stevens	Affirmed Success, 5, 119	Sir Bear, 6, 119	9	1:21.32	150,000
1998	**Affirmed Success**, 4, 115	J. F. Chavez	Receiver, 5, 114	Purple Passion, 4, 114	4	1:21.98	120,000
1997	**Score a Birdie**, 6, 113	W. H. McCauley	Victor Cooley, 4, 120	Royal Haven, 5, 120	8	1:22.47	120,000
1996	**Langfuhr**, 4, 110	J. F. Chavez	Top Account, 4, 115	Lite the Fuse, 5, 121	7	1:21.90	90,000
1995	**Not Surprising**, 5, 121	R. G. Davis	Our Emblem, 4, 113	Lite the Fuse, 4, 123	4	1:21.91	64,200
1994	**American Chance**, 5, 113	P. Day	Evil Bear, 4, 114	Go for Gin, 3, 117	7	1:22.74	66,000
1993	**Birdonthewire**, 4, 117	M. E. Smith	Harlan, 4, 110	Senor Speedy, 6, 117	9	1:21.88	73,080
1992	**Rubiano**, 5, 124	J. A. Krone	Drummond Lane, 5, 115	Diablo, 5, 114	8	1:22.54	70,080
1991	**Housebuster**, 4, 126	C. Perret	Senor Speedy, 4, 112	Clever Trevor, 5, 120	6	1:21.08	69,480
1990	**Lay Down**, 6, 113	C. W. Antley	Quick Call, 6, 120	Traskwood, 4, 112	6	1:22.80	51,840
1989	**Quick Call**, 5, 116	P. Day	Dancing Spree, 4, 117	Sewickley, 4, 119	5	1:21.80	67,920
1988	**Quick Call**, 4, 110	P. Day	Mawsuff (GB), 5, 110	High Brite, 4, 122	6	**1:21.00**	68,520
1987	**Groovy**, 4, 132	A. T. Cordero Jr.	Purple Mountain, 5, 113	Sun Master, 6, 118	6	1:21.80	81,060
1986	**Groovy**, 3, 118	J. A. Santos	Turkoman, 4, 124	Innamorato, 5, 110	8	1:21.20	83,820
1985	**Ziggy's Boy**, 3, 115	A. T. Cordero Jr.	Taylor's Special, 4, 124	Knight of Armor, 5, 112	5	1:21.20	66,510
1984	**Mugatea**, 4, 111	R. G. Davis	Eskimo, 4, 108	I Enclose, 4, 111	6	1:22.40	53,370
1983	**Maudlin**, 5, 119	A. T. Cordero Jr.	Danebo, 4, 115	Singh Tu, 4, 113	5	1:21.60	32,580
1982	**Engine One**, 4, 112	R. Hernandez	Rise Jim, 6, 121	Pass the Tab, 4, 120	5	1:21.20	33,360
1981	**Fappiano**, 4, 119	A. T. Cordero Jr.	Herb Water, 4, 108	Guilty Conscience, 5, 112	5	1:33.80	50,220
1980	**Tanthem**, 5, 114	J. Velasquez	Dr. Patches, 6, 114	Hold Your Tricks, 5, 116	7	1:35.00	51,030

Named for Mrs. Martha Gerry's 1974, '75, '76 Horse of the Year and '74, '75, '76, '77 Woodward H. (G1) winner Forego (1970 g. by *Forli). Grade 3 1983. Grade 2 1984-2000. Forego H. 1980-2004. Held at Belmont Park 1980-'81. 1 mile 1980-'81. 6 furlongs 2000-'02.

Fort Marcy Handicap

Grade 3 in 2006. Aqueduct, three-year-olds and up, 1 1/16 miles, turf. Held April 22, 2006, with a gross value of $109,000. First held in 1975. First graded in 1980. Stakes record 1:40.88 (2000 Spindrift [Ire]).

Year	Winner	Jockey	Second	Third	Strs	Time	1st Purse
2006	**Foreverness**, 7, 115	E. Coa	Pa Pa Da, 5, 114	Sabre d'Argent, 6, 115	6	1:42.99	$65,400
2005	**Better Talk Now**, 6, 123	R. A. Dominguez	Remind, 5, 117	Ecclesiastic, 4, 115	5	1:42.74	65,640
2004	**Chilly Rooster**, 4, 113	S. Uske	Union Place, 5, 113	Slew Valley, 7, 119	8	1:42.47	66,840
2003	**Saint Verre**, 5, 117	J. L. Espinoza	Windsor Castle, 5, 119	Judge's Case, 6, 115	8	1:33.77	70,500
2002	**Pyrus**, 4, 113	E. S. Prado	Proud Man, 4, 116	Capsized, 6, 113	8	1:44.53	67,260
2001	**Strategic Mission**, 6, 118	R. Migliore	Pine Dance, 4, 116	Legal Jousting (Ire), 4, 114	9	1:41.62	67,740
2000	**Spindrift (Ire)**, 5, 115	J. Samyn	Middlesex Drive, 5, 118	Wised Up, 5, 114	9	**1:40.88**	67,680
1999	**Wised Up**, 4, 112	M. J. Luzzi	N B Forrest, 7, 116	La-Faah (Ire), 4, 114	11	1:45.03	69,660
1998	**Subordination**, 4, 118	J. F. Chavez	Fortitude, 5, 116	Crimson Guard, 6, 110	6	1:35.24	67,620
1997	**Influent**, 6, 117	J. Samyn	Slicious (GB), 5, 115	Montjoy, 5, 117	8	1:47.59	67,140
1996	**Warning Glance**, 5, 119	M. E. Smith	Shahid (GB), 4, 115	Grand Continental, 5, 113	10	1:42.48	51,450
1995	**Fourstars Allstar**, 7, 118	J. A. Santos	Chief Master, 5, 112	A in Sociology, 5, 118	8	1:41.69	50,250
1994	**Adam Smith (GB)**, 6, 118	M. E. Smith	Halissee, 4, 113	Nijinsky's Gold, 5, 113	7	1:42.49	49,650
1993	**Adam Smith (GB)**, 5, 112	J. Samyn	Kiri's Clown, 4, 114	Casino Magistrate, 4, 113	11	1:42.30	55,260
1992	**Maxigroom**, 4, 111	J. A. Krone	Colchis Island (Ire), 7, 111	Buchman, 5, 111	6	1:42.66	53,460
1991	**Stage Colony**, 4, 115	C. Perret	Chenin Blanc, 5, 114	Scottish Monk, 8, 116	9	1:42.38	54,630
1990	**Crystal Moment**, 5, 113	S. N. Chavez	Impersonator, 5, 112	Wanderkin, 7, 117	7	1:43.40	53,010
1989	**Arlene's Valentine**, 4, 112	J. A. Krone	Fourstardave, 4, 113	Sunshine Forever, 4, 126	5	1:50.20	52,920
1988	**Equalize**, 6, 115	J. A. Santos	All Hands On Deck, 6, 109	Glaros (Fr), 6, 111	12	1:42.60	89,340
1987	**Dance of Life**, 4, 120	R. P. Romero	Regal Flier, 6, 113	Iroko (GB), 5, 113	7	1:45.00	84,240
	Glaros (Fr), 5, 112	E. Maple	Onyxly, 6, 113	Explosive Dancer, 5, 111	8	1:45.00	85,200
1986	**Onyxly**, 5, 117	J. A. Santos	Equalize, 4, 114	Lieutenant's Lark, 4, 117	9	1:42.20	55,890
1985	**Forzando (GB)**, 4, 120	J. Velasquez	Native Raid, 5, 115	Solidified, 4, 113	7	1:46.00	54,180
1984	**Hero's Honor**, 4, 115	J. D. Bailey	Super Sunrise (GB), 5, 126	Reinvested, 5, 113	9	1:43.60	54,270
1983	**John's Gold**, 4, 108	A. Graell	Acaroid, 5, 115	Beagle (Arg), 5, 105	8	1:47.40	36,600
1982	**Folge**, 4, 110	J. Velasquez	Johnny Dance, 4, 114	St. Brendan, 4, 116	12	1:42.80	36,060
1981	**Masked Marvel (Ire)**, 5, 112	R. I. Encinas	Blue Ensign, 4, 116	Freeo, 4, 113	8	1:44.80	33,300
	Key to Content, 4, 117	J. Fell	Ghazwan (Ire), 4, 114	Contare, 5, 107	7	1:46.00	33,060
1980	**Sten**, 5, 115	C. B. Asmussen	Native Courier, 5, 126	Told, 4, 113	10	1:44.00	35,460
1979	**Uncle Pokey (GB)**, 5, 113	J. Cruguet	Alias Smith, 6, 114	Proud Arion, 5, 111	7	1:45.60	32,550
1978	**True Colors**, 4, 114	E. Maple	Proud Arion, 4, 112	Cinteelo, 5, 119	5	1:42.80	25,410
	Tiller, 4, 112	J. Fell	Noble Dancer (GB), 6, 127	Arachnoid, 5, 111	5	1:41.80	25,410
1976	**Bold Sunrise**, 3, 109	R. W. Cox	Lean To, 3, 113	Scrutiny, 3, 112	10	1:37.60	19,500
1975	***Apollo Nine**, 8, 110	M. Venezia	Silver Badge, 4, 112	Bold Play, 5, 112	11	1:23.00	24,630
	Beau Bugle, 5, 113	J. Cruguet	Ribot Grande, 5, 112	New Alibhai, 7, 112	10	1:22.40	24,510

Named for Rokeby Stable's 1970 Horse of the Year and '70 Man o' War S. winner Fort Marcy (1964 g. by *Amerigo). Held at Belmont Park 1975, 1981, 1987-'88. Not held 1977. 7 furlongs 1975. 1 mile 1998, 2003. Dirt 1998, 2003. Originally scheduled on turf 2003. Two divisions 1975, 1978, 1981, 1987. Nonwinners of a stakes 1975.

Fountain of Youth Stakes

Grade 2 in 2006. Gulfstream Park, three-year-olds, $1\frac{1}{8}$ miles, dirt. Held March 4, 2006, with a gross value of $300,000. First held in 1945. First graded in 1973. Stakes record 1:49 (2006 Corinthian [DQ to third]).

Year	Winner	Jockey	Second	Third	Strs	Time	1st Purse
2006	**‡First Samurai**, 3, 120	E. S. Prado	Flashy Bull, 3, 116	Corinthian, 3, 116	10	**1:49.00**	$180,000
2005	**High Fly**, 3, 120	J. D. Bailey	Bandini, 3, 116	B. B. Best, 3, 120	9	1:49.70	180,000
2004	**Read the Footnotes**, 3, 122	J. D. Bailey	Second of June, 3, 120	Silver Wagon, 3, 120	8	1:42.71	150,000
2003	**Trust N Luck**, 3, 122	C. H. Velasquez	Supah Blitz, 3, 120	Midway Cat, 3, 116	8	1:43.33	120,000
2002	**Booklet**, 3, 122	J. F. Chavez	Harlan's Holiday, 3, 122	Blue Burner, 3, 116	8	1:44.49	120,000
2001	**Songandaprayer**, 3, 117	E. S. Prado	Outofthebox, 3, 114	City Zip, 3, 117	11	1:43.48	120,000
2000	**High Yield**, 3, 117	P. Day	Hal's Hope, 3, 117	Elite Mercedes, 3, 117	11	1:42.56	120,000
1999	**Vicar**, 3, 114	S. J. Sellers	Cat Thief, 3, 119	Certain, 3, 117	10	1:45.64	120,000
1998	**Lil's Lad**, 3, 112	J. D. Bailey	Coronado's Quest, 3, 119	Halory Hunter, 3, 112	4	1:42.63	120,000
1997	**Pulpit**, 3, 112	S. J. Sellers	Blazing Sword, 3, 117	Captain Bodgit, 3, 117	9	1:41.86	120,000
1996	**Built for Pleasure**, 3, 112	G. Boulanger	Unbridled's Song, 3, 119	Victory Speech, 3, 114	9	1:43.64	120,000
1995	**Thunder Gulch**, 3, 119	M. E. Smith	Suave Prospect, 3, 117	Jambalaya Jazz, 3, 119	12	1:43.21	120,000
1994	**Dehere**, 3, 119	C. Perret	Go for Gin, 3, 119	Ride the Rails, 3, 117	6	1:44.70	120,000
1993	**Duc d'Sligovil**, 3, 112	J. A. Krone	Bull Inthe Heather, 3, 113	Silver of Silver, 3, 122	9	1:45.16	113,094
	Storm Tower, 3, 113	R. Wilson	Great Navigator, 3, 117	Kissin Kris, 3, 117	9	1:44.98	113,094
1992	**Dance Floor**, 3, 122	C. W. Antley	‡Pistols and Roses, 3, 119	Tiger Tiger, 3, 112	11	1:45.32	150,258
1991	**Fly So Free**, 3, 122	J. A. Santos	Moment of True, 3, 117	Subordinated Debt, 3, 113	10	1:44.30	73,737
1990	**Shot Gun Scott**, 3, 122	D. Penna	Smelly, 3, 119	Unbridled, 3, 117	13	1:44.60	77,427
1989	**Dixieland Brass**, 3, 122	R. P. Romero	Mercedes Won, 3, 122	Triple Buck, 3, 112	13	1:44.60	78,000
1988	**Forty Niner**, 3, 122	E. Maple	Notebook, 3, 122	Buoy, 3, 119	9	1:43.20	98,991
1987	**Bet Twice**, 3, 122	C. Perret	No More Flowers, 3, 112	Gone West, 3, 114	9	1:43.40	100,482
1986	**Ensign Rhythm**, 3, 112	J. M. Pezua	Jig's Haven, 3, 113	Regal Dreamer, 3, 117	10	1:45.60	57,210
	My Prince Charming, 3, 112	J. A. Santos	Mykawa, 3, 117	Papal Power, 3, 122	10	1:45.00	78,060
1985	**Proud Truth**, 3, 112	J. Velasquez	Stephan's Odyssey, 3, 122	Do It Again Dan, 3, 112	14	1:43.60	106,860
1984	**Darn That Alarm**, 3, 112	M. Venezia	Counterfeit Money, 3, 112	Swale, 3, 122	8	1:43.00	73,200
1983	**Highland Park**, 3, 122	D. Brumfield	Thalassocrat, 3, 117	Chumming, 3, 114	9	1:44.60	45,338
	Copelan, 3, 122	L. A. Pincay Jr.	Current Hope, 3, 117	Blink, 3, 112	8	1:43.60	44,888
1982	**Star Gallant**, 3, 117	S. Hawley	Distinctive Pro, 3, 117	Cut Away, 3, 113	9	1:43.20	54,630
1981	**Akureyri**, 3, 119	E. Maple	Pleasant Colony, 3, 122	Lord Avie, 3, 122	9	1:44.40	47,697
1980	**Naked Sky**, 3, 112	J. D. Bailey	Joanie's Chief, 3, 122	Gold Stage, 3, 122	8	1:43.80	29,820
1979	**Spectacular Bid**, 3, 122	R. J. Franklin	Lot o' Gold, 3, 117	Bishop's Choice, 3, 122	6	1:41.20	35,880
1978	**Sensitive Prince**, 3, 114	M. Solomone	Believe It, 3, 122	Kissing U., 3, 113	11	1:41.00	22,170
1977	**Ruthie's Native**, 3, 122	C. Perret	‡Steve's Friend, 3, 112	Fort Prevel, 3, 117	15	1:42.00	26,010
1976	**Sonkisser**, 3, 117	B. Baeza	Proud Birdie, 3, 122	Archie Beamish, 3, 113	7	1:43.80	22,770
1975	**Greek Answer**, 3, 122	M. Solomone	Decipher, 3, 115	Gatch, 3, 116	8	1:42.80	22,650
1974	**Green Gambados**, 3, 112	C. Baltazar	Judger, 3, 115	Eric's Champ, 3, 112	15	1:42.40	46,440
1973	**Shecky Greene**, 3, 122	B. Baeza	Twice a Prince, 3, 117	My Gallant, 3, 112	6	1:43.80	22,590

Named for the spring that granted eternal youth, sought by Spanish explorer Ponce de Leon in Florida. Grade 3 1973-'81. Grade 1 1999-2003. Fountain of Youth H. 1947-'56, 1958. Not held 1946, 1948, 1952. 1 mile 70 yards 1945, 1947. 6 furlongs 1947. $1\frac{1}{16}$ miles 1949-'51, 1953-2004. Two-year-olds 1945-'47. Two divisions 1983, 1986, 1993. Held in March and December 1947. ‡Fort Prevel finished second, DQ to third, 1977. ‡Careful Gesture finished second, DQ to fifth, 1992. ‡Corinthian finished first, DQ to third, 2006.

Fourstardave Handicap

Grade 2 in 2006. Saratoga Race Course, three-year-olds and up, $1\frac{1}{16}$ miles, turf. Held August 27, 2005, with a gross value of $200,000. First held in 1985. First graded in 1988. Stakes record 1:38.91 (1991 Fourstardave).

Year	Winner	Jockey	Second	Third	Strs	Time	1st Purse
2005	**Leroidesanimaux (Brz)**, 5, 122	J. R. Velazquez	Silver Tree, 5, 117	Steel Light, 4, 117	6	1:39.92	$120,000
2004	**Nothing to Lose**, 4, 117	J. R. Velazquez	Silver Tree, 4, 117	Royal Regalia, 6, 114	10	1:39.50	120,000
2003	**Trademark (SAf)**, 7, 118	R. Migliore	Quest Star, 4, 116	Tap the Admiral, 5, 115	11	1:39.29	120,000
2002	**Capsized**, 6, 115	J. A. Santos	Pure Prize, 4, 119	Pyrus, 4, 113	5	1:50.90	120,000
2001	**Dr. Kashnikow**, 4, 113	J. R. Velazquez	Tubrok, 4, 113	Aly's Alley, 5, 117	12	1:39.30	120,000
2000	**Hap**, 4, 118	J. D. Bailey	Altibr, 5, 115	Weatherbird, 5, 112	11	1:40.24	120,000
1999	**Comic Strip**, 4, 115	P. Day	Divide and Conquer, 5, 114	Bomfim, 6, 113	11	1:41.76	90,000
1998	**Wild Event**, 5, 116	M. Guidry	Bomfim, 5, 114	Rob 'n Gin, 4, 119	11	1:39.25	68,940
1997	**Soviet Line (Ire)**, 7, 118	P. Day	Val's Prince, 5, 114	Outta My Way Man, 5, 114	7	1:39.99	67,500
1996	**Da Hoss**, 4, 113	J. R. Velazquez	Green Means Go, 4, 113	Rare Reason, 5, 118	13	1:40.54	71,100
1995	**Pride of Summer**, 7, 115	E. Maple	Fourstars Allstar, 7, 120	Jaggery John, 4, 120	8	1:40.85	69,240
1994	**A in Sociology**, 4, 115	J. Samyn	Namaqualand, 4, 113	Fourstars Allstar, 6, 120	9	1:41.23	68,340
1993	**Lure**, 4, 122	M. E. Smith	Fourstardave, 8, 122	Scott the Great, 7, 115	6	1:40.84	72,120
1992	**Now Listen**, 5, 119	J. R. Velazquez	Crackedbell, 7, 119	Cold Hoist, 4, 115	5	1:36.64	71,640
1991	**Fourstardave**, 6, 115	M. E. Smith	Who's to Pay, 5, 122	Kate's Valentine, 6, 117	7	**1:38.91**	71,640
1990	**Fourstardave**, 5, 115	M. E. Smith	Foreign Survivor, 5, 119	Wanderkin, 7, 119	8	1:41.20	57,150
1989	**Steinlen (GB)**, 6, 122	A. T. Cordero Jr.	Expensive Decision, 3, 117	Sparkling Wit, 3, 110	8	1:41.00	53,955
	Highland Springs, 5, 122	E. S. Prado	Fourstardave, 4, 122	Soviet Lad, 4, 115	7	1:41.60	53,955
1988	**San's the Shadow**, 4, 115	A. T. Cordero Jr.	My Big Boy, 5, 117	Real Courage, 5, 115	10	1:40.00	56,340
1987	**Persian Mews (Ire)**, 4, 115	J. A. Santos	Island Sun, 5, 115	Explosive Dancer, 5, 115	8	1:42.00	51,120

	Duluth, 5, 117	J. Cruguet	Mourjane (Ire), 7, 115	I'm a Banker, 5, 115	8	1:41.20	$51,120
1986	**Mourjane (Ire)**, 6, 119	J. A. Santos	Island Sun, 4, 117	Little Look, 5, 115	6	1:42.80	33,960
1985	**Roving Minstrel**, 4, 119	A. T. Cordero Jr.	Four Bases, 6, 115	Alev (GB), 6, 117	8	1:45.40	33,540

Named for Richard M. Bomze's local favorite and 1990, '91 Daryl's Joy S. (G3) winner Fourstardave (1985 g. by Compliance); Fourstardave won a race at Saratoga for eight consecutive years and is one of four horses buried on the Saratoga grounds. Formerly named for R. K. C. Goh's multiple SW *Daryl's Joy (1966 c. by Stunning). Grade 3 1988-'99, 2002. Daryl's Joy S. 1985-'93, 1995. Daryl's Joy H. 1994. Fourstardave S. 1996-'97. $1\frac{1}{16}$ miles 1985-'91, 1993-2001. 1 mile 1992. Dirt 1992, 2002. Originally scheduled on turf 2002. Two divisions 1987, 1989.

Frances A. Genter Stakes

Grade 3 in 2006. Calder Race Course, three-year-olds, fillies, $7\frac{1}{2}$ furlongs, turf. Held December 31, 2005, with a gross value of $100,000. First held in 1993. First graded in 2005. Stakes record 1:27.07 (2005 Laurafina).

Year	Winner	Jockey	Second	Third	Strs	Time	1st Purse
2005	**Laurafina**, 3, 116	R. Bejarano	Champagne Ending, 3, 121	More Than Promised, 3, 121	12	**1:27.07**	$60,000
2004	**R Obsession**, 3, 121	M. R. Cruz	Our Exploit, 3, 116	Marina de Chavon, 3, 118	12	1:28.05	60,000
2003	**Changing World**, 3, 118	J. Bravo	Campsie Fells (UAE), 3, 121	Formal Miss, 3, 121	12	1:27.67	60,000
2002	**Cellars Shiraz**, 3, 121	E. Coa	Madeira Mist (Ire), 3, 118	May Gator, 3, 116	12	1:29.45	60,000
2001	**Amelia**, 3, 118	J. Castellano	Sara's Success, 3, 121	Ing Ing (Fr), 3, 118	12	1:28.56	60,000
2000	**Zeiting (Ire)**, 3, 114	R. R. Douglas	Jemima (GB), 3, 113	Golden Saint, 3, 114	11	1:30.08	45,000
1999	**Seducer**, 3, 114	J. A. Santos	Crystal Symphony, 3, 119	Talamanca, 3, 113	11	1:28.67	60,000
1998	**Justenuffheart**, 3, 119	E. Coa	Terreavigne, 3, 114	Robyns Tune, 3, 114	12	1:28.68	60,000
1997	**Oh My Butterfly**, 3, 114	A. R. Toribio	More Silver, 3, 114	Basse Besogne (Ire), 3, 115	12	1:28.40	60,000
1996	**Voy Si No**, 3, 113	E. O. Nunez	Courtlin, 3, 113	Victoria Regia (Ire), 3, 114	11	1:28.19	30,000
1995	**Majestic Dy**, 3, 114	A. Toribio	With a Princess, 3, 114	Reign Dance, 3, 113	10	1:27.90	32,550
1994	**Clean Wager**, 3, 113	A. Toribio	Sunset Gal, 3, 112	Notable Sword, 3, 114	6	1:39.92	19,710
1993	**Putthepowdertoit**, 3, 116	R. R. Douglas	Liberada, 3, 116	Tenacious Tiffany, 3, 114	12	1:28.64	20,970

Named for Frances A. Genter (1898-1992), Eclipse Award-winning Florida breeder.

Frank E. Kilroe Mile Handicap

Grade 1 in 2006. Santa Anita Park, four-year-olds and up, 1 mile, turf. Held March 4, 2006, with a gross value of $300,000. First held in 1955. First graded in 1973. Stakes record 1:31.89 (1997 Atticus).

Year	Winner	Jockey	Second	Third	Strs	Time	1st Purse
2006	**Milk It Mick (GB)**, 5, 116	K. Desormeaux	Aragorn (Ire), 4, 119	Chinese Dragon, 4, 116	13	1:34.49	$180,000
2005	**Leroidesanimaux (Brz)**, 5, 119	J. K. Court	Buckland Manor, 5, 116	Sweet Return (GB), 5, 117	9	1:33.89	180,000
2004	**Sweet Return (GB)**, 4, 119	G. L. Stevens	Singletary, 4, 117	Inesperado (Fr), 5, 116	14	1:33.87	210,000
2003	**Redattore (Brz)**, 8, 120	A. O. Solis	Good Journey, 7, 124	Decarchy, 6, 118	11	1:34.94	240,000
2002	**Decarchy**, 5, 119	K. Desormeaux	Sarafan, 5, 116	Designed for Luck, 5, 117	11	1:34.04	180,000
2001	**Road to Slew**, 6, 117	L. A. Pincay Jr.	Val Royal (Fr), 5, 117	dh-Exchange Rate, 4, 115 dh-Hawksley Hill (Ire), 8, 118	10	1:35.96	240,000
2000	**Commitisize**, 5, 112	V. Espinoza	Chullo (Arg), 6, 117	Sultry Substitute, 5, 114	6	1:36.61	120,000
1999	**Lord Smith (GB)**, 4, 116	G. K. Gomez	Hawksley Hill (Ire), 6, 122	Ladies Din, 4, 120	6	1:34.53	90,000
1998	**Hawksley Hill (Ire)**, 5, 115	P. Day	Via Lombardia (Ire), 6, 117	A Magicman (Fr), 6, 120	10	1:34.84	101,190
1997	**Atticus**, 5, 117	C. S. Nakatani	Pinfloron (Fr), 5, 115	Rainbow Blues (Ire), 4, 121	6	**1:31.89**	97,400
1996	**Tychonic (GB)**, 6, 116	G. L. Stevens	Debutant Trick, 6, 117	Silver Wizard, 6, 117	8	1:35.52	99,400
1995	**College Town**, 4, 117	L. A. Pincay Jr.	Romarin (Brz), 5, 120	Finder's Fortune, 6, 113	5	1:40.62	63,800
1994	**Megan's Interco**, 5, 118	C. A. Black	Tinners Way, 4, 115	Ibero (Arg), 7, 118	7	1:33.86	64,400
1993	**Leger Cat (Arg)**, 7, 114	C. S. Nakatani	Luthier Enchanteur, 6, 116	The Name's Jimmy, 4, 115	12	1:34.19	70,800
1992	**Fly Till Dawn**, 6, 120	L. A. Pincay Jr.	Itsallgreektome, 5, 123	Qathif, 5, 115	11	1:34.69	100,200
1991	**Madjaristan**, 5, 115	E. Delahoussaye	Trebizond, 5, 116	Major Moment, 5, 114	13	1:33.30	105,400
1990	**Prized**, 4, 124	E. Delahoussaye	Happy Toss (Arg), 5, 115	On the Menu, 4, 112	9	1:34.40	67,000
1989	**Bello Horizonte (Ire)**, 6, 116	E. Delahoussaye	Sarhoob, 4, 120	Patchy Groundfog, 6, 117	7	1:36.20	64,700
1988	**Mohamed Abdu (Ire)**, 4, 118	E. Delahoussaye	The Medic, 4, 118	The Scout, 4, 118	10	1:37.00	95,300
1987	**Thrill Show**, 4, 121	W. Shoemaker	Skywalker, 5, 123	Aventino (Ire), 4, 115	9	1:36.00	92,150
1986	**Strawberry Road (Aus)**, 7, 125	G. L. Stevens	Hail Bold King, 5, 116	Schiller, 4, 115	7	2:03.40	76,800
1985	**Fatih**, 5, 116	W. Shoemaker	Tsunami Slew, 4, 119	Swoon, 7, 113	8	1:59.60	64,300
1984	**Sir Pele**, 5, 114	R. Q. Meza	Lucence, 5, 117	Ginger Brink (Fr), 4, 117	6	2:01.20	49,850
1983	**Manantial (Chi)**, 5, 115	K. D. Black	Bohemian Grove, 7, 115	Western, 5, 120	5	2:03.40	46,500
1982	**Perrault (GB)**, 5, 124	L. A. Pincay Jr.	Silveyville, 4, 117	Le Duc de Bar, 5, 111	7	2:04.60	47,700
1981	**Premier Ministre**, 5, 117	L. A. Pincay Jr.	Galaxy Libra (Ire), 5, 119	Bold Tropic (SAf), 6, 126	7	2:02.60	38,350
1980	**Henschel**, 6, 114	W. Shoemaker	Silver Eagle (Ire), 6, 120	Balzac, 5, 112	11	1:58.80	40,900
1979	**Fluorescent Light**, 5, 121	L. A. Pincay Jr.	†Waya (Fr), 5, 123	As de Copas (Arg), 6, 118	9	2:03.60	39,650
1978	**Exceller**, 5, 126	W. Shoemaker	Soldier's Lark, 4, 113	Tacitus, 4, 115	6	2:01.20	31,750
1977	**Caucasus**, 5, 124	F. Toro	dh-Exact Duplicate, 5, 115 dh-Victorian Prince, 7, 116		9	2:00.00	33,900
1976	**Ga Hai**, 5, 115	F. Olivares	Riot in Paris, 5, 120	Copper Mel, 4, 117	10	2:00.40	34,050
1975	**Ga Hai**, 4, 114	J. Vasquez	Indefatigable, 5, 115	Gold Standard, 4, 111	8	2:07.00	32,800
1974	**Court Ruling**, 4, 114	B. Baeza	Scantling, 4, 116	Barrydown, 4, 116	8	2:01.40	32,800
1973	**River Buoy**, 8, 117	D. Pierce	Wing Out, 5, 116	*Mazus, 5, 121	9	2:02.80	20,875
	Kobuk King, 7, 116	J. Lambert	Triggairo, 4, 114	Presidial, 4, 116	8	2:02.80	20,475

Named in honor of Frank E. "Jimmy" Kilroe (1912-'96), longtime racing secretary and handicapper at Santa Anita Park. Formerly named for Arcadia, California, city in which Santa Anita Park is located. Formerly named for the El Camino Real, "the Royal Road" through the California frontier. Grade 3 1973-'83, 1990-'94, 2000. Camino Real H. 1955-'59.

Arcadia H. 1960-2000. 1¼ miles 1955-'71, 1973-'86. About 1¼ miles 1972. Dirt 1975-'76, 1978, 1983, 1995, 2000. Originally scheduled on turf 2000. Three-year-olds and up 1955-'61. Two divisions 1973. Dead heat for second 1977. Dead heat for third 2001. World record 1997. Course record 1997. †Denotes female.

Frank J. De Francis Memorial Dash Stakes

Grade 1 in 2006. Laurel Park, three-year-olds and up, 6 furlongs, dirt. Held November 19, 2005, with a gross value of $300,000. First held in 1990. First graded in 1992. Stakes record 1:07.95 (2000 Richter Scale).

Year	Winner	Jockey	Second	Third	Strs	Time	1st Purse
2005	**I'm the Tiger**, 5, 118	J. D. Bailey	Tiger Heart, 4, 118	Clever Electrician, 6, 118	14	1:09.06	$180,000
2004	**Wildcat Heir**, 4, 119	S. Elliott	Midas Eyes, 4, 123	Clock Stopper, 4, 119	10	1:09.45	180,000
2003	**A Huevo**, 7, 119	R. A. Dominguez	Shake You Down, 5, 123	Gators N Bears, 3, 115	10	1:08.90	180,000
2002	**D'wildcat**, 4, 122	J. F. Chavez	Deer Run, 5, 118	Sassy Hound, 5, 118	8	1:10.81	180,000
2001	**Delaware Township**, 5, 125	J. D. Bailey	Early Flyer, 3, 115	†Xtra Heat, 3, 117	7	1:09.00	180,000
2000	**Richter Scale**, 6, 123	R. Migliore	Just Call Me Carl, 5, 119	Falkenburg, 5, 114	4	**1:07.95**	180,000
1999	**Yes It's True**, 3, 114	J. D. Bailey	Good and Tough, 4, 123	Storm Punch, 4, 114	6	1:08.67	180,000
1998	**Kelly Kip**, 4, 121	J. Samyn	Affirmed Success, 4, 114	Partner's Hero, 4, 114	6	1:08.50	180,000
1997	**Smoke Glacken**, 3, 113	C. Perret	Wise Dusty, 6, 112	†Capote Belle, 4, 110	7	1:09.40	180,000
1996	**Lite the Fuse**, 5, 117	J. A. Krone	Meadow Monster, 5, 119	Prospect Bay, 4, 114	7	1:08.81	180,000
1995	**Lite the Fuse**, 4, 119	J. A. Krone	Crafty Dude, 6, 117	Hot Jaws, 5, 119	7	1:08.89	180,000
1994	**Cherokee Run**, 4, 114	C. Perret	Boom Towner, 6, 119	Fu Man Slew, 3, 107	11	1:08.92	180,000
1993	**Montbrook**, 3, 112	C. J. Ladner III	Lion Cavern, 4, 117	Flaming Emperor, 7, 114	9	1:08.71	180,000
1992	**Superstrike (GB)**, 3, 112	D. Sorenson	†Parisian Flight, 4, 114	King Corrie, 4, 117	12	1:09.90	180,000
1991	**Housebuster**, 4, 126	C. Perret	Clever Trevor, 5, 123	†Safely Kept, 5, 121	6	1:08.76	180,000
1990	**Northern Wolf**, 4, 120	M. J. Luzzi	Glitterman, 5, 124	Sewickley, 5, 126	7	1:09.00	210,000

Named in honor of Frank J. De Francis (1927-'89), president and chairman of Laurel Park and Pimlico Race Course. Grade 3 1992-'93. Grade 2 1994-'98. Held at Pimlico 1990, 2004. Track record 2000. †Denotes female.

Fred W. Hooper Handicap

Grade 3 in 2006. Calder Race Course, three-year-olds and up, 1⅛ miles, dirt. Held December 17, 2005, with a gross value of $100,000. First held in 1938. First graded in 1992. Stakes record 1:46.60 (1960 On-and-On).

Year	Winner	Jockey	Second	Third	Strs	Time	1st Purse
2005	**Andromeda's Hero**, 3, 114	R. Bejarano	Seek Gold, 5, 114	Whos Crying Now, 5, 117	9	1:53.46	$60,000
2004	**Pies Prospect**, 3, 114	E. S. Prado	Twilight Road, 7, 115	Hear No Evil, 4, 112	11	1:50.74	60,000
2003	**Predawn Raid**, 4, 112	J. F. Chavez	Best of the Rest, 8, 122	Deeliteful Guy, 4, 112	9	1:52.47	60,000
2002	**The Judge Sez Who**, 3, 116	C. H. Velasquez	Best of the Rest, 7, 121	Dancing Guy, 7, 112	8	1:50.53	60,000
2001	**Kiss a Native**, 4, 116	C. H. Velasquez	Hal's Hope, 4, 115	Groomstick Stock's, 5, 113	8	1:51.05	60,000
2000	**American Halo**, 4, 111	C. Hunt	General Grant, 3, 112	Sir Bear, 7, 118	8	1:51.68	60,000
1999	**Dancing Guy**, 4, 120	J. C. Ferrer	Wicapi, 7, 118	Loon, 4, 112	8	1:50.83	60,000
1998	**Wicapi**, 6, 113	J. Bravo	Smuggler's Prize, 4, 111	Best of the Rest, 3, 115	5	1:52.15	60,000
1997	**Shrike**, 4, 113	J. D. Bailey	Wicapi, 5, 112	Sir Bear, 4, 113	11	1:51.50	60,000
1996	**Cimarron Secret**, 5, 115	J. A. Velez Jr.	Laughing Dan, 3, 114	Wicapi, 4, 116	8	1:52.70	60,000
1995	**Bound by Honor**, 4, 112	J. A. Krone	Bay Street Star, 4, 113	Halo's Image, 4, 121	10	1:51.81	60,000
1994	**Halo's Image**, 3, 117	G. Boulanger	Fight for Love, 4, 114	Migrating Moon, 4, 120	7	1:51.44	60,000
	Take Me Out, 6, 115	M. E. Smith	Migrating Moon, 4, 119	Meena, 6, 114	11	1:51.80	60,000
1993	**Barkerville**, 5, 114	R. P. Romero	Pistols and Roses, 4, 114	Count the Time, 4, 114	7	1:52.47	45,000
1992	**Classic Seven**, 4, 110	C. E. Lopez Sr.	Honest Ensign, 4, 111	Le Merle Blanc, 4, 114	13	1:53.01	102,960
1990	**Public Account**, 5, 117	H. Castillo Jr.	Zalipour, 3, 114	Cefis, 5, 114	9	1:52.60	49,860
1989	**Primal**, 4, 119	J. A. Velez Jr.	Big Stanley, 3, 122	Falerno (Arg), 7, 111	10	1:51.60	66,960
1988	**Creme Fraiche**, 6, 118	W. A. Guerra	Fast Forward, 4, 114	Primal, 3, 118	7	1:51.80	65,940
	Creme Fraiche, 6, 118	A. T. Cordero Jr.	Cryptoclearance, 4, 122	All Sincerity, 6, 111	8	2:05.80	131,760
	Homebuilder, 4, 115	L. Saumell	All Sincerity, 6, 111	Silver Comet, 5, 116	8	1:53.20	93,000
1987	**Arctic Honeymoon**, 4, 114	C. Perret	Smile, 5, 122	Darn That Alarm, 6, 120	6	1:59.60	92,460
1986	**Racing Star**, 4, 115	E. Fires	Lyphard Line, 3, 114	Show Dancer, 4, 121	12	1:45.20	31,370

Named in honor of Fred W. Hooper (1989-2000), longtime Florida breeder. Formerly named for old Tropical Park, a Miami racetrack that closed in January 1972. Tropical H. 1938-'40, 1942-'58. Tropical Park H. 1941, 1959-'96. Held at Tropical Park 1938-'71. Not held 1943, 1945, 1948, 1951, 1972-'85, 1991. 1$\frac{1}{16}$ miles 1938-'41, 1946-'49, 1987. 1¼ miles 1988. Turf 1986. Three-year-olds 1944. Four-year-olds and up 1949, 1992. Held in January and December 1986. Held in March (twice) and December 1988. Held in January and December 1994. Track record 1960.

Frizette Stakes

Grade 1 in 2006. Belmont Park, two-year-olds, fillies, 1 mile, dirt. Held October 8, 2005, with a gross value of $500,000. First held in 1945. First graded in 1973. Stakes record 1:35.40 (1967 Queen of the Stage; 1978 Golferette; 1990 Meadow Star).

Year	Winner	Jockey	Second	Third	Strs	Time	1st Purse
2005	**Adieu**, 2, 120	J. R. Velazquez	Along the Sea, 2, 120	Keeneland Kat, 2, 120	9	1:38.07	$300,000
2004	**Balletto (UAE)**, 2, 120	C. S. Nakatani	Ready's Gal, 2, 120	Sis City, 2, 120	8	1:43.52	300,000
2003	**Society Selection**, 2, 120	R. Ganpath	Victory U. S. A., 2, 120	Ashado, 2, 120	8	1:43.95	300,000
2002	**Storm Flag Flying**, 2, 120	J. R. Velazquez	Santa Catarina, 2, 120	Appleby Gardens, 2, 120	7	1:44.20	300,000
2001	**You**, 2, 120	E. S. Prado	Cashier's Dream, 2, 120	Riskaverse, 2, 120	5	1:43.94	300,000
2000	**Raging Fever**, 2, 120	J. D. Bailey	Out of Sync, 2, 120	Western Justice, 2, 120	10	1:43.57	300,000
1999	**Surfside**, 2, 119	P. Day	Darling My Darling, 2, 119	March Magic, 2, 119	5	1:43.18	240,000
1998	**Confessional**, 2, 119	J. D. Bailey	Things Change, 2, 119	Pico Teneriffe, 2, 119	5	1:42.88	240,000

1997	**Silver Maiden**, 2, 119	J. D. Bailey	Diamond On the Run, 2, 119	Brac Drifter, 2, 119	6	1:42.74	$240,000
1996	**Storm Song**, 2, 119	C. Perret	Sharp Cat, 2, 119	Aldiza, 2, 119	7	1:42.47	240,000
1995	**Golden Attraction**, 2, 119	G. L. Stevens	My Flag, 2, 119	Flat Fleet Feet, 2, 119	5	1:42.95	150,000
1994	**Flanders**, 2, 119	P. Day	Change Fora Dollar, 2, 119	Pretty Discreet, 2, 119	4	1:43.94	150,000
1993	**Heavenly Prize**, 2, 119	M. E. Smith	Facts of Love, 2, 119	Footing, 2, 119	7	1:35.46	150,000
1992	**Educated Risk**, 2, 119	J. D. Bailey	Standard Equipment, 2, 119	Beal Street Blues, 2, 119	8	1:36.62	150,000
1991	**Preach**, 2, 119	J. A. Krone	Vivano, 2, 119	Anh Duong, 2, 119	12	1:37.20	150,000
1990	**Meadow Star**, 2, 119	J. A. Santos	Champagne Glow, 2, 119	Flawlessly, 2, 119	5	**1:35.40**	171,000
1989	**Stella Madrid**, 2, 119	A. T. Cordero Jr.	Go for Wand, 2, 119	Dance Colony, 2, 119	7	1:38.80	176,700
1988	**Some Romance**, 2, 119	L. A. Pincay Jr.	Open Mind, 2, 119	Ms. Gold Pole, 2, 119	7	1:36.80	209,520
1987	**Classic Crown**, 2, 119	A. T. Cordero Jr.	Tap Your Toes, 2, 119	Justsayno, 2, 119	9	1:37.20	215,640
1986	**Personal Ensign**, 2, 119	R. P. Romero	Collins, 2, 119	Flying Katuna, 2, 119	3	1:36.40	161,400
1985	**Family Style**, 2, 119	L. A. Pincay Jr.	Funistrada, 2, 119	Guadery, 2, 119	7	1:37.20	133,200
1984	**Charleston Rag (Ire)**, 2, 119	D. MacBeth	Tiltalating, 2, 119	Mom's Command, 2, 119	6	1:39.00	130,860
1983	**Miss Oceana**, 2, 119	E. Maple	Life's Magic, 2, 119	Lucky Lucky Lucky, 2, 119	10	1:36.60	68,040
1982	**Princess Rooney**, 2, 119	J. Fell	Winning Tack, 2, 119	Weekend Surprise, 2, 119	13	1:39.00	70,080
1981	**Proud Lou**, 2, 119	D. Beckon	Mystical Mood, 2, 119	Chilling Thought, 2, 119	12	1:38.80	70,920
1980	**Heavenly Cause**, 2, 119	L. A. Pincay Jr.	Sweet Revenge, 2, 119	Prayers'n Promises, 2, 119	8	1:38.00	66,000
1979	**Smart Angle**, 2, 119	S. Maple	Royal Suite, 2, 119	Hardship, 2, 119	11	1:38.20	66,240
1978	**Golferette**, 2, 119	J. Fell	It's in the Air, 2, 119	Terlingua, 2, 119	7	**1:35.40**	63,780
1977	**Lakeville Miss**, 2, 119	R. Hernandez	Misgivings, 2, 119	Itsamaza, 2, 119	8	1:36.20	64,680
1976	**Sensational**, 2, 119	J. Velasquez	Northern Sea, 2, 119	Mrs. Warren, 2, 119	7	1:36.20	64,740
1975	**Optimistic Gal**, 2, 121	B. Baeza	Artfully, 2, 121	Picture Tube, 2, 121	12	1:36.80	69,360
1974	**Molly Ballantine**, 2, 121	L. A. Pincay Jr.	Copernica, 2, 121	Mystery Mood, 2, 121	6	1:37.00	67,140
1973	**Bundler**, 2, 121	J. Vasquez	Chris Evert, 2, 121	I'm a Pleasure, 2, 121	14	1:36.40	72,660

Named for James R. Keene's stakes winner and foundation mare Frizette (1905 f. by Hamburg). Held at Jamaica 1945-'58. Held at Aqueduct 1959-'61, 1963-'67. Not held 1949-'51. 6 furlongs 1945-'47, 1952-'53. 5 furlongs 1948. $1\frac{1}{16}$ miles 1948, 1954-'58, 1994-2004.

Futurity Stakes

Grade 2 in 2006. Belmont Park, two-year-olds, 7 furlongs, dirt. Held September 17, 2005, with a gross value of $294,000. First held in 1888. First graded in 1973. Stakes record 1:21.60 (1977 Affirmed).

Year	Winner	Jockey	Second	Third	Strs	Time	1st Purse
2005	**Private Vow**, 2, 120	J. D. Bailey	Changing Weather, 2, 120	Dixiewink (GB), 2, 120	6	1:24.05	$180,000
2004	**Park Avenue Ball**, 2, 120	J. Castellano	Wallstreet Scandal, 2, 120	Evil Minister, 2, 120	6	1:38.84	180,000
2003	**Cuvee**, 2, 120	J. D. Bailey	Value Plus, 2, 120	El Prado Rob, 2, 120	6	1:35.75	120,000
2002	**Whywhywhy**, 2, 120	E. S. Prado	Pretty Wild, 2, 120	Truckle Feature, 2, 120	7	1:36.33	120,000
2000	**‡Burning Roma**, 2, 122	R. Wilson	City Zip, 2, 122	Scorpion, 2, 122	9	1:37.90	120,000
1999	**Bevo**, 2, 122	J. Bravo	Greenwood Lake, 2, 122	More Than Ready, 2, 122	8	1:36.16	90,000
1998	**Lemon Drop Kid**, 2, 122	J. R. Velazquez	Yes It's True, 2, 122	Medievil Hero, 2, 122	5	1:37.50	90,000
1997	**Grand Slam**, 2, 122	G. L. Stevens	K. O. Punch, 2, 122	Devil's Pride, 2, 122	10	1:35.69	90,000
1996	**Traitor**, 2, 122	J. R. Velazquez	Night in Reno, 2, 122	Harley Tune, 2, 122	9	1:35.29	90,000
1995	**Maria's Mon**, 2, 122	R. G. Davis	Louis Quatorze, 2, 122	Honour and Glory, 2, 122	7	1:35.12	90,000
1994	**Montreal Red**, 2, 122	J. A. Santos	Northern Ensign, 2, 122	Wild Escapade, 2, 122	6	1:36.22	66,180
1993	**Holy Bull**, 2, 122	M. E. Smith	Dehere, 2, 122	Prenup, 2, 122	6	1:23.31	69,360
1992	**Strolling Along**, 2, 122	C. W. Antley	Fight for Love, 2, 122	Caponostro, 2, 122	9	1:23.67	72,120
1991	**Agincourt**, 2, 122	J. F. Chavez	Tri to Watch, 2, 122	Pine Bluff, 2, 122	7	1:23.89	73,140
1990	**Eastern Echo**, 2, 122	J. D. Bailey	Deposit Ticket, 2, 122	Groom's Reckoning, 2, 122	4	1:22.40	69,360
1989	**Senor Pete**, 2, 122	J. A. Santos	Adjudicating, 2, 122	Dawn Quixote, 2, 122	5	1:23.20	75,360
1988	**Trapp Mountain**, 2, 122	A. T. Cordero Jr.	Bio, 2, 122	Fast Play, 2, 122	5	1:23.80	74,280
1987	**Forty Niner**, 2, 122	E. Maple	Tsarbaby, 2, 122	Crusader Sword, 2, 122	5	1:22.60	80,100
1986	**Gulch**, 2, 122	A. T. Cordero Jr.	Demons Begone, 2, 122	Captain Valid, 2, 122	7	1:22.20	82,920
1985	**Ogygian**, 2, 122	W. A. Guerra	Groovy, 2, 122	dh-Mr. Classic, 2, 122 dh-Sovereign Don, 2, 122	6	1:22.40	81,600
1984	**Spectacular Love**, 2, 122	L. A. Pincay Jr.	Chief's Crown, 2, 122	Mugzy's Rullah, 2, 122	8	1:23.20	105,900
1983	**Swale**, 2, 122	E. Maple	Shuttle Jet, 2, 122	Hail Bold King, 2, 122	5	1:24.00	72,915
1982	**Copelan**, 2, 122	J. D. Bailey	Satan's Charger, 2, 122	Pax in Bello, 2, 122	6	1:24.20	97,110
1981	**Irish Martini**, 2, 122	J. Velasquez	Herschelwalker, 2, 122	Timely Writer, 2, 122	8	1:24.40	103,605
1980	**Tap Shoes**, 2, 122	R. Hernandez	Dash o' Pleasure, 2, 122	McCracken, 2, 122	6	1:23.80	85,605
1979	**Rockhill Native**, 2, 122	J. Oldham	Sportful, 2, 122	Gold Stage, 2, 122	8	1:22.00	90,150
1978	**‡Crested Wave**, 2, 122	J. Cruguet	dh-Picturesque, 2, 122 dh-Strike Your Colors, 2, 122		8	1:24.00	75,660
1977	**Affirmed**, 2, 122	S. Cauthen	Alydar, 2, 122	Nasty and Bold, 2, 122	5	**1:21.60**	63,570
1976	**For The Moment**, 2, 122	E. Maple	Banquet Table, 2, 122	Western Wind, 2, 122	10	1:23.20	67,353
1975	**Soy Numero Uno**, 2, 122	J. Vasquez	Jackknife, 2, 122	Beau Talent, 2, 122	7	1:17.80	66,408
1974	**Just the Time**, 2, 122	M. A. Castaneda	High Steel, 2, 122	Valid Appeal, 2, 122	12	1:16.40	66,801
1973	**Wedge Shot**, 2, 122	J. Vasquez	‡Protagonist, 2, 122	Judger, 2, 122	10	1:17.00	82,230

Named for the future nominations, before a foal was born, of early futurity races. Grade 1 1973-2003. Held at Sheepshead Bay 1888-1909. Held at Saratoga Race Course 1910, 1913-'14. Held at Aqueduct 1959-'60, 1963-'67. Not held 1911-'12. Not held due to World Trade Center attack 2001. 6 furlongs 1888-'91, 1902-'09. About 6 furlongs 1892-1901. $6\frac{1}{2}$ furlongs 1910-'24, 1934-'75. About 7 furlongs 1925-'33. 7 furlongs 1976-'93. Colts and fillies 1944. Colts and geldings 1977. Dead heat for second 1978. Dead heat for third 1985. ‡Judger finished second, DQ to third, 1973. ‡Fuzzbuster finished first, DQ to fourth, 1978. ‡City Zip finished first, DQ to second, 2000.

Gallant Bloom Handicap

Grade 2 in 2006. Belmont Park, three-year-olds and up, fillies and mares, 6½ furlongs, dirt. Held October 9, 2005, with a gross value of $147,000. First held in 1992. First graded in 1997. Stakes record 1:15.60 (1998 Catinca).

Year	Winner	Jockey	Second	Third	Strs	Time	1st Purse
2005	**Umpateedle**, 6, 116	A. T. Gryder	Smokey Glacken, 4, 116	Travelator, 5, 115	5	1:16.35	$90,000
2004	**Lady Tak**, 4, 122	J. R. Velazquez	Molto Vita, 4, 115	Zawzooth, 5, 115	7	1:16.04	90,000
2003	**Harmony Lodge**, 5, 117	R. Migliore	House Party, 3, 116	Slews Final Answer, 4, 112	6	1:16.20	90,000
2002	**Nasty Storm**, 4, 114	J. A. Santos	Raging Fever, 4, 120	Shine Again, 5, 118	6	1:17.89	90,000
2001	**Finder's Fee**, 4, 113	J. R. Velazquez	Cedar Knolls, 4, 114	Gold Mover, 3, 115	4	1:17.60	79,928
2000	**Dream Supreme**, 3, 118	P. Day	Finder's Fee, 3, 116	Tropical Punch, 4, 114	5	1:15.86	64,380
1999	**Positive Gal**, 3, 116	J. D. Bailey	Flamingo Way, 5, 114	Torch, 6, 113	6	1:16.86	65,820
1998	**Catinca**, 3, 114	R. Migliore	Dixie Flag, 4, 117	Crab Grass, 4, 114	9	**1:15.60**	50,595
1997	**Top Secret**, 4, 120	J. R. Velazquez	Aldiza, 3, 116	Dixie Flag, 3, 114	7	1:16.00	49,260
1996	**Miss Golden Circle**, 4, 115	R. Migliore	J J'sdream, 3, 119	Nappelon, 4, 117	9	1:16.26	50,040
1995	**Classy Mirage**, 5, 123	J. D. Bailey	Dust Bucket, 4, 114	Fantastic Women, 3, 110	5	1:17.34	48,375
1994	**Vivano**, 5, 116	W. H. McCauley	Ann Dear, 4, 118	Strategic Reward, 5, 113	5	1:10.93	48,255
1992	**Apelia**, 3, 118	L. Attard	Preach, 3, 116	Fretina, 3, 116	8	1:08.97	32,400

Named for King Ranch's 1968 champion two-year-old filly, '69 champion three-year-old filly, '69 champion handicap mare, and '69 Gazelle H. winner Gallant Bloom (1966 f. by *Gallant Man). Grade 3 1997-2000. Not held 1993. 6 furlongs 1994.

Gallorette Handicap

Grade 3 in 2006. Pimlico Race Course, three-year-olds and up, fillies and mares, 1¹⁄₁₆ miles, turf. Held May 20, 2006, with a gross value of $100,000. First held in 1952. First graded in 1973. Stakes record 1:40.85 (2004 Ocean Drive).

Year	Winner	Jockey	Second	Third	Strs	Time	1st Purse
2006	**Ozone Bere (Fr)**, 4, 115	J. Castellano	Humoristic, 5, 115	Art Fan, 5, 114	13	1:42.08	$60,000
2005	**Film Maker**, 5, 121	J. D. Bailey	Briviesca (GB), 4, 115	Humoristic, 4, 114	9	1:44.29	60,000
2004	**Ocean Drive**, 4, 117	J. D. Bailey	Film Maker, 4, 120	With Patience, 5, 112	8	**1:40.85**	60,000
2003	**Carib Lady (Ire)**, 4, 116	P. A. Valenzuela	Affirmed Dancer, 4, 113	Lady of the Future, 5, 114	7	1:50.69	60,000
2002	**Quidnaskra**, 7, 116	C. J. McCarron	De Aar, 5, 111	Step With Style, 5, 115	7	1:46.73	60,000
2001	**License Fee**, 6, 118	P. Day	Starine (Fr), 4, 114	Crystal Sea, 4, 113	8	1:42.81	60,000
2000	**Colstar**, 4, 120	A. Delgado	Melody Queen (GB), 4, 115	Terreavigne, 5, 118	10	1:43.60	60,000
1999	**Winfama**, 6, 114	E. S. Prado	Pleasant Temper, 5, 119	Earth to Jackie, 5, 116	8	1:43.31	60,000
1998	**Tresoriere**, 4, 113	J. A. Santos	Bursting Forth, 4, 114	Starry Dreamer, 4, 114	7	1:45.35	60,000
1997	**Palliser Bay**, 5, 111	C. H. Marquez Jr.	Elusive, 5, 114	Sangria, 4, 117	8	1:43.81	60,000
1996	**Aucilla**, 5, 114	M. E. Smith	Julie's Brilliance, 4, 114	Brushing Gloom, 4, 114	4	1:44.96	60,000
1995	**It's Personal**, 5, 112	J. A. Krone	Churchbell Chimes, 4, 112	Open Toe, 5, 113	6	1:43.72	60,000
1994	**Tribulation**, 4, 117	J. Samyn	McKaymackenna, 5, 118	Fleet Broad, 4, 115	6	1:41.66	60,000
1993	**You'd Be Surprised**, 4, 113	J. D. Bailey	Captive Miss, 4, 117	Dior's Angel, 4, 112	12	1:43.54	60,000
1992	**Brilliant Brass**, 5, 113	E. S. Prado	Spanish Dior, 5, 112	Stem the Tide, 4, 112	6	1:44.81	60,000
1991	**Miss Josh**, 5, 121	E. S. Prado	Splendid Try, 5, 113	Highland Penny, 6, 115	6	1:41.91	60,000
1990	**Highland Penny**, 5, 116	R. I. Rojas	Saphaedra, 6, 112	dh-Channel Three, 4, 112 dh-Double Bunctious, 6, 113	8	1:42.40	60,000
1989	**Dance Teacher**, 4, 115	J. Samyn	Arcroyal, 5, 114	Fortunate Facts, 5, 118	9	1:44.00	60,000
1988	**Just Class (Ire)**, 4, 115	C. Perret	Landaura, 4, 115	Hangin On a Star, 4, 119	8	1:42.80	54,145
1987	**Scotch Heather**, 5, 113	M. G. Pino	Catatonic, 5, 117	Foot Stone, 4, 113	6	1:44.40	54,600
1986	**Natania**, 4, 114	J. W. Edwards	Scotch Heather, 4, 115	Valid Doge, 5, 108	12	1:45.60	71,448
1985	**La Reine Elaine**, 4, 113	G. W. Hutton	Stufida (GB), 4, 115	Lady Emerald, 4, 107	12	1:41.60	58,013
1984	**Kattegat's Pride**, 5, 118	D. A. Miller Jr.	Amanti, 5, 114	Bright Choice, 5, 110	7	1:42.80	55,770
1983	**Wedding Party**, 4, 119	C. Perret	Sunny Sparkler, 4, 122	Bemissed, 3, 110	8	1:50.00	56,648
1982	**Island Charm**, 5, 117	N. Santagata	Lovely Lei, 4, 112	Vibro Vibes, 5, 115	10	1:46.40	57,168
1981	**Exactly So (Ire)**, 4, 112	G. McCarron	Crimson April, 4, 110	Ernestine, 4, 111	8	1:47.20	55,998
1980	**Jamila Kadir**, 6, 109	M. G. Pino	The Very One, 5, 122	Wild Bidder, 4, 108	10	1:44.40	57,428
1979	**Calderina (Ity)**, 4, 121	C. Perret	Dottie O., 5, 105	Warfever (Fr), 4, 116	10	1:44.80	56,875
1978	**Huggle Duggle**, 4, 113	B. Gonzalez	Council House, 4, 118	Nanticious (Ire), 4, 112	10	1:44.20	37,765
1977	**Summertime Promise**, 5, 121	L. Moyers	Summer Session, 4, 111	Siz Ziz Zit, 4, 112	9	1:43.60	37,050
1976	**Redundancy**, 5, 119	R. Broussard	Dos a Dos, 4, 113	Margravine, 4, 112	8	1:42.20	29,575
	***Deesse Du Val**, 5, 119	C. H. Marquez	Summertime Promise, 4, 117	Jabot, 4, 114	9	1:42.20	29,835
1975	**Gulls Cry**, 4, 117	E. Maple	Sarah Percy, 7, 115	Twixt, 6, 127	10	1:46.20	37,960
1974	**Sarre Green**, 6, 113	T. Lee	Unknown Heiress, 3, 103	Out Cold, 4, 112	14	1:44.60	22,295
1973	**Deb Marion**, 3, 107	A. Agnello	dh-Aglimmer, 4, 115 dh-Groton Miss, 4, 115		11	1:44.00	22,068

Named for Mrs. M. A. Moore's 1946 champion handicap female and '45 Pimlico Oaks winner Gallorette (1942 f. by *Challenger II). Gallorette S. 1952-'66. 1⅛ miles 1952-'66. Dirt 1952-'72, 1979-'80, 1984, 1986-'87, 1995-'96. Two divisions 1976. Dead heat for second 1973. Dead heat for third 1990.

Gamely Breeders' Cup Handicap

Grade 1 in 2006. Hollywood Park, three-year-olds and up, fillies and mares, 1⅛ miles, turf. Held May 29, 2006, with a gross value of $349,500. First held in 1939. First graded in 1973. Stakes record 1:45.07 (1993 Toussaud).

Year	Winner	Jockey	Second	Third	Strs	Time	1st Purse
2006	**Shining Energy**, 4, 118	V. Espinoza	Dancing Edie, 4, 116	Argentina (Ire), 4, 116	7	1:46.86	$210,900
2005	**Mea Domina**, 4, 115	T. Baze	Solar Echo, 5, 116	Amorama (Fr), 4, 116	9	1:46.47	276,900

2004	**Noches De Rosa (Chi)**, 6, 115	M. E. Smith	Megahertz (GB), 5, 122	Quero Quero, 4, 115	4	1:48.34	$187,500
2003	**Tates Creek**, 5, 122	P. A. Valenzuela	Dublino, 4, 122	Megahertz (GB), 4, 118	6	1:46.97	263,400
2002	**Astra**, 6, 123	K. Desormeaux	Starine (Fr), 5, 122	Voodoo Dancer, 4, 119	6	1:46.93	300,000
2001	**Happyanunoit (NZ)**, 6, 121	B. Blanc	Tranquility Lake, 6, 124	Beautiful Noise, 5, 116	7	1:47.34	115,710
2000	**Astra**, 4, 117	K. Desormeaux	Happyanunoit (NZ), 5, 121	Tout Charmant, 4, 119	5	1:45.81	157,170
1999	**Tranquility Lake**, 4, 119	E. Delahoussaye	Midnight Line, 4, 117	Green Jewel (GB), 5, 117	5	1:46.04	157,800
1998	**Fiji (GB)**, 4, 123	K. Desormeaux	Kool Kat Katie (Ire), 4, 119	Squeak (GB), 4, 116	6	1:47.40	158,880
1997	**Donna Viola (GB)**, 5, 121	G. L. Stevens	Real Connection, 6, 115	Different (Arg), 5, 121	7	1:47.40	120,000
1996	**Auriette (Ire)**, 4, 118	K. Desormeaux	Flagbird, 5, 118	Didina (GB), 4, 116	6	1:46.59	128,760
1995	**Possibly Perfect**, 5, 123	K. Desormeaux	Lady Affirmed, 4, 114	Don't Read My Lips, 4, 114	6	1:46.99	92,900
1994	**Hollywood Wildcat**, 4, 122	E. Delahoussaye	Mz. Zill Bear, 5, 114	Flawlessly, 6, 124	6	1:46.55	92,900
1993	**Toussaud**, 4, 116	K. Desormeaux	Gold Fleece, 5, 114	Bel's Starlet, 6, 116	9	**1:45.07**	97,700
1992	**Metamorphose**, 4, 114	G. L. Stevens	Guiza, 5, 113	Silvered, 5, 116	6	1:46.56	93,300
1991	**Miss Josh**, 5, 118	L. A. Pincay Jr.	Island Jamboree, 5, 116	Fire the Groom, 4, 120	11	1:47.50	68,000
1990	**Double Wedge**, 5, 112	R. G. Davis	Stylish Star, 4, 116	Beautiful Melody, 4, 115	6	1:47.80	62,700
1989	**Fitzwilliam Place (Ire)**, 5, 119	C. A. Black	Claire Marine (Ire), 4, 119	Ravinella, 4, 121	7	1:47.80	63,400
1988	**Pen Bal Lady (GB)**, 4, 120	E. Delahoussaye	Chapel of Dreams, 4, 117	Galunpe (Ire), 5, 120	3	1:47.00	72,800
1987	**Northern Aspen**, 5, 119	G. L. Stevens	Reloy, 4, 121	Frau Altiva (Arg), 5, 115	6	1:47.60	89,800
1986	**La Koumia (Fr)**, 4, 118	R. Sibille	Estrapade, 6, 123	Tax Dodge, 5, 115	8	1:45.80	92,400
1985	**Estrapade**, 5, 124	C. J. McCarron	Johnica, 4, 115	Possible Mate, 4, 116	6	1:46.60	62,500
1984	**Sabin**, 4, 125	E. Maple	Triple Tipple, 5, 116	Fenny Rough (Ire), 4, 117	8	1:47.40	65,400
1983	**Pride of Rosewood (NZ)**, 5, 115	E. Delahoussaye	Sangue (Ire), 5, 123	Mademoiselle Forli, 4, 119	8	1:48.80	64,800
1982	**Ack's Secret**, 6, 122	L. A. Pincay Jr.	Miss Huntington, 5, 117	Vocalist (GB), 4, 114	9	1:46.80	66,100
1981	**Kilijaro (Ire)**, 5, 127	M. Castaneda	Princess Karenda, 4, 121	Wishing Well, 6, 122	6	1:48.20	62,900
1980	**Wishing Well**, 5, 119	F. Toro	Country Queen, 5, 123	Image of Reality, 4, 118	12	1:47.80	69,600
1979	**Sisterhood**, 4, 118	F. Toro	Country Queen, 4, 118	Camarado, 4, 117	11	1:47.80	50,450
1978	***Lucie Manet**, 5, 119	D. G. McHargue	Sensational, 4, 120	*Glenaris, 4, 113	7	1:48.20	38,975
	***Star Ball**, 6, 122	D. G. McHargue	Up to Juliet, 5, 114	Teisen Lap, 4, 116	7	1:48.80	38,975
1977	**Hail Hilarious**, 4, 123	D. Pierce	Cascapedia, 4, 118	Swingtime, 5, 119	6	1:49.60	31,250
1976	**Katonka**, 4, 121	L. A. Pincay Jr.	Fascinating Girl, 4, 117	*Tizna, 7, 126	5	1:50.40	30,750
1975	**Susan's Girl**, 6, 124	J. E. Tejeira	Bold Ballet, 4, 118	*Dulcia, 6, 121	6	1:48.00	25,200
1974	**Sister Fleet**, 4, 115	A. Pineda	*La Zanzara, 4, 121	*Tizna, 5, 122	7	1:47.40	25,550
1973	**Bird Boots**, 4, 115	E. Belmonte	Susan's Girl, 4, 130	Hill Circus, 5, 120	9	1:47.60	32,950

Named for William Haggin Perry's 1967 champion three-year-old filly, '68, '69 champion older female, and '68 Vanity H. winner Gamely (1964 f. by Bold Ruler). Formerly named for the city of Long Beach, California. Grade 2 1977-'82. Not graded 1976. Long Beach H. 1939-'75. Gamely H. 1976-'97. Not held 1940-'67. 1 mile 1939, 1969. 1$^1/_{16}$ miles 1968, 1970-'72. Dirt 1939-'68, 1978. Both sexes 1968. Two divisions 1978.

Garden City Breeders' Cup Stakes

Grade 1 in 2006. Belmont Park, three-year-olds, fillies, 1$^1/_8$ miles, turf. Held September 10, 2005, with a gross value of $260,000. First held in 1904. First graded in 1985. Stakes record 1:45.62 (2005 Luas Line [Ire]).

Year	Winner	Jockey	Second	Third	Strs	Time	1st Purse
2005	**Luas Line (Ire)**, 3, 116	J. R. Velazquez	Asi Siempre, 3, 116	My Typhoon (Ire), 3, 116	4	**1:45.62**	$180,000
2004	**Lucifer's Stone**, 3, 118	J. A. Santos	Barancella (Fr), 3, 116	Noahs Ark (Ire), 3, 116	7	1:48.88	180,000
2003	**Indy Five Hundred**, 3, 113	P. Day	Dimitrova, 3, 122	Campsie Fells (UAE), 3, 116	8	1:48.44	150,000
2002	**Wonder Again**, 3, 119	E. S. Prado	Riskaverse, 3, 119	Pertuisane (GB), 3, 115	10	1:47.33	150,000
2001	**Voodoo Dancer**, 3, 120	C. S. Nakatani	Shooting Party, 3, 113	Wander Mom, 3, 116	10	1:47.69	150,000
2000	**Gaviola**, 3, 123	J. D. Bailey	Flawly (GB), 3, 115	Millie's Quest, 3, 116	8	1:48.89	150,000
1999	**Perfect Sting**, 3, 120	P. Day	Nordican Inch (GB), 3, 116	Ronda (GB), 3, 121	12	1:49.41	129,900
1998	**Pharatta (Ire)**, 3, 120	C. S. Nakatani	Tenski, 3, 122	Pratella, 3, 115	12	1:47.10	129,720
1997	**Auntie Mame**, 3, 122	J. D. Bailey	Parade Queen, 3, 115	Swearingen, 3, 117	9	1:48.49	128,040
1996	**True Flare**, 3, 121	G. L. Stevens	Henlopen, 3, 113	Zephyr, 3, 114	9	1:42.58	128,460
1995	**Perfect Arc**, 3, 123	J. R. Velazquez	Bail Out Becky, 3, 121	Christmas Gift, 3, 118	8	1:42.35	101,070
1994	**Jade Flush**, 3, 111	R. G. Davis	Lady Affirmed, 3, 117	Saxuality, 3, 117	8	1:46.79	67,140
1993	**Sky Beauty**, 3, 124	M. E. Smith	Fadetta, 3, 112	For all Seasons, 3, 114	6	1:35.76	68,400
1992	**November Snow**, 3, 124	C. W. Antley	Vivano, 3, 112	Easy Now, 3, 124	4	1:35.91	66,480
1991	**Dazzle Me Jolie**, 3, 115	J. A. Santos	Grand Girlfriend, 3, 112	Wide Country, 3, 124	9	1:35.61	72,000
1990	**Aishah**, 3, 115	J. A. Santos	Screen Prospect, 3, 115	Vitola (GB), 3, 112	11	1:35.40	57,690
1989	**Highest Glory**, 3, 115	J. A. Santos	Warfie, 3, 118	Tremolos, 3, 112	7	1:37.20	70,440
1988	**Topicount**, 3, 115	A. T. Cordero Jr.	Toll Fee, 3, 112	Fara's Team, 3, 115	5	1:38.00	82,260
1987	**Personal Ensign**, 3, 115	R. P. Romero	One From Heaven, 3, 118	Key Bid, 3, 118	9	1:36.60	82,140
1986	**Life At the Top**, 3, 118	C. J. McCarron	Lotka, 3, 118	Funistrada, 3, 115	6	1:34.40	51,210
1985	**Kamikaze Rick**, 3, 118	A. T. Cordero Jr.	Wising Up, 3, 115	Videogenic, 3, 118	5	1:36.00	50,490
1984	**Given**, 3, 118	M. J. Vigliotti	Maharadoon, 3, 112	Recharged, 3, 118	9	1:43.40	42,960
1983	**Pretty Sensible**, 3, 112	A. Smith Jr.	High Schemes, 3, 112	Lovin Touch, 3, 115	8	1:37.80	33,600
1982	**Nafees**, 3, 112	J. Velasquez	Middle Stage, 3, 112	Beau Cougar, 3, 112	7	1:38.40	33,120
1981	**Banner Gala**, 3, 113	A. T. Cordero Jr.	Expressive Dance, 3, 112	In True Form, 3, 118	9	1:33.60	33,900
1980	**Mitey Lively**, 3, 113	J. Velasquez	Rose of Morn, 3, 112	Paintbrush, 3, 112	6	1:36.40	33,480
1979	**Danielle B.**, 3, 113	R. Hernandez	Distinct Honor, 3, 114	Seascape, 3, 118	10	1:45.40	33,000

Named for the community of Garden City, located in the heart of New York's Long Island. Formerly named for George D. Widener's 1949 Fashion S. winner Rare Perfume (1947 f. by Eight Thirty). Grade 3 1985-'86. Grade 2 1987-'98. Garden City S. 1904-'13. Garden City Selling S. 1915-'32. Rare Perfume S. 1979-'95. Rare Perfume Breeders' Cup H. 1996-'97. Garden City Breeders' Cup H. 1998-2003. Not held 1908, 1910-'12, 1914, 1933-'78. 1¹/₁₆ miles 1904-'79, 1994-'96. 1 mile 70 yards 1984. Dirt 1904-'93. Three-year-olds and up 1904-'32.

Gardenia Handicap

Grade 3 in 2006. Ellis Park, three-year-olds and up, fillies and mares, 1 mile, dirt. Held August 20, 2005, with a gross value of $150,000. First held in 1982. First graded in 1988. Stakes record 1:35.32 (2005 Dream of Summer).

Year	Winner	Jockey	Second	Third	Strs	Time	1st Purse
2005	**Dream of Summer**, 6, 122	C. S. Nakatani	Halory Leigh, 5, 119	Tempus Fugit, 5, 117	8	**1:35.32**	$90,000
2004	**Angela's Love**, 4, 115	M. Guidry	Miss Fortunate, 4, 116	Bare Necessities, 5, 119	6	1:49.54	120,000
2003	**Bare Necessities**, 4, 119	R. R. Douglas	Desert Gold, 4, 114	So Much More, 4, 115	9	1:50.09	120,000
2002	**Minister's Baby**, 4, 117	C. Perret	Lakenheath, 4, 115	Softly, 4, 114	8	1:49.73	120,000
2001	**Asher**, 4, 115	M. Guidry	Zenith, 4, 112	Royal Fair, 5, 116	8	1:50.16	120,000
2000	**Silent Eskimo**, 5, 116	J. Lopez	Roza Robata, 5, 119	Tap to Music, 5, 120	7	1:50.56	120,000
1999	**Lines of Beauty**, 4, 112	F. Torres	Roza Robata, 4, 113	Castle Blaze, 6, 109	10	1:49.60	120,000
1998	**Meter Maid**, 4, 119	P. A. Johnson	Proper Banner, 4, 114	Three Fanfares, 5, 113	7	1:51.00	120,000
1997	**Three Fanfares**, 4, 113	F. A. Arguello Jr.	Gold n Delicious, 4, 119	Birr, 4, 116	7	1:49.00	120,000
1996	**Country Cat**, 4, 115	D. M. Barton	Bedroom Blues, 5, 111	Alcovy, 6, 116	8	1:49.60	120,000
1995	**Laura's Pistolette**, 4, 115	E. M. Martin Jr.	Sadie's Dream, 5, 112	Cat Appeal, 3, 116	9	1:50.80	120,000
1994	**Alphabulous**, 5, 112	O. Thorwarth	Added Asset, 4, 115	Hey Hazel, 4, 116	10	1:50.00	120,000
1993	**Erica's Dream**, 5, 113	W. Martinez	Fappies Cosy Miss, 5, 111	Hitch, 4, 114	8	1:49.80	120,000
1992	**Bungalow**, 5, 118	F. C. Torres	Forever Fond, 4, 113	Fappies Cosy Miss, 4, 112	11	1:48.60	120,000
1991	**Summer Matinee**, 4, 113	C. A. Black	Blissful Union, 4, 113	Beth Believes, 5, 113	11	1:50.50	90,000
1990	**Evangelical**, 4, 113	L. J. Melancon	Degenerate Gal, 5, 117	Anitas Surprise, 4, 113	10	1:49.80	90,000
1989	**Lawyer Talk**, 5, 114	M. E. Doser	Gallant Ryder, 4, 120	Miss Barbour, 4, 112	10	1:50.00	90,000
1988	**Lt. Lao**, 4, 123	D. Brumfield	Saucy Deb, 4, 118	Silk's Lady, 4, 112	12	1:47.60	90,000
1987	**No Choice**, 4, 113	C. R. Woods Jr.	Layovernite, 5, 112	Firgie's Jule, 4, 112	11	1:49.20	94,500
1986	**Queen Alexandra**, 4, 123	D. E. Foster	Fleet Secretariat, 5, 119	Sherizar, 5, 113	7	1:49.20	63,000
1985	**Crimson Orchid**, 3, 114	S. E. Miller	Electric Fanny, 4, 114	Dusty Gloves, 4, 116	14	1:49.80	41,535
1984	**Rambling Rhythm**, 3, 114	L. J. Martinez	Run Tulle Run, 5, 114	Queen of Song, 5, 122	8	1:50.20	39,325
1983	**Migola**, 3, 115	G. Patterson	Kitchen, 4, 117	Run Tulle Run, 4, 113	14	1:51.60	42,315
1982	**Sweetest Chant**, 4, 121	E. Fires	Muriesk, 3, 111	Run Tulle Run, 3, 112	11	1:49.80	43,778

Named for the flower used in the winner's garland. Formerly sponsored by the Coca-Cola Co. of Atlanta, Georgia 1985-'86. Formerly sponsored by Stroh's Brewery of Minneapolis, Minnesota 1982-'84. Stroh's H. 1982-'84. Coca-Cola Summer Festival H. 1985. Coca-Cola Centennial H. 1986. Gardenia S. 1990, 1997-'98. 1¹/₈ miles 1982-2004.

Gazelle Stakes

Grade 1 in 2006. Belmont Park, three-year-olds, fillies, 1¹/₈ miles, dirt. Held September 10, 2005, with a gross value of $245,000. First held in 1887. First graded in 1973. Stakes record 1:46.80 (1974 Maud Muller).

Year	Winner	Jockey	Second	Third	Strs	Time	1st Purse
2005	**In the Gold**, 3, 117	G. L. Stevens	Leave Me Alone, 3, 119	Yolanda B. Too, 3, 115	5	1:49.75	$150,000
2004	**Stellar Jayne**, 3, 122	R. Albarado	Daydreaming, 3, 115	He Loves Me, 3, 117	6	1:48.25	150,000
2003	**Buy the Sport**, 3, 113	P. Day	Lady Tak, 3, 121	Spoken Fur, 3, 121	8	1:48.57	150,000
2002	**Imperial Gesture**, 3, 117	J. A. Santos	Take Charge Lady, 3, 121	Bella Bellucci, 3, 118	7	1:47.12	150,000
2001	**Exogenous**, 3, 118	J. Castellano	Two Item Limit, 3, 118	Fleet Renee, 3, 122	8	1:47.68	150,000
2000	**Critical Eye**, 3, 115	M. E. Smith	Plenty of Light, 3, 115	Resort, 3, 116	8	1:48.54	120,000
1999	**Silverbulletday**, 3, 124	J. D. Bailey	Queen's Word, 3, 113	Awful Smart, 3, 115	6	1:47.71	120,000
1998	**Tap to Music**, 3, 112	P. Day	Keeper Hill, 3, 122	French Braids, 3, 115	7	1:49.72	120,000
1997	**Royal Indy**, 3, 113	P. Day	Starry Dreamer, 3, 114	Pearl City, 3, 117	7	1:49.11	120,000
1996	**My Flag**, 3, 121	J. D. Bailey	Escena, 3, 121	Top Secret, 3, 117	6	1:48.08	120,000
1995	**Serena's Song**, 3, 124	G. L. Stevens	Miss Golden Circle, 3, 113	Golden Bri, 3, 121	6	1:47.29	90,000
1994	**Heavenly Prize**, 3, 123	M. E. Smith	Cinnamon Sugar (Ire), 3, 118	Sovereign Kitty, 3, 118	5	1:47.20	90,000
1993	**Dispute**, 3, 120	J. D. Bailey	Silky Feather, 3, 117	In Her Glory, 3, 112	8	1:47.20	90,000
1992	**Saratoga Dew**, 3, 120	W. H. McCauley	Vivano, 3, 114	Tiney Toast, 3, 113	6	1:47.63	103,140
1991	**Versailles Treaty**, 3, 123	A. T. Cordero Jr.	Grand Girlfriend, 3, 115	Immerse, 3, 112	8	1:47.47	105,840
1990	**Highland Talk**, 3, 111	J. Samyn	Dance Colony, 3, 116	She Can, 3, 116	7	1:50.80	69,960
1989	**Tactile**, 3, 114	R. Migliore	Dream Deal, 3, 117	Fantastic Find, 3, 114	5	1:48.40	67,440
1988	**Classic Crown**, 3, 117	R. P. Romero	Willa On the Move, 3, 120	Make Change, 3, 118	6	1:49.80	69,360
1987	**Single Blade**, 3, 113	C. W. Antley	Without Feathers, 3, 121	Silent Turn, 3, 114	5	1:48.20	80,100
1986	**Classy Cathy**, 3, 121	E. Fires	Life At the Top, 3, 118	Dynamic Star, 3, 116	4	1:48.40	66,480
1985	**Kamikaze Rick**, 3, 113	A. T. Cordero Jr.	Overwhelming, 3, 112	Fran's Valentine, 3, 121	7	1:48.60	68,880
1984	**Miss Oceana**, 3, 121	E. Maple	Sintra, 3, 117	Life's Magic, 3, 122	5	1:47.60	66,840
1983	**High Schemes**, 3, 121	J. Samyn	Lass Trump, 3, 120	Lady Norcliffe, 3, 115	6	1:48.20	66,720
1982	**Broom Dance**, 3, 121	G. McCarron	Number, 3, 113	Mademoiselle Forli, 3, 114	7	1:47.60	33,360
1981	**Discorama**, 3, 117	R. Hernandez	Secrettame, 3, 114	Tina Tina Too, 3, 114	7	1:48.20	33,300
1980	**Love Sign**, 3, 121	R. Hernandez	Sugar and Spice, 3, 117	Kelley's Day, 3, 112	6	1:49.20	32,580
1979	**Himalayan**, 3, 113	E. Maple	Croquis, 3, 113	Fourdrinier, 3, 112	9	1:48.40	32,580
1978	**Tempest Queen**, 3, 117	J. Velasquez	Lulubo, 3, 116	Terpsichorist, 3, 113	5	1:49.80	31,710
1977	**Pearl Necklace**, 3, 111	S. Cauthen	Sensational, 3, 120	Road Princess, 3, 118	5	1:48.00	31,770
1976	**Revidere**, 3, 124	A. T. Cordero Jr.	Pacific Princess, 3, 112	Ancient Fables, 3, 112	5	1:47.80	31,950
1975	**Land Girl**, 3, 114	J. Vasquez	Hooray Hooray, 3, 108	Let Me Linger, 3, 119	8	1:49.40	33,690

1974	**Maud Muller**, 3, 120	A. T. Cordero Jr.	Raisela, 3, 115	Stage Door Betty, 3, 115	7	**1:46.80**	$33,900
1973	**Desert Vixen**, 3, 126	J. Velasquez	Bag of Tunes, 3, 117	Poker Night, 3, 120	7	1:47.40	33,780

Named for the speedy hooved mammal, the gazelle. Grade 2 1973-'83. Gazelle H. 1922, 1956-2004. Held at Gravesend Park 1887-1909. Held at Aqueduct 1910-'55, 1960, 1963-'68. Not held 1911-'16, 1933-'35. 1$^1/_{16}$ miles 1900-'58. 1 mile 1959-'60. Fillies and mares 1917-'20. Three-year-olds and up 1917-'20.

General George Handicap

Grade 2 in 2006. Laurel Park, three-year-olds and up, 7 furlongs, dirt. Held February 21, 2005, with a gross value of $200,000. First held in 1973. First graded in 1991. Stakes record 1:21.96 (1992 Senor Speedy).

Year	Winner	Jockey	Second	Third	Strs	Time	1st Purse
2005	**Saratoga County**, 4, 114	J. Castellano	Don Six, 5, 118	Gators N Bears, 5, 118	9	1:23.43	$120,000
2004	**Well Fancied**, 6, 115	E. S. Prado	Unforgettable Max, 4, 114	Gators N Bears, 4, 116	9	1:22.49	120,000
2003	**My Cousin Matt**, 4, 113	R. A. Dominguez	Peeping Tom, 6, 114	Disturbingthepeace, 5, 118	11	1:22.12	120,000
2002	**Wrangler**, 4, 115	A. T. Gryder	Rusty Spur, 4, 111	Affirmed Success, 8, 121	8	1:22.53	120,000
2001	**Peeping Tom**, 4, 114	S. Bridgmohan	Delaware Township, 5, 120	Disco Rico, 4, 117	7	1:22.00	120,000
2000	**Affirmed Success**, 6, 121	J. F. Chavez	Young At Heart, 6, 114	Badge, 4, 117	9	1:22.02	120,000
1999	**Esteemed Friend**, 5, 116	M. J. Luzzi	Star of Valor, 6, 114	Purple Passion, 5, 117	9	1:22.54	150,000
1998	**Royal Haven**, 6, 122	R. Migliore	Purple Passion, 4, 116	Wire Me Collect, 5, 117	9	1:23.04	150,000
1997	**Why Change**, 4, 113	M. Guidry	Appealing Skier, 4, 118	Le Grande Pos, 6, 111	10	1:22.41	120,000
1996	**Meadow Monster**, 5, 120	R. Wilson	Splendid Sprinter, 4, 113	Cat Be Nimble, 4, 114	9	1:22.11	120,000
1995	**Who Wouldn't**, 6, 119	J. Rocco	Storm Tower, 5, 116	Powis Castle, 4, 118	8	1:22.08	120,000
1994	**Blushing Julian**, 4, 118	R. E. Colton	Chief Desire, 4, 123	Who Wouldn't, 5, 118	12	1:22.91	120,000
1993	**Majesty's Turn**, 4, 118	A. Delgado	Senor Speedy, 6, 118	Ameri Valay, 4, 123	7	1:22.66	120,000
1992	**Senor Speedy**, 5, 126	J. F. Chavez	Sunny Sunrise, 5, 123	Formal Dinner, 4, 123	12	**1:21.96**	120,000
1991	**Star Touch (Fr)**, 5, 118	M. J. Luzzi	Profit Key, 4, 118	Fire Plug, 8, 118	11	1:22.90	120,000
1990	**King's Nest**, 5, 119	M. T. Hunter	Wind Splitter, 4, 117	Notation, 4, 119	12	1:22.00	120,000
1989	**Little Bold John**, 7, 122	D. A. Miller Jr.	Oraibi, 4, 119	Finder's Choice, 4, 117	13	1:22.80	120,000
1988	**Private Terms**, 3, 116	K. Desormeaux	Dynaformer, 3, 122	Delightful Doctor, 3, 122	13	1:38.80	74,328
1987	**Templar Hill**, 3, 116	G. W. Hutton	Hay Halo, 3, 122	Win Dusty Win, 3, 114	11	1:44.00	74,620
1986	**Broad Brush**, 3, 122	V. A. Bracciale Jr.	Fast Step, 3, 113	Swallow, 3, 116	7	1:44.20	54,373
	‡Lil Tyler, 3, 122	J. Nied Jr.	Fobby Forbes, 3, 116	Fork Union Cadet, 3, 110	6	1:45.60	53,723
1985	**Roo Art**, 3, 122	D. A. Miller Jr.	Joyfull John, 3, 112	I Am the Game, 3, 119	8	1:37.60	55,380
1984	**‡Judge Mc Guire**, 3, 122	C. H. Mendoza	American Artist, 3, 110	S. S. Hot Sauce, 3, 122	9	1:46.60	55,543
1981	**Classic Go Go**, 3, 122	B. Fann	Thirty Eight Paces, 3, 122	Aztec Crown, 3, 115	9	1:23.20	37,115
1980	**Galaxy Road**, 3, 122	G. McCarron	Leader of the Pack, 3, 113	Ashanti Gold, 3, 110	7	1:24.60	36,660
1978	**Ten Ten**, 3, 122	W. J. Passmore	Game Prince, 3, 113	Gala Forecast, 3, 113	8	1:45.80	18,200
1977	**Do the Bump**, 3, 122	C. J. McCarron	John U to Berry, 3, 115	Steel Bandit, 3, 113	6	1:47.20	17,778
1976	**Princely Game**, 3, 119	A. Agnello	On the Sly, 3, 110	Troll By, 3, 116	7	1:44.60	17,940
1975	**Pendulum Sam**, 3, 110	L. Gino	King of Fools, 3, 113	Broadway Reviewer, 3, 110	7	1:48.20	18,005
1974	**Sharp Gary**, 3, 122	C. Barrera	Jolly Johu, 3, 119	Ground Breaker, 3, 110	10	1:46.60	19,045
1973	**Ecole Etage**, 3, 113	G. Cusimano	Big Red L., 3, 113	Select Performance, 3, 110	9	1:44.60	18,265

Named for Gen. George Washington (1731-'99), first president of the United States. General George S. 1973-'94. Held at Bowie 1973-'84. Held at Pimlico 1986. Not held 1979, 1982-'83, 2006. 1$^1/_{16}$ miles 1973-'78, 1984, 1986-'87. 1 mile 1985. Three-year-olds 1973-'88. Two divisions 1986. ‡American Artist finished first, DQ to second, 1984. ‡Fobby Forbes finished first, DQ to second, 1986 (2nd Div.).

Generous Stakes

Grade 3 in 2006. Hollywood Park, two-year-olds, 1 mile, turf. Held November 27, 2004, with a gross value of $100,000. First held in 1982. First graded in 1986. Stakes record 1:34.41 (1991 Contested Bid).

Year	Winner	Jockey	Second	Third	Strs	Time	1st Purse
2004	**Dubleo**, 2, 121	C. S. Nakatani	Littlebitofzip, 2, 116	Sunny Sky (Fr), 2, 116	12	1:37.21	$60,000
2003	**Castledale (Ire)**, 2, 116	J. A. Krone	Dealer Choice (Fr), 2, 116	Lucky Pulpit, 2, 116	12	1:35.43	60,000
2002	**Peace Rules**, 2, 118	V. Espinoza	Lismore Knight, 2, 121	Outta Here, 2, 115	9	1:35.49	120,000
2001	**Mountain Rage**, 2, 116	D. R. Flores	Miesque's Approval, 2, 121	National Park (GB), 2, 117	8	1:40.31	120,000
2000	**Startac**, 2, 118	A. O. Solis	Broadway Moon, 2, 116	Deeliteful Irving, 2, 114	9	1:34.76	120,000
1999	**Jokerman**, 2, 118	P. Day	Purely Cozzene, 2, 121	Kleofus, 2, 121	6	1:35.23	120,000
1998	**Incurable Optimist**, 2, 121	J. R. Velazquez	Company Approval, 2, 114	Brave Gun, 2, 117	8	1:37.72	150,000
1997	**Mantles Star (GB)**, 2, 114	C. J. McCarron	F J's Pace, 2, 116	Commitisize, 2, 121	8	1:36.73	150,000
1996	**Hello (Ire)**, 2, 121	C. J. McCarron	Steel Ruhlr, 2, 114	Divine Insight, 2, 114	12	1:34.77	150,000
1995	**Old Chapel**, 2, 121	G. L. Stevens	Ayrton S, 2, 116	Heza Gone West, 2, 117	10	1:35.11	137,500
1994	**Native Regent**, 2, 121	D. Penna	Dangerous Scenario, 2, 116	Claudius, 2, 121	9	1:37.15	137,500
1993	**Delineator**, 2, 118	R. A. Baze	Devon Port (Fr), 2, 116	Ferrara, 2, 114	8	1:34.73	137,500
1992	**Earl of Barking (Ire)**, 2, 114	A. O. Solis	Devil's Rock, 2, 115	Corby, 2, 118	8	1:34.49	137,500
1991	**Silver Ray**, 2, 114	M. A. Pedroza	Thinkernot, 2, 115	African Colony, 2, 114	9	1:35.00	74,775
	Contested Bid, 2, 114	C. S. Nakatani	Turbulent Kris, 2, 114	Sevengreenpairs, 2, 114	9	**1:34.41**	71,775
1990	**Satis (Fr)**, 2, 115	C. A. Black	What a Spell, 2, 114	Ev for Shir, 2, 114	12	1:35.20	67,800
1989	**Single Dawn**, 2, 114	A. O. Solis	Pleasant Tap, 2, 118	Doyouseewhatisee, 2, 121	12	1:35.60	69,600
1988	**Music Merci**, 2, 121	G. L. Stevens	Double Quick, 2, 121	Crown Collection, 2, 115	9	1:36.40	58,220
	Shipping Time, 2, 114	C. A. Black	Super May, 2, 115	Past Ages, 2, 116	7	1:37.20	58,220
1987	**Purdue King**, 2, 121	C. J. McCarron	Chinese Gold, 2, 121	Blade of the Ball, 2, 115	6	1:36.00	47,500
	White Mischief, 2, 115	J. A. Santos	King Alobar, 2, 115	Texas Typhoon, 2, 115	8	1:35.40	68,750

1986	**Persevered**, 2, 120	G. L. Stevens	Wilderness Bound, 2, 120	Quietly Bold, 2, 115	9	1:41.80	$86,050
	†Sweettuc, 2, 113	G. L. Stevens	Savona Tower, 2, 116	Lord Duckworth, 2, 114	9	1:41.60	68,050
1985	**Darby Fair**, 2, 120	A. L. Castanon	Snow Chief, 2, 120	Acks Lika Ruler, 2, 114	6	1:37.00	119,400
1984	**Overtrump**, 2, 120	C. J. McCarron	Right Con, 2, 120	Herat, 2, 120	11	1:41.80	123,350
1983	**Artichoke**, 2, 120	W. Shoemaker	Nagurski, 2, 114	Fortune's Kingdom, 2, 115	8	1:38.40	50,100
	Precisionist, 2, 116	C. J. McCarron	Fali Time, 2, 120	Tights, 2, 115	8	1:37.60	50,100
1982	**Fifth Division**, 2, 117	L. A. Pincay Jr.	Dominating Dooley, 2, 114	Mezzo, 2, 116	12	1:35.60	33,450

Named for Fahd Salman's 1991 Irish Horse of the Year and dual European classic winner Generous (Ire) (1988 c. by Caerleon [Ire]). Formerly named for Mrs. Stephen C. Clark Jr.'s 1970 champion two-year-old colt and '87 leading North American broodmare sire Hoist the Flag (1968 c. by Tom Rolfe). Grade 2 1988-'89. Hoist the Flag S. 1982-'92. Not held 2005. 1 1/16 miles 1984, 1986. Dirt 1985, 1988. Two divisions 1983, 1986-'88, 1991. †Denotes female.

Genuine Risk Handicap

Grade 2 in 2006. Belmont Park, three-year-olds and up, fillies and mares, 6 furlongs, dirt. Held May 14, 2005, with a gross value of $150,000. First held in 1984. First graded in 1986. Stakes record 1:08.40 (1996 Exotic Wood).

Year	Winner	Jockey	Second	Third	Strs	Time	1st Purse
2005	**Bank Audit**, 4, 117	N. Arroyo Jr.	Sensibly Chic, 5, 115	Forest Music, 4, 115	9	1:09.65	$90,000
2004	**Bear Fan**, 5, 117	J. R. Velazquez	Harmony Lodge, 6, 120	Kitty Knight, 4, 114	5	1:08.85	90,000
2003	**Shine Again**, 6, 119	J. Samyn	Carson Hollow, 4, 122	Harmony Lodge, 5, 116	4	1:09.19	90,000
2002	**Xtra Heat**, 4, 126	H. Vega	Shine Again, 5, 117	La Galerie (Arg), 6, 114	6	1:10.24	90,000
2001	**Katz Me If You Can**, 4, 113	J. Bravo	Lucky Livi, 4, 114	Shine Again, 4, 115	10	1:09.55	90,000
2000	**Imperfect World**, 4, 113	R. G. Davis	Gold Princess, 5, 113	Tropical Punch, 4, 115	7	1:10.00	90,000
1999	**Foil**, 4, 114	J. Samyn	Harpia, 5, 118	Gold Princess, 4, 115	9	1:10.43	90,000
1998	**J J'sdream**, 5, 118	L. C. Reynolds	Tate, 4, 112	Capote Belle, 5, 118	8	1:10.28	83,310
1997	**Miss Golden Circle**, 5, 120	R. Migliore	Start At Once, 4, 111	Nappelon, 5, 110	6	1:09.49	65,040
1996	**Exotic Wood**, 4, 119	M. E. Smith	Lottsa Talc, 6, 118	Miss Golden Circle, 4, 113	6	**1:08.40**	65,100
1995	**Classy Mirage**, 5, 122	J. A. Krone	Through the Door, 5, 112	Lottsa Talc, 5, 117	4	1:11.25	64,080
1994	**Apelia**, 5, 119	L. Attard	Spinning Round, 5, 119	Ann Dear, 4, 114	6	1:09.01	64,680
1993	**Apelia**, 4, 119	L. Attard	Santa Catalina, 5, 117	Reach for Clever, 6, 117	7	1:10.18	69,600
1992	**Parisian Flight**, 4, 117	J. A. Santos	Serape, 4, 117	Devil's Orchid, 5, 119	6	1:09.18	70,680
1991	**Safely Kept**, 5, 122	C. Perret	Missy's Mirage, 3, 109	Token Dance, 4, 117	5	1:10.15	68,400
1990	**Safely Kept**, 4, 122	C. Perret	Diva's Debut, 4, 119	Levitation, 5, 117	4	1:10.20	49,140
1989	**Safely Kept**, 3, 114	A. T. Cordero Jr.	Aptostar, 4, 122	Cagey Exuberance, 5, 122	4	1:09.40	49,410
1988	**Tappiano**, 4, 122	J. Vasquez	Cagey Exuberance, 4, 122	Hedgeabout, 4, 117	4	1:09.00	50,040
1987	**Pine Tree Lane**, 5, 122	A. T. Cordero Jr.	Silent Account, 4, 117	Royal Tali, 4, 117	4	1:10.20	47,970
1986	**Clocks Secret**, 4, 122	W. Shoemaker	Le Slew, 5, 119	Liz Taylor, 3, 109	8	1:10.00	48,900
1985	**Alabama Nana (Ire)**, 4, 117	J. Velasquez	Hare Brain, 5, 119	Two Ours, 4, 119	10	1:10.60	49,260
1984	**On the Bench**, 4, 115	J. Cruguet	Nany, 4, 117	Grateful Friend, 4, 119	6	1:09.60	33,060

Named for Diana Firestone's 1980 champion three-year-old filly and '80 Ruffian H. (G1) winner Genuine Risk (1977 f. by Exclusive Native). Grade 3 1986-'88. Genuine Risk S. 1984-'94.

Glens Falls Handicap

Grade 3 in 2006. Saratoga Race Course, three-year-olds and up, fillies and mares, 1 3/8 miles, turf. Held September 5, 2005, with a gross value of $109,200. First held in 1996. First graded in 1999. Stakes record 2:12.81 (1999 Idle Rich).

Year	Winner	Jockey	Second	Third	Strs	Time	1st Purse
2005	**Honey Ryder**, 4, 120	J. R. Velazquez	Film Maker, 5, 122	Banyu Dewi (Ger), 6, 115	6	2:14.51	$65,520
2004	**Humaita (Ger)**, 4, 114	C. H. Velasquez	Where We Left Off (GB), 4, 116	Savedbythelight, 4, 115	9	2:15.25	66,240
	Arvada (GB), 4, 112	J. R. Velazquez	Spice Island, 5, 118	Film Maker, 4, 121	8	2:14.12	65,580
2003	**Sixty Seconds (NZ)**, 5, 115	J. A. Santos	Primetimevalentine, 4, 113	Alternate, 4, 116	9	2:13.96	67,860
2002	**Owsley**, 4, 116	E. S. Prado	Mot Juste (GB), 4, 116	Sunstone (GB), 4, 114	10	2:15.99	68,100
2001	**Irving's Baby**, 4, 126	J. D. Bailey	New Assembly (Ire), 4, 113	Caveat's Shot, 6, 114	4	2:07.56	65,995
2000	**I'm Indy Mood**, 5, 116	H. Castillo Jr.	Idle Rich, 5, 114	Cybil, 4, 114	6	2:07.41	66,120
1999	**Idle Rich**, 4, 115	J. D. Bailey	Adrian, 5, 114	Bundling, 5, 114	7	**2:12.81**	65,760
1998	**Auntie Mame**, 4, 120	J. R. Velazquez	Yvecrique (Fr), 4, 115	Makethemostofit, 4, 111	6	2:13.15	66,000
1997	**Shemozzle (Ire)**, 4, 115	J. D. Bailey	Picture Hat, 5, 113	Last Approach, 5, 113	5	2:12.89	64,740
1996	**Ampulla**, 5, 113	S. J. Sellers	Look Daggers, 4, 118	Electric Society (Ire), 5, 120	8	2:16.49	67,500

Named for Glens Falls, New York, a town about 15 miles north of Saratoga Springs. Glens Falls S. 1996-'97. 1 1/4 miles 2000-'01. Dirt 2000-'01. Originally scheduled on turf 2001. Two divisions 2004.

Go for Wand Handicap

Grade 1 in 2006. Saratoga Race Course, three-year-olds and up, fillies and mares, 1 1/8 miles, dirt. Held July 31, 2005, with a gross value of $245,000. First held in 1954. First graded in 1973. Stakes record 1:47.86 (2004 Azeri).

Year	Winner	Jockey	Second	Third	Strs	Time	1st Purse
2005	**Ashado**, 4, 121	J. R. Velazquez	Bending Strings, 4, 115	Andujar, 4, 118	5	1:50.30	$150,000
2004	**Azeri**, 6, 120	P. Day	Sightseek, 5, 122	Storm Flag Flying, 4, 117	5	**1:47.86**	150,000
2003	**Sightseek**, 4, 121	J. D. Bailey	She's Got the Beat, 4, 112	Nonsuch Bay, 4, 113	6	1:50.92	150,000
2002	**Dancethruthedawn**, 4, 118	J. D. Bailey	Transcendental, 4, 113	Too Scarlet, 4, 112	7	1:50.21	150,000
2001	**Serra Lake**, 4, 113	E. S. Prado	Pompeii, 4, 114	March Magic, 4, 114	8	1:49.62	150,000
2000	**Heritage of Gold**, 5, 123	S. J. Sellers	Beautiful Pleasure, 5, 125	Roza Robata, 5, 114	5	1:49.84	150,000
1999	**Banshee Breeze**, 4, 124	J. D. Bailey	Beautiful Pleasure, 4, 113	Heritage of Gold, 4, 117	5	1:49.95	150,000
1998	**Aldiza**, 4, 114	M. E. Smith	Escena, 5, 124	Tomisue's Delight, 4, 116	7	1:49.88	150,000

1997	**Hidden Lake**, 4, 123	R. Migliore	Flat Fleet Feet, 4, 120	Clear Mandate, 5, 113	7	1:49.60	$150,000
1996	**Exotic Wood**, 4, 115	C. J. McCarron	Shoop, 5, 118	Frolic, 4, 113	8	1:49.44	105,000
1995	**Heavenly Prize**, 4, 123	P. Day	Forcing Bid, 4, 108	Little Buckles, 4, 111	5	1:49.90	105,000
1994	**Sky Beauty**, 4, 123	M. E. Smith	Link River, 4, 123	Life Is Delicious, 4, 123	5	1:49.47	90,000
1993	**Turnback the Alarm**, 4, 123	C. W. Antley	Nannerl, 6, 116	November Snow, 4, 116	4	1:36.02	120,000
1992	**Easy Now**, 3, 111	J. D. Bailey	‡Train Robbery, 5, 118	Wide Country, 4, 116	5	1:36.13	120,000
1991	**Queena**, 5, 123	A. T. Cordero Jr.	Fit to Scout, 4, 123	Screen Prospect, 4, 116	6	1:34.89	120,000
1990	**Go for Wand**, 3, 118	R. P. Romero	Feel the Beat, 5, 123	Mistaurian, 4, 116	6	1:35.60	68,760
1989	**Miss Brio (Chi)**, 5, 116	J. D. Bailey	Proper Evidence, 4, 116	Aptostar, 4, 123	5	1:35.60	67,080
1988	**Personal Ensign**, 4, 123	R. P. Romero	Winning Colors, 3, 118	Sham Say, 3, 115	4	1:34.20	67,080
1987	**North Sider**, 5, 123	A. T. Cordero Jr.	Wisla, 4, 116	Funistrada, 4, 116	7	1:35.00	85,500
1986	**Lady's Secret**, 4, 125	P. Day	Steal a Kiss, 3, 109	Endear, 4, 120	6	1:33.40	81,060
1985	**Lady's Secret**, 3, 111	J. Velasquez	Dowery, 4, 117	Mrs. Revere, 4, 117	8	1:34.80	85,020
1984	**Miss Oceana**, 3, 120	E. Maple	Paradies (Arg), 4, 114	Nany, 4, 120	6	1:35.20	70,560
1983	**Ambassador of Luck**, 4, 116	A. Graell	A Kiss for Luck, 4, 120	Am Capable, 3, 109	6	1:36.40	67,560
1982	**Too Chic**, 3, 110	R. Hernandez	Ambassador of Luck, 3, 111	Anti Lib, 4, 116	8	1:34.80	67,920
1981	**Jameela**, 5, 123	J. Vasquez	Love Sign, 4, 123	Island Charm, 4, 116	5	1:35.00	65,280
1980	**Bold 'n Determined**, 3, 122	E. Delahoussaye	Genuine Risk, 3, 118	Love Sign, 3, 120	5	1:35.40	49,140
1979	**Blitey**, 3, 112	A. T. Cordero Jr.	It's in the Air, 3, 122	Pearl Necklace, 5, 125	5	1:34.80	48,015
1978	**Pearl Necklace**, 4, 123	R. Hernandez	Ida Delia, 4, 113	Sensational, 4, 117	5	1:33.80	48,195
1977	**What a Summer**, 4, 126	J. Vasquez	Crab Grass, 5, 114	Harvest Girl, 3, 111	8	1:37.40	32,280
1976	**Artfully**, 3, 108	P. Day	Snooze, 4, 108	Land Girl, 4, 109	7	1:34.00	25,920
	Sugar Plum Time, 4, 111	J. Imparato	Pacific Princess, 3, 110	Fleet Victress, 4, 115	9	1:34.00	26,220
1975	**Let Me Linger**, 3, 117	L. A. Pincay Jr.	Honorable Miss, 5, 121	Susan's Girl, 6, 128	8	1:35.20	34,590
1974	**‡Ponte Vecchio**, 4, 118	J. Vasquez	Poker Night, 4, 116	Twixt, 5, 124	12	1:34.60	35,850
1973	**Light Hearted**, 4, 126	E. Nelson	Convenience, 5, 121	Krislin, 4, 111	6	1:34.80	17,040

Named for Christiana Stable's 1989 champion two-year-old filly, '90 champion three-year-old filly, and '90 Maskette S. (G1) winner Go for Wand (1987 f. by Deputy Minister). Go for Wand is buried in Saratoga's infield. Formerly named for James R. Keene's 1908 champion two-year-old filly and Futurity S. winner Maskette (1906 f. by Disguise). Maskette H. 1954-'78. Maskette S. 1979-'91. Go for Wand S. 1992-'97. Held at Belmont Park 1954-'58, 1961, 1969-'93. Held at Aqueduct 1959-'60, 1962-'68. 1 mile 1954-'93. Two divisions 1976. ‡Desert Vixen finished first, DQ to 12th for a positive drug test, 1974. ‡Nannerl finished second, DQ to fifth, 1992.

Golden Gate Fields Handicap

Grade 3 in 2006. Golden Gate Fields, four-year-olds and up, 1⅛ miles, dirt (originally scheduled on the turf). Held March 25, 2006, with a gross value of $150,000. First held in 1947. First graded in 1975. Stakes record 1:48.21 (1993 Val des Bois [Fr]).

Year	Winner	Jockey	Second	Third	Strs	Time	1st Purse
2006	**Cosmonaut**, 4, 113	T. Farina	Adreamisborn, 7, 122	Cheroot, 5, 114	5	1:48.75	$82,500
2004	**Tronare (Chi)**, 6, 115	R. M. Gonzalez	Soud, 6, 118	Aly Bubba, 5, 116	9	1:48.48	41,250
2003	**Ninebanks**, 5, 116	R. J. Warren Jr.	Surprise Halo, 5, 115	Royal Gem, 4, 118	4	1:50.07	82,500
2002	**No Slip (Fr)**, 4, 117	K. Desormeaux	Kerrygold (Fr), 6, 116	Sumitas (Ger), 6, 119	5	1:49.41	82,500
2001	**Northern Quest (Fr)**, 6, 118	V. Espinoza	Eagleton, 5, 114	Entorchado (Ire), 4, 115	6	1:58.58	137,500
2000	**Deploy Venture (GB)**, 4, 115	R. A. Baze	Single Empire (Ire), 6, 121	Bonapartiste (Fr), 6, 119	6	2:19.12	120,000
1999	**Sayarshan (Fr)**, 4, 112	B. Blanc	Alvo Certo (Brz), 6, 117	Plicck (Ire), 4, 115	8	2:15.56	120,000
1998	**Dushyantor**, 5, 118	C. S. Nakatani	Eternity Range, 5, 114	Star Performance, 5, 116	6	2:15.26	150,000
1997	**Irish Wings (Ire)**, 5, 114	D. Carr	Savinio, 7, 117	Mufattish, 4, 114	7	1:49.60	120,000
1996	**Time Star**, 5, 116	C. A. Black	Sand Reef (GB), 5, 116	Bon Point (GB), 6, 117	5	2:16.37	120,000
1995	**Special Price**, 6, 122	E. Delahoussaye	Bluegrass Prince (Ire), 4, 122	Sans Ecocide (GB), 4, 122	6	2:15.14	110,000
1994	**Alex the Great (GB)**, 5, 118	P. A. Valenzuela	Fanmore, 6, 117	Emerald Jig, 5, 113	8	2:15.11	165,000
1993	**Val des Bois (Fr)**, 7, 119	P. A. Valenzuela	Norwich (GB), 6, 116	Never Black, 6, 116	5	**1:48.21**	165,000
1992	**Algenib (Arg)**, 5, 120	L. A. Pincay Jr.	Missionary Ridge (GB), 5, 114	Never Black, 5, 113	7	2:13.96	220,000
1991	**Forty Niner Days**, 4, 115	R. Q. Meza	Aksar, 4, 115	Missionary Ridge (GB), 4, 114	9	2:17.30	220,000
1990	**†Petite Ile (Ire)**, 4, 113	C. A. Black	Valdali (Ire), 4, 114	Pleasant Variety, 6, 116	11	2:15.60	220,000
1989	**Frankly Perfect**, 4, 122	E. Delahoussaye	Pleasant Variety, 5, 114	†Brown Bess, 7, 114	7	2:15.00	165,000
1988	**Great Communicator**, 5, 120	R. Sibille	Putting (Fr), 5, 117	Rivlia, 6, 120	5	2:15.40	165,000
1987	**Rivlia**, 5, 116	C. J. McCarron	Air Display, 4, 115	Reco (Fr), 5, 113	8	2:14.20	165,000
1986	**dh-Le Solaret (Fr)**, 4, 113	M. Castaneda		Complice (Fr), 5, 115	5	2:16.40	113,875
	dh-Val Danseur, 6, 117	G. L. Stevens					
1985	**Fatih**, 5, 119	T. Lipham	†Fact Finder, 6, 115	dh-Nak Ack, 4, 115	9	2:15.40	171,770
				dh-Semillero (Chi), 5, 115			
1984	**John Henry**, 9, 125	C. J. McCarron	Silveyville, 6, 117	Lucence, 5, 116	6	2:13.00	184,200
1983	**Silveyville**, 5, 115	D. Winick	Ask Me, 4, 115	Majesty's Prince, 4, 122	9	2:16.40	165,800
1982	**Regal Bearing (GB)**, 6, 117	R. A. Baze	Visible Pole, 4, 110	Score Twenty Four, 5, 121	5	1:46.00	73,900
1981	**Caterman (NZ)**, 5, 123	M. Castaneda	Opus Dei (Fr), 6, 121	His Honor, 6, 118	9	1:41.40	77,000
1980	**Eagle Toast**, 6, 113	P. A. Valenzuela	Daranstone, 5, 108	Saboulard (Fr), 5, 116	7	1:41.00	63,200
1979	**As de Copas (Arg)**, 6, 120	H. E. Moreno	True Statement, 5, 117	Bywayofchicago, 5, 123	6	1:43.40	62,600
1978	**Bad 'n Big**, 4, 120	A. L. Diaz	Effervescing, 5, 123	Jumping Hill, 6, 124	9	1:44.80	65,500
1977	**Announcer**, 5, 115	M. Castaneda	The Fop, 4, 114	Sir Jason, 6, 116	14	1:40.40	71,700
1976	**Pass the Glass**, 5, 119	F. Olivares	Willie Pleasant, 5, 111	Barrydown, 6, 117	6	1:41.40	31,250
1975	**Pass the Glass**, 4, 115	F. Olivares	Confederate Yankee, 4, 116	Ga Hai, 4, 118	10	1:41.80	33,150

1974	**Acclimatization**, 6, 119	S. Valdez	*Yvetot, 6, 118	Wild World, 5, 111	9	2:27.80	$46,350
1973	**Wing Out**, 5, 124	R. Schacht	Fair Test, 5, 116	*Yvetot, 5, 116	7	1:43.80	30,800

Grade 2 1985-'96. Golden Gate H. 1947-2000. Golden Gate Breeders' Cup H. 2001-'04. Not held 2005. 1¼ miles 1947-'50, 1952, 1955, 1959-'61. 1³⁄₁₆ miles 1953. 1¹⁄₁₆ miles 1962-'64, 1968-'73, 1975-'82. 1½ miles 1974. 1⅜ miles 1983-'92, 1994-'96, 1998-2000. Dirt 1947-'71, 1982, 2006. Originally scheduled on turf 2006. Dead heat for third 1985. Dead heat for first 1986. Course record 1975. Equaled course record 1993. †Denotes female.

Golden Rod Stakes

Grade 2 in 2006. Churchill Downs, two-year-olds, fillies, 1¹⁄₁₆ miles, dirt. Held November 26, 2005, with a gross value of $222,200. First held in 1910. First graded in 1973. Stakes record 1:43.82 (2001 Belterra).

Year	Winner	Jockey	Second	Third	Strs	Time	1st Purse
2005	**French Park**, 2, 122	M. Guidry	She Says It Best, 2, 122	Lady Danza, 2, 118	8	1:47.26	$137,764
2004	**Runway Model**, 2, 122	E. M. Martin Jr.	Kota, 2, 118	Summerly, 2, 116	6	1:45.97	133,548
2003	**Be Gentle**, 2, 122	J. McKee	Lotta Kim, 2, 116	Dynaville, 2, 116	11	1:45.91	142,600
2002	**My Boston Gal**, 2, 117	C. H. Borel	Holiday Lady, 2, 115	My Trusty Cat, 2, 115	7	1:45.00	136,152
2001	**Belterra**, 2, 117	J. K. Court	Take Charge Lady, 2, 122	Lotta Rhythm, 2, 122	5	**1:43.82**	133,424
2000	**Miss Pickums**, 2, 122	J. J. Vitek	Nasty Storm, 2, 113	My White Corvette, 2, 119	9	1:48.84	138,384
1999	**Humble Clerk**, 2, 119	J. K. Court	Cash Run, 2, 122	Secret Status, 2, 111	9	1:45.26	138,880
1998	**Silverbulletday**, 2, 122	G. L. Stevens	Here I Go, 2, 113	Lefty's Dollbaby, 2, 113	6	1:43.87	134,292
1997	**Love Lock**, 2, 119	R. Albarado	Barefoot Dyana, 2, 119	Grechelle, 2, 111	9	1:44.49	139,996
1996	**City Band**, 2, 122	S. J. Sellers	Glitter Woman, 2, 113	Water Street, 2, 122	10	1:46.82	139,996
1995	**Gold Sunrise**, 2, 113	W. Martinez	Birr, 2, 119	Solana, 2, 113	11	1:45.46	97,500
1994	**Lilly Capote**, 2, 113	D. M. Barton	Morris Code, 2, 113	Cat Appeal, 2, 119	8	1:46.66	97,500
1993	**At the Half**, 2, 122	P. Day	Spiritofpocahontas, 2, 115	Mystic Union, 2, 111	9	1:46.83	97,500
1992	**Boots 'n Jackie**, 2, 120	M. A. Lee	Mollie Creek, 2, 115	Dance Account, 2, 113	6	1:47.29	97,500
1991	**Vivid Imagination**, 2, 115	J. M. Johnson	Met Her Dream, 2, 113	Pennant Fever, 2, 113	8	1:46.38	97,500
1990	**Fancy Ribbons**, 2, 114	J. E. Bruin	Nice Assay, 2, 115	Til Forbid, 2, 113	8	1:45.40	97,500
1989	**De La Devil**, 2, 117	J. A. Krone	Crowned, 2, 120	Flew by Em, 2, 117	7	1:44.60	97,500
1988	**Born Famous**, 2, 120	E. Fires	Coax Chelsie, 2, 120	Darby Shuffle, 2, 120	6	1:48.20	97,500
1987	**Darien Miss**, 2, 118	P. A. Johnson	Tap Your Toes, 2, 118	Most Likely, 2, 118	7	1:48.20	83,814
1986	**Stargrass**, 2, 118	K. K. Allen	Zero Minus, 2, 121	Laserette, 2, 113	11	1:46.60	98,358
1985	**Slippin n' Slyding**, 2, 116	C. R. Woods Jr.	Turn and Dance, 2, 110	Bonded Miss, 2, 113	9	1:46.20	95,693
1984	**Kamikaze Rick**, 2, 116	R. Migliore	Boldly Dared, 2, 114	Gallant Libby, 2, 118	9	1:47.80	101,156
1983	**Flippers**, 2, 119	P. Day	Robin's Rob, 2, 116	Mallorca, 2, 116	11	1:47.60	86,158
1982	**Weekend Surprise**, 2, 119	P. Day	National Banner, 2, 116	Quarrel Over, 2, 116	6	1:47.00	77,701
1981	**Betty Money**, 2, 119	D. Brumfield	Hoist Emy's Flag, 2, 116	Subdeb, 2, 119	12	1:45.80	91,669
1980	**Mamzelle**, 2, 116	M. S. Sellers	Switch Point, 2, 116	Brent's Star, 2, 119	7	1:46.20	83,236
1979	**Remote Ruler**, 2, 116	S. Maple	Forever Cordial, 2, 116	Peachblow, 2, 116	10	1:25.00	43,095
1978	**Angel Island**, 2, 119	E. Delahoussaye	Safe, 2, 113	Too Many Sweets, 2, 119	8	1:24.20	36,325
1977	**Bold Rendezvous**, 2, 113	P. Nicolo	Rainy Princess, 2, 116	Silver Spook, 2, 113	10	1:27.00	46,449
1976	**Bring Out the Band**, 2, 114	D. Brumfield	Shady Lou, 2, 116	Ciao, 2, 113	10	1:25.20	38,688
1975	**Old Goat**, 2, 119	M. Hole	Confort Zone, 2, 113	Silent Bidder, 2, 114	7	1:24.80	37,941
1974	**Mirthful Flirt**, 2, 113	W. J. Passmore	Sun and Snow, 2, 119	Yale Coed, 2, 116	10	1:26.60	38,597
1973	**Chris Evert**, 2, 116	L. A. Pincay Jr.	Bundler, 2, 119	Kiss Me Darlin, 2, 116	13	1:25.20	38,200

Named for the state flower of Kentucky, the goldenrod. Grade 3 1973-'82, 1989-'99. Not graded 1983-'88. Not held 1928-'61. 6 furlongs 1910-'18. 1 mile 1919. 7 furlongs 1920-'27, 1962-'79.

Goodwood Breeders' Cup Handicap

Grade 2 in 2006. Oak Tree at Santa Anita, three-year-olds and up, 1⅛ miles, dirt. Held October 1, 2005, with a gross value of $484,000. First held in 1982. First graded in 1982. Stakes record 1:46.72 (1994 Bertrando).

Year	Winner	Jockey	Second	Third	Strs	Time	1st Purse
2005	**Rock Hard Ten**, 4, 121	G. L. Stevens	Roman Ruler, 3, 114	Choctaw Nation, 5, 116	4	1:48.68	$300,000
2004	**Lundy's Liability (Brz)**, 4, 118	D. R. Flores	Total Impact (Chi), 6, 119	Supah Blitz, 4, 117	5	1:48.39	300,000
2003	**Pleasantly Perfect**, 5, 116	A. O. Solis	Fleetstreet Dancer, 5, 113	Star Cross (Arg), 6, 110	8	1:48.37	300,000
2002	**Pleasantly Perfect**, 4, 115	A. O. Solis	Momentum, 4, 119	Reba's Gold, 5, 116	9	1:46.80	300,000
2001	**Freedom Crest**, 5, 116	K. Desormeaux	Skimming, 5, 123	Tiznow, 4, 124	6	1:48.86	300,000
2000	**Tiznow**, 3, 116	C. J. McCarron	Captain Steve, 3, 117	Euchre, 4, 115	7	1:47.38	240,000
1999	**Budroyale**, 6, 119	G. K. Gomez	General Challenge, 3, 120	Old Trieste, 4, 120	6	1:48.31	300,000
1998	**Silver Charm**, 4, 124	G. L. Stevens	Free House, 4, 124	Score Quick, 6, 115	6	1:47.21	262,800
1997	**Benchmark**, 6, 118	E. Delahoussaye	Score Quick, 5, 114	Hesabull, 4, 117	5	1:47.60	158,700
1996	**‡Savinio**, 6, 117	C. S. Nakatani	Dare and Go, 5, 122	Alphabet Soup, 5, 120	4	1:47.88	189,300
1995	**Soul of the Matter**, 4, 121	K. Desormeaux	Tinners Way, 5, 121	Alphabet Soup, 4, 116	5	1:47.54	144,450
1994	**Bertrando**, 5, 120	G. L. Stevens	Dramatic Gold, 3, 115	Tossofthecoin, 4, 115	6	**1:46.72**	124,400
1993	**Lottery Winner**, 4, 115	K. Desormeaux	Region, 4, 116	Pleasant Tango, 3, 115	7	1:47.71	127,200
1992	**Reign Road**, 4, 116	K. Desormeaux	Sir Beaufort, 5, 116	Marquetry, 5, 120	6	1:48.36	125,200
1991	**The Prime Minister**, 4, 115	C. J. McCarron	Marquetry, 4, 119	Pleasant Tap, 4, 117	6	1:47.99	152,300
1990	**Lively One**, 5, 120	A. O. Solis	Miserden, 4, 112	Festin (Arg), 4, 116	7	1:48.00	126,800
1989	**Present Value**, 5, 119	E. Delahoussaye	Rahy, 4, 121	Happy Toss (Arg), 4, 116	8	1:47.20	128,800
1988	**Cutlass Reality**, 6, 124	G. L. Stevens	Lively One, 3, 116	Stylish Winner, 4, 113	8	1:47.20	130,400
1987	**Ferdinand**, 4, 127	W. Shoemaker	Candi's Gold, 3, 117	Skywalker, 5, 123	5	1:50.80	102,500
1986	**Super Diamond**, 6, 122	L. A. Pincay Jr.	Epidaurus, 4, 116	Prince Don B., 5, 115	8	1:41.20	65,500

1985	**Lord At War (Arg)**, 5, 125	W. Shoemaker	Matafao, 4, 106	Last Command, 4, 115	6	1:50.20	$62,800
1984	**Lord At War (Arg)**, 4, 117	W. Shoemaker	Video Kid, 4, 118	Menswear, 6, 117	6	1:42.00	60,150
1983	**Pettrax**, 5, 117	K. D. Black	Konewah, 4, 115	Stancharry, 5, 117	6	1:42.60	46,650
1982	**Cajun Prince**, 5, 115	W. A. Guerra	Caterman (NZ), 6, 122	Rock Softly, 4, 116	6	1:40.20	46,600

Named for Goodwood Race Course in England, the Oak Tree Racing Association's sister track. Grade 3 1982, 1985-'89. Not graded 1983-'84. Goodwood H. 1982-'95. 1 1/16 miles 1982-'84, 1986. ‡Alphabet Soup finished first, DQ to third, 1996.

Gotham Stakes

Grade 3 in 2006. Aqueduct, three-year-olds, 1 1/16 miles. Held March 18, 2006, with a gross value of $200,000. First held in 1953. First graded in 1973. Stakes record 1:43 (1959 Atoll).

Year	Winner	Jockey	Second	Third	Strs	Time	1st Purse
2006	**Like Now**, 3, 116	F. Jara	Keyed Entry, 3, 120	Sweetnorthernsaint, 3, 116	10	1:43.17	$120,000
2005	**Survivalist**, 3, 116	R. Migliore	‡Galloping Grocer, 3, 120	Naughty New Yorker, 3, 120	9	1:35.61	90,000
2004	**Saratoga County**, 3, 116	J. Castellano	Pomeroy, 3, 116	Eddington, 3, 116	8	1:35.53	120,000
2003	**Alysweep**, 3, 120	R. Migliore	Grey Comet, 3, 120	Spite the Devil, 3, 116	9	1:40.60	120,000
2002	**Mayakovsky**, 3, 116	E. S. Prado	Saarland, 3, 120	Parade of Music, 3, 116	7	1:34.90	120,000
2001	**Richly Blended**, 3, 116	R. Wilson	Mr. John, 3, 116	Voodoo, 3, 116	8	1:35.14	120,000
2000	**Red Bullet**, 3, 113	A. O. Solis	Aptitude, 3, 113	Performing Magic, 3, 114	9	1:34.27	120,000
1999	**Badge**, 3, 120	S. Bridgmohan	Apremont, 3, 120	Robin Goodfellow, 3, 113	11	1:34.72	90,000
1998	**Wasatch**, 3, 117	J. D. Bailey	Dr J, 3, 119	Late Edition, 3, 114	10	1:36.56	90,000
1997	**Smokin Mel**, 3, 112	J. R. Velazquez	Ordway, 3, 122	Wild Wonder, 3, 119	11	1:34.38	120,000
1996	**Romano Gucci**, 3, 119	J. A. Krone	Tiger Talk, 3, 117	Feather Box, 3, 114	10	1:34.40	120,000
1995	**Talkin Man**, 3, 122	M. E. Smith	Da Hoss, 3, 117	Devious Course, 3, 117	11	1:36.82	150,000
1994	**Irgun**, 3, 114	J. D. Bailey	Bit of Puddin, 3, 117	Jesse F, 3, 114	12	1:36.27	150,000
1993	**As Indicated**, 3, 114	C. V. Bisono	Itaka, 3, 114	Strolling Along, 3, 121	8	1:36.24	120,000
1992	**dh-Devil His Due**, 3, 114	W. H. McCauley		Best Decorated, 3, 114	8	1:35.63	102,500
	dh-Lure, 3, 114	M. E. Smith					
1991	**Kyle's Our Man**, 3, 121	A. T. Cordero Jr.	King Mutesa, 3, 118	Another Review, 3, 118	8	1:34.69	150,000
1990	**Thirty Six Red**, 3, 114	M. E. Smith	Senor Pete, 3, 121	Burnt Hills, 3, 114	10	1:33.80	182,400
1989	**Easy Goer**, 3, 123	P. Day	Diamond Donnie, 3, 114	Expensive Decision, 3, 118	5	1:32.40	168,300
1988	**Private Terms**, 3, 126	C. W. Antley	Seeking the Gold, 3, 114	Perfect Spy, 3, 121	8	1:34.80	181,500
1987	**Gone West**, 3, 114	R. G. Davis	Shawklit Won, 3, 114	Gulch, 3, 123	9	1:34.60	190,200
1986	**Mogambo**, 3, 121	J. Vasquez	‡Tasso, 3, 123	Zabaleta, 3, 121	9	1:34.60	214,200
1985	**Eternal Prince**, 3, 114	R. Migliore	Pancho Villa, 3, 121	El Basco, 3, 114	7	1:34.40	147,840
1984	**Bear Hunt**, 3, 114	D. MacBeth	Lt. Flag, 3, 123	On the Sauce, 3, 114	5	1:40.40	136,440
1983	**Assault Landing**, 3, 114	V. A. Bracciale Jr.	Bounding Basque, 3, 123	Jacque's Tip, 3, 123	9	1:35.80	50,895
	Chas Conerly, 3, 123	J. Fell	Elegant Life, 3, 123	Law Talk, 3, 114	6	1:36.60	50,535
1982	**Air Forbes Won**, 3, 114	M. Venezia	Shimatoree, 3, 123	Big Brave Rock, 3, 114	8	1:35.60	50,760
1981	**Proud Appeal**, 3, 123	J. Fell	Cure the Blues, 3, 126	Noble Nashua, 3, 123	6	1:33.60	50,040
1980	**Colonel Moran**, 3, 123	J. Velasquez	Dunham's Gift, 3, 114	Bucksplasher, 3, 115	12	1:37.00	53,370
1979	**General Assembly**, 3, 123	J. Vasquez	Belle's Gold, 3, 123	Screen King, 3, 123	8	1:43.60	49,680
1978	**Slap Jack**, 3, 114	J. Velasquez	Quadratic, 3, 123	Shelter Half, 3, 121	9	1:38.60	33,210
1977	**Cormorant**, 3, 123	D. R. Wright	Fratello Ed, 3, 121	Papelote, 3, 114	9	1:43.60	32,850
1976	**Zen**, 3, 116	J. Vasquez	Cojak, 3, 124	Play the Red, 3, 114	10	1:35.60	34,740
1975	**Laramie Trail**, 3, 121	M. Venezia	Lefty, 3, 121	Kalong, 3, 116	5	1:38.00	27,180
	Singh, 3, 121	A. T. Cordero Jr.	Round Stake, 3, 116	Mr. Duds, 3, 116	8	1:37.00	27,630
1974	**Rube the Great**, 3, 119	M. A. Rivera	Hosiery, 3, 116	Cumulo Nimbus, 3, 116	8	1:35.20	27,420
	Stonewalk, 3, 116	M. A. Rivera	L'Amour Rullah, 3, 116	Wing South, 3, 119	9	1:36.00	27,570
1973	**Secretariat**, 3, 126	R. Turcotte	Champagne Charlie, 3, 117	Flush, 3, 117	6	1:33.40	33,330

Named for the unofficial nickname of New York City, "Gotham." Grade 2 1973-'97. Held at Jamaica 1953-'59. 1 mile 70 yards 1984, 2003. 1 mile 1960-'76, 1978, 1980-'83, 1985-2002, 2004-'05. Four-year-olds and up 1958. Two divisions 1974-'75, 1983. Dead heat for first 1992. ‡Groovy finished second, DQ to fifth, 1986. ‡Pavo finished second, DQ to fourth, 2005. Equaled track record 1973. Track record 1989.

Gravesend Handicap

Grade 3 in 2006. Aqueduct, three-year-olds and up, 6 furlongs, dirt. Held December 18, 2005, with a gross value of $112,000. First held in 1959. First graded in 1988. Stakes record 1:08.60 (1973 Petrograd).

Year	Winner	Jockey	Second	Third	Strs	Time	1st Purse
2005	**Banjo Picker**, 5, 114	T. Hemmings	Pioneer Empire, 4, 115	Saay Mi Name, 5, 115	10	1:10.17	$67,200
2004	**Don Six**, 4, 114	M. J. Luzzi	Mr. Whitestone, 4, 114	Papua, 5, 114	6	1:08.97	65,640
2003	**Shake You Down**, 5, 124	M. J. Luzzi	Way to the Top, 5, 114	Gators N Bears, 3, 115	7	1:09.55	65,400
2002	**Multiple Choice**, 4, 118	V. Carrero	Sing Me Back Home, 4, 114	Gold I. D., 3, 113	7	1:09.26	65,520
2001	**Here's Zealous**, 4, 114	E. S. Prado	Peeping Tom, 4, 120	Say Florida Sandy, 7, 120	6	1:10.37	64,740
2000	**Say Florida Sandy**, 6, 116	J. Bravo	Liberty Gold, 6, 115	Lake Pontchartrain, 5, 116	11	1:09.80	51,450
1999	**Cowboy Cop**, 5, 115	A. T. Gryder	Brushed On, 4, 112	Unreal Madness, 4, 116	9	1:09.41	50,370
1998	**Say Florida Sandy**, 4, 117	S. Bridgmohan	Esteemed Friend, 4, 114	Home On the Ridge, 4, 117	8	1:11.17	50,220
1997	**dh-Royal Haven**, 5, 122	R. Migliore		Laredo, 4, 115	7	1:10.08	32,670
	dh-Stalwart Member, 4, 118	A. T. Gryder					
1996	**Victor Avenue**, 3, 119	J. F. Chavez	Royal Haven, 4, 117	Stalwart Member, 3, 114	9	1:09.25	50,325
1995	**Cold Execution**, 4, 116	J. M. Pezua	Crafty Alfel, 7, 117	Golden Tent, 6, 114	10	1:09.50	50,820

1994	**Mining Burrah**, 4, 111	J. R. Velazquez	Golden Pro, 4, 115	Won Song, 4, 111	9	1:10.85	$51,270
1993	**Astudillo (Ire)**, 3, 108	F. A. Arguello Jr.	Fabersham, 5, 113	Ferociously, 3, 110	6	1:11.91	51,300
1992	**Hidden Tomahawk**, 4, 111	J. F. Chavez	Smart Alec, 4, 113	Miner's Dream, 5, 114	8	1:08.65	52,920
1991	**Shuttleman**, 5, 113	A. T. Cordero Jr.	Senor Speedy, 4, 120	Gallant Step, 4, 112	8	1:10.24	52,830
1990	**Mr. Nasty**, 3, 113	J. D. Bailey	Senor Speedy, 3, 114	Dargai, 4, 113	6	1:09.80	41,220
1989	**Never Forgotten**, 5, 117	A. Madrid Jr.	Proud and Valid, 4, 111	Garemma, 3, 113	5	1:12.60	40,980
1988	**High Brite**, 4, 122	A. T. Cordero Jr.	King's Swan, 8, 119	Matter of Honor, 3, 111	6	1:10.60	48,540
1987	**Vinnie the Viper**, 4, 116	J. A. Krone	King's Swan, 7, 122	Best by Test, 5, 117	6	1:09.60	54,360
1986	**Comic Blush**, 3, 106	A. Graell	King's Swan, 6, 122	Cutlass Reality, 4, 117	6	1:09.40	41,100
1985	**Love That Mac**, 3, 111	J. Velasquez	Raja's Shark, 4, 126	Aggressive Bid, 4, 110	6	1:11.00	40,860
1984	**Elegant Life**, 4, 115	J. Velasquez	Tarantara, 5, 120	Top Avenger, 6, 126	8	1:09.40	42,180
1983	**Main Stem**, 5, 109	V. Lopez	Havagreatdate, 5, 119	In From Dixie, 6, 113	10	1:14.00	34,440
1982	**Chan Balum**, 3, 108	J. Samyn	Maudlin, 4, 126	In From Dixie, 5, 120	9	1:11.20	34,320
1981	**Lines of Power**, 4, 116	D. MacBeth	Stiff Sentence, 4, 110	Bayou Black, 5, 115	6	1:09.60	32,760
1980	**Clever Trick**, 4, 117	J. Velasquez	Rise Jim, 4, 119	Dr. Blum, 3, 114	6	1:09.00	32,460
1979	**Shelter Half**, 4, 116	S. A. Boulmetis Jr.	Double Zeus, 4, 114	Tanthem, 4, 126	8	1:11.00	26,220
1978	**Half High**, 5, 113	A. Santiago	Intercontinent, 4, 114	dh-Bold and Stormy, 6, 107 dh-Fratello Ed, 4, 119	6	1:09.60	25,755
1977	**Full Out**, 4, 116	A. T. Cordero Jr.	Great Above, 5, 114	Jackson Square, 5, 114	7	1:10.20	22,065
1976	**Christopher R.**, 5, 131	W. J. Passmore	Mac Corkle, 4, 115	Gallant Bob, 4, 128	8	1:09.80	26,940
1975	**†Honorable Miss**, 5, 123	J. Vasquez	Queen City Lad, 4, 111	Piamem, 5, 118	7	1:10.00	16,485
1974	**Mr. Prospector**, 4, 124	J. Vasquez	Infuriator, 4, 112	Lonetree, 4, 119	8	1:09.00	22,830
1973	**Petrograd**, 4, 120	A. T. Cordero Jr.	Full Pocket, 4, 120	Delta Oil, 4, 111	6	**1:08.60**	16,635

Named for old Gravesend Park, a racetrack located in the Coney Island section of Brooklyn, New York. Held at Jamaica 1959-'60. Held at Belmont Park 1974. 7 furlongs 1962. Dead heat for third 1978. Dead heat for first 1997. ‡Unreal Madness finished third, DQ to ninth, 1999. Equaled track record 1973, 1992. †Denotes female.

Gulfstream Park Breeders' Cup Stakes

Grade 1 in 2006. Gulfstream Park, three-year-olds and up, $1\frac{7}{16}$ miles, turf. Held February 25, 2006, with a gross value of $190,000. First held in 1986. First graded in 1990. Stakes record 2:23.91 (2006 Einstein [Brz]).

Year	Winner	Jockey	Second	Third	Strs	Time	1st Purse
2006	**Einstein (Brz)**, 4, 123	R. Bejarano	Go Deputy, 6, 123	Gun Salute, 4, 123	8	**2:23.91**	$90,000
2005	**Prince Arch**, 4, 119	B. Blanc	Gigli (Brz), 7, 114	Mustanfar, 4, 118	11	2:11.44	150,000
2004	**Hard Buck (Brz)**, 5, 117	E. S. Prado	Balto Star, 6, 122	Kicken Kris, 4, 118	8	2:11.56	90,000
2003	**Man From Wicklow**, 6, 119	J. D. Bailey	Just Listen, 7, 113	Sardaukar (GB), 7, 114	10	2:11.62	120,000
2002	**Cetewayo**, 8, 115	C. H. Velasquez	Band Is Passing, 6, 117	Profit Option, 7, 115	12	2:17.44	120,000
2001	**Subtle Power (Ire)**, 4, 113	P. Day	Whata Brainstorm, 4, 113	Stokosky, 5, 114	9	2:13.50	60,000
2000	**Royal Anthem**, 5, 121	J. D. Bailey	Thesaurus, 6, 112	Band Is Passing, 4, 116	7	2:11.34	120,000
1999	**Yagli**, 6, 121	J. D. Bailey	Wild Event, 6, 117	Unite's Big Red, 5, 115	6	2:10.73	120,000
1998	**Flag Down**, 8, 120	J. A. Santos	Buck's Boy, 5, 115	Copy Editor, 6, 116	12	2:12.59	120,000
1997	**Lassigny**, 6, 116	J. D. Bailey	Flag Down, 7, 117	Awad, 7, 119	11	2:11.33	102,840
1996	**Celtic Arms (Fr)**, 5, 114	M. E. Smith	Broadway Flyer, 5, 117	Flag Down, 6, 118	11	2:13.90	101,880
1995	**Misil**, 7, 119	J. A. Santos	Myrmidon, 4, 113	Star of Manila, 4, 118	11	2:12.41	94,200
1994	**Strolling Along**, 4, 117	J. D. Bailey	Conveyor, 6, 119	Awad, 4, 112	6	2:05.01	93,150
1993	**Stagecraft (GB)**, 6, 115	J. D. Bailey	Social Retiree, 6, 116	Futurist, 5, 116	8	2:13.24	93,600
1992	**†Passagere du Soir (GB)**, 5, 114	J. D. Bailey	Colchis Island (Ire), 7, 111	Crystal Moment, 7, 116	14	2:15.71	95,130
1991	**Shy Tom**, 5, 115	C. Perret	Dr. Root, 4, 112	Runaway Raja, 5, 112	13	2:14.70	94,800
1990	**Youmadeyourpoint**, 4, 112	D. Valiente	Blazing Bart, 6, 118	Iron Courage, 6, 116	10	1:39.60	94,560
1989	**Equalize**, 7, 124	J. A. Santos	Posen, 4, 115	Nisswa, 4, 111	11	1:41.00	93,210
1988	**Salem Drive**, 6, 116	G. St. Leon	Equalize, 6, 112	Kings River (Ire), 6, 113	14	1:40.60	94,530
1987	**Bolshoi Boy**, 4, 116	R. P. Romero	Arctic Honeymoon, 4, 114	Little Bold John, 5, 115	5	1:44.60	80,286
1986	**Sondrio (Ire)**, 5, 113	J. A. Santos	Chief Run Run, 4, 113	Ends Well, 5, 115	10	1:40.60	80,772

Grade 3 1990-'91. Grade 2 1992-'98. Gulfstream Park Budweiser Breeders' Cup H. 1987-'95. Gulfstream Park Breeders' Cup H. 1996-2005. $1\frac{1}{16}$ miles 1986-'90. About $1\frac{3}{8}$ miles 1991. $1\frac{1}{4}$ miles 1994. $1\frac{3}{8}$ miles 1992-'93, 1995-2005. Dirt 1987, 1994. Course record 1993, 1999. Equaled course record 1997. Established course record 2006. †Denotes female.

Gulfstream Park Handicap

Grade 2 in 2006. Gulfstream Park, three-year-olds and up, $1\frac{3}{16}$ miles, dirt. Held March 4, 2006, with a gross value of $300,000. First held in 1946. First graded in 1973. Stakes record 1:54.74 (2005 Eddington).

Year	Winner	Jockey	Second	Third	Strs	Time	1st Purse
2006	**Harlington**, 4, 114	J. R. Velazquez	Contante (Arg), 6, 113	It's No Joke, 4, 116	8	1:55.18	$180,000
2005	**Eddington**, 4, 115	E. Coa	Pies Prospect, 4, 113	Zakocity, 4, 117	8	**1:54.74**	180,000
2004	**Jackpot**, 6, 113	J. Bravo	Newfoundland, 4, 116	The Lady's Groom, 4, 113	6	2:02.80	180,000
2003	**Hero's Tribute**, 5, 115	E. S. Prado	Aeneas, 4, 115	Puzzlement, 4, 114	8	2:04.24	180,000
2002	**Hal's Hope**, 5, 113	R. I. Velez	Mongoose, 4, 115	Sir Bear, 9, 117	5	2:02.91	180,000
2001	**Sir Bear**, 8, 116	E. Coa	Pleasant Breeze, 6, 115	Broken Vow, 4, 114	9	2:02.96	120,000
2000	**Behrens**, 6, 120	J. F. Chavez	Adonis, 4, 115	With Anticipation, 5, 113	6	2:01.79	210,000
1999	**Behrens**, 5, 114	J. F. Chavez	Archers Bay, 4, 114	Sir Bear, 6, 118	8	2:01.91	210,000
1998	**Skip Away**, 5, 127	J. D. Bailey	Unruled, 5, 112	Behrens, 4, 114	6	2:03.21	300,000
1997	**Mt. Sassafras**, 5, 113	J. D. Bailey	Skip Away, 4, 122	Tejano Run, 5, 114	6	2:02.39	300,000
1996	**Wekiva Springs**, 5, 117	J. D. Bailey	Star Standard, 4, 112	Powerful Punch, 7, 113	8	2:03.18	300,000
1995	**Cigar**, 5, 118	J. D. Bailey	Pride of Burkaan, 5, 114	Mahogany Hall, 4, 113	11	2:02.95	300,000

1994 **Scuffleburg**, 5, 113	C. Perret	Migrating Moon, 4, 114	Wallenda, 4, 117	10	2:00.46	$300,000
1993 **Devil His Due**, 4, 113	W. H. McCauley	Offbeat, 4, 112	Pistols and Roses, 4, 114	9	2:01.33	300,000
1992 **Sea Cadet**, 4, 119	A. O. Solis	Strike the Gold, 4, 115	Sunny Sunrise, 5, 114	6	2:01.79	180,000
1991 **Jolie's Halo**, 4, 119	R. Platts	Primal, 6, 117	Chief Honcho, 4, 118	8	2:01.04	180,000
1990 **Mi Selecto**, 5, 114	J. D. Bailey	Tour d'Or, 8, 118	Lay Down, 6, 113	8	2:03.60	180,000
1989 **Slew City Slew**, 5, 117	A. T. Cordero Jr.	Bold Midway, 5, 113	Cryptoclearance, 5, 123	7	2:03.20	180,000
1988 **Jade Hunter**, 4, 113	J. D. Bailey	Cryptoclearance, 4, 122	Creme Fraiche, 6, 120	6	2:01.60	180,000
1987 **Skip Trial**, 5, 118	R. P. Romero	Creme Fraiche, 5, 120	Snow Chief, 4, 124	4	2:02.80	150,000
1986 **Skip Trial**, 4, 121	R. P. Romero	Proud Truth, 4, 125	Important Business, 4, 113	5	2:03.20	180,000
1985 **Dr. Carter**, 4, 119	J. Velasquez	Key to the Moon, 4, 120	Pine Circle, 4, 116	8	2:02.00	171,480
1984 **Mat-Boy (Arg)**, 5, 118	J. Valdivieso	Lord Darnley, 6, 109	Courteous Majesty, 4, 114	7	1:59.00	86,700
1983 **†Christmas Past**, 4, 117	J. Velasquez	Crafty Prospector, 4, 115	Rivalero, 7, 120	12	2:02.60	111,630
1982 **Lord Darnley**, 4, 113	M. Russ	Joanie's Chief, 5, 113	Double Sonic, 4, 111	9	2:01.80	91,200
1981 **Hurry Up Blue**, 4, 119	C. C. Lopez	Yosi Boy, 5, 111	Imperial Dilemma, 4, 113	9	2:03.20	114,888
1980 **Private Account**, 4, 119	J. Fell	Lot o' Gold, 4, 120	Silent Cal, 5, 118	7	2:01.40	100,000
1979 **Sensitive Prince**, 4, 120	J. Vasquez	Jumping Hill, 7, 126	Silent Cal, 4, 119	7	1:59.20	100,000
1978 **Bowl Game**, 4, 112	J. Velasquez	True Statement, 4, 108	Silver Series, 4, 126	11	2:00.60	100,000
1977 **Strike Me Lucky**, 5, 109	J. D. Bailey	Legion, 7, 115	Yamanin, 5, 122	12	2:00.80	88,200
1976 **Hail the Pirates**, 6, 116	B. Baeza	Legion, 6, 113	Packer Captain, 4, 113	7	2:01.80	73,560
1975 **Gold and Myrrh**, 4, 114	W. Blum	Proud and Bold, 5, 120	Buffalo Lark, 5, 117	9	2:01.80	74,520
1974 **Forego**, 4, 127	H. Gustines	True Knight, 5, 123	Golden Don, 4, 118	6	1:59.80	72,360
1973 **West Coast Scout**, 5, 116	L. Adams	Super Sail, 5, 110	Freetex, 4, 113	10	2:01.00	80,880

Grade 1 1975-2002. Gulfstream H. 1946, 1968. 1¼ miles 1946-2004. Four-year-olds and up 1946. †Denotes female. Held as an allowance race 1949-'51.

Hal's Hope Handicap

Grade 3 in 2006. Gulfstream Park, three-year-olds and up, 1⅛ miles, dirt. Held January 7, 2006, with a gross value of $100,000. First held in 1990. First graded in 1993. Stakes record 1:48.05 (2006 On Thin Ice).

Year Winner	Jockey	Second	Third	Strs	Time	1st Purse
2006 **On Thin Ice**, 5, 114	S. Bridgmohan	Network, 4, 114	Seek Gold, 6, 114	9	**1:48.05**	$60,000
2005 **Badge of Silver**, 5, 115	J. D. Bailey	Dynever, 5, 117	Contante (Arg), 5, 114	12	1:48.57	60,000
2004 **Puzzlement**, 5, 116	J. F. Chavez	Bowman's Band, 6, 118	Stockholder, 4, 114	7	1:42.39	60,000
2003 **Windsor Castle**, 5, 115	E. Coa	Saint Verre, 5, 114	Najran, 4, 114	8	1:42.33	60,000
2002 **Hal's Hope**, 5, 112	R. I. Velez	American Halo, 6, 113	Windsor Castle, 4, 112	9	1:42.40	60,000
2000 **Dancing Guy**, 5, 120	J. D. Bailey	Yankee Victor, 4, 113	Midway Magistrate, 6, 117	8	1:44.94	45,000
1999 **Jazz Club**, 4, 114	P. Day	Rock and Roll, 4, 113	Hanarsaan, 6, 113	7	1:42.76	45,000
1998 **K. J.'s Appeal**, 4, 114	J. R. Velazquez	Powerful Goer, 4, 112	Tour's Big Red, 5, 114	8	1:42.34	45,000
1997 **Louis Quatorze**, 4, 121	P. Day	Strawberry Wine, 5, 113	Exalto, 6, 108	5	1:43.43	45,000
1996 **Geri**, 4, 114	J. D. Bailey	Halo's Image, 5, 120	Second Childhood, 4, 113	6	1:41.49	45,000
1995 **Warm Wayne**, 4, 112	J. D. Bailey	Meadow Monster, 4, 113	Silent Lake, 5, 113	9	1:43.11	45,000
1994 **Forever Whirl**, 4, 113	W. H. McCauley	Northern Trend, 6, 113	Royal n Gold, 5, 113	10	1:41.81	45,000
1993 **Classic Seven**, 5, 116	C. E. Lopez Sr.	Devil On Ice, 4, 115	Keratoid, 4, 111	10	1:43.49	60,000
1992 **Peanut Butter Onit**, 6, 114	J. A. Santos	Sunny Sunrise, 5, 117	Honest Ensign, 4, 109	7	1:43.78	45,000
1991 **New York Swell**, 8, 111	J. O. Alferez	Rhythm, 4, 121	Mercedes Won, 5, 112	5	1:42.50	45,000
1990 **Big Sal**, 5, 119	E. Fires	Twice Too Many, 5, 117	Groomstick, 4, 119	6	1:24.80	20,340

Named for Harold Rose's 2000 Florida Derby (G1) and '02 Gulfstream Park H. (G1) winner Hal's Hope (1997 c. by Jolie's Halo). Formerly named for Brushwood Stable's 1986 Donn H. (G2) winner Creme Fraiche (1982 g. by Rich Cream). Creme Fraiche S. 1990. Creme Fraiche H. 1991-2002. Not held 2001. 7 furlongs 1990. Four-year-olds and up 1990. Track record 2006.

Hanshin Cup Handicap

Grade 3 in 2006. Arlington Park, three-year-olds and up, 1 mile, dirt. Held May 27, 2006, with a gross value of $100,000. First held in 1941. First graded in 1983. Stakes record 1:33.20 (1979 Bask).

Year Winner	Jockey	Second	Third	Strs	Time	1st Purse
2006 **‡Gouldings Green**, 5, 118	C. J. Lanerie	Fifteen Rounds, 6, 117	Three Hour Nap, 4, 117	5	1:34.05	$60,000
2005 **Lord of the Game**, 4, 117	E. Razo Jr.	Gouldings Green, 4, 115	Nkosi Reigns, 4, 115	8	1:34.60	60,000
2004 **Crafty Shaw**, 6, 119	C. Perret	Apt to Be, 7, 119	Kodema, 5, 116	7	1:35.36	60,000
2003 **Apt to Be**, 6, 117	E. Razo Jr.	There's Zealous, 5, 116	San Pedro, 5, 116	7	1:34.40	60,000
2002 **Bonapaw**, 6, 121	G. Melancon	Slider, 4, 115	Discreet Hero, 4, 116	7	1:34.00	60,000
2001 **Bright Valour**, 5, 115	R. Albarado	Apt to Be, 4, 114	Castlewood, 4, 115	8	1:36.21	60,000
2000 **‡Bright Valour**, 4, 114	J. Campbell	Desert Demon, 4, 113	Battle Mountain, 6, 114	5	1:34.97	60,000
1997 **Announce**, 5, 116	C. C. Bourque	Victor Cooley, 4, 117	Hunk of Class, 4, 116	7	1:36.95	60,000
1996 **Golden Gear**, 5, 122	M. Guidry	Exclusive Garth, 4, 113	Prospect for Love, 4, 113	10	1:36.13	105,000
1995 **Tarzans Blade**, 4, 115	P. Day	Swank, 4, 114	Come On Flip, 4, 114	9	1:35.64	45,000
1994 **Slerp**, 5, 117	E. Fires	Seattle Morn, 4, 116	Dancing Jon, 6, 113	5	1:35.43	60,000
1993 **Split Run**, 5, 114	E. Fires	Gee Can He Dance, 4, 114	Danc'n Jake, 4, 114	11	1:34.46	60,000
1992 **Katahaula County**, 4, 114	C. C. Bourque	The Great Carl, 5, 111	Stalwars, 7, 116	9	1:37.27	45,000
1991 **Bright Again**, 4, 112	P. Day	Secret Hello, 4, 115	Irish Swap, 4, 112	6	1:35.39	45,000
1990 **Black Tie Affair (Ire)**, 4, 119	J. Velasquez	Bio, 4, 112	New Plymouth, 7, 110	4	1:36.00	47,923
1989 **Present Value**, 5, 114	F. Olivares	Paramount Jet, 4, 114	Sutter's Prospect, 4, 110	8	1:34.40	50,310
1987 **Red Attack**, 5, 116	M. E. Smith	Taylor's Special, 6, 127	Come Summer, 5, 114	5	1:34.20	48,570
1986 **Smile**, 4, 121	J. Vasquez	Taylor's Special, 5, 124	Red Attack, 4, 114	7	1:34.00	69,180

1985	**Timeless Native**, 5, 122	J. E. Tejeira	Par Flite, 4, 115	Harham's Sizzler, 6, 115	7	1:33.80	$49,275
1984	**Win Stat**, 7, 117	D. Pettinger	Le Cou Cou, 4, 116	Harham's Sizzler, 5, 111	8	1:37.80	49,860
1983	**‡Hale Herk**, 4, 113	R. D. Evans	Thumbsucker, 4, 116	Spoonful of Honey, 4, 115	14	1:36.00	52,560
1982	**Summer Advocate**, 5, 117	R. P. Romero	Prince Freddie, 6, 109	Fabulous Find, 4, 110	9	1:36.40	49,860
1981	**J. Burns**, 6, 115	J. D. Bailey	Summer Advocate, 4, 115	Brent's Trans Am, 4, 114	11	1:35.80	68,340
1980	**Prince Majestic**, 6, 113	G. Patterson	Sea Ride, 5, 114	Braze and Bold, 5, 118	12	1:39.20	69,300
1979	**Bask**, 5, 112	M. R. Morgan	Bold Standard, 5, 111	Hold Your Tricks, 4, 120	9	**1:33.20**	22,605
1976	**Visier**, 4, 120	R. Riera Jr.	Dare to Command, 4, 118	Auberge, 3, 112	7	1:47.00	31,650
1975	**Sr. Diplomat**, 4, 113	P. Day	Recaptured, 5, 109	Mike James, 5, 111	10	1:44.40	37,440
1974	**Our Pappa Joe**, 7, 114	R. Cox	Radnor, 4, 113	We're Ready Now, 4, 116	11	1:36.60	45,000
	Henry Tudor, 5, 121	R. Platts	Recaptured, 4, 108	Sharp Gary, 3, 118	10	1:36.00	45,000
1973	**Test Run**, 7, 112	J. Keene	Chateauvira, 5, 120	Fame and Power, 4, 120	12	1:38.20	21,037

Named in honor of the Japan Racing Association, which conducts a race at Hanshin Racecourse in honor of Arlington Park. Formerly named for C. V. Whitney's 1932, '33 Horse of the Year, '42 leading North American sire, and '32 Stars and Stripes H. winner Equipoise (1928 c. by Pennant). Equipoise Mile H. 1941-'97. Hanshin H. 2000. Held at Washington Park 1943-'45. Not held 1977-'78, 1988, 1998-'99. Two divisions 1974. ‡Thumbsucker finished first, DQ to second, 1983. ‡Yankee Victor finished first, DQ to fifth for a positive drug test, 2000. ‡Fifteen Rounds finished first, DQ to second, 2006. Equaled track record 1974 (2nd Div.).

Haskell Invitational Handicap

Grade 1 in 2006. Monmouth Park, three-year-olds, $1\frac{1}{8}$ miles, dirt. Held August 7, 2005, with a gross value of $1,015,000. First held in 1885. First graded in 1973. Stakes record 1:47 (1987 Bet Twice; 1976 Majestic Light).

Year	Winner	Jockey	Second	Third	Strs	Time	1st Purse
2005	**Roman Ruler**, 3, 119	J. D. Bailey	Sun King, 3, 119	Park Avenue Ball, 3, 118	7	1:49.88	$600,000
2004	**Lion Heart**, 3, 121	J. Bravo	My Snookie's Boy, 3, 116	Pies Prospect, 3, 116	8	1:48.95	600,000
2003	**Peace Rules**, 3, 121	E. S. Prado	Sky Mesa, 3, 118	Funny Cide, 3, 123	7	1:49.32	600,000
2002	**War Emblem**, 3, 124	V. Espinoza	Magic Weisner, 3, 118	Like a Hero, 3, 117	5	1:48.21	600,000
2001	**Point Given**, 3, 124	G. L. Stevens	Touch Tone, 3, 115	Burning Roma, 3, 119	6	1:49.77	900,000
2000	**Dixie Union**, 3, 117	A. O. Solis	Captain Steve, 3, 118	Milwaukee Brew, 3, 117	9	1:50.00	600,000
1999	**Menifee**, 3, 124	P. Day	Cat Thief, 3, 123	Forestry, 3, 118	7	1:48.06	600,000
1998	**Coronado's Quest**, 3, 124	M. E. Smith	Victory Gallop, 3, 125	Grand Slam, 3, 118	6	1:48.60	600,000
1997	**Touch Gold**, 3, 125	C. J. McCarron	Anet, 3, 120	Free House, 3, 125	5	1:47.60	850,000
1996	**Skip Away**, 3, 124	J. A. Santos	Dr. Caton, 3, 115	Victory Speech, 3, 121	7	1:47.73	450,000
1995	**†Serena's Song**, 3, 118	G. L. Stevens	Pyramid Peak, 3, 120	Citadeed, 3, 118	11	1:48.94	300,000
1994	**Holy Bull**, 3, 126	M. E. Smith	Meadow Flight, 3, 118	Concern, 3, 118	6	1:48.36	300,000
1993	**Kissin Kris**, 3, 118	J. A. Santos	Storm Tower, 3, 119	Dry Bean, 3, 113	7	1:49.58	300,000
1992	**Technology**, 3, 120	J. D. Bailey	Nines Wild, 3, 112	Scudan, 3, 113	9	1:48.78	300,000
1991	**Lost Mountain**, 3, 118	C. Perret	Corporate Report, 3, 120	Hansel, 3, 126	5	1:48.06	300,000
1990	**Restless Con**, 3, 118	T. T. Doocy	Baron de Vaux, 3, 117	Rhythm, 3, 121	7	1:49.20	300,000
1989	**King Glorious**, 3, 123	C. J. McCarron	Music Merci, 3, 120	Shy Tom, 3, 116	10	1:49.80	300,000
1988	**Forty Niner**, 3, 126	L. A. Pincay Jr.	Seeking the Gold, 3, 125	Primal, 3, 117	5	1:47.60	300,000
1987	**Bet Twice**, 3, 126	C. Perret	Alysheba, 3, 126	Lost Code, 3, 124	5	**1:47.00**	300,000
1986	**Wise Times**, 3, 114	C. P. DeCarlo	Personal Flag, 3, 114	Danzig Connection, 3, 123	9	1:48.60	180,000
1985	**Skip Trial**, 3, 116	J. Samyn	Spend a Buck, 3, 127	Creme Fraiche, 3, 126	7	1:48.60	180,000
1984	**Big Pistol**, 3, 119	G. Patterson	Birdie's Legend, 3, 115	Locust Bayou, 3, 115	6	1:47.80	120,000
1983	**Deputed Testamony**, 3, 124	W. H. McCauley	Bet Big, 3, 116	Parfaitement, 3, 116	10	1:49.20	120,000
1982	**Wavering Monarch**, 3, 117	R. P. Romero	Aloma's Ruler, 3, 126	Lejoli, 3, 112	7	1:47.80	120,000
1981	**Five Star Flight**, 3, 119	C. Perret	Lord Avie, 3, 126	Ornery Odis, 3, 112	6	1:48.40	120,000
1980	**Thanks to Tony**, 3, 111	C. E. Lopez Sr.	Superbity, 3, 124	Amber Pass, 3, 121	8	1:49.40	90,000
1979	**Coastal**, 3, 127	R. Hernandez	Steady Growth, 3, 120	Worthy Piper, 3, 112	5	1:48.80	65,000
1978	**Delta Flag**, 3, 112	D. Nied	Dave's Friend, 3, 120	Special Honor, 3, 118	7	1:53.20	65,000
1977	**Affiliate**, 3, 117	M. A. Rivera	Don Sebastian, 3, 112	Iron Constitution, 3, 118	7	1:50.60	65,000
1976	**Majestic Light**, 3, 122	S. Hawley	Appassionato, 3, 113	Honest Pleasure, 3, 126	10	**1:47.00**	65,000
1975	**Wajima**, 3, 118	B. Baeza	Intrepid Hero, 3, 115	My Friend Gus, 3, 116	8	1:49.60	65,000
1974	**Holding Pattern**, 3, 117	M. Miceli	Little Current, 3, 127	Better Arbitor, 3, 119	10	1:49.80	65,000
1973	**Our Native**, 3, 123	M. A. Rivera	Annihilate 'em, 3, 118	Aljamin, 3, 118	8	1:48.60	65,000

Named for Amory L. Haskell (1894-1966), former president of Monmouth Park. Formerly sponsored by General Motors Corp. of Detroit 1996-'98. Choice S. 1885-'92, 1946-'67. Monmouth Invitational H. 1968-'80. Buick Haskell Invitational H. 1996-'98. Not held 1893-1945. $1\frac{1}{2}$ miles 1885-'92. $1\frac{1}{4}$ miles 1946-'52. $1\frac{1}{16}$ miles 1958-'67. †Denotes female.

Hawthorne Derby

Grade 3 in 2006. Hawthorne Race Course, three-year-olds, $1\frac{1}{8}$ miles, turf. Held October 15, 2005, with a gross value of $250,000. First held in 1965. First graded in 1973. Stakes record 1:44.70 (1991 Rainbows for Life).

Year	Winner	Jockey	Second	Third	Strs	Time	1st Purse
2005	**Gun Salute**, 3, 122	C. H. Velasquez	Cosmic Kris, 3, 116	Embossed (Ire), 3, 114	5	1:47.51	$150,000
2004	**Cool Conductor**, 3, 115	J. A. Santos	Bankruptcy Court, 3, 115	Crown Prince, 3, 113	10	1:47.89	150,000
2003	**False Promises**, 3, 115	C. H. Marquez Jr.	Megoman, 3, 115	Beau Classic, 3, 113	11	1:48.48	150,000
2002	**‡Scooter Roach**, 3, 115	J. M. Campbell	Quest Star, 3, 115	Colorful Tour, 3, 117	7	1:58.88	150,000
2001	**Kalu**, 3, 119	J. A. Santos	Proud Man, 3, 119	Rahy's Secret, 3, 115	7	1:50.49	150,000
2000	**dh-Hymn (Ire)**, 3, 115	L. A. Pincay Jr.		Lonely Place (Ire), 3, 113	10	1:53.79	100,000
	dh-Rumsonontheriver, 3, 115	A. J. Juarez Jr.					

1999	**Minor Wisdom**, 3, 115	R. Zimmerman	Air Rocket, 3, 119	Fred of Gold, 3, 113	12	1:49.06	$150,000
1998	**Stay Sound**, 3, 115	A. J. D'Amico	El Mirasol, 3, 111	Yankee Brass, 3, 114	11	1:47.54	150,000
1997	**River Squall**, 3, 119	C. Perret	Honor Glide, 3, 122	Blazing Sword, 3, 115	6	1:48.20	120,000
1996	**Jaunatxo**, 3, 122	J. L. Diaz	Trail City, 3, 122	Canyon Run, 3, 122	11	1:47.18	120,000
1995	**Cuzzin Jeb**, 3, 117	C. C. Lopez	Hawk Attack, 3, 122	Seven n Seven, 3, 114	9	1:48.90	90,000
1994	**Chrysalis House**, 3, 115	M. Guidry	Unfinished Symph, 3, 122	Marvin's Faith (Ire), 3, 122	11	1:51.88	90,000
1993	**Snake Eyes**, 3, 122	G. K. Gomez	Lt. Pinkerton, 3, 117	Ft. Bent, 3, 115	12	1:50.28	90,000
1992	**Bantan**, 3, 117	C. C. Bourque	†Words of War, 3, 114	Gee Can He Dance, 3, 117	11	1:48.05	60,000
1991	**Rainbows for Life**, 3, 122	D. Penna	Drummer Boy, 3, 117	Kiltartan Cross, 3, 115	11	**1:44.70**	65,370
1990	**Tutu Tobago**, 3, 113	P. A. Johnson	Take That Step, 3, 122	Seti I., 3, 115	11	1:53.60	64,710
1989	**Broto**, 3, 115	S. J. Sellers	Joey Jr., 3, 117	Chenin Blanc, 3, 115	10	1:53.00	94,350
1988	**Pappas Swing**, 3, 119	E. S. Prado	Djedar, 3, 115	Foolish Intent, 3, 117	11	1:55.80	94,200
1987	**Zaizoom**, 3, 119	E. Fires	Sir Bask, 3, 114	Rio's Lark, 3, 116	7	2:09.80	89,280
1986	**Autobot**, 3, 120	E. Fires	Spellbound, 3, 117	Son of the Desert, 3, 115	11	2:00.40	96,360
1985	**Derby Wish**, 3, 123	R. P. Romero	Day Shift, 3, 115	Explosive Darling, 3, 123	8	2:00.20	64,320
1984	**Pass the Line**, 3, 117	C. H. Marquez	Mr. Japan, 3, 117	Bet Blind, 3, 115	12	1:57.60	66,750
1983	**St. Forbes**, 3, 117	E. Fires	His Flower, 3, 117	Saverton, 3, 117	14	1:44.40	67,200
1982	**Drop Your Drawers**, 3, 118	P. Day	Harham's Sizzler, 3, 118	Northern Majesty, 3, 118	9	1:42.80	64,830
1981	**Jeremy Jet**, 3, 112	C. H. Silva	Loose Thoughts, 3, 112	Recusant, 3, 112	14	1:45.60	67,200
1980	**Jaklin Klugman**, 3, 121	C. J. McCarron	Summer Advocate, 3, 115	Hurry Up Blue, 3, 121	7	1:40.80	64,440
1979	**Architect**, 3, 115	S. A. Spencer	Incredible Ease, 3, 112	Door King, 3, 112	9	1:44.60	48,360
1978	**Sensitive Prince**, 3, 118	J. Vasquez	Gordie H., 3, 112	Esops Foibles, 3, 124	8	1:39.60	73,680
1977	**Silver Series**, 3, 114	L. Snyder	Courtly Haste, 3, 114	Affiliate, 3, 112	14	1:41.20	100,800
1976	**Wardlaw**, 3, 117	J. E. Tejeira	Practitioner, 3, 112	Hurricane Ed, 3, 117	8	1:42.80	82,200
1975	**Winter Fox**, 3, 109	B. Fann	Intrepid Hero, 3, 125	American History, 3, 117	14	1:49.20	93,800
1974	**Stonewalk**, 3, 123	R. Turcotte	Tytus Casella, 3, 116	Mr. Door, 3, 114	10	1:40.60	63,150
1973	**‡Golden Don**, 3, 116	M. Manganello	Impecunious, 3, 123	Cades Cove, 3, 114	10	1:41.20	40,600

Hawthorne Diamond Jubilee H. 1965-'68. Hawthorne Derby H. 1969-'75. Held at Sportsman's Park 1979. 1$\frac{1}{16}$ miles 1965-'74, 1976-'84. 1$\frac{3}{16}$ miles 1985-'87. Dirt 1965-'83. Dead heat for first 2000. ‡Impecunious finished first, DQ to second, 1973. ‡Flying Dash (Ger) finished first, DQ to seventh for a positive drug test, 2002. †Denotes female.

Hawthorne Gold Cup Handicap

Grade 2 in 2006. Hawthorne Race Course, three-year-olds and up, 1$\frac{1}{4}$ miles, dirt. Held September 24, 2005, with a gross value of $750,000. First held in 1928. First graded in 1973. Stakes record 1:58.80 (1970 Gladwin; 1974 Group Plan).

Year	Winner	Jockey	Second	Third	Strs	Time	1st Purse
2005	**Super Frolic**, 5, 118	V. Espinoza	Lord of the Game, 4, 117	Desert Boom, 5, 115	10	2:04.66	$450,000
2004	**Freefourinternet**, 6, 112	G. Kuntzweiler	Perfect Drift, 5, 121	Sonic West, 5, 115	7	2:03.34	450,000
2003	**Perfect Drift**, 4, 122	P. Day	Tenpins, 5, 119	Aeneas, 4, 114	6	2:03.63	450,000
2002	**Hail The Chief (GB)**, 5, 114	J. F. Chavez	Dollar Bill, 4, 114	Parade Leader, 5, 115	5	2:02.80	300,000
2001	**Duckhorn**, 4, 112	R. A. Meier	Lido Palace (Chi), 4, 114	Guided Tour, 5, 116	7	2:01.61	300,000
2000	**Dust On the Bottle**, 5, 112	T. T. Doocy	Guided Tour, 4, 113	Golden Missile, 5, 121	8	2:03.09	300,000
1999	**Supreme Sound (GB)**, 5, 112	R. A. Meier	Golden Missile, 4, 115	Beboppin Baby, 6, 113	8	2:01.19	300,000
1998	**Awesome Again**, 4, 123	P. Day	Unruled, 5, 114	Muchacho Fino, 4, 114	8	2:02.71	240,000
1997	**Buck's Boy**, 4, 114	M. Guidry	Cairo Express, 5, 115	Beboppin Baby, 4, 115	7	2:00.54	180,000
1996	**Come On Flip**, 5, 113	C. A. Emigh	Michael's Star, 4, 114	Mt. Sassafras, 4, 120	10	2:03.40	180,000
1995	**Yourmissinthepoint**, 4, 113	M. Guidry	Basqueian, 4, 114	Sky Carr, 5, 112	9	2:01.00	150,000
1994	**Recoup the Cash**, 4, 117	J. L. Diaz	Run Softly, 3, 114	Kissin Kris, 4, 118	11	2:01.99	240,000
1993	**Evanescent**, 6, 115	A. T. Gryder	Marquetry, 6, 123	Valley Crossing, 5, 117	7	2:02.19	240,000
1992	**Irish Swap**, 5, 115	B. E. Poyadou	Sea Cadet, 4, 121	Evanescent, 5, 112	8	2:01.12	240,000
1991	**Sunny Sunrise**, 4, 114	C. W. Antley	Sports View, 4, 116	Discover, 3, 114	14	2:04.10	309,840
1990	**Black Tie Affair (Ire)**, 4, 116	J. L. Diaz	Mi Selecto, 5, 115	Silver Tower, 3, 112	10	2:03.40	307,800
1989	**Cryptoclearance**, 5, 122	J. A. Santos	Proper Reality, 4, 120	Classic Account, 4, 112	7	2:00.40	305,730
1988	**Cryptoclearance**, 4, 117	J. A. Santos	Cutlass Reality, 6, 124	Nostalgia's Star, 6, 113	4	2:00.20	303,690
1987	**Nostalgia's Star**, 5, 117	F. Toro	Savings, 4, 114	Minneapple, 5, 117	9	2:02.00	277,440
1986	**Ends Well**, 5, 121	R. P. Romero	Harham's Sizzler, 7, 115	Inevitable Leader, 7, 113	6	2:00.60	182,340
1985	**Garthorn**, 5, 116	R. Q. Meza	Magic North, 3, 115	Leroy S., 4, 114	10	2:01.80	158,220
1984	**Proof**, 4, 118	E. Delahoussaye	Jack Slade, 4, 119	Bounding Basque, 4, 117	14	2:01.20	160,170
1983	**Water Bank**, 4, 114	C. Lamance	Cad, 5, 116	Gallant Gentleman, 4, 111	13	2:01.40	130,050
1982	**Recusant**, 4, 122	R. J. Hirdes Jr.	Harham's Sizzler, 3, 116	Irish Heart (Ire), 4, 115	12	2:01.80	98,760
1981	**Spruce Bouquet**, 4, 119	K. D. Clark	Lord Gallant, 4, 114	Bill Monroe, 3, 119	16	2:04.20	101,760
1980	**Tunerup**, 4, 125	J. Vasquez	Pole Position, 4, 120	The Trader Man, 4, 112	9	2:00.60	82,590
1979	**Young Bob**, 4, 114	R. L. Turcotte	All the More, 6, 113	Architect, 3, 121	7	1:51.00	62,460
1977	**On the Sly**, 4, 121	G. McCarron	Milwaukee Avenue, 4, 114	Romeo, 4, 111	8	2:01.60	75,072
1976	**Almost Grown**, 4, 110	M. R. Morgan	Teddy's Courage, 3, 113	Romeo, 3, 113	10	2:01.60	86,720
1975	**Royal Glint**, 5, 124	J. E. Tejeira	Buffalo Lark, 5, 123	Group Plan, 5, 126	5	2:02.20	74,480
1974	**Group Plan**, 4, 115	J. Velasquez	Buffalo Lark, 4, 117	Billy Come Lately, 4, 119	5	**1:58.80**	66,120
1973	**Tri Jet**, 4, 117	B. Baeza	Golden Don, 3, 113	Cloudy Dawn, 4, 114	9	2:01.40	75,720

Grade 3 1997-2000. Hawthorne Gold Cup S. 1928-'35. Budweiser-Hawthorne Gold Cup H. 1985-'86, 1988-'91. Hawthorne Budweiser Gold Cup H. 1987, 1992. Not held 1934, 1936, 1940-'45, 1978. Held at Sportsman's Park 1979. 1$\frac{1}{8}$ miles 1979. Equaled track record 1974.

Hawthorne Handicap

Grade 3 in 2006. Hollywood Park, three-year-olds and up, fillies and mares, 1¹/₁₆ miles, dirt. Held May 7, 2006, with a gross value of $100,000. First held in 1974. First graded in 1982. Stakes record 1:41.12 (1993 Freedom Cry).

Year	Winner	Jockey	Second	Third	Strs	Time	1st Purse
2006	**Star Parade (Arg)**, 7, 118	M. A. Pedroza	Hollywood Story, 5, 118	Healthy Addiction, 5, 120	5	1:42.26	$60,000
2005	**Hollywood Story**, 4, 119	V. Espinoza	Siphon Honey, 6, 112	House of Fortune, 4, 117	7	1:42.42	64,980
2004	**Summer Wind Dancer**, 4, 116	V. Espinoza	Pesci, 4, 115	Miss Loren (Arg), 6, 116	7	1:41.56	65,160
2003	**Keys to the Heart**, 4, 115	J. Valdivia Jr.	Rhiana, 6, 116	‡Alexine (Arg), 7, 117	4	1:42.97	63,240
2002	**Queen of Wilshire**, 6, 115	P. A. Valenzuela	Alexine (Arg), 6, 119	Verruma (Brz), 6, 116	5	1:43.16	63,660
2001	**Printemps (Chi)**, 4, 116	C. J. McCarron	Feverish, 6, 119	Brianda (Ire), 4, 109	4	1:43.21	90,000
2000	**Riboletta (Brz)**, 5, 117	C. J. McCarron	Excellent Meeting, 4, 122	Speaking of Time, 4, 111	5	1:42.33	90,000
1999	**Victory Stripes (Arg)**, 5, 115	C. J. McCarron	Magical Allure, 4, 118	Housa Dancer (Fr), 6, 115	4	1:41.73	90,000
1998	**I Ain't Bluffing**, 4, 118	C. J. McCarron	Fun in Excess, 4, 116	Tomorrows Sunshine, 4, 115	5	1:41.49	63,720
1997	**Twice the Vice**, 6, 120	C. J. McCarron	Chile Chatte, 4, 115	Listening, 4, 117	7	1:42.72	64,860
1996	**Borodislew**, 6, 119	C. S. Nakatani	Jewel Princess, 4, 120	Urbane, 4, 118	6	1:41.28	64,200
1995	**Paseana (Arg)**, 8, 122	C. J. McCarron	Pirate's Revenge, 4, 117	Top Rung, 4, 117	7	1:42.40	63,300
1994	**Golden Klair (GB)**, 4, 118	K. Desormeaux	Likeable Style, 4, 119	Andestine, 4, 117	4	1:41.41	60,000
1993	**Freedom Cry**, 5, 117	A. O. Solis	Vieille Vigne (Fr), 6, 114	Miss High Blade, 5, 114	11	**1:41.12**	67,600
1992	**Sacramentada (Chi)**, 6, 117	K. Desormeaux	Brought to Mind, 5, 120	Re Toss (Arg), 5, 116	5	1:43.04	61,600
1991	**Brought to Mind**, 4, 116	P. A. Valenzuela	Fantastic Look, 5, 118	Fit to Scout, 4, 118	6	1:41.50	62,300
1990	**Bayakoa (Arg)**, 6, 125	L. A. Pincay Jr.	Stormy But Valid, 4, 119	Fantastic Look, 4, 115	5	1:34.00	61,400
1989	**Bayakoa (Arg)**, 5, 122	L. A. Pincay Jr.	Goodbye Halo, 4, 123	Behind the Scenes, 5, 114	5	1:32.80	61,400
1988	**Integra**, 4, 120	G. L. Stevens	Invited Guest (Ire), 4, 118	Behind the Scenes, 4, 117	5	1:36.00	59,400
1987	**Seldom Seen Sue**, 4, 114	C. J. McCarron	Clabber Girl, 4, 116	Tiffany Lass, 4, 123	5	1:33.60	59,900
1986	**Dontstop Themusic**, 6, 121	L. A. Pincay Jr.	Till You, 5, 115	Fran's Valentine, 4, 122	6	1:35.40	46,950
1985	**Adored**, 5, 124	L. A. Pincay Jr.	Mitterand, 4, 122	Her Royalty, 4, 118	4	1:34.80	45,350
1984	**Adored**, 4, 117	F. Toro	Holiday Dancer, 4, 116	Princess Rooney, 4, 123	4	1:41.80	36,200
1983	**Marisma (Chi)**, 5, 115	K. D. Black	Sierva (Arg), 5, 115	Matching, 5, 121	5	1:44.80	30,700
1982	**Weber City Miss**, 5, 122	S. Hawley	Miss Huntington, 5, 117	Aduana, 5, 114	7	1:42.40	31,750
1981	**Save Wild Life**, 4, 113	C. J. McCarron	Princess Karenda, 4, 122	Spiffy Laree, 5, 113	6	1:42.80	37,400
1980	**Country Queen**, 5, 122	L. A. Pincay Jr.	Devon Ditty (GB), 4, 117	Wishing Well, 5, 121	6	1:40.60	30,800
1979	**Country Queen**, 4, 118	L. A. Pincay Jr.	Grande Brisa, 5, 113	Sisterhood, 4, 120	9	1:41.20	26,600
1978	**Sensational**, 4, 119	L. A. Pincay Jr.	Up to Juliet, 5, 114	Grand Luxe, 4, 117	10	1:41.80	27,300
1977	**Cascapedia**, 4, 123	S. Hawley	*Bastonera II, 6, 124	*Star Ball, 5, 121	10	1:40.80	26,850
1976	**Swingtime**, 4, 118	W. Shoemaker	Call Me Proper, 4, 116	Tuscarora, 4, 113	5	1:41.80	19,150
	Mia Amore, 4, 116	F. Toro	*Bastonera II, 5, 118	Summertime Promise, 4, 119	7	1:41.80	19,950
1975	***Tizna**, 6, 122	J. Lambert	Modus Vivendi, 4, 121	Lucky Spell, 4, 121	7	1:20.60	22,600
1974	**Tallahto**, 4, 119	L. A. Pincay Jr.	Sister Fleet, 4, 116	Lt.'s Joy, 4, 119	9	1:20.60	23,200

Named for the nearby town of Hawthorne, California. Grade 2 1983-2001. 7 furlongs 1974-'75. 1 mile 1985-'90. Turf 1976-'80. Two divisions 1976. ‡Se Me Acabo finished third, DQ to fourth, 2003.

Herecomesthebride Stakes

Grade 3 in 2006. Gulfstream Park, three-year-olds, fillies, 1¹/₈ miles, turf. Held March 19, 2006, with a gross value of $100,000. First held in 1984. First graded in 1998. Stakes record 1:46.40 (1997 Auntie Mame).

Year	Winner	Jockey	Second	Third	Strs	Time	1st Purse
2006	**Aunt Henny**, 3, 118	J. Castellano	Diamond Spirit, 3, 118	Miss Shop, 3, 118	5	1:46.88	$60,000
2005	**Cape Hope**, 3, 119	J. A. Santos	Dynamite Lass, 3, 117	Dansetta Light, 3, 121	8	1:48.28	60,000
2004	**Lucifer's Stone**, 3, 117	J. A. Santos	Dynamia, 3, 115	Honey Ryder, 3, 117	12	1:52.78	60,000
2003	**Gal O Gal**, 3, 117	C. P. DeCarlo	Formal Miss, 3, 117	Devil At the Wire, 3, 117	8	1:42.38	60,000
2002	**Cellars Shiraz**, 3, 117	C. H. Velasquez	August Storm, 3, 121	She's Vested, 3, 115	10	1:43.21	60,000
2001	**Mystic Lady**, 3, 116	J. D. Bailey	Open Minded, 3, 114	Ruff, 3, 118	7	1:46.73	60,000
2000	**Gaviola**, 3, 114	J. D. Bailey	Solvig, 3, 121	Are You Up, 3, 114	8	1:47.28	45,000
1999	**Pico Teneriffe**, 3, 118	J. D. Bailey	European Rose, 3, 112	Wild Heart Dancing, 3, 114	8	1:48.82	45,000
1998	**Rashas Warning**, 3, 118	M. E. Smith	Quick Lap, 3, 116	Runnaway Dream, 3, 116	7	1:51.44	45,000
1997	**Auntie Mame**, 3, 114	J. D. Bailey	Witchful Thinking, 3, 116	Classic Approval, 3, 114	7	**1:46.40**	45,000
1996	**Lulu's Ransom**, 3, 116	J. D. Bailey	Cymbala (Fr), 3, 114	Vashon, 3, 114	9	1:47.55	30,000
1995	**Clever Thing**, 3, 114	C. Perret	Transient Trend, 3, 114	Palliser Bay, 3, 114	6	1:53.06	30,000
1994	**Cut the Charm**, 3, 116	W. Ramos	Mynameispanama, 3, 113	Tambien Me Voy, 3, 113	11	1:43.72	30,000
1993	**Sigrun**, 3, 116	R. R. Douglas	So Say all of Us, 3, 112	Supah Gem, 3, 116	8	1:45.79	30,000
1992	**Morriston Belle**, 3, 118	D. Penna	Snazzle Dazzle, 3, 113	Miss Jealski, 3, 116	11	1:42.23	30,000
1989	**Darby Shuffle**, 3, 121	C. Perret	Seattle Meteor, 3, 121	Imago, 3, 112	8	1:42.80	36,510
1988	**Topicount**, 3, 112	J. Samyn	Aquaba, 3, 116	Above Special, 3, 113	15	1:43.20	40,350
1987	**Sum**, 3, 121	R. Woodhouse	Easter Mary, 3, 113	Dawandeh, 3, 116	8	1:43.20	25,410
1986	**Judy's Red Shoes**, 3, 114	G. St. Leon	Tea for Top, 3, 112	Minstress, 3, 121	8	1:43.00	35,790
1985	**Debutant Dancer**, 3, 113	G. Gallitano	One Fine Lady, 3, 118	Affirmance, 3, 118	11	1:42.80	38,640
1984	**Delta Mary**, 3, 112	F. A. Pennisi	Vast Domain, 3, 114	Ingot Way, 3, 114	10	1:42.00	14,955
	Oakbrook Lady, 3, 112	J. A. Velez Jr.	Illaka, 3, 112	Rain Devil, 3, 112	8	1:42.80	14,655

Named for Pelican Stable's and Mrs. Warren A. Croll Jr.'s 1977 Bonnie Miss S. winner Herecomesthebride (1974 f. by Al Hattab). Not held 1990-'91. 1¹/₁₆ miles 1984-'89, 1992-'94, 2001-'03. About 1¹/₈ miles 1998. Dirt 1993-'95, 2001. Two divisions 1984. Equaled course record 1997.

Hill 'n' Dale Cigar Mile Handicap

Grade 1 in 2006. Aqueduct, three-year-olds and up, 1 mile, dirt. Held November 26, 2005, with a gross value of $350,000. First held in 1988. First graded in 1990. Stakes record 1:32.80 (1989 Dispersal; 1990 Quiet American).

Year	Winner	Jockey	Second	Third	Strs	Time	1st Purse
2005	**Purge**, 4, 115	G. K. Gomez	Mass Media, 4, 118	Gygistar, 6, 115	11	1:34.26	$210,000
2004	**Lion Tamer**, 4, 115	J. A. Santos	Badge of Silver, 4, 115	Pico Central (Brz), 5, 123	8	1:33.46	210,000
2003	**Congaree**, 5, 124	J. D. Bailey	Midas Eyes, 3, 115	Toccet, 3, 115	7	1:34.30	210,000
2002	**Congaree**, 4, 119	J. D. Bailey	Aldebaran, 4, 116	Crafty C. T., 4, 117	8	1:33.11	210,000
2001	**Left Bank**, 4, 120	J. R. Velazquez	Graeme Hall, 4, 118	Red Bullet, 4, 118	9	1:33.35	210,000
2000	**El Corredor**, 3, 116	J. D. Bailey	Peeping Tom, 3, 111	Affirmed Success, 6, 120	11	1:34.68	210,000
1999	**Affirmed Success**, 5, 118	J. F. Chavez	Adonis, 3, 115	Honorifico (Arg), 5, 113	9	1:34.18	210,000
1998	**Sir Bear**, 5, 116	J. D. Bailey	Affirmed Success, 4, 119	Distorted Humor, 5, 116	8	1:34.05	180,000
1997	**Devious Course**, 5, 112	J. F. Chavez	Lucayan Prince, 4, 114	Basqueian, 6, 115	12	1:34.98	150,000
1996	**Gold Fever**, 3, 115	M. E. Smith	Diligence, 3, 114	Top Account, 4, 117	14	1:34.98	150,000
1995	**Flying Chevron**, 3, 112	R. G. Davis	Wekiva Springs, 4, 117	Dramatic Gold, 4, 120	13	1:34.57	150,000
1994	**Cigar**, 4, 111	J. D. Bailey	Devil His Due, 5, 124	Punch Line, 4, 112	12	1:36.10	150,000
1992	**Ibero (Arg)**, 5, 117	L. A. Pincay Jr.	Irish Swap, 5, 116	Nines Wild, 3, 111	7	1:33.97	300,000
1991	**Rubiano**, 4, 116	J. A. Santos	Sultry Song, 3, 111	Diablo, 4, 112	15	1:33.68	300,000
1990	**Quiet American**, 4, 116	C. J. McCarron	Dancing Spree, 5, 119	Sewickley, 5, 124	12	**1:32.80**	382,800
1989	**Dispersal**, 3, 115	A. T. Cordero Jr.	Sewickley, 4, 120	Speedratic, 4, 117	7	**1:32.80**	348,600
1988	**Forty Niner**, 3, 121	W. I. Fox Jr.	Mawsuff (GB), 5, 115	Precisionist, 7, 124	6	1:34.00	340,200

Sponsored by John G. Sikura's Hill 'n' Dale Farms of Lexington, Kentucky 2005. Named for Allen E. Paulson's 1995, '96 Horse of the Year, '94 NYRA Mile H. (G1) winner, and world's leading earner at his retirement, Cigar (1990 c. by Palace Music). Formerly named for the New York Racing Association 1988-'96. Not held 1993. NYRA Mile H. 1988-'96.

Hill Prince Stakes

Grade 3 in 2006. Belmont Park, three-year-olds, 1 mile, turf. Held June 9, 2006, with a gross value of $115,400. First held in 1975. First graded in 1981. Stakes record 1:34.40 (1977 Forward Charger).

Year	Winner	Jockey	Second	Third	Strs	Time	1st Purse
2006	**Outperformance**, 3, 116	J. Castellano	Spider Power (Ire), 3, 118	Carnera, 3, 116	10	1:36.74	$69,240
2005	**Rey de Cafe**, 3, 123	J. Castellano	Prince Rahy, 3, 116	Classic Campaign, 3, 116	9	1:49.25	68,820
2004	**Artie Schiller**, 3, 120	R. Migliore	Timo, 3, 122	Big Booster, 3, 114	6	1:50.06	66,000
2003	**Happy Trails**, 3, 120	S. Bridgmohan	Traffic Chief, 3, 114	Chilly Rooster, 3, 114	6	1:50.13	67,860
2002	**Van Minister**, 3, 114	M. J. Luzzi	Miesque's Approval, 3, 120	Westcliffe, 3, 114	5	1:54.42	65,580
2001	**Proud Man**, 3, 122	R. R. Douglas	Package Store, 3, 114	Navesink, 3, 118	10	1:48.25	68,760
2000	**Promontory Gold**, 3, 119	E. S. Prado	Rob's Spirit, 3, 113	Avezzano (GB), 3, 115	7	1:49.15	66,540
1999	**Time Off**, 3, 113	J. Samyn	Hoyle, 3, 113	Lenny's Ransom, 3, 113	8	1:47.48	66,720
1998	**Recommended List**, 3, 119	J. F. Chavez	Daniel My Brother, 3, 119	Availability, 3, 119	5	1:49.28	67,800
1997	**Subordination**, 3, 113	J. R. Velazquez	Rob 'n Gin, 3, 119	Tekken (Ire), 3, 119	8	1:45.69	67,200
1996	**Optic Nerve**, 3, 114	J. A. Santos	Fortitude, 3, 117	Allied Forces, 3, 119	7	1:39.70	66,420
1995	**Green Means Go**, 3, 117	J. D. Bailey	Smells and Bells, 3, 114	Debonair Dan, 3, 119	10	1:40.33	68,160
1994	**Pennine Ridge**, 3, 112	J. D. Bailey	Check Ride, 3, 119	Add the Gold, 3, 114	9	1:39.87	50,925
1993	**Halissee**, 3, 121	J. A. Krone	Proud Shot, 3, 117	Logroller, 3, 114	5	1:40.91	52,020
1992	**‡Free At Last**, 3, 126	J. D. Bailey	Casino Magistrate, 3, 123	Kiri's Clown, 3, 114	8	1:41.05	53,190
1991	**Young Daniel**, 3, 114	A. T. Cordero Jr.	Share the Glory, 3, 119	Lech, 3, 114	13	1:39.87	58,050
1990	**Solar Splendor**, 3, 114	E. Maple	Divine Warning, 3, 119	Bismarck Hills, 3, 114	13	1:41.20	57,870
1989	**Slew the Knight**, 3, 121	C. W. Antley	Orange Sunshine, 3, 117	Expensive Decision, 3, 121	10	1:41.00	56,520
1988	**Sunshine Forever**, 3, 114	A. T. Cordero Jr.	Posen, 3, 121	Kris Green, 3, 114	7	1:41.20	85,620
1987	**Forest Fair**, 3, 119	J. A. Santos	Kindly Court, 3, 117	First Patriot, 3, 121	7	1:42.80	86,220
1986	**Double Feint**, 3, 121	J. A. Santos	Glow, 3, 121	Jack of Clubs, 3, 114	7	1:41.40	53,190
1985	**Danger's Hour**, 3, 119	D. MacBeth	Foundation Plan, 3, 119	Exclusive Partner, 3, 114	13	1:40.60	59,310
1984	**A Gift**, 3, 114	D. MacBeth	Is Your Pleasure, 3, 126	Jesse's Hope, 3, 117	7	1:48.40	43,680
1983	**Domynsky (GB)**, 3, 114	J. D. Bailey	White Birch, 3, 114	Macho Duck, 3, 114	11	1:48.80	36,660
1982	**Majesty's Prince**, 3, 114	R. Hernandez	A Real Leader, 3, 114	†Honed Edge, 3, 109	8	1:43.40	33,180
	†Larida, 3, 112	E. Maple	Dew Line, 3, 117	John's Gold, 3, 114	8	1:42.60	33,180
1981	**Summing**, 3, 114	A. T. Cordero Jr.	Stage Door Key, 3, 114	Sportin' Life, 3, 114	10	1:42.40	35,700
1980	**Ben Fab**, 3, 126	J. Cruguet	Vatza, 3, 113	Don Daniello, 3, 117	8	1:43.40	34,800
1979	**Bends Me Mind**, 3, 114	J. Velasquez	Crown Thy Good, 3, 115	T. V. Series, 3, 110	11	1:46.00	34,470
1978	**Darby Creek Road**, 3, 121	A. T. Cordero Jr.	John Henry, 3, 111	Scythian Gold, 3, 111	9	1:35.20	22,605
1977	**Forward Charger**, 3, 115	J. Vasquez	Stir the Embers, 3, 112	Winter Wind, 3, 112	7	**1:34.40**	22,575
1976	**Fifth Marine**, 3, 126	R. Turcotte	Quick Card, 3, 120	Drover's Dawn, 3, 112	9	1:41.20	27,405
1975	**‡Don Jack**, 3, 110	G. Martens	Annie's Brat, 3, 115	Rapid Invader, 3, 113	9	2:23.20	34,650

Named for Christopher T. Chenery's 1950 Horse of the Year and '50 Jockey Club Gold Cup winner Hill Prince (1947 c. by *Princequillo). Hill Prince H. 1975-'80. Held at Aqueduct 1979-'80, 1982. 1$^{3}/_{8}$ miles 1975. 1$^{1}/_{16}$ miles 1976, 1979-'86. 1$^{1}/_{8}$ miles 1987-2005. Dirt 1998. Two divisions 1982. ‡Annie's Brat finished first, DQ to second, 1975. ‡Casino Magistrate finished first, DQ to second, 1992. Course record 1997. †Denotes female.

Hillsborough Stakes

Grade 3 in 2006. Tampa Bay Downs, four-year-olds and up, fillies and mares, about 1$^{1}/_{8}$ miles, turf. Held March 18, 2006, with a gross value of $137,500. First held in 1999. First graded in 2004. Stakes record 1:48.83 (2004 Coney Kitty [Ire]).

Year	Winner	Jockey	Second	Third	Strs	Time	1st Purse
2006	**Ready's Gal**, 4, 116	J. R. Velazquez	Amorama (Fr), 5, 116	Marchonin, 4, 116	12	1:50.50	$75,000

2005	**Rizzi Girl**, 7, 116	O. Castillo	Sister Star, 4, 116	Noisette, 5, 116	9	1:52.59	$75,000
2004	**Coney Kitty (Ire)**, 6, 116	J. A. Santos	Madeira Mist (Ire), 5, 122	Alternate, 5, 116	12	**1:48.83**	60,000
2003	**Strait From Texas**, 4, 118	J. L. Castanon	Dedication (Fr), 4, 118	Stylish, 5, 118	11	1:41.14	60,000
2002	**Platinum Tiara**, 4, 116	M. R. Cruz	Step With Style, 5, 116	Ioya Two, 7, 116	11	1:41.34	60,000
2001	**Song for Annie**, 5, 116	L. J. Melancon	Megans Bluff, 4, 116	Inside Affair, 6, 122	11	1:41.23	60,000
2000	**St Clair Ridge (Ire)**, 4, 117	P. Day	Office Miss, 6, 122	Royal Bloomer, 5, 115	11	1:41.17	45,000
1999	**Pleasant Temper**, 5, 117	P. Day	Sandy Gator, 6, 115	Scatter Buy, 4, 115	10	1:42.62	34,800

Named for Hillsborough County, Florida; the city of Tampa is the county seat. Three-year-olds and up 1999-2001. 1¹⁄₁₆ miles 1999-2003.

Hirsch Jacobs Stakes

Grade 3 in 2006. Pimlico Race Course, three-year-olds, 6 furlongs, dirt. Held May 20, 2006, with a gross value of $100,000. First held in 1975. First graded in 2005. Stakes record 1:09.72 (2006 Songster).

Year	Winner	Jockey	Second	Third	Strs	Time	1st Purse
2006	**Songster**, 3, 116	E. S. Prado	Valid Brush, 3, 116	Urban Guy, 3, 120	6	**1:09.72**	$60,000
2004	**Abbondanza**, 3, 115	R. A. Dominguez	Bwana Charlie, 3, 122	Penn Pacific, 3, 117	9	1:10.72	60,000
2003	**Mt. Carson**, 3, 122	R. A. Dominguez	Gators N Bears, 3, 117	Only the Best, 3, 122	8	1:10.85	60,000
2002	**True Direction**, 3, 117	R. A. Dominguez	Listen Here, 3, 122	It's a Monster, 3, 117	8	1:10.90	45,000
2001	**City Zip**, 3, 122	J. F. Chavez	Sea of Green, 3, 119	Stake Runner, 3, 117	7	1:10.20	45,000
2000	**Max's Pal**, 3, 119	R. Wilson	Ultimate Warrior, 3, 119	Stormin Oedy, 3, 119	8	1:10.32	45,000
1999	**Erlton**, 3, 122	R. Wilson	Jeanies Rob, 3, 122	Jovial Brush, 3, 117	7	1:10.60	45,000
1998	**Klabin's Gold**, 3, 115	R. Wilson	Carnivorous Habit, 3, 115	Greenspring Willy, 3, 122	7	1:11.51	32,760
1997	**Original Gray**, 3, 122	C. H. Marquez Jr.	American Champ, 3, 122	Stroke, 3, 122	9	1:10.85	33,585
1996	**Viv**, 3, 122	M. T. Johnston	Fort Dodge, 3, 122	Big Rut, 3, 115	6	1:12.11	32,805
1995	**Ft. Stockton**, 3, 115	J. D. Bailey	Splendid Sprinter, 3, 115	Sittin Cool, 3, 115	6	1:10.29	32,265
1994	**Foxie G**, 3, 114	E. S. Prado	Distinct Reality, 3, 114	Spartan's Hero, 3, 114	7	1:11.51	32,520
1993	**Montbrook**, 3, 114	M. J. Luzzi	Without Dissent, 3, 122	Mighty Game, 3, 114	7	1:12.10	32,490
1992	**Speakerphone**, 3, 114	C. J. Ladner III	Coin Collector, 3, 122	Golden Phase, 3, 122	7	1:10.52	26,160
1991	**Ameri Run**, 3, 119	G. W. Hutton	Exclusive Dove, 3, 114	Nasty Hero, 3, 122	6	1:10.86	25,860
1990	**Collegian**, 3, 117	H. Vega	Hit the Mahagoney, 3, 117	Bardland, 3, 114	5	1:10.20	26,115
1989	**Pulverizing**, 3, 122	A. T. Stacy	Jimmy Coggins, 3, 114	Midas, 3, 114	6	1:11.20	32,460
1988	**Finder's Choice**, 3, 122	J. A. Santos	†Smarter Than, 3, 117	Royal Highlander, 3, 110	4	1:12.20	27,820
1987	**Green Book**, 3, 122	G. W. Hutton	Judge's Dream, 3, 110	Silano, 3, 122	7	1:11.80	28,730
1986	**Super Delight**, 3, 122	J. Nied Jr.	Part Dutch, 3, 113	Fun Bunch, 3, 115	8	1:11.80	21,515
1985	**Beat Me Daddy**, 3, 122	V. A. Bracciale Jr.	Banjo Dancing, 3, 116	Urigo, 3, 119	7	1:11.80	21,775
1984	**Mickey Mall**, 3, 119	R. Wilson	Moschini, 3, 116	Bold Flunky, 3, 122	7	1:10.80	20,995
1983	**Emperial Age**, 3, 116	J. Nied Jr.	Unreal Zeal, 3, 116	Zeb's Hel Cat, 3, 116	5	1:10.80	20,963
1982	**Mortgage Man**, 3, 122	A. S. Black	Woody's Wish, 3, 116	St. Chrisbee, 3, 122	7	1:10.60	21,353
1981	**Century Prince**, 3, 122	V. A. Bracciale Jr.	J. D. Quill, 3, 116	Irish King, 3, 119	5	1:10.20	21,027
1980	**Amber Pass**, 3, 116	D. MacBeth	Pickett's Charge, 3, 116	Peace for Peace, 3, 119	8	1:10.80	21,418
1979	**Breezing On**, 3, 122	W. J. Passmore	Fearless McGuire, 3, 113	Our Gary, 3, 122	8	1:14.80	21,645
1978	**Shelter Half**, 3, 119	G. Lindberg	Star de Naskra, 3, 122	Game Prince, 3, 116	9	1:11.00	21,645
1977	**Iron Derby**, 3, 119	D. R. Wright	Jeff's Try, 3, 116	Tiny Monk, 3, 116	7	1:11.20	17,875
1976	**Zen**, 3, 116	J. Vasquez	Cojak, 3, 122	Greek Victor, 3, 113	4	1:11.40	17,518
1975	**Bombay Duck**, 3, 122	M. Aristone	Gallant Bob, 3, 122	Ben S., 3, 116	9	1:11.20	18,622

Named for Racing Hall of Fame trainer Hirsch Jacobs (1904-'70); Jacobs was also a leading breeder and owner. Not held 2005. †Denotes female.

Hollywood Breeders' Cup Oaks

Grade 2 in 2006. Hollywood Park, three-year-olds, fillies, 1¹⁄₁₆ miles, dirt. Held June 11, 2006, with a gross value of $152,400. First held in 1946. First graded in 1973. Stakes record 1:41.55 (2004 House of Fortune).

Year	Winner	Jockey	Second	Third	Strs	Time	1st Purse
2006	**Hystericalady**, 3, 119	P. A. Valenzuela	Squallacious, 3, 119	Downthedustyroad, 3, 114	7	1:43.08	$95,040
2005	**Brooke's Halo**, 3, 113	V. Espinoza	Memorette, 3, 116	Cee's Irish, 3, 119	8	1:42.80	111,900
2004	**House of Fortune**, 3, 119	A. O. Solis	Elusive Diva, 3, 115	Hollywood Story, 3, 119	5	**1:41.55**	109,725
2003	**Santa Catarina**, 3, 116	G. L. Stevens	Buffythecenterfold, 3, 113	Princess V., 3, 114	5	1:41.62	127,320
2002	**Adoration**, 3, 115	G. K. Gomez	Sister Girl Blues, 3, 114	Saint Bernadette, 3, 115	7	1:43.73	160,080
2001	**Affluent**, 3, 116	E. Delahoussaye	Collect Call, 3, 115	Secret of Mecca, 3, 116	5	1:49.20	90,000
2000	**Kumari Continent**, 3, 117	K. Desormeaux	Queenie Belle, 3, 119	Saudi Poetry, 3, 115	5	1:49.13	90,000
1999	**Smooth Player**, 3, 117	E. Delahoussaye	Excellent Meeting, 3, 121	Nany's Sweep, 3, 116	5	1:48.17	90,000
1998	**Manistique**, 3, 115	G. L. Stevens	Sweet and Ready, 3, 119	Yolo Lady, 3, 116	5	1:48.40	120,000
1997	**Sharp Cat**, 3, 121	A. O. Solis	Freeport Flight, 3, 121	Really Happy, 3, 121	5	1:49.60	120,000
1996	**Listening**, 3, 121	C. J. McCarron	Antespend, 3, 121	Ocean View, 3, 121	4	1:48.70	110,640
1995	**Sleep Easy**, 3, 121	C. S. Nakatani	‡Bello Cielo, 3, 121	Carsona, 3, 121	5	1:50.24	122,400
1994	**Lakeway**, 3, 121	K. Desormeaux	Sardula, 3, 121	Fancy 'n Fabulous, 3, 121	4	1:46.93	120,000
1993	**Hollywood Wildcat**, 3, 121	E. Delahoussaye	Fit to Lead, 3, 121	Adorydar, 3, 121	9	1:48.48	130,400
1992	**Pacific Squall**, 3, 121	K. Desormeaux	Race the Wild Wind, 3, 121	Alysbelle, 3, 121	7	1:48.07	127,200
1991	**Fowda**, 3, 121	E. Delahoussaye	Grand Girlfriend, 3, 121	Masake, 3, 121	7	1:49.70	94,400
1990	**Patches**, 3, 121	G. L. Stevens	Jefforee, 3, 121	Pampered Star, 3, 121	8	1:49.80	96,100
1989	**Gorgeous**, 3, 121	E. Delahoussaye	Kelly, 3, 121	Lea Lucinda, 3, 121	6	1:47.80	92,700
1988	**Pattern Step**, 3, 121	C. J. McCarron	Super Avie, 3, 121	Comedy Court, 3, 121	7	1:48.60	94,700
1987	**Perchance to Dream**, 3, 121	R. Sibille	Sacahuista, 3, 121	Pen Bal Lady (GB), 3, 121	6	1:48.60	93,200

1986	**Hidden Light**, 3, 121	W. Shoemaker	An Empress, 3, 121	Family Style, 3, 121	4	1:47.80	$116,600
1985	**Fran's Valentine**, 3, 121	C. J. McCarron	Magnificent Lindy, 3, 121	Deal Price, 3, 121	6	1:47.40	120,300
1984	**Moment to Buy**, 3, 121	T. M. Chapman	Mitterand, 3, 121	Lucky Lucky Lucky, 3, 121	9	1:49.20	97,150
1983	**Heartlight No. One**, 3, 121	L. A. Pincay Jr.	Preceptress, 3, 121	Ready for Luck, 3, 121	7	1:49.80	63,900
1982	**Tango Dancer**, 3, 121	L. A. Pincay Jr.	Faneuil Lass, 3, 121	Royal Donna, 3, 121	9	1:49.00	66,100
1981	**Past Forgetting**, 3, 121	C. J. McCarron	Balletomane, 3, 121	Glitter Hitter, 3, 121	7	1:50.00	64,100
1980	**Princess Karenda**, 3, 121	D. Pierce	Secretarial Queen, 3, 121	Disconiz, 3, 121	10	1:48.20	67,400
1979	**Prize Spot**, 3, 121	S. Hawley	It's in the Air, 3, 121	Variety Queen, 3, 124	7	1:48.20	63,300
1978	**B. Thoughtful**, 3, 121	D. Pierce	Country Queen, 3, 121	Grenzen, 3, 121	9	1:47.60	65,400
1977	***Glenaris**, 3, 116	W. Shoemaker	One Sum, 3, 116	Taisez Vous, 3, 121	11	1:48.80	68,100
1976	**Answer**, 3, 121	D. G. McHargue	Franmari, 3, 116	I Going, 3, 115	9	1:48.40	49,200
1975	**Nicosia**, 3, 121	W. Shoemaker	Snap Apple, 3, 112	Mia Amore, 3, 112	9	1:48.40	49,400
1974	**Miss Musket**, 3, 124	L. A. Pincay Jr.	Lucky Spell, 3, 121	Modus Vivendi, 3, 121	8	1:47.80	49,550
1973	**Sandy Blue**, 3, 121	D. Pierce	Cellist, 3, 121	Jungle Princess, 3, 112	10	1:48.00	50,550

Grade 1 1976-'96. Hollywood Oaks 1946-2001. Held at Santa Anita Park 1949. 1 mile 1946, 1948-'50. 7 furlongs 1947. $1\frac{1}{8}$ miles 1954-2001. ‡Predicted Glory finished second, DQ to fifth, 1995.

Hollywood Derby

Grade 1 in 2006. Hollywood Park, three-year-olds, $1\frac{1}{4}$ miles, turf. Held November 28, 2004, with a gross value of $500,000. First held in 1938. First graded in 1973. Stakes record 2:01.53 (2004 Good Reward).

Year	Winner	Jockey	Second	Third	Strs	Time	1st Purse
2004	**Good Reward**, 3, 122	J. D. Bailey	Fast and Furious (Fr), 3, 122	Imperialism, 3, 122	13	**2:01.53**	$300,000
2003	**Sweet Return (GB)**, 3, 122	J. A. Krone	Fairly Ransom, 3, 122	Kicken Kris, 3, 122	13	2:04.27	360,000
2002	**Johar**, 3, 122	A. O. Solis	Mananan McLir, 3, 122	Royal Gem, 3, 122	9	1:48.70	300,000
2001	**Denon**, 3, 122	C. J. McCarron	Sligo Bay (Ire), 3, 122	Aldebaran, 3, 122	12	1:49.28	300,000
2000	**‡Brahms**, 3, 122	P. Day	David Copperfield, 3, 122	Zentsov Street, 3, 122	12	1:46.73	300,000
1999	**Super Quercus (Fr)**, 3, 122	A. O. Solis	Manndar (Ire), 3, 122	Fighting Falcon, 3, 122	14	1:45.82	300,000
1998	**Vergennes**, 3, 122	J. R. Velazquez	Dixie Dot Com, 3, 122	Lone Bid (Fr), 3, 122	10	1:49.44	300,000
1997	**Subordination**, 3, 122	J. D. Bailey	Lasting Approval, 3, 122	Blazing Sword, 3, 122	13	1:50.00	300,000
1996	**Marlin**, 3, 122	J. R. Velazquez	Rainbow Blues (Ire), 3, 122	Devil's Cup, 3, 122	14	1:46.08	300,000
1995	**Labeeb (GB)**, 3, 122	E. Delahoussaye	Helmsman, 3, 122	Da Hoss, 3, 122	13	1:46.42	220,000
1994	**River Flyer**, 3, 122	C. W. Antley	Dare and Go, 3, 122	Fadeyev, 3, 122	13	1:47.48	220,000
1993	**Explosive Red**, 3, 122	C. S. Nakatani	Jeune Homme, 3, 122	Earl of Barking (Ire), 3, 122	14	1:46.88	220,000
1992	**Paradise Creek**, 3, 122	P. Day	Bien Bien, 3, 122	Kitwood, 3, 122	12	1:47.36	220,000
1991	**Eternity Star**, 3, 122	E. Delahoussaye	Native Boundary, 3, 122	Perfectly Proud, 3, 122	11	1:47.30	110,000
	Olympio, 3, 124	E. Delahoussaye	Bistro Garden, 3, 122	River Traffic, 3, 122	10	1:47.10	110,000
1990	**Itsallgreektome**, 3, 122	C. S. Nakatani	Septieme Ciel, 3, 122	Anshan (GB), 3, 122	12	1:46.60	110,000
1989	**Live the Dream**, 3, 122	A. O. Solis	Charlie Barley, 3, 122	River Master, 3, 122	13	1:47.00	110,000
1988	**Silver Circus**, 3, 122	G. L. Stevens	Raykour (Ire), 3, 122	Dr. Death, 3, 122	14	1:48.40	110,000
1987	**Political Ambition**, 3, 122	E. Delahoussaye	The Medic, 3, 122	Light Sabre, 3, 122	7	1:48.20	101,600
	Stately Don, 3, 122	J. Vasquez	Lockton (GB), 3, 122	Noble Minstrel, 3, 122	9	1:47.40	104,600
1986	**Thrill Show**, 3, 122	W. Shoemaker	Air Display, 3, 122	Bold Arrangement (GB), 3, 122	11	1:46.80	146,000
	Spellbound, 3, 122	R. Sibille	Double Feint, 3, 122	Bruiser (GB), 3, 122	12	1:46.80	147,500
1985	**Charming Duke (Fr)**, 3, 122	Y. Saint-Martin	Herat, 3, 122	†La Koumia (Fr), 3, 119	13	1:46.80	171,225
	Slew the Dragon, 3, 122	J. Velasquez	†Savannah Dancer, 3, 119	Catane, 3, 122	12	1:46.40	168,725
1984	**Procida**, 3, 122	C. B. Asmussen	Executive Pride (Ire), 3, 122	†Reine Mathilde, 3, 122	9	1:48.40	139,250
	Foscarini (Ire), 3, 122	D. G. McHargue	Roving Minstrel, 3, 122	Bean Bag, 3, 122	10	1:47.40	140,750
1983	**†Royal Heroine (Ire)**, 3, 119	F. Toro	Interco, 3, 122	Pac Mania, 3, 122	11	1:48.20	87,400
	Ginger Brink (Fr), 3, 122	F. Toro	Fifth Division, 3, 122	Hur Power, 3, 122	10	1:49.20	86,400
1982	**Racing Is Fun**, 3, 122	W. Shoemaker	Prince Spellbound, 3, 122	Uncle Jeff, 3, 122	7	1:47.20	67,150
	Victory Zone, 3, 122	E. Delahoussaye	The Hague, 3, 122	Ask Me, 3, 122	9	1:47.80	70,150
1981	**†De La Rose**, 3, 119	E. Maple	High Counsel, 3, 122	Lord Trendy (Ire), 3, 122	8	1:47.60	68,700
	Silveyville, 3, 122	D. Winick	French Sassafras (GB), 3, 122	Waterway Drive, 3, 122	8	1:48.20	68,700
1980	**Codex**, 3, 122	E. Delahoussaye	Rumbo, 3, 122	Cactus Road, 3, 122	11	1:47.40	195,250
1979	**Flying Paster**, 3, 122	D. Pierce	Switch Partners, 3, 122	Shamgo, 3, 122	7	1:47.60	166,750
1978	**Affirmed**, 3, 122	S. Cauthen	Think Snow, 3, 122	Radar Ahead, 3, 122	9	1:48.20	174,750
1977	**Steve's Friend**, 3, 122	R. Hernandez	Affiliate, 3, 122	*Habitony, 3, 122	10	1:47.80	140,000
1976	**Crystal Water**, 3, 122	W. Shoemaker	Life's Hope, 3, 122	Double Discount, 3, 122	11	1:48.40	152,750
1975	**Intrepid Hero**, 3, 126	D. Pierce	Terete, 3, 126	Sibirri, 3, 126	7	2:29.00	90,000
1974	**Agitate**, 3, 126	W. Shoemaker	Stardust Mel, 3, 126	Top Crowd, 3, 126	9	2:28.20	90,000
1973	***Amen II**, 3, 126	E. Belmonte	Groshawk, 3, 126	Kirrary, 3, 126	11	2:27.80	90,000

Formerly sponsored by the Crown Royal Co. of Stamford, Connecticut 1995-'96. Formerly sponsored by Early Times Distillery Co. of Louisville 1998-2000. Westerner S. 1948-'58. Held at Santa Anita Park 1949. Not held 1942-'44, 2005. $1\frac{1}{8}$ miles 1945, 1950, 1976-2002. $1\frac{1}{2}$ miles 1973-'75. Dirt 1938-'72, 1976-'80. Two divisions 1981-'87, 1991. ‡Designed for Luck finished first, DQ to fifth, 2000. †Denotes female.

Hollywood Futurity

Grade 1 in 2006. Hollywood Park, two-year-olds, $1\frac{1}{16}$ miles, dirt. Held December 17, 2005, with a gross value of $407,250. First held in 1981. First graded in 1983. Stakes record 1:40.74 (1994 Afternoon Deelites).

Year	Winner	Jockey	Second	Third	Strs	Time	1st Purse
2005	**Brother Derek**, 2, 121	A. O. Solis	Your Tent Or Mine, 2, 121	Bob and John, 2, 121	8	1:42.02	$244,350
2004	**Declan's Moon**, 2, 121	V. Espinoza	Giacomo, 2, 121	Wilko, 2, 121	7	1:41.63	269,700
2003	**Lion Heart**, 2, 121	M. E. Smith	St Averil, 2, 121	That's an Outrage, 2, 121	5	1:42.80	225,600
2002	**Toccet**, 2, 121	J. F. Chavez	‡Domestic Dispute, 2, 121	Coax Kid, 2, 121	6	1:41.26	243,900

2001 **Siphonic**, 2, 121	J. D. Bailey	Fonz's, 2, 121	Officer, 2, 121	8	1:42.09	$274,050
2000 **Point Given**, 2, 121	G. L. Stevens	Millennium Wind, 2, 121	Golden Ticket, 2, 121	4	1:42.21	204,300
1999 **Captain Steve**, 2, 121	R. Albarado	High Yield, 2, 121	Cosine, 2, 121	6	1:43.27	245,400
1998 **Tactical Cat**, 2, 121	L. A. Pincay Jr.	Prime Timber, 2, 121	Premier Property, 2, 121	5	1:42.63	235,800
1997 **Real Quiet**, 2, 121	K. Desormeaux	Artax, 2, 121	Nationalore, 2, 121	11	1:41.34	282,120
1996 **Swiss Yodeler**, 2, 121	A. O. Solis	Stolen Gold, 2, 121	In Excessive Bull, 2, 121	13	1:42.70	348,510
1995 **Matty G**, 2, 121	A. O. Solis	Odyle, 2, 121	Ayrton S, 2, 121	7	1:41.75	275,000
1994 **Afternoon Deelites**, 2, 121	K. Desormeaux	Thunder Gulch, 2, 121	A. J. Jett, 2, 121	5	**1:40.74**	275,000
1993 **Valiant Nature**, 2, 121	L. A. Pincay Jr.	Brocco, 2, 121	Flying Sensation, 2, 121	6	1:40.78	275,000
1992 **River Special**, 2, 121	L. A. Pincay Jr.	Stuka, 2, 121	Earl of Barking (Ire), 2, 121	6	1:43.27	275,000
1991 **A.P. Indy**, 2, 121	E. Delahoussaye	Dance Floor, 2, 121	Casual Lies, 2, 121	14	1:42.85	329,780
1990 **Best Pal**, 2, 121	J. A. Santos	General Meeting, 2, 121	Reign Road, 2, 121	9	1:35.40	495,000
1989 **Grand Canyon**, 2, 121	A. T. Cordero Jr.	Farma Way, 2, 121	Silver Ending, 2, 121	9	1:33.00	495,000
1988 **King Glorious**, 2, 121	C. J. McCarron	Music Merci, 2, 121	Hawkster, 2, 121	10	1:35.60	495,000
1987 **Tejano**, 2, 121	L. A. Pincay Jr.	Purdue King, 2, 121	Regal Classic, 2, 121	8	1:34.60	495,000
1986 **Temperate Sil**, 2, 121	W. Shoemaker	Alysheba, 2, 121	Masterful Advocate, 2, 121	12	1:36.20	495,000
1985 **Snow Chief**, 2, 121	A. O. Solis	Electric Blue, 2, 121	Ferdinand, 2, 121	10	1:34.20	589,600
1984 **Stephan's Odyssey**, 2, 121	E. Maple	First Norman, 2, 121	Right Con, 2, 121	13	1:43.40	627,000
1983 **Fali Time**, 2, 121	S. Hawley	Bold T. Jay, 2, 121	†Life's Magic, 2, 118	12	1:41.60	549,849
1982 **Roving Boy**, 2, 121	E. Delahoussaye	Desert Wine, 2, 121	Fifth Division, 2, 121	9	1:41.80	418,770
1981 **Stalwart**, 2, 121	C. J. McCarron	Cassaleria, 2, 121	†Header Card, 2, 118	12	1:47.80	365,805

1 mile 1985-'90. ‡Kafwain finished second, DQ to fourth, 2002. †Denotes female.

Hollywood Gold Cup Handicap

Grade 1 in 2006. Hollywood Park, three-year-olds and up, 1¼ miles, dirt. Held July 9, 2005, with a gross value of $750,000. First held in 1938. First graded in 1973. Stakes record 1:58.20 (1972 Quack).

Year Winner	Jockey	Second	Third	Strs	Time	1st Purse
2005 **Lava Man**, 4, 118	P. A. Valenzuela	Borrego, 4, 115	Congrats, 5, 117	9	1:59.63	$450,000
2004 **Total Impact (Chi)**, 6, 124	M. E. Smith	Olmodavor, 5, 124	Even the Score, 6, 124	7	2:00.72	450,000
2003 **Congaree**, 5, 124	J. D. Bailey	Harlan's Holiday, 4, 124	Kudos, 6, 124	7	2:00.48	450,000
2002 **Sky Jack**, 6, 124	L. A. Pincay Jr.	Momentum, 4, 124	Milwaukee Brew, 5, 124	6	2:01.73	450,000
2001 **‡Aptitude**, 4, 124	L. A. Pincay Jr.	Skimming, 5, 124	Futural, 5, 124	5	2:01.79	450,000
2000 **Early Pioneer**, 5, 124	V. Espinoza	General Challenge, 4, 124	David, 4, 124	9	2:01.40	600,000
1999 **Real Quiet**, 4, 124	J. D. Bailey	Budroyale, 6, 124	Malek (Chi), 6, 124	4	1:59.67	600,000
1998 **Skip Away**, 5, 124	J. D. Bailey	Puerto Madero (Chi), 4, 124	Gentlemen (Arg), 6, 124	8	2:00.16	600,000
1997 **Gentlemen (Arg)**, 5, 124	G. L. Stevens	Siphon (Brz), 6, 124	Sandpit (Brz), 8, 124	6	1:59.26	600,000
1996 **Siphon (Brz)**, 5, 117	D. R. Flores	Geri, 4, 118	Helmsman, 4, 120	8	2:00.50	600,000
1995 **Cigar**, 5, 126	J. D. Bailey	Tinners Way, 5, 118	Tossofthecoin, 5, 118	8	1:59.46	550,000
1994 **Slew of Damascus**, 6, 117	G. L. Stevens	Fanmore, 6, 116	Del Mar Dennis, 4, 116	5	2:00.76	412,500
1993 **Best Pal**, 5, 121	C. A. Black	Bertrando, 4, 118	Major Impact, 4, 114	10	2:00.17	412,500
1992 **Sultry Song**, 4, 113	J. D. Bailey	Marquetry, 5, 118	Another Review, 4, 120	6	2:00.23	550,000
1991 **Marquetry**, 4, 110	D. R. Flores	Farma Way, 4, 122	Itsallgreektome, 4, 119	9	1:59.50	550,000
1990 **Criminal Type**, 5, 121	J. A. Santos	Sunday Silence, 4, 126	Opening Verse, 4, 119	7	1:59.80	550,000
1989 **Blushing John**, 4, 122	P. Day	Sabona, 7, 116	Payant (Arg), 5, 116	7	2:00.40	275,000
1988 **Cutlass Reality**, 6, 116	G. L. Stevens	Alysheba, 4, 126	Ferdinand, 5, 125	6	1:59.40	275,000
1987 **Ferdinand**, 4, 124	W. Shoemaker	dh-Judge Angelucci, 4, 118 dh-Tasso, 4, 115		11	2:00.60	275,000
1986 **Super Diamond**, 6, 118	L. A. Pincay Jr.	Alphabatim, 5, 120	Precisionist, 5, 127	6	2:00.40	275,000
1985 **Greinton (GB)**, 4, 120	L. A. Pincay Jr.	Precisionist, 4, 125	Kings Island (Ire), 4, 112	6	1:58.40	275,000
1984 **Desert Wine**, 4, 122	E. Delahoussaye	John Henry, 9, 125	Sari's Dreamer, 5, 114	8	2:00.40	275,000
1983 **Island Whirl**, 5, 120	E. Delahoussaye	Poley, 4, 116	Prince Spellbound, 4, 120	6	1:59.40	275,000
1982 **Perrault (GB)**, 5, 127	L. A. Pincay Jr.	Erins Isle (Ire), 4, 118	It's the One, 4, 125	8	1:59.20	275,000
1981 **‡Eleven Stitches**, 4, 122	S. Hawley	Caterman (NZ), 5, 120	Super Moment, 4, 117	10	2:00.40	275,000
1980 **Go West Young Man**, 5, 116	E. Delahoussaye	Balzac, 5, 120	Caro Bambino (Ire), 5, 116	10	1:58.80	220,000
1979 **Affirmed**, 4, 132	L. A. Pincay Jr.	Sirlad (Ire), 5, 120	Text, 5, 119	10	1:58.40	275,000
1978 **Exceller**, 5, 128	W. Shoemaker	Text, 4, 118	Vigors, 5, 129	7	1:59.20	192,500
1977 **Crystal Water**, 4, 129	L. A. Pincay Jr.	†Cascapedia, 4, 116	Caucasus, 5, 124	12	2:00.00	210,000
1976 **Pay Tribute**, 4, 117	M. Castaneda	Avatar, 4, 123	Riot in Paris, 5, 123	8	1:58.80	150,000
1975 **Ancient Title**, 5, 125	L. A. Pincay Jr.	Big Band, 5, 115	*El Tarta, 5, 115	7	1:59.20	90,000
1974 **Tree of Knowledge**, 4, 115	W. Shoemaker	Ancient Title, 4, 125	War Heim, 7, 114	10	1:59.80	90,000
1973 **Kennedy Road**, 5, 120	W. Shoemaker	Quack, 4, 127	*Cougar II, 7, 128	6	1:59.40	90,000

Formerly sponsored by Sempra Energy of San Diego, California 2000. Hollywood Gold Cup S. 1997-2004. Hollywood Gold Cup Invitational H. 1972, 1974-'75. Held at Santa Anita Park 1949. Not held 1942-'43. Dead heat for second 1987. ‡Caterman (NZ) finished first, DQ to second, 1981. ‡Futural finished first, DQ to third, 2001. †Denotes female.

Hollywood Juvenile Championship Stakes

Grade 3 in 2006. Hollywood Park, two-year-olds, 6 furlongs, dirt. Held July 16, 2005, with a gross value of $104,500. First held in 1938. First graded in 1973. Stakes record 1:08.60 (1974 Dimaggio).

Year Winner	Jockey	Second	Third	Strs	Time	1st Purse
2005 **What a Song**, 2, 117	V. Espinoza	Bashert, 2, 117	Stevie Wonderboy, 2, 115	5	1:09.55	$62,700
2004 **Chandtrue**, 2, 120	V. Espinoza	Actxecutive, 2, 117	Commandant, 2, 115	4	1:10.88	63,840
2003 **Perfect Moon**, 2, 117	P. A. Valenzuela	Blairs Roarin Star, 2, 117	Ruler's Court, 2, 117	5	1:10.39	61,500
2002 **Crowned Dancer**, 2, 120	A. O. Solis	Outta Here, 2, 117	Chief Planner, 2, 117	7	1:10.10	64,980

2001	**Came Home**, 2, 117	C. J. McCarron	Metatron, 2, 117	A Major Pleasure, 2, 117	6	1:09.20	$64,440
2000	**Squirtle Squirt**, 2, 120	L. A. Pincay Jr.	Legendary Weave, 2, 117	Drumcliff, 2, 117	5	1:09.98	63,540
1999	**Dixie Union**, 2, 117	A. O. Solis	Exchange Rate, 2, 117	High Yield, 2, 115	5	1:09.95	63,780
1998	**Yes It's True**, 2, 120	J. D. Bailey	O'Rey Fantasma, 2, 117	Worldly Manner, 2, 117	7	1:09.58	61,620
1997	**K. O. Punch**, 2, 120	A. O. Solis	Old Topper, 2, 117	Majorbigtimesheet, 2, 120	9	1:09.80	66,120
1996	**Swiss Yodeler**, 2, 120	A. O. Solis	Red, 2, 117	Vermilion, 2, 117	5	1:09.77	61,740
1995	**Hennessy**, 2, 117	G. L. Stevens	Reef Reef, 2, 117	Desert Native, 2, 117	7	1:09.85	57,400
1994	**Mr Purple**, 2, 117	C. J. McCarron	†Serena's Song, 2, 117	Cyrano, 2, 117	7	1:10.16	57,600
1993	**Ramblin Guy**, 2, 117	E. Delahoussaye	Swift Walker, 2, 117	Individual Style, 2, 117	8	1:10.09	57,600
1992	**Altazarr**, 2, 117	E. Delahoussaye	Tatum Canyon, 2, 117	Just Sid, 2, 117	6	1:10.01	58,700
1991	**Scherando**, 2, 117	F. Mena	Prince Wild, 2, 117	Burnished Bronze, 2, 120	7	1:09.70	56,400
1990	**Deposit Ticket**, 2, 117	G. L. Stevens	Avenue of Flags, 2, 117	Stone God, 2, 117	8	1:09.00	56,500
1989	**Magical Mile**, 2, 117	E. Delahoussaye	Forty Niner Days, 2, 117	Willing Worker, 2, 117	7	1:10.00	61,200
1988	**King Glorious**, 2, 120	C. J. McCarron	Bruho, 2, 117	Mountain Ghost, 2, 117	9	1:08.80	64,200
1987	**Mi Preferido**, 2, 117	A. O. Solis	Mixed Pleasure, 2, 120	Purdue King, 2, 117	8	1:10.00	75,900
1986	**Captain Valid**, 2, 117	C. J. McCarron	Qualify, 2, 117	Jazzing Around, 2, 117	12	1:11.60	73,600
1985	**Hilco Scamper**, 2, 120	G. L. Stevens	Little Red Cloud, 2, 117	Exuberant's Image, 2, 117	9	1:09.80	64,400
1984	**Saratoga Six**, 2, 117	A. T. Cordero Jr.	Ten Grand, 2, 117	Spectacular Love, 2, 117	11	1:10.20	90,500
1983	**†Althea**, 2, 117	L. A. Pincay Jr.	Rejected Suitor, 2, 117	Auto Commander, 2, 117	9	1:09.40	66,200
1982	**Desert Wine**, 2, 116	F. Olivares	Ft. Davis, 2, 117	Full Choke, 2, 120	6	1:09.60	57,900
1981	**The Captain**, 2, 117	L. A. Pincay Jr.	Remember John, 2, 115	Helen's Beau, 2, 120	12	1:10.40	64,000
1980	**Loma Malad**, 2, 122	L. A. Pincay Jr.	Motivity, 2, 122	Bold Ego, 2, 122	13	1:10.00	101,150
1979	**Parsec**, 2, 122	W. Shoemaker	Doonesbury, 2, 122	Encino, 2, 122	8	1:10.00	89,350
1978	**†Terlingua**, 2, 119	D. G. McHargue	Flying Paster, 2, 122	Exuberant, 2, 122	8	1:08.80	77,000
1977	**Affirmed**, 2, 122	L. A. Pincay Jr.	He's Dewan, 2, 122	Esops Foibles, 2, 122	8	1:09.20	60,975
	Noble Bronze, 2, 117	S. Hawley	Little Reb, 2, 122	Tally Ho the Fox, 2, 122	10	1:09.80	62,225
1976	**Fleet Dragoon**, 2, 122	F. Olivares	Grey Moon Runner, 2, 122	Red Sensation, 2, 117	13	1:09.60	103,250
1975	**Restless Restless**, 2, 122	S. Hawley	Imacornishprince, 2, 122	Telly's Pop, 2, 122	8	1:09.80	79,350
1974	**Dimaggio**, 2, 122	L. A. Pincay Jr.	The Bagel Prince, 2, 122	George Navonod, 2, 122	12	**1:08.60**	74,500
1973	**Century's Envoy**, 2, 122	J. Lambert	Such a Rush, 2, 122	Tinsley's Image, 2, 122	8	1:09.00	78,550

Grade 2 1973-'96. Starlet Sweepstakes 1938-'39. Starlet S. 1940-'58. Held at Santa Anita 1949. Not held 1942-'43. 5½ furlongs 1938. 7 furlongs 1944. 1¹⁄₁₆ miles 1950. Two divisions 1977. †Denotes female.

Hollywood Prevue Stakes

Grade 3 in 2006. Hollywood Park, two-year-olds, 7 furlongs, dirt. Held November 19, 2005, with a gross value of $100,000. First held in 1981. First graded in 1985. Stakes record 1:20.63 (2003 Lion Heart).

Year	Winner	Jockey	Second	Third	Strs	Time	1st Purse
2005	**Your Tent Or Mine**, 2, 118	P. A. Valenzuela	Da Stoops, 2, 114	The Pharaoh, 2, 114	5	1:21.12	$60,000
2004	**Declan's Moon**, 2, 122	V. Espinoza	Bushwacker, 2, 114	Seize the Day, 2, 117	8	1:21.74	60,000
2003	**Lion Heart**, 2, 114	M. E. Smith	Cooperation, 2, 116	Voladero, 2, 113	5	**1:20.63**	60,000
2002	**Roll Hennessy Roll**, 2, 119	A. O. Solis	Red Apache, 2, 115	Hell Cat, 2, 114	7	1:22.68	75,000
2001	**Fonz's**, 2, 117	L. A. Pincay Jr.	Popular, 2, 113	Labamta Babe, 2, 113	7	1:22.03	60,000
2000	**Proud Tower**, 2, 122	V. Espinoza	Chinook Cat, 2, 116	Yonaguska, 2, 122	8	1:23.01	60,000
1999	**Grey Memo**, 2, 115	M. S. Garcia	Magical Dragon, 2, 115	Cameron Pass, 2, 116	6	1:24.44	60,000
1998	**Premier Property**, 2, 119	D. R. Flores	Select Few, 2, 114	American Spirit, 2, 115	7	1:23.29	60,000
1997	**Commitisize**, 2, 113	D. R. Flores	Buttons N Moes, 2, 122	Search Me, 2, 117	6	1:21.64	60,000
1996	**In Excessive Bull**, 2, 115	C. S. Nakatani	Thisnearlywasmine, 2, 118	Constant Demand, 2, 116	5	1:21.54	61,020
1995	**Cobra King**, 2, 121	C. J. McCarron	Hennessy, 2, 121	Exetera, 2, 116	6	1:21.25	58,800
1994	**Afternoon Deelites**, 2, 115	K. Desormeaux	Valid Wager, 2, 114	Hunt for Missouri, 2, 114	4	1:20.98	57,500
1993	**Individual Style**, 2, 121	C. W. Antley	Egayant, 2, 117	Soul of the Matter, 2, 115	6	1:21.17	46,100
1992	**Stuka**, 2, 115	P. A. Valenzuela	Codified, 2, 114	Altazarr, 2, 121	8	1:21.94	62,350
1991	**Star of the Crop**, 2, 114	G. L. Stevens	Seahawk Gold, 2, 121	Salt Lake, 2, 121	5	1:22.30	57,700
1990	**Olympio**, 2, 116	E. Delahoussaye	Barrage, 2, 115	General Meeting, 2, 114	10	1:21.80	62,600
1989	**Individualist**, 2, 115	R. G. Davis	Top Cash, 2, 122	Tarascon, 2, 115	6	1:22.20	46,600
1988	**King Glorious**, 2, 122	C. J. McCarron	Past Ages, 2, 116	Shipping Time, 2, 115	7	1:21.20	47,150
1986	**Exclusive Enough**, 2, 112	W. Shoemaker	Persevered, 2, 122	Gold On Green, 2, 116	8	1:23.00	45,900
1985	**Judge Smells**, 2, 117	C. J. McCarron	Raised On Stage, 2, 112	Old Bid, 2, 115	8	1:23.00	46,850
1984	**First Norman**, 2, 112	W. Shoemaker	Teddy Naturally, 2, 112	Dan's Diablo, 2, 122	6	1:22.20	63,700
1983	**So Vague**, 2, 115	P. J. Cooksey	Country Manor, 2, 115	French Legionaire, 2, 115	16	1:22.20	76,300
1982	**Copelan**, 2, 122	J. D. Bailey	R. Awacs, 2, 115	Desert Wine, 2, 122	8	1:21.40	62,850
1981	**Sepulveda**, 2, 112	C. J. McCarron	Gato Del Sol, 2, 122	Desert Envoy, 2, 112	6	1:22.00	44,625

Traditionally used as a prep race for the Hollywood Futurity. Formerly sponsored by Jack Daniel's Distillery of Lynchburg, Tennessee 2003. Hollywood Prevue Breeders' Cup S. 1990-'95. Not held 1987.

Hollywood Starlet Stakes

Grade 1 in 2005. Hollywood Park, two-year-olds, fillies, 1¹⁄₁₆ miles, dirt. Held December 18, 2005, with a gross value of $456,000. First held in 1981. First graded in 1983. Stakes record 1:41.82 (2004 Splendid Blended).

Year	Winner	Jockey	Second	Third	Strs	Time	1st Purse
2005	**Diplomat Lady**, 2, 120	T. Baze	Balance, 2, 120	Sabatini, 2, 120	11	1:43.89	$273,600
2004	**Splendid Blended**, 2, 120	K. Desormeaux	Sharp Lisa, 2, 120	Northern Mischief, 2, 120	7	**1:41.82**	233,400
2003	**Hollywood Story**, 2, 120	P. A. Valenzuela	Rahy Dolly, 2, 120	House of Fortune, 2, 120	6	1:42.87	209,700
2002	**Elloluv**, 2, 120	P. A. Valenzuela	Composure, 2, 120	Summer Wind Dancer, 2, 120	7	1:42.88	213,900

2001	**Habibti**, 2, 120	V. Espinoza	You, 2, 120	Tali'sluckybusride, 2, 120	5	1:43.12	$214,800
2000	**I Believe in You**, 2, 120	A. O. Solis	Jetin Excess, 2, 120	Whoopddoo, 2, 120	6	1:43.57	205,050
1999	**Surfside**, 2, 120	P. Day	She's Classy, 2, 120	Abby Girl, 2, 120	5	1:43.51	228,150
1998	**Excellent Meeting**, 2, 120	K. Desormeaux	Lacquaria, 2, 120	Perfect Six, 2, 120	6	1:42.14	240,000
1997	**Love Lock**, 2, 120	K. Desormeaux	Career Collection, 2, 120	Snowberg, 2, 120	6	1:42.17	174,600
1996	**Sharp Cat**, 2, 120	C. S. Nakatani	City Band, 2, 120	High Heeled Hope, 2, 120	8	1:44.69	165,600
1995	**Cara Rafaela**, 2, 120	C. S. Nakatani	Advancing Star, 2, 120	Chile Chatte, 2, 120	5	1:43.10	137,500
1994	**Serena's Song**, 2, 120	C. S. Nakatani	Urbane, 2, 120	Ski Dancer, 2, 120	5	1:41.96	137,500
1993	**Sardula**, 2, 120	E. Delahoussaye	Princess Mitterand, 2, 120	Viz, 2, 120	5	1:42.34	139,095
1992	**Creaking Board (GB)**, 2, 120	C. S. Nakatani	Passing Vice, 2, 120	Madame l'Enjoleur, 2, 120	9	1:43.73	137,500
1991	**Magical Maiden**, 2, 120	G. L. Stevens	Looie Capote, 2, 120	Soviet Sojourn, 2, 120	8	1:42.74	138,105
1990	**Cuddles**, 2, 120	G. L. Stevens	Lite Light, 2, 120	Garden Gal, 2, 120	10	1:36.20	247,500
1989	**Cheval Volant**, 2, 120	A. O. Solis	Annual Reunion, 2, 120	Special Happening, 2, 120	9	1:35.60	247,500
1988	**Stocks Up**, 2, 120	A. O. Solis	Fantastic Look, 2, 120	One of a Klein, 2, 120	8	1:35.00	292,325
1987	**Goodbye Halo**, 2, 120	J. Velasquez	Variety Baby, 2, 120	Jeanne Jones, 2, 120	7	1:36.20	274,505
1986	**Very Subtle**, 2, 120	P. A. Valenzuela	Sacahuista, 2, 120	Infringe, 2, 120	6	1:36.00	267,025
1985	**I'm Splendid**, 2, 120	C. J. McCarron	Trim Colony, 2, 120	Twilight Ridge, 2, 120	9	1:36.00	344,217
1984	**Outstandingly**, 2, 120	W. A. Guerra	Fran's Valentine, 2, 120	Wising Up, 2, 120	16	1:44.00	386,402
1983	**Althea**, 2, 120	L. A. Pincay Jr.	Life's Magic, 2, 120	Spring Loose, 2, 120	6	1:43.00	261,250
1982	**Fabulous Notion**, 2, 120	D. Pierce	O'Happy Day, 2, 120	Stephanie Bryn, 2, 120	9	1:42.40	271,618
1981	**Skillful Joy**, 2, 120	C. J. McCarron	Header Card, 2, 120	Flying Partner, 2, 120	8	1:43.20	221,238

Young actresses in old Hollywood were traditionally known as starlets before reaching full star status. 1 mile 1985-'90.

Hollywood Turf Cup Handicap

Grade 1 in 2006. Hollywood Park, three-year-olds and up, 1½ miles, turf. Held December 4, 2004, with a gross value of $250,000. First held in 1981. First graded in 1983. Stakes record 2:24.80 (1990 Itsallgreektome).

Year	Winner	Jockey	Second	Third	Strs	Time	1st Purse
2004	**Pellegrino (Brz)**, 5, 126	G. L. Stevens	†Megahertz (GB), 5, 123	License To Run (Brz), 4, 126	9	2:29.73	$150,000
2003	**‡Continuously**, 4, 126	A. O. Solis	Bowman Mill, 5, 126	Epicentre, 4, 126	7	2:29.01	150,000
2002	**Sligo Bay (Ire)**, 4, 126	L. A. Pincay Jr.	Grammarian, 4, 126	Delta Form (Aus), 6, 126	11	2:27.22	150,000
2001	**Super Quercus (Fr)**, 5, 126	A. O. Solis	Bonapartiste (Fr), 7, 126	Blazing Fury, 3, 122	9	2:29.86	150,000
2000	**Bienamado**, 4, 126	C. J. McCarron	Northern Quest (Fr), 5, 126	Lazy Lode (Arg), 6, 126	8	2:25.98	240,000
1999	**Lazy Lode (Arg)**, 5, 126	L. A. Pincay Jr.	Public Purse, 5, 126	Single Empire (Ire), 5, 126	7	2:25.85	240,000
1998	**Lazy Lode (Arg)**, 4, 126	C. S. Nakatani	Yagli, 5, 126	Ferrari (Ger), 4, 126	10	2:28.36	300,000
1997	**River Bay**, 4, 126	A. O. Solis	Awad, 7, 126	Flag Down, 7, 126	12	2:26.47	300,000
1996	**Running Flame (Fr)**, 4, 126	C. J. McCarron	Marlin, 3, 122	Talloires, 6, 126	10	2:28.53	300,000
1995	**Royal Chariot**, 5, 126	A. O. Solis	Talloires, 5, 126	Earl of Barking (Ire), 5, 126	14	2:25.18	275,000
1994	**Frenchpark (GB)**, 4, 126	C. A. Black	Dare and Go, 3, 122	Regency (GB), 4, 126	11	2:25.66	275,000
1993	**Fraise**, 5, 126	C. J. McCarron	Know Heights (Ire), 4, 126	Explosive Red, 3, 122	6	2:32.34	275,000
1992	**‡Bien Bien**, 3, 122	C. J. McCarron	Fraise, 4, 126	†Trishyde, 3, 119	6	2:31.28	275,000
1991	**†Miss Alleged**, 4, 123	C. J. McCarron	Itsallgreektome, 4, 126	Quest for Fame (GB), 4, 126	7	2:30.00	275,000
1990	**Itsallgreektome**, 3, 122	C. S. Nakatani	Mashkour, 7, 126	Live the Dream, 4, 126	14	**2:24.80**	275,000
1989	**Frankly Perfect**, 4, 126	C. J. McCarron	Yankee Affair, 7, 126	Pleasant Variety, 5, 126	10	2:26.60	275,000
1988	**Great Communicator**, 5, 126	R. Sibille	Putting (Fr), 5, 126	Nasr El Arab, 3, 122	10	2:34.40	275,000
1987	**Vilzak**, 4, 126	P. Day	Forlitano (Arg), 6, 126	Political Ambition, 3, 122	14	2:27.00	275,000
1986	**Alphabatim**, 5, 126	W. Shoemaker	Dahar, 5, 126	Theatrical (Ire), 4, 126	8	2:25.80	275,000
1985	**Zoffany**, 5, 126	E. Delahoussaye	Win, 5, 126	Vanlandingham, 4, 126	13	2:28.40	275,000
1984	**Alphabatim**, 3, 122	C. J. McCarron	Raami (GB), 3, 122	dh-Both Ends Burning, 4, 126 dh-Scrupules (Ire), 4, 126	12	2:15.80	275,000
1983	**John Henry**, 8, 126	C. J. McCarron	†Zalataia (Fr), 4, 123	Palikaraki (Fr), 5, 126	12	2:16.60	275,000
1982	**Prince Spellbound**, 3, 122	M. Castaneda	Majesty's Prince, 3, 122	Lithan, 4, 126	11	2:14.00	220,000
	The Hague, 3, 122	F. Toro	Caterman (NZ), 6, 126	It's the One, 4, 126	13	2:13.40	220,000
1981	**Providential (Ire)**, 4, 126	A. Lequeux	†Queen to Conquer, 5, 123	Goldiko (Fr), 4, 126	10	2:26.80	325,500

Hollywood Turf Cup S. 1989, 1991-2002. Hollywood Turf Cup Invitational H. 1986-'87. Not held 2005. 1⅜ miles 1982-'84. Two divisions 1982. Dead heat for third 1984. ‡Fraise finished first, DQ to second, 1992. ‡Epicentre finished first, DQ to third, 2003. †Denotes female.

Hollywood Turf Express Handicap

Grade 3 in 2006. Hollywood Park, three-year-olds and up, 5½ furlongs, turf. Held November 26, 2004, with a gross value of $150,000. First held in 1985. First graded in 1994. Stakes record 1:01.40 (1991 Gundaghia [1st Div]; 1991 Answer Do [2nd Div]).

Year	Winner	Jockey	Second	Third	Strs	Time	1st Purse
2004	**Cajun Beat**, 4, 122	R. A. Dominguez	Geronimo (Chi), 5, 117	Mighty Beau, 5, 117	9	1:02.08	$90,000
2003	**King Robyn**, 3, 120	T. Baze	Geronimo (Chi), 4, 116	Golden Arrow, 4, 115	9	1:02.08	90,000
2002	**Texas Glitter**, 6, 119	J. R. Velazquez	Rocky Bar, 4, 114	Malabar Gold, 5, 118	5	1:01.52	120,000
2001	**Swept Overboard**, 4, 122	E. Delahoussaye	Speak in Passing, 4, 117	Blu Air Force (Ire), 4, 118	10	1:01.86	120,000
2000	**El Cielo**, 6, 122	C. S. Nakatani	Texas Glitter, 4, 117	Full Moon Madness, 5, 121	7	1:01.73	120,000
1999	**Mr. Doubledown**, 5, 115	V. Espinoza	Howbaddouwantit, 4, 120	Champ's Star, 4, 115	8	1:01.98	120,000
1998	**Soldier Field**, 3, 117	R. Wilson	Surachai, 5, 118	Bodyguard (GB), 3, 115	10	1:02.19	120,000
1997	**†Advancing Star**, 4, 119	K. Desormeaux	Latin Dancer, 3, 116	Surachai, 4, 117	9	1:02.68	120,000
1996	**Sandtrap**, 3, 114	A. O. Solis	Cyrano Storme (Ire), 6, 118	Suggest, 4, 114	8	1:01.46	120,000
1995	**Cyrano Storme (Ire)**, 5, 116	R. R. Douglas	Lakota Brave, 6, 115	Pembroke, 5, 121	9	1:01.64	110,000

1994	**Rotsaluck**, 3, 118	F. H. Valenzuela	†Marina Park (GB), 4, 116	D'Hallevant, 4, 117	11	1:02.27	$82,500
1993	**Wild Harmony**, 4, 117	C. J. McCarron	Robin des Pins, 5, 119	Monde Bleu (GB), 5, 119	8	1:01.88	110,000
1992	**Answer Do**, 6, 121	E. Delahoussaye	Repriced, 4, 118	Gundaghia, 5, 117	11	1:02.14	110,000
1991	**Gundaghia**, 4, 114	C. S. Nakatani	Club Champ, 3, 116	†Sun Brandy, 4, 115	9	**1:01.40**	61,875
	Answer Do, 5, 120	E. Delahoussaye	Apollo, 3, 115	Cardmania, 5, 116	8	**1:01.40**	61,875
1990	**Answer Do**, 4, 115	R. A. Baze	Waterscape, 4, 115	Yes I'm Blue, 4, 118	11	1:07.00	51,200
1989	**Summer Sale**, 3, 114	B. A. Hernandez	Ofanto, 5, 117	Oraibi, 4, 120	9	1:07.80	51,000
1988	**On the Line**, 4, 121	G. L. Stevens	Little Red Cloud, 5, 115	Faro, 6, 118	6	1:09.20	47,650
1987	**Lord Ruckus**, 4, 117	L. A. Pincay Jr.	Bundle of Iron, 5, 114	Faro, 5, 115	7	1:08.20	49,600
1986	**Zany Tactics**, 5, 117	J. L. Kaenel	Bolder Than Bold, 4, 115	Faro, 4, 113	5	1:07.40	46,100
1985	**Temerity Prince**, 5, 122	W. A. Ward	French Legionaire, 4, 113	Debonaire Junior, 4, 124	5	1:11.40	38,300

Hollywood Turf Sprint Championship 1985. Not held 2005. 6 furlongs 1985-'90. Dirt 1985, 1988. Two divisions 1991. †Denotes female.

Holy Bull Stakes

Grade 3 in 2006. Gulfstream Park, three-year-olds, 1⅛ miles, dirt. Held February 4, 2006, with a gross value of $150,000. First held in 1972. First graded in 1995. Stakes record 1:49.31 (2006 Barbaro).

Year	Winner	Jockey	Second	Third	Strs	Time	1st Purse
2006	**Barbaro**, 3, 122	E. S. Prado	Great Point, 3, 116	My Golden Song, 3, 116	12	**1:49.31**	$90,000
2005	**Closing Argument**, 3, 120	C. H. Velasquez	Kansas City Boy, 3, 118	High Fly, 3, 122	8	1:50.14	90,000
2004	**Second of June**, 3, 122	C. H. Velasquez	Silver Wagon, 3, 120	Friends Lake, 3, 122	9	1:43.00	60,000
2003	**Offlee Wild**, 3, 116	M. Guidry	Powerful Touch, 3, 116	Bham, 3, 118	13	1:43.00	60,000
2002	**Booklet**, 3, 122	E. Coa	Harlan's Holiday, 3, 122	Thiscannonsloaded, 3, 116	7	1:46.16	60,000
2001	**Radical Riley**, 3, 119	E. O. Nunez	Buckle Down Ben, 3, 119	Cee Dee, 3, 117	8	1:46.06	60,000
2000	**Hal's Hope**, 3, 112	R. I. Velez	Personal First, 3, 117	Megacles, 3, 113	11	1:44.52	60,000
1999	**Grits'n Hard Toast**, 3, 114	R. G. Davis	Doneraile Court, 3, 119	Mountain Range, 3, 119	7	1:45.32	60,000
1998	**Cape Town**, 3, 119	J. D. Bailey	Comic Strip, 3, 114	Sweetsouthernsaint, 3, 119	7	1:44.15	60,000
1997	**Arthur L.**, 3, 122	J. R. Velazquez	Acceptable, 3, 114	Captain Bodgit, 3, 119	9	1:42.93	60,000
1996	**Cobra King**, 3, 117	C. J. McCarron	Editor's Note, 3, 119	Tilden, 3, 114	7	1:43.42	45,000
1995	**Suave Prospect**, 3, 119	J. D. Bailey	Bullet Trained, 3, 114	Rush Dancer, 3, 112	8	1:44.03	45,000
1994	**Go for Gin**, 3, 119	J. D. Bailey	Halo's Image, 3, 114	Senor Conquistador, 3, 112	6	1:41.62	45,000
1993	**Pride of Burkaan**, 3, 112	J. D. Bailey	Kassec, 3, 112	Jetting Along, 3, 114	8	1:44.74	45,000
1992	**Waki Warrior**, 3, 114	E. Fires	Scream Machine, 3, 112	Careful Gesture, 3, 113	13	1:44.32	78,258
1991	**Shoot to Kill**, 3, 112	W. S. Ramos	Shotgun Harry J., 3, 114	Cahill Road, 3, 114	5	1:43.54	120,000
1990	**Home At Last**, 3, 118	J. D. Bailey	Run Turn, 3, 122	Sound of Cannons, 3, 118	12	1:53.20	140,160
1979	**Northern Prospect**, 3, 112	J. D. Bailey	Duke of Gansvoort, 3, 114	Coup de Chance, 3, 112	8	1:10.60	18,060
1977	**Smashing Native**, 3, 114	D. Brumfield	Cheeky Cheetah, 3, 113	Caribe Pirate, 3, 111	7	1:12.60	18,480
1974	**Real Supreme**, 3, 110	M. Miceli	Eric's Champ, 3, 113	Lord Rebeau, 3, 112	11	1:09.20	20,220

Named for Warren A. Croll Jr.'s 1994 Horse of the Year and '94 Florida Derby (G1) winner Holy Bull (1991 c. by Great Above). Once named the Preview S., the race was considered a "preview" of or prep for the Florida Derby (G1). Preview S. 1972-'95. Not held 1973, 1975-'76, 1978, 1980-'89. 6 furlongs 1972-'79. 1⅛ miles 1990.

Honey Fox Handicap

Grade 3 in 2006. Gulfstream Park, three-year-olds and up, fillies and mares, 1¹⁄₁₆ miles, turf. Held March 4, 2006, with a gross value of $100,000. First held in 1985. First graded in 1994. Stakes record 1:38.31 (2006 Wend).

Year	Winner	Jockey	Second	Third	Strs	Time	1st Purse
2006	**Wend**, 5, 119	E. S. Prado	Brunilda (Arg), 6, 116	Honey Ryder, 5, 121	7	**1:38.31**	$60,000
2005	**Sand Springs**, 5, 115	J. D. Bailey	Potra Fabulous (Arg), 6, 116	Shaconage, 5, 115	11	1:38.41	60,000
2004	**Delmonico Cat**, 5, 116	J. D. Bailey	Coney Kitty (Ire), 6, 115	Madeira Mist (Ire), 5, 117	10	1:41.30	60,000
2003	**San Dare**, 5, 115	M. Guidry	Calista (GB), 5, 118	Laurica, 6, 114	10	1:46.19	60,000
2002	**Batique**, 6, 117	J. F. Chavez	My Sweet Westly, 6, 115	Silver Bandana, 6, 114	8	1:49.32	60,000
2001	**Spook Express (SAf)**, 7, 115	M. E. Smith	Please Sign In, 5, 116	Lady Dora, 4, 115	12	1:35.60	60,000
2000	**Dominique's Joy**, 5, 113	J. D. Bailey	Circus Charmer, 5, 114	Pico Teneriffe, 4, 117	7	1:39.91	45,000
1999	**Colcon**, 6, 119	J. D. Bailey	Lovers Knot (GB), 4, 115	Tampico, 6, 114	10	1:41.71	45,000
1998	**Parade Queen**, 4, 118	P. Day	Dispersion, 5, 113	Dance Clear (Ire), 5, 114	12	1:42.10	45,000
1997	**Rare Blend**, 4, 118	J. D. Bailey	Queen Tutta, 5, 114	Hurricane Viv, 4, 121	6	1:44.28	45,000
1996	**Apolda**, 5, 116	J. D. Bailey	Class Kris, 4, 116	Alice Springs, 6, 121	11	1:41.55	45,000
1995	**Regal Joy**, 4, 113	D. Penna	Sambacarioca, 6, 119	Sovereign Kitty, 4, 119	6	1:44.79	36,000
1994	**Sambacarioca**, 5, 121	J. D. Bailey	Tiney Toast, 5, 114	Marshua's River, 7, 114	6	1:43.41	36,000
1993	**Hero's Love**, 5, 113	E. Fires	Quilma (Chi), 6, 112	Lady Blessington (Fr), 5, 114	14	1:42.90	30,000
1992	**Explosive Kate**, 5, 113	D. Penna	Indian Fashion, 5, 114	Belleofbasinstreet, 4, 111	14	1:43.37	30,000
1991	**Vigorous Lady**, 5, 116	M. A. Lee	Joyce Azalene, 4, 112	Stacie's Toy, 4, 115	8	1:40.30	30,000
1990	**Fieldy (Ire)**, 7, 120	J. D. Bailey	Betty Lobelia, 5, 115	Leave It Be, 5, 117	12	1:37.60	30,000
1989	**Vana Turns**, 4, 113	R. P. Romero	For Kicks, 4, 112	Stolie, 4, 110	9	1:36.00	30,435
	Fieldy (Ire), 6, 114	C. Perret	Miss Unnameable, 5, 110	Aquaba, 4, 116	8	1:35.80	30,135
1988	**Allegedum**, 5, 114	A. T. Cordero Jr.	Autumn Glitter, 5, 117	Fama, 5, 111	11	1:35.20	31,515
	Shaughnessy Road, 4, 112	J. A. Velez Jr.	Rally for Justice (GB), 5, 112	Fieldy (Ire), 5, 118	10	1:36.00	31,215
1987	**Small Virtue**, 4, 114	J. Vasquez	Thirty Zip, 4, 113	Chaldea, 7, 118	10	1:37.00	27,915
	Top Socialite, 5, 119	C. Perret	Give a Toast, 4, 113	Judy's Red Shoes, 4, 116	9	1:37.40	27,615
1986	**Gypsy Prayer**, 5, 110	R. N. Lester	Four Flings, 5, 112	Isayso, 7, 120	6	1:21.00	29,985
	One Fine Lady, 4, 112	J. A. Velez Jr.	Shocker T., 4, 119	Donna's Dolly, 4, 113	5	1:22.00	29,685

1985	**One Fine Lady**, 3, 116	V. H. Molina	Foxy Deen, 3, 116	Boldly Dared, 3, 114	9	1:34.60	$19,257
	Affirmance, 3, 116	E. Maple	Miss Delice, 3, 114	Deceit Dancer, 3, 116	11	1:35.60	19,617

Named for Dr. Jerome S. Torsney's 1981 Orchid H. (G2) winner Honey Fox (1977 f. by Minnesota Mac). Formerly named for NFL Hall of Fame quarterback Joe Namath. Joe Namath H. 1985-2000. 1 mile 1985, 1987-'89, 2001. 7 furlongs 1986. About 1 mile 1990. 1 mile 70 yards 1991. Dirt 1986, 1991, 1994-'95, 1997. Three-year-olds 1985. Fillies 1985. Two divisions 1985-'89.

Honeymoon Breeders' Cup Handicap

Grade 2 in 2006. Hollywood Park, three-year-olds, fillies, 1⅛ miles, turf. Held June 4, 2006, with a gross value of $137,150. First held in 1952. First graded in 1976. Stakes record 1:46.84 (2005 Three Degrees [Ire]).

Year	Winner	Jockey	Second	Third	Strs	Time	1st Purse
2006	**Attima (GB)**, 3, 118	V. Espinoza	Foxysox (GB), 3, 122	Proxenia (GB), 3, 116	7	1:47.36	$82,290
2005	**Three Degrees (Ire)**, 3, 117	G. L. Stevens	Thatswhatimean, 3, 116	Isla Cozzene, 3, 117	13	**1:46.84**	88,275
2004	**Lovely Rafaela**, 3, 114	V. Espinoza	Western Hemisphere, 3, 114	Sagitta Ra, 3, 116	8	1:49.96	113,355
2003	**Quero Quero**, 3, 113	T. Baze	Atlantic Ocean, 3, 121	Sharpbill (GB), 3, 113	10	1:49.34	130,170
2002	**Megahertz (GB)**, 3, 120	P. A. Valenzuela	Arabic Song (Ire), 3, 117	High Society (Ire), 3, 116	7	1:51.97	97,830
2001	**Innit (Ire)**, 3, 117	C. J. McCarron	Live Your Dreams, 3, 116	Beefeater Baby, 3, 115	9	2:01.28	120,000
2000	**Classy Cara**, 3, 122	I. Puglisi	Kumari Continent, 3, 119	Minor Details, 3, 117	9	1:48.05	90,000
1999	**Sweet Ludy (Ire)**, 3, 116	G. L. Stevens	Tout Charmant, 3, 118	Aviate, 3, 118	7	1:48.05	65,160
1998	**Country Garden (GB)**, 3, 120	K. Desormeaux	Janine Rose, 3, 113	Chenille (Ire), 3, 114	6	1:48.74	64,080
1997	**Famous Digger**, 3, 116	B. Blanc	Freeport Flight, 3, 115	Kentucky Kaper, 3, 117	8	1:47.68	65,460
1996	**Antespend**, 3, 122	C. W. Antley	Clamorosa, 3, 116	Najecam, 3, 113	9	1:47.50	82,410
1995	**Auriette (Ire)**, 3, 117	E. Delahoussaye	Artica, 3, 119	Top Shape (Fr), 3, 118	6	1:41.68	62,100
1994	**Work the Crowd**, 3, 117	C. J. McCarron	Malli Star, 3, 117	Fancy 'n Fabulous, 3, 118	8	1:39.68	64,700
1993	**Likeable Style**, 3, 122	E. Delahoussaye	Adorydar, 3, 114	Vinista, 3, 113	5	1:46.29	62,200
1992	**Pacific Squall**, 3, 115	K. Desormeaux	Miss Turkana, 3, 119	Morriston Belle, 3, 118	10	1:41.02	67,100
1991	**Masake**, 3, 115	M. A. Pedroza	Haunting, 3, 114	Now Showing, 3, 116	4	1:42.10	60,400
1990	**Materco**, 3, 117	E. Delahoussaye	Annual Reunion, 3, 119	Slew of Pearls, 3, 117	9	1:41.40	65,800
1989	**Hot Option**, 3, 116	E. Delahoussaye	Formidable Lady, 3, 118	Black Stockings, 3, 113	6	1:40.20	62,600
1988	**Do So**, 3, 118	A. O. Solis	Pattern Step, 3, 119	Jeanne Jones, 3, 120	5	1:41.80	75,400
1987	**Pen Bal Lady (GB)**, 3, 119	E. Delahoussaye	Some Sensation, 3, 117	Davie's Lamb, 3, 115	10	1:41.20	80,300
1986	**An Empress**, 3, 115	P. A. Valenzuela	Top Corsage, 3, 118	Miraculous, 3, 118	10	1:41.80	66,900
1985	**Sharp Ascent**, 3, 115	E. Delahoussaye	Rose Cream, 3, 117	Akamini (Fr), 3, 119	9	1:41.40	79,400
1984	**Vagabond Gal**, 3, 118	E. Delahoussaye	Heartlight, 3, 119	Allusion, 3, 115	8	1:41.40	65,100
1983	**Stage Door Canteen**, 3, 118	C. J. McCarron	Saucy Bobbie, 3, 117	Hot n Pearly, 3, 115	8	1:42.00	65,200
1982	**Castilla**, 3, 116	R. Sibille	Tango Dancer, 3, 117	Skillful Joy, 3, 121	5	1:40.60	61,400
1981	**Amber Ever**, 3, 114	C. J. McCarron	Verbalize, 3, 117	Bee a Scout, 3, 115	10	1:41.60	50,950
1980	**Lady Roberta**, 3, 116	S. Hawley	Finance Charge, 3, 112	Street Ballet, 3, 123	8	1:41.80	60,050
1979	**Variety Queen**, 3, 118	R. Rosales	Prize Spot, 3, 117	Whydidju, 3, 121	8	1:41.60	32,550
1978	**Country Queen**, 3, 114	M. Castaneda	Collect Call, 3, 116	Equanimity, 3, 121	11	1:43.20	33,700
1977	**Joyous Ways**, 3, 116	L. A. Pincay Jr.	Penny Pueblo, 3, 113	*Glenaris, 3, 119	8	1:43.00	26,150
1976	**Cascapedia**, 3, 121	W. Shoemaker	Go March, 3, 117	Dream of Spring, 3, 118	10	1:42.20	26,750
1975	**Katonka**, 3, 123	L. A. Pincay Jr.	Nicosia, 3, 125	Just a Kick, 3, 118	9	1:42.20	33,150
1974	**Bedknob**, 3, 115	A. Pineda	Bold Tullah, 3, 118	Bold Ballet, 3, 116	11	1:42.20	20,750
1973	**Meilleur**, 3, 118	D. Pierce	Sphere, 3, 118	Goddess Roman, 3, 116	10	1:42.40	20,350

Named for Louis B. Mayer's 1946 Hollywood Derby winner Honeymoon (1943 f. by *Beau Pere), once the leading California-bred distaff earner. Formerly named in honor of the nearby Pacific Ocean. Grade 3 1976-'80, 1983-'97. Sea Breeze S. 1952-'55. Honeymoon S. 1956-'74. Honeymoon H. 1975-2000. Honeymoon Breeders' Cup Invitational H. 2001. 6 furlongs 1952-'53. 7 furlongs 1954. 1 mile 1955-'67, 1970. 1$\frac{1}{16}$ miles 1968-'69, 1971-'95. 1¼ miles 2001. Dirt 1952-'72, 1993. Non-winners of a race worth $12,500 to the winner 1973-'74.

Honorable Miss Handicap

Grade 2 in 2006. Saratoga Race Course, three-year-olds and up, fillies and mares, 6 furlongs, dirt. Held August 5, 2005, with a gross value of $150,000. First held in 1985. First graded in 1996. Stakes record 1:08.93 (2000 Bourbon Belle [2nd Div.]).

Year	Winner	Jockey	Second	Third	Strs	Time	1st Purse
2005	**Forest Music**, 4, 114	J. R. Velazquez	Ebony Breeze, 5, 116	Bank Audit, 4, 120	8	1:10.06	$90,000
2004	**My Trusty Cat**, 4, 115	P. Day	Ebony Breeze, 4, 115	Smok'n Frolic, 5, 116	8	1:10.37	90,000
2003	**Willa On the Move**, 4, 114	E. S. Prado	Shine Again, 6, 120	Smok'n Frolic, 4, 117	6	1:09.92	64,560
2002	**Mandy's Gold**, 4, 116	E. S. Prado	Shine Again, 5, 116	Dat You Miz Blue, 5, 114	6	1:09.24	65,100
2001	**Big Bambu**, 4, 118	J. D. Bailey	Country Hideaway, 5, 118	Dat You Miz Blue, 4, 120	4	1:09.64	63,708
2000	**Debby d'Or**, 5, 114	S. J. Sellers	Tropical Punch, 4, 115	Katz Me If You Can, 3, 113	9	1:10.11	66,450
	Bourbon Belle, 5, 116	W. Martinez	Cassidy, 5, 114	Go to the Ink, 4, 114	8	**1:08.93**	65,850
1999	**Bourbon Belle**, 4, 116	P. A. Johnson	Gold Princess, 4, 116	License Fee, 4, 114	10	1:09.53	67,560
1998	**Furlough**, 4, 113	M. E. Smith	Angel's Tearlet, 5, 114	Dixie Flag, 4, 119	6	1:11.32	48,765
1997	**Dancin Renee**, 5, 116	R. Migliore	Ashboro, 4, 116	Vivace, 4, 113	6	1:09.16	48,465
1996	**Twist Afleet**, 5, 119	M. E. Smith	Broad Smile, 4, 116	In Conference, 4, 113	8	1:09.91	49,005
1995	**Low Key Affair**, 4, 115	P. Day	Classy Mirage, 5, 123	Twist Afleet, 4, 120	5	1:09.67	48,195
1994	**Classy Mirage**, 4, 122	J. A. Krone	Spinning Round, 5, 119	For all Seasons, 4, 117	6	1:09.72	48,675
1993	**Nannerl**, 6, 117	J. D. Bailey	Vivano, 4, 117	Via Dei Portici, 4, 117	6	1:15.19	29,040
1992	**Nice Assay**, 4, 115	C. J. McCarron	Madam Bear, 4, 119	Real Irish Hope, 5, 117	5	1:08.97	31,620
1987	**Funistrada**, 4, 122	R. G. Davis	Tricky Squaw, 4, 122	I'm Sweets, 4, 122	5	1:36.80	33,300

1986 **Wisla**, 3, 113	J. Vasquez	Cherry Jubilee, 4, 122	Dancing Danzig, 3, 113	6	1:36.40	$32,940
1985 **Schematic**, 3, 114	R. G. Davis	Ripley, 5, 116	Tiltalating, 3, 114	7	1:10.20	51,570

Named for Pen-Y-Bryn Farm's 1975, '76 Fall Highweight H. (G2) winner Honorable Miss (1970 f. by Damascus). Grade 3 1996-2003. Honorable Miss S. 1992-'97. Not held 1988-'91. 6½ furlongs 1993. Two divisions 2000.

Hopeful Stakes

Grade 1 in 2006. Saratoga Race Course, two-year-olds, 7 furlongs, dirt. Held August 27, 2005, with a gross value of $245,000. First held in 1903. First graded in 1973. Stakes record 1:21.94 (2001 Came Home).

Year	Winner	Jockey	Second	Third	Strs	Time	1st Purse
2005	**First Samurai**, 2, 120	J. D. Bailey	Henny Hughes, 2, 120	Too Much Bling, 2, 120	5	1:23.25	$150,000
2004	**Afleet Alex**, 2, 122	J. Rose	Devils Disciple, 2, 122	Flamenco, 2, 122	7	1:23.58	150,000
2003	**Silver Wagon**, 2, 122	J. D. Bailey	Chapel Royal, 2, 122	Notorious Rogue, 2, 122	7	1:23.47	120,000
2002	**Sky Mesa**, 2, 122	E. S. Prado	Pretty Wild, 2, 122	Zavata, 2, 122	6	1:23.08	120,000
2001	**Came Home**, 2, 122	C. J. McCarron	Mayakovsky, 2, 122	Thunder Days, 2, 122	7	**1:21.94**	120,000
2000	**dh-City Zip**, 2, 122	J. A. Santos		Macho Uno, 2, 122	11	1:24.52	80,000
	dh-Yonaguska, 2, 122	J. D. Bailey					
1999	**High Yield**, 2, 122	J. D. Bailey	Settlement, 2, 122	Exciting Story, 2, 122	9	1:22.85	120,000
1998	**Lucky Roberto**, 2, 122	R. G. Davis	Tactical Cat, 2, 122	Time Bandit, 2, 122	7	1:23.81	120,000
1997	**Favorite Trick**, 2, 122	P. Day	K. O. Punch, 2, 122	Jess M, 2, 122	7	1:23.87	120,000
1996	**Smoke Glacken**, 2, 122	C. Perret	Ordway, 2, 122	Gun Fight, 2, 122	8	1:23.63	120,000
1995	**Hennessy**, 2, 122	G. L. Stevens	Louis Quatorze, 2, 122	Maria's Mon, 2, 122	7	1:23.44	120,000
1994	**Wild Escapade**, 2, 122	J. F. Chavez	Montreal Red, 2, 122	Law of the Sea, 2, 122	6	1:23.24	120,000
1993	**Dehere**, 2, 122	C. J. McCarron	Slew Gin Fizz, 2, 122	Whitney Tower, 2, 122	7	1:15.97	120,000
1992	**Great Navigator**, 2, 122	A. T. Gryder	Strolling Along, 2, 122	England Expects, 2, 122	8	1:15.71	120,000
1991	**Salt Lake**, 2, 122	M. E. Smith	Slew's Ghost, 2, 122	Caller I. D., 2, 122	9	1:17.74	120,000
1990	**Deposit Ticket**, 2, 122	G. L. Stevens	Hansel, 2, 122	Link, 2, 122	6	1:16.20	139,680
1989	**Summer Squall**, 2, 122	P. Day	Sir Richard Lewis, 2, 122	Eternal Flight, 2, 122	8	1:16.80	140,400
1988	**Mercedes Won**, 2, 122	R. G. Davis	Fast Play, 2, 122	Leading Prospect, 2, 122	6	1:16.60	142,320
1987	**Crusader Sword**, 2, 122	R. P. Romero	Bill E. Shears, 2, 122	Success Express, 2, 122	5	1:18.60	104,580
1986	**Gulch**, 2, 122	A. T. Cordero Jr.	Persevered, 2, 122	Flying Granville, 2, 122	4	1:16.40	126,720
1985	**Papal Power**, 2, 122	D. MacBeth	Danny's Keys, 2, 122	Bullet Blade, 2, 122	10	1:18.40	103,320
1984	**Chief's Crown**, 2, 122	D. MacBeth	Tiffany Ice, 2, 122	Mugzy's Rullah, 2, 122	9	1:16.00	100,440
1983	**Capitol South**, 2, 122	J. D. Bailey	Don Rickles, 2, 122	Swale, 2, 122	13	1:17.40	72,720
1982	**Copelan**, 2, 122	J. D. Bailey	Victorious, 2, 122	Aloha Hawaii, 2, 122	9	1:16.60	69,000
1981	**Timely Writer**, 2, 122	R. Danjean	Out of Hock, 2, 122	Lejoli, 2, 122	8	1:16.20	51,390
1980	**Tap Shoes**, 2, 122	R. Hernandez	Lord Avie, 2, 122	Well Decorated, 2, 122	9	1:17.00	51,750
1979	**‡J. P. Brother**, 2, 122	J. Imparato	Gold Stage, 2, 122	Googolplex, 2, 122	12	1:16.20	50,490
1978	**General Assembly**, 2, 122	D. G. McHargue	Exuberant, 2, 122	Fuzzbuster, 2, 122	6	1:16.40	48,600
1977	**Affirmed**, 2, 122	S. Cauthen	Alydar, 2, 122	Regal and Royal, 2, 122	5	1:15.40	48,105
1976	**Banquet Table**, 2, 122	J. Cruguet	Turn of Coin, 2, 122	P. R. Man, 2, 122	13	1:16.20	51,345
1975	**Jackknife**, 2, 121	J. Cruguet	Ferrous, 2, 121	Whatsyourpleasure, 2, 121	9	1:16.60	41,625
	Eustace, 2, 121	J. Nichols	Iron Bit, 2, 121	Gentle King, 2, 121	9	1:16.40	41,850
1974	**The Bagel Prince**, 2, 121	A. T. Cordero Jr.	Knightly Sport, 2, 121	Cardinal George, 2, 121	7	1:16.80	40,995
	Foolish Pleasure, 2, 121	B. Baeza	Greek Answer, 2, 121	Our Talisman, 2, 121	8	1:16.00	41,445
1973	**Gusty O'Shay**, 2, 121	R. Kotenko	Take by Storm, 2, 121	Prince of Reason, 2, 121	7	1:16.40	50,400

As the first major two-year-old race longer than 6 furlongs, owners are "hopeful" their horses will be able to go a classic distance. Held at Belmont Park 1943-'45. Not held 1911-'12. 6 furlongs 1903-'09. 6½ furlongs 1910-'93. Two divisions 1974-'75. Dead heat for first 2000. ‡Rockhill Native finished first, DQ to sixth, 1979.

Humana Distaff Handicap

Grade 1 in 2006. Churchill Downs, four-year-olds and up, fillies and mares, 7 furlongs, dirt. Held May 6, 2006, with a gross value of $291,000. First held in 1987. First graded in 1990. Stakes record 1:20.70 (2001 Dream Supreme).

Year	Winner	Jockey	Second	Third	Strs	Time	1st Purse
2006	**Pussycat Doll**, 4, 119	G. K. Gomez	Behaving Badly, 5, 122	Bending Strings, 5, 119	8	1:21.62	$175,008
2005	**My Trusty Cat**, 5, 115	J. Castellano	Molto Vita, 5, 115	Puxa Saco, 5, 115	9	1:21.18	174,685
2004	**Mayo On the Side**, 5, 114	P. Day	Azeri, 6, 125	Randaroo, 4, 121	4	1:22.78	174,375
2003	**Sightseek**, 4, 116	J. D. Bailey	Gold Mover, 5, 119	Miss Lodi, 4, 114	8	1:22.12	137,888
2002	**‡Celtic Melody**, 4, 114	M. Guidry	Gold Mover, 4, 115	Hattiesburg, 4, 115	9	1:22.98	141,360
2001	**Dream Supreme**, 4, 120	P. Day	La Feminn, 5, 115	Nany's Sweep, 5, 117	5	**1:20.70**	102,300
2000	**Ruby Surprise**, 5, 114	J. C. Judice	Honest Lady, 4, 119	Cassidy, 5, 113	7	1:21.25	102,951
1999	**Zuppardo Ardo**, 5, 114	S. J. Sellers	French Braids, 4, 114	Prospector's Song, 4, 114	9	1:23.40	105,183
1998	**Colonial Minstrel**, 4, 115	J. R. Velazquez	Stop Traffic, 5, 117	Meter Maid, 4, 114	11	1:22.12	71,300
1997	**Capote Belle**, 4, 118	J. R. Velazquez	Hidden Lake, 4, 115	J J'sdream, 4, 117	8	1:22.38	70,060
1996	**In Conference**, 4, 113	M. E. Smith	Supah Jess, 4, 113	Morris Code, 4, 116	8	1:23.30	72,930
1995	**Laura's Pistolette**, 4, 114	C. S. Nakatani	Morning Meadow, 5, 113	Traverse City, 5, 114	10	1:22.24	74,425
1994	**Roamin Rachel**, 4, 118	M. E. Smith	Arches of Gold, 5, 121	Glory's Ghost, 4, 113	7	1:23.83	72,345
1993	**Court Hostess**, 5, 115	C. J. McCarron	Santa Catalina, 5, 115	Ifyoucouldseemenow, 5, 113	12	1:23.18	56,550
1992	**Ifyoucouldseemenow**, 4, 120	C. Perret	Madam Bear, 4, 114	Magal, 5, 113	10	1:22.22	56,599
1991	**Illeria**, 4, 112	P. Day	Nurse Dopey, 4, 117	Tipsy Girl, 5, 115	10	1:23.26	37,603
1990	**Medicine Woman**, 5, 114	P. Day	Lost Lode, 5, 114	Gallant Ryder, 5, 111	9	1:23.40	36,693
1989	**Sunshine Always**, 5, 113	P. Day	Littlebitapleasure, 7, 115	Lt. Lao, 5, 119	5	1:24.40	35,425

1988	**Le l'Argent**, 6, 119	P. Day	Lady Gretchen, 4, 113	Intently, 5, 117	7	1:22.80	$36,270
1987	**Lazer Show**, 4, 120	P. Day	Weekend Delight, 5, 123	Ten Thousand Stars, 5, 118	7	1:22.80	26,442

Races for females are typically referred to as distaff races. Sponsored by Humana Inc., a major medical corporation headquartered in Louisville 1995-2006. Formerly sponsored by Brown & Williamson Tobacco Corp., also headquartered in Louisville 1987-'94. Grade 3 1990-'98. Grade 2 1999-2001. Brown & Williamson S. 1987. Brown & Williamson H. 1988-'94. ‡Gold Mover finished first, DQ to second, 2002.

Hurricane Bertie Handicap

Grade 3 in 2006. Gulfstream Park, three-year-olds and up, fillies and mares, 6½ furlongs, dirt. Held February 18, 2006, with a gross value of $100,000. First held in 2001. First graded in 2005. Stakes record 1:15.38 (2002 Gold Mover).

Year	Winner	Jockey	Second	Third	Strs	Time	1st Purse
2006	**Smokey Glacken**, 5, 119	J. Castellano	Atlas Valley, 4, 116	Beautiful Bets, 6, 116	10	1:15.47	$60,000
2005	**Lilah**, 8, 114	R. Maragh	Forty Moves, 4, 114	Molto Vita, 5, 118	6	1:15.45	60,000
2004	**House Party**, 4, 117	J. A. Santos	Mooji Moo, 5, 115	Zawzooth, 5, 113	10	1:15.55	60,000
2003	**Gold Mover**, 5, 117	E. S. Prado	Harmony Lodge, 5, 116	Belterra, 4, 116	5	1:15.83	60,000
2002	**Gold Mover**, 4, 116	E. Coa	Celtic Melody, 4, 114	Mandy's Gold, 4, 114	5	**1:15.38**	60,000
2001	**Swept Away**, 4, 121	E. S. Prado	Sahara Gold, 4, 115	Lily's Affair, 5, 115	10	1:09.85	48,720

Named for Richard, Bertram, and Elaine Klein's 2000 First Lady H. (G3) winner Hurricane Bertie (1995 f. by Storm Boot).

Hutcheson Stakes

Grade 2 in 2006. Gulfstream Park, three-year-olds, 7½ furlongs, dirt. Held February 4, 2006, with a gross value of $150,000. First held in 1955. First graded in 1973. Stakes record 1:27.12 (2006 Keyed Entry).

Year	Winner	Jockey	Second	Third	Strs	Time	1st Purse
2006	**Keyed Entry**, 3, 116	J. R. Velazquez	First Samurai, 3, 122	Express News, 3, 118	7	**1:27.12**	$90,000
2005	**Proud Accolade**, 3, 120	J. R. Velazquez	Park Avenue Ball, 3, 120	Vicarage, 3, 118	6	1:29.90	90,000
2004	**Limehouse**, 3, 122	J. R. Velazquez	Deputy Storm, 3, 118	Saratoga County, 3, 116	10	1:22.23	90,000
2003	**Lion Tamer**, 3, 118	J. R. Velazquez	Strength Within, 3, 116	Crafty Guy, 3, 122	6	1:22.60	90,000
2002	**Showmeitall**, 3, 118	J. F. Chavez	Monthir, 3, 116	Royal Lad, 3, 116	6	1:26.07	90,000
2001	**Yonaguska**, 3, 119	J. D. Bailey	City Zip, 3, 122	Sparkling Sabre, 3, 112	11	1:22.63	90,000
2000	**dh-More Than Ready**, 3, 122 **dh-Summer Note**, 3, 113	J. R. Velazquez S. J. Sellers		American Bullet, 3, 114	8	1:21.76	60,000
1999	**Bet Me Best**, 3, 122	J. D. Bailey	Texas Glitter, 3, 119	Cat Thief, 3, 119	7	1:22.33	90,000
1998	**Time Limit**, 3, 119	J. D. Bailey	Coronado's Quest, 3, 122	Zippy Zeal, 3, 114	5	1:22.53	60,000
1997	**Frisk Me Now**, 3, 112	E. L. King Jr.	Confide, 3, 117	Crown Ambassador, 3, 117	8	1:22.51	60,000
1996	**Appealing Skier**, 3, 119	R. Wilson	Unbridled's Song, 3, 119	Gold Fever, 3, 117	5	1:24.72	45,000
1995	**Valid Wager**, 3, 119	M. A. Pedroza	Mr. Greeley, 3, 117	Don Juan A, 3, 114	7	1:23.51	45,000
1994	**Holy Bull**, 3, 122	M. E. Smith	Patton, 3, 113	You and I, 3, 119	5	1:21.23	45,000
1993	**Hidden Trick**, 3, 114	R. P. Romero	‡Great Navigator, 3, 119	Forever Whirl, 3, 113	9	1:23.61	54,108
1992	**My Luck Runs North**, 3, 113	R. D. Lopez	Sneaky Solicitor, 3, 117	Frosted Spy, 3, 117	9	1:24.95	55,008
1991	**Fly So Free**, 3, 122	J. A. Santos	To Freedom, 3, 119	Sunny and Pleasant, 3, 114	10	1:23.30	55,527
1990	**Housebuster**, 3, 119	R. P. Romero	Yonder, 3, 122	Stalker, 3, 114	11	1:24.40	56,787
1989	**Dixieland Brass**, 3, 114	R. P. Romero	Western Playboy, 3, 112	Tricky Creek, 3, 122	12	1:22.80	58,320
1988	**Perfect Spy**, 3, 114	J. Samyn	Forty Niner, 3, 122	Notebook, 3, 122	7	1:23.00	52,335
1987	**Well Selected**, 3, 113	J. Vasquez	Gone West, 3, 114	Faster Than Sound, 3, 119	8	1:23.00	53,376
1986	**Papal Power**, 3, 122	D. MacBeth	Raja's Revenge, 3, 122	Mr. Classic, 3, 112	10	1:23.80	55,440
1985	**Banner Bob**, 3, 114	K. K. Allen	‡Creme Fraiche, 3, 114	Do It Again Dan, 3, 114	12	1:21.60	45,720
1984	**Swale**, 3, 122	E. Maple	For Halo, 3, 114	Darn That Alarm, 3, 112	12	1:22.20	38,790
1983	**Current Hope**, 3, 114	A. O. Solis	Highland Park, 3, 122	Country Pine, 3, 112	13	1:22.80	39,330
1982	**Distinctive Pro**, 3, 117	J. Velasquez	Center Cut, 3, 114	Real Twister, 3, 114	6	1:22.40	34,650
1981	**Lord Avie**, 3, 122	C. J. McCarron	Spirited Boy, 3, 114	Linnleur, 3, 114	7	1:23.40	34,080
1980	**Plugged Nickle**, 3, 122	B. Thornburg	Execution's Reason, 3, 122	One Son, 3, 114	6	1:22.60	17,640
1979	**Spectacular Bid**, 3, 122	R. J. Franklin	Lot o' Gold, 3, 114	Northern Prospect, 3, 114	4	1:21.40	17,766
1978	**Sensitive Prince**, 3, 114	M. Solomone	Kissing U., 3, 114	Pipe Major, 3, 114	11	1:20.80	19,890
1977	**Silver Series**, 3, 112	L. Snyder	Medieval Man, 3, 114	One in a Million, 3, 113	8	1:22.80	20,610
1976	**Sonkisser**, 3, 116	B. Baeza	Gay Jitterbug, 3, 116	Star of the Sea, 3, 122	7	1:21.00	19,350
1975	**Greek Answer**, 3, 122	M. Castaneda	Fashion Sale, 3, 113	Rich Sun, 3, 122	11	1:21.60	20,370
1974	**Frankie Adams**, 3, 114	R. Turcotte	dh-Judger, 3, 110 dh-Training Table, 3, 113		13	1:22.40	31,845
1973	**Shecky Greene**, 3, 122	B. Baeza	Forego, 3, 116	Leo's Pisces, 3, 112	7	1:20.80	19,170

Named for labor leader William Levi Hutcheson (1874-1953), who served as a member of the Gulfstream Park Advisory Board. Formerly sponsored by Danka Office Imaging Co. of St. Petersburg, Florida 1997. Not graded 1975-'81. Hutcheson H. 1955, 1984. 6½ furlongs 1955-'60. Dead heat for second 1974. Dead heat for first 2000. ‡Do It Again Dan finished second, DQ to third, 1985. ‡Demaloot Demashoot finished second, DQ to fourth, 1993. Equaled track record 1973. Track record 2006. Held as an allowance race 1954.

Illinois Derby

Grade 2 in 2006. Hawthorne Race Course, three-year-olds, 1⅛ miles, dirt. Held April 8, 2006, with a gross value of $500,000. First held in 1923. First graded in 1973. Stakes record 1:47.51 (1997 Wild Rush).

Year	Winner	Jockey	Second	Third	Strs	Time	1st Purse
2006	**Sweetnorthernsaint**, 3, 122	K. J. Desormeaux	Mister Triester, 3, 122	Cause to Believe, 3, 122	10	1:49.82	$300,000
2005	**Greeley's Galaxy**, 3, 122	K. Desormeaux	Monarch Lane, 3, 122	Magna Graduate, 3, 122	8	1:49.62	300,000

2004	**Pollard's Vision**, 3, 114	E. Coa	Song of the Sword, 3, 116	Suave, 3, 114	11	1:50.80	$300,000
2003	**Ten Most Wanted**, 3, 114	P. Day	Fund of Funds, 3, 114	Foufa's Warrior, 3, 118	10	1:51.47	300,000
2002	**War Emblem**, 3, 114	L. J. Sterling Jr.	Repent, 3, 124	Fonz's, 3, 117	9	1:49.92	300,000
2001	**Distilled**, 3, 114	M. E. Smith	Saint Damien, 3, 119	Dream Run, 3, 114	8	1:51.37	300,000
2000	**Performing Magic**, 3, 119	S. J. Sellers	Country Only, 3, 117	Country Coast, 3, 114	9	1:50.86	300,000
1999	**Vision and Verse**, 3, 114	H. Castillo Jr.	Prime Directive, 3, 117	Pineaff, 3, 122	10	1:48.47	300,000
1998	**Yarrow Brae**, 3, 114	W. Martinez	‡One Bold Stroke, 3, 117	Orville N Wilbur's, 3, 124	10	1:51.21	300,000
1997	**Wild Rush**, 3, 117	K. Desormeaux	Anet, 3, 124	Saratoga Sunrise, 3, 119	8	**1:47.51**	300,000
1996	**Natural Selection**, 3, 114	R. P. Romero	El Amante, 3, 124	Irish Conquest, 3, 114	13	1:48.60	300,000
1995	**Peaks and Valleys**, 3, 124	J. A. Krone	Da Hoss, 3, 117	Western Echo, 3, 117	13	1:48.99	300,000
1994	**Rustic Light**, 3, 117	E. Fires	Amathos, 3, 114	Seminole Wind, 3, 114	7	1:51.89	300,000
1993	**Antrim Rd.**, 3, 114	A. T. Gryder	Seattle Morn, 3, 114	Secret Negotiator, 3, 114	13	1:48.68	300,000
1992	**Dignitas**, 3, 117	J. D. Bailey	American Chance, 3, 112	Straight to Bed, 3, 114	13	1:49.09	320,100
1991	**Richman**, 3, 124	J. D. Bailey	Doc of the Day, 3, 119	Nowork all Play, 3, 114	14	1:49.36	319,200
1990	**Dotsero**, 3, 117	A. T. Gryder	Sound of Cannons, 3, 112	Hofre, 3, 112	9	1:50.60	190,290
1989	**‡Music Merci**, 3, 124	G. L. Stevens	Notation, 3, 119	Endow, 3, 124	7	1:50.20	310,140
1988	**Proper Reality**, 3, 124	J. D. Bailey	Jim's Orbit, 3, 122	Classic Account, 3, 112	6	1:50.20	321,000
1987	**Lost Code**, 3, 124	G. St. Leon	Blanco, 3, 119	Valid Prospect, 3, 112	7	1:49.60	188,130
1986	**Bolshoi Boy**, 3, 118	R. Migliore	Speedy Shannon, 3, 118	Blue Buckaroo, 3, 116	8	1:52.20	189,432
1985	**Important Business**, 3, 116	J. L. Diaz	Nostalgia's Star, 3, 122	Another Reef, 3, 124	13	1:51.60	192,786
1984	**Delta Trace**, 3, 124	K. K. Allen	Wind Flyer, 3, 122	Birdie's Legend, 3, 124	10	1:51.80	127,530
1983	**Gen'l Practitioner**, 3, 126	J. A. Santiago	Passing Base, 3, 114	Aztec Red, 3, 124	10	1:50.40	127,200
1982	**Star Gallant**, 3, 126	R. Sibille	Drop Your Drawers, 3, 122	Soy Emperor, 3, 119	8	1:52.60	126,420
1981	**Paristo**, 3, 126	D. C. Ashcroft	Pass the Tab, 3, 126	Bitterrook, 3, 114	13	1:49.60	93,300
1980	**Ray's Word**, 3, 124	R. DePass	Mighty Return, 3, 114	Stutz Blackhawk, 3, 121	11	1:52.00	92,970
1979	**Smarten**, 3, 124	S. Maple	Clever Trick, 3, 124	Julie's Dancer, 3, 116	6	1:49.40	91,710
1978	**Batonnier**, 3, 124	R. J. Hirdes Jr.	Raymond Earl, 3, 121	Silver Nitrate, 3, 124	12	1:51.60	62,820
1977	**Flag Officer**, 3, 124	L. Ahrens	Time Call, 3, 116	Cisk, 3, 116	11	1:52.20	62,955
1976	**Life's Hope**, 3, 124	S. Hawley	Wardlaw, 3, 124	New Collection, 3, 116	9	1:51.40	77,295
1975	**Colonel Power**, 3, 124	P. Rubbicco	Ruggles Ferry, 3, 124	Methdioxya, 3, 124	14	1:50.20	63,360
1974	**Sharp Gary**, 3, 124	G. J. Gallitano	Sr. Diplomat, 3, 114	Sports Editor, 3, 119	12	1:50.00	63,060
1973	**Big Whippendeal**, 3, 119	L. Adams	†What Will Be, 3, 121	Golden Don, 3, 126	9	1:50.20	43,491

Named for the home state of Hawthorne Race Course. Grade 3 1973-'87. Held at Sportsman's Park 1924-'32, 1939-'98, 2000-'02. Held at Aurora 1933-'38. Not held 1924-'32, 1939-'62, 1970-'71. 1¼ miles 1923. ‡Notation finished first, DQ to second, 1989. ‡Orville N Wilbur's finished second, DQ to third, 1998. Track record 1997. †Denotes female.

Indiana Breeders' Cup Oaks

Grade 3 in 2006. Hoosier Park, three-year-olds, fillies, 1¹⁄₁₆ miles, dirt. Held September 30, 2005, with a gross value of $405,100. First held in 1995. First graded in 2001. Stakes record 1:42.40 (2000 Humble Clerk).

Year	Winner	Jockey	Second	Third	Strs	Time	1st Purse
2005	**Flying Glitter**, 3, 121	R. Albarado	Eyes On Eddy, 3, 114	Miss Matched, 3, 121	6	1:44.10	$243,060
2004	**Daydreaming**, 3, 118	J. R. Velazquez	Capeside Lady, 3, 121	Stellar Jayne, 3, 121	7	1:43.65	243,780
2003	**Awesome Humor**, 3, 116	R. Albarado	Cloakof Vagueness, 3, 114	Shot Gun Favorite, 3, 118	10	1:45.75	184,140
2002	**Bare Necessities**, 3, 118	J. Valdivia Jr.	Erica's Smile, 3, 121	Tarnished Lady, 3, 118	9	1:45.83	183,840
2001	**Scoop**, 3, 121	R. Albarado	Gold Huntress, 3, 115	Caressing, 3, 121	9	1:44.06	123,480
2000	**Humble Clerk**, 3, 114	L. J. Melancon	Megans Bluff, 3, 121	Miss Seffens, 3, 116	5	**1:42.40**	92,580
1999	**Brushed Halory**, 3, 121	E. M. Martin Jr.	The Happy Hopper, 3, 116	Chelsie's House, 3, 116	10	1:44.64	123,330
1998	**French Braids**, 3, 116	W. Martinez	Remember Ike, 3, 121	Barefoot Dyana, 3, 118	7	1:43.11	124,080
1997	**Cotton Carnival**, 3, 121	E. M. Martin Jr.	Sheepscot, 3, 116	Valid Bonnet, 3, 121	9	1:43.30	64,440
1996	**Princess Eloise**, 3, 118	S. T. Saito	Talking Tower, 3, 116	Shuffle Again, 3, 116	6	1:37.00	33,540
1995	**Niner's Home**, 3, 121	T. J. Hebert	Alltheway Bertie, 3, 118	Graceful Minister, 3, 114	6	1:37.00	24,480

Hoosier Park is located in Anderson, Indiana. Indiana Oaks 1995-'97. 1 mile 1995-'96.

Indiana Derby

Grade 2 in 2006. Hoosier Park, three-year-olds, 1¹⁄₁₆ miles, dirt. Held October 1, 2005, with a gross value of $511,300. First held in 1995. First graded in 2002. Stakes record 1:41.40 (1996 Canyon Run).

Year	Winner	Jockey	Second	Third	Strs	Time	1st Purse
2005	**Don't Get Mad**, 3, 124	B. Blanc	Scrappy T, 3, 124	Thor's Echo, 3, 124	9	1:42.71	$306,780
2004	**Brass Hat**, 3, 124	W. Martinez	Suave, 3, 124	Hasslefree, 3, 115	9	1:44.04	306,780
2003	**Excessivepleasure**, 3, 124	J. K. Court	Grand Hombre, 3, 124	Wando, 3, 124	8	1:43.48	247,080
2002	**Perfect Drift**, 3, 124	J. K. Court	Easyfromthegitgo, 3, 124	Premeditation, 3, 121	12	1:43.50	248,820
2001	**Orientate**, 3, 115	R. Albarado	Saratoga Games, 3, 121	Trion Georgia, 3, 124	11	1:42.22	188,460
2000	**Mister Deville**, 3, 119	L. S. Quinonez	Performing Magic, 3, 122	One Call Close, 3, 119	5	1:41.80	184,500
1999	**Forty One Carats**, 3, 115	J. F. Chavez	Zanetti, 3, 122	First American, 3, 122	12	1:42.24	187,290
1998	**One Bold Stroke**, 3, 122	R. Albarado	Dixie Dot Com, 3, 117	Da Devil, 3, 122	11	1:43.14	188,700
1997	**Dubai Dust**, 3, 113	S. P. LeJeune Jr.	Frisk Me Now, 3, 122	Tansit, 3, 119	8	1:44.00	127,440
1996	**Canyon Run**, 3, 115	F. C. Torres	Broadway Bit, 3, 113	Hunk of Class, 3, 117	10	**1:41.40**	64,560
1995	**Peruvian**, 3, 117	D. Kutz	I Still Believe, 3, 117	Mine Inspector, 3, 119	11	1:43.00	66,900

Hoosier Park is located in Anderson, Indiana. Grade 3 2002-'03.

Inglewood Handicap

Grade 3 in 2006. Hollywood Park, three-year-olds and up, 1$^1/_{16}$ miles, turf. Held April 29, 2006, with a gross value of $100,000. First held in 1938. First graded in 1973. Stakes record 1:38.45 (2004 Leroidesanimaux [Brz]).

Year	Winner	Jockey	Second	Third	Strs	Time	1st Purse
2006	**Willow O Wisp**, 4, 117	V. Espinoza	Artiste Royal (Ire), 5, 116	New Export (Brz), 5, 116	7	1:39.05	$60,000
2005	**King of Happiness**, 6, 117	P. A. Valenzuela	Red Fort (Ire), 5, 117	Just Wonder (GB), 5, 116	6	1:40.67	64,320
2004	**Leroidesanimaux (Brz)**, 4, 114	J. K. Court	Designed for Luck, 7, 118	Devious Boy (GB), 4, 115	9	**1:38.45**	66,540
2003	**Gondolieri (Chi)**, 4, 116	F. T. Alvarado	Truly a Judge, 5, 114	Freefourinternet, 5, 116	4	1:40.32	63,540
2002	**Night Patrol**, 6, 113	V. Espinoza	Redattore (Brz), 7, 120	Seinne (Chi), 5, 117	7	1:39.35	65,820
2001	**Fateful Dream**, 4, 114	D. R. Flores	National Anthem (GB), 5, 115	Casino King (Ire), 6, 115	5	1:41.65	64,260
2000	**Montemiro (Fr)**, 6, 113	V. Espinoza	Bonapartiste (Fr), 6, 118	Takarian (Ire), 5, 118	8	1:40.71	66,300
1999	**Brave Act (GB)**, 5, 120	G. F. Almeida	Lord Smith (GB), 4, 119	Expressionist, 4, 116	8	1:39.13	66,420
1998	**Fantastic Fellow**, 4, 118	C. S. Nakatani	Via Lombardia (Ire), 6, 116	Sharekann (Ire), 6, 113	6	1:38.77	64,740
1997	**El Angelo**, 5, 115	C. S. Nakatani	Irish Wings (Ire), 5, 114	Tychonic (GB), 7, 118	5	1:40.20	63,900
1996	**Fastness (Ire)**, 6, 122	C. S. Nakatani	Helmsman, 4, 120	Tychonic (GB), 6, 120	5	1:39.54	79,470
1995	**Blaze O'Brien**, 8, 116	C. A. Black	Savinio, 5, 118	Stoller, 4, 117	7	1:39.53	79,800
1994	**Gothland (Fr)**, 5, 117	C. S. Nakatani	Rapan Boy (Aus), 6, 116	Johann Quatz (Fr), 5, 117	4	1:39.60	60,700
1993	**The Tender Track**, 6, 116	E. Delahoussaye	Journalism, 5, 118	Johann Quatz (Fr), 4, 117	6	1:40.00	62,500
1992	**Golden Pheasant**, 6, 121	G. L. Stevens	Blaze O'Brien, 5, 114	Native Boundary, 4, 116	7	1:39.86	64,900
1991	**Tight Spot**, 4, 121	L. A. Pincay Jr.	Somethingdifferent, 4, 116	Razeen, 4, 114	6	1:40.30	63,400
1990	**Mohamed Abdu (Ire)**, 6, 117	G. L. Stevens	Peace, 5, 117	Classic Fame, 4, 117	7	1:39.40	64,800
1989	**Steinlen (GB)**, 6, 120	G. L. Stevens	Pasakos, 4, 115	Mi Preferido, 4, 117	7	1:39.60	63,400
1988	**Steinlen (GB)**, 5, 119	G. L. Stevens	Deputy Governor, 4, 120	†Galunpe (Ire), 5, 115	9	1:40.40	66,200
1987	**Le Belvedere**, 4, 113	W. Shoemaker	Sharrood, 4, 118	Barbery, 6, 114	8	1:40.40	65,100
1986	**Zoffany**, 6, 121	E. Delahoussaye	Palace Music, 5, 124	Truce Maker, 8, 112	6	1:45.60	63,300
1985	**Al Mamoon**, 4, 116	E. Delahoussaye	The Noble Player, 5, 118	Swoon, 7, 114	6	1:40.20	62,900
1984	**†Royal Heroine (Ire)**, 4, 116	F. Toro	Bel Bolide, 6, 120	Vin St Benet (GB), 5, 118	13	1:40.20	71,500
1983	**Bold Style**, 4, 115	P. Day	Noalto (GB), 5, 115	Western, 5, 116	8	1:41.40	65,400
1982	**Maipon (Chi)**, 5, 112	D. G. McHargue	Spence Bay (Ire), 7, 122	Wickerr, 7, 116	11	1:40.20	68,900
1981	**Bold Tropic (SAf)**, 6, 124	W. Shoemaker	The Bart, 5, 117	Adraan (GB), 4, 117	11	1:40.00	52,300
1980	**Red Crescent**, 4, 112	C. J. McCarron	Henschel, 6, 118	Numa Pompilius, 6, 115	5	1:40.60	31,300
1979	**Johnny's Image**, 4, 117	C. J. McCarron	Rich Cream, 4, 117	Smoggy (GB), 5, 112	8	1:40.60	26,875
	Star Spangled, 5, 119	L. A. Pincay Jr.	Bywayofchicago, 5, 122	As de Copas (Arg), 6, 121	6	1:40.00	25,875
1978	**Star Spangled**, 4, 116	A. T. Cordero Jr.	Bad 'n Big, 4, 122	No Turning, 5, 116	8	1:39.80	26,800
	Star of Erin (Ire), 4, 117	W. Shoemaker	Landscaper, 6, 113	Life's Hope, 5, 117	7	1:40.60	26,300
1977	**Today 'n Tomorrow**, 4, 117	S. Hawley	Anne's Pretender, 5, 122	Sir Jason, 6, 118	7	1:41.00	32,300
1976	**Riot in Paris**, 5, 121	J. Lambert	Absent Minded, 4, 114	Passionate Pirate, 5, 113	6	1:41.60	25,750
	King Pellinore, 4, 118	W. Shoemaker	Antique, 5, 114	Big Band, 6, 117	7	1:42.00	26,250
1975	***El Botija**, 5, 116	J. E. Tejeira	Kirrary, 5, 115	Against the Snow, 5, 117	8	1:41.60	25,475
	†Gay Style, 5, 120	W. Shoemaker	Out of the East, 5, 116	June's Love, 4, 116	10	1:41.40	26,475
1974	**Shirley's Champion**, 3, 118	H. Grant	Rocket Review, 3, 117	Such a Rush, 3, 121	9	1:14.80	20,100
1973	**Ancient Title**, 3, 122	F. Toro	Groshawk, 3, 122	Pontoise, 3, 114	8	1:21.00	32,550

Named for the city of Inglewood, California, location of Hollywood Park. Formerly sponsored by the Miller Brewing Co. of Milwaukee 1972. Grade 2 1973-'74, 1987-'94. Not graded 1975-'81, 2003. Inglewood Mile H. 1938-'39. Miller High Life Inglewood H. 1972. Held at Santa Anita Park 1949. Not held 1942-'44. 1 mile 1938-'39. 7 furlongs 1945-'47, 1973. 6 furlongs 1948. 1$^1/_8$ miles 1950, 1968-'72. 6$^1/_2$ furlongs 1974. Dirt 1983-'66, 1968-'74, 2003. Originally scheduled on turf 2003. Three-year-olds 1973-'74. Two divisions 1975-'76, 1978-'79. Course record 1998, 2004. †Denotes female.

Iowa Oaks

Grade 3 in 2006. Prairie Meadows, three-year-olds, fillies, 1$^1/_{16}$ miles, dirt. Held July 1, 2005, with a gross value of $122,500. First held in 1989. First graded in 2004. Stakes record 1:41.64 (2003 Wildwood Royal).

Year	Winner	Jockey	Second	Third	Strs	Time	1st Purse
2005	**Whimsy**, 3, 116	C. H. Marquez Jr.	Cee's Irish, 3, 121	Mary Alex, 3, 113	5	1:43.60	$75,000
2004	**He Loves Me**, 3, 118	J. Z. Santana	Prospective Saint, 3, 115	Home Court, 3, 115	8	1:42.80	75,000
2003	**Wildwood Royal**, 3, 121	S. Danush	Golden Reputashn, 3, 112	Tulupai, 3, 112	8	**1:41.64**	75,000
2002	**Lost At Sea**, 3, 115	T. J. Thompson	See How She Runs, 3, 121	Don't Ruffle Me, 3, 115	6	1:42.27	90,000
2001	**Unbridled Elaine**, 3, 115	P. Day	Supreme Song, 3, 115	Sharky's Review, 3, 118	6	1:43.88	90,000
2000	**Trip**, 3, 121	W. Martinez	Lady Melesi, 3, 118	Fiesty Countess, 3, 118	7	1:43.56	90,000
1999	**Golden Temper**, 3, 121	S. J. Sellers	Undermine, 3, 118	Sweeping Story, 3, 121	6	1:42.95	75,000
1998	**Shardona**, 3, 114	K. Shino	Danzig Foxxy Woman, 3, 118	Lady Tamworth, 3, 121	10	1:46.94	43,305
1997	**Bon Ami**, 3, 116	G. W. Corbett	Windy City Raja, 3, 114	Quick n Steady, 3, 121	9	1:44.73	37,317
1996	**Vaguely Who**, 3, 121	V. L. Warhol	Swiss Saphire, 3, 118	Dee's Anny, 3, 117	11	1:43.63	24,439
1995	**Our Gaggy**, 3, 118	D. R. Bickel	Don't Tary Stalker, 3, 121	Melinda Jo, 3, 114	6	1:41.80	17,184
1994	**Punkerdoo**, 3, 121	D. Schroeck	Maria Badria, 3, 118	Chateau Queen, 3, 114	7	1:44.00	9,555
1993	**Medical History**, 3, 114	V. L. Warhol	Millie's Key, 3, 118	Fashioncense, 3, 119	5	1:42.40	8,950
1992	**Giggles Up**, 3, 120	G. A. Schaefer	Chelle Rae, 3, 120	Cobilion, 3, 120	9	1:46.02	10,120
1991	**Chocolate Tuesday**, 3, 121	C. G. Lowrance	Proudest Royal, 3, 121	Amdors Love, 3, 115	7	1:43.10	8,266
1990	**Sixmo**, 3, 115	V. L. Warhol	Dance for the Gold, 3, 115	Pay Her in Gold, 3, 116	12	1:46.60	11,069
1989	**Clickety Click**, 3, 119	K. M. Murray	She's Due Black, 3, 117	Hurry Home, 3, 115	8	1:38.80	15,450

Prairie Meadows is located in Altoona, Iowa. Held at Canterbury Park 1992. 1 mile 1989. 1 mile 70 yards 1990-'98.

Iroquois Stakes

Grade 3 in 2006. Churchill Downs, two-year-olds, 1 mile, dirt. Held November 5, 2005, with a gross value of $116,700. First held in 1982. First graded in 1990. Stakes record 1:35.01 (2001 Harlan's Holiday).

Year	Winner	Jockey	Second	Third	Strs	Time	1st Purse
2005	**Catcominatcha**, 2, 116	R. Bejarano	High Cotton, 2, 118	Mondavi, 2, 118	13	1:36.38	$72,354
2004	**Straight Line**, 2, 122	B. Blanc	Social Probation, 2, 120	Greater Good, 2, 122	7	1:36.62	67,952
2003	**The Cliff's Edge**, 2, 117	S. J. Sellers	Korbyn Gold, 2, 121	Grand Score, 2, 117	9	1:35.57	70,494
2002	**Champali**, 2, 118	P. Day	Alke, 2, 116	What a Bad Day, 2, 118	10	1:37.06	70,804
2001	**Harlan's Holiday**, 2, 121	A. J. D'Amico	Request for Parole, 2, 121	Gold Dollar, 2, 116	10	**1:35.01**	70,184
2000	**Meetyouathebrig**, 2, 118	G. L. Stevens	Hero's Tribute, 2, 114	Keats, 2, 112	13	1:35.24	77,066
1999	**Mighty**, 2, 112	M. St. Julien	Ifitstobeitsuptome, 2, 113	Nature, 2, 114	7	1:35.88	68,758
1998	**Exploit**, 2, 115	C. J. McCarron	Crowning Storm, 2, 114	Olympic Journey, 2, 114	8	1:36.26	71,114
1997	**Keene Dancer**, 2, 121	P. Day	Yarrow Brae, 2, 113	Dawn Exodus, 2, 113	7	1:37.84	68,882
1996	**Global View**, 2, 112	K. Bourque	Partner's Hero, 2, 112	Haint, 2, 121	6	1:36.49	68,200
1995	**Ide**, 2, 121	C. Perret	El Amante, 2, 116	City by Night, 2, 114	8	1:36.89	73,645
1994	**Peruvian**, 2, 121	J. A. Santos	Our Gatsby, 2, 116	Super Jeblar, 2, 116	11	1:36.68	77,025
1993	**Tarzans Blade**, 2, 121	B. E. Bartram	Dove Hunt, 2, 121	Amathos, 2, 114	11	1:37.00	74,945
1992	**Shoal Creek**, 2, 114	B. E. Bartram	Saw Mill, 2, 116	Demaloot Demashoot, 2, 116	13	1:37.51	76,375
1991	**Portroe**, 2, 114	M. E. Smith	Walkie Talker, 2, 121	Richard of England, 2, 121	11	1:37.96	76,570
1990	**Richman**, 2, 121	P. Day	Speedy Cure, 2, 114	Honor Grades, 2, 116	8	1:36.60	36,628
1989	**Insurrection**, 2, 116	P. A. Johnson	Bite the Bullet, 2, 121	Silent Generation, 2, 116	10	1:36.80	37,375
1988	**Dansil**, 2, 118	L. A. Pincay Jr.	Western Playboy, 2, 114	Lorenzoni, 2, 116	9	1:38.20	36,498
1987	**Buoy**, 2, 116	K. K. Allen	Key Voyage, 2, 118	Delightful Doctor, 2, 116	12	1:37.80	32,285
1986	**Icetrain**, 2, 117	M. E. Smith	Grantley, 2, 117	Authentic Hero, 2, 117	12	1:40.20	34,263
1985	**Tile**, 2, 122	P. Day	Bachelor Beau, 2, 117	Dance to the Wire, 2, 117	11	1:37.20	36,062
1984	**Banner Bob**, 2, 117	K. K. Allen	Nordic Scandal, 2, 114	Tasheen, 2, 117	8	1:37.60	18,078
1983	**Taylor's Special**, 2, 117	D. Brumfield	Bello, 2, 119	At the Threshold, 2, 114	9	1:37.20	19,858
1982	**Highland Park**, 2, 122	D. Brumfield	Coax Me Matt, 2, 114	White Fig, 2, 117	8	1:38.20	19,907

Named for the Iroquois Park area of the city of Louisville. Colts and geldings 1982.

Jaipur Handicap

Grade 3 in 2006. Belmont Park, three-year-olds and up, 6 furlongs, turf. Held May 28, 2006, with a gross value of $111,500. First held in 1984. First graded in 1986. Stakes record 1:07.31 (2006 Around the Cape).

Year	Winner	Jockey	Second	Third	Strs	Time	1st Purse
2006	**Around the Cape**, 4, 118	C. H. Velasquez	Bold Decision, 4, 118	Summer Service, 6, 120	7	**1:07.31**	$66,900
2005	**Ecclesiastic**, 4, 118	C. H. Velasquez	Old Forester, 4, 124	Gulch Approval, 5, 120	7	1:20.71	66,960
2004	**Multiple Choice**, 6, 113	J. Castellano	†Dedication (Fr), 5, 114	Geronimo (Chi), 5, 118	8	1:22.32	67,320
2003	**Garnered**, 5, 116	V. Carrero	Speightstown, 5, 121	Whitewaterspritzer, 6, 115	5	1:23.49	67,260
2002	**Shibboleth**, 5, 121	J. D. Bailey	Malabar Gold, 5, 121	†Cozzy Corner, 4, 111	7	1:20.08	67,140
2001	**Affirmed Success**, 7, 123	J. D. Bailey	Texas Glitter, 5, 116	Bought in Dixie, 5, 114	3	1:21.69	66,475
2000	**Gone Fishin**, 4, 114	J. R. Velazquez	Weatherbird, 5, 113	French Envoy, 4, 113	12	1:21.73	52,290
1999	**Notoriety**, 6, 115	J. L. Espinoza	Optic Nerve, 6, 116	Cryptic Rascal, 4, 117	12	1:21.35	52,335
1998	**Elusive Quality**, 5, 115	J. D. Bailey	Bristling, 6, 111	Optic Nerve, 5, 115	11	1:20.99	51,750
1997	**Atraf (GB)**, 4, 116	J. R. Velazquez	Mighty Forum (GB), 6, 115	Play Smart, 5, 112	4	1:23.64	49,635
1996	**Grand Continental**, 5, 114	R. Migliore	Inside the Beltway, 5, 115	Goldmine (Fr), 5, 111	10	1:23.78	51,720
1995	**Inside the Beltway**, 4, 114	J. F. Chavez	Gabr (GB), 5, 117	Golden Cloud, 7, 114	5	1:21.23	49,245
	Mighty Forum (GB), 4, 117	G. L. Stevens	Dominant Prospect, 5, 117	City Nights (Ire), 4, 114	9	1:21.12	49,995
1994	**Nijinsky's Gold**, 5, 114	J. A. Santos	Dominant Prospect, 4, 114	Home of the Free, 6, 122	7	1:20.06	34,905
	A in Sociology, 4, 119	E. Maple	Roman Envoy, 6, 114	Halissee, 4, 119	7	1:20.38	34,905
1993	**Home of the Free**, 5, 117	J. D. Bailey	Wind Symbol (GB), 4, 117	Fourstardave, 8, 117	8	1:20.69	55,080
1992	**To Freedom**, 4, 117	J. A. Krone	Fourstardave, 7, 122	Smart Alec, 4, 117	5	1:22.83	55,710
1991	**Kanatiyr (Ire)**, 5, 117	J. D. Bailey	Senor Speedy, 4, 117	Fourstardave, 6, 122	9	1:23.96	54,630
1990	**Fourstardave**, 5, 122	M. E. Smith	Harperstown, 4, 117	Wanderkin, 7, 119	9	1:21.00	57,240
1989	**Harp Islet**, 4, 117	C. Perret	Fourstardave, 4, 119	†Down Again, 5, 114	10	1:27.00	57,150
1988	**Real Courage**, 5, 117	J. Vasquez	Tinchen's Prince, 5, 117	Spectacularphantom, 4, 117	14	1:22.00	60,570
1987	**Raja's Revenge**, 4, 117	M. Venezia	Trubulare, 4, 117	†Give a Toast, 4, 114	11	1:25.20	52,200
1986	**Red Wing Dream**, 5, 117	J. D. Bailey	Creme Fraiche, 4, 122	Roy, 3, 109	5	1:23.60	48,510
	Basket Weave, 5, 117	R. Migliore	Alev (GB), 7, 117	Judge Costa, 5, 117	4	1:22.80	48,330
1985	**Mt. Livermore**, 4, 119	J. Velasquez	Main Top, 6, 117	Cozzene, 5, 117	7	1:09.20	49,020
1984	**Cannon Shell**, 5, 115	D. J. Murphy	Chan Balum, 5, 115	Believe the Queen, 4, 115	12	1:09.20	35,280

Named for George D. Widener's 1962 champion three-year-old male and '62 Belmont S. winner Jaipur (1959 c. by *Nasrullah). Not graded 1990-'91, 2001, 2003. Jaipur S. 2005. 7 furlongs 1986-2005. Dirt 1984-'86, 1992, 1997, 2001, 2003. Originally scheduled on turf 2001, 2003. Two divisions 1986, 1994-'95. Course record 1993, 1994 (1st Div.). †Denotes female.

Jamaica Handicap

Grade 2 in 2006. Belmont Park, three-year-olds, $1\frac{1}{8}$ miles, dirt (originally scheduled as a Grade 2 on the turf). Held October 8, 2005, with a gross value of $270,000. First held in 1929. First graded in 1978. Stakes record 1:45.50 (2004 Artie Schiller).

Year	Winner	Jockey	Second	Third	Strs	Time	1st Purse
2005	**Watchmon**, 3, 118	J. Castellano	Crown Point, 3, 119	Woodlander, 3, 115	3	1:49.28	$180,000
2004	**Artie Schiller**, 3, 123	R. Migliore	Rousing Victory, 3, 113	Icy Atlantic, 3, 120	6	**1:45.50**	120,000

2003 **Stroll**, 3, 121	J. D. Bailey	Kicken Kris, 3, 121	Joe Bear (Ire), 3, 117	7	1:46.02	$120,000
2002 **Finality**, 3, 116	J. R. Velazquez	Union Place, 3, 115	Chiselling, 3, 121	9	1:46.66	120,000
2001 **Navesink**, 3, 118	E. S. Prado	Strategic Partner, 3, 118	Baptize, 3, 123	7	1:51.53	120,000
2000 **King Cugat**, 3, 123	J. D. Bailey	Mandarin Marsh, 3, 114	Parade Leader, 3, 115	8	1:49.63	120,000
1999 **Monarch's Maze**, 3, 117	J. Bravo	Killer Joe, 3, 112	Monkey Puzzle, 3, 118	8	1:51.66	90,000
1998 **Vergennes**, 3, 115	J. R. Velazquez	Tangazi, 3, 114	Middlesex Drive, 3, 114	10	1:50.42	90,000
1997 **Subordination**, 3, 120	J. F. Chavez	Premier Krischief, 3, 113	Skybound, 3, 121	12	1:49.00	90,000
1996 **Allied Forces**, 3, 119	R. Migliore	Cliptomania, 3, 116	Lite Approval, 3, 114	11	1:40.91	86,325
1994 **Pennine Ridge**, 3, 118	J. R. Velazquez	Holy Mountain, 3, 116	I'm Very Irish, 3, 113	7	1:35.13	66,540
1993 **Mi Cielo**, 3, 116	M. E. Smith	Prospector's Flag, 3, 113	Cherokee Run, 3, 120	8	1:35.20	70,440
1992 **West by West**, 3, 112	J. Samyn	Offbeat, 3, 110	Portroe, 3, 111	7	1:34.27	70,320
1991 **Sultry Song**, 3, 113	C. W. Antley	Honest Ensign, 3, 110	Take Me Out, 3, 116	7	1:34.44	70,320
1990 **Confidential Talk**, 3, 111	J. F. Chavez	Rubiano, 3, 112	Sunshine Jimmy, 3, 114	7	1:35.60	52,470
1989 **Domasca Dan**, 3, 116	S. Hawley	Garemma, 3, 114	Is It True, 3, 120	7	1:35.40	70,920
1988 **Ruhlmann**, 3, 113	G. L. Stevens	Teddy Drone, 3, 112	Din's Dancer, 3, 112	8	1:35.40	84,540
1987 **Stacked Pack**, 3, 110	R. P. Romero	Gulch, 3, 123	Homebuilder, 3, 112	8	1:34.80	67,770
1986 **Waquoit**, 3, 112	R. Migliore	Mogambo, 3, 119	‡Moment of Hope, 3, 110	8	1:34.20	53,280
1985 **Don's Choice**, 3, 114	D. MacBeth	I Enrich, 3, 110	Easton, 3, 109	6	1:36.00	53,010
1984 **Raja's Shark**, 3, 112	R. Migliore	Is Your Pleasure, 3, 116	Leroy S., 3, 117	6	1:36.60	52,560
1983 **Bounding Basque**, 3, 115	G. McCarron	A Phenomenon, 3, 120	Bet Big, 3, 115	8	1:34.00	51,480
1982 **John's Gold**, 3, 113	A. T. Cordero Jr.	Lord Lister, 3, 111	Estoril, 3, 114	5	1:37.00	33,180
1981 **Pass the Tab**, 3, 112	J. Velasquez	Spirited Boy, 3, 117	Counter Espionage, 3, 112	7	1:35.20	33,300
1980 **Far Out East**, 3, 113	C. B. Asmussen	Dunham's Gift, 3, 112	Settlement Day, 3, 111	12	1:34.00	35,100
1979 **Belle's Gold**, 3, 118	L. A. Pincay Jr.	Lean Lad, 3, 107	Gallant Best, 3, 113	10	1:33.60	33,180
1978 **Regal and Royal**, 3, 116	J. Fell	Squire Ambler, 3, 111	Roman Reasoning, 3, 112	8	1:35.00	32,460
1977 **Affiliate**, 3, 124	A. T. Cordero Jr.	Buckfinder, 3, 113	Proud Arion, 3, 115	12	1:35.20	33,660
1976 **Dance Spell**, 3, 119	R. Hernandez	Cojak, 3, 119	Quiet Little Table, 3, 114	9	1:34.00	33,330
1975 **Funalon**, 3, 113	V. A. Bracciale Jr.	Busy Saxon, 3, 114	Precious Elaine, 3, 113	10	1:35.80	34,140

Named for the Jamaica neighborhood of Queens, New York. Jamaica racetrack was located there until it was closed in 1959. Grade 3 1978-'87, 2005. Held at Jamaica 1929-'59. Held at Aqueduct 1960-'77, 1979-'81, 1987. Not held 1933-'35, 1955-'56, 1961-'74, 1995. 6 furlongs 1929-'53, 1957-'60. 1 mile 1975-'94. 1 1/16 miles 1996. Dirt 1929-'93, 2005. Originally scheduled on turf 2005. Three-year-olds and up 1929-'44, 1949-'54, 1960. Fillies 1975. ‡Midnight Call finished third, DQ to fourth, 1986.

Jefferson Cup Stakes

Grade 2 in 2006. Churchill Downs, three-year-olds, 1 1/8 miles, turf. Held June 18, 2005, with a gross value of $220,400. First held in 1977. First graded in 2001. Stakes record 1:47.27 (2000 King Cugat).

Year Winner	Jockey	Second	Third	Strs	Time	1st Purse
2005 **Rush Bay**, 3, 116	R. Albarado	Big Prairie, 3, 116	Gun Salute, 3, 120	7	1:48.75	$136,648
2004 **Prince Arch**, 3, 120	B. Blanc	Kitten's Joy, 3, 122	Cool Conductor, 3, 116	9	1:50.61	140,244
2003 **Senor Swinger**, 3, 120	R. Albarado	Remind, 3, 116	Rapid Proof, 3, 120	7	1:47.54	136,772
2002 **Orchard Park**, 3, 119	M. Guidry	Mr. Mellon, 3, 112	Quest Star, 3, 113	8	1:48.53	172,050
2001 **Indygo Shiner**, 3, 113	L. J. Meche	Strategic Partner, 3, 119	Fast City, 3, 114	9	1:48.81	175,150
2000 **King Cugat**, 3, 122	R. Albarado	Four On the Floor, 3, 122	Field Cat, 3, 122	10	**1:47.27**	177,940
1999 **Special Coach**, 3, 122	C. H. Velasquez	Silver Chadra, 3, 119	Air Rocket, 3, 122	12	1:49.82	180,110
1998 **Buff**, 3, 122	C. H. Borel	Keene Dancer, 3, 122	Ladies Din, 3, 122	7	1:50.80	175,770
1997 **Greed Is Good**, 3, 115	W. Martinez	Royal Strand (Ire), 3, 122	Crimson Classic, 3, 117	5	1:49.47	69,068
1996 **Unruled**, 3, 119	C. Perret	Broadway Beau, 3, 122	Trail City, 3, 122	6	1:50.07	54,210
1995 **Ago**, 3, 115	S. J. Sellers	Michael's Star, 3, 119	Lemon Drop, 3, 113	11	1:49.48	56,550
1994 **Milt's Overture**, 3, 112	P. Day	Jaggery John, 3, 122	Camptown Dancer, 3, 117	6	1:48.21	53,528
1993 **Lt. Pinkerton**, 3, 115	T. J. Hebert	Snake Eyes, 3, 119	Mi Cielo, 3, 117	6	1:48.27	35,555
1992 **Senor Tomas**, 3, 122	P. Day	Coaxing Matt, 3, 112	Black Question, 3, 122	7	1:49.80	35,945
1991 **Hanging Curve**, 3, 119	J. M. Johnson	Wall Street Dancer, 3, 119	Air Force, 3, 112	8	1:50.89	36,368
1990 **Divine Warning**, 3, 117	J. Deegan	Super Abound, 3, 115	Bioblast, 3, 110	8	1:52.20	36,238
1989 **Shy Tom**, 3, 120	E. Fires	Captain Savy, 3, 116	Ruszhinka, 3, 112	4	1:49.20	52,114
1988 **Stop the Stage**, 3, 115	M. McDowell	Cold Cathode, 3, 114	Bates Fay, 3, 115	9	1:51.60	62,310
1987 **Fast Forward**, 3, 120	R. L. Frazier	Unleavened, 3, 118	Gretna Green, 3, 112	5	1:50.00	63,109
1986 **Buffalo Beau**, 3, 110	J. McKnight	Clear Choice, 3, 124	Sumptious, 3, 113	7	1:52.80	53,040
1985 **Avey's Brother**, 3, 110	D. Montoya	La Marseillaise, 3, 110	Hollywood Hackett, 3, 113	10	1:50.00	50,420
1984 **Coax Me Chad**, 3, 119	W. H. McCauley	Fairly Straight, 3, 114	Last Command, 3, 110	7	1:50.60	48,958
1983 **Pron Regard**, 3, 116	C. R. Woods Jr.	Le Cou Cou, 3, 125	Whitesburg Lark, 3, 112	9	1:51.60	36,303
1982 **Wavering Monarch**, 3, 111	R. P. Romero	Forli's Jet, 3, 117	Noted, 3, 111	6	1:44.20	23,026
1981 **Talent Town**, 2, 122	B. Sayler	Helen's Tip, 2, 122	Ken's Revenge, 2, 122	11	1:05.40	19,858
1980 **Golden Derby**, 2, 125	J. C. Espinoza	†Plain Speaking, 2, 119	Bold Tyson, 2, 125	7	1:04.20	19,256
1979 **Rockhill Native**, 2, 122	J. Oldham	Earl of Odessa, 2, 122	Egg's Dynamite, 2, 122	9	1:05.20	19,581
1978 **Future Hope**, 2, 122	A. Rini	Backstabber, 2, 125	Amber White, 2, 117	6	1:05.20	14,073
1977 **Old Jake**, 2, 122	J. C. Espinoza	Bolero's Orphan, 2, 122	Set in My Ways, 2, 122	7	1:04.80	14,219

Named for Jefferson County, Kentucky, home of Churchill Downs. Grade 3 2001-'05. 5 1/2 furlongs 1977-'81. 1 1/16 miles 1982. Dirt 1977-'87. Two-year-olds 1977-'81. †Denotes female.

Jenny Wiley Stakes

Grade 2 in 2006. Keeneland Race Course, four-year-olds and up, fillies and mares, 1¹/₁₆ miles, turf. Held April 15, 2006, with a gross value of $200,000. First held in 1989. First graded in 1995. Stakes record 1:40.78 (1996 Apolda).

Year	Winner	Jockey	Second	Third	Strs	Time	1st Purse
2006	**Wend**, 5, 117	E. S. Prado	Asi Siempre, 4, 117	Mirabilis, 4, 118	8	1:41.34	$124,000
2005	**Intercontinental (GB)**, 5, 123	J. D. Bailey	Delta Princess, 6, 117	Sister Swank, 4, 117	7	1:41.89	124,000
2004	**Intercontinental (GB)**, 4, 116	J. D. Bailey	Ocean Drive, 4, 116	Madeira Mist (Ire), 5, 118	8	1:41.41	68,386
2003	**Sea of Showers**, 4, 116	J. D. Bailey	Magic Mission (GB), 5, 116	Snow Dance, 5, 116	10	1:41.89	70,246
2002	**Tates Creek**, 4, 116	K. Desormeaux	Snow Dance, 4, 123	Step With Style, 5, 116	10	1:42.27	70,432
2001	**Penny's Gold**, 4, 116	J. A. Santos	License Fee, 6, 118	Solvig, 4, 116	9	1:40.93	70,618
2000	**Astra**, 4, 118	C. S. Nakatani	Pratella, 5, 118	Ronda (GB), 4, 116	8	1:42.48	69,688
1999	**Pleasant Temper**, 5, 117	J. D. Bailey	Mingling Glances, 5, 114	Red Cat, 4, 117	8	1:40.93	70,246
1998	**Maxzene**, 5, 114	J. A. Santos	Parade Queen, 4, 121	Rumpipumpy (GB), 5, 114	7	1:42.82	69,192
1997	**Thrilling Day (GB)**, 4, 115	W. Martinez	Romy, 6, 121	Gastronomical, 4, 115	7	1:41.16	68,634
1996	**Apolda**, 5, 121	J. D. Bailey	Mediation (Ire), 4, 118	Luzette (Brz), 6, 121	9	**1:40.78**	69,006
1995	**Romy**, 4, 118	F. C. Torres	Weekend Madness (Ire), 5, 121	Bold Ruritana, 5, 121	9	1:43.32	52,173
1994	**Misspitch**, 4, 118	M. E. Smith	Park Dream (Ire), 5, 112	Sh Bang, 5, 118	10	1:43.83	34,658
1993	**Lady Blessington (Fr)**, 5, 118	P. Day	Radiant Ring, 5, 118	Super Fan, 6, 118	6	1:42.59	34,844
1992	**Indian Fashion**, 5, 115	J. A. Santos	Spanish Parade, 4, 121	Radiant Ring, 4, 121	10	1:41.26	36,514
1991	**Foresta**, 5, 121	A. T. Cordero Jr.	Dance for Lucy, 5, 121	The Caretaker (Ire), 4, 115	10	1:43.88	37,115
1990	**Regal Wonder**, 6, 121	R. D. Lopez	Majestic Legend, 5, 121	Phoenix Sunshine, 5, 115	8	1:46.20	36,043
1989	**Native Mommy**, 6, 121	C. Perret	Blossoming Beauty, 4, 113	Here's Your Silver, 4, 115	8	1:43.60	35,864

Named for Eastern Kentucky heroine Jenny Wiley (1760-1831), a pioneer woman who was captured by Indians and escaped to return to her family. Grade 3 1995-2005. About 1¹/₁₆ miles 1991. Course record 1992, 1996.

Jerome Handicap

Grade 2 in 2006. Belmont Park, three-year-olds, 1 mile, dirt. Held September 11, 2005, with a gross value of $150,000. First held in 1866. First graded in 1973. Stakes record 1:33.20 (1981 Noble Nashua).

Year	Winner	Jockey	Second	Third	Strs	Time	1st Purse
2005	**Silver Train**, 3, 114	E. S. Prado	High Fly, 3, 120	Naughty New Yorker, 3, 115	6	1:34.24	$90,000
2004	**Teton Forest**, 3, 116	S. Bridgmohan	Ice Wynnd Fire, 3, 116	Mahzouz, 3, 112	7	1:35.74	90,000
2003	**During**, 3, 118	J. A. Santos	Tafaseel, 3, 114	Pretty Wild, 3, 116	9	1:36.32	90,000
2002	**Boston Common**, 3, 118	J. F. Chavez	Vinemeister, 3, 115	No Parole, 3, 115	7	1:36.12	90,000
2001	**Express Tour**, 3, 115	J. R. Velazquez	Illusioned, 3, 117	Burning Roma, 3, 120	5	1:34.57	90,000
2000	**Fusaichi Pegasus**, 3, 124	K. Desormeaux	El Corredor, 3, 117	Albert the Great, 3, 120	6	1:34.07	90,000
1999	**Doneraile Court**, 3, 117	C. W. Antley	Vicar, 3, 120	Badger Gold, 3, 115	7	1:35.63	90,000
1998	**Limit Out**, 3, 117	J. Samyn	Grand Slam, 3, 120	Scatmandu, 3, 115	5	1:36.22	90,000
1997	**Richter Scale**, 3, 118	S. J. Sellers	Trafalger, 3, 117	Smokin Mel, 3, 115	8	1:35.88	90,000
1996	**Why Change**, 3, 112	C. C. Lopez	Distorted Humor, 3, 115	Diligence, 3, 117	10	1:34.22	90,000
1995	**French Deputy**, 3, 113	G. L. Stevens	Mr. Greeley, 3, 117	Top Account, 3, 115	6	1:33.53	120,000
1994	**Prenup**, 3, 113	J. D. Bailey	Ulises, 3, 112	End Sweep, 3, 118	8	1:34.59	120,000
1993	**Schossberg**, 3, 113	J. D. Bailey	Williamstown, 3, 118	Mi Cielo, 3, 116	5	1:35.53	120,000
1992	**Furiously**, 3, 113	J. D. Bailey	Colony Light, 3, 111	Dixie Brass, 3, 122	6	1:34.20	120,000
1991	**Scan**, 3, 117	J. A. Santos	Excellent Tipper, 3, 113	King Mutesa, 3, 113	8	1:34.09	120,000
1990	**Housebuster**, 3, 126	C. Perret	Citidancer, 3, 114	D'Parrot, 3, 112	5	1:34.00	102,060
1989	**De Roche**, 3, 108	D. Carr	Fast Play, 3, 116	I'm Influential, 3, 111	5	1:34.40	134,880
1988	**Evening Kris**, 3, 119	J. D. Bailey	dh-Din's Dancer, 3, 113 dh-Parlay Me, 3, 113		7	1:37.80	176,400
1987	**Afleet**, 3, 115	G. Stahlbaum	Stacked Pack, 3, 109	Templar Hill, 3, 117	9	1:33.80	107,640
1986	**Ogygian**, 3, 126	W. A. Guerra	Mogambo, 3, 119	Moment of Hope, 3, 111	5	1:34.00	127,620
1985	**Creme Fraiche**, 3, 124	E. Maple	Pancho Villa, 3, 119	El Basco, 3, 114	8	1:34.60	109,260
1984	**Is Your Pleasure**, 3, 114	D. MacBeth	Track Barron, 3, 124	Concorde Bound, 3, 115	9	1:35.20	109,080
1983	**A Phenomenon**, 3, 116	A. T. Cordero Jr.	Desert Wine, 3, 124	Copelan, 3, 118	8	1:35.00	104,940
1982	**Fit to Fight**, 3, 112	J. D. Bailey	John's Gold, 3, 115	Lord Lister, 3, 107	6	1:35.40	101,880
1981	**Noble Nashua**, 3, 120	C. B. Asmussen	Maudlin, 3, 112	Sing Sing, 3, 109	11	**1:33.20**	69,000
1980	**Jaklin Klugman**, 3, 122	C. J. McCarron	Fappiano, 3, 114	Plugged Nickle, 3, 124	6	1:34.20	67,320
1979	**Czaravich**, 3, 122	J. Cruguet	Valdez, 3, 122	Gallant Best, 3, 112	10	1:35.20	65,580
1978	**Sensitive Prince**, 3, 118	J. Vasquez	Darby Creek Road, 3, 122	Sorry Lookin, 3, 112	5	1:36.00	62,940
1977	**‡Broadway Forli**, 3, 111	P. Day	‡To the Quick, 3, 112	Affiliate, 3, 120	10	1:36.20	66,360
1976	**Dance Spell**, 3, 117	R. Hernandez	Soy Numero Uno, 3, 117	Clean Bill, 3, 112	10	1:35.00	66,600
1975	**Guards Up**, 3, 114	C. C. Lopez	Valid Appeal, 3, 119	Great Above, 3, 114	7	1:34.20	33,720
1974	**Stonewalk**, 3, 126	A. T. Cordero Jr.	Best of It, 3, 117	Heir to the Line, 3, 113	9	1:34.00	34,470
1973	**Step Nicely**, 3, 118	A. T. Cordero Jr.	Forego, 3, 124	Linda's Chief, 3, 126	10	1:34.00	34,800

Named for Leonard Jerome (1817-'91), builder of Jerome Park and president of Coney Island Jockey Club. Jerome was also the maternal grandfather of Sir Winston Churchill. Grade 1 1984-'94. Jerome S. 1866, 1872-'92. Champion S. 1867-'71. Held at Jerome Park 1866-'89. Held at Morris Park 1890-1904. Held at Aqueduct 1960, 1962-'67, 1972-'74. Not held 1910-'13. One mile heats 1866-'70. Two miles 1871-'77. 1³/₄ miles 1878-'89. 1⁵/₁₆ miles 1890-'91, 1903-'09. 1¹/₂ miles 1892. 1¹/₄ miles 1893-'94, 1896, 1914. 1¹/₈ miles 1895. Dead heat for second 1988. ‡To the Quick finished first, DQ to second, 1977. ‡Affiliate finished second, DQ to third, 1977.

Jersey Shore Breeders' Cup Stakes

Grade 3 in 2006. Monmouth Park, three-year-olds, 6 furlongs, dirt. Held July 4, 2005, with a gross value of $130,000. First held in 1992. First graded in 1994. Stakes record 1:08.30 (2005 Joey P.).

Year	Winner	Jockey	Second	Third	Strs	Time	1st Purse
2005	**Joey P.**, 3, 117	J. Bravo	Celtic Innis, 3, 122	Razor, 3, 122	5	**1:08.30**	$75,000
2004	**Pomeroy**, 3, 113	J. Bravo	Gotaghostofachance, 3, 115	Midnight Express, 3, 113	5	1:09.07	60,000
2003	**Gators N Bears**, 3, 115	C. C. Lopez	Mt. Carson, 3, 122	Don Six, 3, 115	6	1:09.80	60,000
2002	**Boston Common**, 3, 117	E. M. Martin Jr.	Listen Here, 3, 117	It's a Monster, 3, 115	6	1:09.35	60,000
2001	**City Zip**, 3, 119	J. C. Ferrer	Sea of Green, 3, 117	Songandaprayer, 3, 122	5	1:09.02	60,000
2000	**Disco Rico**, 3, 115	J. Bravo	Max's Pal, 3, 122	Stormin Oedy, 3, 117	6	1:09.05	60,000
1999	**Yes It's True**, 3, 122	J. D. Bailey	Erlton, 3, 122	Flying Griffoni, 3, 112	4	1:08.59	60,000
1998	**Good and Tough**, 3, 115	W. H. McCauley	Klabin's Gold, 3, 117	El Mirasol, 3, 112	6	1:10.01	45,000
1997	**Smoke Glacken**, 3, 122	C. Perret	Partner's Hero, 3, 115	King Buck, 3, 115	4	1:08.53	45,000
1996	**Swing and Miss**, 3, 112	T. G. Turner	Seacliff, 3, 119	Dixie Connection, 3, 115	6	1:10.00	60,000
1995	**Ft. Stockton**, 3, 115	J. Bravo	Jealous Crusader, 3, 115	Gala Knockout, 3, 115	9	1:22.64	64,050
1994	**End Sweep**, 3, 115	M. E. Smith	Meadow Flight, 3, 122	Foxie G, 3, 115	5	1:21.20	63,450
1993	**Montbrook**, 3, 122	C. J. Ladner III	Evil Bear, 3, 114	Shu Fellow, 3, 114	7	1:21.04	63,420
1992	**Surely Six**, 3, 112	R. Wilson	Superstrike (GB), 3, 122	Salt Lake, 3, 119	8	1:21.94	64,230

Monmouth Park is located on the coast of New Jersey. Jersey Shore Budweiser Breeders' Cup S. 1992-'95. Held at Atlantic City 1992-'96. 7 furlongs 1992-'95.

Jim Dandy Stakes

Grade 2 in 2006. Saratoga Race Course, three-year-olds, 1⅛ miles, dirt. Held July 30, 2005, with a gross value of $490,000. First held in 1964. First graded in 1973. Stakes record 1:47.26 (1996 Louis Quatorze).

Year	Winner	Jockey	Second	Third	Strs	Time	1st Purse
2005	**Flower Alley**, 3, 121	J. R. Velazquez	Reverberate, 3, 115	Andromeda's Hero, 3, 117	5	1:49.50	$300,000
2004	**Purge**, 3, 121	J. R. Velazquez	The Cliff's Edge, 3, 123	‡Niigon, 3, 117	6	1:47.56	300,000
2003	**Strong Hope**, 3, 121	J. R. Velazquez	Empire Maker, 3, 123	Congrats, 3, 115	6	1:48.10	300,000
2002	**Medaglia d'Oro**, 3, 121	J. D. Bailey	‡Gold Dollar, 3, 115	Essence of Dubai, 3, 121	9	1:47.82	300,000
2001	**Scorpion**, 3, 114	J. D. Bailey	Free of Love, 3, 114	Congaree, 3, 123	6	1:48.90	360,000
2000	**Graeme Hall**, 3, 120	J. D. Bailey	Curule, 3, 114	Unshaded, 3, 120	7	1:48.95	240,000
1999	**Ecton Park**, 3, 116	A. O. Solis	Lemon Drop Kid, 3, 124	Badger Gold, 3, 114	7	1:49.52	180,000
1998	**Favorite Trick**, 3, 119	P. Day	Deputy Diamond, 3, 114	Raffie's Majesty, 3, 114	7	1:50.00	150,000
1997	**Awesome Again**, 3, 116	M. E. Smith	Glitman, 3, 114	Affirmed Success, 3, 114	9	1:51.00	150,000
1996	**Louis Quatorze**, 3, 124	P. Day	Will's Way, 3, 114	Secreto de Estado, 3, 114	8	**1:47.26**	90,000
1995	**Composer**, 3, 112	J. D. Bailey	Malthus, 3, 112	Pat n Jac, 3, 112	7	1:51.13	82,575
1994	**Unaccounted For**, 3, 112	J. A. Santos	Tabasco Cat, 3, 126	Ulises, 3, 114	5	1:49.69	80,820
1993	**Miner's Mark**, 3, 117	C. J. McCarron	Virginia Rapids, 3, 121	Colonial Affair, 3, 126	6	1:49.01	90,000
1992	**Thunder Rumble**, 3, 117	W. H. McCauley	Dixie Brass, 3, 126	Devil His Due, 3, 126	8	1:47.53	108,000
1991	**Fly So Free**, 3, 126	J. A. Santos	Upon My Soul, 3, 114	Strike the Gold, 3, 128	8	1:48.88	107,820
1990	**Chief Honcho**, 3, 114	M. E. Smith	Senator to Be, 3, 114	Paradise Found, 3, 114	4	1:51.60	67,680
1989	**Is It True**, 3, 121	J. A. Santos	Fast Play, 3, 114	Roi Danzig, 3, 126	4	1:48.40	99,180
1988	**Brian's Time**, 3, 126	A. T. Cordero Jr.	Evening Kris, 3, 121	Din's Dancer, 3, 114	10	1:48.20	109,980
1987	**Polish Navy**, 3, 117	P. Day	Pledge Card, 3, 117	Cryptoclearance, 3, 126	7	1:48.40	106,740
1986	**Lac Ouimet**, 3, 114	E. Maple	Moment of Hope, 3, 114	Wayar, 3, 114	5	1:48.00	69,360
1985	**Stephan's Odyssey**, 3, 123	L. A. Pincay Jr.	Don's Choice, 3, 114	Government Corner, 3, 121	9	1:48.80	73,080
1984	**Carr de Naskra**, 3, 114	E. Maple	Slew the Coup, 3, 114	Raja's Shark, 3, 114	10	1:47.40	75,720
1983	**A Phenomenon**, 3, 114	A. T. Cordero Jr.	Timeless Native, 3, 126	Head of the House, 3, 114	8	1:49.40	33,900
1982	**Conquistador Cielo**, 3, 128	E. Maple	Lejoli, 3, 114	No Home Run, 3, 114	4	1:48.60	32,700
1981	**Willow Hour**, 3, 117	E. Maple	Lemhi Gold, 3, 117	Silver Supreme, 3, 114	8	1:49.20	34,200
1980	**Plugged Nickle**, 3, 128	J. Fell	Current Legend, 3, 121	Herb Water, 3, 114	8	1:49.40	34,140
1979	**Private Account**, 3, 114	J. Fell	Instrument Landing, 3, 126	Pianist, 3, 114	4	1:48.40	25,500
1978	**Affirmed**, 3, 128	S. Cauthen	Sensitive Prince, 3, 119	Bound Green, 3, 114	5	1:47.80	22,155
1977	**Music of Time**, 3, 114	M. Venezia	Sanhedrin, 3, 114	Super Joy, 3, 114	10	1:50.40	22,830
1976	**Father Hogan**, 3, 114	M. Venezia	Dance Spell, 3, 121	El Portugues, 3, 114	10	1:48.80	22,410
1975	**Forceten**, 3, 126	D. Pierce	Prince Thou Art, 3, 123	Northerly, 3, 114	6	1:48.40	25,725
1974	**Sea Songster**, 3, 114	A. T. Cordero Jr.	‡Hatchet Man, 3, 120	Bobby Murcer, 3, 114	7	1:50.60	22,860
1973	**Cheriepe**, 3, 117	E. Belmonte	Arbees Boy, 3, 120	Bemo, 3, 123	9	1:50.20	17,310

Named for 100-to-1 1930 Travers S. winner Jim Dandy (1927 g. by Jim Gaffney), who upset heavily favored rivals Gallant Fox and Whichone. Grade 3 1973-'83. Grade 1 2001. 1 mile 1964-'70. 7 furlongs 1971. ‡T. V. Newscaster finished second, DQ to fourth, 1974. ‡Quest finished second, DQ to eighth, 2002. ‡Eddington finished third, DQ to fourth, 2004.

Jim Murray Memorial Handicap

Grade 2 in 2006. Hollywood Park, three-year-olds and up, 1½ miles, turf. Held May 13, 2006, with a gross value of $250,000. First held in 1990. First graded in 2005. Stakes record 2:25.31 (2003 Storming Home [GB]).

Year	Winner	Jockey	Second	Third	Strs	Time	1st Purse
2006	**Grey Swallow (Ire)**, 5, 121	A. O. Solis	Brecon Beacon (GB), 4, 118	Runaway Dancer, 7, 115	5	2:27.33	$150,000
2005	**Runaway Dancer**, 6, 115	G. K. Gomez	Vangelis, 6, 117	Exterior, 4, 117	8	2:26.75	210,000
2004	**Rhythm Mad (Fr)**, 4, 116	A. O. Solis	Continental Red, 8, 117	Gassan Royal, 4, 113	7	2:26.73	210,000
2003	**Storming Home (GB)**, 5, 122	G. L. Stevens	Denon, 5, 122	Ballingarry (Ire), 4, 120	8	**2:25.31**	240,000
2002	**Skipping (GB)**, 5, 116	K. Desormeaux	Startac, 4, 120	Our Main Man, 4, 114	7	2:26.23	46,485

2001	**Kudos**, 4, 116	E. Delahoussaye	Indigo Myth, 4, 115	Piranesi (Ire), 5, 113	4	2:26.74	$45,900
2000	**Bienamado**, 4, 121	C. J. McCarron	Casino King (Ire), 5, 117	Adcat, 5, 116	8	1:58.93	47,070
1999	**Lazy Lode (Arg)**, 5, 122	C. S. Nakatani	Musgrave, 4, 116	Astarabad, 5, 121	7	2:01.44	42,690
1998	**Cote d'Azur (Ire)**, 4, 114	C. S. Nakatani	Belgravia (GB), 4, 113	Kaafih Homm (Ire), 7, 115	5	2:30.23	42,990
1997	**Percutant (GB)**, 6, 120	G. L. Stevens	Seaborg (Arg), 6, 119	Big Sky Jim, 5, 116	7	2:26.10	43,800
1996	**Polish Admiral (GB)**, 5, 117	B. Blanc	Big Sky Jim, 4, 116	Bedivere, 4, 115	6	2:26.13	40,500
1995	**Jahafil (GB)**, 7, 117	C. J. McCarron	Talloires, 5, 119	Exalto, 4, 116	7	2:25.45	63,700
1994	**Mashaallah**, 6, 119	L. A. Pincay Jr.	Marfamatic, 5, 114	Samourzakan (Ire), 5, 116	5	2:25.37	46,600
1993	**Toulon (GB)**, 5, 117	E. Delahoussaye	Beyton, 4, 118	Super Chief, 4, 111	4	2:26.67	45,850
1992	**Berillon (GB)**, 5, 115	C. S. Nakatani	Single Dawn, 5, 112	Carnival Baby, 4, 114	7	2:26.80	48,900
1991	**Sahib's Light**, 5, 116	G. L. Stevens	Black Monday (GB), 5, 114	Razeen, 4, 117	12	2:25.90	52,150
1990	**Shotiche**, 4, 114	C. A. Black	Record Boom, 4, 114	Kaboi, 4, 115	12	2:00.60	50,450

Named for Pulitzer Prize-winning Los Angeles *Times* sports columnist Jim Murray (1919-'98). Grade 3 2005.

Jockey Club Gold Cup Stakes

Grade 1 in 2006. Belmont Park, three-year-olds and up, 1¼ miles, dirt. Held October 1, 2005, with a gross value of $1,000,000. First held in 1919. First graded in 1973. Stakes record 1:58.89 (1997 Skip Away).

Year	Winner	Jockey	Second	Third	Strs	Time	1st Purse
2005	**Borrego**, 4, 126	G. K. Gomez	Suave, 4, 126	Sun King, 3, 122	8	2:02.86	$600,000
2004	**Funny Cide**, 4, 126	J. A. Santos	Newfoundland, 4, 126	The Cliff's Edge, 3, 122	7	2:02.44	600,000
2003	**Mineshaft**, 4, 126	R. Albarado	Quest, 4, 126	Evening Attire, 5, 126	5	2:00.25	600,000
2002	**Evening Attire**, 4, 126	S. Bridgmohan	Lido Palace (Chi), 5, 126	Harlan's Holiday, 3, 122	8	1:59.58	600,000
2001	**Aptitude**, 4, 126	J. D. Bailey	Generous Rosi (GB), 6, 126	Country Be Gold, 4, 126	7	2:01.49	600,000
2000	**Albert the Great**, 3, 122	J. F. Chavez	Gander, 4, 126	Vision and Verse, 4, 126	7	1:59.24	600,000
1999	**River Keen (Ire)**, 7, 126	C. W. Antley	Behrens, 5, 126	Almutawakel (GB), 4, 126	8	2:01.40	600,000
1998	**Wagon Limit**, 4, 126	R. G. Davis	Gentlemen (Arg), 6, 126	Skip Away, 5, 126	6	2:00.62	600,000
1997	**Skip Away**, 4, 126	J. D. Bailey	Instant Friendship, 4, 126	Wagon Limit, 3, 121	7	**1:58.89**	600,000
1996	**Skip Away**, 3, 121	S. J. Sellers	Cigar, 6, 126	Louis Quatorze, 3, 121	6	2:00.70	600,000
1995	**Cigar**, 5, 126	J. D. Bailey	Unaccounted For, 4, 126	Star Standard, 3, 121	7	2:01.29	450,000
1994	**Colonial Affair**, 4, 126	J. A. Santos	Devil His Due, 5, 126	Flag Down, 4, 126	8	2:02.19	450,000
1993	**Miner's Mark**, 3, 121	C. J. McCarron	Colonial Affair, 3, 121	Brunswick, 4, 126	5	2:02.79	510,000
1992	**Pleasant Tap**, 5, 126	G. L. Stevens	Strike the Gold, 4, 126	A.P. Indy, 3, 121	7	1:58.95	510,000
1991	**Festin (Arg)**, 5, 126	E. Delahoussaye	Chief Honcho, 4, 126	Strike the Gold, 3, 121	5	2:00.69	510,000
1990	**Flying Continental**, 4, 126	C. A. Black	De Roche, 4, 126	Izvestia, 3, 121	6	2:00.60	503,100
1989	**Easy Goer**, 3, 121	P. Day	Cryptoclearance, 5, 126	Forever Silver, 4, 126	7	2:29.20	659,400
1988	**Waquoit**, 5, 126	J. A. Santos	Personal Flag, 5, 126	Easy N Dirty, 5, 126	4	2:27.60	637,800
1987	**Creme Fraiche**, 5, 126	L. A. Pincay Jr.	Java Gold, 3, 121	Easy N Dirty, 4, 126	6	2:30.80	650,400
1986	**Creme Fraiche**, 4, 126	R. P. Romero	Turkoman, 4, 126	Danzig Connection, 3, 121	6	2:28.00	510,300
1985	**Vanlandingham**, 4, 126	P. Day	Gate Dancer, 4, 126	Creme Fraiche, 3, 121	7	2:27.00	516,600
1984	**Slew o' Gold**, 4, 126	A. T. Cordero Jr.	Hail Bold King, 3, 121	Bounding Basque, 4, 126	5	2:28.80	1,350,400
1983	**Slew o' Gold**, 3, 121	A. T. Cordero Jr.	Highland Blade, 5, 126	Bounding Basque, 3, 121	11	2:26.20	342,000
1982	**Lemhi Gold**, 4, 126	C. J. McCarron	Silver Supreme, 4, 126	†Christmas Past, 3, 118	10	2:31.20	337,800
1981	**John Henry**, 6, 126	W. Shoemaker	Peat Moss, 6, 126	†Relaxing, 5, 123	11	2:28.40	340,800
1980	**Temperence Hill**, 3, 121	E. Maple	John Henry, 5, 126	Ivory Hunter, 6, 126	7	2:30.20	329,400
1979	**Affirmed**, 4, 126	L. A. Pincay Jr.	Spectacular Bid, 3, 121	Coastal, 3, 121	4	2:27.40	225,000
1978	**Exceller**, 5, 126	W. Shoemaker	Seattle Slew, 4, 126	Great Contractor, 5, 126	6	2:27.20	193,080
1977	**On the Sly**, 4, 126	G. McCarron	Great Contractor, 4, 126	Cox's Ridge, 3, 121	13	2:28.20	208,080
1976	**Great Contractor**, 3, 121	P. Day	Appassionato, 3, 121	†Revidere, 3, 118	10	2:28.80	201,360
1975	**Group Plan**, 5, 124	J. Velasquez	Wajima, 3, 119	Outdoors, 6, 124	4	3:23.20	95,850
1974	**Forego**, 4, 124	H. Gustines	*Copte, 4, 124	Group Plan, 4, 124	8	3:21.20	67,140
1973	**Prove Out**, 4, 124	J. Velasquez	Loud, 6, 124	Twice a Prince, 3, 119	6	3:20.00	66,060

Named for the Jockey Club, keeper of the *American Stud Book*, and registrar of North American Thoroughbreds. Jockey Club S. 1919-'20. Held at Aqueduct 1959-'61, 1963-'67, 1969-'74. 1½ miles 1919-'20, 1976-'89. 2 miles 1921-'75. Colts and fillies 1944. †Denotes female. Winner's purse includes $1-million bonus for winning the Woodward S. (G1), Marlboro Cup (G1), and Jockey Club Gold Cup (G1) 1984.

Joe Hirsch Turf Classic Invitational Stakes

Grade 1 in 2006. Belmont Park, three-year-olds and up, 1½ miles, turf. Held October 1, 2005, with a gross value of $750,000. First held in 1977. First graded in 1979. Stakes record 2:24.50 (1992 Sky Classic).

Year	Winner	Jockey	Second	Third	Strs	Time	1st Purse
2005	**Shakespeare**, 4, 126	J. D. Bailey	English Channel, 3, 121	Ace (Ire), 4, 126	7	2:27.22	$450,000
2004	**Kitten's Joy**, 3, 121	J. R. Velazquez	Magistretti, 4, 126	Tycoon (GB), 3, 121	7	2:29.97	450,000
2003	**Sulamani (Ire)**, 4, 126	J. D. Bailey	Deeliteful Irving, 5, 126	Balto Star, 5, 126	7	2:27.51	450,000
2002	**Denon**, 4, 126	E. S. Prado	Blazing Fury, 4, 126	Delta Form (Aus), 6, 126	8	2:28.47	450,000
2001	**Timboroa (GB)**, 5, 126	E. S. Prado	King Cugat, 4, 126	Cetewayo, 7, 126	6	2:29.43	450,000
2000	**John's Call**, 9, 126	J. Samyn	Craigsteel (GB), 5, 126	†Ela Athena (GB), 4, 123	12	2:28.58	450,000
1999	**Val's Prince**, 7, 126	J. F. Chavez	Dream Well (Fr), 4, 126	Fahris (Ire), 5, 126	7	2:28.63	360,000
1998	**Buck's Boy**, 5, 126	S. J. Sellers	Cetewayo, 4, 126	Lazy Lode (Arg), 4, 126	6	2:33.25	300,000
1997	**Val's Prince**, 5, 126	M. E. Smith	Flag Down, 7, 126	Ops Smile, 5, 126	5	2:28.92	300,000
1996	**Diplomatic Jet**, 4, 126	J. F. Chavez	Awad, 6, 126	Marlin, 3, 121	10	2:27.51	300,000
1995	**Turk Passer**, 5, 126	J. R. Velazquez	Hernando (Fr), 5, 126	Celtic Arms (Fr), 4, 126	8	2:36.63	300,000
1994	**Tikkanen**, 3, 121	C. B. Asmussen	Vaudeville, 3, 121	†Yenda (GB), 3, 118	6	2:25.88	300,000

1993 **Apple Tree (Fr)**, 4, 126	M. E. Smith	Solar Splendor, 6, 126	George Augustus, 5, 126	5	2:28.31	$300,000
1992 **Sky Classic**, 5, 126	P. Day	Fraise, 4, 126	Solar Splendor, 5, 126	6	**2:24.50**	300,000
1991 **Solar Splendor**, 4, 126	W. H. McCauley	Dear Doctor (Fr), 4, 126	‡Fortune's Wheel (Ire), 3, 121	9	2:27.89	300,000
1990 **Cacoethes**, 4, 126	R. Cochrane	Alwuhush, 5, 126	With Approval, 4, 126	6	2:25.00	360,000
1989 **Yankee Affair**, 7, 126	J. A. Santos	El Senor, 5, 126	My Big Boy, 6, 126	7	2:27.20	392,550
1988 **Sunshine Forever**, 3, 121	A. T. Cordero Jr.	My Big Boy, 5, 126	Most Welcome (GB), 4, 126	9	2:33.80	360,000
1987 **Theatrical (Ire)**, 5, 126	P. Day	†River Memories, 3, 116	Talakeno, 7, 126	6	2:29.20	360,000
1986 **Manila**, 3, 119	J. A. Santos	Damister, 4, 126	Danger's Hour, 4, 126	9	2:27.80	423,150
1985 **Noble Fighter**, 3, 119	A. Lequeux	Win, 5, 126	Strawberry Road (Aus), 6, 126	12	2:25.40	431,100
1984 **John Henry**, 9, 126	C. J. McCarron	Win, 4, 126	Majesty's Prince, 5, 126	6	2:25.20	375,150
1983 **†All Along (Fr)**, 4, 123	W. R. Swinburn	Thunder Puddles, 4, 126	Erins Isle (Ire), 5, 126	10	2:34.00	351,420
1982 **†April Run (Ire)**, 4, 123	C. B. Asmussen	Naskra's Breeze, 5, 126	Bottled Water, 4, 126	7	2:29.80	286,080
1981 **†April Run (Ire)**, 3, 118	P. Paquet	Galaxy Libra (Ire), 5, 126	†The Very One, 6, 123	9	2:31.20	180,000
1980 **†Anifa**, 4, 123	A. Gilbert	Golden Act, 4, 126	John Henry, 5, 126	8	2:39.60	180,000
1979 **Bowl Game**, 5, 126	J. Velasquez	†Trillion, 5, 123	Native Courier, 4, 126	7	2:28.20	150,000
1978 **†Waya (Fr)**, 4, 123	A. T. Cordero Jr.	Tiller, 4, 126	†Trillion, 4, 123	6	2:26.80	130,000
1977 **Johnny D.**, 3, 122	S. Cauthen	Majestic Light, 4, 126	Crow (Fr), 4, 126	9	2:33.20	130,000

Named in honor of Joe Hirsch, retired executive columnist of the *Daily Racing Form* and dean of American Turf writers. Turf Classic Invitational S. 1977-2003. Held at Aqueduct 1977-'79, 1981-'83. ‡Spinning (Ire) finished third, DQ to fourth, 1991. Course record 1992. †Denotes female.

John B. Connally Breeders' Cup Turf Handicap

Grade 3 in 2006. Sam Houston Race Park, three-year-olds and up, 1⅛ miles, turf. Held April 8, 2006, with a gross value of $193,000. First held in 1995. First graded in 2006. Stakes record 1:47.65 (1999 Chorwon).

Year	Winner	Jockey	Second	Third	Strs	Time	1st Purse
2006	**Fort Prado**, 5, 120	R. Albarado	Dynareign, 6, 116	Dontbotherknocking, 8, 115	11	1:49.41	$103,800
2005	**Rapid Proof**, 5, 118	B. Hernandez Jr.	Warleigh, 7, 117	Dynareign, 5, 111	8	1:51.31	129,600
2004	**Warleigh**, 6, 116	J. Beasley	Skate Away, 5, 117	Gentlemen J J, 4, 109	11	1:53.01	133,200
2003	**Candid Glen**, 6, 113	E. J. Perrodin	Red Mountain, 6, 113	Dynameaux, 5, 114	11	1:53.21	133,800
2002	**Candid Glen**, 5, 114	E. J. Perrodin	Nat's Big Party, 8, 114	El Gran Papa, 5, 116	10	1:50.38	133,200
2001	**Candid Glen**, 4, 114	E. J. Perrodin	Profit Option, 6, 114	Gold Nugget, 6, 114	9	1:50.51	131,400
2000	**Rod and Staff**, 7, 115	R. Albarado	Vilaxy, 5, 114	Tangazi, 5, 115	11	1:51.68	100,350
1999	**Chorwon**, 6, 117	C. H. Borel	El Angelo, 7, 115	Houston Slue, 4, 114	11	**1:47.65**	99,900
1998	**Chorwon**, 5, 115	G. Melancon	Western Trader, 7, 114	Top Seed, 4, 114	10	1:51.86	83,160
1997	**Scott's Scoundrel**, 5, 118	R. D. Ardoin	Western Trader, 6, 119	Volochine (Ire), 6, 121	10	1:53.60	75,000
1996	**Western Trader**, 5, 115	C. Gonzalez	Jury Duty, 4, 114	Mine Inspector, 4, 113	12	1:52.30	75,000
1995	**Marastani**, 5, 122	C. C. Bourque	Glaring, 5, 120	Artema (Ire), 4, 117	12	1:51.25	45,000

Named in honor of John B. Connally Jr. (1917-'93), governor of Texas, Sam Houston Race Park's home state, from 1963-'69; Connally was also U. S. Treasury Secretary from 1971-'72. John B. Connally Jr. Turf Cup H. 1995.

John C. Mabee Handicap

Grade 1 in 2006. Del Mar, three-year-olds and up, fillies and mares, 1⅛ miles, turf. Held July 23, 2005, with a gross value of $400,000. First held in 1945. First graded in 1973. Stakes record 1:47.09 (2004 Musical Chimes).

Year	Winner	Jockey	Second	Third	Strs	Time	1st Purse
2005	**Amorama (Fr)**, 4, 115	M. A. Pedroza	Island Fashion, 5, 117	Intercontinental (GB), 5, 122	8	1:48.01	$240,000
2004	**Musical Chimes**, 4, 116	K. Desormeaux	Moscow Burning, 4, 117	Notting Hill (Brz), 5, 113	6	**1:47.09**	240,000
2003	**Megahertz (GB)**, 4, 116	A. O. Solis	dh-Dublino, 4, 121 dh-Golden Apples (Ire), 5, 122 dh-Tates Creek, 5, 123		5	1:49.09	240,000
2002	**Affluent**, 4, 118	E. Delahoussaye	Golden Apples (Ire), 4, 120	Janet (GB), 5, 118	7	1:48.37	240,000
2001	**Janet (GB)**, 4, 116	D. R. Flores	Tranquility Lake, 6, 123	Minor Details, 4, 112	6	1:48.20	240,000
2000	**Caffe Latte (Ire)**, 4, 117	B. Blanc	Tout Charmant, 4, 120	Alexine (Arg), 4, 115	7	1:47.16	240,000
1999	**Tuzla (Fr)**, 5, 121	D. R. Flores	Happyanunoit (NZ), 4, 115	Spanish Fern, 4, 115	10	1:47.66	240,000
1998	**See You Soon (Fr)**, 4, 114	C. S. Nakatani	Sonja's Faith (Ire), 4, 113	Fiji (GB), 4, 125	8	1:47.40	180,000
1997	**Escena**, 4, 115	P. Day	Real Connection, 6, 115	Different (Arg), 5, 121	7	1:49.80	180,000
1996	**Matiara**, 4, 118	C. S. Nakatani	Alpride (Ire), 5, 119	Pourquoi Pas (Ire), 4, 114	6	1:49.28	193,500
1995	**Possibly Perfect**, 5, 123	C. S. Nakatani	Morgana, 4, 115	Yearly Tour, 4, 116	7	1:49.98	180,600
1994	**Flawlessly**, 6, 124	C. J. McCarron	Hollywood Wildcat, 4, 124	Skimble, 5, 116	5	1:48.25	181,000
1993	**Flawlessly**, 5, 125	C. J. McCarron	Heart of Joy, 6, 114	Let's Elope (NZ), 6, 118	7	1:48.38	186,500
1992	**Flawlessly**, 4, 123	C. J. McCarron	Re Toss (Arg), 5, 115	Polemic, 4, 116	7	1:50.00	187,500
1991	**Campagnarde (Arg)**, 4, 115	J. A. Garcia	Bequest, 5, 118	Somethingmerry, 4, 118	10	1:49.41	196,250
1990	**Double Wedge**, 5, 114	R. G. Davis	Reluctant Guest, 4, 117	Nikishka, 5, 116	8	1:49.00	158,000
1989	**Brown Bess**, 7, 117	J. L. Kaenel	Daring Doone (GB), 6, 117	Galunpe (Ire), 6, 118	7	1:48.80	157,750
1988	**Annoconnor**, 4, 116	C. A. Black	Chapel of Dreams, 4, 118	Short Sleeves (GB), 6, 121	10	1:48.40	134,000
1987	**Short Sleeves (GB)**, 5, 116	E. Delahoussaye	Festivity, 4, 117	Auspiciante (Arg), 6, 120	9	1:50.20	97,900
1986	**Auspiciante (Arg)**, 5, 114	G. L. Stevens	Justicara (Ire), 5, 116	Sauna (Aus), 5, 119	9	1:48.40	81,600
1985	**Daily Busy (Fr)**, 4, 115	W. Shoemaker	Eastland, 4, 114	Envie de Rire (Fr), 4, 116	7	1:48.20	93,500
1984	**Flag de Lune**, 4, 115	F. Olivares	Royal Heroine (Ire), 4, 126	Salt Spring (Arg), 5, 115	9	1:48.40	97,200
1983	**Sangue (Ire)**, 5, 123	W. Shoemaker	Castilla, 4, 121	First Advance, 4, 115	8	1:48.80	80,450
1982	**Honey Fox**, 5, 122	M. Castaneda	Sangue (Ire), 4, 112	French Charmer, 4, 115	10	1:48.80	83,900
1981	**Queen to Conquer**, 5, 120	M. Castaneda	Amber Ever, 3, 112	Track Robbery, 5, 123	10	1:48.80	84,000
1980	**Queen to Conquer**, 4, 115	W. Shoemaker	A Thousand Stars, 5, 118	Wishing Well, 5, 122	13	1:49.40	74,050

1979	**Country Queen**, 4, 121	L. A. Pincay Jr.	More So (Ire), 4, 119	Prize Spot, 3, 116	10	1:48.60	$69,500
1978	**Drama Critic**, 4, 120	D. G. McHargue	Country Queen, 3, 113	B. Thoughtful, 3, 115	8	1:49.20	47,500
1977	**Dancing Femme**, 4, 122	D. G. McHargue	Up to Juliet, 4, 113	Swingtime, 5, 121	11	1:48.40	37,150
1976	**Vagabonda**, 5, 115	S. Hawley	*Stravina, 5, 115	Miss Tokyo, 4, 116	8	1:51.00	34,550
1975	***Dulcia**, 6, 122	W. Shoemaker	*Tizna, 6, 123	Charger's Star, 5, 115	7	1:48.80	33,550
1974	***Tizna**, 5, 120	W. Shoemaker	Modus Vivendi, 3, 118	*La Zanzara, 4, 122	11	1:49.20	29,800
1973	**Minstrel Miss**, 6, 122	D. Pierce	Le Cle, 4, 123	Pallisima, 4, 118	8	1:49.40	19,750

Named for John C. Mabee (1921-2002), owner of Golden Eagle Farm, located in Ramona, California, and longtime chairman of Del Mar Turf Club. Formerly named for the town of Ramona. Grade 3 1973-'79. Grade 2 1980-'83. Ramona H. 1945-2001. John C. Mabee Ramona H. 2002. Not held 1946-'58. 1 mile 1945. Dirt 1945-'69. Triple dead heat for second 2003.

Juddmonte Spinster Stakes

Grade 1 in 2006. Keeneland Race Course, three-year-olds and up, fillies and mares, 1⅛ miles, dirt. Held October 9, 2005, with a gross value of $500,000. First held in 1956. First graded in 1973. Stakes record 1:47 (1990 Bayakoa [Arg]).

Year	Winner	Jockey	Second	Third	Strs	Time	1st Purse
2005	**Pampered Princess**, 5, 123	E. Castro	Pleasant Home, 4, 123	Capeside Lady, 4, 123	11	1:53.91	$310,000
2004	**Azeri**, 6, 123	P. Day	Tamweel, 4, 123	Mayo On the Side, 5, 123	7	1:49.74	310,000
2003	**Take Charge Lady**, 4, 123	E. S. Prado	You, 4, 123	Miss Linda (Arg), 6, 123	6	1:49.57	310,000
2002	**Take Charge Lady**, 3, 120	E. S. Prado	You, 3, 120	Printemps (Chi), 5, 123	7	1:49.90	338,520
2001	**Miss Linda (Arg)**, 4, 123	R. Migliore	Starrer, 3, 120	Printemps (Chi), 4, 123	10	1:49.79	348,440
2000	**Plenty of Light**, 3, 120	G. K. Gomez	Spain, 3, 120	Roza Robata, 5, 123	6	1:48.18	336,970
1999	**Keeper Hill**, 4, 123	K. Desormeaux	Banshee Breeze, 4, 123	A Lady From Dixie, 4, 123	9	1:47.19	344,410
1998	**Banshee Breeze**, 3, 119	R. Albarado	Runup the Colors, 4, 123	Aldiza, 4, 123	8	1:47.04	341,930
1997	**Clear Mandate**, 5, 123	P. Day	Feasibility Study, 5, 123	Naskra Colors, 5, 123	7	1:50.47	336,350
1996	**Different (Arg)**, 4, 123	C. J. McCarron	Top Secret, 3, 119	Belle of Cozzene, 4, 123	6	1:49.74	336,040
1995	**Inside Information**, 4, 123	M. E. Smith	Jade Flush, 4, 123	Mariah's Storm, 4, 123	4	1:50.01	198,276
1994	**Dispute**, 4, 123	P. Day	Lets Be Alert, 3, 119	Miss Dominique, 5, 123	8	1:48.91	204,414
1993	**Paseana (Arg)**, 6, 123	C. J. McCarron	Gray Cashmere, 4, 123	Jacody, 3, 119	9	1:48.46	205,902
1992	**Fowda**, 4, 123	P. A. Valenzuela	Paseana (Arg), 5, 123	Meadow Star, 4, 123	10	1:49.91	209,994
1991	**Wilderness Song**, 3, 119	P. Day	Screen Prospect, 4, 123	Til Forbid, 3, 119	14	1:49.69	226,980
1990	**Bayakoa (Arg)**, 6, 123	L. A. Pincay Jr.	Gorgeous, 4, 123	Luthier's Launch, 4, 123	8	**1:47.00**	174,606
1989	**Bayakoa (Arg)**, 5, 123	L. A. Pincay Jr.	Goodbye Halo, 4, 123	Sharp Dance, 3, 119	6	1:47.80	172,413
1988	**Hail a Cab**, 5, 123	J. Vasquez	Willa On the Move, 3, 119	Integra, 4, 123	5	1:51.00	171,600
1987	**Sacahuista**, 3, 119	R. P. Romero	Ms. Margi, 3, 119	Tall Poppy, 4, 123	13	1:48.60	148,395
1986	**Top Corsage**, 3, 119	S. Hawley	Endear, 4, 123	Life At the Top, 3, 119	8	1:48.20	142,610
1985	**Dontstop Themusic**, 5, 123	L. A. Pincay Jr.	Life's Magic, 4, 123	Dowery, 4, 123	11	1:50.40	110,419
1984	**Princess Rooney**, 4, 123	E. Delahoussaye	Lucky Lucky Lucky, 3, 119	Heatherten, 5, 123	9	1:50.40	123,840
1983	**Try Something New**, 4, 123	P. Day	Dance Number, 4, 123	Miss Huntington, 6, 123	9	1:49.80	107,689
1982	**Track Robbery**, 6, 123	P. A. Valenzuela	Blush With Pride, 3, 119	Our Darling, 3, 119	9	1:47.80	110,517
1981	**Glorious Song**, 5, 123	R. Platts	Truly Bound, 3, 119	Safe Play, 3, 119	7	1:49.20	106,567
1980	**Bold 'n Determined**, 3, 119	E. Delahoussaye	Love Sign, 3, 119	Likely Exchange, 6, 123	6	1:49.20	114,660
1979	**Safe**, 3, 119	E. Fires	Spark of Life, 4, 123	Miss Baja, 4, 123	11	1:49.20	79,852
1978	**Tempest Queen**, 3, 119	J. Velasquez	Northernette, 4, 123	Likely Exchange, 4, 123	10	1:49.00	72,865
1977	**Cum Laude Laurie**, 3, 119	A. T. Cordero Jr.	Mississippi Mud, 4, 123	Ivory Wand, 4, 123	10	1:48.40	54,974
1976	**Optimistic Gal**, 3, 119	C. Perret	Ivory Wand, 3, 119	Rocky Trip, 4, 123	8	1:51.60	53,008
1975	**Susan's Girl**, 6, 123	L. A. Pincay Jr.	Flama Ardiente, 3, 119	Costly Dream, 4, 123	7	1:49.80	37,830
1974	**Summer Guest**, 5, 123	D. Montoya	Desert Vixen, 4, 123	Coraggioso, 4, 123	5	1:48.40	36,953
1973	**Susan's Girl**, 4, 123	B. Baeza	Light Hearted, 4, 123	Coraggioso, 3, 119	6	1:48.80	38,090

A spinster is an unmarried woman beyond the traditional marriage age, hence an appropriate name for a race for females still racing in the fall. Sponsored by Khalid Abdullah's Juddmonte Farms, located in Lexington, Kentucky 2005. Formerly sponsored by the Young family's Overbrook Farm, located in Lexington 2001-'04. Formerly sponsored by Robert N. Clay's Three Chimneys Farm, located in Midway, Kentucky 1996-2000. Spinster S. 1956-'95. Three-, four-, and five-year-olds 1956-'63.

Just a Game Handicap

Grade 2 in 2006. Belmont Park, three-year-olds and up, fillies and mares, 1 mile, turf. Held June 10, 2006, with a gross value of $285,000. First held in 1992. First graded in 1997. Stakes record 1:32.53 (1995 Caress).

Year	Winner	Jockey	Second	Third	Strs	Time	1st Purse
2006	**Gorella (Fr)**, 4, 120	J. R. Leparoux	Pommes Frites, 4, 116	Ozone Bere (Fr), 4, 116	4	1:37.14	$180,000
2005	**Sand Springs**, 5, 117	J. R. Velazquez	Intercontinental (GB), 5, 123	Wonder Again, 6, 121	9	1:33.05	180,000
2004	**Intercontinental (GB)**, 4, 118	J. D. Bailey	Vanguardia (Arg), 6, 113	Etoile Montante, 4, 121	8	1:33.33	150,000
2003	**Mariensky**, 4, 116	J. A. Santos	Riskaverse, 4, 119	Wonder Again, 4, 119	8	1:43.28	128,700
2002	**Babae (Chi)**, 6, 115	J. F. Chavez	Tates Creek, 4, 117	Stylish, 4, 116	8	1:34.57	67,920
2001	**License Fee**, 6, 118	P. Day	Shopping for Love, 4, 114	Veil of Avalon, 4, 115	11	1:32.62	114,780
2000	**Perfect Sting**, 4, 121	J. D. Bailey	Ronda (GB), 4, 116	Snow Polina, 5, 116	7	1:34.48	111,180
1999	**Cozy Blues**, 5, 112	J. F. Chavez	U R Unforgetable, 5, 114	Mysterious Moll, 4, 115	7	1:33.33	94,620
1998	**Witchful Thinking**, 4, 118	C. J. McCarron	Sopran Mariduff (GB), 4, 117	Dixie Ghost, 4, 111	9	1:33.45	95,745
1997	**Memories of Silver**, 4, 120	J. D. Bailey	Dynasty, 4, 113	Elusive, 5, 115	7	1:32.80	95,370
1996	**‡Caress**, 5, 117	R. G. Davis	Class Kris, 4, 122	Upper Noosh, 4, 112	7	1:33.30	94,890
1995	**Caress**, 4, 119	R. G. Davis	Coronation Cup, 4, 119	Grafin, 4, 117	5	**1:32.53**	49,320

1994	**Elizabeth Bay**, 4, 114	M. E. Smith	Tiffany's Taylor, 5, 117	Statuette, 4, 119	5	1:32.85	$33,330
1992	**Lady Lear**, 5, 115	G. Brocklebank	Flaming Torch (Ire), 5, 119	Totemic, 3, 116	5	2:15.90	47,340

Named for Peter M. Brant's 1980 champion grass female and '80 Flower Bowl H. (G2) winner Just a Game (Ire) (1976 f. by Tarboosh). Sponsored by Emirates Airline of Dubai, United Arab Emirates 2005. Grade 3 1997-2003. Just a Game S. 1992-'95. Just a Game Breeders' Cup H. 1996-2005. Not held 1993. Equaled course record 1995. ‡Class Kris finished first, DQ to second, 1996.

Kelso Breeders' Cup Handicap

Grade 2 in 2006. Belmont Park, three-year-olds and up, 1 mile, turf. Held October 2, 2005, with a gross value of $334,200. First held in 1980. First graded in 1984. Stakes record 1:32.40 (1990 Expensive Decision).

Year	Winner	Jockey	Second	Third	Strs	Time	1st Purse
2005	**Funfair (GB)**, 6, 115	E. S. Prado	Artie Schiller, 4, 123	Keep The Faith (Aus), 5, 115	10	1:32.95	$210,000
2004	**Mr O'Brien (Ire)**, 5, 119	E. Coa	Millennium Dragon (GB), 5, 119	Gulch Approval, 4, 114	8	1:32.69	150,000
2003	**Freefourinternet**, 5, 113	J. L. Espinoza	Proud Man, 5, 114	Rouvres (Fr), 4, 115	10	1:34.73	210,000
2002	**Green Fee**, 6, 113	J. R. Velazquez	Forbidden Apple, 7, 121	Moon Solitaire (Ire), 5, 117	7	1:33.83	210,000
2001	**Forbidden Apple**, 6, 118	J. A. Santos	Sarafan, 4, 114	City Zip, 3, 112	9	1:36.77	150,000
2000	**Forbidden Apple**, 5, 116	J. Samyn	Affirmed Success, 6, 120	Johnny Dollar, 4, 113	9	1:34.39	150,000
1999	**Middlesex Drive**, 4, 117	S. J. Sellers	Divide and Conquer, 5, 114	Wised Up, 4, 113	10	1:35.45	150,000
1998	**Dixie Bayou**, 5, 112	J. F. Chavez	Sahm, 4, 115	Let Goodtimes Roll, 5, 112	6	1:36.21	120,000
1997	**Lucky Coin**, 4, 119	R. G. Davis	Hawksley Hill (Ire), 4, 115	†Colcon, 4, 112	12	1:33.72	120,000
1996	**Same Old Wish**, 6, 113	S. J. Sellers	Da Hoss, 4, 120	Volochine (Ire), 5, 116	10	1:34.42	105,000
1995	**Mighty Forum (GB)**, 4, 115	E. Delahoussaye	Fastness (Ire), 5, 119	Dowty, 3, 112	14	1:39.58	120,000
1994	**Nijinsky's Gold**, 5, 114	J. A. Santos	Lure, 5, 128	A in Sociology, 4, 117	7	1:34.18	120,000
1993	**Lure**, 4, 125	M. E. Smith	Paradise Creek, 4, 120	Daarik (Ire), 6, 112	10	1:35.86	120,000
1992	**Roman Envoy**, 4, 117	C. Perret	Lure, 3, 111	Val des Bois (Fr), 6, 118	9	1:36.39	120,000
1991	**Star of Cozzene**, 3, 114	J. A. Santos	Known Ranger (GB), 5, 113	Fourstardave, 6, 117	6	1:33.37	69,720
1990	**Expensive Decision**, 4, 112	J. Samyn	Who's to Pay, 4, 115	Great Commotion, 4, 113	9	**1:32.40**	57,420
1989	**I Rejoice**, 6, 114	J. D. Bailey	Quick Call, 5, 113	Wanderkin, 6, 118	9	1:36.40	75,360
1988	**San's the Shadow**, 4, 116	C. W. Antley	Posen, 3, 117	Tinchen's Prince, 5, 114	7	1:42.00	72,240
1987	**I'm a Banker**, 5, 107	A. Graell	Tertiary Zone, 3, 113	Island Sun, 5, 112	11	2:10.80	76,920
1986	**I'm a Banker**, 4, 111	A. Graell	Duluth, 4, 113	Premier Mister (Mor), 6, 113	9	2:03.20	54,720
1985	**Mourjane (Ire)**, 5, 114	R. Migliore	Cool, 4, 116	Palace Panther (Ire), 4, 116	9	2:02.00	70,560
1984	**Who's for Dinner**, 5, 115	W. A. Guerra	Pin Puller, 5, 112	Norwick, 5, 109	11	2:01.20	71,100
1982	**Worthy Too**, 4, 109	J. Samyn	Nice Pirate, 4, 112	Jadosa Toker, 5, 113	12	3:24.40	69,840
1981	**Peat Moss**, 6, 126	F. Lovato Jr.	Field Cat, 4, 114	Birthday List, 6, 114	8	3:20.80	66,240
1980	**Peat Moss**, 5, 108	F. Lovato Jr.	Ivory Hunter, 6, 114	Ring of Light, 5, 117	10	3:24.60	68,160

Named for Bohemia Stable's 1960, '61, '62, '63, '64 Horse of the Year and '60, '61, '62, '63, '64 Jockey Club Gold Cup winner Kelso (1957 g. by Your Host); Kelso is the only five-time Horse of the Year. Grade 3 1984-'96. Held at Aqueduct 1980-'82. Not held 1983. 2 miles 1980-'82. 1¼ miles 1984-'87. Dirt 1980-'82. †Denotes female.

Kenny Noe Jr. Handicap

Grade 3 in 2006. Calder Race Course, three-year-olds and up, 7 furlongs, dirt. Held December 17, 2005, with a gross value of $100,000. First held in 1975. First graded in 2006. Stakes record 1:22.62 (2004 Medallist).

Year	Winner	Jockey	Second	Third	Strs	Time	1st Purse
2005	**Mister Fotis**, 4, 114	J. F. Chavez	Storm Surge, 3, 113	Silver Wagon, 4, 118	7	1:22.97	$60,000
2004	**Medallist**, 3, 114	J. A. Santos	Paradise Dancer, 4, 113	Hasty Kris, 7, 115	10	**1:22.62**	60,000
2003	**Hasty Kris**, 6, 116	R. R. Douglas	Wake At Noon, 6, 116	Tour of the Cat, 5, 119	10	1:23.82	60,000
2002	**Built Up**, 4, 114	E. Coa	Tour of the Cat, 4, 121	Sea of Tranquility, 6, 118	6	1:23.30	60,000
2001	**Fappie's Notebook**, 4, 117	J. F. Chavez	Kiss a Native, 4, 117	Dancing Guy, 6, 117	6	1:23.31	60,000
2000	**Miners Gamble**, 4, 114	E. O. Nunez	Alice's Notebook, 4, 114	Stormy Do, 7, 114	9	1:22.86	60,000
1999	**Thrillin Discovery**, 4, 112	J. Castellano	Mountain Top, 4, 115	Stormy Do, 6, 113	7	1:23.72	60,000
1998	**Thrillin Discovery**, 3, 114	J. Castellano	Flashing Tammany, 3, 115	Oro de Mexico, 4, 115	7	1:23.19	60,000
1997	**Heckofaralph**, 4, 116	J. A. Velez Jr.	Irish Conquest, 4, 113	Oro de Mexico, 3, 113	11	1:25.77	60,000
1996	**Splendid Sprinter**, 4, 115	J. R. Velazquez	Stormy Do, 3, 112	Ghostly Moves, 4, 114	10	1:23.45	60,000
1995	**Hyroglyphic**, 3, 113	W. H. McCauley	Excelerate, 3, 113	Ponche, 6, 120	10	1:23.53	60,000
1994	**Birdonthewire**, 5, 119	C. Perret	Fortunate Joe, 3, 116	Honest Colors, 3, 113	8	1:23.68	60,000
1993	**Song of Ambition**, 4, 118	R. D. Lopez	American Chance, 4, 114	Swedaus, 6, 115	11	1:23.58	30,000
1992	**Poulain d'Or**, 3, 116	M. A. Lee	Frozen Runway, 5, 115	Groomstick, 6, 116	6	1:23.68	30,000
	Drummond Lane, 5, 112	H. Castillo Jr.	Groomstick, 6, 114	Frozen Runway, 5, 114	8	1:23.08	49,710
1991	**Groomstick**, 5, 120	W. S. Ramos	Swedaus, 4, 110	Greg At Bat, 6, 113	6	1:23.50	32,250
1990	**Groomstick**, 4, 110	W. S. Ramos	Carborundum, 6, 118	The Red Rolls, 6, 113	9	1:24.00	50,475
1988	**Position Leader**, 3, 117	D. Valiente	The Red Rolls, 4, 114	Above Normal, 3, 114	12	1:24.60	52,620
	Princely Lad, 5, 115	L. Saumell	Hail the Ruckus, 5, 112	Baldski's Star, 4, 110	9	1:24.80	67,020
1986	**Chief Steward**, 5, 120	M. A. Lee	Play the King, 3, 114	Mugatea, 6, 117	8	1:25.80	31,080
1985	**Show Dancer**, 3, 114	G. St. Leon	Fortunate Prospect, 4, 119	Opening Lead, 5, 118	10	1:23.60	48,120
1984	**Mo Exception**, 3, 118	V. H. Molina	Jim Bracken, 3, 116	Brother Liam, 4, 118	8	1:24.60	37,695
	For Halo, 3, 118	B. Fann	Forbes' Best, 3, 113	Naskra Drummer, 4, 113	9	1:23.60	37,995
1983	**Eminency**, 5, 121	P. Day	My Mac, 3, 117	Command Attention, 5, 115	11	1:24.20	34,290
1982	**Spirited Boy**, 4, 114	M. Russ	In all Honesty, 3, 110	Moreton Bay, 3, 110	12	1:24.60	27,780
1981	**‡Speedy Prospect**, 4, 114	C. Astorga	Explosive Bid, 3, 115	Wooster Sq., 3, 113	8	1:11.60	22,935
1980	**†Burn's Return**, 4, 120	M. A. Rivera	Speedy Prospect, 3, 113	Southern General, 4, 112	8	1:11.00	16,515
1979	**†Burn's Return**, 3, 113	M. A. Rivera	Dargelo, 3, 112	Soldier Boy, 3, 115	13	1:38.20	17,250

1978	**Robb's Charm**, 3, 115	J. Giovanni	Reggie F., 3, 114	Fleet Gar, 3, 113	10	1:37.80	$18,000
1977	**Jonkiller**, 3, 120	C. Astorga	Jachal II, 3, 118	Haverty, 3, 111	9	1:39.40	17,850
1976	**Irish Captain**, 3, 116	J. Salinas	‡Controller Ike, 3, 122	El Rosillo, 3, 119	8	1:40.20	17,400
1975	**Bad Turn**, 3, 115	R. Perna	Ameri Flyer, 3, 114	American Holme, 3, 114	10	1:39.60	18,000

Named in honor of Kenny Noe Jr. (1928-), former president and general manager of Calder from 1979-'90. Sunny Isles H. 1975-'93. Not held 1987, 1989. 6 furlongs 1980-'81. 1 mile 1975-'79. Three-year-olds 1975-'79. Two divisions 1984. Held in March and December 1988. Held in April and December 1992. ‡El Rosillo finished second, DQ to third, 1976. ‡Explosive Bid finished first, DQ to second, 1981. †Denotes female.

Kent Breeders' Cup Stakes

Grade 3 in 2006. Delaware Park, three-year-olds, $1\frac{1}{8}$ miles, turf. Held June 25, 2005, with a gross value of $501,800. First held in 1937. First graded in 1973. Stakes record 1:47.32 (2005 Seeking Slew).

Year	Winner	Jockey	Second	Third	Strs	Time	1st Purse
2005	**‡Seeking Slew**, 3, 115	R. A. Dominguez	‡Chattahoochee War, 3, 119	Spring House, 3, 115	11	**1:47.32**	$300,000
2004	**Timo**, 3, 117	R. Migliore	Icy Atlantic, 3, 117	Commendation, 3, 115	8	1:55.75	150,000
2003	**Foufa's Warrior**, 3, 115	R. A. Dominguez	Remind, 3, 115	Lismore Knight, 3, 119	7	1:47.44	150,000
2002	**Miesque's Approval**, 3, 115	J. D. Bailey	Regal Sanction, 3, 115	dh-Coco's Madness, 3, 115 dh-Quest Star, 3, 115	8	1:48.81	150,000
2001	**Navesink**, 3, 115	R. A. Dominguez	Bowman Mill, 3, 115	Harrisand (Fr), 3, 115	10	1:49.98	151,000
2000	**Three Wonders**, 3, 115	P. Day	Field Cat, 3, 117	Dawn of the Condor, 3, 115	8	1:48.95	150,000
1999	**North East Bound**, 3, 114	J. A. Velez Jr.	Courtside, 3, 113	Swamp, 3, 119	8	1:51.93	150,000
1998	**Keene Dancer**, 3, 117	P. Day	Red Reef, 3, 115	Danielle's Gray, 3, 117	11	1:50.65	120,000
1997	**Royal Strand (Ire)**, 3, 122	P. Day	Subordination, 3, 122	Broad Choice, 3, 113	7	1:48.00	90,000
1996	**Sir Cat**, 3, 113	J. D. Bailey	Optic Nerve, 3, 122	Fortitude, 3, 116	5	1:52.93	60,000
1982	**Cagey Cougar**, 3, 114	V. A. Bracciale Jr.	King's Dusty, 3, 113	Big Shot (Fr), 3, 113	7	1:43.20	14,495
1979	**T. V. Series**, 3, 116	C. Barrera	Bear Arms, 3, 113	Buck's Chief, 3, 114	11	1:43.60	22,978
1976	**Improve It**, 3, 117	L. Saumell	Return of a Native, 3, 120	Impeccable, 3, 120	7	1:38.00	12,795
	***King Streaker**, 3, 111	H. Pilar	Chati, 3, 117	Parade to Glory, 3, 111	7	1:38.40	12,795
1975	**Talc**, 3, 117	R. Broussard	King of Fools, 3, 117	Leader of the Band, 3, 111	10	1:39.20	15,503
	Grey Beret, 3, 120	J. Canessa	My Friend Gus, 3, 117	Too Easy, 3, 111	10	1:39.40	15,503
1974	**Splitting Headache**, 3, 120	R. Woodhouse	Malaga Bay, 3, 114	Clyde William, 3, 117	12	1:40.80	20,475
1973	**Shane's Prince**, 3, 117	E. Maple	*Amen II, 3, 117	My Darling Boy, 3, 117	12	1:37.60	21,352

Named for Kent County, Delaware. Kent H. 1937-'41. Kent S. 1942-'82. Not held 1943, 1977-'78, 1980-'81, 1983-'95. $1\frac{1}{16}$ miles 1937-'68, 1979, 1982. 1 mile 1969-'76. Dirt 1937-'68. Two divisions 1975-'76. Dead heat for third 2002. ‡Touched by Madness finished first, DQ to fourth, 2005. ‡Spring House finished second, DQ to third, 2005. Course record 1997, 2003, 2005.

Kentucky Breeders' Cup Stakes

Grade 3 in 2006. Churchill Downs, two-year-olds, 5 furlongs, dirt. Held May 4, 2006, with a gross value of $184,250. First held in 1988. First graded in 1999. Stakes record :58.37 (2006 Datrick).

Year	Winner	Jockey	Second	Third	Strs	Time	1st Purse
2006	**Datrick**, 2, 117	S. Bridgmohan	†Pro Pink, 2, 114	Sentry, 2, 117	12	**:58.37**	$109,852
2004	**Lunarpal**, 2, 121	S. J. Sellers	Consolidator, 2, 115	Smoke Warning, 2, 117	4	1:04.07	86,025
2003	**Cuvee**, 2, 117	L. J. Meche	First Money, 2, 117	Exploit Lad, 2, 117	6	1:04.45	109,554
2002	**Posse**, 2, 115	D. J. Meche	Del Diablo, 2, 115	Blackjack Boy, 2, 115	8	1:03.73	102,300
2001	**Leelanau**, 2, 115	J. K. Court	Gygistar, 2, 115	†Lakeside Cup, 2, 112	6	1:03.11	100,812
2000	**†Gold Mover**, 2, 113	C. Perret	City Zip, 2, 115	Unbridled Time, 2, 121	6	1:03.67	101,091
1999	**†Chilukki**, 2, 112	R. Albarado	Barrier, 2, 115	Sky Dweller, 2, 115	7	1:04.01	106,485
1998	**Yes It's True**, 2, 121	S. J. Sellers	Tactical Cat, 2, 115	Alannan, 2, 115	8	1:03.61	85,948
1997	**Favorite Trick**, 2, 121	P. Day	Jess M, 2, 115	†Cutie Luttie, 2, 112	8	1:04.80	68,882
1996	**†Move**, 2, 113	S. J. Sellers	Prairie Junction, 2, 115	†Live Your Best, 2, 112	7	1:05.74	71,175
1995	**†Miraloma**, 2, 112	D. M. Barton	Great Southern, 2, 114	A. V. Eight, 2, 112	9	1:04.04	68,933
1994	**My My**, 2, 116	S. J. Sellers	Wise Affair, 2, 116	Hyroglyphic, 2, 116	11	1:05.96	37,310
1993	**†Astas Foxy Lady**, 2, 118	T. J. Hebert	Dish It Out, 2, 116	Riverinn, 2, 116	9	1:05.51	68,738
1992	**Tempered Halo**, 2, 121	P. A. Johnson	‡Mountain Cat, 2, 116	†Secret Bundle, 2, 113	7	1:05.39	50,326
1991	**Hippomenes**, 2, 112	P. Day	Cold Gate, 2, 118	It's Chemistry, 2, 113	9	1:06.30	50,716
1990	**To Freedom**, 2, 118	J. C. Espinoza	St. Alegis, 2, 112	Maxwell Street, 2, 112	5	1:05.00	17,647
1989	**Summer Squall**, 2, 118	C. R. Woods Jr.	Dr. Bobby A., 2, 118	Wink Road, 2, 118	7	1:05.00	50,294
1988	**†Island Escape**, 2, 115	C. R. Woods Jr.	One That Got Away, 2, 121	Papa Leonard, 2, 114	7	1:04.60	50,456

Churchill Downs is located in Louisville, Kentucky. Kentucky Budweiser Breeders' Cup S. 1988-'95. Not held 2005. $5\frac{1}{2}$ furlongs 1988-2004. Track record 1998, 2001. ‡Exclusive Zone finished second, DQ to fourth, 1992. †Denotes female.

Kentucky Cup Classic Stakes

Grade 2 in 2006. Turfway Park, three-year-olds and up, $1\frac{1}{8}$ miles, dirt. Held September 17, 2005, with a gross value of $342,500. First held in 1994. First graded in 1996. Stakes record 1:47.43 (1996 Atticus).

Year	Winner	Jockey	Second	Third	Strs	Time	1st Purse
2005	**Shaniko**, 4, 118	R. Bejarano	Ball Four, 4, 118	Silver Axe, 8, 118	10	1:49.74	$221,500
2004	**Roses in May**, 4, 118	J. R. Velazquez	Pie N Burger, 6, 117	Sonic West, 5, 113	6	1:49.13	221,500
2003	**Perfect Drift**, 4, 120	P. Day	Congaree, 5, 124	Crafty Shaw, 5, 115	5	1:50.43	221,500
2002	**Pure Prize**, 4, 115	M. E. Smith	Dollar Bill, 4, 117	Hero's Tribute, 4, 113	8	1:51.24	254,000
2001	**Guided Tour**, 5, 119	L. J. Melancon	Balto Star, 3, 114	A Fleets Dancer, 6, 115	6	1:47.90	254,000

2000	**Captain Steve**, 3, 115	S. J. Sellers	Golden Missile, 5, 121	Early Pioneer, 5, 120	6 1:49.95	$314,500
1999	**Da Devil**, 4, 112	C. H. Borel	Social Charter, 4, 115	Cat Thief, 3, 117	8 1:50.54	314,500
1998	**dh-Silver Charm**, 4, 123	G. L. Stevens		Acceptable, 4, 117	5 1:47.48	143,500
	dh-Wild Rush, 4, 117	P. Day				
1997	**Semoran**, 4, 116	K. Desormeaux	Distorted Humor, 4, 116	Coup D' Argent, 5, 114	8 1:48.08	217,000
1996	**Atticus**, 4, 115	C. S. Nakatani	Judge T C, 5, 116	Isitingood, 5, 114	10 **1:47.43**	325,000
1995	**Thunder Gulch**, 3, 121	G. L. Stevens	Judge T C, 4, 112	Bound by Honor, 4, 113	6 1:49.42	260,000
1994	**Tabasco Cat**, 3, 120	P. Day	Mighty Avanti, 4, 115	Best Pal, 6, 115	6 1:50.32	260,000

Turfway Park is located in Florence, Kentucky. Grade 3 1996-'98. Kentucky Cup Classic H. 1994-2004. Dead heat for first 1998.

Kentucky Cup Juvenile Stakes

Grade 3 in 2006. Turfway Park, two-year-olds, 1 1/16 miles, dirt. Held September 17, 2005, with a gross value of $100,000. First held in 1986. First graded in 1989. Stakes record 1:42.89 (1996 Boston Harbor).

Year	Winner	Jockey	Second	Third	Strs	Time	1st Purse
2005	**Stream Cat**, 2, 118	G. L. Stevens	Rungius, 2, 116	Cab, 2, 114	8	1:46.42	$62,000
2004	**Greater Good**, 2, 114	J. McKee	Magna Graduate, 2, 114	Norainonthisparty, 2, 114	6	1:44.96	62,000
2003	**‡Mr. Jester**, 2, 118	R. Bejarano	The Cliff's Edge, 2, 114	Pomeroy, 2, 116	8	1:46.61	62,000
2002	**Vindication**, 2, 116	M. E. Smith	Private Gold, 2, 118	Tito's Beau, 2, 114	8	1:46.70	62,750
2001	**Repent**, 2, 114	A. J. D'Amico	French Assault, 2, 118	Gold Dollar, 2, 114	7	1:43.78	62,750
2000	**Point Given**, 2, 114	S. J. Sellers	Holiday Thunder, 2, 114	The Goo, 2, 116	11	1:47.01	62,600
1999	**Millencolin**, 2, 114	P. Day	Personal First, 2, 118	Deputy Warlock, 2, 118	10	1:47.02	62,600
1998	**Aly's Alley**, 2, 118	P. A. Johnson	Time Bandit, 2, 120	Mac's Rule, 2, 116	9	1:45.63	62,600
1997	**Laydown**, 2, 114	M. E. Smith	Time Limit, 2, 118	Da Devil, 2, 114	7	1:43.17	62,600
1996	**Boston Harbor**, 2, 120	D. M. Barton	Play Waki for Me, 2, 118	Dr. Spine, 2, 112	8	**1:42.89**	65,000
1995	**Editor's Note**, 2, 115	G. L. Stevens	Devil's Honor, 2, 118	Never to Squander, 2, 110	8	1:45.07	65,000
1994	**Tejano Run**, 2, 120	J. D. Bailey	Gold Miner, 2, 120	Bick, 2, 120	7	1:46.10	65,000
1993	**Bibury Court**, 2, 120	S. T. Saito	Moving Van, 2, 120	Durham, 2, 120	11	1:47.75	81,250
1992	**Mountain Cat**, 2, 120	C. R. Woods Jr.	Saw Mill, 2, 120	Shoal Creek, 2, 120	10	1:43.50	97,500
1991	**Star Recruit**, 2, 120	R. D. Lopez	Pick Up the Phone, 2, 120	Battenburg, 2, 120	9	1:45.68	97,500
1990	**Fire in Ice**, 2, 120	A. J. Garcia	Wall Street Dancer, 2, 120	Gold Shoulder, 2, 120	10	1:46.60	81,250
1989	**Fighting Fantasy**, 2, 120	D. W. Cox	Top Snob, 2, 120	Hardburly, 2, 120	9	1:48.40	81,250
1988	**Light Crude**, 2, 120	R. L. Frazier	Bravoure, 2, 120	Revive, 2, 120	8	1:44.80	81,250
1987	**Jim's Orbit**, 2, 120	P. Day	Kingpost, 2, 120	Delightful Doctor, 2, 120	11	1:37.80	81,250
1986	**Rainbow East**, 2, 120	O. B. Aviles	Alysheba, 2, 120	David L.'s Rib, 2, 120	11	1:37.20	78,500

Turfway Park is located in Florence, Kentucky. Formerly sponsored by James McIngvale's Gallery Furniture Co. of Houston, Texas 1998. Formerly named for Dorothy and Pam Scharbauer's 1988 Horse of the Year Alysheba (1984 c. by Alydar); Alysheba placed second in the 1986 In Memoriam S. Formerly named for 1923 champion three-year-old male and '23 Latonia Championship S. winner In Memoriam (1920 c. by *McGee). In Memoriam S. 1986-'88. Alysheba S. 1989-'93. 1 mile 1986-'87. ‡Pomeroy finished first, DQ to third, 2003.

Kentucky Cup Sprint Stakes

Grade 3 in 2006. Turfway Park, three-year-olds, 6 furlongs, dirt. Held September 17, 2005, with a gross value of $100,000. First held in 1994. First graded in 1996. Stakes record 1:08.24 (1996 Appealing Skier).

Year	Winner	Jockey	Second	Third	Strs	Time	1st Purse
2005	**Estate Collection**, 3, 116	P. A. Valenzuela	Humor At Last, 3, 116	Going Wild, 3, 119	7	1:09.75	$62,000
2004	**Level Playingfield**, 3, 116	J. McKee	Cuvee, 3, 116	Swift Attraction, 3, 116	5	1:09.76	62,000
2003	**Cajun Beat**, 3, 122	C. H. Velasquez	Clock Stopper, 3, 116	Champali, 3, 122	11	1:09.54	62,000
2002	**Day Trader**, 3, 118	P. Day	Premier Performer, 3, 114	Ecstatic, 3, 114	11	1:10.01	94,500
2001	**Snow Ridge**, 3, 114	P. Day	City Zip, 3, 122	Dream Run, 3, 117	5	1:09.22	94,500
2000	**Caller One**, 3, 120	K. Desormeaux	Millencolin, 3, 116	Kings Command, 3, 116	6	1:09.46	93,750
1999	**Successful Appeal**, 3, 122	E. S. Prado	Five Star Day, 3, 114	American Spirit, 3, 118	6	1:09.42	74,400
1998	**Reraise**, 3, 116	C. S. Nakatani	Copelan Too, 3, 114	Mr Bert, 3, 114	7	1:08.50	93,900
1997	**Partner's Hero**, 3, 114	P. Day	Oro de Mexico, 3, 116	Prosong, 3, 114	6	1:09.02	74,400
1996	**Appealing Skier**, 3, 118	M. E. Smith	†Capote Belle, 3, 119	Delay of Game, 3, 114	9	**1:08.24**	97,500
1995	**Lord Carson**, 3, 116	M. E. Smith	Ft. Stockton, 3, 122	Evansville Slew, 3, 116	10	1:08.60	97,500
1994	**End Sweep**, 3, 120	C. J. McCarron	Exclusive Praline, 3, 122	Chimes Band, 3, 122	7	1:09.99	97,500

Turfway Park is located in Florence, Kentucky. Grade 2 1996-2001. Equaled track record 1995. †Denotes female.

Kentucky Cup Turf Handicap

Grade 3 in 2006. Kentucky Downs, three-year-olds and up, 1 1/2 miles, turf. Held September 24, 2005, with a gross value of $200,000. First held in 1998. First graded in 2001. Stakes record 2:27.60 (1998 Yaqthan [Ire]).

Year	Winner	Jockey	Second	Third	Strs	Time	1st Purse
2005	**Silverfoot**, 5, 120	R. Bejarano	Rochester, 9, 116	Gallo Del Bar (Chi), 5, 116	8	2:30.30	$124,000
2004	**Sabiango (Ger)**, 6, 119	B. Blanc	Rochester, 8, 117	Gottabeachboy, 4, 115	6	2:33.70	124,000
2003	**‡Rochester**, 7, 116	E. M. Martin Jr.	Quest Star, 4, 116	Art Variety (Brz), 5, 111	8	2:31.39	124,000
2002	**Rochester**, 6, 115	E. M. Martin Jr.	Nowrass (GB), 6, 112	Continental Red, 6, 117	11	2:38.28	186,000
2001	**Chorwon**, 8, 113	J. K. Court	The Knight Sky, 5, 114	Man From Wicklow, 4, 114	7	2:28.68	186,000
2000	**Down the Aisle**, 7, 117	R. Albarado	Crowd Pleaser, 5, 113	Royal Strand (Ire), 6, 115	8	2:27.70	186,000
1999	**Fahris (Ire)**, 5, 116	S. J. Sellers	Yaqthan (Ire), 9, 116	Royal Strand (Ire), 5, 114	12	2:29.60	186,000
1998	**Yaqthan (Ire)**, 8, 115	B. Peck	Perim (Fr), 5, 114	Chorwon, 5, 116	8	**2:27.60**	186,000

Established course record 1998. ‡Art Variety (Brz) finished first, DQ to third, 2003.

Kentucky Derby

Grade 1 in 2006. Churchill Downs, three-year-olds, 1¼ miles, dirt. Held May 6, 2006, with a gross value of $2,213,200. First held in 1875. First graded in 1973. Stakes record 1:59.40 (1973 Secretariat).

(See Triple Crown section for complete history of the Kentucky Derby)

Year	Winner	Jockey	Second	Third	Strs	Time	1st Purse
2006	**Barbaro**, 3, 126	E. S. Prado	Bluegrass Cat, 3, 126	Steppenwolfer, 3, 126	20	2:01.36	$1,453,200
2005	**Giacomo**, 3, 126	M. E. Smith	Closing Argument, 3, 126	Afleet Alex, 3, 126	20	2:02.75	1,639,600
2004	**Smarty Jones**, 3, 126	S. Elliott	Lion Heart, 3, 126	Imperialism, 3, 126	18	2:04.06	884,800
2003	**Funny Cide**, 3, 126	J. A. Santos	Empire Maker, 3, 126	Peace Rules, 3, 126	16	2:01.19	800,200
2002	**War Emblem**, 3, 126	V. Espinoza	Proud Citizen, 3, 126	Perfect Drift, 3, 126	18	2:01.13	1,875,000
2001	**Monarchos**, 3, 126	J. F. Chavez	Invisible Ink, 3, 126	Congaree, 3, 126	17	1:59.97	812,000
2000	**Fusaichi Pegasus**, 3, 126	K. Desormeaux	Aptitude, 3, 126	Impeachment, 3, 126	19	2:01.12	1,038,400
1999	**Charismatic**, 3, 126	C. W. Antley	Menifee, 3, 126	Cat Thief, 3, 126	19	2:03.29	886,200
1998	**Real Quiet**, 3, 126	K. Desormeaux	Victory Gallop, 3, 126	Indian Charlie, 3, 126	15	2:02.38	700,000
1997	**Silver Charm**, 3, 126	G. L. Stevens	Captain Bodgit, 3, 126	Free House, 3, 126	13	2:02.44	700,000
1996	**Grindstone**, 3, 126	J. D. Bailey	Cavonnier, 3, 126	Prince of Thieves, 3, 126	19	2:01.06	869,800
1995	**Thunder Gulch**, 3, 126	G. L. Stevens	Tejano Run, 3, 126	Timber Country, 3, 126	19	2:01.27	707,400
1994	**Go for Gin**, 3, 126	C. J. McCarron	Strodes Creek, 3, 126	Blumin Affair, 3, 126	14	2:03.72	628,800
1993	**Sea Hero**, 3, 126	J. D. Bailey	Prairie Bayou, 3, 126	Wild Gale, 3, 126	19	2:02.42	735,900
1992	**Lil E. Tee**, 3, 126	P. Day	Casual Lies, 3, 126	Dance Floor, 3, 126	18	2:03.04	724,800
1991	**Strike the Gold**, 3, 126	C. W. Antley	Best Pal, 3, 126	Mane Minister, 3, 126	16	2:03.08	655,800
1990	**Unbridled**, 3, 126	C. Perret	Summer Squall, 3, 126	Pleasant Tap, 3, 126	15	2:02.00	581,000
1989	**Sunday Silence**, 3, 126	P. A. Valenzuela	Easy Goer, 3, 126	Awe Inspiring, 3, 126	15	2:05.00	574,200
1988	**†Winning Colors**, 3, 121	G. L. Stevens	Forty Niner, 3, 126	Risen Star, 3, 126	17	2:02.20	611,200
1987	**Alysheba**, 3, 126	C. J. McCarron	Bet Twice, 3, 126	Avies Copy, 3, 126	17	2:03.40	618,600
1986	**Ferdinand**, 3, 126	W. Shoemaker	Bold Arrangement (GB), 3, 126	Broad Brush, 3, 126	16	2:02.80	609,400
1985	**Spend a Buck**, 3, 126	A. T. Cordero Jr.	Stephan's Odyssey, 3, 126	Chief's Crown, 3, 126	13	2:00.20	406,800
1984	**Swale**, 3, 126	L. A. Pincay Jr.	Coax Me Chad, 3, 126	At the Threshold, 3, 126	20	2:02.40	537,400
1983	**Sunny's Halo**, 3, 126	E. Delahoussaye	Desert Wine, 3, 126	Caveat, 3, 126	20	2:02.20	426,000
1982	**Gato Del Sol**, 3, 126	E. Delahoussaye	Laser Light, 3, 126	Reinvested, 3, 126	19	2:02.40	428,850
1981	**Pleasant Colony**, 3, 126	J. Velasquez	Woodchopper, 3, 126	Partez, 3, 126	21	2:02.00	317,200
1980	**†Genuine Risk**, 3, 121	J. Vasquez	Rumbo, 3, 126	Jaklin Klugman, 3, 126	13	2:02.00	250,550
1979	**Spectacular Bid**, 3, 126	R. J. Franklin	General Assembly, 3, 126	Golden Act, 3, 126	10	2:02.40	228,650
1978	**Affirmed**, 3, 126	S. Cauthen	Alydar, 3, 126	Believe It, 3, 126	11	2:01.20	186,900
1977	**Seattle Slew**, 3, 126	J. Cruguet	Run Dusty Run, 3, 126	Sanhedrin, 3, 126	15	2:02.20	214,700
1976	**Bold Forbes**, 3, 126	A. T. Cordero Jr.	Honest Pleasure, 3, 126	Elocutionist, 3, 126	9	2:01.60	165,200
1975	**Foolish Pleasure**, 3, 126	J. Vasquez	Avatar, 3, 126	Diabolo, 3, 126	15	2:02.00	209,600
1974	**Cannonade**, 3, 126	A. T. Cordero Jr.	Hudson County, 3, 126	Agitate, 3, 126	23	2:04.00	274,000
1973	**Secretariat**, 3, 126	R. Turcotte	Sham, 3, 126	Our Native, 3, 126	13	**1:59.40**	155,050

The Kentucky Derby was named for the Derby S. (Eng-G1) in England, commonly known as the Epsom Derby, its predecessor and model. Kentucky is the home state of Churchill Downs. Presented by Yum! Brands of Louisville 2006. 1½ miles 1875-'95. Track record 1973. †Denotes female. Winner's purse includes $1-million bonus for winning the Illinois Derby (G2) and the Kentucky Derby (G1) 2002. Winner's purse includes $5-million bonus from Oaklawn Park 2004.

Kentucky Jockey Club Stakes

Grade 2 in 2006. Churchill Downs, two-year-olds, 1¹⁄₁₆ miles, dirt. Held November 26, 2005, with a gross value of $222,400. First held in 1920. First graded in 1973. Stakes record 1:43.14 (1999 Captain Steve).

Year	Winner	Jockey	Second	Third	Strs	Time	1st Purse
2005	**Private Vow**, 2, 120	S. Bridgmohan	High Cotton, 2, 116	Hyte Regency, 2, 122	7	1:45.80	$137,888
2004	**Greater Good**, 2, 122	J. McKee	Rush Bay, 2, 116	Wild Desert, 2, 118	9	1:45.14	138,384
2003	**The Cliff's Edge**, 2, 122	S. J. Sellers	Gran Prospect, 2, 116	Proper Prado, 2, 118	8	1:45.50	137,764
2002	**Soto**, 2, 117	L. J. Melancon	Ten Cents a Shine, 2, 115	Most Feared, 2, 122	12	1:44.67	143,344
2001	**Repent**, 2, 122	A. J. D'Amico	Request for Parole, 2, 117	High Star, 2, 115	6	1:44.42	134,540
2000	**Dollar Bill**, 2, 113	C. H. Borel	Holiday Thunder, 2, 113	Gift of the Eagle, 2, 113	6	1:47.18	135,656
1999	**Captain Steve**, 2, 122	R. Albarado	Mighty, 2, 122	Personal First, 2, 119	12	**1:43.14**	143,840
1998	**Exploit**, 2, 122	C. J. McCarron	Vicar, 2, 113	Grits'n Hard Toast, 2, 113	11	1:44.16	140,740
1997	**Cape Town**, 2, 113	W. Martinez	Time Limit, 2, 119	Real Quiet, 2, 116	11	1:43.97	142,228
1996	**Concerto**, 2, 119	C. H. Marquez Jr.	Celtic Warrior, 2, 113	Carmen's Baby, 2, 122	11	1:46.91	142,104
1995	**Ide**, 2, 122	C. Perret	Editor's Note, 2, 119	El Amante, 2, 113	5	1:44.31	97,500
1994	**Jambalaya Jazz**, 2, 113	S. Maple	You're the One, 2, 112	Peaks and Valleys, 2, 119	7	1:46.46	97,500
1993	**War Deputy**, 2, 112	G. K. Gomez	Tarzans Blade, 2, 122	Rustic Light, 2, 119	11	1:46.75	97,500
1992	**Wild Gale**, 2, 116	S. J. Sellers	Mi Cielo, 2, 116	Shoal Creek, 2, 121	11	1:45.64	105,918
1991	**Dance Floor**, 2, 121	C. W. Antley	Waki Warrior, 2, 116	Choctaw Ridge, 2, 116	10	1:45.21	104,891
1990	**Richman**, 2, 121	P. Day	Discover, 2, 116	Honor Grades, 2, 116	10	1:45.40	107,718
1989	**Grand Canyon**, 2, 121	A. T. Cordero Jr.	Insurrection, 2, 121	Dusty's Command, 2, 118	6	1:44.60	95,550
1988	**Tricky Creek**, 2, 118	L. J. Melancon	Western Playboy, 2, 116	Revive, 2, 118	10	1:45.40	106,083
1987	**‡Notebook**, 2, 122	J. A. Santos	Buoy, 2, 122	Hey Pat, 2, 119	6	1:47.40	74,701
1986	**Mt. Pleasant**, 2, 116	K. K. Allen	Mondulick, 2, 113	Funny Tunes, 2, 113	11	1:46.40	93,561
1985	**Mustin Lake**, 2, 116	P. Day	Bachelor Beau, 2, 116	Regal Dreamer, 2, 122	10	1:46.80	87,432
1984	**Fuzzy**, 2, 114	D. Brumfield	Banner Bob, 2, 119	Nordic Scandal, 2, 113	13	1:45.00	106,902
1983	**Biloxi Indian**, 2, 119	G. Patterson	Country Manor, 2, 119	Taylor's Special, 2, 119	7	1:46.20	71,721
1982	**Highland Park**, 2, 122	D. Brumfield	Coax Me Matt, 2, 116	Caveat, 2, 122	5	1:47.00	75,869

1981	**El Baba**, 2, 119	R. P. Romero	Crown the King, 2, 116	Talent Town, 2, 119	9	1:45.20	$85,888
1980	**Television Studio**, 2, 119	D. Brumfield	Linnleur, 2, 119	Bear Creek Dam, 2, 116	8	1:47.00	73,226
1979	**King Neptune**, 2, 116	D. Brumfield	Royal Sporan, 2, 119	Silver Shears, 2, 116	7	1:37.80	37,001
1978	**Lot o' Gold**, 2, 119	R. DePass	Arctic Action, 2, 116	Uncle Fudge, 2, 119	12	1:37.80	37,645
1977	**Going Investor**, 2, 119	R. DePass	Jaycean, 2, 119	Silver Nitrate, 2, 116	7	1:38.20	36,121
1976	**Run Dusty Run**, 2, 122	D. G. McHargue	Get the Axe, 2, 116	Silver Series, 2, 116	8	1:37.20	34,831
1975	**Play Boy**, 2, 116	D. Brumfield	Khyber King, 2, 119	Please Find John, 2, 116	9	1:36.80	30,492
	Pastry, 2, 116	B. R. Feliciano	Bold Laddie, 2, 119	Bid to Fame, 2, 116	8	1:36.80	30,329
1974	**Circle Home**, 2, 116	M. Hole	Master Derby, 2, 122	Ruggles Ferry, 2, 116	9	1:36.00	36,748
1973	**Cannonade**, 2, 119	P. Anderson	Satan's Hills, 2, 116	Don't Be Late Jim, 2, 116	15	1:36.80	49,510

Kentucky is the home state of Churchill Downs. Formerly sponsored by Brown & Williamson Tobacco Corp. of Louisville 1987-'93, 1996-2000. Grade 3 1973-'82, 1984-'86, 1989-'97. Not graded 1983. Held at Old Latonia 1931-'33. Not held 1939-'45. 1 mile 1920-'79. Two divisions 1975. ‡Buoy finished first, DQ to second, 1987.

Kentucky Oaks

Grade 1 in 2006. Churchill Downs, three-year-olds, fillies, 1⅛ miles, dirt. Held May 5, 2006, with a gross value of $755,900. First held in 1875. First graded in 1973. Stakes record 1:48.64 (2003 Bird Town).

Year	Winner	Jockey	Second	Third	Strs	Time	1st Purse
2006	**Lemons Forever**, 3, 121	M. Guidry	Ermine, 3, 121	‡Wait a While, 3, 121	14	1:50.07	$426,479
2005	**Summerly**, 3, 121	J. D. Bailey	In the Gold, 3, 121	Gallant Secret, 3, 121	7	1:50.23	343,728
2004	**Ashado**, 3, 121	J. R. Velazquez	Island Sand, 3, 121	Madcap Escapade, 3, 121	11	1:50.81	354,640
2003	**Bird Town**, 3, 121	E. S. Prado	Santa Catarina, 3, 121	Yell, 3, 121	12	**1:48.64**	355,756
2002	**Farda Amiga**, 3, 121	C. J. McCarron	Take Charge Lady, 3, 121	Habibti, 3, 121	9	1:50.41	348,502
2001	**Flute**, 3, 121	J. D. Bailey	Real Cozzy, 3, 121	Collect Call, 3, 121	13	1:48.85	377,704
2000	**Secret Status**, 3, 121	P. Day	Rings a Chime, 3, 121	Classy Cara, 3, 121	14	1:50.30	378,696
1999	**Silverbulletday**, 3, 121	G. L. Stevens	Dreams Gallore, 3, 121	Sweeping Story, 3, 121	7	1:49.92	341,620
1998	**Keeper Hill**, 3, 121	D. R. Flores	Banshee Breeze, 3, 121	Really Polish, 3, 121	13	1:52.06	375,410
1997	**Blushing K. D.**, 3, 121	L. J. Meche	Tomisue's Delight, 3, 121	‡Storm Song, 3, 121	9	1:50.29	362,514
1996	**Pike Place Dancer**, 3, 121	C. S. Nakatani	Escena, 3, 121	Cara Rafaela, 3, 121	6	1:49.88	325,000
1995	**Gal in a Ruckus**, 3, 121	W. H. McCauley	Urbane, 3, 121	Sneaky Quiet, 3, 121	8	1:50.09	235,040
1994	**Sardula**, 3, 121	E. Delahoussaye	Lakeway, 3, 121	Dianes Halo, 3, 121	7	1:51.16	184,340
1993	**Dispute**, 3, 121	J. D. Bailey	Eliza, 3, 121	Quinpool, 3, 121	11	1:52.47	191,230
1992	**Luv Me Luv Me Not**, 3, 121	F. A. Arguello Jr.	Pleasant Stage, 3, 121	Prospectors Delite, 3, 121	6	1:51.41	182,455
1991	**Lite Light**, 3, 121	C. S. Nakatani	Withallprobability, 3, 121	Til Forbid, 3, 121	10	1:48.83	207,285
1990	**Seaside Attraction**, 3, 121	C. J. McCarron	Go for Wand, 3, 121	Bright Candles, 3, 121	10	1:52.80	156,910
1989	**Open Mind**, 3, 121	A. T. Cordero Jr.	Imaginary Lady, 3, 121	Blondeinamotel, 3, 121	5	1:50.60	150,540
1988	**Goodbye Halo**, 3, 121	P. Day	Jeanne Jones, 3, 121	Willa On the Move, 3, 121	10	1:50.40	156,715
1987	**Buryyourbelief**, 3, 121	J. A. Santos	Hometown Queen, 3, 121	Super Cook, 3, 121	8	1:50.40	155,415
1986	**Tiffany Lass**, 3, 121	G. L. Stevens	Life At the Top, 3, 121	Family Style, 3, 121	12	1:50.60	122,103
1985	**Fran's Valentine**, 3, 121	P. A. Valenzuela	Foxy Deen, 3, 121	Rascal Lass, 3, 121	9	1:50.00	118,365
1984	**Lucky Lucky Lucky**, 3, 121	A. T. Cordero Jr.	Miss Oceana, 3, 121	My Darling One, 3, 121	6	1:51.80	112,710
1983	**Princess Rooney**, 3, 121	J. Vasquez	Bright Crocus, 3, 121	Bemissed, 3, 121	7	1:50.80	116,968
1982	**Blush With Pride**, 3, 121	W. Shoemaker	Before Dawn, 3, 121	Flying Partner, 3, 121	7	1:50.20	126,133
1981	**Heavenly Cause**, 3, 121	L. A. Pincay Jr.	De La Rose, 3, 121	Wayward Lass, 3, 121	6	1:43.80	79,300
1980	**Bold 'n Determined**, 3, 121	E. Delahoussaye	Mitey Lively, 3, 121	Honest and True, 3, 121	8	1:44.80	83,915
1979	**Davona Dale**, 3, 121	J. Velasquez	Himalayan, 3, 121	Prize Spot, 3, 121	6	1:47.20	83,590
1978	**White Star Line**, 3, 121	E. Maple	Grenzen, 3, 121	Bold Rendezvous, 3, 121	11	1:45.20	60,889
1977	**Sweet Alliance**, 3, 121	C. J. McCarron	Our Mims, 3, 121	Mrs. Warren, 3, 121	12	1:43.60	60,889
1976	**Optimistic Gal**, 3, 121	B. Baeza	Confort Zone, 3, 121	Carmelita Gibbs, 3, 121	7	1:44.60	40,186
1975	**Sun and Snow**, 3, 121	G. Patterson	Funalon, 3, 121	Funny Cat, 3, 121	11	1:44.60	42,315
1974	**Quaze Quilt**, 3, 121	W. Gavidia	Special Team, 3, 121	Kaye's Commander, 3, 121	14	1:46.60	43,631
1973	**Bag of Tunes**, 3, 121	D. Gargan	La Prevoyante, 3, 121	Coraggioso, 3, 121	13	1:44.20	43,648

Named for the Oaks S. (Eng-G1), commonly known as the Epsom Oaks, its prototype in England. Kentucky is the home state of Churchill Downs. Grade 2 1973-'77. 1½ miles 1875-'90. 1¼ miles 1891-'95. 1¹⁄₁₆ miles 1896-1919, 1942-'81. ‡Sharp Cat finished third, DQ to eighth, 1997. ‡Bushfire finished third, DQ to sixth, 2006.

King's Bishop Stakes

Grade 1 in 2006. Saratoga Race Course, three-year-olds, 7 furlongs, dirt. Held August 27, 2005, with a gross value of $250,000. First held in 1984. First graded in 1987. Stakes record 1:20.99 (2004 Pomeroy).

Year	Winner	Jockey	Second	Third	Strs	Time	1st Purse
2005	**Lost in the Fog**, 3, 123	R. A. Baze	Social Probation, 3, 117	Better Than Bonds, 3, 119	7	1:22.56	$150,000
2004	**Pomeroy**, 3, 121	E. S. Prado	Weigelia, 3, 121	Ice Wynnd Fire, 3, 117	8	**1:20.99**	150,000
2003	**Valid Video**, 3, 121	J. Bravo	Great Notion, 3, 117	Ghostzapper, 3, 117	13	1:22.14	120,000
2002	**Gygistar**, 3, 124	J. R. Velazquez	Boston Common, 3, 121	Thunder Days, 3, 115	8	1:22.85	120,000
2001	**Squirtle Squirt**, 3, 121	J. D. Bailey	Illusioned, 3, 119	City Zip, 3, 124	8	1:21.97	120,000
2000	**More Than Ready**, 3, 124	P. Day	Valiant Halory, 3, 114	Millencolin, 3, 121	6	1:22.49	120,000
1999	**Forestry**, 3, 124	C. W. Antley	Five Star Day, 3, 115	Successful Appeal, 3, 124	12	1:21.00	120,000
1998	**Secret Firm**, 3, 121	E. S. Prado	Mint, 3, 121	Scatmandu, 3, 116	8	1:22.78	120,000
1997	**Tale of the Cat**, 3, 114	J. A. Krone	Oro de Mexico, 3, 116	Trafalger, 3, 121	6	1:21.71	90,000
1996	**Honour and Glory**, 3, 123	J. A. Santos	Elusive Quality, 3, 112	Distorted Humor, 3, 115	6	1:21.78	64,920
1995	**Top Account**, 3, 112	P. Day	Ft. Stockton, 3, 120	Excelerate, 3, 113	10	1:22.50	68,100
1994	**Chimes Band**, 3, 117	J. D. Bailey	End Sweep, 3, 122	Halo's Image, 3, 117	7	1:21.82	65,700

1993	**Mi Cielo**, 3, 115	M. E. Smith	Williamstown, 3, 122	Schossberg, 3, 115	11	1:21.73	$74,280
1992	**Salt Lake**, 3, 117	M. E. Smith	Binalong, 3, 115	Agincourt, 3, 122	10	1:21.53	73,440
1991	**Take Me Out**, 3, 115	M. E. Smith	Joey the Student, 3, 115	To Freedom, 3, 119	10	1:21.73	74,400
1990	**Housebuster**, 3, 122	C. Perret	Poppiano, 3, 115	Sunshine Jimmy, 3, 115	9	1:21.80	54,090
1989	**Houston**, 3, 119	P. Day	Fast Play, 3, 117	Fierce Fighter, 3, 115	6	1:22.00	51,930
1988	**King's Nest**, 3, 115	C. J. McCarron	Tejano, 3, 117	Parlay Me, 3, 115	8	1:21.80	53,280
1987	**Templar Hill**, 3, 119	C. J. McCarron	Mister S. M., 3, 119	Homebuilder, 3, 115	8	1:23.00	51,660
1985	**Pancho Villa**, 3, 122	D. G. McHargue	El Basco, 3, 119	Cullendale, 3, 115	9	1:22.20	33,540
1984	**Commemorate**, 3, 119	F. Lovato Jr.	All Fired Up, 3, 122	Raja's Shark, 3, 115	8	1:22.60	33,900

Named for Bohemia Stable's 1973 Carter H. (G2) winner King's Bishop (1969 c. by Round Table). Grade 3 1987-'91. Grade 2 1992-'98. Not held 1986.

Knickerbocker Handicap

Grade 3 in 2006. Belmont Park, three-year-olds and up, 1$\frac{1}{8}$ miles, turf. Held October 30, 2005, with a gross value of $150,000. First held in 1960. First graded in 1973. Stakes record 1:48.69 (1998 Sahm).

Year	Winner	Jockey	Second	Third	Strs	Time	1st Purse
2005	**Atlando (Ire)**, 4, 116	J. D. Bailey	Certifiably Crazy, 5, 115	Rousing Victory, 4, 115	10	1:50.93	$90,000
2004	**Host (Chi)**, 4, 115	C. P. DeCarlo	Evening Attire, 6, 114	Sailaway, 4, 113	9	1:49.95	90,000
2003	**Better Talk Now**, 4, 116	E. S. Prado	Del Mar Show, 6, 116	Millennium Dragon (GB), 4, 115	12	1:50.53	90,000
2002	**Dawn of the Condor**, 5, 114	J. F. Chavez	Serial Bride, 5, 114	Polish Miner, 5, 114	9	1:52.54	90,000
2001	**Sumitas (Ger)**, 5, 115	E. S. Prado	Manndar (Ire), 5, 116	Crash Course, 5, 115	11	2:02.55	90,000
2000	**Charge d'Affaires (GB)**, 5, 115	J. A. Santos	Devine Wind, 4, 116	Understood, 4, 111	7	1:49.01	90,000
1999	**Charge d'Affaires (GB)**, 4, 114	J. A. Santos	Comic Strip, 4, 119	Nat's Big Party, 5, 113	7	1:49.06	66,480
1998	**Sahm**, 4, 116	J. R. Velazquez	Glok, 4, 113	Let Goodtimes Roll, 5, 112	8	**1:48.69**	67,440
1997	**Sir Cat**, 4, 115	M. E. Smith	Tamhid, 4, 114	Outta My Way Man, 5, 114	5	1:50.02	69,060
1996	**Mr. Bluebird**, 5, 113	M. E. Smith	Devil's Cup, 3, 107	Ops Smile, 4, 116	12	1:49.21	69,660
1995	**Diplomatic Jet**, 3, 113	M. E. Smith	Flag Down, 5, 114	Easy Miner, 4, 110	11	2:04.97	87,870
1994	**Kiri's Clown**, 5, 114	M. J. Luzzi	River Majesty, 5, 117	Red Earth, 3, 111	12	1:49.38	52,335
1993	**River Majesty**, 4, 115	M. E. Smith	Daarik (Ire), 6, 114	Home of the Free, 5, 118	6	1:54.54	52,920
1992	**Binary Light**, 3, 111	J. Cruguet	Share the Glory, 4, 110	Turkey Point, 7, 113	7	1:52.70	56,160
1991	**Home of the Free**, 3, 110	J. R. Velazquez	Turkey Point, 6, 114	Fourstars Allstar, 3, 113	7	1:48.73	56,070
1990	**Who's to Pay**, 4, 115	J. D. Bailey	Yankee Affair, 8, 120	Green Line Express, 4, 121	8	1:49.20	57,240
1989	**Trans Banner**, 4, 112	J. Samyn	Soviet Lad, 4, 112	Impersonator, 4, 114	12	1:53.60	58,770
1988	**Jimmy's Bronco**, 4, 112	J. Cruguet	Coeur de Lion (Fr), 4, 118	†Gai Minois (Fr), 6, 113	11	1:54.80	58,590
1987	**Laser Lane**, 4, 113	J. A. Santos	Yankee Affair, 5, 116	Wanderkin, 4, 112	12	1:51.60	73,260
1986	**Duluth**, 4, 113	J. Cruguet	Dance of Life, 3, 122	Broadway Tommy, 4, 109	8	2:20.80	55,710
1985	**Putting Green**, 5, 112	E. Maple	Domynsky (GB), 5, 113	Capricorn Son (Ire), 3, 109	7	2:23.80	54,405
	Rocamadour (Ire), 6, 109	J. Cruguet	‡Sondrio (Ire), 4, 115	He's Vivacious, 5, 110	7	2:23.80	54,405
1984	**He's Vivacious**, 4, 108	R. G. Davis	Nassipour, 4, 109	Lucky Scott (GB), 3, 107	12	2:26.00	46,440
1983	**Four Bases**, 4, 105	R. J. Thibeau Jr.	Moon Spirit, 3, 114	Ask Me, 4, 117	10	2:17.80	34,230
	Piling, 5, 114	E. Maple	Chem, 4, 116	Charging Through, 3, 110	8	2:19.00	34,470
1982	**Half Iced**, 3, 114	D. MacBeth	No Neck, 7, 109	Erin's Tiger, 4, 113	8	2:18.20	33,330
	†If Winter Comes, 4, 108	M. Venezia	Ten Below, 3, 113	Forkali, 4, 112	8	2:19.60	33,330
1981	**†Euphrosyne**, 5, 110	R. Migliore	Our Captain Willie, 3, 115	Naskra's Breeze, 4, 115	8	2:18.40	33,300
	Ghazwan (Ire), 4, 110	C. Hernandez	Wicked Will (GB), 3, 108	†Hunston (GB), 3, 107	7	2:20.60	33,540
1980	**Foretake**, 4, 112	J. Ruane	El Barril (Chi), 4, 113	Ministrel (Fr), 4, 109	9	2:22.20	33,450
	Lobsang (Ire), 4, 111	M. Venezia	Match the Hatch, 4, 115	King Crimson (Fr), 5, 111	7	2:23.60	33,450
1979	**French Colonial**, 4, 114	J. Vasquez	T. V. Series, 3, 113	Golden Reserve, 5, 112	12	2:21.40	35,880
1978	**Fluorescent Light**, 4, 115	J. Cruguet	Banquet Table, 4, 109	Scythian Gold, 3, 110	10	2:14.20	34,560
1977	**Dance d'Espoir**, 5, 112	J. Cruguet	Java Rajah, 4, 106	Diagramatic, 4, 112	5	2:05.00	26,010
	Keep the Promise, 5, 112	J. Cruguet	Soldier's Lark, 3, 110	Star Spangled, 3, 114	8	2:04.40	26,460
1976	**†Javamine**, 3, 111	J. Velasquez	*Recupere, 6, 112	Banghi, 3, 118	9	2:20.60	26,400
	Oilfield, 3, 112	S. Hawley	Royal Mission, 3, 111	Trumpeter Swan, 5, 112	7	2:22.60	26,100
1975	**Shady Character**, 4, 113	A. T. Cordero Jr.	Blue Times, 4, 115	*Yvetot, 7, 113	8	2:16.20	33,900
1974	**Shady Character**, 3, 115	A. T. Cordero Jr.	John Drew, 3, 111	Crafty Khale, 5, 126	5	2:41.40	33,690
1973	**Astray**, 4, 112	C. Baltazar	Triangular, 6, 114	*Yvetot, 5, 112	11	2:39.80	34,710

Named for a Washington Irving fictional character, Diedrich Knickerbocker; in the 19th century, New Yorkers were often called "Knickerbockers." Grade 3 1973-'97. Held at Aqueduct 1960-'61, 1963-'74, 1976-'94, 1996-2000, 2002-'04. 1$\frac{5}{8}$ miles 1960-'61, 1970-'74. 1$\frac{3}{8}$ miles 1962, 1975-'76, 1978-'86. 1$\frac{3}{16}$ miles 1963-'69. 1$\frac{1}{4}$ miles 1977, 1995, 2001. Dirt 1977, 1992, 1997. Two divisions 1976-'77, 1980-'83, 1985. ‡He's Vivacious finished second, DQ to third, 1985 (2nd Div.). †Denotes female.

La Brea Stakes

Grade 1 in 2006. Santa Anita Park, three-year-olds, fillies, 7 furlongs, dirt. Held December 31, 2005, with a gross value of $250,000. First held in 1974. First graded in 1983. Stakes record 1:20.45 (1993 Mamselle Bebette).

Year	Winner	Jockey	Second	Third	Strs	Time	1st Purse
2005	**Pussycat Doll**, 3, 119	G. K. Gomez	Leave Me Alone, 3, 123	Thrilling Victory, 3, 119	11	1:21.36	$150,000
2004	**Alphabet Kisses**, 3, 117	M. E. Smith	Bending Strings, 3, 121	Elusive Diva, 3, 119	10	1:21.38	150,000
2003	**Island Fashion**, 3, 123	K. Desormeaux	Randaroo, 3, 119	Buffythecenterfold, 3, 119	10	1:21.79	150,000
2002	**Got Koko**, 3, 117	A. O. Solis	Spring Meadow, 3, 119	Erica's Smile, 3, 117	10	1:22.57	120,000
2001	**Affluent**, 3, 121	E. Delahoussaye	Royally Chosen, 3, 119	Love At Noon, 3, 117	12	1:21.29	120,000

2000	**Spain**, 3, 123	V. Espinoza	Cover Gal, 3, 119	Serenita (Arg), 3, 115	6	1:22.27	$120,000
1999	**Hookedonthefeelin**, 3, 119	D. R. Flores	Olympic Charmer, 3, 119	Kalookan Queen, 3, 119	8	1:21.84	120,000
1998	**Magical Allure**, 3, 121	G. L. Stevens	Gourmet Girl, 3, 117	Tranquility Lake, 3, 116	7	1:22.06	120,000
1997	**I Ain't Bluffing**, 3, 119	E. Delahoussaye	Minister's Melody, 3, 119	Praviana (Chi), 3, 115	9	1:21.23	99,540
1996	**Hidden Lake**, 3, 115	C. J. McCarron	Belle's Flag, 3, 119	Tiffany Diamond, 3, 115	7	1:22.00	80,900
1995	**Exotic Wood**, 3, 119	C. J. McCarron	Evil's Pic, 3, 119	Jewel Princess, 3, 119	6	1:21.57	80,250
1994	**Top Rung**, 3, 115	G. L. Stevens	Klassy Kim, 3, 119	Twice the Vice, 3, 119	7	1:21.84	63,700
1993	**Mamselle Bebette**, 3, 115	C. S. Nakatani	Desert Stormer, 3, 116	Island Orchid, 3, 115	9	**1:20.45**	65,900
1992	**Arches of Gold**, 3, 115	E. Delahoussaye	Race the Wild Wind, 3, 121	Terre Haute, 3, 117	8	1:21.28	64,800
1991	**D'Or Ruckus**, 3, 115	C. J. McCarron	Good Potential, 3, 119	Garden Gal, 3, 117	6	1:22.05	48,800
	Teresa Mc, 3, 119	P. A. Valenzuela	Remarkably Easy, 3, 119	Suziqcute, 3, 119	6	1:23.05	48,800
1990	**Brought to Mind**, 3, 117	A. O. Solis	A Wild Ride, 3, 119	Mama Simba, 3, 114	8	1:21.60	65,000
	Akinemod, 4, 117	G. L. Stevens	Fantastic Look, 4, 122	Reluctant Guest, 4, 117	8	1:21.60	62,650
1989	**Variety Baby**, 4, 117	C. A. Black	T. V. of Crystal, 4, 117	Forewarning, 4, 117	8	1:21.60	49,050
1988	**Very Subtle**, 4, 124	P. A. Valenzuela	Saros Brig, 4, 114	Fold the Flag, 4, 117	6	1:21.60	60,300
1987	**Family Style**, 4, 122	G. L. Stevens	Sari's Heroine, 4, 119	Winter Treasure, 4, 117	6	1:22.60	46,700
1985	**Savannah Slew**, 3, 119	W. Shoemaker	Lady's Secret, 3, 124	Ambra Ridge, 3, 114	7	1:22.40	39,150
	Mitterand, 4, 117	E. Delahoussaye	Percipient, 4, 119	Lady Trilby, 4, 117	9	1:21.80	39,950
1983	**Lovlier Linda**, 3, 114	W. Shoemaker	Angel Savage (Mex), 3, 115	Fabulous Notion, 3, 124	9	1:22.20	40,700
1982	**Beautiful Glass**, 3, 114	C. J. McCarron	Skillful Joy, 3, 122	Header Card, 3, 119	11	1:21.00	42,450
	Nell's Briquette, 4, 122	C. J. McCarron	Bannockburn, 4, 115	Bee a Scout, 4, 117	8	1:25.80	40,150
1981	**Dynanite**, 4, 114	W. Shoemaker	Bold 'n Determined, 4, 125	Pachena, 4, 114	5	1:21.40	31,750
1980	**Terlingua**, 4, 121	D. G. McHargue	Glorious Song, 4, 116	Prize Spot, 4, 121	4	1:20.80	31,350
1979	**Great Lady M.**, 4, 117	L. A. Pincay Jr.	dh-B. Thoughtful, 4, 121 dh-Queen Yasna, 4, 114		11	1:22.60	35,850
1978	**Taisez Vous**, 4, 121	D. Pierce	Ida Delia, 4, 114	Sound of Summer, 4, 121	7	1:22.80	26,700
1976	**Kirby Lane**, 3, 117	L. A. Pincay Jr.	Tregillick, 3, 116	Missing Marbles, 3, 116	9	1:45.20	23,750
1975	**Featherfoot**, 3, 114	W. Shoemaker	Banyan Road, 3, 120	Graham Heagney, 3, 114	5	1:43.20	13,025
	Big Destiny, 3, 114	S. Hawley	Bending Away, 3, 120	Mark's Place, 3, 120	6	1:42.80	13,325
	Bobby Murcer, 4, 120	E. Belmonte	Bold Clarion, 4, 120	Roger's Dandy, 4, 117	11	1:43.40	20,800
1974	**Niner Power**, 4, 117	S. Valdez	First Majesty, 4, 117	Handsome Native, 4, 117	10	1:43.80	20,350

Named for Rancho La Brea in Los Angeles County, California; brea means "tar." Grade 3 1983-'93. Grade 2 1994-'96. Not held 1977, 1984, 1986. 1$^{1}/_{16}$ miles 1974-'76. Four-year-olds 1974, 1975 (January), 1978-'81, 1982 (January), 1985 (January), 1987-'89, 1990 (January). Both sexes 1974-'76. Two divisions 1975 (December), 1991. Held in January and December 1975, 1982, 1985, 1990. Dead heat for second 1979. Non-winners of a race worth $10,000 to the winner 1974. Non-winners of a race worth $12,500 to the winner 1975. Non-winners of a race worth $15,000 to the winner 1976.

La Canada Stakes

Grade 2 in 2006. Santa Anita Park, four-year-olds, fillies, 1$^{1}/_{8}$ miles, dirt. Held February 12, 2006, with a gross value of $200,000. First held in 1975. First graded in 1977. Stakes record 1:47.60 (1980 Glorious Song; 1982 Safe Play).

Year	Winner	Jockey	Second	Third	Strs	Time	1st Purse
2006	**Seafree**, 4, 118	P. A. Valenzuela	Play Ballado, 4, 118	Sharp Lisa, 4, 120	5	1:50.04	$120,000
2005	**Tarlow**, 4, 117	P. A. Valenzuela	Sweet Lips, 4, 121	A. P. Adventure, 4, 118	5	1:48.64	120,000
2004	**Cat Fighter**, 4, 115	A. O. Solis	Fencelineneighbor, 4, 116	Tangle (Ire), 4, 116	8	1:50.41	120,000
2003	**Got Koko**, 4, 121	A. O. Solis	Sightseek, 4, 118	Bella Bellucci, 4, 118	5	1:48.41	120,000
2002	**Summer Colony**, 4, 119	G. L. Stevens	Azeri, 4, 115	Ask Me No Secrets, 4, 115	6	1:49.26	120,000
2001	**Spain**, 4, 122	V. Espinoza	Chilukki, 4, 119	Letter of Intent, 4, 116	5	1:49.74	120,000
2000	**Scholars Studio**, 4, 116	C. S. Nakatani	Smooth Player, 4, 117	The Seven Seas, 4, 116	5	1:49.14	120,000
1999	**Manistique**, 4, 119	G. L. Stevens	Magical Allure, 4, 119	Gourmet Girl, 4, 117	7	1:48.81	120,000
1998	**Fleet Lady**, 4, 119	G. K. Gomez	Minister's Melody, 4, 117	I Ain't Bluffing, 4, 117	7	1:48.59	120,000
1997	**Belle's Flag**, 4, 119	C. S. Nakatani	Chile Chatte, 4, 115	Housa Dancer (Fr), 4, 115	8	1:48.26	133,200
1996	**Jewel Princess**, 4, 119	A. O. Solis	Dixie Pearl, 4, 116	Privity, 4, 117	6	1:49.42	129,900
1995	**Dianes Halo**, 4, 115	C. S. Nakatani	Twice the Vice, 4, 119	Klassy Kim, 4, 119	6	1:49.35	123,800
1994	**Stalcreek**, 4, 119	G. L. Stevens	Alyshena, 4, 115	Hollywood Wildcat, 4, 122	4	1:48.85	120,000
1993	**Alysbelle**, 4, 116	E. Delahoussaye	Pacific Squall, 4, 119	Interactive, 4, 117	9	1:49.85	130,850
1992	**Exchange**, 4, 119	L. A. Pincay Jr.	Winglet, 4, 117	Damewood, 4, 116	8	1:49.96	128,250
1991	**Fit to Scout**, 4, 120	J. A. Garcia	Vieille Vigne (Fr), 4, 116	A Wild Ride, 4, 121	7	1:48.50	126,700
1990	**Gorgeous**, 4, 125	E. Delahoussaye	Luthier's Launch, 4, 117	Kelly, 4, 116	5	1:50.00	122,000
1989	**Goodbye Halo**, 4, 126	P. Day	Seattle Smooth, 4, 117	Savannah's Honor, 4, 115	7	1:54.40	125,300
1988	**Hollywood Glitter**, 4, 117	L. A. Pincay Jr.	By Land by Sea, 4, 119	Very Subtle, 4, 126	7	1:49.20	94,200
1987	**Family Style**, 4, 122	G. L. Stevens	Winter Treasure, 4, 117	Sari's Heroine, 4, 121	6	1:49.60	94,800
1986	**Lady's Secret**, 4, 126	C. J. McCarron	Shywing, 4, 119	North Sider, 4, 118	6	1:49.80	120,200
1985	**Mitterand**, 4, 121	E. Delahoussaye	Percipient, 4, 117	Life's Magic, 4, 126	5	1:48.80	90,700
1984	**Sweet Diane**, 4, 120	R. Sibille	Weekend Surprise, 4, 115	Lovlier Linda, 4, 120	4	1:49.20	117,200
1983	**Avigaition**, 4, 117	E. Delahoussaye	Elusive, 4, 115	Etoile Du Matin, 4, 116	11	1:49.80	101,900
1982	**Safe Play**, 4, 119	D. Brumfield	Rainbow Connection, 4, 121	Native Plunder, 4, 117	11	**1:47.60**	100,800
1981	**Summer Siren**, 4, 117	M. Castaneda	Miss Huntington, 4, 115	Tobin's Rose, 4, 118	10	1:48.60	86,250
1980	**Glorious Song**, 4, 118	C. J. McCarron	Prize Spot, 4, 119	It's in the Air, 4, 125	7	**1:47.60**	80,350
1979	**B. Thoughtful**, 4, 119	D. Pierce	Petron's Love, 4, 117	Island Kiss, 4, 115	8	1:48.80	69,900

1978	**Taisez Vous**, 4, 120	D. Pierce	Drama Critic, 4, 116	Table the Rumor, 4, 117	5	1:49.80	$65,000
1977	***Lucie Manet**, 4, 115	W. Shoemaker	Hail Hilarious, 4, 121	Up to Juliet, 4, 115	7	1:48.20	68,300
1976	**Raise Your Skirts**, 4, 119	W. Shoemaker	Fascinating Girl, 4, 117	Our First Delight, 4, 117	8	1:48.40	50,150
1975	**Chris Evert**, 4, 128	J. Velasquez	Mercy Dee, 4, 116	Lucky Spell, 4, 119	7	1:41.60	35,400

Named for Rancho La Canada where the city of La Crescenta, California, is located; canada means "glen" or "dell." Grade 1 1976-'89. 1$^1/_{16}$ miles 1975.

Lady's Secret Breeders' Cup Handicap

Grade 2 in 2006. Oak Tree at Santa Anita, three-year-olds and up, fillies and mares, 1$^1/_{16}$ miles, dirt. Held October 2, 2005, with a gross value of $235,000. First held in 1993. First graded in 1995. Stakes record 1:40.61 (1994 Hollywood Wildcat).

Year	Winner	Jockey	Second	Third	Strs	Time	1st Purse
2005	**Healthy Addiction**, 4, 115	G. K. Gomez	Star Parade (Arg), 6, 114	Island Fashion, 5, 117	6	1:42.23	$150,000
2004	**Island Fashion**, 4, 120	K. John	Miss Loren (Arg), 6, 116	Elloluv, 4, 118	7	1:43.43	150,000
2003	**Got Koko**, 4, 118	A. O. Solis	‡Azeri, 5, 128	Adoration, 4, 115	6	1:42.92	180,000
2002	**Azeri**, 4, 127	M. E. Smith	Starrer, 4, 115	Mystic Lady, 4, 116	7	1:41.10	130,500
2001	**Queenie Belle**, 4, 116	B. Blanc	Letter of Intent, 4, 116	Nany's Sweep, 5, 116	6	1:43.64	126,240
2000	**Smooth Player**, 4, 116	E. Delahoussaye	Speaking of Time, 4, 109	Bordelaise (Arg), 5, 116	6	1:42.27	126,360
1999	**Manistique**, 4, 123	C. S. Nakatani	Cookin Vickie, 4, 111	Kalosca (Fr), 5, 114	5	1:42.39	125,100
1998	**Magical Allure**, 3, 116	D. R. Flores	Victory Stripes (Arg), 4, 114	Housa Dancer (Fr), 5, 117	8	1:42.55	110,280
1997	**Sharp Cat**, 3, 117	A. O. Solis	Twice the Vice, 6, 122	Minister's Melody, 3, 115	5	1:41.40	109,400
1996	**Top Rung**, 5, 116	E. Fires	Jewel Princess, 4, 122	Sleep Easy, 4, 116	5	1:41.84	109,450
1995	**Borodislew**, 5, 120	G. L. Stevens	Top Rung, 4, 116	Golden Klair (GB), 5, 117	6	1:41.61	74,000
1994	**Hollywood Wildcat**, 4, 124	E. Delahoussaye	Exchange, 6, 121	Dancing Mirage, 3, 113	5	**1:40.61**	61,400
1993	**Hollywood Wildcat**, 3, 117	E. Delahoussaye	Re Toss (Arg), 6, 117	Wedding Ring (Ire), 4, 113	5	1:41.05	61,700

Named for Mr. and Mrs. Eugene V. Klein's 1986 Horse of the Year and '86 Breeders' Cup Distaff (G1) (at Santa Anita Park) winner Lady's Secret (1982 f. by Secretariat). Grade 3 1995. Lady's Secret H. 1993-'95. ‡Elloluv finished second, DQ to fourth, 2003.

La Jolla Handicap

Grade 2 in 2006. Del Mar, three-year-olds, 1$^1/_{16}$ miles, turf. Held August 13, 2005, with a gross value of $150,000. First held in 1937. First graded in 1973. Stakes record 1:40.39 (2003 Singletary).

Year	Winner	Jockey	Second	Third	Strs	Time	1st Purse
2005	**Willow O Wisp**, 3, 121	G. K. Gomez	Juliesugardaddy, 3, 119	El Roblar, 3, 120	7	1:41.45	$90,000
2004	**Blackdoun (Fr)**, 3, 120	C. S. Nakatani	Semi Lost, 3, 116	Bedmar (GB), 3, 113	7	1:41.03	90,000
2003	**Singletary**, 3, 118	P. A. Valenzuela	Devious Boy (GB), 3, 117	Senor Swinger, 3, 120	7	**1:40.39**	90,000
2002	**Inesperado (Fr)**, 3, 118	E. Delahoussaye	Regiment, 3, 121	Mountain Rage, 3, 119	4	1:43.92	90,000
2001	**Marine (GB)**, 3, 117	C. S. Nakatani	Romanceishope, 3, 118	Mister Approval, 3, 113	8	1:41.72	90,000
2000	**Purely Cozzene**, 3, 120	D. R. Flores	Duke of Green (GB), 3, 117	Sign of Hope (GB), 3, 115	9	1:41.50	90,000
1999	**Eagleton**, 3, 119	I. D. Enriquez	In Frank's Honor, 3, 117	Zanetti, 3, 117	9	1:41.89	90,000
1998	**Ladies Din**, 3, 120	G. L. Stevens	Success and Glory (Ire), 3, 116	Lucayan Indian (Ire), 3, 116	7	1:41.94	80,670
1997	**Fantastic Fellow**, 3, 118	A. O. Solis	Worldly Ways (GB), 3, 119	Falkenham (GB), 3, 115	7	1:43.43	85,450
1996	**Ambivalent**, 3, 116	R. R. Douglas	The Barking Shark, 3, 114	Caribbean Pirate, 3, 117	10	1:43.34	82,850
1995	**Petionville**, 3, 120	C. S. Nakatani	Private Interview, 3, 115	Beau Temps (GB), 3, 115	7	1:44.26	74,600
1994	**Marvin's Faith (Ire)**, 3, 114	C. W. Antley	Unfinished Symph, 3, 120	Ocean Crest, 3, 114	7	1:42.38	62,800
1993	**Manny's Prospect**, 3, 115	C. J. McCarron	Golden Slewpy, 3, 116	Hawk Spell, 3, 116	9	1:42.12	64,700
1992	**Blacksburg**, 3, 119	K. Desormeaux	Free At Last, 3, 121	Fax News, 3, 114	9	1:41.60	64,700
1991	**Track Monarch**, 3, 116	P. A. Valenzuela	Soweto (Ire), 3, 116	Persianalli (Ire), 3, 115	6	1:41.91	61,400
1990	**Tight Spot**, 3, 118	E. Delahoussaye	Itsallgreektome, 3, 119	Music Prospector, 3, 118	6	1:41.80	62,100
1989	**River Master**, 3, 115	C. J. McCarron	Tokatee, 3, 113	Art Work, 3, 114	8	1:42.60	65,100
1988	**Perfecting**, 3, 116	G. L. Stevens	Roberto's Dancer, 3, 115	Prove Splendid, 3, 115	8	1:41.60	64,800
1987	**The Medic**, 3, 116	C. J. McCarron	Something Lucky, 3, 120	Savona Tower, 3, 117	11	1:42.20	66,250
1986	**Vernon Castle**, 3, 120	E. Delahoussaye	Tripoli Shores, 3, 117	Marvin's Policy, 3, 116	12	1:35.20	64,650
1985	**Floating Reserve**, 3, 117	P. A. Valenzuela	First Norman, 3, 116	Derby Dawning, 3, 119	9	1:34.60	62,750
1984	**Tights**, 3, 120	C. J. McCarron	Ocean View, 3, 113	Refueled (Ire), 3, 115	6	1:35.60	59,150
1983	**Tanks Brigade**, 3, 120	E. Delahoussaye	Dr. Daly, 3, 121	Pair of Aces, 3, 116	7	1:35.80	50,150
1982	**Hugabay**, 3, 115	K. D. Black	Bargain Balcony, 3, 118	The Captain, 3, 118	8	1:35.60	33,050
	Take the Floor, 3, 115	C. J. McCarron	Craelius, 3, 116	Sword Blade, 3, 115	8	1:35.60	33,050
1981	**Minnesota Chief**, 3, 122	C. J. McCarron	High Counsel, 3, 117	Stancharry, 3, 124	11	1:35.20	40,950
1980	**Aristocratical**, 3, 117	C. J. McCarron	Son of a Dodo, 3, 117	Exploded, 3, 117	9	1:36.20	32,850
1979	**Relaunch**, 3, 117	L. A. Pincay Jr.	Hyannis Port, 3, 122	Pole Position, 3, 124	7	1:35.40	25,600
1978	**Singular**, 3, 114	D. G. McHargue	Misrepresentation, 3, 119	Sea Ride, 3, 114	9	1:35.80	23,150
1977	**Stone Point**, 3, 114	M. Castaneda	Pay the Toll, 3, 114	Windy Dancer, 3, 114	6	1:35.80	18,850
1976	**Today 'n Tomorrow**, 3, 114	D. Pierce	Noble Envoy, 3, 114	Wood Green, 3, 115	8	1:35.20	19,400
1975	**Larrikin**, 3, 123	D. Pierce	Wood Carver, 3, 115	Sibirri, 3, 119	9	1:35.00	16,850
1974	**Lightning Mandate**, 3, 125	A. Pineda	Within Hail, 3, 120	Sea Aglo, 3, 113	6	1:34.40	15,800
1973	**Groshawk**, 3, 125	W. Shoemaker	Dancing Papa, 3, 115	Expression, 3, 123	6	1:34.20	16,300

Named for the resort community of La Jolla, California, located in the San Diego area. Grade 3 1973-2003. La Jolla Mile H. 1937-'65, 1982-'86. La Jolla Mile S. 1977-'81. Not held 1939, 1942-'44. 1 mile 1938-'86. Dirt 1937-'74. Three-year-olds and up 1937-'38, 1945-'46, 1949-'50. Two divisions 1982. Course record 1975.

Lake George Stakes

Grade 3 in 2006. Saratoga Race Course, three-year-olds, fillies, 1¹/₁₆ miles, turf. Held July 29, 2005, with a gross value of $111,000. First held in 1996. First graded in 1998. Stakes record 1:40.11 (1999 Nani Rose).

Year	Winner	Jockey	Second	Third	Strs	Time	1st Purse
2005	**Ready's Gal**, 3, 116	J. R. Velazquez	Dream Lady, 3, 116	Who's Cozy, 3, 116	8	1:41.90	$66,600
2004	**Seducer's Song**, 3, 115	J. D. Bailey	Venturi (GB), 3, 119	Fortunate Damsel, 3, 117	10	1:42.01	68,340
2003	**Film Maker**, 3, 115	E. S. Prado	Ocean Drive, 3, 119	Gal O Gal, 3, 122	11	1:41.80	68,700
2002	**Nunatall (GB)**, 3, 115	J. F. Chavez	Guana (Fr), 3, 117	Mariensky, 3, 117	11	1:40.71	69,000
2001	**Light Dancer**, 3, 117	M. Guidry	Owsley, 3, 117	Cozzy Corner, 3, 115	9	1:41.06	67,050
	Voodoo Dancer, 3, 122	J. D. Bailey	Sadler's Sarah, 3, 117	O K to Dance, 3, 122	9	1:41.45	67,350
2000	**Millie's Quest**, 3, 114	J. R. Velazquez	Shopping for Love, 3, 117	Battenkill, 3, 114	9	1:44.52	70,080
1999	**Nani Rose**, 3, 122	S. J. Sellers	Perfect Sting, 3, 122	Intrigued, 3, 122	8	**1:40.11**	67,680
1998	**Caveat Competor**, 3, 116	J. R. Velazquez	Mysterious Moll, 3, 114	Recording, 3, 121	10	1:41.05	50,760
	Tenski, 3, 114	R. Migliore	Pratella, 3, 114	Camella, 3, 114	8	1:40.86	50,070
1997	**Auntie Mame**, 3, 121	J. D. Bailey	Crab Grass, 3, 114	Innovate, 3, 116	9	1:42.80	51,120
1996	**Memories of Silver**, 3, 112	J. D. Bailey	Clamorosa, 3, 118	Captive Number, 3, 113	10	1:42.98	33,780
	Dynasty, 3, 112	J. D. Bailey	River Antoine, 3, 113	Vashon, 3, 116	8	1:42.26	33,630

Named for a favorite summertime resort in upstate New York, just north of Saratoga Springs. Lake George H. 1999. Two divisions 1996, 1998, 2001.

Lake Placid Stakes

Grade 2 in 2006. Saratoga Race Course, three-year-olds, fillies, 1¹/₈ miles, turf. Held August 19, 2005, with a gross value of $150,000. First held in 1984. First graded in 1986. Stakes record 1:46.33 (1998 Tenski).

Year	Winner	Jockey	Second	Third	Strs	Time	1st Purse
2005	**Naissance Royale (Ire)**, 3, 116	E. S. Prado	My Typhoon (Ire), 3, 118	Victory Lap, 3, 118	6	1:47.14	$90,000
2004	**Spotlight (GB)**, 3, 116	J. D. Bailey	Mambo Slew, 3, 120	Fortunate Damsel, 3, 116	7	1:50.54	90,000
2003	**Sand Springs**, 3, 121	M. Guidry	Indy Five Hundred, 3, 114	Film Maker, 3, 119	10	1:49.03	90,000
2002	**Wonder Again**, 3, 114	E. S. Prado	Riskaverse, 3, 120	Miss Marcia, 3, 114	9	1:49.24	90,000
2001	**Snow Dance**, 3, 116	R. Migliore	Wander Mom, 3, 116	Mystic Lady, 3, 117	12	1:47.42	90,000
2000	**Gaviola**, 3, 122	J. D. Bailey	Good Game, 3, 117	Millie's Quest, 3, 117	11	1:48.04	90,000
1999	**Badouizm**, 3, 113	R. G. Davis	Confessional, 3, 115	Emanating, 3, 115	8	1:46.44	90,000
1998	**Tenski**, 3, 119	R. Migliore	Naskra's de Light, 3, 117	Caveat Competor, 3, 118	12	**1:46.33**	90,000
1997	**Witchful Thinking**, 3, 123	S. J. Sellers	Miss Huff n' Puff, 3, 114	Majestic Sunlight, 3, 114	12	1:47.65	90,000
1996	**Memories of Silver**, 3, 115	J. D. Bailey	Unify, 3, 113	Henlopen, 3, 112	9	1:47.80	68,640
1995	**Class Kris**, 3, 112	P. Day	In a Daydream, 3, 112	Shocking Pleasure, 3, 113	9	1:40.90	67,380
	Bail Out Becky, 3, 115	S. J. Sellers	Fashion Star, 3, 112	Grand Charmer, 3, 120	9	1:41.87	67,680
1994	**Alywow**, 3, 121	M. E. Smith	Irish Forever, 3, 121	Knocknock, 3, 114	9	1:43.81	66,660
	Coronation Cup, 3, 114	J. D. Bailey	Stretch Drive, 3, 114	Golden Tajniak (Ire), 3, 118	7	1:43.88	65,760
1993	**Amal Hayati**, 3, 121	J. D. Bailey	Eloquent Silver, 3, 114	Irving's Girl, 3, 114	10	1:40.97	56,940
	Statuette, 3, 114	M. E. Smith	Icy Warning, 3, 114	Dispute, 3, 118	8	1:41.58	55,980
1992	**Shannkara (Ire)**, 3, 114	M. E. Smith	Tiney Toast, 3, 116	Favored Lady, 3, 114	11	1:41.84	73,380
	Heed, 3, 114	M. E. Smith	Captive Miss, 3, 116	Mystic Hawk, 3, 114	10	1:40.98	72,420
1991	**Jinski's World**, 3, 121	J. A. Santos	Belleofbasinstreet, 3, 114	Verbasle, 3, 114	11	1:41.01	59,760
	Grab the Green, 3, 114	A. T. Cordero Jr.	Shareefa, 3, 121	Irish Linnet, 3, 114	11	1:40.20	59,280
1990	**Jefforee**, 3, 114	J. A. Santos	Toffeefee, 3, 114	Colonial Runner, 3, 114	9	1:49.00	60,030
1989	**Capades**, 3, 121	A. T. Cordero Jr.	To the Lighthouse, 3, 116	Vanities, 3, 114	8	1:41.00	55,620
1988	**Betty Lobelia**, 3, 116	J. A. Santos	Curlew, 3, 114	‡Costly Shoes, 3, 121	8	1:41.60	66,780
	Love You by Heart, 3, 114	R. P. Romero	Another Paddock, 3, 116	Flashy Runner, 3, 114	8	1:41.80	66,780
1987	**Graceful Darby**, 3, 116	J. D. Bailey	Spectacular Bev, 3, 114	Token Gift, 3, 114	7	1:41.40	50,760
1986	**An Empress**, 3, 121	J. A. Santos	Fama, 3, 116	Spring Innocence, 3, 114	11	1:42.00	52,200
1985	**Videogenic**, 3, 114	R. G. Davis	My Regrets (Ire), 3, 114	Forever Command, 3, 116	9	1:41.80	33,720
1984	**Possible Mate**, 3, 114	D. MacBeth	Proud Nova, 3, 114	Miss Audimar, 3, 114	6	1:50.00	26,070

Named for the popular Adirondack mountain resort that has hosted the Winter Olympics twice. Formerly named for Cragwood Stable's 1975 Schuylerville S. (G3) winner Nijana (1973 f. by Nijinsky II). Grade 3 1991-'98. Nijana S. 1984-'97. Lake Placid H. 1998-2004. 1¹/₁₆ miles 1984-'89, 1991-'95. Dirt 1990. Two divisions 1988, 1991-'95. ‡Tunita finished third, DQ to fourth, 1988 (1st Div.).

Lane's End Breeders' Futurity

Grade 1 in 2006. Keeneland Race Course, two-year-olds, 1¹/₁₆ miles, dirt. Held October 8, 2005, with a gross value of $500,000. First held in 1910. First graded in 1973. Stakes record 1:42.23 (1993 Polar Expedition).

Year	Winner	Jockey	Second	Third	Strs	Time	1st Purse
2005	**Dawn of War**, 2, 121	J. Jacinto	Catcominatcha, 2, 121	Stream Cat, 2, 121	12	1:48.77	$310,000
2004	**Consolidator**, 2, 121	R. Bejarano	Patriot Act, 2, 121	Diamond Isle, 2, 121	10	1:43.67	310,000
2003	**Eurosilver**, 2, 121	J. Castellano	Tiger Hunt, 2, 121	Limehouse, 2, 121	11	1:43.42	248,000
2002	**Sky Mesa**, 2, 121	E. S. Prado	Lone Star Sky, 2, 121	Truckle Feature, 2, 121	6	1:46.78	269,576
2001	**Siphonic**, 2, 121	C. J. McCarron	Harlan's Holiday, 2, 121	Metatron, 2, 121	11	1:43.79	281,728
2000	**Arabian Light**, 2, 121	S. J. Sellers	Dollar Bill, 2, 121	Holiday Thunder, 2, 121	10	1:43.18	279,744
1999	**Captain Steve**, 2, 121	G. K. Gomez	Graeme Hall, 2, 121	Millencolin, 2, 121	8	1:42.59	274,040
1998	**Cat Thief**, 2, 121	P. Day	Answer Lively, 2, 121	Yes It's True, 2, 121	8	1:44.17	272,552
1997	**Favorite Trick**, 2, 121	P. Day	Time Limit, 2, 121	Laydown, 2, 121	5	1:43.36	265,112
1996	**Boston Harbor**, 2, 121	J. D. Bailey	Blazing Sword, 2, 121	Haint, 2, 121	5	1:45.31	1,166,005

1995	**Honour and Glory**, 2, 121	P. Day	City by Night, 2, 121	Blushing Jim, 2, 121	10	1:43.33	$139,252
1994	**Tejano Run**, 2, 121	J. D. Bailey	Cinch, 2, 121	Gold Miner, 2, 121	11	1:44.71	71,548
1993	**Polar Expedition**, 2, 121	C. C. Bourque	Goodbye Doeny, 2, 121	Solly's Honor, 2, 121	8	**1:42.23**	122,200
1992	**Mountain Cat**, 2, 121	P. Day	Living Vicariously, 2, 121	Boundlessly, 2, 121	4	1:45.42	1,122,200
1991	**Dance Floor**, 2, 121	C. R. Woods Jr.	Star Recruit, 2, 121	Count the Time, 2, 121	7	1:44.37	122,200
1990	**Sir Bordeaux**, 2, 121	W. S. Ramos	Wall Street Dancer, 2, 121	Fire in Ice, 2, 121	6	1:44.40	145,925
1989	**Slavic**, 2, 121	J. A. Santos	Top Snob, 2, 121	Harry, 2, 121	4	1:44.60	159,770
1988	**Fast Play**, 2, 121	A. T. Cordero Jr.	Lorenzoni, 2, 121	Bio, 2, 121	6	1:45.20	129,350
1987	**Forty Niner**, 2, 121	E. Maple	Hey Pat, 2, 121	Sea Trek, 2, 121	7	1:43.80	104,868
1986	**Orono**, 2, 121	S. Hawley	Alysheba, 2, 121	Pledge Card, 2, 121	10	1:45.20	116,711
1985	**Tasso**, 2, 121	L. A. Pincay Jr.	Regal Dreamer, 2, 121	Thundering Force, 2, 121	11	1:46.00	122,424
1984	**Crater Fire**, 2, 121	D. Montoya	Nickel Back, 2, 121	Cullendale, 2, 121	8	1:45.80	110,474
1983	**Swale**, 2, 121	E. Maple	Spender, 2, 121	Back Bay Barrister, 2, 121	8	1:44.00	108,631
1982	**Highland Park**, 2, 121	J. Lively	Caveat, 2, 121	Bright Baron, 2, 121	12	1:43.60	97,825
1981	**D'Accord**, 2, 121	D. G. McHargue	Lets Dont Fight, 2, 121	Shooting Duck, 2, 121	10	1:44.40	94,575
1980	**Fairway Phantom**, 2, 121	J. Lively	Total Pleasure, 2, 121	Quick Ice, 2, 121	7	1:28.80	94,575
1979	**Gold Stage**, 2, 121	D. Brumfield	Degenerate Jon, 2, 121	Tonka Wakhan, 2, 121	5	1:26.80	81,608
1978	**Strike Your Colors**, 2, 122	E. Delahoussaye	Lot o' Gold, 2, 122	Uncle Fudge, 2, 122	13	1:26.20	92,284
1977	**Gonquin**, 2, 122	F. Olivares	Sunny Songster, 2, 122	Jaycean, 2, 122	7	1:28.00	83,866
1976	**Run Dusty Run**, 2, 122	D. G. McHargue	Banquet Table, 2, 122	Get the Axe, 2, 122	10	1:27.40	84,695
1975	**Harbor Springs**, 2, 122	E. Maple	Best Bee, 2, 122	‡Scrutiny, 2, 122	10	1:27.00	82,046
1974	**Packer Captain**, 2, 122	D. Brumfield	Master Derby, 2, 122	Ruggles Ferry, 2, 122	11	1:25.80	53,277
1973	**Provante**, 2, 122	M. Manganello	Training Table, 2, 122	Wage Raise, 2, 122	10	1:27.20	48,327

Named in honor of Kentucky breeders. Sponsored by W. S. Farish's Lane's End, located in Versailles, Kentucky 1997-2005. Grade 3 1973-'75. Grade 2 1976-2003. Held at Kentucky Association 1910-'30. Held at Old Latonia 1931-'33. Held at Churchill Downs 1943-'45. Not held 1934-'37. 4 furlongs 1910-'11. 4½ furlongs 1912. 5 furlongs 1913-'16. About 6 furlongs 1917-'33. 6 furlongs 1938-'49. 7 furlongs 1950-'55. About 7 furlongs 1956-'80. ‡Vuelo finished third, DQ to fourth, 1975. Winner's purse includes $1-million bonus from the Kentucky Thoroughbred Development Fund 1992, 1996.

Lane's End Stakes

Grade 2 in 2006. Turfway Park, three-year-olds, 1⅛ miles, all weather. Held March 25, 2006, with a gross value of $500,000. First held in 1972. First graded in 1984. Stakes record 1:46.70 (1991 Hansel).

Year	Winner	Jockey	Second	Third	Strs	Time	1st Purse
2006	**With a City**, 3, 121	B. Blanc	Seaside Retreat, 3, 121	Malameeze, 3, 121	12	1:51.11	$300,000
2005	**Flower Alley**, 3, 121	J. F. Chavez	Wild Desert, 3, 121	Mr Sword, 3, 121	9	1:50.33	300,000
2004	**Sinister G**, 3, 121	P. R. Toscano	Tricky Taboo, 3, 121	Little Matth Man, 3, 121	11	1:50.71	300,000
2003	**New York Hero**, 3, 121	N. Arroyo Jr.	Eugene's Third Son, 3, 121	Champali, 3, 121	9	1:50.68	300,000
2002	**Perfect Drift**, 3, 121	E. Delahoussaye	Azillion (Ire), 3, 121	Request for Parole, 3, 121	8	1:48.83	300,000
2001	**Balto Star**, 3, 121	M. Guidry	Halo's Stride, 3, 121	Mongoose, 3, 121	9	1:47.23	360,000
2000	**Globalize**, 3, 121	F. C. Torres	Elite Mercedes, 3, 121	Rollin With Nolan, 3, 121	10	1:49.16	360,000
1999	**Stephen Got Even**, 3, 121	S. J. Sellers	K One King, 3, 121	Epic Honor, 3, 121	8	1:49.03	450,000
1998	**Event of the Year**, 3, 121	R. A. Baze	Yarrow Brae, 3, 121	Truluck, 3, 121	10	1:47.12	360,000
1997	**Concerto**, 3, 121	C. H. Marquez Jr.	Jack Flash, 3, 121	Shammy Davis, 3, 121	10	1:48.23	360,000
1996	**Roar**, 3, 121	M. E. Smith	Ensign Ray, 3, 121	Victory Speech, 3, 121	9	1:49.70	360,000
1995	**†Serena's Song**, 3, 116	C. S. Nakatani	Tejano Run, 3, 121	Mecke, 3, 121	8	1:49.65	360,000
1994	**Polar Expedition**, 3, 121	C. C. Bourque	Powis Castle, 3, 121	Chimes Band, 3, 121	11	1:49.03	360,000
1993	**Prairie Bayou**, 3, 121	C. J. McCarron	Proudest Romeo, 3, 121	Miner's Mark, 3, 121	9	1:50.97	360,000
1992	**Lil E. Tee**, 3, 121	P. Day	Vying Victor, 3, 121	Treekster, 3, 121	11	1:53.44	300,000
1991	**Hansel**, 3, 121	J. D. Bailey	Richman, 3, 121	Wilder Than Ever, 3, 121	11	**1:46.70**	300,000
1990	**Summer Squall**, 3, 121	P. Day	Bright Again, 3, 121	Yonder, 3, 121	10	1:49.40	300,000
1989	**Western Playboy**, 3, 121	P. Day	Feather Ridge, 3, 121	Mercedes Won, 3, 121	12	1:49.00	300,000
1988	**Kingpost**, 3, 121	E. J. Sipus Jr.	Stalwars, 3, 121	Brian's Time, 3, 121	11	1:50.80	300,000
1987	**J. T.'s Pet**, 3, 121	P. Day	Faster Than Sound, 3, 121	Homebuilder, 3, 121	12	1:42.80	300,000
1986	**Broad Brush**, 3, 121	V. A. Bracciale Jr.	Miracle Wood, 3, 121	Bachelor Beau, 3, 121	12	1:44.20	210,000
1985	**Banner Bob**, 3, 121	K. K. Allen	Image of Greatness, 3, 121	Roo Art, 3, 121	10	1:42.00	227,500
1984	**At the Threshold**, 3, 121	P. Day	Bold Southerner, 3, 121	The Wedding Guest, 3, 121	12	1:42.80	195,000
1983	**Marfa**, 3, 120	J. Velasquez	Noble Home, 3, 120	Hail to Rome, 3, 120	12	1:42.40	151,515
1982	**Good n' Dusty**, 3, 120	M. T. Moran	Fast Gold, 3, 120	Cupecoy's Joy, 3, 115	12	1:44.60	125,450
1981	**Mythical Ruler**, 3, 114	K. B. Wirth	Classic Go Go, 3, 122	Iron Gem, 3, 115	10	1:38.00	33,210
1980	**Major Run**, 3, 116	M. S. Sellers	Ray's Word, 3, 122	Misty Bell, 3, 113	8	1:37.60	18,740
	Spruce Needles, 3, 116	J. C. Espinoza	Avenger M., 3, 122	Summer Advocate, 3, 113	6	1:36.20	18,440
1979	**Lot o' Gold**, 3, 122	D. Brumfield	Julie's Dancer, 3, 113	Will Henry, 3, 113	8	1:37.60	29,030
1978	**Five Star General**, 3, 113	J. C. Espinoza	As in Elbow, 3, 113	Doc's Rock, 3, 119	9	1:37.80	12,900
	Raymond Earl, 3, 113	J. C. Espinoza	Washington County, 3, 119	Shake Rattl'n Fly, 3, 113	10	1:38.80	12,960
1977	**Smiley's Dream**, 3, 114	W. Destefano	Lighten the Load, 3, 111	Vestry's Best, 3, 111	8	1:39.40	12,788
	Bob's Dusty, 3, 122	J. C. Espinoza	A Letter to Harry, 3, 116	John Washington, 3, 116	9	1:38.80	12,817
1976	**Inca Roca**, 3, 122	W. Nemeti	Here Comes Jo, 3, 116	Brentwood Prince, 3, 116	6	1:37.40	18,780
1975	**Naughty Jake**, 3, 119	G. Vasquez	Promenade Left, 3, 114	Jim Dan Bob, 3, 112	8	1:40.00	15,840
	Ambassador's Image, 3, 122	E. Snell	Clarence Henry, 3, 116	Upper Need, 3, 116	8	1:38.40	15,870
1974	**King of Rome**, 3, 112	K. Wirth	Consigliori, 3, 112	Aroyoport, 3, 116	8	1:44.60	12,204
	Aglorite, 3, 119	J. Beech Jr.	Joint Agreement, 3, 116	Robard, 3, 112	8	1:45.40	12,236

1973	**Jacks Chevron**, 3, 117	B. Phelps	Trip Stop, 3, 116	Mr. Champ, 3, 116	9	1:42.00	$9,785
	Bootlegger's Pet, 3, 116	M. Solomone	Out Ahead, 3, 117	Babingtons Image, 3, 113	8	1:41.00	9,720

Originally designed as a prep race that "spiraled up" to the Blue Grass S. (G1) and the Kentucky Derby (G1). Sponsored by W. S. Farish's Lane's End, located in Versailles, Kentucky 2002-'05. Formerly sponsored by James B. Beam Distilling Co. of Clermont, Kentucky 1982-'98. Formerly sponsored by James McIngvale's Gallery Furniture Co. of Houston 1999. Spiral S. 1972-'81. Jim Beam Spiral S. 1982-'83. Jim Beam S. 1984-'98. Gallery Furniture.com S. 1999. Turfway Spiral S. 2000-'01. Lane's End Spiral S. 2002. Host track known as Latonia Race Course 1972-'85. 1 mile 1972-'81. 1$^1/_{16}$ miles 1982-'87. Dirt 1972-2005. Two divisions 1973-'75, 1977-'78, 1980. †Denotes female.

La Prevoyante Handicap

Grade 2 in 2006. Calder Race Course, three-year-olds and up, fillies and mares, 1$^1/_2$ miles, turf. Held December 17, 2005, with a gross value of $200,000. First held in 1976. First graded in 1982. Stakes record 2:25.20 (1988 Singular Bequest).

Year	Winner	Jockey	Second	Third	Strs	Time	1st Purse
2005	**Film Maker**, 5, 119	E. S. Prado	Kate Winslet, 4, 115	Noble Stella (Ger), 4, 114	12	2:27.75	$120,000
2004	**Arvada (GB)**, 4, 117	E. S. Prado	Humaita (Ger), 4, 119	Honey Ryder, 3, 113	11	2:27.19	120,000
2003	**Volga (Ire)**, 5, 119	R. Migliore	Lady Annaliese (NZ), 4, 116	Lost Appeal, 5, 115	11	2:26.13	120,000
2002	**New Economy**, 4, 113	R. Homeister Jr.	Jennasietta, 4, 112	Tweedside, 4, 114	12	2:28.55	120,000
2001	**Krisada**, 5, 115	P. Day	Sweetest Thing, 3, 115	Great Fever (Fr), 4, 113	10	2:26.63	90,000
2000	**Prospectress**, 5, 114	J. D. Bailey	Innuendo (Ire), 5, 114	Orange Sunset (Ire), 4, 114	10	2:26.97	90,000
1999	**Coretta (Ire)**, 5, 120	J. A. Santos	Idle Rich, 4, 116	St. Bernadette (Per), 3, 114	8	2:27.27	90,000
1998	**Coretta (Ire)**, 4, 117	J. A. Santos	Starry Dreamer, 4, 114	dh-Cuando, 4, 115 dh-Tedarshana (GB), 4, 113	12	2:26.67	90,000
1997	**Last Approach**, 5, 110	J. A. Krone	Flying Concert, 4, 118	Grey Way, 4, 110	6	2:39.13	90,000
1996	**Ampulla**, 5, 122	S. J. Sellers	Miss Caerleona (Fr), 4, 114	Electric Society (Ire), 5, 117	8	2:27.50	90,000
1995	**Interim (GB)**, 4, 116	C. S. Nakatani	Northern Emerald, 5, 116	Caromana, 4, 114	10	2:26.38	90,000
1994	**Abigailthewife**, 5, 114	J. A. Santos	Trampoli, 5, 118	Market Booster, 5, 118	14	2:28.91	90,000
	Trampoli, 5, 120	M. E. Smith	Putthepowdertoit, 4, 115	Adoryphar, 5, 112	14	2:28.14	90,000
1993	**Lemhi Go**, 5, 112	M. A. Gonzalez	Indian Chris (Brz), 6, 112	Silvered, 6, 118	6	2:37.53	60,000
1992	**Sardaniya (Ire)**, 4, 113	J. Cruguet	Flaming Torch (Ire), 5, 112	Expensiveness, 4, 111	9	2:29.62	90,000
1991	**Rigamajig**, 5, 114	J. F. Chavez	Roseate Tern (GB), 5, 117	Ahead (GB), 4, 112	11	2:26.10	60,000
1990	**Yestday's Kisses**, 4, 113	W. H. McCauley	Black Tulip (Fr), 5, 115	Coolawin, 4, 116	11	2:30.80	60,000
1989	**Judy's Red Shoes**, 6, 120	D. Valiente	Gaily Gaily (Ire), 6, 111	Beauty Cream, 6, 118	14	2:26.40	90,000
1988	**Singular Bequest**, 5, 115	E. Fires	Autumn Glitter, 5, 114	Green Oasis (Fr), 6, 114	9	**2:25.20**	120,000
1987	**Lotka**, 4, 121	E. Maple	Bonne Ile (GB), 6, 116	After Party, 5, 112	13	2:36.00	120,000
1986	**Powder Break**, 5, 116	J. A. Santos	Shocker T., 4, 119	Devalois (Fr), 4, 118	9	2:30.40	120,000
1985	**Persian Tiara (Ire)**, 5, 120	J. Terry	Dictina (Fr), 4, 117	Silver in Flight, 5, 115	11	2:28.80	85,335
	Sabin, 5, 126	D. Brumfield	Key Dancer, 4, 118	Burst of Colors, 5, 117	11	2:27.40	72,285
1984	**Bolt From the Blue**, 4, 113	J. Samyn	Bezique (Ire), 7, 112	Gabfest, 5, 110	9	2:33.40	51,960
	Sabin, 4, 120	E. Maple	Grunip (GB), 5, 113	Pat's Joy, 6, 118	10	2:32.80	52,260
1983	**London Lil**, 4, 117	A. Smith Jr.	Dana Calqui (Arg), 5, 114	Middle Stage, 4, 116	14	1:47.40	54,680
	Fact Finder, 4, 115	A. T. Cordero Jr.	Sunny Sparkler, 4, 122	Seaholme, 5, 112	11	1:48.00	53,780
	Canaille (Ire), 5, 118	A. T. Cordero Jr.	Castle Royale, 5, 115	Genuine Diamond, 4, 113	13	1:46.60	54,380
1982	**Judgable Gypsy**, 4, 114	J. O'Driscoll	Castle Royale, 4, 110	Imayrrahtoo, 5, 110	12	1:50.20	42,165
	Just a Game (Ire), 6, 123	A. T. Cordero Jr.	Sweetest Chant, 4, 115	Irish Joy, 4, 114	9	1:50.40	41,655
1981	**Mairzy Doates**, 5, 121	O. B. Aviles	Champagne Ginny, 4, 118	Knightly Noble, 4, 110	11	1:47.20	41,670
	Deuces Over Seven, 4, 114	G. Gallitano	Little Bonny (Ire), 4, 121	Quick as Lightning, 4, 119	8	1:48.00	40,950
1980	**Impetuous Gal**, 5, 113	E. Fires	Tangerine Doll, 4, 118	Highland Gypsy, 4, 116	5	1:52.20	23,775
	Jolie Dutch, 4, 116	B. Thornburg	Reina Del Rulo (Arg), 7, 116	Behave Taurian, 4, 108	6	1:54.60	23,925
1979	**Unreality**, 5, 119	J. D. Bailey	Excitable, 4, 117	Sans Arc, 5, 117	12	1:48.20	37,200
1978	**Len's Determined**, 4, 114	A. Smith Jr.	Regal Gal, 5, 120	Carolina Moon, 6, 114	12	1:48.40	37,200
1976	**Forty Nine Sunsets**, 3, 116	C. Marquez	Cycylya Zee, 3, 121	Satan's Cheer, 4, 116	14	1:46.00	27,510
	Redundancy, 5, 117	A. Haldar	Katonka, 4, 125	Yes Dear Maggy, 4, 121	12	1:41.60	26,040

Named for Jean-Louis Levesque's 1972 Canadian Horse of the Year La Prevoyante (1970 f. by Buckpasser). Grade 3 1982-'87. La Prevoyante Invitational H. 1986-'93. Not held 1977. 1$^1/_{16}$ miles 1976. About 1$^1/_8$ miles 1978-'79, 1981-'83. 1$^1/_8$ miles 1980. About 1$^1/_2$ miles 1992. Dirt 1980, 1987, 1990, 1993, 1997. Two divisions 1980-'82, 1984-'85. Three divisions 1983. Held in January and December 1976, 1994. Dead heat for third 1998.

Las Cienegas Handicap

Grade 3 in 2006. Santa Anita Park, four-year-olds and up, fillies and mares, about 6$^1/_2$ furlongs, turf. Held April 16, 2006, with a gross value of $112,900. First held in 1974. First graded in 1992. Stakes record 1:11.66 (2005 Elusive Diva).

Year	Winner	Jockey	Second	Third	Strs	Time	1st Purse
2006	**Cambiocorsa**, 4, 120	J. K. Court	Lock And Key (Ire), 4, 116	Sandra's Rose, 4, 115	9	1:12.60	$67,740
2005	**Elusive Diva**, 4, 117	P. A. Valenzuela	Quero Quero, 5, 116	Winendynme, 4, 116	9	**1:11.66**	66,660
2004	**Etoile Montante**, 4, 121	J. Santiago	Dedication (Fr), 5, 118	Any for Love (Arg), 6, 115	9	1:13.32	67,680
2003	**Heat Haze (GB)**, 4, 114	J. Valdivia Jr.	Icantgoforthat, 4, 114	Paga (Arg), 6, 116	8	1:13.11	66,000
2002	**Rolly Polly (Ire)**, 4, 119	K. Desormeaux	Penny Marie, 6, 119	Twin Set (Ger), 5, 116	7	1:12.55	65,100
2001	**Go Go**, 4, 118	E. Delahoussaye	Separata (Chi), 5, 118	Dianehill (Ire), 5, 116	8	1:13.54	65,700
2000	**Evening Promise (GB)**, 4, 114	D. Sorenson	La Madame (Chi), 5, 116	Reciclada (Chi), 5, 113	5	1:13.66	63,840
1999	**Desert Lady (Ire)**, 4, 118	C. S. Nakatani	Hula Queen, 5, 112	Bella Chiarra, 4, 115	7	1:13.55	65,640
1998	**Dance Parade**, 4, 119	K. Desormeaux	Advancing Star, 5, 121	Imroz, 4, 115	6	1:13.60	64,800
1997	**Advancing Star**, 4, 116	G. L. Stevens	Ski Dancer, 5, 118	Grab the Prize, 5, 116	6	1:12.50	96,550

1996	**Ski Dancer**, 4, 117	G. L. Stevens	Klassy Kim, 5, 117	Igotrhythm, 4, 117	6	1:14.59	$64,300
1995	**Marina Park (GB)**, 5, 119	A. O. Solis	Pirate's Revenge, 4, 116	Rabiadella, 4, 118	9	1:13.77	63,175
1994	**Mamselle Bebette**, 4, 120	C. J. McCarron	Cool Air, 4, 122	Bel's Starlet, 7, 122	5	1:13.05	45,975
1993	**Glen Kate (Ire)**, 6, 121	C. A. Black	Heart of Joy, 6, 121	Worldly Possession, 5, 115	6	1:12.71	61,225
1992	**Heart of Joy**, 5, 123	C. J. McCarron	Sheltered View, 4, 114	Crystal Gazing, 4, 119	9	1:12.72	63,475
1991	**Flower Girl (GB)**, 4, 116	E. Delahoussaye	Mahaska, 4, 117	Survive, 7, 117	8	1:13.30	49,650
1990	**Stylish Star**, 4, 117	C. J. McCarron	‡Hot Novel, 4, 118	Warning Zone, 5, 116	6	1:13.00	47,100
1989	**Imperial Star (GB)**, 5, 115	R. G. Davis	Down Again, 5, 117	Serve n' Volley (GB), 5, 115	10	1:15.60	50,450
1988	**Hairless Heiress**, 5, 117	G. L. Stevens	Chick Or Two, 5, 115	Aromacor, 5, 113	12	1:15.00	52,050
1987	**Lichi (Chi)**, 7, 115	G. Baze	An Empress, 4, 119	Aromacor, 4, 112	7	1:14.40	38,150
1986	**Shywing**, 4, 120	L. A. Pincay Jr.	Reigning Countess, 4, 114	Her Royalty, 5, 121	4	1:18.00	37,550
1985	**Danzadar**, 4, 114	D. A. Lozoya	Pampas (Ire), 5, 120	Natural Summit, 4, 116	5	1:14.00	37,250
1984	**Tangent (NZ)**, 4, 120	G. Barrera	Irish O'Brien, 6, 118	Frieda Frame, 6, 118	8	1:15.00	39,600
1983	**Faneuil Lass**, 4, 120	L. A. Pincay Jr.	Queen of Song, 4, 115	Waving, 4, 117	9	1:17.40	41,200
1982	**Excitable Lady**, 4, 119	E. Delahoussaye	‡Peppy's Lucky Girl, 5, 117	Glitter Hitter, 4, 119	7	1:14.40	37,450
1981	**Wishing Well**, 6, 122	F. Toro	Back At Two, 4, 114	Peppy's Lucky Girl, 4, 113	9	1:13.40	34,250
1980	**Great Lady M.**, 5, 116	P. A. Valenzuela	Wishing Well, 5, 120	Billie Bets, 4, 115	10	1:14.80	28,100
1979	**Pressing Date**, 5, 114	A. T. Cordero Jr.	Country Queen, 4, 121	Critic, 5, 114	8	1:16.40	27,550
1978	**Drama Critic**, 4, 119	D. G. McHargue	Perils of Pauline, 4, 118	Little Happiness, 4, 120	10	1:14.00	27,800
1977	**Dancing Femme**, 4, 117	W. Shoemaker	Winter Solstice, 5, 123	Katonka, 5, 120	4	1:13.60	24,600
1976	**Life's Hope**, 3, 116	L. A. Pincay Jr.	Sure Fire, 3, 119	Private Signal, 3, 114	7	1:09.40	20,100
1974	**Woodland Pines**, 5, 120	D. Pierce	Pataha Prince, 9, 122	dh-Pontoise, 4, 116 dh-Single Agent, 6, 116	9	1:13.00	18,650

Named for Rancho Las Cienegas in southwestern Los Angeles County, California; las cienegas means "the swamps." Las Cienegas S. 1976. Las Cienegas Breeders' Cup H. 1992-'95. Not held 1975. 6 furlongs 1976. 6½ furlongs 1979, 1982-'83, 1986. Dirt 1976, 1979, 1982-'83, 1986. Three-year-olds 1976. Both sexes 1974-'76. Dead heat for third 1974. ‡Queen of Cornwall finished second, DQ to sixth, 1982. ‡Stormy But Valid finished second, DQ to fifth, 1990.

Las Flores Handicap

Grade 3 in 2006. Santa Anita Park, four-year-olds and up, fillies and mares, 6 furlongs, dirt. Held February 25, 2006, with a gross value of $107,000. First held in 1951. First graded in 1973. Stakes record 1:08.02 (2004 Ema Bovary [Chi]).

Year	Winner	Jockey	Second	Third	Strs	Time	1st Purse
2006	**Behaving Badly**, 5, 120	V. Espinoza	Awesome Lady, 5, 114	Spirit to Spare, 5, 111	6	1:09.09	$64,200
2005	**Miss Terrible (Arg)**, 6, 116	A. O. Solis	Puxa Saco, 5, 115	Mazella, 4, 113	8	1:09.47	65,760
2004	**Ema Bovary (Chi)**, 5, 121	R. M. Gonzalez	Buffythecenterfold, 4, 117	Coconut Girl, 5, 113	6	**1:08.02**	64,380
2003	**Spring Meadow**, 4, 117	C. S. Nakatani	Brisquette, 5, 116	dh-September Secret, 4, 116 dh-Wild Tickle, 5, 117	7	1:10.20	81,300
2002	**Above Perfection**, 4, 117	C. S. Nakatani	Kalookan Queen, 6, 122	Enchanted Woods, 5, 117	4	1:08.65	78,642
2001	**Go Go**, 4, 116	E. Delahoussaye	La Feminn, 5, 120	Cover Gal, 4, 119	6	1:08.83	80,400
2000	**Show Me the Stage**, 4, 118	K. Desormeaux	Theresa's Tizzy, 6, 117	Woodman's Dancer, 6, 115	6	1:08.54	79,440
1999	**Enjoy the Moment**, 4, 117	L. A. Pincay Jr.	Tomorrows Sunshine, 5, 114	Closed Escrow, 6, 116	5	1:08.55	78,720
1998	**Funallover**, 4, 114	A. O. Solis	Advancing Star, 5, 122	Zenda's Diablo, 4, 109	7	1:09.10	79,800
1997	**Our Summer Bid**, 5, 114	J. Silva	Track Gal, 6, 120	Advancing Star, 4, 116	6	1:09.15	80,100
1996	**Igotrhythm**, 4, 115	C. S. Nakatani	Miss L Attack, 6, 115	Little Blue Sheep, 4, 115	7	1:08.88	81,100
1995	**Desert Stormer**, 5, 117	K. Desormeaux	Velvet Tulip, 5, 114	Flying in the Lane, 4, 114	5	1:08.49	59,725
1994	**Mamselle Bebette**, 4, 118	C. S. Nakatani	Arches of Gold, 5, 120	Aspasante, 5, 114	7	1:08.32	47,475
1993	**Bountiful Native**, 5, 121	P. A. Valenzuela	Freedom Cry, 5, 119	Forest Fealty, 6, 112	6	1:09.42	60,325
1992	**Forest Fealty**, 5, 116	M. A. Pedroza	Middlefork Rapids, 4, 118	Phil's Illusion, 5, 113	9	1:08.87	49,350
1991	**Classic Value**, 5, 116	G. L. Stevens	Devil's Orchid, 4, 116	Hasty Pasty, 6, 116	6	1:10.30	60,325
1990	**Stormy But Valid**, 4, 117	E. Delahoussaye	Survive, 6, 117	Warning Zone, 5, 119	7	1:08.20	47,850
1989	**Very Subtle**, 5, 124	L. A. Pincay Jr.	Sadie B. Fast, 4, 113	Comical Cat, 4, 116	3	1:08.60	44,350
1987	**Flying Julia**, 4, 112	F. Olivares	Pine Tree Lane, 5, 122	Le l'Argent, 5, 119	9	1:10.20	48,850
	Pine Tree Lane, 5, 124	A. T. Cordero Jr.	Rangoon Ruby (Ire), 5, 117	Her Royalty, 6, 120	8	1:09.80	38,350
1986	**Baroness Direct**, 5, 120	E. Delahoussaye	Her Royalty, 5, 120	Aerturas (Fr), 5, 113	7	1:08.40	38,850
1985	**Foggy Nation**, 5, 117	L. A. Pincay Jr.	Lovlier Linda, 5, 124	Tangent (NZ), 5, 122	5	1:09.60	37,250
1984	**Bara Lass**, 5, 122	P. A. Valenzuela	Champagne Isle, 4, 116	Bally Knockan, 5, 114	9	1:09.40	40,100
1983	**Matching**, 5, 122	L. A. Pincay Jr.	Bara Lass, 4, 115	Past Forgetting, 5, 122	7	1:09.00	38,650
1982	**Back At Two**, 5, 117	C. J. McCarron	Abisinia (Ven), 5, 116	Excitable Lady, 4, 120	5	1:12.40	37,750
1981	**Shine High**, 5, 114	T. Lipham	Image of Reality, 5, 119	Parsley, 5, 117	7	1:08.60	32,600
1979	**Terlingua**, 3, 121	D. G. McHargue	Powder Room, 4, 113	Ideal Exchange, 3, 116	7	1:08.40	32,800
1978	**Sweet Little Lady**, 3, 117	D. G. McHargue	Grenzen, 3, 122	Great Lady M., 3, 114	8	1:09.00	33,200
1977	**Winter Solstice**, 5, 120	D. G. McHargue	Squander, 3, 114	Don's Music, 3, 115	6	1:11.80	26,100
	My Juliet, 5, 128	A. S. Black	Just a Kick, 5, 121	Juliana F., 4, 115	7	1:10.20	26,750
1976	**Just a Kick**, 4, 114	E. Munoz	Raise Your Skirts, 4, 121	Mismoyola, 6, 115	9	1:09.20	21,550
1975	**Lucky Spell**, 4, 120	J. E. Tejeira	‡*Tizna, 6, 123	Impressive Style, 6, 122	8	1:09.60	21,700
1973	**Sandy Blue**, 3, 120	D. Pierce	Market Again, 5, 112	Impressive Style, 4, 120	10	1:08.60	22,150

Named for the 1844 land grant of Rancho Las Flores, located in Tehama County, California; flores means "flowers." Not graded 1975-'84. Las Flores Breeders' Cup H. 1990-'95. Not held 1953, 1969, 1971, 1974, 1980, 1988. Three-year-olds and up 1951-'52, 1956-'68, 1970, 1977 (December), 1978, 1987 (December). Two-year-olds and up 1972 (December), 1973, 1983. Held in January and December 1977, 1987. Dead heat for third 2003. ‡Modus Vivendi finished second, DQ to fourth, 1975.

Las Palmas Handicap

Grade 2 in 2006. Oak Tree at Santa Anita, three-year-olds and up, fillies and mares, 1 mile, turf. Held November 5, 2005, with a gross value of $150,000. First held in 1969. First graded in 1973. Stakes record 1:33.59 (2005 Mea Domina).

Year	Winner	Jockey	Second	Third	Strs	Time	1st Purse
2005	**Mea Domina**, 4, 118	T. Baze	Elusive Diva, 4, 119	Star Parade (Arg), 6, 115	10	**1:33.59**	$90,000
2004	**Theater R. N.**, 4, 114	R. R. Douglas	Lots of Hope (Brz), 4, 117	Good Student (Arg), 4, 114	7	1:47.81	90,000
2002	**Tates Creek**, 4, 120	J. D. Bailey	Voodoo Dancer, 4, 121	Magic Mission (GB), 4, 113	8	1:47.69	120,000
2001	**Golden Apples (Ire)**, 3, 115	G. K. Gomez	Dancingonice, 5, 113	Janet (GB), 4, 120	9	1:46.61	150,000
2000	**Smooth Player**, 4, 117	E. Delahoussaye	Beautiful Noise, 4, 115	Happyanunoit (NZ), 5, 121	10	1:46.99	105,000
1999	**Sapphire Ring (GB)**, 4, 118	G. L. Stevens	Cyrillic, 4, 117	Country Garden (GB), 4, 113	11	1:48.20	150,000
1998	**Sonja's Faith (Ire)**, 4, 115	E. Ramsammy	See You Soon (Fr), 4, 116	Idealistic Cause, 4, 113	6	1:48.92	90,000
1997	**Real Connection**, 6, 115	G. F. Almeida	Toda Una Dama (Arg), 4, 114	Luna Wells (Ire), 4, 119	9	1:47.60	75,000
1996	**Wandesta (GB)**, 5, 120	C. S. Nakatani	Real Connection, 5, 113	Alpride (Ire), 5, 120	5	1:46.72	79,700
1995	**Onceinabluemamoon**, 4, 116	B. Blanc	Yearly Tour, 4, 117	Don't Read My Lips, 4, 117	9	1:50.34	76,400
1994	**Aube Indienne (Fr)**, 4, 115	K. Desormeaux	Queens Court Queen, 5, 115	Skimble, 5, 116	5	1:49.62	61,300
1993	**Miatuschka**, 5, 114	C. A. Black	Skimble, 4, 115	Potridee (Arg), 4, 115	6	1:47.98	62,600
1992	**Super Staff**, 4, 116	K. Desormeaux	Flawlessly, 4, 124	Re Toss (Arg), 5, 115	7	1:46.89	77,750
1991	**Kostroma (Ire)**, 5, 117	K. Desormeaux	Kikala (GB), 5, 113	Campagnarde (Arg), 4, 118	6	1:43.92	80,750
1990	**Little Brianne**, 5, 115	J. A. Garcia	Double Wedge, 5, 117	Reluctant Guest, 4, 121	5	1:46.80	93,200
1989	**Nikishka**, 4, 116	E. Delahoussaye	No Review, 4, 117	Agirlfromars, 3, 111	7	1:46.60	96,800
1988	**Annoconnor**, 4, 120	C. A. Black	No Review, 3, 114	Goodbye Halo, 3, 120	7	1:47.00	97,800
1987	**Autumn Glitter**, 4, 116	P. Day	Galunpe (Ire), 4, 119	Festivity, 4, 117	8	1:50.40	91,800
1986	**Outstandingly**, 4, 118	G. L. Stevens	Shywing, 4, 118	Justicara (Ire), 5, 118	6	1:47.60	63,400
1985	**Estrapade**, 5, 124	W. Shoemaker	L'Attrayante (Fr), 5, 118	Johnica, 4, 118	11	1:47.20	69,100
1984	**Fenny Rough (Ire)**, 4, 118	K. D. Black	Comedy Act, 5, 117	Pride of Rosewood (NZ), 6, 115	8	1:47.40	78,800
1983	**Castilla**, 4, 121	C. J. McCarron	Night Fire, 4, 113	Berry Bush, 6, 117	7	1:49.20	64,300
1982	**Berry Bush**, 5, 115	M. Castaneda	Satin Ribera, 5, 115	Northern Fable, 4, 115	13	1:47.40	70,400
1981	**Ack's Secret**, 5, 119	D. G. McHargue	Queen to Conquer, 5, 123	Berry Bush, 4, 118	9	1:47.00	50,500
1980	**Ack's Secret**, 4, 114	P. A. Valenzuela	A Thousand Stars, 5, 119	Princess Toby, 5, 117	9	1:46.00	40,400
1979	**High Pheasant**, 4, 114	F. Olivares	Prize Spot, 3, 119	Axe Me Dear, 5, 114	7	1:54.00	39,700
1978	**Grenzen**, 3, 119	L. A. Pincay Jr.	Country Queen, 3, 119	Drama Critic, 4, 123	8	1:48.40	39,400
1977	**Swingtime**, 5, 119	F. Toro	Theia (Fr), 4, 113	Summertime Promise, 5, 118	6	1:47.20	25,650
1976	**Vagabonda**, 5, 118	O. Vergara	*Bastonera II, 5, 122	*Accra II, 4, 115	12	1:48.60	34,500
1975	**Charger's Star**, 5, 116	W. Shoemaker	*Tizna, 6, 126	Hinterland, 5, 116	8	1:47.20	26,000
1974	**Lucky Spell**, 3, 117	J. E. Tejeira	Bold Ballet, 3, 117	Fresh Pepper, 4, 112	10	1:47.40	26,750
1973	**Minstrel Miss**, 6, 123	D. Pierce	*Cruz de Roble, 6, 113	Veiled Desire, 4, 111	10	1:47.80	27,100

Named for Las Palmas (1929 f. by Bon Homme), winner of the first race run at Santa Anita Park on December 25, 1934. Grade 3 1973-'82. Not held 2003. 1 1/16 miles 1969, 1982. 1 1/8 miles 1970-'81, 1983-2004. Dirt 1969, 1979.

Las Virgenes Stakes

Grade 1 in 2006. Santa Anita Park, three-year-olds, fillies, 1 mile, dirt. Held February 11, 2006, with a gross value of $250,000. First held in 1983. First graded in 1985. Stakes record 1:35.14 (1994 Lakeway).

Year	Winner	Jockey	Second	Third	Strs	Time	1st Purse
2006	**Balance**, 3, 120	V. Espinoza	Wild Fit, 3, 120	Itty Bitty Pretty, 3, 120	7	1:36.54	$150,000
2005	**Sharp Lisa**, 3, 119	C. S. Nakatani	Memorette, 3, 119	Charming Colleen, 3, 117	6	1:35.64	150,000
2004	**A. P. Adventure**, 3, 118	A. O. Solis	Hollywood Story, 3, 120	Friendly Michelle, 3, 116	8	1:36.50	150,000
2003	**Composure**, 3, 120	J. D. Bailey	Elloluv, 3, 122	Watching You, 3, 116	6	1:36.13	120,000
2002	**You**, 3, 122	J. D. Bailey	Habibti, 3, 122	Tali'sluckybusride, 3, 120	6	1:36.84	120,000
2001	**Golden Ballet**, 3, 122	C. J. McCarron	Two Item Limit, 3, 120	Affluent, 3, 114	7	1:36.89	120,000
2000	**Surfside**, 3, 122	P. Day	Spain, 3, 115	Rings a Chime, 3, 116	4	1:37.00	120,000
1999	**Excellent Meeting**, 3, 122	K. Desormeaux	Tout Charmant, 3, 116	Weekend Squall, 3, 115	5	1:35.35	120,000
1998	**Keeper Hill**, 3, 114	D. R. Flores	Star of Broadway, 3, 116	Occhi Verdi (Ire), 3, 116	9	1:36.94	120,000
1997	**Sharp Cat**, 3, 122	C. S. Nakatani	High Heeled Hope, 3, 118	Demon Acquire, 3, 116	8	1:35.52	98,800
1996	**Antespend**, 3, 120	C. W. Antley	Cara Rafaela, 3, 122	Hidden Lake, 3, 116	6	1:36.45	96,900
1995	**Serena's Song**, 3, 122	C. S. Nakatani	Cat's Cradle, 3, 118	Urbane, 3, 116	7	1:35.46	92,700
1994	**Lakeway**, 3, 117	K. Desormeaux	Fancy 'n Fabulous, 3, 114	Princess Mitterand, 3, 116	8	**1:35.14**	93,600
1993	**Likeable Style**, 3, 117	G. L. Stevens	Incindress, 3, 117	Blue Moonlight, 3, 119	6	1:36.67	91,000
1992	**Magical Maiden**, 3, 121	G. L. Stevens	Golden Treat, 3, 115	Red Bandana, 3, 115	10	1:36.23	96,800
1991	**Lite Light**, 3, 121	C. S. Nakatani	Garden Gal, 3, 121	Nice Assay, 3, 119	8	1:35.70	93,800
1990	**Cheval Volant**, 3, 123	A. O. Solis	Nasers Pride, 3, 119	Bright Candles, 3, 119	7	1:38.00	78,150
1989	**Kool Arrival**, 3, 121	L. A. Pincay Jr.	Some Romance, 3, 123	Fantastic Look, 3, 115	7	1:36.20	77,200
1988	**Goodbye Halo**, 3, 123	J. Velasquez	Winning Colors, 3, 119	Sadie B. Fast, 3, 115	5	1:36.80	74,750
1987	**Timely Assertion**, 3, 114	G. L. Stevens	Very Subtle, 3, 121	My Turbulent Beau, 3, 114	5	1:36.80	74,900
1986	**Life At the Top**, 3, 114	R. Q. Meza	Twilight Ridge, 3, 121	An Empress, 3, 117	7	1:36.20	77,050
1985	**Fran's Valentine**, 3, 117	P. A. Valenzuela	Rascal Lass, 3, 121	Wising Up, 3, 121	7	1:36.40	77,150
1984	**Althea**, 3, 124	L. A. Pincay Jr.	Vagabond Gal, 3, 117	My Darling One, 3, 114	6	1:37.00	50,500
1983	**Saucy Bobbie**, 3, 114	L. A. Pincay Jr.	A Lucky Sign, 3, 121	Little Hailey, 3, 114	9	1:36.20	50,100

Named for Rancho Las Virgenes, an 1837 land grant located in Los Angeles County, California. Grade 3 1985-'86. Grade 2 1987.

La Troienne Stakes

Grade 3 in 2006. Churchill Downs, three-year-olds, fillies, 7½ furlongs, dirt. Held May 6, 2006, with a gross value of $119,600. First held in 1956. First graded in 1998. Stakes record 1:28.18 (2006 Joint Effort).

Year	Winner	Jockey	Second	Third	Strs	Time	1st Purse
2006	**Joint Effort**, 3, 122	E. S. Prado	Adieu, 3, 122	Smart N Pretty, 3, 117	9	**1:28.18**	$71,186
2005	**Seek a Star**, 3, 116	J. F. Chavez	Cool Spell, 3, 116	Hot Storm, 3, 122	9	1:28.75	70,804
2004	**Friendly Michelle**, 3, 118	A. O. Solis	Ender's Sister, 3, 122	Bohemian Lady, 3, 122	7	1:28.26	69,564
2003	**Final Round**, 3, 116	J. D. Bailey	Lovely Sage, 3, 116	Fast Cookie, 3, 118	6	1:22.13	69,316
2002	**Cashier's Dream**, 3, 121	D. J. Meche	Shameful, 3, 113	Colonial Glitter, 3, 121	5	1:24.83	69,812
2001	**Caressing**, 3, 121	P. Day	Sweet Nanette, 3, 121	Golly Greeley, 3, 116	9	1:22.90	75,020
2000	**Roxelana**, 3, 116	L. J. Melancon	Magicalmysterycat, 3, 121	Watchfull, 3, 116	7	1:21.97	70,308
1999	**Sapphire n' Silk**, 3, 113	P. Day	English Bay, 3, 116	Grand Deed, 3, 121	6	1:23.85	69,936
1998	**Sister Act**, 3, 113	C. H. Borel	Bourbon Belle, 3, 118	Marie J, 3, 114	6	1:24.46	69,874
1997	**Star of Goshen**, 3, 115	A. O. Solis	Pearl City, 3, 115	Flying Lauren, 3, 116	8	1:22.75	70,370
1996	**Rare Blend**, 3, 121	P. Day	Ruby Baby, 3, 113	Prissy One, 3, 113	8	1:23.75	55,624
1995	**Dixieland Gold**, 3, 121	D. Penna	Daylight Ridge, 3, 113	Ivorilla, 3, 121	7	1:22.74	55,088
1994	**Packet**, 3, 113	J. M. Johnson	Golden Braids, 3, 113	Miss Ra He Ra, 3, 121	10	1:24.14	55,770
1993	**Traverse City**, 3, 116	J. A. Krone	Added Asset, 3, 113	Bellewood, 3, 113	10	1:24.38	38,025
1992	**Bell Witch**, 3, 111	J. A. Krone	Take the Cure, 3, 116	Meadow Storm, 3, 121	6	1:24.35	36,497
1991	**Exclusive Bird**, 3, 116	J. D. Bailey	Wilderness Song, 3, 121	Through Flight, 3, 121	8	1:23.64	36,953
1990	**Screen Prospect**, 3, 121	P. Day	Hard Freeze, 3, 116	Windansea, 3, 116	7	1:24.60	37,018
1989	**Top of My Life**, 3, 122	P. Day	Seaquay, 3, 122	Exquisite Mistress, 3, 122	7	1:23.80	36,595
1988	**Gerri n Jo Go**, 3, 122	P. Day	Raging Lady, 3, 114	Whitesburg Express, 3, 114	7	1:25.40	36,205
1987	**Footy**, 3, 122	C. J. McCarron	Sheena Native, 3, 117	Only a Glance, 3, 122	11	1:23.80	38,025
1986	**Lazer Show**, 3, 121	P. Day	Miss Bid, 3, 115	In Full View, 3, 121	6	1:23.60	24,817
1985	**Magnificent Lindy**, 3, 118	E. Delahoussaye	Turn to Wilma, 3, 115	Sewing Classic, 3, 115	8	1:23.40	21,824
1984	**Sintra**, 3, 115	K. K. Allen	Robin's Rob, 3, 121	Tah Dah, 3, 121	7	1:23.20	23,855
1983	**How Clever**, 3, 121	G. Gallitano	Super Belle, 3, 115	Weekend Surprise, 3, 121	8	1:25.40	24,245
1982	**Betty Money**, 3, 121	L. J. Melancon	Avadewan, 3, 112	All Sold Out, 3, 112	9	1:26.20	23,774
	Hoist Emy's Flag, 3, 118	P. Day	Plucky Hussy, 3, 121	Jay Birdie, 3, 115	8	1:26.20	23,579
1981	**Heavenly Cause**, 3, 121	P. Day	Fiddleatune, 3, 121	Roger's Turn, 3, 121	6	1:24.00	17,030
1980	**Ribbon**, 3, 121	R. D. Ardoin	Tilly's Curve, 3, 121	Noble Appeal, 3, 121	12	1:26.60	19,435
1979	**Justa Reflection**, 3, 118	A. L. Fernandez	Hand Creme, 3, 115	Disco Diane, 3, 115	11	1:25.80	17,680
1978	**White Star Line**, 3, 121	E. Maple	Unconscious Doll, 3, 121	Miss Mary Deb, 3, 121	4	1:25.20	13,520
1977	**Sweet Alliance**, 3, 121	C. J. McCarron	Like Ducks, 3, 121	La Lonja, 3, 118	10	1:25.20	14,300
1976	**Moreland Hills**, 3, 121	A. Rini	Thunder Lady, 3, 115	Three Colors, 3, 118	6	1:26.60	13,780
1975	**High Estimate**, 3, 121	E. Delahoussaye	Hoso, 3, 121	My Juliet, 3, 121	6	1:25.60	13,780
1974	**‡Shantung Silk**, 3, 121	A. T. Cordero Jr.	Clemanna, 3, 118	Irish Sonnet, 3, 118	11	1:25.40	14,430
1973	**La Prevoyante**, 3, 121	J. O. LeBlanc	Old Goldie, 3, 115	Coraggioso, 3, 118	8	1:23.80	14,040

Named for Idle Hour Stock Farm's great foundation mare *La Troienne (1926 f. by *Teddy). Formerly held as a prep race for the Kentucky Oaks (G1). Oaks Prep S. 1956-'66. 6 furlongs 1956-'60. 7 furlongs 1961-2003. Two divisions 1982. ‡Clemanna finished first, DQ to second, 1974.

Lazaro Barrera Memorial Stakes

Grade 2 in 2006. Hollywood Park, three-year-olds, 7 furlongs, dirt. Held May 20, 2006, with a gross value of $150,000. First held in 1953. First graded in 2001. Stakes record 1:20.42 (2001 Early Flyer).

Year	Winner	Jockey	Second	Third	Strs	Time	1st Purse
2006	**Northern Soldier**, 3, 115	C. J. Rollins	Remembering Star, 3, 115	Arson Squad, 3, 120	7	1:22.46	$90,000
2005	**Storm Wolf**, 3, 116	A. O. Solis	Dover Dere, 3, 115	Ransom Demanded, 3, 115	6	1:22.26	90,000
2004	**Twice as Bad**, 3, 116	A. O. Solis	Wimplestiltskin, 3, 116	Don'tsellmeshort, 3, 123	8	1:21.57	90,000
2003	**Blazonry**, 3, 115	M. E. Smith	Fly to the Wire, 3, 116	Jimmy O, 3, 115	9	1:22.19	90,000
2002	**Captain Squire**, 3, 123	C. J. Rollins	Fonz's, 3, 123	Kamsack, 3, 117	5	1:21.95	90,000
2001	**Early Flyer**, 3, 123	C. J. McCarron	Squirtle Squirt, 3, 123	Top Hit, 3, 118	7	**1:20.42**	65,160
2000	**Caller One**, 3, 122	C. S. Nakatani	Dixie Union, 3, 122	Swept Overboard, 3, 122	4	1:21.10	60,960
1999	**Love That Red**, 3, 122	G. K. Gomez	Apremont, 3, 118	O'Rey Fantasma, 3, 118	4	1:20.81	56,910
1998	**Reraise**, 3, 116	E. Delahoussaye	Souvenir Copy, 3, 122	Full Moon Madness, 3, 118	6	1:08.51	39,930
1996	**Future Quest**, 3, 122	K. Desormeaux	Slews Royal Son, 3, 119	Tiger Talk, 3, 120	8	1:15.17	35,100
1995	**Flying Standby**, 3, 115	C. W. Antley	Desert Pirate, 3, 119	Boundless Moment, 3, 116	6	1:09.09	40,200

Named for Racing Hall of Fame and Eclipse Award-winning trainer Lazaro S. Barrera (1924-'91), trainer of 1978 Triple Crown winner Affirmed. Formerly named for the city of Playa del Rey, California. Grade 3 2001. Playa del Rey S. 1953-'54, 1995-'96, 1998. Not held 1955-'94, 1997. 6 furlongs 1954, 1995, 1998. 6½ furlongs 1996.

Lecomte Stakes

Grade 3 in 2006. Fair Grounds, three-year-olds, 1 mile, dirt. Held January 15, 2005, with a gross value of $100,000. First held in 1943. First graded in 2003. Stakes record 1:37.60 (1993 Dixieland Heat).

Year	Winner	Jockey	Second	Third	Strs	Time	1st Purse
2005	**Storm Surge**, 3, 122	R. Albarado	Smooth Bid, 3, 122	Kansas City Boy, 3, 114	5	1:39.34	$60,000
2004	**Fire Slam**, 3, 119	S. J. Sellers	Shadowland, 3, 118	Two Down Automatic, 3, 117	7	1:38.48	60,000
2003	**Saintly Look**, 3, 122	S. J. Sellers	Call Me Lefty, 3, 122	Winning Fans, 3, 114	11	1:37.62	60,000
2002	**Easyfromthegitgo**, 3, 114	D. J. Meche	Sky Terrace, 3, 119	It'sallinthechase, 3, 122	11	1:37.98	60,000
2001	**Sam Lord's Castle**, 3, 122	R. Albarado	Wild Hits, 3, 122	Mc Mahon, 3, 119	10	1:37.98	60,000

2000	**Noble Ruler**, 3, 114	L. J. Melancon	Mighty, 3, 122	Peninsula, 3, 114	10	1:39.11	$60,000
1999	**Some Actor**, 3, 114	E. M. Martin Jr.	Desert Demon, 3, 114	Silver Chadra, 3, 114	14	1:38.59	60,000
1998	**Western City**, 3, 112	R. Albarado	Captain Maestri, 3, 116	Slick Report, 3, 112	6	1:37.84	60,000
1997	**Cash Deposit**, 3, 120	R. D. Ardoin	Stroke, 3, 114	Kalispell, 3, 113	5	1:37.97	36,000
1996	**Boomerang**, 3, 116	E. M. Martin Jr.	Commanders Palace, 3, 116	Playing to Win, 3, 115	8	1:39.49	25,845
1995	**Moonlight Dancer**, 3, 112	L. J. Melancon	Beavers Nose, 3, 114	Timeless Honor, 3, 120	8	1:40.13	25,725
1994	**Fly Cry**, 3, 119	R. D. Ardoin	Smilin Singin Sam, 3, 114	Sweet Wager, 3, 115	12	1:39.29	19,905
1993	**Dixieland Heat**, 3, 116	E. J. Perrodin	Apprentice, 3, 117	Masters Windfall, 3, 112	13	**1:37.60**	19,995
1992	**Line In The Sand**, 3, 112	S. P. Romero	Greinton's Dancer, 3, 113	Best Boy's Jade, 3, 116	7	1:39.80	19,215
1991	**Big Courage**, 3, 116	T. L. Fox	Near the Limit, 3, 118	Slick Groom, 3, 111	11	1:48.30	19,725
1990	**Martha's Buck**, 3, 113	B. J. Walker Jr.	Axe It, 3, 115	Arrowhead Al, 3, 112	7	1:47.00	16,050
1989	**Majesty's Imp**, 3, 116	S. R. Rydowski	Nooo Problema, 3, 119	Esker Island, 3, 113	10	1:45.60	16,455
1988	**Pastourelles**, 3, 113	B. J. Walker Jr.	Risen Star, 3, 122	Run Paul Run, 3, 114	7	1:46.60	16,275
1987	**One Tough Cat**, 3, 114	K. P. LeBlanc	Authentic Hero, 3, 118	French 'n Irish, 3, 113	8	1:48.20	17,250
1986	**Timely Albert**, 3, 109	P. Rubbicco	Irish Irish, 3, 114	New Plymouth, 3, 117	9	1:45.60	34,200
1985	**Encolure**, 3, 114	R. D. Ardoin	Northern Bid, 3, 119	Ten Times Ten, 3, 116	11	1:45.80	33,450
1984	**Silent King**, 3, 115	C. Mueller	Taylor's Special, 3, 122	Fairly Straight, 3, 111	8	1:45.20	24,150
1983	**Explosive Wagon**, 3, 116	C. Mueller	Found Pearl Harbor, 3, 116	Pronto Forli, 3, 120	11	1:45.00	26,900
1982	**Linkage**, 3, 120	G. P. Smith	Soy Emperor, 3, 113	Mid Yell, 3, 109	7	1:45.00	23,350
1981	**Law Me**, 3, 113	J. McKnight	Brazen Ruler, 3, 119	Corsicana, 3, 114	10	1:46.40	24,500
1980	**Withholding**, 3, 108	B. Fann	Brent's Trans Am, 3, 120	Bold Source, 3, 107	10	1:44.20	23,650
1979	**Fuego Seguro**, 3, 116	M. R. Morgan	Bo, 3, 114	Will Henry, 3, 116	12	1:46.60	21,175
1978	**Dragon Tamer**, 3, 118	R. Sibille	Batonnier, 3, 110	Traffic Warning, 3, 114	14	1:44.60	22,050
1977	**Clev Er Tell**, 3, 119	R. Broussard	A Letter to Harry, 3, 118	Sea Defier, 3, 110	8	1:44.80	16,725
1976	**Tudor Tambourine**, 3, 117	D. Copling	Glassy Dip, 3, 112	Go East Young Man, 3, 117	12	1:46.20	18,000
1975	**Colonel Power**, 3, 123	P. Rubbicco	Davey Dan, 3, 113	Rustic Ruler, 3, 119	13	1:40.60	18,625
1974	**Crimson Ruler**, 3, 119	K. LeBlanc	Don't Be Late Jim, 3, 116	Heavy Mayonnaise, 3, 120	11	1:43.80	17,650
1973	**Vodika**, 3, 119	T. Barrow	Navajo, 3, 120	Rocket Pocket, 3, 123	14	1:46.00	15,825

Named for Gen. T. J. Wells's Lecomte (1850 c. by Boston); Lecomte was the only horse to defeat Lexington, in a match race at Metairie Race Course near New Orleans. Not held 2006.

Leonard Richards Stakes

Grade 3 in 2006. Delaware Park, three-year-olds, 1$^1/_{16}$ miles, dirt. Held July 17, 2005, with a gross value of $300,000. First held in 1937. First graded in 1973. Stakes record 1:42.41 (2001 Burning Roma).

Year	Winner	Jockey	Second	Third	Strs	Time	1st Purse
2005	**Sun King**, 3, 122	R. Bejarano	Golden Man, 3, 115	High Limit, 3, 122	5	1:43.33	$180,000
2004	**Pollard's Vision**, 3, 122	J. D. Bailey	Britt's Jules, 3, 116	Pies Prospect, 3, 115	7	1:43.85	150,000
2003	**Awesome Time**, 3, 115	A. S. Black	Christine's Outlaw, 3, 115	Cherokee's Boy, 3, 122	8	1:43.26	150,000
2002	**Running Tide**, 3, 115	R. A. Dominguez	Nothing Flat, 3, 115	The Sewickley Kid, 3, 115	8	1:45.10	150,000
2001	**Burning Roma**, 3, 122	R. Wilson	Marciano, 3, 122	Bay Eagle, 3, 115	5	**1:42.41**	120,000
2000	**Grundlefoot**, 3, 113	T. Dunkelberger	Perfect Cat, 3, 114	Mercaldo, 3, 114	8	1:44.04	120,000
1999	**Stellar Brush**, 3, 114	M. J. McCarthy	Smart Guy, 3, 115	Successful Appeal, 3, 122	8	1:42.78	120,000
1998	**Scatmandu**, 3, 114	R. Migliore	Hot Wells, 3, 115	True Silver, 3, 113	7	1:42.43	90,000
1997	**Leestown**, 3, 116	J. A. Velez Jr.	Universe, 3, 113	Bleu Madura, 3, 116	8	1:43.46	90,000
1982	**Northrop**, 3, 113	L. Moyers	Majesty's Prince, 3, 126	Victory Zone, 3, 113	6	1:50.00	14,755
1981	**Sportin' Life**, 3, 116	K. D. Black	Main Stem, 3, 116	Aspro, 3, 113	7	1:49.00	18,801
1980	**Proctor**, 3, 113	V. A. Bracciale Jr.	Poor Dad, 3, 122	Colossal Apostle, 3, 113	12	1:50.20	30,778
1979	**Lucy's Axe**, 3, 126	R. B. Gilbert	Buck's Chief, 3, 114	Idle Jack, 3, 113	8	1:50.80	21,450
1978	**Mac Diarmida**, 3, 122	J. Cruguet	Prince Misko, 3, 122	Strange Proposal, 3, 113	10	1:46.80	22,653
1977	**True Colors**, 3, 113	S. Cauthen	Singleton, 3, 113	Best Person, 3, 113	13	1:43.20	19,663
1976	**Cinteelo**, 3, 117	B. Thornburg	Chati, 3, 117	Babas Fables, 3, 114	12	1:43.40	28,500
1975	**My Friend Gus**, 3, 117	B. Fann	Talc, 3, 120	Too Easy, 3, 114	10	1:42.20	30,290
1974	**Silver Florin**, 3, 122	R. Wilson	Ground Breaker, 3, 116	Clyde William, 3, 116	13	1:47.40	34,450
1973	**London Company**, 3, 122	C. Barrera	Bemo, 3, 119	Warbucks, 3, 119	8	1:47.80	41,798

Named for Leonard P. Richards, second chairman of the Delaware Racing Commission. Formerly named for the Delaware state nickname, the Diamond State. Grade 2 1973-'74. Not graded 1980-'82, 1997-2001. Diamond State S. 1937-'47. Not held 1943, 1983-'96. 1$^1/_8$ miles 1937-'68, 1979-'82. Turf 1970-'80.

Lexington Stakes

Grade 3 in 2006. Belmont Park, three-year-olds, 1$^1/_4$ miles, turf. Held July 10, 2005, with a gross value of $109,700. First held in 1961. First graded in 1973. Stakes record 1:58.93 (2001 Sharp Performance).

Year	Winner	Jockey	Second	Third	Strs	Time	1st Purse
2005	**Woodlander**, 3, 117	E. S. Prado	Reel Legend, 3, 116	Prince Rahy, 3, 115	6	2:01.92	$65,820
2004	**‡Mustanfar**, 3, 114	J. A. Santos	Icy Atlantic, 3, 122	Second Performance, 3, 118	8	2:01.15	66,660
2003	**Sharp Impact**, 3, 114	R. Migliore	Hidden Truth, 3, 118	Urban King (Ire), 3, 114	6	2:02.62	90,000
2002	**Chiselling**, 3, 114	J. D. Bailey	Finality, 3, 114	Irish Colonial, 3, 114	8	2:00.42	90,000
2001	**Sharp Performance**, 3, 114	J. R. Velazquez	Package Store, 3, 114	Whitmore's Conn, 3, 114	8	**1:58.93**	90,000
2000	**Rob's Spirit**, 3, 113	J. D. Bailey	Plato, 3, 113	Rumsonontheriver, 3, 115	6	2:02.87	90,000
1999	**Mythical Gem**, 3, 117	J. F. Chavez	Monkey Puzzle, 3, 113	Bugatti, 3, 114	11	2:01.21	90,000
1998	**Parade Ground**, 3, 117	M. E. Smith	Ay Rouge, 3, 113	La Reine's Terms, 3, 113	8	2:00.55	84,060
1997	**Private Buck Trout**, 3, 119	J. F. Chavez	Red Castle, 3, 112	Renewed, 3, 112	10	2:01.29	90,000
1996	**Ok by Me**, 3, 122	J. F. Chavez	Value Investor, 3, 117	Alzeus (Ire), 3, 113	10	2:03.58	68,160

1995	**Green Means Go**, 3, 119	J. D. Bailey	Nostra, 3, 112	Flitch, 3, 112	9	2:01.69	$66,960
1994	**Holy Mountain**, 3, 112	J. R. Velazquez	Islefaxyou, 3, 112	Check Ride, 3, 117	10	1:59.74	50,850
1993	**Llandaff**, 3, 123	J. A. Krone	Strolling Along, 3, 114	Eastern Memories (Ire), 3, 114	7	2:02.93	52,380
1992	**Spectacular Tide**, 3, 114	J. A. Krone	Preferences, 3, 121	Casino Magistrate, 3, 123	6	2:02.20	69,120
1991	**Lech**, 3, 114	A. T. Cordero Jr.	Fourstars Allstar, 3, 123	Lucky Mathieu, 3, 114	7	1:59.55	71,160
1990	**Solar Splendor**, 3, 123	E. Maple	Rouse the Louse, 3, 123	Apple Current, 3, 114	8	2:01.80	56,640
1989	**Coosaragga**, 3, 114	R. Migliore	Valid Ordinate, 3, 114	Orange Sunshine, 3, 119	8	2:00.80	69,720
1988	**Sunshine Forever**, 3, 123	A. T. Cordero Jr.	Hodges Bay, 3, 114	Ask Not, 3, 114	8	2:03.00	85,500
1987	**Milesius**, 3, 114	E. Maple	Yucca, 3, 117	Rio's Lark, 3, 114	10	2:03.20	89,580
1986	**Manila**, 3, 126	J. A. Santos	Glow, 3, 123	Dance Card Filled, 3, 114	10	2:03.20	88,980
1985	**Danger's Hour**, 3, 123	J. D. Bailey	Foundation Plan, 3, 123	Exclusive Partner, 3, 114	14	2:00.40	71,370
1984	**Onyxly**, 3, 114	J. D. Bailey	Dr. Schwartzman, 3, 126	Vision, 3, 126	13	2:01.20	58,770
1983	**Kilauea**, 3, 114	J. Cruguet	Fortnightly, 3, 126	Top Competitor, 3, 114	10	2:00.60	34,800
1982	**Majesty's Prince**, 3, 126	E. Maple	Lamerok, 3, 114	Flamingo Two, 3, 114	8	2:03.00	50,310
	‡Royal Roberto, 3, 126	J. Fell	Otter Slide, 3, 117	‡Royal Ring, 3, 114	6	2:01.80	50,310
1981	**Acaroid**, 3, 117	C. B. Asmussen	†De La Rose, 3, 121	Wicked Will (GB), 3, 117	11	2:00.20	52,380
1980	**‡Good Bid**, 3, 112	J. Samyn	Proctor, 3, 116	Don Daniello, 3, 122	8	2:01.00	50,310
1979	**Virilify**, 3, 108	R. I. Velez	T. V. Series, 3, 113	Crown Thy Good, 3, 114	11	2:02.40	50,895
1978	**Mac Diarmida**, 3, 126	J. Cruguet	John Henry, 3, 112	Ashikaga, 3, 110	9	1:41.00	34,110
1977	**Swoon Swept**, 3, 112	L. J. Melancon	Stir the Embers, 3, 112	Lynn Davis, 3, 116	8	1:41.20	32,400
	Johnny D., 3, 113	A. T. Cordero Jr.	‡Forward Charger, 3, 117	Best Person, 3, 112	6	1:41.00	32,100
1976	**Fabled Monarch**, 3, 114	J. Vasquez	‡Fighting Bill, 3, 113	Effervescing, 3, 112	8	1:50.00	27,450
	Modred, 3, 117	C. Perret	Dream 'n Be Lucky, 3, 112	Spanish Dagger, 3, 110	7	1:49.40	27,300
1975	**Dr. Emil**, 3, 109	M. Venezia	Martial Law, 3, 109	Le Cypriote, 3, 112	7	2:07.00	27,270
	Brian Boru, 3, 116	B. Baeza	Rapid Invader, 3, 111	Clout, 3, 113	7	2:07.60	27,270
1974	**Jack Sprat**, 3, 112	R. Turcotte	Kin Run, 3, 115	Never Explain, 3, 116	9	1:56.40	28,020
	Hasty Tudor, 3, 112	V. A. Bracciale Jr.	R. Tom Can, 3, 115	Splitting Headache, 3, 118	9	1:56.80	27,870
1973	**London Company**, 3, 125	L. A. Pincay Jr.	Rapid Sage, 3, 112	Bold Nix, 3, 116	13	1:56.00	35,760

Named for champion and leading sire Lexington (1850 c. by Boston). Grade 2 1973-'89. Lexington H. 1961-'80. Held at Aqueduct 1961-'76. 1⅝ miles 1961. 1 mile 1962. 1¹⁄₁₆ miles 1963-'70, 1977-'78. 1³⁄₁₆ miles 1971-'74. 1⅛ miles 1976. Dirt 1962. Two divisions 1970, 1974-'77, 1982. ‡Effervescing finished second, DQ to third, 1976 (1st Div.). ‡True Colors finished second, DQ to sixth, 1977 (2nd Div.). ‡Proctor finished first, DQ to second, 1980. ‡Dew Line finished first, DQ to fifth, 1982 (2nd Div.). ‡Reinvested finished third, DQ to fourth, 1982 (2nd Div.). ‡Icy Atlantic finished first, DQ to second, 2004. †Denotes female.

Locust Grove Handicap

Grade 3 in 2006. Churchill Downs, three-year-olds and up, fillies and mares, 1⅛ miles, turf. Held July 2, 2005, with a gross value of $164,550. First held in 1982. First graded in 1998. Stakes record 1:46.75 (2004 Shaconage).

Year	Winner	Jockey	Second	Third	Strs	Time	1st Purse
2005	**Delta Princess**, 6, 119	B. Blanc	Shaconage, 5, 116	Marwood, 5, 116	6	1:48.90	$102,021
2004	**Shaconage**, 4, 116	B. Blanc	Halory Leigh, 4, 111	Sand Springs, 4, 119	6	**1:46.75**	102,765
2003	**Ipi Tombe (Zim)**, 5, 123	P. Day	Kiss the Devil, 5, 116	Quick Tip, 5, 117	5	1:47.70	101,928
2002	**Voodoo Dancer**, 4, 120	J. A. Santos	Blue Moon (Fr), 5, 116	Solvig, 5, 116	9	1:46.91	104,718
2001	**Colstar**, 5, 121	J. K. Court	Solvig, 4, 115	Megans Bluff, 4, 119	11	1:48.79	107,136
2000	**Colstar**, 4, 121	A. Delgado	Pricearose, 4, 113	Histoire Sainte (Fr), 4, 113	6	1:47.44	102,300
1999	**Shires Ende**, 4, 117	W. Martinez	Formal Tango, 4, 116	Uanme, 4, 112	11	1:49.11	107,508
1998	**Colcon**, 5, 118	S. J. Sellers	Leo's Gypsy Dancer, 4, 113	Mingling Glances, 4, 112	6	1:48.53	103,974
1997	**Romy**, 6, 121	F. Torres	Yokama, 4, 112	Cymbala (Fr), 4, 116	6	1:48.89	68,634
1996	**Bail Out Becky**, 4, 121	C. Perret	Ms. Isadora, 4, 113	Memories (Ire), 5, 117	6	1:47.38	72,670
1995	**Memories (Ire)**, 4, 114	S. J. Sellers	Market Booster, 6, 120	Thread, 4, 115	7	1:47.48	71,760
1994	**Life Is Delicious**, 4, 113	J. R. Martinez Jr.	Eurostorm, 4, 113	Obtain, 4, 112	4	1:53.87	70,850
1993	**Lady Blessington (Fr)**, 5, 121	C. A. Black	Gone Seeking, 4, 109	Crusie, 4, 115	8	1:50.16	74,425
1992	**Behaving Dancer**, 5, 117	D. L. Howard	Firm Stance, 4, 118	Olden Rijn, 4, 112	10	1:47.27	74,750
1991	**Nice Serve**, 4, 111	J. M. Johnson	Super Fan, 4, 118	Behaving Dancer, 4, 113	9	1:51.30	73,840
1990	**Dibs**, 4, 111	A. T. Gryder	City Crowds (Ire), 4, 111	Phillipa Rush (NZ), 4, 116	6	1:50.60	71,435
1989	**Jungle Gold**, 4, 111	C. R. Woods Jr.	Here's Your Silver, 4, 116	Heretic, 4, 115	7	1:43.20	53,381
1988	**Chez Chez Chez**, 4, 111	J. J. Garcia	Lt. Lao, 4, 115	How I Wish, 4, 113	10	1:45.20	55,575
1987	**Luckiest Girl**, 4, 114	D. J. Soto	Slippin n' Slyding, 4, 111	Marianna's Girl, 4, 120	9	1:51.60	36,465
1986	**Glorious View**, 4, 113	C. R. Woods Jr.	Zenobia Empress, 5, 120	Tide, 4, 112	9	1:44.00	36,693
1985	**Sintra**, 4, 123	K. K. Allen	Sweet Missus, 5, 112	Switching Trick, 5, 112	6	1:43.40	21,076
1984	**Heatherten**, 5, 122	S. Maple	Mickey's Echo, 5, 110	Forest Maiden, 4, 113	6	1:43.00	26,462
1983	**Try Something New**, 4, 117	P. Day	Kitchen, 4, 114	Naskra Magic, 4, 117	6	1:45.20	23,156
1982	**Excitable Lady**, 4, 120	D. G. McHargue	Dawn's Beginning, 4, 111	Sweetest Fantasy, 4, 111	9	1:37.20	24,310

Named for the historic landmark Locust Grove, a house once owned by the brother-in-law and surveying partner of George Rogers Clark. Locust Grove S. 1982-'85, 1988. 1 mile 1988. 1¹⁄₁₆ miles 1983-'86, 1988-'89. About 1⅛ miles 1990. Dirt 1982-'86, 1994. Four-year-olds and up 1983-'89.

Lone Star Park Handicap

Grade 3 in 2006. Lone Star Park, three-year-olds and up, 1¹⁄₁₆ miles, dirt. Held May 29, 2006, with a gross value of $400,000. First held in 1997. First graded in 2000. Stakes record 1:40.53 (2001 Dixie Dot Com).

Year	Winner	Jockey	Second	Third	Strs	Time	1st Purse
2006	**Magnum (Arg)**, 5, 119	P. A. Valenzuela	Texcess, 4, 116	Real Dandy, 4, 116	10	1:42.88	$240,000
2005	**Supah Blitz**, 5, 118	J. K. Court	Cryptograph, 4, 116	Absent Friend, 5, 115	10	1:41.90	180,000

2004	**Yessirgeneralsir**, 4, 114	O. Figueroa	Sonic West, 5, 117	Spanish Empire, 4, 117	6	1:41.29	$180,000
2003	**Pie N Burger**, 5, 117	J. Theriot	dh-Bluesthestandard, 6, 120 dh-Maysville Slew, 7, 114		8	1:42.03	180,000
2002	**Congaree**, 4, 119	P. Day	Prince Iroquois, 5, 115	Mercenary, 4, 115	12	1:42.96	180,000
2001	**Dixie Dot Com**, 6, 118	D. R. Flores	Fan the Flame, 4, 113	Big Numbers, 4, 114	8	**1:40.53**	180,000
2000	**Luftikus**, 4, 114	D. R. Flores	Nite Dreamer, 5, 118	Sultry Substitute, 5, 114	11	1:40.87	180,000
1999	**Mocha Express**, 5, 116	M. St. Julien	Littlebitlively, 5, 118	Nite Dreamer, 4, 113	7	1:43.36	183,300
1998	**Mocha Express**, 4, 114	M. St. Julien	Prince of the Mt., 7, 114	Dickey Rickey, 5, 114	5	1:42.17	123,000
1997	**Connecting Terms**, 4, 112	L. J. Melancon	Humble Seven, 5, 112	Isitingood, 6, 122	7	1:41.97	120,000

The track and the race are named for Texas's (Lone Star Park's home state) nickname, the Lone Star State. Equaled track record 2000. Track record 2001. Dead heat for second 2003.

Longacres Mile Handicap

Grade 3 in 2006. Emerald Downs, three-year-olds and up, 1 mile, dirt. Held August 21, 2005, with a gross value of $250,000. First held in 1935. First graded in 1975. Stakes record 1:33 (2003 Sky Jack).

Year	Winner	Jockey	Second	Third	Strs	Time	1st Purse
2005	**No Giveaway**, 4, 117	J. M. Gutierrez	Quiet Cash, 4, 117	Desert Boom, 5, 121	11	1:35.60	$137,500
2004	**Adreamisborn**, 5, 116	R. A. Baze	Demon Warlock, 4, 114	Mr. Makah, 4, 112	12	1:34.80	137,500
2003	**Sky Jack**, 7, 123	R. A. Baze	Poker Brad, 5, 116	Lord Nelson, 6, 116	10	**1:33.00**	137,500
2002	**Sabertooth**, 4, 114	N. J. Chaves	Moonlight Meeting, 7, 119	San Nicolas, 4, 115	12	1:34.60	137,500
2001	**Irisheyesareflying**, 5, 117	I. Puglisi	Handy N Bold, 6, 119	Makors Mark, 4, 118	10	1:35.40	137,500
2000	**Edneator**, 4, 111	G. V. Mitchell	Big Ten (Chi), 5, 119	Crafty Boy, 5, 114	11	1:33.20	137,500
1999	**Budroyale**, 6, 119	G. K. Gomez	Mike K, 5, 117	Kid Katabatic, 6, 116	8	1:34.60	137,500
1998	**Wild Wonder**, 4, 121	E. Delahoussaye	Mocha Express, 4, 115	Hal's Pal (GB), 5, 117	9	1:33.20	110,000
1997	**Kid Katabatic**, 4, 113	C. Loseth	Hesabull, 4, 119	Liberty Road, 4, 114	7	1:34.20	110,000
1996	**Isitingood**, 5, 117	D. R. Flores	Cleante (Arg), 7, 121	Humpty's Hoedown, 6, 114	10	1:35.60	110,000
1995	**L. J. Express**, 5, 119	M. Allen	Funboy, 4, 121	Secret Damascus, 5, 114	10	1:34.60	50,350
1994	**Want a Winner**, 4, 119	V. Belvoir	Sneakin Jake, 7, 118	Forgotten Days, 8, 114	8	1:35.20	48,250
1993	**Adventuresome Love**, 7, 117	G. Baze	Sneakin Jake, 6, 118	For the Children, 3, 115	8	1:34.60	48,050
1992	**Bolulight**, 4, 121	R. D. Hansen	Ibero (Arg), 5, 122	Charmonnier, 4, 118	12	1:34.00	181,300
1991	**Louis Cyphre (Ire)**, 5, 120	G. L. Stevens	Captain Condo, 9, 116	Ever Steady, 4, 113	11	1:36.10	178,500
1990	**Snipledo**, 5, 115	J. R. Corral	Adventuresome Love, 4, 114	dh-Captain Condo, 8, 116 dh-Kent Green, 7, 112	14	1:35.60	187,700
1989	**Simply Majestic**, 5, 122	R. D. Hansen	Crystal Run, 5, 114	Harmony Creek, 3, 113	9	1:34.20	154,000
1988	**Simply Majestic**, 4, 116	R. A. Baze	Kent Green, 5, 113	Chan's Dragon, 4, 113	9	1:33.80	147,800
1987	**Judge Angelucci**, 4, 121	G. Baze	Leading Hour, 4, 111	Slyly Gifted, 4, 117	8	1:34.20	150,000
1986	**Skywalker**, 4, 123	L. A. Pincay Jr.	Bedside Promise, 4, 120	Sir Macamillion, 7, 116	7	1:34.20	177,000
1985	**Chum Salmon**, 5, 122	G. Baze	Dear Rick, 4, 120	M. Double M., 4, 123	9	1:34.20	150,000
1984	**Travelling Victor**, 5, 123	C. Loseth	Night Mover, 4, 121	Iron Billy, 5, 114	10	1:34.80	115,000
1983	**Chinook Pass**, 4, 125	L. A. Pincay Jr.	Travelling Victor, 4, 118	Earthquack, 4, 119	14	1:35.60	115,000
1982	**Pompeii Court**, 5, 121	S. Hawley	Chinook Pass, 3, 113	Police Inspector, 5, 119	11	1:35.60	100,000
1981	**Trooper Seven**, 5, 126	G. Baze	Reb's Golden Ale, 6, 121	Loto Canada, 4, 117	13	1:35.40	100,650
1980	**Trooper Seven**, 4, 123	G. Baze	Island Sultan, 5, 125	Tilt the Balance, 5, 121	10	1:34.40	78,200
1979	**Always Gallant**, 5, 127	D. G. McHargue	Tilt the Balance, 4, 119	Bad 'n Big, 5, 127	13	1:33.80	79,500
1978	**Bad 'n Big**, 4, 128	W. Shoemaker	Smiley's Dream, 4, 118	Run'n Prince, 4, 111	8	1:34.00	75,000
1977	**Theologist**, 4, 118	B. B. Cooper	Ben Adhem, 5, 116	Detrimental, 6, 120	13	1:38.40	65,000
1976	**Yu Wipi**, 4, 123	S. Hawley	Holding Pattern, 5, 121	Ben Adhem, 4, 124	10	1:34.80	55,500
1975	**Jim**, 5, 118	A. Cuthbertson	Times Rush, 7, 121	Whoa Boy, 4, 116	12	1:37.00	39,500
1974	**Times Rush**, 6, 119	B. Frazier	Red Eye Express, 5, 123	Red Wind, 6, 120	13	1:35.20	38,400
1973	**Silver Mallet**, 5, 122	L. Pierce	Pataha Prince, 8, 118	Reluctant Lord, 4, 120	10	1:34.00	30,250

Named for Longacres Park in Renton, Washington; Longacres closed in 1992. Formerly named for Mt. Rainier, which is located in Washington state. Grade 2 1982-'89. Rainier Mile H. 1991. Budweiser Mile H. 1993. Emerald Budweiser Mile H. 1994-'95. Held at Longacres Park 1935-'92. Held at Yakima Meadows 1993-'95. Not held 1943. Four-year-olds and up 1970. Dead heat for third 1990. Established track record 1996. Track record 1998, 2003. Equaled track record 2000.

Long Branch Breeders' Cup Stakes

Grade 3 in 2006. Monmouth Park, three-year-olds, $1\frac{1}{16}$ miles, dirt. Held July 16, 2005, with a gross value of $147,250. First held in 1878. First graded in 1973. Stakes record 1:41 (1956 Skipper Bill).

Year	Winner	Jockey	Second	Third	Strs	Time	1st Purse
2005	**Park Avenue Ball**, 3, 116	C. P. DeCarlo	Chekhov, 3, 113	Golden Man, 3, 114	8	1:41.93	$90,000
2004	**Lion Heart**, 3, 116	J. Bravo	My Snookie's Boy, 3, 115	Royal Assault, 3, 122	7	1:43.51	60,000
2003	**Max Forever**, 3, 113	J. C. Ferrer	Christine's Outlaw, 3, 115	Chilly Rooster, 3, 112	6	1:43.56	60,000
2002	**Puck**, 3, 122	M. Aguilar	Shah Jehan, 3, 114	Stephentown, 3, 114	6	1:44.35	60,000
2001	**Burning Roma**, 3, 122	R. Wilson	This Fleet Is Due, 3, 114	Thunder Blitz, 3, 122	7	1:43.28	60,000
2000	**Thistyranthasclass**, 3, 114	J. A. Velez Jr.	Graeme Hall, 3, 120	Summinitup, 3, 112	9	1:43.60	60,000
1999	**Ghost Story**, 3, 112	R. G. Davis	Unbridled Jet, 3, 114	Clever Gem, 3, 114	6	1:42.64	60,000
1998	**Favorite Trick**, 3, 116	P. Day	Tomorrows Cat, 3, 113	Arctic Sweep, 3, 114	6	1:43.10	60,000
1997	**Jules**, 3, 114	A. T. Gryder	Leestown, 3, 120	Capture the Gold, 3, 114	4	1:42.40	60,000
1996	**Dr. Caton**, 3, 112	J. Bravo	Devil's Honor, 3, 122	Clash by Night, 3, 114	5	1:41.89	45,000
1995	**Pyramid Peak**, 3, 120	W. H. McCauley	Suave Prospect, 3, 120	Mighty Magee, 3, 118	5	1:44.09	47,250
1994	**Meadow Flight**, 3, 120	J. Bravo	Red Tazz, 3, 114	Don's Sho, 3, 114	5	1:43.92	47,370
1993	**Bert's Bubbleator**, 3, 120	E. L. King Jr.	P. J. Higgins, 3, 120	Signoir Valery, 3, 112	5	1:45.92	32,310
1992	**Scudan**, 3, 114	N. Santagata	Pistols and Roses, 3, 122	Munch n' Nosh, 3, 114	8	1:42.18	39,300

1991	**Sultry Song**, 3, 120	N. Santagata	Arrowtown, 3, 114	Zig n' Zag, 3, 116	7	1:42.38	$33,630
1990	**Tees Prospect**, 3, 112	R. Wilson	Sir Richard Lewis, 3, 116	Big Ted K., 3, 114	8	1:42.40	33,660
1989	**Orange Sunshine**, 3, 120	E. L. King Jr.	Slew the Knight, 3, 120	Currently Red, 3, 113	7	1:36.60	34,740
1988	**Mi Selecto**, 3, 120	C. Perret	Blew by Em, 3, 116	Master Speaker, 3, 115	7	1:35.80	40,380
1987	**I'm So Bad**, 3, 112	N. Santagata	Marine Command, 3, 115	Saratoga Sun, 3, 112	6	1:37.40	34,680
1986	**Lyphard Line**, 3, 120	K. Castaneda	Laser Lane, 3, 112	A Blend of Six, 3, 114	8	1:39.20	34,080
1985	**Bea Quality**, 3, 116	C. W. Antley	Sport Jet, 3, 118	Ice and Fire, 3, 114	9	1:38.80	34,980
1984	**Dr. Schwartzman**, 3, 118	C. Perret	Stay the Course, 3, 112	For Halo, 3, 114	8	1:35.00	34,260
1983	**Smart Style**, 3, 120	A. O. Solis	Rocky Marriage, 3, 112	American Diabolo, 3, 114	8	1:36.60	27,855
	Princilian, 3, 113	J. Vasquez	Silent Landing, 3, 113	Northern Ice, 3, 120	6	1:35.60	27,375
1982	**Prince Westport**, 3, 120	D. Brumfield	Cagey Cougar, 3, 114	Our Escapade, 3, 114	10	1:38.40	27,825
	Play for Love, 3, 114	D. Brumfield	†Larida, 3, 115	Colorful Leader, 3, 112	9	1:38.00	27,645
1981	**†De La Rose**, 3, 117	E. Maple	Century Banker, 3, 114	Victorian Double, 3, 114	9	1:35.60	34,410
1980	**No Bend**, 3, 116	W. Nemeti	Dressage, 3, 118	Peaslee, 3, 114	12	1:35.80	27,810
1979	**Commadore C.**, 3, 114	R. Wilson	Quiet Crossing, 3, 124	Durham Ranger, 3, 124	7	1:36.80	21,629
1978	**Mac Diarmida**, 3, 124	J. Cruguet	Noon Time Spender, 3, 118	Morning Frolic, 3, 116	8	1:42.20	21,921
1977	**P. R. Man**, 3, 118	C. Perret	Prince Hagley, 3, 114	Ver-E-Sharp, 3, 114	6	1:37.00	18,298
1976	**Pastry**, 3, 118	M. Solomone	Modred, 3, 114	Noble Surviver, 3, 114	10	1:37.20	18,753
1975	**Lee Gary**, 3, 114	P. I. Grimm	Bombay Duck, 3, 121	Designated Hitter, 3, 114	7	1:36.80	19,143
1974	**Silver Florin**, 3, 124	R. Wilson	I'm On Top, 3, 116	R. Tom Can, 3, 114	10	1:36.60	15,258
	Hat Full, 3, 114	C. Barrera	To the Rescue, 3, 116	Never Explain, 3, 114	9	1:38.00	15,161
1973	**Bemo**, 3, 116	W. J. Passmore	Warbucks, 3, 118	Hey Rube, 3, 116	10	1:36.80	18,753

Named for a popular seaside resort of the 1880s, Long Branch, New Jersey; Long Branch is near Oceanport, Monmouth Park's current location. Not graded 1989-2001. Long Branch H. 1878-1958. Long Branch S. 1963-'91, 1996-'97. Not held 1894-1946, 1959-'62. $1\frac{1}{4}$ miles 1878-'93. 6 furlongs 1963. 1 mile 1964-'70, 1972-'89. Turf 1963-'69, 1971-'74, 1976, 1978-'82, 1984, 1986, 1988-'89. Originally scheduled on turf 1975. Three-year-olds and up 1947-'58. Two divisions 1974, 1982-'83. †Denotes female.

Long Island Handicap

Grade 2 in 2006. Aqueduct, three-year-olds and up, fillies and mares, $1\frac{1}{2}$ miles, turf. Held November 5, 2005, with a gross value of $150,000. First held in 1956. First graded in 1973. Stakes record 2:29.04 (1992 Villandry).

Year	Winner	Jockey	Second	Third	Strs	Time	1st Purse
2005	**Olaya**, 3, 114	E. S. Prado	Spotlight (GB), 4, 116	Kate Winslet, 4, 115	7	2:30.28	$90,000
2004	**Eleusis**, 3, 115	J. A. Santos	Literacy, 4, 114	Arvada (GB), 4, 117	7	2:31.51	90,000
2003	**Spice Island**, 4, 117	V. Carrero	Volga (Ire), 5, 120	Banyu Dewi (Ger), 4, 114	11	2:32.58	90,000
2002	**Uriah (Ger)**, 3, 112	N. Arroyo Jr.	Sunstone (GB), 4, 114	Mot Juste (GB), 4, 119	11	2:42.48	90,000
2001	**Queue**, 4, 115	J. L. Espinoza	Sweetest Thing, 3, 115	Lady Dora, 4, 114	13	2:29.36	90,000
2000	**Moonlady (Ger)**, 3, 114	C. P. DeCarlo	Playact (Ire), 3, 114	La Ville Rouge, 4, 118	11	2:17.94	90,000
1999	**Midnight Line**, 4, 120	J. D. Bailey	Win for Us (Ger), 3, 116	Horatia (Ire), 3, 112	10	2:29.67	90,000
1998	**Coretta (Ire)**, 4, 114	J. A. Santos	Starry Dreamer, 4, 115	Dixie Ghost, 4, 114	11	2:29.73	60,000
	Yokama, 5, 120	J. D. Bailey	Moments of Magic, 3, 113	Bristol Channel (GB), 3, 114	11	2:31.03	60,000
1997	**Sweetzie**, 5, 115	J. F. Chavez	Sweet Sondra, 4, 114	Scenic Point, 4, 120	6	2:16.66	90,000
1996	**Ampulla**, 5, 121	S. J. Sellers	Wandering Star, 3, 118	Beyrouth, 4, 113	12	2:30.70	87,270
1995	**Yenda (GB)**, 4, 114	C. S. Nakatani	Windsharp, 4, 111	Market Booster, 6, 118	10	2:37.15	86,400
1994	**Market Booster**, 5, 115	M. J. Luzzi	Tiffany's Taylor, 5, 114	Lady Affirmed, 3, 113	12	2:31.95	87,495
1993	**Trampoli**, 4, 119	M. E. Smith	Bright Generation (Ire), 3, 114	Northern Emerald, 3, 108	5	2:31.57	68,760
1992	**Villandry**, 4, 115	M. E. Smith	Ratings, 4, 116	Gina Romantica, 4, 113	8	**2:29.04**	71,160
1991	**Shaima**, 3, 115	L. Dettori	Highland Penny, 6, 116	Franc Argument, 5, 111	9	2:31.48	73,560
1990	**Rigamajig**, 4, 110	J. F. Chavez	Narwala (Ire), 3, 115	Roberto's Hope, 3, 112	10	2:29.60	72,120
	Peinture Bleue, 3, 115	J. A. Santos	Franc Argument, 4, 113	Roseate Tern (GB), 4, 119	10	2:29.80	72,600
1989	**Warfie**, 3, 111	W. H. McCauley	River Memories, 5, 113	Noble Links, 4, 111	6	2:14.40	72,480
1988	**Dancing All Night**, 4, 108	J. J. Vazquez	Casey (GB), 3, 113	Gaily Gaily (Ire), 5, 111	10	2:34.20	112,320
1987	**Stardusk**, 3, 109	J. Cruguet	Spruce Fir, 4, 121	Videogenic, 5, 118	13	2:30.40	115,740
1986	**Dismasted**, 4, 120	J. Samyn	Dawn's Curtsey, 4, 113	Anka Germania (Ire), 4, 114	13	2:30.40	115,560
1985	**Videogenic**, 3, 116	J. Cruguet	Duty Dance, 3, 114	Mariella, 3, 110	9	2:29.20	92,175
	Faburola (Fr), 4, 114	E. Legrix	Halloween Queen, 4, 107	Easy to Copy, 4, 114	9	2:29.40	105,675
1984	**Heron Cove**, 4, 114	J. Cruguet	Key Dancer, 3, 115	Secret Sharer, 4, 110	13	2:32.80	109,650
1983	**Hush Dear**, 5, 125	J. Samyn	Mintage (Fr), 4, 111	If Winter Comes, 5, 113	13	2:34.60	70,920
1982	**Hush Dear**, 4, 111	E. Beitia	Canaille (Ire), 4, 112	Mintage (Fr), 3, 111	14	2:31.40	71,160
1981	**Euphrosyne**, 5, 110	R. Migliore	Mairzy Doates, 5, 120	Noble Damsel, 3, 112	12	2:33.00	70,440
1980	**The Very One**, 5, 120	J. Velasquez	Relaxing, 4, 113	Proud Barbara, 3, 113	5	2:35.20	68,400
1979	**Flitalong**, 3, 107	R. I. Encinas	Terpsichorist, 4, 122	Catherine's Bet, 4, 114	10	2:31.40	52,245
1978	**Terpsichorist**, 3, 116	A. T. Cordero Jr.	Leave Me Alone, 5, 109	Proud Event, 4, 113	9	2:34.00	48,555
1977	**Pearl Necklace**, 3, 123	R. Hernandez	Javamine, 4, 121	Leave Me Alone, 4, 113	7	1:43.80	32,430
1976	**Javamine**, 3, 113	J. Velasquez	Nijana, 3, 115	Fun Forever, 3, 112	11	1:41.60	33,270
1975	**Slip Screen**, 3, 115	G. P. Intelisano Jr.	Fleet Victress, 3, 115	Jabot, 3, 115	6	1:42.80	33,930
1974	**D. O. Lady**, 3, 115	M. A. Rivera	Speak Action, 3, 113	Gulls Cry, 3, 116	10	1:43.20	28,080
	Lie Low, 3, 114	J. Velasquez	Victorian Queen, 3, 120	Markhimoff, 3, 115	10	1:42.00	28,080
1973	**Tuerta**, 3, 116	J. Vasquez	North of Venus, 3, 117	Spring in the Air, 3, 118	12	1:43.80	17,850

Named for the largest island in the continental United States, Long Island, New York; Aqueduct is located on Long Island. Grade 3 1973-'80. Held at Jamaica 1956-'58. Held at Belmont Park 1960, 1962, 1968-'69, 1975-'76, 1990-'98, 1995. $1\frac{5}{8}$ miles 1956-'58. $1\frac{3}{16}$ miles 1959, 1961, 1963-'67, 1970-'71. $1\frac{3}{8}$ miles 1960, 1962, 1968-'69, 2000. 1 mile 1972. $1\frac{1}{16}$ miles 1973-'77. Dirt 1956-'58, 1961, 1972, 1989, 1997, 2000. Originally scheduled on turf 1975. Three-year-olds 1972-'76. Both sexes 1956-'71. Fillies 1972-'76. Two divisions 1959, 1962, 1966-'70, 1972, 1974, 1985, 1990, 1998.

Los Angeles Handicap

Grade 3 in 2006. Hollywood Park, three-year-olds and up, 6 furlongs, dirt. Held May 13, 2006, with a gross value of $100,000. First held in 1938. First graded in 1973. Stakes record 1:07.90 (1995 Forest Gazelle).

Year	Winner	Jockey	Second	Third	Strs	Time	1st Purse
2006	**Siren Lure**, 5, 120	A. O. Solis	Areyoutalkintome, 5, 118	Prorunner, 4, 114	8	1:08.57	$60,000
2005	**Forest Grove**, 4, 117	C. S. Nakatani	Areyoutalkintome, 4, 117	Woke Up Dreamin, 5, 115	6	1:08.57	90,000
2004	**Pohave**, 6, 114	J. K. Court	Marino Marini, 4, 119	Summer Service, 4, 117	9	1:08.12	90,000
2003	**Hombre Rapido**, 6, 116	J. Valdivia Jr.	Publication, 4, 116	Giovannetti, 4, 116	8	1:08.49	120,000
2002	**Kona Gold**, 8, 125	A. O. Solis	No Armistice, 5, 116	Komax, 4, 114	6	1:08.72	64,500
2001	**Caller One**, 4, 124	C. S. Nakatani	Stormy Jack, 4, 115	Rapidough, 6, 115	6	1:08.35	64,380
2000	**Highland Gold**, 5, 115	C. J. McCarron	Mellow Fellow, 5, 113	Your Halo, 5, 114	6	1:09.11	64,260
1999	**Son of a Pistol**, 7, 122	A. O. Solis	Men's Exclusive, 6, 118	Ray of Sunshine (Ire), 4, 118	4	1:08.17	63,300
1998	**Gold Land**, 7, 116	K. Desormeaux	Mr. Doubledown, 4, 119	The Exeter Man, 6, 114	7	1:08.06	64,800
1997	**Men's Exclusive**, 4, 117	L. A. Pincay Jr.	‡First Intent, 8, 117	Gold Land, 6, 115	7	1:08.80	80,970
1996	**dh-Abaginone**, 5, 119	G. L. Stevens		Score Quick, 4, 115	6	1:08.33	53,480
	dh-Paying Dues, 4, 115	C. W. Antley					
1995	**Forest Gazelle**, 4, 117	K. Desormeaux	Lucky Forever, 6, 114	Cardmania, 9, 119	10	**1:07.90**	83,650
1994	**J. F. Williams**, 5, 115	C. J. McCarron	Gundaghia, 7, 117	Thirty Slews, 7, 120	6	1:09.03	61,900
1993	**Star of the Crop**, 4, 119	G. L. Stevens	Fabulous Champ, 4, 115	Wild Harmony, 4, 116	7	1:08.78	63,300
1992	**Cardmania**, 6, 118	E. Delahoussaye	Gray Slewpy, 4, 119	Robyn Dancer, 5, 119	5	1:08.73	61,200
1991	**Black Jack Road**, 7, 117	R. A. Baze	Sunny Blossom, 6, 121	Tanker Port, 6, 116	6	1:09.10	62,000
1990	**Timeless Answer**, 4, 114	R. G. Davis	Prospectors Gamble, 5, 116	Sam Who, 5, 120	8	1:08.80	64,500
1989	**Sam Who**, 4, 118	L. A. Pincay Jr.	Prospectors Gamble, 4, 114	Mi Preferido, 4, 119	5	1:09.40	46,200
1988	**Olympic Prospect**, 4, 116	A. O. Solis	Happy in Space, 4, 113	Sylvan Express (Ire), 5, 119	7	1:08.80	47,700
1987	**Bedside Promise**, 5, 126	G. L. Stevens	Bolder Than Bold, 5, 117	Lincoln Park, 5, 115	5	1:08.40	46,200
1986	**Rosie's K.T.**, 5, 116	P. A. Valenzuela	Mane Magic, 4, 116	Much Fine Gold, 5, 112	6	1:10.00	47,050
1985	**Charging Falls**, 4, 114	W. Shoemaker	Fifty Six Ina Row, 4, 117	Premiership, 5, 115	8	1:08.80	48,650
1984	**Night Mover**, 4, 118	E. Delahoussaye	Debonaire Junior, 3, 113	Croeso, 4, 117	6	1:08.40	47,150
1983	**Mr. Prime Minister**, 7, 115	M. A. Pedroza	Poley, 4, 118	Unreal Zeal, 3, 107	4	1:09.80	45,550
1982	**Terresto's Singer**, 5, 113	P. A. Valenzuela	Remember John, 3, 115	Petro D. Jay, 6, 116	7	1:09.20	47,800
1981	**Doonesbury**, 4, 121	S. Hawley	Reb's Golden Ale, 6, 115	Summer Time Guy, 5, 122	7	1:08.80	37,900
1980	**Beau's Eagle**, 4, 123	L. A. Pincay Jr.	Real Soul, 4, 116	Minstrel Grey, 6, 114	8	1:08.20	32,400
1979	**Hawkin's Special**, 4, 117	D. G. McHargue	White Rammer, 5, 117	Whatsyourpleasure, 6, 117	6	1:08.40	31,350
1978	**J. O. Tobin**, 4, 130	S. Cauthen	Maheras, 5, 125	Drapier (Arg), 6, 121	4	1:21.40	30,200
1977	**Beat Inflation**, 4, 120	D. G. McHargue	Full Out, 4, 117	Mark's Place, 5, 126	5	1:20.20	30,500
1976	**Century's Envoy**, 5, 123	S. Hawley	Home Jerome, 6, 116	Sporting Goods, 6, 120	7	1:20.80	31,950
1975	**Big Band**, 5, 117	L. A. Pincay Jr.	Century's Envoy, 4, 121	Shirley's Champion, 4, 120	8	1:20.60	32,300
1974	**Ancient Title**, 4, 126	L. A. Pincay Jr.	Woodland Pines, 5, 118	Soft Victory, 6, 118	8	1:20.40	32,200
1973	**Soft Victory**, 5, 118	D. Pierce	Crusading, 5, 124	†Convenience, 5, 117	7	1:21.00	31,850

Named for the city of Los Angeles. Formerly named for the Los Angeles *Times*, daily newspaper of Los Angeles. Grade 2 1973-'79. Los Angeles Times H. 2003-'05. Not held 1940-'54. 1 1/16 miles 1938-'39. 7 furlongs 1957-'78. Dead heat for first 1996. ‡Surachai finished second, DQ to sixth, 1997. Track record 1995. †Denotes female.

Louisiana Derby

Grade 2 in 2006. Fair Grounds, three-year-olds, 1 1/16 miles, dirt. Held March 12, 2005, with a gross value of $600,000. First held in 1894. First graded in 1973. Stakes record 1:42.60 (1997 Crypto Star).

Year	Winner	Jockey	Second	Third	Strs	Time	1st Purse
2005	**High Limit**, 3, 122	R. A. Dominguez	Vicarage, 3, 122	Storm Surge, 3, 122	9	1:42.74	$360,000
2004	**Wimbledon**, 3, 122	J. Santiago	Borrego, 3, 122	Pollard's Vision, 3, 122	11	1:42.71	360,000
2003	**Peace Rules**, 3, 122	E. S. Prado	‡Funny Cide, 3, 122	Lone Star Sky, 3, 122	10	1:42.67	450,000
2002	**Repent**, 3, 122	J. D. Bailey	Easyfromthegitgo, 3, 122	It'sallinthechase, 3, 122	7	1:43.86	450,000
2001	**Fifty Stars**, 3, 122	D. J. Meche	Millennium Wind, 3, 122	Hero's Tribute, 3, 122	9	1:44.78	450,000
2000	**Mighty**, 3, 122	S. J. Sellers	More Than Ready, 3, 122	Captain Steve, 3, 122	10	1:43.29	450,000
1999	**Kimberlite Pipe**, 3, 122	R. Albarado	Answer Lively, 3, 122	Ecton Park, 3, 122	8	1:43.56	384,000
1998	**Comic Strip**, 3, 122	S. J. Sellers	Nite Dreamer, 3, 122	Captain Maestri, 3, 122	10	1:43.36	300,000
1997	**Crypto Star**, 3, 118	P. Day	Stop Watch, 3, 118	Smoke Glacken, 3, 122	9	**1:42.60**	240,000
1996	**Grindstone**, 3, 118	J. D. Bailey	Zarb's Magic, 3, 122	Commanders Palace, 3, 118	8	1:42.79	222,000
1995	**Petionville**, 3, 122	C. W. Antley	In Character (GB), 3, 118	Moonlight Dancer, 3, 122	11	1:42.96	210,000
1994	**Kandaly**, 3, 118	C. Perret	Game Coin, 3, 118	Argolid, 3, 118	10	1:42.86	195,750
1993	**Dixieland Heat**, 3, 117	R. P. Romero	Offshore Pirate, 3, 117	Tossofthecoin, 3, 115	13	1:44.80	180,000
1992	**‡Line In The Sand**, 3, 117	P. Day	Hill Pass, 3, 117	Colony Light, 3, 112	9	1:43.40	120,000
1991	**Richman**, 3, 122	P. Day	Near the Limit, 3, 114	Far Out Wadleigh, 3, 122	11	1:44.50	120,000
1990	**Heaven Again**, 3, 113	C. S. Nakatani	Big E. Z., 3, 113	Very Formal, 3, 113	9	1:43.80	100,440
1989	**Dispersal**, 3, 118	J. A. Santos	Majesty's Imp, 3, 118	Dansil, 3, 123	9	1:43.80	100,560
1988	**Risen Star**, 3, 120	S. P. Romero	Word Pirate, 3, 118	Pastourelles, 3, 118	7	1:43.20	98,520
1987	**J. T.'s Pet**, 3, 115	P. Day	Authentic Hero, 3, 118	Plumcake, 3, 115	8	1:51.00	70,260
1986	**Country Light**, 3, 123	P. Day	Bolshoi Boy, 3, 118	Lightning Touch, 3, 118	13	1:50.40	112,000
1985	**Violado**, 3, 115	J. Vasquez	Creme Fraiche, 3, 120	Irish Fighter, 3, 113	11	1:50.20	112,000
1984	**Taylor's Special**, 3, 118	S. Maple	Silent King, 3, 120	Fight Over, 3, 123	7	1:49.60	112,000
1983	**Balboa Native**, 3, 118	J. Velasquez	Found Pearl Harbor, 3, 113	Slewpy, 3, 123	8	1:50.60	112,000
1982	**El Baba**, 3, 123	D. Brumfield	Linkage, 3, 120	Spoonful of Honey, 3, 113	8	1:50.60	112,000
1981	**Woodchopper**, 3, 113	J. Velasquez	A Run, 3, 123	Beau Rit, 3, 126	13	1:50.80	125,800

1980	**Prince Valiant**, 3, 115	M. A. Gonzalez	Native Uproar, 3, 118	Brent's Trans Am, 3, 123	10	1:50.40	$97,150
1979	**Golden Act**, 3, 123	S. Hawley	Rivalero, 3, 115	Incredible Ease, 3, 120	9	1:51.20	100,750
1978	**Esops Foibles**, 3, 118	C. J. McCarron	Quadratic, 3, 123	Batonnier, 3, 120	10	1:50.80	79,750
1977	**Clev Er Tell**, 3, 120	R. Broussard	Run Dusty Run, 3, 123	A Letter to Harry, 3, 115	9	1:48.80	61,000
1976	**Johnny Appleseed**, 3, 118	M. Castaneda	Glassy Dip, 3, 113	Gay Jitterbug, 3, 118	15	1:49.80	61,000
1975	**Master Derby**, 3, 123	D. G. McHargue	Colonel Power, 3, 120	Honey Mark, 3, 118	11	1:49.60	61,000
1974	**Sellout**, 3, 118	M. A. Castaneda	Buck's Bid, 3, 115	Beau Groton, 3, 120	12	1:51.20	55,800
1973	**Leo's Pisces**, 3, 115	R. Breen	Navajo, 3, 120	Angle Light, 3, 118	11	1:51.60	50,000

Named in honor of Fair Grounds's home state. Grade 3 1985-'98. Held at Crescent City 1894-1908. Held at Jefferson Park 1920-'31. Not held 1895-'97, 1909-'19, 1921-'22, 1940-'42, 1945, 2006. 1 mile 1894. 1⅛ miles 1898-1987. ‡Colony Light finished first, DQ to third, 1992. ‡Kafwain finished second, DQ to tenth for a positive drug test, 2003.

Louisville Breeders' Cup Handicap

Grade 2 in 2006. Churchill Downs, three-year-olds and up, fillies and mares, 1$^{1}/_{16}$ miles, dirt. Held May 5, 2006, with a gross value of $271,000. First held in 1986. First graded in 1988. Stakes record 1:42.43 (2005 Shadow Cast).

Year	Winner	Jockey	Second	Third	Strs	Time	1st Purse
2006	**Oonagh Maccool (Ire)**, 4, 117	R. Bejarano	La Reason, 6, 114	Gallant Secret, 4, 114	8	1:42.96	$140,127
2005	**Shadow Cast**, 4, 116	R. Albarado	Island Sand, 4, 115	Storm's Darling, 4, 115	9	**1:42.43**	210,366
2004	**Lead Story**, 5, 116	C. H. Borel	Yell, 4, 114	Cat Fighter, 4, 116	6	1:44.37	202,740
2003	**You**, 4, 118	J. D. Bailey	Fly Borboleta, 4, 111	Seven Four Seven, 5, 113	5	1:43.21	201,810
2002	**Spain**, 5, 118	J. D. Bailey	Mystic Lady, 4, 118	De Bertie, 5, 115	6	1:43.93	207,204
2001	**Saudi Poetry**, 4, 112	V. Espinoza	Royal Fair, 5, 113	Dreams Gallore, 5, 114	8	1:42.53	172,980
2000	**Heritage of Gold**, 5, 119	S. J. Sellers	Roza Robata, 5, 112	Bella Chiarra, 5, 116	6	1:42.99	170,655
1999	**Silent Eskimo**, 4, 113	C. H. Borel	Lu Ravi, 4, 118	Leo's Gypsy Dancer, 5, 112	6	1:43.82	169,415
1998	**Escena**, 5, 119	J. D. Bailey	One Rich Lady, 4, 113	Three Fanfares, 5, 109	10	1:44.84	178,405
1997	**Halo America**, 7, 120	C. H. Borel	Escena, 4, 116	Rare Blend, 4, 116	7	1:42.78	138,012
1996	**Jewel Princess**, 4, 118	C. J. McCarron	Serena's Song, 4, 123	Naskra Colors, 4, 113	6	1:42.50	143,000
1995	**Fit to Lead**, 5, 113	K. Desormeaux	Jade Flush, 4, 115	Teewinot, 4, 109	9	1:43.46	138,125
1994	**One Dreamer**, 6, 115	G. L. Stevens	Kalita Melody (GB), 6, 117	Added Asset, 4, 114	7	1:43.73	136,630
1993	**Quilma (Chi)**, 6, 113	J. A. Santos	Looie Capote, 4, 118	Hitch, 4, 113	12	1:44.61	37,570
1992	**Fowda**, 4, 117	P. A. Valenzuela	Dance Colony, 5, 114	Fit for a Queen, 6, 120	7	1:44.16	100,750
1991	**Fit for a Queen**, 5, 113	J. D. Bailey	Crowned, 4, 115	Topsa, 4, 109	8	1:43.13	101,530
1990	**Connie's Gift**, 4, 111	P. Day	Affirmed Classic, 4, 115	Barbarika, 5, 115	6	1:45.80	100,425
1989	**Darien Miss**, 4, 115	P. A. Johnson	Savannah's Honor, 4, 119	Miss Barbour, 4, 109	6	1:46.00	100,750
1988	**By Land by Sea**, 4, 124	F. Toro	Bound, 4, 115	Bestofbothworlds, 4, 113	5	1:43.20	100,198
1987	**Queen Alexandra**, 5, 117	D. Brumfield	Infinidad (Chi), 5, 116	I'm Sweets, 4, 116	6	1:42.80	100,295
1986	**Hopeful Word**, 5, 119	P. Day	Little Missouri, 4, 116	Czar Nijinsky, 4, 121	4	1:49.40	99,808

Named for the city of Louisville, home of Churchill Downs. Grade 3 1988-'89. Louisville Budweiser Breeders' Cup H. 1987-'95. 1⅛ miles 1986. Both sexes 1986.

Louisville Handicap

Grade 3 in 2006. Churchill Downs, three-year-olds and up, 1⅜ miles, turf. Held May 29, 2006, with a gross value of $108,400. First held in 1895. First graded in 2002. Stakes record 2:14.09 (2003 Kim Loves Bucky).

Year	Winner	Jockey	Second	Third	Strs	Time	1st Purse
2006	**Silverfoot**, 6, 118	M. Guidry	Ramazutti, 4, 117	Quest Star, 7, 116	6	2:16.90	$66,537
2005	**Silverfoot**, 5, 117	R. Albarado	Rochester, 9, 115	Epicentre, 6, 116	7	2:18.77	68,448
2004	**Silverfoot**, 4, 114	R. Albarado	Rochester, 8, 116	Ballingarry (Ire), 5, 120	9	2:17.63	69,688
2003	**Kim Loves Bucky**, 6, 117	S. J. Sellers	Rochester, 7, 117	Dr. Kashnikow, 6, 117	8	**2:14.09**	69,440
2002	**‡dh-Classic Par**, 4, 114	D. J. Meche		Red Mountain, 5, 114	9	2:15.82	47,355
	‡dh-Pisces, 5, 116	R. Albarado					
2001	**With Anticipation**, 6, 112	J. K. Court	Profit Option, 6, 112	Gritty Sandie, 5, 115	6	2:16.28	68,138
2000	**Buff**, 5, 113	F. C. Torres	Williams News, 5, 116	Royal Strand (Ire), 6, 115	11	2:14.31	71,734
1999	**Chorwon**, 6, 114	C. H. Borel	Buff, 4, 114	Keats and Yeats, 5, 110	8	2:14.15	69,812
1998	**Chorwon**, 5, 114	P. Day	African Dancer, 6, 117	Thesaurus, 4, 115	5	2:17.10	67,890
1997	**Chorwon**, 4, 113	C. H. Borel	Down the Aisle, 4, 111	Snake Eyes, 7, 116	5	2:19.45	67,952
1996	**Nash Terrace (Ire)**, 4, 105	D. M. Barton	Vladivostok, 6, 117	Hawkeye Bay, 5, 110	6	2:18.82	71,760
1995	**Lindon Lime**, 5, 114	C. Perret	Caesour, 5, 116	Snake Eyes, 5, 116	8	1:48.12	72,800
1994	**L'Hermine (GB)**, 5, 110	L. J. Melancon	Llandaff, 4, 116	Snake Eyes, 4, 118	5	1:48.36	70,525
1993	**Stark South**, 5, 116	R. P. Romero	Cleone, 4, 115	Coaxing Matt, 4, 116	5	1:48.88	71,955
1992	**Lotus Pool**, 5, 115	C. R. Woods Jr.	Buchman, 5, 114	Magesterial Cheer, 4, 111	8	1:47.69	74,230
1991	**Chenin Blanc**, 5, 118	J. A. Krone	Tees Prospect, 4, 109	Cameroon, 4, 113	8	1:52.21	55,120
	Allijeba, 5, 115	D. Kutz	Tutu Tobago, 4, 115	Alaqua, 5, 114	9	1:51.59	55,770
1990	**Silver Medallion**, 4, 114	P. A. Johnson	Spark O'Dan, 5, 113	Mr. Adorable, 4, 111	8	1:50.40	73,125
1989	**El Clipper**, 5, 113	L. J. Melancon	Set a Record, 5, 113	Pollenate (GB), 5, 113	10	1:50.00	55,478
1988	**First Patriot**, 4, 116	E. Fires	Rio's Lark, 4, 118	Uncle Cam, 4, 114	9	1:51.80	54,698
1987	**Icy Groom**, 4, 117	M. McDowell	Niccolo Polo, 4, 108	Blandford Park, 4, 114	9	1:37.80	36,595
1986	**Ten Times Ten**, 4, 114	K. K. Allen	Little Missouri, 4, 114	Fuzzy, 4, 120	11	1:43.60	25,402
1985	**Big Pistol**, 4, 114	P. Day	Hopeful Word, 4, 111	Big Mav, 7, 111	5	1:48.60	35,100
1984	**Le Cou Cou**, 4, 114	D. L. Howard	Big Mav, 6, 111	Jack Slade, 4, 111	5	1:50.80	34,872
1983	**Big Mav**, 5, 111	P. A. Johnson	Eminency, 5, 123	Diverse Dude, 5, 114	6	1:53.80	35,393
1982	**Bobrobbery**, 4, 114	R. P. Romero	Swinging Light, 4, 114	Boys Nite Out, 4, 111	7	1:51.40	38,968
1981	**Dreadnought**, 4, 115	T. Meyers	Oil City, 4, 115	Withholding, 4, 116	5	1:44.60	22,393

1980 **Dr. Riddick**, 6, 117	D. Brumfield	Incredible Ease, 4, 117	King Celebrity, 4, 113	7	1:44.00	$20,703
1979 **Hot Words**, 4, 114	J. McKnight	Prince Majestic, 5, 124	Dr. Riddick, 5, 119	8	1:45.00	22,750
1978 **It's Freezing**, 6, 119	L. J. Melancon	To the Quick, 4, 119	Prince Majestic, 4, 120	6	1:45.40	14,105
1977 **Amano**, 4, 112	L. J. Melancon	‡Inca Roca, 4, 120	Buddy Larosa, 4, 114	8	1:43.80	14,381
1976 **Ski Run**, 4, 115	G. Patterson	Dragset, 5, 117	Yamanin, 4, 117	7	1:44.00	14,203
1975 **Navajo**, 5, 125	J. Nichols	Silver Badge, 4, 110	Vodika, 5, 115	8	1:43.20	14,463
1974 **List**, 6, 115	R. Breen	Royal Knight, 4, 122	Model Husband, 5, 116	12	1:44.40	15,129
1973 **Knight Counter**, 5, 122	D. Brumfield	‡List, 5, 121	Sipin Whiskey, 4, 110	9	1:43.00	14,771

Named for the city of Louisville, home of Churchill Downs. Formerly held as a "special" race; special races are traditonally "winner takes all." Churchill Downs Special 1946. Louisville S. 1982-'86. Not held 1897, 1900-'06, 1914-'37, 1939-'45, 1953-'56. 1$^1/_{16}$ miles 1895-'99, 1938, 1957-'81, 1986. 6 furlongs 1907-'13. 1$^1/_8$ miles 1946-'52, 1982-'85, 1988-'95. 1 mile 1987. Dirt 1895-1986. Four-year-olds and up 1986-'87. Two divisions 1991. Dead heat for first 2002. ‡Sipin Whiskey finished second, DQ to third, 1973. ‡Buddy Larosa finished second, DQ to third, 1977. ‡Two Point Two Mill finished first, DQ to eighth, 2002.

Mac Diarmida Handicap

Grade 3 in 2006. Gulfstream Park, three-year-olds and up, 1$^3/_8$ miles, turf. Held January 29, 2006, with a gross value of $100,000. First held in 1995. First graded in 1997. Stakes record 2:10.90 (2006 Hotstufanthensome).

Year	Winner	Jockey	Second	Third	Strs	Time	1st Purse
2006	**Hotstufanthensome**, 6, 117	R. Maragh	Go Deputy, 6, 112	Honor in War, 7, 118	12	**2:10.90**	$60,000
2005	**Host**, 5, 114	J. Castellano	Navesink River, 4, 112	Burning Sun, 6, 118	12	2:12.83	60,000
2004	**Request for Parole**, 5, 115	J. A. Santos	Slew Valley, 7, 117	Sir Brian's Sword, 6, 113	12	2:12.58	60,000
2003	**Riddlesdown (Ire)**, 6, 113	R. I. Velez	Macaw (Ire), 4, 114	Just Listen, 7, 113	12	2:14.75	60,000
2002	**Crash Course**, 6, 114	J. D. Bailey	Unite's Big Red, 8, 112	Eltawaasul, 6, 113	12	2:16.27	60,000
2000	**Unite's Big Red**, 6, 113	J. F. Chavez	Thesaurus, 6, 112	Carpenter's Halo, 4, 113	8	2:12.14	60,000
1999	**Panama City**, 5, 114	J. D. Bailey	The Kaiser, 4, 113	Notoriety, 6, 111	5	2:20.65	60,000
1998	**Copy Editor**, 6, 114	J. D. Bailey	Inkatha (Fr), 4, 114	Lafitte the Pirate (GB), 5, 112	12	2:16.72	60,000
1997	**Mecke**, 5, 123	J. D. Bailey	Fabulous Frolic, 6, 112	Spicilege, 5, 113	4	2:05.80	45,000
1996	**A Real Zipper**, 3, 114	A. T. Gryder	Tour's Big Red, 3, 114	Shananie's Finale, 3, 114	12	1:42.66	30,000
1995	**Kings Fiction**, 3, 112	R. G. Davis	Ops Smile, 3, 113	Mecke, 3, 119	10	1:43.12	30,000

Named for Dr. Jerome M. Torsney's 1978 champion turf male and '78 Golden Grass H. winner Mac Diarmida (1975 c. by Minnesota Mac). Mac Diarmida S. 1995-'96. Not held 2001. 1 mile 70 yards 1995. 1$^1/_{16}$ miles 1996. 1$^1/_4$ miles 1997. About 1$^3/_8$ miles 1999. Dirt 1995, 1997. Three-year-olds 1995-'96. Course record 2006.

Maker's Mark Mile Stakes

Grade 2 in 2006. Keeneland Race Course, four-year-olds and up, 1 mile, turf. Held April 14, 2006, with a gross value of $250,000. First held in 1989. First graded in 1991. Stakes record 1:33.54 (2004 Perfect Soul [Ire]).

Year	Winner	Jockey	Second	Third	Strs	Time	1st Purse
2006	**Miesque's Approval**, 7, 117	E. Castro	Artie Schiller, 5, 123	Good Reward, 5, 117	6	1:34.06	$155,000
2005	**Artie Schiller**, 4, 121	E. S. Prado	Gulch Approval, 5, 117	Good Reward, 4, 123	10	1:34.09	155,000
2004	**Perfect Soul (Ire)**, 6, 116	E. S. Prado	Burning Roma, 6, 116	Royal Spy, 6, 116	10	**1:33.54**	124,000
2003	**Royal Spy**, 5, 118	R. Albarado	Miesque's Approval, 4, 118	Touch of the Blues (Fr), 6, 117	9	1:35.82	124,000
2002	**Touch of the Blues (Fr)**, 5, 116	K. Desormeaux	Pisces, 5, 123	Boastful, 4, 116	10	1:35.02	124,000
2001	**North East Bound**, 5, 120	J. A. Velez Jr.	Brahms, 4, 123	Strategic Mission, 6, 116	8	1:34.44	140,492
2000	**Conserve**, 4, 116	S. J. Sellers	Marquette, 4, 120	Inkatha (Fr), 6, 116	9	1:35.08	105,927
1999	**Soviet Line (Ire)**, 9, 115	J. R. Velazquez	Trail City, 6, 115	Rob 'n Gin, 5, 120	8	1:35.37	68,696
1998	**Lasting Approval**, 4, 122	R. Albarado	Soviet Line (Ire), 8, 113	Same Old Wish, 8, 122	10	1:35.57	70,060
1997	**Influent**, 6, 116	J. Samyn	Chief Bearhart, 4, 114	Foolish Pole, 4, 113	9	1:34.59	69,936
1996	**Tejano Run**, 4, 113	J. D. Bailey	Sandpit (Brz), 7, 116	Dove Hunt, 5, 116	10	1:35.03	70,618
1995	**Dove Hunt**, 4, 113	J. A. Santos	Road of War, 5, 114	Night Silence, 5, 116	10	1:35.95	53,196
1994	**First and Only**, 7, 116	T. J. Hebert	The Name's Jimmy, 5, 113	Pride of Summer, 6, 116	7	1:36.63	50,685
1993	**Ganges**, 5, 113	J. D. Bailey	Bidding Proud, 4, 119	Rocket Fuel, 6, 114	10	1:35.40	52,731
1992	**Shudanz**, 4, 114	C. Perret	To Freedom, 4, 113	Cudas, 4, 116	9	1:36.52	55,283
1991	**Opening Verse**, 5, 113	J. D. Bailey	Jalaajel, 7, 113	Buchman, 4, 113	8	1:36.17	53,138
1990	**Charlie Barley**, 4, 119	R. Platts	Known Ranger (GB), 4, 113	Careafolie (Ire), 5, 113	10	1:35.80	36,790
1989	**Yankee Affair**, 7, 119	R. P. Romero	Jalaajel, 5, 114	Pollenate (GB), 5, 114	10	1:43.60	36,693

Formerly named for Fort Harrod, located in present-day Harrodsburg, Kentucky, first permanent settlement west of the Allegheny Mountains. Sponsored by Maker's Mark Distillery of Loretto, Kentucky 1997-2006. Grade 3 1991-'99. Fort Harrod S. 1989-'96. About 1$^1/_{16}$ miles 1989. Course record 2004.

Malibu Stakes

Grade 1 in 2006. Santa Anita Park, three-year-olds, 7 furlongs, dirt. Held December 26, 2005, with a gross value of $250,000. First held in 1952. First graded in 1973. Stakes record 1:20 (1980 Spectacular Bid).

Year	Winner	Jockey	Second	Third	Strs	Time	1st Purse
2005	**Proud Tower Too**, 3, 119	D. Cohen	Attila's Storm, 3, 119	Thor's Echo, 3, 121	14	1:21.62	$150,000
2004	**Rock Hard Ten**, 3, 121	G. L. Stevens	Lava Man, 3, 115	Harvard Avenue, 3, 115	10	1:21.89	150,000
2003	**Southern Image**, 3, 115	V. Espinoza	Marino Marini, 3, 115	Midas Eyes, 3, 119	12	1:22.65	150,000
2002	**Debonair Joe**, 3, 119	J. A. Krone	Total Limit, 3, 117	American System, 3, 117	11	1:22.40	120,000
2001	**Mizzen Mast**, 3, 117	K. Desormeaux	Giant Gentleman, 3, 115	I Love Silver, 3, 117	13	1:22.13	120,000
2000	**Dixie Union**, 3, 121	A. O. Solis	Caller One, 3, 119	Wooden Phone, 3, 116	6	1:21.62	120,000
1999	**Love That Red**, 3, 119	G. K. Gomez	Straight Man, 3, 118	Cat Thief, 3, 123	7	1:22.06	120,000
1998	**Run Man Run**, 3, 115	M. J. Luzzi	Artax, 3, 119	Event of the Year, 3, 121	10	1:21.51	120,000

1997	**Lord Grillo (Arg)**, 3, 119	E. Delahoussaye	Silver Charm, 3, 123	Swiss Yodeler, 3, 115	9	1:21.46	$120,000
1996	**King of the Heap**, 3, 116	K. Desormeaux	Hesabull, 3, 118	Northern Afleet, 3, 116	9	1:21.84	134,300
1995	**Afternoon Deelites**, 3, 120	K. Desormeaux	Score Quick, 3, 120	High Stakes Player, 3, 116	9	1:21.73	100,000
1994	**Powis Castle**, 3, 117	P. A. Valenzuela	Ferrara, 3, 116	Numerous, 3, 118	8	1:20.96	64,300
1993	**Diazo**, 3, 120	L. A. Pincay Jr.	Concept Win, 3, 116	Mister Jolie, 3, 116	8	1:21.17	64,700
1992	**Star of the Crop**, 3, 118	G. L. Stevens	The Wicked North, 3, 116	Bertrando, 3, 120	11	1:20.67	67,850
1991	**Olympio**, 3, 122	E. Delahoussaye	Charmonnier, 3, 120	Apollo, 3, 118	10	1:21.28	66,850
1990	**Pleasant Tap**, 3, 117	A. O. Solis	Bedeviled, 3, 120	Due to the King, 3, 117	10	1:21.60	67,600
1989	**Music Merci**, 3, 123	L. A. Pincay Jr.	Exemplary Leader, 3, 117	Doncareer, 3, 114	11	1:21.60	67,300
1988	**Oraibi**, 3, 117	L. A. Pincay Jr.	Perceive Arrogance, 3, 120	Speedratic, 3, 120	13	1:21.60	70,550
1987	**On the Line**, 3, 117	A. T. Cordero Jr.	Temperate Sil, 3, 126	Candi's Gold, 3, 123	9	1:21.00	66,550
1986	**Ferdinand**, 3, 123	W. Shoemaker	Snow Chief, 3, 126	Don B. Blue, 3, 114	12	1:21.60	72,300
1985	**Banner Bob**, 3, 123	G. Baze	Encolure, 3, 120	Carload, 3, 114	9	1:21.00	71,600
1984	**Precisionist**, 3, 126	C. J. McCarron	Bunker, 3, 117	Milord, 3, 115	7	1:21.40	66,700
	Glacial Stream, 4, 120	C. J. McCarron	Total Departure, 4, 120	Hula Blaze, 4, 117	8	1:22.20	43,150
	Pac Mania, 4, 115	P. A. Valenzuela	Retsina Run, 4, 114	Desert Wine, 4, 123	8	1:22.60	43,150
1983	**Time to Explode**, 4, 117	L. A. Pincay Jr.	Prince Spellbound, 4, 123	Wavering Monarch, 4, 123	8	1:21.00	52,550
1982	**Island Whirl**, 4, 123	L. A. Pincay Jr.	Shanekite, 4, 120	It's the One, 4, 120	8	1:26.00	64,000
1981	**Doonesbury**, 4, 117	S. Hawley	Roper, 4, 114	Unalakleet, 4, 114	9	1:20.40	44,100
	Raise a Man, 4, 120	L. A. Pincay Jr.	Just Right Mike, 4, 114	Aristocratical, 4, 117	9	1:20.40	44,400
1980	**Spectacular Bid**, 4, 126	W. Shoemaker	Flying Paster, 4, 123	Rosie's Seville, 4, 117	5	**1:20.00**	47,800
1979	**Little Reb**, 4, 120	F. Olivares	Radar Ahead, 4, 123	Affirmed, 4, 126	5	1:21.00	38,200
1978	**J. O. Tobin**, 4, 123	S. Cauthen	Bad 'n Big, 4, 120	Eagle Ki, 4, 114	9	1:23.00	35,050
1977	**Cojak**, 4, 117	W. Shoemaker	Double Discount, 4, 117	Little Riva, 4, 114	8	1:23.00	26,050
	Romantic Lead, 4, 114	W. Shoemaker	Maheras, 4, 120	Life's Hope, 4, 124	6	1:22.40	24,800
1976	**Forceten**, 4, 123	D. Pierce	Messenger of Song, 4, 120	†My Juliet, 4, 115	8	1:21.20	35,450
1975	**Lightning Mandate**, 4, 120	A. Pineda	Rocket Review, 4, 117	Century's Envoy, 4, 120	8	1:20.60	28,525
	Princely Native, 4, 117	B. Baeza	First Back, 4, 115	Holding Pattern, 4, 123	7	1:20.80	27,775
1974	**Ancient Title**, 4, 120	F. Toro	Linda's Chief, 4, 126	Dancing Papa, 4, 120	7	1:22.80	34,800
1973	**Bicker**, 4, 117	G. Brogan	Royal Owl, 4, 120	Tri Jet, 4, 117	13	1:21.40	39,300

Named for Topanga Malibu Sequit Rancho in Los Angeles County, California. Grade 2 1973-'94. Malibu Sequet S. 1952-'57. Not held 1959, 1964, 1967, 1970. Four-year-olds 1955 (January), 1960 (January), 1965, 1966 (January), 1968-'75, 1977-'83, 1984 (January). Four-year-olds and up 1976. Two divisions 1975, 1977, 1981, 1984 (January). Held in January and December 1984. Equaled track record 1975. Track record 1980. †Denotes female.

Manhattan Handicap

Grade 1 in 2006. Belmont Park, three-year-olds and up, 1¼ miles, turf. Held June 10, 2006, with a gross value of $400,000. First held in 1896. First graded in 1973. Stakes record 1:57.79 (1994 Paradise Creek).

Year	Winner	Jockey	Second	Third	Strs	Time	1st Purse
2006	**Cacique (Ire)**, 5, 120	E. S. Prado	Relaxed Gesture (Ire), 5, 119	Grey Swallow (Ire), 5, 122	7	2:04.10	$240,000
2005	**Good Reward**, 4, 117	J. D. Bailey	Relaxed Gesture (Ire), 4, 116	Artie Schiller, 4, 122	11	2:00.69	240,000
2004	**Meteor Storm (GB)**, 5, 117	J. Valdivia Jr.	Millennium Dragon (GB), 5, 116	Mr O'Brien (Ire), 5, 116	9	1:59.34	240,000
2003	**Denon**, 5, 122	J. D. Bailey	Requete (GB), 4, 116	Dr. Brendler, 5, 116	10	2:14.16	240,000
2002	**Beat Hollow (GB)**, 5, 118	A. O. Solis	Forbidden Apple, 7, 118	Strut the Stage, 4, 117	8	2:01.29	240,000
2001	**Forbidden Apple**, 6, 117	C. S. Nakatani	King Cugat, 4, 120	Tijiyr (Ire), 5, 115	10	2:00.77	240,000
2000	**Manndar (Ire)**, 4, 117	C. S. Nakatani	Boatman, 4, 113	Spindrift (Ire), 5, 116	8	1:59.61	240,000
1999	**Yagli**, 6, 122	J. D. Bailey	Federal Trial, 4, 116	Middlesex Drive, 4, 116	10	1:58.48	180,000
1998	**Chief Bearhart**, 5, 122	J. A. Santos	Devonwood, 4, 113	Buck's Boy, 5, 117	9	1:58.25	150,000
1997	**Ops Smile**, 5, 116	R. G. Davis	Flag Down, 7, 118	Always a Classic, 4, 121	8	1:59.08	120,000
1996	**Diplomatic Jet**, 4, 117	J. F. Chavez	Flag Down, 6, 119	Kiri's Clown, 7, 121	12	2:00.14	120,000
1995	**Awad**, 5, 121	E. Maple	Blues Traveller (Ire), 5, 119	Kiri's Clown, 6, 115	12	1:58.57	120,000
1994	**Paradise Creek**, 5, 124	P. Day	Solar Splendor, 7, 112	River Majesty, 5, 113	7	**1:57.79**	275,000
1993	**Star of Cozzene**, 5, 118	J. A. Santos	Lure, 4, 124	Solar Splendor, 6, 112	8	1:58.99	190,000
1992	**Sky Classic**, 5, 123	P. Day	Roman Envoy, 4, 111	Leger Cat (Arg), 6, 116	11	2:02.42	252,860
1991	**Academy Award**, 5, 117	A. Madrid Jr.	Three Coins Up, 3, 110	Tarsho (Ire), 5, 113	10	1:59.78	111,600
1990	**Phantom Breeze (Ire)**, 4, 113	M. E. Smith	Green Barb, 5, 111	Milesius, 6, 116	6	2:02.60	52,110
1989	**Milesius**, 5, 115	R. Migliore	Salem Drive, 7, 115	My Big Boy, 6, 114	8	2:00.00	73,440
1988	**Milesius**, 4, 112	C. W. Antley	My Big Boy, 5, 114	Maceo, 4, 111	5	2:04.40	71,760
1987	**Silver Voice**, 4, 109	J. M. Pezua	Talakeno, 7, 118	Duluth, 5, 113	9	2:01.40	86,220
1986	**Danger's Hour**, 4, 117	J. D. Bailey	Premier Mister (Mor), 6, 111	Exclusive Partner, 4, 115	8	2:02.60	87,300
1985	**Cool**, 4, 112	J. Vasquez	Win, 5, 126	Sondrio (Ire), 4, 110	13	2:02.00	77,280
1984	**Win**, 4, 114	A. Graell	Fortnightly, 4, 112	Norwick, 5, 110	12	2:00.60	77,520
1983	**Acaroid**, 5, 114	A. T. Cordero Jr.	Craelius, 4, 120	Half Iced, 4, 119	12	2:00.00	72,240
1982	**Sprink**, 4, 113	J. J. Miranda	Naskra's Breeze, 5, 119	Native Courier, 7, 116	8	2:01.00	51,570
1981	**Match the Hatch**, 5, 114	J. Samyn	†Mrs. Penny, 4, 117	Native Courier, 6, 115	8	2:03.00	52,470
1980	**Morold (Fr)**, 5, 113	E. Maple	Match the Hatch, 4, 111	Foretake, 4, 113	13	2:00.20	53,910
1979	**Fluorescent Light**, 5, 121	J. Fell	Tiller, 5, 124	Native Courier, 4, 122	8	2:04.80	51,615
1978	**Fabulous Time**, 4, 112	A. T. Cordero Jr.	Bill Brill, 4, 109	Tiller, 4, 127	8	2:01.40	48,690
1977	**Gentle King**, 4, 111	S. Cauthen	Double Quill, 8, 105	Keep the Promise, 5, 112	6	2:28.40	32,220
	Gallivantor, 5, 112	S. Cauthen	Gallapiat, 4, 112	Togus, 4, 112	5	2:28.00	32,070
1976	**Caucasus**, 4, 120	F. Toro	Trumpeter Swan, 5, 113	*Kamaraan II, 5, 116	13	2:14.40	33,930
1975	**Salt Marsh**, 5, 115	E. Maple	Drollery, 5, 109	London Company, 5, 118	7	2:16.60	33,600
	***Snow Knight**, 4, 123	J. Velasquez	Shady Character, 4, 113	One On the Aisle, 3, 114	3	2:16.20	33,900

1974	**Golden Don**, 4, 119	J. Cruguet	Anono, 4, 112	R. Tom Can, 3, 114	10	2:19.80	$35,970
1973	**London Company**, 3, 116	L. A. Pincay Jr.	Big Spruce, 4, 120	Triangular, 6, 110	13	2:15.60	36,120

Named for the borough of Manhattan, principal borough of New York City. Formerly sponsored by Early Times Distillery Co. of Louisville 1991-'96. Grade 2 1973-'83, 1990-'93. Early Times Manhattan H. 1991-'92. Early Times Manhattan S. 1993-'96. Held at Morris Park 1896-1904. Held at Aqueduct 1959, 1961, 1963-'67. Not held 1897, 1909-'13. 6 furlongs 1898-1908. 7 furlongs 1914-'15. 1 mile 1916-'32. $1\frac{1}{2}$ miles 1933-'58, 1960, 1962-'64, 1968-'69, 1977. $1\frac{5}{8}$ miles 1959, 1965-'67. $1\frac{5}{16}$ miles 1961. $1\frac{3}{8}$ miles 1970-'76. Dirt 1896-1969, 1977, 1988. Two divisions 1975, 1977. Course record 1994. †Denotes female.

Man o' War Stakes

Grade 1 in 2006. Belmont Park, three-year-olds and up, $1\frac{3}{8}$ miles, turf. Held September 10, 2005, with a gross value of $500,000. First held in 1959. First graded in 1973. Stakes record 2:11.65 (2005 Better Talk Now).

Year	Winner	Jockey	Second	Third	Strs	Time	1st Purse
2005	**Better Talk Now**, 6, 126	R. A. Dominguez	King's Drama (Ire), 5, 126	Relaxed Gesture (Ire), 4, 126	11	**2:11.65**	$300,000
2004	**Magistretti**, 4, 126	E. S. Prado	Epalo (Ger), 5, 126	King's Drama (Ire), 4, 126	8	2:14.65	300,000
2003	**Lunar Sovereign**, 4, 126	R. Migliore	Slew Valley, 6, 126	Denon, 5, 126	8	2:17.99	300,000
2002	**With Anticipation**, 7, 126	P. Day	Balto Star, 4, 126	Man From Wicklow, 5, 126	8	2:15.05	300,000
2001	**With Anticipation**, 6, 126	P. Day	Silvano (Ger), 5, 126	†Ela Athena (GB), 5, 123	8	2:15.11	300,000
2000	**Fantastic Light**, 4, 126	J. D. Bailey	†Ela Athena (GB), 4, 123	Drama Critic, 4, 126	8	2:17.44	300,000
1999	**Val's Prince**, 7, 126	J. F. Chavez	Single Empire (Ire), 5, 126	Federal Trial, 4, 126	7	2:16.69	300,000
1998	**Daylami (Ire)**, 4, 126	J. D. Bailey	Buck's Boy, 5, 126	Indy Vidual, 4, 126	9	2:13.18	240,000
1997	**Influent**, 6, 126	J. D. Bailey	Val's Prince, 5, 126	Awad, 7, 126	10	2:11.69	240,000
1996	**Diplomatic Jet**, 4, 126	J. F. Chavez	Mecke, 4, 126	Marlin, 3, 120	8	2:14.37	240,000
1995	**Millkom (GB)**, 4, 126	G. L. Stevens	Kaldounevees (Fr), 4, 126	Signal Tap, 4, 126	12	2:12.80	240,000
1994	**Royal Mountain Inn**, 5, 126	J. A. Krone	Flag Down, 4, 126	Fraise, 6, 126	9	2:11.75	240,000
1993	**Star of Cozzene**, 5, 126	J. A. Santos	Serrant, 5, 126	Dr. Kiernan, 4, 126	8	2:23.14	240,000
1992	**Solar Splendor**, 5, 126	W. H. McCauley	Dear Doctor (Fr), 5, 126	Spinning (Ire), 5, 126	8	2:12.45	240,000
1991	**Solar Splendor**, 4, 126	W. H. McCauley	Dear Doctor (Fr), 4, 126	Beau Sultan, 3, 120	9	2:12.01	240,000
1990	**Defensive Play**, 3, 120	P. Eddery	Shy Tom, 4, 126	†Ode, 4, 123	7	2:17.80	284,160
1989	**Yankee Affair**, 7, 126	J. A. Santos	My Big Boy, 6, 126	Alwuhush, 4, 126	8	2:20.80	282,240
1988	**Sunshine Forever**, 3, 120	A. T. Cordero Jr.	Pay the Butler, 4, 126	My Big Boy, 5, 126	9	2:14.40	357,600
1987	**Theatrical (Ire)**, 5, 126	P. Day	Le Glorieux (GB), 3, 121	Midnight Cousins, 4, 126	8	2:15.40	351,000
1986	**Dance of Life**, 3, 121	P. Day	†Duty Dance, 4, 123	Pillaster, 3, 121	7	2:14.40	201,000
1985	**Win**, 5, 126	R. Migliore	Bob Back, 4, 126	Baillamont, 3, 121	8	2:15.40	183,600
1984	**Majesty's Prince**, 5, 126	V. A. Bracciale Jr.	Win, 4, 126	Cozzene, 4, 126	9	2:14.60	214,200
1983	**Majesty's Prince**, 4, 126	E. Maple	Erins Isle (Ire), 5, 126	L'Emigrant, 3, 121	11	2:23.60	176,700
1982	**Naskra's Breeze**, 5, 126	J. Samyn	Sprink, 4, 126	Thunder Puddles, 3, 121	9	2:13.00	103,860
1981	**Galaxy Libra (Ire)**, 5, 126	W. Shoemaker	Match the Hatch, 5, 126	‡Great Neck, 5, 126	6	2:14.80	99,180
1980	**French Colonial**, 5, 126	J. Vasquez	†Just a Game (Ire), 4, 123	Golden Act, 4, 126	5	2:15.40	84,300
1979	**Bowl Game**, 5, 126	J. Velasquez	Native Courier, 4, 126	Czaravich, 3, 121	4	2:19.00	82,425
1978	**†Waya (Fr)**, 4, 123	A. T. Cordero Jr.	Tiller, 4, 126	Mac Diarmida, 3, 121	5	2:16.20	79,725
1977	**Majestic Light**, 4, 126	S. Hawley	Exceller, 4, 126	Johnny D., 3, 121	11	2:27.60	67,860
1976	**Effervescing**, 3, 121	A. T. Cordero Jr.	Banghi, 3, 121	‡dh-Erwin Boy, 5, 126 ‡dh-Rouge Sang, 4, 126	13	2:31.20	67,500
1975	**‡*Snow Knight**, 4, 126	J. Velasquez	One On the Aisle, 3, 121	Drollery, 5, 126	8	2:29.20	68,400
1974	**†Dahlia**, 4, 123	R. Turcotte	Crafty Khale, 5, 126	London Company, 4, 126	13	2:26.60	71,700
1973	**Secretariat**, 3, 121	R. Turcotte	Tentam, 4, 126	Big Spruce, 4, 126	7	2:24.80	68,160

Named for Samuel D. Riddle's 1920 Horse of the Year, '20 Belmont S. winner, and '26 leading North American sire Man o' War (1917 c. by Fair Play). Man o' War H. 1959, 1961. Held at Aqueduct 1959, 1961, 1963-'67, 1987. $1\frac{1}{2}$ miles 1959-'60, 1962, 1968-'77. $1\frac{5}{8}$ miles 1961, 1963-'67. Dead heat for third 1976. ‡One On the Aisle finished first, DQ to second, 1975. ‡Crackle finished third, DQ to fifth, 1976. ‡Native Courier finished third, DQ to fourth, 1981. Course record 1973. †Denotes female.

Maryland Breeders' Cup Sprint Handicap

Grade 3 in 2006. Pimlico Race Course, three-year-olds and up, 6 furlongs, dirt. Held May 20, 2006, with a gross value of $190,000. First held in 1987. First graded in 1994. Stakes record 1:09.07 (1996 Forest Wildcat).

Year	Winner	Jockey	Second	Third	Strs	Time	1st Purse
2006	**Friendly Island**, 5, 116	G. K. Gomez	Celtic Innis, 4, 111	Gaff, 4, 116	7	1:09.94	$120,000
2005	**Willy o'the Valley**, 4, 114	E. S. Prado	With Distinction, 4, 115	Take Achance On Me, 7, 114	8	1:09.95	120,000
2004	**Gators N Bears**, 4, 117	C. C. Lopez	Highway Prospector, 7, 114	Sassy Hound, 7, 115	9	1:10.84	120,000
2003	**Pioneer Boy**, 5, 113	J. Rose	Sassy Hound, 6, 113	dh-Highway Prospector, 6, 115 dh-Tasty Caberneigh, 5, 114	7	1:10.35	60,000
2002	**Snow Ridge**, 4, 120	M. E. Smith	Smile My Lord, 4, 113	Clever Gem, 6, 116	7	1:10.06	120,000
2001	**Disco Rico**, 4, 118	H. Vega	Flame Thrower, 3, 114	Istintaj, 5, 116	6	1:10.40	120,000
2000	**Dr. Max**, 4, 113	S. J. Sellers	Moon Over Prospect, 4, 114	Crucible, 5, 113	7	1:10.91	60,000
1999	**Yes It's True**, 3, 113	J. D. Bailey	The Trader's Echo, 5, 109	Purple Passion, 5, 114	8	1:09.20	120,000
1998	**Richter Scale**, 4, 117	J. D. Bailey	Trafalger, 4, 115	Original Gray, 4, 112	7	1:09.45	120,000
1997	**Cat Be Nimble**, 5, 118	J. Rocco	Political Whit, 4, 116	Excelerate, 5, 112	7	1:10.12	127,560
1996	**Forest Wildcat**, 5, 109	J. Bravo	Kayrawan, 4, 113	Demaloot Demashoot, 6, 115	9	**1:09.07**	129,720
1995	**Commanche Trail**, 4, 113	M. E. Smith	Goldminer's Dream, 6, 116	Marry Me Do, 6, 114	6	1:09.35	92,850
1994	**Secret Odds**, 4, 119	E. S. Prado	Honor the Hero, 6, 117	Linear, 4, 119	10	1:10.38	93,615
1993	**Senor Speedy**, 6, 117	J. D. Bailey	He Is Risen, 5, 115	Who Wouldn't, 4, 113	7	1:09.69	93,390
1992	**Potentiality**, 6, 117	P. Day	Smart Alec, 4, 114	Boom Towner, 4, 117	9	1:10.25	93,300
1991	**Jeweler's Choice**, 6, 115	C. J. McCarron	Shuttleman, 5, 116	Hadif, 5, 118	5	1:10.38	92,610

1990	**Norquestor**, 4, 115	C. Perret	Kechi, 4, 115	Amerrico's Bullet, 4, 112	9	1:09.40	$93,540
1989	**King's Nest**, 4, 120	J. Rocco	Silano, 5, 115	Regal Intention, 4, 119	6	1:09.60	92,760
1988	**Fire Plug**, 5, 116	J. F. Hampshire Jr.	Harriman, 4, 117	High Brite, 4, 121	6	1:10.60	35,620
1987	**Purple Mountain**, 5, 111	E. Ortiz Jr.	Little Bold John, 5, 120	Berngoo, 5, 106	6	1:24.40	100,100

Sponsored by Emirates airline of Dubai, United Arab Emirates 2005-'06. Maryland Budweiser Breeders' Cup H. 1987-'95. Maryland Breeders' Cup H. 1996-2005. Held at Laurel Park 1987. 7 furlongs 1987. Dead heat for third 2003.

Massachusetts Handicap

Grade 2 in 2006. Suffolk Downs, three-year-olds and up, 1⅛ miles, dirt. Held June 19, 2004, with a gross value of $500,000. First held in 1935. First graded in 1973. Stakes record 1:47.27 (1998 Skip Away).

Year	Winner	Jockey	Second	Third	Strs	Time	1st Purse
2004	**Offlee Wild**, 4, 111	E. S. Prado	Funny Cide, 4, 117	The Lady's Groom, 4, 116	9	1:49.14	$300,000
2002	**Macho Uno**, 4, 117	G. L. Stevens	Evening Attire, 4, 114	Include, 5, 120	9	1:50.52	300,000
2001	**Include**, 4, 118	J. D. Bailey	Sir Bear, 8, 117	Broken Vow, 4, 116	7	1:48.61	300,000
2000	**Running Stag**, 6, 116	J. R. Velazquez	Out of Mind (Brz), 5, 116	David, 4, 113	8	1:49.45	400,000
1999	**Behrens**, 5, 118	J. F. Chavez	Running Stag, 5, 113	Real Quiet, 4, 121	6	1:49.14	400,000
1998	**Skip Away**, 5, 130	J. D. Bailey	Puerto Madero (Chi), 4, 116	K. J.'s Appeal, 4, 113	5	**1:47.27**	500,000
1997	**Skip Away**, 4, 119	S. J. Sellers	Formal Gold, 4, 114	Will's Way, 4, 114	6	1:47.92	500,000
1996	**Cigar**, 6, 130	J. D. Bailey	Personal Merit, 5, 111	Prolanzier, 6, 112	6	1:49.63	400,000
1995	**Cigar**, 5, 124	J. D. Bailey	Poor But Honest, 5, 107	Double Calvados, 5, 113	6	1:48.74	650,000
1989	**Private Terms**, 4, 119	K. Desormeaux	Granacus, 4, 113	Simply Majestic, 5, 120	8	1:49.40	180,000
1988	**Lost Code**, 4, 127	C. Perret	Waquoit, 5, 122	Afleet, 4, 123	5	1:50.20	154,108
1987	**Waquoit**, 4, 117	C. J. McCarron	Broad Brush, 4, 126	Tour d'Or, 5, 114	6	1:49.00	124,560
1986	**Skip Trial**, 4, 123	J. Samyn	Creme Fraiche, 4, 121	El Basco, 4, 118	11	1:49.80	128,040
1985	**Bounding Basque**, 5, 110	A. Graell	Dr. Carter, 4, 122	Hail Bold King, 4, 120	10	1:47.60	124,560
1984	**Dixieland Band**, 4, 115	D. J. Murphy	Ward Off Trouble, 4, 113	Vigumand, 3, 107	13	1:52.00	126,300
1983	**Let Burn**, 4, 115	J. C. Penney	Space Mountain, 4, 110	Bemedalled, 4, 112	11	1:48.80	98,220
1982	**Silver Supreme**, 4, 111	E. Beitia	Reef Searcher, 5, 117	Frost King, 4, 127	13	1:48.80	100,740
1981	**Soldier Boy**, 5, 114	R. Danjean	Niteange, 7, 108	Driving Home, 4, 114	9	1:49.40	97,200
1980	**Ring of Light**, 5, 121	F. Lovato Jr.	Crow's Nest, 4, 114	Niteange, 6, 110	10	1:50.40	68,400
1979	**Island Sultan**, 4, 110	J. Ruane	Western Front, 4, 113	Quiet Jay, 4, 116	13	1:48.60	70,140
1978	**Big John Taylor**, 4, 112	J. Vasquez	Giboulee, 4, 114	Buckfinder, 4, 114	9	1:48.60	67,200
1977	**Blue Times**, 6, 113	A. T. Cordero Jr.	Pension Plan, 7, 109	Nearly On Time, 3, 106	9	1:49.40	42,930
	Swinging Hal, 4, 110	S. R. Pagano	El Pitirre, 5, 113	‡Gentle King, 4, 108	10	1:49.20	43,410
1976	**Dancing Champ**, 4, 118	C. J. McCarron	Rushing Man, 4, 114	El Pitirre, 4, 117	10	1:49.20	60,000
1975	**Stonewalk**, 4, 117	R. Turcotte	Group Plan, 5, 118	Mongongo, 6, 115	9	1:48.60	60,000
1974	**Billy Come Lately**, 4, 109	D. MacBeth	Forage, 5, 114	North Sea, 5, 111	7	1:48.60	45,000
1973	**Riva Ridge**, 4, 125	R. Turcotte	Crafty Khale, 4, 112	Loud, 6, 113	7	1:48.20	36,432

Suffolk Downs is located in East Boston, Massachusetts. Grade 3 1980-'82, 1997-'98. Not graded 1995-'96. Not held 1990-'94, 2003, 2005. 1¼ miles 1948-'69. About 1½ miles 1970-'71. Turf 1970-'71. Equaled track record 1973. Two divisions 1977. ‡Coverack finished third, DQ to fourth, 1977 (2nd Div.). Track record 1998.

Matriarch Stakes

Grade 1 in 2006. Hollywood Park, three-year-olds and up, fillies and mares, 1 mile, turf. Held November 28, 2004, with a gross value of $500,000. First held in 1981. First graded in 1983. Stakes record 1:34.43 (2003 Heat Haze [GB]).

Year	Winner	Jockey	Second	Third	Strs	Time	1st Purse
2004	**Intercontinental (GB)**, 4, 123	J. D. Bailey	Etoile Montante, 4, 123	Ticker Tape (GB), 3, 120	9	1:35.87	$300,000
2003	**Heat Haze (GB)**, 4, 123	J. R. Velazquez	Musical Chimes, 3, 120	Dedication (Fr), 4, 123	14	**1:34.43**	300,000
2002	**Dress To Thrill (Ire)**, 3, 120	P. Smullen	Golden Apples (Ire), 4, 123	Magic Mission (GB), 4, 123	6	1:48.31	300,000
2001	**Starine (Fr)**, 4, 123	J. R. Velazquez	Lethals Lady (GB), 3, 120	Golden Apples (Ire), 3, 120	12	1:50.16	300,000
2000	**Tout Charmant**, 4, 123	C. J. McCarron	Tranquility Lake, 5, 123	Happyanunoit (NZ), 5, 123	9	1:46.06	300,000
1999	**Happyanunoit (NZ)**, 4, 123	B. Blanc	Tuzla (Fr), 5, 123	Spanish Fern, 4, 123	9	1:46.30	300,000
1998	**Squeak (GB)**, 4, 123	A. O. Solis	Real Connection, 7, 123	Green Jewel (GB), 4, 123	8	2:05.08	420,000
1997	**Ryafan**, 3, 120	A. O. Solis	Maxzene, 4, 123	Yokama, 4, 120	8	2:05.80	420,000
1996	**Wandesta (GB)**, 5, 123	C. S. Nakatani	Windsharp, 5, 123	Memories of Silver, 3, 120	12	2:00.14	420,000
1995	**Duda**, 4, 123	J. D. Bailey	Angel in My Heart (Fr), 3, 120	Wandesta (GB), 4, 123	14	2:00.37	385,000
1994	**Exchange**, 6, 123	L. A. Pincay Jr.	Aube Indienne (Fr), 4, 123	Wandesta (GB), 3, 120	8	1:49.42	220,000
1993	**Flawlessly**, 5, 123	C. J. McCarron	Toussaud, 4, 123	Skimble, 4, 123	7	1:46.78	220,000
1992	**Flawlessly**, 4, 123	C. J. McCarron	Super Staff, 4, 123	Kostroma (Ire), 6, 123	9	1:46.14	220,000
1991	**Flawlessly**, 3, 120	C. J. McCarron	Fire the Groom, 4, 123	Free At Last (GB), 4, 123	14	1:46.60	110,000
1990	**Countus In**, 5, 123	C. S. Nakatani	Taffeta and Tulle, 4, 123	Little Brianne, 5, 123	14	1:46.20	110,000
1989	**Claire Marine (Ire)**, 4, 123	C. J. McCarron	General Charge (Ire), 3, 120	Royal Touch (Ire), 4, 123	7	1:47.40	110,000
1988	**Nastique**, 4, 123	W. Shoemaker	Annoconnor, 4, 123	White Mischief (GB), 4, 123	10	1:47.00	110,000
1987	**Asteroid Field**, 4, 123	A. T. Gryder	Nashmeel, 3, 120	Any Song (Ire), 4, 123	10	1:51.00	110,000
1986	**Auspiciante (Arg)**, 5, 123	C. B. Asmussen	Aberuschka (Ire), 4, 123	Reloy, 3, 120	12	1:48.00	110,000
1985	**Fact Finder**, 6, 123	S. Hawley	Tamarinda (Fr), 4, 123	Possible Mate, 4, 123	10	1:48.20	137,000
1984	**Royal Heroine (Ire)**, 4, 123	F. Toro	Reine Mathilde, 3, 120	Sabin, 4, 123	6	1:49.40	164,000
1983	**Sangue (Ire)**, 5, 123	W. Shoemaker	Castilla, 4, 123	Geraldine's Store, 4, 123	10	1:49.40	110,000
1982	**Pale Purple**, 4, 123	R. Sibille	Berry Bush, 5, 123	Ticketed, 3, 120	9	1:48.60	104,600
	Castilla, 3, 120	R. Sibille	Sangue (Ire), 4, 123	Star Pastures (GB), 4, 123	9	1:47.40	104,600
1981	**Kilijaro (Ire)**, 5, 123	L. A. Pincay Jr.	Glorious Song, 5, 123	Bersid, 3, 120	9	1:47.00	131,600

Older women are sometimes known as "matriarchs." Matriarch Invitational S. 1983-'87. Not held 2005. 1⅛ miles 1981-'94, 1999-2002. 1¼ miles 1995-'98. Two divisions 1982.

Matron Stakes

Grade 1 in 2006. Belmont Park, two-year-olds, fillies, 7 furlongs, dirt. Held September 17, 2005, with a gross value of $300,000. First held in 1892. First graded in 1973. Stakes record 1:22.80 (1977 Lakeville Miss; 1990 Meadow Star).

Year	Winner	Jockey	Second	Third	Strs	Time	1st Purse
2005	**Folklore**, 2, 119	E. S. Prado	Miss Norman, 2, 119	Along the Sea, 2, 119	7	1:23.70	$180,000
2004	**Sense of Style**, 2, 119	E. S. Prado	Balletto (UAE), 2, 119	Play With Fire, 2, 119	6	1:37.67	180,000
2003	**Marylebone**, 2, 119	E. S. Prado	Lokoya, 2, 119	Eye Dazzler, 2, 119	8	1:38.02	120,000
2002	**Storm Flag Flying**, 2, 119	J. R. Velazquez	Wild Snitch, 2, 119	Fircroft, 2, 119	7	1:38.52	120,000
2000	**Raging Fever**, 2, 120	J. D. Bailey	Dancinginmydreams, 2, 120	Ilusoria, 2, 120	5	1:38.20	120,000
1999	**Finder's Fee**, 2, 119	H. Castillo Jr.	Darling My Darling, 2, 119	Circle of Life, 2, 119	7	1:36.68	90,000
1998	**Oh What a Windfall**, 2, 119	S. J. Sellers	Arrested Dreams, 2, 119	Marley Vale, 2, 119	6	1:39.29	90,000
1997	**Beautiful Pleasure**, 2, 119	J. D. Bailey	Diamond On the Run, 2, 119	Carrielle, 2, 119	11	1:35.71	90,000
1996	**Sharp Cat**, 2, 119	J. D. Bailey	Storm Song, 2, 119	Fabulously Fast, 2, 119	6	1:36.19	90,000
1995	**Golden Attraction**, 2, 119	G. L. Stevens	Cara Rafaela, 2, 119	My Flag, 2, 119	8	1:36.33	90,000
1994	**‡Stormy Blues**, 2, 119	J. A. Santos	Pretty Discreet, 2, 119	Phone Caller, 2, 119	6	1:35.16	64,740
1993	**Strategic Maneuver**, 2, 119	J. A. Santos	Astas Foxy Lady, 2, 119	Sovereign Kitty, 2, 119	8	1:23.84	70,680
1992	**Sky Beauty**, 2, 119	E. Maple	Educated Risk, 2, 119	Family Enterprize, 2, 119	9	1:23.32	72,480
1991	**Anh Duong**, 2, 119	A. T. Cordero Jr.	Miss Iron Smoke, 2, 119	Vivano, 2, 119	9	1:23.47	81,300
1990	**Meadow Star**, 2, 119	J. A. Santos	Verbasle, 2, 119	Clark Cottage, 2, 119	6	**1:22.80**	93,240
1989	**Stella Madrid**, 2, 119	A. T. Cordero Jr.	Golden Reef, 2, 119	Miss Cox's Hat, 2, 119	7	1:24.40	72,720
1988	**Some Romance**, 2, 119	G. L. Stevens	Seattle Meteor, 2, 119	Dreamy Mimi, 2, 119	3	1:24.80	68,580
1987	**Over All**, 2, 119	A. T. Cordero Jr.	Justsayno, 2, 119	Flashy Runner, 2, 119	6	1:24.80	82,140
1986	**Tappiano**, 2, 119	J. Cruguet	Sea Basque, 2, 119	Daytime Princess, 2, 119	5	1:23.40	72,000
1985	**Musical Lark (Ire)**, 2, 119	D. MacBeth	Family Style, 2, 119	I'm Sweets, 2, 119	5	1:24.00	66,240
1984	**Fiesta Lady**, 2, 119	L. A. Pincay Jr.	Tiltalating, 2, 119	Contredance, 2, 119	4	1:24.80	57,060
1983	**Lucky Lucky Lucky**, 2, 119	A. T. Cordero Jr.	Miss Oceana, 2, 119	Buzz My Bell, 2, 119	9	1:23.60	76,590
1982	**Wings of Jove**, 2, 119	W. H. McCauley	Share the Fantasy, 2, 119	Weekend Surprise, 2, 119	5	1:24.00	72,600
1981	**Before Dawn**, 2, 119	J. Velasquez	Arabian Dancer, 2, 119	Mystical Mood, 2, 119	9	1:23.20	81,210
1980	**Prayers'n Promises**, 2, 119	A. T. Cordero Jr.	Heavenly Cause, 2, 119	Sweet Revenge, 2, 119	8	1:24.60	70,725
1979	**Smart Angle**, 2, 119	S. Maple	Royal Suite, 2, 119	Nuit d'Amour, 2, 119	5	1:23.80	69,075
1978	**Fall Aspen**, 2, 119	R. I. Velez	Fair Advantage, 2, 119	Island Kitty, 2, 119	4	1:23.80	58,980
1977	**Lakeville Miss**, 2, 119	R. Hernandez	Stub, 2, 119	Akita, 2, 119	10	**1:22.80**	49,335
1976	**Mrs. Warren**, 2, 119	E. Maple	Negotiator, 2, 119	Resolver, 2, 119	7	1:24.60	51,162
1975	**Optimistic Gal**, 2, 119	B. Baeza	Pacific Princess, 2, 119	Prowess, 2, 119	8	1:23.00	51,132
1974	**Alpine Lass**, 2, 119	A. T. Cordero Jr.	Copernica, 2, 119	Spring Is Here, 2, 119	13	1:23.00	52,674
1973	**Talking Picture**, 2, 119	R. Turcotte	Dancealot, 2, 119	Raisela, 2, 119	9	1:23.20	64,050

Held at Morris Park 1892-1904. Held at Pimlico 1910. Held at Aqueduct 1960, 1964-'68. Not held 1895-'98, 1911-'13, 1915-'22. Not held due to World Trade Center attack 2001. 6 furlongs 1892-1971. 1 mile 1994-2004. Colts and fillies 1892-1901. Colt and filly divisions 1902-'14. ‡Flanders finished first, DQ to sixth, 1994.

Meadowlands Breeders' Cup Stakes

Grade 2 in 2006. Meadowlands, three-year-olds and up, 1⅛ miles, dirt. Held October 7, 2005, with a gross value of $500,000. First held in 1977. First graded in 1979. Stakes record 1:46.06 (1998 K. J.'s Appeal).

Year	Winner	Jockey	Second	Third	Strs	Time	1st Purse
2005	**Tap Day**, 4, 119	E. Coa	Alumni Hall, 6, 121	Purge, 4, 119	8	1:48.86	$300,000
2004	**Balto Star**, 6, 123	J. R. Velazquez	Dynever, 4, 119	Gygistar, 5, 119	8	1:48.68	300,000
2003	**Bowman's Band**, 5, 119	R. A. Dominguez	Dynever, 3, 120	‡Volponi, 5, 123	6	1:46.84	240,000
2002	**Burning Roma**, 4, 115	E. Coa	Volponi, 4, 116	Windsor Castle, 4, 112	9	1:48.95	240,000
2001	**Gander**, 5, 114	J. R. Velazquez	Broken Vow, 4, 120	Include, 4, 121	5	1:47.11	300,000
2000	**North East Bound**, 4, 116	J. A. Velez Jr.	Lord Sterling, 4, 115	Where's Taylor, 4, 113	10	1:48.84	240,000
1999	**Pleasant Breeze**, 4, 110	J. F. Chavez	Jazz Club, 4, 118	Vision and Verse, 3, 112	8	1:47.17	300,000
1998	**K. J.'s Appeal**, 4, 112	J. R. Velazquez	Hal's Pal (GB), 5, 116	Sir Bear, 5, 119	8	**1:46.06**	300,000
1996	**Dramatic Gold**, 5, 119	K. Desormeaux	Formal Gold, 3, 112	Mt. Sassafras, 4, 114	11	1:48.02	450,000
1995	**Peaks and Valleys**, 3, 116	J. A. Krone	Poor But Honest, 5, 116	Concern, 4, 122	6	1:48.07	300,000
1994	**Conveyor**, 6, 113	M. E. Smith	Personal Merit, 3, 109	Bruce's Mill, 3, 114	11	1:47.96	300,000
1993	**Marquetry**, 6, 120	K. Desormeaux	Michelle Can Pass, 5, 110	Northern Trend, 5, 112	9	1:47.21	300,000
1992	**Sea Cadet**, 4, 120	A. O. Solis	Valley Crossing, 4, 111	American Chance, 3, 109	10	1:48.19	300,000
1991	**Twilight Agenda**, 5, 121	C. J. McCarron	Scan, 3, 116	Sea Cadet, 3, 115	9	1:46.63	300,000
1990	**Great Normand**, 5, 113	C. E. Lopez Sr.	Norquestor, 4, 116	Beau Genius, 5, 122	10	1:47.20	300,000
1989	**Mi Selecto**, 4, 115	J. A. Santos	Make the Most, 4, 110	dh-Master Speaker, 4, 114 dh-Slew City Slew, 5, 116	8	2:00.20	300,000
1988	**Alysheba**, 4, 127	C. J. McCarron	Slew City Slew, 4, 116	Pleasant Virginian, 4, 114	5	1:58.80	360,000
1987	**Creme Fraiche**, 5, 123	L. A. Pincay Jr.	Afleet, 3, 118	Cryptoclearance, 3, 120	7	2:01.80	300,000
1986	**Broad Brush**, 3, 117	A. T. Cordero Jr.	Skip Trial, 4, 122	Little Missouri, 4, 116	10	2:01.60	300,000
1985	**Bounding Basque**, 5, 113	R. G. Davis	Wild Again, 5, 120	Al Mamoon, 4, 115	11	2:00.40	300,000
1984	**Wild Again**, 4, 115	R. Migliore	Canadian Factor, 4, 114	Inevitable Leader, 5, 116	9	2:00.60	300,000
1983	**Slewpy**, 3, 116	A. T. Cordero Jr.	Deputy Minister, 4, 118	Water Bank, 4, 117	9	2:02.40	240,000
1982	**Mehmet**, 4, 118	E. Delahoussaye	Thirty Eight Paces, 4, 113	John Henry, 7, 129	9	2:01.40	240,000
1981	**Princelet**, 3, 110	W. Nemeti	Niteange, 7, 114	Peat Moss, 6, 121	14	2:02.40	202,080
1980	**Tunerup**, 4, 117	J. Vasquez	Dr. Patches, 6, 116	Dewan Keys, 5, 115	12	2:00.40	196,500
1979	**Spectacular Bid**, 3, 126	W. Shoemaker	Smarten, 3, 120	Valdez, 3, 121	5	2:01.20	234,650

1978	**Dr. Patches**, 4, 119	A. T. Cordero Jr.	Do Tell George, 5, 114	Niteange, 4, 115	7	2:01.60	$104,878
1977	**Pay Tribute**, 5, 117	A. T. Cordero Jr.	Father Hogan, 4, 112	Super Boy, 4, 110	11	2:02.60	114,920

Formerly sponsored by General Motors Corp. of Detroit 1996. Grade 1 1983-'98. Meadowlands Cup H. 1977-'95, 1996-2002. Buick Meadowlands Cup H. 1996. Not held 1997. 1¼ miles 1977-'89. Dead heat for third 1989. ‡Unforgettable Max finished third, DQ to fourth, 2003. Track record 1998.

Mede Cahaba All Along Breeders' Cup Stakes

Grade 3 in 2006. Colonial Downs, three-year-olds and up, fillies and mares, 1⅛ miles, turf. Held July 16, 2005, with a gross value of $200,000. First held in 1985. First graded in 1990. Stakes record 1:47.34 (1994 Alice Springs).

Year	Winner	Jockey	Second	Third	Strs	Time	1st Purse
2005	**Stupendous Miss**, 4, 120	G. L. Stevens	Humoristic, 4, 120	Dynamia, 4, 120	10	1:51.10	$120,000
2004	**Film Maker**, 4, 119	E. S. Prado	Noisette, 4, 119	Lady Linda, 6, 119	7	1:50.08	120,000
2003	**Dress To Thrill (Ire)**, 4, 117	E. S. Prado	Lady Linda, 5, 117	Lady of the Future, 5, 117	9	1:49.16	120,000
2002	**Secret River**, 5, 117	H. Karamanos	Golden Corona, 4, 117	Cayman Sunset (Ire), 5, 117	6	1:50.76	90,000
2001	**Colstar**, 5, 121	J. K. Court	Lucky Lune (Fr), 4, 119	Crystal Sea, 4, 119	8	1:47.53	90,000
2000	**Idle Rich**, 5, 115	A. T. Gryder	Emanating, 4, 115	Orange Sunset (Ire), 4, 115	11	1:55.95	60,000
1999	**Tampico**, 6, 122	E. S. Prado	Heavenly Advice, 5, 115	Absolutely Queenie, 6, 115	10	1:47.63	60,000
1998	**Bursting Forth**, 4, 122	E. S. Prado	The Unforgiven, 4, 117	Be Elusive, 4, 115	8	1:48.01	60,000
1997	**Beyrouth**, 5, 115	D. Rice	Hero's Pride (Fr), 4, 117	Palliser Bay, 5, 122	10	1:49.27	67,830
1996	**Another Legend**, 4, 115	C. O. Klinger	Brushing Gloom, 4, 119	Short Time, 4, 115	7	1:58.80	60,000
1994	**Alice Springs**, 4, 120	R. R. Douglas	Via Borghese, 5, 120	Mz. Zill Bear, 5, 116	6	**1:47.34**	150,000
1993	**Lady Blessington (Fr)**, 5, 116	C. A. Black	Via Borghese, 4, 118	Logan's Mist, 4, 116	5	1:51.58	150,000
1992	**Marble Maiden (GB)**, 3, 114	T. Jarnet	Wedding Ring (Ire), 3, 122	Sheba Dancer (Fr), 3, 114	7	1:49.89	180,000
1991	**Sha Tha**, 3, 113	M. E. Smith	Julie La Rousse (Ire), 3, 113	Once in My Life (Ire), 3, 114	11	1:52.59	180,000
1990	**Foresta**, 4, 120	A. T. Cordero Jr.	Miss Josh, 4, 120	Vijaya, 3, 114	10	1:49.40	180,000
1989	**Lady Winner (Fr)**, 3, 112	K. Desormeaux	Capades, 3, 116	Betty Lobelia, 4, 116	8	1:53.60	180,000
1988	**Ravinella**, 3, 120	G. Guignard	Chapel of Dreams, 4, 120	Betty Lobelia, 3, 116	12	1:49.80	150,000
1985	**Bug Eyed Betty**, 2, 118	V. A. Bracciale Jr.	Cosmic Tiger, 2, 118	Eleanor's Best, 2, 118	7	1:36.60	29,185

Named for Daniel Wildenstein's 1983 Horse of the Year and '83 Washington, D.C. International (G1) winner All Along (Fr) (1979 f. by Targowice). Sponsored by Mignon C. Smith's Mede Cahaba Stable of Washington, D.C. 2005. Grade 2 1990-'97. All Along S. 1985, 1988-'94, 1996-2000. Held at Laurel Park 1988-'94, 1996. Held at Delaware Park 1997. Held at Pimlico 1999. Not held 1995, 1986-'87. 1³⁄₁₆ miles 2000. Equaled course record 2001.

Memorial Day Handicap

Grade 3 in 2006. Calder Race Course, three-year-olds and up, 1¹⁄₁₆ miles, dirt. Held May 29, 2006, with a gross value of $100,000. First held in 1971. First graded in 2002. Stakes record 1:44.60 (1985 Rexson's Hope).

Year	Winner	Jockey	Second	Third	Strs	Time	1st Purse
2006	**Siphon City**, 4, 115	E. Trujillo	Congrats, 6, 118	Bob's Proud Moment, 5, 115	7	1:45.87	$60,000
2005	**Twilight Road**, 8, 119	P. Teator	Whos Crying Now, 5, 115	Hear No Evil, 5, 114	8	1:47.71	60,000
2004	**Twilight Road**, 7, 111	P. Teator	Hear No Evil, 4, 115	Gold Dollar, 5, 112	12	1:45.79	60,000
2003	**Dancing Guy**, 8, 113	R. I. Velez	Shotgun Fire, 5, 110	High Ideal, 5, 113	7	1:45.56	60,000
2002	**Best of the Rest**, 7, 123	C. H. Velasquez	High Ideal, 4, 112	Hal's Hope, 5, 117	4	1:44.75	60,000
2001	**Hal's Hope**, 4, 115	R. I. Velez	American Halo, 5, 115	Tahkodha Hills, 4, 118	7	1:45.81	45,000
2000	**Dancing Guy**, 5, 121	J. C. Ferrer	Reporter, 5, 111	Groomstick Stock's, 4, 111	9	1:46.28	45,000
1999	**Wicapi**, 7, 116	E. Coa	Dancing Guy, 4, 114	Golf Game, 4, 112	8	1:46.79	45,000
1998	**Born Mighty**, 4, 114	J. A. Rivera II	Hard Rock Ridge, 5, 113	Auroral, 6, 114	7	1:40.96	30,000
1997	**Vilhelm**, 5, 114	J. C. Ferrer	‡Sir Bear, 4, 113	Donthelumbertrader, 4, 118	9	1:40.80	30,000
1996	**Marcie's Ensign**, 4, 115	E. Coa	Derivative, 5, 114	Halo Bird (Arg), 5, 110	9	1:50.02	30,000
1995	**Mr. Light Tres (Arg)**, 6, 113	K. L. Chapman	Fabulous Frolic, 4, 112	Flying American, 6, 116	11	1:47.17	30,000
1994	**Final Sunrise**, 4, 113	P. A. Rodriguez	Crucial Trial, 4, 114	Bill Mooney, 4, 112	4	1:51.86	30,000
1993	**Boots 'n Buck**, 4, 116	M. Russ	Yankee Axe, 6, 113	Darian's Reason, 5, 113	10	1:53.82	30,000
1992	**Jodi's Sweetie**, 4, 114	J. C. Duarte Jr.	Scottish Ice, 4, 114	Bidding Proud, 3, 113	9	1:44.21	30,000
1991	**S. W. Wildcard**, 5, 116	P. A. Rodriguez	So Dashing, 4, 113	Bold Circle, 5, 114	9	1:46.92	34,110
1990	**Primal**, 5, 122	H. Castillo Jr.	Eagle Watch, 6, 116	Public Account, 5, 113	7	1:47.40	33,180
1989	**Hooting Star**, 4, 116	J. A. Velez Jr.	Val d'Enchere, 6, 116	Bright Balloon, 5, 111	8	1:41.00	33,300
1988	**Billie Osage**, 4, 116	G. St. Leon	Fabulous Devotion, 4, 110	Engrupido II (Uru), 6, 114	7	1:46.20	33,150
1985	**Rexson's Hope**, 4, 113	G. W. Bain	Brother Liam, 5, 121	Amerilad, 4, 115	10	**1:44.60**	33,660
1983	**Bolivar (Chi)**, 6, 116	S. B. Soto	Dallas Express, 5, 114	Grey Adorn, 5, 115	11	1:46.00	23,700
1982	**Two's a Plenty**, 5, 122	A. Smith Jr.	Catch That Pass, 4, 114	Poking, 6, 117	7	1:45.40	19,470
1980	**Poverty Boy**, 5, 119	M. Fromin	J. Rodney G., 5, 115	Irish Swords, 4, 117	11	1:45.60	20,565
1979	**Great Sound (Ire)**, 5, 115	W. A. Guerra	Raymond Earl, 4, 123	Prince Misko, 4, 116	10	1:45.40	20,835
1978	**One Moment**, 5, 114	J. Giovanni	Out Door Johnny, 4, 115	Haverty, 4, 112	8	1:52.20	21,240
1977	**‡Lightning Thrust**, 4, 121	G. St. Leon	Jatski, 3, 110	What a Threat, 5, 116	10	1:45.80	21,780
1976	**Freepet**, 6, 117	R. Broussard	Chilean Chief, 5, 119	Rastaferian, 7, 112	7	1:53.80	20,700
1975	**Plagiarize**, 4, 118	G. St. Leon	*Rimsky II, 4, 115	Trusted, 4, 115	7	1:45.80	13,800
1974	**Snurb**, 4, 121	G. St. Leon	Stairway to Stars, 5, 113	Somewhat Striking, 4, 113	8	1:46.20	14,040
1973	***Correntoso**, 6, 116	R. Danjean	Great Divide, 5, 121	*Asher, 5, 104	9	1:47.80	10,620

Traditionally held during Memorial Day weekend. Memorial H. 1972. Empty Saddles H. 1975. Not held 1981, 1984, 1986-'87. 1 mile 1971. 1⅛ miles 1976, 1978, 1993-'96. About 1⅛ miles 1977, 1992. Turf 1977, 1989, 1992, 1995, 1997-'98. ‡What a Threat finished first, DQ to third, 1977. ‡Donthelumbertrader finished second, DQ to third, 1997.

Mervin H. Muniz Jr. Memorial Handicap

Grade 2 in 2006. Fair Grounds, four-year-olds and up, about 1⅛ miles, turf. Held March 19, 2005, with a gross value of $500,000. First held in 1992. First graded in 1996. Stakes record 1:48.29 (2004 Mystery Giver).

Year	Winner	Jockey	Second	Third	Strs	Time	1st Purse
2005	**‡A to the Z**, 5, 121	V. Espinoza	America Alive, 4, 116	Honor in War, 6, 117	11	1:50.99	$300,000
2004	**Mystery Giver**, 6, 120	R. Albarado	Herculated, 4, 116	Skate Away, 5, 117	10	**1:48.29**	300,000
2003	**Candid Glen**, 6, 114	E. J. Perrodin	Rouvres (Fr), 4, 115	Freefourinternet, 5, 115	11	1:51.15	390,000
2002	**Sarafan**, 5, 116	C. S. Nakatani	Beat Hollow (GB), 5, 115	Even the Score, 4, 116	14	1:48.88	420,000
2001	**Tijiyr (Ire)**, 5, 110	R. Albarado	Northcote Road, 6, 115	King Cugat, 4, 121	13	1:50.72	360,000
2000	**Brave Act (GB)**, 6, 121	C. B. Asmussen	Where's Taylor, 4, 113	Chester House, 5, 114	13	1:48.98	360,000
1999	**Lord Smith (GB)**, 4, 117	G. K. Gomez	Hawksley Hill (Ire), 6, 122	Chorwon, 6, 116	12	1:51.27	398,160
1998	**Joyeux Danseur**, 5, 121	R. Albarado	Martiniquais (Ire), 5, 118	Hollie's Chief, 7, 113	9	1:49.30	223,980
1997	**Always a Classic**, 4, 114	E. M. Martin Jr.	Rainbow Blues (Ire), 4, 120	Snake Eyes, 7, 118	7	1:54.83	131,970
1996	**Kazabaiyn**, 6, 113	K. Desormeaux	Party Season (GB), 5, 116	Coaxing Matt, 7, 112	10	1:50.80	93,195
1995	**Earl of Barking (Ire)**, 5, 115	G. F. Almeida	Kazabaiyn, 5, 114	Coaxing Matt, 6, 113	11	1:52.01	93,375
1994	**Snake Eyes**, 4, 115	B. E. Bartram	Yukon Robbery, 5, 115	dh-Cozzene's Prince, 7, 122 dh-Dipotamos, 6, 111	8	1:49.41	76,305
	Pride of Summer, 6, 113	R. J. King Jr.	Alpine Choice, 6, 114	Empire Pool (GB), 4, 116	10	1:49.59	76,425
1993	**Coaxing Matt**, 4, 114	E. M. Martin Jr.	Dixie Poker Ace, 6, 120	Spending Record, 6, 114	12	1:50.80	47,010
1992	**‡Slick Groom**, 4, 112	K. P. LeBlanc	Little Bro Lantis, 4, 113	Brownsboro, 8, 117	10	1:52.60	31,590

Named for longtime Fair Grounds racing secretary Mervin H. Muniz Jr., who died in 2003. Formerly named for Hawksworth Farm's 1984 Louisiana H. winner Explosive Bid (1978 c. by Explodent). Grade 3 1996-2000. Explosive Bid S. 1992-'94. Explosive Bid H. 1995-2003. Two divisions 1994. Dead heat for third 1994 (2nd Div.). ‡City Ballet finished first, DQ to sixth, 1992. ‡Rapid Proof finished first, DQ to 11th for a positive drug test, 2005. Course record 2004.

Mervyn LeRoy Handicap

Grade 2 in 2006. Hollywood Park, three-year-olds and up, 1¹⁄₁₆ miles, dirt. Held May 13, 2006, with a gross value of $150,000. First held in 1980. First graded in 1980. Stakes record 1:40.20 (1989 Ruhlmann).

Year	Winner	Jockey	Second	Third	Strs	Time	1st Purse
2006	**Surf Cat**, 4, 121	A. O. Solis	Spellbinder, 5, 116	Dixie Meister, 4, 115	5	1:40.65	$90,000
2005	**Ace Blue (Brz)**, 5, 116	D. R. Flores	Ender's Shadow, 5, 116	Borrego, 4, 119	7	1:41.45	90,000
2004	**Even the Score**, 6, 116	D. R. Flores	Ender's Shadow, 4, 113	Total Impact (Chi), 6, 116	8	1:40.81	90,000
2003	**Total Impact (Chi)**, 5, 114	M. E. Smith	Fleetstreet Dancer, 5, 114	Piensa Sonando (Chi), 5, 115	8	1:40.88	90,000
2002	**Sky Jack**, 6, 117	L. A. Pincay Jr.	Bosque Redondo, 5, 117	Devine Wind, 6, 114	6	1:41.36	90,000
2001	**Futural**, 5, 117	C. J. McCarron	Skimming, 5, 119	Moonlight Charger, 6, 114	5	1:42.02	90,000
2000	**Out of Mind (Brz)**, 5, 116	E. Delahoussaye	Early Pioneer, 5, 116	Skimming, 4, 111	7	1:41.82	90,000
1999	**Budroyale**, 6, 118	G. K. Gomez	Moore's Flat, 5, 107	Wild Wonder, 5, 120	6	1:42.12	90,000
1998	**Wild Wonder**, 4, 116	E. Delahoussaye	Budroyale, 5, 116	Flick (GB), 6, 117	7	1:40.92	64,320
1997	**Hesabull**, 4, 116	G. F. Almeida	Region, 8, 112	Kingdom Found, 7, 116	5	1:41.30	63,720
1996	**Siphon (Brz)**, 5, 117	D. R. Flores	Del Mar Dennis, 6, 119	Dramatic Gold, 5, 117	4	1:40.44	61,500
1995	**Tossofthecoin**, 5, 118	C. S. Nakatani	Ferrara, 4, 114	Polar Route, 5, 116	8	1:40.70	64,600
1994	**Del Mar Dennis**, 4, 115	S. Gonzalez Jr.	Tinners Way, 4, 114	Hill Pass, 5, 115	6	1:40.48	93,300
1993	**Marquetry**, 6, 117	K. Desormeaux	Potrillon (Arg), 5, 117	Lottery Winner, 4, 115	6	1:49.10	92,800
1992	**Another Review**, 4, 116	K. Desormeaux	Sir Beaufort, 5, 116	Marquetry, 5, 119	5	1:41.38	87,900
1991	**Louis Cyphre (Ire)**, 5, 114	J. A. Santos	Warcraft, 4, 115	Anshan (GB), 4, 116	6	1:40.90	110,600
1990	**Super May**, 4, 116	R. G. Davis	Charlatan (Chi), 5, 110	Lively One, 5, 122	12	1:40.80	121,600
1989	**Ruhlmann**, 4, 121	L. A. Pincay Jr.	Sabona, 7, 114	Perfec Travel, 7, 115	5	**1:40.20**	122,800
1988	**Judge Angelucci**, 5, 123	E. Delahoussaye	Simply Majestic, 4, 118	Mark Chip, 5, 117	8	1:40.80	129,600
1987	**Zabaleta**, 4, 117	L. A. Pincay Jr.	Nostalgia's Star, 5, 116	Sabona, 5, 114	7	1:34.80	127,000
1986	**Skywalker**, 4, 117	L. A. Pincay Jr.	Sabona, 4, 113	Al Mamoon, 5, 120	8	1:34.80	123,600
1985	**Precisionist**, 4, 126	C. J. McCarron	Greinton (GB), 4, 121	My Habitony, 5, 115	5	1:32.80	118,700
1984	**Sari's Dreamer**, 5, 112	R. Q. Meza	Fighting Fit, 5, 120	Ancestral (Ire), 4, 115	7	1:34.20	95,000
1983	**Fighting Fit**, 4, 115	W. Shoemaker	Island Whirl, 5, 122	Kangroo Court, 6, 116	7	1:35.80	63,600
1982	**Mehmet**, 4, 116	S. Hawley	A Run, 4, 112	Major Sport, 5, 112	6	1:34.60	63,100
1981	**Eleven Stitches**, 4, 115	S. Hawley	†Glorious Song, 5, 121	Summer Time Guy, 5, 114	8	1:36.40	97,100
1980	**Spectacular Bid**, 4, 132	W. Shoemaker	Peregrinator (Ire), 5, 119	Beau's Eagle, 4, 121	6	1:40.40	120,400

Named for Mervyn LeRoy (1900-'87), one of the organizers of Hollywood Park and its president until 1985; LeRoy was a leading Hollywood producer and director. Grade 1 1988-'91. 1 mile 1981-'87. 1⅛ miles 1993. †Denotes female.

Metropolitan Handicap

Grade 1 in 2006. Belmont Park, three-year-olds and up, 1 mile, dirt. Held May 29, 2006, with a gross value of $600,000. First held in 1891. First graded in 1973. Stakes record 1:32.81 (1996 Honour and Glory).

Year	Winner	Jockey	Second	Third	Strs	Time	1st Purse
2006	**Silver Train**, 4, 119	E. S. Prado	Sun King, 4, 118	Mass Media, 5, 116	7	1:34.27	$360,000
2005	**Ghostzapper**, 5, 123	J. Castellano	Silver Wagon, 4, 115	Sir Shackleton, 4, 116	6	1:33.29	450,000
2004	**Pico Central (Brz)**, 5, 119	A. O. Solis	Bowman's Band, 6, 114	Strong Hope, 4, 119	9	1:35.47	450,000
2003	**Aldebaran**, 5, 119	J. D. Bailey	Saarland, 4, 114	Peeping Tom, 6, 114	8	1:34.15	450,000
2002	**Swept Overboard**, 5, 117	J. F. Chavez	Aldebaran, 4, 115	Crafty C. T., 4, 116	10	1:33.34	450,000
2001	**Exciting Story**, 4, 115	P. Husbands	Peeping Tom, 4, 119	Alannan, 5, 118	10	1:37.14	450,000
2000	**Yankee Victor**, 4, 117	H. Castillo Jr.	†Honest Lady, 4, 112	Sir Bear, 7, 117	8	1:34.64	450,000
1999	**Sir Bear**, 6, 117	J. R. Velazquez	Crafty Friend, 6, 114	Liberty Gold, 5, 114	8	1:34.55	300,000

1998	**Wild Rush**, 4, 119	J. D. Bailey	Banker's Gold, 4, 115	Accelerator, 4, 113	9	1:33.50	$300,000
1997	**Langfuhr**, 5, 122	J. F. Chavez	Western Winter, 5, 115	Northern Afleet, 4, 117	10	1:33.11	240,000
1996	**Honour and Glory**, 3, 110	J. R. Velazquez	dh-Afternoon Deelites, 4, 123 dh-Lite the Fuse, 5, 122		9	**1:32.81**	240,000
1995	**You and I**, 4, 112	J. F. Chavez	Lite the Fuse, 4, 113	Our Emblem, 4, 114	9	1:34.63	300,000
1994	**Holy Bull**, 3, 112	M. E. Smith	Cherokee Run, 4, 118	Devil His Due, 5, 122	10	1:33.98	300,000
1993	**Ibero (Arg)**, 6, 119	L. A. Pincay Jr.	Bertrando, 4, 121	Alydeed, 4, 124	9	1:34.29	300,000
1992	**Dixie Brass**, 3, 107	J. M. Pezua	Pleasant Tap, 5, 119	In Excess (Ire), 5, 121	11	1:33.68	300,000
1991	**In Excess (Ire)**, 4, 117	P. A. Valenzuela	Rubiano, 4, 111	Gervazy, 4, 114	14	1:35.45	300,000
1990	**Criminal Type**, 5, 120	J. A. Santos	Housebuster, 3, 113	Easy Goer, 4, 127	9	1:34.40	357,000
1989	**Proper Reality**, 4, 117	J. D. Bailey	Seeking the Gold, 4, 126	Dancing Spree, 4, 113	8	1:34.00	353,400
1988	**Gulch**, 4, 125	J. A. Santos	Afleet, 4, 124	Stacked Pack, 4, 110	8	1:34.60	351,600
1987	**Gulch**, 3, 110	P. Day	King's Swan, 7, 121	Broad Brush, 4, 128	9	1:34.80	360,900
1986	**Garthorn**, 6, 124	R. Q. Meza	Love That Mac, 4, 117	†Lady's Secret, 4, 120	8	1:33.60	179,700
1985	**Forzando (GB)**, 4, 118	D. MacBeth	Mo Exception, 4, 113	Track Barron, 4, 125	8	1:34.40	207,600
1984	**Fit to Fight**, 5, 124	J. D. Bailey	A Phenomenon, 4, 126	Moro, 5, 116	10	1:34.00	209,100
1983	**Star Choice**, 4, 113	J. Velasquez	Tough Critic, 4, 110	John's Gold, 4, 111	13	1:33.80	145,200
1982	**Conquistador Cielo**, 3, 111	E. Maple	Silver Buck, 4, 111	Star Gallant, 3, 111	14	1:33.00	91,800
1981	**Fappiano**, 4, 115	A. T. Cordero Jr.	Irish Tower, 4, 127	Amber Pass, 4, 115	7	1:33.80	85,650
1980	**Czaravich**, 4, 126	L. A. Pincay Jr.	State Dinner, 5, 117	Silent Cal, 5, 120	8	1:35.80	83,850
1979	**State Dinner**, 4, 115	C. J. McCarron	Dr. Patches, 5, 118	Sorry Lookin, 4, 113	9	1:34.00	64,980
1978	**Cox's Ridge**, 4, 130	E. Maple	Buckfinder, 4, 112	Quiet Little Table, 5, 118	9	1:34.60	66,180
1977	**Forego**, 7, 133	W. Shoemaker	Co Host, 5, 111	Full Out, 4, 115	12	1:34.80	68,640
1976	**Forego**, 6, 130	H. Gustines	Master Derby, 4, 126	Lord Rebeau, 5, 119	6	1:34.80	66,660
1975	**Gold and Myrrh**, 4, 121	W. Blum	Stop the Music, 5, 124	Forego, 5, 136	7	1:33.60	66,840
1974	**Arbees Boy**, 4, 112	E. Maple	Forego, 4, 134	Timeless Moment, 4, 109	8	1:34.40	67,200
1973	**Tentam**, 4, 116	J. Velasquez	Key to the Mint, 4, 127	King's Bishop, 4, 118	8	1:35.00	68,580

Held at Morris Park 1891-1904. Held at Aqueduct 1960-'67, 1969, 1975. Not held 1891, 1911-'12. 1⅛ miles 1891-'96. Dead heat for second 1996. †Denotes female.

Miami Mile Breeders' Cup Handicap

Grade 3 in 2006. Calder Race Course, three-year-olds and up, 1 mile, turf. Held April 29, 2006, with a gross value of $150,000. First held in 1987. First graded in 1989. Stakes record 1:33.75 (2001 Mr. Livingston).

Year	Winner	Jockey	Second	Third	Strs	Time	1st Purse
2006	**Gigawatt**, 6, 114	C. Sutherland	dh-Old Forester, 5, 116 dh-Spring House, 4, 116		10	1:34.50	$90,000
2005	**Bob's Proud Moment**, 4, 115	M. R. Cruz	Dancing Master (Ire), 7, 113	Southern Cal, 4, 119	9	1:38.18	45,000
2004	**Twilight Road**, 7, 114	P. Teator	Gold Dollar, 5, 114	Paradise Dancer, 4, 115	9	1:39.56	90,000
2003	**Tour of the Cat**, 5, 115	A. Cabassa Jr.	Last Stand, 4, 113	Lavender's Lad, 5, 114	10	1:38.65	90,000
2002	**Band Is Passing**, 6, 117	C. H. Velasquez	Pisces, 5, 116	Doowaley (Ire), 6, 113	8	1:37.78	90,000
2001	**Mr. Livingston**, 4, 115	A. Castellano Jr.	Honorable Pic, 4, 114	Pisces, 4, 112	8	**1:33.75**	90,000
2000	**Band Is Passing**, 4, 120	E. Coa	Hurrahy, 7, 115	Tiger Shark, 4, 112	9	1:37.28	90,000
1999	**Sharp Appeal**, 6, 114	J. Castellano	Shamrock City, 4, 114	Hurrahy, 6, 115	10	1:35.70	135,000
1998	**Unite's Big Red**, 4, 115	E. O. Nunez	Fig Fest, 5, 113	dh-Copy Editor, 6, 117 dh-Ensign Ray, 5, 113	10	1:36.62	120,000
1997	**Vilhelm**, 5, 114	J. C. Ferrer	Marcie's Ensign, 5, 114	Elite Jeblar, 7, 113	11	1:36.67	120,000
1996	**Satellite Nealski**, 3, 112	J. C. Ferrer	Marcie's Ensign, 4, 115	Copy Editor, 4, 117	10	1:47.63	95,805
1995	**Elite Jeblar**, 5, 113	E. Fires	Myrmidon, 4, 117	Fabulous Frolic, 4, 114	10	1:47.67	94,200
1994	**The Vid**, 4, 114	R. R. Douglas	Mr. Angel, 3, 118	Carterista, 5, 116	9	1:48.28	94,350
1993	**Carterista**, 4, 117	M. A. Lee	Wild Forest, 4, 112	Mr. Explosive, 5, 112	13	1:47.51	95,610
1992	**Jodi's Sweetie**, 4, 115	J. D. Bailey	‡Walkie Talker, 3, 114	‡Futurist, 4, 117	10	1:43.94	94,140
1991	**Run Turn**, 4, 111	G. St. Leon	Scottish Ice, 3, 118	Hidden Tomahawk, 3, 111	6	1:52.96	93,150
1990	**Public Account**, 5, 115	P. A. Rodriguez	Bold Circle, 4, 112	Primal, 5, 126	8	1:52.00	93,300
1989	**Simply Majestic**, 5, 117	H. Castillo Jr.	Maceo, 5, 113	Bold Circle, 3, 110	8	1:48.60	93,510
1988	**Simply Majestic**, 4, 117	J. D. Bailey	Val d'Enchere, 5, 116	Racing Star, 6, 115	8	1:43.60	93,900
1987	**Blazing Bart**, 3, 117	J. A. Santos	Silver Voice, 4, 115	New Colony, 4, 114	9	1:44.20	93,630

Named for the city of Miami, home city of Calder. Miami Budweiser Breeders' Cup H. 1987-'95. Miami Breeders' Cup H. 1996-'98. About 1⅛ miles 1987-'89, 1992-'93. 1⅛ miles 1990-'91, 1994-'96. Dirt 1990-'91. Dead heat for third 1998. Dead heat for second 2006. ‡Futurist finished second, DQ to third, 1992. ‡Say Dance finished third, DQ to fourth, 1992.

Miesque Stakes

Grade 3 in 2006. Hollywood Park, two-year-olds, fillies, 1 mile, turf. Held November 26, 2004 in two divisions, with a gross value of $75,000 for each division. First held in 1990. First graded in 1995. Stakes record 1:34.30 (1995 Antespend).

Year	Winner	Jockey	Second	Third	Strs	Time	1st Purse
2004	**Louvain (Ire)**, 2, 115	R. A. Dominguez	Royal Copenhagen (Fr), 2, 114	La Maitresse (Ire), 2, 114	8	1:37.19	$45,000
	Paddy's Daisy, 2, 121	C. S. Nakatani	Conveyor's Angel, 2, 118	Kenza, 2, 116	8	1:36.92	45,000
2003	**Mambo Slew**, 2, 116	M. E. Smith	Ticker Tape (GB), 2, 116	Winendynme, 2, 116	11	1:36.17	60,000
2002	**Atlantic Ocean**, 2, 121	D. R. Flores	Tangle (Ire), 2, 114	Major Idea, 2, 121	8	1:34.63	120,000
2001	**Forty On Line (GB)**, 2, 117	C. S. Nakatani	Riskaverse, 2, 121	Daisyago, 2, 118	10	1:36.38	120,000
2000	**Fantastic Filly (Fr)**, 2, 116	G. K. Gomez	Smart Timing, 2, 115	Eminent, 2, 118	10	1:35.11	120,000
1999	**Prairie Princess**, 2, 116	A. O. Solis	She's Classy, 2, 118	Mary Kies, 2, 121	6	1:37.30	120,000
1998	**Here's to You**, 2, 116	E. Delahoussaye	Sweet Ludy (Ire), 2, 118	Nausicaa, 2, 116	7	1:36.57	120,000

1997	**Star's Proud Penny**, 2, 116	G. K. Gomez	Superlative, 2, 121	Ransom the Dreamer, 2, 121	9	1:37.42	$120,000
1996	**Ascutney**, 2, 116	E. Delahoussaye	Wealthy, 2, 116	Clever Pilot, 2, 118	8	1:35.16	120,000
1995	**Antespend**, 2, 121	C. W. Antley	Wheatly Special, 2, 121	Platinum Blonde, 2, 121	10	**1:34.30**	110,000
1994	**Bail Out Becky**, 2, 121	K. Desormeaux	Miss Union Avenue, 2, 121	Makin Whopee (Fr), 2, 117	10	1:37.26	110,000
1993	**Tricky Code**, 2, 116	C. S. Nakatani	Irish Forever, 2, 121	Roget's Fact, 2, 114	6	1:35.15	137,500
1992	**Creaking Board (GB)**, 2, 115	K. Desormeaux	Ask Anita, 2, 117	Zoonaqua, 2, 121	10	1:35.62	137,500
1991	**More Than Willing**, 2, 118	E. Delahoussaye	Stormagain, 2, 115	Looie Capote, 2, 114	8	1:35.51	61,875
	Hopeful Amber, 2, 114	D. R. Flores	Storm Ring, 2, 115	Crownette, 2, 114	8	1:36.72	61,875
1990	**Dead Heat**, 3, 114	J. A. Garcia	Bel's Starlet, 3, 114	Somethingmerry, 3, 114	7	1:41.00	35,650

Named for Flaxman Holding's English and French champion, '87, '88 U.S. champion grass female, and '87 Breeders' Cup Mile (at Hollywood Park) winner Miesque (1984 f. by Nureyev). Not held 2005. 1$^1/_{16}$ miles 1990. Three-year-olds 1990. Two divisions 1991, 2004.

Milady Breeders' Cup Handicap

Grade 2 in 2006. Hollywood Park, three-year-olds and up, fillies and mares, 1$^1/_{16}$ miles, dirt. Held June 3, 2006, with a gross value of $168,000. First held in 1952. First graded in 1973. Stakes record 1:40.20 (1980 Image of Reality).

Year	Winner	Jockey	Second	Third	Strs	Time	1st Purse
2006	**Proposed**, 4, 120	P. A. Valenzuela	Star Parade (Arg), 7, 120	Somethinaboutlaura, 4, 115	5	1:42.92	$110,400
2005	**Andujar**, 4, 117	C. S. Nakatani	Hollywood Story, 4, 121	Star Parade (Arg), 6, 115	7	1:41.59	127,290
2004	**Star Parade (Arg)**, 5, 116	V. Espinoza	Quero Quero, 4, 115	Pesci, 4, 114	5	1:41.83	125,670
2003	**Azeri**, 5, 125	M. E. Smith	Enjoy, 4, 114	Tropical Blossom, 5, 111	6	1:41.87	127,080
2002	**Azeri**, 4, 122	M. E. Smith	Affluent, 4, 119	Collect Call, 4, 115	6	1:42.02	126,840
2001	**Lazy Slusan**, 6, 119	V. Espinoza	Lady Melesi, 4, 116	Feverish, 6, 118	6	1:42.25	157,980
2000	**Riboletta (Brz)**, 5, 120	C. J. McCarron	Bordelaise (Arg), 5, 117	Excellent Meeting, 4, 121	6	1:42.01	112,860
1999	**Gourmet Girl**, 4, 115	E. Delahoussaye	Yolo Lady, 4, 115	Victory Stripes (Arg), 5, 117	5	1:40.97	112,440
1998	**I Ain't Bluffing**, 4, 120	C. J. McCarron	Fleet Lady, 4, 119	Real Connection, 7, 112	6	1:42.16	158,640
1997	**Listening**, 4, 116	A. O. Solis	Chile Chatte, 4, 114	Exotic Wood, 5, 118	5	1:41.20	95,220
1996	**Twice the Vice**, 5, 120	C. J. McCarron	Jewel Princess, 4, 120	Urbane, 4, 117	5	1:40.96	110,100
1995	**Pirate's Revenge**, 4, 116	C. W. Antley	Paseana (Arg), 8, 123	Private Persuasion, 4, 116	5	1:41.57	91,000
1994	**Andestine**, 4, 116	C. J. McCarron	Golden Klair (GB), 4, 119	Zarani Sidi Anna, 4, 116	7	1:41.40	94,900
1993	**Paseana (Arg)**, 6, 125	C. J. McCarron	Bold Windy, 4, 114	Re Toss (Arg), 6, 116	7	1:41.67	94,500
1992	**Paseana (Arg)**, 5, 125	C. J. McCarron	Re Toss (Arg), 5, 115	Fowda, 4, 119	7	1:41.46	94,200
1991	**Brought to Mind**, 4, 118	P. A. Valenzuela	Luna Elegante (Arg), 5, 114	Vieille Vigne (Fr), 4, 117	8	1:41.70	95,800
1990	**Bayakoa (Arg)**, 6, 127	L. A. Pincay Jr.	Fantastic Look, 4, 113	Kelly, 4, 110	4	1:41.20	89,700
1989	**Bayakoa (Arg)**, 5, 124	L. A. Pincay Jr.	Flying Julia, 6, 113	Carita Tostada (Chi), 5, 115	5	1:42.00	91,500
1988	**By Land by Sea**, 4, 124	F. Toro	Invited Guest (Ire), 4, 114	Integra, 4, 121	4	1:43.60	89,200
1987	**Seldom Seen Sue**, 4, 117	C. J. McCarron	Tiffany Lass, 4, 120	Frau Altiva (Arg), 5, 115	7	1:48.20	95,000
1986	**Dontstop Themusic**, 6, 122	D. G. McHargue	Magnificent Lindy, 4, 117	Truffles, 5, 110	7	1:48.80	63,500
1985	**Adored**, 5, 125	L. A. Pincay Jr.	Lovlier Linda, 5, 120	Mitterand, 4, 120	4	1:33.60	73,500
1984	**Adored**, 4, 119	L. A. Pincay Jr.	Princess Rooney, 4, 122	Lass Trump, 4, 117	7	1:41.00	63,800
1983	**Marisma (Chi)**, 5, 118	K. D. Black	A Kiss for Luck, 4, 113	Sangue (Ire), 5, 123	7	1:42.20	63,100
1982	**Cat Girl**, 4, 114	C. J. McCarron	Track Robbery, 6, 124	Ack's Secret, 6, 123	6	1:41.60	62,500
1981	**Save Wild Life**, 4, 115	C. J. McCarron	Princess Karenda, 4, 120	Swift Bird, 4, 115	9	1:42.80	65,700
1980	**Image of Reality**, 4, 117	D. G. McHargue	It's in the Air, 4, 122	Fondre, 5, 113	5	**1:40.20**	36,050
1979	**Innuendo**, 5, 113	D. Pierce	It's in the Air, 3, 112	Country Queen, 4, 121	9	1:41.20	32,700
1978	**Taisez Vous**, 4, 127	D. Pierce	Drama Critic, 4, 118	Sensational, 4, 121	8	1:41.80	32,150
1977	**Cascapedia**, 4, 126	S. Hawley	Rocky Trip, 5, 115	Just a Kick, 5, 118	6	1:40.80	31,250
1976	***Bastonera II**, 5, 117	L. A. Pincay Jr.	Swingtime, 4, 120	Just a Kick, 4, 121	6	1:42.00	31,600
1975	**Modus Vivendi**, 4, 121	D. Pierce	*Tizna, 6, 124	Mercy Dee, 4, 111	6	1:42.00	32,100
1974	**Twixt**, 5, 123	W. J. Passmore	Tallahto, 4, 121	*La Zanzara, 4, 121	10	1:41.00	33,900
1973	**Minstrel Miss**, 6, 118	D. Pierce	Susan's Girl, 4, 128	Pallisima, 4, 115	6	1:41.80	38,000

Grade 1 1973-2004. Milady H. 1952-'95. 7 furlongs 1952-'53. 1 mile 1954, 1958-'66, 1970-'72, 1985. 6 furlongs 1955-'57. 1$^1/_8$ miles 1986-'87.

Mineshaft Handicap

Grade 3 in 2006. Fair Grounds, four-year-olds and up, 1$^1/_{16}$ miles, dirt. Held February 12, 2005, with a gross value of $100,000. First held in 1973. First graded in 2003. Stakes record 1:42.55 (1994 Cool Quaker).

Year	Winner	Jockey	Second	Third	Strs	Time	1st Purse
2005	**Wanderin Boy**, 4, 113	L. J. Melancon	Pollard's Vision, 4, 121	‡Gigawatt, 5, 115	9	1:43.08	$60,000
2004	**Olmodavor**, 5, 121	C. J. Lanerie	Spanish Empire, 4, 118	Almuhathir, 6, 114	9	1:45.59	60,000
2003	**Balto Star**, 5, 118	E. M. Martin Jr.	Mineshaft, 4, 116	Bonapaw, 7, 115	8	1:43.74	75,000
2002	**Valhol**, 6, 115	R. Albarado	Parade Leader, 5, 115	Fight for Ally, 5, 113	10	1:42.94	75,000
2001	**Include**, 4, 112	L. J. Meche	Connected, 4, 112	Kombat Kat, 4, 113	8	1:44.01	75,000
2000	**Take Note of Me**, 6, 118	R. Albarado	Crimson Classic, 6, 114	Nite Dreamer, 5, 116	6	1:42.94	75,000
1999	**Precocity**, 5, 117	E. M. Martin Jr.	Prory, 7, 114	Take Note of Me, 5, 117	5	1:43.42	75,000
1998	**Moonlight Dancer**, 6, 114	C. C. Bourque	Precocity, 4, 117	Hot Brush, 4, 113	7	1:44.34	75,000
1997	**Byars**, 4, 114	C. C. Bourque	Bucks Nephew, 7, 117	Clash by Night, 4, 113	7	1:44.47	60,000
1996	**Bucks Nephew**, 6, 116	C. Perret	Prory, 4, 114	Vast Joy, 4, 114	9	1:43.40	38,025
1995	**Adhocracy**, 5, 112	L. J. Melancon	Dynamic Brush, 5, 111	Cool Quaker, 6, 113	7	1:43.10	31,530
1994	**Cool Quaker**, 5, 114	E. M. Martin Jr.	Dixie Poker Ace, 7, 121	Dixieland Heat, 4, 114	6	**1:42.55**	31,005
1993	**West by West**, 4, 117	J. Samyn	Place Dancer, 4, 112	Genuine Meaning, 6, 113	5	1:43.80	18,885

1992	**Irish Swap**, 5, 118	B. E. Poyadou	Jarraar, 5, 113	Wild and Tingley, 5, 113	6	1:43.00	$18,975
1985	**Rapid Gray**, 6, 122	R. P. Romero	Hopeful Word, 4, 113	Silver Diplomat, 4, 118	6	1:43.00	19,250

Named for W. S. Farish's 2003 Horse of the Year and '03 New Orleans H. (G2) winner Mineshaft. Formerly named for Calumet Farm's 1941, '42 Horse of the Year, '41 Triple Crown winner, and '42 Louisiana H. winner Whirlaway (1938 c. by *Blenheim II). Whirlaway H. 1985, 1992, 1998-2004. Whirlaway S. 1993-'97. Not held 1978-'80, 1982-'84, 1986-'91. 1 mile 40 yards 1973-'81. ‡Alumni Hall finished third, DQ to ninth for a positive drug test, 2005. Overnight handicap 1973-'77, 1981.

Mint Julep Handicap

Grade 3 in 2006. Churchill Downs, three-year-olds and up, fillies and mares, $1\frac{1}{16}$ miles, turf. Held June 4, 2005, with a gross value of $110,100. First held in 1977. First graded in 2001. Stakes record 1:40.98 (1994 Words of War).

Year	Winner	Jockey	Second	Third	Strs	Time	1st Purse
2005	**Delta Princess**, 6, 117	R. Albarado	Shaconage, 5, 116	Erhu, 4, 112	7	1:42.43	$68,262
2004	**Stay Forever**, 7, 116	E. Castro	Sand Springs, 4, 120	Eternal Melody (NZ), 4, 115	9	1:42.66	104,346
2003	**Kiss the Devil**, 5, 115	L. J. Meche	Quick Tip, 5, 119	Cellars Shiraz, 4, 120	9	1:41.73	104,346
2002	**Megans Bluff**, 5, 118	C. Perret	Cozy Island, 4, 112	Solvig, 5, 117	8	1:42.87	69,998
2001	**Megans Bluff**, 4, 118	C. Perret	Sitka, 4, 109	Good Game, 4, 116	10	1:42.88	70,432
2000	**Pratella**, 5, 118	L. J. Melancon	Silver Comic, 4, 115	Histoire Sainte (Fr), 4, 113	8	1:43.08	69,378
1999	**Mingling Glances**, 5, 113	L. J. Melancon	Formal Tango, 4, 115	Red Cat, 4, 116	11	1:42.59	70,928
1998	**B. A. Valentine**, 5, 116	F. Torres	Lordy Lordy, 5, 113	Mingling Glances, 4, 112	9	1:41.42	70,804
1997	**‡Valor Lady**, 5, 114	R. Albarado	My Secret, 5, 114	Everhope, 4, 112	11	1:41.20	71,238
1996	**Bail Out Becky**, 4, 118	C. Perret	Country Cat, 4, 117	Fluffkins, 4, 115	8	1:41.86	54,698
1995	**Romy**, 4, 118	J. L. Diaz	Olden Lek, 5, 114	Memories (Ire), 4, 113	6	1:42.69	54,941
1994	**Words of War**, 5, 117	C. H. Marquez Jr.	Freewheel, 5, 116	Eurostorm, 4, 112	10	**1:40.98**	55,673
1993	**Classic Reign**, 4, 115	F. A. Arguello Jr.	Tap Routine, 4, 113	Liz Cee, 5, 114	10	1:42.84	37,375
1992	**Lady Shirl**, 5, 123	P. A. Johnson	Topsa, 5, 112	Behaving Dancer, 5, 119	10	1:41.41	37,083
1991	**Dance for Lucy**, 5, 116	L. J. Melancon	Welsh Muffin (Ire), 4, 113	Super Fan, 4, 118	10	1:43.07	37,148
1990	**Tunita**, 5, 114	R. J. Thibeau Jr.	Port St. Mary (GB), 4, 113	Flags Waving, 4, 112	8	1:43.80	25,821
	Phoenix Sunshine, 5, 116	J. Deegan	Vana Turns, 5, 111	Carousel Baby, 4, 111	8	1:43.20	31,476
1989	**Here's Your Silver**, 4, 115	M. McDowell	Lt. Lao, 5, 117	Danzig's Bride, 4, 114	10	1:50.40	37,115
1988	**How I Wish**, 4, 113	E. Fires	Gaily Gaily (Ire), 5, 113	No Choice, 5, 114	10	1:51.00	36,660
1987	**Thunderdome**, 4, 119	S. H. Bass	Acquire, 5, 119	No Choice, 4, 119	8	1:37.80	26,247
	Innsbruck (GB), 4, 114	S. Hawley	Fantasy Lover, 4, 114	Marianna's Girl, 4, 122	8	1:38.00	21,470
1986	**Zenobia Empress**, 5, 120	E. Fires	Donut's Pride, 4, 120	Ante, 5, 117	7	1:35.80	28,418
1985	**Stave**, 4, 112	C. R. Woods Jr.	Gerrie Singer, 4, 120	Switching Trick, 5, 117	10	1:35.00	21,694
1984	**Lass Trump**, 4, 111	G. Patterson	Lady Hawthorn, 4, 114	Delhousie, 4, 111	7	1:37.00	26,267
1983	**Naskra Magic**, 4, 114	P. Rubbicco	Excitable Lady, 5, 120	Charge My Account, 4, 112	6	1:36.60	23,433
1982	**Kate's Cabin**, 4, 115	E. Snell	Mean Martha, 4, 112	Forever Cordial, 5, 112	8	1:25.20	23,855
1981	**Lillian Russell**, 4, 118	R. J. Hirdes Jr.	Run Ky. Run, 4, 121	Salud, 4, 114	9	1:23.20	19,468
1980	**Likely Exchange**, 6, 118	D. E. Whited	Nauti Lass, 5, 119	Dearyouloveme, 4, 117	11	1:24.40	19,728
1979	**Bold Rendezvous**, 4, 115	A. L. Fernandez	Likely Exchange, 5, 116	Popped Corn, 4, 116	10	1:25.00	17,908
1978	**Time for Pleasure**, 4, 120	T. Barrow	Don't Cry Barbi, 4, 119	Dear Irish, 4, 119	10	1:23.40	14,609
1977	**Satan's Cheer**, 5, 115	M. Manganello	Confort Zone, 4, 117	Decided Lady, 4, 115	7	1:24.00	14,300

Named for the traditional bourbon drink served at the Kentucky Derby. Sponsored by Early Times Distillery Co. of Louisville 2001-'05. Mint Julep S. 1982-'87, 1995-'96, 1998. 7 furlongs 1977-'82. 1 mile 1983-'87. $1\frac{1}{8}$ miles 1988-'89. Three-year-olds and up 1988. Two divisions 1987, 1990. ‡Romy finished first, DQ to fourth, 1997. Course record 1992, 1994.

Modesty Handicap

Grade 3 in 2006. Arlington Park, three-year-olds and up, fillies and mares, $1\frac{3}{16}$ miles, turf. Held July 23, 2005, with a gross value of $150,000. First held in 1942. First graded in 1985. Stakes record 1:55 (1985 Kapalua Butterfly).

Year	Winner	Jockey	Second	Third	Strs	Time	1st Purse
2005	**Noisette**, 5, 116	C. H. Velasquez	Shaconage, 5, 117	Spring Season, 6, 116	11	1:57.30	$90,000
2004	**Bedanken**, 5, 119	D. R. Pettinger	Aud, 4, 116	Shaconage, 4, 118	8	1:57.00	90,000
2003	**Owsley**, 5, 120	R. R. Douglas	Bien Nicole, 5, 119	Beret, 4, 115	7	1:55.06	90,000
2002	**England's Legend (Fr)**, 5, 121	R. R. Douglas	Quick Tip, 4, 114	Innit (Ire), 4, 116	8	1:55.69	90,000
2001	**Ioya Two**, 6, 115	M. Guidry	Megans Bluff, 4, 118	Solvig, 4, 116	11	1:55.47	90,000
2000	**Wade for Me**, 5, 116	C. A. Emigh	Candleinthedark, 5, 113	Wild Heart Dancing, 4, 115	10	1:57.06	60,000
1997	**War Thief**, 5, 116	S. J. Sellers	My Secret (Jpn), 5, 114	Bog Wild, 4, 117	8	1:57.40	60,000
1996	**Belle of Cozzene**, 4, 114	D. R. Pettinger	Trick Attack, 5, 112	Naskra Colors, 4, 113	6	1:58.24	60,000
1994	**‡Assert Oneself**, 4, 115	F. H. Valenzuela	One Dreamer, 6, 117	Seventies, 4, 112	9	1:56.01	60,000
1993	**Hero's Love**, 5, 120	E. Fires	Villandry, 5, 114	Silvered, 6, 120	10	1:55.31	60,000
1992	**Tango Charlie**, 3, 114	A. G. Sorrows Jr.	Alcando (Ire), 6, 114	Hero's Love, 4, 117	13	1:58.79	45,000
1991	**Lady Shirl**, 4, 120	S. J. Sellers	Lyphover, 6, 114	Country Casual, 4, 114	10	1:56.53	45,000
1990	**Gaily Gaily (Ire)**, 7, 114	M. E. Smith	Coolawin, 4, 123	Marsha's Dancer, 4, 114	11	1:55.40	51,405
1989	**Gaily Gaily (Ire)**, 6, 123	J. A. Krone	Baba Cool (Ire), 4, 117	Coolawin, 3, 115	13	1:58.20	52,740
1987	**Spruce Luck**, 6, 114	D. Brumfield	Dancing On a Cloud, 4, 120	Autumn Glitter, 4, 114	9	1:51.60	34,080
1986	**Zenobia Empress**, 5, 118	E. Fires	Navarchus, 4, 112	Flying Girl (Fr), 4, 118	11	1:44.00	53,580
1985	**Kapalua Butterfly**, 4, 115	D. G. McHargue	Trinado, 4, 116	Another Penny, 4, 111	11	**1:55.00**	44,265
1984	**Jay's Sue**, 5, 123	P. Day	Dictina (Fr), 3, 109	Pretty Perfect, 4, 113	9	2:01.20	43,719
1983	**Dana Calqui (Arg)**, 5, 114	F. Lovato Jr.	Unknown Lady, 4, 113	Sarah's a Beauty, 5, 115	12	2:01.40	34,470
1982	**Office Wife**, 5, 113	E. Fires	Sprite Flight, 4, 112	Touch of Glamour, 4, 117	9	1:58.20	33,750

1981	**Innocent Victim**, 3, 108	R. W. Cox	Passolyn, 4, 113	Touch of Glamour, 3, 112	13	1:59.00	$35,040
1980	**Allisons' Gal**, 4, 112	M. R. Morgan	La Bonzo, 4, 112	Jolie Dutch, 4, 114	14	2:01.20	35,160

Named for Modesty (1881 f. by War Dance), first female winner of the American Derby. Modesty S. 1942-'50, 1991-'93. Held at Washington Park 1942-'45, 1958-'61. Held at Hawthorne 1985. Not held 1969-'79, 1988, 1995, 1998-'99. 1 mile 1942, 1944-'46, 1952, 1966. 7 furlongs 1943, 1963-'65. 6 furlongs 1947-'51, 1953-'54, 1959-'62. 1$^1/_{16}$ miles 1955-'58, 1967-'68. 1$^1/_8$ miles 1987. Dirt 1942-'54, 1959-'65, 1996. Three-year-olds 1942. ‡Aube Indienne (Fr) finished first, DQ to seventh, 1994.

Molly Pitcher Breeders' Cup Handicap

Grade 2 in 2006. Monmouth Park, three-year-olds and up, fillies and mares, 1$^1/_{16}$ miles, dirt. Held July 9, 2005, with a gross value of $300,000. First held in 1946. First graded in 1973. Stakes record 1:41.20 (1983 Ambassador of Luck; 1986 Lady's Secret).

Year	Winner	Jockey	Second	Third	Strs	Time	1st Purse
2005	**Capeside Lady**, 4, 116	C. P. DeCarlo	Bending Strings, 4, 117	Emerald Earrings, 4, 114	7	1:41.49	$180,000
2004	**La Reason**, 4, 111	C. C. Lopez	Yell, 4, 114	Bare Necessities, 5, 119	7	1:51.10	180,000
2003	**Summer Colony**, 5, 120	G. L. Stevens	She's Got the Beat, 4, 112	Call an Audible, 4, 110	4	1:51.83	180,000
2002	**Atelier**, 5, 115	E. Coa	Summer Colony, 4, 119	Spain, 5, 122	5	1:48.63	180,000
2001	**March Magic**, 4, 113	M. J. Luzzi	Vivid Sunset, 4, 112	Shine Again, 4, 113	7	1:43.79	180,000
2000	**Lu Ravi**, 5, 116	P. Day	Silverbulletday, 4, 118	Bella Chiarra, 5, 116	7	1:43.17	180,000
1999	**Heritage of Gold**, 4, 114	C. T. Lambert	Harpia, 5, 116	Tap to Music, 4, 116	6	1:41.76	180,000
1998	**Relaxing Rhythm**, 4, 116	P. Day	Minister's Melody, 4, 117	Glitter Woman, 4, 120	6	1:42.30	120,000
1997	**Rare Blend**, 4, 116	M. E. Smith	Top Secret, 4, 116	Chip, 4, 115	5	1:43.60	120,000
1996	**Halo America**, 6, 117	P. Day	Rogues Walk, 4, 116	Why Be Normal, 8, 112	6	1:41.75	120,000
1995	**Inside Information**, 4, 124	M. E. Smith	Jade Flush, 4, 115	Halo America, 5, 118	5	1:43.81	90,000
1994	**Hey Hazel**, 4, 114	R. C. Landry	Ann Dear, 4, 113	Future of Gold, 4, 110	6	1:46.41	120,000
1993	**Wilderness Song**, 5, 119	D. Clark	Quilma (Chi), 6, 117	Looie Capote, 4, 116	6	1:44.79	90,000
1992	**Versailles Treaty**, 4, 120	M. E. Smith	Quick Mischief, 6, 115	Cozzene's Wish, 5, 113	6	1:43.18	90,000
1991	**Valay Maid**, 4, 116	M. Castaneda	Train Robbery, 4, 112	Toffeefee, 4, 116	9	1:43.88	90,000
1990	**A Penny Is a Penny**, 5, 120	A. T. Gryder	Leave It Be, 5, 116	Bodacious Tatas, 5, 117	9	1:43.40	90,000
1989	**Bodacious Tatas**, 4, 111	R. Wilson	Make Change, 4, 112	Grecian Flight, 5, 122	5	1:42.40	90,000
1988	**Personal Ensign**, 4, 125	R. P. Romero	Grecian Flight, 4, 119	Le l'Argent, 6, 117	5	1:41.80	90,000
1987	**Reel Easy**, 4, 112	W. H. McCauley	Lady's Secret, 5, 125	Catatonic, 5, 117	8	1:42.00	99,300
1986	**Lady's Secret**, 4, 126	P. Day	Chaldea, 6, 114	Key Witness, 4, 112	8	**1:41.20**	95,610
1985	**Sefa's Beauty**, 6, 119	P. Day	Mitterand, 4, 119	Dowery, 4, 115	11	1:42.60	69,090
1984	**Sultry Sun**, 4, 116	M. Solomone	Quixotic Lady, 4, 118	Nany, 4, 114	10	1:41.60	68,640
1983	**Ambassador of Luck**, 4, 117	A. Graell	Kattegat's Pride, 4, 122	Dance Number, 4, 115	8	**1:41.20**	67,830
1982	**Jameela**, 6, 120	J. L. Kaenel	Pukka Princess, 4, 114	Prismatical, 4, 117	8	1:42.60	67,620
1981	**Weber City Miss**, 4, 119	R. Hernandez	Jameela, 5, 118	Wistful, 4, 121	6	1:44.00	49,455
1980	**Plankton**, 4, 120	V. A. Bracciale Jr.	Doing It My Way, 4, 114	Whose Bid, 4, 113	12	1:44.20	34,950
1979	**Navajo Princess**, 5, 120	C. Perret	Frosty Skater, 4, 121	Water Malone, 5, 116	8	1:43.40	36,335
1978	**Creme Wave**, 4, 114	D. MacBeth	Pearl Necklace, 4, 123	Flame Lily, 4, 110	8	1:45.20	36,530
1977	**Dottie's Doll**, 4, 113	C. Perret	Proud Delta, 5, 123	Mississippi Mud, 4, 115	11	1:41.80	37,180
1976	**Garden Verse**, 4, 112	F. Lovato Sr.	Spring Is Here, 4, 111	Vodka Time, 4, 112	8	1:46.00	36,433
1975	**Honky Star**, 4, 123	J. E. Tejeira	Twixt, 6, 126	Bundler, 4, 119	9	1:43.00	36,156
1974	**Lady Love**, 4, 117	M. Hole	Ponte Vecchio, 4, 116	Belle Marie, 4, 117	8	1:43.80	28,908
1973	**Light Hearted**, 4, 120	E. Nelson	Wanda, 4, 118	Alma North, 5, 121	7	1:41.40	28,259

Named for Molly Pitcher, famed for firing a cannon during the Battle of Monmouth, New Jersey, during the Revolutionary War. Molly Pitcher H. 1946-'95. 1$^1/_8$ miles 2002-'04.

Monmouth Breeders' Cup Oaks

Grade 3 in 2006. Monmouth Park, three-year-olds, fillies, 1$^1/_{16}$ miles, dirt. Held August 14, 2005, with a gross value of $200,000. First held in 1871. First graded in 1973. Stakes record 1:41.92 (1997 Blushing K. D.).

Year	Winner	Jockey	Second	Third	Strs	Time	1st Purse
2005	**Flying Glitter**, 3, 116	E. Trujillo	Shebelongstoyou, 3, 116	Toll Taker, 3, 119	7	1:44.60	$120,000
2004	**Capeside Lady**, 3, 115	C. P. DeCarlo	Hopelessly Devoted, 3, 118	Habiboo, 3, 115	6	1:42.18	120,000
2002	**Magic Storm**, 3, 112	E. L. King Jr.	Alternate, 3, 114	Bronze Autumn, 3, 114	5	1:51.17	150,000
2001	**Unbridled Elaine**, 3, 121	E. Coa	Unrestrained, 3, 112	Indy Glory, 3, 114	7	1:51.02	150,000
2000	**Spain**, 3, 114	J. A. Velez Jr.	North Lake Jane, 3, 116	Prized Stamp, 3, 114	7	1:42.78	150,000
1999	**Silverbulletday**, 3, 121	J. D. Bailey	Boom Town Girl, 3, 121	Bag Lady Jane, 3, 116	4	1:43.03	150,000
1998	**Kirby's Song**, 3, 121	T. Kabel	Santaria, 3, 114	Brave Deed, 3, 112	6	1:43.31	120,000
1997	**Blushing K. D.**, 3, 121	L. J. Meche	Holiday Ball, 3, 116	Snowy Apparition, 3, 121	7	**1:41.92**	120,000
1996	**Top Secret**, 3, 114	J. Bravo	Yanks Music, 3, 121	Mesabi Maiden, 3, 121	5	1:42.33	120,000
1995	**Kathie's Colleen**, 3, 112	J. McAleney	Gal in a Ruckus, 3, 121	Country Cat, 3, 121	5	1:51.50	90,000
1994	**Two Altazano**, 3, 121	C. Perret	Stellarina, 3, 118	Cavada, 3, 121	5	1:52.19	90,000
1993	**Jacody**, 3, 121	T. G. Turner	Deputy Jane West, 3, 121	Sheila's Revenge, 3, 114	5	1:50.77	90,000
1992	**Diamond Duo**, 3, 121	T. G. Turner	dh-C. C.'s Return, 3, 114 dh-Secretly, 3, 112		8	1:51.40	90,000
1991	**Fowda**, 3, 121	R. Migliore	Shared Interest, 3, 114	Nalees Pin, 3, 116	8	1:50.48	90,000
1990	**Pampered Star**, 3, 121	J. C. Ferrer	Valay Maid, 3, 121	Jefforee, 3, 112	9	1:52.40	90,000
1989	**Dream Deal**, 3, 114	C. Perret	Some Romance, 3, 121	Top of My Life, 3, 121	9	1:49.20	90,000
1988	**Maplejinsky**, 3, 113	C. W. Antley	Make Change, 3, 114	Mother of Eight, 3, 114	6	1:53.60	102,000
1987	**Without Feathers**, 3, 116	C. W. Antley	Single Blade, 3, 121	Grecian Flight, 3, 121	8	1:48.00	66,240
1986	**Fighter Fox**, 3, 114	W. H. McCauley	Toes Knows, 3, 114	Dynamic Star, 3, 118	12	1:49.60	97,170

1985	**Golden Horde**, 3, 116	W. H. McCauley	Koluctoo's Jill, 3, 121	Tabayour, 3, 118	9	1:48.00	$94,380
1984	**Life's Magic**, 3, 121	J. Velasquez	Flippers, 3, 118	Cassowary, 3, 112	10	1:50.00	94,050
1983	**Quixotic Lady**, 3, 116	E. Maple	Am Capable, 3, 114	Pop Rock, 3, 116	5	1:50.40	64,770
1982	**Christmas Past**, 3, 121	J. Vasquez	Milingo, 3, 119	Mademoiselle Forli, 3, 112	9	1:49.40	67,050
1981	**Prismatical**, 3, 117	D. Brumfield	Stunning Native, 3, 112	Privacy, 3, 117	7	1:49.80	49,500
1980	**Rose of Morn**, 3, 114	D. Brumfield	Weber City Miss, 3, 121	Sami Sutton, 3, 117	7	1:50.40	33,030
1979	**Burn's Return**, 3, 117	J. Vasquez	Heavenly Ade, 3, 114	Dominant Dream, 3, 114	8	1:48.80	35,718
1978	**Sharp Belle**, 3, 117	D. B. Thomas	Mucchina, 3, 119	Jevalin, 3, 117	8	1:52.40	35,783
1977	**Small Raja**, 3, 121	M. Solomone	Herecomesthebride, 3, 117	Suede Shoe, 3, 114	8	1:49.60	35,978
1976	**Revidere**, 3, 121	J. Vasquez	Javamine, 3, 112	Quacker, 3, 114	8	1:50.60	36,238
1975	**Aunt Jin**, 3, 119	C. H. Marquez	Let Me Linger, 3, 112	Sarsar, 3, 121	6	1:49.20	35,295
1974	**Honky Star**, 3, 117	W. Blum	Kudara, 3, 117	Raisela, 3, 117	14	1:49.40	38,642
1973	**Desert Vixen**, 3, 114	M. Hole	Ladies Agreement, 3, 111	Lady Love, 3, 111	11	1:49.00	37,473

Monmouth Oaks 1871-'75, 1977-'95. Held at Jerome Park 1891. Not held 1878, 1894-1945, 2003. 1½ miles 1871-'77. 1¼ miles 1879-'93. 1⅛ miles 1953-'95, 2001-'03. Dead heat for second 1992.

Monrovia Handicap

Grade 3 in 2006. Santa Anita Park, three-year-olds and up, fillies and mares, 6½ furlongs, dirt (originally scheduled as a Grade 3 on the turf). Held December 31, 2005, with a gross value of $112,600. First held in 1968. First graded in 1973. Stakes record 1:12.40 (1981 Kilijaro [Ire]).

Year	Winner	Jockey	Second	Third	Strs	Time	1st Purse
2005	**Awesome Lady**, 4, 114	T. Baze	Beneficial Bartok, 4, 118	Allswellthatnswell, 4, 116	9	1:16.77	$67,560
2004	**Resplendency**, 3, 112	C. Fusilier	Puxa Saco, 4, 115	Market Garden, 4, 115	9	1:15.34	68,130
2003	**Icantgoforthat**, 4, 114	T. Baze	Polygreen (Fr), 4, 116	Spring Star (Fr), 4, 119	6	1:13.07	65,580
2002	**Lil Sister Stich**, 5, 117	L. A. Pincay Jr.	Pina Colada (GB), 3, 115	I'm the Business (NZ), 5, 116	12	1:13.81	68,820
2001	**Paga (Arg)**, 4, 117	M. E. Smith	Twin Set (Ger), 4, 115	Impeachable, 4, 115	13	1:15.09	70,890
2000	**Evening Promise (GB)**, 4, 120	K. Desormeaux	Squall Linda, 4, 113	New Heaven (Arg), 6, 119	12	1:12.62	68,640
1999	**Show Me the Stage**, 3, 117	K. Desormeaux	Chichim, 4, 116	Honest Lady, 3, 114	4	1:15.14	64,140
	Desert Lady (Ire), 4, 116	C. S. Nakatani	Sweet Mazarine (Ire), 5, 118	Supercilious, 6, 119	7	1:14.59	65,100
1998	**Madame Pandit**, 5, 118	E. Delahoussaye	Ski Dancer, 6, 115	Dixie Pearl, 6, 117	7	1:15.80	65,700
1997	**Grab the Prize**, 5, 116	A. O. Solis	Finite E. F., 4, 111	Evil's Pic, 5, 116	7	1:16.89	66,900
1996	**Klassy Kim**, 5, 116	G. F. Almeida	Ski Dancer, 4, 116	Baby Diamonds, 5, 114	8	1:14.48	65,650
1995	**Rabiadella**, 4, 117	P. A. Valenzuela	Dezibelle's Star, 4, 113	Las Meninas (Ire), 4, 120	5	1:14.92	47,450
1994	**Mamselle Bebette**, 4, 117	C. S. Nakatani	Shuggleswon, 4, 114	Kalita Melody (GB), 6, 117	6	1:15.35	49,650
1993	**Glen Kate (Ire)**, 6, 118	C. A. Black	Bel's Starlet, 6, 122	Heart of Joy, 6, 121	7	1:12.89	48,650
1992	**Middlefork Rapids**, 4, 116	P. A. Valenzuela	Remarkably Easy, 4, 115	Crystal Gazing, 4, 121	11	1:12.55	51,150
1991	**Wedding Bouquet (Ire)**, 4, 115	K. Desormeaux	Linda Card, 5, 118	Flower Girl (GB), 4, 116	11	1:13.90	51,875
1990	**Down Again**, 6, 117	C. A. Black	Sexy Slew, 4, 111	Hot Novel, 4, 116	9	1:13.00	50,200
1989	**Daloma (Fr)**, 5, 117	F. H. Valenzuela	Valdemosa (Arg), 5, 116	Sadie B. Fast, 4, 116	8	1:16.20	49,550
1988	**Aberuschka (Ire)**, 6, 121	G. L. Stevens	Pen Bal Lady (GB), 4, 118	Aromacor, 5, 114	10	1:14.60	50,050
1987	**Sari's Heroine**, 4, 117	P. A. Valenzuela	Lichi (Chi), 7, 116	Aberuschka (Ire), 5, 124	7	1:15.00	38,400
1986	**Water Crystals**, 5, 116	G. L. Stevens	Baroness Direct, 5, 120	Solva (GB), 5, 116	8	1:15.60	40,100
1985	**Lina Cavalieri (GB)**, 5, 121	E. Delahoussaye	Air Distingue, 5, 117	Tangent (NZ), 5, 121	8	1:14.00	39,650
1984	**Tangent (NZ)**, 4, 117	J. A. Garcia	Irish O'Brien, 6, 115	Frieda Frame, 6, 119	10	1:14.60	41,750
1983	**Matching**, 5, 123	R. Sibille	Irish O'Brien, 5, 115	Night Fire, 4, 115	9	1:13.20	40,600
1982	**Cat Girl**, 4, 117	C. J. McCarron	Excitable Lady, 4, 122	Chateau Dancer, 4, 117	10	1:14.60	41,250
1981	**Kilijaro (Ire)**, 5, 127	M. Castaneda	Love You Dear, 5, 115	She Can't Miss, 4, 119	10	**1:12.40**	34,950
1980	**Fondre**, 5, 113	F. Olivares	Powder Room, 5, 117	Celine, 4, 118	8	1:15.20	27,500
1979	**Camarado**, 4, 119	W. Shoemaker	Pet Label, 6, 115	Sister Julie, 6, 115	11	1:15.40	22,900
	Palmistry, 4, 114	C. J. McCarron	Sing Back, 6, 113	Pressing Date, 5, 114	10	1:15.20	22,500
1978	**Little Happiness**, 4, 116	L. A. Pincay Jr.	Perils of Pauline, 4, 115	Harvest Girl, 4, 119	6	1:16.00	26,200
1977	**Winter Solstice**, 5, 119	M. S. Sellers	Nana Lee, 5, 116	Olive Wreath, 4, 113	9	1:13.60	27,600
1976	**Winter Solstice**, 4, 117	J. Lambert	Miss Tokyo, 4, 121	Exotic Age, 5, 115	7	1:17.60	20,300
1975	**‡Special Goddess**, 4, 119	S. Hawley	Charger's Star, 5, 115	Miss Musket, 4, 124	8	1:13.80	20,700
1974	**Viva La Vivi**, 4, 118	D. Pierce	Impressive Style, 5, 120	Charger's Star, 4, 113	9	1:15.00	17,800
1973	***Tizna**, 4, 119	F. Toro	Generous Portion, 5, 120	‡Soul Mate, 4, 120	11	1:13.80	22,700

Named for railroad pioneer W. N. Monroe (1841-1935), founder of the city of Monrovia, California. Not graded 1975-'89, 2004-'05. 6½ furlongs 1969-'70, 1976, 1978, 1980, 1989, 1994, 1997-'99. Dirt 1969-'70, 1976, 1978, 1980, 1989, 1994, 1997-'99, 2004-'05. Originally scheduled on turf 2004-'05. Four-year-olds and up 1968-'98, 1999 (January). Two divisions 1979. Held in January and December 1999. ‡*Rich Return II finished third, DQ to fourth, 1973. ‡Viva La Vivi finished first, DQ to eighth, 1975.

Morvich Handicap

Grade 3 in 2006. Oak Tree at Santa Anita, three-year-olds and up, 6½ furlongs, turf. Held October 29, 2005, with a gross value of $100,000. First held in 1974. First graded in 1999. Stakes record 1:11.46 (2001 El Cielo).

Year	Winner	Jockey	Second	Third	Strs	Time	1st Purse
2005	**Geronimo (Chi)**, 6, 118	K. Desormeaux	King Robyn, 5, 118	Jungle Prince, 4, 114	8	1:12.10	$60,000
2004	**Leroidesanimaux (Brz)**, 4, 117	J. K. Court	De Valmont (Aus), 7, 115	Cayoke (Fr), 7, 116	6	1:11.76	60,000
2003	**King Robyn**, 3, 117	A. O. Solis	Medecis (GB), 4, 116	Geronimo (Chi), 4, 115	9	1:13.22	66,480
2002	**Master Belt (NZ)**, 4, 114	T. Baze	I Love Silver, 4, 116	Kachamandi (Chi), 5, 117	10	1:12.26	67,020
2001	**El Cielo**, 7, 123	J. Valdivia Jr.	Speak in Passing, 4, 116	Islander, 6, 115	6	**1:11.46**	64,680
2000	**El Cielo**, 6, 119	J. Valdivia Jr.	Kahal (GB), 6, 119	Montemiro (Fr), 6, 116	10	1:12.00	67,020
1999	**‡Riviera (Fr)**, 5, 118	B. Blanc	Kahal (GB), 5, 114	Howbaddouwantit, 4, 121	10	1:12.99	66,840
1998	**Musafi**, 4, 117	G. K. Gomez	Fabulous Guy (Ire), 4, 114	Expelled, 6, 119	8	1:14.54	60,000

1997	**Reality Road**, 5, 115	C. S. Nakatani	Latin Dancer, 3, 116	Torch Rouge (GB), 6, 115	7	1:13.60	$60,000
1996	**Comininalittlehot**, 5, 117	K. Desormeaux	Wild Zone, 6, 116	Wavy Run (Ire), 5, 116	7	1:11.57	65,100
1995	**Score Quick**, 3, 113	G. F. Almeida	Dramatic Gold, 4, 120	Fu Man Slew, 4, 114	7	1:14.64	60,700
1994	**Rotsaluck**, 3, 115	F. H. Valenzuela	D'Hallevant, 4, 118	Didyme, 4, 115	7	1:13.66	47,925
1993	**†Western Approach**, 4, 115	K. Desormeaux	†Yousefia, 4, 116	Exemplary Leader, 7, 115	6	1:12.12	47,025
1992	**Regal Groom**, 5, 118	M. A. Pedroza	Bailarin, 5, 112	Repriced, 4, 118	4	1:16.88	45,150
1991	**Waterscape**, 5, 119	K. Desormeaux	Hollywood Reporter, 5, 113	Anjiz, 3, 115	6	1:11.95	47,250
1990	**Yes I'm Blue**, 4, 116	D. R. Flores	Waterscape, 4, 115	Oraibi, 5, 118	9	1:12.40	49,350
1989	**Basic Rate**, 4, 113	R. Q. Meza	Patchy Groundfog, 6, 118	Major Current, 5, 116	12	1:12.20	52,125
1988	**Dr. Brent**, 3, 115	F. Toro	†Serve n' Volley (GB), 4, 115	Caballo de Oro, 4, 114	12	1:15.80	51,350
1987	**Sabona**, 5, 117	C. J. McCarron	†Aberuschka (Ire), 5, 117	Deputy Governor, 3, 118	8	1:14.80	38,900
1986	**River Drummer**, 4, 121	G. L. Stevens	Prince Sky (Ire), 4, 118	Perfec Travel, 4, 116	11	1:13.80	69,700
1985	**Dear Rick**, 4, 118	C. J. McCarron	Champagne Bid, 6, 121	Hegemony (Ire), 4, 121	8	1:14.20	38,650
1984	**Tsunami Slew**, 3, 119	E. Delahoussaye	Night Mover, 4, 121	Debonaire Junior, 3, 120	8	1:14.00	39,000
1983	**Kangroo Court**, 6, 119	J. J. Steiner	Shanekite, 5, 120	Dave's Friend, 8, 121	7	1:16.00	38,350
1982	**Shanekite**, 4, 115	S. Hawley	Remember John, 3, 120	Smokite, 6, 117	7	1:12.80	37,050
1981	**Forlion**, 5, 116	M. Castaneda	Aristocratical, 4, 117	Syncopate, 6, 122	8	1:13.80	32,800
1980	**To B. Or Not**, 4, 118	M. Castaneda	Someonenoble, 5, 115	†Great Lady M., 5, 119	9	1:13.80	32,200
1979	**Arachnoid**, 6, 119	D. Pierce	He's Dewan, 4, 118	Bywayofchicago, 5, 120	6	1:12.60	25,150
1978	**Impressive Luck**, 5, 119	F. Toro	Bad 'n Big, 4, 126	Eagle in Flight, 7, 114	6	1:13.20	25,250
1977	**Impressive Luck**, 4, 118	F. Toro	Jumping Hill, 5, 120	Key Account, 5, 115	9	1:13.60	19,650
1976	**Cherry River**, 6, 120	L. A. Pincay Jr.	Mark's Place, 4, 119	Uniformity, 4, 117	10	1:13.40	20,400
1975	**Century's Envoy**, 4, 125	J. Lambert	Sir Jason, 4, 117	Cherry River, 5, 123	6	1:13.40	15,900
1974	**Palladium**, 5, 115	A. Pineda	Against the Snow, 4, 118	Soft Victory, 6, 119	6	1:16.20	15,800

Named for Benjamin Block's 1921 champion two-year-old male and '22 Kentucky Derby winner Morvich (1919 c. by Runnymede); Morvich was that race's first California-bred winner. 6½ furlongs 1983, 1992, 1995. Dirt 1983, 1992, 1995. Two-year-olds and up 1974-'92. ‡Kahal (GB) finished first, DQ to second, 1999. †Denotes female.

Mother Goose Stakes

Grade 1 in 2006. Belmont Park, three-year-olds, fillies, 1⅛ miles, dirt. Held June 25, 2005, with a gross value of $300,000. First held in 1957. First graded in 1965. Stakes record 1:46.58 (1994 Lakeway).

Year	Winner	Jockey	Second	Third	Strs	Time	1st Purse
2005	**Smuggler**, 3, 121	E. S. Prado	Spun Sugar, 3, 121	Summerly, 3, 121	6	1:48.55	$180,000
2004	**Stellar Jayne**, 3, 121	R. Albarado	Ashado, 3, 121	Island Sand, 3, 121	6	1:48.13	180,000
2003	**Spoken Fur**, 3, 121	J. D. Bailey	Yell, 3, 121	Final Round, 3, 121	6	1:50.41	180,000
2002	**Nonsuch Bay**, 3, 121	J. D. Bailey	Chamrousse, 3, 121	Seba (GB), 3, 121	4	1:49.09	150,000
2001	**Fleet Renee**, 3, 121	J. R. Velazquez	Real Cozzy, 3, 121	Exogenous, 3, 121	10	1:47.19	150,000
2000	**Secret Status**, 3, 121	P. Day	Jostle, 3, 121	Finder's Fee, 3, 121	7	1:48.03	150,000
1999	**Dreams Gallore**, 3, 121	R. Albarado	Oh What a Windfall, 3, 121	Better Than Honour, 3, 121	6	1:48.69	150,000
1998	**Jersey Girl**, 3, 121	M. E. Smith	Keeper Hill, 3, 121	Banshee Breeze, 3, 121	11	1:47.77	120,000
1997	**Ajina**, 3, 121	M. E. Smith	Sharp Cat, 3, 121	Tomisue's Delight, 3, 121	6	1:48.40	120,000
1996	**Yanks Music**, 3, 121	J. R. Velazquez	Escena, 3, 121	Cara Rafaela, 3, 121	7	1:47.90	120,000
1995	**Serena's Song**, 3, 121	G. L. Stevens	Golden Bri, 3, 121	Forested, 3, 121	6	1:50.37	120,000
1994	**Lakeway**, 3, 121	K. Desormeaux	Cinnamon Sugar (Ire), 3, 121	Inside Information, 3, 121	6	**1:46.58**	120,000
1993	**Sky Beauty**, 3, 121	M. E. Smith	Dispute, 3, 121	Silky Feather, 3, 121	4	1:49.69	120,000
1992	**Turnback the Alarm**, 3, 121	C. W. Antley	Easy Now, 3, 121	Queen of Triumph, 3, 121	7	1:48.80	120,000
1991	**Meadow Star**, 3, 121	J. D. Bailey	Lite Light, 3, 121	Nalees Pin, 3, 121	4	1:48.92	120,000
1990	**Go for Wand**, 3, 121	R. P. Romero	Charon, 3, 121	Stella Madrid, 3, 121	6	1:48.80	136,560
1989	**Open Mind**, 3, 121	A. T. Cordero Jr.	Gorgeous, 3, 121	Nite of Fun, 3, 121	5	1:47.40	136,320
1988	**Goodbye Halo**, 3, 121	J. Velasquez	Make Change, 3, 121	Aptostar, 3, 121	9	1:49.80	142,320
1987	**Fiesta Gal**, 3, 121	A. T. Cordero Jr.	Grecian Flight, 3, 121	Chic Shirine, 3, 121	12	1:50.20	150,240
1986	**Life At the Top**, 3, 121	J. A. Santos	Dynamic Star, 3, 121	Family Style, 3, 121	8	1:49.60	132,300
1985	**Mom's Command**, 3, 121	A. Fuller	Le l'Argent, 3, 121	Willowy Mood, 3, 121	11	1:49.60	109,800
1984	**Life's Magic**, 3, 121	J. Velasquez	Miss Oceana, 3, 121	Wild Applause, 3, 121	5	1:48.80	127,620
1983	**Able Money**, 3, 121	A. Graell	High Schemes, 3, 121	Far Flying, 3, 121	7	1:49.20	84,150
1982	**Cupecoy's Joy**, 3, 121	A. Santiago	Christmas Past, 3, 121	Blush With Pride, 3, 121	12	1:48.40	69,120
1981	**Wayward Lass**, 3, 121	C. B. Asmussen	Heavenly Cause, 3, 121	Banner Gala, 3, 121	8	1:48.80	66,720
1980	**Sugar and Spice**, 3, 121	J. Fell	Bold 'n Determined, 3, 121	Erin's Word, 3, 121	8	1:49.60	68,040
1979	**Davona Dale**, 3, 121	J. Velasquez	Eloquent, 3, 121	Plankton, 3, 121	6	1:48.80	63,960
1978	**Caesar's Wish**, 3, 121	D. R. Wright	Lakeville Miss, 3, 121	Tempest Queen, 3, 121	8	1:47.60	48,600
1977	**Road Princess**, 3, 121	J. Cruguet	Mrs. Warren, 3, 121	Cum Laude Laurie, 3, 121	16	1:48.80	51,480
1976	**Girl in Love**, 3, 121	J. Cruguet	Optimistic Gal, 3, 121	Ancient Fables, 3, 121	5	1:48.80	48,510
1975	**Ruffian**, 3, 121	J. Vasquez	Sweet Old Girl, 3, 121	Sun and Snow, 3, 121	7	1:47.80	50,220
1974	**Chris Evert**, 3, 121	J. Velasquez	Maud Muller, 3, 121	Quaze Quilt, 3, 121	14	1:48.60	53,775
1973	**Windy's Daughter**, 3, 121	E. Belmonte	Lady Love, 3, 121	North Broadway, 3, 121	10	1:48.40	52,965

Named for Harry Payne Whitney's consensus 1924 champion two-year-old filly and '24 Fashion S. winner Mother Goose (1922 f. by *Chicle). Held at Aqueduct 1963-'67, 1969, 1975. 1$^1/_{16}$ miles 1957-'58.

Mr. Prospector Handicap

Grade 3 in 2006. Gulfstream Park, three-year-olds and up, 6 furlongs, dirt. Held January 7, 2006, with a gross value of $100,000. First held in 1946. First graded in 1999. Stakes record 1:08.45 (1997 Punch Line).

Year	Winner	Jockey	Second	Third	Strs	Time	1st Purse
2006	**Gaff**, 4, 113	S. Bridgmohan	War Front, 4, 115	Friendly Island, 5, 116	8	1:08.50	$60,000

2005	**Saratoga County**, 4, 112	J. Castellano	Limehouse, 4, 116	All Hail Stormy, 4, 113	10	1:08.99	$60,000
2004	**Cajun Beat**, 4, 121	C. H. Velasquez	Gygistar, 5, 118	Deer Lake, 5, 115	6	1:09.06	60,000
2003	**Baileys Edge**, 6, 114	G. Boulanger	Friendly Frolic, 4, 114	Out of Fashion, 7, 115	6	1:09.95	60,000
2002	**Hook and Ladder**, 5, 116	J. R. Velazquez	Kipperscope, 5, 114	Red's Honor, 4, 114	8	1:09.69	60,000
2001	**Istintaj**, 5, 116	J. D. Bailey	Miners Gamble, 5, 115	Smokin Pete, 4, 115	13	1:09.63	60,000
2000	**Mountain Top**, 5, 115	J. A. Santos	Lifeisawhirl, 4, 112	Silver Season, 4, 115	6	1:10.80	60,000
1999	**Cowboy Cop**, 5, 114	P. Day	Good and Tough, 4, 115	Mint, 4, 115	6	1:09.65	45,000
1998	**Rare Rock**, 5, 116	P. Day	Heckofaralph, 5, 115	Banjo, 4, 114	8	1:08.67	45,000
1997	**Punch Line**, 7, 116	P. Day	Appealing Skier, 4, 119	Constant Escort, 5, 115	8	**1:08.45**	45,000
1996	**Meadow Monster**, 5, 114	R. Wilson	Lord Carson, 4, 119	Ponche, 7, 118	8	1:09.47	30,000
1995	**Sweet Beast**, 5, 118	M. E. Smith	Exclusive Praline, 4, 119	Distinct Reality, 4, 113	5	1:09.36	30,000
1994	**Binalong**, 5, 116	J. D. Bailey	I Can't Believe, 6, 113	Golden Pro, 4, 113	12	1:09.68	30,000
1993	**Surely Six**, 4, 113	R. Wilson	Groomstick, 7, 114	Poulain d'Or, 4, 117	9	1:21.85	30,000
1992	**Take Me Out**, 4, 115	J. D. Bailey	Gizmo's Fortune, 4, 111	Ocala Flame, 4, 113	10	1:23.75	30,000
1991	**Stalker**, 4, 114	C. Perret	Secret Hello, 4, 117	Shuttleman, 5, 114	11	1:22.50	30,000
1990	**Beau Genius**, 5, 117	W. Shoemaker	The Red Rolls, 6, 112	Norquestor, 4, 116	6	1:23.20	30,000
1989	**Miami Slick**, 4, 112	J. D. Bailey	Dancing Spree, 4, 114	The Red Rolls, 5, 112	6	1:09.20	34,200
1988	**Jato D'Agua (Brz)**, 6, 110	W. A. Guerra	Banbury Cross, 5, 111	Our Happy Warrior, 4, 110	11	1:09.80	37,560
1987	**Uncle Ho**, 4, 111	J. A. Santos	Splendid Catch, 5, 113	Mugatea, 7, 114	7	1:22.60	27,984
1986	**Fortunate Prospect**, 5, 118	R. I. Velez	It's a Done Deal, 4, 113	Basket Weave, 5, 115	8	1:10.40	28,608
1985	**For Halo**, 4, 120	B. Fann	Northern Trader, 4, 115	Rupert's Wing, 4, 111	11	1:09.60	37,620
1984	**D. White**, 3, 112	A. O. Solis	Mo Exception, 3, 112	Reach for More, 3, 117	7	1:44.40	24,276
1983	**Chan Balum**, 4, 111	J. Samyn	Center Cut, 4, 118	Royal Hierarchy, 6, 114	10	1:10.00	25,683
1982	**Noble Warrior**, 6, 119	O. J. Londono	Morold (Fr), 7, 116	San Sal, 4, 110	9	2:27.20	18,585
1980	**Archie Beamish**, 7, 111	W. A. Guerra	Proud Manner, 6, 114	Foretake, 4, 115	10	2:27.20	14,970
1978	**Practitioner**, 5, 121	J. A. Santiago	Unilateral, 4, 110	Odd Man, 7, 113	8	3:18.20	14,520

Named for Aisco Stable's 1987, '88 leading North American sire and nine-time leading North American broodmare sire Mr. Prospector (1970 c. by Raise a Native), who set a six-furlong track record at Gulfstream Park in 1973. Formerly named for Hallandale, Florida, location of Gulfstream Park. Hallandale H. 1946-2000. Not held 1949, 1957-'77, 1979, 1981. 1¹/₁₆ miles 1946, 1984. 1¹/₈ miles 1947-'56. About 2 miles 1978. 1¹/₂ miles 1980, 1982. 7 furlongs 1987, 1990-'93. Turf 1978-'82. Three-year-olds 1946, 1984. Four-year-olds and up 1947. Track record 2006. Held as an allowance race 1950-'55.

Mrs. Revere Stakes

Grade 2 in 2006. Churchill Downs, three-year-olds, fillies, 1¹/₁₆ miles, turf. Held November 12, 2005, with a gross value of $166,950. First held in 1991. First graded in 1995. Stakes record 1:42.86 (2001 Snow Dance).

Year	Winner	Jockey	Second	Third	Strs	Time	1st Purse
2005	**My Typhoon (Ire)**, 3, 120	R. Albarado	Isla Cozzene, 3, 120	Silver Cup (Ire), 3, 120	7	1:43.36	$103,509
2004	**River Belle (GB)**, 3, 120	K. Fallon	Lenatareese, 3, 120	Cape Town Lass, 3, 114	10	1:44.59	106,113
2003	**Hoh Buzzard (Ire)**, 3, 120	R. Fogelsonger	Aud, 3, 120	Gamble to Victory, 3, 116	12	1:45.01	108,903
2002	**Caught in the Rain**, 3, 119	E. L. King Jr.	Glia, 3, 119	Bedanken, 3, 122	11	1:46.25	107,694
2001	**Snow Dance**, 3, 122	C. Perret	Stylish, 3, 115	Cozy Island, 3, 111	10	**1:42.86**	106,950
2000	**Megans Bluff**, 3, 122	M. Guidry	Uncharted Haven (GB), 3, 119	Impending Bear, 3, 119	12	1:43.37	107,973
1999	**Silver Comic**, 3, 115	L. J. Melancon	St Clair Ridge (Ire), 3, 119	Circle of Gold (Ire), 3, 119	12	1:45.13	108,345
1998	**Anguilla**, 3, 119	P. Day	Darling Alice, 3, 119	White Beauty, 3, 119	11	1:45.67	107,601
1997	**Parade Queen**, 3, 122	P. Day	Mystery Code, 3, 117	Starry Dreamer, 3, 122	11	1:45.46	108,624
1996	**Maxzene**, 3, 117	J. A. Krone	Fasta, 3, 117	Turkappeal, 3, 119	12	1:43.78	72,354
1995	**Petrouchka**, 3, 122	D. Penna	Christmas Gift, 3, 122	Ms. Isadora, 3, 117	11	1:44.20	75,725
1994	**Mariah's Storm**, 3, 122	R. N. Lester	Avie's Fancy, 3, 119	Bear Truth, 3, 119	10	1:43.99	75,400
1993	**Weekend Madness (Ire)**, 3, 117	C. R. Woods Jr.	Flower Circle, 3, 117	Amal Hayati, 3, 122	10	1:46.32	74,685
1992	**McKaymackenna**, 3, 119	J. Velasquez	Spinning Round, 3, 122	Aquilegia, 3, 117	10	1:45.04	56,209
1991	**Spanish Parade**, 3, 117	P. Day	Liz Cee, 3, 117	Savethelastdance, 3, 117	10	1:46.19	37,408

Named for Dr. Hiram Polk Jr.'s and Dr. David Richardson's 1984 Dogwood, Edgewood, and Regret S. winner Mrs. Revere (1981 f. by Silver Series). Grade 3 1995-'97.

My Charmer Handicap

Grade 3 in 2006. Calder Race Course, three-year-olds and up, fillies and mares, 1¹/₈ miles, turf. Held December 3, 2005, with a gross value of $100,000. First held in 1984. First graded in 1998. Stakes record 1:45.40 (1988 Sunny Issues).

Year	Winner	Jockey	Second	Third	Strs	Time	1st Purse
2005	**Snowdrops (GB)**, 5, 115	B. Blanc	La Reina, 4, 116	Ticker Tape (GB), 4, 117	9	1:48.33	$60,000
2004	**Something Ventured**, 5, 115	J. R. Velazquez	Snowdrops (GB), 4, 115	Changing World, 4, 117	12	1:46.79	60,000
2003	**New Economy**, 5, 115	R. Homeister Jr.	Something Ventured, 4, 116	Ivanavinalot, 3, 113	12	1:46.97	60,000
2002	**Wander Mom**, 4, 114	E. Coa	Strawberry Blonde (Ire), 4, 114	Babae (Chi), 6, 121	10	1:48.43	60,000
2001	**Batique**, 5, 116	J. F. Chavez	Please Sign In, 5, 114	Wander Mom, 3, 114	12	1:49.85	60,000
2000	**‡Wild Heart Dancing**, 4, 116	J. F. Chavez	Megans Bluff, 3, 116	Orange Sunset (Ire), 4, 114	12	1:47.58	60,000
1999	**Crystal Symphony**, 3, 114	C. H. Velasquez	Winfama, 6, 114	Khumba Mela (Ire), 4, 120	12	1:47.65	60,000
1998	**Colcon**, 5, 118	J. D. Bailey	Cuando, 4, 117	Winfama, 5, 117	12	1:50.51	60,000
1997	**Overcharger**, 5, 116	J. A. Rivera II	Dance Clear (Ire), 4, 113	Hero's Pride (Fr), 4, 116	12	1:48.18	60,000
1996	**Romy**, 5, 114	F. C. Torres	Delta Love, 3, 114	Ms. Mostly, 3, 115	7	1:47.33	60,000
1995	**Danish (Ire)**, 4, 116	J. A. Santos	Cox Orange, 5, 119	Alice Springs, 5, 123	11	1:46.40	60,000
1994	**Caress**, 3, 114	R. G. Davis	Putthepowdertoit, 4, 114	Cox Orange, 4, 116	12	1:50.63	60,000
1993	**Chickasha**, 4, 115	R. D. Lopez	Marshua's River, 6, 113	Always Nettie, 4, 114	14	1:47.36	30,000
1992	**Explosive Kate**, 5, 118	D. Penna	Mia Bird Too, 3, 113	Kiwi Mint, 4, 114	9	1:46.58	30,000

	Julie La Rousse (Ire), 4, 120	J. D. Bailey	Marshua's River, 5, 114	Highland Crystal, 4, 115	10	1:45.78	$30,000
	Lady Shirl, 5, 120	E. Fires	Ratings, 4, 115	Seaquay, 6, 111	11	1:44.74	51,150
1990	**Primetime North**, 3, 112	W. S. Ramos	Igmaar (Fr), 4, 112	Be Exclusive (Ire), 4, 113	11	1:45.60	27,825
1989	**Princess Mora**, 3, 111	M. A. Gonzalez	Coolawin, 3, 118	Yestday's Kisses, 3, 115	13	1:47.60	36,000
1988	**Sunny Issues**, 3, 109	W. A. Guerra	Beauty Cream, 5, 119	Miss Unnameable, 4, 112	10	**1:45.40**	28,830
	Judy's Red Shoes, 5, 117	D. Valiente	Orange Motiff, 3, 113	Chores At Dawn, 4, 113	13	1:45.60	29,130
	Princely Proof, 5, 113	R. Breen	Fraulein Lieber, 4, 112	Judy's Red Shoes, 5, 114	8	1:46.20	33,870
	Fama, 5, 111	J. M. Pezua	Singular Bequest, 5, 116	Ladanum, 4, 115	9	1:44.80	24,570
1986	**Donna's Dolly**, 4, 112	M. A. Lee	Fritzie Bey, 4, 113	Thirty Zip, 3, 117	6	1:55.00	31,010
1985	**Powder Break**, 4, 116	J. A. Santos	Duty Dance, 3, 117	Dictina (Fr), 4, 117	10	1:47.80	20,555
	Shocker T., 3, 119	G. St. Leon	Erin's Dunloe, 3, 109	Spruce Luck, 4, 112	12	1:48.80	20,675
1984	**Our Reverie**, 3, 114	G. St. Leon	Id Am Fac, 3, 114	Break In, 3, 110	13	1:47.20	13,927
	Burst of Colors, 4, 116	J. A. Santos	Ava Romance, 3, 111	Cosmic Sea Queen, 4, 115	13	1:47.60	13,928

Named for Ben S. Castleman's SW My Charmer (1969 f. by Poker), dam of 1977 Horse of the Year and '77 Triple Crown winner Seattle Slew. Not held 1987, 1991. Two divisions 1984-'85, 1988 (March and December), 1992 (December). Held in March and December 1988. Held in April and December (two divisions) 1992. About 1$^1/_8$ miles 1984-'85, 1988-'93. Dirt 1986. ‡Megans Bluff finished first, DQ to second, 2000.

Nashua Stakes

Grade 3 in 2006. Belmont Park, two-year-olds, 1 mile, dirt. Held October 28, 2005, with a gross value of $113,300. First held in 1975. First graded in 1982. Stakes record 1:35.40 (1977 Quadratic).

Year	Winner	Jockey	Second	Third	Strs	Time	1st Purse
2005	**Bluegrass Cat**, 2, 116	J. R. Velazquez	Political Force, 2, 116	Diabolical, 2, 116	10	1:36.02	$67,980
2004	**Rockport Harbor**, 2, 118	S. Elliott	Defer, 2, 116	Better Than Bonds, 2, 116	6	1:36.67	65,700
2003	**Read the Footnotes**, 2, 118	J. D. Bailey	Paddington, 2, 120	Who Is Chris G., 2, 116	9	1:36.48	67,860
2002	**Added Edge**, 2, 122	P. Husbands	Outer Reef, 2, 116	Boston Bull, 2, 122	7	1:36.77	65,820
2001	**Listen Here**, 2, 117	J. D. Bailey	Monthir, 2, 115	Thunder Days, 2, 115	6	1:37.61	65,580
2000	**Ommadon**, 2, 115	A. T. Gryder	Windsor Castle, 2, 117	Griffinite, 2, 115	10	1:36.74	67,920
1999	**Mass Market**, 2, 117	M. E. Smith	Polish Miner, 2, 114	Parade Leader, 2, 117	9	1:38.60	67,020
1998	**Doneraile Court**, 2, 115	J. D. Bailey	Successful Appeal, 2, 122	Exiled Groom, 2, 113	8	1:36.17	66,600
1997	**Coronado's Quest**, 2, 122	M. E. Smith	Not Tricky, 2, 117	Dice Dancer, 2, 119	5	1:37.06	65,100
1996	**Jules**, 2, 114	J. A. Santos	Shammy Davis, 2, 114	Sal's Driver, 2, 114	9	1:36.89	68,340
1994	**Devious Course**, 2, 114	F. T. Alvarado	Mighty Magee, 2, 112	Old Tascosa, 2, 122	7	1:37.50	65,580
1993	**Popol's Gold**, 2, 114	W. H. McCauley	Personal Merit, 2, 117	Sonny's Bruno, 2, 114	11	1:46.68	74,400
1992	**Dalhart**, 2, 114	M. E. Smith	Rohwer, 2, 114	Peace Baby, 2, 114	11	1:44.60	74,640
1991	**Pine Bluff**, 2, 124	C. Perret	Speakerphone, 2, 114	Best Decorated, 2, 114	11	1:46.14	75,960
1990	**Kyle's Our Man**, 2, 114	J. D. Bailey	Oregon, 2, 114	Vouch for Me, 2, 117	11	1:45.40	55,980
1989	**Champagneforashley**, 2, 119	J. Vasquez	Armed for Peace, 2, 114	Flathorn, 2, 114	4	1:45.20	66,480
1988	**Traskwood**, 2, 117	A. T. Cordero Jr.	Doc's Leader, 2, 119	Triple Buck, 2, 117	10	1:45.20	63,240
1987	**Cougarized**, 2, 117	J. A. Santos	Blew by Em, 2, 119	Chicot County, 2, 117	12	1:46.00	104,160
1986	**Bold Summit**, 2, 114	C. W. Antley	Drachma, 2, 114	Perdition's Son, 2, 114	8	1:45.00	72,360
1985	**Raja's Revenge**, 2, 117	R. G. Davis	Royal Doulton, 2, 117	Bordeaux Bob, 2, 114	12	1:44.40	56,610
1984	**Stone White**, 2, 119	R. G. Davis	Banner Bob, 2, 117	Old Main, 2, 114	12	1:38.20	71,550
1983	**Don Rickles**, 2, 114	A. T. Cordero Jr.	Arabian Gift, 2, 114	Raja's Shark, 2, 114	9	1:38.40	34,800
1982	**I Enclose**, 2, 114	R. Hernandez	Loose Cannon, 2, 114	Moment of Joy, 2, 114	11	1:37.60	35,460
1981	**Our Escapade**, 2, 114	D. MacBeth	John's Gold, 2, 114	Hostage, 2, 114	10	1:36.80	35,280
1980	**‡A Run**, 2, 114	C. J. McCarron	Copper Mine, 2, 114	Triocala, 2, 114	12	1:37.20	35,460
1979	**Googolplex**, 2, 117	L. A. Pincay Jr.	Thanks to Tony, 2, 114	Comptroller, 2, 114	8	1:36.40	32,550
1978	**Instrument Landing**, 2, 114	J. Fell	Miroman, 2, 114	Bold Ruckus, 2, 117	12	1:37.00	26,520
1977	**Quadratic**, 2, 119	E. Maple	No Sir, 2, 114	Quip, 2, 114	5	**1:35.40**	21,975
1976	**Nearly On Time**, 2, 114	J. Vasquez	Ruthie's Native, 2, 114	Upper Nile, 2, 114	5	1:35.60	22,005
1975	**Lord Henribee**, 2, 115	E. Maple	Cojak, 2, 120	Expletive Deleted, 2, 115	6	1:35.80	33,030

Named for Belair Stud's 1955 Horse of the Year and '55 Belmont S. winner Nashua (1952 c. by *Nasrullah). Grade 2 1986-'88. Held at Aqueduct 1975-2000, 2002-'04. Not held 1995. 1 mile 70 yards 1985. 1$^1/_{16}$ miles 1986-'93. ‡Willow Hour finished first, DQ to twelfth, 1980.

Nassau County Breeders' Cup Stakes

Grade 2 in 2006. Belmont Park, three-year-olds, fillies, 7 furlongs, dirt. Held May 6, 2006, with a gross value of $205,600. First held in 1996. First graded in 1998. Stakes record 1:22.19 (1996 Star de Lady Ann).

Year	Winner	Jockey	Second	Third	Strs	Time	1st Purse
2006	**Hello Liberty**, 3, 120	N. Arroyo Jr.	Win McCool, 3, 116	Swap Fliparoo, 3, 119	6	1:22.65	$124,560
2005	**Seeking the Ante**, 3, 116	M. J. Luzzi	Slew Motion, 3, 116	Exit to Heaven, 3, 116	7	1:22.86	120,000
2004	**Bending Strings**, 3, 116	J. D. Bailey	Grey Traffic, 3, 116	A Lulu Ofa Menifee, 3, 116	6	1:22.70	120,000
2003	**House Party**, 3, 122	J. A. Santos	Cyber Secret, 3, 122	City Sister, 3, 116	4	1:23.28	120,000
2002	**Nonsuch Bay**, 3, 116	J. Castellano	Wopping, 3, 116	Wilzada, 3, 116	8	1:23.90	120,000
2001	**Cat Chat**, 3, 114	J. R. Velazquez	Xtra Heat, 3, 122	Shooting Party, 3, 114	6	1:23.02	90,000
2000	**C'Est L' Amour**, 3, 115	E. S. Prado	Tugger, 3, 114	Miss Inquistive, 3, 119	6	1:23.46	90,000
1999	**Oh What a Windfall**, 3, 118	M. E. Smith	Paved in Gold, 3, 118	Things Change, 3, 118	8	1:23.59	66,480
1998	**Jersey Girl**, 3, 121	M. E. Smith	Countess Diana, 3, 118	Foil, 3, 114	4	1:22.63	48,831
1997	**Alyssum**, 3, 116	J. A. Santos	Screamer, 3, 121	Sinclara, 3, 112	7	1:22.90	49,065
1996	**Star de Lady Ann**, 3, 114	J. F. Chavez	Stop Traffic, 3, 114	J J'sdream, 3, 121	8	**1:22.19**	49,590

Named for Nassau County, Long Island, New York, where Belmont Park is located. Grade 3 1998-'99. Nassau County S. 1996-2001.

National Jockey Club Handicap

Grade 3 in 2006. Hawthorne Race Course, three-year-olds and up, 1⅛ miles, dirt. Held April 22, 2006, with a gross value of $250,000. First held in 1956. First graded in 1984. Stakes record 1:47.60 (1999 Baytown).

Year	Winner	Jockey	Second	Third	Strs	Time	1st Purse
2006	**Three Hour Nap**, 4, 113	F. C. Torres	Summer Book, 5, 115	Courthouse, 5, 110	6	1:52.48	$150,000
2005	**Pollard's Vision**, 4, 118	J. R. Velazquez	Badge of Silver, 5, 120	Lord of the Game, 4, 117	4	1:49.12	150,000
2004	**Ten Most Wanted**, 4, 121	D. R. Flores	Colonial Colony, 6, 113	New York Hero, 4, 113	6	1:49.54	150,000
2003	**Fight for Ally**, 6, 116	E. Razo Jr.	Colonial Colony, 5, 114	Parrott Bay, 6, 115	8	1:53.46	150,000
2002	**Hail The Chief (GB)**, 5, 114	J. F. Chavez	E Z Glory, 5, 115	Ubiquity, 5, 115	7	1:51.72	120,000
2001	**Chicago Six**, 6, 117	A. J. Juarez Jr.	Guided Tour, 5, 118	Glacial, 6, 114	5	1:48.28	120,000
2000	**Take Note of Me**, 6, 120	R. Albarado	Glacial, 5, 113	Nite Dreamer, 5, 118	8	1:49.91	120,000
1999	**Baytown**, 5, 114	M. Guidry	Precocity, 5, 120	Fred Bear Claw, 5, 116	7	**1:47.60**	120,000
1998	**Polar Expedition**, 7, 117	M. Guidry	Bucks Nephew, 8, 115	Shed Some Light, 6, 114	9	1:49.91	120,000
1997	**Bucks Nephew**, 7, 118	G. K. Gomez	Natural Selection, 4, 114	Gotha, 5, 112	8	1:49.87	120,000
1996	**‡Prory**, 4, 113	C. H. Silva	Polar Expedition, 5, 116	Shed Some Light, 4, 114	9	1:50.83	150,000
1995	**Dusty Screen**, 7, 116	E. Maple	Come On Flip, 4, 114	Adhocracy, 5, 113	8	1:51.57	150,000
1994	**Recoup the Cash**, 4, 113	J. L. Diaz	Dread Me Not, 4, 114	Danc'n Jake, 5, 112	7	1:49.03	150,000
1993	**Stalwars**, 8, 118	J. L. Diaz	Count the Time, 4, 115	Richman, 5, 119	8	1:49.46	150,000
1992	**Stalwars**, 7, 115	M. Guidry	Richman, 4, 122	Sunny Prince, 5, 113	6	1:48.15	156,300
1991	**Allijeba**, 5, 116	S. J. Sellers	Whiz Along, 6, 110	Sound of Cannons, 4, 115	8	1:50.43	157,680
1990	**Dual Elements**, 4, 118	J. L. Diaz	Tricky Creek, 4, 120	Blue Buckaroo, 7, 115	11	1:49.60	143,730
1989	**Present Value**, 5, 112	W. Shoemaker	Super Roberto, 4, 113	Honor Medal, 8, 121	9	1:49.20	126,510
1988	**Lost Code**, 4, 129	C. Perret	Honor Medal, 7, 122	Outlaws Sham, 5, 114	7	1:49.60	125,640
1987	**Honor Medal**, 6, 118	L. E. Ortega	Blue Buckaroo, 4, 115	Coffer Dam, 6, 113	9	1:49.80	95,490
1986	**Magic North**, 4, 117	J. L. Diaz	Rocky Knave, 6, 121	Tuner Jr., 4, 113	7	1:50.00	65,220
1985	**Norwick**, 6, 117	K. Skinner	Harham's Sizzler, 6, 121	Badwagon Harry, 6, 115	9	1:51.20	67,440
1984	**Prince Forli**, 4, 118	R. A. Meier	Full Flame, 8, 119	Spare Card, 4, 117	8	1:52.60	64,080
1983	**Determined Bidder**, 4, 114	C. H. Silva	Thumbsucker, 4, 117	John's Gold, 4, 115	9	1:52.00	64,710
1982	**Frost King**, 4, 127	R. Platts	Dusky Duke, 6, 114	Recusant, 4, 115	12	1:49.80	66,150
1981	**Dusky Duke**, 5, 118	G. E. Louviere	Boyne Valley (Ire), 5, 119	Good and Early, 5, 120	6	1:49.00	46,350
1980	**All the More**, 7, 119	L. Snyder	Hold Your Tricks, 5, 114	Young Bob, 5, 117	9	1:46.20	46,890
1979	**Once Over Lightly**, 6, 113	S. A. Spencer	‡Batonnier, 4, 114	Hold Your Tricks, 4, 114	8	1:45.60	46,800
1978	**Auberge**, 5, 112	O. Sanchez	Bill Bonbright, 5, 121	Brown Cabildo, 4, 116	9	1:41.00	19,305
1977	**Yallah Native**, 4, 112	J. P. Powell	Dare to Command, 5, 119	Brown Cabildo, 3, 109	8	1:37.80	31,860
1976	**Honey Mark**, 4, 124	R. Sibille	Heathen Ways, 6, 114	Chateauvira, 8, 111	7	1:46.80	46,680
1975	***Zografos**, 7, 120	H. Arroyo	Sr. Diplomat, 4, 116	‡Sharp Gary, 4, 118	6	1:44.20	34,410
1974	**Tom Tulle**, 4, 120	L. Snyder	Smooth Dancer, 4, 111	Chateauvira, 6, 117	8	1:43.40	37,800
1973	**Fame and Power**, 4, 118	A. Rini	Full Pocket, 4, 122	Chateauvira, 5, 113	9	1:37.80	21,285

Named for the National Jockey Club, parent company of Sportsman's Park until 2002, when it allied with Hawthorne Race Course to become Hawthorne National LLC. Held at Sportsman's Park 1956-'98, 2000-'02. 1¹⁄₁₆ miles 1956-'71, 1974-'76, 1979-'80. 6½ furlongs 1972. 1 mile 1973, 1977-'78. Four-year-olds and up 1984-2002. ‡Christopher R. finished third, DQ to fourth, 1975. ‡Hold Your Tricks finished second, DQ to third, 1979. ‡Bucks Nephew finished first, DQ to fourth, 1996. Track record 1992, 1993.

National Museum of Racing Hall of Fame Stakes

Grade 2 in 2006. Saratoga Race Course, three-year-olds, 1⅛ miles, turf. Held August 8, 2005, with a gross value of $150,000. First held in 1985. First graded in 1987. Stakes record 1:46.65 (1992 Paradise Creek).

Year	Winner	Jockey	Second	Third	Strs	Time	1st Purse
2005	**T. D. Vance**, 3, 119	T. Kabel	Silver Whistle, 3, 115	Crown Point, 3, 119	9	1:48.15	$90,000
2004	**Artie Schiller**, 3, 122	R. Migliore	Mustanfar, 3, 122	Good Reward, 3, 115	8	1:47.71	90,000
2003	**Stroll**, 3, 117	J. D. Bailey	Urban King (Ire), 3, 115	Saint Stephen, 3, 115	11	1:49.34	90,000
2002	**Quest Star**, 3, 117	P. Day	Union Place, 3, 115	Patrol, 3, 120	5	1:49.66	90,000
2001	**Baptize**, 3, 122	J. D. Bailey	Strategic Partner, 3, 120	Saint Verre, 3, 113	7	1:47.94	90,000
2000	**Turnofthecentury**, 3, 118	A. T. Gryder	Aldo, 3, 118	Polish Miner, 3, 123	5	1:52.35	90,000
1999	**Marquette**, 3, 119	J. D. Bailey	Phi Beta Doc, 3, 118	Good Night, 3, 118	13	1:49.33	90,000
1998	**Parade Ground**, 3, 120	S. J. Sellers	Vergennes, 3, 115	Stay Sound, 3, 115	8	1:47.82	90,000
1997	**Rob 'n Gin**, 3, 120	J. D. Bailey	River Squall, 3, 114	Subordination, 3, 120	6	1:42.09	66,000
1996	**Sir Cat**, 3, 113	J. D. Bailey	Fortitude, 3, 113	Optic Nerve, 3, 120	9	1:40.46	68,340
1995	**Flitch**, 3, 113	M. E. Smith	Diplomatic Jet, 3, 120	Nostra, 3, 112	8	1:48.08	83,700
1994	**Islefaxyou**, 3, 113	E. Maple	Jaggery John, 3, 122	dh-Lahint, 3, 115 dh-Mr. Impatience, 3, 119	13	1:48.61	70,200
1993	**A in Sociology**, 3, 115	C. W. Antley	Strolling Along, 3, 117	Palashall, 3, 117	10	1:48.81	73,080
1992	**Paradise Creek**, 3, 115	M. E. Smith	Smiling and Dancin, 3, 119	Spectacular Tide, 3, 122	8	**1:46.65**	72,600
1991	**Lech**, 3, 122	A. T. Cordero Jr.	Sultry Song, 3, 117	Fourstars Allstar, 3, 122	10	1:49.02	73,920
1990	**Social Retiree**, 3, 115	M. E. Smith	Go Dutch, 3, 115	Divine Warning, 3, 119	7	1:48.20	54,720
1989	**Orange Sunshine**, 3, 117	J. Cruguet	Fast 'n' Gold, 3, 115	Expensive Decision, 3, 122	10	1:49.00	55,980
1988	**Posen**, 3, 122	J. D. Bailey	‡Blew by Em, 3, 119	Harp Islet, 3, 115	9	1:47.00	55,710
1987	**Drachma**, 3, 115	R. G. Davis	Crown the Leader, 3, 115	Major Beard, 3, 115	8	1:49.80	51,480
1986	**Dance of Life**, 3, 115	J. D. Bailey	Southjet, 3, 115	Dance Card Filled, 3, 115	6	1:52.20	49,860
1985	**Duluth**, 3, 115	J. Cruguet	Explosive Dancer, 3, 115	Equalize, 3, 122	8	1:47.60	51,570

Named for the National Museum of Racing and Hall of Fame located in Saratoga Springs, New York. Formerly named for Ralph Lowe's 1957 Travers S. winner *Gallant Man (1954 c. by *Migoli). Gallant Man S. 1985-'91. National Museum of Racing Hall of Fame H. 1998-2003. 1³⁄₁₆ miles 1991. 1¹⁄₁₆ miles 1996-'97. Dirt 2000. Three-year-olds and up 1991. Fillies and mares 1991. Dead heat for third 1994. ‡Fourstardave finished second, DQ to fourth, 1988.

Native Diver Handicap

Grade 3 in 2006. Hollywood Park, three-year-olds and up, 1⅛ miles, dirt. Held December 10, 2005, with a gross value of $100,000. First held in 1979. First graded in 1979. Stakes record 1:45.35 (1996 Gentlemen [Arg]).

Year	Winner	Jockey	Second	Third	Strs	Time	1st Purse
2005	**Trotamondo (Chi)**, 4, 117	G. K. Gomez	Bully Hayes, 5, 116	Spellbinder, 4, 116	10	1:49.92	$60,000
2004	**Truly a Judge**, 6, 115	M. A. Pedroza	Dynever, 4, 119	Calkins Road, 5, 116	8	1:47.06	60,000
2003	**Olmodavor**, 4, 117	A. O. Solis	Nose The Trade (GB), 5, 115	Chinkapin, 7, 118	5	1:49.16	60,000
2002	**Piensa Sonando (Chi)**, 4, 117	L. A. Pincay Jr.	Fleetstreet Dancer, 4, 112	Nose The Trade (GB), 4, 116	8	1:48.43	60,000
2001	**Momentum**, 3, 117	C. S. Nakatani	Euchre, 5, 121	Last Parade (Arg), 5, 117	7	1:48.24	60,000
2000	**Sky Jack**, 4, 118	L. A. Pincay Jr.	Lethal Instrument, 4, 116	Grey Memo, 3, 113	8	1:46.81	60,000
1999	**General Challenge**, 3, 123	C. J. McCarron	Moore's Flat, 5, 117	Koslanin (Arg), 5, 113	6	1:49.07	60,000
1998	**Puerto Madero (Chi)**, 4, 121	K. Desormeaux	Musical Gambler, 4, 117	River Keen (Ire), 6, 114	5	1:48.43	60,000
1997	**Refinado Tom (Arg)**, 4, 119	G. L. Stevens	Steel Ruhlr, 3, 112	Boggle, 5, 114	8	1:47.84	60,000
1996	**Gentlemen (Arg)**, 4, 121	G. L. Stevens	Dramatic Gold, 5, 122	Don't Blame Rio, 3, 113	5	**1:45.35**	63,840
1995	**Alphabet Soup**, 4, 117	C. W. Antley	El Florista (Arg), 5, 118	Regal Rowdy, 6, 116	5	1:47.03	61,400
1994	**Best Pal**, 6, 121	C. J. McCarron	Tossofthecoin, 4, 117	Royal Chariot, 4, 114	7	1:48.44	64,000
1993	**Slew of Damascus**, 5, 118	C. S. Nakatani	Lottery Winner, 4, 117	L'Express (Chi), 4, 115	7	1:47.46	63,300
1992	**Sir Beaufort**, 5, 119	C. J. McCarron	Memo (Chi), 5, 115	Berillon (GB), 5, 115	5	1:47.88	61,700
1991	**Twilight Agenda**, 5, 124	C. J. McCarron	Ibero (Arg), 4, 117	Cobra Classic, 4, 117	4	1:49.00	60,600
1990	**Warcraft**, 3, 117	C. J. McCarron	Pleasant Tap, 3, 115	Go and Go (Ire), 3, 115	7	1:47.40	63,500
1989	**Ruhlmann**, 4, 121	C. J. McCarron	Lively One, 4, 122	Stylish Winner, 5, 116	7	1:48.00	63,100
1988	**Cutlass Reality**, 6, 124	G. L. Stevens	Precisionist, 7, 123	Payant (Arg), 4, 116	7	1:48.60	63,700
1987	**Epidaurus**, 5, 116	P. A. Valenzuela	Midwest King, 4, 116	He's a Saros, 4, 116	8	1:47.60	91,200
1986	**Hopeful Word**, 5, 117	L. A. Pincay Jr.	Epidaurus, 4, 115	Nostalgia's Star, 4, 118	7	1:47.80	90,800
1985	**Innamorato**, 4, 107	S. Hawley	Beldale Lear, 4, 116	Lord At War (Arg), 5, 125	4	1:33.40	87,900
1984	**Lord At War (Arg)**, 4, 120	W. Shoemaker	Fighting Fit, 5, 118	Video Kid, 4, 118	6	1:35.40	62,700
1983	**Menswear**, 5, 115	F. Toro	Fighting Fit, 4, 117	Major Sport, 6, 115	6	1:42.40	63,200
1982	**Native Tactics**, 4, 116	E. Delahoussaye	Belfort (Fr), 5, 116	Rock Softly, 4, 115	10	1:41.60	67,000
1981	**Syncopate**, 6, 117	C. J. McCarron	King Go Go, 6, 115	Wickerr, 6, 121	6	1:38.80	63,500
1980	**Replant**, 6, 111	W. Shoemaker	Relaunch, 4, 120	Flying Paster, 4, 124	6	1:34.20	63,000
1979	**Life's Hope**, 6, 117	L. A. Pincay Jr.	Hawkin's Special, 4, 117	White Rammer, 5, 116	6	1:35.00	31,500

Named for Mr. and Mrs. L. K. Shapiro's 1965, '66, and '67 Hollywood Gold Cup winner Native Diver (1959 g. by Imbros); Native Diver won 34 stakes, a tie with Exterminator for the most stakes wins in North American racing history. Grade 2 1979. 1 mile 1979-'81, 1984-'85. 1$\frac{1}{16}$ miles 1982-'83.

New Orleans Handicap

Grade 2 in 2006. Fair Grounds at Louisiana Downs, four-year-olds and up, 1⅛ miles, dirt. Held January 7, 2006, with a gross value of $435,600. First held in 1918. First graded in 1973. Stakes record 1:48.13 (1998 Phantom On Tour).

Year	Winner	Jockey	Second	Third	Strs	Time	1st Purse
2006	**Brass Hat**, 5, 117	W. Martinez	Dixie Meister, 4, 113	Alumni Hall, 7, 116	8	1:51.35	$261,360
2005	**Badge of Silver**, 5, 118	J. D. Bailey	Limehouse, 4, 115	Second of June, 4, 115	9	1:48.78	300,000
2004	**Peace Rules**, 4, 119	J. D. Bailey	Saint Liam, 4, 114	Funny Cide, 4, 118	8	1:48.61	300,000
2003	**Mineshaft**, 4, 115	R. Albarado	Olmodavor, 4, 117	Strive, 4, 114	11	1:48.92	300,000
2002	**Parade Leader**, 5, 115	C. J. Lanerie	Graeme Hall, 5, 116	Keats, 4, 113	9	1:50.44	300,000
2001	**Include**, 4, 114	J. D. Bailey	Nite Dreamer, 6, 112	Valhol, 5, 116	5	1:49.18	300,000
2000	**Allen's Oop**, 5, 112	W. Martinez	Take Note of Me, 6, 116	Ecton Park, 4, 117	8	1:48.80	300,000
1999	**Precocity**, 5, 118	E. M. Martin Jr.	Real Quiet, 4, 122	Allen's Oop, 4, 108	6	1:49.17	320,640
1998	**Phantom On Tour**, 4, 114	L. J. Melancon	Precocity, 4, 114	Lord Cromby (Ire), 4, 110	8	**1:48.13**	300,000
1997	**Isitingood**, 6, 121	D. R. Flores	Western Trader, 6, 114	Scott's Scoundrel, 5, 113	7	1:48.43	180,000
1996	**Scott's Scoundrel**, 4, 116	R. D. Ardoin	Knockadoon, 4, 113	Patio de Naranjos (Chi), 5, 114	9	1:49.97	162,540
1995	**Concern**, 4, 125	M. E. Smith	Fly Cry, 4, 118	Tossofthecoin, 5, 117	7	1:49.40	120,000
1994	**Brother Brown**, 4, 118	P. Day	Far Out Wadleigh, 6, 112	Eequalsmcsquared, 5, 116	10	1:48.83	120,000
1993	**Latin American**, 5, 112	G. K. Gomez	Delafield, 4, 115	West by West, 4, 119	12	1:49.20	90,000
1992	**Jarraar**, 5, 112	B. J. Walker Jr.	Irish Swap, 5, 120	Bayou Reality, 4, 113	8	1:48.80	60,000
1991	**Silver Survivor**, 5, 120	L. J. Melancon	El Zorzal (Arg), 5, 110	Sangria Time, 4, 115	9	1:50.10	60,000
1990	**Festive**, 5, 117	B. J. Walker Jr.	Majesty's Imp, 4, 116	De Roche, 4, 116	8	1:50.40	60,000
1989	**Galba**, 5, 115	A. L. Castanon	Honor Medal, 8, 123	Position Leader, 4, 116	9	1:51.20	60,000
1988	**Honor Medal**, 7, 121	P. Day	New York Swell, 5, 114	Manzotti, 5, 115	12	1:50.00	60,000
1987	**Honor Medal**, 6, 116	R. A. Baze	Dramatic Desire, 6, 117	Inevitable Leader, 8, 116	10	1:52.20	71,040
1986	**Herat**, 4, 116	R. Q. Meza	Hopeful Word, 5, 120	Kamakura (GB), 4, 108	11	2:01.80	112,000
1985	**Westheimer**, 4, 112	L. Snyder	Inevitable Leader, 6, 116	Vornorco, 4, 108	9	2:01.80	112,000
1984	**Wild Again**, 4, 112	P. Day	Explosive Bid, 6, 112	Crazy Moon, 4, 110	10	2:02.00	112,000
1983	**Listcapade**, 4, 121	E. J. Perrodin	Bold Style, 4, 113	Aspro, 5, 114	9	2:03.20	112,000
1982	**It's the One**, 4, 124	W. A. Guerra	Boys Nite Out, 4, 116	Aspro, 4, 113	11	2:01.80	112,000
1981	**Sun Catcher**, 4, 123	A. Guajardo	Prince Majestic, 7, 118	Yosi Boy, 5, 112	7	2:03.40	103,550
1980	**Pool Court**, 5, 111	R. D. Ardoin	Five Star General, 5, 112	Book of Kings, 6, 113	7	2:04.60	84,500
1979	**A Letter to Harry**, 5, 126	E. Delahoussaye	Prince Majestic, 5, 117	Johnny's Image, 4, 112	6	2:02.60	84,050
1978	**Life's Hope**, 5, 112	C. J. McCarron	Silver Series, 4, 125	Inca Roca, 5, 111	10	2:02.20	77,550
1977	**Tudor Tambourine**, 4, 112	A. J. Trosclair	Inca Roca, 4, 113	Soy Numero Uno, 4, 127	11	1:49.80	65,000
1976	**Master Derby**, 4, 127	D. G. McHargue	Hatchet Man, 5, 118	‡Promised City, 4, 116	9	1:50.00	61,000
1975	**Lord Rebeau**, 4, 116	C. H. Marquez	Warbucks, 5, 113	Diamond Black, 6, 110	16	1:50.60	61,000

1974 **Smooth Dancer**, 4, 116	L. Adams	*Trupan, 7, 108	Rastaferian, 5, 115	12	1:50.60	$56,300
1973 **Combat Ready**, 4, 111	L. Moyers	Hustlin Greek, 4, 111	Guitar Player, 5, 114	9	1:51.00	50,000

Named for the city of New Orleans, home of Fair Grounds. Grade 3 1973-'80, 1990-2000. Held at Louisiana Downs 2006. Not held 1919-'23, 1941-'42, 1945. 1$^1/_{16}$ miles 1918, 1925-'31, 1933, 1936, 1938-'39, 1943-'53. 1 mile 1924, 1935, 1937. 1 mile 70 yards 1940. 1$^1/_4$ miles 1978-'86. Three-year-olds and up 1918-'36, 1939-'78. Three-year-olds 1937-'38. ‡*Zografos finished third, DQ to ninth, 1976. Track record 1997, 1998. Equaled track record 1992, 1994.

New York Handicap

Grade 2 in 2006. Belmont Park, three-year-olds and up, fillies and mares, 1$^1/_4$ miles, turf. Held July 2, 2005, with a gross value of $250,000. First held in 1940. First graded in 1977. Stakes record 1:58.40 (1990 Capades).

Year	Winner	Jockey	Second	Third	Strs	Time	1st Purse
2005	**Wend**, 4, 116	J. D. Bailey	Wonder Again, 6, 120	Film Maker, 5, 121	6	2:02.23	$150,000
2004	**Wonder Again**, 5, 115	E. S. Prado	Stay Forever, 7, 115	Spice Island, 5, 118	7	2:05.60	150,000
2003	**Snow Dance**, 5, 116	R. Migliore	Pertuisane (GB), 4, 115	Riskaverse, 4, 119	8	1:59.63	150,000
2002	**Owsley**, 4, 114	E. S. Prado	Volga (Ire), 4, 116	Janet (GB), 5, 119	7	1:59.81	150,000
2001	**England's Legend (Fr)**, 4, 115	C. S. Nakatani	Gaviola, 4, 119	Spook Express (SAf), 7, 116	7	1:59.63	150,000
2000	**Perfect Sting**, 4, 122	J. D. Bailey	Snow Polina, 5, 116	Pico Teneriffe, 4, 115	8	2:05.36	150,000
1999	**Soaring Softly**, 4, 117	M. E. Smith	Tampico, 6, 116	Anguilla, 4, 119	6	2:02.25	150,000
1998	**Auntie Mame**, 4, 118	J. R. Velazquez	Tresoriere, 4, 115	Cuando, 4, 113	8	1:59.50	120,000
1997	**Maxzene**, 4, 120	M. E. Smith	Memories of Silver, 4, 122	Shemozzle (Ire), 4, 114	6	1:59.80	120,000
1996	**Electric Society (Ire)**, 5, 115	J. F. Chavez	Danish (Ire), 5, 115	Chelsey Flower, 5, 116	7	2:03.79	90,000
1995	**Irish Linnet**, 7, 118	J. R. Velazquez	Danish (Ire), 4, 116	Market Booster, 6, 119	6	1:59.92	65,520
1994	**You'd Be Surprised**, 5, 118	J. D. Bailey	Dahlia's Dreamer, 5, 112	Aquilegia, 5, 115	6	1:59.69	65,340
1993	**Aquilegia**, 4, 114	J. A. Krone	Via Borghese, 4, 117	Ginny Dare, 5, 108	11	1:59.05	74,760
1992	**Plenty of Grace**, 5, 111	J. A. Krone	Dancing Devlette, 5, 111	Flaming Torch (Ire), 5, 115	9	2:00.74	72,720
1991	**Foresta**, 5, 121	A. T. Cordero Jr.	Crockadore, 4, 112	Flaming Torch (Ire), 4, 110	8	1:59.38	72,360
1990	**Capades**, 4, 119	A. T. Cordero Jr.	Laugh and Be Merry, 5, 114	Key Flyer, 4, 109	7	**1:58.40**	71,640
1989	**Miss Unnameable**, 5, 108	R. I. Rojas	‡Love You by Heart, 4, 119	Gaily Gaily (Ire), 6, 113	8	2:05.80	72,000
1988	**Beauty Cream**, 5, 119	P. Day	Antique Mystique, 4, 109	Key to the Bridge, 4, 114	8	2:03.00	70,200
1987	**Anka Germania (Ire)**, 5, 117	C. Perret	Videogenic, 5, 117	Lead Kindly Light, 4, 109	7	2:01.00	83,580
1986	**Possible Mate**, 5, 123	J. Samyn	Lucky Touch, 4, 110	Perfect Point, 4, 113	5	2:02.40	51,750
1985	**Powder Break**, 4, 115	J. D. Bailey	Annie Edge (Ire), 5, 112	Pull the Wool, 5, 107	7	2:03.60	53,280
1984	**Annie Edge (Ire)**, 4, 112	J. Velasquez	Thirty Flags, 4, 114	Geraldine's Store, 5, 121	11	2:02.20	58,950
1983	**Sabin**, 3, 111	E. Maple	If Winter Comes, 5, 113	Doodle, 4, 115	12	2:01.00	53,010
1982	**Noble Damsel**, 4, 114	J. Velasquez	Office Wife, 5, 113	Castle Royale, 4, 111	8	2:07.00	34,620
1981	**Mairzy Doates**, 5, 120	A. T. Cordero Jr.	Love Sign, 4, 114	Wayward Lassie, 4, 107	6	2:04.00	33,960
1980	**Just a Game (Ire)**, 4, 121	D. Brumfield	Poppycock, 4, 112	Please Try Hard, 4, 113	6	2:00.40	33,720
1979	**La Soufriere**, 4, 111	J. Cruguet	Navajo Princess, 5, 118	Emerald Hill (Brz), 5, 120	8	1:41.20	33,600
1978	**Pearl Necklace**, 4, 122	R. Hernandez	Waya (Fr), 4, 116	Dottie's Doll, 5, 118	7	1:40.00	33,360
	Late Bloomer, 4, 115	J. Velasquez	Island Kiss, 3, 108	Fia, 4, 113	9	1:41.20	33,810
1977	**Fleet Victress**, 5, 115	R. Hernandez	Lady Singer (Ire), 4, 113	*Welsh Pearl, 5, 119	9	1:39.20	33,330
1976	**Sugar Plum Time**, 4, 113	A. T. Cordero Jr.	‡*Deesse Du Val, 5, 120	Dos a Dos, 4, 111	9	2:03.20	33,780

Named for New York City, home of Belmont Park. Grade 3 1977-'82. Held at Aqueduct 1940-'60, 1963-'72. Not held 1957, 1973-'75. 2$^1/_4$ miles 1940-'50. 1$^1/_8$ miles 1951-'54, 1959-'60. 1$^3/_8$ miles 1955-'58, 1961. 1$^3/_{16}$ miles 1963, 1968-'71. 1$^1/_{16}$ miles 1965-'67, 1977-'79. 7 furlongs 1972. Dirt 1940-'54, 1972. Three-year-olds 1972. Both sexes 1940-'62. Fillies 1972. Two divisions 1978. ‡Carolerno finished second, DQ to ninth, 1976. ‡Laugh and Be Merry finished second, DQ to fourth, 1989.

Next Move Handicap

Grade 3 in 2006. Aqueduct, three-year-olds and up, fillies and mares, 1$^1/_8$ miles, dirt. Held March 26, 2006, with a gross value of $101,200. First held in 1975. First graded in 1977. Stakes record 1:48.96 (1999 Diggins).

Year	Winner	Jockey	Second	Third	Strs	Time	1st Purse
2006	**Fleet Indian**, 5, 115	J. A. Santos	Flaming Heart, 5, 115	No Sleep, 4, 115	4	1:49.32	$63,720
2005	**Daydreaming**, 4, 119	E. S. Prado	Saintliness, 5, 117	Rare Gift, 4, 116	8	1:50.77	66,000
2004	**Smok'n Frolic**, 5, 119	R. Migliore	Stake, 4, 112	U K Trick, 4, 110	7	1:51.55	65,040
2003	**Smok'n Frolic**, 4, 120	J. R. Velazquez	Ellie's Moment, 5, 116	Pupil, 4, 113	6	1:49.11	64,800
2002	**With Ability**, 4, 113	J. Castellano	Irving's Baby, 5, 117	Diversa, 4, 113	7	1:49.88	65,160
2001	**Atelier**, 4, 117	E. S. Prado	Pompeii, 4, 117	Tax Affair, 4, 114	4	1:50.65	64,264
2000	**Biogio's Rose**, 6, 117	N. Arroyo Jr.	Up We Go, 4, 115	Perlinda (Arg), 5, 114	7	1:51.32	49,875
1999	**Diggins**, 5, 113	J. L. Espinoza	Biogio's Rose, 5, 116	Powerful Nation, 5, 114	7	**1:48.96**	48,915
1998	**Panama Canal**, 4, 113	S. Bridgmohan	Endowment, 4, 110	Dewars Rocks, 4, 116	8	1:51.37	49,455
1997	**Full and Fancy**, 5, 115	R. Migliore	Shoop, 6, 117	Prophet's Warning, 4, 117	8	1:51.12	49,500
1996	**Madame Adolphe**, 4, 110	F. Leon	Shoop, 5, 114	Lotta Dancing, 5, 122	7	1:51.39	49,080
1995	**Restored Hope**, 4, 118	M. J. Luzzi	Cherokee Wonder, 4, 114	Sterling Pound, 4, 114	6	1:52.26	48,975
1994	**Groovy Feeling**, 5, 123	M. J. Luzzi	Broad Gains, 4, 116	Megaroux, 4, 112	7	1:59.79	63,735
1993	**Low Tolerance**, 4, 114	M. E. Smith	Hilbys Brite Flite, 4, 112	Lady Lear, 6, 114	8	1:55.93	67,470
1992	**Spy Leader Lady**, 4, 112	M. E. Smith	Haunting, 4, 117	Grecian Pass, 5, 115	6	2:00.26	67,560
1991	**Buy the Firm**, 5, 119	W. H. McCauley	Overturned, 4, 115	Won Scent, 4, 112	6	1:56.57	65,850
1990	**Bold Wench**, 5, 117	J. Velasquez	Buy the Firm, 4, 112	Dactique, 4, 113	8	1:58.40	53,280
1989	**Rose's Cantina**, 5, 118	E. Maple	To the Hunt, 4, 111	No Butter, 5, 108	5	1:59.80	49,950
1988	**Triple Wow**, 5, 116	R. Migliore	With a Twist, 5, 112	Cuantalamera, 5, 104	5	1:57.60	66,120
1987	**Tricky Squaw**, 4, 110	C. W. Antley	Ms. Eloise, 4, 115	Videogenic, 5, 121	9	1:58.40	70,440
1986	**Cherry Jubilee**, 4, 110	C. H. Marquez Jr.	Madame Called, 4, 109	Lady On the Run, 4, 121	11	1:56.00	68,220
1985	**Flip's Pleasure**, 5, 112	J. Samyn	Sintrillium, 7, 121	Emphatic, 5, 104	7	1:58.20	52,380

1984	**Adept**, 5, 109	M. Venezia	Far Flying, 4, 120	Chieftan's Command, 5, 123	8	1:57.80	$67,860
1983	**Chieftan's Command**, 4, 116	A. Smith Jr.	Noble Damsel, 5, 115	Pert, 4, 113	6	1:53.20	32,880
1982	**Andover Way**, 4, 122	J. Velasquez	Autumn Glory, 4, 111	Who's to Answer, 4, 109	8	1:50.20	50,940
1981	**Plankton**, 5, 123	R. Hernandez	Nalee's Fantasy, 4, 107	Ms. Balding, 5, 109	6	1:53.40	50,130
1980	**Water Lily (Fr)**, 4, 113	M. Castaneda	Plankton, 4, 121	Propitiate, 5, 116	7	1:51.00	49,410
1979	**One Sum**, 5, 116	R. Hernandez	Kit's Double, 6, 111	Municipal Bond, 4, 111	7	1:53.00	48,105
1978	**One Sum**, 4, 121	R. Hernandez	Crab Grass, 6, 121	Sweet Bernice, 5, 114	10	1:52.80	48,690
1977	**Forty Nine Sunsets**, 4, 116	J. Vasquez	Double Quester, 4, 115	Shark's Jaws, 4, 116	11	1:51.00	48,915
1976	**Yes Dear Maggy**, 4, 119	R. Hernandez	Pass a Glance, 5, 115	Mary Queenofscots, 5, 119	8	1:49.40	48,360
1975	**My Juliet**, 3, 125	D. G. McHargue	Channelette, 3, 117	Spring Is Here, 3, 113	7	1:35.60	33,660

Named for Alfred G. Vanderbilt's 1950 champion three-year-old filly, '52 champion older female, and '50, '52 Beldame H. winner Next Move (1947 f. by Bull Lea). Next Move Breeders' Cup H. 1990-'95. 1 mile 1975. 1³⁄₁₆ miles 1984-'94. Three-year-olds 1975. Fillies 1975.

Noble Damsel Handicap

Grade 3 in 2006. Belmont Park, three-year-olds and up, fillies and mares, 1 mile, turf. Held September 24, 2005, with a gross value of $150,000. First held in 1985. First graded in 1988. Stakes record 1:32.79 (2002 Tates Creek).

Year	Winner	Jockey	Second	Third	Strs	Time	1st Purse
2005	**Bright Abundance**, 4, 115	R. Migliore	My Lordship, 4, 116	Asti (Ire), 4, 113	12	1:33.93	$90,000
2004	**Ocean Drive**, 4, 120	J. R. Velazquez	High Court (Brz), 4, 115	Hour of Justice, 4, 116	9	1:34.71	90,000
2003	**Wonder Again**, 4, 117	E. S. Prado	Dancal (Ire), 5, 114	Something Ventured, 4, 115	11	1:33.07	90,000
2002	**Tates Creek**, 4, 119	J. D. Bailey	Amonita (GB), 4, 117	Dat You Miz Blue, 5, 114	8	**1:32.79**	68,640
2001	**Tugger**, 4, 119	J. D. Bailey	Shine Again, 4, 123	Tippity Witch, 4, 113	6	1:35.18	68,280
2000	**Gino's Spirits (GB)**, 4, 114	E. S. Prado	La Ville Rouge, 4, 115	Solar Bound, 4, 114	8	1:36.61	66,720
1999	**Khumba Mela (Ire)**, 4, 118	J. A. Santos	Uanme, 4, 114	Cyrillic, 4, 116	8	1:35.50	67,740
1998	**Oh Nellie**, 4, 116	J. R. Velazquez	Heaven's Command (GB), 4, 116	Irish Daisy, 5, 114	7	1:32.80	50,400
1997	**Colcon**, 4, 113	J. D. Bailey	Antespend, 4, 118	Tiffany's Taylor, 8, 113	11	1:32.80	69,360
1996	**Perfect Arc**, 4, 125	J. R. Velazquez	Fashion Star, 4, 112	Tough Broad, 4, 112	7	1:42.41	60,160
1995	**Irish Linnet**, 7, 121	J. R. Velazquez	Caress, 4, 120	Weekend Madness (Ire), 5, 120	7	1:40.67	60,048
1994	**Irish Linnet**, 6, 117	J. R. Velazquez	Statuette, 4, 113	Cox Orange, 4, 117	10	1:39.59	50,790
1993	**McKaymackenna**, 4, 120	C. W. Antley	La Piaf (Fr), 4, 116	Heed, 4, 116	10	1:43.74	55,620
1992	**Miss Otis**, 5, 115	A. Madrid Jr.	Big Big Affair, 5, 115	Tiney Toast, 3, 115	4	1:43.64	53,460
1991	**Highland Penny**, 6, 116	A. T. Cordero Jr.	Southern Tradition, 4, 116	Virgin Michael, 4, 116	8	1:40.21	50,850
1990	**Christiecat**, 3, 112	E. Maple	Aldbourne (Ire), 4, 120	To the Lighthouse, 4, 116	7	1:43.40	54,090
1989	**Miss Unnameable**, 5, 120	R. I. Rojas	High Browser, 4, 116	Highland Penny, 4, 116	9	1:40.60	55,080
1988	**Glowing Honor**, 3, 115	P. Day	Love You by Heart, 3, 115	Fieldy (Ire), 5, 116	8	1:42.00	55,350
1987	**Fieldy (Ire)**, 4, 116	A. T. Cordero Jr.	Perfect Point, 5, 120	Bailrullah, 5, 123	9	1:43.40	34,500
1986	**Slew's Exceller**, 4, 115	J. Samyn	Tri Argo, 4, 115	Chinguetti (Fr), 4, 115	6	1:42.20	32,460
	Fama, 3, 113	R. P. Romero	Tax Dodge, 5, 119	Anka Germania (Ire), 4, 115	7	1:41.00	32,580
1985	**Alabama Nana (Ire)**, 4, 115	P. A. Valenzuela	Paradies (Arg), 5, 115	Nany, 5, 115	8	1:35.20	34,800

Named for G. Watts Humphrey Jr.'s 1982 New York H. (G3) winner Noble Damsel (1978 f. by *Vaguely Noble). Leixable S. 1985-'88. Noble Damsel S. 1989-'93. 1¹⁄₁₆ miles 1988-'96. Dirt 1992, 2001. Two divisions 1986.

Norfolk Stakes

Grade 2 in 2006. Oak Tree at Santa Anita, two-year-olds, 1¹⁄₁₆ miles, dirt. Held October 2, 2005, with a gross value of $200,000. First held in 1970. First graded in 1973. Stakes record 1:41.27 (2003 Ruler's Court).

Year	Winner	Jockey	Second	Third	Strs	Time	1st Purse
2005	**Brother Derek**, 2, 122	A. O. Solis	A. P. Warrior, 2, 122	Jealous Profit, 2, 122	8	1:44.38	$120,000
2004	**Roman Ruler**, 2, 120	C. S. Nakatani	Boston Glory, 2, 120	Littlebitofzip, 2, 120	4	1:44.27	120,000
2003	**Ruler's Court**, 2, 120	A. O. Solis	Capitano, 2, 120	Perfect Moon, 2, 120	9	**1:41.27**	150,000
2002	**Kafwain**, 2, 120	V. Espinoza	Bull Market, 2, 120	Listen Indy, 2, 120	7	1:42.75	120,000
2001	**Essence of Dubai**, 2, 118	A. O. Solis	Ibn Al Haitham (GB), 2, 118	‡Ecstatic, 2, 118	6	1:37.16	150,000
2000	**Flame Thrower**, 2, 118	V. Espinoza	Street Cry (Ire), 2, 118	Mr Freckles, 2, 118	8	1:34.86	120,000
1999	**Dixie Union**, 2, 118	A. O. Solis	Forest Camp, 2, 118	Anees, 2, 118	6	1:35.79	120,000
1998	**Buck Trout**, 2, 118	E. Delahoussaye	Eagleton, 2, 118	Daring General, 2, 118	9	1:37.55	120,000
1997	**Souvenir Copy**, 2, 118	G. L. Stevens	Old Trieste, 2, 118	Double Honor, 2, 118	7	1:36.00	120,000
1996	**Free House**, 2, 118	K. Desormeaux	Zippersup, 2, 118	Swiss Yodeler, 2, 118	7	1:43.54	120,000
1995	**Future Quest**, 2, 118	K. Desormeaux	Odyle, 2, 118	Exetera, 2, 118	7	1:43.31	120,000
1994	**Supremo**, 2, 118	G. L. Stevens	Desert Mirage, 2, 118	Strong Ally, 2, 118	9	1:43.48	120,000
1993	**Shepherd's Field**, 2, 118	C. J. McCarron	Ramblin Guy, 2, 118	Ferrara, 2, 118	7	1:43.11	120,000
1992	**River Special**, 2, 118	K. Desormeaux	Imperial Ridge, 2, 118	Devil Diamond, 2, 118	5	1:43.58	120,000
1991	**Bertrando**, 2, 118	A. O. Solis	Zurich, 2, 118	Bag, 2, 118	9	1:42.87	164,820
1990	**Best Pal**, 2, 118	P. A. Valenzuela	Pillaring, 2, 118	Formal Dinner, 2, 118	12	1:42.80	178,620
1989	**Grand Canyon**, 2, 118	C. J. McCarron	Single Dawn, 2, 118	Due to the King, 2, 118	7	1:43.20	166,440
1988	**Hawkster**, 2, 118	P. A. Valenzuela	Bold Bryn, 2, 118	Double Quick, 2, 118	9	1:43.40	187,740
1987	**Saratoga Passage**, 2, 118	J. J. Steiner	Purdue King, 2, 118	Bold Second, 2, 118	7	1:45.00	181,140
1986	**Capote**, 2, 118	L. A. Pincay Jr.	Gulch, 2, 118	Gold On Green, 2, 118	6	1:45.20	193,680
1985	**Snow Chief**, 2, 118	A. O. Solis	Lord Allison, 2, 118	Darby Fair, 2, 118	9	1:44.60	167,340
1984	**Chief's Crown**, 2, 118	D. MacBeth	Matthew T. Parker, 2, 118	Viva Maxi, 2, 118	6	1:42.40	201,960
1983	**Fali Time**, 2, 118	S. Hawley	†Life's Magic, 2, 117	Artichoke, 2, 118	10	1:44.20	168,930
1982	**Roving Boy**, 2, 118	E. Delahoussaye	Desert Wine, 2, 118	Aguila, 2, 118	9	1:41.60	181,110
1981	**Stalwart**, 2, 118	C. J. McCarron	Racing Is Fun, 2, 118	Gato Del Sol, 2, 118	9	1:42.20	140,790

1980	**Sir Dancer**, 2, 118	F. Olivares	Chiaroscuro, 2, 118	Partez, 2, 118	8	1:43.80	$100,980
	High Counsel, 2, 118	L. M. Gilligan	Regalberto, 2, 118	Cogency, 2, 118	7	1:42.80	99,780
1979	**The Carpenter**, 2, 118	C. J. McCarron	Rumbo, 2, 118	Idyll, 2, 118	8	1:41.60	119,280
1978	**Flying Paster**, 2, 118	D. Pierce	Golden Act, 2, 118	Knights Choice, 2, 118	6	1:42.20	118,860
1977	**Balzac**, 2, 118	W. Shoemaker	Misrepresentation, 2, 118	Noble Bronze, 2, 118	10	1:45.40	157,230
1976	***Habitony**, 2, 118	W. Shoemaker	Replant, 2, 118	Hey Hey J. P., 2, 118	11	1:42.00	79,290
1975	**Telly's Pop**, 2, 118	F. Mena	Imacornishprince, 2, 118	Thermal Energy, 2, 118	8	1:43.60	74,295
1974	**George Navonod**, 2, 118	D. Pierce	Diabolo, 2, 118	Fleet Velvet, 2, 118	9	1:42.20	77,370
1973	**Money Lender**, 2, 118	J. Lambert	Merry Fellow, 2, 118	Holding Pattern, 2, 118	7	1:42.60	58,050

Named for Theodore Winter's undefeated Norfolk (1861 c. by Lexington), member of the great "triumvirate" of Lexington sons, with Asteroid and Kentucky. Grade 1 1980-'92. 1 mile 1997-2001. Two divisions 1980. ‡Roman Dancer finished third, DQ to fourth, 2001. †Denotes female.

Northern Dancer Breeders' Cup Stakes

Grade 3 in 2006. Churchill Downs, three-year-olds, 1 1/16 miles, dirt. Held June 18, 2005, with a gross value of $217,400. First held in 1998. First graded in 2004. Stakes record 1:42.46 (2005 Don't Get Mad).

Year	Winner	Jockey	Second	Third	Strs	Time	1st Purse
2005	**Don't Get Mad**, 3, 120	G. L. Stevens	Unbridled Energy, 3, 120	Real Dandy, 3, 116	6	**1:42.46**	$134,788
2004	**Suave**, 3, 114	R. Bejarano	J Town, 3, 114	Ecclesiastic, 3, 114	12	1:44.50	144,088
2003	**Champali**, 3, 122	P. Day	Lone Star Sky, 3, 120	During, 3, 114	8	1:34.69	68,882
2002	**Danthebluegrassman**, 3, 119	J. D. Bailey	Stephentown, 3, 113	Sky Terrace, 3, 119	7	1:35.04	67,890

Named for E. P. Taylor's 1964 Canadian Horse of the Year and '64 Kentucky Derby winner Northern Dancer (1961 c. by Nearctic). Northern Dancer S. 2002-'04. 1 mile 2002-'03. Run as an overnight handicap 1998-2001.

Oaklawn Handicap

Grade 2 in 2006. Oaklawn Park, four-year-olds and up, 1 1/8 miles, dirt. Held April 8, 2006, with a gross value of $500,000. First held in 1946. First graded in 1973. Stakes record 1:46.60 (1987 Snow Chief).

Year	Winner	Jockey	Second	Third	Strs	Time	1st Purse
2006	**Buzzards Bay**, 4, 118	J. Valdivia Jr.	Magnum (Arg), 5, 115	Gouldings Green, 5, 116	8	1:48.22	$300,000
2005	**Grand Reward**, 4, 112	J. McKee	Second of June, 4, 117	Eddington, 4, 117	5	1:49.54	300,000
2004	**Peace Rules**, 4, 120	J. D. Bailey	Ole Faunty, 5, 116	Saint Liam, 4, 114	6	1:48.26	300,000
2003	**Medaglia d'Oro**, 4, 122	J. D. Bailey	Slider, 5, 112	Kudos, 6, 117	5	1:47.66	300,000
2002	**Kudos**, 5, 117	E. Delahoussaye	Bowman's Band, 4, 114	Dollar Bill, 4, 114	8	1:48.34	300,000
2001	**Traditionally**, 4, 112	P. Day	Mr Ross, 6, 117	Wooden Phone, 4, 118	7	1:48.15	360,000
2000	**K One King**, 4, 113	C. H. Borel	Almutawakel (GB), 5, 117	Cat Thief, 4, 118	6	1:48.02	360,000
1999	**Behrens**, 5, 116	J. F. Chavez	Littlebitlively, 5, 112	Precocity, 5, 119	7	1:47.77	450,000
1998	**Precocity**, 4, 114	C. Gonzalez	Frisk Me Now, 4, 117	Phantom On Tour, 4, 117	7	1:48.28	450,000
1997	**Atticus**, 5, 114	S. J. Sellers	Isitingood, 6, 120	Tejano Run, 5, 115	8	1:48.20	450,000
1996	**Geri**, 4, 115	J. D. Bailey	Wekiva Springs, 5, 119	Scott's Scoundrel, 4, 113	7	1:47.52	450,000
1995	**Cigar**, 5, 120	J. D. Bailey	Silver Goblin, 4, 119	Concern, 4, 122	7	1:47.22	450,000
1994	**The Wicked North**, 5, 119	K. Desormeaux	Devil His Due, 5, 120	Brother Brown, 4, 116	12	1:47.86	450,000
1993	**Jovial (GB)**, 6, 117	E. Delahoussaye	Lil E. Tee, 4, 123	Best Pal, 5, 123	10	1:48.63	450,000
1992	**Best Pal**, 4, 125	K. Desormeaux	Sea Cadet, 4, 120	Twilight Agenda, 6, 123	7	1:48.10	300,000
1991	**Festin (Arg)**, 5, 115	E. Delahoussaye	Primal, 6, 115	Jolie's Halo, 4, 120	8	1:48.71	300,000
1990	**Opening Verse**, 4, 118	C. J. McCarron	De Roche, 4, 114	Silver Survivor, 4, 116	8	1:47.20	300,000
1989	**Slew City Slew**, 5, 118	A. T. Cordero Jr.	Stalwars, 4, 113	Homebuilder, 5, 115	8	1:49.00	240,000
1988	**Lost Code**, 4, 126	C. Perret	Cryptoclearance, 4, 122	Gulch, 4, 120	8	1:47.00	300,000
1987	**Snow Chief**, 4, 123	A. O. Solis	Red Attack, 5, 112	Vilzak, 4, 108	7	**1:46.60**	163,020
1986	**Turkoman**, 4, 123	C. J. McCarron	Gate Dancer, 5, 123	Red Attack, 4, 114	4	1:47.40	159,180
1985	**Imp Society**, 4, 125	P. Day	Strength in Unity, 4, 109	Pine Circle, 4, 118	11	1:48.40	168,540
1984	**Wild Again**, 4, 115	P. Day	Win Stat, 7, 114	Dew Line, 5, 118	14	1:46.80	173,940
1983	**Bold Style**, 4, 113	P. Day	Eminency, 5, 123	Listcapade, 4, 123	8	1:43.00	165,180
1982	**Eminency**, 4, 116	P. Day	Reef Searcher, 5, 117	Thirty Eight Paces, 4, 120	9	1:44.00	166,740
1981	**Temperence Hill**, 4, 126	E. Maple	Sun Catcher, 4, 123	Uncool, 6, 114	5	1:43.40	128,310
1980	**Uncool**, 5, 116	J. Velasquez	Hold Your Tricks, 5, 111	Braze and Bold, 5, 118	8	1:44.40	103,110
1979	**San Juan Hill**, 4, 114	D. Brumfield	Alydar, 4, 127	A Letter to Harry, 5, 125	7	1:43.60	101,730
1978	**Cox's Ridge**, 4, 128	E. Maple	Prince Majestic, 4, 115	All the More, 5, 120	11	1:43.20	80,190
1977	**Soy Numero Uno**, 4, 123	R. Broussard	Romeo, 4, 119	Dragset, 6, 114	13	1:42.40	80,610
1976	**Master Derby**, 4, 125	D. G. McHargue	Royal Glint, 6, 128	Dragset, 5, 113	6	1:41.60	70,890
1975	**Warbucks**, 5, 121	D. Gargan	Hey Rube, 5, 112	Eastern Pageant, 4, 115	10	1:42.80	37,380
1974	**Royal Knight**, 4, 123	I. Valenzuela	Crimson Falcon, 4, 122	Visualizer, 4, 121	11	1:43.40	38,070
1973	**Prince Astro**, 4, 116	D. W. Whited	Herbalist, 6, 116	Gage Line, 7, 118	8	1:43.60	34,470

Grade 3 1973-'76. Grade 1 1988-2002. Not held 1955-'62. 1 1/16 miles 1946-'83. Three-year-olds and up 1946-'76.

Oak Leaf Stakes

Grade 1 in 2006. Oak Tree at Santa Anita, two-year-olds, fillies, 1 1/16 miles, dirt. Held October 1, 2005, with a gross value of $200,000. First held in 1969. First graded in 1973. Stakes record 1:41.20 (1978 It's in the Air).

Year	Winner	Jockey	Second	Third	Strs	Time	1st Purse
2005	**Diamond Omi**, 2, 122	D. R. Flores	Wild Fit, 2, 122	Golden Silk, 2, 122	7	1:45.57	$120,000
2004	**Sweet Catomine**, 2, 119	C. S. Nakatani	Splendid Blended, 2, 119	Memorette, 2, 119	9	1:42.98	120,000
2003	**Halfbridled**, 2, 119	J. A. Krone	Tarlow, 2, 119	Hollywood Story, 2, 119	7	1:43.72	150,000
2002	**Composure**, 2, 119	M. E. Smith	Buffythecenterfold, 2, 119	Sea Jewel, 2, 119	6	1:42.65	120,000

2001	**Tali'sluckybusride**, 2, 117	J. Valdivia Jr.	Imperial Gesture, 2, 117	Ms Louisett, 2, 117	6	1:37.77	$150,000
2000	**Notable Career**, 2, 118	D. R. Flores	Euro Empire, 2, 118	Cindy's Hero, 2, 118	7	1:36.34	120,000
1999	**Chilukki**, 2, 118	D. R. Flores	Abby Girl, 2, 118	Spain, 2, 118	5	1:36.12	120,000
1998	**Excellent Meeting**, 2, 115	K. Desormeaux	Antahkarana, 2, 115	Stylish Talent, 2, 115	7	1:37.71	120,000
1997	**Vivid Angel**, 2, 116	E. Delahoussaye	Love Lock, 2, 116	Balisian Beauty, 2, 115	9	1:37.33	120,000
1996	**City Band**, 2, 115	J. A. Garcia	Clever Pilot, 2, 115	Wealthy, 2, 115	8	1:44.57	120,000
1995	**Tipically Irish**, 2, 117	L. A. Pincay Jr.	Ocean View, 2, 115	Gastronomical, 2, 117	7	1:42.60	120,000
1994	**Serena's Song**, 2, 115	C. S. Nakatani	Call Now, 2, 115	Mama Mucci, 2, 115	5	1:41.83	120,000
1993	**Phone Chatter**, 2, 117	L. A. Pincay Jr.	Sardula, 2, 116	Tricky Code, 2, 115	6	1:41.78	120,000
1992	**Zoonaqua**, 2, 115	C. J. McCarron	Turkstand, 2, 115	Madame l'Enjoleur, 2, 115	10	1:43.91	120,000
1991	**Pleasant Stage**, 2, 116	E. Delahoussaye	Soviet Sojourn, 2, 116	La Spia, 2, 115	5	1:43.53	156,540
1990	**Lite Light**, 2, 115	R. A. Baze	Garden Gal, 2, 115	Beyond Perfection, 2, 115	4	1:42.80	148,320
1989	**Dominant Dancer**, 2, 116	E. Delahoussaye	Bel's Starlet, 2, 115	Materco, 2, 115	7	1:44.60	153,870
1988	**One of a Klein**, 2, 115	C. J. McCarron	Stocks Up, 2, 115	Lady Lister, 2, 115	7	1:44.00	168,090
1987	**Dream Team**, 2, 115	C. J. McCarron	Lost Kitty, 2, 117	Tomorrow's Child, 2, 115	6	1:44.40	158,910
1986	**Sacahuista**, 2, 115	C. J. McCarron	Silk's Lady, 2, 115	Delicate Vine, 2, 115	7	1:44.60	187,050
1985	**Arewehavingfunyet**, 2, 115	P. A. Valenzuela	Trim Colony, 2, 115	Laz's Joy, 2, 115	8	1:44.60	192,420
1984	**Folk Art**, 2, 117	L. A. Pincay Jr.	Pirate's Glow, 2, 115	Wayward Pirate, 2, 115	6	1:42.60	186,540
1983	**Life's Magic**, 2, 115	C. J. McCarron	Althea, 2, 117	Percipient, 2, 115	9	1:44.40	164,310
1982	**Landaluce**, 2, 117	L. A. Pincay Jr.	Sophisticated Girl, 2, 115	Granja Reina, 2, 115	7	1:41.80	155,610
1981	**Header Card**, 2, 115	D. G. McHargue	A Kiss for Luck, 2, 117	Model Ten, 2, 115	9	1:43.00	144,390
1980	**Astrious**, 2, 115	T. Lipham	Irish Arrival, 2, 115	Bee a Scout, 2, 115	8	1:43.80	90,180
1979	**Bold 'n Determined**, 2, 115	A. T. Cordero Jr.	Hazel R., 2, 115	Arcades Ambo, 2, 115	8	1:46.20	82,440
1978	**It's in the Air**, 2, 115	E. Delahoussaye	Caline, 2, 115	Spiffy Laree, 2, 115	8	**1:41.20**	75,570
1977	**B. Thoughtful**, 2, 115	D. G. McHargue	Grenzen, 2, 115	High Pheasant, 2, 117	7	1:43.80	73,530
1976	**Any Time Girl**, 2, 115	R. Schacht	Lady T. V., 2, 115	*Glenaris, 2, 115	8	1:44.00	73,140
1975	**Answer**, 2, 115	M. Hole	Queen to Be, 2, 115	Awaken, 2, 115	12	1:44.20	84,720
1974	**Cut Class**, 2, 115	F. Toro	Double You Lou, 2, 115	Sweet Old Girl, 2, 115	13	1:42.80	84,300
1973	**Divine Grace**, 2, 115	S. Valdez	Chalk Face, 2, 115	Round Rose, 2, 115	6	1:43.60	59,940

Run at Santa Anita Park's fall Oak Tree Racing Association meet. Grade 2 1973-'79, 1990-'91, 2002-'05. 1 mile 1997-2001.

Oak Tree Breeders' Cup Mile Stakes

Grade 2 in 2006. Oak Tree at Santa Anita, three-year-olds and up, 1 mile, turf. Held October 8, 2005, with a gross value of $249,000. First held in 1986. First graded in 1989. Stakes record 1:32.44 (1996 Urgent Request [Ire]).

Year	Winner	Jockey	Second	Third	Strs	Time	1st Purse
2005	**Singletary**, 5, 119	D. R. Flores	Designed for Luck, 8, 119	Buckland Manor, 5, 119	6	1:34.54	$150,000
2004	**†Musical Chimes**, 4, 118	K. Desormeaux	Buckland Manor, 4, 119	Singletary, 4, 119	6	1:33.29	150,000
2003	**Designed for Luck**, 6, 119	P. A. Valenzuela	Sarafan, 6, 119	Century City (Ire), 4, 119	8	1:32.61	180,000
2002	**Night Patrol**, 6, 119	J. Valdivia Jr.	Kachamandi (Chi), 5, 119	Nicobar (GB), 5, 119	8	1:32.93	150,000
2001	**Val Royal (Fr)**, 5, 119	J. Valdivia Jr.	Thady Quill, 4, 119	I've Decided, 4, 119	6	1:33.21	120,000
2000	**War Chant**, 3, 117	G. L. Stevens	Road to Slew, 5, 119	Sharan (GB), 5, 119	8	1:33.75	172,050
1999	**Silic (Fr)**, 4, 121	C. S. Nakatani	Bouccaneer (Fr), 4, 119	Brave Act (GB), 5, 119	7	1:33.76	150,000
1998	**Hawksley Hill (Ire)**, 5, 123	A. O. Solis	Mr Lightfoot (Ire), 4, 119	Magellan, 5, 119	5	1:36.72	166,200
1997	**Fantastic Fellow**, 3, 115	A. O. Solis	Magellan, 4, 119	Taiki Blizzard, 6, 123	8	1:36.23	165,000
1996	**Urgent Request (Ire)**, 6, 115	C. J. McCarron	Megan's Interco, 7, 119	Felon (Ire), 4, 116	6	**1:32.44**	110,300
1995	**Ventiquattrofogli (Ire)**, 5, 116	G. F. Almeida	Megan's Interco, 6, 119	Debutant Trick, 5, 115	8	1:35.30	76,850
1994	**Bon Point (GB)**, 4, 116	E. Delahoussaye	Journalism, 6, 120	Johann Quatz (Fr), 5, 117	5	1:33.86	62,050
1993	**Johann Quatz (Fr)**, 4, 119	E. Delahoussaye	Myrakalu (Fr), 5, 114	The Tender Track, 6, 117	5	1:36.28	62,350
1992	**Twilight Agenda**, 6, 120	C. J. McCarron	Luthier Enchanteur, 5, 117	Bourgogne (GB), 4, 115	8	1:33.36	65,300
1991	**Ibero (Arg)**, 4, 115	A. O. Solis	Val des Bois (Fr), 5, 118	Tokatee, 5, 116	9	1:33.77	67,000
1990	**Notorious Pleasure**, 4, 117	L. A. Pincay Jr.	Kanatiyr (Ire), 4, 114	Fly Till Dawn, 4, 116	11	1:33.00	68,700
1989	**Political Ambition**, 5, 122	E. Delahoussaye	Mister Wonderful (GB), 6, 118	Sabona, 7, 117	10	1:33.40	67,800
1988	**Mohamed Abdu (Ire)**, 4, 120	G. L. Stevens	Mazilier, 4, 116	Deputy Governor, 4, 121	7	1:34.40	65,550
1987	**Double Feint**, 4, 117	F. Toro	Deputy Governor, 3, 118	Vilzak, 4, 115	10	1:37.00	64,810
1986	**Palace Music**, 5, 122	G. L. Stevens	‡Skywalker, 4, 122	Mangaki, 5, 116	6	1:35.00	59,350

Run at Santa Anita Park's fall Oak Tree Racing Association meet. Formerly named for Col. F. W. Koester, general manager of the California Thoroughbred Breeders' Association. Grade 3 1989, 1996-'99. Col. F. W. Koester H. 1986-'95. Col. F. W. Koester Breeders' Cup H. 1996. Oak Tree Breeders' Cup Mile H. 1997-'98. Course record 1996. ‡Mangaki finished second, DQ to third, 1986. †Denotes female.

Oak Tree Derby

Grade 2 in 2006. Oak Tree at Santa Anita, three-year-olds, 1⅛ miles, turf. Held October 15, 2005, with a gross value of $150,000. First held in 1969. First graded in 1974. Stakes record 1:45.80 (1989 Seven Rivers).

Year	Winner	Jockey	Second	Third	Strs	Time	1st Purse
2005	**Aragorn (Ire)**, 3, 118	P. A. Valenzuela	Eastern Sand, 3, 118	Brecon Beacon (GB), 3, 118	7	1:46.48	$90,000
2004	**Greek Sun**, 3, 118	E. S. Prado	Laura's Lucky Boy, 3, 118	Hendrix, 3, 118	9	1:48.08	90,000
2003	**Devious Boy (GB)**, 3, 118	J. A. Krone	Sweet Return (GB), 3, 118	Urban King (Ire), 3, 118	5	1:48.82	90,000
2002	**Johar**, 3, 118	A. O. Solis	Rock Opera, 3, 118	Mananan McLir, 3, 120	8	1:46.00	90,000
2001	**No Slip (Fr)**, 3, 118	K. Desormeaux	Sligo Bay (Ire), 3, 118	Romanceishope, 3, 122	9	1:46.56	90,000
2000	**Sign of Hope (GB)**, 3, 118	A. O. Solis	David Copperfield, 3, 118	El Gran Papa, 3, 118	5	1:47.71	150,000
1999	**Mula Gula**, 3, 118	G. L. Stevens	Eagleton, 3, 118	Super Quercus (Fr), 3, 118	9	1:46.67	150,000
1998	**Ladies Din**, 3, 120	G. L. Stevens	Dr Fong, 3, 120	Bouccaneer (Fr), 3, 118	7	1:50.24	150,000

1997	**Lasting Approval**, 3, 118	A. O. Solis	Voyagers Quest, 3, 118	Early Colony, 3, 118	7	1:50.84	$150,000
1996	**Odyle**, 3, 117	C. J. McCarron	Lago, 3, 115	Rainbow Blues (Ire), 3, 117	6	1:46.83	80,250
1995	**Helmsman**, 3, 115	C. J. McCarron	Virginia Carnival, 3, 118	Mr Purple, 3, 121	8	1:48.98	75,650
1994	**Run Softly**, 3, 117	L. A. Pincay Jr.	Alphabet Soup, 3, 114	Powis Castle, 3, 118	8	1:49.96	64,800
1993	**Eastern Memories (Ire)**, 3, 113	J. D. Bailey	Cigar, 3, 117	Snake Eyes, 3, 120	9	1:48.03	66,800
1992	**Blacksburg**, 3, 118	A. O. Solis	Siberian Summer, 3, 117	Star Recruit, 3, 115	10	1:48.12	67,700
1991	**General Meeting**, 3, 116	K. Desormeaux	Dominion Gold (GB), 3, 115	Eternity Star, 3, 120	12	1:46.78	69,500
1990	**In Excess (Ire)**, 3, 117	G. L. Stevens	Warcraft, 3, 118	Barton Dene (Ire), 3, 113	8	1:46.60	65,300
1989	**Seven Rivers**, 3, 115	R. G. Davis	Bruho, 3, 117	Raise a Stanza, 3, 121	9	**1:45.80**	66,100
1988	**Coax Me Clyde**, 3, 116	P. A. Valenzuela	Bel Air Dancer, 3, 117	Undercut, 3, 120	11	1:48.40	81,500
1987	**The Medic**, 3, 119	S. Hawley	Temperate Sil, 3, 122	Hot and Smoggy, 3, 115	9	1:47.80	63,800
1986	**Air Display**, 3, 114	G. L. Stevens	Armada (GB), 3, 117	Vernon Castle, 3, 124	9	1:48.00	64,700
1985	**Justoneoftheboys**, 3, 115	A. O. Solis	Floating Reserve, 3, 118	Schiller, 3, 113	8	1:47.60	65,000
1984	**Tights**, 3, 121	C. J. McCarron	Tsunami Slew, 3, 122	Blind Spot, 3, 115	8	1:46.60	65,500
1983	**Mamaison**, 3, 117	C. J. McCarron	Sunny's Halo, 3, 126	Fifth Division, 3, 118	6	1:49.80	63,900
1982	**Lamerok**, 3, 117	L. A. Pincay Jr.	Craelius, 3, 118	Sari's Dreamer, 3, 113	9	1:46.20	66,300
1981	**dh-Seafood**, 3, 118	M. Castaneda		High Counsel, 3, 117	11	1:49.00	33,350
	dh-Waterway Drive, 3, 120	J. D. Bailey					
1980	**Pocketful in Vail**, 3, 115	F. Toro	Son of a Dodo, 3, 118	Always Best, 3, 117	8	1:47.80	39,400
1979	**Hyannis Port**, 3, 118	W. Shoemaker	Red Crescent, 3, 115	Relaunch, 3, 126	7	1:47.60	32,300
1978	**Wayside Station**, 3, 117	L. A. Pincay Jr.	April Axe, 3, 120	John Henry, 3, 122	11	1:47.80	34,600
1977	**Kulak**, 3, 123	W. Shoemaker	Hill Fox, 3, 114	Kaskee, 3, 110	8	1:46.80	19,800
1976	**Today 'n Tomorrow**, 3, 121	L. A. Pincay Jr.	Pocket Park, 3, 115	Kings Cliffe, 3, 115	8	1:46.80	19,450
1975	**Messenger of Song**, 3, 119	J. Lambert	Larrikin, 3, 123	Forceten, 3, 125	6	1:46.80	25,450
1974	**Within Hail**, 3, 124	W. Shoemaker	Orders, 3, 117	Chief Pronto, 3, 113	11	1:48.40	27,250

Run at Santa Anita Park's fall Oak Tree Racing Association meeting. Formerly named for Elias J. "Lucky" Baldwin's American Derby winner Volante, one of four horses whose gravesites were moved to the entrance of the paddock gardens at Santa Anita Park from their original location on Baldwin's ranch across the street from the present-day track. Grade 3 1974-'87, 1990-'95. Volante H. 1969-'96. Not held 1973. Dead heat for first 1981.

Oceanport Stakes

Grade 3 in 2006. Monmouth Park, three-year-olds and up, 1$^{1}/_{16}$ miles, turf. Held August 7, 2005, with a gross value of $150,000. First held in 1947. First graded in 1973. Stakes record 1:39.40 (1999 Mi Narrow).

Year	Winner	Jockey	Second	Third	Strs	Time	1st Purse
2005	**Ay Caramba (Brz)**, 5, 118	G. L. Stevens	Hotstufanthensome, 5, 118	Stormy Roman, 6, 116	9	1:42.53	$90,000
2004	**Gulch Approval**, 4, 117	P. Day	Kathir, 7, 116	Stormy Roman, 5, 115	10	1:42.31	60,000
2003	**Runspastum**, 6, 113	J. Pimentel	Balto Star, 5, 119	Saint Verre, 5, 118	6	1:42.31	60,000
2002	**Tempest Fugit**, 5, 115	J. A. Velez Jr.	Runspastum, 5, 112	One Eyed Joker, 4, 114	3	1:42.72	60,000
2001	**Key Lory**, 7, 111	C. C. Lopez	North East Bound, 5, 121	Crash Course, 5, 115	13	1:40.39	60,000
2000	**North East Bound**, 4, 114	J. A. Velez Jr.	Rize, 4, 112	Selective, 7, 114	6	1:44.70	60,000
1999	**Mi Narrow**, 5, 113	J. Bravo	Hurrahy, 6, 114	Forbidden Apple, 4, 111	8	**1:39.40**	60,000
1998	**Daylight Savings**, 4, 115	H. Castillo Jr.	Mi Narrow, 4, 112	Rob 'n Gin, 4, 120	8	1:42.31	60,000
1997	**Boyce**, 6, 118	J. A. Krone	Foolish Pole, 4, 113	Jambalaya Jazz, 5, 116	7	1:40.20	60,000
1995	**Boyce**, 4, 114	A. S. Black	Myrmidon, 4, 117	Rocket City, 4, 112	9	1:40.91	45,000
1994	**Nijinsky's Gold**, 5, 120	R. G. Davis	Winnetou, 4, 116	Marco Bay, 4, 116	5	1:41.66	45,000
1993	**Furiously**, 4, 119	J. D. Bailey	Adam Smith (GB), 5, 120	Rocket Fuel, 6, 114	5	1:39.60	45,000
1992	**Maxigroom**, 4, 113	R. G. Davis	Rocket Fuel, 5, 112	Go Dutch, 5, 112	9	1:41.77	45,000
1991	**Fiftysevenvette**, 4, 113	J. C. Ferrer	Great Normand, 6, 118	Thunder Regent, 4, 112	6	1:44.94	45,000
1990	**Bill E. Shears**, 5, 118	R. Wilson	Pete the Chief, 4, 115	Timely Warning, 5, 113	9	1:42.80	53,910
1989	**Yankee Affair**, 7, 121	P. Day	River of Sin, 5, 116	Primino (Fr), 4, 110	7	1:43.40	51,870
1988	**Feeling Gallant**, 6, 119	C. W. Antley	Copper Cup, 5, 111	Sovereign Song, 6, 107	8	1:45.20	41,820
1987	**Sovereign Song**, 5, 106	J. A. Krone	Feeling Gallant, 5, 120	Spellbound, 4, 117	8	1:41.60	35,100
1986	**Salem Drive**, 4, 115	D. B. Thomas	Exclusive Partner, 4, 114	Pine Belt, 4, 113	10	1:42.60	34,650
1985	**Cozzene**, 5, 121	W. A. Guerra	Stay the Course, 4, 119	Roving Minstrel, 4, 118	9	1:42.40	34,470
1984	**World Appeal**, 4, 120	C. Perret	Rocca Reale, 5, 109	Castle Guard, 5, 120	8	1:42.80	34,950
1983	**Fray Star (Arg)**, 5, 114	O. Vergara	Domynsky (GB), 3, 112	And More, 5, 117	12	1:43.40	35,190
1982	**McCann**, 4, 114	J. Fell	Sprink, 4, 108	Lord Carnavon, 4, 111	9	1:43.60	27,555
	Erin's Tiger, 4, 114	K. Skinner	Dom Menotti (Fr), 5, 111	War of Words, 5, 114	9	1:43.00	27,555
1981	**Winds of Winter**, 4, 113	G. McCarron	Foretake, 5, 116	No Bend, 4, 115	12	1:43.40	24,225
1980	**North Course**, 5, 114	B. Thornburg	Horatius, 5, 119	Lucy's Axe, 4, 116	11	1:44.00	24,210
1979	**Revivalist**, 5, 117	W. Nemeti	Horatius, 4, 117	Gristle, 4, 112	10	1:38.00	18,866
	Alias Smith, 6, 114	M. Solomone	Qui Native, 5, 114	Fed Funds, 5, 114	9	1:38.00	18,671
1978	**Mr. Red Wing**, 4, 110	W. H. McCauley	Chati, 5, 118	Dan Horn, 6, 116	15	1:43.20	23,514
1977	**Quick Card**, 4, 115	M. Solomone	Bemo, 7, 115	Star of the Sea, 4, 115	12	1:42.60	19,516
1976	**Toujours Pret**, 7, 114	J. W. Edwards	Hat Full, 5, 114	Our Hermis, 5, 113	10	1:43.00	15,072
	Break Up the Game, 5, 114	E. Delahoussaye	Expropriate, 6, 120	Leader of the Band, 4, 118	6	1:44.20	14,682
1975	**R. Tom Can**, 4, 115	D. Brumfield	Prod, 4, 117	Royal Glint, 5, 119	11	1:49.80	15,291
	Haraka, 5, 113	J. Velasquez	London Company, 5, 124	East Sea, 4, 115	9	1:49.80	15,096
1974	**Mo Bay**, 5, 118	W. Tichenor	Shane's Prince, 4, 118	Barbizon Streak, 6, 116	10	1:42.40	18,541
1973	**Lexington Park**, 6, 118	J. Imparato	Prince of Truth, 5, 116	Halo, 4, 117	9	1:45.20	15,056
	Dartsum, 4, 110	M. Cedeno	Dundee Marmalade, 5, 114	Return to Reality, 4, 111	8	1:46.20	14,893

Monmouth Park is located in Oceanport, New Jersey. Grade 3 1984-2001. Not graded 2002. Oceanport H. 1947-2004. Not held 1996. 6 furlongs 1947-'63. 5 furlongs 1964-'67. 1 mile 1968-'72, 1979. Dirt 1947-'63, 1970, 1984, 1990-'91, 2000, 2002. Originally scheduled on turf 2002. Two divisions 1973, 1975-'76, 1979, 1982. Course record 1993, 1999.

Ogden Phipps Handicap

Grade 1 in 2006. Belmont Park, three-year-olds and up, fillies and mares, 1$^1/_{16}$ miles, dirt. Held June 18, 2005, with a gross value of $294,000. First held in 1961. First graded in 1973. Stakes record 1:39.90 (1998 Mossflower).

Year	Winner	Jockey	Second	Third	Strs	Time	1st Purse
2005	**Ashado**, 4, 120	J. R. Velazquez	Society Selection, 4, 119	Bending Strings, 4, 115	5	1:41.02	$180,000
2004	**Sightseek**, 5, 120	J. D. Bailey	Storm Flag Flying, 4, 117	Passing Shot, 5, 116	4	1:41.46	180,000
2003	**Sightseek**, 4, 118	J. D. Bailey	Take Charge Lady, 4, 119	Mandy's Gold, 5, 118	5	1:40.89	180,000
2002	**Raging Fever**, 4, 120	J. R. Velazquez	Transcendental, 4, 113	Two Item Limit, 4, 114	9	1:41.75	180,000
2001	**Critical Eye**, 4, 115	M. J. Luzzi	Jostle, 4, 117	Apple of Kent, 5, 117	7	1:42.18	150,000
2000	**Beautiful Pleasure**, 5, 124	J. F. Chavez	Pentatonic, 5, 112	Roza Robata, 5, 115	6	1:41.54	150,000
1999	**Sister Act**, 4, 117	P. Day	Beautiful Pleasure, 4, 112	Catinca, 4, 122	6	1:40.79	150,000
1998	**Mossflower**, 4, 114	R. G. Davis	Glitter Woman, 4, 120	Colonial Minstrel, 4, 118	6	**1:39.90**	150,000
1997	**Hidden Lake**, 4, 117	R. Migliore	Twice the Vice, 6, 121	Jewel Princess, 5, 124	9	1:40.87	150,000
1996	**Serena's Song**, 4, 125	J. D. Bailey	Shoop, 5, 115	Restored Hope, 5, 114	8	1:41.63	120,000
1995	**Heavenly Prize**, 4, 122	P. Day	Little Buckles, 4, 111	Sky Beauty, 5, 124	4	1:43.37	90,000
1994	**Sky Beauty**, 4, 128	M. E. Smith	You'd Be Surprised, 5, 118	Schway Baby Sway, 4, 109	5	1:47.48	90,000
1993	**Turnback the Alarm**, 4, 119	C. W. Antley	Deputation, 4, 117	You'd Be Surprised, 4, 112	6	1:48.14	90,000
1992	**Missy's Mirage**, 4, 118	E. Maple	Harbour Club, 5, 110	Versailles Treaty, 4, 119	6	1:47.03	120,000
1991	**A Wild Ride**, 4, 120	M. E. Smith	Fit to Scout, 4, 115	Buy the Firm, 5, 121	6	1:49.09	120,000
1990	**Fantastic Find**, 4, 113	C. Perret	Mistaurian, 4, 113	Dreamy Mimi, 4, 113	8	1:50.00	139,680
1989	**Rose's Cantina**, 5, 117	J. Cruguet	Make Change, 4, 111	Colonial Waters, 4, 114	6	1:48.60	135,120
1988	**Personal Ensign**, 4, 123	R. P. Romero	Hometown Queen, 4, 109	Clabber Girl, 5, 118	5	1:47.60	131,760
1987	**Catatonic**, 5, 116	D. A. Miller Jr.	Ms. Eloise, 4, 118	Steal a Kiss, 4, 111	7	1:50.00	137,520
1986	**Endear**, 4, 115	E. Maple	Lady's Secret, 4, 128	Ride Sally, 4, 124	5	1:48.60	97,650
1985	**Heatherten**, 6, 124	R. P. Romero	Life's Magic, 4, 122	Sefa's Beauty, 6, 120	6	1:48.80	84,300
1984	**Heatherten**, 5, 118	S. Maple	Quixotic Lady, 4, 118	Thirty Flags, 4, 114	10	1:49.20	92,400
1983	**Number**, 4, 117	E. Maple	Dance Number, 4, 114	Broom Dance, 4, 121	4	1:48.40	65,880
1982	**Love Sign**, 5, 123	R. Hernandez	Anti Lib, 4, 116	Jameela, 6, 122	4	1:48.00	65,280
1981	**Wistful**, 4, 119	D. Brumfield	Chain Bracelet, 4, 119	Love Sign, 4, 115	5	1:49.80	64,200
1980	**Misty Gallore**, 4, 125	D. MacBeth	Blitey, 4, 115	What'll I Do, 4, 110	6	1:48.80	32,760
1979	**Pearl Necklace**, 5, 122	J. Fell	Miss Baja, 4, 115	Sweet Woodruff, 4, 108	5	1:48.60	31,470
1978	**Dottie's Doll**, 5, 115	J. Vasquez	One Sum, 4, 123	Water Malone, 4, 119	6	1:47.60	32,040
1977	**Pacific Princess**, 4, 112	E. Maple	Mississippi Mud, 4, 114	Fleet Victress, 5, 113	10	1:49.20	32,700
1976	**Proud Delta**, 4, 124	J. Velasquez	Garden Verse, 4, 111	Let Me Linger, 4, 114	8	1:48.40	33,690
1975	**Raisela**, 4, 114	E. Maple	Pass a Glance, 4, 114	Sarsar, 3, 115	7	1:49.20	33,510
1974	**Poker Night**, 4, 114	J. Velasquez	Krislin, 5, 115	Fairway Flyer, 5, 117	8	1:48.60	33,300
1973	**Light Hearted**, 4, 123	E. Nelson	Inca Queen, 5, 116	Blessing Angelica, 5, 117	6	1:48.80	32,880

Named for Ogden Phipps (1908-2002), former chairman of the Jockey Club and New York Racing Association. Formerly named for Hempstead, New York, located in Nassau County, home of Belmont Park. Grade 2 1973-'83. Hempstead H. 1961-2001. Held at Aqueduct 1973-'74. Not held 1910-'60, 1962-'69. 6 furlongs 1970-'71. 1$^1/_2$ miles 1961. 1$^1/_8$ miles 1972-'94. Both sexes 1961.

Ohio Derby

Grade 2 in 2006. Thistledown, three-year-olds, 1$^1/_8$ miles, dirt. Held July 2, 2005, with a gross value of $350,000. First held in 1876. First graded in 1973. Stakes record 1:47.40 (1979 Smarten).

Year	Winner	Jockey	Second	Third	Strs	Time	1st Purse
2005	**Palladio**, 3, 115	R. A. Dos Ramos	Magna Graduate, 3, 117	It's Time to Smile, 3, 115	8	1:51.56	$210,000
2004	**Brass Hat**, 3, 115	W. Martinez	Pollard's Vision, 3, 121	Trieste's Honor, 3, 115	9	1:49.50	210,000
2003	**Wild and Wicked**, 3, 114	S. J. Sellers	Hackendiffy, 3, 112	Midway Road, 3, 114	7	1:50.08	180,000
2002	**Magic Weisner**, 3, 116	R. Migliore	Wiseman's Ferry, 3, 120	The Judge Sez Who, 3, 114	4	1:49.96	195,000
2001	**Western Pride**, 3, 119	D. G. Whitney	Woodmoon, 3, 113	Macho Uno, 3, 119	6	1:48.66	180,000
2000	**Milwaukee Brew**, 3, 116	M. J. McCarthy	Brave Quest, 3, 113	Kiss a Native, 3, 116	10	1:50.58	180,000
1999	**Stellar Brush**, 3, 119	M. J. McCarthy	Ecton Park, 3, 116	Valhol, 3, 114	13	1:49.22	180,000
1998	**Classic Cat**, 3, 122	S. J. Sellers	One Bold Stroke, 3, 118	Hot Wells, 3, 118	10	1:49.92	180,000
1997	**Frisk Me Now**, 3, 122	E. L. King Jr.	Anet, 3, 122	Mr. Groush, 3, 118	7	1:48.28	180,000
1996	**Skip Away**, 3, 122	J. A. Santos	Victory Speech, 3, 118	Clash by Night, 3, 118	10	1:47.86	180,000
1995	**Petionville**, 3, 122	P. Day	Dazzling Falls, 3, 124	Is Sveikatas, 3, 116	6	1:48.93	180,000
1994	**Exclusive Praline**, 3, 118	W. Martinez	Concern, 3, 122	Smilin Singin Sam, 3, 122	8	1:48.54	180,000
1993	**Forever Whirl**, 3, 122	A. Toribio	Boundlessly, 3, 120	Mighty Avanti, 3, 114	10	1:49.44	180,000
1992	**Majestic Sweep**, 3, 117	E. Fires	Technology, 3, 126	Always Silver, 3, 117	8	1:50.07	180,000
1991	**Private Man**, 3, 114	J. R. Velazquez	Richman, 3, 126	Shudanz, 3, 114	9	1:50.30	180,000
1990	**Private School**, 3, 120	J. Vasquez	Restless Con, 3, 123	Real Cash, 3, 123	15	1:51.20	180,000
1989	**King Glorious**, 3, 120	C. J. McCarron	Roi Danzig, 3, 114	Caesar, 3, 114	10	1:50.40	180,000
1988	**Jim's Orbit**, 3, 123	S. P. Romero	Primal, 3, 114	Intensive Command, 3, 114	8	1:50.60	150,000
1987	**Lost Code**, 3, 126	G. St. Leon	Proudest Duke, 3, 117	Homebuilder, 3, 114	9	1:50.60	150,000
1986	**Broad Brush**, 3, 126	G. L. Stevens	Bolshoi Boy, 3, 123	Forty Kings, 3, 114	9	1:51.20	150,000
1985	**Skip Trial**, 3, 114	J. Samyn	Encolure, 3, 123	Jacque l'Heureux, 3, 114	8	1:49.00	120,000
1984	**At the Threshold**, 3, 123	G. Patterson	Biloxi Indian, 3, 123	Perfect Player, 3, 120	7	1:49.60	120,000
1983	**Pax Nobiscum**, 3, 120	R. Platts	Bet Big, 3, 114	Fightin Hill, 3, 114	9	1:50.20	90,000
1982	**Spanish Drums**, 3, 123	J. Vasquez	Air Forbes Won, 3, 126	Lejoli, 3, 114	9	1:49.60	90,000
1981	**Pass the Tab**, 3, 120	A. Graell	Paristo, 3, 123	Classic Go Go, 3, 123	9	1:49.20	90,000
1980	**Stone Manor**, 3, 123	P. Day	Colonel Moran, 3, 123	Hillbizon, 3, 114	13	1:52.00	90,000

1979	**Smarten**, 3, 124	S. Maple	Bold Ruckus, 3, 115	Picturesque, 3, 122	12	**1:47.40**	$90,000
1978	**Special Honor**, 3, 115	R. Breen	Batonnier, 3, 122	Star de Naskra, 3, 120	10	1:47.80	90,000
1977	**Silver Series**, 3, 122	L. Snyder	Cormorant, 3, 122	Pruneplum, 3, 115	12	1:49.20	90,000
1976	**Return of a Native**, 3, 115	G. Patterson	Cojak, 3, 122	Dream 'n Be Lucky, 3, 115	14	1:49.80	75,000
1975	**Brent's Prince**, 3, 115	B. R. Feliciano	Sylvan Place, 3, 112	Canvasser, 3, 115	11	1:49.40	66,780
1974	**Stonewalk**, 3, 120	M. A. Rivera	Better Arbitor, 3, 122	Sharp Gary, 3, 122	9	1:53.20	63,000
1973	**Our Native**, 3, 122	A. Rini	Hearts of Lettuce, 3, 112	Arbees Boy, 3, 115	12	1:50.20	63,882

Thistledown is located in North Randall, Ohio. Held at Chester Park 1876-'83. Held at Maple Heights 1924-'26. Held at Bainbridge Park 1928-'35. Held at Cranwood Park 1952. Held at Randall Park 1961-'62. Not held 1884-1923, 1927, 1933-'34, 1936-'51. 1½ miles 1876-'83. 1¹⁄₁₆ miles 1960-'64.

Old Hat Stakes

Grade 3 in 2006. Gulfstream Park, three-year-olds, fillies, 6½ furlongs, dirt. Held February 4, 2006, with a gross value of $100,000. First held in 1976. First graded in 2005. Stakes record 1:16.03 (2006 Misty Rosette).

Year	Winner	Jockey	Second	Third	Strs	Time	1st Purse
2006	**Misty Rosette**, 3, 115	S. O. Madrid	Swap Fliparoo, 3, 119	Smart N Pretty, 3, 115	6	**1:16.03**	$60,000
2005	**Maddalena**, 3, 115	J. R. Velazquez	Alfonsina, 3, 119	Holy Trinity, 3, 115	7	1:16.31	60,000
2004	**Madcap Escapade**, 3, 115	R. R. Douglas	Sweet Vision, 3, 115	Smokey Glacken, 3, 119	9	1:08.85	60,000
2003	**House Party**, 3, 115	J. A. Santos	Chimichurri, 3, 119	Glorious Miss, 3, 119	5	1:10.81	60,000
2002	**A New Twist**, 3, 115	E. S. Prado	Forest Heiress, 3, 119	French Satin, 3, 115	7	1:10.61	60,000
2000	**Swept Away**, 3, 112	E. Coa	Petite Deputy, 3, 113	Sabre Dance, 3, 118	10	1:09.96	45,000
1999	**Belle's Appeal**, 3, 114	R. Migliore	Extended Applause, 3, 112	Preciosa V., 3, 112	7	1:11.59	45,000
1998	**Evening Hush**, 3, 114	R. G. Davis	Cotton House Bay, 3, 116	Argos Appeal, 3, 116	7	1:10.63	45,000
1997	**Cupids Revenge**, 3, 112	E. Coa	Supah Syble, 3, 112	Witchful Thinking, 3, 116	6	1:09.47	45,000
1996	**J J'sdream**, 3, 116	M. E. Smith	Mindy Gayle, 3, 112	Nic's Halo, 3, 113	8	1:10.60	30,000
1995	**Bluff's Dividend**, 3, 116	J. A. Santos	Mackenzie Slew, 3, 114	Twist a Lime, 3, 112	9	1:10.82	30,000
1994	**Pagofire**, 3, 112	J. D. Bailey	Deaf Power, 3, 116	Vivance, 3, 113	11	1:10.32	30,000
1993	**Sum Runner**, 3, 114	E. Fires	Best in Sale, 3, 114	Hidden Fire, 3, 114	9	1:10.25	30,000
1992	**Super Doer**, 3, 114	R. R. Douglas	Ravensmoor, 3, 114	Miss Valid Pache, 3, 116	7	1:10.99	30,000
1991	**My Own True Love**, 3, 114	H. Castillo Jr.	Flashing Eyes, 3, 116	Parisian Flight, 3, 114	7	1:10.30	30,000
1990	**dh-Sun Luck**, 3, 112	M. A. Gonzalez		Miss Cox's Hat, 3, 113	9	1:12.00	14,000
	dh-Traki Traki, 3, 114	E. Fires					
1989	**Surging**, 3, 114	C. Perret	Royal Snub, 3, 112	Coax Chelsie, 3, 121	6	1:10.40	27,528
1988	**On to Royalty**, 3, 113	J. Vasquez	Willing'n Waiting, 3, 114	Level, 3, 112	9	1:11.40	28,848
1987	**Sheer Ice**, 5, 113	R. Woodhouse	Grand Creation, 5, 110	One Fine Lady, 5, 115	7	1:23.80	20,862
1986	**Noranc**, 3, 112	W. H. McCauley	Spirit of Fighter, 3, 114	Bespeak, 3, 112	15	1:11.00	31,776
1985	**Glorious Glory**, 3, 112	B. Zoppo-Bundy	Sheer Ice, 3, 116	Golden Silence, 3, 112	14	1:11.60	31,752
1984	**Flip for Luck**, 4, 114	G. St. Leon	Pretty as Patty, 4, 115	Amber's Desire, 4, 113	11	1:23.40	13,572
1983	**Unaccompanied**, 3, 112	R. Woodhouse	Lisa's Capital, 3, 114	Masked Romance, 3, 112	11	1:10.80	22,518
1981	**Dame Mysterieuse**, 3, 118	E. Maple	Masters Dream, 3, 112	Irish Joy, 3, 112	9	1:10.20	21,906
1976	**Anne Campbell**, 3, 114	M. Solomone	Veroom Maid, 3, 114	Jet Set Jennifer, 3, 113	8	1:09.80	9,960

Named for Stanley Conrad's 1964, '65 champion older female and '63, '65 Suwannee River H. winner Old Hat (1959 f. by Boston Doge). Not held 1977-'80, 1982, 2001. Dead heat for first 1990.

Orchid Handicap

Grade 3 in 2006. Gulfstream Park, three-year-olds and up, fillies and mares, 1½ miles, turf. Held April 1, 2006, with a gross value of $150,000. First held in 1954. First graded in 1973. Stakes record 2:23.07 (2006 Honey Ryder).

Year	Winner	Jockey	Second	Third	Strs	Time	1st Purse
2006	**Honey Ryder**, 5, 120	J. R. Velazquez	Olaya, 4, 118	Noble Stella (Ger), 5, 116	8	**2:23.07**	$90,000
2005	**Honey Ryder**, 4, 116	J. R. Velazquez	Ellieonthemarch, 4, 114	Pretty Jane, 4, 114	7	2:27.15	90,000
2004	**Meridiana (Ger)**, 4, 114	E. S. Prado	Savedbythelight, 4, 114	Miss Hellie, 5, 114	10	2:26.99	120,000
2003	**Tweedside**, 5, 116	R. R. Douglas	San Dare, 5, 119	Hi Tech Honeycomb, 4, 115	7	2:32.36	120,000
2002	**Julie Jalouse**, 4, 114	J. A. Santos	Sweetest Thing, 4, 115	Refugee, 4, 110	9	2:25.89	120,000
2001	**Innuendo (Ire)**, 6, 116	J. D. Bailey	Windsong, 4, 113	Aiglonne, 4, 114	4	2:25.24	120,000
2000	**Lisieux Rose (Ire)**, 5, 114	J. A. Santos	Champagne Royal, 6, 114	Fly for Avie, 5, 114	10	2:25.64	120,000
1999	**Coretta (Ire)**, 5, 118	J. A. Santos	Delilah (Ire), 5, 117	Almost Skint (Ire), 5, 113	11	2:23.85	120,000
1998	**Colonial Play**, 4, 113	R. G. Davis	Almost Skint (Ire), 4, 114	Gastronomical, 5, 113	11	2:24.75	120,000
1997	**Golden Pond (Ire)**, 4, 116	W. H. McCauley	Tocopilla (Arg), 7, 115	Miss Caerleona (Fr), 5, 114	11	2:26.80	120,000
1996	**Memories (Ire)**, 5, 114	J. A. Santos	Caromana, 5, 112	Curtain Raiser, 4, 113	11	2:31.51	120,000
1995	**Exchange**, 7, 120	L. A. Pincay Jr.	Market Booster, 6, 116	Northern Emerald, 5, 115	10	2:29.02	120,000
1994	**Trampoli**, 5, 121	M. E. Smith	Good Morning Smile, 6, 110	Northern Emerald, 4, 113	7	2:25.42	120,000
1993	**Fairy Garden**, 5, 115	W. S. Ramos	Rougeur, 4, 115	Trampoli, 4, 115	14	2:25.79	120,000
1992	**Crockadore**, 5, 115	M. E. Smith	Indian Fashion, 5, 112	Sardaniya (Ire), 4, 114	10	2:28.32	120,000
1991	**Star Standing**, 4, 114	C. W. Antley	Coolawin, 5, 118	Peinture Bleue, 4, 119	9	2:25.02	120,000
1990	**Coolawin**, 4, 112	J. D. Bailey	Laugh and Be Merry, 5, 113	Gaily Gaily (Ire), 7, 121	10	2:24.20	120,000
1989	**Gaily Gaily (Ire)**, 6, 110	J. A. Krone	Anka Germania (Ire), 7, 120	Laugh and Be Merry, 4, 110	13	2:26.80	120,000
1988	**Beauty Cream**, 5, 115	P. Day	Ladanum, 4, 112	Green Oasis (Fr), 6, 112	14	2:28.40	120,000
1987	**Anka Germania (Ire)**, 5, 117	C. Perret	Singular Bequest, 4, 116	Ivor's Image, 4, 119	14	2:31.40	90,000
1986	**Videogenic**, 4, 121	R. G. Davis	Powder Break, 5, 118	Devalois (Fr), 4, 117	14	2:27.20	118,440
1985	**Pretty Perfect**, 5, 120	G. Gallitano	Early Lunch, 4, 113	Trinado, 4, 112	13	1:41.60	61,980
	Aspen Rose, 5, 116	J. Velasquez	Over Your Shoulder, 4, 114	Dictina (Fr), 4, 117	14	1:42.00	63,180
1984	**Sabin**, 4, 125	E. Maple	Jubilous, 4, 114	Sulemeif, 4, 115	7	1:41.40	70,680

1983	**Sweetest Chant**, 5, 116	E. Fires	Betty Money, 4, 114	Norsan, 4, 115	8	1:43.60	$53,040
	Larida, 4, 118	E. Maple	Syrianna, 4, 116	Promising Native, 4, 115	8	1:44.80	53,640
1982	**Blush**, 4, 112	J. Vasquez	Pine Flower, 4, 114	Honey Fox, 5, 125	12	1:41.00	76,500
1981	**Honey Fox**, 4, 115	J. Vasquez	The Very One, 6, 125	Solo Haina, 5, 114	16	1:41.20	88,530
1980	**Just a Game (Ire)**, 4, 119	D. Brumfield	La Soufriere, 5, 115	La Rouquine (GB), 4, 114	10	1:40.40	80,340
1979	**Sans Arc**, 5, 116	E. Fires	‡Terpsichorist, 4, 122	Time for Pleasure, 5, 119	13	1:41.40	86,093
1978	**Time for Pleasure**, 4, 115	T. Barrow	Late Bloomer, 4, 113	Rich Soil, 4, 116	11	1:41.00	37,800
1977	**Copano**, 5, 122	M. Solomone	Jabot, 5, 117	Carolina Moon, 5, 114	13	1:41.40	43,500
1976	***Deesse Du Val**, 5, 116	C. H. Marquez	Redundancy, 5, 120	K D Princess, 5, 110	12	1:41.80	28,785
1975	***Protectora**, 6, 114	H. Gustines	Zippy Do, 6, 118	Lorraine Edna, 5, 116	7	1:41.20	26,100
1974	**Dogtooth Violet**, 4, 113	D. Brumfield	Dove Creek Lady, 4, 124	Shearwater, 5, 115	8	1:41.00	39,420
1973	**Deb Marion**, 3, 106	F. Iannelli	Tico's Donna, 5, 113	Barely Even, 4, 125	9	1:42.60	27,240

James Donn Sr., Gulfstream Park founder, was a world-renowned florist who developed a special breed of orchid in honor of his wife. Grade 2 1981-2005. Orchid S. 1954-'66. Not held 1955-'64. 6 furlongs 1954. $1\frac{1}{16}$ miles 1965-'66, 1969-'85. 1 mile 1967-'68. About $1\frac{1}{2}$ miles 1992. Dirt 1954-'66, 1983-'84, 2003. Originally scheduled at about $1\frac{1}{2}$ miles on turf 2003. Three-year-olds 1954-'66. Two divisions 1983, 1985. ‡Time for Pleasure finished second, DQ to third, 1979. Course record 1992, 2006.

Pacific Classic Stakes

Grade 1 in 2006. Del Mar, three-year-olds and up, $1\frac{1}{4}$ miles, dirt. Held August 21, 2005, with a gross value of $1,000,000. First held in 1991. First graded in 1993. Stakes record 1:59.11 (2003 Candy Ride [Arg]).

Year	Winner	Jockey	Second	Third	Strs	Time	1st Purse
2005	**Borrego**, 4, 124	G. K. Gomez	Perfect Drift, 6, 124	Lava Man, 4, 124	11	2:00.71	$600,000
2004	**Pleasantly Perfect**, 6, 124	J. D. Bailey	Perfect Drift, 5, 124	Total Impact (Chi), 6, 124	8	2:01.17	600,000
2003	**Candy Ride (Arg)**, 4, 124	J. A. Krone	Medaglia d'Oro, 4, 124	Fleetstreet Dancer, 5, 124	4	**1:59.11**	600,000
2002	**Came Home**, 3, 117	M. E. Smith	Momentum, 4, 124	Milwaukee Brew, 5, 124	14	2:01.45	600,000
2001	**Skimming**, 5, 124	G. K. Gomez	Dixie Dot Com, 6, 124	Dig for It, 6, 124	6	1:59.96	600,000
2000	**Skimming**, 4, 124	G. K. Gomez	Tiznow, 3, 117	Ecton Park, 4, 124	7	2:01.22	600,000
1999	**General Challenge**, 3, 117	D. R. Flores	River Keen (Ire), 7, 124	Barter Town, 4, 124	8	2:00.57	700,000
1998	**Free House**, 4, 124	C. J. McCarron	Gentlemen (Arg), 6, 124	Pacificbounty, 4, 124	9	2:00.29	600,000
1997	**Gentlemen (Arg)**, 5, 124	G. L. Stevens	Siphon (Brz), 6, 124	Crafty Friend, 4, 124	5	2:00.56	600,000
1996	**Dare and Go**, 5, 124	A. O. Solis	Cigar, 6, 124	Siphon (Brz), 5, 124	6	1:59.85	600,000
1995	**Tinners Way**, 5, 124	E. Delahoussaye	Soul of the Matter, 4, 124	Blumin Affair, 4, 124	6	1:59.63	550,000
1994	**Tinners Way**, 4, 124	E. Delahoussaye	Best Pal, 6, 124	Dramatic Gold, 3, 117	9	1:59.43	550,000
1993	**Bertrando**, 4, 124	G. L. Stevens	Missionary Ridge (GB), 6, 124	Best Pal, 5, 124	7	1:59.55	550,000
1992	**Missionary Ridge (GB)**, 5, 124	K. Desormeaux	Defensive Play, 5, 124	Claret (Ire), 4, 124	7	2:00.87	550,000
1991	**Best Pal**, 3, 116	P. A. Valenzuela	Twilight Agenda, 5, 124	Unbridled, 4, 124	8	1:59.86	550,000

Named for the Pacific Ocean, where Del Mar's "turf meets the surf." Track record 1993-'94, 2003.

Palm Beach Stakes

Grade 3 in 2006. Gulfstream Park, three-year-olds, $1\frac{1}{8}$ miles, turf. Held March 12, 2006, with a gross value of $100,000. First held in 1987. First graded in 1990. Stakes record 1:45.94 (2006 Go Between).

Year	Winner	Jockey	Second	Third	Strs	Time	1st Purse
2006	**Go Between**, 3, 118	E. S. Prado	Up an Octave, 3, 122	Papal Crown, 3, 118	7	**1:45.94**	$60,000
2005	**Interpatation**, 3, 116	T. G. Turner	Tadreeb, 3, 118	Fishy Advice, 3, 118	8	1:47.12	60,000
2004	**Kitten's Joy**, 3, 122	J. D. Bailey	Prince Arch, 3, 118	Pa Pa Da, 3, 118	12	1:48.76	60,000
2003	**Nothing to Lose**, 3, 122	J. D. Bailey	White Cat, 3, 118	Imitation, 3, 118	12	1:48.28	60,000
2002	**Orchard Park**, 3, 118	J. D. Bailey	Lord Juban, 3, 118	Red's Top Gun, 3, 116	12	1:49.80	60,000
2001	**Proud Man**, 3, 119	R. R. Douglas	One Eyed Joker, 3, 114	Strategic Partner, 3, 112	12	1:48.32	90,000
2000	**Mr. Livingston**, 3, 114	S. J. Sellers	Powerful Appeal, 3, 114	Gateman (GB), 3, 117	11	1:48.04	45,000
1999	**Swamp**, 3, 114	R. Migliore	Marquette, 3, 114	Valid Reprized, 3, 119	12	1:48.38	45,000
1998	**Cryptic Rascal**, 3, 119	M. E. Smith	The Kaiser, 3, 113	American Odyssey, 3, 114	8	1:55.01	45,000
1997	**Unite's Big Red**, 3, 117	R. A. Hernandez	Trample, 3, 112	Tekken (Ire), 3, 117	7	1:47.32	45,000
1996	**Harrowman**, 3, 114	M. E. Smith	A Real Zipper, 3, 117	Ok by Me, 3, 119	6	1:49.22	45,000
1995	**Admiralty**, 3, 114	J. A. Krone	Nostra, 3, 114	Smells and Bells, 3, 114	4	1:51.03	30,000
1994	**Mr. Angel**, 3, 112	W. H. McCauley	Clint Essential, 3, 114	Fabulous Frolic, 3, 119	9	1:44.66	30,000
1993	**Kissin Kris**, 3, 112	D. Penna	Pride Prevails, 3, 112	Awad, 3, 119	10	1:46.41	38,760
1992	**Preferences**, 3, 114	J. C. Duarte Jr.	Doo You, 3, 112	Stress Buster, 3, 114	12	1:42.64	38,940
1991	**Magic Interlude**, 3, 114	C. W. Antley	Island Delay, 3, 117	Explosive Jeff, 3, 114	11	1:43.10	38,310
1990	**Dawn Quixote**, 3, 119	C. Perret	Rowdy Regal, 3, 119	Always Running, 3, 115	9	1:23.40	30,000
1989	**Shy Tom**, 3, 113	R. P. Romero	Verbatree, 3, 114	Group Process, 3, 114	8	1:37.20	29,835
	Storm Predictions, 3, 119	S. Gaffalione	Mercedes Won, 3, 122	Ocean Mistery, 3, 113	10	1:36.20	30,735
1988	**Tanzanid**, 3, 115	D. Valiente	Cefis, 3, 113	Denomination (GB), 3, 113	12	1:35.60	39,420
1987	**Racing Star**, 5, 114	S. B. Soto	Explosive Darling, 5, 118	New Colony, 4, 109	9	1:34.80	36,390

Named in honor of the residents of West Palm Beach and Palm Beach County, Florida. Palm Beach H. 1987. 1 mile 1987-'89. 7 furlongs 1990. $1\frac{1}{16}$ miles 1991-'93. About $1\frac{1}{16}$ miles 1994. About $1\frac{1}{8}$ miles 1998. Dirt 1990, 1993, 1995. Three-year-olds and up 1987. Two divisions 1989.

Palomar Breeders' Cup Handicap

Grade 2 in 2006. Del Mar, three-year-olds and up, fillies and mares, $1\frac{1}{16}$ miles, turf. Held September 3, 2005, with a gross value of $180,000. First held in 1945. First graded in 1981. Stakes record 1:39.84 (2005 Intercontinental [GB]).

Year	Winner	Jockey	Second	Third	Strs	Time	1st Purse
2005	**Intercontinental (GB)**, 5, 122	J. D. Bailey	Amorama (Fr), 4, 119	Ticker Tape (GB), 4, 118	5	**1:39.84**	$120,000

2004	**Etoile Montante**, 4, 120	J. Valdivia Jr.	Katdogawn (GB), 4, 117	Tangle (Ire), 4, 117	7	1:40.59	$120,000
2003	**Spring Star (Fr)**, 4, 116	A. O. Solis	Magic Mission (GB), 5, 117	Garden in the Rain (Fr), 6, 114	5	1:40.78	120,000
2002	**Voodoo Dancer**, 4, 120	K. Desormeaux	I'm the Business (NZ), 5, 114	Skywriting, 4, 114	7	1:41.56	90,000
2001	**Tranquility Lake**, 6, 123	E. Delahoussaye	La Ronge, 4, 116	Al Desima (GB), 4, 113	6	1:41.94	90,000
2000	**Tranquility Lake**, 5, 121	E. Delahoussaye	Tout Charmant, 4, 121	Miss of Wales (Chi), 5, 114	7	1:41.01	82,170
1999	**Happyanunoit (NZ)**, 4, 113	B. Blanc	Tuzla (Fr), 5, 123	Isle de France, 4, 118	6	1:41.28	80,520
1998	**Tuzla (Fr)**, 4, 117	C. S. Nakatani	Ecoute, 5, 114	Call Me (GB), 5, 116	7	1:42.28	80,970
1997	**Blushing Heiress**, 5, 117	C. J. McCarron	Traces of Gold, 5, 115	Listening, 4, 120	6	1:43.32	83,200
1996	**Yearly Tour**, 5, 116	C. J. McCarron	Slewvera, 4, 115	Real Connection, 5, 114	8	1:42.56	81,350
1995	**Morgana**, 4, 118	G. L. Stevens	Yearly Tour, 4, 118	Lady Affirmed, 4, 117	7	1:42.41	74,450
1994	**Shir Dar (Fr)**, 4, 114	C. S. Nakatani	Baby Diamonds, 3, 110	Prying (Arg), 6, 117	7	1:42.95	63,600
1993	**Heart of Joy**, 6, 119	D. R. Flores	Kalita Melody (GB), 5, 114	Amal Hayati, 3, 114	8	1:42.07	63,000
1992	**Super Staff**, 4, 114	C. J. McCarron	Odalea (Arg), 6, 114	Only Yours (GB), 4, 115	10	1:42.20	64,900
1991	**Guiza**, 4, 114	G. L. Stevens	Agirlfromars, 5, 114	Run to Jenny (Ire), 5, 113	8	1:42.11	49,300
	Somethingmerry, 4, 117	L. A. Pincay Jr.	Countus In, 6, 117	Sweet Roberta (Fr), 7, 115	7	1:41.84	48,800
1990	**Jabalina Brown (Arg)**, 5, 112	J. A. Garcia	Stylish Star, 4, 116	Nikishka, 5, 117	8	1:42.60	64,200
1989	**Claire Marine (Ire)**, 4, 122	R. G. Davis	Galunpe (Ire), 6, 118	Daring Doone (GB), 6, 116	8	1:43.20	64,800
1988	**Chapel of Dreams**, 4, 117	E. Delahoussaye	Short Sleeves (GB), 6, 121	Davie's Lamb, 4, 117	7	1:42.60	78,000
1987	**Festivity**, 4, 115	A. O. Solis	Adorable Micol, 4, 117	Secuencia (Chi), 5, 117	9	1:35.80	64,850
1986	**Aberuschka (Ire)**, 4, 118	P. A. Valenzuela	Sauna (Aus), 5, 118	Fran's Valentine, 4, 119	9	1:34.40	62,750
1985	**Capichi**, 5, 116	R. A. Baze	L'Attrayante (Fr), 5, 119	Gala Event (Ire), 4, 115	8	1:35.20	50,150
1984	**‡Moment to Buy**, 3, 115	T. M. Chapman	L'Attrayante (Fr), 4, 120	Royal Heroine (Ire), 4, 125	8	1:35.20	50,550
1983	**Triple Tipple**, 4, 118	C. J. McCarron	Castilla, 4, 121	First Advance, 4, 115	10	1:35.60	52,050
1982	**Northern Fable**, 4, 114	S. Hawley	Sangue (Ire), 4, 114	Princess Gayle (Ire), 4, 116	8	1:35.20	33,500
	Star Pastures (GB), 4, 117	W. Shoemaker	Honey Fox, 5, 122	Cannon Boy, 5, 111	9	1:35.40	34,000
1981	**Kilijaro (Ire)**, 5, 129	M. Castaneda	Lisawan, 4, 115	Satin Ribera, 4, 118	9	1:35.40	40,700
1980	**A Thousand Stars**, 5, 115	E. Delahoussaye	Wishing Well, 5, 121	Devon Ditty (GB), 4, 120	9	1:34.80	34,150
1979	**More So (Ire)**, 4, 115	W. Shoemaker	Giggling Girl, 5, 119	Wishing Well, 4, 118	8	1:35.40	34,150
1978	**Drama Critic**, 4, 118	D. Pierce	Afifa, 4, 119	Fact (Arg), 5, 115	9	1:36.40	26,550
1977	**Dancing Femme**, 4, 120	D. Pierce	Swingtime, 5, 121	Dacani (Ire), 4, 115	12	1:35.60	17,250
1976	**Just a Kick**, 4, 120	L. A. Pincay Jr.	Our First Delight, 4, 114	Effusive, 5, 113	5	1:29.40	15,900
1975	**Modus Vivendi**, 4, 122	F. Toro	Move Abroad, 4, 113	*Tizna, 6, 124	10	1:28.80	14,100
1974	**Sphere**, 4, 114	S. Valdez	Lt.'s Joy, 4, 121	Modus Vivendi, 3, 122	10	1:28.40	14,050
1973	**Meilleur**, 3, 114	D. Pierce	Lady Debbie, 5, 116	Probation, 4, 113	9	1:28.80	10,775
	Belle Marie, 3, 114	W. Shoemaker	Best Go, 5, 115	Chargerette, 4, 116	5	1:28.80	9,975

Named for Palomar and Mt. Palomar, California, located near San Diego; Mt. Palomar was once the site of the world's largest telescope. Grade 3 1981-'84, 1997-2000. 6 furlongs 1945-'69. 7½ furlongs 1970-'76. 1 mile 1977-'87. Dirt 1945-'69. Two divisions 1973, 1982, 1991. ‡Royal Heroine (Ire) finished first, DQ to third, 1984.

Palos Verdes Handicap

Grade 2 in 2006. Santa Anita Park, four-year-olds and up, 6 furlongs, dirt. Held January 21, 2006, with a gross value of $150,000. First held in 1951. First graded in 1973. Stakes record 1:07.20 (1989 Sunny Blossom).

Year	Winner	Jockey	Second	Third	Strs	Time	1st Purse
2006	**Major Success**, 5, 114	T. Baze	Jet West, 5, 118	Attila's Storm, 4, 119	7	1:09.23	$90,000
2005	**Saint Afleet**, 4, 117	P. A. Valenzuela	Hombre Rapido, 8, 116	Bluesthestandard, 8, 116	8	1:09.15	90,000
2004	**Bluesthestandard**, 7, 117	M. E. Smith	Marino Marini, 4, 115	Our New Recruit, 5, 114	7	1:08.13	90,000
2003	**Avanzado (Arg)**, 6, 116	T. Baze	Mellow Fellow, 8, 117	Disturbingthepeace, 5, 120	6	1:07.85	90,000
2002	**Snow Ridge**, 4, 116	M. E. Smith	Squirtle Squirt, 4, 122	Ceeband, 5, 117	7	1:07.70	90,000
2001	**Men's Exclusive**, 8, 116	L. A. Pincay Jr.	Big Jag, 8, 120	Freespool, 5, 116	6	1:08.33	120,000
2000	**Kona Gold**, 6, 121	A. O. Solis	Big Jag, 7, 121	Freespool, 4, 115	5	1:08.85	120,000
1999	**Big Jag**, 6, 116	J. Valdivia Jr.	Kona Gold, 5, 121	Swiss Yodeler, 5, 114	5	1:08.05	120,000
1998	**Funontherun**, 4, 113	G. F. Almeida	Red, 4, 116	Elmhurst, 8, 119	9	1:08.93	120,000
1997	**High Stakes Player**, 5, 118	C. S. Nakatani	Rotsaluck, 6, 114	Larry the Legend, 5, 116	7	1:08.44	131,600
1996	**Lit de Justice**, 6, 122	E. Delahoussaye	Siphon (Brz), 5, 119	Lakota Brave, 7, 115	9	1:08.88	135,100
1995	**D'Hallevant**, 5, 117	C. S. Nakatani	Cardmania, 9, 120	Subtle Trouble, 4, 115	10	1:08.44	94,400
1994	**Concept Win**, 4, 115	G. L. Stevens	J. F. Williams, 5, 117	Scherando, 5, 116	6	1:07.71	62,100
1993	**Music Merci**, 7, 114	D. R. Flores	Star of the Crop, 4, 119	Cardmania, 7, 117	7	1:08.82	63,700
1992	**Individualist**, 5, 117	L. A. Pincay Jr.	High Energy, 5, 114	Rushmore, 5, 114	9	1:08.66	65,600
1990	**Frost Free**, 5, 119	C. J. McCarron	Valiant Pete, 4, 117	Kipper Kelly, 3, 112	5	1:08.60	61,400
1989	**Sunny Blossom**, 4, 115	G. L. Stevens	Olympic Prospect, 5, 123	Sam Who, 4, 122	6	**1:07.20**	62,400
1988	**On the Line**, 4, 124	G. L. Stevens	Claim, 3, 118	Basic Rate, 3, 115	6	1:07.60	62,700
1987	**High Brite**, 3, 116	G. L. Stevens	Hilco Scamper, 4, 117	Zany Tactics, 6, 123	6	1:09.00	62,500
1986	**Bedside Promise**, 4, 123	G. L. Stevens	Bolder Than Bold, 4, 116	Rocky Marriage, 6, 115	6	1:08.40	60,000
1985	**Phone Trick**, 3, 121	L. A. Pincay Jr.	Five North, 4, 112	Debonaire Junior, 4, 123	6	1:08.00	50,100
1984	**Debonaire Junior**, 3, 120	C. J. McCarron	Charging Falls, 3, 112	Premiership, 4, 117	7	1:10.20	51,700
1983	**Fighting Fit**, 4, 122	E. Delahoussaye	Expressman, 3, 115	Gemini Dreamer, 3, 117	5	1:09.00	38,150
1982	**Chinook Pass**, 3, 120	L. A. Pincay Jr.	General Jimmy, 3, 112	Unpredictable, 3, 122	8	1:07.60	40,050
1981	**I'm Smokin**, 5, 119	P. A. Valenzuela	To B. Or Not, 5, 121	Solo Guy, 3, 119	7	1:08.00	39,200
1980	**To B. Or Not**, 4, 121	M. Castaneda	Unalakleet, 3, 115	Syncopate, 5, 123	9	1:08.20	34,000
1979	**Beau's Eagle**, 3, 122	S. Hawley	Always Gallant, 5, 124	‡Charley Sutton, 5, 115	7	1:10.00	32,750
1978	**Little Reb**, 3, 116	F. Olivares	Crash Program, 3, 112	Bad 'n Big, 4, 125	9	1:08.60	33,900
1977	**Impressive Luck**, 4, 119	S. Hawley	Maheras, 4, 120	Current Concept, 3, 117	6	1:10.40	26,000
1976	**Maheras**, 3, 119	L. A. Pincay Jr.	Sure Fire, 3, 116	Ancient Title, 6, 126	13	1:08.60	29,400
1975	**Messenger of Song**, 3, 125	J. Lambert	Willmar, 7, 115	Rise High, 5, 118	6	1:08.60	19,800

1974 **Ancient Title**, 4, 126	L. A. Pincay Jr.	Princely Native, 3, 116	King of the Blues, 5, 113	8	1:08.80	$20,900
1973 **Woodland Pines**, 4, 115	D. Pierce	Tragic Isle, 4, 117	Ancient Title, 3, 122	8	1:09.00	20,800

Named for the 1824 California land grant named Los Palos Verdes Ranchos; palos verdes means "green trees." Grade 3 1973-'74, 1988-'97. Not held 1969-'70, 1991. Three-year-olds and up 1951-'66, 1971 (January). Two-year-olds and up 1967-'68, 1971 (December) 1972-'89. ‡Grand Alliance finished third, DQ to fourth, 1979.

Pan American Handicap

Grade 3 in 2006. Gulfstream Park, three-year-olds and up, 1½ miles, turf. Held April 1, 2006, with a gross value of $150,000. First held in 1962. First graded in 1973. Stakes record 2:23.15 (1999 Unite's Big Red).

Year	Winner	Jockey	Second	Third	Strs	Time	1st Purse
2006	**Silver Whistle**, 4, 115	E. S. Prado	Ramazutti, 4, 113	Go Deputy, 6, 118	8	2:24.35	$90,000
2005	**Navesink River**, 4, 114	J. R. Velazquez	Quest Star, 6, 114	Deputy Lad, 5, 115	8	2:25.95	90,000
2004	**Quest Star**, 5, 114	P. Day	Request for Parole, 5, 115	Megantic, 6, 112	7	2:26.46	120,000
2003	**Quest Star**, 4, 113	E. S. Prado	Man From Wicklow, 6, 122	Reduit (GB), 5, 114	9	2:28.45	120,000
2002	**Deeliteful Irving**, 4, 113	C. P. DeCarlo	Cetewayo, 8, 118	Mr. Livingston, 5, 114	9	2:24.14	120,000
2001	**Whata Brainstorm**, 4, 114	J. R. Velazquez	Subtle Power (Ire), 4, 115	Craigsteel (GB), 6, 114	7	2:23.75	150,000
2000	**Buck's Boy**, 7, 120	E. S. Prado	Thesaurus, 6, 113	‡Epistolaire (Ire), 5, 114	7	2:24.80	150,000
1999	**Unite's Big Red**, 5, 114	M. E. Smith	African Dancer, 7, 116	Panama City, 5, 116	7	**2:23.15**	150,000
1998	**Buck's Boy**, 5, 115	E. Fires	African Dancer, 6, 115	Royal Strand (Ire), 4, 114	9	2:23.43	150,000
1997	**Flag Down**, 7, 117	J. A. Santos	Lassigny, 6, 117	Awad, 7, 117	6	2:27.00	180,000
1996	**Celtic Arms (Fr)**, 5, 115	M. E. Smith	Broadway Flyer, 5, 116	Flag Down, 6, 117	7	2:25.71	180,000
1995	**Awad**, 5, 114	E. Maple	Misil, 7, 120	Frenchpark (GB), 5, 117	9	2:29.44	180,000
1994	**Fraise**, 6, 124	M. E. Smith	Summer Ensign, 5, 113	†Fairy Garden, 6, 115	10	2:24.65	180,000
1993	**Fraise**, 5, 124	P. A. Valenzuela	Stagecraft (GB), 6, 117	Futurist, 5, 114	8	2:32.86	180,000
1992	**Wall Street Dancer**, 4, 114	J. Velasquez	†Passagere du Soir (GB), 5, 116	Missionary Ridge (GB), 5, 115	14	2:25.53	210,000
1991	**Phantom Breeze (Ire)**, 5, 116	J. A. Krone	Dr. Root, 4, 114	Runaway Raja, 5, 111	11	2:29.55	180,000
1990	**My Big Boy**, 7, 112	H. Castillo Jr.	Marksmanship, 5, 113	Turfah, 7, 115	12	2:29.20	180,000
1989	**Mi Selecto**, 4, 114	J. A. Santos	Pay the Butler, 5, 121	Fabulous Indian, 4, 112	8	2:01.60	180,000
1988	**†Carotene**, 5, 115	D. J. Seymour	†Ladanum, 4, 110	Salem Drive, 6, 117	13	2:25.00	180,000
1987	**Iroko (GB)**, 5, 112	E. Fires	Akabir, 6, 113	Glaros (Fr), 5, 112	13	2:26.40	150,000
1986	**†Powder Break**, 5, 112	S. B. Soto	Uptown Swell, 4, 116	Flying Pidgeon, 5, 118	11	2:25.00	180,000
1985	**Selous Scout**, 4, 112	R. Platts	Norclin, 5, 111	Nassipour, 5, 115	13	2:25.20	185,280
1984	**Tonzarun**, 6, 112	W. H. McCauley	Ayman, 4, 114	Nassipour, 4, 110	9	2:26.80	109,275
1983	**Highland Blade**, 5, 121	J. Vasquez	Tonzarun, 5, 108	Dhausli (Fr), 6, 113	10	2:29.20	80,295
	Field Cat, 6, 110	J. Samyn	Pin Puller, 4, 112	Santo's Joe, 6, 109	11	2:29.60	82,095
1982	**Robsphere**, 5, 117	J. Velasquez	Come Rain Or Shine, 5, 110	The Bart, 6, 126	16	2:26.00	102,150
1981	**†Little Bonny (Ire)**, 4, 114	E. Maple	Lobsang (Ire), 5, 115	Buckpoint (Fr), 5, 124	12	2:32.40	121,030
1980	**†Flitalong**, 4, 110	R. I. Encinas	Morning Frolic, 5, 119	Novel Notion, 5, 117	12	2:28.40	100,000
1979	**Noble Dancer (GB)**, 7, 129	J. Vasquez	Fleet Gar, 4, 116	†Warfever (Fr), 4, 113	9	2:25.20	100,000
1978	**Bowl Game**, 4, 117	J. Velasquez	That's a Nice, 4, 116	Court Open, 4, 112	10	2:30.20	100,000
1977	**Gravelines (Fr)**, 5, 124	J. D. Bailey	Le Cypriote, 5, 110	Gay Jitterbug, 4, 124	9	2:24.80	80,400
1976	**Improviser**, 4, 114	J. Cruguet	Green Room, 6, 109	Pampered Jabneh, 6, 113	13	2:26.60	86,880
1975	**Buffalo Lark**, 5, 120	L. Snyder	London Company, 5, 123	Duke Tom, 5, 115	6	2:27.60	84,120
1974	**London Company**, 4, 119	A. T. Cordero Jr.	Outdoors, 5, 112	*Bush Fleet, 5, 113	12	2:26.40	84,720
1973	**Lord Vancouver**, 5, 112	W. Blum	Life Cycle, 4, 118	Windtex, 4, 116	11	2:26.60	83,520

Named in honor of the multicultural heritage of South Florida's residents. Formerly sponsored by the Crown Royal Co. of Stamford, Connecticut 1996. Grade 1 1983-'89. Grade 2 1973-'82, 1990-2005. Crown Royal Pan American H. 1996. 1⅛ miles 1989. About 1½ miles 1993, 2003. Dirt 1962-'64, 1975, 1989. Two divisions 1983. ‡Beautiful Dancer finished third, DQ to sixth, 2000. Track record 1975. Course record 1999. †Denotes female.

Pat O'Brien Breeders' Cup Handicap

Grade 2 in 2006. Del Mar, three-year-olds and up, 7 furlongs, dirt. Held August 21, 2005, with a gross value of $280,000. First held in 1986. First graded in 1994. Stakes record 1:20.06 (1995 Lit de Justice).

Year	Winner	Jockey	Second	Third	Strs	Time	1st Purse
2005	**Imperialism**, 4, 117	V. Espinoza	Gotaghostofachance, 4, 114	Taste of Paradise, 6, 115	8	1:21.70	$180,000
2004	**Kela**, 6, 116	T. Baze	Domestic Dispute, 4, 116	Pico Central (Brz), 5, 122	5	1:21.17	120,000
2003	**Disturbingthepeace**, 5, 116	V. Espinoza	Rushin' to Altar, 4, 117	Full Moon Madness, 8, 119	10	1:21.53	90,000
2002	**Disturbingthepeace**, 4, 119	V. Espinoza	Hot Market, 4, 115	I Love Silver, 4, 117	5	1:21.89	90,000
2001	**El Corredor**, 4, 119	V. Espinoza	Swept Overboard, 4, 117	Ceeband, 4, 114	7	1:20.42	90,000
2000	**Love That Red**, 4, 118	C. S. Nakatani	Cliquot, 4, 117	Son of a Pistol, 8, 117	5	1:21.89	90,000
1999	**Regal Thunder**, 5, 116	C. W. Antley	Christmas Boy, 6, 118	Bet On Sunshine, 7, 116	9	1:21.13	90,000
1998	**Old Topper**, 3, 116	E. Delahoussaye	Son of a Pistol, 6, 123	Uncaged Fury, 7, 115	5	1:21.51	95,220
1997	**Tres Paraiso**, 5, 115	G. L. Stevens	High Stakes Player, 5, 119	Gold Land, 6, 114	7	1:21.45	68,200
1996	**Alphabet Soup**, 5, 118	C. W. Antley	Boundless Moment, 4, 116	Lit de Justice, 6, 123	8	1:20.79	65,450
1995	**Lit de Justice**, 5, 118	C. S. Nakatani	D'Hallevant, 5, 117	Pembroke, 5, 119	7	**1:20.06**	60,400
1994	**D'Hallevant**, 4, 115	C. S. Nakatani	Minjinsky, 4, 115	J. F. Williams, 5, 117	5	1:20.25	59,725
1993	**Slerp**, 4, 117	A. D. Lopez	Portoferraio (Arg), 5, 114	Cardmania, 7, 116	7	1:21.36	47,850
1992	**Light of Morn**, 6, 116	E. Delahoussaye	Three Peat, 3, 116	Slerp, 3, 114	12	1:20.65	66,025
1991	**Bruho**, 5, 118	C. S. Nakatani	Burn Annie, 6, 115	Due to the King, 4, 116	5	1:21.45	46,350
1990	**Sensational Star**, 6, 116	R. Q. Meza	Frost Free, 5, 116	Earn Your Stripes, 6, 116	9	1:20.60	49,275
1989	**Olympic Native**, 4, 116	R. G. Davis	On the Line, 5, 126	Sam Who, 4, 121	4	1:20.20	44,850
1988	**Sebrof**, 4, 116	G. L. Stevens	Synastry, 5, 116	Epidaurus, 6, 119	9	1:20.40	39,350

1987	**Zany Tactics**, 6, 123	J. L. Kaenel	Bold Smoocher, 5, 114	Bolder Than Bold, 5, 120	7	1:21.20	$31,750
1986	**Bold Brawley**, 3, 115	P. A. Valenzuela	First Norman, 4, 115	American Legion, 6, 121	5	1:20.40	30,850

Named in honor of actor Pat O'Brien (1899-1983), co-founder with Bing Crosby of the Del Mar Turf Club. Grade 3 1994-'98. Pat O'Brien H. 1986-'89, 1996-2003.

Pegasus Stakes

Grade 3 in 2006. Meadowlands, three-year-olds, $1\frac{1}{8}$ miles, dirt. Held September 30, 2005, with a gross value of $250,000. First held in 1980. First graded in 1983. Stakes record 1:45.50 (1999 Forty One Carats).

Year	Winner	Jockey	Second	Third	Strs	Time	1st Purse
2005	**Magna Graduate**, 3, 120	J. R. Velazquez	Crown Point, 3, 118	Network, 3, 120	8	1:47.47	$150,000
2004	**Pies Prospect**, 3, 118	E. S. Prado	Eddington, 3, 118	Zakocity, 3, 118	8	1:48.57	180,000
2002	**Regal Sanction**, 3, 115	J. A. Santos	No Parole, 3, 117	This Guns for Hire, 3, 115	6	1:49.87	210,000
2001	**Volponi**, 3, 114	S. Bridgmohan	Burning Roma, 3, 119	Giant Gentleman, 3, 116	6	1:46.55	150,000
2000	**Kiss a Native**, 3, 119	M. K. Walls	Cool N Collective, 3, 115	Pine Dance, 3, 121	7	1:48.33	150,000
1999	**Forty One Carats**, 3, 120	J. F. Chavez	Unbridled Jet, 3, 116	Talk's Cheap, 3, 118	6	**1:45.50**	240,000
1998	**Tomorrows Cat**, 3, 113	J. Bravo	Limit Out, 3, 115	Comic Strip, 3, 119	6	1:46.95	300,000
1997	**Behrens**, 3, 117	J. D. Bailey	Anet, 3, 120	Frisk Me Now, 3, 119	4	1:46.61	600,000
1996	**Allied Forces**, 3, 116	R. Migliore	Lite Approval, 3, 112	Defacto, 3, 116	9	1:47.19	120,000
1995	**Flying Chevron**, 3, 112	R. G. Davis	Da Hoss, 3, 122	Ghostly Moves, 3, 113	4	1:40.27	120,000
1994	**Brass Scale**, 3, 114	E. S. Prado	Hello Chicago, 3, 114	Serious Spender, 3, 111	9	1:49.27	120,000
1993	**Diazo**, 3, 117	L. A. Pincay Jr.	Press Card, 3, 116	Schossberg, 3, 116	7	1:47.18	150,000
1992	**Scuffleburg**, 3, 111	J. A. Krone	Nines Wild, 3, 113	Agincourt, 3, 115	11	1:49.09	300,000
1991	**Scan**, 3, 119	J. A. Santos	Sea Cadet, 3, 119	Sultry Song, 3, 114	8	1:46.53	180,000
1990	**Silver Ending**, 3, 119	E. Delahoussaye	Music Prospector, 3, 116	Runaway Stream, 3, 113	12	1:47.20	180,000
1989	**Norquestor**, 3, 114	J. A. Krone	Rampart Road, 3, 113	Fast Play, 3, 116	12	1:49.60	180,000
1988	**Brian's Time**, 3, 121	A. T. Cordero Jr.	Festive, 3, 110	Congeleur, 3, 112	14	1:47.00	180,000
1987	**Cryptoclearance**, 3, 122	J. A. Santos	Lost Code, 3, 122	Templar Hill, 3, 118	8	1:48.60	180,000
1986	**Danzig Connection**, 3, 122	P. Day	Broad Brush, 3, 122	Ogygian, 3, 124	5	1:49.00	180,000
1985	**Skip Trial**, 3, 123	J. Samyn	Stephan's Odyssey, 3, 123	Violado, 3, 117	7	1:51.00	200,040
1984	**Hail Bold King**, 3, 115	J. Velasquez	Carr de Naskra, 3, 122	dh-Jyp, 3, 115 dh-Morning Bob, 3, 119	8	1:49.20	131,040
1983	**World Appeal**, 3, 114	A. Graell	Hyperborean, 3, 118	Bounding Basque, 3, 115	10	1:46.60	135,360
1982	**Fast Gold**, 3, 110	J. Samyn	Muttering, 3, 120	Exclusive One, 3, 116	8	1:49.00	131,160
1981	**Summing**, 3, 122	G. Martens	Johnny Dance, 3, 114	Maudlin, 3, 112	11	1:51.00	133,620
1980	**Dr. Blum**, 3, 115	R. Hernandez	Bill Wheeler, 3, 115	Peace for Peace, 3, 115	7	1:11.00	15,150

Named for the winged horse of Greek mythology. Formerly sponsored by the General Motors Corp. of Detroit, Michigan 1997-'98. Grade 1 1987-'93. Grade 2 1994-2002. Pegasus H. 1981-'95, 1997-2002. Pegasus Breeders' Cup H. 1996. Buick Pegasus H. 1997-'98. Not held 2003. 6 furlongs 1980. $1\frac{1}{16}$ miles 1995-'96. Turf 1996. Dead heat for third 1984. Track record 1999.

Pennsylvania Derby

Grade 2 in 2006. Philadelphia Park, three-year-olds, $1\frac{1}{8}$ miles, dirt. Held September 5, 2005, with a gross value of $750,000. First held in 1979. First graded in 1981. Stakes record 1:47.60 (1989 Western Playboy).

Year	Winner	Jockey	Second	Third	Strs	Time	1st Purse
2005	**Sun King**, 3, 122	R. Bejarano	Southern Africa, 3, 122	Smokescreen, 3, 114	14	1:49.43	$397,500
2004	**Love of Money**, 3, 116	R. Albarado	Pollard's Vision, 3, 122	Swingforthefences, 3, 119	12	1:48.42	450,000
2003	**Grand Hombre**, 3, 114	J. Bravo	Gimmeawink, 3, 122	Ashmore, 3, 114	10	1:49.03	450,000
2002	**Harlan's Holiday**, 3, 122	E. S. Prado	Essence of Dubai, 3, 122	Make the Bend, 3, 119	5	1:51.10	300,000
2001	**Macho Uno**, 3, 116	G. L. Stevens	†Unbridled Elaine, 3, 119	Touch Tone, 3, 122	6	1:49.69	300,000
2000	**Pine Dance**, 3, 122	M. J. McCarthy	Mass Market, 3, 122	Cherokeeinthehills, 3, 114	10	1:49.03	180,000
1999	**Smart Guy**, 3, 119	R. E. Colton	Ghost Ring, 3, 114	Pineaff, 3, 122	10	1:49.40	180,000
1998	**Rock and Roll**, 3, 114	H. Castillo Jr.	Tomorrows Cat, 3, 114	Black Blade, 3, 119	11	1:47.69	150,000
1997	**Frisk Me Now**, 3, 122	E. L. King Jr.	Envy of the Crown, 3, 114	Christian Soldier, 3, 114	8	1:48.14	120,000
1996	**Devil's Honor**, 3, 122	A. S. Black	Formal Gold, 3, 117	Clash by Night, 3, 119	7	1:48.58	120,000
1995	**Pineing Patty**, 3, 122	L. J. Melancon	Royal Haven, 3, 117	Tenants Harbor, 3, 117	12	1:48.05	120,000
1994	**Meadow Flight**, 3, 122	J. Bravo	Red Tazz, 3, 117	Kandaly, 3, 122	9	1:49.08	120,000
1993	**Wallenda**, 3, 114	W. H. McCauley	Press Card, 3, 117	Saintly Prospector, 3, 122	9	1:49.33	120,000
1992	**Thelastcrusade**, 3, 114	V. H. Molina	Ecstatic Ride, 3, 114	Nines Wild, 3, 117	10	1:49.47	90,000
1991	**Valley Crossing**, 3, 119	A. J. Seefeldt	Gala Spinaway, 3, 122	Riflery, 3, 117	11	1:50.10	90,000
1990	**Summer Squall**, 3, 122	P. Day	Challenge My Duty, 3, 122	Sports View, 3, 122	9	1:48.20	180,000
1989	**Western Playboy**, 3, 122	K. D. Clark	Roi Danzig, 3, 122	Tricky Creek, 3, 122	12	**1:47.60**	180,000
1988	**Cefis**, 3, 122	L. Saumell	Congeleur, 3, 119	Ballindaggin, 3, 122	10	1:49.60	180,000
1987	**Afleet**, 3, 122	G. Stahlbaum	Lost Code, 3, 122	Homebuilder, 3, 119	8	1:48.20	180,000
1986	**Broad Brush**, 3, 122	A. T. Cordero Jr.	Sumptious, 3, 122	Glow, 3, 122	7	1:50.80	180,000
1985	**Skip Trial**, 3, 122	J. Samyn	El Basco, 3, 122	Jacque l'Heureux, 3, 119	13	1:50.20	180,000
1984	**Morning Bob**, 3, 122	G. McCarron	At the Threshold, 3, 122	dh-Biloxi Indian, 3, 122 dh-Raja's Shark, 3, 122	7	1:49.40	132,240
1983	**Dixieland Band**, 3, 122	W. J. Passmore	Jacque's Tip, 3, 122	Intention, 3, 122	9	1:49.40	136,500
1982	**Spanish Drums**, 3, 122	J. Vasquez	Air Forbes Won, 3, 122	A Magic Spray, 3, 122	11	1:49.00	101,460
1981	**Summing**, 3, 122	G. Martens	Sportin' Life, 3, 122	Classic Go Go, 3, 122	9	1:49.00	100,380
1980	**Lively King**, 3, 122	C. J. Baker	Mutineer, 3, 122	Stutz Blackhawk, 3, 122	7	1:48.80	99,480
1979	**Smarten**, 3, 122	S. Maple	Incredible Ease, 3, 122	Incubator, 3, 122	6	1:49.20	68,880

Philadelphia Park is located in Bensalem, Pennsylvania. Grade 3 1981-'84, 1996-2003. Not held 2006. Dead heat for third 1984. †Denotes female.

Perryville Stakes

Grade 3 in 2006. Keeneland Race Course, three-year-olds, 7 furlongs, dirt. Held October 14, 2005, with a gross value of $200,000. First held in 1999. First graded in 2005. Stakes record 1:25.19 (2004 Commentator).

Year	Winner	Jockey	Second	Third	Strs	Time	1st Purse
2005	**Vicarage**, 3, 120	J. R. Velazquez	Straight Line, 3, 123	Social Probation, 3, 117	8	1:26.06	$124,000
2004	**Commentator**, 3, 117	R. Bejarano	Eurosilver, 3, 123	Weigelia, 3, 123	7	**1:25.19**	69,812
2003	**Clock Stopper**, 3, 117	R. Albarado	Ballado Chieftan, 3, 117	Champali, 3, 123	6	1:25.33	67,146
2002	**Najran**, 3, 118	P. Day	Flying Free, 3, 118	Premier Performer, 3, 118	9	1:26.00	52,127
2001	**Dream Run**, 3, 118	P. Day	Strawberry Affair, 3, 118	Solingen, 3, 120	5	1:27.25	50,360
2000	**Smokin Pete**, 3, 118	S. J. Sellers	Classic Appeal, 3, 120	Chervy, 3, 118	6	1:25.38	44,020
1999	**National Saint**, 3, 118	R. Albarado	Moon Over Prospect, 3, 118	Hidden City, 3, 120	6	1:25.21	36,674

Named for Perryville, Kentucky. The largest Civil War battle in the state was fought there on October 8, 1862. Sponsored by the Anheuser-Busch Co. of St. Louis, Missouri 2005.

Personal Ensign Handicap

Grade 1 in 2006. Saratoga Race Course, three-year-olds and up, fillies and mares, 1¼ miles, dirt. Held August 26, 2005, with a gross value of $400,000. First held in 1948. First graded in 1973. Stakes record 2:02.07 (2005 Shadow Cast).

Year	Winner	Jockey	Second	Third	Strs	Time	1st Purse
2005	**Shadow Cast**, 4, 118	R. Albarado	Personal Legend, 5, 116	Two Trail Sioux, 4, 118	6	**2:02.07**	$240,000
2004	**Storm Flag Flying**, 4, 116	J. R. Velazquez	Azeri, 6, 122	Nevermore, 4, 114	5	2:03.63	240,000
2003	**Passing Shot**, 4, 114	J. A. Santos	Wild Spirit (Chi), 4, 122	Miss Linda (Arg), 6, 114	5	2:03.33	240,000
2002	**Summer Colony**, 4, 120	J. R. Velazquez	Transcendental, 4, 114	Dancethruthedawn, 4, 120	6	2:03.15	240,000
2001	**Pompeii**, 4, 117	R. Migliore	Beautiful Pleasure, 6, 117	Irving's Baby, 4, 117	7	2:04.60	240,000
2000	**Beautiful Pleasure**, 5, 124	J. F. Chavez	‡Heritage of Gold, 5, 124	Pentatonic, 5, 113	5	2:03.77	240,000
1999	**Beautiful Pleasure**, 4, 113	J. F. Chavez	Banshee Breeze, 4, 124	Keeper Hill, 4, 118	6	2:02.57	240,000
1998	**Tomisue's Delight**, 4, 115	P. Day	Tuzia, 4, 114	One Rich Lady, 4, 114	8	2:04.08	240,000
1997	**Clear Mandate**, 5, 115	M. E. Smith	Shoop, 6, 111	Power Play, 5, 117	6	2:03.71	210,000
1996	**Urbane**, 4, 119	A. O. Solis	Shoop, 5, 114	Frolic, 4, 113	8	2:03.05	180,000
1995	**Heavenly Prize**, 4, 127	P. Day	Forcing Bid, 4, 108	Cinnamon Sugar (Ire), 4, 114	8	2:04.16	120,000
1994	**Link River**, 4, 114	J. A. Krone	You'd Be Surprised, 5, 120	Dispute, 4, 119	7	1:50.46	120,000
1993	**You'd Be Surprised**, 4, 115	J. D. Bailey	Avian Assembly, 4, 111	Gray Cashmere, 4, 114	8	1:48.59	90,000
1992	**Quick Mischief**, 6, 113	C. Perret	Versailles Treaty, 4, 122	Shared Interest, 4, 111	7	1:47.96	120,000
1991	**Fit to Scout**, 4, 114	C. W. Antley	Train Robbery, 4, 112	Her She Shawklit, 4, 111	7	1:50.30	120,000
1990	**Personal Business**, 4, 111	C. W. Antley	Buy the Firm, 4, 112	Lady Hoolihan, 4, 110	8	1:51.20	70,200
1989	**Colonial Waters**, 4, 116	A. T. Cordero Jr.	Topicount, 4, 116	Rose's Cantina, 5, 119	5	1:50.00	67,080
1988	**Rose's Cantina**, 4, 111	J. A. Santos	Ms. Eloise, 5, 115	Clabber Girl, 5, 120	4	1:49.80	67,080
1987	**Coup de Fusil**, 5, 116	A. T. Cordero Jr.	Clabber Girl, 4, 113	I'm Sweets, 4, 118	7	1:49.20	83,700
1986	**Shocker T.**, 4, 124	G. St. Leon	Bharal, 5, 113	Natania, 4, 115	5	1:50.00	66,840
1985	**Lady On the Run**, 3, 115	A. T. Cordero Jr.	Verbality, 3, 112	Halloween Queen, 4, 112	6	1:52.00	51,210
1984	**Solar Halo**, 3, 110	R. G. Davis	It's Fine, 4, 109	Quixotic Lady, 4, 115	8	1:49.20	53,640
1983	**Chieftan's Command**, 4, 117	A. T. Cordero Jr.	Adept, 4, 110	Sintrillium, 5, 116	7	1:51.60	34,440
1982	**Number**, 3, 114	E. Maple	Sintrillium, 4, 112	Norsan, 3, 112	5	1:51.40	32,340
1981	**Tina Tina Too**, 3, 114	D. MacBeth	Explorare, 4, 114	Office Wife, 4, 113	8	1:51.00	33,060
1980	**Relaxing**, 4, 118	J. Velasquez	Sugar and Spice, 3, 115	Plankton, 4, 121	8	1:49.20	33,540
1979	**Catherine's Bet**, 4, 113	D. Montoya	Water Malone, 5, 117	Miss Baja, 4, 114	7	1:50.20	32,340
1978	**Mrs. Warren**, 4, 113	J. Velasquez	Water Malone, 4, 121	One Sum, 4, 121	7	1:51.40	32,190
1977	**Water Malone**, 3, 121	J. Samyn	Northernette, 3, 120	Sweet Bernice, 4, 113	8	1:50.40	32,280
1976	**Sugar Plum Time**, 4, 113	A. T. Cordero Jr.	Ten Cents a Dance, 3, 110	Quacker, 3, 111	9	1:51.00	32,610
1975	**Lie Low**, 4, 115	J. Velasquez	Princesse Grey, 4, 114	Carolerno, 4, 112	12	2:15.20	35,910
1974	**Lie Low**, 3, 116	J. Velasquez	Aglimmer, 5, 116	D. O. Lady, 3, 115	8	1:49.00	27,840
	Twixt, 5, 121	W. J. Passmore	Garland of Roses, 5, 114	Fairway Flyer, 5, 124	10	1:49.80	28,290
1973	**Aglimmer**, 4, 115	M. Venezia	Garland of Roses, 4, 111	Cathy Baby, 4, 120	13	1:49.40	36,150

Named for Ogden Phipps's undefeated 1988 champion older female, '88 Whitney H. (G1) winner, and '96 Broodmare of the Year Personal Ensign (1984 f. by Private Account). Formerly named for John A. Morris (1892-1985), former president of the Thoroughbred Racing Association and Jamaica racetrack. Formerly named for James Ben Ali Haggin's multiple SW Firenze (1884 f. by Glenelg). Grade 2 1983-'86. Firenze H. 1948-'85. John A. Morris H. 1986-'97. Held at Jamaica 1948-'57. Held at Aqueduct 1958-'74, 1976-'85. Held at Belmont Park 1975. 1¹⁄₁₆ miles 1948-'51, 1958. 1⅛ miles 1952-'57, 1959, 1962-'74, 1976-'94. 1 mile 1960-'61. 1⅜ miles 1975. Turf 1972-'75. Two divisions 1974. ‡Back in Shape finished second, DQ to fourth, 2000. Equaled track record 1980.

Peter Pan Stakes

Grade 2 in 2006. Belmont Park, three-year-olds, 1⅛ miles, dirt. Held May 20, 2006, with a gross value of $200,000. First held in 1940. First graded in 1978. Stakes record 1:46.35 (2005 Oratory).

Year	Winner	Jockey	Second	Third	Strs	Time	1st Purse
2006	**Sunriver**, 3, 116	R. Bejarano	Lewis Michael, 3, 116	Strong Contender, 3, 116	9	1:49.39	$120,000
2005	**Oratory**, 3, 116	J. D. Bailey	Reverberate, 3, 116	Golden Man, 3, 116	8	**1:46.35**	120,000
2004	**Purge**, 3, 115	J. R. Velazquez	Swingforthefences, 3, 115	Master David, 3, 115	10	1:47.98	120,000
2003	**Go Rockin' Robin**, 3, 117	S. Bridgmohan	Alysweep, 3, 123	Supervisor, 3, 115	6	1:48.47	120,000
2002	**Sunday Break (Jpn)**, 3, 121	G. L. Stevens	Puzzlement, 3, 115	Deputy Dash, 3, 115	7	1:48.10	120,000
2001	**Hero's Tribute**, 3, 117	J. F. Chavez	E Dubai, 3, 123	Dayton Flyer, 3, 115	7	1:47.47	120,000
2000	**Postponed**, 3, 113	E. S. Prado	Unshaded, 3, 123	Globalize, 3, 123	9	1:49.71	120,000

1999 **Best of Luck**, 3, 113	J. Samyn	Treasure Island, 3, 114	Lemon Drop Kid, 3, 120	9	1:47.94	$90,000
1998 **Grand Slam**, 3, 120	J. D. Bailey	Rubiyat, 3, 113	Parade Ground, 3, 120	7	1:49.14	90,000
1997 **Banker's Gold**, 3, 113	E. Maple	Zede, 3, 120	Prince Guistino, 3, 114	4	1:48.60	90,000
1996 **Jamies First Punch**, 3, 118	J. R. Velazquez	Unbridled's Song, 3, 123	Diligence, 3, 118	5	1:47.32	90,000
1995 **Citadeed**, 3, 112	E. Maple	Pat n Jac, 3, 113	Treasurer (GB), 3, 115	10	1:50.03	90,000
1994 **Twining**, 3, 122	J. A. Santos	Lahint, 3, 112	Gash, 3, 119	5	1:49.11	90,000
1993 **Virginia Rapids**, 3, 114	E. Maple	Colonial Affair, 3, 117	Itaka, 3, 114	6	1:48.48	90,000
1992 **A.P. Indy**, 3, 126	E. Delahoussaye	Colony Light, 3, 114	Berkley Fitz, 3, 114	7	1:47.49	106,380
1991 **Lost Mountain**, 3, 114	C. Perret	Man Alright, 3, 114	Scan, 3, 126	6	1:49.47	106,380
1990 **Profit Key**, 3, 117	J. A. Santos	Country Day, 3, 114	Paradise Found, 3, 114	8	1:47.20	106,560
1989 **Imbibe**, 3, 117	A. T. Cordero Jr.	Irish Actor, 3, 126	Pro Style, 3, 117	9	1:48.60	110,160
1988 **Seeking the Gold**, 3, 120	P. Day	Tejano, 3, 126	Gay Rights, 3, 117	7	1:47.60	140,880
1987 **Leo Castelli**, 3, 114	J. A. Santos	Gone West, 3, 126	Shawklit Won, 3, 114	9	1:48.00	132,360
1986 **Danzig Connection**, 3, 117	P. Day	Clear Choice, 3, 123	Parade Marshal, 3, 117	8	1:48.40	85,380
1985 **Proud Truth**, 3, 126	J. Velasquez	Cutlass Reality, 3, 114	Salem Drive, 3, 114	7	1:47.60	67,050
1984 **Back Bay Barrister**, 3, 117	D. MacBeth	Gallant Hour, 3, 114	Romantic Tradition, 3, 114	9	1:50.00	57,330
1983 **Slew o' Gold**, 3, 126	A. T. Cordero Jr.	I Enclose, 3, 123	Foyt, 3, 117	5	1:46.80	34,380
1982 **Wolfie's Rascal**, 3, 120	A. T. Cordero Jr.	John's Gold, 3, 114	Illuminate, 3, 117	6	1:48.80	34,020
1981 **Tap Shoes**, 3, 126	R. Hernandez	Willow Hour, 3, 117	West On Broad, 3, 120	7	1:48.40	34,080
1980 **Comptroller**, 3, 114	R. I. Encinas	Bar Dexter, 3, 117	Suzanne's Star, 3, 114	9	1:49.20	34,080
1979 **Coastal**, 3, 120	R. Hernandez	Lucy's Axe, 3, 123	Pianist, 3, 117	6	1:47.00	32,820
1978 **Buckaroo**, 3, 114	J. Velasquez	Darby Creek Road, 3, 117	Star de Naskra, 3, 123	8	1:48.00	32,520
1977 **Spirit Level**, 3, 114	A. Graell	Sanhedrin, 3, 114	Lynn Davis, 3, 114	9	1:49.20	32,910
1976 **Sir Lister**, 3, 114	J. Velasquez	‡Jamming, 3, 117	El Portugues, 3, 114	9	1:36.00	34,620
1975 **Singh**, 3, 114	E. Maple	Majestic One, 3, 114	Sir Paulus, 3, 115	8	1:35.20	33,420

Named for James R. Keene's champion and 1907 Belmont S. winner Peter Pan (1904 c. by Commando). Grade 3 1978-'82. Grade 1 1984-'86. Peter Pan H. 1940-'60. Held at Aqueduct 1940-'43, 1945-'49, 1952-'55, 1958-'60, 1975. Not held 1961-'74. 1 mile 1975-'76. Three-year-olds and up 1979. ‡El Portugues finished second, DQ to third, 1976.

Philip H. Iselin Breeders' Cup Handicap

Grade 3 in 2005. Monmouth Park, three-year-olds and up, 1⅛ miles, dirt. Held August 28, 2005, with a gross value of $190,000. First held in 1884. First graded in 1973. Stakes record 1:46.80 (1985 Spend a Buck; 1992 Jolie's Halo).

Year Winner	Jockey	Second	Third	Strs	Time	1st Purse
2005 **West Virginia**, 4, 115	J. A. Velez Jr.	Zoffinger, 5, 114	Purge, 4, 118	8	1:50.83	$90,000
2004 **Ghostzapper**, 4, 120	J. Castellano	Presidentialaffair, 5, 117	Zoffinger, 4, 115	4	1:47.66	120,000
2003 **Tenpins**, 5, 119	R. Albarado	Aeneas, 4, 114	Jersey Giant, 4, 115	9	1:50.35	120,000
2002 **Cat's At Home**, 5, 116	J. A. Velez Jr.	Bowman's Band, 4, 117	Runspastum, 5, 114	7	1:49.10	210,000
2001 **Broken Vow**, 4, 119	R. A. Dominguez	First Lieutenant, 4, 115	Sir Bear, 8, 117	5	1:49.55	210,000
2000 **Rize**, 4, 112	J. C. Ferrer	Sir Bear, 7, 118	Talk's Cheap, 4, 114	6	1:48.42	210,000
1999 **Frisk Me Now**, 5, 117	E. L. King Jr.	Call Me Mr. Vain, 5, 110	Black Cash, 4, 112	6	1:49.00	210,000
1998 **Skip Away**, 5, 131	J. D. Bailey	Stormin Fever, 4, 113	‡Devil's Fire, 6, 113	7	1:47.33	300,000
1997 **Formal Gold**, 4, 121	K. Desormeaux	Skip Away, 4, 124	Distorted Humor, 4, 115	4	1:40.20	250,000
1996 **Smart Strike**, 4, 115	C. Perret	Eltish, 4, 116	†Serena's Song, 4, 115	7	1:41.59	180,000
1995 **Schossberg**, 5, 118	D. Penna	Poor But Honest, 5, 115	Mickeray, 4, 114	10	1:49.22	180,000
1994 **Taking Risks**, 4, 115	M. T. Johnston	Valley Crossing, 6, 117	Proud Shot, 4, 112	9	1:48.33	150,000
1993 **Valley Crossing**, 5, 113	C. W. Antley	Devil His Due, 4, 123	Bertrando, 4, 119	8	1:49.20	300,000
1992 **Jolie's Halo**, 5, 116	E. S. Prado	Out of Place, 5, 113	Valley Crossing, 4, 111	11	**1:46.80**	300,000
1991 **Black Tie Affair (Ire)**, 5, 119	P. Day	Farma Way, 4, 122	Chief Honcho, 4, 115	8	1:47.80	300,000
1990 **Beau Genius**, 5, 122	R. D. Lopez	Tricky Creek, 4, 112	De Roche, 4, 115	10	1:48.20	150,000
1989 **Proper Reality**, 4, 119	J. D. Bailey	Bill E. Shears, 4, 112	Mi Selecto, 4, 114	9	1:48.00	150,000
1988 **Alysheba**, 4, 124	C. J. McCarron	Bet Twice, 4, 123	Gulch, 4, 122	6	1:47.80	300,000
1987 **Bordeaux Bob**, 4, 115	C. W. Antley	Silver Comet, 4, 114	Lost Code, 3, 117	7	1:48.20	163,920
1986 **Roo Art**, 4, 117	W. Shoemaker	Precisionist, 5, 125	†Lady's Secret, 4, 120	5	1:48.80	188,280
1985 **Spend a Buck**, 3, 118	L. A. Pincay Jr.	Carr de Naskra, 4, 120	‡Valiant Lark, 5, 115	6	**1:46.80**	162,180
1984 **Believe the Queen**, 4, 120	D. A. Miller Jr.	World Appeal, 4, 121	Bet Big, 4, 117	9	1:48.20	194,040
1983 **Bates Motel**, 4, 124	T. Lipham	Island Whirl, 5, 124	Linkage, 4, 115	9	1:47.20	167,520
1982 **Mehmet**, 4, 115	E. Delahoussaye	†Pukka Princess, 4, 108	Summer Advocate, 5, 117	13	1:48.20	174,240
1981 **Amber Pass**, 4, 117	C. B. Asmussen	Joanie's Chief, 4, 108	Ring of Light, 6, 114	10	1:47.40	170,580
1980 **Spectacular Bid**, 4, 132	W. Shoemaker	†Glorious Song, 4, 117	The Cool Virginian, 4, 112	8	1:48.00	158,160
1979 **‡Text**, 5, 118	W. Shoemaker	Cox's Ridge, 5, 120	Silent Cal, 4, 115	6	1:47.40	70,948
1978 **Life's Hope**, 5, 115	C. Perret	Wise Philip, 5, 114	Father Hogan, 5, 115	7	2:03.20	72,183
1977 **Majestic Light**, 4, 124	S. Hawley	Capital Idea, 4, 108	Peppy Addy, 5, 116	6	2:00.40	71,143
1976 **Hatchet Man**, 5, 112	V. A. Bracciale Jr.	Intrepid Hero, 4, 119	Forego, 6, 136	8	2:00.60	71,793
1975 **Royal Glint**, 5, 121	C. Perret	Proper Bostonian, 5, 118	Stonewalk, 4, 121	6	2:00.60	70,948
1974 **True Knight**, 5, 124	M. A. Rivera	Ecole Etage, 4, 112	Hey Rube, 4, 111	9	2:02.00	72,215
1973 **West Coast Scout**, 5, 114	L. Adams	Tentam, 4, 118	Windtex, 4, 113	11	2:01.20	74,295

Named for Philip H. Iselin (1902-'76), president and chairman of the board of Monmouth Park (1966-'77). Formerly named for Amory L. Haskell (1894-1966), former president of Monmouth Park. Grade 1 1973-'96. Grade 2 1997-2002. Monmouth H. 1884-'93, 1946-'66, 1981-'85. Amory L. Haskell H. 1967-'80. Not held 1894-1945. 1½ miles 1884-'93. 1¼ miles 1956-'78. 1¹⁄₁₆ miles 1996-'97. Two-year-olds and up 1884-'86. ‡Cox's Ridge finished first, DQ to second, 1979. ‡Rumptious finished third, DQ to sixth, 1985. ‡Testafly finished third, DQ to seventh for a positive drug test, 1998. Track record 1974. Equaled track record 1992. †Denotes female.

Phoenix Breeders' Cup Stakes

Grade 3 in 2006. Keeneland Race Course, three-year-olds and up, 6 furlongs, dirt. Held October 8, 2005, with a gross value of $266,500. First held in 1831. First graded in 2000. Stakes record 1:07.78 (1993 Anjiz).

Year	Winner	Jockey	Second	Third	Strs	Time	1st Purse
2005	**Elusive Jazz**, 4, 118	R. Albarado	Wild Tale, 4, 118	Premium Saltine, 6, 118	8	1:11.60	$165,230
2004	**Champali**, 4, 122	R. Bejarano	Gold Storm, 4, 118	Clock Stopper, 4, 118	11	1:08.72	168,175
2003	**Najran**, 4, 122	J. Castellano	Ethan Man, 4, 118	Take Achance On Me, 5, 118	8	1:08.32	169,880
2002	**†Xtra Heat**, 4, 123	H. Vega	Day Trader, 3, 120	Touch Tone, 4, 119	5	1:10.13	155,000
2001	**Bet On Sunshine**, 9, 123	C. H. Borel	Robin de Nest, 4, 121	Erlton, 5, 119	5	1:09.65	166,470
2000	**Five Star Day**, 4, 119	G. K. Gomez	Istintaj, 4, 119	Bet On Sunshine, 8, 123	6	1:07.90	167,245
1999	**Richter Scale**, 5, 117	K. Desormeaux	Bet On Sunshine, 7, 117	Vicar, 3, 121	6	1:08.40	166,780
1998	**Partner's Hero**, 4, 117	C. H. Borel	Pyramid Peak, 6, 117	High Stakes Player, 6, 123	6	1:09.25	100,533
1997	**Bet On Sunshine**, 5, 123	F. Torres	Receiver, 4, 117	Valid Expectations, 4, 117	5	1:08.70	97,464
1996	**Forest Wildcat**, 5, 121	J. Bravo	Valid Expectations, 3, 119	Bet On Sunshine, 4, 115	10	1:09.57	101,246
1995	**Golden Gear**, 4, 124	C. Perret	Hello Paradise, 4, 115	Mississippi Chat, 3, 113	6	1:08.96	67,456
1994	**Lost Pan**, 4, 114	D. M. Barton	Pacific West, 4, 112	Fort Chaffee, 4, 116	5	1:09.45	33,728
1993	**Anjiz**, 5, 114	D. A. Miller Jr.	Gold Spring (Arg), 5, 124	Friendly Lover, 5, 121	9	**1:07.78**	50,251
1992	**British Banker**, 4, 114	D. Kutz	Megas Vukefalos, 4, 124	Binalong, 3, 113	6	1:09.20	49,693
1991	**Deposit Ticket**, 3, 114	P. Day	Tom Cobbley, 5, 114	Hammocker, 7, 113	6	1:10.38	51,838
1990	**Hadif**, 4, 120	D. Penna	Fighting Fantasy, 3, 115	Raise a Tradition, 4, 114	11	1:09.40	52,796
1989	**Momsfurrari**, 5, 114	M. E. Smith	Hammocker, 5, 114	Irish Open, 5, 118	9	1:10.60	36,319
1988	**Carload**, 6, 114	E. Fires	Conquer, 4, 117	Carborundum, 4, 117	8	1:09.80	45,275
1987	**Diapason**, 7, 112	P. A. Johnson	Hail the Ruckus, 4, 116	Dr. Koch, 5, 114	9	1:09.80	35,783
1986	**Lucky North**, 5, 115	P. Day	Clever Wake, 4, 114	Fortunate Prospect, 5, 121	5	1:11.00	34,613
1985	**Harry 'n Bill**, 5, 115	M. Russ	Irish Freeze, 4, 116	Diapason, 5, 113	9	1:09.60	35,913
1984	**Timeless Native**, 4, 121	D. Brumfield	Euathlos, 4, 116	Runderbar, 4, 112	10	1:10.80	36,286
1983	**Shot n' Missed**, 6, 115	L. Moyers	Gallant Gentleman, 4, 114	†Excitable Lady, 5, 115	6	1:09.00	35,214
1982	**Golden Derby**, 4, 115	J. C. Espinoza	Shot n' Missed, 5, 117	Aristocratical, 5, 119	13	1:10.00	40,853
1981	**Turbulence**, 5, 115	J. C. Espinoza	Final Tribute, 5, 114	It's a Rerun, 5, 114	9	1:09.40	35,783
	Zuppardo's Prince, 5, 116	J. C. Espinoza	Convenient, 5, 118	Done Well, 4, 116	8	1:09.40	38,870
1980	**Zuppardo's Prince**, 4, 116	J. C. Espinoza	Cregan's Cap, 5, 111	Cabrini Green, 5, 116	9	1:09.00	35,165
1979	**Shelter Half**, 4, 116	S. A. Boulmetis Jr.	Cabrini Green, 4, 118	Going Investor, 4, 115	12	1:09.20	29,494
1978	**Amadevil**, 4, 117	S. Maple	It's Freezing, 6, 121	See the U. S. A., 8, 118	11	1:09.40	22,539
1977	**It's Freezing**, 5, 118	E. Maple	Harbor Springs, 4, 114	Dixmart, 5, 113	13	1:09.60	19,143
1976	**Gallant Bob**, 4, 126	D. Brumfield	Real Value, 4, 120	Amerrico, 4, 115	12	1:08.40	18,736
1975	**Delta Oil**, 6, 118	R. Breen	Jazziness, 5, 117	Hasty Flyer, 4, 116	12	1:09.40	19,468
1974	**Penholder**, 5, 116	B. Thornburg	List, 6, 118	Grocery List, 5, 118	12	1:09.40	18,330
1973	**Honey Jay**, 5, 123	J. C. Espinoza	Three Martinis, 5, 116	Mighty Mackie, 4, 110	12	1:11.40	18,493

Named for the old Phoenix Hotel in Lexington, Kentucky; oldest recognized race in North America. The race has also been known as the Brennan, Chiles, Association, and Phoenix Hotel S. Not held 1898-1904, 1906-'10, 1914-'16, 1929, 1931-'36. Phoenix H. 1937-'80. Phoenix Breeders' Cup H. 1990-'91. Phoenix S. 1994-'95. Held at Kentucky Association 1831-1930. Held at Churchill Downs 1943-'45. Two divisions 1981. Track record 1993. †Denotes female. Held as a heat race 1831-'77.

Pimlico Special Handicap

Grade 1 in 2006. Pimlico Race Course, four-year-olds and up, 1$^3/_{16}$ miles, dirt. Held May 19, 2006, with a gross value of $500,000. First held in 1937. First graded in 1990. Stakes record 1:52.55 (1991 Farma Way).

Year	Winner	Jockey	Second	Third	Strs	Time	1st Purse
2006	**Invasor (Arg)**, 4, 116	R. A. Dominguez	Wanderin Boy, 5, 117	West Virginia, 5, 115	5	1:54.40	$300,000
2005	**Eddington**, 4, 116	E. Coa	Pollard's Vision, 4, 117	Presidentialaffair, 6, 115	7	1:58.05	300,000
2004	**Southern Image**, 4, 120	V. Espinoza	Midway Road, 4, 116	Bowman's Band, 6, 114	6	1:55.89	300,000
2003	**Mineshaft**, 4, 121	R. Albarado	Western Pride, 5, 116	Judge's Case, 6, 113	9	1:56.16	400,000
2001	**Include**, 4, 114	J. D. Bailey	Albert the Great, 4, 121	Pleasant Breeze, 6, 114	6	1:55.61	450,000
2000	**Golden Missile**, 5, 116	K. Desormeaux	Pleasant Breeze, 5, 111	Lemon Drop Kid, 4, 120	8	1:54.65	450,000
1999	**Real Quiet**, 4, 120	G. L. Stevens	Free House, 5, 124	Fred Bear Claw, 5, 113	5	1:54.31	300,000
1998	**Skip Away**, 5, 128	J. D. Bailey	Precocity, 4, 115	Hot Brush, 4, 113	5	1:54.26	450,000
1997	**Gentlemen (Arg)**, 5, 122	G. L. Stevens	Skip Away, 4, 119	Tejano Run, 5, 114	8	1:53.03	360,000
1996	**Star Standard**, 4, 111	P. Day	Key of Luck, 5, 120	Geri, 4, 118	4	1:54.46	360,000
1995	**Cigar**, 5, 122	J. D. Bailey	Devil His Due, 6, 121	Concern, 4, 121	6	1:53.72	360,000
1994	**As Indicated**, 4, 120	R. G. Davis	Devil His Due, 5, 121	Valley Crossing, 6, 113	6	1:55.08	360,000
1993	**Devil His Due**, 4, 120	W. H. McCauley	Valley Crossing, 5, 112	Pistols and Roses, 4, 114	6	1:55.53	510,000
1992	**Strike the Gold**, 4, 114	C. Perret	Fly So Free, 4, 116	Twilight Agenda, 6, 122	7	1:54.86	420,000
1991	**Farma Way**, 4, 119	G. L. Stevens	Summer Squall, 4, 120	Jolie's Halo, 4, 119	7	**1:52.55**	450,000
1990	**Criminal Type**, 5, 117	J. A. Santos	Ruhlmann, 5, 124	De Roche, 4, 114	10	1:53.00	600,000
1989	**Blushing John**, 4, 117	P. Day	Proper Reality, 4, 118	Granacus, 4, 113	12	1:53.20	420,000
1988	**Bet Twice**, 4, 124	C. Perret	Lost Code, 4, 126	Cryptoclearance, 4, 121	6	1:54.20	425,000

In the past, "special" races were "winner takes all" (the winner got all of the purse money). Not held 1959-'87, 2002. Three-year-olds 1937, 1954. Four-year-olds and up 1988-'97. Winner's share included mid-series bonus of $150,000 from ACRS 1993.

Pocahontas Stakes

Grade 3 in 2006. Churchill Downs, two-year-olds, fillies, 1 mile, dirt. Held November 5, 2005, with a gross value of $120,600. First held in 1969. First graded in 2005. Stakes record 1:34.82 (2000 Unbridled Elaine).

Year	Winner	Jockey	Second	Third	Strs	Time	1st Purse
2005	**French Park**, 2, 118	M. Guidry	Trippi Street, 2, 118	Coolwind, 2, 118	12	1:37.19	$74,772
2004	**Punch Appeal**, 2, 122	P. Day	Holy Trinity, 2, 118	Kota, 2, 122	7	1:37.77	67,890
2003	**Stellar Jayne**, 2, 119	C. H. Velasquez	Turn to Lass, 2, 119	Sister Star, 2, 117	9	1:38.97	69,626
2002	**Belle of Perintown**, 2, 116	M. Guidry	Star of Atticus, 2, 116	Souris, 2, 121	8	1:36.52	68,882
2001	**Lotta Rhythm**, 2, 116	M. St. Julien	Cunning Play, 2, 116	Joanies Bella, 2, 121	8	1:37.96	69,130
2000	**Unbridled Elaine**, 2, 113	S. J. Sellers	Ilusoria, 2, 112	Gold Mover, 2, 121	8	**1:34.82**	70,060
1999	**Crown of Crimson**, 2, 112	R. Albarado	Maddie's Promise, 2, 121	Dance for Dixie, 2, 114	8	1:37.81	69,812
1998	**The Happy Hopper**, 2, 121	W. Martinez	Tutorial, 2, 112	Gold From the West, 2, 112	9	1:37.73	70,556
1997	**Mission Park**, 2, 113	C. H. Borel	Rave, 2, 113	So Generous, 2, 112	10	1:38.55	70,432
1996	**Water Street**, 2, 112	C. Perret	Cotton Carnival, 2, 114	Private Pursuit, 2, 114	9	1:36.90	69,936
1995	**Birr**, 2, 112	P. Day	Gold Sunrise, 2, 116	Classy 'n' Bold, 2, 114	8	1:36.84	73,580
1994	**Minister Wife**, 2, 116	P. Day	Valor Lady, 2, 114	Musical Cat, 2, 114	6	1:38.64	73,385
1993	**At the Half**, 2, 121	S. J. Sellers	Footing, 2, 116	Mystic Union, 2, 112	12	1:38.13	75,660
1992	**Coni Bug**, 2, 121	S. J. Sellers	Sock City, 2, 121	Far Out Countess, 2, 114	8	1:37.85	54,698
1991	**Fretina**, 2, 116	J. E. Bruin	Pleasant Baby, 2, 116	Vivid Imagination, 2, 116	9	1:40.25	55,478
1990	**Middlefork Rapids**, 2, 116	R. M. Gonzalez	Dark Stage, 2, 116	Til Forbid, 2, 114	10	1:38.00	37,700
1989	**Crowned**, 2, 116	M. E. Smith	Charitable Gift, 2, 114	Truly My Style, 2, 114	6	1:39.80	36,010
1988	**Solid Eight**, 2, 121	R. P. Romero	Box Office Gold, 2, 114	Northern Wife, 2, 114	8	1:40.60	36,270
1987	**Epitome**, 2, 114	P. Day	Darien Miss, 2, 114	Cushion Cut, 2, 118	9	1:38.20	34,589
1986	**Bestofbothworlds**, 2, 112	P. J. Cooksey	Laserette, 2, 114	Combative, 2, 117	12	1:42.60	34,649
1985	**Prime Union**, 2, 119	D. E. Foster	Northern Maiden, 2, 112	Whirl Series, 2, 117	8	1:38.40	22,133
1984	**Gallant Libby**, 2, 119	P. Day	Off Shore Breeze, 2, 117	Gallants Gem, 2, 122	10	1:41.80	18,460
1983	**Geevilla**, 2, 114	P. Day	Robin's Rob, 2, 119	Sintra, 2, 114	11	1:40.20	18,403
	Flippers, 2, 117	P. Day	Shelbiana, 2, 114	Jay Paree, 2, 117	8	1:39.80	19,703
1982	**Brindy Brindy**, 2, 117	J. C. Espinoza	Roberto's Doll, 2, 119	Issues n' Answers, 2, 122	7	1:38.20	19,500
	Weekend Surprise, 2, 122	D. Brumfield	Decision, 2, 119	Quarrel Over, 2, 117	9	1:37.80	19,663
1981	**Majestic Gold**, 2, 118	J. C. Espinoza	I See Spring, 2, 112	Golden Try, 2, 112	15	1:26.80	20,768
	Taylor Park, 2, 121	J. McKnight	Ecole d'Humanite, 2, 118	Dreamtide, 2, 112	14	1:26.40	20,605
1980	**Kathy T.**, 2, 118	L. J. Melancon	Silver Doll, 2, 115	Fleet Pocket, 2, 114	10	1:27.60	18,476
	Masters Dream, 2, 118	G. Gallitano	Taralina, 2, 118	Singing Rockett, 2, 118	11	1:27.40	20,101
1979	**Dancing Blade**, 2, 121	A. S. Black	Champagne Ginny, 2, 115	Ribbon, 2, 115	13	1:26.80	17,258
1978	**Starclock**, 2, 121	R. DePass	Silver Oaks, 2, 114	Sensuous Sinnamon, 2, 115	9	1:25.40	14,820
	Safe, 2, 118	E. Fires	Sexy, 2, 115	Fair Advantage, 2, 121	10	1:25.60	14,983
1977	**Rainy Princess**, 2, 118	L. Snyder	Silver Spook, 2, 121	Irish Agate, 2, 118	8	1:25.20	14,909
	Plains and Simple, 2, 118	A. L. Fernandez	Salzburg, 2, 118	She's Debonair, 2, 112	9	1:26.20	14,909
1976	**Ciao**, 2, 121	W. Gavidia	Shady Lou, 2, 121	Every Move, 2, 112	9	1:27.00	14,812
	Sweet Alliance, 2, 115	C. J. McCarron	Pocket Princess, 2, 115	My Bold Beauty, 2, 118	8	1:25.60	14,649
1975	**Alvarada**, 2, 118	D. Brumfield	Confort Zone, 2, 121	Bells and Blades, 2, 121	11	1:27.60	15,941
1974	**My Juliet**, 2, 121	A. Hill	Channelette, 2, 115	Yale Coed, 2, 121	12	1:23.60	15,941
1973	**Shoo Dear**, 2, 121	D. Brumfield	Escrolla, 2, 118	Snow Peak, 2, 115	10	1:27.80	15,308
	Fairway Fable, 2, 118	D. E. Whited	Clemanna, 2, 121	Passing Look, 2, 118	9	1:26.00	15,308

Named for Pocahontas (1837 f. by *Glencoe), one of the great foundation mares of all time and ancestress of numerous American classic winners. Two divisions 1973, 1976-'78, 1980-'83. Non-winners of a stakes worth $7,500 to the winner 1973. Non-winners of a stakes 1975.

Poker Handicap

Grade 3 in 2006. Belmont Park, three-year-olds and up, 1 mile, turf. Held July 3, 2005, with a gross value of $111,800. First held in 1983. First graded in 1988. Stakes record 1:31.63 (1998 Elusive Quality).

Year	Winner	Jockey	Second	Third	Strs	Time	1st Purse
2005	**Mr. Light (Arg)**, 6, 117	C. H. Velasquez	Willard Straight, 5, 115	Remind, 5, 117	7	1:32.18	$67,080
2004	**Christine's Outlaw**, 4, 113	S. Bridgmohan	Millennium Dragon (GB), 5, 120	Silver Tree, 4, 117	9	1:32.46	67,560
2003	**War Zone**, 4, 117	J. Castellano	Trademark (SAf), 7, 114	Saint Verre, 5, 112	11	1:32.81	69,720
2002	**Volponi**, 4, 115	S. Bridgmohan	Saint Verre, 4, 112	Navesink, 4, 117	7	1:32.24	66,720
2001	**Affirmed Success**, 7, 121	J. D. Bailey	In Frank's Honor, 5, 114	Union One, 4, 114	6	1:34.60	66,240
2000	**Affirmed Success**, 6, 117	J. F. Chavez	Rabi (Ire), 5, 114	Weatherbird, 5, 113	10	1:34.06	68,280
1999	**Rob 'n Gin**, 5, 118	J. F. Chavez	Bomfim, 6, 115	Wised Up, 4, 115	8	1:32.81	69,120
1998	**Elusive Quality**, 5, 117	J. D. Bailey	Za-Im (GB), 4, 114	Fortitude, 5, 114	9	**1:31.63**	51,240
1997	**Draw Shot**, 4, 118	C. W. Antley	Val's Prince, 5, 114	Fortitude, 4, 112	10	1:33.08	51,345
1996	**Smooth Runner**, 5, 113	J. A. Krone	Mighty Forum (GB), 5, 116	Da Hoss, 4, 119	10	1:33.62	51,600
1995	**†Caress**, 4, 117	R. G. Davis	Fourstars Allstar, 7, 119	Pennine Ridge, 4, 119	9	1:34.20	51,030
1994	**Dominant Prospect**, 4, 114	J. F. Chavez	Fourstardave, 9, 114	Nijinsky's Gold, 5, 114	8	1:32.69	49,905
1993	**Fourstardave**, 8, 117	R. Migliore	Adam Smith (GB), 5, 122	Lech, 5, 117	7	1:33.02	53,190
1992	**Scott the Great**, 6, 117	J. Samyn	Kate's Valentine, 7, 117	Cigar Toss (Arg), 5, 117	7	1:33.27	54,810
1991	**Who's to Pay**, 5, 117	J. D. Bailey	Scott the Great, 5, 117	Senor Speedy, 4, 117	10	1:33.55	56,160
1990	**Scottish Monk**, 7, 117	A. T. Cordero Jr.	Quick Call, 6, 117	Yankee Affair, 8, 122	5	1:33.40	52,110
1989	**Fourstardave**, 4, 117	J. A. Santos	Feeling Gallant, 7, 117	Valid Fund, 4, 117	9	1:33.20	56,610
1988	**Wanderkin**, 5, 122	J. A. Santos	Kings River (Ire), 6, 122	dh-My Prince Charming, 5, 117 dh-Silver Voice, 5, 117	7	1:35.60	54,720
1987	**Double Feint**, 4, 117	J. A. Santos	Onyxly, 6, 117	Island Sun, 5, 117	8	1:35.20	34,320

1986	**Island Sun**, 4, 119	R. Migliore	Divulge, 4, 119	Equalize, 4, 119	10	2:02.40	$33,300
1985	**Mr. Chromacopy**, 4, 119	J. Cruguet	Roving Minstrel, 4, 121	Regal Humor, 4, 119	6	1:42.40	33,420
1983	**Freon**, 6, 115	R. G. Davis	Nadasdy (Ire), 3, 113	Kentucky River, 5, 117	5	2:03.20	24,870

Named for Ogden Phipps's 1967 Bowling Green H. winner Poker (1963 c. by Round Table), broodmare sire of Seattle Slew and Silver Charm. Poker S. 1985-'95. Not held 1984. Dead heat for third 1988. Course record 1998. World record 1998. †Denotes female.

Potrero Grande Breeders' Cup Handicap

Grade 2 in 2006. Santa Anita Park, four-year-olds and up, 6½ furlongs, dirt. Held April 2, 2006, with a gross value of $128,000. First held in 1983. First graded in 1988. Stakes record 1:13.71 (1998 Son of a Pistol).

Year	Winner	Jockey	Second	Third	Strs	Time	1st Purse
2006	**Surf Cat**, 4, 119	A. O. Solis	Grinding It Out, 6, 116	Oceanus (Brz), 7, 114	5	1:15.00	$60,000
2005	**Harvard Avenue**, 4, 115	G. K. Gomez	Rushin' to Altar, 6, 116	Roi Charmant, 4, 114	9	1:16.12	120,000
2004	**McCann's Mojave**, 4, 116	J. Valdivia Jr.	Unfurl the Flag, 4, 114	Bluesthestandard, 7, 118	5	1:15.60	66,840
2003	**Bluesthestandard**, 6, 115	M. E. Smith	Joey Franco, 4, 116	Kona Gold, 9, 121	7	1:14.86	72,000
2002	**†Kalookan Queen**, 6, 116	A. O. Solis	Ceeband, 5, 116	Elaborate, 7, 115	8	1:15.31	130,620
2001	**Kona Gold**, 7, 126	A. O. Solis	dh-Explicit, 4, 116 dh-Hollycombe, 7, 114		4	1:15.03	123,000
2000	**Kona Gold**, 6, 122	A. O. Solis	Old Topper, 5, 116	Your Halo, 5, 116	4	1:14.75	123,060
1999	**Big Jag**, 6, 119	J. Valdivia Jr.	‡Gold Land, 8, 117	Son of a Pistol, 7, 120	5	1:15.09	123,720
1998	**Son of a Pistol**, 6, 114	G. K. Gomez	White Bronco, 4, 114	Gold Land, 7, 115	9	**1:13.71**	66,420
1997	**First Intent**, 8, 114	R. R. Douglas	Hesabull, 4, 117	Northern Afleet, 4, 118	6	1:14.60	64,250
1996	**Abaginone**, 5, 115	G. L. Stevens	Dramatic Gold, 5, 117	Kingdom Found, 6, 118	6	1:14.59	124,400
1995	**Lit de Justice**, 5, 115	C. S. Nakatani	Cardmania, 9, 119	Phone Roberto, 6, 116	6	1:14.65	63,000
1994	**Sir Hutch**, 4, 117	P. A. Valenzuela	Concept Win, 4, 117	Furiously, 5, 117	5	1:14.48	61,100
1993	**Gray Slewpy**, 5, 118	K. Desormeaux	Cardmania, 7, 117	Star of the Crop, 4, 119	8	1:14.91	64,700
1992	**Cardmania**, 6, 117	E. Delahoussaye	Frost Free, 7, 117	Answer Do, 6, 123	4	1:17.16	60,200
1991	**Jacodra**, 4, 111	C. S. Nakatani	Answer Do, 5, 118	Bruho, 5, 117	6	1:15.10	62,300
1990	**Olympic Prospect**, 6, 121	P. A. Valenzuela	Raise a Stanza, 4, 118	Doncareer, 4, 114	4	1:14.20	60,400
1989	**On the Line**, 5, 125	G. L. Stevens	Ron Bon, 4, 116	Jamoke, 5, 114	10	1:14.00	66,500
1988	**Gulch**, 4, 123	E. Delahoussaye	†Very Subtle, 4, 120	Gallant Sailor, 5, 111	3	1:15.00	44,050
1987	**Zabaleta**, 4, 117	L. A. Pincay Jr.	Zany Tactics, 6, 120	Bedside Promise, 5, 125	4	1:15.00	44,850
1986	**Halo Folks**, 5, 124	C. J. McCarron	Bozina, 5, 111	American Legion, 6, 112	5	1:15.60	43,050
1985	**Fifty Six Ina Row**, 4, 117	L. A. Pincay Jr.	Hula Blaze, 5, 120	Coyotero, 7, 114	6	1:15.40	44,650
1984	**Honeyland**, 5, 117	W. Shoemaker	American Legion, 4, 113	Shecky Blue, 4, 116	9	1:15.40	40,450
1983	**Chinook Pass**, 4, 123	L. A. Pincay Jr.	Haughty But Nice, 5, 115	The Captain, 4, 114	5	1:14.60	37,050

Named for Potrero Grande Rancho, near present-day El Monte, California; potrero grande means "big pasture." Grade 3 1988-'96. Potrero Grande H. 1983-'95. Dead heat for second 2001. ‡Early Pioneer finished second, DQ to fourth, 1999. Track record 1998. †Denotes female.

Prairie Meadows Cornhusker Breeders' Cup Handicap

Grade 2 in 2006. Prairie Meadows, three-year-olds and up, 1⅛ miles, dirt. Held July 2, 2005, with a gross value of $300,000. First held in 1966. First graded in 1973. Stakes record 1:46.62 (1998 Beboppin Baby).

Year	Winner	Jockey	Second	Third	Strs	Time	1st Purse
2005	**Lord of the Game**, 4, 117	E. Razo Jr.	Silver Axe, 8, 113	Mambo Train, 4, 115	8	1:49.94	$180,000
2004	**Roses in May**, 4, 115	M. Guidry	Perfect Drift, 5, 119	Crafty Shaw, 6, 117	6	1:46.63	180,000
2003	**Tenpins**, 5, 118	R. Albarado	Bowman's Band, 5, 116	Woodmoon, 5, 116	6	1:48.39	210,000
2002	**Mr. John**, 4, 114	M. Guidry	Unshaded, 5, 115	Fajardo, 5, 113	10	1:47.97	240,000
2001	**Euchre**, 5, 116	G. K. Gomez	Dixie Dot Com, 6, 119	Sure Shot Biscuit, 5, 115	7	1:47.72	240,000
2000	**Sir Bear**, 7, 116	E. Coa	Skimming, 4, 111	Ecton Park, 4, 117	5	1:48.49	240,000
1999	**Nite Dreamer**, 4, 113	R. Albarado	Mocha Express, 5, 117	Worldly Ways (GB), 5, 116	7	1:48.85	231,000
1998	**Beboppin Baby**, 5, 114	J. Campbell	Acceptable, 4, 116	Pacificbounty, 4, 113	8	**1:46.62**	150,000
1997	**Semoran**, 4, 117	D. R. Flores	Mister Fire Eyes (Ire), 5, 115	Come On Flip, 6, 114	9	1:48.40	120,000
1995	**Powerful Punch**, 6, 115	C. C. Bourque	All Gone, 5, 115	Glaring, 5, 116	8	1:49.80	90,000
1994	**Zeeruler**, 6, 116	R. N. Lester	Powerful Punch, 5, 118	Dancing Jon, 6, 114	8	1:50.20	75,000
1993	**Link**, 5, 114	R. D. Ardoin	Rapid World, 5, 115	Flying Continental, 7, 117	9	1:50.40	75,000
1992	**Irish Swap**, 5, 117	B. E. Poyadou	Zeeruler, 4, 115	Stalwars, 7, 116	11	1:47.80	75,000
1991	**Black Tie Affair (Ire)**, 5, 124	P. Day	Bedeviled, 4, 117	Whodam, 6, 113	5	1:48.70	75,000
1990	**Dispersal**, 4, 122	J. Velasquez	No More Cash, 4, 114	Protect Yourself, 8, 113	9	1:50.00	90,000
1989	**Blue Buckaroo**, 6, 115	S. J. Sellers	Henbane, 4, 115	Advancing Ensign, 4, 112	10	1:49.40	120,000
1988	**Palace March (Ire)**, 4, 118	J. A. Krone	Outlaws Sham, 5, 114	Galba, 4, 112	9	1:49.00	120,000
1987	**Bolshoi Boy**, 4, 117	C. W. Antley	Forkintheroad, 5, 112	Honor Medal, 6, 119	10	1:48.40	120,000
1986	**Gourami**, 4, 116	T. T. Doocy	Honor Medal, 5, 114	Smile, 4, 120	7	1:49.40	150,000
1985	**Gate Dancer**, 4, 126	C. J. McCarron	Badwagon Harry, 6, 114	Eminency, 7, 119	8	1:48.60	100,800
1984	**Timeless Native**, 4, 122	D. Brumfield	‡Inevitable Leader, 5, 120	Wild Again, 4, 121	12	1:49.40	90,000
1983	**Win Stat**, 6, 111	D. Pettinger	†Bersid, 5, 116	Aspro, 5, 121	11	1:53.20	92,978
1982	**Recusant**, 4, 118	R. J. Hirdes Jr.	Plaza Star, 4, 121	Vodika Collins, 4, 118	10	1:51.60	92,895
1981	**Summer Advocate**, 4, 118	K. Jones Jr.	Sun Catcher, 4, 121	Brent's Trans Am, 4, 116	11	1:48.20	93,143
1980	**Hold Your Tricks**, 5, 116	D. Pettinger	Overskate, 5, 126	Daring Damascus, 4, 117	10	1:49.20	88,688
1979	**Star de Naskra**, 4, 125	J. Fell	Prince Majestic, 5, 119	Quiet Jay, 4, 117	13	1:48.40	90,613
1978	**True Statement**, 4, 118	B. Fann	Big John Taylor, 4, 115	Giboulee, 4, 116	9	1:48.20	60,913
1977	**Private Thoughts**, 4, 118	R. R. Perez	Latimer, 5, 114	Dragset, 6, 113	12	1:48.00	62,782

1976	**Dragset**, 5, 112	S. Maple	Sharp Gary, 5, 113	Methdioxya, 4, 114	7	1:49.00	$60,500
1975	**Stonewalk**, 4, 120	R. Turcotte	Sharp Gary, 4, 115	Rooter, 5, 114	14	1:48.40	59,290
1974	**Blazing Gypsey**, 5, 114	S. Burgos	Tom Tulle, 4, 122	Super Sail, 6, 117	10	1:49.60	57,963
1973	**Joey Bob**, 5, 118	L. Moyers	Haveago, 6, 121	Prince Astro, 4, 114	12	1:42.80	30,828

The Cornhusker Handicap was formerly held at Ak-Sar-Ben in Nebraska, the "Cornhusker State." Cornhusker H. 1966-'72, 1985-'95. Ak-Sar-Ben Cornhusker H. 1973-'84. Prairie Meadows Cornhusker H. 1997. Held at Ak-Sar-Ben 1966-'95. Not held 1996. $1\frac{1}{16}$ miles 1966-'73. ‡Pron Regard finished second, DQ to sixth, 1984. Track record 1998. †Denotes female.

Preakness Stakes

Grade 1 in 2006. Pimlico Race Course, three-year-olds, $1\frac{3}{16}$ miles, dirt. Held May 20, 2006, with a gross value of $1,000,000. First held in 1873. First graded in 1924. Stakes record 1:53.40 (1985 Tank's Prospect).

(See Triple Crown section for complete history of the Preakness Stakes)

Year	Winner	Jockey	Second	Third	Strs	Time	1st Purse
2006	**Bernardini**, 3, 126	J. Castellano	Sweetnorthernsaint, 3, 126	Hemingway's Key, 3, 126	9	1:54.65	$600,000
2005	**Afleet Alex**, 3, 126	J. Rose	Scrappy T, 3, 126	Giacomo, 3, 126	14	1:55.04	650,000
2004	**Smarty Jones**, 3, 126	S. Elliott	Rock Hard Ten, 3, 126	Eddington, 3, 126	10	1:55.59	650,000
2003	**Funny Cide**, 3, 126	J. A. Santos	Midway Road, 3, 126	Scrimshaw, 3, 126	10	1:55.61	650,000
2002	**War Emblem**, 3, 126	V. Espinoza	Magic Weisner, 3, 126	Proud Citizen, 3, 126	13	1:56.36	650,000
2001	**Point Given**, 3, 126	G. L. Stevens	A P Valentine, 3, 126	Congaree, 3, 126	11	1:55.51	650,000
2000	**Red Bullet**, 3, 126	J. D. Bailey	Fusaichi Pegasus, 3, 126	Impeachment, 3, 126	8	1:56.04	650,000
1999	**Charismatic**, 3, 126	C. W. Antley	Menifee, 3, 126	Badge, 3, 126	13	1:55.32	650,000
1998	**Real Quiet**, 3, 126	K. Desormeaux	Victory Gallop, 3, 126	Classic Cat, 3, 126	10	1:54.75	650,000
1997	**Silver Charm**, 3, 126	G. L. Stevens	Free House, 3, 126	Captain Bodgit, 3, 126	10	1:54.84	488,150
1996	**Louis Quatorze**, 3, 126	P. Day	Skip Away, 3, 126	Editor's Note, 3, 126	12	1:53.43	458,120
1995	**Timber Country**, 3, 126	P. Day	Oliver's Twist, 3, 126	Thunder Gulch, 3, 126	11	1:54.45	446,810
1994	**Tabasco Cat**, 3, 126	P. Day	Go for Gin, 3, 126	Concern, 3, 126	10	1:56.47	447,720
1993	**Prairie Bayou**, 3, 126	M. E. Smith	Cherokee Run, 3, 126	El Bakan, 3, 126	12	1:56.61	471,835
1992	**Pine Bluff**, 3, 126	C. J. McCarron	Alydeed, 3, 126	Casual Lies, 3, 126	14	1:55.60	484,120
1991	**Hansel**, 3, 126	J. D. Bailey	Corporate Report, 3, 126	Mane Minister, 3, 126	8	1:54.05	432,770
1990	**Summer Squall**, 3, 126	P. Day	Unbridled, 3, 126	Mister Frisky, 3, 126	9	1:53.60	445,900
1989	**Sunday Silence**, 3, 126	P. A. Valenzuela	Easy Goer, 3, 126	Rock Point, 3, 126	8	1:53.80	438,230
1988	**Risen Star**, 3, 126	E. Delahoussaye	Brian's Time, 3, 126	†Winning Colors, 3, 121	9	1:56.20	413,700
1987	**Alysheba**, 3, 126	C. J. McCarron	Bet Twice, 3, 126	Cryptoclearance, 3, 126	9	1:55.80	421,100
1986	**Snow Chief**, 3, 126	A. O. Solis	Ferdinand, 3, 126	Broad Brush, 3, 126	7	1:54.80	411,900
1985	**Tank's Prospect**, 3, 126	P. Day	Chief's Crown, 3, 126	Eternal Prince, 3, 126	11	**1:53.40**	423,200
1984	**Gate Dancer**, 3, 126	A. T. Cordero Jr.	Play On, 3, 126	Fight Over, 3, 126	10	1:53.60	243,600
1983	**Deputed Testamony**, 3, 126	D. A. Miller Jr.	Desert Wine, 3, 126	High Honors, 3, 126	12	1:55.40	251,200
1982	**Aloma's Ruler**, 3, 126	J. L. Kaenel	Linkage, 3, 126	Cut Away, 3, 126	7	1:55.40	209,900
1981	**Pleasant Colony**, 3, 126	J. Velasquez	Bold Ego, 3, 126	Paristo, 3, 126	13	1:54.60	200,800
1980	**Codex**, 3, 126	A. T. Cordero Jr.	†Genuine Risk, 3, 121	Colonel Moran, 3, 126	8	1:54.20	180,600
1979	**Spectacular Bid**, 3, 126	R. J. Franklin	Golden Act, 3, 126	Screen King, 3, 126	5	1:54.20	165,300
1978	**Affirmed**, 3, 126	S. Cauthen	Alydar, 3, 126	Believe It, 3, 126	7	1:54.40	136,200
1977	**Seattle Slew**, 3, 126	J. Cruguet	Iron Constitution, 3, 126	Run Dusty Run, 3, 126	9	1:54.40	138,600
1976	**Elocutionist**, 3, 126	J. Lively	Play the Red, 3, 126	Bold Forbes, 3, 126	6	1:55.00	129,700
1975	**Master Derby**, 3, 126	D. G. McHargue	Foolish Pleasure, 3, 126	Diabolo, 3, 126	10	1:56.40	158,100
1974	**Little Current**, 3, 126	M. A. Rivera	Neapolitan Way, 3, 126	Cannonade, 3, 126	13	1:54.60	156,500
1973	**Secretariat**, 3, 126	R. Turcotte	Sham, 3, 126	Our Native, 3, 126	6	1:54.40	129,900

Named for M. H. Sanford's Preakness (1867 c. by Lexington), first winner of the Dinner Party S. (now the Dixie S. [G2]) at Pimlico. Held at Morris Park, New York 1890. Held at Gravesend Park, New York 1894-1908. Not held 1891-'93. $1\frac{1}{2}$ miles 1894. $1\frac{1}{4}$ miles 1889. $1\frac{1}{16}$ miles 1894-1900, 1908. 1 mile 70 yards 1901-'07. 1 mile 1909-'10. $1\frac{1}{8}$ miles 1911-'24. ‡Dancer's Image finished third, DQ to eighth, 1968. †Denotes female. In 1973 *Daily Racing Form* reported the time as $1{:}53\frac{2}{5}$, a track and stakes record; official time is recorded as $1{:}54\frac{2}{5}$.

Princess Rooney Handicap

Grade 1 in 2006. Calder Race Course, three-year-olds and up, fillies and mares, 6 furlongs, dirt. Held July 10, 2005, with a gross value of $500,000. First held in 1985. First graded in 1999. Stakes record 1:09.93 (2005 Madcap Escapade).

Year	Winner	Jockey	Second	Third	Strs	Time	1st Purse
2005	**Madcap Escapade**, 4, 120	J. D. Bailey	Happy Ticket, 4, 117	Savorthetime, 6, 117	6	**1:09.93**	$294,000
2004	**Ema Bovary (Chi)**, 5, 119	R. M. Gonzalez	Bear Fan, 5, 122	Lady Tak, 4, 119	6	1:10.81	294,000
2003	**Gold Mover**, 5, 118	J. D. Bailey	Vision in Flight, 4, 113	Harmony Lodge, 5, 116	8	1:11.31	294,000
2002	**Gold Mover**, 4, 115	J. D. Bailey	Xtra Heat, 4, 127	Fly Me Crazy, 4, 112	6	1:10.21	240,000
2001	**Dream Supreme**, 4, 122	P. Day	Hidden Assets, 4, 114	Sugar N Spice, 6, 114	9	1:10.48	240,000
2000	**Hurricane Bertie**, 5, 117	P. Day	Bourbon Belle, 5, 116	Cassidy, 5, 115	7	1:11.43	240,000
1999	**Princess Pietrina**, 5, 114	R. Homeister Jr.	Hurricane Bertie, 4, 118	U Can Do It, 6, 119	8	1:10.49	180,000
1998	**U Can Do It**, 5, 118	E. Coa	Closed Escrow, 5, 117	Colonial Minstrel, 4, 118	9	1:10.12	150,000
1997	**Vivace**, 4, 117	R. P. Romero	Ashboro, 4, 119	Special Request, 4, 115	9	1:10.94	150,000
1996	**Chaposa Springs**, 4, 126	L. A. Pincay Jr.	Reign Dance, 4, 113	Supah Jess, 4, 113	6	1:23.54	60,000
1995	**Miss Gibson County**, 4, 115	G. Boulanger	Goldarama, 5, 113	Sigrun, 5, 116	7	1:23.18	60,000
1994	**Roamin Rachel**, 4, 119	W. S. Ramos	Sigrun, 4, 113	Goldarama, 4, 110	10	1:24.01	60,000
1993	**Lady Sonata**, 4, 115	M. A. Lee	Fortune Forty Four, 4, 112	Treasured, 6, 112	5	1:23.00	30,000
1992	**Magal**, 5, 117	R. Hernandez	Fortune Forty Four, 3, 111	My Own True Love, 4, 116	8	1:23.60	30,000

1991	**Magal**, 4, 112	R. Hernandez	Joyce Azalene, 4, 110	Wekive Run, 3, 112	7	1:24.62	$32,550
1990	**Sweet Proud Polly**, 3, 112	P. A. Rodriguez	Legend One, 4, 110	Love's Exchange, 4, 117	6	1:25.00	32,040
1989	**Ana T.**, 4, 113	R. N. Lester	‡Ells Once Again, 5, 111	My Sweet Replica, 5, 112	8	1:24.80	48,990
1988	**Spirit of Fighter**, 5, 121	O. J. Londono	Stanleys Run, 3, 111	Sheer Ice, 6, 117	7	1:24.60	32,550
1987	**Classy Tricks**, 4, 115	M. C. Suckie	Sheer Ice, 5, 117	Spirit of Fighter, 4, 123	5	1:25.00	32,040
1986	**Classy Tricks**, 3, 112	R. N. Lester	Fleur de Soleil, 3, 113	Southern Velvet, 5, 113	6	1:25.00	28,130
1985	**Birdie Belle**, 4, 121	J. A. Santiago	Private Secretary, 4, 119	T. V. Snow, 5, 118	8	1:24.40	33,240

Named for Paula J. Tucker's 1984 champion older female and '82 Melaleuca S. winner Princess Rooney (1980 f. by Verbatim). Grade 3 1999-2001. Grade 2 2002-'05. 7 furlongs 1985-'96. ‡Spirit of Fighter finished second, DQ to fifth, 1989.

Prioress Stakes

Grade 1 in 2006. Belmont Park, three-year-olds, fillies, 6 furlongs, dirt. Held July 9, 2005, with a gross value of $250,000. First held in 1948. First graded in 1973. Stakes record 1:08.26 (2001 Xtra Heat).

Year	Winner	Jockey	Second	Third	Strs	Time	1st Purse
2005	**Acey Deucey**, 3, 119	D. Nelson	Maddalena, 3, 119	Sense of Style, 3, 121	7	1:10.37	$150,000
2004	**Friendly Michelle**, 3, 119	C. S. Nakatani	Feline Story, 3, 121	Forest Music, 3, 119	9	1:09.09	150,000
2003	**House Party**, 3, 121	J. A. Santos	Chimichurri, 3, 119	Princess V., 3, 115	8	1:09.45	120,000
2002	**Carson Hollow**, 3, 114	J. R. Velazquez	Spring Meadow, 3, 121	Proper Gamble, 3, 121	7	1:08.79	120,000
2001	**Xtra Heat**, 3, 121	R. Wilson	Above Perfection, 3, 116	Harmony Lodge, 3, 116	7	**1:08.26**	120,000
2000	**I'm Brassy**, 3, 113	M. J. Luzzi	Dat You Miz Blue, 3, 114	Lucky Livi, 3, 121	9	1:09.53	90,000
1999	**Sapphire n' Silk**, 3, 121	P. Day	Marley Vale, 3, 112	Confessional, 3, 118	8	1:09.55	90,000
1998	**Hurricane Bertie**, 3, 121	P. Day	Catinca, 3, 114	Foil, 3, 114	11	1:08.85	68,220
1997	**Pearl City**, 3, 118	J. D. Bailey	Alyssum, 3, 121	Vegas Prospector, 3, 121	5	1:09.40	64,680
1996	**Capote Belle**, 3, 112	J. R. Velazquez	Flat Fleet Feet, 3, 118	Miss Maggie, 3, 116	10	1:08.81	67,200
1995	**Scotzanna**, 3, 121	R. Platts	Culver City, 3, 116	Miss Golden Circle, 3, 118	9	1:10.61	66,840
1994	**Penny's Reshoot**, 3, 116	J. R. Velazquez	Heavenly Prize, 3, 121	Beckys Shirt, 3, 114	6	1:09.07	64,500
1993	**Classy Mirage**, 3, 114	J. A. Krone	Missed the Storm, 3, 118	Educated Risk, 3, 118	5	1:08.89	67,680
1992	**American Royale**, 3, 118	J. A. Santos	Debra's Victory, 3, 121	Preach, 3, 118	6	1:09.36	68,280
1991	**Zama Hummer**, 3, 114	G. L. Stevens	Missy's Mirage, 3, 114	Devilish Touch, 3, 118	10	1:09.88	74,760
1990	**Token Dance**, 3, 114	E. Maple	Stella Madrid, 3, 121	Charging Fire, 3, 114	4	1:09.40	49,770
1989	**Safely Kept**, 3, 118	A. T. Cordero Jr.	Cojinx, 3, 114	The Way It's Binn, 3, 114	5	1:11.60	49,770
1988	**Fara's Team**, 3, 114	J. D. Bailey	Lake Valley, 3, 112	Raging Lady, 3, 114	8	1:10.20	65,700
1987	**Firey Challenge**, 3, 114	R. Migliore	Up the Apalachee, 3, 118	Monogram, 3, 114	12	1:10.60	69,300
1986	**Religiosity**, 3, 112	J. A. Santos	Fighter Fox, 3, 112	Tromphe de Naskra, 3, 114	8	1:11.00	54,450
1985	**Clocks Secret**, 3, 115	J. Nied Jr.	Lady's Secret, 3, 118	Ride Sally, 3, 112	8	1:10.00	53,010
1984	**Proud Clarioness**, 3, 115	J. Samyn	Dumdedumdedum, 3, 112	Suavite, 3, 112	6	1:10.40	41,400
1983	**Able Money**, 3, 112	A. Graell	Quixotic Lady, 3, 118	Captivating Grace, 3, 118	10	1:11.00	34,440
1982	**Trove**, 3, 118	M. Venezia	Larida, 3, 114	Dearly Too, 3, 112	8	1:10.00	34,380
1981	**Tina Tina Too**, 3, 118	C. B. Asmussen	Sweet Revenge, 3, 121	Ruler's Dancer, 3, 112	8	1:11.20	33,420
1980	**Lien**, 3, 115	E. Maple	Cybele, 3, 112	Nuit d'Amour, 3, 115	10	1:11.00	27,390
1979	**Fall Aspen**, 3, 121	R. I. Velez	Spanish Fake, 3, 118	Too Many Sweets, 3, 115	7	1:11.40	25,740
1978	**Tempest Queen**, 3, 118	J. Velasquez	Sweet Joyce, 3, 112	Silver Ice, 3, 115	5	1:11.40	25,320
1977	**Ring O'Bells**, 3, 116	A. T. Cordero Jr.	Road Princess, 3, 118	Pearl Necklace, 3, 116	10	1:10.40	22,410
1976	**Dearly Precious**, 3, 121	B. Baeza	Old Goat, 3, 118	Answer, 3, 118	4	1:09.80	22,110
1975	**Sarsar**, 3, 118	W. Shoemaker	Stulcer, 3, 114	Gallant Trial, 3, 114	8	1:10.80	17,070
1974	**Clear Copy**, 3, 115	D. Montoya	Heartful, 3, 118	Talking Picture, 3, 115	12	1:10.20	17,745
1973	**Windy's Daughter**, 3, 121	B. Baeza	Voler, 3, 115	Waltz Fan, 3, 115	9	1:10.20	17,355

Named for the first American Thoroughbred to ever win a race in England, Prioress (1853 f. by *Sovereign). Grade 3 1973-'74, 1985-'87. Not graded 1975-'84. Grade 2 1988-2000. Held at Jamaica 1948-'59. Held at Aqueduct 1960-'86.

Providencia Stakes

Grade 3 in 2006. Santa Anita Park, three-year-olds, fillies, 1 mile, turf. Held April 8, 2006, with a gross value of $109,400. First held in 1981. First graded in 2005. Stakes record 1:34.55 (2004 Ticker Tape [GB]).

Year	Winner	Jockey	Second	Third	Strs	Time	1st Purse
2006	**Foxysox (GB)**, 3, 119	A. Bisono	Harriett Lane, 3, 119	Chosen Royalty, 3, 116	8	1:34.88	$65,640
2005	**Berbatim**, 3, 116	A. O. Solis	Royal Copenhagen (Fr), 3, 117	Thatswhatimean, 3, 119	10	1:47.66	66,960
2004	**Ticker Tape (GB)**, 3, 118	K. Desormeaux	Amorama (Fr), 3, 114	Winendynme, 3, 115	12	**1:34.55**	68,220
2003	**Star Vega (GB)**, 3, 114	M. E. Smith	Makeup Artist, 3, 115	Shapes and Shadows, 3, 115	6	1:47.89	90,000
2002	**Megahertz (GB)**, 3, 118	A. O. Solis	La Martina (GB), 3, 118	Ayzal (GB), 3, 114	7	1:47.34	48,690
2001	**Dynamous**, 3, 114	V. Espinoza	Heads Will Roll (GB), 3, 114	Little Firefly (Ire), 3, 116	7	1:50.13	48,915
2000	**Kumari Continent**, 3, 116	D. R. Flores	Minor Details, 3, 118	Velvet Morning, 3, 115	5	1:48.37	47,790
1999	**Sweet Life**, 3, 118	A. O. Solis	Lady At Peace, 3, 116	Smittenby (Ire), 3, 116	6	1:49.85	48,375
1998	**Country Garden (GB)**, 3, 118	K. Desormeaux	Star's Proud Penny, 3, 120	Marie J, 3, 115	8	1:50.84	49,050
1997	**Famous Digger**, 3, 114	B. Blanc	Cerita, 3, 114	Clever Pilot, 3, 114	7	1:49.85	48,160
1996	**Gastronomical**, 3, 116	K. Desormeaux	Wish You, 3, 114	Staffin (GB), 3, 114	6	1:50.40	47,880
1995	**Artica**, 3, 117	L. A. Pincay Jr.	Kindred Soul, 3, 114	One Hot Mama, 3, 115	6	1:49.36	46,725
1994	**Fancy 'n Fabulous**, 3, 114	A. O. Solis	Rabiadella, 3, 117	Espadrille, 3, 117	7	1:49.02	47,700
1993	**On the Catwalk (Ire)**, 3, 116	E. Delahoussaye	Amal Hayati, 3, 118	Voluptuous, 3, 114	6	1:50.35	46,650
1992	**Miss Turkana**, 3, 115	A. L. Castanon	Red Bandana, 3, 114	More Than Willing, 3, 120	7	1:47.32	47,475
1991	**Fantastic Ways**, 3, 115	C. J. McCarron	Island Shuffle, 3, 114	Saucy Lady B, 3, 115	9	1:49.50	49,425

1990	**Materco**, 3, 120	E. Delahoussaye	Somethingmerry, 3, 120	Nijinsky's Lover, 3, 120	9	1:47.40	$48,900
1989	**Formidable Lady**, 3, 117	G. L. Stevens	General Charge (Ire), 3, 117	Kelly, 3, 117	10	1:50.60	49,350
1988	**Pattern Step**, 3, 120	C. J. McCarron	Do So, 3, 117	Twice Titled, 3, 117	8	1:48.00	48,000
1987	**Some Sensation**, 3, 117	L. A. Pincay Jr.	Davie's Lamb, 3, 113	Pink Slipper, 3, 113	7	1:48.20	37,950
1986	**Miraculous**, 3, 113	G. L. Stevens	Top Corsage, 3, 116	Roberto's Key, 3, 115	8	1:47.80	38,350
1985	**Soft Dawn**, 3, 113	W. Shoemaker	Rose Cream, 3, 114	Charming Susan, 3, 117	7	1:49.60	37,850
1984	**Class Play**, 3, 117	L. A. Pincay Jr.	Pronto Miss, 3, 115	Powder Break, 3, 113	7	1:50.20	37,850
1983	**Spruce Song**, 3, 115	S. Hawley	Yours Or Mine, 3, 114	Stage Door Canteen, 3, 115	10	1:47.40	39,850
1982	**Phaedra**, 3, 117	L. A. Pincay Jr.	Northern Style, 3, 115	Carry a Tune, 3, 115	10	1:47.00	39,800
1981	**Flying Baton**, 3, 113	T. Lipham	Ice Princess, 3, 115	Bee a Scout, 3, 115	11	1:47.60	34,050

Named for an 1843 California land grant, Rancho Providencia, located near present-day Burbank; providencia means "providence" or "foresight." 1 1/8 miles 1981-2003, 2005.

Pucker Up Stakes

Grade 3 in 2006. Arlington Park, three-year-olds, fillies, 1 1/8 miles, turf. Held September 17, 2005, with a gross value of $200,000. First held in 1961. First graded in 1973. Stakes record 1:47.58 (1991 Jinski's World).

Year	Winner	Jockey	Second	Third	Strs	Time	1st Purse
2005	**Royal Copenhagen (Fr)**, 3, 116	S. Bridgmohan	Singhalese (GB), 3, 122	Isla Cozzene, 3, 116	11	1:48.76	$120,000
2004	**Ticker Tape (GB)**, 3, 122	K. Desormeaux	Spotlight (GB), 3, 122	Sister Swank, 3, 116	11	1:48.63	120,000
2003	**Aud**, 3, 118	B. D. Peck	Hail Hillary, 3, 116	Julie's Prize, 3, 120	12	1:49.16	105,000
2002	**Little Treasure (Fr)**, 3, 122	R. R. Douglas	Cellars Shiraz, 3, 122	Kathy K D, 3, 116	11	1:49.92	90,000
2001	**Snow Dance**, 3, 122	C. Perret	Kiss the Devil, 3, 116	Twilite Tryst, 3, 116	12	1:47.93	90,000
2000	**Solvig**, 3, 121	P. Day	Zoftig, 3, 118	Impending Bear, 3, 118	6	1:52.40	90,000
1997	**Witchful Thinking**, 3, 121	G. K. Gomez	Swearingen, 3, 116	Cozy Blues, 3, 116	8	1:48.80	75,000
1996	**Ms. Mostly**, 3, 114	R. P. Romero	Mountain Affair, 3, 116	Clamorosa, 3, 121	9	1:51.18	90,000
1995	**Grand Charmer**, 3, 116	P. Day	Upper Noosh, 3, 116	Set Me Straight, 3, 114	8	1:49.59	60,000
1994	**Work the Crowd**, 3, 118	A. T. Gryder	Irish Forever, 3, 116	Looking for Heaven, 3, 116	14	1:49.32	60,000
1993	**Amal Hayati**, 3, 113	W. S. Ramos	Warside, 3, 113	Future Starlet, 3, 111	11	1:53.39	60,000
1992	**Ziggy's Act**, 3, 116	G. Boulanger	Bernique, 3, 111	Luv Me Luv Me Not, 3, 121	10	1:48.79	60,000
1991	**Jinski's World**, 3, 111	A. Madrid Jr.	Ms. Aerosmith, 3, 116	Radiant Ring, 3, 121	9	**1:47.58**	60,000
1990	**Southern Tradition**, 3, 116	E. Fires	Virgin Michael, 3, 116	Slew of Pearls, 3, 116	11	1:49.20	70,140
1989	**Oczy Czarnie**, 3, 112	C. A. Black	Adira, 3, 112	Vanities, 3, 115	9	1:55.00	67,680
1987	**Sum**, 3, 118	E. Fires	Spectacular Bev, 3, 118	Lucie's Bower, 3, 113	10	1:51.80	47,790
1986	**Top Corsage**, 3, 120	S. Hawley	Marianna's Girl, 3, 115	Innsbruck (GB), 3, 114	10	1:44.20	34,620
1985	**Itsagem**, 3, 118	K. K. Allen	Miss Ultimo, 3, 121	Tide, 3, 112	7	1:57.60	35,520
1984	**Witwatersrand**, 3, 112	E. Fires	Madam Flutterby, 3, 118	Mr. T.'s Tune, 3, 112	9	1:52.40	48,885
	Dictina (Fr), 3, 112	J. L. Diaz	Nettie Cometti, 3, 121	Princess Moran, 3, 116	7	1:51.40	48,285
1983	**Decision**, 3, 121	E. Fires	Narrate, 3, 118	Won'tyoucomehome, 3, 116	15	1:51.20	35,310
1982	**Rose Bouquet**, 3, 121	R. P. Romero	Stay a Leader, 3, 116	Smart Heiress, 3, 121	11	1:53.60	34,710
1981	**Melanie Frances**, 3, 116	R. Sibille	Safe Play, 3, 121	Touch of Glamour, 3, 116	9	1:51.80	33,660
1980	**Ribbon**, 3, 114	P. Day	Satin Ribera, 3, 121	Cannon Boy, 3, 113	14	1:52.20	35,250
1979	**Allisons' Gal**, 3, 112	M. R. Morgan	Safe, 3, 121	Cup of Honey, 3, 116	12	2:00.40	34,500
1978	**Key to the Saga**, 3, 119	J. Samyn	Pretty Delight, 3, 119	Xandu, 3, 122	13	1:51.40	34,650
1977	**Rich Soil**, 3, 122	M. A. Rivera	New Scent, 3, 114	Ivory Castle, 3, 122	12	1:50.40	34,530
1976	**T. V. Vixen**, 3, 122	M. Manganello	Three Colors, 3, 119	True Reality, 3, 113	8	1:48.40	36,600
1975	**Kissapotamus**, 3, 118	D. Stover	Miami Game, 3, 118	Be Victorious, 3, 113	11	1:45.60	21,400
1974	**Tappahannock**, 3, 113	W. Gavidia	Pot Roast Billie, 3, 112	Miss Indian Chief, 3, 115	13	1:47.60	22,350
1973	**Eleven Pleasures**, 3, 112	H. Arroyo	Princess Doubleday, 3, 121	Guided Missle, 3, 112	9	1:37.60	16,150

Named for Mrs. Ada L. Rice's 1957 champion older female and '57 Washington Park H. winner Pucker Up (1953 f. by Olympia). Not graded 1979. Grade 2 1996-'97. Pucker Up H. 1961, 1963-'73. Held at Hawthorne Race Course 1985. Not held 1988, 1998-'99. 1 mile 1961, 1966-'73. 1 1/16 miles 1962-'65, 1974-'75, 1986. 1 3/16 miles 1979. Dirt 1961-'74, 1976. Originally scheduled at 1 1/8 miles on turf 1973. Originally scheduled at 1 1/16 miles on turf 1974. Two divisions 1984.

Queen Elizabeth II Challenge Cup Stakes

Grade 1 in 2006. Keeneland Race Course, three-year-olds, fillies, 1 1/8 miles, turf. Held October 15, 2005, with a gross value of $500,000. First held in 1984. First graded in 1986. Stakes record 1:45.81 (1996 Memories of Silver).

Year	Winner	Jockey	Second	Third	Strs	Time	1st Purse
2005	**Sweet Talker**, 3, 121	R. Bejarano	Karen's Caper, 3, 121	Gorella (Fr), 3, 121	7	1:51.20	$310,000
2004	**Ticker Tape (GB)**, 3, 121	K. Desormeaux	Barancella (Fr), 3, 121	River Belle (GB), 3, 121	7	1:51.35	310,000
2003	**Film Maker**, 3, 121	E. S. Prado	Maiden Tower (GB), 3, 121	Casual Look, 3, 121	10	1:47.82	310,000
2002	**Riskaverse**, 3, 121	M. Guidry	Zenda (GB), 3, 121	Lush Soldier, 3, 121	9	1:49.84	310,000
2001	**Affluent**, 3, 121	E. Delahoussaye	Golden Apples (Ire), 3, 121	Snow Dance, 3, 121	10	1:50.03	310,000
2000	**Collect the Cash**, 3, 121	S. J. Sellers	Blue Moon (Fr), 3, 121	Theoretically, 3, 121	9	1:47.94	310,000
1999	**Perfect Sting**, 3, 121	P. Day	Tout Charmant, 3, 121	Wannabe Grand (Ire), 3, 121	9	1:50.66	310,000
1998	**Tenski**, 3, 121	R. Migliore	Shires Ende, 3, 121	Sierra Virgen, 3, 121	9	1:48.54	248,000
1997	**Ryafan**, 3, 121	A. O. Solis	Auntie Mame, 3, 121	Golden Arches (Fr), 3, 121	8	1:46.64	248,000
1996	**Memories of Silver**, 3, 121	R. G. Davis	Shake the Yoke (GB), 3, 121	Antespend, 3, 121	10	**1:45.81**	248,000
1995	**Perfect Arc**, 3, 121	J. R. Velazquez	Auriette (Ire), 3, 121	Country Cat, 3, 121	8	1:49.84	155,000
1994	**Danish (Ire)**, 3, 121	J. A. Krone	Eternal Reve, 3, 121	Avie's Fancy, 3, 121	10	1:48.89	124,000
1993	**Tribulation**, 3, 121	J. Samyn	Miami Sands (Ire), 3, 121	Possibly Perfect, 3, 121	9	1:53.62	124,000

1992	**Captive Miss**, 3, 121	J. A. Krone	Suivi, 3, 121	Trampoli, 3, 121	10	1:48.66	$124,000
1991	**La Gueriere**, 3, 121	B. D. Peck	Satin Flower, 3, 121	Radiant Ring, 3, 121	9	1:49.86	130,000
1990	**Plenty of Grace**, 3, 121	J. D. Bailey	Christiecat, 3, 121	My Girl Jeannie, 3, 121	10	1:51.40	65,000
1989	**Coolawin**, 3, 121	J. A. Velez Jr.	To the Lighthouse, 3, 121	Songlines, 3, 121	8	1:43.20	65,000
1988	**Love You by Heart**, 3, 121	R. P. Romero	Siggebo, 3, 121	Glowing Honor, 3, 121	8	1:44.80	65,000
1987	**Graceful Darby**, 3, 121	J. D. Bailey	Shot Gun Bonnie, 3, 121	Sum, 3, 121	10	1:47.20	65,000
1986	**Lotka**, 3, 121	W. A. Guerra	Minstress, 3, 121	Top Corsage, 3, 121	9	1:50.00	65,000
1985	**Contredance**, 3, 112	E. Maple	Debutant Dancer, 3, 115	Folk Art, 3, 120	10	1:47.00	55,608
1984	**Sintra**, 3, 112	K. K. Allen	Solar Halo, 3, 112	Mr. T.'s Tune, 3, 112	12	1:43.40	69,644

Named in honor of the 1984 visit of Queen Elizabeth II of England to Central Kentucky; she presented the first winner's trophy. Grade 3 1986-'87. Grade 2 1988-'90. 1$^1/_{16}$ miles 1987. Dirt 1984-'86.

Queens County Handicap

Grade 3 in 2006. Aqueduct, three-year-olds and up, 1$^3/_{16}$ miles. Held December 10, 2005, with a gross value of $105,400. First held in 1902. First graded in 1973. Stakes record 1:54.40 (1972 Sunny and Mild).

Year	Winner	Jockey	Second	Third	Strs	Time	1st Purse
2005	**Philanthropist**, 4, 115	E. Coa	West Virginia, 4, 115	We Can Seek (Chi), 4, 113	5	1:56.99	$64,440
2004	**Classic Endeavor**, 6, 117	A. T. Gryder	Evening Attire, 6, 123	Colita, 4, 115	9	1:57.13	67,260
2003	**Thunder Blitz**, 5, 114	J. F. Chavez	Evening Attire, 5, 123	Seattle Fitz (Arg), 4, 115	6	1:55.90	64,980
2002	**Snake Mountain**, 4, 117	J. A. Santos	Docent, 4, 115	Cat's At Home, 5, 115	7	1:56.84	66,000
2001	**Evening Attire**, 3, 113	S. Bridgmohan	Balto Star, 3, 118	Top Official, 6, 113	8	1:55.08	67,140
2000	**Boston Party**, 4, 114	N. Arroyo Jr.	Talk's Cheap, 4, 115	Turnofthecentury, 3, 116	9	1:56.32	50,340
1999	**Early Warning**, 4, 116	J. F. Chavez	Doc Martin, 4, 112	Yankee Victor, 3, 114	7	1:55.03	49,230
1998	**Fire King**, 5, 113	F. Lovato Jr.	Las Vegas Ernie, 4, 112	Mr. Sinatra, 4, 119	7	1:56.88	49,140
1997	**Mr. Sinatra**, 3, 115	R. Migliore	Delay of Game, 4, 118	Draw, 4, 113	8	1:55.68	49,725
1996	**Topsy Robsy**, 4, 111	P. Keim-Bruno	More to Tell, 5, 114	Colonial Secretary, 4, 116	5	1:55.30	48,705
1995	**Aztec Empire**, 5, 113	J. Samyn	Mighty Magee, 3, 115	More to Tell, 4, 115	9	1:55.56	50,340
1994	**Federal Funds**, 5, 112	D. Carr	Jacksonport, 5, 110	Contract Court, 4, 116	8	1:56.42	49,665
1993	**Repletion**, 4, 111	M. E. Smith	Dibbs n' Dubbs, 5, 111	Primitive Hall, 4, 113	8	1:44.35	53,010
1992	**Shots Are Ringing**, 5, 117	J. R. Velazquez	A Call to Rise, 4, 111	Jacksonport, 3, 111	6	1:54.90	51,120
1991	**Nome**, 5, 112	E. Maple	Runaway Stream, 4, 116	Challenge My Duty, 4, 114	5	1:56.18	51,390
1990	**Sports View**, 3, 114	C. Perret	I'm Sky High, 4, 115	dh-Killer Diller, 3, 115 dh-Lost Opportunity, 4, 112	8	1:57.00	53,550
1989	**Its Acedemic**, 5, 115	J. D. Bailey	Homebuilder, 5, 113	Ole Atocha, 4, 113	7	1:58.00	52,290
1988	**Lay Down**, 4, 109	J. Samyn	Nostalgia's Star, 6, 113	Pleasant Virginian, 4, 113	6	1:57.20	64,980
1987	**Personal Flag**, 4, 116	R. P. Romero	Easy N Dirty, 4, 113	Gold Alert, 4, 114	5	1:59.00	64,170
1986	**Pine Belt**, 4, 111	E. Maple	Scrimshaw, 3, 108	Cost Conscious, 4, 111	6	1:57.20	55,260
1985	**Late Act**, 6, 118	E. Maple	Lightning Leap, 3, 110	Morning Bob, 4, 113	8	1:55.40	52,380
1984	**Puntivo**, 4, 114	R. G. Davis	High Honors, 4, 114	Moro, 5, 121	9	1:58.00	44,640
1983	**Country Pine**, 3, 118	J. D. Bailey	Count Normandy, 4, 108	Megaturn, 3, 113	8	1:58.00	33,240
1982	**Bar Dexter**, 5, 112	J. Fell	Castle Knight, 4, 111	Nice Pirate, 4, 110	5	1:58.20	32,880
1981	**French Cut**, 4, 112	D. MacBeth	Bar Dexter, 4, 110	Alla Breva, 4, 109	11	1:56.40	35,040
1980	**Fool's Prayer**, 5, 112	J. Velasquez	Ring of Light, 5, 115	Picturesque, 4, 114	7	1:56.00	33,360
1979	**Dewan Keys**, 4, 112	E. Maple	Mr. International, 6, 108	Gallant Best, 3, 116	8	1:56.80	32,940
1978	**†Cum Laude Laurie**, 4, 114	A. T. Cordero Jr.	Wise Philip, 5, 112	Do Tell George, 5, 112	8	1:55.80	32,580
1977	**Cox's Ridge**, 3, 126	E. Maple	Father Hogan, 4, 111	Popular Victory, 5, 115	7	1:55.80	32,670
1976	**It's Freezing**, 4, 113	J. Vasquez	Distant Land, 4, 111	Nalees Rialto, 4, 108	8	1:56.60	32,640
1975	**Hail the Pirates**, 5, 111	R. Turcotte	‡Sharp Gary, 4, 110	Herculean, 4, 111	10	1:55.60	34,560
1974	**Free Hand**, 4, 109	J. Amy	Arbees Boy, 4, 121	Group Plan, 4, 123	8	1:55.00	33,780
1973	**True Knight**, 4, 126	A. T. Cordero Jr.	Triangular, 6, 110	North Sea, 4, 117	12	1:55.00	35,070

Named for Queens County, New York, where Aqueduct is located. Grade 2 1973-'74. Not graded 1980. Held at Belmont Park 1946. Held at Jamaica 1956-'58. Not held 1909, 1911-'13. 1 mile 70 yards 1902-'03. 1 mile 1904-'39, 1959-'62. 1$^1/_{16}$ miles 1940-'58, 1993. 1$^1/_8$ miles 1963-'71. Dead heat for third 1990. ‡Festive Mood finished second, DQ to tenth, 1975. †Denotes female.

Railbird Stakes

Grade 3 in 2006. Hollywood Park, three-year-olds, fillies, 7 furlongs, dirt. Held May 6, 2006, with a gross value of $100,000. First held in 1963. First graded in 1973. Stakes record 1:20.60 (1979 Eloquent).

Year	Winner	Jockey	Second	Third	Strs	Time	1st Purse
2006	**Bettarun Fast**, 3, 120	A. T. Gryder	Mystery Girl, 3, 115	So Long Sonoma, 3, 118	6	1:23.29	$60,000
2005	**Short Route**, 3, 118	P. A. Valenzuela	Inspiring, 3, 123	Off the Richter, 3, 115	8	1:22.99	65,820
2004	**Elusive Diva**, 3, 118	P. A. Valenzuela	M. A. Fox, 3, 116	Speedy Falcon, 3, 123	8	1:21.36	65,760
2003	**Buffythecenterfold**, 3, 123	V. Espinoza	Honest Answer, 3, 117	Dash for Money, 3, 115	6	1:22.54	64,320
2002	**September Secret**, 3, 118	P. A. Valenzuela	Affairs of State, 3, 118	Fun House, 3, 118	5	1:22.95	63,780
2001	**Golden Ballet**, 3, 123	C. J. McCarron	Starrer, 3, 115	Pretty 'n Smart, 3, 115	6	1:21.57	90,000
2000	**‡Cover Gal**, 3, 122	L. A. Pincay Jr.	Wired to Fly, 3, 122	Classic Olympio, 3, 122	5	1:22.57	90,000
1999	**Olympic Charmer**, 3, 115	C. J. McCarron	Dianehill (Ire), 3, 115	Fee Fi Foe, 3, 116	9	1:21.18	90,000
1998	**Brulay**, 3, 115	G. L. Stevens	Gourmet Girl, 3, 119	Unreal Squeal, 3, 116	6	1:20.84	64,260
1997	**I Ain't Bluffing**, 3, 118	E. Delahoussaye	Really Happy, 3, 121	Montecito, 3, 114	7	1:22.60	65,100
1996	**Supercilious**, 3, 121	C. S. Nakatani	Tiffany Diamond, 3, 118	Raw Gold, 3, 121	6	1:22.55	64,260

1995	**Sleep Easy**, 3, 113	C. S. Nakatani	Texinadress, 3, 118	Laguna Seca, 3, 115	8	1:22.42	$64,600
1994	**Sportful Snob**, 3, 118	P. A. Valenzuela	Pirate's Revenge, 3, 121	Accountable Lady, 3, 116	5	1:21.94	61,400
1993	**Afto**, 3, 114	P. Atkinson	Fit to Lead, 3, 121	Nijivision, 3, 113	8	1:22.48	64,500
1992	**She's Tops**, 3, 114	K. Desormeaux	Race the Wild Wind, 3, 121	Magical Maiden, 3, 121	9	1:22.78	66,500
1991	**Suziqcute**, 3, 119	C. J. McCarron	Zama Hummer, 3, 117	Ifyoucouldseemenow, 3, 122	6	1:21.90	62,800
1990	**Forest Fealty**, 3, 114	J. A. Garcia	Patches, 3, 122	Golden Reef, 3, 122	8	1:21.60	48,950
1989	**Imaginary Lady**, 3, 122	G. L. Stevens	Kiwi, 3, 114	Stormy But Valid, 3, 122	7	1:21.40	47,800
1988	**Sheesham**, 3, 122	L. A. Pincay Jr.	Affordable Price, 3, 114	Super Avie, 3, 116	9	1:22.60	49,700
1987	**Very Subtle**, 3, 122	W. Shoemaker	Joey the Trip, 3, 117	Sacahuista, 3, 122	4	1:22.60	45,750
1986	**Melair**, 3, 114	P. A. Valenzuela	Comparability, 3, 119	Silent Arrival, 3, 122	7	1:22.40	48,600
1985	**Reigning Countess**, 3, 122	G. L. Stevens	Window Seat, 3, 122	Charming Susan, 3, 115	6	1:22.40	38,300
1984	**Mitterand**, 3, 115	E. Delahoussaye	Gene's Lady, 3, 122	Lucky Lucky Lucky, 3, 122	10	1:22.20	40,000
1983	**Ski Goggle**, 3, 122	C. J. McCarron	Madam Forbes, 3, 115	Gatita, 3, 117	9	1:23.40	33,150
1982	**Faneuil Lass**, 3, 117	T. Lipham	Jones Time Machine, 3, 119	Hasty Hannah, 3, 119	8	1:23.20	32,400
1981	**Cherokee Frolic**, 3, 119	G. Cohen	Strangeways, 3, 114	Terra Miss, 3, 115	8	1:22.20	32,400
1980	**Cinegita**, 3, 114	T. Lipham	Thundertee, 3, 122	Back At Two, 3, 119	6	1:20.80	31,450
1979	**Eloquent**, 3, 122	D. Pierce	Celine, 3, 122	Joy's Jewel, 3, 114	9	**1:20.60**	26,800
1978	**Eximious**, 3, 119	W. Shoemaker	B. Thoughtful, 3, 122	Joe's Bee, 3, 114	7	1:22.20	25,550
1977	**Taisez Vous**, 3, 115	F. Toro	Wavy Waves, 3, 122	Silent Wisdom, 3, 114	8	1:22.60	22,650
1976	**Hail Hilarious**, 3, 114	D. Pierce	Doc Shah's Siren, 3, 119	I Going, 3, 115	10	1:21.40	20,550
1975	**Raise Your Skirts**, 3, 118	W. Mahorney	Miss Tokyo, 3, 117	Fascinating Girl, 3, 119	7	1:20.80	19,350
1974	**Modus Vivendi**, 3, 121	D. Pierce	Fleet Peach, 3, 118	Fresno Star, 3, 118	9	1:21.60	19,800
1973	**Sandy Blue**, 3, 118	D. Pierce	Sphere, 3, 113	Goddess Roman, 3, 113	9	1:21.80	20,250

Named for racing fans who watch races from along the rail, known as "railbirds." Grade 2 1988, 1991-2001. Railbird H. 1963-'64. Both sexes 1963. ‡Abby Girl finished first, DQ to fifth for a positive drug test, 2000.

Rampart Handicap

Grade 2 in 2006. Gulfstream Park, three-year-olds and up, fillies and mares, 1$^1/_8$ miles, dirt. Held March 25, 2006, with a gross value of $200,000. First held in 1976. First graded in 1986. Stakes record 1:47.92 (2003 Allamerican Bertie).

Year	Winner	Jockey	Second	Third	Strs	Time	1st Purse
2006	**Oonagh Maccool (Ire)**, 4, 114	R. Bejarano	Sweet Symphony, 4, 119	Classy Charm, 4, 116	6	1:49.99	$120,000
2005	**D' Wildcat Speed**, 5, 113	M. R. Cruz	Isola Piu Bella (Chi), 5, 118	Pampered Princess, 5, 116	5	1:48.92	120,000
2004	**Sightseek**, 5, 121	J. D. Bailey	Redoubled Miss, 5, 113	Lead Story, 5, 117	4	1:51.07	120,000
2003	**Allamerican Bertie**, 4, 122	J. R. Velazquez	Smok'n Frolic, 4, 118	Softly, 5, 115	6	**1:47.92**	120,000
2002	**Forest Secrets**, 4, 117	P. Day	Summer Colony, 4, 118	Happily Unbridled, 4, 114	6	1:49.83	120,000
2001	**De Bertie**, 4, 116	J. F. Chavez	Apple of Kent, 5, 114	Scratch Pad, 4, 116	7	1:50.48	120,000
2000	**Bella Chiarra**, 5, 116	S. J. Sellers	Lines of Beauty, 5, 114	Up We Go, 4, 113	8	1:43.27	120,000
1999	**Banshee Breeze**, 4, 122	J. D. Bailey	Glitter Woman, 5, 119	Timely Broad, 5, 114	5	1:42.83	120,000
1998	**Dance for Thee**, 4, 113	J. Bravo	Escena, 5, 119	Glitter Woman, 4, 121	6	1:44.73	120,000
1997	**Chip**, 4, 114	J. Bravo	Rare Blend, 4, 122	Hurricane Viv, 4, 116	9	1:42.51	120,000
1996	**Investalot**, 5, 114	S. J. Sellers	Queen Tutta, 4, 113	Alcovy, 6, 117	9	1:43.99	120,000
1995	**Educated Risk**, 5, 126	M. E. Smith	Recognizable, 4, 117	Jade Flush, 4, 113	5	1:43.09	120,000
1994	**Nine Keys**, 4, 113	M. E. Smith	Educated Risk, 4, 120	Traverse City, 4, 113	6	1:42.12	120,000
1993	**Girl On a Mission**, 4, 112	J. D. Bailey	‡Luv Me Luv Me Not, 4, 116	Haunting, 5, 114	8	1:45.47	120,000
1992	**Fit for a Queen**, 6, 119	J. D. Bailey	Firm Stance, 4, 111	Nannerl, 5, 113	12	1:43.66	120,000
1991	**Charon**, 4, 121	C. Perret	Wortheroatsingold, 4, 112	Train Robbery, 4, 113	8	1:43.10	120,000
1990	**Barbarika**, 5, 113	C. Perret	Fit for a Queen, 4, 112	Natala, 4, 112	11	1:44.20	120,000
1989	**Colonial Waters**, 4, 112	W. H. McCauley	Savannah's Honor, 4, 113	Haiati, 4, 112	12	1:44.80	120,000
1988	**By Land by Sea**, 4, 118	F. Toro	Queen Alexandra, 6, 120	Bound, 4, 113	10	1:43.80	120,000
1987	**Life At the Top**, 4, 122	R. P. Romero	I'm Sweets, 4, 119	Natania, 5, 113	7	1:44.00	97,440
1986	**Endear**, 4, 113	E. Maple	Isayso, 7, 118	Natania, 4, 112	11	1:45.80	103,080
1985	**Isayso**, 6, 113	E. Maple	Pretty Perfect, 5, 122	Basie, 4, 114	7	1:44.20	70,080
1984	**Thinghatab**, 4, 118	C. Perret	National Banner, 4, 117	Vestris, 5, 112	10	1:43.80	36,870
1983	**Flag Waver**, 4, 108	A. O. Solis	Prime Prospect, 5, 118	Our Darling, 4, 112	13	1:44.00	57,960
1982	**Sweetest Chant**, 4, 117	E. Fires	Deby's Willing, 5, 115	Pretorienne (Fr), 6, 114	10	1:43.40	25,662
1981	**Wistful**, 4, 117	D. Brumfield	Lillian Russell, 4, 109	Deby's Willing, 4, 112	9	1:44.60	54,180
1976	**Moon Glitter**, 4, 110	E. Fires	Regal Quillo, 3, 112	K D Princess, 5, 111	8	1:22.20	9,960

Named for Mrs. H. Haggerty's 1948 Gulfstream Park H. winner Rampart (1942 f. by Trace Call); Rampart was the race's first female winner. Formerly sponsored by Johnnie Walker Scotch Whisky 1989-'90. Grade 3 1986-'87. Johnnie Walker Black Classic H. 1989-'90. Not held 1977-'80. 7 furlongs 1976. 1$^1/_{16}$ miles 1981-2000. ‡Now Dance finished second, DQ to fifth, 1993.

Rancho Bernardo Handicap

Grade 3 in 2006. Del Mar, three-year-olds and up, fillies and mares, 6$^1/_2$ furlongs, dirt. Held August 19, 2005, with a gross value of $150,000. First held in 1967. First graded in 1988. Stakes record 1:14.28 (1995 Track Gal).

Year	Winner	Jockey	Second	Third	Strs	Time	1st Purse
2005	**Behaving Badly**, 4, 113	V. Espinoza	Freakin Streakin, 4, 117	Dee Dee's Diner, 5, 118	8	1:15.32	$90,000
2004	**Dream of Summer**, 5, 118	M. E. Smith	Barbara Orr, 4, 113	Cyber Slew, 4, 117	7	1:15.85	90,000
2003	**Secret Liaison**, 5, 116	C. S. Nakatani	Lacie Girl, 4, 116	Spring Meadow, 4, 117	8	1:15.53	90,000
2002	**Kalookan Queen**, 6, 123	A. O. Solis	Warren's Whistle, 4, 116	Fancee Bargain, 6, 112	5	1:16.40	90,000
2001	**Kalookan Queen**, 5, 119	A. O. Solis	Go Go, 4, 125	Warren's Whistle, 3, 111	6	1:15.52	90,000

2000	**Theresa's Tizzy**, 6, 117	L. A. Pincay Jr.	Nany's Sweep, 4, 117	Hookedonthefeelin, 4, 119	6	1:16.23	$90,000
1999	**Enjoy the Moment**, 4, 119	D. R. Flores	Snowberg, 4, 117	Stop Traffic, 6, 121	6	1:15.97	90,000
1998	**Advancing Star**, 5, 120	C. J. McCarron	Closed Escrow, 5, 115	Tiffany Diamond, 5, 116	6	1:14.64	64,140
1997	**Track Gal**, 6, 120	G. L. Stevens	Madame Pandit, 4, 118	Advancing Star, 4, 116	8	1:15.64	69,125
1996	**Track Gal**, 5, 122	C. J. McCarron	Tricky Code, 5, 116	Evil's Pic, 4, 117	5	1:14.64	63,550
1995	**Track Gal**, 4, 118	C. J. McCarron	Desert Stormer, 5, 119	Lakeway, 4, 122	5	**1:14.28**	58,650
1994	**Desert Stormer**, 4, 116	E. Delahoussaye	Magical Maiden, 5, 120	Booklore, 4, 117	9	1:14.81	62,800
1993	**Knight Prospector**, 4, 119	K. Desormeaux	Interactive, 4, 119	Bountiful Native, 5, 120	5	1:16.14	45,675
1992	**Bountiful Native**, 4, 117	P. A. Valenzuela	Devil's Orchid, 5, 120	She's Tops, 3, 114	9	1:15.30	63,400
1991	**Cascading Gold**, 5, 117	L. A. Pincay Jr.	Survive, 7, 120	Suziqcute, 3, 114	5	1:15.42	60,100
1990	**Hot Novel**, 4, 118	K. Desormeaux	Sexy Slew, 4, 116	Down Again, 6, 115	9	1:14.60	62,875
1989	**Kool Arrival**, 3, 117	L. A. Pincay Jr.	Super Avie, 4, 117	Survive, 5, 116	7	1:15.20	47,625
1988	**Clabber Girl**, 5, 120	L. A. Pincay Jr.	Queen Forbes, 4, 113	Behind the Scenes, 4, 117	8	1:14.60	38,750
1987	**Julie the Flapper**, 3, 114	C. J. McCarron	Clabber Girl, 4, 117	Sari's Heroine, 4, 119	10	1:15.00	33,200
1986	**Bold n Special**, 3, 115	C. J. McCarron	Rangoon Ruby (Ire), 4, 116	Eloquack, 4, 117	5	1:14.60	30,850
1985	**Take My Picture**, 3, 114	F. Olivares	Sales Bulletin, 4, 118	Mimi Baker, 4, 112	10	1:09.20	33,200
1984	**Pleasure Cay**, 4, 121	L. A. Pincay Jr.	Lovlier Linda, 4, 120	Pride of Rosewood (NZ), 6, 115	8	1:08.60	32,250
1983	**Bara Lass**, 4, 120	C. J. McCarron	Excitable Lady, 5, 124	Milingo, 4, 113	7	1:09.40	31,800
1982	**Lucky Lady Ellen**, 3, 117	L. A. Pincay Jr.	Glitter Hitter, 4, 118	Excitable Lady, 4, 125	7	1:08.60	31,850
1981	**Forluvofiv**, 4, 118	E. Delahoussaye	Untamed Spirit, 4, 122	Ack's Secret, 5, 118	8	1:09.40	31,400
1980	**Great Lady M.**, 5, 121	L. A. Pincay Jr.	Sal's High, 4, 118	Western Hand, 3, 110	8	1:08.60	25,800
1979	**Fantastic Girl**, 3, 112	W. Shoemaker	Happy Holme, 5, 120	Delice, 4, 122	8	1:09.20	22,850
1978	**Happy Holme**, 4, 120	C. J. McCarron	Telferner, 4, 117	Dallas Deb, 3, 114	5	1:13.00	18,200
1977	**Lullaby Song**, 4, 120	L. A. Pincay Jr.	Miss Rising Market, 4, 113	Honeyhugger, 4, 117	7	1:09.00	16,550
1976	**Mama Kali**, 5, 117	L. A. Pincay Jr.	Mismoyola, 6, 119	Vol Au Vent, 4, 120	6	1:09.20	16,400
1975	**Mama Kali**, 4, 120	J. Lambert	Hooley Ruley, 5, 117	Modus Vivendi, 4, 124	8	1:08.40	17,050
1974	**Impressive Style**, 5, 117	R. Rosales	Fleet Peach, 3, 115	Lt.'s Joy, 4, 120	10	1:08.60	16,300
1973	**Fairly Certain**, 4, 121	S. Valdez	Tannyhill, 4, 117	Normandy Grey, 4, 115	8	1:42.80	10,400
	dh-D. B. Carm, 4, 119	F. Toro		Dr. Kerlan, 4, 118	5	1:43.20	6,400
	dh-Dollar Discount, 4, 119	S. Valdez					

Named for the city of Rancho Bernardo, California. Rancho Bernardo Breeders' Cup H. 1990-'95. Not held 1968-'72. 1 mile 1967. 1$^1/_{16}$ miles 1973. 6 furlongs 1974-'85. Turf 1973. Both sexes 1967-'73. Two divisions 1973. Dead heat for first 1973 (2nd Div.). Non-winners of a race worth $10,000 to the winner 1973.

Raven Run Stakes

Grade 2 in 2006. Keeneland Race Course, three-year-olds, fillies, 7 furlongs, dirt. Held October 22, 2005, with a gross value of $300,000. First held in 1999. First graded in 2002. Stakes record 1:20.88 (2000 Darling My Darling).

Year	Winner	Jockey	Second	Third	Strs	Time	1st Purse
2005	**For All We Know**, 3, 116	S. Bridgmohan	Flying Glitter, 3, 118	Career Oriented, 3, 116	11	1:23.74	$186,000
2004	**Josh's Madelyn**, 3, 118	J. Shepherd	Vision of Beauty, 3, 116	Feline Story, 3, 118	10	1:22.86	139,004
2003	**Yell**, 3, 123	P. Day	Ebony Breeze, 3, 123	Tina Bull, 3, 117	12	1:21.75	108,159
2002	**Sightseek**, 3, 117	J. D. Bailey	Miss Lodi, 3, 123	Respectful, 3, 117	12	1:23.98	106,578
2001	**Nasty Storm**, 3, 123	P. Day	Hattiesburg, 3, 123	Forest Secrets, 3, 123	7	1:23.30	68,138
2000	**Darling My Darling**, 3, 117	M. E. Smith	Surfside, 3, 123	Cat Cay, 3, 117	6	**1:20.88**	51,104
1999	**Dreamy Maiden**, 3, 117	P. Day	Golden Illusion, 3, 117	Cosmic Wing, 3, 117	6	1:22.64	37,076

Named for the Raven Run nature sanctuary located outside Lexington, Kentucky. Sponsored by the Lexus Division of Toyota Motor Manufacturing Co. of Georgetown, Kentucky 2005. Grade 3 2002-'03.

Razorback Breeders' Cup Handicap

Grade 3 in 2006. Oaklawn Park, four-year-olds and up, 1$^1/_{16}$ miles, dirt. Held March 12, 2006, with a gross value of $150,000. First held in 1976. First graded in 1978. Stakes record 1:40.40 (1988 Lost Code).

Year	Winner	Jockey	Second	Third	Strs	Time	1st Purse
2006	**Purim**, 4, 116	R. Albarado	Arch Hall, 5, 115	Thunder Mission, 4, 116	8	1:43.77	$90,000
2005	**Added Edge**, 5, 115	L. S. Quinonez	Mauk Four, 5, 112	Absent Friend, 5, 115	10	1:43.88	75,000
2004	**Sonic West**, 5, 113	W. Martinez	Crafty Shaw, 6, 117	Pie N Burger, 6, 119	7	1:43.56	60,000
2003	**Colorful Tour**, 4, 118	L. S. Quinonez	Crafty Shaw, 5, 119	Windward Passage, 4, 118	7	1:43.53	60,000
2002	**Mr Ross**, 7, 120	D. R. Pettinger	Remington Rock, 8, 115	Big Numbers, 5, 116	8	1:44.13	60,000
2001	**Mr Ross**, 6, 119	D. R. Pettinger	Graeme Hall, 4, 120	Maysville Slew, 5, 117	9	1:42.60	75,000
2000	**Well Noted**, 5, 112	T. T. Doocy	Crimson Classic, 6, 115	Mr Ross, 5, 115	7	1:43.21	75,000
1999	**Desert Air**, 4, 113	C. J. Lanerie	Magnify, 6, 113	Black Tie Dinner, 6, 112	7	1:44.75	75,000
1998	**Brush With Pride**, 6, 115	T. T. Doocy	Littlebitlively, 4, 112	Krigeorj's Gold, 5, 115	7	1:43.55	75,000
1997	**No Spend No Glow**, 5, 115	R. N. Lester	Illesam, 5, 114	Come On Flip, 6, 115	8	1:43.20	90,000
1996	**Juliannus**, 7, 113	R. Albarado	Judge T C, 5, 121	Dazzling Falls, 4, 118	5	1:43.37	90,000
1995	**Silver Goblin**, 4, 124	D. W. Cordova	Joseph's Robe, 4, 111	Wooden Ticket, 5, 115	6	1:42.79	120,000
1994	**Prize Fight**, 5, 113	P. A. Johnson	Brother Brown, 4, 120	Country Store, 4, 113	8	1:43.70	90,000
1993	**Lil E. Tee**, 4, 123	P. Day	Zeeruler, 5, 115	Senor Tomas, 4, 114	7	1:41.55	90,000
1992	**Tokatee**, 6, 115	G. K. Gomez	On the Edge, 5, 112	Total Assets, 7, 110	9	1:42.87	90,000
1991	**Bedeviled**, 4, 115	D. L. Howard	Din's Dancer, 6, 117	Black Tie Affair (Ire), 5, 118	7	1:42.50	90,000
1990	**Opening Verse**, 4, 116	P. Day	Primal, 5, 121	Silver Survivor, 4, 118	7	1:41.40	90,000
1989	**Blushing John**, 4, 117	P. Day	Lyphard's Ridge, 6, 111	Proper Reality, 4, 123	5	1:43.00	60,000

1988 **Lost Code**, 4, 123	C. Perret	Red Attack, 6, 112	Demons Begone, 4, 121	7	**1:40.40**	$73,500
1987 **Bolshoi Boy**, 4, 119	R. P. Romero	Lyphard's Ridge, 4, 110	Sun Master, 6, 119	7	1:40.80	86,520
1986 **Red Attack**, 4, 111	L. Snyder	Vanlandingham, 5, 125	Inevitable Leader, 7, 111	9	1:42.00	96,900
1985 **Imp Society**, 4, 126	P. Day	Introspective, 4, 113	Strength in Unity, 4, 109	10	1:42.60	97,740
1984 **Dew Line**, 5, 116	S. Maple	Passing Base, 4, 112	Win Stat, 7, 115	14	1:41.60	74,520
1983 **Eminency**, 5, 120	P. Day	Cassaleria, 4, 115	Bold Style, 4, 113	10	1:43.60	70,740
1982 **Eminency**, 4, 111	P. Day	Reef Searcher, 5, 119	Tally Ho the Fox, 7, 115	15	1:45.20	76,200
1981 **Temperence Hill**, 4, 124	E. Maple	Blue Ensign, 4, 113	Belle's Ruler, 6, 112	6	1:44.20	66,660
1980 **All the More**, 7, 114	L. Snyder	Prince Majestic, 6, 116	Breaker Breaker, 4, 117	11	1:45.40	56,400
1979 **Cisk**, 5, 120	G. Patterson	Droll's Reason, 4, 113	Prince Majestic, 5, 121	8	1:45.40	53,700
1978 **Cox's Ridge**, 4, 125	E. Maple	Dr. Riddick, 4, 116	Mark's Place, 6, 124	12	1:43.00	37,110
1977 **Dragset**, 6, 111	J. Kunitake	Romeo, 4, 120	Last Buzz, 4, 115	9	1:44.40	35,910
1976 **Royal Glint**, 6, 126	J. E. Tejeira	Marauding, 4, 115	Heaven Forbid, 5, 112	8	1:42.40	35,550

Named for the unofficial state animal and University of Arkansas mascot, the razorback pig. Grade 2 1985-'96. Razorback H. 1976-2004.

Rebel Stakes

Grade 3 in 2006. Oaklawn Park, three-year-olds, 1$^1/_{16}$ miles, dirt. Held March 18, 2006, with a gross value of $300,000. First held in 1976. First graded in 1990. Stakes record 1:41 (1984 Vanlandingham).

Year	Winner	Jockey	Second	Third	Strs	Time	1st Purse
2006	**Lawyer Ron**, 3, 122	J. McKee	Red Raymond, 3, 117	Steppenwolfer, 3, 118	10	1:44.09	$180,000
2005	**Greater Good**, 3, 122	J. McKee	Rockport Harbor, 3, 119	Batson Challenge, 3, 117	6	1:44.92	150,000
2004	**Smarty Jones**, 3, 122	S. Elliott	Purge, 3, 117	Pro Prado, 3, 117	9	1:42.07	120,000
2003	**Crowned King**, 3, 115	C. R. Rennie	Great Notion, 3, 119	Comic Truth, 3, 117	7	1:44.00	75,000
2002	**Windward Passage**, 3, 116	D. J. Meche	Ocean Sound (Ire), 3, 114	Dusty Spike, 3, 114	8	1:45.06	60,000
2001	**Crafty Shaw**, 3, 113	J. M. Johnson	Arctic Boy, 3, 114	Strike It Smart, 3, 114	9	1:43.82	60,000
2000	**Snuck In**, 3, 119	C. B. Asmussen	Big Numbers, 3, 114	Fan the Flame, 3, 113	12	1:42.99	60,000
1999	**Etbauer**, 3, 112	M. E. Smith	Desert Demon, 3, 119	Kutsa, 3, 112	11	1:44.02	75,000
1998	**Victory Gallop**, 3, 119	E. Coa	Robinwould, 3, 114	Whataflashyactor, 3, 114	10	1:44.72	75,000
1997	**Phantom On Tour**, 3, 117	L. J. Melancon	Direct Hit, 3, 119	River Squall, 3, 117	12	1:42.80	75,000
1996	**Ide**, 3, 122	C. Perret	Blow Out, 3, 112	Bunker Hill Road, 3, 113	7	1:44.10	60,000
1995	**Mystery Storm**, 3, 122	C. Perret	Rich Man's Gold, 3, 112	Valid Advantage, 3, 113	7	1:44.41	75,000
1994	**Judge T C**, 3, 119	J. M. Johnson	Concern, 3, 112	Milt's Overture, 3, 114	11	1:44.14	75,000
1993	**Dalhart**, 3, 122	M. E. Smith	Foxtrail, 3, 122	Mi Cielo, 3, 114	8	1:42.31	75,000
1992	**Pine Bluff**, 3, 122	J. D. Bailey	Desert Force, 3, 117	Looks Like Money, 3, 113	7	1:42.83	75,000
1991	**Quintana**, 3, 112	D. Guillory	Corporate Report, 3, 114	Far Out Wadleigh, 3, 119	8	1:42.70	60,000
1990	**Nuits St. Georges**, 3, 114	J. E. Bruin	Maverick Miner, 3, 114	Tarascon, 3, 122	11	1:46.00	60,000
1989	**Manastash Ridge**, 3, 119	A. L. Castanon	Big Stanley, 3, 122	Double Quick, 3, 122	14	1:43.00	60,000
1988	**Sea Trek**, 3, 112	P. A. Johnson	Din's Dancer, 3, 114	Notebook, 3, 122	10	1:42.60	73,500
1987	**Demons Begone**, 3, 119	P. Day	Fast Forward, 3, 114	You're No Bargain, 3, 112	6	1:41.40	86,520
1986	**Rare Brick**, 3, 119	M. E. Smith	Clear Choice, 3, 112	The Flats, 3, 114	8	1:43.20	68,760
1985	**Clever Allemont**, 3, 119	P. Day	Bonham, 3, 113	Proper Native, 3, 114	7	1:44.40	95,100
1984	**Vanlandingham**, 3, 115	P. Day	Wind Flyer, 3, 118	Leavesumdouble, 3, 112	10	**1:41.00**	70,740
1983	**Sunny's Halo**, 3, 121	L. Snyder	Sligh Jet, 3, 117	Le Cou Cou, 3, 115	11	1:42.20	68,850
1982	**Bold Style**, 3, 116	L. Snyder	Majesty's Prince, 3, 115	Lost Creek, 3, 114	8	1:43.80	51,420
1981	**Bold Ego**, 3, 122	J. Lively	Catch That Pass, 3, 117	Chapel Creek, 3, 112	10	1:41.40	35,580
1980	**Temperence Hill**, 3, 114	D. Haire	Royal Sporan, 3, 111	Be a Prospect, 3, 123	15	1:42.80	38,430
1979	**Lucy's Axe**, 3, 121	E. Maple	Tunerup, 3, 115	Arctic Action, 3, 118	8	1:42.80	35,070
1978	**Chop Chop Tomahawk**, 3, 116	L. Snyder	Abidan, 3, 114	Forever Casting, 3, 124	10	1:42.40	36,150
1977	**United Holme**, 3, 120	J. E. Tejeira	J. J. Battle, 3, 124	Tinsley's Affair, 3, 115	12	1:42.20	36,810
1976	**Riverside Sam**, 3, 113	G. Patterson	Elocutionist, 3, 121	Klen Klitso, 3, 113	14	1:41.60	37,710

Named for the nickname of Southerners, "rebels"; the nickname is derived from the South's rebellion against the United States during the Civil War. Rebel H. 1976-'83. Not graded 2003-'04.

Red Bank Handicap

Grade 3 in 2006. Monmouth Park, three-year-olds and up, 1 mile, turf. Held May 28, 2005, with a gross value of $150,000. First held in 1974. First graded in 1986. Stakes record 1:33.34 (1991 Double Booked).

Year	Winner	Jockey	Second	Third	Strs	Time	1st Purse
2005	**American Freedom**, 7, 115	J. A. Velez Jr.	Spruce Run, 7, 113	Royal Affirmed, 7, 112	8	1:43.12	$90,000
2004	**Burning Roma**, 6, 120	J. L. Castanon	Remind, 4, 117	American Freedom, 6, 115	11	1:34.73	60,000
2003	**Just Le Facts**, 4, 111	J. Bravo	Saint Verre, 5, 118	Runspastum, 6, 114	4	1:37.73	20,000
2002	**Key Lory**, 8, 117	H. Vega	Sardaukar (GB), 6, 113	Spruce Run, 4, 113	8	1:35.92	60,000
2001	**Pavillon (Brz)**, 7, 112	J. Bravo	Western Summer, 4, 114	Runspastum, 4, 114	10	1:36.38	90,000
2000	**Mi Narrow**, 6, 114	C. H. Velasquez	Deep Gold, 4, 114	Inkatha (Fr), 6, 117	9	1:34.84	90,000
1999	**Inkatha (Fr)**, 5, 114	H. Castillo Jr.	Rob 'n Gin, 5, 119	Soviet Line (Ire), 9, 118	8	1:33.95	90,000
1998	**Statesmanship**, 4, 117	J. A. Santos	Rob 'n Gin, 4, 120	Bomfim, 5, 114	11	1:35.00	60,000
1997	**Basqueian**, 6, 118	R. Wilson	Wild Night Out, 5, 111	Jambalaya Jazz, 5, 117	6	1:35.20	60,000
1996	**Joker**, 4, 113	J. A. Velez Jr.	Rare Reason, 5, 118	Diplomatic Jet, 4, 116	8	1:35.90	60,000
1995	**Dove Hunt**, 4, 118	W. H. McCauley	Rare Reason, 4, 115	Winnetou, 5, 113	9	1:33.95	45,000
1994	**Adam Smith (GB)**, 6, 120	J. A. Krone	Discernment, 5, 113	Fourstardave, 9, 118	8	1:34.43	45,000

1993	**Adam Smith (GB)**, 5, 116	J. Samyn	Fourstars Allstar, 5, 116	Rinka Das, 5, 115	8	1:34.39	$45,000
1992	**Daarik (Ire)**, 5, 114	L. Saumell	Leger Cat (Arg), 6, 116	Kate's Valentine, 7, 114	8	1:34.07	45,000
1991	**Double Booked**, 6, 122	J. C. Ferrer	Great Normand, 6, 118	Now Listen, 4, 112	10	**1:33.34**	45,000
1990	**Norquestor**, 4, 118	J. Samyn	Master Speaker, 5, 120	Grande Jette, 5, 111	5	1:36.00	52,980
1989	**Arlene's Valentine**, 4, 115	J. C. Ferrer	Yankee Affair, 7, 121	Alwasmi, 5, 114	6	1:40.20	52,290
1988	**Iron Courage**, 4, 113	W. H. McCauley	Spellbound, 5, 112	Ioskeha, 5, 113	7	1:35.40	42,210
1987	**Feeling Gallant**, 5, 117	C. W. Antley	Hi Ideal, 5, 114	Racing Star, 5, 117	5	1:37.20	35,610
1986	**†Mazatleca (Mex)**, 6, 112	C. W. Antley	Feeling Gallant, 4, 114	Hi Ideal, 4, 113	8	1:35.80	34,800
1985	**Castelets**, 6, 115	V. A. Bracciale Jr.	Evzone, 4, 117	Gothic Revival, 4, 112	8	1:37.00	27,885
	Ends Well, 4, 116	M. R. Morgan	Domynsky (GB), 5, 117	Bold Southerner, 4, 115	9	1:35.60	28,065
1984	**Tough Mickey**, 4, 118	K. Skinner	Fortnightly, 4, 117	Roman Bend, 4, 108	9	1:36.40	28,470
	Castle Guard, 5, 118	J. C. Ferrer	Super Sunrise (GB), 5, 123	Fray Star (Arg), 6, 117	10	1:35.80	28,530
1983	**Sun and Shine (GB)**, 4, 115	J. Terry	St. Brendan, 5, 116	Mr. Dreamer, 6, 113	11	1:36.60	24,480
1982	**Alhambra Joe**, 5, 111	W. Nemeti	Pepper's Segundo, 5, 117	Timely Counsel, 4, 112	5	1:38.60	23,265
1981	**Colonel Moran**, 4, 116	G. W. Donahue	Dan Horn, 9, 115	Contare, 5, 108	12	1:35.20	24,570
1980	**Horatius**, 5, 117	D. MacBeth	Pipedreamer (GB), 5, 116	North Course, 5, 114	11	1:35.00	24,495
1979	**Navajo Princess**, 5, 122	J. Vasquez	La Soufriere, 4, 116	Sans Arc, 5, 115	10	1:43.20	22,441
1978	**Love Jenny**, 4, 108	M. A. Gomez	Table Hopper, 5, 111	Chanctonbury, 4, 114	5	1:46.20	28,308
1977	**Playin' Footsie**, 4, 110	R. D. Ardoin	Desiree, 4, 110	Artfully, 4, 112	10	1:44.40	29,510
1976	**Collegiate**, 4, 116	J. W. Edwards	Show Me How, 4, 110	Four Bells, 5, 114	11	1:40.20	25,919
1975	**Kudara**, 4, 118	D. MacBeth	Enchanted Native, 4, 111	Twixt, 6, 121	11	1:42.20	18,850
1974	**‡Mystery Mood**, 2, 115	J. E. Tejeira	Molly Ballantine, 2, 121	Lucky Leslie, 2, 117	11	1:45.20	18,672

Named for the town of Red Bank, New Jersey. Not graded 2003. Red Bank S. 1974. 1$^1/_{16}$ miles 1974-'75, 1977-'79. 1 mile 70 yards 1976. Dirt 1974-'78, 1982, 1987, 1990, 1997, 2003. Originally scheduled on turf 2003. Two-year-olds 1974. Fillies and mares 1975-'79. Two divisions 1984-'85. ‡Molly Ballantine finished first, DQ to second, 1974. Course record 1999. †Denotes female.

Red Smith Handicap

Grade 2 in 2006. Aqueduct, three-year-olds and up, 1$^3/_8$ miles, turf. Held November 12, 2005, with a gross value of $150,000. First held in 1960. First graded in 1973. Stakes record 2:14.44 (1999 Monarch's Maze).

Year	Winner	Jockey	Second	Third	Strs	Time	1st Purse
2005	**King's Drama (Ire)**, 5, 122	E. S. Prado	Rousing Victory, 4, 114	Dreadnaught, 5, 117	8	2:15.37	$90,000
2004	**Dreadnaught**, 4, 115	J. Samyn	Certifiably Crazy, 4, 112	Alost (Fr), 4, 116	10	2:18.87	90,000
2003	**Balto Star**, 5, 120	J. R. Velazquez	Macaw (Ire), 4, 118	Cetewayo, 9, 116	11	2:18.86	90,000
2002	**Evening Attire**, 4, 126	S. Bridgmohan	Fisher Pond, 3, 116	Pleasant Breeze, 7, 120	6	2:14.81	90,000
2001	**Mr. Pleasentfar (Brz)**, 4, 115	J. A. Santos	Eltawaasul, 5, 114	Regal Dynasty, 5, 113	12	2:16.94	90,000
2000	**Cetewayo**, 6, 114	R. Migliore	Understood, 4, 113	Val's Prince, 8, 118	13	2:17.93	90,000
1999	**Monarch's Maze**, 3, 113	J. Bravo	Williams News, 4, 114	Gritty Sandie, 3, 114	14	**2:14.44**	90,000
1998	**Musical Ghost**, 6, 115	J. R. Velazquez	Rice, 6, 115	Plato's Love, 3, 109	12	2:15.53	90,000
1997	**Instant Friendship**, 4, 123	J. R. Velazquez	Demi's Bret, 4, 117	Trample, 3, 112	5	2:17.08	150,000
1996	**Mr. Bluebird**, 5, 116	M. E. Smith	Ops Smile, 4, 116	Raintrap (GB), 6, 117	13	2:15.35	87,750
1995	**Flag Down**, 5, 114	J. A. Santos	‡Party Season (GB), 4, 116	Proceeded, 4, 110	11	2:22.03	69,900
1994	**Franchise Player**, 5, 109	D. V. Beckner	Red Bishop, 6, 119	Same Old Wish, 4, 112	14	2:20.53	72,120
1993	**Royal Mountain Inn**, 4, 110	J. A. Krone	Spectacular Tide, 4, 113	Share the Glory, 5, 111	8	1:59.82	71,760
1992	**Montserrat**, 4, 118	J. A. Krone	Preferences, 3, 110	First Rate (Ire), 7, 111	7	2:00.32	70,920
1991	**Who's to Pay**, 5, 117	J. D. Bailey	Simili (Fr), 5, 114	Solar Splendor, 4, 114	8	1:58.18	71,160
1990	**Yankee Affair**, 8, 122	J. A. Santos	Hodges Bay, 5, 116	Phantom Breeze (Ire), 4, 112	7	2:00.20	70,560
1989	**Rambo Dancer**, 5, 113	J. A. Santos	El Senor, 5, 117	Salem Drive, 7, 116	8	2:01.00	72,360
1988	**Pay the Butler**, 4, 110	R. G. Davis	Equalize, 6, 116	Yankee Affair, 6, 120	15	2:01.40	118,620
1987	**Theatrical (Ire)**, 5, 122	P. Day	Dance of Life, 4, 122	Equalize, 5, 112	11	2:00.80	116,460
1986	**Divulge**, 4, 116	J. Cruguet	Tri for Size, 5, 113	Island Sun, 4, 118	9	1:59.00	88,950
	Equalize, 4, 114	W. A. Guerra	Palace Panther (Ire), 5, 116	Entitled To, 4, 112	8	2:02.20	103,650
1985	**Sharannpour (Ire)**, 5, 112	A. T. Cordero Jr.	Inevitable Leader, 6, 116	Cold Feet (Fr), 4, 110	13	2:04.20	114,600
1984	**Hero's Honor**, 4, 117	J. D. Bailey	Win, 4, 114	Eskimo, 4, 112	5	2:02.20	102,900
1983	**Super Sunrise (GB)**, 4, 114	C. Perret	Mariacho (Ire), 5, 116	Field Cat, 6, 111	7	2:06.80	67,200
	Thunder Puddles, 4, 117	J. Samyn	John's Gold, 4, 112	Open Call, 5, 124	7	2:06.40	67,200
1982	**Highland Blade**, 4, 124	J. Vasquez	Dom Menotti (Fr), 5, 109	Open Call, 4, 125	8	2:06.40	69,000
1981	**Match the Hatch**, 5, 114	K. Skinner	Passing Zone, 4, 108	Great Neck, 5, 114	9	1:59.60	68,160
1980	**Marquee Universal (Ire)**, 4, 121	H. Pilar	Match the Hatch, 4, 114	Lyphard's Wish (Fr), 4, 122	8	1:58.80	67,680
1978	**Tiller**, 4, 114	J. Fell	True Colors, 4, 116	Tacitus, 4, 113	8	2:00.20	33,960
1977	**Clout**, 5, 114	G. Martens	Chati, 4, 117	Gay Jitterbug, 4, 122	8	1:40.00	25,927
	Quick Card, 4, 112	A. T. Cordero Jr.	Bemo, 7, 115	Noble Dancer (GB), 5, 119	6	1:39.60	25,687
1976	**Erwin Boy**, 5, 116	R. Turcotte	Clout, 4, 111	Quick Card, 3, 110	10	2:01.20	28,110
1975	***Telefonico**, 4, 120	C. Perret	Drollery, 5, 114	Barcas, 4, 114	9	2:03.00	17,400
1974	**Take Off**, 5, 117	R. Turcotte	Jogging, 7, 112	Red Reality, 8, 112	7	2:00.40	23,070
1973	**Red Reality**, 7, 122	J. Velasquez	Malwak, 5, 114	New Hope, 4, 113	5	2:13.20	16,890

Named in honor of Walter "Red" Smith, Pulitzer Prize-winning sports columnist. Formerly named for Edgemere, New York, a Queens neighborhood. Grade 3 1973-'80, 2002. Edgemere H. 1960-'73, 1976-'81. Edgemere S. 1974-'75. Held at Belmont Park 1960-'62, 1968-'78, 1980-'93. Not held 1979. 1$^3/_{16}$ miles 1963-'67. 1$^1/_4$ miles 1972-'76, 1978, 1980-'93. 1$^1/_{16}$ miles 1977. Dirt 1960-'64, 1984, 1997, 2002. Originally scheduled on turf 2002. Two divisions 1977, 1983, 1986. ‡Boyce finished second, DQ to 11th, 1995. Track record 1940.

Regret Stakes

Grade 3 in 2006. Churchill Downs, three-year-olds, fillies, 1⅛ miles, turf. Held June 18, 2005, with a gross value of $225,000. First held in 1970. First graded in 1999. Stakes record 1:48.78 (2003 Sand Springs).

Year	Winner	Jockey	Second	Third	Strs	Time	1st Purse
2005	**Rich in Spirit**, 3, 120	G. L. Stevens	Sweet Talker, 3, 120	Royal Bean, 3, 116	8	1:49.76	$139,500
2004	**Sister Star**, 3, 116	B. Blanc	Western Ransom, 3, 120	Jinny's Gold, 3, 118	7	1:51.40	137,516
2003	**Sand Springs**, 3, 118	M. Guidry	Personal Legend, 3, 116	Achnasheen, 3, 116	12	**1:48.78**	143,220
2002	**Distant Valley (GB)**, 3, 119	J. D. Bailey	Peace River Lady, 3, 115	Stylelistick, 3, 122	9	1:42.71	104,811
2001	**Casual Feat**, 3, 115	L. J. Melancon	Amaretta, 3, 117	La Vida Loca (Ire), 3, 119	8	1:42.75	103,695
2000	**Solvig**, 3, 122	P. Day	Trip, 3, 117	Miss Chief, 3, 115	9	1:42.95	104,439
1999	**Nani Rose**, 3, 115	S. J. Sellers	Solar Bound, 3, 122	Suffragette, 3, 115	8	1:42.40	104,439
1998	**Formal Tango**, 3, 115	C. R. Woods Jr.	Adel, 3, 122	Pratella, 3, 112	10	1:48.73	105,927
1997	**Starry Dreamer**, 3, 122	W. Martinez	Cozy Blues, 3, 115	Swearingen, 3, 122	8	1:42.77	69,378
1996	**Daylight Come**, 3, 117	C. C. Bourque	Fleur de Nuit, 3, 112	Esquive (GB), 3, 115	9	1:45.72	55,526
1995	**Christmas Gift**, 3, 122	C. R. Woods Jr.	Bail Out Becky, 3, 122	Grand Charmer, 3, 117	7	1:45.00	54,210
1994	**Packet**, 3, 117	J. M. Johnson	Thread, 3, 122	Slew Kitty Slew, 3, 112	7	1:42.14	54,551
1993	**Lovat's Lady**, 3, 112	B. D. Peck	Warside, 3, 122	Mari's Key, 3, 112	8	1:42.95	36,595
1992	**Tiney Toast**, 3, 122	S. P. Payton	Shes Just Super, 3, 122	Riverjinsky, 3, 115	10	1:42.06	37,440
1991	**Maria Balastiere**, 3, 117	A. T. Gryder	Savethelastdance, 3, 119	Lady Be Great, 3, 119	7	1:44.40	35,718
1990	**Secret Advice**, 3, 119	B. E. Bartram	Super Fan, 3, 122	Screen Prospect, 3, 119	6	1:44.40	35,815
1989	**Justice Will Come**, 3, 119	S. H. Bass	Luthier's Launch, 3, 119	Motion in Limine, 3, 117	10	1:46.20	36,693
1988	**Lets Do Lunch**, 3, 114	K. K. Allen	Stolie, 3, 119	Lucky Lydia, 3, 117	8	1:45.60	44,208
1987	**Jonowo**, 3, 119	M. McDowell	Lt. Lao, 3, 122	Sum, 3, 119	10	1:39.20	37,115
1986	**Rosemont Risk**, 3, 114	P. Day	Prime Union, 3, 122	Hail a Cab, 3, 122	8	1:36.80	25,090
1985	**Weekend Delight**, 3, 122	J. McKnight	Gallants Gem, 3, 122	Turn to Wilma, 3, 117	6	1:35.60	21,028
1984	**Mrs. Revere**, 3, 111	L. J. Melancon	Dusty Gloves, 3, 119	Robin's Rob, 3, 122	6	1:36.60	21,873
1983	**Rosy Spectre**, 3, 112	J. McKnight	Princesse Rapide, 3, 119	Fiesty Belle, 3, 111	8	1:37.80	19,939
1982	**Amazing Love**, 3, 116	L. J. Melancon	Jay Birdie, 3, 113	Noon Balloon, 3, 116	7	1:37.00	19,289
	Sefa's Beauty, 3, 113	M. S. Sellers	Mystical Mood, 3, 116	Smooth Fleet, 3, 113	5	1:37.60	19,143
1981	**Contrefaire**, 3, 121	T. Barrow	Solo Disco, 3, 121	Sweet Granny, 3, 118	13	1:11.60	16,705
1980	**Forever Cordial**, 3, 118	R. DePass	Missile Masquerade, 3, 118	Sweetladyroll, 3, 118	10	1:12.00	15,966
	No No Nona, 3, 115	M. A. Holland	Cerada Ridge, 3, 121	Romper, 3, 121	7	1:12.00	15,575
1979	**Fearless Dame**, 3, 121	R. DePass	Im for Joy, 3, 121	Shawn's Gal, 3, 121	10	1:10.80	16,120
1978	**Unconscious Doll**, 3, 121	E. Delahoussaye	Swervy, 3, 118	White Song, 3, 121	11	1:10.60	14,853
1977	**‡Shady Lou**, 3, 121	E. Delahoussaye	Time for Pleasure, 3, 121	Welsung, 3, 121	8	1:10.60	14,528
1976	**Carmelita Gibbs**, 3, 121	R. Breen	Sunny Romance, 3, 118	Island Venture, 3, 121	9	1:12.80	14,504
	Confort Zone, 3, 121	J. C. Espinoza	Rough Girl, 3, 121	My Fair Maid, 3, 115	6	1:12.80	14,114
1975	**Red Cross**, 3, 121	D. Brumfield	Flama Ardiente, 3, 121	Jill the Terrible, 3, 121	10	1:09.60	15,243
1974	**Clemanna**, 3, 121	J. C. Espinoza	Sarah Babe, 3, 121	Quick Sea, 3, 121	9	1:11.20	14,763
	Mary Dugan, 3, 121	J. McKnight	Princess Teamiga, 3, 118	Miss Orevent, 3, 121	12	1:10.40	15,153
1973	**Juke Joint**, 3, 118	W. Soirez	La Gentillesse, 3, 118	Never Ask, 3, 121	12	1:11.80	15,535

Named for Harry Payne Whitney's 1915 champion three-year-old filly and '15 Kentucky Derby winner Regret (1912 f. by Broomstick); Regret was the first filly to win the Derby. 6 furlongs 1970-'81. 1 mile 1982-'87. 1¹⁄₁₆ miles 1988-2002. Dirt 1970-'86. Two divisions 1974, 1976, 1980, 1982. ‡Time for Pleasure finished first, DQ to second, 1977. Nonwinners of a stakes worth $7,500 to the winner 1973-'75.

Remsen Stakes

Grade 2 in 2006. Aqueduct, two-year-olds, 1⅛ miles, dirt. Held November 26, 2005, with a gross value of $200,000. First held in 1904. First graded in 1973. Stakes record 1:47.80 (1977 Believe It).

Year	Winner	Jockey	Second	Third	Strs	Time	1st Purse
2005	**Bluegrass Cat**, 2, 120	J. R. Velazquez	Flashy Bull, 2, 116	Parkhimonbroadway, 2, 116	8	1:52.20	$120,000
2004	**Rockport Harbor**, 2, 120	S. Elliott	Galloping Grocer, 2, 120	Killenaule, 2, 120	6	1:48.88	120,000
2003	**Read the Footnotes**, 2, 122	J. D. Bailey	Master David, 2, 116	West Virginia, 2, 116	11	1:50.62	120,000
2002	**Toccet**, 2, 122	J. F. Chavez	Bham, 2, 116	Empire Maker, 2, 116	8	1:50.40	120,000
2001	**Saarland**, 2, 116	J. R. Velazquez	Nokoma, 2, 116	Silent Fred, 2, 116	9	1:51.28	120,000
2000	**Windsor Castle**, 2, 116	R. G. Davis	Ommadon, 2, 122	Buckle Down Ben, 2, 122	8	1:51.92	120,000
1999	**Greenwood Lake**, 2, 122	J. Samyn	Un Fino Vino, 2, 113	Polish Miner, 2, 113	8	1:50.63	120,000
1998	**Comeonmom**, 2, 113	J. Bravo	Millions, 2, 122	Wondertross, 2, 113	9	1:49.84	120,000
1997	**Coronado's Quest**, 2, 122	M. E. Smith	Halory Hunter, 2, 115	Brooklyn Nick, 2, 115	7	1:52.27	120,000
1996	**The Silver Move**, 2, 114	R. Migliore	Jules, 2, 122	Accelerator, 2, 122	8	1:53.54	120,000
1995	**Tropicool**, 2, 112	J. F. Chavez	Skip Away, 2, 112	Crafty Friend, 2, 113	11	1:50.30	170,000
1994	**Thunder Gulch**, 2, 115	G. L. Stevens	Western Echo, 2, 119	Mighty Magee, 2, 114	10	1:53.80	120,000
1993	**Go for Gin**, 2, 117	J. D. Bailey	Arrovente, 2, 113	Linkatariat, 2, 113	7	1:52.79	120,000
1992	**Silver of Silver**, 2, 122	J. Vasquez	Dalhart, 2, 115	Wild Gale, 2, 115	11	1:50.25	120,000
1991	**Pine Bluff**, 2, 113	C. Perret	Offbeat, 2, 113	Cheap Shades, 2, 113	8	1:50.80	120,000
1990	**Scan**, 2, 119	J. D. Bailey	Subordinated Debt, 2, 115	Kyle's Our Man, 2, 113	8	1:52.40	106,560
1989	**Yonder**, 2, 115	E. Maple	Roanoke, 2, 122	Armed for Peace, 2, 113	10	1:51.20	145,680
1988	**Fast Play**, 2, 122	A. T. Cordero Jr.	Fire Maker, 2, 115	Silver Sunsets, 2, 122	15	1:50.60	197,400
1987	**Batty**, 2, 113	J. A. Santos	Old Stories, 2, 115	Three Engines, 2, 113	8	1:52.40	176,400
1986	**Java Gold**, 2, 113	P. Day	Talinum, 2, 115	Drachma, 2, 113	8	1:49.60	172,680
1985	**Pillaster**, 2, 119	A. T. Cordero Jr.	Mr. Classic, 2, 113	Dance of Life, 2, 113	10	1:49.00	175,800

1984	**‡Mighty Appealing**, 2, 122	G. P. Smith	Hot Debate, 2, 117	Bolting Holme, 2, 115	11	1:53.20	$178,680
1983	**Dr. Carter**, 2, 113	J. Velasquez	Secret Prince, 2, 117	Hail Bold King, 2, 113	8	1:49.00	134,700
1982	**Pax in Bello**, 2, 113	J. Fell	Chumming, 2, 115	Primitive Pleasure, 2, 113	11	1:50.20	141,300
1981	**Laser Light**, 2, 113	E. Maple	Real Twister, 2, 115	Wolfie's Rascal, 2, 113	11	1:50.80	103,500
1980	**‡Pleasant Colony**, 2, 116	V. A. Bracciale Jr.	Foolish Tanner, 2, 113	Akureyri, 2, 117	8	1:50.20	67,920
1979	**Plugged Nickle**, 2, 122	B. Thornburg	Googolplex, 2, 117	Proctor, 2, 113	8	1:50.40	64,560
1978	**Instrument Landing**, 2, 119	J. Fell	Lucy's Axe, 2, 117	Picturesque, 2, 117	9	1:50.20	48,375
1977	**Believe It**, 2, 122	E. Maple	Alydar, 2, 122	Quadratic, 2, 116	5	**1:47.80**	48,015
1976	**Royal Ski**, 2, 122	J. Kurtz	Nostalgia, 2, 122	Hey Hey J. P., 2, 116	9	1:50.40	49,545
1975	**Hang Ten**, 2, 116	L. A. Pincay Jr.	Dance Spell, 2, 113	Play the Red, 2, 113	12	1:49.20	52,290
1974	**El Pitirre**, 2, 112	M. Venezia	Bombay Duck, 2, 118	Circle Home, 2, 115	10	1:49.40	34,380
1973	**Heavy Mayonnaise**, 2, 112	C. Baltazar	Hegemony, 2, 112	Flip Sal, 2, 112	13	1:51.40	17,925

Named for Col. Joremus Remsen (1735-'90), leader of the Revolutionary forces at the battle of Long Island, New York. Grade 1 1981-'88. Remsen H. 1904-'53. Held at Jamaica 1904-'58. Not held 1908, 1910-'17, 1951. 5$^1/_2$ furlongs 1904-'09. 6 furlongs 1918-'45, 1949-'50. 1$^1/_{16}$ miles 1946-'47, 1952-'58. 5 furlongs 1948. 1 mile 1959-'72. Colts 1954-'57. Colts and geldings 1958-'60. ‡Akureyri finished first, DQ to third, 1980. ‡Stone White finished first, DQ to 11th, 1984.

Richter Scale Breeders' Cup Sprint Championship Handicap

Grade 2 in 2006. Gulfstream Park, three-year-olds and up, 7 furlongs, dirt. Held March 4, 2006, with a gross value of $189,000. First held in 1972. First graded in 1996. Stakes record 1:21.15 (2003 Tour of the Cat).

Year	Winner	Jockey	Second	Third	Strs	Time	1st Purse
2006	**Mister Fotis**, 5, 115	R. Bejarano	Sir Greeley, 4, 116	Universal Form, 5, 116	9	1:21.73	$120,000
2005	**Sir Shackleton**, 4, 116	J. Castellano	Lion Tamer, 5, 119	Clock Stopper, 5, 117	6	1:21.64	120,000
2004	**Lion Tamer**, 4, 116	J. R. Velazquez	Coach Jimi Lee, 4, 115	Wacky for Love, 4, 114	7	1:21.52	120,000
2003	**Tour of the Cat**, 5, 116	A. Cabassa Jr.	Burning Roma, 5, 116	Highway Prospector, 6, 114	8	**1:21.15**	120,000
2002	**Dream Run**, 4, 113	P. Day	Binthebest, 5, 114	Burning Roma, 4, 118	8	1:22.30	120,000
2001	**Hook and Ladder**, 4, 115	R. Migliore	Trippi, 4, 120	Rollin With Nolan, 4, 116	6	1:21.85	120,000
2000	**Richter Scale**, 6, 118	R. Migliore	Forty One Carats, 4, 116	Kelly Kip, 6, 120	10	1:23.30	120,000
1999	**Frisk Me Now**, 5, 117	E. L. King Jr.	Young At Heart, 5, 113	Good and Tough, 4, 115	6	1:22.86	60,000
1998	**Rare Rock**, 5, 117	P. Day	Irish Conquest, 5, 114	Frisco View, 5, 118	7	1:22.00	120,000
1997	**Frisco View**, 4, 116	J. D. Bailey	El Amante, 4, 114	Templado (Ven), 4, 114	7	1:23.14	98,160
1996	**Patton**, 5, 113	R. G. Davis	Forty Won, 5, 115	Our Emblem, 5, 115	10	1:21.81	100,140
1995	**Cherokee Run**, 5, 122	M. E. Smith	Waldoboro, 4, 113	Evil Bear, 5, 116	6	1:21.70	60,000
1994	**I Can't Believe**, 6, 113	E. Maple	American Chance, 5, 114	British Banker, 6, 114	8	1:22.55	60,000
1993	**Binalong**, 4, 112	J. D. Bailey	Loach, 5, 114	Richman, 5, 113	6	1:22.35	60,000
1992	**Groomstick**, 6, 112	W. S. Ramos	Ocala Flame, 4, 111	Cold Digger, 5, 113	9	1:23.98	60,000
1991	**Gervazy**, 4, 115	W. S. Ramos	Shuttleman, 5, 114	Swedaus, 4, 110	7	1:21.46	60,000
1990	**‡Dancing Spree**, 5, 126	A. T. Cordero Jr.	Pentelicus, 6, 114	Shuttleman, 4, 111	7	1:10.00	30,000
1989	**Claim**, 4, 115	C. Perret	Position Leader, 4, 117	Prospector's Halo, 5, 115	7	1:23.40	41,904
1988	**Royal Pennant**, 5, 113	J. A. Santos	dh-Grantley, 4, 112 dh-Real Forest, 5, 113		12	1:23.20	45,612
1987	**Dwight D.**, 5, 116	R. N. Lester	Splendid Catch, 5, 113	Uncle Ho, 4, 112	7	1:10.80	27,816
1986	**Hot Cop**, 4, 115	J. Samyn	Dwight D., 4, 114	Opening Lead, 6, 115	12	1:22.80	45,324
1985	**Key to the Moon**, 4, 122	R. Platts	For Halo, 4, 123	Northern Ocean, 5, 112	8	1:22.60	42,552
1984	**Number One Special**, 4, 116	E. Fires	Ward Off Trouble, 4, 116	El Perico, 4, 114	6	1:21.80	23,793
1983	**Deputy Minister**, 4, 122	D. MacBeth	Wipe 'em Out, 4, 109	Center Cut, 4, 118	12	1:22.80	38,040
1981	**King's Fashion**, 6, 122	J. Samyn	Jaklin Klugman, 4, 124	Joanie's Chief, 4, 108	7	1:22.60	34,920
1977	**Yamanin**, 5, 122	W. Gavidia	Full Out, 4, 119	Rexson, 4, 114	6	1:22.80	37,860
1974	**Cheriepe**, 4, 115	J. Velasquez	Shecky Greene, 4, 127	Gay Pierre, 5, 112	4	1:22.40	25,236

Named for Wafare Farm's and Richard S. and Nancy Kaster's 2000 Gulfstream Park Breeders' Cup Sprint Championship H. (G2) winner Richter Scale (1994 c. by *Habitony). Grade 3 1996-'98. Sprint Championship H. 1972, 1974, 1977, 1981. Gulfstream Sprint Championship H. 1983-'90. Gulfstream Park Sprint Championship H. 1991-'93. Gulfstream Park Sprint H. 1994-'95. Gulfstream Park Breeders' Cup Sprint Championship H. 1996-2002. Richter Scale Breeders' Cup Sprint Championship S. 2003. Not held 1973, 1975-'76, 1978-'80, 1982. 6 furlongs 1987, 1990. Dead heat for second 1988. ‡Pentelicus finished first, DQ to second, 1990.

Risen Star Stakes

Grade 3 in 2006. Fair Grounds at Louisiana Downs, three-year-olds, 1$^1/_{16}$ miles, dirt. Held January 14, 2006, with a gross value of $268,000. First held in 1988. First graded in 2002. Stakes record 1:42.98 (1996 Zarb's Magic).

Year	Winner	Jockey	Second	Third	Strs	Time	1st Purse
2006	**Lawyer Ron**, 3, 118	J. McKee	Mark of Success, 3, 116	Hyte Regency, 3, 116	7	1:43.13	$160,800
2005	**Scipion**, 3, 117	G. L. Stevens	Real Dandy, 3, 118	Storm Surge, 3, 122	11	1:44.54	90,000
2004	**Gradepoint**, 3, 116	R. Albarado	Mr. Jester, 3, 122	Nightlifeatbigblue, 3, 118	6	1:45.36	90,000
2003	**Badge of Silver**, 3, 116	R. Albarado	Lone Star Sky, 3, 122	Defrere's Vixen, 3, 114	12	1:42.99	90,000
2002	**Repent**, 3, 122	A. J. D'Amico	Bob's Image, 3, 115	Easyfromthegitgo, 3, 122	9	1:43.17	90,000
2001	**Dollar Bill**, 3, 122	C. J. McCarron	Gracie's Dancer, 3, 114	Rahy's Secret, 3, 122	10	1:43.45	75,000
2000	**Exchange Rate**, 3, 119	C. S. Nakatani	Mighty, 3, 122	Ifitstobeitsuptome, 3, 114	8	1:44.25	75,000
1999	**Ecton Park**, 3, 114	S. J. Sellers	Answer Lively, 3, 122	Kimberlite Pipe, 3, 122	12	1:44.83	75,000
1998	**Comic Strip**, 3, 119	S. J. Sellers	Captain Maestri, 3, 122	Time Limit, 3, 122	7	1:44.27	75,000
1997	**Open Forum**, 3, 117	D. M. Barton	Crypto Star, 3, 117	Cash Deposit, 3, 122	5	1:44.20	60,000

1996	**Zarb's Magic**, 3, 122	E. J. Perrodin	Imminent First, 3, 114	Palikar, 3, 122	9	**1:42.98**	$37,950
1995	**Knockadoon**, 3, 114	W. Martinez	Key to Malagra, 3, 114	Scott's Scoundrel, 3, 122	9	1:45.44	31,882
	Beavers Nose, 3, 117	K. Bourque	Moonlight Dancer, 3, 122	Fuzzy Me, 3, 114	8	1:45.22	31,792
1994	**Fly Cry**, 3, 122	R. D. Ardoin	Smilin Singin Sam, 3, 122	Little Jazz Boy, 3, 122	7	1:43.02	31,155
1993	**Dixieland Heat**, 3, 119	R. P. Romero	O'Star, 3, 114	Gold Angle, 3, 114	7	1:43.20	16,080
	Dry Bean, 3, 117	A. T. Gryder	Apprentice, 3, 119	Grand Jewel, 3, 114	6	1:43.80	16,020
1992	**Line In The Sand**, 3, 119	S. P. Romero	Hill Pass, 3, 119	Sheik to Sheik, 3, 114	11	1:45.00	19,635
1991	**Big Courage**, 3, 119	T. L. Fox	Slick Groom, 3, 114	Denizen, 3, 115	8	1:46.70	19,230
1990	**Genuine Meaning**, 3, 122	J. Hirdes	Very Formal, 3, 114	Diamond Prospector, 3, 114	12	1:40.80	16,740
1989	**Nooo Problema**, 3, 117	S. P. Romero	Alota Strawberry, 3, 114	Majesty's Imp, 3, 119	8	1:42.40	13,163
	Dispersal, 3, 114	B. J. Walker Jr.	Island Alibi, 3, 114	Major Prospect, 3, 114	7	1:42.20	13,103
1988	**Risen Star**, 3, 120	S. P. Romero	Pastourelles, 3, 115	Jim's Orbit, 3, 122	12	1:40.00	13,890

Named for Lamarque Racing Stable's and Louie J. Roussel III's 1988 champion three-year-old male and '88 Louisiana Derby (G3) winner Risen Star (1985 c. by Secretariat). Originally designed as a prep for the Louisiana Derby (G2). Louisiana Derby Trial S. 1988. Held at Louisiana Downs 2006. 1 mile 40 yards 1988-'90. Two divisions 1989, 1993, 1995.

River City Handicap

Grade 3 in 2006. Churchill Downs, three-year-olds and up, $1\frac{1}{8}$ miles, turf. Held November 20, 2005, with a gross value of $167,700. First held in 1978. First graded in 1996. Stakes record 1:47.90 (2001 Dr. Kashnikow).

Year	Winner	Jockey	Second	Third	Strs	Time	1st Purse
2005	**America Alive**, 4, 119	R. Albarado	G P Fleet, 5, 117	Shaniko, 4, 116	8	1:50.78	$103,974
2004	**G P Fleet**, 4, 115	J. R. Martinez Jr.	Cloudy's Knight, 4, 115	Ay Caramba (Brz), 4, 115	12	1:51.26	108,066
2003	**Hard Buck (Brz)**, 4, 118	B. Blanc	Warleigh, 5, 117	Rowans Park, 3, 114	10	1:51.60	107,136
2002	**Dr. Kashnikow**, 5, 116	R. Albarado	Foster's Landing, 4, 109	Roxinho (Brz), 4, 115	11	1:51.44	108,903
2001	**Dr. Kashnikow**, 4, 116	R. Albarado	Tijiyr (Ire), 5, 117	Strategic Mission, 6, 115	8	**1:47.90**	109,926
2000	**Brahms**, 3, 112	P. Day	Vergennes, 5, 115	Super Quercus (Fr), 4, 116	9	1:48.09	111,879
1999	**Comic Strip**, 4, 119	P. Day	Keats and Yeats, 5, 112	Aboriginal Apex, 6, 114	10	1:50.71	106,113
1998	**Wild Event**, 5, 116	S. J. Sellers	Buff, 3, 113	Floriselli, 4, 114	13	1:49.18	116,436
1997	**Same Old Wish**, 7, 117	S. J. Sellers	Aboriginal Apex, 4, 113	Joyeux Danseur, 4, 114	9	1:50.90	106,578
1996	**Same Old Wish**, 6, 119	S. J. Sellers	Jet Freighter, 5, 113	Franchise Player, 7, 111	7	1:49.21	70,122
1995	**Homing Pigeon**, 5, 113	R. P. Romero	Hawk Attack, 3, 115	Dusty Asher, 5, 111	8	1:51.00	73,320
1994	**Lindon Lime**, 4, 113	S. J. Sellers	Torch Rouge (GB), 3, 114	Jaggery John, 3, 115	11	1:49.30	75,660
1993	**Secreto's Hideaway**, 4, 110	W. Martinez	Little Bro Lantis, 5, 115	Ganges, 5, 113	5	1:53.83	72,670
1992	**Cozzene's Prince**, 5, 117	D. Penna	Lotus Pool, 5, 118	Stagecraft (GB), 5, 114	8	1:49.31	73,060
1991	**Spending Record**, 4, 114	P. Day	Stage Colony, 4, 113	Silver Medallion, 5, 118	10	1:50.34	75,075
1990	**Silver Medallion**, 4, 118	C. Perret	Blair's Cove, 5, 114	Rushing Raj, 4, 114	10	1:50.80	56,550
1989	**Spark O'Dan**, 4, 113	J. M. Johnson	Exclusive Greer, 8, 115	Air Worthy, 4, 118	10	1:50.80	55,429
1988	**Ile de Jinsky**, 4, 113	E. J. Sipus Jr.	Stop the Stage, 3, 114	Herakles, 5, 117	7	1:53.20	44,618
1987	**Kings River (Ire)**, 5, 114	M. E. Smith	Lord Grundy (Ire), 5, 119	Boulder Run, 4, 117	10	1:45.40	37,148
1986	**Taylor's Special**, 5, 123	P. Day	Doonesbear, 3, 116	Sumptious, 3, 121	8	1:36.20	30,007
1985	**Banner Bob**, 3, 118	K. K. Allen	Rapid Gray, 6, 123	Cullendale, 3, 116	6	1:36.60	29,348
1984	**Eminency**, 6, 115	P. Day	Thumbsucker, 5, 123	Bayou Hebert, 3, 116	8	1:38.40	18,103
1983	**Northern Majesty**, 4, 120	S. Maple	Shot n' Missed, 6, 123	Straight Flow, 5, 115	8	1:37.00	18,249
1982	**Pleasing Times**, 3, 110	P. Day	Hechizado (Arg), 6, 115	Rackensack, 4, 118	13	1:38.20	20,719
1981	**Suliman**, 4, 113	L. Snyder	Tiger Lure, 7, 121	Senate Chairman, 3, 113	12	1:10.60	20,199
1980	**Tinsley's Hope**, 6, 113	J. C. Espinoza	Go With the Times, 4, 122	Withholding, 3, 114	6	1:11.00	19,208
1979	**Go With the Times**, 3, 120	G. Gallitano	Cossett Charlie, 6, 112	Bask, 5, 117	7	1:10.20	19,435
1978	**Inca Roca**, 5, 118	J. C. Espinoza	Perplext, 4, 114	Raymond Earl, 3, 115	8	1:10.40	17,859

Named for one of the nicknames of Louisville: the "River City." River City S. 1983-'86. 6 furlongs 1978-'81. 1 mile 1982-'86. $1\frac{1}{16}$ miles 1987. Dirt 1978-'86, 1988, 1993.

Robert F. Carey Memorial Handicap

Grade 3 in 2006. Hawthorne Race Course, three-year-olds and up, 1 mile, turf. Held September 24, 2005, with a gross value of $150,000. First held in 1983. First graded in 1986. Stakes record 1:33.40 (1998 Soviet Line [Ire]).

Year	Winner	Jockey	Second	Third	Strs	Time	1st Purse
2005	**Spruce Run**, 7, 115	R. A. Stokes III	Fort Prado, 4, 121	Remind, 5, 118	9	1:39.97	$90,000
2004	**Scooter Roach**, 5, 115	J. M. Campbell	Gin and Sin, 4, 116	Cloudy's Knight, 4, 116	9	1:34.51	90,000
2003	**Mystery Giver**, 5, 120	C. H. Marquez Jr.	Al's Dearly Bred, 6, 118	Major Rhythm, 4, 116	8	1:34.70	90,000
2002	**Kimberlite Pipe**, 6, 115	C. A. Emigh	Aslaaf, 4, 114	Major Omansky, 6, 115	10	1:35.94	90,000
2001	**Galic Boy**, 6, 115	R. Sibille	Where's Taylor, 5, 121	Good Journey, 5, 115	10	1:35.10	90,000
2000	**Where's Taylor**, 4, 117	C. J. Lanerie	Dernier Croise (Fr), 5, 113	Associate, 5, 115	11	1:36.31	90,000
1999	**Ray's Approval**, 6, 114	E. Fires	Stay Sound, 4, 115	Inkatha (Fr), 5, 115	9	1:37.01	90,000
1998	**Soviet Line (Ire)**, 8, 115	S. J. Sellers	Fun to Run, 5, 110	Wild Event, 5, 115	10	**1:33.40**	90,000
1997	**Trail City**, 4, 119	J. D. Bailey	Power of Opinion, 4, 113	Da Bull, 5, 114	8	1:36.04	90,000
1996	**Homing Pigeon**, 6, 114	R. Albarado	Joker, 4, 115	Why Change, 3, 115	12	1:36.58	90,000
1995	**Homing Pigeon**, 5, 114	R. Albarado	Gilder, 4, 113	Rare Reason, 4, 119	9	1:38.09	60,000
1994	**Recoup the Cash**, 4, 119	J. L. Diaz	Road of War, 4, 115	Glenfiddich Lad, 5, 114	7	1:40.91	60,000
1993	**High Habitation**, 5, 114	G. C. Retana	Beau Fasa, 7, 114	Glenfiddich Lad, 4, 114	12	1:35.33	60,000
1992	**Double Booked**, 7, 115	J. C. Ferrer	Evanescent, 5, 113	That's Sunny, 7, 114	11	1:39.82	60,000

1991	**Slew the Slewor**, 4, 114	G. K. Gomez	Jalaajel, 7, 118	The Great Carl, 4, 118	9	1:38.72	$96,090
1990	**Allijeba**, 4, 118	K. D. Clark	Wave Wise, 4, 114	Expensive Decision, 4, 118	9	1:39.20	86,070
1989	**Iron Courage**, 5, 121	R. R. Pena	Saint Oxford, 5, 112	Do Loop, 6, 109	10	1:47.00	94,080
1988	**New Colony**, 5, 114	R. R. Douglas	Rio's Lark, 4, 115	Bank Fast, 4, 111	9	1:47.60	93,900
1987	**The Sassman**, 4, 113	K. D. Clark	Zaizoom, 3, 115	Zuppardo's Love, 6, 111	6	2:05.40	89,130
1986	**Pass the Line**, 5, 117	J. L. Diaz	Explosive Darling, 4, 117	Salem Drive, 4, 116	8	2:01.00	94,500
1985	**River Lord**, 6, 111	R. A. Meier	Harham's Sizzler, 6, 118	Attaway to Go, 4, 111	4	2:06.20	63,370
1984	**Ronbra**, 4, 115	C. H. Marquez	Grazie, 4, 115	Bold Run (Fr), 5, 115	12	2:03.80	66,540
1983	**Sir Pele**, 4, 112	O. Vergara	John's Gold, 4, 120	Energetic King, 4, 111	7	1:55.00	64,800

Named for Robert F. Carey (1904-'80), managing director of Hawthorne Race Course (1947-'80). Formerly sponsored by United Airlines of Chicago 1995. Not graded 1990-'97. Robert F. Carey H. 1984-'85. $1\frac{3}{16}$ miles 1983. $1\frac{1}{4}$ miles 1984-'87. $1\frac{1}{8}$ miles 1988-'89. 1 mile 70 yards 1994. Dirt 1985, 1994.

Ruffian Handicap

Grade 1 in 2006. Belmont Park, three-year-olds and up, fillies and mares, $1\frac{1}{16}$ miles, dirt. Held September 11, 2005, with a gross value of $300,000. First held in 1976. First graded in 1976. Stakes record 1:40.35 (2000 Riboletta [Brz]).

Year	Winner	Jockey	Second	Third	Strs	Time	1st Purse
2005	**Stellar Jayne**, 4, 119	J. D. Bailey	Society Selection, 4, 118	Halory Leigh, 5, 116	6	1:41.87	$180,000
2004	**Sightseek**, 5, 122	J. R. Velazquez	Pocus Hocus, 6, 114	Miss Loren (Arg), 6, 117	5	1:41.51	180,000
2003	**Wild Spirit (Chi)**, 4, 121	J. D. Bailey	You, 4, 118	Passing Shot, 4, 115	6	1:41.23	180,000
2002	**Mandy's Gold**, 4, 116	J. A. Santos	You, 3, 117	Shine Again, 5, 117	5	1:42.57	180,000
2000	**Riboletta (Brz)**, 5, 125	C. J. McCarron	Gourmet Girl, 5, 114	Country Hideaway, 4, 114	7	**1:40.35**	150,000
1999	**Catinca**, 4, 119	J. D. Bailey	Furlough, 5, 116	Keeper Hill, 4, 118	5	1:41.94	150,000
1998	**Sharp Cat**, 4, 124	C. S. Nakatani	Furlough, 4, 115	Stop Traffic, 5, 119	8	1:42.48	150,000
1997	**Tomisue's Delight**, 3, 113	J. D. Bailey	Clear Mandate, 5, 119	Mil Kilates, 4, 114	9	1:44.43	150,000
1996	**Yanks Music**, 3, 116	J. R. Velazquez	Serena's Song, 4, 126	Head East, 4, 108	6	1:41.84	150,000
1995	**Inside Information**, 4, 125	M. E. Smith	Unlawful Behavior, 5, 110	Incinerate, 5, 112	6	1:40.98	120,000
1994	**Sky Beauty**, 4, 130	M. E. Smith	Dispute, 4, 117	Educated Risk, 4, 114	5	1:41.79	120,000
1993	**Shared Interest**, 5, 114	R. G. Davis	Dispute, 3, 115	Turnback the Alarm, 4, 123	5	1:41.92	120,000
1992	**Versailles Treaty**, 4, 120	M. E. Smith	Quick Mischief, 6, 116	Nannerl, 5, 119	6	1:41.41	120,000
1991	**Queena**, 5, 120	A. T. Cordero Jr.	Sharp Dance, 5, 114	Lady d'Accord, 4, 113	7	1:41.65	120,000
1990	**Quick Mischief**, 4, 111	R. I. Rojas	Personal Business, 4, 113	Mistaurian, 4, 115	9	1:42.80	144,480
1989	**Bayakoa (Arg)**, 5, 125	L. A. Pincay Jr.	Colonial Waters, 4, 118	Open Mind, 3, 120	6	1:48.40	135,840
1988	**Sham Say**, 3, 113	J. Vasquez	Classic Crown, 3, 115	Make Change, 3, 114	11	1:48.00	146,400
1987	**‡Coup de Fusil**, 5, 117	A. T. Cordero Jr.	Clabber Girl, 4, 112	Sacahuista, 3, 114	12	1:48.60	149,760
1986	**Lady's Secret**, 4, 129	P. Day	Steal a Kiss, 3, 109	Endear, 4, 119	6	1:46.80	165,240
1985	**Lady's Secret**, 3, 116	J. Velasquez	Isayso, 6, 115	Sintrillium, 7, 118	6	1:47.40	128,880
1984	**Heatherten**, 5, 118	R. P. Romero	Miss Oceana, 3, 119	Adored, 4, 123	7	1:48.20	103,320
1983	**Heartlight No. One**, 3, 117	L. A. Pincay Jr.	Mochila, 4, 113	Try Something New, 4, 116	12	1:47.20	103,140
1982	**Christmas Past**, 3, 117	J. Vasquez	Mademoiselle Forli, 3, 112	Love Sign, 5, 123	8	1:48.60	100,080
1981	**Relaxing**, 5, 123	A. T. Cordero Jr.	Love Sign, 4, 120	Jameela, 5, 122	4	1:47.60	97,020
1980	**Genuine Risk**, 3, 118	J. Vasquez	Misty Gallore, 4, 124	It's in the Air, 4, 118	6	1:49.20	81,900
1979	**It's in the Air**, 3, 122	L. A. Pincay Jr.	Blitey, 3, 113	Waya (Fr), 5, 126	4	1:47.40	79,875
1978	**Late Bloomer**, 4, 122	J. Velasquez	Pearl Necklace, 4, 124	Tempest Queen, 3, 117	9	1:47.00	64,860
1977	**Cum Laude Laurie**, 3, 114	A. T. Cordero Jr.	Mississippi Mud, 4, 123	Cascapedia, 4, 128	12	1:52.20	66,480
1976	**Revidere**, 3, 118	J. Vasquez	*Bastonera II, 5, 123	Optimistic Gal, 3, 118	5	2:01.00	79,425

Named for Locust Hill Farm's 1974 champion two-year-old filly, '75 champion three-year-old filly, and '75 filly triple crown winner Ruffian (1972 f. by Reviewer); Ruffian is buried in the Belmont infield. Ruffian S. 1976. Not held due to World Trade Center attack 2001. $1\frac{1}{4}$ miles 1976. $1\frac{1}{8}$ miles 1977-'89. ‡Sacahuista finished first, DQ to third, 1987.

Sabin Handicap

Grade 3 in 2006. Gulfstream Park, three-year-olds and up, fillies and mares, $1\frac{1}{8}$ miles, dirt. Held February 18, 2006, with a gross value of $100,000. First held in 1991. First graded in 1994. Stakes record 1:50.49 (2006 Taittinger Rose).

Year	Winner	Jockey	Second	Third	Strs	Time	1st Purse
2006	**Taittinger Rose**, 5, 115	E. S. Prado	Mocita, 4, 119	Darling Daughter, 5, 116	6	**1:50.49**	$60,000
2005	**Isola Piu Bella (Chi)**, 5, 116	J. R. Velazquez	Pampered Princess, 5, 117	Adobe Gold, 4, 116	5	1:50.68	60,000
2004	**Roar Emotion**, 4, 116	J. R. Velazquez	Nonsuch Bay, 5, 115	Lead Story, 5, 119	9	1:43.32	60,000
2003	**Allamerican Bertie**, 4, 120	J. D. Bailey	Small Promises, 5, 112	Redoubled Miss, 4, 114	11	1:42.49	60,000
2002	**Miss Linda (Arg)**, 5, 119	R. Migliore	Forest Secrets, 4, 117	Tap Dance, 4, 113	12	1:42.61	60,000
2001	**De Bertie**, 4, 115	J. F. Chavez	Royal Fair, 5, 113	Frankly My Dear, 4, 116	8	1:44.74	60,000
2000	**Brushed Halory**, 4, 115	M. E. Smith	Roza Robata, 5, 115	Mop Squeezer, 4, 113	5	1:41.84	45,000
1999	**Timely Broad**, 5, 115	N. J. Petro	Highfalutin, 5, 116	Mudslinger, 4, 116	9	1:42.50	45,000
1998	**Radiant Megan**, 5, 113	J. A. Krone	Escena, 5, 119	Biding Time, 4, 113	7	1:41.25	45,000
1997	**Rare Blend**, 4, 120	J. D. Bailey	Golden Gale, 4, 113	Termly, 4, 112	7	1:41.28	45,000
1996	**Lindsay Frolic**, 4, 117	P. Day	Investalot, 5, 114	Queen Tutta, 4, 113	8	1:43.70	45,000
1995	**Recognizable**, 4, 115	M. E. Smith	Jade Flush, 4, 113	Sambacarioca, 6, 118	8	1:42.50	45,000
1994	**Hunzinga**, 5, 113	J. E. Felix	Nine Keys, 4, 114	Pleasant Jolie, 6, 112	9	1:39.57	45,000
1993	**Now Dance**, 4, 113	M. Guidry	Spinning Round, 4, 115	Luv Me Luv Me Not, 4, 117	10	1:41.68	30,000
1992	**Lemhi Go**, 4, 113	R. N. Lester	Trumpet's Blare, 5, 114	Tappanzee, 4, 114	8	1:44.79	45,000
1991	**Fit for a Queen**, 5, 114	J. D. Bailey	Trumpet's Blare, 4, 114	Express Star, 5, 116	9	1:42.50	46,020

Named for Henryk de Kwiatkowski's 1984 Orchid H. (G2) winner Sabin (1980 f. by Lyphard). Sabin Breeders' Cup H. 1991. 1 mile 70 yards 1993-2000. $1\frac{1}{16}$ miles 1991-'92, 2001-'04.

Safely Kept Breeders' Cup Stakes

Grade 3 in 2006. Laurel Park, three-year-olds, fillies, 6 furlongs, dirt. Held October 16, 2005, with a gross value of $131,500. First held in 1986. First graded in 1990. Stakes record 1:09.21 (1999 Godmother).

Year	Winner	Jockey	Second	Third	Strs	Time	1st Purse
2005	**Trickle of Gold**, 3, 116	J. Rose	Maddalena, 3, 120	Partners Due, 3, 116	5	1:10.45	$90,000
2004	**Bending Strings**, 3, 119	H. Karamanos	Smokey Glacken, 3, 119	Then She Laughs, 3, 117	6	1:10.11	90,000
2003	**Randaroo**, 3, 119	H. Castillo Jr.	Follow Me Home, 3, 117	Awesome Charm, 3, 115	8	1:10.54	90,000
2002	**Miss Lodi**, 3, 117	R. Fogelsonger	For Rubies, 3, 117	Wilzada, 3, 117	8	1:11.20	60,000
2000	**Swept Away**, 3, 122	J. Beasley	Another, 3, 115	Cat Cay, 3, 117	8	1:09.51	60,000
1999	**Godmother**, 3, 117	M. G. Pino	Superduper Miss, 3, 117	Rills, 3, 113	7	**1:09.21**	60,000
1998	**Hair Spray**, 3, 117	J. A. Velez Jr.	Expensive Issue, 3, 115	Ninth Inning, 3, 119	8	1:10.67	66,390
1997	**Weather Vane**, 3, 119	M. G. Pino	Vegas Prospector, 3, 117	Requesting More, 3, 115	7	1:10.21	64,800
1996	**J J'sdream**, 3, 122	M. G. Pino	Flat Fleet Feet, 3, 119	Rare Blend, 3, 122	5	1:09.45	60,000
1995	**Broad Smile**, 3, 117	J. Brown	Scotzanna, 3, 122	Shebatim's Trick, 3, 115	7	1:10.30	60,000
1994	**Twist Afleet**, 3, 117	D. Carr	Penny's Reshoot, 3, 117	Our Royal Blue, 3, 114	7	1:10.88	60,000
1993	**Miss Indy Anna**, 3, 113	D. B. Thomas	Ann Dear, 3, 113	Lily of the North, 3, 113	7	1:10.12	60,000
1992	**Meafara**, 3, 119	B. Swatuk	Squirm, 3, 122	Super Doer, 3, 122	6	1:10.55	60,000
1991	**Missy's Mirage**, 3, 119	W. H. McCauley	Withallprobability, 3, 122	Corporate Fund, 3, 114	5	1:10.53	60,000
1990	**Voodoo Lily**, 3, 117	K. Desormeaux	Miss Spentyouth, 3, 119	Catchamenot, 3, 114	8	1:10.60	60,000
1989	**Safely Kept**, 3, 122	C. Perret	Cojinx, 3, 119	Kathleen the Queen, 3, 117	5	1:11.20	60,000
1988	**Clever Power**, 3, 120	J. A. Krone	Lake Valley, 3, 120	Ready Jet Go, 3, 120	8	1:16.40	65,000
1987	**Endless Surprise**, 4, 118	K. Desormeaux	Bea Quality, 5, 120	Miracle Wood, 4, 111	7	1:17.40	28,340
1986	**Debtor's Prison**, 5, 108	D. Byrnes	Night Above, 4, 117	Bea Quality, 4, 114	6	1:11.40	28,178

Named for Jayeff "B" Stables's and Barry Weisbord's 1989 champion sprinter and '89 Columbia S. winner Safely Kept (1986 f. by Horatius). Formerly named for the nearby city of Columbia, Maryland. Columbia H. 1986-'87. Columbia S. 1988-'95. Held at Laurel Park 1988, 1990, 1998-2000. Held at Colonial Downs 1997. Not held 2001. 6½ furlongs 1988.

Salvator Mile Handicap

Grade 3 in 2006. Monmouth Park, three-year-olds and up, 1 mile, dirt. Held July 24, 2005, with a gross value of $150,000. First held in 1894. First graded in 1973. Stakes record 1:34.46 (1991 Peanut Butter Onit).

Year	Winner	Jockey	Second	Third	Strs	Time	1st Purse
2005	**Cherokee's Boy**, 5, 117	A. T. Gryder	Aggadan, 6, 117	Gygistar, 6, 119	5	1:36.79	$90,000
2004	**Presidentialaffair**, 5, 117	S. Elliott	Unforgettable Max, 4, 117	Roaring Fever, 4, 115	5	1:35.27	60,000
2003	**Vinemeister**, 4, 114	J. A. Velez Jr.	Jersey Giant, 4, 117	Highway Prospector, 6, 113	6	1:35.89	60,000
2002	**‡Sea of Tranquility**, 6, 120	J. C. Ferrer	Free of Love, 4, 117	First Lieutenant, 5, 114	8	1:36.12	60,000
2001	**Sea of Tranquility**, 5, 115	J. C. Ferrer	Knock Again, 4, 112	Hal's Hope, 4, 117	7	1:36.74	90,000
2000	**Leave It to Beezer**, 7, 120	R. E. Alvarado Jr.	Delaware Township, 4, 112	Prime Directive, 4, 114	5	1:37.29	90,000
1999	**Truluck**, 4, 115	J. Bravo	Rock and Roll, 4, 119	Siftaway, 4, 114	6	1:35.18	90,000
1998	**El Amante**, 5, 119	J. A. Krone	Stormin Fever, 4, 117	Gold Token, 5, 114	8	1:34.95	60,000
1997	**Distorted Humor**, 4, 114	J. A. Krone	Wild Deputy, 4, 114	Smooth the Loot, 4, 113	4	1:36.03	60,000
1996	**Smart Strike**, 4, 113	S. Hawley	Cozy Drive, 4, 113	November Sunset, 4, 115	10	1:36.28	60,000
1995	**Schossberg**, 5, 116	D. Penna	Cast Iron, 4, 110	Relentless Star, 5, 109	9	1:35.86	45,000
1994	**Storm Tower**, 4, 119	R. Wilson	Cold Digger, 7, 113	Koluctoo Jimmy Al, 4, 114	6	1:36.26	45,000
1993	**Dusty Screen**, 5, 117	E. L. King Jr.	Count New York, 4, 112	Root Boy, 5, 118	8	1:35.86	45,000
1992	**Peanut Butter Onit**, 6, 120	A. T. Gryder	Root Boy, 4, 114	He Is Risen, 4, 118	7	1:36.21	45,000
1991	**Peanut Butter Onit**, 5, 115	W. S. Ramos	Private School, 4, 114	Runaway Stream, 4, 116	8	**1:34.46**	45,000
1990	**Shy Tom**, 4, 115	J. A. Krone	Bill E. Shears, 5, 121	Pete the Chief, 4, 115	5	1:36.00	49,020
1989	**Bill E. Shears**, 4, 112	R. Hernandez	Festive, 4, 110	Mi Selecto, 4, 117	6	1:35.40	49,890
1988	**Slew City Slew**, 4, 116	M. Castaneda	Bet Twice, 4, 125	Matthews Keep, 4, 116	5	1:35.00	38,880
1987	**Moment of Hope**, 4, 118	M. Venezia	Owens Troupe, 4, 117	Entitled To, 5, 116	6	1:34.60	33,270
1986	**Jyp**, 5, 115	J. Rocco	Minneapple, 4, 119	Valiant Lark, 6, 117	7	1:35.80	33,300
1985	**Valiant Lark**, 5, 116	V. A. Bracciale Jr.	Pat's Addition, 5, 115	Rumptious, 5, 116	10	1:36.00	33,990
1984	**Rumptious**, 4, 115	W. H. McCauley	English Master, 4, 112	World Appeal, 4, 122	10	1:34.60	34,260
1983	**Naughty Jimmy**, 6, 114	L. Saumell	Castle Guard, 4, 115	Star Gallant, 4, 120	7	1:37.00	33,510
1982	**Count His Fleet**, 4, 116	W. Nemeti	Explosive Bid, 4, 117	Accipiter's Hope, 4, 116	12	1:35.40	35,070
1981	**Colonel Moran**, 4, 117	C. Perret	Sun Catcher, 4, 120	Pikotazo (Mex), 4, 117	12	1:35.60	35,190
1980	**Convenient**, 4, 114	V. A. Bracciale Jr.	Tunerup, 4, 113	Foretake, 4, 113	8	1:36.60	26,640
1979	**‡Revivalist**, 5, 122	D. MacBeth	Horatius, 4, 120	Nice Catch, 5, 120	9	1:35.40	25,578
1978	**Do Tell George**, 5, 113	B. Mize	Buckfinder, 4, 118	Get Permission, 5, 114	5	1:36.40	17,664
1977	**Peppy Addy**, 5, 120	B. Phelps	Resound, 5, 115	Break Up the Game, 6, 117	8	1:36.00	18,168
1976	**Royal Glint**, 6, 126	J. E. Tejeira	Talc, 4, 113	Peppy Addy, 4, 118	9	1:35.20	18,395
1975	**Proper Bostonian**, 5, 117	M. Miceli	Rastaferian, 6, 113	Orbit Round, 4, 110	8	1:36.20	14,576
	Mongongo, 6, 119	B. Thornburg	Good John, 5, 114	Silver Hope, 4, 116	8	1:36.20	14,576
1974	**Okavango**, 4, 112	W. Blum	Hey Rube, 4, 114	Escaped, 5, 113	9	1:35.80	18,265
1973	**Prince of Truth**, 5, 117	W. Blum	Windtex, 4, 116	New Alibhai, 5, 115	7	1:35.80	17,761

Named for James Ben Ali Haggin's 1890 Monmouth Cup winner Salvator (1886 c. by *Prince Charlie); in 1890 he set an American record for one mile at Monmouth Park that stood for 28 years. Salvator Mile S. 1957, 1997. Two divisions 1975. ‡Nice Catch finished first, DQ to third, 1979. ‡First Lieutenant finished first, DQ to third, 2002.

San Antonio Handicap

Grade 2 in 2006. Santa Anita Park, four-year-olds and up, 1⅛ miles, dirt. Held February 5, 2006, with a gross value of $250,000. First held in 1935. First graded in 1973. Stakes record 1:46.20 (1978 Vigors).

Year	Winner	Jockey	Second	Third	Strs	Time	1st Purse
2006	**Spellbinder**, 5, 114	M. A. Pedroza	With Distinction, 5, 115	Wilko, 4, 116	8	1:48.84	$150,000
2005	**Lundy's Liability (Brz)**, 5, 119	D. R. Flores	Truly a Judge, 7, 118	Congrats, 5, 116	9	1:49.05	150,000
2004	**Pleasantly Perfect**, 6, 121	A. O. Solis	Star Cross (Arg), 7, 114	Fleetstreet Dancer, 6, 116	4	1:47.25	150,000
2003	**Congaree**, 5, 123	J. D. Bailey	Milwaukee Brew, 6, 120	Pleasantly Perfect, 5, 117	6	1:47.60	150,000
2002	**Redattore (Brz)**, 7, 116	A. O. Solis	Euchre, 6, 119	Irisheyesareflying, 6, 117	7	1:48.66	150,000
2001	**Guided Tour**, 5, 115	L. J. Melancon	Lethal Instrument, 5, 116	Moonlight Charger, 6, 113	8	1:48.70	180,000
2000	**Budroyale**, 7, 121	G. K. Gomez	Cat Thief, 4, 120	Elaborate, 5, 116	5	1:48.70	180,000
1999	**Free House**, 5, 123	C. J. McCarron	Malek (Chi), 6, 119	Dramatic Gold, 8, 116	4	1:48.54	180,000
1998	**Gentlemen (Arg)**, 6, 124	G. L. Stevens	Da Bull, 6, 115	Refinado Tom (Arg), 5, 120	5	1:47.60	180,000
1997	**Gentlemen (Arg)**, 5, 122	G. L. Stevens	Alphabet Soup, 6, 122	Kingdom Found, 7, 116	5	1:47.38	180,300
1996	**Alphabet Soup**, 5, 119	C. W. Antley	Soul of the Matter, 5, 121	Dare and Go, 5, 119	5	1:49.96	184,900
1995	**Best Pal**, 7, 121	C. J. McCarron	Slew of Damascus, 7, 119	Tossofthecoin, 5, 117	10	1:47.43	148,500
1994	**The Wicked North**, 5, 116	K. Desormeaux	‡Region, 5, 117	Hill Pass, 5, 116	9	1:47.48	155,500
1993	**Marquetry**, 6, 117	E. Delahoussaye	Sir Beaufort, 6, 120	Reign Road, 5, 116	6	1:48.96	155,500
1992	**Ibero (Arg)**, 5, 115	A. O. Solis	In Excess (Ire), 5, 123	Cobra Classic, 5, 114	8	1:47.05	189,750
1991	**Farma Way**, 4, 118	G. L. Stevens	Anshan (GB), 4, 116	dh-Festin (Arg), 5, 116 dh-Louis Cyphre (Ire), 5, 111	9	1:47.30	196,750
1990	**Criminal Type**, 5, 117	A. O. Solis	Stylish Winner, 6, 113	Ruhlmann, 5, 122	7	1:49.00	190,500
1989	**Super Diamond**, 9, 121	L. A. Pincay Jr.	Frankly Perfect, 4, 116	Cherokee Colony, 4, 120	7	1:48.80	159,600
1988	**Judge Angelucci**, 5, 122	E. Delahoussaye	Ferdinand, 5, 128	Crimson Slew, 4, 115	6	1:48.60	156,700
1987	**Bedside Promise**, 5, 121	G. L. Stevens	Hopeful Word, 6, 118	Bruiser (GB), 4, 114	9	1:47.20	129,600
1986	**Hatim**, 5, 117	L. A. Pincay Jr.	Right Con, 4, 117	Nostalgia's Star, 4, 118	8	1:47.40	128,700
1985	**Lord At War (Arg)**, 5, 122	W. Shoemaker	Al Mamoon, 4, 114	Hail Bold King, 4, 122	7	1:48.20	125,200
1984	**Poley**, 5, 120	C. J. McCarron	Water Bank, 5, 117	Danebo, 5, 122	9	1:48.00	156,900
1983	**Bates Motel**, 4, 114	T. Lipham	Time to Explode, 4, 121	It's the One, 5, 124	10	1:47.00	132,300
1982	**Score Twenty Four**, 5, 115	P. A. Valenzuela	Super Moment, 5, 124	High Counsel, 4, 114	6	1:47.80	124,200
1981	**Flying Paster**, 5, 126	C. J. McCarron	‡Doonesbury, 4, 121	King Go Go, 6, 119	5	1:46.60	91,700
1980	**Beau's Eagle**, 4, 121	D. Pierce	Relaunch, 4, 117	Double Discount, 7, 114	6	1:48.40	79,650
1979	**Tiller**, 5, 121	A. T. Cordero Jr.	Painted Wagon, 6, 114	‡Life's Hope, 6, 120	6	1:47.00	65,800
1978	**Vigors**, 5, 121	D. G. McHargue	Ancient Title, 8, 120	Double Discount, 5, 116	7	**1:46.20**	67,100
1977	**Ancient Title**, 7, 119	S. Hawley	Double Discount, 4, 115	Properantes, 4, 114	10	1:47.80	72,500
1976	**Lightning Mandate**, 5, 118	A. T. Cordero Jr.	Dancing Papa, 6, 117	Messenger of Song, 4, 122	10	1:48.20	54,350
1975	**Cheriepe**, 5, 120	A. Santiago	First Back, 4, 117	Ancient Title, 5, 128	9	1:46.80	52,850
1974	**Prince Dantan**, 4, 116	L. A. Pincay Jr.	Forage, 5, 119	Dancing Papa, 4, 116	8	1:47.60	51,550
1973	**Kennedy Road**, 5, 119	D. Pierce	Crusading, 5, 119	Big Spruce, 4, 117	6	1:47.60	49,400

Named for seven California land grants, each of which was called Rancho San Antonio; two were in Los Angeles County, one is now Beverly Hills. Grade 1 1983-'89. San Antonio S. 1968-'82. Not held 1941-'45. 1¹⁄₁₆ miles 1940. Three-year-olds and up 1946, 1948, 1950-'52, 1956, 1958, 1960. Dead heat for third 1991. ‡Mr. Redoy finished third, DQ to sixth, 1979. ‡King Go Go finished second, DQ to third, 1981. ‡Hill Pass finished second, DQ to third, 1994. Equaled track record 1940.

San Carlos Handicap

Grade 2 in 2006. Santa Anita Park, four-year-olds and up, 7 furlongs, dirt. Held February 18, 2006, with a gross value of $150,000. First held in 1935. First graded in 1973. Stakes record 1:20.20 (1981 Flying Paster).

Year	Winner	Jockey	Second	Third	Strs	Time	1st Purse
2006	**Surf Cat**, 4, 117	A. O. Solis	Major Success, 5, 118	Oceanus (Brz), 7, 114	8	1:22.09	$90,000
2005	**Hasty Kris**, 8, 115	R. R. Douglas	Harvard Avenue, 4, 115	Perfect Moon, 4, 117	8	1:21.42	90,000
2004	**Pico Central (Brz)**, 5, 116	D. R. Flores	Publication, 5, 116	Pohave, 6, 112	10	1:21.16	90,000
2003	**Aldebaran**, 5, 116	J. Valdivia Jr.	Crafty C. T., 5, 116	Grey Memo, 6, 116	6	1:21.53	120,000
2002	**Snow Ridge**, 4, 118	M. E. Smith	Alyzig, 5, 112	Grey Memo, 5, 114	6	1:22.02	90,000
2001	**Kona Gold**, 7, 125	A. O. Solis	Blade Prospector (Brz), 6, 113	Grey Memo, 4, 115	7	1:21.35	90,000
2000	**Son of a Pistol**, 8, 117	G. K. Gomez	Kona Gold, 6, 122	Old Topper, 5, 116	6	1:22.11	96,930
1999	**Big Jag**, 6, 118	J. Valdivia Jr.	Kona Gold, 5, 120	Dramatic Gold, 8, 117	5	1:21.18	90,000
1998	**Reality Road**, 6, 116	C. J. McCarron	Gold Land, 7, 116	Son of a Pistol, 6, 114	10	1:21.62	100,530
1997	**Northern Afleet**, 4, 117	C. J. McCarron	Hesabull, 4, 117	High Stakes Player, 5, 120	7	1:21.45	97,700
1996	**Kingdom Found**, 6, 116	C. J. McCarron	Lakota Brave, 7, 114	Lit de Justice, 6, 123	8	1:22.23	98,850
1995	**Softshoe Sure Shot**, 9, 113	A. O. Solis	Ferrara, 4, 115	Subtle Trouble, 4, 113	7	1:21.46	91,600
1994	**Cardmania**, 8, 122	E. Delahoussaye	The Wicked North, 5, 117	Portoferraio (Arg), 6, 115	7	1:21.23	63,900
1993	**Sir Beaufort**, 6, 120	C. J. McCarron	Cardmania, 7, 117	Excavate, 5, 114	6	1:22.22	62,900
1992	**Answer Do**, 6, 120	G. L. Stevens	Individualist, 5, 115	Media Plan, 4, 116	7	1:21.23	63,700
1991	**Farma Way**, 4, 115	G. L. Stevens	Yes I'm Blue, 5, 117	Tanker Port, 6, 117	7	1:21.50	63,500
1990	**Raise a Stanza**, 4, 117	R. A. Baze	Oraibi, 5, 119	Tanker Port, 5, 117	8	1:21.60	64,500
1989	**Cherokee Colony**, 4, 119	R. Q. Meza	On the Line, 5, 126	Happy in Space, 5, 116	6	1:20.60	62,800
1988	**Epidaurus**, 6, 117	P. A. Valenzuela	Super Diamond, 8, 125	Lord Ruckus, 5, 118	7	1:22.00	63,500
1987	**Zany Tactics**, 6, 118	J. L. Kaenel	Bolder Than Bold, 5, 116	Epidaurus, 5, 115	8	1:22.40	65,600
1986	**Phone Trick**, 4, 125	L. A. Pincay Jr.	Temerity Prince, 6, 122	My Habitony, 6, 117	6	1:20.80	78,200
1985	**Debonaire Junior**, 4, 125	C. J. McCarron	Tennessee Rite, 4, 112	Fifty Six Ina Row, 4, 116	6	1:21.60	64,300

1984	**Danebo**, 5, 117	L. A. Pincay Jr.	Pac Mania, 4, 118	Poley, 5, 119	7	1:21.00	$54,900
1983	**Kangroo Court**, 6, 118	J. J. Steiner	Dave's Friend, 8, 117	Shanekite, 5, 118	6	1:21.00	49,550
1982	**Solo Guy**, 4, 118	W. Shoemaker	‡Smokite, 6, 116	King Go Go, 7, 119	8	1:20.80	60,700
1981	**Flying Paster**, 5, 124	C. J. McCarron	To B. Or Not, 5, 123	Double Discount, 8, 115	8	**1:20.20**	51,550
1980	**Handsomeness**, 4, 118	L. A. Pincay Jr.	Relaunch, 4, 121	Beau's Eagle, 4, 125	5	1:24.00	49,100
1979	**O Big Al**, 4, 120	D. G. McHargue	Maheras, 6, 122	Bad 'n Big, 5, 124	7	1:22.20	40,800
1978	**Double Discount**, 5, 117	F. Mena	Impressive Luck, 5, 120	Romantic Lead, 5, 117	6	1:22.00	32,650
1977	**Uniformity**, 5, 115	F. Toro	†My Juliet, 5, 123	Messenger of Song, 5, 122	7	1:21.60	34,050
1976	**No Bias**, 6, 120	L. A. Pincay Jr.	Century's Envoy, 5, 126	Bahia Key, 6, 120	5	1:21.80	32,200
1975	**Ancient Title**, 5, 128	L. A. Pincay Jr.	dh-Bahia Key, 5, 117 dh-Hudson County, 4, 116		12	1:21.20	37,750
1974	**Royal Owl**, 5, 117	L. A. Pincay Jr.	Soft Victory, 6, 116	Against the Snow, 4, 112	9	1:23.40	35,600
1973	**‡Crusading**, 5, 119	F. Toro	Kennedy Road, 5, 117	*Figonero, 8, 114	8	1:20.80	33,850

Named for Rancho El Potrero de San Carlos in Monterey County, California. Grade 1 2001-'03. Not held 1942-'45, 1960. 1$^1/_{16}$ miles 1935-'39. Three-year-olds and up 1946, 1949-'52, 1954-'59. Dead heat for second 1975. ‡Kennedy Road finished first, DQ to second, 1973. ‡King Go Go finished second, DQ to third, 1982. †Denotes female.

San Clemente Handicap

Grade 2 in 2006. Del Mar, three-year-olds, fillies, 1 mile, turf. Held July 30, 2005, with a gross value of $150,000. First held in 1950. First graded in 1994. Stakes record 1:33.62 (2003 Katdogawn [GB]).

Year	Winner	Jockey	Second	Third	Strs	Time	1st Purse
2005	**Shining Energy**, 3, 117	R. R. Douglas	dh-Memorette, 3, 119 dh-Royal Copenhagen (Fr), 3, 117		10	1:34.25	$90,000
2004	**Sweet Win**, 3, 114	V. Espinoza	Miss Vegas (Ire), 3, 121	Victory U. S. A., 3, 119	5	1:34.11	90,000
2003	**Katdogawn (GB)**, 3, 116	J. A. Krone	Atlantic Ocean, 3, 120	Buffythecenterfold, 3, 118	9	**1:33.62**	90,000
2002	**Little Treasure (Fr)**, 3, 117	K. Desormeaux	Pina Colada (GB), 3, 115	Arabic Song (Ire), 3, 118	9	1:33.97	90,000
2001	**Reine de Romance (Ire)**, 3, 116	E. Delahoussaye	Gabriellina Giof (GB), 3, 116	La Vida Loca (Ire), 3, 116	8	1:34.88	90,000
2000	**Uncharted Haven (GB)**, 3, 116	A. O. Solis	Automated, 3, 117	Islay Mist (GB), 3, 118	10	1:35.13	90,000
1999	**Sweet Ludy (Ire)**, 3, 118	C. S. Nakatani	Caffe Latte (Ire), 3, 115	Sweet Life, 3, 117	10	1:35.02	90,000
1998	**Sicy d'Alsace (Fr)**, 3, 115	C. S. Nakatani	Miss Hot Salsa, 3, 117	Tranquility Lake, 3, 114	10	1:34.97	67,500
1997	**Famous Digger**, 3, 120	B. Blanc	Cozy Blues, 3, 116	Really Happy, 3, 119	10	1:36.00	71,725
1996	**True Flare**, 3, 116	C. S. Nakatani	Gastronomical, 3, 119	Najecam, 3, 114	10	1:35.59	67,200
1995	**Jewel Princess**, 3, 115	C. J. McCarron	Auriette (Ire), 3, 119	Scratch Paper, 3, 119	6	1:36.12	59,650
1994	**Work the Crowd**, 3, 120	C. J. McCarron	Pharma, 3, 116	Dancing Mirage, 3, 115	8	1:36.07	48,550
1993	**Hollywood Wildcat**, 3, 120	E. Delahoussaye	Miami Sands (Ire), 3, 116	Beal Street Blues, 3, 117	10	1:34.89	49,950
1992	**Golden Treat**, 3, 121	K. Desormeaux	Morriston Belle, 3, 118	Alysbelle, 3, 118	8	1:35.20	49,350
1991	**Flawlessly**, 3, 120	C. J. McCarron	Gold Fleece, 3, 114	Miss High Blade, 3, 117	9	1:34.88	64,600
1990	**Nijinsky's Lover**, 3, 118	G. L. Stevens	Bimbo (GB), 3, 113	Slew of Pearls, 3, 116	9	1:36.40	50,300
	Lonely Girl, 3, 116	P. A. Valenzuela	Bel's Starlet, 3, 114	Bidder Cream, 3, 113	9	1:36.20	50,300
1989	**Darby's Daughter**, 3, 120	G. L. Stevens	Sticky Wile, 3, 117	Bel Darling, 3, 116	9	1:36.60	66,000
1988	**Do So**, 3, 121	A. O. Solis	Affordable Price, 3, 115	Variety Baby, 3, 117	8	1:35.80	50,650
1987	**Davie's Lamb**, 3, 115	F. Toro	Develop, 3, 114	Wild Manor, 3, 116	7	1:42.80	25,500
	Future Bright, 3, 114	P. A. Valenzuela	Chapel of Dreams, 3, 114	Down Again, 3, 116	7	1:44.60	25,300
1986	**Our Sweet Sham**, 3, 114	S. B. Soto	Mille Et Une, 3, 115	T. V. Residual, 3, 115	10	1:43.20	33,450
1985	**Mint Leaf**, 3, 122	C. J. McCarron	Queen of Bronze, 3, 115	Stakes to Win, 3, 117	10	1:42.60	33,650
1984	**Fashionably Late**, 3, 117	C. J. McCarron	Auntie Betty, 3, 117	Patricia James, 3, 114	8	1:43.20	32,800
1983	**Eastern Bettor**, 3, 113	R. Q. Meza	Nice 'n Proper, 3, 117	Olympic Bronze, 3, 116	9	1:44.00	25,875
	Lituya Bay, 3, 121	L. A. Pincay Jr.	Corselette, 3, 116	Capitalization, 3, 115	8	1:43.80	25,375
1982	**Northern Style**, 3, 114	M. Castaneda	Mama Tia, 3, 116	Marl Lee Ann, 3, 115	7	1:43.40	32,200
1981	**French Charmer**, 3, 118	D. G. McHargue	Tap Dancer (Fr), 3, 113	I Got Speed, 3, 121	9	1:44.20	26,850
1980	**Plenty O'Toole**, 3, 116	T. Lipham	Potter, 3, 115	Swift Bird, 3, 113	10	1:44.20	27,050
1979	**Ancient Art**, 3, 121	F. Toro	Our Suiti Pie, 3, 116	Double Deceit, 3, 117	9	1:44.20	23,550
1978	**Miss Magnetic**, 3, 117	M. Castaneda	Secala, 3, 112	Agree, 3, 114	9	1:44.20	13,550
	Joe's Bee, 3, 120	L. A. Pincay Jr.	Fairy Dance, 3, 117	Carrie's Angel, 3, 115	7	1:44.40	13,150
1977	**Teisen Lap**, 3, 113	D. G. McHargue	Goldfilled, 3, 112	Lullaby, 3, 120	8	1:44.80	12,850
1976	**Go March**, 3, 114	D. Pierce	Granja Sueno, 3, 112	I Going, 3, 115	8	1:42.80	13,150
1975	**Miss Francesca**, 3, 113	D. G. McHargue	Summer Evening, 3, 115	Bradley's Pago, 3, 113	8	1:43.20	10,475
	‡Princess Papulee, 3, 121	F. Toro	Mia Amore, 3, 121	Miracolo, 3, 113	7	1:43.80	10,275
1974	**Bold Ballet**, 3, 121	F. Toro	Shah's Envoy, 3, 121	Sweet Ramblin Rose, 3, 116	9	1:44.00	13,350
1973	**Button Top**, 3, 112	S. Valdez	Merry Madeleine, 3, 120	Gourmet Lark, 3, 117	5	1:43.80	12,750

Named for San Clemente, California, located in Orange County. Grade 3 1994-'95. Not held 1951-'69. 1$^1/_{16}$ miles 1950, 1970-'87. Dirt 1950. Two divisions 1975, 1978, 1983, 1987, 1990. Dead heat for second 2005. ‡Mia Amore finished first, DQ to second, 1975 (2nd Div.). Non-winners of a race worth $10,000 to the winner 1973-'74. Non-winners of a race worth $12,500 to the winner 1975.

San Diego Handicap

Grade 2 in 2006. Del Mar, three-year-olds and up, 1$^1/_{16}$ miles, dirt. Held July 24, 2005, with a gross value of $250,000. First held in 1937. First graded in 1983. Stakes record 1:40 (1965 Native Diver).

Year	Winner	Jockey	Second	Third	Strs	Time	1st Purse
2005	**Choctaw Nation**, 5, 115	V. Espinoza	Ace Blue (Brz), 5, 117	Preachinatthebar, 4, 115	6	1:42.40	$150,000
2004	**Choctaw Nation**, 4, 114	V. Espinoza	Pleasantly Perfect, 6, 124	During, 4, 118	7	1:42.32	150,000
2003	**Taste of Paradise**, 4, 113	V. Espinoza	Gondolieri (Chi), 4, 117	Reba's Gold, 6, 116	8	1:42.62	150,000

2002	**Grey Memo**, 5, 116	E. Delahoussaye	Euchre, 6, 116	Congaree, 4, 120	8	1:43.48	$150,000
2001	**Skimming**, 5, 120	G. K. Gomez	Futural, 5, 120	Captain Steve, 4, 122	7	1:41.62	150,000
2000	**Skimming**, 4, 112	G. K. Gomez	Prime Timber, 4, 116	National Saint, 4, 117	7	1:41.06	150,000
1999	**Mazel Trick**, 4, 117	C. J. McCarron	River Keen (Ire), 7, 116	Tibado, 5, 116	4	1:40.68	150,000
1998	**Mud Route**, 4, 117	C. J. McCarron	Hal's Pal (GB), 5, 113	Benchmark, 7, 117	5	1:41.11	150,300
1997	**Northern Afleet**, 4, 118	C. J. McCarron	Benchmark, 6, 117	New Century, 5, 114	9	1:41.80	100,300
1996	**Savinio**, 6, 116	C. W. Antley	Misnomer, 4, 114	Nonproductiveasset, 6, 118	6	1:40.82	95,350
1995	**Blumin Affair**, 4, 116	C. J. McCarron	Rapan Boy (Aus), 7, 116	Luthier Fever, 4, 115	4	1:41.29	87,200
1994	**Kingdom Found**, 4, 116	C. J. McCarron	Tossofthecoin, 4, 117	Rapan Boy (Aus), 6, 115	6	1:41.21	75,850
1993	**Fanatic Boy (Arg)**, 6, 115	C. J. McCarron	Memo (Chi), 6, 116	Missionary Ridge (GB), 6, 116	5	1:48.59	74,450
1992	**Another Review**, 4, 120	L. A. Pincay Jr.	Claret (Ire), 4, 116	Quintana, 4, 114	6	1:47.00	76,050
1991	**Twilight Agenda**, 5, 118	C. S. Nakatani	Roanoke, 4, 118	Louis Cyphre (Ire), 5, 118	7	1:47.65	90,900
1990	**Quiet American**, 4, 115	K. Desormeaux	†Bayakoa (Arg), 6, 122	Bosphorus (Arg), 5, 112	6	1:40.40	89,800
1989	**Lively One**, 4, 120	R. G. Davis	Mi Preferido, 4, 115	Hot Operator, 4, 114	5	1:40.80	76,200
1988	**Cutlass Reality**, 6, 123	G. L. Stevens	Simply Majestic, 4, 115	Nostalgia's Star, 6, 116	7	1:41.40	63,700
1987	**Super Diamond**, 7, 123	L. A. Pincay Jr.	Nostalgia's Star, 5, 116	Good Command, 4, 114	7	1:40.80	48,050
1986	**Skywalker**, 4, 121	L. A. Pincay Jr.	Nostalgia's Star, 4, 118	Epidaurus, 4, 113	13	1:40.80	65,350
1985	**Super Diamond**, 5, 115	R. Q. Meza	M. Double M., 4, 119	French Legionaire, 4, 115	7	1:41.40	48,550
1984	**Ancestral (Ire)**, 4, 116	E. Delahoussaye	Retsina Run, 4, 117	Slew's Royalty, 4, 117	8	1:41.20	60,550
1983	**Bates Motel**, 4, 122	T. Lipham	The Wonder (Fr), 5, 123	Runaway Groom, 4, 117	6	1:41.00	47,650
1982	**Wickerr**, 7, 117	E. Delahoussaye	Cajun Prince, 5, 117	Drouilly (Fr), 6, 114	9	1:41.40	50,350
1981	**Summer Time Guy**, 5, 115	S. Hawley	Shamgo, 5, 117	Exploded, 4, 115	7	1:41.00	48,550
1980	**Island Sultan**, 5, 114	M. Castaneda	Summer Time Guy, 4, 116	Borzoi, 4, 120	6	1:41.80	38,000
1979	**Always Gallant**, 5, 118	D. G. McHargue	Bad 'n Big, 5, 120	Blondie's Dancer, 4, 117	6	1:41.00	33,050
1978	**Vic's Magic**, 5, 116	F. Toro	Mr. Redoy, 4, 119	Clout, 6, 117	6	1:40.20	25,300
1977	**Mark's Place**, 5, 124	W. Shoemaker	Austin Mittler, 5, 113	Confederate Yankee, 6, 114	5	1:40.60	18,450
1976	**‡Good Report**, 6, 116	L. A. Pincay Jr.	Austin Mittler, 4, 117	Holding Pattern, 5, 115	7	1:42.40	19,000
1975	**Chesapeake**, 6, 116	F. Olivares	Top Command, 4, 116	Against the Snow, 5, 123	6	1:40.60	16,800
1974	***Matun**, 5, 121	W. Shoemaker	Chesapeake, 5, 113	Imaginative, 8, 115	4	1:41.00	16,150
1973	**Kennedy Road**, 5, 126	W. Shoemaker	Imaginative, 7, 117	New Prospect, 4, 120	5	1:41.40	15,700

Named for the city of San Diego, California; the track is located in the nearby town of Del Mar, which means "by the sea." Grade 3 1983-2000. Not held 1939-'40, 1942-'44. 6 furlongs 1937, 1945-'47. 1 mile 1941. $1\frac{1}{8}$ miles 1991-'93. ‡Mark's Place finished first, DQ to seventh, 1976. †Denotes female.

Sands Point Stakes

Grade 3 in 2006. Belmont Park, three-year-olds, fillies, $1\frac{1}{8}$ miles, dirt (originally scheduled on the turf). Held June 3, 2006, with a gross value of $104,200. First held in 1995. First graded in 1998. Stakes record 1:47.50 (2005 Melhor Ainda).

Year	Winner	Jockey	Second	Third	Strs	Time	1st Purse
2006	**Wait a While**, 3, 115	G. K. Gomez	Diamond Spirit, 3, 115	Hostess, 3, 115	4	1:49.25	$65,520
2005	**Melhor Ainda**, 3, 123	J. R. Velazquez	Laurafina, 3, 115	My Typhoon (Ire), 3, 121	7	**1:47.50**	66,720
2004	**Mambo Slew**, 3, 122	E. S. Prado	Lucifer's Stone, 3, 122	Vous, 3, 119	10	1:47.24	68,880
2003	**Savedbythelight**, 3, 115	R. Migliore	Virgin Voyage, 3, 117	Little Bonnet, 3, 115	5	1:49.18	68,760
2002	**Riskaverse**, 3, 119	R. G. Davis	Cyclorama, 3, 115	She's Vested, 3, 115	11	1:51.63	69,660
2001	**Tweedside**, 3, 119	R. Migliore	Owsley, 3, 114	Platinum Tiara, 3, 122	4	1:50.43	66,674
2000	**Gaviola**, 3, 121	J. D. Bailey	Shopping for Love, 3, 121	Millie's Quest, 3, 113	8	1:47.77	66,780
1999	**Perfect Sting**, 3, 118	P. Day	Pico Teneriffe, 3, 121	Illiquidity, 3, 113	6	1:46.99	65,160
1998	**Recording**, 3, 113	J. F. Chavez	Royal Ransom, 3, 114	Naskra's de Light, 3, 116	11	1:48.93	69,600
1997	**Auntie Mame**, 3, 121	J. D. Bailey	Hoochie Coochie, 3, 114	Sagasious, 3, 113	8	1:46.65	66,720
1996	**Merit Wings**, 3, 120	R. G. Davis	Unify, 3, 113	Turkappeal, 3, 117	10	1:45.83	51,885
1995	**Perfect Arc**, 3, 117	J. R. Velazquez	Miss Union Avenue, 3, 123	Transient Trend, 3, 110	5	1:43.14	49,395

Named for the community of Sands Point, New York, located on Long Island. Not graded 2001, 2003. Sands Point H. 1995-'98, 2000, 2003. $1\frac{1}{16}$ miles 1995-'96. Dirt 2001, 2003, 2005. Originally scheduled on turf 2001, 2003, 2005.

San Felipe Stakes

Grade 2 in 2006. Santa Anita Park, three-year-olds, $1\frac{1}{16}$ miles, dirt. Held March 18, 2006, with a gross value of $250,000. First held in 1935. First graded in 1973. Stakes record 1:40.11 (2005 Consolidator).

Year	Winner	Jockey	Second	Third	Strs	Time	1st Purse
2006	**A. P. Warrior**, 3, 119	C. S. Nakatani	Point Determined, 3, 116	Bob and John, 3, 122	9	1:42.40	$150,000
2005	**Consolidator**, 3, 116	R. Bejarano	Giacomo, 3, 116	Don't Get Mad, 3, 116	8	**1:40.11**	150,000
2004	**Preachinatthebar**, 3, 116	J. Santiago	St Averil, 3, 122	Harvard Avenue, 3, 116	9	1:42.87	150,000
2003	**Buddy Gil**, 3, 119	G. L. Stevens	Atswhatimtalknbout, 3, 116	Brancusi, 3, 116	10	1:43.64	150,000
2002	**Medaglia d'Oro**, 3, 116	L. A. Pincay Jr.	U S S Tinosa, 3, 116	Siphonic, 3, 122	6	1:41.95	150,000
2001	**Point Given**, 3, 122	G. L. Stevens	I Love Silver, 3, 116	Jamaican Rum, 3, 119	8	1:41.94	150,000
2000	**Fusaichi Pegasus**, 3, 116	K. Desormeaux	The Deputy (Ire), 3, 122	Anees, 3, 119	7	1:42.66	150,000
1999	**Prime Timber**, 3, 116	D. R. Flores	Exploit, 3, 122	High Wire Act, 3, 116	7	1:42.16	150,000
1998	**Artax**, 3, 122	C. J. McCarron	Real Quiet, 3, 119	Prosperous Bid, 3, 116	5	1:41.73	150,000
1997	**Free House**, 3, 119	D. R. Flores	Silver Charm, 3, 122	King Crimson, 3, 116	9	1:42.49	152,400
1996	**Odyle**, 3, 116	C. S. Nakatani	Smithfield, 3, 116	Cavonnier, 3, 122	7	1:42.43	152,400
1995	**Afternoon Deelites**, 3, 119	K. Desormeaux	Timber Country, 3, 122	Lake George, 3, 116	4	1:42.11	117,200

1994	**Soul of the Matter**, 3, 116	K. Desormeaux	Brocco, 3, 119	Valiant Nature, 3, 119	5	1:44.68	$118,500
1993	**Corby**, 3, 116	C. J. McCarron	Personal Hope, 3, 116	Devoted Brass, 3, 122	6	1:42.11	121,100
1992	**Bertrando**, 3, 122	A. O. Solis	Arp, 3, 116	Hickman Creek, 3, 116	6	1:42.76	120,800
1991	**Sea Cadet**, 3, 119	C. J. McCarron	Scan, 3, 119	Compelling Sound, 3, 116	8	1:41.90	124,200
1990	**Real Cash**, 3, 113	A. O. Solis	Warcraft, 3, 117	Music Prospector, 3, 117	12	1:42.00	102,600
1989	**Sunday Silence**, 3, 119	P. A. Valenzuela	Flying Continental, 3, 118	Music Merci, 3, 124	5	1:42.60	91,800
1988	**Mi Preferido**, 3, 119	C. J. McCarron	Purdue King, 3, 119	Tejano, 3, 122	8	1:42.20	96,300
1987	**Chart the Stars**, 3, 116	E. Delahoussaye	Alysheba, 3, 120	Temperate Sil, 3, 122	8	1:43.00	107,450
1986	**Variety Road**, 3, 120	C. J. McCarron	Big Play, 3, 114	Dancing Pirate, 3, 116	5	1:45.40	75,350
1985	**Image of Greatness**, 3, 120	L. A. Pincay Jr.	Skywalker, 3, 120	Nostalgia's Star, 3, 117	9	1:43.20	106,350
1984	**Fali Time**, 3, 122	S. Hawley	Gate Dancer, 3, 117	Commemorate, 3, 117	6	1:42.60	103,450
1983	**‡Desert Wine**, 3, 124	C. J. McCarron	Naevus, 3, 115	Fifth Division, 3, 120	6	1:41.60	62,900
1982	**Advance Man**, 3, 117	C. J. McCarron	Gato Del Sol, 3, 118	Cassaleria, 3, 123	7	1:42.20	77,550
1981	**Stancharry**, 3, 118	F. Toro	Splendid Spruce, 3, 116	Flying Nashua, 3, 121	12	1:42.00	69,900
1980	**Raise a Man**, 3, 119	W. Shoemaker	The Carpenter, 3, 123	Rumbo, 3, 119	7	1:41.60	64,300
1979	**Pole Position**, 3, 119	S. Hawley	Switch Partners, 3, 114	Flying Paster, 3, 127	7	1:41.20	48,500
1978	**Affirmed**, 3, 126	S. Cauthen	Chance Dancer, 3, 117	Tampoy, 3, 118	6	1:42.60	38,100
1977	**Smasher**, 3, 115	S. Hawley	*Habitony, 3, 122	Miami Sun, 3, 115	5	1:42.60	32,850
1976	**Crystal Water**, 3, 117	W. Shoemaker	Beau Talent, 3, 117	Double Discount, 3, 113	6	1:42.60	34,000
1975	**Fleet Velvet**, 3, 120	F. Toro	George Navonod, 3, 122	Diabolo, 3, 124	6	1:42.40	33,200
1974	**Aloha Mood**, 3, 118	D. Pierce	Money Lender, 3, 124	Triple Crown, 3, 124	10	1:42.40	43,700
1973	**Linda's Chief**, 3, 126	B. Baeza	Ancient Title, 3, 120	Out of the East, 3, 115	9	1:41.80	42,700

Named for the Rancho Valle de San Felipe located in present-day San Diego County, California. Grade 1 1984-'88. San Felipe H. 1935-'41, 1952-'90. Not held 1942-'44. 1 mile 1935-'36. 7 furlongs 1937, 1941, 1947-'51. 6 furlongs 1938-'40, 1945-'46. Three-year-olds and up 1935-'40. Colts and geldings 1935-'51. ‡Naevus finished first, DQ to second, 1983.

San Fernando Breeders' Cup Stakes

Grade 2 in 2006. Santa Anita Park, four-year-olds, 1$^1/_{16}$ miles, dirt. Held January 14, 2006, with a gross value of $194,000. First held in 1952. First graded in 1973. Stakes record 1:40.80 (1955 *Poona II).

Year	Winner	Jockey	Second	Third	Strs	Time	1st Purse
2006	**Unbridled Energy**, 4, 116	G. K. Gomez	Canteen, 4, 118	Greeley's Galaxy, 4, 120	9	1:44.33	$120,000
2005	**Minister Eric**, 4, 116	R. R. Douglas	Mass Media, 4, 118	Skipaslew, 4, 116	9	1:42.14	120,000
2004	**During**, 4, 120	D. R. Flores	Toccet, 4, 116	Touch the Wire, 4, 117	10	1:41.63	134,280
2003	**Pass Rush**, 4, 116	C. S. Nakatani	Tracemark, 4, 116	Tizbud, 4, 116	8	1:42.37	131,760
2002	**Western Pride**, 4, 122	G. K. Gomez	Orientate, 4, 120	Fancy As, 4, 120	10	1:41.30	134,640
2001	**Tiznow**, 4, 122	C. J. McCarron	Walkslikeaduck, 4, 120	Wooden Phone, 4, 116	6	1:42.05	98,880
2000	**Saint's Honor**, 4, 117	K. Desormeaux	Cat Thief, 4, 122	Mr. Broad Blade, 4, 118	7	1:41.94	190,200
1999	**Dixie Dot Com**, 4, 116	D. R. Flores	Event of the Year, 4, 122	Old Topper, 4, 118	8	1:41.06	190,800
1998	**Silver Charm**, 4, 122	G. L. Stevens	Mud Route, 4, 116	Lord Grillo (Arg), 4, 120	4	1:41.94	125,520
1997	**Northern Afleet**, 4, 116	C. J. McCarron	Ambivalent, 4, 116	Ready to Order, 4, 116	9	1:48.59	194,000
1996	**Helmsman**, 4, 118	C. J. McCarron	Gold and Steel (Fr), 4, 120	The Key Rainbow (Ire), 4, 116	9	1:48.87	134,500
1995	**Wekiva Springs**, 4, 118	K. Desormeaux	Dramatic Gold, 4, 120	Dare and Go, 4, 116	7	1:48.59	126,800
1994	**Zignew**, 4, 116	C. J. McCarron	Nonproductiveasset, 4, 116	Pleasant Tango, 4, 116	12	1:47.87	135,400
1993	**Bertrando**, 4, 120	C. J. McCarron	Star Recruit, 4, 120	The Wicked North, 4, 116	8	1:51.22	127,800
1992	**Best Pal**, 4, 122	K. Desormeaux	Olympio, 4, 122	Dinard, 4, 120	9	1:48.25	130,000
1991	**In Excess (Ire)**, 4, 126	G. L. Stevens	Warcraft, 4, 120	Go and Go (Ire), 4, 123	9	1:46.70	128,800
1990	**Flying Continental**, 4, 120	C. A. Black	Splurger, 4, 114	Secret Slew, 4, 114	8	1:47.20	128,600
1989	**Mi Preferido**, 4, 123	C. J. McCarron	Speedratic, 4, 120	Perceive Arrogance, 4, 120	12	1:47.40	138,200
1988	**On the Line**, 4, 120	J. A. Santos	Candi's Gold, 4, 123	Grand Vizier, 4, 114	5	1:49.00	122,400
1987	**Variety Road**, 4, 123	L. A. Pincay Jr.	Broad Brush, 4, 126	Snow Chief, 4, 126	8	1:49.00	96,300
1986	**Right Con**, 4, 117	R. Q. Meza	Nostalgia's Star, 4, 120	Fast Account, 4, 114	10	1:48.40	101,800
1985	**Precisionist**, 4, 126	C. J. McCarron	Greinton (GB), 4, 120	Gate Dancer, 4, 126	7	1:47.40	123,350
1984	**Interco**, 4, 123	P. A. Valenzuela	Desert Wine, 4, 123	Paris Prince, 4, 120	12	1:48.60	92,850
1983	**Wavering Monarch**, 4, 123	E. Delahoussaye	Water Bank, 4, 120	Prince Spellbound, 4, 126	9	1:50.00	88,400
1982	**It's the One**, 4, 120	W. A. Guerra	Princelet, 4, 123	Rock Softly, 4, 114	9	1:47.60	84,650
1981	**Doonesbury**, 4, 120	S. Hawley	Raise a Man, 4, 120	Idyll, 4, 117	11	1:47.00	74,300
1980	**Spectacular Bid**, 4, 126	W. Shoemaker	Flying Paster, 4, 126	Relaunch, 4, 120	4	1:48.00	63,300
1979	**Radar Ahead**, 4, 123	D. G. McHargue	Affirmed, 4, 126	Little Reb, 4, 120	8	1:48.00	69,200
1978	**Text**, 4, 120	F. Toro	J. O. Tobin, 4, 123	Centennial Pride, 4, 114	5	1:49.40	65,500
1977	**Kirby Lane**, 4, 120	L. A. Pincay Jr.	Double Discount, 4, 117	Rajab, 4, 114	10	1:47.60	39,000
	‡Pocket Park, 4, 114	S. Cauthen	Properantes, 4, 114	Crystal Water, 4, 123	9	1:48.60	38,500
1976	**Messenger of Song**, 4, 120	J. Lambert	Avatar, 4, 123	Larrikin, 4, 120	11	1:48.20	54,350
1975	**Stardust Mel**, 4, 120	W. Shoemaker	Century's Envoy, 4, 120	Princely Native, 4, 120	8	1:48.60	36,700
	First Back, 4, 114	J. Vasquez	Lightning Mandate, 4, 120	Confederate Yankee, 4, 117	9	1:46.80	37,700
1974	**Ancient Title**, 4, 120	L. A. Pincay Jr.	Linda's Chief, 4, 123	*Mariache II, 4, 114	7	1:47.60	50,250
1973	**Bicker**, 4, 120	G. Brogan	Royal Owl, 4, 120	Commoner, 4, 114	14	1:48.20	58,350

Named for San Fernando, California, west of Santa Anita Park. Grade 1 1981-'89. San Fernando S. 1952-'96. Not held 1970. 1$^1/_8$ miles 1960-'97. Four-year-olds and up 1981. Two divisions 1975, 1977. ‡Properantes finished first, DQ to second, 1977 (2nd Div.).

Sanford Stakes

Grade 2 in 2006. Saratoga Race Course, two-year-olds, 6 furlongs, dirt. Held July 29, 2004, with a gross value of $150,000. First held in 1913. First graded in 1973. Stakes record 1:09.32 (2004 Afleet Alex).

Year	Winner	Jockey	Second	Third	Strs	Time	1st Purse
2004	**Afleet Alex**, 2, 120	J. Rose	Flamenco, 2, 122	Consolidator, 2, 118	11	**1:09.32**	$90,000
2003	**Chapel Royal**, 2, 122	J. R. Velazquez	Blushing Indian, 2, 118	Flushing Meadows, 2, 118	7	1:10.74	90,000
2002	**Whywhywhy**, 2, 122	E. S. Prado	Wildcat Heir, 2, 118	Spite the Devil, 2, 118	9	1:10.40	90,000
2001	**Buster's Daydream**, 2, 122	J. R. Velazquez	Seeking the Money, 2, 117	Heavyweight Champ, 2, 117	6	1:10.55	64,680
2000	**City Zip**, 2, 119	J. A. Santos	Yonaguska, 2, 119	Scorpion, 2, 114	7	1:10.69	65,220
1999	**More Than Ready**, 2, 122	J. R. Velazquez	Mighty, 2, 114	Bulling, 2, 114	5	1:09.65	64,560
1998	**Time Bandit**, 2, 119	P. Day	Prime Directive, 2, 117	Texas Glitter, 2, 117	9	1:11.59	66,480
1997	**Polished Brass**, 2, 116	P. Day	Double Honor, 2, 116	Jigadee, 2, 116	7	1:10.23	65,520
1996	**Kelly Kip**, 2, 118	J. Samyn	Boston Harbor, 2, 118	Say Florida Sandy, 2, 115	8	1:10.31	66,840
1995	**Maria's Mon**, 2, 115	R. G. Davis	Seeker's Reward, 2, 115	Frozen Ice, 2, 112	11	1:10.80	68,340
1994	**Montreal Red**, 2, 115	J. A. Santos	Boone's Mill, 2, 115	De Niro, 2, 122	5	1:10.56	64,620
1993	**Dehere**, 2, 122	C. J. McCarron	Prenup, 2, 115	Distinct Reality, 2, 122	6	1:10.48	68,520
1992	**Mountain Cat**, 2, 119	P. Day	‡Satellite Signal, 2, 115	Rule Sixteen, 2, 122	10	1:10.62	73,440
1991	**Caller I. D.**, 2, 122	J. D. Bailey	Pick Up the Phone, 2, 119	Money Run, 2, 115	6	1:10.92	69,000
1990	**Formal Dinner**, 2, 115	J. A. Santos	Beaudaspic, 2, 115	Link, 2, 117	10	1:10.20	55,260
1989	**Bite the Bullet**, 2, 115	J. A. Santos	Graf, 2, 115	For Really, 2, 113	9	1:09.80	54,720
1988	**Mercedes Won**, 2, 119	R. G. Davis	Leading Prospect, 2, 115	Fire Maker, 2, 115	11	1:10.00	55,440
1987	**Forty Niner**, 2, 115	E. Maple	Once Wild, 2, 115	Velvet Fog, 2, 115	6	1:10.00	65,340
1986	**Persevered**, 2, 115	A. T. Cordero Jr.	Perdition's Son, 2, 115	Bucks Best, 2, 115	5	1:10.60	51,120
1985	**Sovereign Don**, 2, 122	J. Velasquez	Roy, 2, 115	Cause for Pause, 2, 119	9	1:10.60	54,000
1984	**Tiffany Ice**, 2, 115	G. McCarron	Vindaloo, 2, 115	Fortunate Dancer, 2, 113	4	1:10.80	51,300
1983	**Big Walt**, 2, 115	J. Fell	Fill Ron's Pockets, 2, 122	Agile Jet, 2, 115	8	1:11.00	34,260
1982	**Copelan**, 2, 115	J. D. Bailey	Smart Style, 2, 115	Safe Ground, 2, 117	5	1:10.40	33,660
1981	**Mayanesian**, 2, 115	J. Vasquez	Shipping Magnate, 2, 115	Lejoli, 2, 115	10	1:11.20	35,280
1980	**Tap Shoes**, 2, 115	R. Hernandez	Triocala, 2, 115	Painted Shield, 2, 117	10	1:10.00	34,260
1979	**I Speedup**, 2, 122	J. Fell	Muckraker, 2, 122	My Pal Jeff, 2, 117	7	1:10.40	26,175
1978	**Fuzzbuster**, 2, 115	J. Velasquez	Make a Mess, 2, 115	Turnbuckle, 2, 115	6	1:10.80	22,230
1977	**Affirmed**, 2, 124	S. Cauthen	Tilt Up, 2, 122	Jet Diplomacy, 2, 124	6	1:09.60	22,290
1976	**Turn of Coin**, 2, 122	A. T. Cordero Jr.	Hey Hey J. P., 2, 115	Super Joy, 2, 115	7	1:10.20	22,395
1975	**Turn to Turia**, 2, 121	E. Maple	Iron Bit, 2, 121	Gentle King, 2, 121	5	1:10.80	22,575
1974	**Ramahorn**, 2, 121	C. Baltazar	Prop Man, 2, 121	Knightly Sport, 2, 121	8	1:11.00	17,205
1973	**Az Igazi**, 2, 121	M. Venezia	Prince of Reason, 2, 121	Totheend, 2, 121	6	1:10.60	16,680

Named for the Sanford family, owners of Hurricane Stud in Amsterdam, New York. Grade 3 1990-'98. Sanford Memorial S. 1913-'26. Held at Belmont Park 1943-'45. Not held 1961, 2005. 5½ furlongs 1962-'68. ‡Thirty Two Slew finished second, DQ to fourth, 1992.

San Francisco Breeders' Cup Mile Stakes

Grade 2 in 2006. Golden Gate Fields, four-year-olds and up, 1 mile, turf. Held April 29, 2006, with a gross value of $330,000. First held in 1948. First graded in 1987. Stakes record 1:33.40 (1980 Don Alberto).

Year	Winner	Jockey	Second	Third	Strs	Time	1st Purse
2006	**Charmo (Fr)**, 5, 122	M. A. Pedroza	Aragorn (Ire), 4, 122	Place Cowboy (Ire), 5, 122	8	1:34.28	$165,000
2005	**Castledale (Ire)**, 4, 118	R. R. Douglas	Adreamisborn, 6, 119	Aly Bubba, 6, 116	9	1:37.40	55,000
2004	**Singletary**, 4, 119	J. Valdivia Jr.	Captain Squire, 5, 116	Gold Ruckus, 6, 116	7	1:35.16	82,500
2003	**Ninebanks**, 5, 117	R. J. Warren Jr.	Nicobar (GB), 6, 116	National Anthem (GB), 7, 116	8	1:37.20	110,000
2002	**Suances (GB)**, 5, 116	D. R. Flores	Decarchy, 5, 121	The Tin Man, 4, 116	4	1:35.19	110,000
2001	**Redattore (Brz)**, 6, 115	J. P. Lumpkins	Hawksley Hill (Ire), 8, 119	Kerrygold (Fr), 5, 116	9	1:35.14	137,500
2000	**Ladies Din**, 5, 120	K. Desormeaux	Fighting Falcon, 4, 116	Self Feeder (Ire), 6, 116	10	1:35.46	150,000
1999	**†Tuzla (Fr)**, 5, 112	B. Blanc	Poteen, 5, 116	Rob 'n Gin, 5, 117	10	1:35.46	180,000
1998	**Hawksley Hill (Ire)**, 5, 119	G. L. Stevens	Fantastic Fellow, 4, 121	Uncaged Fury, 7, 117	6	1:34.33	120,000
1997	**Wavy Run (Ire)**, 6, 116	B. Blanc	Savinio, 7, 118	Romarin (Brz), 7, 118	7	1:37.11	120,000
1996	**Gold and Steel (Fr)**, 4, 114	A. O. Solis	Savinio, 6, 115	Debutant Trick, 6, 117	7	1:35.07	120,000
1995	**Unfinished Symph**, 4, 118	C. W. Antley	Vaudeville, 4, 119	Torch Rouge (GB), 4, 115	9	1:34.14	110,000
1994	**Gothland (Fr)**, 5, 115	C. S. Nakatani	Emerald Jig, 5, 113	The Tender Track, 7, 116	11	1:35.46	110,000
1993	**Norwich (GB)**, 6, 114	K. Desormeaux	Qathif, 6, 115	Luthier Enchanteur, 6, 117	8	1:35.57	137,500
1992	**Tight Spot**, 5, 125	L. A. Pincay Jr.	Notorious Pleasure, 6, 116	Forty Niner Days, 5, 116	9	1:35.57	110,000
1991	**Forty Niner Days**, 4, 112	T. T. Doocy	Exbourne, 5, 116	Blaze O'Brien, 4, 116	6	1:38.90	110,000
1990	**Colway Rally (GB)**, 6, 116	C. A. Black	River Master, 4, 115	Miswaki Tern, 5, 117	10	1:35.80	110,000
1989	**Patchy Groundfog**, 6, 116	F. Olivares	No Commitment, 4, 113	Mazilier, 5, 115	7	1:38.20	82,500
1988	**Ifrad**, 6, 115	T. M. Chapman	The Medic, 4, 118	Blanco, 4, 117	9	1:36.40	82,500
1987	**Dormello (Arg)**, 6, 113	A. L. Diaz	Air Display, 4, 116	Barbery, 6, 115	8	1:36.20	82,500
1986	**Hail Bold King**, 5, 117	M. Castaneda	Right Con, 4, 119	Lucky n Green (Ire), 4, 114	12	1:36.40	69,900
1985	**Truce Maker**, 7, 112	J. A. Garcia	†Lina Cavalieri (GB), 5, 115	Baron O'Dublin, 5, 116	11	1:35.20	69,500
1984	**Drumalis (Ire)**, 4, 117	E. Delahoussaye	Silveyville, 6, 117	Ten Below, 5, 115	8	1:35.60	43,275
	Icehot, 4, 115	M. Castaneda	Major Sport, 7, 117	Otter Slide, 5, 114	8	1:35.40	34,275
1983	**King's County (Ire)**, 4, 112	E. Munoz	Police Inspector, 6, 118	Silveyville, 5, 121	12	1:37.60	48,950
1982	**Silveyville**, 4, 121	D. Winick	Visible Pole, 4, 110	A Sure Hit, 4, 113	10	1:36.80	51,050

1981	**Opus Dei (Fr)**, 6, 119	F. Olivares	Drouilly (Fr), 5, 116	His Honor, 6, 117	13 1:34.80	$41,850
1980	**Don Alberto**, 5, 114	R. M. Gonzalez	Saboulard (Fr), 5, 116	Capt. Don, 5, 121	10 **1:33.40**	33,300
1979	**Struttin' George**, 5, 117	T. M. Chapman	Crafty Native, 6, 111	Foreign Power, 5, 115	8 1:37.40	32,950
1978	**Jumping Hill**, 6, 121	J. Lambert	Boy Tike, 5, 115	Dr. Henry K., 4, 109	6 1:38.40	32,500
1977	**Crafty Native**, 4, 112	M. James	Cojak, 4, 122	Money Lender, 6, 119	8 1:38.40	26,350
1975	**Whoa Boy**, 4, 113	G. Baze	Ocala Boy, 5, 113	Star of Kuwait, 7, 116	7 1:39.00	18,100
1974	**Visualizer**, 4, 114	F. Mena	Roka Zaca, 4, 117	*Larkal II, 6, 110	10 1:38.00	21,900
1973	**New Prospect**, 4, 118	J. Sellers	Masked, 4, 116	Rock Bath, 5, 113	6 1:43.20	22,150

Named for the city of San Francisco. Grade 3 1987-'93. San Francisco Mile H. 1948-'98. San Francisco Breeders' Cup Mile H. 1999-2005. Held at Bay Meadows 2001-'05. Not held 1960, 1976. Dirt 1948-'65, 1974. Originally scheduled on turf 1974. Three-year-olds and up 1948-'67, 1969-2005. Two divisions 1984. †Denotes female.

San Gabriel Handicap

Grade 2 in 2006. Santa Anita Park, four-year-olds and up, 1⅛ miles, turf. Held January 1, 2006, with a gross value of $150,000. First held in 1935. First graded in 1973. Stakes record 1:46.20 (1989 Wretham [GB]).

Year	Winner	Jockey	Second	Third	Strs	Time	1st Purse
2006	**Badge of Silver**, 6, 118	P. A. Valenzuela	Atlando (Ire), 5, 116	Toasted, 5, 117	9	1:50.02	$90,000
2005	**Truly a Judge**, 7, 116	M. A. Pedroza	Star Cross (Arg), 8, 112	Continental Red, 9, 116	6	1:48.90	90,000
2003	**Redattore (Brz)**, 8, 122	A. O. Solis	Continental Red, 7, 116	Denied, 5, 116	9	1:48.17	90,000
2002	**Grammarian**, 4, 117	J. Valdivia Jr.	David Copperfield, 5, 117	Decarchy, 5, 119	9	1:48.12	90,000
2001	**Irish Prize**, 5, 121	G. L. Stevens	Sligo Bay (Ire), 3, 117	El Gran Papa, 4, 114	11	1:50.56	90,000
	Irish Prize, 5, 117	K. Desormeaux	Manndar (Ire), 5, 121	Here Comes Big C, 6, 110	8	1:47.88	90,000
2000	**Brave Act (GB)**, 6, 120	A. O. Solis	Native Desert, 7, 116	Manndar (Ire), 4, 116	6	1:49.25	97,470
1998	**Brave Act (GB)**, 4, 118	G. F. Almeida	Mash One (Chi), 4, 116	Fabulous Guy (Ire), 4, 113	8	1:46.78	90,000
1997	**Martiniquais (Ire)**, 4, 116	C. S. Nakatani	Bienvenido (Arg), 4, 115	Da Bull, 5, 115	8	1:48.42	99,180
	Rainbow Blues (Ire), 4, 119	G. L. Stevens	River Deep, 6, 116	Via Lombardia (Ire), 5, 116	7	1:46.89	81,500
1996	**Romarin (Brz)**, 6, 119	C. S. Nakatani	Virginia Carnival, 4, 116	Silver Wizard, 6, 117	8	1:49.69	82,050
1995	**Romarin (Brz)**, 5, 119	C. S. Nakatani	Inner City (Ire), 6, 117	Ianomami (Ire), 5, 116	6	1:49.36	62,900
1994	**Earl of Barking (Ire)**, 4, 118	C. J. McCarron	Fanmore, 6, 116	Navarone, 6, 119	8	1:48.64	65,300
1993	**Star of Cozzene**, 5, 118	G. L. Stevens	Bistro Garden, 5, 114	Leger Cat (Arg), 7, 115	9	1:48.33	66,100
1992	**Classic Fame**, 6, 118	E. Delahoussaye	Super May, 6, 119	Defensive Play, 5, 116	6	1:46.69	64,300
1990	**In Excess (Ire)**, 3, 117	G. L. Stevens	Rouvignac (Fr), 4, 113	Kanatiyr (Ire), 4, 115	11	1:47.20	68,100
1989	**Wretham (GB)**, 4, 117	L. A. Pincay Jr.	Patchy Groundfog, 6, 117	In Extremis, 4, 117	10	**1:46.20**	67,700
1988	**Conquering Hero**, 5, 115	G. L. Stevens	Hot and Smoggy, 4, 117	Ten Keys, 4, 116	9	1:50.60	66,500
	Simply Majestic, 4, 120	J. D. Bailey	Payant (Arg), 4, 118	Dr. Death, 3, 115	8	1:47.40	66,100
1987	**Nostalgia's Star**, 5, 118	L. A. Pincay Jr.	Inevitable Leader, 8, 112	Spellbound, 4, 116	5	1:51.20	61,550
1986	**Yashgan (GB)**, 5, 124	C. J. McCarron	Tights, 5, 118	Rivlia, 4, 116	8	1:49.60	51,800
1985	**Dahar**, 4, 120	F. Toro	Paris Prince, 5, 116	Massera (Chi), 7, 116	7	1:47.60	50,750
1984	**Prince Florimund (SAf)**, 6, 118	P. A. Valenzuela	Ten Below, 5, 113	Ginger Brink (Fr), 4, 118	8	1:48.20	40,225
	Beldale Lustre, 5, 118	L. A. Pincay Jr.	I'll See You (GB), 6, 112	Color Bearer, 6, 111	7	1:48.80	39,425
1983	**Greenwood Star (GB)**, 6, 119	D. Pierce	Tell Again, 5, 118	Western, 5, 115	12	1:47.20	51,450
1981	**The Bart**, 5, 125	E. Delahoussaye	Irish Heart (Ire), 3, 115	Forlion, 5, 114	7	1:48.00	48,050
1980	**Premier Ministre**, 4, 113	L. A. Pincay Jr.	Galaxy Libra (Ire), 4, 117	Fast, 4, 118	7	1:48.20	38,250
	John Henry, 5, 123	D. G. McHargue	Smasher, 6, 111	As de Copas (Arg), 7, 117	9	1:49.80	39,300
1979	**Fluorescent Light**, 5, 118	A. T. Cordero Jr.	As de Copas (Arg), 6, 118	Tiller, 5, 127	7	1:47.60	32,200
1978	**Mr. Redoy**, 4, 110	S. Hawley	Dr. Krohn, 5, 116	Papelote, 4, 113	9	1:48.40	33,100
1977	**Riot in Paris**, 6, 125	W. Shoemaker	Distant Land, 5, 115	Ribot Grande, 7, 113	7	1:50.00	34,000
1975	**Zanthe**, 6, 117	S. Hawley	Copper Mel, 3, 115	Riot in Paris, 4, 124	9	1:47.40	26,550
1974	**Fair Test**, 6, 113	A. Santiago	Indefatigable, 4, 118	Montmartre, 4, 118	6	1:50.60	25,750
1973	**Astray**, 4, 115	J. Vasquez	Golden Doc Ray, 3, 114	Kirrary, 3, 117	8	1:48.20	26,250
	Kentuckian, 4, 114	J. Lambert	Artaxerxes, 5, 113	Harkville, 5, 112	10	1:47.60	26,950

Named for the nearby city of San Gabriel, California; the city is named for a Spanish mission. Grade 3 1973-'93, 2005. Not held 1936, 1939-'44, 1947-'51, 1970, 1976, 1982, 1991, 1999, 2004. 3 furlongs 1935-'38. 6 furlongs 1945-'46. 7 furlongs 1952-'54. 1¼ miles 1955-'59. Dirt 1935-'54, 1965, 1972, 1974, 1977, 1987, 2005. Originally scheduled on turf 2005. Two-year-olds 1935-'38. Three-year-olds and up 1945-'46, 1975-'77, 1981, 1988-'90, 1997-'98, 2001-'02. Three-year-olds 1952-'54. Two divisions 1984. Held in January and December 1973, 1980, 1988, 1997, 2001.

San Gorgonio Handicap

Grade 2 in 2006. Santa Anita Park, four-year-olds and up, fillies and mares, 1⅛ miles, turf. Held January 8, 2006, with a gross value of $150,000. First held in 1968. First graded in 1983. Stakes record 1:46.40 (1983 Castilla).

Year	Winner	Jockey	Second	Third	Strs	Time	1st Purse
2006	**Silver Cup (Ire)**, 4, 114	V. Espinoza	Ticker Tape (GB), 5, 117	Royal Copenhagen (Fr), 4, 116	11	1:47.46	$90,000
2005	**Fencelineneighbor**, 5, 115	L. H. Jauregui	Uraib (Ire), 5, 115	Dolly Wells (Arg), 5, 113	5	1:49.82	90,000
2004	**Megahertz (GB)**, 5, 119	A. O. Solis	Garden in the Rain (Fr), 7, 116	Firth of Lorne (Ire), 5, 116	4	1:49.51	90,000
2003	**Tates Creek**, 5, 121	P. A. Valenzuela	Megahertz (GB), 4, 117	Double Cat, 5, 114	7	1:46.91	90,000
2002	**Tout Charmant**, 6, 120	C. J. McCarron	Janet (GB), 5, 119	Vencera (Fr), 5, 115	8	1:47.22	90,000
2001	**Uncharted Haven (GB)**, 4, 115	A. O. Solis	Brianda (Ire), 4, 110	Beautiful Noise, 5, 116	12	1:50.02	90,000
2000	**Lady At Peace**, 4, 115	G. K. Gomez	Spanish Fern, 5, 119	Riboletta (Brz), 5, 116	5	1:48.75	90,000
1999	**See You Soon (Fr)**, 5, 118	K. Desormeaux	Sonja's Faith (Ire), 5, 118	Verinha (Brz), 5, 115	6	1:49.14	90,000
1998	**Golden Arches (Fr)**, 4, 120	C. J. McCarron	Ecoute, 5, 115	‡Real Connection, 7, 116	6	1:49.42	96,870
1997	**Sixieme Sens**, 5, 116	C. S. Nakatani	Alpride (Ire), 6, 120	Grafin, 6, 116	9	1:47.16	82,950
1996	**Wandesta (GB)**, 5, 119	C. S. Nakatani	Matiara, 4, 118	Yearly Tour, 5, 117	6	1:49.13	80,550

1995	**Queens Court Queen**, 6, 117	C. S. Nakatani	Wende, 5, 116	Vinista, 5, 115	5	1:48.70	$62,000
1994	**Hero's Love**, 6, 119	L. A. Pincay Jr.	Skimble, 5, 118	Miss Turkana, 5, 118	10	1:47.65	66,800
1993	**Southern Truce**, 5, 114	C. S. Nakatani	Laura Ly (Arg), 7, 114	Lite Light, 5, 115	5	1:51.28	67,100
1992	**Paseana (Arg)**, 5, 118	C. J. McCarron	Laura Ly (Arg), 6, 112	Reluctant Guest, 6, 117	4	1:53.88	77,250
1991	**Royal Touch (Ire)**, 6, 118	C. J. McCarron	Countus In, 6, 119	Marsha's Dancer, 5, 113	10	1:47.90	83,850
1990	**Invited Guest (Ire)**, 6, 117	R. A. Baze	White Mischief (GB), 6, 115	Oeilladine (Fr), 4, 115	10	1:46.40	83,750
1989	**No Review**, 4, 117	R. Q. Meza	Annoconnor, 5, 122	White Mischief (GB), 5, 116	6	1:48.80	79,950
1988	**Miss Alto**, 5, 116	E. Delahoussaye	Top Corsage, 5, 119	My Virginia Reel, 6, 115	6	1:49.20	63,200
1987	**Frau Altiva (Arg)**, 5, 117	L. A. Pincay Jr.	Auspiciante (Arg), 6, 122	Solva (GB), 6, 119	7	1:50.20	63,100
1986	**Mountain Bear (GB)**, 5, 118	E. Delahoussaye	Royal Regatta (NZ), 7, 115	Justicara (Ire), 5, 117	11	1:48.40	67,150
1985	**Fact Finder**, 6, 118	F. Toro	Capichi, 5, 118	Comedy Act, 6, 119	7	1:48.20	62,500
1984	**First Advance**, 5, 115	M. Castaneda	Avigaition, 5, 120	L'Attrayante (Fr), 4, 121	11	1:48.80	53,950
1983	**Castilla**, 4, 122	C. J. McCarron	Star Pastures (GB), 5, 119	Cat Girl, 5, 115	11	**1:46.40**	50,800
1982	**Track Robbery**, 6, 123	E. Delahoussaye	Rainbow Connection, 4, 117	Targa, 5, 114	5	1:52.60	45,700
1981	**Kilijaro (Ire)**, 5, 128	W. Shoemaker	Queen to Conquer, 5, 122	Refinish, 4, 117	4	1:49.20	36,300
1980	**Miss Magnetic**, 5, 111	L. E. Ortega	Maytide, 4, 112	Persona, 4, 113	9	1:50.00	39,700
1979	**Via Maris (Fr)**, 4, 113	A. T. Cordero Jr.	Drama Critic, 5, 122	Donna Inez, 4, 114	10	1:52.60	33,550
1977	***Lucie Manet**, 4, 121	W. Shoemaker	Theia (Fr), 4, 116	Claire Valentine (Ire), 4, 114	4	1:54.00	30,250
	***Merry Lady III**, 5, 119	L. A. Pincay Jr.	Our First Delight, 5, 117	*Pacara, 5, 114	10	1:50.80	36,200
1976	***Tizna**, 7, 132	F. Alvarez	Miss Tokyo, 4, 120	Charger's Star, 6, 121	8	1:47.20	25,800
1975	***Madison Palace**, 7, 119	D. Pierce	Grotonian, 6, 115	At the Dance, 6, 115	9	1:48.40	21,400
1974	**Margum**, 5, 115	W. Shoemaker	Harbor Point, 6, 117	Expediter, 5, 115	10	1:50.60	22,500
1973	**Extra Hand**, 7, 118	L. A. Pincay Jr.	Timoteo, 5, 122	Dundee Marmalade, 5, 115	8	1:49.00	23,200

Named for San Gorgonio Mountain, highest mountain in Southern California. Grade 3 1983-'84, 2005. San Gorgonio Claiming S. 1969-'75. Not held 1970, 1978. 6½ furlongs 1968. Dirt 1969-'71, 1973-'74, 1977-'80, 1982, 1988-'89, 1992-'93, 1995, 2005. Originally scheduled on turf 1973, 2005. Three-year-olds and up 1977. Both sexes 1968-'75. Held in January and December 1977. ‡Escabiosa (Arg) finished third, DQ to fourth, 1998.

San Juan Capistrano Invitational Handicap

Grade 2 in 2006. Santa Anita Park, four-year-olds and up, about 1¾ miles, turf. Held April 23, 2006, with a gross value of $250,000. First held in 1935. First graded in 1973. Stakes record 2:42.96 (2001 Bienamado).

Year	Winner	Jockey	Second	Third	Strs	Time	1st Purse
2006	**T. H. Approval**, 5, 117	A. O. Solis	One Off (GB), 6, 114	Quinquin the King (Fr), 4, 118	12	2:45.29	$150,000
2005	**T. H. Approval**, 4, 115	R. R. Douglas	Exterior, 4, 116	Fitz Flag (Arg), 5, 113	8	2:45.02	150,000
2004	**Meteor Storm (GB)**, 5, 116	J. Valdivia Jr.	Rhythm Mad (Fr), 4, 115	Runaway Dancer, 5, 115	9	2:45.98	150,000
2003	**Passinetti**, 7, 111	B. Blanc	All the Boys, 6, 115	Champion Lodge (Ire), 6, 117	9	2:46.97	240,000
2002	**Ringaskiddy**, 6, 116	E. Delahoussaye	Staging Post, 4, 115	Continental Red, 6, 117	8	2:44.49	240,000
2001	**Bienamado**, 5, 122	C. J. McCarron	Persianlux (GB), 5, 114	Blueprint (Ire), 6, 116	11	**2:42.96**	240,000
2000	**Sunshine Street**, 5, 115	J. D. Bailey	Single Empire (Ire), 6, 118	Chelsea Barracks (GB), 4, 109	5	2:49.06	240,000
1999	**Single Empire (Ire)**, 5, 118	K. Desormeaux	Le Paillard (Ire), 5, 115	Lucayan Indian (Ire), 4, 113	9	2:45.93	240,000
1998	**Amerique**, 4, 116	E. Delahoussaye	Star Performance, 5, 115	Kessem Power (NZ), 6, 116	10	2:47.08	240,000
1997	**Marlin**, 4, 119	E. Delahoussaye	dh-African Dancer, 5, 114 dh-Sunshack (GB), 6, 118		7	2:44.56	240,000
1996	**Raintrap (GB)**, 6, 115	A. O. Solis	†Windsharp, 5, 116	Awad, 6, 120	7	2:48.40	240,000
1995	**Red Bishop**, 7, 119	M. E. Smith	Special Price, 6, 116	Liyoun (Ire), 7, 112	8	2:48.02	220,000
1994	**Bien Bien**, 5, 122	C. J. McCarron	Grand Flotilla, 7, 116	Alex the Great (GB), 5, 114	9	2:46.69	220,000
1993	**Kotashaan (Fr)**, 5, 121	K. Desormeaux	Bien Bien, 4, 119	Fraise, 5, 123	5	2:45.00	220,000
1992	**Fly Till Dawn**, 6, 121	P. A. Valenzuela	†Miss Alleged, 5, 118	Wall Street Dancer, 4, 114	9	2:46.53	275,000
1991	**Mashkour**, 8, 115	C. J. McCarron	River Warden, 5, 115	Aksar, 4, 116	11	2:47.70	275,000
1990	**Delegant**, 6, 115	K. Desormeaux	Valdali (Ire), 4, 114	Hawkster, 4, 123	7	2:46.60	275,000
1989	**Nasr El Arab**, 4, 123	P. A. Valenzuela	Pleasant Variety, 5, 117	Academic (Ire), 4, 113	8	2:51.40	220,000
1988	**Great Communicator**, 5, 119	R. Sibille	Fiction, 4, 116	†Carotene, 5, 115	7	2:51.60	220,000
1987	**Rosedale**, 4, 117	L. A. Pincay Jr.	Wylfa (GB), 6, 115	Rivlia, 5, 115	6	2:49.00	220,000
1986	**Dahar**, 5, 124	A. O. Solis	†Mountain Bear (GB), 5, 115	Jupiter Island (GB), 7, 123	10	2:48.20	220,000
1985	**Prince True**, 4, 124	C. J. McCarron	†Estrapade, 5, 120	Swoon, 7, 117	7	2:26.40	180,000
1984	**Load the Cannons**, 4, 119	L. A. Pincay Jr.	Jenkins Ferry, 4, 114	Norwick, 5, 115	9	2:48.00	180,000
1983	**Erins Isle (Ire)**, 5, 125	L. A. Pincay Jr.	Wolver Heights (Ire), 5, 118	Victory Zone, 4, 115	12	2:48.60	180,000
1982	**Lemhi Gold**, 4, 121	W. A. Guerra	Exploded, 5, 118	Perrault (GB), 5, 129	9	2:45.60	180,000
1981	**Obraztsovy**, 6, 121	P. A. Valenzuela	Exploded, 4, 115	Singularity, 4, 115	9	2:50.40	120,000
1980	**John Henry**, 5, 126	D. G. McHargue	Fiestero (Chi), 5, 114	†The Very One, 5, 113	11	2:46.80	120,000
1979	**Tiller**, 5, 126	A. T. Cordero Jr.	Exceller, 6, 127	Noble Dancer (GB), 7, 128	11	2:48.00	120,000
1978	**Exceller**, 5, 126	W. Shoemaker	Noble Dancer (GB), 6, 125	Xmas Box, 4, 115	11	2:51.00	120,000
1977	**Properantes**, 4, 120	D. G. McHargue	Top Crowd, 6, 118	Caucasus, 5, 128	8	2:47.60	85,000
1976	**One On the Aisle**, 4, 119	S. Hawley	*Elaborado, 5, 113	Top Crowd, 5, 121	10	2:50.00	75,000
1975	**†*La Zanzara**, 5, 114	D. Pierce	Astray, 6, 125	Stardust Mel, 4, 126	12	2:52.20	75,000
1974	**Astray**, 5, 126	J. Vasquez	*El Rey, 6, 113	Big Spruce, 5, 125	6	2:45.40	75,000
1973	**Queen's Hustler**, 4, 115	R. Rosales	Big Spruce, 4, 119	*Cougar II, 7, 127	7	2:46.40	75,000

Named for San Juan Capistrano, California, which took its name from the mission. San Juan Capistrano H. 1935-'64. Grade 1 1973-2003. Not held 1942-'44, 1947-'48. 1⅛ miles 1935-'38. 1½ miles 1939, 1941, 1945-'46, 1949, 1954. 1$^{1}/_{16}$ miles 1940. 1¾ miles 1950-'53. Dirt 1935-'53. Three-year-olds and up 1935-'39, 1941-'67. Three-year-olds 1940. Dead heat for second 1997. Course record 1993, 2001. †Denotes female.

San Luis Obispo Handicap

Grade 2 in 2006. Santa Anita Park, four-year-olds and up, 1½ miles, turf. Held February 26, 2006, with a gross value of $150,000. First held in 1952. First graded in 1973. Stakes record 2:23.80 (1974 Captain Cee Jay [1st Div.]).

Year	Winner	Jockey	Second	Third	Strs	Time	1st Purse
2006	**Atlando (Ire)**, 5, 115	M. A. Pedroza	T. H. Approval, 5, 116	King's Drama (Ire), 6, 122	8	2:23.95	$90,000
2005	**License To Run (Brz)**, 5, 117	P. A. Valenzuela	Californian (GB), 5, 114	T. H. Approval, 4, 115	8	2:28.72	90,000
2004	**Puerto Banus**, 5, 115	V. Espinoza	Continuously, 5, 116	Continental Red, 8, 117	12	2:28.00	120,000
2003	**The Tin Man**, 5, 121	M. E. Smith	Special Matter, 5, 113	Harrisand (Fr), 5, 116	5	2:31.22	120,000
2002	**Nazirali (Ire)**, 5, 112	B. Blanc	Continental Red, 6, 116	Bonapartiste (Fr), 8, 114	7	2:26.09	120,000
2001	**Persianlux (GB)**, 5, 113	T. Baze	Devon Deputy, 5, 114	Falcon Flight (Fr), 5, 116	10	2:27.70	120,000
2000	**Dark Moondancer (GB)**, 5, 120	C. J. McCarron	The Fly (GB), 6, 115	Casino King (Ire), 5, 116	5	2:39.61	120,000
1999	**Kessem Power (NZ)**, 7, 115	G. L. Stevens	Brave Act (GB), 5, 121	Lazy Lode (Arg), 5, 120	7	2:28.02	120,000
1998	**Bienvenido (Arg)**, 5, 115	C. J. McCarron	Prize Giving (GB), 5, 116	Callisthene (Fr), 6, 115	6	2:29.34	120,000
1997	**Shanawi (Ire)**, 5, 111	B. Blanc	Rainbow Dancer (Fr), 6, 117	Bon Point (GB), 7, 117	7	2:24.51	132,100
1996	**†Windsharp**, 5, 115	E. Delahoussaye	†Wandesta (GB), 5, 114	Virginia Carnival, 4, 115	6	2:30.33	130,800
1995	**Square Cut**, 6, 114	C. W. Antley	Ianomami (Ire), 5, 115	River Rhythm, 8, 111	10	2:26.04	133,200
1994	**Fanmore**, 6, 116	K. Desormeaux	Bien Bien, 5, 124	Navire (Fr), 5, 114	9	2:27.03	131,400
1993	**Kotashaan (Fr)**, 5, 114	K. Desormeaux	Carnival Baby, 5, 112	The Name's Jimmy, 4, 115	8	2:27.64	129,600
1992	**Quest for Fame (GB)**, 5, 121	G. L. Stevens	Cool Gold Mood, 5, 114	†Miss Alleged, 5, 121	9	2:28.79	158,500
1991	**Rial (Arg)**, 6, 118	J. Velasquez	Intelligently, 5, 113	Royal Reach, 5, 113	9	2:24.10	163,400
1990	**Frankly Perfect**, 5, 124	C. J. McCarron	Delegant, 6, 116	Just as Lucky, 5, 114	12	2:28.00	171,100
1989	**Great Communicator**, 6, 124	R. Sibille	Vallotton (Fr), 4, 117	Roberto's Dancer, 4, 114	5	2:30.20	122,800
1988	**Great Communicator**, 5, 117	R. Sibille	Trokhos, 5, 116	†Ivor's Image, 5, 114	10	2:27.60	133,800
1987	**Louis Le Grand**, 5, 118	W. Shoemaker	Zoffany, 7, 125	Schiller, 5, 115	8	2:28.40	96,600
1986	**Talakeno**, 6, 115	P. A. Valenzuela	Foscarini (Ire), 5, 117	Strawberry Road (Aus), 7, 126	12	2:33.20	123,750
1985	**Western**, 7, 114	G. L. Stevens	Scrupules (Ire), 5, 121	Strong Dollar (Ire), 5, 115	5	2:26.00	89,250
1984	**Sir Pele**, 5, 118	R. Q. Meza	Lucence, 5, 118	Debonair Herc, 4, 114	9	2:27.40	79,375
1983	**Pelerin (Fr)**, 6, 116	W. Shoemaker	Western, 5, 118	Massera (Chi), 5, 118	10	2:24.60	67,200
1982	**Regal Bearing (GB)**, 6, 114	J. J. Steiner	Le Duc de Bar, 5, 114	Goldiko (Fr), 5, 119	10	2:27.20	80,450
1981	**John Henry**, 6, 127	L. A. Pincay Jr.	Galaxy Libra (Ire), 5, 119	Zor, 8, 115	6	2:24.00	62,800
1980	**Silver Eagle (Ire)**, 6, 120	W. Shoemaker	Balzac, 5, 123	Friuli (Arg), 7, 114	8	2:30.20	65,100
1979	**Fluorescent Light**, 5, 124	L. A. Pincay Jr.	As de Copas (Arg), 6, 118	dh-Alpha Boy, 5, 112 dh-Nostalgia, 5, 112	8	2:28.20	48,950
1978	**Copper Mel**, 6, 115	S. Hawley	Avodire, 5, 110	Tacitus, 4, 115	11	2:28.00	42,300
1977	***Royal Derby II**, 8, 126	W. Shoemaker	Gallivantor, 5, 115	Anne's Pretender, 5, 123	10	2:24.80	41,700
1976	**Announcer**, 4, 118	F. Toro	Top Crowd, 5, 123	Zanthe, 7, 121	6	2:30.80	38,200
1975	***Madison Palace**, 7, 120	L. A. Pincay Jr.	Toujours Pret, 6, 121	*Barclay Joy, 5, 118	8	2:30.20	40,100
1974	**Captain Cee Jay**, 4, 113	F. Alvarez	Court Ruling, 4, 112	*El Rey, 6, 112	8	**2:23.80**	28,150
	Astray, 5, 118	J. Vasquez	Scantling, 4, 112	Wichita Oil, 6, 115	8	2:24.40	28,150
1973	**Queen's Hustler**, 4, 112	R. Rosales	China Silk, 4, 115	River Buoy, 8, 117	9	2:27.20	40,800

Named for St. Louis of Toulouse, a Franciscan bishop and Catholic saint. Formerly named in honor of George Washington's birthday; the race was held on that holiday. Grade 3 1990-'91. Washington's Birthday H. 1952-'62. Not held 1963-'67. 7 furlongs 1952-'53. 1¼ miles 1954, 1970. About 1½ miles 1968, 1972. Dirt 1952-'53, 1973, 1980, 2005. Originally scheduled on turf 2005. Two divisions 1974. Dead heat for third 1979. Track record 1973. †Denotes female.

San Luis Rey Handicap

Grade 2 in 2006. Santa Anita Park, four-year-olds and up, 1½ miles, turf. Held March 25, 2006, with a gross value of $200,000. First held in 1952. First graded in 1973. Stakes record 2:23 (1970 Fiddle Isle; 1980 John Henry).

Year	Winner	Jockey	Second	Third	Strs	Time	1st Purse
2006	**King's Drama (Ire)**, 6, 121	J. K. Court	T. H. Approval, 5, 116	Wild Buddy, 7, 113	7	2:26.50	$120,000
2005	**Stanley Park**, 5, 116	G. L. Stevens	Meteor Storm (GB), 6, 118	Epicentre, 6, 115	10	2:24.45	120,000
2004	**Meteor Storm (GB)**, 5, 115	J. Valdivia Jr.	Labirinto, 6, 114	Gene de Campeao (Brz), 5, 114	10	2:26.03	120,000
2003	**Champion Lodge (Ire)**, 6, 116	A. O. Solis	Special Matter, 5, 113	Adminniestrator, 6, 116	7	2:33.48	150,000
2002	**Continental Red**, 6, 116	P. A. Valenzuela	†Keemoon (Fr), 6, 115	Speedy Pick, 4, 112	8	2:26.81	150,000
2001	**Blueprint (Ire)**, 6, 116	G. L. Stevens	Devon Deputy, 5, 114	Kerrygold (Fr), 5, 116	8	2:28.57	150,000
2000	**Dark Moondancer (GB)**, 5, 122	C. J. McCarron	Single Empire (Ire), 6, 122	Bonapartiste (Fr), 6, 122	6	2:26.00	150,000
1999	**Single Empire (Ire)**, 5, 122	K. Desormeaux	Kessem Power (NZ), 7, 122	Alvo Certo (Brz), 6, 122	7	2:27.97	150,000
1998	**Kessem Power (NZ)**, 6, 122	L. Dettori	Storm Trooper, 5, 122	Star Performance, 5, 122	12	2:28.40	150,000
1997	**Marlin**, 4, 122	C. J. McCarron	Sunshack (GB), 6, 122	Peckinpah's Soul (Fr), 5, 122	10	2:28.14	166,600
1996	**†Windsharp**, 5, 117	E. Delahoussaye	†Wandesta (GB), 5, 117	Silver Wizard, 6, 122	7	2:27.91	161,900
1995	**Sandpit (Brz)**, 6, 124	C. S. Nakatani	River Rhythm, 8, 124	Square Cut, 6, 124	7	2:27.15	155,000
1994	**Bien Bien**, 5, 124	C. J. McCarron	Navire (Fr), 5, 124	Grand Flotilla, 7, 124	5	2:26.65	149,500
1993	**Kotashaan (Fr)**, 5, 124	K. Desormeaux	Bien Bien, 4, 124	Fast Cure, 4, 124	4	2:23.91	148,250
1992	**Fly Till Dawn**, 6, 124	L. A. Pincay Jr.	Provins, 4, 124	Quest for Fame (GB), 5, 124	6	2:27.26	179,000
1991	**Pleasant Variety**, 7, 126	G. L. Stevens	Royal Reach, 5, 126	Mashkour, 8, 126	10	2:24.50	188,250
1990	**Prized**, 4, 126	E. Delahoussaye	Hawkster, 4, 126	Frankly Perfect, 5, 126	6	2:25.20	180,000
1989	**Frankly Perfect**, 4, 126	E. Delahoussaye	Great Communicator, 6, 126	Payant (Arg), 5, 126	5	2:32.80	152,400
1988	**Rivlia**, 6, 126	C. J. McCarron	Great Communicator, 5, 126	Swink, 5, 126	7	2:27.20	158,400
1987	**Zoffany**, 7, 126	E. Delahoussaye	Louis Le Grand, 5, 126	Long Mick (Fr), 6, 126	5	2:25.20	121,200
1986	**Dahar**, 5, 126	A. O. Solis	Strawberry Road (Aus), 7, 126	Alphabatim, 5, 126	7	2:26.40	148,600
1985	**Prince True**, 4, 126	C. J. McCarron	Western, 7, 126	Dahar, 4, 126	6	2:25.40	147,300

1984	**Interco**, 4, 126	P. A. Valenzuela	Gato Del Sol, 5, 126	John Henry, 9, 126	10	2:26.80	$127,200
1983	**Erins Isle (Ire)**, 5, 126	L. A. Pincay Jr.	Prince Spellbound, 4, 126	Majesty's Prince, 4, 126	6	2:26.20	120,900
1982	**Perrault (GB)**, 5, 126	L. A. Pincay Jr.	Exploded, 5, 126	John Henry, 7, 126	5	2:24.00	116,200
1981	**John Henry**, 6, 126	L. A. Pincay Jr.	Obraztsovy, 6, 126	Fiestero (Chi), 6, 126	6	2:25.20	93,900
1980	**John Henry**, 5, 126	D. G. McHargue	Relaunch, 4, 126	Silver Eagle (Ire), 6, 126	7	**2:23.00**	94,800
1979	**Noble Dancer (GB)**, 7, 126	J. Vasquez	Tiller, 5, 126	Good Lord (NZ), 8, 126	7	2:34.60	95,300
1978	**Noble Dancer (GB)**, 6, 126	S. Cauthen	Properantes, 5, 126	Text, 4, 126	7	2:24.00	64,400
1977	**Caucasus**, 5, 126	F. Toro	King Pellinore, 5, 126	Top Crowd, 6, 126	7	2:25.60	64,400
1976	**Avatar**, 4, 126	L. A. Pincay Jr.	‡Top Crowd, 5, 126	Top Command, 5, 126	7	2:24.80	64,300
1975	**Trojan Bronze**, 4, 126	J. E. Tejeira	Okavango, 5, 126	Montmartre, 5, 126	6	2:29.60	63,500
1974	**Astray**, 5, 126	J. Vasquez	Big Spruce, 5, 126	Quack, 5, 126	10	2:24.40	67,000
1973	**Big Spruce**, 4, 126	D. Pierce	*Cicero's Court, 4, 126	*Cougar II, 7, 126	10	2:27.60	66,800

Named for the San Luis Rey Mission; the California mission was named in honor of King and Catholic St. Louis IX of France. Grade 1 1973-'96. San Luis Rey S. 1952-'53, 1973-2000. 7 furlongs 1952. 6 furlongs 1953. 1 mile 1954. Dirt 1952-'54, 1962, 1975. Originally scheduled on turf 1975. Three-year-olds and up 1958-'59. ‡Ga Hai finished second, DQ to fourth, 1976. †Denotes female. California-breds 1952-'54.

San Marcos Stakes

Grade 2 in 2006. Santa Anita Park, four-year-olds and up, 1¼ miles, turf. Held January 22, 2006, with a gross value of $150,000. First held in 1952. First graded in 1973. Stakes record 1:57.92 (2003 Johar).

Year	Winner	Jockey	Second	Third	Strs	Time	1st Purse
2006	**The Tin Man**, 8, 115	V. Espinoza	Milk It Mick (GB), 5, 115	Whilly (Ire), 5, 119	11	1:58.39	$90,000
2005	**Whilly (Ire)**, 4, 117	F. F. Martinez	Puppeteer (GB), 5, 116	T. H. Approval, 4, 117	6	2:00.68	90,000
2004	**Sweet Return (GB)**, 4, 121	G. L. Stevens	Nothing to Lose, 4, 116	Blue Steller (Ire), 6, 116	9	1:58.82	90,000
2003	**Johar**, 4, 120	A. O. Solis	The Tin Man, 5, 122	Grammarian, 5, 122	7	**1:57.92**	90,000
2002	**Irish Prize**, 6, 122	G. L. Stevens	Continental Red, 6, 116	Cagney (Brz), 5, 119	6	2:01.27	90,000
2001	**Bienamado**, 5, 122	C. J. McCarron	Kerrygold (Fr), 5, 116	Northern Quest (Fr), 6, 122	7	2:02.75	90,000
2000	**Public Purse**, 6, 119	A. O. Solis	Dark Moondancer (GB), 5, 120	The Fly (GB), 6, 114	7	1:59.58	98,280
1999	**Brave Act (GB)**, 5, 120	G. F. Almeida	Ferrari (Ger), 5, 117	Native Desert, 6, 117	7	2:04.25	90,000
1998	**Prize Giving (GB)**, 5, 114	A. O. Solis	Bienvenido (Arg), 5, 115	Martiniquais (Ire), 5, 118	6	2:04.41	97,380
1997	**Sandpit (Brz)**, 8, 123	C. S. Nakatani	River Deep, 6, 116	‡Shanawi (Ire), 5, 112	8	2:00.61	99,000
1996	**Urgent Request (Ire)**, 6, 115	C. W. Antley	Bon Point (GB), 6, 114	Virginia Carnival, 4, 116	6	2:02.26	97,000
1995	**River Flyer**, 4, 118	C. W. Antley	Silver Wizard, 5, 117	Savinio, 5, 116	7	2:05.61	92,200
1994	**Bien Bien**, 5, 122	L. A. Pincay Jr.	Explosive Red, 4, 116	Myrakalu (Fr), 6, 113	6	2:00.55	75,850
1993	**Star of Cozzene**, 5, 120	G. L. Stevens	Kotashaan (Fr), 5, 116	Carnival Baby, 5, 112	7	2:01.71	77,650
1992	**Classic Fame**, 6, 120	E. Delahoussaye	Fly Till Dawn, 6, 120	French Seventyfive, 5, 115	6	1:58.02	90,600
1991	**Fly Till Dawn**, 5, 120	L. A. Pincay Jr.	Vaguely Hidden, 6, 115	The Medic, 7, 115	8	1:58.70	97,350
1990	**Putting (Fr)**, 7, 114	C. A. Black	Colway Rally (GB), 6, 115	Live the Dream, 4, 119	13	1:58.20	105,600
1989	**Trokhos**, 6, 117	L. A. Pincay Jr.	Vallotton (Fr), 4, 117	Roberto's Dancer, 4, 113	8	2:02.00	97,200
1988	**Great Communicator**, 5, 115	R. Sibille	Schiller, 6, 113	Bello Horizonte (Ire), 5, 113	10	2:02.60	100,400
1987	**Zoffany**, 7, 123	E. Delahoussaye	Louis Le Grand, 5, 117	Strawberry Road (Aus), 8, 122	8	2:00.80	64,100
1986	**Silveyville**, 8, 120	C. J. McCarron	Strawberry Road (Aus), 7, 125	Nasib (Ire), 4, 116	7	2:00.80	63,200
1985	**Dahar**, 4, 121	F. Toro	Scrupules (Ire), 5, 122	Alphabatim, 4, 124	6	2:01.20	61,900
1984	**Lucence**, 5, 114	P. A. Valenzuela	Ginger Brink (Fr), 4, 117	Sir Pele, 5, 114	11	2:01.80	54,200
1983	**Western**, 5, 116	C. J. McCarron	Handsome One, 5, 116	Tell Again, 5, 117	7	2:04.00	47,950
1982	**Super Moment**, 5, 125	L. A. Pincay Jr.	Forlion, 6, 114	Le Duc de Bar, 5, 111	5	2:00.60	45,900
1981	**Galaxy Libra (Ire)**, 5, 116	A. T. Cordero Jr.	Bold Tropic (SAf), 6, 127	Mike Fogarty (Ire), 6, 115	9	2:00.20	40,300
1980	**John Henry**, 5, 124	D. G. McHargue	El Fantastico, 5, 113	Conmemorativo, 5, 110	5	2:01.60	37,350
1979	**Tiller**, 5, 126	A. T. Cordero Jr.	Palton (Chi), 6, 121	How Curious, 5, 112	6	1:58.80	37,700
1978	**Vigors**, 5, 121	D. G. McHargue	Pay Tribute, 6, 122	Jumping Hill, 6, 123	9	1:46.60	33,350
1977	***Royal Derby II**, 8, 124	W. Shoemaker	Anne's Pretender, 5, 123	Teddy's Courage, 4, 116	10	1:58.20	34,150
1976	**Announcer**, 4, 115	F. Toro	Zanthe, 7, 122	Top Crowd, 5, 123	9	1:58.40	32,800
1975	**Trojan Bronze**, 4, 117	W. Shoemaker	Indefatigable, 5, 115	*El Botija, 5, 114	11	1:59.80	34,550
1974	**Triangular**, 7, 118	D. Pierce	Big Spruce, 5, 124	Kentuckian, 5, 118	9	2:04.80	33,000
1973	***Tuqui II**, 6, 114	L. A. Pincay Jr.	*Soudard, 5, 115	Aggressively, 6, 114	9	2:02.20	27,000

Named for Rancho San Marcos, which was located in Santa Barbara County, California. Grade 3 1973-'92. San Marcos H. 1952-2000. Not held 1970. 1 mile 1952-'53. 1⅛ miles 1978. Dirt 1952-'53, 1956, 1962, 1969, 1973, 1975, 1978-'83, 1996. Originally scheduled on turf 1973. Three-year-olds and up 1955-'59. ‡Marlin finished third, DQ to fifth, 1997.

San Pasqual Handicap

Grade 2 in 2006. Santa Anita Park, four-year-olds and up, 1$\frac{1}{16}$ miles, dirt. Held January 7, 2006, with a gross value of $150,000. First held in 1935. First graded in 1973. Stakes record 1:40.20 (1978 Ancient Title; 1980 Valdez).

Year	Winner	Jockey	Second	Third	Strs	Time	1st Purse
2006	**High Limit**, 4, 118	P. A. Valenzuela	Buckland Manor, 6, 116	Spellbinder, 5, 115	7	1:43.64	$90,000
2005	**Congrats**, 5, 114	T. Baze	Total Impact (Chi), 7, 120	Sigfreto, 7, 111	5	1:41.97	90,000
2004	**Star Cross (Arg)**, 7, 113	V. Espinoza	Nose The Trade (GB), 6, 115	Olmodavor, 5, 118	7	1:42.22	90,000
2003	**Congaree**, 5, 121	J. D. Bailey	Kudos, 6, 119	Hot Market, 5, 116	9	1:41.04	90,000

2002	**Wooden Phone**, 5, 119	D. R. Flores	Euchre, 6, 120	Red Eye, 6, 112	7	1:41.83	$120,000
2001	**Freedom Crest**, 5, 116	G. L. Stevens	Bosque Redondo, 4, 114	Sultry Substitute, 6, 114	8	1:41.94	120,000
2000	**Dixie Dot Com**, 5, 118	P. A. Valenzuela	Budroyale, 7, 122	Six Below, 5, 116	6	1:40.95	120,000
1999	**Silver Charm**, 5, 125	G. L. Stevens	Malek (Chi), 6, 119	Crafty Friend, 6, 118	5	1:41.78	120,000
1998	**Hal's Pal (GB)**, 5, 113	B. Blanc	Malek (Chi), 5, 116	Flick (GB), 6, 116	9	1:41.89	120,000
1997	**Kingdom Found**, 7, 115	G. L. Stevens	Savinio, 7, 117	Eltish, 5, 113	4	1:40.74	122,200
1996	**Alphabet Soup**, 5, 118	C. W. Antley	Luthier Fever, 5, 115	Cezind, 6, 114	9	1:41.66	130,100
1995	**Del Mar Dennis**, 5, 118	A. O. Solis	Slew of Damascus, 7, 120	Tossofthecoin, 5, 116	6	1:41.23	116,100
1994	**Hill Pass**, 5, 113	C. J. McCarron	Best Pal, 6, 122	Lottery Winner, 5, 116	7	1:41.00	87,800
1993	**Jovial (GB)**, 6, 115	M. Walls	‡Marquetry, 6, 118	Provins, 5, 115	7	1:41.94	91,400
1992	**Twilight Agenda**, 6, 125	K. Desormeaux	Ibero (Arg), 5, 116	Answer Do, 6, 118	5	1:42.32	89,000
1991	**Farma Way**, 4, 116	G. L. Stevens	Flying Continental, 5, 122	Stylish Stud, 5, 114	6	1:40.90	93,100
1990	**Criminal Type**, 5, 114	C. J. McCarron	Lively One, 5, 122	Present Value, 6, 121	8	1:42.40	96,300
1989	**On the Line**, 5, 123	G. L. Stevens	Mark Chip, 6, 114	Stylish Winner, 5, 113	6	1:41.00	93,300
1988	**Super Diamond**, 8, 125	L. A. Pincay Jr.	Judge Angelucci, 5, 122	He's a Saros, 5, 114	5	1:43.00	92,300
1987	**Epidaurus**, 5, 116	G. Baze	Ascension, 5, 114	Nostalgia's Star, 5, 120	7	1:42.40	90,800
1986	**Precisionist**, 5, 126	C. J. McCarron	Bare Minimum, 5, 113	My Habitony, 6, 116	6	1:41.20	90,000
1985	**Hula Blaze**, 5, 115	P. A. Valenzuela	Video Kid, 5, 117	Tennessee Rite, 4, 112	11	1:42.00	95,300
1984	**Danebo**, 5, 120	L. A. Pincay Jr.	Water Bank, 5, 118	Honeyland, 5, 116	8	1:41.80	91,900
1983	**Regal Falcon**, 5, 115	E. Delahoussaye	Time to Explode, 4, 121	West On Broad, 5, 113	7	1:43.20	63,900
1982	**Five Star Flight**, 4, 120	L. A. Pincay Jr.	Tahitian King (Ire), 6, 122	King Go Go, 7, 119	8	1:40.80	65,000
1981	**Flying Paster**, 5, 127	C. J. McCarron	King Go Go, 6, 117	Fiestero (Chi), 6, 113	6	1:41.20	47,150
1980	**Valdez**, 4, 125	L. A. Pincay Jr.	Prenotion, 5, 111	Balzac, 5, 122	4	**1:40.20**	46,350
1979	**Mr. Redoy**, 5, 117	A. T. Cordero Jr.	Life's Hope, 6, 116	Big John Taylor, 5, 115	8	1:42.20	38,900
1978	**Ancient Title**, 8, 124	D. G. McHargue	Mark's Place, 6, 120	Double Discount, 5, 120	4	**1:40.20**	30,250
1977	**Uniformity**, 5, 117	F. Toro	Distant Land, 5, 116	*Pisistrato, 5, 117	8	1:41.00	35,500
1976	**Lightning Mandate**, 5, 118	S. Hawley	Guards Up, 4, 113	Ga Hai, 5, 116	5	1:48.40	32,250
1975	**Okavango**, 5, 114	F. Toro	†Tallahto, 5, 118	Cheriepe, 5, 114	12	1:41.40	38,400
1974	**Tri Jet**, 5, 121	W. Shoemaker	Forage, 5, 121	†Susan's Girl, 5, 119	10	1:41.40	36,550
1973	**Single Agent**, 5, 119	J. Lambert	Kennedy Road, 5, 119	Autobiography, 5, 125	6	1:41.80	33,850

Named for El Rancho San Pasqual, which encompassed almost all of what is now the Pasadena, California, area. Not held 1942-'44. 6 furlongs 1935-'36. 7 furlongs 1938. 1⅛ miles 1939-'41. 1¼ miles 1955. Three-year-olds 1935-'36. Three-year-olds and up 1937-'53, 1958. ‡Best Pal finished second, DQ to fifth, 1993. †Denotes female.

San Rafael Stakes

Grade 2 in 2006. Santa Anita Park, three-year-olds, 1 mile, dirt. Held January 14, 2006, with a gross value of $147,000. First held in 1975. First graded in 1983. Stakes record 1:34.40 (1982 Prince Spellbound).

Year	Winner	Jockey	Second	Third	Strs	Time	1st Purse
2006	**Brother Derek**, 3, 122	A. O. Solis	Stevie Wonderboy, 3, 122	Wanna Runner, 3, 116	4	1:36.11	$90,000
2005	**Spanish Chestnut**, 3, 116	G. L. Stevens	Iced Out, 3, 115	Texcess, 3, 121	5	1:36.69	90,000
2004	**Imperialism**, 3, 118	V. Espinoza	Lion Heart, 3, 121	Consecrate, 3, 115	10	1:36.11	120,000
2003	**Rojo Toro**, 3, 115	J. D. Bailey	Spensive, 3, 118	Crowned Dancer, 3, 118	7	1:35.89	120,000
2002	**Came Home**, 3, 118	C. J. McCarron	Easy Grades, 3, 116	Werblin, 3, 115	7	1:36.24	120,000
2001	**Crafty C. T.**, 3, 116	E. Delahoussaye	Palmeiro, 3, 117	Early Flyer, 3, 118	9	1:35.79	120,000
2000	**War Chant**, 3, 116	K. Desormeaux	Archer City Slew, 3, 118	Cocky, 3, 115	6	1:36.45	120,000
1999	**Desert Hero**, 3, 116	C. S. Nakatani	Prime Timber, 3, 115	Capsized, 3, 115	9	1:36.45	120,000
1998	**Orville N Wilbur's**, 3, 115	C. S. Nakatani	Souvenir Copy, 3, 121	Futuristic, 3, 115	6	1:35.96	120,000
1997	**Funontherun**, 3, 115	G. F. Almeida	Inexcessivelygood, 3, 116	Hello (Ire), 3, 121	10	1:36.01	121,800
1996	**Honour and Glory**, 3, 121	G. L. Stevens	Halo Sunshine, 3, 115	Matty G, 3, 121	8	1:36.45	122,000
1995	**Larry the Legend**, 3, 118	K. Desormeaux	Fandarel Dancer, 3, 118	Timber Country, 3, 121	5	1:37.61	88,600
1994	**Tabasco Cat**, 3, 121	P. Day	Powis Castle, 3, 115	Shepherd's Field, 3, 121	5	1:36.39	89,700
1993	**Devoted Brass**, 3, 115	K. Desormeaux	Union City, 3, 115	Stuka, 3, 118	6	1:35.13	90,000
1992	**A.P. Indy**, 3, 121	E. Delahoussaye	Treekster, 3, 116	Prince Wild, 3, 118	6	1:35.41	90,300
1991	**Dinard**, 3, 118	C. J. McCarron	Apollo, 3, 118	Best Pal, 3, 121	5	1:35.90	91,900
1990	**Mister Frisky**, 3, 115	G. L. Stevens	Tight Spot, 3, 115	Land Rush, 3, 115	7	1:36.60	80,300
1989	**Music Merci**, 3, 121	G. L. Stevens	Manastash Ridge, 3, 118	Past Ages, 3, 118	5	1:34.80	76,300
1988	**What a Diplomat**, 3, 115	G. L. Stevens	Flying Victor, 3, 121	Success Express, 3, 121	9	1:38.00	79,350
1987	**Masterful Advocate**, 3, 122	L. A. Pincay Jr.	Chart the Stars, 3, 116	Hot and Smoggy, 3, 116	7	1:35.80	90,500
1986	**Variety Road**, 3, 116	C. J. McCarron	Ferdinand, 3, 116	Jetting Home, 3, 116	9	1:35.60	68,300
1985	**Smarten Up**, 3, 122	R. Q. Meza	Fast Account, 3, 122	Stan's Bower, 3, 118	9	1:36.20	94,500
1984	**Precisionist**, 3, 120	C. J. McCarron	Fali Time, 3, 122	Commemorate, 3, 118	6	1:35.00	91,600
1983	**Desert Wine**, 3, 119	C. J. McCarron	Naevus, 3, 114	Balboa Native, 3, 116	7	1:35.60	65,900
1982	**Prince Spellbound**, 3, 119	M. Castaneda	Muttering, 3, 121	Unpredictable, 3, 119	9	**1:34.40**	68,200
1981	**Johnlee n' Harold**, 3, 119	M. Castaneda	Minnesota Chief, 3, 115	A Run, 3, 119	10	1:36.00	51,500
1978	**Little Happiness**, 4, 116	S. Cauthen	*Merry Lady III, 6, 114	Up to Juliet, 5, 118	7	1:35.40	16,975
1976	**Vagabonda**, 5, 114	W. Shoemaker	*Bastonera II, 5, 117	Mia Amore, 4, 117	9	1:48.20	16,825
1975	**Donna B Quick**, 4, 114	W. Shoemaker	In Prosperity, 5, 115	Take Powder, 5, 122	10	1:09.60	11,300

Named for Rancho San Rafael, a 1785 land grant where Burbank, Glendale, and Montrose, California, are now located. Grade 3 1983. Not held 1977, 1979-'80. 6 furlongs 1975. 1⅛ miles 1976. Turf 1976. Four-year-olds and up 1975-'78. Fillies and mares 1975-'78.

San Simeon Handicap

Grade 3 in 2006. Santa Anita Park, four-year-olds and up, about 6½ furlongs, turf. Held April 22, 2006, with a gross value of $109,400. First held in 1968. First graded in 1973. Stakes record 1:11.46 (2004 Glick).

Year	Winner	Jockey	Second	Third	Strs	Time	1st Purse
2006	**Pure as Gold**, 4, 118	P. A. Valenzuela	Saint Buddy, 6, 114	Siren Lure, 5, 122	8	1:12.56	$65,640
2005	**Shadow of Illinois**, 5, 116	M. Guidry	Geronimo (Chi), 6, 117	Golden Arrow, 6, 116	6	1:12.62	64,200
2004	**Glick**, 8, 117	A. O. Solis	Cayoke (Fr), 7, 116	Summer Service, 4, 117	6	**1:11.46**	64,380
2003	**Speak in Passing**, 6, 118	D. R. Flores	Spinelessjellyfish, 7, 115	Rocky Bar, 5, 116	8	1:12.87	82,500
2002	**Malabar Gold**, 5, 117	C. J. McCarron	Astonished (GB), 6, 117	Nuclear Debate, 7, 118	9	1:11.73	82,825
2001	**Lake William**, 5, 114	V. Espinoza	Macward, 5, 117	Touch of the Blues (Fr), 4, 116	6	1:12.34	80,175
2000	**El Cielo**, 6, 117	J. Valdivia Jr.	King Slayer (GB), 5, 116	Scooter Brown, 5, 117	6	1:12.66	79,440
1999	**Naninja**, 6, 115	C. J. McCarron	Expressionist, 4, 116	Indian Rocket (GB), 5, 119	7	1:13.32	65,220
1998	**Labeeb (GB)**, 6, 120	K. Desormeaux	Surachai, 5, 118	Captain Collins (Ire), 4, 115	11	1:12.94	67,860
1997	**Sandtrap**, 4, 117	A. O. Solis	‡Daggett Peak, 6, 113	Tychonic (GB), 7, 120	6	1:12.50	96,850
1996	**†Ski Dancer**, 4, 114	G. L. Stevens	Daggett Peak, 5, 115	Boulderdash Bay, 6, 118	6	1:13.98	64,200
1995	**Finder's Fortune**, 6, 117	P. A. Valenzuela	Rotsaluck, 4, 117	Pembroke, 5, 117	7	1:13.65	64,550
1994	**Rapan Boy (Aus)**, 6, 114	G. L. Stevens	The Berkeley Man, 4, 115	Artistic Reef (GB), 5, 116	7	1:13.16	63,100
1993	**Exemplary Leader**, 7, 113	M. A. Pedroza	Prince Ferdinand (GB), 4, 119	Wild Harmony, 4, 117	8	1:13.98	64,300
1992	**†Heart of Joy**, 5, 119	C. J. McCarron	Regal Groom, 5, 115	Time Gentlemen (GB), 4, 117	10	1:12.94	69,600
1991	**Forest Glow**, 4, 116	J. A. Garcia	Answer Do, 5, 119	‡Shirkee, 6, 117	9	1:12.50	63,900
1990	**Coastal Voyage**, 6, 118	A. O. Solis	Patchy Groundfog, 7, 117	Raise a Stanza, 4, 119	4	1:12.20	60,000
1989	**Mazilier**, 5, 116	P. A. Valenzuela	†Imperial Star (GB), 5, 112	Caballo de Oro, 5, 116	8	1:15.80	48,750
1988	**Caballo de Oro**, 4, 112	R. Q. Meza	Gallant Sailor, 5, 112	Sylvan Express (Ire), 5, 121	5	1:15.40	46,700
1987	**Bolder Than Bold**, 5, 117	G. Baze	Prince Bobby B., 4, 122	†Lichi (Chi), 7, 112	9	1:13.60	49,800
1986	**Estate**, 7, 114	A. L. Castanon	Will Dancer (Fr), 4, 118	Exclusive Partner, 4, 116	8	1:13.80	52,150
1985	**Champagne Bid**, 6, 121	R. Sibille	Forzando (GB), 4, 122	Smart and Sharp, 6, 118	8	1:13.60	52,150
1984	**Champagne Bid**, 5, 121	R. Sibille	Retsina Run, 4, 115	Famous Star (GB), 5, 115	9	1:14.40	53,350
1983	**Chinook Pass**, 4, 124	L. A. Pincay Jr.	Shanekite, 5, 118	Earthquack, 4, 121	7	1:15.40	39,100
1982	**Shagbark**, 7, 122	L. A. Pincay Jr.	Shanekite, 4, 118	Belfort (Fr), 5, 116	8	1:13.00	39,850
1981	**Syncopate**, 6, 119	D. Pierce	Parsec, 4, 116	Matsadoon's Honey, 4, 115	4	1:16.40	31,450
1980	**Dragon Command (NZ)**, 6, 115	E. Delahoussaye	Numa Pompilius, 6, 115	Bywayofchicago, 6, 115	11	1:12.60	29,050
1979	**Bywayofchicago**, 5, 120	D. G. McHargue	Maheras, 6, 118	Whatsyourpleasure, 6, 117	9	1:21.80	33,850
1978	**Maheras**, 5, 122	L. A. Pincay Jr.	dh-Bad 'n Big, 4, 119 dh-Yu Wipi, 6, 114		6	1:22.80	25,650
1977	**Mark's Place**, 5, 122	S. Hawley	Maheras, 4, 124	Painted Wagon, 4, 114	7	1:21.00	26,250
1976	**Pay Tribute**, 4, 118	L. A. Pincay Jr.	Against the Snow, 6, 118	King Pellinore, 4, 122	6	1:35.20	25,650
1975	**Century's Envoy**, 4, 121	J. E. Tejeira	First Back, 4, 121	Rocket Review, 4, 120	5	1:22.40	19,700
1974	***Matun**, 5, 118	S. Valdez	‡Selecting, 5, 115	Forage, 5, 123	8	1:21.20	21,200
1973	**Soft Victory**, 5, 115	D. Pierce	Selecting, 4, 115	dh-Andrew Feeney, 4, 116 dh-Goalie, 4, 113	12	1:21.40	23,050

Named for Rancho San Simeon, California, originally attached to the San Miguel Mission. Not graded 1975-'83. 7 furlongs 1968-'75, 1977-'79. 1 mile 1976. 6½ furlongs 1980-'85, 1987-'90. Dirt 1968-'79, 1981, 1983, 1988. Dead heat for third 1973. Dead heat for second 1978. ‡Forage finished second, DQ to third, 1974. ‡Coastal Voyage finished third, DQ to fourth, 1991. ‡Destiny's Venture finished second, DQ to fourth, 1997. Course record 2004. †Denotes female.

Santa Ana Handicap

Grade 2 in 2006. Santa Anita Park, four-year-olds and up, fillies and mares, 1⅛ miles, turf. Held March 26, 2006, with a gross value of $150,000. First held in 1968. First graded in 1981. Stakes record 1:46.23 (1993 Exchange).

Year	Winner	Jockey	Second	Third	Strs	Time	1st Purse
2006	**Silver Cup (Ire)**, 4, 118	V. Espinoza	Argentina (Ire), 4, 116	Beautyandthebeast (GB), 4, 116	8	1:48.13	$90,000
2005	**Megahertz (GB)**, 6, 122	A. O. Solis	Katdogawn (GB), 5, 117	Valentine Dancer, 5, 117	7	1:47.95	90,000
2004	**‡Katdogawn (GB)**, 4, 117	M. E. Smith	Fun House, 5, 118	Arabic Song (Ire), 5, 117	7	1:47.36	90,000
2003	**Noches De Rosa (Chi)**, 5, 115	M. E. Smith	Garden in the Rain (Fr), 6, 116	Megahertz (GB), 4, 117	8	1:48.31	90,000
2002	**Golden Apples (Ire)**, 4, 119	G. K. Gomez	Starine (Fr), 5, 122	Astra, 6, 122	9	1:47.05	90,000
2001	**Beautiful Noise**, 5, 115	C. J. McCarron	High Walden, 4, 114	Matiere Grise (Fr), 4, 113	12	1:47.27	90,000
2000	**Spanish Fern**, 5, 119	V. Espinoza	Virginie (Brz), 6, 120	Country Garden (GB), 5, 116	7	1:49.30	97,830
1999	**See You Soon (Fr)**, 5, 119	K. Desormeaux	Blending Element (Ire), 6, 116	La Madame (Chi), 4, 116	6	1:49.46	90,000
1998	**Fiji (GB)**, 4, 115	K. Desormeaux	Shake the Yoke (GB), 5, 116	Golden Arches (Fr), 4, 120	6	1:49.85	96,480
1997	**Windsharp**, 6, 121	E. Delahoussaye	Wheatly Special, 4, 113	Donna Viola (GB), 5, 120	7	1:49.47	97,750
1996	**Pharma**, 5, 116	C. J. McCarron	Angel in My Heart (Fr), 4, 120	Matiara, 4, 120	5	1:49.14	95,650
1995	**Wandesta (GB)**, 4, 115	C. S. Nakatani	Yearly Tour, 4, 116	Aube Indienne (Fr), 5, 120	7	1:50.18	90,700
1994	**Possibly Perfect**, 4, 119	K. Desormeaux	Hero's Love, 6, 120	‡Lady Blessington (Fr), 6, 120	7	1:51.05	91,000
1993	**Exchange**, 5, 120	L. A. Pincay Jr.	Party Cited, 4, 115	Villandry, 5, 116	5	**1:46.23**	89,700
1992	**Gravieres (Fr)**, 4, 116	G. L. Stevens	Appealing Missy, 5, 117	Explosive Ele, 5, 115	8	1:47.75	94,900
1991	**dh-Annual Reunion**, 4, 116 **dh-Noble and Nice**, 5, 113	G. L. Stevens K. Desormeaux		Bequest, 5, 117	8	1:46.70	63,400
1990	**Annoconnor**, 6, 119	C. A. Black	Royal Touch (Ire), 5, 121	Brown Bess, 8, 123	7	1:47.80	94,500
1989	**Maria Jesse (Fr)**, 4, 116	G. L. Stevens	Fieldy (Ire), 6, 117	Claire Marine (Ire), 4, 115	8	1:47.20	97,100
1988	**‡Pen Bal Lady (GB)**, 4, 118	E. Delahoussaye	Fitzwilliam Place (Ire), 4, 119	Galunpe (Ire), 5, 119	10	1:47.20	94,900
1987	**Reloy**, 4, 116	W. Shoemaker	Northern Aspen, 5, 119	North Sider, 5, 120	7	1:48.00	91,300
1986	**Videogenic**, 4, 120	R. G. Davis	Capichi, 6, 118	Water Crystals, 5, 114	6	1:48.40	62,800

1985	**Estrapade**, 5, 123	F. Toro	Fact Finder, 6, 119	Air Distingue, 5, 116	10	1:47.00	$67,100
1984	**Avigaition**, 5, 118	W. Shoemaker	Pride of Rosewood (NZ), 6, 116	L'Attrayante (Fr), 4, 122	9	1:48.40	93,600
1983	**Happy Bride (Ire)**, 5, 116	C. J. McCarron	Avigaition, 4, 121	Miss Huntington, 6, 115	6	1:47.80	63,400
1982	**Track Robbery**, 6, 123	E. Delahoussaye	Manzanera (Arg), 6, 117	Ack's Secret, 6, 123	8	1:47.20	65,100
1981	**Queen to Conquer**, 5, 121	L. A. Pincay Jr.	Track Robbery, 5, 119	Ack's Secret, 5, 123	7	1:48.00	46,900
1980	**The Very One**, 5, 117	C. Cooke	Sisterhood, 5, 118	Mairzy Doates, 4, 116	8	1:48.40	37,300
1979	**Waya (Fr)**, 5, 127	A. T. Cordero Jr.	Amazer, 4, 123	Shua, 4, 115	10	1:48.20	38,450
1978	**Kittyluck**, 5, 115	F. Toro	Innuendo, 4, 111	‡Belle o' Reason, 5, 120	9	1:53.00	26,750
1977	**Up to Juliet**, 4, 120	L. A. Pincay Jr.	Quintas Fannie, 4, 114	Belle o' Reason, 4, 115	11	1:48.00	27,550
1976	**Sun Festival**, 7, 116	D. Pierce	Quaze Quilt, 5, 122	Cut Class, 4, 117	9	1:48.40	25,450
1975	**Move Abroad**, 4, 115	S. Hawley	Joli Vert, 4, 114	Bold Ballet, 4, 122	6	1:51.40	19,500
1974	**Belle Marie**, 4, 118	W. Shoemaker	Grasping, 5, 114	Flying Fur, 5, 115	12	1:46.60	26,800
1973	**Bird Boots**, 4, 115	E. Belmonte	Best Go, 5, 119	Resolutely, 6, 115	9	1:47.00	15,600
	Minstrel Miss, 6, 119	D. Pierce	*Rich Return II, 6, 118	Hill Circus, 5, 124	8	1:46.80	15,300

Named for the Rancho Santa Ana, located in present-day Ventura County, California. Grade 3 1981. Grade 1 1984-'96. 1$^1/_{16}$ miles 1971. Dirt 1981-'83, 1986. Two divisions 1973. Dead heat for first 1991. ‡Ida Delia finished third, DQ to fifth, 1978. ‡Fitzwilliam Place (GB) finished first, DQ to second, 1988. ‡Waitryst (NZ) finished third, DQ to seventh, 1994. ‡Megahertz (GB) finished first, DQ to seventh, 2004. Non-winners of a race worth $12,500 to the winner 1973.

Santa Anita Derby

Grade 1 in 2006. Santa Anita Park, three-year-olds, 1$^1/_8$ miles, dirt. Held April 8, 2006, with a gross value of $750,000. First held in 1935. First graded in 1973. Stakes record 1:47 (1965 Lucky Debonair; 1973 Sham; 1998 Indian Charlie).

Year	Winner	Jockey	Second	Third	Strs	Time	1st Purse
2006	**Brother Derek**, 3, 122	A. O. Solis	Point Determined, 3, 122	A. P. Warrior, 3, 122	5	1:48.00	$450,000
2005	**Buzzards Bay**, 3, 122	M. Guidry	General John B, 3, 122	Wilko, 3, 122	11	1:49.18	450,000
2004	**Castledale (Ire)**, 3, 122	J. Valdivia Jr.	‡Imperialism, 3, 122	Rock Hard Ten, 3, 122	7	1:49.24	450,000
2003	**Buddy Gil**, 3, 122	G. L. Stevens	Indian Express, 3, 122	Kafwain, 3, 122	9	1:49.36	450,000
2002	**Came Home**, 3, 122	C. J. McCarron	Easy Grades, 3, 122	Lusty Latin, 3, 122	8	1:50.02	450,000
2001	**Point Given**, 3, 122	G. L. Stevens	Crafty C. T., 3, 122	I Love Silver, 3, 122	6	1:47.77	450,000
2000	**The Deputy (Ire)**, 3, 120	C. J. McCarron	War Chant, 3, 120	Captain Steve, 3, 120	6	1:49.08	600,000
1999	**General Challenge**, 3, 120	G. L. Stevens	Prime Timber, 3, 120	Desert Hero, 3, 120	8	1:48.92	450,000
1998	**Indian Charlie**, 3, 120	G. L. Stevens	Real Quiet, 3, 120	Artax, 3, 120	7	**1:47.00**	450,000
1997	**Free House**, 3, 120	K. Desormeaux	Silver Charm, 3, 120	Hello (Ire), 3, 120	10	1:47.60	450,000
1996	**Cavonnier**, 3, 120	C. J. McCarron	‡Honour and Glory, 3, 120	Corker, 3, 120	8	1:48.81	600,000
1995	**Larry the Legend**, 3, 122	G. L. Stevens	Afternoon Deelites, 3, 122	Jumron (GB), 3, 122	8	1:47.99	385,000
1994	**Brocco**, 3, 122	G. L. Stevens	Tabasco Cat, 3, 122	Strodes Creek, 3, 122	6	1:48.33	275,000
1993	**Personal Hope**, 3, 122	G. L. Stevens	Union City, 3, 122	†Eliza, 3, 117	7	1:49.03	275,000
1992	**A.P. Indy**, 3, 122	E. Delahoussaye	Bertrando, 3, 122	Casual Lies, 3, 122	7	1:49.25	275,000
1991	**Dinard**, 3, 122	C. J. McCarron	Best Pal, 3, 122	Sea Cadet, 3, 122	9	1:48.10	275,000
1990	**Mister Frisky**, 3, 122	G. L. Stevens	Video Ranger, 3, 122	Warcraft, 3, 122	8	1:49.00	275,000
1989	**Sunday Silence**, 3, 122	P. A. Valenzuela	Flying Continental, 3, 122	Music Merci, 3, 122	6	1:47.60	275,000
1988	**†Winning Colors**, 3, 117	G. L. Stevens	Lively One, 3, 122	Mi Preferido, 3, 122	9	1:47.80	275,000
1987	**Temperate Sil**, 3, 122	W. Shoemaker	Masterful Advocate, 3, 122	Something Lucky, 3, 122	6	1:49.00	278,250
1986	**Snow Chief**, 3, 122	A. O. Solis	Icy Groom, 3, 122	Ferdinand, 3, 122	7	1:48.60	275,000
1985	**Skywalker**, 3, 122	L. A. Pincay Jr.	Fast Account, 3, 122	Nostalgia's Star, 3, 122	9	1:48.40	219,500
1984	**Mighty Adversary**, 3, 120	E. Delahoussaye	Precisionist, 3, 120	Prince True, 3, 120	8	1:49.00	189,700
1983	**Marfa**, 3, 120	J. Velasquez	My Habitony, 3, 120	Naevus, 3, 120	10	1:49.40	198,000
1982	**Muttering**, 3, 120	L. A. Pincay Jr.	Prince Spellbound, 3, 120	Journey At Sea, 3, 120	9	1:47.60	188,800
1981	**Splendid Spruce**, 3, 120	D. G. McHargue	Johnlee n' Harold, 3, 120	Hoedown's Day, 3, 120	13	1:49.00	180,600
1980	**Codex**, 3, 120	P. A. Valenzuela	Rumbo, 3, 120	Bic's Gold, 3, 120	9	1:47.60	117,200
1979	**Flying Paster**, 3, 120	D. Pierce	Beau's Eagle, 3, 120	Switch Partners, 3, 120	10	1:48.00	124,900
1978	**Affirmed**, 3, 120	L. A. Pincay Jr.	Balzac, 3, 120	Think Snow, 3, 120	12	1:48.00	127,300
1977	***Habitony**, 3, 120	W. Shoemaker	For The Moment, 3, 120	Steve's Friend, 3, 120	15	1:48.20	131,000
1976	**An Act**, 3, 120	L. A. Pincay Jr.	Double Discount, 3, 120	Life's Hope, 3, 120	9	1:48.00	97,700
1975	**Avatar**, 3, 120	J. E. Tejeira	Rock of Ages, 3, 120	Diabolo, 3, 120	7	1:47.60	82,900
1974	**Destroyer**, 3, 120	I. Valenzuela	Aloha Mood, 3, 120	Agitate, 3, 120	8	1:48.80	85,200
1973	**Sham**, 3, 120	L. A. Pincay Jr.	Linda's Chief, 3, 120	Out of the East, 3, 120	6	**1:47.00**	79,400

The race and the track are both named in honor of Rancho Santa Anita, the name of the land when it was purchased by E. J. "Lucky" Baldwin. Not held 1942-'44. 1$^1/_{16}$ miles 1935-'37. 1$^1/_4$ miles 1947. ‡Alyrob finished second, DQ to eighth, 1996. ‡Rock Hard Ten finished second, DQ to third, 2004. †Denotes female.

Santa Anita Handicap

Grade 1 in 2006. Santa Anita Park, four-year-olds and up, 1$^1/_4$ miles, dirt. Held March 4, 2006, with a gross value of $1,000,000. First held in 1935. First graded in 1973. Stakes record 1:58.60 (1979 Affirmed).

Year	Winner	Jockey	Second	Third	Strs	Time	1st Purse
2006	**Lava Man**, 5, 120	C. S. Nakatani	Magnum (Arg), 5, 113	Wilko, 4, 115	9	2:00.57	$600,000
2005	**Rock Hard Ten**, 4, 119	G. L. Stevens	Congrats, 5, 115	Borrego, 4, 115	11	2:01.20	600,000

2004	**Southern Image**, 4, 118	V. Espinoza	†Island Fashion, 4, 115	Saint Buddy, 4, 111	8	2:01.64	$600,000
2003	**Milwaukee Brew**, 6, 119	E. S. Prado	Congaree, 5, 124	Kudos, 6, 117	6	1:59.80	600,000
2002	**Milwaukee Brew**, 5, 115	K. Desormeaux	Western Pride, 4, 116	Kudos, 5, 116	14	2:01.02	600,000
2001	**Tiznow**, 4, 122	C. J. McCarron	Wooden Phone, 4, 117	Tribunal, 4, 116	12	2:01.55	600,000
2000	**General Challenge**, 4, 121	C. S. Nakatani	Budroyale, 7, 122	Puerto Madero (Chi), 6, 118	8	2:01.49	600,000
1999	**Free House**, 5, 123	C. J. McCarron	Event of the Year, 4, 119	Silver Charm, 5, 124	6	2:00.67	600,000
1998	**Malek (Chi)**, 5, 115	A. O. Solis	Bagshot, 4, 113	Don't Blame Rio, 5, 117	4	2:02.26	600,000
1997	**Siphon (Brz)**, 6, 120	D. R. Flores	Sandpit (Brz), 8, 121	Gentlemen (Arg), 5, 123	11	2:00.23	600,000
1996	**Mr Purple**, 4, 116	E. Delahoussaye	Luthier Fever, 5, 114	Just Java, 5, 114	11	2:02.04	600,000
1995	**Urgent Request (Ire)**, 5, 116	G. L. Stevens	Best Pal, 7, 122	Dare and Go, 4, 120	10	1:59.25	550,000
1994	**‡Stuka**, 4, 115	C. W. Antley	Bien Bien, 5, 120	Myrakalu (Fr), 6, 114	8	2:00.17	550,000
1993	**Sir Beaufort**, 6, 119	P. A. Valenzuela	Star Recruit, 4, 117	Major Impact, 4, 114	11	2:00.55	550,000
1992	**Best Pal**, 4, 124	K. Desormeaux	Twilight Agenda, 6, 124	Defensive Play, 5, 115	7	1:59.08	550,000
1991	**Farma Way**, 4, 120	G. L. Stevens	Festin (Arg), 5, 115	Pleasant Tap, 4, 115	10	2:00.30	550,000
1990	**Ruhlmann**, 5, 121	G. L. Stevens	Criminal Type, 5, 119	Flying Continental, 4, 121	10	2:01.20	550,000
1989	**Martial Law**, 4, 113	M. A. Pedroza	Triteamtri, 4, 116	Stylish Winner, 5, 113	11	1:58.80	550,000
1988	**Alysheba**, 4, 126	C. J. McCarron	Ferdinand, 5, 127	Super Diamond, 8, 124	4	1:59.80	550,000
1987	**Broad Brush**, 4, 122	A. T. Cordero Jr.	Ferdinand, 4, 125	Hopeful Word, 6, 117	9	2:00.60	550,000
1986	**Greinton (GB)**, 5, 122	L. A. Pincay Jr.	Herat, 4, 112	Hatim, 5, 118	13	2:00.00	689,500
1985	**Lord At War (Arg)**, 5, 125	W. Shoemaker	Greinton (GB), 4, 120	Gate Dancer, 4, 125	7	2:00.60	275,600
1984	**Interco**, 4, 121	P. A. Valenzuela	Journey At Sea, 5, 117	Gato Del Sol, 5, 117	12	2:00.60	298,650
1983	**Bates Motel**, 4, 118	T. Lipham	It's the One, 5, 123	Wavering Monarch, 4, 121	17	1:59.60	317,350
1982	**‡John Henry**, 7, 130	W. Shoemaker	Perrault (GB), 5, 126	It's the One, 4, 120	11	1:59.00	318,800
1981	**John Henry**, 6, 128	L. A. Pincay Jr.	King Go Go, 6, 117	Exploded, 4, 115	11	1:59.40	238,150
1980	**Spectacular Bid**, 4, 130	W. Shoemaker	Flying Paster, 4, 123	Beau's Eagle, 4, 122	5	2:00.60	190,000
1979	**Affirmed**, 4, 128	L. A. Pincay Jr.	Tiller, 5, 127	dh-Exceller, 6, 127 dh-Painted Wagon, 6, 115	8	**1:58.60**	192,800
1978	**Vigors**, 5, 127	D. G. McHargue	Mr. Redoy, 4, 120	Jumping Hill, 6, 115	10	2:01.20	180,000
1977	**Crystal Water**, 4, 122	L. A. Pincay Jr.	Faliraki (Ire), 4, 114	King Pellinore, 5, 130	13	1:59.20	173,550
1976	**Royal Glint**, 6, 124	J. E. Tejeira	Ancient Title, 6, 124	Lightning Mandate, 5, 120	15	2:00.40	155,900
1975	**Stardust Mel**, 4, 123	W. Shoemaker	Out of the East, 5, 112	Okavango, 5, 116	8	2:06.40	105,000
1974	**Prince Dantan**, 4, 119	R. Turcotte	Ancient Title, 4, 125	Big Spruce, 5, 122	11	2:03.60	105,000
1973	***Cougar II**, 7, 126	L. A. Pincay Jr.	Kennedy Road, 5, 119	Cabin, 5, 110	10	2:00.00	105,000

The race and the track are both named in honor of Rancho Santa Anita, the name of the land when it was purchased by E. J. "Lucky" Baldwin. Not held 1942-'44. Three-year-olds and up 1935-'68. Dead heat for third 1979. ‡Perrault (GB) finished first, DQ to second, 1982. ‡The Wicked North finished first, DQ to fourth, 1994. Track record 1940. †Denotes female.

Santa Anita Oaks

Grade 1 in 2006. Santa Anita Park, three-year-olds, fillies, 1$^{1}/_{16}$ miles, dirt. Held March 12, 2006, with a gross value of $300,000. First held in 1935. First graded in 1973. Stakes record 1:41.20 (1980 Bold 'n Determined).

Year	Winner	Jockey	Second	Third	Strs	Time	1st Purse
2006	**Balance**, 3, 122	V. Espinoza	Quiet Kim, 3, 122	Wild Fit, 3, 122	9	1:42.99	$180,000
2005	**Sweet Catomine**, 3, 121	C. S. Nakatani	Memorette, 3, 121	She Sings, 3, 121	7	1:44.44	180,000
2004	**Silent Sighs**, 3, 117	D. R. Flores	Halfbridled, 3, 117	A. P. Adventure, 3, 117	7	1:42.84	180,000
2003	**Composure**, 3, 117	J. D. Bailey	Elloluv, 3, 117	Go for Glamour, 3, 117	5	1:43.34	180,000
2002	**You**, 3, 117	J. D. Bailey	Habibti, 3, 117	Ile de France, 3, 117	9	1:42.70	180,000
2001	**Golden Ballet**, 3, 117	C. J. McCarron	Flute, 3, 117	Affluent, 3, 117	8	1:41.83	180,000
2000	**Surfside**, 3, 117	P. Day	Kumari Continent, 3, 117	Classy Cara, 3, 117	5	1:44.03	180,000
1999	**Excellent Meeting**, 3, 117	K. Desormeaux	Tout Charmant, 3, 117	Gleefully, 3, 117	6	1:43.26	150,000
1998	**Hedonist**, 3, 117	K. Desormeaux	Keeper Hill, 3, 117	Nijinsky's Passion, 3, 117	7	1:44.14	150,000
1997	**Sharp Cat**, 3, 117	C. S. Nakatani	Queen of Money, 3, 117	Double Park (Fr), 3, 117	5	1:42.22	128,800
1996	**Antespend**, 3, 117	C. W. Antley	Cara Rafaela, 3, 117	Hidden Lake, 3, 117	5	1:43.04	128,600
1995	**Serena's Song**, 3, 117	C. S. Nakatani	Urbane, 3, 117	Mari's Sheba, 3, 117	5	1:42.71	121,600
1994	**Lakeway**, 3, 117	K. Desormeaux	Dianes Halo, 3, 117	Flying in the Lane, 3, 117	6	1:41.66	122,800
1993	**Eliza**, 3, 117	P. A. Valenzuela	Stalcreek, 3, 117	Dance for Vanny, 3, 117	9	1:42.97	129,200
1992	**Golden Treat**, 3, 117	K. Desormeaux	Magical Maiden, 3, 117	Queens Court Queen, 3, 117	8	1:43.20	129,300
1991	**Lite Light**, 3, 117	C. S. Nakatani	Garden Gal, 3, 117	Ifyoucouldseemenow, 3, 117	5	1:42.50	122,100
1990	**Hail Atlantis**, 3, 117	G. L. Stevens	Bright Candles, 3, 117	Fit to Scout, 3, 117	6	1:43.00	122,800
1989	**Imaginary Lady**, 3, 117	G. L. Stevens	Some Romance, 3, 117	Kool Arrival, 3, 117	7	1:43.40	125,400
1988	**Winning Colors**, 3, 117	G. L. Stevens	Jeanne Jones, 3, 117	Goodbye Halo, 3, 117	4	1:42.00	89,900
1987	**Timely Assertion**, 3, 117	G. L. Stevens	Buryyourbelief, 3, 117	Very Subtle, 3, 117	7	1:43.60	95,100
1986	**Hidden Light**, 3, 117	W. Shoemaker	Twilight Ridge, 3, 117	An Empress, 3, 117	6	1:42.40	120,200
1985	**Fran's Valentine**, 3, 117	P. A. Valenzuela	Rascal Lass, 3, 117	Wising Up, 3, 117	7	1:42.40	122,100
1984	**Althea**, 3, 117	L. A. Pincay Jr.	Personable Lady, 3, 115	Life's Magic, 3, 115	5	1:43.60	118,500
1983	**Fabulous Notion**, 3, 115	D. Pierce	Capichi, 3, 115	O'Happy Day, 3, 115	6	1:43.60	93,900
1982	**Blush With Pride**, 3, 115	W. Shoemaker	Skillful Joy, 3, 115	Carry a Tune, 3, 115	10	1:45.80	100,400
1981	**Nell's Briquette**, 3, 115	W. Shoemaker	Bee a Scout, 3, 115	Ice Princess, 3, 115	8	1:42.80	82,550
1980	**Bold 'n Determined**, 3, 115	E. Delahoussaye	Street Ballet, 3, 115	Table Hands, 3, 115	7	**1:41.20**	67,100
1979	**Caline**, 3, 115	W. Shoemaker	Terlingua, 3, 115	It's in the Air, 3, 117	8	1:41.60	69,000
1978	**Grenzen**, 3, 115	D. G. McHargue	Equanimity, 3, 115	Mashteen, 3, 115	7	1:43.80	47,800

1977 **Sound of Summer**, 3, 115	F. Toro	Wavy Waves, 3, 115	Lady T. V., 3, 115	9	1:42.20	$33,200
1976 **Girl in Love**, 3, 115	F. Toro	I'm a Charmer, 3, 115	Queen to Be, 3, 115	8	1:43.20	32,700
1975 **Sarsar**, 3, 115	W. Shoemaker	Double You Lou, 3, 115	Fascinating Girl, 3, 115	8	1:42.80	33,100
1974 **Miss Musket**, 3, 115	W. Shoemaker	Out to Lunch, 3, 115	Special Team, 3, 115	7	1:47.00	32,800
1973 **Belle Marie**, 3, 115	L. A. Pincay Jr.	Tallahto, 3, 115	Waltz Fan, 3, 115	6	1:41.80	31,800

The race and the track are both named in honor of Rancho Santa Anita, the name of the land when it was purchased by E. J. "Lucky" Baldwin. Formerly named for the community of Santa Susana, California. Santa Susana S. 1951-'85. Grade 2 1973-'78. Not held 1936, 1942-'44, 1955. 3 furlongs 1935. 6 furlongs 1937-'38, 1946. 7 furlongs 1939-'45, 1947-'51, 1956. 1 mile 1954, 1957. Two-year-olds 1935.

Santa Barbara Handicap

Grade 2 in 2006. Santa Anita Park, four-year-olds and up, fillies and mares, 1¼ miles, turf. Held April 22, 2006, with a gross value of $200,000. First held in 1935. First graded in 1973. Stakes record 1:57.50 (1991 Bequest).

Year Winner	Jockey	Second	Third	Strs	Time	1st Purse
2006 **Sharp Lisa**, 4, 118	C. S. Nakatani	Eternal Melody (NZ), 6, 114	Cissy (Arg), 6, 114	6	2:02.17	$120,000
2005 **Megahertz (GB)**, 6, 123	A. O. Solis	Nadeszhda (GB), 5, 114	Hoh Buzzard (Ire), 5, 117	7	1:59.76	120,000
2004 **Megahertz (GB)**, 5, 121	A. O. Solis	Noches De Rosa (Chi), 6, 116	Mandela (Ger), 4, 111	5	2:00.71	120,000
2003 **Megahertz (GB)**, 4, 117	A. O. Solis	Trekking, 4, 111	Noches De Rosa (Chi), 5, 117	5	2:00.08	150,000
2002 **Astra**, 6, 121	K. Desormeaux	Golden Apples (Ire), 4, 121	Polaire (Ire), 6, 115	6	2:01.48	150,000
2001 **Astra**, 5, 118	K. Desormeaux	Beautiful Noise, 5, 116	Uncharted Haven (GB), 4, 116	7	2:01.33	150,000
2000 **Caffe Latte (Ire)**, 4, 116	C. S. Nakatani	Happyanunoit (NZ), 5, 121	Country Garden (GB), 5, 116	6	2:00.51	150,000
1999 **Tranquility Lake**, 4, 116	E. Delahoussaye	Virginie (Brz), 5, 118	Midnight Line, 4, 118	7	2:01.06	150,000
1998 **Fiji (GB)**, 4, 119	K. Desormeaux	Pomona (GB), 5, 115	Ecoute, 5, 114	5	2:00.35	150,000
1997 **Donna Viola (GB)**, 5, 120	G. L. Stevens	Fanjica (Ire), 5, 114	Windsharp, 6, 122	8	1:59.85	197,200
1996 **Auriette (Ire)**, 4, 116	K. Desormeaux	Angel in My Heart (Fr), 4, 119	Wandesta (GB), 5, 121	5	2:02.10	190,900
1995 **Wandesta (GB)**, 4, 118	C. S. Nakatani	Yearly Tour, 4, 116	Morgana, 4, 116	7	2:01.77	126,400
1994 **Possibly Perfect**, 4, 121	K. Desormeaux	Pracer, 4, 115	Waitryst (NZ), 5, 114	5	2:00.56	122,800
1993 **Exchange**, 5, 121	L. A. Pincay Jr.	Trishyde, 4, 120	Revasser, 4, 118	4	2:02.26	120,400
1992 **Kostroma (Ire)**, 6, 121	K. Desormeaux	Miss Alleged, 5, 124	Free At Last (GB), 5, 117	6	1:59.63	152,700
1991 **Bequest**, 5, 117	E. Delahoussaye	Noble and Nice, 5, 114	Annual Reunion, 4, 117	6	**1:57.50**	126,400
1990 **Brown Bess**, 8, 123	J. L. Kaenel	Royal Touch (Ire), 5, 121	Double Wedge, 5, 111	5	1:58.40	122,000
1989 **No Review**, 4, 116	E. Delahoussaye	Galunpe (Ire), 6, 117	Annoconnor, 5, 121	8	2:02.60	128,800
1988 **Pen Bal Lady (GB)**, 4, 119	E. Delahoussaye	Carotene, 5, 121	Galunpe (Ire), 5, 119	8	1:59.60	95,800
1987 **Reloy**, 4, 120	W. Shoemaker	Northern Aspen, 5, 119	Ivor's Image, 4, 119	9	2:00.00	97,600
1986 **Mountain Bear (GB)**, 5, 119	C. J. McCarron	Estrapade, 6, 124	Royal Regatta (NZ), 7, 116	8	2:01.00	119,300
1985 **Fact Finder**, 6, 118	G. L. Stevens	Love Smitten, 4, 117	Salt Spring (Arg), 6, 114	6	2:01.60	116,600
1984 **Comedy Act**, 5, 116	C. J. McCarron	L'Attrayante (Fr), 4, 122	Lido Isle, 4, 114	10	2:00.40	121,200
1983 **Avigaition**, 4, 121	E. Delahoussaye	Happy Bride (Ire), 5, 120	Comedy Act, 4, 116	8	1:59.80	78,650
1982 **Ack's Secret**, 6, 122	L. A. Pincay Jr.	Landresse (Fr), 4, 116	Plenty O'Toole, 5, 114	8	2:00.60	78,550
1981 **The Very One**, 6, 122	J. Velasquez	Mairzy Doates, 5, 117	Ack's Secret, 5, 121	9	2:01.20	65,900
1980 **Sisterhood**, 5, 118	L. A. Pincay Jr.	Petron's Love, 5, 114	Relaxing, 4, 118	10	2:00.40	67,600
1979 **Waya (Fr)**, 5, 131	A. T. Cordero Jr.	Petron's Love, 4, 117	Island Kiss, 4, 111	8	2:01.00	49,350
1978 **Kittyluck**, 5, 116	L. A. Pincay Jr.	Countess Fager, 4, 117	Sensational, 4, 120	9	2:00.60	40,400
1977 **Desiree**, 4, 110	V. Centeno	Swingtime, 5, 120	Charger's Star, 7, 113	6	2:02.60	38,100
1976 ***Stravina**, 5, 109	W. Shoemaker	Katonka, 4, 122	*Tizna, 7, 127	7	1:59.60	38,600
1975 **Gay Style**, 5, 125	W. Shoemaker	Move Abroad, 4, 113	*La Zanzara, 5, 117	6	2:01.40	31,600
1974 **Tallahto**, 4, 118	L. A. Pincay Jr.	*La Zanzara, 4, 120	*Tizna, 5, 122	8	1:59.20	39,600
1973 **Susan's Girl**, 4, 129	L. A. Pincay Jr.	Veiled Desire, 4, 110	Gray Mirage, 4, 112	5	2:03.60	37,600

Named for Santa Barbara, California, where an 1841 tax was the first on racing wagers. Grade 1 1973-'95. Not held 1939-'40, 1942-'45, 1947-'51, 1959-'61. 3 furlongs 1935-'41. 7 furlongs 1946-'52. 6 furlongs 1953-'54, 1958. 1¹⁄₁₆ miles 1955-'57. About 1¼ miles 1968. Dirt 1935-'58, 1973, 1977, 1982. Originally scheduled on turf 1973. Two-year-olds 1937-'41. Three-year-olds 1952-'54. Three-year-olds and up 1955-'65. California-breds 1935-'54.

Santa Catalina Stakes

Grade 2 in 2006. Santa Anita Park, three-year-olds, 1¹⁄₁₆ miles, dirt. Held March 4, 2006, with a gross value of $200,000. First held in 1935. First graded in 1998. Stakes record 1:41.40 (1981 Stancharry).

Year Winner	Jockey	Second	Third	Strs	Time	1st Purse
2006 **Brother Derek**, 3, 122	A. O. Solis	Sacred Light, 3, 115	Latent Heat, 3, 118	8	1:41.96	$120,000
2005 **Declan's Moon**, 3, 122	V. Espinoza	Going Wild, 3, 122	Spanish Chestnut, 3, 122	6	1:42.41	120,000
2004 **St Averil**, 3, 113	T. Baze	Lucky Pulpit, 3, 115	Master David, 3, 113	9	1:41.62	90,000
2003 **Domestic Dispute**, 3, 113	D. R. Flores	Our Bobby V., 3, 113	Scrimshaw, 3, 115	8	1:42.20	90,000
2002 **Labamta Babe**, 3, 115	K. Desormeaux	Siphonic, 3, 123	Cottonwood Cowboy, 3, 115	6	1:42.50	90,000
2001 **Millennium Wind**, 3, 114	C. J. McCarron	Palmeiro, 3, 117	Denied, 3, 116	6	1:42.38	64,620
2000 **The Deputy (Ire)**, 3, 115	C. J. McCarron	High Yield, 3, 117	Captain Steve, 3, 123	6	1:43.04	64,380
1999 **General Challenge**, 3, 117	G. L. Stevens	Buck Trout, 3, 120	Brilliantly, 3, 115	5	1:42.93	63,900
1998 **Artax**, 3, 114	C. J. McCarron	Souvenir Copy, 3, 120	Allen's Oop, 3, 117	6	1:42.32	64,320
1997 **Hello (Ire)**, 3, 120	C. J. McCarron	Bagshot, 3, 116	Carmen's Baby, 3, 120	8	1:42.60	65,950
1996 **Prince of Thieves**, 3, 113	G. L. Stevens	Smithfield, 3, 116	Matty G, 3, 124	6	1:42.94	64,250
1995 **Larry the Legend**, 3, 117	K. Desormeaux	In Character (GB), 3, 115	Awesome Thought, 3, 119	5	1:42.93	45,975
1994 **Wekiva Springs**, 3, 121	K. Desormeaux	Gracious Ghost, 3, 116	Dream Trapp, 3, 117	5	1:41.94	45,900
1993 **Art of Living**, 3, 115	G. L. Stevens	Tossofthecoin, 3, 115	Glowing Crown, 3, 115	5	1:43.48	45,900

1992	**Vying Victor**, 3, 115	C. A. Black	Turbulent Kris, 3, 114	Al Sabin, 3, 117	11	1:44.33	$51,000
1991	**Mane Minister**, 3, 114	D. R. Flores	Conveyor, 3, 114	Famed Devil, 3, 114	8	1:42.70	48,375
1990	**Music Prospector**, 3, 114	F. Olivares	Senegalaise, 3, 114	Tsu's Dawning, 3, 120	6	1:43.60	46,950
1989	**Flying Continental**, 3, 117	L. A. Pincay Jr.	Very Personably, 3, 114	Morlando, 3, 114	9	1:43.60	48,750
1988	**Lively One**, 3, 120	W. Shoemaker	Stalwars, 3, 114	Havanaffair, 3, 114	9	1:43.40	48,650
1987	**Stylish Winner**, 3, 114	G. L. Stevens	Prince Sassafras, 3, 117	Barb's Relic, 3, 116	7	1:43.80	38,200
1986	**Ferdinand**, 3, 114	W. Shoemaker	Variety Road, 3, 114	Grand Allegiance, 3, 117	8	1:43.00	38,750
1985	**Floating Reserve**, 3, 117	L. A. Pincay Jr.	Brecons Charge, 3, 117	Bolder Than Bold, 3, 114	11	1:42.60	40,450
1984	**Tights**, 3, 120	R. Q. Meza	Prince True, 3, 117	Gate Dancer, 3, 120	10	1:43.60	40,150
1983	**Fast Passage**, 3, 116	E. Delahoussaye	Hyperborean, 3, 114	My Habitony, 3, 114	8	1:42.60	38,900
1982	**Water Bank**, 3, 115	D. G. McHargue	Bargain Balcony, 3, 117	Crystal Star, 3, 115	8	1:42.40	38,850
1981	**‡Stancharry**, 3, 117	L. A. Pincay Jr.	Minnesota Chief, 3, 117	Litigator, 3, 120	8	**1:41.40**	31,900
1980	**Super Moment**, 3, 115	D. Pierce	Executive Counsel, 3, 117	Decent Davey, 3, 120	7	1:44.40	20,075
	Rumbo, 3, 117	W. Shoemaker	Idyll, 3, 114	Bold 'n Rulling, 3, 117	6	1:44.60	19,675
1979	**Pole Position**, 3, 120	C. J. McCarron	Grand Alliance, 3, 114	Shamgo, 3, 115	8	1:42.00	26,100
1978	**Johnny's Image**, 3, 115	S. Hawley	Kamehameha, 3, 115	Go Forth, 3, 115	8	1:44.00	26,350
1977	**Text**, 3, 118	D. Pierce	Cuzwuzwrong, 3, 118	Nordic Prince, 3, 118	9	1:42.00	24,600
1976	**An Act**, 3, 118	L. A. Pincay Jr.	Life's Hope, 3, 118	First Return, 3, 118	8	1:42.00	20,800
1975	**Kinalmeaky**, 3, 118	W. Shoemaker	Rock of Ages, 3, 118	Looks Impressive, 3, 118	10	1:42.80	22,400
1974	**Rube the Great**, 3, 118	A. Santiago	Aloha Mood, 3, 118	L'Amour Rullah, 3, 118	10	1:43.00	18,700
1973	**Sham**, 3, 118	L. A. Pincay Jr.	Out of the East, 3, 118	Scantling, 3, 118	5	1:45.00	19,800

Named for Rancho Santa Catalina Island, which occupied the entire island of Santa Catalina off the California coast. Grade 3 1998. Santa Catalina H. 1935, 1941-'63, 1997. Santa Catalina California-Bred Championship 1937-'39. Santa Catalina Nursery S. 1940. Not held 1936, 1942-'44. 1 mile 1935. 1⅛ miles 1939, 1947-'52, 1954-'63. 3 furlongs 1940. 7 furlongs 1970. Three-year-olds and up 1937-'38, 1941-'46, 1991. Two-year-olds 1940. Four-year-olds and up 1947-'63. Two divisions 1980. ‡Minnesota Chief finished first, DQ to second, 1981. California-foaled 1963. Non-winners of a race worth $12,500 to the winner 1973-'75. Non-winners of a race worth $25,000 to the winner 1990, 1992. California-breds 1937-'39.

Santa Margarita Invitational Handicap

Grade 1 in 2006. Santa Anita Park, four-year-olds and up, fillies and mares, 1⅛ miles, dirt. Held March 11, 2006, with a gross value of $300,000. First held in 1935. First graded in 1973. Stakes record 1:47 (1954 Cerise Reine; 1986 Lady's Secret).

Year	Winner	Jockey	Second	Third	Strs	Time	1st Purse
2006	**Healthy Addiction**, 5, 116	J. K. Court	Dream of Summer, 7, 120	Seafree, 4, 115	8	1:48.18	$180,000
2005	**Tarlow**, 4, 117	P. A. Valenzuela	Dream of Summer, 6, 116	Miss Loren (Arg), 7, 118	9	1:49.41	180,000
2004	**Adoration**, 5, 118	M. E. Smith	Star Parade (Arg), 5, 115	Bare Necessities, 5, 118	5	1:48.85	180,000
2003	**Starrer**, 5, 121	P. A. Valenzuela	Sightseek, 4, 116	Bella Bellucci, 4, 116	5	1:48.20	180,000
2002	**Azeri**, 4, 115	M. E. Smith	Spain, 5, 118	Printemps (Chi), 5, 116	7	1:49.01	180,000
2001	**Lazy Slusan**, 6, 116	D. R. Flores	Spain, 4, 122	Critikola (Arg), 6, 116	7	1:48.59	180,000
2000	**Riboletta (Brz)**, 5, 115	C. S. Nakatani	Bordelaise (Arg), 5, 114	Snowberg, 5, 114	5	1:50.40	180,000
1999	**Manistique**, 4, 122	G. L. Stevens	Magical Allure, 4, 118	India Divina (Chi), 5, 116	4	1:48.31	180,000
1998	**Toda Una Dama (Arg)**, 5, 114	G. F. Almeida	Exotic Wood, 6, 123	Praviana (Chi), 4, 114	10	1:48.87	180,000
1997	**Jewel Princess**, 5, 125	C. S. Nakatani	Top Rung, 6, 116	Hidden Lake, 4, 114	6	1:49.30	180,000
1996	**Twice the Vice**, 5, 117	C. J. McCarron	Sleep Easy, 4, 115	Jewel Princess, 4, 119	8	1:49.53	180,000
1995	**Queens Court Queen**, 6, 120	C. S. Nakatani	Paseana (Arg), 8, 123	Klassy Kim, 4, 116	5	1:48.81	180,000
1994	**Paseana (Arg)**, 7, 123	C. J. McCarron	Kalita Melody (GB), 6, 117	Stalcreek, 4, 119	9	1:49.12	180,000
1993	**Southern Truce**, 5, 115	C. S. Nakatani	Paseana (Arg), 6, 125	Guiza, 6, 114	9	1:49.46	180,000
1992	**Paseana (Arg)**, 5, 122	C. J. McCarron	Laramie Moon (Arg), 5, 116	Colour Chart, 5, 118	5	1:47.48	180,000
1991	**Little Brianne**, 6, 119	J. A. Garcia	Bayakoa (Arg), 7, 126	A Wild Ride, 4, 119	7	1:48.50	180,000
1990	**Bayakoa (Arg)**, 6, 127	C. J. McCarron	Gorgeous, 4, 125	Luthier's Launch, 4, 113	4	1:48.40	180,000
1989	**Bayakoa (Arg)**, 5, 118	L. A. Pincay Jr.	Goodbye Halo, 4, 125	No Review, 4, 117	7	1:48.40	180,000
1988	**Flying Julia**, 5, 114	F. Olivares	Hollywood Glitter, 4, 118	Clabber Girl, 5, 118	10	1:50.40	180,000
1987	**North Sider**, 5, 117	A. T. Cordero Jr.	Winter Treasure, 4, 115	Frau Altiva (Arg), 5, 117	12	1:48.80	180,000
1986	**Lady's Secret**, 4, 125	J. Velasquez	Johnica, 5, 120	Dontstop Themusic, 6, 122	9	**1:47.00**	180,000
1985	**Lovlier Linda**, 5, 119	C. J. McCarron	Mitterand, 4, 123	Percipient, 4, 116	8	1:48.00	180,000
1984	**Adored**, 4, 114	F. Toro	High Haven, 5, 118	Weekend Surprise, 4, 114	11	1:48.60	150,000
1983	**Marimbula (Chi)**, 5, 119	S. Hawley	Avigaition, 4, 120	Sintrillium, 5, 114	11	1:48.20	150,000
1982	**Ack's Secret**, 6, 118	L. A. Pincay Jr.	Track Robbery, 6, 123	Past Forgetting, 4, 122	10	1:47.60	150,000
1981	**Princess Karenda**, 4, 118	L. A. Pincay Jr.	Glorious Song, 5, 130	Ack's Secret, 5, 122	10	1:47.20	120,000
1980	**Glorious Song**, 4, 120	C. J. McCarron	The Very One, 5, 116	Kankam (Arg), 5, 125	11	1:48.40	82,500
1979	**Sanedtki (Ire)**, 5, 124	W. Shoemaker	‡Surera (Arg), 6, 115	Ida Delia, 5, 117	11	1:47.80	75,000
1978	**Taisez Vous**, 4, 120	D. Pierce	Sensational, 4, 118	*Merry Lady III, 6, 114	11	1:49.00	60,000
1977	***Lucie Manet**, 4, 119	D. G. McHargue	*Bastonera II, 6, 126	Hope of Glory, 5, 114	9	1:48.40	60,000
1976	**Fascinating Girl**, 4, 115	F. Toro	Summertime Promise, 4, 114	Charger's Star, 6, 114	8	1:49.40	60,000
1975	***Tizna**, 6, 120	D. Pierce	Susan's Girl, 6, 123	Gay Style, 5, 125	12	1:48.60	60,000
1974	***Tizna**, 5, 117	F. Toro	Penny Flight, 4, 113	Tallahto, 4, 119	12	1:50.80	60,000
1973	**Susan's Girl**, 4, 127	L. A. Pincay Jr.	Convenience, 5, 123	Minstrel Miss, 6, 115	8	1:47.80	60,000

Named for the 1841 California land grant Rancho Santa Margarita y Las Flores. Santa Margarita H. 1935-'67. Not held 1942-'44. 7 furlongs 1935-'36. 6 furlongs 1937. 1¹⁄₁₆ miles 1938-'48, 1953-'54. Three-year-olds and up 1935-'40, 1945-'60. Both sexes 1935-'37. ‡Queen Yasna finished second, DQ to seventh, 1979.

Santa Maria Handicap

Grade 1 in 2006. Santa Anita Park, four-year-olds and up, fillies and mares, 1 1/16 miles, dirt. Held February 11, 2006, with a gross value of $250,000. First held in 1934. First graded in 1973. Stakes record 1:40.95 (1998 Exotic Wood).

Year	Winner	Jockey	Second	Third	Strs	Time	1st Purse
2006	**Star Parade (Arg)**, 7, 116	M. A. Pedroza	Proposed, 4, 118	Hollywood Story, 5, 117	7	1:42.31	$150,000
2005	**Miss Loren (Arg)**, 7, 117	J. Valdivia Jr.	Good Student (Arg), 5, 114	Hollywood Story, 4, 117	8	1:42.42	150,000
2004	**Star Parade (Arg)**, 5, 114	V. Espinoza	Bare Necessities, 5, 118	La Tour (Chi), 5, 115	6	1:43.87	150,000
2003	**Starrer**, 5, 119	P. A. Valenzuela	You, 4, 118	Rhiana, 6, 112	5	1:42.75	120,000
2002	**Favorite Funtime**, 5, 116	G. L. Stevens	Verruma (Brz), 6, 114	Printemps (Chi), 5, 116	7	1:44.15	120,000
2001	**Lovellon (Arg)**, 5, 116	G. L. Stevens	Feverish, 6, 119	Critikola (Arg), 6, 115	5	1:43.37	120,000
2000	**Manistique**, 5, 125	C. S. Nakatani	Snowberg, 5, 114	Gourmet Girl, 5, 116	8	1:42.60	120,000
1999	**India Divina (Chi)**, 5, 114	G. K. Gomez	Victory Stripes (Arg), 5, 115	Belle's Flag, 6, 117	5	1:42.71	120,000
1998	**Exotic Wood**, 6, 121	C. J. McCarron	Toda Una Dama (Arg), 5, 115	Tuxedo Junction, 5, 115	5	**1:40.95**	120,000
1997	**Jewel Princess**, 5, 123	C. S. Nakatani	Cat's Cradle, 5, 118	Top Rung, 6, 117	7	1:41.72	97,900
1996	**Serena's Song**, 4, 124	G. L. Stevens	Twice the Vice, 5, 118	Real Connection, 5, 114	5	1:42.21	95,800
1995	**Queens Court Queen**, 6, 118	C. S. Nakatani	Paseana (Arg), 8, 123	Key Phrase, 4, 117	5	1:41.61	89,300
1994	**Supah Gem**, 4, 116	C. S. Nakatani	Paseana (Arg), 7, 124	Alysbelle, 5, 116	7	1:41.83	90,700
1993	**Race the Wild Wind**, 4, 117	K. Desormeaux	Paseana (Arg), 6, 126	Southern Truce, 5, 116	6	1:41.27	90,500
1992	**Paseana (Arg)**, 5, 120	C. J. McCarron	Colour Chart, 5, 118	Campagnarde (Arg), 5, 117	5	1:41.94	89,100
1991	**Little Brianne**, 6, 117	J. A. Garcia	Luna Elegante (Arg), 5, 114	Somethingmerry, 4, 114	4	1:41.70	89,700
1990	**Bayakoa (Arg)**, 6, 126	C. J. McCarron	Nikishka, 5, 117	Carita Tostada (Chi), 6, 112	4	1:43.00	90,200
1989	**Miss Brio (Chi)**, 5, 119	E. Delahoussaye	Bayakoa (Arg), 5, 118	Annoconnor, 5, 122	7	1:41.00	79,000
1988	**Mausie (Arg)**, 6, 114	G. L. Stevens	Miss Alto, 5, 118	Novel Sprite, 5, 115	7	1:43.60	63,800
1987	**Fran's Valentine**, 5, 121	P. A. Valenzuela	North Sider, 5, 118	Infinidad (Chi), 5, 113	8	1:42.60	91,700
1986	**Love Smitten**, 5, 120	C. J. McCarron	Johnica, 5, 121	North Sider, 4, 118	9	1:44.60	65,600
1985	**Adored**, 5, 124	L. A. Pincay Jr.	Dontstop Themusic, 5, 121	Lovlier Linda, 5, 122	5	1:42.40	88,800
1984	**Marisma (Chi)**, 6, 117	L. A. Pincay Jr.	Brindy Brindy, 4, 114	Sierva (Arg), 6, 118	7	1:44.20	69,850
	High Haven, 5, 116	R. Sibille	Castilla, 5, 122	Avigaition, 5, 120	8	1:42.40	50,600
1983	**Star Pastures (GB)**, 5, 119	W. Shoemaker	Sintrillium, 5, 116	Viga (Chi), 6, 112	7	1:42.60	49,650
	Sangue (Ire), 5, 124	L. A. Pincay Jr.	Cat Girl, 5, 115	Happy Bride (Ire), 5, 116	8	1:41.00	50,650
1982	**Targa**, 5, 114	F. Olivares	Jameela, 6, 124	Track Robbery, 6, 124	8	1:42.00	65,100
1981	**Glorious Song**, 5, 127	C. J. McCarron	Track Robbery, 5, 117	Miss Huntington, 4, 113	4	1:43.20	45,450
1980	**Kankam (Arg)**, 5, 123	E. Delahoussaye	Flaming Leaves, 5, 123	Miss Magnetic, 5, 117	5	1:41.80	47,400
1979	**Grenzen**, 4, 124	L. A. Pincay Jr.	Ida Delia, 5, 118	Drama Critic, 5, 122	6	1:47.20	37,650
1978	**Swingtime**, 6, 122	F. Toro	Winter Solstice, 6, 124	Granja Sueno, 5, 113	6	1:41.40	37,500
1977	**Hail Hilarious**, 4, 122	D. Pierce	Swingtime, 5, 120	*Bastonera II, 6, 126	10	1:42.00	36,050
1976	**Gay Style**, 6, 127	D. Pierce	Raise Your Skirts, 4, 120	*Tizna, 7, 127	9	1:41.40	35,100
1975	**Gay Style**, 5, 122	W. Shoemaker	*Tizna, 6, 120	Susan's Girl, 6, 124	8	1:42.00	34,650
1974	**Convenience**, 6, 121	L. A. Pincay Jr.	*Tizna, 5, 117	Tallahto, 4, 119	8	1:42.80	34,750
1973	**Susan's Girl**, 4, 125	L. A. Pincay Jr.	Convenience, 5, 123	Hill Circus, 5, 119	6	1:42.00	32,900

Named for the city of Santa Maria, California, located in Santa Barbara County. Grade 2 1973-'89. Santa Maria S. 1934-'47. Not held 1937, 1942-'45, 1948-'51. 6 furlongs 1934-'60. 3 furlongs 1941. 1 mile 1946-'53. 7 furlongs 1954-'56. Two-year-olds and up 1934-'35. Three-year-olds 1936-'40, 1946-'47. Two-year-olds 1941. Three-year-olds and up 1952-'59. Fillies 1936-'47. Two divisions 1983-'84. California-breds 1941.

Santa Monica Handicap

Grade 1 in 2006. Santa Anita Park, four-year-olds and up, fillies and mares, 7 furlongs, dirt. Held January 29, 2006, with a gross value of $250,000. First held in 1957. First graded in 1973. Stakes record 1:20.60 (1982 Past Forgetting).

Year	Winner	Jockey	Second	Third	Strs	Time	1st Purse
2006	**Behaving Badly**, 5, 115	V. Espinoza	Miss Terrible (Arg), 7, 117	Leave Me Alone, 4, 119	8	1:21.93	$150,000
2005	**Salt Champ (Arg)**, 5, 116	G. L. Stevens	Island Fashion, 5, 120	Resplendency, 4, 114	9	1:22.14	150,000
2004	**Island Fashion**, 4, 120	K. Desormeaux	Buffythecenterfold, 4, 114	Got Koko, 5, 119	6	1:21.37	150,000
2003	**Affluent**, 5, 119	A. O. Solis	Sightseek, 4, 115	Secret of Mecca, 5, 110	7	1:22.17	120,000
2002	**Kalookan Queen**, 6, 119	A. O. Solis	Leading Light, 7, 115	Spain, 5, 120	5	1:22.37	120,000
2001	**Nany's Sweep**, 5, 117	K. Desormeaux	Serenita (Arg), 4, 115	Surfside, 4, 121	7	1:22.50	120,000
2000	**Honest Lady**, 4, 114	C. S. Nakatani	Kalookan Queen, 4, 116	Enjoy the Moment, 5, 118	9	1:21.45	132,840
1999	**Stop Traffic**, 6, 120	C. A. Black	Belle's Flag, 6, 118	Closed Escrow, 6, 116	8	1:22.17	120,000
1998	**Exotic Wood**, 6, 121	C. J. McCarron	Madame Pandit, 5, 119	Advancing Star, 5, 121	8	1:21.07	120,000
1997	**Toga Toga Toga**, 5, 114	J. A. Garcia	Ski Dancer, 5, 117	Grab the Prize, 5, 116	6	1:23.27	96,750
1996	**Serena's Song**, 4, 123	G. L. Stevens	Exotic Wood, 4, 118	Klassy Kim, 5, 116	6	1:21.56	96,800
1995	**Key Phrase**, 4, 116	C. W. Antley	Flying in the Lane, 4, 114	Desert Stormer, 5, 117	9	1:22.82	93,100
1994	**Southern Truce**, 6, 116	G. L. Stevens	Arches of Gold, 5, 119	Mamselle Bebette, 4, 115	9	1:21.44	93,100
1993	**Freedom Cry**, 5, 114	A. O. Solis	Devil's Orchid, 6, 119	Mama Simba, 6, 114	7	1:21.78	91,200
1992	**Laramie Moon (Arg)**, 5, 116	E. Delahoussaye	D'Or Ruckus, 4, 114	Ifyoucouldseemenow, 4, 118	10	1:22.66	94,700
1991	**Devil's Orchid**, 4, 116	R. A. Baze	‡Stormy But Valid, 5, 121	Classic Value, 5, 118	7	1:21.90	90,800
1990	**Stormy But Valid**, 4, 119	G. L. Stevens	Survive, 6, 118	Hot Novel, 4, 117	5	1:22.40	61,300
1989	**Miss Brio (Chi)**, 5, 117	E. Delahoussaye	Valdemosa (Arg), 5, 116	Josette, 4, 115	8	1:21.60	64,800
1988	**Pine Tree Lane**, 6, 121	G. L. Stevens	Fairly Old, 5, 115	Le l'Argent, 6, 120	6	1:23.00	60,000
1987	**Pine Tree Lane**, 5, 125	A. T. Cordero Jr.	Balladry, 5, 116	Her Royalty, 6, 119	6	1:21.80	58,140
1986	**Her Royalty**, 5, 120	C. J. McCarron	North Sider, 4, 119	Take My Picture, 4, 117	8	1:21.60	51,300
1985	**Lovlier Linda**, 5, 123	W. Shoemaker	Dontstop Themusic, 5, 123	Foggy Nation, 5, 119	5	1:22.80	48,900
1984	**Bara Lass**, 5, 124	W. A. Guerra	Holiday Dancer, 4, 117	Bally Knockan, 5, 113	9	1:22.00	52,250
1983	**Past Forgetting**, 5, 123	C. J. McCarron	‡Sierva (Arg), 5, 119	Bara Lass, 4, 115	10	1:23.40	49,850

1982	**Past Forgetting**, 4, 122	W. Shoemaker	Nell's Briquette, 4, 118	In True Form, 4, 117	9	**1:20.60**	$49,250
1981	**Parsley**, 5, 116	A. T. Cordero Jr.	Ack's Secret, 5, 125	Splendid Girl, 5, 118	7	1:23.40	40,050
1980	**Flack Flack**, 5, 117	W. Shoemaker	Shine High, 4, 115	Flaming Leaves, 5, 123	6	1:23.80	39,100
1979	**Grenzen**, 4, 122	L. A. Pincay Jr.	Dottie's Doll, 6, 116	Bidding Bold, 4, 116	8	1:21.60	40,600
1978	**Winter Solstice**, 6, 123	D. G. McHargue	Little Happiness, 4, 115	Splendid Size, 4, 117	7	1:21.20	27,200
1977	**Hail Hilarious**, 4, 119	D. Pierce	*Bastonera II, 6, 125	Modus Vivendi, 6, 121	8	1:22.60	28,150
1976	**Gay Style**, 6, 125	D. Pierce	Raise Your Skirts, 4, 123	*Tizna, 7, 129	6	1:22.00	26,650
1975	**Sister Fleet**, 5, 115	F. Toro	Susan's Girl, 6, 125	Modus Vivendi, 4, 123	13	1:21.40	31,250
1974	***Tizna**, 5, 116	F. Toro	Susan's Girl, 5, 127	Impressive Style, 5, 118	7	1:24.00	28,050
1973	**Chou Croute**, 5, 128	J. L. Rotz	Generous Portion, 5, 114	Minstrel Miss, 6, 115	7	1:23.60	27,800

Named for the city of Santa Monica, California. Grade 2 1973-'83, 1988-'89. Grade 3 1984-'87. Not held 1970. Three-year-olds and up 1957-'59. ‡Marimbula (Chi) finished second, DQ to sixth, 1983. ‡Classic Value finished second, DQ to third, 1991.

Santa Paula Stakes

Grade 3 in 2006. Santa Anita Park, three-year-olds, fillies, 6½ furlongs, dirt. Held April 1, 2006, with a gross value of $105,650. First held in 1968. First graded in 1973. Stakes record 1:15.02 (1994 Sardula).

Year	Winner	Jockey	Second	Third	Strs	Time	1st Purse
2006	**Bettarun Fast**, 3, 116	A. T. Gryder	El Mirage Queen, 3, 116	Acceleration, 3, 116	7	1:15.08	$63,390
2005	**No Bull Baby**, 3, 118	V. Espinoza	Leave Me Alone, 3, 114	Inspiring, 3, 118	6	1:15.79	48,240
2004	**Friendly Michelle**, 3, 116	T. Baze	Lyin Goddess, 3, 116	Very Vegas, 3, 118	5	1:17.34	48,690
2003	**Buffythecenterfold**, 3, 121	V. Espinoza	Watching You, 3, 116	Tavy's Plan, 3, 114	5	1:16.56	47,655
2002	**Bella Bellucci**, 3, 118	M. E. Smith	Shameful, 3, 116	Spring Meadow, 3, 117	5	1:16.36	47,745
2001	**Starrer**, 3, 114	C. J. McCarron	Skywriting, 3, 117	Warren's Whistle, 3, 121	7	1:16.46	49,920
2000	**Abby Girl**, 3, 116	C. S. Nakatani	Mintly Fresh, 3, 114	Classic Olympio, 3, 118	5	1:15.47	47,700
1999	**Perfect Six**, 3, 116	D. R. Flores	Olympic Charmer, 3, 116	Kalookan Queen, 3, 116	4	1:15.41	47,295
1998	**Loveontheroad**, 3, 117	K. Desormeaux	Holy Nola, 3, 118	Tippytoe Cat, 3, 116	7	1:16.07	48,690
1997	**Lavender**, 3, 118	A. O. Solis	Silken Magic, 3, 117	Soiree, 3, 116	6	1:16.34	64,300
1996	**Raw Gold**, 3, 121	C. W. Antley	Sheza Valentine, 3, 114	Supercilious, 3, 116	6	1:15.63	64,200
1995	**Made to Perfection**, 3, 114	A. O. Solis	Embroidered, 3, 116	Comstock Queen, 3, 114	5	1:16.24	45,975
1994	**Sardula**, 3, 121	E. Delahoussaye	Ballerina Gal, 3, 117	Serena's World, 3, 117	5	**1:15.02**	61,000
1992	**Peaceful Road**, 3, 116	M. A. Pedroza	Jetinwith Kennedy, 3, 115	Wicked Wit, 3, 118	9	1:16.33	65,200
1974	**Viva La Vivi**, 4, 121	D. Pierce	Miss Rebound, 6, 113	Sister Fleet, 4, 116	3	1:24.00	21,300
1973	***Tizna**, 4, 124	F. Toro	Minstrel Miss, 6, 121	Judith, 5, 109	3	1:21.60	19,100

Named for the Santa Paula y Saticoy Rancho, site of present-day Saticoy, California. Saticoy is the Chumash Indian name for a native village. Not graded 1992-2005. Santa Paula H. 1968-'74. Not held 1975-'91, 1993. 7 furlongs 1968-'74. Four-year-olds and up 1968-'74. Fillies and mares 1968-'74.

Santa Ynez Stakes

Grade 2 in 2006. Santa Anita Park, three-year-olds, fillies, 7 furlongs, dirt. Held January 16, 2006, with a gross value of $150,000. First held in 1952. First graded in 1973. Stakes record 1:21.11 (2004 Yearly Report).

Year	Winner	Jockey	Second	Third	Strs	Time	1st Purse
2006	**Dance Daily**, 3, 114	J. K. Court	Talullah Lula, 3, 115	Folklore, 3, 123	6	1:23.34	$90,000
2005	**Sharp Lisa**, 3, 114	T. Baze	No Bull Baby, 3, 121	Hot Attraction, 3, 114	7	1:23.10	90,000
2004	**Yearly Report**, 3, 114	J. D. Bailey	House of Fortune, 3, 121	Papa to Kinzie, 3, 115	8	**1:21.11**	90,000
2003	**Elloluv**, 3, 121	P. A. Valenzuela	Watching You, 3, 116	Himalayan, 3, 116	5	1:23.03	90,000
2002	**Dancing (GB)**, 3, 116	G. L. Stevens	Respectful, 3, 116	Lady George, 3, 123	8	1:23.07	90,000
2001	**Golden Ballet**, 3, 123	C. J. McCarron	Affluent, 3, 114	Warren's Whistle, 3, 116	9	1:22.30	90,000
2000	**Penny Blues**, 3, 118	E. Delahoussaye	Classic Olympio, 3, 121	Mean Imogene, 3, 117	5	1:23.38	63,600
1999	**Honest Lady**, 3, 115	K. Desormeaux	Rayelle, 3, 118	Controlled, 3, 123	4	1:21.67	63,240
1998	**Nijinsky's Passion**, 3, 121	C. A. Black	Well Chosen, 3, 115	Vivid Angel, 3, 123	7	1:23.15	64,980
1997	**Queen of Money**, 3, 116	D. R. Flores	Goodnight Irene, 3, 116	High Heeled Hope, 3, 121	8	1:22.55	65,650
1996	**Raw Gold**, 3, 121	C. W. Antley	Pareja, 3, 121	Hidden Lake, 3, 116	6	1:22.66	64,550
1995	**Serena's Song**, 3, 123	C. S. Nakatani	Cat's Cradle, 3, 121	Call Now, 3, 121	5	1:21.45	59,800
1994	**Tricky Code**, 3, 121	C. S. Nakatani	Fancy 'n Fabulous, 3, 114	Sophisticatedcielo, 3, 116	5	1:22.16	59,575
1993	**Fit to Lead**, 3, 116	C. S. Nakatani	Nijivision, 3, 114	Booklore, 3, 115	8	1:22.55	62,500
1992	**Looie Capote**, 3, 114	K. Desormeaux	Icy Eyes, 3, 118	Soviet Sojourn, 3, 121	7	1:23.42	61,450
1991	**Brazen**, 3, 121	C. J. McCarron	Fowda, 3, 116	Ifyoucouldseemenow, 3, 121	5	1:23.70	46,050
1990	**Fit to Scout**, 3, 118	C. J. McCarron	Bright Candles, 3, 114	Heaven for Bid, 3, 116	6	1:23.80	60,625
1989	**Hot Novel**, 3, 121	E. Delahoussaye	Fantastic Look, 3, 114	Agotaras, 3, 121	6	1:22.80	46,950
1988	**Goodbye Halo**, 3, 123	J. Velasquez	Bolchina, 3, 116	Floral Magic, 3, 114	8	1:23.40	47,900
1987	**Very Subtle**, 3, 122	W. Shoemaker	Chic Shirine, 3, 119	Young Flyer, 3, 122	5	1:22.60	46,200
1986	**Sari's Heroine**, 3, 119	A. O. Solis	An Empress, 3, 117	Life At the Top, 3, 115	8	1:23.40	52,000
1985	**Wising Up**, 3, 119	E. Delahoussaye	Rascal Lass, 3, 122	Reigning Countess, 3, 119	9	1:23.40	52,700
1984	**Gene's Lady**, 3, 117	L. A. Pincay Jr.	Kennedy Express, 3, 115	Natural Summit, 3, 117	9	1:23.80	41,600
	Boo La Boo, 3, 122	L. A. Pincay Jr.	Personable Lady, 3, 122	Costly Array, 3, 117	7	1:23.20	39,900
1983	**A Lucky Sign**, 3, 121	C. J. McCarron	Sophisticated Girl, 3, 116	Fabulous Notion, 3, 124	8	1:23.40	49,050
1982	**Flying Partner**, 3, 114	R. Sibille	Skillful Joy, 3, 124	Carry a Tune, 3, 114	8	1:22.80	49,300
1981	**Past Forgetting**, 3, 119	S. Hawley	Rosie Doon, 3, 119	Nell's Briquette, 3, 121	11	1:22.40	41,800
1980	**Table Hands**, 3, 117	W. Shoemaker	Street Ballet, 3, 119	Hazel R., 3, 119	7	1:22.40	38,700

1979	**Terlingua**, 3, 121	L. A. Pincay Jr.	Caline, 3, 119	It's in the Air, 3, 121	5	1:21.20	$37,900
1978	**Grenzen**, 3, 119	D. G. McHargue	Extravagant, 3, 121	Happy Kin, 3, 114	9	1:22.20	27,600
1977	**Wavy Waves**, 3, 121	L. A. Pincay Jr.	Don's Music, 3, 119	Any Time Girl, 3, 121	11	1:22.80	29,550
1976	**Daisy Do**, 3, 114	S. Hawley	Girl in Love, 3, 115	Windy Welcome, 3, 117	6	1:22.40	20,300
1975	**Raise Your Skirts**, 3, 117	W. Mahorney	Fascinating Girl, 3, 115	Miss Francesca, 3, 117	13	1:22.40	23,350
1974	**Modus Vivendi**, 3, 119	D. Pierce	Donna Chere, 3, 114	Special Team, 3, 121	9	1:22.40	28,500
1973	**Tallahto**, 3, 117	J. E. Tejeira	Waltz Fan, 3, 117	Windy's Daughter, 3, 121	5	1:21.40	25,800

Named for the city of Santa Ynez, California, which takes its name from an 1804 mission. Grade 3 1975-'80, 1984-'98. Santa Ynez Breeders' Cup S. 1990-'95. Not held 1953. 6 furlongs 1952, 1956-'57. $6\frac{1}{2}$ furlongs 1958-'66. Two-year-olds 1952 (December). Two divisions 1984.

Santa Ysabel Stakes

Grade 3 in 2006. Santa Anita Park, three-year-olds, fillies, $1\frac{1}{16}$ miles, dirt. Held January 7, 2006, with a gross value of $109,200. First held in 1968. First graded in 1998. Stakes record 1:41.34 (1997 Sharp Cat).

Year	Winner	Jockey	Second	Third	Strs	Time	1st Purse
2006	**Itty Bitty Pretty**, 3, 118	P. A. Valenzuela	Sabatini, 3, 115	Horse B With You, 3, 118	6	1:44.60	$65,520
2005	**Sweet Catomine**, 3, 124	D. R. Flores	Pussycat Doll, 3, 115	On London Time, 3, 115	5	1:43.77	64,800
2004	**A. P. Adventure**, 3, 115	A. O. Solis	Salty Romance, 3, 120	Wildwood Flower, 3, 115	6	1:44.27	64,080
2003	**Atlantic Ocean**, 3, 120	D. R. Flores	Sea Jewel, 3, 115	Summer Wind Dancer, 3, 120	6	1:43.25	66,540
2002	**Bella Bella Bella**, 3, 115	C. J. McCarron	Tamarack Bay, 3, 116	No Turbulence, 3, 116	4	1:44.14	64,550
2001	**Collect Call**, 3, 115	A. O. Solis	Irguns Angel, 3, 115	Eminent, 3, 115	8	1:44.69	65,580
2000	**Surfside**, 3, 123	P. Day	Rings a Chime, 3, 115	She's Classy, 3, 118	4	1:43.53	62,880
1999	**Holywood Picture**, 3, 115	O. Vergara	Exbourne Free, 3, 115	Gleefully, 3, 116	7	1:43.48	64,860
1998	**‡Nonies Dancer Ali**, 3, 114	G. K. Gomez	Mamaison Miss, 3, 116	Continental Lea, 3, 113	5	1:44.14	63,660
1997	**Sharp Cat**, 3, 120	C. S. Nakatani	Clever Pilot, 3, 115	Guthrie, 3, 116	6	**1:41.34**	64,300
1996	**Antespend**, 3, 120	C. W. Antley	Dancing Prism, 3, 114	Rumpipumpy (GB), 3, 116	6	1:43.87	64,950
1995	**Ski Dancer**, 3, 115	K. Desormeaux	Dixie Pearl, 3, 117	Wilga, 3, 115	5	1:44.24	45,750
1994	**Princess Mitterand**, 3, 119	C. J. McCarron	Dianes Halo, 3, 115	Jacodra's Devil, 3, 115	4	1:43.25	44,925
1993	**Likeable Style**, 3, 115	G. L. Stevens	Fit to Lead, 3, 117	Amandari, 3, 117	5	1:44.74	45,900
1992	**Crownette**, 3, 116	P. A. Valenzuela	Golden Treat, 3, 114	Looie Capote, 3, 114	9	1:44.33	48,975
1991	**Nice Assay**, 3, 117	L. A. Pincay Jr.	Assombrie, 3, 117	Ms. Aerosmith, 3, 115	9	1:43.70	49,275
1990	**Bright Candles**, 3, 114	G. L. Stevens	Heaven for Bid, 3, 117	Annual Reunion, 3, 117	7	1:45.60	47,175
1989	**Gorgeous**, 3, 116	E. Delahoussaye	My Glamorous One, 3, 117	April Mon, 3, 114	6	1:42.40	46,450
1988	**Jeanne Jones**, 3, 114	W. Shoemaker	Pattern Step, 3, 120	Affordable Price, 3, 116	8	1:43.60	48,100
1987	**Perchance to Dream**, 3, 117	R. Sibille	Buryyourbelief, 3, 117	My Turbulent Beau, 3, 114	7	1:43.40	37,900
1986	**Trim Colony**, 3, 117	G. L. Stevens	Fashion Book, 3, 115	Top Corsage, 3, 117	5	1:44.80	36,900
1985	**Savannah Dancer**, 3, 120	W. Shoemaker	Pink Sapphire, 3, 117	Ed's Bold Lady (Ire), 3, 117	6	1:44.20	37,350
1984	**Sales Bulletin**, 3, 115	C. J. McCarron	Spring Loose, 3, 115	Agitated Miss, 3, 115	9	1:44.00	39,300
1983	**Ski Goggle**, 3, 115	C. J. McCarron	Sophisticated Girl, 3, 116	Saucy Bobbie, 3, 115	7	1:41.60	38,100
1982	**Avigaition**, 3, 115	E. Delahoussaye	Blush With Pride, 3, 117	Carry a Tune, 3, 114	10	1:42.40	39,750
1981	**Lovely Robbery**, 3, 117	L. A. Pincay Jr.	Bee a Scout, 3, 117	Ice Princess, 3, 117	10	1:44.20	33,350
1980	**Back At Two**, 3, 117	F. Toro	Thundertee, 3, 117	Regretfully, 3, 114	4	1:45.20	24,250
1979	**Maytide**, 3, 114	A. T. Cordero Jr.	Smile On Me, 3, 117	Smaller Bicker, 3, 114	7	1:44.00	19,875
	Top Soil, 3, 115	D. Pierce	Reporting Act, 3, 114	To the Top, 3, 114	9	1:44.00	20,675
1978	**Palmistry**, 3, 115	W. Shoemaker	Equanimity, 3, 115	My Buck, 3, 115	8	1:44.40	26,050
1977	**Geothermal**, 3, 116	M. Castaneda	*Glenaris, 3, 116	Sound of Summer, 3, 116	8	1:43.00	23,550
1976	**Flunsa**, 3, 116	S. Hawley	Girl in Love, 3, 116	Go March, 3, 116	7	1:43.80	20,100
1975	**Double You Lou**, 3, 116	S. Hawley	Fascinating Girl, 3, 116	Miss Francesca, 3, 116	10	1:44.80	21,300
1974	**Miss Musket**, 3, 116	W. Shoemaker	Acknowledge Me, 3, 116	Lucky Spell, 3, 116	9	1:41.80	17,800
1973	**Belle Marie**, 3, 116	L. A. Pincay Jr.	Wind Gap, 3, 116	Flo's Pleasure, 3, 116	7	1:45.40	20,800

Named for two California land grants called Rancho Santa Ysabel, home of the Santa Ysabel mission. 7 furlongs 1970. Two divisions 1979. ‡Love Lock finished first, DQ to fifth for a positive drug test, 1998. Non-winners of a race worth $12,500 to the winner 1973. Non-winners of a race worth $25,000 to the winner 1992.

San Vicente Stakes

Grade 2 in 2006. Santa Anita Park, three-year-olds, 7 furlongs, dirt. Held February 12, 2006, with a gross value of $150,000. First held in 1935. First graded in 1973. Stakes record 1:21 (1973 Ancient Title).

Year	Winner	Jockey	Second	Third	Strs	Time	1st Purse
2006	**Too Much Bling**, 3, 116	G. K. Gomez	Peace Chant, 3, 115	New Joysey Jeff, 3, 116	8	1:22.50	$90,000
2005	**Fusaichi Rock Star**, 3, 116	D. R. Flores	Don't Get Mad, 3, 115	Kirkendahl, 3, 116	4	1:22.59	90,000
2004	**Imperialism**, 3, 116	V. Espinoza	Hosco, 3, 120	Consecrate, 3, 116	6	1:22.34	90,000
2003	**Kafwain**, 3, 123	V. Espinoza	Sum Trick, 3, 120	Southern Image, 3, 117	5	1:21.12	90,000
2002	**Came Home**, 3, 123	C. J. McCarron	Jack's Silver, 3, 116	Werblin, 3, 116	6	1:21.92	90,000
2001	**Early Flyer**, 3, 114	C. J. McCarron	Lasersport, 3, 120	D'wildcat, 3, 117	5	1:21.51	90,000
2000	**Archer City Slew**, 3, 117	K. Desormeaux	Joopy Doopy, 3, 116	Gibson County, 3, 120	6	1:22.18	90,000
1999	**Exploit**, 3, 123	C. J. McCarron	Aristotle, 3, 116	Yes It's True, 3, 123	3	1:22.00	90,000
1998	**Sea of Secrets**, 3, 116	K. Desormeaux	Late Edition, 3, 115	Pleasant Drive, 3, 116	5	1:22.00	64,080
1997	**Silver Charm**, 3, 120	C. J. McCarron	Free House, 3, 120	Funontherun, 3, 114	9	1:21.07	66,400
1996	**Afleetaffair**, 3, 116	C. S. Nakatani	Honour and Glory, 3, 123	Ready to Order, 3, 120	5	1:22.28	63,850
1995	**Afternoon Deelites**, 3, 120	K. Desormeaux	Mr Purple, 3, 116	Fandarel Dancer, 3, 117	5	1:21.35	59,725

1994	**Fly'n J. Bryan**, 3, 114	C. A. Black	Gracious Ghost, 3, 114	Cois Na Tine (Ire), 3, 116	6	1:22.32	$60,700
1993	**Yappy**, 3, 116	P. A. Valenzuela	Denmars Dream, 3, 118	Devoted Brass, 3, 116	9	1:22.33	63,100
1992	**Mineral Wells**, 3, 116	P. A. Valenzuela	Star of the Crop, 3, 116	Prince Wild, 3, 118	7	1:21.28	61,450
1991	**Olympio**, 3, 120	E. Delahoussaye	Dinard, 3, 118	Scan, 3, 123	6	1:21.50	61,075
1990	**Mister Frisky**, 3, 118	G. L. Stevens	Tarascon, 3, 120	Top Cash, 3, 120	6	1:22.60	47,325
1989	**Gum**, 3, 117	L. A. Pincay Jr.	Yes I'm Blue, 3, 120	Roman Avie, 3, 114	7	1:22.40	47,600
1988	**Mi Preferido**, 3, 120	A. O. Solis	No Commitment, 3, 120	Success Express, 3, 123	5	1:22.60	45,900
1987	**Stylish Winner**, 3, 119	G. L. Stevens	Prince Sassafras, 3, 116	Mount Laguna, 3, 116	6	1:23.80	46,750
1986	**Grand Allegiance**, 3, 114	R. Hernandez	Royal Treasure, 3, 114	Dancing Pirate, 3, 119	7	1:23.20	51,050
1985	**The Rogers Four**, 3, 124	C. J. McCarron	Teddy Naturally, 3, 119	Michadilla, 3, 122	5	1:22.80	49,400
1984	**Fortunate Prospect**, 3, 119	D. Pierce	Precisionist, 3, 122	Tights, 3, 117	5	1:22.80	49,700
1983	**Shecky Blue**, 3, 114	S. Hawley	Full Choke, 3, 117	Naevus, 3, 115	7	1:22.40	48,200
1982	**Unpredictable**, 3, 122	E. Delahoussaye	Prince Spellbound, 3, 122	Sepulveda, 3, 119	10	1:21.20	50,700
1981	**Flying Nashua**, 3, 114	A. T. Cordero Jr.	Minnesota Chief, 3, 117	Torso, 3, 117	9	1:23.40	40,450
1980	**Raise a Man**, 3, 114	W. Shoemaker	Super Moment, 3, 114	Bold 'n Rulling, 3, 117	8	1:21.40	39,550
1979	**Flying Paster**, 3, 124	D. Pierce	Oats and Corn, 3, 119	Infusive, 3, 122	5	1:21.20	37,300
1978	**Chance Dancer**, 3, 122	R. Culberson	O Big Al, 3, 122	Reb's Golden Ale, 3, 114	6	1:22.20	25,600
1977	**Replant**, 3, 117	D. G. McHargue	Current Concept, 3, 122	Smasher, 3, 122	8	1:21.20	29,750
1976	**Thermal Energy**, 3, 117	W. Shoemaker	Stained Glass, 3, 122	Bold Forbes, 3, 119	7	1:21.80	20,200
1975	**Boomie S.**, 3, 114	S. Hawley	George Navonod, 3, 122	Udonegood, 3, 114	8	1:22.00	21,350
1974	**Triple Crown**, 3, 114	B. Baeza	El Espanoleto, 3, 114	Destroyer, 3, 114	8	1:22.60	28,000
1973	**Ancient Title**, 3, 122	F. Toro	Linda's Chief, 3, 122	Out of the East, 3, 114	9	**1:21.00**	28,150

Named for El Rancho San Vicente, California; early horse races were held there on a mesa. Grade 3 1973-'82, 1984-'97. San Vicente H. 1956-'66. San Vicente Breeders' Cup S. 1990-'95. Not held 1942-'44, 1949-'51, 1970. 6 furlongs 1935-'36, 1952-'54. 1 mile 1940-'46. $1\frac{1}{16}$ miles 1947-'48. Three-year-olds and up 1935-'36. Colts and geldings 1935-'53.

Sapling Stakes

Grade 3 in 2006. Monmouth Park, two-year-olds, 6 furlongs, dirt. Held August 20, 2005, with a gross value of $150,000. First held in 1883. First graded in 1973. Stakes record 1:07.84 (1992 Gilded Time).

Year	Winner	Jockey	Second	Third	Strs	Time	1st Purse
2005	**He's Got Grit**, 2, 121	A. T. Gryder	Diabolical, 2, 121	Confront, 2, 121	6	1:09.69	$90,000
2004	**Evil Minister**, 2, 120	J. Pimentel	Park Avenue Ball, 2, 120	Upscaled, 2, 120	8	1:11.21	60,000
2003	**Dashboard Drummer**, 2, 120	J. C. Ferrer	Deputy Storm, 2, 120	Charming Jim, 2, 120	7	1:10.84	60,000
2002	**Valid Video**, 2, 120	C. C. Lopez	Farno, 2, 120	Boston Park, 2, 120	8	1:09.88	60,000
2001	**Pure Precision**, 2, 120	E. Coa	Truman's Raider, 2, 120	Wild Navigator, 2, 120	8	1:10.82	90,000
2000	**Shooter**, 2, 119	J. Bravo	Snow Ridge, 2, 119	T P Louie, 2, 119	7	1:10.63	120,000
1999	**Dont Tell the Kids**, 2, 122	J. E. Tejeira	Outrigger, 2, 122	House Burner, 2, 122	6	1:10.18	120,000
1998	**Yes It's True**, 2, 122	S. J. Sellers	Erlton, 2, 122	Heroofthegame, 2, 122	7	1:10.09	120,000
1997	**Double Honor**, 2, 122	J. Bravo	Jigadee, 2, 122	E Z Line, 2, 122	8	1:09.75	120,000
1996	**Smoke Glacken**, 2, 122	C. Perret	Harley Tune, 2, 122	Country Rainbow, 2, 122	10	1:10.16	120,000
1995	**Hennessy**, 2, 122	D. M. Barton	Built for Pleasure, 2, 122	Cashier Coyote, 2, 122	7	1:10.84	120,000
1994	**Boone's Mill**, 2, 122	P. Day	Enlighten, 2, 122	Western Echo, 2, 122	6	1:10.46	120,000
1993	**Sacred Honour**, 2, 122	C. E. Lopez Sr.	Meadow Flight, 2, 122	Solly's Honor, 2, 117	6	1:11.19	120,000
1992	**Gilded Time**, 2, 122	C. J. McCarron	Wild Zone, 2, 122	Great Navigator, 2, 122	8	**1:07.84**	120,000
1991	**Big Sur**, 2, 122	R. Migliore	Never Wavering, 2, 122	Dr Fountainstein, 2, 122	8	1:10.92	120,000
1990	**Deposit Ticket**, 2, 122	G. L. Stevens	Alaskan Frost, 2, 122	Hansel, 2, 122	9	1:11.00	120,000
1989	**Carson City**, 2, 122	J. A. Krone	Mr. Nasty, 2, 122	Adjudicating, 2, 122	7	1:10.40	120,000
1988	**Bio**, 2, 122	P. A. Johnson	Truely Colorful, 2, 122	Light My Fuse, 2, 122	8	1:10.40	111,600
1987	**Tejano**, 2, 122	J. Vasquez	Unzipped, 2, 122	Jim's Orbit, 2, 122	8	1:09.00	111,600
1986	**Bet Twice**, 2, 122	C. W. Antley	Faster Than Sound, 2, 122	Homebuilder, 2, 122	5	1:10.20	120,000
1985	**Hilco Scamper**, 2, 122	G. L. Stevens	Danny's Keys, 2, 122	Mr. Spiffy, 2, 122	9	1:10.80	114,555
1984	**Doubly Clear**, 2, 122	J. R. Garcia	†Tiltalating, 2, 119	Do It Again Dan, 2, 122	10	1:10.40	120,150
1983	**Smart n Slick**, 2, 122	D. A. Miller Jr.	Tonto, 2, 122	Triple Sec, 2, 122	9	1:10.80	120,615
1982	**O. K. by You**, 2, 122	C. Perret	Willow Drive, 2, 122	Love to Laugh, 2, 122	8	1:10.80	82,032
1981	**Out of Hock**, 2, 122	D. Brumfield	T. Dykes, 2, 122	What a Wabbit, 2, 122	9	1:10.20	90,591
1980	**Travelling Music**, 2, 122	C. Perret	Lord Avie, 2, 122	Timeless Event, 2, 122	8	1:11.00	78,438
1979	**Rockhill Native**, 2, 122	J. Oldham	Antique Gold, 2, 122	Gold Stage, 2, 122	7	1:08.80	75,366
1978	**Tim the Tiger**, 2, 122	J. Fell	Groton High, 2, 122	Spartan Emperor, 2, 116	7	1:11.80	86,682
1977	**Alydar**, 2, 122	E. Maple	Noon Time Spender, 2, 122	Dominant Ruler, 2, 122	5	1:10.60	65,829
1976	**Ali Oop**, 2, 122	L. Saumell	Ahoy Mate, 2, 122	First Ambassador, 2, 122	10	1:09.80	84,636
1975	**Full Out**, 2, 122	B. Thornburg	Riverside Sam, 2, 116	Eustace, 2, 122	13	1:11.60	82,227
1974	**Foolish Pleasure**, 2, 122	J. Vasquez	The Bagel Prince, 2, 122	Bombay Duck, 2, 122	15	1:10.40	86,997
1973	**Tisab**, 2, 122	W. Blum	Wedge Shot, 2, 122	Go for Love, 2, 122	11	1:10.20	77,721

Young trees are referred to as saplings. Grade 1 1973-'83. Grade 2 1984-'96. Not held 1894-1945. $5\frac{1}{2}$ furlongs 1893. Track record 1992. †Denotes female.

Saranac Stakes

Grade 3 in 2006. Saratoga Race Course, three-year-olds, $1\frac{3}{16}$ miles, turf. Held September 4, 2005, with a gross value of $111,900. First held in 1901. First graded in 1973. Stakes record 1:51.61 (1999 Phi Beta Doc).

Year	Winner	Jockey	Second	Third	Strs	Time	1st Purse
2005	**Jambalaya**, 3, 121	J. C. Jones	Silver Whistle, 3, 115	Woodlander, 3, 121	9	1:54.20	$67,140
2004	**Prince Arch**, 3, 123	J. Castellano	Mustanfar, 3, 121	Catch the Glory, 3, 115	6	1:53.89	64,920

2003	**Shoal Water**, 3, 116	J. R. Velazquez	Urban King (Ire), 3, 115	Sharp Impact, 3, 116	6	1:55.43	$65,280
2002	**Ibn Al Haitham (GB)**, 3, 114	R. Migliore	Finality, 3, 116	Irish Colonial, 3, 115	9	1:55.30	66,900
2001	**Blazing Fury**, 3, 113	J. Castellano	Fast City, 3, 114	Rapid Ryan, 3, 114	9	1:54.88	67,500
2000	**Rob's Spirit**, 3, 120	J. D. Bailey	Whata Brainstorm, 3, 117	Dawn of the Condor, 3, 117	9	1:55.47	68,280
1999	**Phi Beta Doc**, 3, 118	R. A. Dominguez	Monarch's Maze, 3, 114	Big Rascal, 3, 113	8	**1:51.61**	67,020
1998	**Crowd Pleaser**, 3, 115	J. Samyn	Parade Ground, 3, 122	Reformer Rally, 3, 115	7	1:53.42	66,060
1997	**River Squall**, 3, 114	C. Perret	Daylight Savings, 3, 114	Inkatha (Fr), 3, 114	10	1:52.82	68,460
1996	**Harghar**, 3, 113	P. Day	Sir Cat, 3, 123	Defacto, 3, 115	11	1:48.58	69,180
1995	**Debonair Dan**, 3, 112	J. F. Chavez	Crimson Guard, 3, 122	Treasurer (GB), 3, 114	7	1:33.65	50,400
1994	**†Casa Eire**, 3, 114	J. Bravo	Warn Me (GB), 3, 114	Presently, 3, 117	8	1:34.67	66,480
1993	**Halissee**, 3, 114	J. A. Krone	Forest Wind, 3, 117	Compadre, 3, 114	9	1:34.34	74,280
1992	**Casino Magistrate**, 3, 120	E. Maple	Restless Doctor, 3, 114	Smiling and Dancin, 3, 117	10	1:39.37	76,440
1991	**Club Champ**, 3, 114	A. T. Cordero Jr.	Share the Glory, 3, 117	Young Daniel, 3, 114	15	1:34.34	81,480
1990	**Rouse the Louse**, 3, 114	J. D. Bailey	†My Girl Jeannie, 3, 118	V. J.'s Honor, 3, 114	12	1:37.00	78,600
1989	**Expensive Decision**, 3, 114	J. Samyn	Ninety Years Young, 3, 114	Valid Ordinate, 3, 114	8	1:36.00	55,140
	Slew the Knight, 3, 114	J. Samyn	Verbatree, 3, 114	Luge (GB), 3, 123	8	1:36.00	55,620
1988	**Posen**, 3, 123	D. Brumfield	Sunshine Forever, 3, 114	Blew by Em, 3, 117	8	1:38.40	73,560
1987	**Lights and Music**, 3, 114	E. Maple	Forest Fair, 3, 114	First Patriot, 3, 117	10	1:34.80	73,560
1986	**Glow**, 3, 114	E. Maple	Manila, 3, 114	Pillaster, 3, 120	11	1:34.60	72,270
1985	**Equalize**, 3, 114	R. G. Davis	Verification, 3, 114	Danger's Hour, 3, 114	9	1:39.00	71,820
1984	**Is Your Pleasure**, 3, 114	A. T. Cordero Jr.	Onyxly, 3, 114	Loft, 3, 123	12	1:35.20	61,470
1983	**†Sabin**, 3, 113	E. Maple	Fortnightly, 3, 117	Domynsky (GB), 3, 123	10	1:39.60	36,600
1982	**Prince Westport**, 3, 114	J. D. Bailey	Four Bases, 3, 114	A Real Leader, 3, 114	8	1:39.00	35,040
1981	**†De La Rose**, 3, 112	E. Maple	Stage Door Key, 3, 114	Color Bearer, 3, 114	7	1:34.40	35,400
1980	**Key to Content**, 3, 114	G. Martens	Current Legend, 3, 114	Ben Fab, 3, 123	13	1:33.80	36,300
1979	**Told**, 3, 114	J. Cruguet	Crown Thy Good, 3, 114	Quiet Crossing, 3, 123	10	1:34.40	35,250
1978	**Buckaroo**, 3, 123	J. Velasquez	Junction, 3, 123	Quadratic, 3, 123	5	1:35.00	31,950
1977	**Bailjumper**, 3, 114	A. T. Cordero Jr.	Lynn Davis, 3, 114	Gift of Kings, 3, 114	9	1:35.20	32,910
1976	**Dance Spell**, 3, 114	A. T. Cordero Jr.	Zen, 3, 123	Quiet Little Table, 3, 114	6	1:34.20	33,030
1975	**Bravest Roman**, 3, 114	E. Maple	Wajima, 3, 114	Valid Appeal, 3, 114	9	1:34.80	34,380
1974	**Accipiter**, 3, 123	A. Santiago	Best of It, 3, 117	Hosiery, 3, 117	11	1:36.40	34,980
1973	**Linda's Chief**, 3, 126	B. Baeza	Step Nicely, 3, 123	Illberightback, 3, 117	4	1:34.00	33,150

Named for an Adirondack mountain village in Clinton County, New York. Grade 2 1973-'89. Saranac H. 1901-'70, 1998-2004. Held at Jamaica 1948-'56. Held at Aqueduct 1957-'61, 1963-'67, 1972-'74, 1976. Held at Belmont Park 1962, 1968-'71, 1975, 1977-'95. Not held 1911-'12, 1944, 1946-'47. 1⅛ miles 1901-'08, 1996-'97. 1 mile 1909, 1913-'42, 1960-'95. 1 1/16 miles 1948-'59. Dirt 1901-'79. Two divisions 1989. †Denotes female. Held as an allowance race 1943, 1945.

Saratoga Breeders' Cup Handicap

Grade 2 in 2006. Saratoga Race Course, three-year-olds and up, 1¼ miles, dirt. Held August 21, 2005, with a gross value of $250,000. First held in 1865. First graded in 1996. Stakes record 2:00.83 (2004 Evening Attire).

Year	Winner	Jockey	Second	Third	Strs	Time	1st Purse
2005	**Suave**, 4, 114	J. R. Velazquez	Royal Assault, 4, 116	Tap Day, 4, 115	5	2:03.38	$150,000
2004	**Evening Attire**, 6, 115	C. H. Velasquez	Funny Cide, 4, 118	Bowman's Band, 6, 116	7	**2:00.83**	150,000
2003	**Puzzlement**, 4, 113	J. F. Chavez	Volponi, 5, 122	Iron Deputy, 4, 115	8	2:03.54	180,000
2002	**Evening Attire**, 4, 115	S. Bridgmohan	Abreeze, 7, 113	Dollar Bill, 4, 117	10	2:02.95	180,000
2001	**Aptitude**, 4, 122	J. D. Bailey	Perfect Cat, 4, 115	A Fleets Dancer, 6, 115	7	2:01.55	180,000
2000	**Pleasant Breeze**, 5, 116	J. F. Chavez	Catienus, 6, 114	Gander, 4, 114	7	2:02.17	180,000
1999	**Running Stag**, 5, 122	S. J. Sellers	Catienus, 5, 115	Golden Missile, 4, 115	8	2:01.11	180,000
1998	**Awesome Again**, 4, 120	P. Day	Concerto, 4, 114	Early Warning, 3, 110	7	2:03.14	180,000
1997	**Cairo Express**, 5, 111	J. Samyn	Golden Larch, 6, 111	Instant Friendship, 4, 108	9	2:03.99	180,000
1996	**L'Carriere**, 5, 114	J. F. Chavez	Peaks and Valleys, 4, 121	Mahogany Hall, 5, 116	8	2:01.67	130,000
1995	**L'Carriere**, 4, 113	J. D. Bailey	Yourmissinthepoint, 4, 108	Unaccounted For, 4, 120	6	2:02.87	120,000
1994	**Thunder Rumble**, 5, 112	R. Migliore	West by West, 5, 113	Wallenda, 4, 117	8	1:48.52	150,000

The race and the track are named for the town of Saratoga Springs, New York. Grade 3 1996-'97. Saratoga Cup H. 1865-'96. Held at Belmont Park 1943-'45. Not held 1887-'90, 1892-1900, 1908, 1911-'12, 1956-'62, 1964-'93. 2¼ miles 1865-'86. 2 miles 1891. 1⅝ miles 1901, 1963. 1¾ miles 1902-'55. 1⅛ miles 1994.

Saratoga Special Stakes

Grade 2 in 2006. Saratoga Race Course, two-year-olds, 6 furlongs, dirt. Held July 28, 2005, with a gross value of $150,000. First held in 1901. First graded in 1973. Stakes record 1:09 (1978 General Assembly).

Year	Winner	Jockey	Second	Third	Strs	Time	1st Purse
2005	**Henny Hughes**, 2, 121	G. L. Stevens	Master of Disaster, 2, 117	Union Course, 2, 117	6	1:10.38	$90,000
2003	**Cuvee**, 2, 122	J. D. Bailey	Pomeroy, 2, 118	Limehouse, 2, 122	8	1:15.97	90,000
2002	**Zavata**, 2, 122	J. D. Bailey	Lone Star Sky, 2, 122	Spite the Devil, 2, 116	5	1:17.65	90,000
2001	**Jump Start**, 2, 115	P. Day	Heavyweight Champ, 2, 115	Booklet, 2, 117	6	1:17.35	90,000
2000	**City Zip**, 2, 122	J. A. Santos	Scorpion, 2, 114	Standard Speed, 2, 117	8	1:16.88	90,000
1999	**Bevo**, 2, 117	E. S. Prado	Afternoon Affair, 2, 114	Settlement, 2, 114	6	1:17.78	90,000
1998	**Prime Directive**, 2, 114	J. F. Chavez	Silk Broker, 2, 114	Tactical Cat, 2, 117	4	1:17.18	90,000
1997	**Favorite Trick**, 2, 122	P. Day	Case Dismissed, 2, 114	K. O. Punch, 2, 119	5	1:17.15	90,000
1996	**All Chatter**, 2, 113	J. F. Chavez	Gray Raider, 2, 114	Just a Cat, 2, 113	10	1:16.37	84,375
1995	**Bright Launch**, 2, 112	J. A. Santos	Devil's Honor, 2, 114	Severe Clear, 2, 113	8	1:17.98	66,540
1994	**Montreal Red**, 2, 122	J. A. Santos	Flitch, 2, 115	Law of the Sea, 2, 115	5	1:17.96	64,800

1993 **Dehere**, 2, 117	E. Maple	Slew Gin Fizz, 2, 117	Whitney Tower, 2, 117	9	1:09.92	$71,760
1992 **Tactical Advantage**, 2, 117	J. A. Krone	Strolling Along, 2, 117	Mi Cielo, 2, 117	10	1:10.59	72,600
1991 **Caller I. D.**, 2, 117	J. D. Bailey	Pick Up the Phone, 2, 122	Coin Collector, 2, 122	8	1:09.55	71,040
1990 **To Freedom**, 2, 124	A. T. Cordero Jr.	Fighting Affair, 2, 117	Eugene Eugene, 2, 117	6	1:11.40	52,740
1989 **Summer Squall**, 2, 124	P. Day	Dr. Bobby A., 2, 117	Graf, 2, 117	8	1:09.80	53,370
1988 **Trapp Mountain**, 2, 117	J. D. Bailey	Bio, 2, 122	Leading Prospect, 2, 117	7	1:10.80	66,240
1987 **Crusader Sword**, 2, 117	R. G. Davis	Tejano, 2, 117	Endurance, 2, 119	8	1:10.20	66,420
1986 **Gulch**, 2, 122	A. T. Cordero Jr.	Jazzing Around, 2, 117	Java Gold, 2, 117	10	1:10.00	54,990
1985 **Sovereign Don**, 2, 122	J. Velasquez	Hagley Mill, 2, 117	Bullet Blade, 2, 117	9	1:11.40	43,200
1984 **Chief's Crown**, 2, 117	D. MacBeth	Do It Again Dan, 2, 117	Sky Command, 2, 122	6	1:10.20	42,060
1983 **Swale**, 2, 117	E. Maple	Shuttle Jet, 2, 117	Big Walt, 2, 117	7	1:12.60	33,720
1982 **Victorious**, 2, 122	A. T. Cordero Jr.	Pappa Riccio, 2, 124	Safe Ground, 2, 119	7	1:10.60	33,960
1981 **Conquistador Cielo**, 2, 117	E. Maple	Herschelwalker, 2, 117	Timely Writer, 2, 122	10	1:10.60	33,900
1980 **Well Decorated**, 2, 117	M. Venezia	Tap Shoes, 2, 117	Motivity, 2, 119	10	1:10.20	34,320
1979 **J. P. Brother**, 2, 122	E. Maple	Native Moment, 2, 117	Muckraker, 2, 122	5	1:12.00	25,365
1978 **General Assembly**, 2, 117	D. G. McHargue	‡Turnbuckle, 2, 117	Make a Mess, 2, 117	8	**1:09.00**	22,350
1977 **Darby Creek Road**, 2, 117	A. T. Cordero Jr.	Jet Diplomacy, 2, 122	Quadratic, 2, 122	10	1:10.00	22,470
1976 **Banquet Table**, 2, 122	J. Vasquez	Turn of Coin, 2, 122	May I Rule, 2, 117	9	1:11.60	22,455
1975 **Bold Forbes**, 2, 120	J. Velasquez	Family Doctor, 2, 117	Gentle King, 2, 120	5	1:09.80	22,680
1974 **Our Talisman**, 2, 117	M. Venezia	Valid Appeal, 2, 117	Knightly Sport, 2, 120	10	1:10.40	17,430
1973 **Az Igazi**, 2, 117	M. Venezia	Gusty O'Shay, 2, 117	Lakeville, 2, 117	8	1:11.00	17,025

The race and the track are named for the town of Saratoga Springs, New York. In the past, "special" races were "winner takes all." Saratoga Special Sweepstakes 1901-'58. Held at Belmont Park 1943-'45. Not held 1911-'12, 2004. 5½ furlongs 1901-'05. 6½ furlongs 1994-2003. ‡Smarten finished second, DQ to eighth, 1978.

Schuylerville Stakes

Grade 3 in 2006. Saratoga Race Course, two-year-olds, fillies, 6 furlongs, dirt. Held July 28, 2004, with a gross value of $150,000. First held in 1918. First graded in 1973. Stakes record 1:09.80 (1974 Laughing Bridge [2nd Div.]; 1988 Wonders Delight).

Year Winner	Jockey	Second	Third	Strs	Time	1st Purse
2004 **Classic Elegance**, 2, 122	P. Day	Angel Trumpet, 2, 118	Wild Chick, 2, 118	10	1:12.48	$90,000
2003 **Ashado**, 2, 118	E. S. Prado	Maple Syrple, 2, 122	Hermione's Magic, 2, 118	7	1:12.12	90,000
2002 **Freedom's Daughter**, 2, 118	J. R. Velazquez	Miss Mary Apples, 2, 118	Mymich, 2, 116	7	1:12.14	90,000
2001 **Touch Love**, 2, 119	J. F. Chavez	Lakeside Cup, 2, 117	Lost Expectations, 2, 117	6	1:11.12	65,460
2000 **Gold Mover**, 2, 122	C. Perret	Seeking It All, 2, 114	Miss Doolittle, 2, 114	5	1:10.33	64,920
1999 **Magicalmysterycat**, 2, 122	P. Day	Circle of Life, 2, 114	Regally Appealing, 2, 114	7	1:10.91	65,700
1998 **Call Me Up**, 2, 117	J. F. Chavez	Brittons Hill, 2, 117	Fantasy Lake, 2, 117	8	1:12.89	66,060
1997 **Countess Diana**, 2, 116	S. J. Sellers	Love Lock, 2, 119	Sequence, 2, 116	6	1:10.39	64,800
1996 **How About Now**, 2, 115	R. Migliore	Exclusive Hold, 2, 115	City College, 2, 115	11	1:12.37	68,220
1995 **Golden Attraction**, 2, 121	D. M. Barton	Daylight Come, 2, 112	Western Dreamer, 2, 121	8	1:10.84	65,940
1994 **Changing Ways**, 2, 114	M. E. Smith	Unacceptable, 2, 119	Artic Experience, 2, 114	10	1:12.66	67,980
1993 **Strategic Maneuver**, 2, 114	J. A. Santos	Astas Foxy Lady, 2, 119	She Rides Tonite, 2, 114	11	1:11.15	73,560
1992 **Distinct Habit**, 2, 119	J. D. Bailey	Tourney, 2, 114	Lily La Belle, 2, 114	9	1:11.03	72,480
1991 **Turnback the Alarm**, 2, 114	D. Carr	Speed Dialer, 2, 119	Teddy's Top Ten, 2, 114	13	1:12.04	76,200
1990 **Meadow Star**, 2, 119	C. W. Antley	Garden Gal, 2, 119	Prayerful Miss, 2, 114	7	1:11.20	53,010
1989 **Golden Reef**, 2, 114	J. A. Santos	Lucy's Glory, 2, 119	Miss Cox's Hat, 2, 114	10	1:10.40	54,360
1988 **Wonders Delight**, 2, 114	J. A. Santos	Coax Chelsie, 2, 114	Attu, 2, 112	9	**1:09.80**	67,680
1987 **Over All**, 2, 119	A. T. Cordero Jr.	Joe's Tammie, 2, 119	Flashy Runner, 2, 119	10	1:10.60	68,850
1986 **Sacahuista**, 2, 114	C. J. McCarron	Our Little Margie, 2, 114	Collins, 2, 114	9	1:10.60	54,540
1985 **I'm Splendid**, 2, 114	A. T. Cordero Jr.	Musical Lark (Ire), 2, 114	Famous Speech, 2, 114	6	1:10.80	41,820
1984 **Weekend Delight**, 2, 119	C. R. Woods Jr.	Resembling, 2, 114	Winters' Love, 2, 114	8	1:11.60	42,840
1983 **Bottle Top**, 2, 114	D. Brumfield	Officer's Ball, 2, 114	Ark, 2, 114	7	1:11.40	34,020
1982 **Weekend Surprise**, 2, 114	J. Velasquez	Share the Fantasy, 2, 116	Flying Lassie, 2, 114	7	1:11.00	34,620
1981 **Mystical Mood**, 2, 114	J. Vasquez	Aga Pantha, 2, 114	Trove, 2, 116	8	1:11.80	34,320
1980 **Sweet Revenge**, 2, 114	J. Velasquez	Companionship, 2, 114	Heavenly Cause, 2, 114	11	1:10.40	34,980
1979 **Damask Fan**, 2, 114	E. Maple	Jet Rating, 2, 114	Lovin' Lass, 2, 112	7	1:10.20	25,860
1978 **Palm Hut**, 2, 121	R. I. Velez	Hermanville, 2, 114	Please Try Hard, 2, 114	7	1:10.40	22,215
1977 **L'Alezane**, 2, 121	R. Turcotte	Akita, 2, 121	Lakeville Miss, 2, 114	8	1:11.80	22,350
1976 **Mrs. Warren**, 2, 114	E. Maple	Tickle My Toes, 2, 116	Spy Flag, 2, 112	12	1:11.80	22,980
1975 **Nijana**, 2, 112	J. Velasquez	Future Tense, 2, 116	Crown Treasure, 2, 116	7	1:12.20	22,680
1974 **Our Dancing Girl**, 2, 116	V. A. Bracciale Jr.	Secret's Out, 2, 119	But Exclusive, 2, 116	7	1:11.20	16,575
Laughing Bridge, 2, 117	B. Baeza	Molly Ballantine, 2, 116	Fair Wind, 2, 119	7	**1:09.80**	16,500
1973 **Talking Picture**, 2, 116	B. Baeza	Imajoy, 2, 116	Celestial Lights, 2, 119	10	1:10.80	17,760

Named for a town located 12 miles east of Saratoga Springs in upstate New York. Grade 3 1975-'86. Held at Belmont Park 1943-'45. Held at Jamaica 1952. Not held 2005. 5½ furlongs 1918-'59, 1962-'68. Two divisions 1974.

Secretariat Stakes

Grade 1 in 2006. Arlington Park, three-year-olds, 1¼ miles, turf. Held August 13, 2005, with a gross value of $400,000. First held in 1974. First graded in 1975. Stakes record 1:59.65 (2004 Kitten's Joy).

Year Winner	Jockey	Second	Third	Strs	Time	1st Purse
2005 **Gun Salute**, 3, 123	C. H. Velasquez	English Channel, 3, 126	Chattahoochee War, 3, 121	8	2:03.79	$240,000

2004	**Kitten's Joy**, 3, 123	J. D. Bailey	Greek Sun, 3, 121	Moscow Ballet (Ire), 3, 119	7	**1:59.65**	$240,000
2003	**Kicken Kris**, 3, 116	J. Castellano	Joe Bear (Ire), 3, 116	Lismore Knight, 3, 121	11	2:02.53	240,000
2002	**Chiselling**, 3, 121	K. Desormeaux	Jazz Beat (Ire), 3, 117	Extra Check, 3, 116	7	2:04.16	240,000
2001	**Startac**, 3, 121	A. O. Solis	Strut the Stage, 3, 123	Sharp Performance, 3, 121	11	2:04.91	240,000
2000	**Ciro**, 3, 120	M. J. Kinane	King Cugat, 3, 123	Guillamou City (Fr), 3, 117	8	2:01.64	240,000
1997	**Honor Glide**, 3, 123	G. K. Gomez	Casey Tibbs (Ire), 3, 116	Glok, 3, 114	9	2:02.74	240,000
1996	**Marlin**, 3, 114	S. J. Sellers	Trail City, 3, 126	Dancing Fred, 3, 114	10	2:01.09	300,000
1995	**Hawk Attack**, 3, 120	P. Day	Mecke, 3, 117	Petit Poucet (GB), 3, 114	10	2:00.17	240,000
1994	**Vaudeville**, 3, 123	G. L. Stevens	Dare and Go, 3, 114	Jaggery John, 3, 120	13	2:01.11	240,000
1993	**Awad**, 3, 120	J. Velasquez	Explosive Red, 3, 123	Brazany, 3, 114	14	2:08.74	240,000
1992	**Ghazi**, 3, 114	R. G. Davis	Paradise Creek, 3, 123	†Tango Charlie, 3, 117	10	2:01.18	180,000
1991	**Jackie Wackie**, 3, 123	P. Day	Olympio, 3, 126	Sultry Song, 3, 114	8	2:01.27	180,000
1990	**Super Abound**, 3, 114	R. P. Romero	Unbridled, 3, 126	†Super Fan, 3, 117	8	2:01.60	150,000
1989	**Hawkster**, 3, 123	P. A. Valenzuela	Chenin Blanc, 3, 114	Ninety Years Young, 3, 114	8	2:04.00	150,000
1987	**Stately Don**, 3, 113	J. Vasquez	The Medic, 3, 120	Zaizoom, 3, 120	11	2:04.60	103,590
1986	**Southjet**, 3, 113	J. A. Santos	Glow, 3, 120	Tripoli Shores, 3, 115	10	2:02.00	102,510
1985	**Derby Wish**, 3, 114	R. P. Romero	‡Day Shift, 3, 114	Duluth, 3, 123	12	2:01.00	146,880
1984	**Vision**, 3, 114	G. McCarron	Mr. Japan, 3, 114	Pine Circle, 3, 114	8	2:38.40	117,240
1983	**Fortnightly**, 3, 117	P. Day	Jack Slade, 3, 114	Reap, 3, 114	13	2:32.40	102,360
1982	**Half Iced**, 3, 114	D. MacBeth	Dew Line, 3, 114	Continuing, 3, 114	8	2:31.20	90,000
1981	**Sing Sing**, 3, 114	M. Venezia	Television Studio, 3, 117	Jungle Tough, 3, 114	11	2:53.60	96,240
1980	**Spruce Needles**, 3, 123	J. C. Espinoza	Proctor, 3, 120	The Messanger, 3, 123	6	2:40.80	99,960
1979	**Golden Act**, 3, 126	S. Hawley	Smarten, 3, 120	Flying Dad, 3, 120	6	2:32.80	91,080
1978	**Mac Diarmida**, 3, 120	J. Cruguet	April Axe, 3, 120	The Liberal Member, 3, 114	11	2:29.80	99,600
1977	**Text**, 3, 120	M. Castaneda	Run Dusty Run, 3, 126	Flag Officer, 3, 123	7	1:42.00	73,140
1976	**Joachim**, 3, 123	S. Maple	Romeo, 3, 112	L'Heureux, 3, 117	10	1:50.80	88,400
1975	**Intrepid Hero**, 3, 123	A. T. Cordero Jr.	Gab Bag, 3, 117	Larrikin, 3, 117	14	1:49.80	94,000
1974	**Glossary**, 3, 114	A. Santiago	Stonewalk, 3, 123	Talkative Turn, 3, 117	13	1:42.80	96,400

Named for Meadow Stable's 1972, '73 Horse of the Year and '73 Triple Crown winner Secretariat (1970 c. by Bold Ruler); he made his first start after the Belmont S. (G1) in a stakes race at Arlington Park. Grade 2 1975-'83. Held at Hawthorne Race Course 1985. Not held 1988, 1998-'99. 1$\frac{1}{16}$ miles 1974, 1977. 1$\frac{1}{8}$ miles 1975-'76. 1$\frac{1}{2}$ miles 1978-'84. Dirt 1977. ‡Racing Star finished second, DQ to fourth, 1985. †Denotes female.

Senator Ken Maddy Handicap

Grade 3 in 2006. Oak Tree at Santa Anita, three-year-olds and up, fillies and mares, about 6$\frac{1}{2}$ furlongs, turf. Held September 28, 2005, with a gross value of $100,000. First held in 1969. First graded in 1973. Stakes record 1:11.56 (2005 Elusive Diva).

Year	Winner	Jockey	Second	Third	Strs	Time	1st Purse
2005	**Elusive Diva**, 4, 119	P. A. Valenzuela	Chasethegold, 5, 116	Abounding Truth, 5, 116	11	**1:11.56**	$60,000
2004	**Belleski**, 5, 118	C. S. Nakatani	Intercontinental (GB), 4, 120	Acago, 4, 116	9	1:12.86	60,000
2003	**Belleski**, 4, 117	V. Espinoza	Buffythecenterfold, 3, 116	Icantgoforthat, 4, 115	10	1:12.37	67,200
2002	**Rolly Polly (Ire)**, 4, 119	P. A. Valenzuela	I'm the Business (NZ), 5, 117	Nanogram, 5, 113	12	1:12.86	68,460
2001	**A La Reine**, 4, 115	A. O. Solis	Nanogram, 4, 111	Global, 4, 113	8	1:13.27	66,240
2000	**Evening Promise (GB)**, 4, 118	K. Desormeaux	Strawberry Way, 5, 114	Southern House (Ire), 4, 114	10	1:13.05	67,020
1999	**Hula Queen**, 5, 116	A. O. Solis	Desert Lady (Ire), 4, 121	Ecudienne, 5, 117	11	1:13.05	67,740
1998	**Dance Parade**, 4, 120	K. Desormeaux	Advancing Star, 5, 121	Green Jewel (GB), 4, 116	8	1:13.87	60,000
1997	**Madame Pandit**, 4, 118	E. Delahoussaye	Advancing Star, 4, 120	Highest Dream (Ire), 4, 116	10	1:13.82	60,000
1996	**Dixie Pearl**, 4, 116	E. Delahoussaye	Ski Dancer, 4, 119	Cat's Cradle, 4, 118	9	1:12.33	66,400
1995	**Denim Yenem**, 3, 115	C. J. McCarron	Miss L Attack, 5, 116	Jacodra's Devil, 4, 116	7	1:14.92	60,400
1994	**Starolamo**, 5, 117	K. Desormeaux	Sophisticatedcielo, 3, 114	Beautiful Gem, 3, 115	6	1:16.07	47,475
1993	**Toussaud**, 4, 122	K. Desormeaux	Best Dress, 3, 113	Yousefia, 4, 116	6	1:14.32	46,950
1992	**Bel's Starlet**, 5, 120	K. Desormeaux	Glen Kate (Ire), 5, 117	Brisa de Mar, 4, 117	9	1:11.63	49,575
1991	**Bel's Starlet**, 4, 115	K. Desormeaux	Sun Brandy, 4, 117	Bright Asset, 5, 115	12	1:11.89	52,125
1990	**Stylish Star**, 4, 118	E. Delahoussaye	Tasteful T. V., 3, 115	Linda Card, 4, 113	11	1:12.00	51,525
1989	**Warning Zone**, 4, 119	R. Q. Meza	Down Again, 5, 119	Stormy But Valid, 3, 116	11	1:12.80	51,675
1988	**Jeanne Jones**, 3, 118	A. T. Gryder	Native Paster, 4, 116	Serve n' Volley (GB), 4, 116	14	1:14.80	53,100
1987	**Aberuschka (Ire)**, 5, 120	P. A. Valenzuela	Luisant (Arg), 5, 118	Down Again, 3, 113	11	1:14.80	41,050
1986	**Shywing**, 4, 120	L. A. Pincay Jr.	Her Royalty, 5, 119	Water Crystals, 5, 119	9	1:14.80	31,075
	Lichi (Chi), 6, 115	G. Baze	Tax Dodge, 5, 119	Outstandingly, 4, 120	7	1:14.60	29,875
1985	**Love Smitten**, 4, 119	G. L. Stevens	Danzadar, 4, 116	Sales Bulletin, 4, 117	7	1:15.40	29,725
1984	**Irish O'Brien**, 6, 116	J. J. Steiner	Mel's Whisper, 4, 111	Foggy Nation, 4, 116	11	1:14.60	32,200
	Lina Cavalieri (GB), 4, 116	E. Delahoussaye	Betty Money, 5, 115	Percipient, 3, 116	8	1:14.40	30,400
1983	**Matching**, 5, 122	R. Sibille	Excitable Lady, 5, 123	Nan's Dancer, 4, 113	6	1:17.00	37,850
1982	**Maple Tree**, 4, 115	E. Delahoussaye	Northern Fable, 4, 116	A Kiss for Luck, 3, 115	7	1:15.60	30,650
	Jones Time Machine, 3, 117	L. A. Pincay Jr.	Rosy Cloud, 5, 115	Manzanera (Arg), 6, 117	9	1:16.00	31,950
1981	**Kilijaro (Ire)**, 5, 130	L. A. Pincay Jr.	Ack's Secret, 5, 118	Miss Huntington, 4, 110	9	1:13.80	28,650
	Save Wild Life, 4, 121	M. Castaneda	Disconiz, 4, 115	I Got Speed, 3, 112	11	1:14.20	29,750
1980	**Great Lady M.**, 5, 122	P. A. Valenzuela	Evyostling, 5, 115	Conveniently, 4, 117	11	1:13.60	29,400
1979	**Palmistry**, 4, 115	C. J. McCarron	Splendid Size, 5, 116	Terresto's Dream, 4, 113	10	1:12.80	22,325
	Wishing Well, 4, 117	F. Toro	Great Lady M., 4, 116	Habeebti (GB), 5, 115	8	1:12.60	21,425
1978	**Happy Holme**, 4, 118	C. J. McCarron	Stellar Envoy, 4, 114	Pet Label, 5, 116	10	1:14.20	22,300
	‡Country Queen, 3, 118	F. Toro	Sweet Little Lady, 3, 116	Rich Soil, 4, 119	9	1:14.20	21,900

1977	**Dancing Femme**, 4, 125	D. G. McHargue	Lullaby Song, 4, 117	Swingtime, 5, 121	12	1:13.20	$22,250
1976	**If You Prefer**, 5, 118	L. A. Pincay Jr.	*Accra II, 4, 115	Vagabonda, 5, 121	7	1:13.00	15,750
	Dancing Liz, 4, 114	W. Shoemaker	Miss Tokyo, 4, 120	Lucky Spell, 5, 113	8	1:12.40	16,050
1975	***Tizna**, 6, 125	D. Pierce	Mama Kali, 4, 121	Modus Vivendi, 4, 122	9	1:12.80	17,700
1974	**Impressive Style**, 5, 123	R. Rosales	Modus Vivendi, 3, 121	*Tizna, 5, 124	12	1:13.80	19,150
1973	***New Moon II**, 6, 116	W. Shoemaker	Minstrel Miss, 6, 124	Meilleur, 3, 116	11	1:13.20	19,200

Named for California state Sen. Kenneth L. Maddy (1935-2000), a longtime racing enthusiast. The race is held during the autumn Oak Tree Racing Association meet at Santa Anita Park. Autumn Days S. 1969. Autumn Days H. 1970-'98. 6½ furlongs 1983, 1994. Dirt 1983, 1994. Two-year-olds and up 1975, 1988-'89. Both sexes 1969-'70. Two divisions 1976, 1978-'79, 1981-'82, 1984, 1986. ‡Sweet Little Lady finished first, DQ to second, 1978 (2nd Div.).

Senorita Stakes

Grade 3 in 2006. Hollywood Park, three-year-olds, fillies, 1 mile, turf. Held May 6, 2006, with a gross value of $100,000. First held in 1968. First graded in 1990. Stakes record 1:33.66 (1992 Charm a Gendarme).

Year	Winner	Jockey	Second	Third	Strs	Time	1st Purse
2006	**Foxysox (GB)**, 3, 121	A. Bisono	Arlene, 3, 119	Shermeen (Ire), 3, 116	5	1:35.28	$60,000
2005	**Virden**, 3, 119	O. Figueroa	Three Degrees (Ire), 3, 116	Thatswhatimean, 3, 117	10	1:35.37	67,140
2004	**Miss Vegas (Ire)**, 3, 115	A. O. Solis	Ticker Tape (GB), 3, 121	Amorama (Fr), 3, 116	7	1:34.25	65,340
2003	**Makeup Artist**, 3, 117	V. Espinoza	Rutters Renegade (Ire), 3, 117	Shapes and Shadows, 3, 117	7	1:36.54	68,100
2002	**Adoration**, 3, 117	G. K. Gomez	High Society (Ire), 3, 115	Nunatall (GB), 3, 115	6	1:34.91	64,380
2001	**Fantastic Filly (Fr)**, 3, 123	G. K. Gomez	Innit (Ire), 3, 115	Blushing Bride (GB), 3, 115	8	1:35.13	65,880
2000	**Islay Mist (GB)**, 3, 116	D. R. Flores	Fire Sale Queen, 3, 118	Miss Pixie, 3, 114	10	1:34.16	67,080
1999	**Coracle**, 3, 116	K. Desormeaux	Aviate, 3, 118	Dianehill (Ire), 3, 115	11	1:34.04	67,740
1998	**Dancing Rhythm**, 3, 117	K. Desormeaux	Phone Alex (Ire), 3, 115	Star's Proud Penny, 3, 122	7	1:35.39	64,860
1997	**Kentucky Kaper**, 3, 114	R. R. Douglas	Ascutney, 3, 120	Ava Knowsthecode, 3, 115	10	1:34.74	66,780
1996	**To B. Super**, 3, 118	C. W. Antley	Gastronomical, 3, 118	Ribot's Secret (Ire), 3, 116	13	1:34.36	68,940
1995	**Top Shape (Fr)**, 3, 114	C. S. Nakatani	Artica, 3, 118	Auriette (Ire), 3, 116	10	1:34.79	63,900
1994	**Rabiadella**, 3, 118	L. A. Pincay Jr.	Magical Avie, 3, 116	Fancy 'n Fabulous, 3, 118	6	1:34.84	60,800
1993	**Likeable Style**, 3, 121	K. Desormeaux	Adorydar, 3, 113	Icy Warning, 3, 118	7	1:34.56	61,250
1992	**Charm a Gendarme**, 3, 116	R. Q. Meza	Moonlight Elegance, 3, 116	Morriston Belle, 3, 118	13	**1:33.66**	67,250
1991	**Paula Revere**, 3, 117	J. A. Santos	Shy Trick, 3, 114	Island Shuffle, 3, 119	7	1:35.50	61,850
1990	**Brought to Mind**, 3, 114	A. O. Solis	Tasteful T. V., 3, 119	She's a V. P., 3, 117	8	1:34.40	62,600
1989	**Reluctant Guest**, 3, 114	C. J. McCarron	Formidable Lady, 3, 119	General Charge (Ire), 3, 117	9	1:34.00	50,200
1988	**Do So**, 3, 117	A. O. Solis	Pattern Step, 3, 119	Sheesham, 3, 117	4	1:34.20	45,950
1987	**Pen Bal Lady (GB)**, 3, 117	E. Delahoussaye	Sweettuc, 3, 119	Davie's Lamb, 3, 115	6	1:35.40	61,350
1986	**Nature's Way**, 3, 117	C. J. McCarron	An Empress, 3, 115	Miraculous, 3, 119	7	1:42.60	39,200
1985	**Akamini (Fr)**, 3, 117	F. Toro	Charming Susan, 3, 115	Sharp Ascent, 3, 114	6	1:35.40	32,250
	Shywing, 3, 117	T. Lipham	Delaware Ginny, 3, 117	Savannah Dancer, 3, 119	8	1:35.60	33,450
1984	**Heartlight**, 3, 117	L. A. Pincay Jr.	Table Ten, 3, 115	Dear Carrie, 3, 115	8	1:35.60	38,900
1983	**Stage Door Canteen**, 3, 114	C. J. McCarron	I'm Prestigious, 3, 116	O'Happy Day, 3, 115	6	1:35.60	25,675
	Preceptress, 3, 115	M. Castaneda	Madam Forbes, 3, 114	Toga, 3, 116	6	1:36.60	25,675
1982	**Skillful Joy**, 3, 119	C. J. McCarron	Phaedra, 3, 122	Faneuil Lass, 3, 122	5	1:34.00	31,050
1981	**Shimmy**, 3, 114	P. A. Valenzuela	Queen of Prussia (Ire), 3, 117	Bee a Scout, 3, 114	6	1:36.20	37,450
1980	**Ballare**, 3, 117	C. J. McCarron	Street Ballet, 3, 122	Cinegita, 3, 114	6	1:35.00	31,600
1979	**Variety Queen**, 3, 117	R. Rosales	Top Soil, 3, 119	Whydidju, 3, 122	7	1:37.00	25,850
1978	**Blue Blood**, 3, 117	D. Pierce	Equanimity, 3, 122	Eximious, 3, 119	6	1:37.00	25,000
1977	***Glenaris**, 3, 114	W. Shoemaker	Countess Fager, 3, 119	Shop Windows, 3, 114	7	1:36.00	19,300
1976	**Now Pending**, 3, 117	D. Pierce	Cascapedia, 3, 115	Queen to Be, 3, 119	11	1:35.80	20,650
1975	**Raise Your Skirts**, 3, 119	W. Mahorney	Fresno Flyer, 3, 117	Vol Au Vent, 3, 117	7	1:36.40	19,050
1973	**Cellist**, 3, 119	J. L. Rotz	Jungle Princess, 3, 120	Meilleur, 3, 119	10	1:42.20	20,250

Young, unmarried women are known as senoritas in Spanish. Senorita Breeders' Cup S. 1992-'95. Not held 1974. 1$^{1}/_{16}$ miles 1973, 1986. Dirt 1973. Two divisions 1983, 1985. Non-winners of a race worth $10,000 to the winner 1973.

Shadwell Turf Mile Stakes

Grade 1 in 2006. Keeneland Race Course, three-year-olds and up, 1 mile, turf. Held October 8, 2005, with a gross value of $600,000. First held in 1986. First graded in 1988. Stakes record 1:33.72 (2000 Altibr).

Year	Winner	Jockey	Second	Third	Strs	Time	1st Purse
2005	**Host (Chi)**, 5, 126	R. Bejarano	Vanderlin (GB), 6, 126	Gulch Approval, 5, 126	10	1:37.67	$372,000
2004	**Nothing to Lose**, 4, 126	R. Albarado	Honor in War, 5, 126	Silver Tree, 4, 126	9	1:35.55	372,000
2003	**Perfect Soul (Ire)**, 5, 126	E. S. Prado	Honor in War, 4, 126	Touch of the Blues (Fr), 6, 126	10	1:36.01	372,000
2002	**Landseer (GB)**, 3, 123	E. S. Prado	Touch of the Blues (Fr), 5, 126	Beat Hollow (GB), 5, 126	8	1:35.55	372,000
2001	**Hap**, 5, 126	J. D. Bailey	Where's Taylor, 5, 126	Aly's Alley, 5, 126	9	1:35.98	346,270
2000	**Altibr**, 5, 126	R. Migliore	Strategic Mission, 5, 126	Quiet Resolve, 5, 126	9	**1:33.72**	279,744
1999	**Kirkwall (GB)**, 5, 126	V. Espinoza	Delay of Game, 6, 126	Ladies Din, 4, 126	10	1:37.96	281,232
1998	**Favorite Trick**, 3, 123	P. Day	Soviet Line (Ire), 8, 126	Wild Event, 5, 126	5	1:35.00	168,795
1997	**Wild Event**, 4, 126	M. Guidry	Trail City, 4, 126	Soviet Line (Ire), 7, 126	10	1:34.66	134,075
1996	**Dumaani**, 5, 126	J. A. Krone	Desert Waves, 6, 126	Dove Hunt, 5, 126	9	1:35.68	133,843
1995	**Dumaani**, 4, 126	J. A. Krone	Holy Mountain, 4, 126	Mr Purple, 3, 123	10	1:38.78	116,514
1994	**†Weekend Madness (Ire)**, 4, 123	S. J. Sellers	†Words of War, 5, 123	Pennine Ridge, 3, 123	10	1:38.73	116,328
1993	**Coaxing Matt**, 4, 126	E. M. Martin Jr.	Adam Smith (GB), 5, 126	Mr. Light Tres (Arg), 4, 126	9	1:53.16	116,421
1992	**Lotus Pool**, 5, 126	C. R. Woods Jr.	Thunder Regent, 5, 126	Chenin Blanc, 6, 126	6	1:48.36	114,902

1991	**Itsallgreektome**, 4, 126	J. Velasquez	Opening Verse, 5, 126	Super Abound, 4, 126	6	1:48.42	$119,600
1990	**Silver Medallion**, 4, 126	C. Perret	Shot Gun Scott, 3, 122	†Coolawin, 4, 123	9	1:52.20	121,973
1989	**Steinlen (GB)**, 6, 126	J. A. Santos	Crystal Moment, 4, 126	Posen, 4, 126	10	1:52.40	122,103
1988	**Niccolo Polo**, 5, 126	D. Brumfield	Pollenate (GB), 4, 126	Eve's Error (Ire), 5, 126	10	1:53.00	101,823
1987	**Storm On the Loose**, 4, 126	J. C. Espinoza	Uptown Swell, 5, 126	Vilzak, 4, 126	9	1:52.60	101,855
1986	**Leprechauns Wish**, 4, 126	J. D. Bailey	Ingot's Ruler, 4, 126	Wop Wop, 4, 126	7	1:51.80	100,848

Sponsored by Sheikh Hamdan bin Rashid al Maktoum's Shadwell Farm, located a short distance from Keeneland in Lexington. Grade 3 1991-'97. Grade 2 1998-2001. Keeneland Breeders' Cup S. 1991-'95. Keeneland Breeders' Cup Mile S. 1996-'98. Shadwell Keeneland Turf Mile S. 1999-2002. 1⅛ miles 1991-'93. †Denotes female.

Shakertown Stakes

Grade 3 in 2006. Keeneland Race Course, three-year-olds and up, 5½ furlongs, turf. Held April 14, 2006, with a gross value of $115,000. First held in 1995. First graded in 2003. Stakes record 1:01.78 (2004 Soaring Free).

Year	Winner	Jockey	Second	Third	Strs	Time	1st Purse
2006	**Atticus Kristy**, 5, 119	G. K. Gomez	Around the Cape, 4, 119	Man Of Illusion (Aus), 5, 119	12	1:01.83	$71,300
2005	**Soaring Free**, 6, 121	J. D. Bailey	Mighty Beau, 6, 121	Parker Run, 4, 119	11	1:02.22	70,246
2004	**Soaring Free**, 5, 120	S. J. Sellers	Chosen Chief, 5, 118	Banned in Boston, 4, 118	12	**1:01.78**	71,362
2003	**No Jacket Required**, 6, 118	B. Blanc	Testify, 6, 120	Abderian (Ire), 6, 120	10	1:03.25	70,494
2002	**Morluc**, 6, 118	R. Albarado	Mighty Beau, 3, 116	Grangeville, 7, 118	10	1:03.25	52,731
2001	**Airbourne Command**, 6, 118	J. F. Chavez	Final Row (GB), 4, 118	Grangeville, 6, 118	10	1:02.71	52,824
2000	**Bold Fact**, 5, 115	R. Migliore	Howbaddouwantit, 5, 118	Claire's Honor, 6, 115	10	1:02.61	46,800
1999	**Prankster**, 6, 115	S. J. Sellers	Tyaskin, 6, 120	Howbaddouwantit, 4, 123	10	1:02.43	43,850
1998	**Sesaro**, 6, 123	S. J. Sellers	Brave Pancho, 4, 114	Claire's Honor, 4, 114	9	1:02.35	43,850
1997	**G H's Pleasure**, 5, 114	J. A. Santos	Louie the Lucky, 6, 114	Parklo, 5, 117	10	1:03.00	34,410
1995	**Cinch**, 3, 112	R. P. Romero	Hollywood Flash, 3, 115	Ikickedthehabit, 3, 112	4	1:47.69	38,168

Named for Shakertown, a Shaker village located at Pleasant Hill, Kentucky, near Harrodsburg. Formerly named for Robert E. Sangster's 1977 English Horse of the Year The Minstrel (1974 c. by Northern Dancer). The Minstrel S. 1995, 1997. Not held 1996. Course record 1997, 1998.

Sham Stakes

Grade 3 in 2006. Santa Anita Park, three-year-olds, 1⅛ miles, dirt. Held February 4, 2006, with a gross value of $102,500. First held in 2001. First graded in 2006. Stakes record 1:48.39 (2003 Man Among Men).

Year	Winner	Jockey	Second	Third	Strs	Time	1st Purse
2006	**Bob and John**, 3, 120	V. Espinoza	Hawkinsville, 3, 118	Sacred Light, 3, 118	5	1:49.15	$61,500
2005	**Going Wild**, 3, 117	V. Espinoza	Papi Chullo, 3, 117	Giacomo, 3, 117	9	1:50.18	61,380
2004	**Master David**, 3, 116	A. O. Solis	Borrego, 3, 120	Preachinatthebar, 3, 116	7	1:49.20	48,840
2003	**Man Among Men**, 3, 120	A. O. Solis	Empire Maker, 3, 115	Spensive, 3, 120	7	**1:48.39**	48,600
2002	**U S S Tinosa**, 3, 120	K. Desormeaux	Puerto Banus, 3, 116	Hot Contest, 3, 115	6	1:49.11	47,190
2001	**Wild and Wise**, 3, 117	V. Espinoza	Swordfish, 3, 116	Special Times, 3, 116	6	1:50.51	60,750

Named for Sigmund Sommer's 1973 Santa Anita Derby (G1) winner Sham (1970 c. by Pretense).

Sheepshead Bay Handicap

Grade 2 in 2006. Belmont Park, three-year-olds and up, fillies and mares, 1⅜ miles, turf. Held May 27, 2006, with a gross value of $150,000. First held in 1959. First graded in 1973. Stakes record 2:11.57 (1997 Maxzene).

Year	Winner	Jockey	Second	Third	Strs	Time	1st Purse
2006	**Honey Ryder**, 5, 121	G. K. Gomez	Noble Stella (Ger), 5, 116	Angara (GB), 5, 119	7	2:12.98	$90,000
2005	**Sauvage (Fr)**, 4, 115	J. Castellano	Angara (GB), 4, 118	Barancella (Fr), 4, 116	8	2:15.65	90,000
2004	**Moscow Burning**, 4, 114	M. E. Smith	Spice Island, 5, 119	Meridiana (Ger), 4, 119	7	2:18.24	90,000
2003	**Mariensky**, 4, 114	J. R. Velazquez	Owsley, 5, 119	Silent Crystal, 4, 112	8	2:28.19	90,000
2002	**Tweedside**, 4, 114	J. R. Velazquez	Sweetest Thing, 4, 119	Golden Corona, 4, 114	10	2:13.63	90,000
2001	**Critical Eye**, 4, 122	M. J. Luzzi	Playact (Ire), 4, 115	Janet (GB), 4, 116	5	2:18.18	90,000
2000	**Lisieux Rose (Ire)**, 5, 116	J. A. Santos	Melody Queen (GB), 4, 113	La Ville Rouge, 4, 113	7	2:14.16	90,000
1999	**Soaring Softly**, 4, 114	M. E. Smith	Starry Dreamer, 5, 114	Pinafore Park, 4, 113	6	2:15.11	90,000
1998	**Maxzene**, 5, 121	J. A. Santos	Sweetzie, 6, 111	Colonial Play, 4, 115	6	2:14.17	90,000
1997	**Maxzene**, 4, 117	M. E. Smith	Fanjica (Ire), 5, 117	Future Act, 5, 112	8	**2:11.57**	90,000
1996	**Chelsey Flower**, 5, 114	R. G. Davis	Look Daggers, 4, 114	Transient Trend, 4, 113	10	2:12.64	67,320
1995	**Duda**, 4, 112	J. D. Bailey	Danish (Ire), 4, 116	Chelsey Flower, 4, 112	7	2:13.69	65,700
1994	**Market Booster**, 5, 114	J. A. Santos	Irish Linnet, 6, 115	Fairy Garden, 6, 120	9	2:11.69	66,960
1993	**Trampoli**, 4, 116	M. E. Smith	Aquilegia, 4, 116	Revasser, 4, 114	4	2:14.08	67,680
1992	**Ratings**, 4, 112	J. Cruguet	Ristna (GB), 4, 110	Dancing Devlette, 5, 113	12	2:15.14	75,000
1991	**Crockadore**, 4, 112	M. E. Smith	Rigamajig, 5, 114	Star Standing, 4, 114	8	2:14.95	71,760
1990	**Destiny Dance**, 4, 111	J. A. Santos	Key Flyer, 4, 108	Yestday's Kisses, 4, 112	5	2:19.20	55,080
1989	**Love You by Heart**, 4, 118	J. Cruguet	Nastique, 5, 117	Laugh and Be Merry, 4, 112	10	2:12.60	72,480
1988	**Nastique**, 4, 111	R. G. Davis	Princely Proof, 5, 115	Anka Germania (Ire), 6, 124	9	2:16.40	71,040
1987	**Steal a Kiss**, 4, 111	E. Maple	Videogenic, 5, 117	Graceful Darby, 3, 112	5	2:23.80	87,180
1986	**Possible Mate**, 5, 124	J. Samyn	Tremulous, 4, 112	Dawn's Curtsey, 4, 113	9	2:14.00	75,480
1985	**Persian Tiara (Ire)**, 5, 116	J. Velasquez	Key Dancer, 4, 118	Dictina (Fr), 4, 112	10	2:16.00	86,820
1984	**Sabin**, 4, 125	E. Maple	Thirty Flags, 4, 114	Double Jeux, 4, 111	9	2:12.80	71,880

1983 **Sabin**, 3, 112	E. Maple	First Approach, 5, 118	Mintage (Fr), 4, 114	9	2:13.80	$67,920
1982 **Castle Royale**, 4, 110	J. J. Miranda	Trevita (Ire), 5, 118	So Pleasantly, 4, 113	8	2:13.00	66,060
Dana Calqui (Arg), 4, 110	A. T. Cordero Jr.	If Winter Comes, 4, 110	Noble Damsel, 4, 115	7	2:14.20	66,060
1981 **Love Sign**, 4, 114	R. Hernandez	Rokeby Rose, 4, 115	Mairzy Doates, 5, 122	8	2:13.00	67,680
1980 **The Very One**, 5, 116	C. Cooke	Euphrosyne, 4, 114	Baby Sister, 5, 115	15	2:13.00	71,520
1979 **Terpsichorist**, 4, 117	E. Maple	Late Bloomer, 5, 123	Warfever (Fr), 4, 110	10	2:01.60	67,200
1978 **Late Bloomer**, 4, 118	J. Velasquez	Waya (Fr), 4, 115	Pearl Necklace, 4, 124	11	2:01.00	68,880
1977 **Glowing Tribute**, 4, 118	J. Velasquez	Fleet Victress, 5, 119	Dottie's Doll, 4, 116	7	1:59.60	65,700
1976 **Glowing Tribute**, 3, 110	P. Day	Bubbling, 4, 119	Carmelize, 4, 109	6	1:49.20	50,700
Fleet Victress, 4, 115	P. Day	‡Redundancy, 5, 123	Summertime Promise, 4, 119	8	1:49.00	51,600
1975 **Gems and Roses**, 5, 112	M. Venezia	Hinterland, 5, 113	Carolerno, 4, 110	11	2:01.60	34,740
1974 **North Broadway**, 4, 116	A. T. Cordero Jr.	Lorraine Edna, 4, 117	Gnome Home, 4, 109	10	1:56.20	35,190
1973 **Shearwater**, 4, 112	A. T. Cordero Jr.	Inca Queen, 5, 118	Aglimmer, 4, 115	13	1:59.80	35,610

Named for the old Brooklyn, New York, racetrack Sheepshead Bay, which closed in 1911 with the ban of racing in New York and never reopened. Grade 3 1991-'94. Held at Jamaica 1959. Held at Aqueduct 1960-'74, 1976. 1$^{1}/_{16}$ miles 1959, 1963-'64. 1$^{1}/_{8}$ miles 1960-'61, 1976. 1 mile 1962. 1$^{3}/_{16}$ miles 1965-'74. 1$^{1}/_{4}$ miles 1975, 1977-'79. Dirt 1959, 1962, 1974, 1990, 2001. Originally scheduled on turf 1990, 2001. Both sexes 1959-'61. Two divisions 1976, 1982. ‡Summertime Promise finished second, DQ to third, 1976 (2nd Div.). Course record 1997.

Shirley Jones Breeders' Cup Handicap

Grade 2 in 2006. Gulfstream Park, three-year-olds and up, fillies and mares, 7 furlongs, dirt. Held March 18, 2006, with a gross value of $187,000. First held in 1976. First graded in 1988. Stakes record 1:21.42 (2004 Randaroo).

Year	Winner	Jockey	Second	Third	Strs	Time	1st Purse
2006	**Splendid Blended**, 4, 117	M. R. Cruz	Beautiful Bets, 6, 116	Injustice, 5, 116	10	1:21.62	$120,000
2005	**Madcap Escapade**, 4, 118	J. D. Bailey	Alix M, 5, 115	D' Wildcat Speed, 5, 114	7	1:22.06	90,000
2004	**Randaroo**, 4, 118	J. R. Velazquez	Harmony Lodge, 6, 121	Halory Leigh, 4, 114	8	**1:21.42**	60,000
2003	**Harmony Lodge**, 5, 114	J. R. Velazquez	Gold Mover, 5, 117	Nonsuch Bay, 4, 117	6	1:22.35	60,000
2002	**Cat Cay**, 5, 118	P. Day	Raging Fever, 4, 120	Vague Memory, 5, 112	7	1:22.31	60,000
2001	**Hidden Assets**, 4, 114	J. D. Bailey	Another, 4, 115	Dream Supreme, 4, 120	6	1:22.40	60,000
2000	**Marley Vale**, 4, 118	J. R. Velazquez	Cassidy, 5, 113	Class On Class, 5, 113	8	1:22.24	60,000
1999	**Harpia**, 5, 118	R. Migliore	Scotzanna, 7, 115	Memories of Gold, 4, 113	5	1:22.17	60,000
1998	**U Can Do It**, 5, 116	S. J. Sellers	Glitter Woman, 4, 123	Flashy n Smart, 5, 118	5	1:23.33	60,000
1997	**Chip**, 4, 114	J. Bravo	Steady Cat, 4, 113	Flat Fleet Feet, 4, 117	7	1:22.24	60,000
1996	**Dust Bucket**, 5, 112	R. G. Davis	Russian Flight (Ire), 4, 110	Culver City, 4, 115	5	1:25.97	60,000
1995	**Educated Risk**, 5, 125	M. E. Smith	Elizabeth Bay, 5, 115	Clever Act, 4, 114	5	1:22.94	60,000
1994	**Santa Catalina**, 6, 115	P. Day	Jeano, 6, 113	Traverse City, 4, 113	11	1:21.94	60,000
1993	**Jeano**, 5, 113	S. J. Sellers	Santa Catalina, 5, 115	Miss Jealski, 4, 111	13	1:23.56	39,060
1992	**Nannerl**, 5, 111	J. A. Krone	Withallprobability, 4, 120	Fit for a Queen, 6, 119	10	1:23.23	36,600
1991	**Love's Exchange**, 5, 126	H. Castillo Jr.	Peach of It, 5, 116	Tipsy Girl, 5, 114	8	1:23.30	35,820
1990	**Love's Exchange**, 4, 112	E. Fires	Fantastic Find, 4, 113	Fit for a Queen, 4, 112	9	1:23.60	36,720
1989	**Social Pro**, 4, 110	J. F. Chavez	Haiati, 4, 113	Costly Shoes, 4, 114	8	1:23.60	35,640
1988	**Tappiano**, 4, 115	J. Cruguet	Cadillacing, 4, 111	Bound, 4, 115	13	1:23.00	52,110
1987	**Life At the Top**, 4, 121	R. P. Romero	I'm Sweets, 4, 120	Jose's Bomb, 4, 112	8	1:22.80	35,640
1986	**Soli**, 4, 113	J. D. Bailey	Bessarabian, 4, 123	Nany, 6, 117	14	1:23.80	39,390
1985	**Mickey's Echo**, 6, 117	W. A. Guerra	Sugar's Image, 4, 117	Nany, 5, 122	10	1:23.60	37,110
1984	**Chic Belle**, 4, 114	C. Perret	Promising Native, 5, 114	First Flurry, 5, 115	9	1:22.40	25,578
1983	**Meringue Pie**, 5, 115	J. Velasquez	Cherokee Frolic, 5, 118	Mara Mia, 5, 109	8	1:24.20	24,717
	Secrettame, 5, 116	J. Vasquez	Prime Prospect, 5, 120	Miss Hitch, 7, 114	9	1:23.60	25,158
1982	**Bushmaid**, 4, 112	J. D. Bailey	Expressive Dance, 4, 124	Sweetest Chant, 4, 117	11	1:23.20	19,470
1981	**Sober Jig**, 4, 112	J. P. Souter	‡Likely Exchange, 7, 116	Island Charm, 4, 115	12	1:23.20	27,153
1979	**Candy Eclair**, 3, 122	A. S. Black	Davona Dale, 3, 122	Drop Me a Note, 3, 114	4	1:08.60	17,766
1976	**Regal Quillo**, 3, 114	C. Baltazar	Forty Nine Sunsets, 3, 112	Tristana, 3, 112	10	1:42.20	10,200

Named for James V. Tigani's SW Shirley Jones (1956 f. by Double Jay); Shirley Jones, the horse, was named for the actress. Grade 3 1988-2004. Shirley Jones S. 1976, 1979. Shirley Jones H. 1981-2005. Not held 1977-'78, 1980. 1$^{1}/_{16}$ miles 1976. 6 furlongs 1979. Two divisions 1983. ‡Cherry Berry finished second, DQ to fourth, 1981.

Shoemaker Breeders' Cup Mile Stakes

Grade 1 in 2006. Hollywood Park, three-year-olds and up, 1 mile, turf. Held May 29, 2006, with a gross value of $321,000. First held in 1938. First graded in 1973. Stakes record 1:32.64 (1994 Megan's Interco).

Year	Winner	Jockey	Second	Third	Strs	Time	1st Purse
2006	**Aragorn (Ire)**, 4, 124	C. S. Nakatani	Charmo (Fr), 5, 124	Silent Name (Jpn), 4, 124	6	1:32.95	$204,600
2005	**Castledale (Ire)**, 4, 124	R. R. Douglas	King of Happiness, 6, 124	Fast and Furious (Fr), 4, 124	7	1:33.17	205,800
2004	**Designed for Luck**, 7, 124	P. A. Valenzuela	Singletary, 4, 124	Tsigane (Fr), 5, 124	8	1:32.81	282,000
2003	**Redattore (Brz)**, 8, 124	A. O. Solis	Special Ring, 6, 124	Touch of the Blues (Fr), 6, 124	9	1:33.37	225,000
2002	**Ladies Din**, 7, 124	P. A. Valenzuela	Redattore (Brz), 7, 124	Spinelessjellyfish, 6, 124	10	1:33.39	240,000
2001	**Irish Prize**, 5, 124	G. L. Stevens	Touch of the Blues (Fr), 4, 124	Brahms, 4, 124	9	1:33.68	285,000
2000	**Silic (Fr)**, 5, 124	C. S. Nakatani	Ladies Din, 5, 124	Sharan (GB), 5, 124	11	1:33.36	304,800
1999	**Silic (Fr)**, 4, 124	C. S. Nakatani	Ladies Din, 4, 124	Hawksley Hill (Ire), 6, 124	8	1:32.95	280,200
1998	**Labeeb (GB)**, 6, 124	K. Desormeaux	Fantastic Fellow, 4, 124	Hawksley Hill (Ire), 5, 124	7	1:33.29	319,200

1997	**Pinfloron (Fr)**, 5, 124	D. R. Flores	Surachai, 4, 124	Helmsman, 5, 124	14	1:34.40	$353,400
1996	**Fastness (Ire)**, 6, 124	C. S. Nakatani	Romarin (Brz), 6, 124	Atticus, 4, 124	7	1:32.74	420,000
1995	**Unfinished Symph**, 4, 121	C. W. Antley	Rapan Boy (Aus), 7, 115	Journalism, 7, 117	9	1:33.14	98,400
1994	**Megan's Interco**, 5, 119	C. A. Black	Furiously, 5, 116	Rapan Boy (Aus), 6, 115	6	**1:32.64**	63,200
1993	**Journalism**, 5, 114	A. O. Solis	Lomitas (GB), 5, 118	Brief Truce, 4, 122	7	1:32.89	63,800
1991	**Exbourne**, 5, 118	G. L. Stevens	Super May, 5, 117	Dansil, 5, 111	7	1:33.50	65,300
1990	**Shining Steel (GB)**, 4, 114	C. J. McCarron	Super May, 4, 117	Brave Capade, 5, 111	5	1:34.00	63,000
1989	**Peace**, 4, 115	W. Shoemaker	Steinlen (GB), 6, 121	Political Ambition, 5, 122	8	1:33.00	65,700
1988	**Steinlen (GB)**, 5, 119	G. L. Stevens	Siyah Kalem, 6, 115	Neshad, 4, 115	8	1:33.20	80,200
1987	**Clever Song**, 5, 119	F. Toro	Al Mamoon, 6, 122	Le Belvedere, 4, 114	5	1:41.20	61,900
1986	**Clever Song**, 4, 116	F. Toro	Poly Test (Fr), 6, 115	Both Ends Burning, 6, 124	7	1:38.80	49,400
1985	**dh-Capture Him**, 4, 120	C. J. McCarron		Val Danseur, 5, 113	8	1:33.40	26,500
	dh-Retsina Run, 5, 116	E. Delahoussaye					
	Native Charmer (GB), 4, 113	S. Hawley	Gato Del Sol, 6, 120	Both Ends Burning, 5, 123	8	1:33.60	41,000
1984	**Massera (Chi)**, 6, 115	E. Delahoussaye	Sari's Dreamer, 5, 112	Barberstown, 4, 119	7	1:34.20	33,350
	Drumalis (Ire), 4, 119	E. Delahoussaye	Bel Bolide, 6, 122	Hula Blaze, 4, 114	8	1:33.80	33,950
1980	**Peregrinator (Ire)**, 5, 119	C. J. McCarron	Dragon Command (NZ), 6, 117	Life's Hope, 7, 117	7	1:41.60	31,850
1979	**Farnesio (Arg)**, 5, 119	W. Shoemaker	Harry's Love, 4, 114	Star Spangled, 5, 120	5	1:41.60	31,100
1978	**J. O. Tobin**, 4, 125	S. Cauthen	Mr. Redoy, 4, 121	Miami Sun, 4, 115	5	1:41.40	30,600
1977	**Barrera**, 4, 119	L. A. Pincay Jr.	Beat Inflation, 4, 120	Maheras, 4, 124	5	1:07.40	24,650
1976	**Sporting Goods**, 6, 115	F. Toro	Century's Envoy, 5, 124	Money Lender, 5, 115	10	1:08.20	20,500
1975	**Rise High**, 5, 116	S. Hawley	‡Selecting, 6, 117	Money Lender, 4, 115	6	1:09.00	18,900
1974	**Beira**, 5, 115	W. Mahorney	Woodland Pines, 5, 119	Linda's Chief, 4, 124	8	1:07.80	19,700
1973	**Diplomatic Agent**, 5, 115	R. Rosales	Rough Night, 5, 111	Selecting, 4, 116	9	1:09.00	20,150

Named for Racing Hall of Fame jockey William Shoemaker (1931-2003), who retired as leading rider by number of wins. Formerly named in honor of Hollywood's film industry. Formerly sponsored by the Miller Brewing Co. of Milwaukee, Wisconsin 1971. Grade 3 1987-'89. Not graded 1975-'86. Grade 2 1990-'99. Hollywood Premiere H. 1938-'63. Premiere H. 1964-'70, 1972-'80, 1984-'89. Miller High Life Premiere H. 1971. Shoemaker H. 1990-'95. Held at Santa Anita Park 1949. Not held 1942-'43, 1948, 1981-'83, 1992. 6 furlongs 1938-'49, 1951-'77. 7 furlongs 1950. $1^1/_{16}$ miles 1978-'80, 1986-'87. Dirt 1938-'80. Two-year-olds and up 1944. Two divisions 1984-'85. Dead heat for first 1985 (1st Div.). ‡Shirley's Champion finished second, DQ to fourth, 1975. Equaled track record 1940. Equaled course record 1993, 1996. Course record 1994.

Shuvee Handicap

Grade 2 in 2006. Belmont Park, three-year-olds and up, fillies and mares, 1 mile, dirt. Held May 21, 2006, with a gross value of $147,000. First held in 1976. First graded in 1978. Stakes record 1:34.23 (2005 Society Selection).

Year	Winner	Jockey	Second	Third	Strs	Time	1st Purse
2006	**Take D'Tour**, 5, 115	C. H. Velasquez	Balletto (UAE), 4, 116	Smuggler, 4, 120	5	1:36.10	$90,000
2005	**Society Selection**, 4, 118	E. Coa	Daydreaming, 4, 119	Bohemian Lady, 4, 114	5	**1:34.23**	120,000
2004	**Storm Flag Flying**, 4, 116	J. R. Velazquez	Passing Shot, 5, 117	Roar Emotion, 4, 117	6	1:36.10	120,000
2003	**Wild Spirit (Chi)**, 4, 115	J. Castellano	Smok'n Frolic, 4, 119	You, 4, 120	6	1:34.51	120,000
2002	**Shiny Band**, 4, 113	R. G. Davis	Raging Fever, 4, 121	Victory Ride, 4, 118	5	1:34.95	120,000
2001	**Apple of Kent**, 5, 114	R. Migliore	March Magic, 4, 113	Country Hideaway, 5, 118	5	1:35.16	120,000
2000	**Beautiful Pleasure**, 5, 122	J. F. Chavez	Biogio's Rose, 6, 115	Up We Go, 4, 114	5	1:35.65	120,000
1999	**Catinca**, 4, 121	R. Migliore	Sister Act, 4, 117	Tap to Music, 4, 115	6	1:34.38	90,000
1998	**Colonial Minstrel**, 4, 117	J. R. Velazquez	Dixie Flag, 4, 120	Hidden Reserve, 4, 113	5	1:36.20	90,000
1997	**Hidden Lake**, 4, 115	R. Migliore	Flat Fleet Feet, 4, 120	Escena, 4, 116	9	1:35.27	90,000
1996	**Clear Mandate**, 4, 111	J. A. Krone	Smooth Charmer, 4, 111	Restored Hope, 5, 115	7	1:35.01	90,000
1995	**Inside Information**, 4, 119	J. A. Santos	Sky Beauty, 5, 126	Restored Hope, 4, 115	4	1:35.10	80,220
1994	**Sky Beauty**, 4, 125	M. E. Smith	For all Seasons, 4, 113	Looie Capote, 5, 112	4	1:40.60	90,000
1993	**Turnback the Alarm**, 4, 117	C. W. Antley	Shared Interest, 5, 113	Vivano, 4, 112	9	1:43.11	90,000
1992	**Missy's Mirage**, 4, 116	E. Maple	Harbour Club, 5, 110	Versailles Treaty, 4, 119	6	1:40.74	102,960
1991	**A Wild Ride**, 4, 119	M. E. Smith	Buy the Firm, 5, 122	Degenerate Gal, 6, 117	6	1:42.52	103,140
1990	**Tis Juliet**, 4, 113	R. Migliore	Survive, 6, 119	Dreamy Mimi, 4, 114	7	1:43.00	102,780
1989	**Banker's Lady**, 4, 122	A. T. Cordero Jr.	Rose's Cantina, 5, 117	Grecian Flight, 5, 117	7	1:40.80	104,580
1988	**Personal Ensign**, 4, 121	R. P. Romero	Clabber Girl, 5, 118	Bishop's Delight, 5, 111	6	1:41.60	102,060
1987	**Ms. Eloise**, 4, 117	R. G. Davis	North Sider, 5, 120	Clemanna's Rose, 6, 114	10	1:41.80	107,820
1986	**Lady's Secret**, 4, 126	P. Day	Endear, 4, 115	Ride Sally, 4, 125	6	1:41.80	81,780
1985	**Life's Magic**, 4, 121	J. Velasquez	Heatherten, 6, 126	Some for All, 4, 109	7	1:42.40	83,820
1984	**Queen of Song**, 5, 117	S. Maple	Try Something New, 5, 121	Narrate, 4, 116	10	1:43.00	86,340
1983	**Dance Number**, 4, 113	A. T. Cordero Jr.	Number, 4, 117	May Day Eighty, 4, 116	4	1:40.40	49,500
1982	**Anti Lib**, 4, 113	J. Vasquez	Tina Tina Too, 4, 112	Funny Bone, 4, 108	7	1:41.60	33,420
1981	**Chain Bracelet**, 4, 117	R. Hernandez	Weber City Miss, 4, 118	Wistful, 4, 120	5	1:42.80	32,700
1980	**Alada**, 4, 115	J. Fell	Lady Lonsdale, 5, 115	Blitey, 4, 116	5	1:43.00	32,460
1979	**Pearl Necklace**, 5, 121	J. Fell	Tingle Stone, 4, 120	Kit's Double, 6, 109	8	1:41.40	32,280
1978	**One Sum**, 4, 121	R. Hernandez	Sparkling Topaz, 4, 107	Charming Story, 4, 113	5	1:44.00	31,830
1977	**‡Mississippi Mud**, 4, 113	J. Vasquez	Sweet Bernice, 4, 109	Secret Lanvin, 4, 111	10	1:43.60	32,760
1976	**Proud Delta**, 4, 122	J. Velasquez	Snooze, 4, 108	Let Me Linger, 4, 115	8	1:35.00	33,810

Named for Mrs. Whitney Stone's 1970, '71 champion older female and '69 Coaching Club American Oaks winner Shuvee (1966 f. by Nashua). Grade 1 1986-'96. $1^1/_{16}$ miles 1977-'94. ‡Secret Lanvin finished first, DQ to third, 1977.

Silky Sullivan Stakes

Grade 3 in 2006. Golden Gate Fields, three-year-olds, 1⅛ miles, turf. Held November 5, 2005, with a gross value of $100,000. First held in 1954. First graded in 1983. Stakes record 1:47.60 (1986 Le Belvedere).

Year	Winner	Jockey	Second	Third	Strs	Time	1st Purse
2005	**Eastern Sand**, 3, 115	V. Espinoza	Mr. Splash, 3, 115	Eager Pharisien, 3, 117	6	1:49.03	$55,000
2004	**Congressionalhonor**, 3, 115	R. A. Baze	Talaris, 3, 116	‡On the Acorn (GB), 3, 116	8	1:48.92	55,000
2003	**Stanley Park**, 3, 116	E. Saint-Martin	Bis Repetitas, 3, 118	Kewen, 3, 116	8	1:48.97	55,000
2002	**Royal Gem**, 3, 119	R. A. Baze	Aly Bubba, 3, 114	Century City (Ire), 3, 122	8	1:48.38	55,000
2001	**Blue Steller (Ire)**, 3, 119	A. O. Solis	Sir Alfred, 3, 116	Sea to See, 3, 116	8	1:46.81	55,000
2000	**Walkslikeaduck**, 3, 122	E. Delahoussaye	Jokerman, 3, 119	Calamari, 3, 115	5	1:46.57	82,500
1999	**Mula Gula**, 3, 117	R. Q. Meza	†Miss Chryss (Ire), 3, 111	Fighting Falcon, 3, 120	10	1:45.34	82,500
1998	**Takarian (Ire)**, 3, 116	C. A. Black	I. M. Bzy, 3, 115	Prevalence (GB), 3, 114	8	1:46.80	82,500
1997	**Shellbacks**, 3, 113	R. Q. Meza	Brave Act (GB), 3, 122	Zippersup, 3, 115	7	1:49.01	82,500
1996	**†Ocean Queen**, 3, 110	J. A. Garcia	Mateo, 3, 115	Mystic Knight (GB), 3, 116	8	1:47.80	110,000
1995	**Virginia Carnival**, 3, 115	R. J. Warren Jr.	Helmsman, 3, 113	Tabor, 3, 116	10	1:46.17	55,000
1994	**Marvin's Faith (Ire)**, 3, 116	M. Castaneda	Western Trader, 3, 116	Turbo Fan, 3, 115	8	1:48.88	55,000
1993	**Ranger (Fr)**, 3, 114	G. Boulanger	El Atroz, 3, 113	Guide (Fr), 3, 120	9	1:48.90	55,000
1992	**Star Recruit**, 3, 116	R. D. Hansen	Siberian Summer, 3, 116	Fax News, 3, 115	6	1:49.13	55,000
1991	**Bistro Garden**, 3, 120	M. Castaneda	Dominion Gold (GB), 3, 116	Fraise, 3, 115	8	1:46.70	82,500
1990	**Sekondi (Fr)**, 3, 114	R. M. Gonzalez	Courtesy Title, 3, 115	†Appealing Missy, 3, 113	12	1:48.80	55,000
1989	**Irish**, 3, 115	M. A. Espindola	Polar Boy, 3, 115	Two Moccasins, 3, 113	12	1:48.20	55,000
1988	**Coax Me Clyde**, 3, 118	R. J. Warren Jr.	Gran Judgement, 3, 116	Literati, 3, 117	11	1:49.00	68,500
1987	**Hot and Smoggy**, 3, 117	J. Vasquez	Wolsey, 3, 116	Lucky Harold H., 3, 115	9	1:48.60	66,400
1986	**Le Belvedere**, 3, 113	W. Shoemaker	Santella Mac (Ire), 3, 115	Grand Exchange, 3, 116	11	**1:47.60**	81,300
1985	**Minutes Away**, 3, 115	C. R. Hummel	Charming Duke (Fr), 3, 124	Lucky n Green (Ire), 3, 115	10	1:51.40	66,800
1984	**Mangaki**, 3, 115	C. Lamance	Refueled (Ire), 3, 117	Foscarini (Ire), 3, 120	11	1:52.00	68,400
1983	**Interco**, 3, 116	J. C. Judice	Bang Bang Bang, 3, 112	Baron O'Dublin, 3, 120	6	1:49.60	63,500
1982	**Ask Me**, 3, 120	F. Toro	Water Bank, 3, 120	Take the Floor, 3, 121	10	1:46.00	66,100
1981	**Silveyville**, 3, 120	D. Winick	Sunshine Swag, 3, 113	Tempo's Tiger, 3, 117	10	1:48.20	67,000
1980	**Fleet Tempo**, 3, 114	R. M. Gonzalez	Super Moment, 3, 123	Aliyoun (Ire), 3, 112	9	1:44.60	32,750
1979	**Nain Bleu (Fr)**, 3, 113	C. Baltazar	Bends Me Mind, 3, 118	Gummaka, 3, 115	9	1:45.40	32,300
1978	**Quip**, 3, 115	T. Lipham	Shagbark, 3, 115	Kamehameha, 3, 123	11	1:45.20	34,250

Named for Tom Ross's and Phil Klipstein's 1957 Golden Gate Futurity winner Silky Sullivan (1955 c. by *Sullivan). Silky Sullivan was a local favorite and is buried at Golden Gate. Bay Meadows Derby 1954, 1957, 1978-'95, 2001-'04. Bay Meadows Breeders' Cup Derby 1996-2000. Held at Bay Meadows 1954, 1957, 1978-2004. Not held 1955-'56, 1958-'77. 1$^1/_{16}$ miles 1957, 1978-'82. About 1⅛ miles 1983-'84, 1986, 1988-'91, 1994-'95, 1997-2002. Dirt 1992. ‡Hendrix finished third, DQ to eighth, 2004. †Denotes female.

Silverbulletday Stakes

Grade 3 in 2006. Fair Grounds at Louisiana Downs, three-year-olds, fillies, 1$^1/_{16}$ miles, dirt. Held January 14, 2006, with a gross value of $269,200. First held in 1982. First graded in 1999. Stakes record 1:42.09 (2002 Take Charge Lady).

Year	Winner	Jockey	Second	Third	Strs	Time	1st Purse
2006	**Baghdaria**, 3, 116	M. C. Berry	French Park, 3, 122	Capozzene, 3, 116	8	1:46.07	$161,520
2005	**Summerly**, 3, 118	D. J. Meche	Eyes On Eddy, 3, 112	Enduring Will, 3, 122	9	1:43.79	90,000
2004	**Shadow Cast**, 3, 116	R. Albarado	Quick Temper, 3, 113	Sister Swank, 3, 117	6	1:46.82	90,000
2003	**Belle of Perintown**, 3, 122	C. H. Borel	Afternoon Dreams, 3, 112	Rebridled Dreams, 3, 117	8	1:44.48	90,000
2002	**Take Charge Lady**, 3, 122	J. K. Court	Charmed Gift, 3, 119	Chamrousse, 3, 115	5	**1:42.09**	90,000
2001	**Lakenheath**, 3, 119	C. J. Lanerie	Morning Sun, 3, 112	Beloved by All, 3, 114	5	1:46.09	75,000
2000	**Shawnee Country**, 3, 122	D. J. Meche	Chilukki, 3, 122	Humble Clerk, 3, 122	9	1:45.11	75,000
1999	**Silverbulletday**, 3, 122	G. L. Stevens	Brushed Halory, 3, 114	On a Soapbox, 3, 119	8	1:44.36	75,000
1998	**Cool Dixie**, 3, 122	R. D. Ardoin	Lu Ravi, 3, 114	Silent Eskimo, 3, 112	9	1:43.38	75,000
1997	**Blushing K. D.**, 3, 122	L. J. Meche	Tomisue's Delight, 3, 119	Morelia, 3, 122	6	1:42.48	60,000
1996	**Up Dip**, 3, 114	C. C. Bourque	Brush With Tequila, 3, 113	Not Likely, 3, 122	8	1:44.61	37,635
1995	**Legendary Priness**, 3, 113	C. A. Emigh	Broad Smile, 3, 122	Hero's Valor, 3, 114	9	1:44.42	25,875
1994	**Playcaller**, 3, 119	R. D. Ardoin	Two Altazano, 3, 112	Briar Road, 3, 112	7	1:44.31	31,095
1993	**Bright Penny**, 3, 114	R. D. Ardoin	She's a Little Shy, 3, 114	Wakerup, 3, 112	7	1:44.80	19,095
1992	**Prospectors Delite**, 3, 117	B. J. Walker Jr.	Royal Med, 3, 112	Glitzi Bj, 3, 119	7	1:43.80	19,020
1991	**Nalees Pin**, 3, 122	K. Bourque	Oxford Screen, 3, 112	Lady Blockbuster, 3, 119	7	1:46.50	19,065
1990	**Windansea**, 3, 112	R. P. Romero	Everlasting Lady, 3, 119	A Hula, 3, 114	11	1:46.40	16,560
1989	**Exquisite Mistress**, 3, 114	C. H. Borel	Jewel Bid, 3, 117	Lunar Princess, 3, 112	6	1:46.80	16,065
1988	**False Glitter**, 3, 114	S. P. Romero	Part Native, 3, 117	Quite a Gem, 3, 114	10	1:47.40	16,710
1987	**Out of the Bid**, 3, 112	K. Bourque	Trapped, 3, 115	Quick Closing, 3, 122	7	1:47.20	25,170
1986	**Tiffany Lass**, 3, 122	R. L. Frazier	Super Set, 3, 122	Port of Departure, 3, 117	10	1:46.00	25,200
1985	**Marshua's Echelon**, 3, 122	R. J. Franklin	Turn to Wilma, 3, 114	Not Again Debbie, 3, 114	8	1:45.20	19,150
1984	**Texas Cowgirl Nite**, 3, 122	K. Bourque	Only Bid, 3, 114	Runny Nose, 3, 114	8	1:42.00	18,950
1983	**Duped**, 3, 122	J. C. Espinoza	Shamivor, 3, 117	Juliet's Pet, 3, 117	5	1:43.00	14,100
1982	**Linda North**, 3, 122	R. J. Franklin	‡Mickey's Echo, 3, 117	Rose Bouquet, 3, 122	9	1:42.80	13,950

Named for Mike Pegram's 1998 champion two-year-old filly, '99 champion three-year-old filly, and '99 Davona Dale S. (G3) winner Silverbulletday (1996 f. by Silver Deputy). Formerly named for Calumet Farm's 1979 champion three-year-old filly and filly triple crown winner Davona Dale (1976 f. by Best Turn). Davona Dale S. 1982-2000. Held at Louisiana Downs 2006. 1 mile 40 yards 1982-'84. ‡Avadewan finished second, DQ to fifth, 1982.

Sir Beaufort Stakes

Grade 3 in 2006. Santa Anita Park, three-year-olds, 1 mile, turf. Held December 26, 2005, in two divisions, with a gross value of $84,500 for the first division, and $86,500 for the second division. First held in 2000. First graded in 2006. Stakes record 1:34.34 (2005 Tedo [Ger] [2nd Div.]).

Year	Winner	Jockey	Second	Third	Strs	Time	1st Purse
2005	**Tedo (Ger)**, 3, 122	C. S. Nakatani	Eastern Sand, 3, 122	Follow the Rainbow, 3, 122	10	**1:34.34**	$51,900
	Chinese Dragon, 3, 118	K. Desormeaux	Hockey the General, 3, 118	Becrux (Ity), 3, 118	8	1:35.09	50,700
2004	**Whilly (Ire)**, 3, 118	F. F. Martinez	We All Love Aleyna, 3, 120	Cozy Guy, 3, 122	9	1:34.60	67,620
2003	**Buckland Manor**, 3, 120	C. S. Nakatani	Saint Buddy, 3, 116	Kewen, 3, 118	8	1:36.08	46,800
2002	**Inesperado (Fr)**, 3, 122	P. A. Valenzuela	Music's Storm, 3, 120	Golden Arrow, 3, 118	8	1:35.82	46,020
2001	**Orientate**, 3, 122	C. J. McCarron	Sigfreto, 3, 122	Blue Steller (Ire), 3, 122	10	1:36.39	46,440
2000	**Fateful Dream**, 3, 118	K. Desormeaux	Designed for Luck, 3, 122	†Vencera (Fr), 3, 116	8	1:35.03	45,705

Named for Victoria Calantoni's 1993 Santa Anita H. (G1) winner Sir Beaufort (1987 c. by Pleasant Colony). Dirt 2003. Originally scheduled on turf 2003. Two divisions 2005. †Denotes female.

Sixty Sails Handicap

Grade 3 in 2006. Hawthorne Race Course, three-year-olds and up, fillies and mares, 1⅛ miles, dirt. Held April 22, 2006, with a gross value of $250,000. First held in 1976. First graded in 1984. Stakes record 1:46.69 (1999 Crafty Oak).

Year	Winner	Jockey	Second	Third	Strs	Time	1st Purse
2006	**Fleet Indian**, 5, 116	J. A. Santos	Silver Highlight, 4, 114	Platinum Ballet, 5, 115	8	1:49.37	$150,000
2005	**Isola Piu Bella (Chi)**, 5, 118	J. R. Velazquez	Rare Gift, 4, 115	Ghostly Gate, 4, 117	7	1:49.58	150,000
2004	**Allspice**, 4, 115	C. A. Emigh	Bare Necessities, 5, 122	Mavoreen, 4, 114	6	1:50.66	150,000
2003	**Bare Necessities**, 4, 118	R. R. Douglas	Jaramar Rain, 4, 114	Lakenheath, 5, 114	9	1:52.84	150,000
2002	**With Ability**, 4, 115	J. Castellano	Lakenheath, 4, 115	Katy Kat, 4, 116	7	1:51.37	180,000
2001	**License Fee**, 6, 116	L. J. Melancon	Lady Melesi, 4, 116	Megans Bluff, 4, 116	8	1:49.11	180,000
2000	**Lu Ravi**, 5, 116	P. Day	Tap to Music, 5, 120	Batuka, 4, 116	8	1:49.15	180,000
1999	**Crafty Oak**, 5, 114	R. Sibille	Highfalutin, 5, 115	Lines of Beauty, 4, 114	7	**1:46.69**	180,000
1998	**Glitter Woman**, 4, 118	G. L. Stevens	Top Secret, 5, 115	dh-Im Out First, 5, 112 dh-Tuxedo Junction, 5, 115	7	1:50.49	180,000
1997	**Top Secret**, 4, 115	C. Perret	Hurricane Viv, 4, 119	Gold n Delicious, 4, 114	9	1:49.71	180,000
1996	**Alcovy**, 6, 119	W. Martinez	Shoop, 5, 118	Lotta Dancing, 5, 120	13	1:50.70	180,000
1995	**Eskimo's Angel**, 6, 114	M. Guidry	Little Buckles, 4, 113	Norfolk Lavender, 4, 112	13	1:51.53	180,000
1994	**Princess Polonia**, 4, 113	W. S. Ramos	Eskimo's Angel, 5, 115	Joyous Melody, 4, 113	8	1:51.88	180,000
1993	**Pleasant Baby**, 4, 112	J. L. Diaz	Miss Jealski, 4, 113	Steff Graf (Brz), 5, 115	9	1:49.30	180,000
1992	**Peach of It**, 6, 114	E. T. Baird	Bungalow, 5, 115	Zend to Aiken, 4, 113	13	1:51.28	162,090
1991	**Balotra**, 4, 112	R. A. Meier	Charon, 4, 122	Beth Believes, 5, 113	8	1:50.98	157,860
1990	**Leave It Be**, 5, 119	H. A. Sanchez	Anitas Surprise, 4, 114	Degenerate Gal, 5, 116	8	1:53.40	156,510
1989	**Valid Vixen**, 4, 116	J. L. Diaz	Scorned Lass, 5, 115	Arcroyal, 5, 116	8	1:52.60	156,480
1988	**Top Corsage**, 5, 118	P. A. Valenzuela	Yukon Dolly, 4, 114	Inspiracion (Uru), 7, 110	6	1:52.00	125,010
1987	**Queen Alexandra**, 5, 123	D. Brumfield	My Gallant Duchess, 5, 116	Happy Hollow Miss, 4, 113	7	1:49.60	126,330
1986	**Sefa's Beauty**, 7, 124	R. P. Romero	Flying Heat, 4, 122	Farer Belle Lee, 7, 118	10	1:50.00	112,290
1985	**Sefa's Beauty**, 6, 122	P. Day	Farer Belle Lee, 6, 115	Princess Moran, 4, 113	12	1:52.60	113,580
1984	**Queen of Song**, 5, 122	R. J. Hirdes Jr.	Frosty Tail, 4, 120	Herb Wine, 5, 118	11	1:46.60	97,710
1983	**Queen of Song**, 4, 115	R. J. Hirdes Jr.	Bersid, 5, 121	Sefa's Beauty, 4, 120	9	1:43.80	96,630
1982	**Targa**, 5, 116	R. D. Evans	Really Royal, 4, 115	Knights Beauty, 5, 115	12	1:45.00	98,040
1981	**Karla's Enough**, 4, 120	E. Fires	Favorite Prospect, 4, 117	Romantic Mood, 4, 113	9	1:37.60	46,890
	Gold Treasure, 4, 118	J. L. Diaz	Sissy's Time, 4, 120	Satin Ribera, 4, 120	10	1:38.00	47,040
1980	**Doing It My Way**, 4, 115	R. J. Hirdes Jr.	Powerless, 4, 118	Cookie Puddin, 4, 116	8	1:40.20	40,335
	Conga Miss, 4, 118	G. Gallitano	Century Type, 6, 120	Royal Villa, 3, 115	7	1:40.20	40,215
1979	**Strate Sunshine**, 5, 113	R. Lindsay	Timeforaturn, 4, 114	Century Type, 5, 112	9	1:40.80	46,830
1978	**Drop the Pigeon**, 4, 118	J. L. Diaz	Evelyn's Time, 5, 113	Creation, 5, 119	11	1:39.40	16,320
1977	**Kissapotamus**, 5, 115	G. Baze	Kittyluck, 4, 116	Lady B. Gay, 4, 116	10	1:38.80	22,470
1976	**Enchanted Native**, 5, 115	L. Snyder	Honky Star, 5, 121	Regal Rumor, 4, 118	11	1:40.00	31,650

Named for John J. Petre's and Chris Vodanovich's 1974 Louis S. Meen Memorial H. winner Sixty Sails (1970 f. by Creme dela Creme). Held at Sportsman's Park 1976-'89, 2000-'02. 1 mile 1976-'81. 1$^1/_{16}$ miles 1982-'84. Four-year-olds and up 1984-'87. Two divisions 1980-'81. Dead heat for third 1998. Track record 1993. Equaled track record 1999.

Skip Away Handicap

Grade 3 in 2006. Gulfstream Park, three-year-olds and up, 1⅛ miles, dirt. Held April 1, 2006, with a gross value of $100,000. First held in 1987. First graded in 1992. Stakes record 1:48.10 (1991 Chief Honcho).

Year	Winner	Jockey	Second	Third	Strs	Time	1st Purse
2006	**Bandini**, 4, 117	J. R. Velazquez	We Can Seek (Chi), 5, 113	O'Connell's (Brz), 5, 116	8	1:49.11	$60,000
2005	**Eurosilver**, 4, 113	J. Castellano	Twilight Road, 8, 114	Zakocity, 4, 117	10	1:49.29	60,000
2004	**Newfoundland**, 4, 116	J. R. Velazquez	Supah Blitz, 4, 114	Bowman's Band, 6, 117	10	1:43.26	60,000
2003	**Best of the Rest**, 8, 121	E. Coa	Consistency, 4, 114	Roger E, 4, 114	5	1:42.72	60,000
2002	**Sir Bear**, 9, 116	E. S. Prado	Red Bullet, 5, 118	Hal's Hope, 5, 114	8	1:43.98	60,000
2001	**American Halo**, 5, 114	R. G. Davis	Vision and Verse, 5, 114	Pleasant Breeze, 6, 118	10	1:42.31	60,000
2000	**Horse Chestnut (SAf)**, 5, 117	M. E. Smith	Isaypete, 4, 116	Rock and Roll, 5, 120	6	1:42.78	60,000
1999	**Sir Bear**, 6, 119	J. D. Bailey	Behrens, 5, 113	Hanarsaan, 6, 110	8	1:43.66	60,000
1998	**Sir Bear**, 5, 112	E. M. Jurado	Black Forest, 4, 113	Kiridashi, 6, 116	7	1:43.27	60,000

1997 **Crafty Friend**, 4, 114	M. E. Smith	Diligence, 4, 116	Ghostly Moves, 5, 114	8	1:42.27	$45,000
1996 **Halo's Image**, 5, 119	P. Day	Wekiva Springs, 5, 119	Flying Chevron, 4, 116	7	1:42.71	45,000
1995 **Fight for Love**, 5, 113	J. D. Bailey	‡Danville, 4, 113	Pride of Burkaan, 5, 113	7	1:43.98	45,000
1994 **Devil His Due**, 5, 121	M. E. Smith	Migrating Moon, 4, 116	Northern Trend, 6, 111	8	1:43.17	45,000
1993 **Technology**, 4, 118	J. D. Bailey	Barkerville, 5, 117	Bidding Proud, 4, 114	8	1:42.47	45,000
1992 **Honest Ensign**, 4, 109	J. Cruguet	Peanut Butter Onit, 6, 114	Strike the Gold, 4, 117	7	1:49.41	45,000
1991 **Chief Honcho**, 4, 116	M. E. Smith	No Marker, 7, 113	Barkada, 5, 114	8	**1:48.10**	45,000
1990 **Primal**, 5, 120	E. Fires	Ole Atocha, 5, 113	Wonderloaf, 4, 113	10	1:43.40	60,000
1987 **Big Blowup**, 3, 115	C. Baltazar	Micanopy Boy, 3, 113	Jim Bowie, 3, 113	6	1:44.40	34,290

Named for Carolyn Hine's 1998 Horse of the Year and '98 Donn H. (G1) winner Skip Away (1993 c. by Skip Trial). Formerly named for Broward County, Florida, location of Gulfstream Park. Broward H. 1987-2000. Not held 1988-'89. 1¹⁄₁₆ miles 1987, 1993-2004. Turf 1987. Three-year-olds 1987. ‡Northern Trend finished second, DQ to fifth, 1995.

Smile Sprint Handicap

Grade 2 in 2006. Calder Race Course, three-year-olds and up, 6 furlongs, dirt. Held July 10, 2005, with a gross value of $500,000. First held in 1958. First graded in 2003. Stakes record 1:08.95 (2000 Forty One Carats).

Year	Winner	Jockey	Second	Third	Strs	Time	1st Purse
2005	**Woke Up Dreamin**, 5, 117	M. E. Smith	Toscani, 5, 113	Nightmare Affair, 4, 113	9	1:09.80	$294,000
2004	**Champali**, 4, 117	J. D. Bailey	Clock Stopper, 4, 115	Built Up, 6, 114	10	1:10.14	294,000
2003	**Shake You Down**, 5, 119	M. J. Luzzi	Private Horde, 4, 113	My Cousin Matt, 4, 116	13	1:10.03	294,000
2002	**Orientate**, 4, 119	M. E. Smith	Echo Eddie, 5, 117	Crafty C. T., 4, 117	7	1:09.98	240,000
2001	**Fappie's Notebook**, 4, 116	J. F. Chavez	Thrillin Discovery, 6, 112	Salty Glance, 6, 115	12	1:09.89	120,000
2000	**Forty One Carats**, 4, 116	J. Castellano	Personal First, 3, 114	Alice's Notebook, 4, 111	7	**1:08.95**	180,000
1999	**Silver Season**, 3, 112	E. Coa	Son of a Pistol, 7, 119	My Jeff's Mombo, 5, 116	7	1:10.03	180,000
1998	**Heckofaralph**, 5, 115	W. Ramos	Thunder Breeze, 4, 113	Nicholas Ds, 4, 115	13	1:11.48	180,000
1997	**†Vivace**, 4, 114	R. P. Romero	Score a Birdie, 6, 113	Valid Expectations, 4, 117	9	1:10.65	150,000
1996	**Constant Escort**, 4, 114	E. O. Nunez	Honest Colors, 5, 114	Excelerate, 4, 113	10	1:21.82	60,000
1995	**Request a Star**, 4, 113	A. Toribio	Thats Our Buck, 5, 113	Halo's Image, 4, 118	11	1:23.69	60,000
1994	**Exclusive Praline**, 3, 117	W. S. Ramos	Migrating Moon, 4, 118	Fortunate Joe, 3, 114	10	1:22.29	60,000
1993	**Song of Ambition**, 4, 116	R. D. Lopez	Coolin It, 4, 113	Daniel's Boy, 5, 117	12	1:22.52	45,000
1992	**My Luck Runs North**, 3, 114	R. D. Lopez	Groomstick, 6, 119	Cigar Toss (Arg), 5, 112	9	1:17.57	45,000
1991	**Greg At Bat**, 6, 114	J. Vasquez	Sunny and Pleasant, 3, 113	Perfection, 4, 115	11	1:24.26	51,105
1990	**Groomstick**, 4, 113	P. A. Rodriguez	Country Isle, 3, 113	Medieval Victory, 5, 119	7	1:24.20	49,170
1989	**Glitterman**, 4, 119	W. A. Guerra	Doddle Bug Mel, 4, 112	Proud and Valid, 4, 112	7	1:10.40	32,970
1988	**Position Leader**, 3, 112	D. Valiente	Medieval Victory, 3, 112	Hooting Star, 3, 113	9	1:24.80	49,635
1987	**Princely Lad**, 4, 110	B. Green	Rilial, 6, 113	Ward Off Trouble, 7, 114	6	1:23.80	32,580
1986	**Jeblar**, 4, 123	J. A. Velez Jr.	Power Plan, 4, 116	Mugatea, 6, 115	9	1:24.80	32,790
1985	**Opening Lead**, 5, 117	J. M. Pezua	Rexson's Hope, 4, 121	King of Bridlewood, 5, 115	7	1:24.00	32,760
1984	**I Really Will**, 4, 120	G. St. Leon	Mo Exception, 3, 120	El Kaiser, 4, 112	11	1:12.00	33,840
1978	**J. Burns**, 3, 114	N. B. Navarro	Jungle Adam, 4, 113	Forward Charger, 4, 114	8	1:45.20	17,400
1977	**Ilefetchit**, 5, 115	M. A. Rivera	‡Super Boy, 4, 110	Coverack, 4, 121	9	1:44.60	17,700
1974	**Canvasser**, 2, 116	M. Solomone	Hunka Papa, 2, 120	What a Threat, 2, 112	12	1:47.60	14,880
1973	**Tai G. T.**, 2, 117	R. Hernandez	Mr. Sad, 2, 118	Neapolitan Way, 2, 118	12	1:46.40	14,880

Named for Frances A. Genter's 1986 champion sprinter and '85 Carry Back S. winner Smile (1982 c. by In Reality); Smile is the broodmare sire of 2004 champion three-year-old male Smarty Jones. Formerly named for the city of Miami Beach. Grade 3 2003-'04. City of Miami Beach S. 1958-'62. City of Miami Beach H. 1963-'69, 1978. Miami Beach H. 1970-'77, 1984-'93. Miami Beach Sprint H. 1994-'98. Not held 1975-'76, 1979-'83. 7 furlongs 1985-'88, 1990-'91, 1993-'96. 1¹⁄₁₆ miles 1958-'60. 6¹⁄₂ furlongs 1992. Two divisions 1958, 1961. ‡Coverack finished second, DQ to third, 1977. †Denotes female.

Sorrento Stakes

Grade 3 in 2006. Del Mar, two-year-olds, fillies, 6¹⁄₂ furlongs, dirt. Held August 6, 2005, with a gross value of $150,000. First held in 1967. First graded in 1986. Stakes record 1:15.26 (1995 Batroyale).

Year	Winner	Jockey	Second	Third	Strs	Time	1st Purse
2005	**Bully Bones**, 2, 119	R. R. Douglas	Acceleration, 2, 117	Slick Road, 2, 119	9	1:17.36	$90,000
2004	**Inspiring**, 2, 118	D. R. Flores	Souvenir Gift, 2, 122	Hello Lucky, 2, 118	8	1:18.29	90,000
2003	**Tizdubai**, 2, 118	D. R. Flores	Dirty Diana, 2, 122	Solar Fire, 2, 118	8	1:17.15	90,000
2002	**Buffythecenterfold**, 2, 121	M. S. Garcia	Tricks Her, 2, 115	Indy Groove, 2, 117	8	1:17.39	90,000
2001	**Tempera**, 2, 117	D. R. Flores	Respectful, 2, 115	Roaring Blaze, 2, 117	8	1:16.13	90,000
2000	**Give Praise**, 2, 116	L. A. Pincay Jr.	Sea Reel, 2, 115	Fort Lauderdale, 2, 117	7	1:17.88	90,000
1999	**Chilukki**, 2, 121	D. R. Flores	November Slew, 2, 117	She's Classy, 2, 117	6	1:16.40	90,000
1998	**Silverbulletday**, 2, 121	G. L. Stevens	Excellent Meeting, 2, 117	Colorado Song, 2, 117	7	1:17.56	64,980
1997	**Career Collection**, 2, 121	C. S. Nakatani	Griselle, 2, 117	Bent Creek City, 2, 121	7	1:17.83	67,825
1996	**Desert Digger**, 2, 116	E. Delahoussaye	Silken Magic, 2, 117	Montecito, 2, 117	9	1:16.03	65,950
1995	**Batroyale**, 2, 119	G. L. Stevens	Cosmic Fire, 2, 117	Waycross, 2, 117	6	**1:15.26**	59,200
1994	**How So Oiseau**, 2, 117	P. A. Valenzuela	Ski Dancer, 2, 117	Serena's Song, 2, 121	8	1:15.89	47,100
1993	**Phone Chatter**, 2, 117	L. A. Pincay Jr.	Rhapsodic, 2, 121	Noassemblyrequired, 2, 117	6	1:16.23	45,900
1992	**Zoonaqua**, 2, 117	E. Delahoussaye	Eliza, 2, 117	Medici Bells, 2, 117	11	1:22.67	49,125
1991	**Soviet Sojourn**, 2, 121	C. S. Nakatani	La Spia, 2, 117	She's Tops, 2, 117	4	1:22.38	44,475
1990	**Lite Light**, 2, 115	R. A. Baze	Beyond Perfection, 2, 117	Dragonetta, 2, 117	8	1:22.00	47,100
1989	**Cheval Volant**, 2, 117	L. A. Pincay Jr.	Breezing Dixie, 2, 115	Dancing Jamie, 2, 115	6	1:23.80	46,575
1988	**Stocks Up**, 2, 117	G. L. Stevens	Approved to Fly, 2, 116	Lea Lucinda, 2, 117	8	1:23.40	49,100

1987	**Hasty Pasty**, 2, 121	L. A. Pincay Jr.	Lost Kitty, 2, 121	Torch the Track, 2, 117	6	1:23.00	$37,200
1986	**Brave Raj**, 2, 117	P. A. Valenzuela	Breech, 2, 117	Footy, 2, 121	10	1:22.60	33,250
1985	**Arewehavingfunyet**, 2, 120	P. A. Valenzuela	Life At the Top, 2, 116	Python, 2, 117	11	1:37.00	34,250
1984	**Wayward Pirate**, 2, 114	W. Shoemaker	Doon's Baby, 2, 120	Trunk, 2, 116	6	1:37.20	31,350
1983	**Leading Ladybug**, 2, 115	P. A. Valenzuela	Bright Orphan, 2, 118	Lapidist, 2, 116	6	1:40.20	31,150
1982	**Time of Sale**, 2, 113	W. Shoemaker	Sharili Brown, 2, 117	Infantes, 2, 115	8	1:38.40	32,300
1981	**First Advance**, 2, 113	W. Shoemaker	Merry Sport, 2, 115	Skillful Joy, 2, 113	8	1:38.60	26,100
1980	**Native Fancy**, 2, 117	L. A. Pincay Jr.	Raja's Delight, 2, 115	Wedding Reception, 2, 114	8	1:38.80	22,950
1979	**Hazel R.**, 2, 117	C. J. McCarron	Arcades Ambo, 2, 113	Princess Karenda, 2, 114	6	1:35.80	19,100
1978	**Beauty Hour**, 2, 114	M. Castaneda	Hand Creme, 2, 117	Top Soil, 2, 114	8	1:37.00	19,150
1977	**My Little Maggie**, 2, 114	W. Shoemaker	Extravagant, 2, 114	Short Stanza, 2, 114	8	1:36.40	16,150
1976	**Telferner**, 2, 114	L. A. Pincay Jr.	Lullaby, 2, 117	Asterisca, 2, 114	9	1:36.60	16,150
1975	**Queen to Be**, 2, 113	D. G. McHargue	T. V. Terese, 2, 114	Pet Label, 2, 116	8	1:36.80	13,350
1974	**Spout**, 2, 115	A. Pineda	Just a Kick, 2, 115	Cut Class, 2, 113	11	1:36.80	14,000
1973	**Fleet Peach**, 2, 113	D. Pierce	Calaki, 2, 116	Poona's Double, 2, 116	5	1:09.20	12,600

Named for Sorrento, California, and the Sorrento Valley region. Grade 2 1994-2003. Not held 1968-'69. About $7\frac{1}{2}$ furlongs 1967. 6 furlongs 1970-'73. 1 mile 1974-'85. 7 furlongs 1986-'92. Turf 1967. Non-winners of a race worth $10,000 to the winner 1974-'75.

Spend a Buck Handicap

Grade 3 in 2006. Calder Race Course, three-year-olds and up, $1\frac{1}{16}$ miles, dirt. Held October 15, 2005, with a gross value of $100,000. First held in 1991. First graded in 2003. Stakes record 1:42.59 (2001 Best of the Rest).

Year	Winner	Jockey	Second	Third	Strs	Time	1st Purse
2005	**Supervisor**, 5, 116	A. Toribio Jr.	B. B. Best, 3, 114	Apalachian Thunder, 5, 118	6	1:46.94	$60,000
2004	**Built Up**, 6, 115	E. Coa	Super Frolic, 4, 117	Gold Dollar, 5, 115	11	1:45.86	60,000
2003	**Tour of the Cat**, 5, 116	A. Cabassa Jr.	Best of the Rest, 8, 122	Dancing Guy, 8, 116	8	1:46.30	60,000
2002	**Pay the Preacher**, 4, 114	C. H. Velasquez	Best of the Rest, 7, 121	Built Up, 4, 112	8	1:44.91	60,000
2001	**Best of the Rest**, 6, 116	E. Coa	Dancing Guy, 6, 117	Sir Bear, 8, 117	7	**1:42.59**	60,000
2000	**Groomstick Stock's**, 4, 111	R. Homeister Jr.	Reporter, 5, 113	Broadway Tune, 4, 113	8	1:44.82	60,000
1999	**Best of the Rest**, 4, 114	E. Coa	Dancing Guy, 4, 113	High Security (Ven), 4, 114	10	1:44.67	60,000
1998	**Unruled**, 5, 116	G. Boulanger	Sir Bear, 5, 124	Laughing Dan, 5, 113	6	1:45.68	60,000
1997	**Derivative**, 6, 116	J. C. Ferrer	Shan's Ready, 6, 114	Sur Irish's Secret, 4, 114	8	1:45.65	30,000
1996	**King Rex**, 4, 116	R. D. Lopez	Derivative, 5, 113	Leave'm Inthedark, 4, 114	6	1:52.92	48,945
1995	**Pride of Burkaan**, 5, 119	R. R. Douglas	Crafty Chris, 5, 114	Dauntless Gem, 5, 114	10	1:51.96	60,000
1994	**Daniel's Boy**, 6, 111	P. A. Rodriguez	It'sali'lknownfact, 4, 110	Aggressive Chief, 4, 115	8	1:52.68	60,000
1991	**Higgler**, 3, 112	D. Nied	Jodi's Sweetie, 3, 115	Treblestaff, 3, 112	9	1:48.38	50,505

Named for Hunter Farm's 1985 Horse of the Year Spend a Buck (1982 c. by Buckaroo); Spend a Buck broke his maiden at Calder. Spend a Buck Breeders' Cup H. 1996. Not held 1993. $1\frac{1}{8}$ miles 1994-'96. Three-year-olds 1991. Held as an overnight handicap 1992.

Spinaway Stakes

Grade 1 in 2006. Saratoga Race Course, two-year-olds, fillies, 7 furlongs, dirt. Held August 26, 2005, with a gross value of $250,000. First held in 1881. First graded in 1973. Stakes record 1:23.18 (1994 Flanders).

Year	Winner	Jockey	Second	Third	Strs	Time	1st Purse
2005	**Adieu**, 2, 119	J. R. Velazquez	Folklore, 2, 119	Along the Sea, 2, 119	7	1:23.68	$150,000
2004	**Sense of Style**, 2, 121	E. S. Prado	Miss Matched, 2, 121	Play With Fire, 2, 121	7	1:23.83	150,000
2003	**Ashado**, 2, 121	E. S. Prado	Be Gentle, 2, 121	Daydreaming, 2, 121	6	1:24.08	120,000
2002	**Awesome Humor**, 2, 121	P. Day	Forever Partners, 2, 121	Midnight Cry, 2, 121	12	1:24.36	120,000
2001	**Cashier's Dream**, 2, 121	D. J. Meche	Smok'n Frolic, 2, 121	Magic Storm, 2, 121	7	1:23.47	120,000
2000	**Stormy Pick**, 2, 121	J. C. Ferrer	Nasty Storm, 2, 121	Seeking It All, 2, 121	9	1:24.33	120,000
1999	**Circle of Life**, 2, 121	J. R. Velazquez	Surfside, 2, 121	Miss Wineshine, 2, 121	6	1:23.25	120,000
1998	**Things Change**, 2, 121	J. A. Santos	Extended Applause, 2, 121	Miss Jennifer Lynn, 2, 121	7	1:24.82	120,000
1997	**Countess Diana**, 2, 121	S. J. Sellers	Brac Drifter, 2, 121	Aunt Anne, 2, 121	5	1:24.17	120,000
1996	**Oath**, 2, 121	S. J. Sellers	Pearl City, 2, 121	Fabulously Fast, 2, 121	9	1:23.71	120,000
1995	**Golden Attraction**, 2, 121	G. L. Stevens	Flat Fleet Feet, 2, 121	Western Dreamer, 2, 121	8	1:23.85	120,000
1994	**Flanders**, 2, 119	P. Day	Sea Breezer, 2, 119	Stormy Blues, 2, 119	6	**1:23.18**	120,000
1993	**Strategic Maneuver**, 2, 119	J. A. Santos	Astas Foxy Lady, 2, 119	Delta Lady, 2, 119	9	1:10.34	120,000
1992	**‡Family Enterprize**, 2, 119	P. Day	Standard Equipment, 2, 119	‡Sky Beauty, 2, 119	5	1:09.82	120,000
1991	**Miss Iron Smoke**, 2, 119	M. A. Pedroza	Turnback the Alarm, 2, 119	Preach, 2, 119	10	1:10.68	120,000
1990	**Meadow Star**, 2, 119	J. A. Santos	Garden Gal, 2, 119	Good Potential, 2, 119	8	1:10.20	143,040
1989	**Stella Madrid**, 2, 119	A. T. Cordero Jr.	Golden Reef, 2, 119	Saratoga Sizzle, 2, 119	7	1:10.40	141,840
1988	**Seattle Meteor**, 2, 119	R. P. Romero	Love and Affection, 2, 119	Moonlight Martini, 2, 119	6	1:12.60	141,120
1987	**Over All**, 2, 119	A. T. Cordero Jr.	Bold Lady Anne, 2, 119	Flashy Runner, 2, 119	4	1:11.00	101,340
1986	**Tappiano**, 2, 119	J. Cruguet	Our Little Margie, 2, 119	Daytime Princess, 2, 119	4	1:11.40	130,680
1985	**Family Style**, 2, 119	D. MacBeth	Musical Lark (Ire), 2, 119	Nervous Baba, 2, 119	7	1:12.00	97,680
1984	**Tiltalating**, 2, 119	A. T. Cordero Jr.	Sociable Duck, 2, 119	Contredance, 2, 119	7	1:11.00	85,380
1983	**Buzz My Bell**, 2, 119	J. Velasquez	Demetria, 2, 119	Bottle Top, 2, 119	10	1:13.20	52,740
1982	**Share the Fantasy**, 2, 119	J. Fell	Singing Susan, 2, 119	Midnight Rapture, 2, 119	6	1:09.80	50,040
1981	**Before Dawn**, 2, 119	G. McCarron	Betty Money, 2, 119	Take Lady Anne, 2, 119	10	1:09.40	52,920
1980	**Prayers'n Promises**, 2, 119	A. T. Cordero Jr.	Fancy Naskra, 2, 119	Companionship, 2, 119	9	1:11.00	50,850
1979	**Smart Angle**, 2, 119	S. Maple	Jet Rating, 2, 119	Marathon Girl, 2, 119	6	1:10.60	48,510

1978	**Palm Hut**, 2, 119	R. I. Velez	Himalayan, 2, 119	Golferette, 2, 119	5	1:10.60	$31,770
1977	**Sherry Peppers**, 2, 119	A. T. Cordero Jr.	Akita, 2, 119	Stub, 2, 119	8	1:10.80	32,340
1976	**Mrs. Warren**, 2, 119	E. Maple	Exerene, 2, 119	Sensational, 2, 119	10	1:10.40	33,060
1975	**Dearly Precious**, 2, 120	M. Hole	Optimistic Gal, 2, 120	Quintas Vicki, 2, 120	6	1:10.60	47,880
1974	**Ruffian**, 2, 120	V. A. Bracciale Jr.	Laughing Bridge, 2, 120	Scottish Melody, 2, 120	4	1:08.60	33,060
1973	**Talking Picture**, 2, 120	R. Turcotte	Special Team, 2, 120	Raisela, 2, 120	10	1:10.00	35,040

Named for 1880 consensus champion two-year-old filly Spinaway (1878 f. by *Leamington). Grade 2 2004-'05. Held at Belmont Park 1943-'45. Not held 1892-1900, 1911-'12. 5 furlongs 1881-'91. $5\frac{1}{2}$ furlongs 1901-'22. 6 furlongs 1923-'93. ‡Sky Beauty finished first, DQ to third, 1992. ‡Try in the Sky finished third, DQ to fourth, 1992.

Sport Page Handicap

Grade 3 in 2006. Belmont Park, three-year-olds and up, 7 furlongs, dirt. Held October 29, 2005, with a gross value of $281,500. First held in 1953. First graded in 1984. Stakes record 1:21.10 (2004 Mass Media).

Year	Winner	Jockey	Second	Third	Strs	Time	1st Purse
2005	**Gotaghostofachance**, 4, 118	J. K. Court	Captain Squire, 6, 121	Wild Tale, 4, 116	9	1:23.16	$168,900
2004	**Mass Media**, 3, 113	J. Castellano	Lion Tamer, 4, 118	Gygistar, 5, 120	9	**1:21.10**	66,720
2003	**Voodoo**, 5, 114	J. F. Chavez	Bowman's Band, 5, 120	Highway Prospector, 6, 114	9	1:22.18	67,620
2002	**Multiple Choice**, 4, 113	V. Carrero	Bowman's Band, 4, 118	‡Gold I. D., 3, 112	8	1:23.28	66,840
2001	**Yonaguska**, 3, 116	C. J. McCarron	Silky Sweep, 5, 116	Big E E, 4, 114	6	1:15.54	65,640
2000	**Stalwart Member**, 7, 117	N. Arroyo Jr.	Istintaj, 4, 117	Mister Tricky (GB), 5, 112	6	1:21.97	48,690
1999	**Scatmandu**, 4, 115	A. T. Gryder	Aristotle, 3, 114	Watchman's Warning, 4, 112	8	1:22.68	50,250
1998	**Stormin Fever**, 4, 120	R. Migliore	Olympic Cat, 4, 113	Adverse, 4, 113	9	1:21.49	50,115
1997	**Stalwart Member**, 4, 114	A. T. Gryder	Basqueian, 6, 116	Why Change, 4, 115	10	1:22.15	68,640
1996	**Valid Expectations**, 3, 117	C. B. Asmussen	Diligence, 3, 116	Blissful State, 4, 117	8	1:21.80	68,040
1995	**Siphon (Brz)**, 4, 117	K. Desormeaux	In Case, 5, 113	Ft. Stockton, 3, 111	13	1:22.08	71,460
1994	**Man's Hero**, 4, 111	M. J. Luzzi	Itaka, 4, 117	Storm Tower, 4, 118	10	1:22.10	51,045
1993	**Boom Towner**, 5, 117	F. Lovato Jr.	†Raise Heck, 5, 115	Fabersham, 5, 113	9	1:10.62	53,730
1992	**R. D. Wild Whirl**, 4, 114	R. G. Davis	Senor Speedy, 5, 122	Burn Fair, 5, 114	6	1:09.93	51,570
1991	**Senor Speedy**, 4, 119	J. F. Chavez	Shuttleman, 5, 113	Gallant Step, 4, 113	9	1:09.34	55,080
1990	**Senor Speedy**, 3, 113	A. Santiago	Brave Adventure, 4, 116	Dargai, 4, 115	8	1:10.00	53,190
1989	**Garemma**, 3, 111	J. F. Chavez	Proud and Valid, 4, 111	Born to Shop, 5, 117	6	1:10.20	51,120
1988	**High Brite**, 4, 120	A. T. Cordero Jr.	Proud and Valid, 3, 109	Matter of Honor, 3, 112	7	1:09.60	64,980
1987	**Vinnie the Viper**, 4, 115	J. A. Krone	King's Swan, 7, 123	Banker's Jet, 5, 118	10	1:10.40	67,500
1986	**Best by Test**, 4, 112	F. Lovato Jr.	King's Swan, 6, 118	Sun Master, 5, 117	7	1:08.80	66,870
1985	**Raja's Shark**, 4, 120	A. T. Cordero Jr.	Love That Mac, 3, 110	Whoop Up, 5, 115	6	1:09.60	51,120
1984	**Tarantara**, 5, 117	R. Migliore	Muskoka Wyck, 5, 114	New Connection, 3, 113	13	1:10.80	46,140
1983	**Fast as the Breeze**, 4, 110	M. Toro	Maudlin, 5, 120	Swelegant, 5, 117	8	1:10.60	33,180
1982	**Maudlin**, 4, 115	J. D. Bailey	‡Top Avenger, 4, 115	Duke Mitchell, 3, 115	11	1:09.40	34,200
1981	**Well Decorated**, 3, 117	R. Hernandez	Engine One, 3, 116	Guilty Conscience, 5, 126	6	1:10.60	32,760
1980	**Dave's Friend**, 5, 126	V. A. Bracciale Jr.	Tilt Up, 5, 114	Hawkin's Special, 5, 114	8	1:08.20	34,380
1979	**Amadevil**, 5, 113	W. H. McCauley	Tanthem, 4, 123	Dave's Friend, 4, 119	7	1:09.40	32,580
1978	**Topsider**, 4, 109	M. Venezia	†What a Summer, 5, 124	Affiliate, 4, 118	6	1:10.20	32,400
1977	**Affiliate**, 3, 124	A. T. Cordero Jr.	Intercontinent, 3, 112	Gitche Gumee, 5, 117	4	1:10.00	31,560
1976	**Amerrico**, 4, 111	S. Hawley	†Honorable Miss, 6, 115	Relent, 5, 113	9	1:09.80	32,610
1975	**Lonetree**, 5, 122	E. Maple	Petrograd, 6, 119	Piamem, 5, 114	8	1:09.40	26,805
1974	**Startahemp**, 4, 114	J. Velasquez	Nostrum, 3, 114	Frankie Adams, 3, 121	7	1:09.60	22,950
1973	**Timeless Moment**, 3, 116	B. Baeza	Tap the Tree, 4, 122	North Sea, 4, 124	5	1:09.20	16,350

Named for Royce Martin's 1948 East View S. winner Sport Page (1946 c. by Our Boots). Held at Jamaica 1953-'58. Held at Aqueduct 1959-'67, 1969-'70, 1972-'94, 1996-2000, 2002. 6 furlongs 1953-'93. $6\frac{1}{2}$ furlongs 2001. Two-year-olds and up 1953-'58. ‡King's Fashion finished second, DQ to fifth, 1982. ‡Sing Me Back Home finished third, DQ to eighth for a positive drug test, 2002. †Denotes female.

Stage Door Betty Handicap

Grade 3 in 2006. Calder Race Course, three-year-olds and up, fillies and mares, $1\frac{1}{16}$ miles, dirt. Held December 31, 2005, with a gross value of $100,000. First held in 2001. First graded in 2006. Stakes record 1:44.08 (2002 Stormy Frolic).

Year	Winner	Jockey	Second	Third	Strs	Time	1st Purse
2005	**Mocita**, 3, 118	E. Castro	Special Report, 4, 116	Pitanga, 3, 119	9	1:48.56	$60,000
	Personal Legend, 5, 116	J. D. Bailey	Pampered Princess, 5, 118	Shady Woman, 5, 115	7	1:45.12	60,000
2003	**Redoubled Miss**, 4, 116	E. Coa	Grab Bag, 4, 112	Pampered Princess, 3, 114	9	1:46.78	60,000
2002	**Stormy Frolic**, 3, 114	J. A. Santos	Small Promises, 4, 113	Redoubled Miss, 3, 114	7	**1:44.08**	60,000
2001	**Extend**, 3, 112	E. Coa	Happily Unbridled, 3, 114	Halo Reality, 3, 114	9	1:46.74	60,000

Named for Betty Sessa's 1973 Vizcaya S. winner Stage Door Betty (1971 f. by Stage Door Johnny); Stage Door Betty won three races as a two-year-old at Calder. Not held 2004. Held in January and December 2005.

Stanford Breeders' Cup Handicap

Grade 3 in 2006. Bay Meadows, three-year-olds and up, $1\frac{1}{16}$ miles, turf. Held March 19, 2005, with a gross value of $113,750. First held in 1934. First graded in 1981. Stakes record 1:46.28 (2005 Adreamisborn).

Year	Winner	Jockey	Second	Third	Strs	Time	1st Purse
2005	**Adreamisborn**, 6, 117	R. A. Baze	Night Bokbel (Ire), 6, 116	Fantastic Spain, 5, 112	8	**1:46.28**	$68,750
2004	**Needwood Blade (GB)**, 6, 116	D. Carr	Seinne (Chi), 7, 116	Balestrini (Ire), 4, 117	7	1:46.55	55,000

2003	**Mister Acpen (Chi)**, 5, 116	R. M. Gonzalez	Fateful Dream, 6, 117	Ninebanks, 5, 118	10	1:46.94	$55,000
2002	**David Copperfield**, 5, 117	J. P. Lumpkins	Ninebanks, 4, 115	Little Ghazi, 6, 115	5	1:48.95	110,000
2001	**Super Quercus (Fr)**, 5, 117	R. A. Baze	Most Likely (Arg), 5, 112	Sign of Hope (GB), 4, 116	6	1:47.50	55,000
2000	**Devine Wind**, 4, 114	G. K. Gomez	Irish Prize, 4, 115	Deploy Venture (GB), 4, 117	6	1:47.19	110,000
1999	**Kirkwall (GB)**, 5, 114	V. Espinoza	Special Quest (Fr), 4, 115	Game Ploy (Pol), 7, 113	8	1:47.13	110,000
1998	**Hawksley Hill (Ire)**, 5, 120	A. O. Solis	Magellan, 5, 117	Floriselli, 4, 115	5	1:45.49	110,000
1997	**El Angelo**, 5, 119	A. O. Solis	Via Lombardia (Ire), 5, 115	Dreamer, 5, 115	5	1:45.47	110,000
1996	**Gentlemen (Arg)**, 4, 117	C. S. Nakatani	Party Season (GB), 5, 116	Petit Poucet (GB), 4, 119	5	1:45.90	110,000
1995	**Caesour**, 5, 115	R. A. Baze	Johann Quatz (Fr), 6, 115	Canaska Dancer (Ire), 4, 113	6	1:45.45	110,000
1994	**Blues Traveller (Ire)**, 4, 116	G. L. Stevens	Fastness (Ire), 4, 116	Wharf, 4, 114	6	1:46.03	110,000
1993	**Slew of Damascus**, 5, 114	T. M. Chapman	Fast Cure, 4, 112	Lissitki (Fr), 4, 112	7	1:45.91	110,000
1992	**Forty Niner Days**, 5, 115	C. S. Nakatani	Bistro Garden, 4, 116	Luthier Enchanteur, 5, 118	8	1:46.58	137,500
1991	**French Seventyfive**, 4, 112	G. Boulanger	Forty Niner Days, 4, 116	Batshoof (Ire), 5, 116	9	1:49.40	137,500
1990	**Robinski (NZ)**, 7, 112	J. Velasquez	Sekondi (Fr), 3, 113	Rushing Raj, 4, 113	12	1:50.80	137,500
1989	**Ten Keys**, 5, 118	K. Desormeaux	Colway Rally (GB), 5, 116	Nediym (Ire), 4, 113	12	1:46.60	137,500
1988	**Wait Till Monday (Ire)**, 4, 113	R. E. Dominguez	Miswaki Tern, 3, 113	Skip Out Front, 6, 117	12	1:46.00	137,500
1987	**Show Dancer**, 5, 113	M. Castaneda	Skip Out Front, 5, 114	Exclusive Partner, 5, 116	10	1:47.80	165,000
1986	**Palace Music**, 5, 123	F. Toro	Nugget Point (Ire), 4, 113	Barbery, 5, 116	10	1:50.60	165,000
1985	**Drumalis (Ire)**, 5, 116	R. Q. Meza	Silveyville, 7, 121	Talakeno, 5, 115	8	1:47.00	165,000
1984	**Scrupules (Ire)**, 4, 118	E. Delahoussaye	Raami (GB), 3, 120	Both Ends Burning, 4, 123	8	2:17.20	178,500
1983	**Interco**, 3, 115	J. C. Judice	Super Sunrise (GB), 4, 116	Floriano, 4, 114	15	1:55.40	179,200
1982	**Super Moment**, 5, 120	R. A. Baze	†Buchanette, 3, 113	Les Aspres (Fr), 6, 112	10	1:51.60	132,400
1981	**Super Moment**, 4, 124	L. A. Pincay Jr.	Tahitian King (Ire), 5, 121	The Bart, 5, 126	8	1:53.60	98,400
1980	**Super Moment**, 3, 116	F. Toro	Fleet Tempo, 3, 114	Mike Fogarty (Ire), 5, 118	12	1:46.20	68,600
1979	**Leonotis (NZ)**, 6, 118	R. M. Gonzalez	John Henry, 4, 123	Capt. Don, 4, 117	14	1:49.60	69,900
1978	**Bywayofchicago**, 4, 122	F. Toro	Noble Bronze, 3, 113	As de Copas (Arg), 5, 119	16	1:50.80	72,000
1977	**Painted Wagon**, 4, 120	M. S. Sellers	Sudanes (Arg), 4, 117	Mark's Place, 5, 123	12	1:41.40	51,000
1976	**Life's Hope**, 3, 118	D. G. McHargue	Fighting Bill, 3, 113	Podium, 4, 117	7	1:43.40	31,400
1975	**Bahia Key**, 5, 122	F. Olivares	Fleet Velvet, 3, 120	Holding Pattern, 4, 120	7	1:43.00	31,700
1974	**Indefatigable**, 4, 117	D. Pierce	Star of Kuwait, 6, 116	Confederate Yankee, 3, 115	8	1:41.40	31,900
1973	**Partner's Hope**, 4, 117	A. L. Diaz	Ipse, 5, 116	Woodland Pines, 4, 118	6	1:43.20	17,525

Named for Stanford University, located in nearby Palo Alto, California. Grade 2 1982-'84, 1986-'95. Not graded 1985. Bay Meadows H. 1934-2000. Bay Meadows Breeders' Cup H. 2001-'04. Not held 2006. 1⅛ miles 1934-'35, 1938, 1940-'51, 1953, 1959, 1961, 1970-'72, 1978-'83, 1985-2004. 1¼ miles 1952. 1⅜ miles 1984. Dirt 1934-'77, 1980. Two-year-olds and up 1935-'40, 1942, 1947-'50, 1953. Course record 1993, 1995. †Denotes female.

Stars and Stripes Breeders' Cup Turf Handicap

Grade 3 in 2006. Arlington Park, three-year-olds and up, 1½ miles, turf. Held July 3, 2005, with a gross value of $197,750. First held in 1929. First graded in 1973. Stakes record 2:27.50 (2002 Cetewayo).

Year	Winner	Jockey	Second	Third	Strs	Time	1st Purse
2005	**Revved Up**, 7, 114	B. Blanc	Cloudy's Knight, 5, 117	Swagger Stick, 4, 115	8	2:28.29	$120,000
2004	**Ballingarry (Ire)**, 5, 120	R. R. Douglas	‡Grey Beard, 5, 117	Art Variety (Brz), 6, 116	8	2:36.30	120,000
2003	**Ballingarry (Ire)**, 4, 121	R. R. Douglas	Dr. Brendler, 5, 118	Jack's Own Time, 4, 112	9	2:28.30	131,520
2002	**Cetewayo**, 8, 118	R. R. Douglas	Private Son, 4, 115	Pisces, 5, 117	9	**2:27.50**	137,475
2001	**Falcon Flight (Fr)**, 5, 114	R. R. Douglas	Langston, 4, 114	Williams News, 6, 116	11	2:27.86	96,300
2000	**Williams News**, 5, 115	R. Albarado	Profit Option, 5, 110	Buff, 5, 114	12	2:31.22	148,425
1997	**Lakeshore Road**, 4, 114	C. H. Borel	Chief Bearhart, 4, 119	Awad, 7, 119	9	2:29.57	140,025
1996	**Vladivostok**, 6, 116	C. Perret	Raintrap (GB), 6, 118	Special Price, 7, 118	8	2:30.23	138,075
1995	**Snake Eyes**, 5, 116	R. Albarado	Coaxing Matt, 6, 115	Bucks Nephew, 5, 114	7	1:56.46	45,000
1994	**Marastani**, 4, 113	A. T. Gryder	‡Snake Eyes, 4, 117	The Vid, 4, 113	12	1:54.64	60,000
1993	**Little Bro Lantis**, 5, 114	C. C. Bourque	Stark South, 5, 119	Coaxing Matt, 4, 115	12	1:56.92	60,000
1992	**Plate Dancer**, 7, 114	E. Fires	Little Bro Lantis, 4, 114	Stark South, 4, 114	9	1:55.00	60,000
1991	**Blair's Cove**, 6, 115	G. K. Gomez	Opening Verse, 5, 118	Cameroon, 4, 112	9	1:55.95	60,000
1990	**Mister Sicy (Fr)**, 4, 114	C. A. Black	Silver Medallion, 4, 115	Careafolie (Ire), 5, 113	12	1:54.40	69,900
1989	**Salem Drive**, 7, 116	P. Day	Green Barb, 4, 115	Delegant, 5, 115	10	1:55.20	69,660
1987	**Sharrood**, 4, 120	F. Toro	Explosive Darling, 5, 121	Santella Mac (Ire), 4, 115	11	1:56.20	52,080
1986	**Explosive Darling**, 4, 115	E. Fires	Clever Song, 4, 120	Forkintheroad, 4, 113	13	1:48.40	70,560
1985	**Drumalis (Ire)**, 5, 118	P. Day	Best of Both, 5, 116	Lofty (Ire), 5, 117	13	1:42.20	91,920
1984	**Tough Mickey**, 4, 119	J. Samyn	Fortnightly, 4, 115	Jack Slade, 4, 113	15	1:41.40	80,460
1983	**Rossi Gold**, 7, 122	P. Day	Who's for Dinner, 4, 110	Lucence, 4, 115	7	1:48.80	70,860
1982	**Rossi Gold**, 6, 124	P. Day	Johnny Dance, 4, 115	Don Roberto, 5, 118	7	1:46.00	70,560
1981	**‡dh-Ben Fab**, 4, 122	G. Stahlbaum		Opus Dei (Fr), 6, 116	8	1:43.80	48,600
	‡dh-Rossi Gold, 5, 123	P. Day					
1980	**Told**, 4, 114	J. Samyn	Rossi Gold, 4, 111	Overskate, 5, 130	8	1:43.00	72,960
1979	**Overskate**, 4, 125	R. Platts	That's a Nice, 5, 119	Bold Standard, 5, 111	8	1:44.00	33,360
1978	**Old Frankfort**, 6, 112	R. Turcotte	Capt. Stevens, 8, 114	That's a Nice, 4, 122	10	1:50.20	34,380
1977	**Quick Card**, 4, 118	M. Solomone	dh-Emperor Rex, 6, 116		14	1:43.00	35,640
			dh-Proponent, 5, 116				
1976	**Passionate Pirate**, 5, 114	H. Arroyo	Improviser, 4, 122	*Zografos, 8, 115	11	1:43.00	39,500
1975	**Buffalo Lark**, 5, 121	L. Snyder	*Kuryakin, 5, 111	‡*Zografos, 7, 115	7	1:43.00	40,600

1974 ***Zografos**, 6, 113	W. Gavidia	Smooth Dancer, 4, 111	Fun Co K., 5, 109	10	1:50.80	$45,600
1973 **Triumphant**, 4, 119	A. Rini	Super Sail, 5, 116	Vegas Vic, 5, 114	11	1:34.80	36,400

Traditionally held during the July 4 holiday, celebrating the birth of the United States and its flag, the "stars and stripes." Grade 2 1973-'89. Stars and Stripes H. 1929-'95. Stars and Stripes Breeders' Cup H. 2000-'01. Held at Washington Park 1958-'59. Not held 1988, 1998-'99. 1⅛ miles 1929-'41, 1943-'72, 1974-'75, 1986. 1³⁄₁₆ miles 1942, 1987-'95. 1 mile 1973. 1¹⁄₁₆ miles 1976-'85. Dirt 1929-'49, 1956-'58, 1960-'64, 1968-'74. Originally scheduled at 1¹⁄₁₆ miles on the turf 1973. Originally scheduled at 1⅛ miles on the turf 1974. Three-year-olds 1958. Dead heat for second 1977. Dead heat for first 1981. ‡*Nevermore II finished third, DQ to seventh, 1975. ‡Key to Content finished first, DQ to fourth, 1981. ‡Kazabaiyn finished second, DQ to fifth, 1994. ‡Silverfoot finished second, DQ to fourth, 2004.

Stephen Foster Handicap

Grade 1 in 2006. Churchill Downs, three-year-olds and up, 1⅛ miles, dirt. Held June 18, 2005, with a gross value of $828,000. First held in 1982. First graded in 1988. Stakes record 1:47.28 (1999 Victory Gallop).

Year	Winner	Jockey	Second	Third	Strs	Time	1st Purse
2005	**Saint Liam**, 5, 121	E. S. Prado	Eurosilver, 4, 113	Perfect Drift, 6, 117	8	1:47.52	$513,360
2004	**Colonial Colony**, 6, 111	R. Bejarano	Southern Image, 4, 122	Perfect Drift, 5, 119	6	1:50.40	502,665
2003	**Perfect Drift**, 4, 115	P. Day	Mineshaft, 4, 123	Aldebaran, 5, 120	10	1:47.55	531,030
2002	**Street Cry (Ire)**, 4, 120	J. D. Bailey	Dollar Bill, 4, 114	Tenpins, 4, 115	8	1:47.84	516,615
2001	**Guided Tour**, 5, 113	L. J. Melancon	Captain Steve, 4, 123	Brahms, 4, 114	8	1:47.74	515,220
2000	**Golden Missile**, 5, 118	K. Desormeaux	Ecton Park, 4, 114	Cat Thief, 4, 117	6	1:49.56	502,200
1999	**Victory Gallop**, 4, 120	J. D. Bailey	Nite Dreamer, 4, 110	Littlebitlively, 5, 115	7	**1:47.28**	512,895
1998	**Awesome Again**, 4, 113	P. Day	Silver Charm, 4, 127	Semoran, 5, 114	7	1:48.61	495,690
1997	**City by Night**, 4, 113	S. J. Sellers	Victor Cooley, 4, 115	Semoran, 4, 113	6	1:50.40	101,649
1996	**Tenants Harbor**, 4, 112	F. C. Torres	Pleasant Tango, 6, 113	Mt. Sassafras, 4, 115	8	1:49.94	107,933
1995	**Recoup the Cash**, 5, 119	A. T. Gryder	Tyus, 5, 114	Powerful Punch, 6, 114	9	1:49.39	109,298
1994	**Recoup the Cash**, 4, 112	J. L. Diaz	Taking Risks, 4, 113	Dignitas, 5, 113	7	1:49.46	106,275
1993	**Root Boy**, 5, 113	T. G. Turner	Discover, 5, 114	Flying Continental, 7, 117	11	1:50.80	74,100
1992	**Discover**, 4, 116	B. E. Bartram	Barkerville, 4, 113	Classic Seven, 4, 113	13	1:50.14	75,335
1991	**Black Tie Affair (Ire)**, 5, 119	J. L. Diaz	Private School, 4, 114	Greydar, 4, 115	5	1:49.81	70,915
1990	**No Marker**, 6, 115	A. T. Gryder	Western Playboy, 4, 117	Lucky Peach, 5, 114	10	1:49.80	72,930
1989	**Air Worthy**, 4, 115	D. J. Soto	J. T.'s Pet, 5, 115	Present Value, 5, 114	9	1:49.60	73,255
1988	**Honor Medal**, 7, 123	L. E. Ortega	Outlaws Sham, 5, 115	Momsfurrari, 4, 109	10	1:50.60	82,655
1987	**Red Attack**, 5, 119	J. L. Kaenel	Sir Naskra, 5, 116	Blue Buckaroo, 4, 117	9	1:51.20	65,254
1986	**Hopeful Word**, 5, 123	K. K. Allen	Dramatic Desire, 5, 114	Ten Gold Pots, 5, 122	7	1:49.40	64,133
1985	**Vanlandingham**, 4, 121	P. Day	Manantial (Chi), 7, 112	Sovereign Exchange, 4, 113	7	1:48.80	35,263
1984	**Mythical Ruler**, 6, 117	J. McKnight	Fairly Straight, 3, 114	Le Cou Cou, 4, 121	5	1:49.60	34,808
1983	**Vodika Collins**, 5, 118	L. Moyers	Mythical Ruler, 5, 120	Northern Majesty, 4, 114	7	1:49.20	35,588
1982	**Vodika Collins**, 4, 116	T. Barrow	Mythical Ruler, 4, 113	Two's a Plenty, 5, 115	7	1:51.80	38,610

Named for composer Stephen Foster (1826-'64), who wrote Kentucky's state song, "My Old Kentucky Home." Grade 3 1988-'94. Grade 2 1995-2001. Four-year-olds and up 1983, 1985-'87. Track record 1999.

Stonerside Beaumont Stakes

Grade 2 in 2006. Keeneland Race Course, three-year-olds, fillies, about 7 furlongs, dirt. Held April 13, 2006, with a gross value of $250,000. First held in 1986. First graded in 1990. Stakes record 1:25.61 (1999 Swingin On Ice).

Year	Winner	Jockey	Second	Third	Strs	Time	1st Purse
2006	**Diplomat Lady**, 3, 123	C. H. Velasquez	Lake Alice, 3, 117	Wildcat Bettie B, 3, 117	10	1:27.97	$155,000
2005	**In the Gold**, 3, 117	R. Bejarano	Holy Trinity, 3, 117	Hot Storm, 3, 119	5	1:26.04	155,000
2004	**Victory U. S. A.**, 3, 118	J. D. Bailey	Halfbridled, 3, 123	Wildwood Flower, 3, 118	8	1:27.06	155,000
2003	**My Boston Gal**, 3, 120	P. Day	Bird Town, 3, 118	Midnight Cry, 3, 118	9	1:26.87	155,000
2002	**Proper Gamble**, 3, 118	J. Castellano	Respectful, 3, 116	Vicki Vallencourt, 3, 118	7	1:28.79	155,000
2001	**Xtra Heat**, 3, 120	R. Wilson	Mountain Bird, 3, 116	Raging Fever, 3, 123	5	1:27.86	155,000
2000	**Sahara Gold**, 3, 123	J. D. Bailey	Swept Away, 3, 118	Darling My Darling, 3, 116	6	1:26.58	84,847
1999	**Swingin On Ice**, 3, 115	R. Albarado	Secret Hills, 3, 115	Appealing Phylly, 3, 123	7	**1:25.61**	83,917
1998	**Star of Broadway**, 3, 119	P. Day	Santaria, 3, 119	Bourbon Belle, 3, 119	12	1:26.67	91,140
1997	**dh-Make Haste**, 3, 112	P. Day		Move, 3, 121	7	1:28.08	57,042
	dh-Screamer, 3, 112	R. Albarado					
1996	**Golden Gale**, 3, 115	M. E. Smith	Birr, 3, 115	Bright Time, 3, 115	7	1:26.10	84,398
1995	**Dixieland Gold**, 3, 118	D. Penna	Niner's Home, 3, 113	Conquistadoress, 3, 118	10	1:27.42	69,874
1994	**Her Temper**, 3, 112	P. Day	Lotta Dancing, 3, 113	Term Limits, 3, 121	6	1:28.41	67,456
1993	**Roamin Rachel**, 3, 122	C. W. Antley	Added Asset, 3, 114	Fit to Lead, 3, 122	10	1:26.48	69,998
1992	**Fluttery Danseur**, 3, 122	S. J. Sellers	Miss Iron Smoke, 3, 119	Spinning Round, 3, 122	8	1:27.46	53,918
1991	**Ifyoucouldseemenow**, 3, 122	M. A. Pedroza	Versailles Treaty, 3, 114	Ever a Lady, 3, 114	6	1:27.01	54,275
1990	**Go for Wand**, 3, 122	R. P. Romero	Trumpet's Blare, 3, 119	Seaside Attraction, 3, 119	6	1:26.40	53,983
1989	**Exquisite Mistress**, 3, 117	D. Brumfield	Love's Exchange, 3, 114	Up, 3, 114	10	1:28.60	36,774
1988	**On to Royalty**, 3, 121	C. Perret	Plate Queen, 3, 121	Tilt My Halo, 3, 121	9	1:26.60	46,680
1987	**Fold the Flag**, 3, 113	S. Hawley	Bound, 3, 113	Arctic Cloud, 3, 118	6	1:28.20	43,428
1986	**Classy Cathy**, 3, 112	E. Fires	She's a Mystery, 3, 119	Close Tolerance, 3, 112	13	1:27.60	37,408

Named for Hal Price Headley's Beaumont Farm; Headley was one of Keeneland's founders and the track's first president. Sponsored by Robert and Janice McNair's Stonerside Stables of Paris, Kentucky 2000-'06. Grade 3 1990-'92. Beaumont S. 1986-'99. Dead heat for first 1997.

Stonerside Forward Gal Stakes

Grade 2 in 2006. Gulfstream Park, three-year-olds, fillies, 7 furlongs, dirt. Held March 5, 2006, with a gross value of $150,000. First held in 1981. First graded in 1986. Stakes record 1:21.76 (1997 Glitter Woman).

Year	Winner	Jockey	Second	Third	Strs	Time	1st Purse
2006	**Miraculous Miss**, 3, 120	J. Rose	India, 3, 116	Misty Rosette, 3, 120	10	1:22.78	$90,000
2005	**Letgomyecho**, 3, 115	J. Castellano	Little Money Down, 3, 115	Hot Storm, 3, 121	7	1:23.24	90,000
2004	**Madcap Escapade**, 3, 121	J. D. Bailey	La Reina, 3, 121	Frenchglen, 3, 115	5	1:22.97	90,000
2003	**Midnight Cry**, 3, 117	E. S. Prado	Final Round, 3, 117	Chimichurri, 3, 121	8	1:22.55	60,000
2002	**Take the Cake**, 3, 117	R. R. Douglas	A New Twist, 3, 121	Cherokee Girl, 3, 117	7	1:25.47	60,000
2001	**Gold Mover**, 3, 121	J. D. Bailey	Hazino, 3, 114	Thunder Bertie, 3, 118	5	1:22.43	60,000
2000	**Miss Inquistive**, 3, 114	T. G. Turner	Swept Away, 3, 118	Regally Appealing, 3, 118	9	1:22.25	45,000
1999	**China Storm**, 3, 114	P. Day	Three Ring, 3, 121	Extended Applause, 3, 112	5	1:23.69	45,000
1998	**Uanme**, 3, 113	S. J. Sellers	Diamond On the Run, 3, 114	Holy Capote, 3, 112	7	1:24.56	45,000
1997	**Glitter Woman**, 3, 114	M. E. Smith	City Band, 3, 121	Southern Playgirl, 3, 121	6	**1:21.76**	45,000
1996	**Mindy Gayle**, 3, 112	J. A. Krone	Marfa's Finale, 3, 113	Supah Jen, 3, 114	7	1:24.54	45,000
1995	**Chaposa Springs**, 3, 114	H. Castillo Jr.	Culver City, 3, 113	Mackenzie Slew, 3, 114	7	1:24.18	44,580
1994	**Mynameispanama**, 3, 113	M. Castaneda	Frigid Coed, 3, 116	Wonderlan, 3, 114	9	1:22.97	45,960
1993	**Sum Runner**, 3, 118	R. P. Romero	Boots 'n Jackie, 3, 121	Lunar Spook, 3, 118	9	1:23.67	45,270
1992	**Spinning Round**, 3, 118	J. A. Santos	Patty's Princess, 3, 116	Super Doer, 3, 118	5	1:24.85	44,550
1991	**Withallprobability**, 3, 114	C. Perret	Private Treasure, 3, 118	Far Out Nurse, 3, 112	8	1:22.50	48,240
1990	**Charon**, 3, 112	E. Fires	Trumpet's Blare, 3, 121	De La Devil, 3, 121	8	1:24.80	36,180
1989	**Open Mind**, 3, 121	A. T. Cordero Jr.	Surging, 3, 114	Georgies Doctor, 3, 118	9	1:24.20	36,780
1988	**On to Royalty**, 3, 114	C. Perret	Social Pro, 3, 122	Most Likely, 3, 112	10	1:23.20	37,020
1987	**Added Elegance**, 3, 121	J. Vasquez	Beau Love Flowers, 3, 112	Easter Mary, 3, 112	11	1:24.60	37,380
1986	**Noranc**, 3, 116	W. H. McCauley	Dancing Danzig, 3, 112	I'm Sweets, 3, 121	8	1:23.80	36,000
1985	**Lucy Manette**, 3, 114	C. Perret	Grand Glory, 3, 112	Boldly Dared, 3, 112	13	1:23.40	39,690
1984	**Miss Oceana**, 3, 121	E. Maple	Katrinka, 3, 112	Scorched Panties, 3, 121	5	1:22.40	24,108
1983	**Unaccompanied**, 3, 114	R. Woodhouse	Lisa's Capital, 3, 114	Quixotic Lady, 3, 113	15	1:23.40	28,203
1982	**Trove**, 3, 116	L. Saumell	Here's to Peg, 3, 112	Wendy's Ten, 3, 113	8	1:22.80	17,828
	All Manners, 3, 116	O. J. Londono	Acharmer, 3, 114	Smart Heiress, 3, 112	9	1:23.00	17,978
1981	**Dame Mysterieuse**, 3, 118	J. Samyn	Heavenly Cause, 3, 121	Masters Dream, 3, 113	10	1:22.20	26,040

Named for Aisco Stable's 1970 Florida-bred champion two-year-old filly Forward Gal (1968 f. by Native Charger). Sponsored by Robert and Janice McNair's Stonerside Stable of Paris, Kentucky 2004-'06. Grade 3 1986-'90, 1997-2003. Forward Gal Breeders' Cup S. 1991-'95. Forward Gal S. 1996-2002. Two divisions 1982.

Strub Stakes

Grade 2 in 2006. Santa Anita Park, four-year-olds, 1⅛ miles, dirt. Held February 4, 2006, with a gross value of $300,000. First held in 1948. First graded in 1973. Stakes record 1:47.25 (2002 Mizzen Mast).

Year	Winner	Jockey	Second	Third	Strs	Time	1st Purse
2006	**High Limit**, 4, 121	P. A. Valenzuela	Top This and That, 4, 117	Giacomo, 4, 123	11	1:49.14	$180,000
2005	**Rock Hard Ten**, 4, 121	G. L. Stevens	Imperialism, 4, 119	Love of Money, 4, 123	9	1:49.24	180,000
2004	**Domestic Dispute**, 4, 117	K. Desormeaux	During, 4, 121	Buckland Manor, 4, 117	11	1:49.08	180,000
2003	**Medaglia d'Oro**, 4, 123	J. D. Bailey	Olmodavor, 4, 117	Tracemark, 4, 117	6	1:48.04	240,000
2002	**Mizzen Mast**, 4, 121	K. Desormeaux	Giant Gentleman, 4, 117	Fancy As, 4, 119	11	**1:47.25**	240,000
2001	**Wooden Phone**, 4, 117	C. S. Nakatani	Tiznow, 4, 123	Jimmy Z, 4, 117	6	1:48.43	300,000
2000	**General Challenge**, 4, 123	C. S. Nakatani	Luftikus, 4, 117	Saint's Honor, 4, 121	4	1:48.81	300,000
1999	**Event of the Year**, 4, 119	C. S. Nakatani	Dr Fong, 4, 121	Hanuman Highway (Ire), 4, 117	7	1:47.65	300,000
1998	**Silver Charm**, 4, 123	G. L. Stevens	Mud Route, 4, 117	Bagshot, 4, 117	6	1:47.27	300,000
1997	**Victory Speech**, 4, 124	J. D. Bailey	The Barking Shark, 4, 118	Ambivalent, 4, 118	9	2:01.50	300,000
1996	**Helmsman**, 4, 122	C. J. McCarron	Afternoon Deelites, 4, 120	Mr Purple, 4, 118	9	2:02.76	300,000
1995	**Dare and Go**, 4, 118	A. O. Solis	Dramatic Gold, 4, 124	Wekiva Springs, 4, 122	5	2:00.15	275,000
1994	**Diazo**, 4, 120	L. A. Pincay Jr.	Nonproductiveasset, 4, 118	Stuka, 4, 118	11	2:00.33	275,000
1993	**Siberian Summer**, 4, 118	C. S. Nakatani	Bertrando, 4, 122	Major Impact, 4, 118	8	2:00.78	275,000
1992	**Best Pal**, 4, 124	K. Desormeaux	Dinard, 4, 120	Reign Road, 4, 118	8	1:59.95	275,000
1991	**Defensive Play**, 4, 122	J. A. Santos	My Boy Adam, 4, 117	In Excess (Ire), 4, 121	7	2:00.90	275,000
1990	**Flying Continental**, 4, 119	C. A. Black	Quiet American, 4, 114	Hawkster, 4, 126	10	2:01.40	275,000
1989	**Nasr El Arab**, 4, 123	P. A. Valenzuela	Perceive Arrogance, 4, 117	Silver Circus, 4, 120	7	2:02.20	275,000
1988	**Alysheba**, 4, 126	C. J. McCarron	Candi's Gold, 4, 117	On the Line, 4, 119	6	2:00.40	275,000
1987	**Snow Chief**, 4, 126	P. A. Valenzuela	Ferdinand, 4, 126	Broad Brush, 4, 126	8	2:00.00	291,750
1986	**Nostalgia's Star**, 4, 116	F. Toro	Roo Art, 4, 117	Fast Account, 4, 115	12	2:03.60	314,250
1985	**Precisionist**, 4, 125	C. J. McCarron	Greinton (GB), 4, 117	Gate Dancer, 4, 126	5	2:00.20	189,300
1984	**Desert Wine**, 4, 117	E. Delahoussaye	Load the Cannons, 4, 115	Silent Fox, 4, 114	11	2:02.20	221,400
1983	**Swing Till Dawn**, 4, 115	P. A. Valenzuela	Wavering Monarch, 4, 121	Water Bank, 4, 117	10	2:02.00	178,000
1982	**It's the One**, 4, 118	W. A. Guerra	Dorcaro (Fr), 4, 115	Rock Softly, 4, 115	8	2:00.40	172,700
1981	**Super Moment**, 4, 116	F. Toro	Exploded, 4, 116	Doonesbury, 4, 118	10	2:01.20	145,000
1980	**Spectacular Bid**, 4, 126	W. Shoemaker	Flying Paster, 4, 121	Valdez, 4, 121	4	1:57.80	124,500
1979	**Affirmed**, 4, 126	L. A. Pincay Jr.	Johnny's Image, 4, 115	Quip, 4, 115	9	2:01.00	142,500
1978	**Mr. Redoy**, 4, 116	D. G. McHargue	Text, 4, 121	J. O. Tobin, 4, 122	9	2:01.00	140,200
1977	**Kirby Lane**, 4, 118	S. Hawley	Properantes, 4, 114	Double Discount, 4, 115	14	2:00.40	90,900
1976	**George Navonod**, 4, 115	F. Toro	Larrikin, 4, 118	Dancing Gun, 4, 115	8	2:12.00	76,900
1975	**Stardust Mel**, 4, 120	W. Shoemaker	Confederate Yankee, 4, 116	Rube the Great, 4, 122	9	2:04.20	86,300

1974	**Ancient Title**, 4, 121	L. A. Pincay Jr.	Dancing Papa, 4, 116	Prince Dantan, 4, 115	9	2:00.80	$85,200
1973	**Royal Owl**, 4, 116	J. Sellers	Big Spruce, 4, 117	New Prospect, 4, 117	10	2:04.00	82,800

Originally named for Charles H. Strub (1884-1958), founder of the modern Santa Anita Park. Race name shortened in 1993 to also honor Robert P. Strub (1919-'93), his son and former track president. Formerly the Santa Anita Maturity; maturities are typically for four-year-old and older horses. Grade 1 1973-'97. Santa Anita Maturity 1948-'62. Charles H. Strub S. 1963-'93. 1¼ miles 1948-'69, 1971-'97.

Stuyvesant Handicap

Grade 3 in 2006. Aqueduct, three-year-olds and up, 1⅛ miles, dirt. Held November 19, 2005, with a gross value of $108,600. First held in 1916. First graded in 1973. Stakes record 1:47 (1973 Riva Ridge).

Year	Winner	Jockey	Second	Third	Strs	Time	1st Purse
2005	**Evening Attire**, 7, 116	J. A. Santos	West Virginia, 4, 115	Aggadan, 6, 116	6	1:51.38	$65,160
2004	**Classic Endeavor**, 6, 114	E. S. Prado	Colita, 4, 115	Snake Mountain, 6, 115	7	1:49.70	65,940
2003	**Presidentialaffair**, 4, 115	R. Migliore	Thunder Blitz, 5, 114	Gander, 7, 115	8	1:50.86	66,180
2002	**Snake Mountain**, 4, 114	J. A. Santos	Windsor Castle, 4, 115	Docent, 4, 115	10	1:50.56	68,040
2001	**Graeme Hall**, 4, 119	J. R. Velazquez	Country Be Gold, 4, 115	Cat's At Home, 4, 114	6	1:47.95	64,620
2000	**Lager**, 6, 116	H. Castillo Jr.	Top Official, 5, 113	Fire King, 7, 115	6	1:50.03	64,860
1999	**Best of Luck**, 3, 114	M. E. Smith	Wild Imagination, 5, 115	Durmiente (Chi), 5, 113	9	1:49.77	67,200
1998	**Mr. Sinatra**, 4, 115	A. T. Gryder	Rock and Roll, 3, 114	Accelerator, 4, 114	5	1:48.16	65,280
1997	**Delay of Game**, 4, 114	J. Samyn	Concerto, 3, 118	Mr. Sinatra, 3, 117	8	1:47.72	66,060
1996	**Poor But Honest**, 6, 116	J. F. Chavez	Flitch, 4, 115	Admiralty, 4, 117	8	1:49.44	66,480
1995	**Silver Fox**, 4, 113	M. E. Smith	Yourmissinthepoint, 4, 111	Earth Colony, 4, 114	7	1:48.03	68,940
1994	**Wallenda**, 4, 118	W. H. McCauley	Lost Soldier, 4, 109	Pistols and Roses, 5, 117	6	1:50.69	64,560
1993	**Michelle Can Pass**, 5, 115	J. R. Velazquez	Key Contender, 5, 115	Primitive Hall, 4, 113	8	1:51.07	70,200
1992	**Shots Are Ringing**, 5, 114	J. R. Velazquez	Key Contender, 4, 111	Timely Warning, 7, 115	7	1:49.36	69,120
1991	**Montubio (Arg)**, 6, 110	J. M. Pezua	Mountain Lore, 4, 112	Timely Warning, 6, 114	9	1:48.30	72,480
1990	**I'm Sky High**, 4, 111	M. E. Smith	Silver Survivor, 4, 113	Lost Opportunity, 4, 111	7	1:48.20	71,760
1989	**Its Acedemic**, 5, 110	J. D. Bailey	Congeleur, 4, 115	Homebuilder, 5, 114	8	1:48.80	70,560
1988	**Talinum**, 4, 112	M. Castaneda	Nostalgia's Star, 6, 113	Pleasant Virginian, 4, 113	9	1:51.20	111,240
1987	**Moment of Hope**, 4, 118	M. Venezia	Wind Chill, 4, 110	I Rejoice, 4, 111	9	1:49.60	109,080
1986	**Little Missouri**, 4, 116	R. G. Davis	Waquoit, 3, 115	Let's Go Blue, 5, 118	10	1:50.00	125,280
1985	**Garthorn**, 5, 112	R. Q. Meza	Morning Bob, 4, 114	Waitlist, 6, 118	7	1:48.40	70,320
1984	**Valiant Lark**, 4, 112	V. A. Bracciale Jr.	Puntivo, 4, 112	Bounding Basque, 4, 117	8	1:51.40	70,080
1983	**Fit to Fight**, 4, 117	J. D. Bailey	Deputy Minister, 4, 119	Sing Sing, 5, 115	7	1:49.00	68,280
1982	**Engine One**, 4, 123	R. Hernandez	Bar Dexter, 5, 112	Fit to Fight, 3, 118	6	1:49.60	67,200
1981	**Idyll**, 4, 114	C. B. Asmussen	Spoils of War, 4, 113	Silver Buck, 3, 112	12	1:48.80	68,280
1980	**Plugged Nickle**, 3, 122	C. B. Asmussen	Dr. Patches, 6, 115	Ring of Light, 5, 116	10	1:50.20	68,880
1979	**Music of Time**, 5, 114	J. Fell	What a Gent, 5, 111	Dewan Keys, 4, 112	6	1:50.40	65,220
1978	**Seattle Slew**, 4, 134	A. T. Cordero Jr.	Jumping Hill, 6, 115	Wise Philip, 5, 113	5	1:47.40	62,310
1977	**Cox's Ridge**, 3, 124	E. Maple	Wise Philip, 4, 114	Gentle King, 4, 112	8	1:48.40	32,760
1976	**Distant Land**, 4, 111	H. Gustines	Blue Times, 5, 114	It's Freezing, 4, 115	9	1:49.00	32,610
1975	**Festive Mood**, 6, 115	H. Hinojosa	‡Step Nicely, 5, 124	Stonewalk, 4, 122	6	1:48.40	33,210
1974	**Crafty Khale**, 5, 121	J. Cruguet	Stop the Music, 4, 120	True Knight, 5, 121	10	1:48.00	34,890
1973	**Riva Ridge**, 4, 130	E. Maple	Forage, 4, 116	True Knight, 4, 122	9	**1:47.00**	34,470

Named for the Bedford-Stuyvesant neighborhood in the borough of Brooklyn, New York. Held at Jamaica 1916-'24, 1937-'39. Held at Belmont Park 1990, 1995, 2001. Not held 1925-'36, 1940-'62. 6 furlongs 1916-'17. 1 mile 1919-'24, 1965-'72, 1988. Three-year-olds 1916-'24. ‡Herculean finished second, DQ to sixth, 1975. Track record 1973.

Suburban Handicap

Grade 1 in 2006. Belmont Park, three-year-olds and up, 1¼ miles, dirt. Held July 2, 2005, with a gross value of $500,000. First held in 1884. First graded in 1973. Stakes record 1:58.33 (1991 In Excess [Ire]).

Year	Winner	Jockey	Second	Third	Strs	Time	1st Purse
2005	**Offlee Wild**, 5, 116	E. S. Prado	Tap Day, 4, 115	Pollard's Vision, 4, 118	8	2:00.50	$300,000
2004	**Peace Rules**, 4, 120	J. D. Bailey	Newfoundland, 4, 114	Funny Cide, 4, 117	8	1:59.52	300,000
2003	**Mineshaft**, 4, 121	R. Albarado	Volponi, 5, 121	Dollar Bill, 5, 115	8	2:01.57	300,000
2002	**E Dubai**, 4, 116	J. R. Velazquez	Lido Palace (Chi), 5, 119	Macho Uno, 4, 119	7	2:00.95	300,000
2001	**Albert the Great**, 4, 123	J. F. Chavez	Lido Palace (Chi), 4, 115	Include, 4, 122	6	2:00.39	300,000
2000	**Lemon Drop Kid**, 4, 122	E. S. Prado	Behrens, 6, 122	Lager, 6, 113	6	1:58.97	300,000
1999	**Behrens**, 5, 121	J. F. Chavez	Catienus, 5, 113	Social Charter, 4, 113	8	2:01.06	240,000
1998	**Frisk Me Now**, 4, 118	E. L. King Jr.	Ordway, 4, 110	Sir Bear, 5, 117	8	2:00.45	210,000
1997	**Skip Away**, 4, 122	S. J. Sellers	Will's Way, 4, 116	Formal Gold, 4, 120	6	2:02.39	210,000
1996	**Wekiva Springs**, 5, 122	M. E. Smith	Mahogany Hall, 5, 114	L'Carriere, 5, 118	7	2:02.78	300,000
1995	**Key Contender**, 7, 115	J. D. Bailey	Kissin Kris, 5, 113	Federal Funds, 6, 107	10	2:02.30	210,000
1994	**Devil His Due**, 5, 124	M. E. Smith	Valley Crossing, 6, 113	Federal Funds, 5, 110	5	2:02.52	210,000
1993	**Devil His Due**, 4, 121	W. H. McCauley	Pure Rumor, 4, 110	West by West, 4, 116	8	2:01.25	180,000
1992	**Pleasant Tap**, 5, 119	E. Delahoussaye	Strike the Gold, 4, 119	Defensive Play, 5, 115	7	2:00.33	337,500
1991	**In Excess (Ire)**, 4, 119	G. L. Stevens	Chief Honcho, 4, 115	Killer Diller, 4, 113	7	**1:58.33**	300,000
1990	**Easy Goer**, 4, 126	P. Day	De Roche, 4, 113	Montubio (Arg), 5, 113	7	2:00.00	239,400
1989	**Dancing Spree**, 4, 114	A. T. Cordero Jr.	Forever Silver, 4, 116	Easy N Dirty, 6, 114	12	2:02.40	258,720
1988	**Personal Flag**, 5, 117	P. Day	Waquoit, 5, 121	Bet Twice, 4, 126	4	2:01.40	228,060
1987	**Broad Brush**, 4, 126	A. T. Cordero Jr.	Set Style (Chi), 4, 112	Bordeaux Bob, 4, 112	5	2:03.00	232,260
1986	**Roo Art**, 4, 116	P. Day	Proud Truth, 4, 121	Creme Fraiche, 4, 121	6	2:01.20	197,700
1985	**Vanlandingham**, 4, 115	D. MacBeth	Carr de Naskra, 4, 120	Dramatic Desire, 4, 109	9	2:01.00	180,600

1984 **Fit to Fight**, 5, 126	J. D. Bailey	Canadian Factor, 4, 116	Wild Again, 4, 116	7	2:00.60	$201,300
1983 **Winter's Tale**, 7, 120	J. Fell	Sing Sing, 5, 119	Highland Blade, 5, 119	8	2:01.60	168,600
1982 **Silver Buck**, 4, 111	D. MacBeth	It's the One, 4, 124	Aloma's Ruler, 3, 112	8	1:59.60	100,620
1981 **Temperence Hill**, 4, 127	D. MacBeth	Ring of Light, 6, 115	Highland Blade, 3, 113	8	2:02.00	100,620
1980 **Winter's Tale**, 4, 114	J. Fell	State Dinner, 5, 117	Czaravich, 4, 127	7	2:00.60	97,920
1979 **State Dinner**, 4, 118	J. Velasquez	Mister Brea (Arg), 5, 120	Alydar, 4, 126	5	2:01.60	79,125
1978 **Upper Nile**, 4, 113	J. Velasquez	Nearly On Time, 4, 109	Great Contractor, 5, 114	6	2:01.80	63,840
1977 **Quiet Little Table**, 4, 114	E. Maple	Forego, 7, 138	Nearly On Time, 3, 104	6	2:03.00	63,840
1976 **Foolish Pleasure**, 4, 125	E. Maple	Forego, 6, 134	Lord Rebeau, 5, 116	4	1:55.40	65,280
1975 **Forego**, 5, 134	H. Gustines	Arbees Boy, 5, 118	Loud, 8, 114	7	2:27.80	66,840
1974 **True Knight**, 5, 127	A. T. Cordero Jr.	Plunk, 4, 114	Forego, 4, 131	10	2:01.40	68,880
1973 **Key to the Mint**, 4, 126	B. Baeza	True Knight, 4, 118	Cloudy Dawn, 4, 113	6	2:00.80	65,700

Named after the City and Suburban Handicap in England, won by Parole, one of the first American horses to win a major English stakes race. Grade 2 1997-2002. Held at Sheepshead Bay 1884-1910. Held at Aqueduct 1961-'74, 1976. Not held 1911-'12, 1914. 1½ miles 1975. 1³⁄₁₆ miles 1976.

Sunset Breeders' Cup Handicap

Grade 2 in 2006. Hollywood Park, three-year-olds and up, 1½ miles, turf. Held July 17, 2005, with a gross value of $165,300. First held in 1938. First graded in 1973. Stakes record 2:23.55 (1996 Talloires).

Year	Winner	Jockey	Second	Third	Strs	Time	1st Purse
2005	**Always First (GB)**, 4, 113	V. Espinoza	dh-Runaway Dancer, 6, 118 dh-T. H. Approval, 4, 116		8	2:27.00	$99,180
2004	**Star Over the Bay**, 6, 113	T. Baze	Continuously, 5, 116	Leprechaun Kid, 5, 114	7	2:26.47	90,000
2003	**Puerto Banus**, 4, 113	V. Espinoza	Cagney (Brz), 6, 116	Continental Red, 7, 116	8	2:26.95	90,000
2002	**Grammarian**, 4, 112	B. Blanc	Continental Red, 6, 116	Lord Flasheart, 5, 115	7	2:26.59	150,000
2001	**Blueprint (Ire)**, 6, 116	G. L. Stevens	Kudos, 4, 116	Northern Quest (Fr), 6, 116	5	2:26.16	120,000
2000	**Bienamado**, 4, 122	C. J. McCarron	Deploy Venture (GB), 4, 115	Single Empire (Ire), 6, 120	5	2:25.06	150,000
1999	**Plicck (Ire)**, 4, 116	D. R. Flores	River Bay, 6, 121	Lazy Lode (Arg), 5, 120	8	2:26.97	150,000
1998	**River Bay**, 5, 121	A. O. Solis	Lazy Lode (Arg), 4, 115	Devonwood, 4, 114	6	2:27.40	210,000
1997	**Marlin**, 4, 120	D. R. Flores	Flyway (Fr), 4, 117	Percutant (GB), 6, 118	6	2:25.20	240,000
1996	**Talloires**, 6, 116	K. Desormeaux	Awad, 6, 117	Sandpit (Brz), 7, 125	7	**2:23.55**	420,000
1995	**Sandpit (Brz)**, 6, 124	C. S. Nakatani	Special Price, 6, 122	Liyoun (Ire), 7, 115	5	2:25.50	464,700
1994	**Grand Flotilla**, 7, 119	G. L. Stevens	Semillon (GB), 4, 116	Emerald Jig, 5, 115	7	2:26.35	158,000
1993	**Bien Bien**, 4, 122	C. J. McCarron	Emerald Jig, 4, 114	Beyton, 4, 116	6	2:25.69	154,300
1992	**Qathif**, 5, 114	A. O. Solis	Seven Rivers, 6, 114	Stark South, 4, 116	5	2:26.72	153,600
1991	**Black Monday (GB)**, 5, 112	C. S. Nakatani	Super May, 5, 117	Razeen, 4, 116	7	2:26.10	158,400
1990	**†Petite Ile (Ire)**, 4, 115	C. A. Black	Live the Dream, 4, 116	Soft Machine, 5, 110	9	2:25.60	163,600
1989	**Pranke (Arg)**, 5, 117	P. A. Valenzuela	Frankly Perfect, 4, 123	Pleasant Variety, 5, 117	7	2:28.00	157,200
1988	**Roi Normand**, 5, 114	F. Toro	Putting (Fr), 5, 117	Circus Prince, 5, 114	11	2:24.60	170,000
1987	**Swink**, 4, 112	W. Shoemaker	Forlitano (Arg), 6, 122	Rivlia, 5, 122	10	2:25.00	165,300
1986	**Zoffany**, 6, 122	E. Delahoussaye	Dahar, 5, 125	Flying Pidgeon, 5, 121	8	2:24.40	161,500
1985	**Kings Island (Ire)**, 4, 116	F. Toro	Greinton (GB), 4, 122	Val Danseur, 5, 114	5	2:25.80	148,800
1984	**John Henry**, 9, 126	C. J. McCarron	Load the Cannons, 4, 118	Pair of Deuces, 6, 113	9	2:24.80	129,800
1983	**Craelius**, 4, 118	C. J. McCarron	Palikaraki (Fr), 5, 115	Decadrachm, 4, 115	12	2:26.40	137,600
1982	**Erins Isle (Ire)**, 4, 118	A. T. Cordero Jr.	Don Roberto, 5, 117	Exploded, 5, 119	8	2:25.60	129,600
1981	**Galaxy Libra (Ire)**, 5, 119	W. Shoemaker	Caterman (NZ), 5, 122	The Bart, 5, 117	11	2:25.80	136,050
1980	**Inkerman**, 5, 115	W. Shoemaker	Balzac, 5, 120	Obraztsovy, 5, 121	7	2:24.40	94,700
1979	**Sirlad (Ire)**, 5, 122	D. G. McHargue	Ardiente, 4, 115	Inkerman, 4, 119	12	2:24.00	102,000
1978	**Exceller**, 5, 130	W. Shoemaker	Diagramatic, 5, 122	Effervescing, 5, 122	8	2:27.00	96,600
1977	**Today 'n Tomorrow**, 4, 116	W. Shoemaker	Hunza Dancer, 5, 122	Copper Mel, 5, 117	13	2:27.60	104,450
1976	**Caucasus**, 4, 121	F. Toro	King Pellinore, 4, 124	Riot in Paris, 5, 123	10	2:26.40	81,350
1975	***Barclay Joy**, 5, 117	W. Shoemaker	Captain Cee Jay, 5, 118	Top Crowd, 4, 115	8	2:26.80	50,450
	***Cruiser II**, 6, 114	F. Olivares	Pass the Glass, 4, 119	Kirrary, 5, 116	7	2:27.00	49,450
1974	***Greco II**, 5, 113	W. Shoemaker	Big Whippendeal, 4, 120	Scantling, 4, 118	12	2:27.00	69,600
1973	***Cougar II**, 7, 128	W. Shoemaker	Life Cycle, 4, 120	Rock Bath, 5, 114	7	2:26.00	80,100

The Sunset is traditionally one of the last races run at the Hollywood Park spring meeting. Formerly named for the Hawaiian word for "goodbye," aloha. Formerly sponsored by Caesars International's hotel, Caesars Palace 1995-'96. Grade 1 1973-'89. Aloha H. 1938-'39. Caesars Palace Turf Championship H. 1995-'96. Sunset H. 1940-'94, 1997-2004. Held at Santa Anita Park 1949. Not held 1942-'45. 1⅛ miles 1938, 1950. 1⅝ miles 1941-'49, 1952, 1955-'59, 1961-'66. 2 miles 1969-'72. Dirt 1938-'66. Two divisions 1975. Dead heat for second 2005. Course record 1996. †Denotes female.

Super Derby

Grade 2 in 2006. Louisiana Downs, three-year-olds, 1¼ miles, dirt. Held October 1, 2005, with a gross value of $750,000. First held in 1980. First graded in 1982. Stakes record 1:59.84 (2000 Tiznow).

Year	Winner	Jockey	Second	Third	Strs	Time	1st Purse
2005	**The Daddy**, 3, 124	P. Morales	A. P. Arrow, 3, 124	Nolan's Cat, 3, 124	10	2:03.15	$450,000
2004	**Fantasticat**, 3, 124	G. Melancon	Borrego, 3, 124	Britt's Jules, 3, 124	9	1:51.40	300,000
2003	**Ten Most Wanted**, 3, 124	P. Day	Soto, 3, 124	Crowned King, 3, 124	6	1:50.77	300,000
2002	**Essence of Dubai**, 3, 124	J. F. Chavez	Walk in the Snow, 3, 124	A. P. Five Hundred, 3, 124	8	1:49.43	300,000
2001	**Outofthebox**, 3, 124	L. J. Meche	E Dubai, 3, 124	Quadrophonic Sound, 3, 124	9	2:06.20	300,000
2000	**Tiznow**, 3, 124	C. J. McCarron	Commendable, 3, 124	Mass Market, 3, 124	6	**1:59.84**	300,000
1999	**Ecton Park**, 3, 126	A. O. Solis	Menifee, 3, 126	Pineaff, 3, 126	8	2:00.59	300,000
1998	**Arch**, 3, 126	C. S. Nakatani	Classic Cat, 3, 126	Sir Tiff, 3, 126	7	2:01.51	300,000

1997	**Deputy Commander**, 3, 126	C. J. McCarron	Precocity, 3, 126	Blazing Sword, 3, 126	6	2:00.80	$300,000
1996	**Editor's Note**, 3, 126	G. L. Stevens	The Barking Shark, 3, 126	Devil's Honor, 3, 126	11	2:02.37	450,000
1995	**Mecke**, 3, 126	J. D. Bailey	Pineing Patty, 3, 126	Scott's Scoundrel, 3, 126	12	2:00.34	450,000
1994	**Soul of the Matter**, 3, 126	K. Desormeaux	Concern, 3, 126	Bay Street Star, 3, 126	6	2:03.57	450,000
1993	**Wallenda**, 3, 126	W. H. McCauley	Saintly Prospector, 3, 126	Peteski, 3, 126	12	2:02.71	450,000
1992	**Senor Tomas**, 3, 126	A. T. Gryder	Count the Time, 3, 126	Orbit's Revenge, 3, 126	14	2:04.09	450,000
1991	**Free Spirit's Joy**, 3, 126	C. H. Borel	Olympio, 3, 126	Zeeruler, 3, 126	7	2:00.96	600,000
1990	**Home At Last**, 3, 126	J. D. Bailey	Unbridled, 3, 126	Cee's Tizzy, 3, 126	9	2:02.00	600,000
1989	**Sunday Silence**, 3, 126	P. A. Valenzuela	‡Awe Inspiring, 3, 126	Dispersal, 3, 126	8	2:03.20	600,000
1988	**Seeking the Gold**, 3, 126	P. Day	Happyasalark Tomas, 3, 126	Lively One, 3, 126	9	2:03.80	600,000
1987	**Alysheba**, 3, 126	C. J. McCarron	Candi's Gold, 3, 126	Parochial, 3, 126	8	2:03.20	600,000
1986	**Wise Times**, 3, 126	E. Maple	dh-Cheapskate, 3, 126		7	2:04.00	300,000
			dh-Southern Halo, 3, 126				
1985	**Creme Fraiche**, 3, 126	E. Maple	Encolure, 3, 126	Government Corner, 3, 126	8	2:02.80	300,000
1984	**Gate Dancer**, 3, 126	L. A. Pincay Jr.	Precisionist, 3, 126	Big Pistol, 3, 126	8	2:00.20	300,000
1983	**Sunny's Halo**, 3, 126	L. A. Pincay Jr.	Play Fellow, 3, 126	My Habitony, 3, 126	6	2:01.60	300,000
1982	**Reinvested**, 3, 126	J. Velasquez	El Baba, 3, 126	Drop Your Drawers, 3, 126	10	2:01.60	300,000
1981	**Island Whirl**, 3, 126	L. A. Pincay Jr.	Summing, 3, 126	Willow Hour, 3, 126	12	2:03.20	300,000
1980	**Temperence Hill**, 3, 126	E. Maple	First Albert, 3, 126	Cactus Road, 3, 126	8	2:06.60	300,000

Formerly sponsored by the Isle of Capri Casino in Bossier City, Louisiana, location of Louisiana Downs 1995-'96. Super Derby Invitational 1980-'86. Grade 1 1983-2001. Isle of Capri Casino Super Derby 1995-'96. 1⅛ miles 2002-'04. Dead heat for second 1986. ‡Big Earl finished second, DQ to eighth, 1989.

Suwannee River Handicap

Not graded in 2006. Gulfstream Park, three-year-olds and up, fillies and mares, 1⅛ miles, dirt (originally scheduled as a Grade 3 on the turf). Held February 4, 2006, with a gross value of $100,000. First held in 1947. First graded in 1973. Stakes record 1:46.40 (2005 Snowdrops [GB]).

Year	Winner	Jockey	Second	Third	Strs	Time	1st Purse
2006	**Eyes On Eddy**, 4, 114	R. Bejarano	Taittinger Rose, 5, 115	Marchonin, 4, 114	5	1:49.56	$60,000
2005	**Snowdrops (GB)**, 5, 116	E. S. Prado	Angela's Love, 5, 117	High Court (Brz), 5, 116	10	**1:46.40**	60,000
2004	**Wishful Splendor**, 5, 114	J. A. Santos	May Gator, 5, 113	Mymich, 4, 113	5	1:54.86	60,000
2003	**Amonita (GB)**, 5, 117	J. Samyn	What a Price, 5, 114	Calista (GB), 5, 118	9	1:47.90	60,000
2002	**Snow Dance**, 4, 119	P. Day	Step With Style, 5, 114	Windsong, 5, 113	6	1:49.04	60,000
2001	**Spook Express (SAf)**, 7, 116	M. E. Smith	Gaviola, 4, 120	Windsong, 4, 113	8	1:47.28	60,000
2000	**Pico Teneriffe**, 4, 115	J. F. Chavez	Dominique's Joy, 5, 114	Crystal Symphony, 4, 115	8	1:47.83	45,000
1999	**Winfama**, 6, 114	R. Migliore	Circus Charmer, 4, 113	Colcon, 6, 120	10	1:52.38	45,000
1998	**Seebe**, 4, 114	D. Rice	Colcon, 5, 115	Parade Queen, 4, 119	10	1:47.58	45,000
1997	**Golden Pond (Ire)**, 4, 115	J. D. Bailey	Rumpipumpy (GB), 4, 114	Elusive, 5, 113	11	1:47.87	45,000
1996	**Class Kris**, 4, 116	P. Day	Apolda, 5, 118	Majestic Dy, 4, 113	5	1:49.17	45,000
1995	**Cox Orange**, 5, 116	J. D. Bailey	Irving's Girl, 5, 113	Alice Springs, 5, 120	7	1:47.43	45,000
1994	**Marshua's River**, 7, 114	J. A. Santos	Sheila's Revenge, 4, 118	Icy Warning, 4, 115	12	1:46.68	45,000
1993	**Via Borghese**, 4, 116	J. D. Bailey	Marshua's River, 6, 113	Blue Daisy, 5, 114	14	1:48.22	40,230
1992	**Julie La Rousse (Ire)**, 4, 115	J. D. Bailey	Christiecat, 5, 117	Grab the Green, 4, 120	11	1:48.48	38,670
1991	**Vigorous Lady**, 5, 117	M. A. Lee	Yen for Gold, 5, 111	Premier Question, 4, 116	5	1:45.10	36,120
1990	**Princess Mora**, 4, 111	M. A. Gonzalez	Fieldy (Ire), 7, 121	Northling, 6, 113	12	1:41.20	38,970
1989	**Love You by Heart**, 4, 117	R. P. Romero	Native Mommy, 6, 118	Aquaba, 4, 115	10	1:41.60	37,275
	Fieldy (Ire), 6, 116	C. Perret	Summer Secretary, 4, 110	Chapel of Dreams, 5, 122	9	1:41.60	36,975
1988	**Go Honey Go (Ire)**, 5, 110	J. M. Pezua	Princely Proof, 5, 115	Fieldy (Ire), 5, 119	11	1:41.80	38,490
	Anka Germania (Ire), 6, 122	C. Perret	Sum, 4, 114	Fama, 5, 112	12	1:41.80	39,090
1987	**dh-Fama**, 4, 114	R. P. Romero		Navarchus, 5, 114	8	1:44.20	17,810
	dh-Fieldy (Ire), 4, 114	C. Perret					
	Singular Bequest, 4, 114	E. Fires	Cadabra Abra, 4, 114	Duckweed, 5, 112	7	1:43.60	26,415
1986	**Chesire Kitten**, 4, 112	J. Samyn	Chaldea, 6, 111	Four Flings, 5, 113	10	1:44.80	30,990
	Videogenic, 4, 120	R. G. Davis	Contredance, 4, 117	Verbality, 4, 112	9	1:44.60	30,690
1985	**Early Lunch**, 4, 112	W. A. Guerra	Eva G., 5, 114	Maidenhead, 6, 111	11	1:35.60	28,521
	Sherizar, 4, 113	J. McKnight	Madam Flutterby, 4, 114	Melanie Frances, 7, 115	12	1:36.40	28,820
	Burst of Colors, 5, 117	J. A. Santos	Queen of Song, 6, 121	Silver in Flight, 5, 115	12	1:35.60	28,820
1984	**Sulemeif**, 4, 113	J. D. Bailey	Jubilous, 4, 115	Melanie Frances, 6, 113	13	1:36.80	39,330
1983	**Norsan**, 4, 113	J. D. Bailey	Dana Calqui (Arg), 5, 114	Colatina, 4, 111	12	1:38.20	28,890
	Syrianna, 4, 114	J. Vasquez	Meringue Pie, 5, 115	Plenty O'Toole, 6, 114	8	1:24.20	27,390
	Promising Native, 4, 113	D. MacBeth	Avowal, 4, 117	Our Darling, 4, 112	7	1:23.80	27,060
1982	**Pine Flower**, 4, 113	C. Perret	Sweetest Chant, 4, 116	Fair Davina (Ire), 6, 110	9	1:35.40	27,000
	Teacher's Pet (GB), 5, 114	C. H. Marquez	Shark Song (GB), 4, 114	Blush, 4, 113	9	1:35.20	27,300
1981	**Honey Fox**, 4, 111	J. Samyn	Racquette (Ire), 4, 115	Pompoes (Den), 4, 110	9	1:35.20	22,568
	Exactly So (Ire), 4, 109	J. Samyn	Draw In, 5, 114	Champagne Ginny, 4, 118	9	1:35.80	22,568
1980	**Ouro Verde**, 4, 112	R. I. Encinas	No Disgrace (Ire), 4, 110	Anna Yrrah D., 4, 112	10	1:37.20	18,870
	Just a Game (Ire), 4, 117	D. Brumfield	La Soufriere, 5, 113	La Voyageuse, 5, 120	10	1:35.20	18,870
1979	**Navajo Princess**, 5, 124	C. Perret	La Soufriere, 4, 119	Unreality, 5, 121	13	1:35.20	19,650
	Calderina (Ity), 4, 117	J. Fell	Terpsichorist, 4, 122	She Can Dance, 4, 113	11	1:36.20	19,200
1978	**Len's Determined**, 4, 119	J. Cruguet	What a Summer, 5, 122	Late Bloomer, 4, 113	9	1:35.60	19,260
1977	**Bronze Point**, 4, 120	H. Arroyo	Funny Peculiar, 5, 114	Collegiate, 5, 114	7	1:24.20	21,390
1976	**Jabot**, 4, 112	H. Gustines	Redundancy, 5, 119	*Deesse Du Val, 5, 117	14	1:34.60	21,330
1975	***Deesse Du Val**, 4, 115	M. Hole	North of Venus, 5, 118	Lorraine Edna, 5, 118	11	1:35.40	20,400

1974	**Dove Creek Lady**, 4, 121	M. A. Rivera	North Broadway, 4, 120	North of Venus, 4, 119	13	1:36.40	$21,960
1973	**Ziba Blue**, 6, 110	M. Miceli	Cathy Baby, 4, 113	dh-Barely Even, 4, 127 dh-Tico's Donna, 5, 114	13	1:35.80	21,270

Named for Stephen Foster's song "Old Folks at Home (Suwannee River)," Florida's state song. Not graded 1979-'81, 2004. Not held 1949. 7 furlongs 1947, 1961-'66, 1977, 1983 (two divisions). 6 furlongs 1948. 1$^1/_{16}$ miles 1953-'60, 1967-'68, 1986-'91. 1 mile 1969-'76, 1978-'79, 1981-'82, 1983 (one division), 1984-'85. About 1$^1/_8$ miles 1999. Dirt 1965-'66, 1977, 1983 (two divisions), 1986, 1991, 2004, 2006. Originally scheduled on turf 2004, 2006. Four-year-olds and up 1994. Two divisions 1979-'82, 1986-'89. Three divisions 1983, 1985. Dead heat for third 1973. Dead heat for first 1987 (1st Div.). Equaled course record 1992. Held as an overnight handicap 1950-'52.

Swale Stakes

Grade 2 in 2006. Gulfstream Park, three-year-olds, 7 furlongs, dirt. Held March 4, 2006, with a gross value of $150,000. First held in 1985. First graded in 1990. Stakes record 1:21.06 (2003 Midas Eyes).

Year	Winner	Jockey	Second	Third	Strs	Time	1st Purse
2006	**Sharp Humor**, 3, 118	M. Guidry	Noonmark, 3, 116	Court Folly, 3, 116	11	1:22.14	$90,000
2005	**Lost in the Fog**, 3, 120	R. A. Baze	Around the Cape, 3, 116	More Smoke, 3, 118	10	1:22.21	90,000
2004	**Wynn Dot Comma**, 3, 120	E. S. Prado	Eurosilver, 3, 120	Dashboard Drummer, 3, 120	5	1:22.87	90,000
2003	**Midas Eyes**, 3, 116	J. D. Bailey	Posse, 3, 120	Whywhywhy, 3, 122	8	**1:21.06**	90,000
2002	**Ethan Man**, 3, 116	P. Day	Listen Here, 3, 120	Governor Hickel, 3, 116	5	1:22.29	90,000
2001	**D'wildcat**, 3, 116	C. S. Nakatani	Tarek, 3, 112	Yonaguska, 3, 122	6	1:22.25	90,000
2000	**Trippi**, 3, 113	J. D. Bailey	Ultimate Warrior, 3, 117	Harlan Traveler, 3, 114	8	1:23.43	60,000
1999	**Yes It's True**, 3, 122	J. D. Bailey	Texas Glitter, 3, 117	Lucky Roberto, 3, 119	5	1:22.29	60,000
1998	**Favorite Trick**, 3, 122	P. Day	Good and Tough, 3, 114	Dice Dancer, 3, 113	9	1:22.86	60,000
1997	**Confide**, 3, 117	M. E. Smith	Country Rainbow, 3, 112	The Silver Move, 3, 119	9	1:23.35	45,000
1996	**Roar**, 3, 113	M. E. Smith	Gomtuu, 3, 119	Dixie Connection, 3, 112	6	1:22.46	45,000
1995	**Mr. Greeley**, 3, 114	J. A. Krone	Devious Course, 3, 119	Pyramid Peak, 3, 114	6	1:22.18	45,000
1994	**Arrival Time**, 3, 115	C. J. McCarron	Senor Conquistador, 3, 113	Meadow Monster, 3, 112	7	1:22.53	45,000
1993	**Premier Explosion**, 3, 114	D. Penna	Demaloot Demashoot, 3, 113	Cherokee Run, 3, 114	8	1:23.23	53,520
1992	**D. J. Cat**, 3, 114	J. D. Bailey	Binalong, 3, 114	Always Silver, 3, 112	10	1:23.39	71,250
1991	**Chihuahua**, 3, 112	J. O. Alferez	To Freedom, 3, 119	Greek Costume, 3, 114	7	1:23.47	51,060
1990	**Housebuster**, 3, 122	C. Perret	Summer Squall, 3, 122	Thirty Six Red, 3, 113	6	1:22.20	34,350
1989	**Easy Goer**, 3, 122	P. Day	Trion, 3, 112	Tricky Creek, 3, 122	6	1:22.20	34,290
1988	**Seeking the Gold**, 3, 114	R. P. Romero	Above Normal, 3, 114	Perfect Spy, 3, 122	7	1:21.60	35,100
1986	**One Magic Moment**, 3, 113	C. Perret	Admiral's Image, 3, 122	Two Punch, 3, 113	11	1:25.40	31,230
1985	**Chief's Crown**, 3, 122	D. MacBeth	Creme Fraiche, 3, 117	Cherokee Fast, 3, 113	9	1:22.40	30,792

Named for Claiborne Farm's 1984 champion three-year-old male and '84 Florida Derby (G1) winner Swale (1981 c. by Seattle Slew). Grade 3 1990-2004. Not held 1987.

Swaps Breeders' Cup Stakes

Grade 2 in 2006. Hollywood Park, three-year-olds, 1$^1/_8$ miles, dirt. Held July 9, 2005, with a gross value of $361,000. First held in 1974. First graded in 1975. Stakes record 1:45.80 (1997 Free House).

Year	Winner	Jockey	Second	Third	Strs	Time	1st Purse
2005	**Surf Cat**, 3, 115	A. O. Solis	Dover Dere, 3, 117	Indian Ocean, 3, 118	6	1:48.07	$192,600
2004	**Rock Hard Ten**, 3, 116	C. S. Nakatani	Suave, 3, 120	Boomzeeboom, 3, 118	6	1:47.47	252,780
2003	**During**, 3, 115	J. D. Bailey	Ten Most Wanted, 3, 122	dh-Eye of the Tiger, 3, 118 dh-Outta Here, 3, 120	6	1:49.38	240,000
2002	**Came Home**, 3, 122	M. E. Smith	Like a Hero, 3, 114	Fonz's, 3, 116	7	1:48.28	300,000
2001	**Congaree**, 3, 122	G. L. Stevens	Until Sundown, 3, 118	Jamaican Rum, 3, 118	6	1:48.61	300,000
2000	**Captain Steve**, 3, 120	C. S. Nakatani	Tiznow, 3, 118	Spacelink, 3, 118	6	1:48.01	300,000
1999	**Cat Thief**, 3, 120	P. Day	General Challenge, 3, 122	Walk That Walk, 3, 117	4	1:47.87	300,000
1998	**Old Trieste**, 3, 118	C. J. McCarron	Grand Slam, 3, 120	Old Topper, 3, 117	6	1:47.00	300,000
1997	**Free House**, 3, 122	K. Desormeaux	Deputy Commander, 3, 118	Wild Rush, 3, 122	6	**1:45.80**	300,000
1996	**Victory Speech**, 3, 118	J. D. Bailey	Prince of Thieves, 3, 118	Hesabull, 3, 118	5	1:48.28	300,000
1995	**Thunder Gulch**, 3, 126	G. L. Stevens	Da Hoss, 3, 118	Petionville, 3, 120	7	1:49.09	275,000
1994	**Silver Music**, 3, 119	C. W. Antley	Dramatic Gold, 3, 119	Valiant Nature, 3, 121	6	2:00.76	123,800
1993	**Devoted Brass**, 3, 123	L. A. Pincay Jr.	Future Storm, 3, 119	Codified, 3, 123	6	2:00.64	124,000
1992	**Bien Bien**, 3, 119	C. J. McCarron	Treekster, 3, 123	Sevengreenpairs, 3, 119	5	2:02.91	123,400
1991	**Best Pal**, 3, 116	P. A. Valenzuela	Corporate Report, 3, 114	Compelling Sound, 3, 123	4	2:00.70	120,000
1990	**Jovial (GB)**, 3, 120	G. L. Stevens	Silver Ending, 3, 126	Stalwart Charger, 3, 126	4	2:01.20	120,000
1989	**Prized**, 3, 120	E. Delahoussaye	Sunday Silence, 3, 126	Endow, 3, 123	5	2:01.80	232,400
1988	**Lively One**, 3, 120	W. Shoemaker	Blade of the Ball, 3, 114	Iz a Saros, 3, 123	9	2:01.00	131,200
1987	**Temperate Sil**, 3, 123	W. Shoemaker	Candi's Gold, 3, 123	Pledge Card, 3, 115	6	2:02.20	124,400
1986	**Clear Choice**, 3, 120	C. J. McCarron	Southern Halo, 3, 114	Jota, 3, 116	9	2:03.60	137,000
1985	**Padua**, 3, 115	P. A. Valenzuela	Turkoman, 3, 115	Don't Say Halo, 3, 120	8	2:01.40	123,500
1984	**Precisionist**, 3, 123	C. J. McCarron	Prince True, 3, 120	Majestic Shore, 3, 114	7	1:59.80	121,300
1983	**Hyperborean**, 3, 115	F. Toro	My Habitony, 3, 120	Tanks Brigade, 3, 120	9	2:01.00	97,500
1982	**Journey At Sea**, 3, 120	C. J. McCarron	West Coast Native, 3, 114	Cassaleria, 3, 123	5	2:00.20	91,300
1981	**Noble Nashua**, 3, 123	L. A. Pincay Jr.	Dorcaro (Fr), 3, 115	Stancharry, 3, 123	7	2:01.20	127,000
1980	**First Albert**, 3, 123	F. Mena	Amber Pass, 3, 123	Mr. Mud, 3, 114	11	2:00.80	162,200
1979	**Valdez**, 3, 120	L. A. Pincay Jr.	Shamgo, 3, 114	Paint King, 3, 114	6	1:59.40	124,250
1978	**Radar Ahead**, 3, 120	D. G. McHargue	Batonnier, 3, 123	Poppy Popowich, 3, 115	10	2:00.00	133,300
1977	**J. O. Tobin**, 3, 120	W. Shoemaker	Affiliate, 3, 117	Text, 3, 120	7	1:58.60	194,900
1976	**Majestic Light**, 3, 114	S. Hawley	Crystal Water, 3, 123	Double Discount, 3, 115	9	1:59.20	98,200

1975	**Forceten**, 3, 120	D. Pierce	Sibirri, 3, 114	Diabolo, 3, 123	8	1:59.80	$119,800
1974	**Agitate**, 3, 123	W. Shoemaker	Stardust Mel, 3, 120	Master Music, 3, 114	9	1:59.60	66,300

Named for Rex Ellsworth's 1956 Horse of the Year and '56 Hollywood Gold Cup H. winner Swaps (1952 c. by *Khaled). Grade 1 1975-'88, 1999-2001. Swaps S. 1974-2003. 1¼ miles 1974-'94. Dead heat for third 2003.

Sword Dancer Invitational Stakes

Grade 1 in 2005. Saratoga Race Course, three-year-olds and up, 1½ miles, turf. Held August 13, 2005, with a gross value of $500,000. First held in 1975. First graded in 1981. Stakes record 2:23.20 (1997 Awad).

Year	Winner	Jockey	Second	Third	Strs	Time	1st Purse
2005	**King's Drama (Ire)**, 5, 116	J. F. Chavez	Relaxed Gesture (Ire), 4, 116	Vangelis, 6, 118	8	2:27.38	$300,000
2004	**Better Talk Now**, 5, 118	R. A. Dominguez	Request for Parole, 5, 123	Balto Star, 6, 120	6	2:28.49	300,000
2003	**Whitmore's Conn**, 5, 115	J. Samyn	Macaw (Ire), 4, 114	Slew Valley, 6, 114	11	2:28.14	300,000
2002	**With Anticipation**, 7, 120	P. Day	Denon, 4, 118	Volponi, 4, 115	11	2:24.06	300,000
2001	**With Anticipation**, 6, 114	P. Day	King Cugat, 4, 120	Slew Valley, 4, 114	9	2:26.41	300,000
2000	**John's Call**, 9, 114	J. Samyn	Aly's Alley, 4, 114	Single Empire (Ire), 6, 119	8	2:32.17	300,000
1999	**Honor Glide**, 5, 116	J. A. Santos	Val's Prince, 7, 115	Chorwon, 6, 114	7	2:28.23	240,000
1998	**Cetewayo**, 4, 115	J. R. Velazquez	Val's Prince, 6, 113	Dushyantor, 5, 119	6	2:29.56	180,000
1997	**Awad**, 7, 117	P. Day	Fahim (GB), 4, 110	Val's Prince, 5, 112	10	**2:23.20**	150,000
1996	**Broadway Flyer**, 5, 118	M. E. Smith	Kiri's Clown, 7, 113	Flag Down, 6, 119	9	2:32.08	150,000
1995	**Kiri's Clown**, 6, 114	M. J. Luzzi	Awad, 5, 121	King's Theatre (Ire), 4, 113	13	2:25.45	150,000
1994	**Alex the Great (GB)**, 5, 118	P. A. Valenzuela	Kiri's Clown, 5, 112	L'Hermine (GB), 5, 112	10	2:28.66	150,000
1993	**Spectacular Tide**, 4, 112	J. A. Krone	Square Cut, 4, 112	Dr. Kiernan, 4, 117	9	2:30.39	120,000
1992	**Fraise**, 4, 113	J. D. Bailey	Wall Street Dancer, 4, 116	Montserrat, 4, 112	8	2:25.88	150,000
1991	**Dr. Root**, 4, 109	J. Samyn	Karmani, 6, 113	El Senor, 7, 116	7	2:25.43	150,000
1990	**El Senor**, 6, 119	A. T. Cordero Jr.	With Approval, 4, 124	Hodges Bay, 5, 114	7	2:28.00	140,400
1989	**El Senor**, 5, 118	W. H. McCauley	Nediym (Ire), 4, 113	My Big Boy, 6, 115	7	2:27.00	139,920
1988	**†Anka Germania (Ire)**, 6, 117	C. Perret	Sunshine Forever, 3, 114	†Carotene, 5, 114	7	2:32.20	141,120
1987	**‡Theatrical (Ire)**, 5, 124	P. Day	Dance of Life, 4, 122	Akabir, 6, 114	4	2:26.00	133,080
1986	**Southern Sultan**, 4, 109	R. G. Davis	Talakeno, 6, 114	Tri for Size, 5, 111	8	2:39.40	143,460
1985	**Tri for Size**, 4, 110	R. J. Thibeau Jr.	Talakeno, 5, 112	†Persian Tiara (Ire), 5, 113	9	2:33.20	151,320
1984	**Majesty's Prince**, 5, 124	E. Maple	Nassipour, 4, 109	Four Bases, 5, 112	11	2:31.00	176,820
1983	**Majesty's Prince**, 4, 120	E. Maple	‡Thunder Puddles, 4, 118	Erins Isle (Ire), 5, 128	9	2:34.40	141,600
1982	**Lemhi Gold**, 4, 126	C. J. McCarron	Erins Isle (Ire), 4, 126	Field Cat, 5, 126	5	2:26.00	99,000
1981	**John Henry**, 6, 126	W. Shoemaker	Passing Zone, 4, 126	Peat Moss, 6, 126	5	2:26.80	97,380
1980	**Tiller**, 6, 126	R. Hernandez	John Henry, 5, 126	Sten, 5, 126	4	2:25.20	96,660
1979	**Darby Creek Road**, 4, 119	A. T. Cordero Jr.	John Henry, 4, 119	Poison Ivory, 4, 119	8	1:41.60	34,320
1978	**True Colors**, 4, 114	M. Venezia	Bill Brill, 4, 107	Blue Baron, 4, 114	12	1:41.00	34,020
1977	**Effervescing**, 4, 117	A. T. Cordero Jr.	Gentle King, 4, 110	Cinteelo, 4, 116	9	1:39.60	33,690
1976	**Arabian Law**, 3, 112	J. Vasquez	Full Out, 3, 118	Half High, 3, 111	7	1:10.60	26,535
1975	**Gallant Bob**, 3, 126	G. Gallitano	Our Hero, 3, 113	Due Diligence, 3, 113	9	1:09.60	27,630

Named for Brookmeade Stable's 1959 Horse of the Year and '59 Jockey Club Gold Cup winner Sword Dancer (1956 c. by Sunglow). Grade 3 1981. Grade 2 1982-'83. Sword Dancer H. 1975-'78, 1983-'93. Sword Dancer S. 1979-'82. Sword Dancer Invitational H. 1994-2004. Held at Aqueduct 1975-'76. Held at Belmont Park 1977-'91. 6 furlongs 1975-'76. 1¹⁄₁₆ miles 1977-'79. Dirt 1975-'76. Three-year-olds 1975-'76. ‡Hush Dear finished second, DQ to fourth, 1983. ‡Dance of Life finished first, DQ to second, 1987. †Denotes female.

Sycamore Breeders' Cup Stakes

Grade 3 in 2006. Keeneland Race Course, three-year-olds and up, 1½ miles, turf. Held October 7, 2005, with a gross value of $161,100. First held in 1995. First graded in 2003. Stakes record 2:29.55 (2003 Sharbayan [Ire]).

Year	Winner	Jockey	Second	Third	Strs	Time	1st Purse
2005	**Rochester**, 9, 120	G. L. Stevens	Dreadnaught, 5, 122	Vangelis, 6, 122	8	2:34.30	$99,882
2004	**Mustanfar**, 3, 118	J. A. Santos	Deputy Strike, 6, 120	Rochester, 8, 122	9	2:30.88	100,626
2003	**Sharbayan (Ire)**, 5, 120	P. Day	Cetewayo, 9, 122	Deputy Strike, 5, 120	10	**2:29.55**	73,904
2002	**Rochester**, 6, 125	P. Day	Roxinho (Brz), 4, 120	Lord Flasheart, 5, 120	7	2:30.48	101,928
2001	**Rochester**, 5, 119	P. Day	Chorwon, 8, 125	Regal Dynasty, 5, 119	7	2:31.29	103,044
2000	**Crowd Pleaser**, 5, 118	C. H. Borel	Dixie's Crown, 4, 122	Kim Loves Bucky, 3, 114	7	2:44.00	44,439
1999	**Royal Strand (Ire)**, 5, 117	P. Day	Arizona Storm, 4, 117	Magest, 4, 117	6	2:38.68	42,315
1998	**Royal Strand (Ire)**, 4, 116	S. J. Sellers	Thesaurus, 4, 116	Lakeshore Road, 5, 116	5	2:41.93	33,015
1997	**Gleaming Key**, 5, 116	S. J. Sellers	Double Leaf (GB), 4, 116	Seattle Blossom, 4, 116	5	2:45.86	33,015
1996	**Gleaming Key**, 4, 114	R. Albarado	Nash Terrace (Ire), 4, 120	Hawkeye Bay, 5, 114	4	2:44.49	32,860
1995	**Lindon Lime**, 5, 123	C. Perret	Hyper Shu, 5, 114	Lordly Prospect, 6, 114	9	2:42.11	39,098

Named for the sycamore tree at the entrance to Keeneland's walking ring. Sycamore S. 1995-2000.

Tampa Bay Derby

Grade 3 in 2006. Tampa Bay Downs, three-year-olds, 1¹⁄₁₆ miles, dirt. Held March 18, 2006, with a gross value of $250,000. First held in 1981. First graded in 1984. Stakes record 1:43.66 (2002 Equality).

Year	Winner	Jockey	Second	Third	Strs	Time	1st Purse
2006	**Deputy Glitters**, 3, 116	J. Lezcano	Bluegrass Cat, 3, 122	Winnies Tigger Too, 3, 116	9	1:44.26	$150,000
2005	**Sun King**, 3, 116	E. S. Prado	Forever Wild, 3, 116	Global Trader, 3, 116	7	1:43.98	150,000
2004	**Limehouse**, 3, 118	P. Day	Mustanfar, 3, 116	Swingforthefences, 3, 116	8	1:43.99	150,000
2003	**Region of Merit**, 3, 120	E. Coa	Aristocat, 3, 118	Hear No Evil, 3, 123	8	1:44.61	150,000

2002	**Equality**, 3, 118	R. A. Dominguez	Tails of the Crypt, 3, 123	Political Attack, 3, 123	9	**1:43.66**	$120,000
2001	**Burning Roma**, 3, 123	R. Migliore	American Prince, 3, 123	Paging, 3, 116	11	1:44.30	120,000
2000	**Wheelaway**, 3, 116	R. Migliore	Impeachment, 3, 116	Perfect Cat, 3, 116	10	1:43.90	90,000
1999	**Pineaff**, 3, 122	J. A. Santos	Menifee, 3, 120	Doneraile Court, 3, 122	6	1:45.33	90,000
1998	**Parade Ground**, 3, 118	P. Day	Middlesex Drive, 3, 118	Rock and Roll, 3, 116	8	1:44.20	90,000
1997	**Zede**, 3, 118	J. D. Bailey	Brisco Jack, 3, 116	Favorable Regard, 3, 118	12	1:44.80	90,000
1996	**Thundering Storm**, 3, 118	J. A. Guerra	El Amante, 3, 118	Natural Selection, 3, 116	10	1:43.80	90,000
1995	**Gadzook**, 3, 116	G. Boulanger	Composer, 3, 116	Bet Your Bucks, 3, 116	10	1:45.20	90,000
1994	**Prix de Crouton**, 3, 120	M. Walls	Able Buck, 3, 120	Parental Pressure, 3, 122	7	1:46.60	90,000
1993	**Marco Bay**, 3, 120	R. D. Allen Jr.	Thriller Chiller, 3, 116	Tunecke Charlie, 3, 118	12	1:44.40	90,000
1992	**Careful Gesture**, 3, 118	R. N. Lester	Chief Speaker, 3, 116	Clipper Won, 3, 116	12	1:45.93	120,000
1991	**Speedy Cure**, 3, 118	R. D. Lopez	Link, 3, 118	Shudanz, 3, 116	9	1:46.26	90,000
1990	**Champagneforashley**, 3, 122	J. Vasquez	Slew of Angels, 3, 120	Always Running, 3, 116	10	1:44.60	90,000
1989	**Storm Predictions**, 3, 120	S. Gaffalione	With Approval, 3, 120	Mercedes Won, 3, 122	11	1:43.80	90,000
1988	**Cefis**, 3, 116	E. Maple	Buck Forbes, 3, 118	Twice Too Many, 3, 118	9	1:44.40	90,000
1987	**Phantom Jet**, 3, 122	K. K. Allen	Homebuilder, 3, 116	You're No Bargain, 3, 116	10	1:43.80	90,000
1986	**My Prince Charming**, 3, 122	C. Perret	Lucky Rebeau, 3, 120	Major Moran, 3, 116	13	1:46.60	98,100
1985	**Regal Remark**, 3, 122	J. Fell	Verification, 3, 122	Sport Jet, 3, 118	14	1:46.80	95,400
1984	**Bold Southerner**, 3, 116	W. Crews	Rexson's Hope, 3, 122	Stickler, 3, 120	13	1:44.60	95,400
1983	**Morganmorganmorgan**, 3, 118	W. Rodriguez	Slew o' Gold, 3, 118	Quick Dip, 3, 118	14	1:47.20	60,000
1982	**Reinvested**, 3, 114	R. D. Luhr	Stage Reviewer, 3, 120	Real Twister, 3, 120	12	1:45.20	40,140
1981	**Paristo**, 3, 112	D. C. Ashcroft	Bravestofall, 3, 120	Darby Gillic, 3, 122	14	1:45.40	43,560

The race and the track are named for the city of Tampa, Florida, and the bay on which it is located. Formerly sponsored by the Anheuser-Busch Co. of St. Louis, Missouri 1981-'86. Not graded 1990-2001. Budweiser Tampa Bay Derby 1981-'86.

Taylor Made Matchmaker Stakes

Grade 3 in 2006. Monmouth Park, three-year-olds and up, fillies and mares, 1⅛ miles, turf. Held August 7, 2005, with a gross value of $150,000. First held in 1967. First graded in 1973. Stakes record 1:46.19 (2001 Batique).

Year	Winner	Jockey	Second	Third	Strs	Time	1st Purse
2005	**Love Match**, 5, 116	J. Castellano	Cat Alert, 5, 118	Emerald Earrings, 4, 116	10	1:50.38	$90,000
2004	**Where We Left Off (GB)**, 4, 118	C. S. Nakatani	Mrs. M, 5, 118	Spin Control, 4, 116	9	1:48.80	60,000
2003	**Volga (Ire)**, 5, 116	J. Bravo	Something Ventured, 4, 117	Cocktailsandreams, 6, 115	10	1:48.22	60,000
2002	**Clearly a Queen**, 5, 115	E. Coa	Siringas (Ire), 4, 116	Platinum Tiara, 4, 115	7	1:47.76	60,000
2001	**Batique**, 5, 113	J. C. Ferrer	Melody Queen (GB), 5, 114	Lucky Lune (Fr), 4, 114	8	**1:46.19**	60,000
2000	**Horatia (Ire)**, 4, 114	J. A. Santos	Camella, 5, 120	Champagne Royal, 6, 114	11	1:47.52	60,000
1999	**Natalie Too**, 5, 116	J. Bravo	Saralea (Fr), 4, 116	U R Unforgetable, 5, 120	6	1:46.81	60,000
1998	**Bursting Forth**, 4, 116	M. E. Verge	French Buster, 4, 116	Gastronomical, 5, 113	9	1:48.46	60,000
1997	**Fleur de Nuit**, 4, 113	J. A. Krone	Flame Valley, 4, 113	Overcharger, 5, 113	7	1:48.97	60,000
1996	**Powder Bowl**, 4, 113	D. S. Rice	Class Kris, 4, 120	Turkish Tryst, 5, 114	6	1:54.71	60,000
1995	**Avie's Fancy**, 4, 113	W. H. McCauley	Plenty of Sugar, 4, 118	Northern Emerald, 5, 113	8	1:54.19	60,000
1994	**Alice Springs**, 4, 118	J. A. Krone	Hero's Love, 6, 118	Cox Orange, 4, 118	8	1:55.21	60,000
1993	**Fairy Garden**, 5, 120	M. E. Smith	Saratoga Source, 4, 118	Logan's Mist, 4, 118	8	1:57.81	60,000
1992	**Radiant Ring**, 4, 115	R. E. Colton	Highland Crystal, 4, 118	La Gueriere, 4, 118	8	1:55.92	60,000
1991	**Miss Josh**, 5, 123	L. A. Pincay Jr.	Whip Cream, 5, 113	Le Famo, 5, 113	7	1:54.18	90,000
1990	**Capades**, 4, 120	A. T. Cordero Jr.	Gaily Gaily (Ire), 7, 115	Summer Secretary, 5, 115	7	1:55.60	90,000
1989	**Spruce Fir**, 6, 113	D. B. Thomas	Ravinella, 4, 120	Native Mommy, 6, 120	8	1:53.40	90,000
1988	**Magdelaine (NZ)**, 5, 120	E. Maple	Spruce Fir, 5, 115	Carotene, 5, 120	7	1:56.20	60,000
1987	**Carotene**, 4, 118	D. J. Seymour	Spruce Fir, 4, 115	Cadabra Abra, 4, 120	10	1:56.60	73,500
1986	**Lake Country**, 5, 118	V. A. Bracciale Jr.	Capo Di Monte (Ire), 4, 120	Top Socialite, 4, 120	11	1:54.60	60,000
1985	**Key Dancer**, 4, 118	J. D. Bailey	Forest Maiden, 5, 118	Dictina (Fr), 4, 115	7	2:02.40	30,000
1984	**Sabin**, 4, 123	E. Maple	Doblique, 5, 113	Virgin Bride, 4, 113	8	1:53.80	30,000
1983	**Luminaire**, 4, 113	B. Thornburg	Vestris, 4, 113	Lonely Balladier, 5, 113	8	1:56.80	25,000
1982	**Hunston (GB)**, 4, 113	J. Samyn	Trevita (Ire), 5, 118	Kuja Happa, 4, 115	9	1:58.60	35,000
1981	**Mairzy Doates**, 5, 120	C. B. Asmussen	Honey Fox, 4, 120	Little Bonny (Ire), 4, 120	7	1:56.00	35,000
1980	**Just a Game (Ire)**, 4, 120	D. Brumfield	La Soufriere, 5, 115	Record Acclaim, 4, 115	10	1:57.60	25,000
1979	**Warfever (Fr)**, 4, 113	J. Samyn	Smooth Journey, 3, 106	La Soufriere, 4, 118	10	2:03.20	25,000
1978	**Queen Lib**, 3, 112	D. MacBeth	Debby's Turn, 4, 114	Dottie's Doll, 5, 117	8	1:56.40	25,000
1977	**Mississippi Mud**, 4, 119	J. E. Tejeira	Vodka Time, 5, 114	*Lucie Manet, 4, 124	8	1:54.20	30,000
1976	**Dancers Countess**, 4, 119	C. J. McCarron	Vodka Time, 4, 114	Garden Verse, 4, 119	8	1:56.00	20,000
1975	**Susan's Girl**, 6, 121	R. Broussard	Aunt Jin, 3, 114	Pink Tights, 4, 114	6	1:54.20	20,000
1974	**Desert Vixen**, 4, 123	L. A. Pincay Jr.	Coraggioso, 4, 115	Twixt, 5, 123	9	1:55.20	30,000
1973	**Alma North**, 5, 118	F. Lovato	Light Hearted, 4, 121	Susan's Girl, 4, 125	9	1:55.20	30,000

The first three finishers of this race are awarded future breeding seasons; named for "matchmaking" between stallions and mares. Sponsored by Taylor Made Farm of Nicholasville, Kentucky 2005. Formerly sponsored by Vinery of Lexington 1996, 1998-2001. Formerly sponsored by Gainesway of Lexington 1997. Grade 1 1973-'79. Grade 2 1980-'96. Matchmaker S. 1967-2001. Matchmaker H. 2002-'04. Held at Atlantic City Race Course 1967-'96. 1³⁄₁₆ miles 1967-'96. Dirt 1967-'78, 1983. Track record 1975. Course record 2001.

Tempted Stakes

Grade 3 in 2006. Belmont Park, two-year-olds, fillies, 1 mile, dirt. Held October 30, 2005, with a gross value of $110,000. First held in 1975. First graded in 1980. Stakes record 1:35.40 (1975 Secret Lanvin).

Year	Winner	Jockey	Second	Third	Strs	Time	1st Purse
2005	**Better Now**, 2, 115	J. Castellano	Capote's Crown, 2, 115	Wonder Lady Anne L, 2, 115	7	1:38.35	$66,000

2004	**Summer Raven**, 2, 115	S. Elliott	K. D.'s Shady Lady, 2, 115	Salute, 2, 115	5	1:36.09	$63,960
2003	**La Reina**, 2, 115	J. R. Velazquez	Eye Dazzler, 2, 115	Sisti's Pride, 2, 115	8	1:36.15	66,420
2002	**Chimichurri**, 2, 119	J. R. Velazquez	Reheat, 2, 115	Bonay, 2, 115	8	1:37.52	66,240
2001	**Smok'n Frolic**, 2, 119	J. R. Velazquez	Saintly Action, 2, 115	Wopping, 2, 117	8	1:37.77	66,900
2000	**Two Item Limit**, 2, 117	R. Migliore	Celtic Melody, 2, 115	Twining Star, 2, 115	6	1:38.53	65,520
1999	**Shawnee Country**, 2, 116	J. F. Chavez	To Marquet, 2, 114	Marigalante, 2, 116	5	1:38.60	65,460
1998	**Oh What a Windfall**, 2, 121	J. D. Bailey	La Ville Rouge, 2, 114	Honour a Bull, 2, 114	8	1:39.84	66,120
1997	**Dancing With Ruth**, 2, 118	T. G. Turner	Soft Senorita, 2, 118	Aunt Anne, 2, 116	6	1:37.40	65,340
1996	**Ajina**, 2, 112	J. D. Bailey	Glitter Woman, 2, 114	Aldiza, 2, 114	7	1:36.59	66,240
1994	**Special Broad**, 2, 114	J. A. Krone	Carson Creek, 2, 114	Golden Bri, 2, 114	7	1:37.20	66,000
1993	**Sovereign Kitty**, 2, 112	J. R. Velazquez	Seeking the Circle, 2, 112	Her Temper, 2, 112	8	1:46.84	69,720
1992	**True Affair**, 2, 121	J. Bravo	Broad Gains, 2, 121	Touch of Love, 2, 114	6	1:47.48	68,520
1991	**Deputation**, 2, 114	D. W. Lidberg	Turnback the Alarm, 2, 121	Bless Our Home, 2, 114	9	1:46.74	72,600
1990	**Flawlessly**, 2, 121	J. D. Bailey	Debutant's Halo, 2, 121	Slept Thru It, 2, 114	12	1:46.60	56,250
1989	**Worth Avenue**, 2, 113	R. P. Romero	Crown Quest, 2, 119	Voodoo Lily, 2, 114	6	1:46.80	69,480
1988	**Box Office Gold**, 2, 116	J. A. Santos	Dreamy Mimi, 2, 116	Surging, 2, 116	5	1:46.20	57,600
1987	**Thirty Eight Go Go**, 2, 121	K. Desormeaux	Best Number, 2, 114	Dangerous Type, 2, 116	9	1:44.60	100,920
1986	**Silent Turn**, 2, 119	C. W. Antley	Grecian Flight, 2, 119	Chase the Dream, 2, 119	11	1:46.20	74,400
1985	**Cosmic Tiger**, 2, 121	E. Maple	Tracy's Espoir, 2, 114	Roses for Avie, 2, 114	10	1:46.80	68,580
1984	**Willowy Mood**, 2, 121	J. Velasquez	Koluctoo's Jill, 2, 114	Easy Step, 2, 116	12	1:46.20	57,330
1983	**Surely Georgie's**, 2, 113	R. Hernandez	Baroness Direct, 2, 114	Dumdedumdedum, 2, 114	8	1:39.60	34,320
1982	**Only Queens**, 2, 114	M. A. Rivera	Future Fun, 2, 113	Blue Garter, 2, 114	6	1:37.00	33,180
1981	**Choral Group**, 2, 121	J. Velasquez	Michelle Mon Amour, 2, 114	Middle Stage, 2, 113	7	1:38.00	33,000
1980	**Tina Tina Too**, 2, 114	C. B. Asmussen	Prayers'n Promises, 2, 121	Explosive Kingdom, 2, 114	6	1:38.40	32,580
1979	**Genuine Risk**, 2, 114	J. Vasquez	Street Ballet, 2, 117	Tell a Secret, 2, 114	9	1:36.00	33,060
1978	**Whisper Fleet**, 2, 119	A. T. Cordero Jr.	Run Cosmic Run, 2, 114	Distinct Honor, 2, 113	6	1:36.20	25,665
1977	**Caesar's Wish**, 2, 116	G. McCarron	Itsamaza, 2, 116	Lucinda Lea, 2, 114	13	1:36.20	22,635
1976	**Pearl Necklace**, 2, 114	A. T. Cordero Jr.	Our Mims, 2, 113	Road Princess, 2, 115	10	1:39.60	22,380
1975	**Secret Lanvin**, 2, 113	J. Cruguet	Free Journey, 2, 121	Imaflash, 2, 113	9	**1:35.40**	33,600

Named for Mrs. Philip duPont's 1959 champion older female and '59 Ladies H. winner Tempted (1955 f. by *Half Crown). Grade 2 1981-'82, 1988. Held at Aqueduct 1975-'94, 1996-2000, 2002-'04. Not held 1995. $1\frac{1}{16}$ miles 1984-'93.

Test Stakes

Grade 1 in 2006. Saratoga Race Course, three-year-olds, fillies, 7 furlongs, dirt. Held August 6, 2005, with a gross value of $250,000. First held in 1922. First graded in 1973. Stakes record 1:20.83 (2003 Lady Tak).

Year	Winner	Jockey	Second	Third	Strs	Time	1st Purse
2005	**Leave Me Alone**, 3, 118	K. Desormeaux	Hide and Chic, 3, 116	In the Gold, 3, 120	9	1:22.76	$150,000
2004	**Society Selection**, 3, 120	E. S. Prado	Bending Strings, 3, 120	Forest Music, 3, 118	12	1:23.69	150,000
2003	**Lady Tak**, 3, 122	J. D. Bailey	Bird Town, 3, 122	House Party, 3, 122	7	**1:20.83**	150,000
2002	**You**, 3, 123	J. D. Bailey	Carson Hollow, 3, 120	Spring Meadow, 3, 120	7	1:22.84	150,000
2001	**Victory Ride**, 3, 116	E. S. Prado	Xtra Heat, 3, 123	Nasty Storm, 3, 120	8	1:21.72	150,000
2000	**Dream Supreme**, 3, 115	P. Day	Big Bambu, 3, 118	Finder's Fee, 3, 123	11	1:22.66	150,000
1999	**Marley Vale**, 3, 114	J. R. Velazquez	Awful Smart, 3, 114	Emanating, 3, 114	11	1:22.77	150,000
1998	**Jersey Girl**, 3, 123	M. E. Smith	Brave Deed, 3, 114	Catinca, 3, 114	11	1:23.02	120,000
1997	**Fabulously Fast**, 3, 114	J. D. Bailey	Aldiza, 3, 114	Pearl City, 3, 117	9	1:21.65	90,000
1996	**Capote Belle**, 3, 115	J. R. Velazquez	Flat Fleet Feet, 3, 115	J J'sdream, 3, 123	8	1:21.08	90,000
1995	**Chaposa Springs**, 3, 120	J. D. Bailey	Miss Golden Circle, 3, 114	Daijin, 3, 123	9	1:21.81	90,000
1994	**Twist Afleet**, 3, 114	J. D. Bailey	Penny's Reshoot, 3, 118	Heavenly Prize, 3, 121	8	1:22.08	90,000
1993	**Missed the Storm**, 3, 114	M. E. Smith	Miss Indy Anna, 3, 114	Educated Risk, 3, 114	5	1:22.12	90,000
1992	**November Snow**, 3, 116	C. W. Antley	Meafara, 3, 114	Preach, 3, 116	8	1:21.33	105,480
1991	**Versailles Treaty**, 3, 114	A. T. Cordero Jr.	Ifyoucouldseemenow, 3, 121	‡Classy Women, 3, 116	7	1:22.85	104,040
1990	**Go for Wand**, 3, 124	R. P. Romero	Screen Prospect, 3, 118	Token Dance, 3, 118	10	1:21.00	73,440
1989	**Safely Kept**, 3, 121	C. Perret	Fantastic Find, 3, 114	Cojinx, 3, 116	5	1:21.40	101,520
1988	**Fara's Team**, 3, 121	J. D. Bailey	Lake Valley, 3, 114	Classic Crown, 3, 121	10	1:22.60	109,980
1987	**Very Subtle**, 3, 121	P. A. Valenzuela	Up the Apalachee, 3, 121	Silent Turn, 3, 121	14	1:21.00	116,280
1986	**Storm and Sunshine**, 3, 118	C. Perret	Classy Cathy, 3, 121	I'm Sweets, 3, 121	7	1:22.80	103,500
1985	**Lady's Secret**, 3, 121	J. Velasquez	Mom's Command, 3, 124	Majestic Folly, 3, 118	10	1:21.60	99,600
1984	**Sintra**, 3, 116	K. K. Allen	Wild Applause, 3, 121	Lucky Lucky Lucky, 3, 124	9	1:22.60	101,040
1983	**Lass Trump**, 3, 114	P. Day	Medieval Moon, 3, 121	Chic Belle, 3, 114	9	1:22.20	34,380
1982	**Gold Beauty**, 3, 116	D. Brumfield	Ambassador of Luck, 3, 121	Number, 3, 114	12	1:22.80	35,940
1981	**Cherokee Frolic**, 3, 121	G. Cohen	Maddy's Tune, 3, 114	Discorama, 3, 118	6	1:23.20	34,140
1980	**Love Sign**, 3, 116	A. T. Cordero Jr.	Weber City Miss, 3, 124	Andrea F., 3, 114	7	1:22.20	33,900
1979	**Blitey**, 3, 114	A. T. Cordero Jr.	Jameela, 3, 118	Spanish Fake, 3, 121	10	1:22.60	25,987
	Clef d'Argent, 3, 114	R. Hernandez	Alada, 3, 114	Syncopating Lady, 3, 114	10	1:22.20	25,988
1978	**White Star Line**, 3, 121	J. Fell	Silken Delight, 3, 114	Zerelda, 3, 114	8	1:21.40	22,095
	Tingle Stone, 3, 114	R. Hernandez	Mucchina, 3, 121	Summer Fling, 3, 116	7	1:22.00	22,020
1977	**Small Raja**, 3, 124	M. Solomone	Pressing Date, 3, 114	Pearl Necklace, 3, 116	9	1:21.80	22,275
	Northern Sea, 3, 121	J. Velasquez	Northernette, 3, 121	Flying Above, 3, 114	8	1:22.40	22,200
1976	**Ivory Wand**, 3, 114	P. Day	Doc Shah's Siren, 3, 116	Pacific Princess, 3, 114	10	1:23.00	22,500
1975	**Hot n Nasty**, 3, 122	J. E. Tejeira	A Charm, 3, 113	Alpine Lass, 3, 116	7	1:22.00	19,665
	My Juliet, 3, 116	J. Vasquez	Slip Screen, 3, 113	‡Funalon, 3, 113	7	1:22.00	19,590
1974	**Quaze Quilt**, 3, 121	J. Vasquez	Maud Muller, 3, 113	Clear Copy, 3, 121	11	1:22.40	20,385
	Maybellene, 3, 116	D. Meade Jr.	Raisela, 3, 116	Stage Door Betty, 3, 121	11	1:23.60	20,385

1973	**Desert Vixen**, 3, 121	J. Velasquez	Full of Hope, 3, 118	Clandenita, 3, 118	5	1:23.00	$13,470
	Waltz Fan, 3, 118	J. Velasquez	Gallant Davelle, 3, 116	Tuerta, 3, 116	7	1:23.60	13,545

Sometimes used as a prep or "test" for the Alabama S. (G1) later in the meet. Grade 2 1973-'74, 1979-'87. Grade 3 1975-'78. Held at Belmont Park 1943-'45. Not held 1923-'25, 1961. 1¼ miles 1922. Two divisions 1973-'75, 1977-'79. ‡Fleet Victress finished third, DQ to fourth, 1975 (2nd Div.). ‡Zama Hummer finished third, DQ to sixth, 1991.

Texas Mile Stakes

Grade 3 in 2006. Lone Star Park, three-year-olds and up, 1 mile, dirt. Held April 29, 2006, with a gross value of $300,000. First held in 1997. First graded in 1999. Stakes record 1:34.44 (1997 Isitingood).

Year	Winner	Jockey	Second	Third	Strs	Time	1st Purse
2006	**Preachinatthebar**, 5, 120	J. K. Court	Stockholder, 6, 116	Texcess, 4, 116	11	1:36.81	$165,000
2005	**High Strike Zone**, 5, 118	R. J. Faul	Supah Blitz, 5, 120	Twilight Road, 8, 118	6	1:35.34	185,000
2004	**Kela**, 6, 119	D. C. Nuesch	Supah Blitz, 4, 116	Yessirgeneralsir, 4, 114	8	1:35.64	175,000
2003	**Bluesthestandard**, 6, 120	M. A. Pedroza	Bonapaw, 7, 116	Compendium, 5, 116	9	1:35.68	170,000
2002	**Unrullah Bull**, 5, 116	A. J. Lovato	Reba's Gold, 5, 118	Compendium, 4, 116	9	1:37.78	170,000
2001	**Dixie Dot Com**, 6, 116	D. R. Flores	Mr Ross, 6, 120	Five Straight, 4, 115	7	1:34.72	180,000
2000	**Sir Bear**, 7, 116	E. Coa	Lexington Park, 4, 118	Luftikus, 4, 118	9	1:35.98	170,000
1999	**Littlebitlively**, 5, 116	C. Gonzalez	Real Quiet, 4, 116	Allen's Oop, 4, 113	8	1:35.65	145,000
1998	**Littlebitlively**, 4, 118	C. Gonzalez	Anet, 4, 116	Scott's Scoundrel, 6, 118	5	1:37.07	160,000
1997	**Isitingood**, 6, 123	D. R. Flores	Spiritbound, 5, 116	Skip Away, 4, 116	7	**1:34.44**	150,000

Texas is the home state of Lone Star Park.

The Very One Handicap

Grade 3 in 2006. Gulfstream Park, three-year-olds and up, fillies and mares, 1$\frac{7}{16}$ miles, turf. Held March 4, 2006, with a gross value of $100,000. First held in 1987. First graded in 1996. Stakes record 2:18.81 (2006 Dynamite Lass).

Year	Winner	Jockey	Second	Third	Strs	Time	1st Purse
2006	**Dynamite Lass**, 4, 114	R. Bejarano	Olaya, 4, 118	Noble Stella (Ger), 5, 116	10	**2:18.81**	$60,000
2005	**Honey Ryder**, 4, 114	J. R. Velazquez	Briviesca (GB), 4, 114	Vous, 4, 113	10	2:11.71	60,000
2004	**Binya (Ger)**, 5, 114	J. R. Velazquez	Ocean Silk, 4, 115	Boana (Ger), 6, 114	12	2:19.65	60,000
2003	**San Dare**, 5, 116	M. Guidry	Tweedside, 5, 115	Hi Tech Honeycomb, 4, 113	12	2:13.76	60,000
2002	**Moon Queen (Ire)**, 4, 118	J. D. Bailey	Jennasietta, 4, 114	Sweetest Thing, 4, 115	6	2:18.38	60,000
2001	**Innuendo (Ire)**, 6, 115	J. D. Bailey	Lucky Lune (Fr), 4, 114	Silver Bandana, 5, 114	10	2:13.62	60,000
2000	**My Sweet Westly**, 4, 110	P. Day	I'm Indy Mood, 5, 114	Manoa, 5, 114	6	2:06.79	45,000
1999	**Delilah (Ire)**, 5, 116	J. D. Bailey	Starry Dreamer, 5, 114	Justenuffheart, 4, 113	8	2:13.45	45,000
1998	**Shemozzle (Ire)**, 5, 114	J. R. Velazquez	Turkappeal, 5, 114	Yokama, 5, 119	8	2:19.06	45,000
1997	**Tocopilla (Arg)**, 7, 114	B. D. Peck	Ampulla, 6, 123	Beyrouth, 5, 113	6	2:14.35	45,000
1996	**Electric Society (Ire)**, 5, 113	M. E. Smith	Northern Emerald, 6, 117	Chelsey Flower, 5, 114	13	2:15.23	30,000
1995	**P J Floral**, 6, 113	S. J. Sellers	Trampoli, 6, 118	Memories (Ire), 4, 113	6	2:14.44	30,000
1994	**Russian Tango**, 4, 112	J. D. Bailey	Maxamount, 6, 116	Camiunch, 5, 112	6	2:02.58	30,000
1993	**Fairy Garden**, 5, 113	W. S. Ramos	Trampoli, 4, 115	Tango Charlie, 4, 114	11	2:14.67	30,000
1992	**Bungalow**, 5, 112	S. J. Sellers	Raffinierte (Ire), 4, 110	Lover's Quest, 4, 109	7	2:05.79	30,000
1991	**Rigamajig**, 5, 116	R. P. Romero	Star Standing, 4, 114	Ahead (GB), 4, 112	11	2:15.10	30,000
1990	**Storm of Glory**, 6, 113	J. D. Bailey	Tukwila, 4, 110	Topicount, 5, 113	8	1:25.00	30,000
1987	**First Prediction**, 5, 114	J. M. Pezua	Thirty Zip, 4, 113	Lady of the North, 4, 110	11	1:35.20	37,620

Named for Mrs. Helen M. Polinger's 1981 Orchid H. (G2) winner The Very One (1975 f. by One for All). Not graded 2000. Not held 1988-'89. 1 mile 1987. 7 furlongs 1990. 1¼ miles 1992, 1994, 2000. About 1⅜ miles 1998, 2002. 1⅜ miles 1988-'89, 1991, 1993, 1995-'97, 1999-2001, 2003-'05. Dirt 1990, 1992, 1994, 2000. Four-year-olds and up 1996. Course record 2006.

Thoroughbred Club of America Stakes

Grade 3 in 2006. Keeneland Race Course, three-year-olds and up, fillies and mares, 6 furlongs, dirt. Held October 16, 2005, with a gross value of $300,000. First held in 1981. First graded in 1988. Stakes record 1:08.70 (1998 Bourbon Belle).

Year	Winner	Jockey	Second	Third	Strs	Time	1st Purse
2005	**Reunited**, 3, 116	R. Albarado	Miss Terrible (Arg), 6, 122	Savorthetime, 6, 118	10	1:11.59	$186,000
2004	**Molto Vita**, 4, 122	R. Bejarano	My Trusty Cat, 4, 124	My Boston Gal, 4, 118	6	1:09.92	77,500
2003	**Summer Mis**, 4, 122	R. R. Douglas	Don't Countess Out, 4, 122	Born to Dance, 4, 122	10	1:09.77	77,500
2002	**French Riviera**, 3, 116	D. J. Meche	Don't Countess Out, 3, 120	Away, 5, 122	10	1:09.75	77,500
2001	**Cat Cay**, 4, 118	P. Day	Spanish Glitter, 3, 120	Another, 4, 124	7	1:09.24	67,580
2000	**Katz Me If You Can**, 3, 115	J. F. Chavez	Hurricane Bertie, 5, 123	My Alibi, 4, 117	6	1:09.42	67,394
1999	**‡Cinemine**, 4, 120	E. M. Martin Jr.	Bourbon Belle, 4, 122	Lucky Again, 3, 114	5	1:08.86	62,000
1998	**Bourbon Belle**, 3, 111	W. Martinez	J J'sdream, 5, 121	Meter Maid, 4, 121	8	**1:08.70**	62,000
1997	**Sky Blue Pink**, 3, 111	P. Day	Bluffing Girl, 3, 114	Mama's Pro, 4, 116	7	1:10.06	62,000
1996	**Surprising Fact**, 3, 110	P. Day	Morris Code, 4, 118	Mama's Pro, 3, 113	9	1:10.14	62,000
1995	**Cat Appeal**, 3, 116	D. M. Barton	Russian Flight (Ire), 3, 113	Traverse City, 5, 118	9	1:10.02	46,500
1994	**Tenacious Tiffany**, 4, 113	C. Perret	Roamin Rachel, 4, 120	Jeano, 6, 120	7	1:11.00	46,500
1993	**Jeano**, 5, 120	P. Day	Apelia, 4, 117	Fluttery Danseur, 4, 120	6	1:09.39	46,500
1992	**Ifyoucouldseemenow**, 4, 120	C. Perret	Harbour Club, 5, 117	Madam Bear, 4, 117	8	1:09.67	48,750
1991	**Avie Jane**, 7, 117	C. Perret	Amen, 4, 114	Hoga, 5, 114	6	1:10.24	48,750
1990	**Safely Kept**, 4, 123	C. Perret	Volterra, 5, 112	Medicine Woman, 5, 117	5	1:10.40	48,750
1989	**Plate Queen**, 4, 117	R. P. Romero	Degenerate Gal, 4, 114	Social Pro, 4, 123	8	1:11.20	48,750
1988	**Tappiano**, 4, 123	J. Vasquez	Bound, 4, 117	Pine Tree Lane, 6, 123	7	1:10.20	48,750

1987	**‡There Are Rainbows**, 7, 120	R. Fletcher	Weekend Delight, 5, 123	Ten Thousand Stars, 5, 120	7	1:11.00	$32,500
1986	**Zenobia Empress**, 5, 117	E. Fires	Endear, 4, 120	Weekend Delight, 4, 123	11	1:11.80	32,500
1985	**Boldara**, 4, 114	P. Rubbicco	Shamrock Boat, 4, 114	Space Angel, 5, 120	8	1:10.80	32,500
1984	**Bids and Blades**, 3, 114	D. Brumfield	Lass Trump, 4, 123	Grecian Comedy, 4, 123	8	1:11.60	32,500
1983	**Excitable Lady**, 5, 111	P. Day	Wendy's Ten, 4, 114	A Status Symbol, 4, 111	4	1:09.80	31,250
1982	**Excitable Lady**, 4, 123	D. G. McHargue	Privacy, 4, 117	Arbutus Toehold, 4, 114	10	1:09.20	27,350
1981	**Gold Treasure**, 4, 111	M. S. Sellers	Sweet Revenge, 3, 109	Weber City Miss, 4, 114	8	1:10.20	21,250

Named for the Thoroughbred Club of America, whose headquarters is a short distance from Keeneland. Thoroughbred Club Dinner S. 1981-'82. ‡Zigbelle finished first, DQ to fourth, 1987. ‡Bourbon Belle finished first, DQ to second, 1999.

Toboggan Handicap

Grade 3 in 2006. Aqueduct, three-year-olds and up, 6 furlongs. Held March 11, 2006, with a gross value of $107,400. First held in 1890. First graded in 1973. Stakes record 1:09.09 (2003 Affirmed Success).

Year	Winner	Jockey	Second	Third	Strs	Time	1st Purse
2006	**Kazoo**, 8, 116	R. Migliore	Bishop Court Hill, 6, 117	Wild Jam, 5, 115	6	1:09.22	$64,440
2005	**Primary Suspect**, 4, 115	P. Fragoso	Shake You Down, 7, 122	Houston's Prayer, 5, 115	6	1:09.47	64,260
2004	**Well Fancied**, 6, 118	E. Coa	Gators N Bears, 4, 115	Don Six, 4, 113	10	1:22.06	67,320
2003	**Affirmed Success**, 9, 118	R. Migliore	Peeping Tom, 6, 117	Captain Red, 6, 115	6	**1:09.09**	65,460
2002	**Affirmed Success**, 8, 119	R. Migliore	Vodka, 5, 114	Multiple Choice, 4, 111	6	1:22.87	64,920
2001	**Peeping Tom**, 4, 118	S. Bridgmohan	Say Florida Sandy, 7, 117	Lake Pontchartrain, 6, 113	6	1:21.25	64,380
2000	**Brutally Frank**, 6, 114	S. Bridgmohan	Master O Foxhounds, 5, 114	Watchman's Warning, 5, 113	8	1:20.77	49,410
1999	**Wouldn't We All**, 5, 114	R. Migliore	Brushed On, 4, 115	Esteemed Friend, 5, 120	7	1:20.95	48,900
1998	**Home On the Ridge**, 4, 114	W. H. McCauley	Wire Me Collect, 5, 118	King Roller, 7, 116	7	1:23.01	49,650
1997	**Royal Haven**, 5, 115	R. Migliore	Jamies First Punch, 4, 115	Cold Execution, 6, 113	6	1:22.40	48,600
1996	**Placid Fund**, 4, 112	J. F. Chavez	Valid Wager, 4, 116	Pat n Jac, 4, 112	12	1:22.92	51,480
1995	**Boom Towner**, 7, 117	F. Lovato Jr.	Virginia Rapids, 5, 113	Won Song, 5, 112	6	1:23.77	49,080
1994	**Blare of Trumpets**, 5, 112	D. Carr	Preporant, 5, 117	Fabersham, 6, 115	6	1:09.70	49,200
1993	**Argyle Lake**, 7, 109	D. Carr	The Great M. B., 4, 111	Regal Conquest, 5, 110	12	1:10.11	55,530
1992	**Boom Towner**, 4, 115	D. Nelson	Real Minx, 5, 112	Gallant Step, 5, 114	8	1:10.03	52,740
1991	**Bravely Bold**, 5, 115	M. E. Smith	True and Blue, 6, 116	Proud and Valid, 6, 110	8	1:10.71	52,020
1990	**Sunny Blossom**, 5, 117	E. Maple	Diamond Donnie, 4, 111	Once Wild, 5, 123	6	1:09.60	51,300
1989	**Lord of the Night**, 6, 114	J. Velasquez	Teddy Drone, 4, 117	Vinnie the Viper, 6, 115	7	1:10.40	52,290
1988	**Afleet**, 4, 123	G. Stahlbaum	Pinecutter, 4, 115	Vinnie the Viper, 5, 122	4	1:09.20	66,480
1987	**Play the King**, 4, 112	R. Hernandez	Comic Blush, 4, 117	Best by Test, 5, 124	6	1:09.60	50,400
1986	**Rexson's Bishop**, 4, 114	R. R. Baez	Green Shekel, 4, 126	Cullendale, 4, 116	5	1:11.40	50,760
1985	**Fighting Fit**, 6, 123	R. Migliore	Entropy, 5, 123	Shadowmar, 6, 107	6	1:09.60	51,210
1984	**Top Avenger**, 6, 120	A. Graell	Main Stem, 6, 109	Elegant Life, 4, 116	9	1:10.40	43,080
1983	**Mouse Corps**, 5, 111	R. X. Alvarado Jr.	Top Avenger, 5, 123	Prince Valid, 4, 115	7	1:09.40	33,000
1982	**Always Run Lucky**, 4, 110	J. J. Miranda	Swelegant, 4, 113	In From Dixie, 5, 125	7	1:10.00	33,180
1981	**Dr. Blum**, 4, 123	R. Hernandez	Guilty Conscience, 5, 115	Dunham's Gift, 4, 118	4	1:11.20	32,340
1980	**Tilt Up**, 5, 116	J. Fell	Ardaluan (Ire), 4, 111	Double Zeus, 5, 123	5	1:11.00	33,660
1979	**Vencedor**, 5, 127	M. A. Rivera	Jet Diplomacy, 4, 113	Al Battah, 4, 125	8	1:10.00	32,280
1978	**Barrera**, 5, 126	R. Hernandez	Pumpkin Moonshine, 4, 106	Fratello Ed, 4, 121	5	1:08.80	31,890
1977	**Great Above**, 5, 112	S. Cauthen	Full Out, 4, 117	Patriot's Dream, 4, 126	9	1:09.40	32,490
1976	**Due Diligence**, 4, 111	J. Velasquez	*Pompini, 6, 113	Gallant Bob, 4, 129	11	1:10.20	34,740
1975	**†Honorable Miss**, 5, 117	J. Vasquez	Frankie Adams, 4, 116	Startahemp, 5, 121	6	1:09.00	16,350
1974	**Mike John G.**, 4, 112	V. A. Bracciale Jr.	Tap the Tree, 5, 115	Delta Champ, 4, 113	6	1:08.60	16,575
1973	**Tentam**, 4, 122	J. Velasquez	Spanish Riddle, 4, 115	Tap the Tree, 4, 118	7	1:09.40	16,710

Originally the Toboggan Slide H., held on the downhill course at Old Morris Park in the Bronx, New York. Not graded 1975-'83, 1996-2002. Toboggan Slide H. 1890-'94. Held at Morris Park 1890-'94. Held at Belmont Park 1896-1961. Not held 1891, 1895, 1911-'12. 7 furlongs 1896-1909, 1995-2002, 2004. †Denotes female.

Tokyo City Handicap

Grade 3 in 2006. Santa Anita Park, four-year-olds and up, 1⅛ miles, dirt. Held April 1, 2006, with a gross value of $110,600. First held in 1957. First graded in 1973. Stakes record 1:45.80 (1975 Royal Glint; 1976 Zanthe; 1979 Star Spangled).

Year	Winner	Jockey	Second	Third	Strs	Time	1st Purse
2006	**Preachinatthebar**, 5, 116	J. K. Court	Texcess, 4, 116	Melanyhasthepapers, 5, 116	9	1:48.14	$66,360
2005	**Supah Blitz**, 5, 116	V. Espinoza	Outta Here, 5, 116	Ender's Shadow, 5, 114	5	1:48.90	63,600
2004	**Dynever**, 4, 117	C. S. Nakatani	Total Impact (Chi), 6, 116	Even the Score, 6, 116	7	1:48.07	66,360
2003	**Western Pride**, 5, 116	P. A. Valenzuela	Total Impact (Chi), 5, 113	Fleetstreet Dancer, 5, 112	8	1:48.56	90,000
2002	**Bosque Redondo**, 5, 114	C. J. McCarron	Mysterious Cat, 4, 111	Freedom Crest, 6, 116	6	1:49.11	90,000
2001	**Futural**, 5, 115	G. K. Gomez	Irisheyesareflying, 5, 117	Tribunal, 4, 117	5	1:47.87	90,000
2000	**Early Pioneer**, 5, 113	M. S. Garcia	David, 4, 113	General Challenge, 4, 123	5	1:49.08	95,490
1999	**Classic Cat**, 4, 122	G. L. Stevens	Budroyale, 6, 119	Klinsman (Ire), 5, 115	4	1:47.77	90,000
1998	**Budroyale**, 5, 112	M. S. Garcia	Don't Blame Rio, 5, 114	Bagshot, 4, 116	10	1:48.48	100,530
1997	**Benchmark**, 6, 114	C. J. McCarron	Kingdom Found, 7, 115	Private Song, 4, 112	7	1:48.26	97,650
1996	**Del Mar Dennis**, 6, 118	K. Desormeaux	Just Java, 5, 116	Regal Rowdy, 7, 115	6	1:48.37	96,650
1995	**Del Mar Dennis**, 5, 117	C. W. Antley	Wharf, 5, 113	Stoller, 4, 115	8	1:47.27	130,000
1994	**Del Mar Dennis**, 4, 112	S. Gonzalez Jr.	Hill Pass, 5, 115	Tinners Way, 4, 115	8	1:48.36	129,400
1993	**Memo (Chi)**, 6, 114	P. Atkinson	Charmonnier, 5, 117	Marquetry, 6, 118	7	1:47.49	125,800

1992	**Another Review**, 4, 114	K. Desormeaux	Defensive Play, 5, 115	Loach, 4, 116	11	1:47.33	$163,100
1991	**Anshan (GB)**, 4, 115	C. S. Nakatani	Louis Cyphre (Ire), 5, 112	Pleasant Tap, 4, 116	9	1:47.10	158,900
1990	**Ruhlmann**, 5, 123	G. L. Stevens	Criminal Type, 5, 119	Stylish Winner, 6, 113	6	1:47.20	240,800
1989	**Ruhlmann**, 4, 119	L. A. Pincay Jr.	Lively One, 4, 120	Saratoga Passage, 4, 116	6	1:47.20	185,600
1988	**Alysheba**, 4, 127	C. J. McCarron	Ferdinand, 5, 127	Good Taste (Arg), 6, 113	5	1:47.20	350,000
1987	**Judge Angelucci**, 4, 115	W. Shoemaker	Iron Eyes, 4, 116	Grecian Wonder, 4, 113	8	1:48.40	129,400
1986	**Precisionist**, 5, 126	C. J. McCarron	Greinton (GB), 5, 126	Encolure, 4, 116	4	1:47.60	148,200
1985	**Greinton (GB)**, 4, 120	L. A. Pincay Jr.	Precisionist, 4, 127	Al Mamoon, 4, 115	6	1:47.00	117,300
1984	**Journey At Sea**, 5, 122	W. A. Guerra	My Habitony, 4, 118	Fighting Fit, 5, 121	5	1:48.00	102,050
1983	**The Wonder (Fr)**, 5, 122	W. Shoemaker	Konewah, 4, 112	Swing Till Dawn, 4, 119	6	1:49.20	62,500
1982	**Super Moment**, 5, 124	C. J. McCarron	Mehmet, 4, 116	It's the One, 4, 126	5	1:48.60	75,450
1981	**Borzoi**, 5, 118	W. Shoemaker	Shamgo, 5, 117	King Go Go, 6, 122	8	1:46.20	64,700
1980	**Peregrinator (Ire)**, 5, 115	C. J. McCarron	Lunar Probe (NZ), 6, 116	Henschel, 6, 120	8	1:47.80	65,300
1979	**Star Spangled**, 5, 117	L. A. Pincay Jr.	Farnesio (Arg), 5, 118	State Dinner, 4, 118	6	**1:45.80**	46,900
1978	**J. O. Tobin**, 4, 123	S. Cauthen	Henschel, 4, 115	Riot in Paris, 7, 119	6	1:47.80	31,950
1977	**Today 'n Tomorrow**, 4, 112	S. Hawley	Exact Duplicate, 5, 115	Rajab, 4, 114	9	1:46.40	35,300
1976	**Zanthe**, 7, 118	S. Hawley	Riot in Paris, 5, 121	Mateor, 5, 114	6	**1:45.80**	34,300
1975	**Royal Glint**, 5, 120	W. Shoemaker	Against the Snow, 5, 115	June's Love, 4, 115	8	**1:45.80**	34,800
1974	**Court Ruling**, 4, 117	B. Baeza	Captain Cee Jay, 4, 119	Acclimatization, 6, 115	8	1:48.40	25,900
	Wichita Oil, 6, 116	L. A. Pincay Jr.	*Madison Palace, 6, 117	Woodland Pines, 5, 118	8	1:47.60	25,800
1973	**Quack**, 4, 125	D. Pierce	River Buoy, 8, 119	Curious Course, 4, 112	8	1:49.00	36,500

Named for Tokyo City Racecourse in Japan, one of Santa Anita's sister racetracks. Formerly named for Rancho San Bernardino, location of the present-day city of San Bernardino, California. San Bernardino H. 1957-2004. Grade 2 1973-'77, 1979-2000. Not graded 1978. 1$^{1}/_{16}$ miles 1957-'66, 1974. Turf 1957-'72, 1974-'78. Originally scheduled on turf 1973. Three-year-olds 1957. Three-year-olds and up 1958-'67. Two divisions 1974, 2004. Equaled course record 1975.

Tom Fool Handicap

Grade 2 in 2006. Belmont Park, three-year-olds and up, 7 furlongs, dirt. Held July 17, 2005, with a gross value of $150,000. First held in 1975. First graded in 1981. Stakes record 1:20.17 (2002 Left Bank).

Year	Winner	Jockey	Second	Third	Strs	Time	1st Purse
2005	**Smokume**, 4, 115	C. Sutherland	Willy o'the Valley, 4, 115	Clever Electrician, 6, 114	6	1:21.92	$90,000
2004	**Ghostzapper**, 4, 119	J. Castellano	Aggadan, 5, 114	Unforgettable Max, 4, 114	4	1:20.42	90,000
2003	**Aldebaran**, 5, 122	J. D. Bailey	Peeping Tom, 6, 117	State City, 4, 118	7	1:22.54	90,000
2002	**Left Bank**, 5, 121	J. R. Velazquez	Affirmed Success, 8, 120	Summer Note, 5, 113	6	**1:20.17**	90,000
2001	**Exchange Rate**, 4, 114	J. D. Bailey	Say Florida Sandy, 7, 117	Here's Zealous, 4, 112	5	1:21.24	90,000
2000	**Trippi**, 3, 112	J. D. Bailey	Cornish Snow, 7, 113	Sailor's Warning, 4, 111	6	1:21.69	90,000
1999	**Crafty Friend**, 6, 116	R. Migliore	Affirmed Success, 5, 119	Artax, 4, 117	5	1:20.62	90,000
1998	**Banker's Gold**, 4, 115	J. F. Chavez	Boundless Moment, 6, 115	Partner's Hero, 4, 114	6	1:21.04	90,000
1997	**Diligence**, 4, 116	J. A. Santos	Royal Haven, 5, 118	Elusive Quality, 4, 114	7	1:22.40	90,000
1996	**Kayrawan**, 4, 113	R. Migliore	Cold Execution, 5, 112	Lite the Fuse, 5, 122	5	1:22.95	64,860
1995	**Lite the Fuse**, 4, 117	J. A. Krone	Our Emblem, 4, 115	Evil Bear, 5, 118	6	1:21.72	65,220
1994	**Virginia Rapids**, 4, 124	J. Samyn	Cherokee Run, 4, 121	Boundary, 4, 119	5	1:22.27	64,380
1993	**Birdonthewire**, 4, 119	C. Perret	Fly So Free, 5, 119	Take Me Out, 5, 119	5	1:20.93	67,680
1992	**Rubiano**, 5, 126	J. A. Krone	Take Me Out, 4, 119	Arrowtown, 4, 119	8	1:21.70	70,920
1991	**Mr. Nasty**, 4, 119	A. T. Cordero Jr.	Rubiano, 4, 121	Senor Speedy, 4, 119	4	1:21.79	67,800
1990	**Quick Call**, 6, 119	J. F. Chavez	Sewickley, 5, 123	Traskwood, 4, 119	5	1:21.40	52,680
1989	**Sewickley**, 4, 119	R. P. Romero	Houston, 3, 114	Crusader Sword, 4, 119	6	1:24.00	67,920
1988	**King's Swan**, 8, 128	A. T. Cordero Jr.	Gulch, 4, 128	Abject, 4, 119	4	1:22.40	100,980
1987	**Groovy**, 4, 128	A. T. Cordero Jr.	Sun Master, 6, 121	Moment of Hope, 4, 119	6	1:22.40	81,900
1986	**Groovy**, 3, 112	J. A. Santos	Phone Trick, 4, 126	Basket Weave, 5, 119	5	1:21.60	80,460
1985	**Track Barron**, 4, 123	A. T. Cordero Jr.	Mt. Livermore, 4, 126	Cannon Shell, 6, 126	6	1:22.00	82,260
1984	**Believe the Queen**, 4, 126	J. Velasquez	A Phenomenon, 4, 119	Cannon Shell, 5, 121	6	1:22.40	70,680
1983	**Deputy Minister**, 4, 126	D. MacBeth	Fit to Fight, 4, 119	Maudlin, 5, 126	9	1:22.20	52,020
1982	**Rise Jim**, 6, 119	A. T. Cordero Jr.	Maudlin, 4, 119	And More, 4, 119	5	1:23.80	32,940
1981	**Rise Jim**, 5, 119	A. T. Cordero Jr.	Proud Appeal, 3, 121	Rivalero, 5, 119	6	1:21.20	32,820
1980	**Plugged Nickle**, 3, 121	J. Fell	Dr. Patches, 6, 119	Isella, 5, 119	6	1:22.20	33,060
1979	**Cox's Ridge**, 5, 119	E. Maple	Nice Catch, 5, 121	Tilt Up, 4, 119	5	1:22.20	25,500
1978	**J. O. Tobin**, 4, 129	J. Fell	White Rammer, 4, 119	It's Freezing, 6, 116	8	1:20.80	25,950
1977	**Mexican General**, 4, 115	C. Perret	Full Out, 4, 119	Sticky Situation, 4, 110	9	1:22.00	22,605
1976	**El Pitirre**, 4, 114	A. T. Cordero Jr.	Nalees Knight, 5, 110	†Honorable Miss, 6, 118	6	1:24.40	26,550
1975	**Kinsman Hope**, 5, 116	J. Ruane	Lonetree, 5, 125	Right Mind, 4, 113	9	1:21.40	26,925

Named for Greentree Stable's 1953 Horse of the Year and '53 Carter H. winner Tom Fool (1949 c. by Menow). Grade 3 1981. Tom Fool S. 1979-'95. Held at Aqueduct 1975-'76. †Denotes female.

Top Flight Handicap

Grade 2 in 2006. Aqueduct, three-year-olds and up, fillies and mares, 1 mile, dirt. Held November 25, 2005, with a gross value of $150,000. First held in 1940. First graded in 1973. Stakes record 1:34.96 (1994 Educated Risk).

Year	Winner	Jockey	Second	Third	Strs	Time	1st Purse
2005	**Stellar Jayne**, 4, 123	J. D. Bailey	Bohemian Lady, 4, 115	Seeking the Ante, 3, 116	8	1:35.94	$90,000
2004	**Daydreaming**, 3, 117	J. D. Bailey	Bending Strings, 3, 118	Roar Emotion, 4, 116	6	1:35.29	90,000
2003	**Randaroo**, 3, 116	H. Castillo Jr.	Beauty Halo (Arg), 4, 115	Pocus Hocus, 5, 116	12	1:36.49	90,000
2002	**Sightseek**, 3, 113	J. D. Bailey	Zonk, 4, 116	Nasty Storm, 4, 116	9	1:35.46	90,000

2001	**Cat Cay**, 4, 117	J. R. Velazquez	Tugger, 4, 116	Atelier, 4, 120	9	1:35.45	$90,000
2000	**Reciclada (Chi)**, 5, 116	J. D. Bailey	Country Hideaway, 4, 120	Critical Eye, 3, 120	8	1:35.54	90,000
1999	**Belle Cherie**, 3, 113	J. R. Velazquez	dh-Furlough, 5, 118 dh-Harpia, 5, 117		7	1:35.46	90,000
1998	**Catinca**, 3, 119	R. Migliore	Furlough, 4, 115	Glitter Woman, 4, 120	5	1:35.81	90,000
1997	**Dixie Flag**, 3, 117	M. J. Luzzi	Aldiza, 3, 114	Mil Kilates, 4, 117	9	1:35.34	90,000
1996	**Flat Fleet Feet**, 3, 116	M. E. Smith	Queen Tutta, 4, 114	Miss Golden Circle, 4, 116	9	1:37.00	90,000
1995	**Twist Afleet**, 4, 123	M. E. Smith	Chaposa Springs, 3, 118	Lotta Dancing, 4, 114	8	1:35.26	90,000
1994	**Educated Risk**, 4, 120	M. E. Smith	Triumph At Dawn, 4, 111	Imah, 4, 111	8	**1:34.96**	90,000
1993	**You'd Be Surprised**, 4, 112	J. D. Bailey	Looie Capote, 4, 115	Shared Interest, 5, 114	7	1:48.82	90,000
1992	**Firm Stance**, 4, 114	P. Day	Haunting, 4, 112	Lady d'Accord, 5, 117	14	1:50.55	120,000
1991	**Buy the Firm**, 5, 119	J. A. Krone	Colonial Waters, 6, 118	Sharp Dance, 5, 113	5	1:52.30	120,000
1990	**Dreamy Mimi**, 4, 111	J. D. Bailey	She Can, 3, 108	Survive, 6, 120	7	1:50.40	136,800
1989	**Banker's Lady**, 4, 121	A. T. Cordero Jr.	Colonial Waters, 4, 114	Aptostar, 4, 117	5	1:51.20	133,680
1988	**Clabber Girl**, 5, 117	J. A. Santos	Psyched, 5, 112	Cadillacing, 4, 113	9	1:49.40	141,840
1987	**Ms. Eloise**, 4, 116	R. G. Davis	Beth's Song, 5, 111	Clemanna's Rose, 6, 115	8	1:50.20	138,480
1986	**Ride Sally**, 4, 123	W. A. Guerra	Squan Song, 5, 124	Leecoo, 5, 107	6	1:49.20	148,140
1985	**Flip's Pleasure**, 5, 117	J. Samyn	Sintrillium, 7, 119	Some for All, 4, 110	5	1:51.00	101,160
1984	**Sweet Missus**, 4, 103	R. J. Thibeau Jr.	Lady Norcliffe, 4, 115	Adept, 5, 110	7	1:50.20	104,040
1983	**Adept**, 4, 109	K. L. Rogers	Broom Dance, 4, 122	Dance Number, 4, 115	6	1:50.00	65,160
1982	**Andover Way**, 4, 121	J. Velasquez	Anti Lib, 4, 113	Discorama, 4, 116	9	1:50.00	66,360
1981	**Chain Bracelet**, 4, 115	R. Hernandez	Lady Oakley (Ire), 4, 115	Weber City Miss, 4, 118	5	1:49.60	64,680
1980	**Glorious Song**, 4, 123	J. Velasquez	Misty Gallore, 4, 126	Blitey, 4, 117	7	1:49.60	66,360
1979	**Waya (Fr)**, 5, 128	A. T. Cordero Jr.	Pearl Necklace, 5, 120	Island Kiss, 4, 112	8	1:50.80	64,680
1978	**Northernette**, 4, 121	J. Fell	One Sum, 4, 121	Dottie's Doll, 5, 116	8	1:49.40	48,330
1977	**Shawi**, 4, 111	M. Venezia	Proud Delta, 5, 124	Mississippi Mud, 4, 114	9	1:49.80	48,285
1976	**Proud Delta**, 4, 120	J. Velasquez	Let Me Linger, 4, 116	Spring Is Here, 4, 108	7	1:49.00	49,455
1975	**Twixt**, 6, 125	W. J. Passmore	Heloise, 4, 109	Something Super, 5, 116	8	1:50.60	33,240
1974	**Lady Love**, 4, 114	E. Maple	Krislin, 5, 111	Penny Flight, 4, 115	7	1:48.60	33,120
1973	**Poker Night**, 3, 110	R. Woodhouse	Summer Guest, 4, 123	Roba Bella, 4, 113	7	1:48.20	33,420

Named for C. V. Whitney's 1931 champion two-year-old filly, '32 champion three-year-old filly, and '32 Coaching Club American Oaks winner Top Flight (1929 f. by *Dis Donc). Sponsored by Delta Airlines of Atlanta 1996-2000, 2003, 2005. Grade 1 1973-'96. Delta Top Flight H. 1996-2000, 2003. Held at Belmont Park 1940-'61, 1993. 1$^1/_{16}$ miles 1940-'60. 1$^1/_8$ miles 1961-'93. Four-year-olds and up 1988, 1990. Dead heat for second 1999.

Transylvania Stakes

Grade 3 in 2006. Keeneland Race Course, three-year-olds, 1 mile, turf. Held April 7, 2006, with a gross value of $150,000. First held in 1989. First graded in 2003. Stakes record 1:34.65 (1998 Dog Watch [GB]).

Year	Winner	Jockey	Second	Third	Strs	Time	1st Purse
2006	**Chin High**, 3, 117	S. Bridgmohan	Le Plaix (Fr), 3, 117	Wherethewestbegins, 3, 117	10	1:37.87	$93,000
2005	**Chattahoochee War**, 3, 121	J. D. Bailey	Guillaume Tell (Ire), 3, 117	Rey de Cafe, 3, 121	8	1:35.28	93,000
2004	**Timo**, 3, 123	E. S. Prado	Mr. J. T. L., 3, 116	America Alive, 3, 116	9	1:36.52	70,308
2003	**White Cat**, 3, 116	S. J. Sellers	Deep Shadow, 3, 118	Christmas Away, 3, 116	9	1:34.98	62,000
2002	**Flying Dash (Ger)**, 3, 116	J. D. Bailey	Back Packer, 3, 116	Political Attack, 3, 120	8	1:35.69	62,000
2001	**Baptize**, 3, 120	J. D. Bailey	Dynameaux, 3, 116	Act of Reform, 3, 116	9	1:35.28	70,556
2000	**Field Cat**, 3, 116	M. E. Smith	Lendell Ray, 3, 116	Go Lib Go, 3, 123	9	1:35.19	70,618
1999	**Good Night**, 3, 114	S. J. Sellers	Air Rocket, 3, 114	Make Your Mark, 3, 114	10	1:35.00	70,308
1998	**Dog Watch (GB)**, 3, 116	R. G. Davis	Reformer Rally, 3, 118	American Odyssey, 3, 114	10	**1:34.65**	45,781
1997	**Near the Bank**, 3, 118	P. Day	Daylight Savings, 3, 114	Song for James, 3, 113	6	1:36.40	44,249
1996	**More Royal**, 3, 112	J. A. Krone	Defacto, 3, 121	Rough Opening, 3, 121	5	1:35.92	43,202
1995	**‡Crimson Guard**, 3, 118	M. E. Smith	Dixie Dynasty, 3, 114	‡Nostra, 3, 118	9	1:44.04	42,259
1994	**Star of Manila**, 3, 121	S. J. Sellers	Prix de Crouton, 3, 118	Carpet, 3, 118	6	1:42.87	33,635
1993	**Proud Shot**, 3, 118	W. H. McCauley	Explosive Red, 3, 121	Awad, 3, 121	7	1:44.17	34,364
1992	**Casino Magistrate**, 3, 121	R. D. Lopez	Coaxing Matt, 3, 112	Trans Caribbean, 3, 115	7	1:46.62	35,636
1991	**Eastern Dude**, 3, 121	S. J. Sellers	Magic Interlude, 3, 121	January Man, 3, 112	10	1:42.94	36,514
1990	**Izvestia**, 3, 112	R. P. Romero	Scattered, 3, 115	Divine Warning, 3, 112	9	1:43.80	36,043
1989	**Shy Tom**, 3, 121	R. P. Romero	Once Over Knightly, 3, 118	Ringerman, 3, 121	6	1:50.00	35,133

Named for Transylvania University, the oldest college west of the Allegheny Mountains, founded in 1780 in Lexington. Sponsored by Central Bank of Lexington 2005-'06. 1$^1/_{16}$ miles 1989-'95. ‡Ops Smile finished first, DQ to eighth, 1995. ‡Hawk Attack finished third, DQ to seventh, 1995.

Travers Stakes

Grade 1 in 2006. Saratoga Race Course, three-year-olds, 1$^1/_4$ miles, dirt. Held August 27, 2005, with a gross value of $1,000,000. First held in 1864. First graded in 1973. Stakes record 2:00 (1979 General Assembly).

Year	Winner	Jockey	Second	Third	Strs	Time	1st Purse
2005	**Flower Alley**, 3, 126	J. R. Velazquez	Bellamy Road, 3, 126	Roman Ruler, 3, 126	7	2:02.76	$600,000
2004	**Birdstone**, 3, 126	E. S. Prado	The Cliff's Edge, 3, 126	Eddington, 3, 126	7	2:02.45	600,000
2003	**Ten Most Wanted**, 3, 126	P. Day	Peace Rules, 3, 126	Strong Hope, 3, 126	6	2:02.14	600,000
2002	**Medaglia d'Oro**, 3, 126	J. D. Bailey	Repent, 3, 126	Nothing Flat, 3, 126	9	2:02.53	600,000
2001	**Point Given**, 3, 126	G. L. Stevens	E Dubai, 3, 126	Dollar Bill, 3, 126	9	2:01.40	600,000
2000	**Unshaded**, 3, 126	S. J. Sellers	Albert the Great, 3, 126	Commendable, 3, 126	9	2:02.59	600,000
1999	**Lemon Drop Kid**, 3, 126	J. A. Santos	Vision and Verse, 3, 126	Menifee, 3, 126	8	2:02.19	600,000
1998	**Coronado's Quest**, 3, 126	M. E. Smith	Victory Gallop, 3, 126	Raffie's Majesty, 3, 126	7	2:03.40	450,000
1997	**Deputy Commander**, 3, 126	C. J. McCarron	Behrens, 3, 126	Awesome Again, 3, 126	8	2:04.08	450,000

1996 **Will's Way**, 3, 126	J. F. Chavez	Louis Quatorze, 3, 126	Skip Away, 3, 126	7	2:02.55	$450,000
1995 **Thunder Gulch**, 3, 126	G. L. Stevens	Pyramid Peak, 3, 126	Malthus, 3, 126	7	2:03.70	450,000
1994 **Holy Bull**, 3, 126	M. E. Smith	Concern, 3, 126	Tabasco Cat, 3, 126	5	2:02.03	450,000
1993 **Sea Hero**, 3, 126	J. D. Bailey	Kissin Kris, 3, 126	Miner's Mark, 3, 126	11	2:01.95	600,000
1992 **Thunder Rumble**, 3, 126	W. H. McCauley	Devil His Due, 3, 126	Dance Floor, 3, 126	10	2:00.99	600,000
1991 **Corporate Report**, 3, 126	C. J. McCarron	Hansel, 3, 126	Fly So Free, 3, 126	6	2:01.20	600,000
1990 **Rhythm**, 3, 126	C. Perret	Shot Gun Scott, 3, 126	Sir Richard Lewis, 3, 126	13	2:02.60	707,100
1989 **Easy Goer**, 3, 126	P. Day	Clever Trevor, 3, 126	Shy Tom, 3, 126	6	2:00.80	653,100
1988 **Forty Niner**, 3, 126	C. J. McCarron	Seeking the Gold, 3, 126	Brian's Time, 3, 126	6	2:01.40	653,100
1987 **Java Gold**, 3, 126	P. Day	Cryptoclearance, 3, 126	Polish Navy, 3, 126	9	2:02.00	673,800
1986 **Wise Times**, 3, 126	J. D. Bailey	‡Danzig Connection, 3, 126	Personal Flag, 3, 126	7	2:03.40	203,700
1985 **Chief's Crown**, 3, 126	A. T. Cordero Jr.	Turkoman, 3, 126	Skip Trial, 3, 126	7	2:01.20	202,800
1984 **Carr de Naskra**, 3, 126	L. A. Pincay Jr.	Pine Circle, 3, 126	Morning Bob, 3, 126	9	2:02.60	211,500
1983 **Play Fellow**, 3, 126	P. Day	Slew o' Gold, 3, 126	Hyperborean, 3, 126	7	2:01.00	135,000
1982 **Runaway Groom**, 3, 126	J. Fell	Aloma's Ruler, 3, 126	Conquistador Cielo, 3, 126	5	2:02.60	132,900
1981 **Willow Hour**, 3, 126	E. Maple	Pleasant Colony, 3, 126	Lord Avie, 3, 126	10	2:03.80	135,600
1980 **Temperence Hill**, 3, 126	E. Maple	First Albert, 3, 126	Amber Pass, 3, 126	9	2:02.80	100,980
1979 **General Assembly**, 3, 126	J. Vasquez	Smarten, 3, 126	Private Account, 3, 126	7	**2:00.00**	80,850
1978 **‡Alydar**, 3, 126	J. Velasquez	Affirmed, 3, 126	Nasty and Bold, 3, 126	4	2:02.00	62,880
1977 **‡Jatski**, 3, 126	S. Maple	Run Dusty Run, 3, 126	Silver Series, 3, 126	14	2:01.60	68,160
1976 **Honest Pleasure**, 3, 126	C. Perret	Romeo, 3, 126	Dance Spell, 3, 126	8	2:00.20	65,040
1975 **Wajima**, 3, 126	B. Baeza	Media, 3, 126	Prince Thou Art, 3, 126	5	2:02.00	65,220
1974 **Holding Pattern**, 3, 121	M. Miceli	Little Current, 3, 126	†Chris Evert, 3, 121	11	2:05.20	69,660
1973 **Annihilate 'em**, 3, 120	R. Turcotte	Stop the Music, 3, 122	See the Jaguar, 3, 120	8	2:01.60	68,280

Named for the first president of Saratoga Race Course, William R. Travers; he won the inaugural running with Kentucky. Travers Midsummer Derby 1927-'32. Held at Belmont Park 1943-'45. Not held 1896, 1898, 1900, 1911-'12. 1¾ miles 1864-'89. 1½ miles 1890-'92. 1⅛ miles 1895, 1901-'03. ‡Run Dusty Run finished first, DQ to second, 1977. ‡Affirmed finished first, DQ to second, 1978. ‡Broad Brush finished second, DQ to fourth, 1986. †Denotes female.

Triple Bend Invitational Handicap

Grade 1 in 2006. Hollywood Park, three-year-olds and up, 7 furlongs, dirt. Held July 3, 2005, with a gross value of $350,000. First held in 1952. First graded in 1988. Stakes record 1:19.40 (1980 Rich Cream).

Year Winner	Jockey	Second	Third	Strs	Time	1st Purse
2005 **Unfurl the Flag**, 5, 117	C. S. Nakatani	dh-Bear in the Woods, 4, 112 dh-McCann's Mojave, 5, 117		13	1:20.95	$210,000
2004 **Pohave**, 6, 116	V. Espinoza	Rojo Toro, 4, 115	Revello, 6, 110	13	1:21.06	180,000
2003 **Joey Franco**, 4, 118	P. A. Valenzuela	Publication, 4, 116	‡Primerica, 5, 113	9	1:21.56	180,000
2002 **Disturbingthepeace**, 4, 113	V. Espinoza	D'wildcat, 4, 115	Mellow Fellow, 7, 120	9	1:21.09	180,000
2001 **Ceeband**, 4, 110	M. S. Garcia	Squirtle Squirt, 3, 114	Elaborate, 6, 118	10	1:21.17	180,000
2000 **Elaborate**, 5, 114	V. Espinoza	Cliquot, 4, 116	Lexicon, 5, 117	10	1:21.19	180,000
1999 **Mazel Trick**, 4, 115	C. J. McCarron	Christmas Boy, 6, 111	Regal Thunder, 5, 115	8	1:19.97	180,000
1998 **Son of a Pistol**, 6, 118	A. O. Solis	The Exeter Man, 6, 114	Benchmark, 7, 118	11	1:20.81	120,000
1997 **Score Quick**, 5, 113	G. F. Almeida	Elmhurst, 7, 115	First Intent, 8, 116	11	1:21.00	100,980
1996 **Letthebighossroll**, 8, 116	C. J. McCarron	Score Quick, 4, 116	Comininalittlehot, 5, 116	7	1:21.43	125,460
1995 **Concept Win**, 5, 118	P. A. Valenzuela	Gold Land, 4, 116	Lucky Forever, 6, 119	6	1:21.09	63,100
1994 **Memo (Chi)**, 7, 120	P. Atkinson	Minjinsky, 4, 115	Slerp, 5, 119	6	1:20.52	62,400
1993 **Now Listen**, 6, 116	K. Desormeaux	Cardmania, 7, 116	Star of the Crop, 4, 120	10	1:20.83	66,400
1992 **Slew the Surgeon**, 4, 111	M. G. Linares	Softshoe Sure Shot, 6, 114	Record Boom, 6, 112	8	1:21.44	64,600
1991 **Robyn Dancer**, 4, 118	L. A. Pincay Jr.	Bruho, 5, 117	Black Jack Road, 7, 118	6	1:21.10	62,700
1990 **Prospectors Gamble**, 5, 114	J. A. Garcia	Raise a Stanza, 4, 117	Hot Operator, 5, 113	8	1:21.40	64,200
1989 **Sensational Star**, 5, 114	R. Q. Meza	Oraibi, 4, 120	Hot Operator, 4, 113	9	1:21.40	49,700
1988 **Perfec Travel**, 6, 115	C. A. Black	Reconnoitering, 4, 115	Don's Irish Melody, 5, 115	9	1:22.20	49,600
1987 **Bedside Promise**, 5, 124	R. Q. Meza	Zabaleta, 4, 118	Bolder Than Bold, 5, 118	5	1:21.00	46,500
1986 **Sabona**, 4, 114	C. J. McCarron	Innamorato, 5, 113	Michadilla, 4, 115	6	1:21.00	47,150
1985 **Fifty Six Ina Row**, 4, 117	L. A. Pincay Jr.	Premiership, 5, 115	French Legionaire, 4, 117	7	1:20.80	38,500
1984 **Debonaire Junior**, 3, 114	C. J. McCarron	Croeso, 4, 116	Night Mover, 4, 120	7	1:21.20	37,980
1983 **Regal Falcon**, 5, 117	E. Delahoussaye	Island Whirl, 5, 123	Kangroo Court, 6, 118	5	1:23.40	30,700
1982 **Never Tabled**, 5, 112	C. J. McCarron	Shanekite, 4, 117	Pompeii Court, 5, 116	7	1:21.00	31,750
1981 **Summer Time Guy**, 5, 118	C. J. McCarron	Back'n Time, 4, 118	Life's Hope, 8, 115	6	1:20.20	37,400
1980 **Rich Cream**, 5, 118	W. Shoemaker	I'm Smokin, 4, 115	Dragon Command (NZ), 6, 116	10	**1:19.40**	32,250
1979 **White Rammer**, 5, 120	W. Shoemaker	Arachnoid, 6, 124	Bad 'n Big, 5, 122	5	1:21.20	24,650
1978 **Drapier (Arg)**, 6, 120	F. Toro	Voy Por Uno (Mex), 5, 114	Prince of Saron, 5, 115	4	1:21.20	24,200
1977 **Painted Wagon**, 4, 115	C. Baltazar	Beat Inflation, 4, 122	L'Natural, 4, 115	7	1:20.20	25,750
1976 **Home Jerome**, 6, 115	M. Castaneda	Shirley's Champion, 5, 116	Money Lender, 5, 116	6	1:21.20	25,050
1975 **Messenger of Song**, 3, 115	J. Lambert	Century's Envoy, 4, 122	Chesapeake, 6, 115	10	1:20.60	26,650
1974 **Woodland Pines**, 5, 119	L. A. Pincay Jr.	Soft Victory, 6, 118	Finalista, 5, 123	8	1:20.60	19,800
1973 **Briartic**, 5, 122	W. Shoemaker	New Prospect, 4, 121	Silver Mallet, 5, 115	8	1:21.20	25,950

Named for Frank McMahon's 1972 Los Angeles H. winner Triple Bend (1968 c. by Never Bend). Formerly named for Hollywood Park's nickname, "The Track of Lakes and Flowers." Grade 3 1988-'97. Grade 2 1998-2002. Lakes and Flowers H. 1952-'78. Triple Bend H. 1979-'95. Triple Bend Breeders' Cup H. 1996-'97. Triple Bend Breeders' Cup Invitational H. 1998-2004. 6 furlongs 1956-'72. Equaled track record 1993. Track record 1994, 1999. Dead heat for second 2005. ‡Bluesthestandard finished third, DQ to sixth, 2003.

Tropical Park Derby

Grade 3 in 2006. Calder Race Course, three-year-olds, 1⅛ miles, turf. Held January 1, 2006, with a gross value of $100,000. First held in 1976. First graded in 1978. Stakes record 1:46.60 (1983 My Mac; 1985 Irish Sur; 2000 Go Lib Go).

Year	Winner	Jockey	Second	Third	Strs	Time	1st Purse
2006	**Barbaro**, 3, 119	E. S. Prado	Wise River, 3, 117	Lewis Michael, 3, 119	12	1:46.65	$60,000
2005	**Lord Robyn**, 3, 117	E. Coa	Fire Path, 3, 114	Crown Point, 3, 119	12	1:47.18	60,000
2004	**Kitten's Joy**, 3, 119	J. D. Bailey	Broadway View, 3, 112	Soverign Honor, 3, 117	11	1:46.95	60,000
2003	**Nothing to Lose**, 3, 115	J. D. Bailey	Millennium Storm, 3, 119	Supah Blitz, 3, 115	12	1:50.45	60,000
2002	**Political Attack**, 3, 119	M. Guidry	The Judge Sez Who, 3, 115	Deeliteful Guy, 3, 114	8	1:51.71	60,000
2001	**Proud Man**, 3, 115	R. R. Douglas	Mr Notebook, 3, 119	Cee Dee, 3, 119	11	1:47.95	60,000
2000	**Go Lib Go**, 3, 119	J. A. Santos	Mr. Livingston, 3, 115	Granting, 3, 115	12	**1:46.60**	60,000
1999	**Valid Reprized**, 3, 115	J. Castellano	Mr. Roark, 3, 115	Wertz, 3, 119	12	1:53.58	60,000
1998	**Draw Again**, 3, 117	J. Bravo	Buddha's Delight, 3, 115	Daddy's Dream, 3, 117	11	1:51.28	60,000
1997	**Arthur L.**, 3, 119	E. Coa	Unite's Big Red, 3, 117	Keep It Strait, 3, 117	12	1:46.93	60,000
1996	**Ok by Me**, 3, 117	J. D. Bailey	Darn That Erica, 3, 114	Tour's Big Red, 3, 117	12	1:47.25	60,000
1995	**Mecke**, 3, 117	H. Castillo Jr.	Val's Prince, 3, 112	Claudius, 3, 119	14	1:51.12	60,000
1994	**Fabulous Frolic**, 3, 112	J. Cruguet	Wake Up Alarm, 3, 117	Gator Back, 3, 119	14	1:46.99	60,000
1993	**Summer Set**, 3, 112	M. A. Gonzalez	Duc d'Sligovil, 3, 112	Silver of Silver, 3, 122	10	1:53.87	60,000
1992	**Technology**, 3, 119	J. D. Bailey	Majestic Sweep, 3, 114	Always Silver, 3, 114	10	1:53.01	134,160
1991	**Jackie Wackie**, 3, 119	H. Castillo Jr.	Gizmo's Fortune, 3, 119	Paulrus, 3, 114	13	1:51.90	69,120
1990	**Run Turn**, 3, 117	E. Fires	Country Day, 3, 112	Shot Gun Scott, 3, 119	8	1:52.40	66,420
1989	**Big Stanley**, 3, 114	J. Vasquez	Appealing Pleasure, 3, 114	Prized, 3, 114	8	1:52.40	100,170
1988	**Digress**, 3, 117	E. Maple	Intensive Command, 3, 117	Granacus, 3, 117	11	1:54.60	176,460
1987	**Baldski's Star**, 3, 117	C. Perret	Manhattan's Woody, 3, 112	Schism, 3, 117	13	1:54.80	139,920
1986	**Strong Performance**, 3, 117	J. Cruguet	Dr. Dan Eyes, 3, 114	Real Forest, 3, 117	12	1:54.40	143,760
1985	**Irish Sur**, 3, 121	J. A. Santos	Artillerist, 3, 121	Banner Bob, 3, 121	16	**1:46.60**	107,370
1984	**Morning Bob**, 3, 121	E. Maple	‡Don Rickles, 3, 121	Papa Koo, 3, 121	15	1:46.00	89,310
1983	**My Mac**, 3, 121	D. MacBeth	Caveat, 3, 121	Blink, 3, 121	11	**1:46.60**	100,350
1982	**Victorian Line**, 3, 121	A. Smith Jr.	North Cat, 3, 121	Sandy Bee's Baby, 3, 121	10	1:45.40	68,280
1981	**Double Sonic**, 3, 121	A. Smith Jr.	Akureyri, 3, 121	Might Be Home, 3, 121	14	1:46.40	70,740
1980	**Superbity**, 3, 121	J. Vasquez	Ray's Word, 3, 121	Irish Tower, 3, 121	11	1:45.60	69,600
1979	**Bishop's Choice**, 3, 111	D. MacBeth	Lot o' Gold, 3, 119	Smarten, 3, 119	12	1:44.20	74,400
1978	**Dr. Valeri**, 3, 116	R. Riera Jr.	Quadratic, 3, 119	Galimore, 3, 119	11	1:45.20	73,200
1977	**Ruthie's Native**, 3, 112	L. Saumell	Fort Prevel, 3, 121	Dreaming of Moe, 3, 112	12	1:44.40	55,800
1976	**Star of the Sea**, 3, 115	C. Perret	Controller Ike, 3, 114	Great Contractor, 3, 121	12	1:44.00	55,800

Named for the old Tropical Park racetrack in Miami, which closed in 1972. Grade 2 1983-'89. 1¹⁄₁₆ miles 1976-'85. About 1⅛ miles 1994. Dirt 1978-'93, 2002. ‡Rexson's Hope finished second, DQ to fifth, 1984.

Tropical Turf Handicap

Grade 3 in 2006. Calder Race Course, three-year-olds and up, 1⅛ miles, turf. Held December 3, 2005, with a gross value of $100,000. First held in 1935. First graded in 1981. Stakes record 1:44.99 (1995 The Vid).

Year	Winner	Jockey	Second	Third	Strs	Time	1st Purse
2005	**Silver Tree**, 5, 116	J. D. Bailey	Demeteor, 6, 114	Settle Up, 5, 115	11	1:46.28	$60,000
2004	**Host (Chi)**, 4, 118	J. R. Velazquez	Silver Tree, 4, 118	Demeteor, 5, 114	12	1:45.74	60,000
2003	**Political Attack**, 4, 116	R. R. Douglas	Millennium Dragon (GB), 4, 116	Sforza (Fr), 4, 115	12	1:45.81	60,000
2002	**Krieger**, 4, 113	E. Coa	Stokosky, 6, 113	Serial Bride, 5, 114	12	1:47.02	60,000
2001	**Band Is Passing**, 5, 118	C. Gonzalez	Crash Course, 5, 116	Groomstick Stock's, 5, 114	12	1:46.90	60,000
2000	**Stokosky**, 4, 114	C. A. Hernandez	dh-Band Is Passing, 4, 119 dh-Special Coach, 4, 114		11	1:48.77	60,000
1999	**Hibernian Rhapsody (Ire)**, 4, 114	R. R. Douglas	Garbu, 5, 117	Shamrock City, 4, 114	12	1:46.17	60,000
1998	**Unite's Big Red**, 4, 115	E. O. Nunez	N B Forrest, 6, 115	Glok, 4, 115	8	1:48.96	60,000
1997	**Sir Cat**, 4, 116	J. A. Rivera II	Foolish Pole, 4, 115	Written Approval, 5, 112	6	1:54.08	60,000
1996	**Mecke**, 4, 124	R. G. Davis	Satellite Nealski, 3, 113	Elite Jeblar, 6, 114	10	1:46.51	60,000
1995	**The Vid**, 5, 120	W. H. McCauley	Elite Jeblar, 5, 114	Scannapieco, 5, 113	12	**1:44.99**	60,000
1994	**The Vid**, 4, 116	R. R. Douglas	Country Coy, 4, 113	Gone for Real, 3, 113	10	1:49.06	60,000
1993	**Carterista**, 4, 121	W. S. Ramos	Rinka Das, 5, 113	Daarik (Ire), 6, 114	12	1:44.95	45,000
1992	**Carterista**, 3, 112	M. A. Lee	Rinka Das, 4, 114	Pidgeon's Promise, 3, 110	11	1:46.35	30,000
	Bidding Proud, 3, 115	J. A. Santos	Buckhar, 4, 118	Plate Dancer, 7, 116	7	1:46.02	30,000
1990	**Stolen Rolls**, 4, 112	P. A. Rodriguez	Gay's Best Boy, 3, 111	Seasabb, 3, 111	13	1:45.20	35,700
1989	**Vaguely Double**, 4, 118	W. A. Guerra	Mr. Adorable, 3, 113	Highland Springs, 5, 120	12	1:48.80	35,490
1988	**Equalize**, 6, 122	J. A. Santos	Val d'Enchere, 5, 116	Racing Star, 6, 114	10	1:45.00	35,010
1986	**Arctic Honeymoon**, 3, 111	R. N. Lester	Lover's Cross, 3, 121	Darn That Alarm, 5, 122	7	1:54.00	32,550
1985	**Ban the Blues**, 6, 114	G. St. Leon	Jim Bracken, 4, 112	Bold Southerner, 4, 112	11	1:53.20	34,140
1984	**Biloxi Indian**, 3, 114	B. Fann	Key to the Moon, 3, 122	Di Roma Feast, 3, 114	7	1:54.00	32,700
1983	**‡Eminency**, 5, 122	P. Day	World Appeal, 3, 118	Ready to Prove, 3, 110	13	1:51.20	34,770
1982	**Rivalero**, 6, 120	J. Vasquez	Current Blade, 4, 115	In all Honesty, 3, 110	9	1:53.60	33,270
1981	**The Liberal Member**, 6, 115	J. D. Bailey	Jayme G., 5, 116	Recusant, 3, 112	14	1:51.80	35,130
1980	**Yosi Boy**, 4, 111	A. Smith Jr.	Two's a Plenty, 3, 120	Von Clausewitz, 5, 119	8	1:51.80	33,180
1979	**Lot o' Gold**, 3, 123	D. Brumfield	King Celebrity, 3, 117	J. Rodney G., 4, 114	8	1:52.60	33,330
1975	**Proud Birdie**, 2, 117	J. Fieselman	Controller Ike, 2, 117	†Noble Royalty, 2, 115	13	1:47.00	18,900

1974	**L. Grant Jr.**, 4, 121	J. Combest	Super Sail, 6, 118	El Tordillo, 4, 115	11	1:45.80	$18,300
1973	**Proud and Bold**, 3, 121	R. Woodhouse	Outatholme, 4, 116	Seminole Joe, 5, 112	7	1:45.60	17,100

Named for the old Tropical Park racetrack in Miami, which closed in 1972. Formerly run on or about December 25. Christmas H. 1935-'71. Christmas Day H. 1972-'92. Held at Tropical Park 1935-'71. Not held 1939-'45, 1947, 1950-'51, 1976-'78, 1987, 1991. 1 mile 1935-'36. 6 furlongs 1949. 1$^1/_{16}$ miles 1960-'75. 1 mile 70 yards 1971. About 1$^1/_8$ miles 1988-'93, 2003. Dirt 1972-'86, 1997. Two-year-olds and up 1935-'36. Two-year-olds 1975. Two divisions 1964, 1967, 1969, 1992. Dead heat for second 2000. ‡World Appeal finished first, DQ to second, 1983. †Denotes female.

True North Handicap

Grade 2 in 2006. Belmont Park, three-year-olds and up, 6 furlongs, dirt. Held June 10, 2006, with a gross value of $200,000. First held in 1979. First graded in 1983. Stakes record 1:07.80 (1987 Groovy).

Year	Winner	Jockey	Second	Third	Strs	Time	1st Purse
2006	**Anew**, 5, 113	A. Garcia	Tiger, 5, 116	Spanish Chestnut, 4, 117	8	1:08.10	$120,000
2005	**Woke Up Dreamin**, 5, 116	M. E. Smith	Voodoo, 7, 113	Mass Media, 4, 117	10	1:08.38	128,220
2004	**Speightstown**, 6, 119	J. R. Velazquez	Cat Genius, 4, 116	Pohave, 6, 117	9	1:08.04	126,840
2003	**Shake You Down**, 5, 118	M. J. Luzzi	Highway Prospector, 6, 115	Vodka, 6, 114	6	1:09.59	90,000
2002	**Explicit**, 5, 119	L. J. Meche	Entepreneur, 5, 115	Late Carson, 6, 114	7	1:09.98	150,000
2001	**Say Florida Sandy**, 7, 116	A. T. Gryder	Wake At Noon, 4, 117	Explicit, 4, 115	8	1:08.77	90,000
2000	**Intidab**, 7, 117	R. G. Davis	Brutally Frank, 6, 119	Oro de Mexico, 6, 113	7	1:10.22	90,000
1999	**Kashatreya**, 5, 110	J. Samyn	Artax, 4, 119	The Trader's Echo, 5, 111	9	1:09.63	90,000
1998	**Richter Scale**, 4, 119	J. D. Bailey	Trafalger, 4, 114	Kelly Kip, 4, 122	8	1:08.83	83,160
1997	**Punch Line**, 7, 122	R. G. Davis	Cold Execution, 6, 112	Jamies First Punch, 4, 116	7	1:08.96	66,180
1996	**Not Surprising**, 6, 121	R. G. Davis	Prospect Bay, 4, 113	Forest Wildcat, 5, 114	8	1:09.17	66,720
1995	**Waldoboro**, 4, 112	E. Maple	Corma Ray, 5, 111	Mining Burrah, 5, 117	8	1:09.62	66,300
1994	**Friendly Lover**, 6, 114	R. Wilson	Boundary, 4, 117	Birdonthewire, 5, 119	9	1:09.65	67,380
1993	**Lion Cavern**, 4, 116	J. A. Krone	Arrowtown, 5, 115	Codys Key, 4, 111	7	1:10.33	69,120
1992	**Shining Bid**, 4, 112	E. Maple	Arrowtown, 4, 113	To Freedom, 4, 117	9	1:08.28	71,880
1991	**Diablo**, 4, 112	J. A. Krone	Sunny Blossom, 6, 120	Bravely Bold, 5, 119	7	1:08.24	69,720
1990	**Mr. Nickerson**, 4, 119	C. W. Antley	Sewickley, 5, 117	Dancing Spree, 5, 123	4	1:10.40	51,360
1989	**Dancing Spree**, 4, 113	A. T. Cordero Jr.	Dr. Carrington, 4, 109	Pok Ta Pok, 4, 118	6	1:09.40	68,160
1988	**High Brite**, 4, 120	A. T. Cordero Jr.	Irish Open, 4, 115	King's Swan, 8, 122	6	1:10.00	81,300
1987	**Groovy**, 4, 123	A. T. Cordero Jr.	King's Swan, 7, 120	Sun Master, 6, 117	4	**1:07.80**	78,780
1986	**Phone Trick**, 4, 127	J. Velasquez	Love That Mac, 4, 117	Cullendale, 4, 111	5	1:09.00	66,480
1985	**Cannon Shell**, 6, 114	D. J. Murphy	Basket Weave, 4, 114	Mt. Livermore, 4, 126	6	1:10.80	52,200
1984	**Believe the Queen**, 4, 114	J. Velasquez	Muskoka Wyck, 5, 112	Cannon Shell, 5, 115	5	1:09.80	52,110
1983	**†Gold Beauty**, 4, 121	D. Brumfield	Singh Tu, 4, 111	Fit to Fight, 4, 113	8	1:10.40	50,760
1982	**Shimatoree**, 3, 117	M. G. Pino	Pass the Tab, 4, 121	Will of Iron, 4, 112	8	1:08.60	49,590
1981	**Joanie's Chief**, 4, 109	J. Samyn	Proud Appeal, 3, 117	Guilty Conscience, 5, 113	7	1:09.00	33,480
1980	**Syncopate**, 5, 120	L. A. Pincay Jr.	Isella, 5, 117	Double Zeus, 5, 116	6	1:09.20	33,000
1979	**Moleolus**, 4, 110	J. Samyn	Jet Diplomacy, 4, 118	Northern Prospect, 3, 116	7	1:10.40	25,335

Named for Derring Howe's 1945 Fall Highweight H. winner True North (1940 g. by Only One). Grade 3 1983-'84. True North Breeders' Cup H. 2003-'05. †Denotes female.

Turfway Breeders' Cup Stakes

Grade 3 in 2006. Turfway Park, three-year-olds and up, fillies and mares, 1$^1/_{16}$ miles, dirt. Held September 17, 2005, with a gross value of $175,000. First held in 1986. First graded in 1990. Stakes record 1:41.67 (1995 Mariah's Storm).

Year	Winner	Jockey	Second	Third	Strs	Time	1st Purse
2005	**Miss Fortunate**, 5, 120	L. J. Melancon	Sheer Luck, 4, 118	Whoopi Cat, 4, 116	9	1:44.48	$108,500
2004	**Susan's Angel**, 3, 116	R. Bejarano	Mayo On the Side, 5, 120	Angela's Love, 4, 122	6	1:44.21	108,500
2003	**Smok'n Frolic**, 4, 122	E. S. Prado	Awesome Humor, 3, 112	So Much More, 4, 118	9	1:44.98	108,500
2002	**Trip**, 5, 116	P. Day	Mystic Lady, 4, 118	Red n'Gold, 4, 118	9	1:43.01	125,500
2001	**Trip**, 4, 118	C. Perret	Precious Feather, 4, 114	Spain, 4, 122	7	1:42.47	125,500
2000	**Spain**, 3, 118	P. Day	Ruby Surprise, 5, 118	Undermine, 4, 118	9	1:44.85	156,500
1999	**Ruby Surprise**, 4, 118	W. Martinez	Let, 4, 118	French Braids, 4, 114	8	1:44.95	162,886
1998	**Biding Time**, 4, 117	C. S. Nakatani	Meter Maid, 4, 121	Dancing Gulch, 4, 119	7	1:43.13	162,266
1997	**Feasibility Study**, 5, 119	M. E. Smith	City Band, 3, 114	Gold n Delicious, 4, 121	5	1:42.50	161,522
1996	**Golden Attraction**, 3, 114	G. L. Stevens	Bedroom Blues, 5, 117	Betty Van, 4, 119	8	1:42.53	205,920
1995	**Mariah's Storm**, 4, 117	R. N. Lester	Serena's Song, 3, 119	Alcovy, 5, 117	5	**1:41.67**	116,415
1994	**Pennyhill Park**, 4, 123	C. J. McCarron	Roamin Rachel, 4, 123	Hey Hazel, 4, 123	10	1:44.20	118,073
1993	**Gray Cashmere**, 4, 117	D. Kutz	Deputation, 4, 120	November Snow, 4, 113	8	1:43.39	117,130
1992	**Fit for a Queen**, 6, 123	R. D. Lopez	Auto Dial, 4, 120	Hitch, 3, 112	9	1:43.30	117,975
1991	**Fit for a Queen**, 5, 123	R. D. Lopez	Til Forbid, 3, 118	Screen Prospect, 4, 114	8	1:43.22	117,358
1990	**Barbarika**, 5, 123	A. T. Gryder	Colonial Waters, 5, 114	Luthier's Launch, 4, 112	11	1:44.00	119,015
1989	**Winning Colors**, 4, 115	C. J. McCarron	Grecian Flight, 5, 123	Lawyer Talk, 5, 123	7	1:44.80	101,368
1988	**Darien Miss**, 3, 115	P. A. Johnson	Integra, 4, 123	Ms. Eloise, 5, 120	9	1:43.60	101,758
1987	**In Neon**, 5, 111	M. McDowell	Northern Maiden, 4, 122	Just Barely Able, 5, 113	7	1:45.20	50,180
1986	**Gypsy Prayer**, 5, 111	M. W. Bryan	Queen Alexandra, 4, 114	Donut's Pride, 4, 111	10	1:43.20	19,180

Grade 2 1992-'98. Latonia Breeders' Cup S. 1986. Turfway Park Budweiser Breeders' Cup S. 1987-'88, 1991-'95. Turfway Park Breeders' Cup H. 1989-'90. Host track known as Latonia Race Course 1986.

Turfway Park Fall Championship Stakes

Grade 3 in 2006. Turfway Park, three-year-olds and up, 1 mile, all weather. Held October 1, 2005, with a gross value of $100,000. First held in 1919. First graded in 1997. Stakes record 1:36.89 (2003 Crafty Shaw).

Year	Winner	Jockey	Second	Third	Strs	Time	1st Purse
2005	**Artemus Sunrise**, 4, 116	J. L. Castanon	Mr. Krisley, 7, 115	Mighty Military, 4, 117	12	1:37.31	$62,000
2004	**Cappuchino**, 5, 115	D. A. Sarvis	Crafty Shaw, 6, 122	Added Edge, 4, 119	7	1:37.19	62,000
2003	**Crafty Shaw**, 5, 117	C. Perret	Cat Tracker, 5, 117	Cappuchino, 4, 119	8	**1:36.89**	62,000
2002	**Crafty Shaw**, 4, 117	J. Lopez	Rock Slide, 4, 117	Deferred Comp, 4, 115	7	1:52.29	62,750
2001	**Generous Rosi (GB)**, 6, 115	L. J. Meche	Storm Day, 4, 117	Jadada, 6, 117	6	1:49.83	46,500
2000	**Mount Lemon**, 6, 117	R. Albarado	Unloosened, 5, 114	Phil the Grip, 6, 117	7	1:51.14	62,600
1999	**Phil the Grip**, 5, 112	R. Albarado	Part the Waters, 5, 111	Metatonia, 4, 110	5	1:52.15	49,600
1998	**Acceptable**, 4, 116	C. Perret	Magnify, 5, 114	Muchacho Fino, 4, 112	6	1:51.95	62,600
1997	**Tejano Run**, 5, 122	W. Martinez	Short Stay, 5, 114	Thesaurus, 3, 112	7	1:49.44	46,950
1996	**Strawberry Wine**, 4, 114	B. D. Peck	Kiridashi, 4, 121	Prospect for Love, 4, 114	8	1:50.15	65,000
1995	**Bound by Honor**, 4, 113	R. P. Romero	Lord Gordon, 5, 113	Lordly Prospect, 6, 112	6	1:51.54	48,750
1994	**Meena**, 6, 114	W. Martinez	Powerful Punch, 5, 122	It'sali'lknownfact, 4, 111	4	1:52.92	27,284
1993	**Powerful Punch**, 4, 116	C. C. Bourque	Medium Cool, 5, 114	Benburb, 4, 121	7	1:50.51	41,048
1992	**Flying Continental**, 6, 122	J. Velasquez	Alyten, 4, 116	Regal Affair, 6, 113	5	1:48.67	27,511
1991	**Allijeba**, 5, 116	J. E. Bruin	D. C. Tenacious, 4, 113	Discover, 3, 116	9	1:49.63	41,421
1990	**Aly Mar**, 4, 112	D. Kutz	Cefis, 5, 120	Cantrell Road, 4, 116	7	1:49.20	34,531
1989	**Currentsville Lane**, 4, 112	J. Neagle	Air Worthy, 4, 121	Loyal Pal, 6, 118	8	1:51.60	28,031
1988	**Mr. Odie**, 4, 110	S. Neff	Boyish Charm, 5, 115	Government Corner, 6, 114	11	1:52.40	28,795
1987	**Lord Glacier**, 4, 114	M. Solomone	Aggies Best, 5, 117	Ten Times Ten, 5, 115	12	1:43.60	28,860
1986	**Big Pistol**, 5, 123	L. J. Melancon	Exit Five B., 5, 119	Something Cool, 4, 117	6	1:42.80	19,565
1985	**Country Hick**, 4, 113	J. C. Espinoza	Turn Here, 4, 114	McShane, 6, 117	10	1:43.00	20,215
1984	**Immediate Reaction**, 4, 118	M. McDowell	Fairly Straight, 3, 120	Never Company, 4, 113	9	1:43.80	18,541
1983	**Cad**, 5, 115	D. Brumfield	His Flower, 3, 113	Noted, 4, 112	9	1:44.00	18,444
1982	**Leader Jet**, 4, 117	C. R. Woods Jr.	Rock Steady, 3, 113	Diverse Dude, 4, 118	10	1:44.00	13,680
1981	**Exterminate**, 4, 114	D. E. Foster	Kentucky Scout, 4, 119	Withholding, 4, 120	9	1:44.40	13,080
1980	**Silver Shears**, 3, 110	R. R. Matias	Penalty Declined, 6, 119	One Lucky Devil, 6, 124	9	1:43.20	12,975
1979	**†Lotta Honey**, 4, 116	J. C. Espinoza	Penalty Declined, 5, 113	One Lucky Devil, 5, 114	12	1:42.40	18,005
1978	**†Likely Exchange**, 4, 114	M. S. Sellers	Pirogue, 4, 113	Mr. Pitty Pat, 5, 110	8	1:45.60	16,020
1977	**Certain Roman**, 4, 111	M. McDowell	*The Pepe, 5, 114	Payne Street, 4, 120	9	1:44.80	12,855
1976	**Brustigert**, 6, 113	A. F. Herrera	Faneuil Boy, 5, 118	Visier, 4, 120	12	1:45.40	13,155
1975	**Eager Wish**, 6, 119	C. Bramble	*Zografos, 7, 124	†Princess Jillo, 4, 106	6	1:44.40	12,765
1974	**Bootlegger's Pet**, 4, 116	G. Solomon	Lester's Jester, 5, 113	Babingtons Image, 4, 111	8	1:47.60	13,878
1973	**Knight Counter**, 5, 123	D. Brumfield	Divorce Trial, 4, 114	On the Money, 5, 116	10	1:46.80	9,962

Traditionally held during Turfway Park's fall meet. Latonia Championship S. 1919-'33, 1964-'86. Turfway Championship S. 1987-'90. Turfway Championship H. 1991-'95, 1997. Kentucky Cup Classic Preview H. 1996, 1998-'99. Turfway Park Fall Championship H. 2000. Held at Old Latonia 1919-'33. Host track known as Latonia Race Course 1964-'86. Not held 1934-'63, 1972. 1 1/8 miles 1913-'18, 1934-'63, 1988-2002. 1 3/4 miles 1919-'33. 1 1/16 miles 1964-'87. Dirt 1919-'33, 1964-'71, 1973-2004. Three-year-olds 1919-'33. †Denotes female.

Turnback the Alarm Handicap

Grade 3 in 2006. Aqueduct, three-year-olds and up, fillies and mares, 1 1/8 miles, dirt. Held November 5, 2005, with a gross value of $105,800. First held in 1995. First graded in 1999. Stakes record 1:48.89 (1995 Incinerate).

Year	Winner	Jockey	Second	Third	Strs	Time	1st Purse
2005	**Indian Vale**, 3, 112	J. R. Velazquez	Taittinger Rose, 4, 116	Asti (Ire), 4, 115	5	1:49.83	$64,680
2004	**Personal Legend**, 4, 115	J. D. Bailey	Roar Emotion, 4, 117	Fast Cookie, 4, 114	9	1:51.27	66,420
2003	**Pocus Hocus**, 5, 114	J. A. Santos	Nonsuch Bay, 4, 115	Miss Linda (Arg), 6, 118	6	1:50.67	64,500
2002	**Svea Dahl**, 5, 114	R. Migliore	Mystic Lady, 4, 119	Critical Eye, 5, 115	5	1:50.42	64,800
2001	**Rochelle's Terms**, 4, 113	R. G. Davis	Resort, 4, 113	Strolling Belle, 5, 118	6	1:51.19	65,100
2000	**Atelier**, 3, 113	E. S. Prado	Tap to Music, 5, 119	Pentatonic, 5, 115	10	1:48.95	67,920
1999	**Belle Cherie**, 3, 112	J. R. Velazquez	Brushed Halory, 3, 114	Sweet Misty, 5, 116	8	1:50.03	66,000
1998	**Snit**, 4, 117	J. R. Velazquez	Manoa, 3, 112	Shoop, 7, 114	8	1:51.30	49,740
1997	**Mil Kilates**, 4, 116	J. Bravo	Radiant Megan, 4, 110	Shoop, 6, 114	5	1:49.40	48,330
1996	**Shoop**, 5, 121	J. D. Bailey	Queen Tutta, 4, 116	Madame Adolphe, 4, 113	4	1:51.35	48,420
1995	**Incinerate**, 5, 115	F. Leon	Lotta Dancing, 4, 115	Pretty Discreet, 3, 110	7	**1:48.89**	49,005

Named for Valley View Farm's and Dr. Richard Coburn's 1992 Coaching Club American Oaks (G1) winner Turnback the Alarm (1989 f. by Darn That Alarm).

United Nations Stakes

Grade 1 in 2006. Monmouth Park, three-year-olds and up, 1 3/8 miles, turf. Held July 2, 2005, with a gross value of $750,000. First held in 1953. First graded in 1973. Stakes record 2:12.78 (2003 Balto Star).

Year	Winner	Jockey	Second	Third	Strs	Time	1st Purse
2005	**Better Talk Now**, 6, 118	R. A. Dominguez	Silverfoot, 5, 118	Request for Parole, 6, 118	9	2:20.57	$450,000
2004	**Request for Parole**, 5, 118	E. S. Prado	Mr O'Brien (Ire), 5, 120	Nothing to Lose, 4, 118	11	2:13.37	450,000
2003	**Balto Star**, 5, 117	J. A. Velez Jr.	The Tin Man, 5, 121	Lunar Sovereign, 4, 112	7	**2:12.78**	450,000
2002	**With Anticipation**, 7, 119	P. Day	Denon, 4, 118	Sarafan, 5, 117	7	2:12.81	300,000
2001	**‡Senure**, 5, 116	R. G. Davis	With Anticipation, 6, 113	Gritty Sandie, 5, 112	8	2:13.56	300,000
2000	**Down the Aisle**, 7, 114	R. G. Davis	Aly's Alley, 4, 111	Honor Glide, 6, 116	7	2:13.63	210,000
1999	**Yagli**, 6, 124	J. D. Bailey	Supreme Sound (GB), 5, 113	Amerique, 5, 115	6	2:16.02	150,000

1997	**Influent**, 6, 117	J. Samyn	Geri, 5, 113	Flag Down, 7, 118	4	1:53.72	$240,000
1996	**Sandpit (Brz)**, 7, 122	C. S. Nakatani	Diplomatic Jet, 4, 117	Northern Spur (Ire), 5, 122	8	1:55.71	300,000
1995	**Sandpit (Brz)**, 6, 122	C. S. Nakatani	Celtic Arms (Fr), 4, 118	†Alice Springs, 5, 115	9	1:57.25	300,000
1994	**Lure**, 5, 123	M. E. Smith	Fourstars Allstar, 6, 117	Star of Cozzene, 6, 121	5	1:52.66	300,000
1993	**Star of Cozzene**, 5, 120	J. A. Santos	Lure, 4, 123	Finder's Choice, 8, 113	7	1:53.22	300,000
1992	**Sky Classic**, 5, 123	P. Day	Chenin Blanc, 6, 115	Lotus Pool, 5, 114	9	1:52.53	300,000
1991	**Exbourne**, 5, 122	C. J. McCarron	Forty Niner Days, 4, 116	Goofalik, 4, 114	7	1:52.75	300,000
1990	**Steinlen (GB)**, 7, 124	J. A. Santos	†Capades, 4, 112	Alwuhush, 5, 121	8	1:52.00	300,000
1989	**Yankee Affair**, 7, 121	P. Day	Salem Drive, 7, 117	Simply Majestic, 5, 119	5	1:53.20	120,000
1988	**Equalize**, 6, 116	J. A. Santos	Wanderkin, 5, 115	Bet Twice, 4, 124	9	1:52.60	120,000
1987	**Manila**, 4, 124	J. Vasquez	Racing Star, 5, 115	Air Display, 4, 110	5	1:58.80	90,000
1986	**Manila**, 3, 114	J. A. Santos	Uptown Swell, 4, 116	Lieutenant's Lark, 4, 121	8	1:52.60	104,040
1985	**Ends Well**, 4, 114	M. R. Morgan	Who's for Dinner, 6, 116	Cool, 4, 110	11	1:54.60	107,820
1984	**Hero's Honor**, 4, 123	J. D. Bailey	Cozzene, 4, 114	Who's for Dinner, 5, 110	11	1:54.00	106,200
1983	**Acaroid**, 5, 113	A. T. Cordero Jr.	†Trevita (Ire), 6, 116	Majesty's Prince, 4, 120	13	1:53.40	90,000
1982	**Naskra's Breeze**, 5, 117	J. Samyn	Acaroid, 4, 115	Don Roberto, 5, 116	10	1:55.60	90,000
1981	**Key to Content**, 4, 121	G. Martens	Ben Fab, 4, 123	Quality T. V., 4, 110	9	1:52.80	82,500
1980	**Lyphard's Wish (Fr)**, 4, 118	A. T. Cordero Jr.	Match the Hatch, 4, 115	Scythian Gold, 5, 111	9	1:53.80	82,500
1979	**Noble Dancer (GB)**, 7, 125	J. Vasquez	Dom Alaric (Fr), 5, 120	Overskate, 4, 128	6	1:56.60	75,000
1978	**Noble Dancer (GB)**, 6, 127	S. Cauthen	Upper Nile, 4, 118	Dan Horn, 6, 117	5	1:56.40	81,250
1977	**Bemo**, 7, 116	D. Brumfield	Quick Card, 4, 124	Alias Smith, 4, 112	5	1:54.00	65,000
1976	**Intrepid Hero**, 4, 125	S. Hawley	Improviser, 4, 116	Break Up the Game, 5, 120	8	1:53.40	65,000
1975	**Royal Glint**, 5, 120	J. E. Tejeira	Stonewalk, 4, 120	R. Tom Can, 4, 116	9	1:57.00	65,000
1974	**Halo**, 5, 118	J. Velasquez	London Company, 4, 123	Scantling, 4, 115	10	1:56.80	65,000
1973	**Tentam**, 4, 123	J. Velasquez	Star Envoy, 5, 116	Return to Reality, 4, 113	12	1:54.60	75,000

Named for the United Nations, headquartered in New York City. Formerly sponsored by Caesars Palace Hotel of Atlantic City, New Jersey 1990-'97. Grade 2 1990-'93. United Nations Invitational H. 1953-'81. Caesars International H. 1990-'97. United Nations H. 1953-'72, 1975-'89, 1999-2003. Held at Atlantic City 1953-'97. Not held 1998. 1³/₁₆ miles 1953-'97. Dirt 1969. ‡With Anticipation finished first, DQ to second, 2001. Equaled course record 1999. Course record 2000, 2003. †Denotes female.

Vagrancy Handicap

Grade 2 in 2006. Belmont Park, three-year-olds and up, fillies and mares, 6½ furlongs, dirt. Held June 11, 2006, with a gross value of $150,000. First held in 1948. First graded in 1973. Stakes record 1:14.46 (2004 Bear Fan).

Year	Winner	Jockey	Second	Third	Strs	Time	1st Purse
2006	**Dubai Escapade**, 4, 120	E. S. Prado	High Button Shoes, 4, 114	Magnolia Jackson, 4, 117	6	1:15.39	$90,000
2005	**Sensibly Chic**, 5, 116	J. R. Velazquez	Bank Audit, 4, 120	Ender's Sister, 4, 116	9	1:16.31	90,000
2004	**Bear Fan**, 5, 121	J. R. Velazquez	Smok'n Frolic, 5, 117	Aspen Gal, 3, 109	9	**1:14.46**	90,000
2003	**Shawklit Mint**, 4, 115	R. Migliore	Shine Again, 6, 121	Gold Mover, 5, 118	3	1:15.38	90,000
2002	**Xtra Heat**, 4, 127	H. Vega	Gold Mover, 4, 115	Shine Again, 5, 117	5	1:16.44	90,000
2001	**Dat You Miz Blue**, 4, 116	J. R. Velazquez	Dream Supreme, 4, 122	Katz Me If You Can, 4, 115	5	1:15.32	64,080
2000	**Country Hideaway**, 4, 117	J. D. Bailey	Hurricane Bertie, 5, 118	Imperfect World, 4, 115	7	1:17.05	65,640
1999	**‡Gold Princess**, 4, 114	J. R. Velazquez	Hurricane Bertie, 4, 114	Delta Music, 4, 113	5	1:16.57	63,840
1998	**Chip**, 5, 115	J. Bravo	Furlough, 4, 114	Parlay, 4, 115	6	1:15.69	48,945
1997	**Inquisitive Look**, 4, 111	J. F. Chavez	Flat Fleet Feet, 4, 123	Mama Dean, 4, 114	6	1:22.07	64,800
1996	**Twist Afleet**, 5, 122	J. A. Krone	Smooth Charmer, 4, 111	Lottsa Talc, 6, 120	8	1:20.94	66,300
1995	**Sky Beauty**, 5, 125	M. E. Smith	Aly's Conquest, 4, 114	Through the Door, 5, 110	4	1:21.56	47,865
1994	**Sky Beauty**, 4, 122	M. E. Smith	For all Seasons, 4, 114	Pamzig, 4, 107	6	1:21.67	48,855
1993	**Spinning Round**, 4, 112	J. F. Chavez	Reach for Clever, 6, 114	Nannerl, 6, 118	8	1:24.52	52,740
1992	**Nannerl**, 5, 116	J. A. Santos	Serape, 4, 115	Makin Faces, 4, 112	6	1:22.55	51,210
1991	**Queena**, 5, 115	M. E. Smith	Missy's Mirage, 3, 109	Gottagetitdone, 6, 111	10	1:22.07	55,080
1990	**Mistaurian**, 4, 113	W. H. McCauley	Feel the Beat, 5, 118	Fantastic Find, 4, 116	5	1:25.20	50,040
1989	**Aptostar**, 4, 118	A. T. Cordero Jr.	Toll Fee, 4, 110	Lambros, 4, 109	7	1:22.80	51,570
1988	**Grecian Flight**, 4, 121	C. Perret	Nasty Affair, 4, 114	Tappiano, 4, 123	7	1:20.80	66,240
1987	**North Sider**, 5, 121	A. T. Cordero Jr.	Storm and Sunshine, 4, 117	Funistrada, 4, 114	6	1:24.20	64,440
1986	**Le Slew**, 5, 113	J. A. Santos	Clocks Secret, 4, 121	Willowy Mood, 4, 114	8	1:23.80	54,630
1985	**Nany**, 5, 121	J. Velasquez	Sugar's Image, 4, 120	Brindy Brindy, 5, 113	6	1:23.80	52,020
1984	**Grateful Friend**, 4, 114	A. T. Cordero Jr.	Pleasure Cay, 4, 118	Sweet Laughter, 7, 108	7	1:24.00	52,470
1983	**Broom Dance**, 4, 121	G. McCarron	Syrianna, 4, 114	Sprouted Rye, 6, 115	7	1:22.80	33,480
1982	**Westport Native**, 4, 115	J. Velasquez	Tell a Secret, 5, 115	Raise 'n Dance, 4, 113	6	1:22.60	32,580
1981	**Island Charm**, 4, 110	R. Migliore	Contrary Rose, 5, 114	The Wheel Turns, 4, 114	5	1:23.60	32,520
1980	**Lady Lonsdale**, 5, 114	L. Saumell	Peaceful Banner, 4, 108	Worthy Poise, 6, 112	6	1:24.40	32,700
1979	**Frosty Skater**, 4, 119	D. MacBeth	Hagany, 5, 114	Skipat, 5, 126	10	1:23.20	33,240
1978	**Dainty Dotsie**, 4, 124	B. Phelps	What a Summer, 5, 127	Navajo Princess, 4, 110	6	1:21.80	32,160
1977	**Shy Dawn**, 6, 119	A. T. Cordero Jr.	Reasonable Win, 5, 118	Secret Lanvin, 4, 111	5	1:23.80	31,590
1976	**My Juliet**, 4, 127	J. Velasquez	Shy Dawn, 5, 119	Kudara, 5, 116	5	1:22.00	32,790
1975	**Honorable Miss**, 5, 120	J. Vasquez	Viva La Vivi, 5, 126	Coraggioso, 5, 121	8	1:22.20	34,020
1974	**Coraggioso**, 4, 119	D. Brumfield	Ponte Vecchio, 4, 114	‡Lady Love, 4, 118	14	1:22.40	35,940
1973	**Krislin**, 4, 113	M. A. Castaneda	Numbered Account, 4, 120	Fairway Flyer, 4, 115	8	1:22.60	16,845

Named for Belair Stud's 1942 champion three-year-old filly, '42 champion handicap female, and '42 Beldame H. winner Vagrancy (1939 f. by *Sir Gallahad III). Held at Aqueduct 1948-'55, 1960, 1963-'67, 1975, 1977-'86, 1997. Not held 1949-'51. 1¹/₁₆ miles 1948-'52. 7 furlongs 1953-'97. ‡Wanda finished third, DQ to fourteenth, 1974. ‡Hurricane Bertie finished first, DQ to second, 1999.

Valley Stream Stakes

Grade 3 in 2006. Aqueduct, two-year-olds, fillies, 6 furlongs, dirt. Held November 20, 2005, with a gross value of $105,200. First held in 1995. First graded in 2001. Stakes record 1:08.66 (2001 Forest Heiress).

Year	Winner	Jockey	Second	Third	Strs	Time	1st Purse
2005	**Miraculous Miss**, 2, 118	R. A. Dominguez	Diamond Spirit, 2, 116	India, 2, 116	5	1:11.13	$64,320
2004	**Megascape**, 2, 122	J. R. Velazquez	Alfonsina, 2, 118	More Moonlight, 2, 118	5	1:10.38	63,900
2003	**Smokey Glacken**, 2, 118	J. A. Santos	Baldomera, 2, 118	Stoic, 2, 118	9	1:11.18	67,320
2002	**Randaroo**, 2, 116	J. R. Velazquez	House Party, 2, 116	Fast Cookie, 2, 116	8	1:09.46	66,780
2001	**Forest Heiress**, 2, 122	R. Migliore	A New Twist, 2, 116	On Parade, 2, 116	6	**1:08.66**	48,465
2000	**Astrapi**, 2, 116	D. Nelson	Major Wager, 2, 116	Look of the Lynx, 2, 118	5	1:10.66	48,570
1999	**Magicalmysterycat**, 2, 121	M. E. Smith	Sahara Gold, 2, 121	Silentlea, 2, 121	8	1:10.53	49,815
1998	**Paula's Girl**, 2, 116	J. R. Velazquez	President's Girl, 2, 114	Godmother, 2, 121	5	1:11.99	38,700
1997	**Cotton House Bay**, 2, 114	J. F. Chavez	Foil, 2, 116	Kate Again, 2, 114	10	1:10.11	33,990
1996	**Dixie Flag**, 2, 116	J. Samyn	Alyssum, 2, 114	Nimble Tread, 2, 114	6	1:10.13	32,490
1995	**Oxford Scholar**, 2, 112	J. D. Bailey	Zee Lady, 2, 120	Stormy Krissy, 2, 112	5	1:12.13	32,430

Named for Valley Stream, a Long Island town in Nassau County, New York. Held at Belmont Park 1995.

Valley View Stakes

Grade 3 in 2006. Keeneland Race Course, three-year-olds, fillies, 1$^1/_{16}$ miles, turf. Held October 21, 2005, with a gross value of $125,000. First held in 1991. First graded in 1999. Stakes record 1:41.51 (1992 Spinning Round).

Year	Winner	Jockey	Second	Third	Strs	Time	1st Purse
2005	**Asi Siempre**, 3, 120	G. L. Stevens	Dynamite Lass, 3, 116	Victory Lap, 3, 120	9	1:45.37	$77,500
2004	**Sister Swank**, 3, 116	P. Day	Jinny's Gold, 3, 116	Shadow Cast, 3, 119	12	1:46.75	72,106
2003	**Dyna Da Wyna**, 3, 119	P. Day	Mexican Moonlight, 3, 116	Derrianne, 3, 123	10	1:43.54	69,998
2002	**Bedanken**, 3, 119	D. R. Pettinger	Mariensky, 3, 119	High Maintenance (GB), 3, 119	10	1:44.24	71,734
2001	**dh-Chausson Poire**, 3, 119	R. W. Woolsey		Quick Tip, 3, 123	10	1:42.93	46,576
	dh-Cozzy Corner, 3, 119	L. J. Meche					
2000	**Good Game**, 3, 119	P. Day	Impending Bear, 3, 119	Soccory, 3, 119	10	1:45.69	71,176
1999	**Gimmeakissee**, 3, 115	P. J. Cooksey	The Happy Hopper, 3, 119	Celestialbutterfly, 3, 119	9	1:42.05	70,122
1998	**White Beauty**, 3, 113	C. H. Borel	Shires Ende, 3, 117	Leaveemlaughing, 3, 117	8	1:43.09	56,591
1997	**Mingling Glances**, 3, 117	J. Bravo	Majestic Sunlight, 3, 113	Fluid Move, 3, 113	9	1:44.51	52,592
1996	**Turkappeal**, 3, 117	D. M. Barton	Inner Circle, 3, 113	Mariuka, 3, 117	9	1:46.10	52,126
1995	**Country Cat**, 3, 121	D. M. Barton	Appointed One, 3, 121	Petrouchka, 3, 121	10	1:44.88	51,150
1994	**Pharma**, 3, 121	C. W. Antley	Mariah's Storm, 3, 121	Thread, 3, 121	9	1:42.48	50,747
1993	**Weekend Madness (Ire)**, 3, 121	C. R. Woods Jr.	Life Is Delicious, 3, 121	Augusta Springs, 3, 121	10	1:43.06	23,870
1992	**Spinning Round**, 3, 121	F. A. Arguello Jr.	Shes Just Super, 3, 121	Enticed, 3, 121	9	**1:41.51**	23,870
1991	**La Gueriere**, 3, 121	B. D. Peck	Dance O'My Life, 3, 121	Spanish Parade, 3, 121	9	1:43.49	29,250

Named for the Valley View ferry, Kentucky's oldest recorded commerical business. Valley View Breeders' Cup S. 1994-'95. Dead heat for first 2001.

Vanity Invitational Handicap

Grade 1 in 2006. Hollywood Park, three-year-olds and up, fillies and mares, 1$^1/_8$ miles, dirt. Held July 3, 2005, with a gross value of $300,000. First held in 1940. First graded in 1973. Stakes record 1:46.20 (1984 Princess Rooney).

Year	Winner	Jockey	Second	Third	Strs	Time	1st Purse
2005	**Splendid Blended**, 3, 115	J. D. Bailey	Island Fashion, 5, 117	Andujar, 4, 121	8	1:49.33	$180,000
2004	**Victory Encounter**, 4, 116	A. O. Solis	Adoration, 5, 122	Star Parade (Arg), 5, 117	4	1:48.28	150,000
2003	**Azeri**, 5, 127	M. E. Smith	Sister Girl Blues, 4, 111	Bare Necessities, 4, 118	7	1:48.48	150,000
2002	**Azeri**, 4, 125	M. E. Smith	Affluent, 4, 119	dh-Collect Call, 4, 115	5	1:48.88	150,000
				dh-Starrer, 4, 117			
2001	**Gourmet Girl**, 6, 119	G. L. Stevens	Lazy Slusan, 6, 122	Setareh, 4, 114	5	1:49.21	150,000
2000	**Riboletta (Brz)**, 5, 123	C. J. McCarron	Speaking of Time, 4, 108	Excellent Meeting, 4, 120	6	1:48.54	180,000
1999	**Manistique**, 4, 122	C. J. McCarron	Yolo Lady, 4, 115	Bella Chiarra, 4, 116	6	1:48.06	240,000
1998	**Escena**, 5, 124	J. D. Bailey	Housa Dancer (Fr), 5, 115	Different (Arg), 6, 119	7	1:48.13	210,000
1997	**Twice the Vice**, 6, 121	K. Desormeaux	Real Connection, 6, 114	Jewel Princess, 5, 123	5	1:46.40	240,000
1996	**Jewel Princess**, 4, 120	C. S. Nakatani	Serena's Song, 4, 125	Top Rung, 5, 116	6	1:47.17	150,000
1995	**Private Persuasion**, 4, 114	G. L. Stevens	Top Rung, 4, 116	Wandesta (GB), 4, 119	7	1:48.30	165,000
1994	**Potridee (Arg)**, 5, 114	A. O. Solis	Exchange, 6, 118	Golden Klair (GB), 4, 119	8	1:48.08	165,000
1993	**Re Toss (Arg)**, 6, 116	E. Delahoussaye	Paseana (Arg), 6, 126	Guiza, 6, 114	8	1:47.92	165,000
1992	**Paseana (Arg)**, 5, 127	C. J. McCarron	Fowda, 4, 118	Re Toss (Arg), 5, 115	6	1:48.06	165,000
1991	**Brought to Mind**, 4, 120	P. A. Valenzuela	Fit to Scout, 4, 115	Luna Elegante (Arg), 5, 114	6	1:48.50	110,000
1990	**Gorgeous**, 4, 124	E. Delahoussaye	Fantastic Look, 4, 112	Kelly, 4, 110	5	1:48.20	110,000
1989	**Bayakoa (Arg)**, 5, 125	L. A. Pincay Jr.	Flying Julia, 6, 112	Goodbye Halo, 4, 122	6	1:47.20	110,000
1988	**Annoconnor**, 4, 114	C. A. Black	Pen Bal Lady (GB), 4, 119	Abloom (Arg), 4, 113	7	1:49.20	110,000
1987	**Infinidad (Chi)**, 5, 113	C. A. Black	North Sider, 5, 121	Clabber Girl, 4, 115	7	2:00.60	110,000
1986	**Magnificent Lindy**, 4, 116	C. J. McCarron	Dontstop Themusic, 6, 124	Outstandingly, 4, 118	5	2:02.00	137,000
1985	**Dontstop Themusic**, 5, 118	A. T. Cordero Jr.	Salt Spring (Arg), 6, 114	Estrapade, 5, 119	7	1:47.80	110,000
1984	**Princess Rooney**, 4, 120	E. Delahoussaye	Adored, 4, 120	Salt Spring (Arg), 5, 113	7	**1:46.20**	150,500
1983	**A Kiss for Luck**, 4, 114	C. J. McCarron	Try Something New, 4, 118	Sangue (Ire), 5, 122	11	1:49.20	110,000
1982	**Sangue (Ire)**, 4, 120	W. Shoemaker	Track Robbery, 6, 123	Cat Girl, 4, 117	7	1:48.00	110,000
1981	**Track Robbery**, 5, 120	P. A. Valenzuela	Princess Karenda, 4, 118	Save Wild Life, 4, 117	7	1:47.00	110,000
1980	**It's in the Air**, 4, 120	L. A. Pincay Jr.	Conveniently, 4, 111	Image of Reality, 4, 119	7	1:47.00	94,600
1979	**It's in the Air**, 3, 113	W. Shoemaker	Country Queen, 4, 121	Innuendo, 5, 116	8	1:47.40	77,950
1978	**Afifa**, 4, 113	W. Shoemaker	Drama Critic, 4, 117	Dottie's Doll, 5, 117	7	1:46.40	77,050

1977 **Cascapedia**, 4, 129	S. Hawley	*Bastonera II, 6, 122	Swingtime, 5, 117	9	1:47.60	$65,500
1976 **Miss Toshiba**, 4, 120	F. Toro	*Bastonera II, 5, 121	Bold Baby, 4, 115	11	1:48.00	67,200
1975 ***Dulcia**, 6, 118	W. Shoemaker	Susan's Girl, 6, 123	*La Zanzara, 5, 120	11	1:47.40	67,500
1974 **Tallahto**, 4, 126	L. A. Pincay Jr.	*La Zanzara, 4, 120	Dogtooth Violet, 4, 118	10	1:47.00	66,500
1973 **Convenience**, 5, 121	J. L. Rotz	Minstrel Miss, 6, 121	Susan's Girl, 4, 127	8	1:47.80	64,500

Vanity H. 1945-'80, 1997, 1999-2004. Held at Santa Anita Park 1949. Not held 1942-'43. 1 mile 1940. 1$^1/_{16}$ miles 1941-'53. 1$^1/_4$ miles 1986-'87. Dead heat for third 2002.

Vernon O. Underwood Stakes

Grade 3 in 2006. Hollywood Park, three-year-olds and up, 6 furlongs, dirt. Held December 3, 2005, with a gross value of $98,000. First held in 1981. First graded in 1984. Stakes record 1:08.04 (2004 Taste of Paradise).

Year	Winner	Jockey	Second	Third	Strs	Time	1st Purse
2005	**Bordonaro**, 4, 120	P. A. Valenzuela	Turnbolt, 4, 120	Captain Squire, 6, 124	4	1:08.11	$60,000
2004	**Taste of Paradise**, 5, 122	J. Valdivia Jr.	Watchem Smokey, 4, 116	My Master (Arg), 5, 116	7	**1:08.04**	60,000
2003	**Watchem Smokey**, 3, 112	J. A. Krone	Our New Recruit, 4, 114	Hasty Kris, 6, 116	6	1:08.93	60,000
2002	**Debonair Joe**, 3, 112	J. A. Krone	F J's Pace, 7, 116	American System, 3, 116	9	1:09.17	60,000
2001	**Men's Exclusive**, 8, 120	L. A. Pincay Jr.	Tavasco, 4, 114	Caller One, 4, 124	7	1:09.04	60,000
2000	**Men's Exclusive**, 7, 116	L. A. Pincay Jr.	Love All the Way, 5, 117	Lexicon, 5, 122	7	1:09.02	60,000
1999	**Five Star Day**, 3, 120	A. O. Solis	Your Halo, 4, 122	Son of a Pistol, 7, 122	5	1:09.91	60,000
1998	**†Love That Jazz**, 4, 117	K. Desormeaux	Peyrano (Arg), 6, 116	Swiss Yodeler, 4, 120	8	1:08.79	60,000
1997	**Tower Full**, 5, 118	C. S. Nakatani	Trafalger, 3, 118	Swiss Yodeler, 3, 114	4	1:08.17	60,000
1996	**Paying Dues**, 4, 124	P. Day	Men's Exclusive, 3, 114	Kern Ridge, 5, 114	7	1:08.24	64,860
1995	**Powis Castle**, 4, 114	G. L. Stevens	Lucky Forever, 6, 122	Plenty Zloty, 5, 116	8	1:08.40	62,300
1994	**Wekiva Springs**, 3, 118	K. Desormeaux	Cardmania, 8, 120	Gundaghia, 7, 120	9	1:08.37	63,750
1993	**†Meafara**, 4, 119	G. L. Stevens	†Arches of Gold, 4, 121	Davy Be Good, 5, 116	6	1:10.01	60,900
1992	**Gundaghia**, 5, 116	G. L. Stevens	Gray Slewpy, 4, 124	Cardmania, 6, 124	5	1:09.33	61,300
1991	**Individualist**, 4, 114	K. Desormeaux	Thirty Slews, 4, 117	Cardmania, 5, 120	8	1:08.86	64,500
1990	**Frost Free**, 5, 120	C. J. McCarron	Timebank, 3, 112	Sam Who, 5, 114	9	1:08.20	65,300
1989	**Olympic Prospect**, 5, 120	A. O. Solis	Sam Who, 4, 122	Order, 4, 122	4	1:08.80	60,200
1988	**Gallant Sailor**, 5, 116	F. Olivares	Reconnoitering, 4, 116	†Very Subtle, 4, 117	7	1:09.60	63,400
1987	**Hilco Scamper**, 4, 114	C. A. Black	Reconnoitering, 3, 112	Zabaleta, 4, 122	6	1:09.60	62,800
1986	**Bedside Promise**, 4, 122	G. L. Stevens	Bolder Than Bold, 4, 114	†Pine Tree Lane, 4, 117	10	1:08.80	127,200
	Nasib (Ire), 4, 116	E. Delahoussaye	Will Dancer (Fr), 4, 116	Barbery, 5, 115	8	1:40.40	66,900
1985	**Pancho Villa**, 3, 122	L. A. Pincay Jr.	Charging Falls, 4, 122	Temerity Prince, 5, 122	6	1:08.80	121,900
1984	**Fifty Six Ina Row**, 3, 112	S. Hawley	Debonaire Junior, 3, 120	Charging Falls, 3, 112	11	1:09.40	91,975
	†Lovlier Linda, 4, 121	W. Shoemaker	Sonrie Jorge (Arg), 4, 116	Fali Time, 3, 122	9	1:10.00	89,475
1983	**Fighting Fit**, 4, 120	E. Delahoussaye	Expressman, 3, 112	†Matching, 5, 119	10	1:09.60	101,950
1982	**Mad Key**, 5, 116	E. Delahoussaye	Shanekite, 4, 120	Dave's Friend, 7, 114	9	1:08.20	70,600
	Unpredictable, 3, 120	K. D. Black	Remember John, 3, 120	Chinook Pass, 3, 112	8	1:08.60	69,100
1981	**Shanekite**, 3, 114	S. Hawley	Syncopate, 6, 122	Big Presentation, 5, 114	8	1:08.20	50,500
	Smokite, 5, 116	D. C. Hall	I'm Smokin, 5, 120	Stand Pat, 6, 114	8	1:08.60	50,500

Named for Vernon O. Underwood, chief executive officer and chairman of the board of Hollywood Park (1972-'85). National Sprint Championship S. 1981-'89. Vernon O. Underwood Breeders' Cup S. 1993-'95. Two divisions 1981-'82, 1984, 1986. †Denotes female.

Victory Ride Stakes

Grade 3 in 2006. Saratoga Race Course, three-year-olds, fillies, 6 furlongs, dirt. Held August 25, 2005, with a gross value of $81,500. First held in 2003. First graded in 2006. Stakes record 1:09.62 (2003 Country Romance).

Year	Winner	Jockey	Second	Third	Strs	Time	1st Purse
2005	**Nothing But Fun**, 3, 116	R. Migliore	Maddalena, 3, 123	Reunited, 3, 118	6	1:09.86	$48,900
2004	**Smokey Glacken**, 3, 120	J. Bravo	Grand Prayer, 3, 116	Feline Story, 3, 120	7	1:09.64	46,080
2003	**Country Romance**, 3, 116	J. F. Chavez	She's Zealous, 3, 114	Ebony Breeze, 3, 122	9	**1:09.62**	45,720

Named for G. Watts Humphrey Jr.'s 2001 Test S. (G1) winner Victory Ride (1998 f. by Seeking the Gold).

Vinery Madison Stakes

Grade 2 in 2006. Keeneland Race Course, four-year-olds and up, fillies and mares, about 7 furlongs, dirt. Held April 12, 2006, with a gross value of $200,000. First held in 2002. First graded in 2005. Stakes record 1:22.34 (2006 Dubai Escapade).

Year	Winner	Jockey	Second	Third	Strs	Time	1st Purse
2006	**Dubai Escapade**, 4, 117	E. S. Prado	Josh's Madelyn, 5, 117	Ever Elusive, 4, 117	9	**1:22.34**	$124,000
2005	**Madcap Escapade**, 4, 123	J. D. Bailey	My Trusty Cat, 5, 117	Molto Vita, 5, 119	7	1:23.33	124,000
2004	**Ema Bovary (Chi)**, 5, 120	R. M. Gonzalez	Harmony Lodge, 6, 123	Yell, 4, 116	6	1:23.41	108,500
2003	**A New Twist**, 4, 116	P. Day	Flaxen Flyer, 4, 116	Forest Secrets, 5, 116	4	1:24.32	84,863
2002	**Victory Ride**, 4, 116	E. S. Prado	Celtic Melody, 4, 116	Away, 5, 116	7	1:23.70	69,006

Named for Madison County, Kentucky. Sponsored by Vinery of Lexington 2004-'06. Grade 3 2005. Madison S. 2002-'03.

Violet Stakes

Grade 3 in 2006. Meadowlands, three-year-olds and up, fillies and mares, 1$^1/_{16}$ miles, turf. Held October 21, 2005, with a gross value of $150,000. First held in 1977. First graded in 1983. Stakes record 1:39.60 (1989 Gather The Clan [Ire]).

Year	Winner	Jockey	Second	Third	Strs	Time	1st Purse
2005	**Humoristic**, 4, 117	H. Vega	Delta Princess, 6, 123	Brunilda (Arg), 5, 119	11	1:42.23	$90,000
2004	**Changing World**, 4, 113	P. Fragoso	High Court (Brz), 4, 117	Ocean Drive, 4, 121	7	1:41.53	120,000

2003	**Dancal (Ire)**, 5, 116	J. Castellano	Madeira Mist (Ire), 4, 116	Something Ventured, 4, 116	8	1:43.69	$90,000
2002	**Babae (Chi)**, 6, 119	J. F. Chavez	Platinum Tiara, 4, 115	Stylish, 4, 119	10	1:41.17	90,000
2001	**Clearly a Queen**, 4, 115	J. F. Chavez	Queue, 4, 115	Paga (Arg), 4, 117	12	1:43.56	90,000
2000	**Follow the Money**, 4, 116	C. J. McCarron	Melody Queen (GB), 4, 116	Fickle Friends, 4, 114	7	1:42.65	90,000
1999	**Tookin Down**, 4, 113	E. S. Prado	Proud Run, 5, 115	Darling Alice, 4, 113	7	1:42.39	90,000
1998	**Heaven's Command (GB)**, 4, 115	R. Migliore	Maxzene, 5, 123	Oh Nellie, 4, 116	7	1:40.71	60,000
1997	**Sangria**, 4, 114	R. Wilson	Fasta, 4, 11	Shemozzle (Ire), 4, 117	8	1:42.02	60,000
1996	**Plenty of Sugar**, 5, 117	R. E. Colton	Brushing Gloom, 4, 121	Hello Mom, 4, 115	6	1:48.62	60,000
1995	**Symphony Lady**, 5, 116	J. Bravo	Kira's Dancer, 6, 115	Irish Linnet, 7, 122	8	1:45.48	60,000
1994	**It's Personal**, 4, 111	J. R. Velazquez	Carezza, 5, 115	Artful Pleasure, 4, 109	11	1:42.61	45,000
1993	**Mz. Zill Bear**, 4, 113	E. S. Prado	Vivano, 4, 115	Topsa, 6, 113	4	1:44.55	45,000
1992	**Highland Crystal**, 4, 116	E. S. Prado	Irish Actress, 5, 116	Navarra, 4, 111	7	1:41.26	45,000
1991	**Southern Tradition**, 4, 116	J. A. Santos	Songlines, 5, 115	Memories of Pam, 4, 114	7	1:43.68	45,000
1990	**Miss Josh**, 4, 116	M. G. Pino	Summer Secretary, 5, 117	Leave It Be, 5, 118	13	1:40.00	54,750
1989	**Gather The Clan (Ire)**, 4, 117	C. Perret	Sweet Blow Pop, 5, 119	Summer Secretary, 4, 117	10	**1:39.60**	55,260
1988	**Just Class (Ire)**, 4, 117	C. W. Antley	Shadowfay, 5, 109	Flying Katuna, 4, 115	8	1:40.20	53,400
	Graceful Darby, 4, 115	R. P. Romero	Mystical Lass, 4, 112	Kim Kimmie, 5, 111	10	1:41.00	42,900
1987	**Videogenic**, 5, 118	J. Cruguet	Spruce Fir, 4, 119	Cadabra Abra, 4, 120	7	1:42.00	45,180
	Dismasted, 5, 118	J. Samyn	Small Virtue, 4, 118	Country Recital, 4, 113	6	1:41.60	44,790
1986	**Lake Country**, 5, 118	V. A. Bracciale Jr.	Duckweed, 4, 111	Anka Germania (Ire), 4, 114	8	1:41.20	68,310
1985	**Possible Mate**, 4, 119	J. Samyn	Eastern Dawn, 4, 112	Carlypha (Ire), 4, 116	9	1:42.20	52,665
	Vers La Caisse, 4, 116	R. Migliore	Cato Double, 5, 117	Forest Maiden, 5, 117	10	1:43.00	63,240
1984	**Rash But Royal**, 4, 114	J. L. Kaenel	High Schemes, 4, 115	Candlelight Affair, 3, 110	8	1:42.20	49,020
	Aspen Rose, 4, 114	J. Velasquez	It's Fine, 4, 112	If Winter Comes, 6, 113	8	1:42.00	49,020
1983	**Twosome**, 4, 113	J. D. Bailey	Princess Roberta, 5, 115	Svarga, 4, 112	8	1:41.20	26,535
	Geraldine's Store, 4, 117	J. Samyn	Maidenhead, 4, 110	Mistretta (Fr), 4, 116	7	1:40.60	26,355
1982	**Pat's Joy**, 4, 114	J. D. Bailey	Prismatical, 4, 115	Kuja Happa, 4, 113	9	1:42.20	26,670
	Dearly Too, 3, 114	J. Samyn	Tableaux, 4, 112	Dance Troupe, 5, 114	9	1:42.20	26,670
1981	**Honey Fox**, 4, 120	J. Samyn	Adlibber, 4, 117	Hemlock, 4, 116	11	1:41.40	33,690
1980	**Producer**, 4, 119	J. Fell	Champagne Ginny, 3, 116	Cannon Boy, 3, 113	8	1:41.60	26,325
	The Very One, 5, 117	J. Velasquez	Hey Babe, 4, 115	Poppycock, 4, 113	7	1:42.40	26,145
1979	**Terpsichorist**, 4, 122	M. Venezia	Spark of Life, 4, 111	Sisterhood, 4, 117	11	1:43.20	36,010
1978	**Navajo Princess**, 4, 115	C. Perret	Pressing Date, 4, 114	Fun Forever, 5, 118	6	1:44.00	35,360
1977	**Lady Singer (Ire)**, 4, 113	A. T. Cordero Jr.	Sans Arc, 3, 111	Jolly Song, 5, 112	6	1:48.40	35,035

Named for New Jersey's state flower, the common violet. Formerly sponsored by the Sheraton Meadowlands in East Rutherford, New Jersey 1995. Sheraton Meadowlands Violet H. 1995. Violet H. 1977-'94, 1996-2005. Dirt 1977, 1993, 1999. Two divisions 1980, 1982-'85, 1987-'88.

Virginia Derby

Grade 2 in 2006. Colonial Downs, three-year-olds, 1¼ miles, turf. Held July 16, 2005, with a gross value of $750,000. First held in 1998. First graded in 2004. Stakes record 1:59.97 (1999 Phi Beta Doc).

Year	Winner	Jockey	Second	Third	Strs	Time	1st Purse
2005	**English Channel**, 3, 120	J. R. Velazquez	Chattahoochee War, 3, 120	Rebel Rebel (Ire), 3, 116	9	2:02.57	$450,000
2004	**Kitten's Joy**, 3, 117	E. S. Prado	Artie Schiller, 3, 117	Prince Arch, 3, 119	8	2:01.22	300,000
2003	**Silver Tree**, 3, 115	E. S. Prado	Kicken Kris, 3, 115	King's Drama (Ire), 3, 115	8	2:01.11	300,000
2002	**Orchard Park**, 3, 119	E. S. Prado	Flying Dash (Ger), 3, 119	Touring England, 3, 115	6	2:03.10	300,000
2001	**Potaro (Ire)**, 3, 115	B. E. Bartram	Bay Eagle, 3, 115	Confucius Say, 3, 115	9	2:02.17	120,000
2000	**Lightning Paces**, 3, 115	G. W. Hutton	Sunspot, 3, 115	Blaze and Blues, 3, 115	10	2:02.18	120,000
1999	**Phi Beta Doc**, 3, 117	R. A. Dominguez	Passinetti, 3, 115	North East Bound, 3, 119	13	**1:59.97**	120,000
1998	**Crowd Pleaser**, 3, 117	J. Samyn	Distant Mirage (Ire), 3, 115	Errant Escort, 3, 115	10	2:00.28	150,000

Colonial Downs is located in New Kent, Virginia. Grade 3 2004-'05.

Vosburgh Stakes

Grade 1 in 2006. Belmont Park, three-year-olds and up, 6 furlongs, dirt. Held October 1, 2005, with a gross value of $500,000. First held in 1940. First graded in 1973. Stakes record 1:08.82 (2005 Taste of Paradise).

Year	Winner	Jockey	Second	Third	Strs	Time	1st Purse
2005	**Taste of Paradise**, 6, 124	G. K. Gomez	Tiger Heart, 4, 124	Lion Tamer, 5, 124	10	**1:08.82**	$300,000
2004	**Pico Central (Brz)**, 5, 124	V. Espinoza	Voodoo, 6, 124	Speightstown, 6, 124	5	1:09.74	300,000
2003	**Ghostzapper**, 3, 123	J. Castellano	Aggadan, 4, 126	Posse, 3, 123	10	1:14.72	300,000
2002	**Bonapaw**, 6, 126	G. Melancon	Aldebaran, 4, 126	Voodoo, 4, 126	6	1:22.34	180,000
2001	**Left Bank**, 4, 126	J. R. Velazquez	Squirtle Squirt, 3, 123	Big E E, 4, 126	6	1:20.73	180,000
2000	**Trippi**, 3, 123	J. D. Bailey	More Than Ready, 3, 123	One Way Love, 5, 126	10	1:21.66	180,000
1999	**Artax**, 4, 126	J. F. Chavez	Stormin Fever, 5, 126	Mountain Top, 4, 126	6	1:21.65	150,000
1998	**Affirmed Success**, 4, 126	J. F. Chavez	Stormin Fever, 4, 126	Tale of the Cat, 4, 126	7	1:21.99	150,000
1997	**Victor Cooley**, 4, 126	J. F. Chavez	Score a Birdie, 6, 126	Tale of the Cat, 3, 122	12	1:22.05	150,000
1996	**Langfuhr**, 4, 126	J. F. Chavez	Honour and Glory, 3, 122	Lite the Fuse, 5, 126	8	1:21.25	120,000
1995	**Not Surprising**, 5, 126	R. G. Davis	You and I, 4, 126	Our Emblem, 4, 126	13	1:22.48	120,000
1994	**Harlan**, 5, 126	J. D. Bailey	American Chance, 5, 126	Cherokee Run, 4, 126	10	1:21.82	120,000
1993	**Birdonthewire**, 4, 126	M. E. Smith	Take Me Out, 5, 126	Lion Cavern, 4, 126	6	1:22.28	120,000
1992	**Rubiano**, 5, 126	J. A. Krone	Sheikh Albadou (GB), 4, 126	Salt Lake, 3, 123	8	1:22.80	120,000
1991	**Housebuster**, 4, 126	C. Perret	Senator to Be, 4, 126	Sunshine Jimmy, 4, 126	6	1:21.85	120,000
1990	**Sewickley**, 5, 126	A. T. Cordero Jr.	Sunshine Jimmy, 3, 122	Glitterman, 5, 126	9	1:21.00	142,080
1989	**Sewickley**, 4, 126	R. P. Romero	Once Wild, 4, 126	Mr. Nickerson, 3, 123	5	1:23.00	135,120

1988	**Mining**, 4, 126	R. P. Romero	Gulch, 4, 126	High Brite, 4, 126	4	1:22.40	$133,920
1987	**Groovy**, 4, 126	A. T. Cordero Jr.	Moment of Hope, 4, 126	Sun Master, 6, 126	8	1:22.60	139,680
1986	**King's Swan**, 6, 126	J. A. Santos	Love That Mac, 4, 126	Cutlass Reality, 4, 126	8	1:21.80	141,840
1985	**Another Reef**, 3, 124	N. Santagata	Pancho Villa, 3, 124	Whoop Up, 5, 126	6	1:21.80	102,420
1984	**Track Barron**, 3, 123	A. T. Cordero Jr.	Timeless Native, 4, 126	Raja's Shark, 3, 123	9	1:22.00	109,800
1983	**A Phenomenon**, 3, 123	A. T. Cordero Jr.	Fit to Fight, 4, 126	Deputy Minister, 4, 126	8	1:21.00	69,000
1982	**Engine One**, 4, 126	R. Hernandez	‡†Gold Beauty, 3, 120	Maudlin, 4, 126	6	1:23.80	65,760
1981	**Guilty Conscience**, 5, 126	C. B. Asmussen	Rise Jim, 5, 126	Well Decorated, 3, 123	8	1:22.00	67,920
1980	**Plugged Nickle**, 3, 123	C. B. Asmussen	Jaklin Klugman, 3, 123	Dave's Friend, 5, 126	9	1:21.40	67,440
1979	**General Assembly**, 3, 123	J. Vasquez	Dr. Patches, 5, 126	Syncopate, 4, 126	6	1:21.00	48,195
1978	**Dr. Patches**, 4, 117	A. T. Cordero Jr.	†What a Summer, 5, 124	Sorry Lookin, 3, 109	8	1:21.00	48,960
1977	**Affiliate**, 3, 114	C. Perret	Broadway Forli, 3, 118	Great Above, 5, 112	9	1:21.00	49,905
1976	**†My Juliet**, 4, 120	A. S. Black	‡It's Freezing, 4, 113	Bold Forbes, 3, 126	6	1:21.80	31,980
1975	**No Bias**, 5, 116	A. Santiago	Step Nicely, 5, 126	Lonetree, 5, 117	11	1:22.80	34,590
1974	**Forego**, 4, 131	H. Gustines	Stop the Music, 4, 118	Prince Dantan, 4, 119	12	1:21.60	35,550
1973	**Aljamin**, 3, 118	A. T. Cordero Jr.	Highbinder, 5, 115	Timeless Moment, 3, 112	8	1:21.20	33,660

Named for Walter S. Vosburgh (1855-1938), official handicapper for the Jockey Club and various racing associations. Grade 2 1973-'79. Vosburgh H. 1940-'78. Held at Aqueduct 1959, 1961-'74, 1976-'77, 1979-'83, 1985-'86. 7 furlongs 1940-2002. Two-year-olds and up 1940-'57. ‡Bold Forbes finished second, DQ to third, 1976. ‡Duke Mitchell finished second, DQ to fourth, 1982. †Denotes female.

Walmac Lone Star Derby

Grade 3 in 2006. Lone Star Park, three-year-olds, 1$^1/_{16}$ miles, dirt. Held May 13, 2006, with a gross value of $300,000. First held in 1997. First graded in 2002. Stakes record 1:40.88 (1997 Anet).

Year	Winner	Jockey	Second	Third	Strs	Time	1st Purse
2006	**Wanna Runner**, 3, 122	V. Espinoza	Wait in Line, 3, 122	Admiral's Arch, 3, 122	6	1:43.71	$185,000
2005	**Southern Africa**, 3, 122	J. K. Court	Shamoan (Ire), 3, 122	Real Dandy, 3, 122	11	1:41.92	165,000
2004	**Pollard's Vision**, 3, 122	J. R. Velazquez	Cryptograph, 3, 122	Flamethrowintexan, 3, 122	12	1:42.10	150,000
2003	**Dynever**, 3, 122	E. S. Prado	Most Feared, 3, 122	Commander's Affair, 3, 122	12	1:50.43	277,500
2002	**Wiseman's Ferry**, 3, 122	J. F. Chavez	Tracemark, 3, 122	Peekskill, 3, 122	14	1:49.92	277,500
2001	**Percy Hope**, 3, 122	J. K. Court	Fifty Stars, 3, 122	Gift of the Eagle, 3, 122	8	1:50.27	292,500
2000	**Tahkodha Hills**, 3, 122	E. Coa	Jeblar Sez Who, 3, 122	Big Numbers, 3, 122	7	1:44.05	180,000
1999	**T. B. Track Star**, 3, 122	E. M. Martin Jr.	Desert Demon, 3, 122	Congratulate, 3, 122	11	1:42.92	165,000
1998	**Smolderin Heart**, 3, 122	T. T. Doocy	Shot of Gold, 3, 122	Troy's Play, 3, 122	8	1:46.29	145,000
1997	**Anet**, 3, 122	D. R. Flores	Frisk Me Now, 3, 122	Holzmeister, 3, 122	9	**1:40.88**	140,000

Sponsored by John T. L. Jones III's and Bobby Trussell's Walmac Farm of Lexington 2004-'05. The track and the race are named for Texas's (Lone Star Park's home state) nickname, the Lone Star State. Lone Star Derby 1997-2003. 1$^1/_{16}$ miles 1997-2000.

Washington Park Handicap

Grade 2 in 2006. Arlington Park, three-year-olds and up, 1$^3/_{16}$ miles, dirt. Held July 30, 2005, with a gross value of $300,000. First held in 1926. First graded in 1973. Stakes record 1:54.27 (2005 Perfect Drift).

Year	Winner	Jockey	Second	Third	Strs	Time	1st Purse
2005	**Perfect Drift**, 6, 120	M. Guidry	Mambo Train, 4, 115	Home of Stars, 5, 114	7	**1:54.27**	$180,000
2004	**Eye of the Tiger**, 4, 116	E. Razo Jr.	Olmodavor, 5, 121	Congrats, 4, 116	5	1:56.87	210,000
2003	**Perfect Drift**, 4, 120	P. Day	Aeneas, 4, 115	Flatter, 4, 114	5	1:55.49	240,000
2002	**Tenpins**, 4, 116	R. Albarado	Generous Rosi (GB), 7, 115	Bonus Pack, 4, 115	5	1:55.07	240,000
2001	**Guided Tour**, 5, 116	L. J. Melancon	A Fleets Dancer, 6, 115	Duckhorn, 4, 114	5	2:00.76	240,000
2000	**Blazing Sword**, 6, 113	J. A. Rivera II	Mula Gula, 4, 114	Nite Dreamer, 5, 116	8	1:50.59	150,000
1997	**Beboppin Baby**, 4, 112	G. K. Gomez	City by Night, 4, 116	Stephanotis, 4, 118	5	1:49.00	90,000
1996	**Polar Expedition**, 5, 115	M. Guidry	Knockadoon, 4, 115	Tejano Run, 4, 117	8	1:49.97	120,000
1994	**Brother Brown**, 4, 117	P. Day	Eequalsmcsquared, 5, 113	Antrim Rd., 4, 113	11	1:49.77	120,000
1993	**Powerful Punch**, 4, 114	C. C. Bourque	Memo (Chi), 6, 115	Northern Trend, 5, 113	13	1:50.19	120,000
1992	**Irish Swap**, 5, 118	B. E. Poyadou	Clever Trevor, 6, 119	Barkerville, 4, 113	7	1:47.83	90,000
1991	**Black Tie Affair (Ire)**, 5, 120	S. J. Sellers	Summer Squall, 4, 119	Secret Hello, 4, 114	4	1:49.45	150,000
1990	**Lay Down**, 6, 115	W. H. McCauley	Sir Wesley, 6, 112	Mercedes Won, 4, 112	6	1:48.40	64,680
1989	**Blushing John**, 4, 124	P. Day	Grantley, 5, 112	Paramount Jet, 4, 113	5	1:50.80	48,030
1987	**Taylor's Special**, 6, 118	J. Lively	Blue Buckaroo, 4, 120	Fuzzy, 5, 114	6	1:51.60	61,965
1985	**Par Flite**, 4, 112	E. Fires	Big Pistol, 4, 122	Timeless Native, 5, 122	6	1:47.60	78,300
1984	**Thumbsucker**, 5, 115	S. Maple	Timeless Native, 4, 122	Le Cou Cou, 4, 122	10	1:48.60	80,940
1983	**Harham's Sizzler**, 4, 112	J. L. Diaz	Listcapade, 4, 122	Stage Reviewer, 4, 112	9	1:49.80	67,620
1982	**Summer Advocate**, 5, 115	P. Day	Mythical Ruler, 4, 112	Law Me, 4, 112	6	1:49.80	64,920
1981	**Rossi Gold**, 5, 119	P. Day	John's Monster, 4, 112	Lord Gallant, 4, 114	7	1:48.60	81,870
1980	**Spectacular Bid**, 4, 130	W. Shoemaker	Hold Your Tricks, 5, 119	Architect, 4, 119	6	1:46.20	155,880
1979	**That's a Nice**, 5, 117	I. J. Jimenez	†Calderina (Ity), 4, 113	Me Good Man, 5, 112	10	1:50.00	52,320
1978	**That's a Nice**, 4, 116	D. Richard	Court Open, 4, 115	Improviser, 6, 117	9	1:50.60	53,160
1977	**Majestic Light**, 4, 120	M. Venezia	Fifth Marine, 4, 122	Improviser, 5, 122	10	1:48.00	54,180
1976	**Double Edge Sword**, 6, 116	V. A. Bracciale Jr.	*Zografos, 8, 113	Proponent, 4, 109	5	1:48.20	70,400
1975	**Hasty Flyer**, 4, 115	H. Arroyo	Group Plan, 5, 116	Yaki King, 4, 113	6	1:48.60	38,100
1974	**Super Sail**, 6, 118	W. Gavidia	Smooth Dancer, 4, 112	Jesta Dream Away, 4, 111	7	2:03.00	38,300
1973	**Burning On**, 5, 114	D. Richard	New Hope, 4, 113	Vegas Vic, 5, 109	7	2:02.20	32,800

Named for the old Washington Park racetrack near Chicago. Grade 3 1973-'81. Washington H. 1964. Held at Washington Park 1926-'57. Not held 1928, 1937, 1986, 1988, 1995, 1998-'99. 1$^1/_4$ miles 1926, 1935-'36, 1940-'50, 1973-'74,

2001. 6 furlongs 1927-'34, 1938. 1 mile 1939, 1951-'58, 1960-'62, 1965-'72. 1⅛ miles 1959, 1963-'64, 1975-2000. Turf 1977-'79. Track record 2005. †Denotes female.

Westchester Handicap

Grade 3 in 2006. Belmont Park, three-year-olds and up, 1 mile, dirt. Held May 3, 2006, with a gross value of $108,800. First held in 1918. First graded in 1973. Stakes record 1:32.24 (2003 Najran [track record and equaled world record]).

Year	Winner	Jockey	Second	Third	Strs	Time	1st Purse
2006	**Sir Greeley**, 4, 117	E. Coa	Love of Money, 5, 117	Happy Hunting, 5, 116	6	1:33.69	$65,280
2005	**Gygistar**, 6, 118	J. Castellano	Swingforthefences, 4, 115	Value Plus, 4, 117	7	1:33.50	65,700
2004	**Gygistar**, 5, 115	J. Bravo	Saarland, 5, 114	Black Silk (GB), 8, 113	7	1:35.89	65,700
2003	**Najran**, 4, 113	E. S. Prado	Saarland, 4, 114	Justification, 6, 113	7	**1:32.24**	65,820
2002	**Free of Love**, 4, 114	J. D. Bailey	Dayton Flyer, 4, 112	Country Be Gold, 5, 114	9	1:35.56	67,500
2001	**Cat's At Home**, 4, 114	F. Leon	Little Hans, 4, 113	Milwaukee Brew, 4, 117	6	1:33.60	64,920
2000	**Yankee Victor**, 4, 115	H. Castillo Jr.	Golden Missile, 5, 116	Watchman's Warning, 5, 113	7	1:34.37	66,000
1999	**Mr. Sinatra**, 5, 116	C. C. Lopez	Laredo, 6, 114	Brushing Up, 6, 113	4	1:35.04	64,202
1998	**Wagon Limit**, 4, 114	J. Samyn	Draw, 5, 113	Lucayan Prince, 5, 116	8	1:34.06	66,420
1997	**Pacific Fleet**, 5, 114	F. T. Alvarado	Circle of Light, 4, 110	Stalwart Member, 4, 114	7	1:33.80	65,940
1996	**Valid Wager**, 4, 115	J. M. Pezua	Pat n Jac, 4, 111	More to Tell, 5, 118	7	1:34.74	66,240
1995	**Mr. Shawklit**, 4, 112	M. J. Luzzi	Devil His Due, 6, 124	Our Emblem, 4, 112	6	1:34.66	65,760
1994	**Virginia Rapids**, 4, 116	J. Samyn	Colonial Affair, 4, 121	Cherokee Run, 4, 119	7	1:34.52	65,640
1993	**Bill Of Rights**, 4, 110	J. Samyn	Fly So Free, 5, 118	Loach, 5, 113	10	1:34.69	72,720
1992	**Rubiano**, 5, 117	J. A. Santos	Out of Place, 5, 115	Wild Away, 5, 111	6	1:34.83	68,880
1991	**Rubiano**, 4, 111	J. D. Bailey	Senor Speedy, 4, 113	Killer Diller, 4, 115	9	1:34.94	71,520
1990	**Once Wild**, 5, 121	A. T. Cordero Jr.	dh-Its Acedemic, 6, 116 dh-King's Swan, 10, 113		5	1:35.00	67,800
1989	**Lord of the Night**, 6, 115	J. Velasquez	Dancing Spree, 4, 112	Congeleur, 4, 112	8	1:35.60	71,040
1988	**Faster Than Sound**, 4, 113	J. A. Krone	Ron Stevens, 4, 111	King's Swan, 8, 133	9	1:34.40	108,000
1987	**King's Swan**, 7, 122	J. A. Santos	Cutlass Reality, 5, 114	Landing Plot, 4, 115	6	1:36.20	69,120
1986	**Garthorn**, 6, 120	R. Q. Meza	Ends Well, 5, 115	Grand Rivulet, 5, 110	11	1:33.80	75,240
1985	**Verbarctic**, 5, 114	G. McCarron	Moro, 6, 122	Fighting Fit, 6, 124	7	1:36.60	53,460
1984	**Jacque's Tip**, 4, 114	A. T. Cordero Jr.	Minstrel Glory, 4, 107	Havagreatdate, 6, 111	8	1:41.80	55,440
1983	**Singh Tu**, 4, 109	J. Samyn	Master Digby, 4, 114	Fabulous Find, 5, 114	10	1:35.20	33,780
1982	**John Casey**, 5, 114	J. Fell	Brasher Doubloon, 4, 111	Accipiter's Hope, 4, 120	9	1:38.00	33,090
	Fabulous Find, 4, 109	J. O. Cintron	In From Dixie, 5, 122	Princelet, 4, 126	7	1:38.00	33,330
1981	**Dunham's Gift**, 4, 115	M. Venezia	Ring of Light, 6, 114	Dr. Blum, 4, 124	6	1:35.00	33,000
1980	**Nice Catch**, 6, 120	J. Fell	Ardaluan (Ire), 4, 119	Lark Oscillation (Fr), 5, 115	8	1:36.80	34,020
1979	**Vencedor**, 5, 126	R. Hernandez	Don Aronow, 5, 108	Coverack, 6, 114	10	1:44.00	33,060
1978	**Pumpkin Moonshine**, 4, 105	D. A. Borden	Lynn Davis, 4, 115	Sharpstone, 4, 111	7	1:44.40	32,250
1977	**Cinteelo**, 4, 113	E. Maple	Turn and Count, 4, 124	Cojak, 4, 120	9	1:43.40	33,090
1976	**Double Edge Sword**, 6, 114	A. T. Cordero Jr.	Dr. Emil, 4, 116	Bold and Fancy, 5, 111	8	1:33.40	34,170
1975	**Step Nicely**, 5, 126	J. Velasquez	*Tambac, 5, 116	Onion, 6, 119	9	1:34.00	33,900
1974	**Dundee Marmalade**, 6, 113	M. Hole	Infuriator, 4, 113	Prove Out, 5, 126	6	1:36.00	32,940
1973	**North Sea**, 4, 117	R. C. Smith	Forage, 4, 116	†Summer Guest, 4, 118	9	1:33.60	33,990

Named for Westchester County, New York, located north of the Bronx. Formerly named in honor of the Allied victory in World War I and the signing of the Versailles Peace Treaty in 1919. Formerly named for Yorktown, New York, a community located in Westchester County. Grade 2 1973-'79. Yorktown H. 1918, 1920-'39. Victory H. 1919. Westchester S. 1953-'71. Held at Empire City 1918-'42. Held at Jamaica 1943-'59. Held at Aqueduct 1960-2001. Not held 1932-'33, 1954-'58. 1⅛ miles 1918, 1922-'39, 1951-'53. 1¼ miles 1919-'21. 1³⁄₁₆ miles 1940-'50. 1¹⁄₁₆ miles 1977-'79. 1 mile 70 yards 1984. Four-year-olds and up 1959-'71. Two divisions 1982. Dead heat for second 1990. Track record 2003. Equaled world record 2003. †Denotes female.

West Virginia Derby

Grade 3 in 2006. Mountaineer Race Track, three-year-olds, 1⅛ miles, dirt. Held August 14, 2005, with a gross value of $750,000. First held in 1958. First graded in 2002. Stakes record 1:46.29 (2003 Soto).

Year	Winner	Jockey	Second	Third	Strs	Time	1st Purse
2005	**Real Dandy**, 3, 114	M. Guidry	Magna Graduate, 3, 113	Anthony J., 3, 115	11	1:50.29	$450,000
2004	**Sir Shackleton**, 3, 117	R. Bejarano	Pollard's Vision, 3, 119	Britt's Jules, 3, 115	7	1:49.16	363,000
2003	**Soto**, 3, 111	R. A. Dominguez	Dynever, 3, 117	Colita, 3, 111	9	**1:46.29**	360,000
2002	**Wiseman's Ferry**, 3, 122	J. F. Chavez	The Judge Sez Who, 3, 115	Captain Squire, 3, 115	9	1:49.63	360,000
2001	**Western Pride**, 3, 113	D. G. Whitney	Saratoga Games, 3, 115	Thunder Blitz, 3, 119	9	1:47.20	300,000
2000	**Mass Market**, 3, 115	R. Wilson	Hal's Hope, 3, 122	Bet On Red, 3, 122	10	1:49.94	180,000
1999	**Stellar Brush**, 3, 122	J. V. Stokes	American Spirit, 3, 113	Harry's Halo, 3, 119	11	1:49.02	150,000
1998	**Da Devil**, 3, 113	J. K. Court	One Bold Stroke, 3, 122	Jess M, 3, 115	12	1:48.84	120,000
1990	**Challenge My Duty**, 3, 113	I. B. Ayarza	My Other Brother, 3, 115	Gay's Best Boy, 3, 115	8	1:49.60	60,000
1989	**Doc's Leader**, 3, 114	W. I. Fox Jr.	Halo Hansom, 3, 117	Downtown Davey, 3, 117	7	1:50.00	60,000
1988	**Old Stories**, 3, 114	R. Hernandez	Viva Deputy, 3, 117	Rising Colors, 3, 112	10	1:52.20	60,000
1981	**Park's Policy**, 3, 115	J. S. Lloyd	Diverse Dude, 3, 115	Iron Gem, 3, 115	9	1:49.60	22,750
	Johnny Dance, 3, 115	F. Lovato Jr.	Master Tommy, 3, 115	Amasham, 3, 115	8	1:47.80	22,750
1980	**Summer Advocate**, 3, 115	W. L. Floyd	Lucky Pluck, 3, 115	Foolish Move, 3, 115	11	1:50.80	32,500
1979	**Architect**, 3, 115	S. A. Spencer	Sir Prince P., 3, 115	Lt. Bert, 3, 115	11	1:51.00	32,500
1978	**Beau Sham**, 3, 115	P. Day	Silent Cal, 3, 115	Morning Frolic, 3, 115	9	1:48.60	32,500
1977	**Best Person**, 3, 115	V. A. Bracciale Jr.	Swoon Swept, 3, 115	A Letter to Harry, 3, 115	9	1:48.60	32,500
1976	**Wardlaw**, 3, 121	J. E. Tejeira	American Trader, 3, 115	Joachim, 3, 121	7	1:47.60	32,500
1975	**At the Front**, 3, 117	A. Santiago	My Friend Gus, 3, 117	Packer Captain, 3, 117	10	1:48.60	32,500

1974	**Park Guard**, 3, 124	B. M. Feliciano	Sea Songster, 3, 126	Sahib Nearco, 3, 124	11	1:47.40	$32,500
1973	**Blue Chip Dan**, 3, 118	M. Solomone	Dr. Pantano, 3, 121	Double Edge Sword, 3, 124	8	1:49.20	20,930

Mountaineer Race Track is located in Chester, West Virginia. Held at Wheeling Downs 1958-'61. Held at Waterford Park 1963-'81. Not held 1960, 1962, 1982-'87, 1991-'97. Two divisions 1981. Track record 2001, 2003.

Whitney Handicap

Grade 1 in 2006. Saratoga Race Course, three-year-olds and up, 1⅛ miles, dirt. Held August 6, 2005, with a gross value of $750,000. First held in 1928. First graded in 1973. Stakes record 1:47 (1974 Tri Jet).

Year	Winner	Jockey	Second	Third	Strs	Time	1st Purse
2005	**Commentator**, 4, 116	G. L. Stevens	Saint Liam, 5, 122	Sir Shackleton, 4, 115	8	1:48.33	$450,000
2004	**Roses in May**, 4, 114	E. S. Prado	Perfect Drift, 5, 117	Bowman's Band, 6, 114	9	1:48.54	450,000
2003	**Medaglia d'Oro**, 4, 123	J. D. Bailey	Volponi, 5, 120	Evening Attire, 5, 118	7	1:47.69	450,000
2002	**Left Bank**, 5, 118	J. R. Velazquez	Street Cry (Ire), 4, 123	Lido Palace (Chi), 5, 119	6	1:47.04	450,000
2001	**Lido Palace (Chi)**, 4, 115	J. D. Bailey	Albert the Great, 4, 124	Gander, 5, 113	7	1:47.94	540,000
2000	**Lemon Drop Kid**, 4, 123	E. S. Prado	Cat Thief, 4, 117	Behrens, 6, 122	6	1:48.30	680,000
1999	**Victory Gallop**, 4, 123	J. D. Bailey	Behrens, 5, 123	Catienus, 5, 113	8	1:48.66	360,000
1998	**Awesome Again**, 4, 117	P. Day	Tale of the Cat, 4, 114	Crypto Star, 4, 116	8	1:49.71	240,000
1997	**Will's Way**, 4, 117	J. D. Bailey	Formal Gold, 4, 120	Skip Away, 4, 125	6	1:48.37	210,000
1996	**Mahogany Hall**, 5, 113	J. A. Santos	†Serena's Song, 4, 116	Peaks and Valleys, 4, 121	9	1:48.65	210,000
1995	**Unaccounted For**, 4, 114	P. Day	L'Carriere, 4, 111	Silver Fox, 4, 112	9	1:49.29	210,000
1994	**Colonial Affair**, 4, 117	J. A. Santos	Devil His Due, 5, 125	West by West, 5, 113	7	1:48.61	210,000
1993	**Brunswick**, 4, 112	M. E. Smith	West by West, 4, 115	Devil His Due, 4, 122	7	1:47.41	150,000
1992	**Sultry Song**, 4, 115	J. D. Bailey	Out of Place, 5, 115	Chief Honcho, 5, 116	9	1:47.29	150,000
1991	**In Excess (Ire)**, 4, 121	G. L. Stevens	Chief Honcho, 4, 115	Killer Diller, 4, 112	7	1:48.01	150,000
1990	**Criminal Type**, 5, 126	G. L. Stevens	Dancing Spree, 5, 121	Mi Selecto, 5, 117	6	1:48.60	140,640
1989	**Easy Goer**, 3, 119	P. Day	Forever Silver, 4, 120	Cryptoclearance, 5, 122	6	1:47.40	172,500
1988	**†Personal Ensign**, 4, 117	R. P. Romero	Gulch, 4, 124	King's Swan, 8, 123	3	1:47.80	162,300
1987	**Java Gold**, 3, 113	P. Day	Gulch, 3, 117	Broad Brush, 4, 127	7	1:48.40	173,100
1986	**†Lady's Secret**, 4, 119	P. Day	Ends Well, 5, 116	Fuzzy, 4, 110	7	1:49.80	202,500
1985	**Track Barron**, 4, 124	A. T. Cordero Jr.	Carr de Naskra, 4, 120	Vanlandingham, 4, 124	5	1:47.60	160,680
1984	**Slew o' Gold**, 4, 126	A. T. Cordero Jr.	Track Barron, 3, 117	Thumbsucker, 5, 115	3	1:48.60	165,744
1983	**Island Whirl**, 5, 123	E. Delahoussaye	Bold Style, 4, 114	Sunny's Halo, 3, 116	9	1:48.40	103,860
1982	**Silver Buck**, 4, 115	D. MacBeth	Winter's Tale, 6, 119	Tap Shoes, 4, 113	6	1:47.80	99,000
1981	**Fio Rito**, 6, 113	L. Hulet	Winter's Tale, 5, 121	Ring of Light, 6, 114	8	1:48.00	105,300
1980	**State Dinner**, 5, 120	R. Hernandez	Dr. Patches, 6, 114	Czaravich, 4, 123	8	1:48.20	99,540
1979	**Star de Naskra**, 4, 120	J. Fell	Cox's Ridge, 5, 117	The Liberal Member, 4, 120	6	1:47.60	65,040
1978	**Alydar**, 3, 123	J. Velasquez	Buckaroo, 3, 112	Father Hogan, 5, 114	9	1:47.40	49,545
1977	**Nearly On Time**, 3, 103	S. Cauthen	American History, 5, 112	Dancing Gun, 5, 112	7	1:49.40	49,545
1976	**Dancing Gun**, 4, 108	R. I. Velez	American History, 4, 109	Erwin Boy, 5, 116	7	1:50.00	48,825
1975	**Ancient Title**, 5, 128	S. Hawley	Group Plan, 5, 115	Arbees Boy, 5, 118	3	1:48.20	50,085
1974	**Tri Jet**, 5, 123	L. A. Pincay Jr.	Infuriator, 4, 120	Stop the Music, 4, 120	6	**1:47.00**	33,390
1973	**Onion**, 4, 119	J. Vasquez	Secretariat, 3, 119	Rule by Reason, 6, 119	5	1:49.20	32,310

Named for the Whitney family, one of the most influential families of 20th-century American racing. Grade 2 1973-'80. Whitney S. 1928-'53, 1955-'59, 1961-'65, 1967-'74, 1978-'80. Held at Belmont Park 1943-'45. 1¼ miles 1928-'54. Four-year-olds and up 1957-'69. Colts and fillies 1928-'40. †Denotes female.

William Donald Schaefer Handicap

Grade 3 in 2006. Pimlico Race Course, three-year-olds and up, 1⅛ miles, dirt. Held May 20, 2006, with a gross value of $100,000. First held in 1994. First graded in 2001. Stakes record 1:48.19 (1995 Tidal Surge).

Year	Winner	Jockey	Second	Third	Strs	Time	1st Purse
2006	**Master Command**, 4, 115	G. K. Gomez	Andromeda's Hero, 4, 117	Funny Cide, 6, 117	6	1:49.42	$60,000
2005	**Zakocity**, 4, 117	J. D. Bailey	Clays Awesome, 5, 114	Royal Assault, 4, 112	8	1:49.19	60,000
2004	**Seattle Fitz (Arg)**, 5, 116	R. Migliore	The Lady's Groom, 4, 115	Roaring Fever, 4, 114	8	1:49.43	60,000
2003	**Windsor Castle**, 5, 117	J. A. Santos	Changeintheweather, 4, 113	Tempest Fugit, 6, 116	8	1:50.08	60,000
2002	**Tenpins**, 4, 114	R. Albarado	Bowman's Band, 4, 117	Tactical Side, 5, 113	7	1:50.20	60,000
2001	**Perfect Cat**, 4, 115	J. D. Bailey	Rize, 5, 115	Judge's Case, 4, 115	8	1:49.55	60,000
2000	**Ecton Park**, 4, 116	P. Day	The Groom Is Red, 4, 111	Crosspatch, 6, 116	4	1:49.21	60,000
1999	**Perfect to a Tee**, 7, 112	A. C. Cortez	Allen's Oop, 4, 113	Smile Again, 4, 114	7	1:49.20	60,000
1998	**Acceptable**, 4, 118	J. D. Bailey	Littlebitlively, 4, 118	Testafly, 4, 114	8	1:48.76	60,000
1997	**Western Echo**, 5, 116	E. S. Prado	Suave Prospect, 5, 114	Mary's Buckaroo, 6, 120	5	1:49.41	60,000
1996	**Canaveral**, 5, 115	S. J. Sellers	Michael's Star, 4, 114	Rugged Bugger, 5, 113	7	1:49.03	45,000
1995	**Tidal Surge**, 5, 112	J. D. Carle	Mary's Buckaroo, 4, 113	Ameri Valay, 6, 119	5	**1:48.19**	60,000
1994	**Taking Risks**, 4, 117	M. T. Johnston	Frottage, 5, 115	Super Memory, 4, 112	6	1:49.53	45,000

Named for William Donald Schaefer, governor of Maryland (1987-'95) and mayor of Baltimore (1971-'86).

Will Rogers Stakes

Grade 3 in 2006. Hollywood Park, three-year-olds, 1 mile, turf. Held May 21, 2006, with a gross value of $100,000. First held in 1938. First graded in 1973. Stakes record 1:33.45 (2004 Laura's Lucky Boy).

Year	Winner	Jockey	Second	Third	Strs	Time	1st Purse
2006	**Stratham (Ire)**, 3, 121	D. Cohen	New Joysey Jeff, 3, 116	Obrigado (Fr), 3, 119	7	1:34.19	$60,000
2005	**Osidy**, 3, 116	A. O. Solis	Willow O Wisp, 3, 119	Eastern Sand, 3, 117	8	1:34.67	65,940
2004	**Laura's Lucky Boy**, 3, 119	P. A. Valenzuela	Toasted, 3, 121	Street Theatre, 3, 117	8	**1:33.45**	65,640

2003	**Private Chef**, 3, 115	V. Espinoza	Banshee King, 3, 115	Singletary, 3, 117	6	1:35.57	$67,560
2002	**Doc Holiday (Ire)**, 3, 116	D. R. Flores	Johar, 3, 119	Golden Arrow, 3, 115	5	1:34.64	63,900
2001	**dh-Dr. Park**, 3, 117	T. Baze		Learing At Kathy, 3, 116	8	1:35.10	43,920
	dh-Media Mogul (GB), 3, 116	A. O. Solis					
2000	**Purely Cozzene**, 3, 120	V. Espinoza	Duke of Green (GB), 3, 116	Silver Axe, 3, 115	8	1:34.67	66,000
1999	**Eagleton**, 3, 118	C. A. Black	Hidden Magic (GB), 3, 115	Mr. Reignmaker, 3, 115	11	1:34.38	67,800
1998	**Magical (GB)**, 3, 114	R. R. Douglas	Commitisize, 3, 119	Son's Corona, 3, 114	8	1:33.98	65,820
1997	**Brave Act (GB)**, 3, 117	C. J. McCarron	P. T. Indy, 3, 118	Without Doubt (Ire), 3, 116	12	1:34.01	68,520
1996	**Let Bob Do It**, 3, 118	K. Desormeaux	Nightcapper, 3, 114	Dr. Sardonica, 3, 116	10	1:34.05	67,140
1995	**Via Lombardia (Ire)**, 3, 117	E. Delahoussaye	Mr Purple, 3, 119	Bee El Tee, 3, 117	9	1:34.15	63,650
1994	**Unfinished Symph**, 3, 116	G. Baze	Silver Music, 3, 118	Valiant Nature, 3, 122	8	1:40.60	64,600
1993	**Future Storm**, 3, 116	K. Desormeaux	Lykatill Hil, 3, 119	Earl of Barking (Ire), 3, 122	12	1:40.01	68,900
1992	**The Name's Jimmy**, 3, 116	D. Sorenson	Bold Assert, 3, 117	Prospect for Four, 3, 114	7	1:40.99	63,600
1991	**Compelling Sound**, 3, 119	P. A. Valenzuela	Stark South, 3, 116	Persianalli (Ire), 3, 117	9	1:40.70	66,100
1990	**Itsallgreektome**, 3, 114	C. S. Nakatani	Warcraft, 3, 120	Balla Cove (Ire), 3, 116	9	1:40.20	66,500
1989	**Notorious Pleasure**, 3, 117	L. A. Pincay Jr.	Advocate Training, 3, 115	First Play, 3, 116	10	1:40.20	66,900
1988	**Word Pirate**, 3, 119	E. Delahoussaye	Perfecting, 3, 115	Roberto's Dancer, 3, 116	9	1:40.20	50,400
1987	**Something Lucky**, 3, 117	L. A. Pincay Jr.	The Medic, 3, 115	Persevered, 3, 119	9	1:43.00	49,600
1986	**‡Mazaad (Ire)**, 3, 120	W. Shoemaker	Autobot, 3, 119	He's a Saros, 3, 115	7	1:42.40	48,800
1985	**Pine Belt**, 3, 113	R. Q. Meza	Rich Earth, 3, 119	Academy Road, 3, 116	10	1:41.00	40,700
1984	**Tsunami Slew**, 3, 119	L. A. Pincay Jr.	Swinging Scobie (GB), 3, 115	Tights, 3, 122	6	1:39.80	37,550
1983	**Barberstown**, 3, 116	F. Toro	Lover Boy Leslie, 3, 117	Tanks Brigade, 3, 120	13	1:41.40	35,200
1982	**Give Me Strength**, 3, 116	J. Samyn	Ask Me, 3, 115	Accoustical, 3, 113	8	1:40.60	26,500
	Sword Blade, 3, 112	D. G. McHargue	Art Director, 3, 113	Lucky Ship, 3, 114	7	1:41.80	26,050
1981	**Splendid Spruce**, 3, 123	D. G. McHargue	Seafood, 3, 119	Surprise George, 3, 115	8	1:41.40	38,900
1980	**Stiff Diamond**, 3, 113	T. Lipham	Naked Sky, 3, 117	Big Doug, 3, 115	11	1:41.40	34,300
1979	**Ibacache (Chi)**, 3, 118	D. G. McHargue	Beau's Eagle, 3, 121	David's Gotcha (Ire), 3, 111	8	1:40.80	32,550
1978	**April Axe**, 3, 115	C. J. McCarron	Poppy Popowich, 3, 115	He's Dewan, 3, 117	9	1:41.60	33,100
1977	**Nordic Prince**, 3, 117	S. Hawley	Sonny Collins, 3, 119	Bad 'n Big, 3, 123	10	1:41.40	33,950
1976	**Madera Sun**, 3, 116	L. A. Pincay Jr.	An Act, 3, 126	‡Today 'n Tomorrow, 3, 115	7	1:42.00	32,100
1975	**Uniformity**, 3, 115	W. Shoemaker	Dusty County, 3, 117	Exact Duplicate, 3, 115	8	1:42.00	32,150
1974	**Stardust Mel**, 3, 120	F. Toro	Agitate, 3, 122	El Seetu, 3, 114	8	1:40.80	32,800
1973	**Groshawk**, 3, 123	W. Shoemaker	Ancient Title, 3, 124	dh-Mug Punter, 3, 113	10	1:35.60	33,600
				dh-Out of the East, 3, 118			

Named for actor and American humorist Will Rogers (1879-1935); Rogers was killed in a plane crash in Alaska. Grade 2 1973-'82, 1988-'89. Will Rogers Memorial H. 1938-'40. Will Rogers H. 1941-'51, 1973-'94, 1996-2000. Will Rogers Breeders' Cup H. 1995. Held at Santa Anita Park 1949. Not held 1942-'43, 1950. 7 furlongs 1938-'44, 1946-'47. 6 furlongs 1948-'54. 1 1/16 miles 1974-'94. Dirt 1938-'68. Three-year-olds and up 1938, 1944. Colts and geldings 1953-'73. Two divisions 1982. Dead heat for third 1973. Dead heat for first 2001. ‡Sure Fire finished third, DQ to fourth, 1976. ‡Sovereign Don finished first, DQ to fifth, 1986.

Wilshire Handicap

Grade 3 in 2006. Hollywood Park, three-year-olds and up, fillies and mares, 1 mile, turf. Held April 26, 2006, with a gross value of $100,000. First held in 1953. First graded in 1975. Stakes record 1:33.14 (2006 Heavenly Ransom).

Year	Winner	Jockey	Second	Third	Strs	Time	1st Purse
2006	**Heavenly Ransom**, 4, 116	J. K. Court	Ticker Tape (GB), 5, 119	Flip Flop (Fr), 5, 115	6	**1:33.14**	$60,000
2005	**Pickle (GB)**, 4, 114	J. K. Court	Makeup Artist, 5, 114	Amorama (Fr), 4, 117	8	1:33.85	65,760
2004	**Spring Star (Fr)**, 5, 117	A. O. Solis	Quero Quero, 4, 115	Dublino, 5, 120	9	1:33.41	66,540
2003	**Dublino**, 4, 120	K. Desormeaux	Southern Oasis, 5, 116	Final Destination (NZ), 5, 118	9	1:33.62	66,600
2002	**Eurolink Raindance (Ire)**, 5, 115	C. J. McCarron	Crazy Ensign (Arg), 6, 118	Impeachable, 5, 115	5	1:34.31	63,960
2001	**Tranquility Lake**, 6, 123	E. Delahoussaye	Dianehill (Ire), 5, 116	Out of Reach (GB), 4, 117	7	1:34.69	65,160
2000	**Tout Charmant**, 4, 121	C. J. McCarron	Penny Marie, 4, 117	Perfect Copy, 4, 117	6	1:33.86	64,740
1999	**Sapphire Ring (GB)**, 4, 119	G. L. Stevens	Bella Chiarra, 4, 116	Green Jewel (GB), 5, 118	7	1:33.86	65,160
1998	**Shake the Yoke (GB)**, 5, 118	E. Delahoussaye	Traces of Gold, 6, 116	Cozy Blues, 4, 115	9	1:34.10	66,240
1997	**Blushing Heiress**, 5, 115	C. J. McCarron	Real Connection, 6, 115	De Puntillas (GB), 5, 117	7	1:40.80	65,040
1996	**Pharma**, 5, 118	C. S. Nakatani	Didina (GB), 4, 116	Matiara, 4, 120	5	1:40.96	79,770
1995	**Possibly Perfect**, 5, 121	K. Desormeaux	Morgana, 4, 116	Aube Indienne (Fr), 5, 119	5	1:40.37	76,600
1994	**Skimble**, 5, 118	E. Delahoussaye	Bel's Starlet, 7, 117	Miami Sands (Ire), 4, 116	6	1:41.39	62,800
1993	**Toussaud**, 4, 116	K. Desormeaux	Visible Gold, 5, 117	Wedding Ring (Ire), 4, 115	7	1:40.14	63,500
1992	**Kostroma (Ire)**, 6, 123	K. Desormeaux	Danzante, 4, 114	Appealing Missy, 5, 116	6	1:41.35	62,600
1991	**Fire the Groom**, 4, 118	G. L. Stevens	Odalea (Arg), 5, 115	Agirlfromars, 5, 114	6	1:40.10	63,000
1990	**Reluctant Guest**, 4, 114	R. G. Davis	Beautiful Melody, 4, 115	Estrella Fuega, 4, 114	6	1:39.40	62,400
1989	**Claire Marine (Ire)**, 4, 117	C. J. McCarron	Fitzwilliam Place (Ire), 5, 119	Galunpe (Ire), 6, 119	6	1:39.00	62,700
1988	**Chapel of Dreams**, 4, 115	G. L. Stevens	Fitzwilliam Place (Ire), 4, 119	Invited Guest (Ire), 4, 116	8	1:39.40	64,700
1987	**Galunpe (Ire)**, 4, 118	F. Toro	Top Socialite, 5, 119	Perfect Match (Fr), 5, 116	6	1:41.00	75,900
1986	**Outstandingly**, 4, 117	G. L. Stevens	La Koumia (Fr), 4, 118	Estrapade, 6, 124	5	1:41.60	75,600
1985	**Johnica**, 4, 114	C. J. McCarron	Tamarinda (Fr), 4, 119	Salt Spring (Arg), 6, 113	6	1:40.60	63,100
1984	**Triple Tipple**, 5, 114	L. A. Pincay Jr.	Comedy Act, 5, 121	Nan's Dancer, 5, 116	7	1:41.20	48,900
1983	**Mademoiselle Forli**, 4, 118	P. A. Valenzuela	Night Fire, 4, 117	Nan's Dancer, 4, 115	5	1:44.80	47,300
1982	**Miss Huntington**, 5, 115	P. A. Valenzuela	Mi Quimera (Arg), 5, 114	French Charmer, 4, 116	10	1:41.40	51,250
1981	**Track Robbery**, 5, 118	P. A. Valenzuela	Luth Music (Fr), 4, 115	Save Wild Life, 4, 116	6	1:40.80	47,550
1980	**Wishing Well**, 5, 120	F. Toro	Sisterhood, 5, 119	Love You Dear, 4, 113	9	1:41.60	38,500
1979	**Country Queen**, 4, 121	L. A. Pincay Jr.	Giggling Girl, 5, 116	Camarado, 4, 119	8	1:40.40	33,100
1978	***Lucie Manet**, 5, 119	C. J. McCarron	Swingtime, 6, 118	Drama Critic, 4, 119	6	1:49.00	30,950

1977	**Now Pending**, 4, 114	R. Campas	Swingtime, 5, 116	Up to Juliet, 4, 116	10	1:48.80	$33,550
1976	**Miss Toshiba**, 4, 117	F. Toro	Charger's Star, 6, 116	Swingtime, 4, 120	8	1:49.20	32,300
1975	***Tizna**, 6, 123	J. Lambert	Susan's Girl, 6, 123	*Dulcia, 6, 120	10	1:48.60	33,300
1974	**Tallahto**, 4, 121	L. A. Pincay Jr.	Ready Wit, 4, 113	Dogtooth Violet, 4, 119	11	1:47.60	33,650
1973	**Balcony's Babe**, 5, 116	J. Lambert	Ground Song, 4, 118	Dating, 6, 111	8	1:48.60	17,250
	Convenience, 5, 124	J. L. Rotz	Pallisima, 4, 120	Veiled Desire, 4, 109	7	1:49.00	16,900

Named for Wilshire, a historic district of Los Angeles. Grade 2 1983-'97. Wilshire S. 1953, 1970-'72. Not held 1954-'62. 7 furlongs 1963-'69. 1$^1/_8$ miles 1970-'78. 1$^1/_{16}$ miles 1979-'97. Dirt 1953-'69, 1983. Three-year-olds 1953, 1970. Four-year-olds and up 1971-'72. Fillies 1953, 1970. Two divisions 1973. Non-winners of a race worth $10,000 to the winner 1973.

WinStar Distaff Handicap

Grade 3 in 2006. Lone Star Park, three-year-olds and up, fillies and mares, 1 mile, turf. Held May 29, 2006, with a gross value of $200,000. First held in 1999. First graded in 2003. Stakes record 1:35.98 (2004 Academic Angel).

Year	Winner	Jockey	Second	Third	Strs	Time	1st Purse
2006	**Sweet Talker**, 4, 120	R. A. Dominguez	Joint Aspiration (GB), 4, 115	Stretching, 4, 116	10	1:38.66	$120,000
2005	**Katdogawn (GB)**, 5, 120	J. D. Bailey	Valentine Dancer, 5, 120	Voz De Colegiala (Chi), 6, 115	11	1:39.53	120,000
2004	**Academic Angel**, 5, 117	S. J. Sellers	Janeian (NZ), 6, 119	Katdogawn (GB), 4, 120	12	**1:35.98**	120,000
2003	**Eagle Lake**, 5, 116	G. Melancon	Little Treasure (Fr), 4, 117	Magic Mission (GB), 5, 116	9	1:43.02	120,000
2002	**Queen of Wilshire**, 6, 117	D. R. Flores	Pleasant State, 7, 115	Blushing Bride (GB), 4, 115	12	1:38.96	120,000
2001	**Voladora**, 6, 114	M. C. Berry	Dyna Likes Bingo, 6, 109	Iftiraas (GB), 4, 118	10	1:42.23	120,000
2000	**Mumtaz (Fr)**, 4, 113	V. Espinoza	Evening Promise (GB), 4, 117	Really Polish, 5, 114	9	1:37.28	120,000
1999	**Heritage of Gold**, 4, 114	C. T. Lambert	Red Cat, 4, 116	Nalynn, 5, 114	10	1:37.75	90,000

Races for females are typically referred to as distaff races. Sponsored by Bill Casner's and Kenny Troutt's WinStar Farm of Versailles, Kentucky 2000-'05. Formerly sponsored by Prestonwood Farm (predecessor of WinStar Farm) of Versailles, Kentucky 1999. Prestonwood Distaff H. 1999.

WinStar Galaxy Stakes

Grade 2 in 2006. Keeneland Race Course, three-year-olds and up, fillies and mares, 1 mile, turf. Held October 9, 2005, with a gross value of $400,000. First held in 1998. First graded in 2000. Stakes record 1:37.40 (2005 Intercontinental [GB]).

Year	Winner	Jockey	Second	Third	Strs	Time	1st Purse
2005	**Intercontinental (GB)**, 5, 123	J. D. Bailey	Wend, 4, 123	Katdogawn (GB), 5, 121	9	**1:37.40**	$248,000
2004	**Stay Forever**, 7, 121	E. Castro	Super Brand (SAf), 5, 119	Shaconage, 4, 121	9	1:57.08	310,000
2003	**Bien Nicole**, 5, 121	D. R. Pettinger	Approach (GB), 3, 116	New Economy, 5, 121	6	1:55.87	310,000
2002	**Owsley**, 4, 122	E. S. Prado	Snow Dance, 4, 120	Surya, 4, 118	6	1:56.72	337,590
2001	**Spook Express (SAf)**, 7, 120	M. E. Smith	Solvig, 4, 118	Veil of Avalon, 4, 118	9	1:54.24	349,370
2000	**Tout Charmant**, 4, 117	C. J. McCarron	Perfect Sting, 4, 121	License Fee, 5, 119	7	1:54.74	343,480
1999	**Happyanunoit (NZ)**, 4, 119	B. Blanc	Pleasant Temper, 5, 119	Fiji (GB), 5, 117	9	1:53.91	346,270
1998	**Witchful Thinking**, 4, 115	C. J. McCarron	Memories of Silver, 5, 120	Starry Dreamer, 4, 115	6	1:54.24	169,415

Sponsored by Bill Casner's and Kenny Troutt's WinStar Farm of Versailles, Kentucky 2000-'04. Formerly sponsored by Vinery of Lexington 1998-'99. Grade 3 2000. Vinery First Lady S. 1998-'99. 1$^3/_{16}$ miles 1998-2005.

Withers Stakes

Grade 3 in 2006. Aqueduct, three-year-olds, 1 mile, dirt. Held April 29, 2006, with a gross value of $142,500. First held in 1874. First graded in 1973. Stakes record 1:32.79 (1993 Williamstown).

Year	Winner	Jockey	Second	Third	Strs	Time	1st Purse
2006	**Bernardini**, 3, 116	J. Castellano	Doc Cheney, 3, 116	Luxembourg, 3, 116	4	1:35.07	$90,000
2005	**Scrappy T**, 3, 120	N. Arroyo Jr.	Park Avenue Ball, 3, 120	War Plan, 3, 116	7	1:35.74	90,000
2004	**Medallist**, 3, 116	J. F. Chavez	Forest Danger, 3, 123	Two Down Automatic, 3, 120	5	1:34.49	90,000
2003	**Spite the Devil**, 3, 116	L. Chavez	Alysweep, 3, 123	Stanislavsky, 3, 116	8	1:35.89	90,000
2002	**Fast Decision**, 3, 116	J. A. Santos	Shah Jehan, 3, 118	Listen Here, 3, 120	5	1:36.41	90,000
2001	**Richly Blended**, 3, 123	R. Wilson	Le Grande Danseur, 3, 120	Telescam, 3, 116	7	1:35.66	90,000
2000	**Big E E**, 3, 116	H. Castillo Jr.	Precise End, 3, 123	Port Herman, 3, 116	8	1:35.69	90,000
1999	**Successful Appeal**, 3, 120	J. L. Espinoza	Best of Luck, 3, 116	Treasure Island, 3, 116	8	1:35.18	90,000
1998	**Dice Dancer**, 3, 123	J. F. Chavez	Rubiyat, 3, 123	Limit Out, 3, 123	7	1:34.48	90,000
1997	**Statesmanship**, 3, 123	W. H. McCauley	Cryp Too, 3, 123	Stormin Fever, 3, 123	7	1:35.30	67,140
1996	**Appealing Skier**, 3, 123	R. Wilson	Jamies First Punch, 3, 123	Roar, 3, 123	5	1:35.02	66,120
1995	**Blu Tusmani**, 3, 123	J. A. Santos	Pat n Jac, 3, 123	‡Slice of Reality, 3, 123	9	1:35.19	67,260
1994	**Twining**, 3, 123	J. A. Santos	Able Buck, 3, 123	Presently, 3, 123	8	1:34.75	67,140
1993	**Williamstown**, 3, 124	C. Perret	Virginia Rapids, 3, 124	Farmonthefreeway, 3, 124	12	**1:32.79**	76,800
1992	**Dixie Brass**, 3, 126	J. M. Pezua	Big Sur, 3, 126	Superstrike (GB), 3, 126	8	1:33.71	73,080
1991	**Subordinated Debt**, 3, 126	J. A. Krone	Scan, 3, 126	Kyle's Our Man, 3, 126	9	1:34.03	73,920
1990	**Housebuster**, 3, 126	C. Perret	Profit Key, 3, 126	Sunny Serve, 3, 126	6	1:34.80	71,040
1989	**Fire Maker**, 3, 126	J. D. Bailey	Imbibe, 3, 126	Manastash Ridge, 3, 126	8	1:36.40	73,800
1988	**Once Wild**, 3, 126	P. Day	Tejano, 3, 126	Perfect Spy, 3, 126	5	1:35.20	69,360
1987	**Gone West**, 3, 126	E. Maple	High Brite, 3, 126	Mister S. M., 3, 126	6	1:36.40	82,620
1986	**Clear Choice**, 3, 126	J. Velasquez	Tasso, 3, 126	Landing Plot, 3, 126	10	1:35.60	71,550
1985	**El Basco**, 3, 126	J. Vasquez	Another Reef, 3, 126	Concert, 3, 126	12	1:36.60	72,990
1984	**Play On**, 3, 126	J. Samyn	Morning Bob, 3, 126	Back Bay Barrister, 3, 126	10	1:36.40	69,750
1983	**Country Pine**, 3, 126	J. D. Bailey	I Enclose, 3, 126	Megaturn, 3, 126	10	1:35.60	52,380
1982	**Aloma's Ruler**, 3, 126	J. L. Kaenel	Spanish Drums, 3, 126	John's Gold, 3, 126	6	1:35.40	33,300

1981	**Spirited Boy**, 3, 126	A. T. Cordero Jr.	Willow Hour, 3, 126	A Run, 3, 126	7	1:36.80	$33,600
1980	**Colonel Moran**, 3, 126	J. Velasquez	Temperence Hill, 3, 126	J. P. Brother, 3, 126	7	1:34.40	34,200
1979	**Czaravich**, 3, 126	J. Cruguet	Instrument Landing, 3, 126	Strike the Main, 3, 126	9	1:35.60	33,330
1978	**Junction**, 3, 126	M. Solomone	Star de Naskra, 3, 126	Buckaroo, 3, 126	8	1:36.80	32,520
1977	**Iron Constitution**, 3, 126	J. Velasquez	Cormorant, 3, 126	Affiliate, 3, 126	8	1:37.00	33,360
1976	**Sonkisser**, 3, 126	B. Baeza	El Portugues, 3, 126	Full Out, 3, 126	6	1:35.00	32,760
1975	**†Sarsar**, 3, 121	W. Shoemaker	Laramie Trail, 3, 126	Ramahorn, 3, 126	13	1:34.60	36,360
1974	**Accipiter**, 3, 126	A. Santiago	Best of It, 3, 126	Hosiery, 3, 126	12	1:35.60	36,240
1973	**Linda's Chief**, 3, 126	J. Velasquez	Stop the Music, 3, 126	Forego, 3, 126	6	1:34.80	33,120

Named for David Dunham Withers (1821-'72), a founder of Jerome Park and president of Monmouth Park. Grade 2 1973-'99. Held at Jerome Park 1874-'89. Held at Morris Park 1890-1904. Held at Belmont Park 1905-'55, 1957-'59, 1972-'74, 1976, 1981, 1984-'85, 1987-'96. Held at Jamaica 1956. Not held 1911-'12. 1$^1/_{16}$ miles 1956. Colts and fillies 1944. ‡Northern Ensign finished third, DQ to ninth, 1995. Track record 1993. †Denotes female.

W. L. McKnight Handicap

Grade 2 in 2006. Calder Race Course, three-year-olds and up, 1½ miles, turf. Held December 17, 2005, with a gross value of $200,000. First held in 1973. First graded in 1975. Stakes record 2:24.11 (1995 Flag Down).

Year	Winner	Jockey	Second	Third	Strs	Time	1st Purse
2005	**Meteor Storm (GB)**, 6, 118	J. Castellano	Revved Up, 7, 117	Scooter Roach, 6, 114	12	2:25.91	$120,000
2004	**Dreadnaught**, 4, 116	J. Samyn	Demeteor, 5, 112	Scooter Roach, 5, 115	12	2:26.60	120,000
2003	**Balto Star**, 5, 121	J. R. Velazquez	Continuously, 4, 116	Rowans Park, 3, 114	11	2:24.87	120,000
2002	**Man From Wicklow**, 5, 118	J. D. Bailey	Serial Bride, 5, 114	Rochester, 6, 117	12	2:28.05	120,000
2001	**Profit Option**, 6, 115	M. Guidry	Deeliteful Irving, 3, 113	Eltawaasul, 5, 114	12	2:27.95	90,000
2000	**A Little Luck**, 6, 114	M. E. Smith	Stokosky, 4, 115	Whata Brainstorm, 3, 113	12	2:29.01	90,000
1999	**‡Wicapi**, 7, 114	C. H. Velasquez	Special Coach, 3, 114	King's Jewel, 3, 112	12	2:26.28	90,000
1998	**Wild Event**, 5, 116	S. J. Sellers	N B Forrest, 6, 114	Glok, 4, 114	8	2:26.93	90,000
1997	**Panama City**, 3, 117	P. Day	Slicious (GB), 5, 114	Skillington, 4, 113	12	2:27.19	90,000
1996	**Diplomatic Jet**, 4, 123	J. F. Chavez	Marcie's Ensign, 4, 113	dh-Identity, 4, 114 dh-Lassigny, 5, 116	12	2:24.20	90,000
1995	**Flag Down**, 5, 116	J. A. Santos	Mecke, 3, 118	Green Means Go, 3, 115	12	**2:24.11**	90,000
1994	**Star of Manila**, 3, 116	C. Perret	Spectacular Tide, 5, 114	Kissin Kris, 4, 117	13	2:28.43	90,000
	Cobblestone Road, 5, 113	J. C. Ferrer	Daarik (Ire), 7, 113	Fraise, 6, 126	12	2:27.89	90,000
1993	**Antartic Wings**, 5, 113	R. R. Douglas	Cigar Toss (Arg), 6, 112	Luv U. Jodi, 6, 110	9	2:33.44	60,000
1992	**Bye Union Ave.**, 6, 113	R. R. Douglas	†Crockadore, 5, 113	Skate On Thin Ice, 5, 111	9	2:27.23	90,000
1991	**Stolen Rolls**, 5, 115	P. A. Rodriguez	Runaway Raja, 5, 112	Gallant Mel, 6, 110	13	2:27.10	60,000
1990	**Drum Taps**, 4, 114	J. A. Santos	†Black Tulip (Fr), 5, 112	Turfah, 7, 115	12	2:29.80	60,000
1989	**Mataji**, 5, 113	D. Valiente	Mi Selecto, 4, 118	Creme Fraiche, 7, 118	13	2:25.60	90,000
1988	**All Sincerity**, 6, 111	C. Hernandez	Blazing Bart, 4, 118	Creme Fraiche, 6, 118	8	2:25.40	120,000
1987	**Creme Fraiche**, 5, 115	E. Maple	Flying Pidgeon, 6, 120	Akabir, 6, 113	10	2:27.00	120,000
1986	**Flying Pidgeon**, 5, 117	J. A. Santos	Creme Fraiche, 4, 115	Amerilad, 5, 112	7	2:39.60	120,000
1985	**Jack Slade**, 5, 120	G. Gallitano	Rake (Fr), 5, 116	Rilial, 4, 120	9	2:26.20	69,900
	Flying Pidgeon, 4, 114	J. A. Santos	Pass the Line, 4, 114	Selous Scout, 4, 110	10	2:25.80	70,800
1984	**Open Call**, 6, 120	J. Velasquez	Dom Cimarosa (Ire), 5, 114	Bold Frond, 5, 113	10	2:30.20	63,075
	Nijinsky's Secret, 6, 124	J. A. Velez Jr.	Dom Menotti (Fr), 7, 112	Four Bases, 5, 114	11	2:31.20	63,675
1983	**Current Blade**, 5, 114	J. D. Bailey	Half Iced, 4, 122	Leader Jet, 5, 115	12	2:29.20	70,020
1982	**Ghazwan (Ire)**, 5, 120	C. Hernandez	Gleaming Channel, 4, 116	Beyond Recall, 5, 110	11	2:28.80	61,920
	Russian George (Fr), 6, 114	M. A. Rivera	†Euphrosyne, 6, 117	Nar, 7, 113	10	2:29.80	61,920
1981	**El Barril (Chi)**, 5, 118	J. Vasquez	Lord Bawlmer, 5, 115	Lobsang (Ire), 5, 117	9	2:28.40	51,630
	Buckpoint (Fr), 5, 122	J. D. Bailey	Scythian Gold, 6, 116	Proud Manner, 7, 112	10	2:28.00	52,230
1980	**Old Crony**, 5, 117	D. Brumfield	Once Over Lightly, 7, 114	Houdini, 5, 125	11	1:48.40	35,565
	Drum's Captain (Ire), 5, 118	J. Fell	Lot o' Gold, 4, 125	Scythian Gold, 5, 116	9	1:48.00	34,875
1979	**Bob's Dusty**, 5, 119	R. DePass	Prince Misko, 4, 116	Bridewell, 4, 112	12	1:48.00	55,800
1978	**Practitioner**, 5, 118	J. S. Rodriguez	Fort Prevel, 4, 111	Bob's Dusty, 4, 118	12	1:48.80	56,250
1977	**Hall of Reason**, 4, 119	M. Solomone	Visier, 5, 120	Lightning Thrust, 4, 116	8	1:47.20	52,200
1976	**Toonerville**, 5, 119	G. St. Leon	Ameri Flyer, 4, 117	Emperor Rex, 5, 115	12	1:44.60	55,800
1975	**Snurb**, 5, 119	G. St. Leon	Buffalo Lark, 5, 121	Lord Rebeau, 4, 116	13	1:46.00	37,800
1974	**Shane's Prince**, 4, 116	E. Maple	Star Envoy, 6, 125	Return to Reality, 5, 119	9	1:46.00	35,700
1973	**Getajetholme**, 4, 121	J. Imparato	Daring Young Man, 4, 120	Outdoors, 4, 116	14	1:47.20	38,700

Named for William L. McKnight (1881-1978), co-founder of Calder Race Course and founder of Tartan Farms. Grade 3 1976-'81. W. L. McKnight Invitational H. 1986-'93. 1⅛ miles 1973-'75, 1977-'80. About 1⅛ miles 1976. Dirt 1993. Two divisions 1980-'82, 1984-'85. Held in January and December 1994. Dead heat for third 1996. ‡Just Listen finished first, DQ to ninth, 1999. Course record 1976. †Denotes female.

Woodford Reserve Turf Classic Stakes

Grade 1 in 2006. Churchill Downs, three-year-olds and up, 1⅛ miles, turf. Held May 6, 2006, with a gross value of $454,900. First held in 1987. First graded in 1989. Stakes record 1:46.34 (1993 Lure).

Year	Winner	Jockey	Second	Third	Strs	Time	1st Purse
2006	**English Channel**, 4, 122	G. K. Gomez	Cacique (Ire), 5, 122	Milk It Mick (GB), 5, 126	10	1:47.15	$267,937
2005	**America Alive**, 4, 117	R. Albarado	Meteor Storm (GB), 6, 119	Quest Star, 6, 115	10	1:47.34	291,648
2004	**Stroll**, 4, 121	J. D. Bailey	Sweet Return (GB), 4, 123	Mystery Giver, 6, 123	11	1:53.00	281,418
2003	**Honor in War**, 4, 116	D. R. Flores	Requete (GB), 4, 116	Patrol, 4, 114	8	1:46.67	276,086
2002	**Beat Hollow (GB)**, 5, 115	A. O. Solis	With Anticipation, 7, 123	Hap, 6, 123	10	1:47.35	280,550

2001	**White Heart (GB)**, 6, 116	G. L. Stevens	King Cugat, 4, 120	Brahms, 4, 123	8	1:48.75	$216,938
2000	**Manndar (Ire)**, 4, 114	C. S. Nakatani	Falcon Flight (Fr), 4, 118	Yagli, 7, 120	8	1:47.91	217,310
1999	**Wild Event**, 6, 120	S. J. Sellers	Garbu, 5, 116	Hawksley Hill (Ire), 6, 120	7	1:47.25	206,646
1998	**Joyeux Danseur**, 5, 123	R. Albarado	Lasting Approval, 4, 120	Hawksley Hill (Ire), 5, 120	8	1:48.14	174,282
1997	**Always a Classic**, 4, 120	J. D. Bailey	Labeeb (GB), 5, 118	Down the Aisle, 4, 114	8	1:49.29	145,328
1996	**Mecke**, 4, 123	P. Day	Petit Poucet (GB), 4, 116	Winged Victory, 6, 116	11	1:49.48	165,230
1995	**Romarin (Brz)**, 5, 118	C. S. Nakatani	Blues Traveller (Ire), 5, 120	Hasten To Add, 5, 120	12	1:46.86	160,095
1994	**Paradise Creek**, 5, 118	P. Day	Lure, 5, 123	Yukon Robbery, 5, 116	7	1:48.34	152,068
1993	**Lure**, 4, 123	M. E. Smith	Star of Cozzene, 5, 118	Cleone, 4, 116	8	**1:46.34**	117,683
1992	**Cudas**, 4, 117	P. A. Valenzuela	Sky Classic, 5, 123	Fourstars Allstar, 4, 118	12	1:46.56	124,703
1991	**Opening Verse**, 5, 116	C. J. McCarron	Itsallgreektome, 4, 123	Pedro the Cool, 5, 112	11	1:47.22	125,060
1990	**Ten Keys**, 6, 120	K. Desormeaux	Yankee Affair, 8, 120	Stellar Rival, 7, 113	5	1:50.80	110,435
1989	**Equalize**, 7, 118	J. A. Santos	Yankee Affair, 7, 116	Gallant Mel, 4, 114	8	1:51.40	114,140
1988	**Yankee Affair**, 6, 118	P. Day	Yucca, 4, 112	First Patriot, 4, 112	10	1:50.00	121,225
1987	**Manila**, 4, 120	J. Vasquez	Vilzak, 4, 112	Lieutenant's Lark, 5, 120	4	1:48.80	110,045

Sponsored by Woodford Reserve Distillery of Versailles, Kentucky 2000-'06. Sponsored by Early Times Distillery of Louisville 1987-'99. Grade 3 1989-'93. Grade 2 1994-'95. Early Times Turf Classic S. 1987-'99. Four-year-olds and up 1987-'91. Course record 1992, 1993.

Wood Memorial Stakes

Grade 1 in 2006. Aqueduct, three-year-olds, 1⅛ miles, dirt. Held April 8, 2006, with a gross value of $750,000. First held in 1925. First graded in 1973. Stakes record 1:47.16 (2005 Bellamy Road).

Year	Winner	Jockey	Second	Third	Strs	Time	1st Purse
2006	**Bob and John**, 3, 123	G. K. Gomez	Jazil, 3, 123	Keyed Entry, 3, 123	9	1:51.54	$450,000
2005	**Bellamy Road**, 3, 123	J. Castellano	Survivalist, 3, 123	Scrappy T, 3, 123	7	**1:47.16**	450,000
2004	**Tapit**, 3, 123	R. A. Dominguez	Master David, 3, 123	Eddington, 3, 123	11	1:49.70	450,000
2003	**Empire Maker**, 3, 123	J. D. Bailey	Funny Cide, 3, 123	Kissin Saint, 3, 123	8	1:48.70	450,000
2002	**Buddha**, 3, 123	P. Day	Medaglia d'Oro, 3, 123	Sunday Break (Jpn), 3, 123	8	1:48.61	450,000
2001	**Congaree**, 3, 123	V. Espinoza	Monarchos, 3, 123	Richly Blended, 3, 123	6	1:47.96	450,000
2000	**Fusaichi Pegasus**, 3, 123	K. Desormeaux	Red Bullet, 3, 123	Aptitude, 3, 123	12	1:47.92	450,000
1999	**Adonis**, 3, 123	J. F. Chavez	Best of Luck, 3, 123	Cliquot, 3, 123	11	1:47.71	360,000
1998	**Coronado's Quest**, 3, 123	R. G. Davis	Dice Dancer, 3, 123	Parade Ground, 3, 123	11	1:47.47	300,000
1997	**Captain Bodgit**, 3, 123	A. O. Solis	Accelerator, 3, 123	Smokin Mel, 3, 123	10	1:48.39	300,000
1996	**Unbridled's Song**, 3, 123	M. E. Smith	In Contention, 3, 123	Romano Gucci, 3, 123	6	1:49.80	300,000
1995	**Talkin Man**, 3, 123	S. J. Sellers	‡Is Sveikatas, 3, 123	Candy Cone, 3, 123	8	1:49.24	300,000
1994	**Irgun**, 3, 123	G. L. Stevens	Go for Gin, 3, 123	Shiprock, 3, 123	9	1:49.07	300,000
1993	**Koluctoo Jimmy Al**, 3, 116	P. Day	Too Wild, 3, 113	Bounding Daisy, 3, 116	8	1:48.09	49,140
	Storm Tower, 3, 126	R. Wilson	Tossofthecoin, 3, 126	Marked Tree, 3, 126	12	1:48.50	300,000
1992	**Devil His Due**, 3, 126	M. E. Smith	West by West, 3, 126	Rokeby (GB), 3, 126	12	1:49.32	300,000
	Al Sabin, 3, 117	K. Desormeaux	Justfortherecord, 3, 117	Jay Gee, 3, 117	8	1:49.24	49,086
1991	**Cahill Road**, 3, 126	C. Perret	Lost Mountain, 3, 126	Happy Jazz Band, 3, 126	10	1:48.44	300,000
1990	**Thirty Six Red**, 3, 126	M. E. Smith	Burnt Hills, 3, 126	Champagneforashley, 3, 126	10	1:50.40	362,400
1989	**Easy Goer**, 3, 126	P. Day	Rock Point, 3, 126	Triple Buck, 3, 126	6	1:50.60	340,800
1988	**Private Terms**, 3, 126	C. W. Antley	Seeking the Gold, 3, 126	Cherokee Colony, 3, 126	10	1:47.20	359,400
1987	**Gulch**, 3, 126	J. A. Santos	Gone West, 3, 126	Shawklit Won, 3, 126	8	1:49.00	354,300
1986	**Broad Brush**, 3, 126	V. A. Bracciale Jr.	Mogambo, 3, 126	Groovy, 3, 126	7	1:50.60	178,500
1985	**Eternal Prince**, 3, 126	R. Migliore	Proud Truth, 3, 126	Rhoman Rule, 3, 126	6	1:48.80	204,900
1984	**Leroy S.**, 3, 126	J. Cruguet	Raja's Shark, 3, 126	Bear Hunt, 3, 126	7	1:51.40	207,000
1983	**Bounding Basque**, 3, 126	G. McCarron	Country Pine, 3, 126	Aztec Red, 3, 126	8	1:51.40	100,980
	Slew o' Gold, 3, 126	E. Maple	Parfaitement, 3, 126	High Honors, 3, 126	7	1:51.00	101,700
1982	**Air Forbes Won**, 3, 126	A. T. Cordero Jr.	Shimatoree, 3, 126	Laser Light, 3, 126	10	1:51.00	105,120
1981	**Pleasant Colony**, 3, 126	J. Fell	Highland Blade, 3, 126	Cure the Blues, 3, 126	6	1:49.60	98,280
1980	**Plugged Nickle**, 3, 126	B. Thornburg	Colonel Moran, 3, 126	†Genuine Risk, 3, 121	11	1:50.80	87,300
1979	**Instrument Landing**, 3, 126	A. T. Cordero Jr.	Screen King, 3, 126	Czaravich, 3, 126	10	1:49.20	85,650
1978	**Believe It**, 3, 126	E. Maple	Darby Creek Road, 3, 126	Track Reward, 3, 126	11	1:49.80	65,940
1977	**Seattle Slew**, 3, 126	J. Cruguet	Sanhedrin, 3, 126	Catalan, 3, 126	7	1:49.60	66,180
1976	**Bold Forbes**, 3, 126	A. T. Cordero Jr.	On the Sly, 3, 126	Sonkisser, 3, 126	7	1:47.40	67,560
1975	**Foolish Pleasure**, 3, 126	J. Vasquez	Bombay Duck, 3, 126	Media, 3, 126	15	1:48.80	72,840
1974	**Flip Sal**, 3, 126	A. T. Cordero Jr.	Triple Crown, 3, 126	Sharp Gary, 3, 126	11	1:51.40	69,360
	Rube the Great, 3, 126	M. A. Rivera	Friendly Bee, 3, 126	Hudson County, 3, 126	11	1:49.60	69,660
1973	**Angle Light**, 3, 126	J. Vasquez	Sham, 3, 126	Secretariat, 3, 126	8	1:49.80	68,940

Named for Eugene D. Wood (d. 1924), one of the founders of Jamaica racetrack. Grade 2 1995-2001. Wood S. 1925-'26. Wood Memorial Invitational S. 1984-'93. Held at Jamaica 1925-'59. 1 mile 70 yards 1925-'39. 1¹⁄₁₆ miles 1940-'51. Two divisions 1974, 1983, 1992-'93. ‡Knockadoon finished second, DQ to eighth, 1995. †Denotes female.

Woodward Stakes

Grade 1 in 2006. Belmont Park, three-year-olds and up, 1⅛ miles, dirt. Held September 10, 2005, with a gross value of $490,000. First held in 1954. First graded in 1973. Stakes record 1:45.80 (1976 Forego; 1990 Dispersal).

Year	Winner	Jockey	Second	Third	Strs	Time	1st Purse
2005	**Saint Liam**, 5, 126	J. D. Bailey	Sir Shackleton, 4, 126	Commentator, 4, 126	5	1:49.07	$300,000
2004	**Ghostzapper**, 4, 126	J. Castellano	Saint Liam, 4, 126	Bowman's Band, 6, 126	7	1:46.38	300,000
2003	**Mineshaft**, 4, 126	R. Albarado	Hold That Tiger, 3, 122	Puzzlement, 4, 126	5	1:46.21	300,000

2002	**Lido Palace (Chi)**, 5, 126	J. F. Chavez	Gander, 6, 126	Express Tour, 4, 126	6	1:47.75	$300,000
2001	**Lido Palace (Chi)**, 4, 126	J. D. Bailey	Albert the Great, 4, 126	Tiznow, 4, 126	5	1:47.42	300,000
2000	**Lemon Drop Kid**, 4, 126	E. S. Prado	Behrens, 6, 126	Gander, 4, 126	5	1:50.53	300,000
1999	**River Keen (Ire)**, 7, 126	C. W. Antley	Almutawakel (GB), 4, 126	Stephen Got Even, 3, 121	7	1:46.85	300,000
1998	**Skip Away**, 5, 126	J. D. Bailey	Gentlemen (Arg), 6, 126	Running Stag, 4, 126	5	1:47.80	300,000
1997	**Formal Gold**, 4, 126	K. Desormeaux	Skip Away, 4, 126	Will's Way, 4, 126	5	1:47.51	300,000
1996	**Cigar**, 6, 126	J. D. Bailey	L'Carriere, 5, 126	Golden Larch, 5, 126	5	1:47.06	300,000
1995	**Cigar**, 5, 126	J. D. Bailey	Star Standard, 3, 121	Golden Larch, 4, 126	6	1:47.07	300,000
1994	**Holy Bull**, 3, 121	M. E. Smith	Devil His Due, 5, 126	Colonial Affair, 4, 126	8	1:46.89	300,000
1993	**Bertrando**, 4, 126	G. L. Stevens	Devil His Due, 4, 126	Valley Crossing, 5, 126	6	1:47.00	525,000
1992	**Sultry Song**, 4, 126	J. D. Bailey	Pleasant Tap, 5, 126	Out of Place, 5, 126	8	1:47.05	300,000
1991	**In Excess (Ire)**, 4, 126	G. L. Stevens	Farma Way, 4, 126	Festin (Arg), 5, 126	6	1:46.33	300,000
1990	**Dispersal**, 4, 123	C. W. Antley	Quiet American, 4, 117	Rhythm, 3, 120	8	**1:45.80**	354,000
1989	**Easy Goer**, 3, 122	P. Day	Its Acedemic, 5, 109	Forever Silver, 4, 119	5	2:01.00	485,400
1988	**Alysheba**, 4, 126	C. J. McCarron	Forty Niner, 3, 119	Waquoit, 5, 122	8	1:59.40	498,600
1987	**Polish Navy**, 3, 116	R. P. Romero	Gulch, 3, 118	Creme Fraiche, 5, 119	9	1:47.00	357,000
1986	**Precisionist**, 5, 126	C. J. McCarron	†Lady's Secret, 4, 121	Personal Flag, 3, 110	5	1:46.00	199,200
1985	**Track Barron**, 4, 123	A. T. Cordero Jr.	Vanlandingham, 4, 123	Chief's Crown, 3, 121	6	1:46.60	200,400
1984	**Slew o' Gold**, 4, 126	A. T. Cordero Jr.	Shifty Sheik, 5, 116	Bet Big, 4, 116	6	1:47.80	175,200
1983	**Slew o' Gold**, 3, 118	A. T. Cordero Jr.	Bates Motel, 4, 123	Sing Sing, 5, 119	10	1:46.60	138,900
1982	**Island Whirl**, 4, 123	A. T. Cordero Jr.	Silver Buck, 4, 126	Silver Supreme, 4, 126	7	1:46.80	136,500
1981	**Pleasant Colony**, 3, 123	A. T. Cordero Jr.	Amber Pass, 4, 126	Herb Water, 4, 116	9	1:47.20	137,400
1980	**Spectacular Bid**, 4, 126	W. Shoemaker			1	2:02.40	73,300
1979	**Affirmed**, 4, 126	L. A. Pincay Jr.	Coastal, 3, 120	Czaravich, 3, 120	5	2:01.60	114,600
1978	**Seattle Slew**, 4, 126	A. T. Cordero Jr.	Exceller, 5, 126	It's Freezing, 6, 126	5	2:00.00	97,800
1977	**Forego**, 7, 133	W. Shoemaker	Silver Series, 3, 114	Great Contractor, 4, 115	10	1:48.00	105,000
1976	**Forego**, 6, 135	W. Shoemaker	Dance Spell, 3, 115	dh-Honest Pleasure, 3, 121 dh-Stumping, 6, 109	10	**1:45.80**	103,920
1975	**Forego**, 5, 126	H. Gustines	Wajima, 3, 119	Group Plan, 5, 126	6	2:27.20	64,920
1974	**Forego**, 4, 126	H. Gustines	Arbees Boy, 4, 126	Group Plan, 4, 126	11	2:27.40	69,240
1973	**Prove Out**, 4, 126	J. Velasquez	Secretariat, 3, 119	*Cougar II, 7, 126	5	2:25.80	64,920

Named for William Woodward (1876-1953), chairman of the Jockey Club from 1930-'50; Woodward also owned Belair Stud. Woodward H. 1955, 1976-'77, 1988-'90. Held at Aqueduct 1959-'60, 1962-'67. 1 mile 1954. 1¼ miles 1956-'71, 1978-'80, 1988-'89. 1½ miles 1972-'75. Dead heat for third 1976. †Denotes female. Won in a walkover 1980.

Woody Stephens Breeders' Cup Stakes

Grade 2 in 2006. Belmont Park, three-year-olds, 7 furlongs, dirt. Held June 10, 2006, with a gross value of $250,000. First held in 1985. First graded in 1988. Stakes record 1:20.33 (1994 You and I).

Year	Winner	Jockey	Second	Third	Strs	Time	1st Purse
2006	**Songster**, 3, 123	E. S. Prado	Too Much Bling, 3, 123	Noonmark, 3, 115	7	1:21.45	$150,000
2005	**Lost in the Fog**, 3, 123	E. S. Prado	Egg Head, 3, 119	Middle Earth, 3, 116	8	1:21.54	90,000
2004	**Fire Slam**, 3, 123	P. Day	Teton Forest, 3, 115	Abbondanza, 3, 123	7	1:20.94	120,000
2003	**Posse**, 3, 123	C. J. Lanerie	Midas Eyes, 3, 123	Halo Homewrecker, 3, 123	8	1:22.03	120,000
2002	**Gygistar**, 3, 119	P. Day	Draw Play, 3, 115	True Direction, 3, 119	9	1:22.61	120,000
2001	**Put It Back**, 3, 120	N. A. Wynter	Flame Thrower, 3, 120	Touch Tone, 3, 123	6	1:21.76	90,000
2000	**Trippi**, 3, 123	J. D. Bailey	Bevo, 3, 120	Sun Cat, 3, 116	6	1:23.68	90,000
1999	**Yes It's True**, 3, 123	J. D. Bailey	Lion Hearted, 3, 114	Silver Season, 3, 113	8	1:22.35	90,000
1998	**Coronado's Quest**, 3, 123	M. E. Smith	Mellow Roll, 3, 113	Flashing Tammany, 3, 120	7	1:22.50	82,050
1997	**Smoke Glacken**, 3, 123	C. Perret	Trafalger, 3, 123	Wild Wonder, 3, 120	6	1:20.98	66,060
1996	**Gold Fever**, 3, 118	M. E. Smith	Gameel, 3, 114	Bright Launch, 3, 120	9	1:23.30	67,620
1995	**Western Larla**, 3, 119	G. L. Stevens	Mr. Greeley, 3, 122	Blu Tusmani, 3, 122	8	1:24.24	66,960
1994	**You and I**, 3, 122	C. J. McCarron	End Sweep, 3, 114	Slew Gin Fizz, 3, 122	9	**1:20.33**	67,080
1993	**Montbrook**, 3, 117	C. J. Ladner III	As Indicated, 3, 122	Forever Whirl, 3, 122	10	1:23.34	74,160
1992	**Superstrike (GB)**, 3, 115	J. A. Santos	Three Peat, 3, 122	Windundermywings, 3, 115	7	1:22.41	70,560
1991	**Fly So Free**, 3, 122	J. D. Bailey	Formal Dinner, 3, 122	Dodge, 3, 122	11	1:23.13	74,040
1990	**Adjudicating**, 3, 122	J. Vasquez	Silent Generation, 3, 115	Bayou Blurr, 3, 115	7	1:23.80	68,040
1989	**Is It True**, 3, 122	C. W. Antley	Mr. Nickerson, 3, 115	Fierce Fighter, 3, 115	8	1:22.20	70,200
1988	**Evening Kris**, 3, 117	L. A. Pincay Jr.	Perfect Spy, 3, 122	King's Nest, 3, 115	7	1:22.80	69,120
1987	**Jazzing Around**, 3, 115	J. A. Santos	dh-High Brite, 3, 119 dh-Polish Navy, 3, 122		7	1:22.40	48,240
1986	**Ogygian**, 3, 122	W. A. Guerra	Wayar, 3, 115	Landing Plot, 3, 122	5	1:23.40	48,900
1985	**Ziggy's Boy**, 3, 115	A. T. Cordero Jr.	Tiffany Ice, 3, 122	Huddle Up, 3, 115	6	1:22.20	48,960

Named for Hall of Fame trainer Woodford C. Stephens (1913-'98); Stephens-trained horses won the Belmont S. (G1) five consecutive years (1982-'86). Formerly named for Meadow Stable's 1971 champion two-year-old male, '73 champion older male, and '72 Belmont S. winner Riva Ridge (1969 c. by First Landing). Grade 3 1988-'97. Riva Ridge S. 1985-2002. Riva Ridge Breeders' Cup S. 2003-'05. Dead heat for second 1987. Track record 1994.

Yellow Ribbon Stakes

Grade 1 in 2006. Oak Tree at Santa Anita, three-year-olds and up, fillies and mares, 1¼ miles, turf. Held October 1, 2005, with a gross value of $500,000. First held in 1977. First graded in 1979. Stakes record 1:57.60 (1989 Brown Bess).

Year	Winner	Jockey	Second	Third	Strs	Time	1st Purse
2005	**Megahertz (GB)**, 6, 123	A. O. Solis	Flip Flop (Fr), 4, 123	Halo Ola (Arg), 5, 123	7	2:00.50	$300,000
2004	**Light Jig (GB)**, 4, 123	R. R. Douglas	Tangle (Ire), 4, 123	Katdogawn (GB), 4, 123	10	1:59.28	300,000

2003	**Tates Creek**, 5, 123	P. A. Valenzuela	Musical Chimes, 3, 118	Crazy Ensign (Arg), 7, 123	8	2:00.77	$300,000
2002	**Golden Apples (Ire)**, 4, 123	P. A. Valenzuela	Voodoo Dancer, 4, 123	Banks Hill (GB), 4, 123	6	1:59.72	300,000
2001	**Janet (GB)**, 4, 123	D. R. Flores	Tranquility Lake, 6, 123	Al Desima (GB), 4, 123	8	1:58.64	300,000
2000	**Tranquility Lake**, 5, 123	E. Delahoussaye	Spanish Fern, 5, 123	Polaire (Ire), 4, 123	6	2:02.98	300,000
1999	**Spanish Fern**, 4, 123	C. J. McCarron	Caffe Latte (Ire), 3, 118	Shabby Chic, 3, 118	7	1:59.52	300,000
1998	**Fiji (GB)**, 4, 122	K. Desormeaux	‡Sonja's Faith (Ire), 4, 122	Pomona (GB), 5, 122	10	2:05.23	300,000
1997	**Ryafan**, 3, 118	A. O. Solis	Fanjica (Ire), 5, 122	Memories of Silver, 4, 122	8	2:03.89	300,000
1996	**Donna Viola (GB)**, 4, 122	G. L. Stevens	Real Connection, 5, 122	Dixie Pearl, 4, 122	8	2:00.62	360,000
1995	**Alpride (Ire)**, 4, 122	C. J. McCarron	Angel in My Heart (Fr), 3, 118	Bold Ruritana, 5, 122	12	2:01.68	360,000
1994	**Aube Indienne (Fr)**, 4, 122	K. Desormeaux	Fondly Remembered, 4, 122	Zoonaqua, 4, 122	11	2:02.32	240,000
1993	**Possibly Perfect**, 3, 118	C. S. Nakatani	Tribulation, 3, 118	Miatuschka, 5, 122	13	2:02.91	240,000
1992	**Super Staff**, 4, 123	K. Desormeaux	Flawlessly, 4, 123	Campagnarde (Arg), 5, 123	9	1:59.36	240,000
1991	**Kostroma (Ire)**, 5, 123	K. Desormeaux	Flawlessly, 3, 119	Fire the Groom, 4, 123	13	2:01.01	240,000
1990	**Plenty of Grace**, 3, 119	W. H. McCauley	Petite Ile (Ire), 4, 123	Royal Touch (Ire), 5, 123	13	1:58.40	240,000
1989	**Brown Bess**, 7, 123	J. L. Kaenel	Darby's Daughter, 3, 119	Colorado Dancer (Ire), 3, 119	11	**1:57.60**	240,000
1988	**Delighter**, 3, 119	C. J. McCarron	Nastique, 4, 123	No Review, 3, 119	12	2:02.40	240,000
1987	**Carotene**, 4, 123	J. A. Santos	Nashmeel, 3, 119	Khariyda (Fr), 3, 119	12	2:03.80	240,000
1986	**Bonne Ile (GB)**, 5, 123	F. Toro	Top Corsage, 3, 118	Carotene, 3, 118	12	2:01.40	240,000
1985	**Estrapade**, 5, 123	W. Shoemaker	Alydar's Best, 3, 118	La Koumia (Fr), 3, 118	11	2:00.40	240,000
1984	**Sabin**, 4, 123	E. Maple	Grise Mine (Fr), 3, 118	Estrapade, 4, 123	8	2:00.00	240,000
1983	**Sangue (Ire)**, 5, 123	W. Shoemaker	L'Attrayante (Fr), 3, 119	Infinite, 3, 119	12	2:02.20	240,000
1982	**‡Castilla**, 3, 119	R. Sibille	Avigaition, 3, 119	Sangue (Ire), 4, 123	12	1:58.60	180,000
1981	**Queen to Conquer**, 5, 123	M. Castaneda	Star Pastures (GB), 3, 119	Ack's Secret, 5, 123	11	1:58.60	180,000
1980	**Kilijaro (Ire)**, 4, 123	A. Lequeux	Ack's Secret, 4, 123	Queen to Conquer, 4, 123	10	1:59.20	120,000
1979	**Country Queen**, 4, 123	L. A. Pincay Jr.	Prize Spot, 3, 119	Giggling Girl, 5, 123	10	2:00.20	90,000
1978	**Amazer**, 3, 119	W. Shoemaker	Drama Critic, 4, 123	Surera (Arg), 5, 123	9	1:59.20	90,000
1977	***Star Ball**, 5, 123	H. Grant	Swingtime, 5, 123	Theia (Fr), 4, 123	11	2:02.60	60,000

Named for the song, "Tie a Yellow Ribbon," which refers to tying a ribbon around the "old oak tree." The Yellow Ribbon is run at the Oak Tree Racing Association meet. Yellow Ribbon Invitational S. 1979-'87, 1989-'94. ‡Avigaition finished first, DQ to second, 1982. ‡See You Soon (Fr) finished second, DQ to fourth, 1998.

Yerba Buena Breeders' Cup Handicap

Grade 3 in 2006. Golden Gate Fields, four-year-olds and up, fillies and mares, 1⅛ miles, turf. Held May 7, 2006, with a gross value of $125,625. First held in 1973. First graded in 1978. Stakes record 1:47.76 (2006 Hallowed Dream [Ire]).

Year	Winner	Jockey	Second	Third	Strs	Time	1st Purse
2006	**Hallowed Dream (Ire)**, 4, 118	D. Carr	Sky Dreams, 5, 116	Dreams Come True (Fr), 5, 115	10	**1:47.76**	$68,750
2005	**Pickle (GB)**, 4, 118	R. A. Baze	Marla Bay, 4, 116	Midwife, 4, 117	6	1:41.72	41,250
2004	**A B Noodle**, 5, 116	J. M. Castro	Marwood, 4, 116	Hooked On Niners, 5, 116	6	1:46.66	68,750
2003	**Chiming (Ire)**, 5, 116	C. S. Nakatani	Noches De Rosa (Chi), 5, 119	Lindsay Jean, 5, 118	7	1:45.41	55,000
2002	**Peu a Peu (Ger)**, 4, 115	R. A. Baze	Janet (GB), 5, 122	Racene, 5, 115	6	2:16.39	55,000
2001	**Janet (GB)**, 4, 115	D. R. Flores	Keemoon (Fr), 5, 121	Alexine (Arg), 5, 119	4	2:17.09	82,500
2000	**Gleefully**, 4, 113	R. Q. Meza	Country Garden (GB), 5, 116	Marie de Bayeux (Fr), 4, 113	8	2:15.99	110,000
1999	**Blending Element (Ire)**, 6, 117	G. K. Gomez	Queen Douna (Fr), 6, 113	Midnight Line, 4, 117	6	2:17.26	120,000
1998	**Miss Universal (Ire)**, 5, 114	P. Mercado	Proud Fillie (Fr), 4, 115	Squeak (GB), 4, 118	12	2:15.72	75,000
1997	**De Puntillas (GB)**, 5, 116	V. Espinoza	Dynatar, 5, 117	Tricky Code, 6, 116	11	1:46.71	60,000
1996	**Fanjica (Ire)**, 4, 114	D. Carr	Nimble Mind, 4, 115	Dynatar, 4, 113	8	2:17.42	60,000
1995	**Work the Crowd**, 4, 123	R. A. Baze	Late Sailing, 5, 116	Ask Anita, 5, 117	5	1:49.27	68,750
1994	**Ask Anita**, 4, 116	V. Belvoir	Miami Sands (Ire), 4, 115	Oxava (Fr), 4, 115	7	2:15.55	55,000
1993	**Party Cited**, 4, 117	R. J. Warren Jr.	Silvered, 6, 115	Rougeur, 4, 115	6	2:15.11	55,000
1992	**Flaming Torch (Ire)**, 5, 114	R. A. Baze	Indian Chris (Brz), 5, 116	Silvered, 5, 114	8	2:16.26	82,500
1991	**Free At Last (GB)**, 4, 120	R. D. Hansen	Noble and Nice, 5, 117	Louve Bleue, 4, 113	6	2:15.10	82,500
1990	**Petite Ile (Ire)**, 4, 118	C. A. Black	Double Wedge, 5, 112	Brown Bess, 8, 124	5	2:15.60	82,500
1989	**Brown Bess**, 7, 119	J. L. Kaenel	Carmanetta, 5, 114	Flattering News, 4, 111	10	2:15.60	82,500
1988	**Magdelaine (NZ)**, 5, 113	T. T. Doocy	Sweet Roberta (Fr), 4, 115	Top Corsage, 5, 118	7	2:14.40	82,500
1987	**Ivor's Image**, 4, 119	C. J. McCarron	Micenas (Arg), 5, 115	Royal Regatta (NZ), 8, 114	5	2:29.60	82,500
1986	**Scythe (GB)**, 5, 113	T. M. Chapman	Heat Spell, 4, 115	Lock's Dream, 4, 114	11	2:32.20	85,000
1985	**Salt Spring (Arg)**, 6, 115	T. M. Chapman	High Spruce, 5, 111	L'Attrayante (Fr), 5, 120	7	2:30.20	95,800
1984	**Fact Finder**, 5, 115	M. Castaneda	Lido Isle, 4, 114	Her Decision, 5, 115	7	2:30.20	107,200
1983	**Dilmoun (Ire)**, 4, 111	J. J. Steiner	Latrone, 6, 112	Berry Bush, 6, 119	10	2:31.60	82,350
1982	**Sangue (Ire)**, 4, 117	T. M. Chapman	Berry Bush, 5, 119	Mademoiselle Ivor, 4, 112	10	2:16.40	78,400
1981	**Mairzy Doates**, 5, 120	F. Mena	Princess Karenda, 4, 123	Princess Toby, 6, 117	10	2:15.80	78,550
1980	**Mairzy Doates**, 4, 116	F. Mena	Sisterhood, 5, 121	Smaller Bicker, 4, 113	11	2:15.00	66,900
1978	***Star Ball**, 6, 124	D. G. McHargue	Up to Juliet, 5, 114	Surera (Arg), 5, 112	8	2:13.60	63,800
1977	***Star Ball**, 5, 121	J. L. Vargas	*Bastonera II, 6, 124	Up to Juliet, 4, 117	8	2:14.80	48,350
1976	**Our First Delight**, 4, 120	E. Munoz	Graceful Banner, 4, 112	Larking Party, 4, 113	11	2:16.40	33,400
1975	**Joli Vert**, 4, 115	F. Olivares	Lucky Spell, 4, 122	Gentleweave, 4, 106	6	2:16.80	31,000
1974	**Merry Madeleine**, 4, 113	F. Mena	Hurry Countess, 4, 110	Hum Dum, 6, 111	9	2:31.40	17,625
1973	***Live Forever**, 4, 112	J. T. Gonzalez	Fleet Ahead, 6, 112	Homespun, 4, 111	9	2:19.60	12,050

Named for Yerba Buena Island in San Francisco Bay, California; Yerba Buena was once known as Goat Island, for the herd of wild goats living there. Grade 2 1982-'83. Not graded 1990-'92. Yerba Buena H. 1973-'98. Held at Bay Meadows 2001-'04. Not held 1979. 1⅜ miles 1973, 1975-'82, 1988-'94, 1996, 1998-2002. 1½ miles 1974, 1983-'87. 1$^1/_{16}$ miles 1997, 2003-'05. About 1⅛ miles 2003-'04. Three-year-olds and up 1973-2005.

Previously Graded Stakes

Race	Last Grade	Track	Year Last Graded
Affectionately H.	3	Aqueduct	2004
AKsarben Oaks	3	AKsarben	1997
Alabama Derby	3	Lousiana Downs	1997
Alibhai H.	3	Santa Anita Park	1985
Allegheny S.	3	Keystone	1977
Anne Arundel S.	3	Pimlico	2004
Anoakia S.	3	Santa Anita Park	1987
Ark-La-Tex H.	3	Louisiana Downs	1999
Ascot H.	3	Bay Meadows	2002
Assault H.	3	Aqueduct	1997
Astoria Breeders' Cup S.	3	Belmont Park	1994
Bahamas S.	3	Hialeah	1974
Baltimore Breeders' Cup H.	3	Pimlico	2003
Bay Meadows Oaks	3	Bay Meadows	1998
Bel Air H.	2	Hollywood Park	2001
Benjamin Franklin H.	3	Garden State	1974
Best Turn S.	3	Aqueduct	1996
Betsy Ross H.	3	Garden State	1995
Black Helen H.	2	Hialeah	2001
Board of Governors' H.	3	AKsarben	1993
Boardwalk S.	3	Atlantic City	1975
Bold Reason H.	3	Saratoga	1988
Bougainvillea H.	3	Hialeah	2001
Brandywine Turf H.	3	Delaware Park	1973
Brighton Beach H.	3	Belmont Park	1983
Brown Bess H.	3	Golden Gate Fields	2004
Bryn Mawr S.	3	Keystone	1975
Budweiser H.	3	Fairmount Park	1989
Busher S.	3	Aqueduct	1998
Caballero H.	3	Hollywood Park	1978
Cabrillo H.	3	Del Mar	1990
California Derby	3	Golden Gate Fields	1999
California Jockey Club H.	3	Bay Meadows	1996
California Juvenile S.	3	Bay Meadows	2000
Camden H.	3	Garden State	1974
Canadian Turf H.	3	Gulfstream Park	2004
Canterbury Oaks	3	Canterbury	1989
Carousel H.	3	Laurel Park	1992
Chaposa Springs H.	3	Calder Race Course	2004
Cherry Hill Mile S.	3	Garden State	1996
Chesapeake H.	3	Bowie	1975
Choice H.	3	Monmouth	1995
Chrysanthemum H.	3	Laurel Park	1989
Coaltown Breeders' Cup H.	3	Aqueduct	1995
Colin S.	3	Belmont Park	1994
Colleen S.	3	Monmouth	1974
Colonial H.	3	Garden State	1976
Columbiana H.	3	Hialeah	1989
Correction H.	3	Aqueduct	1982
Countess Fager H.	3	Golden Gate Fields	1994
Cowdin S.	3	Belmont Park	2002
Cradle S.	3	River Downs	2004
Cygnet S.	3	Hollywood Park	1974
Dade Turf Classic	3	Calder Race Course	1975
De La Rose H.	3	Gulfstream Park	2002
Delaware Valley H.	3	Garden State	1974
Derby Trial S.	3	Churchill Downs	2004
Desert Stormer H.	3	Hollywood Park	2005
Display H.	3	Aqueduct	1989
Donald LeVine Memorial H.	3	Philadelphia Park	2004
Donald P. Ross H.	3	Delaware Park	1981
Dover S.	3	Delaware Park	1974
Dragoon S.	3	Liberty Bell	1974

Race	Last Grade	Track	Year Last Graded
El Camino Real S.	3	Bay Meadows	1984
El Dorado H.	3	Hollywood Park	1981
Endurance S.	3	Meadowlands	1995
Everglades S.	3	Hialeah	2001
Fair Grounds Classic	3	Fair Grounds	1987
Fairmount Derby	3	Fairmount Park	1995
Fall Highweight H.	3	Aqueduct	2004
Fashion S.	3	Belmont Park	1974
Fastness H.	3	Hollywood Park	2001
Federico Tesio S.	3	Pimlico	1997
Finger Lakes Breeders' Cup S.	3	Finger Lakes	1999
Flamingo S.	3	Hialeah	2001
Flash S.	3	Belmont	2005
Flintlock S.	3	Keystone	1974
Flirtation S.	3	Pimlico	1974
Florida Oaks	3	Tampa Bay Downs	2003
Florida Turf Cup H.	3	Calder Race Course	1989
Forerunner S.	3	Keeneland	1998
Forest Hills H.	2	Belmont Park	2002
Ft. Lauderdale H.	3	Gulfstream Park	2002
Gallant Fox H.	3	Aqueduct	2002
Garden State Breeders' Cup H.	3	Garden State	1995
Garden State S.	3	Garden State	1994
Golden Gate Derby	3	Golden Gate Fields	2004
Golden Harvest H.	3	Louisiana Downs	1993
Golden Poppy H.	3	Golden Gate Fields	1994
Gold Rush Futurity	3	Arapahoe Park	1984
Governor S.	1	Belmont Park	1975
Governor's Cup H.	3	Bowie	1985
Governor's Cup H.	3	Arlington Park	1974
Great American S.	3	Aqueduct	1974
Grey Lag H.	3	Aqueduct	1999
Haggin S.	3	Hollywood Park	1974
Hall of Fame Breeders' Cup H.	3	Thistledown	2000
Harold C. Ramser Sr. H.	3	Santa Anita Park	1989
Hawthorne Breeders' Cup H.	3	Hawthorne	1993
Hawthorne Juvenile S.	3	Hawthorne	1982
Heirloom H.	3	Liberty Bell	1974
Heritage S.	2	Keystone	1978
Hessian H.	3	Keystone	1974
Hialeah Turf Cup H.	2	Hialeah	2001
Hibiscus S.	3	Hialeah	1973
Hillsborough H.	3	Bay Meadows	2000
Hobson H.	2	Keystone	1977
Hollywood Express H.	3	Hollywood Park	1974
Honey Bee H.	3	Meadowlands	2001
Honeybee S.	3	Oaklawn Park	2002
Indian Maid H.	3	Hawthorne	1978
Interborough H.	3	Aqueduct	2000
Island Whirl H.	3	Louisiana Downs	1989
Jasmine S.	3	Hialeah	1974
Jersey Belle H.	3	Garden State	1977
Jersey Derby	3	Monmouth Park	2004
John B. Campbell H.	3	Pimlico	1999
John Henry H.	2	Hollywood Park	1994
Junior League S.	3	Hollywood Park	1974
Junior Miss S.	3	Del Mar	1992
Juvenile S.	3	AKsarben	1988
Kelly-Olympic H.	3	Atlantic City	1979
Keystone H.	3	Liberty Bell	1974
Kindergarten S.	3	Liberty Bell	1974
Ladies H.	3	Aqueduct	2004
Lady Canterbury H.	3	Canterbury	1991

Race	Last Grade	Track	Year Last Graded
Lafayette S.	3	Keeneland	2005
Lakeside H.	2	Hollywood Park	1980
Lamplighter H.	3	Monmouth Park	1998
Laurance Armour H.	3	Arlington Park	1996
Laurel Dash S.	3	Laurel Park	2000
Laurel Futurity	3	Laurel Park	2004
Laurel Turf Cup S.	3	Laurel Park	2000
Lazaro S. Barrera H.	3	Hollywood Park	1998
Letellier Memorial H.	3	Fair Grounds	1974
Linda Vista H.	3	Santa Anita Park	1996
Little Silver H.	3	Monmouth Park	1988
Longacres Derby	3	Longacres	1988
Longfellow H.	3	Monmouth Park	1997
Long Look Breeders' Cup H.	3	Meadowlands	1997
Louisiana Downs H.	3	Lousiana Downs	1996
Louis R. Rowan H.	3	Santa Anita Park	1998
Magnolia S.	3	Oaklawn Park	1974
Margate H.	3	Atlantic City	1978
Maria H.	3	Garden State	1996
Marlboro Cup Invitational H.	1	Belmont Park	1987
Marylander H.	3	Pimlico	1981
Mermaid S.	3	Atlantic City	1975
Michigan Mile and One-Eighth H.	2	Detroit	1993
Militia S.	3	Keystone	1975
Mimosa S.	3	Hialeah	1973
Minnesota Derby S.	2	Canterbury	1991
Minuteman H.	3	Keystone	1978
Miss America H.	3	Golden Gate Fields	1996
Miss Grillo S.	3	Belmont Park	2000
Miss Woodford S.	3	Monmouth Park	1974
Monmouth Park Breeders' Cup H.	3	Monmouth Park	1992
Morven S.	3	Meadowlands	1987
Nassau County H.	1	Belmont Park	1993
New Hampshire Sweepstakes H.	3	Rockingham	2002
New Hope S.	3	Keystone	1975
New Jersey Turf Classic S.	3	Meadowlands	1993
Norristown H.	3	Philadelphia Park	1993
Oil Capitol H.	3	Hawthorne	1975
Oklahoma Derby	3	Remington Park	2004
Omaha Gold Cup S.	3	AKsarben	1994
Open Fire S.	3	Delaware Park	1978
Pageant S.	3	Atlantic City	1975
Pasadena S.	3	Santa Anita Park	1974
Paterson H.	3	Meadowlands	1995
Patriot S.	3	Keystone	1978
Paumonok H.	3	Aqueduct	1978
Pebbles H.	3	Belmont Park	2004
Pennsylvania Governor's Cup H.	3	Penn National	1989
Philadelphia H.	3	Monmouth Park	1974
Phoenix Gold Cup S.	3	Turf Paradise	1997
Pilgrim S.	3	Belmont Park	2000
Pimlico Oaks	3	Pimlico	1991
Pimlico S.	3	Pimlico	1974
Poinsettia S.	3	Hialeah	1989
Polynesian H.	3	Pimlico	1994
Post-Deb S.	2	Monmouth Park	1993
President's Cup S.	3	AKsarben	1988
Princess S.	2	Hollywood Park	2001
Princeton S.	3	Garden State	1974
Quaker H.	3	Liberty Bell	1974
Queen Charlotte H.	3	Monmouth Park	1992
Queen's H.	3	AKsarben	1993
Rare Treat H.	3	Aqueduct	2002
Reeve Schley Jr. S.	3	Monmouth Park	2001
Regret H.	3	Monmouth Park	1974
Riggs H.	3	Pimlico	1992
River Cities Breeders' Cup S.	3	Lousiana Downs	1998
Roamer H.	3	Aqueduct	1983
Rolling Green H.	3	Golden Gate Fields	1994
Roseben H.	3	Belmont Park	1995
Rosemont S.	2	Delaware Park	1976
Round Table S.	3	Arlington Park	2001
Royal Palm H.	3	Hialeah	1999
Rutgers H.	3	Meadowlands	1996
Ruthless S.	3	Aqueduct	1982
San Jacinto S.	2	Santa Anita Park	1977
San Miguel S.	3	Santa Anita Park	2004
Santa Anita Breeders' Cup H.	3	Santa Anita Park	1995
Saul Silberman H.	3	Calder	1979
Schuylkill S.	3	Liberty Bell	1974
Sea O Erin H.	3	Arlington Park	1994
Seashore H.	3	Atlantic City	1973
Select H.	3	Monmouth Park	1974
Selima S.	3	Laurel	1999
Seminole H.	2	Hialeah Park	19889
Seneca H.	3	Saratoga	1997
Sentinel S.	3	Liberty Bell	1974
Sheridan S.	3	Arlington Park	1996
Sierra Madre H.	3	Santa Anita Park	1990
Sierra Nevada H.	3	Santa Anita Park	1985
Signature S.	3	Keystone	1976
Snow Goose H.	3	Laurel	1996
Sorority S.	3	Monmouth Park	2003
Southwest S.	3	Oaklawn Park	1999
Spicy Living H.	3	Rockingham	1994
Spotlight Breeders' Cup H.	3	Hollywood Park	1994
Stymie H.	3	Aqueduct	2002
Suffolk Downs Sprint H.	3	Suffolk Downs	1988
Sunny Slope S.	3	Santa Anita	1984
Sunrise H.	3	Atlantic City	1973
Super Bowl S.	3	Gulfstream Park	1997
Susquehanna H.	3	Keystone	1978
Sussex Turf H.	3	Delaware Park	1975
Sweetest Chant S.	3	Gulfstream Park	2000
Swift S.	3	Aqueduct	1989
Swoon's Son H.	3	Arlington Park	1996
Tanforan H.	3	Golden Gate Fields	2002
Thanksgiving Day H.	3	Bay Meadows	1979
Thomas D. Nash Memorial H.	3	Sportsman's Park	1993
Tidal H.	2	Belmont Park	1993
Tremont S.	3	Belmont Park	2003
Trenton H.	3	Garden State	1994
Tyro S.	3	Monmouth Park	1974
Valley Forge H.	3	Garden State	1974
Ventnor H.	3	Monmouth Park	1975
Villager S.	3	Keystone	1977
Vineland H.	3	Garden State	1996
Virginia Belle S.	3	Bowie	1974
Washington, D.C., International S.	1	Laurel Park	1994
Week of Fame Fortune H.	3	Fair Grounds	1990
What a Pleasure S.	3	Calder	2000
Whitemarsh H.	3	Keystone	1977
Widener H.	3	Hialeah	2001
William du Pont Jr. H.	3	Delaware Park	1981
William P. Kyne H.	3	Bay Meadows	1999
Windy City H.	3	Sportsman's Park	1973
Woodlawn S.	3	Pimlico	1988
World's Playground S.	3	Atlantic City	1979
Young America Breeders' Cup S.	3	Meadowlands	1995
Youthful S.	3	Belmont Park	1974

2005 North American Stakes Races

Absent Russian S., Calder Race Course, Aug. 20, $40,000, 3&up, 1 1/8mT, 1:46.73, KEEP COOL, Texas Red, Go Directlyto Jail, 11 started.

Accordant H. (R), Meadowlands, Nov. 1, $55,000, 3&up, New Jersey-bred, 6f, 1:08.28, MIDNIGHT EXPRESS, Monsterinmyroom, Jay's Wish, 7 started.

Achievement H. (R), Woodbine, July 1, $129,424, 3yo, Ontario-bred, 6f, 1:11.68, QUICK IN DEED, Dave the Knave, Lake Secret, 5 started.

Ack Ack H., Hollywood Park, June 11, $91,350, 3&up, 7 1/2f, 1:27.23, MCCANN'S MOJAVE, Congrats, St Averil, 8 started.

ACK ACK H. (G3), Churchill Downs, Oct. 30, $112,200, 3&up, 7 1/2f, 1:28.34, STRAIGHT LINE, Vicarage, Level Playingfield, 9 started.

A. C. Kemp H., The Downs at Albuquerque, Sept. 21, $30,000, 2yo, 7f, 1:23.87, MIGHT BE HOOKED, Ima Highway Star, Afternoon Smooch, 8 started.

ACORN S. (G1), Belmont Park, June 4, $250,000, 3yo, f, 1m, 1:35.33, ROUND POND, Smuggler, In the Gold, 6 started.

ACTRA S., Grand Prairie, Aug. 21, $3,170, 3yo, 5 1/2f, 1:09, FORGOTTEN WEEKEND, Scruffy, Cool N Cautious, 4 started.

ACTRA S. (R), Grand Prairie, Aug. 6, $5,373, 3&up, f&m, Alberta-bred, 6f, 1:12.60, CERTAINLY REGAL, Ali's Glori, Bonus Parlay, 7 started.

ACTRA S. (R), Grand Prairie, Aug. 12, $5,331, 3&up, c&g, Alberta-bred, 6f, 1:12.80, EZEE TARGET, Dr. Mo, Waitin for Pete, 5 started.

Adena Springs Matchmaker Turf Sprint S., Remington Park, Aug. 5, $40,000, 3&up, f&m, 5fT, :56.98, TIMELESS DREAMER, Runs Naked, Queena Corrina, 10 started.

Adena Springs Oakley S. (R), Colonial Downs, June 19, $60,000, 3yo, f, Virginia-bred and/or -sired, 1 1/16mT, 1:45.72, CHERRY HILL LADY, Joyous Song, Maria's Dance, 7 started.

ADENA STALLIONS' MISS PREAKNESS S. (G3), Pimlico Race Course, May 20, $100,000, 3yo, f, 6f, 1:12.40, BURNISH, Partners Due, Hot Storm, 7 started.

ADIRONDACK S. (G2), Saratoga Race Course, July 27, $150,000, 2yo, f, 6f, 1:13.66, FOLKLORE, Fifth Avenue, Truart, 7 started.

Adoration H. (R), Del Mar, Sept. 1, $80,775, 3&up, f&m, non-winners of a stakes of $50,000 other than state-bred at one mile or over since February 1, 1m, 1:35.26, HEALTHY ADDICTION, Fencelineneighbor, Seeking the Heart, 5 started.

AEGON TURF SPRINT S. (G3), Churchill Downs, May 6, $113,500, 3&up, 5fT, :56.18, MIGHTY BEAU, Chosen Chief, Sgt. Bert, 10 started.

Affectionately H., Aqueduct, Jan. 15, $81,275, 3&up, f&m, 1 1/16m, 1:44.89, SAINTLINESS, Miss Fortunate, Mariakel, 6 started.

AFFIRMED H. (G3), Hollywood Park, June 18, $102,998, 3yo, 1 1/16m, 1:42.53, INDIAN OCEAN, Surf Cat, Dover Dere, 4 started.

Affirmed S., Zia Park, Nov. 19, $41,500, 3yo, 1m, 1:38, BOOM BOOM, Devon Rules, Devious Choice, 6 started.

Affirmed S. (R), Calder Race Course, Sept. 3, $125,000, 2yo, progeny of stallions standing in Florida, 7f, 1:24.87, IN SUMMATION, Blazing Rate, Old Town Pond, 7 started.

African Prince S. (R), Suffolk Downs, June 18, $40,000, 3yo, Massachusetts-bred, 6f, 1:13.65, STYLISH SULTANA, Spectacular Orage, Reprized Strike, 13 started.

Agassiz S., Assiniboia Downs, Aug. 20, $33,016, 3&up, 1m, 1:38.60, ALBARINO, Gus Again, His Money, 6 started.

A GLEAM INVITATIONAL H. (G2), Hollywood Park, July 9, $150,000, 3&up, f&m, 7f, 1:21.67, ALPHABET KISSES, Valentine Dancer, Muir Beach, 9 started.

Ahwatukee Express S., Turf Paradise, Oct. 22, $40,000, 3yo, f, 6f, 1:08.99, SHESA PRIVATE I, Katy Smiles, Kresgeville, 9 started.

Airline S., Louisiana Downs, July 16, $54,540, 3yo, 6f, 1:10.17, J. D.'S BLUE BAYOU, Logan's Draw, Dreamsandvisions, 7 started.

A. J. Foyt S. (R), Indiana Downs, June 18, $40,000, 3&up, Indiana-bred, 1 1/16mT, 1:42.58, LAC A ROCK, Call Roy, Sir Traver, 11 started.

Ajina S. (R), Belmont Park, Oct. 23, $70,500, 3&up, f&m, non-winners of an open stakes in 2005, 1m, 1:38.38, LAST SONG, Fait Accompli, Provincial, 7 started.

Alabama Belle S. (R), Louisiana Downs, Sept. 16, $55,000, 3&up, f&m, Alabama-bred, 6f, 1:12.10, COMALAGOLD, She's a Punter, Fancy Empire, 12 started.

ALABAMA S. (G1), Saratoga Race Course, Aug. 20, $750,000, 3yo, f, 1 1/4m, 2:04.45, SWEET SYMPHONY, Spun Sugar, R Lady Joy, 7 started.

Aladdin Resort and Casino H., Del Mar, Aug. 21, $77,125, 3yo, f, 1mT, 1:33.18, BINASUCCESS, Conveyor's Angel, Brooke's Halo, 10 started.

Alameda County Fillies and Mares H., Pleasanton, July 4, $51,000, 3&up, f&m, 1 1/16m, 1:42.11, SECRET CORSAGE, Platinum Princess, Lucky Sabre, 7 started.

Alamedan H., Pleasanton, July 10, $50,750, 3&up, 1 1/16m, 1:41.48, YOUGOTTAWANNA, Adreamisborn, Easy Million, 6 started.

Albany S., Golden Gate Fields, Oct. 23, $58,275, 3&up, f&m, 6f, 1:08.44, THRILLING VICTORY, Heavenly Humor, Yerevan Star, 6 started.

Albany S. (R), Saratoga Race Course, Aug. 24, $150,000, 3yo, New York-bred, 1 1/8m, 1:50.88, NAUGHTY NEW YORKER, Carminooch, Gold and Roses, 6 started.

Alberta-Bred Thoroughbreds Fall S., Lethbridge, Oct. 29, $11,207, 3&up, c&g, Alberta-bred, 7f, 1:25, DR. MO, Royal Group, Bridal Creek, 8 started.

Alberta Breeders' H. (R), Northlands Park, Sept. 24, $64,035, 3&up, Alberta-bred, 1 1/16m, 1:44, FUHR ORE, Beau Brass, Royalty Boy, 5 started.

Alberta Centennial H., Northlands Park, Aug. 13, $83,550, 3yo, f, 1 1/16m, 1:45.60, WILD BENDER, Secrets Galore, After the Knight, 5 started.

ALBERTA DERBY (Can-G3), Stampede Park, June 18, $101,700, 3yo, 1 1/16m, 1:48.40, KNIGHT'S COVENANT, Blackjack Willy, Tommy's Topper, 7 started.

Alberta Oaks (R), Northlands Park, Sept. 24, $42,690, 3yo, f, Alberta-bred, 1m, 1:39.20, SPEEDY GONE SALLY, Wild Bender, Tas Force, 5 started.

Alberta Premier's Futurity (R), Northlands Park, Sept. 24, $42,690, 2yo, Alberta-bred, 1m, 1:40, TEAGUES FIGHT, Mocha John, Wye Red, 5 started.

Albert Dominguez Invitational Starter Distance Series S., Ruidoso Downs, Sept. 5, $16,900, 3&up, 1 1/4m, 2:11.60, SWELTER, Mr. Excitement, Ink Grimsley, 7 started.

Albuquerque Derby, The Downs at Albuquerque, Sept. 18, $30,000, 3yo, 1 1/16m, 1:46.30, HOPE FOR PEACE, Julie's Wild Child, Lizard King, 6 started.

Alcatraz Breeders' Cup S., Golden Gate Fields, May 15, $86,875, 3yo, 1mT, 1:37, CHINESE DRAGON, Leo Getz, Mighty Empire (Ire), 4 started.

Alex M. Robb H. (R), Aqueduct, Dec. 28, $84,875, 3&up, New York-bred, 1 1/16m, 1:43.55, TWO SIXTY FOUR, Naughty New Yorker, Carminooch, 10 started.

ALFRED G. VANDERBILT H. (G2), Saratoga Race Course, Aug. 13, $200,000, 3&up, 6f, 1:08.69, POMEROY, I'm the Tiger, Voodoo, 7 started.

Algoma S. (R), Woodbine, Sept. 4, $105,599, 3&up, f&m, Canadian-bred, 1 1/16m, 1:44.24, ONE FOR ROSE, Kissed by a Prince, Bay Sweetie Babe, 6 started.

All Brandy S. (R), Laurel Park, Oct. 29, $50,000, 3&up, f&m, Maryland-bred, 1 1/8mT, 1:49.54, LARRUPIN GAL, Lucrezia, Rowdy, 7 started.

Allen Bogan Memorial S. (R), Lone Star Park, July 9, $100,000, 3&up, f&m, Texas-bred, 1m, 1:38.52, SLEWPY'S STORM, Sheza Lucky Son'so, This Man's Darling, 8 started.

Alliance S., Louisiana Downs, April 30, $49,000, 3&up, 1 1/16mT, 1:42.60, CROWNED KING, Run to the Border, Northern Scene, 5 started.

All Sold Out S. (R), Fairmount Park, Sept. 5, $41,000, 2yo, f, Illinois-bred, 6f, 1:13.20, TROUT RIVER RED, Lovely Love, Pretti Frosti, 9 started.

Alma North S. (R), Timonium, Sept. 3, $50,000, 3&up, f&m, Maryland-bred, a6 1/2f, 1:17.73, GRANT'S MOON, Niclie, Leavn Ona Jetplane, 10 started.

A. L. (Red) Erwin S. (R), Louisiana Downs, Aug. 21, $73,750, 3yo, Louisiana-bred, a1mT, 1:37.06, CHIP HUNTER, Badtotheboneandrew, Z Storm, 12 started.

Al Swihart Memorial H., Fonner Park, April 30, $26,500, 3&up, f&m, 6 1/2f, 1:19.20, UP 'N BLUMIN, Burning Memories, Missy Can Do, 10 started.

Alysheba Breeders' Cup S., Lone Star Park, July 2, $97,000, 3yo, 6f, 1:08.52, SANTANA STRINGS, War Bridle, Logan's Draw, 5 started.

Alysheba S., Churchill Downs, May 6, $112,900, 3&up, 1 1/16m, 1:42.32, LIMEHOUSE, Skipaslew, Missme, 8 started.

Alysheba S., Meadowlands, Oct. 29, $63,600, 3&up, 1 1/16m, 1:41.60, RICARDO A, Trueamericanspirit, Pushed, 6 started.

Alyssa H. (R), Beulah Park, May 7, $20,000, 3&up, f&m, starters at Beulah Park in 2005, 6f, 1:10.27, JUST MICHEL, Ask Linda, Red Hot Helen, 7 started.

Alywow S., Woodbine, June 12, $90,765, 3yo, f, 6 1/2fT, 1:16.31, HATPIN, Elle Runaway, Miss Venturous, 11 started.

Amadevil H. (R), Columbus Races, Aug. 13, $15,600, 3&up, Nebraska-bred, 6f, 1:13.40, DOUG'S SHADOW, Mortrump, High Dice, 6 started.

Ambassador of Luck H. (R), Philadelphia Park, July 23, $50,000, 3&up, f&m, Pennsylvania-bred, 7f, 1:24.28, VALLEY OF THE GODS, S W Aly'svalentine, Defrere's Venture, 9 started.

Ambehaving S., Calder Race Course, Sept. 10, $40,000, 3&up, 1 1/16m, 1:46.51, WHOS CRYING NOW, Lawbook, Supervisor, 8 started.

Amelia Peabody S. (R), Suffolk Downs, Nov. 5, $40,000, 2yo, f, Massachusetts-bred, 6f, 1:15.71, AUNTIE MILLIE, Sassy Splash, Strawbrysundance, 11 started.

American Beauty S., Oaklawn Park, Jan. 22, $50,000, 4&up, f&m, 6f, 1:10.83, SOURIS, Saltwater Runner, Southern Surprise, 8 started.

AMERICAN DERBY (G2), Arlington Park, July 23, $250,000, 3yo, 1 3/16mT, 1:55.31, GUN SALUTE, Purim, Exceptional Ride, 8 started.

American Dreamer S., Calder Race Course, Aug. 21, $40,000, 3yo, 1m, 1:40.34, HAL'S IMAGE, Talented Prince, Dazzling Dr. Cevin, 6 started.

AMERICAN INVITATIONAL H. (G2), Hollywood Park, July 3, $250,000, 3&up, 1 1/8mT, 1:46.30, WHILLY (IRE), King of Happiness, Fourty Niners Son, 8 started.

AMERICAN INVITATIONAL OAKS (G1), Hollywood Park, July 3, $750,000, 3yo, f, 1 1/4mT, 1:59.03, CESARIO (JPN), Melhor Ainda, Singhalese (GB), 12 started.

AMERICAN TURF S. (G3), Churchill Downs, May 6, $114,700, 3yo, 1 1/16mT, 1:42, REY DE CAFE, Rush Bay, Guillaume Tell (Ire), 9 started.

AMSTERDAM S. (G2), Saratoga Race Course, Aug. 7, $150,000, 3yo, 6f, 1:10.18, SANTANA STRINGS, Social Probation, Silver Train, 9 started.

ANCIENT TITLE BREEDERS' CUP S. (G1), Oak Tree at Santa Anita, Oct. 8, $236,000, 3&up, 6f, 1:08.85, CAPTAIN SQUIRE, Zanzibar (Arg), Indian Country, 7 started.

Anderson Fowler S., Monmouth Park, July 23, $55,000, 3yo, 5fT, :56.46, SILVER MOOSE, Yes Yes Yes, Swissle Stick, 8 started.

Anet S., Lone Star Park, June 4, $40,000, 3yo, 5 1/2f, 1:02.56, WAR BRIDLE, Moody Goose, Lord of the Track, 6 started.

Angel Island S., Golden Gate Fields, Dec. 3, $59,050, 3yo, f, 6f, 1:09.32, THRILLING VICTORY, Lunachick, Double D Appeal, 6 started.

Angenora S. (R), Thistledown, April 30, $40,000, 3&up, f&m, Ohio-bred, 6f, 1:12.16, JUST MICHEL, Bubble Dourbon, Spring Cat, 7 started.

Angie C. S., Emerald Downs, July 24, $43,650, 2yo, f, 6f, 1:12.40, CELTIC CROWN, Nite Moon, Fergie's Fantasy, 9 started.

Anna M. Fisher Debutante S., Ellis Park, Aug. 20, $62,000, 2yo, f, 7f, 1:23.97, SHE SAYS IT BEST, Claremont, Swept Gold, 5 started.

Ann Arbor S. (R), Great Lakes Downs, Aug. 20, $50,000, 3yo, f, Michigan-bred, 1m, 1:45.52, CREATIVE MISS, Maxie Match, Valor Within, 8 started.

Anne Arundel S., Laurel Park, Nov. 19, $100,000, 3yo, f, 1m, 1:37.01, TRICKLE OF GOLD, Sticky, Lexi Star, 10 started.

Ann Owens Distaff H. (R), Turf Paradise, April 30, $40,000, 3&up, f&m, Arizona-bred, 6f, 1:09.60, SOCIETY CAT, Lil Easy, Foolofit, 11 started.

Anoakia S., Oak Tree at Santa Anita, Oct. 23, $82,125, 2yo, f, 6f, 1:09.59, PRIVATE WORLD, Bettarun Fast, Make Mine Minnie, 8 started.

Answer Do S., Turf Paradise, Dec. 9, $23,700, 3&up, 6f, 1:09.01, COCOA LATTE, Red Creek, Il Colosseo (Ire), 6 started.

Answer Do S., Turf Paradise, Jan. 11, $21,800, 4&up, 6f, 1:08.46, PALMERTON, Flying Supercon, Bang, 8 started.

Anthony Fair H., Anthony Downs, July 24, $4,150, 3&up, a6 1/2f, 1:21.90, PINT O' STOUT, Puckerupbuttercup, Marlin's Ruler, 7 started.

Anthony Thoroughbred Futurity, Anthony Downs, July 24, $11,000, 2yo, 5f, 1:01.25, KELLY CARSON, Texas Charm, Hadley's Note, 7 started.

Appalachian S., Keeneland Race Course, April 24, $112,800, 3yo, f, 1mT, 1:37.69, MELHOR AINDA, Paddy's Daisy, Sweet Talker, 8 started.

APPLE BLOSSOM H. (G1), Oaklawn Park, April 9, $500,000, 4&up, f&m, 1 1/16m, 1:43.86, DREAM OF SUMMER, Star Parade (Arg), Shadow Cast, 7 started.

APPLETON H. (G3), Gulfstream Park, Feb. 12, $100,000, 3&up, 1mT, 1:32.98, MR. LIGHT (ARG), Host (Chi), Millennium Dragon (GB), 8 started.

Appleton Hurdle S., Far Hills, Oct. 22, $50,000, 4&up, a2 1/8mT, 4:36.43, ERIN GO BRAGH (NZ), Mauritania, Jazzitupgeorge, 10 started.

April Run S., Laurel Park, Nov. 19, $75,000, 3&up, f&m, 1 1/8mT, 1:47.96, SMART N CLASSY, Art Fan, Moon Dazzle, 13 started.

A. P. Smithwick Memorial Steeplechase S., Saratoga Race Course, Aug. 8, $79,550, 4&up, a2 1/16mT, 3:43.83, PARADISE'S BOSS, Serazzo, Hirapour (Ire), 8 started.

AQUEDUCT H. (G3), Aqueduct, Jan. 30, $110,300, 3&up, 1 1/16m, 1:44.80, COUNTRY BE GOLD, Aggadan, Mahzouz, 8 started.

Arapahoe Park Sprint H., Arapahoe Park, June 12, $27,975, 3&up, 6f, 1:09.50, COCOA LATTE, Lukfata Louis, Sharm, 6 started.

ARCADIA H. (G2), Santa Anita Park, April 9, $150,000, 4&up, 1mT, 1:33.52, SINGLETARY, Sweet Return (GB), Buckland Manor, 5 started.

Arcadia S. (R), Louisiana Downs, June 5, $50,000, 3yo, Louisiana-bred, 6f, 1:10.12, J. D.'S BLUE BAYOU, Crawfish King, Mr. Barracuda, 11 started.

Arctic Queen H. (R), Finger Lakes, July 4, $50,000, 3&up, f&m, New York-bred, 6f, 1:10.66, KEESLER, Perty Number, Ava Marisa, 7 started.

ARISTIDES BREEDERS' CUP H. (G3), Churchill Downs, June 25, $162,450, 3&up, 6f, 1:07.59 (NTR), KELLY'S LANDING, Battle Won, Jet Prospector, 6 started.

Arizona Breeders' Derby (R), Turf Paradise, April 30, $49,272, 3yo, Arizona-bred, 1 1/16m, 1:45.12, TIPTON, Rowdy Creek, Special Truce, 6 started.

Arizona Breeders' Futurity (R), Turf Paradise, Dec. 3, $49,454, 2yo, f, Arizona-bred, 6f, 1:11.63, RESTRIDE, Stellar Babe, Instantly Right, 12 started.

Arizona Breeders' Futurity (R), Turf Paradise, Dec. 3, $51,580, 2yo, c&g, Arizona-bred, 6f, 1:10.57, LEVELLED, Corporal Tillman, Captain Strider, 12 started.

Arizona County Fair Distance Series S., Cochise County Fair, April 24, $2,447, 3&up, 1m70y, 1:46.40, DYNA KING, Chehalis, Cosmic High, 8 started.

Arizona County Fair Distance Series S. (1st Div.), Graham County Fair, April 10, $2,121, 3&up, 1m, 1:45.80, WE BE CUZZINS, Shoot the Loot, Jaffa, 7 started.

Arizona County Fair Distance Series S. (2nd Div.), Graham County Fair, April 10, $2,121, 3&up, 1m, 1:43.60, CHEHALIS, Valtry, Cabreo, 8 started.

Arizona County Fair Distance Series S. (1st Div.), Greenlee County Fair, March 20, $2,247, 3&up, 7f, 1:28.40, POLITICAL STORM, Radical Reality, Valtry, 6 started.

Arizona County Fair Distance Series S. (2nd Div.), Greenlee County Fair, March 20, $2,247, 3&up, 7f, 1:29.40, FAST MACHINE, Cabreo, High Smoke, 6 started.

Arizona County Fair Distance Series S., Mohave County Fair, May 22, $2,390, 3&up, 1 1/8m, 1:53 (NTR), COLOREADO (CHI), Wind Talkin, Proud General, 6 started.

Arizona County Fair Distance Series S., Santa Cruz County Fair, May 8, $2,439, 3&up, 1 1/16m, 1:49.80, CHEHALIS, Coloreado (Chi), Cabreo, 8 started.

Arizona County Fair Speed Series S., Cochise County Fair, April 23, $2,447, 3&up, a3f, 37.80, BRITE NITE, Zippin Zane, Soaring an Action, 8 started.

Arizona County Fair Speed Series S., Graham County Fair, April 9, $2,145, 3&up, 4f, :46.60, STRANGER AMONG US, Cherry Martini, Starship, 8 started.

Arizona County Fair Speed Series S., Graham County Fair, April 9, $2,145, 3&up, 4f, :46.40, BRITE NITE, From A to Z, Duke of Haz, 8 started.

Arizona County Fair Speed Series S., Greenlee County Fair, March 19, $2,297, 3&up, 5f, 1:01.80, BRITE NITE, Honest Ridge, From A to Z, 8 started.

Arizona County Fair Speed Series S., Mohave County Fair, May 22, $2,438, 3&up, 6f, 1:13.80, A J DUSTDEVIL, J J Thedotcom Man, Uncle Johnny, 6 started.

Arizona County Fair Speed Series S., Santa Cruz County Fair, May 7, $2,439, 3&up, 5 1/2f, 1:05.80, FROM A TO Z, Brite Nite, Starship, 8 started.

Arizona Juvenile S., Turf Paradise, Dec. 26, $40,000, 2yo, 6 1/2f, 1:16.68, KEAGAN, Mining Gold, Hey Slick, 9 started.

Arizona Juvenile S., Turf Paradise, Dec. 31, $40,000, 2yo, f, 6 1/2f, 1:14.79, BULLY BONES, Toppisme, Along Came Jones, 9 started.

Arizona Oaks, Turf Paradise, Feb. 12, $75,000, 3yo, f, 1 1/16m, 1:43.85, SHE SINGS, Virden, Mi Luna Nueva, 7 started.

Arizona Stallion S. (R), Turf Paradise, April 9, $36,000, 3yo, progeny of stallions standing in Arizona, 7 1/2fT, 1:30.53, DESERT PROSPECTOR, Buck's Wine, Special Truce, 7 started.

ARKANSAS DERBY (G2), Oaklawn Park, April 16, $1,000,000, 3yo, 1 1/8m, 1:48.80, AFLEET ALEX, Flower Alley, Andromeda's Hero, 10 started.

Ark-La-Tex H., Louisiana Downs, June 18, $50,000, 3&up, 1 1/16m, 1:43.93, HIGH STRIKE ZONE, Akanti (Ire), Majestic Thief, 7 started.

Arlington Breeders' Cup Sprint H., Arlington Park, Aug. 27, $150,000, 3&up, 6f, 1:08.51, FIFTEEN ROUNDS, Elusive Jazz, Level Playingfield, 6 started.

ARLINGTON CLASSIC S. (G3), Arlington Park, July 2, $150,000, 3yo, 1 1/16mT, 1:42.65, PURIM, United, Cosmic Kris, 9 started.

ARLINGTON H. (G3), Arlington Park, July 23, $200,000, 3&up, 1 1/4mT, 2:02.26, COOL CONDUCTOR, Vangelis, Major Rhythm, 7 started.

ARLINGTON MATRON H. (G3), Arlington Park, Sept. 3, $150,000, 3&up, f&m, 1 1/8m, 1:49.87, QUICK TEMPER, Diavla, For Gillian, 7 started.

ARLINGTON MILLION S. (G1), Arlington Park, Aug. 13, $1,000,000, 3&up, 1 1/4mT, 2:03.38, POWERSCOURT (GB), Kitten's Joy, Fourty Niners Son, 10 started.

Arlington Oaks, Arlington Park, Aug. 20, $100,000, 3yo, f, 1 1/8m, 1:49.39, MISS MATCHED, Gallant Secret, Tappin for Gold, 8 started.

ARLINGTON-WASHINGTON BREEDERS' CUP FUTURITY (G3), Arlington Park, Sept. 18, $198,500, 2yo, 1m, 1:35.16, SORCEROR'S STONE, Charley Tango, Red Raymond, 9 started.

ARLINGTON-WASHINGTON BREEDERS' CUP LASSIE S. (G3), Arlington Park, Sept. 18, $147,000, 2yo, f, 1m, 1:35.93, ORIGINAL SPIN, Ex Caelis, Coolwind, 9 started.

Artax H., Gulfstream Park, April 2, $100,000, 3&up, 7 1/2f, 1:28.42, VALUE PLUS, Gygistar, Super Frolic, 7 started.

Arthur I. Appleton Juvenile Turf S. (R), Calder Race Course, Nov. 12, $100,000, 2yo, Florida-bred, 1 1/16mT, 1:42.50, MR. SILVER, Gin Rummy King, Full In, 7 started.

Art Smith Memorial S., Crooked River Roundup, July 9, $3,900, 3&up, a7f, 1:32.10, DREAMONEIR, Black Canyon Bart, Mon T. Hauls, 7 started.

Ascot Graduation S., Hastings Race Course, Oct. 23, $101,779, 2yo, 1 1/16m, 1:47.58, REGAL REQUEST, Mighty Cahill, Celtic Warrior, 9 started.

Ashford Stud Coolmore Daniel Van Clief S. (R), Colonial Downs, July 3, $60,000, 3&up, Virginia-bred and/or -sired, 1 1/16mT, 1:42.34, RAHY'S CHANCE, Run the Light, Ouagadougou, 9 started.

ASHLAND S. (G1), Keeneland Race Course, April 9, $500,000, 3yo, f, 1 1/16m, 1:46.35, SIS CITY, Runway Model, Memorette, 6 started.

Ashley T. Cole H. (R), Belmont Park, Sept. 18, $112,900, 3&up, New York-bred, 1 1/8mT, 1:48.78, CERTIFIABLY CRAZY, Continental Reins, Gryffindor, 10 started.

Aspen Cup H., Ruidoso Downs, June 25, $25,000, 3yo, f, 6f, 1:10, REVOLVING DOOR, Dixie Kiss, Lite Write, 8 started.

Aspen H. (R), Arapahoe Park, July 17, $30,675, 3&up, Colorado-bred, 6f, 1:08.36, COCOA LATTE, Cajun Pepper, Tank Two, 8 started.

Aspidistra H., Calder Race Course, Sept. 5, $100,000, 3&up, f&m, 1mT, 1:39.39, CHANCEY LIGHT, Skip Command, Silver Lace, 8 started.

Aspirant S. (R), Finger Lakes, Aug. 20, $128,275, 2yo, New York-bred, 6f, 1:10.24, ONE WAY FLIGHT, Speed of Sound, Nunzionic, 8 started.

Assault S. (R), Lone Star Park, July 9, $125,000, 3&up, Texas-bred, 1 1/16m, 1:44.26, GOOSEY MOOSE, Agrivating General, Charming Socialite, 7 started.

Assiniboia Oaks, Assiniboia Downs, Sept. 4, $33,684, 3yo, f&m, 1 1/16m, 1:48.40, J D'S DEELITES, Oxford Joy, Wautega Light, 6 started.

ASTARITA S. (G3), Belmont Park, Oct. 2, $108,400, 2yo, f, 6 1/2f, 1:16.90, SENSATION, Swap Fliparoo, Unobstructed View, 6 started.

Astoria S., Belmont Park, July 3, $109,500, 2yo, f, 5 1/2f, 1:04.02, ADIEU, Folklore, Wonder Lady Anne L, 6 started.

ATBA Fall Sales S. (R), Turf Paradise, Oct. 15, $73,195, 2yo, c&g, consigned to a 2004 ATBA sale, 6f, 1:10.74, IBETIWIN, Keagan, Corporal Tillman, 11 started.

ATBA Fall Sales S. (R), Turf Paradise, Oct. 15, $67,202, 2yo, f, consigned to a 2004 ATBA sale, 6f, 1:12.21, SNOWBOUND N DELMAR, Queen Razyana, Caros Foxy Lady, 11 started.

ATBA Spring Sales S. (R), Turf Paradise, May 22, $67,161, 2yo, consigned to a 2004 ATBA sale, 5f, :58.13, BORDER SWINGER, Ibetiwin, Rachel's Smokey, 12 started.

Atchison Topeka and Santa Fe S., The Woodlands, Oct. 8, $20,000, 3&up, 6f, 1:10.80, ROAROFVICTORY, Subsequently, dh-Bay of Love, dh-Just Add Water, 11 started.

Athenia H., Belmont Park, Oct. 15, $111,300, 3&up, f&m, 1 1/16m (originally scheduled as a Grade 3 on the turf), 1:42.57, ASTI (IRE), Bohemian Lady, Zosima, 6 started.

ATTO MILE S. (Can-G1), Woodbine, Sept. 18, $849,757, 3&up, 1mT, 1:35.08, LEROIDESANIMAUX (BRZ), Mobil, Le Cinquieme Essai, 9 started.

Auburn S., Emerald Downs, May 1, $40,000, 3yo, c&g, 6f, 1:09.40, BEAU MAGGIE, One Special Hoss, J D's Date, 7 started.

Audrey Skirball-Kenis S., Hollywood Park, Nov. 13, $72,150, 3yo, f, 1 1/16m, 1:42.15, PUSSYCAT DOLL, Skipping Court, A Classic Life, 5 started.

Audubon Oaks, Ellis Park, Aug. 6, $75,000, 3yo, f, 1 1/16mT, 1:41.24, UNBRIDLED DANZ, Royal Bean, Mrs. Debbie M, 12 started.

Auntie Mame S. (R), Belmont Park, Sept. 21, $67,750, 3yo, f, nonwinners of a stakes on the turf, 1mT, 1:35.58, CONNIE BELLE, Silver Charades, Forever Smart, 8 started.

Au Revoir H., Sun Downs, May 8, $2,300, 3&up, 7f, 1:26, PERCIPITATE, Here's Your Ticket, Tender Offer (Ire), 6 started.

Autotote Derby, Lethbridge, Oct. 30, $13,754, 3yo, 1 1/16m, 1:51, ALLRIGHT, Bold Position, Derby Drifter, 6 started.

Autumn Leaves H., Bay Meadows Race Course, Oct. 8, $75,000, 3&up, f&m, 1 1/16mT, 1:44.68, ALOZAINA (IRE), Sparkling Humor, Penny Ante, 10 started.

Autumn Leaves S., Mountaineer Race Track, Oct. 18, $75,000, 3&up, f&m, 1 1/16m, 1:47.19, PLUMLAKE LADY, Monument Valley, Quick Temper, 9 started.

Aventura S., Gulfstream Park, Jan. 8, $125,000, 3yo, 1m, 1:35.88, HIGH FLY, Drum Major, Magna Graduate, 12 started.

Awad S., Arlington Park, June 4, $42,250, 3yo, 1mT, 1:37.68, EXCEPTIONAL RIDE, Raving Rocket, Ready Ruler, 8 started.

AZALEA BREEDERS' CUP S. (G3), Calder Race Course, July 10, $248,250, 3yo, f, 6f, 1:10.32, LEAVE ME ALONE, Hide and Chic, Midtown Miss, 6 started.

Azalea S. (R), Delta Downs, March 25, $50,000, 3yo, f, Louisiana-bred, 5f, 1:00.85, INDIGO GIRL, Actress E, Maid in China, 6 started.

AZERI BREEDERS' CUP S. (G3), Oaklawn Park, March 12, $175,000, 3&up, f&m, 1 1/16m, 1:43.40, INJUSTICE, Colony Band, Island Sand, 6 started.

Aztec Oaks (R), SunRay Park, Sept. 3, $60,200, 3yo, f, New Mexico-bred, 6 1/2f, 1:17.40, MY DESERT LADY, La Mamie, Slewsflight, 7 started.

Bachman S., Fonner Park, Feb. 26, $10,625, 3yo, 4f, :46.40, S C KING, Slews in Oz Now, Slotsfan, 7 started.

Baldwin S., Santa Anita Park, March 5, $110,450, 3yo, 6 1/2f (originally scheduled as a Grade 3 at a6 1/2f on the turf), 1:16.16, HIGH STANDARDS, Talking to John, Run Thruthe Sun, 7 started.

Ballade S. (R), Woodbine, June 8, $100,696, 3&up, f&m, progeny of stallions standing in Ontario, 6f, 1:11.38, BELIEVE IN MISSY, Roman Romance, Kissed by a Prince, 6 started.

BALLERINA BREEDERS' CUP S. (Can-G3), Hastings Race Course, Oct. 15, $150,456, 3&up, f&m, 1 1/8m, 1:50.40, MONASHEE, Socorro County, Pretty Meadow, 11 started.

BALLERINA S. (G1), Saratoga Race Course, Aug. 28, $250,000, 3&up, f&m, 7f, 1:24.53, HAPPY TICKET, Pleasant Home, Molto Vita, 7 started.

BALLSTON SPA BREEDERS' CUP H. (G3), Saratoga Race Course, Aug. 29, $135,966, 3&up, f&m, 1 1/16mT, 1:40.30, ALINGHI (AUS), Que Puntual (Arg), Delta Princess, 11 started.

Band is Passing S., Calder Race Course, June 18, $40,000, 3&up, 1 1/16mT, 1:45.49, FINAL PROPHECY, Dancing Master (Ire), Lord Robyn, 9 started.

Bangles and Beads S., Fairplex Park, Sept. 26, $59,700, 3&up, f&m, 6 1/2f, 1:15.92, TIALINGA, Awesome Lady, Crowded Room, 9 started.

Banshee Breeze S., Gulfstream Park, Jan. 23, $60,000, 3&up, f&m, 1 1/8m, 1:51.25, PAMPERED PRINCESS, Adobe Gold, Isola Piu Bella (Chi), 8 started.

Bara Lass S. (R), Sam Houston Race Park, Nov. 19, $50,000, 2yo, f, Texas-bred, 7f, 1:25.88, ANNIE SAVOY, Betty Garr, Perfect Ruby, 11 started.

BARBARA FRITCHIE H. (G2), Laurel Park, Feb. 19, $200,000, 3&up, f&m, 7f, 1:23.64, CATIVA, Sensibly Chic, Silmaril, 10 started.

Barbara Shinpoch S., Emerald Downs, Sept. 10, $89,290, 2yo, f, 1m, 1:38.60, CHESTNUT LADY, Carrie With a C, She's All Silk, 10 started.

Barb's Dancer S. (R), Calder Race Course, Aug. 7, $40,000, 3&up, f&m, non-winners of a stakes of $25,000 since January 2, 6f, 1:11.42, PROSPECTIVE SAINT, Clearly A. K. O., So Much More, 8 started.

Barksdale H., Louisiana Downs, May 30, $49,000, 3&up, 1m70y, 1:43.73, CROWNED KING, Roar On Tour, Virginia Pride, 5 started.

Barretts Debutante S. (R), Fairplex Park, Sept. 17, $110,733, 2yo, f, sold at a Barretts sale, 6 1/2f, 1:17.01, CATCH MY FANCY, Acceleration, Itty Bitty Pretty, 8 started.

Barretts Juvenile S. (R), Fairplex Park, Sept. 18, $115,400, 2yo, sold at a Barretts sale, 6 1/2f, 1:17.85, DIRECT CONNECT, Bengal Lore, Musical Meeting, 10 started.

Barretts S. (R), Hollywood Park, April 24, $70,000, 3&up, California-bred non-winners of $3,000 other than maiden, claiming, or starter or non-winners of two races, 7f, 1:22.35, TRAIL MIX, K C Nite Mayr, Steel Cutlass, 13 started.

BASHFORD MANOR S. (G3), Churchill Downs, July 10, $176,250, 2yo, 6f, 1:11.38, DEPUTY G, R Loyal Man, Honor Due, 10 started.

Bassinet S., River Downs, Sept. 3, $100,000, 2yo, f, 6f, 1:09.60, DIXIE DREAMER, She Says It Best, High Heritage, 7 started.

Battlefield S., Monmouth Park, June 11, $60,000, 3&up, 1$^1/_8$mT, 1:48.24, REVVED UP, Tam's Terms, Cacht Wells (Arg), 9 started.

Battler Star H. (R), Fair Grounds, Feb. 27, $75,000, 3yo, f, Louisiana-bred, 6f, 1:11.02, THE BETER MAN CAN, Maid in China, My Foriels On, 9 started.

Baxter S., Fonner Park, March 19, $17,125, 3yo, 6$^1/_2$f, 1:21.40, CORK THE BARBER, The Straw Man, My Hobby, 7 started.

BAYAKOA H. (G2), Hollywood Park, Dec. 11, $150,000, 3&up, f&m, 1$^1/_{16}$m, 1:41.96, STAR PARADE (ARG), Dream of Summer, Island Fashion, 9 started.

Bayakoa S., Oaklawn Park, April 10, $100,000, 4&up, f&m, 1$^1/_{16}$m, 1:43.61, TWO TRAIL SIOUX, Platinum Ballet, Casual Attitude, 9 started.

BAY MEADOWS BREEDERS' CUP H. (G3), Bay Meadows Race Course, Oct. 1, $121,250, 3&up, a1$^1/_8$mT, 1:46.94, ADREAMISBORN, Shadow Raider, Hatif (Brz), 5 started.

Bay Meadows Juvenile S., Bay Meadows Race Course, Oct. 15, $68,200, 2yo, 1m, 1:37.50, CAUSE TO BELIEVE, Crafty Ang, M. J. Pkay, 7 started.

Bay Meadows Oaks, Bay Meadows Race Course, April 16, $69,725, 3yo, f, 1$^1/_{16}$mT, 1:44.68, THRILLING VICTORY, Jill's Sky, Laguna Pointe, 7 started.

Bay Meadows Speed H., Bay Meadows Race Course, Oct. 1, $100,000, 3&up, 6f, 1:08.05, LOST IN THE FOG, Halo Cat, Jeffries Bay, 5 started.

BAYOU BREEDERS' CUP H. (G3), Fair Grounds, Feb. 19, $125,000, 4&up, f&m, a1$^1/_8$mT, 1:53.75, SHADOW CAST, Bijou, Sister Swank, 8 started.

Bayouland Sales S. (R), Evangeline Downs, Dec. 2, $50,000, 2yo, passed through the sales ring at the Louisiana Thoroughbred Breeders' Sale Co., 6f, 1:11.74, VOODOO GOLD, Lexi's Luck, Unofficial, 10 started.

Bayou State S. (R), Delta Downs, March 12, $50,000, 4&up, Louisiana-bred, 6$^1/_2$f, 1:20.30, BELIEVE IM SPECIAL, Kim's Gem, Mister Ajax, 8 started.

BAY SHORE S. (G3), Aqueduct, April 9, $150,000, 3yo, 7f, 1:21.33, LOST IN THE FOG, White Socks, Big Top Cat, 6 started.

B. B. Sixty Rayburn S. (R), Evangeline Downs, July 30, $50,000, 3yo, c&g, Louisiana-bred, 1m, 1:39.89, MR. BARRACUDA, J. D.'s Blue Bayou, Jacob V and G A, 7 started.

B Cup Classic S., Lethbridge, Oct. 16, $14,004, 3&up, 1$^1/_8$m, 1:55.60, LARRY THE LONGSHOT, Chief Joseph, Horizon Weekend, 8 started.

B Cup Fillies and Mares S., Lethbridge, Oct. 16, $11,009, 3&up, f&m, 7f, 1:25.80, GUILTYBYSUPISCION, Selita's Dream, Nindawayma, 7 started.

B Cup Fillies and Mares Sprint S., Lethbridge, Oct. 16, $11,136, 3&up, f&m, 5$^1/_2$f, 1:08.40, HIGHLAND LORE, Getta Klew, Highness, 8 started.

B Cup S., Lethbridge, Oct. 16, $10,882, 3&up, 7f, 1:25, LAFLEUR, Dr. Mo, Arctic Horizon, 6 started.

B Cup S., Lethbridge, Oct. 16, $11,136, 2yo, a6f, 1:11.80, BLACK EYED MONTE, Coming Back, She's Twenty Below, 8 started.

B Cup S., Lethbridge, Oct. 16, $11,009, 3yo, a6f, 1:10.40, RUMBLE RIVER, John's Magic, Cool Yer Boots, 7 started.

B Cup Sprint S., Lethbridge, Oct. 16, $11,136, 3&up, 5$^1/_2$f, 1:08.20, FROSTY PRINCE, Allys Thunder, Starr's Future, 8 started.

Beau Brummel S., Fairplex Park, Sept. 14, $58,200, 2yo, 6$^1/_2$f, 1:17.75, THE THOUGHT OCCURS, Don Jaun Con, At a Boy Russ, 6 started.

Beaufort S. (R), Northlands Park, Sept. 24, $42,690, 3yo, Alberta-bred, 1$^1/_{16}$m, 1:45, DING DONG DANDY, Newport Road, Knight's Covenant, 10 started.

BEAUGAY H. (G3), Aqueduct, April 30, $112,800, 3&up, f&m, 1$^1/_{16}$mT, 1:44.56, FINERY, Changing World, Asti (Ire), 9 started.

Beau Genius H., Churchill Downs, July 3, $68,850, 3yo, 5fT, :57.02, SMOKE SMOKE SMOKE, British Attitude, Silent Bid, 6 started.

Beau's Eagle S. (R), Hollywood Park, June 29, $63,590, 3yo, non-winners of a stakes, 5$^1/_2$fT, 1:01.87, CHARMVICTOR, I'll Prey for You, Talking to John, 6 started.

Beautiful Day S., Delaware Park, July 9, $58,600, 3yo, f, 6f, 1:11.26, ALL PLATINUM, Coastal Strike, Contrast, 5 started.

Beck Auto Group Turf Sprint H., Lone Star Park, May 30, $100,000, 3&up, 5fT, :57.63, ONCEAROUNDTWICE, Top Commander, Orphan Brigade, 6 started.

BED O' ROSES BREEDERS' CUP H. (G3), Aqueduct, April 23, $153,200, 3&up, f&m, 1m, 1:36.72, PLEASANT HOME, Traci Girl, Cativa, 7 started.

BELDAME S. (G1), Belmont Park, Oct. 1, $750,000, 3&up, f&m, 1$^1/_8$m, 1:48.88, ASHADO, Happy Ticket, Society Selection, 7 started.

Belle Roberts S. (R), Emerald Downs, Oct. 2, $47,750, 3&up, f&m, Washington-bred, 1$^1/_{16}$m, 1:43.40, HALONATOR, Carrie's a Jewel, La Belle Fleur, 6 started.

BELMONT BREEDERS' CUP H. (G2), Belmont Park, Sept. 11, $197,200, 3&up, 1$^1/_8$mT, 1:45.06 (NCR), SHAKESPEARE, Meteor Storm (GB), Muqbil, 4 started.

BELMONT S. (G1), Belmont Park, June 11, $1,000,000, 3yo, 1$^1/_2$m, 2:28.75, AFLEET ALEX, Andromeda's Hero, Nolan's Cat, 11 started.

BEN ALI S. (G3), Keeneland Race Course, April 28, $150,000, 4&up, 1$^1/_8$m, 1:51.29, ALUMNI HALL, Pies Prospect, Go Now, 8 started.

Ben Cohen S., Pimlico Race Course, May 28, $50,000, 3&up, 5fT, :57.99, TACIRRING, Midwatch, Yankee Wildcat, 9 started.

Bergen County S., Meadowlands, Oct. 21, $50,000, 3yo, 5fT, :56.82, KING'S SCHOLAR, Silver Moose, North Potomac, 9 started.

BERKELEY H. (G3), Golden Gate Fields, June 11, $100,000, 3&up, 1$^1/_{16}$m, 1:40.94, DESERT BOOM, Easy Million, Yougottawanna, 7 started.

BERNARD BARUCH H. (G2), Saratoga Race Course, Aug. 1, $147,000, 3&up, 1$^1/_8$mT, 1:47.65, ARTIE SCHILLER, Silver Tree, America Alive, 5 started.

Bernie Dowd H. (R), Monmouth Park, June 19, $60,000, 3&up, New Jersey-bred, 1m70y, 1:42.12, UPTURN, Brucker's Brother, Quiet Desperation, 8 started.

Bersid S., Turf Paradise, Oct. 14, $23,600, 3&up, f&m, 1m, 1:36.87, HILLSDALE, Relaxing Green, Robyn's Day, 6 started.

Bertram F. Bongard S. (R), Belmont Park, Sept. 25, $107,700, 2yo, New York-bred, 7f, 1:24.20, SHARP HUMOR, Saint Paddy's Pro, Parkhimonbroadway, 6 started.

BESSARABIAN H. (Can-G3), Woodbine, Dec. 3, $154,474, 3&up, f&m, 7f, 1:25, MISS CONCERTO, Colonial Surprise, Hatpin, 12 started.

Best of Ohio Distaff S. (R), Beulah Park, Oct. 1, $50,000, 3&up, f&m, Ohio-bred, 1$^1/_8$m, 1:53.03, WHITEWATER WAY, Barnsy, Golden Tour, 13 started.

Best of Ohio Endurance S. (R), Beulah Park, Oct. 1, $75,000, 3&up, Ohio-bred, 1$^1/_4$m, 2:01.80, READY FOR ROSES, Go Johnny Go, Count On My Word, 11 started.

Best of Ohio Sprint S. (R), Beulah Park, Oct. 1, $50,000, 3&up, Ohio-bred, 6f, 1:10.38, BEN'S REFLECTION, Catlaunch, I Cant Refuse, 8 started.

BEST PAL S. (G2), Del Mar, Aug. 14, $147,000, 2yo, 6$^1/_2$f, 1:15.64, WHAT A SONG, Bashert, Plug Me In, 4 started.

Betsy Ross Overnight H., Emerald Downs, July 4, $25,000, 3&up, f&m, 6f, 1:09.20, MARVA JEAN, Strollin Slew, Melba Jewel, 6 started.

Better Bee S., Arlington Park, July 3, $41,750, 3&up, 6f, 1:08.80, FIFTEEN ROUNDS, Apalachian Thunder, Without a Doubt, 7 started.

Bettie Bullock Memorial Derby, Wyoming Downs, Aug. 21, $8,350, 3yo, 5$^1/_2$f, 1:04.23, GAL'S HUNTER, Iza Reckless, Valiant Soldier, 5 started.

BEVERLY D. S. (G1), Arlington Park, Aug. 13, $750,000, 3&up, f&m, 1$^3/_{16}$mT, 1:58.30, ANGARA (GB), Megahertz (GB), Melhor Ainda, 9 started.

BEVERLY HILLS H. (G2), Hollywood Park, June 25, $200,000, 3&up, f&m, 1$^1/_4$mT, 2:01.78, MEGAHERTZ (GB), Winendynme, Halo Ola (Arg), 6 started.

BEWITCH S. (G3), Keeneland Race Course, April 27, $109,300, 4&up, f&m, 1$^1/_2$mT, 2:36.24, ANGARA (GB), Cape Town Lass, Strike Me Lucky, 7 started.

Bien Bien S. (R), Hollywood Park, Nov. 12, $70,250, 3yo, non-winners of $60,000 at one mile or over, 1$^1/_{16}$m, 1:43.30, CHIPS ARE DOWN, Yes He's a Pistol, Becrux (Ity), 4 started.

Bienvenidos S., Turf Paradise, Sept. 30, $24,000, 3&up, 1m, 1:36.16, SUSPICIOUS MINDS, Point Dume, Gospodin, 9 started.

Big Red Mile H. (R), Lincoln State Fair, May 30, $20,900, 3&up, Nebraska-bred, 1m, 1:38.20, WHAT ABOUT DAVID, Cassanova Kid, High Dice, 9 started.

Big Sky H., Great Falls, July 31, $7,500, 3&up, 1m70y, 1:48, SHOULDBEVICTORY, Lost Again, Streak a Roani, 6 started.

Bill Callihan H., Columbus Races, Sept. 4, $10,350, 3&up, f&m, 6$^1/_2$f, 1:20.20, BURNING MEMORIES, Missy Can Do, Jay's Impact, 5 started.

Bill Thomas Memorial H., Sunland Park, March 5, $54,100, 3&up, $6\frac{1}{2}$f, 1:15.21, PROUD CARDENAL, This Chris, Beyond Brilliant, 8 started.

Bill Wheeler H. (R), Monmouth Park, Aug. 27, $60,000, 3&up, New Jersey-bred, 6f, 1:10.45, TRUEAMERICANSPIRIT, Jay's Wish, War's Prospect, 6 started.

Bill Wineberg S. (R), Portland Meadows, Nov. 19, $21,650, 2yo, c&g, Oregon-bred, 6f, 1:13.02, TOM TWO, Cascadians Cuttie, Newberg Gold, 11 started.

Billy Powell Claiming H., The Downs at Albuquerque, June 12, $15,600, 3&up, $1\frac{1}{2}$m, 2:37.86, JULIE'S WILD CHILD, Cryptotune, Power Strokin, 7 started.

BING CROSBY H. (G1), Del Mar, July 31, $300,000, 3&up, 6f, 1:08.04, GREG'S GOLD, Battle Won, Taste of Paradise, 9 started.

Birdcatcher S., Northlands Park, Sept. 5, $42,105, 2yo, c&g, $6\frac{1}{2}$f, 1:19.40, BELL N' GONE, Teagues Fight, Bear Character, 8 started.

Bird of Pay S., Northlands Park, Sept. 3, $42,105, 2yo, f, $6\frac{1}{2}$f, 1:18.80, KAYLEE'S MAGIC, Sassy Sarah, Tartan Star, 6 started.

Birdonthewire S., Calder Race Course, July 10, $75,000, 2yo, $5\frac{1}{2}$f, 1:05.67, IN SUMMATION, The Pharaoh, Tizzys No Saint, 6 started.

Birmingham Maiden S. (R), River Downs, June 4, $22,500, 3&up, Alabama-bred, 6f, 1:12.20, SWOON ME BABY, Ruben John, Ability Springs, 11 started.

Bison City S. (R), Fort Erie, July 4, $201,425, 3yo, f, Canadian-bred, $1\frac{1}{16}$m, 1:43.15, READY AND ALLURING, Skippingall Theway, Victorious Ami, 6 started.

BLACK-EYED SUSAN S. (G2), Pimlico Race Course, May 20, $200,000, 3yo, f, $1\frac{1}{8}$m, 1:53.27, SPUN SUGAR, R Lady Joy, Pleasant Chimes, 6 started.

Black Gold H., Fair Grounds, Jan. 29, $50,000, 3yo, 1m, 1:39.30, STRAW HAT, Medigating (Fr), Krises Bells, 5 started.

Black Mesa S. (R), Remington Park, Aug. 27, $40,000, 3&up, f&m, Oklahoma-bred, 6f, 1:10.48, PASSION FEVER, Racing Sundown, Rammers Best, 9 started.

Black Mountain H., Turf Paradise, Dec. 10, $40,000, 3&up, $1\frac{1}{16}$m, 1:42.99, STRATEGICALLY, Lydia's Legacy, Point Dume, 6 started.

Black Swan S., Fairplex Park, Sept. 21, $59,400, 2yo, f, $1\frac{1}{16}$m, 1:46.14, I CAN SEE, More Angels, Kalookan Lessie, 8 started.

Black Tie Affair H. (R), Arlington Park, June 25, $86,950, 3&up, Illinois-conceived and/or -foaled, $1\frac{1}{16}$mT, 1:41.72, FORT PRADO, Scooter Roach, Home of Stars, 11 started.

Blair's Cove S. (R), Canterbury Park, July 2, $40,000, 3&up, Minnesota-bred, $1\frac{1}{16}$mT, 1:44.14, WALLY'S CHOICE, Now Playing, Bassant, 6 started.

Blaze O'Brien S., Turf Paradise, April 12, $23,900, 3&up, $1\frac{1}{16}$mT, 1:42.53, CUT OF MUSIC, Strategically, Hero's Pleasure, 9 started.

Blazing Sword S., Calder Race Course, June 5, $40,000, 3&up, 1m, 1:39.54, CERVELO, Nightmare Affair, Unbridels King, 7 started.

Blazing Sword S., Calder Race Course, Nov. 19, $40,000, 3yo, $1\frac{1}{16}$m, 1:47.92, SIR JACKIE, Notgonagetemtoday, Talented Prince, 7 started.

B L's Sweep S., Calder Race Course, June 20, $40,000, 2yo, $5\frac{1}{2}$f, 1:04.78, IN SUMMATION, Tizzys No Saint, With a City, 9 started.

Bluegrass H., Lincoln State Fair, June 4, $12,813, 3&up, f&m, 6f, 1:11.60, MISSY CAN DO, Up 'n Blumin, Starlord, 6 started.

BLUE GRASS S. (G1), Keeneland Race Course, April 16, $750,000, 3yo, $1\frac{1}{8}$m, 1:50.16, BANDINI, High Limit, Closing Argument, 7 started.

Blue Hen S., Delaware Park, Oct. 22, $100,900, 2yo, f, $1\frac{1}{16}$m, 1:47.37, LOVE LOCKET, Stylish Yankee, She's Indy Money, 8 started.

Blue Jay Way S. (R), Oak Tree at Santa Anita, Oct. 1, $71,000, 3&up, non-winners of a stakes worth $50,000 since May 15, a$6\frac{1}{2}$fT, 1:11.95, SIREN LURE, Geronimo (Chi), Crystal Castle, 10 started.

Blue Mountain Juvenile S. (R), Penn National Race Course, Nov. 25, $52,750, 2yo, f, Pennsylvania-bred, 6f, 1:13, HAILIE'S GIRL, D. D. Night Star, Whim's Gem, 7 started.

Blue Norther S., Santa Anita Park, Jan. 14, $92,600, 3yo, f, 1mT, 1:38.37, CEE'S IRISH, Royal Copenhagen (Fr), Conveyor's Angel, 6 started.

Blue Skies H., Louisiana Downs, Aug. 7, $40,000, 3&up, 1m70y, 1:41.93, MAJESTIC THIEF, Crowned King, Agrivating General, 6 started.

Blue Sparkler S., Monmouth Park, Sept. 18, $60,000, 3&up, f&m, 6f, 1:10.26, COMOCINA, Traci Girl, Every Trick, 6 started.

Bobbie Bricker Memorial H. (R), Beulah Park, Oct. 22, $40,000, 3&up, f&m, Ohio-bred, $1\frac{1}{16}$m, 1:46.76, PATTI'S CLOWN, Misty Tab, Imahoneytoo, 8 started.

Bob Bryant S. (R), Prairie Meadows, May 28, $60,130, 3yo, f, Iowa-bred, 6f, 1:10.22, SUNRISEONTHEOASIS, Camela Carson, French Clu, 10 started.

Bob Harding S., Monmouth Park, Sept. 5, $60,000, 3&up, 1mT, 1:35.38, STORMY ROMAN, Ballonenostrikes, Foreverness, 10 started.

Bob Johnson Memorial S., Lone Star Park, July 17, $75,000, 3&up, 1m, 1:36.32, SHAKY TOWN, Majestic Thief, Runaway Choice, 5 started.

Bob Slater S., Gulfstream Park, April 16, $50,000, 3&up, f&m, 5fT, :55.04, MISS VICTORY (ARG), Adreality, Platinum Perfect, 10 started.

Bob Weems Memorial S., Turf Paradise, March 25, $23,900, 3&up, $1\frac{1}{8}$m, 1:50.86, HERO'S PLEASURE, Cut of Music, Geririg, 9 started.

Boeing H., Emerald Downs, July 30, $40,000, 3&up, f&m, $1\frac{1}{16}$m, 1:42.60, KARIS MAKAW, Summer Symphony, Ruby Dawn, 7 started.

Boiling Springs S., Monmouth Park, May 29, $136,500, 3yo, f, $1\frac{1}{16}$m (originally scheduled as a Grade 3 on the turf), 1:44.36, TOLL TAKER, Pleasant Lyrics, Ruby Martini, 3 started.

Bold Accent H., Fonner Park, Feb. 12, $10,625, 3&up, f&m, 4f, :44.40, MISSY CAN DO, Tee Times Two, Starlord, 8 started.

Bold Ego H., Sunland Park, Dec. 22, $50,000, 3&up, f&m, $5\frac{1}{2}$f, 1:03.47, SANDIA'S FLICKA, Red Lifesaver, Culpeper Moon, 9 started.

Bold Ego H., Sunland Park, Jan. 2, $53,250, 3&up, f&m, $5\frac{1}{2}$f, 1:03.01, SOURIS, Sandia's Flicka, Yet Anothernatalie, 7 started.

Bold Ruckus S. (R), Woodbine, June 15, $101,027, 3yo, progeny of stallions standing in Ontario, 6fT, 1:13.26, QUICK IN DEED, Flat Rock, Archers Alyancer, 9 started.

BOLD RULER H. (G3), Belmont Park, May 7, $104,600, 3&up, 6f, 1:08.67, UNCLE CAMIE, Don Six, Thunder Touch, 5 started.

Bold Venture H., Woodbine, July 9, $112,907, 3&up, $6\frac{1}{2}$f, 1:15.41, JUDITHS WILD RUSH, High Blitz, Ministers Wild Cat, 7 started.

Bold World S., Calder Race Course, Nov. 6, $40,000, 3&up, f&m, 6f, 1:10.68, MIDTOWN MISS, Lady in Pink, Wise and Precious, 7 started.

Bonnie Heath Turf Cup H. (R), Calder Race Course, Nov. 12, $150,000, 3&up, Florida-bred, $1\frac{1}{8}$mT, 1:45.89, REVVED UP, Silver Tree, Gin and Sin, 9 started.

BONNIE MISS S. (G2), Gulfstream Park, March 5, $150,000, 3yo, f, $1\frac{1}{8}$m, 1:53.12, JILL ROBIN L, In the Gold, Holy Trinity, 7 started.

Boomer S. (R), Fair Meadows at Tulsa, July 2, $38,400, 3&up, f&m, Oklahoma-bred, $5\frac{1}{2}$f, 1:05.80, TICKIN' OKIE, Rammers Best, Arthel, 9 started.

Borderland Derby, Sunland Park, Feb. 27, $104,800, 3yo, $1\frac{1}{16}$m, 1:43.18, SOUTHERN AFRICA, Thor's Echo, Dover Dere, 12 started.

Born Famous S., Calder Race Course, Jan. 2, $40,000, 4&up, f&m, 5fT, :56.11, WHENTHEDOVEFLIES, Mooji Moo, Unhurried, 8 started.

Bossier City H., Louisiana Downs, June 11, $50,180, 3yo, a$1\frac{1}{16}$mT, 1:43.40, SILVER HAZE, Bob O's Boy, South Beach Boy, 6 started.

Bourbon County S., Keeneland Race Course, Oct. 28, $125,000, 2yo, $1\frac{1}{16}$mT, 1:43.85, YANKEE MASTER, Wedding Singer, Desert Wheat, 8 started.

Bourbonette Breeders' Cup S., Turfway Park, March 26, $150,000, 3yo, f, 1m, 1:37.52, DANCE AWAY CAPOTE, Gallant Secret, Amazing Buy, 11 started.

Bouwerie S. (R), Belmont Park, May 8, $116,000, 3yo, f, New York-bred, 7f, 1:23.83, SWEET SWEET, Brushme On, Party Maker, 11 started.

BOWLING GREEN H. (G2), Belmont Park, July 16, $150,000, 3&up, $1\frac{3}{8}$mT, 2:15.49, CACHT WELLS (ARG), Relaxed Gesture (Ire), Dreadnaught, 7 started.

Brandywine H., Delaware Park, June 11, $100,600, 3&up, $1\frac{1}{16}$m, 1:44.30, CHEROKEE'S BOY, Separato, Ouagadougou, 7 started.

Brave Raj Breeders' Cup S., Calder Race Course, Sept. 24, $138,375, 2yo, f, 1m70y, 1:47.79, MIA'S REFLECTION, A Sea Trippi, Prospect of Love, 7 started.

BREEDERS' CUP CLASSIC (G1), Belmont Park, Oct. 29, $4,291,560, 3&up, $1\frac{1}{4}$m, 2:01.49, SAINT LIAM, Flower Alley, Perfect Drift, 13 started.

BREEDERS' CUP DISTAFF (G1), Belmont Park, Oct. 29, $1,834,000, 3&up, f&m, $1\frac{1}{8}$m, 1:48.34, PLEASANT HOME, Society Selection, Ashado, 13 started.

BREEDERS' CUP FILLY AND MARE TURF (G1), Belmont Park, Oct. 29, $972,020, 3&up, f&m, $1\frac{1}{4}$mT, 2:02.34, INTERCONTINENTAL (GB), Ouija Board (GB), Film Maker, 14 started.

BREEDERS' CUP JUVENILE (G1), Belmont Park, Oct. 29, $1,458,030, 2yo, c&g, $1\frac{1}{16}$m, 1:41.64, STEVIE WONDERBOY, Henny Hughes, First Samurai, 14 started.

BREEDERS' CUP JUVENILE FILLIES (G1), Belmont Park, Oct. 29, $972,020, 2yo, f, $1\frac{1}{16}$m, 1:43.85, FOLKLORE, Wild Fit, Original Spin, 10 started.

BREEDERS' CUP MILE (G1), Belmont Park, Oct. 29, $1,856,925, 3&up, 1mT, 1:36.10, ARTIE SCHILLER, Leroidesanimaux (Brz), Gorella (Fr), 12 started.

BREEDERS' CUP SPRINT (G1), Belmont Park, Oct. 29, $972,020, 3&up, 6f, 1:08.86, SILVER TRAIN, Taste of Paradise, Lion Tamer, 11 started.

Breeders' Cup Steeplechase S., Far Hills, Oct. 22, $188,250, 4&up, a2$^5/_8$mT, 5:46.65, MCDYNAMO, Three Carat, Hirapour (Ire), 5 started.

BREEDERS' CUP TURF (G1), Belmont Park, Oct. 29, $2,090,760, 3&up, 1$^1/_2$mT, 2:29.30, SHIROCCO (GER), Ace (Ire), Azamour (Ire), 13 started.

Breeders' S. (R), Woodbine, Aug. 7, $412,466, 3yo, Canadian-bred, 1$^1/_2$mT, 2:27.86, JAMBALAYA, Area Limits, See the Wind, 9 started.

Breeders' Special S. (R), Lincoln State Fair, July 9, $20,550, 3yo, f, Nebraska-bred, 6f, 1:12.80, MY HOBBY, Dress Right, Peppermint Swirl, 5 started.

Brent's Princess S. (R), Thistledown, May 28, $40,000, 3&up, f&m, Ohio-bred, 6f, 1:12.04, JUST MICHEL, Southbound Katie, Imahoney-too, 9 started.

Brian Barenscheer Juvenile S., Canterbury Park, July 23, $40,000, 2yo, 5$^1/_2$f, 1:03.59, DAWN OF WAR, Counterfeit Gold, Casper Who, 8 started.

Brickyard S. (R), Hoosier Park, Oct. 23, $40,000, 3&up, Indiana-bred, 6f, 1:09.60, MR. MINK, Pass Rush, Bruce On the Loose, 12 started.

Brighouse Belles S., Hastings Race Course, June 11, $32,121, 3&up, f&m, 1$^1/_{16}$m, 1:46.10, LA BELLE FLEUR, Spirit to Spare, You and Nelly, 8 started.

BRITISH COLUMBIA BREEDERS' CUP OAKS (Can-G3), Hastings Race Course, Sept. 4, $150,009, 3yo, f, 1$^1/_8$m, 1:50.84, MONASHEE, Queenledo, A Classic Life, 12 started.

British Columbia Cup Classic H. (R), Hastings Race Course, Aug. 1, $59,318, 3&up, British Columbia-bred, 1$^1/_8$m, 1:49.54, ROSCOE PITO, Coeur Joie, Trick of the North, 5 started.

British Columbia Cup Debutante S. (R), Hastings Race Course, Aug. 1, $51,390, 2yo, f, British Columbia-bred, 6$^1/_2$f, 1:18.30, EXCITED MISS, No Ka Oi, Jittery Julia, 9 started.

British Columbia Cup Distaff H. (R), Hastings Race Course, Aug. 1, $45,523, 3&up, f&m, British Columbia-bred, 1$^1/_8$m, 1:50.93, SO-CORRO COUNTY, Victor's Secret, Galica, 5 started.

British Columbia Cup Nursery S. (R), Hastings Race Course, Aug. 1, $47,955, 2yo, c&g, British Columbia-bred, 6$^1/_2$f, 1:18.31, LUKIN AWESOME, Feu Express, Regal Request, 9 started.

British Columbia Cup Sprint H. (R), Hastings Race Course, Aug. 1, $45,629, 3&up, British Columbia-bred, 6$^1/_2$f, 1:16.51, COMMODORE CRAIG, Five Point Star, Silver Donn, 5 started.

British Columbia Cup Stallion H. (R), Hastings Race Course, Aug. 1, $45,417, 3yo, c&g, British Columbia-bred, 1$^1/_{16}$m, 1:45.29, AL-ABAMA RAIN, He's So Regal, Lone Link, 7 started.

British Columbia Cup Stallion H. (R), Hastings Race Course, Aug. 1, $45,417, 3yo, f, British Columbia-bred, 1$^1/_{16}$m, 1:44.83, SLEW-PAST, After the Knight, Backseat Becka, 7 started.

BRITISH COLUMBIA DERBY (Can-G3), Hastings Race Course, Sept. 24, $288,329, 3yo, 1$^1/_8$m, 1:49.30, SPAGHETTI MOUSE, Bull Ranch, Timeless Passion, 11 started.

British Columbia Lottery Corporation S., Kamloops, Oct. 23, $10,457, 3&up, a1m, 1:38.25, EAGER LEE, Bullinsky, Everyone's N. V., 6 started.

British Columbia Lottery Purse S., Kin Park, July 31, $8,170, 3&up, a1$^1/_{16}$m, 1:45.37, DR CHIANG MAI, Colondelivery, Slew's Alibi, 6 started.

Broadway H. (R), Aqueduct, March 12, $82,350, 3&up, f&m, New York-bred, 6f, 1:10.44, HIGH PEAKS, Travelator, Schemer, 8 started.

BROOKLYN H. (G2), Belmont Park, June 11, $250,000, 3&up, 1$^1/_8$m, 1:46.69, LIMEHOUSE, Gygistar, Royal Assault, 9 started.

Brooks Fields S., Canterbury Park, June 11, $50,000, 3&up, 7$^1/_2$fT, 1:29.53, LOAN ME A FEN, Dontbotherknocking, Our Best Man, 9 started.

Brother Brown S., Remington Park, Aug. 6, $40,000, 3&up, 5fT, :56.52, PROVEN CURE, Orphan Brigade, The Niner Account, 10 started.

Brown Bess H., Golden Gate Fields, Jan. 30, $100,000, 4&up, f&m, 1$^1/_{16}$mT, 1:44.68, HOH BUZZARD (IRE), Uraib (Ire), Hooked On Niners, 8 started.

Brumbeau S., Turf Paradise, April 10, $23,800, 3yo, f, 6f, 1:09.26, UDRIGA, Lady Bertrando, Kresgeville, 6 started.

Bryan Station S., Keeneland Race Course, Oct. 13, $150,000, 3yo, 1mT, 1:34.65, T.D. VANCE, Rey de Cafe, Therecomesatiger, 8 started.

B. Thoughtful S. (R), Hollywood Park, April 24, $150,000, 4&up, f&m, California-bred, 7f, 1:22.06, ALPHABET KISSES, Thunder's Echo, Tucked Away, 8 started.

Bucharest S., Sam Houston Race Park, Jan. 29, $40,000, 3yo, 6f, 1:12.06, BLAZING EXPLOIT, Dwight Polite, Count the Bucks, 8 started.

Buckeye Native S. (R), River Downs, Aug. 14, $40,000, 3&up, Ohio-bred, 1$^1/_{16}$mT, 1:44.80, DAWN'S REVENGE, The Potters Hand, Scout Me, 13 started.

Buckland S., Colonial Downs, June 25, $70,000, 3&up, f&m, 5$^1/_2$fT, 1:02.21, BRIGHT GOLD, Tight Spin, Spring Kitten, 11 started.

Budweiser H., Sunland Park, Jan. 29, $53,400, 3&up, 5f, :57.20, CAT BUSTER, Hecamefromaclaim, Racing Nut, 6 started.

BUENA VISTA H. (G3), Santa Anita Park, Feb. 21, $150,000, 4&up, f&m, 1m (originally scheduled as a Grade 2 on the turf), 1:33.72, URAIB (IRE), Resplendency, Elusive Diva, 5 started.

Bueno S., Turf Paradise, April 3, $24,200, 3&up, f&m, 5$^1/_2$f, 1:02.65, TOP PENNY, Fun'ngames Toknite, Marquet First, 10 started.

Bueno S., Turf Paradise, Dec. 18, $23,800, 3yo, f, 6f, 1:10.45, MEET YOU AT T'S, Cosmic Lady, Royal B, 8 started.

Buffalo Bayou S., Sam Houston Race Park, Nov. 5, $40,000, 3&up, 1$^1/_{16}$mT, 1:44.54, CHARMING SOCIALITE, Shakethemhatersoff, Middleweight, 12 started.

Buffalo S. (R), Assiniboia Downs, Sept. 18, $33,936, 2yo, Manitoba-bred, 1m, 1:44.60, DREAM EXTREME, Callie's Wisdom, Miss Dou-bletrouble, 4 started.

Bull Dog S., Fresno, Oct. 16, $51,300, 3&up, 1m, 1:35.36, EASY MIL-LION, Apollo King, Traffic Update, 7 started.

Bullet S. (R), Hollywood Park, May 27, $63,150, 3&up, non-winners of $60,000 in 2004-'05, 5fT, :55.62 (NCR), STORMIN' LYON, Golden Arrow, Billy's Echo, 6 started.

Bull Page S. (R), Woodbine, Oct. 15, $106,800, 2yo, c&g, progeny of stallions standing in Ontario, 6f, 1:12.63, FOXY MONEY, Trail Fox, Duffin's Creek, 9 started.

Bullys Futurity, Lethbridge, Oct. 29, $11,079, 2yo, a6f, 1:12, BLACK EYED MONTE, She's Italian, Native Remark, 7 started.

Bungalow H. (R), Fairmount Park, July 9, $40,700, 3&up, f&m, Illinois-bred, 1m, 1:39.60, LADY RISS, Defuhr, Cart's Turn, 7 started.

Bunty Lawless S. (R), Woodbine, Oct. 30, $107,483, 3&up, progeny of stallions standing in Ontario, 1mT, 1:37.37, TUSAYAN, Decew Falls, Arch Hall, 9 started.

Burlingame S., Bay Meadows Race Course, Feb. 19, $70,250, 3yo, f, 1$^1/_{16}$m, 1:44.07, COSMIC LADY, Tense Wager, Hold the Game, 7 started.

Burnaby Breeders' Cup H., Hastings Race Course, June 5, $54,617, 3yo, 1$^1/_{16}$m, 1:46.72, SPAGHETTI MOUSE, Alabama Rain, One Spe-cial Hoss, 8 started.

Busanda S., Aqueduct, Jan. 16, $80,550, 3yo, f, 1m70y, 1:44.59, AMAZ-ING BUY, Pelham Bay, Pretty Partisan, 6 started.

Busher S., Aqueduct, Feb. 27, $80,700, 3yo, f, 1$^1/_{16}$m, 1:44.63, AMAZ-ING BUY, Neverlacken, Winning Season, 6 started.

Bustles and Bows S., Fairplex Park, Sept. 15, $58,800, 2yo, f, 6$^1/_2$f, 1:19.40, DANCIN OLIVIA, I Can See, Aloha Mangos Kitty, 7 started.

Caballos del Sol H., Turf Paradise, Oct. 8, $40,000, 3&up, 6f, 1:09.06, SCOTTSBLUFF, Cocoa Latte, Grimm, 5 started.

Cab Calloway S. (R), Saratoga Race Course, Aug. 3, $250,000, 3yo, progeny of stallions standing in New York, 1$^1/_8$m, 1:53.09, GOLD AND ROSES, Galloping Grocer, Western Galaxy, 7 started.

Cactus Cup H., Turf Paradise, March 13, $40,000, 3yo, f, 6$^1/_2$f, 1:15.60, ISLAND ESCAPE, Virden, Skyline Gal, 5 started.

Cactus Flower H., Turf Paradise, April 16, $40,000, 3&up, f&m, 6f, 1:08.91, FUN'NGAMES TOKNITE, Sawtelle Belle, Coke's Melody, 7 started.

Cactus Wren H. (R), Turf Paradise, Jan. 1, $40,000, 4&up, Arizona-bred, 6$^1/_2$f, 1:17.86, GRIMM, Charm Attack, Red Creek, 5 started.

Cactus Wren H. (R), Turf Paradise, Dec. 31, $40,000, 3&up, Arizona-bred, 6$^1/_2$f, 1:15.62, MOORES BRIDGE, Komax, Blackbird, 7 started.

Caesar Rodney H., Delaware Park, Sept. 3, $194,000, 3&up, 1$^1/_8$mT, 1:48.05, AY CARAMBA (BRZ), Mr O'Brien (Ire), Cottage (Arg), 4 started.

Cajun S. (R), Louisiana Downs, Sept. 17, $78,600, 3&up, Louisiana-bred, 6f, 1:10.25, ZARB'S DAHAR, Runners Name, Mister Ajax, 8 started.

Calder Derby, Calder Race Course, Oct. 15, $200,000, 3yo, 1$^1/_8$m (originally scheduled as a Grade 3 on the turf), 1:52.44, DAZZLING DR. CEVIN, Dream On Dream On, Talented Prince, 7 started.

Calder Oaks, Calder Race Course, Oct. 15, $200,000, 3yo, f, 1$^1/_8$m (originally scheduled on the turf), 1:53.95, TIGER BELLE, My Ty-phoon (Ire), Fast Lisa, 10 started.

Calder Turf Sprint H., Calder Race Course, July 10, $100,000, 3&up, 5fT, :58.12, SOUTHERN CAL, Gin Rummy Champ, True Love's Se-cret, 11 started.

California Breeders' Champion S. (R), Santa Anita Park, Dec. 26, $135,250, 2yo, California-bred, 7f, 1:21.63, DA STOOPS, Direct Con-nect, Brite Maneuvers, 7 started.

California Breeders' Champion S. (R), Santa Anita Park, Dec. 28, $139,750, 2yo, f, California-bred, 7f, 1:23.45, SIERRA SWEETIE, She's an Eleven, Unchanged Melody, 10 started.

California Cup Classic H. (R), Oak Tree at Santa Anita, Nov. 6, $250,000, 3&up, California-bred, 1 1/8m, 1:48.31, MCCANN'S MOJAVE, Desert Boom, Cheroot, 8 started.

California Cup Distaff H. (R), Oak Tree at Santa Anita, Nov. 6, $150,000, 3&up, f&m, California-bred, a6 1/2fT, 1:12.40, TEMPTING DATE, Beneficial Bartok, Resident Alien, 13 started.

California Cup Distance H. (R), Oak Tree at Santa Anita, Nov. 6, $100,000, 3&up, f&m, California-bred, 1 1/4mT, 2:00.72, MOSCOW BURNING, Dancing General, Fortunate Event, 6 started.

California Cup Juvenile Fillies S. (R), Oak Tree at Santa Anita, Nov. 6, $125,000, 2yo, f, California-bred, 1 1/16m, 1:44.89, BAI AND BAI, Sierra Sweetie, Fun Logic, 9 started.

California Cup Juvenile S. (R), Oak Tree at Santa Anita, Nov. 6, $125,000, 2yo, c&g, California-bred, 1 1/16m, 1:45.23, BRITE MANEUVERS, Catouttathebag, Moonlite Romance, 10 started.

California Cup Matron H. (R), Oak Tree at Santa Anita, Nov. 6, $150,000, 3&up, f&m, California-bred, 1 1/16m, 1:42.21, DREAM OF SUMMER, House of Fortune, Proposed, 7 started.

California Cup Mile H. (R), Oak Tree at Santa Anita, Nov. 6, $175,000, 3&up, California-bred, 1mT, 1:33.85, DRAKE'S VICTORY, Orbits World, Running Free, 11 started.

California Cup Sprint H. (R), Oak Tree at Santa Anita, Nov. 6, $150,000, 3&up, California-bred, 6f, 1:08.63, JET WEST, Areyoutalkintome, Thor's Echo, 11 started.

California Cup Starter H. (R), Oak Tree at Santa Anita, Nov. 6, $50,000, 3&up, California-bred starters for a claiming price of $40,000 or less in 2005, 1 1/2mT, 2:27.46, TIME TO HONOR, Top This and That, It's Quite Unusual, 11 started.

California Cup Starter Sprint H. (R), Oak Tree at Santa Anita, Nov. 6, $50,000, 3&up, California-bred starters for a claiming price of $32,000 or less in 2005, 6f, 1:08.11, BORDONARO, Hello Fame, Stalking Tiger, 9 started.

CALIFORNIAN S. (G2), Hollywood Park, June 18, $250,000, 3&up, 1 1/8m, 1:47.83, LAVA MAN, Anziyan Royalty, Skukuza, 7 started.

California Thoroughbred Breeders' Association S. (R), Del Mar, July 22, $125,000, 2yo, f, California-bred, 5 1/2f, 1:04.51, DEVONS SMOKIN, Harbor's Halo, Chulla Isabella, 7 started.

California Turf Championship H. (R), Bay Meadows Race Course, Sept. 5, $100,000, 3&up, California-bred, 1mT, 1:36.48, EL DON, Shadow Raider, Hemet Thought, 5 started.

California Turf Sprint Championship H. (R), Bay Meadows Race Course, Sept. 24, $100,000, 3&up, California-bred, 5fT, :56.84, EXCEEDING, Bonfante, McManus, 8 started.

Camelia S. (R), Delta Downs, Jan. 8, $50,000, 4&up, f&m, Louisiana-bred, 7f, 1:28.51, LEGS O'NEAL, Midnight Delight, Misty Glo, 6 started.

Camilla Urso S., Golden Gate Fields, May 22, $58,712, 3&up, f&m, 6f, 1:09.16, YEREVAN STAR, Our Mango, Platinum Princess, 5 started.

Canada Day S., Assiniboia Downs, July 1, $32,652, 3&up, f&m, 1m, 1:40.40, OLA DOCURA, Ericka's Lass, Remiewaterbluz, 8 started.

Canada Day S., Lethbridge, July 1, $13,551, 3&up, 1 1/8m, 1:54, LOST AGAIN, Larry the Longshot, Diamond Passer, 7 started.

CANADIAN DERBY (Can-G3), Northlands Park, Aug. 27, $250,260, 3yo, 1 3/8m, 2:20.80, ALABAMA RAIN, Ding Dong Dandy, Knight's Covenant, 11 started.

CANADIAN H. (Can-G2), Woodbine, Sept. 18, $316,538, 3&up, f&m, a1 1/8mT, 1:47.25, CLASSIC STAMP, Ambitious Cat, Mona Rose, 9 started.

CANADIAN INTERNATIONAL S. (Can-G1), Woodbine, Oct. 23, $1,684,883, 3&up, 1 1/2mT, 2:32.64, RELAXED GESTURE (IRE), Meteor Storm (GB), Electrocutionist, 10 started.

Canadian Juvenile S., Northlands Park, Oct. 10, $63,810, 2yo, 1 1/16m, 1:47.20, BELL N' GONE, Beau Run, Teagues Fight, 4 started.

Canadian Turf H., Gulfstream Park, March 13, $100,000, 3&up, 1 1/16mT, 1:38.20, OLD FORESTER, Gulch Approval, Muqbil, 11 started.

Candy Eclair S., Monmouth Park, June 4, $55,000, 3&up, f&m, 5f, :57.24, TRAVELATOR, Platinum Perfect, She Is Raging, 7 started.

Canterbury Park Lassie S., Canterbury Park, July 23, $38,800, 2yo, f, 5 1/2f, 1:05.37, BOUNTEMPO, Sentimental Charm, Jb's Golden Regret, 5 started.

Cape Henlopen S., Delaware Park, July 17, $59,300, 3&up, 1 1/2m, 2:32.38, HYDROGEN, Stage Call (Ire), Private Lap, 5 started.

Capital City H. (R), Penn National Race Course, Sept. 2, $41,000, 3&up, Pennsylvania-bred, 1 1/16mT, 1:42.64, R. EARL, Yo, Watchman's Warning, 8 started.

Capital Request S., Calder Race Course, Oct. 2, $40,000, 3&up, f&m, 1m, 1:40.49, TIGI, Silver Lace, Leona's Knight, 6 started.

Capitol City Futurity, Lincoln State Fair, June 26, $12,688, 2yo, 4 1/2f, :52.20, THOUGHTUWASATOAD, Slew Lucky, Speed Aly, 8 started.

Captain Condo S. (R), Emerald Downs, Oct. 2, $40,000, 2yo, c&g, Washington-bred, 6f, 1:08, FAST PARADE, Tom Two, Tusko T., 8 started.

Captain Stanley Harrison H., Marquis Downs, July 9, $4,921, 3yo, f, 6f, 1:16.35, SIMILKAMEEN BREW, Chipaway, Bermuda Rose, 9 started.

Capt. Billy Boogie S., Turf Paradise, May 15, $22,944, 3&up, 1m, 1:35.06, LYDIA'S LEGACY, Suspicious Minds, Cut of Music, 4 started.

CARDINAL H. (G3), Churchill Downs, Nov. 19, $175,050, 3&up, f&m, 1 1/8mT, 1:50.10, SUNDROP (JPN), Delta Princess, Finery, 12 started.

Caressing H., Churchill Downs, Nov. 19, $71,800, 2yo, f, 1 1/16mT, 1:45.22, FOR ALWAYS, Special Heritage, Performing Diva, 10 started.

CARLETON F. BURKE H. (G3), Oak Tree at Santa Anita, Oct. 30, $100,000, 3&up, 1 1/2mT, 2:27.02, GOLDEN RAHY, Wild Buddy, Stage Shy, 6 started.

Carl G. Rose Classic H. (R), Calder Race Course, Nov. 12, $200,000, 3&up, Florida-bred, 1 1/8m, 1:52.68, WHOS CRYING NOW, Supervisor, Dazzling Dr. Cevin, 10 started.

Carlos Salazar S. (R), The Downs at Albuquerque, May 14, $37,600, 3&up, f&m, New Mexico-bred, 6 1/2f, 1:18.33, LATENITE SPECIAL, Janna's Gold, Spirit de Azure, 9 started.

Carmel H., Bay Meadows Race Course, Oct. 9, $74,500, 2yo, f, 1m, 1:37.49, SIERRA SWEETIE, Bai and Bai, Talverna, 6 started.

Carolina Cup Hurdle S., Camden, April 2, $46,500, 4&up, a2 3/8mT, 4:33, SUR LA TETE, Hirapour (Ire), Preemptive Strike, 4 started.

Carotene S. (R), Woodbine, Oct. 8, $139,531, 3yo, f, Ontario-bred, 1 1/8mT, 1:49.39, INVITATIONAL, Silver Impulse, The Queen's Stamp, 7 started.

Carousel S., Oaklawn Park, April 2, $49,000, 4&up, f&m, 6f, 1:09.57, SAVORTHETIME, Boston Express, Dance Tune, 5 started.

CARRY BACK S. (G2), Calder Race Course, July 10, $300,000, 3yo, 6f, 1:09.30, LOST IN THE FOG, Qureall, Hot Space, 6 started.

CARTER H. (G1), Aqueduct, April 9, $350,000, 3&up, 7f, 1:20.46, FOREST DANGER, Medallist, Don Six, 6 started.

Carterista H., Calder Race Course, April 30, $75,000, 3&up, 1 1/16mT, 1:40.44, FINAL PROPHECY, He's Crafty, Miesque's Approval, 12 started.

Carter McGregor Jr. Memorial S. (R), Lone Star Park, May 28, $50,000, 3&up, Texas-bred, 6f, 1:09.24, LIGHTS ON BROADWAY, Charming Socialite, Smile Away, 6 started.

Casey Darnell Pony Express H. (R), The Downs at Albuquerque, May 14, $37,600, 3&up, New Mexico-bred, 5 1/2f, 1:03.50, BOLD NXS, B. G. Tiger, Gulchrunssweet, 5 started.

Cassidy S., Calder Race Course, July 10, $75,000, 2yo, f, 5 1/2f, 1:06.21, MYKINDASAINT, Good Intentions, Running Lass, 9 started.

Catcharisingstar S., Calder Race Course, Sept. 3, $50,000, 2yo, f, 5fT, :58.59, BETTARUN FAST, Little Right Dove, Road Track's Joy, 12 started.

Cat's Cradle H. (R), Hollywood Park, Dec. 4, $99,300, 3&up, f&m, California-bred, 7 1/2f, 1:27.24, HOUSE OF FORTUNE, Western Hemisphere, Strut Your Stuff, 7 started.

Cavada West Virginia Breeders' Classic S. (R), Charles Town Races, Oct. 8, $225,000, 3&up, f&m, West Virginia-bred, 7f, 1:26.06, ORIGINAL GOLD, Alaska Ash, Cedar Slew, 10 started.

Cavonnier Juvenile S., Santa Rosa, Aug. 7, $52,625, 2yo, 5 1/2f, 1:03.76, CAUSE TO BELIEVE, Fast Parade, Hunter's Fortune, 9 started.

Cavonnier S. (R), Oak Tree at Santa Anita, Oct. 9, $79,650, 2yo, California-bred, 7f, 1:23.32, DIRECT CONNECT, Moonlite Romance, At a Boy Russ, 5 started.

Cellars Shiraz S., Gulfstream Park, April 23, $48,600, 3yo, f, 5fT, :56.74, WINSOME, Memories of Pa, Lady in Pink, 6 started.

Centennial S., Remington Park, Nov. 28, $40,000, 2yo, c&g, 1mT, 1:38.43, TEST BOY, Hot Foot Slew, Unruly, 11 started.

Central Iowa S., Prairie Meadows, Sept. 10, $40,700, 3&up, f&m, 1 1/16m, 1:43.84, BEAU WATCH, Candybedandy, Valliant Dancer, 7 started.

Centre Stage Anne Cup S. (R), Fort Erie, Sept. 5, $25,263, 3&up, f&m, starters at Fort Erie twice in 2005, 1 1/16mT, 1:47.87, KIRLAN, Clubay, Iwontstopdancing, 12 started.

CERF H. (R), Del Mar, Sept. 7, $83,120, 3&up, f&m, non-winners of a stakes other than state-bred since March 1, 6f, 1:08.57, SIMPLY BECAUSE, Abounding Truth, Freakin Streakin, 9 started.

Challenger S., Tampa Bay Downs, March 12, $65,000, 4&up, 1 1/16m, 1:44.58, TAP DAY, Above the Wind, Attack the Books, 9 started.

Chamisa H., The Downs at Albuquerque, May 1, $40,000, 3&up, f&m,

6$^{1}/_{2}$f, 1:16.68, BLUE SONG, Bar Bailey, Water Park, 8 started.

CHAMPAGNE S. (G1), Belmont Park, Oct. 8, $500,000, 2yo, 1m, 1:36.29, FIRST SAMURAI, Henny Hughes, Superfly, 6 started.

Chandler H., Turf Paradise, Nov. 12, $40,000, 3yo, f, 7$^{1}/_{2}$fT, 1:29.15, HEAVENLY RANSOM, Shesa Private I, Kick the Can, 8 started.

Chantilly S., Assiniboia Downs, June 5, $32,064, 3yo, f, 6f, 1:14.20, RICH RUBIES, Wautega Light, Hold On Heather, 10 started.

Chapel Belle S., Louisiana Downs, May 28, $51,550, 3yo, f, 1mT, 1:38.87, VICTORY LAP, Miriam L., Phone Affair, 8 started.

Chaposa Springs H., Calder Race Course, Dec. 31, $100,000, 3&up, f&m, 7f, 1:24.97, MALIBU MINT, Tigi, Lilah, 9 started.

Chariot Chaser H., Northlands Park, Oct. 14, $42,270, 3yo, f, 6$^{1}/_{2}$f, 1:18.80, SLEWPAST, Nessarose, Avenging Kat, 7 started.

Charles H. Hadry S., Laurel Park, Sept. 10, $83,500, 3&up, 1m, 1:36.77, HONORABLE MAN, Saay Mi Name, Cherokee's Boy, 8 started.

Charles Taylor Derby, The Downs at Albuquerque, June 5, $40,000, 3yo, 1$^{1}/_{16}$m, 1:45.62, HOPE FOR PEACE, Western Act, On Ice, 8 started.

CHARLES WHITTINGHAM MEMORIAL H. (G1), Hollywood Park, June 11, $350,000, 3&up, 1$^{1}/_{4}$mT, 2:01.35, SWEET RETURN (GB), Red Fort (Ire), Vangelis, 9 started.

Charlie Barley S., Woodbine, June 26, $90,877, 3yo, 1mT, 1:33.64, GAMBLERS SLEW, Stag Nation, Silver Charades, 10 started.

Charlie Iles Express H., The Downs at Albuquerque, April 24, $40,000, 4&up, 6f, 1:10.24, BALDWIN COUNTY, Artesian, Sharm, 6 started.

Charlie Palmer Starter H. (R), Ferndale, Aug. 13, $6,990, 3&up, f&m, starters for a claiming price of $12,500 or less in 2005, 6$^{1}/_{2}$f, 1:19.68, MOM LIKED YOU BEST, In Love With Loot, Lill Trina, 5 started.

Charon S. (R), Calder Race Course, June 12, $40,000, 3&up, f&m, non-winners of a stakes of $55,000 at one mile or over during 2004-'05, 1$^{1}/_{16}$m, 1:45.06, PAMPERED PRINCESS, So Much More, American Miss, 6 started.

Charon S., Calder Race Course, Dec. 11, $40,000, 3&up, f&m, 1$^{1}/_{16}$m, 1:48.15, POTRA CLASICA (ARG), Palaestra, Aesculus, 8 started.

Chaves County S., Zia Park, Nov. 24, $83,800, 3&up, f&m, 1m, 1:37.20, BLUE SONG, Show Me Your Glory, Good Humor Gal, 8 started.

Chenery S., Colonial Downs, July 31, $60,000, 2yo, 5$^{1}/_{2}$fT, 1:04.59, TOMPEST, Warrior Within, Black Snake, 12 started.

Cherokee Frolic S., Calder Race Course, Dec. 10, $100,000, 2yo, f, 1$^{1}/_{16}$mT, 1:45.38, CHRISTMAS STOCKING, Sprightly, Warrior Girl, 12 started.

Cherokee River Stables Turf Classic S., Tampa Bay Downs, April 9, $85,100, 4&up, a1$^{1}/_{8}$mT, 1:49.62, REVVED UP, Admiral Lance, Attack the Books, 11 started.

Cherokee Run H., Churchill Downs, Nov. 6, $69,000, 3&up, 5fT, :57.73, ATTICUS KRISTY, Ridge Runner (GB), Chosen Chief, 11 started.

Chesapeake S., Colonial Downs, Aug. 6, $60,000, 3&up, 6f, 1:08.87, SAAY MI NAME, Founding Chairman, Abbondanza, 5 started.

CHICAGO BREEDERS' CUP H. (G3), Arlington Park, June 18, $175,000, 3&up, f&m, 7f, 1:22.54, HAPPY TICKET, Savorthetime, Injustice, 7 started.

Chicagoland H. (R), Hawthorne Race Course, April 30, $88,250, 4&up, Illinois-conceived and/or -foaled, 6f, 1:10.55, TAKE ACHANCE ON ME, Silver Bid, Shandy, 5 started.

Chick Lang Jr. Memorial S., Retama Park, Sept. 10, $40,000, 3&up, 1m, 1:37.74, WISHINGITWAS, Charming Socialite, Agrivating General, 6 started.

Chief Bearhart S., Woodbine, Oct. 29, $92,881, 3&up, 1$^{1}/_{4}$mT, 2:05.42, SEATTLESPECTACULAR, Sky Conqueror, Lenny the Lender, 6 started.

Chief Narbona S. (R), The Downs at Albuquerque, May 14, $37,600, 3yo, f, New Mexico-bred, 6f, 1:11.46, HOLLYWOOD GONE, Strange Devil, Greene for Todd, 10 started.

CHILUKKI H. (G2), Churchill Downs, Nov. 6, $169,350, 3&up, f&m, 1m, 1:35.19, BENDING STRINGS, Prospective Saint, Miss Fortunate, 11 started.

China Doll S., Santa Anita Park, March 12, $85,300, 3yo, f, 1mT, 1:34.44, THATSWHATIMEAN, Cee's Irish, On London Time, 7 started.

CHINESE CULTURAL CENTRE S. (Can-G2), Woodbine, July 24, $283,565, 3&up, 1$^{3}/_{8}$mT, 2:15.94, A BIT O'GOLD, Mobil, Last Answer, 11 started.

Chinook Pass Sprint S. (R), Emerald Downs, Oct. 2, $38,200, 3&up, Washington-bred, 6f, 1:08.60, POLO BENDER, Wasserman, Starbird Road, 6 started.

Chippewa Downs Open Thoroughbred Futurity, Chippewa Downs, June 26, $2,500, 2yo, a4$^{1}/_{2}$f, WINSOME CAT, Busi Boy, Rough Knight, 7 started.

Chippewa Downs Open Thoroughbred S., Chippewa Downs, June 26, $2,800, 4&up, a1m70y, 1:54, BOONE AVIE, Crimson Island, Grand Mister, 7 started.

Choice S., Monmouth Park, Aug. 28, $60,000, 3yo, 1$^{1}/_{8}$mT, 1:51.24, CLASSIC CAMPAIGN, Doctor Voodoo, One Good Man, 5 started.

Chou Croute H., Fair Grounds, Feb. 20, $75,000, 4&up, f&m, 1$^{1}/_{16}$m, 1:44.32, STORM'S DARLING, Spectacular Lisa, Oneofacat, 8 started.

Chris Thomas Turf Classic S., Tampa Bay Downs, May 7, $75,000, 3&up, a1$^{1}/_{8}$mT, 1:49.40, HEAR NO EVIL, Revved Up, Headline, 9 started.

Christopher Elser Memorial S. (R), Philadelphia Park, Nov. 5, $57,000, 2yo, have spent 90 days in South Carolina and paid a nomination fee to the South Carolina Thoroughbred Owners' and Breeders' Association, 6$^{1}/_{2}$f, 1:18.10, LIQUOREUX, Voo Kan Do, Guru Pasha, 6 started.

Chuck N Luck S., Turf Paradise, Dec. 7, $23,900, 3yo, a1mT, 1:36.43 (NCR), NIGHT DASH, Desert Prospector, Western Act, 9 started.

Chuck N Luck S., Turf Paradise, Jan. 28, $21,800, 4&up, 1m, 1:37.23, CUT OF MUSIC, No Toro, His Way, 8 started.

Chuck Taliaferro Memorial S., Remington Park, Sept. 10, $40,650, 3&up, 6f, 1:09.01, THE NINER ACCOUNT, Herecomesthemannow, Lumbre, 5 started.

CHURCHILL DOWNS H. (G2), Churchill Downs, May 7, $231,000, 4&up, 7f, 1:20.56, BATTLE WON, Level Playingfield, Pomeroy, 11 started.

Cicada S., Delaware Park, Oct. 3, $60,900, 3&up, f&m, 1$^{1}/_{8}$mT, 1:49.40, SPOTLIGHT (GB), With Affection, Latice (Ire), 8 started.

CICADA S. (G3), Aqueduct, March 19, $109,800, 3yo, f, 7f, 1:23.04, DIXIE TALKING, Acey Deucey, Alfonsina, 8 started.

Cigar S., Arlington Park, Aug. 13, $47,100, 3&up, 1m, 1:35.10, NKOSI REIGNS, Bodgiteer, Courthouse, 7 started.

Cimarron S., Remington Park, Nov. 19, $40,390, 2yo, f, 7$^{1}/_{2}$fT, 1:29.84, BROWNIE POINTS, Jazzy Okie, Sky Miles, 9 started.

Cincinnatian S. (R), River Downs, July 3, $40,000, 3yo, f, Ohio-bred, 1$^{1}/_{16}$mT, 1:44.60, MISTY TAB, Marketable, Annie's Award, 11 started.

Cinderella S., Hollywood Park, June 4, $94,125, 2yo, f, 5$^{1}/_{2}$f, 1:04.30, RIVER'S PRAYER, My Lucky Free, Slick Road, 8 started.

CINEMA BREEDERS' CUP H. (G3), Hollywood Park, June 26, $153,450, 3yo, 1$^{1}/_{8}$mT, 1:48.59, WILLOW O WISP, Osidy, Honorable Coach, 5 started.

Cinnamon Girl S., Calder Race Course, Sept. 23, $40,000, 3&up, f&m, 1$^{1}/_{16}$m, 1:48.94, APPEALING POND, La Sami (Per), Shady Woman, 7 started.

Circle C Classic H., Fairmount Park, Aug. 6, $50,700, 4&up, 1$^{1}/_{8}$m, 1:51, BEABASQUE, Ask the Lord, Little More, 4 started.

Citgo S., Sam Houston Race Park, Feb. 26, $40,000, 4&up, f&m, 5f, :57.56, AMBITION UNBRIDLED, Peace Symbol, Seneca Song, 5 started.

City Centre Bingo H., Marquis Downs, Sept. 9, $5,077, 3&up, f&m, 1m, 1:41.75, CELTIC DANCE, She's Nifty, Astrel Angel, 5 started.

City of Anderson S. (R), Hoosier Park, Sept. 30, $40,000, 2yo, f, Indiana-bred, 5$^{1}/_{2}$f, 1:06.33, LIL BROAD TEE, Spotless Mind, Dixie Dell, 12 started.

City of Bridges Sophomore S. (R), Marquis Downs, Aug. 6, $5,345, 3yo, c&g, Saskatchewan-bred, 1m, 1:39.25, FARGO FORBES, Wind Dancer, Axe Em All, 7 started.

City of Edmonton Distaff H., Northlands Park, Aug. 28, $62,565, 3&up, f&m, 1$^{1}/_{16}$m, 1:44.20, RAYLENE, Gold Accent, Ice Girl, 6 started.

City of Phoenix H., Turf Paradise, Oct. 1, $40,000, 3&up, f&m, 6f, 1:09.83, KATY SMILES, Lyndee's Pearl, Kathryns Birthday, 6 started.

City of Roses H., Portland Meadows, Dec. 10, $10,950, 3&up, f&m, 1m, 1:40.98, CHANCY CHANCY, Rbeei, Our Girl Pearl, 7 started.

City Zip S., Monmouth Park, Sept. 25, $70,800, 3yo, 6f, 1:09.04, WHO'S THE COWBOY, Euro Code, Caribbean Cruiser, 5 started.

C. J. Hindley Humboldt County Marathon H. (R), Ferndale, Aug. 21, $13,340, 3&up, starters for a claiming price of $12,500 or less in 2005, 1$^{5}/_{8}$m, 2:47.50, BLACK HORSE MONEY, Janzig Warrior, Power Star, 7 started.

Claiming Crown Emerald S. (R), Canterbury Park, July 16, $122,500, 3&up, starters for a claiming price of $20,000 or less since July 15, 2004, 1$^{1}/_{16}$mT, 1:41.77, MR. MABEE, Sigfreto, Rockhurst, 12 started.

Claiming Crown Express S. (R), Canterbury Park, July 16, $46,500, 3&up, starters for a claiming price of $7,500 or less since July 15, 2004, 6f, 1:08.04 (NTR), ONLYNURIMAGINATION, Cicero Grimes, Landler, 7 started.

Claiming Crown Glass Slipper S. (R), Canterbury Park, July 16, $72,000, 3&up, f&m, starters for a claiming price of $12,500 or less since July 15, 2004, 6$^1/_2$f, 1:16.31, ELLS EDITOR, I Will Survive, Peekaboo Cat, 10 started.

Claiming Crown Iron Horse S. (R), Canterbury Park, July 16, $49,000, 3&up, starters for a claiming price of $5,000 or less since July 15, 2004, 1$^1/_{16}$m, 1:43.91, MY EXTOLLED HONOR, King of Chicago, Sacsahuaman (Chi), 12 started.

Claiming Crown Jewel S. (R), Canterbury Park, July 16, $138,000, 3&up, starters for a claiming price of $25,000 or less since July 15, 2004, 1$^1/_8$m, 1:47.32, DESERT BOOM, Lord of the Game, Habaneros, 6 started.

Claiming Crown Rapid Transit S. (R), Canterbury Park, July 16, $93,000, 3&up, starters for a claiming price of $16,000 or less since July 15, 2004, 6$^1/_2$f, 1:14.54, PROCREATE, The Student (Arg), Crafty Player, 7 started.

Claiming Crown Tiara S. (R), Canterbury Park, July 16, $93,000, 3&up, f&m, starters for a claiming price of $20,000 or less since July 15, 2004, 1$^1/_{16}$mT, 1:43.51, INHONOROFJOHNNIE, O. K. Corral, Secret Lies, 7 started.

Claire Marine S., Arlington Park, Sept. 4, $41,750, 3&up, f&m, 1$^1/_2$mT, 2:33.39, STRIKE ME LUCKY, Beau Happy, Cape Town Lass, 7 started.

Clarendon S. (R), Woodbine, July 9, $131,626, 2yo, Ontario-bred, 5$^1/_2$f, 1:05.06, VIBANK, Moon Worship, Atlas Shrugs, 5 started.

CLARK H. (G2), Churchill Downs, Nov. 25, $573,500, 3&up, 1$^1/_8$m, 1:50.89, MAGNA GRADUATE, Suave, Perfect Drift, 12 started.

Classy Mirage S. (R), Aqueduct, April 8, $60,600, 4&up, f&m, non-winners of an open stakes, 6f, 1:09.95, FORESTIER, Storm Minstrel, Lovethatlegend, 6 started.

Classy 'n Smart S. (R), Woodbine, Oct. 10, $106,350, 3&up, f&m, progeny of stallions standing in Ontario, 1$^1/_{16}$m, 1:46.03, SCHOONER BAY, Kissed by a Prince, Spanish Decree, 4 started.

CLEMENT L. HIRSCH H. (G2), Del Mar, Aug. 7, $300,000, 3&up, f&m, 1$^1/_{16}$m, 1:42.82, TUCKED AWAY, Hollywood Story, Valentine Dancer, 8 started.

CLEMENT L. HIRSCH MEMORIAL TURF CHAMPIONSHIP S. (G1), Oak Tree at Santa Anita, Oct. 2, $250,000, 3&up, 1$^1/_4$mT, 2:01.17, FOURTY NINERS SON, Leprechaun Kid, Laura's Lucky Boy, 8 started.

Cleveland Gold Cup S. (R), Thistledown, July 2, $75,000, 3yo, Ohio-bred, 1$^1/_8$m, 1:53.84, PYRITE SPRINGS, Ready for Roses, Bug Hunter, 14 started.

Cleveland Kindergarten S. (R), Thistledown, Aug. 12, $40,000, 2yo, Ohio-bred, 6f, 1:12.34, DINNER CHOICE, Tri Uimet, Fisticuff, 7 started.

Clever Trevor S., Remington Park, Sept. 5, $40,390, 2yo, 6f, 1:10.23, BRICK CREW, Out Our Way, Paltu, 7 started.

CLIFF HANGER S. (G3), Meadowlands, Oct. 22, $150,000, 3&up, 1$^1/_{16}$mT, 1:54.32, HOTSTUFANTHENSOME, Icy Atlantic, Stormy Ray, 8 started.

Club House Special S., Columbus Races, Aug. 27, $10,625, 2yo, 6f, 1:14.80, KELLY CARSON, Thoughtuwasatoad, Slew Lucky, 7 started.

Clyde B. Stephens Memorial S. (R), Delta Downs, March 26, $50,000, 3yo, Louisiana-bred, 5f, :58.72, ALL WIRED UP, J. D.'s Blue Bayou, Grande Diablo, 7 started.

COACHING CLUB AMERICAN OAKS (G1), Belmont Park, July 23, $500,000, 3yo, f, 1$^1/_4$m, 2:04.39, SMUGGLER, Summerly, Spun Sugar, 7 started.

Colin S., Woodbine, July 23, $111,301, 2yo, 6f, 1:11.04, EDENWOLD, Key West Breeze, Top Authority, 6 started.

Colleen S., Monmouth Park, Aug. 6, $60,000, 2yo, f, 5$^1/_2$f, 1:04.56, LIVERMORE VALLEY, Ten Halos, Fantast, 6 started.

Colonel E. R. Bradley H., Fair Grounds, Jan. 15, $100,000, 4&up, a1$^1/_{16}$mT, 1:44.43, AMERICA ALIVE, Honor in War, Rapid Proof, 11 started.

Colonel E. R. Bradley H., Fair Grounds at Louisiana Downs, Dec. 18, $75,000, 3&up, 1$^1/_{16}$mT, 1:44.17, ONTHEDEANSLIST, Fort Prado, Middleweight, 6 started.

Colonel Power H., Fair Grounds, Jan. 9, $58,200, 4&up, 6f, 1:09.19, GOLD STORM, Clock Stopper, Ole Rebel, 4 started.

Colonial Cup Steeplechase S., Camden, Nov. 26, $150,000, 4&up, a2$^3/_4$mT, 5:14.40, MCDYNAMO, Hirapour (Ire), Erin Go Bragh (NZ), 9 started.

Colonial Minstrel S. (R), Belmont Park, Sept. 29, $68,250, 3yo, f, non-winners of an open stakes, 1m, 1:38.46, CLASSY CHARM, Carlow, Lady Pegasus, 7 started.

Colonial Turf Cup S., Colonial Downs, June 25, $500,000, 3yo, 1$^3/_{16}$mT, 1:56.37, ENGLISH CHANNEL, Exceptional Ride, Interpatation, 6 started.

Colorado Derby, Arapahoe Park, July 31, $27,750, 3yo, 1$^1/_{16}$m, 1:46.57, HECKOFALOTOFCASH, Hope for Peace, Tanya's Beau, 10 started.

Colts Neck H. (R), Monmouth Park, July 17, $60,000, 3&up, New Jersey-bred, 6f, 1:08.30, WAR'S PROSPECT, Jay's Wish, Upturn, 7 started.

Columbia River S., Portland Meadows, Dec. 4, $10,750, 2yo, 6f, 1:12.19, TOM TWO, Cascadians Cuttie, Two Fourteen, 5 started.

Columbus Breeders' Special H. (R), Columbus Races, Sept. 2, $13,000, 3yo, f, Nebraska-bred, 6$^1/_2$f, 1:22.20, MY HOBBY, Dabney, Seville's Lil Sis, 5 started.

Columbus Breeders' Special H. (R), Columbus Races, Sept. 2, $13,100, 3yo, c&g, Nebraska-bred, 6$^1/_2$f, 1:20.60, CORK THE BARBER, Uncle Beno, Will Rein, 6 started.

Columbus Debutante S. (R), Columbus Races, Sept. 11, $13,150, 2yo, f, Nebraska-bred, 6f, 1:16, ANY DREAM WILL DO, Mini Whinny, Phil's Little Girl, 6 started.

Columbus Futurity (R), Columbus Races, Sept. 11, $13,400, 2yo, c&g, Nebraska-bred, 6f, 1:15.80, SKWHIRL, My Halo, Hero in My Heart, 9 started.

COMELY S. (G2), Aqueduct, April 16, $150,000, 3yo, f, 1m, 1:35.95, ACEY DEUCEY, Seeking the Ante, Pleasant Chimes, 8 started.

Come Summer S., Canterbury Park, June 18, $50,000, 3yo, a1mT, 1:36.59, COSMIC KRIS, Honour Our Troops, Departing Now, 9 started.

COMMONWEALTH BREEDERS' CUP S. (G2), Keeneland Race Course, April 16, $424,900, 3&up, 7f, 1:22.06, CLOCK STOPPER, Gators N Bears, Silver Wagon, 6 started.

Commonwealth Turf S., Churchill Downs, Nov. 13, $174,900, 3yo, 1$^1/_{16}$mT, 1:43.94, THERECOMESATIGER, Cosmonaut, Drum Major, 9 started.

COMPUSA TURF MILE S. (G3), Churchill Downs, May 7, $112,200, 3&up, f&m, 1mT, 1:35.89, MISS TERRIBLE (ARG), Sand Springs, Shaconage, 7 started.

Con Jackson Claiming H., The Downs at Albuquerque, Sept. 25, $10,000, 3&up, 1$^{13}/_{16}$m, 3:11.61, BILLY BIRD, Cadillac Key, Hold Down the Fort, 10 started.

CONNAUGHT CUP S. (Can-G3), Woodbine, May 29, $119,929, 4&up, 1$^1/_{16}$mT, 1:40.79, LE CINQUIEME ESSAI, Tusayan, Silver Ticket, 6 started.

Connecting Terms S. (R), Lone Star Park, June 17, $40,000, 3&up, Texas-bred non-winners of a stakes in 2005, 7$^1/_2$fT, 1:30.74, CHARMING SOCIALITE, Agrivating General, Goosey Moose, 8 started.

Connecting Terms S. (R), Lone Star Park, May 7, $40,000, 3&up, non-winners of a stakes in 2005, 1$^1/_{16}$mT, 1:42.87, WAUPACA, Seinne (Chi), Sea Dub, 9 started.

Connie Ann S., Calder Race Course, Dec. 18, $40,000, 3&up, f&m, 1$^1/_{16}$mT, 1:42.21, MY LORDSHIP, Brunilda (Arg), Present Danger, 12 started.

Conniver S. (R), Laurel Park, March 12, $50,000, 3&up, f&m, Maryland-bred, 7f, 1:26.11, CHRUSCIKI, Glory of Love, Richetta, 8 started.

Conroe S., Sam Houston Race Park, Dec. 3, $40,000, 3yo, 7f, 1:23.18, DREAMSANDVISIONS, Leaving On My Mind, Andanight, 7 started.

Continental Mile S., Monmouth Park, Sept. 4, $60,115, 2yo, 1m (originally scheduled on the turf), 1:39.43, REAFFIRMED, First Class Guy, That Magic Moment, 8 started.

Cool Air S., Calder Race Course, May 15, $40,000, 3&up, f&m, 5fT, :56.30, COVINCING, Tchula Miss, Lady in Pink, 11 started.

COOLMORE LEXINGTON S. (G2), Keeneland Race Course, April 23, $325,000, 3yo, 1$^1/_{16}$m, 1:45.76, COIN SILVER, Sort It Out, Storm Surge, 7 started.

Copano S., Calder Race Course, Nov. 5, $40,000, 3&up, f&m, 7$^1/_2$fT, 1:30.73, RIDE HER OUT, Pattiano, Silver Lace, 10 started.

Copper Case S. (R), Zia Park, Nov. 24, $42,250, 2yo, New Mexico-bred, 5$^1/_2$f, 1:04.80, MANOLITO, Mister Yates, Dig a Dare, 8 started.

Copper Top Futurity (R), Sunland Park, April 3, $216,063, 2yo, New Mexico-bred, 4$^1/_2$f, :51.18, MANOLITO, Da Candy Man, Hometown Ghost, 9 started.

Cormorant S. (R), Aqueduct, Nov. 6, $100,000, 3&up, c&g, New York-bred, 1mT, 1:37.33, RETRIBUTION, Unnerving, Red Down South, 10 started.

Cornerstone H., Finger Lakes, June 10, $20,500, 3&up, 5$^1/_2$f, 1:04.06, TOP SHOTER, Hey Rube, Trumpster, 6 started.

Cornucopia H., Louisiana Downs, Oct. 9, $40,300, 3&up, f&m, a1$^1/_{16}$mT, 1:41.95, PAZ CIUDADANA (CHI), Rose Hunter, Due to Win Again, 12 started.

Coronado's Quest S., Monmouth Park, June 11, $60,000, 3yo, 6f, 1:09.63, CELTIC INNIS, Miracle Man, Diamond Isle, 6 started.

Coronation Futurity (R), Woodbine, Nov. 10, $214,434, 2yo, Canadian-bred, $1\frac{1}{8}$m, 1:54.84, THINKING OUT LOUD, Pyramid Park, Shillelagh Slew, 11 started.

Correction H., Aqueduct, Feb. 5, $78,375, 3&up, f&m, 6f, 1:12.86, LAVENDER LASS, Bank Audit, Santa Croce, 5 started.

COTILLION H. (G2), Philadelphia Park, Oct. 1, $300,000, 3yo, f, $1\frac{1}{16}$m, 1:46.64, NOTHING BUT FUN, Yolanda B. Too, Shebelongstoyou, 6 started.

Cotton Fitzsimmons H., Turf Paradise, Jan. 8, $50,000, 4&up, 1mT, 1:36.66, GRIMM, Pure, Paladin Power, 8 started.

Count Fleet S., Aqueduct, Jan. 15, $83,175, 3yo, 1m70y, 1:42.41, SCRAPPY T, Naughty New Yorker, Tani Maru, 9 started.

COUNT FLEET SPRINT H. (G3), Oaklawn Park, April 14, $150,000, 4&up, 6f, 1:08.74, TOP COMMANDER, Forest Grove, That Tat, 8 started.

Count Lathum S., Northlands Park, Aug. 6, $41,115, 3yo, $1\frac{1}{16}$m, 1:47.60, FOREVER RASCAL, Courtney Bay, Dakota Duke, 11 started.

Country Life Farm S. (R), Pimlico Race Course, April 23, $65,500, 3yo, f, Maryland-bred and/or Maryland Million-nominated, $1\frac{1}{16}$m, 1:48.06, ONLY IN PHILLY, Hear Us Roar, Lucky Slevin, 6 started.

Cover Gal S. (R), Oak Tree at Santa Anita, Oct. 10, $81,150, 2yo, f, California-bred, 7f, 1:23.92, OH YUM, Bless Idbyour Name, River's Prayer, 7 started.

Cover Girl H., Hastings Race Course, Aug. 21, $32,816, 3&up, f&m, $6\frac{1}{2}$f, 1:16.47, PRETTY MEADOW, Regal Red, La Belle Fleur, 4 started.

Cowdin S., Belmont Park, Oct. 2, $77,150, 2yo, $6\frac{1}{2}$f, 1:17.75, HE'S GOT GRIT, Dr. Pleasure, Jimmy's Pride, 5 started.

Coyote H., Turf Paradise, Feb. 26, $40,000, 4&up, 6f, 1:07.45, FLYING SUPERCON, Newark, Vigilant Site, 7 started.

Coyote Lakes S., Aqueduct, Dec. 7, $67,000, 3&up, $1\frac{5}{8}$m, 2:48.43, NAVESINK RIVER, Loving (Brz), Diligent Gambler, 6 started.

Cradle S., River Downs, Sept. 5, $200,000, 2yo, $1\frac{1}{16}$m, 1:43.60, LAITY, Dawn of War, Acts Like a King, 8 started.

Crafty Drone S., Hawthorne Race Course, Nov. 6, $49,725, 3&up, 5f (originally scheduled on the turf), :57.19, WITHOUT A DOUBT, Danieltown, Marley's Revenge, 9 started.

Crank It Up S., Monmouth Park, June 18, $55,000, 3yo, f, 5fT, :56, LAKES TUNE, Wild Chick, Tiger Fever, 9 started.

Crescent City Derby (R), Fair Grounds, Jan. 8, $75,000, 3yo, Louisiana-bred, $1\frac{1}{16}$m, 1:46.77, CRIMSON STAG, Zarb's Music Man, Prince T., 7 started.

Criterium S., Calder Race Course, Oct. 15, $100,000, 2yo, 6f, 1:10.67, GIN RUMMY KING, Forest Danz, Lord of the Flame, 9 started.

Crown Royal Hurdle S., Pine Mountain, Calloway Garden, Nov. 5, $50,000, 3&up, f&m, a$2\frac{1}{4}$mT, 3:56.40, GUELPH, Feeling So Pretty, Tepee Tot, 10 started.

Crystal Water H. (R), Santa Anita Park, March 12, $109,800, 4&up, California-bred, 1mT, 1:33.50, COZY GUY, Early Snow, Running Free, 8 started.

CTBA Breeders' Oaks S. (R), Arapahoe Park, Aug. 7, $30,400, 3yo, f, Colorado-bred, 1m70y, 1:43.65, FUZDAISY, Skyline Gal, Java Jolene, 8 started.

CTBA Derby (R), Arapahoe Park, Aug. 27, $32,200, 3yo, Colorado-bred, $1\frac{1}{16}$m, 1:46.12, SKYLINE GAL, Heck Ofalotof Cash, Beckabase, 9 started.

CTBA Futurity (R), Arapahoe Park, Aug. 13, $34,425, 2yo, Colorado-bred, $5\frac{1}{2}$f, 1:06.68, GLIDININTHECASH, Takeittothebank, Sunday Romeo, 9 started.

CTBA Lassie S. (R), Arapahoe Park, Aug. 14, $35,825, 2yo, f, Colorado-bred, 6f, 1:18.41, SKIP'S BET, Assante Sana, Neyla's Day, 9 started.

CTBA Marian S. (R), Fairplex Park, Sept. 19, $59,400, 3yo, f, California-bred, $1\frac{1}{16}$m, 1:43.90, GN. GROUP MEETING, Fortunate Event, One Inde Gal, 8 started.

CTHS Sales S. (R), Assiniboia Downs, Sept. 5, $42,527, 2yo, sold at a CTHS sale, 6f, 1:14.40, DREAM EXTREME, Missing Fortune, Miss Doubletrouble, 7 started.

CTHS Sales S. (R), Hastings Race Course, Sept. 11, $55,999, 2yo, f, Canadian-bred sold at the CTHS sale, $6\frac{1}{2}$f, 1:19.70, MISS ME NOT, Star's Sassy Girl, Regal Roo, 11 started.

CTHS Sales S. (R), Hastings Race Course, Sept. 10, $56,662, 2yo, c&g, Canadian-bred sold at a CTHS sale, $6\frac{1}{2}$f, 1:17.73, FEU EXPRESS, Yoodaman, Arizona Drifter, 6 started.

CTHS Sales S. (R), Hastings Race Course, June 18, $36,098, 3yo, f, Canadian-bred sold at a CTHS sale, $6\frac{1}{2}$f, 1:18.48, AVENGING KAT, La Pistola, After the Knight, 8 started.

CTHS Sales S. (R), Hastings Race Course, June 19, $36,267, 3yo, c&g, Canadian-bred sold at a CTHS sale, $6\frac{1}{2}$f, 1:18.26, NO SOX FOX, Forecastor, Alabama Rain, 6 started.

CTT and Thoroughbred Owners of California H., Del Mar, Aug. 26, $84,085, 3&up, f&m, $1\frac{3}{8}$mT, 2:12.59, COLD COLD WOMAN (GB), Secret Charm (Ire), Beneficial Bartok, 5 started.

Cup and Saucer S. (R), Woodbine, Oct. 16, $213,600, 2yo, Canadian-bred, $1\frac{1}{16}$mT, 1:41.43, PYRAMID PARK, River Heights, French Beret, 13 started.

Curious Clover S. (R), Hollywood Park, July 8, $64,688, 4&up, f&m, non-winners of a race other than closed, claiming, or starter since April 22, $5\frac{1}{2}$fT, 1:01.68, VERY VEGAS, Fortunately (GB), Gathering Storm (SAf), 7 started.

Curribot H., Sunland Park, Feb. 5, $53,200, 3&up, $1\frac{1}{16}$m, 1:46.52, SKIP AND GO, Bayou the Moon, Fin Entertainment, 7 started.

C. W. "Doc" Pardee Starter S. (R), Turf Paradise, April 30, $17,500, 3&up, f&m, Arizona-bred starters for a claiming price of $8,000 or less since September 30, 2004 and have not won for more since that date, 1m, 1:39.26, LUCKY AUTUM, Shesgonnabeastar, Strawberry Ice, 9 started.

Cyclones H. (R), Prairie Meadows, June 18, $70,000, 3&up, c&g, Iowa-bred, $1\frac{1}{16}$m, 1:42.97, SCOOTER RAINS, Rubianos Image, Take Me Up, 10 started.

Cypress S. (R), Delta Downs, Jan. 14, $50,000, 4&up, Louisiana-bred, 7f, 1:27.81, NITRO CHIP, Sanctuary's Omooni, Spritely Walker, 8 started.

Czaria H., Sunland Park, Feb. 20, $54,400, 3&up, f&m, 6f, 1:08.99, BAR BAILEY, Savorthetime, Elegant Mercedes, 7 started.

Da Hoss S., Colonial Downs, July 9, $60,000, 3&up, 1mT, 1:35.85, RUNNING TIDE, Mt. Carson, Foufa's Warrior, 6 started.

Da Hoss S., Turf Paradise, April 16, $23,800, 3yo, 1mT, 1:37.02, WESTERN ACT, Night Gig, Raging Wind, 7 started.

Daisycutter H., Del Mar, July 29, $76,225, 3&up, f&m, 5fT, :55.48, FORTUNATELY (GB), Abounding Truth, Bella Banissa, 8 started.

Dallas Turf Cup H., Lone Star Park, June 18, $200,000, 3&up, $1\frac{1}{8}$mT, 1:48.82, SEA DUB, Fullbridled, Major Rhythm, 11 started.

Damon Runyon S. (R), Aqueduct, Dec. 11, $85,250, 2yo, New York-bred, $1\frac{1}{16}$m, 1:46.70, PLATINUM COUPLE, Building New Era, Stolen Thunder, 11 started.

Dance Director S., Turf Paradise, May 21, $24,000, 3&up, $4\frac{1}{2}$fT, :49.74, KING JUSTIN, Grimm, Top Boot, 10 started.

DANCE SMARTLY H. (Can-G3), Woodbine, July 16, $279,184, 3&up, f&m, $1\frac{1}{8}$mT, 1:49.95, NOBLE STELLA (GER), Classic Stamp, Juliet's Kiss, 7 started.

Dance Trainer S. (R), Zia Park, Dec. 2, $41,500, 3&up, New Mexico-bred, 1m, 1:37.80, DEAR BULL, Boom Boom, Tietjen, 5 started.

Dancing Count S., Pimlico Race Course, Jan. 1, $50,000, 3yo, 6f, 1:11.81, MORE SMOKE, Timely Impulse, Primal Storm, 6 started.

Dancin Renee S. (R), Belmont Park, June 15, $59,300, 3yo, f, New York-bred non-winners of an open stakes, $6\frac{1}{2}$f, 1:16.86, SLEW MOTION, What's Your Point, Speed Bag, 5 started.

Danzig S. (R), Penn National Race Course, May 20, $40,700, 3yo, c&g, Pennsylvania-bred, 6f, 1:10.46, LINGLESTOWN, No Passing Zone, Mr. Good Stuff, 5 started.

Daring Doone S., Turf Paradise, Dec. 26, $23,800, 3&up, f&m, a1mT, 1:37.14, SAWTELLE BELLE, Allbow, Madison Meadows, 8 started.

DARLEY ALCIBIADES S. (G2), Keeneland Race Course, Oct. 7, $400,000, 2yo, f, $1\frac{1}{16}$m, 1:49.07, SHE SAYS IT BEST, Ex Caelis, Performing Diva, 11 started.

Darrell Ost Memorial S., Western Montana Fair and Races, Aug. 11, $4,450, 3&up, f&m, $6\frac{1}{2}$f, 1:23.80, EVITAN NATIVE, A Step Beyond, Flying Lady Cue, 7 started.

Daryl Wells Sr. Memorial S. (R), Fort Erie, July 4, $80,570, 3&up, Canadian-bred, $1\frac{1}{16}$mT, 1:42.07, LE CINQUIEME ESSAI, Tamara, Lenny the Lender, 5 started.

Dating Game S., Lethbridge, Oct. 30, $11,079, 3&up, f&m, 7f, 1:26.40, GUILTYBYSUPISCION, Hallas, A Rainbow Princess, 7 started.

Dave Feldman S., Gulfstream Park, Feb. 27, $60,000, 3yo, $1\frac{1}{16}$mT, 1:40.72, DUBLEO, Tadreeb, Crown Point, 10 started.

Dave's Friend S., Laurel Park, Oct. 29, $75,000, 3&up, $5\frac{1}{2}$f, 1:03.70, ABBONDANZA, Forest Park, Dale's Prospect, 6 started.

David L. "Zeke" Ferguson Memorial Hurdle S., Colonial Downs, July 17, $50,000, 3&up, a$2\frac{1}{4}$mT, 4:30.87, PARADISE'S BOSS, McDynamo, Understood, 5 started.

DAVONA DALE S. (G2), Gulfstream Park, Feb. 5, $150,000, 3yo, f, $1\frac{1}{8}$m, 1:50.20, SIS CITY, In the Gold, Jill Robin L, 6 started.

Daytona H., Santa Anita Park, Feb. 20, $78,600, 4&up, $6\frac{1}{2}$f (originally scheduled on the turf), 1:14.03, ROYAL PLACE, Forest Grove, Indian Country, 5 started.

Dayton Andrews Dodge Sophomore Turf S., Tampa Bay Downs, April 9, $85,000, 3yo, $1^{1}/_{16}$mT, 1:41.73, NICANDRO, Rich in Spirit, Shoot Out, 12 started.

Dean Kutz S., Canterbury Park, Aug. 13, $40,000, 3&up, f&m, $6^{1}/_{2}$f, 1:16.68, KATY SMILES, Ells Editor, Mamboalot, 7 started.

Dearly Precious S., Aqueduct, Feb. 21, $81,200, 3yo, f, 6f, 1:10.68, ACEY DEUCEY, Phyllis Sassy Girl, Megascape, 6 started.

DEBUTANTE S. (G3), Churchill Downs, July 9, $112,600, 2yo, f, $5^{1}/_{2}$f, 1:03.95, EFFECTUAL, Joint Effort, Swept Gold, 9 started.

Debutante S., Assiniboia Downs, July 17, $32,768, 2yo, f, $5^{1}/_{2}$f, 1:08.60, CAT RUSH, Hey Hey Renee, Say Maybe Baby, 7 started.

Decathlon S., Monmouth Park, May 14, $65,000, 3&up, 6f, 1:09.85, SMOKUME, Vinemeister, Bold Days, 8 started.

Decoration Day H., Mountaineer Race Track, May 30, $75,000, 3&up, f&m, 1mT, 1:38.16, KAYLAN'S ROSE, Beau Watch, Chef's Choice, 7 started.

De La Rose S. (1st Div.) (R), Saratoga Race Course, Aug. 11, $67,100, 4&up, f&m, non-winners of $50,000 on the turf in 2004-'05, 1mT, 1:36.83, PATH OF THUNDER, With Patience, Sharp Needle (GB), 10 started.

De La Rose S. (2nd Div.) (R), Saratoga Race Course, Aug. 11, $66,900, 4&up, f&m, non-winners of $50,000 on the turf in 2004-'05, 1mT, 1:34.71, CLOAKOF VAGUENESS, My Lordship, Banyu Dewi (Ger), 8 started.

Delaware Certified Distaff S. (R), Delaware Park, Oct. 2, $48,500, 3&up, f&m, Delaware-certified, 6f, 1:10.71, EBONY STAR, Weeks, True Gold, 4 started.

Delaware Certified S. (R), Delaware Park, Oct. 2, $50,600, 3&up, Delaware-certified, 6f, 1:10.89, MAGICAL GEM, Fear the Cape, Scary Bob, 7 started.

DELAWARE H. (G2), Delaware Park, July 17, $1,001,800, 3&up, f&m, $1^{1}/_{4}$m, 2:02.89, ISLAND SAND, Two Trail Sioux, Personal Legend, 11 started.

DELAWARE OAKS (G2), Delaware Park, July 16, $500,300, 3yo, f, $1^{1}/_{16}$m, 1:43.25, R LADY JOY, Round Pond, Dance Away Capote, 6 started.

Delicada S., Louisiana Downs, July 24, $50,000, 3&up, f&m, $1^{1}/_{16}$m, 1:44.73, SLEWPY'S STORM, Red Lifesaver, Boomboomgirl, 9 started.

DEL MAR BREEDERS' CUP H. (G2), Del Mar, Sept. 4, $338,000, 3&up, 1mT, 1:32.21 (NCR), THREE VALLEYS, We All Love Aleyna, Wild Buddy, 10 started.

DEL MAR DEBUTANTE S. (G1), Del Mar, Aug. 27, $250,000, 2yo, f, 7f, 1:23.20, WILD FIT, Mystery Girl, River's Prayer, 11 started.

DEL MAR DERBY (G2), Del Mar, Sept. 5, $400,000, 3yo, $1^{1}/_{8}$mT, 1:45.85 (NCR), WILLOW O WISP, Tedo (Ger), Osidy, 10 started.

DEL MAR FUTURITY (G2), Del Mar, Sept. 7, $250,000, 2yo, 7f, 1:22.43, STEVIE WONDERBOY, The Pharaoh, Jealous Profit, 11 started.

DEL MAR H. (G2), Del Mar, Aug. 28, $250,000, 3&up, $1^{3}/_{8}$mT, 2:12.81, LEPRECHAUN KID, Laura's Lucky Boy, Exterior, 10 started.

DEL MAR OAKS (G1), Del Mar, Aug. 20, $300,000, 3yo, f, $1^{1}/_{8}$mT, 1:46.29, SINGHALESE (GB), Three Degrees (Ire), Dancing Edie, 9 started.

Delta Mile S., Delta Downs, March 4, $50,000, 4&up, 1m, 1:38.39, HIGH STRIKE ZONE, Mauk Four, Golden Glen, 8 started.

DEMOISELLE S. (G2), Aqueduct, Nov. 26, $196,000, 2yo, f, $1^{1}/_{8}$m, 1:52.85, WONDER LADY ANNE L, Cinderella's Dream, Wait a While, 5 started.

Denise Rhudy Memorial S., Delaware Park, July 2, $75,300, 3yo, f, $1^{1}/_{8}$mT, 1:50.43, DYNAMIST, Grat, Toll Taker, 6 started.

Deputed Testamony S. (R), Pimlico Race Course, June 11, $50,000, 3yo, Maryland-bred, $1^{1}/_{16}$m, 1:45.80, LEGAL CONTROL, Monster Chaser, It's Time to Smile, 6 started.

DEPUTY MINISTER H. (G3), Gulfstream Park, Feb. 5, $100,000, 3&up, $6^{1}/_{2}$f, 1:15.62, MEDALLIST, Mister Fotis, Kela, 6 started.

Deputy Minister S. (R), Woodbine, July 20, $102,538, 3yo, progeny of stallions standing in Ontario, 7f, 1:22.74, BOLD GRENADIER, Flat Rock, Quick in Deed, 4 started.

Derby Day H., Blue Ribbon Downs, May 7, $10,925, 3&up, 6f, 1:10.55, SOONER PRIDE, Final Draft, Harry the Prince, 7 started.

Derby Trial S., Assiniboia Downs, July 10, $32,804, 3yo, $1^{1}/_{16}$m, 1:46, STORMY BUSINESS, Prime Time T. V., Raggidy Rowe, 7 started.

Derby Trial S., Churchill Downs, April 30, $113,100, 3yo, 1m, 1:36.16, DON'T GET MAD, Gallardo, Vicarage, 7 started.

Derby Trial S., Fairplex Park, Sept. 12, $58,800, 3yo, $1^{1}/_{16}$m, 1:44.79, TAKE A CHANCE, Chummin, Top This and That, 7 started.

Desert Rose H., Ruidoso Downs, Aug. 14, $25,000, 3&up, f&m, 6f, 1:11.40, BLUE SONG, Sabrina Slew, Culpeper Moon, 6 started.

Desert Sky H. (R), Turf Paradise, May 7, $40,000, 3&up, f&m, starters at the 2004-'05 Turf Paradise meet, 1mT, 1:37.49, KICK THE CAN, V'ville Lady, Sawtelle Belle, 8 started.

DESERT STORMER H. (G3), Hollywood Park, June 5, $106,400, 3&up, f&m, 6f, 1:09.79, PUXA SACO, Tucked Away, Ramatuelle (Chi), 5 started.

Desert Vixen S. (R), Calder Race Course, Aug. 13, $75,000, 2yo, f, progeny of stallions standing in Florida, 6f, 1:12.45, RUNNING LASS, Note to Diane, Five Star Susan, 7 started.

Dessie and Fern Sawyer Futurity (R), The Downs at Albuquerque, Sept. 25, $68,686, 2yo, f, New Mexico-bred, 6f, 1:10.86, BO CHIME, Fern's Free Spirit, McMolly, 11 started.

Devil's Honor H. (R), Philadelphia Park, July 23, $50,000, 3&up, Pennsylvania-bred, 7f, 1:24.52, SENOR CIELO TWO, Banjo Picker, Billy Gilman, 6 started.

Diamondback S. (R), Yavapai Downs, Aug. 13, $11,900, 3&up, Arizona-bred, 6f, 1:10.20, INSTANTLY, Barricade Point, Wishinonastar, 9 started.

Diamond Jo S., Evangeline Downs, Dec. 31, $100,000, 2yo, 1m, 1:39.19, LAWYER RON, Desert Wheat, Premier Dance, 5 started.

DIANA S. (G1), Saratoga Race Course, July 30, $500,000, 3&up, f&m, $1^{1}/_{8}$mT, 1:46.91, SAND SPRINGS, Que Puntual (Arg), Angara (GB), 7 started.

Diane Kem H., Portland Meadows, Oct. 29, $10,925, 3&up, f&m, 6f, 1:12.28, BULLISHDEMANDS, Corona Del Hielo, Wine At Dawn, 6 started.

Diane Kem S. (R), Emerald Downs, Oct. 2, $39,200, 2yo, f, Washington-bred, 6f, 1:10.20, CINDERELLA LIBERTY, Musical Wine, She's All Silk, 7 started.

Dine S. (R), SunRay Park, Sept. 4, $59,400, 3yo, c&g, New Mexico-bred, $6^{1}/_{2}$f, 1:17.20, TRICKEY TODD, Ring of the Run, Abullwithapurpose, 7 started.

DISCOVERY H. (G3), Belmont Park, Oct. 29, $287,250, 3yo, $1^{1}/_{16}$m, 1:41.35, MAGNA GRADUATE, Scrappy T, Buzzards Bay, 11 started.

Display S., Woodbine, Nov. 26, $120,540, 2yo, $1^{1}/_{16}$m, 1:43.90, SEASIDE RETREAT, Ports N Porsches, Bridgecut, 8 started.

DISTAFF BREEDERS' CUP H. (G2), Aqueduct, March 26, $148,900, 3&up, f&m, 7f, 1:22.07, BANK AUDIT, Sensibly Chic, Travelator, 7 started.

Distaff H., Blue Ribbon Downs, May 7, $9,625, 3&up, f&m, $7^{1}/_{2}$f, 1:33.69, R NANEE, Bow Time, Free B's Flying, 8 started.

DISTAFF H. (G1), Churchill Downs, May 7, $281,750, 4&up, f&m, 7f, 1:21.18, MY TRUSTY CAT, Molto Vita, Puxa Saco, 9 started.

Distaff S., Assiniboia Downs, Sept. 5, $33,684, 3&up, f&m, 1m, 1:42, CINDY EMBERS, Gold With Honor, Buck a Shot, 9 started.

Distorted Humor H., Churchill Downs, Nov. 25, $70,320, 3&up, $6^{1}/_{2}$f, 1:15.90, STRENGTH AND HONOR, With Distinction, Social Probation, 8 started.

Dixie Belle S., Oaklawn Park, Jan. 29, $50,000, 3yo, f, 6f, 1:12.33, MORE MOONLIGHT, True Tails, Dimple Pinch, 6 started.

Dixieland S., Oaklawn Park, Jan. 21, $50,000, 3yo, $5^{1}/_{2}$f, 1:05.16, RAZOR, Smoke Smoke Smoke, Cherokee Path, 8 started.

Dixie Miss S., Louisiana Downs, May 21, $50,000, 3yo, f, 6f, 1:12.07, KETCHMEWHEREYOUCAN, Risen Empress, Kera's Kitty Cat, 7 started.

Dixie Poker Ace H. (R), Fair Grounds, March 5, $75,000, 4&up, Louisiana-bred, a$7^{1}/_{2}$fT, 1:33.61, MR. SULU, Bebe Garcon, Spritely Walker, 9 started.

Dixie S., Pimlico Race Course, May 21, $200,000, 3&up, $1^{1}/_{8}$mT, 1:52.79, COOL CONDUCTOR, Artie Schiller, Good Reward, 5 started.

DOGWOOD BREEDERS' CUP S. (G3), Churchill Downs, June 11, $162,900, 3yo, f, $1^{1}/_{16}$m, 1:43.49, MISS MATCHED, Culinary, Catta Pilosa, 7 started.

DOMINION DAY H. (G3), Woodbine, July 1, $176,484, 3&up, $1^{1}/_{4}$m, 2:07.55, A BIT O'GOLD, Niigon, Just in Case Jimmy, 6 started.

Donada Farm H., Fairmount Park, Aug. 6, $30,600, 3&up, 6f, 1:09, BUBBA GUM, Mr. Mink, Knowwhatimean, 6 started.

Donald LeVine Memorial H., Philadelphia Park, May 28, $100,000, 3&up, 7f, 1:21.27, GADACE'S KHAMSEH, Saay Mi Name, Polish Pride, 5 started.

Don Bernhardt S., Ellis Park, July 30, $75,000, 3&up, $6^{1}/_{2}$f, 1:16.29, STERLING GOLD, Level Playingfield, Private Horde, 7 started.

Don Juan de Onate S. (R), The Downs at Albuquerque, May 14, $37,600, 3yo, New Mexico-bred, 6f, 1:09.70, TRICKEY TODD, Ring of the Run, Tricky Tactics, 9 started.

Donna Freyer S. (R), Philadelphia Park, Nov. 5, $57,100, 2yo, f, have spent 90 days in South Carolina and paid a nomination fee to the South Carolina Thoroughbred Owners' and Breeders' Association, 6½f, 1:18.67, SMART AND FANCY, D. D. Night Star, One Slick Chick, 6 started.

Donna Reed S. (R), Prairie Meadows, Aug. 27, $79,200, 4&up, f&m, Iowa-bred, 1m70y, 1:43.39, GAMBLERS PASSION, Switch Lanes, Blanchetta, 7 started.

DONN H. (G1), Gulfstream Park, Feb. 5, $500,000, 3&up, 1⅛m, 1:48.43, SAINT LIAM, Roses in May, Eddington, 6 started.

Donnie Wilhite Memorial H., Louisiana Downs, Oct. 1, $50,000, 3yo, 1mT, 1:36.25, DREAMSANDVISIONS, Ready Ruler, Classical Affirm, 11 started.

Donthelumbertrader S., Calder Race Course, July 17, $40,000, 3yo, 7½fT, 1:29.59, LORD ROBYN, Talented Prince, Tibo, 9 started.

Don Valliere Memorial Cup S. (R), Fort Erie, Aug. 7, $24,669, 3&up, starters at Fort Erie twice in 2005, 6f, 1:09.53, ONTARIO ROAD, Sparkman, Russian Hand, 7 started.

Double Delta S., Arlington Park, June 19, $42,000, 3yo, f, 1mT, 1:36.50, RUGULA, More Than Promised, Mrs. Debbie M, 7 started.

Doubledogdare S., Keeneland Race Course, April 20, $109,700, 4&up, f&m, 1¹⁄₁₆m, 1:46.15, COLONY BAND, La Reason, Ender's Sister, 7 started.

Double Your Flavor S. (R), Sam Houston Race Park, March 26, $40,000, 4&up, f&m, Texas-bred, 7f, 1:24.60, NATIVE ANNIE, Lady Sonya, Shannons Valentine, 8 started.

Dover S., Delaware Park, Oct. 8, $100,000, 2yo, 1¹⁄₁₆m, 1:46.71, SOUTHERN SUCCESS, Mister Alimony, Charming Image, 5 started.

Dowd Mile H., Fonner Park, April 2, $30,000, 3&up, 1m, 1:40.60, PRINEVILLE, Robin Zee, Loan Me a Fen, 8 started.

Dowling S. (R), Great Lakes Downs, Aug. 23, $50,000, 3yo, c&g, Michigan-bred, 1m, 1:44.52, ITS HIS TIME, Meadow Vespers, Demagoguery, 7 started.

Down the Isle S., Turf Paradise, March 7, $23,700, 4&up, 1m, 1:36.73, OUR BEST MAN, Cut of Music, Grog, 6 started.

Dr. A. B. Leggio Memorial Breeders' Cup S., Fair Grounds at Louisiana Downs, Dec. 3, $73,500, 3&up, f&m, 7f, 1:23.34, SILVER CROWN, Red Lifesaver, Josh's Madelyn, 10 started.

Dr. A. B. Leggio Memorial H., Fair Grounds, Jan. 15, $100,000, 4&up, f&m, a5½fT, 1:04.10, AMBITION UNBRIDLED, Tara's Touch (SAf), Our Love, 13 started.

Draw In S., Calder Race Course, Sept. 10, $40,000, 3&up, f&m, 1¹⁄₁₆m, 1:45.90, PAMPERED PRINCESS, D'Wildcat Speed, Appealing Pond, 5 started.

Dream Supreme H., Churchill Downs, Nov. 26, $71,800, 3&up, f&m, 6½f, 1:17.58, INJUSTICE, Savorthetime, Ten Carat Ruby, 9 started.

Dr. Ernest Benner S. (R), Charles Town Races, Sept. 17, $41,500, 2yo, nominated to the West Virginia Breeders' Classic, 6½f, 1:21.57, KING COHL, Brother Banks, Hold On Tight, 9 started.

Dr. Fager S., Arlington Park, July 9, $40,050, 3&up, 1⅛m, 1:48.42, STORMY IMPACT, Nkosi Reigns, Ole Faunty, 4 started.

Dr. Fager S. (R), Calder Race Course, Aug. 13, $75,000, 2yo, progeny of stallions standing in Florida, 6f, 1:10.90, IN SUMMATION, B L's a Runner, Old Town Pond, 7 started.

Dr. James Penny Memorial H., Philadelphia Park, July 2, $100,000, 3&up, f&m, 1¹⁄₁₆mT, 1:46.37, SPRING SEASON, Sunup, Ernabel, 10 started.

Dr. O. G. Fischer Memorial H., SunRay Park, Aug. 6, $32,700, 3&up, f&m, 7f, 1:27.20, MISS NOTEWORTHY, Striptease, Mystic Melissa, 5 started.

D. S. "Shine" Young Memorial Futurity (R), Evangeline Downs, July 30, $100,000, 2yo, Louisiana-bred, 5f, :59.89, VOODOO GOLD, Justin's Magic, Poppa Duke, 10 started.

DTHA Owners' Day H. (R), Delaware Park, Sept. 10, $100,300, 3&up, starters at Delaware Park in 2005, 1⅛m, 1:50.55, TRAPPED AGAIN, Separato, Play Bingo, 6 started.

Duchess H., Marquis Downs, Sept. 2, $5,071, 3yo, f, 1m, 1:42.45, CHIPAWAY, Arctic Taliyah, Fractious Lady, 5 started.

Duchess of York S., Stampede Park, June 11, $40,020, 3&up, f&m, 1¹⁄₁₆m, 1:43.80, GOLD ACCENT, A Shaky Start, Socorro County, 4 started.

DUCHESS S. (Can-G3), Woodbine, Aug. 13, $138,317, 3yo, f, 7f, 1:22.03, LEMON MAID, Hatpin, Roving Angel, 6 started.

Duncan F. Kenner Breeders' Cup H., Fair Grounds, March 19, $125,000, 4&up, 6f, 1:08.99, GOLD STORM, Ole Rebel, Premier Performer, 5 started.

Duncan Hopeful S., Greenlee County Fair, March 20, $4,933, 3&up, 5½f, 1:08.60, C'EST SEA BUN, Major Barker, Slumberjack, 6 started.

DURHAM CUP H. (Can-G3), Woodbine, Oct. 15, $135,862, 3&up, 1⅛m, 1:52.51, CRYPTOGRAPH, Niigon, Forever Rush, 6 started.

Dust Commander S., Turfway Park, Feb. 19, $50,000, 4&up, 1m, 1:38.93, BONUS PACK, Paging, Alpha to Omega, 7 started.

Dwight D. Patterson H. (R), Turf Paradise, April 30, $40,000, 3&up, Arizona-bred, 1¹⁄₁₆mT, 1:43.14, NICE CHOICE, Overland Road, Imdabossau, 10 started.

DWYER S. (G2), Belmont Park, July 4, $150,000, 3yo, 1¹⁄₁₆m, 1:40.83, ROMAN RULER, Flower Alley, Proud Accolade, 6 started.

Earlene McCabe Derby (R), Bay Meadows Race Course, Sept. 4, $70,400, 3yo, California-bred, 6f, 1:09.94, THIRSTY GUY'S, Funny Flyer, Wind Water, 6 started.

Early's Top Seeded H., Marquis Downs, June 25, $4,868, 3&up, 6f, 1:13.35, DOUBLETIME, Always a Houston, Rouge Royale, 7 started.

East View S. (R), Aqueduct, Dec. 4, $83,450, 2yo, f, New York-bred, 1¹⁄₁₆m, 1:47.95, HOME AND AWAY, Zippy Missy, Bee in a Bonnet, 9 started.

EATONTOWN H. (G3), Monmouth Park, July 3, $150,000, 3&up, f&m, 1¹⁄₁₆mT, 1:46.22, SMART N CLASSY, Lentil, Spotlight (GB), 7 started.

E. B. Johnston S., Fairplex Park, Sept. 11, $60,000, 3&up, f&m, 1¹⁄₁₆m, 1:46.92, WILLOW RUSH, Ligacao Direta (Brz), Bend, 7 started.

ECLIPSE H. (Can-G3), Woodbine, May 23, $131,163, 4&up, 1¹⁄₁₆m, 1:43.77, HONOLUA STORM, Cuba, Judiths Wild Rush, 8 started.

EDDIE READ H. (G1), Del Mar, July 24, $400,000, 3&up, 1⅛mT, 1:46.53, SWEET RETURN (GB), Fourty Niners Son, Singletary, 6 started.

Eddy County S., Zia Park, Nov. 25, $82,100, 2yo, 1m, 1:38.20, PREMIER DANCE, Wait in Line, Might Be Hooked, 6 started.

Edgewood S., Churchill Downs, May 6, $112,400, 3yo, f, 1¹⁄₁₆mT, 1:41.94, SWEET TALKER, Rich in Spirit, Insan Mala (Ire), 8 started.

Edmonton Juvenile S., Northlands Park, July 29, $40,585, 2yo, c&g, 6f, 1:12, BEAR CHARACTER, Hidden Speed, Explosion, 8 started.

Edward Babst Memorial H. (R), Beulah Park, April 16, $40,000, 3&up, Ohio-bred, 6f, 1:09.91, CAT SINGER, Catch My Cat, Catlaunch, 9 started.

Edward J. DeBartolo Sr. Memorial Breeders' Cup H., Remington Park, Sept. 5, $125,000, 3&up, 1⅛mT, 1:46.46, DONTBOTHERKNOCKING, Waupaca, Runaway Choice, 7 started.

Eight Thirty S., Delaware Park, May 30, $52,900, 3&up, 1⅛m, 1:52.10, THE LADY'S GROOM, Cherokee's Boy, Lusty Latin, 5 started.

Eillo S., Meadowlands, Sept. 30, $54,600, 3&up, 6f, 1:09.40, TWO DOWN AUTOMATIC, The Student (Arg), Abbondanza, 3 started.

Eillo S., Zia Park, Oct. 31, $42,000, 3&up, 5f, :56.60 (NTR), ORPHAN BRIGADE, Lorenzon, Absolutely True, 7 started.

E. K. Rolfson Mile H., North Dakota Horse Park, Aug. 27, $8,500, 4&up, 1m, 1:40.20 (NTR), MADDIES BLUES, Suntana, Dakota Dixie, 5 started.

El Cajon S., Del Mar, Sept. 3, $100,000, 3yo, 1m, 1:36.34, FOLLOW THE RAINBOW, Chips Are Down, Khyber Pass, 8 started.

EL CAMINO REAL DERBY (G3), Bay Meadows Race Course, March 12, $200,000, 3yo, 1¹⁄₁₆m, 1:42.22, UNCLE DENNY, Wannawinemall, Buzzards Bay, 10 started.

EL CONEJO H. (G3), Santa Anita Park, Jan. 2, $110,500, 4&up, 5½f, 1:02.52, AREYOUTALKINTOME, Hombre Rapido, Woke Up Dreamin, 9 started.

Eleanor M. Casey Memorial S. (R), Charles Town Races, Dec. 3, $41,600, 2yo, f, West Virginia-bred, 6½f, 1:23.09, MALIBU SUE, Cross Creek Rosie, Aye Robbin, 10 started.

EL ENCINO S. (G2), Santa Anita Park, Jan. 16, $150,000, 4yo, f, 1¹⁄₁₆m, 1:42.76, GIRL WARRIOR, A. P. Adventure, Tarlow, 7 started.

Eleven North H. (R), Monmouth Park, Sept. 17, $100,000, 3&up, f&m, New Jersey-bred, 6f, 1:09.89, TOTALLY PRECIOUS, Summer Sting, Eastern Gale, 7 started.

E. L. Gaylord Memorial S., Remington Park, Oct. 15, $40,650, 2yo, f, 6½f, 1:16.46, JAZZY OKIE, Brownie Points, Yaddo Cat, 12 started.

Elge Rasberry S. (R), Louisiana Downs, Aug. 20, $70,000, 3yo, f, Louisiana-bred, a1mT, 1:37.01, EQUESTRIAN GIRLS, Leestown Fantasie, Zarba the Great, 9 started.

Elgin S. (R), Woodbine, Sept. 4, $105,263, 3&up, Canadian-bred, 1¹⁄₁₆m, 1:44.33, BARBEAU RUCKUS, Ever So Free, Ablo, 4 started.

El Joven S., Retama Park, Sept. 3, $100,000, 2yo, 1m (originally scheduled on the turf), 1:40.37, ALMOST CERTAIN, Desert Wheat, Counterfeit Gold, 12 started.

ELKHORN S. (G3), Keeneland Race Course, April 29, $200,000, 4&up, 1½mT, 2:32.62, MACAW (IRE), European (Ire), Rochester, 12 started.

Elko County Thoroughbred Futurity, Elko County Fair, Sept. 5, $21,000, 2yo, 5½f, 1:11.20, LOMARD, Renos Premier City, Seattle Bound Baby, 7 started.

Elko Thoroughbred Derby, Elko County Fair, Sept. 4, $20,000, 3yo, 7f, 1:24.30, HANDSOMCHAMP, Gal's Hunter, Weekend Bar Talk, 7 started.

Elkwood S., Monmouth Park, July 16, $60,000, 3&up, 1 1/16mT, 1:42.54, HOTSTUFANTHENSOME, Cottage (Arg), Stormy Roman, 6 started.

Ellis Park Breeders' Cup Turf S., Ellis Park, Aug. 20, $100,000, 3&up, f&m, 1 1/16mT, 1:45.12, SHACONAGE, Sheer Luck, Victoire Bataille, 7 started.

Elmer Heubeck Distaff H. (R), Calder Race Course, Nov. 12, $200,000, 3&up, f&m, Florida-bred, 1 1/16m, 1:46.43, AMERICAN MISS, Special Report, Appealing Pond, 9 started.

El Paso Times H., Sunland Park, Feb. 12, $54,200, 3yo, f, 6 1/2f, 1:18.76, MERGER TALK, Dixie Kiss, Time to Divorce, 9 started.

Ema Bovary S., Calder Race Course, June 14, $40,000, 3&up, f&m, 6f, 1:11.25, WILD SPEED, Really Royal, French Village, 6 started.

Emerald Breeders' Cup Distaff H., Emerald Downs, Aug. 21, $98,125, 3&up, f&m, 1m, 1:36.80, SECRET CORSAGE, Karis Makaw, Strollin Slew, 9 started.

Emerald Downs Breeders' Cup Derby, Emerald Downs, Sept. 5, $95,000, 3yo, 1 1/8m, 1:49, ALEXANDERSRUN, Norm's Nephew, Timeless Passion, 12 started.

Emerald Downs H., Hastings Race Course, May 29, $35,069, 3yo, f, 6 1/2f, 1:18.22, REGAL PUSHER, Backseat Becka, Virtuous Lady, 7 started.

Emerald Express S., Emerald Downs, July 30, $43,650, 2yo, c&g, 6f, 1:09.60, TUSKO T., Courting Seattle, Whiteriver Gold, 9 started.

Emerald H., Emerald Downs, June 19, $75,000, 3&up, 1m, 1:35.80, MR. MAKAH, Sabertooth, R. Associate, 7 started.

Emerald Necklace S. (R), Thistledown, Sept. 17, $40,000, 2yo, f, Ohio-bred, 6f, 1:13.54, DOUBLE DIVA, Mercy, Tommeyesgold, 8 started.

Emergency Nurse S., Calder Race Course, May 8, $40,000, 3&up, f&m, 1 1/16m, 1:47.35, PAMPERED PRINCESS, Miracle Runner, Gentille Alouette, 6 started.

Emirates S. (R), Belmont Park, June 11, $69,300, 4&up, f&m, non-winners of an open stakes in 2004-'05, 1 1/16m, 1:42.91, MADONNA LILY, Judy Soda, Strategy, 5 started.

Empire Classic H. (R), Belmont Park, Oct. 22, $250,000, 3&up, New York-bred, 1 1/8m, 1:50.86, SPITE THE DEVIL, Organizer, Carminooch, 10 started.

Endeavour S., Tampa Bay Downs, Feb. 26, $100,000, 4&up, f&m, 1 1/16mT, 1:43.54, DELTA PRINCESS, Fast Cookie, Lentil, 11 started.

ENDINE H. (G3), Delaware Park, Sept. 10, $200,900, 3&up, f&m, 6f, 1:10.18, UMPATEEDLE, Sensibly Chic, Ebony Breeze, 8 started.

England's Legend S. (R), Belmont Park, June 8, $60,950, 4&up, f&m, non-winners of a stakes in 2004-'05, 1 1/8mT, 1:48.97, NATALIE BEACH (ARG), Broad Hopes, La Reina, 7 started.

E. P. TAYLOR S. (Can-G1), Woodbine, Oct. 23, $843,956, 3&up, f&m, 1 1/4mT, 2:06.70, HONEY RYDER, Latice (Ire), Ambitious Cat, 12 started.

Ernest Finley H., Santa Rosa, July 31, $65,625, 3&up, 6f, 1:09.17, BONFANTE, Tonco, Tenth Street, 7 started.

Ernie Samuel Memorial S. (R), Fort Erie, July 17, $81,920, 3&up, f&m, Canadian-bred, 1 1/16m (originally scheduled on the turf), 1:44.62, SPANISH DECREE, Tamara, Miss Filibuster, 6 started.

Escondido H. (R), Del Mar, Aug. 3, $82,450, 3&up, non-winners of a stakes of $50,000 other than state-bred at one mile or over in 2005, 1 3/8mT, 2:12.06 (NCR), LAURA'S LUCKY BOY, Sarafan, Continental Red, 7 started.

ESSEX H. (G3), Oaklawn Park, Feb. 12, $100,000, 4&up, 1 1/16m, 1:43.66, ABSENT FRIEND, Mauk Four, Separato, 10 started.

Eternal Search S. (R), Woodbine, Aug. 31, $105,261, 3yo, f, progeny of stallions standing in Ontario, 1 1/16m, 1:44.57, WHISKEY AND LOW, Coastal Fortress, Cherry Grove, 6 started.

E. T. Springer S. (R), The Downs at Albuquerque, Sept. 10, $30,000, 3&up, New Mexico-bred, 7f, 1:23.59, ROMEOS WILSON, Local Case, Rocky Gulch, 7 started.

Evangeline Mile H., Evangeline Downs, Aug. 13, $100,000, 3&up, 1m, 1:38.60, SHAKY TOWN, Drill Hall, Chippewa Trail, 5 started.

Evan Shipman H. (R), Belmont Park, July 24, $109,900, 3&up, New York-bred, 1 1/16m, 1:43.52, YANKEE MON, West Virginia, Chowder's First, 8 started.

Evanston Mayor's Derby, Wyoming Downs, July 9, $3,700, 3&up, 6f, 1:12.20, POORBOYS PLAYBOY, Oughta Be Illegal, Alyjam, 7 started.

Evanston Speed H., Wyoming Downs, July 9, $3,450, 3&up, 4 1/2f, :51.14 (NTR), DR. TOM B, Restrictions Apply, Popescu (Brz), 9 started.

Everett Nevin Alameda County Futurity (R), Pleasanton, July 3, $53,600, 2yo, California-bred, 5f, :56.31, DON JAUN CON, Momotombo, From Above, 8 started.

Excalibur S., Louisiana Downs, May 15, $50,000, 3yo, a1mT, 1:36.62, SILVER HAZE, Hopkins, South Beach Boy, 6 started.

EXCELSIOR BREEDERS' CUP H. (G3), Aqueduct, April 2, $196,000, 3&up, 1 1/8m, 1:50.41, OFFLEE WILD, Rogue Agent, Cuba, 5 started.

Excess Energy S., Turf Paradise, Dec. 3, $23,600, 3&up, f&m, 5 1/2f, 1:02.32, LIL EASY, Sawtelle Belle, Kresgeville, 6 started.

Excitable Lady H., Churchill Downs, June 11, $69,150, 3&up, f&m, 5fT, :57.31, SINGIT, Nicole's Dream, Mocha Queen, 12 started.

Exotic Wood S. (R), Hollywood Park, June 3, $65,332, 4&up, f&m, non-winners of $40,000 in 2005, 5 1/2fT, 1:01.69, STARKAY (NZ), Navaja (NZ), Fun'ngames Toknite, 6 started.

Express S., Lone Star Park, May 14, $75,000, 3&up, 6f, 1:07.85, RODEO'S CASTLE, Joe Six Pack, Two Down Automatic, 5 started.

Fain Road S., Yavapai Downs, Sept. 6, $10,500, 3&up, 4 1/2f, :49.80 (ETR), BOBAWAY, Jack Dugan, Persee Joe, 9 started.

Fairfield S., Solano County Fair, July 23, $54,250, 3yo, f, 6f, 1:10.09, LUCK AND FAME, Two to Get Ready, Charming Colleen, 6 started.

Fair Grounds Breeders' Cup H., Fair Grounds, Feb. 26, $125,000, 4&up, a1 1/8mT, 1:53.79, G P FLEET, Honor in War, Rapid Proof, 9 started.

FAIR GROUNDS OAKS (G2), Fair Grounds, March 12, $300,000, 3yo, f, 1 1/16m, 1:43.79, SUMMERLY, Carlea, Runway Model, 6 started.

Fair Grounds Sales S. (R), Fair Grounds, March 20, $73,000, 3yo, offered for sale at the 2004 Fair Grounds Sales Co. two-year-olds in training sale, 1m, 1:38.47, PRESSED, Catquit, Drew Lil Slew, 10 started.

Fair Lady S. (R), Hastings Race Course, April 17, $44,576, 3yo, f, British Columbia-bred, 6 1/2f, 1:19.66, SLEWPAST, Vic's Sweety, Vice, 6 started.

Fair Queen H., The Downs at Albuquerque, Sept. 16, $30,000, 3yo, f, 6 1/2f, 1:16.90, SHESA PRIVATE I, Desert House, Shadows N Dust, 12 started.

Fall Classic Distaff H. (R), Northlands Park, Sept. 24, $64,035, 3&up, f&m, Alberta-bred, 1 1/16m, 1:46, S. L. CHARMER, Banjo Babe, dh-To Dream Again, dh-Weekend Ceilidh, 8 started.

Fall Highweight H., Aqueduct, Nov. 24, $112,500, 3&up, 6f, 1:09.30, ATTILA'S STORM, Voodoo, Super Fuse, 9 started.

Fall Overnight S., Lethbridge, Sept. 17, $11,199, 3&up, 5 1/2f, 1:09, RUGGED CLIFF, Nattandyahoo, Sizzlin Hot Summer, 8 started.

Fall S., Mountaineer Race Track, Oct. 4, $75,000, 3&up, 1 1/8m, 1:48.33, DISCREET HERO, Silver Axe, Azucar (Per), 7 started.

Falls Amiss H. (R), Horsemen's Park, July 22, $28,600, 4&up, f&m, Nebraska-bred, 1m, 1:40.80, UP 'N BLUMIN, Shawklit Premiere, Magic Trump, 6 started.

FALLS CITY H. (G2), Churchill Downs, Nov. 24, $338,700, 3&up, f&m, 1 1/8m, 1:50.25, INDIAN VALE, Pampered Princess, Miss Fortunate, 10 started.

Fanfreluche S. (R), Woodbine, Oct. 29, $141,995, 2yo, f, Ontario-bred, 6f, 1:10.09, GUMBOOTS, Devil's Bride, Salty Surprise, 8 started.

Fantango Lady S. (R), Horsemen's Park, July 21, $29,500, 3yo, f, Nebraska-bred, 1m, 1:42.80, CERVEZA LITE, Dress Right, Peppermint Swirl, 9 started.

Fantasia S. (R), Louisiana Downs, May 1, $50,000, 3yo, f, Louisiana-bred, 6f, 1:11.49, SWEET MACARONI, Courtneys Doll, Raspberry Wine, 7 started.

Fantasy S., Hastings Race Course, Oct. 22, $91,586, 2yo, f, 1 1/16m, 1:47.96, LANGARA LASS, Miss Me Not, No Ka Oi, 7 started.

FANTASY S. (G2), Oaklawn Park, April 15, $250,000, 3yo, f, 1 1/16m, 1:43.49, ROUND POND, Rugula, R Lady Joy, 7 started.

Farer Belle Lee H. (R), Great Lakes Downs, Sept. 17, $50,000, 3&up, f&m, Michigan-bred, 1 1/16m, 1:50.67, DEB'S FAVOITE GIFT, Lunes Grito, Reasonable Code, 9 started.

Fargo Thoroughbred Futurity, North Dakota Horse Park, Aug. 27, $10,000, 2yo, 6f, 1:15.60, CAROL D, Substancial Lyric, Rough Knight, 7 started.

Fargo Thoroughbred Open H., North Dakota Horse Park, Sept. 5, $9,400, 4&up, 1m, 1:40.80, ROBIN ZEE, Maddies Blues, Exciting Trick, 6 started.

Fashion S., Belmont Park, June 9, $81,000, 2yo, f, 5f, :58.24, FIFTH AVENUE, Blissful Trip, Successful Romance, 6 started.

Fasig-Tipton Turf Dash S., Calder Race Course, Sept. 3, $50,000, 2yo, 5f (originally scheduled on the turf), :58.97, FOREST DANZ, Connoisseur, Golden Flame, 10 started.

FAYETTE S. (G3), Keeneland Race Course, Oct. 29, $150,000, 3&up, 1 1/8m, 1:51.37, ALUMNI HALL, On Thin Ice, M B Sea, 9 started.

Federal Way H., Emerald Downs, May 15, $43,150, 3yo, f, 6 1/2f, 1:16, QUEENLEDO, No Fences, Debbie's Assault, 9 started.

Federico Tesio S., Pimlico Race Course, April 23, $100,000, 3yo, 1 1/8m, 1:53.31, MALIBU MOONSHINE, Hello Jerry, December Treasure, 6 started.

Fiesta Mile S. (R), Retama Park, Oct. 1, $40,000, 3&up, f&m, Texas-bred, 1mT, 1:36.25, CLAUDIA'S AGENDA, Leo's Baroness, Lady Mallory, 8 started.

Fifth Avenue S. (R), Aqueduct, Nov. 6, $125,000, 2yo, f, New York-bred, 6f, 1:11.60, PRINCESS SWEET, No Reason, Little Miss Zip, 9 started.

FIFTH SEASON S. (G3), Oaklawn Park, April 13, $100,000, 4&up, $1^1/_{16}$m, 1:42.89, MAUK FOUR, Clays Awesome, Absent Friend, 8 started.

Filly Sale S. (R), Northlands Park, Aug. 20, $48,534, 2yo, f, Canadian-bred sold at the CTHS sale, $6^1/_2$f, 1:19.80, TARTAN STAR, Kaylee's Magic, Ain't No Options, 9 started.

Finale H., Marquis Downs, Sept. 10, $5,096, 3&up, 1m, 1:44.45, BULLINSKY, Dick's Hunter, Beauzak, 4 started.

Find H. (R), Laurel Park, Oct. 29, $50,000, 3&up, Maryland-bred, $1^1/_8$mT, 1:49.03, PRIVATE SCANDAL, Tam's Terms, Bingobear, 8 started.

Finger Lakes Juvenile Fillies S., Finger Lakes, Oct. 1, $50,000, 2yo, f, 6f, 1:11.85, PRECISEPURSUIT, Blushing Marian, Bella Dorato, 9 started.

Finger Lakes Juvenile S., Finger Lakes, Oct. 22, $50,000, 2yo, 6f, 1:12.67, FLY TO ME, Judge Tommy D., Imperial Zip, 8 started.

FIRECRACKER BREEDERS' CUP H. (G2), Churchill Downs, July 4, $274,000, 3&up, 1mT, 1:35.25, KITTEN'S JOY, Old Forester, America Alive, 6 started.

Firecracker S., Mountaineer Race Track, July 4, $75,000, 3&up, f&m, 1mT, 1:34.49, LADY GRACE, Modena Bay (NZ), Melody Maiden, 7 started.

First Episode S. (R), Suffolk Downs, Aug. 6, $39,200, 3&up, f&m, Massachusetts-bred, $1^1/_{16}$m, 1:46.05, ASK QUEENIE, African Princess, Papa Dancer, 5 started.

FIRST FLIGHT H. (G2), Belmont Park, Oct. 30, $150,000, 3&up, f&m, 7f, 1:23.98, GREAT INTENTIONS, Habiboo, Smokey Glacken, 8 started.

First Lady H., Ruidoso Downs, June 18, $25,000, 3&up, f&m, 6f, 1:09, BLUE SONG, Miss Noteworthy, Culpeper Moon, 6 started.

FIRST LADY H. (G3), Gulfstream Park, Jan. 22, $100,000, 3&up, f&m, 6f, 1:09.21, SAVORTHETIME, Cologny, Ebony Breeze, 7 started.

First Lady S. (R), Indiana Downs, May 30, $40,000, 3yo, f, Indiana-bred, $7^1/_2$fT, 1:33.39, CONGRATULATING, Black Eyed Susie, Free Bonus, 6 started.

First Snowbound S., Yavapai Downs, Aug. 15, $10,200, 3&up, f&m, $5^1/_2$f, 1:05.60, PAINLESS, Mirando, Little Pursuit, 5 started.

Fit for a Queen S., Arlington Park, May 21, $42,000, 3&up, f&m, 6f, 1:10.03, MY RO, Rich City Girl, Liz On Polk Street, 7 started.

Flag Officer S., Hawthorne Race Course, March 12, $42,000, 3yo, $1^1/_{16}$m, 1:49.19, RAVING ROCKET, Win Me Over, Royal Flyer, 5 started.

Flame Thrower S. (R), Hollywood Park, June 17, $63,050, 3&up, non-winners of $40,000 twice in 2004-'05, $5^1/_2$fT, 1:02.29, BILLY'S ECHO, Golden Arrow, Moth Ball (GB), 5 started.

Flaming Page S., Woodbine, Sept. 25, $94,430, 3&up, f&m, $1^1/_2$mT, 2:27.29, NOBLE STELLA (GER), Nomistakeaboutit, Sheer Enchantment, 9 started.

FLASH S. (G3), Belmont Park, June 10, $105,100, 2yo, 5f, :58.39, BEACON SHINE, Union Course, Speed of Sound, 5 started.

Flatterer Hurdle H. (R), Philadelphia Park, July 23, $50,000, 3&up, Pennsylvania-bred, a$2^1/_{16}$mT, 3:44.43, PARTY AIRS, Three Carat, Mixed Up, 6 started.

Flawlessly S., Arlington Park, Sept. 11, $41,750, 3&up, f&m, $1^1/_{16}$mT, 1:42.20, ANEGADA, Unbridled Echo, Lenatareese, 7 started.

Flawlessly S., Hollywood Park, July 4, $112,900, 3yo, f, 1mT, 1:34.49, LOUVAIN (IRE), Royal Copenhagen (Fr), Island Escape, 11 started.

Fleet Treat S. (R), Del Mar, July 23, $100,000, 3yo, f, California-bred, 7f, 1:22.50, SOLDIER'S KISS, Gn. Group Meeting, Short Route, 10 started.

FLEUR DE LIS H. (G2), Churchill Downs, June 18, $330,000, 3&up, f&m, $1^1/_8$m, 1:48.53, TWO TRAIL SIOUX, Storm's Darling, Rare Gift, 7 started.

Fleur de Lis S., Louisiana Downs, June 19, $40,000, 3&up, f&m, 1m70y, 1:42.57, SOUTHERN SURPRISE, Salzurita (Arg), Boomboomgirl, 8 started.

Floor Show S., Delaware Park, June 21, $59,100, 3yo, $1^1/_{16}$m, 1:45.50, LETTERMAN'S HUMOR, Malibu Moonshine, Killenaule, 6 started.

FLORAL PARK H. (G3), Belmont Park, Sept. 17, $109,100, 3&up, f&m, 6f, 1:10.26, SMOKEY GLACKEN, Areek, Baldomera, 6 started.

Florence Henderson S. (R), Indiana Downs, June 17, $40,000, 3&up, f&m, Indiana-bred, $1^1/_{16}$mT, 1:43.18, MY SWEET SUG, Ellens Lucky Star, Speedy Tiffany, 9 started.

Florida Breeders' Distaff S., Ocala Training Center, March 21, $40,000, 3&up, f&m, $1^1/_{16}$m, 1:47.20, STORMIN' DAINA, Miracle Runner, Family Favorite, 7 started.

FLORIDA DERBY (G1), Gulfstream Park, April 2, $1,000,000, 3yo, $1^1/_8$m, 1:49.43, HIGH FLY, Noble Causeway, B. B. Best, 9 started.

Florida Oaks, Tampa Bay Downs, March 19, $150,000, 3yo, f, $1^1/_{16}$m, 1:44.58, R LADY JOY, Toll Taker, Gotta Rush, 9 started.

Florida Thoroughbred Charities S. (R), Ocala Training Center, March 21, $40,000, 3&up, progeny of stallions whose seasons have been offered to the 2001 Florida Thoroughbred Charities live auction, 5f, :57.40, BOG HUNTER, Above the Wind, Carey's Gold, 10 started.

FLOWER BOWL INVITATIONAL S. (G1), Belmont Park, Oct. 1, $750,000, 3&up, f&m, $1^1/_4$mT, 2:00.27, RISKAVERSE, Wonder Again, Film Maker, 9 started.

Flying Lark S., Portland Meadows, Jan. 29, $7,500, 3yo, 6f, 1:11.83, TYPHOON AARON, Palanca, Top Toad, 11 started.

Flying Pidgeon H., Calder Race Course, Oct. 1, $100,000, 3&up, $1^1/_8$mT, 1:50.22, DANCING MASTER (IRE), Keep Cool, Magic Mecke, 10 started.

Fly So Free S. (R), Aqueduct, Dec. 7, $65,850, 3yo, non-winners of an open stakes, 6f, 1:11.31, SIR GREELEY, Tashdeed, December Treasure, 5 started.

Folklore H., Louisiana Downs, Aug. 27, $56,600, 3&up, $6^1/_2$f, 1:16.69, ZARB'S DAHAR, That Tat, Nuttyboom, 7 started.

Fonner Park Special S. (R), Fonner Park, April 16, $31,000, 3yo, c&g, Nebraska-bred, 6f, 1:14.80, THE STRAW MAN, Cork the Barber, Uncle Beno, 9 started.

Fonner Park Special S. (R), Fonner Park, April 17, $30,900, 3yo, f, Nebraska-bred, 6f, 1:14.40, DRESS RIGHT, My Hobby, Lovely Jewel, 9 started.

Foolish Pleasure Breeders' Cup S., Calder Race Course, Sept. 24, $126,375, 2yo, 1m70y, 1:45.76, BLAZING RATE, D' broken Speed, Tizzys No Saint, 7 started.

Fool the Experts S., Turf Paradise, Nov. 28, $23,700, 2yo, $6^1/_2$f, 1:16.25, KEAGAN, Rachel's Smokey, Soft Seventeen, 7 started.

Foothill S., Fairplex Park, Sept. 9, $60,000, 3yo, $6^1/_2$f, 1:16.10, DILIGENT PROSPECT, Ninety Fine, Ransom Demanded, 6 started.

Forego S., Turfway Park, Feb. 4, $49,500, 4&up, $6^1/_2$f, 1:14.35, PRIVATE HORDE, Deer Lake, Paging, 3 started.

FOREGO S. (G1), Saratoga Race Course, Sept. 3, $250,000, 3&up, 7f, 1:22.59, MASS MEDIA, Battle Won, Silver Wagon, 6 started.

Forerunner S., Keeneland Race Course, April 21, $110,500, 3yo, $1^1/_8$mT, 1:48.51, GUN SALUTE, Mad Adam, Cosmic Kris, 8 started.

Fort Bend County S. (R), Sam Houston Race Park, April 2, $40,000, 3yo, Texas-bred, 7f, 1:23.55, LEAVING ON MY MIND, General Charley, Dixie Meister, 8 started.

Fort Erie Slots Cup S. (R), Fort Erie, Aug. 21, $24,762, 3&up, f&m, starters at Fort Erie twice in 2005, 5fT, :59.02, DECADENT DASH, Clubay, Glitter Cove, 10 started.

FORT MARCY H. (G3), Aqueduct, April 23, $107,400, 3&up, $1^1/_{16}$mT, 1:42.74, BETTER TALK NOW, Remind, Ecclesiastic, 5 started.

Fort Monmouth S., Monmouth Park, May 30, $60,000, 3&up, f&m, 1mT, 1:36.87, BRUNILDA (ARG), Bright Abundance, Krasnaya, 8 started.

Forty-Niner H., Golden Gate Fields, Nov. 25, $100,000, 3&up, $1^1/_{16}$m, 1:41.32, TRICKEY TREVOR, Melanyhasthepapers, My Creed, 6 started.

Forward Pass S., Arlington Park, Aug. 13, $48,000, 3yo, 7f, 1:22.77, STRAIGHT LINE, Wonone, Rocky River, 10 started.

Foster City H., Bay Meadows Race Course, March 5, $55,550, 3&up, f&m, 1m, 1:36.38, UNINHIBITED SONG, Secret Corsage, Platinum Princess, 5 started.

FOUNTAIN OF YOUTH S. (G2), Gulfstream Park, March 5, $300,000, 3yo, $1^1/_8$m, 1:49.70, HIGH FLY, Bandini, B. B. Best, 9 started.

Four Seasons H., Blue Ribbon Downs, Oct. 29, $9,575, 3&up, 1m, 1:38.60, SHEIK OF WAGONER, Plenty Lucky, Neuf de Coeur, 7 started.

FOURSTARDAVE H. (G2), Saratoga Race Course, Aug. 27, $200,000, 3&up, $1^1/_{16}$mT, 1:39.92, LEROIDESANIMAUX (BRZ), Silver Tree, Steel Light, 6 started.

Foxbrook Supreme Hurdle S. (R), Far Hills, Oct. 22, $100,000, 4&up, non-winners over hurdles prior to June 1, 2004, a$2^1/_2$mT, 5:20.75, MOVE WEST, Bulawayo, Irish Actor, 11 started.

Fox Sports Network H., Emerald Downs, May 22, $40,000, 3&up, $6^1/_2$f, 1:13 (NTR), SABERTOOTH, Best On Tap, Random Memo, 8 started.

Foxy J. G. S. (R), Philadelphia Park, June 25, $53,250, 3yo, f, Pennsylvania-bred, 7f, 1:24.65, REDASPEN, S W Aly'svalentine, J. D. Safari, 5 started.

FRANCES A. GENTER S. (G3), Calder Race Course, Dec. 31, $100,000, 3yo, f, 7½fT, 1:27.07, LAURAFINA, Champagne Ending, More Than Promised, 12 started.

Frances Genter S. (R), Canterbury Park, July 9, $42,800, 3yo, f, Minnesota-bred, 6f, 1:09.98, OH YOU AGAIN, Isle See You Later, Glitter Star, 10 started.

Frances Slocum S. (R), Hoosier Park, Nov. 19, $40,000, 3&up, f&m, Indiana-bred, 1¹/₁₆m, 1:47.08, MY SWEET SUG, Lady Blue Sky, Jessica Proud, 5 started.

Francis "Jock" LaBelle Memorial S., Delaware Park, May 7, $77,138, 3yo, 6f, 1:11.28, EGG HEAD, Lieutenant Danz, Shmooo, 9 started.

Frank A. "Buddy" Abadie Memorial S. (R), Evangeline Downs, July 30, $50,000, 3yo, f, Louisiana-bred, 1m, 1:42.34, PHONE AFFAIR, Zarba the Great, Miriam L., 5 started.

Frank Arnason Sire S. (R), Assiniboia Downs, July 30, $32,680, 2yo, Manitoba-bred, 6f, 1:15, MISSING FORTUNE, Clairebell, Farm Team, 5 started.

FRANK E. KILROE MILE H. (G1), Santa Anita Park, March 5, $300,000, 4&up, 1mT, 1:33.89, LEROIDESANIMAUX (BRZ), Buckland Manor, Sweet Return (GB), 9 started.

Frank Gall Memorial H. (R), Charles Town Races, Nov. 5, $50,950, 3&up, West Virginia-bred, 7f, 1:26.07, ADAMS TRIBE, Brigader, Earth Power, 6 started.

Frankie Figueroa Memorial S., Santa Cruz County Fair, May 1, $2,712, 3&up, 6f, 1:12.20, FROM A TO Z, Onceinafullmoon, Cosmic High, 7 started.

FRANK J. DE FRANCIS MEMORIAL DASH S. (G1), Laurel Park, Nov. 19, $300,000, 3&up, 6f, 1:09.06, I'M THE TIGER, Tiger Heart, Clever Electrician, 14 started.

Franklin County S., Keeneland Race Course, Oct. 20, $113,300, 3&up, f&m, 5½fT, 1:02.53, BRIGHT GOLD, Tara's Touch (SAf), Mocha Queen, 10 started.

Fran's Valentine S. (R), Hollywood Park, April 24, $150,000, 4&up, f&m, California-bred, 1¹/₁₆mT, 1:40.53, VALENTINE DANCER, Smokegetenyoureyes, Scrofa, 5 started.

Fred "Cappy" Capossela S., Aqueduct, Feb. 19, $80,550, 3yo, 6f, 1:10.96, DISTINCTIVE TRICK, Pavo, Benjamin Baby, 6 started.

Fred Drysdale S., Grand Prairie, Aug. 14, $5,691, 3&up, f&m, 6½f, 1:19, WILD COUNTY, She's Shameless, Real Sterling, 6 started.

Fred Mendel Memorial H., Marquis Downs, July 23, $4,923, 3&up, 1m, 1:39.29, SAND RUSH, Rouge Royale, Bullinsky, 9 started.

FRED W. HOOPER H. (G3), Calder Race Course, Dec. 17, $100,000, 3&up, 1⅛m, 1:53.46, ANDROMEDA'S HERO, Seek Gold, Whos Crying Now, 9 started.

Freedom of the City S., Northlands Park, Oct. 8, $42,540, 2yo, f, 1m, 1:41.20, AWESOME DEAL, Hilltop Neddy, Mia Cat Dancer, 6 started.

Free Press S., Assiniboia Downs, June 19, $32,544, 3&up, 6f, 1:12, IWOODIFICOULD, Simply Regal, Sand Rush, 8 started.

Free Spirits H., Ruidoso Downs, June 26, $25,000, 3&up, 6f, 1:09.20, TOUGH PILGRIM, Baldwin County, Absolutely True, 6 started.

Fresa S. (R), Lone Star Park, July 1, $40,000, 3&up, f&m, non-winners of a stakes in 2005, 1¹/₁₆mT, 1:46.09, VOZ DE COLEGIALA (CHI), Bonnie J., Touch of Creme, 7 started.

Fresa S. (R), Lone Star Park, July 1, $40,000, 3&up, f&m, non-winners of a stakes in 2005, 1¹/₁₆mT, 1:45.91, HIGH PIONEER, Bridal Gal, Chitchat Chitchat, 6 started.

Friendly Lover H. (R), Monmouth Park, Sept. 17, $100,000, 3&up, New Jersey-bred, 6f, 1:08.59, JOEY P., War's Prospect, Second Collection, 6 started.

Frisk Me Now S., Monmouth Park, May 29, $65,000, 3&up, 1m70y, 1:40.64, TAP DAY, Ricardo A, Sinister G, 5 started.

FRIZETTE S. (G1), Belmont Park, Oct. 8, $500,000, 2yo, f, 1m, 1:38.07, ADIEU, Along the Sea, Keeneland Kat, 9 started.

Frontier H. (R), Great Lakes Downs, Sept. 19, $50,000, 3&up, Michigan-bred, 1⅛m, 1:55, DORTHYS CHAMP, Rockem Sockem, Equi Power, 10 started.

Front Range H., Arapahoe Park, July 4, $27,425, 3&up, 7f, 1:22.70, KOMAX, Cocoa Latte, Cut of Music, 8 started.

Frost King S. (R), Woodbine, Nov. 23, $106,413, 2yo, progeny of stallions standing in Ontario, 7f, 1:24.75, BAD HAT, Initforthemoney, Atlas Shrugs, 5 started.

Ft. Lauderdale S., Gulfstream Park, Jan. 9, $60,000, 4&up, 1¹/₁₆mT, 1:38.26, UNION PLACE, Freefourinternet, Stormy Roman, 12 started.

Full Choke S. (R), Zia Park, Nov. 20, $42,000, 3&up, New Mexico-bred, 5½f, 1:03.20, NINETY NINE JACK, C. G's Dollar, Bold Nxs, 8 started.

Furl Sail H., Fair Grounds at Louisiana Downs, Dec. 17, $75,000, 3&up, f&m, 1m70y (originally scheduled at a 1m on the turf), 1:43.69, CULINARY, Glitteration, Go Girlfriend Go, 10 started.

Fury S. (R), Woodbine, May 8, $133,881, 3yo, f, Ontario-bred, 7f, 1:24.53, RIVER NORE, Time Saver, Silver Impulse, 7 started.

FUTURITY S. (G2), Belmont Park, Sept. 17, $294,000, 2yo, 7f, 1:24.05, PRIVATE VOW, Changing Weather, Dixiewink (GB), 6 started.

Gaily Gaily S., Gulfstream Park, Feb. 20, $60,000, 3yo, f, 1¹/₁₆mT, 1:39.31, CAPE HOPE, Dynamite Lass, Paddy's Daisy, 9 started.

GALLANT BLOOM H. (G2), Belmont Park, Oct. 9, $147,000, 3&up, f&m, 6½f, 1:16.35, UMPATEEDLE, Smokey Glacken, Travelator, 5 started.

Gallant Bob H., Philadelphia Park, Oct. 1, $100,000, 3yo, 6f, 1:10.29, JOEY CARSON, Pavo, Euro Code, 7 started.

Gallant Fox H., Aqueduct, Dec. 31, $83,100, 3&up, 1⅝m, 2:44.96, NAVESINK RIVER, India Halo (Arg), Chilly Rooster, 9 started.

GALLORETTE H. (G3), Pimlico Race Course, May 21, $100,000, 3&up, f&m, 1¹/₁₆mT, 1:44.29, FILM MAKER, Briviesca (GB), Humoristic, 9 started.

GAMELY BREEDERS' CUP H. (G1), Hollywood Park, May 30, $441,500, 3&up, f&m, 1⅛mT, 1:46.47, MEA DOMINA, Solar Echo, Amorama (Fr), 9 started.

Gander S. (R), Aqueduct, Nov. 30, $67,700, 3&up, New York-bred, 1m70y, 1:41.54, CARMINOOCH, Coined for Success, Naughty New Yorker, 10 started.

GARDEN CITY BREEDERS' CUP S. (G1), Belmont Park, Sept. 10, $260,000, 3yo, f, 1⅛mT, 1:45.62, LUAS LINE (IRE), Asi Siempre, My Typhoon (Ire), 4 started.

Garden City Futurity, Western Montana Fair and Races, Aug. 12, $4,550, 2yo, a5¼f, 1:07.40, BOUND TO BE FREE, Double Dedawn, Pingston Creek, 3 started.

GARDENIA H. (G3), Ellis Park, Aug. 20, $150,000, 3&up, f&m, 1m, 1:35.32, DREAM OF SUMMER, Halory Leigh, Tempus Fugit, 8 started.

Garland of Roses H., Aqueduct, Dec. 3, $84,300, 3&up, f&m, 6f, 1:11.13, LILAH, Secret Forest, Bank Audit, 10 started.

Gasparilla S., Tampa Bay Downs, Feb. 5, $60,000, 3yo, f, 7f, 1:24.36, COOL SPELL, Sherrie Belle, Gallant Secret, 13 started.

Gate Dancer S., Delaware Park, Aug. 20, $58,900, 3&up, 1¹/₁₆m, 1:43.93, SEPARATO, Blue Finally, Major Mecke, 6 started.

Gateway to Glory S., Fairplex Park, Sept. 22, $57,000, 2yo, 1¹/₁₆m, 1:43.64, IRISH BAR, Say Tomorrow, Eastwood, 5 started.

Gaviola S. (R), Belmont Park, Oct. 30, $69,950, 3yo, f, non-winners of a stakes on the turf, 1¹/₁₆mT, 1:44.35, JOINT ASPIRATION (GB), Half Heaven, Mountain Mambo, 10 started.

GAZELLE S. (G1), Belmont Park, Sept. 10, $245,000, 3yo, f, 1⅛m, 1:49.75, IN THE GOLD, Leave Me Alone, Yolanda B. Too, 5 started.

Geisha H. (R), Laurel Park, Dec. 10, $75,000, 3&up, f&m, Maryland-bred, 1⅛m, 1:51.49, PROMENADE GIRL, Take a Check, Dance Fee, 8 started.

Gene and Wanda June Johnson S., Turf Paradise, April 16, $23,900, 3&up, 4½fT, :50.14, GRIMM, Snowbound Writer, Ransome Road, 8 started.

Gene Francis and Associates H., Anthony Downs, July 23, $4,150, 3&up, 1¹/₁₆m, 1:51.87 (NTR), DEVIL'S BANDIT, Coffee Bubbles, Overprint, 8 started.

General Douglas MacArthur H. (R), Belmont Park, Sept. 9, $104,500, 3&up, New York-bred, 7f, 1:22.77, CLEVER ELECTRICIAN, Papua, Yankee Mon, 5 started.

GENERAL GEORGE H. (G2), Laurel Park, Feb. 21, $200,000, 3&up, 7f, 1:23.43, SARATOGA COUNTY, Don Six, Gators N Bears, 9 started.

Generous Portion S. (R), Del Mar, Aug. 31, $100,000, 2yo, f, California-bred, 6f, 1:11.46, SIERRA SWEETIE, Princess McLean, Bid of Genius, 7 started.

Gene's Big Sky S., Calder Race Course, July 24, $40,000, 3yo, f, 5fT, :56.57, MERTIE M, Wise and Precious, Arrepio, 8 started.

Genesee Valley Breeders' H. (R), Finger Lakes, Sept. 10, $50,000, 3&up, New York-bred, 1¹/₁₆m, 1:43.57, SINDBAD THE SAILOR, S. Cherry Legacy, Top Shoter, 9 started.

Genesee Valley Hunt Cup Timber S., Genesee Valley, Oct. 8, $22,000, 4&up, a3½mT, ALBERT'S CROSSING, Hall of Angels, Bubble Economy, 6 started.

Genesis S., Delta Downs, Jan. 22, $50,000, 3yo, f, 6½f, 1:23.78, GLORIOUS PROSPECT, Lil Cream Puff, Short Leg Sue, 6 started.

Gentilly H. (R), Fair Grounds, March 19, $100,000, 3yo, Louisiana-bred, a1mT, 1:39.64, PRINCE T., Encinal, Betnow, 10 started.

Gentilly S. (R), Fair Grounds at Louisiana Downs, Nov. 19, $50,000, 2yo, Louisiana-bred, a1mT, 1:38.22, DESERT WHEAT, Willtosucceed, Waystogeaux, 10 started.

GENUINE RISK H. (G2), Belmont Park, May 14, $150,000, 3&up, f&m, 6f, 1:09.65, BANK AUDIT, Sensibly Chic, Forest Music, 9 started.

Genuine Risk S., Zia Park, Oct. 30, $43,000, 3yo, f, 6f, 1:10, MATTIE CAKES, Merger Talk, Ellen's Foxy Girl, 9 started.

GEORGE C. HENDRIE H. (Can-G3), Woodbine, May 15, $167,464, 4&up, f&m, 6$^1/_2$f, 1:16.49, NASHINDA, One for Rose, Silver Bird, 7 started.

George Lewis Memorial S. (R), Thistledown, July 29, $45,000, 3&up, Ohio-bred, 1$^1/_8$m, 1:52.68, FOREST PICNIC, Ready for Roses, Bernard's Candy, 8 started.

George Maloof Futurity (R), The Downs at Albuquerque, Sept. 25, $66,561, 2yo, c&g, New Mexico-bred, 6f, 1:11.35, LATENITE BAND, Park Echols, Oh Three Jack, 11 started.

George Rosenberger Memorial S. (R), Delaware Park, Sept. 10, $102,100, 3&up, f&m, starters at Delaware Park in 2005, 1$^1/_{16}$mT, 1:40.92, COHERENT, Louve Royale (Ire), Margarita Maggie, 12 started.

George Royal S., Hastings Race Course, April 16, $41,297, 3&up, 6$^1/_2$f, 1:17.41, BLOWIN IN THE WIND, Lord Nelson, Metatron, 7 started.

George W. Barker H. (R), Finger Lakes, May 30, $50,000, 3&up, New York-bred, 6f, 1:09.49, TOP SHOTER, Gotham Limited, One N Three, 6 started.

Georgia Cup Hurdle S., Atlanta, April 16, $75,000, 4&up, a2mT, 3:40.80, PREEMPTIVE STRIKE, Understood, Najjm, 7 started.

Gerry Howard Inaugural H., Yavapai Downs, May 28, $20,000, 3&up, 6f, 1:09, KOMAX, No Toro, Snowbound Writer, 6 started.

Gerry Howard Memorial S., Turf Paradise, May 2, $23,700, 3&up, 6f, 1:10.03, VIGILANT SITE, Flying Supercon, Skeeman, 7 started.

Ghost and Goblins S., Delaware Park, Oct. 31, $57,020, 3yo, f, 6f, 1:09.96, TRICKLE OF GOLD, Madame Diva, Ebony Star, 4 started.

Gilded Time S., Monmouth Park, June 25, $55,000, 3yo, 5fT, :55.17 (NCR), CONCORDE'S EDGE, Silver Moose, Yes Yes Yes, 7 started.

Girl Powder H. (R), Monmouth Park, Aug. 21, $60,000, 3&up, f&m, New Jersey-bred, 1m, 1:38.86, I'MTOOGOODTOBETRUE, Lord Billy, Avery Hall, 7 started.

Glacial Princess S. (R), Beulah Park, Nov. 19, $40,000, 2yo, f, Ohio-bred, 1m, 1:40.87, TOMMEYESGOLD, Sybles Angel, Mercy, 8 started.

Gladstone Hurdle S., Far Hills, Oct. 22, $50,000, 3yo, a2$^1/_8$mT, 4:42.71, GINZ, Kilbride Rd, Haddix, 12 started.

Glendale H., Turf Paradise, Feb. 26, $50,000, 4&up, f&m, 1$^1/_{16}$mT, 1:44.63, SHEZSOSPIRITUAL, Muir Beach, V'ville Lady, 7 started.

Glenda Perez Memorial H., Blue Ribbon Downs, April 2, $10,250, 3&up, f&m, 5$^1/_2$f, 1:05.65, SHARI BANK, Hide N Watch, Rammers Best, 9 started.

GLENS FALLS H. (G3), Saratoga Race Course, Sept. 5, $109,200, 3&up, f&m, 1$^3/_8$mT, 2:14.51, HONEY RYDER, Film Maker, Banyu Dewi (Ger), 6 started.

Glorious Song S., Woodbine, Nov. 20, $123,167, 2yo, f, 7f, 1:23.86, TOP NOTCH LADY, Angel On Watch, Gumboots, 8 started.

Glowing Tribute S. (R), Aqueduct, Nov. 8, $68,250, 3&up, f&m, non-winners of an open stakes on the turf, 1$^1/_{16}$mT, 1:43.13, JOYFUL CHAOS, La Reina, Lady Bi Bi, 7 started.

Goddess Breeders' Cup S., Delta Downs, April 1, $95,750, 4&up, f&m, 1$^1/_{16}$m, 1:45.96, STORM'S DARLING, Miss Confusion, Legs O'Neal, 5 started.

Go for Gin S. (R), Aqueduct, Dec. 4, $64,950, 3yo, non-winners of an open stakes, 1m70y, 1:42.07, SPANISH MISSION, Gold and Roses, Mr Sword, 5 started.

GO FOR WAND H. (G1), Saratoga Race Course, July 31, $245,000, 3&up, f&m, 1$^1/_8$m, 1:50.30, ASHADO, Bending Strings, Andujar, 5 started.

Go for Wand S., Delaware Park, May 28, $100,300, 3yo, f, 1$^1/_{16}$m, 1:47.14, DANCE AWAY CAPOTE, Gotta Rush, Last Toots, 6 started.

Gold Breeders' Cup S., Assiniboia Downs, Sept. 25, $54,003, 3&up, 1$^1/_8$m, 1:53.20, ALBARINO, Indy Lead, Deputy Country, 8 started.

Golden Bear Breeders' Cup S., Golden Gate Fields, May 14, $90,000, 3yo, 6f, 1:07.32, LOST IN THE FOG, Wind Water, Olympic Miler, 3 started.

Golden Boy S., Assiniboia Downs, June 4, $32,064, 3yo, 6f, 1:11, PRIME TIME T. V., S C King, Cherokee Dancer, 6 started.

Golden Circle S., Prairie Meadows, April 23, $50,000, 3yo, 6f, 1:10.05, RAVING ROCKET, Semaphore Man, S C King, 7 started.

Golden Gate Derby, Golden Gate Fields, Jan. 15, $90,000, 3yo, 1$^1/_{16}$m, 1:43.69, BUZZARDS BAY, Sharp Writer, Dover Dere, 3 started.

Golden Gull Chris Brown Memorial S. (R), Charles Town Races, Sept. 17, $41,850, 2yo, f, nominated to the West Virginia Breeders' Classic, 4$^1/_2$f, :53.64, CROSS CREEK ROSIE, Aye Robbin, Time to Go, 10 started.

Golden Horseshoe Cup S. (R), Fort Erie, Aug. 14, $25,065, 3&up, f&m, starters at Fort Erie twice in 2005, 1$^1/_{16}$m, 1:46.93, ORIENTAL-SPRINGHOPE, Roman Romance, March Valley Girl, 5 started.

Golden Poppy Breeders' Cup S., Golden Gate Fields, May 30, $86,250, 3yo, f, 1mT, 1:37.33, CONVEYOR'S ANGEL, Island Escape, Thrilling Victory, 8 started.

GOLDEN ROD S. (G2), Churchill Downs, Nov. 26, $222,200, 2yo, f, 1$^1/_{16}$m, 1:47.26, FRENCH PARK, She Says It Best, Lady Danza, 8 started.

Golden Sylvia H., Mountaineer Race Track, June 21, $75,000, 3&up, f&m, 1m, 1:38.03, TEMPUS FUGIT, Indy Groove, Catboat, 7 started.

Goldfinch H. (R), Monmouth Park, July 4, $60,000, 3&up, f&m, New Jersey-bred, 6f, 1:09.70, EASTERN GALE, I'mtoogoodtobetrue, Dressed for Succes, 7 started.

Goldfinch S., Monmouth Park, Sept. 4, $56,815, 3&up, f&m, 1$^1/_8$mT, 1:50.05, BRIVIESCA (GB), Bright Abundance, Smart N Classy, 10 started.

Goldfinch S., Prairie Meadows, April 22, $53,000, 3yo, f, 6f, 1:11.70, SWEDE, Queansco, Tally Ho Dixie, 7 started.

Gold Nugget S. (R), Lone Star Park, June 17, $40,000, 3&up, Texas-bred non-winners of a stakes in 2005, 7$^1/_2$fT, 1:30.74, CHARMING SOCIALITE, Agrivating General, Goosey Moose, 8 started.

Gold Rush Futurity, Arapahoe Park, Aug. 28, $44,900, 2yo, 6f, 1:10.83, IMA HIGHWAY STAR, Might Be Hooked, Glidininthecash, 11 started.

GOODWOOD BREEDERS' CUP H. (G2), Oak Tree at Santa Anita, Oct. 1, $484,000, 3&up, 1$^1/_8$m, 1:48.68, ROCK HARD TEN, Roman Ruler, Choctaw Nation, 4 started.

Goshen Farm Punch Line S. (R), Colonial Downs, July 24, $58,200, 3&up, Virginia-bred and/or -sired, 5fT, :55.98, SATAN'S CODE, Silver Flower, Burning Rambo, 5 started.

GOTHAM S. (G3), Aqueduct, March 19, $150,000, 3yo, 1m, 1:35.61, SURVIVALIST, Galloping Grocer, Naughty New Yorker, 9 started.

Got Koko S. (R), Lone Star Park, April 30, $125,000, 3yo, f, nominated to the Texas Stallion Stakes, 1$^1/_{16}$m, 1:45.37, TIMBER JONES, Rockin' Kate, Tizzy Girl, 10 started.

Go to Will S., Calder Race Course, Oct. 22, $40,000, 3&up, 7f, 1:24, ANJIZ CRYPTO (ARG), Precocious Unity, Paradise Dancer, 8 started.

Gottstein Futurity, Emerald Downs, Oct. 15, $100,000, 2yo, 1$^1/_{16}$m, 1:42.80, SCHOOLIN YOU, Raise the Bluff, Coastal King, 10 started.

Governor's Buckeye Cup S. (R), Thistledown, Sept. 5, $75,000, 3&up, Ohio-bred, 1$^1/_4$m, 2:05.24, READY FOR ROSES, Bernard's Candy, Count On My Word, 10 started.

Governor's Cup H., Fairplex Park, Sept. 25, $58,800, 3&up, 6$^1/_2$f, 1:15.18 (NTR), JUNGLE PRINCE, Bonus Pack, King Robyn, 7 started.

Governor's Cup H., Wyoming Downs, July 9, $4,000, 3&up, 1m, 1:38.80, SHOTMO, Sarawat, Lookn East, 10 started.

Governor's Cup S., Remington Park, Nov. 26, $41,300, 3&up, 1m70y, 1:41.64, ZEE OH SIX, Outlaw Cowboy, Notable Okie, 10 started.

Governor's H., Ellis Park, Aug. 27, $50,000, 3&up, 1m, 1:36.87, NAKAYAMA KUN, Paging, Artemus Sunrise, 7 started.

Governor's H., Emerald Downs, July 31, $39,000, 3&up, 6$^1/_2$f, 1:15, NO GIVEAWAY, Diamond View, Random Memo, 4 started.

Governor's Lady H. (R), Hawthorne Race Course, April 30, $91,625, 4&up, f&m, Illinois-conceived and/or -foaled, 6f, 1:12.11, FIGHTING FEVER, Dutchie, Deno's Connection, 8 started.

Governor's S. (R), Indiana Downs, May 31, $40,000, 3yo, Indiana-bred, 7$^1/_2$fT, 1:32.46, COMMANDING HEIGHTS, Bruce On the Loose, War Tracer, 10 started.

Governor's S., Zia Park, Oct. 30, $56,700, 2yo, 6f, 1:10.20, PREMIER DANCE, Might Be Hooked, Down Home Boy, 7 started.

Governor's Speed H., Portland Meadows, March 19, $7,500, 4&up, 6f, 1:11.46, MY FRIEND DAVE, Crimson Design, Freedom Fair, 8 started.

Gowell S., Turfway Park, Dec. 26, $49,500, 2yo, f, 6f, AW, 1:13.60, SEEN DANCING, Mighty Martha, Unbridled Tale, 10 started.

Graceful Klinchit H., Marquis Downs, Aug. 26, $5,032, 3&up, f&m, 1$^1/_{16}$m, 1:48.35, CELTIC DANCE, All About Elsie, She's Nifty, 6 started.

Graduation S. (R), Del Mar, July 27, $125,000, 2yo, California-bred, 5$^1/_2$f, 1:04.23, COUGAR MTN LODGE, Blaze It, Irish Bar, 7 started.

Grand Canyon H., Churchill Downs, Nov. 20, $71,500, 2yo, 1$^1/_{16}$mT, 1:44.71, LEWIS MICHAEL, Smart Sherif, Wise River, 7 started.

Grand National Timber S., Grand National, April 23, $27,900, 5&up, a3$^1/_4$mT, 6:15.20, ROSBRIAN (IRE), Bug River, Lil Starvin Marvin, 7 started.

Grand Prairie Derby, Grand Prairie, Aug. 14, $8,925, 3yo, 1m, 1:42.40, COOL YER BOOTS, Forgotten Weekend, Bold Position, 6 started.

Grand Prairie Turf Challenge S., Lone Star Park, April 30, $75,000,

3yo, 1mT, 1:36.37, JAZZY GALLOP, Smooth Bid, Justa Red Bird, 8 started.

Grasmick H., Fonner Park, Feb. 19, $10,750, 3&up, 4f, :46, LUKFATA LOUIS, Blue Eyed Tiger, Nakayama Jazz, 8 started.

GRAVESEND H. (G3), Aqueduct, Dec. 18, $112,000, 3&up, 6f, 1:10.17, BANJO PICKER, Pioneer Empire, Saay Mi Name, 10 started.

Gray's Lake S. (R), Prairie Meadows, May 29, $58,330, 3yo, c&g, Iowa-bred, 6f, 1:09.81, WILL E SCAT, King Freddie, Five Rubies, 7 started.

Great Canadian H., Hastings Race Course, July 31, $61,275, 3&up, 1 1/16m, 1:42.97, QUIET CASH, Tobe Suave, Royal Place, 6 started.

Great White Way S. (R), Aqueduct, Nov. 6, $122,500, 2yo, c&g, New York-bred, 6f, 1:11.30, CLASSIC PACK, Surfing Ian, Trick Meeting, 6 started.

Green Carpet S. (R), River Downs, June 4, $45,000, 3yo, Ohio-bred, 1 1/16mT, 1:43.40, CAST NO SHADOW, Pyrite Springs, I'lltellyounolies, 11 started.

Green Flash H., Del Mar, Aug. 17, $76,300, 3&up, 5fT, :55.11, COURAGEOUS KING, Roi Charmant, Siren Lure, 8 started.

Green Oaks S., Delta Downs, March 18, $50,000, 3yo, f, 1m, 1:41.49, SEA SIREN, Gold Case Motel, Urge to Splurge, 9 started.

Gregson Foundation Sprint S., Bay Meadows Race Course, April 30, $75,850, 3yo, 6f, 1:10.06, WIND WATER, Family Guy, Elegant Ice, 5 started.

GREY BREEDERS' CUP S. (Can-G3), Woodbine, Oct. 10, $235,289, 2yo, 1 1/16m, 1:46.50, UNIFICATION, Badge of Truth, Seaside Retreat, 7 started.

Groomstick H., Calder Race Course, July 30, $75,000, 3&up, 6 1/2f, 1:17.04, NIGHTMARE AFFAIR, Lawbook, Swift Replica, 6 started.

Groovy S. (R), Sam Houston Race Park, Nov. 19, $50,000, 2yo, Texas-bred, 7f, 1:24.62, GUACAMOLE, Minstrel Runner, Gambling Wolfe, 12 started.

GTOBA Debutante S. (R), Calder Race Course, Dec. 24, $50,000, 2yo, f, progeny of GTOBA-nominated stallions, 1 1/16mT, 1:40.46, PROSPECT OF LOVE, Survicat, Hold Your Conduct, 9 started.

GTOBA Georgia Peaches S. (R), Calder Race Course, Aug. 6, $50,000, 3&up, f&m, progeny of sires with a donated season to the GTOBA stallion auction, 1mT, 1:36.33, CHANCEY LIGHT, Spicy Light, Wekiva Mist, 10 started.

GTOBA Juvenile Filly Turf Dash S. (R), Calder Race Course, July 23, $50,000, 2yo, f, progeny of GTOBA-nominated stallions, 5fT, :56.76, RUNNING LASS, Time Banshee, Southern Fortune, 12 started.

GTOBA Oaks (R), Calder Race Course, May 6, $50,000, 3yo, f, progeny of GTOBA-nominated stallions, 1 1/16mT, 1:44.71, WISE BRIANA, More Than Promised, Amoramente, 10 started.

Gulf Coast Breeders' Cup Classic S., Delta Downs, April 2, $125,000, 4&up, 1 1/16m, 1:46, ROAR ON TOUR, High Strike Zone, Mauk Four, 7 started.

GULFSTREAM PARK BREEDERS' CUP H. (G1), Gulfstream Park, March 6, $230,000, 3&up, 1 3/8mT, 2:11.44, PRINCE ARCH, Gigli (Brz), Mustanfar, 11 started.

GULFSTREAM PARK H. (G2), Gulfstream Park, March 5, $300,000, 3&up, 1 3/16m, 1:54.74, EDDINGTON, Pies Prospect, Zakocity, 8 started.

Gus Fonner S., Fonner Park, April 23, $100,000, 3&up, 1 1/16m, 1:45.60, STORMY IMPACT, Skip and Go, Robin Zee, 9 started.

Gus Grissom S. (R), Hoosier Park, Oct. 1, $40,000, 3&up, Indiana-bred and/or -sired, 1 1/16m, 1:44.60, PASS RUSH, Liepers Fork, Commanding Heights, 8 started.

H. A. Hindmarsh S. (R), Fort Erie, July 11, $29,524, 3&up, f&m, passed through the ring at a CTHS or CBS sale, 1 1/16m, 1:44.96, KISSED BY A PRINCE, Oblivious, Young and Restless, 3 started.

Hall of Fame H., Columbus Races, Aug. 6, $10,350, 3yo, 6f, 1:13.80, CHASIN THE WIND, Glorious Future, S C King, 6 started.

Hallowed Dreams S., Evangeline Downs, April 15, $50,000, 3yo, f, 5 1/2f, 1:05.09, INDIGO GIRL, Maid in China, Rubian Star, 7 started.

Hallowed Dreams S. (R), Louisiana Downs, July 17, $50,000, 3&up, f&m, Louisiana-bred, 6f, 1:11.28, WHERE IS MY DADDY, Glorious Quest, Dear Alicia, 8 started.

HAL'S HOPE H. (G3), Gulfstream Park, Jan. 8, $100,000, 3&up, 1 1/8m, 1:48.57, BADGE OF SILVER, Dynever, Contante (Arg), 12 started.

Halton S. (R), Woodbine, Sept. 4, $105,263, 3&up, Canadian-bred, 1 1/8mT, 1:49.06, MOBIL, Lenny the Lender, Sextet, 5 started.

Hancock County H., Mountaineer Race Track, May 17, $75,000, 3&up, f&m, 5f, :57.10, HOSTILITY, Revolutionary Act, Cobra Lady, 8 started.

Hank Mills Sr. Memorial H., Wyoming Downs, Aug. 20, $4,100, 3&up, f&m, 5f, :56.90, EXCLUSIVE GLORY, Cheese Puff, Never Been Caught, 7 started.

Hansel S., Turfway Park, March 26, $49,500, 3yo, 6f, 1:09.64, CALL THE LORD, Eyeforglory, Carnival Show, 8 started.

HANSHIN CUP H. (G3), Arlington Park, May 28, $100,000, 3&up, 1m, 1:34.60, LORD OF THE GAME, Gouldings Green, Nkosi Reigns, 8 started.

Happy New Year S., Calder Race Course, Jan. 1, $50,000, 3yo, f, 5fT, :56.43, LADY IN PINK, Running Bobcats, Glittering Tax, 9 started.

Harmony Lodge S., Calder Race Course, May 13, $40,000, 3yo, f, 6 1/2f, 1:19.20, MIDTOWN MISS, Mocita, Babaganush, 7 started.

Harold C. Ramser Sr. H., Oak Tree at Santa Anita, Oct. 16, $100,000, 3yo, f, 1mT, 1:35.14, LOUVAIN (IRE), Shining Energy, Thatswhatimean, 10 started.

Harold V. Goodman Memorial S. (R), Lone Star Park, July 9, $50,000, 3yo, Texas-bred, 6 1/2f, 1:16.21, LIGHTSNATCHER, P F Deco, War Bridle, 5 started.

Harper County H., Anthony Downs, July 17, $5,000, 3&up, a5f, 1:02.08, D D DOT COMM, Ama Missprint, Marlin's Ruler, 6 started.

Harper County H., Anthony Downs, July 17, $4,600, 3&up, a5f, 1:01.94, CLEVER RED, Triage, Grand Strand, 6 started.

Harrison E. Johnson Memorial H., Laurel Park, March 19, $50,000, 4&up, 1 1/8m, 1:52.03, LUSTY LATIN, Ouagadougou, Jim Thirds Bolero, 7 started.

Harry F. Brubaker H. (R), Del Mar, Aug. 18, $89,400, 3&up, non-winners of a stakes of $45,000 other than state-bred at one mile or over since March 1, 1 1/16mT, 1:41.39, RUNNING FREE, Terroplane (Fr), Kilkea Castle, 6 started.

Harry Henson S., Hollywood Park, April 22, $92,925, 3yo, 5 1/2fT, 1:01.87, JULIESUGARDADDY, Osidy, Dover Dere, 10 started.

Harry Jeffrey S., Assiniboia Downs, Aug. 28, $33,368, 3yo, 1 1/8m, 1:53.40, RAGGIDY ROWE, Arthurlooksgood, Resurgent, 8 started.

Harry W. Henson H., Sunland Park, April 2, $104,350, 3&up, f&m, 1m, 1:35.61, BLUE SONG, Resplendency, Homemaker, 4 started.

Harvest Festival Futurity, Fresno, Oct. 13, $53,300, 2yo, 6f, 1:08.53, WESTERN SOVEREIGN, Don Jaun Con, Tormento de Oro, 7 started.

Harvey Arneault Memorial Breeders' Cup H., Mountaineer Race Track, Aug. 14, $125,000, 3&up, 6f, 1:09.96, WILD TALE, Sterling Gold, Areyoutalkintome, 8 started.

HASKELL INVITATIONAL H. (G1), Monmouth Park, Aug. 7, $1,015,000, 3yo, 1 1/8m, 1:49.88, ROMAN RULER, Sun King, Park Avenue Ball, 7 started.

Hasta La Vista H., Turf Paradise, May 22, $50,000, 3&up, 1 7/8mT, 3:16.76, BALUSTRADE, Paladin Power, Geririg, 9 started.

Hastings Park H., Emerald Downs, May 8, $40,000, 3&up, f&m, 6f, 1:09, MARVA JEAN, Sariano, Ruby Dawn, 8 started.

Hastings Sophomore S., Hastings Race Course, Sept. 24, $45,766, 3yo, 1 1/16m, 1:44.62, NOTIS OTIS, Gold Bridle, Tommy's Topper, 7 started.

Hatoof S., Arlington Park, Aug. 27, $42,375, 3yo, f, 1 1/16mT, 1:43.57, DEAREST QUEEN, Special Grayce, Unbridled Danz, 8 started.

Hawkeyes H. (R), Prairie Meadows, June 18, $70,000, 3&up, f&m, Iowa-bred, 1 1/16m, 1:42.97, SCOOTER RAINS, Rubianos Image, Take Me Up, 10 started.

Hawkeyes H. (R), Prairie Meadows, June 25, $70,000, 3&up, f&m, Iowa-bred, 1 1/16m, 1:44.21, GAMBLERS PASSION, Traveler, Hollywood and Wine, 6 started.

HAWTHORNE DERBY (G3), Hawthorne Race Course, Oct. 15, $250,000, 3yo, 1 1/8mT, 1:47.51, GUN SALUTE, Cosmic Kris, Embossed (Ire), 5 started.

HAWTHORNE GOLD CUP S. (G2), Hawthorne Race Course, Sept. 24, $750,000, 3&up, 1 1/4m, 2:04.66, SUPER FROLIC, Lord of the Game, Desert Boom, 10 started.

HAWTHORNE H. (G3), Hollywood Park, May 7, $108,300, 3&up, f&m, 1 1/16m, 1:42.42, HOLLYWOOD STORY, Siphon Honey, House of Fortune, 7 started.

Hawthorne Oaks, Hawthorne Race Course, Oct. 15, $150,000, 3yo, f, 1 1/16mT, 1:40.54, ISLA COZZENE, You Dancing Devil, Baena, 10 started.

HBPA and WVRC S. (R), Charles Town Races, July 31, $41,300, 3&up, most starts at Charles Town in the last four starts, 1 1/8m, 1:53.05, DONALD'S PRIDE, Longfield Spud, Clays Awesome, 7 started.

HBPA Au Revoir H., Grants Pass, July 4, $3,923, 3&up, 6 1/2f, 1:19.40, SEVENEIGHTONE EAST, Harvey's Delight, Mon T. Hauls, 8 started.

HBPA City of Charles Town H., Charles Town Races, Oct. 7, $50,875, 3&up, 4 1/2f, :50.99, OUTCASHEM, Bishoftu, General Tommy, 4 started.

HBPA City of Ranson H., Charles Town Races, Oct. 7, $51,300, 3&up, f&m, 7f, 1:25.46, MISS HAMMA, Thermal Ablasion, Cedar Runs Case, 6 started.

HBPA Dash S. (R), Charles Town Races, July 31, $41,200, 3&up, most starts at Charles Town in the last four starts, 4 1/2f, :50.83, OUT-

CASHEM, Lothar, Not for Sam, 7 started.

HBPA Governor's Cup H., Charles Town Races, Oct. 9, $51,150, 3&up, 1 1/8m, 1:49.88 (NTR), CHEROKEE'S BOY, Donald's Pride, Miner Moss, 7 started.

HBPA H., Ellis Park, July 16, $75,000, 3&up, f&m, 1mT, 1:39.05, KAYLAN'S ROSE, Strike Me Lucky, May Gator, 11 started.

HBPA H., Grants Pass, June 5, $3,879, 3&up, 6 1/2f, 1:19.80, FULL GALLOP, D Devil, I Wood Be a Winner, 7 started.

HBPA Horsemen's S. (R), Charles Town Races, July 31, $41,500, 3&up, f&m, most starts at Charles Town in the last four starts, 4 1/2f, :52.52, MISS HAMMA, Katotrick, Lilias Trotter, 10 started.

HBPA West Virginia S. (R), Charles Town Races, July 31, $41,400, 3&up, f&m, most starts at Charles Town in the last four starts, 7f, 1:27.31, SARDIS, Lady Aflair, Ketch a Hello, 9 started.

Heavenly Cause S., Churchill Downs, July 9, $72,800, 3yo, f, 1m, 1:35.51, FLYING GLITTER, Culinary, She's That Cat, 7 started.

Heckofaralph S., Calder Race Course, June 11, $40,000, 3&up, 5f, :57.95, SCRUBS, Paradise Dancer, Love That Moon, 8 started.

Helen Anthony Memorial S., Yavapai Downs, Aug. 7, $15,000, 3yo, f, 6f, 1:11, REDS FLING, Missingrbueno, Kideeakey, 6 started.

Henry P. Mercer Memorial S. (R), Charles Town Races, Dec. 31, $40,800, 2yo, West Virginia-bred, 7f, 1:30.14, RHYTHMIC MOVES, Star Jubilee, Hold On Tight, 8 started.

Henry S. Clark S., Pimlico Race Course, May 7, $50,000, 3&up, 1mT, 1:34.25, GUNNING FOR, Package Store, Rubi Echo, 9 started.

Herald Gold Plate H., Stampede Park, June 12, $40,020, 3&up, 1 1/16m, 1:43.80, FIVE POINT STAR, Lord Samarai, Rindanica, 6 started.

HERECOMESTHEBRIDE S. (G3), Gulfstream Park, March 19, $100,000, 3yo, f, 1 1/8mT, 1:48.28, CAPE HOPE, Dynamite Lass, Dansetta Light, 8 started.

Hidden Light S. (R), Oak Tree at Santa Anita, Nov. 2, $67,500, 2yo, f, non-winners of a stakes at one mile or over, 1mT, 1:37.84, CROSS, Golden Silk, Balance, 8 started.

High Alexander H. (R), Hawthorne Race Course, Nov. 12, $105,950, 3&up, Illinois-conceived and/or -foaled, 1 1/16m, 1:44.96, WIGGINS, High Expectations, Beabasque, 8 started.

HIGHLANDER H. (Can-G3), Woodbine, June 26, $182,890, 3&up, 6fT, 1:08.03, SOARING FREE, Worldwind Romance, All Star Lover, 9 started.

HILL 'N' DALE CIGAR MILE H. (G1), Aqueduct, Nov. 26, $350,000, 3&up, 1m, 1:34.26, PURGE, Mass Media, Gygistar, 11 started.

Hill 'n' Dale S., Woodbine, June 25, $86,333, 3yo, f, 1 1/16m, 1:47.81, LEMON MAID, Warm Rain, Charming Ruckus, 4 started.

HILL PRINCE S. (G3), Belmont Park, June 10, $114,700, 3yo, 1 1/8mT, 1:49.25, REY DE CAFE, Prince Rahy, Classic Campaign, 9 started.

Hill Rise S., Santa Anita Park, Jan. 15, $83,550, 3yo, 1mT, 1:37.38, CHATTAHOOCHEE WAR, Eastern Sand, Littlebitofzip, 9 started.

Hillsborough H., Bay Meadows Race Course, Sept. 3, $72,200, 3&up, f&m, 1mT, 1:37.77, PENNY ANTE, Pickle (GB), Lucky Sabre, 9 started.

HILLSBOROUGH S. (G3), Tampa Bay Downs, March 19, $125,000, 4&up, f&m, a1 1/8mT, 1:52.59, RIZZI GIRL, Sister Star, Noisette, 9 started.

Hillsdale S. (R), Hoosier Park, Oct. 1, $40,000, 2yo, c&g, Indiana-bred, 5 1/2f, 1:05.29, FATHER ART, Randall, Call in Advance, 7 started.

Hilltop Breeders' Cup S., Pimlico Race Course, May 14, $75,000, 3yo, f, 1 1/16mT, 1:44.38, MY TYPHOON (IRE), Flashy Three (GB), Rutledge Ballado, 7 started.

Hilton Garden Inn Sprint S., Tampa Bay Downs, April 9, $83,900, 4&up, 6f, 1:10.15, NIGHTMARE AFFAIR, Scrubs, Hi Time Scott, 9 started.

H. J. Addison Jr. S. (R), Fort Erie, July 12, $32,876, 3&up, c&g, passed through the ring at a CTHS or CBS sale, 1 1/16m, 1:45.22, CHIVAS, Hunter Jay, Thank You Sir, 5 started.

Hockessin S., Delaware Park, Aug. 29, $57,900, 3&up, 6f, 1:09.91, SAAY MI NAME, Pisgah, Founding Chairman, 5 started.

Hoist Her Flag S., Canterbury Park, June 4, $40,000, 3&up, f&m, 6f, 1:10.76, SPARKLING SABIA, Offshore News, Two Bayou, 6 started.

Holiday Cheer S., Turfway Park, Dec. 31, $50,000, 3&up, 6f, AW, 1:11.03, SAINTLY LOOK, Sgt. Bert, Private Horde, 11 started.

Holiday Cheer S., Turfway Park, Jan. 1, $50,000, 4&up, 6f, 1:09.58, DEER LAKE, Private Horde, Saintly Look, 10 started.

Holiday Inaugural S., Turfway Park, Dec. 3, $43,500, 3&up, f&m, 6f, AW, 1:11.60, HOT STORM, Dewey's Trick, Mocha Queen, 9 started.

Holiday Inn Express S., Tampa Bay Downs, March 19, $75,000, 3&up, 5fT, :57.62, WHENTHEDOVEFLIES, Scattering Breezes, Relaunch Star, 10 started.

Holiday Turf H., Bay Meadows Race Course, Dec. 26, $75,000, 3&up, 1 1/16m (originally scheduled on the turf), 1:41.09, TRICKEYTREVOR, Adreamisborn, Desert Boom, 5 started.

Hollie Hughes H. (R), Aqueduct, Feb. 20, $80,975, 3&up, New York-bred, 6f, 1:09.76, PAPUA, Show Boot, Citizenship, 6 started.

Holly S., Meadowlands, Oct. 28, $50,000, 2yo, f, 6f, 1:09.52, CELESTIAL LEGEND, Wild and Proud, Primary Motive, 7 started.

HOLLYWOOD BREEDERS' CUP OAKS (G2), Hollywood Park, June 12, $177,500, 3yo, f, 1 1/16m, 1:42.80, BROOKE'S HALO, Memorette, Cee's Irish, 8 started.

HOLLYWOOD FUTURITY (G1), Hollywood Park, Dec. 17, $407,250, 2yo, 1 1/16m, 1:42.02, BROTHER DEREK, Your Tent Or Mine, Bob and John, 8 started.

HOLLYWOOD GOLD CUP H. (G1), Hollywood Park, July 9, $750,000, 3&up, 1 1/4m, 1:59.63, LAVA MAN, Borrego, Congrats, 9 started.

HOLLYWOOD JUVENILE CHAMPIONSHIP S. (G3), Hollywood Park, July 16, $104,500, 2yo, 6f, 1:09.55, WHAT A SONG, Bashert, Stevie Wonderboy, 5 started.

HOLLYWOOD PREVUE S. (G3), Hollywood Park, Nov. 19, $100,000, 2yo, 7f, 1:21.12, YOUR TENT OR MINE, Da Stoops, The Pharaoh, 5 started.

HOLLYWOOD STARLET S. (G1), Hollywood Park, Dec. 18, $456,000, 2yo, f, 1 1/16m, 1:43.89, DIPLOMAT LADY, Balance, Sabatini, 11 started.

Hollywood Wildcat Breeders' Cup H., Calder Race Course, April 30, $150,000, 3&up, f&m, 1 1/16mT, 1:40.73, WEND, Minge Cove, Hymn of Love (Ire), 12 started.

HOLY BULL S. (G3), Gulfstream Park, Feb. 5, $150,000, 3yo, 1 1/8m, 1:50.14, CLOSING ARGUMENT, Kansas City Boy, High Fly, 8 started.

Home of the Free S. (R), Belmont Park, May 20, $59,500, 3yo, non-winners of a stakes on the turf, 1 1/16mT, 1:43.33, TINSELTOWN, Touched by Madness, Prince Rahy, 5 started.

Honest Pleasure S., Arlington Park, July 31, $46,950, 2yo, 5 1/2f, 1:04.46, SORCEROR'S STONE, Cole Express, M Lee, 6 started.

Honey Bee S., Meadowlands, Nov. 5, $60,000, 3&up, f&m, 1 1/16m, 1:44.09, SCHEDULE (GB), Defrere's Venture, Ask Queenie, 8 started.

Honeybee S., Oaklawn Park, March 20, $75,000, 3yo, f, 1 1/16m, 1:45.16, ROUND POND, Rugula, Southern, 6 started.

HONEY FOX H. (G3), Gulfstream Park, March 13, $100,000, 3&up, f&m, 1 1/16mT, 1:38.41, SAND SPRINGS, Potra Fabulous (Arg), Shaconage, 11 started.

Honey Jay S. (R), Thistledown, Sept. 9, $40,000, 3&up, Ohio-bred, 6f, 1:09.70, I CANT REFUSE, Ben's Reflection, Pyrite Springs, 5 started.

HONEYMOON BREEDERS' CUP H. (G2), Hollywood Park, June 5, $163,125, 3yo, f, 1 1/8mT, 1:46.84, THREE DEGREES (IRE), Thatswhatimean, Isla Cozzene, 13 started.

Honeymoon S., Louisiana Downs, May 7, $50,000, 3&up, f&m, 1mT, 1:35.15, PAZ CIUDADANA (CHI), Yoursmineours, Chitchat Chitchat, 9 started.

Hong Kong Jockey Club Sprint H., Hastings Race Course, May 7, $35,676, 3&up, 6 1/2f, 1:16.34, LORD NELSON, Commodore Craig, Five Point Star, 6 started.

HONORABLE MISS H. (G2), Saratoga Race Course, Aug. 5, $150,000, 3&up, f&m, 6f, 1:10.06, FOREST MUSIC, Ebony Breeze, Bank Audit, 8 started.

Honorary Mile H., Wyoming Downs, Aug. 21, $4,525, 3&up, 1m, 1:37.47, TIZWAR, Air Forbes Too, Sarawat, 5 started.

Honor the Hero S., Turf Paradise, Feb. 11, $24,000, 4&up, 6 1/2f, 1:17.27, COCOA LATTE, Fonz's, His Way, 6 started.

Honor the Hero Turf Express S., Canterbury Park, May 30, $40,000, 3&up, 5fT, :56.01 (NCR), ROCKHURST, Rapid Raj, Marley's Revenge, 9 started.

Hoofprint on My Heart H., Stampede Park, May 28, $39,870, 3yo, 1m, 1:37.40, DAKOTA DUKE, Forever Rascal, Blackjack Willy, 5 started.

Hoosier Silver Cup S. (R), Hoosier Park, Oct. 16, $40,000, 2yo, f, nominated through the ITOBA auction sale, 6f, 1:15.67, NORTHERN LADY, Detailed, All Night Affair, 5 started.

Hoosier Silver Cup S. (R), Hoosier Park, Oct. 16, $40,000, 2yo, c&g, nominated through the ITOBA auction sale, 6f, 1:15.93, EWELL, Medieval Dreams, My Guy Ely, 5 started.

Hooting Star S., Calder Race Course, Oct. 8, $40,000, 3&up, 5f, :58.12, SCRUBS, Gregson, Bow Out, 7 started.

Hoover S., Laurel Park, April 9, $50,000, 3&up, 6f, 1:09.99, TAKE ACHANCE ON ME, Dale's Prospect, Excellent Band, 8 started.

Hoover S. (R), River Downs, July 17, $40,000, 2yo, Ohio-bred, 5 1/2f, 1:04.60, ACTS LIKE A KING, M and Em, Too Much Bling, 14 started.

HOPEFUL S. (G1), Saratoga Race Course, Aug. 27, $245,000, 2yo, 7f, 1:23.25, FIRST SAMURAI, Henny Hughes, Too Much Bling, 5 started.

Horatius S., Laurel Park, March 5, $50,000, 3yo, 6f, 1:11.91, DIAMOND WILDCAT, Distinctive Trick, Monster Chaser, 8 started.

Horizon S. (R), River Downs, July 24, $40,000, 3yo, Ohio-bred, 1$^{1}/_{16}$mT, 1:43, MISTY TAB, Brooks Blach, Hero Act, 10 started.

Hot Springs S., Oaklawn Park, March 26, $49,000, 4&up, 6f, 1:10.23, THAT TAT, Level Playingfield, Engineered, 5 started.

House Party S., Aqueduct, Nov. 13, $65,950, 4&up, f&m, 6f, 1:10.47, BANK AUDIT, Baldomera, Lilah, 5 started.

Houston Chronicle S., Sam Houston Race Park, Oct. 29, $40,000, 3&up, f&m, 1$^{1}/_{16}$mT, 1:43.56, ROSE HUNTER, Pad the Wallet, Voz De Colegiala (Chi), 9 started.

Howard B. Noonan S. (R), Beulah Park, March 26, $40,000, 3yo, Ohio-bred, 6f, 1:10.80, MARCH DANCER, Dontshootthemsngr, Hurricane Rib, 11 started.

HRA Marathon S., Grand Prairie, July 10, $4,466, 3&up, 1m, 1:41.80, CHIEF JOSEPH, Lafleur, Gomka, 7 started.

H. Steward Mitchell S., Laurel Park, Nov. 26, $53,500, 2yo, 7f, 1:26.45, NINE BEST, Dancehall Fever, Creve Coeur, 8 started.

Hudson H. (R), Belmont Park, Oct. 22, $125,000, 3&up, New York-bred, 6f, 1:10.35, FRIENDLY ISLAND, Introspect, Papua, 8 started.

Hula Chief S., Hawthorne Race Course, Feb. 26, $42,000, 4&up, 6f, 1:11.10, SILVER BID, Stormy Impact, Silver Zipper, 5 started.

Humphrey S. Finney S. (R), Pimlico Race Course, Aug. 13, $50,000, 3yo, Maryland-bred, 1$^{1}/_{8}$mT, 1:56.66, LEARNING, Easy Red, Seize, 6 started.

Huntington S., Aqueduct, Nov. 13, $81,350, 2yo, 6f, 1:11.03, SAINT DAIMON, Urban Guy, Justawalkinthepark, 6 started.

HURRICANE BERTIE H. (G3), Gulfstream Park, March 20, $100,000, 3&up, f&m, 6$^{1}/_{2}$f, 1:15.45, LILAH, Forty Moves, Molto Vita, 6 started.

HUTCHESON S. (G2), Gulfstream Park, Feb. 5, $150,000, 3yo, 7$^{1}/_{2}$f, 1:29.90, PROUD ACCOLADE, Park Avenue Ball, Vicarage, 6 started.

Icecapade S., Monmouth Park, Sept. 5, $72,750, 3&up, 6f, 1:09.31, FOREST PARK, Spooky Mulder, Abbondanza, 4 started.

I. C. Light Memorial Day H., Mountaineer Race Track, May 30, $75,000, 3&up, 1mT, 1:37.84, PACKAGE STORE, Gunning For, One Nice Cat, 10 started.

Idaho Cup Claiming S., Les Bois Park, Aug. 27, $5,000, 3&up, 7f, 1:26.30, SARAWAT, Fall for Me, Regal Dr. Stuart, 6 started.

Idaho Cup Classic S. (R), Les Bois Park, Aug. 27, $20,000, 4&up, c&g, Idaho-bred, 1m, 1:39.10, SILENT SNOW, Shotmo, Crooked Key, 7 started.

Idaho Cup Derby (R), Les Bois Park, Aug. 27, $20,000, 3yo, c&g, Idaho-bred, 1m, 1:41.30, POORBOYS PLAYBOY, Kingsgeneralissimo, Valid Sex Appeal, 4 started.

Idaho Cup Distaff Derby (R), Les Bois Park, Aug. 27, $20,000, 3yo, f&m, Idaho-bred, 1m, 1:42.40, GIG'S STAR, Tiffany Window, Conquestindadesert, 6 started.

Idaho Cup Distaff Maturity (R), Les Bois Park, Aug. 27, $20,000, 4&up, Idaho-bred, 1m, 1:40.10, PARADISE WILD, Ruready, Opal's Song, 6 started.

Idaho Cup Juvenile S. (R), Les Bois Park, Aug. 27, $20,000, 2yo, Idaho-bred, 5f, 1:00.30, DANGEROUSLY DUNN, Dancing Buckaroo, Magical Slew, 6 started.

Idaho Cup Juvenile S. (R), Les Bois Park, Aug. 27, $20,000, 2yo, Idaho-bred, 5f, 1:02, COW TRADER, Blackjack Robber, Ruffinas Orphan, 5 started.

Idaho Cup Sprint S. (R), Les Bois Park, Aug. 27, $7,500, 3&up, Idaho-bred, 5f, :59.20, BOBBIBLUE BAYOU, Dun Ringill, Quiet Syns, 5 started.

Illini Princess H. (R), Hawthorne Race Course, Nov. 12, $84,450, 3&up, f&m, Illinois-conceived and/or-foaled, 1$^{1}/_{16}$m, 1:45.02, MEADOW BRIDE, Jaguar City, Ms. Lydonia, 5 started.

ILLINOIS DERBY (G2), Hawthorne Race Course, April 9, $500,000, 3yo, 1$^{1}/_{8}$m, 1:49.62, GREELEY'S GALAXY, Monarch Lane, Magna Graduate, 8 started.

Illinois Thoroughbred Breeders' and Owners' Foundation Sales Graduate S. (R), Hawthorne Race Course, April 10, $42,450, 3yo, f, consigned to the 2004 Illinois Thoroughbred Breeders' and Owners' Foundation two-year-old in training sale, 6$^{1}/_{2}$f, 1:19.15, KICKAPOO PRINCESS, Bewitching Miss, Miss Classified, 10 started.

Illinois Thoroughbred Breeders' and Owners' Foundation Sales Graduate S. (R), Hawthorne Race Course, April 10, $41,900, 3yo, c&g, consigned to the 2004 Illinois Thoroughbred Breeders' and Owners' Foundation two-year-old in training sale, 6$^{1}/_{2}$f, 1:20.86, LUKE'S WARTORTLE, Morning Gold, Shanty Hill Road, 8 started.

Imperial Cup Hurdle S., Aiken, March 26, $35,000, 4&up, a2$^{1}/_{8}$mT, 4:42.20, BARZULU (NZ), Shady Valley, Unalienable Right, 7 started.

Impressive Style S. (R), Hollywood Park, July 1, $54,100, 3yo, f, non-winners of a stakes, 5$^{1}/_{2}$fT, 1:02.46, BINASUCCESS, Haka Girl, Spring of Pearls (Ire), 6 started.

I'm Smokin S. (R), Del Mar, Sept. 5, $100,000, 2yo, California-bred, 6f, 1:08.78, BRO LO, Moonlite Romance, Brother Derek, 5 started.

Inaugural H., Evangeline Downs, April 7, $50,000, 3yo, 6f, 1:10.30, J. D.'S BLUE BAYOU, Smilin Fine, All Wired Up, 7 started.

Inaugural H., Grants Pass, May 21, $3,205, 3&up, 5f, 1:00, JEHOSAPHAT, West Saratoga, Sizzlin Hot Summer, 6 started.

Inaugural H., Les Bois Park, Aug. 26, $5,000, 3&up, 7f, 1:25.30, FIND MY HALTER, Twentyonthenose, Mountain Mustang, 7 started.

Inaugural H., North Dakota Horse Park, Aug. 5, $9,000, 3&up, 6f, 1:12.60, MADDIES BLUES, Robin Zee, Exciting Trick, 5 started.

Inaugural H., Portland Meadows, Oct. 22, $10,800, 3&up, 6f, 1:11.65, EASTERN ACCENT, Tamper, My Friend Dave, 5 started.

Inaugural H., SunRay Park, July 2, $30,000, 3&up, 6$^{1}/_{2}$f, 1:17.60, ISLANDS SUCESS, Ceetart, Stone Canyon, 7 started.

Inaugural H., Wyoming Downs, June 25, $4,375, 3&up, 6f, 1:09.86, BOSTWICK, Sherroyal, Shotmo, 10 started.

Inaugural S., Arapahoe Park, June 11, $27,075, 3yo, 6f, 1:11.50, CAJUN PEPPER, Bueno Indio, Tanya's Beau, 7 started.

Inaugural S., Columbus Races, July 29, $10,350, 3yo, f, 6f, 1:15.60, PEPPER LANG, Justahamsandwich, Piano Girl, 6 started.

Inaugural S., Evangeline Downs, Dec. 1, $75,000, 3&up, 5f, :57.58, ALL WIRED UP, Believe Im Special, Zarb's Luck, 9 started.

Inaugural S., Tampa Bay Downs, Dec. 10, $60,000, 2yo, 6f, 1:11.91, R LOYAL MAN, Forestry Prince, Neverbeendancin', 12 started.

Incredible Revenge S., Monmouth Park, Aug. 27, $55,000, 3&up, f&m, 5f (originally scheduled on the turf), :57.82, GILDED GOLD, Clay's Rocket, Pretty Imposing, 8 started.

Independence Day H., Emerald Downs, July 3, $39,000, 3&up, 1$^{1}/_{16}$m, 1:41, POKER BRAD, Flamethrowintexan, Mr. Makah, 4 started.

Independence Day S., Mountaineer Race Track, July 4, $75,000, 3&up, 1mT, 1:33.96, GIN AND SIN, Package Store, Doctorate (GB), 5 started.

Independence H., Louisiana Downs, July 4, $50,770, 3&up, 1$^{1}/_{16}$mT, 1:43.73, WAUPACA, Gigawatt, Spruce's Prince, 9 started.

INDIANA BREEDERS' CUP OAKS (G3), Hoosier Park, Sept. 30, $405,100, 3yo, f, 1$^{1}/_{16}$m, 1:44.10, FLYING GLITTER, Eyes On Eddy, Miss Matched, 6 started.

INDIANA DERBY (G2), Hoosier Park, Oct. 1, $511,300, 3yo, 1$^{1}/_{16}$m, 1:42.71, DON'T GET MAD, Scrappy T, Thor's Echo, 9 started.

Indiana Stallion S. (R), Hoosier Park, Nov. 25, $40,000, 2yo, Indiana-bred and -sired, 6f, 1:15.38, LOVE THIS TRICK, Play Smart, Page's Buddy, 9 started.

Indian Maid Breeders' Cup H., Hawthorne Race Course, Sept. 24, $171,500, 3&up, f&m, 1$^{1}/_{16}$mT, 1:48.79, NOISETTE, Sister Swank, Samantha B., 6 started.

INGLEWOOD H. (G3), Hollywood Park, April 30, $107,200, 3&up, 1$^{1}/_{16}$mT, 1:40.67, KING OF HAPPINESS, Red Fort (Ire), Just Wonder (GB), 6 started.

Ingrid Knotts H. (R), Arapahoe Park, July 3, $29,700, 3&up, f&m, Colorado-bred, 6f, 1:10.43, LADYSGOTTHELOOKS, Kranky Karol, Bar Bailey, 7 started.

In Reality S. (R), Calder Race Course, Oct. 15, $400,000, 2yo, progeny of stallions standing in Florida, 1$^{1}/_{16}$m, 1:47.45, BLAZING RATE, In Summation, Lucky Chief, 11 started.

Instant Racing Breeders' Cup S., Oaklawn Park, April 16, $98,000, 3yo, f, 1$^{1}/_{16}$m, 1:45.87, DIBOLL DILLY, Maise and Blue, Kota, 6 started.

Interborough H., Aqueduct, Jan. 1, $81,225, 3&up, f&m, 6f, 1:10.55, BANK AUDIT, Mariakel, Belong to Sea, 7 started.

International Gold Cup Timber S., Great Meadows, Oct. 15, $30,800, 4&up, a3$^{1}/_{2}$mT, 7:32, FIELDS OF OMAGH, Lord Kenneth, Fast Steppin Man, 10 started.

Iowa Breeders' Derby (R), Prairie Meadows, Aug. 27, $73,900, 3yo, c&g, Iowa-bred, 1$^{1}/_{16}$m, 1:45.20, COUNT ROCK, King Freddie, Mingo Mohawk, 8 started.

Iowa Breeders' Oaks (R), Prairie Meadows, Aug. 27, $79,630, 3yo, f, Iowa-bred, 1m70y, 1:43.48, QUEANSCO, Camela Carson, Cheer Girl, 8 started.

Iowa Cradle S. (R), Prairie Meadows, Aug. 27, $74,700, 2yo, c&g, Iowa-bred, 6f, 1:10.85, TIMETOBOOK, Casper Who, Hesluckytoo, 10 started.

Iowa Derby, Prairie Meadows, July 1, $250,000, 3yo, 1$^{1}/_{16}$m, 1:43.14, SHAMOAN (IRE), Apache Point, Thor's Echo, 7 started.

Iowa Distaff Breeders' Cup S., Prairie Meadows, July 2, $125,000, 3&up, f&m, 1$^{1}/_{16}$m, 1:43.76, PLATINUM BALLET, Josh's Madelyn, Ide Be a Lady, 7 started.

IOWA OAKS (G3), Prairie Meadows, July 1, $122,500, 3yo, f, 1$^{1}/_{16}$m,

1:43.60, WHIMSY, Cee's Irish, Mary Alex, 5 started.

Iowa Sorority S. (R), Prairie Meadows, Aug. 27, $75,800, 2yo, f, Iowa-bred, 6f, 1:12.09, LOUIS LEGGS, Thekatcamehome, L D's Shes Special, 11 started.

Iowa Sprint H., Prairie Meadows, July 4, $122,500, 3&up, 6f, 1:09.10, COACH JIMI LEE, Premium Saltine, Super Fuse, 5 started.

Iowa Stallion Futurity (R), Prairie Meadows, Aug. 13, $88,397, 2yo, progeny of eligible Iowa stallions, 6f, 1:11.18, JAZZY OKIE, Concert King, Hesluckytoo, 10 started.

Iowa Stallion S. (R), Prairie Meadows, July 23, $81,305, 3yo, progeny of stallions standing in Iowa, 1m70y, 1:42.63, MINGO MOHAWK, Okie Dozer, One Fine Affair, 7 started.

Iowa State Fair S., Prairie Meadows, Aug. 20, $40,000, 3&up, f&m, 6f, 1:09.63, CANDYBEDANDY, Swede, Silver Crown, 8 started.

Irish Day H., Emerald Downs, June 12, $40,000, 3yo, f, 1m, 1:36.60, QUEENLEDO, Gins Majesty, Brite Luci, 6 started.

Irish O'Brien S. (R), Santa Anita Park, March 17, $140,625, 4&up, f&m, California-bred, a6 1/2fT, 1:13.08, SCROFA, Blind Ambition, Our Mango, 11 started.

Irish Sonnet S., Delaware Park, Sept. 24, $58,500, 2yo, f, 1m, 1:41.69, LOVE LOCKET, Gorgeous Mistress, Missy's Advantage, 6 started.

Iroquois H. (R), Belmont Park, Oct. 22, $125,000, 3&up, f&m, New York-bred, 7f, 1:25.40, SEEKING THE ANTE, Travelator, Star Celebrity, 12 started.

Iroquois H. (R), Philadelphia Park, July 23, $50,000, 3&up, Pennsylvania-bred, 1 1/16m, 1:46.22, NITTANY EXPRESS, Yo, Valleyman, 5 started.

Iroquois Hurdle S., Percy Warner, May 14, $160,000, 4&up, a3mT, 5:47.40, SUR LA TETE, McDynamo, Seafaring Man, 8 started.

IROQUOIS S. (G3), Churchill Downs, Nov. 5, $116,700, 2yo, 1m, 1:36.38, CATCOMINATCHA, High Cotton, Mondavi, 13 started.

Irving Distaff S., Lone Star Park, April 16, $75,000, 3&up, f&m, 7 1/2fT, 1:31.08, QUEENA CORRINA, Janeian (NZ), My Misty Princess, 10 started.

Isaac Murphy H. (R), Arlington Park, June 25, $85,700, 3&up, f&m, Illinois-conceived and/or -foaled, 6f, 1:10.82, JAGUAR CITY, Miss Outrageous, Piano Tunner, 10 started.

Isadorable S. (R), Suffolk Downs, May 28, $40,000, 3&up, f&m, Massachusetts-bred, 6f, 1:12.42, ASK QUEENIE, Glory Be Good, African Princess, 7 started.

Isi Newborn Memorial S., Thistledown, July 2, $40,000, 3&up, 6f, 1:10.24, BERNIE BLUE, Cayenne Red, Majestic Dinner, 10 started.

Island Whirl H., Louisiana Downs, July 30, $50,000, 3&up, 6f, 1:09.47, GRAND BANK, Rodeo's Castle, That Tat, 6 started.

ITBOA Sales Futurity (R), Prairie Meadows, July 16, $50,737, 2yo, graduates of the 2004 ITBOA two-year-olds-in-training sale, 5 1/2f, 1:04.84, THE K B KID, Concert King, Sharkille O'Neal, 10 started.

Jack Betta Be Rite H. (R), Finger Lakes, Sept. 10, $50,000, 3&up, f&m, New York-bred, 1 1/16m, 1:44.19, RUBY'S ROCKET, New York Gold, Buck Mountain, 6 started.

Jack Diamond Futurity (R), Hastings Race Course, Oct. 2, $91,857, 2yo, c&g, Canadian-bred, 6 1/2f, 1:19.42, FASTRAC KAT, Lukin Awesome, Power Chip, 10 started.

Jack Dudley Sprint H. (R), Calder Race Course, Nov. 12, $150,000, 3&up, Florida-bred, 6f, 1:09.40, WEIGELIA, Mister Fotis, Qureall, 10 started.

Jack Hammer Memorial H., Blue Ribbon Downs, April 30, $9,625, 3&up, 5f, :57.95, SOONER PRIDE, Shadow's Image, Speakster, 7 started.

Jack Hardy S., Assiniboia Downs, Aug. 1, $32,680, 3yo, f, 1m, 1:42.20, ALY'S FLYER, Wautega Light, Hold On Heather, 6 started.

Jack Price Juvenile S. (R), Calder Race Course, Nov. 12, $150,000, 2yo, Florida-bred, 7f, 1:23.03, ELECTRIFY, Big Lover, Cab, 6 started.

Jack Shoemaker Memorial S., Rillito Park, Feb. 26, $3,667, 3&up, f&m, 5 1/2f, 1:05.60, GREETING CARD, Winatbingo, Major Brat Angela, 8 started.

Jacques Cartier S., Woodbine, April 16, $140,475, 4&up, 6f, 1:09.67, MINISTERS WILD CAT, Judiths Wild Rush, Wando, 9 started.

JAIPUR S. (G3), Belmont Park, May 29, $111,600, 3&up, 7fT, 1:20.71, ECCLESIASTIC, Old Forester, Gulch Approval, 7 started.

JAMAICA H. (G3), Belmont Park, Oct. 8, $270,000, 3yo, 1 1/8m (originally scheduled as a Grade 2 on the turf), 1:49.28, WATCHMON, Crown Point, Woodlander, 3 started.

James C. Ellis Juvenile S., Ellis Park, Aug. 20, $75,000, 2yo, 7f, 1:23.59, RED RAYMOND, Catcominatcha, Deputy G, 6 started.

James Leakos Sophomore S. (R), Marquis Downs, Aug. 5, $5,356, 3yo, f, Saskatchewan-bred, 1m, 1:41.35, ARCTIC TALIYAH, Sheen Sky, Bold Invader, 5 started.

Jammed Lovely S. (R), Woodbine, Nov. 13, $142,238, 3yo, f, Ontario-bred, 7f, 1:23.49, CHARMING RUCKUS, Simply Lovely, River Nore, 10 started.

Jane Driggers Debutante S. (R), Portland Meadows, Dec. 31, $10,000, 2yo, f, Oregon-bred, 6f, 1:14.15, CASCADES EXPRESS, Truly Jest, Top Diamond Dancer, 7 started.

Janet Wineberg S. (R), Portland Meadows, Nov. 19, $25,500, 2yo, f, Oregon-bred, 6f, 1:14.55, CASCADES EXPRESS, Delecana, Fettles Klan, 10 started.

Japan Racing Association S., Laurel Park, Oct. 22, $60,000, 3yo, 1 1/16mT, 1:44.28, SPRING HOUSE, Ramazutti, Sly One, 14 started.

J. Archie Sebastien Memorial S. (R), Evangeline Downs, July 30, $50,000, 4&up, f&m, Louisiana-bred, 1 1/16m, 1:48.65, K BROWN, Agree to Disagree, Legs O'Neal, 9 started.

JEFFERSON CUP S. (G3), Churchill Downs, June 18, $220,400, 3yo, 1 1/8mT, 1:48.75, RUSH BAY, Big Prairie, Gun Salute, 7 started.

JEH Stallion Station S. (R), Lone Star Park, May 21, $50,000, 3&up, f&m, Texas-bred, 6 1/2f, 1:15.67, RHOME MAGIC, Hay Madison, Rockin' Kate, 11 started.

Jena Jena S. (R), Belmont Park, July 22, $61,600, 3yo, f, New York-bred non-winners of a stakes in 2005, 1 1/16mT, 1:41.65, HIS BEAUTY, Cayuga's Waters, Half Heaven, 8 started.

Jennings H. (R), Laurel Park, Dec. 3, $75,000, 3&up, Maryland-bred, 1 1/8m, 1:52.49, CHEROKEE'S BOY, George's Gain, Water Cannon, 6 started.

JENNY WILEY S. (G3), Keeneland Race Course, April 17, $200,000, 4&up, f&m, 1 1/16mT, 1:41.89, INTERCONTINENTAL (GB), Delta Princess, Sister Swank, 7 started.

JEROME H. (G2), Belmont Park, Sept. 11, $150,000, 3yo, 1m, 1:34.24, SILVER TRAIN, High Fly, Naughty New Yorker, 6 started.

Jerry & Eileen Towslee Memorial H., Tillamook County Fair, Aug. 13, $3,637, 3&up, a5f, 1:03, MOUNTAIN MUSTANG, Larron, Seven-eightone East, 5 started.

Jersey Breeders' H. (R), Monmouth Park, Sept. 17, $100,000, 3&up, New Jersey-bred, 1 1/16m, 1:43.72, CARROTS ONLY, Upturn, Cuba, 8 started.

Jersey Derby, Monmouth Park, May 30, $100,000, 3yo, 1 1/16mT, 1:43.54, TOUCHED BY MADNESS, Spring House, Hole in the Head, 10 started.

Jersey Girl H. (R), Monmouth Park, Sept. 17, $100,000, 3&up, f&m, New Jersey-bred, 1m70y, 1:42.62, PICNIC THEME, Final Assault, I'mtoogoodtobetrue, 8 started.

Jersey Lilly S., Sam Houston Race Park, April 9, $50,000, 4&up, f&m, 1 1/16mT, 1:45.45, PEACE SYMBOL, Bonnie J., Dancing Liebling, 8 started.

JERSEY SHORE BREEDERS' CUP S. (G3), Monmouth Park, July 4, $130,000, 3yo, 6f, 1:08.30, JOEY P., Celtic Innis, Razor, 5 started.

Jersey Village S. (R), Sam Houston Race Park, Feb. 5, $40,000, 4&up, Texas-bred, 1 1/16mT, 1:49.17, TWILIGHT VISION, Oncearoundtwice, Goosey Moose, 10 started.

Jessamine County S., Keeneland Race Course, Oct. 27, $112,000, 2yo, f, 1 1/16mT, 1:45.57, J'RAY, Beau Dare, Dyna's Destiny, 8 started.

Jim Bowie S., Retama Park, Aug. 27, $40,000, 3yo, 7 1/2fT, 1:29.27, WHISKEY FOR ME, Ready Ruler, Justa Red Bird, 8 started.

Jim Coleman Province H., Hastings Race Course, July 3, $35,184, 3yo, 1 1/16m, 1:44.05, ALABAMA RAIN, Timeless Passion, Spaghetti Mouse, 8 started.

JIM DANDY S. (G2), Saratoga Race Course, July 30, $490,000, 3yo, 1 1/8m, 1:49.50, FLOWER ALLEY, Reverberate, Andromeda's Hero, 5 started.

Jim Edgar Illinois Futurity (R), Hawthorne Race Course, Dec. 17, $105,950, 2yo, c&g, Illinois-conceived and/or -foaled, 1 1/16m, 1:46.75, CREATIVE FORCE, Last Gran Standing, Princeton Hills, 10 started.

Jim E. Weir Memorial S., Turf Paradise, April 23, $23,800, 3yo, f, 7 1/2fT, 1:29.96, KICK THE CAN, Tall Pines, Skyline Gal, 7 started.

Jim McKay Breeders' Cup H., Pimlico Race Course, April 23, $150,000, 3&up, 1 1/8m, 1:49.62, PRESIDENTIALAFFAIR, Classic Endeavor, Hydrogen, 5 started.

JIM MURRAY MEMORIAL H. (G3), Hollywood Park, May 14, $350,000, 3&up, 1 1/2mT, 2:26.75, RUNAWAY DANCER, Vangelis, Exterior, 8 started.

Jimmy Winkfield S., Aqueduct, Jan. 17, $80,400, 3yo, 6f, 1:11.43, MADDY'S LION, More Smoke, Lieutenant Danz, 6 started.

Jim Rasmussen Memorial S., Prairie Meadows, May 30, $50,000, 3&up, 1 1/16m, 1:42.93, SILVER AXE, Dusty Spike, Tricky Mocha, 8 started.

Jim's Orbit S. (R), Sam Houston Race Park, Feb. 19, $125,000, 3yo, c&g, nominated and eligible for the Texas Stallion Stakes, 1m, 1:38.86, DIXIE MEISTER, General Charley, Leaving On My Mind, 7 started.

J J'sdream S., Arlington Park, July 24, $47,250, 3&up, f&m, 5fT, :56.41,

NICOLE'S DREAM, Dharma Girl, Rich City Girl, 5 started.

J J'sdream S., Calder Race Course, Oct. 15, $100,000, 2yo, f, 6f, 1:13.24, LAKE ALICE, No Hear Say, Zooming By, 10 started.

JOCKEY CLUB GOLD CUP S. (G1), Belmont Park, Oct. 1, $1,000,000, 3&up, 1¼m, 2:02.86, BORREGO, Suave, Sun King, 8 started.

JOE HIRSCH TURF CLASSIC INVITATIONAL S. (G1), Belmont Park, Oct. 1, $750,000, 3&up, 1½mT, 2:27.22, SHAKESPEARE, English Channel, Ace (Ire), 7 started.

Joe O'Farrell Juvenile Fillies S. (R), Calder Race Course, Nov. 12, $150,000, 2yo, f, Florida-bred, 7f, 1:24.42, PEACH FLAMBE, Stolen Prayer, Secret Brook, 8 started.

John and Kitty Fletcher S. (R), Emerald Downs, Oct. 2, $39,200, 3yo, f, Washington-bred, 1m, 1:36.20, GOLDEN PINE, Queenledo, Roanaway Bride, 7 started.

John Battaglia Memorial S., Turfway Park, March 5, $100,000, 3yo, 1 1/16m, 1:43.94, MAGNA GRADUATE, Pavo, Collegiate Honor, 9 started.

John B. Campbell Breeders' Cup H., Laurel Park, Feb. 19, $122,000, 3&up, 1⅛m, 1:50.09, COAST LINE, Offlee Wild, Ole Faunty, 7 started.

John B. Connally Breeders' Cup Turf H., Sam Houston Race Park, April 9, $216,000, 3&up, 1⅛mT, 1:51.31, RAPID PROOF, Warleigh, Dynareign, 8 started.

John Bullit S., Canterbury Park, Aug. 6, $75,000, 3&up, 1 1/16mT, 1:42.52, SCOOTER ROACH, Dontbotherknocking, Wally's Choice, 8 started.

JOHN C. MABEE H. (G1), Del Mar, July 23, $400,000, 3&up, f&m, 1⅛mT, 1:48.01, AMORAMA (FR), Island Fashion, Intercontinental (GB), 8 started.

John D. Schapiro Memorial Breeders' Cup H., Laurel Park, Sept. 17, $150,000, 3&up, 1⅛mT, 1:46, BATTLE CHANT, Dr. Kashnikow, Proud Man, 7 started.

John Franks Juvenile Fillies Turf S. (R), Calder Race Course, Nov. 12, $100,000, 2yo, f, Florida-bred, 1 1/16mT, 1:43.34, dh-SURVICAT, dh-GOOD INTENTIONS, Mia's Reflection, 8 started.

John Franks Memorial S. (R), Louisiana Downs, April 29, $50,000, 3&up, Louisiana-bred, 1mT, 1:35.02, SCREEN IDOL, Spritely Walker, Bebe Garcon, 9 started.

John Franks Memorial Sales S. (R), Evangeline Downs, Aug. 20, $75,000, 2yo, sold at the Evangeline Downs March sale, 5f, :59.53, VOODOO GOLD, Triple S Gold, C S C Grand Slam, 9 started.

John Henry S., Arlington Park, Sept. 10, $42,000, 3&up, 1 1/16mT, 1:42.11, HOME OF STARS, Lacer, Ole Faunty, 8 started.

John Henry S., Meadowlands, Nov. 5, $60,000, 3&up, 1⅜mT, 2:14.31, RUMOR HAS IT, Westmoreland Road, Publisher's Phil, 8 started.

Johnie L. Jamison H. (R), Sunland Park, Dec. 11, $125,000, 3&up, New Mexico-bred, 6½f, 1:16.15, NINETY NINE JACK, Rocky Gulch, Bold Nxs, 10 started.

John J. Reilly H. (R), Monmouth Park, May 28, $60,000, 3&up, New Jersey-bred, 6f, 1:09.84, WAR'S PROSPECT, Quiet Desperation, Upturn, 8 started.

John Kirby S. (R), Suffolk Downs, Oct. 22, $40,000, 3yo, Massachusetts-bred, 1m, 1:39.95, REPRIZED STRIKE, Stylish Sultana, Feathertop, 9 started.

John Longden "6000" H., Hastings Race Course, June 4, $39,223, 3&up, 1 1/16m, 1:44.13, LORD NELSON, R. Associate, Illusive Force, 8 started.

John McSorley S., Monmouth Park, July 10, $55,000, 3&up, 5f, :56.48, TACIRRING, Choose, Weigelia, 5 started.

John Morrissey S. (R), Saratoga Race Course, Aug. 18, $66,500, 3&up, New York-bred, 6½f, 1:18.53, CHOWDER'S FIRST, Clever Electrician, Papua, 7 started.

John Patrick H., Northlands Park, July 23, $41,025, 3&up, f&m, 1m, 1:39.20, GOLD ACCENT, Stole One, Overact, 7 started.

John's Call S. (R), Saratoga Race Course, Aug. 15, $66,600, 4&up, non-winners of graded stakes in 2004-'05, 1⅝mT, 2:40.94, ROUSING VICTORY, Stage Call (Ire), Muqbil, 7 started.

John Wayne S. (R), Prairie Meadows, May 21, $60,000, 3&up, c&g, Iowa-bred, 6f, 1:09.79, WILD WILD WEST, Scooter Rains, Asailortorember, 7 started.

John W. Galbreath Memorial S. (R), Beulah Park, Oct. 1, $60,000, 2yo, f, Ohio-bred, 1 1/16m, 1:49.19, CRYPTOVILLE, Lillians Choice, Tommeyesgold, 11 started.

John W. Rooney Memorial H., Delaware Park, June 4, $91,000, 3&up, f&m, 1⅛m (originally scheduled on the turf), 1:52.27, RACING LUCK, Spring Season, Summer Rainbow, 3 started.

Joseph A. Gimma S. (R), Belmont Park, Sept. 25, $113,500, 2yo, f, New York-bred, 7f, 1:26.29, ARTISTIC EXPRESS, Fly to Me, Zippy Missy, 10 started.

Joseph T. Grace H., Santa Rosa, Aug. 6, $98,000, 3&up, 1 1/16mT, 1:41.32, ADREAMISBORN, Charbonnier, Kilgowan, 5 started.

Journal H., Northlands Park, June 25, $40,570, 3&up, 6½f, 1:17.60, SIXTHIRTYJOE, Hot Talk, Rindanica, 9 started.

Journal Star S., Lincoln State Fair, May 22, $12,687, 3yo, 6f, 1:11.80, S C KING, Sooner Pride, The Straw Man, 6 started.

Joy to the World S. (R), Calder Race Course, Dec. 26, $40,000, 3&up, f&m, non-winners of a stakes in 2005 at one mile or over, 1 1/16mT, 1:42.20, MARCHONIN, Cloon, Formal Miss, 10 started.

J. R. Straus Memorial S., Retama Park, Aug. 5, $40,000, 3&up, 6f, 1:09.77, RUN ZEAL RUN, War Bridle, Charming Socialite, 7 started.

Juan Gonzalez Memorial S. (R), Pleasanton, July 2, $49,500, 2yo, f, California-bred, 5f, :57.43, HYSTERICALADY, Bid of Genius, Smart Kitten, 10 started.

JUDDMONTE SPINSTER S. (G1), Keeneland Race Course, Oct. 9, $500,000, 3&up, f&m, 1⅛m, 1:53.91, PAMPERED PRINCESS, Pleasant Home, Capeside Lady, 11 started.

Judy's Red Shoes S., Calder Race Course, Sept. 24, $75,000, 3yo, f, 1 1/16mT, 1:43.60, ACLASSYSASSYLASSY, Ragtime Hope, Flying Circle, 9 started.

Junior Champion S., Monmouth Park, Aug. 21, $55,000, 2yo, f, 1m, 1:40.38, CAPOZZENE, Leesburg Express, Cosmo Queen, 7 started.

Junius Delahoussaye Memorial Sprint S. (R), Evangeline Downs, July 30, $50,000, 3&up, Louisiana-bred, 5½f, 1:03.84, MAJESTIC COMMANDER, Zarb's Dahar, Lac Laronge, 6 started.

JUST A GAME BREEDERS' CUP H. (G2), Belmont Park, June 11, $300,000, 3&up, f&m, 1mT, 1:33.05, SAND SPRINGS, Intercontinental (GB), Wonder Again, 9 started.

Justakiss S., Delaware Park, Nov. 13, $60,500, 3&up, f&m, 1 1/16m, 1:45, DANCE FEE, Racing Luck, Summer Rainbow, 8 started.

Just Smashing S., Monmouth Park, May 22, $60,000, 3yo, f, 6f, 1:10.23, PORTSEA, Golden Locket, All Platinum, 5 started.

Juvenile Breeders' Cup S., Louisiana Downs, Oct. 1, $87,000, 2yo, 1 1/16mT, 1:43.19, HYTE REGENCY, Desert Wheat, Test Boy, 12 started.

Juvenile Mile S., Portland Meadows, Dec. 31, $40,000, 2yo, 1m, 1:42.75, TOM TWO, Cascadians Cuttie, Newberg Gold, 9 started.

Juvenile S. (R), Beulah Park, Oct. 1, $60,000, 2yo, Ohio-bred, 1 1/16m, 1:46.43, DINNER CHOICE, Acts Like a King, Chop Spats, 7 started.

J. William (Bill) Petro Memorial H. (R), Thistledown, June 11, $45,000, 3yo, f, Ohio-bred, 1 1/16m, 1:47.26, FLIP SIDE, Nitty Gritty, Cho Chang, 9 started.

J. W. Sifton S. (R), Assiniboia Downs, Sept. 17, $33,936, 3yo, Manitoba-bred, 1⅛m, 1:54.20, RESURGENT, Brinello, Cindy Embers, 10 started.

Kabbendjian S., Fairmount Park, Aug. 6, $40,900, 3yo, f, 1m, 1:39.60, MEADOW BRIDE, Galactic Cat, Special Grayce, 7 started.

Kachina H., Turf Paradise, Jan. 15, $40,000, 4&up, f&m, 1m, 1:37.20, MUIR BEACH, Arch Lady, Very Vegas, 7 started.

Kachina S., Zia Park, Oct. 22, $65,800, 3&up, 1m, 1:36.60, MR. TRISTE, Go Kitty Go, Bayou the Moon, 6 started.

Kalispell Claiming S., Kalispell, Aug. 28, $3,050, 3&up, 1m70y, 1:52.40, BORN WILD AGAIN, Flying Catman, Up Mim's Aly, 7 started.

Kalispell Thoroughbred Derby, Kalispell, Aug. 28, $3,000, 3yo, 7f, 1:29.40, REALITY BELLE, Secret Victory, She Ledo Target, 6 started.

Kalookan Queen H., Santa Anita Park, Jan. 5, $81,450, 4&up, f&m, 6½f, 1:16.26, TIZAKITTY, Mazella, Dream of Summer, 6 started.

Kansas-bred H. (R), Anthony Downs, July 23, $11,000, 3&up, Kansas-bred, a5f, 1:01.90, CLEVER RED, D D Dot Comm, Rapid Baby, 6 started.

Kansas Oaks, The Woodlands, Oct. 23, $20,000, 3yo, f, 1m70y, 1:45.60, LEGENDARY SMILE, Pepper Lang, Bad Little Bernie, 9 started.

Kansas Thoroughbred Association Derby (R), The Woodlands, Oct. 1, $20,000, 3yo, c&g, sired by eligible stallions, 1m70y, 1:47.20, dh-PROPER DECREE, dh-SCARLET JEFF, Discreet Ways, 8 started.

Kansas Thoroughbred Association Futurity (R), The Woodlands, Oct. 15, $18,000, 2yo, c&g, progeny of eligible Kansas stallions, 5½f, 1:06.40, MANOVAN, Sir Regent, Murphy's Magic, 7 started.

Kansas Thoroughbred Association Futurity (R), The Woodlands, Oct. 16, $18,000, 2yo, f, progeny of eligible Kansas stallions, 5½f, 1:07, SHELBY DEE, Regan Rules, Flicka My Bicka, 5 started.

Kansas Thoroughbred Association Oaks (R), The Woodlands, Oct. 2, $18,000, 3yo, f, sired by eligible stallions, 1m70y, 1:46.20, LADY LEGEND, Lost in L. A., Asplashtoremember, 6 started.

Karl Flaman Mile S., Yorkton Exh. Assoc., July 9, $2,050, 3&up, 1m, 1:45.40, HERB E, Makewayforbighoss, Detained, 4 started.

Kathryn's Doll S., Turf Paradise, Jan. 23, $22,000, 4&up, f&m, 4½fT, :50.45, ROYAL AGAIN, North of Rio, Melba Jewel, 10 started.

Kathryn's Doll S., Turf Paradise, Nov. 15, $24,000, 3&up, f&m, 4½fT, :51.24, LIL EASY, Queen Creek, Society Cat, 9 started.

Kattegat's Pride S., Laurel Park, Nov. 5, $60,750, 3&up, f&m, 5fT,

:55.70 (NCR), GILDED GOLD, Tight Spin, Ambition Unbridled, 11 started.

Keddie's Track & Western Wear S., Grand Prairie, July 24, $4,893, 3&up, 1$^1/_{16}$m, 1:48.80, EZEE TARGET, Lafleur, Bolywood, 7 started.

Keith Anderson Memorial S. (R), Turf Paradise, Dec. 27, $23,600, 3&up, non-winners of $20,000 or more in 2005, 1m, 1:37.01, CUT OF MUSIC, Point Dume, Brazen n' Bold, 6 started.

KELSO BREEDERS' CUP H. (G2), Belmont Park, Oct. 2, $334,200, 3&up, 1mT, 1:32.95, FUNFAIR (GB), Artie Schiller, Keep The Faith (Aus), 10 started.

Kelso H., Delaware Park, Oct. 1, $100,900, 3&up, 1$^3/_{16}$m, 1:55.41 (NTR), TRAPPED AGAIN, Navesink River, Separato, 8 started.

Kendal Pipeline and Oilfield Service S., Grand Prairie, Aug. 13, $5,571, 3&up, 6$^1/_2$f, 1:19.40, SECRET ONE, Bolywood, Gentle John, 5 started.

Ken Maddy Sprint S. (R), Golden Gate Fields, May 28, $75,000, 3&up, California-bred, 6f, 1:08.33, BONFANTE, Flying Supercon, Kool Suggestion, 6 started.

Kennedy Road S., Woodbine, Dec. 10, $122,782, 3&up, 6f, 1:09.55, ARE YOU SERIOUS, dh-Bishop Court Hill, dh-Gangster, 10 started.

Kenny Noe Jr. H., Calder Race Course, Dec. 17, $100,000, 3&up, 7f, 1:22.97, MISTER FOTIS, Storm Surge, Silver Wagon, 7 started.

Kenora S. (R), Woodbine, Sept. 4, $105,936, 3&up, Canadian-bred, 6f, 1:09.41, DAVE THE KNAVE, Nyuk Nyuk Nyuk, Mister Coop, 7 started.

Ken Pearson Memorial H., Stampede Park, May 23, $39,495, 3&up, f&m, 1m, 1:38, SUMMER SYMPHONY, Unforgettable Too, A Shaky Start, 5 started.

KENT BREEDERS' CUP S. (G3), Delaware Park, June 25, $501,800, 3yo, 1$^1/_8$mT, 1:47.32 (NCR), SEEKING SLEW, Chattahoochee War, Spring House, 11 started.

Kent H., Emerald Downs, July 10, $40,450, 3yo, f, 1$^1/_{16}$m, 1:42.80, GINS MAJESTY, Queenledo, M K Beck, 10 started.

KENTUCKY CUP CLASSIC S. (G2), Turfway Park, Sept. 17, $342,500, 3&up, 1$^1/_8$m, 1:49.74, SHANIKO, Ball Four, Silver Axe, 10 started.

Kentucky Cup Juvenile Fillies S., Turfway Park, Sept. 17, $100,000, 2yo, f, 1m, 1:38.93, BEAU DARE, Delicate Dynamite, Joint Effort, 10 started.

KENTUCKY CUP JUVENILE S. (G3), Turfway Park, Sept. 17, $100,000, 2yo, 1$^1/_{16}$m, 1:46.42, STREAM CAT, Rungius, Cab, 8 started.

Kentucky Cup Ladies Turf S., Kentucky Downs, Sept. 24, $100,000, 3&up, f&m, 1mT, 1:39.25, MISS WELLSPRING, Juliet's Kiss, Fast Cookie, 10 started.

KENTUCKY CUP SPRINT S. (G3), Turfway Park, Sept. 17, $100,000, 3yo, 6f, 1:09.75, ESTATE COLLECTION, Humor At Last, Going Wild, 7 started.

Kentucky Cup Turf Dash S., Kentucky Downs, Sept. 24, $100,000, 3&up, 6fT, 1:10.30, DURBAN THUNDER (BRZ), Atticus Kristy, Super Fuse, 8 started.

KENTUCKY CUP TURF H. (G3), Kentucky Downs, Sept. 24, $200,000, 3&up, 1$^1/_2$mT, 2:30.30, SILVERFOOT, Rochester, Gallo Del Bar (Chi), 8 started.

KENTUCKY DERBY (G1), Churchill Downs, May 7, $2,399,600, 3yo, 1$^1/_4$m, 2:02.75, GIACOMO, Closing Argument, Afleet Alex, 20 started.

KENTUCKY JOCKEY CLUB S. (G2), Churchill Downs, Nov. 26, $222,400, 2yo, 1$^1/_{16}$m, 1:45.80, PRIVATE VOW, High Cotton, Hyte Regency, 7 started.

KENTUCKY OAKS (G1), Churchill Downs, May 6, $554,400, 3yo, f, 1$^1/_8$m, 1:50.23, SUMMERLY, In the Gold, Gallant Secret, 7 started.

Khaled S. (R), Hollywood Park, April 24, $150,000, 4&up, California-bred, 1$^1/_8$mT, 1:48, RUNNING FREE, Continental Red, Legal Logic, 7 started.

Kimscountrydiamond S., Calder Race Course, May 22, $40,000, 3&up, f&m, 6$^1/_2$f, 1:18.52, PROSPECTIVE SAINT, French Village, So Much More, 7 started.

Kingarvie S. (R), Woodbine, Dec. 11, $108,679, 2yo, progeny of stallions standing in Ontario, 1$^1/_{16}$m, 1:48.98, BAD HAT, Pressac, Shivaree, 7 started.

King Cotton S., Oaklawn Park, Feb. 5, $50,000, 4&up, 6f, 1:10.32, DEPUTY STORM, Engineered, Level Playingfield, 8 started.

King County H, Emerald Downs, July 3, $40,000, 3&up, f&m, 1m, 1:36.20, KARIS MAKAW, Ruby Dawn, Summer Symphony, 8 started.

KING EDWARD BREEDERS' CUP H. (Can-G2), Woodbine, July 3, $265,950, 3&up, 1$^1/_8$mT, 1:47.54, SILVER TICKET, Mobil, Colorful Judgement, 5 started.

King Knocker S., Fairmount Park, Aug. 6, $45,900, 3yo, c&g, 1$^1/_{16}$m, 1:44.80, TEPEXPAN, Wise Diplomat, Jazzy Gallop, 8 started.

KING'S BISHOP S. (G1), Saratoga Race Course, Aug. 27, $250,000, 3yo, 7f, 1:22.56, LOST IN THE FOG, Social Probation, Better Than Bonds, 7 started.

Kings Court S., Louisiana Downs, May 29, $50,100, 3&up, 6f, 1:10.85, RODEO'S CASTLE, Watchem Smokey, Stormy But Crafty, 7 started.

Kings Point H. (R), Aqueduct, May 1, $75,950, 3&up, New York-bred, 1$^1/_8$m, 1:51.44, CHOWDER'S FIRST, Spite the Devil, Rogue Agent, 4 started.

Kingston H. (R), Belmont Park, May 15, $113,100, 3&up, New York-bred, 1$^1/_8$mT, 1:45.35 (NCR), GOLDEN COMMANDER, Sicilian Boy, Save the Profit, 10 started.

Kissapotamus S., Hawthorne Race Course, March 5, $42,800, 4&up, f&m, 6f, 1:10.49, DUTCHIE, Pass the Pepper, Wildwood Royal, 7 started.

KLAQ H., Sunland Park, Dec. 3, $50,000, 3&up, 5$^1/_2$f, 1:04.59, DAY TRADER, Boots Are Walking, Absolutely True, 5 started.

Klassy Briefcase S., Monmouth Park, July 30, $55,000, 3&up, f&m, 5fT, :55.89, WHENTHEDOVEFLIES, Melody of Colors, Letthefreedomroar, 10 started.

Klondike H., Hastings Race Course, May 15, $34,828, 3yo, 6$^1/_2$f, 1:18.14, HALL DANCER, Spaghetti Mouse, Alabama Rain, 7 started.

Klondike H., Northlands Park, July 30, $40,850, 3&up, 1$^1/_{16}$m, 1:43.80, DEPUTY COUNTRY, Beau Brass, Rindanica, 6 started.

KNICKERBOCKER H. (G3), Belmont Park, Oct. 30, $150,000, 3&up, 1$^1/_8$mT, 1:50.93, ATLANDO (IRE), Certifiably Crazy, Rousing Victory, 10 started.

Knights Choice S. (R), Emerald Downs, Aug. 20, $43,200, 2yo, f, progeny of stallions standing in Washington, 6$^1/_2$f, 1:17.80, CINDERELLA LIBERTY, Nite Moon, Fergie's Fantasy, 8 started.

Kris S. S., Calder Race Course, Dec. 10, $100,000, 2yo, 1$^1/_{16}$mT, 1:44.11, UP AN OCTAVE, Yankee Master, Mr. Silver, 11 started.

Kudzu Juvenile S. (R), Evangeline Downs, Dec. 16, $50,000, 2yo, Alabama-bred, 5$^1/_2$f, 1:07.78, VALID RUN, Big Fred, Cameroon Kid, 10 started.

Ky Alta H., Northlands Park, July 16, $40,960, 3yo, 1m, 1:41, HOTENUFORYOO, Gusso, Lonesome Leo, 8 started.

Labeeb S., Woodbine, Nov. 10, $97,619, 3&up, 1m70y, 1:42.78, ESTEVAN, Vegas Venture, Sky Diamond, 7 started.

Labor Day H., Columbus Races, Sept. 5, $10,650, 3&up, 6$^1/_2$f, 1:20.40, LALI'S CAT, Hez Comin Thru, Subsequently, 10 started.

Labor Day S., Mountaineer Race Track, Sept. 5, $75,000, 3&up, 1mT, 1:33.74, SPRUCE RUN, Beau Classic, Midnight Arrival, 8 started.

LA BREA S. (G1), Santa Anita Park, Dec. 31, $250,000, 3yo, f, 7f, 1:21.36, PUSSYCAT DOLL, Leave Me Alone, Thrilling Victory, 11 started.

LA CANADA S. (G2), Santa Anita Park, Feb. 12, $200,000, 4yo, f, 1$^1/_8$m, 1:48.64, TARLOW, Sweet Lips, A. P. Adventure, 5 started.

La Coneja H. (R), Sunland Park, Dec. 17, $125,000, 3yo, f, New Mexico-bred, 5$^1/_2$f, 1:05.27, HOLLYWOOD GONE, La Mamie, Windy Storm'n Rose, 9 started.

Ladies H., Aqueduct, Dec. 17, $82,750, 3&up, f&m, 1$^1/_4$m, 2:05.26, INDIA HALO (ARG), Bohemian Lady, Taittinger Rose, 8 started.

Ladies Secret S., Zia Park, Nov. 14, $41,750, 3&up, f&m, 5$^1/_2$f, 1:03.80, DEE DEE'S DINER, Sandia's Flicka, Ladysgotthelooks, 7 started.

Ladnesian S., Hastings Race Course, July 10, $33,317, 2yo, 6$^1/_2$f, 1:19.03, BOUND TO BE M V P, One Special Browny, Red's Memories, 7 started.

Lady Angela S. (R), Woodbine, May 28, $99,675, 3yo, f, progeny of stallions standing in Ontario, 7f, 1:23.88, BOSSKIRI, Baby Lou, Whiskey and Low, 5 started.

Lady Canterbury Breeders' Cup S., Canterbury Park, June 19, $100,000, 3&up, f&m, a1mT, 1:36.25, RUE DES REVES, Ghostly Gate, Noisette, 6 started.

Lady Fingers S. (R), Finger Lakes, Aug. 20, $132,575, 2yo, f, New York-bred, 6f, 1:10.83, LITTLE MISS ZIP, Oprah Winney, Doll Baby, 12 started.

Lady Hallie S. (R), Hawthorne Race Course, April 30, $94,125, 3yo, f, Illinois-conceived and/or -foaled, 6f, 1:12.97, PRETTY JENNY, Li'l-bito'sunshine, Meadow Bride, 11 started.

Lady Luck S., Louisiana Downs, Oct. 8, $50,000, 2yo, f, a1mT, 1:36.90, PARIS RETURN, Double Faced, Silver Navasha, 12 started.

Lady Razorback Futurity (R), Louisiana Downs, Sept. 29, $45,000, 2yo, f, Arkansas-bred, 6f, 1:11.39, LOVE THE BEACH, Angel's Are Due, Beautiful Rainbows, 10 started.

Lady Slipper S. (R), Canterbury Park, May 22, $40,000, 3&up, f&m, Minnesota-bred, 6f, 1:10.88, ISLE SEE YOU LATER, Shakopee, Demiparfait, 10 started.

Lady Sonata S., Calder Race Course, Oct. 16, $40,000, 3yo, f, 6f, 1:10.74, FLYING CIRCLE, Midtown Miss, Mertie M, 8 started.

LADY'S SECRET BREEDERS' CUP H. (G2), Oak Tree at Santa Anita, Oct. 2, $235,000, 3&up, f&m, 1$^1/_{16}$m, 1:42.23, HEALTHY ADDICTION, Star Parade (Arg), Island Fashion, 6 started.

Lady's Secret S., Monmouth Park, Aug. 7, $100,000, 3&up, f&m, 1 1/16m, 1:45.09, FRIEL'S FOR REAL, Diavla, La Reason, 11 started.

Lady's Secret S. (R), Remington Park, Nov. 12, $40,650, 3&up, f&m, Oklahoma-bred, 7f, 1:22.94, D FINE OKIE, Red Lifesaver, Shady Caller, 11 started.

Lafayette H., Golden Gate Fields, Jan. 1, $78,150, 4&up, 1m, 1:35.73, JAKE SKATE, Adreamisborn, Yougottawanna, 4 started.

Lafayette S., Evangeline Downs, Sept. 5, $100,000, 2yo, 6f, 1:13.01, PREMIER DANCE, Zarb's Pleasure, Costa Rising, 6 started.

LAFAYETTE S. (G3), Keeneland Race Course, April 10, $103,887, 3yo, 6f, 1:09.88, MORE SMOKE, Crimson Stag, Razor, 4 started.

La Fiesta H., The Downs at Albuquerque, April 10, $40,000, 3yo, f, 5 1/2f, 1:05.25, TIME TO DIVORCE, Dixie Kiss, Revolving Door, 8 started.

La Habra S., Santa Anita Park, March 6, $111,400, 3yo, f, a6 1/2fT, 1:13.61, SHINING ENERGY, Kohar, dh-Berbatim, dh-Royal Wave, 9 started.

LA JOLLA H. (G2), Del Mar, Aug. 13, $150,000, 3yo, 1 1/16mT, 1:41.45, WILLOW O WISP, Juliesugardaddy, El Roblar, 7 started.

LAKE GEORGE S. (G3), Saratoga Race Course, July 29, $111,000, 3yo, f, 1 1/16mT, 1:41.90, READY'S GAL, Dream Lady, Who's Cozy, 8 started.

LAKE PLACID S. (G2), Saratoga Race Course, Aug. 19, $150,000, 3yo, f, 1 1/8mT, 1:47.14, NAISSANCE ROYALE (IRE), My Typhoon (Ire), Victory Lap, 6 started.

Lakeway S., Retama Park, Aug. 20, $40,000, 3yo, f, 6f, 1:10.55, HELLO LUCKY, Ellen's Foxy Girl, Texas Spice, 9 started.

La Lorgnette S., Woodbine, Sept. 24, $146,662, 3yo, f, 1 1/16m, 1:45.18, COASTAL FORTRESS, Roving Angel, Simply Again, 6 started.

Lambholm South Brookmeade S. (R), Colonial Downs, July 2, $60,000, 3&up, f&m, Virginia-bred and/or -sired, 1 1/16mT, 1:42.40, WITH PATIENCE, Old Fashion Girl, Miswes, 6 started.

Lamplighter S., Monmouth Park, Aug. 7, $100,000, 3yo, 1mT, 1:35.96, NETWORK, Touched by Madness, Spring House, 6 started.

Landaluce S., Hollywood Park, July 2, $104,800, 2yo, f, 6f, 1:10.91, INDIAN BREEZE, River's Prayer, Mystery Girl, 7 started.

Land of Enchantment H. (R), Ruidoso Downs, July 31, $45,000, 3&up, New Mexico-bred, 7 1/2f, 1:32.40, DANCING MOVES, Some Ghost, B. G. Tiger, 10 started.

Land of Jazz S. (R), Ferndale, Aug. 19, $6,645, 3&up, starters for a claiming price of $12,500 or less in 2005, 7f, 1:25.65, RED SEATTLE, Wisenheimer, Totalitarian, 4 started.

Land of Lincoln S. (R), Hawthorne Race Course, April 30, $90,950, 3yo, Illinois-conceived and/or -foaled, 6f, 1:11.99, TOP KICK, Humor At Last, Dress for Success, 7 started.

LANE'S END BREEDERS' FUTURITY (G1), Keeneland Race Course, Oct. 8, $500,000, 2yo, 1 1/16m, 1:48.77, DAWN OF WAR, Catcominatcha, Stream Cat, 12 started.

LANE'S END S. (G2), Turfway Park, March 26, $500,000, 3yo, 1 1/8m, 1:50.33, FLOWER ALLEY, Wild Desert, Mr Sword, 9 started.

Langley H., Hastings Race Course, Aug. 14, $34,279, 3yo, 1 1/16m, 1:45.25, APPEARANCE FEE, He's So Regal, Timely Brush, 7 started.

Lang Michener Matriarch H., Hastings Race Course, July 30, $32,680, 3&up, f&m, 1 1/16m, 1:45.07, STORMENTED, Champagne Royale, See Me Through, 8 started.

Lansing S. (R), Great Lakes Downs, June 13, $45,000, 3yo, c&g, Michigan-bred, 6f, 1:16.18, SPEAK OF KINGS, Demagoguery, Rodrigues, 7 started.

La Paz S., Turf Paradise, Nov. 28, $23,800, 2yo, f, 6f, 1:09.94, HOLY FASHION, Silly Little Mama, Queen Razyana, 7 started.

LA PREVOYANTE H. (G2), Calder Race Course, Dec. 17, $200,000, 3&up, f&m, 1 1/2mT, 2:27.75, FILM MAKER, Kate Winslet, Noble Stella (Ger), 12 started.

La Prevoyante S. (R), Woodbine, Sept. 17, $106,729, 3yo, f, progeny of stallions standing in Ontario, 1mT, 1:40.55, TOP TEN LIST, Simply Lovely, Wisdomisgold, 7 started.

La Puente S., Santa Anita Park, April 16, $109,800, 3yo, 1 1/8mT, 1:48.02, CHINESE DRAGON, Eastern Sand, Shamoan (Ire), 5 started.

Larkspur H. (R), Great Lakes Downs, June 18, $50,000, 3&up, f&m, Michigan-bred, 6f, 1:14.25, BORN TO DANCE, Charlies Indian, Deb's Favoite Gift, 7 started.

Larkspur S., Golden Gate Fields, Dec. 10, $60,800, 3yo, 6f, 1:08.59, LOYALTON, Seattles Best Joe, Wilko, 7 started.

Larry R. Riviello President's Cup S., Philadelphia Park, Aug. 6, $97,000, 3yo, 1m70y, 1:43.83, TANI MARU, Letterman's Humor, Russian Bay, 4 started.

LAS CIENEGAS H. (G3), Santa Anita Park, April 10, $111,100, 4&up, f&m, a6 1/2fT, 1:11.66, ELUSIVE DIVA, Quero Quero, Winendynme, 9 started.

La Senora H. (R), Sunland Park, Jan. 22, $132,200, 3yo, f, New Mexico-bred, 6f, 1:12.30, HOLLYWOOD GONE, Bay View Sue, My Desert Lady, 12 started.

La Senorita S., Retama Park, Sept. 3, $100,000, 2yo, f, 1m (originally scheduled on the turf), 1:42.79, JB'S GOLDEN REGRET, Cancel the Wedding, Lady Cosmo, 11 started.

LAS FLORES H. (G3), Santa Anita Park, Feb. 27, $109,600, 4&up, f&m, 6f, 1:09.47, MISS TERRIBLE (ARG), Puxa Saco, Mazella, 8 started.

Las Madrinas H., Fairplex Park, Sept. 23, $98,000, 3&up, f&m, 1 1/16m, 1:43.28, BROOKE'S HALO, Mini Skirt, Santa Candida (Arg), 7 started.

LAS PALMAS H. (G2), Oak Tree at Santa Anita, Nov. 5, $150,000, 3&up, f&m, 1mT, 1:33.59, MEA DOMINA, Elusive Diva, Star Parade (Arg), 10 started.

Lassie S., Portland Meadows, Dec. 4, $11,175, 2yo, f, 6f, 1:14.30, ROYAL SNOWFLIGHT, Cascades Express, Wings Are the Way, 8 started.

Last Chance Derby, Turf Paradise, Dec. 31, $23,800, 3yo, a1 1/16mT, 1:42.93 (NCR), WESTERN ACT, Night Dash, Desert Prospector, 8 started.

Last Dance S. (R), Suffolk Downs, July 4, $40,000, 3&up, Massachusetts-bred, 1 1/16m, 1:46.46, JINI'S JET, Ask Queenie, African Princess, 9 started.

Last Don B. S., Turf Paradise, May 15, $23,700, 3yo, 6 1/2f, 1:14.38, QUINTONS RELAUNCH, Aluringact, Peripatetic, 6 started.

Last Don B. S., Turf Paradise, Nov. 22, $23,800, 3&up, 6 1/2f, 1:14.32, COCOA LATTE, Aces of Gold, Moores Bridge, 7 started.

LAS VIRGENES S. (G1), Santa Anita Park, Feb. 12, $250,000, 3yo, f, 1m, 1:35.64, SHARP LISA, Memorette, Charming Colleen, 6 started.

LA TROIENNE S. (G3), Churchill Downs, May 5, $114,200, 3yo, f, 7 1/2f, 1:28.75, SEEK A STAR, Cool Spell, Hot Storm, 9 started.

Laurel Futurity, Laurel Park, Nov. 19, $125,000, 2yo, 1 1/16mT, 1:40.17, BARBARO, Diabolical, Exton, 13 started.

Laurel Lane S. (R), Louisiana Downs, Sept. 17, $80,700, 2yo, f, Louisiana-bred, 6f, 1:11.41, TORTUGA FLATS, Leesa Lee, Gracie's Gem, 11 started.

Laurel Turf Cup S., Laurel Park, Nov. 19, $75,000, 3&up, 1 1/8mT, 1:47.50, DREADNAUGHT, Major Rhythm, Patrol, 13 started.

La Verendrye S., Assiniboia Downs, June 12, $32,016, 3&up, f&m, 6f, 1:13, ERICKA'S LASS, Remiewaterbluz, Ruby Slew, 11 started.

Lawrence Realization S., Belmont Park, Oct. 23, $79,250, 3yo, 1 1/8m (originally scheduled at 1 1/2m on the turf), 1:49.72, TAMING THE TIGER, Angliana, Crown Point, 5 started.

LAZARO BARRERA MEMORIAL S. (G2), Hollywood Park, May 21, $150,000, 3yo, 7f, 1:22.26, STORM WOLF, Dover Dere, Ransom Demanded, 6 started.

Lazer Show H., Churchill Downs, July 2, $70,350, 3&up, f&m, 6 1/2f, 1:16.42, MY RO, Souris, Edge Sweep, 6 started.

Lea County Sprint S., Zia Park, Nov. 5, $59,860, 3yo, 6f, 1:09.80, ASHBY HILL, Dangerous Devon, Devon Rules, 10 started.

LECOMTE S. (G3), Fair Grounds, Jan. 15, $100,000, 3yo, 1m, 1:39.34, STORM SURGE, Smooth Bid, Kansas City Boy, 5 started.

Left the Latch S., Turf Paradise, May 20, $24,200, 3yo, f, 6 1/2f, 1:15.51, KRESGEVILLE, Udriga, Meet You At T's, 10 started.

Legal Light S., Delaware Park, April 30, $75,300, 3yo, f, 6f, 1:11.68, MADDALENA, All Platinum, Broadway Gold, 6 started.

LEONARD RICHARDS S. (G3), Delaware Park, July 17, $300,000, 3yo, 1 1/16m, 1:43.33, SUN KING, Golden Man, High Limit, 5 started.

Les Mackin H., Yavapai Downs, June 21, $15,000, 3&up, 1m, 1:35 (NTR), SUSPICIOUS MINDS, Henry Higgins, Chory Four, 9 started.

Les Mademoiselle S., Ferndale, Aug. 20, $11,120, 3&up, f&m, 1 1/16m, 1:46.73, SCATTERING, Total Arrogance, One Flew Over, 8 started.

Letellier Memorial S., Fair Grounds, Jan. 1, $48,500, 3yo, f, 6f, 1:10.81, MORE MOONLIGHT, Hot Storm, Steal the Show, 4 started.

Lethbridge Alberta-Bred S. (R), Lethbridge, July 3, $10,653, 3&up, f&m, Alberta-bred, 5 1/2f, 1:08.60, GUILTYBYSUPISCION, Wild County, Bonus Parlay, 7 started.

Lethbridge Alberta-Bred S. (R), Lethbridge, July 3, $10,775, 3&up, c&g, Alberta-bred, a6f, 1:09.80, DEVIL'S FLAME, Nattandyahoo, Ezee Target, 8 started.

Lethbridge Alberta-Bred S. (R), Lethbridge, Oct. 2, $10,969, 2yo, Alberta-bred, 5f, 1:01.80, I'MAMAGICIANTOO, She's Twenty Below, Black Eyed Monte, 5 started.

Lethbridge Alberta-Bred S. (R), Lethbridge, Oct. 9, $10,975, 3&up, f&m, Alberta-bred, 7f, 1:26, A RAINBOW PRINCESS, Guiltybysupiscion, Katty Du, 6 started.

Lethbridge Alberta-Bred S. (R), Lethbridge, Sept. 18, $11,072, 3yo, f, Alberta-bred, a6f, 1:12.20, JOHN'S MAGIC, Blazing Wings, Bushmill Girl, 7 started.

Lethbridge Alberta-Bred S. (R), Lethbridge, Sept. 18, $11,072, 3yo, c&g, Alberta-bred, a6f, 1:11.60, COOL YER BOOTS, Native Jive, Chelseas Point, 7 started.

Lethbridge Fillies and Mares S., Lethbridge, Sept. 17, $11,199, 3&up, a6f, 1:12, HALLAS, Wild County, Guiltybysupiscion, 8 started.

Lethbridge Fillies and Mares Spring S., Lethbridge, June 12, $10,565, 3&up, f&m, a6f, 1:11.20, SPECIAL ERA, Flying Lady Cue, Guiltybysupiscion, 8 started.

Lethbridge Fillies Oaks, Lethbridge, Oct. 2, $11,356, 3yo, a6f, 1:11.40, JOHN'S MAGIC, Cascade Jazz, Hollywood Hustle, 8 started.

Lethbridge Marathon Series First Leg S., Lethbridge, Oct. 2, $9,377, 3&up, $1\frac{1}{16}$m, 1:49.20, ARCTIC HORIZON, Horizon Weekend, Lost Again, 6 started.

Lethbridge Marathon Series Second Leg S., Lethbridge, Oct. 30, $9,254, 3&up, $1\frac{1}{8}$m, 1:54.80, SHADY REMARK, Sweet Beau, Deriga Bay, 6 started.

Lethbridge Open S., Lethbridge, Sept. 18, $11,199, 3&up, 7f, 1:24.80, LAFLEUR, Dr. Mo, Sefapianos Way, 8 started.

Lethbridge Starter Allowance Third Leg S., Lethbridge, Oct. 1, $5,850, 3&up, $1\frac{3}{16}$m, 2:03.20, DERIGA BAY, Larry the Longshot, Bid N Battle, 8 started.

Lewis and Clark Thoroughbred Derby, Great Falls, July 31, $9,200, 3yo, 7f, 1:26, HANDSOMCHAMP, A Leo Thing, Pakawalup, 8 started.

LEXINGTON S. (G3), Belmont Park, July 10, $109,700, 3yo, $1\frac{1}{4}$mT, 2:01.92, WOODLANDER, Reel Legend, Prince Rahy, 6 started.

Liberation H. (R), Hastings Race Course, July 16, $35,698, 3yo, f, British Columbia-bred and/or -owned, $1\frac{1}{16}$m, 1:45.12, SLEWPAST, Vickies Song, Country Kat, 7 started.

LIEUTENANT GOVERNORS' H. (Can-G3), Hastings Race Course, July 1, $104,703, 3&up, $1\frac{1}{8}$m, 1:48.94, R. ASSOCIATE, Roscoe Pito, Quiet Cash, 10 started.

Light Hearted H., Delaware Park, July 17, $101,200, 3&up, f&m, 6f, 1:09.85, UMPATEEDLE, Storm Minstrel, Schedule (GB), 9 started.

Lighthouse S., Monmouth Park, Sept. 10, $60,000, 3&up, f&m, 1m70y, 1:43.34, FREEROLL, Palaestra, Ballroom Deputy, 9 started.

Lightning City S., Tampa Bay Downs, May 7, $83,150, 3&up, f&m, 5fT, :56.54, WHENTHEDOVEFLIES, Inhonorofjohnnie, Impressive Star, 10 started.

Lightning Jet H. (R), Hawthorne Race Course, Nov. 12, $114,050, 3&up, Illinois-conceived and/or -foaled, 6f, 1:11.39, KNOWWHATIMEAN, Silver Bid, Out for a Spin, 12 started.

Likely Exchange S., Turfway Park, Feb. 12, $50,000, 4&up, f&m, 1m, 1:37.85, TEMPUS FUGIT, Golden Marlin, Evil Eye Aly, 10 started.

Lilac H., Stampede Park, May 29, $39,870, 3yo, f, 1m, 1:38.20, KATHERN'S CAT, Speedy Gone Sally, Wild Bender, 7 started.

Lincoln H. (R), Ruidoso Downs, July 31, $45,000, 4&up, f&m, New Mexico-bred, 6f, 1:11.60, FLIPSIDER, Bendalee, Ringthatbellagain, 12 started.

Lincoln Heritage H. (R), Arlington Park, June 25, $88,400, 3&up, f&m, Illinois-conceived and/or -foaled, $1\frac{1}{16}$mT, 1:43.17, BEAU HAPPY, Arsen Annie, Cashmere Miss, 12 started.

Lincroft H. (R), Monmouth Park, Aug. 7, $60,000, 3&up, New Jersey-bred, 1m70y, 1:42.92, TRUEAMERICANSPIRIT, Hurricane Shockey, Quiet Desperation, 8 started.

Lindsay Frolic S., Calder Race Course, Sept. 3, $50,000, 2yo, f, 1m, 1:41.61, MIA'S REFLECTION, A Sea Trippi, Ensign Appeal, 8 started.

Lineage S. (R), The Downs at Albuquerque, May 14, $37,600, 3&up, New Mexico-bred, $1\frac{1}{16}$m, 1:45.07, SOME GHOST, M. R. Books, Romeos Wilson, 7 started.

Lite the Fuse S. (R), Belmont Park, May 18, $60,950, 3yo, non-winners of a graded stakes, $6\frac{1}{2}$f, 1:15.25, TANI MARU, Tashdeed, Silver Train, 6 started.

Littlebitlively S. (R), Lone Star Park, April 22, $40,000, 3&up, non-winners of a stakes in 2005, 5fT, :57.85, ORPHAN BRIGADE, Savonarola (GB), Charming Socialite, 9 started.

Little Everglades Hurdle S., Little Everglades, March 6, $33,950, 4&up, $a2\frac{1}{8}$mT, 3:53.20 (NCR), RAISE A STORM (IRE), Little Hurt, Il Capitano (GB), 5 started.

Little Ones S. (R), Great Lakes Downs, Sept. 4, $50,000, 2yo, c&g, Michigan-bred, 6f, 1:18.42, DAT FING GOTA HEMI, Mt. Factor, Shoot With Pride, 9 started.

Little Silver S., Monmouth Park, June 26, $60,000, 3yo, f, $1\frac{1}{16}$mT, 1:40.49, READY'S GAL, Who's Cozy, Connie Belle, 7 started.

Little Sister S., Calder Race Course, May 2, $35,000, 3&up, f&m, 6f, 1:11.42, WILD SPEED, Sorbet, Starship Dame, 8 started.

LOCUST GROVE H. (G3), Churchill Downs, July 2, $164,550, 3&up, f&m, $1\frac{1}{8}$mT, 1:48.90, DELTA PRINCESS, Shaconage, Marwood, 6 started.

Lone Star Oaks, Lone Star Park, July 2, $100,000, 3yo, f, $1\frac{1}{16}$mT, 1:44.62, VICTORY LAP, Mybrowneyedgal, Prospectors Spirit, 8 started.

LONE STAR PARK H. (G3), Lone Star Park, May 30, $300,000, 3&up, $1\frac{1}{16}$m, 1:41.90, SUPAH BLITZ, Cryptograph, Absent Friend, 10 started.

LONGACRES MILE H. (G3), Emerald Downs, Aug. 21, $250,000, 3&up, 1m, 1:35.60, NO GIVEAWAY, Quiet Cash, Desert Boom, 11 started.

LONG BRANCH BREEDERS' CUP S. (G3), Monmouth Park, July 16, $147,250, 3yo, $1\frac{1}{16}$m, 1:41.93, PARK AVENUE BALL, Chekhov, Golden Man, 8 started.

Longfellow S., Monmouth Park, June 11, $65,000, 3&up, 6f, 1:09.03, DON SIX, Bold Days, Dashboard Drummer, 6 started.

LONG ISLAND H. (G2), Aqueduct, Nov. 5, $150,000, 3&up, f&m, $1\frac{1}{2}$mT, 2:30.28, OLAYA, Spotlight (GB), Kate Winslet, 7 started.

Long Look S., Meadowlands, Oct. 7, $60,000, 3&up, f&m, $1\frac{1}{8}$m, 1:50.38, AFTERTHETONE, Taittinger Rose, Becky in Pink, 5 started.

Longshots OTB Cup S. (R), Fort Erie, Aug. 28, $25,026, 3&up, f&m, starters at Fort Erie twice in 2005, 6f, 1:10.14, ROMAN ROMANCE, Huckleberry's Gal, Decadent Dash, 6 started.

Lord Juban S., Calder Race Course, June 25, $40,000, 3yo, $1\frac{1}{16}$m, 1:46.47, SIR JACKIE, Talented Prince, Dream On Dream On, 6 started.

Lorelei S., Louisiana Downs, July 9, $56,020, 3yo, f, $1\frac{1}{16}$m, 1:44.99, RASPBERRY WINE, Zarba the Great, Snipper Lou, 7 started.

LOS ANGELES TIMES H. (G3), Hollywood Park, May 14, $150,000, 3&up, 6f, 1:08.57, FOREST GROVE, Areyoutalkintome, Woke Up Dreamin, 6 started.

Lost Code Breeders' Cup S., Hawthorne Race Course, April 9, $143,650, 3yo, 6f, 1:09.45, SMOKE SMOKE SMOKE, Santana Strings, Around the Cape, 8 started.

Louise Kimball S. (R), Suffolk Downs, Oct. 8, $40,000, 3yo, f, Massachusetts-bred, 1m, 1:43.07, STYLISH SULTANA, Branded in Gold, Dale's Desire, 8 started.

Louisiana Breeders' Derby (R), Louisiana Downs, Sept. 17, $105,400, 3yo, Louisiana-bred, $1\frac{1}{16}$m, 1:44.29, BADTOTHEBONEANDREW, Z Storm, Isle of Silver, 8 started.

Louisiana Breeders' Oaks (R), Louisiana Downs, Sept. 17, $104,850, 3yo, f, Louisiana-bred, $1\frac{1}{16}$m, 1:45.72, MIRIAM L., Leestown Fantasie, Tensas Star, 7 started.

Louisiana Champions Day Classic S. (R), Fair Grounds at Louisiana Downs, Dec. 10, $150,000, 3&up, Louisiana-bred, $1\frac{1}{8}$m, 1:53.69, BADTOTHEBONEANDREW, Nitro Chip, Sanctuary's Omooni, 7 started.

Louisiana Champions Day Juvenile S. (R), Fair Grounds at Louisiana Downs, Dec. 10, $100,000, 2yo, Louisiana-bred, 6f, 1:13.19, NOB HILL DEELITE, Hud's Playmate, Voodoo Gold, 8 started.

Louisiana Champions Day Ladies S. (R), Fair Grounds at Louisiana Downs, Dec. 10, $100,000, 3&up, f&m, Louisiana-bred, $1\frac{1}{16}$m, 1:46.13, THE BETER MAN CAN, Bonita's Reinbeau, Destiny Calls, 10 started.

Louisiana Champions Day Lassie S. (R), Fair Grounds at Louisiana Downs, Dec. 10, $100,000, 2yo, f, Louisiana-bred, 6f, 1:13.21, TORTUGA FLATS, Grand Facile, Leesa Lee, 7 started.

Louisiana Champions Day Sprint S. (R), Fair Grounds at Louisiana Downs, Dec. 10, $100,000, 3&up, Louisiana-bred, 6f, 1:10.90, ZARB'S DAHAR, Zarb's Luck, Meteor Impact, 8 started.

Louisiana Champions Day Starter H. (R), Fair Grounds at Louisiana Downs, Dec. 10, $50,000, 3&up, Louisiana-bred starters for a claiming price of $20,000 or less in 2005, $1\frac{1}{16}$m, 1:49.76, PONOPAAN, Sacrament, Stratford On Avon, 8 started.

Louisiana Champions Day Turf S. (R), Fair Grounds at Louisiana Downs, Dec. 10, $100,000, 3&up, Louisiana-bred, $1\frac{1}{16}$mT, 1:44.83, MR. SULU, Spruce's Prince, Sevenapriladthirty, 6 started.

LOUISIANA DERBY (G2), Fair Grounds, March 12, $600,000, 3yo, $1\frac{1}{16}$m, 1:42.74, HIGH LIMIT, Vicarage, Storm Surge, 9 started.

Louisiana Downs Breeders' Cup H., Louisiana Downs, Oct. 2, $121,000, 3&up, $1\frac{1}{16}$mT, 1:41.69, DONTBOTHERKNOCKING, Waupaca, Middleweight, 12 started.

Louisiana Futurity (R), Fair Grounds at Louisiana Downs, Dec. 31, $75,740, 2yo, f, Louisiana-bred, 6f, 1:10.97, TORTUGA FLATS, Hottamolly, Leesa Lee, 5 started.

Louisiana Futurity (R), Fair Grounds at Louisiana Downs, Dec. 31, $79,140, 2yo, c&g, Louisiana-bred, 6f, 1:11.80, NOB HILL DEELITE, Carson Bay, Cut Off Time, 7 started.

Louisiana HBPA S., Evangeline Downs, Dec. 3, $75,000, 3&up, f&m,

5 1/2f, 1:03.70, INDIGO GIRL, Shes Dixies Eskimo, Living Lavida Lisa, 7 started.

Louisiana Premier Night Bon Temps Starter S. (R), Delta Downs, Feb. 5, $45,000, 4&up, f&m, Louisiana-bred starters for a claiming price of $7,500 in 2004-'05, 5f, 1:01.06, ADIEU AND FAREWELL, Bewitching Hour, Victorious Hour, 7 started.

Louisiana Premier Night Championship S. (R), Delta Downs, Feb. 5, $200,000, 4&up, Louisiana-bred, 1 1/16m, 1:45.86, NITRO CHIP, Witt Ante, Meteor Impact, 9 started.

Louisiana Premier Night Distaff S. (R), Delta Downs, Feb. 5, $150,000, 4&up, f&m, Louisiana-bred, 1m, 1:40.81, DESTINY CALLS, Legs O'Neal, Cute N Noble, 6 started.

Louisiana Premier Night Gentlemen Starter S. (R), Delta Downs, Feb. 5, $55,000, 4&up, Louisiana-bred starters for a claiming price of $15,000 or less in 2004-'05, 1 1/16m, 1:48.15, SUNUP SUNDOWN, Huttutrefo, Kriss Is School, 8 started.

Louisiana Premier Night Ladies Starter S. (R), Delta Downs, Feb. 5, $55,000, 4&up, f&m, Louisiana-bred starters for a claiming price of $15,000 or less in 2004-'05, 1m, 1:43.29, RICH'N RESTLESS, Goodbye Beautiful, Agree to Disagree, 9 started.

Louisiana Premier Night Matron S. (R), Delta Downs, Feb. 5, $100,000, 4&up, f&m, Louisiana-bred, 5f, :59.28, WHERE IS MY DADDY, Crypto Em, Kylers Midge, 10 started.

Louisiana Premier Night Prince S. (R), Delta Downs, Feb. 5, $125,000, 3yo, Louisiana-bred, 7f, 1:28.21, CRIMSON STAG, St. Roch, Grande Diablo, 10 started.

Louisiana Premier Night Ragin Cajun Starter S. (R), Delta Downs, Feb. 5, $45,000, 4&up, Louisiana-bred starters for a claiming price of $7,500 in 2004-'05, 5f, :59.80, LED BY THE LIGHT, Screamin Demon, Heller, 10 started.

Louisiana Premier Night Sprint S. (R), Delta Downs, Feb. 5, $100,000, 4&up, Louisiana-bred, 5f, :59.59, LAC LARONGE, Believe Im Special, Rent a Prince, 8 started.

Louisiana Premier Night Starlet S. (R), Delta Downs, Feb. 5, $125,000, 3yo, f, Louisiana-bred, 7f, 1:28.52, SWEET MACARONI, Indigo Girl, Equestrian Girls, 10 started.

LOUISVILLE BREEDERS' CUP H. (G2), Churchill Downs, May 6, $336,300, 3&up, f&m, 1 1/16m, 1:42.43, SHADOW CAST, Island Sand, Storm's Darling, 9 started.

LOUISVILLE H. (G3), Churchill Downs, May 30, $110,400, 3&up, 1 3/8mT, 2:18.77, SILVERFOOT, Rochester, Epicentre, 7 started.

Loyalty S. (R), Thistledown, Sept. 4, $40,000, 2yo, Ohio-bred, 6f, 1:12.54, TOMMY PANACHE, Cruzable, Fisticuff, 11 started.

Lulu's Ransom S., Calder Race Course, June 26, $40,000, 3yo, f, 1m, 1:39.66, DARLUNA, Ragtime Hope, Wise Briana, 7 started.

Lure S., Gulfstream Park, Jan. 15, $60,000, 4&up, 7 1/2f, 1:29, QUEST, Judiths Wild Rush, Gran Cesare (Arg), 8 started.

Luther Burbank H., Santa Rosa, July 30, $60,750, 3&up, f&m, 1 1/16mT, 1:43.37, PENNY ANTE, Pickle (GB), Lucky Sabre, 7 started.

Lyman Sprint Championship H. (R), Philadelphia Park, July 2, $54,900, 3&up, Pennsylvania-bred, 7f, 1:23.28, BANJO PICKER, Nittany Express, North Potomac, 7 started.

Lyrique H., Louisiana Downs, Sept. 3, $50,000, 3yo, f, 1 1/16mT, 1:42.21, MALIKA'S GOLD, Prospectors Spirit, Where's Bailey, 10 started.

MAC DIARMIDA H. (G3), Gulfstream Park, Jan. 30, $100,000, 3&up, 1 3/8mT, 2:12.83, HOST, Navesink River, Burning Sun, 12 started.

Mack Hall Starter H. (R), Turf Paradise, Oct. 15, $20,000, 3&up, consigned to and passed through the sales ring at any ATBA sale and started for a claiming price of $8,000 or less since September 30, 2004, 6 1/2f, 1:15.25, BARRICADED, Rapid Dance, Sunnys Siren, 7 started.

Mackinac H. (R), Great Lakes Downs, Sept. 21, $50,000, 3yo, c&g, Michigan-bred, 1 1/16m, 1:49.15, DEMAGOGUERY, Its His Time, Buscando Fortuna, 9 started.

Mademoiselle H., Hastings Race Course, June 17, $35,964, 3yo, f, 1 1/16m, 1:46.66, REGAL PUSHER, Slewpast, Country Kat, 6 started.

Mademoiselle H., Marquis Downs, July 22, $4,927, 3&up, f&m, 1m, 1:40.75, PICTURE THE ANSWER, She's Nifty, Celtic Dance, 9 started.

Madamoiselle H., Northlands Park, Aug. 12, $41,640, 3&up, f&m, 1 1/16m, 1:44.80, ICE GIRL, dh-Raylene, dh-Weekend Ceilidh, 7 started.

Mademoiselle S. (R), Delta Downs, March 11, $50,000, 4&up, f&m, Louisiana-bred, 6 1/2f, 1:20.68, WHERE IS MY DADDY, Living Lavida Lisa, Midnight Delight, 9 started.

Magic City Classic S. (R), River Downs, June 4, $55,000, 3&up, Alabama-bred, 1m70y, 1:41.80, CHIEF TUDOR, Fancy Empire, Bama Royal, 13 started.

Magnolia State H. (R), Fair Grounds, March 27, $20,000, 3&up, Mississippi-owned, 6f, 1:11.27, SMALLTOWN SLEW, Cheery Hour, Driftwood Lodge, 7 started.

Maid of the Mist S. (R), Belmont Park, Oct. 22, $100,000, 2yo, f, New York-bred, 1m, 1:39.33, CINDERELLA'S DREAM, Zippy Missy, Little Miss Zip, 12 started.

Majorette H., Louisiana Downs, Oct. 2, $40,000, 3&up, f&m, a5fT, :55.62, COMALAGOLD, Nicole's Dream, Runs Naked, 10 started.

Major Moran S., Calder Race Course, Aug. 28, $40,000, 3&up, 6f, 1:10.89, NIGHTMARE AFFAIR, Paradise Dancer, Swift Replica, 6 started.

Make Me Conquer S., Delaware Park, Aug. 6, $59,900, 3&up, f&m, 6f, 1:10.28, THERMAL ABLASION, Valley of the Gods, Clay's Rocket, 7 started.

MAKER'S MARK MILE S. (G2), Keeneland Race Course, April 15, $250,000, 4&up, 1mT, 1:34.09, ARTIE SCHILLER, Gulch Approval, Good Reward, 10 started.

Malcolm Anderson S., Golden Gate Fields, June 18, $75,000, 2yo, 5f, :57.83, COUSINS LEW, Cause to Believe, Don Jaun Con, 9 started.

MALIBU S. (G1), Santa Anita Park, Dec. 26, $250,000, 3yo, 7f, 1:21.62, PROUD TOWER TOO, Attila's Storm, Thor's Echo, 14 started.

Mamie Eisenhower S. (R), Prairie Meadows, May 14, $60,000, 3&up, f&m, Iowa-bred, 6f, 1:11.68, SWITCH LANES, Traveler, Only At Night, 6 started.

Mamzelle S., Churchill Downs, May 5, $112,100, 3&up, f&m, 5fT, :56.41, NICOLE'S DREAM, Mocha Queen, Singit, 8 started.

Manatee S., Tampa Bay Downs, Feb. 12, $60,000, 4&up, f&m, 7f, 1:24.22, GRAB BAG, Ebony Breeze, Habiboo, 12 started.

Manhattan Beach S., Hollywood Park, May 29, $94,350, 3yo, f, 5 1/2fT, 1:03.17, KRESGEVILLE, Brooke's Halo, Private Banking (Fr), 11 started.

MANHATTAN H. (G1), Belmont Park, June 11, $400,000, 3&up, 1 1/4mT, 2:00.69, GOOD REWARD, Relaxed Gesture (Ire), Artie Schiller, 11 started.

Manhattan S. (R), The Woodlands, Sept. 25, $25,000, 3&up, f&m, Kansas-bred, 6f, 1:11.80, LADY LEGEND, Missy Can Do, Onda Ray, 5 started.

Manitoba Derby, Assiniboia Downs, Aug. 1, $81,700, 3yo, 1 1/8m, 1:52.20, PRIME TIME T. V., Wayzata Bay, Stormy Business, 11 started.

Manitoba Maturity S., Assiniboia Downs, July 9, $32,804, 4yo, 1 1/16m, 1:47.40, ALBARINO, Simply Regal, Stonewall Harris, 4 started.

Manitoba S., Assiniboia Downs, June 25, $32,456, 3yo, 1m, 1:41.80, RESURGENT, Whiskey Drive, Your Excellence, 12 started.

Manor Downs Thoroughbred Futurity, Manor Downs, April 24, $20,000, 2yo, 4 1/2f, :53.84, GOLD BEACON, Kim Impossible, Katekari, 8 started.

MAN O'WAR S. (G1), Belmont Park, Sept. 10, $500,000, 3&up, 1 3/8mT, 2:11.65, BETTER TALK NOW, King's Drama (Ire), Relaxed Gesture (Ire), 11 started.

MAPLE LEAF S. (Can-G3), Woodbine, Nov. 12, $176,568, 3&up, f&m, 1 1/4m, 2:05.77, BALLROOM DEPUTY, Quick Temper, Silver Impulse, 12 started.

Marathon Series Final S., Turf Paradise, March 1, $25,200, 4&up, 1 5/8m, 2:44.82, HAMMERIN, Rasty, Ive Got the Rhythm, 11 started.

Marcellus Frost Hurdle S., Percy Warner, May 14, $48,500, 4&up, a2mT, 3:51.20, UNDERSTOOD, Three Carat, Party Airs, 6 started.

March Madness Starter H. (R), Santa Anita Park, March 26, $44,786, 4&up, starters for a claiming price of $40,000 or less since February 1, 2004, 1mT, 1:34.74, FAIL ME NOT (ARG), Sigfreto, Right Proof, 4 started.

Mardi Gras H., Fair Grounds, Feb. 8, $50,000, 4&up, a7 1/2fT, 1:31.86, WARLEIGH, Shiloh Bound, Social King, 10 started.

Marfa S., Turfway Park, Sept. 24, $75,000, 3&up, 6 1/2f, AW, 1:17.08 (NTR), LEVEL PLAYINGFIELD, Korbyn Gold, With Distinction, 8 started.

Margaret Currey Henley Sport of Queens Hurdle S., Percy Warner, May 14, $29,100, 4&up, f&m, a2 1/4mT, 4:20.60, FEELING SO PRETTY, Orchid Princess, Class Yankee, 8 started.

Margarita Breeders' Cup H., Retama Park, Aug. 6, $29,250, 3&up, f&m, 1 1/16mT, 1:41.99, PAZ CIUDADANA (CHI), Rose Hunter, Topango, 9 started.

Mariah's Storm S., Arlington Park, Aug. 12, $47,100, 3&up, f&m, 1 1/8m, 1:49.68, INDY GROOVE, For Gillian, Catboat, 7 started.

Marie G. Krantz Memorial H., Fair Grounds, March 12, $100,000, 4&up, f&m, a7 1/2fT, 1:31.29, WARNING ZONE (SAF), Sister Swank, Gamble to Victory, 12 started.

Marie P. DeBartolo Oaks, Louisiana Downs, Oct. 1, $76,100, 3yo, f,

1$^1/_{16}$mT, 1:42.75, MORE THAN PROMISED, Enduring Will, Equestrian Girls, 11 started.

Marina De Chavon S., Calder Race Course, Dec. 4, $40,000, 3&up, f&m, 6$^1/_2$f, 1:18.31, KUANYAN, Midtown Miss, Tigi, 8 started.

MARINE S. (Can-G3), Woodbine, May 21, $131,676, 3yo, 1$^1/_{16}$m, 1:46, UNBRIDLED ENERGY, Wholelottabourbon, Palladio, 7 started.

Marshua S., Pimlico Race Course, Jan. 8, $50,000, 3yo, f, 6f, 1:12.53, ELLAJEAN, Maysville, Promenade Girl, 6 started.

Marshua's River S., Gulfstream Park, Jan. 9, $60,000, 3&up, f&m, 1$^1/_{16}$mT, 1:39.39, ANGELA'S LOVE, Delta Princess, Snowdrops (GB), 12 started.

Martanza S. (R), Sam Houston Race Park, Nov. 19, $75,000, 3&up, f&m, Texas-bred, 1m, 1:40.38, SLEWPY'S STORM, Shons Secret, Cookin's Cast, 7 started.

Martha Washington Breeders' Cup S., Laurel Park, Sept. 24, $150,000, 3yo, f, 1$^1/_{16}$mT, 1:41.63, SWEET TALKER, Lucrezia, Dynamite Lass, 7 started.

Martha Washington S., Oaklawn Park, Feb. 21, $50,000, 3yo, f, 1m, 1:39.11, ISABELL'S SHOES, Carlea, Kota, 6 started.

Mary Goldblatt S. (R), Portland Meadows, March 5, $8,000, 3yo, f, Oregon-bred, 1m, 1:42.47, QUARTERN, Yourgoldgirl, Gordys Sweet Jordy, 9 started.

MARYLAND BREEDERS' CUP H. (G3), Pimlico Race Course, May 21, $189,000, 3&up, 6f, 1:09.95, WILLY O'THE VALLEY, With Distinction, Take Achance On Me, 8 started.

Maryland Hunt Cup Timber S., Glyndon, April 30, $60,450, 5&up, a4mT, 9:48.80, MAKE ME A CHAMP, Bug River, Lil Starvin Marvin, 7 started.

Maryland Juvenile Championship S. (R), Laurel Park, Dec. 31, $75,000, 2yo, Maryland-bred, 1m, 1:40.94, VEGAS PLAY, Creve Coeur, Travelin Leroy, 9 started.

Maryland Juvenile Filly Championship S. (R), Laurel Park, Dec. 26, $75,000, 2yo, f, Maryland-bred, 1m, 1:41.04, SOMETHINABOUTBETTY, Don't Tell Susan, Keep On Talking, 5 started.

Maryland Million Classic S. (R), Laurel Park, Oct. 15, $237,500, 3&up, Maryland-bred, 1$^3/_{16}$m, 1:59.08, PLAY BINGO, Aggadan, Five Steps, 6 started.

Maryland Million Distaff S. (R), Laurel Park, Oct. 15, $142,500, 3&up, f&m, Maryland-bred, 7f, 1:25.34, VALLEY OF THE GODS, Blind Canyon, Spirited Game, 9 started.

Maryland Million Distaff Starter H. (R), Laurel Park, Oct. 15, $47,500, 3&up, f&m, Maryland-bred starters for a claiming price of $12,500 or less since October 9, 2004, 1m, 1:40.16, MARLEY HART, Seventeen Above, Bo's Typhoon, 10 started.

Maryland Million Ladies S. (R), Laurel Park, Oct. 15, $142,500, 3&up, f&m, Maryland-bred, 1$^1/_8$mT, 1:51.95 (NCR), SURF LIGHT, Sassy Love, Rowdy, 7 started.

Maryland Million Lassie S. (R), Laurel Park, Oct. 15, $118,750, 2yo, f, Maryland-bred, 7f, 1:25.98, SMART AND FANCY, Who Was, Swear to It, 8 started.

Maryland Million Nursery S. (R), Laurel Park, Oct. 15, $118,750, 2yo, Maryland-bred, 7f, 1:26.21, CREVE COEUR, X Marks the Spot, Preferred Lender, 10 started.

Maryland Million Oaks (R), Laurel Park, Oct. 15, $142,500, 3yo, f, Maryland-bred, 1$^1/_8$m, 1:54.20, STICKY, Lexi Star, Unbridled Grace, 7 started.

Maryland Million Sprint S. (R), Laurel Park, Oct. 15, $142,500, 3&up, Maryland-bred, 6f, 1:10.68, SAAY MI NAME, Cherokee's Boy, American Proud, 9 started.

Maryland Million Sprint Starter H. (R), Laurel Park, Oct. 15, $28,500, 3&up, Maryland-bred starters for a claiming price of $12,500 or less since October 9, 2004, 6f, 1:11.96, FOXS GOLD DIGGER, Summer Carnival, Dixie Rap, 8 started.

Maryland Million Starter H. (R), Laurel Park, Nov. 19, $50,000, 3&up, starters for a claiming price of $10,000 or less since November 20, 2004, 1m, 1:38.82, SUM MARVAL, Summer Carnival, Johns Rush, 7 started.

Maryland Million Starter H. (R), Laurel Park, Oct. 15, $47,500, 3&up, Maryland-bred, 1$^1/_8$m, 1:54.09, DIXIE COLONY, Mr Song and Dance, All Irish, 8 started.

Maryland Million Turf S. (R), Laurel Park, Oct. 15, $142,500, 3&up, Maryland-bred, 1$^1/_8$mT, 1:51.60, LA REINE'S TERMS, Dr Detroit, Rubi Echo, 9 started.

Maryland Million Turf Sprint S. (R), Laurel Park, Oct. 15, $95,000, 3&up, Maryland-bred, 5fT, :56.53, SARAH'S PROSPECT, Love Antics, Mr Mutter, 11 started.

Maryland My Maryland S. (R), Calder Race Course, May 21, $50,000, 3&up, non-winners of two races other than maiden, claiming, or starter as of April 22, 2005 or $25,000 claiming or a starter for $16,000 or less in 2004-'05, 1$^3/_{16}$m, 2:04.12, SIR RAY, Perspicacious (Arg), Sir Jackie, 8 started.

Maryland Racing Media H., Laurel Park, Feb. 26, $50,000, 3&up, f&m, 1$^1/_8$m, 1:52.81, FRIEL'S FOR REAL, Pour It On, Summer Rainbow, 7 started.

Maryland Stallion Station S. (R), Pimlico Race Course, April 23, $97,000, 3yo, Maryland-bred and/or Maryland Million-nominated, 6f, 1:12.30, CELTIC INNIS, Mojodajo, Monster Chaser, 7 started.

Mason Houghland Memorial Timber S., Percy Warner, May 14, $48,500, 4&up, a3mT, 6:25.80, ALBERT'S CROSSING, Bubble Economy, No Fast Moves, 8 started.

Matchmaker H. (R), Lincoln State Fair, June 18, $20,700, 3&up, f&m, Nebraska-bred, 1m, 1:38.60, UP 'N BLUMIN, Magic Trump, Sheso, 7 started.

Matron Breeders' Cup S., Assiniboia Downs, Sept. 24, $53,363, 3&up, f&m, 1$^1/_8$m, 1:53.80, RAYLENE, J D's Deelites, Ice Girl, 7 started.

Matron H., Evangeline Downs, Sept. 3, $50,000, 3&up, f&m, 1m, 1:41.66, MISTY GLO, Phone Affair, Leestown Lib, 6 started.

Matron H., Marquis Downs, June 24, $4,871, 3&up, f&m, 6f, 1:14.35, BRITE STEEL, Bonnie Bo, Picture the Answer, 8 started.

MATRON S. (G1), Belmont Park, Sept. 17, $300,000, 2yo, f, 7f, 1:23.70, FOLKLORE, Miss Norman, Along the Sea, 7 started.

Matt Winn S., Churchill Downs, May 14, $109,700, 3yo, 6f, 1:09.48, RAZOR, Crimson Stag, Sir Laff Alot, 7 started.

Maxine M. Piggott S. (R), Turf Paradise, April 30, $40,000, 3yo, f, Arizona-bred, 6$^1/_2$f, 1:17.73, MISSINGRBUENO, Lite Write, Lil Blue Sky, 8 started.

Maxxam Gold Cup H., Sam Houston Race Park, Jan. 22, $100,000, 4&up, 1$^1/_8$m, 1:51.10, ALUMNI HALL, Colonial Colony, Toratora, 7 started.

MAZARINE BREEDERS' CUP S. (Can-G3), Woodbine, Oct. 1, $232,625, 2yo, f, 1$^1/_{16}$m, 1:43.15, KNIGHTS TEMPLAR, Sudsy Baby, Top Notch Lady, 11 started.

McFadden Memorial S. (R), Portland Meadows, Feb. 19, $9,000, 3yo, c&g, Oregon-bred, 1$^1/_{16}$m, 1:50.08, RAGGIDY ROWE, Big Tuff and Ugly, A Colt Named Sue, 7 started.

Meadow Brook Hurdle S. (R), Belmont Park, June 12, $80,350, 4&up, non-winners over hurdles prior to March 1, 2004, a2$^1/_2$mT, 4:33.95 (NCR), PARADISE'S BOSS, Class Yankee, Mixed Up, 14 started.

MEADOWLANDS BREEDERS' CUP S. (G2), Meadowlands, Oct. 7, $500,000, 3&up, 1$^1/_8$m, 1:48.86, TAP DAY, Alumni Hall, Purge, 8 started.

Meadow Star S. (R), Belmont Park, June 18, $57,550, 3yo, f, non-winners of an open stakes, 6f, 1:09.11, PARTNERS DUE, Exit to Heaven, Exploivacious, 4 started.

Meafara Breeders' Cup S., Hawthorne Race Course, April 9, $144,000, 3yo, f, 6f, 1:10.92, PORTSEA, Megascape, Angel Trumpet, 8 started.

Mecke H., Calder Race Course, July 4, $100,000, 3&up, 1$^1/_8$mT, 1:49.87, KEEP COOL, Bob's Proud Moment, Demeteor, 12 started.

MEDE CAHABA ALL ALONG BREEDERS' CUP S. (G3), Colonial Downs, July 16, $200,000, 3&up, f&m, 1$^1/_8$mT, 1:51.10, STUPENDOUS MISS, Humoristic, Dynamia, 10 started.

Melair S. (R), Hollywood Park, April 24, $200,000, 3yo, f, California-bred, 1$^1/_{16}$m, 1:43.07, LEAVE ME ALONE, Cee's Irish, Two Times Won, 10 started.

Mel's Hope S., Calder Race Course, Dec. 14, $40,000, 3yo, 1$^1/_{16}$mT, 1:41.28, DREAM ON DREAM ON, Zurich (Ire), Holy Ground, 8 started.

MEMORIAL DAY H. (G3), Calder Race Course, May 30, $100,000, 3&up, 1$^1/_{16}$m, 1:47.71, TWILIGHT ROAD, Whos Crying Now, Hear No Evil, 8 started.

Memories of Silver S. (R), Belmont Park, Sept. 25, $68,450, 4&up, f&m, non-winners of a stakes on the turf, 1$^1/_{16}$mT, 1:42.25, SHARP NEEDLE (GB), Louve Royale (Ire), La Reina, 7 started.

Merrillville S. (R), Hoosier Park, Oct. 22, $40,000, 3&up, f&m, Indiana-bred, 6f, 1:10.68, LADY BLUE SKY, My Sweet Sug, A Fine One, 10 started.

Merry Colleen S., Hawthorne Race Course, April 1, $42,000, 4&up, f&m, 1$^1/_{16}$m, 1:45.51, GHOSTLY GATE, Julie's Prize, Catboat, 5 started.

Merry Time S. (R), Thistledown, June 18, $45,000, 3&up, f&m, Ohio-bred, 1$^1/_{16}$m, 1:47.08, OH SO EASY, Spring Cat, Imahoneytoo, 8 started.

MERVIN H. MUNIZ JR. MEMORIAL H. (G2), Fair Grounds, March 19, $500,000, 4&up, a1$^1/_8$mT, 1:50.99, A TO THE Z, America Alive, Honor in War, 11 started.

Mervin Muniz Memorial S. (R), Evangeline Downs, July 30, $25,000, 3&up, Louisiana-bred starters for a claiming price of $10,000 or less in 2004-'05, 1m70y, 1:46.68, J D MAN, Seemeloadandfire, Coastal Cat, 6 started.

MERVYN LEROY H. (G2), Hollywood Park, May 14, $150,000, 3&up, 1$^1/_{16}$m, 1:41.45, ACE BLUE (BRZ), Ender's Shadow, Borrego, 7 started.

Mesa H., Turf Paradise, Dec. 17, $40,000, 3&up, f&m, 6$^1/_2$f, 1:16.65, MISS HESTER, Kresgeville, Smarty Me, 10 started.

METROPOLITAN H. (G1), Belmont Park, May 30, $750,000, 3&up, 1m, 1:33.29, GHOSTZAPPER, Silver Wagon, Sir Shackleton, 6 started.

MIAMI MILE BREEDERS' CUP H. (G3), Calder Race Course, Sept. 5, $85,500, 3&up, 1mT, 1:38.18, BOB'S PROUD MOMENT, Dancing Master (Ire), Southern Cal, 9 started.

Mia's Hope S. (R), Calder Race Course, Nov. 25, $40,000, 3&up, f&m, non-winners of a stakes of $15,000 twice at one mile or over since September 15, 1$^1/_{16}$m, 1:48.56, MENIFEEQUE, Pitanga, Leona's Knight, 5 started.

Michael G. Schaefer Mile S., Hoosier Park, Nov. 19, $104,100, 3&up, 1m, 1:37.52, IOSILVER, Artemus Sunrise, Private Horde, 7 started.

Michigan Breeders' H. (R), Great Lakes Downs, July 26, $50,000, 3&up, Michigan-bred, 1$^1/_{16}$m, 1:49.54, DORTHYS CHAMP, Rockem Sockem, Jaguar Joe, 10 started.

Michigan Futurity (R), Great Lakes Downs, Nov. 2, $41,250, 2yo, c&g, Michigan-bred, 7f, 1:28.74, ZEPHYR CHARLIE, Magical Powers, Gulch It's Hot, 7 started.

Michigan Futurity (R), Great Lakes Downs, Nov. 2, $41,250, 2yo, c&g, Michigan-bred, 7f, 1:29.24, GRRRIFECK, Kyle's Treasury, Out With a Bang, 7 started.

Michigan Juvenile Fillies S. (R), Great Lakes Downs, Nov. 1, $73,800, 2yo, f, Michigan-bred, 7f, 1:28.10, CHAREDI'S PEAK, Summer Cyclone, Brick by Brick, 8 started.

Michigan Oaks (R), Great Lakes Downs, Sept. 20, $50,000, 3yo, f, Michigan-bred, 1$^1/_{16}$m, 1:49.52, CREATIVE MISS, Maxie Match, Half a Glance, 8 started.

Michigan Sire S. (R), Great Lakes Downs, Oct. 15, $144,587, 4&up, c&g, progeny of eligible Michigan sires, 1$^1/_8$m, 1:57.35, ROCKEM SOCKEM, Lite Up, Kid Attitude, 10 started.

Michigan Sire S. (R), Great Lakes Downs, Oct. 15, $140,887, 2yo, f, progeny of eligible Michigan sires, 6f, 1:17.45, EASY ELLIE, Silent Sunset, Summer Cyclone, 7 started.

Michigan Sire S. (R), Great Lakes Downs, Oct. 15, $141,887, 3yo, f, progeny of eligible Michigan sires, 1$^1/_{16}$m, 1:52.21, CREATIVE MISS, Steel Bond, Half a Glance, 8 started.

Michigan Sire S. (R), Great Lakes Downs, Oct. 15, $143,987, 4&up, f&m, progeny of eligible Michigan sires, 1$^1/_8$m, 2:00.18, SWEETWATER PROMISE, Deb's Favoite Gift, Ima Bender Boo, 10 started.

Michigan Sire S. (R), Great Lakes Downs, Oct. 15, $144,587, 2yo, c&g, progeny of eligible Michigan sires, 6f, 1:13.36, WEATHERSTORM, Kyle's Treasury, Stover, 10 started.

Michigan Sire S. (R), Great Lakes Downs, Oct. 15, $144,587, 3yo, c&g, progeny of eligible Michigan sires, 1$^1/_{16}$m, 1:50, MEADOW VESPERS, Buscando Fortuna, Q Big Top, 10 started.

Middleground Breeders' Cup S., Lone Star Park, July 16, $73,500, 2yo, c&g, 6f, 1:10.96, PREMIER DANCE, Don't Tell Mommy, Out Our Way, 6 started.

Midland Odessa Sprint Series S. (1st Div.), Zia Park, Nov. 11, $14,000, 3&up, 6f, 1:09.80, SWEEPINGLY, Janzig Affair, Prideov Fappiano, 7 started.

Midland Odessa Sprint Series S. (2nd Div.), Zia Park, Nov. 11, $14,000, 3&up, 6f, 1:10.60, STEW'S STONE, Skeeman, Windsor Lodge, 6 started.

Midland/Odessa Sprint Series S., Zia Park, Nov. 28, $41,700, 3&up, 6$^1/_2$f, 1:15.80, PRIDEOV FAPPIANO, Skeeman, Sweepingly, 10 started.

Mike Lee S. (R), Belmont Park, June 26, $108,000, 3yo, New York-bred, 7f, 1:23.05, NAUGHTY NEW YORKER, Sort It Out, Blue Sunday, 6 started.

Mike Rowland Memorial H. (R), Thistledown, May 14, $40,000, 3&up, Ohio-bred, 6f, 1:12.20, CATCH MY CAT, Catlaunch, Cruzcat, 5 started.

MILADY BREEDERS' CUP H. (G2), Hollywood Park, June 4, $205,150, 3&up, f&m, 1$^1/_{16}$m, 1:41.59, ANDUJAR, Hollywood Story, Star Parade (Arg), 7 started.

Mile Hi H., Yavapai Downs, Aug. 28, $20,000, 3&up, 1$^1/_{16}$m, 1:43.60, NICE CHOICE, Acting Report, Gospodin, 11 started.

Miles City Thoroughbred Maiden S., Cow Capital Turf Club, May 22, $4,600, 3&up, 5$^1/_2$f, 1:09.40, RILEYS KNIGHT, A Leo Thing, Sweet Stories, 7 started.

Millard Harrell Memorial S. (R), Charles Town Races, Sept. 10, $41,200, 3yo, West Virginia-bred, 7f, 1:27.51, BRYCESLITTLESECRET, Raggedy Andy, Hello Out There, 9 started.

Millarville Derby, Millarville Race Society, Sept. 4, $26,610, 3&up, 1$^1/_8$m, 2:01.40, LOST AGAIN, Tata Pantoja, Ezee Target, 8 started.

Millarville Sprint S., Millarville Race Society, Sept. 4, $13,642, 3&up, 5f, 1:03.60, WARTOCK, Shootin for Gold, Dr. Mo, 8 started.

Miller Lite S., Lone Star Park, June 25, $50,000, 3&up, f&m, 5fT, :56.21, QUEENA CORRINA, Timeless Dreamer, Twice a Deelite, 9 started.

Mill Valley S., Golden Gate Fields, Nov. 26, $50,600, 2yo, 6f, 1:09.22, CAUSE TO BELIEVE, Barber, John Hennessy, 10 started.

Milwaukee Avenue H. (R), Hawthorne Race Course, April 30, $92,700, 3&up, Illinois-conceived and/or -foaled, 1$^1/_{16}$m, 1:45.87, HOME OF STARS, Magic Doe, Garesche, 11 started.

Minaret S., Tampa Bay Downs, Jan. 8, $60,000, 4&up, f&m, 6f, 1:10.54, SLEWS FINAL ANSWER, Diablosangeleyes, Beautiful Honor, 13 started.

MINESHAFT H. (G3), Fair Grounds, Feb. 12, $100,000, 4&up, 1$^1/_{16}$m, 1:43.08, WANDERIN BOY, Pollard's Vision, Gigawatt, 9 started.

Minneapolis S., Canterbury Park, Sept. 5, $40,000, 3&up, 1m70y, 1:40.75, WALLY'S CHOICE, Diligent Won, Wayzata Bay, 7 started.

Minnesota Classic Championship S. (R), Canterbury Park, Aug. 21, $43,650, 3&up, Minnesota-bred, 1$^1/_{16}$m, 1:42.51, WALLY'S CHOICE, Bisquik, Blue Dancer, 4 started.

Minnesota Derby (R), Canterbury Park, July 30, $62,800, 3yo, c&g, Minnesota-bred, 1m70y, 1:41.16, KEY ISSUES, Bisquik, Roust About, 11 started.

Minnesota Distaff Classic Championship S. (R), Canterbury Park, Aug. 21, $45,000, 3&up, f&m, Minnesota-bred, 1$^1/_{16}$m, 1:44.88, GLITTER STAR, Play N Fare, Ma Home Cat, 8 started.

Minnesota Distaff Sprint Championship S. (R), Canterbury Park, Aug. 21, $40,000, 3&up, f&m, Minnesota-bred, 6f, 1:11.15, BLEU'S APPARITION, Maywood's Jill, Swasti, 6 started.

Minnesota HBPA Mile S., Canterbury Park, July 4, $40,000, 3&up, f&m, 1mT, 1:35.42, GHOSTLY GATE, Lost Bride, Music Way, 6 started.

Minnesota HBPA Sprint S., Canterbury Park, July 4, $40,000, 3&up, 6$^1/_2$f, 1:15.52, DILIGENT WON, Wimplestiltskin, Vazandar, 6 started.

Minnesota Oaks (R), Canterbury Park, July 30, $61,800, 3yo, f, Minnesota-bred, 1m70y, 1:42.22, GLITTER STAR, Oh You Again, Ma Home Cat, 9 started.

Minnesota Sprint Championship S. (R), Canterbury Park, Aug. 21, $40,000, 3&up, Minnesota-bred, 6f, 1:09.19, TOGA SWITCH, Vazandar, Sahab, 7 started.

Minnesota Turf Championship S. (R), Canterbury Park, Aug. 21, $40,000, 3&up, Minnesota-bred, a1mT, 1:38.90, LT. SAMPSON, Sajjan, Bassant, 7 started.

Minstrel S., Louisiana Downs, Aug. 13, $50,000, 2yo, 6f, 1:10.71, PREMIER DANCE, Smart 'n Salty, Noble Texas, 6 started.

MINT JULEP H. (G3), Churchill Downs, June 4, $110,100, 3&up, f&m, 1$^1/_{16}$mT, 1:42.43, DELTA PRINCESS, Shaconage, Erhu, 7 started.

Miracle Wood S., Laurel Park, Feb. 5, $58,500, 3yo, 1m, 1:40.25, MALIBU MOONSHINE, Legal Control, Seize, 11 started.

Miss America H., Bay Meadows Race Course, April 9, $64,875, 3&up, f&m, 1$^1/_{16}$mT, 1:44.88, FIRST DRAFT, Marla Bay, Pickle (GB), 6 started.

Miss America H., Golden Gate Fields, Oct. 30, $100,000, 3&up, f&m, 1$^1/_8$mT, 1:50.67, dh-UNINHIBITED SONG, dh-GIRL WARRIOR, First Draft, 9 started.

Miss Gibson County S., Turf Paradise, Oct. 31, $23,800, 2yo, f, 6f, 1:10.60, SILLY LITTLE MAMA, Coffeeinparis, Old Fashion Desire, 7 started.

Miss Grillo S., Belmont Park, Oct. 23, $82,550, 2yo, f, 1$^1/_8$m (originally scheduled on the turf), 1:52.87, WAIT A WHILE, Swap Fliparoo, Interpretation, 6 started.

Miss Indiana S. (R), Hoosier Park, Nov. 11, $40,000, 2yo, f, Indiana-bred, 6f, 1:12.80, SPOTLESS MIND, Lil Broad Tee, Dixie Dell, 6 started.

Miss Kansas City S., The Woodlands, Oct. 9, $20,000, 3&up, f&m, 1$^1/_{16}$m, 1:48.20, VANNACIDE, Defuhr, Reprized Angel, 8 started.

Miss Liberty S., Meadowlands, Nov. 8, $55,000, 3yo, f, 1m 70yT., 1:40.29, CROISIERE, Forever Smart, British Event, 8 started.

Miss Oceana S. (R), Aqueduct, Nov. 2, $66,650, 3yo, f, non-winners of an open stakes in 2005, 1m, 1:36.92, PLAY BALLADO, Classy Charm, Quail Run, 5 started.

Miss Ohio S. (R), Thistledown, Aug. 26, $40,000, 2yo, f, Ohio-bred, 6f, 1:12.14, LILLIANS CHOICE, Fight Girl, Lady Zora, 8 started.

Miss Woodford S., Monmouth Park, Aug. 20, $60,000, 3yo, f, 6f, 1:10.31, CAREER ORIENTED, Lady Dynasty, Neverlacken, 5 started.

Miss Yankee Doodle Starter H., Turf Paradise, Oct. 31, $10,650, 3&up,

f&m, 6f, 1:11.08, IN LOVE WITH LOOT, Chubby Is Ready, Coup de Foudre, 6 started.

Missy Good S. (R), Penn National Race Course, Aug. 26, $40,900, 3&up, f&m, Pennsylvania-bred, 6f, 1:10.80, DEFRERE'S VENTURE, Tigress Bythetail, Connie's Passion, 9 started.

Mister Diz S. (R), Pimlico Race Course, Aug. 20, $50,000, 3&up, Maryland-bred, 5fT, :56.87, YANKEE WILDCAT, Procreate, Spring Kitten, 8 started.

Mister Gus S., Arlington Park, May 30, $42,000, 3&up, a1mT, 1:36.87, FORT PRADO, Major Rhythm, Cloudy's Knight, 8 started.

Misty Galore S. (R), Belmont Park, July 2, $62,950, 4&up, f&m, nonwinners of an open stakes on dirt in 2005, 7½f, 1:28.13, STELLAR JAYNE, Provincial, Summer Rainbow, 4 started.

Mo Bay S., Delaware Park, July 4, $58,700, 3&up, 6f, 1:10.53, FOREST PARK, Dale's Prospect, Silver Flower, 6 started.

Moccasin S., Hollywood Park, Nov. 20, $100,000, 2yo, f, 7f, 1:22.39, PRIVATE WORLD, True Xena, Cotton Bay, 7 started.

MODESTY H. (G3), Arlington Park, July 23, $150,000, 3&up, f&m, 1³⁄₁₆mT, 1:57.30, NOISETTE, Shaconage, Spring Season, 11 started.

Mohawk H. (R), Belmont Park, Oct. 22, $150,000, 3&up, New York-bred, 1⅛m (originally scheduled on the turf), 1:51.22, WIN WITH BECK, Continental Reins, Chestertown Slew, 13 started.

Molly Brown H., Arapahoe Park, June 19, $27,250, 3&up, f&m, 6f, 1:09.22, HUMBLE ROANNIE, Shesa Private I, Bar Bailey, 6 started.

MOLLY PITCHER BREEDERS' CUP H. (G2), Monmouth Park, July 9, $300,000, 3&up, f&m, 1¹⁄₁₆m, 1:41.49, CAPESIDE LADY, Bending Strings, Emerald Earrings, 7 started.

Moment to Buy S., Golden Gate Fields, Nov. 12, $82,750, 3yo, f, 1¹⁄₁₆mT, 1:44.52, JILL'S SKY, Private Banking (Fr), Island Escape, 11 started.

Mongo Queen S., Monmouth Park, Sept. 25, $60,000, 3yo, f, 6f, 1:10.13, MISSILE BAY, Career Oriented, Partners Due, 6 started.

Monmouth Beach S., Monmouth Park, June 18, $70,000, 3&up, f&m, 1¹⁄₁₆m, 1:45.08, CAPESIDE LADY, Twist and Pop, Chrusciki, 8 started.

MONMOUTH BREEDERS' CUP OAKS (G3), Monmouth Park, Aug. 14, $200,000, 3yo, f, 1¹⁄₁₆m, 1:44.60, FLYING GLITTER, Shebelongstoyou, Toll Taker, 7 started.

Monmouth Park NATC Futurity (R), Monmouth Park, Sept. 24, $200,000, 2yo, f, offered for sale during 2005 and paid 2005 advertising fee fund, 6f, 1:11.20, SPARKLING PINK, More Than Pretty, Good Conduct, 8 started.

Monmouth Park NATC Futurity (R), Monmouth Park, Sept. 24, $200,000, 2yo, c&g, offered for sale during 2005 and paid 2005 advertising fee fund, 6f, 1:08.99, ATLANTIC BREEZE, Diabolical, Rock Creek Pass, 10 started.

Monrovia H., Santa Anita Park, Dec. 31, $112,600, 3&up, f&m, 6½f (originally scheduled as a Grade 3 at a6½f on the turf), 1:16.77, AWESOME LADY, Beneficial Bartok, Allswellthatnswell, 9 started.

Montauk H. (R), Aqueduct, Nov. 27, $80,400, 3&up, f&m, New York-bred, 1⅛m, 1:53.87, FLEET INDIAN, Star Celebrity, Shady Lane, 6 started.

Montclair State University S., Meadowlands, Nov. 11, $60,000, 3&up, f&m, 6f, 1:09.29, WELCOME HOME, Fortress Hill, Smartlee Away, 7 started.

Monterey H., Bay Meadows Race Course, Sept. 10, $67,300, 3&up, f&m, 5fT, :57.46, AWESOME LADY, Beezer, Our Mango, 8 started.

Moonbeam H. (R), Great Lakes Downs, July 23, $50,000, 3&up, f&m, Michigan-bred, 1m, 1:45.92, SWEETWATER PROMISE, Deb's Favoite Gift, Reasonable Code, 8 started.

Moonsplash S., Turf Paradise, Nov. 15, $23,700, 3&up, 4½fT, :50.80, BOBAWAY, Quintons Relaunch, Adroitly Superb, 7 started.

Morgan's Ford Farm Somethingroyal S. (R), Colonial Downs, July 23, $60,000, 3&up, f&m, Virginia-bred and/or -sired, 5½fT, 1:02.22, BRIGHT GOLD, With Patience, Neigh Highs, 6 started.

MORVICH H. (G3), Oak Tree at Santa Anita, Oct. 29, $100,000, 3&up, a6½fT, 1:12.10, GERONIMO (CHI), King Robyn, Jungle Prince, 8 started.

MOTHER GOOSE S. (G1), Belmont Park, June 25, $300,000, 3yo, f, 1⅛m, 1:48.55, SMUGGLER, Spun Sugar, Summerly, 6 started.

Mother's Day H., Finger Lakes, May 8, $20,500, 3&up, f&m, 5½f, 1:05.01, BLUE RIDGE LINDA, Elhew Midway, Flora Mac Flimsey, 7 started.

Mountaineer Juvenile Fillies S., Mountaineer Race Track, Aug. 14, $85,000, 2yo, f, 6f, 1:12.52, LIZZY'S TOWNSHIP, More Than Pretty, Dixie Dreamer, 6 started.

Mountaineer Juvenile S., Mountaineer Race Track, Aug. 14, $85,000, 2yo, 6f, 1:12.20, CRAFTY TRICKER, Gallows, Neverbeendancin', 7 started.

Mountaineer Mile H., Mountaineer Race Track, Nov. 12, $125,000, 3&up, 1m, 1:40.81, PRESIDENTIALAFFAIR, Discreet Hero, Seattle Schifty, 4 started.

Mountain Valley S., Oaklawn Park, March 5, $50,000, 3yo, 6f, 1:09.52, AFLEET ALEX, Razor, Smoke Smoke Smoke, 6 started.

Mount Elbert H. (R), Arapahoe Park, Aug. 6, $32,125, 3&up, c&g, Colorado-bred, 1¹⁄₁₆m, 1:44.91, LONG RANGE, Cut of Music, Tank Two, 7 started.

Mount Royal H., Stampede Park, May 8, $40,265, 3yo, f, 6f, 1:11.40, RUMBEAU RUCKUS, R Lucinda, Silver Seven, 7 started.

Mount Vernon H. (1st Div.) (R), Belmont Park, June 19, $84,100, 3&up, f&m, New York-bred, 1⅛mT, 1:49.12, LADY BI BI, Little Buttercup, Sabellina, 7 started.

Mount Vernon H. (2nd Div.) (R), Belmont Park, June 19, $85,100, 3&up, f&m, New York-bred, 1⅛mT, 1:49.06, KEVIN'S DECISION, Nurse Culkin, The Lamp Is Lit, 8 started.

M. R. Jenkins Memorial H., Stampede Park, May 1, $39,735, 4&up, f&m, 6f, 1:10.40, STOLE ONE, Unforgettable Too, Kellys Guest, 6 started.

Mr. Pappion S., Turf Paradise, Oct. 18, $23,600, 3&up, 1m, 1:39.22, POINT DUME, Brazen n' Bold, Cut of Music, 5 started.

MR. PROSPECTOR H. (G3), Gulfstream Park, Jan. 8, $100,000, 3&up, 6f, 1:08.99, SARATOGA COUNTY, Limehouse, All Hail Stormy, 10 started.

Mr. Prospector S., Monmouth Park, July 3, $65,000, 3&up, 6f, 1:09.46, PRETTY WILD, Trueamericanspirit, Kazoo, 6 started.

Mrs. Penny S. (R), Philadelphia Park, July 23, $50,000, 3&up, f&m, Pennsylvania-bred, 1¹⁄₁₆mT, 1:43.42, DYNAMIC CAT, All Dolled Up, Redaspen, 12 started.

MRS. REVERE S. (G2), Churchill Downs, Nov. 12, $166,950, 3yo, f, 1¹⁄₁₆mT, 1:43.36, MY TYPHOON (IRE), Isla Cozzene, Silver Cup (Ire), 7 started.

Ms. Brookski S., Calder Race Course, July 3, $40,000, 3&up, f&m, 7½fT, 1:33.48, R OBSESSION, You Glitter Girl, Shesadorabull, 10 started.

Ms Brookski S., Calder Race Course, Oct. 23, $40,000, 3&up, f&m, 7f, 1:24.51, KUANYAN, So Much More, Wild Speed, 8 started.

Ms. S., Portland Meadows, Feb. 5, $7,500, 3yo, f, 6f, 1:13.70, QUARTERN, One Fast Cowgirl, Secret Victory, 6 started.

Ms. Southern Ohio S. (R), River Downs, Aug. 6, $40,000, 3&up, f&m, Ohio-bred, 1¹⁄₁₆m (originally scheduled on the turf), 1:46.60, PATTI'S CLOWN, dh-Imahoneytoo, dh-Oh So Easy, 9 started.

MTA Stallion Auction Laddie S. (R), Canterbury Park, Sept. 3, $39,790, 3&up, c&g, progeny of stallion seasons sold at the MTA auction, 6½f, 1:17.75, BISQUIK, Tez Taran, Roust About, 5 started.

MTA Stallion Auction Lassie S. (R), Canterbury Park, Sept. 3, $42,040, 3yo, f, progeny of stallions whose services were sold at the 2000 MTA stallion auction, 6½f, 1:18.87, WA WA WINDY, Chance to Bet, Bings Fine Silk, 10 started.

Mt. Cristo Rey H. (R), Sunland Park, March 27, $102,850, 3&up, New Mexico-bred, 4½f, :50.65, ROCKY GULCH, Hecamefromaclaim, Jonnygetachex, 5 started.

MTOBA Joy S. (R), Great Lakes Downs, Oct. 29, $47,500, 3yo, f, progeny of a stallion season purchased through the 2001 MTOBA stallion auction, 1m, 1:43.45, TRUE KISS, Loot Tooten Trudy, Tickle Bug, 5 started.

MTOBA Pride S. (R), Great Lakes Downs, Oct. 29, $48,500, 3yo, c&g, progeny of a stallion season purchased through the 2001 MTOBA stallion auction, 1m, 1:42.91, DEMOLITION ZONE, Dangerous Guy, Demagoguery, 6 started.

Mt. Rainier Breeders' Cup H., Emerald Downs, July 31, $98,750, 3&up, 1⅛m, 1:47.40, FLAMETHROWINTEXAN, Poker Brad, R. Associate, 6 started.

Mt. Sassafras S. (R), Woodbine, Oct. 8, $68,915, 3&up, Ontario-bred, 7f, 1:23.73, MISTER COOP, Nyuk Nyuk Nyuk, Millfleet, 5 started.

Mt. St. Helens S., Portland Meadows, March 26, $7,500, 3yo, f, 1m, 1:41.86, EASY VOTE, Yourgoldgirl, My Emy My Amy, 8 started.

Muckleshoot Tribal Classic S. (R), Emerald Downs, Oct. 2, $46,250, 3&up, Washington-bred, 1¹⁄₁₆m, 1:42.40, MR. MAKAH, Best Game in Town, Skyrider, 5 started.

Murmur Farm Starter H. (R), Pimlico Race Course, May 21, $50,000, 3&up, Maryland Million-nominated starters for a claiming price of $16,000 or less since May 15, 2004, 1¹⁄₁₆m, 1:44.55, TESTY GUY, Yo Can Do, All Irish, 8 started.

Muscogee (Creek) Nation S., Fair Meadows at Tulsa, July 23, $32,375, 3&up, f&m, 6½f, 1:19.80, TICKIN' OKIE, Shishkbob Hay, Racing Sundown, 7 started.

Muskoka S. (R), Woodbine, Sept. 4, $107,620, 2yo, f, Canadian-bred, 7f, 1:25.71, SILENT COURSE, London Snow, Sweet Afton, 12 started.

MY CHARMER H. (G3), Calder Race Course, Dec. 3, $100,000, 3&up,

f&m, 1 1/8mT, 1:48.33, SNOWDROPS (GB), La Reina, Ticker Tape (GB), 9 started.

My Charmer S. (1st Div.), Turfway Park, Dec. 10, $48,000, 3&up, f&m, 1 1/16m, AW, 1:48.19, EYES ON EDDY, Malaysia (GB), Miss Wellspring, 11 started.

My Charmer S. (2nd Div.), Turfway Park, Dec. 10, $50,000, 3&up, f&m, 1 1/16m, AW, 1:48.82, TAPPIN FOR GOLD, Lenatareese, Stavinsky's Gal, 10 started.

My Dear Girl S. (R), Calder Race Course, Oct. 15, $400,000, 2yo, f, progeny of stallions standing in Florida, 1 1/16m, 1:47.76, CONSIDER THESOURCE, Stolen Prayer, Note to Diane, 10 started.

My Dear S., Woodbine, July 2, $137,587, 2yo, f, 5f, :59.52, WANNA-TALKABOUTME, Sudsy Baby, Howaboutrightnow, 7 started.

My Fair Lady Breeders' Cup S., Suffolk Downs, Aug. 13, $50,000, 3&up, f&m, a1m 70yT., 1:42.69, BRITISH EVENT, Plenty, Unthinkable, 6 started.

My Juliet S., Philadelphia Park, June 25, $100,000, 3&up, f&m, 6f, 1:10.43, EBONY BREEZE, Storm Minstrel, Umpateedle, 5 started.

My Lady's Manor Timber S., Monkton, April 16, $23,250, 5&up, a3mT, 6:24 (NCR), PLEASANT PARCEL, Make Me a Champ, Narrow River, 6 started.

My Melanie S., Calder Race Course, Dec. 22, $40,000, 3&up, f&m, 5fT, :55.57, WHENTHEDOVEFLIES, Melody of Colors, Wildcard Cat, 10 started.

My Old Kentucky Home S. (R), Calder Race Course, May 7, $50,000, 3&up, non-winners of two races other than maiden, claiming, or starter as of April 22, 2005 or $25,000 claiming or starters for $16,000 or less in 2004-'05, 1 1/4m, 2:09.13, PERSPICACIOUS (ARG), Sir Ray, The Man, 11 started.

Mystery Jet S. (R), Suffolk Downs, July 30, $40,000, 3yo, f, Massachusetts-bred, 6f, 1:12.95, PAPA DANCER, Stylish Sultana, Branded in Gold, 8 started.

Naked Greed S., Calder Race Course, April 29, $40,000, 3yo, 6f, 1:11.49, GOWER, Nicandro, Hostile Witness, 5 started.

Nanaimo H., Hastings Race Course, Aug. 20, $34,458, 3yo, f, 1 1/16m, 1:44.99, WIND SURF, Miss Rainier, Avenging Kat, 8 started.

Nancy's Glitter H., Calder Race Course, July 16, $75,000, 3&up, f&m, 1 1/16m, 1:47.44, AMERICAN MISS, Pampered Princess, Gentille Alouette, 7 started.

Nandi S. (R), Woodbine, Aug. 6, $103,445, 2yo, f, progeny of stallions standing in Ontario, 6f, 1:11.45, U R FLASHY, To the Brim, Bajan Princess, 7 started.

NASHUA S. (G3), Belmont Park, Oct. 28, $113,300, 2yo, 1m, 1:36.02, BLUEGRASS CAT, Political Force, Diabolical, 10 started.

NASSAU COUNTY BREEDERS' CUP S. (G2), Belmont Park, May 7, $192,000, 3yo, f, 7f, 1:22.86, SEEKING THE ANTE, Slew Motion, Exit to Heaven, 7 started.

NASSAU S. (Can-G2), Woodbine, June 4, $286,332, 3&up, f&m, 1 1/16mT, 1:41.96, QUE PUNTUAL (ARG), Ambitious Cat, Mona Rose, 12 started.

NATALMA S. (Can-G3), Woodbine, Sept. 11, $152,637, 2yo, f, 1mT, 1:35.73, ARRAVALE, Top Notch Lady, Tasha's Delight, 11 started.

National Hunt Cup Hurdle S. (R), Malvern, May 21, $75,000, 4&up, non-winners over hurdles prior to March 1, 2004, a2 3/8mT, MIXED UP, Charlie Whiskey, Move West, 12 started.

NATIONAL JOCKEY CLUB H. (G3), Hawthorne Race Course, April 23, $242,500, 3&up, 1 1/8m, 1:49.12, POLLARD'S VISION, Badge of Silver, Lord of the Game, 4 started.

NATIONAL MUSEUM OF RACING HALL OF FAME S. (G2), Saratoga Race Course, Aug. 8, $150,000, 3yo, 1 1/8mT, 1:48.15, T. D. VANCE, Silver Whistle, Crown Point, 9 started.

Native Dancer S., Arlington Park, June 26, $42,000, 3yo, 1 1/8m, 1:49.84, THREE HOUR NAP, Devilment, Pressed, 7 started.

Native Dancer S., Pimlico Race Course, Jan. 15, $50,000, 4&up, 1 1/16m, 1:44.48, JIM THIRDS BOLERO, Little Matth Man, Tidal Wave, 6 started.

NATIVE DIVER H. (G3), Hollywood Park, Dec. 10, $100,000, 3&up, 1 1/8m, 1:49.92, TROTAMONDO (CHI), Bully Hayes, Spellbinder, 10 started.

Navajo Princess S. (1st Div.), Meadowlands, Sept. 30, $60,000, 3&up, f&m, 1 1/16mT, 1:42.26, BRUNILDA (ARG), The Lamp Is Lit, Relaxed, 8 started.

Navajo Princess S. (2nd Div.), Meadowlands, Sept. 30, $60,000, 3&up, f&m, 1 1/16mT, 1:41.21, MOVIE STAR (BRZ), Briviesca (GB), Snowdrops (GB), 6 started.

NEARCTIC H. (Can-G2), Woodbine, Oct. 23, $423,156, 3&up, a6fT, 1:12.14, STEEL LIGHT, Sophia's Prince, Atticus Kristy, 12 started.

Nebraska Derby, Fonner Park, May 7, $26,500, 3yo, 1m, 1:41.20, THE STRAW MAN, Count the Bucks, Chasin the Wind, 8 started.

Needles S., Calder Race Course, Sept. 24, $75,000, 3yo, 1 1/16mT, 1:43.37, DREAM ON DREAM ON, Looks Good Junic, Lord Robyn, 10 started.

Nellie Morse S., Laurel Park, Jan. 29, $71,500, 4&up, f&m, 1m, 1:39.51, SILMARIL, Richetta, Points West, 10 started.

Never Miss T. V. S., Yavapai Downs, Aug. 9, $9,500, 3&up, 4 1/2f, :49.80 (NTR), RIVER ADVENTURE (BRZ), Vibod, Chronic Tychonic, 5 started.

Nevill S. (R), Lone Star Park, June 4, $40,000, 3yo, non-winners of a stakes in 2005, 5 1/2f, 1:02.56, WAR BRIDLE, Moody Goose, Lord of the Track, 6 started.

New Braunfels S., Retama Park, Sept. 17, $40,000, 3&up, f&m, 6f, 1:10.73, BRIDAL GAL, Shannons Valentine, Aclevershadeofjade, 6 started.

New Jersey Futurity (R), Meadowlands, Nov. 4, $61,639, 2yo, c&g, New Jersey-bred, 6f, 1:09.85, FIRST CLASS GUY, Fagedaboudit Sal, Defrere the Smile, 6 started.

New Jersey Futurity (R), Meadowlands, Nov. 4, $57,991, 2yo, f, New Jersey-bred, 6f, 1:10.62, PURE DISCO, Highland Lass, Morgan's Wish, 6 started.

New Jersey Hunt Cup S., Far Hills, Oct. 22, $46,500, 4&up, a3 1/4mT, 7:48.40, THARI, Bubble Economy, Hall of Angels, 9 started.

New Mexico Breeders' Association H. (R), SunRay Park, July 17, $57,700, 3&up, New Mexico-bred, 1m, 1:38.80, J J MYSTIQUE, Tietjen, Local Case, 9 started.

New Mexico Breeders' Derby (R), Sunland Park, April 2, $104,450, 3yo, New Mexico-bred, 1m, 1:39.35, C. G'S DOLLAR, Spelling Bee Jones, My Desert Lady, 9 started.

New Mexico Cup Classic S. (R), Zia Park, Nov. 6, $147,200, 3&up, New Mexico-bred, 1m, 1:39, ROCKY GULCH, Cattleman Prospect, Off Shore Prospect, 8 started.

New Mexico Cup Colts Championship S. (R), Zia Park, Nov. 6, $115,800, 3yo, c&g, New Mexico-bred, 6 1/2f, 1:16.40, MARRONE, C. G's Dollar, Spelling Bee Jones, 12 started.

New Mexico Cup Fillies & Mares S. (R), Zia Park, Nov. 6, $125,800, 3&up, f&m, New Mexico-bred, 6 1/2f, 1:16.80, LATENITE SPECIAL, Hat Creek, Betsy N, 12 started.

New Mexico Cup Filly Championship S. (R), Zia Park, Nov. 6, $115,800, 3yo, f, New Mexico-bred, 6 1/2f, 1:18, DESERT PRIDE, La Mamie, Bay View Sue, 12 started.

New Mexico Cup Juvenile Fillies S. (R), Zia Park, Nov. 6, $115,300, 2yo, f, New Mexico-bred, 6 1/2f, 1:17.40, PEPPERS PRIDE, Bo Chime, Price of Hope, 11 started.

New Mexico Cup Juvenile S. (R), Zia Park, Nov. 6, $115,800, 2yo, New Mexico-bred, 6 1/2f, 1:17.60, IN UNITY, Mister Yates, Copelan's Mask, 12 started.

New Mexico Distaff H. (R), SunRay Park, July 9, $57,200, 3&up, f&m, New Mexico-bred, 6 1/2f, 1:18.40, LATENITE SPECIAL, Mystic Melissa, Ruthless Kitten, 7 started.

New Mexico Racing Commission H. (R), Sunland Park, Dec. 4, $125,000, 3&up, f&m, New Mexico-bred, 6f, 1:11.65, SHEMOVES-LIKEAGHOST, Mystic Melissa, Latenite Special, 11 started.

New Mexico Sprint S. (R), Zia Park, Nov. 6, $124,900, 3&up, New Mexico-bred, 6f, 1:09.20, ROMEOS WILSON, Jonnygetachex, Bold Nxs, 11 started.

New Mexico State Fair Breeders' Derby (R), The Downs at Albuquerque, Sept. 24, $51,609, 3yo, New Mexico-bred, 1 1/16m, 1:47.60, MOJO MUNDO, Devil's Justice, Spelling Bee Jones, 9 started.

New Mexico State Fair H., The Downs at Albuquerque, Sept. 25, $30,000, 3&up, 1 1/8m, 1:49.69, BAYOU THE MOON, Skip and Go, Long Range, 6 started.

New Mexico State University H. (R), Sunland Park, Feb. 19, $130,400, 4&up, New Mexico-bred, 1m, 1:36.48, ROCKY GULCH, Cattleman Prospect, Some Ghost, 9 started.

NEW ORLEANS H. (G2), Fair Grounds, March 12, $500,000, 4&up, 1 1/8m, 1:48.78, BADGE OF SILVER, Limehouse, Second of June, 9 started.

New Providence S. (R), Woodbine, May 14, $100,368, 3&up, progeny of stallions standing in Ontario, 6f, 1:10.56, MISTER COOP, Barbeau Ruckus, Dillinger, 10 started.

New Westminster H., Hastings Race Course, Aug. 28, $36,726, 2yo, 6 1/2f, 1:19.07, LUKIN AWESOME, Regal Request, T. J. Hennessy, 5 started.

New York Breeders' Futurity (R), Finger Lakes, Sept. 5, $248,400, 2yo, New York-bred, 6f, 1:09.85, CLASSIC PACK, Fly to Me, Sharp Humor, 6 started.

New York Derby (R), Finger Lakes, July 16, $168,400, 3yo, New York-bred, 1$^1/_{16}$m, 1:43.78, ACCOUNTFORTHEGOLD, Gold and Roses, Naughty New Yorker, 10 started.

NEW YORK H. (G2), Belmont Park, July 2, $250,000, 3&up, f&m, 1$^1/_4$mT, 2:02.23, WEND, Wonder Again, Film Maker, 6 started.

New York New York S. (R), Calder Race Course, June 11, $50,000, 3&up, non-winners of two races other than maiden, claiming, or starter as of April 22 or $25,000 claiming or a starter for $16,000 or less in 2004-'05, 1$^1/_2$m, 2:39.13, PERSPICACIOUS (ARG), Stars of Silver, Sir Stack, 7 started.

New York Oaks (R), Finger Lakes, Sept. 5, $75,000, 3yo, f, New York-bred, 1$^1/_{16}$m, 1:45.59, CARLOW, Line Memory, Milly La Foret B B, 8 started.

New York Turf Writers Cup Steeplechase H., Saratoga Race Course, Sept. 2, $159,200, 4&up, 2$^3/_8$mT, 4:24.90, HIRAPOUR (IRE), Three Carat, Party Airs, 9 started.

NEXT MOVE H. (G3), Aqueduct, March 25, $110,000, 3&up, f&m, 1$^1/_8$m, 1:50.77, DAYDREAMING, Saintliness, Rare Gift, 8 started.

NIAGARA BREEDERS' CUP H. (Can-G2), Woodbine, Sept. 5, $282,777, 3&up, 1$^1/_2$mT, 2:27.13, REVVED UP, Strut the Stage, A Bit O'Gold, 9 started.

Niagara S. (R), Finger Lakes, July 4, $50,000, 3yo, f, New York-bred, 6f, 1:10.67, CARLOW, Speed Bag, Champagne Ending, 9 started.

Nick Shuk Memorial S., Delaware Park, June 5, $75,900, 3yo, 1$^1/_{16}$m (originally scheduled on the turf), 1:44.30, MIGHTY MECKE, Letterman's Humor, Killenaule, 8 started.

Nicole S., Hawthorne Race Course, May 8, $42,600, 4&up, f&m, 1$^1/_{16}$m, 1:46.93, SUNSET KISSES, Samantha B., Arsen Annie, 5 started.

NOBLE DAMSEL H. (G3), Belmont Park, Sept. 24, $150,000, 3&up, f&m, 1mT, 1:33.93, BRIGHT ABUNDANCE, My Lordship, Asti (Ire), 12 started.

Noble Robyn S., Calder Race Course, July 29, $40,000, 3yo, f, 1$^1/_{16}$mT, 1:43, RAGTIME HOPE, Statue, Crafty Judy, 9 started.

Noel Laing Steeplechase S., Montpelier, Nov. 5, $29,100, 4&up, a2$^1/_2$mT, 5:09.80, MON VILLEZ (FR), Understood, Noble Bob, 7 started.

No Le Hace S., Retama Park, Oct. 15, $40,000, 3&up, 7$^1/_2$fT, 1:29.19, SPRUCE'S PRINCE, Oncearoundtwice, Charming Socialite, 11 started.

NORFOLK S. (G2), Oak Tree at Santa Anita, Oct. 2, $200,000, 2yo, 1$^1/_{16}$m, 1:44.38, BROTHER DEREK, A. P. Warrior, Jealous Profit, 8 started.

Norgor Derby, Ruidoso Downs, May 29, $25,000, 3yo, 6f, 1:10.80, SLEW OF ENERCHI, C. G's Dollar, Trickey Todd, 8 started.

Norman Hall S. (R), Suffolk Downs, Nov. 19, $40,000, 2yo, assachusetts-bred, 6f, 1:13.12, SPRINKLE OF GOLD, Caller Sara Kate, Flirt for Fame, 7 started.

Northampton S. (R), Northampton Fair, Sept. 4, $14,950, 3&up, Massachusetts-bred, a6$^1/_2$f, 1:22.57, JILL'S JUMPSHOT, dh-Storm Quest, dh-Abit Eratic, 6 started.

Northbound Pride S., Canterbury Park, June 25, $40,000, 3yo, f, a1$^1/_{16}$mT, 1:43.56, STORMY VENUS, Camela Carson, Malika's Gold, 9 started.

North Dakota-Bred Derby (R), North Dakota Horse Park, Sept. 4, $23,568, 3yo, North Dakota-bred, 1m, 1:44, NORTHRNIMPROVEMENT, Firehawk, Could've Been Mine, 8 started.

North Dakota-Bred Futurity (R), North Dakota Horse Park, Aug. 7, $24,738, 2yo, North Dakota-bred, 6f, 1:16.80, J DAM STRIKE, Liberty Reigns, Iron Aries, 8 started.

North Dakota Derby, Assiniboia Downs, July 3, $16,326, 3yo, 1m, 1:44.60, NORTHRNIMPROVEMENT, Firehawk, Peacefull Sammy, 7 started.

North Dakota Futurity, Assiniboia Downs, Sept. 4, $20,421, 2yo, 6f, 1:14.40, J DAM STRIKE, Dakota Long Legs, Tiger Jet, 6 started.

North Dakota Stallion S. (R), Assiniboia Downs, Aug. 21, $24,762, 2yo, North Dakota-bred, 6f, 1:15, BARNSTORM, Missing Fortune, Catch Me Talkin, 8 started.

North Dakota Stallion S. (R), Assiniboia Downs, July 29, $15,171, 3yo, North Dakota-bred, 1$^1/_{16}$m, 1:49.20, YOUR EXCELLENCE, Northrnimprovement, Illalwaysbethere, 5 started.

NORTHERN DANCER BREEDERS' CUP S. (G3), Churchill Downs, June 18, $217,400, 3yo, 1$^1/_{16}$m, 1:42.46, DON'T GET MAD, Unbridled Energy, Real Dandy, 6 started.

Northern Dancer S. (R), Laurel Park, Nov. 12, $75,000, 3yo, Maryland-bred, 1$^1/_8$m, 1:53.18, GOLD CASING, Promenade Girl, Serious Lightning, 8 started.

Northern Lights Debutante S. (R), Canterbury Park, Aug. 21, $55,100, 2yo, f, Minnesota-bred, 6f, 1:11.76, SENTIMENTAL CHARM, Gazette, Speed Wagon, 7 started.

Northern Lights Futurity (R), Canterbury Park, Aug. 21, $56,400, 2yo, Minnesota-bred, 6f, 1:10.97, THE K B KID, Eddie Rascal, Audiahvo, 9 started.

Northern Metallic S., Grand Prairie, July 17, $3,649, 3&up, 6f, 1:14.60, HIGHLAND ROAD, Gentle John, Native Gambler, 7 started.

Northern Spur Breeders' Cup S., Oaklawn Park, April 16, $75,000, 3yo, 1$^1/_{16}$m, 1:43.91, JONESBORO, Prince T., Jazzy Gallop, 6 started.

Northlands Oaks, Northlands Park, July 15, $41,245, 3yo, f, 1m, 1:39.80, NESSAROSE, Speedy Gone Sally, Kathern's Cat, 9 started.

North Randall S. (R), Thistledown, Aug. 5, $40,000, 3yo, Ohio-bred, 6f, 1:11.32, RUBIUS, Turn the Page, Pyrite Springs, 10 started.

Northview Stallion Station/M.Tyson Gilpin S. (R), Laurel Park, Dec. 18, $50,000, 2yo, Virginia-bred, 6f, 1:14.09, NORTH BEACH CONDO, Patterson, First to Rome, 6 started.

Northview Stallion Station S. (R), Pimlico Race Course, April 23, $100,000, 3&up, f&m, Maryland-bred and/or Maryland Million-nominated, 1$^1/_8$m, 1:53.71, SILMARIL, Grant's Moon, Chrusciki, 5 started.

Northwest Stallion Strong Ruler S. (R), Emerald Downs, Aug. 20, $41,850, 2yo, progeny of stallions standing in Washington, 6$^1/_2$f, 1:17.80, TOM TWO, Tougher'n Owljuice, Gucci for You, 9 started.

NTRA S. (R), Hollywood Park, April 24, $60,000, 3&up, f&m, California-bred maidens, 6$^1/_2$f, 1:15.28, SOLDIER'S KISS, Membership Coffee, Passionate Heat, 13 started.

Nursery S., Hollywood Park, May 15, $98,625, 2yo, f, 5f, :58.42, LIL' SISTER SWISS, Walkonkaydeeavenue, Slick Road, 9 started.

NWMF H., Kalispell, Aug. 21, $3,000, 3&up, 7f, 1:28.20, DREAMONEIR, Regal Maxim, Larron, 6 started.

NWMF Matron H., Kalispell, Aug. 21, $3,200, 3&up, f&m, 6f, 1:14, CRISSY'S CRICKET, C C Sky Dancer, Alibi Expert, 4 started.

OAKLAWN H. (G2), Oaklawn Park, April 9, $490,000, 4&up, 1$^1/_8$m, 1:49.54, GRAND REWARD, Second of June, Eddington, 5 started.

OAK LEAF S. (G2), Oak Tree at Santa Anita, Oct. 1, $200,000, 2yo, f, 1$^1/_{16}$m, 1:45.57, DIAMOND OMI, Wild Fit, Golden Silk, 7 started.

OAK TREE BREEDERS' CUP MILE S. (G2), Oak Tree at Santa Anita, Oct. 8, $249,000, 3&up, 1mT, 1:34.54, SINGLETARY, Designed for Luck, Buckland Manor, 6 started.

OAK TREE DERBY (G2), Oak Tree at Santa Anita, Oct. 15, $150,000, 3yo, 1$^1/_8$mT, 1:46.48, ARAGORN (IRE), Eastern Sand, Brecon Beacon (GB), 7 started.

Obeah H., Delaware Park, June 18, $100,000, 3&up, f&m, 1$^1/_8$m, 1:53.68, ISOLA PIU BELLA (CHI), City Fire, Becky in Pink, 5 started.

Ocala Breeders' Sales Championship S. (R), Ocala Training Center, March 21, $97,000, 3yo, f, offered for sale at an OBS sale, 1$^1/_{16}$m, 1:45.80, NEVERLACKEN, Miami Princess, Airizon, 4 started.

Ocala Breeders' Sales Championship S. (R), Ocala Training Center, March 21, $100,000, 3yo, c&g, offered for sale at an OBS sale, 1$^1/_{16}$m, 1:44.40, MIGHTY MECKE, Favre, Casey's Biscuit, 6 started.

Ocala Breeders' Sales Sophomore S., Tampa Bay Downs, April 9, $83,650, 3yo, 7f, 1:24.20, BERNIE BLUE, Lite Brigade, Roman Candles, 10 started.

Ocala Breeders' Sales Sprint S. (R), Ocala Training Center, March 21, $50,000, 3yo, f, offered for sale at an OBS sale, 6f, 1:11.80, BABAGANUSH, Higher World, Pick Five, 11 started.

Ocala Breeders' Sales Sprint S. (R), Ocala Training Center, March 21, $50,000, 3yo, c&g, offered for sale at an OBS sale, 6f, 1:10, GOWER, Hostile Witness, Rompburger, 7 started.

Ocean Bay S., Turf Paradise, Jan. 1, $21,800, 4&up, f&m, 1m (originally scheduled on the turf), 1:39.57, ARCH LADY, Cal's Baby, Royal Again, 6 started.

OCEANPORT S. (G3), Monmouth Park, Aug. 7, $150,000, 3&up, 1$^1/_{16}$mT, 1:42.53, AY CARAMBA (BRZ), Hotstufanthensome, Stormy Roman, 9 started.

Oceanside S. (1st Div.) (R), Del Mar, July 20, $85,400, 3yo, non-winners of a stakes of $50,000 in 2005, 1mT, 1:33.91, BECRUX (ITY), Legal Precedent, Leo Getz, 9 started.

Oceanside S. (2nd Div.) (R), Del Mar, July 20, $85,400, 3yo, non-winners of a stakes of $50,000 in 2005, 1mT, 1:33.67, EL ROBLAR, In Excelsis, Juliesugardaddy, 8 started.

Office Queen S., Calder Race Course, June 4, $100,000, 3yo, f, 1$^1/_{16}$m, 1:47.77, SNUG HARBOUR, Leona's Knight, Crazy Caro, 7 started.

Ogataul H. (R), Fonner Park, March 12, $25,600, 3&up, Nebraska-bred, 6f, 1:12, THUNDERING VERZY, What About David, Mortrump, 6 started.

OGDEN PHIPPS H. (G1), Belmont Park, June 18, $294,000, 3&up, f&m, 1$^1/_{16}$m, 1:41.02, ASHADO, Society Selection, Bending Strings, 5 started.

Ogle and Company Turf Distaff S., Tampa Bay Downs, April 9, $85,500, 4&up, f&m, 1$^1/_{16}$mT, 1:42.05, JOYFUL BALLAD, Marwood, Vidlocity, 12 started.

Ohio Debutante H. (R), Thistledown, Sept. 3, $40,000, 3yo, f, Ohio-bred, 6f, 1:11.60, PYRITE BONDS, Bold Passage, Noon Win, 13 started.

OHIO DERBY (G2), Thistledown, July 2, $350,000, 3yo, 1 1/8m, 1:51.56, PALLADIO, Magna Graduate, It's Time to Smile, 8 started.

Ohio Freshman S. (R), Beulah Park, Nov. 5, $40,000, 2yo, Ohio-bred, 1m70y, 1:45.12, TURNPIKE MIKE, Major Mark, Red George, 8 started.

Ohio Valley H., Mountaineer Race Track, May 31, $75,000, 3&up, f&m, 6f, 1:09.67, COBRA LADY, Ready and Tough, Shannons Valentine, 5 started.

Oh Say S., Delaware Park, July 23, $58,100, 3yo, 6f, 1:09.86, EURO CODE, Captain Corelli, Pointsman, 5 started.

Oh What a Windfall S. (R), Belmont Park, Sept. 25, $65,150, 3yo, f, non-winners of a stakes, 6 1/2f, 1:16.41, dh-GREAT INTENTIONS, dh-REUNITED, Hot Attraction, 5 started.

Oklahoma Classics Day Classic S. (R), Remington Park, Sept. 24, $75,000, 3&up, Oklahoma-bred, 1 1/16m, 1:42.46, ZEE OH SIX, George Taylor, Presto Ridge, 5 started.

Oklahoma Classics Day Distaff S. (R), Remington Park, Sept. 24, $40,000, 3&up, f&m, Oklahoma-bred, 1m70y, 1:41.97, THE PENGUIN, Juanitas Babe, Racing Sundown, 8 started.

Oklahoma Classics Day Filly & Mare Turf S. (R), Remington Park, Sept. 24, $40,000, 3&up, f&m, Oklahoma-bred, 7 1/2fT, 1:28.41, GOODIE GOOD GIRL, D Fine Okie, Gentle Fun, 11 started.

Oklahoma Classics Day Juvenile S. (R), Remington Park, Sept. 24, $40,000, 2yo, c&g, Oklahoma-bred, 6f, 1:10.63, OUT OUR WAY, Here Comes Deplane, Rubiano's Twin, 8 started.

Oklahoma Classics Day Lassie S. (R), Remington Park, Sept. 24, $40,000, 2yo, f, Oklahoma-bred, 6f, 1:12.10, CHYNA STAR, Spooky Okie, Cherokee Diva, 11 started.

Oklahoma Classics Day Sprint S. (R), Remington Park, Sept. 24, $40,000, 3&up, Oklahoma-bred, 6f, 1:09.80, DUDON, Sooner Risk, Sooner Pride, 7 started.

Oklahoma Classics Day Turf S. (R), Remington Park, Sept. 24, $40,000, 3&up, Oklahoma-bred, 1mT, 1:34.61, NOTABLE OKIE, Outlaw Cowboy, April's Lucky Boy, 7 started.

Oklahoma Derby, Remington Park, Oct. 21, $150,000, 3yo, 1 1/8m, 1:49.49, MILITARY MAJOR, Real Dandy, Golden Rainbow, 10 started.

Old Dutch H., Marquis Downs, Aug. 27, $5,005, 3&up, 1 1/16m, 1:47.55, DICK'S HUNTER, Bullinsky, Double Time, 7 started.

Old Glory Overnight H., Emerald Downs, July 4, $25,000, 3&up, 6f, 1:08.60, DIAMOND VIEW, No Giveaway, Commodore Craig, 7 started.

OLD HAT S. (G3), Gulfstream Park, Feb. 5, $100,000, 3yo, f, 6 1/2f, 1:16.31, MADDALENA, Alfonsina, Holy Trinity, 7 started.

Old Ironsides Breeders' Cup S., Suffolk Downs, June 18, $50,000, 3&up, a1m 70yT, 1:43.80, MIESQUE'S APPROVAL, Canyon's Way, Tom the River Rat, 8 started.

Old South H., Louisiana Downs, June 4, $50,180, 3&up, f&m, 1 1/16mT, 1:45.83, PAD THE WALLET, Chitchat Chitchat, Janeian (NZ), 6 started.

Old Timers' S., Grand Prairie, Aug. 5, $3,752, 8&up, 7f, 1:22 (NTR), GOMKA, Last One Standing, Past Time, 7 started.

Oliver S., Indiana Downs, June 18, $43,600, 3yo, f, 1mT, 1:38.39, AYLA BELLA, Flexible Princess, Black Eyed Susie, 8 started.

Omaha S., Horsemen's Park, July 24, $100,000, 3&up, 1m, 1:37.40, MISSME, Stormy Impact, Big Glori, 6 started.

Omnibus S., Monmouth Park, Aug. 27, $63,600, 3&up, f&m, 1 1/16mT, 1:45.15, KRASNAYA, Smart N Classy, My Limit, 6 started.

Ontario Colleen H. (R), Woodbine, Sept. 3, $139,536, 3yo, f, progeny of stallions standing in Ontario, 1mT, 1:36.11, ELLE RUNAWAY, Count to Three, Playwild, 13 started.

Ontario County S. (R), Finger Lakes, June 19, $50,000, 3yo, New York-bred, 6f, 1:10.95, CARIBBEAN CRUISER, Pinky Freud, Freddy the Cap, 8 started.

Ontario Damsel S. (R), Woodbine, July 10, $136,424, 3yo, f, Canadian-bred, 6 1/2fT, 1:15.75, TOP TEN LIST, See the Wind, Simply Lovely, 8 started.

Ontario Debutante S., Woodbine, Aug. 20, $113,637, 2yo, f, 6f, 1:09.75, KNIGHTS TEMPLAR, Truly Blushed, Tasha's Delight, 7 started.

Ontario Derby, Woodbine, Oct. 9, $141,020, 3yo, 1 1/8m, 1:50.67, PALLADIO, Gold and Roses, Ever So Free, 8 started.

Ontario Fashion H., Woodbine, Nov. 5, $129,403, 3&up, f&m, 6f, 1:10.89, COLONIAL SURPRISE, Search the Church, Tamara, 7 started.

Ontario Jockey Club S. (R), Woodbine, July 24, $67,117, 3&up, Ontario-bred, 7fT, 1:22.27, AWESOME ACTION, Soaring Free, Riva's Tribute, 7 started.

Ontario Lassie S. (R), Woodbine, Dec. 4, $140,004, 2yo, f, Ontario-bred, 1 1/16m, 1:49.26, OUR MADISON, Like a Gem, Sugar Swirl, 6 started.

Ontario Matron H., Woodbine, June 18, $134,753, 3&up, f&m, 1 1/16m, 1:45.28, ONE FOR ROSE, Ballroom Deputy, Raylene, 5 started.

On Trust H. (R), Hollywood Park, Dec. 4, $101,000, 3&up, California-bred, 7 1/2f, 1:27.37, PROUD TOWER TOO, Jack's Wild, Areyoutalkintome, 7 started.

Opening Verse H., Churchill Downs, June 18, $111,200, 3&up, 1 1/16mT, 1:42.07, SENOR SWINGER, G P Fleet, Seeking Answers (Ire), 8 started.

Open Mind H. (R), Monmouth Park, May 15, $60,000, 3&up, f&m, New Jersey-bred, 6f, 1:11.33, AVERY HALL, Cigno d'Oro, Smart N Classy, 11 started.

Open Mind S., Churchill Downs, May 21, $111,000, 3yo, f, 5fT, :56.97, FLYING CIRCLE, Angel Trumpet, Harmonic Miss, 9 started.

Open Mind S. (R), Aqueduct, Nov. 20, $67,500, 3yo, f, non-winners of an open stakes in 2005, 6f, 1:10.59, MYSTIC CHANT, Holy Trinity, Pelham Bay, 8 started.

Open S., Lethbridge, June 19, $10,495, 3&up, 7f, 1:26.40, LAFLEUR, Candid Remark, Streak a Roani, 6 started.

ORCHID H. (G2), Gulfstream Park, April 2, $150,000, 3&up, f&m, 1 1/2mT, 2:27.15, HONEY RYDER, Ellieonthemarch, Pretty Jane, 7 started.

Oregon Derby, Portland Meadows, April 2, $15,000, 3yo, 1 1/8m, 1:54.91, J D'S DATE, Typhoon Aaron, City Fox, 11 started.

Oregon HBPA H., Portland Meadows, Jan. 1, $7,000, 3yo, f, 5 1/2f, 1:07.48, GORDYS SWEET JORDY, Wice O Kat, Sassy Sushi, 6 started.

Oregon HBPA Invitational H., Portland Meadows, Jan. 2, $7,000, 4&up, 1m, 1:39.72, MY FRIEND DAVE, Mt. Vista, Yesss, 6 started.

Oregon HBPA Invitational H., Portland Meadows, Jan. 8, $7,000, 4&up, f&m, 1m, 1:41.30, CHANCY CHANCY, Misty Leader, Quiz the Maid, 6 started.

Oregon Hers S. (R), Portland Meadows, Dec. 31, $10,000, 3yo, f, Oregon-bred, 1m, 1:42.53, WICE O KAT, Mi Pet Rock, My Emy My Amy, 7 started.

Oregon His S. (R), Portland Meadows, Dec. 31, $10,000, 3yo, c&g, Oregon-bred, 1 1/16m, 1:48.31, RAGGIDY ROWE, Oregon Merlot, D Devil, 9 started.

Oregon Oaks, Portland Meadows, April 16, $7,500, 3yo, f, 1 1/16m, 1:48.06, EASY VOTE, Miss Bliss, Yourgoldgirl, 6 started.

Oregon Sprint Championship S. (R), Portland Meadows, Dec. 31, $10,000, 3&up, Oregon-bred, 6f, 1:12.94, MY FRIEND DAVE, Stately Jack Flash, Red Watch, 6 started.

Orphan Kist H. (R), Fonner Park, March 5, $25,800, 3&up, f&m, Nebraska-bred, 6f, 1:13, UP 'N BLUMIN, Magic Trump, Shantac, 8 started.

Osage Hills S. (R), Remington Park, Oct. 29, $40,000, 3&up, Oklahoma-bred, 5fT, :56.23, APRIL'S LUCKY BOY, Notable Okie, Ranger B., 10 started.

Osunitas H. (R), Del Mar, Aug. 10, $81,500, 3&up, f&m, non-winners of a stakes of $50,000 at one mile or over in 2005, 1 1/16mT, 1:40.73, HEALTHY ADDICTION, Cotopaxi, Ticker Tape (GB), 10 started.

OS West Oregon Futurity (R), Portland Meadows, Dec. 31, $40,000, 2yo, Oregon-bred, 1m, 1:42.75, TOM TWO, Cascadians Cuttie, Newberg Gold, 9 started.

OTBA Sales S. (R), Portland Meadows, Nov. 5, $12,000, 2yo, passed through the OTBA sales ring, 6f, 1:14.33, RILEY BEAVER, Mountain Band, Tracy's Nitemare, 7 started.

OTBA Stallion S. (R), Portland Meadows, Jan. 1, $10,000, 3yo, progeny of stallions standing in Oregon, 6f, 1:13.04, QUARTERN, One Tuft Woeman, Truth Buster, 6 started.

Our Dear Peggy S., Calder Race Course, Dec. 26, $40,000, 3&up, 1 1/8mT, 1:46.84, EVERYTHING TO GAIN, Stormy Roman, Cottage (Arg), 10 started.

Outlook S. (R), Delta Downs, Jan. 1, $40,000, 4&up, non-winners of a stakes, 1m, 1:40.76, GO STAR BUSTER, Monty Man, Seainsky, 9 started.

Overskate S. (R), Woodbine, Sept. 21, $107,192, 3&up, progeny of stallions standing in Ontario, 7f, 1:21.30, MISTER COOP, Arch Hall, Barbeau Ruckus, 6 started.

Owner's Appreciation Sprint S. (R), Delta Downs, Feb. 19, $40,000, 4&up, starters in an overnight race at the 2004-'05 Delta Downs meet, 5f, :58.93, NOBLE DECISION, Kim's Gem, Believe Im Special, 7 started.

PACIFIC CLASSIC S. (G1), Del Mar, Aug. 21, $1,000,000, 3&up, 1 1/4m, 2:00.71, BORREGO, Perfect Drift, Lava Man, 11 started.

Pago Hop S., Fair Grounds at Louisiana Downs, Nov. 26, $75,000, 3yo, f, a1 1/16mT, 1:42.98, MORE THAN PROMISED, Enduring

Will, Leestown Fantasie, 8 started.

PALM BEACH S. (G3), Gulfstream Park, March 26, $100,000, 3yo, 1 1/8mT, 1:47.12, INTERPATATION, Tadreeb, Fishy Advice, 8 started.

Palo Alto H., Bay Meadows Race Course, Sept. 17, $75,650, 3yo, f, 1 1/16mT, 1:43.30, SOMETHINABOUTLAURA, Conveyor's Angel, Apology Accepted, 10 started.

PALOMAR BREEDERS' CUP H. (G2), Del Mar, Sept. 3, $180,000, 3&up, f&m, 1 1/16mT, 1:39.84, INTERCONTINENTAL (GB), Amorama (Fr), Ticker Tape (GB), 5 started.

PALOS VERDES H. (G2), Santa Anita Park, Jan. 23, $150,000, 4&up, 6f, 1:09.15, SAINT AFLEET, Hombre Rapido, Bluesthestandard, 8 started.

Palo Verde H., Turf Paradise, March 6, $40,000, 3yo, 6 1/2f, 1:15.49, RAGING WIND, Quintons Relaunch, Silent Exploit, 9 started.

PAN AMERICAN H. (G2), Gulfstream Park, April 2, $150,000, 3&up, 1 1/2mT, 2:25.95, NAVESINK RIVER, Quest Star, Deputy Lad, 8 started.

Panhandle H., Mountaineer Race Track, May 7, $75,000, 3&up, 5f, :56.11, BERNIE BLUE, Danieltown, Top Shoter, 6 started.

Panthers S., Prairie Meadows, June 10, $50,750, 3yo, f, 1m, 1:35.51, WHIMSY, Swede, Khayelitsha, 9 started.

Pan Zareta H., Fair Grounds, Feb. 5, $60,000, 4&up, f&m, 6f, 1:10.26, SOURIS, Silver Crown, Crow Jane, 5 started.

Paradise Creek S., Arlington Park, Sept. 17, $42,375, 3yo, 1 1/16mT, 1:43.42, COSMIC KRIS, Thunder Mission, Earths Vain Shadow, 9 started.

Paradise Valley H., Turf Paradise, Nov. 19, $40,000, 3yo, 7 1/2fT, 1:29.96, RAGING WIND, Chinese Dragon, Desert Prospector, 10 started.

Park Avenue S. (R), Aqueduct, April 24, $150,000, 3yo, f, progeny of stallions standing in New York, 1m, 1:36.75, PRETTY SUZI, Dynamo Hum, Ms Litigator, 11 started.

Parkland Heritage S. (R), Marquis Downs, Aug. 20, $8,254, 3yo, f, Saskatchewan-bred, 1 1/16m, 1:51.53, SHEEN SKY, Arctic Taliyah, Bold Invader, 4 started.

Parnitha Cup S. (R), Fort Erie, Aug. 21, $24,762, 3&up, starters at Fort Erie twice in 2005, 5fT, :58.02, WIRE EDITOR, Krz Ruckus, Ontario Road, 9 started.

Parts Unknown S., Hawthorne Race Course, March 18, $42,400, 3yo, f, 6f, 1:14.72, CART'S TURN, Im a Dixie Girl, Spanning, 5 started.

Pasadena S., Santa Anita Park, March 19, $82,300, 3yo, 1mT, 1:35.36, CHINESE DRAGON, Eastern Sand, Shamoan (Ire), 12 started.

Pasco S., Tampa Bay Downs, Jan. 22, $60,000, 3yo, 7f, 1:23.67, ELECTRIC LIGHT, Captain Lindsay, Dazzling Dr. Cevin, 14 started.

Paseana H., Santa Anita Park, Jan. 14, $85,300, 4&up, f&m, 1 1/16m, 1:43.08, MISS LOREN (ARG), Valentine Dancer, Bartok's Blithe, 5 started.

Passing Mood S. (R), Woodbine, July 27, $101,663, 3yo, f, progeny of stallions standing in Ontario, 7fT, 1:25.93, TOP TEN LIST, Simply Lovely, Archer's Dreamer, 5 started.

Pass the Line S., Calder Race Course, Nov. 26, $40,000, 3&up, 7 1/2fT, 1:27.94, WIRE BOUND, Pulpit Talk, Cervelo, 7 started.

Patchy Groundfog S., Turf Paradise, Nov. 21, $24,000, 3&up, 1mT, 1:35.75, STRATEGICALLY, Brazen n' Bold, Talaris, 8 started.

Pat Hosie Memorial S., Yorkton Exh. Assoc., July 8, $2,035, 3&up, f&m, 5f, 1:04.60, SWINGNLISA, Ruanwar, Party in the Park, 7 started.

PAT O'BRIEN BREEDERS' CUP H. (G2), Del Mar, Aug. 21, $280,000, 3&up, 7f, 1:21.70, IMPERIALISM, Gotaghostofachance, Taste of Paradise, 8 started.

Patrick Wood S. (R), Great Lakes Downs, Sept. 26, $50,000, 2yo, c&g, Michigan-bred, 6f, 1:15.73, OUT WITH A BANG, Domestic Oil, Lil Perfect Storm, 10 started.

Pat Whitworth Illinois Debutante S. (R), Hawthorne Race Course, Dec. 10, $104,375, 2yo, f, Illinois-conceived and/or -foaled, 1 1/16m, 1:45.08, ROLLING SEA, Cause She's Crafty, Lampoon, 8 started.

Paul Cacci Eel River Sprint S. (R), Ferndale, Aug. 14, $7,218, 3&up, starters for a claiming price of $12,500 or less in 2005, 5f, :58.76, RED SEATTLE, Truly a Runner, Janzig Warrior, 6 started.

Paumonok H., Aqueduct, Jan. 29, $82,700, 3&up, 6f, 1:08.86, DON SIX, Gators N Bears, Mr. Whitestone, 8 started.

Peace Bridge Cup S., Fort Erie, Aug. 14, $25,065, 3&up, 1 1/16m, 1:43.29, SAILOR KNOT, Pleasant Hall, Open Lock, 6 started.

Peach of It H. (R), Hawthorne Race Course, April 30, $91,500, 3&up, f&m, Illinois-conceived and/or -foaled, 1 1/16m, 1:46.64, MS. LYDONIA, Cashmere Miss, Di's Delight, 9 started.

Peapack Hurdle S., Far Hills, Oct. 22, $50,000, 3&up, f&m, a2 1/8mT, 4:30.25, GUELPH, Vente, Classic Gale, 12 started.

Pearl Necklace S. (R), Pimlico Race Course, June 4, $50,000, 3yo, f, Maryland-bred, 1 1/16mT, 1:47.95, FROST PRINCESS, Cozy Gain, Sweetsoutherndessa, 7 started.

Pebbles S., Belmont Park, Oct. 10, $110,900, 3yo, f, 1m (originally scheduled on the turf), 1:37.19, CAYUGA'S WATERS, Wait It Out, Quail Run, 7 started.

Pecos S. (R), Zia Park, Nov. 28, $41,500, 3&up, f&m, New Mexico-bred, 1m, 1:39.40, RUN LOOKER RUN, Rylie Cheyenne, Policy Cat, 6 started.

PEGASUS S. (G3), Meadowlands, Sept. 30, $250,000, 3yo, 1 1/8m, 1:47.47, MAGNA GRADUATE, Crown Point, Network, 8 started.

Pelican S., Tampa Bay Downs, Jan. 1, $60,000, 4&up, 6f, 1:10.04, ABOVE THE WIND, Ranger Chance, Sing Me Back Home, 13 started.

PENNSYLVANIA DERBY (G2), Philadelphia Park, Sept. 5, $750,000, 3yo, 1 1/8m, 1:49.43, SUN KING, Southern Africa, Smokescreen, 14 started.

Pennsylvania Governor's Cup H., Penn National Race Course, Aug. 5, $50,000, 3&up, 5fT, :54.80, TACIRRING, Worldwind Romance, Shades of Sunny, 9 started.

Pennsylvania Hunt Cup Steeplechase S., Unionville, Nov. 6, $24,250, 5&up, a4mT, 9:09, NORTHERNTHINKING, Bubble Economy, Ghost Valley, 7 started.

Pennsylvania Nursery S. (R), Philadelphia Park, Nov. 19, $56,350, 2yo, Pennsylvania-bred, 7f, 1:26.41, ESCROW ACCOUNT, Valay Night, Evening Meadow, 10 started.

Pennsylvania Oaks, Philadelphia Park, Sept. 5, $100,000, 3yo, f, 1m70y, 1:42.19, AMAZING BUY, Hide and Chic, Cozy Gain, 6 started.

Penny Ridge S., Northlands Park, June 26, $40,570, 3yo, f, 1 1/16m, 1:46.60, WILD BENDER, Speedy Gone Sally, Nessarose, 4 started.

Pent Up Kiss H., Churchill Downs, Nov. 12, $72,000, 3&up, f&m, 5fT, :56.67, ANGEL TRUMPET, Unbridled Sidney, Very Vegas, 12 started.

Pepper Oaks Farm S. (R), Hollywood Park, April 24, $60,000, 3&up, c&g, California-bred maidens, 6 1/2f, 1:15.36, KING OF L. A., Perfect Mode, Maximum Heat, 12 started.

Peppy Addy S. (R), Philadelphia Park, June 11, $54,100, 3yo, Pennsylvania-bred, 7f, 1:22.18, UNITED, North Potomac, Moonshine Man, 6 started.

Pepsi-Cola H., Emerald Downs, May 30, $45,175, 3yo, c&g, 6 1/2f, 1:16, NORM'S NEPHEW, Marsh Creek, Idabetabuck, 5 started.

Pepsi-Cola H. (R), Sunland Park, Jan. 15, $132,450, 3yo, New Mexico-bred, 6f, 1:11.19, MR. BOOMER, C. G's Dollar, Abullwithapurpose, 12 started.

Pepsi S., Fonner Park, April 3, $15,850, 3yo, f, 6f, 1:14.80, YESTERDAY'S ROSE, Donaren, Pepper Lang, 9 started.

Perfect Arc S. (R), Aqueduct, Nov. 6, $100,000, 3&up, f&m, New York-bred, 1mT, 1:36.95, CHAMPAGNE ENDING, Forbidden Sea, Square Dancing, 9 started.

Permian Basin S., Zia Park, Oct. 29, $58,500, 2yo, f, 6f, 1:10.20, YADDO CAT, Ms. Glacken, Shezmorethanready, 9 started.

PERRYVILLE S. (G3), Keeneland Race Course, Oct. 14, $200,000, 3yo, a7f, 1:26.06, VICARAGE, Straight Line, Social Probation, 8 started.

PERSONAL ENSIGN S. (G1), Saratoga Race Course, Aug. 26, $400,000, 3&up, f&m, 1 1/4m, 2:02.07, SHADOW CAST, Personal Legend, Two Trail Sioux, 6 started.

Pete Axthelm S., Calder Race Course, Dec. 31, $100,000, 3yo, 7 1/2fT, 1:26.83, DRUM MAJOR, Dream On Dream On, Therecomesatiger, 12 started.

Pete Condellone Memorial H. (R), Fairmount Park, July 23, $40,800, 3&up, Illinois-bred, 1m, 1:37.60, LADY RISS, Beabasque, Afleet Buck, 8 started.

PETER PAN S. (G2), Belmont Park, May 28, $200,000, 3yo, 1 1/8m, 1:46.35, ORATORY, Reverberate, Golden Man, 8 started.

Pete's Buckeye H., Thistledown, June 10, $20,000, 3&up, 6f, 1:10.12, COOGAMONGA, Majestic Dinner, Bernard's Candy, 8 started.

P. G. Johnson S., Meadowlands, Oct. 22, $50,000, 3yo, f, 5f (originally scheduled on the turf), :57.46, MEGASCAPE, Waytotheleft, More Moonlight, 7 started.

P. G. Johnson S. (R), Saratoga Race Course, Sept. 2, $67,700, 2yo, f, non-winners of a stakes, 1 1/16mT, 1:44.61, MAY NIGHT, My Interpretation, Dressed to Kill, 10 started.

Phil D. Shepherd S., Fairplex Park, Sept. 10, $60,000, 3&up, 1 1/16m, 1:44.42, MELANYHASTHEPAPERS, Intelligent Male, R. Baggio, 9 started.

PHILIP H. ISELIN BREEDERS' CUP H. (G3), Monmouth Park, Aug. 28, $190,000, 3&up, 1 1/8m, 1:50.83, WEST VIRGINIA, Zoffinger, Purge, 8 started.

PHOENIX BREEDERS' CUP S. (G3), Keeneland Race Course, Oct. 8, $266,500, 3&up, 6f, 1:11.60, ELUSIVE JAZZ, Wild Tale, Premium Saltine, 8 started.

Phoenix Gold Cup H., Turf Paradise, March 19, $100,000, 3&up, 6f, 1:08.42, PROUD CARDENAL, Flying Supercon, Indian Country, 8 started.

Phoenix S., Meadowlands, Oct. 7, $50,000, 3&up, f&m, 5f (originally scheduled on the turf), :56.47, SPRING RUSH, Ensenada, Chez Audra, 5 started.

Piedmont S., Golden Gate Fields, Nov. 13, $57,125, 2yo, f, 6f, 1:10.18, TALVERNA, Seam Seeker, Aloha Mangos Kitty, 9 started.

Pierre LeBlanc Memorial Ladies Sprint S. (R), Evangeline Downs, July 30, $50,000, 3&up, f&m, Louisiana-bred, 5$^1/_2$f, 1:05.72, MIDNIGHT JUDGE, Shes Dixies Eskimo, Living Lavida Lisa, 9 started.

Pilgrim S., Belmont Park, Oct. 23, $82,575, 2yo, 1$^1/_8$m (originally scheduled on the turf), 1:52.11, FAGAN'S LEGACY, Church Service, Go Between, 6 started.

PIMLICO BREEDERS' CUP DISTAFF H. (G3), Pimlico Race Course, May 20, $107,400, 3&up, f&m, 1$^1/_{16}$m, 1:44.87, SILMARIL, Ashado, Friel's for Real, 4 started.

PIMLICO SPECIAL H. (G1), Pimlico Race Course, May 20, $500,000, 4&up, 1$^3/_{16}$m, 1:58.05, EDDINGTON, Pollard's Vision, Presidentialaffair, 7 started.

Pine Tree Lane S. (R), Oak Tree at Santa Anita, Oct. 23, $67,990, 3&up, f&m, non-winners of a stakes of $50,000 since June 15 other than state-bred, 6$^1/_2$f, 1:14.90, RESPLENDENCY, Freakin Streakin, Soldier's Kiss, 5 started.

Pinjara S. (R), Oak Tree at Santa Anita, Oct. 30, $65,121, 2yo, non-winners of a stakes at one mile or over, 1mT, 1:35.38, STRATHAM (IRE), Class of Fifty, Sensational Score, 4 started.

Pin Oak Stud/Hildene S. (R), Laurel Park, Dec. 11, $50,000, 2yo, f, Virginia-bred and -sired, 6f, 1:13.31, CINNAMON CHARLIE, Scholastic Giant, Virginia Baby, 6 started.

Pin Oak Stud USA S., Lone Star Park, May 30, $200,000, 3yo, 1$^1/_{16}$mT, 1:47.08, MAD ADAM, Justa Red Bird, Smooth Bid, 9 started.

Pioneer S., Louisiana Downs, June 26, $41,400, 2yo, 5f, :59.23, DON'T TELL MOMMY, Kubwa, Rowdy Profit, 6 started.

Pio Pico S. (R), Fairplex Park, Sept. 16, $58,800, 3&up, f&m, California-bred, 6$^1/_2$f, 1:17.32, TWO TO GET READY, Dee Dee's Diner, Wendy's On to Me, 7 started.

Pippin S., Oaklawn Park, Feb. 20, $50,000, 4&up, f&m, 1$^1/_{16}$m, 1:45.43, CASUAL ATTITUDE, Island Sand, Catboat, 7 started.

Pirate's Bounty H. (R), Del Mar, Sept. 7, $87,315, 3&up, non-winners of a stakes other than state-bred since March 1, 6f, 1:08.93, INDIAN COUNTRY, Areyoutalkintome, Smoocher, 8 started.

Pistol Packer H. (R), Philadelphia Park, Oct. 8, $53,800, 3&up, f&m, Pennsylvania-bred, 1$^1/_{16}$m, 1:46.34, VALLEY OF THE GODS, Immune to Gloom, Mae and Ree, 5 started.

Plate Trial S. (R), Woodbine, June 5, $131,703, 3yo, Canadian-bred, 1$^1/_8$m, 1:52.52, THREE IN THE BAG, Get Down, Out From Africa, 7 started.

PLAY THE KING H. (Can-G2), Woodbine, Aug. 27, $195,203, 3&up, 7fT, 1:21.18, VANDERLIN (GB), Le Cinquieme Essai, Frank's Selection, 13 started.

Pleasant Temper S., Kentucky Downs, Sept. 17, $40,000, 3&up, f&m, 1mT, 1:36.70, VERY VERY, Singit, Miss Wellspring, 12 started.

Plenty of Grace S. (R), Belmont Park, July 4, $61,100, 4&up, f&m, non-winners of a stakes other than state-bred, 1mT, 1:33.38, BRIGHT ABUNDANCE, Asti (Ire), Lady Cheyne, 6 started.

Plymouth S. (R), Great Lakes Downs, July 16, $50,000, 3yo, f, Michigan-bred, 7f, 1:31.62, MAXIE MATCH, Sheza Match, Musical Factor, 10 started.

POCAHONTAS S. (G3), Churchill Downs, Nov. 5, $120,600, 2yo, f, 1m, 1:37.19, FRENCH PARK, Trippi Street, Coolwind, 12 started.

POKER H. (G3), Belmont Park, July 3, $111,800, 3&up, 1mT, 1:32.18, MR. LIGHT (ARG), Willard Straight, Remind, 7 started.

Pola Benoit Memorial S. (R), Evangeline Downs, July 30, $50,000, 4&up, Louisiana-bred, 1$^1/_{16}$m, 1:47.31, SANCTUARY'S OMOONI, Sunny Brick, Walk This Way, 7 started.

Politely S., Monmouth Park, June 12, $60,000, 3&up, f&m, 1$^1/_{16}$mT, 1:42.62, SNOWDROPS (GB), Dynamia, Smart N Classy, 9 started.

Polly's Jet S., Delaware Park, Aug. 13, $66,077, 3yo, f, 1m, 1:39.86, GOTTA RUSH, Redaspen, Ebony Star, 8 started.

Polynesian S., Colonial Downs, Aug. 7, $60,000, 3&up, 1$^1/_{16}$m, 1:41.61, ONE NICE CAT, River Mountain Rd, Marina Minister, 7 started.

Pomona Derby, Fairplex Park, Sept. 24, $98,000, 3yo, a1$^1/_8$m, 1:49.96, DOVER DERE, Chummin, Ninety Fine, 7 started.

Ponche H., Calder Race Course, April 30, $75,000, 3&up, 6f, 1:11.65, NIGHTMARE AFFAIR, Toscani, Paradise Dancer, 5 started.

Portland Meadows Mile H., Portland Meadows, April 9, $20,000, 3&up, 1m, 1:37.92, DEMON WARLOCK, My Friend Dave, Crimson Design, 8 started.

Possibly Perfect S., Arlington Park, July 4, $42,500, 3&up, f&m, 1$^1/_8$mT, 1:51.63, MAKE MY HEART SING, Atlantic Frost, Humorous Miss, 9 started.

POTRERO GRANDE BREEDERS' CUP H. (G2), Santa Anita Park, April 3, $194,000, 4&up, 6$^1/_2$f, 1:16.12, HARVARD AVENUE, Rushin' to Altar, Roi Charmant, 9 started.

Powerless H. (R), Hawthorne Race Course, Nov. 12, $100,025, 3&up, f&m, Illinois-conceived and/or -foaled, 6f, 1:10.90, DENOUN N DEVERB, Dharma Girl, Lady Riss, 8 started.

Prairie Bayou S., Turfway Park, Dec. 17, $50,000, 3&up, 1$^1/_8$m, AW, 1:52.50, BRASS HAT, On the Border, dh-Paging, dh-Discreet Hero, 10 started.

Prairie Express S., Prairie Meadows, May 7, $51,500, 3&up, 5$^1/_2$f, 1:02.64, PREMIUM SALTINE, Coach Jimi Lee, Roarofvictory, 6 started.

Prairie Gold Juvenile S., Prairie Meadows, July 3, $50,000, 2yo, 5f, :57.92, COUNTERFEIT GOLD, Dawn of War, Hello Liberty, 7 started.

Prairie Gold Lassie S., Prairie Meadows, July 3, $50,750, 2yo, f, 5f, :58.07, WHATSITGONNATAKE, Sentimental Charm, Jazzy Okie, 9 started.

Prairie Lily Sales S. (R), Marquis Downs, Sept. 3, $18,947, 2yo, sold at the Prairie Lily sales, 7f, 1:29.45, CRAZY CARSON, Shadazzle, Sofisticated Humor, 8 started.

PRAIRIE MEADOWS CORNHUSKER BREEDERS' CUP H. (G2), Prairie Meadows, July 2, $300,000, 3&up, 1$^1/_8$m, 1:49.94, LORD OF THE GAME, Silver Axe, Mambo Train, 8 started.

Prairie Meadows Debutante S., Prairie Meadows, Sept. 3, $48,400, 2yo, f, 6f, 1:11.64, THEKATCAMEHOME, Bountempo, Sentimental Charm, 6 started.

Prairie Meadows Derby, Prairie Meadows, Sept. 24, $89,250, 3yo, 1$^1/_{16}$m, 1:44.92, MINGO MOHAWK, Bisquik, Yak the Desert Rat, 5 started.

Prairie Meadows Freshman S., Prairie Meadows, Sept. 5, $40,600, 2yo, 6f, 1:10.33, TEMPTING TREAT, Magnus One, Timetobook, 5 started.

Prairie Meadows H., Prairie Meadows, July 30, $76,313, 3&up, 1$^1/_8$m, 1:50.09, SILVER AXE, Azucar (Per), Tricky Mocha, 6 started.

Prairie Meadows Oaks, Prairie Meadows, Sept. 17, $75,000, 3yo, f, 1$^1/_{16}$m, 1:44.07, TAPPIN FOR GOLD, Dearest Queen, Whimsy, 7 started.

Prairie Meadows Sprint S., Prairie Meadows, Aug. 6, $50,750, 3&up, 6f, 1:09.26, PREMIUM SALTINE, Two Down Automatic, Silver Dollar, 7 started.

Prairie Mile S., Prairie Meadows, June 11, $50,750, 3yo, 1m, 1:36.67, WAYZATA BAY, Quiet Money, Three Elevens, 8 started.

Prairie Rose S., Prairie Meadows, April 30, $50,000, 3&up, f&m, 6f, 1:09.31, ABOUNDING TRUTH, Wildwood Royal, Glitterbdancing, 7 started.

PREAKNESS S. (G1), Pimlico Race Course, May 21, $1,000,000, 3yo, 1$^3/_{16}$m, 1:55.04, AFLEET ALEX, Scrappy T, Giacomo, 14 started.

Prelude S., Louisiana Downs, Sept. 5, $50,000, 3yo, 1$^1/_{16}$m, 1:44.17, ROYAL SAINT, Key Issues, Silver Haze, 7 started.

Premiere S. (R), Lone Star Park, April 14, $50,000, 3&up, Texas-bred, 1m, 1:37.15, RARE CURE, Yessirgeneralsir, Agrivating General, 8 started.

Premier S., Zia Park, Sept. 23, $56,700, 3&up, 6f, 1:10.80, LORENZON, Dangerous Devon, Go Kitty Go, 7 started.

PREMIER'S H. (Can-G3), Hastings Race Course, Oct. 16, $108,824, 3&up, 1$^3/_8$m, 2:18.25, BULL RANCH, Alabama Rain, Trick of the North, 9 started.

President's Cup H., Lincoln State Fair, June 19, $13,750, 3&up, 6f, 1:11.60, THUNDERING VERZY, Mortrump, Doug's Shadow, 7 started.

President's H., Stampede Park, May 7, $40,265, 3yo, c&g, 6f, 1:10.40, GOLDEN HUNT, Blackjack Willy, Dakota Duke, 8 started.

Preview S., Portland Meadows, March 12, $7,500, 3yo, 1$^1/_{16}$m, 1:49.51, J D'S DATE, American Poet, A Colt Named Sue, 11 started.

Primonetta S., Laurel Park, April 16, $50,000, 3&up, f&m, 6f, 1:10.59, FOREST MUSIC, Spirited Game, Gelli, 9 started.

Princelet S. (R), Belmont Park, Oct. 10, $65,350, 3yo, non-winners of an open stakes, 1$^1/_{16}$m, 1:41.79, WAR FRONT, Skagway, Funk, 5 started.

Prince of Wales S. (R), Fort Erie, July 17, $409,600, 3yo, Canadian-bred, 1$^3/_{16}$m, 1:56.90, ABLO, Autumn Snow, Wild Desert, 6 started.

Princess Elaine S. (R), Canterbury Park, July 3, $40,000, 3&up, f&m, Minnesota-bred, 1$^1/_{16}$mT, 1:43.75, GRAND RAPIDS MISS, Demiparfait, Play N Fare, 12 started.

Princess Elizabeth S. (R), Woodbine, Oct. 22, $211,747, 2yo, f, Canadian-bred, 1$^1/_{16}$m, 1:50, SUGAR SWIRL, Kimchi, Classical Miss, 9 started.

Princess H., Sunland Park, Dec. 6, $50,000, 2yo, f, 6f, 1:11.10, YADDO CAT, Visual Effect, Ms. Glacken, 5 started.

Princess Margaret S., Northlands Park, July 31, $40,850, 2yo, f, 6f, 1:12.40, KAYLEE'S MAGIC, Docalady, Sassy Sarah, 8 started.

Princess of Palms H. (R), Turf Paradise, Feb. 5, $40,000, 4&up, f&m, starters at the Turf Paradise 2004-'05 meet, 6f, 1:09.50, MUIR BEACH, Fun'ngames Toknite, Sawtelle Belle, 7 started.

PRINCESS ROONEY H. (G2), Calder Race Course, July 10, $500,000, 3&up, f&m, 6f, 1:09.93, MADCAP ESCAPADE, Happy Ticket, Savorthetime, 6 started.

Princess S., Lincoln State Fair, May 14, $12,813, 3yo, f, 6f, 1:13.60, SQUAWK TALK, More Monkey Time, Pepper Lang, 7 started.

Princess S., Louisiana Downs, Aug. 28, $50,000, 2yo, f, 6f, 1:12.56, MYKINDASAINT, Love the Beach, Kathy's Rocket, 8 started.

PRIORESS S. (G1), Belmont Park, July 9, $250,000, 3yo, f, 6f, 1:10.37, ACEY DEUCEY, Maddalena, Sense of Style, 7 started.

Private Terms S., Laurel Park, March 26, $50,000, 3yo, 1m, 1:40.04, MALIBU MOONSHINE, Hello Jerry, Monster Chaser, 10 started.

Prospectors Gamble H., Arapahoe Park, Aug. 21, $27,700, 3&up, $1\frac{1}{8}$m, 1:52.06, PERSONAL BEAU, Cut of Music, Spirit Gulch, 9 started.

Proud Puppy H., Finger Lakes, Aug. 20, $50,000, 3&up, f&m, 6f, 1:11.25, SPEAK OUT, Ruby's Rocket, Keesler, 9 started.

PROVIDENCIA S. (G3), Santa Anita Park, April 9, $111,600, 3yo, f, $1\frac{1}{8}$mT, 1:47.66, BERBATIM, Royal Copenhagen (Fr), Thatswhatimean, 10 started.

PUCKER UP S. (G3), Arlington Park, Sept. 17, $200,000, 3yo, f, $1\frac{1}{8}$mT, 1:48.76, ROYAL COPENHAGEN (FR), Singhalese (GB), Isla Cozzene, 11 started.

Purple Violet S. (R), Arlington Park, June 25, $86,200, 3yo, f, Illinois-conceived and/or -foaled, 1m, 1:37.07, PRETTY JENNY, Meadow Bride, Li'lbito'sunshine, 10 started.

Puss n Boots Cup S., Fort Erie, Sept. 5, $25,263, 3&up, $1\frac{1}{16}$mT, 1:45.44, Sandspit, Irish Dave, KRIS'S DANCER, 12 started.

Queen City Oaks (R), River Downs, July 30, $75,000, 3yo, f, Ohio-bred, $1\frac{1}{8}$m, 1:53, FLIP SIDE, Bold Passage, Bring Spring, 7 started.

QUEEN ELIZABETH II CHALLENGE CUP S. (G1), Keeneland Race Course, Oct. 15, $500,000, 3yo, f, $1\frac{1}{8}$mT, 1:51.20, SWEET TALKER, Karen's Caper, Gorella (Fr), 7 started.

Queen Lib H. (R), Meadowlands, Nov. 1, $55,000, 3&up, f&m, New Jersey-bred, 6f, 1:09, CIGNO D'ORO, Totally Precious, Pickin Laurel, 7 started.

Queen of the Green H., Turf Paradise, Nov. 26, $40,000, 3&up, f&m, 1mT, 1:36.14, BENEFICIAL BARTOK, Allbow, Moonlight Cruise, 7 started.

Queen S., Turfway Park, March 26, $50,000, 4&up, f&m, 6f, 1:09.71, REVOLUTIONARY ACT, Plumlake Lady, Moonlit Romance, 8 started.

QUEENS COUNTY H. (G3), Aqueduct, Dec. 10, $105,400, 3&up, $1\frac{3}{16}$m, 1:56.99, PHILANTHROPIST, West Virginia, We Can Seek (Chi), 5 started.

Queen's H., Horsemen's Park, July 23, $40,000, 3&up, f&m, 1m, 1:38, FEISTY PRINCESS, Switch Lanes, My Time Now, 8 started.

Queen's Plate S. (R), Woodbine, June 26, $812,700, 3yo, Canadian-bred, $1\frac{1}{4}$m, 2:07.37, WILD DESERT, King of Jazz, Gold Strike, 9 started.

Queenston S. (R), Woodbine, May 7, $130,459, 3yo, Ontario-bred, 7f, 1:23.40, VERNE'S BABY, Enough Is Enough, Moonshine Justice, 5 started.

Quick Card S., Delaware Park, May 14, $53,300, 3&up, 1m, 1:37.73, POLISH PRIDE, On Thin Ice, The Lady's Groom, 5 started.

Quicken Tree S. (R), Hollywood Park, June 18, $78,600, 4&up, California-bred, $1\frac{1}{2}$mT, 2:27.10, CONTINENTAL RED, Perfect Mode, Running Free, 8 started.

Quill S., Delaware Park, Oct. 17, $59,900, 3&up, f&m, 1m, 1:38.35, SUMMER RAINBOW, Becky in Pink, Thermal Ablasion, 8 started.

Radar Love S., Calder Race Course, Nov. 27, $40,000, 3&up, $6\frac{1}{2}$f, 1:18.63, UNIVERSAL FORM, Champagne Account, B. B. Best, 7 started.

Radnor Hunt Cup Timber S., Malvern, May 21, $40,000, 4&up, a$3\frac{1}{4}$mT, MILES AHEAD, Hall of Angels, Sham Aciss, 8 started.

Rage Starter H. (R), Turf Paradise, Dec. 7, $6,050, 3&up, starters for a claiming price of $3,000 or less in 2005, 5f, :56.27, WHITE RINO, Kid Courageous, Kolinor, 6 started.

Railbird S., Hollywood Park, May 1, $109,700, 3yo, f, 7f, 1:22.99, SHORT ROUTE, Inspiring, Off the Richter, 8 started.

Rainbow Connection S. (R), Fort Erie, July 24, $102,563, 3&up, f&m, progeny of stallions standing in Ontario, 5fT, :57.23, DEPUTY CURES BLUES, Cricket Wicket, On Silent Wings, 7 started.

Rainbow Miss S. (R), Oaklawn Park, April 3, $50,000, 3yo, f, Arkansas-bred, 6f, 1:11.52, DOLL AND A HALF, Ritas Wampus Cat, Maggio, 9 started.

Rainbow S. (R), Oaklawn Park, April 3, $50,000, 3yo, c&g, Arkansas-bred, 6f, 1:10.97, STORMY BUT CRAFTY, Leon's Best, Wow Yao, 7 started.

Ralph Hayes S. (R), Prairie Meadows, Aug. 27, $81,600, 4&up, c&g, Iowa-bred, $1\frac{1}{16}$m, 1:44.27, SUR SANDPIT, Rubianos Image, Take Me Up, 11 started.

Ralph M. Hinds Invitational H., Fairplex Park, Sept. 25, $98,000, 3&up, a$1\frac{1}{8}$m, 1:49.81, COURTLY JAZZ, Robledo, Melanyhasthepapers, 7 started.

RAMPART H. (G2), Gulfstream Park, March 26, $200,000, 3&up, f&m, $1\frac{1}{8}$m, 1:48.92, D'WILDCAT SPEED, Isola Piu Bella (Chi), Pampered Princess, 5 started.

RANCHO BERNARDO H. (G3), Del Mar, Aug. 19, $150,000, 3&up, f&m, $6\frac{1}{2}$f, 1:15.32, BEHAVING BADLY, Freakin Streakin, Dee Dee's Diner, 8 started.

Randaroo S., Aqueduct, Dec. 14, $67,450, 2yo, f, 6f, 1:10.80, OPRAH WINNEY, Silvestris, Livermore Valley, 9 started.

Randy Bailey Memorial H. (R), Blue Ribbon Downs, Feb. 20, $9,925, 3&up, 4f, :46.23, SOONER PRIDE, Final Draft, Really Tough, 8 started.

Rare Treat H., Aqueduct, Feb. 26, $78,575, 3&up, f&m, $1\frac{1}{8}$m, 1:51.17, MISS FORTUNATE, Lady Libby, Rare Gift, 5 started.

Rattlesnake S., Turf Paradise, Jan. 23, $40,000, 3yo, 1m, 1:37.25, LEAD FOR SPEED, Scottsbluff, Night Gig, 7 started.

RAVEN RUN S. (G2), Keeneland Race Course, Oct. 22, $300,000, 3yo, f, 7f, 1:23.74, FOR ALL WE KNOW, Flying Glitter, Career Oriented, 11 started.

Ravolia S., Calder Race Course, Sept. 4, $40,000, 3yo, f, 1m, 1:40.68, FAST LISA, Ragtime Hope, Flying Circle, 8 started.

RAZORBACK BREEDERS' CUP H. (G3), Oaklawn Park, March 13, $125,000, 4&up, $1\frac{1}{16}$m, 1:43.88, ADDED EDGE, Mauk Four, Absent Friend, 10 started.

Razorback Futurity (R), Louisiana Downs, Sept. 30, $45,000, 2yo, c&g, Arkansas-bred, 6f, 1:11.52, BRASSIE PRINCE, Storm Is Due, Pourthecoaltoit, 10 started.

R. C. Anderson S. (R), Assiniboia Downs, July 16, $32,768, 3yo, f, Manitoba-bred, 1m, 1:42.20, CINDY EMBERS, Danger Pay, Black Teddie, 8 started.

Real Good Deal S. (R), Del Mar, Aug. 12, $100,000, 3yo, California-bred, 7f, 1:22.09, THOR'S ECHO, Scottsbluff, Ninety Fine, 9 started.

Real Prize S., Aqueduct, Nov. 27, $67,500, 3&up, f&m, $1\frac{1}{8}$m, 1:54.68, STRATEGY, Freeroll, Taittinger Rose, 6 started.

Real Quiet S., Hollywood Park, Nov. 26, $100,000, 2yo, $1\frac{1}{16}$m, 1:43.99, GENRE (GB), Kissin Knight, Bob and John, 5 started.

Reappeal S., Calder Race Course, May 14, $40,000, 3&up, 5fT, :55.75, PLACIDO, True Love's Secret, Simmer, 10 started.

REBEL S. (G3), Oaklawn Park, March 19, $250,000, 3yo, $1\frac{1}{16}$m, 1:44.92, GREATER GOOD, Rockport Harbor, Batson Challenge, 6 started.

RED BANK H. (G3), Monmouth Park, May 28, $150,000, 3&up, 1mT, 1:43.12, AMERICAN FREEDOM, Spruce Run, Royal Affirmed, 8 started.

Red Camelia H. (R), Fair Grounds, March 27, $100,000, 4&up, f&m, Louisiana-bred, a1mT, 1:39.68, MERRY MARY, Autobesarah, Destiny Calls, 10 started.

Red Cross S., Monmouth Park, July 17, $59,150, 3&up, f&m, 6f, 1:09.30, AREEK, Thermal Ablasion, Welcome Home, 3 started.

Red Diamond Express H. (R), Northlands Park, Sept. 24, $42,690, 3&up, Alberta-bred, $6\frac{1}{2}$f, 1:17.60, COOL BENDER, Fly Esteem, Winspear, 6 started.

Red Hedeman Mile H. (R), Sunland Park, Dec. 18, $125,000, 2yo, New Mexico-bred, 1m, 1:39.05, LATENITE BAND, Matchstick Man, Manolito, 9 started.

Red McCombs S. (R), Retama Park, Oct. 1, $40,000, 3yo, Texas-bred, 5fT, :55.75 (NCR), K D KING, Jonsey Rabbit, Leaving On My Mind, 7 started.

Red Smith H., Aqueduct, Nov. 12, $150,000, 3&up, $1\frac{3}{8}$mT, 2:15.37, KING'S DRAMA (IRE), Rousing Victory, Dreadnaught, 8 started.

Red White and Blue Overnight H., Emerald Downs, July 4, $25,000, 3yo, f, $5\frac{1}{2}$f, 1:03, LIGHT MY DUCKS, Roanaway Bride, America's Girl, 7 started.

Regaey Island S., Ellis Park, July 23, $75,000, 3yo, $1\frac{1}{16}$mT, 1:43.66, PIRATES BITE, Giambi, Mesawmi, 11 started.

Regal Gal S., Calder Race Course, Aug. 22, $40,000, 3yo, f, 1m, 1:40.71, ALISA'S HOPE, Leona's Knight, Midtown Miss, 7 started.

Regret S., Monmouth Park, Aug. 7, $100,000, 3&up, f&m, 6f, 1:10.11, AREEK, My Trusty Cat, Silver Bird, 8 started.

REGRET S. (G3), Churchill Downs, June 18, $225,000, 3yo, f, 1$^1/_8$mT, 1:49.76, RICH IN SPIRIT, Sweet Talker, Royal Bean, 8 started.

Regret S. (R), Great Lakes Downs, June 11, $45,000, 3yo, f, Michigan-bred, 6f, 1:16.71, MUSICAL FACTOR, Sheza Match, Valor Within, 10 started.

Reluctant Guest S., Arlington Park, May 29, $42,375, 3&up, f&m, a1mT, 1:38.07, VITAMIN BAG, Ghostly Gate, Ms. Lydonia, 9 started.

Reluctant Guest S., Arlington Park, May 29, $42,625, 3&up, f&m, a1mT, 1:37.78, ATLANTIC FROST, Samantha B., Sunset Kisses, 10 started.

Remington Green S., Remington Park, Oct. 21, $50,000, 3&up, 1$^1/_{16}$mT, 1:40.40, DONTBOTHERKNOCKING, Missme, Wishingitwas, 12 started.

Remington Mile S., Remington Park, Oct. 21, $75,390, 2yo, 1m, 1:38.26, TEST BOY, Out Our Way, Ioway Indian, 11 started.

Remington Park Oaks, Remington Park, Oct. 21, $40,000, 3yo, f, 1mT, 1:34.89, MORE THAN PROMISED, Stormin Gold, Swift Wings, 9 started.

Remington Park Oaks, Remington Park, Oct. 21, $40,650, 3yo, f, 1mT, 1:35.32, WHERE'S BAILEY, D Fine Okie, Goodie Good Girl, 11 started.

REMSEN S. (G2), Aqueduct, Nov. 26, $200,000, 2yo, 1$^1/_8$m, 1:52.20, BLUEGRASS CAT, Flashy Bull, Parkhimonbroadway, 8 started.

Restoration S., Monmouth Park, June 19, $60,000, 3yo, 1$^1/_{16}$mT, 1:42.07, HOUSEOFROYALHEARTS, T. D. Vance, All Trumps, 7 started.

Retama Park Turf Breeders' Cup H., Retama Park, Aug. 13, $50,000, 3&up, 1$^1/_{16}$mT, 1:45.14, A R CRACKERS, Waupaca, Seainsky, 6 started.

Revidere S., Monmouth Park, June 4, $60,000, 3yo, f, 1m70y, 1:42.59, BAYOU BREEZE, Sense of Style, Smokestack, 5 started.

Richard King H. (R), Sam Houston Race Park, Nov. 19, $50,000, 3&up, Texas-bred, 1$^1/_8$mT, 1:51.84, LEAVING ON MY MIND, Northern Scene, Blinding Prospect, 9 started.

Richmond Derby Trial H., Hastings Race Course, Sept. 5, $43,513, 3yo, 1$^1/_{16}$m, 1:44.56, APPEARANCE FEE, Spaghetti Mouse, Notis Otis, 8 started.

Richmond H., Golden Gate Fields, Jan. 17, $53,500, 3&up, f&m, 6f, 1:09.43, STORMICA, Vaca City Flyer, Yerevan Star, 6 started.

Richmond S. (R), Hoosier Park, Sept. 30, $40,000, 3&up, f&m, Indiana-bred, 1$^1/_{16}$m, 1:45.41, ELLENS LUCKY STAR, Lady Blue Sky, Black Eyed Susie, 10 started.

RICHTER SCALE BREEDERS' CUP SPRINT CHAMPIONSHIP H. (G2), Gulfstream Park, March 12, $200,000, 3&up, 7f, 1:21.64, SIR SHACKLETON, Lion Tamer, Clock Stopper, 6 started.

Ricks Memorial S., Remington Park, Sept. 5, $40,000, 3&up, f&m, 1mT, 1:34.16, PAZ CIUDADANA (CHI), Queena Corrina, Claudia's Agenda, 9 started.

Ride Sally S. (R), Aqueduct, Dec. 15, $66,750, 3yo, f, non-winners of an open stakes, 1m70y, 1:43.48, SPUN SILK, Victory Pool, Pleasant Laughter, 7 started.

Riley Allison Futurity, Sunland Park, Dec. 31, $166,933, 2yo, 6$^1/_2$f, 1:18.55, DISAPPEARING TRICK, Forrest G., Cab, 10 started.

Rio Grande Senor Futurity (R), Ruidoso Downs, July 31, $97,952, 2yo, c&g, New Mexico-bred, 5$^1/_2$f, 1:05.20, IN UNITY, Silver City Jones, Mr. Band Time, 10 started.

Rio Grande Senorita Futurity (R), Ruidoso Downs, July 31, $87,541, 2yo, f, New Mexico-bred, 5$^1/_2$f, 1:05, PEPPERS PRIDE, Zzzs Ghost, Hang Glide, 8 started.

Rise Jim S. (R), Suffolk Downs, May 30, $40,000, 3&up, Massachusetts-bred, 6f, 1:11.13, JINI'S JET, Storm Quest, Gun Is Set, 7 started.

RISEN STAR S. (G3), Fair Grounds, Feb. 12, $150,000, 3yo, 1$^1/_{16}$m, 1:44.54, SCIPION, Real Dandy, Storm Surge, 11 started.

RIVA RIDGE BREEDERS' CUP S. (G2), Belmont Park, June 11, $170,000, 3yo, 7f, 1:21.54, LOST IN THE FOG, Egg Head, Middle Earth, 8 started.

River Cities Breeders' Cup S., Louisiana Downs, Sept. 10, $68,000, 3&up, f&m, a1$^1/_{16}$mT, 1:42.40, DUETOWINAGAIN, Chitchat Chitchat, Go Girlfriend Go, 5 started.

RIVER CITY H. (G3), Churchill Downs, Nov. 20, $167,700, 3&up, 1$^1/_8$mT, 1:50.78, AMERICA ALIVE, G P Fleet, Shaniko, 8 started.

River Memories S., Woodbine, Nov. 5, $93,266, 3&up, f&m, 1m70y (originally scheduled at 1m on the turf), 1:44.46, CAN IHAVETHISDANCE, Kabul, Juliet's Kiss, 6 started.

River Oaks S., Sam Houston Race Park, Jan. 15, $40,000, 3yo, f, 6f, 1:11.82, CORONADO ROSE, Texas Spirit, Lip Gloss, 8 started.

R. J. Speers S., Assiniboia Downs, Sept. 3, $33,684, 3&up, 1$^1/_{16}$m, 1:47.60, ALBARINO, Nugrayontheblock, Northern Affair, 8 started.

Road Runner H. (R), Ruidoso Downs, July 31, $45,000, 3yo, c&g, New Mexico-bred, 5$^1/_2$f, 1:03.20, C. G'S DOLLAR, Ring of the Run, Cherokee Tyger, 7 started.

ROBERT F. CAREY MEMORIAL H. (G3), Hawthorne Race Course, Sept. 24, $150,000, 3&up, 1mT, 1:39.97, SPRUCE RUN, Fort Prado, Remind, 9 started.

Robert G. Dick Memorial Breeders' Cup H., Delaware Park, July 16, $296,000, 3&up, f&m, 1$^3/_8$mT, 2:20.58, HONEY RYDER, Sweet Science, Natalie Beach (Arg), 10 started.

Robert G. Leavitt Memorial H. (R), Charles Town Races, Aug. 13, $41,500, 3yo, West Virginia-bred, 7f, 1:26.78, BRYCESLITTLESECRET, Wild Remarks, Raggedy Andy, 10 started.

Robert K. Kerlan Memorial H., Hollywood Park, July 10, $79,500, 3&up, 5$^1/_2$fT, 1:01.82, SIREN LURE, Stormin' Lyon, Golden Arrow, 7 started.

Robert R. Hilton Memorial S. (R), Charles Town Races, Sept. 10, $41,150, 3&up, West Virginia-bred, 7f, 1:27.08, BRIGADER, Longfield Spud, Kokando, 10 started.

Robert W. Camac Memorial S. (R), Philadelphia Park, July 23, $50,000, 3&up, Pennsylvania-bred, 5fT, :57.55, SHADES OF SUNNY, Namequest, Mad Anthony, 8 started.

Rocket Bar S., Turf Paradise, Dec. 21, $23,700, 3yo, 6f, 1:09.22, PRORUNNER, Gold Rush Banker, Raging Wind, 6 started.

Rocket Man S., Calder Race Course, July 10, $50,000, 2&up, 2f, :21.21, THATS THE PROBLEM, Caller One, Love My Mountain, 11 started.

Roger Van Hoozer Memorial S. (R), Charles Town Races, Sept. 10, $41,400, 3&up, f&m, West Virginia-bred, 7f, 1:27.51, ORIGINAL GOLD, Ketch a Hello, Alaska Ash, 10 started.

Rolling Green Breeders' Cup H., Golden Gate Fields, June 4, $95,625, 3&up, 1$^1/_8$mT, 1:49.46, CAPITANO, Gold Ruckus, Courtly Jazz, 4 started.

Rood and Riddle Dowager S., Keeneland Race Course, Oct. 23, $150,000, 3&up, f&m, 1$^1/_2$mT, 2:38.77, BRIVIESCA (GB), Cape Town Lass, Louve Royale (Ire), 8 started.

Rose Blossom H., Western Montana Fair and Races, Aug. 13, $4,750, 3&up, f&m, 1$^1/_{16}$m, 1:53, SNOWBOUND STAR, Suprisingly, Game Princess, 7 started.

Rose DeBartolo Memorial S. (R), Thistledown, July 16, $75,000, 3&up, f&m, Ohio-bred, 1$^1/_8$m, 1:52.76, GIRLISH GIGGLE, Barnsy, Golden Tour, 7 started.

Rossi Gold S., Arlington Park, Sept. 3, $41,500, 3&up, 1$^1/_2$mT, 2:29.64, CLOUDY'S KNIGHT, Come On Jazz, Delafield, 6 started.

Rotsaluck Starter H., Turf Paradise, Oct. 30, $10,600, 3&up, 6f, 1:09.71, BARRICADED, White Rino, Ty the Score, 8 started.

Round Table S., Arlington Park, July 16, $100,000, 3yo, 1$^1/_8$m, 1:47.73, DEVILMENT, Real Dandy, High Expectations, 8 started.

Route 66 S. (R), Fair Meadows at Tulsa, July 16, $37,225, 3&up, Oklahoma-bred, 6$^1/_2$f, 1:18, HERECOMESTHEMANNOW, Sooner Pride, Proper Prospect, 7 started.

Royal Chase for the Sport of Kings S., Keeneland Race Course, April 22, $159,250, 4&up, a2$^1/_2$mT, 4:42.08, HIRAPOUR (IRE), Sur La Tete, McDynamo, 8 started.

ROYAL HEROINE INVITATIONAL S. (G3), Hollywood Park, July 3, $200,000, 3&up, f&m, 1mT, 1:34.33, INTERCONTINENTAL (GB), Ticker Tape (GB), Navaja (NZ), 5 started.

ROYAL NORTH H. (Can-G3), Woodbine, Aug. 1, $144,445, 3&up, f&m, 6fT, 1:09.79, TARA'S TOUCH (SAF), Saint Etienne (Ire), Unbridled Sidney, 9 started.

Royal North S. (R), Beulah Park, April 9, $40,000, 3yo, f, Ohio-bred, 6f, 1:10.45, NOON WIN, Queens Over Jacks, Cloud Forty Nine, 6 started.

R. R. M. Carpenter Jr. Memorial H., Delaware Park, July 16, $100,300, 3&up, 1$^1/_{16}$m, 1:43.53, ROYAL ASSAULT, Trapped Again, Super Frolic, 6 started.

Rudy Baez Breeders' Cup S., Suffolk Downs, June 11, $47,750, 3yo, 6f, 1:12.26, ACCURATE, Ed Miracle, Lucky Sherman, 5 started.

Ruffian H., Arapahoe Park, July 17, $27,275, 3yo, f, 7f, 1:23.11, SHESA PRIVATE I, Adance, Skyline Gal, 8 started.

RUFFIAN H. (G1), Belmont Park, Sept. 11, $300,000, 3&up, f&m, 1$^1/_{16}$m, 1:41.87, STELLAR JAYNE, Society Selection, Halory Leigh, 6 started.

Ruffian S., Zia Park, Nov. 18, $42,000, 3yo, f, 1m, 1:37.20, MERGER TALK, Mattie Cakes, Superior Deputy, 8 started.

Ruff/Kirchberg Memorial H. (R), Beulah Park, Nov. 12, $40,000, 3&up, Ohio-bred, 1$^1/_4$m, 2:05.84, COUNT ON MY WORD, Go Johnny Go, R S Express, 7 started.

Ruidoso Mile H., Ruidoso Downs, Aug. 6, $25,000, 3&up, 1m, 1:42, BALDWIN COUNTY, Fin Entertainment, Don't Strike Out, 6 started.

Ruidoso Throughbred Championship S., Ruidoso Downs, Sept. 5, $37,100, 3&up, 1$^1/_{16}$m, 1:45, DON'T STRIKE OUT, Bayou the Moon, Baldwin County, 7 started.

Ruidoso Thoroughbred Derby, Ruidoso Downs, Sept. 4, $26,900, 3yo, 1$^{1}/_{16}$m, 1:52.80, PHANTOM ACCOUNT, C. G's Dollar, Devious Choice, 6 started.

Ruidoso Thoroughbred Overnight S., Ruidoso Downs, Aug. 28, $15,000, 3yo, f, 7$^{1}/_{2}$f, 1:35.40, MERGER TALK, Superior Deputy, I'm N Clover, 8 started.

RuidosoThoroughbred Overnite S., Ruidoso Downs, July 17, $15,000, 3yo, f, 7$^{1}/_{2}$f, 1:36.60, MERGER TALK, Lite Write, So Still, 6 started.

RuidosoThoroughbred Overnite S., Ruidoso Downs, July 17, $15,000, 3yo, c&g, 5$^{1}/_{2}$f, 1:03.40, C. G'S DOLLAR, Trickey Todd, Beccas' Shoulder, 6 started.

RuidosoThoroughbred Overnite S., Ruidoso Downs, Sept. 5, $15,000, 2yo, 6f, 1:12, COWBOYED UP, Skookum Man, She's Stormin, 7 started.

RuidosoThoroughbred Overnite S., Ruidoso Downs, Sept. 2, $15,000, 3yo, 5$^{1}/_{2}$f, 1:05, DANGEROUS DEVON, Takin Issue, Cajun Pepper, 6 started.

Ruidoso Thoroughbred Sale Futurity (R), Ruidoso Downs, June 18, $110,303, 2yo, New Mexico-bred, 5f, 58, SILVER CITY JONES, Ryejee's Prancer, Gone Extra, 9 started.

Rumson S., Monmouth Park, Aug. 14, $70,800, 3yo, 6f, 1:09.13, WHO'S THE COWBOY, Caribbean Cruiser, Euro Code, 5 started.

Runza H., Fonner Park, March 26, $16,375, 3&up, f&m, 6f, 1:13.40, PRINCESS OF HOLME, Up 'n Blumin, Burning Memories, 7 started.

Rushaway S., Turfway Park, March 26, $100,000, 3yo, 1$^{1}/_{16}$m, 1:44.49, CAT SHAKER, Daddy Joe, Catch Me, 10 started.

Rutgers S., Meadowlands, Nov. 12, $70,800, 3&up, 6f, 1:08.21, JOEY P., Slam Bammy, Two Down Automatic, 9 started.

Ruth C. Funkhouser S. (R), Charles Town Races, Sept. 17, $41,200, 3yo, f, nominated to the West Virginia Breeders' Classic, 7f, 1:27.71, BRAVURA, Karate Kat, Melissa's Melody, 9 started.

Ruthless S., Aqueduct, Jan. 2, $76,450, 3yo, f, 6f, 1:11.45, MEGASCAPE, Pelham Bay, Academy Brass, 4 started.

SABIN H. (G3), Gulfstream Park, Feb. 26, $100,000, 3&up, f&m, 1$^{1}/_{8}$m, 1:50.68, ISOLA PIU BELLA (CHI), Pampered Princess, Adobe Gold, 5 started.

Sadie Diamond Futurity (R), Hastings Race Course, Oct. 1, $91,779, 2yo, f, Canadian-bred, 6$^{1}/_{2}$f, 1:18.51, NO KA OI, Starlite Strike, Miss Me Not, 11 started.

Sadie Hawkins H. (R), Charles Town Races, Aug. 20, $41,450, 3&up, f&m, West Virginia-bred, 7f, 1:27.30, CARNIVAL CHROME, Cedar Runs Case, Alaska Ash, 9 started.

SAFELY KEPT BREEDERS' CUP S. (G3), Laurel Park, Oct. 16, $131,500, 3yo, f, 6f, 1:10.45, TRICKLE OF GOLD, Maddalena, Partners Due, 5 started.

Safely Kept S., Arlington Park, Sept. 5, $41,750, 3&up, f&m, 6f, 1:09.41, LIZ ON POLK STREET, Beautiful Bets, Silver Crown, 7 started.

Saguaro S., Turf Paradise, Oct. 29, $40,000, 3yo, 6f, 1:08.76, SCOTTSBLUFF, Thirsty Guy's, Night Dash, 6 started.

Sail On By S., Turf Paradise, Nov. 1, $23,600, 2yo, 6f, 1:11.09, IBETIWIN, Dufourspitze, Rebuck, 6 started.

Salem County S., Meadowlands, Oct. 1, $50,000, 2yo, f, 1m 70yT., 1:40.81, ART SHOW, Dressed to Kill, Perilous Pursuit, 8 started.

Sale S. (R), Northlands Park, Aug. 20, $48,534, 2yo, c&g, Canadian-bred sold at the CTHS sale, 6$^{1}/_{2}$f, 1:19.40, TEAGUES FIGHT, Blue Storm, Sweetwood, 8 started.

Sales H. (R), Stampede Park, April 16, $39,308, 4&up, f&m, Canadian-bred sold at the CTHS sale, 6f, 1:12, A SHAKY START, Tantoo, Code's Decree, 7 started.

Sales H. (R), Stampede Park, April 16, $39,308, 4&up, c&g, Canadian-bred sold at the CTHS sale, 6f, 1:11.20, CODE NAME FRED, Rokeby's Nugget, Boldanzar, 9 started.

Sales S. (R), Marquis Downs, July 23, $6,154, 3yo, passed through the 2003 Prairie Lily Sale, 7f, 1:27.45, WIND DANCER, Fargo Forbes, Lambrose, 6 started.

SALVATOR MILE H. (G3), Monmouth Park, July 24, $150,000, 3&up, 1m, 1:36.79, CHEROKEE'S BOY, Aggadan, Gygistar, 5 started.

Sambacarioca S., Calder Race Course, Aug. 19, $40,000, 3&up, f&m, 1$^{1}/_{16}$m, 1:46.47, AMERICAN MISS, Shady Woman, Cute Connie, 9 started.

Sam F. Davis S., Tampa Bay Downs, Feb. 26, $100,000, 3yo, 1$^{1}/_{16}$m, 1:46.63, ANDROMEDA'S HERO, Summer Legacy, Captain Lindsay, 12 started.

Sam Houston Distaff H., Sam Houston Race Park, Jan. 22, $50,000, 4&up, f&m, 1$^{1}/_{16}$m, 1:46.14, ACADEMIC ANGEL, Native Annie, Bonnie J., 10 started.

Sam Houston Oaks, Sam Houston Race Park, March 12, $40,000, 3yo, f, 1m, 1:40.87, THUNDERDOLL, Parisparis, Timber Jones, 6 started.

Sam Houston Sprint H., Sam Houston Race Park, Jan. 22, $50,000, 4&up, 7f, 1:24.02, TWO DOWN AUTOMATIC, High Strike Zone, Charming Socialite, 9 started.

Sam Houston Turf Sprint Cup S., Sam Houston Race Park, April 9, $50,000, 4&up, 5fT, :57.92, PROVEN CURE, Hortense (Chi), Charming Socialite, 10 started.

Sam J. Whiting Memorial H., Pleasanton, July 9, $53,550, 3&up, 6f, 1:08.71, BONFANTE, Flying Supercon, Kool Suggestion, 8 started.

Samuel H. (R), Beulah Park, Dec. 17, $20,000, 3&up, starters at the Beulah Park fall 2005 meet, 6f, 1:09.63, JUST MICHEL, City Rapid, Catlaunch, 7 started.

SAN ANTONIO H. (G2), Santa Anita Park, Feb. 6, $250,000, 4&up, 1$^{1}/_{8}$m, 1:49.05, LUNDY'S LIABILITY (BRZ), Truly a Judge, Congrats, 9 started.

SAN CARLOS H. (G2), Santa Anita Park, Feb. 26, $150,000, 4&up, 7f, 1:21.42, HASTY KRIS, Harvard Avenue, Perfect Moon, 8 started.

San Carlos H., Bay Meadows Race Course, March 26, $57,925, 3&up, 6f, 1:08.25, TRICKEY TREVOR, Verkade, Ice Legend, 5 started.

SAN CLEMENTE H. (G2), Del Mar, July 30, $150,000, 3yo, f, 1mT, 1:34.25, SHINING ENERGY, dh-Royal Copenhagen (Fr), dh-Memorette, 10 started.

Sandia H., The Downs at Albuquerque, Sept. 17, $30,000, 3&up, 5$^{1}/_{2}$f, 1:02.94, ABSOLUTELY TRUE, Las Devious, Beyond Brilliant, 5 started.

SAN DIEGO H. (G2), Del Mar, July 24, $250,000, 3&up, 1$^{1}/_{16}$m, 1:42.40, CHOCTAW NATION, Ace Blue (Brz), Preachinatthebar, 6 started.

Sandpiper S., Tampa Bay Downs, Dec. 31, $60,000, 2yo, f, 6f, 1:10.33, MISTY ROSETTE, Runaway in Love, Running Lass, 12 started.

Sandpiper S., Tampa Bay Downs, Jan. 15, $60,000, 3yo, f, 6f, 1:11.26, PORTSEA, Lady in Pink, Joyous Song, 13 started.

Sandra Hall Grand Canyon H. (R), Turf Paradise, April 30, $40,000, 3&up, Arizona-bred, 6f, 1:08.30, KING JUSTIN, Komax, Grimm, 8 started.

SANDS POINT S. (G3), Belmont Park, June 5, $111,200, 3yo, f, 1$^{1}/_{8}$mT, 1:47.50, MELHOR AINDA, Laurafina, My Typhoon (Ire), 7 started.

San Felipe S., Sam Houston Race Park, Jan. 8, $40,000, 4&up, f&m, 6f, 1:11.60, RACING SUNDOWN, Questionable Past, Hay Madison, 9 started.

SAN FELIPE S. (G2), Santa Anita Park, March 19, $250,000, 3yo, 1$^{1}/_{16}$m, 1:40.11, CONSOLIDATOR, Giacomo, Don't Get Mad, 8 started.

SAN FERNANDO BREEDERS' CUP S. (G2), Santa Anita Park, Jan. 15, $198,000, 4yo, 1$^{1}/_{16}$m, 1:42.14, MINISTER ERIC, Mass Media, Skipaslew, 9 started.

SAN FRANCISCO BREEDERS' CUP MILE H. (G2), Bay Meadows Race Course, April 23, $111,250, 3&up, 1mT, 1:37.40, CASTLEDALE (IRE), Adreamisborn, Aly Bubba, 9 started.

SAN GABRIEL H. (G3), Santa Anita Park, Jan. 1, $150,000, 4&up, 1$^{1}/_{8}$m (originally scheduled on the turf), 1:48.90, TRULY A JUDGE, Star Cross (Arg), Continental Red, 6 started.

SAN GORGONIO H. (G3), Santa Anita Park, Jan. 8, $150,000, 4&up, f&m, 1$^{1}/_{8}$m (originally scheduled on the turf), 1:49.82, FENCELINENEIGHBOR, Uraib (Ire), Dolly Wells (Arg), 5 started.

Sangue H., Louisiana Downs, Aug. 14, $56,930, 3&up, f&m, 7$^{1}/_{2}$fT, 1:27.96 (NCR), OUR LOVE, Chitchat Chitchat, Due to Win Again, 8 started.

San Jacinto S. (R), Sam Houston Race Park, Nov. 19, $50,000, 3&up, f&m, Texas-bred, 1$^{1}/_{16}$mT, 1:46.53, MARFA'S TAXES, Bea's Gal, Leo's Baroness, 10 started.

SAN JUAN CAPISTRANO INVITATIONAL H. (G2), Santa Anita Park, April 16, $250,000, 4&up, a1$^{3}/_{4}$mT, 2:45.02, T. H. APPROVAL, Exterior, Fitz Flag (Arg), 8 started.

San Juan County Commission H., SunRay Park, Sept. 5, $77,800, 3&up, 1$^{1}/_{8}$m, 1:50, MR. TRIESTE, Suspicious Minds, Skip and Go, 8 started.

San Juan Invitational S., SunRay Park, Sept. 5, $35,800, 3yo, 1m, 1:38.20, MAYBEFIRST, Julie's Wild Child, Lizard King, 8 started.

SAN LUIS OBISPO H. (G3), Santa Anita Park, Feb. 19, $150,000, 4&up, 1$^{1}/_{2}$m (originally scheduled on the turf), 2:28.72, LICENSE TO RUN (BRZ), Californian (GB), T. H. Approval, 8 started.

SAN LUIS REY H. (G2), Santa Anita Park, March 27, $200,000, 4&up, 1$^{1}/_{2}$mT, 2:24.45, STANLEY PARK, Meteor Storm (GB), Epicentre, 10 started.

SAN MARCOS S. (G2), Santa Anita Park, Jan. 22, $150,000, 4&up, 1$^{1}/_{4}$mT, 2:00.68, WHILLY (IRE), Puppeteer (GB), T. H. Approval, 6 started.

San Mateo Mile S., Bay Meadows Race Course, Feb. 12, $100,000, 3yo, 1m, 1:35.57, STELLAR MAGIC, Texcess, King Mobay, 7 started.

San Miguel S., Santa Anita Park, Jan. 17, $104,762, 3yo, 6f, 1:09.62,

GOING WILD, So Long Birdie, General John B, 4 started.

SAN PASQUAL H. (G2), Santa Anita Park, Jan. 8, $150,000, 4&up, 1 1/16m, 1:41.97, CONGRATS, Total Impact (Chi), Sigfreto, 5 started.

San Pedro S., Santa Anita Park, March 26, $95,475, 3yo, 6 1/2f, 1:16.58, HIGH STANDARDS, Ransom Demanded, Talking to John, 6 started.

SAN RAFAEL S. (G2), Santa Anita Park, Jan. 15, $150,000, 3yo, 1m, 1:36.69, SPANISH CHESTNUT, Iced Out, Texcess, 5 started.

SAN SIMEON H. (G3), Santa Anita Park, April 18, $107,000, 4&up, a6 1/2fT, 1:12.62, SHADOW OF ILLINOIS, Geronimo (Chi), Golden Arrow, 6 started.

SANTA ANA H. (G2), Santa Anita Park, March 20, $150,000, 4&up, f&m, 1 1/8mT, 1:47.95, MEGAHERTZ (GB), Katdogawn (GB), Valentine Dancer, 7 started.

SANTA ANITA DERBY (G1), Santa Anita Park, April 9, $750,000, 3yo, 1 1/8m, 1:49.18, BUZZARDS BAY, General John B, Wilko, 11 started.

SANTA ANITA H. (G1), Santa Anita Park, March 5, $1,000,000, 4&up, 1 1/4m, 2:01.20, ROCK HARD TEN, Congrats, Borrego, 11 started.

SANTA ANITA OAKS (G1), Santa Anita Park, March 13, $300,000, 3yo, f, 1 1/16m, 1:44.44, SWEET CATOMINE, Memorette, She Sings, 7 started.

SANTA BARBARA H. (G2), Santa Anita Park, April 17, $200,000, 4&up, f&m, 1 1/4mT, 1:59.76, MEGAHERTZ (GB), Nadeszhda (GB), Hoh Buzzard (Ire), 7 started.

SANTA CATALINA S. (G2), Santa Anita Park, March 5, $200,000, 3yo, 1 1/16m, 1:42.41, DECLAN'S MOON, Going Wild, Spanish Chestnut, 6 started.

SANTA MARGARITA INVITATIONAL H. (G1), Santa Anita Park, March 12, $300,000, 4&up, f&m, 1 1/8m, 1:49.41, TARLOW, Dream of Summer, Miss Loren (Arg), 9 started.

SANTA MARIA H. (G1), Santa Anita Park, Feb. 13, $250,000, 4&up, f&m, 1 1/16m, 1:42.42, MISS LOREN (ARG), Good Student (Arg), Hollywood Story, 8 started.

SANTA MONICA H. (G1), Santa Anita Park, Jan. 30, $250,000, 4&up, f&m, 7f, 1:22.14, SALT CHAMP (ARG), Island Fashion, Resplendency, 9 started.

Santana Mile H., Santa Anita Park, March 13, $79,850, 4&up, 1m, 1:36.93, SKIPASLEW, Silver Traffic, Ender's Shadow, 8 started.

Santa Paula S., Santa Anita Park, April 2, $86,250, 3yo, f, 6 1/2f, 1:15.79, NO BULL BABY, Leave Me Alone, Inspiring, 6 started.

Santa Teresa H., Sunland Park, March 13, $52,850, 3&up, f&m, 6 1/2f, 1:15.83, BAR BAILEY, Red Lifesaver, Sexy Boots, 5 started.

SANTA YNEZ S. (G2), Santa Anita Park, Jan. 17, $150,000, 3yo, f, 7f, 1:23.10, SHARP LISA, No Bull Baby, Hot Attraction, 7 started.

SANTA YSABEL S. (G3), Santa Anita Park, Jan. 16, $108,000, 3yo, f, 1 1/16m, 1:43.77, SWEET CATOMINE, Pussycat Doll, On London Time, 5 started.

SAN VICENTE S. (G2), Santa Anita Park, Feb. 13, $147,000, 3yo, 7f, 1:22.59, FUSAICHI ROCK STAR, Don't Get Mad, Kirkendahl, 4 started.

SAPLING S. (G3), Monmouth Park, Aug. 20, $150,000, 2yo, 6f, 1:09.69, HE'S GOT GRIT, Diabolical, Confront, 6 started.

Sarah Lane's Oates H. (R), Fair Grounds, March 26, $100,000, 3yo, f, Louisiana-bred, a1mT, 1:41.78, MIRIAM L., The Beter Man Can, Blueyed Lass, 10 started.

Sarah Lane's Oates H. (R), Fair Grounds at Louisiana Downs, Nov. 20, $50,000, 2yo, f, Louisiana-bred, a1mT, 1:38.59, LEESTOWN LIGHT, Royal Madame, Supreme Trick, 11 started.

SARANAC S. (G3), Saratoga Race Course, Sept. 4, $111,900, 3yo, 1 3/16mT, 1:54.20, JAMBALAYA, Silver Whistle, Woodlander, 9 started.

Sara's Success S., Calder Race Course, May 29, $40,000, 3&up, f&m, 7 1/2fT, 1:27.89, YOU GLITTER GIRL, Covincing, R Obsession, 11 started.

SARATOGA BREEDERS' CUP H. (G2), Saratoga Race Course, Aug. 21, $245,000, 3&up, 1 1/4m, 2:03.38, SUAVE, Royal Assault, Tap Day, 5 started.

Saratoga Dew S. (R), Saratoga Race Course, Sept. 1, $66,500, 3&up, f&m, New York-bred non-winners of an open stakes at one mile or over in 2005, 1 1/8m, 1:52.02, JUDY SODA, So Sweet a Cat, South Wing, 6 started.

SARATOGA SPECIAL S. (G2), Saratoga Race Course, July 28, $150,000, 2yo, 6f, 1:10.38, HENNY HUGHES, Master of Disaster, Union Course, 6 started.

Sarco S., Hawthorne Race Course, April 2, $42,600, 4&up, 1 1/16m, 1:44.73, STORMY IMPACT, Cat Tracker, Ask the Lord, 6 started.

Saskatchewan Derby, Marquis Downs, Sept. 10, $12,741, 3yo, 1 1/16m, 1:50.45, WIND DANCER, Second Time Clever, Fargo Forbes, 5 started.

Saskatchewan Futurity (R), Marquis Downs, July 30, $13,378, 2yo, Canadian-bred, 6f, 1:17.25, EXCESSIVELY SWEET, Shadazzle, Crazy Carson, 9 started.

Saskatoon H., Marquis Downs, July 8, $4,884, 3yo, 6f, 1:13.25, WIND DANCER, Lambrose, Fargo Forbes, 7 started.

Sausalito S., Golden Gate Fields, Oct. 29, $50,700, 3&up, 6f, 1:08.59, SEATTLES BEST JOE, Stormin' Lyon, Siphonizer, 5 started.

Say Florida Sandy S. (R), Belmont Park, June 4, $60,750, 3yo, New York-bred non-winners of a stakes, 6f, 1:11.80, BOLD DECISION, Freddy the Cap, Be Wild Again, 6 started.

Saylorville S., Prairie Meadows, July 4, $100,000, 3&up, f&m, 6f, 1:09.22, INJUSTICE, Johns Place, Silver Crown, 6 started.

Scarlet and Gray H. (R), Beulah Park, Oct. 29, $40,000, 3&up, f&m, Ohio-bred, 6f, 1:11.27, THE GREAT TYLER, Just Michel, Kisses for Kara, 8 started.

Scarlet Carnation S., Thistledown, July 2, $40,000, 3&up, f&m, 6f, 1:10.60, COBRA LADY, Fly Away Angel, Shannons Valentine, 7 started.

Schenectady H. (R), Belmont Park, Sept. 18, $109,800, 3&up, f&m, New York-bred, 6f, 1:09.96, TRAVELATOR, High Peaks, Royal Fudge, 8 started.

Scottsdale H., Turf Paradise, April 2, $40,000, 3yo, f, 1mT, 1:35.87, VIRDEN, Kick the Can, Regal Boot, 9 started.

SEABISCUIT BREEDERS' CUP H. (G3), Bay Meadows Race Course, Feb. 5, $86,250, 4&up, 1 1/16m, 1:41.42, YOUGOTTAWANNA, Jake Skate, Adreamisborn, 7 started.

Seacliff S., Calder Race Course, Sept. 3, $50,000, 2yo, 1m, 1:42.91, WEEKEND WEATHER, Gin Rummy King, He's a Lumberjack, 10 started.

SEAGRAM CUP S. (Can-G3), Woodbine, July 30, $131,946, 3&up, 1 1/16m, 1:44.18, ONE FOR ROSE, Honolua Storm, Cuba, 6 started.

Sea O Erin Breeders' Cup Mile H., Arlington Park, Aug. 6, $117,000, 3&up, 1mT, 1:36.18, FORT PRADO, Old Deuteronomy, Remind, 5 started.

Seattle H., Emerald Downs, April 24, $40,000, 3&up, 6f, 1:08.60, SLEWICIDE CRUISE, Sabertooth, Best On Tap, 9 started.

Seattle Slew Breeders' Cup H., Emerald Downs, Aug. 7, $60,625, 3yo, c&g, 1 1/16m, 1:41.60, ALEXANDERSRUN, Confidential Call, Norm's Nephew, 11 started.

SEAWAY S. (Can-G3), Woodbine, Sept. 10, $149,324, 3&up, f&m, 7f, 1:21.88, FIFTH OVERTURE, Silver Bird, La Trillium, 7 started.

Secretariat Memorial S., Santa Cruz County Fair, May 7, $3,985, 3&up, 6f, 1:11.80, SAXMEAMEMO, Let George Do It, Onceinafullmoon, 7 started.

SECRETARIAT S. (G1), Arlington Park, Aug. 13, $400,000, 3yo, 1 1/4mT, 2:03.79, GUN SALUTE, English Channel, Chattahoochee War, 8 started.

Select S., Monmouth Park, May 21, $60,000, 3yo, 6f, 1:10.04, MORE SMOKE, Lieutenant Danz, Miracle Man, 5 started.

SELENE S. (Can-G3), Woodbine, May 22, $221,488, 3yo, f, 1 1/16m, 1:45.80, GOLD STRIKE, Lemon Maid, Charming Ruckus, 6 started.

Selima S., Laurel Park, Nov. 19, $125,000, 2yo, f, 1 1/16mT, 1:41.87, J'RAY, Nice Nelly, Rasta Farian, 11 started.

Selma S. (R), Retama Park, Oct. 1, $40,000, 3yo, f, Texas-bred, 5fT, :55.48 (NCR), ROCKIN' KATE, Martys Expectation, Magic Power, 12 started.

Senate Appointee H., Hastings Race Course, July 2, $33,416, 3&up, f&m, 1 1/8m, 1:51.20, LA BELLE FLEUR, Victor's Secret, Gold Accent, 5 started.

SENATOR KEN MADDY H. (G3), Oak Tree at Santa Anita, Sept. 28, $100,000, 3&up, f&m, a6 1/2fT, 1:11.56, ELUSIVE DIVA, Chasethegold, Abounding Truth, 11 started.

Senorita S., Louisiana Downs, Aug. 6, $50,000, 3yo, f, a1 1/16mT, 1:44.58, ALEX'S ALLURE, Malika's Gold, Our Leading Lady, 7 started.

SENORITA S. (G3), Hollywood Park, May 8, $111,900, 3yo, f, 1mT, 1:35.37, VIRDEN, Three Degrees (Ire), Thatswhatimean, 10 started.

Sensational Star H. (R), Santa Anita Park, Feb. 20, $137,875, 4&up, California-bred, 6 1/2f, 1:14.56, GRAND APPOINTMENT, Red Warrior, Excessivepleasure, 9 started.

Serena S., Zia Park, Dec. 3, $42,000, 2yo, f, 5 1/2f, 1:03.20, LUNARGAL, Legally Wild, Princess Patricia, 6 started.

Serena's Song S., Monmouth Park, July 24, $60,000, 3yo, f, 1m70y, 1:41.98, GOLDEN LOCKET, Toll Taker, Capitulation, 5 started.

SHADWELL TURF MILE S. (G1), Keeneland Race Course, Oct. 8, $600,000, 3&up, 1mT, 1:37.67, HOST (CHI), Vanderlin (GB), Gulch Approval, 10 started.

Shady Well S. (R), Woodbine, July 17, $133,407, 2yo, f, Ontario-bred, 5 1/2f, 1:05.52, WANNATALKABOUTME, Queen's College, Seductively, 6 started.

SHAKERTOWN S. (G3), Keeneland Race Course, April 16, $113,300,

3&up, 5$^{1}/_{2}$fT, 1:02.22, SOARING FREE, Mighty Beau, Parker Run, 11 started.

Shakopee S., Canterbury Park, Sept. 5, $40,000, 3&up, f&m, 1m70y, 1:42.26, PHONE THE DIVA, Sippin' Devil, Ells Editor, 6 started.

Sham S., Santa Anita Park, Feb. 5, $102,300, 3yo, 1$^{1}/_{8}$m, 1:50.18, GOING WILD, Papi Chullo, Giacomo, 9 started.

Sharp Cat S., Hollywood Park, Nov. 27, $100,000, 2yo, f, 1$^{1}/_{16}$m, 1:42.58, BALANCE, Sweet Fourty, Talullah Lula, 8 started.

Shecky Greene S., Delaware Park, Nov. 12, $59,500, 3&up, 1$^{1}/_{16}$m, 1:44.07, SILVER AXE, Trapped Again, Separato, 6 started.

SHEEPSHEAD BAY H. (G2), Belmont Park, May 22, $150,000, 3&up, f&m, 1$^{3}/_{8}$mT, 2:15.65, SAUVAGE (FR), Angara (GB), Barancella (Fr), 8 started.

Shelby County S. (R), Indiana Downs, May 6, $40,000, 3&up, f&m, Indiana-sired, 6f, 1:10.79, FREE BONUS, Down by the Sea, Ellens Lucky Star, 6 started.

Shepperton S. (R), Woodbine, Aug. 7, $103,774, 3&up, progeny of stallions standing in Ontario, 6$^{1}/_{2}$f, 1:14.56 (NTR), SOPHIA'S PRINCE, Dave the Knave, Mister Coop, 8 started.

Shine Again S. (R), Belmont Park, July 16, $63,150, 4&up, f&m, non-winners of a graded stakes in 2004-'05, 6f, 1:11.09, SOURIS, High Peaks, Don't Tell Ashlie, 4 started.

SHIRLEY JONES H. (G2), Gulfstream Park, Feb. 19, $150,000, 3&up, f&m, 7f, 1:22.06, MADCAP ESCAPADE, Alix M, D' Wildcat Speed, 7 started.

Shiskabob S. (R), Louisiana Downs, Sept. 17, $103,145, 3&up, Louisiana-bred, 1$^{1}/_{16}$mT, 1:42.20, SPRUCE'S PRINCE, Witt Ante, Chip Hunter, 5 started.

Shocker T. H., Calder Race Course, Oct. 15, $100,000, 3&up, f&m, 1$^{1}/_{16}$m, 1:47.18, PROSPECTIVE SAINT, Tigi, India Halo (Arg), 6 started.

SHOEMAKER BREEDERS' CUP MILE S. (G1), Hollywood Park, May 30, $369,000, 3&up, 1mT, 1:33.17, CASTLEDALE (IRE), King of Happiness, Fast and Furious (Fr), 7 started.

Shortgrass Heritage S. (R), Marquis Downs, Aug. 20, $8,254, 3yo, c&g, Saskatchewan-bred, 1$^{1}/_{16}$m, 1:47.28, WIND DANCER, Fargo Forbes, Lambrose, 5 started.

Shot of Gold S., Canterbury Park, May 7, $40,000, 3&up, 6f, 1:09.35, VAZANDAR, Twentythreejaybird, Classy Sheikh, 6 started.

Showtime Deb S. (R), Hawthorne Race Course, Nov. 12, $92,300, 2yo, f, Illinois-conceived and/or -foaled, 6f, 1:12.02, RICH FANTASY, Lovely Love, Unreal Rocket, 9 started.

SHUVEE H. (G2), Belmont Park, May 21, $196,000, 3&up, f&m, 1m, 1:34.23, SOCIETY SELECTION, Daydreaming, Bohemian Lady, 5 started.

Sickle's Image S. (R), Great Lakes Downs, Sept. 24, $50,000, 2yo, f, Michigan-bred, 6f, 1:15.46, FIJI ISLAND, Money Code, Easy Ellie, 7 started.

Sierra Starlet H. (R), Ruidoso Downs, July 31, $45,000, 3yo, f, New Mexico-bred, 5$^{1}/_{2}$f, 1:05.20, SKIRT ALERT, Alley's Lady, Hollywood Gone, 12 started.

Silk Stockings S., Yavapai Downs, June 6, $10,500, 3yo, f, 6f, 1:11.20, EXCUSABULL, Meet You At T's, Reds Fling, 10 started.

SILKY SULLIVAN S. (G3), Golden Gate Fields, Nov. 5, $100,000, 3yo, 1$^{1}/_{8}$mT, 1:49.03, EASTERN SAND, Mr. Splash, Eager Pharisien, 6 started.

SILVERBULLETDAY S. (G3), Fair Grounds, Feb. 12, $150,000, 3yo, f, 1$^{1}/_{16}$m, 1:43.79, SUMMERLY, Eyes On Eddy, Enduring Will, 9 started.

Silver Cup Futurity, Arapahoe Park, Aug. 27, $27,950, 2yo, 5$^{1}/_{2}$f, 1:07.12, THE COMPANY VAN, Lake Cide Girl, Ahead of His Class, 12 started.

Silver Deputy S., Woodbine, Sept. 5, $89,599, 2yo, 6$^{1}/_{2}$f, 1:17.98, BRIGHT N GOLDEN, Victoria's Boy, Doc O Dynamite, 6 started.

Silver Goblin S. (R), Remington Park, Aug. 20, $40,000, 3&up, Oklahoma-bred, 6$^{1}/_{2}$f, 1:15, ZEE OH SIX, Herecomesthemannow, Notable Okie, 8 started.

Silver Spur Breeders' Cup S., Lone Star Park, July 16, $70,000, 2yo, f, 6f, 1:11.96, HOSANNA HIT, Yaddo Cat, Slewpy's Star, 4 started.

Silvey's Image S., Turf Paradise, April 17, $24,000, 3yo, 4$^{1}/_{2}$fT, :50.66, THRESHER, Quintons Relaunch, Smoke Magic, 9 started.

Simcoe S. (R), Woodbine, Sept. 4, $106,273, 2yo, c&g, Canadian-bred, 7f, 1:24.45, EDENWOLD, Seeking Shelter, Grey Mirage, 8 started.

Similkameen Cup S., Sunflower Downs, June 30, $8,142, 3&up, 1$^{1}/_{8}$m, 1:48.20, FAREWELL COWBOYS, River Run, Golden Niblet, 6 started.

Simply Majestic S., Calder Race Course, May 28, $75,000, 3yo, 1$^{1}/_{16}$mT, 1:40.64, DREAM ON DREAM ON, Magic Speed, Talented Prince, 11 started.

Singspiel S., Woodbine, June 26, $92,013, 3&up, 1$^{1}/_{2}$mT, 2:27.66, DADDY COOL, Shop Hill, More Bourb, 11 started.

Sir Barton S., Pimlico Race Course, May 21, $100,000, 3yo, 1$^{1}/_{16}$m, 1:44.43, PINPOINT, Smokescreen, Killenaule, 8 started.

Sir Barton S. (R), Woodbine, Nov. 27, $106,900, 3&up, progeny of stallions standing in Ontario, 1$^{1}/_{16}$m, 1:44.13, ARCH HALL, Moonshine Justice, Barbeau Ruckus, 5 started.

Sir Beaufort S. (1st Div.), Santa Anita Park, Dec. 26, $84,500, 3yo, 1mT, 1:35.09, CHINESE DRAGON, Hockey the General, Becrux (Ity), 8 started.

Sir Beaufort S. (2nd Div.), Santa Anita Park, Dec. 26, $86,500, 3yo, 1mT, 1:34.34, TEDO (GER), Eastern Sand, Follow the Rainbow, 10 started.

Sir Cat S. (R), Saratoga Race Course, Aug. 6, $67,650, 3yo, non-winners of a stakes on the turf, 1mT, 1:34.43, ALL TRUMPS, Classic Campaign, United, 9 started.

Sir Winston Churchill H., Hastings Race Course, Sept. 24, $43,454, 3&up, 1$^{1}/_{8}$m, 1:49.74, FLAMETHROWINTEXAN, Quiet Cash, Trick of the North, 9 started.

Sissy Woolums Memorial S. (R), Colonial Downs, Aug. 6, $40,000, 3&up, f&m, progeny of stallions donated to the 2005 Virginia Stallion Season Auction and the 2004 South Carolina Season Auction or registered Virginia-bred/-sired, South Carolina-bred/-sired, or North Carolina-bred/-sired, 7f, 1:23.82, PARTNERS DUE, Rumbling Girl, Plumpish, 6 started.

Six Perfections S. (R), Belmont Park, July 9, $63,950, 3yo, f, non-winners of an open stakes, 1$^{1}/_{16}$m (originally scheduled on the turf), 1:46.07, IF IT'S MEANT TO B, Merrill Gold, K. D.'s Shady Lady, 4 started.

SIXTY SAILS H. (G3), Hawthorne Race Course, April 23, $250,000, 3&up, f&m, 1$^{1}/_{8}$m, 1:49.58, ISOLA PIU BELLA (CHI), Rare Gift, Ghostly Gate, 7 started.

Skipat S., Pimlico Race Course, June 12, $50,000, 3&up, f&m, 6f, 1:10.24, SPRING RUSH, Princess Pelona, Forestier, 7 started.

SKIP AWAY H. (G3), Gulfstream Park, April 2, $100,000, 3&up, 1$^{1}/_{8}$m, 1:49.29, EUROSILVER, Twilight Road, Zakocity, 10 started.

Skip Away S., Monmouth Park, July 2, $70,000, 3&up, 1$^{1}/_{16}$m, 1:42.40, CHEROKEE'S BOY, Aggadan, Cherokee Spook, 6 started.

Ski Roundtop Timber S., Shawan Downs, Sept. 24, $23,250, 4&up, a3$^{3}/_{4}$mT, HALL OF ANGELS, Albert's Crossing, Chef Bear, 4 started.

Skunktail S. (R), Horsemen's Park, July 24, $29,800, 3yo, c&g, Nebraska-bred, 1m, 1:40.60, dh-BIG RED FANTASY, dh-WILL REIN, Cork the Barber, 8 started.

Sky Beauty S. (R), Belmont Park, Sept. 22, $67,400, 3&up, f&m, non-winners of a stakes in 2005, 1$^{1}/_{16}$m, 1:44.08, TAITTINGER ROSE, A Song in A Minor, Taygete, 8 started.

SKY CLASSIC H. (Can-G2), Woodbine, Oct. 2, $283,297, 3&up, 1$^{3}/_{8}$mT, 2:17.17, A BIT O'GOLD, Revved Up, Lenny the Lender, 7 started.

Sleepy Hollow S. (R), Belmont Park, Oct. 22, $100,000, 2yo, New York-bred, 1m, 1:39.55, SHARP HUMOR, Parkhimonbroadway, Classic Pack, 14 started.

Slight in the Rear S. (R), Fairmount Park, June 11, $40,700, 3yo, f, Illinois-bred, 6f, 1:12.40, CART'S TURN, Denoun N Deverb, Li'lbito'-sunshine, 5 started.

Slipton Fell H., Mountaineer Race Track, June 11, $75,000, 3&up, 1m70y, 1:41.32, DISCREET HERO, X Country, Be Like Mike, 6 started.

Smart Deb S., Arlington Park, Aug. 13, $48,000, 3yo, f, 6f, 1:10.43, BLUESBDANCING, Loramateal, Bold Passage, 10 started.

Smart Halo S., Laurel Park, April 2, $50,000, 3yo, f, 6f, 1:12.70, JET SET CITI, Missile Bay, Flashy Three (GB), 6 started.

Smile S., Arlington Park, July 17, $47,250, 3&up, 5fT, :56.50, LUCKY PULPIT, So Gifted, Rapid Raj, 7 started.

SMILE SPRINT H. (G2), Calder Race Course, July 10, $500,000, 3&up, 6f, 1:09.80, WOKE UP DREAMIN, Toscani, Nightmare Affair, 9 started.

Smoke Glacken S. (R), Belmont Park, July 15, $63,350, 3yo, non-winners of an open stakes of $50,000 in 2005, 6f, 1:09.66, VICARAGE, Big Apple Daddy, Storm Creek Rising, 4 started.

Smokin Albert S., Turf Paradise, Dec. 12, $23,700, 2yo, 6f, 1:08.61, SNOWBOUND HALO, Mining Gold, Storm War, 7 started.

Sneakbox S., Monmouth Park, Aug. 13, $55,000, 3&up, 5fT, :56.26, TACIRRING, Midwatch, Gulch Approval, 6 started.

Snow Chief S. (R), Hollywood Park, April 24, $250,000, 3yo, California-bred, 1$^{1}/_{8}$m, 1:49.40, ROBADOR, Lucky J. H., Top This and That, 12 started.

Snurb S., Calder Race Course, April 25, $35,000, 3yo, f, 6f, 1:12.32, FLYING CIRCLE, Midtown Miss, Running Bobcats, 5 started.

Soaring Softly S. (R), Aqueduct, Nov. 19, $68,000, 3yo, f, non-winners of a stakes on the turf, 1$^{1}/_{16}$mT, 1:45.81, MOUNTAIN MAMBO, Half Heaven, Quick Queen, 10 started.

Solana Beach H. (R), Del Mar, Sept. 4, $125,000, 3&up, f&m, California-bred, 1mT, 1:33.36 (NCR), CANDY FACTORY, Valentine Dancer, Smokegetenyoureyes, 6 started.

Solano County Juvenile Filly S. (R), Solano County Fair, July 24, $52,300, 2yo, f, California-bred, 5 1/2f, 1:04.78, COUNTRY VISION, Sierra Sweetie, I Apologize, 6 started.

Somerset Medical Center Steeplechase Race for Cancer Awareness H., Meadowlands, Oct. 1, $75,000, 4&up, a2 1/2mT, 4:17.60, PREEMPTIVE STRIKE, McDynamo, Three Carat, 7 started.

Sonny Hine S., Laurel Park, Oct. 1, $60,000, 3yo, 6f, 1:11.86, DISTINCTIVE TRICK, Favalora, Salary Cap, 5 started.

Sorie S. (R), Zia Park, Dec. 4, $42,000, 2yo, f, New Mexico-bred, 5 1/2f, 1:04.80, BO CHIME, Cozzenetime, Grand Majestic, 7 started.

Sorority S., Monmouth Park, Sept. 3, $103,000, 2yo, f, 6f, 1:11.23, KEENELAND KAT, Unobstructed View, Pure Disco, 11 started.

SORRENTO S. (G3), Del Mar, Aug. 6, $150,000, 2yo, f, 6 1/2f, 1:17.36, BULLY BONES, Acceleration, Slick Road, 9 started.

Southern Beau S. (R), Louisiana Downs, July 31, $50,000, 2yo, Louisiana-bred, 5 1/2f, 1:05.88, HERE TIGER, Willtosucceed, Carroll's Delight, 6 started.

Southern Belle H., Grants Pass, May 29, $3,723, 3&up, f&m, 5 1/2f, 1:06.80, CHARLEE CHOP CHOP, Springs Goldengirl, Crown of Pearls, 8 started.

Southern Belle S. (R), Louisiana Downs, July 23, $50,000, 2yo, f, Louisiana-bred, 5 1/2f, 1:05.64, SIXTEEN GRAND, Tortuga Flats, Kourtneysfirst, 6 started.

South Mississippi Owners' and Breeders' S. (R), Fair Grounds, Feb. 4, $42,500, 3yo, Mississippi-owned, 6f, 1:10.63, BILOXI BREEZE, Hello Mo, Spiritridge, 10 started.

South Ocean S. (R), Woodbine, Nov. 9, $107,061, 2yo, f, progeny of stallions standing in Ontario, 1 1/16m, 1:48.64, LA GRAN MARYLIN, Questuary, Perigee Girl, 10 started.

Southwest S., Oaklawn Park, Feb. 19, $100,000, 3yo, 1m, 1:39.09, GREATER GOOD, Munificence, Humor At Last, 7 started.

Soviet Problem H., Bay Meadows Race Course, Feb. 26, $59,725, 3&up, f&m, 6f, 1:09.04, HEAVENLY HUMOR, Cryptos' Best, Our Mango, 6 started.

Spangled Jimmy H., Northlands Park, July 9, $41,005, 3&up, 1m, 1:37.20, DEPUTY COUNTRY, Beau Brass, Sixthirtyjoe, 9 started.

Spartan S. (R), Great Lakes Downs, July 19, $50,000, 3yo, c&g, Michigan-bred, 7f, 1:29.51, DEMAGOGUERY, Its His Time, Meadow Vespers, 7 started.

Speed H., Lincoln State Fair, May 21, $12,500, 3&up, 4 1/2f, :51, LUKFATA LOUIS, Tonight Rainbow, Trackem 'n' Wackem, 7 started.

Speed H., Louisiana Downs, Sept. 18, $39,200, 3&up, 6f, 1:09.66, THAT TAT, Skin Flint, Nuttyboom, 5 started.

Speed to Spare Championship S., Northlands Park, Sept. 10, $84,940, 3&up, 1 3/8m, 2:17.80, BEAU BRASS, Raylene, Royalty Boy, 8 started.

SPEND A BUCK H. (G3), Calder Race Course, Oct. 15, $100,000, 3&up, 1 1/16m, 1:46.94, SUPERVISOR, B. B. Best, Apalachian Thunder, 6 started.

Spend a Buck S., Monmouth Park, July 9, $60,000, 3yo, 1 1/16m, 1:43.49, NETWORK, Alexandersrun, Miracle Man, 6 started.

Spicy H. (R), Arapahoe Park, Aug. 28, $30,450, 3&up, f&m, Colorado-bred, 1 1/16m, 1:46.33, LADYSGOTTHELOOKS, Tricky Transaction, Fuzdaisy, 7 started.

SPINAWAY S. (G2), Saratoga Race Course, Aug. 26, $250,000, 2yo, f, 7f, 1:23.68, ADIEU, Folklore, Along the Sea, 7 started.

Spirit of Texas S. (R), Sam Houston Race Park, Nov. 19, $50,000, 3&up, Texas-bred, 6f, 1:10.87, RED BIRD'S MEISTER, Smile Away, Charming Socialite, 8 started.

Sport City H., Louisiana Downs, Sept. 4, $50,000, 3&up, 1 1/4mT, 2:02.76 (NCR), MIDDLEWEIGHT, Crowned King, Tromp, 8 started.

Sport of Queens Filly and Mare Hurdle S., Camden, Nov. 26, $29,100, 3&up, f&m, a2 1/4mT, 4:16.80 (NCR), GUELPH, Vente, Orchid Princess, 9 started.

SPORT PAGE H. (G3), Belmont Park, Oct. 29, $281,500, 3&up, 7f, 1:23.16, GOTAGHOSTOFACHANCE, Captain Squire, Wild Tale, 9 started.

Sportsman's Paradise S., Delta Downs, March 19, $50,000, 3yo, 1m, 1:40.67, MUNIFICENCE, Reno Bob, El Batallon, 7 started.

Spring Fever S., Oaklawn Park, Feb. 26, $50,000, 4&up, f&m, 5 1/2f, 1:03.78, SOURIS, Forest Music, Saltwater Runner, 7 started.

Springfield S. (R), Arlington Park, June 25, $88,900, 3yo, Illinois-conceived and/or -foaled, 1m, 1:36.09, HIGH EXPECTATIONS, Northern Gent, Sir Winzalot, 13 started.

Spring S. (R), Sam Houston Race Park, March 19, $40,000, 4&up, Texas-bred, 7f, 1:23.05, R B J'S BLAZE, Nuttyboom, Giant Bellyache, 11 started.

Spring Sprint S., Lethbridge, June 5, $10,581, 3&up, 5 1/2f, 1:10, BOO ROO, Arctic Horizon, Chief Swan, 7 started.

Spring Thoroughbred Futurity (R), The Downs at Albuquerque, May 14, $57,154, 2yo, New Mexico-bred, 5f, :58.27, HOMETOWN GHOST, Acute Angle, Mo's Doll, 7 started.

Spruce Fir H. (R), Monmouth Park, June 12, $60,000, 3&up, f&m, New Jersey-bred, 1m70y, 1:44.29, CIGNO D'ORO, Avery Hall, Key to Love, 7 started.

Squan Song S. (R), Laurel Park, Dec. 17, $50,000, 3&up, f&m, Maryland-bred non-winners of a stakes, 7f, 1:26.55, MAGICAL BROAD, Starleena, Experts Only, 9 started.

Stage Door Betty H., Calder Race Course, Dec. 31, $100,000, 3&up, f&m, 1 1/16m, 1:48.56, MOCITA, Special Report, Pitanga, 9 started.

Stage Door Betty H., Calder Race Course, Jan. 1, $100,000, 3&up, f&m, 1 1/16m, 1:45.12, PERSONAL LEGEND, Pampered Princess, Shady Woman, 7 started.

Stallion Company W. Meredith Bailes Memorial S. (R), Colonial Downs, July 10, $60,000, 3&up, Virginia-bred and/or -sired, 6f, 1:10.12, SATAN'S CODE, Slavic's Gold, Standing Room Only, 6 started.

Stampede Park Sprint Championship H., Stampede Park, April 30, $39,735, 4&up, 6f, 1:10, CHIEF MTN, Rindanica, Sixthirtyjoe, 7 started.

STANFORD BREEDERS' CUP H. (G3), Bay Meadows Race Course, March 19, $113,750, 3&up, 1 1/16mT, 1:46.28, ADREAMISBORN, Night Bokbel (Ire), Fantastic Spain, 8 started.

Stanton S., Delaware Park, Aug. 27, $56,454, 3yo, 1 1/8m (originally scheduled on the turf), 1:55.19, HOLY GROUND, Touched by Madness, Seize, 4 started.

Stardust S. (R), Louisiana Downs, Sept. 17, $79,900, 2yo, Louisiana-bred, 6f, 1:11.58, HERETIGER, Poppa Duke, Carson Bay, 10 started.

Star of Texas S. (R), Sam Houston Race Park, Nov. 19, $100,000, 3&up, Texas-bred, 1 1/16m, 1:44.95, DIXIE MEISTER, Agrivating General, Dreamsandvisions, 9 started.

STARS AND STRIPES BREEDERS' CUP TURF H. (G3), Arlington Park, July 3, $197,750, 3&up, 1 1/2mT, 2:28.29, REVVED UP, Cloudy's Knight, Swagger Stick, 8 started.

Stars and Stripes Overnight H., Emerald Downs, July 4, $25,000, 3yo, 5 1/2f, 1:02.20, ANOTHER BOB, The Great Face, Wasserman, 7 started.

Star Shoot S., Woodbine, April 24, $114,533, 3yo, f, 6f, 1:10.60, LEMON MAID, Gold Strike, Hatpin, 8 started.

State Fair Board H., Lincoln State Fair, July 4, $16,500, 3&up, 1m70y, 1:43, HIGH DICE, What About David, Thundering Verzy, 8 started.

State Fair Breeders' Special S. (R), Lincoln State Fair, June 11, $20,700, 3yo, Nebraska-bred, 1m, 1:41.20, THE STRAW MAN, My Hobby, Cork the Barber, 6 started.

State Fair Derby, Lincoln State Fair, June 25, $16,125, 3yo, 1m, 1:38.60, THE STRAW MAN, Chasin the Wind, My Hobby, 5 started.

State Fair Futurity (R), Lincoln State Fair, July 17, $16,000, 2yo, Nebraska-bred, 4 1/2f, :52.60, SKWHIRL, C. O. Rascal, Hero in My Heart, 10 started.

Statue of Liberty S. (R), Saratoga Race Course, Aug. 4, $250,000, 3yo, f, progeny of stallions standing in New York, 1 1/8m, 1:53.85, INDY WOODS, Avery Hall, Fountain'sprincess, 6 started.

Steady Growth S. (R), Woodbine, June 11, $101,331, 3&up, progeny of stallions standing in Ontario, 1 1/16m, 1:45.69, BARBEAU RUCKUS, Mister Coop, Kent Ridge, 9 started.

Stefanita S., Laurel Park, Nov. 19, $75,000, 3&up, f&m, 7f, 1:24.27, PRINCESS PELONA, Traci Girl, Sensibly Chic, 5 started.

STEPHEN FOSTER H. (G1), Churchill Downs, June 18, $828,000, 3&up, 1 1/8m, 1:47.52, SAINT LIAM, Eurosilver, Perfect Drift, 8 started.

Steve Van Buren H., Philadelphia Park, Sept. 5, $75,000, 3&up, f&m, 7f, 1:22.75, ANNIKA LASS, Valley of the Gods, Tamweel, 9 started.

St. Georges S., Delaware Park, June 13, $54,900, 3yo, f, a1 1/16mT, 1:44.58, MORE FOR ME, Defensa (Ger), Rutledge Ballado, 7 started.

Stonehedge Farm South Sophomore Fillies S., Tampa Bay Downs, April 9, $85,250, 3yo, f, 7f, 1:24.87, RUNNING BOBCATS, Forever Brilliant, British Event, 12 started.

STONERSIDE BEAUMONT S. (G2), Keeneland Race Course, April 14, $250,000, 3yo, f, a7f, 1:26.04, IN THE GOLD, Holy Trinity, Hot Storm, 5 started.

STONERSIDE FORWARD GAL S. (G2), Gulfstream Park, March 5, $150,000, 3yo, f, 7f, 1:23.24, LETGOMYECHO, Little Money Down, Hot Storm, 7 started.

Stonerside S., Lone Star Park, May 30, $145,500, 3yo, f, 7f, 1:23.31, R FAST LADY, Forever Brilliant, True Tails, 4 started.

Storm Cat S., Meadowlands, Nov. 5, $50,000, 2yo, 1 1/16m, 1:44.19, PEGASUSBYSTORM, Wilentz, Saint Augustus, 7 started.

Stormy Frolic S., Calder Race Course, Nov. 20, $40,000, 3yo, f, 1 1/16m,

1:47.75, MOCITA, Fast Lisa, Sheila's Gin Fizz, 6 started.

St. Paul S., Canterbury Park, May 28, $36,400, 3yo, 6f, 1:10.21, STORMY BUSINESS, Smoke Smoke Smoke, Raging Wind, 3 started.

Stravinsky S., Keeneland Race Course, April 23, $114,700, 3&up, f&m, 5½fT, 1:04.52, TARA'S TOUCH (SAF), Shaunavon, Singit, 12 started.

Strawberry Morn S., Hastings Race Course, April 23, $34,775, 3&up, f&m, 6½f, 1:17.22, REGAL RED, Overact, Pretty Meadow, 5 started.

STRUB S. (G2), Santa Anita Park, Feb. 5, $300,000, 4yo, 1⅛m, 1:49.24, ROCK HARD TEN, Imperialism, Love of Money, 9 started.

Sturgeon River S. (R), Northlands Park, Sept. 24, $42,690, 2yo, f, Alberta-bred, 1m, 1:42.40, KAYLEE'S MAGIC, Intenionally Dear, Sierra Center, 4 started.

STUYVESANT H. (G3), Aqueduct, Nov. 19, $108,600, 3&up, 1⅛m, 1:51.38, EVENING ATTIRE, West Virginia, Aggadan, 6 started.

Stymie H., Aqueduct, March 5, $79,450, 3&up, 1⅛m, 1:50.82, HYDROGEN, Aggadan, Song of the Sword, 5 started.

Subordination S. (R), Belmont Park, Sept. 23, $68,250, 3yo, non-winners of a stakes on the turf, 1⅛mT, 1:47.25, GRAND RESERVE, Fishy Advice, Tadreeb, 7 started.

SUBURBAN H. (G1), Belmont Park, July 2, $500,000, 3&up, 1¼m, 2:00.50, OFFLEE WILD, Tap Day, Pollard's Vision, 8 started.

Summer Finale S., Mountaineer Race Track, Sept. 5, $75,000, 3&up, f&m, 1mT, 1:35.27, TEMPUS FUGIT, Rue des Reves, Lady Grace, 8 started.

SUMMER S. (Can-G2), Woodbine, Sept. 18, $241,200, 2yo, 1mT, 1:40.35, BEAR'S KID, Badge of Truth, Wedding Singer, 7 started.

Sumter S., Calder Race Course, May 7, $35,000, 3&up, 1¹⁄₁₆m, 1:46.22, SUPER FROLIC, Whos Crying Now, Supervisor, 6 started.

Sun City H., Turf Paradise, March 19, $40,000, 3&up, f&m, 1mT, 1:36.51, MUIR BEACH, Pleasant Gulch, Peace Symbol, 8 started.

Suncoast S., Tampa Bay Downs, Feb. 26, $60,000, 3yo, f, 1¹⁄₁₆m, 1:46.15, TOLL TAKER, Gotta Rush, Gallant Secret, 7 started.

Sun Devil S., Turf Paradise, Jan. 22, $40,000, 3yo, f, 1m, 1:37.01, VIRDEN, She Sings, Country Kat, 7 started.

Sunflower S. (R), The Woodlands, Sept. 25, $25,000, 3&up, Kansas-bred, 6f, 1:11.20, SCARLET LAD, Polar Barron, Nick Missed, 6 started.

Sun H., Hastings Race Course, May 14, $32,520, 3&up, f&m, 6½f, 1:17.45, PRETTY MEADOW, Victor's Secret, Overact, 7 started.

Sunland Park Fall Thoroughbred Derby, Sunland Park, Dec. 10, $50,000, 3yo, 6½f, 1:16.25, TAKIN ISSUE, Dangerous Devon, Slew of Enerchi, 5 started.

Sunland Park H., Sunland Park, March 26, $105,900, 3&up, 1⅛m, 1:50.44, FIN ENTERTAINMENT, Skip and Go, Cozzen Vinny, 8 started.

Sunny Slope S., Oak Tree at Santa Anita, Oct. 22, $81,675, 2yo, 6f, 1:09.19, WITHIN REASON, Bengal Lore, Say Tomorrow, 6 started.

Sun Power S. (R), Hawthorne Race Course, Nov. 12, $92,975, 2yo, c&g, Illinois-conceived and/or -foaled, 6f, 1:12.06, LAST GRAN STANDING, Silver Titan, Cartlets, 9 started.

SUNSET BREEDERS' CUP H. (G2), Hollywood Park, July 17, $165,300, 3&up, 1½mT, 2:27, ALWAYS FIRST (GB), dh-T. H. Approval, dh-Runaway Dancer, 8 started.

Sunset Gun S. (R), Suffolk Downs, Sept. 5, $40,000, 3&up, f&m, Massachusetts-bred, a1¹⁄₁₆mT, 1:48.48, ASK QUEENIE, Papa Dancer, Deerwood Lass, 6 started.

Sunshine Millions Barretts/CTBA Distaff S. (R), Santa Anita Park, Jan. 29, $500,000, 4&up, f&m, California- or Florida-bred, 1¹⁄₁₆m, 1:42.64, SWEET LIPS, Fencelineneighbor, Dream of Summer, 10 started.

Sunshine Millions Cloverleaf Farms Filly and Mare Turf S. (R), Gulfstream Park, Jan. 29, $500,000, 4&up, f&m, California- or Florida-bred, 1⅛mT, 1:47.20, VALENTINE DANCER, Marwood, Changing World, 12 started.

Sunshine Millions Oaks (R), Santa Anita Park, Jan. 29, $250,000, 3yo, f, California- or Florida-bred, 6f, 1:09.16, HOT STORM, Binasuccess, Memorette, 12 started.

Sunshine Millions Ocala Breeders' Sales Classic S. (R), Gulfstream Park, Jan. 29, $1,000,000, 4&up, California- or Florida-bred, 1⅛m, 1:49.17, MUSIQUE TOUJOURS, Zakocity, Classic Endeavor, 12 started.

Sunshine Millions Ocala Stud Dash S. (R), Gulfstream Park, Jan. 29, $250,000, 3yo, California- or Florida-bred, 6f, 1:09.96, LOST IN THE FOG, Santana Strings, Lucky Frolic, 10 started.

Sunshine Millions Padua Stables Filly and Mare Sprint S. (R), Gulfstream Park, Jan. 29, $300,000, 4&up, f&m, California- or Florida-bred, 6f, 1:10.40, ALIX M, Bear Fan, Double Scoop, 6 started.

Sunshine Millions Vinery Farms Sprint S. (R), Santa Anita Park, Jan. 29, $300,000, 4&up, California- or Florida-bred, 6f, 1:08.84, RED WARRIOR, Full Moon Madness, Areyoutalkintome, 11 started.

Sunshine Millions Warren's Thoroughbred Turf S. (R), Santa Anita Park, Jan. 29, $500,000, 4&up, California- or Florida-bred, 1⅛mT, 1:48.40, STAR OVER THE BAY, A to the Z, Silver Tree, 12 started.

Sun Sprint Championship H., Northlands Park, Aug. 1, $40,850, 3&up, 6½f, 1:17.80, SIXTHIRTYJOE, Mr Don, Chief Mtn, 6 started.

SUPER DERBY (G2), Louisiana Downs, Oct. 1, $750,000, 3yo, 1¼m, 2:03.15, THE DADDY, A. P. Arrow, Nolan's Cat, 10 started.

Supernaturel H., Hastings Race Course, May 8, $35,160, 3yo, f, 6½f, 1:17.43, SLEWPAST, After the Knight, Virtuous Lady, 6 started.

Super S., Tampa Bay Downs, Jan. 29, $50,000, 4&up, 7f, 1:22.60 (ETR), ABOVE THE WIND, Avid Skier, Attack the Books, 13 started.

Super Test Starter H. (R), Turf Paradise, Dec. 13, $10,400, 3&up, f&m, starters for a claiming price of $6,250 or less in 2005, 1m, 1:38.02, CHUBBY IS READY, Passionate Kiss, Hillsdale, 7 started.

Susan B. Anthony H. (R), Finger Lakes, May 30, $50,000, 3&up, f&m, New York-bred, 6f, 1:10.59, RUBY'S ROCKET, Buck Mountain, Flora Mac Flimsey, 8 started.

Susan's Girl Breeders' Cup S., Delaware Park, June 18, $170,800, 3yo, f, 1¹⁄₁₆m, 1:47.76, PLEASANT CHIMES, Dance Away Capote, Capitulation, 6 started.

Susan's Girl S. (R), Calder Race Course, Sept. 3, $125,000, 2yo, f, progeny of stallions standing in Florida, 7f, 1:26.09, RUNNING LASS, Prospect of Love, Note to Diane, 7 started.

Sussex H., Delaware Park, July 30, $97,000, 3&up, 1¹⁄₁₆mT, 1:41.24, L'OISEAU D'ARGENT, Stage Call (Ire), Mr O'Brien (Ire), 4 started.

Suthern Accent S., Louisiana Downs, May 14, $50,000, 3&up, f&m, 6f, 1:09.57, HAPPY TICKET, Southern Surprise, Red Lifesaver, 6 started.

SUWANNEE RIVER H. (G3), Gulfstream Park, Feb. 12, $100,000, 3&up, f&m, 1⅛mT, 1:46.40, SNOWDROPS (GB), Angela's Love, High Court (Brz), 10 started.

SWALE S. (G2), Gulfstream Park, March 5, $150,000, 3yo, 7f, 1:22.21, LOST IN THE FOG, Around the Cape, More Smoke, 10 started.

SWAPS BREEDERS' CUP S. (G2), Hollywood Park, July 9, $361,000, 3yo, 1⅛m, 1:48.07, SURF CAT, Dover Dere, Indian Ocean, 6 started.

Sweet and Sassy H., Delaware Park, May 21, $76,200, 3&up, f&m, 6f, 1:11.06, ANNIKA LASS, Fortress Hill, Storm Minstrel, 9 started.

Sweet Briar Too S., Woodbine, July 3, $89,140, 3&up, f&m, 7f, 1:23.81, FIFTH OVERTURE, Deputy Cures Blues, Expect an Angel, 8 started.

Sweetest Chant S., Arlington Park, July 29, $46,950, 3yo, f, 1m, 1:35.53, EYES ON EDDY, Modjadji, Miss Matched, 6 started.

Sweetheart H., Portland Meadows, Feb. 12, $7,313, 4&up, f&m, 1¹⁄₁₆m, 1:48.47, QUIZ THE MAID, Pete's Dolly, Chancy Chancy, 4 started.

Sweetheart S., Delta Downs, Feb. 26, $50,000, 4&up, f&m, 1m, 1:39.65, MISS CONFUSION, So Much More, Cute N Noble, 5 started.

Sweettrickydancer S., Calder Race Course, July 12, $40,000, 3yo, f, 7½fT, 1:31.49, STATUE, Ragtime Hope, Darluna, 9 started.

Swept Away S., Calder Race Course, June 17, $40,000, 3yo, f, 6f, 1:11.02, HIDE AND CHIC, Princess Samala, Lady in Pink, 7 started.

Swift S., Turf Paradise, Jan. 29, $40,000, 4&up, 5½f, 1:03.41, NEWARK, Palmerton, Ransome Road, 7 started.

Swingtime S. (R), Oak Tree at Santa Anita, Oct. 7, $74,040, 3&up, f&m, non-winners of a stakes worth $50,000 at one mile or over in 2005 other than state-bred, 1mT, 1:34.62, DREAM'S (CHI), House of Fortune, Cotopaxi, 8 started.

Swoon's Bid Starter H. (R), Turf Paradise, Nov. 27, $14,050, 3&up, f&m, starters for a claiming price of $10,000 or less in 2005, 1mT, 1:38.94, PASSIONATE KISS, Stormi Sounds, Fool's Detente, 8 started.

SWORD DANCER INVITATIONAL S. (G1), Saratoga Race Course, Aug. 13, $500,000, 3&up, 1½mT, 2:27.38, KING'S DRAMA (IRE), Relaxed Gesture (Ire), Vangelis, 8 started.

S.W. Randall Plate H., Hastings Race Course, Aug. 28, $36,352, 3&up, 1⅛m, 1:50, COEUR JOIE, Illusive Force, Royal Place, 7 started.

Swynford S., Woodbine, Sept. 25, $113,342, 2yo, 7f, 1:23.83, BEAR CHARACTER, Ballado Dancer, Bright N Golden, 4 started.

SYCAMORE BREEDERS' CUP S. (G3), Keeneland Race Course, Oct. 7, $161,100, 3&up, 1½mT, 2:34.30, ROCHESTER, Dreadnaught, Vangelis, 8 started.

Sydney Gendelman Memorial H. (R), River Downs, June 19, $45,000, 3&up, Ohio-bred, 1¹⁄₁₆mT, 1:41.80, DEVIL TIME, Ben's Reflection, Altura, 12 started.

Sydney Valentini H. (R), Sunland Park, March 12, $105,100, 3&up, f&m, New Mexico-bred, 1m, 1:38.51, LATENITE SPECIAL, Betsy N, My Desert Lady, 11 started.

Sylvia Bishop Memorial S. (R), Charles Town Races, Nov. 26, $41,700,

3yo, f, West Virginia-bred, 7f, 1:27.98, CABER'S CUTIE, Melissa's Melody, Karate Kat, 9 started.

Tacoma H., Emerald Downs, June 26, $53,950, 3yo, c&g, 1m, 1:37.80, THIRSTY GUY'S, Datzig, Confidential Call, 8 started.

Tah Dah S. (R), River Downs, July 31, $40,000, 2yo, f, Ohio-bred, 5½f, 1:05, LILLIANS CHOICE, Fight Girl, Tommeyesgold, 9 started.

Taking Risks S. (R), Timonium, Sept. 5, $50,000, 3&up, Maryland-bred, a6½f, 1:17.08, DALE'S PROSPECT, Hands On, Captain Chessie, 6 started.

Tampa Bay Breeders' Cup S., Tampa Bay Downs, Feb. 19, $100,000, 3&up, 1$^1/_{16}$mT, 1:40.14, WIRE BOUND, Remind, Above the Wind, 12 started.

TAMPA BAY DERBY (G3), Tampa Bay Downs, March 19, $250,000, 3yo, 1$^1/_{16}$m, 1:43.98, SUN KING, Forever Wild, Global Trader, 7 started.

Tampa Turf Test H., Tampa Bay Downs, Jan. 18, $18,212, 4&up, 1mT, 1:35.73, DRY ICE, Skipteaser, King Cassia, 10 started.

Tampa Turf Test H., Tampa Bay Downs, Jan. 25, $17,150, 4&up, f&m, 1mT, 1:36.10, TWISTED CORD, Rizzi Girl, Sweeping Cat, 12 started.

Tampa Turf Test H., Tampa Bay Downs, Feb. 1, $20,212, 4&up, 1$^1/_{16}$mT, 1:43.69, DRY ICE, Wauwinet, Severado (Brz), 10 started.

Tampa Turf Test H., Tampa Bay Downs, Feb. 8, $19,150, 4&up, f&m, 1$^1/_{16}$mT, 1:42.07, RIZZI GIRL, Phone the Diva, Twisted Cord, 7 started.

Tampa Turf Test H. (1st Div.), Tampa Bay Downs, March 26, $21,000, 4&up, 1$^3/_8$m (originally scheduled on the turf), 2:20.30, BANSHEE BRAD, Rupert's Kuetch, Mesne Process, 11 started.

Tampa Turf Test H. (2nd Div.), Tampa Bay Downs, March 26, $20,150, 4&up, f&m, 1$^3/_8$m (originally scheduled on the turf), 2:22.09, BELLA BELLA BAILEY, Miss Bradford Co, Special Version, 7 started.

Tanforan H., Golden Gate Fields, Oct. 22, $100,000, 3&up, 1$^3/_8$mT, 2:17.77, ADREAMISBORN, Noble Masterpiece, Secret Charm (Ire), 9 started.

TAYLOR MADE MATCHMAKER S. (G3), Monmouth Park, Aug. 7, $150,000, 3&up, f&m, 1$^1/_8$mT, 1:50.38, LOVE MATCH, Cat Alert, Emerald Earrings, 10 started.

Taylor's Special H., Fair Grounds, Feb. 12, $100,000, 4&up, a5½fT, 1:03.70, WRZESZCZ, Mighty Beau, Chosen Chief, 9 started.

Taylor's Special S., Arlington Park, Sept. 18, $42,500, 3&up, 5½fT, 1:02.54, NICOLE'S DREAM, Justice for Auston, Lucky Pulpit, 10 started.

Teddy Drone S., Monmouth Park, Aug. 7, $100,000, 3&up, 6f, 1:08.59, WILDCAT HEIR, Forest Park, Judiths Wild Rush, 8 started.

Teeworth Plate H., Stampede Park, May 21, $39,495, 3&up, 1m, 1:36.20, BLOWIN IN THE WIND, Rindanica, Bubblegum Kid, 7 started.

Tejano Run S., Turfway Park, March 19, $50,000, 4&up, 1$^1/_8$m, 1:49.50, DISCREET HERO, Paging, Regal Reproach, 6 started.

Tellike H., Evangeline Downs, July 4, $50,000, 3&up, f&m, 6f, 1:11.57, KEEP THIS CAT, Midnight Delight, Living Lavida Lisa, 10 started.

Tempe H., Turf Paradise, March 26, $40,000, 3yo, 1mT, 1:37.39, CLAYMONT, Western Act, Night Gig, 9 started.

Temple Gwathmey Hurdle S. (R), Middleburg, April 23, $75,000, 4&up, non-winners over hurdles prior to March 1, 2004, a2$^1/_8$mT, 4:01, TOUGHKENAMON, Erin Go Bragh (NZ), Paradise's Boss, 10 started.

TEMPTED S. (G3), Belmont Park, Oct. 30, $110,000, 2yo, f, 1m, 1:38.35, BETTER NOW, Capote's Crown, Wonder Lady Anne L, 7 started.

Temptress S. (R), Great Lakes Downs, Sept. 3, $50,000, 2yo, f, Michigan-bred, 6f, 1:18.05, FIJI ISLAND, Giddy Up Girl, Rockem S'more, 6 started.

Tenski S. (R), Saratoga Race Course, Aug. 28, $68,000, 3yo, f, non-winners of a stakes on the turf, 1$^1/_{16}$mT, 1:43.32, INSAN MALA (IRE), Connie Belle, Who's Cozy, 9 started.

Ten Thousand Lakes S. (R), Canterbury Park, May 21, $40,000, 3&up, Minnesota-bred, 6f, 1:09.56, VAZANDAR, Adroitly Superb, Timberwolf Power, 7 started.

TEST S. (G1), Saratoga Race Course, Aug. 6, $250,000, 3yo, f, 7f, 1:22.76, LEAVE ME ALONE, Hide and Chic, In the Gold, 9 started.

Texas Glitter H., Churchill Downs, June 12, $72,800, 3&up, 5f (originally scheduled on the turf), :57.80, BAYOU BUSTER, Artemus Sunrise, Deer Lake, 5 started.

Texas Heritage S., Sam Houston Race Park, March 5, $40,000, 3yo, 1m, 1:39.22, LEAVING ON MY MIND, Major League, Smooth Bid, 10 started.

Texas Horse Racing Hall of Fame S. (R), Retama Park, Oct. 1, $100,000, 3&up, Texas-bred, 1$^1/_{16}$mT, 1:40.95, NORTHERN SCENE, Charming Socialite, Agrivating General, 9 started.

TEXAS MILE S. (G3), Lone Star Park, April 30, $300,000, 3&up, 1m, 1:35.34, HIGH STRIKE ZONE, Supah Blitz, Twilight Road, 6 started.

Texas Stallion S. (R), Lone Star Park, April 30, $125,000, 3yo, progeny of stallions standing in Texas, 1$^1/_{16}$m, 1:41.76, GENERAL CHARLEY, Dixie Meister, War Bridle, 8 started.

Texas Stallion S. (R), Lone Star Park, April 30, $125,000, 3yo, f, progeny of stallions standing in Texas, 1$^1/_{16}$m, 1:45.37, TIMBER JONES, Rockin' Kate, Tizzy Girl, 10 started.

Texas Stallion S. (R), Lone Star Park, July 9, $125,000, 2yo, f, progeny of stallions standing in Texas, 5½f, 1:04.69, FINAL TRICK, Cats Legend, Sauternes, 7 started.

Texas Stallion S. (R), Lone Star Park, July 9, $125,000, 2yo, c&g, progeny of stallions standing in Texas, 5½f, 1:04.55, PALTU, Gambling Wolfe, Fast Fashion, 12 started.

Texas Stallion Two-Year-Old Colts and Geldings S. (R), Retama Park, Oct. 1, $125,000, 2yo, c&g, progeny of stallions standing in Texas, 6f, 1:11.53, LAKE MAC MAC, Upstream, Noble Texas, 14 started.

Texas Stallion Two-Year-Old Fillies S. (R), Retama Park, Oct. 1, $125,000, 2yo, f, progeny of stallions standing in Texas, 6f, 1:12.05, KATHY'S ROCKET, Cats Legend, She's Open Minded, 13 started.

Tex's Zing S. (R), Fairmount Park, Aug. 27, $40,700, 3yo, c&g, Illinois-bred, 6f, 1:10.80, HUMOR AT LAST, Yukon's Gambler, Foxie's Boy, 7 started.

Thanksgiving Breeders' Cup H., Fair Grounds at Louisiana Downs, Nov. 24, $57,750, 3&up, 6f, 1:10.07, ZARB'S DAHAR, Rodeo's Castle, Premier Performer, 5 started.

The Downs at Albuquerque H., The Downs at Albuquerque, June 12, $60,000, 3&up, 1$^1/_8$m, 1:50.51, BAYOU THE MOON, Fin Entertainment, Skip and Go, 12 started.

THE VERY ONE H. (G3), Gulfstream Park, March 6, $100,000, 3&up, f&m, 1$^3/_8$mT, 2:11.71, HONEY RYDER, Briviesca (GB), Vous, 10 started.

The Very One S., Pimlico Race Course, May 20, $75,000, 3&up, f&m, 5fT, :59.69, GABIANNA, Feisty Bull, Nicole's Dream, 11 started.

The Vid S., Calder Race Course, July 31, $40,000, 3&up, 1mT, 1:35.77, SOUTHERN CAL, Bob's Proud Moment, Final Prophecy, 12 started.

Thomas Edison S., Meadowlands, Nov. 4, $50,000, 3&up, 5f (originally scheduled on the turf), :56.19, TACIRRING, Special Judge, Old Dodge (Brz), 5 started.

Thomas F. Moran S. (R), Suffolk Downs, Aug. 20, $40,000, 3&up, Massachusetts-bred, a1$^1/_{16}$mT, 1:47.18, ASK QUEENIE, Jini's Jet, Murray's Dream, 7 started.

Thomas J. Malley S., Monmouth Park, Sept. 4, $55,000, 3yo, f, 5f (originally scheduled on the turf), :57.89, COASTAL STRIKE, Lady Dynasty, Water Walker, 7 started.

Thoroughbred Bettors H., Grants Pass, June 26, $4,425, 3&up, 6½f, 1:19.80, DREAMONEIR, Jehosaphat, Speakin Britt, 8 started.

THOROUGHBRED CLUB OF AMERICA S. (G3), Keeneland Race Course, Oct. 16, $300,000, 3&up, f&m, 6f, 1:11.59, REUNITED, Miss Terrible (Arg), Savorthetime, 10 started.

Thoroughbred Queens Derby, Eastern Oregon Livestock Show, June 12, $3,500, 3&up, 1$^1/_{16}$m, 1:48.80, TENDER OFFER (IRE), Zee Chalupa, Sir Bay Sky, 5 started.

Three Chimneys Juvenile S., Churchill Downs, May 7, $120,000, 2yo, 5f, :57.07, HALF OURS, Five Star Holding, Beacon Shine, 6 started.

Three Coins Up S. (R), Aqueduct, Nov. 12, $69,400, 3yo, non-winners of an open stakes on the turf, 1$^1/_{16}$mT, 1:43.85, FISHY ADVICE, Key Event, Spanish Mission, 10 started.

Three Ring S., Calder Race Course, Dec. 3, $100,000, 2yo, f, 1$^1/_{16}$m, 1:50.01, STOLEN PRAYER, Capozzene, El Bank Robber, 6 started.

Three-Year-Old Filly Sales S. (R), Northlands Park, Sept. 9, $41,459, 3yo, f, Canadian-bred sold at a CTHS sale, 1m, 1:38.40, SPEEDY GONE SALLY, Howsitgoin, Saucy Ciano, 5 started.

Three-Year-Old Sales S. (R), Northlands Park, Sept. 11, $41,621, 3yo, c&g, Canadian-bred sold at a CTHS sale, 1m, 1:39.60, CINDERCHANCE, Blinkanhesgone, Northtown Will, 7 started.

Thunder Road H., Santa Anita Park, Feb. 9, $78,650, 4&up, 1mT, 1:34.39, LAURA'S LUCKY BOY, Silver Traffic, King's County (Ire), 6 started.

Ticonderoga H. (R), Belmont Park, Oct. 22, $150,000, 3&up, f&m, New York-bred, 1$^1/_8$m (originally scheduled on the turf), 1:51.32, RAHYS' APPEAL, The Lamp Is Lit, Sweeping Glance, 9 started.

Tiffany Lass S., Fair Grounds, Jan. 15, $100,000, 3yo, f, 1m, 1:39.59, THE BETER MAN CAN, Enduring Will, Punch Appeal, 6 started.

Timber Music S. (R), Hastings Race Course, July 9, $33,305, 2yo, f, British Columbia-bred and/or-owned, 6½f, 1:19.45, LANGARA LASS, Pewterville, Jittery Julia, 8 started.

Timeless Prince S. (R), Canterbury Park, July 31, $40,000, 2yo, Minnesota-bred, 5½f, 1:05.01, THE K B KID, Bow River, C C Tat, 7 started.

Times Square S. (R), Aqueduct, April 24, $150,000, 3yo, progeny of stallions standing in New York, 1m, 1:36.05, GOLD AND ROSES, Big Apple Daddy, Galloping Grocer, 7 started.

Tippett S., Colonial Downs, July 30, $60,000, 2yo, f, 5$^1/_2$fT, 1:04.54, LEESBURG EXPRESS, Whiteface, Red Liquor n' Lace, 10 started.

Tiznow S. (R), Hollywood Park, April 24, $150,000, 4&up, California-bred, 7$^1/_2$f, 1:27.49, UNFURL THE FLAG, El Don, Greg's Gold, 10 started.

TOBOGGAN H. (G3), Aqueduct, March 12, $107,100, 3&up, 6f, 1:09.47, PRIMARY SUSPECT, Shake You Down, Houston's Prayer, 6 started.

Toddler S., Laurel Park, Nov. 26, $50,000, 2yo, f, 7f, 1:25.73, CELESTIAL LEGEND, Sea Pines, Painted Rose, 7 started.

TOKYO CITY H. (G3), Santa Anita Park, April 2, $106,000, 4&up, 1$^1/_8$m, 1:48.90, SUPAH BLITZ, Outta Here, Ender's Shadow, 5 started.

Tomball S. (R), Sam Houston Race Park, Feb. 12, $40,000, 4&up, f&m, Texas-bred, 1$^1/_{16}$mT, 1:49.20, NATIVE ANNIE, Lady Mallory, Won Ton Win, 8 started.

Tom Bane Starter Allowance S. (R), Turf Paradise, April 30, $17,500, 3&up, Arizona-bred starters for a claiming price of $8,000 or less since September 30, 2004 and have not won for more since that date, 6f, 1:09.84, FAST FORCE, Basically Radical, Sunnys Siren, 10 started.

Tomboy S. (R), River Downs, May 21, $45,000, 3yo, f, Ohio-bred, 1$^1/_{16}$mT, 1:45, FLIP SIDE, Marketable, Nitty Gritty, 12 started.

TOM FOOL H. (G2), Belmont Park, July 17, $150,000, 3&up, 7f, 1:21.92, SMOKUME, Willy o'the Valley, Clever Electrician, 6 started.

To Much Coffee S. (R), Hoosier Park, Nov. 20, $40,000, 3&up, Indiana-bred, 1$^1/_{16}$m, 1:45.68, PASS RUSH, Mr. Mink, Liepers Fork, 8 started.

Tondi H., Fonner Park, April 9, $26,000, 3&up, 6f, 1:12.80, LUKFATA LOUIS, What About David, Thundering Verzy, 8 started.

Tony Sanchez Memorial Mile S., Manor Downs, April 24, $18,000, 3&up, 1m, 1:38.68, EASY TOO EASY, One Special Judge, Salem Times, 9 started.

TOP FLIGHT H. (G2), Aqueduct, Nov. 25, $150,000, 3&up, f&m, 1m, 1:35.94, STELLAR JAYNE, Bohemian Lady, Seeking the Ante, 8 started.

Top Hat S., Yavapai Downs, June 7, $10,200, 3yo, 6f, 1:09.60, LUTE OATSON, Cover Now, Peripatetic, 6 started.

Topsider S., Suffolk Downs, Aug. 27, $32,500, 3&up, 1m70y, 1:42.85, DHAFFIR (CHI), Itsawonderfulife, Trapped Again, 10 started.

Toronto Cup H., Woodbine, July 16, $132,096, 3yo, 1$^1/_8$mT, 1:51.39, T. D. VANCE, Area Limits, Bestowed, 5 started.

Torrey Pines S., Del Mar, Sept. 2, $100,000, 3yo, f, 1m, 1:36.21, PUSSYCAT DOLL, Bella Banissa, Soldier's Kiss, 5 started.

Totah Futurity (R), SunRay Park, Aug. 21, $83,787, 2yo, New Mexico-bred, 6$^1/_2$f, 1:20.60, COPELAN'S MASK, Banishment, Aint He a Bull, 10 started.

To the Post S., Turf Paradise, Dec. 13, $24,100, 2yo, f, 6f, 1:09.92, BLUMIN BEAUTY, Alpine Secret, Queen Razyana, 10 started.

To the Post S., Turf Paradise, May 20, $24,000, 3&up, f&m, 4$^1/_2$fT, :50.21, FUN'NGAMES TOKNITE, Lil Easy, Shimmering Heat, 10 started.

Tranquility Lake S. (R), Hollywood Park, May 28, $65,600, 4&up, f&m, non-winners of $40,000 twice since November 15, 2004, 1mT, 1:35.24, WINENDYNME, Fencelineneighbor, Alozaina (Ire), 9 started.

TRANSYLVANIA S. (G3), Keeneland Race Course, April 8, $150,000, 3yo, 1mT, 1:35.28, CHATTAHOOCHEE WAR, Guillaume Tell (Ire), Rey de Cafe, 8 started.

TRAVERS S. (G1), Saratoga Race Course, Aug. 27, $1,000,000, 3yo, 1$^1/_4$m, 2:02.76, FLOWER ALLEY, Bellamy Road, Roman Ruler, 7 started.

Treasure State Thoroughbred Futurity, Great Falls, July 30, $4,000, 2yo, 5f, 1:02.20, DANCING BUCKAROO, Pingston Creek, Double Dedawn, 5 started.

Tremont S., Belmont Park, July 4, $107,700, 2yo, 5$^1/_2$f, 1:03.67, HENNY HUGHES, Short Circuit, Caleb Pond, 6 started.

Trenton S., Monmouth Park, July 31, $56,815, 3yo, f, 5fT, :56.22, COASTAL STRIKE, Mecke's Queen, Big City Danse, 8 started.

TRIPLE BEND INVITATIONAL H. (G1), Hollywood Park, July 3, $350,000, 3&up, 7f, 1:20.95, UNFURL THE FLAG, dh-Bear in the Woods, dh-McCann's Mojave, 13 started.

Triple Crown Nutrition West Virginia Breeders' Classic S. (R), Charles Town Races, Oct. 8, $67,500, 2yo, f, West Virginia-bred, 4$^1/_2$f, :52.88, STANDING FOR PEACE, Aye Robbin, Cross Creek Rosie, 10 started.

Triple Sec S., Delta Downs, Jan. 28, $50,000, 3yo, 6$^1/_2$f, 1:21.61, MUNIFICENCE, Mechanic, Buddys Rebel, 5 started.

Trippi S. (R), Belmont Park, Oct. 2, $66,100, 3yo, non-winners of a stakes, 6f, 1:09.36, DECEMBER TREASURE, Run Thruthe Sun, Upscaled, 5 started.

Tri-State Futurity (R), Charles Town Races, Oct. 22, $80,650, 2yo, Maryland-, Virginia-, or West Virginia-bred, 7f, 1:28.51, SOUND MOON, Standing for Peace, Shesagrumptoo, 6 started.

Tri-State H., Ellis Park, Sept. 5, $50,000, 3&up, 1$^1/_{16}$mT, 1:39.11, ONTHEDEANSLIST, Mighty Military, Saturday Deelites, 7 started.

Trooper Seven S. (R), Emerald Downs, Oct. 2, $40,000, 3yo, c&g, Washington-bred, 1m, 1:36.60, INDIAN WEAVER, Confidential Call, Rusty Rolls, 10 started.

TROPICAL PARK DERBY (G3), Calder Race Course, Jan. 1, $100,000, 3yo, 1$^1/_8$mT, 1:47.18, LORD ROBYN, Fire Path, Crown Point, 12 started.

Tropical Park Oaks, Calder Race Course, Jan. 1, $100,000, 3yo, f, 1$^1/_{16}$mT, 1:42.06, DANSETTA LIGHT, Dynamite Lass, Silver Stage, 11 started.

TROPICAL TURF H. (G3), Calder Race Course, Dec. 3, $100,000, 3&up, 1$^1/_8$mT, 1:46.28, SILVER TREE, Demeteor, Settle Up, 11 started.

Troy Our Boy S. (R), Fairmount Park, Sept. 3, $41,000, 2yo, c&g, Illinois-bred, 6f, 1:13.60, MR. CANYON RUN, Tazi's Brother, Slew Creek Slew, 7 started.

Troy S. (R), Saratoga Race Course, Aug. 20, $67,200, 4&up, non-winners of an open stakes on the turf in 2004-'05, 1mT, 1:38.13, FUNFAIR (GB), Diamond Green (Fr), Provincetown, 6 started.

TRUE NORTH BREEDERS' CUP H. (G2), Belmont Park, June 11, $212,900, 3&up, 6f, 1:08.38, WOKE UP DREAMIN, Voodoo, Mass Media, 10 started.

Truly Bound Breeders' Cup H., Fair Grounds at Louisiana Downs, Dec. 24, $75,000, 3&up, f&m, 1$^1/_{16}$m, 1:45.32, PRIVATE GIFT, Freei, La Reason, 7 started.

Truly Bound H., Fair Grounds, Jan. 22, $60,000, 4&up, f&m, 1$^1/_{16}$m, 1:44.09, SHADOW CAST, Family Business, Miss Confusion, 6 started.

TTA Sales Futurity (R), Lone Star Park, June 11, $131,500, 2yo, f, passed through the ring at a TTA sale, 5f, .69, COVERED IN CLOVER, September in Texas, Final Trick, 10 started.

TTA Sales Futurity (R), Lone Star Park, June 11, $135,450, 2yo, c&g, passed through the ring at a TTA sale, 5f, :57.54, FORREST G., Lord Vicar, D Denton, 10 started.

Tulsa Dash S., Fair Meadows at Tulsa, June 18, $33,175, 3&up, 4f, :45, OKLAHOMA NATURAL, Harry the Prince, Shadow's Image, 10 started.

Turbulent World Starter H. (R), Turf Paradise, Nov. 20, $15,300, 3&up, starters for a claiming price of $12,500 or less in 2005, 1$^3/_8$mT, 2:18.14, GERIRIG, Hammerin, Max's Ace, 8 started.

Turf Distance Series Final S. (R), Turf Paradise, April 24, $42,650, 3&up, horses must have competed in all divisions offered to be eligible to advance to the final, 1$^3/_8$mT, 2:16.72, BACKONBABYSIDE, Henry Higgins, Tenaja Trail, 11 started.

Turf Monster H., Philadelphia Park, May 30, $100,000, 3&up, 5fT, :57.07, WORLDWIND ROMANCE, Cumby Texas, Nolimosforyou, 6 started.

Turf Paradise Breeders' Cup H., Turf Paradise, Feb. 12, $98,500, 3&up, 1$^1/_{16}$mT, 1:44.39, NIGHT PATROL, Vigilant Site, Paladin Power, 9 started.

Turf Paradise Derby, Turf Paradise, Feb. 12, $100,000, 3yo, 1$^1/_{16}$m, 1:45.48, GENERAL JOHN B, Quiet Money, Lead for Speed, 6 started.

TURFWAY BREEDERS' CUP S. (G3), Turfway Park, Sept. 17, $175,000, 3&up, f&m, 1$^1/_{16}$m, 1:44.48, MISS FORTUNATE, Sheer Luck, Whoopi Cat, 9 started.

TURFWAY PARK FALL CHAMPIONSHIP S. (G3), Turfway Park, Oct. 1, $100,000, 3&up, 1m, AW, 1:37.31, ARTEMUS SUNRISE, Mr. Krisley, Mighty Military, 12 started.

Turfway Prevue S., Turfway Park, Jan. 8, $41,500, 3yo, 6$^1/_2$f, 1:17.53, SNACK, Truly Native, Cat Shaker, 11 started.

TURNBACK THE ALARM H. (G3), Aqueduct, Nov. 5, $105,800, 3&up, f&m, 1$^1/_8$m, 1:49.83, INDIAN VALE, Taittinger Rose, Asti (Ire), 5 started.

Tuzla H., Santa Anita Park, Jan. 27, $79,350, 4&up, f&m, 1mT, 1:37.38, GOOD STUDENT (ARG), Belle Ange (Fr), Katdogawn (GB), 7 started.

Tuzla S. (R), Hollywood Park, May 6, $63,250, 4&up, f&m, non-winners of $60,000 since August 1, 2004, 5$^1/_2$fT, 1:01.75, WINENDYNME, Very Vegas, Solar Echo, 7 started.

Twist Afleet S. (R), Aqueduct, Dec. 11, $66,750, 3yo, f, non-winners of an open stakes, 6f, 1:10.17, GRECIAN WINGS, Popular Delusions, Pelham Bay, 7 started.

Twist Afleet S. (R), Belmont Park, May 29, $60,750, 3yo, f, non-winners of a stakes, 6f, 1:09.83, TALENTED, Secrets Galore, Song of the Saints, 6 started.

Twixt S. (R), Laurel Park, Sept. 7, $75,000, 3yo, f, Maryland-bred,

1m, 1:38.52, PROMENADE GIRL, Magical Broad, Sticky, 10 started.

Two Altazano S. (R), Sam Houston Race Park, Feb. 19, $125,000, 3yo, f, nominated and eligible for the Texas Stallion Stakes, 1m, 1:40.73, TIMBER JONES, Angela Marjorie, Ms Seneca Rock, 5 started.

Tyro S., Monmouth Park, July 30, $60,000, 2yo, 5$^1/_2$f, 1:03.97, HE'S GOT GRIT, Confront, Creve Coeur, 9 started.

U Can Do It H., Calder Race Course, Sept. 17, $75,000, 3&up, f&m, 6$^1/_2$f, 1:18.43, WILD SPEED, Midtown Miss, Tigi, 7 started.

Unbridled S., Calder Race Course, April 30, $100,000, 3yo, 1$^1/_{16}$m, 1:48.89, HAL'S IMAGE, Talented Prince, Captain Lindsay, 10 started.

Union Avenue S. (R), Saratoga Race Course, Aug. 22, $66,600, 3&up, f&m, New York-bred non-winners of an open stakes in 2005, 6f, 1:11.44, LAPIS, Slew Motion, High Peaks, 8 started.

UNITED NATIONS S. (G1), Monmouth Park, July 2, $750,000, 3&up, 1$^3/_8$mT, 2:20.57, BETTER TALK NOW, Silverfoot, Request for Parole, 9 started.

U. S. Bank S., Emerald Downs, April 17, $40,000, 3yo, f, 6f, 1:09.80, QUEENLEDO, Debbie's Assault, Kelly's Princess, 10 started.

U. S. Championship Supreme Hurdle S. (R), Pine Mountain, Calloway Garden, Nov. 5, $100,000, 4&up, non-winners over hurdles prior to June 1, 2004, a2$^1/_4$mT, 3:58.20, BON FLEUR, Good Night Shirt, Thegooddieyoung, 9 started.

Vacaville H., Solano County Fair, July 16, $51,500, 3&up, f&m, 6f, 1:09.93, BEEZER, Yerevan Star, Mahalo, 9 started.

VAGRANCY H. (G2), Belmont Park, June 12, $150,000, 3&up, f&m, 6$^1/_2$f, 1:16.31, SENSIBLY CHIC, Bank Audit, Ender's Sister, 9 started.

Valdale S., Turfway Park, Feb. 26, $50,000, 3yo, f, 1m, 1:40.89, BRETT'S FAVRETTE, Patty Seattle, Touch of Splendor, 8 started.

Valedictory H., Woodbine, Dec. 11, $121,572, 3&up, 1$^3/_4$m, 3:01.81, SEATTLESPECTACULAR, Last Answer, Vegas Venture, 9 started.

Valentine Memorial Sport of Queen's Hurdle S., Fair Hill, May 28, $29,100, 4&up, f&m, a2$^1/_4$mT, 4:35.90, FOOTLIGHTS, Feeling So Pretty, Guelph, 5 started.

Valid Expectations S., Lone Star Park, May 30, $100,000, 3&up, f&m, 6f, 1:08.38, BOSTON EXPRESS, Savorthetime, Miss Smart Strike, 6 started.

Valid Leader S., Turf Paradise, Oct. 29, $23,700, 3&up, f&m, 6$^1/_2$f, 1:16.85, POP THE LATCH, Miss Catalina, Arch Lady, 6 started.

Valid Video S., Calder Race Course, June 19, $40,000, 3yo, 6f, 1:11.48, DAZZLING DR. CEVIN, Precocious Unity, Gower, 6 started.

Valkyr S. (R), Hollywood Park, July 16, $76,875, 3&up, f&m, California-bred, 6f, 1:09.55, DEE DEE'S DINER, Tucked Away, Crowded Room, 5 started.

Vallejo S., Golden Gate Fields, May 29, $55,412, 3yo, f, 6f, 1:08.42, LUNACHICK, Hello Lucky, Binasuccess, 6 started.

VALLEY STREAM S. (G3), Aqueduct, Nov. 20, $105,200, 2yo, f, 6f, 1:11.13, MIRACULOUS MISS, Diamond Spirit, India, 5 started.

VALLEY VIEW S. (G3), Keeneland Race Course, Oct. 21, $125,000, 3yo, f, 1$^1/_{16}$mT, 1:45.37, ASI SIEMPRE, Dynamite Lass, Victory Lap, 9 started.

Valor Farm S. (R), Lone Star Park, July 9, $50,000, 3yo, f, Texas-bred, 6f, 1:10.17, BODY BY KATRINA, Tizzy Girl, Texas Spice, 9 started.

Van Berg Derby, Columbus Races, Aug. 20, $10,775, 3yo, 1m70y, 1:46.60, CHASIN THE WIND, Uncle Beno, Goldust Wishes, 6 started.

Vandal S. (R), Woodbine, Aug. 14, $133,596, 2yo, Ontario-bred, 6f, 1:10.29, EDENWOLD, Victoria's Boy, Moon Worship, 5 started.

VANITY INVITATIONAL H. (G1), Hollywood Park, July 3, $300,000, 3&up, f&m, 1$^1/_8$m, 1:49.33, SPLENDID BLENDED, Island Fashion, Andujar, 8 started.

Vector Communications S., Grand Prairie, July 9, $3,481, 3&up, 7f, 1:28, WELDER'S FLASH, Badolstory, Native Gambler, 5 started.

VERNON O. UNDERWOOD S. (G3), Hollywood Park, Dec. 3, $98,000, 3&up, 6f, 1:08.11, BORDONARO, Turnbolt, Captain Squire, 4 started.

Veteran S., Zia Park, Nov. 12, $81,600, 3&up, 1$^1/_{16}$m, 1:43, MR. TRIESTE, Don't Strike Out, R. Associate, 6 started.

Vice Regent S. (R), Woodbine, Aug. 28, $105,276, 3yo, progeny of stallions standing in Ontario, 1mT, 1:39.38, DECEW FALLS, Miracle Alley, Flat Rock, 8 started.

Victoriana S. (R), Woodbine, Aug. 21, $103,835, 3&up, f&m, progeny of stallions standing in Ontario, 1$^1/_{16}$mT, 1:48.03, SPANISH DECREE, Bay Sweetie Babe, Top Ten List, 7 started.

Victorian Queen S. (R), Woodbine, Oct. 5, $106,979, 2yo, f, progeny of stallions standing in Ontario, 6f, 1:11.83, PERIGEE GIRL, La Gran Marylin, U R Flashy, 6 started.

Victoria Park S., Woodbine, June 12, $109,275, 3yo, 1$^1/_8$m, 1:51.95, PALLADIO, Ablo, Commander Pat, 6 started.

Victoria S., Woodbine, June 19, $109,836, 2yo, 5f, :59.26, VIBANK, Edenwold, Fifty Seven Flat, 5 started.

Victoria S. (R), Louisiana Downs, Sept. 17, $79,150, 3&up, f&m, Louisiana-bred, 6f, 1:10.38, ZARBA THE GREAT, Destiny Calls, Shes Dixies Eskimo, 7 started.

Victor S. Myers Jr. S. (R), Canterbury Park, July 9, $42,300, 3yo, c&g, Minnesota-bred, 6f, 1:09.18, KEY ISSUES, George L Brown, Roust About, 9 started.

Victory Ride S., Saratoga Race Course, Aug. 25, $81,500, 3yo, f, 6f, 1:09.86, NOTHING BUT FUN, Maddalena, Reunited, 6 started.

VIGIL H. (Can-G3), Woodbine, April 30, $132,000, 4&up, 7f, 1:23.19, JUDITHS WILD RUSH, Mobil, A Bit O'Gold, 7 started.

Vincent A. Moscarelli Memorial H., Delaware Park, Oct. 15, $100,300, 3&up, 6f, 1:10.45, THUNDER TOUCH, Forest Park, Banjo Picker, 6 started.

VINERY MADISON S. (G3), Keeneland Race Course, April 13, $200,000, 4&up, f&m, 7f, 1:23.33, MADCAP ESCAPADE, My Trusty Cat, Molto Vita, 7 started.

VIOLET S. (G3), Meadowlands, Oct. 21, $150,000, 3&up, f&m, 1$^1/_{16}$mT, 1:42.23, HUMORISTIC, Delta Princess, Brunilda (Arg), 11 started.

VIRGINIA DERBY (G3), Colonial Downs, July 16, $750,000, 3yo, 1$^1/_4$mT, 2:02.57, ENGLISH CHANNEL, Chattahoochee War, Rebel Rebel (Ire), 9 started.

Virginia Gold Cup Timber S., Great Meadows, May 7, $50,000, 5&up, a4mT, 8:40.80, MILES AHEAD, Chinese Whisper, Dr. Ramsey, 7 started.

Virginia Oaks, Colonial Downs, July 16, $200,000, 3yo, f, 1$^1/_8$mT, 1:49.63, MY TYPHOON (IRE), Masseuse, Rich in Spirit, 8 started.

Vivacious H. (R), River Downs, Aug. 21, $45,000, 3&up, f&m, Ohio-bred, 1$^1/_{16}$mT, 1:43, RHYTHM IN SHOES, Always Dreaming, Golden Tour, 11 started.

Voodoo Dancer S. (R), Belmont Park, May 12, $60,850, 4&up, f&m, non-winners of a graded stakes on the turf, 1mT, 1:33.95, MY LORDSHIP, With Patience, Asti (Ire), 6 started.

VOSBURGH S. (G1), Belmont Park, Oct. 1, $500,000, 3&up, 6f, 1:08.82, TASTE OF PARADISE, Tiger Heart, Lion Tamer, 10 started.

Vulcan S. (R), Fair Grounds, March 25, $50,000, 3yo, Alabama-bred, 6f, 1:11.81, WEST SCOTTIE, Commited Right, Pops Return, 8 started.

Wadsworth Memorial H., Finger Lakes, June 19, $50,000, 3&up, 1$^1/_8$m, 1:51.73, SINISTER G, Noble Adversary, S. Cherry Legacy, 9 started.

Wafare Farm S., Lone Star Park, April 23, $50,000, 3yo, f, 6f, 1:08.76, TRUE TAILS, Ketchmewhereyoucan, Lady Carmen, 7 started.

Wagon Yard S., Grand Prairie, July 31, $3,443, 3&up, 5$^1/_2$f, 1:06.80, LADY'S LIL' RINGER, Highland Road, Secret One, 6 started.

Waldo Williams/W. O. Edwards Memorial H., Western Montana Fair and Races, Aug. 14, $4,400, 3&up, 1$^1/_8$m, HIGH RIVER HANK, Tender Offer (Ire), Excellenceinmotion, 6 started.

Walla Walla Thoroughbred H., Walla Walla, Sept. 3, $2,275, 3&up, a5f, 1:03 (NTR), GAME CADILLAC, Les Crime, Larron, 5 started.

Walla Walla Thoroughbred Queen's Derby H., Walla Walla, Sept. 4, $2,250, 3&up, 1$^1/_8$m, 1:58.20, TENDER OFFER (IRE), Dark Fool, Zee Chalupa, 4 started.

Walmac Farm Matchmaker S. (R), Louisiana Downs, Sept. 17, $106,000, 3&up, f&m, Louisiana-bred, 1$^1/_{16}$mT, 1:42.69, OUR LOVE, Intractabie, Butter Head, 8 started.

WALMAC LONE STAR DERBY (G3), Lone Star Park, May 14, $300,000, 3yo, 1$^1/_{16}$m, 1:41.92, SOUTHERN AFRICA, Shamoan (Ire), Real Dandy, 11 started.

Walter R. Cluer Memorial H., Turf Paradise, Nov. 5, $40,000, 3&up, 7$^1/_2$fT, 1:29.42, STRATEGICALLY, Brazen n' Bold, Cocoa Latte, 9 started.

Warren's Thoroughbreds S. (R), Hollywood Park, April 24, $70,000, 3&up, f&m, California-bred non-winners of $3,000 other than maiden, claiming, or starter or non-winners of two races, 7f, 1:23.35, WENDY'S ON TO ME, Del Mar Miss, Valid's Valid, 12 started.

Washington Breeders' Cup Oaks, Emerald Downs, Aug. 20, $98,125, 3yo, f, 1$^1/_8$m, 1:49.60, A CLASSIC LIFE, Gins Majesty, Gentle Flow, 6 started.

WASHINGTON PARK H. (G2), Arlington Park, July 30, $300,000, 3&up, 1$^3/_{16}$m, 1:54.27 (NTR), PERFECT DRIFT, Mambo Train, Home of Stars, 7 started.

Washington State Legislators H., Emerald Downs, June 5, $40,000, 3&up, f&m, 6$^1/_2$f, 1:15.60, MARVA JEAN, Ruby Dawn, Arco Iris, 7 started.

Washington Thoroughbred Breeders' Association Lads S., Emerald Downs, Sept. 11, $53,910, 2yo, c&g, 1m, 1:37.20, SCHOOLIN YOU, Raise the Bluff, Coastal King, 7 started.

Waterford Park H., Mountaineer Race Track, May 21, $75,000, 3&up, 6f, 1:09.05, DANIELTOWN, Super Fuse, Tour the Hive, 7 started.

Waya S. (R), Saratoga Race Course, Aug. 12, $66,700, 4&up, f&m, non-winners of a graded stakes in 2005, $1^1/_2$mT, 2:28.70, LATICE (IRE), A Lulu Ofa Menifee, Theater R. N., 7 started.

Wayward Lass S., Tampa Bay Downs, March 5, $60,000, 4&up, f&m, $1^1/_{16}$m, 1:44.71, JOYFUL BALLAD, Slews Final Answer, Grab Bag, 8 started.

WEBN S., Turfway Park, Feb. 5, $43,500, 3yo, 1m, 1:38.06, SNACK, Catch Me, Cat Shaker, 8 started.

Weekend Delight S., Turfway Park, Sept. 10, $63,750, 3&up, f&m, 6f, 1:11.54, HOT STORM, Dewey's Trick, Born to Dance, 9 started.

Wende S., Turf Paradise, Nov. 5, $23,800, 3&up, f&m, $7^1/_2$fT, 1:30.67, ALLBOW, Sawtelle Belle, Lookingforpleasure, 6 started.

WESTCHESTER H. (G3), Belmont Park, May 4, $109,500, 3&up, 1m, 1:33.50, GYGISTAR, Swingforthefences, Value Plus, 7 started.

Western Canada H., Northlands Park, Oct. 15, $42,180, 3yo, $6^1/_2$f, 1:17.80, GOLDEN HUNT, Ding Dong Dandy, Smudgeledo, 9 started.

Westerner H., Northlands Park, Aug. 21, $41,270, 3&up, $1^1/_{16}$m, 1:44.60, DEPUTY COUNTRY, Beau Brass, Candid Remark, 6 started.

Western Heritage S. (R), Marquis Downs, Aug. 20, $8,254, 2yo, c&g, Saskatchewan-bred, $6^1/_2$f, 1:23.35, CRAZY CARSON, Stage Finale, Artic Melt Down, 4 started.

Western Montana Fair Derby, Western Montana Fair and Races, Aug. 14, $5,000, 3&up, $6^1/_2$f, 1:24.20, PAKAWALUP, A Leo Thing, Big Creek Cowboy, 6 started.

Western Montana Fair Maiden Derby, Western Montana Fair and Races, Aug. 9, $4,400, 3yo, a$5^1/_4$f, 1:07.40, NORTHERN VOYAGE, Man At Arms, Lucky Lucas, 8 started.

West Long Branch S., Monmouth Park, June 25, $65,000, 3&up, f&m, 6f, 1:09.79, TRAVELATOR, Fortress Hill, Areek, 7 started.

West Mesa H., The Downs at Albuquerque, Sept. 23, $30,000, 3&up, f&m, 7f, 1:21.62, BLUE SONG, Ladysgotthelooks, Mystic Melissa, 6 started.

West Point H. (R), Saratoga Race Course, Aug. 14, $113,600, 3&up, New York-bred, $1^1/_8$mT, 1:48.11, DAVE, Provincetown, Certifiably Crazy, 9 started.

West Virginia Breeders' Classic S. (R), Charles Town Races, Oct. 8, $450,000, 3&up, West Virginia-bred, $1^1/_8$m, 1:52.65, SPEED WHIZ, Slew's Smile, Sheckatoo, 10 started.

West Virginia Dash for Cash Breeders' Classic S. (R), Charles Town Races, Oct. 8, $67,500, 3&up, West Virginia-bred, $4^1/_2$f, :52.10, NOT FOR SAM, Missacity Luke, Three Aces, 7 started.

WEST VIRGINIA DERBY (G3), Mountaineer Race Track, Aug. 14, $750,000, 3yo, $1^1/_8$m, 1:50.29, REAL DANDY, Magna Graduate, Anthony J., 11 started.

West Virginia Division of Tourism Breeders' Classic S. (R), Charles Town Races, Oct. 8, $67,500, 3yo, f, West Virginia-bred, 7f, 1:26.72, BRAVURA, Miss Angel, Carnival Chrome, 9 started.

West Virginia Futurity (1st Div.) (R), Charles Town Races, Nov. 12, $42,725, 2yo, West Virginia-bred, 7f, 1:30.59, SHESAGRUMPTOO, Dandy Topper, Cross Creek Rosie, 8 started.

West Virginia Futurity (2nd Div.) (R), Charles Town Races, Nov. 12, $42,725, 2yo, West Virginia-bred, 7f, 1:28.91, KING COHL, Hold On Tight, Kandy Kard, 8 started.

West Virginia Governor's S., Mountaineer Race Track, Aug. 14, $125,000, 3&up, $1^1/_{16}$m, 1:43.82, M B SEA, Artemus Sunrise, Bound for Fame, 6 started.

West Virginia House of Delegates Speaker's Cup S., Mountaineer Race Track, Aug. 14, $85,000, 3&up, 1mT, 1:33.69, IMMEDIATE REACTION, Cloudy's Knight, Gin and Sin, 11 started.

West Virginia Legislature Chairman's Cup S., Mountaineer Race Track, Aug. 14, $85,000, 3&up, $4^1/_2$f, :51.09, OUTCASHEM, Korbyn Gold, Hassledontheborder, 7 started.

West Virginia Lottery Breeders' Classic S. (R), Charles Town Races, Oct. 8, $67,500, 3yo, West Virginia-bred, 7f, 1:26.26, BRYCESLITTLESECRET, Cielo's Edge, Raggedy Andy, 10 started.

West Virginia "Onion Juice" Breeders' Classic S. (R), Charles Town Races, Oct. 8, $67,500, 3yo, c&g, West Virginia-bred, 7f, 1:25.76, SPINDINI, Five Star Account, Earth Power, 10 started.

West Virginia Secretary of State S., Mountaineer Race Track, Aug. 14, $85,000, 3&up, f&m, 6f, 1:09.89, COBRA LADY, Injustice, No Affair, 6 started.

West Virginia Senate President's Breeders' Cup S., Mountaineer Race Track, Aug. 14, $120,200, 3&up, f&m, 1mT, 1:33.74, LADY GRACE, Pretty Jane, Kaylan's Rose, 11 started.

West Virginia Vincent Moscarelli Memorial Breeders' Classic S. (R), Charles Town Races, Oct. 8, $67,500, 2yo, West Virginia-bred, $6^1/_2$f, 1:20.86, KING COHL, Alphabet Plunge, Brother Banks, 9 started.

What a Pleasure S., Calder Race Course, Dec. 3, $100,000, 2yo, $1^1/_{16}$m, 1:47.94, SAINT AUGUSTUS, Big Lover, Rehoboth, 7 started.

What a Summer S., Laurel Park, Jan. 29, $50,000, 4&up, f&m, 6f, 1:09.84, SENSIBLY CHIC, Wallop, Bronze Abe, 8 started.

Wheat City S., Assiniboia Downs, Aug. 1, $32,680, 3&up, 1m, 1:40.60, KAT KOOL, Northern Affair, I'm a Gem, 8 started.

Whimsical S., Woodbine, April 17, $184,100, 4&up, f&m, 6f, 1:11.80, NASHINDA, Silver Bird, Whispertoascream, 9 started.

Whippleton S., Calder Race Course, Sept. 25, $40,000, 3&up, 6f, 1:11.71, APALACHIAN THUNDER, Eternal Look, Paradise Dancer, 7 started.

Whirlaway S., Aqueduct, Feb. 12, $84,150, 3yo, $1^1/_{16}$m, 1:43.32, SORT IT OUT, Naughty New Yorker, Scrappy T, 10 started.

Whirling Ash S., Delaware Park, Sept. 17, $57,700, 2yo, 1m, 1:38.11, SUPERFLY, Kid Lemonade, Vegas Play, 5 started.

White Carnation S. (R), Belmont Park, June 11, $69,300, 4&up, f&m, non-winners of an open stakes in 2004-'05, $1^1/_{16}$m, 1:42.91, MADONNA LILY, Judy Soda, Strategy, 5 started.

White Oak H. (R), Arlington Park, June 25, $83,550, 3&up, Illinois-conceived and/or -foaled, 6f, 1:09.60, TAKE ACHANCE ON ME, Big Bold Sweep, Silver Bid, 8 started.

WHITNEY H. (G1), Saratoga Race Course, Aug. 6, $750,000, 3&up, $1^1/_8$m, 1:48.33, COMMENTATOR, Saint Liam, Sir Shackleton, 8 started.

Who Doctor Who H. (R), Horsemen's Park, July 23, $29,800, 4&up, Nebraska-bred, 1m, 1:38.80, HIGH DICE, What About David, Mortrump, 8 started.

Wickerr H. (R), Del Mar, July 30, $76,325, 3&up, non-winners of a stakes of $50,000 other than state-bred at one mile or over since May 1, 1mT, 1:32.23, TSIGANE (FR), Geronimo (Chi), Terroplane (Fr), 9 started.

Wide Country S., Laurel Park, Feb. 12, $55,750, 3yo, f, 1m, 1:40.70, AMAZING BUY, Take a Check, Rutledge Ballado, 6 started.

Wildcat H., Turf Paradise, May 1, $40,000, 3&up, $1^3/_8$mT, 2:16.34, J J WANTSTHEFRONT, Habaneros, Paladin Power, 9 started.

Wild Rose H., Northlands Park, July 1, $40,815, 3&up, f&m, $6^1/_2$f, 1:17.80, STOLE ONE, Unforgettable Too, Robyn's Request, 8 started.

Wild Rose S., Prairie Meadows, June 4, $62,000, 3&up, f&m, $1^1/_{16}$m, 1:44.61, SWITCH LANES, Gamblers Passion, Platinum Ballet, 8 started.

Willard L. Proctor Memorial S. (R), Hollywood Park, May 22, $94,725, 2yo, non-winners of two races, 5f, :58.85, WILD UNCLE KURT, The Missile Came, June's Prince, 6 started.

WILLIAM DONALD SCHAEFER H. (G3), Pimlico Race Course, May 21, $100,000, 3&up, $1^1/_8$m, 1:49.19, ZAKOCITY, Clays Awesome, Royal Assault, 8 started.

William Henry Harrison S. (R), Indiana Downs, May 7, $40,000, 3&up, Indiana-sired, 6f, 1:10.12, HONOR PURSUIT, Pass Rush, Sir Traver, 7 started.

William Kyne H., Portland Meadows, Nov. 26, $10,700, 3&up, $1^1/_{16}$m, 1:47.27, TAMPER, My Friend Dave, Silent Exploit, 5 started.

Willow Lake H., Yavapai Downs, July 31, $15,000, 3&up, f&m, 1m, 1:36.60, PAINLESS, Hillsdale, Pleasant Gulch, 6 started.

WILL ROGERS S. (G3), Hollywood Park, May 28, $109,900, 3yo, 1mT, 1:34.67, OSIDY, Willow O Wisp, Eastern Sand, 8 started.

WILSHIRE H. (G3), Hollywood Park, April 23, $109,600, 3&up, f&m, 1mT, 1:33.85, PICKLE (GB), Makeup Artist, Amorama (Fr), 8 started.

Windsor Ford S., Grand Prairie, Aug. 21, $6,148, 3&up, $1^1/_8$m, 1:53.60, LAFLEUR, Stage Door Jade, Chief Joseph, 7 started.

Windy Sands H., Del Mar, Sept. 5, $86,225, 3&up, 1m, 1:35.62, TOTAL IMPACT (CHI), Anziyan Royalty, Truly a Judge, 7 started.

Wine Country H. (R), Finger Lakes, July 16, $50,000, 3&up, New York-bred, 6f, 1:08.49, TOP SHOTER, Karakorum Patriot, Scary Bob, 7 started.

Winners' Foundation Sprint S., Bay Meadows Race Course, April 24, $62,365, 3yo, f, 6f, 1:09.74, R FAST LADY, Lunachick, Jewels of Bagdad, 7 started.

Winning Colors S., Churchill Downs, May 28, $107,200, 3&up, f&m, 6f, 1:09.50, MOLTO VITA, Heavenly Humor, Born to Dance, 5 started.

Winnipeg Futurity, Assiniboia Downs, Aug. 1, $32,680, 2yo, 6f, 1:13.20, HEY HEY RENEE, Thunderacchi, Gone Wild, 5 started.

Winnipeg Sun S., Assiniboia Downs, July 31, $32,680, 3&up, f&m,

1 1/16m, 1:47, ERICKA'S LASS, Ola Docura, Remiewaterbluz, 7 started.

Winsham Lad H., Sunland Park, Jan. 8, $53,900, 3&up, 1m, 1:36.28, SKIP AND GO, Two Down Automatic, Beyond Brilliant, 9 started.

WinStar Derby, Sunland Park, April 2, $500,000, 3yo, 1 1/8m, 1:49.59, THOR'S ECHO, Southern Africa, Sort It Out, 8 started.

WINSTAR DISTAFF H. (G3), Lone Star Park, May 30, $200,000, 3&up, f&m, 1mT, 1:39.53, KATDOGAWN (GB), Valentine Dancer, Voz De Colegiala (Chi), 11 started.

WINSTAR GALAXY S. (G2), Keeneland Race Course, Oct. 9, $400,000, 3&up, f&m, 1mT, 1:37.40, INTERCONTINENTAL (GB), Wend, Katdogawn (GB), 9 started.

WinStar Sunland Park Oaks, Sunland Park, April 2, $259,000, 3yo, f, 1 1/16m, 1:44.66, CEE'S IRISH, Dayglogreen, Island Escape, 8 started.

Wintergreen H. (R), Thistledown, May 7, $45,000, 3yo, Ohio-bred, 1 1/16m, 1:45.92, DONTSHOOTTHEMSNGR, Circulator, Pyrite Springs, 8 started.

Wintergreen S., Turfway Park, March 12, $50,000, 4&up, f&m, 1m, 1:34.95, TEMPUS FUGIT, Plumlake Lady, Honorable Cat, 7 started.

Winter Melody S., Delaware Park, May 23, $51,216, 3&up, f&m, 1 1/16m, 1:46.07, INDIA HALO (ARG), City Fire, Essence, 4 started.

Win the Honors Starter H. (R), Turf Paradise, Dec. 11, $11,400, 3&up, starters for a claiming price of $7,500 or less in 2005, a1 1/8mT, 1:50.89 (NCR), WAILEA WARRIOR, Fellner, Hammerin, 8 started.

Wishing Well H., Santa Anita Park, Jan. 30, $81,000, 4&up, f&m, a6 1/2fT, 1:13.14, ELUSIVE DIVA, Solar Echo, Any for Love (Arg), 10 started.

Wishing Well S., Turfway Park, Jan. 15, $50,000, 4&up, f&m, 6f, 1:09.11, GOLDEN MARLIN, Jinny's Gold, Moonlit Romance, 8 started.

Witches Brew S., Meadowlands, Oct. 29, $50,000, 3&up, f&m, 5f (originally scheduled on the turf), :55.45 (NTR), PLATINUM PERFECT, Spring Rush, Chez Audra, 6 started.

With Anticipation S. (R), Saratoga Race Course, Sept. 3, $67,200, 2yo, non-winners of a stakes, 1 1/16mT, 1:45.20, STREAM CAT, Metro Meteor, Immersed in Gold, 10 started.

WITHERS S. (G3), Aqueduct, April 30, $150,000, 3yo, 1m, 1:35.74, SCRAPPY T, Park Avenue Ball, War Plan, 7 started.

Without Feathers S., Monmouth Park, Sept. 11, $60,000, 3yo, f, 1m70y, 1:42.28, SHEBELONGSTOYOU, Redaspen, Golden Locket, 6 started.

W. L. MCKNIGHT H. (G2), Calder Race Course, Dec. 17, $200,000, 3&up, 1 1/2mT, 2:25.91, METEOR STORM (GB), Revved Up, Scooter Roach, 12 started.

W. M. Koepplin Memorial S., Western Montana Fair and Races, Aug. 10, $4,275, 3&up, a5 1/4f, 1:05.60, RODEO CHAMP, Seattle Cue, White Pass, 7 started.

Wolf Hill S., Monmouth Park, June 5, $55,000, 3&up, 5f, :56.65, CHOOSE, Procreate, Introspect, 9 started.

Wolverine S. (R), Great Lakes Downs, June 20, $50,000, 3&up, Michigan-bred, 6f, 1:15.59, ROCKEM SOCKEM, Dangel, Above the Wind, 10 started.

Wonders Delight S. (R), Penn National Race Course, May 27, $41,050, 3yo, f, Pennsylvania-bred, 6f, 1:10.95, S W ALY'SVALENTINE, Unlawful Spirit, Redaspen, 10 started.

Wonder Where S. (R), Woodbine, July 31, $206,211, 3yo, f, Canadian-bred, 1 1/4mT, 2:03.69, SILVER HIGHLIGHT, Invitational, See the Wind, 11 started.

Woodbine Oaks (R), Woodbine, June 12, $401,801, 3yo, f, Canadian-bred, 1 1/8m, 1:51.63, GOLD STRIKE, Ready and Alluring, Victorious Ami, 10 started.

WOODBINE SLOTS CUP H. (Can-G3), Woodbine, Nov. 19, $139,154, 3&up, 1 1/16m, 1:43.96, CRYPTOGRAPH, Niigon, Powerful Touch, 8 started.

Woodchopper S., Fair Grounds at Louisiana Downs, Nov. 27, $75,000, 3yo, 1 1/16m (originally scheduled at a1 1/16m on the turf), 1:46.58, SILVER HAZE, Zetetic, Charming Kid, 6 started.

WOODFORD RESERVE TURF CLASSIC S. (G1), Churchill Downs, May 7, $470,400, 3&up, 1 1/8mT, 1:47.34, AMERICA ALIVE, Meteor Storm (GB), Quest Star, 10 started.

Woodford S., Keeneland Race Course, Oct. 9, $112,800, 3&up, 5 1/2fT, 1:04.06, SGT. BERT, Atticus Kristy, Midwatch, 10 started.

Woodland Heritage S. (R), Marquis Downs, Aug. 20, $8,254, 2yo, f, Saskatchewan-bred, 6 1/2f, 1:23.25, EXCESSIVELY SWEET, Shadazzle, Mexican Cutie, 6 started.

Woodlands Derby, The Woodlands, Oct. 22, $20,000, 3yo, 1 1/16m, 1:47.60, PROPER CARSON, Crypto Dynamo, Slew of Love, 9 started.

Woodlands Juvenile S., The Woodlands, Oct. 29, $20,000, 2yo, 6f, 1:12.60, SLEW LUCKY, All About Us, Nikki Nine, 11 started.

Woodlands S., The Woodlands, Oct. 29, $20,000, 3&up, 1 1/16m, 1:45.20, MATCHED, Canyon de Oro, Pay Check, 8 started.

Woodlawn S., Pimlico Race Course, May 21, $100,000, 3yo, 1 1/16mT, 1:45.55, ENGLISH CHANNEL, United, Holy Ground, 8 started.

WOOD MEMORIAL S. (G1), Aqueduct, April 9, $750,000, 3yo, 1 1/8m, 1:47.16, BELLAMY ROAD, Survivalist, Scrappy T, 7 started.

Woodside H., Bay Meadows Race Course, April 2, $60,400, 3&up, f&m, 6f, 1:09.46, HEAVENLY HUMOR, Puxa Saco, Yerevan Star, 6 started.

Woodstock S., Woodbine, April 23, $109,127, 3yo, 6f, 1:12.89, WHOLELOTTABOURBON, Accountforthegold, Promontory, 6 started.

WOODWARD S. (G1), Belmont Park, Sept. 10, $490,000, 3&up, 1 1/8m, 1:49.07, SAINT LIAM, Sir Shackleton, Commentator, 5 started.

World Appeal S., Meadowlands, Oct. 4, $53,000, 2yo, 1m 70yT., 1:42.18, LAST BEST PLACE, Eagle River, Ernie Bogen, 8 started.

Xtra Heat S., Pimlico Race Course, April 30, $50,000, 3yo, f, 5f, :58.58, MISSILE BAY, Coastal Strike, Partners Due, 7 started.

Yaddo H. (1st Div.) (R), Saratoga Race Course, Aug. 17, $82,650, 3&up, f&m, New York-bred, 1 1/8mT, 1:48.19, ON THE BUS, Finlandia, Beebe Lake, 8 started.

Yaddo H. (2nd Div.) (R), Saratoga Race Course, Aug. 17, $83,050, 3&up, f&m, New York-bred, 1 1/8mT, 1:49.10, KATE WINSLET, Rahys' Appeal, The Lamp Is Lit, 9 started.

Yankee Affair S., Gulfstream Park, April 9, $50,000, 3&up, 5fT, :53.79 (NCR), PROCREATE, True Love's Secret, Shake the Bank, 9 started.

Yaqthan S., Kentucky Downs, Sept. 24, $50,000, 3&up, 1mT, 1:37.80, SEEKING ANSWERS (IRE), Missme, Tempered Steel, 8 started.

Yavapai Classic H., Yavapai Downs, June 5, $15,000, 3&up, f&m, 6f, 1:09.40, DYSFUNCTIONAL LADY, Pegalee, Pleasant Gulch, 9 started.

Yavapai County Arizona Breeders' Futurity (R), Yavapai Downs, June 26, $25,165, 2yo, Arizona-bred, 5f, :58.80, DESERT GLORY, Rebuck, Flying Bill, 5 started.

Yavapai Downs Derby (1st Div.), Yavapai Downs, Aug. 20, $20,000, 3yo, 1 1/16m, 1:45.40, WE BROTHERS, Lion D'Art, Threat From Above, 8 started.

Yavapai Downs Derby (2nd Div.), Yavapai Downs, Aug. 20, $20,000, 3yo, 1 1/16m, 1:46.20, CAPTAIN BARBOSSO, Go Wild Willie, Fool's Destiny, 7 started.

Yavapai Downs Futurity, Yavapai Downs, Sept. 5, $43,350, 2yo, 6f, 1:10.60, MINING GOLD, Queen Razyana, Peeples Valley, 11 started.

Yavapai Downs H., Yavapai Downs, July 12, $15,000, 3&up, 5 1/2f, 1:02.60, PEGALEE, River Adventure (Brz), Ground Zero Hero, 7 started.

Yavapai Downs Triathlon Series S., Yavapai Downs, Aug. 2, $12,700, 3&up, 1m, 1:38.40, MASTERFULLY'S GAME, Folton, Pirate's Fleet, 7 started.

YELLOW RIBBON S. (G1), Oak Tree at Santa Anita, Oct. 1, $500,000, 3&up, f&m, 1 1/4mT, 2:00.50, MEGAHERTZ (GB), Flip Flop (Fr), Halo Ola (Arg), 7 started.

Yellow Rose S. (R), Sam Houston Race Park, Nov. 19, $50,000, 3&up, f&m, Texas-bred, 6f, 1:11.59, EXPECTANT DIVA, Shannons Valentine, Dodd, 9 started.

Yellowstone Downs Thoroughbred H., Yellowstone Downs, Sept. 11, $3,600, 3&up, 7f, 1:26.40, STREAK A ROANI, Harbour Axe, Fruit Rapport, 7 started.

YERBA BUENA BREEDERS' CUP H. (G3), Golden Gate Fields, May 21, $80,625, 3&up, f&m, 1 1/16mT, 1:41.72, PICKLE (GB), Marla Bay, Midwife, 6 started.

Yo Tambien S., Hawthorne Race Course, Nov. 5, $49,050, 3&up, f&m, 1 1/16mT, 1:42.98, ATLANTIC FROST, Tisket a Tasket, Chic Dancer, 8 started.

Zadracarta S. (R), Woodbine, June 19, $65,617, 3&up, f&m, Ontario-bred, 6fT, 1:11.95, CRICKET WICKET, Velvet Snow, Financing-available, 6 started.

Zenobia Empress H., Churchill Downs, July 9, $71,600, 3&up, f&m, 5fT, :55.54 (NCR), UNBRIDLED SIDNEY, Mocha Queen, Final Discount, 10 started.

Zia Park Derby, Zia Park, Dec. 3, $107,600, 3yo, 1 1/16m, 1:45.60, REAL DANDY, Lumbre, Broke Sharply, 6 started.

Zia Park Distaff S., Zia Park, Oct. 8, $50,750, 3&up, f&m, 6f, 1:10.20, CULPEPER MOON, Dee Dee's Diner, Ladysgotthelooks, 7 started.

Zia Park Distance Championship H., Zia Park, Dec. 4, $106,000, 3&up, 1 1/8m, MR. TRIESTE, Silver Axe, Don't Strike Out, 5 started.

Zia Park Express H., Zia Park, Dec. 4, $80,400, 3&up, 6 1/2f, 1:15, JUNGLE PRINCE, Nuttyboom, Komax, 4 started.

Zip Pocket S., Turf Paradise, Oct. 30, $23,700, 3&up, 5 1/2f, 1:03.55, MOORES BRIDGE, Adroitly Superb, Offshore News, 6 started.

Oldest Stakes Races

Although horse racing in North America dates from the Colonial period, stakes races did not become popular until the mid-1800s.

The oldest continually run stakes in North America—meaning that it has been run every year since its inception—is the Queen's Plate Stakes at Woodbine. First run in 1860, the race was named for Queen Victoria, then in the 23rd year of her 64-year reign, and was for horses of all ages foaled in the province of Ontario. The winner of that first Queen's Plate was Don Juan, a five-year-old Sir Tatton Sykes gelding. (Another Queen's Plate, restricted to horses foaled in Quebec, dated from 1836 and was discontinued after World War II.) From 1902 through '51, the race was known as the King's Plate, for a succession of English male monarchs.

North America's oldest stakes race still in existence is the Phoenix Breeders' Cup Stakes (G3), first run in 1831 at the Kentucky Association track in Lexington. Known at various times as the Phoenix Hotel S., Phoenix S., Brennan S., Chiles S., Association S., and the Phoenix H., the race was discontinued in 1930. It was revived with the first spring race meeting of Keeneland Race Course in 1937.

Oldest Continuously Run Stakes

Race	Track	First Running	First Winner
Queen's Plate	Woodbine	1860	Don Juan
Kentucky Derby	Churchill	1875	Aristides
Kentucky Oaks	Churchill	1875	Vinaigrette
Clark H.	Churchill	1875	Voltigeur
Bashford Manor S.	Churchill	1902	Von Rouse
Fall Highweight H.	Aqueduct	1914	Comely
Coaching Club American Oaks	Belmont	1917	Wistful
Jockey Club Gold Cup S.	Belmont	1919	Purchase
Cowdin S.	Belmont	1923	Mr. Mutt
Wood Memorial S.	Aqueduct	1925	Backbone
Selima S.	Laurel	1926	Fair Star
Whitney H.	Saratoga	1928	Black Maria
Canadian Derby	Northlands	1930	Jack Whittier

Oldest Stakes Races

Race	Track	First Running	First Winner

PHOENIX BREEDERS' CUP S. **Keeneland 1831 McDonough**
1831-'77, run as a heat race; 1898-1904,1906-'10, 1914-'16, 1929, 1931-'36, not run; before 1937, held at the Kentucky Association track; 1943-'45, held at Churchill Downs; 1972, 1981, run in two divisions; before 1989, held during the spring meeting; inaugurated in 1831 as the Phoenix Hotel S.; has also been run as Brennan S., Chiles S., Phoenix S., Association S., and Phoenix H.

QUEEN'S PLATE S. Woodbine 1860 Don Juan
Before 1887, run at 1½ miles; 1924-'56, run at 1⅛ miles; before 1938, for three-year-olds and up; 1938, for three- and four-year-olds; 1902-'51, run as the King's Plate; before 1956, held at Old Woodbine; before 1959, for three-year-olds bred and owned in Canada

TRAVERS S. Saratoga 1864 Kentucky
1943, 1944, 1945, held at Belmont Park; 1896, 1898, 1899, 1900, 1911, 1912, not run; before 1890, run at 1¾ miles; 1890-'92, run at 1½ miles; 1895, 1901-'03, run at 1⅛ miles; 1927-'32, run as the Travers Midsummer Derby

JEROME H. Belmont 1866 Watson
1866-'89, held at Jerome Park; 1890-1905, held at Morris Park; 1960, 1962-'67, held at Aqueduct; 1910-'13, not run; 1866-'70, run in two divisions; 1871-'77, run at two miles; 1878-'89, run at 1¾ miles; 1890, 1891, 1903, run at 1 5/16 miles; 1892, run at 1½ miles; 1893, 1894, 1896-1909, run at 1¼ miles; 1895, run at 1⅛ miles

BELMONT S. Belmont 1867 Ruthless
1867-'89, held at Jerome Park; 1890-1904, held at Morris Park; 1963-'67, held at Aqueduct; 1911-'12, not run; 1867-'73, run at 1⅝ miles; 1890-'92, 1895, 1904-'05, run at 1¼ miles; 1893-'94, run at 1⅛ miles; 1896-1903, 1906-'25, run at 1⅜ miles; 1895, 1913, run as a handicap stakes

CHAMPAGNE S. Belmont 1867 Sarah B.
Before 1890, held at Jerome Park; 1890-1905, held at Morris Park; 1959, 1963-'67, 1984, held at Aqueduct; 1910-'13, 1956, not run; 1871-'80, run at six furlongs; 1891-1904, run at seven furlongs; 1905-'32, run on the Widener course (165 feet less than seven furlongs); 1933-'39, run on the Widener course at 6½ furlongs; 1940-'83, 1985-'93, run at one mile; 1984, run at 1⅛ miles; 1973, run in two divisions

LADIES H. Aqueduct 1868 Bonnie Braes
Before 1913, for three-year-old fillies; 1931-'34,1940-2001, for fillies and mares all ages, three-year-olds and up; before 1890, held at Jerome Park; 1890-1904, held at Morris Park; 1950-'58, 1960, held at Belmont Park; 1895, 1911, 1912, not run; before 1874, run at 1⅝ miles; 1889, 1892, run at 1⅛ miles; 1890, 1891, run at 1,400 yards; 1893, 1894, run at 1 1/16 miles; 1896-1939, run at one mile; 1961, 1962, run at 1 5/16 miles; 1874-'85, 1940-'58, 1960, 1963, 1964, run at 1½ miles.

FLASH S. Belmont 1869 Remorseless
1869-1942, 1946-'71, held at Saratoga; 1943-'45, held at Belmont Park on the Widener course; 1981, 1982, held at Belmont Park; 1896, 1898-1900, 1911, 1912, 1960, 1972-'80, 1983-'98, not run; before 1901, run at four furlongs; 1901, run at five furlongs; 1969-'71, run at six furlongs; 1981, 1982, run at 5½ furlongs

DIXIE S. Pimlico 1870 Preakness
1870, run as Dinner Party S.; 1871, run as Reunion S.; 1903-'04, held at Benning, Washington, D.C., at 1¾ miles for three-year-olds; 1870-'88, run at two miles for three-year-olds; 1924-'52, run at 1 3/16 miles; 1960-'87, 1989, 1990, run at 1½ miles; 1955-'59, run at 1⅜ miles; 1988, run at 1⅝ miles; before 1955, 1988, run on dirt; 1889-1901, 1905-'23, not run; 1965-'78, run in two divisions

MONMOUTH PARK BREEDERS' CUP OAKS **Monmouth 1871 Salina**
1871-'77, run at 1½ miles; 1879-'93, run at 1¼ miles; 1946-'52, 1996-2001, run at 1 1/16 miles; 1953-'95, run at 1⅛ miles; 1891, held at Jerome Park; 1878, 1894-1945, 2003, not run; 1976, run as Monmouth Bicentennial Oaks

ALABAMA S. Saratoga 1872 Woodbine
1943-'45, held at Belmont Park; 1893-'96, 1898-1900, 1911, 1912, not run; before 1901, 1904, 1906-'16, run at 1⅛ miles; 1901-'03, run at 1 1/16 miles; 1903, run on turf; 1905, run at 1 5/16 miles

CALIFORNIA DERBY Bay Meadows 1873 Camilla Urso
1897-1909, run at 1¼ miles; 1923, run at 1½ miles; 1936-'48, 1976-'81, run at 1 1/16 miles; 1874, 1891-'96, 1900, 1911-'22, 1924-'34, 1939, 1940, 1942, 1943, 1945, 1947, 1949-'53, 1957, not run; 1873-1959, 1962, held at Tanforan; 1961, 1964-2000, held at Golden Gate Fields

Race	Track	First Running	First Winner
PREAKNESS S.	**Pimlico**	**1873**	**Survivor**

Before 1894, run at 1½ miles; 1889, run at 1¼ miles; 1894-1900, 1908, run at 1$\frac{1}{16}$ miles; 1901-'07, run at one mile and 70 yards; 1909, 1910, run at one mile; 1911-'24, run at 1⅛ miles; 1891-'93, not run; 1890, for three-year-olds and up; 1890, held at Morris Park, New York; 1894-1908, held at Gravesend, New York; 1918, run in two divisions

Race	Track	First Running	First Winner
WITHERS S.	**Aqueduct**	**1874**	**Dublin**

1847-'89, held at Jerome Park; 1890-1904, held at Morris Park; 1956, held at Jamaica; 1984-'96, held at Belmont Park; 1911, 1912, not run; 1956, run at 1$\frac{1}{16}$ miles

Race	Track	First Running	First Winner
CLARK H.	**Churchill**	**1875**	**Voltigeur**

1875-1901, run as three-year-old stakes; 1902-2001, run as a handicap for three-year-olds and up; 1875-'80, run at two miles; 1881-'95, run at 1¼ miles; 1902-'21, 1925-'54, run at 1$\frac{1}{16}$ miles; 1953, run in two divisions

Race	Track	First Running	First Winner
KENTUCKY DERBY	**Churchill**	**1875**	**Aristides**

Before 1896, run at 1½ miles

Race	Track	First Running	First Winner
KENTUCKY OAKS	**Churchill**	**1875**	**Vinaigrette**

1875-'90, run at 1½ miles; 1891-'95, run at 1¼ miles; 1896-1919, 1942-'81, run at 1$\frac{1}{16}$ miles

Fastest Times of 2005

Dirt

Dist.	Time	Winner, Age, Sex	Track	Date	Cond.
1½f	:17.06	Abuela Yiya, 2	El Comandante	Aug. 1	my
2f	:21.21	Thats the Problem, 6	Calder Race Course	July 10	ft
2½f	:28.08	Snap Count, 2	Evangeline Downs	April 29	ft
3f	:31.01	Eclat, 5	Remington Park	Nov. 28	ft
3½f	:39.60	Nashwaak Dancer, 2	Northlands Park	July 22	ft
4f	:43.80	Golden Hunt, 3	Stampede Park	April 1	ft
4½f	:49.80	Bobaway, 6	Yavapai Downs	Sept. 6	ft
		River Adventure (Brz), 5	Yavapai Downs	Aug. 9	ft
5f	:55.45	Platinum Perfect, 4	Meadowlands	Oct. 29	ft
5¼f	1:03.00	Bobski, 4	Yellowstone Downs	Sept. 10	ft
		Evitan Native, 6	Yellowstone Downs	Sept. 4	ft
		King of Adventure, 8	Yellowstone Downs	Sept. 4	ft
		Restrictions Apply, 5	Yellowstone Downs	Sept. 11	ft
5½f	1:01.65	Frisco Star, 2	Santa Rosa	Aug. 6	ft
6f	1:07.32	Lost in the Fog, 3	Golden Gate Fields	May 14	ft
6½f	1:13.00	Sabertooth, 7	Emerald Downs	May 22	ft
7f	1:20.23	Commentator, 4	Belmont Park	June 29	ft
7½f	1:27.23	McCann's Mojave, 5	Hollywood Park	June 11	ft
1m	1:33.29	Ghostzapper, 5	Belmont Park	May 30	ft
1m 40y	1:40.40	Pushed, 5	Fair Grounds	Jan. 17	ft
1m 70y	1:37.90	With Probability, 4	Meadowlands	Oct. 28	ft
1$\frac{1}{16}$m	1:40.11	Consolidator, 3	Santa Anita Park	March 19	wf
1⅛m	1:46.35	Oratory, 3	Belmont Park	May 28	ft
1$\frac{3}{16}$m	1:54.27	Perfect Drift, 6	Arlington Park	July 30	ft
1¼m	1:59.63	Lava Man, 4	Hollywood Park	July 9	ft
1$\frac{5}{16}$m	2:11.80	Jiffyjimmygee, 5	Northlands Park	Aug. 26	ft
1⅜m	2:16.28	Golden Rahy, 6	Hollywood Park	Dec. 1	ft
1$\frac{7}{16}$m	2:25.80	Watchmon, 3	Gulfstream Park	April 8	sy
1½m	2:28.72	License To Run (Brz), 5	Santa Anita Park	Feb. 19	sy
1$\frac{9}{16}$m	2:42.36	Anthem Hill, 6	Hoosier Park	Nov. 12	ft
1⅝m	2:44.82	Hammerin, 5	Turf Paradise	March 1	ft
1¾m	3:01.81	Seattlespectacular, 5	Woodbine	Dec. 11	ft
1$\frac{13}{16}$m	3:11.61	Billy Bird, 5	The Downs at Albuquerque	Sept. 25	ft
1⅞m	3:16.71	Dancer's Guest, 6	Woodbine	Dec. 11	ft
2m	3:25.00	Horatio, 6	Emerald Downs	Oct. 16	ft
2m 70y	3:35.52	Dancer's Guest, 6	Fort Erie	Nov. 1	sy
2⅛m	3:47.84	Crescent Remark, 6	Hastings Race Course	Nov. 12	sy

All Weather

Dist.	Time	Winner, Age	Track	Date	Cond.
5½f	1:04.72	Cayenne Red, 4	Turfway Park	Dec. 30	ft
1¼m	2:08.56	Leonard's Shaker, 4	Turfway Park	Dec. 18	ft

Turf

Dist.	Time	Winner, Age	Track	Date	Cond.
4½f	:49.74	King Justin, 4	Turf Paradise	May 21	fm
		Lill's Fame, 4	Turf Paradise	Dec. 17	fm
5f	:53.79	Procreate, 7	Gulfstream Park	April 9	fm
5½f	1:01.17	Actual, 3	Ellis Park	Sept. 3	fm
6f	1:06.82	Keep The Faith (Aus), 5	Belmont Park	July 24	fm
6½f	1:13.97	My Lucky Strike, 6	Woodbine	Aug. 7	fm
7f	1:20.21	Lucky Tom, 5	Woodbine	Oct. 21	fm
7½f	1:26.83	Drum Major, 3	Calder Race Course	Dec. 31	fm
1m	1:31.41	Mr. Light (Arg), 6	Gulfstream Park	Jan. 3	fm
1m 70y	1:38.56	Crete (Aus), 9	Penn National Race Course	Aug. 24	fm
1$\frac{1}{16}$m	1:38.20	Old Forester, 4	Gulfstream Park	March 13	fm
1⅛m	1:44.69	Saint Stephen, 5	Gulfstream Park	Feb. 19	fm
1$\frac{3}{16}$m	1:53.13	Tempered Steel, 5	Saratoga Race Course	Aug. 4	fm
1¼m	1:59.03	Cesario (Jpn), 3	Hollywood Park	July 3	fm
1⅜m	2:11.44	Prince Arch, 4	Gulfstream Park	March 6	fm
1½m	2:24.45	Stanley Park, 5	Santa Anita Park	March 27	fm
1⅝m	2:40.94	Rousing Victory, 4	Saratoga Race Course	Aug. 15	fm

Dist.	Time	Winner, Age	Track	Date	Cond.
$1\frac{3}{4}$m	2:53.35	Inaugural Address, 6	Mountaineer Race Track	Aug. 15	fm
$1\frac{13}{16}$m	3:08.09	Earnest Storm, 7	Remington Park	Nov. 28	fm
$1\frac{7}{8}$m	3:11.20	Convexity, 5	River Downs	Sept. 5	fm
2m	3:38.80	Studio Time, 6	Shawan Downs	Sept. 24	fm
$2\frac{1}{16}$m	3:43.04	Mr Perkolater, 7	Saratoga Race Course	Aug. 3	fm
$2\frac{1}{2}$m	4:17.60	Preemptive Strike, 7	Meadowlands	Oct. 1	fm

North American Records

Dirt

Dist.	Time	Winner, Age Sex	Track	Date
2f	:20.71	Pensglitter, 7 h.	Penn National Race Course	10/9/2004
$2\frac{1}{2}$f	:26.53	Yes He Will, 4 g.	Lone Star Park	11/7/1997
3f	:31.20	Raisable Adversary, 11 g.	Remington Park	8/29/1999
$3\frac{1}{2}$f	:38.00	Primero Del Anno, 5 g.	Flagstaff	7/4/1998
4f	:43.10	Slewofrainbows, 7 g.	Mohave County Fair	5/23/1999
$4\frac{1}{2}$f	:49.20	Valiant Pete, 4 c.	Los Alamitos Race Course	8/11/1990
5f	:55.20	Chinook Pass, 3 c.	Longacres	9/17/1982
$5\frac{1}{2}$f	1:01.10	Plenty Zloty, 5 g.	Turf Paradise	4/18/1998
6f	1:06.60	G Malleah, 4 g.	Turf Paradise	4/8/1995
$6\frac{1}{4}$f	1:15.80	Montanic, 4 g.	Washington Park	7/20/1901
$6\frac{1}{2}$f	1:13.00	Sabertooth, 7 g.	Emerald Downs	5/22/2005
7f	1:19.40	Rich Cream, 5 h.	Hollywood Park	5/28/1980
		Time to Explode, 3 c.	Hollywood Park	6/26/1982
$7\frac{1}{2}$f	1:26.26	Awesome Daze, 5 g.	Hollywood Park	11/23/1997
1m	$1:32\frac{1}{5}$	Dr. Fager, 4 c.	Arlington Park	8/24/1968
	1:32.24	Najran, 4 c.	Belmont Park	5/7/2003
1m 20y	1:39.00	Froglegs, 4 c.	Churchill Downs	5/13/1913
1m 40y	1:38.20	Zaffarancho (Arg), 5 h.	Rockingham	6/19/1987
1m 70y	1:37.90	Schedule (GB), 3 f.	Meadowlands	10/15/2004
		With Probability, 4 c.	Meadowlands	10/28/2005
1m 100y	1:43.80	Old Honesty, 3 c.	Empire City	8/20/1907
$1\frac{1}{16}$m	1:38.40	Hoedown's Day, 5 h.	Bay Meadows Race Course	10/23/1983
$1\frac{1}{8}$m	1:45.00	Simply Majestic, 4 c.	Golden Gate Fields	4/2/1988
$1\frac{3}{16}$m	1:52.40	Riva Ridge, 4 c.	Aqueduct	7/4/1973
$1\frac{1}{4}$m	1:57.80	Spectacular Bid, 4 c.	Santa Anita Park	2/3/1980
$1\frac{5}{16}$m	2:07.32	Gold Star Deputy, 5 g.	Aqueduct	4/10/1999
$1\frac{3}{8}$m	2:12.31	Demi's Bret, 4 g.	Aqueduct	10/26/1997
$1\frac{7}{16}$m	2:23.00	Who's In Command, 5 h.	Hastings Race Course	8/10/1987
$1\frac{1}{2}$m	2:24.00	Secretariat, 3 c.	Belmont Park	6/9/1973
$1\frac{9}{16}$m	2:35.77	Well Lit, 5 g.	Sportsman's Park	4/25/1992
$1\frac{5}{8}$m	2:38.20	Swaps, 4 c.	Hollywood Park	7/25/1956
$1\frac{3}{4}$m	2:52.60	Major Pots, 5 g.	Woodbine	12/8/1994
$1\frac{7}{8}$m	3:11.56	Asserche, 6 g.	Laurel Park	3/20/1994
2m	3:19.20	Kelso, 7 g.	Aqueduct	10/31/1964
$2\frac{1}{4}$m	3:47.00	Fenelon, 4 c.	Belmont Park	10/4/1941
$2\frac{1}{2}$m	4:14.60	*Miss Grillo, 6 m.	Pimlico Race Course	11/12/1948

Turf

Dist.	Time	Winner, Age	Track	Date
4f	:46.60	Fine Tassles, 5 m.	Rillito	1/30/1994
$4\frac{1}{2}$f	:49.26	Dan's Groovy, 7 g.	Turf Paradise	4/13/2003
5f	:53.79	Procreate, 7 g.	Gulfstream park	4/9/2005
$5\frac{1}{2}$f	1:00.46	Pembroke, 5 h.	Hollywood Park	7/15/1995
6f	1:06.82	Keep The Faith (Aus), 5 h.	Belmont Park	7/24/2005
$6\frac{1}{2}$f	1:13.97	My Luck Strike, 6 g.	Woodbine	8/7/2005
a$6\frac{1}{2}$f	1:11.13	Lennyfromalibu, 5 g.	Santa Anita Park	1/22/2004
7f	1:19.38	Soaring Free, 5 g.	Woodbine	7/24/2004
$7\frac{1}{2}$f	1:26.54	Court Lark, 6 g.	Calder Race Course	7/16/1994
1m	1:31.41	Mr. Light (Arg), 6 h.	Gulfstream Park	1/3/2005
1m 40y	1:38.08	Castaneto (Arg), 7 g.	Atlantic City Race Course	6/28/1991
1m 70y	1:37.20	Aborigine, 6 h.	Penn National Race Course	8/20/1978
$1\frac{1}{16}$m	1:38.00	Told, 4 c.	Penn National Race Course	9/14/1980
$1\frac{1}{8}$m	1:43.92	Kostroma (Ire), 5 m.	Santa Anita Park	10/20/1991
$1\frac{3}{16}$m	1:51.40	Toonerville, 4 g.	Hialeah Park	2/7/1976
$1\frac{1}{4}$m	1:57.40	Double Discount, 4 c.	Santa Anita Park	10/9/1977
$1\frac{5}{16}$m	2:06.00	Ruff Mack, 5 m.	Mountaineer Race Track	8/25/1962
$1\frac{3}{8}$m	2:10.20	With Approval, 4 c.	Belmont Park	6/17/1990
$1\frac{7}{16}$m	2:25.00	Dina's Playmate, 11 g.	River Downs	8/30/1969
$1\frac{1}{2}$m	2:22.80	Hawkster, 3 c.	Santa Anita Park	10/14/1989
$1\frac{9}{16}$m	2:40.26	To the Floor, 7 g.	Fair Grounds	3/29/1999
$1\frac{5}{8}$m	2:37.00	Tom Swift, 5 h.	Saratoga Race Course	8/23/1978
$1\frac{3}{4}$m	2:53.35	Inaugural Address, 6 g.	Mountaineer Race Track	8/15/2005
$1\frac{7}{8}$m	3:08.23	Code's Best, 6 g.	Mountaineer Race Track	9/4/2000
2m	3:18.00	*Petrone, 5 h.	Hollywood Park	7/23/1969
$2\frac{1}{4}$m	3:48.40	Buteo, 6 g.	River Downs	9/3/1990

Progression of Fastest Times on Dirt

Six Furlongs

Time	Horse	YOB Sex, Sire	Date	Track	Weight
1:06.60	G Malleah	1991 g., Fool the Experts	4/8/1995	Turf Paradise	120
1:06⅘	Zany Tactics	1981 h., Zanthe	3/8/1987	Turf Paradise	126
1:07⅕	Petro D. Jay	1976 h., *Grey Tudor	5/9/1982	Turf Paradise	120
1:07⅕	Grey Papa	1967 g., Grey Eagle	9/4/1972	Longacres	116
1:07⅖	Vale of Tears	1963 h., *Royal Vale	6/7/1969	Ak-Sar-Ben	120
1:07⅖	Zip Pocket	1964 h., Nantallah	12/4/1966	Turf Paradise	126
1:07⅘	Admirably	1962 m., *Oceanus II	4/7/1965	Golden Gate Fields	118
1:07⅘	Crazy Kid	1958 h., Krakatao	8/18/1962	Del Mar	118
1:08	*Dumpty Humpty	1953 h., Stalino	11/2/1957	Golden Gate Fields	115
1:08⅕	Bolero	1946 h., Eight Thirty	5/27/1950	Golden Gate Fields	122
1:08⅖	*Fair Truckle	1943 h., Fair Trial	10/4/1947	Golden Gate Fields	119
1:09⅕	Polynesian	1942 h., Unbreakable	9/16/1946	Atlantic City Race Course	126
1:09⅕	*Mafosta	1942 h., Fair Trial	7/14/1946	Longacres	116
1:09⅕	Clang	1932 g., Stimulus	10/12/1935	Coney Island (Oh.)	110
1:09⅗	Iron Mask	1908 g., Disguise	1/4/1914	Juarez (Mex)	115
1:10⅘	Orb	1911 h., Luck and Charity	12/9/1913	Juarez (Mex)	90
1:10⅘	Leochares	1910 g., Broomstick	10/3/1913	Douglas Park	109
1:10⅘	Iron Mask	1908 g., Disguise	9/23/1913	Douglas Park	127
1:11	Priscillian	1905 g., Hastings	6/19/1911	Hamilton (Can)	113
1:11	Prince Ahmed	1904 h., King Hanover	7/29/1909	Empire City	117
1:11	Chapultepec	1905 h., *Gerolstein	12/28/1908	Santa Anita (old)	112
1:11⅗	Col. Bob	1905 h., Cesarion	12/27/1907	Santa Anita (old)	92
1:11⅗	Roseben	1901 g., *Ben Strome	10/6/1905	Belmont Park	147
1:11⅘	Ivan the Terrible	1902 h., *Pirate of Penzance	10/27/1904	Worth (Il.)	92
1:11⅘	Dick Welles	1900 h., King Eric	6/30/1903	Washington Park	109
1:12	*Lux Casta	1899 m., Donovan	7/23/1902	Brighton Beach	111
1:12	Bummer II	1896 h., Register	10/17/1900	Kinloch (Mo.)	80
1:12⅕	*Voter	1894 h., Friar's Balsam	7/6/1900	Brighton Beach	123
1:12¼	Mary Black	1895 m., *Islington	7/16/1898	Washington Park	93
1:12¼	Flora Louise	1895 m., *Florist	9/30/1897	Harlem (Il.)	88
1:12¼	O'Connell	1890 g., Harry o' Fallon	7/18/1895	Oakley (Oh.)	121
1:13	Tom Hood	1884 h., Virgil	9/19/1888	Louisville	115
1:13	Force	1878 h., West Roxbury	9/24/1883	Louisville	121
1:14	Monarch	1879 h., Monarchist	8/22/1882	Saratoga	91
1:14	Knight Templar	1877 g., Fellowcraft	9/18/1880	Gravesend	77
1:14	Barrett	1878 h., *Bonnie Scotland	8/14/1880	Monmouth Park	110
1:15	First Chance	1871 g., Baywood	10/17/1876	Philadelphia	110
1:15½	Bill Bruce	1872 h., Enquirer	5/12/1776	Lexington (Ky.)	108
1:15¾	Madge	1871 m., *Australian	8/21/1874	Saratoga	87
1:16	Alarm	1869 h., *Eclipse	7/15/1872	Saratoga	90
1:16¾	Tom Bowling	1870 h., Lexington	8/6/1872	Long Branch (N.J.)	100

Seven Furlongs

Time	Horse	YOB Sex, Sire	Date	Track	Weight
1:19⅖	Time to Explode	1979 h., Explodent	6/26/1982	Hollywood Park	117
1:19⅖	Rich Cream	1975 h., Creme dela Crème	5/28/1980	Hollywood Park	118
1:19⅘	Triple Bend	1968 h., Never Bend	5/6/1972	Hollywood Park	123
1:20	Native Diver	1959 g., Imbros	5/22/1965	Hollywood Park	126
1:20	El Drag	1951 h., *Khaled	5/21/1955	Hollywood Park	115
1:20⅗	Imbros	1950 h., Polynesian	1/2/1954	Santa Anita Park	118
1:21	Bolero	1946 h., Eight Thirty	1/1/1951	Santa Anita Park	121
1:21⅖	Ky. Colonel	1946 h., Balladier	8/10/1949	Washington Park	116
1:21⅘	Buzfuz	1942 g., Zacaweista	6/20/1947	Hollywood Park	120
1:21⅘	Honeymoon	1943 m., *Beau Pere	6/3/1947	Hollywood Park	114
1:22	High Resolve	1941 g., Zacaweista	10/17/1945	Hollywood Park	126
1:22	Clang	1932 g., Stimulus	7/19/1935	Arlington Park	105
1:22	Roseben	1901 g., *Ben Strome	10/16/1906	Belmont Park	126
1:25	The Musketeer	1898 h., *Masetto	8/18/1902	Saratoga	108
1:25⅖	Clifford	1890 h., Bramble	8/29/1894	Sheepshead Bay	127
1:26⅖	Britannic	1884 h., Plevna	9/5/1889	Sheepshead Bay	110
1:27¼	Kingston	1884 h., Spendthrift	9/1/1887	Sheepshead Bay	118
1:28½	Joe Murray	1879 h., Rebel	7/17/1884	Chicago	117
1:28¾	Little Phil	1878 h., Enquirer	7/3/1882	Monmouth Park	111
1:30	Brambaletta	1878 m., *Bonnie Scotland	9/24/1881	Brighton Beach	92
1:30	Reporter	1877 g., King Ernest	8/13/1881	Brighton Beach	95

One Mile

Time	Horse	YOB Sex, Sire	Date	Track	Weight
1:32.24	Najran	1999 c., Runaway Groom	5/7/2003	Belmont Park	113
1:32⅕	Dr. Fager	1964 h., Rough 'n Tumble	8/24/1968	Arlington Park	134
1:32⅗	Buckpasser	1963 h., Tom Fool	6/25/1966	Arlington Park	125
1:33⅕	Hedevar	1962 h., Count of Honor	6/18/1966	Arlington Park	116

Time	Horse	YOB Sex, Sire	Date	Track	Weight
1:33⅕	Pia Star	1961 h., Olympia	6/19/1965	Arlington Park	112
1:33⅕	Intentionally	1956 h., Intent	6/27/1959	Washington Park	121
1:33⅕	Swaps	1952 h., *Khaled	6/9/1956	Hollywood Park	128
1:33⅗	Citation	1945 h., Bull Lea	6/3/1950	Golden Gate Fields	128
1:34	Coaltown	1945 h., Bull Lea	8/20/1949	Washington Park	130
1:34⅖	Prevaricator	1943 g., Omaha	10/2/1948	Golden Gate Fields	118
1:34⅖	Equipoise	1928 h., Pennant	6/30/1932	Arlington Park	128
1:34⅘	Roamer	1911 g., Knight Errant	8/21/1918	Saratoga	110
1:36⅕	*Sun Briar	1915 h., Sundridge	8/6/1918	Saratoga	113
1:36¼	Amalfi	1908 g., The Scribe	9/3/1914	Syracuse (N.Y.)	107
1:36⅘	Christophine	1911 m., Plaudit	3/11/1914	Juarez (Mex.)	102
1:37	Bonne Chance	1909 g., Orsini	1/18/1914	Juarez	98
1:37⅕	Vested Rights	1910 g., Abe Frank	12/25/1913	Juarez	105
1:37⅕	Manasseh	1909 f., *Star Shoot	12/12/1913	Juarez	93
1:37⅕	Centre Shot	1905 f., *Sain	12/22/1908	Santa Anita (old)	105
1:37⅖	Kiamesha	1902 f., *Esher	10/9/1905	Belmont Park	104
1:37⅖	Dick Welles	1900 h., King Eric	8/14/1903	Harlem (Il.)	112
1:37⅗	Alan-a-Dale	1899 h., Halma	7/1/1903	Washington Park	110
1:37⅘	Brigadier	1897 g., *Rayon d'Or	6/22/1901	Sheepshead Bay	112
1:38	Orimar	1894 h., Sir Dixon	7/21/1900	Washington Park	109
1:38	*Voter	1894 h., Friar's Balsam	7/17/1900	Brighton Beach	122
1:38¾	Libertine	1891 h., Leonatus	10/24/1894	Harlem (Il.)	90
1:39	Arab	1886 g., *Dalnacardoch	6/11/1894	Morris Park	93
1:39¼	Chorister	1890 h., Falsetto	6/1/1893	Morris Park	112
1:39½	Racine	1887 h., Bishop	6/28/1890	Washington Park	107
1:39¾*	Ten Broeck	1872 h., *Phaeton	5/24/1877	Louisville	110
1:41¼	Kadi	1870 g., Lexington	9/2/1875	Hartford (Ct.)	90
1:41⅗	Searcher	1872 h., Enquirer	5/13/1875	Lexington (Ky.)	90
1:42½*	Grey Planet	1869 h., Planet	8/13/1874	Saratoga	110
1:42¾	Springbok	1870 h., *Australian	6/25/1874	Utica (N.Y.)	108
1:42¾	Alarm	1869 h., *Eclipse	7/17/1872	Saratoga	90
1:43½	Herzog	1866 h., Vandal	5/25/1869	Cincinnati	—

*Against time

1⅛ Miles

Time	Horse	YOB Sex, Sire	Date	Track	Weight
1:45	Simply Majestic	1984 h., Majestic Light	4/2/1988	Golden Gate Fields	114
1:45⅖	Secretariat	1970 h., Bold Ruler	9/15/1973	Belmont Park	124
1:46⅕	Canonero II	1968 h., *Pretendre	9/20/1972	Belmont Park	110
1:46⅕	*Figonero	1965 h., Idle Hour	9/1/1969	Del Mar	124
1:46⅖	Ole Bob Bowers	1963 h., Prince Blessed	10/12/1968	Bay Meadows Race Course	114
1:46⅖	Quicken Tree	1963 g., Royal Orbit	9/2/1968	Del Mar	120
1:46⅖	*Colorado King	1959 h., *Grand Rapids II	7/4/1964	Hollywood Park	119
1:46⅖	Bug Brush	1955 m., *Nasrullah	2/14/1959	Santa Anita Park	113
1:46⅘	Round Table	1954 h., *Princequillo	2/25/1958	Santa Anita Park	130
1:46⅘	Gen. Duke	1954 h., Bull Lea	3/30/1957	Gulfstream Park	122
1:46⅘	Swaps	1952 h., *Khaled	7/4/1956	Hollywood Park	130
1:46⅘	Alidon	1951 g., *Alibhai	7/4/1955	Hollywood Park	116
1:46⅘	*Noor	1945 h., *Nasrullah	6/17/1950	Golden Gate Fields	123
1:47⅗	Coaltown	1945 h., Bull Lea	2/14/1949	Hialeah Park	114
1:47⅗	*Shannon II	1941 h., Midstream	10/9/1948	Golden Gate Fields	124
1:47⅗	Indian Broom	1933 h., Brooms	4/11/1936	Tanforan	94
1:48⅕	Discovery	1931 h., Display	6/22/1935	Aqueduct	123
1:48⅖	Blessed Event	1930 g., Happy Argo	3/10/1934	Hialeah Park	111
1:48⅖	Hot Toddy	1926 g., Ed Crump	9/13/1929	Belmont Park	110
1:48⅗	Peanuts	1922 h., *Ambassador IV	9/18/1926	Aqueduct	114
1:48⅘	Chilhowee	1921 h., Ballot	10/14/1924	Latonia	115
1:49	Grey Lag	1918 h., *Star Shoot	7/7/1921	Aqueduct	123
1:49	*Goaler	1916 h., Duke Michael	6/10/1921	Belmont Park	94
1:49⅕	Man o' War	1917 h., Fair Play	7/10/1920	Aqueduct	126
1:49⅖	Boots	1911 g., *Hessian	7/7/1917	Aqueduct	127
1:49⅖	Borrow	1908 g., Hamburg	6/25/1917	Aqueduct	117
1:49⅗	Roamer	1911 g., Knight Errant	10/10/1914	Laurel Park	124
1:50	Vox Populi	1904 h., *Voter	12/19/1908	Santa Anita (old)	110
1:50⅗	Charles Edward	1904 h., *Golden Garter	7/10/1907	Brighton Beach	126
1:51	Bonnibert	1898 h., *Albert	7/30/1902	Brighton Beach	120
1:51⅕	Roehampton	1898 h., *Bathampton	7/26/1901	Brighton Beach	94
1:51⅕	Watercure	1897 g., *Watercress	6/18/1900	Brighton Beach	100
1:51½	Tristan	1885 h., *Glenelg	6/2/1891	Morris Park	114
1:53	Terra Cotta	1884 h., Harry o' Fallon	6/23/1888	Sheepshead Bay	124
1:53¼	Grover Cleveland	1883 h., Monday	10/12/1887	Los Angeles	118
1:53¼	Spalding	1882 g., *Billet	7/1/1886	Washington Park	97
1:53¼	Rosalie	1877 m., *Leamington	8/13/1881	Brighton Beach	80
1:54	Bob Woolley	1872 h., *Leamington	9/6/1875	Lexington	90
1:56	Fadladeen	1867 h., War Dance	8/19/1874	Saratoga	101
1:56	Picolo	1871 h., Concord	8/15/1874	Saratoga	83
1:56½	Fanny Ludlow	1865 m., *Eclipse	8/10/1869	Saratoga	105

All-Time Leading North American-Raced Earners

Horse, YOB Sex, Sire	Years Raced	Starts	Wins	Stakes Wins	Earnings
Cigar, 1990 h., by Palace Music	4	33	19	15	$9,999,815
Skip Away, 1993 h., by Skip Trial	4	38	18	16	9,616,360
Fantastic Light, 1996 h., by Rahy	4	25	12	10	8,486,957
Pleasantly Perfect, 1998 h., by Pleasant Colony	4	18	9	6	7,789,880
Smarty Jones, 2001 h., by Elusive Quality	2	9	8	7	7,613,155
Silver Charm, 1994 h., by Silver Buck	4	24	12	11	6,944,369
Captain Steve, 1997 h., by Fly So Free	3	25	9	8	6,828,356
Alysheba, 1984 h., by Alydar	3	26	11	10	6,679,242
John Henry, 1975 g., by Ole Bob Bowers	8	83	39	30	6,591,860
Tiznow, 1997 h., by Cee's Tizzy	2	15	8	7	6,427,830
Singspiel (Ire), 1992 h., by In the Wings (GB)	4	20	9	8	5,952,825
Falbrav (Ire), 1998 h., by Fairy King	4	26	13	8	5,825,517
Medaglia d'Oro, 1999 h., by El Prado (Ire)	4	17	8	7	5,754,720
Best Pal, 1988 g., by *Habitony	7	47	18	17	5,668,245
Taiki Blizzard, 1991 h., by Seattle Slew	4	23	6	3	5,523,549
Roses in May, 2000 h., by Devil His Due	3	13	8	4	5,490,187
High Chaparral (Ire), 1999 h., by Sadler's Wells	3	13	10	9	5,331,231
Street Cry (Ire), 1998 h., by Machiavellian	3	12	5	3	5,150,837
Jim and Tonic (Fr), 1994 g., by Double Bed (Fr)	7	39	13	9	4,975,807
Sunday Silence, 1986 h., by Halo	3	14	9	7	4,968,554
Easy Goer, 1986 h., by Alydar	3	20	14	12	4,873,770
Daylami (Ire), 1994 h., by Doyoun	4	21	11	8	4,614,762
Behrens, 1994 h., by Pleasant Colony	4	27	9	7	4,563,500
Unbridled, 1987 h., by Fappiano	3	24	8	5	4,489,475
Saint Liam, 2000 h., by Saint Ballado	3	20	9	5	4,456,995
Awesome Again, 1994 h., by Deputy Minister	2	12	9	7	4,374,590
Moon Ballad (Ire), 1999 h., by Singspiel (Ire)	3	14	5	4	4,364,791
Perfect Drift, 1999 g., by Dynaformer	5	35	11	8	4,290,190
Spend a Buck, 1982 h., by Buckaroo	2	15	10	7	4,220,689
Sulamani (Ire), 1999 h., by Hernando (Fr)	3	17	9	8	5,252,368
Pilsudski (Ire), 1992 h., by Polish Precedent	4	22	10	8	4,080,297
Azeri, 1998 m., by Jade Hunter	4	24	17	14	4,079,820
Creme Fraiche, 1982 g., by Rich Cream	6	64	17	14	4,024,727
Seeking the Pearl, 1994 m., by Seeking the Gold	4	21	8	7	4,021,716
Point Given, 1998 h., by Thunder Gulch	2	13	9	8	3,968,500
Cat Thief, 1996 h., by Storm Cat	3	30	4	3	3,951,012
Ashado, 2001 m., by Saint Ballado	3	21	12	11	3,931,440
Devil His Due, 1989 h., by Devil's Bag	4	41	11	9	3,920,405
Sandpit (Brz), 1989 h., by Baynoun (Ire)	7	40	14	12	3,812,597
Swain (Ire), 1992 h., by Nashwan	4	22	10	7	3,797,566
Ferdinand, 1983 h., by Nijinsky II	4	29	8	7	3,777,978
Almutawakel (GB), 1995 h., by Machiavellian	4	19	4	2	3,643,021
Harlan's Holiday, 1999 h., by Harlan	3	22	9	8	3,632,664
Gentlemen (Arg), 1992 h., by Robin des Bois	5	24	13	11	3,608,558
Spain, 1997 m., by Thunder Gulch	4	35	9	7	3,540,542
Slew o' Gold, 1980 h., by Seattle Slew	3	21	12	8	3,533,534
Victory Gallop, 1995 h., by Cryptoclearance	3	17	9	7	3,505,895
War Emblem, 1999 h., by Our Emblem	2	13	7	4	3,491,000
Precisionist, 1981 h., by Crozier	5	46	20	17	3,485,398
Strike the Gold, 1988 h., by Alydar	4	31	6	4	3,457,026
Ghostzapper, 2000 h., by Awesome Again	4	11	9	6	3,446,120
Lando (Ger), 1990 h., by Acatenango	4	24	10	8	3,438,727
Paradise Creek, 1989 h., by Irish River (Fr)	4	25	14	10	3,401,416
Snow Chief, 1983 h., by Reflected Glory	3	24	13	12	3,383,210
Chief Bearhart, 1993 h., by Chief's Crown	4	26	12	9	3,381,557
Cryptoclearance, 1984 h., by Fappiano	4	44	12	9	3,376,327
Black Tie Affair (Ire), 1986 h., by Miswaki	4	45	18	13	3,370,694
Agnes World, 1995 h., by Danzig	4	20	8	5	3,365,680
Sky Classic, 1987 h., by Nijinsky II	4	29	15	13	3,320,398
Paseana (Arg), 1987 m., by Ahmad	6	36	19	17	3,317,427
Bet Twice, 1984 h., by Sportin' Life	3	26	10	7	3,308,599
Steinlen (GB), 1983 h., by Habitat	5	45	20	16	3,297,169
Serena's Song, 1992 m., by Rahy	3	38	18	17	3,283,388
Real Quiet, 1995 h., by Quiet American	3	20	6	5	3,271,802
Awad, 1990 h., by Caveat	7	70	14	11	3,270,131
Congaree, 1998 h., by Arazi	5	25	12	10	3,267,490
Dance Smartly, 1988 m., by Danzig	3	17	12	10	3,263,835
Sakhee, 1997 h., by Bahri	4	14	8	5	3,253,253
Lemon Drop Kid, 1996 h., by Kingmambo	3	24	10	7	3,245,370
Funny Cide, 2000 g., by Distorted Humor	4	24	8	6	3,220,319
Caller One, 1997 g., by Phone Trick	6	22	10	8	3,200,000
Volponi, 1998 h., by Cryptoclearance	4	31	7	4	3,187,232
Bertrando, 1989 h., by Skywalker	5	24	9	8	3,185,610
Free House, 1994 h., by Smokester	4	22	9	8	3,178,971
Montjeu (Ire), 1996 h., by Sadler's Wells	3	16	11	10	3,178,177
Ouija Board (GB), 2001 m., by Cape Cross (Ire)	3	13	7	6	3,163,126
Siphon (Brz), 1991 h., by Itajara	5	25	12	9	3,136,428
Gulch, 1984 h., by Mr. Prospector	3	32	13	11	3,095,521
Silverbulletday, 1996 m., by Silver Deputy	3	23	15	14	3,093,207
Peace Rules, 2000 h., by Jules	3	19	9	8	3,084,278
Concern, 1991 h., by Broad Brush	3	30	7	4	3,079,350
Giant's Causeway, 1997 h., by Storm Cat	2	13	9	8	3,078,989
Lady's Secret, 1982 m., by Secretariat	4	45	25	22	3,021,325
Albert the Great, 1997 h., by Go for Gin	2	22	8	5	3,012,490
Alphabet Soup, 1991 h., by Cozzene	4	24	10	7	2,990,270
A.P. Indy, 1989 r., by Seattle Slew	2	11	8	6	2,979,815
Escena, 1993 m., by Strawberry Road (Aus)	4	29	11	7	2,962,639
Theatrical (Ire), 1982 h., by Nureyev	4	22	10	8	2,940,036
Hansel, 1988 h., by Woodman	2	14	7	6	2,936,586
Sea Hero, 1990 h., by Polish Navy	3	24	6	3	2,929,869
Great Communicator, 1983 g., by Key to the Kingdom	6	56	14	9	2,922,615
Thunder Gulch, 1992 h., by Gulch	2	16	9	8	2,915,086
Farma Way, 1987 h., by Marfa	3	23	8	6	2,897,175
Milwaukee Brew, 1997 h., by Wild Again	4	24	8	5	2,879,612
General Challenge, 1996 g., by General Meeting	4	21	9	8	2,877,178
Dance in the Mood (Jpn), 2001 m., by Sunday Silence	3	17	4	2	3,339,410
With Approval, 1986 h., by Caro (Ire)	3	23	13	9	2,863,540
Bayakoa (Arg), 1984 m., by Consultant's Bid	6	39	21	17	2,861,701
Rough Habit (NZ), 1986 g., by Roughcast	7	66	28	21	2,861,579
Marquetry, 1987 h., by Conquistador Cielo	5	36	10	7	2,857,886
Budroyale, 1993 g., by Cee's Tizzy	7	52	17	7	2,840,810
Kotashaan (Fr), 1988 h., by Darshaan	4	22	10	8	2,812,114
Banshee Breeze, 1995 m., by Unbridled	3	18	10	8	2,784,798
Spectacular Bid, 1976 h., by Bold Bidder	3	30	26	23	2,781,608
Afleet Alex, 2002 h., by Northern Afleet	2	12	8	6	2,765,800
Symboli Rudolf (Jpn), 1981 h., by Partholon	4	16	13	10	2,764,980
Buck's Boy, 1993 g., by Bucksplasher	5	30	16	9	2,750,148
Beautiful Pleasure, 1995 m., by Maudlin	5	25	10	7	2,734,078
Forty Niner, 1985 h., by Mr. Prospector	2	19	11	9	2,726,000
Pleasant Tap, 1987 h., by Pleasant Colony	4	32	9	6	2,721,169
Lido Palace (Chi), 1997 h., by Rich Man's Gold	4	23	11	8	2,705,865
Izvestia, 1987 h., by Icecapade	3	21	11	10	2,702,527
Manila, 1983 h., by Lyphard	3	18	12	10	2,692,799
With Anticipation, 1995 g., by Relaunch	8	48	15	8	2,660,543
Broad Brush, 1983 h., by Ack Ack	3	27	14	12	2,656,793
Trinycarol (Ven), 1979 m., by Velvet Cap	4	29	18	0	2,644,392
Dynever, 2000 h., by Dynaformer	3	19	4	3	2,640,444
Better Talk Now, 1999 g., by Talkin Man	5	32	11	7	2,622,077
Sarafan, 1997 g., by Lear Fan	7	49	10	6	2,617,621
Fraise, 1988 h., by Strawberry Road (Aus)	4	34	10	6	2,613,105
Flawlessly, 1988 m., by Affirmed	5	28	16	15	2,572,536
Dramatic Gold, 1991 g., by Slew o' Gold	6	39	9	4	2,567,630
Wando, 2000 h., by Langfuhr	4	23	11	8	2,563,038
Sir Bear, 1993 g., by Sir Leon	8	71	19	11	2,538,422
Let's Elope (NZ), 1987 m., by Nassipour	5	26	11	8	2,528,902
Lure, 1989 h., by Danzig	4	25	14	10	2,515,289
Cesario (Jpn), 2002 f., by Special Week	2	6	5	3	2,578,568
Gate Dancer, 1981 h., by Sovereign Dancer	4	28	7	4	2,501,705
Evening Attire, 1998 g., by Black Tie Affair (Ire)	6	46	12	8	2,488,796
Holy Bull, 1991 h., by Great Above	3	16	13	11	2,481,760
Take Charge Lady, 1999 m., by Dehere	3	22	11	9	2,480,377
Mecke, 1992 h., by Maudlin	4	40	12	9	2,470,550
Golden Pheasant, 1986 h., by Caro (Ire)	4	22	7	5	2,453,958
Paolini (Ger), 1997 h., by Lando (Ger)	6	28	5	4	3,253,469
Marlin, 1993 h., by Sword Dance (Ire)	3	26	9	6	2,448,880
Sightseek, 1999 m., by Distant View	3	20	12	10	2,445,216
Flower Alley, 2002 c., by Distorted Humor	2	10	4	3	2,437,660
Affirmed, 1975 h., by Exclusive Native	3	29	22	19	2,393,818
Xtra Heat, 1998 m., by Dixieland Heat	4	35	26	25	2,389,635
Malek (Chi), 1993 h., by Mocito Guapo	6	23	10	7	2,382,623
Heritage of Gold, 1995 m., by Gold Legend	4	28	16	11	2,381,762
Balto Star, 1998 g., by Glitterman	5	38	12	7	2,363,780
Criminal Type, 1985 h., by Alydar	4	24	10	6	2,351,274
Tabasco Cat, 1991 h., by Storm Cat	2	18	8	6	2,347,671

Horse, YOB Sex, Sire	Years Raced	Starts	Wins	Stakes Wins	Earnings
Quiet Resolve, 1995 g., by Affirmed	5	31	10	5	2,346,768
Bien Bien, 1989 h., by Manila	3	26	9	8	2,331,875
Fly So Free, 1988 h., by Time for a Change	4	33	12	8	2,330,954
Silvano (Ger), 1996 h., by Lomitas (GB)	4	18	7	5	2,321,024
Triptych, 1982 m., by Riverman	5	41	14	12	2,318,946
Star of Cozzene, 1988 h., by Cozzene	5	38	14	9	2,308,923
Seeking the Gold, 1985 h., by Mr. Prospector	3	15	8	4	2,307,000
Soul of the Matter, 1991 h., by Private Terms	4	16	7	4	2,302,818
Kona Gold, 1994 g., by Java Gold	6	30	14	11	2,293,384
Skimming, 1996 h., by Nureyev	4	20	8	5	2,286,601
Affirmed Success, 1994 g., by Affirmed	7	42	17	10	2,285,315
Mineshaft, 1999 h., by A.P. Indy	2	18	10	7	2,283,402
Yankee Affair, 1982 h., by Northern Fling	5	55	22	15	2,282,156
Polish Summer (GB), 1997 h., by Polish Precedent	6	27	6	4	2,277,871
Prized, 1986 h., by Kris S.	4	17	9	6	2,262,555
Megahertz (GB), 1999 m., by Pivotal	5	34	14	13	2,261,594
Festin (Arg), 1986 h., by Mat-Boy (Arg)	4	24	9	4	2,256,295
Pine Bluff, 1989 h., by Danzig	2	13	6	5	2,255,884
Life's Magic, 1981 m., by Cox's Ridge	3	32	8	7	2,255,218
Galileo (Ire), 1998 h., by Sadler's Wells	2	8	6	5	2,245,373
Skywalker, 1982 h., by Relaunch	4	20	8	5	2,226,750
Waquoit, 1983 h., by Relaunch	4	30	19	13	2,225,360
Wild Again, 1980 h., by Icecapade	4	28	8	4	2,204,829
Perfect Sting, 1996 m., by Red Ransom	4	21	14	11	2,202,042
Proud Truth, 1982 h., by Graustark	3	21	10	6	2,198,895
Golden Missile, 1995 h., by A.P. Indy	4	25	7	5	2,194,510
Safely Kept, 1986 m., by Horatius	4	31	24	22	2,194,206
Chief's Crown, 1982 h., by Danzig	2	21	12	10	2,191,168
Riskaverse, 1999 m., by Dynaformer	5	32	9	6	2,182,429
Twilight Agenda, 1986 h., by Devil's Bag	5	32	13	9	2,174,529
Nostalgia's Star, 1982 h., by Nostalgia	5	59	9	7	2,154,827
Kalanisi (Ire), 1996 h., by Doyoun	3	11	6	4	2,148,836
Turkoman, 1982 h., by Alydar	3	22	8	5	2,146,924
Caitano (GB), 1994 h., by Niniski	7	44	9	7	2,137,459
All Along (Fr), 1979 m., by Targowice	4	21	9	7	2,125,828
Daliapour (Ire), 1996 h., by Sadler's Wells	5	26	7	5	2,123,763
Val's Prince, 1992 g., by Eternal Prince	7	52	13	4	2,118,785
Soaring Free, 1999 g., by Smart Strike	4	26	15	10	2,110,371
You, 1999 m., by You and I	3	23	9	8	2,101,353
Say Florida Sandy, 1994 h., by Personal Flag	8	98	33	19	2,085,408
Lost Code, 1984 h., by Codex	3	27	15	12	2,085,396
Sunshine Forever, 1985 h., by Roberto	3	23	8	5	2,084,800
Hernando (Fr), 1990 h., by Niniski	3	20	7	6	2,081,978
Majesty's Prince, 1979 h., by His Majesty	4	43	12	9	2,077,796
Kitten's Joy, 2001 h., by El Prado (Ire)	3	14	9	7	2,075,791
Miesque, 1984 m., by Nureyev	3	16	12	11	2,070,163
Louis Quatorze, 1993 h., by Sovereign Dancer	3	18	7	4	2,054,434
Borrego, 2001 h., by El Prado (Ire)	3	20	5	2	2,052,090
Adoration, 1999 m., by Honor Grades	3	20	8	7	2,051,160
Coronado's Quest, 1995 h., by Forty Niner	2	17	10	8	2,046,190
Charismatic, 1996 h., by Summer Squall	2	17	5	3	2,038,064
Sharp Cat, 1994 m., by Storm Cat	3	22	15	14	2,032,575

Progression of Leading Earner

North America

Because of the paucity and unreliability of published records of Thoroughbred racing before the Civil War, the earliest leading North American earner whose record can be reliably verified is the great American Eclipse, who became an American popular hero in the 1820s. More than 20 years later, the baton was handed to the giant filly Peytona, who collected the largest purse on the continent to that date, $41,000, for her victory in the Peyton Stakes at Nashville, Tennessee, in 1843. Her owner promptly changed her name from the unwieldy Glumdalclitch and named her after her most famous win.

The pace of change on the leading earner list has quickened since antebellum days. Perhaps the most exciting exchange occurred in 1947, when Racing Hall of Fame members Assault, Armed, and Stymie batted Whirlaway's previous record around like a badminton shuttlecock. Stymie's durability finally outlasted the other two, and he ended his career with earnings of $918,485. Citation, who became the leading earner in 1950, moved the mark above $1-million the following year.

The great two-year-old and epochal sire Domino held the torch for the longest period, 27 years, from 1893 until supplanted by Man o' War in 1920. Assault and Stymie each held the title for the shortest period, seven days, during their duel in 1947. The only stallion to sire two leading North American money earners is Bull Lea. Peytona and Miss Woodford are the only females to hold the title.

International racing has always complicated the issue. Parole's record earnings include about $20,000 earned on his sojourn in England in 1879-'80. Cigar's earnings similarly include the $2.4-million earned in his Dubai World Cup victory.

Chronology of Leading American Money Winners

1823—American Eclipse, 1814 ch. h., Duroc—Millers Damsel, by Messenger. 8-8-0-0, **$56,700.**

1845—Peytona, 1839 ch. f., *Glencoe—Giantess, by *Leviathan. 8-6-1-0, **$62,400.**

1861—Planet, 1855 ch. h., Revenue—Nina, by Boston. 31-27-4-0, **$69,700.**

1881—Hindoo, 1878 b. h., Virgil—Florence, by Lexington. 35-30-3-2, **$71,875.**

1881—Parole, 1873 br. h., *Leamington—Maiden, by Lexington. 129-59-22-16, **$82,816.**

1885—Miss Woodford, 1880 br. f., *Billet—Fancy Jane, by Neil Robinson. 48-37-7-2, **$118,270.**

1889—Hanover, 1884 ch. h., Hindoo—Bourbon Belle, by *Bonnie Scotland. 50-32-14-2, **$118,887.**

1892—Kingston, 1884 dk. b. or br. h., Spendthrift—*Kapanga, by Victorious. 138-89-33-12, **$138,917.**

1893—Domino, 1891 br. h., Himyar—Mannie Gray, by Enquirer. 25-19-3-1, **$193,550.**

1920—Man o' War, 1917 ch. h., Fair Play—Mahubah, by *Rock Sand. 21-20-1-0, **$249,465.**

1923—Zev, 1920 dk. b. or br. h., The Finn—Miss Kearney, by *Planudes. 43-23-8-5, **$313,639.**

1930—Gallant Fox, 1927 b. h., *Sir Gallahad III—Marguerite, by Celt. 17-11-3-2, **$328,165.**

1931—Sun Beau, 1925 b. h., *Sun Briar—Beautiful Lady, by Fair Play. 74-33-12-10, **$376,744.**

1940—Seabiscuit, 1933 b. h., Hard Tack—Swing On, by Whisk Broom II. 89-33-15-13, **$437,730.**

1942—Whirlaway, 1938 ch. h., *Blenheim II—Dustwhirl, by Sweep. 60-32-15-9, **$561,161.**

1947 (June 21)—Assault, 1943 ch. h., Bold Venture—Igual, by Equipoise. 42-18-6-7, **$576,670.**

1947 (July 5)—Stymie, 1941 ch. h., Equestrian—Stop Watch, by On Watch. 131-35-33-28, **$595,510.**

1947 (July 12)—Assault, $613,370 (career $675,470).

1947 (July 19)—Stymie, $678,510.

1947 (October 9)—Armed, 1941 dk. b. or br. g., Bull Lea—Armful, by Chance Shot. 81-41-20-10, **$761,500 (career $817,475).**

1947 (October 25)—Stymie $816,060 (career $918,485).

1950—Citation, 1945 b. h., Bull Lea—*Hydroplane II, by Hyperion. 45-32-10-2, **$1,085,760.**

1956—Nashua, 1952 b. h., *Nasrullah—Segula, by Johnstown. 30-22-4-1, **$1,288,565.**

1958—Round Table, 1954 b. h., *Princequillo—*Knight's Daughter, by Sir Cosmo. 66-43-8-5, **$1,749,869.**

1965—Kelso, 1957 dk. b. or br. g., Your Host—Maid of Flight, by Count Fleet. 63-39-12-2, **$1,977,896.**

1979—Affirmed, 1975 ch. h., Exclusive Native—Won't Tell You, by Crafty Admiral. 29-22-5-1, **$2,393,818.**

1980—Spectacular Bid, 1976 gr. h., Bold Bidder—Spectacular, by Promised Land. 30-26-2-1, **$2,781,608.**

1981—John Henry, 1975 b. g., Ole Bob Bowers—Once Double, by Double Jay. 83-39-15-9, **$6,591,860.**

1988—Alysheba, 1984 b. h., Alydar—Bel Sheba, by Lt. Stevens. 26-11-8-2, **$6,679,242.**

1996—Cigar, 1990 b. h., Palace Music—Solar Slew, by Seattle Slew. 33-19-4-5, **$9,999,815.**

International

In the 20th century, America became so accustomed to being the home of the world's leading money-winning racehorse that it did not even notice when Japanese-bred and -trained Oguri Cap soared past American leader Alysheba in 1990.

Since organized Thoroughbred racing originated in England in the early 18th century, it is obvious that the earliest leading earners must have resided there as well. Determining the first world's richest Thoroughbred is all but impossible because early records are nonexistent or unclear on purse awards.

English record-keepers recorded that in 1889 Donovan broke the record previously held by the French-bred Gladiateur. In turn, Gladiateur had broken the previous record of England's The Flying Dutchman.

The earliest horse who can reliably be accorded the palm of world's leading earner is the undefeated Highflyer, who was foaled in 1774. Based on the exchange rate of $5 to £1 that prevailed in the 19th century (America was still a British colony in 1774), Highflyer earned the equivalent of $38,395 by winning all 12 of his races.

By that standard, American Eclipse surpassed Highflyer, but 1830 Epsom Derby winner *Priam earned more money by the same exchange rate. The title remained in Europe until 1923, when Zev's victory over *Papyrus propelled him past Isinglass, who remained England's leading earner for more than 60 years.

Zev began a 67-year reign for American horses at the same time the American economy began to dominate the world. Only the huge increases in Japanese purses beginning in the 1980s changed that equation. As shown by the accompanying list of the world's current leading earners, the earnings of T.M.Opera O far exceed any American horse.

Chronology of Leading International Money Winners

1780—Highflyer, 1774 b. h., Herod—Rachel, by Blank. 12-12-0-0, **$38,395.**

1823—American Eclipse, 1814 ch. h., Duroc—Miller's Damsel, by *Messenger. 8-8-0-0, **$56,700.**

1830—*Priam, 1827 br. h., Emilius—Cressida, by Whiskey. 16-14-1-1, **$65,100.**

1850—The Flying Dutchman, 1846 b. h., Bay Middleton—Barbelle, by Sandbeck. 15-14-1-0, **$93,900.**

1865—Gladiateur, 1862 b. h., Monarque—Miss Gladiator, by Gladiator. 19-16-0-1, **$236,537.**

1889—Donovan, 1886 b. h., Galopin—Mowerina, by The Scottish Chief. 21-18-2-1, **$275,775.**

1895—Isinglass, 1890 b. h., Isonomy—Dead Lock, by Wenlock. 12-11-1-0, **$287,275.**

1923—Zev, 1920 dk. b. or br. h., The Finn—Miss Kearney, by *Planudes. 43-23-8-5, **$313,639.**

1930—Gallant Fox, 1927 b. h., *Sir Gallahad III—Marguerite, by Celt. 17-11-3-2, **$328,165.**

1931—Sun Beau, 1925 b. h., *Sun Briar—Beautiful Lady, by Fair Play. 74-33-12-10, **$376,744.**

1940—Seabiscuit, 1933 b. h., Hard Tack—Swing On, by Whisk Broom II. 89-33-15-13, **$437,730.**

1942—Whirlaway, 1938 ch. h., *Blenheim II—Dustwhirl, by Sweep. 60-32-15-9, **$561,161.**

1947 (June 21)—Assault, 1943 ch. h., Bold Venture—Igual, by Equipoise. 42-18-6-7, **$576,670.**

1947 (July 5)—Stymie, 1941 ch. h., Equestrian—Stop Watch, by On Watch. 131-35-33-28, **$595,510.**

1947 (July 12)—Assault, $613,370 (career $675,470).

1947 (July 19)—Stymie, $678,510.

1947 (October 9)—Armed, 1941 dk. b. or br. g., Bull Lea—Armful, by Chance Shot. 81-41-20-10, **$761,500 (career $817,475).**

1947 (October 25)—Stymie $816,060 (career $918,485).

1950—Citation, 1945 b. h., Bull Lea—*Hydroplane II, by Hyperion. 45-32-10-2, **$1,085,760.**

1956—Nashua, 1952 b. h., *Nasrullah—Segula, by Johnstown. 30-22-4-1, **$1,288,565.**

1958—Round Table, 1954 b. h., *Princequillo—*Knight's Daughter, by Sir Cosmo. 66-43-8-5, **$1,749,869.**

1965—Kelso, 1957 dk. b. or br. g., Your Host—Maid of Flight, by Count Fleet. 63-39-12-2, **$1,977,896.**

1979—Affirmed, 1975 ch. h., Exclusive Native—Won't Tell You, by Crafty Admiral. 29-22-5-1, **$2,393,818.**

1980—Spectacular Bid, 1976 gr. h., Bold Bidder—Spectacular, by Promised Land. 30-26-2-1, **$2,781,608.**

1981—John Henry, 1975 b. g., Ole Bob Bowers—Once Double, by Double Jay. 83-39-15-9, **$6,591,860.**
1988—Alysheba, 1984 b. h., Alydar—Bel Sheba, by Lt. Stevens. 26-11-8-2, **$6,679,242.**
1990—Oguri Cap, 1985 gr. h., Dancing Cap—White Narubi, by *Silver Shark. 32-22-6-1, **$6,919,201.**
1993—Mejiro McQueen, 1987 gr. h., Mejiro Titan—Mejiro Aurola, by Remand. 14-9-3-0, **$7,618,803.**
1995—Narita Brian, 1991 dk b. or br. h., Brian's Time—Pacificus, by Northern Dancer. 21-12-3-1, **$9,296,552.**
1996—Cigar, 1990 b. h., Palace Music—Solar Slew, by Seattle Slew. 33-19-4-5, **$9,999,815.**
2000—T.M.Opera O, 1996 ch. h., Opera House (GB)—Once Wed, by Blushing Groom (Fr). 26-14-6-3, **$16,200,337.**

World's Leading Earners

Through February 25, 2006

Rank	Horse	YOB, Color, Sex, Pedigree	Country	Earnings (in Dollars)
1.	T.M.Opera O	1996 ch. h., Opera House (GB)—Once Wed, by Blushing Groom (Fr)	Jpn	$16,200,337
2.	Makybe Diva	1999 b. m., Desert King—Tugela, by Riverman	Aus	10,767,186
3.	Zenno Rob Roy	2000 dk. b. or br. h., Sunday Silence—Roamin Rachel, by Mining	Jpn	10,483,242
4.	Cigar	1990 b. h., Palace Music—Solar Slew, by Seattle Slew	USA	9,999,815
5.	Skip Away	1993 gr. h., Skip Trial—Ingot Way, by Diplomat Way	USA	9,616,360
6.	Tap Dance City	1997 b. h., Pleasant Tap—All Dance, by Northern Dancer	Jpn	9,586,479
7.	Special Week	1995 dk. b. or br. h., Sunday Silence—Campaign Girl, by Maruzensky	Jpn	9,346,435
8.	Narita Brian	1991 dk. b. or br. h., Brian's Time—Pacificus, by Northern Dancer	Jpn	9,296,552
9.	Stay Gold	1994 dk. b. or br. h., Sunday Silence—Golden Sash, by Dictus		8,682,142
10.	Fantastic Light	1996 b. h., Rahy—Jood, by Nijinsky II	GB	8,486,957
11.	Symboli Kris S	1999 dk. b. or br. h., Kris S.—Tee Kay, by Gold Meridian	Jpn	8,401,282
12.	Narita Top Road	1996 ch. h., Soccer Boy—Floral Magic, by Affirmed	Jpn	8,389,594
13.	Hokuto Vega	1990 b. m., Nagurski—Takeno Falcon, by Philip of Spain	Jpn	8,300,301
14.	Agnes Digital	1997 ch. h., Crafty Prospector—Chancey Squaw, by Chief's Crown	Jpn	8,095,160
15.	Meisho Doto	1996 b. h., Bigstone (Ire)—Princess Reema, by Affirmed	Jpn	8,088,202
16.	Time Paradox	1998 ch. h., Brian's Time—Jolie Zaza, by Alzao	Jpn	7,821,520
17.	Pleasantly Perfect	1998 b. h., Pleasant Colony—Regal State, by Affirmed	USA	7,789,880
18.	Admire Don	1999 b. h., Timber Country—Vega, by Tony Bin	Jpn	7,712,841
19.	Mejiro Mc Queen	1987 gr. h., Mejiro Titan—Mejiro Aurola, by Remand	Jpn	7,618,803
20.	Smarty Jones	2001 ch. h., Elusive Quality—I'll Get Along, by Smile	USA	7,613,155
21.	Biwa Hayahide	1990 gr. h., Sharrood—Pacificus, by Northern Dancer	Jpn	7,555,480
22.	Mayano Top Gun	1992 ch. h., Brian's Time—Alp Me Please, by Blushing Groom (Fr)	Jpn	7,463,557
23.	Eishin Preston	1997 dk. b. or br. h., Green Dancer—Warranty Applied, by Monteverdi (Ire)	Jpn	7,408,086
24.	Hishi Amazon	1991 dk. b. or br. m., Theatrical (Ire)—Katies (Ire), by Nonoalco	Jpn	6,981,102
25.	Silver Charm	1994 gr. h., Silver Buck—Bonnie's Poker, by Poker	USA	6,944,369
26.	Oguri Cap	1985 gr. h., Dancing Cap—White Narubi, by *Silver Shark	Jpn	6,940,077
27.	Mejiro Bright	1994 b. h., Mejiro Ryan—Reru du Temps, by Maruzensky	Jpn	6,848,423
28.	Air Groove	1993 b. m., Tony Bin—Dyna Carle, by Northern Taste	Jpn	6,832,242
29.	Captain Steve	1997 ch. h., Fly So Free—Sparkling Delite, by Vice Regent	USA	6,828,356
30.	Alysheba	1984 b. h., Alydar—Bel Sheba, by Lt. Stevens	USA	6,679,242
31.	Sunline	1995 b. m., Desert Sun (GB)—Songline, by Western Symphony	Aus	6,625,105
32.	John Henry	1975 b. g., Ole Bob Bowers—Once Double, by Double Jay	USA	6,591,860
33.	Tiznow	1997 b. h., Cee's Tizzy—Cee's Song, by Seattle Song	USA	6,427,830
34.	Wing Arrow	1995 b. h., Assatis—Sanyo Arrow, by Mr C B	Jpn	6,273,733
35.	Mejiro Dober	1994 b. m., Mejiro Ryan—Mejiro Beauty, by Partholon	Jpn	6,240,681
36.	Deep Impact	2002 b. c., Sunday Silence—Wind in Her Hair (Ire), by Alzao	Jpn	6,191,041
37.	Rice Shower	1989 dk. b. or br. h., Real Shadai—Lilac Point, by Maruzensky	Jpn	6,070,429
38.	Grass Wonder	1995 ch. h., Silver Hawk—Ameriflora, by Danzig	Jpn	5,987,405
39.	Dance Partner (Jpn)	1992 b. m., Sunday Silence—Dancing Key, by Nijinsky II	Jpn	5,973,652
40.	Singspiel (Ire)	1992 b. h., In the Wings (GB)—Glorious Song, by Halo	GB	5,952,825
41.	Fast Friend	1994 ch. m., Ines Fujin—The Last Word, by Northern Taste	Jpn	5,896,693
42.	Silent Witness	1999 b. g., El Moxie—Jade Tiara, by Bureaucracy	HK	5,885,654
43.	Nobo True	1996 b. h., Broad Brush—Nastique, by Naskra	Jpn	5,828,240
44.	Falbrav (Ire)	1998 b. h., Fairy King—Gift of the Night, by Slewpy	GB	5,825,517
45.	Jungle Pocket	1998 b. h., Tony Bin—Dance Charmer, by Nureyev	Jpn	5,788,198
46.	Medaglia d'Oro	1999 dk. b. or br. h., El Prado (Ire)—Cappucino Bay, by Bailjumper	USA	5,754,720
47.	Sakura Laurel	1991 b. h., Rainbow Quest—Lola Lola, by Saint Cyrien	Jpn	5,751,390
48.	Black Hawk (GB)	1994 b. h., Nureyev—Silver Lane, by Silver Hawk	Jpn	5,750,386
49.	Best Pal	1988 b. g., *Habitony—Ubetshedid, by King Pellinore	USA	5,668,245
50.	Kyoto City	1991 b. h., Soccer Boy—Mountain Queen, by Nizon	Jpn	5,622,437

Leading North American Earners by Year

North American Racing Only

Year	Horse, YOB Sex, Pedigree	Earnings
2005	Saint Liam, 2000 h., Saint Ballado—Quiet Dance, by Quiet American	$3,696,960
2004	Smarty Jones, 2001 c., Elusive Quality—I'll Get Along, by Smile	7,563,535
2003	Pleasantly Perfect, 1998 h., Pleasant Colony—Regal State, by Affirmed	2,470,000
2002	War Emblem, 1999 c., Our Emblem—Sweetest Lady, by Lord At War (Arg)	3,455,000
2001	Point Given, 1998 c., Thunder Gulch—Turko's Turn, by Turkoman	3,350,000
2000	Tiznow, 1997 c., Cee's Tizzy—Cee's Song, by Seattle Song	3,445,950
1999	Cat Thief, 1996 c., Storm Cat—Train Robbery, by Alydar	3,020,500
1998	Awesome Again, 1994 c., Deputy Minister—Primal Force, by Blushing Groom (Fr)	3,845,990
1997	Skip Away, 1993 c., Skip Trial—Ingot Way, by Diplomat Way	4,089,000
1996	Skip Away, 1993 c., Skip Trial—Ingot Way, by Diplomat Way	2,699,280
1995	Cigar, 1990 h., Palace Music—Solar Slew, by Seattle Slew	4,819,800
1994	Concern, 1991 c., Broad Brush—Fara's Team, by Tunerup	2,541,670
1993	Sea Hero, 1990 c., Polish Navy—Glowing Tribute, by Graustark	2,484,190
1992	A.P. Indy, 1989 c., Seattle Slew—Weekend Surprise, by Secretariat	2,622,560
1991	Dance Smartly, 1988 f., Danzig—Classy 'n Smart, by Smarten	2,876,821
1990	Unbridled, 1987 c., Fappiano—Gana Facil, by *Le Fabuleux	3,718,149
1989	Sunday Silence, 1986 c., Halo—Wishing Well, by Understanding	4,578,454
1988	Alysheba, 1984 c., Alydar—Bel Sheba, by Lt. Stevens	3,808,600
1987	Alysheba, 1984 c., Alydar—Bel Sheba, by Lt. Stevens	2,511,156
1986	Snow Chief, 1983 c., Reflected Glory—Miss Snowflake, by *Snow Sporting	1,875,200
1985	Spend a Buck, 1982 c., Buckaroo—Belle de Jour, by Speak John	3,552,704
1984	Slew o' Gold, 1980 c., Seattle Slew—Alluvial, by Buckpasser	2,627,944
1983	Sunny's Halo, 1980 c., Halo—Mostly Sunny, by Sunny	1,011,962
1982	Perrault (GB), 1977 h., Djakao—Innocent Air, by *Court Martial	1,197,400
1981	John Henry, 1975 g., Ole Bob Bowers—Once Double, by Double Jay	1,798,030
1980	Temperence Hill, 1977 c., Stop the Music—Sister Shannon, by Etonian	1,130,452
1979	Spectacular Bid, 1976 c., Bold Bidder—Spectacular, by Promised Land	1,279,334
1978	Affirmed, 1975 c., Exclusive Native—Won't Tell You, by Crafty Admiral	901,541
1977	Seattle Slew, 1974 c., Bold Reasoning—My Charmer, by Poker	641,370
1976	Forego, 1970 g., *Forli—Lady Golconda, by Hasty Road	491,701
1975	Foolish Pleasure, 1972 c., What a Pleasure—Fool-Me-Not, by Tom Fool	716,278
1974	Chris Evert, 1971 f., Swoon's Son—Miss Carmie, by T. V. Lark	551,063
1973	Secretariat, 1970 c., Bold Ruler—Somethingroyal, by *Princequillo	860,404
1972	Droll Role, 1968 c., Tom Rolfe—*Pradella, by Preciptic	471,633
1971	Riva Ridge, 1969 c., First Landing—Iberia, by *Heliopolis	503,263
1970	Personality, 1967 c., Hail to Reason—Affectionately, by Swaps	444,049
1969	Arts and Letters, 1966 c., *Ribot—All Beautiful, by Battlefield	555,604
1968	Forward Pass, 1965 c., On-and-On—Princess Turia, by *Heliopolis	546,674
1967	Damascus, 1964 c., Sword Dancer—Kerala, by *My Babu	817,941
1966	Buckpasser, 1963 c., Tom Fool—Busanda, by War Admiral	669,078
1965	Buckpasser, 1963 c., Tom Fool—Busanda, by War Admiral	568,096
1964	Gun Bow, 1960 c., Gun Shot—Ribbons and Bows, by War Admiral	580,100
1963	Candy Spots, 1960 c., *Nigromante—Candy Dish, by *Khaled	604,481
1962	Never Bend, 1960 c., *Nasrullah—Lalun, by *Djeddah	402,969
1961	Carry Back, 1958 c., Saggy—Joppy, by Star Blen	565,349
1960	Bally Ache, 1957 c., *Ballydam—Celestial Blue, by Supremus	455,045
1959	Sword Dancer, 1956 c., Sunglow—Highland Fling, by By Jimminy	537,004
1958	Round Table, 1954 c., *Princequillo—*Knight's Daughter, by Sir Cosmo	662,780
1957	Round Table, 1954 c., *Princequillo—*Knight's Daughter, by Sir Cosmo	600,383
1956	Needles, 1953 c., Ponder—Noodle Soup, by Jack High	440,850
1955	Nashua, 1952 c., *Nasrullah—Segula, by Johnstown	752,550
1954	Determine, 1951 c., *Alibhai—Koubis, by *Mahmoud	328,700
1953	Native Dancer, 1950 c., Polynesian—Geisha, by Discovery	513,425
1952	Crafty Admiral, 1948 c., Fighting Fox—Admiral's Lady, by War Admiral	277,225
1951	Counterpoint, 1948 c., Count Fleet—Jabot, by *Sickle	250,525
1950	*Noor, 1945 h., *Nasrullah—Queen of Baghdad, by *Bahram	346,940
1949	Ponder, 1946 c., Pensive—Miss Rushin, by *Blenheim II	321,825
1948	Citation, 1945 c., Bull Lea—*Hydroplane II, by Hyperion	709,470
1947	Armed, 1941 g., Bull Lea—Armful, by Chance Shot	376,325
1946	Assault, 1943 c., Bold Venture—Igual, by Equipoise	424,195
1945	Busher, 1942 f., War Admiral—Baby League, by Bubbling Over	273,735
1944	Pavot, 1942 c., Case Ace—Coquelicot, by Man o' War	179,040
1943	Count Fleet, 1940 c., Reigh Count—Quickly, by Haste	174,055
1942	Shut Out, 1939 c., Equipoise—Goose Egg, by *Chicle	238,972
1941	Whirlaway, 1938 c., *Blenheim II—Dustwhirl, by Sweep	272,386
1940	Bimelech, 1937 c., Black Toney—*La Troienne, by *Teddy	110,005
1939	Challedon, 1936 c., *Challenger II—Laura Gal, by *Sir Gallahad III	184,535
1938	Stagehand, 1935 c., *Sickle—Stagecraft, by Fair Play	189,710
1937	Seabiscuit, 1933 c., Hard Tack—Swing On, by Whisk Broom II	168,580
1936	Granville, 1933 c., Gallant Fox—Gravita, by *Sarmatian	110,295
1935	Omaha, 1932 c., Gallant Fox—Flambino, by *Wrack	142,255
1934	Cavalcade, 1931 c., *Lancegaye—*Hastily, by Hurry On	111,235
1933	Singing Wood, 1931 c., *Royal Minstrel—Glade, by Touch Me Not	88,050
1932	Gusto, 1929 c., American Flag—Daylight Saving, by *Star Shoot	145,940
1931	Top Flight, 1929 f., *Dis Donc—Flyatit, by Peter Pan	219,000
1930	Gallant Fox, 1927 c., *Sir Gallahad III—Marguerite, by Celt	308,275

Leading Earners in North America

North American Racing Only

Horse, YOB Sex, Sire	Wins	SWs	Earnings
Skip Away, 1993 h., by Skip Trial	18	16	$9,616,360
Smarty Jones, 2001 c., by Elusive Quality	8	7	7,613,155
Cigar, 1990 h., by Palace Music	18	14	7,599,815
Alysheba, 1984 h., by Alydar	11	10	6,679,242
John Henry, 1975 g., by Ole Bob Bowers	39	30	6,591,860
Tiznow, 1997 h., by Cee's Tizzy	8	7	6,427,830
Best Pal, 1988 g., by *Habitony	18	17	5,668,245
Sunday Silence, 1986 h., by Halo	9	7	4,968,554
Easy Goer, 1986 h., by Alydar	14	12	4,873,770
Medaglia d'Oro, 1999 c., by El Prado (Ire)	8	7	4,554,720
Unbridled, 1987 h., by Fappiano	8	5	4,489,475
Saint Liam, 2000 h., by Saint Ballado	9	5	4,456,995
Silver Charm, 1994 h., by Silver Buck	11	10	4,444,369
Awesome Again, 1994 h., by Deputy Minister	9	7	4,374,590
Perfect Drift, 1999 g., by Dynaformer	11	8	4,290,190
Spend a Buck, 1982 h., by Buckaroo	10	7	4,220,689
Pleasantly Perfect, 1998 h., by Pleasant Colony	8	5	4,189,880
Azeri, 1998 m., by Jade Hunter	17	14	4,079,820
Creme Fraiche, 1982 h., by Rich Cream	17	14	4,024,727
Point Given, 1998 h., by Thunder Gulch	9	8	3,968,500
Cat Thief, 1996 h., by Storm Cat	4	3	3,951,012
Ashado, 2001 f., by Saint Ballado	12	11	3,931,440
Devil His Due, 1989 h., by Devil's Bag	11	9	3,920,405
Ferdinand, 1983 h., by Nijinsky II	8	7	3,777,978
Spain, 1997 m., by Thunder Gulch	9	7	3,540,542
Slew o' Gold, 1980 h., by Seattle Slew	12	8	3,533,534
War Emblem, 1999 c., by Our Emblem	7	4	3,491,000
Precisionist, 1981 h., by Crozier	20	17	3,485,398
Strike the Gold, 1988 h., by Alydar	6	4	3,457,026
Ghostzapper, 2000 h., by Awesome Again	9	6	3,446,120
Snow Chief, 1983 h., by Reflected Glory	13	12	3,383,210
Cryptoclearance, 1984 h., by Fappiano	12	9	3,376,327
Gentlemen (Arg), 1992 h., by Robin des Bois	9	8	3,374,890
Black Tie Affair (Ire), 1986 h., by Miswaki	18	13	3,370,694
Sky Classic, 1987 h., by Nijinsky II	15	13	3,320,398
Bet Twice, 1984 h., by Sportin' Life	10	7	3,308,599
Serena's Song, 1992 m., by Rahy	18	17	3,283,388
Real Quiet, 1995 h., by Quiet American	6	5	3,271,802
Congaree, 1998 h., by Arazi	12	10	3,267,490
Dance Smartly, 1988 m., by Danzig	12	10	3,263,835
Lemon Drop Kid, 1996 h., by Kingmambo	10	7	3,245,370
Behrens, 1994 h., by Pleasant Colony	9	7	3,243,500
Steinlen (GB), 1983 h., by Habitat	16	14	3,229,752
Captain Steve, 1997 h., by Fly So Free	8	7	3,228,356
Funny Cide, 2000 g., by Distorted Humor	8	6	3,220,319
Chief Bearhart, 1993 h., by Chief's Crown	12	9	3,219,017
Volponi, 1998 h., by Cryptoclearance	7	4	3,187,232
Bertrando, 1989 h., by Skywalker	9	8	3,185,610
Free House, 1994 h., by Smokester	9	8	3,178,971
Sandpit (Brz), 1989 h., by Baynoun (Ire)	9	8	3,147,973
Paseana (Arg), 1987 m., by Ahmad	14	14	3,111,292
Gulch, 1984 h., by Mr. Prospector	13	11	3,095,521
Silverbulletday, 1996 m., by Silver Deputy	15	14	3,093,207
Peace Rules, 2000 c., by Jules	9	8	3,084,278
Concern, 1991 h., by Broad Brush	7	4	3,079,350
Lady's Secret, 1982 m., by Secretariat	25	22	3,021,325
Albert the Great, 1997 h., by Go for Gin	8	5	3,012,490
Victory Gallop, 1995 h., by Cryptoclearance	9	7	3,005,895

Leading Female Earners in North America

Horse, YOB Sex, Sire	Wins	Stakes Wins	Earnings
Azeri, 1998 m., Jade Hunter	17	14	$4,079,820
Ashado, 2001 m., Saint Ballado	12	11	3,931,440
Spain, 1997 m., Thunder Gulch	9	7	3,540,542
Serena's Song, 1992 m., Rahy	18	17	3,283,388
Dance Smartly, 1988 m., Danzig	12	10	3,263,835
Paseana (Arg), 1987 m., Ahmad	14	14	3,111,292
Silverbulletday, 1996 m., Silver Deputy	15	14	3,093,207
Lady's Secret, 1982 m., Secretariat	25	22	3,021,325
Escena, 1993 m., Strawberry Road (Aus)	11	7	2,962,639
Bayakoa (Arg), 1984 m., Consultant's Bid	18	16	2,785,259
Banshee Breeze, 1995 m., Unbridled	10	8	2,784,798
Beautiful Pleasure, 1995 m., Maudlin	10	7	2,734,078
Flawlessly, 1988 m., Affirmed	16	15	2,572,536
Take Charge Lady, 1999 m., Dehere	11	9	2,480,377
Sightseek, 1999 m., Distant View	12	10	2,445,216
Heritage of Gold, 1995 m., Gold Legend	16	11	2,381,762
Life's Magic, 1981 m., Cox's Ridge	8	7	2,255,218
Megahertz (GB), 1999 m., Pivotal	13	13	2,237,160
Perfect Sting, 1996 m., Red Ransom	14	11	2,202,042
Safely Kept, 1986 m., Horatius	24	22	2,194,206
Xtra Heat, 1998 m., Dixieland Heat	26	25	2,189,635
Riskaverse, 1999 m., Dynaformer	9	6	2,182,429
You, 1999 m., You and I	9	8	2,101,353
Adoration, 1999 m., Honor Grades	8	7	2,051,160
Sharp Cat, 1994 m., Storm Cat	15	14	2,032,575
Society Selection, 2001 m., Coronado's Quest	6	5	1,984,200
Island Fashion, 2000 m., Petionville	6	6	1,965,970
Storm Flag Flying, 2000 m., Storm Cat	7	5	1,951,828
Jewel Princess, 1992 m., Key to the Mint	13	10	1,904,060
Intercontinental (GB), 2000 m., Danehill	9	8	1,863,586
Surfside, 1997 m., Seattle Slew	8	6	1,852,987
Open Mind, 1986 m., Deputy Minister	12	11	1,844,372
Estrapade, 1980 m., *Vaguely Noble	8	7	1,834,600
Heavenly Prize, 1991 m., Seeking the Gold	9	8	1,825,940
Lu Ravi, 1995 m., A.P. Indy	11	8	1,819,781
Tout Charmant, 1996 m., Slewvescent	9	7	1,781,879
Unbridled Elaine, 1998 m., Unbridled's Song	6	4	1,770,740
Goodbye Halo, 1985 m., Halo	11	10	1,706,702
Personal Ensign, 1984 m., Private Account	13	10	1,679,880
Tranquility Lake, 1995 m., Rahy	11	9	1,662,390
Keeper Hill, 1995 m., Deputy Minister	4	3	1,661,281
Golden Apples (Ire), 1998 m., Pivotal	5	5	1,652,346

North American Leaders by Graded Stakes Earnings

North American Racing Only

Horse, YOB Sex, Sire	Years Raced	Graded Stakes Wins	Graded Stakes Earnings
Skip Away, 1993 h., by Skip Trial	4	16	$9,548,100
Smarty Jones, 2001 h., by Elusive Quality	2	3	7,334,800
Alysheba, 1984 h., by Alydar	3	10	6,616,417
Tiznow, 1997 h., by Cee's Tizzy	2	7	6,382,830
Cigar, 1990 h., by Palace Music	4	11	5,695,000
John Henry, 1975 g., by Ole Bob Bowers	8	25	4,953,417
Sunday Silence, 1986 h., by Halo	3	7	4,929,254
Easy Goer, 1986 h., by Alydar	3	10	4,775,280
Best Pal, 1988 g., by *Habitony	7	12	4,713,795
Medaglia d'Oro, 1999 h., by El Prado (Ire)	4	7	4,535,000
Silver Charm, 1994 h., by Silver Buck	4	10	4,416,619
Saint Liam, 2000 h., by Saint Ballado	3	5	4,292,920
Unbridled, 1987 h., by Fappiano	3	3	4,105,529
Perfect Drift, 1999 g., by Dynaformer	5	7	4,103,440
Pleasantly Perfect, 1998 h., by Pleasant Colony	4	5	4,070,000
Awesome Again, 1994 h., by Deputy Minister	2	6	4,065,590
Azeri, 1998 m., by Jade Hunter	4	14	3,999,420
Point Given, 1998 h., by Thunder Gulch	2	8	3,930,900
Cat Thief, 1996 h., by Storm Cat	3	3	3,909,952
Ashado, 2001 m., by Saint Ballado	3	11	3,905,640
Devil His Due, 1989 h., by Devil's Bag	4	9	3,895,265
Spend a Buck, 1982 h., by Buckaroo	2	4	3,809,004
Creme Fraiche, 1982 h., by Rich Cream	6	11	3,689,091
Ferdinand, 1983 h., by Nijinsky II	4	5	3,619,978
Spain, 1997 m., by Thunder Gulch	4	7	3,490,307
Slew o' Gold, 1980 h., by Seattle Slew	3	8	3,454,694
War Emblem, 1999 h., by Our Emblem	2	4	3,425,000
Strike the Gold, 1988 h., by Alydar	4	4	3,391,210
Ghostzapper, 2000 h., by Awesome Again	4	6	3,362,000
Gentlemen (Arg), 1992 h., by Robin des Bois	3	8	3,324,140
Serena's Song, 1992 m., by Rahy	3	17	3,260,353
Behrens, 1994 h., by Pleasant Colony	4	7	3,204,500
Real Quiet, 1995 h., by Quiet American	3	5	3,195,740
Lemon Drop Kid, 1996 h., by Kingmambo	3	7	3,168,900
Cryptoclearance, 1984 h., by Fappiano	4	8	3,162,157
Snow Chief, 1983 h., by Reflected Glory	3	9	3,162,110
Free House, 1994 h., by Smokester	4	8	3,153,021
Precisionist, 1981 h., by Crozier	5	13	3,136,608
Black Tie Affair (Ire), 1986 h., by Miswaki	4	11	3,132,547
Bertrando, 1989 h., by Skywalker	5	7	3,131,320
Paseana (Arg), 1987 m., by Ahmad	5	14	3,074,292

North American Leaders by Grade 1 Earnings

North American Racing Only

Horse, YOB Sex, Sire	Years Raced	Grade 1 Stakes Wins	Grade 1 Stakes Earnings
Skip Away, 1993 h., by Skip Trial	4	10	$7,310,920
Smarty Jones, 2001 h., by Elusive Quality	2	2	6,734,800
Alysheba, 1984 h., by Alydar	3	9	6,230,506
Tiznow, 1997 h., by Cee's Tizzy	2	4	5,815,400
Cigar, 1990 h., by Palace Music	4	11	5,660,000
Sunday Silence, 1986 h., by Halo	3	6	4,757,454
Easy Goer, 1986 h., by Alydar	3	9	4,606,980
John Henry, 1975 g., by Ole Bob Bowers	8	16	4,125,680
Unbridled, 1987 h., by Fappiano	3	3	4,039,360
Best Pal, 1988 g., by *Habitony	7	6	3,841,870
Saint Liam, 2000 h., by Saint Ballado	3	4	3,796,960
Point Given, 1998 h., by Thunder Gulch	2	6	3,718,300
Medaglia d'Oro, 1999 h., by El Prado (Ire)	4	3	3,545,000
Devil His Due, 1989 h., by Devil's Bag	4	5	3,466,000
Slew o' Gold, 1980 h., by Seattle Slew	3	7	3,420,314
Azeri, 1998 m., by Jade Hunter	4	11	3,408,920
Cat Thief, 1996 h., by Storm Cat	3	2	3,366,500
Ashado, 2001 f., by Saint Ballado	3	7	3,335,640
Ferdinand, 1983 h., by Nijinsky II	4	3	3,326,678
Pleasantly Perfect, 1998 h., by Pleasant Colony	4	2	3,240,000
Ghostzapper, 2000 h., by Awesome Again	4	4	3,152,000
War Emblem, 1999 h., by Our Emblem	2	3	3,125,000
Awesome Again, 1994 h., by Deputy Minister	2	2	2,999,900
Real Quiet, 1995 h., by Quiet American	3	5	2,920,920
Creme Fraiche, 1982 g., by Rich Cream	6	7	2,897,068
Strike the Gold, 1988 h., by Alydar	4	2	2,800,876
Paseana (Arg), 1987 m., by Ahmad	5	10	2,753,942
A.P. Indy, 1989 r., by Seattle Slew	2	4	2,725,660
Theatrical (Ire), 1982 h., by Nureyev	3	6	2,724,040
Silver Charm, 1994 h., by Silver Buck	4	2	2,716,350
Gulch, 1984 h., by Mr. Prospector	3	7	2,683,496
Sea Hero, 1990 h., by Polish Navy	3	3	2,635,900
Lemon Drop Kid, 1996 h., by Kingmambo	3	5	2,630,400
Gentlemen (Arg), 1992 h., by Robin des Bois	3	3	2,610,000
Bet Twice, 1984 h., by Sportin' Life	3	4	2,573,337
Funny Cide, 2000 g., by Distorted Humor	4	3	2,566,034
Bertrando, 1989 h., by Skywalker	5	3	2,554,820
Fantastic Light, 1996 h., by Rahy	2	2	2,507,400
Spain, 1997 m., by Thunder Gulch	4	2	2,499,900
Beautiful Pleasure, 1995 m., by Maudlin	5	6	2,467,500
Volponi, 1998 h., by Cryptoclearance	4	1	2,406,000
Sandpit (Brz), 1989 h., by Baynoun (Ire)	4	5	2,396,000
Concern, 1991 h., by Broad Brush	3	2	2,375,780
Bayakoa (Arg), 1984 m., by Consultant's Bid	4	12	2,345,509
Farma Way, 1987 h., by Marfa	3	2	2,340,000
Chief Bearhart, 1993 h., by Chief's Crown	4	3	2,321,000
Cryptoclearance, 1984 h., by Fappiano	4	4	2,317,732
Lady's Secret, 1982 m., by Secretariat	4	11	2,314,731
Banshee Breeze, 1995 m., by Unbridled	3	5	2,311,680
Daylami (Ire), 1994 h., by Doyoun	2	2	2,280,000
With Anticipation, 1995 g., by Relaunch	8	5	2,246,859
Serena's Song, 1992 m., by Rahy	3	11	2,244,400
Albert the Great, 1997 h., by Go for Gin	2	1	2,237,120
Free House, 1994 h., by Smokester	4	3	2,229,361
Hansel, 1988 h., by Woodman	2	2	2,226,466
Precisionist, 1981 h., by Crozier	5	6	2,207,810
Snow Chief, 1983 h., by Reflected Glory	3	6	2,181,590
Escena, 1993 m., by Strawberry Road (Aus)	4	4	2,172,000
Better Talk Now, 1999 g., by Talkin Man	5	4	2,165,000
Great Communicator, 1983 g., by Key to the Kingdom	6	4	2,162,000
Affirmed, 1975 h., by Exclusive Native	3	14	2,158,031
Gate Dancer, 1981 h., by Sovereign Dancer	4	2	2,137,245
Flawlessly, 1988 m., by Affirmed	5	9	2,130,900
Manila, 1983 h., by Lyphard	3	5	2,117,190
General Challenge, 1996 g., by General Meeting	4	3	2,110,000
Perfect Drift, 1999 g., by Dynaformer	5	1	2,094,970
Pleasant Tap, 1987 h., by Pleasant Colony	4	2	2,090,000
Milwaukee Brew, 1997 h., by Wild Again	4	2	2,087,500
Alphabet Soup, 1991 h., by Cozzene	4	1	2,080,000
Chief's Crown, 1982 h., by Danzig	2	8	2,075,158
Thunder Gulch, 1992 h., by Gulch	2	4	2,064,080
Life's Magic, 1981 m., by Cox's Ridge	3	5	2,060,998

North American Leading Males by Turf Earnings

North American Racing Only

Horse, YOB Sex, Sire	Years Raced	Turf Wins	Turf Earnings
John Henry, 1975 g., by Ole Bob Bowers	8	30	$5,269,212
Steinlen (GB), 1983 h., by Habitat	4	16	3,229,752
Sky Classic, 1987 h., by Nijinsky II	4	14	3,176,638
Chief Bearhart, 1993 h., by Chief's Crown	4	11	3,164,509
Great Communicator, 1983 g., by Key to the Kingdom	6	13	2,908,485
Awad, 1990 h., by Caveat	7	13	2,871,645
Theatrical (Ire), 1982 h., by Nureyev	3	7	2,840,500
Sandpit (Brz), 1989 h., by Baynoun (Ire)	4	9	2,752,973
Manila, 1983 h., by Lyphard	3	11	2,676,299
Paradise Creek, 1989 h., by Irish River (Fr)	4	14	2,675,514
Fraise, 1988 h., by Strawberry Road (Aus)	4	10	2,613,105
Better Talk Now, 1999 g., by Talkin Man	5	11	2,605,717
Fantastic Light, 1996 h., by Rahy	2	2	2,507,400
Buck's Boy, 1993 g., by Bucksplasher	5	10	2,493,520
Lure, 1989 h., by Danzig	4	11	2,348,839
Quiet Resolve, 1995 g., by Affirmed	5	10	2,346,768
With Anticipation, 1995 g., by Relaunch	8	7	2,332,512
Daylami (Ire), 1994 h., by Doyoun	2	2	2,280,000
Marlin, 1993 h., by Sword Dance (Ire)	3	8	2,262,255
With Approval, 1986 h., by Caro (Ire)	3	7	2,254,760
Yankee Affair, 1982 h., by Northern Fling	5	18	2,204,524
Sunshine Forever, 1985 h., by Roberto	3	8	2,083,700
Kitten's Joy, 2001 h., by El Prado (Ire)	3	9	2,065,241
High Chaparral (Ire), 1999 h., by Sadler's Wells	2	2	2,021,600
Kotashaan (Fr), 1988 h., by Darshaan	2	7	2,017,050
Star of Cozzene, 1988 h., by Cozzene	5	11	2,015,039
Sulamani (Ire), 1999 h., by Hernando (Fr)	2	3	2,013,600
Bien Bien, 1989 h., by Manila	3	8	1,998,725
Artie Schiller, 2001 h., by El Prado (Ire)	3	10	1,982,705
Majesty's Prince, 1979 h., by His Majesty	4	11	1,942,922
Soaring Free, 1999 g., by Smart Strike	4	11	1,916,789
Ladies Din, 1995 g., by Din's Dancer	6	11	1,894,710
Itsallgreektome, 1987 g., by Sovereign Dancer	5	7	1,821,893
El Senor, 1984 h., by Valdez	5	12	1,767,245
Singletary, 2000 h., by Sultry Song	4	8	1,753,192
Good Journey, 1996 h., by Nureyev	4	7	1,722,965
Yagli, 1993 h., by Jade Hunter	5	10	1,702,121
Leroidesanimaux (Brz), 2000 h., by Candy Stripes	2	8	1,650,900
Denon, 1998 h., by Pleasant Colony	4	4	1,647,269
Val's Prince, 1992 g., by Eternal Prince	7	10	1,585,940
Sarafan, 1997 g., by Lear Fan	5	6	1,578,413
Strut the Stage, 1998 h., by Theatrical (Ire)	5	10	1,568,555
Da Hoss, 1992 g., by Gone West	4	8	1,559,780
John's Call, 1991 g., by Lord At War (Arg)	7	14	1,542,130
Redattore (Brz), 1995 h., by Roi Normand	3	8	1,536,927
Fly Till Dawn, 1986 h., by Swing Till Dawn	5	9	1,536,150
Native Desert, 1993 g., by Desert Classic	8	14	1,532,834
Perfect Soul (Ire), 1998 h., by Sadler's Wells	3	7	1,527,764
Mecke, 1992 h., by Maudlin	4	6	1,522,080
Touch of the Blues (Fr), 1997 h., by Cadeaux Genereux	5	3	1,517,540
Sweet Return (GB), 2000 h., by Elmaamul	3	6	1,501,060

North American Leading Females by Turf Earnings

North American Racing Only

Horse, YOB Sex, Sire	Years Raced	Turf Wins	Turf Earnings
Flawlessly, 1988 m., by Affirmed	5	14	$2,459,250
Megahertz (GB), 1999 m., by Pivotal	4	13	2,237,160
Perfect Sting, 1996 m., by Red Ransom	4	13	2,163,673
Riskaverse, 1999 m., by Dynaformer	5	8	2,096,299
Intercontinental (GB), 2000 m., by Danehill	2	9	1,863,586
Estrapade, 1980 m., by *Vaguely Noble	3	8	1,789,600
Golden Apples (Ire), 1998 m., by Pivotal	3	5	1,652,346
Tout Charmant, 1996 m., by Slewvescent	5	7	1,607,219
Starine (Fr), 1997 m., by Mendocino	2	4	1,560,189
Miss Alleged, 1987 m., by Alleged	2	2	1,532,500
Happyanunoit (NZ), 1995 m., by Yachtie	3	6	1,481,892
Tates Creek, 1998 m., by Rahy	3	11	1,470,834
Memories of Silver, 1993 m., by Silver Hawk	3	9	1,435,140
Wonder Again, 1999 m., by Silver Hawk	4	7	1,434,762
Voodoo Dancer, 1998 m., by Kingmambo	4	11	1,427,952

Horse, YOB Sex, Sire	Years Raced	Turf Wins	Turf Earnings
Tranquility Lake, 1995 m., by Rahy	4	9	1,420,770
Astra, 1996 m., by Theatrical (Ire)	4	11	1,378,424
Film Maker, 2000 m., by Dynaformer	4	7	1,371,090
Possibly Perfect, 1990 m., by Northern Baby	3	11	1,367,050
All Along (Fr), 1979 m., by Targowice	2	3	1,337,146
Sand Springs, 2000 m., by Dynaformer	4	9	1,270,058
Tuzla (Fr), 1994 m., by Panoramic (GB)	4	11	1,266,079
Ticker Tape (GB), 2001 m., by Royal Applause (GB)	3	5	1,257,855
Carotene, 1983 m., by Great Nephew	4	10	1,242,126
Brown Bess, 1982 m., by *Petrone	6	13	1,224,265
Soaring Softly, 1995 m., by Kris S.	3	7	1,193,450
Irish Linnet, 1988 m., by Seattle Song	6	18	1,191,980
Windsharp, 1991 m., by Lear Fan	3	6	1,191,600
Fieldy (Ire), 1983 m., by Northfields	4	18	1,182,530
Wandesta (GB), 1991 m., by Nashwan	3	6	1,170,650
Heat Haze (GB), 1999 m., by Green Desert	2	5	1,135,660
Royal Heroine (Ire), 1980 m., by Lypheor (GB)	2	5	1,110,900
Bold Ruritana, 1990 m., by Bold Ruckus	6	14	1,102,790
Kostroma (Ire), 1986 m., by Caerleon	3	7	1,093,275
Banks Hill (GB), 1998 m., by Danehill	2	1	1,068,800
Maxzene, 1993 m., by Cozzene	3	11	1,067,587
Volga (Ire), 1998 m., by Caerleon	3	4	1,067,320
Honey Ryder, 2001 m., by Lasting Approval	3	8	1,054,810
Colstar, 1996 m., by Opening Verse	4	11	1,053,056
Dimitrova, 2000 m., by Swain (Ire)	2	2	1,045,404
Janet (GB), 1997 m., by Emperor Jones	3	7	1,004,585
Sabin, 1980 m., by Lyphard	4	15	998,235
Capades, 1986 m., by Overskate	3	9	991,516
Sangue (Ire), 1978 m., by Lyphard	3	8	974,900
Ryafan, 1994 m., by Lear Fan	1	3	968,000
Six Perfections (Fr), 2000 m., by Celtic Swing	2	1	964,800
Auntie Mame, 1994 m., by Theatrical (Ire)	3	10	961,480
Real Connection, 1991 m., by Vigors	5	5	956,438
Hatoof, 1989 m., by Irish River (Fr)	3	2	950,960
Ouija Board (GB), 2001 m., by Cape Cross (Ire)	2	1	945,200
Spook Express (SAf), 1994 m., by Comic Blush	3	5	932,270
Bien Nicole, 1998 m., by Bien Bien	3	9	917,570
England's Legend (Fr), 1997 m., by Lure	2	4	917,480
Gaily Gaily (Ire), 1983 m., by Cure the Blues	4	11	914,939
Stay Forever, 1997 m., by Stack	4	10	910,399
Valentine Dancer, 2000 m., by In Excess (Ire)	4	6	906,966
Anka Germania (Ire), 1982 m., by Malinowski	4	11	903,554
Miesque, 1984 m., by Nureyev	2	2	900,000
Pebbles (GB), 1981 m., by Sharpen Up (GB)	1	1	900,000
Snow Dance, 1998 m., by Forest Wildcat	4	7	894,457
Moscow Burning, 2000 m., by Moscow Ballet	3	7	888,810
The Very One, 1975 m., by One for All	5	18	888,523
Fiji (GB), 1994 m., by Rainbow Quest	3	6	871,410
Lady Shirl, 1987 m., by That's a Nice	6	14	863,973
Sweetest Thing, 1998 m., by Candy Stripes	2	6	857,094
Sarah Lane's Oates, 1994 m., by Sunshine Forever	7	20	855,834
Classic Stamp, 2000 m., by Regal Classic	3	5	845,774
Inish Glora, 1998 m., by Regal Classic	5	6	830,101
Fact Finder, 1979 m., by Staff Writer	6	9	822,669
Snow Polina, 1995 m., by Trempolino	2	4	816,143
Owsley, 1998 m., by Harlan	3	7	811,964
Katdogawn (GB), 2000 m., by Bahhare	3	6	807,488

Leading Two-Year-Old Males by North American Earnings

North American Racing Only

Horse, YOB Sex, Sire	Starts	Wins	Stakes Wins	Earnings
Boston Harbor, 1994 c., by Capote	7	6	5	$1,928,605
Mountain Cat, 1990 c., by Storm Cat	8	6	5	1,460,627
Favorite Trick, 1995 c., by Phone Trick	8	8	7	1,231,998
Tejano, 1985 c., by Caro (Ire)	10	5	4	1,177,189
Stevie Wonderboy, 2003, c., by Stephen Got Even	5	3	2	1,028,940
Best Pal, 1988 g., by *Habitony	8	6	5	1,026,195
Grand Canyon, 1987 c., by Fappiano	8	4	3	1,019,540
Snow Chief, 1983 c., by Reflected Glory	9	5	4	935,740
Timber Country, 1992 c., by Woodman	7	4	3	928,590
Chief's Crown, 1982 c., by Danzig	9	6	5	920,890
Fly So Free, 1988 c., by Time for a Change	6	4	2	872,580
Gilded Time, 1990 c., by Timeless Moment	4	4	3	855,980
Wilko, 2002, c., by Awesome Again	2	1	1	833,580
Action This Day, 2001, c., by Kris S.	3	2	1	817,200
Regal Classic, 1985 c., by Vice Regent	8	4	4	812,500
Roving Boy, 1980 c., by Olden Times	7	5	4	800,425
Macho Uno, 1998 c., by Holy Bull	4	3	2	768,803
Tasso, 1983 c., by Fappiano	7	5	3	761,534
Toccet, 2000, c., by Awesome Again	8	6	4	755,610
Fali Time, 1981 c., by Faliraki (Ire)	7	3	2	748,829
Captain Steve, 1997 c., by Fly So Free	8	4	3	744,880
Officer, 1999, c., by Bertrando	8	5	4	740,010
Success Express, 1985 c., by Hold Your Peace	8	4	3	737,207
Mr. Jester, 2001, c., by Silver Deputy	6	4	3	730,800
Texcess, 2002 g., by In Excess (Ire)	4	3	2	725,427
Siphonic, 1999, c., by Siphon (Brz)	4	3	2	703,978
Easy Goer, 1986 c., by Alydar	6	4	2	697,500
Answer Lively, 1996 c., by Lively One	7	4	2	695,296
Bet Twice, 1984 c., by Sportin' Life	7	5	3	690,565
First Samurai, 2003, c., by Giant's Causeway	5	4	2	682,575
Vindication, 2000, c., by Seattle Slew	4	4	2	680,950
Afleet Alex, 2002, c., by Northern Afleet	6	4	2	680,800
Spend a Buck, 1982 c., by Buckaroo	8	5	2	667,985
River Special, 1990 c., by Riverman	6	3	3	663,900
Capote, 1984 c., by Seattle Slew	4	3	2	654,680
Brocco, 1991 c., by Kris S.	4	3	1	653,550
Stephan's Odyssey, 1982 c., by Danzig	4	3	1	651,100
King Glorious, 1986 c., by Naevus	5	5	4	646,100
Henny Hughes, 2003, c., by Hennessy	6	3	2	644,820
Forty Niner, 1985 c., by Mr. Prospector	6	5	4	634,908
Point Given, 1998 c., by Thunder Gulch	6	3	2	618,500
Swiss Yodeler, 1994 c., by Eastern Echo	9	6	5	617,200
Rhythm, 1987 c., by Mr. Prospector	5	3	1	612,920
Anees, 1997 c., by Unbridled	4	2	1	609,200
Music Merci, 1986 g., by Stop the Music	9	5	3	607,220
Is It True, 1986 c., by Raja Baba	6	2	1	605,342
Dehere, 1991 c., by Deputy Minister	7	5	4	595,912
Hennessy, 1993 c., by Storm Cat	9	4	3	580,400
Bertrando, 1989 c., by Skywalker	4	3	2	570,865
Buckpasser, 1963 c., by Tom Fool	11	9	6	568,096
Unbridled's Song, 1993 c., by Unbridled	3	2	1	568,000
Storm Cat, 1983 c., by Storm Bird	6	3	1	557,080
Temperate Sil, 1984 c., by Temperence Hill	5	3	2	549,625
Kafwain, 2000, c., by Cherokee Run	8	3	2	535,848
Sir Oscar, 2001, c., by Halo's Image	6	6	5	528,800
Stalwart, 1979 c., by Hoist the Flag	5	4	2	528,595
Johannesburg, 1999, c., by Hennessy	1	1	1	520,000
Arazi, 1989 c., by Blushing Groom (Fr)	1	1	1	520,000
Declan's Moon, 2002 g., by Malibu Moon	4	4	3	507,300
Adjudicating, 1987 c., by Danzig	8	4	2	506,232
Riva Ridge, 1969 c., by First Landing	9	7	5	503,263
Brother Derek, 2003, c., by Benchmark	5	3	2	502,080
Maria's Mon, 1993 c., by Wavering Monarch	5	4	3	498,340
Sadair, 1962 c., by *Petare	12	8	5	498,216
Swale, 1981 c., by Seattle Slew	7	5	4	491,950
Purdue King, 1985 c., by Dimaggio	10	5	4	489,730
Chapel Royal, 2001, c., by Montbrook	6	3	2	484,755
Consolidator, 2002, c., by Storm Cat	7	2	1	480,260

Leading Two-Year-Old Females by North American Earnings

North American Racing Only

Horse, YOB Sex, Sire	Starts	Wins	Stakes Wins	Earnings
Silverbulletday, 1996 f., by Silver Deputy	7	6	5	$1,114,110
Countess Diana, 1995 f., by Deerhound	6	5	4	1,019,785
Meadow Star, 1988 f., by Meadowlake	7	7	6	992,250
Storm Flag Flying, 2000 f., by Storm Cat	4	4	3	967,000
Brave Raj, 1984 f., by Rajab	9	6	5	933,650
Folklore, 2003 f., by Tiznow	7	4	3	927,500
Storm Song, 1994 f., by Summer Squall	7	4	3	898,205
Outstandingly, 1982 f., by Exclusive Native	6	3	2	867,872
Halfbridled, 2001 f., by Unbridled	4	4	3	849,400
Eliza, 1990 f., by Mt. Livermore	5	4	3	808,000
Family Style, 1983 f., by State Dinner	10	4	3	805,809
Flanders, 1992 f., by Seeking the Gold	5	4	3	805,000
Sweet Catomine, 2002 f., by Storm Cat	4	3	3	799,800
Excellent Meeting, 1996 f., by General Meeting	8	4	3	773,824
Chilukki, 1997 f., by Cherokee Run	7	6	5	762,723
Phone Chatter, 1991 f., by Phone Trick	6	4	3	753,500
Open Mind, 1986 f., by Deputy Minister	6	4	3	724,064

Horse, YOB Sex, Sire	Starts	Wins	Stakes Wins	Earnings
Althea, 1981 f., by Alydar	9	5	4	692,625
Caressing, 1998 f., by Honour and Glory	5	3	2	690,642
Pleasant Stage, 1989 f., by Pleasant Colony	4	2	2	687,240
Surfside, 1997 f., by Seattle Slew	6	4	2	677,350
Golden Attraction, 1993 f., by Mr. Prospector	8	6	5	675,588
Tempera, 1999 f., by A.P. Indy	5	3	2	670,240
Cash Run, 1997 f., by Seeking the Gold	6	3	1	653,352
Twilight Ridge, 1983 f., by Cox's Ridge	5	3	2	617,808
My Flag, 1993 f., by Easy Goer	6	2	1	614,614
Balletto (UAE), 2002 f., by Timber Country	5	3	1	614,000
Ashado, 2001 f., by Saint Ballado	6	4	3	610,800
Raging Fever, 1998 f., by Storm Cat	6	5	4	598,500
Serena's Song, 1992 f., by Rahy	10	4	3	597,335
Runway Model, 2002 f., by Petionville	10	4	2	580,598
Boots 'n Jackie, 1990 f., by Major Moran	12	4	3	579,820
Tappiano, 1984 f., by Fappiano	5	4	3	572,820
Sacahuista, 1984 f., by Raja Baba	9	4	3	564,965
I'm Splendid, 1983 f., by Our Native	7	4	3	560,857
Adieu, 2003 f., by El Corredor	6	4	3	554,470
Go for Wand, 1987 f., by Deputy Minister	4	3	1	548,390
Cara Rafaela, 1993 f., by Quiet American	9	3	2	546,962
You, 1999 f., by You and I	6	3	2	540,440
Life's Magic, 1981 f., by Cox's Ridge	7	2	1	537,259
Epitome, 1985 f., by Summing	8	3	2	534,805
Sardula, 1991 f., by Storm Cat	5	3	2	532,545
Be Gentle, 2001 f., by Tale of the Cat	7	4	3	523,078
Stella Madrid, 1987 f., by Alydar	7	4	3	519,096
Sharp Cat, 1994 f., by Storm Cat	7	4	3	505,950
Lost Kitty, 1985 f., by Magesterial	11	4	3	499,038
Aclassysassylassy, 2002 f., by Wild Event	7	5	4	498,800
She's a Devil Due, 1998 f., by Devil His Due	5	4	2	495,320
Love Lock, 1995 f., by Silver Ghost	9	4	3	483,122
Career Collection, 1995 f., by General Meeting	8	4	3	482,005
Arewehavingfunyet, 1983 f., by Sham	9	5	5	475,730
Nancy's Glitter, 1995 f., by Glitterman	8	5	4	464,460
Lea Lucinda, 1986 f., by Secreto	9	3	2	459,962
Three Ring, 1996 f., by Notebook	5	3	2	458,440
Private Treasure, 1988 f., by Explodent	8	3	2	457,242
Tiltalating, 1982 f., by Tilt Up	10	4	3	454,944
Numbered Account, 1969 f., by Buckpasser	10	8	7	446,594
Ruling Angel, 1984 f., by Vice Regent	9	6	5	433,952
Wild Fit, 2003 f., by Wild Wonder	4	2	1	432,600
Goodbye Halo, 1985 f., by Halo	4	3	2	431,585
Composure, 2000 f., by Touch Gold	6	2	1	431,300
La Spia, 1989 f., by Capote	7	2	1	428,008
Stocks Up, 1986 f., by Kris S.	6	3	2	418,751
Ivanavinalot, 2000 f., by West Acre	6	5	3	418,300
La Prevoyante, 1970 f., by Buckpasser	12	12	10	417,109
Sweet Roberta, 1987 f., by Roberto	3	2	1	415,800
Sez Fourty, 1986 f., by Sezyou	11	5	3	414,678
Dominant Dancer, 1987 f., by Moscow Ballet	9	5	4	412,470
Skillful Joy, 1979 f., by Nodouble	8	4	2	411,312
Over All, 1985 f., by Mr. Prospector	10	6	5	406,500
Stormy Blues, 1992 f., by Cure the Blues	6	4	3	403,740
Collins, 1984 f., by Majestic Light	7	3	2	400,806
Strategic Maneuver, 1991 f., by Cryptoclearance	6	5	4	398,340
Educated Risk, 1990 f., by Mr. Prospector	5	2	1	396,256
Habibti, 1999 f., by Tabasco Cat	4	3	2	393,000
Delicate Vine, 1984 f., by Knights Choice	5	4	3	390,370
Punch Appeal, 2002 f., by Successful Appeal	9	6	5	389,840
Darby Shuffle, 1986 f., by Darby Creek Road	10	3	2	389,627
Special Happening, 1987 f., by Relaunch	6	3	2	386,455
Cicada, 1959 f., by Bryan G.	16	11	8	384,676
Chatter Chatter, 2001 f., by Lost Soldier	7	3	2	383,470
She Says It Best, 2003 f., by Stormy Atlantic	8	4	2	382,918
Cheval Volant, 1987 f., by Kris S.	7	3	2	379,762

Horse, YOB Sex, Sire	Starts	Wins	Stakes Wins	Earnings
Unbridled, 1987 c., by Fappiano	11	4	3	3,718,149
Spend a Buck, 1982 c., by Buckaroo	7	5	5	3,552,704
War Emblem, 1999 c., by Our Emblem	10	5	4	3,455,000
Tiznow, 1997 c., by Cee's Tizzy	9	5	4	3,445,950
Point Given, 1998 c., by Thunder Gulch	7	6	6	3,350,000
Cat Thief, 1996 c., by Storm Cat	13	2	2	3,020,500
Skip Away, 1993 c., by Skip Trial	12	6	5	2,699,280
Thunder Gulch, 1992 c., by Gulch	10	7	7	2,644,080
A.P. Indy, 1989 r., by Seattle Slew	7	5	5	2,622,560
Hansel, 1988 c., by Woodman	9	4	4	2,565,680
Concern, 1991 c., by Broad Brush	14	3	2	2,541,670
Alysheba, 1984 c., by Alydar	10	3	3	2,511,156
Izvestia, 1987 c., by Icecapade	11	8	8	2,486,667
Sea Hero, 1990 c., by Polish Navy	9	2	2	2,484,190
Flower Alley, 2002 c., by Distorted Humor	9	4	3	2,435,200
Medaglia d'Oro, 1999 c., by El Prado (Ire)	9	4	3	2,260,600
Tabasco Cat, 1991 c., by Storm Cat	12	5	5	2,164,334
Seeking the Gold, 1985 c., by Mr. Prospector	12	6	4	2,145,620
Holy Bull, 1991 c., by Great Above	10	8	8	2,095,000
Forty Niner, 1985 c., by Mr. Prospector	13	6	5	2,091,092
Afleet Alex, 2002 c., by Northern Afleet	6	4	4	2,085,000
Sunshine Forever, 1985 c., by Roberto	12	8	5	2,032,636
Wando, 2000 c., by Langfuhr	8	5	5	2,017,323
Charismatic, 1996 c., by Summer Squall	10	4	3	2,007,404
Fusaichi Pegasus, 1997 c., by Mr. Prospector	8	6	4	1,987,800
Victory Gallop, 1995 c., by Cryptoclearance	8	3	3	1,981,720
Pine Bluff, 1989 c., by Danzig	6	3	3	1,970,896
Funny Cide, 2000 g., by Distorted Humor	8	2	2	1,963,200
Risen Star, 1985 c., by Secretariat	8	6	5	1,958,368
Empire Maker, 2000 c., by Unbridled	6	3	3	1,936,200
Proud Truth, 1982 c., by Graustark	11	7	5	1,926,327
Bet Twice, 1984 c., by Sportin' Life	9	3	3	1,922,642
Prized, 1986 c., by Kris S.	7	4	4	1,888,705
Captain Steve, 1997 c., by Fly So Free	11	3	3	1,882,276
Snow Chief, 1983 c., by Reflected Glory	9	6	6	1,875,200
Louis Quatorze, 1993 c., by Sovereign Dancer	12	4	2	1,854,908
Peace Rules, 2000 c., by Jules	7	3	3	1,850,000
Deputy Commander, 1994 c., by Deputy Minister	10	4	3	1,849,440
Giacomo, 2002 c., by Holy Bull	6	1	1	1,846,876
Manila, 1983 c., by Lyphard	10	8	6	1,814,729
Real Quiet, 1995 c., by Quiet American	6	2	2	1,788,800
With Approval, 1986 c., by Caro (Ire)	10	6	5	1,772,150
Coronado's Quest, 1995 c., by Forty Niner	11	5	5	1,739,950
Monarchos, 1998 c., by Maria's Mon	7	4	2	1,711,600
Menifee, 1996 c., by Harlan	9	3	2	1,695,400
General Challenge, 1996 g., by General Meeting	11	6	6	1,658,100
Silver Charm, 1994 c., by Silver Buck	7	3	3	1,638,750
Kitten's Joy, 2001 c., by El Prado (Ire)	8	6	6	1,625,796
Came Home, 1999 c., by Gone West	8	6	6	1,624,500
Java Gold, 1984 c., by Key to the Mint	8	6	4	1,621,300
Harlan's Holiday, 1999 c., by Harlan	10	3	3	1,606,000
Ten Most Wanted, 2000 c., by Deputy Commander	10	4	3	1,544,860
Touch Gold, 1994 c., by Deputy Minister	7	4	3	1,522,313
Strike the Gold, 1988 c., by Alydar	12	2	2	1,443,850
Broad Brush, 1983 c., by Ack Ack	14	7	7	1,409,778
Prairie Bayou, 1990 g., by Little Missouri	8	5	5	1,405,521
Cryptoclearance, 1984 c., by Fappiano	15	4	4	1,367,150
Lemon Drop Kid, 1996 c., by Kingmambo	9	3	2	1,349,400
Kissin Kris, 1990 c., by Kris S.	12	2	2	1,341,292
Tikkanen, 1991 c., by Cozzene	2	2	2	1,340,000
Free House, 1994 c., by Smokester	10	3	3	1,336,910
Peaks and Valleys, 1992 c., by Mt. Livermore	8	5	4	1,323,750
Gulch, 1984 c., by Mr. Prospector	14	3	3	1,297,171
Dramatic Gold, 1991 g., by Slew o' Gold	10	4	2	1,294,850
Creme Fraiche, 1982 g., by Rich Cream	15	5	5	1,291,397

Leading Three-Year-Old Males by North American Earnings in Single Season

North American Racing Only

Horse, YOB Sex, Sire	Starts	Wins	Stakes Wins	Earnings
Smarty Jones, 2001 c., by Elusive Quality	7	6	6	$7,563,535
Sunday Silence, 1986 c., by Halo	9	7	6	4,578,454
Easy Goer, 1986 c., by Alydar	11	8	8	3,837,150

Leading Three-Year-Old Females by North American Earnings in Single Season

North American Racing Only

Horse, YOB Sex, Sire	Starts	Wins	Stakes Wins	Earnings
Dance Smartly, 1988 f., by Danzig	8	8	8	$2,876,821
Ashado, 2001 f., by Saint Ballado	8	5	5	2,259,640
Spain, 1997 f., by Thunder Gulch	13	5	4	1,979,500
Silverbulletday, 1996 f., by Silver Deputy	11	8	8	1,707,640

Horse, YOB Sex, Sire	Starts	Wins	Stakes Wins	Earnings
Unbridled Elaine, 1998 f., by Unbridled's Song	8	4	3	1,663,175
Serena's Song, 1992 f., by Rahy	13	9	9	1,524,920
Banshee Breeze, 1995 f., by Unbridled	10	6	4	1,425,980
Take Charge Lady, 1999 f., by Dehere	10	6	6	1,388,635
Winning Colors, 1985 f., by Caro (Ire)	10	4	4	1,347,746
Farda Amiga, 1999 f., by Broad Brush	6	3	2	1,248,902
Ticker Tape (GB), 2001 f., by Royal Applause (GB)	10	5	5	1,159,075
Surfside, 1997 f., by Seattle Slew	7	4	4	1,147,637
Open Mind, 1986 f., by Deputy Minister	11	8	8	1,120,308
Island Fashion, 2000 f., by Petionville	10	4	4	1,112,970
Flute, 1998 f., by Seattle Slew	7	4	2	1,094,104
Dancethruthedawn, 1998 f., by Mr. Prospector	6	3	2	1,045,039
Xtra Heat, 1998 f., by Dixieland Heat	13	9	9	1,012,040
Lady's Secret, 1982 f., by Secretariat	17	10	10	994,349
Stellar Jayne, 2001 f., by Wild Rush	13	3	3	992,169
Ajina, 1994 f., by Strawberry Road (Aus)	9	3	3	979,175
Elloluv, 2000 f., by Gilded Time	8	2	2	978,775
Jostle, 1997 f., by Brocco	9	4	4	975,570
Ryafan, 1994 f., by Lear Fan	3	3	3	968,000
Dimitrova, 2000 f., by Swain (Ire)	4	2	2	950,000
Keeper Hill, 1995 f., by Deputy Minister	8	3	2	949,410
Very Subtle, 1984 f., by Hoist the Silver	12	6	6	947,135
My Flag, 1993 f., by Easy Goer	10	4	4	933,043
Society Selection, 2001 f., by Coronado's Quest	9	3	3	929,700
Sharp Cat, 1994 f., by Storm Cat	11	7	7	911,300
Exogenous, 1998 f., by Unbridled	7	4	2	901,500
Hollywood Wildcat, 1990 f., by Kris S.	9	5	5	893,330
You, 1999 f., by You and I	9	4	4	883,805
Life's Magic, 1981 f., by Cox's Ridge	12	4	4	873,956
Imperial Gesture, 1999 f., by Langfuhr	5	3	2	873,600
Blushing K. D., 1994 f., by Blushing John	8	6	6	845,040
Secret Status, 1997 f., by A.P. Indy	9	5	3	842,796
Go for Wand, 1987 f., by Deputy Minister	9	7	7	824,948
Life At the Top, 1983 f., by Seattle Slew	18	6	5	821,349
Bird Town, 2000 f., by Cape Town	8	3	3	815,976
Lite Light, 1988 f., by Majestic Light	9	5	5	804,685
Goodbye Halo, 1985 f., by Halo	11	5	5	789,117
Yearly Report, 2001 f., by General Meeting	7	5	5	787,500
Summerly, 2002 f., by Summer Squall	7	4	3	786,728
Six Perfections (Fr), 2000 f., by Celtic Swing	1	1	1	780,000
Mystic Lady, 1998 f., by Thunder Gulch	11	6	6	775,000
Yanks Music, 1993 f., by Air Forbes Won	7	5	4	751,000
Dispute, 1990 f., by Danzig	11	6	4	750,226
Ouija Board (GB), 2001 f., by Cape Cross (Ire)	1	1	1	733,200
Affluent, 1998 f., by Affirmed	10	4	3	725,200
Sacahuista, 1984 f., by Raja Baba	9	2	2	724,857
Banks Hill (GB), 1998 f., by Danehill	1	1	1	722,800

Leading Males Four or Older by North American Earnings in Single Season

North American Racing Only

Horse, YOB Sex, Sire	Age	Starts	Wins	Stakes Wins	Earnings
Cigar, 1990 h., by Palace Music	5	10	10	9	$4,819,800
Skip Away, 1993 h., by Skip Trial	4	11	4	4	4,089,000
Awesome Again, 1994 h., by Deputy Minister	4	6	6	5	3,845,990
Alysheba, 1984 h., by Alydar	4	9	7	7	3,808,600
Saint Liam, 2000 h., by Saint Ballado	5	6	4	4	3,696,960
Tiznow, 1997 h., by Cee's Tizzy	4	6	3	3	2,981,880
Skip Away, 1993 h., by Skip Trial	5	9	7	7	2,740,000
Slew o' Gold, 1980 h., by Seattle Slew	4	6	5	4	2,627,944
Farma Way, 1987 h., by Marfa	4	11	5	5	2,598,350
Ghostzapper, 2000 h., by Awesome Again	4	4	4	4	2,590,000
Alphabet Soup, 1991 h., by Cozzene	5	7	4	4	2,536,450
Cigar, 1990 h., by Palace Music	6	7	4	4	2,510,000
Black Tie Affair (Ire), 1986 h., by Miswaki	5	10	7	7	2,483,540
Pleasantly Perfect, 1998 h., by Pleasant Colony	5	4	2	2	2,470,000
Volponi, 1998 h., by Cryptoclearance	4	8	3	2	2,389,200
John Henry, 1975 g., by Ole Bob Bowers	9	9	6	6	2,336,650
Silver Charm, 1994 h., by Silver Buck	4	8	5	5	2,296,506
Criminal Type, 1985 h., by Alydar	5	11	7	6	2,270,290
Theatrical (Ire), 1982 h., by Nureyev	5	9	7	7	2,235,500
Bertrando, 1989 h., by Skywalker	4	9	3	3	2,217,800
Mineshaft, 1999 h., by A.P. Indy	4	9	7	7	2,209,686
Ferdinand, 1983 h., by Nijinsky II	4	10	4	4	2,185,150
Gentlemen (Arg), 1992 h., by Robin des Bois	5	6	4	4	2,125,300
Fantastic Light, 1996 h., by Rahy	5	1	1	1	2,112,800
Wild Again, 1980 h., by Icecapade	4	16	6	4	2,054,409
Daylami (Ire), 1994 h., by Doyoun	5	1	1	1	2,040,000
Great Communicator, 1983 g., by Key to the Kingdom	5	11	6	6	2,017,950
Chief Bearhart, 1993 h., by Chief's Crown	4	7	5	5	2,011,259
Festin (Arg), 1986 h., by Mat-Boy (Arg)	5	11	3	3	2,003,250
Medaglia d'Oro, 1999 h., by El Prado (Ire)	4	5	3	3	1,990,000
Kotashaan (Fr), 1988 h., by Darshaan	5	9	6	6	1,984,100
Pleasant Tap, 1987 h., by Pleasant Colony	5	10	4	4	1,959,914
Devil His Due, 1989 h., by Devil's Bag	4	11	4	4	1,939,120
Paradise Creek, 1989 h., by Irish River (Fr)	5	10	8	8	1,920,872
Strike the Gold, 1988 h., by Alydar	4	13	2	2	1,920,176
Buck's Boy, 1993 g., by Bucksplasher	5	10	6	6	1,874,020
Skywalker, 1982 h., by Relaunch	4	9	4	4	1,811,400
John Henry, 1975 g., by Ole Bob Bowers	6	10	8	8	1,798,030
Albert the Great, 1997 h., by Go for Gin	4	9	3	3	1,740,000
Budroyale, 1993 g., by Cee's Tizzy	6	11	4	4	1,735,640
Sky Classic, 1987 h., by Nijinsky II	5	9	5	5	1,735,482
Behrens, 1994 h., by Pleasant Colony	5	9	4	4	1,735,000
Roses in May, 2000 h., by Devil His Due	4	6	5	3	1,723,277
Lemon Drop Kid, 1996 h., by Kingmambo	4	9	5	4	1,673,900
Best Pal, 1988 g., by *Habitony	4	5	4	4	1,672,000
Star of Cozzene, 1988 h., by Cozzene	5	11	6	6	1,620,744
Southern Image, 2000 h., by Halo's Image	4	4	3	3	1,612,150
Congaree, 1998 h., by Arazi	5	9	5	5	1,608,000
Milwaukee Brew, 1997 h., by Wild Again	5	7	2	2	1,590,000
Twilight Agenda, 1986 h., by Devil's Bag	5	11	6	5	1,563,600
Arcangues, 1988 h., by Sagace (Fr)	5	1	1	1	1,560,000
Borrego, 2001 h., by El Prado (Ire)	4	8	3	2	1,536,600
Fraise, 1988 h., by Strawberry Road (Aus)	4	10	5	2	1,534,720
Turkoman, 1982 h., by Alydar	4	8	4	4	1,531,664
Marlin, 1993 h., by Sword Dance (Ire)	4	10	4	4	1,521,600
Steinlen (GB), 1983 h., by Habitat	6	11	7	6	1,521,378
With Anticipation, 1995 g., by Relaunch	7	8	3	3	1,507,700
Perfect Drift, 1999 g., by Dynaformer	4	8	5	4	1,505,388
Artie Schiller, 2001 h., by El Prado (Ire)	4	6	3	3	1,448,000
Waquoit, 1983 h., by Relaunch	5	7	3	3	1,441,444
Beat Hollow (GB), 1997 h., by Sadler's Wells	5	8	4	3	1,437,150
Include, 1997 h., by Broad Brush	4	9	5	5	1,435,400
Orientate, 1998 h., by Mt. Livermore	4	10	6	6	1,412,970
Chester House, 1995 h., by Mr. Prospector	5	6	1	1	1,408,500
Better Talk Now, 1999 g., by Talkin Man	5	8	2	2	1,407,000
Guided Tour, 1996 g., by Hansel	5	8	4	4	1,384,220
Gulch, 1984 h., by Mr. Prospector	4	11	5	4	1,360,840
Sandpit (Brz), 1989 h., by Baynoun (Ire)	6	8	4	3	1,342,700
Yankee Affair, 1982 h., by Northern Fling	7	13	5	5	1,333,813
Evening Attire, 1998 g., by Black Tie Affair (Ire)	4	9	5	4	1,332,720
Skimming, 1996 h., by Nureyev	5	6	3	3	1,330,000

Leading Females Four and Older by North American Earnings in a Single Season

North American Racing Only

Horse, YOB Sex, Sire	Age	Starts	Wins	Stakes Wins	Earnings
Azeri, 1998 m., by Jade Hunter	4	9	8	7	$2,181,540
Escena, 1993 m., by Strawberry Road (Aus)	5	9	5	5	2,032,425
Lady's Secret, 1982 m., by Secretariat	4	15	10	10	1,871,053
Beautiful Pleasure, 1995 m., by Maudlin	4	7	4	3	1,716,404
Paseana (Arg), 1987 m., by Ahmad	5	9	7	7	1,518,290
Bayakoa (Arg), 1984 m., by Consultant's Bid	5	11	9	8	1,406,403
Riboletta (Brz), 1995 m., by Roi Normand	5	11	7	7	1,384,860
Perfect Sting, 1996 m., by Red Ransom	4	6	5	5	1,367,000
Banshee Breeze, 1995 m., by Unbridled	4	7	4	4	1,358,818
Miss Alleged, 1987 m., by Alleged	4	3	2	2	1,345,000
Heritage of Gold, 1995 m., by Gold Legend	5	8	5	5	1,332,282
Pleasant Home, 2001 m., by Seeking the Gold	4	8	3	2	1,316,420
Intercontinental (GB), 2000 m., by Danehill	5	7	5	5	1,271,200
Bayakoa (Arg), 1984 m., by Consultant's Bid	6	10	7	7	1,234,406
Personal Ensign, 1984 m., by Private Account	4	7	7	7	1,202,640
Soaring Softly, 1995 m., by Kris S.	4	8	7	5	1,193,450
Estrapade, 1980 m., by *Vaguely Noble	6	9	3	3	1,184,800
Sightseek, 1999 m., by Distant View	4	8	4	4	1,171,888
Serena's Song, 1992 m., by Rahy	4	15	5	5	1,161,133
Adoration, 1999 m., by Honor Grades	4	5	2	2	1,160,750

Horse, YOB Sex, Sire	Age	Starts	Wins	Stakes Wins	Earnings
Inside Information, 1991 m., by Private Account	4	8	7	6	1,160,408
Jewel Princess, 1992 m., by Key to the Mint	4	9	5	5	1,150,800
Golden Apples (Ire), 1998 m., by Pivotal	4	7	3	3	1,111,680
Heat Haze (GB), 1999 m., by Green Desert	4	7	4	4	1,101,460
Tout Charmant, 1996 m., by Slewvescent	4	7	3	3	1,089,044
Ashado, 2001 m., by Saint Ballado	4	7	3	3	1,061,000
Azeri, 1998 m., by Jade Hunter	6	8	3	3	1,035,000
Royal Heroine (Ire), 1980 m., by Lypheor (GB)	4	8	4	4	1,023,500
Sightseek, 1999 m., by Distant View	5	7	4	4	1,011,350
Summer Colony, 1998 m., by Summer Squall	4	8	4	4	992,500
Storm Flag Flying, 2000 m., by Storm Cat	4	8	3	2	963,248
Safely Kept, 1986 m., by Horatius	4	10	8	7	959,280
Paseana (Arg), 1987 m., by Ahmad	6	8	3	3	950,402
Manistique, 1995 m., by Unbridled	4	9	6	6	935,100
Lu Ravi, 1995 m., by A.P. Indy	5	8	3	3	918,200
Honey Ryder, 2001 m., by Lasting Approval	4	7	5	5	910,980
Pebbles (GB), 1981 m., by Sharpen Up (GB)	4	1	1	1	900,000
Heavenly Prize, 1991 m., by Seeking the Gold	4	7	4	4	895,900
Tuzla (Fr), 1994 m., by Panoramic (GB)	5	8	4	4	889,080
Flawlessly, 1988 m., by Affirmed	5	5	4	4	886,700
Spook Express (SAf), 1994 m., by Comic Blush	7	8	3	3	866,870
Happyanunoit (NZ), 1995 m., by Yachtie	4	8	4	3	862,792
Princess Rooney, 1980 m., by Verbatim	4	9	6	5	854,791
Heritage of Gold, 1995 m., by Gold Legend	4	10	6	5	853,680
North Sider, 1982 m., by Topsider	5	17	7	6	847,107
Life's Magic, 1981 m., by Cox's Ridge	4	13	2	2	844,003
Different (Arg), 1992 m., by Candy Stripes	4	5	4	3	839,290
One Dreamer, 1988 m., by Relaunch	6	8	4	4	837,730
Spain, 1997 m., by Thunder Gulch	4	9	1	1	837,705
Wild Spirit (Chi), 1999 m., by Hussonet	4	4	3	3	830,000
Starine (Fr), 1997 m., by Mendocino	5	4	1	1	820,600
Azeri, 1998 m., by Jade Hunter	5	5	4	4	817,080
All Along (Fr), 1979 m., by Targowice	4	3	3	3	813,631
Fiji (GB), 1994 m., by Rainbow Quest	4	7	6	4	805,560
Claire Marine (Ire), 1985 m., by What A Guest	4	12	7	6	801,565
Megahertz (GB), 1999 m., by Pivotal	6	6	4	4	780,000
Smok'n Frolic, 1999 m., by Smoke Glacken	4	11	3	3	776,856
Snow Polina, 1995 m., by Trempolino	5	10	3	2	772,943
Xtra Heat, 1998 m., by Dixieland Heat	4	10	7	7	765,485
Sangue (Ire), 1978 m., by Lyphard	5	13	6	6	764,600
Honest Lady, 1996 m., by Seattle Slew	4	8	3	3	762,350
Astra, 1996 m., by Theatrical (Ire)	6	5	3	3	758,000

Winningest Horses of All Time

North American Racing Only

Through 2005

Horse, YOB Sex, Sire	Starts	Wins	Earnings
Kingston, 1884 h., by Spendthrift	138	89	$140,195
Bankrupt, 1883 g., by Spendthrift	348	86	41,260
King Crab, 1885 g., by Kingfisher	310	85	55,682
Little Minch, 1880 h., by Glenelg	222	85	58,225
Hiblaze, 1935 h., by Blazes	406	79	32,647
Tippity Witchet, 1915 g., by Broomstick	265	78	88,241
Pan Zareta, 1910 m., by Abe Frank	151	76	39,082
Badge, 1885 h., by *Ill-Used	167	70	73,253
Raceland, 1885 g., by *Billet	130	70	116,391
Geraldine, 1885 m., by Grinstead	185	69	43,020
Care Free, 1918 g., by Colin	227	67	59,873
Welsh Lad, 1934 g., by Prince of Wales	329	67	25,317
Shot One, 1941 g., by Shoeless Joe	360	65	29,982
Worthowning, 1935 g., by *Longworth	339	63	41,830
Back Bay, 1908 g., by Rubicon	289	62	40,377
Banquet, 1887 g., by *Rayon d'Or	166	62	118,872
Ed R., 1948 g., by Donnay	248	62	63,552
Imp, 1894 m., by *Wagner	171	62	70,069
Leochares, 1910 g., by Broomstick	175	62	68,867
Seth's Hope, 1924 h., by Seth	327	62	74,341
Vantime, 1939 g., by Playtime	295	62	46,290
Brandon Prince, 1929 h., by *Axenstein	280	61	47,287
Irene's Bob, 1929 h., by The Turk	237	61	58,010
Kenilworth, 1898 h., by *Sir Modred	163	61	28,255
Molasses Bill, 1933 g., by *Challenger II	262	61	50,699
Mucho Gusto, 1932 h., by Marvin May	217	61	101,880
Shuchor, 1936 g., by Haste	261	61	33,607
Vantryst, 1936 h., by Tryster	334	61	31,971
Frank Fogarty, 1918 g., by Wrack	270	60	47,651
George de Mar, 1922 h., by *Colonel Vennie	333	60	69,091
Indiantown, 1930 h., by Trojan	224	60	55,455
Lewis A. D., 1947 h., by Galway	212	60	65,482
Noah's Pride, 1929 g., by Noah	317	60	41,507
Parole, 1873 g., by Leamington	127	59	82,111
Strathmeath, 1888 g., by Strathmore	133	59	114,958
Charlie Boy, 1955 h., by Graphic	241	58	207,642
Flag Bearer, 1926 h., by *Porte Drapeau	222	58	37,683
Golden Arrow, 1961 h., by Fort Salonga	176	58	167,264
Top o' the Morning, 1912 h., by Peep o'Day	217	58	48,120
Columcille, 1948 h., by Alaking	182	57	89,665
El Puma, 1929 h., by *Spanish Prince II	242	57	44,807
End of Street, 1963 h., by Bunty's Flight	202	57	67,686
Bulwark, 1933 h., by *Bull Dog	252	56	65,125
Matchup, 1936 h., by Misstep	229	55	58,528
Tommy Whelan, 1936 g., by Enoch	233	55	33,279
Vote Boy, 1932 g., by Torchilla	304	55	39,240
Argos, 1937 g., by *Happy Argo	215	54	37,507
Bee Golly, 1942 m., by Bee Line	183	53	54,544
Crying for More, 1965 h., by I'm For More	192	53	183,685
Door Prize, 1952 g., by Eight Thirty	131	53	109,920
Hamburger Jim, 1928 h., by Whiskaway	212	53	24,383
Onus, 1933 g., by Jack High	344	53	32,039
Post War Style, 1941 m., by Burgoo King	179	53	52,600
Agrarian-U, 1942 g., by Agrarian	236	52	199,345
Alviso, 1932 h., by *Hand Grenade	193	52	41,898
Billy Brier, 1953 g., by Bunty Lawless	231	52	83,168
Cloudy Weather, 1934 g., by Mud	294	52	53,487
Fleet Argo, 1947 g., by *Happy Argo	243	52	149,000
Float Away, 1936 g., by Whiskaway	265	52	61,365
My Blaze, 1930 h., by Big Blaze	338	52	32,707
Old Kickapoo, 1924 h., by Runnymede	217	52	35,827
Port Conway Lane, 1969 h., by Bold Commander	242	52	431,593
Air Patrol, 1941 h., by Sun Teddy	146	51	163,100
Blenweed, 1938 g., by *Blenheim II	202	51	105,415
Commendable, 1935 g., by Insco	163	51	30,583
Dr. Johnson, 1940 h., by *Boswell	256	51	54,422
Estin, 1923 g., by Westy Hogan	205	51	46,901
Gay Parisian, 1924 g., by *Parisian Diamond	209	51	49,197
Sagely, 1970 h., by Sage and Sand	124	51	116,196
Small Change, 1930 h., by Aromatic	200	51	18,495
Talked About, 1934 h., by The Porter	235	51	49,447
Big Devil, 1963 h., by Call Over	237	50	222,715
Brownskin, 1946 h., by Martinus	224	50	77,913
Exterminator, 1915 g., by *McGee	100	50	221,227
Frosty Admiral, 1961 h., by Ace Admiral	151	50	166,305
Go Lite, 1960 h., by Go Lightly	211	50	96,938
Live One, 1928 g., by Sweep On	218	50	38,965
Misty Eye, 1938 m., by Dunlin	220	50	25,236
The Break, 1928 h., by Star Master	264	50	31,030
Time to Bid, 1975 h., by Jig Time	179	50	241,247
Ahba's Bull, 1949 h., by Bull Reigh	157	49	97,057
Candle Wood, 1949 h., by Easy Mon	253	49	171,127
Cruising, 1930 h., by Whiskalong	222	49	38,857
Golden Fate, 1930 h., by *The Satrap	216	49	42,570
Imahead, 1955 h., by *Beau Gem	246	49	69,884

Most Wins by Decade by Year of Birth

North American Racing Only

1931-1940

Horse, YOB Sex, Sire	Yrs. Raced	Starts	Wins	Earnings
Hiblaze, 1935 h., by Blazes	14	406	**79**	$32,647
Welsh Lad, 1934 g., by Prince of Wales	13	329	**67**	25,317
Worthowning, 1935 g., by *Longworth	14	339	**63**	41,830
Vantime, 1939 g., by Playtime	13	295	**62**	46,290
Molasses Bill, 1933 g., by *Challenger II	13	262	**61**	50,699
Mucho Gusto, 1932 h., by Marvin May	9	217	**61**	101,880
Shuchor, 1936 g., by Haste	13	261	**61**	33,607
Vantryst, 1936 h., by Tryster	13	334	**61**	31,971
Bulwark, 1933 h., by *Bull Dog	14	252	**56**	65,125
Matchup, 1936 h., by Misstep	12	229	**55**	58,528

1941-1950

Horse, YOB Sex, Sire	Yrs. Raced	Starts	Wins	Earnings
Shot One, 1941 g., by Shoeless Joe	13	360	**65**	$29,982
Ed R., 1948 g., by Donnay	14	248	**62**	63,552
Lewis A. D., 1947 h., by Galway	12	212	**60**	65,482
Columcille, 1948 h., by Alaking	11	182	**57**	89,665
Bee Golly, 1942 m., by Bee Line	11	183	**53**	54,544
Post War Style, 1941 m., by Burgoo King	10	179	**53**	52,600
Agrarian-U, 1942 g., by Agrarian	12	236	**52**	199,345
Fleet Argo, 1947 g., by *Happy Argo	12	243	**52**	149,000
Air Patrol, 1941 h., by Sun Teddy	10	146	**51**	163,100
Brownskin, 1946 h., by Martinus	10	224	**50**	77,913

1951-1960

Horse, YOB Sex, Sire	Yrs. Raced	Starts	Wins	Earnings
Charlie Boy, 1955 h., by Graphic	11	241	**58**	$207,642
Door Prize, 1952 g., by Eight Thirty	10	131	**53**	109,920
Billy Brier, 1953 g., by Bunty Lawless	12	231	**52**	83,168
Go Lite, 1960 h., by Go Lightly	11	211	**50**	96,938
Imahead, 1955 h., by *Beau Gem	13	246	**49**	69,884
Apple, 1958 g., by *Ambiorix	15	195	**48**	102,385
Bill Pac, 1951 h., by Billings	10	272	**48**	73,374
Annette G., 1951 m., by Holdall	10	237	**47**	68,932
Aquanotte, 1960 h., by Decathlon	10	142	**47**	80,603
Grand Wizard, 1956 g., by Poised	13	220	**47**	222,312

1961-1970

Horse, YOB Sex, Sire	Yrs. Raced	Starts	Wins	Earnings
Golden Arrow, 1961 h., by Fort Salonga	16	176	**58**	$167,264
End of Street, 1963 h., by Bunty's Flight	11	202	**57**	67,686
Crying for More, 1965 h., by I'm For More	11	192	**53**	183,685
Port Conway Lane, 1969 h., by Bold Commander	13	242	**52**	431,593
Sagely, 1970 h., by Sage and Sand	14	124	**51**	116,196
Big Devil, 1963 h., by Call Over	12	237	**50**	222,715
Frosty Admiral, 1961 h., by Ace Admiral	9	151	**50**	166,305
Bayou Teche, 1961 g., by Bryan G.	12	281	**48**	107,577
Flyingphere, 1961 g., by Mr. Hemisphere	14	213	**48**	85,683
Saturnina, 1967 m., by *Ballydonnell	5	107	**47**	392,195

1971-1980

Horse, YOB Sex, Sire	Yrs. Raced	Starts	Wins	Earnings
Time to Bid, 1975 h., by Jig Time	12	179	**50**	$241,247
Dot the T., 1972 h., by *Notable II	12	261	**48**	227,033
Dobi's Knight, 1971 g., by Dobi Deenar	12	219	**45**	178,996
Guy, 1974 h., by Golden Ruler	11	161	**45**	281,085
Chrystal Gail, 1973 m., by Special Dunce	11	137	**43**	154,910
Flying Hitch, 1972 h., by Double Hitch	8	125	**43**	124,352
Kintla's Folly, 1972 g., by Run Like Mad	10	130	**43**	397,761
Norman Prince, 1974 h., by Skookum	11	161	**43**	169,947
Missouri Brave, 1972 h., by *Indian Chief II	13	137	**42**	116,717
Moxeytown, 1977 h., by L'Aiglon	10	116	**41**	216,652

1981-1990

Horse, YOB Sex, Sire	Yrs. Raced	Starts	Wins	Earnings
Win Man, 1985 g., by Con Man	9	178	**48**	$416,316
Jilsie's Gigalo, 1984 g., by Gallant Knave	11	136	**45**	315,456
Boca Ratony, 1988 g., by Boca Rio	12	139	**41**	133,715
Best Boy's Jade, 1989 g., by Raja's Best Boy	12	175	**40**	223,983
Last Don B., 1987 g., by Don B.	9	104	**40**	471,461
Noble But Nasty, 1981 g., by Nasty and Bold	11	200	**40**	325,588
Sawmill Run, 1988 g., by It's Freezing	12	160	**40**	253,744
Inspector Moomaw, 1987 g., by Entropy	10	179	**38**	269,052
Little Bold John, 1982 g., by John Alden	9	105	**38**	1,956,406
The Hive Five, 1983 g., by Raja Baba	10	159	**38**	178,907

1991-2000

Horse, YOB Sex, Sire	Yrs. Raced	Starts	Wins	Earnings
Bandit Bomber, 1991 h., by Prosperous	5	49	**39**	$471,445
Shotgun Pro, 1993 g., by Shot Gun Scott	9	137	**39**	250,862
Oh So Fabulous, 1992 g., by Singular	10	125	**38**	286,339
Secret Service Man, 1992 g., by Shot Gun Scott	9	132	**37**	364,263
Lightning Al, 1993 h., by Fortunate Prospect	7	63	**36**	680,146
J V Bennett, 1993 g., by Key to the Mint	11	109	**35**	438,431
Maybe Jack, 1993 g., by Classic Account	10	122	**35**	534,715
Cumberland Gap, 1992 g., by Allen's Prospect	12	156	34	323,345
Say Florida Sandy, 1994 h., by Personal Flag	8	98	**33**	2,085,408
King Kenny Roberts, 1991 g., by Slew Machine	9	107	**32**	166,306

2001-2005

Horse, YOB Sex, Sire	Yrs. Raced	Starts	Wins	Earnings
Code of Justice, 2001 m., by Double Honor	3	34	**15**	$253,073
Cocoa Latte, 2001 g., by Demidoff	3	25	**13**	211,683
Danieltown, 2001 g., by Pioneering	3	37	**13**	487,141
Lady Riss, 2001 m., by Unreal Zeal	3	26	**13**	263,385
Rocky Gulch, 2001 g., by Dry Gulch	3	20	**13**	798,608
Ask Queenie, 2001 m., by Key Contender	3	24	**12**	296,910
Blue Song, 2001 m., by Sultry Song	3	26	**12**	262,889
Joann Jr, 2001 m., by Wheaton	2	30	**12**	189,170
Moment of Song, 2001 g., by Hazaam	3	39	**12**	131,372
Painter's Creek, 2001 g., by Salt Lake	3	28	**12**	92,737

Most Consecutive Victories

Camarero, an unfamiliar name to almost all racing fans, holds the record for the most consecutive victories by a Thoroughbred. His 56 straight wins were not registered in the sport's sometimes murky and poorly documented distant past, however. He raced in the 1950s, going undefeated until his 57th career start. All of his races were in Puerto Rico and were against other Puerto Rican-bred horses. Camarero broke the win mark set by undefeated Kincsem, a Hungarian-bred mare who raced in the late 19th century. Boston made the list of most consecutive wins twice, with 19 wins from 1839-'42 and 17 straight wins from 1836-'38.

Citation and Cigar share the modern North American record for most consecutive victories, 16, along with Louisiana-bred mare Hallowed Dreams, who won many of her races against overmatched state-breds. Citation and Cigar competed at the highest level of the sport in North America while compiling their win skeins.

Cons. Wins	Horse	YOB	Where Raced
56	Camarero	1951	Puerto Rico
54	Kincsem	1874	Hungary, England
39	Galgo Jr.	1928	Puerto Rico
23	Leviathan	1793	United States
22	Miss Petty	1981	Australia
	Pooker T.	1957	Puerto Rico
21	Bond's First Consul	1798	United States
	Lottery	1803	United States
	Meteor	1783	England
	Picnic In The Park	1979	Australia
20	Filch	1773	Ireland
	Fashion	1837	United States
	Kentucky	1861	United States
19	Boston	1833	United States
	Skiff	1821	Scotland
18	Hindoo	1878	United States
	Karayel	1970	Turkey
17	Alice Hawthorn	1838	England
	Beeswing	1835	United States
	Boston	1833	United States
	Careless	1751	England
	Dudley	1914	England
	Gradisco	1957	Venezuela
	Harkaway	1834	Ireland
	Hanover	1884	United States
	Mainbrace	1947	New Zealand
	Sir Ken	1947	England
16	Cigar	1990	United States
	Citation	1945	United States
	Hallowed Dreams	1997	United States
	Luke Blackburn	1877	United States
	Master Bagot	1787	Ireland
	Minimo	1968	Turkey
	Miss Woodford	1880	United States
	Mister Frisky	1987	Puerto Rico, United States
	*Ormonde	1883	England

Cons. Wins	Horse	YOB	Where Raced
16	Prestige	1903	France
	*Ribot	1952	Europe
	The Bard	1883	England
15	Bayardo	1906	England
	*Bernborough	1939	Australia
	Brigadier Gerard	1968	England
	Buckpasser	1963	United States
	Carbine	1885	New Zealand, Australia
	Colin	1905	United States
	Macon	1922	Argentina
	Pretty Polly	1901	England, France
	Rattler	1816	United States
15	Squanderer	1973	India
	Thebais	1878	England
	Vander Pool	1928	United States
14	Friponnier	1864	England
	Harry Bassett	1868	United States
	Lucifer	1813	Scotland
	Man o' War	1917	United States
	Nearco	1935	Europe
	*Phar Lap	1926	New Zealand, Australia, Mexico
	*Prince Charlie	1869	England
	Springfield	1873	England
13	Dungannon	1780	England
	Effie Deans	1815	England
	Grano de Oro	1937	Ireland, Venezuela
	Hippolitus	1767	Ireland
	Kingston	1884	United States
	Limerick	1923	New Zealand, Australia
	Personal Ensign	1984	United States
	Phenomenom	1780	England
	Planet	1855	United States
	Polar Star	1904	England
	Rockingham	1781	England
	Sweet Wall	1925	Ireland
	The Flying Dutchman	1846	England
	Timoleon	1814	United States
	Tremont	1884	United States
	Weimar	1968	Italy

Leading Unbeaten Racehorses

A rare breed indeed is the racehorse that completes its career without a defeat on its record. No modern horse can ever expect to equal the record of Kincsem, who went unbeaten in 54 starts over five racing seasons in Hungary. Although her pedigree was largely English, she was bred in Hungary; her name derives from the Magyar "kincs," which means treasure or jewel. The word itself means "my treasure," and she indeed was a jewel.

Following are some of the best-known horses who have retired unbeaten after careers at the top levels of their divisions. Eclipse's record, in particular, is worth noting because 18th-century records are unreliable. He is attributed in various sources with anywhere from ten to 18 victories. In this listing, he is assigned the highest number, and the one fact for certain is that he never was beaten.

Wins, Horse, YOB Sex, Pedigree

54 **Kincsem,** 1874 m., Cambuscan—Waternymph, by Cotswold

18 **Eclipse,** 1764 h., Marske—Spiletta, by Regulus

16 ***Ormonde,** 1883 h., Bend Or—Lily Agnes, by Macaroni

***Ribot,** 1952 h., Tenerani—Romanella, by El Greco

15 **Colin,** 1905 h., Commando—*Pastorella, by Springfield

14 **Nearco,** 1935 h., Pharos—Nogara, by Havresac II

13 **Personal Ensign,** 1984 m., Private Account—Grecian Banner, by Hoist the Flag

Tremont, 1884 h., Virgil—Ann Fief, by Alarm

12 **Asteroid,** 1861 h., Lexington—Nebula, by *Glencoe

Barcaldine, 1878 h., Solon—Ballyroe, by Belladrum

Crucifix, 1837 m., *Priam—Octaviana, by Octavian

9 ***Bahram,** 1932 h., Blandford—Friar's Daughter, by Friar Marcus

St. Simon, 1881 h., Galopin—St. Angela, by King Tom

8 **American Eclipse,** 1814 h., Duroc—Millers Damsel, by *Messenger

Rare Brick, 1983 h., Rare Performer—Windy Brick, by Mr. Brick

Sensation, 1877, h., *Leamington—Susan Beane, by Lexington

7 **El Rio Rey,** 1887 h., Norfolk—Marian, by Malcolm

Regulus, 1739 h., Godolphin Arabian—Grey Robinson, by Bald Galloway

The Tetrarch, 1911 h., Roi Herode—Vahren, by Bona Vista

5 **Ajax,** 1901 h., Flying Fox—Amie, by Clamart

Bay Middleton, 1833 h., Sultan—Cobweb, by Phantom

Landaluce, 1980 f., Seattle Slew—Strip Poker, by Bold Bidder

Norfolk, 1861 h., Lexington—Novice, by *Glencoe

4 **Golden Fleece,** 1979 h., Nijinsky II—Exotic Treat, by *Vaguely Noble

Lammtarra, 1992 h., Nijinsky II—Snow Bride, by Blushing Groom (Fr)

Raise a Native, 1961 h., Native Dancer—Raise You, by Case Ace

Vindication, 2000 h., Seattle Slew—Strawberry Reason, by Strawberry Road (Aus)

Leading Winners of Million-Dollar Races in North America

Horse, YOB Sex	Starts in $1-M Races	Wins in $1-M Races	Earnings in $1-M Races
Skip Away, 1993 h.	8	5	$4,798,000
Point Given, 1998 h.	5	4	2,750,000
Funny Cide, 2000 g.	7	3	2,360,200
Afleet Alex, 2002 h.	5	3	2,350,000
Smarty Jones, 2001 h.	4	3	2,334,800
Tiznow, 1997 h.	4	3	5,360,400
Easy Goer, 1986 h.	4	3	2,401,020
Cigar, 1990 h.	6	3	3,740,000
Lemon Drop Kid, 1996 h.	8	3	2,035,400
Real Quiet, 1995 h.	3	2	1,550,000
Manila, 1983 h.	2	2	1,500,000
Gentlemen (Arg), 1992 h.	7	2	1,840,000
John Henry, 1975 g.	2	2	1,200,000
Sulamani (Ire), 1999 h.	3	2	1,563,600
War Emblem, 1999 h.	5	2	2,525,000
A.P. Indy, 1989, r.	3	2	2,048,880
Tinners Way, 1990 h.	7	2	1,330,000
Best Pal, 1988 g.	11	2	2,237,000
Monarchos, 1998 h.	4	2	1,522,000
Borrego, 2001 h.	7	2	1,520,000
Free House, 1994 h.	4	2	1,385,000
Charismatic, 1996 h.	3	2	1,646,200
Dance Smartly, 1988 m.	2	2	1,782,140
Milwaukee Brew, 1997 h.	7	2	1,900,000
Chief Bearhart, 1993 h.	6	2	2,162,000
Snow Chief, 1983 h.	3	2	1,214,600
Sunday Silence, 1986 h.	4	2	3,301,624
Prized, 1986 h.	5	2	1,565,940
High Chaparral (Ire), 1999 h.	2	2	2,021,600

Horse, YOB Sex	Starts in $1-M Races	Wins in $1-M Races	Earnings in $1-M Races
Alysheba, 1984 h.	5	2	2,657,916
Bertrando, 1989 h.	6	2	1,675,000
Pleasantly Perfect, 1998 h.	5	2	3,240,000
General Challenge, 1996 g.	6	2	1,560,000
Birdstone, 2001 h.	4	2	1,200,000
Izvestia, 1987 h.	5	2	1,813,600
Skimming, 1996 h.	3	2	1,200,000
Southern Image, 2000 h.	2	2	1,150,000
Empire Maker, 2000 h.	3	2	1,370,000
Siphon (Brz), 1991 h.	6	2	1,780,000
Criminal Type, 1985 h.	3	2	1,350,000

Leading Winners of Grade 1 Races in North America

Horse, YOB Sex	Wins	G1 SWs	SWs	Earnings
John Henry, 1975 g.	39	**16**	30	$6,591,860
Affirmed, 1975 h.	22	**14**	19	2,393,818
Forego, 1970 g.	34	**14**	24	1,938,957
Spectacular Bid, 1976 h.	26	**13**	23	2,781,608
Bayakoa (Arg), 1984 m.	18	**12**	16	2,785,259
Azeri, 1998 m.	17	**11**	14	4,079,820
Cigar, 1990 h.	18	**11**	14	7,599,815
Lady's Secret, 1982 m.	25	**11**	22	3,021,325
Serena's Song, 1992 m.	18	**11**	17	3,283,388
Paseana (Arg), 1987 m.	14	**10**	14	3,111,292
Skip Away, 1993 h.	18	**10**	16	9,616,360
Alysheba, 1984 h.	11	**9**	10	6,679,242
Easy Goer, 1986 h.	14	**9**	12	4,873,770
Flawlessly, 1988 m.	16	**9**	15	2,572,536
Sky Beauty, 1990 m.	15	**9**	13	1,336,000
Chief's Crown, 1982 h.	12	**8**	10	2,191,168
Heavenly Prize, 1991 m.	9	**8**	8	1,825,940
Personal Ensign, 1984 m.	13	**8**	10	1,679,880
Seattle Slew, 1974 h.	14	**8**	9	1,208,726
Susan's Girl, 1969 m.	29	**8**	24	1,251,668
Ashado, 2001 m.	12	**7**	11	3,931,440
Creme Fraiche, 1982 g.	17	**7**	14	4,024,727
Exceller, 1973 h.	8	**7**	8	1,125,772
Foolish Pleasure, 1972 h.	16	**7**	12	1,216,705
Go for Wand, 1987 f.	10	**7**	8	1,373,338
Goodbye Halo, 1985 m.	11	**7**	10	1,706,702
Gulch, 1984 h.	13	**7**	11	3,095,521
Honest Pleasure, 1973 h.	12	**7**	9	839,997
Open Mind, 1986 m.	12	**7**	11	1,844,372
Sharp Cat, 1994 m.	15	**7**	14	2,032,575
Sightseek, 1999 m.	12	**7**	10	2,445,216
Slew o' Gold, 1980 h.	12	**7**	8	3,533,534
Alydar, 1975 h.	14	**6**	11	957,195
Beautiful Pleasure, 1995 m.	10	**6**	7	2,734,078
Best Pal, 1988 g.	18	**6**	17	5,668,245
Bold 'n Determined, 1977 m.	16	**6**	11	949,599
Desert Vixen, 1970 m.	13	**6**	9	421,538
Holy Bull, 1991 h.	13	**6**	11	2,481,760
Inside Information, 1991 m.	14	**6**	9	1,641,806
Meadow Star, 1988 m.	11	**6**	10	1,445,740
Miss Oceana, 1981 m.	11	**6**	9	1,010,385
Optimistic Gal, 1973 m.	13	**6**	10	686,861
Point Given, 1998 h.	9	**6**	8	3,968,500
Possibly Perfect, 1990 m.	11	**6**	8	1,367,050
Precisionist, 1981 h.	20	**6**	17	3,485,398
Snow Chief, 1983 h.	13	**6**	12	3,383,210
Sunday Silence, 1986 h.	9	**6**	7	4,968,554
Theatrical (Ire), 1982 h.	7	**6**	7	2,840,500

Leading Winners of Graded Stakes in North America

Horse, YOB Sex	Wins	Graded SWs	SWs	Earnings
John Henry, 1975 g.	39	**25**	30	$6,591,860
Forego, 1970 g.	34	**23**	24	1,938,957
Spectacular Bid, 1976 h.	26	**21**	23	2,781,608
Affirmed, 1975 h.	22	**18**	19	2,393,818
Ancient Title, 1970 g.	24	**17**	20	1,252,791
Serena's Song, 1992 m.	18	**17**	17	3,283,388
Skip Away, 1993 h.	18	**16**	16	9,616,360
Bayakoa (Arg), 1984 m.	18	**15**	16	2,785,259
Lady's Secret, 1982 m.	25	**15**	22	3,021,325
Azeri, 1998 m.	17	**14**	14	4,079,820
Paseana (Arg), 1987 m.	14	**14**	14	3,111,292
Flawlessly, 1988 m.	16	**13**	15	2,572,536
Precisionist, 1981 h.	20	**13**	17	3,485,398
Silverbulletday, 1996 m.	15	**13**	14	3,093,207
Sky Beauty, 1990 m.	15	**13**	13	1,336,000
Best Pal, 1988 g.	18	**12**	17	5,668,245
Sabin, 1980 m.	18	**12**	14	1,098,341
Safely Kept, 1986 m.	24	**12**	22	2,194,206
Sharp Cat, 1994 m.	15	**12**	14	2,032,575
Steinlen (GB), 1983 h.	16	**12**	14	3,229,752
Susan's Girl, 1969 m.	29	**12**	24	1,251,668
Ashado, 2001 m.	12	**11**	11	3,931,440
Black Tie Affair (Ire), 1986 h.	18	**11**	13	3,370,694
Cigar, 1990 h.	18	**11**	14	7,599,815
Creme Fraiche, 1982 g.	17	**11**	14	4,024,727
Foolish Pleasure, 1972 h.	16	**11**	12	1,216,705
Gulch, 1984 h.	13	**11**	11	3,095,521
Housebuster, 1987 h.	15	**11**	14	1,229,696
Royal Glint, 1970 h.	21	**11**	15	1,004,816
Xtra Heat, 1998 m.	26	**11**	25	2,389,635
Alysheba, 1984 h.	11	**10**	10	6,679,242
Congaree, 1998 h.	12	**10**	10	3,267,490
Easy Goer, 1986 h.	14	**10**	12	4,873,770
Goodbye Halo, 1985 m.	11	**10**	10	1,706,702
King's Swan, 1980 g.	31	**10**	12	1,924,845
Kona Gold, 1994 g.	14	**10**	11	2,293,384
Lure, 1989 h.	14	**10**	10	2,515,289
Optimistic Gal, 1973 m.	13	**10**	10	686,861
Personal Ensign, 1984 m.	13	**10**	10	1,679,880
Sightseek, 1999 m.	12	**10**	10	2,445,216
Silver Charm, 1994 h.	11	**10**	10	4,444,369
Sir Bear, 1993 g.	19	**10**	11	2,538,422

Leading Winners of Stakes Races in North America

Horse, YOB Sex	Wins	Graded SWs	SWs	Earnings
Exterminator, 1915 g.	50	0	**34**	$221,227
Native Diver, 1959 h.	37	0	**34**	1,026,500
Miss Woodford, 1880 m.	37	0	**33**	118,270
Firenze, 1884 m.	47	0	**32**	112,471
Round Table, 1954 h.	43	0	**32**	1,749,869
Kelso, 1957 g.	39	0	**31**	1,977,896
Kingston, 1884 h.	89	0	**31**	140,195
John Henry, 1975 g.	39	25	**30**	6,591,860
Hanover, 1884 h.	32	0	**27**	118,887
Roamer, 1911 g.	39	0	**27**	98,828
Seabiscuit, 1933 h.	33	0	**27**	437,730
Who Doctor Who, 1983 g.	33	1	**26**	813,870
Hindoo, 1878 h.	30	0	**25**	71,875
Little Bold John, 1982 g.	38	5	**25**	1,956,406
Stymie, 1941 h.	35	0	**25**	918,485
Xtra Heat, 1998 m.	26	11	**25**	2,389,635
Equipoise, 1928 h.	29	0	**24**	338,610
Forego, 1970 g.	34	23	**24**	1,938,957
Susan's Girl, 1969 m.	29	12	**24**	1,251,668
Whirlaway, 1938 h.	32	0	**24**	561,161
Citation, 1945 h.	32	0	**23**	1,085,760
Spectacular Bid, 1976 h.	26	21	**23**	2,781,608
Curribot, 1977 g.	37	0	**22**	491,527
Discovery, 1931 h.	27	0	**22**	195,287
Lady's Secret, 1982 m.	25	15	**22**	3,021,325
Royal Harmony, 1964 h.	38	0	**22**	587,164

Horse, YOB Sex	Wins	Graded SWs	SWs	Earnings
Safely Kept, 1986 m.	24	12	**22**	2,194,206
Swoon's Son, 1953 h.	30	0	**22**	970,605
Armed, 1941 g.	41	0	**21**	817,475
Buckpasser, 1963 h.	25	0	**21**	1,462,014
Frost King, 1978 h.	26	2	**21**	1,033,260
Rosy Way, 1989 g.	28	0	**21**	97,389
Amadevil, 1974 h.	33	0	**20**	653,534
Ancient Title, 1970 g.	24	17	**20**	1,252,791
Chilcoton Blaze, 1980 h.	31	0	**20**	490,862
Hidden Treasure, 1957 h.	24	0	**20**	187,734
Judy's Red Shoes, 1983 m.	25	1	**20**	1,085,668
Sarazen, 1921 g.	27	0	**20**	225,000
Affirmed, 1975 h.	22	18	**19**	2,393,818
Alsab, 1939 h.	25	0	**19**	350,015
Ben Brush, 1893 h.	25	0	**19**	65,217
Decathlon, 1953 h.	25	0	**19**	269,530
Delta Colleen, 1985 m.	23	0	**19**	810,798
Man o' War, 1917 h.	20	0	**19**	249,465
Nashua, 1952 h.	22	0	**19**	1,288,565
Police Inspector, 1977 h.	25	1	**19**	713,707
Rapido Dom, 1978 h.	25	0	**19**	466,974
Say Florida Sandy, 1994 h.	33	5	**19**	2,085,408
Scott's Scoundrel, 1992 h.	22	2	**19**	1,270,052
Spirit of Fighter, 1983 m.	33	0	**19**	847,454
Affectionately, 1960 m.	28	0	**18**	546,659
Arctic Laur, 1988 h.	21	0	**18**	634,809
Cicada, 1959 m.	23	0	**18**	783,674
Copper Case, 1977 g.	33	0	**18**	365,374
Devil Diver, 1939 h.	22	0	**18**	261,064
Dixie Poker Ace, 1987 g.	27	0	**18**	850,126
Energetic King, 1979 h.	35	0	**18**	765,776
Fantango Lady, 1994 m.	22	0	**18**	279,295
Grey Lag, 1918 h.	25	0	**18**	136,715
In Rem, 1975 g.	21	0	**18**	307,742
Orphan Kist, 1984 m.	28	0	**18**	631,997
Overskate, 1975 h.	24	3	**18**	791,634
Parole, 1873 g.	59	0	**18**	82,111
Polynesian, 1942 h.	27	0	**18**	310,410
Timely Ruckus, 1993 g.	25	0	**18**	618,004
Tom Fool, 1949 h.	21	0	**18**	570,165
Twixt, 1969 m.	26	7	**18**	619,141
Victorian Era, 1962 h.	23	0	**18**	198,410
Best Pal, 1988 g.	18	12	**17**	5,668,245
Bewitch, 1945 m.	20	0	**17**	462,605
Bold Ruler, 1954 h.	23	0	**17**	764,204
Cagey Exuberance, 1984 m.	18	3	**17**	765,017
Challedon, 1936 h.	20	0	**17**	334,660
Coaltown, 1945 h.	23	0	**17**	415,675
Damascus, 1964 h.	21	0	**17**	1,176,781
Dance Trainer, 1983 g.	27	0	**17**	276,262
Dave's Friend, 1975 g.	35	2	**17**	1,079,915
Foncier, 1976 h.	29	0	**17**	323,515
Full Pocket, 1969 h.	27	1	**17**	424,031
Gallant Bob, 1972 g.	23	2	**17**	489,992
Glacial Princess, 1981 m.	27	0	**17**	542,792
Hallowed Dreams, 1997 m.	25	0	**17**	740,144
Henry of Navarre, 1891 h.	29	0	**17**	68,985
Imp, 1894 m.	62	0	**17**	70,119
Isadorable, 1983 m.	19	0	**17**	415,018
Leaping Plum, 1991 g.	29	0	**17**	371,584
My Juliet, 1972 m.	24	6	**17**	548,859
Native Dancer, 1950 h.	21	0	**17**	785,240
Precisionist, 1981 h.	20	13	**17**	3,485,398
Secret Romeo, 1998 h.	23	0	**17**	865,790
Sefa's Beauty, 1979 m.	25	5	**17**	1,171,628
Serena's Song, 1992 m.	18	17	**17**	3,283,388
Special Intent, 1981 h.	30	0	**17**	438,558
Spicy, 1955 m.	33	0	**17**	135,233
Sun Beau, 1925 h.	33	0	**17**	376,744
Tosmah, 1961 m.	23	0	**17**	612,588

Most Stakes Wins by Decade by Year of Birth

1931-1940

Horse, YOB Sex, Sire	Yrs. Raced	Starts	Wins	Stk. Wins	Earnings
Seabiscuit, 1933 h., by Hard Tack	6	89	33	**27**	$437,730
Discovery, 1931 h., by Display	4	63	27	**22**	195,287
Alsab, 1939 h., by Good Goods	4	51	25	**19**	350,015
Devil Diver, 1939 h., by *St. Germans	5	47	22	**18**	261,064
Whirlaway, 1938 h., by *Blenheim II	4	60	32	**24**	561,161
Challedon, 1936 h., by *Challenger II	5	44	20	**17**	334,660
War Admiral, 1934 h., by Man o' War	4	26	21	**15**	273,240
Eight Thirty, 1936 h., by Pilate	4	27	16	**13**	155,475
Marriage, 1936 h., by *Strolling Player	8	99	35	**11**	216,090
Parasang, 1937 h., by Halcyon	10	134	29	**11**	102,627

1941-1950

Horse, YOB Sex, Sire	Yrs. Raced	Starts	Wins	Stk. Wins	Earnings
Stymie, 1941 h., by Equestrian	7	131	35	**25**	$918,485
Citation, 1945 h., by Bull Lea	4	45	32	**23**	1,085,760
Armed, 1941 g., by Bull Lea	7	81	41	**21**	817,475
Polynesian, 1942 h., by Unbreakable	4	58	27	**18**	310,410
*Miss Grillo, 1942 m., by Rolando	7	43	16	**17**	250,930
Bewitch, 1945 m., by Bull Lea	5	55	20	**17**	462,605
Native Dancer, 1950 h., by Polynesian	3	22	21	**17**	785,240
Coaltown, 1945 h., by Bull Lea	4	39	23	**17**	415,675
Delegate, 1944 g., by Maeda	9	134	31	**16**	277,530
My Request, 1945 h., by Requested	4	52	22	**16**	385,495

1951-1960

Horse, YOB Sex, Sire	Yrs. Raced	Starts	Wins	Stk. Wins	Earnings
Native Diver, 1959 h., by Imbros	7	81	37	**34**	$1,026,500
Kelso, 1957 g., by Your Host	8	63	39	**31**	1,977,896
Round Table, 1954 h., by *Princequillo	4	66	43	**32**	1,749,869
Swoon's Son, 1953 h., by The Doge	4	51	30	**22**	970,605
Hidden Treasure, 1957 h., by Dark Star	5	65	24	**20**	187,734
Nashua, 1952 h., by *Nasrullah	3	30	22	**19**	1,288,565
Affectionately, 1960 m., by Swaps	4	52	28	**18**	546,659
Cicada, 1959 m., by Bryan G.	4	42	23	**18**	783,674
Decathlon, 1953 h., by Olympia	3	42	25	**19**	269,530
Bold Ruler, 1954 h., by *Nasrullah	3	33	23	**17**	764,204

1961-1970

Horse, YOB Sex, Sire	Yrs. Raced	Starts	Wins	Stk. Wins	Earnings
Forego, 1970 g., by *Forli	6	57	34	**24**	$1,938,957
Susan's Girl, 1969 m., by Quadrangle	5	63	29	**24**	1,251,668
Royal Harmony, 1964 h., by Royal Note	6	105	38	**22**	587,164
Buckpasser, 1963 h., by Tom Fool	3	31	25	**21**	1,462,014
Ancient Title, 1970 g., by Gummo	7	57	24	**20**	1,252,791
Twixt, 1969 m., by Restless Native	4	70	26	**18**	619,141
Victorian Era, 1962 h., by Victoria Park	4	48	23	**18**	198,410
Damascus, 1964 h., by Sword Dancer	3	32	21	**17**	1,176,781
Full Pocket, 1969 h., by Olden Times	4	47	27	**17**	424,031

1971-1980

Horse, YOB Sex, Sire	Yrs. Raced	Starts	Wins	Stk. Wins	Earnings
John Henry, 1975 g., by Ole Bob Bowers	8	83	39	**30**	$6,591,860
Spectacular Bid, 1976 h., by Bold Bidder	3	30	26	**23**	2,781,608
Curribot, 1977 g., by Little Current	12	139	37	**22**	491,527
Frost King, 1978 h., by Ruritania	4	55	27	**21**	1,196,954
Amadevil, 1974 h., by Jungle Savage	7	93	33	**20**	653,534
Chilcoton Blaze, 1980 h., by Victorian Host	10	83	31	**20**	490,862
Affirmed, 1975 h., by Exclusive Native	3	29	22	**19**	2,393,818
Police Inspector, 1977 h., by Police Car	6	71	25	**19**	713,707
Rapido Dom, 1978 h., by Sir Dom	8	105	25	**19**	466,974

1981-1990

Horse, YOB Sex, Sire	Yrs. Raced	Starts	Wins	Stk. Wins	Earnings
Who Doctor Who, 1983 g., by Doctor Stat	8	64	33	**26**	$813,870
Little Bold John, 1982 g., by John Alden	9	105	38	**25**	1,956,406
Lady's Secret, 1982 m., by Secretariat	4	45	25	**22**	3,021,325

Horse, YOB Sex, Sire	Yrs. Raced	Starts	Wins	Stk. Wins	Earnings
Safely Kept, 1986 m., by Horatius	4	31	24	**22**	2,194,206
Rosy Way, 1989 g., by Lord Avie	8	51	28	**21**	97,389
Judy's Red Shoes, 1983 m., by Hold Your Tricks	6	83	25	**20**	1,085,668
Delta Colleen, 1985 m., by Golden Reserve	7	71	23	**19**	810,798
Spirit of Fighter, 1983 m., by Gallant Knave	8	72	33	**19**	847,454
Arctic Laur, 1988 h., by Son of Briartic	7	60	21	**18**	634,809
Dixie Poker Ace, 1987 g., by Patriotically	8	86	27	**18**	850,126

1991-2000

Horse, YOB Sex, Sire	Yrs. Raced	Starts	Wins	Stk. Wins	Earnings
Xtra Heat, 1998 m., by Dixieland Heat	4	35	26	**25**	$2,389,635
Say Florida Sandy, 1994 h., by Personal Flag	8	98	33	**19**	2,085,408
Scott's Scoundrel, 1992 h., by L'Enjoleur	6	50	22	**19**	1,270,052
Fantango Lady, 1994 m., by Lytrump	5	55	22	**18**	279,295
Timely Ruckus, 1993 g., by Bold Executive	8	68	25	**18**	618,004
Hallowed Dreams, 1997 m., by Malagra	4	30	25	**17**	740,144
Leaping Plum, 1991 g., by Lightning Leap	12	66	29	**17**	371,584
Secret Romeo, 1998 h., by Service Stripe	5	55	23	**17**	865,790
Serena's Song, 1992 m., by Rahy	3	38	18	**17**	3,283,388

2001-2005

Horse, YOB Sex, Sire	Yrs. Raced	Starts	Wins	Stk. Wins	Earnings
Ashado, 2001 m., by Saint Ballado	3	21	12	**11**	$3,931,440
Rocky Gulch, 2001 g., by Dry Gulch	3	20	13	**11**	798,608
Lost in the Fog, 2002 c., by Lost Soldier	2	11	10	**9**	889,075
Rockem Sockem, 2001 g., by Ulises	3	21	9	**9**	391,824
A Bit O'Gold, 2001 g., by Gold Fever	3	18	10	**8**	1,788,256
Cocoa Latte, 2001 g., by Demidoff	3	25	13	**8**	211,683
Happy Ticket, 2001 m., by Anet	2	13	10	**8**	782,260
Thundering Verzy, 2001 g., by Verzy	3	24	9	**8**	110,142
Latenite Special, 2001 m., by Super Special	2	16	10	**7**	367,283
Smarty Jones, 2001 h., by Elusive Quality	2	9	8	**7**	7,613,155

North American Leading Runners by Most Stakes Placings

Horse, YOB Sex	Wins	Stakes Wins	Stakes Placings	Earnings
Stymie, 1941 h.	35	25	**38**	918,485
Pampas Host, 1972 h.	19	13	**32**	310,922
Major Presto, 1963 g.	24	12	**30**	125,694
Tick Tock, 1953 g.	20	10	**30**	386,951
Alerted, 1948 h.	20	12	**29**	440,485
Orphan Kist, 1984 m.	28	18	**28**	631,997
Talent Show, 1955 g.	16	7	**28**	507,038
Exterminator, 1915 g.	50	34	**27**	252,596
Gene's Lady, 1981 m.	14	10	**27**	946,190
Royal Harmony, 1964 h.	38	22	**27**	587,164
Ruhe, 1948 g.	11	6	**27**	294,490
Gallorette, 1942 m.	21	13	**26**	445,535
Love Your Host, 1966 h.	22	16	**26**	160,683
*Grey Monarch, 1955 h.	13	7	**25**	216,146
Creme Fraiche, 1982 h.	17	14	**25**	4,024,727
Delegate, 1944 g.	31	15	**25**	277,530
Delta Colleen, 1985 m.	23	19	**25**	810,798
Military Hawk, 1987 g.	18	12	**25**	686,128
Nostalgia's Star, 1982 h.	9	7	**25**	2,154,827
Special Intent, 1981 h.	30	17	**25**	438,558
Stranglehold, 1949 g.	25	9	**25**	289,190
Fiftieth Star, 1972 h.	19	6	**24**	167,035
Armed, 1941 g.	41	19	**23**	817,475
Double B Express, 1975 g.	31	13	**23**	246,013
Eddie Schmidt, 1953 h.	20	12	**23**	526,292
Fourstardave, 1985 g.	21	13	**23**	1,636,737
In the Curl, 1984 m.	26	10	**23**	749,891
Ky Alta, 1977 h.	14	9	**23**	313,885
On Trust, 1944 h.	23	11	**23**	554,145
Straight Deal, 1962 m.	21	13	**23**	733,020
Arctic Laur, 1988 h.	21	18	**22**	634,809
Buzfuz, 1942 g.	35	11	**22**	286,740
Chompion, 1965 h.	14	10	**22**	604,401
Foncier, 1976 h.	29	17	**22**	323,515
Homebuilder, 1984 h.	11	8	**22**	1,172,153
Honor Medal, 1981 h.	19	9	**22**	1,347,073
Judy's Red Shoes, 1983 m.	25	20	**22**	1,085,668
Lucky Salvation, 1980 h.	22	5	**22**	467,891
Ruler's Whirl, 1966 h.	27	8	**22**	116,354
Say Florida Sandy, 1994 h.	33	19	**22**	2,085,408
Sir Bear, 1993 g.	19	11	**22**	2,538,422
Susan's Girl, 1969 m.	29	24	**22**	1,251,668
Adventuresome Love, 1986 h.	16	9	**21**	436,244
Bye and Near, 1963 h.	21	10	**21**	202,040
Charlie Chalmers, 1985 g.	9	6	**21**	378,715
Dixie Poker Ace, 1987 g.	27	18	**21**	850,126
First Fiddle, 1939 h.	23	10	**21**	398,610
Fort Marcy, 1964 g.	21	16	**21**	1,109,791
High Dice, 1995 g.	20	15	**21**	320,672
Kent Green, 1983 g.	13	8	**21**	395,469
King's Swan, 1980 h.	31	12	**21**	1,924,845
Pongo Boy, 1992 g.	22	12	**21**	776,184

North American Leading Runners by Most Stakes Placings Without a Stakes Win

Horse, YOB Sex, Sire	Years Raced	Starts	Wins	Stakes Plcgs	Earnings
Guadalcanal, 1958 h., by Citation	8	91	7	**13**	$243,337
Stunning Native, 1978 m., by Our Native	3	35	3	**13**	155,312
Grand Galop, 1962 g., by Victoria Park	7	119	20	**12**	115,744
Big Numbers, 1997 h., by Numerous	6	54	5	**11**	342,904
Blue Trumpeter, 1949 h., by Thumbs Up	6	106	15	**11**	120,912
Gat's Girl, 1975 m., by Lurullah	5	70	6	**11**	119,242
Milk Wood (GB), 1995 g., by Zafonic	6	45	7	**11**	298,966
Mistress Fletcher, 1992 m., by Sovereign Don	6	71	9	**11**	260,638
Aces Court, 1981 m., by Know Your Aces	6	75	8	**10**	112,740
Behind the Scenes, 1984 m., by Hurry Up Blue	4	41	7	**10**	331,095
Dance Play, 1988 m., by Sovereign Dancer	3	42	4	**10**	168,431
Distinctive Moon, 1979 m., by Distinctive	3	36	4	**10**	124,086
Hold the Beans, 1977 h., by Northern Fling	10	186	18	**10**	175,528
Ladies Agreement, 1970 m., by Royal Union	5	68	14	**10**	295,193
Little Buckles, 1991 m., by Buckley Boy	5	43	9	**10**	466,755
Lonny's Secret, 1966 h., by Terrang	4	38	6	**10**	107,542
Lotta Tike, 1974 m., by Skin Head	5	58	10	**10**	91,760
March of Kings, 1993 g., by River of Kings (Ire)	9	95	17	**10**	497,643
Patti L., 1987 m., by Lyphard's Wish (Fr)	5	55	9	**10**	211,995
Phyxius, 1999 m., by Broad Brush	3	32	3	**10**	220,146
Rule by Reason, 1967 h., by Hail to Reason	5	91	15	**10**	263,547
Sharethetime, 1998 h., by Local Time	5	49	6	**10**	209,626
Sweets, 1985 g., by Mr. Redoy	8	85	8	**10**	196,524
Vaunted Vamp, 1992 m., by Racing Star	6	78	21	**10**	419,641
A Call to Rise, 1988 g., by Poles Apart	8	124	18	**9**	600,441
Autobesarah, 1998 m., by Autocracy	6	63	6	**9**	338,060
Beth Believes, 1986 m., by Believe It	5	44	10	**9**	357,936
Cup o' Shine, 1977 m., by Raise a Cup	4	77	9	**9**	95,556
Dance Card Filled, 1983 h., by Dance Bid	5	71	10	**9**	398,706
Dewans Mischief, 1984 m., by Dewan	4	55	18	**9**	256,399
Dusty Heather, 1996 m., by M. Double M.	4	42	5	**9**	464,887
*Elegant Heir, 1965 h., by Pharamond	5	93	23	**9**	163,435
Fappies Cosy Miss, 1988 m., by Fappiano	3	35	4	**9**	304,885
Golden Arrow, 1999 h., by Rahy	4	32	5	**9**	397,119
Habby's Stuff, 1995 m., by Habitonia	6	68	7	**9**	212,343
Intensitivo, 1966 h., by *Sensitivo	9	143	25	**9**	292,535
Iron Becky, 1977 m., by Iron Anthony	4	61	6	**9**	85,781
Judy's Joe, 1964 h., by *Ben Lomond	5	78	10	**9**	34,102
Lenny the Lender, 1996 g., by Lac Ouimet	8	58	6	**9**	475,761
Naskra Colors, 1992 m., by Star de Naskra	5	28	5	**9**	411,437
Paladin Power, 1998 g., by Blush Rambler	6	53	3	**9**	111,762
Princess Tiree, 1989 m., by Main Debut	6	59	10	**9**	87,601
River Bank Kid, 1989 m., by Eskimo	5	40	6	**9**	142,865
Runaway Magic, 1997 m., by Runaway Groom	3	18	3	**9**	131,305
Sensitive Music, 1969 h., by *Sensitivo	5	68	10	**9**	159,111
Sentosa, 1991 g., by Northern Supremo	12	93	13	**9**	54,879
Shed Some Light, 1992 g., by Homebuilder	9	105	20	**9**	569,638
She's Content, 1983 m., by Restivo	4	47	9	**9**	225,501
Shuttered, 1993 m., by Wild Again	4	26	7	**9**	226,918
Todd's Orphan, 1966 m., by Ambehaving	6	86	6	**9**	60,809
Treachery, 1960 m., by Promised Land	5	105	11	**9**	182,071
Whiz Along, 1985 h., by Cormorant	6	80	9	**9**	581,115

Losingest Horses of All Time
(Without a Win)

Thrust, a chestnut gelding by Bold Salute out of Stitching, by Sting, had very little thrust and lost 105 consecutive races before being retired from the field of battle in 1956.

Thrust finished second five times and was third on seven occasions, with career earnings of $8,180.

Zippy Chippy, a foal of 1991, is notable for the length of time he tried and failed to win. He raced his 11th season in 2004, a longer career than any other horse with more than 58 defeats. He was retired at the end of that year with 100 consecutive losses. Following is a list of the sport's leading losers from 1930 through 2005.

Losses	Horse, YOB	Years Raced	Earnings
105	Thrust, 1950	5	$8,180
100	Zippy Chippy, 1991	11	30,834
92	Star Time, 1943	5	7,215
89	Good Get, 1940	5	2,805
86	Fagrace, 1943	5	6,200
85	Maker of Trouble, 1922	4	565
84	Western Holiday, 1929	5	620
83	City Limit, 1934	5	1,105
82	Giant's Heel, 1943	6	1,560
	Master Mark, 1941	6	290
81	Jibberty Bell, 1955	4	4,802
79	Arvella, 1957	4	2,531
	Omashane, 1942	5	1,475
77	Fred Whitham, 1925	7	1,100
	Space, 1942	5	3,070
76	Prima Whisk, 1936	4	670
	Sure Its Legal, 1988	5	9,772
75	War Bull, 1980	4	10,568
73	*Cafre II, 1951	7	2,339
	Gray Leaves, 1961	4	1,424
	Judgaville, 1981	3	12,965
72	Lattanzio, 1991	5	19,163
	Winnie's Pride, 1988	6	6,790
71	Lady Jule, 1925	3	1,095
	Ninon, 1923	3	1,360
	Roman Sandal, 1924	4	990
	Stark Mad, 1946	4	2,950
70	Red Alley Cat, 1990	6	7,610
69	Buddugie, 1920	4	1,865
	Tuff Nuggets, 1980	4	8,120
68	Buck Flares, 1955	4	6,100
	Lucky Change, 1941	4	3,930
	Right Chief, 1961	4	3,689
67	Bengal Dancer, 1954	4	5,240
	Jimmy What, 1987	6	14,036
	Tchadar, 1924	6	480
66	Dominate'em, 1978	4	5,860
	Doug's Dame, 1965	4	3,558
	Filly Gumbo, 1970	3	4,667
	Really Rushing, 1995	5	17,184
	Rosette, 1926	4	243
	Unclebuck, 1939	7	730
65	Alpha's Star, 1990	6	12,530
	Amarushka, 1981	5	24,336
	Brill Lon, 1956	4	1,420
	Flashy Lark, 1981	5	14,510
	Goodyear, 1927	5	20
	Icy Ethel, 1948	5	3,215
	Jacinto's Arky, 1980	4	4,536
	Petulant, 1928	4	690
	Sam's Tip, 1975	4	14,344
	Tarbucket, 1932	3	945
64	Able Archer, 1957	3	1,847
	Clay K., 1965	6	2,570
	Dawn's Debbie, 1982	3	7,292
	Gosport, 1936	5	465
	Junior T., 1948	4	1,160
	Pacific Star, 1946	7	1,000
	Truckin, 1936	5	865
63	Bell's Luck, 1961	4	867
	Castle Rock, 1927	4	625
	Double Our Flag, 1994	5	22,175
	Dusky Boy, 1928	5	1,310
	Mail Plane, 1948	3	1,805
	Performance Critic, 1996	4	16,475
	Ruby's Crystal, 1980	4	5,575
	Sweet Bernice, 1935	8	995
62	Colonel Titus, 1939	9	605
	Indiana Spa, 1935	5	635
	Kitty Leon, 1939	7	595
	Navy Bean Soup, 1952	4	3,705
	Rebel Girl, 1951	4	4,005
	Suspended Star, 1954	3	3,040
	War O'Gold, 1966	3	4,313
	White Hoops, 1928	6	350
61	Dengee, 1936	4	200
	El Toro Rey, 1943	5	300
	Grimsby, 1957	5	1,114
	Jackson Better, 1982	3	5,572
	Last Ditch, 1971	4	4,344
	Total Mayhem, 1992	4	12,735
	West River, 1959	4	4,765

Leading Horses of All Time By Starts

Horse, YOB Sex, Sire	Years Raced	Starts	Wins	2nds	3rds	Stakes Wins	Earnings
Hiblaze, 1935 h., by Blazes	14	**406**	79	73	52	0	$32,647
*Galley Sweep, 1933 g., by Aga Khan	14	**399**	19	34	46	0	10,677
Shot One, 1941 g., by Shoeless Joe	13	**360**	65	65	68	0	29,982
Onus, 1933 g., by Jack High	15	**344**	53	58	63	0	32,039
Worthowning, 1935 g., by *Longworth	14	**339**	63	62	64	0	41,830
My Blaze, 1930 h., by Big Blaze	11	**338**	52	35	51	1	32,707
Agreed, 1950 g., by Revoked	14	**338**	39	50	49	0	68,004
Marabou, 1925 h., by *Hourless	10	**337**	41	61	44	0	27,458
Vantryst, 1936 h., by Tryster	13	**334**	61	78	48	0	31,971
George de Mar, 1922 h., by *Colonel Vennie	13	**333**	60	54	64	0	69,091
Welsh Lad, 1934 g., by Prince of Wales	13	**329**	67	54	49	0	25,317
Buffoon, 1937 h., by St. Brideaux	10	**329**	37	36	45	0	11,538
Seth's Hope, 1924 h., by Seth	11	**327**	62	51	50	0	74,341
Panjab, 1937 g., by *Kiev	11	**327**	21	32	44	0	17,929
Copin, 1937 h., by Mate	13	**323**	42	40	53	0	27,926
Commission, 1935 h., by Banstar	13	**319**	41	36	39	0	25,626
Higher Bracket, 1936 h., by *Rolls Royce	11	**318**	37	50	51	0	15,661
Golden Sweep, 1923 h., by Flittergold	10	**318**	46	47	58	0	32,285
Noah's Pride, 1929 g., by Noah	12	**317**	60	50	61	1	41,507

Horse, YOB Sex, Sire	Years Raced	Starts	Wins	2nds	3rds	Stakes Wins	Earnings
Champ Sorter, 1952 h., by Four Freedoms	12	**315**	35	43	51	0	62,747
Bee's Little Man, 1961 h., by *Iceberg II	12	**315**	42	32	31	0	108,675
Appease Not, 1946 g., by King Cole	13	**314**	42	44	46	0	122,802
Easiest Way, 1931 g., by *Waygood	11	**311**	27	38	44	0	24,375
Mister Snow Man, 1959 g., by *Iceberg II	14	**310**	43	37	36	0	104,074
Shannon's Hope, 1956 h., by *Shannon II	12	**309**	29	36	43	0	39,848
Port o' Play, 1926 h., by The Porter	9	**308**	44	47	34	1	39,234
Behavin Jerry, 1964 h., by Ambehaving	14	**307**	38	25	48	0	72,259
Star Soldier, 1934 g., by Son o' Battle	11	**305**	37	22	50	0	8,307
Vote Boy, 1932 g., by Torchilla	11	**304**	55	37	48	1	39,240
It's No Use, 1950 h., by *Basileus II	11	**304**	25	40	52	0	68,326
Dr. Jillson, 1930 h., by *Kiev	12	**304**	27	42	37	0	12,522
Mr. Minx, 1952 h., by *Mafosta	12	**302**	36	48	34	0	87,072
Chronology, 1935 g., by *Donnacona	13	**302**	44	41	46	0	14,632
Call Mac, 1965 g., by Loukenmac	13	**301**	13	61	58	0	82,664
Bull Market, 1932 g., by Happy Time	14	**301**	28	49	39	0	19,275
Mantados, 1932 h., by Rock Man	14	**299**	32	47	50	0	19,840
Nine-O-Two, 1936 g., by Sweep By	11	**298**	48	48	40	0	13,915
Huppy, 1931 g., by *Donnacona	10	**297**	12	31	34	0	7,535

Most Starts by Decade by Year of Birth

1931-1940

Horse, YOB Sex, Sire	Yrs. Raced	Starts	Wins	Earnings
Hiblaze, 1935 h., by Blazes	14	**406**	79	$32,647
*Galley Sweep, 1933 g., by Aga Khan	14	**399**	19	10,677
Onus, 1933 g., by Jack High	15	**344**	53	32,039
Worthowning, 1935 g., by *Longworth	14	**339**	63	41,830
Vantryst, 1936 h., by Tryster	13	**334**	61	31,971
Buffoon, 1937 h., by St. Brideaux	10	**329**	37	11,538
Welsh Lad, 1934 g., by Prince of Wales	13	**329**	67	25,317
Panjab, 1937 g., by *Kiev	11	**327**	21	17,929
Copin, 1937 h., by Mate	13	**323**	42	27,926
Commission, 1935 h., by Banstar	13	**319**	41	25,626

1941-1950

Horse, YOB Sex, Sire	Yrs. Raced	Starts	Wins	Earnings
Shot One, 1941 g., by Shoeless Joe	13	**360**	65	29,982
Agreed, 1950 g., by Revoked	14	**338**	39	68,004
Appease Not, 1946 g., by King Cole	13	**314**	42	122,802
It's No Use, 1950 h., by *Basileus II	11	**304**	25	68,326
Bobs Ace, 1947 g., by War Jeep	10	**286**	31	56,957
Eagle Speed, 1946 g., by Sun Again	12	**284**	40	66,337
Shadow Shot, 1944 h., by Chance Shot	11	**279**	35	68,585
Royal Bones, 1947 g., by Mr. Bones	8	**274**	33	70,670
Quatrefoil, 1945 h., by *Quatre Bras II	10	**273**	18	46,994
Bee Lee Tee, 1947 h., by Roy T.	12	**270**	47	104,805

1951-1960

Horse, YOB Sex, Sire	Yrs. Raced	Starts	Wins	Earnings
Champ Sorter, 1952 h., by Four Freedoms	12	**315**	35	62,747
Mister Snow Man, 1959 g., by *Iceberg II	14	**310**	43	104,074
Shannon's Hope, 1956 h., by *Shannon II	12	**309**	29	39,848
Mr. Minx, 1952 h., by *Mafosta	12	**302**	36	87,072
Ole Sarge, 1956 g., by Carrara Marble	12	**296**	24	36,373
Easy Knight, 1955 g., by Easy Mon	12	**294**	22	48,099
Asking, 1952 h., by Pry	12	**287**	27	46,442
Black Jet, 1957 h., by Lord Boswell	12	**281**	21	51,077
Knight-King, 1957 g., by Tuscany	12	**277**	26	79,141
Bell's Range, 1954 g., by Ramillies	13	**274**	41	65,100

1961-1970

Horse, YOB Sex, Sire	Yrs. Raced	Starts	Wins	Earnings
Bee's Little Man, 1961 h., by *Iceberg II	12	**315**	42	108,675
Behavin Jerry, 1964 h., by Ambehaving	14	**307**	38	72,259
Call Mac, 1965 g., by Loukenmac	13	**301**	13	82,664
Royal Doctor, 1961 g., by *Royal Vale	12	**286**	21	50,793
Bayou Teche, 1961 g., by Bryan G.	12	**281**	48	107,577
Dandier, 1961 h., by Mohammedan	11	**278**	31	74,523
Pin Pan Dan, 1966 h., by Pan Dancer	12	**278**	33	86,330
Wild Wink, 1969 h., by Quickasawink	13	**275**	40	129,004
Bucket O'Suds, 1965 h., by Rattle Dancer	13	**273**	38	158,017
Candy Top, 1964 h., by Top Double	13	**273**	35	94,990

1971-1980

Horse, YOB Sex, Sire	Yrs. Raced	Starts	Wins	Earnings
Dot the T., 1972 h., by *Notable II	12	**261**	48	227,033
Legrand, 1974 h., by Delta Judge	11	**255**	13	104,322
Mr. Turnabout, 1971 h., by Reverse	11	**252**	25	89,061
Magic Flash, 1971 g., by *Babieca II	10	**250**	22	63,175
Catch Poppy, 1973 h., by Poppy Jay	12	**246**	30	122,346
Arrowsmith, 1976 h., by Briartic	12	**243**	20	166,106
One Purpose, 1978 g., by Sinister Purpose	13	**242**	13	145,894
Dan Dan, 1975 g., by Tumiga	11	**238**	29	171,438
Troy Knight, 1973 h., by Nashwood	12	**235**	38	143,287
Uhrich Enzurich, 1972 g., by *Semillant	13	**234**	21	60,247

1981-1990

Horse, YOB Sex, Sire	Yrs. Raced	Starts	Wins	Earnings
Z. Z. Quickfoot, 1982 g., by Master Derby	12	**266**	27	122,752
Sharon Caper, 1983 g., by Cartesian	13	**244**	33	109,685
Passive Loss, 1987 m., by Highland Blade	13	**225**	22	121,356
Side Winding, 1985 g., by Shananie	12	**218**	26	121,648
Our Legal Eagle, 1990 g., by Exuberant	13	**217**	10	100,892
Valley Cat, 1985 g., by Valdez	14	**216**	29	123,612
Wicked Wike, 1982 g., by Olden Times	11	**212**	11	318,561
Callisto, 1987 g., by Nasty and Bold	11	**210**	28	329,002
Playing Politics, 1982 g., by In Reality	15	**203**	25	187,639
Noble But Nasty, 1981 g., by Nasty and Bold	11	**200**	40	325,588

1991-2000

Horse, YOB Sex, Sire	Yrs. Raced	Starts	Wins	Earnings
Smart And Regal, 1991 g., by Regal Classic	11	**188**	21	$148,253
Talc of Dreams, 1992 g., by Talc	11	**172**	11	110,421
He Makes Cents, 1992 g., by Narcotics Squad	9	**171**	7	99,747
Motion to Suppress, 1992 g., by Timeless Native	12	**161**	20	164,156
Mr. Butterscotch, 1992 g., by Compliance	10	**161**	12	116,614
Lindapinda, 1992 m., by Unite	7	**158**	14	104,473
Cumberland Gap, 1992 g., by Allen's Prospect	12	**156**	34	323,345
Desiard, 1993 g., by Nalees Man	11	**155**	21	200,635
Francis Albert, 1992 g., by Cross Canal	11	**155**	27	267,055
Mahrally, 1991 g., by Ballydoyle	11	**154**	32	168,440

2001-2005

Horse, YOB Sex, Sire	Yrs. Raced	Starts	Wins	Earnings
Smart Confidence, 2001 g., by Confide	3	**56**	6	$65,211
Haillye's Brother, 2001 g., by Wayne's Crane	3	**53**	6	63,603
Emilin, 2001 g., by Scatmandu	3	**52**	3	40,876
Real Town Guy, 2001 h., by Real Quiet	3	**52**	3	48,264
Dandy Belle, 2001 f., by Boone's Mill	3	**51**	4	61,883
Dble Diamond Norma, 2001 m., by Name for Norm	3	**49**	6	26,627
Lady Irene, 2001 m., by Traitor	3	**49**	8	98,871
Booming Sound, 2001 g., by Line In The Sand	3	**48**	3	29,983
Buck's Shar, 2001 m., by Buck Strider	3	**48**	7	36,207
Formal Fanny, 2001 m., by Formal Dinner	3	**48**	7	104,235

All-Time Leading Earners by Deflated Dollars

Comparing horses of different eras is always an entertaining exercise. Was Secretariat a better racehorse than Citation? That question will never be answered definitively because they never met on the track, so comparing horses of one era to another is subjective.

Earnings are one measure of performance, though that yardstick also has its drawbacks because the purses of yesteryear do not compare with the purses of today. There is a way to use earnings as a measure of productivity, however, by deflating the earnings; that is, adjusting earnings to account for the effects of inflation.

In the tables presented on this page and the following two pages are deflated earnings of the all-time leaders in Thoroughbred racing since 1929. Considered for inclusion on the list is any horse that started at least once in North America. Horses that raced at least once in North America and also raced overseas have all their earnings included, all being converted to United States dollars and then deflated by racing year.

All-time leading money winner adjusted for inflation is two-time Horse of the Year John Henry, who raced 83 times from 1977 through '84. The durable gelding won the first $1-million Thoroughbred race in the U.S., the 1981 Arlington Million Stakes (G1), and his career ended the year in which the Breeders' Cup was inaugurated. Second on the list is two-time Horse of the Year Cigar, the all-time leading earner in North America in current dollars.

The deflator used to convert all earnings is the Gross Domestic Product implicit price deflator published by the U.S. Bureau of Economic Analysis.

On the first two pages are the all-time leaders by deflated dollars regardless of sex. On the third page is a list of the all-time leading female earners by deflated dollars. Statistics are through December 31, 2005.

All-Time Leading Earners by Deflated Dollars

Horse, YOB Sex, Sire	Yrs. Raced	Starts	1st	2nd	3rd	Nominal Earnings	Deflated Earnings
John Henry, 1975 g., by Ole Bob Bowers	8	83	39	15	9	$6,591,860	$12,077,802
Cigar, 1990 h., by Palace Music	4	33	19	4	5	9,999,815	12,069,840
Skip Away, 1993 h., by Skip Trial	4	38	18	10	6	9,616,360	11,320,575
Kelso, 1957 g., by Your Host	8	63	39	12	2	1,977,896	10,258,907
Alysheba, 1984 h., by Alydar	3	26	11	8	2	6,679,242	10,052,999
Round Table, 1954 h., by *Princequillo	4	66	43	8	5	1,749,869	9,641,509
Fantastic Light, 1996 h., by Rahy	4	25	12	5	3	8,486,957	9,428,770
Pleasantly Perfect, 1998 h., by Pleasant Colony	4	18	9	3	2	7,789,880	8,095,048
Silver Charm, 1994 h., by Silver Buck	4	24	12	7	2	6,944,369	8,089,992
Smarty Jones, 2001 h., by Elusive Quality	2	9	8	1	0	7,613,155	7,824,819
Nashua, 1952 h., by *Nasrullah	3	30	22	4	1	1,288,565	7,659,296
Captain Steve, 1997 h., by Fly So Free	3	25	9	3	7	6,828,356	7,564,488
Citation, 1945 h., by Bull Lea	4	45	32	10	2	1,085,760	7,410,317
Best Pal, 1988 g., by *Habitony	7	47	18	11	4	5,668,245	7,374,411
Stymie, 1941 h., by Equestrian	7	131	35	33	28	918,485	7,289,621
Tiznow, 1997 h., by Cee's Tizzy	2	15	8	4	2	6,427,830	7,128,941
Buckpasser, 1963 h., by Tom Fool	3	31	25	4	1	1,462,014	7,117,967
Sunday Silence, 1986 h., by Halo	3	14	9	5	0	4,968,554	7,072,606
Singspiel (Ire), 1992 h., by In the Wings (GB)	4	20	9	8	0	5,952,825	7,060,102
Easy Goer, 1986 h., by Alydar	3	20	14	5	1	4,873,770	6,975,354
Spend a Buck, 1982 h., by Buckaroo	2	15	10	3	2	4,220,689	6,820,424
Taiki Blizzard, 1991 h., by Seattle Slew	4	23	6	8	2	5,523,549	6,646,689
Carry Back, 1958 h., by Saggy	4	62	21	11	11	1,241,165	6,525,114
Creme Fraiche, 1982 g., by Rich Cream	6	64	17	12	13	4,024,727	6,286,651
Armed, 1941 g., by Bull Lea	7	81	41	20	10	817,475	6,285,368
Spectacular Bid, 1976 h., by Bold Bidder	3	30	26	2	1	2,781,608	6,155,696
Unbridled, 1987 h., by Fappiano	3	24	8	6	6	4,489,475	6,150,546
Medaglia d'Oro, 1999 h., by El Prado (Ire)	4	17	8	7	0	5,754,720	6,077,251
Slew o' Gold, 1980 h., by Seattle Slew	3	21	12	5	1	3,533,534	5,913,367
Whirlaway, 1938 h., by *Blenheim II	4	60	32	15	9	561,161	5,903,600
Ferdinand, 1983 h., by Nijinsky II	4	29	8	9	6	3,777,978	5,819,538
Forego, 1970 g., by *Forli	6	57	34	9	7	1,938,957	5,804,947
Affirmed, 1975 h., by Exclusive Native	3	29	22	5	1	2,393,818	5,709,082
High Chaparral (Ire), 1999 h., by Sadler's Wells	3	13	10	1	2	5,331,231	5,703,377
Jim and Tonic (Fr), 1994 g., by Double Bed (Fr)	7	39	13	13	4	4,975,807	5,596,895
Street Cry (Ire), 1998 h., by Machiavellian	3	12	5	6	1	5,150,837	5,565,088
Swoon's Son, 1953 h., by The Doge	4	51	30	10	3	970,605	5,555,731
Precisionist, 1981 h., by Crozier	5	46	20	10	4	3,485,398	5,548,228
Roses in May, 2000 h., by Devil His Due	3	13	8	4	0	5,490,187	5,541,724
Damascus, 1964 h., by Sword Dancer	3	32	21	7	3	1,176,781	5,461,590
Snow Chief, 1983 h., by Reflected Glory	3	24	13	3	5	3,383,210	5,332,058
Daylami (Ire), 1994 h., by Doyoun	4	21	11	3	4	4,614,762	5,311,859

Horse, YOB Sex, Sire	Yrs. Raced	Starts	1st	2nd	3rd	Nominal Earnings	Deflated Earnings
Assault, 1943 h., by Bold Venture	6	42	18	6	7	$ 675,470	$5,227,546
Behrens, 1994 h., by Pleasant Colony	4	27	9	8	3	4,563,500	5,213,796
Awesome Again, 1994 h., by Deputy Minister	2	12	9	0	2	4,374,590	5,090,654
Bet Twice, 1984 h., by Sportin' Life	3	26	10	6	4	3,308,599	5,061,460
Native Diver, 1959 h., by Imbros	7	81	37	7	12	1,026,500	5,055,667
Cryptoclearance, 1984 h., by Fappiano	4	44	12	10	7	3,376,327	5,015,748
Swaps, 1952 h., by *Khaled	3	25	19	2	2	848,900	4,997,914
Seabiscuit, 1933 h., by Hard Tack	6	89	33	15	13	437,730	4,962,473
Devil His Due, 1989 h., by Devil's Bag	4	41	11	12	3	3,920,405	4,955,400
Dahlia, 1970 m., by *Vaguely Noble	5	48	15	3	7	1,489,105	4,851,139
Native Dancer, 1950 h., by Polynesian	3	22	21	1	0	785,240	4,840,691
Pilsudski (Ire), 1992 h., by Polish Precedent	4	22	10	6	2	4,080,297	4,830,750
T. V. Lark, 1957 h., by *Indian Hemp	4	72	19	13	6	902,194	4,796,231
Lady's Secret, 1982 m., by Secretariat	4	45	25	9	3	3,021,325	4,793,721
Fort Marcy, 1964 g., by *Amerigo	6	75	21	18	14	1,109,791	4,785,424
Roman Brother, 1961 g., by Third Brother	4	42	16	10	5	943,473	4,771,915
Secretariat, 1970 h., by Bold Ruler	2	21	16	3	1	1,316,808	4,724,986
Seeking the Pearl, 1994 m., by Seeking the Gold	4	21	8	2	3	4,021,716	4,709,213
Steinlen (GB), 1983 h., by Habitat	5	45	20	10	7	3,297,169	4,708,779
Gulch, 1984 h., by Mr. Prospector	3	32	13	8	4	3,095,521	4,690,870
Trinycarol (Ven), 1979 m., by Velvet Cap	4	29	18	3	1	2,644,392	4,680,133
Dr. Fager, 1964 h., by Rough'n Tumble	3	22	18	2	1	1,002,642	4,642,980
Find, 1950 g., by Discovery	8	110	22	27	27	803,615	4,619,267
Sandpit (Brz), 1989 h., by Baynoun (Ire)	7	40	14	11	6	3,812,597	4,589,642
Theatrical (Ire), 1982 h., by Nureyev	4	22	10	4	2	2,940,036	4,535,454
Black Tie Affair (Ire), 1986 h., by Miswaki	4	45	18	9	6	3,370,694	4,530,182
Strike the Gold, 1988 h., by Alydar	4	31	6	8	5	3,457,026	4,528,813
Symboli Rudolf (Jpn), 1981 h., by Partholon	4	16	13	1	1	2,764,980	4,527,373
Cat Thief, 1996 h., by Storm Cat	3	30	4	9	8	3,951,012	4,521,147
Saint Liam, 2000 h., by Saint Ballado	3	20	9	6	1	4,456,995	4,481,808
Sword Dancer, 1956 h., by Sunglow	3	39	15	7	4	829,610	4,468,952
Swain (Ire), 1992 h., by Nashwan	4	22	10	4	6	3,797,566	4,461,503
Perfect Drift, 1999 g., by Dynaformer	5	35	11	9	6	4,290,190	4,453,482
Sulamani (Ire), 1999 h., by Hernando (Fr)	2	11	5	2	1	4,215,365	4,402,147
Sky Classic, 1987 h., by Nijinsky II	4	29	15	6	1	3,320,398	4,401,251
*Cougar II, 1966 h., by Tale of Two Cities	6	50	20	7	17	1,172,625	4,388,146
Point Given, 1998 h., by Thunder Gulch	2	13	9	3	0	3,968,500	4,362,146
Dance Smartly, 1988 m., by Danzig	3	17	12	2	3	3,263,835	4,337,482
Azeri, 1998 m., by Jade Hunter	4	24	17	4	0	4,079,820	4,323,410
Great Communicator, 1983 h., by Key to the Kingdom	6	56	14	10	7	2,922,615	4,319,461
Susan's Girl, 1969 m., by Quadrangle	5	63	29	14	11	1,251,668	4,309,420
Bold Ruler, 1954 h., by *Nasrullah	3	33	23	4	2	764,204	4,275,245
Exceller, 1973 h., by *Vaguely Noble	5	33	15	5	6	1,674,587	4,267,352
Paradise Creek, 1989 h., by Irish River (Fr)	4	25	14	7	1	3,401,416	4,264,491
Paseana (Arg), 1987 m., by Ahmad	6	36	19	10	2	3,317,427	4,257,916
Gentlemen (Arg), 1992 h., by Robin des Bois	5	24	13	4	2	3,608,558	4,246,791
Lando (Ger), 1990 h., by Acatenango	4	24	10	3	1	3,438,727	4,244,132
Candy Spots, 1960 h., by *Nigromante	3	22	12	5	1	824,718	4,239,976
First Landing, 1956 h., by *Turn-to	3	37	19	9	2	779,577	4,217,107
Mongo, 1959 h., by *Royal Charger	4	46	22	10	4	820,766	4,209,800
Manila, 1983 h., by Lyphard	3	18	12	5	0	2,692,799	4,201,186
Allez France, 1970 m., by *Sea-Bird	4	21	13	3	1	1,262,801	4,184,601
Almutawakel (GB), 1995 h., by Machiavellian	4	19	4	4	1	3,643,021	4,171,906
Riva Ridge, 1969 h., by First Landing	3	30	17	3	1	1,111,497	4,170,356
Crimson Satan, 1959 h., by Spy Song	4	58	18	9	9	796,077	4,137,030
Broad Brush, 1983 h., by Ack Ack	3	27	14	5	5	2,656,793	4,131,578
Cicada, 1959 m., by Bryan G.	4	42	23	8	6	783,674	4,095,253
Gate Dancer, 1981 h., by Sovereign Dancer	4	28	7	8	7	2,501,705	4,078,930
Bertrando, 1989 h., by Skywalker	5	24	9	6	2	3,185,610	4,077,427
Forty Niner, 1985 h., by Mr. Prospector	2	19	11	5	0	2,726,000	4,069,666
Bally Ache, 1957 h., by *Ballydam	2	31	16	9	4	758,522	4,064,240
Victory Gallop, 1995 h., by Cryptoclearance	3	17	9	5	1	3,505,895	4,052,719
With Approval, 1986 h., by Caro (Ire)	3	23	13	5	1	2,863,540	4,033,936
Gun Bow, 1960 h., by Gun Shot	3	42	17	8	4	798,722	4,033,321
Ashado, 2001 m., by Saint Ballado	3	21	12	4	3	3,931,440	4,027,237
Bayakoa (Arg), 1984 m., by Consultant's Bid	6	39	21	9	0	2,861,701	4,024,253
Social Outcast, 1950 g., by Shut Out	5	58	18	9	6	668,300	4,017,968
Serena's Song, 1992 m., by Rahy	3	38	18	11	3	3,283,388	3,985,181
Awad, 1990 h., by Caveat	7	70	14	10	11	3,270,131	3,977,718
Chief Bearhart, 1993 h., by Chief's Crown	4	26	12	5	3	3,381,557	3,970,701
Spain, 1997 m., by Thunder Gulch	4	35	9	9	7	3,540,542	3,925,736

Female All-Time Leading Earners by Deflated Dollars

Horse, YOB Sex, Sire	Yrs. Raced	Starts	1st	2nd	3rd	Nominal Earnings	Deflated Earnings
Dahlia, 1970 m., by *Vaguely Noble	5	48	15	3	7	$1,489,105	$4,851,139
Lady's Secret, 1982 m., by Secretariat	4	45	25	9	3	3,021,325	4,793,721
Seeking the Pearl, 1994 m., by Seeking the Gold	4	21	8	2	3	4,021,716	4,709,213
Trinycarol (Ven), 1979 m., by Velvet Cap	4	29	18	3	1	2,644,392	4,680,133
Dance Smartly, 1988 m., by Danzig	3	17	12	2	3	3,263,835	4,337,482
Azeri, 1998 m., by Jade Hunter	4	24	17	4	0	4,079,820	4,323,410
Susan's Girl, 1969 m., by Quadrangle	5	63	29	14	11	1,251,668	4,309,420
Paseana (Arg), 1987 m., by Ahmad	6	36	19	10	2	3,317,427	4,257,916
Allez France, 1970 m., by *Sea-Bird	4	21	13	3	1	1,262,801	4,184,601
Cicada, 1959 m., by Bryan G.	4	42	23	8	6	783,674	4,095,253
Ashado, 2001 m., by Saint Ballado	3	21	12	4	3	3,931,440	4,027,237
Bayakoa (Arg), 1984 m., by Consultant's Bid	6	39	21	9	0	2,861,701	4,024,253
Serena's Song, 1992 m., by Rahy	3	38	18	11	3	3,283,388	3,985,181
Spain, 1997 m., by Thunder Gulch	4	35	9	9	7	3,540,542	3,925,736
Shuvee, 1966 m., by Nashua	4	44	16	10	6	890,445	3,750,645
Life's Magic, 1981 m., by Cox's Ridge	3	32	8	11	6	2,255,218	3,729,320
All Along (Fr), 1979 m., by Targowice	4	21	9	4	2	2,125,809	3,642,400
Triptych, 1982 m., by Riverman	5	41	14	5	11	2,318,946	3,580,271
Silverbulletday, 1996 m., by Silver Deputy	3	23	15	3	1	3,093,207	3,555,273
Straight Deal, 1962 m., by Hail to Reason	6	99	21	21	9	733,020	3,495,757
Gallorette, 1942 m., by *Challenger II	5	72	21	20	13	445,535	3,490,553
Escena, 1993 m., by Strawberry Road (Aus)	4	29	11	9	3	2,962,639	3,466,110
Let's Elope (NZ), 1987 m., by Nassipour	5	26	11	0	5	2,528,902	3,346,745
Flawlessly, 1988 m., by Affirmed	5	28	16	4	3	2,572,536	3,321,173
Banshee Breeze, 1995 m., by Unbridled	3	18	10	5	2	2,784,798	3,213,772
Bewitch, 1945 m., by Bull Lea	5	55	20	10	11	462,605	3,209,763
Ouija Board (GB), 2001 m., by Cape Cross (Ire)	3	13	7	1	3	3,163,126	3,197,175
Miesque, 1984 m., by Nureyev	3	16	12	3	1	2,070,163	3,138,782
Beautiful Pleasure, 1995 m., by Maudlin	5	25	10	5	2	2,734,078	3,115,086
Estrapade, 1980 m., by *Vaguely Noble	4	30	12	5	5	1,937,142	3,085,624
Top Flight, 1929 m., by *Dis Donc	2	16	12	0	0	275,900	3,074,324
Tosmah, 1961 m., by Tim Tam	4	39	23	6	2	612,588	3,074,305
Safely Kept, 1986 m., by Horatius	4	31	24	2	3	2,194,206	3,040,879
Busher, 1942 m., by War Admiral	3	21	15	3	1	334,035	3,012,787
Honeymoon, 1943 m., by *Beau Pere	6	78	20	14	9	387,760	2,964,523
Dance in the Mood (Jpn), 2001 m., by Sunday Silence	3	17	4	3	1	3,339,410	2,946,182
Old Hat, 1959 m., by Boston Doge	6	80	35	18	9	556,401	2,794,880
Affectionately, 1960 m., by Swaps	4	52	28	8	6	546,659	2,783,420
Heritage of Gold, 1995 m., by Gold Legend	4	28	16	2	4	2,381,762	2,691,103
Open Mind, 1986 m., by Deputy Minister	3	19	12	2	2	1,844,372	2,671,309
Take Charge Lady, 1999 m., by Dehere	3	22	11	7	0	2,480,377	2,660,722
Next Move, 1947 m., by Bull Lea	4	46	17	11	3	398,550	2,630,920
Xtra Heat, 1998 m., by Dixieland Heat	4	35	26	5	2	2,389,635	2,599,316
Sickle's Image, 1948 m., by Sickletoy	5	73	27	13	16	413,275	2,593,104
Gamely, 1964 m., by Bold Ruler	3	41	16	9	6	574,961	2,572,885
Sightseek, 1999 m., by Distant View	3	20	12	5	0	2,445,216	2,557,112
Bed o' Roses, 1947 m., by Rosemont	4	46	18	8	6	383,925	2,552,077
Politely, 1963 m., by *Amerigo	4	49	21	9	5	552,972	2,543,309
Goodbye Halo, 1985 m., by Halo	3	24	11	5	4	1,706,702	2,523,445
Personal Ensign, 1984 m., by Private Account	3	13	13	0	0	1,679,880	2,519,556
Cesario (Jpn), 2002 f., by Special Week	2	6	5	1	0	2,578,568	2,511,053
Perfect Sting, 1996 m., by Red Ransom	4	21	14	3	0	2,202,042	2,484,499
Very Subtle, 1984 m., by Hoist the Silver	4	29	12	6	4	1,608,360	2,455,392
Family Style, 1983 m., by State Dinner	3	35	10	8	7	1,537,118	2,432,684
Sharp Cat, 1994 m., by Storm Cat	3	22	15	3	0	2,032,575	2,390,274
Convenience, 1968 m., by Fleet Nasrullah	4	35	15	9	4	648,933	2,369,597
Megahertz (GB), 1999 m., by Pivotal	5	34	14	6	5	2,261,594	2,347,688
Hatoof, 1989 m., by Irish River (Fr)	4	21	9	4	1	1,841,070	2,335,635
Miss Alleged, 1987 m., by Alleged	3	15	5	4	3	1,757,342	2,335,165
Gallant Bloom, 1966 m., by *Gallant Man	3	22	16	1	1	535,739	2,328,108
Numbered Account, 1969 m., by Buckpasser	3	22	14	3	2	607,048	2,323,333
Trillion, 1974 m., by Hail to Reason	3	32	9	14	3	957,413	2,304,510
Pebbles (GB), 1981 m., by Sharpen Up (GB)	3	15	8	4	0	1,419,632	2,297,876
Outstandingly, 1982 m., by Exclusive Native	4	28	10	4	3	1,412,206	2,296,195
The Very One, 1975 m., by One for All	5	71	22	12	9	1,104,623	2,295,445
User Friendly (GB), 1989 m., by Slip Anchor	3	16	8	1	2	1,764,938	2,278,748
Riskaverse, 1999 m., by Dynaformer	5	32	9	6	4	2,182,429	2,274,998
Princess Rooney, 1980 m., by Verbatim	3	21	17	2	1	1,343,339	2,271,699
Jewel Princess, 1992 m., by Key to the Mint	4	29	13	4	7	1,904,060	2,271,073

Leading Earners by Foal Crop

YOB	MALE, Sex, Sire	Yrs. Raced	Strts	Wins	St. Wins	Earnings	FEMALE, Sex, Sire	Yrs. Raced	Strts	Wins	St. Wins	Earnings
2003	**Stevie Wonderboy**, c., Stephen Got Even	2	5	3	2	$1,028,940	**Folklore**, f., Tiznow	2	7	4	3	$927,500
2002	**Afleet Alex**, h., Northern Afleet	2	12	8	6	2,765,800	**Sweet Catomine**, f., Storm Cat	2	7	5	5	1,059,600
2001	**Smarty Jones**, h., Elusive Quality	2	9	8	7	7,613,155	**Ashado**, m., Saint Ballado	3	21	12	11	3,931,440
2000	**Roses in May**, h., Devil His Due	3	13	8	4	5,490,187	**Island Fashion**, m., Petionville	3	27	6	6	1,965,970
1999	**Medaglia d'Oro**, h., El Prado (Ire)	4	17	8	7	5,754,720	**Take Charge Lady**, m., Dehere	3	22	11	9	2,480,377
1998	**Pleasantly Perfect**, h., Pleasant Colony	4	18	9	6	7,789,880	**Azeri**, m., Jade Hunter	4	24	17	14	4,079,820
1997	**Captain Steve**, h., Fly So Free	3	25	9	8	6,828,356	**Spain**, m., Thunder Gulch	4	35	9	7	3,540,542
1996	**Fantastic Light**, h., Rahy	4	25	12	10	8,486,957	**Silverbulletday**, m., Silver Deputy	3	23	15	14	3,093,207
1995	**Victory Gallop**, h., Cryptoclearance	3	17	9	7	3,505,895	**Banshee Breeze**, m., Unbridled	3	18	10	8	2,784,798
1994	**Silver Charm**, h., Silver Buck	4	24	12	11	6,944,369	**Seeking the Pearl**, m., Seeking the Gold	4	21	8	7	4,021,716
1993	**Skip Away**, h., Skip Trial	4	38	18	16	9,616,360	**Escena**, m., Strawberry Road (Aus)	4	29	11	7	2,962,639
1992	**Thunder Gulch**, h., Gulch	2	16	9	8	2,915,086	**Serena's Song**, m., Rahy	3	38	18	17	3,283,388
1991	**Taiki Blizzard**, h., Seattle Slew	4	23	6	3	5,523,549	**Heavenly Prize**, m., Seeking the Gold	4	18	9	8	1,825,940
1990	**Cigar**, h., Palace Music	4	33	19	15	9,999,815	**Ski Paradise**, m., Lyphard	3	20	6	5	1,470,588
1989	**Devil His Due**, h., Devil's Bag	4	41	11	9	3,920,405	**Hatoof**, m., Irish River (Fr)	4	21	9	8	1,841,070
1988	**Best Pal**, g., *Habitony	7	47	18	17	5,668,245	**Dance Smartly**, m., Danzig	3	17	12	10	3,263,835
1987	**Unbridled**, h., Fappiano	3	24	8	5	4,489,475	**Miss Alleged**, m., Alleged	3	15	5	4	1,757,342
1986	**Sunday Silence**, h., Halo	3	14	9	7	4,968,554	**Safely Kept**, m., Horatius	4	31	24	22	2,194,206
1985	**Forty Niner**, h., Mr. Prospector	2	19	11	9	2,726,000	**Goodbye Halo**, m., Halo	3	24	11	10	1,706,702
1984	**Alysheba**, h., Alydar	3	26	11	10	6,679,242	**Miesque**, m., Nureyev	3	16	12	11	2,070,163
1983	**Ferdinand**, h., Nijinsky II	4	29	8	7	3,777,978	**Family Style**, m., State Dinner	3	35	10	9	1,537,118
1982	**Spend a Buck**, h., Buckaroo	2	15	10	7	4,220,689	**Lady's Secret**, m., Secretariat	4	45	25	22	3,021,325
1981	**Precisionist**, h., Crozier	5	46	20	17	3,485,398	**Life's Magic**, m., Cox's Ridge	3	32	8	7	2,255,218
1980	**Slew o' Gold**, h., Seattle Slew	3	21	12	8	3,533,534	**Estrapade**, m., *Vaguely Noble	4	30	12	10	1,937,142
1979	**Majesty's Prince**, h., His Majesty	4	43	12	9	2,077,796	**Sefa's Beauty**, m., Lt. Stevens	5	52	25	17	1,171,628
1978	**Silveyville**, h., *Petrone	8	56	19	14	1,282,880	**Sintrillium**, m., Sinister Purpose	5	46	14	9	743,602
1977	**Temperence Hill**, h., Stop the Music	3	31	11	9	1,567,650	**Bold 'n Determined**, m., Bold and Brave	3	20	16	11	949,599
1976	**Spectacular Bid**, h., Bold Bidder	3	30	26	23	2,781,608	**Track Robbery**, m., No Robbery	6	59	22	13	1,098,537
1975	**John Henry**, g., Ole Bob Bowers	8	83	39	30	6,591,860	**The Very One**, m., One for All	5	71	22	13	1,104,623
1974	**Seattle Slew**, h., Bold Reasoning	3	17	14	9	1,208,726	**Trillion**, m., Hail to Reason	3	32	9	8	957,413
1973	**Exceller**, h., *Vaguely Noble	5	33	15	13	1,674,587	**Optimistic Gal**, m., Sir Ivor	2	21	13	10	686,861
1972	**Foolish Pleasure**, h., What a Pleasure	3	26	16	12	1,216,705	**Ivanjica**, m., Sir Ivor	3	15	6	5	626,682
1971	**Sharp Gary**, g., Carry Back	7	115	16	8	535,198	**Chris Evert**, m., Swoon's Son	3	15	10	7	679,475
1970	**Forego**, g., *Forli	6	57	34	24	1,938,957	**Dahlia**, m., *Vaguely Noble	5	48	15	14	1,489,105
1969	**Riva Ridge**, h., First Landing	3	30	17	13	1,111,497	**Susan's Girl**, m., Quadrangle	5	63	29	24	1,251,668
1968	**Run the Gantlet**, h., Tom Rolfe	3	21	9	7	559,079	**Convenience**, m., Fleet Nasrullah	4	35	15	8	648,933
1967	**Loud**, g., *Herbager	7	88	12	3	527,779	**Saturnina**, m., *Ballydonnell	5	107	47	8	392,195
1966	**Ack Ack**, h., Battle Joined	4	27	19	13	636,641	**Shuvee**, m., Nashua	4	44	16	15	890,445
1965	**Nodouble**, h., *Noholme II	4	42	13	9	846,749	**Gay Matelda**, m., Sir Gaylord	3	37	9	5	409,945
1964	**Damascus**, h., Sword Dancer	3	32	21	17	1,176,781	**Gamely**, m., Bold Ruler	3	41	16	13	574,961
1963	**Buckpasser**, h., Tom Fool	3	31	25	21	1,462,014	**Politely**, m., *Amerigo	4	49	21	13	552,972
1962	**Tom Rolfe**, h., *Ribot	3	32	16	9	671,297	**Straight Deal**, m., Hail to Reason	6	99	21	13	733,020
1961	**Roman Brother**, g., Third Brother	4	42	16	10	943,473	**Tosmah**, m., Tim Tam	4	39	23	16	612,588
1960	**Candy Spots**, h., *Nigromante	3	22	12	9	824,718	**Affectionately**, m., Swaps	4	52	28	18	546,659
1959	**Native Diver**, h., Imbros	7	81	37	33	1,026,500	**Cicada**, m., Bryan G.	4	42	23	18	783,674
1958	**Carry Back**, h., Saggy	4	62	21	14	1,241,165	**Bowl of Flowers**, m., Sailor	2	16	10	6	398,504
1957	**Kelso**, g., Your Host	8	63	39	31	1,977,896	**Airmans Guide**, m., One Count	3	20	13	8	315,673
1956	**Sword Dancer**, h., Sunglow	3	39	15	10	829,610	**Royal Native**, m., *Royal Charger	4	49	18	11	422,769
1955	**Bald Eagle**, h., *Nasrullah	4	29	12	12	692,946	**Idun**, m., *Royal Charger	3	30	17	9	392,490
1954	**Round Table**, h., *Princequillo	4	66	43	31	1,749,869	**Endine**, m., *Rico Monte	3	45	10	4	306,547
1953	**Swoon's Son**, h., The Doge	4	51	30	22	970,605	**Dotted Line**, m., *Princequillo	5	67	11	5	324,159
1952	**Nashua**, h., *Nasrullah	3	30	22	19	1,288,565	**High Voltage**, m., *Ambiorix	3	45	13	10	362,240
1951	**Determine**, h., *Alibhai	3	44	18	16	573,360	**Queen Hopeful**, m., Roman	5	65	18	10	365,044
1950	**Find**, g., Discovery	8	110	22	13	803,615	**Grecian Queen**, m., *Heliopolis	4	53	12	9	323,575
1949	**Mark-Ye-Well**, h., Bull Lea	4	40	14	11	581,910	**Real Delight**, m., Bull Lea	2	15	12	10	261,822
1948	**Crafty Admiral**, h., Fighting Fox	4	39	18	12	499,200	**Sickle's Image**, m., Sickletoy	5	73	27	10	413,275
1947	**Oil Capitol**, h., *Mahmoud	5	80	19	14	580,756	**Next Move**, m., Bull Lea	4	46	17	12	398,550
1946	**Ponder**, h., Pensive	4	41	14	11	541,275	**Two Lea**, m., Bull Lea	4	26	15	9	309,250
1945	**Citation**, h., Bull Lea	4	45	32	22	1,085,760	**Bewitch**, m., Bull Lea	5	55	20	15	462,605
1944	**On Trust**, h., *Alibhai	7	88	23	11	554,145	**But Why Not**, m., Blue Larkspur	5	46	12	8	295,155
1943	**Assault**, h., Bold Venture	6	42	18	15	675,470	**Honeymoon**, m., *Beau Pere	6	78	20	13	387,760
1942	**Pavot**, h., Case Ace	4	32	14	12	373,365	**Gallorette**, m., *Challenger II	5	72	21	13	445,535
1941	**Stymie**, h., Equestrian	7	131	35	25	918,485	**Twilight Tear**, m., Bull Lea	3	24	18	10	202,165
1940	**Count Fleet**, h., Reigh Count	2	21	16	9	250,300	**Happy Issue**, m., Bow to Me	9	157	27	5	225,424
1939	**First Fiddle**, h., *Royal Minstrel	6	95	23	10	398,610	**Vagrancy**, m., *Sir Gallahad III	3	42	15	9	102,480
1938	**Whirlaway**, h., *Blenheim II	4	60	32	22	561,161	**Moon Maiden**, m., *Challenger II	6	109	19	1	76,780
1937	**Bimelech**, h., Black Toney	3	15	11	8	248,745	**Fairy Chant**, m., Chance Shot	3	42	10	7	81,985
1936	**Challedon**, h., *Challenger II	5	44	20	17	334,660	**Loveday**, m., Petee-Wrack	6	85	17	5	56,225
1935	**Stagehand**, h., *Sickle	3	25	9	6	200,110	**Jacola**, m., *Jacopo	3	25	11	4	70,060
1934	**War Admiral**, h., Man o' War	4	26	21	15	273,240	**Dawn Play**, m., Clock Tower	2	14	4	3	50,800
1933	**Seabiscuit**, h., Hard Tack	6	89	33	26	437,730	**Columbiana**, m., Petee-Wrack	4	28	11	1	60,925
1932	**Rosemont**, h., The Porter	4	23	7	5	168,750	**Esposa**, m., Espino	7	96	19	15	132,055
1931	**Top Row**, h., Peanuts	5	42	14	11	213,870	**Mata Hari**, m., Peter Hastings	2	16	7	5	66,699
1930	**Ladysman**, h., Pompey	5	22	8	5	134,310	**Swivel**, m., *Swift and Sure	2	24	5	2	74,955

All-Time Leading Earners by State Where Bred 1954-2005

Alabama

MALE, YOB Sex, Sire	Yrs Raced	Strts	Wins	SWs	Earnings
Winonly, 1957 h., Olympia	5	64	21	11	$326,264
Lombardi Time, 1987 g., Lombardi	6	68	25	5	270,933
Alpena Magic, 1990 g., L'Enjoleur	14	154	16	0	206,482
Sky Gem, 1960 h., *Quibu	4	63	12	2	197,573
Chief Tudor, 1997 g., Chief Persuasion	7	55	9	4	194,430
Alagon, 1989 g., Rajab	6	80	10	3	169,353
He's a Duster, 1991 g., Stark Duster	10	112	11	0	146,364
Ezgo, 1954 g., Olympia	6	72	12	4	135,731
King Oasis, 1974 h., Island Kingdom	8	102	32	0	134,508
Knight Tres, 1994 g., Knight of Old	8	107	16	0	130,693

FEMALE, YOB Sex, Sire	Yrs Raced	Strts	Wins	SWs	Earnings
My Portrait, 1958 m., Olympia	5	94	17	3	$261,275
Comalagold, 2000 m., Royal Empire	4	26	8	4	199,670
Blacksher, 1995 m., Reack Boldly	8	93	19	0	167,232
Rocky Turn, 1995 m., Rocky Mountain	6	62	10	0	158,335
Vicki's Ryde, 1987 m., Society Max	7	81	24	1	130,758
Teacher's Art, 1964 m., *Quibu	3	15	5	2	121,494
Georges Cherub, 1985 m., If This Be So	5	76	11	0	101,905
Darling's Bid, 1993 m., Prospector's Bid	4	37	7	0	101,141
Jem Klip, 1988 m., Luck's Reality	8	102	12	0	81,835
Sun Block, 2000 m., Shot Block	3	12	4	1	80,417

Alaska

MALE, YOB Sex, Sire	Years Raced	Strts	Wins	SWs	Earnings
Austin Texas, 1988 g., Tom Tulle	7	76	9	0	$27,778
Cope Stetic, 1983 h., Romeo	3	36	3	0	9,157
Whistling Johnny, 1975 h., Whistling Kettle	2	15	1	0	3,202

FEMALE, YOB Sex, Sire	Years Raced	Strts	Wins	SWs	Earnings
Ice Blue Moon, 1979 m., *Hard Water	4	60	4	0	$15,146
Murph's Pet, 1979 m., J. R.'s Pet	3	21	2	0	7,911
Princess Will Win, 1988 m., Will Win	2	6	1	0	2,970

Arizona

MALE, YOB Sex, Sire	Years Raced	Strts	Wins	SWs	Earnings
Coyote Lakes, 1994 g., Society Max	8	63	20	5	$728,337
First Intent, 1989 g., Prima Voce	7	63	12	2	524,357
Last Don B., 1987 g., Don B.	9	104	40	15	471,461
Faro, 1982 h., Crafty Drone	7	59	20	6	460,103
G Malleah, 1991 g., Fool the Experts	10	61	17	13	439,613
Peaked, 1985 h., Drone	6	43	16	11	398,338
Tropic Ruler, 1979 g., Key Rulla	4	21	11	4	395,898
Radar Ahead, 1975 h., *Repicado II	5	17	9	4	390,125
Hyder, 1997 g., Calumar	7	58	13	0	354,318
Mad Key, 1977 h., Key Rulla	7	62	21	8	288,779

FEMALE, YOB Sex, Sire	Years Raced	Strts	Wins	SWs	Earnings
Monrow, 1996 m., Fool the Experts	5	43	17	3	$287,344
Knoll Lake, 1998 m., Benton Creek	5	26	12	9	270,155
Nervous John, 1976 m., Nervous Energy	4	44	14	11	257,686
To the Post, 1989 m., Bold Ego	4	22	11	7	241,912
Bueno, 1992 m., Society Max	6	49	14	9	233,130
Left the Latch, 1991 m., Society Max	6	40	16	5	207,848
Carte Madera, 1999 m., Society Max	5	35	8	0	180,835
Reatta Pass, 1999 m., Benton Creek	5	36	14	1	180,679
The Lord's Tune, 1997 m., Relaunch a Tune	3	26	12	0	176,305
Hugafool, 1994 m., Fool the Experts	5	29	9	4	175,653

Arkansas

MALE, YOB Sex, Sire	Years Raced	Strts	Wins	SWs	Earnings
Nodouble, 1965 h., *Noholme II	4	42	13	9	$846,749
Dust On the Bottle, 1995 h., Temperence Hill	7	81	11	4	683,312
Beau's Town, 1998 g., Beau Genius	4	21	12	8	611,930
Never Forgotten, 1984 g., Bold L. B.	8	119	15	6	499,606
E J Harley, 1992 g., Beat Inflation	10	54	17	4	456,915
Lanyons Star, 1988 g., Suzanne's Star	10	127	21	4	450,915
Temperence Time, 1996 g., Temperence Hill	6	39	10	6	436,860
Dirty Mike, 1995 g., Temperence Hill	9	93	18	2	431,063
Be a Agent, 1984 h., Be a Prospect	7	81	16	0	355,362
Up Limit, 1978 g., Decimator	7	68	23	4	353,216

FEMALE, YOB Sex, Sire	Years Raced	Strts	Wins	SWs	Earnings
Humble Clerk, 1997 m., Humble Eleven	3	17	6	4	$503,545
Ruddy Eagle, 1990 m., Beau's Leader	6	82	15	5	468,680
Nurse Dopey, 1987 m., Dr. Blum	4	32	16	11	456,362
Stoney Jody, 1994 m., Silver Survivor	3	39	14	1	384,813
Biolage, 1989 m., Hurricane Ed	7	122	12	1	294,983
Jay's Sue, 1979 m., Jahan	5	51	18	5	282,560
Humble Eight, 1992 m., Seattle Battle	4	34	6	4	278,450
Tsu Tsu Won, 1993 m., Air Forbes Won	10	117	18	0	270,878
Cato Double, 1980 m., Nodouble	4	56	10	3	265,869
Turn to the Queen, 1993 m., Lyphard's Ridge	4	25	6	1	263,905

California

MALE, YOB Sex, Sire	Years Raced	Strts	Wins	SWs	Earnings
Tiznow, 1997 h., Cee's Tizzy	2	15	8	7	$6,427,830
Best Pal, 1988 g., *Habitony	7	47	18	17	5,668,245
Snow Chief, 1983 h., Reflected Glory	3	24	13	12	3,383,210
Bertrando, 1989 h., Skywalker	5	24	9	8	3,185,610
Free House, 1994 h., Smokester	4	22	9	8	3,178,971
General Challenge, 1996 g., General Meeting	4	21	9	8	2,877,178
Budroyale, 1993 g., Cee's Tizzy	7	52	17	7	2,840,810
Nostalgia's Star, 1982 h., Nostalgia	5	59	9	7	2,154,827
Native Desert, 1993 g., Desert Classic	8	74	21	15	1,828,177

FEMALE, YOB Sex, Sire	Years Raced	Strts	Wins	SWs	Earnings
Fran's Valentine, 1982 m., Saros (GB)	4	34	13	12	$1,375,465
Brown Bess, 1982 m., *Petrone	6	36	16	11	1,300,920
Gourmet Girl, 1995 m., Cee's Tizzy	5	33	9	6	1,255,373
Lazy Slusan, 1995 m., Slewvescent	5	47	12	10	1,150,410
Valentine Dancer, 2000 m., In Excess (Ire)	5	28	8	5	1,144,126
Dream of Summer, 1999 m., Siberian Summer	4	18	10	6	1,071,150
Feverish, 1995 m., Pirate's Bounty	4	42	12	8	908,983
Soviet Problem, 1990 m.,	4	20	15	10	905,546

MALE, YOB Sex, Sire	Years Raced	Strts	Wins	SWs	Earnings
Flying Continental, 1986 h., Flying Paster	6	51	12	8	1,815,938

FEMALE, YOB Sex, Sire	Years Raced	Strts	Wins	SWs	Earnings
Moscow Ballet					
Moscow Burning, 2000 m., Moscow Ballet	4	24	9	4	902,535
Summer Wind Dancer, 2000 m., Siberian Summer	3	18	5	4	898,762

Colorado

MALE, YOB Sex, Sire	Years Raced	Strts	Wins	SWs	Earnings
To Erin, 1976 h., Epic Journey	7	104	28	1	$392,707
Rusty Canyon, 1975 h., Sound Off	9	94	16	5	372,935
Personal Beau, 1996 g., Personal Flag	8	50	17	10	336,213
Lewistown, 1992 g., Strike Gold	10	64	21	0	308,547
Moro Grande, 1995 g., Fuzzy	8	43	7	5	247,119
Defrere's Vixen, 2000 g., Defrere	5	34	6	0	240,150
High Rover, 1965 g., Star Rover	10	110	33	10	215,701
Cocoa Latte, 2001 g., Demidoff	4	25	13	8	211,683
Cut of Music, 2000 g., Coverallbases	5	55	11	6	201,852
Bitterrook, 1978 h., *David II	5	60	9	2	201,212

FEMALE, YOB Sex, Sire	Years Raced	Strts	Wins	SWs	Earnings
Prairie Maiden, 1993 m., Badger Land	4	30	10	5	$294,784
Bar Bailey, 2000 m., Bates Motel	4	26	10	2	187,582
She's Finding Time, 1999 m., Ragtime Rascal	5	33	13	5	185,072
Windic, 1975 m., Dancing Dervish	5	55	9	1	144,097
Jennaly, 1995 m., Alydarmer	5	48	9	3	135,263
Gentle Gil, 1981 m., Gilligan	5	53	14	2	134,828
Broncomania, 1977 m., Marv 'n Jeff	7	58	19	7	130,418
Astral Girl, 1988 m., The Astonisher	8	88	20	2	126,527
Miss Bob O Lark, 1975 m., My Lark	4	58	8	0	109,255
Slewannavan, 1997 m., Slewacide	6	36	7	2	109,053

Connecticut

MALE, YOB Sex, Sire	Years Raced	Strts	Wins	SWs	Earnings
Nantucketeer, 1998 h., Departing Prints	6	48	12	0	$198,849
Fast Smile, 1970 h., Fast Gun	6	105	32	1	142,795
Belle's Brat, 1974 h., Precision	8	173	27	0	131,872
Reserve Native, 1974 h., Native Admiral	9	146	21	0	114,496
Lonesome Dawn, 1994 g., Fly Till Dawn	5	43	5	0	114,235
President Jim, 1960 g., *Good Shot	7	84	20	1	101,722
More Coins, 1960 g., Royal Visitor	9	193	23	0	92,858
Chapel Creek, 1978 h., Our Native	3	28	4	0	84,456
Peace Isle, 1956 g., *Good Shot	7	117	19	0	65,579
Gisele's Banker, 1969 h., My Banker	11	115	25	0	64,499

FEMALE, YOB Sex, Sire	Years Raced	Strts	Wins	SWs	Earnings
Skipat, 1974 m., Jungle Cove	5	45	26	14	$614,215
Leave No Prints, 1995 m., Departing Prints	5	53	8	1	232,377
Onyx Fox, 1974 m., Mr. Hasty	7	105	20	0	109,451
Poker's Thunder, 1992 m., Honest Turn	6	92	17	0	108,877
Pation, 1977 m., Patrician	7	96	17	0	91,313
Naskrahoney, 1974 m., Naskra	4	38	6	1	83,201
Diplomatic King, 1984 m., Diplomatic Note	3	40	12	0	75,429
Good Jane, 1961 m., *Good Shot	4	45	9	1	70,563
Lady Petee, 1983 m., Hairy Business	7	63	10	0	69,977
Clown's Gal, 1977 m., The Clown	5	88	10	0	66,893

Delaware

MALE, YOB Sex, Sire	Years Raced	Strts	Wins	SWs	Earnings
Baitman, 1961 g., Assemblyman	8	113	27	3	$298,198
Golden Immigrant, 1981 g., Medaille d'Or	5	47	6	0	161,380
Whale, 1969 g., Impressive	10	123	18	0	119,663
Proudest Doon, 1982 h., Matsadoon	3	11	4	2	104,620
Space to Kevin, 1984 h., Travelling Music	5	78	9	0	96,530
Great Depths, 1962 h., *King of the Tudors	7	125	15	1	96,521
Brixton Road, 1963 h., Great Captain	8	133	13	0	58,472
Parish Judge, 1968 g., Delta Judge	4	85	16	0	52,301
Devilfish, 1953 g., Greek Song	7	109	12	0	50,237
Frank's Ace, 1973 h., Rock Talk	5	78	5	0	49,600

FEMALE, YOB Sex, Sire	Years Raced	Strts	Wins	SWs	Earnings
Pokey Lady, 1984 m., Georgeandthedragon	5	74	20	0	$155,275
Wing Flutter, 1969 m., Sunrise Flight	6	86	13	0	90,894
Shoe Off, 1972 m., Rambunctious	4	64	10	0	76,316
Wild Beat, 1979 m., Iron Ruler	2	7	4	0	52,980
Appear, 1969 m., Loom	3	39	7	0	47,689
Double Hold, 1981 m., Hold Your Peace	4	28	4	0	41,915
Foamy, 1954 m., Tide Rips	7	133	21	0	36,233
Tacky Lady, 1973 m., Nail	3	50	5	0	35,834
Wedge, 1969 m., Fulcrum	3	60	12	0	32,172
Oh She May, 1979 m., Oceans Reward	5	64	7	0	25,555

Florida

MALE, YOB Sex, Sire	Years Raced	Strts	Wins	SWs	Earnings
Skip Away, 1993 h., Skip Trial	4	38	18	16	$9,616,360
Silver Charm, 1994 h., Silver Buck	4	24	12	11	6,944,369
Unbridled, 1987 h., Fappiano	3	24	8	5	4,489,475
Precisionist, 1981 h., Crozier	5	46	20	17	3,485,398
Peace Rules, 2000 h., Jules	3	19	9	8	3,084,278
Afleet Alex, 2002 h., Northern Afleet	2	12	8	6	2,765,800
Sir Bear, 1993 g., Sir Leon	8	71	19	11	2,538,422
Gate Dancer, 1981 h., Sovereign Dancer	4	28	7	4	2,501,705
Holy Bull, 1991 h., Great Above	3	16	13	11	2,481,760
Mecke, 1992 h., Maudlin	4	40	12	9	2,470,550

FEMALE, YOB Sex, Sire	Years Raced	Strts	Wins	SWs	Earnings
Beautiful Pleasure, 1995 m., Maudlin	5	25	10	7	$2,734,078
Jewel Princess, 1992 m., Key to the Mint	4	29	13	10	1,904,060
Smok'n Frolic, 1999 m., Smoke Glacken	4	33	9	8	1,534,720
Halo America, 1990 m., Waquoit	5	40	15	9	1,460,992
Meadow Star, 1988 m., Meadowlake	3	20	11	10	1,445,740
Hollywood Wildcat, 1990 m., Kris S.	4	21	12	11	1,432,160
Tappiano, 1984 m., Fappiano	4	34	17	14	1,305,522
One Dreamer, 1988 m., Relaunch	4	25	12	7	1,266,067
Glitter Woman, 1994 m., Glitterman	4	23	10	5	1,256,805
Susan's Girl, 1969 m., Quadrangle	5	63	29	24	1,251,668

Georgia

MALE, YOB Sex, Sire	Years Raced	Strts	Wins	SWs	Earnings
Bluesthestandard, 1997 g., American Standard	5	44	17	3	$1,014,218
Maybe Jack, 1993 g., Classic Account	10	122	35	1	534,715
Southern Slew, 1986 h., Slew Machine	6	41	13	0	207,610
Fortunate Lance, 1988 g., Fortunate Prospect	6	53	11	0	186,499
More Tell, 1996 g., Reach for More	7	58	15	0	161,542
Rise Higher, 1991 g., Reach for More	10	119	20	0	156,289
My Mac Flashys, 1986 g., Flashy Mac	4	28	8	1	139,195
Jeshurun, 1986 h., First Sea Lord	7	73	14	0	115,333
Reach for Ameri, 1996 g., Reach for More	7	64	9	1	109,786
Finally Class, 1985 h., Finally Gotcha	6	41	8	1	102,808

FEMALE, YOB Sex, Sire	Years Raced	Strts	Wins	SWs	Earnings
Vivace, 1993 m., Shot Gun Scott	5	40	20	15	$1,037,671
Ayrial Delight, 1992 m., Quick Dip	6	63	18	6	458,992
Bobbyrea, 1994 m., Classic Account	4	39	13	0	262,106
Miss Hamma, 1999 m., Roaring Camp	4	23	7	2	183,98
Tia's Orphan Annie, 1995 m., Prospector's Halo	8	93	12	0	163,910
Rose Darling, 1996 m., Roaring Camp	6	77	11	0	158,800
Prime to Go, 1991 m., Classic Go Go	7	72	19	0	142,223
Sarcasm, 1987 m., Noon Time Spender	8	87	11	0	136,154
Rabs Lil Brit Brit, 1991 m., Classic Account	5	47	7	0	123,044
Paddy's Princess, 1975 m., Irish Dude	5	64	8	0	120,750

Idaho

MALE, YOB Sex, Sire	Years Raced	Strts	Wins	SWs	Earnings
Gratteau, 1995 g., Synastry	8	50	14	4	$366,644
L'Effaceur, 1997 g., Jestic	6	30	10	1	324,064
Lookn East, 1998 g., Eastern Echo	4	34	8	2	259,416
Northern Provider, 1982 g., Staff Writer	7	51	8	2	231,619
Mining for Fun, 1998 g., L. B. Jaklin	6	69	7	0	213,439
San Diego Pete, 1995 g., Santiago Peak	7	63	16	4	199,210
Bojima's Majesty, 1990 g., Bojima	6	84	20	1	189,143
Schuyler Road, 1992 g., Synastry	9	75	14	1	173,399
Hooten Harry, 1992 g., Unable	6	64	13	0	171,367
Curt's First Bid, 1999 g., Digression	4	35	11	0	170,224

FEMALE, YOB Sex, Sire	Years Raced	Strts	Wins	SWs	Earnings
Angi Go, 1990 m., Idaho's Majesty	5	36	15	8	$437,493
Lookn Mighty Fine, 1997 m., Peterhof	6	54	12	2	300,851
Lethal Leta, 1991 m., Synastry	5	32	12	8	300,602
Just Lookn, 1994 m., Synastry	2	18	8	4	213,675
Princess in Charge, 1991 m., Prince Card	5	46	7	0	193,105
Thou Shalt Not Lie, 1990 m., El Baba	4	39	8	1	183,687
Printasity, 1983 m., Growler	8	81	20	0	170,279
Riband, 1996 m., Lord of the Apes	6	50	11	0	166,671
Ladys Lil Cruiser, 1992 m., Key to the Carr	5	50	11	1	161,975
Somer Wonders, 1995 m., Synastry	6	65	13	2	161,571

Illinois

MALE, YOB Sex, Sire	Years Raced	Strts	Wins	SWs	Earnings
Buck's Boy, 1993 g., Bucksplasher	5	30	16	9	$2,750,148
Polar Expedition, 1991 g., Kodiack	7	49	20	14	1,491,071
Mystery Giver, 1998 g., Dynaformer	4	33	11	8	1,165,900
Western Playboy, 1986 h., Play Fellow	5	45	8	4	1,128,449
Bucks Nephew, 1990 g., Bucksplasher	5	45	15	8	853,618
Harham's Sizzler, 1979 h., Good Behaving	7	73	24	14	843,406
Beboppin Baby, 1993 g., Hatchet Man	8	64	13	3	842,540
Magic Doe, 1995 g., Fast Gold	9	90	17	6	788,128
Tic N Tin, 1995 g., Lac Ouimet	9	97	29	9	771,570
Chicago Six, 1995 h., Wild Again	5	39	16	9	733,347

FEMALE, YOB Sex, Sire	Years Raced	Strts	Wins	SWs	Earnings
Two Item Limit, 1998 m., Twining	3	28	7	4	$1,060,585
Lady Shirl, 1987 m., That's a Nice	6	41	18	10	951,523
Bungalow, 1987 m., Lord Avie	3	42	17	9	850,141
Peach of It, 1986 m., Navajo	5	53	15	9	625,721
Summer Mis, 1999 m., Summer Squall	4	23	11	6	542,662
Your Ladyship, 1990 m., Moment of Hope	5	47	17	6	539,328
Darley Dancer, 1988 m., Play Fellow	6	48	17	5	516,098
Valid Vixen, 1985 m., Valid Appeal	4	27	10	6	492,655
Faccia Bella, 1996 m., Dixie Brass	7	57	8	4	488,442
My Own Lovely Lee, 1992 m., Bucksplasher	4	34	13	6	487,149

Indiana

MALE, YOB Sex, Sire	Years Raced	Strts	Wins	SWs	Earnings
Hillsdale, 1955 h., Take Away	3	41	23	14	$646,935
Pass Rush, 1999 h., Crown Ambassador	5	34	7	4	576,335
Fight for Ally, 1997 g., Fit to Fight	7	32	12	6	546,559
Navajo, 1970 h., *Grey Dawn II	5	48	22	6	351,982
Red's Honor, 1998 h., Glitterman	6	37	12	4	332,830
Vic's Rebel, 1994 g., Lac Ouimet	5	34	11	4	304,682
Pelican Beach, 1998 g., Air Forbes Won	4	34	17	11	277,817
Joanies No Phony, 1997 g., Buckhar	7	77	14	1	242,157
Cancion Alegre, 1997 g., Smilin Singin Sam	6	63	13	0	241,922
Mr. Mink, 2000 g., Gold Case	4	23	14	5	229,580

FEMALE, YOB Sex, Sire	Years Raced	Strts	Wins	SWs	Earnings
Honky Star, 1971 m., Bupers	4	39	18	10	$353,012
Marciann, 1997 m., Speedy Cure	5	29	11	5	278,806
Ellens Lucky Star, 1999 m., Crown Ambassador	4	26	10	7	249,155
Senorita Ziggy, 1998 m., Senor Speedy	5	28	9	4	226,080
Maggie's Dream, 1998 m., Philadream	6	37	9	3	182,073
Lighting Bopers, 1996 m., Cape Storm	3	8	5	4	178,455
Amanda's Crown, 1999 m., Crown Ambassador	3	21	5	3	161,152
Miss Dakota, 2000 m., Never Wavering	3	21	6	3	148,600
Atractiva, 1981 m., Navajo	4	22	13	1	145,145
Lady's Legal Ma Ja, 1997 m., Legalmumblejumble	5	43	2	1	138,678

Iowa

MALE, YOB Sex, Sire	Years Raced	Strts	Wins	SWs	Earnings
Sure Shot Biscuit, 1996 g., Miracle Heights	6	54	23	13	$1,025,480
Take Me Up, 1998 g., Take Me Out	5	41	12	5	512,579

FEMALE, YOB Sex, Sire	Years Raced	Strts	Wins	SWs	Earnings
Sharky's Review, 1998 m., Sharkey	4	36	15	10	$685,425
Nut N Better, 1997 m., Miracle Heights	4	28	14	9	572,828
Lady Tamworth, 1995 m., No Louder	6	68	15	3	567,058

MALE, YOB Sex, Sire	Years Raced	Strts	Wins	SWs	Earnings
Cowboy Stuff, 1999 h., Evansville Slew	4	23	11	4	428,280
Le Numerous, 1998 g., Numerous	6	60	11	1	340,418
Country Warrior, 1999 g., Ghazi	6	45	12	0	296,385
Fleet Flyer, 1994 g., Wind Flyer	9	57	14	3	279,348
Reuben, 1997 h., Rubiano	6	41	7	1	276,708
Deputy Flag, 1996 h., Personal Flag	4	23	6	2	274,586
Rubianos Image, 2000 g., Rubiano	4	38	7	1	273,879
Cmego, 2000 g., Gold Case	4	50	8	1	259,633

FEMALE, YOB Sex, Sire	Years Raced	Strts	Wins	SWs	Earnings
Switch Lanes, 1999 m., Deerhound	4	38	11	3	381,411
Vaguely Who, 1993 m., Hittias (GB)	6	48	12	5	333,745
Sumthintotalkabout, 1997 m., Kyle's Our Man	4	25	9	2	313,928
Danzig Foxxy Woman, 1995 m., Dr. Danzig	4	28	6	4	268,707
Sound of Gold, 1998 m., Mutakddim	5	40	13	4	268,243
One Fine Shweetie, 1999 m., Shuailaan	4	30	5	2	260,587
Only At Night, 1999 m., Olympio	5	30	7	1	245,475

Kansas

MALE, YOB Sex, Sire	Years Raced	Strts	Wins	SWs	Earnings
I Dancer, 1995 g., I Enclose	7	68	15	1	$270,862
Gay Revoke, 1958 h., Blue Gay	9	128	27	5	251,251
Kangaroo King, 1993 g., Tarsal	6	53	14	4	211,719
Cheryl's Gazelle, 1995 g., Discover	7	70	11	0	179,306
Polar Barron, 1996 g., Track Barron	8	59	14	3	175,721
Scarlet Lad, 1998 g., Big Splash	6	70	11	3	169,472
Rio Gambler, 1990 g., Boca Rio	8	92	17	2	168,904
Jim Dunham, 1991 g., Dunham's Gift	11	109	17	2	168,455
Morning Merry, 2000 g., Scarlet 'n Gray	4	21	7	3	168,210
Liberated Pleasure, 1990 g., Pleasure Prize	7	91	18	4	161,141

FEMALE, YOB Sex, Sire	Years Raced	Strts	Wins	SWs	Earnings
Sunnie Do It, 1994 m., Do It Again Dan	8	83	16	9	$316,722
Queena Corrina, 1999 m., Here We Come	5	31	10	0	267,770
Tiney Toast, 1989 m., Blue Jester	4	28	6	3	217,614
Shero, 1993 m., Glorious Flag	6	63	9	0	164,203
Swinging Janie Gal, 1997 m., A. M. Swinger	6	36	5	0	157,815
Bonnie J., 2000 m., Arab Speaker	4	26	6	0	149,975
Discreetly Irish, 1998 m., Big Splash	6	67	11	4	144,485
Amberaja, 1985 m., Kibe	7	90	23	0	141,868
Lady Take the Gold, 1989 m., Gold Ruler	8	116	17	0	137,492
Scarlet Rumor, 1995 m., Scarlet 'n Gray	5	36	9	5	126,310

Kentucky

MALE, YOB Sex, Sire	Years Raced	Strts	Wins	SWs	Earnings
Fantastic Light, 1996 h., Rahy	4	25	12	10	$8,486,957
Pleasantly Perfect, 1998 h., Pleasant Colony	4	18	9	6	7,789,880
Captain Steve, 1997 h., Fly So Free	3	25	9	8	6,828,356
Alysheba, 1984 h., Alydar	3	26	11	10	6,679,242
John Henry, 1975 g., Ole Bob Bowers	8	83	39	30	6,591,860
Medaglia d'Oro, 1999 h., El Prado (Ire)	4	17	8	7	5,754,720
Taiki Blizzard, 1991 h., Seattle Slew	4	23	6	3	5,523,549
Roses in May, 2000 h., Devil His Due	3	13	8	4	5,490,187
Sunday Silence, 1986 h., Halo	3	14	9	7	4,968,554
Easy Goer, 1986 h., Alydar	3	20	14	12	4,873,770

FEMALE, YOB Sex, Sire	Years Raced	Strts	Wins	SWs	Earnings
Azeri, 1998 m., Jade Hunter	4	24	17	14	$4,079,820
Ashado, 2001 m., Saint Ballado	3	21	12	11	3,931,440
Spain, 1997 m., Thunder Gulch	4	35	9	7	3,540,542
Serena's Song, 1992 m., Rahy	3	38	18	17	3,283,388
Silverbulletday, 1996 m., Silver Deputy	3	23	15	14	3,093,207
Escena, 1993 m., Strawberry Road (Aus)	4	29	11	7	2,962,639
Banshee Breeze, 1995 m., Unbridled	3	18	10	8	2,784,798
Flawlessly, 1988 m., Affirmed	5	28	16	15	2,572,536
Take Charge Lady, 1999 m., Dehere	3	22	11	9	2,480,377
Sightseek, 1999 m., Distant View	3	20	12	10	2,445,216

Louisiana

MALE, YOB Sex, Sire	Years Raced	Strts	Wins	SWs	Earnings
Scott's Scoundrel, 1992 h., L'Enjoleur	6	50	22	19	$1,270,052
Zarb's Magic, 1993 g., Zarbyev	8	69	23	5	893,946
King Roller, 1991 g., Silent King	9	107	21	5	883,588
Dixie Poker Ace, 1987 g., Patriotically	8	86	27	18	850,126
Free Spirit's Joy, 1988 h., Joey Bob	5	32	8	5	841,277
Oak Hall, 1996 g., Olympio	7	43	18	9	635,067
Nijinsky's Gold, 1989 g., Lot o' Gold	7	45	10	7	622,160
Zarb's Luck, 1997 g., Zarbyev	7	52	12	6	611,850
Caro's Royalty, 1993 g., Spruce Bouquet	9	84	20	3	587,743
Witt Ante, 2000 g., Upping the Ante	5	29	10	6	584,057

FEMALE, YOB Sex, Sire	Years Raced	Strts	Wins	SWs	Earnings
Sarah Lane's Oates, 1994 m., Sunshine Forever	7	77	21	15	$888,296
Happy Ticket, 2001 m., Anet	2	13	10	8	782,260
Fit to Scout, 1987 m., Fit to Fight	3	30	8	6	767,600
Hallowed Dreams, 1997 m., Malagra	4	30	25	17	740,144
Eskimo's Angel, 1989 m., Eskimo	5	39	11	8	701,539
Zuppardo Ardo, 1994 m., Zuppardo's Prince	5	39	14	10	667,886
Leslie's Love, 1997 m., Combat Ready	6	56	22	6	642,484
Hope List, 1990 m., List	6	81	20	7	601,475
Up the Apalachee, 1984 m., Apalachee	3	28	14	8	595,935
I Ain't Bluffing, 1994 m., Pine Bluff	3	13	8	6	582,069

Maine

MALE, YOB Sex, Sire	Years Raced	Strts	Wins	SWs	Earnings
Seboomook, 1976 h., Sunny South	7	96	22	0	$124,837
My Secret Love, 1965 g., Busy Harvest	10	172	24	0	69,853
Sokokis, 1971 h., Midland Man	2	32	5	0	54,232

FEMALE, YOB Sex, Sire	Years Raced	Strts	Wins	SWs	Earnings
North of Boston, 1972 m., Midland Man	4	25	4	0	$40,693
Louisa Midland, 1975 m., George Lewis	3	20	5	0	40,149
Amblast, 1973 m., Blasting Charge	4	36	6	0	31,632

Maryland

MALE, YOB Sex, Sire	Years Raced	Strts	Wins	SWs	Earnings
Cigar, 1990 h., Palace Music	4	33	19	15	$9,999,815
Awad, 1990 h., Caveat	7	70	14	11	3,270,131
Concern, 1991 h., Broad Brush	3	30	7	4	3,079,350
Broad Brush, 1983 h., Ack Ack	3	27	14	12	2,656,793

FEMALE, YOB Sex, Sire	Years Raced	Strts	Wins	SWs	Earnings
Safely Kept, 1986 m., Horatius	4	31	24	22	$2,194,206
Shine Again, 1997 m., Wild Again	5	34	14	7	1,271,840
Jameela, 1976 m., Rambunctious	4	58	27	16	1,038,704
Urbane, 1992 m., Citidancer	3	18	8	7	1,018,568

MALE, YOB Sex, Sire	Years Raced	Strts	Wins	SWs	Earnings
Little Bold John, 1982 g., John Alden	9	105	38	25	1,956,406
Include, 1997 h., Broad Brush	4	20	10	7	1,659,560
Valley Crossing, 1988 h., Private Account	5	48	8	4	1,616,490
Our New Recruit, 1999 h., Alphabet Soup	3	19	6	2	1,470,915
Ten Keys, 1984 h., Sir Ivor Again	5	54	21	16	1,209,211
Homebuilder, 1984 h., Mr. Prospector	4	60	11	8	1,172,153

FEMALE, YOB Sex, Sire	Years Raced	Strts	Wins	SWs	Earnings
Squan Song, 1981 m., Exceller	5	36	18	14	898,444
Thirty Eight Go Go, 1985 m., Thirty Eight Paces	5	46	10	8	871,229
Wide Country, 1988 m., Magesterial	3	26	12	11	819,728
Brilliant Brass, 1987 m., Marine Brass	4	27	16	9	767,051
In the Curl, 1984 m., Shelter Half	8	85	26	10	749,891
Mz. Zill Bear, 1989 m., Salutely	6	41	15	10	740,423

Massachusetts

MALE, YOB Sex, Sire	Years Raced	Strts	Wins	SWs	Earnings
Rise Jim, 1976 h., Jim J.	5	52	27	12	$528,789
Jini's Jet, 1998 g., A. P Jet	6	57	22	11	427,380
Garemma, 1986 g., Shananie	5	43	16	1	395,583
Stylish Sultan, 1999 h., Sundance Ridge	5	36	14	10	314,195
Galloping Gael, 1994 h., Lost Code	6	50	9	3	297,317
Second Episode, 1992 h., Potentiate	7	68	17	13	274,277
Papa Ho Ho, 1993 g., On to Glory	8	87	18	6	265,882
Tonights the Night, 1978 h., Great Mystery	8	115	13	8	258,532
Josiah W., 1977 h., Heat of Battle	7	104	18	2	193,244
But Jim, 1987 h., Rise Jim	10	84	12	5	188,699

FEMALE, YOB Sex, Sire	Years Raced	Strts	Wins	SWs	Earnings
Isadorable, 1983 m., Moleolus	4	39	19	17	$415,018
Big Miss, 1996 m., Chief Honcho	5	76	16	5	357,834
Sunlit Ridge, 1998 m., Sundance Ridge	6	64	16	10	347,780
Ask Queenie, 2001 m., Key Contender	4	24	12	7	296,910
Land Ahoy, 1993 m., Oh Say	7	74	14	7	242,765
Lt'l Miss D. S., 1990 m., Hiromi the Great	4	54	12	7	220,064
African Princess, 1999 m., Sundance Ridge	4	42	7	5	205,790
Potential Fire, 1991 m., Potentiate	6	46	10	5	202,938
Weepecket, 1997 m., Mr. Sparkles	6	56	8	3	184,775
Potential Dreamer, 1991 m., Potentiate	6	76	12	4	184,247

Michigan

MALE, YOB Sex, Sire	Years Raced	Strts	Wins	SWs	Earnings
Tenpins, 1998 h., Smart Strike	4	17	9	5	$1,133,449
Secret Romeo, 1998 h., Service Stripe	5	55	23	17	865,790
Pongo Boy, 1992 g., Matchlite	9	87	22	12	776,184
Badwagon Harry, 1979 h., Ole Bob Bowers	9	121	19	10	742,412
Xclusive Imp, 1994 g., Majesty's Imp	8	87	12	9	584,130
Thumbsucker, 1979 h., Great Sun	4	31	16	10	525,553
Wind Chill, 1983 h., It's Freezing	7	73	15	6	502,492
That Gift, 1997 h., Monetary Gift	7	62	19	6	466,905
Solo Matt, 1986 h., Bucksplasher	4	47	12	5	453,249
Grand Circus Park, 1988 h., Apalachee	8	43	22	13	442,713

FEMALE, YOB Sex, Sire	Years Raced	Strts	Wins	SWs	Earnings
Peppen, 1994 m., Pep Up	4	37	15	11	$623,417
Karate Miss, 1995 m., Chicanery Slew	4	38	17	14	602,465
Born to Dance, 1999 m., Service Stripe	5	36	11	9	566,139
Sefas Rose, 1997 m., Sefapiano	5	32	13	7	488,815
Cashier's Dream, 1999 m., Service Stripe	2	7	5	3	423,042
Agiftfrom Bertie, 1993 m., Monetary Gift	4	38	10	9	408,378
Sweetwater Promise, 1999 m., Service Stripe	5	39	9	5	361,919
Farer Belle Lee, 1979 m., Seafarer	5	62	17	9	334,700
My Show, 1986 m., Tilt Up	6	77	19	6	331,408
North Rustim, 1978 m., Northern Native	5	61	19	15	328,002

Minnesota

MALE, YOB Sex, Sire	Years Raced	Strts	Wins	SWs	Earnings
Blair's Cove, 1985 h., Bucksplasher	6	58	17	10	$533,528
Super Abound, 1987 h., Superbity	4	36	6	2	398,418
Cocoboy, 1988 g., Cozzene	13	196	30	1	371,567
Crocrock, 1997 g., North Prospect	7	42	16	9	359,977
Wally's Choice, 2001 g., Quick Cut	3	24	11	7	340,590
Timeless Prince, 1987 g., Prince Forli	7	69	16	6	326,977
It's Truly Obvious, 1992 g., Mufti	8	96	20	2	325,204
Ashar, 1995 g., Bucksplasher	8	53	9	5	274,654
Bleu Victoriate, 1996 g., Victoriate	6	43	11	5	262,154
Buchman, 1987 h., Bucksplasher	3	32	8	1	254,929

FEMALE, YOB Sex, Sire	Years Raced	Strts	Wins	SWs	Earnings
Courtly Kathy, 1991 m., Lost Code	8	89	18	4	$277,950
Fortunate Faith, 1990 m., Fortunate Prospect	3	14	5	1	251,635
Princess Elaine, 1985 m., Providential (Ire)	4	27	9	6	232,240
Northbound Pride, 1986 m., Proud Pocket	5	38	11	4	213,983
Samdanya, 1995 m., Northern Prospect	4	27	9	6	192,747
Plana Dance, 1993 m., Northern Flagship	5	26	11	5	171,216
Shabana, 1991 m., Nasty and Bold	5	48	10	2	169,412
Wishek's Kid, 1989 m., Pappa Riccio	7	67	18	3	167,359
Sweet Sum, 1990 m., Scroll	7	51	12	3	167,025
Nidari, 1996 m., Northern No Trump	6	32	6	5	165,553

Mississippi

MALE, YOB Sex, Sire	Years Raced	Strts	Wins	SWs	Earnings
American Cowboy, 1994 g., Gold Crest	5	56	9	1	$174,867
Lotsa Honey, 1981 h., Turn and Count	5	20	4	0	122,125
Dollars and Sense, 1991 g., Dollar Away	11	139	17	0	113,800
Nick's Palace, 1988 g., Palace Music	7	97	9	0	112,299
Ruben Wizznat, 1986 h., North Rock	6	111	19	0	110,753
Smalltown Slew, 2001 g., Evansville Slew	4	20	4	2	108,680
Go Star Buster, 2000 g., Blushing Star	5	33	5	1	107,665
Pajima, 1985 h., Wajima	4	47	8	0	98,061
Jobaker, 1981 h., Heir to the Line	3	15	7	3	85,119
Question of Gold, 1994 g., Gold Angle	9	82	7	0	83,589

FEMALE, YOB Sex, Sire	Years Raced	Strts	Wins	SWs	Earnings
Real Irish Hope, 1987 m., Tilt Up	5	49	15	3	$433,190
Miss Needlework, 1970 m., Needles	5	65	11	0	71,053
Miss Corinne, 1976 m., Grand Premiere	5	76	7	0	64,907
Cocoa Baker, 1994 m., Jobaker	4	39	10	0	62,478
Pass the Money, 1987 m., Pass the Tab	5	57	10	0	59,178
Proclaiming, 1973 m., Full Value	5	89	17	0	51,700
Claire's Secret, 1991 m., Happy Hooligan	5	37	3	0	40,590
Sweet Debbie, 2000 m., Sekari (GB)	4	26	3	0	34,050
Peaches Galore, 1984 m., Hold Your Tricks	6	80	10	0	32,855
Kerosene Prospect, 2001 m., Kerosene	3	24	5	1	31,321

Missouri

MALE, YOB Sex, Sire	Years Raced	Strts	Wins	SWs	Earnings
Carjack, 1981 h., Cojak	5	72	20	0	$469,181
Fort Metfield, 1994 g., Metfield	10	107	23	0	441,847
Page Two, 1994 g., Victorious	9	111	18	0	253,006
Missouri Ace, 1985 g., Taxachusetts	7	48	12	3	244,152
Mr. Springfield, 1989 g., Taxachusetts	11	107	24	0	216,230
Pilot Knob, 1965 h., Gun Shot	10	164	37	1	186,139
Hold Me Together, 1994 g., Comet Kat	9	109	19	0	168,611
Minor Flaw, 1986 h., Rolfson	6	47	6	3	154,418
Campinout, 1999 g., Victorious	4	52	10	0	151,330
Uncle Zip, 1967 h., Bergamot	9	151	38	0	149,950

FEMALE, YOB Sex, Sire	Years Raced	Strts	Wins	SWs	Earnings
Peaceful River, 1979 m., Peaceful Tom	5	72	14	4	$250,990
Redoy's Drive, 1994 m., Mr. Redoy	6	51	11	0	224,534
Arctic Quest, 1995 m., Yukon	4	53	8	0	146,511
My Sister Kate, 1993 m., Haileys Tropic	6	56	17	0	146,489
Simply So, 1988 m., Gold Ruler	6	48	8	1	136,634
Shared Reflections, 1986 m., Pursuit	6	67	12	1	114,601
Caban Monere, 1992 m., Indian Detail	6	56	12	0	112,861
Shergars Best Shot, 1989 m., Shergar's Best (Ire)	7	90	20	0	107,596
Trip the Load, 1989 m., Positiveness	7	89	19	0	106,466
Silly Girl, 1998 m., Mandamus	5	53	10	0	104,330

Montana

MALE, YOB Sex, Sire	Years Raced	Strts	Wins	SWs	Earnings
Payday Mackee, 1990 g., Black Mackee	9	79	17	5	$214,668
River Lord, 1979 h., Eastern Lord	8	96	15	2	204,451
Toseek, 1993 g., Cave Creek	7	96	17	2	149,793
Big Sky Rusher, 1994 g., Cave Creek	6	49	9	3	131,714
Sonabove, 1992 g., Son of Briartic	8	79	11	0	117,204
Kelsos Kin, 1968 h., Scotsmans Bond	11	152	20	2	104,952
Dublin's Woodwin, 1999 g.,	5	37	8	0	104,541
Blazing Zulu, 1980 h., Zulu Tom	7	73	12	0	96,855
No Name Trail, 1991 g., Mr. Badger Black Mackee	8	56	15	2	92,558
Flying Whitesocks, 1990 g., Blushing Guest	9	93	18	0	91,914

FEMALE, YOB Sex, Sire	Years Raced	Strts	Wins	SWs	Earnings
Hallelujah Angel, 1991 m., Dance Centre	6	55	12	1	$197,496
Mickey's Hot Stuff, 1995 m., Mickey Le Moussev	6	65	10	2	174,667
Hatti, 1985 m., One More Slew	3	38	6	2	139,545
Montani, 1988 m., Kotani	8	92	20	1	121,780
Breath of Dawn, 1993 m., Black Mackee	7	75	13	0	121,437
Jocko Miss, 1997 m., Black Mackee	4	37	10	0	102,217
Belle of Nassau, 1993 m., Nassau Square	6	53	14	0	101,728
Mission Gem, 1976 m., Prince Alert	4	35	11	1	101,223
Dancing River, 1975 m., Marketable	5	74	17	0	99,812
Happy Ann, 1989 m., Fiesty Fouts	7	61	11	0	88,145

Nebraska

MALE, YOB Sex, Sire	Years Raced	Strts	Wins	SWs	Earnings
Dazzling Falls, 1992 h., Taylor's Falls	3	20	9	7	$904,622
Who Doctor Who, 1983 g., Doctor Stat	8	64	33	26	813,870
Amadevil, 1974 h., Jungle Savage	7	93	33	20	653,534
Darla's Charge, 1987 g., Ragtime Band	10	141	30	1	447,766
Roman Zipper, 1972 h., Zip Line	9	128	31	13	392,782
Skunktail, 1989 g., Music Prince	11	103	20	12	380,075
Plaza Star, 1978 h., Lt. Stevens	9	108	20	7	361,742
High Dice, 1995 g., Lytrump	8	69	20	15	320,672
Irish Villon, 1990 g., Verzy	7	66	17	11	311,016
Wandarous, 1984 g., Replant	10	103	23	9	302,051

FEMALE, YOB Sex, Sire	Years Raced	Strts	Wins	SWs	Earnings
Orphan Kist, 1984 m., Fort Prevel	8	100	28	18	$631,997
Falls Amiss, 1986 m., Taylor's Falls	4	29	15	9	312,301
G. U. Dreamer, 1985 m., Tarsal	4	39	14	4	289,219
Fantango Lady, 1994 m., Lytrump	5	55	22	18	279,295
Clever Kat, 1986 m., Comet Kat	6	59	23	9	260,170
Oglala Sue, 1998 m., Verzy	4	29	8	3	235,232
Face the Verdict, 1979 m., Executioner	5	66	10	1	228,799
St. Patty Day, 1982 m., Majestic Red	8	67	24	3	202,610
Robbers Doll, 1982 m., No Robbery	7	85	13	4	199,635
Nasty and Brave, 1994 m., Nasty and Bold	8	80	19	0	192,516

Nevada

MALE, YOB Sex, Sire	Years Raced	Strts	Wins	SWs	Earnings
Y Flash, 1960 h., Flash o' Night	2	28	6	3	$226,635
Times Rush, 1968 h., Indian Rush	6	75	15	7	215,332
Port of the Sea, 1971 h., Port Wine	7	61	13	3	113,649
Washoe Lea, 1977 h., Double Lea	8	58	17	0	101,979
Arvoicsal, 1996 g., King Alobar	5	61	8	0	90,431
Noti, 1960 h., Leisure Time	1	12	3	2	89,150
Import Wine, 1975 h., Port Wine	7	68	9	0	82,928
First Estimate, 1969 h., Windy Sands	4	47	9	0	71,337
Crow Creek, 1968 g., *Rapido	6	63	17	0	62,170
Pee Jay Kit, 1970 g., Nevada P. J.	5	39	11	0	61,853

FEMALE, YOB Sex, Sire	Years Raced	Strts	Wins	SWs	Earnings
Wood and Wine, 1975 m., Fleet Allied	5	54	18	4	$261,119
High Estimate, 1972 m., Windy Sands	5	45	16	5	164,749
Nevada Bond, 1955 m., Bymeabond	4	40	6	1	49,250
Petrones Own, 1972 m., *Petrone	4	38	8	1	45,219
Snow Spirit, 1985 m., Feather Dollar	2	18	1	0	44,110
Bingo Bets, 1981 m., Art's Classy Jet	5	44	10	3	39,529
Ingrid H., 1969 m., Mr. Busher	3	54	5	0	38,027
Orbit Rose, 1995 m., Pencil Point (Ire)	2	16	6	0	34,792
Dharita, 1960 m., Dharan	8	143	23	0	32,631
Fun Finder, 1978 m., Pleasure Seeker	2	11	4	0	32,555

New Hampshire

MALE, YOB Sex, Sire	Years Raced	Strts	Wins	SWs	Earnings
Road to Rock, 1963 g., Ross Sea	9	187	36	2	$248,113
Trim Clipper, 1963 g., *Pallestrelli	11	127	21	0	72,419
Mystic Clown, 1972 h., The Clown	6	23	11	0	56,230
Easter Gloves, 1958 h., Golden Gloves	9	197	24	0	55,786
Ruff Enuff, 1971 h., *Arrebato II	7	90	18	0	51,737

FEMALE, YOB Sex, Sire	Years Raced	Strts	Wins	SWs	Earnings
Lite Ft., 1981 m., Last Dance	6	71	15	0	$137,000
A Wish for Abby, 1993 m., Maudlin's Pleasure	6	40	9	0	40,644
Frost Heaves, 1979 m., Buck Run	6	67	6	0	36,896
Toy Party, 1962 m., Pan	11	199	22	0	34,665
Sunapee, 1990 m., Iron Brigade	5	57	8	0	32,478

New Jersey

MALE, YOB Sex, Sire	Years Raced	Strts	Wins	SWs	Earnings
Friendly Lover, 1988 h., Cutlass	7	66	22	12	$1,247,670
Zoffany, 1980 h., Our Native	6	36	15	11	1,225,569
Sewickley, 1985 h., Star de Naskra	4	32	11	5	1,017,517

FEMALE, YOB Sex, Sire	Years Raced	Strts	Wins	SWs	Earnings
Open Mind, 1986 m., Deputy Minister	3	19	12	11	$1,844,372
Missy's Mirage, 1988 m., Stop the Music	4	28	14	9	838,894
Classy Mirage, 1990 m., Storm Bird	3	25	13	7	716,712

MALE, YOB Sex, Sire	Years Raced	Strts	Wins	SWs	Earnings
Dance Floor, 1989 h., Star de Naskra	2	16	4	3	863,299
Gators N Bears, 2000 h., Stormy Atlantic	4	32	10	6	804,393
Sea of Tranquility, 1996 h., Heff	8	76	23	13	784,902
Frugal Doc, 1987 g., Baederwood	9	113	29	4	782,547
Loaded Gun, 1995 h., Prosper Fager	6	58	13	8	633,272
Park Avenue Ball, 2002 c., Citidancer	2	12	4	3	629,600
Johnny Legit, 1994 g., Double Negative	5	67	19	0	616,808

FEMALE, YOB Sex, Sire	Years Raced	Strts	Wins	SWs	Earnings
Spruce Fir, 1983 m., Big Spruce	5	40	16	12	698,703
Private Treasure, 1988 m., Explodent	2	19	5	4	603,189
Jersey Girl, 1995 m., Belong to Me	2	11	9	7	571,136
Just Smashing, 1982 m., Explodent	5	61	25	8	532,383
Eleven North, 1994 m., Northern Idol	6	40	16	6	459,755
Girl Powder, 1983 m., Talc	4	44	18	10	449,447
Wild Palm, 1994 m., My Prince Charming	6	74	17	0	428,061

New Mexico

MALE, YOB Sex, Sire	Years Raced	Strts	Wins	SWs	Earnings
Rocky Gulch, 2001 g., Dry Gulch	3	20	13	11	$798,608
Ciento, 1998 h., Prospector Jones	5	32	19	14	776,014
Run Johnny, 1992 g., Johnny Blade	7	52	14	6	518,790
Bold Ego, 1978 h., Bold Tactics	3	35	15	5	511,648
Runmore Mema, 1997 h., Jack Wilson	7	58	14	5	442,927
Star Smasher, 1999 h., Full Choke	3	24	12	10	437,992
Ninety Nine Jack, 1999 g., Jack Wilson	5	33	16	8	415,644
Copper Case, 1977 g., Hopeful Venture	9	92	33	18	365,374
Boulderdash Bay, 1990 g., Spotter Bay	7	47	16	5	331,885
B. G.'s Drone, 1989 h., Full Choke	7	57	14	3	294,470

FEMALE, YOB Sex, Sire	Years Raced	Strts	Wins	SWs	Earnings
Shemoveslikeaghost, 2000 m., Ghostly Moves	4	20	11	8	$533,441
Yulla Yulla, 1995 m., Look See	5	27	21	14	443,022
Latenite Special, 2001 m., Super Special	3	16	10	7	367,283
Frosty Tail, 1980 m., It's Freezing	3	28	11	3	361,078
Espeedytoo, 1999 m., Ghost Ranch	3	24	10	6	340,564
Fearless Ego, 1985 m., Bold Ego	4	43	16	6	325,377
Bold n Special, 1983 m., Bold River (Fr)	3	22	7	3	265,541
Scarzane, 1999 m., Devon Lane	4	25	6	2	248,265
Peachy Manners, 1981 m., Well Mannered	6	51	17	8	239,085
Hollywood Gone, 2002 f., Gone Hollywood	2	12	6	3	238,974

New York

MALE, YOB Sex, Sire	Years Raced	Strts	Wins	SWs	Earnings
Funny Cide, 2000 g., Distorted Humor	4	24	8	6	$3,220,319
Say Florida Sandy, 1994 h., Personal Flag	8	98	33	19	2,085,408
Gander, 1996 g., Cormorant	7	60	15	6	1,824,011
L'Carriere, 1991 g., Carr de Naskra	3	23	8	2	1,726,175
Fourstardave, 1985 g., Compliance	9	100	21	13	1,636,737
Fourstars Allstar, 1988 h., Compliance	6	59	14	9	1,596,760
Win, 1980 g., Barachois	5	44	14	7	1,408,980
Victory Speech, 1993 h., Deputy Minister	3	27	9	5	1,289,020
Thunder Rumble, 1989 h., Thunder Puddles	3	19	8	6	1,047,552
More to Tell, 1991 h., Moro	7	85	18	7	995,804

FEMALE, YOB Sex, Sire	Years Raced	Strts	Wins	SWs	Earnings
Grecian Flight, 1984 m., Cormorant	5	40	21	14	$1,320,215
Fit for a Queen, 1986 m., Fit to Fight	5	51	13	8	1,226,429
Irish Linnet, 1988 m., Seattle Song	6	62	19	13	1,220,180
Lottsa Talc, 1990 m., Talc	6	65	21	16	1,206,248
Critical Eye, 1997 m., Dynaformer	4	38	14	5	1,060,984
Capades, 1986 m., Overskate	3	27	11	8	1,051,006
Queen Alexandra, 1982 m., Determined King	5	46	19	14	1,034,144
Dat You Miz Blue, 1997 m., Cure the Blues	4	33	14	7	806,291
Biogio's Rose, 1994 m., Polish Numbers	6	52	16	6	797,959
Capeside Lady, 2001 m., Cape Town	3	17	7	6	694,760

North Carolina

MALE, YOB Sex, Sire	Years Raced	Strts	Wins	SWs	Earnings
Bold Circle, 1986 h., Circle Home	4	55	11	3	$372,488
G H's Pleasure, 1992 g., Foolish Pleasure	7	52	9	3	356,293
Triangular, 1967 g., Blue Prince	8	72	15	3	240,059
Insideangle, 1992 h., Allen's Prospect	4	60	10	0	233,738
Moment of Triumph, 1984 h., Timeless Moment	5	50	17	1	230,427
Dump Truck, 1973 h., Four Strings	10	188	31	0	211,930
R. T. Rise n Shine, 1984 g., Secretary of War	8	132	18	0	186,887
We're Just Bluff, 1987 g., Fairway Phantom	8	86	15	0	180,435
Ben Ali's Rullah, 1989 h., Clever Trick	4	58	9	0	175,365
Gold Candy Too, 1990 g., Goldlust	4	38	11	1	172,550

FEMALE, YOB Sex, Sire	Years Raced	Strts	Wins	SWs	Earnings
Top Socialite, 1982 m., Topsider	5	34	10	7	$521,944
Amanti, 1979 m., Anticipating	5	53	15	4	306,981
See Your Point, 1992 m., Rock Point	3	37	12	3	283,985
Family Effort, 1991 m., Goldlust	5	69	13	0	252,855
Hadee Mae, 1991 m., Goldlust	3	37	9	2	178,294
Flashy Concorde, 1988 m., Super Concorde	4	59	19	0	176,032
Clever Tune, 1992 m., Tricky Tab	7	96	15	0	149,597
One More Sue, 1990 m., One More Slew	6	91	16	0	148,091
Lark's Impression, 1998 m., I Above Norma	3	34	9	0	141,133
Flying Hope, 1982 m., Inverness Drive	7	85	9	0	139,808

North Dakota

MALE, YOB Sex, Sire	Years Raced	Strts	Wins	SWs	Earnings
Dakota Prospect, 1997 g., Slewdledo	5	52	8	1	$131,159
Northern Ace, 1998 g., Northern Prospect	6	49	14	1	121,855
Bold Aferd, 1994 g., Aferd	5	29	6	5	107,388
Stilaferd, 1994 g., Aferd	9	63	9	2	96,994
Breaker Breaker, 1997 h., Power Break	3	16	4	3	91,322
Suntana, 2000 g., Sun Man	3	23	6	4	81,242
Maddies Blues, 2000 g., Aferd	4	28	9	7	75,310
Leeaferd, 1995 g., Aferd	9	89	9	0	74,629
Hub Cap, 1981 h., Aferd	6	50	16	4	70,597
Jo Pelouse, 1970 h., Pelouse	9	127	17	0	58,715

FEMALE, YOB Sex, Sire	Years Raced	Strts	Wins	SWs	Earnings
Hoist Her Flag, 1982 m., Aferd	5	43	19	11	$290,849
Creel Ribot, 1979 m., Domian	7	86	19	0	93,175
Patty Kim, 1989 m., Aferd	4	23	6	4	87,944
Strike an Image, 2001 m., Patriot Strike	3	21	4	3	73,969
Can I Lead, 1986 m., Lead Astray	8	98	23	0	60,700
Penny Bolinas, 1976 m., Bolinas Intent	6	80	11	0	49,862
Music Time, 1993 m., Ragtime Reign	7	56	8	1	44,651
Milk N Cookies, 1996 m., Continental Morn	6	53	6	0	41,745
Sheza Broad, 1989 m., Au Point	5	46	15	0	40,637
Quillos Bolinas, 1978 m., Bolinas Intent	6	91	11	0	36,785

Ohio

MALE, YOB Sex, Sire	Years Raced	Strts	Wins	SWs	Earnings
Harlan's Holiday, 1999 h., Harlan	3	22	9	8	$3,632,664
Phantom On Tour, 1994 h., Tour d'Or	4	20	7	6	724,605
Kingpost, 1985 g., Stalwart	2	20	3	1	598,966
One Bold Stroke, 1995 h., Broad Brush	3	16	5	4	595,662
Royal Harmony, 1964 h., Royal Note	6	105	38	22	587,164
Stormy Deep, 1987 g., Diamond Shoal (GB)	5	53	17	8	565,672
Devil Time, 1997 g., Devil His Due	7	48	14	9	490,351
Majestic Dinner, 1997 g., Formal Dinner	6	41	17	7	473,923
Bill Monroe, 1978 g., Brent's Prince	6	65	24	15	466,824
Major Adversary, 1992 g., Mighty Adversary	9	87	21	10	458,708

FEMALE, YOB Sex, Sire	Years Raced	Strts	Wins	SWs	Earnings
Tougaloo, 1983 m., Lot o' Gold	5	33	13	11	$583,030
Ashwood C C, 1998 m., Cryptoclearance	6	52	17	7	581,329
Lady Cherie, 1997 m., Al Sabin	5	39	17	13	552,095
Glacial Princess, 1981 m., Brent's Prince	4	52	27	17	542,792
Sadie's Dream, 1990 m., Rare Performer	5	37	10	6	488,529
Cut the Cuteness, 1992 m., Cut Throat (GB)	5	38	13	12	411,459
Extended Applause, 1996 m., Exbourne	4	23	4	1	408,520
Safe Play, 1978 m., Sham	3	27	11	7	393,085
Crypto's Redjet, 1992 m., Cryptoclearance	5	39	17	8	364,640
Princess Hawkins, 1981 m., Brent's Prince	6	74	12	5	354,593

Oklahoma

MALE, YOB Sex, Sire	Years Raced	Strts	Wins	SWs	Earnings
Clever Trevor, 1986 g., Slewacide	5	30	15	9	$1,388,841
Mr Ross, 1995 g., Slewacide	6	44	18	14	1,091,046
Silver Goblin, 1991 g., Silver Ghost	6	26	16	11	1,083,895
Brother Brown, 1990 g., Eminency	3	20	14	8	791,448
Darrell Darrell, 1987 g., Boca Rio	7	53	23	13	591,646
That Tat, 1998 g., Faltaat	5	48	16	7	560,985
Brush With Pride, 1992 g., Broad Brush	5	35	14	9	548,615
Mighty Beau, 1999 g., Rainbow Prospect	6	41	9	2	519,809
Perfec Travel, 1982 g., Inverness Drive	8	52	14	10	514,747
Highland Ice, 1993 g., Highland Blade	7	48	16	9	474,090

FEMALE, YOB Sex, Sire	Years Raced	Strts	Wins	SWs	Earnings
Lady's Secret, 1982 m., Secretariat	4	45	25	22	$3,021,325
Voladora, 1995 m., Hickory Ridge	4	53	20	10	548,622
Belle of Cozzene, 1992 m., Cozzene	4	22	9	7	522,455
Slide Show, 1991 m., Slewacide	4	25	12	8	347,917
Fullasatick, 1993 m., Derby Wish	5	43	9	3	289,611
Mean Martha, 1978 m., Menocal	4	40	8	3	276,985
Caznire, 1989 m., Bold Ego	5	30	14	8	271,582
Southern Etiquette, 1988 m., Slewacide	4	27	10	6	259,459
Muhammad's Baby, 1986 m., Ask Muhammad	6	76	15	6	257,186
She's a Bullet, 1991 m., T. H. Bend	6	56	13	4	254,865

Oregon

MALE, YOB Sex, Sire	Years Raced	Strts	Wins	SWs	Earnings
Polynesian Flyer, 1982 h., Flying Lark	5	54	14	11	$346,525
Lethal Grande, 1999 g., Corslew	5	56	17	5	294,556
Lark's Legacy, 1981 g., Flying Lark	8	104	24	8	240,199
Eternal Secrecy, 1997 g., Black Tie Affair (Ire)	7	52	13	1	203,545
Annie's Turn, 1977 h., Joyous Turn	6	64	16	4	203,516
Weinhard, 1996 g., Falstaff	5	69	8	0	202,688
Family Fox, 1979 h., Bob Mathias	6	95	17	0	196,973
Strong Award, 1965 h., Strong Ruler	11	118	29	3	189,361
Supreme Lark, 1977 h., Flying Lark	8	112	24	5	186,799
Praise Jay, 1964 h., Jaybil	5	54	12	6	186,578

FEMALE, YOB Sex, Sire	Years Raced	Strts	Wins	SWs	Earnings
Revillew Slew, 1996 m., Can't Be Slew	6	46	13	3	$383,824
Moonlit Maddie, 1998 m., Abstract	5	38	12	6	207,358
La Famille, 1981 m., Bob Mathias	8	80	14	0	193,105
Valeri's Delight, 1984 m., Dr. Valeri	4	28	10	1	181,415
Solda Holme, 1986 m., Jeff's Companion	7	47	21	2	163,977
Cruisin' Two Su, 1983 m., Dr. Valeri	4	30	10	2	155,380
Solamente Un Vez, 1983 m., Relaunch	3	17	6	3	126,470
Just Out Run, 1988 m., Just the Time	6	64	11	4	125,976
So Happy Together, 2001 m., Corslew	4	24	7	1	117,962
Swoon's Bid, 1990 m., Swoon	7	81	14	0	116,999

Pennsylvania

MALE, YOB Sex, Sire	Years Raced	Strts	Wins	SWs	Earnings
Smarty Jones, 2001 h., Elusive Quality	2	9	8	7	$7,613,155
Alphabet Soup, 1991 h., Cozzene	4	24	10	7	2,990,270
With Anticipation, 1995 g., Relaunch	8	48	15	8	2,660,543
Yankee Affair, 1982 h., Northern Fling	5	55	22	15	2,282,156
Tikkanen, 1991 h., Cozzene	3	17	4	3	1,599,335
Lil E. Tee, 1989 h., At the Threshold	3	13	7	3	1,437,506
Rochester, 1996 g., Green Dancer	8	46	11	6	1,184,309
High Yield, 1997 h., Storm Cat	2	14	4	3	1,170,196
Unaccounted For, 1991 h., Private Account	2	17	6	2	998,468
Selkirk, 1988 h., Sharpen Up (GB)	3	15	6	6	843,661

FEMALE, YOB Sex, Sire	Years Raced	Strts	Wins	SWs	Earnings
Go for Wand, 1987 f., Deputy Minister	2	13	10	8	$1,373,338
Bessarabian, 1982 m., Vice Regent	3	37	18	14	1,032,640
Alice Springs, 1990 m., Val de l'Orne (Fr)	5	26	9	5	768,889
Mrs. Penny, 1977 m., Great Nephew	3	22	6	6	689,609
Classy Cathy, 1983 m., Private Account	3	15	7	4	537,970
Contredance, 1982 m., Danzig	3	21	8	5	492,700
Ambassador of Luck, 1979 m., What Luck	4	23	14	9	489,583
Wonders Delight, 1986 m., Icecapade	3	36	9	4	481,521
My Pal Lana, 2000 m., Kris S.	4	25	6	2	465,538
After the Glitter, 1989 m., Screen King	6	51	17	8	456,786

Rhode Island

MALE, YOB Sex, Sire	Years Raced	Strts	Wins	SWs	Earnings
Beau Britches, 1975 h., Oxford Accent	6	89	8	2	$121,145
Gulio Cesere, 1956 h., Mel Hash	4	59	16	2	106,308
Troll By, 1973 h., Military Plume	4	28	10	3	89,914
Tullo, 1956 h., Bull Dandy	9	202	23	1	81,680

FEMALE, YOB Sex, Sire	Years Raced	Strts	Wins	SWs	Earnings
Good Musical, 1977 m., Rock Talk	3	45	12	0	$155,580
Dandy Blitzen, 1955 m., Bull Dandy	4	48	14	4	131,499
Venomous, 1953 m., Mel Hash	4	32	15	4	107,932
Dandy Princess, 1958 m., Bull Dandy	4	58	15	0	80,533

MALE, YOB Sex, Sire	Years Raced	Strts	Wins	SWs	Earnings
New 'tricia, 1966 h., New Rullah	9	128	22	0	68,489
Rival Hunter, 1978 h., Oxford Accent	8	123	12	0	53,358
Melpet, Jr., 1954 g., Bull Dandy	4	66	13	0	53,325
Bandito Billy, 1978 h., Banderilla	5	69	14	0	51,127

FEMALE, YOB Sex, Sire	Years Raced	Strts	Wins	SWs	Earnings
Musical Sadie, 1967 m., *Good Shot	6	90	16	0	51,094
Farrago, 1977 m., Oxford Accent	3	22	5	0	47,153
Helipat, 1954 m., Bull Dandy	5	84	6	1	45,871
Distinctive Lady, 1970 m., Times Roman	4	36	8	0	44,41

South Carolina

MALE, YOB Sex, Sire	Years Raced	Strts	Wins	SWs	Earnings
Big Rut, 1993 g., Kokand	9	91	22	7	$570,488
Normandy Beach, 1996 g., Sewickley	7	80	18	1	450,319
American Prince, 1998 g., Miner	6	56	10	1	414,001
Intelligent Male, 2000 g., Ride the Storm	4	34	7	2	308,339
Kiss and Run, 1968 h., Double Hitch	8	144	40	7	295,681
Double Quill, 1969 h., Double Hitch	8	152	30	3	283,890
Roman Report, 1983 g., Greatest Roman	7	94	23	0	256,369
Race 'N Brace, 1984 h., Hard Crush	5	63	19	2	242,459
No Complaints, 1995 g., Personal Flag	6	83	16	0	219,340
Dressy Time, 1977 h., Canmore	8	108	20	0	219,250

FEMALE, YOB Sex, Sire	Years Raced	Strts	Wins	SWs	Earnings
Double Stake, 1993 m., Kokand	4	37	11	4	$343,480
Running Cousin, 1978 m., Double Hitch	5	86	22	8	291,440
Has Beauty, 1991 m., Kokand	10	106	25	0	232,156
Frills and Ribbons, 1978 m., Double Hitch	5	77	15	1	199,354
Sea Trip, 1981 m., Sea Songster	5	76	12	2	194,479
Frezil, 1978 m., Double Hitch	7	88	17	1	189,019
Raise a Prince, 1988 m., Raise a Bid	5	54	13	2	188,653
Crushem, 1979 m., Hard Crush	4	62	12	1	178,283
Miss Hitch, 1976 m., Double Hitch	6	54	13	3	174,470
Winter's Work, 1989 m., Cool Corn	6	90	22	0	162,781

South Dakota

MALE, YOB Sex, Sire	Years Raced	Strts	Wins	SWs	Earnings
Little Bro Lantis, 1988 g., Lost Atlantis	9	120	23	8	$719,866
Win Stat, 1977 h., Doctor Stat	8	84	22	6	438,378
Disarco's Rib, 1980 h., Libra's Rib	5	40	10	1	125,558
Atlantis Blend, 1989 g., Lost Atlantis	10	68	17	6	117,680
Right Key, 1971 h., Key Issue	8	97	22	1	108,279
Streaking On, 1975 h., Hi-Hasty	11	123	26	3	93,788
Shekmatyar, 1980 h., Bon Mot (Fr)	3	50	12	0	92,340
Officer's Call, 1971 g., Jet Man	5	53	13	3	88,543
John Jet, 1966 h., Jet Man	10	131	29	5	86,627
Rosedale Boy, 1971 h., Hi-Hasty	6	90	16	2	74,790

FEMALE, YOB Sex, Sire	Years Raced	Strts	Wins	SWs	Earnings
Reen Aferd, 1985 m., Aferd	6	78	13	1	$96,107
Ferns Image, 1986 m., Aferd	8	75	15	0	82,242
Pro Raja, 1970 m., Semi-pro	4	46	15	7	74,510
Rajaja, 1978 m., Jacinto	2	29	6	1	70,330
Hi-Mini, 1969 m., Hi-Hasty	3	41	7	1	60,463
Palacity Jet, 1971 m., Jet Man	4	44	15	5	60,289
Rio Nite, 1981 m., Aferd	5	41	12	1	57,685
Dakota Diamond, 1977 m., Four Way Split	5	62	12	1	51,053
Beturio, 1979 m., *Centurio	5	62	10	0	47,893
Beautitious, 1978 m., Restitious	5	51	8	3	44,077

Tennessee

MALE, YOB Sex, Sire	Years Raced	Strts	Wins	SWs	Earnings
Slew of Damascus, 1988 g., Slewacide	7	48	16	12	$1,420,350
Startahemp, 1970 g., Hempen	8	72	25	1	282,153
Shot n' Missed, 1977 h., Naskra	3	29	12	3	228,711
Act It Out, 1979 h., An Act	5	41	11	0	211,983
Bold Ruddy, 1978 g., Captain Cee Jay	8	75	10	2	206,886
Jay Bar Toughie, 1980 h., Full Pocket	10	126	26	0	205,232
Temperence Week, 1984 g., Temperence Hill	7	117	15	0	185,026
Hold the Beans, 1977 h., Northern Fling	10	186	18	0	175,528
Charlie Jr., 1966 h., Charlevoix	9	144	25	1	159,262
Big Rock Candy, 1962 h., Morning Line	6	54	17	1	151,013

FEMALE, YOB Sex, Sire	Years Raced	Strts	Wins	SWs	Earnings
Fancy Naskra, 1978 m., Naskra	5	26	8	2	$291,769
Tanya's Tuition, 1987 m., D'Accord	5	25	8	3	246,225
Tipper Time, 1992 m., Forward	6	78	13	1	171,282
Tourforsure, 1969 m., Above the Law	4	76	16	0	160,379
Alda's Will, 1993 m., Gallapiat	5	71	13	1	143,172
Southern Sweet, 1998 m., Tethra	5	29	5	0	142,642
Jay Bar Pet, 1971 m., Bold and Brave	4	65	11	0	132,240
Valieo, 2001 m., Evansville Slew	3	26	4	0	120,550
Cellar's Best, 1985 m., Band Practice	5	59	10	1	112,800
Flee the Storm, 1979 m., Forceten	3	49	8	0	106,388

Texas

MALE, YOB Sex, Sire	Years Raced	Strts	Wins	SWs	Earnings
Groovy, 1983 h., Norcliffe	3	26	12	12	$1,346,956
Mocha Express, 1994 h., Java Gold	4	34	16	10	960,216
Feeling Gallant, 1982 h., Gallant Gambler	6	86	19	10	846,145
Top Avenger, 1978 h., Staunch Avenger	6	57	23	11	721,237
Gold Nugget, 1995 g., Gold Legend	7	46	14	6	633,821
Jim's Orbit, 1985 h., Orbit Dancer	2	19	5	3	600,720
Appealing Breeze, 1987 h., Breezing On	2	14	9	8	553,327
Lights On Broadway, 1997 g., Majestic Light	6	62	13	6	540,980
Rare Cure, 1998 g., Rare Brick	6	59	12	7	512,410
Beverly Greedy, 1995 g., Raja's Best Boy	8	70	18	1	482,898

FEMALE, YOB Sex, Sire	Years Raced	Strts	Wins	SWs	Earnings
Got Koko, 1999 m., Signal Tap	3	15	7	5	$960,946
Two Altazano, 1991 m., Manzotti	3	20	9	6	709,725
Traces of Gold, 1992 m., Strike Gold	5	48	12	10	664,672
Bara Lass, 1979 m., Barachois	4	60	17	7	542,362
Take My Picture, 1982 m., Tyrant	3	28	13	7	541,273
Eagle Lake, 1998 m., Desert Royalty	4	43	13	7	477,877
Grab the Green, 1988 m., Cozzene	4	26	9	6	454,023
Darby's Daughter, 1986 m., Darby Creek Road	3	15	5	4	435,104
Sweet Misty, 1994 m., Lucky So n' So	4	45	15	8	422,005
Mastery's Gamble, 1992 m., Mastery	7	55	16	7	406,943

Utah

MALE, YOB Sex, Sire	Years Raced	Strts	Wins	SWs	Earnings
Pharaoh's Heart, 1990 g., Persevered	7	67	10	2	$340,470
R Friar Tuck, 1991 g., Religiously	4	24	4	1	236,641
Indian Express, 2000 h., Indian Charlie	4	7	3	0	174,628
Charley Mc, 1993 g., High Counsel	5	25	5	2	141,813
Pierces Homeremedy, 1988 g., Humbaba	11	102	27	3	128,693
Raise a Kitten, 1985 h., Humbaba	7	78	16	2	119,102

FEMALE, YOB Sex, Sire	Years Raced	Strts	Wins	SWs	Earnings
Jones Time Machine, 1979 m., Current Concept	3	26	13	7	$329,500
Let's Get Raced, 1980 m., Joduke	5	67	14	0	137,664
Ancient River, 1983 m., Upper Nile	6	47	14	3	134,964
Lovehermadly, 1997 m., Regal Groom	7	61	13	0	96,217
Lady Supreme, 1996 m., Four Seasons (GB)	4	58	6	0	80,311

MALE, YOB Sex, Sire	Years Raced	Strts	Wins	SWs	Earnings
Nintyfiver, 1995 g., Navegante (Chi)	9	108	19	0	94,869
Startinover, 1995 g., Regal Intention	7	89	8	0	93,377
Chory Four, 1999 g., Four Seasons (GB)	4	47	5	0	91,689
Force of Habit, 1996 g., Four Seasons (GB)	5	43	5	0	88,077

FEMALE, YOB Sex, Sire	Years Raced	Strts	Wins	SWs	Earnings
Seasons Promise, 2000 m., Four Seasons (GB)	4	33	4	0	79,275
Miss Table Talk, 1994 m., Never Tabled	5	64	8	0	71,950
Synaster Angel, 1993 m., Synastry	4	29	3	0	69,495
Bay Heart, 1973 m., *Epicuro	4	35	6	0	53,655
K J Lucky Seven, 1997 m., Four Seasons (GB)	3	17	4	0	50,528

Virginia

MALE, YOB Sex, Sire	Years Raced	Strts	Wins	SWs	Earnings
Paradise Creek, 1989 h., Irish River (Fr)	4	25	14	10	$3,401,416
Hansel, 1988 h., Woodman	2	14	7	6	2,936,586
Sea Hero, 1990 h., Polish Navy	3	24	6	3	2,929,869
Pleasant Tap, 1987 h., Pleasant Colony	4	32	9	6	2,721,169
Majesty's Prince, 1979 h., His Majesty	4	43	12	9	2,077,796
Java Gold, 1984 h., Key to the Mint	2	15	9	5	1,908,832
Simply Majestic, 1984 h., Majestic Light	4	44	18	14	1,667,713
Colonial Affair, 1990 h., Pleasant Colony	3	20	7	4	1,635,228
Secretariat, 1970 h., Bold Ruler	2	21	16	14	1,316,808
Chief Honcho, 1987 h., Chief's Crown	5	34	10	4	1,265,719

FEMALE, YOB Sex, Sire	Years Raced	Strts	Wins	SWs	Earnings
Seeking the Pearl, 1994 m., Seeking the Gold	4	21	8	7	$4,021,716
Sabin, 1980 m., Lyphard	4	25	18	14	1,098,341
Mandy's Gold, 1998 m., Gilded Time	4	24	11	7	1,081,744
Miss Oceana, 1981 m., Alydar	2	19	11	9	1,010,385
Love Sign, 1977 m., Spanish Riddle	4	39	16	10	934,827
Shuvee, 1966 m., Nashua	4	44	16	15	890,445
Possible Mate, 1981 m., King's Bishop	3	29	14	9	675,999
Dismasted, 1982 m., Restless Native	3	36	14	6	629,803
Zoonaqua, 1990 m., Silver Hawk	6	28	5	4	611,225
Topicount, 1985 m., Private Account	4	43	9	5	607,618

Washington

MALE, YOB Sex, Sire	Years Raced	Strts	Wins	SWs	Earnings
Saratoga Passage, 1985 g., Pirateer	4	22	6	4	$800,212
Military Hawk, 1987 g., Colonel Stevens	9	86	18	12	686,128
Captain Condo, 1982 g., Captain Courageous	8	70	30	16	511,695
Chinook Pass, 1979 h., Native Born	3	25	16	11	480,073
Funboy, 1991 h., Gumboy	5	49	13	11	478,180
Refried Dreams, 1993 g., Lac Ouimet	5	51	15	0	453,570
Sneakin Jake, 1987 g., Table Run	8	76	16	12	439,590
Moscow M D, 1989 g., Moscow Ballet	8	69	16	0	435,843
Makors Mark, 1997 h., Son of Briartic	5	29	11	6	430,753
Snipledo, 1985 g., Slewdledo	6	45	17	5	409,905

FEMALE, YOB Sex, Sire	Years Raced	Strts	Wins	SWs	Earnings
Peterhof's Patea, 1988 m., Peterhof	5	52	16	14	$623,367
Rings a Chime, 1997 m., Metfield	2	13	4	2	606,315
Run Away Stevie, 1989 m., Table Run	6	40	12	9	468,267
Cadette Stevens, 1988 m., Colonel Stevens	4	30	11	10	453,539
Belle of Rainier, 1979 m., Windy Tide	4	43	17	14	424,526
Classy Cara, 1997 m., General Meeting	2	10	4	3	405,847
Jazznwithwindy, 1994 m., Jazzing Around	7	71	18	0	391,739
Delicate Vine, 1984 m., Knights Choice	1	5	4	3	390,370
Bonne Nuite, 1989 m., Knights Choice	5	65	16	7	376,161
Firesweeper, 1983 m., Drum Fire	4	34	13	13	363,394

West Virginia

MALE, YOB Sex, Sire	Years Raced	Strts	Wins	SWs	Earnings
Soul of the Matter, 1991 h., Private Terms	4	16	7	4	$2,302,818
Afternoon Deelites, 1992 h., Private Terms	3	12	7	6	1,061,193
Confucius Say, 1998 g., Eastover Court	3	23	12	7	527,897
Rebellious Dreamer, 1996 h., My Boy Adam	5	53	10	6	407,918
Ardent Arab, 1992 g., Weshaam	9	77	24	2	407,475
A Huevo, 1996 g., Cool Joe	4	12	6	2	389,750
Coolmars, 1995 g., Glide	9	65	13	1	344,925
Slew's Smile, 1997 g., Native Slew	7	78	12	1	339,306
Me No Sissy, 1988 g., Light Years	11	123	18	2	336,011
Coin Collector, 1989 g., Weshaam	5	43	12	6	328,115

FEMALE, YOB Sex, Sire	Years Raced	Strts	Wins	SWs	Earnings
Evil's Pic, 1992 m., Piccolino	5	31	10	7	$437,877
Original Gold, 2000 m., Slavic	3	15	7	3	371,124
Shes a Caper Too, 1993 m., Feel the Power	6	78	12	1	291,089
Fancy Buckles, 2000 m., My Boy Adam	3	17	9	4	278,188
Mongo Queen, 1976 m., Mongo	3	40	8	2	277,837
Sweet Annuity, 1997 m., Oh Say	5	37	9	5	260,052
Longfield Star, 1996 m., Allen's Prospect	5	41	8	3	254,077
Peacomb Hen, 1995 m., Glide	8	78	17	0	242,525
Shesanothergrump, 1999 m., Weshaam	5	43	7	3	226,699
Who's Ya Mama, 1998 m., Allen's Prospect	5	32	10	1	219,056

Wisconsin

MALE, YOB Sex, Sire	Years Raced	Strts	Wins	SWs	Earnings
Chad's Boy, 1965 h., Disdainful	9	106	31	1	$73,871
Hope to Sea, 1986 g., Captain Seaweed	8	86	7	0	73,400
Sekao, 1974 h., Oakesun	7	77	10	0	65,124
Home Swiftly, 1975 h., Swift Pursuit	7	99	18	0	63,251
Island Command, 1975 h., Command Decision	3	32	6	0	61,459
Hard Liquor, 1972 g., Nahr Love	9	140	25	0	53,125
Racers Dream, 1984 h., Captain Seaweed	7	92	13	0	51,583

FEMALE, YOB Sex, Sire	Years Raced	Strts	Wins	SWs	Earnings
Cheetah Chick, 1977 m., Captain Seaweed	5	36	10	0	$43,882
Theresadon, 1974 m., Ocala Kid	9	116	18	0	38,689
Autumn Eagle, 1993 m., Curfew	6	50	6	0	32,745
Jami Pari, 1996 m., Bold James	6	79	5	0	30,717
Solaratee, 2001 m., Armed Truce	3	14	3	0	29,870
Weeds for Jennifer, 1978 m., Captain Seaweed	3	44	9	0	28,134
Connie's Fashion, 1980 m., Best Award	5	76	8	0	27,105

Wyoming

MALE, YOB Sex, Sire	Years Raced	Strts	Wins	SWs	Earnings
Peter Glory, 1956 h., New World	12	197	35	0	$81,319
Pappa Jeff, 1987 g., Pappagallo (Fr)	5	65	10	0	59,298
Toe to Toe, 1973 h., *Leandro	6	75	21	0	52,394

FEMALE, YOB Sex, Sire	Years Raced	Strts	Wins	SWs	Earnings
Zip Pouch, 1990 m., Destroyer (SAf)	4	16	7	2	$48,981
Vicsrose, 1972 m., Emma's Orphan	4	31	11	1	47,475
Sterling Memory, 1989 m., Hoist the Silver	3	24	6	0	36,517

Leading 2005 Earners by State Where Bred

State	MALE, YOB Sex, Sire	Strts	Wns	SWns	Earnings	FEMALE, YOB Sex, Sire	Strts	Wns	SWns	Earnings
Alabama	**Valid Run**, 2003 g., Valid Victorious	2	2	1	$35,180	**Comalagold**, 2000 m., Royal Empire	6	2	2	$64,130
Arizona	**Grimm**, 1999 g., Hansel	11	4	3	142,140	**Reatta Pass**, 1999 m., Benton Creek	12	6	0	54,726
Arkansas	**Quote Me Later**, 2000 g., Bold Anthony	5	3	0	66,390	**Rememberthecowgirl**, 2000 m., Remember Hope	16	6	0	80,330
California	**Lava Man**, 2001 g., Slew City Slew	9	3	2	774,103	**Dream of Summer**, 1999 m., Siberian Summer	9	3	3	658,650
Colorado	**Cocoa Latte**, 2001 g., Demidoff	13	7	5	121,283	**Bar Bailey**, 2000 m., Bates Motel	9	4	2	113,956
Florida	**Afleet Alex**, 2002 c., Northern Afleet	6	4	4	2,085,000	**Wild Fit**, 2003 f., Wild Wonder	4	2	1	432,600
Georgia	**Bluesthestandard**, 1997 g., American Standard	11	2	0	74,400	**Miss Hamma**, 1999 m., Roaring Camp	7	3	2	94,880
Idaho	**Robs Coin**, 2001 g., Hey Rob	12	5	0	68,570	**Free Rent**, 2001 m., Renteria	13	3	0	79,020
Illinois	**Fort Prado**, 2001 h., El Prado (Ire)	9	5	3	245,888	**Original Spin**, 2003 f., Distorted Humor	3	2	1	222,800
Indiana	**Mr. Mink**, 2000 g., Gold Case	8	5	1	72,320	**Lady Blue Sky**, 2002 f., Bidding Proud	13	5	1	99,877
Iowa	**Mingo Mohawk**, 2002 g., Mercedes Won	11	3	2	154,226	**Switch Lanes**, 1999 m., Deerhound	9	4	2	153,800
Kansas	**Scarlet Lad**, 1998 g., Big Splash	19	4	1	63,900	**Queena Corrina**, 1999 m., Here We Come	8	3	2	113,600
Kentucky	**Saint Liam**, 2000 h., Saint Ballado	6	4	4	3,696,960	**Pleasant Home**, 2001 m., Seeking the Gold	8	3	2	1,316,420
Louisiana	**Badtotheboneandrew**, 2002 c., On the Sauce	14	3	2	224,210	**Happy Ticket**, 2001 m., Anet	6	3	3	535,000
Maryland	**Cherokee's Boy**, 2000 h., Citidancer	12	7	5	368,050	**Maddalena**, 2002 f., Good and Tough	9	3	2	223,100
Massachusetts	**Jini's Jet**, 1998 g., A. P Jet	14	6	2	98,560	**Ask Queenie**, 2001 m., Key Contender	11	7	4	165,210
Michigan	**Mad Adam**, 2002 c., Service Stripe	5	1	1	145,850	**Creative Miss**, 2002 f., Creative	8	5	3	164,797
Minnesota	**Wally's Choice**, 2001 g., Quick Cut	11	4	3	112,500	**Glitter Star**, 2002 f., Glitterman	7	3	2	85,766
Mississippi	**Go Star Buster**, 2000 g., Blushing Star	12	2	1	51,355	**Blushing Starlite**, 2001 m., Blushing Star	9	1	0	14,215
Missouri	**Campinout**, 1999 g., Victorious	10	2	0	25,410	**Pass the Luck**, 1999 m., Lucky South	13	2	0	14,828
Montana	**Backonbabyside**, 2000 g., Baby I Lied	8	3	1	37,960	**Tabitango**, 2000 m., Snowbound	11	1	0	6,542
Nebraska	**The Straw Man**, 2002 g., Canaveral	9	5	4	68,130	**Up 'n Blumin**, 2001 m., Blumin Affair	8	5	4	72,400
Nevada	**Arvoicsal Two**, 2002 g., Distinctive Cat	7	2	0	12,150	**Hyatopthehills**, 2002 f., Presidents Summit	7	2	0	8,360
New Jersey	**Park Avenue Ball**, 2002 c., Citidancer	7	1	1	351,000	**Smart N Classy**, 2000 m., Smart Strike	9	2	2	193,565
New Mexico	**Rocky Gulch**, 2001 g., Dry Gulch	5	3	3	257,520	**Latenite Special**, 2001 m., Super Special	7	5	4	224,820
New York	**Commentator**, 2001 g., Distorted Humor	4	2	1	529,400	**Seeking the Ante**, 2002 f., Seeking the Gold	12	5	2	362,280
North Carolina	**Chief's Spokesman**, 2001 g., Dove Hunt	11	1	0	38,521	**Mizz Joclyne**, 1999 m., Othello	11	1	0	16,357
North Dakota	**J Dam Strike**, 2003 g., Patriot Strike	5	2	2	25,303	**Liberty Reigns**, 2003 f., Patriot Strike	5	0	0	7,723
Ohio	**Ready for Roses**, 2002 g., More Than Ready	10	4	2	136,480	**Just Michel**, 2000 m., Pacific Waves	11	6	4	108,132
Oklahoma	**Mighty Beau**, 1999 g., Rainbow Prospect	9	2	1	169,848	**Before Midnight**, 2002 f., Gilded Time	10	4	0	107,911
Oregon	**Tom Two**, 2003 g., Free At Last	11	5	4	86,913	**So Happy Together**, 2001 m., Corslew	11	4	0	80,007
Pennsylvania	**Presidentialaffair**, 1999 g., Not For Love	7	2	2	269,198	**Valley of the Gods**, 2000 m., Valley Crossing	11	4	3	207,874
South Carolina	**American Prince**, 1998 g., Miner	15	4	0	67,630	**Havin' a Moan**, 2002 f., Ride the Storm	15	5	0	76,070
South Dakota	**Barnstorm**, 2003 g., Storm of the Night	2	2	1	16,416	**Platinum Sky**, 2000 m., Pioneering	10	2	0	17,600
Tennessee	**Approved by Dylan**, 2002 c., With Approval	11	4	0	128,532	**Valieo**, 2001 m., Evansville Slew	11	1	0	50,670
Texas	**Dixie Meister**, 2002 g., Holzmeister	7	2	2	173,850	**Slewpy's Storm**, 2001 m., Storm Creek	12	4	3	165,950
Utah	**Maybefirst**, 2002 c., Cahill Road	2	2	1	25,440	**Seasons Promise**, 2000 m., Four Seasons (GB)	14	2	0	31,225
Virginia	**Tap Day**, 2001 h., Pleasant Tap	8	3	3	498,800	**Bank Audit**, 2001 m., Wild Rush	12	5	4	400,691
Washington	**No Giveaway**, 2001 g., He's Tops	7	3	2	182,723	**Storminbayoubabe**, 2000 m., Storm Blast	11	6	0	111,550
West Virginia	**Speed Whiz**, 2001 g., Weshaam	12	3	1	272,520	**Original Gold**, 2000 m., Slavic	5	3	2	164,427
Wisconsin	**R's Star**, 2003 g., Hacker	5	1	0	11,760	**Solaratee**, 2001 m., Armed Truce	11	3	0	27,770
Wyoming	**Thurber**, 2000 g., Aide Memoire	7	0	0	1,793	**Cat N Dolls**, 2002 f., Distinctive Cat	5	0	0	336

Performance Rates for 2005

Performance Rates are an objective measurement of racetrack performance developed by the Jockey Club Information Systems. Performance Rates were first published in *The Thoroughbred Record* in the 1960s. Performance Rates assign a rate to horses based on beaten lengths—who beat whom and by how much—with some adjustments made to standardize beaten distances to account for horses that were not pressed or were eased in large fields. Races in which individual horses did not finish are not counted for those horses.

Time is not a factor in Performance Rates, which are based on every start by every horse in North America in 2005. Performance Rates are expressed in lengths around a theoretical mean of zero. The average performances of the best horses in a given year are generally about 30 lengths better than an average performance of the average horse.

Two-Year-Old Males

Rank	Horse	Starts	Rating
1.	Henny Hughes	6	25.28
2.	First Samurai	5	25.22
3.	Fagan's Legacy	4	23.77
4.	Superfly	5	23.38
5.	Church Service	3	22.87
6.	In Summation	6	22.22
7.	Blazing Rate	4	20.46
8.	Dr. Pleasure	3	20.29
9.	Parkhimonbroadway	6	20.04
10.	Brother Derek	5	20.00
11.	Sorcerer's Stone	4	19.24
12.	High Cotton	5	19.23
13.	He's Got Grit	4	19.04
14.	Well Said	4	19.00
15.	Diabolical	5	18.99
16.	Stevie Wonderboy	5	18.92
17.	A. P. Warrior	5	18.42
18.	Achilles of Troy	4	17.92
19.	Sharp Humor	5	17.88
20.	Bluegrass Cat	4	17.79
21.	Yankee Master	3	17.73
22.	Your Tent Or Mine	3	17.68
23.	Glidininthecash	4	17.26
24.	Go Between	3	17.24
25.	Bob and John	5	17.16
26.	Up an Octave	4	17.15
27.	Travelin Leroy	3	17.15
28.	Broadway Ridge	4	16.85
29.	Groovy Luck	3	16.81
30.	Bell n' Gone	4	16.70
31.	Southern Success	3	16.68
32.	Private Vow	6	16.62
33.	Right Place N Time	3	16.57
34.	Save Big Money	4	16.53
35.	Mondavi	3	16.52
36.	Hyte Regency	5	16.48
37.	Ima Highway Star	5	16.45
38.	Laity	5	16.44
39.	Hesanoldsalt	3	16.41
40.	Steel the Glory	3	16.34
41.	Catcominatcha	7	16.33

Rank	Horse	Starts	Rating
42.	Electrify	4	16.27
43.	Flashy Bull	6	15.95
44.	B L's a Runner	4	15.92
45.	Midway Man	3	15.91
46.	Weatherstorm	3	15.88
47.	D' broken Speed	4	15.86
48.	Park Avenue Prince	5	15.86
49.	Storm Treasure	3	15.70
50.	Da Stoops	7	15.69

Two-Year-Old Fillies

Rank	Horse	Starts	Rating
1.	French Park	3	26.06
2.	Cinderella's Dream	4	25.11
3.	Along the Sea	5	23.67
4.	Celestial Legend	4	23.36
5.	Folklore	7	23.06
6.	Kimchi	3	22.15
7.	Adieu	6	21.91
8.	Wild Fit	4	21.27
9.	Sensation	5	21.10
10.	Ex Caelis	5	20.63
11.	Keeneland Kat	3	20.18
12.	Balance	4	19.92
13.	Halo Humor	3	19.82
14.	Bully Bones	4	19.78
15.	Catch My Fancy	4	19.60
16.	Your Quote	4	19.41
17.	Sugar Swirl	4	19.39
18.	Bo Chime	6	19.37
19.	Peppers Pride	3	19.19
20.	Tortuga Flats	6	19.04
21.	Wait a While	4	19.04
22.	Zippy Missy	5	19.01
23.	Original Spin	3	18.99
24.	Stolen Prayer	6	18.98
25.	Amandatude	4	18.58
26.	Love Locket	5	18.48
27.	Racing Bridgett	3	18.45
28.	Incumbent	3	18.38
29.	Sugar Cookie	4	18.28
30.	Siren Cove	4	18.22
31.	The Case Queen	3	18.11
32.	Performing Diva	5	18.09
33.	Livermore Valley	4	18.05
34.	Sea Pines	4	18.03
35.	She Says It Best	8	18.01
36.	River's Prayer	6	17.76
37.	Coolwind	4	17.73
38.	Peach Flambe	3	17.36
39.	Loosends	4	17.35
40.	Better Now	6	17.33
41.	Oprah Winney	5	17.10
42.	Effectual	3	17.10
43.	Diplomat Lady	5	17.07
44.	Rgirldoesn'tbluff	3	16.97
45.	Gumboots	3	16.92
46.	Keep On Talking	6	16.84
47.	Like a Gem	3	16.82
48.	Love the Beach	4	16.73
49.	Smart and Fancy	5	16.70
50.	Zzzs Ghost	4	16.62

Three-Year-Old Males

Rank	Horse	Starts	Rating
1.	Bellamy Road	4	38.6
2.	Afleet Alex	6	31.43
3.	Flower Alley	9	30.97
4.	Scrappy T	8	30.02
5.	Closing Argument	4	29.95
6.	Sun King	10	29.46
7.	Monarch Lane	3	29.08
8.	High Fly	7	28.41
9.	Giacomo	6	28.05
10.	Survivalist	6	27.32
11.	Andromeda's Hero	12	26.65
12.	Harlington	3	26.41
13.	Bandini	5	26.38
14.	Park Avenue Ball	7	26.13
15.	Magna Graduate	10	26.10
16.	Noble Causeway	6	25.71
17.	Don't Get Mad	9	25.34
18.	Wild Desert	5	24.91
19.	Lost in the Fog	9	24.18
20.	English Channel	8	24.14
21.	Coin Silver	5	23.85
22.	Gold and Roses	11	23.55
23.	Galloping Grocer	7	23.16
24.	Consolidator	3	22.95
25.	Naughty New Yorker	14	22.94
26.	Carminooch	6	22.85
27.	Roman Ruler	5	22.81
28.	Southern Africa	8	22.36
29.	Greeley's Galaxy	7	22.35
30.	War Front	5	22.23
31.	Chekhov	8	22.23
32.	Smokescreen	9	22.20
33.	Oratory	5	22.13
34.	Golden Rainbow	7	21.97
35.	Proud Accolade	5	21.95
36.	Sort It Out	11	21.93
37.	Rikman	5	21.90
38.	Thor's Echo	10	21.77
39.	Thunderprince	3	21.74
40.	Vicarage	11	21.62
41.	Real Dandy	12	21.61
42.	Spanish Mission	9	21.60
43.	More Smoke	6	21.46
44.	Spanish Chestnut	5	21.42
45.	Watchmon	10	21.35
46.	C. G's Dollar	11	21.23
47.	Defer	3	21.19
48.	Sir Halory	3	21.13
49.	High Limit	7	21.06
50.	Malibu Moonshine	7	20.96

Three-Year-Old Fillies

Rank	Horse	Starts	Rating
1.	Nature's Dowry	3	35.32
2.	Spun Sugar	6	31.86
3.	Sis City	5	29.80
4.	Smuggler	4	29.57
5.	In the Gold	9	28.90
6.	Shebelongstoyou	5	28.85
7.	Indian Vale	6	28.60
8.	Summerly	7	28.30
9.	Aspen Tree	7	26.88
10.	Dance Away Capote	6	26.80
11.	R Lady Joy	8	26.20
12.	Sweet Catomine	3	26.06
13.	Lexi Star	5	25.99
14.	Sweet Symphony	6	25.56
15.	Pussycat Doll	5	25.5
16.	Gold Strike	4	25.3
17.	Maddalena	9	25.17
18.	Contrast	3	25.01
19.	Play Ballado	4	24.91
20.	Seafree	3	24.59
21.	Amazing Buy	9	24.54
22.	Nothing But Fun	5	24.01
23.	For All We Know	6	24.01
24.	Promenade Girl	7	23.90
25.	Talented	4	23.85
26.	Leave Me Alone	10	23.67
27.	Letgomyecho	4	23.66
28.	Trickle of Gold	8	23.37
29.	Round Pond	6	23.26
30.	Only in Philly	4	23.21
31.	Portsea	4	23.03
32.	The Beter Man Can	7	23.03
33.	Reunited	8	22.69
34.	Hot Storm	11	22.65
35.	Take a Check	7	22.62
36.	Jill Robin L	4	22.57
37.	Acey Deucey	8	22.48
38.	Sharp Lisa	4	22.38
39.	Great Intentions	6	22.35
40.	Seeking the Ante	12	22.29
41.	Burnish	5	22.19
42.	My Typhoon (Ire)	7	22.05
43.	Melhor Ainda	5	22.01
44.	Party Maker	3	21.79
45.	Memorette	8	21.75
46.	Atlas Valley	10	21.65
47.	Pleasant Chimes	8	21.60
48.	Lady Pegasus	8	21.53
49.	Proposed	6	21.48
50.	Lemon Maid	5	21.44

Males, Four-Year-Olds and Older

Rank	Horse	Starts	Rating
1.	Saint Liam	6	32.05
2.	Commentator	4	29.78
3.	Suave	5	27.20
4.	Dwango	4	26.82
5.	Sir Shackleton	9	24.13
6.	Eddington	5	24.04
7.	Zakocity	4	23.66
8.	Rock Hard Ten	3	23.43
9.	Mr. Trieste	5	23.07
10.	Swingforthefences	4	22.82
11.	I'm the Tiger	4	22.76
12.	King's Drama (Ire)	5	22.52
13.	Relaxed Gesture (Ire)	7	22.29
14.	Whale	3	22.06
15.	Borrego	8	22.05
16.	Eurosilver	5	21.97
17.	Maytown	3	21.94
18.	Badge of Silver	5	21.84
19.	Alumni Hall	10	21.59
20.	Botanical	3	21.40
21.	Gouldings Green	5	21.33
22.	Better Talk Now	6	21.28
23.	Cherokee's Boy	12	21.14
24.	Yankee Mon	9	21.07
25.	Summer Book	6	21.02
26.	Super Frolic	8	20.96
27.	Iosilver	7	20.85
28.	Perfect Drift	8	20.75
29.	Wanderin Boy	3	20.62
30.	Gygistar	8	20.34
31.	Lord of the Game	12	20.26
32.	Funfair (GB)	3	20.22
33.	Silverfoot	7	19.99
34.	Purge	6	19.99
35.	Pollard's Vision	6	19.96
36.	Tiger Heart	6	19.92
37.	Desert Patrol	4	19.85
38.	Offlee Wild	5	19.83
39.	Mauk Four	8	19.76
40.	Silver Wagon	9	19.75
41.	Presidentialaffair	7	19.74
42.	A Golden Time	3	19.70
43.	Debating	6	19.69
44.	Rousing Victory	6	19.66
45.	West Virginia	7	19.64
46.	Zarb's Dahar	6	19.62
47.	Limehouse	10	19.49
48.	Wild Notions	3	19.39
49.	Five Steps	7	19.31
50.	Forest Danger	4	19.27

Females, Four-Year-Olds and Older

Rank	Horse	Starts	Rating
1.	Stellar Jayne	4	26.49
2.	Colony Band	3	25.24
3.	Supah Sensation	3	24.10
4.	Pampered Princess	10	23.64
5.	Flaming Heart	8	23.27
6.	Pleasant Home	8	23.08
7.	Bohemian Lady	9	23.01
8.	Ashado	7	22.85
9.	D' Wildcat Speed	3	21.98
10.	Happy Ticket	6	21.84
11.	Madcap Escapade	4	21.29
12.	Taittinger Rose	7	21.22
13.	Moon Dolly (GB)	7	21.19
14.	Lady Grace	6	21.10
15.	Film Maker	7	21.08
16.	Isola Piu Bella (Chi)	7	20.85
17.	Capeside Lady	6	20.74
18.	Personal Legend	8	20.67
19.	Plata	3	20.60

Rank	Horse	Starts	Rating
20.	Miss Fortunate	8	20.07
21.	Diavla	7	19.97
22.	Society Selection	7	19.90
23.	Patriots Image	7	19.86
24.	Wonder Again	5	19.73
25.	Xtra Tough	3	19.72
26.	For Gillian	8	19.71
27.	Wadena	4	19.53
28.	Shadow Cast	7	19.49
29.	Fortress Hill	7	19.46
30.	My Sweet Sug	6	19.36
31.	Essence	3	19.35
32.	Cammy's Jet	4	19.32
33.	Habiboo	7	19.31
34.	Chic Dancer	7	19.25
35.	Twist and Pop	3	19.15
36.	Rare Gift	5	19.13
37.	Storm's Darling	6	19.11
38.	Friel's for Real	9	19.08
39.	Smokey Glacken	6	19.07
40.	Dance Fee	15	19.06
41.	Beau Watch	8	19.04
42.	Bay Sweetie Babe	3	19.02
43.	Fast Navy (Brz)	3	19.01
44.	Miss Loren (Arg)	3	19.00
45.	Taygete	6	18.88
46.	Sanibel Sunset	4	18.85
47.	Mrs. Doyle	8	18.77
48.	La Reason	11	18.75
49.	Sensibly Chic	9	18.70
50.	Two Trail Sioux	7	18.68

Sprint Males, Three-Year-Olds and Older

Rank	Horse	Starts	Rating
1.	Lost in the Fog	9	24.18
2.	I'm the Tiger	4	22.76
3.	Maytown	3	21.94
4.	Egg Head	5	21.83
5.	More Smoke	6	21.46
6.	Botanical	3	21.40
7.	Better Than Bonds	3	21.37
8.	Middle Earth	5	21.18
9.	C. G's Dollar	9	21.06
10.	Vicarage	8	20.91
11.	Blue Sunday	5	20.84
12.	Awesome Twist	6	20.42
13.	The Daddy	3	20.34
14.	Yankee Mon	6	20.28
15.	Cherokee's Boy	4	19.96
16.	Tiger Heart	6	19.92
17.	Northern Gent	3	19.87
18.	Big Apple Daddy	7	19.83
19.	A Golden Time	3	19.70
20.	Zarb's Dahar	6	19.62
21.	Qureall	6	19.41
22.	Forest Danger	3	19.36
23.	Thor's Echo	4	19.27
24.	Ultimate	5	19.25
25.	Gotaghostofachance	3	19.04
26.	Clever Electrician	6	18.96
27.	Attila's Storm	9	18.90
28.	British Attitude	5	18.77
29.	Around the Cape	6	18.75
30.	Crimson Stag	3	18.75
31.	Social Probation	8	18.68
32.	Take Achance On Me	4	18.66
33.	Busted Trust	4	18.22
34.	Northern Stag	4	18.16
35.	Razor	5	18.15
36.	Lion Tamer	4	18.15
37.	Silver Wagon	7	18.13
38.	Santana Strings	8	18.01
39.	Patriot Act	3	18.00
40.	With Distinction	10	17.93
41.	Mr. Boomer	6	17.89
42.	Value Plus	4	17.78
43.	Joey P.	6	17.77
44.	Runingforpresident	3	17.74
45.	Potrisunrise (Arg)	7	17.72
46.	Wonone	3	17.69
47.	Elusive Jazz	14	17.68
48.	Byanosejoe	6	17.65
49.	Sunshinenbeer	4	17.62
50.	Scat Cat Jamey	4	17.57

Sprint Females, Three-Year-Olds and Older

Rank	Horse	Starts	Rating
1.	Aspen Tree	6	27.01
2.	For All We Know	3	26.37
3.	Maddalena	9	25.17
4.	Seeking the Ante	3	25.16
5.	Contrast	3	25.01
6.	Seafree	3	24.59
7.	Letgomyecho	3	23.91
8.	Talented	4	23.85
9.	Leave Me Alone	7	23.46
10.	Karakorum Splendor	3	23.13
11.	Seek a Star	4	23.11
12.	Portsea	4	23.03
13.	Happy Ticket	4	22.91
14.	Trickle of Gold	7	22.84
15.	Reunited	8	22.69
16.	Hot Storm	11	22.65
17.	Great Intentions	6	22.35
18.	Burnish	5	22.19
19.	Acey Deucey	7	22.11
20.	Flaming Heart	4	22.08
21.	Party Maker	3	21.79
22.	Cool Spell	3	21.71
23.	Lady Pegasus	3	21.43
24.	Alfonsina	4	21.43
25.	Madcap Escapade	4	21.29
26.	Forever Brilliant	6	20.54
27.	Nothing But Fun	3	20.44
28.	Exit to Heaven	6	20.10
29.	Jet Set Citi	4	19.92
30.	Xtra Tough	3	19.72
31.	Flying Glitter	5	19.61
32.	Wadena	4	19.53
33.	Ten Carat Ruby	8	19.51
34.	Fortress Hill	7	19.46
35.	Cammy's Jet	4	19.32
36.	Whimsy	4	19.28
37.	Lemon Maid	3	19.19
38.	Smokey Glacken	6	19.07
39.	Ender's Sister	3	19.04
40.	Hide and Chic	8	18.98
41.	Partners Due	10	18.93
42.	Naughty Is	3	18.86
43.	Blue Song	5	18.80
44.	Sensibly Chic	9	18.70
45.	Wild Speed	4	18.67
46.	Cupid's Dixie	3	18.64
47.	Thermal Ablasion	7	18.61
48.	Secrets Galore	4	18.56
49.	True Tails	4	18.55
50.	Mantova Run	3	18.53

Turf Males, Three-Year-Olds and Older

Rank	Horse	Starts	Rating
1.	English Channel	8	24.14
2.	King's Drama (Ire)	5	22.52
3.	Relaxed Gesture (Ire)	7	22.29
4.	Whale	3	22.06
5.	Better Talk Now	6	21.28
6.	Gun Salute	7	20.78
7.	Funfair (GB)	3	20.22
8.	Touched by Madness	5	20.09
9.	Silverfoot	7	19.99
10.	Rousing Victory	6	19.66
11.	Jambalaya	5	19.47
12.	Crown Point	7	19.20
13.	Rebel Rebel (Ire)	3	19.05
14.	Artie Schiller	6	19.04
15.	Leroidesanimaux (Brz)	4	18.88
16.	Vanderlin (GB)	4	18.86
17.	Milky Way Guy	3	18.84
18.	Host (Chi)	3	18.79
19.	Holy Ground	5	18.41
20.	Republican Hawk	3	18.35
21.	Certifiably Crazy	7	18.28
22.	Therecomesatiger	5	18.22
23.	Drum Major	5	18.20
24.	Tadreeb	7	18.15
25.	Seattlespectacular	3	18.07
26.	Ole Faunty	3	17.99
27.	Tinseltown	3	17.92
28.	Dreadnaught	8	17.90
29.	Chattahoochee War	7	17.89
30.	United	4	17.82
31.	Dubleo	4	17.79
32.	Spring House	9	17.75
33.	Lac a Rock	5	17.67
34.	Inaugural Address	6	17.61
35.	Vangelis	6	17.54
36.	Dontbotherknocking	6	17.54
37.	Revved Up	8	17.51
38.	Rochester	7	17.50
39.	Purim	4	17.47
40.	Rey de Cafe	6	17.46
41.	Meteor Storm (GB)	9	17.46
42.	Kilbride Rd	5	17.29
43.	Salic Law	4	17.19
44.	Fort Prado	9	17.19
45.	Speed of Light (Ire)	5	17.12
46.	Shredded	4	17.08
47.	Le Cinquieme Essai	4	17.03
48.	Witt Ante	3	17.02
49.	Shakespeare	4	17.02
50.	Mad Adam	3	16.95

Turf Females, Three-Year-Olds and Older

Rank	Horse	Starts	Rating
1.	Melhor Ainda	5	22.01
2.	Sweet Talker	6	21.30
3.	Lady Grace	6	21.10
4.	Film Maker	7	21.08
5.	Asi Siempre	3	20.99
6.	My Typhoon (Ire)	6	20.91
7.	Cape Hope	5	19.93
8.	Wonder Again	5	19.73
9.	Beau Watch	4	19.47
10.	Masseuse	3	19.27
11.	Chic Dancer	7	19.25
12.	Rich in Spirit	6	19.20
13.	Unbridled Danz	4	19.02
14.	Intercontinental (GB)	7	18.65
15.	Cayuga's Waters	4	18.55
16.	Singhalese (GB)	7	18.28
17.	Luas Line (Ire)	4	18.15
18.	Wend	8	18.09
19.	Cat Alert	5	18.05
20.	Brag (Ire)	6	18.04
21.	Ellens Lucky Star	3	18.02
22.	More Than Promised	8	18.01
23.	Unbridled Sidney	4	17.92
24.	Joyful Chaos	6	17.82
25.	Yes Beth	10	17.80
26.	Who's Cozy	5	17.76
27.	Victory Lap	8	17.75
28.	Louve Royale (Ire)	5	17.72
29.	Defensa (Ger)	5	17.61
30.	Champagne Ending	3	17.35
31.	Silver Cup (Ire)	4	17.28
32.	Dynamite Lass	9	17.17
33.	Humoristic	8	17.12
34.	Enduring Will	3	17.11
35.	Dream Lady	5	17.04
36.	Berbatim	3	17.03
37.	Sweet Science	5	16.97
38.	La Reina	8	16.91
39.	Dynamia	6	16.87
40.	Three Degrees (Ire)	7	16.85
41.	Queen Supreme	3	16.82
42.	Art Fan	9	16.82
43.	Finery	6	16.81
44.	Sheer Enchantment	6	16.79
45.	Invitational	4	16.79
46.	Equestrian Girls	3	16.78
47.	Paddy's Daisy	6	16.77
48.	My Lordship	6	16.67
49.	Delta Princess	9	16.62
50.	Latice (Ire)	4	16.52
	Noble Stella (Ger)	9	16.52

Experimental Free Handicap

The Experimental Free Handicap, published annually by the Jockey Club, is based on a hypothetical $1\frac{1}{16}$-mile race for two-year-olds on dirt. Walter S. Vosburgh, the legendary Jockey Club handicapper, compiled the first Experimental Free Handicap in 1933. He placed Sanford Stakes winner First Minstrel atop his list at 126 pounds, although the filly Mata Hari at 122 pounds effectively was the highweight when considering the five-pound sex allowance then in effect. The 126-pound high weight became the standard impost for a champion of average accomplishment.

Vosburgh, who had been the racing secretary at New York tracks since 1894, retired in 1934, and no Experimental Free Handicap was prepared for that year. John B. Campbell assumed the task in 1935 and continued to compile the list until his death in '54.

Campbell, also racing secretary at the New York tracks, wrote in a 1943 letter that his Experimental Free Handicap was intended primarily as a forecast of how the horses would perform as three-year-olds. The Experimental, he wrote, "is based mainly upon my opinion of what the two-year-olds will accomplish as three-year-olds and at distances of a mile and a furlong or greater."

Following Campbell's death, Frank E. "Jimmy" Kilroe assigned the weights through 1960. Thomas Trotter, who compiled the list through 1972, followed him.

Starting in 1969, at the behest of the Jockey Club, the thrust of the Experimental was changed from a prediction of future performance to a measure of accomplishment during the two-year-old season exclusively.

Kenneth Noe Jr. prepared the Experimental Free Handicap from 1972 through '75, and Trotter resumed the task in '76. Beginning in 1979, a committee of three racing secretaries was chosen to establish the Experimental weights. In 1985, for the first time, separate lists were compiled for males and fillies. The 2005 Experimental Free Handicap was prepared by Ben Huffman of Keeneland Race Course, P. J. Campo of the New York Racing Association, and Tom Robbins of Del Mar.

The highest Experimental weight ever assigned was 132 pounds to Count Fleet in 1942; the following year, he won the Triple Crown.

Past Experimental Free Handicap Highweights

Year	Male	Female
2005	Stevie Wonderboy (126)	Folklore (123)
2004	Declan's Moon (126)	Sweet Catomine (124)
	Wilko (126)	
2003	Action This Day (126)	Halfbridled (124)
	Cuvee (126)	
	Ruler's Court (126)	
2002	Vindication (126)	Storm Flag Flying (123)
2001	Johannesburg (126)	Tempera (123)
2000	Macho Uno (126)	Caressing (123)
1999	Anees (126)	Cash Run (123)
		Chilukki (123)
		Surfside (123)
1998	Answer Lively (126)	Silverbulletday (123)
1997	Favorite Trick (128)	Countess Diana (125)
1996	Boston Harbor (126)	Storm Song (124)
1995	Maria's Mon (126)	My Flag (123)
	Unbridled's Song (126)	
1994	Timber Country (126)	Flanders (124)
1993	Brocco (126)	Phone Chatter (123)
	Dehere (126)	
1992	Gilded Time (126)	Eliza (123)
1991	Arazi (130)	Pleasant Stage (123)
1990	Fly So Free (126)	Meadow Star (123)
1989	Rhythm (126)	Go for Wand (123)
1988	Easy Goer (126)	Open Mind (123)
1987	Forty Niner (126)	Epitome (123)
		Over All (123)
1986	Capote (126)	Brave Raj (123)
1985†	Ogygian (126)	I'm Splendid (123)
	Tasso (126)	
1984	Chief's Crown (126)	Outstandingly (118)
1983	Devil's Bag (128)	Miss Oceana (120)
1982	Copelan (126)	Landaluce (121)
	Roving Boy (126)	Princess Rooney (121)
1981	Deputy Minister (126)	Before Dawn (120)
	Timely Writer (126)	
1980	Lord Avie (126)	Heavenly Cause (120)
1979	Rockhill Native (126)	Smart Angle (120)
1978	Spectacular Bid (126)	Candy Eclair (119)
		It's in the Air (119)
1977	Affirmed (126)	Lakeville Miss (119)
1976	Seattle Slew (126)	Sensational (119)
1975	Honest Pleasure (126)	Dearly Precious (119)
		Optimistic Gal (119)
1974	Foolish Pleasure (127)	Ruffian (122)
1973	Protagonist (126)	Talking Picture (121)
1972	Secretariat (129)	La Prevoyante (121)
1971	Riva Ridge (126)	Numbered Account (119)
1970	Hoist the Flag (126)	Forward Gal (118)

Year	Male	Female
1969	Silent Screen (128)	Fast Attack (116)
1968	Top Knight (126)	Gallant Bloom (118)
		Process Shot (118)
1967	Vitriolic (126)	Queen of the Stage (117)
1966	Successor (126)	Regal Gleam (116)
1965	Buckpasser (126)	Moccasin (120)
1964	Bold Lad (130)	Queen Empress (118)
1963	Raise a Native (126)	Castle Forbes (115)
		Tosmah (115)
1962	Never Bend (126)	Affectionately (115)
		Smart Deb (115)
1961	Crimson Satan (126)	Cicada (118)
1960	Hail to Reason (126)	Bowl of Flowers (120)
1959	Warfare (126)	My Dear Girl (117)
1958	First Landing (126)	Quill (117)
1957	Jewel's Reward (126)	Idun (120)
1956	Barbizon (126)	Alanesian (117)
1955	Career Boy (126)	Doubledogdare (116)
		Nasrina (116)
1954	Summer Tan (128)	HIgh Voltage (117)
1953	Porterhouse (126)	Evening Out (118)
	*Turn-to (126)	
1952	Native Dancer (130)	Bubbley (116)
		Sweet Patootie (116)
1951	Tom Fool (126)	Rose Jet (115)
1950	Uncle Miltie (126)	Aunt Jinny (115)
		How (115)
1949	Middleground (126)	Bed o' Roses (119)
1948	Blue Peter (126)	Myrtle Charm (121)
1947	Citation (126)	Bewitch (121)
1946	Cosmic Bomb (126)	First Flight (126)
	Double Jay (126)	
1945	Lord Boswell (128)	Beaugay (121)
1944	Free for All (126)	Busher (119)
	Pavot (126)	
1943	Pukka Gin (126)	Durazna (121)
		Miss Keeneland (121)
1942	Count Fleet (132)	Askmenow (119)
		Good Morning (119)
1941	Alsab (130)	Chiquita Mia (115)
		Ficklebush (115)
1940	Whirlaway (126)	Level Best (121)
1939	Bimelech (130)	Now What (119)
1938	El Chico (126)	Inscoelda (116)
1937	Menow (126)	Jacola (116)
1936	Brooklyn (126)	Rifted Clouds (115)
1935	Red Rain (126)	Forever Yours (116)
1933	First Minstrel (126)	Mata Hari (122)

†Starting in 1985, fillies were weighted separately.
No weights assigned in 1934.

2005 Experimental Free Handicap Colts and Geldings

Wt.	Horse	Sire—Dam, Broodmare Sire	Sts	1st	2nd	3rd	Earnings
126	Stevie Wonderboy	Stephen Got Even—Heat Lightning, by Summer Squall	5	3	1	1	$1,028,940
124	First Samurai	Giant's Causeway—Freddie Frisson, by Dixieland Band	5	4	0	1	682,575
123	Henny Hughes	Hennessy—Meadow Flyer, by Meadowlake	6	3	3	0	644,820
121	Brother Derek	Benchmark—Miss Soft Sell, by Siyah Kalem	5	3	0	1	502,080
119	Private Vow	Broken Vow—Smooth as Silk, by Deputy Minister	6	4	1	0	382,508
	Your Tent Or Mine	Forest Camp—Shes Got the Look, by Prospector's Music	3	2	1	0	173,250
118	What a Song	Songandaprayer—What a Knight, by Tough Knight	3	3	0	0	179,700
115	Bluegrass Cat	She's a Winner, by A.P. Indy	4	3	0	0	213,780
	He's Got Grit	Songandaprayer—Hollow Miss, by With Approval	4	4	0	0	191,900
	Sorcerer's Stone	Gulch—Magical Holiday, by Slew o' Gold	4	3	0	0	177,645
114	Barbaro	Dynaformer—La Ville Rouge, by Carson City	2	2	0	0	99,000
	Bob and John	Seeking the Gold—Minister's Melody, by Deputy Minister	5	1	1	2	107,370
	Dawn of War	Catienus—Hillary Step, by Chimes Band	7	3	3	0	403,800
113	A. P. Warrior	A.P. Indy—Warrior Queen, by Quiet American	5	2	1	0	118,435
112	Bashert	Tiger Ridge—Caught Ree, by Eastern Echo	5	1	2	1	83,300
111	Yankee Master	Yankee Victor—Ghazo, by Ghazi	3	2	1	0	123,900
110	Half Ours	Unbridled's Song—Zing, by Storm Cat	2	2	0	0	105,670
	High Cotton	Dixie Union—Happy Tune, by A.P. Indy	5	1	2	1	98,120
	Laity	Pulpit—Tour, by Forty Niner	5	2	0	0	151,200
	Lawyer Ron	Langfuhr—Donation, by Lord Avie	10	3	1	3	129,208
	Stream Cat	Black Minnaloushe—Water Course, by Irish River (Fr)	5	2	0	1	153,670
	Within Reason	Five Star Day—Pretty Reason, by Fly So Free	3	2	1	0	86,005
109	Bengal Lore	Tale of the Cat—Sew and Sew, by Ogygian	7	1	3	1	86,907
	Deputy G	Matty G—French Lady, by French Deputy	4	2	0	1	146,800
	Gin Rummy King	Double Honor—Ginny Auxier, by Racing Star	8	3	4	0	138,860
	Hyte Regency	Diligence—Silvery Lace, by Silver Buck	5	2	1	1	92,690
	In Summation	Put It Back—Fiesta Baby, by Dayjur	6	5	1	0	285,800
	Political Force	Unbridled's Song—Glitter Woman, by Glitterman	5	1	3	0	66,285
	Saint Augustus	Saint Ballado—Lorie Darlin, by West by West	5	2	0	1	90,650
	Superfly	Fusaichi Pegasus—Marozia, by Storm Bird	5	1	1	2	145,820
108	Blazing Rate	Exchange Rate—Blazing Alarmiss, by Mr. Prospector	4	3	1	0	351,300
	Catcominatcha	Tale of the Cat—Certainly a Star, by Red Ransom	7	2	2	0	206,706
	Fagan's Legacy	Monarchos—Erie Dearie, by Kris S.	4	2	1	0	82,745
	R Loyal Man	More Than Ready—Wildwife, by Wild Gale	6	3	1	0	88,050
107	Beacon Shine	Montbrook—Unlimited Pleasure, by Valid Appeal	3	2	0	1	101,680
	Flashy Bull	Holy Bull—Iridescence, by Mt. Livermore	6	1	3	1	90,650
	Mr. Silver	Concorde's Tune—Clever Lou, by Tri Jet	7	3	0	1	112,680
	The Pharaoh	Forest Camp—Touche de Velours, by Meadowlake	5	1	2	1	97,800
	Up an Octave	Brahms—Afleet Change, by Time for a Change	4	2	0	0	89,500
106	Diabolical	Artax—Bonnie Byerly, by Dayjur	5	1	3	1	128,130
	Premier Dance	Premiership—Vilshedance, by Vilzak	9	6	1	1	245,380
	Red Raymond	Deputy Commander—Win Right Now, by Waquoit	6	2	0	1	109,735
	Saint Daimon	Saint Ballado—Daimon, by Strike Gold	4	2	0	1	81,060
	Too Much Bling	Rubiano—Rose Colored Lady, by Formal Dinner	5	1	0	2	53,954
	Union Course	Dixie Union—Sweetest Smile, by Dehere	4	1	1	1	77,220
105	Almost Certain	Favorite Trick—Wishes and Roses, by Greinton (GB)	4	2	0	0	81,300
	Da Stoops	Distorted Humor—Glamorous Lady, by Kingdom of Spain	7	2	3	1	163,970
	Jealous Profit	Trippi—Fast Profit, by Tejano	6	0	2	2	67,460
	Speed of Sound	Phone Trick—Lark Creek, by Meadowlake	4	1	1	1	65,467
104	Church Service	Pulpit—To Be Approved, by With Approval	3	1	1	0	47,475
	Genre (GB)	Orpen—Blue Indigo (Fr), by Pistolet Bleu (Ire)	9	3	1	2	94,461
	Southern Success	Dixieland Band—My Success, by A.P. Indy	3	2	0	0	84,454
103	Crafty Tricker	Favorite Trick—Crafty Personality, by Crafty Prospector	9	3	0	1	95,636
	Desert Wheat	Wheaton—Absoluta (Ire), by Royal Academy	8	2	3	1	111,210
	Dr. Pleasure	Thunder Gulch—Beautiful Pleasure, by Maudlin	3	1	1	0	43,298
	Honor Due	Proud and True—Atrial Flutter, by Lear Fan	3	1	0	1	43,085
	Master of Disaster	Dance Master—More d'Amour, by Tour d'Or	5	2	1	0	87,640
	Old Thunder	Fusaichi Pegasus—Enjoy the Moment, by Slew's Royalty	6	1	0	2	57,065
	One Union	Dixie Union—Onceinabluemamoon, by Al Mamoon	2	1	0	0	45,600
	Out Our Way	New Way—Insight to Cope, by Copelan	7	3	2	1	86,123
	Plug Me In	Hold for Gold—Karaoke Kid, by Fast Play	6	0	0	1	36,460
	Rungius	Cat Thief—Remuda, by Gilded Time	9	2	2	3	64,510
	Test Boy	Brahms—Soundproof (Ire), by Ela-Mana-Mou (Ire)	5	3	1	1	92,300
102	Cause to Believe	Maria's Mon—Imaginary Cat, by Storm Cat	6	4	2	0	126,825
	Congo King	Horse Chestnut (SAf)—Sweet Nostalgia, by Mr. Redoy	3	1	0	0	33,999
	D' broken Speed	Broken Vow—Velvet Panther, by Pentaquod	5	1	2	0	47,250
	Disappearing Trick	Favorite Trick—Missuma, by Procida	3	2	1	0	96,215
	Ioway Indian	Indian Charlie—Emily's Treat, by State Dinner	3	1	0	1	20,625
	Kissin Knight	Kissin Kris—Super Princess, by Super May	6	1	2	1	62,240
	Say Tomorrow	Tomorrows Cat—Belsay, by Leo Castelli	7	1	1	1	47,921
	Wait in Line	Line In The Sand—Long Wait, by Classic Go Go	10	2	2	2	63,582
	Wedding Singer	Songandaprayer—Diamond of Forever, by Diamond Prospect	5	1	1	2	82,897
101	Creve Coeur	Lion Hearted—Imposing Light, by Majestic Light	8	3	1	2	150,185
	Don't Tell Mommy	Capote—My Meggie Meg, by French Deputy	3	2	1	0	54,900
	Might Be Hooked	Mighty—Hooked On Candy, by Lit de Justice	8	3	2	1	59,388
	Nine Best	Crafty Friend—Kwik as a Wink, by De Niro	5	3	2	0	70,640
100	Big Lover	Ecton Park—Love On the Rail, by Meadowlake	6	1	3	1	77,160
	Cab	Trippi—Lovely Cabrini, by Cabrini Green	7	1	1	4	83,382
	Counterfeit Gold	Twining—Counterfeit Bid, by Sheikh Albadou (GB)	4	2	1	1	58,000
	Cousins Lew	Slew Gin Fizz—Sofisticada, by Northern Jove	1	1	0	0	41,250
	Don Jaun Con	Suggest—Nifty Slew, by Slewdledo	7	2	2	1	79,075
	Mondavi	Maria's Mon—Senate Appointee, by Storm Cat	3	1	0	1	22,700
	Schoolin You	You and I—Home School, by Pine Bluff	6	2	1	0	90,781
	Tizzys No Saint	Cee's Tizzy—Karon's Relentless, by Saint Ballado	6	1	1	2	53,650
	Value Fund	Valid Expectations—Velenta, by Theatrical (Ire)	5	1	0	1	19,144

2005 Experimental Free Handicap Fillies

Wt.	Horse	Sire—Dam, Broodmare Sire	Sts	1st	2nd	3rd	Earnings
123	Folklore	Tiznow—Contrive, by Storm Cat	7	4	3	0	$927,500
122	Adieu	El Corredor—Irene's Talkin, by At the Threshold	6	4	0	0	554,470
120	Wild Fit	Wild Wonder—Grannies Feather, by At Full Feather	4	2	2	0	432,600
117	Along the Sea	Anees—Russian Flight (Ire), by Siberian Express	5	1	1	2	168,800
	Diamond Omi	Giant's Causeway—Hum Along, by Fappiano	5	2	0	1	160,740
116	Diplomat Lady	Forestry—Playcaller, by Saratoga Six	5	3	0	0	334,800
115	Wonder Lady Anne L	Real Quiet—Ancho, by Wild Zone	7	2	0	3	160,780
114	Balance	Thunder Gulch—Vertigineux, by Kris S.	4	2	1	1	183,300
	French Park	Ecton Park—Alarming Prospect, by Darn That Alarm	3	3	0	0	243,761
	Original Spin	Distorted Humor—We Love Granny, by Home At Last	3	2	0	1	222,800
	Private World	Thunder Gulch—Rita Rucker, by Dmitri	4	3	0	0	141,075
	Sensation	Dixie Union—Ryn, by Mr. Prospector	5	3	0	0	163,340
	She Says It Best	Stormy Atlantic—Bestsayes, by Marsayas	8	4	2	0	382,918
113	Bully Bones	Hesabull—Anniversary Wish, by Beau's Eagle	4	3	0	0	141,000
	Fifth Avenue	Monarchos—Shop Here, by Dehere	5	2	1	0	109,900
	Mystery Girl	Stormy Atlantic—A B C Amanda, by Alphabet Soup	5	1	1	1	119,876
	River's Prayer	Devon Lane—Cozzy Flyer, by Cozzene	6	2	1	2	156,683
112	Better Now	Thunder Gulch—Scenic Point, by Unbridled	6	2	1	1	136,900
	J'ray	Distant View—Bubbling Heights (Fr), by Darshaan (GB)	4	3	0	0	157,245
111	Beau Dare	Military—Gen Corp Purposes, by Beau Genius	5	2	1	0	108,316
	Cinderella's Dream	Prime Timber—Broadway Hoofer, by Belong to Me	4	2	2	0	133,600
	Ex Caelis	Fusaichi Pegasus—La Barberina, by Nijinsky II	5	1	2	1	201,920
	Miraculous Miss	Mr. Greeley—No Small Miracle, by Silver Deputy	3	3	0	0	114,120
	Wait a While	Maria's Mon—Flirtatious, by A.P. Indy	4	2	0	1	97,280
110	Bettarun Fast	Kelly Kip—Split Decision, by Dispersal	5	3	1	0	83,225
	Effectual	Carson City—Hooklineandsinker, by Skywalker	3	2	0	0	108,582
	Indian Breeze	Indian Charlie—Pulaski Countess, by Fluorescent Light	4	2	0	0	89,880
	Keeneland Kat	Hennessy—Meadow Victory, by Ogygian	3	2	0	1	132,200
	Sabatini	Five Star Day—Play Date, by Geiger Counter	2	1	0	1	84,865
	Sweet Fourty	Sweetsouthernsaint—Majestic Fourty, by Majestic Venture	6	2	1	0	59,000
109	Capozzene	Capote—Lady Cozzene, by Cozzene	5	2	1	0	79,110
	Stolen Prayer	Songandaprayer—Stolen Skates, by Overskate	6	3	2	0	211,230
108	Blissful Trip	Trippi—Bright Bliss, by Well Decorated	5	1	1	1	41,275
	Mykindasaint	Saint Ballado—Sabu, by Deputy Minister	5	3	0	0	69,400
	Truart	Yes It's True—Artistic One, by Copelan	3	1	1	1	49,400
	True Xena	Yes It's True—Miss Xena, by Unbridled	3	1	1	0	44,000
107	Golden Silk	Songandaprayer—Sharp Call, by Sharpen Up (GB)	6	1	2	1	80,100
	Love Locket	Thunder Gulch—Love Lock, by Silver Ghost	5	3	0	0	127,249
	Mia's Reflection	Halo's Image—Mia's Hope, by Rexson's Hope	7	2	0	1	138,150
	Sprightly	Wild Rush—Worthy of Silver, by Silver Ghost	3	1	1	0	52,255
	Trippi Street	Trippi—Ten Downing Street, by Alleged	2	1	1	0	40,920
106	Acceleration	Vision and Verse—Epithet, by Gulch	9	2	3	1	93,728
	Lil' Sister Swiss	Swiss Yodeler—Nell's Key to Mint, by Sharper One	2	1	1	0	71,955
	Meetmeinthewoods	General Meeting—Star of the Woods, by Woodman	2	1	0	0	58,560
105	Christmas Stocking	Ops Smile—Christmas Shoes, by Valley Crossing	6	2	1	2	85,540
	Dixie Dreamer	Mutakddim—Dixieland Fantasy, by Dixieland Band	5	2	0	1	86,600
	Performing Diva	Storm Cat—Bunting, by Private Account	5	1	0	2	74,630
	Princess Sweet	Precise End—Princess Meadowlak, by Meadowlake	3	2	0	0	105,032
104	Capote's Crown	Capote—Majesty's Crown, by Magesterial	2	1	1	0	47,800
	Coolwind	Forest Wildcat—Scoop, by Gone West	4	1	0	2	64,760
	Dyna's Destiny	Dynaformer—Arjunand, by Diesis (GB)	5	1	0	2	40,590
	Hosanna Hit	Formal Gold—Solid Hit, by Time for a Change	3	1	2	0	53,300
	Lady Danza	Cryptoclearance—Danzalert, by Gold Alert	6	2	0	2	51,719
	Nice Nelly	Seattle Slew—Pleasant Temper, by Storm Cat	3	1	1	0	46,025
	Unobstructed View	Yes It's True—Thimble Island, by Kissin Kris	3	1	1	1	56,840
	Yaddo Cat	Forest Wildcat—Kombat Kate, by Fit to Fight	6	3	1	1	110,370
103	A Sea Trippi	Trippi—Best of the Sea, by Lord of the Sea	6	2	2	0	67,300
	Categorize	Menifee—Catechism, by St. Jovite	2	1	0	0	26,400
	Cotton Bay	El Corredor—One Bad Cat, by Mountain Cat	2	1	0	1	36,000
	Dance Daily	Five Star Day—Dance Alexa, by Southern Halo	7	2	0	1	81,292
	Diamond Spirit	Holy Bull—Ransom Dance, by Red Ransom	5	1	3	0	66,590
	Joint Effort	Runaway Groom—C. C. Princess, by Conquistador Cielo	8	2	3	1	99,240
	Lake Alice	Mt. Livermore—Comfort a Belle, by Red Ransom	6	2	1	0	88,360
	Lizzy's Township	Delaware Township—Tarahumara, by Black Tie Affair (Ire)	3	2	0	1	70,800
	Rasta Farian	Holy Bull—Chic Corine, by Nureyev	5	1	1	1	43,280
102	Art Show	Out of Place—Art Student, by El Prado (Ire)	6	2	3	0	75,150
	Carrie With a C	Beau Genius—Nevercomesagain, by Ascot Knight	3	1	2	0	31,052
	Jb's Golden Regret	Banker's Gold—Golden Gazelle, by Meadowlake	5	2	1	1	78,432
	Miss Norman	Artax—Cajun Cat, by Storm Cat	5	1	2	0	118,300
	Pure Disco	Disco Rico—V for Vera, by Concorde's Tune	5	2	0	1	78,155
	Warrior Girl	War Chant—Carefree Cheetah, by Trempolino	4	1	0	2	34,800
101	Perilous Pursuit	Lemon Drop Kid—Name of Love (Ire), by Petardia (GB)	3	1	0	1	38,100
	Slick Road	Mud Route—Slim 'n Fast, by Distinctive Cat	6	1	0	4	74,448
100	Chestnut Lady	Horse Chestnut (SAf)—Its a Girl, by Thunder Gulch	3	2	0	0	56,111
	Delicate Dynamite	Old Trieste—Majestic Dy, by Dynaformer	4	1	2	1	46,350
	India	Hennessy—Misty Hour, by Miswaki	4	1	1	1	49,392
	More Than Pretty	More Than Ready—Pretty Livia, by Forest Wildcat	8	1	3	0	102,450
	My Lucky Free	Mazel Trick—Fair Margarita, by Crafty Prospector	4	1	1	0	53,283
	No Hear Say	Impeachment—Si Si Sezyou, by Sezyou	9	2	3	0	67,800
	Running Lass	Running Stag—Shannon's Storm, by Future Storm	9	4	1	2	199,480
	She's Indy Money	A.P. Indy—Nany's Sweep, by End Sweep	2	1	0	1	28,200
	Swap Fliparoo	Exchange Rate—Fliparoo, by Buckaroo	8	2	5	0	119,890
	Talullah Lula	Old Trieste—McConnell Springs, by Deputy Minister	6	1	0	3	50,940
	Walkonkaydeeavenue	Avenue of Flags—Kaydee Classic, by Regal Classic	3	0	2	0	28,885

American Match Races

Match races, a prominent part of American Thoroughbred racing through the mid-1970s, slowed to a trickle after Ruffian's fatal showdown with Foolish Pleasure at Belmont Park on July 6, 1975. Of all the match races in North America during the 20th century, very few were contested after the undefeated filly shattered her right front ankle and was euthanized the next day. Only nine of those 13 were in the United States, and none of them commanded the national attention given the Ruffian–Foolish Pleasure match and such earlier match races as Seabiscuit–War Admiral and Nashua–Swaps.

Match races in America were mostly winner take all and trace back to the early 1820s, when American Eclipse engaged in and won two matches. Similarly, the great sire Lexington won twice in head-to-head competition in the 1850s. Since Domino defeated Clifford by three-quarters of a length in a one-mile match race at Sheepshead Bay Racetrack in New York on September 6, 1894, 15 match races have contained at least one starter who was recognized officially or unofficially as a champion. (*Daily Racing Form* first designated champions in 1936.) Thirteen of the 15 races offered wagering, and favorites lost nine of them. None was more noteworthy than War Admiral's loss to Seabiscuit in 1938, and none was more one-sided than Miss Musket's 50-length loss to Chris Evert on July 20, 1974, at Hollywood Park.

To appreciate America's greatest match races, it is necessary to understand the hype and expectations heading into them. For more than a year, racing fans had clamored for a match-up of Seabiscuit and War Admiral, the two dominant horses of the late 1930s. When the two finally met, they were the only entrants in the 1 3/16-mile Pimlico Special Stakes on November 1, 1938. A record crowd of 40,000 turned out to see Seabiscuit, a five-year-old grandson of Man o' War, take on War Admiral, a four-year-old son of Man o' War who had won the 1937 Triple Crown and 16 of 17 starts prior to the match.

Seabiscuit, breaking from the second post position, was sent off at 2.20-to-1 under George Woolf; War Admiral, thought to be the quicker from the gate, was 0.25-to-1 under Charley Kurtsinger. War Admiral was expected to lead at the start, but Seabiscuit outbroke him. Seabiscuit had been on the lead in just one of his previous 13 starts.

War Admiral made several moves at his opponent and once drew within a nose, but Seabiscuit had plenty left and won by four lengths in track-record time of 1:56.60.

Nearly 17 years later, Kentucky Derby winner Swaps went off as the 3-to-10 favorite against Preakness and Belmont Stakes winner Nashua in the $100,000 Washington Park Match Race at 1¼ miles on August 31, 1955. Swaps was undefeated as a three-year-old and owner-breeder Rex Ellsworth had returned him to California after he defeated Nashua by 1½ lengths in the 1955 Derby. Nashua's only loss in 11 starts had been in the Derby. Swaps was the favorite under Bill Shoemaker, while Nashua was 6-to-5 with Eddie Arcaro. Nashua won by 6½ lengths, leading from start to finish.

The race that effectively ended top-level match races pitted Foolish Pleasure, 1975 Kentucky Derby winner, against undefeated Ruffian, a three-year-old filly who never had been headed in ten career starts, all against other fillies. Jacinto Vasquez was the regular rider of both horses and chose to ride Frank Whiteley-trained Ruffian in the nationally televised race. Ruffian went off at 0.40-to-1; Foolish Pleasure was 0.90-to-1.

Ruffian broke from the rail and narrowly led Foolish Pleasure through a blazing first quarter-mile in :22⅕ on Belmont's deep 1¼-mile chute. Shortly after they entered the main track, however, Ruffian broke down and swerved to the outside. Foolish Pleasure finished the race under Braulio Baeza. Ruffian, who fought her handlers when coming out of anesthetic after surgery, reinjured her leg, and was euthanized early on July 7. Match races since then never have been the same.—*Bill Heller*

Match Races, 1820 to Present

Winner, Age, Sex	Loser, Age, Sex	Race	Date	Track	Distance	Time
Soviet Problem, 4, f.	Mamselle Bebette, 4, f.	Match Race	August 21, 1994	Del Mar	5fT	:56.58
Soviet Problem, 4, f.	Lazor, 4, g.	Match Race	May 12, 1994	Golden Gate Fields	6f	1:08.55
Who Doctor Who, 5, g.	Explosive Girl, 4, f.	Match Race	July 23, 1988	Ak-Sar-Ben	1m 70y	1:42.00
Foolish Pleasure, 3, c.	Ruffian, 3, f.	Great Match Race	July 6, 1975	Belmont Park	1¼m	2:02.80
Chris Evert, 3, f.	Miss Musket, 3, f.	Hollywood Special S.	July 20, 1974	Hollywood Park	1¼m	2:02.00
Jovial John, 4, g.	Blunt Man, 9, h.	Match Race	November 16, 1972	Cahokia Downs	5f	1:00.80
Convenience, 4, f.	Typecast, 6, m.	Hollywood Park Match Race	June 17, 1972	Hollywood Park	1⅛m	1:47.60
Nasharco, 4, c.	Nancycee, 4, f.	Match Race	April 10, 1966	Turf Paradise	5½f	1:10.20
Nancycee, 4, f.	Nasharco, 4, c.	Match Race	March 20, 1966	Turf Paradise	5f	:56.20
Short Nail, 2, c.	Florida Cracker, 2, c.	Match Race	December 4, 1962	Garden State	6f	1:13.40
Cesca, 2, f.	Aim n Fire, 2, c.	Match Race	July 7, 1962	Woodbine	5½f	1:04.60
Wichita Maid, 4, f.	Gilhooley, 5, m.	Australian Welcome Inv. Match Race	August 19, 1961	Centennial	5½f	1:04.40
Routeen, 2, f.	Modest Step, 2, f.	Latonia Match Race	October 1, 1960	Latonia	6f	1:13.60
Roman Colonel, 4, c.	Benedicto, 5, g.	Special Match Race	June 11, 1960	Detroit Race Course	6f	1:10.40
Lori Lynn, 4, f.	*Salmon Peter, 9, g.	Inv. Match Race	August 22, 1959	Centennial	1¼m	2:05.00
Wildoath, 3, c.	War Marshal, 4, c.	Special Match Race	October 12, 1957	Fresno	1 1/16m	1:43.60
Noorahge, 4, c.	Early Bull, 7, h.	Dapper Dan Match Race	September 14, 1957	Wheeling Downs	6½f	1:24.00
Queen Doris, 3, f.	Molly Darling, 4, f.	Inv. Match Race	July 28, 1956	Centennial	5½f	1:05.60
Nashua, 3, c.	Swaps, 3, c.	Washington Park Match Race	August 31, 1955	Washington Park	1¼m	2:04.20
Virginia Fair, 2, f.	Virden, 2, f.	Inv. Match Race	August 15, 1952	Edmonton	abt 5f	1:00.40
Capot, 3, c.	Coaltown, 4, c.	Pimlico Special	October 28, 1949	Pimlico	1 3/16m	1:56.80
Armed, 6, g.	Assault, 4, c.	The Special	September 27, 1947	Belmont Park	1¼m	2:02.80
Busher, 3, f.	Durazna, 4, f.	Match Race	August 29, 1945	Washington Park	1m	1:37.80
Alsab, 3, c.	Whirlaway, 4, c.	Narragansett Championship	September 19, 1942	Narragansett	1 3/16m	1:56.40
Lavengro, 7, g.	*Sir Winsome, 4, c.	Pacific Coast Sprint Championship	August 16, 1942	Longacres	6f	1:10.00
Wise Moss, 3, f.	Sweet Willow, 4, f.	New Hampshire Special	November 22, 1941	Rockingham	6f	1:11.20
Alsab, 2, c.	Requested, 2, c.	Match Race	September 23, 1941	Belmont Park	6½f	1:16.00
Unerring, 3, f.	Flying Lill, 3, f.	Match Race	August 31, 1939	Washington Park	1m	1:37.80
Seabiscuit, 5, h.	War Admiral, 4, c.	Pimlico Special	November 1, 1938	Pimlico	1 3/16m	1:56.60
Seabiscuit, 5, h.	*Ligaroti, 6, h.	Special Stake Race	August 12, 1938	Del Mar	1⅛m	1:49.00

Winner, Age, Sex	Loser, Age, Sex	Race	Date	Track	Distance	Time
Myrtlewood, 4, f.	Miss Merriment, 5, m.	Special Sweepstakes	October 24, 1936	Keeneland	6f	1:11.80
Clang, 3, g.	Myrtlewood, 3, f.	Match Race	October 12, 1935	Coney Island	6f	1:09.20
Myrtlewood, 3, f.	Clang, 3, g.	Match Race	September 25, 1935	Hawthorne	6f	1:10.80
*Winooka, 5, c.	Onrush, 3, g.	International Match Race	September 16, 1933	Longacres	6f	1:14.00
Zev, 3, c.	In Memoriam, 4, c.	Match Race	November 17, 1923	Churchill Downs	1¼m	2:06.60
Sarazen, 2, g.	Happy Thoughts, 2, f.	Laurel Special	October 26, 1923	Laurel Park	6f	1:14.00
Zev, 3, c.	*Papyrus, 3, c.	International Race	October 20, 1923	Belmont Park	1½m	2:35.40
Man o' War, 3, c.	Sir Barton, 4, c.	Kenilworth Park Gold Cup	October 12, 1920	Kenilworth	1¼m	2:03.00
*Hourless, 3, c.	*Omar Khayyam, 3, c.	American Champion S.	October 18, 1917	Laurel Park	1¼m	2:02.00
Novelty, 2, c.	Textile, 2, c.	Two-Year-Old Special	August 17, 1910	Saratoga	6f	1:13.20
Dick Welles, 3, c.	Grand Opera, 4, c.	Special Race	August 14, 1903	Harlem	1m	1:37.40
Ethelbert, 4, c.	Jean Beraud, 4, c.	Special Sweepstakes	June 2, 1900	Gravesend	1¼m	2:08.20
Admiration, 3, f.	May Hempstead, 3, f.	Match Race	July 1, 1899	Coney Island	1m	1:40.20
dh-Domino, 3, c.	dh-Henry of Navarre, 3, c.	The Third Special	September 15, 1894	Brooklyn	1⅛m	1:55.50
dh-Domino, 2, c.	dh-Dobbins, 2, c.	Match Race	August 31, 1893	Coney Island	abt 6f	1:12.60
Kingston, 7, h.	Van Buren, 3, c.	Match Race	August 31, 1891	Garfield Park, Chicago	1¹⁄₁₆m	1:50.75
Longstreet, 5, h.	Tenny, 5, h.	Match Race	August 1, 1891	Morris Park	1¼m	2:07.50
Salvator, 4, c.	Tenny, 4, c.	Match Race	June 25, 1890	Sheepshead Bay	1¼m	2:05.00
Troubadour, 4, c.	Miss Woodford, 5, m.	Special Race	June 29, 1886	Coney Island	1¼m	2:08.75
Miss Woodford, 5, m.	Freeland, 6, g.	Match Race	August 20, 1885	Monmouth Park	1¼m	2:09.50
Miss Woodford, 4, f.	Drake Carter, 4, g.	Match Race	September 18, 1884	Sheepshead Bay	2½m	4:28.75
Crickmore, 3, g.	Hindoo, 3, c.	Brighton Beach Purse	September 17, 1881	Sheepshead Bay	1½m	2:36.25
Hiawassa, 2, f.	Memento, 2, f.	Match Race	August 20, 1881	Monmouth Park	6f	1:16.50
Eole, 3, c.	Getaway, 3, c.	Match Race	August 12, 1881	Saratoga	1⅝m	2:52.25
Onondaga, 2, c.	Sachem, 2, c.	Match Race	June 25, 1881	Sheepshead Bay	6f	1:15.50
Geranium, 3, f.	Marathon, 3, g.	Match Race	June 23, 1881	Sheepshead Bay	1m	1:45.00
Marathon, 3, g.	Geranium, 3, f.	Match Race	June 4, 1881	Jerome Park	1m	1:53.00
Luke Blackburn, 3, c.	Uncas, 4, c.	Match Race	September 14, 1880	Gravesend Park	1½m	2:42.50
Spartan, 3, c.	Bramble, 3, c.	Match Race	July 6, 1878	Monmouth Park	1¼m	2:16.00
Ten Broeck, 6, h.	Mollie McCarthy, 5, m.	Match Race	July 4, 1878	Louisville	4m	heats
Mollie McCarthy, 5, m.	Jake, 5, h.	Match Race	March 2, 1878	Sacramento	2m	heats
Jake, 4, c.	Madge Duke, 3, f.	Match Race	November 29, 1877	San Francisco	2m	heats
Rappahannock, 4, c.	Kilburn, 6, g.	Match Race	October 26, 1877	Pimlico	2m	heats
Bazil, 3, g.	Cloverbrook, 3, c.	Match Race	June 18, 1877	Jerome Park	1¼m	2:12.75
Shirley, 3, g.	Resolute, 6, h.	Match Race	October 28, 1876	Pimlico	2m	3:44.50
Shylock, 5, h.	Vaultress, 3, f.	Match Race	July 18, 1874	Monmouth Park	2m	3:46.50
Joe Daniels, 4, c.	Nell Flaherty, 6, m.	Match Race	December 25, 1873	San Francisco	1½m	2:46.00
Girl of the Period, 4, f.	Ophelia, 4, f.	Match Race	October 4, 1873	Jerome Park	4f	heats
Shylock, 4, c.	M. A. B., 4, f.	Match Race	October 4, 1873	Jerome Park	1½m	heats
Survivor, 3, c.	Aerolite, 3, c.	Match Race	July 21, 1873	Monmouth Park	1m	1:46.00
Thad Stevens, 8, h.	Ben Wade, 4, c.	Match Race	June 28, 1873	Oakland	2m	heats
Nell Flaherty, 6, m.	Abi, 4, f.	Match Race	June 28, 1873	Oakland	1m	heats
Thad Stevens, 8, h.	Nettie Brown, 5, m.	Match Race	March 1, 1873	San Francisco	1m	heats
Alarm, 2, c.	Inverary, 2, f.	Match Race	August 16, 1871	Saratoga	1m	1:47.50
Virgil, 6, h.	Chalmette, 6, h.	Match Race	May 20, 1871	New Orleans	2m	heats
Nannie McNairy, 7, m.	Sarah McDonald, 4, f.	Match Race	December 4, 1869	New Orleans	6f	1:20.00
Finesse, 2, f.	Intrigue, 2, f.	Match Race	October 6, 1869	Jerome Park	1m	1:52.25
Intrigue, 2, f.	El Dorado, 2, c.	Match Race	June 6, 1869	Jerome Park	6f	1:25.75
Glenelg, 3, c.	Rapture, 3, f.	Match Race	June 3, 1869	Jerome Park	1m	1:49.25
Miss Alice, 2, f.	c. by Censor, 2	Match Race	June 3, 1869	Jerome Park	1m	1:54.25
Nannie McNairy, 6, m.	Lewis E. Smith, 5, h.	Match Race	April 8, 1869	New Orleans	4f	:49.75
Nannie McNairy, 5, m.	Le Noir, 6, m.	Match Race	December 7, 1868	New Orleans	4f	:54.50
Maid of Honor, 4, f.	Trovatore, 5, m.	Match Race	November 7, 1868	Jerome Park	1m	1:51.25
Raquette, 3, c.	Redwing, 3, f.	Match Race	November 9, 1867	Jerome Park	1m	1:48.50
DeCourcy, 3, c.	Maid of Honor, 3, f.	Match Race	May 25, 1867	Jerome Park	1m	heats
Tornado, 6, h.	Minnie C., 6, m.	Match Race	January 22, 1867	New Orleans	1m	1:52.50
Derringer, 4, c.	Susie B. Moore, 5, m.	Match Race	January 14, 1867	San Francisco	1m	heats
Maid of Honor, 2, f.	Redwing, 2, f.	Match Race	October 3, 1866	Jerome Park	6f	1:21.00
Mike Edwards, 5, g.	Red Oak, 11, g.	Match Race	May 15, 1866	St. Louis	2m	3:20.25
Lewis E. Smith, 2, c.	Maiden, 3, f.	Match Race	April 20, 1866	New Orleans	1m	heats
Ooltawa, 5, h.	Muggins, 4, c.	Match Race	January 13, 1866	Nashville	1m	heats
Flora, 5, m.	Pele, 6, m.	Match Race	January 6, 1866	San Francisco	4m	heats
Norfolk, 4, c.	Lodi, 5, h.	Match Race	September 23, 1865	Sacramento	3m	heats
Norfolk, 4, c.	Lodi, 5, h.	Match Race	September 18, 1865	Sacramento	2m	heats
Norfolk, 4, c.	Lodi, 5, h.	Match Race	May 23, 1865	San Francisco	2m	heats
Kentucky, 3, c.	Aldebaran, 4, c.	Match Race	September 17, 1864	Paterson, New Jersey	2m	heats
Lexington, 5, h.	Lecomte, 5, h.	Jockey Club Purse	April 14, 1855	New Orleans	4m	heats
Lexington, 3, c.	Sallie Waters, 4, f.	Match Race	May 27, 1853	New Orleans	3m	heats
Peytona, 6, m.	Fashion, 8, m.	Great Sectional Match Race	May 13, 1845	Union Course	4m	heats
Fashion, 5, m.	Boston, 9, h.	North vs. South Match Race	May 10, 1842	Union Course	4m	heats
Boston, 7, h.	Gano	Match Race	December 7, 1840	Augusta, Georgia	4m	heats
Black Maria	Brilliant		October 23, 1839	Union Course		
Portsmouth, h.	Boston, 6, h.	Match Race	April 16, 1839	Petersburg, Virginia	2m	heats
Arietta, f.	Ariel, 8, m.	Match Race	May 8, 1830	Union Course	2m	3:44.00
Flirtilla, f.	Ariel, 3, f.	Match Race	October 31, 1825	Union Course	3m	heats
Ariel, 3, f.	Lafayette, 3, c.	Match Race	October 3, 1825	Union Course	1m	heats
American Eclipse, 9, h.	Henry, 4, c.	Match Race	May 27, 1823	Union Course	4m	heats
American Eclipse, 8, h.	Sir Charles, c.	Match Race	November 20, 1822	Washington, D.C.	4m	heats

Notable Walkovers Since 1930

Walkovers are rare in Thoroughbred racing if only because competition is at the heart of the sport. The most recent walkover occurred in 1997 when Sharp Cat's two opponents, Alzora and Toda Una Dama (Arg) were scratched from the Bayakoa Handicap (G2) after December rains turned Hollywood Park's track muddy. Prior to that, champion Spectacular Bid walked over when Winter's Tale, Temperence Hill, and Dr. Patches were scratched from the 1980 Woodward Stakes (G1).

In consecutive years, Calumet Farm champions Coaltown and Citation walked over in Maryland races. Coaltown was unopposed in the 1949 Edward Burke Handicap at Havre de Grace, and Citation had no opponents entered against him in the 1948 Pimlico Special.

Although walkovers usually involve only one horse, two horses with the same owner may walk over if they are entered in a race and no horses oppose them. Here are several of the most important walkovers since 1930.

Walkovers, 1930 to Present

Horse, Age, Sex	Race (Grade)	Date	Track	Distance	Time
Sharp Cat, 3, f.	Bayakoa H. (G2)	December 7, 1997	Hollywood Park	1 1/16m	1:42.68
Spectacular Bid, 4, c.	Woodward S. (G1)	September 20, 1980	Belmont Park	1¼m	2:02.40
Coaltown, 4, c.	Edward Burke H.	April 23, 1949	Havre De Grace	1 1/16m	1:52.20
Citation, 3, c.	Pimlico Special	October 29, 1948	Pimlico	1 3/16m	1:59.80
Stymie, 5, h.	Saratoga Cup	August 31, 1946	Saratoga Race Course	1¾m	3:07.40

Scale of Weights

The scale of weights provides a guideline to the weights that horses carry at different ages and over different distances. As in many standards in Thoroughbred racing, the current scale of weights evolved over time.

The earliest Thoroughbred races in the 17th century were run at catch weights—whatever the rider, usually the owner, weighed. As racing became more sophisticated, various methods were tried to make contests more fair as well as more competitive, including assigning different weights according to the height of the horse, known as "give-and-take" weights.

That concept eventually evolved into assigning different weights to horses of differing perceived abilities. The first recorded handicap race was the Subscription Handicap Plate at Newmarket in 1785.

In 1740, the English Parliament established minimum weights for horses of different ages. Those weights were not meant to be assigned to horses of different ages in the same race, however.

In the mid-19th century, Admiral Henry Rous, British racing's de facto dictator, applied and expanded the concept to horses of different ages in the same race. Rous published the world's first weight-for-age scale in his 1850 book *On the Laws and Practice of Horse Racing.* Rous's scale also recognized that Thoroughbreds mature steadily from ages two through four; he assigned different weights at different distances for every month of the year.

All subsequent scales essentially have been refinements of Rous's work. The scale of weights listed below is the official scale used by American racing secretaries.

Distance and Age	Jan.	Feb.	Mar.	Apr.	May	June	July	Aug.	Sept.	Oct.	Nov.	Dec.
Half mile												
2 years	x	x	x	x	x	x	x	105	108	111	114	114
3 years	117	117	119	119	121	123	125	126	127	128	129	129
4 years	130	130	130	130	130	130	130	130	130	130	130	130
5 years & up	130	130	130	130	130	130	130	130	130	130	130	130
6 furlongs												
2 years	x	x	x	x	x	x	x	102	105	108	111	111
3 years	114	114	117	117	119	121	123	125	126	127	128	128
4 years	129	129	130	130	130	130	130	130	130	130	130	130
5 years & up	130	130	130	130	130	130	130	130	130	130	130	130
1 mile												
2 years	x	x	x	x	x	x	x	x	96	99	102	102
3 years	107	107	111	111	113	115	117	119	121	122	123	123
4 years	127	127	128	128	127	126	126	126	126	126	126	126
5 years & up	128	128	128	128	127	126	126	126	126	126	126	126
1¼ miles												
2 years	x	x	x	x	x	x	x	x	x	x	x	x
3 years	101	101	107	107	111	113	116	118	120	121	122	122
4 years	125	125	127	127	127	126	126	126	126	126	126	126
5 years & up	127	127	127	127	127	126	126	126	126	126	126	126
1½ miles												
2 years	x	x	x	x	x	x	x	x	x	x	x	x
3 years	98	98	104	104	108	111	114	117	119	121	122	122
4 years	124	124	126	126	126	126	126	126	126	126	126	126
5 years & up	126	126	126	126	126	126	126	126	126	126	126	126
2 miles												
3 years	96	96	102	102	106	109	112	114	117	119	120	120
4 years	124	124	126	126	126	126	126	125	125	124	124	124
5 years & up	126	126	126	126	126	126	126	125	125	124	124	124

(a) In races of intermediate lengths, the weights for the shorter distance are carried.
(b) In races exclusively for three-year-olds or four-year-olds, the weight is 126 lbs., and in races exclusively for two-year-olds, it is 122 lbs.
(c) In all races except handicaps and races where the conditions expressly state to the contrary, the scale of weights is less, by the following: for two-year-old fillies, 3 lbs.; for three-year-old and up fillies and mares, 5 lbs. before September 1, and 3 lbs. thereafter.
(d) In all handicaps that close more than 72 hours prior to the race the top weight shall not be less than 126 lbs., except in handicaps for fillies and mares, the top weight shall not be less than 126 lbs. less the sex allowance at the time of the race.

Oldest Male Grade 1 Stakes Winners Since 1976

Age	Horse, YOB Sex, Sire	Year, Race
9	John Henry, 1975 g., by Ole Bob Bowers	1984 Budweiser Million, Hollywood Inv. H., Sunset H., Turf Classic
	John's Call, 1991 g., by Lord At War (Arg)	2000 Sword Dancer Inv. H., Turf Classic Inv. S.
	Super Diamond, 1980 h., by Pass the Glass	1989 San Antonio H.
8	Affirmed Success, 1994 g., by Affirmed	2002 Carter H.
	Cetewayo, 1994 h., by His Majesty	2002 Gulfstream Park Breeders' Cup H.
	John Henry, 1975 g., by Ole Bob Bowers	1983 Hollywood Turf Cup
	Mashkour, 1983 h., by Irish River (Fr)	1991 San Juan Capistrano Inv. H.
	Redattore (Brz), 1995 h., by Roi Normand	2003 Shoemaker Breeders' Cup Mile S.
	Sir Bear, 1993 g., by Sir Leon	2001 Gulfstream Park H.
7	A Huevo, 1996 g., by Cool Joe	2003 Frank J. De Francis Memorial Dash S.
	Ancient Title, 1970 h., by Gummo	1977 San Antonio S.
	Awad, 1990 h., by Caveat	1997 Sword Dancer Inv. H.
	Bemo, 1970 g., by Maribeau	1977 United Nations H.
	Cardmania, 1986 g., by Cox's Ridge	1993 Breeders' Cup Sprint
	Designed for Luck, 1997 g., by Rahy	2004 Shoemaker Breeders' Cup Mile S.
	Down the Aisle, 1993 h., by Runaway Groom	2000 United Nations H.
	Elmhurst, 1990 g., by Wild Again	1997 Breeders' Cup Sprint
	Forego, 1970 g., by *Forli	1977 Metropolitan H., Woodward H.
	Grand Flotilla, 1987 h., by Caro (Ire)	1994 Hollywood Turf H.
	John Henry, 1975 g., by Ole Bob Bowers	1982 Oak Tree Inv. H., Santa Anita H.
	Jumping Hill, 1972 h., by Hillary	1979 Widener H.
	Key Contender, 1988 h., by Fit to Fight	1995 Suburban H.
	Kona Gold, 1994 g., by Java Gold	2001 San Carlos H.
	Ladies Din, 1995 g., by Din's Dancer	2002 Shoemaker Breeders' Cup Mile S.
	Noble Dancer (GB), 1972 h., by Prince de Galles	1979 San Luis Rey S., United Nations H.
	Passinetti, 1996 g., by Slew o' Gold	2003 San Juan Capistrano Inv. H.
	Pleasant Variety, 1984 h., by Pleasant Colony	1991 San Luis Rey S.
	Red Bishop, 1988 h., by Silver Hawk	1995 San Juan Capistrano Inv. H.
	River Keen (Ire), 1992 h., by Keen	1999 Jockey Club Gold Cup, Woodward S.
	Sabona, 1982 h., by Exclusive Native	1989 Californian S.
	Sandpit (Brz), 1989 h., by Baynoun (Ire)	1996 Caesars International H., Hollywood Turf H.
	Special Ring, 1997 g., by Nureyev	2004 Eddie Read H.
	Steinlen (GB), 1983 h., by Habitat	1990 Hollywood Turf H.
	Val's Prince, 1992 g., by Eternal Prince	1999 Man o' War S., Turf Classic Inv. S.
	Winter's Tale, 1976 g., by Arts and Letters	1983 Suburban H.
	With Anticipation, 1995 g., by Relaunch	2002 Man o' War S., Sword Dancer Inv. H., United Nations H.
	Yankee Affair, 1982 h., by Northern Fling	1989 Man o' War S., Turf Classic, United Nations H.
	Zoffany, 1980 h., by Our Native	1987 San Luis Rey S.

Oldest Female Grade 1 Stakes Winners Since 1976

Age	Horse, YOB Sex, Sire	Year, Race
8	Brown Bess, 1982 m., by *Petrone	1990 Santa Barbara H.
7	Brown Bess, 1982 m., by *Petrone	1989 Ramona H., Yellow Ribbon Inv. S.
	Halo America, 1990 m., by Waquoit	1997 Apple Blossom H.
	Miss Loren (Arg), 1998 m., by Numerous	2005 Santa Maria H.
	Paseana (Arg), 1987 m., by Ahmad	1994 Santa Margarita Inv. H.
6	Ack's Secret, 1976 m., by Ack Ack	1982 Santa Barbara H., Santa Margarita Inv. H.
	Anka Germania (Ire), 1982 m., by Malinowski	1988 Sword Dancer H.
	Annoconnor, 1984 m., by Nureyev	1990 Santa Ana H.
	Astra, 1996 m., by Theatrical (Ire)	2002 Beverly Hills H., Gamely Breeders' Cup H.
	Azeri, 1998 m., by Jade Hunter	2004 Apple Blossom H., Go for Wand H., Overbrook Spinster S.
	Bayakoa (Arg), 1984 m., by Consultant's Bid	1990 Breeders' Cup Distaff, Milady H., Santa Margarita H., Santa Maria H., Spinster S.
	Dahlia, 1970 m., by *Vaguely Noble	1976 Hollywood Inv. H.
	Dream of Summer, 1999 m., by Siberian Summer	2005 Apple Blossom H.
	Estrapade, 1980 m., by *Vaguely Noble	1986 Arlington Million, Oak Tree Inv. S.
	Exchange, 1988 m., by Explodent	1994 Matriarch S.
	Exotic Wood, 1992 m., by Rahy	1998 Santa Maria H., Santa Monica H.
	Fact Finder, 1979 m., by Staff Writer	1985 Matriarch Inv. S., Santa Barbara H.
	Far Out Beast, 1987 m., by Far Out East	1993 Flower Bowl H.
	Flawlessly, 1988 m., by Affirmed	1994 Ramona H.
	Gourmet Girl, 1995 m., by Cee's Tizzy	2001 Apple Blossom H., Vanity H.
	Happyanunoit (NZ), 1995 m., by Yachtie	2001 Gamely Breeders' Cup H.
	Heatherten, 1979 m., by Forceten	1985 Hempstead H.
	Jameela, 1976 m., by Rambunctious	1982 Delaware H.
	Kalookan Queen, 1996 m., by Lost Code	2002 Ancient Title Breeders' Cup H., Santa Monica H.
	Kostroma (Ire), 1986 m., by Caerleon	1992 Beverly D. S., Santa Barbara H.
	Lazy Slusan, 1995 m., by Slewvescent	2001 Milady Breeders' Cup H., Santa Margarita Inv. H.
	Little Brianne, 1985 m., by Coastal	1991 Santa Margarita Inv. H., Santa Maria H.

Age	Horse, YOB Sex, Sire	Year, Race
6	Megahertz (GB), 1999 m., by Pivotal	2005 Yellow Ribbon S.
	Miss Huntington, 1977 m., by Torsion	1983 Apple Blossom H.
	Noches De Rosa (Chi), 1998 m., by Stagecraft (GB)	2004 Gamely Breeders' Cup H.
	One Dreamer, 1988 m., by Relaunch	1994 Breeders' Cup Distaff
	Paseana (Arg), 1987 m., by Ahmad	1993 Apple Blossom H., Milady H., Spinster S.
	Queens Court Queen, 1989 m., by Lyphard	1995 Santa Margarita Inv. H., Santa Maria H.
	Quick Mischief, 1986 m., by Distinctive Pro	1992 John A. Morris H.
	Re Toss (Arg), 1987 m., by Egg Toss	1993 Vanity H.
	Riskaverse, 1999 m., by Dynaformer	2005 Flower Bowl Inv. S.
	Sefa's Beauty, 1979 m., by Lt. Stevens	1985 Apple Blossom H.
	Southern Truce, 1988 m., by Truce Maker	1994 Santa Monica H.
	Stop Traffic, 1993 m., by Cure the Blues	1999 Santa Monica H.
	The Very One, 1975 m., by One for All	1981 Santa Barbara H.
	Track Robbery, 1976 m., by No Robbery	1982 Apple Blossom H., Spinster S.
	Twice the Vice, 1991 m., by Vice Regent	1997 Vanity H.
	Windsharp, 1991 m., by Lear Fan	1997 Beverly Hills H.

Oldest Male Graded Stakes Winners Since 1976

Age	Horse, YOB Sex, Sire	Year, Race
9	Affirmed Success, 1994 g., by Affirmed	2003 Toboggan H. (G3)
	Bet On Sunshine, 1992 g., by Bet Big	2001 Aristides H. (G3), Phoenix Breeders' Cup S. (G3)
	Desert Waves, 1990 g., by Alysheba	1999 King Edward Breeders' Cup H. (Can-G2)
	John Henry, 1975 g., by Ole Bob Bowers	1984 Budweiser Million (G1), Hollywood Invitational H. (G1), Sunset H. (G1), Turf Classic (G1), Golden Gate H. (G3)
	John's Call, 1991 g., by Lord At War (Arg)	2000 Sword Dancer Invitational H. (G1), Turf Classic Invitational S. (G1)
	Kona Gold, 1994 g., by Java Gold	2003 El Conejo H. (G3)
	Parose, 1994 g., by Parlay Me	2003 Durham Cup H. (Can-G3)
	Rochester, 1996 g., by Green Dancer	2005 Sycamore Breeders' Cup S. (G3)
	Sir Bear, 1993 g., by Sir Leon	2002 Skip Away H. (G3)
	Softshoe Sure Shot, 1986 g., by Bolger	1995 San Carlos H. (G2)
	Soviet Line (Ire), 1990 g., by Soviet Star	1999 Maker's Mark Mile S. (G3)
	Sunny Sunrise, 1987 g., by Sunny's Halo	1996 John B. Campbell H. (G3)
	Super Diamond, 1980 h., by Pass the Glass	1989 San Antonio H. (G1)
8	*Royal Derby II, 1969 h., by Bally Royal	1977 San Luis Obispo H. (G2), San Marcos H. (G3)
	Affirmed Success, 1994 g., by Affirmed	2002 Carter H. (G1)
	Ancient Title, 1970 g., by Gummo	1978 San Pasqual H. (G2)
	Best of the Rest, 1995 h., by Skip Trial	2003 Skip Away H. (G3)
	Bet On Sunshine, 1992 g., by Bet Big	2000 Aristides H. (G3)
	Blaze O'Brien, 1987 g., by Interco	1995 Inglewood H. (G3)
	Cardmania, 1986 g., by Cox's Ridge	1994 San Carlos H. (G2)
	Cetewayo, 1994 h., by His Majesty	2002 Gulfstream Park Breeders' Cup H. (G1), Stars and Stripes Breeders' Cup Turf H. (G3)
	Chorwon, 1993 g., by Cozzene	2001 Kentucky Cup Turf H. (G3)
	Country Be Gold, 1997 h., by Summer Squall	2005 Aqueduct H. (G3)
	Coyote Lakes, 1994 g., by Society Max	2002 Gallant Fox H. (G3)
	Dancing Guy, 1995 g., by Robyn Dancer	2003 Memorial Day H. (G3)
	Deputy Inxs, 1991 g., by Silver Deputy	1999 Durham Cup H. (Can-G3), Vigil H. (Can-G3)
	First Intent, 1989 g., by Prima Voce	1997 Potrero Grande Breeders' Cup H. (G2), Bing Crosby Breeders' Cup H. (G3)
	Flag Down, 1990 h., by Deputy Minister	1998 Gulfstream Park Breeders' Cup H. (G2)
	Forlitano (Arg), 1981 h., by Good Manners	1989 Bougainvillea H. (G2)
	Fourstardave, 1985 g., by Compliance	1993 Poker S. (G3)
	Friendly Lover, 1988 h., by Cutlass	1996 Philadelphia Park Breeders' Cup H. (G3)
	Glick, 1996 h., by Theatrical (Ire)	2004 San Simeon H. (G3)
	Hasty Kris, 1997 g., by Kissin Kris	2005 San Carlos H. (G2)
	Inevitable Leader, 1979 h., by Mr. Leader	1987 Ark-La-Tex H. (G3)
	John Henry, 1975 g., by Ole Bob Bowers	1983 Hollywood Turf Cup (G1), American H. (G2)
	John's Call, 1991 g., by Lord At War (Arg)	1999 Laurel Turf Cup S. (G3)
	Key Lory, 1994 h., by Key to the Mint	2002 Red Bank H. (G3)
	King's Swan, 1980 g., by King's Bishop	1988 Bold Ruler S. (G2), Tom Fool S. (G2), Assault H. (G3), Grey Lag H. (G3), Stymie H. (G3)
	Kona Gold, 1994 g., by Java Gold	2002 Los Angeles H. (G3)
	Letthebighossroll, 1988 g., by Flying Paster	1996 Triple Bend Breeders' Cup H. (G3)
	Mashkour, 1983 h., by Irish River (Fr)	1991 San Juan Capistrano Invitational H. (G1)
	Men's Exclusive, 1993 g., by Exclusive Ribot	2001 Palos Verdes H. (G2), Vernon O. Underwood S. (G3)
	P Day, 1995 g., by Private Terms	2003 Baltimore Breeders' Cup H. (G3)
	Parose, 1994 g., by Parlay Me	2002 Woodbine Slots Cup H. (Can-G3)
	Punch Line, 1990 g., by Two Punch	1998 Fall Highweight H. (G2), Forest Hills H. (G2)
	Redattore (Brz), 1995 h., by Roi Normand	2003 Shoemaker Breeders' Cup Mile S. (G1), Citation H. (G2), Frank E. Kilroe Mile H. (G2), San Gabriel H. (G2)
	Sandpit (Brz), 1989 h., by Baynoun (Ire)	1997 San Marcos H. (G2)
	Silveyville, 1978 h., by *Petrone	1986 San Marcos H. (G3)

Age	Horse, YOB Sex, Sire	Year, Race
8	Sir Bear, 1993 g., by Sir Leon	2001 Gulfstream Park H. (G1)
	Son of a Pistol, 1992 g., by Big Pistol	2000 San Carlos H. (G2)
	Soviet Line (Ire), 1990 g., by Soviet Star	1998 Robert F. Carey Memorial H. (G3)
	Stalwars, 1985 h., by Stalwart	1993 National Jockey Club H. (G3)
	Super Diamond, 1980 h., by Pass the Glass	1988 San Pasqual H. (G2)
	Truce Maker, 1978 h., by Ack Ack	1986 Tanforan H. (G3)
	Twilight Road, 1997 g., by Cahill Road	2005 Memorial Day H. (G3)
	Variety Road, 1983 h., by Kennedy Road	1991 William P. Kyne H. (G3)
	Yankee Affair, 1982 h., by Northern Fling	1990 Red Smith H. (G2)

Oldest Female Graded Stakes Winners Since 1976

Age	Horse, YOB Sex, Sire	Year, Race
8	Brown Bess, 1982 m., by *Petrone	1990 Santa Barbara H. (G1)
	Lilah, 1997 m., by Defrere	2005 Hurricane Bertie H. (G3)
	Paseana (Arg), 1987 m., by Ahmad	1995 Hawthorne H. (G2)
	Avie Jane, 1984 m., by Lord Avie	1991 Thoroughbred Club of America S. (G3)
7	Brown Bess, 1982 m., by *Petrone	1989 Ramona H. (G1), Yellow Ribbon Inv. S. (G1), California Jockey Club H. (G3), Countess Fager H. (G3), Yerba Buena H. (G3)
	Exchange, 1988 m., by Explodent	1995 Orchid H. (G2)
	Fieldy (Ire), 1983 m., by Northfields	1990 Beaugay H. (G3), Lady Canterbury H. (G3)
	Gaily Gaily (Ire), 1983 m., by Cure the Blues	1990 Modesty H. (G3)
	Halo America, 1990 m., by Waquoit	1997 Apple Blossom H. (G1), Louisville Breeders' Cup H. (G2)
	Irish Linnet, 1988 m., by Seattle Song	1995 New York H. (G2), Noble Damsel H. (G3)
	Marshua's River, 1987 m., by Riverman	1994 Buckram Oak H. (G3), Suwannee River H. (G3)
	Miss Loren (Arg), 1998 m., by Numerous	2005 Santa Maria H. (G1)
	Miss Unnameable, 1984 m., by Great Neck	1991 Bewitch S. (G3)
	Paseana (Arg), 1987 m., by Ahmad	1994 Santa Margarita Inv. H. (G1), Chula Vista H. (G2)
	Quidnaskra, 1995 m., by Halo	2002 Gallorette H. (G3)
	Rizzi Girl, 1998 m., by Rizzi	2005 Hillsborough S. (G3)
	Scotzanna, 1992 m., by Silver Deputy	1999 First Lady H. (G3)
	Sefa's Beauty, 1979 m., by Lt. Stevens	1986 Sixty Sails H. (G3)
	Sintrillium, 1978 m., by Sinister Purpose	1985 Affectionately H. (G3)
	Skipat, 1974 m., by Jungle Cove	1981 Barbara Fritchie H. (G3)
	Spook Express (SAf), 1994 m., by Comic Blush	2001 WinStar Galaxy S. (G2), Honey Fox H. (G3), Suwannee River H. (G3)
	Stay Forever, 1997 m., by Stack	2004 WinStar Galaxy S. (G2), Mint Julep H. (G3)
	Survive, 1984 m., by Pass the Glass	1991 A Gleam H. (G2)
	Tocopilla (Arg), 1990 m., by El Basco	1997 The Very One H. (G3)

Oldest Male Stakes Winners Since 1976

Age	Horse, YOB Sex, Sire	Year, Race
12	Bold Sundance, 1989 g., by Bold Ryan	2001 Gene Francis & Associates S.
	Island Day Break, 1985 g., by Time to Explode	1997 Claiming Series #2 H., Cowboy Bar Claiming H., OMO Construction H.
	Leaping Plum, 1991 g., by Lightning Leap	2003 Grasmick H.
	Mayruncouldfly, 1974 h., by Cheapers' David	1986 Rocking Chair Inv. H.
11	Antiash, 1978 h., by Anticipating	1989 Memorial Day H.
	Bad Toda Bone, 1992 g., by Taj Alriyadh	2003 Keddie's Track & Western Wear S.
	Brush Count, 1968 h., by Fleet Burn	1979 Governor's H.
	Curribot, 1977 g., by Little Current	1988 Albuquerque H., Sunland Park H.
	Dobi Pay, 1971 h., by Dobi Deenar	1982 Buck Buchanan Memorial H.
	Lost Again, 1994 g., by Lost Code	2005 Canada Day S., Millarville Derby
	Major Zee, 1993 g., by Dayjur	2004 Parnitha S.
	Prexy Machree, 1970 h., by Prexy	1981 Vernon Sayler Memorial S.
	Proven Cure, 1994 g., by Cure the Blues	2005 Brother Brown S., Sam Houston Turf Sprint Cup S.
	Sir Echo, 1991 g., by Herat	2002 Yankee Affair S.
	Spend, 1985 g., by Draconic	1996 Pinon H.
10	Alias Jake, 1979 h., by Ingrained	1989 San Juan Downs H.
	All American Kid, 1972 g., by Count of Honor	1982 Centennial H.
	Aran Island, 1994 g., by Irish River (Fr)	2004 Old Timers S.
	Bay Rocket, 1987 g., by Forbidden Pleasure	1997 Independence Day H.
	Better Choice, 1994 g., by Variety Road	2004 Inaugural H.
	Blue Mercenary, 1972 h., by Blue Serenade	1982 Robert Hall H.
	Brush Count, 1968 h., by Fleet Burn	1978 Governor's H.
	Caro's Royalty, 1993 g., by Spruce Bouquet	2003 Brother Brown S.
	Castelets, 1979 g., by King's Bishop	1989 Viburnum S.
	Clarinet King, 1976 h., by His Majesty	1986 Royal Vale S.
	Crimson Victory, 1968 h., by Crimson Satan	1978 Gemini H.
	Curribot, 1977 g., by Little Current	1987 Clyde Tingley H., Sunland Park H.
	D. Guilford, 1986 g., by Guilford Road	1996 Basil Hall S.
	Doug's Shadow, 1995 g., by Verzy	2005 Amadevil H.
	Energetic King, 1979 h., by On the Sly	1989 Doublrab H.
	Fluid Gold, 1992 g., by Strike Gold	2002 Chippewa Downs Open S.
	Galic Boy, 1995 h., by Irish River (Fr)	2005 Tampa Turf Test H.

Age	Horse, YOB Sex, Sire	Year, Race
10	Groovy Add Vice, 1991 g., by Groovy	2001 Georgia Bragging Rights S.
	High Dice, 1995 g., by Lytrump	2005 State Fair Board H., Who Doctor Who H.
	Highland Road, 1995 g., by Highland Ruckus	2005 Northern Metallic Sales S.
	John's Call, 1991 g., by Lord At War (Arg)	2001 Cape Henlopen H.
	La Reine's Terms, 1995 h., by Private Terms	2005 Maryland Million Turf S.
	Leaping Plum, 1991 g., by Lightning Leap	2001 Grasmick H.
	Lost Again, 1994 g., by Lost Code	2004 Dempsey Gibbons Thoroughbred H.
	March Speed, 1980 h., by Curra Boy	1990 Wyoming Centennial Series S. #1
	Mr. I R S, 1992 g., by Minshaanshu Amad	2002 B Cup S.
	Nosho, 1991 g., by Falstaff	2001 Frank Figueroa Memorial Starter S.
	Oil Man, 1994 g., by Black Tie Affair (Ire)	2004 Arizona County Fair Distance Series S.
	Olden Ring, 1988 g., by Silver Ring (Fr)	1998 FSIN/SIGA Mile H.
	On the Edge, 1987 g., by L'Enjoleur	1997 I-80 S., Prairie Meadows H.
	Papa Ho Ho, 1993 g., by On to Glory	2003 Rise Jim S.
	Passport Money, 1982 g., by Dogwood Passport	1992 Early Bird Allowance S.
	Polar Ridge, 1988 g., by Cox's Ridge	1998 Con Jackson Claiming H.
	Prolanzier, 1990 g., by Copelan	2000 Private Terms S., Waquoit S.
	Quiet I'm Thinking, 1986 g., by Zen	1996 Ten Thousand Lakes S.
	Quite a Day, 1968 g., by Prince Khaled	1978 Pomona H.
	Rebuff, 1985 g., by Cold Reception	1995 Chieftain H.
	Right Ribot, 1976 h., by Right Reason	1986 Au Revoir H., Buck Buchanan Memorial H.
	Rosy Way, 1989 g., by Lord Avie	1999 Carl "Cub" Klahr Memorial H., City of Trees H., Govenor's Cup H., Stars And Stripes H.
	Shady Remark, 1995 g., by Regal Remark	2005 Marathon Series 2nd Leg S.
	Sir Echo, 1991 g., by Herat	2001 Yankee Affair S.
	Skunktail, 1989 g., by Music Prince	1999 Dowd Mile H., Nebraskaland H.
	Smile for Action, 1971 h., by Fleet Action	1981 Brown Palace H.
	Stilaferd, 1994 g., by Aferd	2004 Chippewa Downs Open Thoroughbred S.
	Thou Art Handy, 1974 h., by Captain Courageous	1984 Yakima Speed H.
	Tonights the Night, 1978 h., by Great Mystery	1988 Massachusetts Stallion S.
	We Be Cuzzins, 1995 g., by Gallant Prospector	2005 Arizona County Fair Distance Series S.
	Wilkes, 1985 g., by Traffic Cop	1995 Independence Day H.
	Willy Fiddle, 1976 h., by Roan Will	1986 Inaugural H., Stars and Stripes H.
	Wise Dusty, 1991 g., by Bishop Northcraft	2001 HBPA Kelly Kip S.

Oldest Female Stakes Winners Since 1976

Age	Horse, YOB Sex, Sire	Year, Race
10	Alex Marie, 1992 m., by Trooper Seven	2002 Buttons and Bows S.
	Chrystal Gail, 1973 m., by Special Dunce	1983 Carlton Cup, Dale Buick H.
	Favorite Pleasure, 1966 m., by *Favorite Prince	1976 Vicki Merrill H.
	Judge Smiles, 1991 m., by Judge Smells	2001 Matron H.
	Physical Law, 1982 m., by Wardlaw	1992 Merrimack Valley H.
9	All That Glitters, 1994 m., by Goldlust	2003 Buckland S., Somethingroyal S.
	Astral Moon, 1973 m., by *The Knack II	1982 Anniversary S.
	Crystal Cinders, 1994 m., by Incinderator	2003 Ralph Taylor/Vance Davenport Memorial S.
	Due to Win, 1995 m., by Lac Ouimet	2004 Cornucopia H., Fleur de Lis S., Matron H.
	Ghetto Doll, 1976 m., by Dendron	1985 Red Camelia H.
	Judge Smiles, 1991 m., by Judge Smells	2000 Matron H.
	Just Like Mama, 1975 m., by *Tenerosa	1984 Ladies H.
	Okie Miss, 1989 m., by Competitiveness	1998 Interior Royal Bank Futurity
	Orientalspringhope, 1996 m., by Raj Waki	2005 Golden Horseshoe Cup S.
	Petrina Above, 1995 m., by Great Above	2004 Barb's Dancer S., U Can Do It H.
	Run Around Sue, 1995 m., by Coach George	2004 Falls Amiss H.
	Sea Kindly, 1973 m., by Night Invader	1982 Bed of Roses S.
	St. Patty Day, 1982 m., by Majestic Red	1991 South Sioux City H.
	Sum Day Flowers, 1981 m., by Jenny's Boy	1990 Raton Mile H.
	Swingnlisa, 1996 m., by Nickel Slot	2005 Pat Hosie Memorial S.
	Wychnor (NZ), 1985 m., by Truly Vain	1994 Toolie's Country H.

Oldest Male Winners Since 1976

Age	Horse, YOB Sex, Sire	Track	Date	Race Condition
17	Behavin Jerry, 1964 h., Ambehaving	Com	9/7/1981	$1,500 clm
	Golden Arrow, 1961 h., Fort Salonga	GBF	9/25/1978	1,500 clm
16	Double Express, 1980 g., Viking Ruler	GF	7/6/1996	1,600 clm
	Maxwell G., 1961 h., Author	TuP	1/22/1977	2,000 clm
	Playing Politics, 1982 g., In Reality	Suf	1/4/1998	4,000 clm
	Silver Fir, 1963 h., Swoon's Son	FL	10/24/1979	2,000 clm
	Stonehenge, 1960 h., Call Over	Com	8/13/1976	1,500 clm
15	Beaver Cat, 1962 g., Brown Beaver	Bil	9/10/1977	1,000 clm
	Best Beau, 1962 h., Beauguerre	Poc	5/27/1977	1,500 clm
	Double Express, 1980 g., Viking Ruler	GF	7/29/1995	1,600 clm
		MeP	8/19/1995	1,600 clm

Age	Horse, YOB Sex, Sire	Track	Date	Race Condition
15	Dr. Hecker, 1967 g., Clem Pac	MF	8/23/1982	$1,500 clm
	Flyingphere, 1961 g., Mr. Hemisphere	FL	11/21/1976	1,500 clm
	Golden Arrow, 1961 h., Fort Salonga	LD	6/28/1976	2,000 clm
	Jymfyg, 1965 h., Beau Max	FL	10/28/1980	2,000 clm
	Lexington Park, 1967 g., Quadrangle	Com	5/22/1982	2,000 clm
	Lindsey-Jan, 1965 h., *Silver King II	GBF	7/23/1980	2,000 clm
	Maxwell G., 1961 h., Author	Haw	5/6/1976	4,000 clm
	Mayruncouldfly, 1974 h., Cheapers' David	SJD	8/5/1989	2,000 clm
	Montana Winds, 1967 h., Windy Sands	Com	7/24/1982	2,000 clm
	Nellies Joy, 1977 g., Immediate Joy	MeP	8/16/1992	1,250 clm
	Northern Broadway, 1988 g., Northern Magus	Beu	4/3/2003	3,500 clm
	Playing Politics, 1982 g., In Reality	Suf	4/23/1997	4,000 clm
	Royal Rouser, 1968 g., Speed Rouser	Bil	8/18/1983	1,600 clm
	Sagely, 1970 h., Sage and Sand	FL	5/12/1985	3,500 clm
	Sailawayin, 1967 g., Bal Harbour	FP	9/18/1982	2,500 clm
	Satans Story, 1968 h., Crimson Satan	MF	8/24/1983	2,000 clm
	Sharon Caper, 1983 g., Cartesian	Nmp	9/6/1998	4,000 clm
	Silver Fir, 1963 h., Swoon's Son	FL	10/28/1978	1,500 clm
	Snappy Nashville, 1964 h., Nashville	YM	2/17/1979	1,600 clm
14	Alpena Magic, 1990 g., L'Enjoleur	InD	5/27/2004	4,000 clm
	Ariel Beau, 1967 h., Ariel Streak	Beu	9/26/1981	2,500 clm
	Northern Broadway, 1988 g., Northern Magus	Beu	10/16/2002	3,500 clm
	Rhinasti, 1988 g., Rinoso	Eur	6/16/2002	2,500 clm
	Son Coming, 1986 g., Son of Briartic	NP	9/3/2000	3,000 clm

Oldest Female Winners Since 1976

Age	Horse, YOB Sex, Sire	Track	Date	Race Condition
14	Gloriella, 1964 m., *Nathoo	GBF	9/14/1978	$1,500 clm
		GBF	9/18/1978	1,500 clm
13	Double the Count, 1980 m., Gala Double	BGD	10/27/1993	3,200 clm
	Fuzzy White, 1964 m., Roman Line	FD	1/21/1977	2,000 clm
		FD	1/28/1977	2,000 clm
	Gather Round, 1963 m., Blenban	GBF	9/22/1976	1,500 clm
	Gloriella, 1964 m., *Nathoo	MF	8/25/1977	1,500 clm
	Jackie H., 1965 m., Greek Star	Nar	8/3/1978	1,500 clm
	Johns Sis, 1965 m., Be Joyful	Bil	10/1/1978	1,000 clm
	Mabel My Love, 1970 m., *Puerto Madero	GBF	9/20/1983	2,000 clm
	Passive Loss, 1987 m., Highland Blade	Suf	5/21/2000	4,000 clm
	Vain Lass, 1964 m., *Newbus	LaD	1/29/1977	2,500 clm
12	Brandy Star, 1968 m., *Northern Star	CT	7/19/1980	1,600 clm
		CT	8/17/1980	1,600 clm
	Carla Sparkles, 1993 m., Mr. Sparkles	MNR	5/24/2005	5,000 clm
	Chotin, 1967 m., *Belliqueux	GBF	9/12/1979	1,500 clm
	College Fiddler, 1966 m., College Boy	PJ	8/19/1978	1,250 clm
	Culottes, 1965 m., *Khaled	Boi	5/25/1977	700 alw
	Doge Hill, 1967 m., Boston Doge	MF	8/25/1979	2,000 clm
		Nmp	9/2/1979	1,500 clm
	Everfast, 1966 m., Gordian Knot	FL	5/10/1978	1,500 clm
		GBF	9/16/1978	1,500 clm
		GBF	10/2/1978	1,500 clm
	Favorite Pleasure, 1966 m., *Favorite Prince	AsD	6/11/1978	2,000 clm
	Flash Thru, 1967 m., Nir Thru	Reg	6/23/1979	3,200 clm
		Reg	7/7/1979	4,000 clm
		Reg	7/21/1979	2,200 str
		MD	8/1/1979	2,200 str
	Gambolak, 1964 m., Sid's Gambol	Nmp	9/2/1976	1,500 clm
	Gene's Hobby, 1974 m., Fincastle	MD	9/13/1986	1,500 clm
	Gloriella, 1964 m., *Nathoo	BD	9/24/1976	1,500 clm
	Johns Sis, 1965 m., Be Joyful	MD	7/5/1977	1,500 clm
		Reg	9/13/1977	1,500 clm
	Lindarella, 1966 m., *Bel Canto II	ElP	7/28/1978	2,500 clm
	Mabel My Love, 1970 m., *Puerto Madero	MF	8/20/1982	1,500 clm
	Mama Doc, 1964 m., Double Brandy	CT	3/27/1976	1,500 clm
	My Encore, 1964 m., Encore Fer	GM	7/5/1976	1,500 clm
	Old Toy, 1975 m., Obsolete	ErD	5/16/1987	2,500 clm
	Platters Honey, 1965 m., Platter	FL	6/25/1977	1,500 clm
	Polyego, 1965 m., Egotistical	FL	3/19/1977	1,500 clm
	Rainbow Gold, 1966 m., *Mont d'Or	MF	8/25/1978	1,500 clm
	Serenity Empress, 1986 m., Klassy Charger	FE	8/17/1998	5,000 clm
	Shore to Shore, 1987 m., Proctor	ElP	7/1/1999	4,000 clm
	Sis Jane, 1966 m., Hay Hook	RD	6/25/1978	2,500 clm
	Texas Toy, 1969 m., Green Hornet	RD	5/30/1981	2,500 clm
	Troublesome Sal, 1964 m., War Trouble	ElP	8/20/1976	2,000 clm

The Claiming Game

Claiming races are the heart of almost every racing meet in America. In 2003, nearly two-thirds of all races (66.5%) were either straight claiming or maiden claiming. The horses that populate those races are an eclectic band of warriors whose common bond is their owners' willingness to lose them for a specified price as soon as the race is over.

The claimers are typified by such horses as Creme de La Fete, a chestnut gelding who went to post with a price on his head in all but 20 of his 151 career starts in the late 1970s and early '80s. His claiming prices ranged from $7,000 to $72,500.

Creme de La Fete was so well known that he was saluted in a ceremony at Aqueduct. The National Horsemen's Benevolent and Protective Association annually selects a claimer of the year, and the Claiming Crown held each summer has given more attention to the sport's foot soldiers.

But publicity for claimers is rare, accorded usually to horses that were claimed early in their careers and developed into champions, as Stymie did in the 1940s. Or, the attention goes to horses that ran in claiming races but were not taken, such as two-time Horse of the Year John Henry or 1999 Horse of the Year Charismatic.

Most claimers toil in anonymity, week after week, start after start, battling their infirmities as much as the competition. Most males are geldings and race well past their prime.

Claiming races have been a part of Thoroughbred racing for more than three centuries, though they began in England in a much different fashion and were called selling races.

In a story in the January 1972 issue of *The Thoroughbred of California*, Barry H. Irwin uncovered the original set of horse racing rules used in England in 1698, '99, and 1700 for races "at Thettford in the Countys of Norfolke and Suffolke" for the last Friday in September of each year. Eight noblemen and 11 commoners wrote 15 conditions for the races. One was that every owner would sell every horse entered for "Thirty Guineys" and that the "Contributors present shall throw dice" and that "the Purchaser will be he who throwes most at three."

More than 300 years later, if more than one claim is entered on a particular horse, the winner is determined by lot by the stewards. Getting to that point took several revisions once racing became established in the United States.

According to the Jockey Club's 1828 *Racing Calendar*, the owner of the second-place finisher in a selling race was entitled to purchase the winner for a specified sum. That rule was modified to allow all losing owners in a race to buy the winner, with the option to purchase determined by the order of finish. If the owner of the second-place horse did not want the winner, the option to buy passed to the third-place finisher.

In the early 1900s, Canadian racetracks introduced the concept of sealed bids for the winner being submitted within 15 minutes after the race. A similar rule was approved by the Kentucky Association on September 1, 1916, and used at the 1917 spring race meeting in Lexington.

On opening day that spring, April 28, the Kentucky Association approved a Claiming Race Rule that allowed all horses in a claiming race to be purchased, and it set down the chilling reality for the person making a claim. The purchaser would become the owner of the horse "whether he be alive or dead, sound or unsound, or injured during the race or after it." To this day, the claim takes effect as soon as the starting gate opens. If a claimed horse dies during the race, the person who claimed it must not only buy the horse but also pay to remove the horse from the track and pay its burial fees.

Claiming races were well received and soon spread to East Coast tracks in the 1920s. However, selling races remained a part of the Jockey Club's rules of racing to the 1950s. By the 1940s, the selling race had become a variation of a claiming race in which only the winner was auctioned off for at least the offering price. All other horses in the race were eligible to be claimed for the stated claiming price.

Claiming rules today vary modestly from one racing jurisdiction to another, but two basic concepts apply in almost all of them. First, any licensed trainer or owner who has had at least one starter at a race meeting may claim any horse at that meeting, although an owner or trainer who lost the last horse of his stable on a claim at the previous meeting is eligible to make a claim. Second, for a period of 30 days, the horse must race for at least 25% more than the price for which it was claimed. For example, a horse claimed for $10,000 cannot start in a claiming race for less than $12,500 for 30 days. Under those restrictions, the horse is frequently referred to as being "in jail," ostensibly because the new owner does not have the freedom to place him at any claiming price. Some racing jurisdictions have experimented with eliminating jail time. In addition, the claimed horse cannot be sold privately to another party in the 30-day period, and the horse cannot race at another track until the end of the race meet at which it was claimed.

For every claimer, there is a claiming trainer, and, like their horses, some have risen to prominence. Hirsch Jacobs, who led the nation in victories 11 times between 1933 and '44, may have been the first great claiming trainer. Jacobs claimed Stymie from a maiden claimer for $1,500 on June 8, 1943, and Stymie rewarded him by winning more than $900,000.

On the West Coast, one of the most prominent claiming trainers was R. H. "Red" McDaniel, who led the nation in victories from 1950 through 1954. In 1955, McDaniel saddled a winner at Golden Gate Fields and a few minutes later jumped to his death from the San Francisco Bay Bridge.

Claimers have been an integral part of the success of father-son Racing Hall of Fame members Marion and Jack Van Berg. Jack Van Berg led the nation's trainers in victories nine times, including a still-record 496 wins in 1976.

Frank "Pancho" Martin won 11 New York training titles, the first in 1971 and then ten straight from 1973 through 1982. The Cuban-born Martin explained his training philosophy in a 1972 magazine article: "The most important thing to remember is to treat your cheapest horse as good as your best," Martin said. "Give a claimer the same care you give a stakes horse, and he'll win for you in his own class. If you improve a horse, move him up in company, but never ask him to do the impossible."

Three of Martin's greatest claimers were Manassa Mauler, a $12,800 claim who won the 1959 Wood Memorial Stakes and earned $359,171; Autobiography, a $29,000 claim who won the '72 Jockey Club Gold Cup over Key to the Mint and Riva Ridge; and *Big Shot II, a $25,000 claim who won a $100,000 stakes, the '71 Century Handicap.

Though Bobby Frankel shifted his base of operations to California in 1972, he had considerable success with claimers in his six New York seasons before heading west. In that period, Frankel developed claimers Barometer, Baitman, and Pataha Prince into stakes winners. Barometer, claimed for $15,000, won the 1970 Suburban Handicap and earned $174,584. Baitman, who was seven years old when Frankel claimed him for $15,000, earned more than $150,000 after the claim. In California, Frankel claimed Wickerr for $50,000 and then won the 1981 and '82 Eddie Read Handicaps (G1) with him. Wickerr also won the 1981 Del Mar Handicap (G2).

West Virginia-based Dale Baird led the nation's trainers in victories 15 times from 1971 through '99, almost exclusively with claimers. He was displaced as America's top trainer by victories in 2000 and '01 by Scott Lake, who races simultaneously at several tracks in the Northeast. Steve Asmussen was the 2002 leader by wins.

Fifty-two years after Stymie was claimed for $1,500, a first-time starter at Hollywood Park named Budroyale was claimed in a maiden race for $32,000 by trainer Dan Hendricks for Decourcy W. Graham. Budroyale was subsequently claimed twice more for $40,000 and for $50,000 before he matured to win several graded stakes, finish second in the 1999 Breeders' Cup Classic (G1), and earn more than $2.8-million, most of it for small-scale owner Jeffrey Sengara. Such horses as Stymie and Budroyale are the exceptions, but the hope of finding a diamond in the rough keeps many owners and trainers in the claiming game.

—Bill Heller

North American Claiming Races in 2005

While claiming races remain a vitally important part of Thoroughbred racing, the core of most racing programs underwent a significant decline in several measures in 2005. Most important, the number and total value of claiming races dived sharply in the 2005 season. Total claiming races declined to 37,793 in 2005, a 3.1% drop from 39,010 in the previous year. The percentage of claiming races fell to 66% of all races from 66.5% in 2004.

All purses declined in 2005, and claiming races constituted a large part of the drop. Purses for all claiming races totaled $426,168,889 in 2005, which was a 4.6% drop from $446,836,040 a year earlier. The proportion of purse money going into claiming races fell to 37.1% from 37.9%. The average claiming purse declined to $11,276 from $11,454 in 2004.

Because of fewer claims, the average claiming price advanced to $13,303 from $12,853 in 2004. The highest average claiming price was $13,792 in 2000.

Claiming Races in North America, 1997-2005

Year	Number of Races	Percent of Races	Total Claiming Purses	Percent of Purses	Average Purse	Number of Claims	Value of All Claims	Average Claim Price
2005	37,793	66.0%	$426,168,889	37.1%	$11,276	15,381	$200,467,775	$13,303
2004	39,010	66.5%	446,836,040	37.9%	11,454	16,307	209,586,963	12,853
2003	39,111	66.5%	436,172,397	37.8%	11,152	14,777	202,646,625	13,714
2002	39,351	65.9%	444,901,718	38.0%	11,306	15,912	207,807,725	13,060
2001	39,655	65.5%	428,916,774	37.4%	10,816	14,974	200,883,275	13,415
2000	39,103	64.5%	393,469,977	36.0%	10,062	14,682	202,498,225	13,792
1999	39,420	65.6%	367,718,557	36.5%	9,328	13,909	177,754,863	12,780
1998	40,194	65.7%	354,541,816	36.6%	8,821	12,466	150,608,500	12,080
1997	42,368	66.7%	327,460,399	36.8%	7,729	11,703	136,154,325	11,634

Claims by Category at United States Tracks in 2005

Claiming Price Range	No. of Starts	No. Claims	% of Claimed	% of All of Claims	Total Value of Claims	Average Claim Price
Less than $1,000	1	0	0.0%	0.0%	$0	—
$1,000 to $2,499	1,816	68	3.7%	0.5%	116,600	$1,715
$2,500 to $4,999	68,880	2,072	3.0%	14.5%	7,390,900	3,567
$5,000 to $7,499	70,484	3,472	4.9%	24.2%	18,508,250	5,331
$7,500 to $9,999	30,817	1,540	5.0%	10.7%	11,876,500	7,712
$10,000 to $14,999	47,452	2,843	6.0%	19.8%	31,309,000	11,013
$15,000 to $19,999	22,062	1,456	6.6%	10.2%	23,071,500	15,846
$20,000 to $29,999	26,199	1,481	5.7%	10.3%	33,996,500	22,955
$30,000 to $39,999	11,424	659	5.8%	4.6%	21,109,000	32,032
$40,000 to $49,999	5,589	395	7.1%	2.8%	15,930,000	40,329
$50,000 to $74,999	3,976	279	7.0%	1.9%	14,820,000	53,118
$75,000 and up	1,089	66	6.1%	0.5%	5,275,000	79,924
TOTALS	**289,789**	**14,331**	**4.9%**	**100.0%**	**183,403,250**	**12,798**

Claims by Category at Canadian Tracks in 2005

Claiming Price Range	No. of Starts	No. Claims	% of Claimed	% of All of Claims	Total Value of Claims	Average Claim Price
Less than $1,000	0	0	0	0.0%	$0	—
$1,000 to $2,499	607	10	1.6%	1.0%	21,500	$2,150
$2,500 to $4,999	3,236	65	2.0%	6.2%	236,900	3,645
$5,000 to $7,499	8,125	197	2.4%	18.8%	1,052,250	5,341
$7,500 to $9,999	3,898	121	3.1%	11.5%	958,375	7,920
$10,000 to $14,999	4,703	169	3.6%	16.1%	1,955,500	11,571
$15,000 to $19,999	3,298	138	4.2%	13.1%	2,280,500	16,525
$20,000 to $29,999	2,958	200	6.8%	19.0%	4,467,000	22,335
$30,000 to $39,999	1,445	61	4.2%	5.8%	1,950,000	31,967
$40,000 to $49,999	923	56	6.1%	5.3%	2,250,000	40,179
$50,000 to $74,999	631	28	4.4%	2.7%	1,502,500	53,661
$75,000 and up	119	5	4.2%	0.5%	390,000	78,000
TOTALS	**29,943**	**1,050**	**3.5%**	**100.0%**	**17,064,525**	**16,252**

United States Claiming Activity by State and Track in 2005

	No. of Horses Claimed	Total Value of Claims	Avg. Price of Claim
Arizona			
Cochise County Fair	1	$1,000	$1,000
Flagstaff	4	4,250	1,063
Gila County Fair	3	3,250	1,083
Graham County Fair	3	3,000	1,000
Greenlee County Fair	1	1,000	1,000
Mohave County Fair	4	4,500	1,125
Rillito Park	6	8,500	1,417
Santa Cruz County Fair	2	3,500	1,750
Turf Paradise	485	2,935,550	6,053
Yavapai Downs	61	191,600	3,141
Total Arizona	**570**	**3,156,150**	**5,537**
Arkansas			
Oaklawn Park	264	$4,120,500	$15,608
Total Arkansas	**264**	**4,120,500**	**15,608**
California			
Bay Meadows Fair	45	$360,700	$8,016
Bay Meadows Race Course	536	6,474,750	12,080
Del Mar	348	10,383,000	29,836
Fairplex Park	58	866,750	14,944
Fresno	8	44,400	5,550
Golden Gate Fields	449	5,579,500	12,427
Hollywood Park	387	10,409,000	26,897
Los Alamitos Race Course	239	740,200	3,097
Oak Tree at Santa Anita	128	3,467,000	27,086
Pleasanton	44	431,150	9,799
Santa Anita Park	321	8,766,500	27,310
Santa Rosa	27	208,500	7,722
Solano County Fair	44	282,500	6,420
Stockton	18	85,950	4,775
Total California	**2,652**	**48,099,900**	**18,137**
Colorado			
Arapahoe Park	21	$113,250	$5,393
Total Colorado	**21**	**113,250**	**5,393**
Delaware			
Delaware Park	646	$7,261,000	$11,240
Total Delaware	**646**	**7,261,000**	**11,240**
Florida			
Calder Race Course	381	$6,516,250	$17,103
Gulfstream Park	442	10,212,750	23,106
Tampa Bay Downs	215	1,919,500	8,928
Total Florida	**1,038**	**18,648,500**	**17,966**
Idaho			
Les Bois Park	2	$6,400	$3,200
Total Idaho	**2**	**6,400**	**3,200**
Illinois			
Arlington Park	430	$6,972,000	$16,214
Fairmount Park	54	260,250	4,819
Hawthorne Race Course	458	5,427,000	11,849
Total Illinois	**942**	**12,659,250**	**13,439**
Indiana			
Hoosier Park	106	$546,250	$5,153
Indiana Downs	22	114,000	5,182
Total Indiana	**128**	**660,250**	**5,158**
Iowa			
Prairie Meadows	86	$1,196,250	$13,910
Total Iowa	**86**	**1,196,250**	**13,910**
Kansas			
The Woodlands	16	$64,500	$4,031
Total Kansas	**16**	**64,500**	**4,031**
Kentucky			
Churchill Downs	441	$7,918,750	$17,956
Ellis Park	66	553,000	8,379
Keeneland Race Course	124	2,412,500	19,456
Kentucky Downs	1	17,500	17,500
Turfway Park	214	2,430,500	11,357
Total Kentucky	**846**	**13,332,250**	**15,759**
Louisiana			
Delta Downs	147	$1,133,000	$7,707
Evangeline Downs	282	1,792,500	6,356
Fair Grounds Race Course	276	5,056,500	18,321
Louisiana Downs	253	3,151,000	12,455
Total Louisiana	**958**	**11,133,000**	**11,621**

	No. of Horses Claimed	Total Value of Claims	Avg. Price of Claim
Maryland			
Laurel Park	384	$5,325,500	$13,868
Pimlico Race Course	169	2,298,500	13,601
Timonium	10	133,000	13,300
Total Maryland	**563**	**7,757,000**	**13,778**
Massachusetts			
Suffolk Downs	127	$859,500	$6,768
Total Massachusetts	**127**	**859,500**	**6,768**
Michigan			
Great Lakes Downs	29	$209,000	$7,207
Total Michigan	**29**	**209,000**	**7,207**
Minnesota			
Canterbury Park	68	$579,500	$8,522
Total Minnesota	**68**	**579,500**	**8,522**
Montana			
Great Falls	3	$6,500	$2,167
Total Montana	**3**	**6,500**	**2,167**
Nebraska			
Columbus Races	12	$38,500	$3,208
Fonner Park	48	163,000	3,396
Horsemen's Atokad Downs	2	9,000	4,500
Horsemen's Park	11	52,000	4,727
Lincoln State Fair	41	170,000	4,146
Total Nebraska	**114**	**432,500**	**3,794**
New Jersey			
Meadowlands	30	$502,000	$16,733
Monmouth Park	275	4,377,750	15,919
Total New Jersey	**305**	**4,879,750**	**15,999**
New Mexico			
Ruidoso Downs	36	$237,450	$6,596
Sunland Park	186	1,622,000	8,720
SunRay Park	8	44,000	5,500
The Downs at Albuquerque	10	67,750	6,775
Zia Park	51	387,500	7,598
Total New Mexico	**291**	**2,358,700**	**8,105**
New York			
Aqueduct	262	$7,335,500	$27,998
Belmont Park	143	4,660,500	32,591
Finger Lakes Gaming and Race Track	128	726,250	5,674
Saratoga Race Course	72	2,972,500	41,285
Total New York	**605**	**15,694,750**	**25,942**
North Dakota			
Chippewa Downs	1	$2,500	$2,500
North Dakota Horse Park	1	3,500	3,500
Total North Dakota	**2**	**6,000**	**3,000**
Ohio			
Beulah Park	39	$200,500	$5,141
River Downs	67	394,500	5,888
Thistledown	120	509,000	4,242
Total Ohio	**226**	**1,104,000**	**4,885**
Oklahoma			
Blue Ribbon Downs	2	$8,500	$4,250
Fair Meadows at Tulsa	15	84,500	5,633
Remington Park	53	341,000	6,434
Total Oklahoma	**70**	**434,000**	**6,200**
Oregon			
Eastern Oregon Livestock Show	1	$2,500	$2,500
Portland Meadows	75	267,000	3,560
Tillamook County Fair	1	1,600	1,600
Total Oregon	**77**	**271,100**	**3,521**
Pennsylvania			
Penn National Race Course	275	$1,639,500	$5,962
Philadelphia Park	754	7,256,500	9,624
Total Pennsylvania	**1029**	**8,896,000**	**8,645**
Texas			
Lone Star Park	173	$2,232,500	$12,905
Manor Downs	2	10,000	5,000
Retama Park	24	302,000	12,583
Sam Houston Race Park	73	615,000	8,425
Total Texas	**272**	**3,159,500**	**11,616**
Virginia			
Colonial Downs	38	$553,000	$14,553
Great Meadows	1	15,000	15,000
Morven Park	2	27,500	13,750
Total Virginia	**41**	**595,500**	**14,524**
Washington			
Emerald Downs	282	$2,297,750	$8,148
Sun Downs	1	2,500	2,500
Total Washington	**283**	**2,300,250**	**8,128**
West Virginia			
Charles Town Races	1,580	$10,133,000	$6,413
Mountaineer Race Track	475	3,263,000	6,869
Total West Virginia	**2,055**	**13,396,000**	**6,519**
Wyoming			
Wyoming Downs	1	$2,500	$2,500
Total Wyoming	**1**	**2,500**	**2,500**

Canadian Claiming Activity by Province and Track in 2005

	No. of Horses Claimed	Total Value of Claims	Avg. Price of Claim
Alberta			
Lethbridge	16	$46,500	$2,906
Northlands Park	139	2,051,000	14,755
Stampede Park	115	1,643,000	14,287
Total Alberta	**270**	**3,740,500**	**13,854**
British Columbia			
Hastings Race Course	186	$2,143,000	$11,522
Kin Park	1	3,000	3,000
Total British Columbia	**187**	**$2,146,000**	**$11,476**
Manitoba			
Assiniboia Downs	87	$461,188	$5,301
Total Manitoba	**87**	**$461,188**	**$5,301**
Ontario			
Fort Erie	131	$1,052,500	$8,034
Woodbine	411	10,764,500	26,191
Total Ontario	**542**	**$11,817,000**	**$21,803**
Saskatchewan			
Marquis Downs	19	$50,225	$2,643
Total Saskatchewan	**19**	**$50,225**	**$2,643**

Horses With Highest Earnings After First Claim in 2005

Horse, YOB Sex, Sire	Claiming Price	Wins After Claim	Earnings After Claim
Silver Axe, 1997 g., Silver Ghost	$35,000	5	$288,900
Speed Whiz, 2001 g., Weshaam	15,000	3	257,500
Network, 2002 g., Pulpit	62,500	5	244,160
Seattlespectacular, 2000 g., Seattle Slew	40,000	4	217,487
Blue Song, 2001 m., Sultry Song	20,000	7	202,564
Leprechaun Kid, 1999 g., Alphabet Soup	80,000	1	200,000
Miss Concerto, 2001 m., Concerto	30,000	4	198,866
The Student (Arg), 1999 g., Mutakddim	35,000	6	194,600
Siren Lure, 2001 g., Joyeux Danseur	50,000	5	186,111

Horse, YOB Sex, Sire	Claiming Price	Wins After Claim	Earnings After Claim
Outcashem, 2001 g., Mazel Trick	25,000	8	185,631
Sierra Bella, 2002 f., Montbrook	25,000	8	181,572
Dark Beauty, 2002 f., Bertrando	32,000	4	179,496
Morine's Victory, 2001 g., Victory Gallop	30,000	8	176,400
Trickey Trevor, 1999 h., Demaloot Demashoot	62,500	5	176,150
Willy o'the Valley, 2001 g., Will's Way	100,000	1	156,411
Artemus Sunrise, 2001 h., Tale of the Cat	40,000	2	156,300
Bull Ranch, 2002 g., Real Quiet	40,000	2	151,697
Jet West, 2001 h., Western Fame	62,500	3	150,480
Penny Ante, 2001 m., Fabulous Champ	32,000	4	150,375
Top This and That, 2002 g., Old Topper	40,000	3	149,040
Slew's Smile, 1997 g., Native Slew	16,000	3	148,173
Golden Man, 2002 g., Suave Prospect	60,000	1	147,500
Royal Kleven, 2000 m., Kleven	10,000	3	147,005
Spring Rush, 2000 m., Wild Rush	62,500	5	146,495
Our Madison, 2003 f., Tactical Cat	40,000	2	141,140
Do Da Princess, 2002 f., Scatmandu	40,000	6	141,000
Red Crusader, 2001 g., Explosive Red	20,000	5	139,690
Stetter Jr, 2001 g., Tejano Run	14,000	5	138,610
Code of Justice, 2001 m., Double Honor	16,000	8	136,180
Spooky Mulder, 1998 g., Brunswick	50,000	3	134,048
Geronimo (Chi), 1999 g., Gold Tribute	80,000	1	131,397
Brite Maneuvers, 2003 g., High Brite	40,000	3	130,990
Guidebook, 2000 m., Notebook	40,000	4	130,356
Nyuk Nyuk Nyuk, 2001 g., Mutakddim	50,000	2	129,286
With Due Respect, 2002 f., Devil His Due	35,000	4	127,706
Missile Bay, 2002 f., Yes It's True	75,000	3	126,701
Scat Cat Jamey, 2000 g., Wild Rush	7,500	6	126,340
Orphan Brigade, 2001 g., Roar	40,000	4	126,000

Leading Earners After First Claim, 1991-2005

Horse, YOB Sex, Sire	Initial Claim Price	Date of Claim	Starts After Claim	Wins After Claim	Earnings After Claim
Budroyale, 1993 g., by Cee's Tizzy	$32,000	12/9/1995	52	17	$2,837,610
Ladies Din, 1995 g., by Din's Dancer	32,000	7/30/1997	35	11	1,896,854
Native Desert, 1993 g., by Desert Classic	32,000	10/10/1996	72	20	1,815,827
Say Florida Sandy, 1994 h., by Personal Flag	70,000	9/14/1997	85	27	1,774,748
Peeping Tom, 1997 g., by Eagle Eyed	40,000	3/24/2000	55	15	1,384,397
River Keen (Ire), 1992 h., by Keen	100,000	12/4/1998	16	3	1,338,880
One for Rose, 1999 m., by Tejano Run	40,000	10/4/2002	26	14	1,296,943
Shake You Down, 1998 g., by Montbrook	65,000	3/12/2003	28	14	1,218,224
Full Moon Madness, 1995 g., by Half a Year	32,000	6/25/1997	58	17	1,199,953
Lazy Slusan, 1995 m., by Slewvescent	20,000	10/22/1997	45	11	1,142,196
Recoup the Cash, 1990 g., by Copelan	15,000	6/3/1993	67	22	1,090,713
License Fee, 1995 m., by Black Tie Affair (Ire)	75,000	9/2/1998	34	13	1,084,276
Early Pioneer, 1995 g., by Rahy	62,500	10/25/1998	22	7	1,068,815
Parose, 1994 g., by Parlay Me	15,000	7/22/1998	82	19	1,056,875
Mr. Epperson, 1995 g., by Cabrini Green	50,000	7/10/1998	68	15	1,029,820
Bluesthestandard, 1997 g., by American Standard	22,500	4/25/2001	43	16	1,004,618
Designed for Luck, 1997 g., by Rahy	62,500	12/17/1999	25	9	951,100
Elated Guy, 1989 g., by Brave Shot (GB)	40,000	8/22/1991	63	9	941,904
One Way Love, 1995 h., by Regal Classic	50,000	11/1/1997	37	14	937,095
Lava Man, 2001 g., by Slew City Slew	50,000	8/13/2004	14	4	936,103
Pie N Burger, 1998 g., by Twining	62,500	9/13/2000	42	14	920,533
Dancing Guy, 1995 g., by Robyn Dancer	18,000	11/25/1997	90	21	912,953
Shoop, 1991 m., by Double Sonic	25,000	8/26/1995	70	11	911,515
Moscow Burning, 2000 m., by Moscow Ballet	25,000	8/7/2003	20	6	871,550
Tour of the Cat, 1998 g., by Tour d'Or	25,000	11/11/2000	46	13	867,861
Classic Endeavor, 1998 h., by Silver Buck	75,000	9/2/2000	59	16	853,693
Royal Haven, 1992 g., by Hail Emperor	75,000	8/6/1995	37	16	847,161
Beboppin Baby, 1993 g., by Hatchet Man	32,000	7/13/1996	64	13	830,990
Judge T C, 1991 h., by Judge Smells	30,000	6/11/1993	27	11	825,960
Arromanches, 1993 h., by Relaunch	12,500	6/24/1996	75	30	800,224
Adminniestrator, 1997 g., by Incinderator	32,000	3/31/2000	40	9	761,716
Sis City, 2002 f., by Slew City Slew	50,000	8/5/2004	9	4	758,220
Chris's Bad Boy, 1997 g., by Marquetry	10,000	11/13/2001	39	17	744,211
Truly a Judge, 1998 g., by Judge T C	50,000	3/7/2001	42	12	742,072

Horse, YOB Sex, Sire	Initial Claim Price	Date of Claim	Starts After Claim	Wins After Claim	Earnings After Claim
Presidentialaffair, 1999 g., by Not For Love	20,000	6/28/2003	22	9	732,778
Coyote Lakes, 1994 g., by Society Max	12,500	10/26/1996	59	19	724,337
Sharp Appeal, 1993 h., by World Appeal	50,000	7/14/1995	39	12	712,346
Irisheyesareflying, 1996 h., by Flying Continental	12,500	2/20/1999	36	8	711,736
Star Over the Bay, 1998 g., by Cozzene	80,000	5/16/2004	8	4	709,000
Musique Toujours, 2000 g., by Musique d'Enfer	40,000	11/21/2003	12	3	707,600
Ninebanks, 1998 g., by Smokester	50,000	8/3/2001	30	10	698,283
Umpateedle, 1999 m., by Suave Prospect	40,000	5/27/2002	44	16	688,930
Praise From Dixie, 1996 g., by Dixie Brass	62,500	5/7/2000	61	13	685,403
My Cousin Matt, 1999 g., by Matty G	85,000	9/25/2002	31	4	682,443
Esteemed Friend, 1994 g., by Gulch	50,000	8/21/1997	51	17	677,417
Same Old Wish, 1990 g., by Lyphard's Wish (Fr)	35,000	8/4/1994	49	5	675,935
Chicago Six, 1995 h., by Wild Again	18,000	9/2/1999	29	15	675,147
Golden Tent, 1989 g., by Shelter Half	50,000	5/15/1994	105	17	673,903
Mr. Sinatra, 1994 h., by Mining	75,000	8/22/1997	53	10	667,205
Boom Towner, 1988 g., by Obligato	50,000	9/1/1993	56	16	663,070
Tic N Tin, 1995 g., by Lac Ouimet	25,000	10/2/1999	81	25	656,125
Wicapi, 1992 g., by Waquoit	20,000	1/11/1996	54	17	651,601
Halory Leigh, 2000 m., by Halory Hunter	75,000	6/5/2003	20	6	647,312
Judge's Case, 1997 g., by Montbrook	32,000	3/2/2000	74	11	646,661
Iron Gavel, 1990 g., by Time for a Change	15,500	11/18/1993	77	24	646,408
Freedom Crest, 1996 g., by To Freedom	32,000	6/10/1999	28	7	641,400
Watchman's Warning, 1995 g., by Carnivalay	35,000	6/28/1998	84	15	639,170
Oro de Mexico, 1994 g., by Well Decorated	80,000	3/14/1997	60	9	638,950
Devine Wind, 1996 g., by American Chance	40,000	5/10/2000	46	13	633,885
Morluc, 1996 h., by Housebuster	50,000	1/15/1999	34	10	628,088
Echo Eddie, 1997 g., by Restless Con	20,000	11/20/1999	27	8	627,084
Lil Personalitee, 1997 g., by Personal Flag	62,500	8/4/2000	51	12	625,016
Sassy Hound, 1997 g., by Deerhound	14,500	1/6/2000	43	14	619,298
Theresa's Tizzy, 1994 m., by Cee's Tizzy	20,000	7/25/1997	31	13	612,171
Zarb's Luck, 1997 g., by Zarbyev	25,000	12/31/1999	50	12	611,400
Boston Common, 1999 g., by Boston Harbor	50,000	6/23/2001	32	12	605,317

Horses With Most Wins After First Claim in 2005

Horse, YOB Sex, Sire	Claiming Price	Wins After Claim	Earnings After Claim
Outcashem, 2001 g., Mazel Trick	$25,000	8	$185,631
Sierra Bella, 2002 f., Montbrook	25,000	8	181,572
Morine's Victory, 2001 g., Victory Gallop	30,000	8	176,400
Code of Justice, 2001 m., Double Honor	16,000	8	136,180
O. K. Corral, 2000 m., Allied Forces	12,500	8	121,500
Moment of Song, 2001 g., Hazaam	6,250	8	61,534
Les Crime, 2000 g., Really Golden	2,500	8	15,856
Blue Song, 2001 m., Sultry Song	20,000	7	202,564
My Buddy Richie, 2002 c., Double Honor	40,000	7	119,480
Beer Stien, 2002 g., Fabulous Champ	10,000	7	104,910
My Extolled Honor, 1998 g., My Mike	10,000	7	95,740
Set to Sparkle, 2000 m., Lite the Fuse	15,000	7	89,480
Salty N Sassy, 2001 m., Salt Lake	5,000	7	77,701
The Student (Arg), 1999 g., Mutakddim	35,000	6	194,600
Do Da Princess, 2002 f., Scatmandu	40,000	6	141,000
Scat Cat Jamey, 2000 g., Wild Rush	7,500	6	126,340
Onlynurimagination, 1999 g., Marfa	35,000	6	104,164
Unbridled's Evie, 2001 m., Unbridled Success	10,000	6	98,300
Mae and Ree, 2000 m., Waquoit	10,000	6	80,428
Tooth Doctor, 1999 g., Cresting Water	10,000	6	73,940
Evening Clinic, 2000 g., Ball's Bluff	5,000	6	65,881
Truely a Trooper, 2001 g., Is It True	10,000	6	61,879
Reatta Pass, 1999 m., Benton Creek	10,000	6	51,926
Cassie's Casper, 1997 g., Jog My Memory	6,250	6	47,735
Pal's Pro, 2002 g., Distinctive Pro	25,000	6	45,981
Painter's Creek, 2001 g., Salt Lake	4,000	6	45,051
Dr Chiang Mai, 2000 h., Dr. Adagio	5,000	6	43,901
Firey New Love, 2001 g., Fiery Best	5,000	6	38,413
Continuum, 2000 g., Saint Ballado	5,000	6	33,615
Colony Lane, 1999 g., Majesterian	15,000	6	28,689
I've Decided, 1997 g., Bertrando	3,000	6	23,963

Horses With Most Wins After First Claim, 1991-2005

Horse, YOB Sex, Sire	Initial Claim Price	Date of Claim	Starts After Claim	Wins After Claim	Earnings After Claim
Sawmill Run, 1988 g., by It's Freezing	$4,000	6/28/1992	125	35	$224,514
Mankato, 1988 g., by Meadowlake	15,000	3/17/1992	145	34	330,856
Maybe Jack, 1993 g., by Classic Account	15,000	4/18/1997	107	33	512,395
Oh So Fabulous, 1992 g., by Singular	6,250	2/21/1997	97	33	229,402
It's the Wind, 1989 g., by Contare	5,000	3/1/1992	123	32	202,300
J V Bennett, 1993 g., by Key to the Mint	32,000	6/20/1996	99	32	384,370
Meine Empress, 1989 m., by Rex Imperator	14,000	9/12/1992	75	32	145,190
The Mighty Zip, 1988 g., by Fire Dancer	5,000	10/5/1992	121	32	223,453
Adorable Racer, 1992 g., by Two's a Plenty	3,500	2/13/1996	103	30	333,622
Arromanches, 1993 h., by Relaunch	12,500	6/24/1996	75	30	800,224
Belle's Ruckus, 1985 g., by Bold Ruckus	5,000	7/11/1992	106	30	156,856
Out for Gold, 1990 g., by Gold Crest	35,000	1/6/1993	179	30	284,711
Sgt. Ivor, 1990 g., by Ivor Street	5,000	1/28/1994	157	30	165,012
Tate Express, 1992 g., by Naevus	12,500	12/29/1995	137	30	236,159
Bell Buzzer, 1990 g., by Sauce Boat	4,000	11/17/1994	101	29	111,630
Cope With Peace, 1988 h., by Copelan	10,000	2/20/1992	109	29	182,749
Mahrally, 1991 g., by Ballydoyle	6,250	8/1/1994	142	29	146,535
Secret Service Man, 1992 g., by Shot Gun Scott	18,000	8/2/1996	98	29	290,043
Boca Ratony, 1988 g., by Boca Rio	14,000	7/31/1993	103	28	75,934
Cumberland Gap, 1992 g., by Allen's Prospect	14,500	3/4/1996	132	28	248,972
Fearless Peer, 1994 g., by Overpeer	5,000	8/1/1998	95	28	244,032
Gold Digs, 1987 g., by Regal and Royal	4,000	4/5/1992	103	28	150,206
Spacemaker, 1988 g., by Sunny Clime	5,000	10/11/1992	83	28	148,711
Victory Tower, 1990 g., by Singular	10,000	8/20/1993	152	28	151,654
Exuberant's Tip, 1990 g., by Exuberant	30,000	6/26/1992	87	27	116,315
Fit for Royalty, 1988 g., by Fighting Fit	9,000	4/9/1993	135	27	206,439
Northern Broadway, 1988 g., by Northern Magus	5,000	5/10/1992	160	27	108,542
Rosy Way, 1989 g., by Lord Avie	20,000	8/22/1993	46	27	88,779
Say Florida Sandy, 1994 h., by Personal Flag	70,000	9/14/1997	85	27	1,774,748
Scent a Grade, 1992 g., by Foolish Pleasure	5,000	7/20/1995	86	27	172,910
Win Man, 1985 g., by Con Man	8,250	2/23/1992	66	27	262,792

Horses With Most Claiming Wins in 2005

Horse, YOB Sex, Sire	Starts	Claiming Wins	Claiming Earnings
Senor Cielo Two, 2000 g., by Partner's Hero	18	7	$147,700
Code of Justice, 2001 m., by Double Honor	17	7	120,605
O. K. Corral, 2000 m., by Allied Forces	17	7	91,025
Set to Sparkle, 2000 m., by Lite the Fuse	13	7	88,380
Corpus Sand, 2002 c., by Sand Tunnel	18	7	83,120
Drill Hall, 1999 g., by Saint Ballado	14	7	82,660
Cassie's Casper, 1997 g., by Jog My Memory	9	7	56,135
Pancho, 2002 g., by Hazaam	13	7	52,660
Ringofdiamonds, 2001 m., by Diamond	15	7	47,130
Sailor's Dream, 2000 m., by Iron Cat	17	7	43,197
Zany Northwestern, 2001 g., by West Acre	15	7	37,542
Red Hot Fox, 1999 g., by Foxhound	17	7	21,692
Savanna's Folley, 1999 m., by Live At the Half	14	7	13,955
Frankie Grande, 1997 g., by End Sweep	19	7	13,697

Horses With Most Claiming Wins, 1991-2005

No. Claiming Wins	Horse, YOB Sex, Sire	Claiming Starts	Claiming Earnings	Total Earnings
36	Boca Ratony, 1988 g., by Boca Rio	117	$107,020	$123,587
34	Best Boy's Jade, 1989 g., by Raja's Best Boy	134	170,982	223,983
32	Mankato, 1988 g., by Meadowlake	139	299,146	381,821
	Spacemaker, 1988 g., by Sunny Clime	91	145,020	174,097
31	Sawmill Run, 1988 g., by It's Freezing	123	195,437	251,404
	Smart Graustark, 1990 h., by Special Graustark	94	51,057	52,487
30	Dundee Maverick, 1989 g., by Implore	110	112,638	125,220
	Gold Digs, 1987 g., by Regal and Royal	107	$151,805	$182,566
	Halo Round My Head, 1988 m., by Gregorian	97	112,852	130,383
29	Thar He Blows, 1988 g., by Dewan Keys	143	75,020	80,867
	The Mighty Zip, 1988 g., by Fire Dancer	114	183,953	265,341
28	Inspector Moomaw, 1987 g., by Entropy	128	184,689	207,948
	It's the Wind, 1989 g., by Contare	102	163,627	207,100
	Northern Broadway, 1988 g., by Northern Magus	163	119,212	127,096
	Sgt. Ivor, 1990 g., by Ivor Street	151	143,856	173,316
	Son Coming., 1986 g., by Son of Briartic	130	128,806	136,579

No. Claiming Wins	Horse, YOB Sex, Sire	Claiming Starts	Claiming Earnings	Total Earnings
	Two the Twist, 1987 g., by Two's a Plenty	141	292,975	496,488
	Wilowy's Image, 1989 m., by Mongo's Image	70	130,208	154,698
27	Bon to Run, 1992 g., by Search for Gold	130	119,427	132,833
	J V Bennett, 1993 G., by Key to the Mint	69	296,731	438,431
	Elegant Bo, 1987 g., by Swelegant	121	153,132	199,284
	Monsignor K., 1987 g., by Gala Harry	158	130,434	138,286
	Oh So Fabulous, 1992, g., by Singular	88	173,081	286,339
	Out for Gold, 1990 g., by Gold Crest	169	253,929	313,896
	Primetime Pirate, 1991 g., by Word Pirate	114	65,705	71,368
	Regal Peace, 1988 m., by Peace for Peace	112	113,460	115,383
	Sheila K., 1988 m., by Family Doctor	127	117,413	117,833

Horses Claimed Most Times, 1991-2005

No. Times Claimed	Horse, YOB Sex, Sire	Aggregate Claim Price	Average Claim Price	Starts	Wins	Earnings
22	Sound System, 1993 g., by Waquoit	$170,000	$7,727	105	28	$306,101
21	T. V. Secretary, 1998 m., by Wheaton	189,000	9,000	84	16	219,029
20	Above the Crowd, 1993 g., by Housebuster	541,500	27,075	88	24	461,886
	Game Skipper, 1992 g., by Skip Trial	165,000	8,250	128	19	237,043
	Tour of the Rose, 1997 m., by Tour d'Or	130,500	6,525	74	20	273,810
19	North Salem, 1994 h., by Badger Land	243,500	12,816	106	17	297,236
18	Brisa, 1995 m., by Prince of Fame	84,500	4,694	99	10	149,426
	Erhard, 1996 g., by Gallant Prospector	157,000	8,722	75	13	111,011
	Nauset Flash, 1987 g., by Parfaitement	204,000	11,333	164	20	299,579
	Out for Gold, 1990 g., by Gold Crest	171,500	9,528	187	33	313,896
	Sharp n Strong, 1992 m., by Stalwart	226,000	12,556	86	14	290,071
	Storm's Secret, 1998 m., by Storm Creek	106,000	5,889	71	17	197,216
	Tenfortynine, 1998 g., by Ide	92,000	5,111	57	12	163,061
17	Euroclydon, 1995 g., by Momsfurrari	235,000	13,824	97	17	343,928
	Halos Wonder, 1993 m., by Hay Halo	109,750	6,456	77	18	140,509
	Imua Keoki, 1991 g., by Qui Native	178,500	10,500	86	17	201,224
	Palace Heroine, 1996 m., by Fort Chaffee	94,000	5,529	77	10	173,574
	Retail Sales, 1995 m., by Tour d'Or	171,500	10,088	96	19	205,712
	Rich Coins, 1998 h., by Rizzi	335,500	19,735	72	12	315,111
	Shot On Stage, 1991 g., by Gold Stage	154,000	9,059	129	12	184,274
	Takeitlikeaman, 1991 g., by Exuberant	148,000	8,706	111	14	291,699
	Wings of Jones, 1996 g., by Seneca Jones	146,000	8,588	102	19	361,682

Horses Claimed Most Times in 2005

No. Times Claimed	Horse, YOB Sex, Sire	Average Claim Price	Tracks Where Claimed	2004 Race Record
11	Suave Line, 2001 m., Suave Prospect	17,045	Crc, GP, Tam	16-3-5-3, $75,816
10	Friday's a Comin', 1998 g., Wheaton	6,850	CT	16-3-1-2, 44,565
9	And Nobody Knows, 2000 m., Colonial Affair	6,167	CT, Lrl	11-4-3-2, 53,340
	Bold Trick, 2000 g., Phone Trick	7,222	CT, Pha	19-2-3-5, 37,785
9	Busher's Chad, 2000 g., Fortunate Prospect	7,500	AP, CD, Haw, OP	15-4-4-1, 45,720
	Red Hot Secret, 2000 g., Mr. Greeley	5,361	CT	14-6-2-1, 71,980
8	Bet the Ranch, 2000 h., Dixie Brass	7,688	CT	14-4-4-2, 61,500
	Booster, 2000 g., Boone's Mill	8,063	AP, Haw	17-3-4-0, 47,070
	Doc's Treasure, 1999 m., Demaloot Demashoot	8,938	CT, Del, Tam	18-4-4-3, 57,389
	Millennium Song, 1998 h., Maudlin	8,875	CT	14-1-2-4, 28,510
	Poppy's Courage, 1999 g., Ole'	6,344	CT	15-4-3-1, 51,340
	Rocket Wager, 1999 g., Valid Wager	9,875	CT, Lrl	15-4-3-2, 61,050
7	Banker Boy, 2000 g., Banker's Gold	10,107	BM, GG, Haw, PrM	15-4-5-2, 52,068
	Classy Lover, 2002 g., Friendly Lover	12,786	BM, Dmr, GG, Hol, OSA	16-4-3-2, 52,793
	Clever Comique, 2001 m., Comic Strip	21,429	AP, Haw	10-4-1-2, 59,490
	Grand Piano, 2001 m., Suave Prospect	5,429	CT	14-4-1-2, 31,465
	Millenniummillions, 2000 g., Rubiano	10,071	Del, Pen	18-4-2-7, 59,915
	Monkey Junior, 2000 h., Dr. Caton	12,143	CT	15-2-4-3, 59,370
	Morethanastar, 1999 g., Mt. Livermore	5,500	CT	10-2-3-3, 28,200
	Reatta Pass, 1999 m., Benton Creek	11,857	Hst, SA	12-6-3-1, 54,726
	Ruling Star, 1999 g., Stark Ridge	6,179	Del	13-3-3-2, 43,019
	Short Fuse, 1998 g., Lite the Fuse	5,429	CT	14-2-8-2, 43,800
	T. V. Secretary, 1998 m., Wheaton	4,429	CT	17-3-1-2, 30,430

Horses Claimed Most Times Consecutively in 2005

Cons. Claims	Horse, YOB Sex, Sire	Starts	Wins	Earnings
8	Busher's Chad, 2000 g., Fortunate Prospect	15	4	$45,720
	Millennium Song, 1998 h., Maudlin	14	1	28,510

Cons. Claims	Horse, YOB Sex, Sire	Starts	Wins	Earnings
7	Bold Trick, 2000 g., Phone Trick	19	2	37,785
	Short Fuse, 1998 g., Lite the Fuse	14	2	43,800
6	Fastnloose, 2001 m., Clever Trick	12	3	28,130
	Red Hot Secret, 2000 g., Mr. Greeley	14	6	71,980
	Suave Line, 2001 m., Suave Prospect	16	3	75,816
	Waving Monarch, 2001 g., Wavering Monarch	16	5	37,375
5	Actcentric, 2001 m., Noactor	10	2	27,470
	Calamiamine, 2001 m., Montbrook	12	2	22,250
	Clear Terms, 2000 h., Arch	15	6	80,800
	Dandy Squall, 2000 g., Summer Squall	17	4	57,170
	Diamond Bullet, 2000 g., Awesome Again	15	4	24,500
	Editorial, 2000 g., Editor's Note	9	5	39,548
	Forbidden Gold, 1998 g., Gold Meridian	8	1	19,030
	Fumph Around, 2001 g., Meadowlake	16	2	23,340
	Glorious Raj, 2001 m., Big Jewel	10	0	10,980
	Grand Piano, 2001 m., Suave Prospect	14	4	31,465
	Internal Revenue, 1999 g., End Sweep	14	5	55,620
	Morethanastar, 1999 g., Mt. Livermore	10	2	28,200
	Pleasant Hope, 1999 m., Pleasant Dancer	10	3	38,325
	Reatta Pass, 1999 m., Benton Creek	12	6	54,726
	Rocket Wager, 1999 g., Valid Wager	15	4	61,050
	Ruling Star, 1999 g., Stark Ridge	13	3	43,019
	Shake Salt, 1998 g., Salt Lake	11	2	28,160
	Shamiza, 2001 m., Cobra King	13	6	60,040
	Show Me Tazz, 1997 g., Crystal Tas	11	4	25,113
	Sidekick, 1997 g., Gold Saga	17	4	43,330
	So Far Go, 2001 g., Fargo	20	2	46,327
	Todds Volcano, 2000 g., Cherokee Run	11	2	9,082

Horses Claimed Most Consecutive Times, 1991-2005

Horse, YOB Sex, Sire	Cons Claims	Initial Claim Price	Date	Wins During Claim Period	Earnings During Claim Period
I Wood Be a Winner, 1995 g., by Knight Skiing	9	$ 6,250	11/21/1998	22	$281,352
Red Hot Secret, 2000 g., by Mr. Greeley	9	7,500	2/18/2004	8	121,360
Adjustable Note, 1993 g., by Native Prospector	8	5,000	8/7/1998	2	22,230
Busher's Chad, 2000 g., by Fortunate Prospect	8	10,000	2/5/2005	4	42,500
Millennium Song, 1998 h., by Maudlin	8	16,000	4/3/2002	8	131,385
Blazing Wind, 1997 g., by Zero for Conduct	7	4,000	7/14/2002	2	49,491
Bold Trick, 2000 g., by Phone Trick	7	5,000	2/19/2005	2	33,845
Dirty Harryette, 1999 m., by Unaccounted For	7	12,500	5/30/2002	6	138,018
Magicleigh, 1999 m., by Magic Prospect	7	5,000	11/21/2002	3	45,364
Mapeb, 1997 h., by Wallenda	7	3,500	6/21/2001	8	72,960
Mr. Sundancer, 1995 g., by Allen's Prospect	7	17,500	6/4/1999	12	129,521
Opus Won, 1997 h., by Fit to Fight	7	40,000	1/21/2002	6	70,890
Personal Stash, 1998 g., by Air Forbes Won	7	7,500	9/21/2002	4	67,117
Rally Mode, 1999 g., by Hasty Spirit	7	10,000	10/10/2003	3	39,624
Short Fuse, 1998 g., by Lite the Fuse	7	25,000	1/24/2003	3	67,785
Silver Mystery, 1994 m., by Norquestor	7	16,000	2/21/1999	8	126,247
Well Travelled, 1999 h., by Fortunate Prospect	7	25,000	11/22/2001	7	92,290
Castlebright, 1998 m., by Bagdad Road	6	20,000	10/5/2000	7	123,880
Catch If You Can, 1990 g., by Big Burn	6	8,000	12/1/1994	11	57,238
Cien Seas, 1997 g., by Cien Fuegos	6	7,500	8/23/2001	4	44,984
Crijinsky, 1989 g., by Sir Jinsky	6	8,000	9/7/1995	7	53,330
Fastnloose, 2001 m., by Clever Trick	6	4,500	4/15/2005	2	16,330
Foyt Sparkler, 1988 g., by Foyt	6	12,500	7/30/1996	6	59,342
Fumph Around, 2001 g., by Meadowlake	6	20,000	6/19/2004	2	28,270
Imablazinbeauty, 2000 m., by Semoran	6	10,000	12/18/2002	11	105,183
Just Wyatt, 1995 g., by Claim	6	17,500	6/3/1998	15	56,555
Lambourne, 1995 g., by Exbourne	6	12,500	5/5/2001	3	46,294
Milky Bar (Chi), 1996 g., by The Great Shark	6	20,000	12/29/2001	9	152,715
Nasty Newt, 1989 g., by Nasty and Bold	6	10,000	2/19/1994	9	53,691
Parlay Cory, 1995 g., by Parlay Me	6	5,500	8/4/2001	4	28,161
Pell Mell, 1998 g., by Press Card	6	2,500	4/19/2002	9	82,933
Remission, 1997 m., by Superbity	6	8,000	5/19/2002	5	40,734
Rustic, 1999 m., by Schossberg	6	20,000	8/5/2002	4	61,193
Sabalucious, 2000 g., by Northern Afleet	6	32,000	5/21/2003	6	94,570
Show Me Tazz, 1997 g., by Crystal Tas	6	6,250	5/19/2002	8	54,934
Sound System, 1993 g., by Waquoit	6	18,500	9/15/1996	26	261,930
Sox On Top, 1995 g., by Black Moonshine	6	35,000	11/29/1998	10	223,917
Stroker, 1999 g., by Forest Wildcat	6	5,000	1/30/2003	4	48,034
Suave Line, 2001 m., by Suave Prospect	6	12,500	3/3/2005	1	30,945

Horse, YOB Sex, Sire	Cons Claims	Initial Claim Price	Date	Wins During Claim Period	Earnings During Claim Period
Tender Hearted, 1995 m., by Bello	6	20,000	5/7/1999	2	87,268
Tenfortynine, 1998 g., by Ide	6	4,000	9/1/2002	7	104,398
U. R. My Hope, 1997 g., by Sir Leon	6	20,000	10/10/1999	5	90,496
Waving Monarch, 2001 g., by Wavering Monarch	6	4,000	4/11/2005	3	23,967
Where's Sally, 1996 m., by Mi Cielo	6	12,500	12/8/1998	8	86,994

Claiming Crown

The Claiming Crown, started in 1999 by the Thoroughbred Owners and Breeders Association and the National Horsemen's Benevolent and Protective Association, is promoted as a championship event for the sport's hard-working claimers, and it certainly offers generous purses, a total of $550,000 spread over six races. The event has been described as the "granddaddy of all starter allowances," which are races limited to horses that have started for a specific claiming price or less within a specified period of time. To be eligible for the Claiming Crown races, the horse must have made at least one start at the stated claiming price or lower within the prior year. The claiming prices range from $5,000 or less for the $50,000 Claiming Crown Iron Horse to $25,000 or less for the $150,000 Claiming Crown Jewel. All races are for horses three years old and up, with weight allowances made to three-year-olds and females. A seventh race, the $100,000 Claiming Crown Tiara, was run in 1999 and 2000.

Owners must nominate their horses to the Claiming Crown program for $100 by April 15 or $500 by May 27, with a race specified by the latter date. Supplemental entries, at 5% of the purse, are permitted until July 1. Pre-entries are made 11 days before the races, and entries are taken three days in advance of the event. A maximum of 14 horses can start in each race; if more than 14 horses are entered for a race, winners of official preview races will be given preference to start, as will the two highest-ranked Canterbury Park-based horses in each category. The remainder of the field will be selected according to a points system based on finish position and quality of races. For instance, a winner of a graded stakes race will receive 12 points, and the third finisher in a claimer or starter race with a price below that of the Claiming Crown contest will receive one point. Pre-entry, entry, and starting fees range from $1,000 for the Iron Horse to $3,000 for the Jewel.

The Claiming Crown has been held each year at Canterbury Park near Minneapolis with the exception of 2002, when the races were held at Philadelphia Park. The 2006 Claiming Crown was scheduled for July 15 at Canterbury.

Claiming Crown Emerald S.

Canterbury Park, three-year-olds and up, starters for a claiming price of $20,000 or less, 1¹⁄₁₆ miles, turf. Held July 16, 2005, with a gross value of $122,500. First held in 2000. Stakes record 1:41.66 (2000 P. D. Lucky).

Year	Winner	Jockey	Second	Third	Strs	Time	1st Purse
2005	**Mr. Mabee**, 4, 120	D. Bell	Sigfreto, 7	Rockhurst, 6	12	1:41.77	$68,750
2004	**Stage Player**, 5, 124	T. A. Baze	Bristolville, 8	He Flies, 6	14	1:42.20	68,750
2003	**Image**, 5, 122	J. A. Krone	W. W. Robin de Hood, 5	Mega Gift, 6	10	1:42.12	68,750
2002	**Nowrass (GB)**, 6, 122	J. Valdivia Jr.	Grade One, 6	Taylorman (NZ), 7	9	1:46.66	68,750
2001	**Al's Dearly Bred**, 4, 120	S. Martinez	Metatonia, 6	Concielo, 5	11	1:42.22	68,750
2000	**P. D. Lucky**, 5, 124	R. Perez	Felite Patet, 6	G. R. Rabbit, 7	8	**1:41.66**	55,000.

Sponsored by the *Daily Racing Form* 2001. Held at Philadelphia Park 2002.

Claiming Crown Express S.

Canterbury Park, three-year-olds and up, starters for a claiming price of $7,500 or less, 6 furlongs, dirt. Held July 16, 2005, with a gross value of $46,500. First held in 1999. Stakes record 1:08.04 (2005 Onlynurimagination).

Year	Winner	Jockey	Second	Third	Strs	Time	1st Purse
2005	**Onlynurimagination, 6, 124**	B. Walker Jr.	Cicero Grimes, 6	Landler, 6	7	**1:08.04**	$27,500
2004	**Chisholm**, 7, 124	J. Campbell	Setthehook, 5	Devil's Con, 5	8	1:10.10	27,500
2003	**Landler**, 4, 122	R. Fogelsonger	Pelican Peach, 5	Spooky Mulder, 5	10	1:09.65	27,500
2002	**Talknow**, 5, 124	E. Trujillo	Danny E, 4	Wise Sweep, 6	8	1:09.29	27,500
2001	**The Maccabee**, 5, 122	J. Flores	Lord of Time, 4	Hot Affair, 5	10	1:09.68	27,500
2000	**Spit Polish**, 8, 122	J. Flores	Modesto, 5	Citizen's Arrest, 5	10	1:10.74	27,500
1999	**Pioneer Spirit**, 5, 120	W. Martinez	Satchmo, 5	Exclusive Example, 5	10	1:10.45	33,000

Sponsored by Winticket.com 2001. Held at Philadelphia Park 2002. Track record 2005.

Claiming Crown Glass Slipper S.

Canterbury Park, three-year-olds and up, fillies and mares, starters for a claiming price of $12,500 or less, 6½ furlongs, dirt. Held July 16, 2005, with a gross value of $72,000. First held in 1999. Stakes record 1:16.31 (2005 Ells Editor).

Year	Winner	Jockey	Second	Third	Strs	Time	1st Purse
2005	**Ells Editor**, 4, 118	S. Stevens	I Will Survive, 6	Peekaboo Cat, 4	10	**1:16.31**	$41,250
2004	**Banished Lover**, 6, 124	T. Clifton	Moving Fever, 4	Flaming Night, 5	8	1:17.29	41,250
2003	**Mum's Gold**, 4, 124	N. Santagata	Margarita's Garden, 4	Sentimentalromance, 7	9	1:16.82	41,500
2002	**Won Moro**, 5, 122	G. Melancon	Dandy Dulce, 4	Playmera, 5	9	1:17.01	41,500
2001	**French Teacher**, 5, 120	M. Johnston	Beauty's Due, 4	Lost Judgement, 5	13	1:16.68	41,250
2000	**A Lot of Mary**, 5, 124	J. Flores	Pretty Lilly, 5	Cinderella Island, 7	10	1:16.75	33,000
1999	**You're a Lady**, 5, 124	W. Martinez	Castle Blaze, 6	Dazzling Danielle, 6	8	1:44.33	41,250

Held at Philadelphia Park 2002. 1¹⁄₁₆ miles 1999.

Claiming Crown Iron Horse S.

Canterbury Park, three-year-olds and up, starters for a claiming price of $5,000 or less, 1⅙ miles, dirt. Held July 16, 2005, with a gross value of $49,000. First held in 1999. Stakes record 1:43.45 (2000 Gingerboy).

Year	Winner	Jockey	Second	Third	Strs	Time	1st Purse
2005	**My Extolled Honor**, 7, 122	H. Castillo Jr.	King of Chicago, 5	Sacsahuaman (Chi), 7	12	1:43.91	$27,500
2004	**Superman Can**, 4, 122	S. Stevens	Rough Draft, 7	Gram's Folly, 6	11	1:44.26	27,500
2003	**Ghoastly Prize**, 5, 120	B. Walker Jr.	Entrepreneurship, 6	Shut Out Time, 7	12	1:44.99	27,500
2002	**Ruskin**, 9, 120	J. Flores	Regal Tour, 4	Entrepreneurship, 5	7	1:45.37	27,500
2001	**Secret Squall**, 6, 122	L. Quinonez	Home a Winner, 7	Gothard, 4	13	1:45.75	27,500
2000	**Gingerboy**, 6, 122	M. Guidry	Irish Bacon, 7	Your Draw, 5	9	**1:43.45**	27,500
1999	**A Point Well Made**, 6, 120	D. Bell	Higher Desire, 7	Unruly Zeal, 7	9	1:45.65	27,500

Sponsored by Vetrap 2001. Held at Philadelphia Park 2002.

Claiming Crown Jewel S.

Canterbury Park, three-year-olds and up, starters for a claiming price of $25,000 or less, 1⅛ miles, dirt. Held July 16, 2005, with a gross value of $138,000. First held in 1999. Stakes record 1:47.32 (2005 Desert Boom).

Year	Winner	Jockey	Second	Third	Strs	Time	1st Purse
2005	**Desert Boom**, 5, 124	R. Gonzalez	Lord of the Game, 4	Habaneros, 6	6	**1:47.32**	$82,500
2004	**Intelligent Male**, 4, 120	E. M. Martin Jr.	Musique Toujours, 4	Rize, 8	11	1:49.62	82,500
2003	**Daunting**, 5, 122	J. A. Krone	Freeze Alert, 6	Patton's Victory, 5	8	1:49.17	82,500
2002	**Truly a Judge**, 4, 122	J. Valdivia Jr.	Quiet Mike, 5	Prince Iroquois, 5	9	1:50.39	85,500
2001	**Sing Because**, 8, 124	J. Valdivia Jr.	Halo Kris, 4	Banner Salute, 4	8	1:50.74	82,500
2000	**B Flat Major**, 5, 126	R. Madrigal Jr.	Shot of Gold, 5	Snohomish Loot, 5	7	1:49.72	68,750
1999	**One Brick Shy**, 4, 120	E. M. Martin Jr.	Honest Venture, 6	Captain Ripperton, 4	14	1:50.79	82,500

Held at Philadelphia Park 2002.

Claiming Crown Rapid Transit S.

Canterbury Park, three-year-olds and up, starters for a claiming price of $16,000 or less, 6½ furlongs, dirt. Held July 16, 2005, with a gross value of $93,000. First held in 1999. Stakes record 1:14.54 (2005 Procreate).

Year	Winner	Jockey	Second	Third	Strs	Time	1st Purse
2005	**Procreate**, 7, 124	H. Castillo Jr.	The Student (Arg), 6	Crafty Player, 4	7	**1:14.54**	$55,000
2004	**Heroic Sight**, 6, 124	T. Glasser	Quote Me Later, 4	Satan's Code, 6	8	1:15.56	55,000
2003	**Pioneer Boy**, 5, 124	R. Wilson	Debonair Joe, 4	Bensalem, 6	10	1:15.47	55,000
2002	**Risen Warrior**, 6, 124	S. Elliott	Yavapai, 6	Largenadincharge, 6	9	1:16.10	55,000
2001	**Sassy Hound**, 4, 124	M. Johnston	Crowns Runner, 8	Exert, 4	13	1:16.18	55,000
2000	**Teddy Boy**, 5, 122	M. Guidry	Bion, 6	Taylor's Day, 6	9	1:16.90	41,250
1999	**Aplomado**, 6, 120	L. A. Pincay Jr.	Emperor Tigere, 5	Oto No Icy, 5	12	1:16.27	55,000

Held at Philadelphia Park 2002.

Claiming Crown Tiara S.

Canterbury Park, three-year-olds and up, fillies and mares, starters for a claiming price of $20,000 or less, 1⅙ miles, turf. Held July 16, 2005, with a gross value of $93,000. First held in 1999. Stakes record 1:42.14 (2000 Look to the Day).

Year	Winner	Jockey	Second	Third	Strs	Time	1st Purse
2005	**Inhonorofjohnnie**, 4, 122	M. Ziegler	O. K. Corral, 5	Secret Lies, 3	7	1:43.51	$55,000
2000	**Look to the Day**, 6, 118	P. Nolan	Vengeful Val, 7	Pine Baroness, 4	10	**1:42.14**	55,000
1999	**Taffy**, 4, 120	T. T. Doocy	Partial Prift, 4	Frosty Peace, 4	14	1:17.37	68,750

Not held 2001-'04. 6½ furlongs 1999. Dirt 1999.

Some of the Best Claimers

Following are some of the most prominent horses who either were claimed prior to outstanding careers on the racetrack or at stud or started in claiming races but went unclaimed:

ASPIDISTRA—1954 b. m., Better Self—Tilly Rose, by Bull Brier. 14-2-2-2, $5,115. Bred by King Ranch, Aspidistra was purchased by William L. McKnight's Minnesota Mining & Manufacturing Co. employees as a 70th birthday gift in 1957. Aspidistra, named for a hardy house plant, then was in the midst of a nondescript racing career that did not improve after her purchase. For McKnight, she raced for a $6,500 claiming tag. Retired after one racing season at age three, she became the foundation of McKnight's Tartan Farms in Florida, producing 1968 Horse of the Year Dr. Fager and champion sprinter Ta Wee.

BOOM TOWNER—1988 b. g., Obligato—Perfect Profile, by Stop the Music. 82-29-16-14, $962,391. Boom Towner began his eight-year career in a $5,000 maiden claimer at Rockingham Park, winning by 10¾ lengths. He won the 1992 Toboggan Handicap (G3) and was claimed the following year for $50,000 by trainer Mike Hushion for Barry Schwartz. In Hushion's care, Boom Towner won the 1993 Boojum (G3) and Sport Page (G3) Handicaps, both at Aqueduct. He won the Toboggan again in 1995.

BROWN BESS—1982 dk. b. or br. m., *Petrone—Chickadee, by Windy Sands. 36-16-8-6, $1,300,920. Brown Bess's owner-breeder, Calbourne Farm, put her at risk only once, for $50,000 in a Bay Meadows Race Course claimer on September 28, 1986. It was her first start on grass, and she finished second by a nose. Brown Bess would thrive on the grass, winning the 1989 Yellow Ribbon Invitational Stakes (G1) and the Ramona Handicap (G1) on her way to an Eclipse Award as champion turf female.

BUDROYALE—1993 b. g., Cee's Tizzy—Cee's Song, by Seattle Song. 52-17-12-2, $2,840,810. First-time starter Budroyale was taken for $32,000 by trainer Dan Hendricks from breeder/co-owner Cecilia Straub-Rubens on December 9, 1995, at Hollywood Park. Budroyale was subsequently claimed for $40,000 by trainer Nick Canani on August 17, 1997, and for $50,000 by trainer Ted West for Jeffrey Sengara on February 15, 1998. He won the 1998 San Bernardino Handicap (G2) and in '99 scored victories in the Goodwood Breeders' Cup Handicap (G2), the Mervyn LeRoy Handicap (G2), and the Longacres Mile Handicap (G3). He was second five times, including the Breeders' Cup Classic (G1). In 2000, Budroyale won the

San Antonio Handicap (G2) the same year his full brother Tiznow won the first of his two Breeders' Cup Classics.

CHARISMATIC—1996 ch. h., Summer Squall—Bail Babe, by Drone. 17-5-2-4, $2,038,064. Charismatic won only one of his first 13 starts and only raced four more times in his career. Trained by D. Wayne Lukas and owned by Robert and Beverly Lewis, Charismatic was placed first in a $62,500 claimer at Santa Anita Park on February 11, 1999. After finishing second in the El Camino Real Derby (G3) at Bay Meadows Race Course, Charismatic was a soundly beaten fourth in the Santa Anita Derby (G1). He subsequently won the Coolmore Lexington Stakes (G2), the Kentucky Derby (G1), and the Preakness Stakes (G1) before finishing third in the Belmont Stakes (G1), in which he sustained two fractures of his right foreleg. He was voted 1999 champion three-year-old male and Horse of the Year.

CREME DE LA FETE—1976 ch. g., Creme Dela Creme—Bridge Day, by *Tudor Minstrel. 151-40-27-16, $460,350. After winning his career debut by a nose as a two-year-old at Keeneland Race Course in 1978, Creme de La Fete finished fifth of six in the Bashford Manor Stakes at Churchill Downs. Unlike many two-year-olds that fade from the racing scene, Creme de La Fete would make 149 more starts. His two best years were in 1981, when he won 12 of 26 starts and $123,180, and in '83, when he won nine of 30 starts and earned $127,240.

DEPUTED TESTAMONY—1980 b. h., Traffic Cop—Proof Requested, by Prove It. 20-11-3-0, $674,329. Owned by Francis Sears and trained by J. William Boniface, Deputed Testamony was not competitive in his first start, finishing sixth by 12¾ lengths in a $25,000 maiden claimer at Bowie Race Course on September 21, 1982. In his next start, the colt won a $22,500 maiden claimer at Keystone Race Track, and Boniface put him at risk once more, in a $40,000 open claimer at the Meadowlands. Deputed Testamony won by three lengths and was not claimed. The following year, he won the Preakness Stakes (G1) and Monmouth Park's Haskell Invitational Handicap (G1). He won his two 1984 starts, including a track-record effort in the City of Baltimore Handicap, before retiring to stud at Boniface's Bonita Farm, the place of his birth.

GAIL'S BRUSH—1991 b. m., Broad Brush—Parade of Roses, by Blues Parade. 39-11-5-4, $250,701. Claimed by John E. Salzman Jr. on November 25, 1995, for $25,000, Gail's Brush made only two starts for the Maryland trainer before she was picked up by owner-trainer Edwin T. Broome from a $40,000 claimer on grass at Gulfstream Park in early 1996. Gail's Brush, whose performance had improved dramatically when switched to grass, made only six starts for Broome, but they included consecutive victories in the 1996 Eatontown Handicap (G3), Columbiana Handicap, Politely Stakes, and Rumson Stakes.

GOLDEN TENT—1989 dk. b. or br. g., Shelter Half—Jump for Gold, by Search for Gold. 114-21-27-17, $732,793. By the standards of racing in the new century, Golden Tent is made of iron. He started once at three and then made 113 starts through 2001. Golden Tent was claimed seven times, four within a little more than four months in 1999 at the age of ten. Trainer Mike Hushion claimed Golden Tent three times for Barry Schwartz, for whom the gelding finished second in the 1998 Bold Ruler Handicap (G3) and third in the Fall Highweight Handicap (G2) that year.

JEWEL PRINCESS—1992 b. m., Key to the Mint—Jewell Ridge, by Melyno (Ire). 29-13-4-7, $1,904,060. An Eclipse Award winner as outstanding older female after winning the 1996 Breeders' Cup Distaff (G1), Jewel Princess began her career with a third-place finish in a $20,000 maiden claimer at Calder Race Course on October 27, 1994. She won her next start in a $30,000 maiden claimer and never looked back. In the care of Wally Dollase, Jewel Princess won the 1996 Vanity Invitational Handicap (G1) in addition to the Distaff, and in '97 she won the Santa Maria (G1) and Santa Margarita Invitational (G1) Handicaps. At the 2000 Keeneland November breeding stock sale, she was sold for $4.9-million to Coolmore Stud principal owner John Magnier.

JOHN HENRY—1975 b. g., Old Bob Bowers—Once Double, by Double Jay. 83-39-15-9, $6,591,860. John Henry raced five times in claiming races in 1978 but was not claimed. Purchased privately for $27,500 by Sam Rubin in 1978, he made his final claiming start for Sam and Dorothy Rubin's Dotsam Stable at $35,000 on June 28, 1978, at Belmont Park and won by 14 lengths. Trained by Robert Donato, Victor "Lefty" Nickerson, and Ron McAnally, he was Horse of the Year in 1981 and '84 as well as a four-time champion turf male and once champion older male. He retired as the richest North American Thoroughbred of all time.

KING COMMANDER—1949 dk. b. or br. g., Brown King—Guinea Egg, by *Cohort. 67-17-15-6, $100,295. King Commander made 27 of his first 31 starts in claimers although he was claimed only once, for $5,000 at Aqueduct in 1952. Converted to steeplechasing after winning three of 32 starts on the flat, King Commander won 14 of 35 starts over fences and was voted champion steeplechase horse in 1954.

KING'S SWAN—1980 b. h., King's Bishop—Royal Cygnet, by *Sea-Bird. 107-31-19-18, $1,924,845. King's Swan already had won 11 of 44 starts and $212,350 when he was claimed in 1985 for $80,000 by trainer Richard Dutrow. The following year, King's Swan won eight of 15 starts, including the Vosburgh Stakes (G1) and Boojum Handicap (G3), and earned $451,207. At seven, he won three Grade 3 stakes in 12 starts and earned $477,218. He was even better at eight, winning five graded stakes, including the Bold Ruler (G2) and Tom Fool (G2) Stakes in 14 starts and banking $539,681.

KOBUK KING—1966 dk. b. or br. h., One-Eyed King—Winby, by Crafty Admiral. 68-12-10-11, $173,921. After showing considerable promise as a two-year-old in 1968, winning three of 13 starts and finishing second in the El Camino Stakes at Bay Meadows Race Course, Kobuk King went zero-for-three as a three-year-old and zero-for-19 at four. Claimed for $15,000 in 1971, Kobuk King found himself and scored consecutive victories in the Cabrillo Handicap at Del Mar, the Tanforan Handicap at Bay Meadows, and Santa Anita Park's Carleton F. Burke Invitational Handicap for co-owners Allegre Stable and Ron McAnally, who trained the horse.

LADY MARYLAND—1934 gr. m., Sir Greysteel—Palestra, by *Prince Palatine. 82-18-14-14, $31,067. The 1939 champion handicap mare, Lady Maryland made 19 of her 82 starts in claimers and was taken for $2,500 in her 28th career start by B. B. Archer. Her final start in a claimer was as a four-year-old for $4,500 at Havre de Grace. She was not claimed and quickly improved in her five-year-old season, winning the Carroll and Ritchie Handicaps at Pimlico Race Course.

LAKEVILLE MISS—1975 dk. b. or br. m., Rainy Lake—Hew, by Blue Prince. 14-7-4-1, $371,582. While Affirmed and Alydar slugged it out for two-year-old male honors in 1977, the juvenile filly championship was taken by the strapping Lakeville Miss, who possessed a blue-collar pedigree and started her career as a $25,000 maiden claimer for owner-breeder Randolph Weinsier. She won a 5½-furlong claiming race at Belmont Park by four lengths on June 30 and never started again for a claiming tag. Trained by Jose Martin, Lakeville Miss won the Matron (G1) and Frizette (G1) Stakes at Belmont and the Selima Stakes (G1) at Laurel Race Course. She concluded her career with a four-length win in the 1978 Coaching Club American Oaks (G1).

LAVA MAN—2001 dk. b. or br. g., Slew City Slew—Li'l Ms. Leonard, by Nostalgia's Star. 30-10-7-3, $2,274,706. Lava Man was by no means a cheap claim. Trainer Doug O'Neill haltered the California-bred as a three-year-old for $50,000 out of a Del Mar grass race on August 13, 2004. To that point in his career, Lava Man had won three races in Northern California for a partnership that included trainer Lonnie Arterburn, the gelding's co-breeder. Switched to dirt, Lava Man won the Derby Trial Stakes at Fairplex Park but did not win again until he went on a tear the following spring, when he won an optional claiming race, the Californian Stakes (G2), and the Hollywood Gold Cup Handicap (G1). He went off form after finishing third in the Pacific Classic Stakes (G1) as the 3-to-2 favorite but came back strongly in the winter of 2006 with consecutive victories in the Sunshine Millions Classic Stakes, the Santa Anita Handicap (G1), and, back on grass again, the restricted TVG Khaled Stakes.

LEAVE IT TO BEEZER—1993 b. g., Henbane—Blue Shocker, by Copelan. 75-22-11-13, $587,086. Although he had lost ten straight races, six-year-old Leave It to Beezer was claimed for $32,000 by trainer Scott Lake for Leo Gaspari Racing Stable on December 22, 1999. His third-place finish that day extended his losing streak to 11. Lake backed off on the gelding's training regimen, and Leave It to Beezer responded by winning nine of 15 starts, including the Salvator Mile Handicap (G3) at Monmouth Park and the Baltimore Breeders' Cup Handicap (G3) at Pimlico on the way to earning $350,830 in 2000.

McKAYMACKENNA—1989 b. m., Ends Well—Amuse, by Secretariat. 38-15-6-2, $581,322. R Kay Stable claimed McKaymackenna for $35,000 from a Belmont Park race in which she was beaten by more than 35 lengths. Sloppy tracks like the one she encountered at Belmont on May 16, 1992, were not to her liking; turf racing was her game. After trainer Gary Sciacca claimed her, she won seven grass stakes, including the 1993 Beaugay Handicap (G3) and Noble Damsel Stakes (G3).

PARKA—1958 br. g., *Arctic Prince—Manchon, by *Blenheim II. 93-27-14-18, $446,236. Bred by Marion duPont Scott and unraced at two, Parka was claimed for $10,000 in his 11th career start by Warren A. "Jimmy" Croll Jr. for client Rachel Carpenter. Parka won that Atlantic City Race Course race by a head, and Croll entered him in a $13,000 claimer 15 days later. He won that race by eight lengths and never raced in a claimer again. He was 1965 champion grass horse off victories in the Bougainvillea Handicap at Hialeah Park, the Kelly-Olympic and United Nations Handicaps at Atlantic City, and Aqueduct's Long Island Handicap in his final career start.

PEAT MOSS—1975 b. g., *Herbager—Moss, by Round Table. 55-15-7-9, $635,517. A little more than one year after winning a $10,000 claimer, Claiborne Farm-bred Peat Moss came within a head of upsetting John Henry in the 1981 Jockey Club Gold Cup (G1). Owned and trained by Murray Garren, Peat Moss loved to go a distance, winning the 1980 Display Handicap (G3) at 2¼ miles and the 1980 and '81 Kelso Handicap at two miles.

PORT CONWAY LANE—1969 gr. h., Bold Commander—*Grey Taffety, by Grey Sovereign. 242-52-39-36, $431,593. Port Conway Lane spent most of his lengthy career in claimers, although he started his career in allowance and stakes races, including a second-place finish in the 1971 Marlboro Nursery Stakes. He won Pimlico Race Course's City of Baltimore Handicap twice, in 1974 and '75, as well as Bowie Race Course's '74 Bowie Handicap and '75 Terrapin Handicap. By the end of 1976, however, he was racing principally in claimers and continued to do so through '83.

***PRINCEQUILLO**—1940 b. h., by Prince Rose—*Cosquilla, by *Papyrus. 33-12-5-7, $96,550. Exported from England in 1941, *Princequillo was offered for a $2,500 claiming price by owner Anthony Pelleteri on August 20, 1942. Taking him for Boone Hall Stable was Horatio Luro, who would develop *Princequillo into a multiple stakes winner during World War II. At Claiborne Farm, he proved to be an outstanding stallion, leading the general sire list in 1957 and '58 and topping the broodmare sire list eight times in North America and once in England.

SEABISCUIT—1933 b. h., Hard Tack—Swing On, by Whisk Broom II. 89-33-15-13, $437,730. Long before he became a top handicap horse, Seabiscuit lost the first 17 races of his career, including three defeats in $2,500 claimers and a loss in a $4,000 claimer at Havre de Grace in April 1935. Nobody took him, and later Wheatley Stable sold him to Charles Howard. Under the care of Racing Hall of Fame trainer Tom Smith, Seabiscuit went on to spectacular success, including a seven-stakes win streak in 1937, when he was champion handicap horse. The following year, he was voted Horse of the Year and handicap champion.

STYMIE—1941 ch. h., Equestrian—Stop Watch, by On Watch. 131-35-33-28, $918,485. Taken in his third lifetime start for $1,500 by Hirsch Jacobs, Stymie became the richest Thoroughbred of all time by his retirement in 1949, a record that only lasted until Citation moved past him in 1950. In his prime from ages four through seven, he won 28 of 69 starts, including the Saratoga Cup Stakes and the Gallant Fox, Metropolitan, Grey Lag, Aqueduct, and Sussex Handicaps twice each.

TIMELY WRITER—1979 b., c., Staff Writer—Timely Roman, by Sette Bello. 15-9-1-2, $605,491. A $13,000 yearling purchase owned by Peter and Francis Martin and trained by Dominic Imprescia, Timely Writer made his debut with an eight-length victory in a $30,000 maiden claimer at Monmouth Park. He subsequently won Saratoga Race Course's Hopeful Stakes (G1) and the Champagne Stakes (G1) at Belmont Park, earning him co-highweight with Eclipse Award champion Deputy Minister on the 1981 Experimental Free Handicap. At three, he won the Flamingo Stakes (G1) and Florida Derby (G1), but surgery for an intestinal blockage knocked him out of the Triple Crown races. He returned in the fall but sustained a fatal breakdown in the Jockey Club Gold Cup (G1).

VIDEOGENIC—1982 b. m., Caucasus—Video Babe, by T.V. Commercial. 73-20-9-10, $1,154,360. Trainer Gasper Moschera convinced owner Albert Davis to claim Videogenic for $100,000 on May 24, 1985. She was not much to look at, but she could run, winning 11 stakes races after the claim, including the 1985 Ladies Handicap (G1) at Aqueduct and the 1986 Santa Ana Handicap (G1) at Santa Anita Park. She won more than $1-million for Davis on the racetrack and was sold as a broodmare prospect for $625,000 at the 1988 Keeneland November breeding stock sale.

RACETRACKS

Racetracks of North America

Arizona

Apache County Fair

Location: 825 W. 4th St. N., Box 357, Saint Johns, Az. 85936-0357
Phone: (928) 337-4469
Year Founded: 1954
Abbreviation: SJ

Ownership

Apache County

Officers

President: Monty Long
General Manager: Herman Mineer
Director of Racing: Herman Mineer
Director of Marketing: Herman Mineer
Director of Publicity: Herman Mineer
Track Photographer: Double B Photography
Track Superintendent: Herman Mineer

Racing Dates

2005: September 17-September 25, 4 days
2006: September 16-September 24, 4 days
2007: September 15-September 23, 4 days

Attendance

Average Daily Recent Meeting: 550, 2005
Total Attendance Recent Meeting: 2,200, 2005

Leaders

Recent Meeting, Leading Jockey: Rick J. Oliver, 3, 2005; Terry Lee Gard, 3, 2005
Recent Meeting, Leading Trainer: Wiley Aker, 2, 2005; Ceasar J. Lopez, 2, 2005

Fastest Times of 2005 (Dirt)

4 furlongs: Ex Pirate, :45, September 25, 2005; Stranger Among Us, :45, September 24, 2005
5½ furlongs: Gold Fevers Gift, 1:07, September 24, 2005
6 furlongs: Frankie Grande, 1:12.40, September 25, 2005
6½ furlongs: Realignment, 1:19.40, September 18, 2005
7 furlongs: Lord of the Sun, 1:24.40, September 18, 2005
1 mile: King Vic, 1:41.80, September 17, 2005

Cochise County Fair

Location: 3677 N. Leslie Canyon Rd., Douglas, Az. 85607-6304
Phone: (520) 364-3819
Fax: (520) 364-1175
E-Mail: cochisefair@theriver.com
Year Founded: 1924
Abbreviation: DG

Ownership

Cochise County Fair Association

Officers

Chairman: Bob Ford
President: Nick Forsythe
General Manager: Karen Strongin
Director of Racing: Geoffrey E. Gonsher
Racing Secretary: Doreen Rawls
Treasurer: Dennis McAvoy
Director of Mutuels: Jerry Doolittle
Vice President: Howard Henderson
Director of Publicity: Howard Henderson
Stewards: Floyd Campbell, Melanie Campbell
Track Announcer: Jim Collins
Track Photographer: Double B Photography
Asst. Racing Secretary: Dodie Rawls
Horsemen's Bookkeeper: Connie Haggard

Racing Dates

2005: April 16-April 24, 4 days
2006: April 8-April 23, 4 days

Attendance

Average Daily Recent Meeting: 1,225, 2005
Total Attendance Recent Meeting: 4,900, 2005

Handle

Average On-Track Recent Meeting: $29,119, 2005
Total On-Track Recent Meeting: $116,475, 2005

Leaders

Recent Meeting, Leading Jockey: Stephen Michael Karr, 2, 2005; Jess Chance, 2, 2005; Alfredo Torres, 3, 2006

Fastest Times of 2005 (Dirt)

a3 furlongs: Brite Nite, :37.80, April 23, 2005
5½ furlongs: Areallyniceguy, 1:06.80, April 16, 2005
6 furlongs: A J Dustdevil, 1:14.20, April 24, 2005
7 furlongs: Potri Burn (Arg), 1:26.60, April 17, 2005
1 mile: Honest Ridge, 1:43.40, April 23, 2005
1m 70 yds: Dyna King, 1:46.40, April 24, 2005

Coconino County Fair

Location: HC 39 Box 3A, Flagstaff, Az. 86001
Phone: (928) 774-5139
Fax: (928) 774-2572
Website: *www.co.coconino.az.us/parks*
E-Mail: parks2@co.coconino.az.us
Year Founded: 1954
Abbreviation: Flg
Acreage: 400
Number of Stalls: 320
Seating Capacity: 3,500

Ownership

Coconino County Parks and Recreation

Officers

General Manager: Linda Kellogg
Racing Secretary: Jim Davis
Director of Operations: Linda Kellogg
Director of Finance: Kelly Burkhart
Director of Marketing: Jennifer Hartin
Director of Mutuels: Jerry Doolittle
Stewards: Robert Clink, Rita Fresquez, Violet Smith
Track Announcer: Craig Willis
Track Photographer: Double B Photography
Track Superintendent: Dave Stewart

Racing Dates

2005: July 1-4, 4 days
2006: June 30-July 3, 4 days

Track Layout

Main Circumference: 5 furlongs
Main Width: 75 Feet

Fastest Times of 2005 (Dirt)

a3 furlongs: Twilight Career, :40, July 3, 2005
5½ furlongs: Step Outside, 1:08.80, July 1, 2005
6 furlongs: Buck's Shar, 1:14.20, July 1, 2005
7 furlongs: Realignment, 1:27.40, July 1, 2005
1 mile: King Vic, 1:44.20, July 4, 2005

Gila County Fair

Location: P.O. Box 2193, Globe, Az. 85502-2193
Phone: (928) 425-0348
E-Mail: flivingood@cybertrails.com
Abbreviation: GCF

Officers

Chairman: Floyd Livingood

Racing Dates

2005: October 1-October 9, 4 days
2006: September 30-October 8, 4 days

Leaders

Recent Meeting, Leading Jockey: Jess Chance, 3, 2005; Don Lee French, 3, 2005
Recent Meeting, Leading Trainer: Robert M. Pledge, 2, 2005; Sandra Ehret, 2, 2005

Fastest Times of 2005 (Dirt)

3 furlongs: Aledo Cougar, :34.80, October 1, 2005; Northern Morning, :34.80, October 8, 2005
5 furlongs: Gold Fevers Gift, 1:00.60, October 9, 2005
5½ furlongs: Jazzy Man, 1:07.40, October 1, 2005; Lucky Mussell, 1:07.40, October 8, 2005; Natural Cat, 1:07.40, October 1, 2005; Occupied, 1:07.40, October 8, 2005
6 furlongs: Joggy Told, 1:13.60, October 8, 2005
7 furlongs: Nintyfiver, 1:28.80, October 8, 2005
1 1/16 miles: Slick Dude, 1:49.80, October 9, 2005

Graham County Fair

Location: 527 E. Armory Rd., Safford, Az. 85546-2231
Phone: (928) 428-7180
Fax: (928) 348-0023
E-Mail: cfaunce@graham.az.gov
Year Founded: 1965
Abbreviation: Saf
Acreage: 220

Officers

President: Phil Curtis
General Manager: Casey Faunce
Director of Racing: Casey Faunce
Racing Secretary: Jim Collins
Secretary: Jessie Hines
Director of Operations: Larry Jensen
Director of Mutuels: Jerome Doolittle
Vice President: Jon Haralson
Horsemen's Liaison: Robert Pledge
Stewards: Robert Clink, Roy Snedigar, Violet Smith
Track Announcer: Red Davis
Track Photographer: Double D
Track Superintendent: Jim Gutierrez

Racing Dates

2005: April 2-April 10, 4 days
2006: March 25-April 2, 4 days

Attendance

Average Daily Recent Meeting: 1,725, 2005
Total Attendance Recent Meeting: 6,900, 2005

Handle

Average On-Track Recent Meeting: $31,835, 2005
Total On-Track Recent Meeting: $127,338, 2005

Leaders

Recent Meeting, Leading Jockey: Jess Chance, 2, 2005; Anna M. Barrio, 2, 2005
Recent Meeting, Leading Trainer: Lowell N. Bunyard, 2, 2005

Track Records, Main Dirt

4 furlongs: Red Spark, :44.60, March 25, 2006
6 furlongs: Tooties Teddy, 1:12.40, March 31, 2002
7 furlongs: Mr. Machine, 1:26, March 26, 2006
1 mile: Mudslide, 1:41.80, April 2, 2006
1 1/16 miles: Cop Out, 1:46.60, March 31, 2001
Other: 3 furlongs, Aledo Cougar, :33.20, April 2, 2006

Fastest Times of 2005 (Dirt)

4 furlongs: Brite Nite, :46.40, April 9, 2005
5½ furlongs: Muy Pronto, 1:08, April 9, 2005; Pickled Bay, 1:08, April 3, 2005
6 furlongs: White Rino, 1:14, April 3, 2005
7 furlongs: Tooties Teddy, 1:26.40, April 2, 2005
1 mile: Chehalis, 1:43.60, April 10, 2005

Greenlee County Fair

Location: 1258 Fairgrounds Rd., P.O. Box 123, Duncan, Az. 85534-0123
Phone: (928) 359-2032
Fax: (928) 359-2721
E-Mail: fairnracing@co.greenlee.az.us
Abbreviation: Dun

Ownership

Greenlee County

Officers

Chairman: Mike Looby
Director of Racing: Douglas D. Barlow
Racing Secretary: James Collins
Secretary: Karla Ellis
Director of Mutuels: Jerry Doolittle
Stewards: Floyd Campbell, Melanie Posey, Violet Smith
Track Announcer: James Collins
Track Photographer: Double B Photography
Asst. Racing Secretary: Dodie Rawls
Horsemen's Bookkeeper: Connie Haggard

Racing Dates

2005: March 12-March 20, 4 days
2006: March 11-March 19, 4 days

Attendance

Average Daily Recent Meeting: 419, 2005
Total Attendance Recent Meeting: 1,675, 2005

Handle

Average On-Track Recent Meeting: $21,512, 2005
Total On-Track Recent Meeting: $86,048, 2005

Leaders

Recent Meeting, Leading Jockey: Steve Hancock, 2, 2005; Jess Chance, 2, 2005; Anna M. Barrio, 2, 2005

Fastest Times of 2005 (Dirt)

5 furlongs: Brite Nite, 1:01.80, March 19, 2005
5½ furlongs: J J Thedotcom Man, 1:06.60, March 20, 2005
a6 furlongs: Get Off the Phone, 1:12.60, March 19, 2005
7 furlongs: Tooties Teddy, 1:27.20, March 19, 2005

Mohave County Fair

Location: 2600 Fairgrounds Blvd., Kingman, Az. 86401-4169
Phone: (928) 753-2636
Fax: (928) 753-8383
Website: *www.mcfafairgrounds.org*
E-Mail: info@mcfafairgrounds.org
Abbreviation: MoF

Racing Dates

2005: May 14-May 22, 4 days
2006: May 13-May 21, 4 days

Attendance

Average Daily Recent Meeting: 663, 2005
Total Attendance Recent Meeting: 2,653, 2005

Handle

Average On-Track Recent Meeting: $26,703, 2005
Total On-Track Recent Meeting: $106,813, 2005

Leaders

Recent Meeting, Leading Jockey: Fernando Manuel Gamez, 3, 2005; Daniel W. Gutierrez, 3, 2006
Recent Meeting, Leading Owner: Lowell N. Bunyard, 2, 2005; Terry S. Roberts, 2, 2005

Fastest Times of 2005 (Dirt)

4 furlongs: C Bs Deposit, :45.60, May 21, 2005
5½ furlongs: Mountain Falls, 1:07, May 15, 2005
6 furlongs: Magnum Mac, 1:13, May 15, 2005
7 furlongs: Summer Prince, 1:26.40, May 15, 2005
1 mile: Monroe Doctrine (Ire), 1:41.60, May 14, 2005
1⅛ miles: Coloreado (Chi), 1:53, May 22, 2005

Rillito Park

Location: 4502 N. 1st Ave., P.O. Box 65132, Tucson, Az. 85728
Phone: (520) 293-5011
Fax: (520) 887-6726
E-Mail: pawhite@yahoo.com
Year Founded: 1946
Dates of Inaugural Meeting: November 1, 1953
Abbreviation: Ril
Number of Stalls: 500
Seating Capacity: 2,500

Ownership

Pima County

Officers

Chairman: Steve Brody
President: Timothy Kelly
General Manager: Patricia White
Director of Racing: Patricia White
Racing Secretary: Josephine Stavers
Secretary/Treasurer: Patricia White
Director of Operations: Timothy Kelly
Director of Marketing: Jim Collins
Director of Mutuels: Patrick E. Kelly
Vice President: Patricia Shirley
Director of Publicity: Jim Collins
Horsemen's Liaison: Patricia Shirley
Steward: Robert Allison
Track Announcer: Jim Collins
Track Photographer: Coady Photography
Track Superintendent: Kevin Hancock
Horsemen's Bookkeeper: Mickey Ybarra
Security: Lisa Pina

Racing Dates

2005: January 22-March 6, 13 days
2006: January 21-March 5, 13 days

Track Layout

Main Circumference: 5 furlongs
Main Track Chute: 6 furlongs and 1¼ miles
Main Width: 80 feet
Main Length of Stretch: 660 feet

Attendance

Average Daily Recent Meeting: 4,107, 2005; 4,508, 2006
Total Attendance Recent Meeting: 53,388, 2005; 58,605, 2006
Lowest Single-Day Record: 1,782, February 8, 2003

Handle

Average On-Track Recent Meeting: $82,291, 2005; $84,158, 2006
Total On-Track Recent Meeting: $1,069,781, 2005; $1,094,059, 2006
Highest Single-Day On-Track Record Recent Meet: $117,537, March 6, 2005; $136,712, March 5, 2006

Leaders

Recent Meeting, Leading Jockey: Fernando Manuel Gamez, 15, 2005; Alfredo Torres, 11, 2006
Recent Meeting, Leading Trainer: Ceasar J. Lopez, 2005; L. Wayne Brasher, 6, 2006
Recent Meeting, Leading Horse: Onceinafullmoon, 4, 2005; Shoot the Loot, 3, 2006

Track Records, Main Dirt

4 furlongs: Blushing God, :44.40, February 3, 2001
5½ furlongs: Cornino Bay, 1:04.60, February 4, 2001
6 furlongs: Turf's Bounty, 1:10⅕, November 25, 1989
6½ furlongs: Club Champ, 1:15.80, February 18, 1996
7 furlongs: Stalk the Table, 1:22.60, January 29, 1994
Other: 3 furlongs, Alice Be Gay, :36, March 2, 1974; 3½ furlongs, Slow Dancing, :40⅗, March 22, 1981; a6 furlongs, Loomis Trail, 1:20, February 15, 2000

Notable Events

Rillito Park Weiner Cup

Fastest Times of 2005 (Dirt)

4 furlongs: Stranger Among Us, :45.20, February 6, 2005; Tobin's Clue, :45.20, February 26, 2005
5½ furlongs: From A to Z, 1:05, February 6, 2005
6 furlongs: Areallyniceguy, 1:11, February 27, 2005
6½ furlongs: Awesome Prospect, 1:19, February 5, 2005
7 furlongs: Onceinafullmoon, 1:23.60, February 27, 2005
1¹⁄₁₆ miles: Cabreo, 1:48, March 6, 2005

Santa Cruz County Fair

Location: 3142 S. Highway 83, P.O. Box 85, Sonoita, Az. 85637-0085
Phone: (520) 455-5553
Fax: (520) 455-5330
Website: *www.sonoitafairgrounds.com*
E-Mail: sccfra@theriver.com
Abbreviation: Son
Acreage: 36.5
Number of Stalls: 180
Seating Capacity: 2,200

Officers

Chairman: Burton S. Kruglick
President: John Titus
General Manager: Tina Letarte
Director of Racing: Geoffrey Gonsher
Racing Secretary: James Collins
Secretary: Charlie Hadden
Treasurer: Tom Boisvert
Director of Mutuels: Jerry Doolittle
Vice President: Ray Schock
Director of Publicity: Scott McDaniel
Stewards: Melanie Posey, Violet Smith
Track Announcer: James Collins
Track Photographer: Double B Photography
Track Superintendent: Harold Hager

Racing Dates

2005: April 30-May 8, 4 days
2006: April 29-May 7, 4 days

Track Layout

Main Circumference: 4 furlongs

Attendance

Average Daily Recent Meeting: 2,538, 2005
Total Attendance Recent Meeting: 10,150, 2005

Handle

Average On-Track Recent Meeting: $43,889, 2005
Total On-Track Recent Meeting: $175,557, 2005

Leaders

Recent Meeting, Leading Jockey: Anna M. Barrio, 4, 2005; Rob Scanlon, 3, 2006
Recent Meeting, Leading Trainer: Laurie Jones, 2, 2005, Laurie Jones, 2, 2006

Fastest Times of 2005 (Dirt)

5 furlongs: Semi Annual, :59.80, May 7, 2005
5½ furlongs: Pointed, 1:05.60, May 8, 2005
6 furlongs: Pointed, 1:11.60, April 30, 2005
7 furlongs: Saxmeamemo, 1:27.20, April 30, 2005
1¹⁄₁₆ miles: Chehalis, 1:49.80, May 8, 2005

Turf Paradise

A Phoenix tradition for a half-century, Turf Paradise has survived several ownership changes and a dramatic reshaping of wagering and gaming options in Arizona to remain a vital part of the winter racing scene. Turf Paradise was the vision of businessman Walter Cluer, who purchased 1,400 acres of desert land in 1954 and transformed it into a racetrack, which opened its doors on January 7, 1956. Cluer owned the track until 1980. The track's next two owners, Herb Owens and Robert Walker, added a turf course and off-track betting, respectively. Hollywood Park purchased the track in 1994 and weathered an influx of Native American casino gambling in Arizona before selling the track to Phoenix developer Jerry Simms in June 2000. In November 2002, Arizona voters rejected slot machines at the state's racetracks and approved more machines at Native American casinos.

Location: 1501 W. Bell Rd., Phoenix, Az. 85023-3411
Phone: (602) 942-1101
Fax: (602) 942-8659
Website: *www.turfparadise.com*
E-Mail: turf@turfparadise.net
Year Founded: 1955
Dates of Inaugural Meeting: January 7, 1956
Abbreviation: TuP
Acreage: 1,400
Number of Stalls: 1,700
Seating Capacity: 7,284

Ownership

Jerry Simms

Officers

General Manager: Eugene Joyce
Director of Racing: Shawn Swartz
Racing Secretary: Shawn Swartz
Director of Marketing: Vincent Francia
Director of Mutuels: Ray Land
Vice President: Dave Johnson
Director of Publicity: Vincent Francia
Director of Sales: Myrah Aiello
Director of Simulcasting: Shilo Demoney
Horsemen's Liaison: Bucky Huff
Steward: Hank Mills
Track Announcer: Luke Kruytbosch
Track Photographer: Coady Photography
Track Superintendent: Terry Brown
Security: Gordon French

Racing Dates

2005: October 1, 2004-May 22, 2005, 160 days
2006: September 30, 2005-May 21, 2006, 166 days
2007: October 6, 2006-May 6, 2007, 156 days

Track Layout

Main Circumference: 1 mile
Main Track Chute: 3 furlongs and 6$^1/_2$ furlongs
Main Width: Homestretch: 80 feet; Backstretch: 70 feet; Turns: 100 feet
Main Length of Stretch: 990 feet
Main Turf Circumference: 7 furlongs
Main Turf Chute: $^1/_8$ mile
Main Turf Width: 73 feet
Main Turf Length of Stretch: 999 feet

Attendance

Average Daily Recent Meeting: 2,128, 2004/2005; 2,154, 2005/2006
Highest Single-Day Record: 16,000 est., March 18, 1984
Total Attendance Recent Meeting: 340,473, 2004/2005; 357,566, 2005/2006

Handle

Average All Sources Recent Meeting: $1,320,169, 2004/2005; $1,403,735, 2005/2006
Average On-Track Recent Meeting: $96,048, 2004/2005; $95,546, 2005/2006
Total All Sources Recent Meeting: $211,227,066, 2004/2005; $233,019,960, 2005/2006
Total On-Track Recent Meeting: $15,367,663, 2004/2005; $15,860,655, 2005/2006

Mutuel Records

Highest Win: $287.60, Gaye Rest, May 23, 1974
Highest Exacta: $17,092.20, May 8, 1988
Highest Trifecta: $42,774, October 18, 1987
Highest Daily Double: $5,355, April 24, 1985
Highest Pick 6: $137,372, March 3, 1986

Leaders

Career, Leading Jockey by Titles: Sam Powell, 16
Career, Leading Owner by Titles: Dennis Weir, 10
Career, Leading Trainer by Titles: Richard Hazelton, 27
Recent Meeting, Leading Jockey: Wilson Omar Diequez, 127, 2004/2005; Glenn W. Corbett, 117, 2005/2006
Recent Meeting, Leading Owner: Buddy Lee Racing Stable, 46, 2004/2005
Recent Meeting, Leading Trainer: Troy Bainum, 68, 2004/2005; Troy Bainum, 68, 2005/2006
Recent Meeting, Leading Horse: Frostmark, 7, 2005/2006; Of Course, 7, 2005/2006

Records

Single-Day Jockey Wins: Marty Wentz, 7; Ray York, 7
Single Meet, Leading Jockey by Wins: Pat Steinberg, 225
Single Meet, Leading Trainer by Wins: Bart Hone, 88

Track Records, Main Dirt

4 furlongs: Beau Madison, :45, March 30, 1957
4$^1/_2$ furlongs: Jazz Hot, :50.20, April 18, 1995
5 furlongs: Zip Pocket, :55$^2/_5$, April 22, 1967
5$^1/_2$ furlongs: Plenty Zloty, 1:01.10, April 18, 1995
6 furlongs: G Malleah, 1:06.60, April 8, 1995
6$^1/_2$ furlongs: G Malleah, 1:13.80, December 3, 1994
7 furlongs: Free Duty, 1:26$^1/_5$, January 23, 1985
1 mile: Mr. Pappion, 1:33.20, January 30, 1993
1$^1/_{16}$ miles: Down the Isle, 1:39$^1/_5$, February 11, 1987
1$^1/_8$ miles: Our Forbes, 1:47.60, November 29, 1996
1$^3/_{16}$ miles: Erin Glen, 1:55$^3/_5$, January 15, 1967
1$^1/_4$ miles: Truly a Pleasure, 2:01.40, March 26, 1995
1$^3/_8$ miles: Bloom n Character, 2:15$^2/_5$, April 12, 1980
1$^1/_2$ miles: Spinney, 2:29$^2/_5$, April 30, 1961
1$^5/_8$ miles: Masked Rider, 2:44.40, February 10, 2002
1$^3/_4$ miles: Arsenal, 2:55$^2/_5$, February 7, 1971
2 miles: Vermejo, 3:24, April 20, 1969
Other: 2 furlongs, Wandering Boy, :21$^1/_5$, December 5, 1965; 3 furlongs, Never Shamed, :31.60, April 1, 1996

Track Records, Main Turf

4$^1/_2$ furlongs: Dan's Groovy, :49.26, April 13, 2003
5 furlongs: Honor the Hero, :56.20, February 5, 1995; Amersham, :56.29, February 2, 2002
7 furlongs: Lord Pleasant, 1:22.80, October 12, 1992
7$^1/_2$ furlongs: Briartic Gold, 1:28.18, April 13, 2003
1 mile: Prose (Ire), 1:34.83, March 27, 2001
1$^1/_{16}$ miles: Caesour, 1:40.40, February 5, 1995
1$^1/_8$ miles: Narghile, 1:48, February 1, 1987
1$^3/_8$ miles: Free Corona, 2:15.17, April 27, 2003
1$^1/_2$ miles: Senator McGuire, 2:29$^3/_5$, May 22, 1988
Other: a5 furlongs, J. Zac, :57.80, February 18, 1990; a7 furlongs, Faro, 1:25$^1/_5$, November 23, 1986; a7$^1/_2$ furlongs, Aza, 1:29.42, December 5, 2005; a1 mile, Night Dash, 1:36.43, December 7, 2005; a1$^1/_{16}$ miles, Western Act, 1:42.93, December 31, 2005; a1$^1/_8$ miles, Wailea Warrior, 1:50.89, December 11, 2005; a1$^3/_8$ miles, Doctor Trotter, 2:16.80, April 18, 1998; a1$^1/_2$ miles, Estonia, 2:34, April 5, 1997; a1$^7/_8$ miles, Amapour, 3:15$^1/_5$, May 18, 1986; 1$^7/_8$ miles, Shadows Fall, 3:09$^2/_5$, May 17, 1987

Principal Races

Turf Paradise Derby, Phoenix Gold Cup H., Arizona Oaks, Turf Paradise H.

Fastest Times of 2005 (Dirt)

2 furlongs: Snowbound Halo, :21.80, April 3, 2005
4$^1/_2$ furlongs: Friendship Avenue, :50.43, February 21, 2005
5 furlongs: White Rino, :56.27, December 7, 2005
5$^1/_2$ furlongs: Lil Easy, 1:02.32, December 3, 2005
6 furlongs: Flying Supercon, 1:07.45, February 26, 2005
6$^1/_2$ furlongs: Cocoa Latte, 1:14.32, November 22, 2005
a6$^1/_2$ furlongs: Duddly Doo Run, 1:16.36, March 1, 2005
1 mile: Hero's Pleasure, 1:34.75, February 21, 2005
1$^1/_{16}$ miles: Tangled Up In Blue (Ire), 1:42.73, May 22, 2005
1$^1/_8$ miles: Hero's Pleasure, 1:50.86, March 25, 2005
1$^1/_4$ miles: Hammerin, 2:07.52, February 11, 2005
1$^5/_8$ miles: Hammerin, 2:44.82, March 1, 2005

Fastest Times of 2005 (Turf)

4$^1/_2$ furlongs: King Justin, :49.74, May 21, 2005
a4$^1/_2$ furlongs: Auroraz, :50.77, December 3, 2005; Lill's Fame, :50.77, December 17, 2005
7$^1/_2$ furlongs: Heavenly Ransom, 1:29.15, November 12, 2005
a7$^1/_2$ furlongs: Aza, 1:29.42, December 5, 2005
1 mile: Super Highway (Brz), 1:35.53, May 15, 2005
a1 miles: Night Dash, 1:36.43, December 7, 2005
1$^1/_{16}$ miles: Cut of Music, 1:42.53, April 12, 2005
a1$^1/_{16}$ miles: Western Act, 1:42.93, December 31, 2005
1$^1/_8$ miles: Backonbabyside, 1:49.28, April 5, 2005
a1$^1/_8$ miles: Wailea Warrior, 1:50.89, December 11, 2005
1$^3/_8$ miles: J J Wantsthefront, 2:16.34, May 1, 2005
1$^1/_2$ miles: Mondeville (Fr), 2:33.16, March 7, 2005
1$^7/_8$ miles: Balustrade, 3:16.76, May 22, 2005

Yavapai Downs

The story of Yavapai Downs actually involves two

tracks. Located in Arizona's Prescott Valley region, Yavapai opened its doors in 2001, replacing Prescott Downs, a half-mile oval that had been in operation since 1913. While Prescott was known for its rustic atmosphere and occasionally wild bullring racing, Yavapai quickly established a reputation as a more refined track, with modern amenities and a one-mile oval. The $23-million facility was completed in 13 months, almost one year ahead of schedule, allowing it to open in May 2001. The physical plant features a three-story clubhouse and grandstand with Arizona's Mingus Mountains as a backdrop. The backstretch offers stabling for 1,200 horses. During its first five meets, average purses exceeded $30,000 per day. Prescott, Arizona's summer racing home for the better part of nine decades, was the site of Racing Hall of Fame jockey Pat Day's first victory.

Location: 10401 Highway 89A, P.O. Box 26557, Prescott Valley, Az. 86312-6557
Phone: (928) 775-8000
Fax: (928) 445-0408
Website: *www.yavapaidownsatpv.com*
Year Founded: 2001
Dates of Inaugural Meeting: May 26, 2001
Abbreviation: Yav
Acreage: 200
Number of Stalls: 1,300
Seating Capacity: 5,000

Ownership

Yavapai County Fair Association

Officers

President: Bob Gray
General Manager: James Grundy
Director of Racing: Hank Demoney
Racing Secretary: Hank Demoney
Secretary: James Pickering
Treasurer: Jim Pickering
Director of Operations: Gary Spiker
Director of Admissions: Janet Howard
Director of Finance: Sharon Fischer
Director of Marketing: James Grundy
Director of Mutuels: Bob Chisholm
Vice President: Jean Knight
Director of Publicity: Sharon Fischer
Director of Sales: James Grundy
Director of Simulcasting: Don Rogers
Track Announcer: Greg Wry
Track Photographer: Coady Photography
Track Superintendent: Bubba French

Racing Dates

2005: May 28-September 6, 60 days
2006: May 27-September 5, 60 days

Track Layout

Main Circumference: 1 mile
Main Track Chute: 2 furlongs and 6 furlongs
Main Width: 75 feet
Main Length of Stretch: 1,020 feet

Leaders

Recent Meeting, Leading Jockey: Miguel Luis Gaeta Hernandez, 68, 2005
Recent Meeting, Leading Trainer: Justin Evans, 35, 2005
Recent Meeting, Leading Horse: Eddienojado, 4, 2005; I've Decided, 4, 2005; Mint Royale, 4, 2005

Track Records, Main Dirt

4½ furlongs: River Adventure (Brz), :49.80, August 9, 2005
5 furlongs: Canyon's Wildcat, :56.40, August 9, 2004
5½ furlongs: At Sunrise, 1:02.20, August 8, 2005
6 furlongs: Miss Pixie, 1:08.12, August 24, 2002
1 mile: Suspicious Minds, 1:35, June 21, 2005
1 1/16 miles: Gusto Forzado, 1:42.63, June 24, 2002
1⅛ miles: Moonray, 1:49.40, June 25, 2002
1¼ miles: Cajun Bound, 2:03.20, August 18, 2003

Principal Races

Yavapai Downs Thoroughbred Futurity, Yavapai H., Mile Hi H., Yavapai Classic H.

Interesting Facts

Previous Names and Dates: Prescott Downs

Fastest Times of 2005 (Dirt)

4½ furlongs: Bobaway, :49.80, September 6, 2005; River Adventure (Brz), :49.80, August 9, 2005
5 furlongs: White Rino, :56.60, August 2, 2005
5½ furlongs: At Sunrise, 1:02.20, August 8, 2005; Rapid Dance, 1:02.20, August 21, 2005
6 furlongs: Lute Oatson, 1:08.20, August 29, 2005
1 mile: Suspicious Minds, 1:35, June 21, 2005
1 1/16 miles: Crazy Larrys, 1:43.40, August 8, 2005

Arkansas

Oaklawn Park

Arkansas's leading tourist attraction is Oaklawn Park in the resort community of Hot Springs. The track first opened in 1905 but closed two years later due to political problems in the state. The track reopened in 1916 under the ownership of Louis Cella, whose great-nephew, Charles Cella, is the track's current president and board chairman. Oaklawn, which offers live racing from January to mid-April, attracts runners from across the United States for its Racing Festival of the South. The festival features at least one stakes race each day on the final eight days of the meet, ending with the $500,000 Arkansas Derby (G2), which was first run in 1936. Other major races include the Apple Blossom Handicap (G1) for fillies and mares and the $500,000-guaranteed Oaklawn Handicap (G2) for older horses. In 2004, Oaklawn Park and the Cella family received the Eclipse Award of Merit for their contributions to racing.

Location: 2705 Central Ave., Hot Springs, Ar. 71901-7515
Phone: (501) 623-4411
Phone: (800) 625-5296
Website: *www.oaklawn.com*
E-Mail: winning@oaklawn.com
Year Founded: 1904
Dates of Inaugural Meeting: February 24, 1905
Abbreviation: OP
Acreage: 120
Number of Stalls: 1,600
Seating Capacity: 26,200

Officers

Chairman: Charles J. Cella
President: Charles J. Cella
General Manager: R. Eric Jackson
Racing Secretary: Patrick J. Pope
Treasurer: William L. Cravens
Director of Operations: John Hopkins
Director of Marketing: Kim Baron
Director of Mutuels: Bobby Geiger
Director of Publicity: Terry Wallace
Director of Simulcasting: Bobby Geiger
Horsemen's Liaison: Deborah Keene
Stewards: Johnnie Johnson, Larry Snyder, Gary Wilfert
Track Announcer: Terry Wallace
Track Photographer: Coady Photography
Track Superintendent: Steve Breckling

Racing Dates

2005: January 21-April 16, 55 days
2006: January 20-April 15, 53 days

Track Layout

Main Circumference: 1 mile
Main Track Chute: 6 furlongs
Main Width: Straightaways: 70 feet; Turns: 80 feet
Main Length of Stretch: 1,155 feet

Attendance
Average Daily Recent Meeting: 12,842, 2005; 12,161, 2006
Highest Single-Day Record: 71,203, April 19, 1986
Record Daily Average for Single Meet: 23,271, 1983
Highest Single-Meet Record: 1,419,650, 1984
Total Attendance Recent Meeting: 706,328, 2005; 644,535, 2006

Handle
Average All Sources Recent Meeting: $4,009,669, 2005; $4,501,416, 2006
Average On-Track Recent Meeting: $1,437,255, 2005; $1,394,990, 2006
Single-Day Total Handle All Sources: $15,133,537, April 15, 2000
Total All Sources Recent Meeting: $220,531,775, 2005; $238,575,044, 2006
Total On-Track Recent Meeting: $79,049,041, 2005; $73,934,490, 2006
Record Average All Sources Single Meet: $5,189,245, 2002
Highest Single-Day Record Recent Meet: $13,736,650, April 16, 2005; $14,700,492, April 15, 2006

Mutuel Records
Highest Win: $350.80, Phaltup, March 7, 1950
Highest Exacta: $3,915.20, April 8, 1994
Highest Trifecta: $17,925.40, March 19, 2005
Highest Daily Double: $6,902, March 30, 1971
Highest Pick 3: $36,686.80, February 17, 1996
Highest Pick 6: $818,693.40, February 15, 1995

Leaders
Career, Leading Jockey by Titles: Pat Day, 12
Career, Leading Trainer by Titles: Henry Forest, 11
Recent Meeting, Leading Jockey: Jeremy Rose, 48, 2005; John Jacinto, 45, 2006
Recent Meeting, Leading Owner: Michael Gill, 17, 2005; Gary Owens, 17, 2005; Ken Murphy Thoroughbreds Ltd., 11, 2006
Recent Meeting, Leading Trainer: Cole Norman, 62, 2005; Cole Norman, 41, 2006
Recent Meeting, Leading Horse: Texas Best, 4, 2006; Couldudance, 4, 2006; No Better Chance, 4, 2006

Records
Single-Day Jockey Wins: Larry Snyder, 6, April 1, 1969; Pat Day, 6, February 17, 1986; Pat Day, 6, March 11, 1993; Pat Day, 6, February 20, 1995
Single Meet, Leading Jockey by Wins: Pat Day, 137, 1986
Single Meet, Leading Trainer by Wins: Cole Norman, 62, 2005

Track Records, Main Dirt
4 furlongs: Crimson Saint, :44⁴⁄₅, April 1, 1971
4½ furlongs: Montague, :53, March 29, 1937
5 furlongs: Miss Brendy, :57³⁄₅, February 22, 1966
5½ furlongs: Sis Pleasure Fager, 1:02³⁄₅, February 15, 1984
6 furlongs: Karen's Tom, 1:07⁴⁄₅, April 16, 1990
1 mile: Whitebrush, 1:34²⁄₅, March 10, 1984
1m 70 yds: Win Stat, 1:38²⁄₅, March 7, 1984
1¹⁄₁₆ miles: Heatherten, 1:40¹⁄₅, April 18, 1984; Hang On Slewpy, 1:40¹⁄₅, April 20, 1991
1⅛ miles: Snow Chief, 1:46³⁄₅, April 17, 1987
1³⁄₁₆ miles: Brassy, 1:57²⁄₅, March 29, 1952
1¼ miles: Out of Fire, 2:04, March 31, 1937
1⅜ miles: Dapper, 2:31³⁄₅, March 30, 1957
1½ miles: Dapper, 2:31³⁄₅, March 30, 1957
1¾ miles: Flag Carrier, 2:58, April 18, 1987
Other: 3 furlongs, Gay Whip, :33²⁄₅, March 7, 1967; Hempen's Song, :33²⁄₅, February 16, 1971; 2m 70 yds, Turntable, 3:34, March 27, 1942

Principal Races
Apple Blossom H. (G1), Arkansas Derby (G2), Azeri Breeders' Cup S. (G3), Rebel S. (G3), Count Fleet Sprint H. (G3)

Fastest Times of 2005 (Dirt)
5½ furlongs: Blazing Count, 1:03.73, April 2, 2005
6 furlongs: Top Commander, 1:08.74, April 14, 2005
1 mile: Free Thinking, 1:37.61, March 25, 2005
1¹⁄₁₆ miles: Mauk Four, 1:42.89, April 13, 2005
1⅛ miles: Afleet Alex, 1:48.80, April 16, 2005
1³⁄₁₆ miles: Boyum, 1:59.78, March 30, 2005
1¾ miles: Tubby Cat, 3:03.41, April 16, 2005

California

Bay Meadows Fair

Location: 2600 South Delaware St., P.O. Box 1027, San Mateo, Ca. 94403-1902
Phone: (650) 574-7223
Fax: (650) 574-3985
Website: *www.sanmateocountyfair.com*
Abbreviation: BMF
Number of Stalls: 900
Seating Capacity: 20,000

Ownership
San Mateo County Fair

Officers
President: Tony Clifford
General Manager: Chris Carpenter
Director of Racing: Chris Carpenter
Racing Secretary: Tom Doutrich
Secretary/Treasurer: Melanie Hildebrand
Director of Mutuels: Bryan Wayte
Vice President: Jack Olsen
Director of Publicity: Tom Ferrall
Director of Simulcasting: Kay Webb
Asst. Racing Secretary: C. Gregory Brent Jr.

Racing Dates
2005: August 10-August 25, 12 days
2006: August 9-August 24, 12 days

Track Layout
Main Circumference: 1 mile
Main Track Chute: 6 furlong and 1¼ mile
Main Width: Homestretch: 85 feet; Backstretch: 75 feet
Main Length of Stretch: 990 feet
Main Turf Circumference: 7 furlongs, 32 feet
Main Turf Width: 75 feet

Attendance
Average Daily Recent Meeting: 2,119, 2005
Total Attendance Recent Meeting: 25,428, 2005

Handle
Average All Sources Recent Meeting: $2,630,683, 2005
Average On-Track Recent Meeting: $581,129, 2005
Total All Sources Recent Meeting: $31,568,199, 2005
Total On-Track Recent Meeting: $6,973,546, 2005

Leaders
Recent Meeting, Leading Jockey: Russell Baze, 13, 2005
Recent Meeting, Leading Trainer: Art Sherman, 16, 2005

Fastest Times of 2005 (Dirt)
5 furlongs: Thayre Goes Money, :59.20, August 21, 2005
5½ furlongs: Somethinaboutlaura, 1:02.67, August 19, 2005
6 furlongs: Brand Name, 1:10.21, August 18, 2005
1 mile: Pronto One, 1:36.89, August 11, 2005
1¹⁄₁₆ miles: Copper Mist, 1:44.44, August 10, 2005

Fastest Times of 2005 (Turf)
5 furlongs: Yakima River, :57.58, August 14, 2005
7½ furlongs: Aizarunner, 1:29.88, August 11, 2005
1 mile: Shadow Raider, 1:36.78, August 14, 2005

Bay Meadows Race Course

Located 20 miles south of San Francisco in San Mateo, Bay Meadows Race Course was founded in 1934 by the innovative William P. Kyne, who helped to bring about the legalization of pari-mutuel wagering in California that year. At Bay Meadows, Kyne introduced the totalizator system, photo-finish camera, and the still-popular daily double wager. Bay Meadows also was the site of the first all-enclosed starting gate in America in 1939 and, on October 27, 1945, the destination point of the first equine air passenger when El Lobo, a Thoroughbred, was flown from Los Angeles to an airstrip adjacent to Bay Meadows. Bay Meadows was the only California racetrack allowed to operate during World War II as Kyne pledged all profits to various war relief projects. In 1951, Coaltown captured the Children's Hospital Handicap, another charity fund-raiser. Bay Meadows introduced the El Camino Real Derby (G3) in 1982 as a prep for the Kentucky Derby (G1), and 17 years later Charismatic finished second by a head in the race (to Cliquot) before winning the Derby and Preakness Stakes (G1). Magna Entertainment Corp. leased the track from 2001 through '04, and Bay Meadows Land Co., which owns the property, resumed operation of the facility in 2005.

Location: 2600 South Delaware St., P.O. Box 5050, San Mateo, Ca. 94402
Phone: (650) 574-7223
Fax: (925) 803-8168
Website: *www.baymeadows.com*
E-Mail: info@baymeadows.com
Year Founded: 1934
Dates of Inaugural Meeting: November 3, 1934
Abbreviation: BM
Acreage: 90
Number of Stalls: 900
Seating Capacity: 20,000

Ownership

Bay Meadows Land Co.

Officers

President: F. Jack Liebau
General Managers: Bernie Thurman, Mike Ziegler
Director of Racing: Richard J. Lewis
Racing Secretary: Tom Doutrich
Treasurer: Daniel Newman
Director of Mutuels: Bryan Wayte
Vice Presidents: Dyan Grealish, Mike Scalzo
Director of Publicity: Tom Ferrall
Director of Simulcasting: Kay Webb
Track Announcer: Tony Calo
Track Photographer: William Vassar
Track Superintendent: Robert Turman
Asst. Racing Secretaries: Linda Anderson, C. Gregory Brent Jr.
Security: Jerry Gonzalez
Promotions/Events: Robin McHargue

Racing Dates

2005: February 2-May 8, 72 days; August 26-October 16, 33 days
2006: May 10-June 18, 28 days; October 18-December 18, 44 days

Track Layout

Main Circumference: 1 mile
Main Track Chute: 6 furlongs and $1^1/_4$ miles
Main Width: Homestretch: 85 feet; Backstretch: 75 feet
Main Length of Stretch: 990 feet
Main Turf Circumference: 7 furlongs, 32 feet
Main Turf Width: 75 feet

Attendance

Average Daily Recent Meeting: 2,882, Winter/Spring 2005; 3,665, Summer/Fall 2005
Highest Single-Day Record: 29,300, April 17, 1948
Total Attendance Recent Meeting: 207,507, Winter/Spring 2005; 120,939, Summer/Fall 2005
Highest Single-Day Recent Meet: 8,314, October 1, 2005

Handle

Average All Sources Recent Meeting: $3,684,220, Winter/Spring 2005; $3,509,088, Summer/Fall 2005
Average On-Track Recent Meeting: $724,282, Winter/Spring 2005; $724,152, Summer/Fall 2005
Single-Day Total Handle All Sources: $8,660,396, November 6, 1999
Total All Sources Recent Meeting: $265,263,819, Winter/Spring 2005; $115,799,888, Summer/Fall 2005
Total On-Track Recent Meeting: $52,148,334, Winter/Spring 2005; $23,897,000, Summer/Fall 2005

Mutuel Records

Highest Win: $599.80
Highest Exacta: $2,108
Highest Daily Double: $5,231
Highest Pick 6: $1,132,466
Highest Other Exotics: $1,298.80, Quinella; $347,970.40, Pick Nine

Leaders

Career, Leading Jockey by Titles: Russell Baze, 34
Career, Leading Trainer by Titles: Jerry Hollendorfer, 31
Recent Meeting, Leading Jockey: Russell Baze, 119, Winter/Spring 2005; Russell Baze, 67, Summer/Fall 2005
Recent Meeting, Leading Trainer: Jerry Hollendorfer, 71, Winter/Spring 2005; Jerry Hollendorfer, 45, Summer/Fall 2005

Records

Single-Day Jockey Wins: John Adams, 6, April 7, 1938; John Longden, 6, November 22, 1947; Bill Shoemaker, 6, October 13, 1950; William Harmatz, 6, September 23, 1954; Ralph Neves, 6, October 24, 1961; Russell Baze, 6, September 1, 1984; Russell Baze, 6, January 31, 1999

Track Records, Main Dirt

4 furlongs: Ima Dear, :$46^2/_5$, April 2, 1935
$4^1/_2$ furlongs: Metatron, :50.59, May 24, 2001
5 furlongs: Trickey Trevor, :56.01, October 27, 2004
$5^1/_2$ furlongs: Rio Oro, 1:01.69, October 7, 2001
6 furlongs: Black Jack Road, 1:$07^1/_5$, October 28, 1990
$7^1/_2$ furlongs: Lookabout, 1:$30^2/_5$, November 26, 1936
1 mile: Aristocratical, 1:$33^3/_5$, September 10, 1983
1m 70 yds: Redress, 1:$41^3/_5$, December 10, 1934
$1^1/_{16}$ miles: Hoedown's Day, 1:$38^2/_5$, October 23, 1983
$1^1/_8$ miles: Super Moment, 1:$46^1/_5$, December 13, 1980
$1^3/_{16}$ miles: Force of Reason, 1:$52^4/_5$, November 5, 1983
$1^1/_4$ miles: Ask Father, 2:$00^2/_5$, September 28, 1968
$1^1/_2$ miles: Cattle Creek, 2:$27^3/_5$, December 12, 1979
$1^5/_8$ miles: Rag King, 2:$43^1/_5$, December 15, 1990
$1^3/_4$ miles: Tornillo, 2:$57^3/_5$, November 21, 1936
Other: 2 furlongs, Lady Las Vegas, :21, March 20, 1997; 2 furlongs, Royalette, :21.11, April 12, 2002; $3^1/_2$ furlongs, Harrogate, :$40^4/_5$, March 16, 1935

Track Records, Main Turf

$4^1/_2$ furlongs: Santano, :50.38, May 17, 2001
5 furlongs: Excessive Barb, :56.32, May 30, 2004
7 furlongs: First Flyer, 1:24.35, September 25, 1997
$7^1/_2$ furlongs: Hegemony (Ire), 1:$28^4/_5$, October 12, 1985
1 mile: Position's Best, 1:$34^3/_5$, September 6, 1987; Staff Rider, 1:34.68, August 28, 1993
$1^1/_{16}$ miles: Dreamer, 1:40.21, August 17, 1997
$1^1/_8$ miles: Ocean Queen, 1:47.80, October 12, 1996
$1^3/_8$ miles: Peu a Peu, 2:16.39, May 18, 2002
$1^1/_2$ miles: Swiss Conviction, 2:31.46, October 12, 1998
2 miles: Lighting Star, 3:28.39, March 23, 1997
Other: a$1^1/_8$ miles, Mula Gula, 1:45.34, September 25, 1999; a$1^3/_8$ miles, Handsome Weed, 2:17.10, October 24, 1991

Principal Races

Bay Meadows Breeders' Cup Sprint H. (G3), Bay Meadows Breeders' Cup Oaks, California Turf Sprint Championship H.

Interesting Facts

Bay Meadows is the longest continually operating racetrack in California and is home to the longest-running stakes race in the state, the Bay Meadows H. (G3).

Notable Events

Labor Day Family Day Infield Party

Fastest Times of 2005 (Dirt)

2 furlongs: Tippy Toe Terri, :21.65, April 21, 2005
5 furlongs: Another Variety, :57.67, December 30, 2005
$5^1/_2$ furlongs: Welcome Aboard, 1:02.33, February 4, 2005
6 furlongs: Lost in the Fog, 1:08.05, October 1, 2005
1 mile: Smoocher, 1:34.40, April 23, 2005
$1^1/_{16}$ miles: Trickey Trevor, 1:41.09, December 26, 2005
$1^1/_8$ miles: Especialista (Arg), 1:50.24, April 8, 2005
$1^1/_4$ miles: Destined to Win, 2:03.19, April 29, 2005

Fastest Times of 2005 (Turf)

5 furlongs: No Derby, :56.65, August 28, 2005
$7^1/_2$ furlongs: Motivus, 1:30.91, October 10, 2005
1 mile: My Onomatopoeia, 1:35.77, April 13, 2005
$1^1/_{16}$ miles: Drought Breaker, 1:42.80, April 13, 2005
$1^1/_8$ miles: Calster, 1:49.78, September 21, 2005
a$1^1/_8$ miles: Adreamisborn, 1:46.94, October 1, 2005
$1^3/_8$ miles: Eager Pharisien, 2:18.65, October 16, 2005

Del Mar

Known as the track "where the surf meets the turf," Del Mar is renowned for its laid-back atmosphere and rich purses. The Del Mar style is a legacy of the film stars who helped build it, principally Bing Crosby and Pat O'Brien. But the track's beginnings were rocky. In the mid-1930s, the 22nd District Agricultural Association began to build a fairgrounds with a one-mile racetrack and grandstand north of San Diego, and Crosby formed the Del Mar Turf Club to lease the facility for ten years. But the agricultural district soon ran out of money, and Crosby and O'Brien borrowed almost $600,000 to complete the project. The track opened on July 3, 1937, with Crosby greeting the first patron through the turnstiles. The following year, the crooner wrote "Where the Surf Meets the Turf" and sang it on opening day; it still is played every day at the track. Del Mar was closed during World War II, serving as a Marine training center and an assembly center for B-17 wing ribs. It reopened in 1945, and the lease was extended through 1959. In 1970, a group of prominent California owners and breeders formed the Del Mar Thoroughbred Club and leased the facility for 20 years. The lease was extended for another 20 years in 1990. A rebuilt Del Mar grandstand and clubhouse costing $80-million were completed in 1993, two years after the first running of the track's now-signature event, the Pacific Classic Stakes (G1).

Location: 2260 Jimmy Durante Blvd., P.O. Box 700, Del Mar, Ca. 92014
Phone: (858) 755-1141
Fax: (858) 792-4269
Website: *www.delmarracing.com*
E-Mail: marys@dmtc.com
Year Founded: 1937
Dates of Inaugural Meeting: July 3-July 31, 1937
Abbreviation: Dmr
Acreage: 350
Number of Stalls: 2,100
Seating Capacity: 14,304

Ownership

Del Mar Thoroughbred Club

Officers

Chief Executive Officer: Joe Harper
Chairman: Robert S. Strauss
President: Joe Harper
General Manager: Joe Harper
Director of Racing: Thomas S. Robbins
Racing Secretary: Thomas S. Robbins
Director of Operations: Tim Read
Director of Finance: Michael R. Ernst
Director of Marketing: Josh Rubinstein
Director of Mutuels: William D. Navarro
Vice President: Craig R. Fravel
Director of Publicity: Daniel G. Smith
Director of Sales: Kathleen McDonald
Director of Simulcasting: Paul Porter
Horsemen's Liaison: Lisa Iaria
Stewards: Dennis Nevin, Gina Powell, Kim Sawyer, George Slender
Track Announcer: Trevor Denman
Track Photographer: Benoit and Associates
Track Superintendent: Steve Wood
Security: Bill Sullivan
Asst. Racing Secretaries: Rick Hammerle, Zachary Soto
Clerk of the Course: Melanie Stubblefield

Racing Dates

2005: July 20-September 7, 43 days
2006: July 19-September 6, 43 days

Track Layout

Main Circumference: 1 mile
Main Track Chute: 7 furlongs and $1\frac{1}{4}$ miles
Main Width: 80 feet
Main Length of Stretch: 919 feet
Main Turf Circumference: $7\frac{1}{2}$ furlongs
Main Turf Chute: $1\frac{1}{8}$ miles diagonal
Main Turf Width: 63 feet
Main Turf Length of Stretch: 761 feet
Training Track: $\frac{1}{2}$ mile

Attendance

Average Daily Recent Meeting: 17,007, 2005
Highest Single-Day Record: 44,181, August 10, 1996
Record Daily Average for Single Meet: 19,776, 1985
Highest Single-Meet Record: 846,495, 1987
Total Attendance Recent Meeting: 731,287, 2005
Highest Single-Day Recent Meet: 40,046, July 20, 2005

Handle

Average All Sources Recent Meeting: $14,143,449, 2005
Average On-Track Recent Meeting: $2,532,740, 2005
Record Daily Average for Single Meet: $3,861,247, 1987
Single-Day On-Track Handle: $5,657,840, August 15, 1987
Single-Day Total Handle All Sources: $24,004,733, August 21, 2005
Total All Sources Recent Meeting: $608,168,297, 2005
Total On-Track Recent Meeting: $108,907,839, 2005
Highest Single-Day Record Recent Meet: $24,004,733, August 21, 2005
Highest Single-Day On-Track Record Recent Meet: $5,188,886, August 21, 2005
Record Total All Sources for Single Meet: $608,168,297, 2005
Record Average All Sources Single Meet: $14,143,449, 2005

Mutuel Records

Highest Win: $263.40, Cipria, September 1, 1955
Highest Exacta: $2,383, August 7, 1987
Highest Trifecta: $13,405.50, July 28, 1997
Highest Daily Double: $7,720, August 27, 2004
Highest Pick 3: $20,080.30, August 20, 2000
Highest Pick 6: $2,100,017, August 1, 2004
Highest Other Exotics: $133,013.40, Superfecta, September 6, 1998; $43,602.40, Place Pick All, September 8, 2002
Highest Quinella: $1,374, July 28, 1997
Highest Pick 4: $49,571.60, July 23, 2003

Leaders

Career, Leading Jockey by Titles: William Shoemaker, 7
Career, Leading Owner by Titles: Golden Eagle Farm, 6
Career, Leading Trainer by Titles: Farrell W. Jones, 11
Career, Leading Jockey by Stakes Wins: Chris McCarron, 134
Career, Leading Trainer by Stakes Wins: Charles Whittingham, 74, Bob Baffert, 74
Career, Leading Jockey by Wins: Laffit Pincay Jr., 1,011
Career, Leading Trainer by Wins: Ron McAnally, 419
Recent Meeting, Leading Jockey: Victor Espinoza, 53, 2005
Recent Meeting, Leading Owner: Robert Bone, 9, 2005
Recent Meeting, Leading Trainer: Jeff Mullins, 23, 2005

Records

Single-Day Jockey Wins: William Shoemaker, 6, September 4, 1954; Rudy Rosales, 6, September 6, 1969; Laffit Pincay Jr., 6, July 28, 1976; Laffit Pincay Jr., 6, July 29, 1978
Single-Day Trainer Wins: R. H. "Red" McDaniel, 4, September 4, 1954; R. H. "Red" McDaniel, 4, September 6, 1954; Farrell W. Jones, 4, August 13, 1963; Ron McAnally, 4, August 20, 1989; Jack Van Berg, 4, August 3, 1995
Single Meet, Leading Jockey by Wins: Bill Shoemaker, 94, 1954
Single Meet, Leading Trainer by Wins: R. H. "Red" McDaniel, 47, 1954
Single Meet, Leading Trainer by Stakes Wins: Bob Baffert, 13, 2000
Single Meet, Leading Jockey by Stakes Wins: Laffit Pincay Jr., 12, 1976; Chris McCarron, 12, 1995; Gary Stevens, 12, 1997; Corey Nakatani, 12, 1998

Track Records, Main Dirt

5 furlongs: Soldier Girl, :$56\frac{2}{5}$, August 13, 1964; Bro Lo, :56.46, July 20, 2005
$5\frac{1}{2}$ furlongs: Ack Ack, 1:$02\frac{1}{5}$, September 12, 1970; Lakeside Trail, 1:$02\frac{1}{5}$, August 18, 1974; Little Mustard, 1:$02\frac{1}{5}$, September 5, 1974; King's Sea Rullah, 1:$02\frac{1}{5}$, August 12, 1977; World Pleasure, 1:$02\frac{1}{5}$, August 24, 1977; Brainstorming, 1:$02\frac{1}{5}$, August 28, 1991; Captain Squire, 1:02.26, August 24, 2005
6 furlongs: King of Cricket, 1:$07\frac{3}{5}$, August 22, 1973
$6\frac{1}{2}$ furlongs: Native Paster, 1:$13\frac{3}{5}$, September 4, 1988

7 furlongs: Solar Launch, 1:20, August 10, 1990; Lit de Justice, 1:20, August 19, 1995
1 mile: Precisionist, $1{:}33^1/_5$, August 1, 1988
$1^1/_{16}$ miles: Windy Sands, 1:40, August 4, 1962; Native Diver, 1:40, August 7, 1965; Matching, 1:40, August 18, 1982
$1^1/_8$ miles: Latin Touch, 1:46, September 1, 1979
$1^3/_{16}$ miles: Four By Five, $1{:}56^2/_5$, August 16, 1954
$1^1/_4$ miles: Candy Ride (Arg), 1:59.11, August 24, 2003
$1^1/_2$ miles: Spring Boy, $2{:}29^2/_5$, August 16, 1958
$1^5/_8$ miles: Ormolu, 2:45, August 24, 1957
$1^3/_4$ miles: Lurline B., $2{:}57^2/_5$, August 26, 1949
2 miles: Pilot Anne, $3{:}24^1/_5$, September 2, 1949
Other: a$1^3/_{16}$ miles, Ancient Title, $1{:}55^2/_5$, September 5, 1977

Track Records, Main Turf

5 furlongs: Whata Soldier, :55, August 5, 2005
$7^1/_2$ furlongs: Syncopate, $1{:}27^4/_5$, August 24, 1981
1 mile: Three Valleys, 1:32.21, September 4, 2005
$1^1/_{16}$ miles: Cheroot, 1:39.68, August 19, 2005
$1^1/_8$ miles: Willow O Wisp, 1:45.85, September 5, 2005
$1^3/_8$ miles: Laura's Lucky Boy, 2:12.06, August 3, 2005
Other: a$7^1/_2$ furlongs, Buck Price, $1{:}27^2/_5$, September 8, 1975

Principal Races

Pacific Classic (G1), Del Mar Oaks (G1), Eddie Read H. (G1), John C. Mabee H. (G1), Bing Crosby H. (G1), Del Mar Debutante (G1)

Fastest Times of 2005 (Dirt)

5 furlongs: Bro Lo, :56.46, July 20, 2005
$5^1/_2$ furlongs: Captain Squire, 1:02.26, August 24, 2005
6 furlongs: Greg's Gold, 1:08.04, July 31, 2005
$6^1/_2$ furlongs: Beau Soleil, 1:14.71, July 31, 2005
7 furlongs: Imperialism, 1:21.70, August 21, 2005
1 mile: Healthy Addiction, 1:35.26, September 1, 2005
$1^1/_{16}$ miles: Choctaw Nation, 1:42.40, July 24, 2005
$1^1/_8$ miles: Lord Mussi (Arg), 1:49.96, August 28, 2005
$1^1/_4$ miles: Borrego, 2:00.71, August 21, 2005

Fastest Times of 2005 (Turf)

5 furlongs: Whata Soldier, :55, August 5, 2005
1 mile: Three Valleys, 1:32.21, September 4, 2005
$1^1/_{16}$ miles: Cheroot, 1:39.68, August 19, 2005
$1^1/_8$ miles: Willow O Wisp, 1:45.85, September 5, 2005
$1^3/_8$ miles: Laura's Lucky Boy, 2:12.06, August 3, 2005

Fairplex Park

For more than 80 years, the Los Angeles County Fair Association has offered racing at Fairplex Park. In recent decades, the fair meeting has given the major Southern California circuit a welcome break between the Del Mar and Oak Tree at Santa Anita meets in September. The inaugural Los Angeles County Fair was conducted in 1922, a five-day meet over a half-mile track. By the mid-1930s, after pari-mutuel wagering had been legalized in California, the fair was extended to a 17-day meeting. With minor changes over the years, the meet has remained essentially the same. The Barretts Ltd. sales pavilion is located adjacent to the track.

Location: 1101 W. McKinley Ave., Pomona, Ca. 91768-1639
Phone: (909) 623-3111
Fax: (909) 865-3602
Website: *www.fairplex.com*
E-Mail: info@fairplex.com
Year Founded: 1922
Abbreviation: Fpx
Acreage: 487
Number of Stalls: 1,306
Seating Capacity: 10,000

Officers

Chairman: Stephen C. Morgan
President: James E. Henwood
Director of Racing: Terry Gilligan
Racing Secretary: Richard Wheeler
Director of Mutuels: William D. Navarro
Vice President: Michael Seder
Director of Publicity: Wendy Talarico
Stewards: Violet Smith, Nancy Ury, Thomas Ward
Track Announcer: Trevor Denman
Track Photographer: Benoit & Asssociates
Track Superintendent: Steve Wood
Asst. Racing Secretary: Zachary Soto
Clerk of the Course: Lisa Jones

Racing Dates

2005: September 9-September 26, 16 days
2006: September 8-September 25, 16 days

Track Layout

Main Circumference: 5 furlongs
Main Track Chute: $^1/_4$ mile and $1^1/_8$ miles
Main Width: 75 feet
Main Length of Stretch: 660 feet

Attendance

Average Daily Recent Meeting: 5,531, 2005
Highest Single-Day Record: 28,300, September 25, 1948
Highest Single-Meet Record: 337,491, 1998
Record Daily Average for Single Meet: 18,749, 1998
Total Attendance Recent Meeting: 88,494, 2005

Handle

Average All Sources Recent Meeting: $5,682,662, 2005
Average On-Track Recent Meeting: $738,431, 2005
Single-Day On-Track Handle: $4,112,091, September 27, 1987
Single-Day Total Handle All Sources: $10,200,000, September 27, 2003
Total All Sources Recent Meeting: $90,922,589, 2005
Total On-Track Recent Meeting: $11,814,889, 2005
Highest Single-Day Record Recent Meet: $9,291,538, September 17, 2005
Record Total All Sources for Single Meet: $90,922,589, 2005

Mutuel Records

Highest Win: $182.20, Uncle Fox, September 21, 1976
Highest Exacta: $5,645, September 13, 1986
Highest Trifecta: $29,278.80, September 30, 1996
Highest Daily Double: $4,362.40, September 17, 1990
Highest Pick 6: $199,346.60, September 13, 1999
Highest Other Exotics: $78.20, Place, October 5, 1992; $51.40, Showm September 18, 1933; $30,497, Superfecta, September 19, 2000; $155,602.50, Daily Triple, October 1, 1993

Leaders

Career, Leading Jockey by Stakes Wins: David Flores, 53
Career, Leading Trainer by Stakes Wins: Mel Stute, 43
Career, Leading Jockey by Wins: Martin Pedroza, 433
Career, Leading Trainer by Wins: Mel Stute, 179
Recent Meeting, Leading Jockey: Martin Pedroza, 26, 2005
Recent Meeting, Leading Trainer: Doug O'Neill, 13, 2005
Recent Meeting, Leading Horse: More Angels, 2, 2005; Ultimate Summer, 2, 2005; Mylilchickade, 2, 2005; Dark Past, 2, 2005; Inanewyorksecond, 2, 2005; Rivatear, 2, 2005

Records

Single-Day Jockey Wins: David Flores, 6, September 20, 1992; David Flores, 6, September 30, 1992
Single-Day Trainer Wins: Gordon Campbell, 4, September 30, 1967; Jerry Fanning, 4, September 24, 1984
Single Meet, Leading Jockey by Wins: Martin Pedroza, 51, 2004
Single Meet, Leading Trainer by Wins: Doug O'Neill, 16, 2004

Track Records, Main Dirt

4 furlongs: Nashua's Asset, :45.55, September 15, 2002
6 furlongs: Ultimate Summer, 1:08.62, September 26, 2005
$6^1/_2$ furlongs: Jungle Prince, 1:15.18, September 25, 2005
7 furlongs: Irish Honor, 1:22.25, September 25, 2005
$1^1/_{16}$ miles: Monte Parnes (Arg), $1{:}41^3/_5$, September 29, 1990
$1^3/_8$ miles: Mummy's Pleasure, 2:15, September 28, 1986
Other: a$1^1/_8$ miles, Dachi's Folly, $1{:}48^2/_5$, September 29, 1990

Principal Races

Barretts Juvenile S., Barretts Debutante S., Ralph M. Hinds Pomona Invitational H., Las Madrinas H., Pomona Derby

Interesting Facts

Achievements/Milestones: Track was expanded to $^5/_8$ mile in 1986

Notable Events

Mel Stute inaugural inductee into Fairplex Park Hall of Fame, September 27, 2003
Julie Krone rode in and won Pomona Derby, September 27, 2003.

Fastest Times of 2005 (Dirt)

a4 furlongs: Olympic Moment, :44.48, September 19, 2005
6 furlongs: Ultimate Summer, 1:08.62, September 26, 2005
6$\frac{1}{2}$ furlongs: Jungle Prince, 1:15.18, September 25, 2005
7 furlongs: Irish Honor, 1:22.25, September 25, 2005
1$\frac{1}{16}$ miles: Brooke's Halo, 1:43.28, September 23, 2005
a1$\frac{1}{8}$ miles: Courtly Jazz, 1:49.81, September 25, 2005
1$\frac{3}{8}$ miles: Potri Cacho (Arg), 2:17.29, September 25, 2005

Ferndale

Location: 1250 Fifth St., P.O. Box 637, Ferndale, Ca. 95536-9712
Phone: (707) 786-5533
Fax: (707) 786-0724
Website: *www.humboldtcountyfair.org*
E-Mail: humcofair@frontiernet.net
Year Founded: 1896
Abbreviation: Fer
Number of Stalls: 258 permanent, 200 portable
Seating Capacity: 1,800

Ownership

County of Humboldt

Officers

President: Irv Parlato
General Manager: Stuart Titus
Director of Racing: Stuart Titus
Racing Secretary: Ella Robinson
Director of Mutuels: Dominick DePrenzio
Vice President: Bill Branstetter
Track Announcer: Frank Mirahmadi
Asst. Racing Secretary: Lisa Jones

Racing Dates

2005: August 11-August 21, 10 days
2006: August 10-August 20, 10 days

Track Layout

Main Circumference: 4 furlongs
Main Track Chute: 5 furlongs and 7 furlongs
Main Length of Stretch: 530 feet

Attendance

Average Daily Recent Meeting: 2,281, 2005
Total Attendance Recent Meeting: 22,811, 2005

Handle

Average All Sources Recent Meeting: $215,873, 2005
Average On-Track Recent Meeting: $77,517, 2005
Total All Sources Recent Meeting: $2,158,729, 2005
Total On-Track Recent Meeting: $775,170, 2005

Leaders

Recent Meeting, Leading Jockey: Victor Miranda, 9, 2005
Recent Meeting, Leading Trainer: Santiago C. Rodriquez, 6, 2005
Recent Meeting, Leading Horse: Miss Feather River, 2, 2005; Red Seattle, 2, 2005; Decision Time, 2, 2005; Warlago, 2, 2005; Town Gambler, 2, 2005; Orchy Star, 2, 2005

Principal Races

Les Mademoiselle S.

Fastest Times of 2005 (Dirt)

5 furlongs: Royal Night Out, :58.37, August 14, 2005; Truly a Runner, :58.37, August 20, 2005
6$\frac{1}{2}$ furlongs: Miss Feather River, 1:19.51, August 21, 2005
7 furlongs: Red Seattle, 1:25.65, August 19, 2005
1$\frac{1}{16}$ miles: Scattering, 1:46.73, August 20, 2005
1$\frac{5}{8}$ miles: Black Horse Money, 2:47.50, August 21, 2005

Fresno

Location: 1121 S. Chance Ave., Fresno, Ca. 93702-3707
Phone: (559) 650-3247
Fax: (559) 650-3226
Website: *www.fresnofair.com*
E-Mail: info@fresnofair.com
Year Founded: 1883
Dates of Inaugural Meeting: September 1935
Abbreviation: Fno
Number of Stalls: 634 permanent, 200 portable
Seating Capacity: 5,125

Ownership

State of California

Officers

Chief Executive Officer: John C. Alkire
Chairman: Ardie Der Manouel
President: Debbie Jacobsen
General Manager: John Alkire
Director of Racing: Dan White
Racing Secretary: Zachary Soto
Director of Operations: Larry Swartzlander
Director of Marketing: Debbie Nalchajian-Cohen
Director of Mutuels: Richard Horner
Director of Publicity: Debbie Nalchajian-Cohen
Director of Simulcasting: Kay Webb
Stewards: Smith, Nicolo, Sawyer
Track Announcer: Frank Mirahmadi
Track Photographer: Photos By Frank
Track Superintendent: Chuck George
Asst. Racing Secretary: Ella Robinson
Clerk of the Course: Dawn Schmid

Racing Dates

2005: October 5-October 16, 11 days
2006: October 4-October 15, 11 days
2007: October 3-October 14, 11 days

Track Layout

Main Circumference: 1 mile
Main Track Chute: 2 furlongs and 6 furlongs
Main Length of Stretch: 979 feet

Attendance

Average Daily Recent Meeting: 7,438, 2005
Total Attendance Recent Meeting: 81,823, 2005

Handle

Average All Sources Recent Meeting: $626,973, 2005
Average On-Track Recent Meeting: $312,933, 2005
Total All Sources Recent Meeting: $6,896,707, 2005
Total On-Track Recent Meeting: $3,442,260.50, 2005
Highest Single-Day On-Track Record Recent Meet: $429,545.50, October 16, 2005

Leaders

Recent Meeting, Leading Jockey: Jorge Ayarza, 22, 2005
Recent Meeting, Leading Trainer: Michael Lenzini, 9, 2005
Recent Meeting, Leading Horse: Summer Guide, 2, 2005; Victory Roar, 2, 2005; Sheza Cats Meow, 2, 2005; Parisian, 2, 2005

Track Records, Main Dirt

4 furlongs: Nellie's Girl, :44$\frac{4}{5}$, October 7, 1978; King Stephen, :44$\frac{4}{5}$, October 7, 1978
4$\frac{1}{2}$ furlongs: Rio Linda Flo, :52$\frac{4}{5}$, May 14, 1981
5 furlongs: Big Volume, :55$\frac{2}{5}$, November 15, 1977
5$\frac{1}{2}$ furlongs: Knight in Savannah, 1:01$\frac{2}{5}$, November 13, 1990
6 furlongs: Tolemeo, 1:07$\frac{2}{5}$, November 12, 1997
1 mile: The Ayes Have It, 1:33$\frac{4}{5}$, November 11, 1986
1$\frac{1}{16}$ miles: Dimaggio, 1:39$\frac{4}{5}$, October 16, 1976
1$\frac{1}{8}$ miles: Minutes Away, 1:46$\frac{2}{5}$, November 20, 1985
1$\frac{1}{4}$ miles: Capt. Quicksilver, 1:59$\frac{4}{5}$, October 18, 1992
1$\frac{1}{2}$ miles: El Maduro, 2:30$\frac{2}{5}$, September 17, 1980
2 miles: Nina's Flag, 3:29$\frac{2}{5}$, October 9, 1954
Other: a6 furlongs, Tia Ping, 1:10$\frac{1}{5}$, October 11, 1963; 1$\frac{1}{16}$ miles, Bull Patch, 2:56, October 5, 1954

Principal Races

Bulldog S., Harvest Futurity

Fastest Times of 2005 (Dirt)

5 furlongs: Shi'ahs Devil, :56.04, October 12, 2005
5$\frac{1}{2}$ furlongs: Nighthunter, 1:03.46, October 10, 2005
6 furlongs: Summer Guide, 1:07.98, October 6, 2005
1 mile: Another Gear, 1:34.76, October 6, 2005

Golden Gate Fields

On April 29, 1949, a 19-year-old apprentice jockey from Texas named Bill Shoemaker rode Shafter V. to victory in the second race at Golden Gate Fields in Albany, California. That win marked the first of a then-record 8,833 career victories for Shoemaker, a Racing Hall of Fame jockey. Several famous horses also have raced at the San Francisco-area track. Citation, the 1948 Triple Crown winner, defeated champion handicap male *Noor in the '50 Golden Gate Mile Handicap, setting a world record for one mile in the process. Silky Sullivan captured his first stakes victory in the 1957 Golden Gate Futurity and went on to win 12 of 27 career starts and earned more than $150,000. In February 1941, entrepreneur Edward "Slip" Madigan opened the track, then known as the Albany Turf Club. The track closed after its first five days of racing due to flooding from heavy rains. During World War II, the United States Navy used Golden Gate as a landing base for amphibious craft. Racing resumed in 1947 after the water problem was solved, and in '71 the track added a turf course. In 1989, Ladbroke Group purchased Golden Gate for $41-million. As it wound down its North American racing operations, Ladbroke sold the facility to Magna Entertainment Corp. in 1999.

Location: 1100 Eastshore Highway, Albany, Ca. 94710
Phone: (510) 559-7300
Fax: (510) 559-7467
Website: *www.goldengatefields.com*
E-Mail: help@goldengatefields.com
Year Founded: 1941
Dates of Inaugural Meeting: February 1, 1941, 5 Days
Abbreviation: GG
Acreage: 225
Number of Stalls: 1,420
Seating Capacity: 14,750

Ownership

Magna Entertainment Corp.

Officers

Chairman: Frank Stronach
Director of Racing: Richard Lewis
Racing Secretary: Tom Doutrich
Secretary: Gary Cohn
Treasurer: Barbara Helm
Director of Mutuels: Bryan Wayte
Vice Presidents: Bernie Thurman, Calvin Rainey, Michael A. Scalzo, Michael Ziegler
Director of Publicity: Tom Ferrall
Director of Sales: Dyan Grealish
Director of Simulcasting: Kay Webb
Horsemen's Liaison: Jenny Scullin
Stewards: Dennis Nevin, John Herbuveaux, Darrel McHargue
Track Announcer: Tony Calo
Track Photographer: William Vassar
Track Superintendent: Juan Meza
Security: Jerry Gonzalez
Promotions/Events: Robin McHargue

Racing Dates

2005: November 10, 2004-January 30, 2005, 59 days; May 11-June 19, 29 days; October 19-December 19, 46 days
2006: February 8-May 7, 65 days; August 24-October 15, 36 days

Track Layout

Main Circumference: 1 mile
Main Width: Homestretch: 78 feet; Backstretch: 75 feet
Main Length of Stretch: 1,000 feet
Main Turf Circumference: 9/10 mile
Main Turf Chute: 3/16 mile
Main Turf Width: 65 feet

Attendance

Average Daily Recent Meeting: 2,235, Fall/Winter 2004/2005; 2,957, Spring 2005; 2,035, Fall 2005
Highest Single-Day Record: 34,967, May 5, 1990
Total Attendance Recent Meeting: 131,879, Fall/Winter 2004/2005; 85,740, Spring 2005; 93,626, Fall 2005

Handle

Average All Sources Recent Meeting: $3,784,767, Fall/Winter 2004/2005; $4,185,744, Spring 2005; $3,630,862, Fall 2005
Average On-Track Recent Meeting: $561,837, Fall/Winter 2004/2005; $714,788, Spring 2005; $505,382, Fall 2005
Single-Day Total Handle All Sources: $6,638,222, January 31, 2004
Total All Sources Recent Meeting: $223,301,272.20, Fall/Winter 2004/2005; $121,386,576, Spring 2005; $167,019,655, Fall 2005
Total On-Track Recent Meeting: $33,148,373.10, Fall/Winter 2004/2005; $20,728,862, Spring 2005; $23,247,554, Fall 2005

Mutuel Records

Highest Win: $322.60, Pasadena Slim, October 28, 1957
Highest Exacta: $2,270.20, January 18, 1997
Highest Trifecta: $38,689.20, January 18, 1997
Highest Daily Double: $8,711.40, November 16, 1960
Highest Pick 3: $18,851, December 13, 1998
Highest Pick 6: $1,074,405.80, May 23, 1990
Highest Other Exotics: $63,954, Superfecta, March 2, 2002

Leaders

Career, Leading Jockey by Titles: Russell Baze, 27
Career, Leading Trainer by Titles: Jerry Hollendorfer, 27
Recent Meeting, Leading Jockey: Martin Garcia, 78, 2006
Recent Meeting, Leading Owner: Jerry Hollendorfer and George Todaro, 17, 2006
Recent Meeting, Leading Trainer: Jerry Hollendorfer, 44, 2006
Recent Meeting, Leading Horse: Pragmatico (Arg), 3, 2006; Sneaky Dip, 3, 2006

Records

Single-Day Jockey Wins: Russell Baze, 7, April 16, 1992
Single-Day Trainer Wins: Walter Greenman, 5, November 25, 1970; Ace Gibson, 5, February 24, 1971; Jerry Hollendorfer, 5, May 1, 1996; Jerry Hollendorfer, 5, January 23, 1997
Single Meet, Leading Jockey by Wins: Russell Baze, 178, 1992
Single Meet, Leading Trainer by Wins: Jerry Hollendorfer, 89, 1990

Track Records, Main Dirt

4 furlongs: Glenbar, :47, March 12, 1952; Giddy Up, :47, March 25, 1952
4½ furlongs: Victory Found, :50.30, April 30, 1992
5 furlongs: Contradiction, :56.12, January 1, 2003
5½ furlongs: Proudest Hour, 1:02, May 30, 1986
6 furlongs: Lost in the Fog, 1:07.32, May 14, 2005
1 mile: Caros Love, 1:33, February 13, 1988
1 1/16 miles: Restless Con, 1:39.50, June 24, 1991
1 1/8 miles: Simply Majestic, 1:45, April 2, 1988
1 3/16 miles: Fleet Bird, 1:52 3/5, October 24, 1953
1¼ miles: *Noor, 1:58 1/5, June 24, 1950
1 3/8 miles: Forin Sea, 2:18 3/5, October 3, 1959
1½ miles: Bo Donna, 2:29 2/5, June 8, 1979
1¾ miles: Sirmark, 2:57 1/5, October 16, 1948
2 miles: Mantourist, 3:25 4/5, October 23, 1948
Other: 2 furlongs, The Money Doctor, :21 4/5, February 21, 1975

Track Records, Main Turf

4½ furlongs: Bonne Nuite, :50.58, May 22, 1994
5 furlongs: Black Tornado, :56, May 10, 1975; L'Natural, :56, May 28, 1977; Goldie's Goldian, :56, May 27, 1978; Prime Time Event, :56.03, May 22, 2005
7½ furlongs: Struttin' George, 1:28, May 5, 1979; His Honor, 1:28, April 25, 1981; Clever Song, 1:28, May 25, 1986
1 mile: Don Alberto, 1:33 2/5, March 22, 1980
1 1/16 miles: Announcer, 1:40 2/5, April 16, 1977
1 1/8 miles: Blues Traveller (Ire), 1:47.71, May 14, 1994
1 3/8 miles: John Henry, 2:13, May 6, 1984
1½ miles: Silveyville, 2:27 2/5, June 10, 1984; Kings Island (Ire), 2:27 2/5, June 9, 1985; Val Danseur, 2:27 2/5, June 8, 1986
2 miles: Never-Rust, 3:25 3/5, June 26, 1988
Other: 1 7/8 miles, Paired and Painted, 3:12 1/5, June 28, 1987; 2 3/8 miles, Situada (Chi), 4:10 4/5, June 25, 1990

Principal Races

San Francisco Breeders' Cup Mile S. (G2), All American H. (G3), Golden Gate Fields H. (G3), Yerba Buena Breeders' Cup H. (G3)

Notable Events

Crab and wine festival for charity, Beer Fest for charity.

Fastest Times of 2005 (Dirt)

4½ furlongs: Cause to Believe, :51.02, June 5, 2005
5 furlongs: Forest Ruler, :56.74, October 26, 2005
5½ furlongs: Onebadshark, 1:02.34, November 27, 2005
6 furlongs: Lost in the Fog, 1:07.32, May 14, 2005

1 mile: Thames, 1:35.45, October 29, 2005
1$^1/_{16}$ miles: Desert Boom, 1:40.94, June 11, 2005
1$^1/_8$ miles: Sharpster, 1:49.23, December 9, 2005
1$^1/_4$ miles: Ghost Actor, 2:02.26, January 14, 2005
1$^1/_2$ miles: Sharp Marc, 2:32.68, December 18, 2005

Fastest Times of 2005 (Turf)

5 furlongs: Prime Time Event, :56.03, May 22, 2005
1 mile: First Rate Event, 1:35.35, May 22, 2005
1$^1/_{16}$ miles: Pickle (GB), 1:41.72, May 21, 2005
1$^1/_8$ miles: Eastern Sand, 1:49.03, November 5, 2005
1$^3/_8$ miles: San Remy (Ire), 2:17.15, May 21, 2005

Hollywood Park

Hollywood Park sprung to life in 1938 when the Hollywood Turf Club was formed with Warner Brothers executive Jack L. Warner as its chairman. Several Hollywood power brokers, including actors (Ralph Bellamy), singers (Bing Crosby), and studio executives (Walt Disney, Darryl Zanuck) were among the original shareholders. Not everything has had a Hollywood ending at the track, however. A fire in 1949 destroyed the club's physical plant and forced racing over to Santa Anita Park for one year. The track reopened in time for a typical Hollywood finish when Citation won the 1951 Hollywood Gold Cup and became racing's first equine millionaire in the process. Hollywood again was the backdrop of history 28 years later when Affirmed won the Hollywood Gold Cup (G1) to break racing's $2-million barrier. In 1983, John Henry became the first $4-million earner when he won the Hollywood Turf Cup (G1). The first Breeders' Cup championship day was staged at Hollywood in 1984. The event returned in 1987 and again in '97. Hollywood has not been immune from controversy. An expensive rebuilding of the track—including an extension of the track to 1⅛ miles and construction of a new clubhouse structure, the Pavilion of the Stars—preceded the first Breeders' Cup, and fans resented the move of the finish line toward the new facility. A bitter fight for control of the track raged in the late 1980s and early '90s, and the struggle was resolved in February '91 when R. D. Hubbard wrested control from longtime executive Marjorie Lindheimer Everett in a proxy fight. Hubbard immediately launched a multimillion-dollar renovation program that spruced up the track and transformed the clubhouse pavilion into a card-club casino. As part of that project, the finish line was returned to its original location. In 1999, Churchill Downs Inc. bought Hollywood Park (excluding the card club) for $140-million. On December 10, 1999, Laffit Pincay Jr. became the winningest rider in racing history with a triumph at Hollywood. Churchill sold the track to the Bay Meadows Land Co. in 2005 for $257.5-million.

Location: 1050 South Prairie Ave., P.O. Box 369, Inglewood, Ca. 90306-0369
Phone: (310) 419-1500
Fax: (310) 672-4664
Website: *www.hollywoodpark.com*
E-Mail: customerservice@hollywoodpark.com
Year Founded: 1938
Dates of Inaugural Meeting: June 10, 1938
Abbreviation: Hol
Acreage: 240
Number of Stalls: 1,958
Seating Capacity: 35,000

Ownership

Bay Meadows Land Co.

Officers

President: F. Jack Liebau
General Manager: Eual G. Wyatt Jr.
Director of Racing: Martin Panza
Racing Secretary: Martin Panza
Director of Communications: Michael P. Mooney
Vice Presidents: Eual G. Wyatt Jr., Tim Barden, Michael Ziegler, Martin Panza
Director of Publicity: Michael P. Mooney
Director of Simulcasting: Tim Barden
Horsemen's Liaison: Diana Hudak
Track Announcer: Vic Stauffer
Track Photographer: Benoit & Associates
Horsemen's Bookkeeper: Susan Winter

Racing Dates

2005: April 20-July 17, 64 days; November 9-December 19, 27 days
2006: April 26-July 16, 58 days; November 1-December 18, 36 days

Track Layout

Main Circumference: 1$^1/_8$ miles
Main Track Chute: 7$^1/_2$ furlongs
Main Width: Homestretch: 92 feet; Backstretch: 82 feet
Main Length of Stretch: 990 feet
Main Turf Circumference: 1 mile and 165 feet
Main Turf Width: 64 feet
Main Turf Length of Stretch: 990 feet
Training Track: 4 furlongs

Attendance

Average Daily Recent Meeting: 7,773, Spring/Summer 2005; 5,417, Fall 2005
Highest Single-Day Record: 80,348, May 4, 1980
Highest Single-Meet Record: 2,398,528, Spring/Summer 1980
Record Daily Average for Single Meet: 34,516, 1965
Total Attendance Recent Meeting: 497,465, Spring/Summer 2005; 146,261, Fall 2005

Handle

Average All Sources Recent Meeting: $8,864,466, Spring/Summer 2005; $7,530,670, Fall 2005
Average On-Track Recent Meeting: $1,727,792, Spring/Summer 2005; $1,356,609, Fall 2005
Record Daily Average for Single Meet: $5,486,172, 1985
Single-Day Total Handle All Sources: $67,096,242, November 8, 1997
Total All Sources Recent Meeting: $567,325,817, Spring/Summer 2005; $203,328,084, Fall 2005
Total On-Track Recent Meeting: $110,578,658, Spring/Summer 2005; $36,628,437, Fall 2005

Mutuel Records

Highest Win: $361.80, Family Flair, June 29, 1989
Highest Exacta: $6,989.40, May 11, 1991
Highest Trifecta: $28,294, July 17, 1997
Highest Daily Double: $6,141.60, July 10, 1962
Highest Pick 3: $137,200.20, December 17, 1993
Highest Pick 6: $1,312,808.60, May 19, 2004
Highest Other Exotics: $148, Place, June 5, 1956; $87.20, Show, May 13, 1989; $190,769.80, Superfecta, November 11, 1994; $54,276.80, Place Pick All, July 4, 2001
Highest Pick 4: $90,470.50, June 20, 2004
Highest Stakes Win: $180.60, Perizade, July 1, 1961
Highest Quinella: $1,588, July 17, 1997

Leaders

Career, Leading Jockey by Titles: William Shoemaker, 18
Career, Leading Owner by Titles: Juddmonte Farms, 8
Career, Leading Trainer by Titles: Robert Frankel, 13
Career, Leading Jockey by Stakes Wins: Laffit A. Pincay Jr., 288
Career, Leading Trainer by Stakes Wins: Charles Whittingham, 222
Career, Leading Horse by Stakes Wins: Native Diver, 10
Career, Leading Jockey by Wins: Laffit A. Pincay Jr., 3,049
Career, Leading Trainer by Wins: Robert Frankel, 897
Recent Meeting, Leading Jockey: Martin A. Pedroza, 31, Fall 2005
Recent Meeting, Leading Trainer: Jeff Mullins, 13, Fall 2005
Recent Meeting, Leading Horse: Crowned Dancer, 3, Fall 2005

Records

Single-Day Jockey Wins: William Shoemaker, 6, June 20, 1953; Laffit A. Pincay Jr., 6, April 27, 1968; William Shoemaker, 6, June 24, 1970; Kent J. Desormeaux, 6, July 3, 1992

Single-Day Owner Wins: Robert D. Bone, 4, November 16, 2005
Single-Day Trainer Wins: Allen Drumheller Sr., 5, July 4, 1955
Single Meet, Leading Jockey by Wins: Laffit A. Pincay Jr., 148, 1974
Single Meet, Leading Owner by Wins: Marion R. Frankel, 55, 1972
Single Meet, Leading Trainer by Wins: Robert Frankel, 60, 1972
Single Meet, Leading Trainer by Stakes Wins: Charles Whittingham, 14, 1971
Single Meet, Leading Jockey by Stakes Wins: William Shoemaker, 18, 1971
Single Meet, Leading Horse by Stakes Wins: Honeymoon, 5, 1946; A Gleam, 5, 1952; Swaps, 5, 1956; Round Table, 5, 1957; Hillsdale, 5, 1959; Turkish Trousers, 5, 1971
Single Meet, Leading Horse by Wins: Flying Jean, 6, 1940; Kay Diane, 6, 1941; Security Check, 6, 1968

Track Records, Main Dirt

4½ furlongs: Bridge of Royalty, :50.59, May 4, 1995
5 furlongs: Diligent Prospect, :56.29, May 30, 2004
5½ furlongs: Hombre Rapido, 1:01.67, December 20, 2002
6 furlongs: Apalachee Ridge, 1:07.52, December 12, 1997
6½ furlongs: Lucky Forever, 1:13.24, May 20, 1995
7 furlongs: Mazel Trick, 1:19.97, June 27, 1999
7½ furlongs: Awesome Daze, 1:26.26, November 23, 1997
1 mile: Greinton (GB), 1:32⅗, June 9, 1985
1¹⁄₁₆ miles: Power Forward, 1:40, December 19, 1987; New Journey, 1:40.06, November 27, 1997
1⅛ miles: Gentlemen (Arg), 1:45.35, December 22, 1996
1³⁄₁₆ miles: Dig for It, 1:54.85, May 30, 2001
1¼ miles: Greinton (GB), 1:58⅖, June 23, 1985
1⅜ miles: Golden Ticket, 2:13.42, December 21, 2002
1⅝ miles: Ol' Henry, 2:42.50, June 27, 1997
1¾ miles: Roman Cuzzin, 2:56.77, July 21, 1997

Track Records, Main Turf

5 furlongs: Stormin' Lyon, :55.62, May 27, 2005
5½ furlongs: Scottsbluff, 1:00.26, May 15, 2006
6 furlongs: Answer Do, 1:07, December 15, 1990
1 mile: Megan's Interco, 1:32.64, May 22, 1994
1¹⁄₁₆ miles: Leroidesanimaux, 1:38.45, May 1, 2004
1⅛ miles: Lava Man, 1:44.26, April 30, 2006
1³⁄₁₆ miles: Kudos, 1:51.99, April 25, 2001
1¼ miles: Bien Bien, 1:57.75, May 31, 1993
1½ miles: Talloires, 2:23.55, July 21, 1996
Other: a1⅛ miles, Zoffany, 1:44⅘, November 16, 1985; a1¾ miles, Big Warning, 2:50⅖, December 22, 1990

Principal Races

Fall: Hollywood Derby (G1), Matriarch S. (G1), Citation H. (G1), Hollywood Turf Cup H. (G1), Hollywood Futurity (G1), Hollywood Starlet S. (G1)

Spring/Summer: Hollywood Gold Cup H. (G1), American Oaks Invitational (G1), Shoemaker Breeders' Cup Mile S. (G1), Charles Whittingham Memorial H. (G1), Gamely Breeders' Cup H. (G1), Triple Bend Invitational H. (G1), Vanity Invitational H. (G1)

Notable Events

Gold Rush in April, Autumn Turf Festival on Thanksgiving weekend

Fastest Times of 2005 (Dirt)

4½ furlongs: Bully Bones, :51.31, April 23, 2005
5 furlongs: Calamity June, :57.70, June 29, 2005
5½ furlongs: Brooker, 1:03.25, November 17, 2005
6 furlongs: Bordonaro, 1:08.11, December 3, 2005
6½ furlongs: Surf Cat, 1:14.44, May 15, 2005
7 furlongs: Unfurl the Flag, 1:20.95, July 3, 2005
7½ furlongs: McCann's Mojave, 1:27.23, June 11, 2005
1¹⁄₁₆ miles: Ace Blue (Brz), 1:41.45, May 14, 2005
1⅛ miles: Lava Man, 1:47.83, June 18, 2005
1¼ miles: Lava Man, 1:59.63, July 9, 2005
1⅜ miles: Golden Rahy, 2:16.28, December 1, 2005

Fastest Times of 2005 (Turf)

5 furlongs: Stormin' Lyon, :55.62, May 27, 2005
5½ furlongs: Astonished (GB), 1:01.42, April 30, 2005
1 mile: Castledale (Ire), 1:33.17, May 30, 2005
1¹⁄₁₆ miles: Fourty Niners Son, 1:40.43, June 8, 2005
1⅛ miles: Whilly (Ire), 1:46.30, July 3, 2005
1³⁄₁₆ miles: Qsar (Ger), 1:55.49, May 29, 2005
1¼ miles: Cesario (Jpn), 1:59.03, July 3, 2005
1½ miles: Republican Hawk, 2:25.14, June 26, 2005

Los Alamitos Race Course

Thoroughbreds have competed at Los Alamitos Race Course in Cypress, California, since 1994, when the track received permission to begin offering races for the breed. Los Alamitos primarily had been known as a Quarter Horse track since 1947, when nonpari-mutuel racing debuted at the track built by Frank Vessels on his ranch. In 1951, Los Alamitos received approval to begin holding pari-mutuel racing. After Vessels's death in 1963, his son Frank Vessels Jr. took over operation of the track, which five years later began offering night racing. After Vessels Jr.'s death in 1974, his wife, Millie, assumed the track's presidency and became one of the first women to hold a leadership position in Thoroughbred racing. In 1984, Los Alamitos was sold to Hollywood Park and entered a period of decline. Five years later, businessmen and harness-racing enthusiasts Lloyd Arnold and Chris Bardis bought the facility. Edward C. Allred, a physician and the all-time leading breeder of Quarter Horses by earnings, then purchased a majority interest in Los Alamitos and today is sole owner of the track, which also offers Paint, Appaloosa, and Arabian racing.

Location: 4961 Katella Ave., Los Alamitos, Ca. 90720-2721
Phone: (714) 820-2800
Fax: (714) 820-2689
Website: *www.losalamitos.com*
E-Mail: larace@losalamitos.com
Year Founded: 1946
Dates of Inaugural Meeting: December 4, 1951
Abbreviation: LA
Number of Stalls: 1,400
Seating Capacity: 7,500

Ownership

Edward C. Allred

Officers

Chairman: Edward C. Allred
Chief Executive Officer: Edward C. Allred
President: Edward C. Allred
General Manager: Edward C. Allred
Director of Racing: Ronald Church
Racing Secretary: Ronald Church
Secretary: G. Michael Lyon
Treasurer: Kathleen Chavez
Director of Operations: Howard Knuchell
Director of Finance: Robert M. Passero
Director of Marketing: Orlando Gutierrez
Director of Mutuels: Robert DiGiovanni
Vice President: John T. Seibly
Director of Publicity: Orlando Gutierrez
Director of Simulcasting: Melodie Knuchell
Horsemen's Liaison: Rene Catania
Stewards: Albert Christiansen, Martin Hamilton, George Slender
Track Announcer: Ed Burgart
Track Photographer: Scott Martinez
Track Superintendent: Rick Hughes
Promotions/Events: Vandi Ekins
Security: Rick Castaneda
Asst. Racing Secretary: Edward Reese

Racing Dates

2005: December 26, 2004-December 18, 2005, 200 days
2006: December 26, 2005- December 17, 2006, 200 days
2007: December 28, 2006-December 16, 2007

Track Layout

Main Circumference: 5 furlongs
Main Track Chute: 550 yards and 4½ furlongs
Main Width: Homestretch: 100 feet; Backstretch: 90 feet
Main Length of Stretch: 558 feet

Attendance

Highest Single-Day Record: 19,970, May 6, 1983

Highest Single-Meet Record: 1,046,158, 1994
Record Daily Average for Single Meet: 9,492, 1970

Handle

Average All Sources Recent Meeting: $1,281,367, 2005
Average On-Track Recent Meeting: $239,781, 2005
Record Daily Average for Single Meet: $1,281,868, 2004
Single-Day Total Handle All Sources: $2,379,112, November 1, 2003
Total All Sources Recent Meeting: $256,273,335, 2005
Total On-Track Recent Meeting: $47,956,200, 2005
Record Total All Sources for Single Meet: $260,219,285, 2004
Highest Single-Day Record Recent Meet: $2,195,064, November 5, 2005

Mutuel Records

Highest Exacta: $8,650.30, August 30, 1996
Highest Trifecta: $27,386.10, July 27, 1996
Highest Daily Double: $2,107.90, June 12, 1997
Highest Pick 3: $12,017.60, August 21, 1991
Highest Other Exotics: $21,198, Superfecta, July 12, 1997

Leaders

Career, Leading Jockey by Titles: Alex Bautista, 3
Career, Leading Trainer by Titles: Charles S. Treece, 6
Career, Leading Jockey by Wins: Alex Bautista, 426
Career, Leading Trainer by Wins: Charles S. Treece, 348
Recent Meeting, Leading Jockey: Agapito Delgadillo, 76, 2005
Recent Meeting, Leading Owner: Edward C. Allred, 46, 2005
Recent Meeting, Leading Trainer: Jesus Nunez, 53, 2005
Recent Meeting, Leading Horse: That Close, 5, 2005

Track Records, Main Dirt

4½ furlongs: Valiant Pete, :49⅕, August 11, 1990

Principal Races

Los Alamitos Million Futurity, Golden State Million, Ed Burke Million Futurity, Champion of Champions

Interesting Facts

Achievements/Milestones: Los Alamitos is the home of the richest horse race of any breed in California—the $1.3-million Los Alamitos Million

Notable Events

California Breeders Champions Night, Wiener Dog Nationals

Fastest Times of 2005 (Dirt)

4½ furlongs: Walker, :50.45, November 10, 2005

Oak Tree Racing Association at Santa Anita

In 1968, Southern California horsemen Clement Hirsch, Jack K. Robbins, and Louis R. Rowan approached Santa Anita Park President Robert P. Strub with a proposal for a brief, high-quality fall meeting at the Arcadia track. Except for the brief Fairplex Park meet, the Southern California racing calendar was empty between the close of Del Mar in September and the opening of Santa Anita's winter-spring meet each December 26. (Hollywood Park then had only a spring-summer meet.) Strub initially resisted, but Santa Anita officials finally agreed to try a fall meet under the auspices of the Oak Tree Racing Association, headed by Hirsch, in October 1969. In case the idea flopped, Oak Tree's directors had to guarantee the first day's purses. The initial 20-day fall meet was a success, and Oak Tree has become an important part of the racing scene in Southern California and nationally. Oak Tree secured rights to stage the third Breeders' Cup championship day in 1986, and the event attracted an on-track crowd of 69,155, the largest crowd to that time. Oak Tree hosted the championship day in 1993 and 2003. In addition, Oak Tree's stakes serve as leading prep races for the Breeders' Cup championship events. Hirsch died in 2000 and was succeeded as Oak Tree president by Robbins.

Location: 285 W. Huntington Dr., Arcadia, Ca. 91007-3439
Phone: (626) 574-6345
Fax: (626) 447-2940
Website: *www.oaktreeracing.com*
E-Mail: oaktreeracing@yahoo.com
Year Founded: 1968
Dates of Inaugural Meeting: October 7, 1969
Abbreviation: OSA

Ownership

Oak Tree Racing Association

Officers

President: Dr. Jack K. Robbins
General Manager: George Haines
Director of Racing: Michael J. Harlow
Racing Secretary: Rick Hammerle
Secretary: Thomas R. Capehart
Director of Operations: Richard Price
Director of Marketing: Allen Gutterman
Director of Mutuels: Randy Hartzell
Vice President: Sherwood C. Chillingworth
Director of Publicity: Michael Willman
Director of Simulcasting: Aaron Vercruysse
Horsemen's Liaison: Nancy Wallen
Stewards: Martin Hamilton, John Herbuveaux, Kim Sawyer, George Slender
Track Announcer: Trevor Denman
Track Photographer: Benoit & Associates
Track Superintendent: Steve Wood
Asst. Racing Secretary: Richard D. Wheeler
Security: Dick Honaker
Clerk of the Course: Melanie Stubblefield

Racing Dates

2005: September 28-November 6, 31 days
2006: September 27-October 29, 26 days

Attendance

Average Daily Recent Meeting: 8,507, 2005
Highest Single-Day Record: 69,155, November 1, 1986
Highest Single-Meet Record: 858,652, 1985
Record Daily Average for Single Meet: 28,822, 1982
Total Attendance Recent Meeting: 263,719, 2005

Handle

Average All Sources Recent Meeting: $7,108,162, 2005
Average On-Track Recent Meeting: $1,950,220, 2005
Record Daily Average for Single Meet: $5,607,928, 1986
Single-Day On-Track Handle: $17,171,128, October 25, 2003
Single-Day Total Handle All Sources: $120,788,128, October 25, 2003
Total All Sources Recent Meeting: $220,353,024, 2005
Total On-Track Recent Meeting: $60,456,834.20, 2005
Record Total All Sources for Single Meet: $327,591,053, 1998
Record Total for Single Meet: $169,252,456, 1987
Highest Single-Day Record Recent Meet: $19,548,155, October 29, 2005
Record Average All Sources Single Meet: $10,647,918, 2002

Mutuel Records

Highest Win: $269.20, Arcangues, November 6, 1993
Highest Exacta: $3,022.20, September 26, 2001
Highest Trifecta: $52,892.50, September 26, 2001
Highest Daily Double: $5,000, October 13, 1990
Highest Pick 3: $174,331.80, October 18, 1991
Highest Pick 6: $1,010,221.20, October 19, 1994
Highest Other Exotics: $98.20, Place, October 12, 1990; $42.60, Show, October 4, 1985; $91,543.90, Superfecta, November 6, 2003; $57,062.50, Place Pick All, November 11, 1995
Highest Pick 4: $58,803.30, September 26, 2001
Highest Quinella: $1,949.60, September 26, 2001

Leaders

Career, Leading Jockey by Titles: Laffit Pincay Jr., 6
Career, Leading Owner by Titles: Elmendorf, 3; Juddmonte Farms, 3
Career, Leading Trainer by Titles: Robert Frankel, 6
Career, Leading Jockey by Stakes Wins: Chris McCarron, 74
Career, Leading Trainer by Stakes Wins: Charles Whittingham, 68
Career, Leading Jockey by Wins: Laffit Pincay Jr., 671
Career, Leading Trainer by Wins: Robert Frankel, 257

Recent Meeting, Leading Jockey: Garrett Gomez, 44, 2005
Recent Meeting, Leading Owner: Robert Bone, 6, 2005
Recent Meeting, Leading Trainer: Steve Knapp, 16, 2005
Recent Meeting, Leading Horse: Brite Maneuvers, 3, 2005

Records

Single-Day Jockey Wins: Steve Valdez, 6, October 15, 1973; Darrel McHargue, 6, October 25, 1979; Patrick Valenzuela, 6, October 21, 1988; Martin Pedroza, 6, October 31, 1992

Track Records, Main Dirt

5 furlongs: Zero Henry, :57.78, October 23, 1996
5$^1/_2$ furlongs: Davy Be Good, 1:02.17, November 14, 1993
6 furlongs: Beira, 1:07$^4/_5$, October 13, 1974; Grenzen, 1:07$^4/_5$, October 7, 1978; Hawkin's Special, 1:07$^4/_5$, October 27, 1978
6$^1/_2$ furlongs: Enjoy the Moment, 1:14.15, October 8, 1998
7 furlongs: Ancient Title, 1:20$^4/_5$, October 18, 1972
1 mile: Salud y Pesetas, 1:33$^4/_5$, October 7, 1987
1$^1/_{16}$ miles: Cajun Prince, 1:40$^1/_5$, October 9, 1982
1$^1/_8$ miles: My Sonny Boy, 1:46, November 3, 1990
1$^1/_4$ miles: King Pellinore, 2:00, November 6, 1976
1$^1/_2$ miles: Whisk Spree, 2:29.17, October 16, 1993

Track Records, Main Turf

1 mile: Urgent Request (Ire), 1:32.44, October 5, 1996
1$^1/_8$ miles: Kostroma (Ire), 1:43.92, October 20, 1991
1$^1/_4$ miles: Double Discount, 1:57$^2/_5$, October 9, 1977
1$^1/_2$ miles: Hawkster, 2:22$^4/_5$, October 14, 1989
Other: a6$^1/_2$ furlongs, El Cielo, 1:11.46, November 3, 2001

Principal Races

Yellow Ribbon S. (G1), Clement L. Hirsch Memorial Turf Championship S. (G1), Ancient Title Breeders' Cup S. (G1), Oak Tree Breeders' Cup Mile S. (G2), Goodwood Breeders' Cup H. (G2)

Notable Events

California Cup

Fastest Times of 2005 (Dirt)

5$^1/_2$ furlongs: Scotty's Ladd, 1:02.90, October 29, 2005
6 furlongs: Bordonaro, 1:08.11, November 6, 2005
6$^1/_2$ furlongs: Resplendency, 1:14.90, October 23, 2005
7 furlongs: Proud Tower Too, 1:21.44, October 12, 2005
1 mile: Deputy Doc Renzi, 1:35.65, October 14, 2005
1$^1/_{16}$ miles: Surf Cat, 1:41.65, October 10, 2005
1$^1/_8$ miles: McCann's Mojave, 1:48.31, November 6, 2005

Fastest Times of 2005 (Turf)

a6$^1/_2$ furlongs: Selvatica, 1:11.50, October 13, 2005
1 mile: Mea Domina, 1:33.59, November 5, 2005
1$^1/_8$ miles: Urban King (Ire), 1:46.47, October 6, 2005
1$^1/_4$ miles: Like a Tiger, 1:59.95, October 9, 2005
1$^1/_2$ miles: Golden Rahy, 2:27.02, October 30, 2005

Pleasanton

Location: 4501 Pleasanton Ave., Pleasanton, Ca. 94566
Phone: (925) 426-7600
Fax: (925) 426-7599
Website: *www.alamedacountyfair.com*
E-Mail: info@alamedacountyfair.com
Year Founded: 1939
Dates of Inaugural Meeting: August 10, 1939
Abbreviation: Pln
Number of Stalls: 700
Seating Capacity: 6,608

Officers

Chief Executive Officer: Rick K. Pickering
Chairman: DeWitt Wilson
President: Tony Macchiano
General Manager: Rick K. Pickering
Director of Racing: Rick K. Pickering
Racing Secretary: Billie Sherwood, Bob Moreno
Treasurer: Ted Holder
Director of Mutuels: Bryan Wayte
Director of Simulcasting: Jeanne Wasserman
Track Announcer: Frank Mirahmadi
Track Photographer: Photos by Frank
Track Superintendent: Toni Applebee

Racing Dates

2005: June 29-July 10, 11 days
2006: June 28-July 9, 11 days

Track Layout

Main Circumference: 1 mile
Main Track Chute: 2 furlongs and 6 furlongs
Main Width: 60 feet
Main Length of Stretch: 1,085 feet

Attendance

Average Daily Recent Meeting: 5,206, 2005
Total Attendance Recent Meeting: 57,262, 2005

Handle

Average All Sources Recent Meeting: $3,085,009, 2005
Average On-Track Recent Meeting: $627,781, 2005
Single-Day On-Track Handle: $908,604, July 6, 2003
Single-Day Total Handle All Sources: $4,586,825, July 3, 2004
Total All Sources Recent Meeting: $33,935,100, 2005
Total On-Track Recent Meeting: $6,905,586, 2005

Leaders

Recent Meeting, Leading Jockey: Roberto M. Gonzalez, 14, 2005; Chad Phillip Schvaneveldt, 14, 2005
Recent Meeting, Leading Trainer: Jerry Hollendorfer, 11, 2005

Track Records, Main Dirt

4$^1/_2$ furlongs: French Invader, :51.20, June 27, 1996
5 furlongs: Don Jaun Con, :56.31, July 3, 2005
5$^1/_2$ furlongs: Boundary Ridge, 1:02, June 29, 1993
6 furlongs: Black Jack Road, 1:08.20, July 10, 1993
1m 70 yds: Call It, 1:38.01, July 5, 2003
1$^1/_{16}$ miles: Aunt Sophie, 1:40.34, July 5, 2003

Principal Races

Juan Gonzalez Memorial S., Everett Nevin Alameda County Futurity, Sam J. Whiting Memorial H., Alameda County Fillies and Mares H., Alamedan H.

Fastest Times of 2005 (Dirt)

4$^1/_2$ furlongs: Bold Bobo, :51.29, July 3, 2005
5 furlongs: Don Jaun Con, :56.31, July 3, 2005
5$^1/_2$ furlongs: Bad Anne, 1:02.71, July 10, 2005
6 furlongs: Bonfante, 1:08.71, July 9, 2005
1m 70 yds: Bells Fool, 1:39.07, July 4, 2005
1$^1/_{16}$ miles: Yougottawanna, 1:41.48, July 10, 2005

Sacramento

Location: 1600 Exposition Blvd., Sacramento, Ca. 95815-5104
Phone: (916) 263-3279
Fax: (916) 263-3198
Website: *www.bigfun.org*
E-Mail: horseracing@calexpo.com
Year Founded: 1963
Abbreviation: Sac
Number of Stalls: 1,000
Seating Capacity: 7,100

Ownership

State of California

Officers

Chairman: Ed Phillips
General Manager: Norbert Bartosik
Director of Racing: David Elliott
Racing Secretary: Grant Baker
Director of Operations: Kate Snider
Director of Marketing: Sally Ash
Director of Mutuels: George Vidak
Director of Publicity: Alex Traverso
Stewards: Pam Berg, Thomas Ward, Will Meyers
Track Announcer: John McGary
Track Photographer: Vassar Photography
Track Superintendent: Steve Wood

Track Layout

Main Circumference: 1 mile
Main Track Chute: 6 furlongs and 1$^1/_4$ miles
Main Width: 80 feet
Main Length of Stretch: 990 feet

Attendance

Highest Single-Day Record: 18,722, September 1, 1975

Handle

Single-Day Total Handle All Sources: $4,223,537, August 23, 2003

Principal Races

Governor's H., Earlene McCabe Derby

Notable Events

Dachshund Derby

Santa Anita Park

With the San Bernardino Mountains as a backdrop, an undulating downhill turf course, and an abundance of quality racing, Santa Anita Park symbolizes racing's possibilities. On a big race day, with a sizable crowd in the stands and quality Thoroughbreds on the track, the Arcadia track is one of the world's finest facilities. The story of Santa Anita is told in two parts. The first part is the original track, the dream of early 20th-century California entrepreneur E. J. "Lucky" Baldwin. Opened in 1907, the track gave Los Angeles racing fans a tantalizing glimpse of racing as an opulent spectacle. But Baldwin's death two years later and the lack of legal pari-mutuel wagering in California postponed the Santa Anita dream until the 1930s. When pari-mutuel wagering was legalized in 1933, the Los Angeles Turf Club was organized under the leadership of Dr. Charles H. Strub, and it built a $1-million facility near the site of Baldwin's track. Opened in 1934, the track's inaugural 1934-'35 racing season featured two races that immediately had an impact on the national racing calendar, the Santa Anita Handicap and the Santa Anita Derby. Now Grade 1 races, they continue to have important places on the spring schedule. With a $100,000 purse for its inaugural running, the Big 'Cap immediately became one of America's best-known races. The race and its $1-million purse today draw some of the best handicap runners from around North America. The Santa Anita Derby is one of the top Kentucky Derby (G1) prep races and has been utilized by recent Kentucky Derby winners Silver Charm, Real Quiet, and Charismatic. Legendary jockey Bill Shoemaker rode in his final race at Santa Anita in February 1990. The track hosts the important Oak Tree Racing Association meet each fall. Magna Entertainment Corp. purchased the track in December 1998 for $126-million.

Location: 285 W. Huntington Dr., Arcadia, Ca. 91007-3439
Phone: (626) 574-7223
Fax: (626) 574-6682
Website: *www.santaanita.com*
E-Mail: comments@santaanita.com
Year Founded: 1934
Dates of Inaugural Meeting: December 25, 1934
Abbreviation: SA
Acreage: 320
Number of Stalls: 2,000
Seating Capacity: 26,000

Ownership

Magna Entertainment Corp.

Officers

Chairman: Tom Hodgson
Chief Executive Officer: Ron Charles
President: Ron Charles
General Manager: George Haines
Director of Racing: Michael J. Harlow
Racing Secretary: Rick Hammerle
Secretary: Gary M. Cohn
Treasurer: Barbara Helm
Director of Operations: Richard Price
Director of Finance: Douglas R. Tatters
Director of Marketing: Stuart A. Zanville
Director of Mutuels: Randy Hartzell
Vice Presidents: Frank DeMarco Jr., Allen Gutterman, George Haines
Director of Publicity: Mike Willman
Director of Sales: Dyan Grealish
Director of Simulcasting: Aaron Vercruysse
Track Announcer: Trevor Denman
Track Photographer: Benoit & Associates
Track Superintendent: Steve Wood
Asst. Racing Secretary: Richard D. Wheeler
Security: Dick Honaker

Racing Dates

2005: December 26, 2004-April 18, 2005, 85 days
2006: December 26, 2005-April 23, 2006, 86 days

Track Layout

Main Circumference: 1 mile
Main Track Chute: 7 furlongs and 1¼ miles
Main Width: Homestretch: 85 feet; Backstretch: 80 feet
Main Length of Stretch: 990 feet
Main Turf Circumference: 7 furlongs
Main Turf Chute: a6½ furlongs or a1¾ miles

Attendance

Average Daily Recent Meeting: 7,967, 2004/2005; 9,341, 2005/2006
Highest Single-Day Record: 85,527, March 3, 1985
Highest Single-Meet Record: 2,936,086, 1983/1984
Record Daily Average for Single Meet: 35,247, 1946/1947
Total Attendance Recent Meeting: 677,193, 2004/2005; 803,326 est., 2005/2006

Handle

Average All Sources Recent Meeting: $9,310,351, 2004/2005
Average On-Track Recent Meeting: $2,031,838, 2004/2005; $2,245,531, 2005/2006
Record Daily Average for Single Meet: $6,176,295, 1986/1987
Single-Day Total Handle All Sources: $25,282,789, April 8, 2000
Total All Sources Recent Meeting: $791,379,796, 2004/2005
Total On-Track Recent Meeting: $172,706,230, 2004/2005; $193,115,666 est., 2005/2006

Mutuel Records

Highest Win: $673.40, Playmay, February 4, 1938
Highest Exacta: $1,502.50, February 15, 2002
Lowest Exacta: $1.60, April 1, 2001
Highest Trifecta: $21,771.80, February 6, 1999
Lowest Trifecta: $2.90, December 29, 2004
Highest Daily Double: $4,330, January 31, 2001
Lowest Daily Double: $4.40, March 29, 1996; $4.40, April 5, 2002
Highest Pick 3: $73,527.30, February 16, 1997
Lowest Pick 3: $2, March 9, 1997
Highest Pick 6: $1,567,984.60, March 3, 2004
Lowest Pick 6: $106.20, March 16, 1986
Highest Other Exotics: $148, Place, February 4, 1938; $104.60, Show, February 4, 1938; $187,651.20, Superfecta, February 21, 1999; $47,393.10, Place Pick All, March 7, 1998
Lowest Other Exotics: $8.70, Superfecta, February 12, 2005; $23.90, Place Pick All, February 11, 2005
Lowest Pick 4: $31.10, March 4, 2001
Highest Quinella: $1,482.80, February 3, 2000
Lowest Quinella: $2.20, March 8, 2003; $2.20, April 13, 2003
Highest Stakes Win: $55.60, Debonair Joe, December 26, 2002
Highest Pick 4: $124,199.10, December 27, 2003

Leaders

Career, Leading Jockey by Titles: William Shoemaker, 17
Career, Leading Owner by Titles: Elmendorf, 4; Golden Eagle Farm, 4
Career, Leading Trainer by Titles: Farrell W. Jones, 8; Bob Baffert, 8
Career, Leading Jockey by Stakes Wins: William Shoemaker, 260
Career, Leading Trainer by Stakes Wins: Charles Whittingham, 204
Career, Leading Jockey by Wins: Laffit Pincay Jr., 2,860
Career, Leading Trainer by Wins: Charles Whittingham, 869
Recent Meeting, Leading Jockey: Patrick A. Valenzuela, 69, 2004/2005; Patrick A. Valenzuela, 77, 2005/2006
Recent Meeting, Leading Owner: Robert D. Bone, 11, 2004/2005; Robert D. Bone, 17, 2005/2006

Recent Meeting, Leading Trainer: Doug F. O'Neill, 54, 2004/2005; Doug F. O'Neill, 50, 2005/2006
Recent Meeting, Leading Horse: Cambiocorsa, 5, 2005/2006; Fly to the Wire, 5, 2005/2006

Records

Single-Day Jockey Wins: Laffit Pincay Jr., 7, March 14, 1987
Single-Day Trainer Wins: Clyde Van Dusen, 4, February 6, 1941; Farrell W. Jones, 4, January 5, 1962; M. E. "Buster" Millerick, 4, December 29, 1965; Charles Whittingham, 4, February 9, 1967; Bobby Frankel, 4, January 3, 1976; Bobby Frankel, 4, March 26, 1981; Mike Mitchell, 4, January 13, 1995; Doug O'Neill, 4, January 2, 2005
Single Meet, Leading Jockey by Wins: Laffit Pincay Jr., 138, 1970/1971
Single Meet, Leading Trainer by Wins: Doug F. O'Neill, 54, 2004/2005

Track Records, Main Dirt

4 furlongs: Valiant Pete, :44$\frac{1}{5}$, April 20, 1991
$4\frac{1}{2}$ furlongs: Willy Float, :51$\frac{2}{5}$, March 23, 1972
5 furlongs: Zero Henry, :57.78, October 23, 1996
$5\frac{1}{2}$ furlongs: Kona Gold, 1:01.74, January 3, 1999
6 furlongs: Sunny Blossom, 1:07$\frac{1}{5}$, December 30, 1989
$6\frac{1}{2}$ furlongs: Son of a Pistol, 1:13.71, April 4, 1998
7 furlongs: Spectacular Bid, 1:20, January 5, 1980
1 mile: Ruhlmann, 1:33$\frac{2}{5}$, March 5, 1989
$1\frac{1}{16}$ miles: Efervescente (Arg), 1:39.18, January 6, 1993
$1\frac{1}{8}$ miles: Star Spangled, 1:45$\frac{4}{5}$, March 24, 1979
$1\frac{1}{4}$ miles: Spectacular Bid, 1:57$\frac{4}{5}$, February 3, 1980
$1\frac{3}{8}$ miles: Be Faithful, 2:15$\frac{1}{5}$, February 9, 1946
$1\frac{1}{2}$ miles: Queen's Hustler, 2:27$\frac{1}{5}$, February 19, 1973
$1\frac{5}{8}$ miles: Ace Admiral, 2:39$\frac{4}{5}$, July 23, 1949
$1\frac{3}{4}$ miles: *Noor, 2:52$\frac{4}{5}$, March 4, 1950
2 miles: Durango, 3:26$\frac{1}{5}$, February 2, 1935; Fuego, 3:26$\frac{1}{5}$, June 30, 1945; Jimmy John, 3:26$\frac{1}{5}$, March 9, 1946
Other: 2 furlongs, Beautiful Moment, :21, April 3, 1996; 3 furlongs, King Rhymer, :32, February 27, 1947; $2\frac{1}{4}$ miles, English Harry, 3:55$\frac{3}{5}$, February 16, 1940; $2\frac{1}{2}$ miles, Big Ed, 4:22, February 23, 1940; 3 miles, English Harry, 5:20$\frac{1}{5}$, March 1, 1940

Track Records, Main Turf

1 mile: Atticus, 1:31.89, March 1, 1997
$1\frac{1}{8}$ miles: Kostroma (Ire), 1:43.92, October 20, 1991
$1\frac{1}{4}$ miles: Double Discount, 1:57$\frac{3}{5}$, October 9, 1977; Bequest, 1:57.50, March 31, 1991
$1\frac{1}{2}$ miles: Hawkster, 2:22$\frac{4}{5}$, October 14, 1989
Other: a$6\frac{1}{2}$ furlongs, Lennyfromalibu, 1:11.13, January 22, 2004; a$1\frac{1}{2}$ miles, *Practicante, 2:26$\frac{2}{5}$, February 21,1972; a$1\frac{3}{4}$ miles, Bienamado, 2:42.96, April 14, 2001

Principal Races

Santa Anita H. (G1), Santa Anita Derby (G1), Santa Anita Oaks (G1), Santa Margarita Invitational H. (G1), Frank E. Kilroe Mile H. (G1)

Notable Events

Sunshine Millions

Fastest Times of 2005 (Dirt)

2 furlongs: Angel One, :21.30, March 30, 2005
$5\frac{1}{2}$ furlongs: Family Guy, 1:01.80, March 19, 2005
6 furlongs: Areyoutalkintome, 1:08.13, March 20, 2005
$6\frac{1}{2}$ furlongs: Royal Place, 1:14.03, February 20, 2005
7 furlongs: Pussycat Doll, 1:21.36, December 31, 2005
1 mile: Uraib (Ire), 1:33.72, February 21, 2005
$1\frac{1}{16}$ miles: Consolidator, 1:40.11, March 19, 2005
$1\frac{1}{8}$ miles: Tarlow, 1:48.64, February 12, 2005
$1\frac{1}{4}$ miles: Rock Hard Ten, 2:01.20, March 5, 2005
$1\frac{1}{2}$ miles: License To Run (Brz), 2:28.72, February 19, 2005

Fastest Times of 2005 (Turf)

a$6\frac{1}{2}$ furlongs: Elusive Diva, 1:11.66, April 10, 2005
1 mile: Cozy Guy, 1:33.50, March 12, 2005
$1\frac{1}{8}$ miles: Fullbridled, 1:45.92, March 31, 2005
$1\frac{1}{4}$ miles: Ring of Friendship, 1:59.42, February 2, 2005
$1\frac{1}{2}$ miles: Stanley Park, 2:24.45, March 27, 2005
a$1\frac{3}{4}$ miles: T. H. Approval, 2:45.02, April 16, 2005

Santa Rosa

Location: 1350 Bennett Valley Rd., Santa Rosa, Ca. 95403
Phone: (707) 545-4200
Fax: (707) 573-9342
Website: *www.sonomacountyfair.com*
E-Mail: info@sonomacountyfair.com
Year Founded: 1936
Dates of Inaugural Meeting: October 8, 1936
Abbreviation: SR
Number of Stalls: 1,022

Officers

Chairman: Tony Withington
President: John Serres
Director of Racing: Jim Moore
Racing Secretary: C. Gregory Brent Jr.
Director of Mutuels: Bryan Wayte
Track Announcer: Vic Stauffer
Asst. Racing Secretary: Linda Anderson

Racing Dates

2005: July 27-August 8, 12 days
2006: July 26-August 7, 12 days

Track Layout

Main Circumference: 1 mile
Main Track Chute: 6 furlongs and $1\frac{1}{4}$ miles
Main Length of Stretch: 1,145.8 feet
Main Turf Circumference: 7 furlongs
Main Turf Width: 60 feet

Attendance

Average Daily Recent Meeting: 5,367, 2005
Total Attendance Recent Meeting: 64,400, 2005

Handle

Average All Sources Recent Meeting: $3,088,957, 2005
Average On-Track Recent Meeting: $516,971, 2005
Single-Day Total Handle All Sources: $4,128,001, August 2, 2003
Total All Sources Recent Meeting: $37,067,483, 2005
Total On-Track Recent Meeting: $6,203,650, 2005

Leaders

Recent Meeting, Leading Jockey: Russell A. Baze, 19, 2005
Recent Meeting, Leading Trainer: William E. Morey, 9, 2005

Principal Races

Joseph T. Grace H., Luther Burbank H., Ernest Finley H., Cavonnier Juvenile S.

Fastest Times of 2005 (Dirt)

$4\frac{1}{2}$ furlongs: Siberian Slew, :51.37, August 4, 2005
5 furlongs: Cinderella Liberty, :57.35, July 27, 2005
$5\frac{1}{2}$ furlongs: Frisco Star, 1:01.65, August 6, 2005
6 furlongs: Bonfante, 1:09.17, July 31, 2005
1 mile: Stormy Zone, 1:37.04, July 27, 2005
$1\frac{1}{16}$ miles: Huka's Diamond, 1:42.61, August 7, 2005

Fastest Times of 2005 (Turf)

5 furlongs: Military Academy, :57.42, August 7, 2005
1 mile: River Bend Ladd, 1:37.10, July 31, 2005
$1\frac{1}{16}$ miles: Adreamisborn, 1:42.20, August 6, 2005
a$1\frac{3}{8}$ miles: San Remy (Ire), 2:17.12, August 3, 2005

Stockton

Location: 1658 S. Airport Way, Stockton, Ca. 95206
Phone: (209) 466-5041
Fax: (209) 466-5739
Website: *www.sanjoaquinfair.com*
E-Mail: fun@sanjoaquinfair.com
Year Founded: 1933
Dates of Inaugural Meeting: August 1934
Abbreviation: Stk
Number of Stalls: 800
Seating Capacity: 5,660

Officers

Chief Executive Officer: Forrest J. White
President: Greg O'Leary
Director of Racing: Forrest J. White
Racing Secretary: Robert Moreno
Director of Mutuels: Annette Snezek
Vice President: Wayne Watanabe
Track Announcer: Frank Mirahmadi
Track Photographer: Photos by Frank

Racing Dates

2005: June 15-June 26, 10 days
2006: June 14-June 25, 10 days

Track Layout

Main Circumference: 1 mile
Main Track Chute: 6 furlongs and $1\frac{1}{4}$ miles
Main Width: 80 feet
Main Length of Stretch: 1,003 feet

Attendance

Average Daily Recent Meeting: 4,534, 2005
Total Attendance Recent Meeting: 45,338, 2005

Handle

Average All Sources Recent Meeting: $1,610,851, 2005
Average On-Track Recent Meeting: $218,119, 2005
Total All Sources Recent Meeting: $16,108,510, 2005
Total On-Track Recent Meeting: $2,181,189, 2005

Leaders

Recent Meeting, Leading Jockey: David G. Lopez, 17, 2005
Recent Meeting, Leading Trainer: John F. Martin, 5, 2005
Recent Meeting, Leading Horse: Stylish Gal, 2, 2005; Never Lost a Wager, 2, 2005

Track Records, Main Dirt

5 furlongs: Shining Prince, :55.80, June 26, 1994
$5\frac{1}{2}$ furlongs: Colonel Courtney, 1:02.03, June 16, 2005
6 furlongs: Lynn's Notebook, 1:07.80, June 25, 1995
1 mile: Flying Cuantal, 1:33.40, June 15, 1997
$1\frac{1}{16}$ miles: Athenia Green (GB), 1:40.40, June 28, 1992
$1\frac{1}{8}$ miles: Episodic, 1:49.20, June 27, 1993
$1\frac{1}{4}$ miles: Ali Kato, 2:01$\frac{3}{5}$, August 17, 1986

Fastest Times of 2005 (Dirt)

$4\frac{1}{2}$ furlongs: Bold Bobo, :50.86, June 17, 2005
5 furlongs: Decision Time, :58.20, June 15, 2005
$5\frac{1}{2}$ furlongs: Colonel Courtney, 1:02.03, June 16, 2005
6 furlongs: Truckee Warrior, 1:09.45, June 22, 2005
1 mile: Ghost Actor, 1:35.68, June 22, 2005

Vallejo

Location: 900 Fairgrounds Dr., Vallejo, Ca. 94589
Phone: (707) 551-2066
Fax: (707) 554-8045
Website: *www.scfair.com*
E-Mail: pskelton@scfair.org
Year Founded: 1950
Dates of Inaugural Meeting: June 16, 1951
Abbreviation: Sol
Number of Stalls: 864
Seating Capacity: 6,500

Ownership

County of Solano

Officers

Chairman: Raymond Simonds
President: William Luiz
General Manager: Joe Barkett
Director of Racing: Joe Barkett
Racing Secretary: C. Gregory Brent Jr.
Director of Operations: Stephen Hales
Director of Mutuels: Richard Horner
Vice President: Cyndy Gill
Track Announcer: Frank Mirahmadi
Track Photographer: Photos by Frank
Track Superintendent: Trackmasters Inc.
Asst. Racing Secretary: Linda Anderson
Promotions/Events: Emanuel Lorenzana
Security: Mark Coffman

Racing Dates

2005: July 13-July 25, 11 days
2006: July 12-July 24, 11 days

Track Layout

Main Circumference: 7 furlongs
Main Track Chute: 6 furlongs
Main Length of Stretch: 1,085 feet

Attendance

Average Daily Recent Meeting: 1,504, 2005
Highest Single-Day Record: 18,127, June 14, 1980
Total Attendance Recent Meeting: 16,539, 2005

Handle

Average All Sources Recent Meeting: $2,655,681, 2005
Average On-Track Recent Meeting: $261,002, 2005
Total All Sources Recent Meeting: $29,212,493, 2005
Total On-Track Recent Meeting: $2,871,017, 2005

Leaders

Recent Meeting, Leading Jockey: David G. Lopez, 14, 2005
Recent Meeting, Leading Trainer: Art Sherman, 8, 2005

Track Records, Main Dirt

$4\frac{1}{2}$ furlongs: Notorious One, :51.26, July 25, 2005
5 furlongs: One Bad Shark, :56.60, July 14, 2002
$5\frac{1}{2}$ furlongs: Ridgewood High, 1:02$\frac{1}{5}$, July 18, 1982
6 furlongs: Salta's Pride, 1:07.80, July 13, 1996
1 mile: Kamalii King, 1:34$\frac{4}{5}$, July 18, 1982
$1\frac{1}{16}$ miles: Hoedown's Day, 1:39$\frac{4}{5}$, July 24, 1983
$1\frac{1}{8}$ miles: Baffi's Eagle, 1:48$\frac{2}{5}$, July 17, 1984
$1\frac{1}{4}$ miles: Super Sonet, 2:03$\frac{2}{5}$, June 20, 1974
$1\frac{3}{8}$ miles: Rain Storm, 2:15$\frac{4}{5}$, June 22, 1973
$1\frac{1}{2}$ miles: Always King, 2:32$\frac{3}{5}$, June 24, 1978

Principal Races

Solano County Juvenile Filly S., Vacaville H., Fairfield S.

Fastest Times of 2005 (Dirt)

$4\frac{1}{2}$ furlongs: Notorious One, :51.26, July 25, 2005
5 furlongs: Playgirl, :57.90, July 22, 2005
$5\frac{1}{2}$ furlongs: Red Seattle, 1:03.93, July 17, 2005
6 furlongs: Colonel Courtney, 1:09.87, July 16, 2005
1 mile: We Will Prevail, 1:37.79, July 17, 2005
$1\frac{1}{16}$ miles: Bells Fool, 1:42.39, July 17, 2005

Colorado

Arapahoe Park

One of racing's quiet survivors, Denver-area Arapahoe Park has survived a disastrous launch, increased gambling competition, and disputes with horsemen to remain a summer racing fixture in the Rocky Mountains region. The track opened in the mid-1980s, replacing longtime Denver track Centennial Park. But its location southeast of Denver was far from any interstate highways; interest in the track was negligible, and it was closed for several years after its opening. The track reopened in the early 1990s but struggled to develop a fan base amid competition from a state lottery and Native American casinos, which were legalized in the state in the early '90s. A dispute between the track's former owner, Wembley USA, and horsemen over racing dates nearly forced the cancellation of the 2000 race meet. Arapahoe and other Wembley properties were sold to BLB Investors for $455-million in 2005.

Location: 26000 E. Quincy Ave., P.O. Box 460370, Aurora, Co. 80016-2026
Phone: (303) 690-2400
Fax: (303) 690-6730
Website: *www.mihiracing.com*
Dates of Inaugural Meeting: May 24, 1984
Abbreviation: Arp
Acreage: 297
Number of Stalls: 1,400
Seating Capacity: 7,500

Ownership

BLB Investors

Officers

General Manager: Bruce Seymore
Director of Racing: Bill Powers
Racing Secretary: Bill Powers

Director of Marketing: Sean Beirne
Track Announcer: Sean Beirne
Track Superintendent: William Byers

Racing Dates

2005: June 10-August 28, 37 days
2006: June 10-September 4, 39 days

Track Layout

Main Circumference: 1 mile
Main Track Chute: 6 furlongs, 7 furlongs and 1 5/16 miles
Main Width: 90 feet
Main Length of Stretch: 1,029 feet

Handle

Average All Sources Recent Meeting: $94,236, 2005
Single-Day Total Handle All Sources: $361,000, August 5, 2003
Total All Sources Recent Meeting: $3,486,747, 2005

Leaders

Recent Meeting, Leading Jockey: Wilson Omar Dieguez, 45, 2005
Recent Meeting, Leading Trainer: Jon G. Arnett, 26, 2005
Recent Meeting, Leading Horse: Cocoa Latte, 4, 2005

Track Records, Main Dirt

4 furlongs: Et Tu Brutus, :44.60, July 26, 2004
4 1/2 furlongs: V G's Catch, :50.40, June 23, 2002; Hugs Legacy, :50.40, July 19, 2004
5 furlongs: Nycity, :56, July 13, 2002
5 1/2 furlongs: Choppers Passion, 1:02.20, June 22, 2001; Ribot Line, 1:02.20, June 30, 2002
6 furlongs: Absolutely True, 1:08.20, July 11, 2004
6 1/2 furlongs: Pray for Booger, 1:18.60, August 25, 1995
7 furlongs: Daring Pegasus, 1:21.20, July 4, 2003
1 mile: Honor Bright, 1:35.20, August 7, 1993
1m 70 yds: Naskra's Advocate, 1:38.20, July 23, 1993
1 1/16 miles: Run At Night, 1:42.40, August 14, 2004
1 1/8 miles: Maysville Slew, 1:49, September 1, 2002
1 1/4 miles: Builder's Boy, 2:05.40, June 26, 1992
1 1/2 miles: Calgary Classic, 2:33.20, July 24, 1993
1 3/4 miles: Read My Mind, 3:02, August 9, 1992
2 miles: Little Reeves, 3:28.40, August 27, 1994

Principal Races

Gold Rush Futurity, Colorado Derby, Inaugural S., Arapahoe Park Sprint H., Molly Brown H.

Fastest Times of 2005 (Dirt)

4 furlongs: Glidininthecash, :46.13, June 11, 2005
4 1/2 furlongs: Appleton (Mex), :51, July 30, 2005
5 furlongs: Stormy Town, :56.74, July 3, 2005
5 1/2 furlongs: Lorenzon, 1:02.78, July 24, 2005
6 furlongs: Cocoa Latte, 1:08.36, July 17, 2005
7 furlongs: Komax, 1:22.70, July 4, 2005
1 mile: Continuum, 1:36.81, July 16, 2005
1m 70 yds: Fuzdaisy, 1:43.65, August 7, 2005
1 1/16 miles: Beaverton, 1:44.25, July 2, 2005
1 1/8 miles: Personal Beau, 1:52.06, August 21, 2005
1 1/2 miles: Huckleberry Prize, 2:36.49, August 28, 2005

Delaware

Delaware Park

Competition from racetracks in neighboring Pennsylvania, Maryland, and New Jersey forced the closure of historic Delaware Park in Stanton in September 1982. In late 1983, Maryland developer William Rickman Sr. acquired Delaware Park in partnership with Maryland horseman William Christmas, and the track ran abbreviated meets in the spring and fall of '84. Rickman's son, William Rickman Jr., managed track operations and in 1994 helped to secure state approval for installing slot machines at the track. Delaware's slots facility opened in December 1995, and revenues from the slots have more than tripled purses. The Wilmington-area track was designed by banker and horseman William duPont Jr. and became a haven for summer racing fans throughout the Mid-Atlantic region. The track's richest race, the Delaware Handicap (G2), debuted in 1937 as the New Castle Handicap and has been won by some of the sport's leading fillies and mares.

Location: 777 Delaware Park Blvd., Wilmington, De. 19804
Phone: (302) 994-2521
Fax: (302) 994-3567
Website: *www.delawarepark.com*
E-Mail: programs@delawarepark.com
Year Founded: 1937
Abbreviation: Del

Ownership

Delaware Racing Association

Officers

Chief Executive Officer: William M. Rickman Jr.
President: William M. Rickman Jr.
Racing Secretary: Sam Abbey
Director of Operations: William Fasy
Director of Communications: Mike McGinnis
Director of Marketing: Pam Cunningham
Director of Mutuels: Scott Loomis
Vice Presidents: Greg Petkiewicz, Joseph Rudisill, Ray Spera, Nancy Myshko, Christer Farr
Director of Publicity: Jennifer Oberle
Horsemen's Liaison: Joe'Lyn Rigione
Stewards: Fritz Burkhardt, Jack Houghton Jr., Dennis Lima
Track Announcer: John Curran
Track Photographer: Hoofprints Inc.
Track Superintendent: Ken Brown
Security: Kathy Harer
Horsemen's Bookkeeper: Cindy Houghton
Asst. Racing Secretary: Chris Camac

Racing Dates

2005: April 30-November 13, 137 days
2006: April 22-November 19, 136 days

Track Layout

Main Circumference: 1 mile
Main Track Chute: 6 furlongs and 1 1/4 miles
Main Width: 100 feet
Main Length of Stretch: 995 feet
Main Turf Circumference: 7 furlongs

Attendance

Average Daily Recent Meeting: 3,498, 2005
Total Attendance Recent Meeting: 479,198, 2005

Handle

Average All Sources Recent Meeting: $1,717,370, 2005
Average On-Track Recent Meeting: $135,546, 2005
Total All Sources Recent Meeting: $235,279,675, 2005
Total On-Track Recent Meeting: $18,569,775, 2005
Highest Single-Day Record Recent Meet: $3,901,467, July 17, 2005

Mutuel Records

Highest Win: $403.20, Gerabon, June 16, 1949
Lowest Win: $2.10, Spectacular Bid, August 26, 1979
Highest Exacta: $4,565.60, July 21, 1972
Lowest Exacta: $3.80, August 7, 1977; $3.80, August 26, 1979
Highest Trifecta: $50,870.80, May 25, 1974
Highest Daily Double: $5,507.80, July 4, 1941
Lowest Daily Double: $6.40, June 11, 1976
Highest Other Exotics: $699,100, Twin-Trifecta, June 13, 1986
Highest Quinella: $623.40, June 13, 1968
Lowest Quinella: $5.40, July 1, 1968

Leaders

Recent Meeting, Leading Jockey: Ramon A. Dominquez, 188, 2005
Recent Meeting, Leading Owner: Michael Gill, 44, 2005
Recent Meeting, Leading Trainer: Scott A. Lake, 126, 2005
Recent Meeting, Leading Horse: Sierra Bella, 7, 2005

Records

Single-Day Jockey Wins: Eldon Nelson, 6, June 20, 1958; George Cusimano, 6, July 16, 1968; Greg McCarron, 6, July 6, 1974; Jimmy Edwards, 6, May 28, 1984; Michael McCarthy, 6, November 2, 1997; Michael McCarthy, 6, May 20, 1998

Single Meet, Leading Jockey by Wins: Michael McCarthy, 218, 1997
Single Meet, Leading Trainer by Wins: Scott A. Lake, 126, 2005
Single Meet, Leading Horse by Wins: Fionnghal, 10, 1988

Track Records, Main Dirt

$4\frac{1}{2}$ furlongs: Erlton, :51.80, May 5, 1998
5 furlongs: Milky Way Gal, :56.20, July 29, 1989
$5\frac{1}{2}$ furlongs: Trickle of Gold, 1:02.68, May 6, 2006
6 furlongs: Pisgah, 1:07.92, April 25, 2006
1 mile: Ashlar, 1:35.20, June 25, 1960
1m 70 yds: Distinct Vision, 1:39.20, August 25, 2003
$1\frac{1}{16}$ miles: Lies of Omission, 1:41.20, July 4, 1998
$1\frac{1}{8}$ miles: Victoria Park, 1:47.40, June 18, 1960
$1\frac{3}{16}$ miles: Trapped Again, 1:55.41, October 1, 2005
$1\frac{1}{4}$ miles: Coup de Fusil, 1:59.80, July 25, 1987
$1\frac{1}{2}$ miles: Bam, 2:31, June 26, 1948
$1\frac{5}{8}$ miles: Flying Restina Run, 2:45.40, September 4, 2000
$1\frac{3}{4}$ miles: Cer Vantes, 2:56.40, June 27, 1951
2 miles: Dixies Act, 3:29.40, August 10, 1975
Other: 2 furlongs, Glitter River, :21.60, September 5, 2000; 2m 70 yds, Wolfe Tone, 3:34, November 7, 1993; $2\frac{1}{4}$ miles, Sanguine Sword, 3:58.60, July 2, 1986

Track Records, Main Turf

5 furlongs: Beer Stien, :55.84, June 29, 2005
1 mile: Hanover Hollywood, 1:34.74, August 3, 2002
$1\frac{1}{16}$ miles: Charablanc, 1:40.20, July 20, 1963
$1\frac{1}{8}$ miles: Seeking Slew, 1:47.32, June 25, 2005
$1\frac{3}{8}$ miles: Cool Prince, 2:12.40, July 3, 1965
$1\frac{1}{2}$ miles: Revved Up, 2:26.46, July 20, 2003
2 miles: Verdance, 3:24.40, September 21, 1986
Other: $1\frac{7}{8}$ miles, El Moro, 3:11.80, July 22, 1963; $2\frac{3}{8}$ miles, Lively London, 4:09, July 25, 1986; $2\frac{7}{8}$ miles, Call Louis, 5:08.20, August 24, 1986

Principal Races

Delaware H. (G2), Delaware Oaks (G2), Kent Breeders' Cup S. (G3), Leonard Richards S. (G3), Endine H. (G3)

Notable Events

Delaware Handicap Festival of Racing, Owners Day

Fastest Times of 2005 (Dirt)

2 furlongs: Don't Be Long, :22.52, May 17, 2005
$4\frac{1}{2}$ furlongs: Master of Disaster, :51.86, May 10, 2005
5 furlongs: Hold the Salt, :57.71, September 18, 2005
$5\frac{1}{2}$ furlongs: Western Times, 1:03.95, July 31, 2005
6 furlongs: Toscani, 1:08.51, September 19, 2005
1 mile: Gadace's Khamseh, 1:36.97, June 21, 2005
1m 70 yds: Indian Lotus (Arg), 1:40.49, October 1, 2005
$1\frac{1}{16}$ miles: R Lady Joy, 1:43.25, July 16, 2005
$1\frac{1}{8}$ miles: Trapped Again, 1:50.55, September 10, 2005
$1\frac{3}{16}$ miles: Trapped Again, 1:55.41, October 1, 2005
$1\frac{1}{4}$ miles: Island Sand, 2:02.89, July 17, 2005
$1\frac{1}{2}$ miles: Hydrogen, 2:32.38, July 17, 2005

Fastest Times of 2005 (Turf)

5 furlongs: Beer Stien, :55.84, June 29, 2005
a5 furlongs: Tune of the Spirit, :56.76, June 15, 2005
1 mile: Go Ricky Go, 1:35.53, October 4, 2005; He's Impressive, 1:35.53, July 3, 2005
a1 miles: Grady N, 1:37.73, June 12, 2005
$1\frac{1}{16}$ miles: Whale, 1:40.51, June 25, 2005
a$1\frac{1}{16}$ miles: Bingobear, 1:43.38, September 25, 2005
$1\frac{1}{8}$ miles: Seeking Slew, 1:47.32, June 25, 2005
a$1\frac{1}{8}$ miles: Learning, 1:50.38, June 11, 2005
$1\frac{3}{8}$ miles: Margarita Maggie, 2:16.91, August 13, 2005

Florida

Calder Race Course

Calder Race Course, which offers racing from late April through early January, is located in Miami next to Pro Player Stadium, home of the National Football League's Miami Dolphins. Built by real-estate businessman Stephen A. Calder, the track was granted summer racing dates for 1970. Because the track was under construction, those dates were run at Tropical Park. Calder officially opened on May 6, 1971, debuting an all-weather synthetic track surface designed by 3M that remained in place until 1992. In 1972, Tropical Park closed and began holding its meet at Calder; the last several weeks of each year's season are known as the Tropical Park meet. From 1980-'84, Calder underwent $10.5-million in improvements. In 1988, Thoroughbred owner-breeder Bertram R. Firestone bought Calder. Three years later, Kawasaki Leasing Inc. assumed control of the track. The track underwent a $1-million renovation of its first floor, and in 1995 it added full-card simulcasting. In 1999, Churchill Downs Inc. bought Calder for approximately $86-million. Today, Calder features three racing events: the Florida Stallion Stakes, a series of races for offspring of Florida stallions; Festival of the Sun, a $1.6-million day of racing highlighted by the finals of the Florida Stallion Stakes series; and Summit of Speed, sprint stakes races with combined purses totaling $1.9-million.

Location: 21001 N.W. 27th Ave., Miami Gardens, Fl. 33056
Phone: (305) 625-1311
Fax: (305) 620-2569
Website: *www.calderracecourse.com*
E-Mail: blanco@calderracecourse.com
Year Founded: 1971
Dates of Inaugural Meeting: May 6, 1971
Abbreviation: Crc
Acreage: 220
Number of Stalls: 1,850
Seating Capacity: 15,585

Ownership

Churchill Downs Inc.

Officers

Chairman: Thomas H. Meeker
President: C. Kenneth Dunn
General Manager: Michael Abes
Racing Secretary: Michael Anifantis
Secretary: Rebecca C. Reed
Treasurer: Michael Abes
Director of Admissions: Bill Keers
Director of Marketing: Michael Cronin
Director of Mutuels: Edward Mackie Sr.
Vice President: Michael Abes, Michael Cronin
Director of Publicity: Michele Blanco
Director of Simulcasting: Diane Stoess
Horsemen's Liaison: Janet Kownacke
Stewards: Charles Camac, Jeffrey Noe, Kevin Scheen
Track Announcer: Bobby Neuman
Track Photographer: Jim Lisa
Track Superintendent: Steve Cross
Security: Tony Otero

Racing Dates

2005: April 25-October 16, 120 days
2006: April 25-October 15, 112 days

Track Layout

Main Circumference: 1 mile
Main Track Chute: 7 furlongs and $1\frac{1}{4}$ miles
Main Width: Homestretch: 80 feet; Backstretch: 75 feet
Main Length of Stretch: 990 feet
Main Turf Circumference: 7 furlongs
Main Turf Chute: $1\frac{1}{8}$ miles
Main Turf Width: 67 feet
Main Turf Length of Stretch: 986 feet

Attendance

Average Daily Recent Meeting: 4,250, 2005
Highest Single-Day Record: 23,103, May 4, 1985
Record Daily Average for Single Meet: 9,401, 1976
Highest Single-Meet Record: 1,113,017, 1975
Total Attendance Recent Meeting: 509,958, 2005
Lowest Single-Meet Record: 509,958, 2005
Highest Single-Day Recent Meet: 11,567, October 15, 2005

Handle

Average All Sources Recent Meeting: $2,770,554, 2005
Average On-Track Recent Meeting: $361,489, 2005
Record Daily Average for Single Meet: $1,206,739, 1986
Single-Day On-Track Handle: $2,954,162, May 7, 1988
Single-Day Total Handle All Sources: $10,843,994, July 10, 2004
Total All Sources Recent Meeting: $332,466,453, 2005
Total On-Track Recent Meeting: $43,378,733, 2005
Highest Single-Day Record Recent Meet: $7,020,071, July 10, 2005
Record Total for Single Meet: $152,326,480, 1990
Record Total All Sources for Single Meet: $452,540,885, 2002
Record Average All Sources Single Meet: $3,535,476, 2002

Mutuel Records

Highest Win: $345.40, Lou Glory, September 12, 1991
Lowest Win: $2.10, Isle O'Style, June 12, 1974; $2.10, June 16, 2001
Highest Exacta: $31,133.20, November 3, 1972
Lowest Exacta: $3.40, August 16, 1989
Highest Trifecta: $58,432.40, October 25, 1986
Lowest Trifecta: $10.40, July 31, 1994
Highest Daily Double: $2,671, July 2, 1976
Lowest Daily Double: $3.20, September 16, 1992
Highest Pick 3: $39,548.80, April 26, 2004
Lowest Pick 3: $9, September 12, 2000
Highest Other Exotics: $74,622, Superfecta, October 26, 1996; $222, Place, October 17, 1975; $97.80, Show, December 31, 2004
Lowest Other Exotics: $33.40, Superfecta, August 7, 1995
Highest Pick 4: $10,846.70, April 26, 2004
Lowest Pick 4: $59.10, October 12, 2002

Leaders

Career, Leading Jockey by Titles: Eibar Coa, 4
Career, Leading Trainer by Titles: William P. White, 9
Career, Leading Jockey by Stakes Wins: Gene St. Leon, 73
Career, Leading Trainer by Stakes Wins: Frank Gomez, 93
Career, Leading Jockey by Wins: Gene St. Leon, 1,310
Career, Leading Trainer by Wins: Emanuel Tortora, 1001
Recent Meeting, Leading Jockey: Eddie Castro, 218, 2005
Recent Meeting, Leading Owner: Steve Dwoskin, 22, 2005; Michael Sherman, 22, 2005
Recent Meeting, Leading Trainer: Tim Ritvo, 45, 2005
Recent Meeting, Leading Horse: Burley A, 5, 2005

Records

Single-Day Jockey Wins: Eddie Castro, 9, June 4, 2005
Single-Day Trainer Wins: Arnold N. Winick, 5, September 16, 1972; Stanley Hough, 5, May 12, 1977
Single Meet, Leading Jockey by Wins: Eddie Castro, 218, 2005
Single Meet, Leading Trainer by Wins: Stanley Hough, 110, 1977
Single Meet, Leading Trainer by Stakes Wins: Frank Gomez, 10, 1979
Single Meet, Leading Jockey by Stakes Wins: Jose Velez Jr., 14, 1986

Track Records, Main Dirt

4 furlongs: Diamond Studs, :46.21, July 14, 2001
4½ furlongs: Gold Phantom, :51.86, September 16, 2001
5 furlongs: Honest, :57.61, July 1, 1996
5½ furlongs: Bernard's Candy, 1:04.39, August 9, 2002
6 furlongs: Forty One Carats, 1:08.95, October 7, 2000
6½ furlongs: Tour of the Cat, 1:15.99, August 17, 2002
7 furlongs: Constant Escort, 1:21.82, September 28, 1996
1 mile: High Ideal, 1:36.25, September 15, 2001
1m 70 yds: Halo's Image, 1:41.78, October 31, 1995
1$^1/_{16}$ miles: Castlebrook, 1:42.55, September 15, 2001
1⅛ miles: Jumping Hill, 1:50, December 30, 1978
1$^3/_{16}$ miles: Arctic Honeymoon, 1:59⅗, January 3, 1987
1¼ miles: Wicapi, 2:05.08, June 24, 1996
1½ miles: Lead'm Home, 2:32⅗, December 31, 1977
1⅝ miles: Timberlea Tune, 2:50⅕, October 16, 1971
1¾ miles: *Detective II, 3:03⅕, October 23, 1971
2 miles: *Detective II, 3:30⅕, November 11, 1971
Other: 2 furlongs, Baby Shark, :20.81, July 13, 2002

Track Records, Main Turf

5 furlongs: Whenthedoveflies, :54.78, May 23, 2004
7 furlongs: Carterista, 1:22.36, June 19, 1993
7½ furlongs: Court Lark, 1:26.54, July 16, 1994
1 mile: Mr. Explosive, 1:33⅗, October 17, 1992; Dillonmyboy, 1:33.66, October 30, 2000
1$^1/_{16}$ miles: He's Crafty, 1:39.27, December 28, 2004
1⅛ miles: The Vid, 1:44.99, November 25, 1995
1⅜ miles: King's Design, 2:13.18, July 23, 1999
1½ miles: Flag Down, 2:24.11, December 16, 1995
2 miles: Skate On Thin Ice, 3:21.89, January 2, 1996

Principal Races

Princess Rooney H. (G1), Smile Sprint H. (G2), Carry Back S. (G2), Calder Derby (G3), Miami Mile Breeders' Cup H. (G3)

Notable Events

Summit of Speed, Festival of the Sun, Juvenile Showcase

Fastest Times of 2005 (Dirt)

2 furlongs: Thats the Problem, :21.21, July 10, 2005
4½ furlongs: The Pharaoh, :52.51, June 25, 2005
5 furlongs: Scrubs, :57.95, June 11, 2005
5½ furlongs: Sugarcane Road, 1:04.54, November 13, 2005
6 furlongs: Lost in the Fog, 1:09.30, July 10, 2005
6½ furlongs: Mister Fotis, 1:16.79, January 1, 2005
7 furlongs: Mister Fotis, 1:22.97, December 17, 2005
1 mile: Current Niner, 1:38.69, November 12, 2005
1m 70 yds: Blazing Rate, 1:45.76, September 24, 2005
1$^1/_{16}$ miles: Pampered Princess, 1:45.06, June 12, 2005
1⅛ miles: Siphon City, 1:52.42, October 8, 2005
1$^3/_{16}$ miles: Sir Ray, 2:04.12, May 21, 2005
1¼ miles: Uncivil, 2:08.32, December 19, 2005
1½ miles: Perspicacious (Arg), 2:39.13, June 11, 2005

Fastest Times of 2005 (Turf)

5 furlongs: Placido, :55.36, January 2, 2005
7½ furlongs: Drum Major, 1:26.83, December 31, 2005
1 mile: Devine Wind, 1:33.98, December 31, 2005
1$^1/_{16}$ miles: Wood Be Willing, 1:39.80, December 27, 2005
1⅛ miles: Revved Up, 1:45.89, November 12, 2005
1⅜ miles: Hup Two, 2:19.47, September 18, 2005
1½ miles: Meteor Storm (GB), 2:25.91, December 17, 2005

Gulfstream Park

Since the 1940s, Gulfstream Park, located north of Miami in Hallandale, Florida, has been a favorite winter destination for horsemen and annually offers high-quality winter racing. Gulfstream opened in February 1939 but went bankrupt and closed after four days of racing. In 1944, James Donn Sr., who owned a local floral shop and was a creditor of the track, reopened Gulfstream. In 1952, the Florida Derby (now G1) debuted and became a major stop on the road to the Kentucky Derby (G1). Eleven winners of the race, including Northern Dancer, Unbridled, Thunder Gulch, and Barbaro, went on to win the Kentucky Derby. Gulfstream in 1989 held the first of the track's three Breeders' Cup championship days. In 1999, Frank Stronach-led Magna Entertainment Corp. purchased Gulfstream for $95-million. In 2003, Magna opened Palm Meadows Training Center, a 304-acre training facility located near Boynton Beach, approximately 35 miles north of the track. The track's grandstand was lavishly rebuilt for $171-million and reopened in 2006.

Location: 901 S. Federal Hwy., Hallandale Beach, Fl. 33009-7199
Phone: (954) 454-7000, (800) 771-TURF
Fax: (954) 454-7827
Website: *www.gulfstreampark.com*
E-Mail: tsweeney@gulfstreampark.com
Year Founded: 1939
Dates of Inaugural Meeting: February 1-4, 1939
Abbreviation: GP
Seating Capacity: 4,350

Ownership

Magna Entertainment Corp.

Officers

Chairman: Frank Stronach
President: Paul Micucci
General Manager: Paul Micucci

Director of Racing: David F. Bailey
Director of Operations: Dennis Testa
Director of Admissions: Tanessa Sweeney
Director of Finance: Richard Odum
Director of Mutuels: Edward Mackie
Vice President: Tom Dillon
Horsemen's Liaison: Raina Chingos-Gunderson
Stewards: Charles Camac, Jeffrey Noe, Kevin Sheen
Track Announcer: Vic Stauffer
Track Photographer: Equi-Photo/Bill Denver
Track Superintendents: John Grillon (main track); Doug Kickbush (turf)
Other Officials: Director of Media, Mike Mullaney
Security: Rick Buhrmaster

Racing Dates

2005: January 3-April 23, 86 days
2006: January 4-April 23, 86 days

Track Layout

Main Circumference: 1⅛ miles
Main Turf Circumference: 1 mile
Main Turf Width: 170 feet
Training Track: Palm Meadows

Attendance

Average Daily Recent Meeting: 5,087, 2005; 4,782 est., 2006
Highest Single-Day Record: 33,864, March 4, 1989; 51,342, November 4, 1989 (Breeders' Cup Day)
Highest Single-Meet Record: 1,096,404, 1991
Total Attendance Recent Meeting: 437,452, 2005; 416,000 est., 2006
Highest Single-Day Recent Meet: 15,064, April 24, 2005

Handle

Average All Sources Recent Meeting: $9,271,530, 2005
Average On-Track Recent Meeting: $1,761,022, 2005; $1,403,559, 2006
Record Daily Average for Single Meet: $2,121,121, 1998
Single-Day On-Track Handle: $7,993,485, March 12, 1994; $15,377,709, November 6, 1999 (Breeders' Cup Day)
Single-Day Total Handle All Sources: $24,482,519, March 11, 2001
Total All Sources Recent Meeting: $797,351,561, 2005
Total On-Track Recent Meeting: $151,447,851, 2005; $120,706,069, 2006
Highest Single-Day Record Recent Meet: $19,073,314, April 2, 2005
Record Total All Sources for Single Meet: $825,343,874, 2003

Mutuel Records

Highest Win: $404, Concert Grand, February 14, 1993
Lowest Win: $2.10, Honest Pleasure, April 3, 1976; $2.10, Spectacular Bid, February 7, 1979; $2.10, Spectacular Bid, March 6, 1979
Highest Exacta: $8,948.80, March 13, 1987
Lowest Exacta: $3.80, March 6, 1979; $3.80, March 10, 1991
Highest Trifecta: $96,751.80, January 31, 1993
Lowest Trifecta: $6.40, January 19, 1997
Highest Daily Double: $6,683.60, January 28, 1972
Lowest Daily Double: $6, January 14, 1995
Highest Pick 3: $63,737.60, January 26, 1995
Lowest Pick 3: $9.80, February 22, 1994
Highest Pick 6: $799,191, February 3, 2005
Highest Other Exotics: $127,737, Superfecta, February 17, 2001

Leaders

Career, Leading Jockey by Titles: Walter Blum, 4; Jorge Chavez, 4
Career, Leading Trainer by Titles: Arnold Winick, 12
Career, Leading Jockey by Stakes Wins: Jerry Bailey, 147
Recent Meeting, Leading Jockey: Edgar Prado, 62, 2005; John Velazquez, 86, 2006
Recent Meeting, Leading Owner: Olympia Stables, 10, 2005; Frank Carl Calabrese, 10, 2005; Darley Stable, 14, 2006; Frank Carl Calabrese, 14, 2006
Recent Meeting, Leading Trainer: Todd Pletcher, 36, 2005; Todd Pletcher, 60, 2006
Recent Meeting, Leading Horse: My Buddy Richie, 4, 2005; Unforgettable Gal, 4, 2005; Necropolis, 4, 2006

Records

Single-Day Jockey Wins: Jerry Bailey, 7, March 11, 1995
Single Meet, Leading Jockey by Wins: Julio Pezua, 97, 1987; Wigberto Ramos, 97, 1991; Jerry Bailey, 97, 1996
Single Meet, Leading Trainer by Wins: Mark Shuman, 87, 2003
Single Meet, Leading Horse by Wins: Shir-Tee, 5, 1971

Track Records, Main Dirt

5½ furlongs: Shane Jules, 1:03.03, March 19, 2006
6 furlongs: Tiger, 1:08.46, February 16, 2006
6½ furlongs: Forest Danger, 1:14.44, February 14, 2005
7 furlongs: Exclusive Quality, 1:21.11, March 4, 2006
7½ furlongs: Keyed Entry, 1:27.12, February 4, 2006
1 mile: Showing Up, 1:34.05, March 11, 2006
1⅛ miles: Brass Hat, 1:47.79, February 4, 2006
1 3/16 miles: Eddington, 1:54.74, March 5, 2005
Other: 1 7/16 miles, Watchmon, 2:25.80, April 8, 2005

Track Records, Main Turf

5 furlongs: Procreate, :53.79, April 9, 2005
7½ furlongs: Paula Smith, 1:27.72, January 13, 2005
1 mile: Mr. Light (Arg), 1:31.41, January 3, 2005
1 1/16 miles: Congleve, 1:38.17, January 20, 2006
1⅛ miles: Saint Stephen, 1:44.69, February 19, 2005
1⅜ miles: Prince Arch, 2:11.44, March 6, 2005
1½ miles: Honey Ryder, 2:23.07, April 1, 2006
Other: 1 7/16 miles, Giant Hope, 2:17.64, March 12, 2006

Principal Races

Florida Derby (G1), Donn H. (G1), Gulfstream Park Breeders' Cup S. (G1), Gulfstream Park H. (G2), Fountain of Youth S. (G2)

Interesting Facts

Trivia: Bill Shoemaker rode the last winner of his career (Beau Genius) in the 1990 Hallandale Handicap. Turf course opened in 1959.

Notable Events

Sunshine Millions

Fastest Times of 2005 (Dirt)

2½ furlongs: Rolling Honor, :28.13, April 22, 2005
5½ furlongs: Harbor Chief, 1:03.50, January 9, 2005
6 furlongs: Saratoga County, 1:08.99, January 8, 2005
6½ furlongs: Forest Danger, 1:14.44, February 14, 2005
7 furlongs: Sir Shackleton, 1:21.64, March 12, 2005
7½ furlongs: Value Plus, 1:28.42, April 2, 2005
1 mile: Nakayama Kun, 1:34.25, April 6, 2005
1⅛ miles: Saint Liam, 1:48.43, February 5, 2005
1 3/16 miles: Eddington, 1:54.74, March 5, 2005
1 7/16 miles: Watchmon, 2:25.80, April 8, 2005

Fastest Times of 2005 (Turf)

5 furlongs: Procreate, :53.79, April 9, 2005
7½ furlongs: Paula Smith, 1:27.72, January 13, 2005
1 mile: Mr. Light (Arg), 1:31.41, January 3, 2005
1 1/16 miles: Old Forester, 1:38.20, March 13, 2005
1⅛ miles: Saint Stephen, 1:44.69, February 19, 2005
1⅜ miles: Prince Arch, 2:11.44, March 6, 2005
1½ miles: Navesink River, 2:25.95, April 2, 2005

Hialeah Park

Location: 105 E. 21st St., P.O. Box 158, Hialeah, Fl. 33010
Phone: (305) 885-8000, (708) 614-1830
Fax: (305) 887-8006
Website: *www.hialeahpark.com*
Year Founded: 1924
Dates of Inaugural Meeting: January 25, 1925
Abbreviation: Hia
Acreage: 220
Number of Stalls: 1,631
Seating Capacity: 20,000

Officers

President: John Brunetti Jr.
General Manager: David Romanik
Director of Racing: Stephen Brunetti
Racing Secretary: J. Sam Abbey
Director of Operations: Sergio Lopez
Director of Finance: Rene Leoncio
Director of Marketing: Steve Bovo
Director of Mutuels: Ed Mackie
Director of Publicity: Joe Savage
Director of Simulcasting: Ed Mackie Jr.
Horsemen's Liaison: Rhonda Soth

Track Layout

Main Circumference: 1 1/8 miles
Main Track Chute: 3 furlongs
Main Track Chute: 7 furlongs
Main Width: 80 feet
Main Length of Stretch: 1,410 feet
Main Turf Circumference: 7 1/2 furlongs
Main Turf Width: 90 feet
Main Turf Length of Stretch: 975 feet

Attendance

Highest Single-Day Record: 42,366, February 18, 1956

Handle

Single-Day On-Track Handle: $4,822,601, February 28, 1987
Single-Day Total Handle All Sources: $8,421,464, April 1,1995

Mutuel Records

Highest Win: $325.60, Robber, 1950
Lowest Win: $2.10, Coaltown, 1949; $2.10, Cure the Blues, March 26, 1981
Highest Exacta: $5,583.80, February 4, 1984
Lowest Exacta: $4, February 17, 1982
Highest Trifecta: $67,432, February 15, 1987
Lowest Trifecta: $8.20, April 22, 1995
Highest Daily Double: $5,919,20, January 25, 1987
Lowest Daily Double: $5.80, May 2, 1981
Highest Pick 3: $19,186, December 28, 1991
Lowest Pick 3: $16.20, March 20, 1995; $16.20, April 17, 1995
Highest Pick 6: $382,344.80, January 25, 1982

Leaders

Career, Leading Jockey by Titles: Bobby Ussery, 5
Career, Leading Trainer by Titles: H. A. "Jimmy" Jones, 7

Records

Single-Day Jockey Wins: Angel Cordero Jr., 6, February 28, 1968; Craig Perret, 6, March 9, 1989
Single-Day Trainer Wins: Ben A. Jones, 4, January 17, 1940; Dan Hurtak, 4, May 17, 1996
Single Meet, Leading Jockey by Wins: Jorge Chavez, 93, 1989
Single Meet, Leading Trainer by Wins: John Tammaro, 71, 1986

Track Records, Main Dirt

4 1/2 furlongs: Elvis On Velvet, :53.53, April 29, 2001
5 furlongs: Barnacle Jim, :56.54, May 16, 1997
5 1/2 furlongs: Lover's Trust, 1:02 3/5, May 6, 1989
6 furlongs: Earthmover, 1:08, March 7, 1985
7 furlongs: Seattle Slew, 1:20 3/5, March 9, 1977
1 1/16 miles: A P Valentine, 1:40.39, March 24, 2001
1 1/8 miles: Albert the Great, 1:45.52, March 24, 2001
1 3/16 miles: Swoon's Plume, 1:55 4/5, March 4, 1978
1 1/4 miles: Turkoman, 1:58 3/5, March 29, 1986
Other: 3 furlongs, Cherokee Road, :32, April 30, 2001

Track Records, Main Turf

5 1/2 furlongs: Glitterman, 1:01 3/5, May 20, 1989
1 1/16 miles: Judge Connelly, 1:38.78, April 2, 1995
1 1/8 miles: Signal Tap, 1:46, March 31, 1996
1 3/16 miles: Toonerville, 1:51 2/5, February 7, 1976
1 1/2 miles: Out of the Realm, 2:24.43, March 26, 1995

Ocala Training Center

Location: 1701 S.W. 60th Ave., P.O. Box 99, Ocala, Fl. 34478
Phone: (352) 237-2154
Fax: (352) 237-3566
Website: *www.obssales.com*
E-Mail: obs@obssales.com
Abbreviation: OTC

Officers

General Manager: Tom Ventura
Director of Auctions: Tom Ventura
Director of Publicity: Jay Friedman
Track Announcer: Phil Saltzman
Track Superintendent: John Barbazon

Racing Dates

2005: March 21, 1 day
2006: March 20, 1 day

Fastest Times of 2005 (Dirt)

5 furlongs: Bog Hunter, :57.40, March 21, 2005
6 furlongs: Gower, 1:10, March 21, 2005
1 1/16 miles: Mighty Mecke, 1:44.40, March 21, 2005

Tampa Bay Downs

Tampa Bay Downs, the only Thoroughbred track on Florida's Gulf Coast, opened on February 18, 1926, as Tampa Downs. The initial 39-day meet was orchestrated by Harvey Mayers, a businessman from Ohio, and Churchill Downs executive Col. Matt J. Winn. Renamed Sunshine Park in 1947, it became known as the "Santa Anita of the South" in the '50s, a nickname provided by legendary sportswriters Grantland Rice, Red Smith, and Arthur Daley, who frequented the track while covering baseball spring training. Following the sale of the track, its name was changed to Florida Downs in 1965 and to Tampa Bay Downs in '80. On February 12, 1981, jockey Julie Krone scored the first victory of her Racing Hall of Fame career on Lord Farkle. Tampa Bay Downs was sold again in 1986 and has since added a picnic area, year-round simulcasting, a seven-furlong turf course, a luxurious Sports Gallery featuring an extensive video racing library, an updated grandstand with private work stations, central air conditioning, and a renovated deli, bar, and pizza area. In 2004, the track opened a card room.

Location: 11225 Racetrack Rd., P.O. Box 2007, Oldsmar, Fl. 34677-7007
Phone: (813) 855-4401, (866) 823-6967
Fax: (813) 261-1832
Website: *www.tampabaydowns.com*
E-Mail: customerservice@tampabaydowns.com
Year Founded: 1926
Dates of Inaugural Meeting: February 18, 1926
Abbreviation: Tam
Acreage: 450
Number of Stalls: 1,462
Seating Capacity: 6,000

Ownership

Stella Thayer and Howell Ferguson

Officers

President: Stella F. Thayer
General Manager: Peter N. Berube
Secretary: Howell Ferguson
Treasurer: Stella F. Thayer
Director of Operations: Bob Cassanese
Director of Admissions: Melissa Wirth
Director of Finance: Greg Gelyon
Director of Marketing: Margo Flynn
Director of Mutuels: Frank White
Vice President: Peter N. Berube, Howell Ferguson
Director of Publicity: Margo Flynn
Director of Sales: Nicole McGill
Director of Simulcasting: Cathy Dwyer
Stewards: Robert Clark, Dennis Lima, Charles Miranda
Track Announcer: Richard Grunder
Track Photographer: Tom Cooley
Track Superintendent: Tom McLaughlin
Clerk of the Course: Judy Clark
Asst. Racing Secretary: Stanley Shina
Horsemen's Bookkeeper: Nerissa Steward

Racing Dates

2005: December 11, 2004-May 8, 2005, 94 days
2006: December 10, 2005-May 7, 2006, 94 days

Track Layout

Main Circumference: 1 mile
Main Track Chute: 3 furlongs and 7 furlongs
Main Width: 75 feet
Main Length of Stretch: 976 feet
Main Turf Circumference: 7 furlongs

Main Turf Chute: 1/4 mile
Main Turf Width: 80 feet

Attendance

Average Daily Recent Meeting: 3,513, 2004/2005; 3,501, 2005/2006
Highest Single-Day Record: 10,451, March 18, 2006
Highest Single-Meet Record: 457,414, 1988/1989
Total Attendance Recent Meeting: 330,248, 2004/2005; 329,097, 2005/2006

Handle

Average All Sources Recent Meeting: $3,410,115, 2004/2005; $3,900,061, 2005/2006
Average On-Track Recent Meeting: $300,530, 2004/2005; 321,202, 2005/2006
Single-Day Total Handle All Sources: $10,500,000, March 18, 2006
Total All Sources Recent Meeting: $320,550,814, 2004/2005; $366,605,761, 2005/2006
Total On-Track Recent Meeting: $28,249,856, 2004/2005; $30,192,981, 2005/2006
Highest Single-Day Record Recent Meet: $6,889,834, March 19, 2005; $10,500,000, March 18, 2006

Mutuel Records

Highest Win: $249, March 23, 1988
Highest Trifecta: $50,617, January 26, 1999
Highest Daily Double: $3,320, January 17, 1950
Highest Pick 3: $12,913.40, January 9, 2001
Highest Other Exotics: $9,754, Perfecta, February 8, 1973; $34,632.80, Superfecta, March 18, 2006
Highest Quinella: $5,067.60, February 21, 1995

Leaders

Career, Leading Jockey by Titles: William Henry, 4
Career, Leading Trainer by Titles: Don R. Rice, 8
Career, Leading Jockey by Stakes Wins: William Henry, 22
Career, Leading Owner by Stakes Wins: Harold Queen, 6
Career, Leading Trainer by Stakes Wins: Don R. Rice, 11
Recent Meeting, Leading Jockey: Jesus Lopez Castanon, 101, 2004/2005; Jose Lezcano, 92, 2005/2006
Recent Meeting, Leading Owner: Michael F. Buccina, 17, 2004/2005; Richard Averill, 17, 2005/2006
Recent Meeting, Leading Trainer: Don R. Rice, 35, 2004/2005; Kirk Ziadie, 34, 2005/2006
Recent Meeting, Leading Horse: Skip's Singer, 5, 2004/2005; Java Wit, 5, 2004/2005; Voodoomon, 5, 2005/2006; Forli's Con Man, 5, 2005/2006

Records

Single-Day Jockey Wins: Richard DePass, 7, March 15, 1980
Single-Day Owner Wins: Christos Gatis, 3, April 10, 2001
Single-Day Trainer Wins: Kathleen O'Connell, 4, February 23, 2003
Single Meet, Leading Jockey by Wins: Willie Martinez, 123, 1991/1992; William Henry, 123, 1992/1993
Single Meet, Leading Trainer by Wins: Don R. Rice, 44, 2001/2002

Track Records, Main Dirt

4 furlongs: Camp Izard, :46.80, May 1, 1993
4 1/2 furlongs: Geronimo J., :52 4/5, March 16, 1984
5 furlongs: Arion Fair, :57 1/5, March 20, 1982; We Can Do, :57.26, March 22, 2005
5 1/2 furlongs: Schmoopy, 1:03.55, March 17, 2000
6 furlongs: Bootlegger's Pet, 1:09, January 26, 1974
6 1/2 furlongs: Ebony Breeze, 1:16.41, January 21, 2006
7 furlongs: Sir Shackleton, 1:22.28, February 11, 2006
7 1/2 furlongs: Secret Romeo, 1:22.62, January 22, 2002
1 mile: Double Prince, 1:42 3/5, February 8, 1966; Rianan, 1:42 3/5, February 11, 1966
1m 40 yds: Mistum, 1:41 1/5, March 21, 1981
1m 70 yds: Deep Thought, 1:41 4/5, January 21, 1956
1 1/16 miles: Cherokee Prince, 1:43.13, February 11, 2006
1 1/8 miles: Las Olas, 1:48 2/5, November 21, 1968
1 3/16 miles: Warning Flag, 1:59 3/5, January 25, 1986
1 1/4 miles: Finale Puer, 2:07 2/5, March 7, 1959
1 3/8 miles: Banshee Brad, 2:20.30, March 26, 2005
1 1/2 miles: Royal Jacopo, 2.33, March 12, 1955
1 5/8 miles: Most Valiant, 2:48.20, March 29, 1997
1 3/4 miles: Our Day, 3:00 2/5, March 20, 1957
2 miles: Boss Man Jarett, 3:30.30, April 24, 1999
Other: 2 furlongs, Silver Dollar Boy, :21 4/5, January 18, 1990; 3 furlongs, Hot Star, :33 2/5, February 14, 1980; 3 furlongs, Wynn Dot Comma, :33.40, April 21, 2003; 1 7/8 miles, Best Hearted, 3:18 3/5, March 22, 1986; 2m 70 yds, Turkey Foot Road, 3:39 4/5, March 22, 1969; 2 1/16 miles, Mystic Fox, 3:37 3/5, March 27, 1988

Track Records, Main Turf

5 furlongs: Atticus Kristy, :55.02, February 21, 2006
1 mile: Lucky J J, 1:33.79, February 12, 2000
1 1/16 miles: Legs Galore, 1:39.65, February 20, 1999
1 1/8 miles: Lilys Cousin, 1:46.34, May 6, 2000
1 3/8 miles: Fun n' Gun, 2:24.06, March 30, 2002
Other: a5 furlongs, Dirtymoposse, :56.94, March 29, 2005; a1 mile, Headline, 1:36.80, April 5, 2005; a1 1/16 miles, Ben's Quitoxe, 1:41.23, December 28, 1999; a1 1/8 miles, Guardianofthegate, 1:48.33, April 6, 2003; a1 1/2 miles, Top Senor, 2:31.60, February 26, 2002

Principal Races

Tampa Bay Derby (G3), Hillsborough S. (G3), Florida Oaks

Interesting Facts

Previous Names and Dates: Tampa Downs (1926-1946), Sunshine Park (1947-1964), Florida Downs (1965-1979)

Notable Events

Florida Cup Day

Fastest Times of 2005 (Dirt)

5 furlongs: We Can Do, :57.26, March 22, 2005
5 1/2 furlongs: Blades Hill, 1:03.71, April 5, 2005
6 furlongs: Above the Wind, 1:10.04, January 1, 2005
6 1/2 furlongs: Glittering Tax, 1:17.09, January 22, 2005
7 furlongs: Briefton, 1:22.37, May 8, 2005
1 1/16 miles: Sun King, 1:43.98, March 19, 2005
1 1/8 miles: Access Approved, 1:51.67, March 22, 2005
1 3/8 miles: Banshee Brad, 2:20.30, March 26, 2005

Fastest Times of 2005 (Turf)

5 furlongs: Mighty Patriot, :55.81, January 25, 2005
a5 furlongs: Eva's Prospector, :57.47, April 17, 2005
1 mile: Native Hawk, 1:35.27, February 5, 2005
a1 miles: Boastful, 1:38.33, April 19, 2005
1 1/16 miles: Wire Bound, 1:40.14, February 19, 2005
a1 1/16 miles: Starlight Serenade, 1:44.40, April 17, 2005
a1 1/8 miles: Galic Boy, 1:48.45, February 22, 2005

Tropical Park

Tropical Park no longer has a physical presence but remains alive as the late fall-early winter meeting at Calder Race Course in northwest Miami. The Tropical Park meet at Calder Race Course runs from late October until the first days of January, which approximates the traditional Tropical Park spot in the South Florida rotation. Starting in the late 1940s, Tropical operated from late November until mid-January. Tropical Park first was a greyhound track and opened as a Thoroughbred track on December 26, 1931, in Coral Gables, a suburb southwest of Miami. The track was sold in 1941 and went through two ownership changes in the early '50s. Tropical was host for the first Calder meeting in 1970 and for that season used an experimental synthetic Tartan track, developed by Minnesota Mining and Manufacturing Co., inside the main, one-mile oval. Calder's investors, including 3M Chairman William L. McKnight, bought out Tropical with the intention of moving its dates to the new track. Tropical closed on January 15, 1972, and was transformed into a municipal park. Several of Calder's graded stakes races are held during the Tropical Park meeting. Tropical Park still maintains separate meet records from Calder for leading jockey, trainer, and other categories, although track records are the same for both.

Location: 21001 N.W. 27th Ave., Miami Gardens, Fl. 33056
Phone: (305) 625-1311
Fax: (305) 620-2569

Website: *www.calderracecourse.com*
E-Mail: blanco@calderracecourse.com
Year Founded: 1972
Abbreviation: Crc
Number of Stalls: 1,850
Seating Capacity: 15,585

Ownership

Churchill Downs Inc.

Officers

Chairman: Thomas H. Meeker
President: C. Kenneth Dunn
General Manager: Michael Abes
Racing Secretary: Michael Anifantis
Secretary: Rebecca C. Reed
Treasurer: Michael Abes
Director of Marketing: Michael Cronin
Director of Mutuels: Edward Mackie, Sr.
Vice Presidents: Michael Abes, Michael Cronin
Director of Publicity: Michele Blanco
Director of Simulcasting: Diane Stoess
Horsemen's Liaison: Janet Kownacke
Stewards: Charles Camac, Jeffrey Noe, Kevin Scheen
Track Announcer: Bobby Neuman
Track Photographer: Jim Lisa
Track Superintendent: Steve Cross
Security: Tony Otero

Racing Dates

2005: October 17, 2005-January 2, 2006, 55 days
2006: October 16, 2006-January 2, 2007, 60 days

Track Layout

Main Circumference: 1 mile
Main Track Chute: 7 furlongs and $1\frac{1}{4}$ miles
Main Width: Homestretch: 80 feet; Backstretch: 75 feet
Main Length of Stretch: 990 feet
Main Turf Circumference: 7 furlongs
Main Turf Chute: $1\frac{1}{8}$ miles
Main Turf Width: 67 feet
Main Turf Length of Stretch: 986 feet

Attendance

Average Daily Recent Meeting: 4,122, 2005/2006
Highest Single-Day Record: 17,671, January 14, 1978
Highest Single-Meet Record: 514,496, 1979/1980
Record Daily Average for Single Meet: 10,324, 1975/1976
Total Attendance Recent Meeting: 226,709, 2005/2006
Lowest Single-Meet Record: 226,709, 2005/2006
Highest Single-Day Recent Meet: 9,837, November 12, 2005

Handle

Average All Sources Recent Meeting: $3,971,536, 2005/2006
Average On-Track Recent Meeting: $400,886, 2005/2006
Record Daily Average for Single Meet: $1,475,680, 1988
Single-Day On-Track Handle: $2,793,767, January 7, 1989
Single-Day Total Handle All Sources: $9,461,604, December 29, 2001
Total All Sources Recent Meeting: $218,434,499, 2005/2006
Total On-Track Recent Meeting: $22,048,727, 2005/2006
Record Total for Single Meet: $73,784,024, 1988
Highest Single-Day Record Recent Meet: $8,013,475, December 31, 2005
Record Total All Sources for Single Meet: $240,373,189, 2004/2005

Mutuel Records

Highest Win: $447.40, December 23, 1986
Lowest Win: $2.20, December 18, 1972
Highest Exacta: $10,837.20, December 18, 1988
Lowest Exacta: $4.80, December 18, 1972
Highest Trifecta: $63,599, November 13, 2005
Lowest Trifecta: $11.40, December 9, 1993
Highest Daily Double: $7,907.80, December 14, 1973
Lowest Daily Double: $6.40, April 18, 1992
Highest Pick 3: $28,275, December 21, 1993
Lowest Pick 3: $15.80, December 17, 1988
Highest Other Exotics: $68,684.20, Superfecta, November 16, 1996; $97.80, Show, December 31, 2004
Lowest Other Exotics: $37.80, Superfecta, November 16, 1995
Lowest Pick 4: $52.50, November 16, 2002
Highest Pick 4: $77,762.40, December 30, 2000

Leaders

Career, Leading Jockey by Titles: Jacinto Vasquez, 5
Career, Leading Trainer by Titles: Stanley Hough, 5; William White, 5
Career, Leading Jockey by Stakes Wins: Jerry Bailey, 27
Career, Leading Trainer by Stakes Wins: Martin D. Wolfson, 20
Career, Leading Jockey by Wins: Eibar Coa, 537
Career, Leading Trainer by Wins: Emanuel Tortora, 373
Recent Meeting, Leading Jockey: Manoel Cruz, 68, 2005/2006
Recent Meeting, Leading Owner: Live Oak Plantation, 9, 2005/2006
Recent Meeting, Leading Trainer: Henry Collazo, 17, 2005/2006
Recent Meeting, Leading Horse: Malibu Mint, 3, 2005/2006

Records

Single-Day Jockey Wins: Jacinto Vasquez, 6, December 22, 1990; Rene Douglas, 6, December 8, 1993; Javier Castellano, 6, December 31, 2000; Eddie Castro, 6, October 17, 2005; Manoel Cruz, 6, November 27, 2005
Single Meet, Leading Jockey by Wins: Cornelio Velasquez, 84, 2002/2003
Single Meet, Leading Trainer by Wins: Stanley Hough, 35, 1978/1979; John Tammaro, 35, 1988
Single Meet, Leading Trainer by Stakes Wins: George Gianos, 7, 1988/1989
Single Meet, Leading Jockey by Stakes Wins: Douglas Valiente, 8, 1988/1989; Heberto Castillo Jr., 8, 1990/1991

Track Records, Main Dirt

4 furlongs: Diamond Studs, :46.21, July 14, 2001
$4\frac{1}{2}$ furlongs: Gold Phantom, :51.86, September 16, 2001
5 furlongs: Honest, :57.61, July 1, 1996
$5\frac{1}{2}$ furlongs: Bernard's Candy, 1:04.39, August 9, 2002
6 furlongs: Forty One Carats, 1:08.95, October 7, 2000
$6\frac{1}{2}$ furlongs: Tour of the Cat, 1:15.99, August 17, 2002
7 furlongs: Constant Escort, 1:21.82, September 28, 1996
1 mile: High Ideal, 1:36.25, September 15, 2001
1m 70 yds: Halo's Image, 1:41.78, October 31, 1995
$1\frac{1}{16}$ miles: Castlebrook, 1:42.55, September 15, 2001
$1\frac{1}{8}$ miles: Jumping Hill, 1:50, December 30, 1978
$1\frac{3}{16}$ miles: Arctic Honeymoon, 1:59$\frac{3}{5}$, January 3, 1987
$1\frac{1}{4}$ miles: Wicapi, 2:05.08, June 24, 1996
$1\frac{1}{2}$ miles: Lead'm Home, 2:32$\frac{3}{5}$, December 31, 1977
$1\frac{5}{8}$ miles: Timberlea Tune, 2:50$\frac{1}{5}$, October 16, 1971
$1\frac{3}{4}$ miles: *Detective II, 3:03$\frac{1}{5}$, October 23, 1971
2 miles: *Detective II, 3:30$\frac{1}{5}$, November 11, 1971
Other: 2 furlongs, Baby Shark, :20.81, July 13, 2002

Track Records, Main Turf

5 furlongs: Whenthedoveflies, :54.78, May 23, 2004
7 furlongs: Carterista, 1:22.36, June 19, 1993
$7\frac{1}{2}$ furlongs: Court Lark, 1:26.54, July 16, 1994
1 mile: Mr. Explosive, 1:33$\frac{3}{5}$, October 17, 1992; Dillonmyboy, 1:33.66, October 30, 2000
$1\frac{1}{16}$ miles: He's Crafty, 1:39.27, December 28, 2004
$1\frac{1}{8}$ miles: The Vid, 1:44.99, November 25, 1995
$1\frac{3}{8}$ miles: King's Design, 2:13.18, July 23, 1999
$1\frac{1}{2}$ miles: Flag Down, 2:24.11, December 16, 1995
2 miles: Skate On Thin Ice, 3:21.89, January 2, 1996

Principal Races

La Prevoyante H. (G2), W. L. McKnight H. (G2), Tropical Park Derby (G3), Frances A. Genter S. (G3), Fred W. Hooper H. (G3)

Notable Events

Florida Million, Grand Slam I, II, and III

Fastest Times of 2005 (Dirt)

2 furlongs: Thats the Problem, :21.21, July 10, 2005
$4\frac{1}{2}$ furlongs: The Pharaoh, :52.51, June 25, 2005
5 furlongs: Scrubs, :57.95, June 11, 2005
$5\frac{1}{2}$ furlongs: Sugarcane Road, 1:04.54, November 13, 2005
6 furlongs: Lost in the Fog, 1:09.30, July 10, 2005
$6\frac{1}{2}$ furlongs: Mister Fotis, 1:16.79, January 1, 2005
7 furlongs: Mister Fotis, 1:22.97, December 17, 2005
1 mile: Current Niner, 1:38.69, November 12, 2005
1m 70 yds: Blazing Rate, 1:45.76, September 24, 2005
$1\frac{1}{16}$ miles: Pampered Princess, 1:45.06, June 12, 2005
$1\frac{1}{8}$ miles: Siphon City, 1:52.42, October 8, 2005
$1\frac{3}{16}$ miles: Sir Ray, 2:04.12, May 21, 2005
$1\frac{1}{4}$ miles: Uncivil, 2:08.32, December 19, 2005
$1\frac{1}{2}$ miles: Perspicacious (Arg), 2:39.13, June 11, 2005

Fastest Times of 2005 (Turf)

5 furlongs: Placido, :55.36, January 2, 2005

7½ furlongs: Drum Major, 1:26.83, December 31, 2005
1 mile: Devine Wind, 1:33.98, December 31, 2005
1¹⁄₁₆ miles: Wood Be Willing, 1:39.80, December 27, 2005
1⅛ miles: Revved Up, 1:45.89, November 12, 2005
1⅜ miles: Hup Two, 2:19.47, September 18, 2005
1½ miles: Meteor Storm (GB), 2:25.91, December 17, 2005

Idaho

Eastern Idaho State Fair

Location: P.O. Box 250, Blackfoot, Id. 83221-0250
Phone: (208) 785-2480
Fax: (208) 785-2483
Website: *www.idaho-state-fair.com*
E-Mail: thefair@idaho-state-fair.com
Abbreviation: BKF

Racing Dates

2005: September 5-September 10, 4 days
2006: September 4-September 9, 4 days

Jerome Racing

Location: 200 N. Fir, Jerome, Id. 83338-2319
Phone: (208) 324-7209
E-Mail: jerome@fair.myrf.net
Abbreviation: Jrm

Racing Dates

2005: June 18- June 25, 3 days
2006: June 17- June 25, 3 days

Les Bois Park

Located in Boise on the Western Idaho Fairgrounds, Les Bois Park is one of the largest racetracks in the Northwest and annually holds the Idaho Cup for state-bred Thoroughbreds, Quarter Horses, Paints, and Appaloosas. Les Bois, which is French for "the woods," opened in May 1970, six years after pari-mutuel wagering was legalized in Idaho. The track had difficult times in the late 1980s, when a downturn in horse racing caused the track owners, the Ada County Commission, to put the Les Bois lease up for auction. A group of horsemen led by veterinarian Chris Christian won the lease for $100 per month and successfully lobbied for full-card simulcasting, which turned the track around and allowed it to increase its purses. In April 2002, the track was leased to former professional basketball player Arnell Jones and his wife, Lanae, but their Lariat Productions defaulted on payments, and the property was sold to Capitol Racing in 2005. The track features Thoroughbreds, Quarter Horses, Appaloosas, and Paints racing from early May to mid-August. Les Bois was the launching pad for Racing Hall of Fame jockey Gary Stevens, who scored his first career victory at the track aboard Little Star in 1979.

Location: 5610 N. Glenwood St., Garden City, Id. 83714-1338
Phone: (208) 321-0222
Fax: (208) 321-4820
Website: www.lesboisracing.com
E-Mail: alanhorowitz@sprintmail.com
Year Founded: 1970
Dates of Inaugural Meeting: May 15, 1970
Abbreviation: Boi

Ownership

Capitol Racing

Officers

President: Steve Bieri
General Manager: Alan Horowitz
Racing Secretary: Tracey Barker
Director of Operations: Matt Heggli
Director of Marketing: Melinda Nothern
Director of Mutuels: Diana Fairchild
Vice President: Barbara Bieri
Director of Publicity: Melinda Nothern
Stewards: Jack Baker, Terry Crystal, Doug Standlee
Track Announcer: Tracey Barker
Track Photographer: Linda Bernsten
Track Superintendent: Ken Anderson

Racing Dates

2005: August 24-August 26, 3 days
2006: May 5-August 12, 46 days

Track Layout

Main Circumference: 6 furlongs
Main Track Chute: 5 furlongs and 1 mile
Main Width: 80 feet
Main Length of Stretch: 660 feet

Attendance

Average Daily Recent Meeting: 2,618, 2005
Total Attendance Recent Meeting: 7,853, 2005

Handle

Average On-Track Recent Meeting: $72,046, 2005
Total On-Track Recent Meeting: $216,138, 2005
Highest Single-Day On-Track Record Recent Meet: $84,224, August 2005

Leaders

Recent Meeting, Leading Jockey: Melissa Marshall, 4, 2005
Recent Meeting, Leading Trainer: Jim Hanson, 4, 2005

Principal Races

Idaho Cup Juvenile Championship S., Idaho Cup Classic S., Idaho Cup Derby, Idaho Cup Distaff Maturity S., Idaho Cup Distaff Derby

Notable Events

Idaho Cup Day

Fastest Times of 2005 (Dirt)

5 furlongs: Smokin' Freddy, :58.20, August 28, 2005
6½ furlongs: Jac Four Girls, 1:21.10, August 26, 2005
7 furlongs: Find My Halter, 1:25.30, August 26, 2005
1 mile: Silent Snow, 1:39.10, August 27, 2005

Oneida County Fair

Location: P.O. Box 13, Malad City, Id. 83252-0013
Phone: (208) 766-4706, (805) 565-1125
Fax: (208) 766-4707
Abbreviation: One
Acreage: 30
Number of Stalls: 93
Seating Capacity: 1,000

Officers

President: David Moss
Director of Racing: Deon Jones
Secretary: Deon Jones
Director of Marketing: Jim Moss
Vice President: Bob Hobson
Director of Publicity: Jim Moss
Director of Simulcasting: Linda Daniels

Track Layout

Main Circumference: ½ mile
Main Width: 60 feet
Main Length of Stretch: 300 yds

Pocatello Downs

Location: 10588 Fairgrounds Rd., Pocatello, Id. 83204
Phone: (208) 238-1721
Fax: (208) 238-1763
Abbreviation: PoD

Racing Dates

2005: May 14-June 5, 9 days
2006: May 13-June 4, 9 days

Rupert Downs

Location: P.O. Box 263, Rupert, Id. 83350-0263
Phone: (208) 436-9748
Fax: (208) 436-8063
Abbreviation: Rup

Racing Dates

2005: July 2-July 10, 5 days
2006: July 1-July 9, 5 days

Illinois

Arlington Park

Arlington Park first opened on October 13, 1927, and has been home to many firsts in Thoroughbred racing. Located northwest of Chicago in Arlington Heights, the track became the first in Illinois to offer turf races in 1934. In 1966, Laffit Pincay Jr. recorded his first United States victory there on his way to a place in the Racing Hall of Fame and a record 9,530 victories. In 1981, Arlington became the world's first track to host a $1-million race for Thoroughbreds when it inaugurated the Arlington Million Stakes (G1). The first running was won by John Henry, who returned to win the race in 1984. Today, the Million is part of Arlington's International Festival of Racing, which also includes the Beverly D. (G1) and Secretariat (G1) Stakes. On July 31, 1985, fire destroyed Arlington's clubhouse, causing the track to shift most of its remaining races to Hawthorne Race Course. The exception was the Million, which was held on August 25 at Arlington, and more than 35,000 fans watched the race from tents and temporary facilities during what would be dubbed the "Miracle Million." Those efforts led to Arlington becoming the first racetrack to earn an Eclipse Award. Arlington was rebuilt lavishly by Chicago-area industrialist Richard Duchossois, who closed the track for two seasons—1998 and '99—due to unfavorable economic and regulatory conditions. Arlington reopened in 2000 and the Arlington Million was resumed. Also in 2000, Churchill Downs Inc. purchased the track and assumed about $80-million in loans, while Duchossois received close to 4-million shares of common stock in Churchill.

Location: 2200 W. Euclid Ave., Arlington Heights, Il. 60006
Phone: (847) 385-7500
Fax: (847) 385-7251
Website: *www.arlingtonpark.com*
E-Mail: track@arlingtonpark.com
Year Founded: 1926
Dates of Inaugural Meeting: October 13, 1927
Abbreviation: AP
Number of Stalls: 2,140
Seating Capacity: 35,000

Ownership

Churchill Downs Inc.

Officers

Chairman: Richard L. Duchossois
President: Roy A. Arnold
Director of Racing: Kevin Greely
Racing Secretary: Kevin Greely
Treasurer: Dan Peters
Director of Operations: Anthony Petrillo
Director of Admissions: Bill Adams
Director of Communications: Dan Leary
Director of Finance: Michael Cody
Director of Marketing: Keith Darby
Director of Mutuels: Jack Lisowski
Vice President: William A. Thayer Jr.
Director of Sales: Tom Maloney
Stewards: Eddie Arroyo, Joseph K. Lindeman, Steve Morgan, Peter Kosiba Jr.
Track Announcer: John G. Dooley
Track Photographer: Benoit & Associates
Track Superintendent: Javier Barajas
Security: Dan Centracchio
Asst. Racing Secretary: Christian A. Polzin

Racing Dates

2005: May 13-September 18, 94 days
2006: May 5-September 12, 95 days

Track Layout

Main Circumference: 1$^1/_8$ miles
Main Track Chute: 6$^1/_2$ furlongs, 7 furlongs, 7$^1/_2$ furlongs and 1 mile
Main Width: 92 feet
Main Length of Stretch: 1,028 feet
Main Turf Circumference: 1 mile
Main Turf Width: 150 feet
Main Turf Length of Stretch: 1,020 feet
Training Track: a5 furlongs

Attendance

Average Daily Recent Meeting: 7,607, 2005
Highest Single-Day Record: 50,638, July 4, 1938
Total Attendance Recent Meeting: 715,023, 2005

Handle

Average All Sources Recent Meeting: $4,312,728, 2005
Average On-Track Recent Meeting: $575,213, 2005
Single-Day On-Track Handle: $13,568,209, October 26, 2002
Single-Day Total Handle All Sources: $116,059,574, October 26, 2002
Total All Sources Recent Meeting: $405,396,420, 2005
Total On-Track Recent Meeting: $54,070,047, 2005
Highest Single-Day Record Recent Meet: $20,987,021, August 13, 2005 (Arlington Million Day)

Mutuel Records

Highest Win: $382, Ivalinda, August 12, 1963
Highest Exacta: $6267, August 7, 1991
Highest Trifecta: $58,116.20, September 14, 2001
Highest Daily Double: $3,835.20, July 5, 1939
Highest Pick 3: $21,775.40, June 11, 1990
Highest Pick 6: $269,253.60, September 25, 1984
Highest Other Exotics: $52,686, Superfecta, August 13, 1995; $2,701, Quinella, September 3, 2000; $16,349.30, Pick 5, October 26, 2002

Leaders

Career, Leading Jockey by Titles: Earlie Fires, 6
Career, Leading Owner by Titles: Calumet Farm, 9
Career, Leading Trainer by Titles: Richard Hazelton, 8; William Hal Bishop, 8
Career, Leading Jockey by Stakes Wins: Earlie Fires, 101
Career, Leading Owner by Stakes Wins: Calumet Farm, 57
Career, Leading Trainer by Stakes Wins: Harry Trotsek, 44
Career, Leading Jockey by Wins: Earlie Fires, 2,801
Career, Leading Trainer by Wins: Richard P. Hazelton, 1,149
Recent Meeting, Leading Jockey: Shaun Bridgmohan, 132, 2005
Recent Meeting, Leading Owner: Frank C. Calabrese, 64, 2005
Recent Meeting, Leading Trainer: Wayne Catalano, 69, 2005
Recent Meeting, Leading Horse: Fifteen Rounds, 5, 2005

Records

Single-Day Jockey Wins: Pat Day, 8, September 13, 1989
Single Meet, Leading Jockey by Wins: Shane Sellers, 219, 1991
Single Meet, Leading Owner by Wins: Frank Calabrese, 66, 2002
Single Meet, Leading Trainer by Wins: Wayne Catalano, 69, 2005

Track Records, Main Dirt

4$^1/_2$ furlongs: Wheat Penny, :51.64, June 8, 2000; Bold America, :51.64, June 28, 2002
5 furlongs: Staunch Avenger, :57$^1/_5$, June 29, 1970; Heisanative, :57$^1/_5$, June 12, 1971; Shecky Greene, :57$^1/_5$, June 15, 1972; Zarb's Magic, :57.31, September 7, 2002
5$^1/_2$ furlongs: Hey That's Great, 1:02$^3/_5$, June 27, 1992
6 furlongs: Taylor's Special, 1:08, August 22, 1986
6$^1/_2$ furlongs: Pentelicus, 1:14$^1/_5$, July 14, 1990
7 furlongs: Tumiga, 1:20$^2/_5$, July 13, 1968
7$^1/_2$ furlongs: Land Mine, 1:28.45, August 4, 2005
1 mile: Dr. Fager, 1:32$^1/_5$, August 24, 1968
1m 70 yds: Geo. Groom, 1:42$^4/_5$, October 25, 1927

$1\frac{1}{16}$ miles: Kindly Manner, 1:41$\frac{2}{5}$, August 22, 1977; Mojave, 1:41$\frac{2}{5}$, June 30, 1981
$1\frac{1}{8}$ miles: Spectacular Bid, 1:46$\frac{1}{5}$, July 19, 1980
$1\frac{3}{16}$ miles: Perfect Drift, 1:54.27, July 30, 2005
$1\frac{1}{4}$ miles: Private Thoughts, 1:59$\frac{2}{5}$, August 20, 1977
$1\frac{3}{8}$ miles: Playdale, 2:15$\frac{2}{5}$, July 19, 1932
$1\frac{1}{2}$ miles: El Misterio, 2:28$\frac{1}{5}$, September 5, 1960
$1\frac{5}{8}$ miles: Fool's Robbery, 2:45$\frac{3}{5}$, July 5, 1973
$1\frac{3}{4}$ miles: *Deux-Moulins, 2:59$\frac{2}{5}$, July 14, 1955
2 miles: Swede Of Norfolk, 3:26$\frac{2}{5}$, August 15, 1970
Other: a$1\frac{1}{16}$ miles, Ashleigh's Jet, 1:44.10, June 14, 2001; $1\frac{5}{16}$ miles, Rush Home, 2:10, August 7, 1971; $1\frac{5}{16}$ miles, Evanescent, 2:10, July 18, 1993; $2\frac{1}{4}$ miles, *Djem, 4:05$\frac{3}{5}$, July 30, 1953

Track Records, Main Turf

5 furlongs: Distinctive Mr. B, :56.36, September 15, 2001
$5\frac{1}{2}$ furlongs: Marley's Revenge, 1:02.44, September 19, 2004
1 mile: Gee Can He Dance, 1:34.50, September 4, 1995
1m 70yds: Pass the Brandy, 1:38$\frac{4}{5}$, July 25, 1970
$1\frac{1}{16}$ miles: Zeeruler, 1:41, September 7, 1992
$1\frac{1}{8}$ miles: Mr. Leader, 1:47$\frac{2}{5}$, July 4, 1970; Jinski's World, 1:47$\frac{2}{5}$, July 6, 1991; World Class Splash, 1:47.40, July 11, 1992
$1\frac{3}{16}$ miles: Reluctant Guest, 1:53$\frac{1}{5}$, September 1, 1990
$1\frac{1}{4}$ miles: Awad, 1:58.69, August 27, 1995
$1\frac{1}{2}$ miles: Cetewayo, 2:27.50, July 6, 2002
$1\frac{5}{8}$ miles: Coincident, 2:45, July 26, 1951
$1\frac{3}{4}$ miles: *Pennsburg, 3:02$\frac{3}{5}$, July 5, 1941
2 miles: Penaway, 3:25$\frac{2}{5}$, July 24, 1953
Other: a5 furlongs, Nicole's Dream, :56.38, September 18, 2003; a$5\frac{1}{2}$ furlongs, Loco Kid, 1:01$\frac{3}{5}$, May 28, 1969; a6 furlongs, Mr. Sam A., 1:05$\frac{4}{5}$, July 12, 1966; a1 mile, Soaking Smoking, 1:34.92, July 24, 1991; a1m 70yds, Elegant Heir, 1:41$\frac{2}{5}$, August 11, 1970; a$1\frac{1}{16}$ miles, Top Floor, 1:40$\frac{2}{5}$, June 18, 1969; a$1\frac{1}{16}$ miles, Crafty Bee, 1:40$\frac{2}{5}$, June 21, 1969; a$1\frac{1}{8}$ miles, Lotus Pool, 1:47.22, August 1, 1991; a$1\frac{3}{16}$ miles, Duckaroo, 1:57.51, June 10, 1992; a$1\frac{3}{16}$ miles, Quintillion, 1:57.51, August 20, 1990; a$1\frac{1}{2}$ miles, Noble Savage, 2:22$\frac{1}{5}$, July 20, 1991; a$1\frac{5}{8}$ miles, Roman Leader, 2:51, August, 19, 1972; $2\frac{1}{16}$ miles, *Deux-Moulins, 3:30$\frac{4}{5}$, July 28, 1955; $2\frac{1}{8}$ miles, English Harry, 3:45, July 30, 1941

Principal Races

Arlington Million (G1), Beverly D. S. (G1), Secretariat S. (G1), Washington Park H. (G2), American Derby (G2)

Interesting Facts

Trivia: June 24, 2003, jockey Rene Douglas won seven races, including first five on the card, from nine mounts.
Previous Names and Dates: Arlington International Racecourse
Achievements/Milestones: July 13, 1985, destroyed by fire. June 28, 1989, track reopened. June 16, 2003, third consecutive year with highest Father's Day attendance in U.S. (26,101).

Notable Events

International Festival of Racing (Arlington Million Day)

Fastest Times of 2005 (Dirt)

$4\frac{1}{2}$ furlongs: Cole Express, :51.74, June 8, 2005
5 furlongs: Silver Fortune, :57.60, August 18, 2005
$5\frac{1}{2}$ furlongs: Lizzy's Township, 1:03.34, July 23, 2005
6 furlongs: Fifteen Rounds, 1:08.46, August 5, 2005
$6\frac{1}{2}$ furlongs: Number Juan, 1:15.80, August 31, 2005
7 furlongs: Just See James, 1:21.76, June 5, 2005
$7\frac{1}{2}$ furlongs: Land Mine, 1:28.45, August 4, 2005
1 mile: Lord of the Game, 1:34.60, May 28, 2005
$1\frac{1}{8}$ miles: Devilment, 1:47.73, July 16, 2005
$1\frac{3}{16}$ miles: Perfect Drift, 1:54.27, July 30, 2005
$1\frac{1}{4}$ miles: Tejano Who, 2:04.33, July 23, 2005

Fastest Times of 2005 (Turf)

5 furlongs: Ridge Runner (GB), :56.37, September 11, 2005
a5 furlongs: Durban Thunder (Brz), :56.45, August 24, 2005
$5\frac{1}{2}$ furlongs: Nicole's Dream, 1:02.54, September 18, 2005
1 mile: Lord of the Game, 1:35.63, September 4, 2005
a1 miles: Chic Dancer, 1:36.22, August 24, 2005
$1\frac{1}{16}$ miles: Fort Prado, 1:41.72, June 25, 2005
a$1\frac{1}{16}$ miles: Baena, 1:42.15, August 26, 2005
$1\frac{1}{8}$ miles: Royal Copenhagen (Fr), 1:48.76, September 17, 2005
a$1\frac{1}{8}$ miles: Slew Slayer, 1:49.01, September 2, 2005
$1\frac{3}{16}$ miles: Gun Salute, 1:55.31, July 23, 2005
$1\frac{1}{4}$ miles: Cool Conductor, 2:02.26, July 23, 2005
$1\frac{1}{2}$ miles: Revved Up, 2:28.29, July 3, 2005
a$1\frac{1}{2}$ miles: Delafield, 2:31.11, August 10, 2005

Fairmount Park

Fairmount Park, located in Collinsville, about 30 minutes east of St. Louis, opened on September 26, 1925. The track was built to resemble a small Churchill Downs by Col. E. R. Bradley, who owned four Kentucky Derby winners, and Col. Matt Winn, who made the Kentucky Derby at Churchill a sporting institution. In 1947, Fairmount became the first one-mile oval racetrack in the world to provide lighting for night Thoroughbred racing. Fairmount's most famous horseman is jockey Dave Gall, who retired in 1999 with 7,396 wins, placing him among Thoroughbred racing's winningest jockeys. Fairmount, which has been owned since 1969 by Ogden Services Corp., has struggled to compete against riverboat gambling casinos throughout the St. Louis area in recent years.

Location: 9301 Collinsville Rd., Collinsville, Il. 62234-1729
Phone: (618) 345-4300
Fax: (618) 344-8218
Website: *www.fairmountpark.com*
E-Mail: fmtpark@fairmountpark.com
Year Founded: 1924
Dates of Inaugural Meeting: September 26, 1925
Abbreviation: FP
Acreage: 190
Number of Stalls: 1,000
Seating Capacity: 5,500

Ownership

Fairmount Park Inc.

Officers

President: Brian F. Zander
General Manager: Brian F. Zander
Director of Racing: Bobby Pace
Racing Secretary: Bobby Pace
Treasurer: Joe Ruppert
Director of Operations: Joe Ruppert
Director of Admissions: Gregory G. Graves
Director of Marketing: Gregg Smith
Director of Mutuels: Michael L. Heidemann
Vice President: Joe Ruppert
Director of Publicity: Jon Sloane
Director of Simulcasting: Gregory G. Graves
Horsemen's Liaison: Lanny Brooks
Stewards: Jeffrey Bowen, David A. Smith, Roger Duff
Track Announcer: John Scully
Track Photographer: Jim Ainsley
Track Superintendent: Gale Franklin
Security: Steve Chambliss
Horsemen's Bookkeeper: Barbara Randazzo
Asst. Racing Secretary: Darrel Cassity

Racing Dates

2005: March 25-September 17, 102 days
2006: March 14-September 4, 90 days

Track Layout

Main Circumference: 1 mile
Main Track Chute: 6 furlongs and $1\frac{1}{4}$ miles
Main Width: Homestretch: 80 feet; Backstretch: 70 feet
Main Length of Stretch: 1,050 feet

Attendance

Average Daily Recent Meeting: 2,148, 2005
Highest Single-Day Record: 13,898, September 7, 1953
Total Attendance Recent Meeting: 219,104, 2005

Handle

Average All Sources Recent Meeting: $279,541, 2005
Average On-Track Recent Meeting: $126,566, 2005
Single-Day Total Handle All Sources: $1,380,880, May 5, 1990
Total All Sources Recent Meeting: $28,513,196, 2005
Total On-Track Recent Meeting: $12,909,597, 2005
Highest Single-Day On-Track Record Recent Meet: $277,099, May 7, 2005
Highest Single-Day Record Recent Meet: $538,003, May 17, 2005

Leaders

Recent Meeting, Leading Jockey: Rafael Manuel Hernandez, 122, 2005
Recent Meeting, Leading Trainer: Ralph Martinez, 131, 2005
Recent Meeting, Leading Horse: Lady Riss, 6, 2005

Records

Single Meet, Leading Trainer by Wins: Ralph Martinez, 157, 2001

Track Records, Main Dirt

4 furlongs: Aledo, :45.60, June 2, 1994; Nextquestor, :45.60, March 25, 2005
4½ furlongs: Vague Promise, :51⅗, May 19, 1978
5 furlongs: Slight in the Rear, :56⅘, July 25, 1989
5½ furlongs: Sarof Jr., 1:03⅖, June 5, 1980
6 furlongs: Ye Country, 1:08⅗, November 26, 1977
1 mile: Dusty Appeal, 1:37.40, June 20, 1992
1m 70 yds: Dusty Appeal, 1:39⅘, July 30, 1989
1¹⁄₁₆ miles: Lt. Lao, 1:40⅘, July 22, 1989
1⅛ miles: Andover Man, 1:47⅗, August 26, 1989
1¼ miles: Leaddrop, 2:03, July 22, 1989
1½ miles: *Firth of Tay, 2:33, September 21, 1927
1⅝ miles: Monthazar, 2:48, November 3, 1973
1¾ miles: Lightin Bill, 3:02⅘, October 14, 1939
2 miles: East Royalty, 3:32.60, December 1, 1991
Other: 2 furlongs, Fantan Sam, :21⅖, November 22, 1989; 2 furlongs, Sammy the Champ, :21.40, April 12, 2002; 2m 70 yds, King Boogie, 3:33⅗, September 1, 1984; 2¹⁄₁₆ miles, Tim Trefle, 3:38⅘, September 10, 1983; 2⅛ miles, Lucrest, 3:46⅕, September 24, 1983; 2¼ miles, Baye Dawn, 4:00, October 8, 1983; 2½ miles, Cat Walk, 4:29, October 22, 1983

Principal Races

St. Louis Derby, King Knocker S., Circle C Classic H., Slight in the Rear S., Pete Condellone S.

Interesting Facts

Previous Names and Dates: Cahokia Downs

Notable Events

Party at the Park, Ultra Thursdays

Fastest Times of 2005 (Dirt)

2 furlongs: Hazzari, :21.60, September 15, 2005
4 furlongs: Nextquestor, :45.60, March 25, 2005
4½ furlongs: True Monarch, :52.80, September 5, 2005
5 furlongs: Tee to Green, :58.80, March 26, 2005
5½ furlongs: Crazy Debutante, 1:04.80, July 22, 2005
6 furlongs: Bubba Gum, 1:09, August 6, 2005
1 mile: Lady Riss, 1:37.60, July 23, 2005
1m 70 yds: Moe B Dick, 1:41.80, July 22, 2005
1¹⁄₁₆ miles: Tepexpan, 1:44.80, August 6, 2005
1⅛ miles: Beabasque, 1:51, August 6, 2005
1¼ miles: Butterscotch Dave, 2:04.20, July 22, 2005
1½ miles: Mount Tora Bora, 2:36, September 2, 2005

Hawthorne Race Course

For nearly 100 years, members of the Carey family have overseen Hawthorne Race Course in the near Chicago suburb of Stickney. In 1909, Thomas Carey bought the track from horseman and noted gambler Ed Corrigan, who had opened the track in 1891. Under Corrigan's ownership, Hawthorne closed when the state Senate banned racing in Chicago in 1905, and new owner Carey attempted over the next several years to revive racing. He finally succeeded in 1922. In 1928, the track's most notable race, the Hawthorne Gold Cup Handicap (G2), debuted. Among the winners of the Hawthorne Gold Cup are five-time Horse of the Year Kelso, 1968 Horse of the Year Dr. Fager, and '91 Horse of the Year Black Tie Affair (Ire). In 1977, a fire destroyed Hawthorne's grandstand, and the remainder of its meet was held at Sportsman's Park, located a block away. Racing returned to the track in 1980 when a new grandstand was built. Over the years, Hawthorne also has conducted harness racing. In late 2002, Hawthorne merged with Sportsman's Park to form a new operating entity, Hawthorne National. Sportsman's Park was sold for development, and its racing dates and major races are now run at Hawthorne.

Location: 3501 S. Laramie Ave., Cicero, Il. 60804-4503
Phone: (708) 780-3700
Fax: (708) 780-3753
Website: *www.hawthorneracecourse.com*
E-Mail: jim@hawthorneracecourse.com
Year Founded: 1890
Dates of Inaugural Meeting: May 20, 1891
Abbreviation: Haw
Acreage: 119
Number of Stalls: 2,400
Seating Capacity: 18,000

Officers

Chairman: Patricia Bidwell
President: Tim Carey
General Manager: Ed Duffy
Director of Racing: Gary M. Duch
Racing Secretary: Gary M. Duch
Secretary: P. J. Mudro
Director of Operations: Thomas F. Carey III
Director of Admissions: Mike Harris
Director of Communications: Jim Miller
Director of Marketing: Joe Scurto
Director of Mutuels: Michael P. Hart
Vice President: Mary Patton Pitocchelli
Director of Publicity: Jim Miller
Director of Sales: Pam Dorr
Director of Simulcasting: Lorene Heninger
Horsemen's Liaison: Tim Becker
Stewards: Eddie Arroyo, Joseph K. Lindeman, Steve Morgan
Track Announcer: Peter Galassi
Track Photographer: Four Footed Fotos
Track Superintendent: Gregorio Cardenas
Security: Dennis Taylor
Asst. Racing Secretary: Christian Polzin

Racing Dates

2005: February 25-May 10, 54 days; September 23, 2005-January 2, 2006, 72 days
2006: February 24-May 2, 48 days; September 15, 2006-January 2, 2007, 86 days

Track Layout

Main Circumference: 1 mile
Main Track Chute: 6½ furlongs
Main Width: 75 feet
Main Length of Stretch: 1,320 feet
Main Turf Circumference: 7 furlongs, 148 feet

Attendance

Highest Single-Day Record: 37,792, September 6, 1937

Handle

Average All Sources Recent Meeting: $2,215,265, Spring 2005; $3,103,147, Fall 2005; $2,400,138, Spring 2006
Average On-Track Recent Meeting: $191,050, Spring 2005; $179,414, Fall 2005; $160,188, Spring 2006
Single-Day Total Handle All Sources: $10,300,640, May 5, 2001
Total All Sources Recent Meeting: $119,624,310, Spring 2005; $223,426,584, Fall 2005; $115,206,624, Spring 2006
Total On-Track Recent Meeting: $10,316,700, Spring 2005; $12,917,808, Fall 2005; $7,689,024, Spring 2006
Record Average All Sources Single Meet: $3,575,861, 1996

Leaders

Recent Meeting, Leading Jockey: Chris Emigh, Spring 2005; Chris Emigh, 65, Fall 2005; Chris Emigh, 56, Spring 2006
Recent Meeting, Leading Owner: Frank Calabrese, Spring 2005; Frank Calabrese, 35, Fall 2005; Frank Calabrese, 20, Spring 2006
Recent Meeting, Leading Trainer: Wayne Catalano, 35, Fall 2005; Tom Tomillo, 28, Spring 2006

Records

Single-Day Jockey Wins: Johnny Heckman, 7, October 1, 1956
Single-Day Trainer Wins: Mike Reavis, 5, November 2, 2002
Single Meet, Leading Jockey by Wins: Mark Guidry, 137, 1995
Single Meet, Leading Trainer by Wins: Richard Hazelton, 48, 1976

Track Records, Main Dirt

4½ furlongs: Joanies Bella, :51.80, May 28, 2001
5 furlongs: De La Concorde, :57, November 11, 1992

5$^1/_2$ furlongs: Marluel's Troy, 1:02$^2/_5$, November 2, 1976
6 furlongs: Satan's Poppy, 1:08$^1/_5$, October 21, 1978
6$^1/_2$ furlongs: Dee Lance, 1:14$^2/_5$, August 27, 1988
1 mile: Actuary, 1:37$^1/_5$, July 17, 1923; Hopeless, 1:37$^1/_5$, August 29, 1925
1m 70 yds: Soldat Bleu, 1:39$^1/_5$, July 27, 1988
1$^1/_{16}$ miles: Sensitive Prince, 1:39$^3/_5$, September 23, 1978
1$^1/_8$ miles: *Zografos, 1:46$^3/_5$, October 9, 1974
1$^3/_{16}$ miles: Lindy's Lad, 1:59$^2/_5$, November 12, 1980; Steal the Account, 1:59.40, August 28, 1999
1$^1/_4$ miles: Gladwin, 1:58$^4/_5$, October 1, 1970; Group Plan, 1:58$^4/_5$, October 19, 1974
1$^1/_2$ miles: David II, 2:29$^3/_5$, October 1, 1969
1$^5/_8$ miles: Viale (Uru), 2:47.02, December 10, 2000
1$^3/_4$ miles: America Fore, 3:02$^1/_5$, October 2, 1943
Other: 2 furlongs, Minty Flavors, :20.88, May 14, 1999; 2m 70yds, Sun 'N Shine, 3:30$^2/_5$, October 19, 1974; 2$^1/_{16}$ miles, Revoque, 3:35$^2/_5$, October 5, 1963; 2$^1/_8$ miles, Hallandale, 3:41$^1/_5$, October 12, 1963

Track Records, Main Turf

5 furlongs: Sulemark, :56, October 25, 1992
7 furlongs: Glassy Dip, 1:22$^3/_5$, May 30, 1977
7$^1/_2$ furlongs: Joey Jr., 1:27$^1/_5$, November 5, 1989
1 mile: Soviet Line (Ire), 1:33.40, July 25, 1998
1$^1/_{16}$ miles: Bendecida, 1:40.53, September 6, 1999
1$^1/_8$ miles: Rainbows for Life, 1:44$^3/_5$, October 13, 1991
1$^3/_{16}$ miles: Royal Glint, 1:54$^2/_5$, September 28, 1974; Sari's Baba, 1:54$^2/_5$, September 24, 1985
1$^1/_4$ miles: Pass the Line, 2:00$^2/_5$, August 10, 1985
1$^3/_8$ miles: Shayzari (Ire), 2:15$^1/_5$, September 3, 1988
1$^1/_2$ miles: Lord Comet, 2:26.87, October 27, 1999
1$^3/_4$ miles: Neverest, 2:58$^4/_5$, August 31, 1973

Principal Races

Hawthorne Gold Cup H. (G2), Illinois Derby (G2), National Jockey Club H. (G3), Sixty Sails H. (G3), Hawthorne Derby (G3)

Interesting Facts

Trivia: First major U.S. track to use an electric timer (1931). Track announcer Phil Georgeff entered the Guiness Book of World Records when he called his 85,000th race on August 13, 1988.

Fastest Times of 2005 (Dirt)

4$^1/_2$ furlongs: Whatsitgonnatake, :52.50, May 9, 2005
5 furlongs: Without a Doubt, :57.19, November 6, 2005
6 furlongs: Orphan Brigade, 1:08.98, October 12, 2005
6$^1/_2$ furlongs: Ohwhataparade, 1:15.46, December 21, 2005
1m 70 yds: Radiant Gold, 1:40.43, November 17, 2005
1$^1/_{16}$ miles: Precocious Kat, 1:41.64, November 17, 2005
1$^1/_8$ miles: Pollard's Vision, 1:49.12, April 23, 2005
1$^1/_4$ miles: Super Frolic, 2:04.66, September 24, 2005

Fastest Times of 2005 (Turf)

7$^1/_2$ furlongs: Tio Lupe, 1:28.57, October 10, 2005
1 mile: Spider the Glider, 1:34.90, October 22, 2005
1$^1/_{16}$ miles: Isla Cozzene, 1:40.54, October 15, 2005
1$^1/_8$ miles: Gun Salute, 1:47.51, October 15, 2005
1$^1/_2$ miles: A Team Leader, 2:32.99, November 3, 2005

Sportsman's Park

Location: 3301 S. Laramie Ave., Cicero, Il. 60804-4520
Phone: (773) 242-1121
Fax: (773) 242-0775
Website: *www.sportsmanspark.com*
Year Founded: 1932
Abbreviation: Spt
Number of Stalls: 1,900
Seating Capacity: 65,000

Track Layout

Main Circumference: 7 furlongs
Main Length of Stretch: 1,463 feet

Leaders

Career, Leading Jockey by Titles: Tony Skoronski, 11
Career, Leading Trainer by Titles: Richard Hazelton, 20
Career, Leading Jockey by Wins: Randall Meier, 1,074

Records

Single-Day Jockey Wins: Randall Meier, 4, April 1, 2001; Chris Valovich, 4, March 11, 2001
Single Meet, Leading Jockey by Wins: Mark Guidry, 134, 1992
Single Meet, Leading Trainer by Wins: Richard Hazelton, 59, 1981

Track Records, Main Dirt

5 furlongs: Hez Comin Thru, :58.06, March 3, 2001
5$^1/_2$ furlongs: Faultless Appeal, 1:03.78, April 8, 2001
6 furlongs: Linear, 1:08.85, March 26, 1994
6$^1/_2$ furlongs: Bold Favorite, 1:15$^2/_5$, October 2, 1971
1 mile: Tabasco Cid, 1:36, March 30, 1994
1$^1/_{16}$ miles: Humble Eight, 1:42.29, June 3, 1995
1$^1/_8$ miles: Wild Rush, 1:47.51, May 10, 1997
1$^3/_8$ miles: Skinny C., 2:17$^3/_5$, May 27, 1974
1$^5/_8$ miles: Ball Hawk, 2:48$^2/_5$, October 24, 1956
2 miles: Tri for Charlie, 3:37$^3/_5$, May 8, 1990
Other: 2 furlongs, Nervous Moment, :20.98, June 8, 1998; 1$^7/_{16}$ miles, Theoretic, 2:24$^1/_5$, October 15, 1973; 1$^9/_{16}$ miles, Well Lit, 2:35.77, April 25, 1992

Indiana

Hoosier Park

In 1989, Indiana approved pari-mutuel wagering, and the state's first pari-mutuel racetrack, Hoosier Park, opened its inaugural season of Standardbred racing in 1994. Thoroughbred racing debuted at Hoosier in 1995. Located northeast of Indianapolis in Anderson, the $10-million track was developed by majority owner Churchill Downs Inc. as the company's first racing interest outside Kentucky. Hoosier annually holds a Thoroughbred meet. For 2004, Hoosier hosted two graded stakes, the $500,000 Indiana Derby (G2) and the $350,000 Indiana Breeders' Cup Oaks (G3). A competitor, Indiana Downs, opened on April 1, 2003, only 40 miles from its facility.

Location: 4500 Dan Patch Circle, Anderson, In. 46013-3165
Phone: (765) 642-7223, (800) 526-7223
Fax: (765) 644-0467
Website: *www.hoosierpark.com*
E-Mail: info@hoosierpark.com
Year Founded: 1994
Dates of Inaugural Meeting: September 1-October 28, 1995
Abbreviation: Hoo
Acreage: 105
Number of Stalls: 1,080
Seating Capacity: 15,000

Ownership

Churchill Downs Inc.

Officers

Chairman: Thomas H. Meeker
President: Richard B. Moore
General Manager: Richard B. Moore
Director of Racing: Raymond "Butch" Cook
Racing Secretary: Raymond "Butch" Cook
Secretary: Rebecca C. Reed
Treasurer: Steven L. Wilkening
Director of Operations: Kevin Mack
Director of Admissions: Sue Walters
Director of Communications: Thomas F. Bannon
Director of Finance: Steven L. Wilkening
Director of Marketing: Donna R. Smith
Director of Mutuels: Randy Westerman
Vice Presidents: Thomas F. Bannon, Steven L. Wilkening, Donna R. Smith
Director of Publicity: Tammy Knox
Director of Sales: Jim Garrett
Director of Simulcasting: Randy Westerman
Horsemen's Liaison: Gayle Christman
Stewards: Gary I. Wilfert, James Higginbottom, Mike Manganello
Track Announcer: Steve Cross
Track Photographer: Jim Linscott
Track Superintendent: John Betts
Security: James Leist
Horsemen's Bookkeeper: Karen Baker
Asst. Racing Secretary: Michael Smith

Racing Dates
2005: September 3-November 25, 57 days
2006: September 2-November 25, 61 days

Track Layout
Main Circumference: 7 furlongs
Main Track Chute: 6 furlongs
Main Width: 90 feet
Main Length of Stretch: 1,255 feet

Attendance
Average Daily Recent Meeting: 1,178, 2005
Highest Single-Day Record: 10,827, October 7, 2000
Highest Single-Meet Record: 95,468, 1995
Record Daily Average for Single Meet: 2,273, 1995
Total Attendance Recent Meeting: 67,166, 2005
Lowest Single-Meet Record: 56,345, 2004

Handle
Average All Sources Recent Meeting: $1,764,065, 2005
Average On-Track Recent Meeting: $52,873, 2005
Record Daily Average for Single Meet: $153,786, 1995
Single-Day Total Handle All Sources: $3,083,764, November 23, 2005
Total All Sources Recent Meeting: $100,551,680, 2005
Total On-Track Recent Meeting: $3,013,753, 2005
Record Total for Single Meet: $6,459,004, 1995
Record Total All Sources for Single Meet: $100,551,680, 2005
Record Average All Sources Single Meet: $1,764,065, 2005
Highest Single-Day Record Recent Meet: $3,083,764, November 23, 2005

Mutuel Records
Highest Win: $291.40, Mi Serenade, October 19, 2001
Highest Exacta: $3,212.60, September 10, 2000
Highest Trifecta: $34,077.20, November 22, 2002
Highest Daily Double: $5,986.40, October 17, 2002
Highest Pick 3: $8,952, November 22, 2002
Highest Other Exotics: $107.60, Place, October 7, 1996; $36.60, Show, November 19, 2003; $128,485.60, Superfecta, September 14, 2005; $4,270.95, 50 Cent Trifecta, September 4, 2005; $6,424.28, 10 Cent Superfecta, September 14, 2005
Highest Pick 4: $10,405.80, November 2, 2005

Leaders
Career, Leading Jockey by Titles: Jon Court, 3
Career, Leading Owner by Titles: Highway 1 Racing, 3; Louis O'Brien, 3
Career, Leading Trainer by Titles: Ralph Martinez, 3
Career, Leading Jockey by Stakes Wins: Jon Court, 14
Career, Leading Owner by Stakes Wins: McKee Stables, 9
Career, Leading Trainer by Stakes Wins: Dale Romans, 18
Career, Leading Jockey by Wins: Terry Thompson, 397
Career, Leading Owner by Wins: Louis O'Brien, 171
Career, Leading Trainer by Wins: Gary Patrick, 189
Recent Meeting, Leading Jockey: Rodney A. Prescott, 81, 2005
Recent Meeting, Leading Owner: Louis O'Brien, 40, 2005
Recent Meeting, Leading Trainer: Ralph Martinez, 40, 2005

Records
Single-Day Jockey Wins: Terry Thompson, 7, November 18, 2001
Single-Day Owner Wins: Louis O'Brien, 4, October 21, 2004
Single-Day Trainer Wins: Ralph Martinez, 4, October 21, 2004
Single Meet, Leading Jockey by Wins: Terry Thompson, 122, 2001
Single Meet, Leading Owner by Wins: Louis O'Brien, 66, 2003
Single Meet, Leading Trainer by Wins: Ralph Martinez, 66, 2003
Single Meet, Leading Horse by Wins: Green Appeal, 5, 1997

Track Records, Main Dirt
5 furlongs: Geruase, :57.73, November 10, 2005
5½ furlongs: Moro Oro, 1:02.20, September 20, 1996; Chukker Creek, 1:02.20, November 24, 1996
6 furlongs: Moro Oro, 1:07.40, November 16, 1996
1 mile: Vic's Rebel, 1:33.99, October 13, 1998
1$^{1}/_{16}$ miles: Alydar's Rib, 1:41, November 1, 1996
1⅛ miles: Stay Forever Young, 1:51.86, October 12, 2005
1⅜ miles: Mount Tora Bora, 2:22, October 29, 2005
1½ miles: Got Brass, 2:36.88, October 30, 2004
1⅝ miles: Open Space, 2:41.20, November 16, 1996
Other: 1$^{9}/_{16}$ miles, Our Forbes, 2:39.20, November 7, 1997; 1⅞ miles, Raw New, 3:16.20, December 1, 2000

Principal Races
Indiana Derby (G2), Indiana Breeders' Cup Oaks (G3), Michael Schaefer Mile S.

Notable Events
Indiana Derby Gala, Ladies' Night

Fastest Times of 2005 (Dirt)
5 furlongs: Geruase, :57.73, November 10, 2005
5½ furlongs: Mr. Sass, 1:04.17, November 23, 2005
6 furlongs: Mr. Mink, 1:09.60, October 23, 2005
1 mile: Iosilver, 1:37.52, November 19, 2005
1$^{1}/_{16}$ miles: Don't Get Mad, 1:42.71, October 1, 2005
1⅛ miles: Stay Forever Young, 1:51.86, October 12, 2005
1⅜ miles: Mount Tora Bora, 2:22, October 29, 2005
1$^{9}/_{16}$ miles: Anthem Hill, 2:42.36, November 12, 2005
1⅞ miles: Mannie's Mistake, 3:27.12, November 25, 2005

Indiana Downs

Located in Shelbyville, about 40 miles southeast of Indianapolis, Indiana Downs held its inaugural Thoroughbred meet in 2003. Construction of the $35-million track was opposed by Hoosier Park, but the red-and-white grandstand facility opened on schedule for its inaugural 2002 Standardbred meet. Owned by Oliver Racing LLC and LHT Capital LLC, the track opened its first off-track betting facility in February 2003 in Evansville, near Churchill-owned Ellis Park, and in '04 opened an OTB facility across the Ohio River from Louisville, home of Churchill Downs. Beginning in 2003, Indiana Downs and Hoosier split the state subsidy generated by a tax on riverboat admissions.

Location: 4200 N. Michigan Rd., Shelbyville, In. 46176-8515
Phone: (317) 421-0000, (866) 478-7223
Fax: (317) 421-0100
Website: *www.indianadowns.com*
E-Mail: info@indianadowns.com
Year Founded: 2002
Dates of Inaugural Meeting: April 11-May 26, 2003
Abbreviation: InD
Acreage: 152

Ownership
Oliver Racing LLC; LHT Capital LLC

Officers
Chairman: Ross Mangano
General Manager: Jonathan Schuster
Director of Racing: Jim Ewart
Racing Secretary: Raymond "Butch" Cook
Director of Operations: Eddie Matson
Director of Marketing: John Droghei Jr.
Director of Mutuels: Jamie Dean
Director of Simulcasting: Joe Melek
Horsemen's Liaison: Joe Thompson
Track Announcer: Dominic Polito
Track Photographer: Coady Photography
Security: Dave Scranton

Racing Dates
2005: April 15-June 20, 48 days
2006: April 21-June 28, 49 days

Track Layout
Main Circumference: 1 mile
Main Turf Circumference: 7 furlongs

Handle
Average All Sources Recent Meeting: $417,193, 2005
Average On-Track Recent Meeting: $46,709, 2005
Total All Sources Recent Meeting: $20,025,282, 2005
Total On-Track Recent Meeting: $2,242,011, 2005
Highest Single-Day Record Recent Meet: $755,219, May 24, 2005

Mutuel Records
Highest Pick 6: $322,561.40, August 9, 2004

Leaders

Recent Meeting, Leading Jockey: Rodney A. Prescott, 68, 2005
Recent Meeting, Leading Trainer: Barbara I. McBride, 28, 2005
Recent Meeting, Leading Horse: Rebecca G Dianne, 3, 2005; Resurrect, 3, 2005; Life Sayver, 3, 2005; Flying Nuggets, 3, 2005; Ayla Bella, 3, 2005; Congratulating, 3, 2005; Moment of Song, 3, 2005

Track Records, Main Dirt

5 furlongs: Cinnapie, :57, May 13, 2005
5½ furlongs: Speak of Kings, 1:03.16, May 17, 2005
6 furlongs: Call Roy, 1:09.38, May 18, 2005
1 mile: Image of Approval, 1:37.44, June 4, 2005
1m 70 yds: K K Avey, 1:41.56, May 7, 2003
1 1/16 miles: Brass Punch, 1:42.70, May 30, 2005
1⅛ miles: A Secret Scoop, 1:50.62, May 15, 2003

Track Records, Main Turf

5 furlongs: Don Manuel, :55.79, May 29, 2006
7½ furlongs: Chasing the Ghosts, 1:29.06, May 23, 2006
1 mile: Private Horde, 1:36.03, May 10, 2005
1 1/16 miles: Luckymata, 1:42.34, May 22, 2004

Principal Races

Shelby County S., William Henry Harrison S., Indiana First Lady S., Governor's S., Florence Henderson S., A. J. Foyt S.

Fastest Times of 2005 (Dirt)

4½ furlongs: Flying Nuggets, :51.53, June 11, 2005
5 furlongs: Cinnapie, :57, May 13, 2005
5½ furlongs: Speak of Kings, 1:03.16, May 17, 2005
6 furlongs: Call Roy, 1:09.38, May 18, 2005
1 mile: Image of Approval, 1:37.44, June 4, 2005
1m 70 yds: Woodsnwaters, 1:41.77, June 4, 2005
1 1/16 miles: Brass Punch, 1:42.70, May 30, 2005
1¼ miles: Pleasant Italian, 2:05.54, May 13, 2005

Fastest Times of 2005 (Turf)

5 furlongs: Chaotic Achiever, :57.53, May 28, 2005
a5 furlongs: Mighty Picture Too, :58.85, June 7, 2005
7½ furlongs: Ayla Bella, 1:30.98, June 1, 2005
a7½ furlongs: Cold N Evil, 1:34.01, June 8, 2005
1 mile: Private Horde, 1:36.03, May 10, 2005
a1 miles: Lee's Receivable, 1:39.67, June 10, 2005
1 1/16 miles: Lac a Rock, 1:42.58, June 18, 2005
a1 1/16 miles: Waffle Head, 1:46.27, June 9, 2005

Iowa

Prairie Meadows Racetrack

The Thoroughbred industry in Iowa received a boost when Prairie Meadows Racetrack in Altoona, not far from Des Moines, opened in 1989. But financial difficulties forced the track to file for bankruptcy in 1991 and to close for live racing in '92. The following year, Prairie Meadows became the property of Polk County, which today leases the facility to the not-for-profit Racing Association of Central Iowa. The track's future was secured in 1995 when slot machines were installed, with a portion of revenues significantly increasing race purses. Today, Prairie Meadows's live racing schedule begins with a Thoroughbred meet that is followed by a mixed meet for Thoroughbreds and Quarter Horses, and concludes with a harness racing season. One of the track's most popular events is the Iowa Classic, a ten-race event for state-bred Thoroughbreds and Quarter Horses.

Location: 1 Prairie Meadows Dr., Altoona, Ia. 50009-0901
Phone: (515) 967-1000, (800) 325-9015
Fax: (859) 288-1081
Website: *www.prairiemeadows.com*
E-Mail: marylou.coady@prairiemeadows.com
Year Founded: July 19, 1984
Dates of Inaugural Meeting: March 1-15, 1989
Abbreviation: PrM
Acreage: 233
Number of Stalls: 1,400
Seating Capacity: 7,000

Officers

Chairman: Jack Bishop
Senior Vice President: Gary Palmer
Director of Racing: Derron D. Heldt
Racing Secretary: Daniel J. Doocy
Secretary: Shirley Kleywegt
Director of Finance: Pat Fox
Director of Marketing: Julie Stewart
Director of Mutuels: Mark Loewe
Director of Publicity: Mary Lou Coady
Director of Simulcasting: Mark Loewe
Horsemen's Bookkeeper: Tami Burns
Horsemen's Liaison: Chuck Schott
Stewards: Gerald Hobby, Ralph D'Amico, Rick Sackett
Track Announcer: Jim McAulay
Track Photographer: Jack Coady Jr.
Track Superintendent: Lamont Marks
Clerk of Course: Carmen Bish
Asst. Racing Secretary: Chad Keller

Racing Dates

2005: April 21-July 4, 47 days; July 8-September 24, 48 days
2006: April 21-July 3, 45 days; July 13-September 9, 36 days

Track Layout

Main Circumference: 1 mile
Main Track Chute: 2 furlongs and 6 furlongs
Main Width: Homestretch: 90 feet; Backstretch: 60 feet
Main Length of Stretch: 1,033 feet
Training Track: 5 furlongs

Handle

Record Daily Average for Single Meet: $580,430, Fall 2002

Mutuel Records

Lowest Win: $2.20
Highest Exacta: $2,424.20, May 19, 1997
Lowest Exacta: $3.60, July 28, 1994
Highest Trifecta: $35,761.40, August 31, 2002
Lowest Trifecta: $7.80, July 22, 2000
Highest Daily Double: $2,216, September 24, 1998
Lowest Daily Double: $3.00, August 28, 2004

Leaders

Career, Leading Jockey by Titles: Glenn Corbett, 6
Career, Leading Owner by Titles: River Ridge Ranch, 6
Career, Leading Trainer by Titles: Dick R. Clark, 17
Career, Leading Owner by Wins: Maggi Moss, 206
Career, Leading Trainer by Wins: Dick R. Clark, 593
Recent Meeting, Leading Jockey: Timothy Doocy, 62, Spring 2005; Glenn Corbett, 55, Summer 2005
Recent Meeting, Leading Trainer: Dick R. Clark, 52, Spring 2005; Dick R. Clark, 36, Summer 2005

Records

Single-Day Jockey Wins: Terry Thompson, 6, May 20, 2002
Single Meet, Leading Jockey by Wins: Kelly Murray, 101, 1989
Single Meet, Leading Owner by Wins: Maggi Moss, 35, 2004
Single Meet, Leading Trainer by Wins: Gary Ryan, 76, 1989

Track Records, Main Dirt

4 furlongs: Straight Fever, :46.20, July 16, 1993
4½ furlongs: Southern Alert, :51.24, May 7, 2002
5 furlongs: Dayjob, :56, May 1, 1999
5½ furlongs: Leaping Plum, 1:02.50, August 5, 1997
6 furlongs: Coach Jimi Lee, 1:07.85, July 4, 2004
1 mile: Tartine, 1:35, August 11, 1998
1m 70 yds: Northwest Hill, 1:39.69, July 4, 2003
1 1/16 miles: Excessivepleasure, 1:40.82, July 5, 2003
1⅛ miles: Beboppin Baby, 1:46.62, July 4, 1998
1¼ miles: Famous Event, 2:02.60, June 23, 1995
1½ miles: Famous Event, 2:32, July 9, 1995
1⅝ miles: Sir Star, 2:44.3, May 12, 1989
2 miles: Gritti Marco, 3:26, July 28, 1995
Other: 2 furlongs, Dashboard Drummer, :22.20, May 9, 2003

Principal Races

Prairie Meadows Cornhusker Breeders' Cup H. (G2), Iowa Oaks (G3), Iowa Derby, Iowa Sprint H., Iowa Distaff Breeders' Cup S.

Fastest Times of 2005 (Dirt)

4½ furlongs: Jazzy Okie, :52.09, May 21, 2005
5 furlongs: Counterfeit Gold, :57.92, July 3, 2005
5½ furlongs: Premium Saltine, 1:02.64, May 7, 2005

6 furlongs: Silver Dollar, 1:08.45, June 10, 2005
1 mile: Whimsy, 1:35.51, June 10, 2005
1m 70 yds: Act of Reform, 1:39.81, June 16, 2005
1 1/16 miles: Silver Axe, 1:42.93, May 30, 2005
1 1/8 miles: Lord of the Game, 1:49.94, July 2, 2005
2 miles: Scarlet Lad, 3:31.73, July 4, 2005

Kansas

Anthony Downs

Location: 523 East Sherman, P.O. Box 444, Anthony, Ks. 67003-0444
Phone: (620) 842-3796
Fax: (620) 842-3797
Website: *www.anthonydownsraces.com*
Year Founded: 1904
Abbreviation: AnF

Ownership

Anthony Fair Association

Officers

Chairman: Dan Bird
President: Dan Bird
Director of Racing: Norris E. Gwin
Secretary: Terry Allen
Treasurer: Niel Kitts
Director of Mutuels: Connie Shellhammer
Vice President: Allen Thomas
Stewards: Trudie Lyons, Robert Stovall, Samuel Lato
Track Announcer: Jerry McNamar
Asst. Racing Secretary: Rita Osborn
Security: John Blevins

Racing Dates

2005: July 15-July 24, 6 days
2006: July 14-July 23, 6 days
2007: July 13-July 22, 6 days

Track Layout

Main Circumference: 4 furlongs

Attendance

Average Daily Recent Meeting: 948, 2005
Total Attendance Recent Meeting: 5,690, 2005

Handle

Average On-Track Recent Meeting: $26,667, 2005
Total On-Track Recent Meeting: $160,000, 2005
Highest Single-Day Record Recent Meet: $35,051, July 24, 2005

Leaders

Recent Meeting, Leading Jockey: Gary Worst, 4, 2005
Recent Meeting, Leading Owner: Hector Espino, 2005
Recent Meeting, Leading Trainer: Jose Ibarra, 2, 2005
Recent Meeting, Leading Horse: Clever Red, 2, 2005; Devil's Bandit, 2, 2005

Principal Races

Anthony Downs Derby, Anthony Thoroughbred Futurity, Harper County H., Anthony Fair H., Gene Francis and Associates S., Kansas Bred Centennial H.

Notable Events

Kansas City BBQ Society Contest

Fastest Times of 2005 (Dirt)

5 furlongs: Puckerupbuttercup, 1:00.36, July 16, 2005
a5 furlongs: Clever Red, 1:01.90, July 23, 2005
a6 1/2 furlongs: Pint o' Stout, 1:21.90, July 24, 2005
7 furlongs: Captain Comet, 1:30.50, July 16, 2005
1 1/16 miles: Devil's Bandit, 1:51.87, July 23, 2005

Eureka Downs

Eureka Downs, located 60 miles east of Wichita, runs a mixed horse meet on weekends and holidays from the first week of May through July 4. The five-furlong track, which dates to 1872, raced Standardbreds in the late 1940s and was the site of Kansas's first pari-mutuel race for Thoroughbreds on September 3, 1988. The track closed in 1991 and reopened in '93 with the Greenwood County Fair Association and the Kansas Quarter Horse Racing Association co-licensed as operators. Eureka Downs races Thoroughbreds, Quarter Horses, Appaloosas, Paints, and mules. Non-betting mule contests began in the late 1990s and proved so popular that they were added to the pari-mutuel menu.

Location: 210 N. Jefferson St., P.O. Box 228, Eureka, Ks. 67045
Phone: (620) 583-5528
Fax: (620) 583-5381
Website: *www.eurekadowns.com*
E-Mail: info@eurekadowns.com
Year Founded: 1993
Abbreviation: Eur

Officers

General Manager: Lee Smith

Racing Dates

2005: May 7-July 10, 20 days
2006: May 6-July 4, 18 days

Track Layout

Main Circumference: 5 furlongs

Leaders

Recent Meeting, Leading Jockey: Mike J. Bishop, 9, 2005
Recent Meeting, Leading Trainer: Joe Frederick Thomas Sr., 8, 2005
Recent Meeting, Leading Horse: Crane Away, 3, 2005

Fastest Times of 2005 (Dirt)

4 furlongs: D D Dot Comm, :45.97, May 29, 2005
6 furlongs: Devious Kyle, 1:14.18, May 30, 2005
7 furlongs: Crane Away, 1:28.48, June 18, 2005
1 1/16 miles: Goldstar Night, 1:56, July 4, 2005

The Woodlands

Opened in September 1989 for greyhound racing, The Woodlands began Thoroughbred racing on May 24, 1990. The track, located in the northwest corner of Kansas City, offers a 26-day mixed horse racing meet for Thoroughbreds and Quarter Horses in October and year-round greyhound racing on a separate track. The three types of racing have been conducted concurrently since 1990. The Woodlands set a single-day attendance record of 22,015 in its first year of Thoroughbred operation with a wallet giveaway. The track's then-parent company filed for bankruptcy protection from its creditors in 1996. The track was sold in 1998 to William M. Grace, principal owner of the St. Jo Frontier Casino in St. Joseph, Missouri.
Location: 9700 Leavenworth Rd., Kansas City, Ks. 66109-3551
Phone: (913) 299-9797, (800) 695-7223
Fax: (913) 299-9804
Website: *www.woodlandskc.com*
E-Mail: info@woodlandskc.com
Year Founded: 1989
Dates of Inaugural Meeting: May 24, 1990
Abbreviation: Wds
Acreage: 700
Number of Stalls: 1,250
Seating Capacity: 4,250

Ownership

Kansas Racing LLC

Officers

Chairman: Carol Sader
President: Stephen F. Rehm
General Manager: James Gartland
Director of Racing: Doug Schoepf
Racing Secretary: Doug Schoepf

Secretary: William M. Epperheimer
Treasurer: Randall P. Kancel
Director of Operations: Kevin King
Director of Finance: Charles Wheeler
Director of Marketing: Connie Loebsack
Director of Mutuels: Carl Schroll
Vice President: Patricia Quinlan
Director of Simulcasting: Jayme LaRocca
Stewards: Sam Lato, Trudy Lyons, Robert Stovall
Track Announcer: Keith Nelson
Track Photographer: Gene Wilson and Associates
Track Superintendent: Curtis Jardon
Horsemen's Bookkeeper: Judy Laster
Security: Robert Fritz

Racing Dates

2005: September 24-October 29, 26 days
2006: September 18-October 29, 30 days

Track Layout

Main Circumference: 1 mile
Main Track Chute: 6 furlongs
Main Length of Stretch: 1,030 feet

Attendance

Average Daily Recent Meeting: 1,338, 2005
Highest Single-Day Record: 22,015, July 22, 1990
Total Attendance Recent Meeting: 34,781, 2005

Handle

Average All Sources Recent Meeting: $256,012.68, 2005
Average On-Track Recent Meeting: $56,087.60, 2005
Total All Sources Recent Meeting: $6,656,329.70, 2005
Total On-Track Recent Meeting: $1,458,277.70, 2005
Highest Single-Day Record Recent Meet: $564,585, October 25, 2005

Leaders

Recent Meeting, Leading Jockey: Alex Birzer, 57, 2005
Recent Meeting, Leading Trainer: Timothy Mark Gleason, 24, 2005
Recent Meeting, Leading Horse: Melody Ruth, 4, 2005

Track Records, Main Dirt

4 furlongs: King of Diamonds, :45.80, October 10, 2001
4$\frac{1}{2}$ furlongs: Lanyons Star, :51$\frac{2}{5}$, June 29, 1990
5 furlongs: Jungle Merit, :57.40, October 29, 1993
5$\frac{1}{2}$ furlongs: Axe Age, 1:03.20, August 15, 1993
6 furlongs: Great Immunity, 1:08.50, June 30, 1991
1 mile: French Fritter, 1:36, June 1, 1991
1m 70 yds: Holly's Wind, 1:40$\frac{2}{5}$, June 24, 1990
1$\frac{1}{16}$ miles: Axle Lode, 1:42.80, September 22, 1996
1$\frac{1}{8}$ miles: Model Age, 1:49$\frac{4}{5}$, July 18, 1990
1$\frac{3}{16}$ miles: Old Man's Delite, 1:58, October 21, 2003
1$\frac{1}{4}$ miles: Midway Mail, 2:03.20, September 10, 1993
1$\frac{1}{2}$ miles: He's a Valentine, 2:33.20, October 14, 1994
1$\frac{3}{4}$ miles: Mark of Strength, 3:02, November 5, 1993

Principal Races

Woodlands Derby, Manhattan S., Sunflower S., Kansas Oaks, Woodlands S.

Fastest Times of 2005 (Dirt)

5 furlongs: Manovan, :59.40, September 27, 2005
5$\frac{1}{2}$ furlongs: Makesyourheadspin, 1:05, October 29, 2005; Zealian, 1:05, October 26, 2005
6 furlongs: Denoun N Deverb, 1:10, October 4, 2005
1 mile: Raw Roy, 1:40.40, October 26, 2005; Was a Zeal, 1:40.40, September 25, 2005
1m 70 yds: Game Day, 1:42.80, September 26, 2005
1$\frac{1}{16}$ miles: Matched, 1:45.20, October 29, 2005
1$\frac{1}{8}$ miles: Game Day, 1:54, October 15, 2005
1$\frac{3}{4}$ miles: Diamond Roo, 3:05.60, October 29, 2005

Kentucky

Churchill Downs

Churchill Downs in Louisville is arguably the world's best-known racetrack, and its premier event, the Kentucky Derby (G1), is widely recognized as the sport's best-known race. First staged in 1875, the Derby is one of America's oldest continually run races and annually attracts an on-track throng exceeding 140,000, the nation's largest crowd for a Thoroughbred race, as well as worldwide television audience in the millions. The Derby has been held at Churchill since the track opened on its current site in 1875. Col. M. Lewis Clark Jr., the track's founder, built the first grandstand on land he secured from uncles John and Henry Churchill. Churchill Downs had financial problems for the first 28 years of its existence, forcing its sale by Clark and subsequent owners until Col. Matt Winn and partners bought the track in 1902. The track, whose famous Twin Spires date from 1895, today is owned by Churchill Downs Inc., which also owns Arlington Park near Chicago, Calder Race Course in Miami, Ellis Park in Western Kentucky, and Fair Grounds in New Orleans. It also is part-owner of Hoosier Park in Indiana. Churchill has hosted five runnings of the Breeders' Cup, beginning in 1988 and was scheduled to be the host of the 2006 Breeders' Cup. In 2005, Churchill completed a $121-million renovation project, including a $95-million rebuilding of the track's clubhouse.

Location: 700 Central Ave., Louisville, Ky. 40208-1200
Phone: (502) 636-4400, (800) 28-DERBY
Fax: (502) 636-4430
Website: *www.churchilldowns.com*
E-Mail: info@kyderby.com
Year Founded: 1875
Dates of Inaugural Meeting: May 17, 1875
Abbreviation: CD
Acreage: 147
Number of Stalls: 1,404
Seating Capacity: 48,500

Ownership

Churchill Downs Inc.

Officers

Chief Executive Officer: Thomas H. Meeker
Chairman: Carl F. Pollard
President: Steve Sexton
General Manager: Jim Gates
Director of Racing: Doug Bredar
Racing Secretary: Doug Bredar
Director of Operations: David Sweazy
Director of Admissions: Ray Pait Jr.
Director of Communications: John Asher
Director of Marketing: Stacey Meier
Director of Mutuels: Rick Smith
Vice Presidents: John Asher, Scott Graff, Raymond Lehr Jr., Thomas Schneider, David Sweazy
Director of Publicity: Tony Terry
Horsemen's Liaison: J. L. "Buck" Wheat
Stewards: Butch Becraft, Richard S. Leigh, John Veitch
Track Announcer: Luke Kruytbosch
Track Photographer: Four Footed Fotos
Track Superintendent: Raymond Lehr Jr.

Racing Dates

2005: April 30-July 10, 52 days; October 30-November 26, 21 days
2006: April 29-July 16, 57 days; October 29-November 25, 21 days

Track Layout

Main Circumference: 1 mile
Main Track Chute: 1$\frac{1}{4}$ miles
Main Width: Homestretch: 80 feet; Backstretch: 79 feet
Main Length of Stretch: 1,234.5 feet
Main Turf Circumference: 7 furlongs
Main Turf Width: 80 feet

Attendance

Average Daily Recent Meeting: 13,813, Spring 2005; 7,820, Fall 2005
Highest Single-Day Record: 163,628, May 4, 1974; 80,452, November 7, 1998

Highest Single-Meet Record: 811,446, Spring 1988; 337,977, Fall 1988
Record Daily Average for Single Meet: 20,066, Spring 1944; 14,082, Fall 1988
Total Attendance Recent Meeting: 718,270, Spring 2005; 164,214, Fall 2005
Highest Single-Day Recent Meet: 156,435, May 7, 2005; 14,864, November 5, 2005

Handle

Average All Sources Recent Meeting: $11,255,342, Spring 2005; $8,676,904, Fall 2005
Average On-Track Recent Meeting: $1,539,157, Spring 2005; $921,796, Fall 2005
Record Daily Average for Single Meet: $2,054,901, Spring 1997; $1,945,058, Fall 1988
Total All Sources Recent Meeting: $585,277,784, Spring 2005; $182,214,993, Fall 2005
Total On-Track Recent Meeting: $80,036,165, Spring 2005; $19,357,722, Fall 2005
Highest Single-Day Record Recent Meet: $155,133,631, May 7, 2005; $15,527,121, November 19, 2005
Record Total for Single Meet: $102,302,494, Spring 2000; $46,945,394, Fall 1988

Mutuel Records

Highest Win: $495.60, Gold and Rubies, November 21, 1978
Highest Exacta: $9,814.80, May 7, 2005
Highest Trifecta: $133,134.80, May 7, 2005
Highest Daily Double: $6,818.20, October 29, 1984
Highest Pick 3: $114,156, November 4, 2000
Highest Pick 6: $1,168,136, June 25, 2003
Highest Other Exotics: $864,253, Superfecta, May 7, 2005
Highest Pick 4: $164,168, May 7, 2005

Leaders

Career, Leading Jockey by Titles: Pat Day, 34
Career, Leading Owner by Titles: Kenneth and Sarah Ramsey, 10
Career, Leading Trainer by Titles: D. Wayne Lukas, 11
Career, Leading Jockey by Stakes Wins: Pat Day, 155
Career, Leading Owner by Stakes Wins: Calumet Farm, 32
Career, Leading Trainer by Stakes Wins: William I. Mott, 69
Career, Leading Jockey by Wins: Pat Day, 2,481
Career, Leading Trainer by Wins: William I. Mott, 561
Recent Meeting, Leading Jockey: Rafael Bejarano, 64, Spring 2005; Rafael Bejarano, 26, Fall 2005; Mark Guidry, 26, Fall 2005
Recent Meeting, Leading Owner: Billy Hays, 19, Spring 2005; Kenneth and Sarah Ramsey, 7, Fall 2005
Recent Meeting, Leading Trainer: Dale Romans, 36, Spring 2005; Dale Romans, 16, Fall 2005
Recent Meeting, Leading Horse: Ellen's Foxy Girl, 4, Spring 2005; French Park, 2, Fall 2005; Moonshine Gal, 2, Fall 2005; Three Steps Ahead, 2, Fall 2005; Fabulosity, 2, Fall 2005; Mr. Kimbo, 2, Fall 2005; Arch Assault, 2, Fall 2005

Records

Single-Day Jockey Wins: Pat Day, 7, June 20, 1984
Single Meet, Leading Jockey by Wins: Pat Day, 169, Spring 1983; Pat Day, 55, Fall 1985
Single Meet, Leading Trainer by Wins: William I. Mott, 54, Spring 1984; Dale Romans, 20, Fall, 2003

Track Records, Main Dirt

4 furlongs: Fair Phantom, :46$^{3}/_{5}$, May 7, 1921; Casey :46$^{3}/_{5}$, May 9, 1921; Miss Joy, :46$^{3}/_{5}$, May 10, 1921
$4^{1}/_{2}$ furlongs: He's Got Grit, :50.73, June 26, 2005
5 furlongs: Wildcat Shoes, :56.49, May 20, 2005
$5^{1}/_{2}$ furlongs: Cashier's Dream, 1:02.52, July 7, 2001
6 furlongs: Kelly's Landing, 1:07.59, June 25, 2005
$6^{1}/_{2}$ furlongs: Love At Noon, 1:14.34, May 5, 2001
7 furlongs: Alannan, 1:20.50, May 5, 2001
$7^{1}/_{2}$ furlongs: Miss Lodi, 1:28.08, June 1, 2002
1 mile: Chilukki, 1:33.57, November 4, 2000
1m 70 yds: The Porter, 1:41$^{3}/_{5}$, May 30, 1919
$1^{1}/_{16}$ miles: Yes Sir, 1:41$^{3}/_{5}$, November 25, 1970
$1^{1}/_{8}$ miles: Victory Gallop, 1:47.28, June 12, 1999
$1^{3}/_{16}$ miles: Bonnie Andrew, 1:58$^{3}/_{5}$, November 14, 1942
$1^{1}/_{4}$ miles: Secretariat, 1:59$^{2}/_{5}$, May 5, 1973
$1^{3}/_{8}$ miles: Elliott, 2:20$^{3}/_{5}$, October 15, 1906
$1^{1}/_{2}$ miles: A Storm Is Brewing, 2:32.02, June 17, 2001
$1^{5}/_{8}$ miles: Tupolev (Arg), 2:49$^{2}/_{5}$, July 23, 1983
$1^{3}/_{4}$ miles: Caslon Bold, 2:59.64, July 4, 1995
2 miles: Libertarian, 3:22.26, November 28, 1998
Other: 1m 20 yds, Frog Legs, 1:39, May 13, 1913; 1m 50 yds, Hodge, 1:41$^{4}/_{5}$, October 4, 1916; 1m 100 yds, The Caxton, 1:49$^{1}/_{5}$, May 16, 1902; $2^{1}/_{16}$ miles, Hi Neighbor, 3:40$^{4}/_{5}$, November 11, 1949; $2^{1}/_{4}$ miles, Raincoat, 3:53, October 7, 1915; 3 miles, Ten Broeck, 5:26$^{1}/_{5}$, September 3, 1876; 4 miles, Sotemia, 7:10$^{4}/_{5}$, October 7, 1912

Track Records, Main Turf

5 furlongs: Unbridled Sidney, :55.54, July 9, 2005
1 mile: Jaggery John, 1:33.78, July 4, 1995
$1^{1}/_{16}$ miles: Ever With You, 1:40.82, November 7, 2001
$1^{1}/_{8}$ miles: Lure, 1:46.34, April 30, 1993
$1^{3}/_{8}$ miles: Snake Eyes, 2:13, May 22, 1997
$1^{1}/_{2}$ miles: Tikkanen, 2:26.50, November 5, 1994

Principal Races

Spring Meet: Kentucky Derby (G1), Kentucky Oaks (G1), Woodford Reserve Turf Classic S. (G1), Humana Distaff H. (G1), Stephen Foster H. (G1)
Fall Meet: Clark H. (G2), Falls City H. (G2), Kentucky Jockey Club S. (G2), Golden Rod S. (G2), Chilukki S. (G2)

Notable Events

Fall Meet: Churchill Downs Chili Cook-Off
Spring Meet: Kentucky Derby, Festival in the Field, Brew and Barbecue Fest

Fastest Times of 2005 (Dirt)

$4^{1}/_{2}$ furlongs: He's Got Grit, :50.73, June 26, 2005
5 furlongs: Wildcat Shoes, :56.49, May 20, 2005
$5^{1}/_{2}$ furlongs: Forever Bertie, 1:03.88, June 9, 2005
6 furlongs: Kelly's Landing, 1:07.59, June 25, 2005
$6^{1}/_{2}$ furlongs: Cap'n Capote, 1:15.26, May 7, 2005
7 furlongs: Battle Won, 1:20.56, May 7, 2005
$7^{1}/_{2}$ furlongs: Straight Line, 1:28.34, October 30, 2005
1 mile: Elijah's Song, 1:34.22, June 8, 2005
$1^{1}/_{16}$ miles: Wiggins, 1:42.18, July 8, 2005
$1^{1}/_{8}$ miles: Saint Liam, 1:47.52, June 18, 2005
$1^{1}/_{4}$ miles: Giacomo, 2:02.75, May 7, 2005

Fastest Times of 2005 (Turf)

5 furlongs: Unbridled Sidney, :55.54, July 9, 2005
1 mile: Everything to Gain, 1:34.33, July 10, 2005
$1^{1}/_{16}$ miles: Mythical Conquest, 1:41.66, July 7, 2005
$1^{1}/_{8}$ miles: America Alive, 1:47.34, May 7, 2005
$1^{3}/_{8}$ miles: Triple X., 2:17.85, June 4, 2005

Ellis Park

Ellis Park holds the distinction of being the only racetrack where soybeans are grown in the infield. Built in 1922 and designed after Saratoga Race Course, the track located on an island in the Ohio River near Evansville, Indiana, was originally named Dade Park and intended for harness racing. Within one month of its opening, the track replaced harness racing with Thoroughbred racing. Dade Park was plagued with financial problems and, in 1923 and '24, the only racing held was for race cards on Labor Day weekend. In 1924, James C. Ellis, who owned construction and oil enterprises, purchased the track for $35,100 and reopened it for Thoroughbred racing in 1925. In 1954, two years before Ellis's death, the track's name was changed to James C. Ellis Park. In 1998, Churchill Downs Inc. purchased Ellis, and its purses benefited from full-card simulcasting revenues. The track sustained significant damage in a 2005 tornado and was rebuilt. Ellis's richest race each year is the $200,000 Gardenia Handicap (G3) for fillies and mares.

Location: 3300 US Hwy. 41 N., P.O. Box 33, Henderson, Ky. 42419
Phone: (812) 425-1456, (800) 333-8110
Fax: (812) 425-0146
Website: *www.ellisparkracing.com*

Year Founded: 1922 (as Dade Park)
Dates of Inaugural Meeting: November 8, 1922
Abbreviation: EIP
Acreage: 214
Number of Stalls: 1,142
Seating Capacity: 7,750

Ownership

Churchill Downs Inc.

Officers

Chairman: Thomas H. Meeker
President: Steven P. Sexton
General Manager: Brian Elmore
Director of Racing: Douglas Bredar
Racing Secretary: Douglas Bredar
Director of Operations: Robert A. Jackson
Director of Admissions: Marianne Wagner
Director of Marketing: Jennifer Ray
Director of Mutuels: Jeff Hall
Vice President: Brian Elmore
Director of Publicity: Josh Abner
Director of Simulcasting: Robert A. Jackson
Horsemen's Liaison: Kathy Griffith
Stewards: Brooks A. Becraft, Barbara Borden, John Veitch
Track Announcer: Luke Kruytbosch
Track Photographer: Reed Palmer Photography
Track Superintendent: Glenn Thompson
Security: Darrell Williams
Horsemen's Bookkeeper: Lana Murphy
Asst. Racing Secretary: Dan Bork

Racing Dates

2005: July 13-September 5, 41 days
2006: July 19-September 4, 36 days

Track Layout

Main Circumference: 1 1/8 miles
Main Track Chute: 7 furlongs and 1 mile
Main Width: Homestretch: 100 feet; Backstretch: 85 feet
Main Length of Stretch: 1,175 feet
Main Turf Circumference: 1 mile

Attendance

Average Daily Recent Meeting: 2,937, 2005
Highest Single-Day Record: 15,500 est., September 4, 1967
Total Attendance Recent Meeting: 120,430, 2005

Handle

Average All Sources Recent Meeting: $2,707,421, 2005
Average On-Track Recent Meeting: $195,434, 2005
Total All Sources Recent Meeting: $111,004,246, 2005
Total On-Track Recent Meeting: $8,012,806, 2005
Highest Single-Day Record Recent Meet: $3,615,229, August 20, 2005

Leaders

Career, Leading Jockey by Titles: Leroy Tauzin, 7
Career, Leading Owner by Titles: George "Hoolie" Hudson, 5
Career, Leading Trainer by Titles: Bernard S. Flint, 11
Recent Meeting, Leading Jockey: Jesus Lopez Castanon, 53, 2005
Recent Meeting, Leading Owner: R and G Stables, 6, 2005
Recent Meeting, Leading Trainer: Steven M. Asmussen, 19, 2005
Recent Meeting, Leading Horse: Set to Sparkle, 4, 2005

Records

Single-Day Jockey Wins: Willie Martinez, 7
Single-Day Trainer Wins: Wayne Bearden, 5, August 7, 1997
Single Meet, Leading Jockey by Wins: Mike McDowell, 89, 1986
Single Meet, Leading Owner by Wins: Tom Dorris, 20, 1978
Single Meet, Leading Trainer by Wins: Angel Montano, 34, 1976

Track Records, Main Dirt

5 furlongs: White Image, :57 3/5, July 9, 1988
5 1/2 furlongs: Mount Forloon, 1:03 2/5, July 17, 1988
6 furlongs: Stubilem, 1:09, July 1, 1982
6 1/2 furlongs: American Chance, 1:15, July 16, 1994
7 furlongs: Josh's Madelyn, 1:21.37, September 5, 2004
1 mile: Still Waving, 1:34 3/5, August 13, 1988
1 1/8 miles: Lt. Lao, 1:47 3/5, August 27, 1988
1 1/4 miles: Won Du Loup, 2:03, September 4, 1988
1 3/8 miles: Ramona Jay, 2:23, August 24, 1985
1 1/2 miles: Unaccountable, 2:29 3/5, July 23, 1988
1 5/8 miles: Sir Lightning, 2:45 4/5, August 9, 1992
1 3/4 miles: Bondi, 3:00, August 27, 1966
2 miles: Classic Deal, 3:25 3/5, August 21, 1988
Other: 2 1/4 miles, Bondi, 3:54, September 5, 1966

Track Records, Main Turf

5 1/2 furlongs: Bettybird, 1:00.52, August 21, 2002
1 mile: Slewper Imp, 1:32 3/5, July 16, 1995; Suffragette, 1:32 3/5, July 24, 1999
1 1/16 miles: Onthedeanslist, 1:39.11, September 5, 2005
1 1/8 miles: Yaqthan (Ire), 1:44 3/5, September 2, 1996
1 1/4 miles: Ye Slew, 1:59 3/5, August 6, 1994
1 1/2 miles: Our Forbes, 2:25 2/5, August 10, 1994
2 miles: Irish Harbour, 3:20 1/5, September 2, 1996

Principal Races

Gardenia H. (G3), Ellis Park Breeders' Cup Turf S., HBPA H., Don Bernhardt S., Regaey Island S.

Interesting Facts

Previous Names and Dates: Dade Park

Notable Events

Family Day, Year-Round Simulcasting

Fastest Times of 2005 (Dirt)

5 furlongs: Salty Surprise, :58.32, September 2, 2005
5 1/2 furlongs: Seattle Smoke, 1:04.06, August 31, 2005
6 furlongs: Danieltown, 1:09.97, August 20, 2005
6 1/2 furlongs: Sterling Gold, 1:16.29, July 30, 2005
7 furlongs: Southern Surprise, 1:22.48, July 24, 2005
1 mile: Dream of Summer, 1:35.32, August 20, 2005
1 1/8 miles: Big Squeeze, 1:51.12, August 28, 2005
1 1/2 miles: Pueblo de Spain, 2:33.25, August 19, 2005

Fastest Times of 2005 (Turf)

5 1/2 furlongs: Actual, 1:01.17, September 3, 2005
1 mile: Wayuphi, 1:32.94, September 4, 2005
1 1/16 miles: Onthedeanslist, 1:39.11, September 5, 2005
1 1/8 miles: Cantbeattheprice, 1:48.23, September 5, 2005

Keeneland Race Course

Some tracks offer nothing more than an endless procession of live and simulcast races. But a few American tracks offer a sense of history and a state of mind. Keeneland Race Course falls into the latter category. Since its opening meet in October 1936, the Lexington track has developed a unique identity. The stately facility offers two short, marquee meetings—including races such as the Blue Grass Stakes (G1) in the spring and the Juddmonte Spinster Stakes (G1) in the fall—in an attractive setting. Profits from Keeneland's lucrative sales arm help to finance purses and make them among the highest in the country. The Keeneland Association was incorporated in 1935 and purchased 147.5 acres of land, including an ornate training track, from J. O. "Jack" Keene, to build the facility. Lexington, bereft of racing after the Kentucky Association track closed earlier in the 1930s, quickly embraced the new facility, and more than 25,000 people attended the inaugural nine-day meeting. Crowds in excess of 25,000 on a Single-Day are common at Keeneland, whose meets attract a wide range of spectators, including veteran racegoers, local business executives, breeders, and college students.

Location: 4201 Versailles Rd., P.O. Box 1690, Lexington, Ky. 40588-1690
Phone: (859) 254-3412, (800) 456-3412
Fax: (859) 255-2484
Website: *www.keeneland.com*
E-Mail: webmaster@keeneland.com
Year Founded: 1935
Dates of Inaugural Meeting: October 15-24, 1936
Abbreviation: Kee
Acreage: 907

Number of Stalls: 1,845
Seating Capacity: 7,000

Ownership

Keeneland Association Inc.

Officers

Chief Executive Officer: Nick Nicholson
President: Nick Nicholson
Director of Racing: W. B. Rogers Beasley
Racing Secretary: D. Ben Huffman
Secretary: William T. Bishop III
Treasurer: Jessica A. Green
Director of Operations: James A. Perry
Director of Auctions: Geoffrey G. Russell
Director of Communications: R. James Williams
Director of Finance: Jessica A. Green
Director of Marketing: Fran Taylor
Director of Mutuels: Robert A. Butcher
Vice President: Harvie B. Wilkinson
Stewards: Ronald L. Herbstreit, R. Spencer Leigh III, John Veitch
Track Announcer: Kurt Becker
Track Photographer: Patrick Lang
Track Superintendents: Sammy Garland, Jerry Huff, Jimmy Young
Asst. Racing Secretary: Allison A. DeLuca
Horsemen's Bookkeeper: Pam Barker
Security: James A. Perry

Racing Dates

2005: April 8-April 29, 16 days; October 7-October 29, 17 days
2006: April 7-April 28, 15 days; October 6-October 28, 17 days

Track Layout

Main Circumference: 1$^{1}/_{16}$ miles
Main Track Chute: 4$^{1}/_{2}$ furlongs and 7 furlongs
Main Width: 77 feet
Main Length of Stretch: 1,174 ft.
Main Turf Circumference: 7$^{1}/_{2}$ furlongs
Main Turf Length of Stretch: 1,190 ft.
Training Track: 5 furlongs

Attendance

Average Daily Recent Meeting: 14,701, Spring 2005; 13,672, Fall 2005; 16,276, Spring 2006
Highest Single-Day Record: 33,621, April 16, 2005; 28,788, Fall 1989
Record Daily Average for Single Meet: 16,276, Spring 2006; 14,177, Fall 1992
Highest Single-Meet Record: 244,145, Spring 2006; 232,499, Fall 2003
Total Attendance Recent Meeting: 235,220, Spring 2005; 232,429, Fall 2005; 244,145, Spring 2006
Lowest Single-Day Record: 1,294, October 16, 1936

Handle

Average All Sources Recent Meeting: $7,699,867, Spring 2005; $6,975,899, Fall 2005; $9,210,834, Spring 2006
Average On-Track Recent Meeting: $1,349,956, Spring 2005; $1,195,400, Fall 2005; $1,455,534, Spring 2006
Record Daily Average for Single Meet: $1,558,917, Spring 1988; $1,373,329, Fall 1992
Single-Day On-Track Handle: $2,902,234, April 16, 2005
Single-Day Total Handle All Sources: $17,347,623, April 16, 2005
Total All Sources Recent Meeting: $123,197,871, Spring 2005; $118,590,290, Fall 2005; $138,162,512, Spring 2006
Total On-Track Recent Meeting: $21,599,291, Spring 2005; $20,321,797, Fall 2005; $21,833,015, Spring 2006
Highest Single-Day Record Recent Meet: $3,599,647, April 16, 2005; $2,678,067, October 29, 2005

Mutuel Records

Highest Win: $255.40, Rip Dabbs, October 8, 1988
Lowest Win: $2.10, Spectacular Bid, April 26, 1979
Highest Exacta: $5,200.40, October 27, 1993
Lowest Exacta: $3.60, April 13, 1988
Highest Trifecta: $37,832, October 28, 1995
Lowest Trifecta: $7.80, April 3, 2004
Highest Daily Double: $5,796.40, April 19, 1961
Lowest Daily Double: $4.60, October 12, 1983
Highest Pick 3: $49,628.60, April 6, 1997
Lowest Pick 3: $8.80, April 21, 1990
Highest Pick 6: $160,628.90, October 16, 2003
Lowest Pick 6: $74.80, October 9, 1991
Highest Other Exotics: Pick Five, $7,172.30, October 18, 2001; Superfecta, $120,550, October 24, 2001
Lowest Other Exotics: Pick Five, $375.80, October 12, 2001; Superfecta, $43, April 21, 2004
Lowest Quinella: $2.60, October 5, 2003
Highest Stakes Win: $222.60, Foxy Dean, October 13, 1984, Alcibiades S.
Highest Pick 4: $56,235.80, October 11, 2003
Highest Quinella: $1,535.40, October 8, 2004
Lowest Pick 4: $21.50, April 19, 2001

Leaders

Career, Leading Jockey by Titles: Pat Day, 22
Career, Leading Owner by Titles: T. A. and J. E. Grissom, 14
Career, Leading Trainer by Titles: D. Wayne Lukas, 16
Career, Leading Jockey by Stakes Wins: Pat Day, 95
Career, Leading Owner by Stakes Wins: Claiborne Farm, 25
Career, Leading Trainer by Stakes Wins: D. Wayne Lukas, 50
Career, Leading Jockey by Wins: Pat Day, 918
Career, Leading Owner by Wins: William S. Farish, 183
Career, Leading Trainer by Wins: D. Wayne Lukas, 260
Recent Meeting, Leading Jockey: John R. Velazquez, 21, Spring 2005; Rafael Bejarano, 30, Fall 2005; Julien R. Leparoux, 17, Spring 2006; Rafael Bejarano, 17, Spring 2006
Recent Meeting, Leading Owner: Augustin Stable, 4, Spring 2005; William S. Farish (includes partners), 4, Spring 2005; William S. Farish (includes partners), 5, Fall 2005; Kenneth L. and Sarah K. Ramsey, 6, Spring 2006
Recent Meeting, Leading Trainer: Todd A. Pletcher, 16, Spring 2005; Nicholas P. Zito, 9, Fall 2005; Nicholas P. Zito, 12, Spring 2006
Recent Meeting, Leading Horse: Alumni Hall, 2, Spring 2005; Angara (GB), 2, Spring 2005; Dynamic Cat, 2, Spring 2005; Psych, 2, Spring 2005; Nine Chimes, 2, Spring 2005; Brian's Echo, 2, Spring 2005; Asi Siempre, 2, Fall 2005, Smokin' John, 2, Fall 2005; Fotogenic (Arg), 2, Fall 2005; Wanderin Boy, 2, Spring 2006

Records

Single-Day Jockey Wins: Randy Romero, 6, April 7, 1990; Craig Perret, 6, April 18, 1990
Single-Day Trainer Wins: William I. Mott, 4, April 9, 1995
Single Meet, Leading Jockey by Wins: Randy Romero, 32; Spring 1990; Pat Day, 45, Fall 1991
Single Meet, Leading Owner by Wins: Calumet Farm, 12, Spring 1941; Mr. and Mrs. Robert F. Roberts, 12, Fall 1968
Single Meet, Leading Trainer by Wins: Todd A. Pletcher, 16, Spring 2005; D. Wayne Lukas, 22, Fall 1989

Track Records, Main Dirt

4$^{1}/_{2}$ furlongs: Quick Swoon, :51, April 20, 1966; Royality Note, :51, April 23, 1968; Bend the Times, :51, April 8, 1980; City Street, :51.04, April 20, 2001; Heckle, :51.04, April 18, 2003
6 furlongs: Anjiz, 1:07.78, October 9, 1993
6$^{1}/_{2}$ furlongs: Number One Sheikh, 1:14.70, October 11, 2000
7 furlongs: Binalong, 1:20.39, October 13, 1993
1$^{1}/_{16}$ miles: Din's Dancer, 1:40$^{4}/_{5}$, October 9, 1990
1$^{1}/_{8}$ miles: Midway Road, 1:46.78, April 22, 2004
1$^{3}/_{16}$ miles: Arch, 1:53.87, October 11, 1998
1$^{1}/_{4}$ miles: Political Fact, 2:02.21, October 15, 1993
1$^{5}/_{8}$ miles: Put-in-Bay, 2:45, October 13, 1967; Mr. Copy Chief, 2:45, October 20, 1971
Other: 7 furlongs 184 feet, Lamb Chop, 1:24$^{3}/_{5}$, October 10, 1963

Track Records, Main Turf

5$^{1}/_{2}$ furlongs: Chris's Thunder, 1:01.72, October 8, 2000
1 mile: Perfect Soul (Ire), 1:33.54, April 9, 2004
1$^{1}/_{16}$ miles: Quiet Resolve, 1:40.30, April 27, 2000
1$^{1}/_{8}$ miles: Memories of Silver, 1:45.81, October 5, 1996
1$^{3}/_{16}$ miles: Happyanunoit (NZ), 1:53.91, October 15, 1999
1$^{1}/_{2}$ miles: Bursting Forth, 2:27.54, April 22, 1999
1$^{5}/_{8}$ miles: Royal Strand (Ire), 2:38.68, October 24, 1999

Principal Races

Fall: Shadwell Turf Mile S. (G1), Lane's End Breeders' Futurity (G1), Juddmonte Spinster S. (G1), Queen Elizabeth II Challenge Cup S. (G1), Darley Alcibiades S. (G2)
Spring: Blue Grass S. (G1), Ashland S. (G1), Commonwealth Breeders' Cup S. (G2), Coolmore Lexington S. (G2), Stonerside Beaumont S. (G2), Maker's Mark Mile S. (G2).

Fastest Times of 2005 (Dirt)

4$^{1}/_{2}$ furlongs: Half Ours, :51.61, April 17, 2005
6 furlongs: More Smoke, 1:09.88, April 10, 2005

6$^1/_2$ furlongs: Ender's Sister, 1:16.05, October 22, 2005
7 furlongs: Clock Stopper, 1:22.06, April 16, 2005
a7 furlongs: In the Gold, 1:26.04, April 14, 2005
1$^1/_{16}$ miles: Gold Mask, 1:44.72, April 16, 2005; Spun Sugar, 1:44.72, April 16, 2005
1$^1/_8$ miles: Bandini, 1:50.16, April 16, 2005
1$^3/_{16}$ miles: Desert Patrol, 2:00.75, April 21, 2005
1$^1/_4$ miles: A Table for Three, 2:12.14, October 12, 2005

Fastest Times of 2005 (Turf)

5$^1/_2$ furlongs: Soaring Free, 1:02.22, April 16, 2005
1 mile: Artie Schiller, 1:34.09, April 15, 2005
a1 miles: Chattahoochee War, 1:35.28, April 8, 2005
1$^1/_{16}$ miles: Que Puntual (Arg), 1:40.51, April 16, 2005
a1$^1/_{16}$ miles: Dynamic Cat, 1:41.86, April 10, 2005
1$^1/_8$ miles: Path of Thunder, 1:47.93, April 14, 2005
a1$^1/_8$ miles: On the Acorn (GB), 1:48.68, April 9, 2005
1$^3/_{16}$ miles: Joyful Chaos, 1:58.69, April 20, 2005
1$^1/_2$ miles: Pace Yourself, 2:30.81, October 26, 2005
a1$^1/_2$ miles: Cape Town Lass, 2:29.18, April 9, 2005
2$^1/_2$ miles: Hirapour (Ire), 4:42.08, April 22, 2005

Kentucky Downs

Straddling the Kentucky-Tennessee state border adjacent to Interstate 65, Kentucky Downs has enjoyed a short, colorful history. Opened in 1990 as Dueling Grounds Race Course—the track site was reputed to be the scene of several 19th century duels—the turf-only racecourse was conceived as a simulcasting facility with one day of live steeplechase racing a year. But ownership controversies dogged the facility until the late 1990s, when businessman Brad Kelley, Turfway Park, and Churchill Downs purchased the facility. Kelley owns 52%, and the tracks each hold 24%. Track officials have found ways to make Kentucky Downs's turf-only status pay off. The track now offers a series of turf stakes on the flat to coincide partly with the Kentucky Cup series of races at Turfway Park in Florence, Kentucky.

Location: 5629 Nashville Rd., P.O. Box 405, Franklin, Ky. 42134
Phone: (270) 586-7778
Fax: (270) 586-8080
Website: *www.kentuckydowns.com*
Dates of Inaugural Meeting: April 22, 1990
Abbreviation: KD

Ownership

Kentucky Downs LLC

Officers

General Manager: Ryan Driscoll
Racing Secretary: Richard S. Leigh
Director of Operations: Jon Goodman
Director of Mutuels: Shelley Spears
Director of Simulcasting: Mary Troilo
Track Superintendent: Tommy Sullivan
Asst. Racing Secretary: Brook Hawkins

Racing Dates

2005: September 17-September 27, 6 days
2006: September 16-September 26, 7 days

Track Layout

Main Turf Circumference: 1$^3/_8$ miles

Handle

Average All Sources Recent Meeting: $1,528,491, 2005
Average On-Track Recent Meeting: $63,095, 2005
Total All Sources Recent Meeting: $9,170,947, 2005
Total On-Track Recent Meeting: $378,567, 2005

Leaders

Career, Leading Jockey by Titles: Jon Court, 2
Recent Meeting, Leading Jockey: Calvin H. Borel, 4, 2005
Recent Meeting, Leading Trainer: William I. Mott, 5, 2005

Records

Single Meet, Leading Jockey by Wins: Jon Court, 8

Track Records, Main Turf

6 furlongs: Testify, 1:09.46, September 19, 2005
7 furlongs: Bastille, 1:22.68, September 20, 2005
1 mile: Rob 'n Gin, 1:35, September 19, 1998
1$^1/_2$ miles: Yaqthan (Ire), 2:27.60, September 19, 1998

Principal Races

Kentucky Cup Turf H. (G3), Kentucky Cup Turf Dash S., Kentucky Cup Ladies Turf S.

Interesting Facts

Previous Names and Dates: Dueling Grounds 1990-'96

Fastest Times of 2005 (Turf)

6 furlongs: Testify, 1:09.46, September 19, 2005
7 furlongs: Bastille, 1:22.68, September 20, 2005
1 mile: Lady Offense, 1:36.47, September 20, 2005
1$^1/_2$ miles: Silverfoot, 2:30.30, September 24, 2005

Turfway Park

Turfway Park is the Northern Kentucky successor to Old Latonia, a track that opened in the Latonia section of Covington in 1883 and shut down in 1939. In the late 1950s, an investor group built a new Latonia Race Course in Florence, approximately ten miles from the former site, and it opened on August 27, 1959. On April 9, 1986, Nashville real-estate developer Jerry Carroll and partners bought Latonia for $13.5-million and renamed it Turfway Park. Carroll undertook an extensive renovation program and raised the purse of the track's spring race for three-year-old Triple Crown prospects, the Jim Beam Stakes (G2), to $500,000 in 1987. The race's purse would peak at $750,000 when the Jim Beam sponsorship ended and the race became the Galleryfurniture.com Stakes for 1999 only. In 2002, the race became the Lane's End Spiral Stakes, and in 2003 it was renamed the Lane's End Stakes. During Carroll's tenure, Turfway was a leader in offering intertrack wagering in Kentucky (1988) and in promoting legislation for full-card simulcasting in '94. Also in 1994, Turfway launched its Kentucky Cup Day of Champions, a September event featuring five stakes races. Carroll and partners sold the track to a partnership led by the Keeneland Association for $37-million on January 15, 1999. For its 2005 fall meeting, Turfway renovated its track by putting in Polytrack, becoming the first track in North America to install the synthetic surface as its main track.

Location: 7500 Turfway Rd., P.O. Box 8, Florence, Ky. 41022
Phone: (859) 371-0200, (800) 733-0200
Fax: (859) 647-4730
Website: *www.turfway.com*
E-Mail: info@turfway.com
Year Founded: 1959 as Latonia Race Track; 1986 as Turfway Park
Dates of Inaugural Meeting: August 27, 1959 (Latonia Race Track); April 9, 1986 (Turfway Park)
Abbreviation: TP
Acreage: 197
Number of Stalls: 1,000

Ownership

Keeneland Association and Harrah's Entertainment

Officers

Chief Executive Officer: Robert N. Elliston
President: Robert N. Elliston
General Manager: Greg Schmitz
Director of Racing: Richard S. Leigh
Racing Secretary: Richard S. Leigh
Treasurer: Clifford Reed
Director of Operations: Greg Schmitz
Director of Marketing: Jack Gordon
Director of Mutuels: Kenny Kramer
Vice President: Clifford Reed

Director of Publicity: Sherry Pinson
Director of Simulcasting: Mary Troilo
Horsemen's Liaison: W. Randolf Wehrman
Stewards: Brooks A. Becraft III, Ronald Herbstreit, John Veitch
Track Announcer: Mike Battaglia
Track Photographer: Patrick Lang
Track Superintendent: Daniel Chapman
Horsemen's Bookkeeper: Terry Moore
Asst. Racing Secretary: Tyler B. Picklesimer

Racing Dates

2005: January 1-April 7, 61 days; September 7-October 6, 22 days; November 27-December 31, 24 days
2006: January 1-April 6, 69 days; September 6-October 5, 22 days; November 26-December 31, 26 days

Track Layout

Main Circumference: 1 mile
Main Track Chute: 6½ furlongs and 1¼ miles
Main Width: Homestretch: 90 feet; Backstretch: 50 feet
Main Length of Stretch: 970 feet

Attendance

Average Daily Recent Meeting: 1,884 est., Winter/Spring 2005; 2,018 est., Fall 2005; 1,315 est., Holiday 2005
Highest Single-Day Record: 22,747, March 26, 2005
Highest Single-Meet Record: 354,867, Spring 1988
Record Daily Average for Single Meet: 5,377, Spring 1988
Total Attendance Recent Meeting: 114,916 est., Winter/Spring 2005; 44,396 est., Fall 2005; 31,549 est., Holiday 2005

Handle

Average All Sources Recent Meeting: $2,011,005, Winter/Spring 2005; $2,153,593, Fall 2005; $3,097,188, Holiday 2005; $2,874,546, Winter/Spring 2006
Average On-Track Recent Meeting: $124,010, Winter/Spring 2005; $132,070, Fall 2005; $134,905, Holiday 2005; $131,001, Winter/Spring 2006
Single-Day On-Track Handle: $3,223,778, April 2, 1994
Total All Sources Recent Meeting: $122,671,290, Winter/Spring 2005; $47,379,056, Fall 2005; $74,332,516, Holiday 2005; $198,343,642, Winter/Spring 2006
Total On-Track Recent Meeting: $7,564,630, Winter/Spring 2005; $2,905,545, Fall 2005; $3,237,724, Holiday 2005; $9,039,053, Winter/Spring 2006
Highest Single-Day Record Recent Meet: $7,545,734, March 26, 2005 (Winter/Spring); $6,164,738, September 17, 2005 (Fall); $4,587,578, December 23, 2005 (Holiday)

Mutuel Records

Highest Win: $267.60, Ante a Gold Penny, January 21, 1999
Highest Exacta: $6,777.20, January 29, 1988
Lowest Exacta: $3.20, September 26, 1998
Highest Trifecta: $50,847.40, February 21, 1996
Lowest Trifecta: $5.20, September 26, 1998
Highest Daily Double: $4,575.80, December 12, 1986
Lowest Daily Double: $5, September 24, 1994
Highest Pick 3: $12,376.20, December 16, 1993
Lowest Pick 3: $8.60, March 3, 2005
Highest Pick 6: $1,474,380, March 23, 1988
Highest Other Exotics: $106,848.20, Superfecta, March 20, 2004
Highest Pick 4: $40,027.20, March 26, 2005

Leaders

Career, Leading Jockey by Titles: Willie Martinez, 9
Career, Leading Trainer by Titles: Bernard S. Flint, 20
Career, Leading Jockey by Stakes Wins: Pat Day, 37
Career, Leading Trainer by Stakes Wins: D. Wayne Lukas, 35
Recent Meeting, Leading Jockey: Dean Sarvis, 91, Winter/Spring 2005; Dane Kobiskie, 20, Fall 2005; Jesus Lopez Castanon, 27, Holiday 2005; Julien R. Leparoux, 167, Winter/Spring 2006
Recent Meeting, Leading Owner: Louis D. O'Brien, 8, Winter/Spring 2005; Silverton Hill LLC, 3, Fall 2005; Nancy R. and Richard S. Kaster, 3, Fall 2005; Arthur B. Hancock III, 3, Fall 2005; Herman Van Den Broeck, 3, Fall 2005; Stan E. Fulton, 3, Fall 2005; Joseph F. Schrage, 3, Fall 2005; Everest Stables Inc., 3, Holiday 2005; Donamire Farm, 3, Holiday 2005; AFM Stables Ltd., 3, Holiday 2005; Jackie Christenson, 3, Holiday 2005; Wayne Bearden, 15, Winter/Spring 2006
Recent Meeting, Leading Trainer: Gregory Foley, 25, Winter/Spring 2005; D. Wayne Lukas, 8, Fall 2005; S. Joseph Cain, 8, Holiday 2005; Gregory Foley, 30, Winter/Spring 2006
Recent Meeting, Leading Horse: My Dear Jazz, 4, Winter/Spring 2005; Indy Energy, 6, Winter/Spring 2006

Records

Single-Day Jockey Wins: Rafael Bejarano, 7, March 12, 2004
Single-Day Trainer Wins: Bernard S. Flint, 4; George Isaacs, 4; D. Wayne Lukas, 4; Harry Trotsek, 4; V. R. Wright, 4
Single Meet, Leading Jockey by Wins: Julien R. Leparoux, 167, Winter/Spring 2006; Glen Brogan, 37, Fall 1968; Rafael Bejarano, 46, Holiday 2003
Single Meet, Leading Trainer by Wins: Bernard S. Flint, 44, Winter/Spring 2003; D. Wayne Lukas, 24, Fall 1995; D. Wayne Lukas, 21, Holiday 1995

Track Records, Main Dirt

5 furlongs: Indy Energy, :58.90, April 1, 2006
5½ furlongs: Cayenne Red, 1:04.46, March 10, 2006
6 furlongs: Estate Collection, 1:09.75, September 17, 2005
6½ furlongs: Level Playingfield, 1:17.08, September 24, 2005
1 mile: Artemus Sunrise, 1:37.31, October 1, 2005
1¹⁄₁₆ miles: Miss Fortunate, 1:44.48, September 17, 2005
1⅛ miles: Shaniko, 1:49.74, September 17, 2005
1¼ miles: Leonard's Shaker, 2:08.56, December 18, 2005
1⅝ miles: Anthem Hill, 2:53.59, April 5, 2006

Principal Races

Winter/Spring: Lane's End S. (G2), Bourbonette Breeders' Cup S., John Battaglia Memorial S., Rushaway S.
Fall: Kentucky Cup Classic H. (G2), Kentucky Cup Juvenile S. (G3), Kentucky Cup Sprint S. (G3), Turfway Breeders' Cup S. (G3), Turfway Park Fall Championship S. (G3), Kentucky Cup Juvenile Fillies S.

Interesting Facts

Previous Names and Dates: Latonia Race Track (1959-'86)
Achievements/Milestones: Became the first track in North America to install Polytrack as a racing surface. Polytrack opened for training on August 3, 2005, and racing commenced on the surface on September 7, 2005

Notable Events

Kentucky Cup Day of Champions

Fastest Times of 2005 (Dirt and All Weather)

5 furlongs: Dues for the Blues, :59.13, February 26, 2005
5½ furlongs (AW): Cayenne Red, 1:04.72, December 30, 2005
6 furlongs: Lil Red Flyer, 1:07.97, March 30, 2005
6½ furlongs: Private Horde, 1:14.35, February 4, 2005
1 mile: Tempus Fugit, 1:34.95, March 12, 2005
1¹⁄₁₆ miles: Count On the Tuna, 1:43.69, March 6, 2005
1⅛ miles: Discreet Hero, 1:49.50, March 19, 2005
1¼ miles (AW): Leonard's Shaker, 2:08.56, December 18, 2005
1½ miles: Watch Your Pennies, 2:41.58, January 21, 2005

Louisiana

Delta Downs

Lee Berwick, a prominent Quarter Horse breeder and owner and a former president of the American Quarter Horse Association, opened the first Delta Downs as a nonpari-mutuel match track on his farm at St. Joseph, Louisiana, on the banks of the Mississippi River. He moved the operation to Vinton, Louisiana, two hours northeast of Houston, Texas, and opened Delta Downs in 1973. Berwick served as track president until 1997, when his daughter, Kathryn, succeeded him in the position. In 1999, the Berwicks sold Delta Downs for more than $10-million to Shaun Scott and Jinho Cho, who began renovating the facility in hopes of installing slot machines. In 2001, the track was sold for $125-million to Las Vegas-based Boyd Gaming Corp., which owns casinos in Louisiana, Nevada, Illinois, and Mississippi. In October 2001, Boyd received approval from the Louisiana Gaming Control Board to operate 1,700 slot machines. Delta Downs offers racing for Thoroughbreds as well as a separate season for Quarter Horses and Paints. The slots have resulted in sizable increases in Thoroughbred purses. A portion of the 2005-'06 season was run at Evangeline Downs because of extensive damage by Hurricane Rita.

Location: 2717 Delta Downs Dr., Vinton, La. 70668-6025
Phone: (337) 589-7441, (800) 589-7441
Fax: (337) 589-9195
Website: *www.deltadowns.com*
E-Mail: racefans@boydgaming.com
Year Founded: 1973
Abbreviation: DeD
Acreage: 240
Number of Stalls: 1200
Seating Capacity: 3,400

Ownership

Boyd Gaming Corp.

Officers

General Manager: Jack Bernsmeier
Director of Racing: Chris Warren
Racing Secretary: Trent McIntosh
Director of Operations: Jack Bernsmeier
Director of Marketing: Adrian King
Vice President: Jack Bernsmeier
Director of Publicity: Don Stevens
Director of Simulcasting: Chris Warren
Horsemen's Liaison: Trent McIntosh
Stewards: Duane Domingue, Julian Dupuy, Sam Lato
Track Announcer: Don Stevens
Track Photographer: Coady Photography
Track Superintendent: Darald Wilfer

Racing Dates

2005: October 1, 2004-April 2, 2005, 101 days
2006: November 1, 2006-March 31, 2007, 88 days

Track Layout

Main Circumference: 6 furlongs
Main Track Chute: 5 furlongs and $1\frac{1}{16}$ miles
Main Width: Homestretch: 80 feet; Backstretch: 70 feet
Main Length of Stretch: 660 feet

Handle

Average All Sources Recent Meeting: $1,393,824, 2004/2005
Average On-Track Recent Meeting: $39,452, 2004/2005
Total All Sources Recent Meeting: $140,776,251, 2004/2005
Total On-Track Recent Meeting: $3,984,683, 2004/2005
Highest Single-Day Record Recent Meet: $2,206,902, December 30, 2004

Leaders

Recent Meeting, Leading Jockey: Guy Smith, 119, 2004/2005
Recent Meeting, Leading Owner: Carrol Castille, 18, 2004/2005
Recent Meeting, Leading Trainer: Keith Bourgeois, 53, 2004/2005
Recent Meeting, Leading Horse: Starofmynight, 6, 2004/2005

Track Records, Main Dirt

4 furlongs: Rock Afire, :$46\frac{1}{5}$, December 10, 1994
$4\frac{1}{2}$ furlongs: Raisable Adversary, :51, February 15, 1992
5 furlongs: Britt's Jules, :57.49, November 5, 2003
$6\frac{1}{2}$ furlongs: Chief Okie Dokie, 1:18.76, February 8, 2002
7 furlongs: Norms Promise, 1:$24\frac{3}{5}$, March 2, 1975
$7\frac{1}{2}$ furlongs: Junior Gent, 1:$33\frac{1}{5}$, March 14, 1974
1 mile: Freon Flier, 1:37.52, March 10, 2002
1m 70 yds: Thriller, 1:$42\frac{2}{5}$, September 27, 1973
$1\frac{1}{16}$ miles: Norms Promise, 1:$43\frac{1}{5}$, March 23, 1975
$1\frac{1}{8}$ miles: Lucky Silence, 1:$55\frac{2}{5}$, February 18, 1994
$1\frac{3}{16}$ miles: Ponderosa Lark, 2:$03\frac{3}{5}$, October 31, 1975
$1\frac{1}{4}$ miles: Shy Bull, 2:$10\frac{1}{5}$, November 3, 1974
$1\frac{3}{8}$ miles: Ponderosa Lark, 2:$27\frac{1}{5}$, December 15, 1974
$1\frac{1}{2}$ miles: Art Work, 2:$41\frac{1}{5}$, January 11, 1974
2 miles: Can 'em, 3:$43\frac{4}{5}$, December 10, 1988
Other: $2\frac{1}{2}$ furlongs, Mrs. Deville, :27, February 19, 1976; $2\frac{1}{2}$ furlongs, Cajun Two Step, :27, February 10, 1985; $1\frac{5}{16}$ miles, Gentleman Mike, 2:$17\frac{3}{5}$, December 1, 1974; $1\frac{9}{16}$ miles, Landing Officer, 2:$51\frac{4}{5}$, January 15, 1989

Principal Races

Delta Jackpot S. (G3), Delta Princess S., Gulf Coast Breeders' Cup Classic S., Goddess Breeders' Cup S., Gold Cup S.

Interesting Facts

Trivia: Three alligators live in the infield

Notable Events

Louisiana Premier Night

Fastest Times of 2005 (Dirt)

$4\frac{1}{2}$ furlongs: Painter's Creek, :52.64, February 17, 2005
5 furlongs: All Wired Up, :58.72, March 26, 2005
$6\frac{1}{2}$ furlongs: Believe Im Special, 1:20.30, March 12, 2005
7 furlongs: Mr. Barracuda, 1:26.77, February 3, 2005
$7\frac{1}{2}$ furlongs: Aspirin, 1:35.55, January 8, 2005
1 mile: High Strike Zone, 1:38.39, March 4, 2005
$1\frac{1}{16}$ miles: Nitro Chip, 1:45.86, February 5, 2005
$1\frac{1}{4}$ miles: Aceinthebag, 2:11.45, January 13, 2005
$1\frac{3}{8}$ miles: Valentino Bob, 2:27.50, February 3, 2005

Evangeline Downs

Located in Louisiana's colorful Cajun country, Evangeline Downs is known as the cradle of jockeys. Racing Hall of Fame members Eddie Delahoussaye and Kent Desormeaux as well as leading jockeys Shane Sellers and Mark Guidry all won their first races at the track. Several nationally known horses also have competed at Evangeline. In 1977, a two-year-old named John Henry won two of three starts at Evangeline and scored his first stakes win in the Lafayette Futurity. From that beginning, John Henry went on to earn more than $6.5-million and was voted Horse of the Year in 1981 and '84. In 1999 and 2000, Louisiana-bred Hallowed Dreams won 16 consecutive races, including six at Evangeline. The track, which offers some Quarter Horse racing, conducts live racing from mid-April to early September. Slot machines began generating purse money in December 2003. In 2005, the track moved to Opelousas to take advantage of a state law that permits slot machines at racetracks if authorized by local parishes. The new track has a grandstand that seats nearly 6,000 fans, a one-mile dirt oval, and a turf course inside the main track.

Location: 2235 Creswell Ln. Ext, Opelousas, La. 70570
Phone: (337) 594-3000, (866) 349-0687
Fax: (337) 594-3166
Website: *www.evangelinedowns.com*
E-Mail: evdinfo@evangelinedowns.com
Year Founded: 1966
Dates of Inaugural Meeting: April 28, 1966
Abbreviation: EvD
Acreage: 750
Number of Stalls: 1,000

Ownership

Peninsula Gaming

Officers

Chief Executive Officer: M. Brent Stevens
President: Michael S. Luzich
General Manager: Michael Howard
Director of Racing: David A. Yount
Racing Secretary: Jason M. Boulet
Director of Finance: Steve Darbonne
Director of Mutuels: Rachel Conway
Horsemen's Liaison: Dayne Dugas
Track Photographer: S.C.I. Photography
Security: Joseph Albarado

Racing Dates

2005: April 7-September 24, 86 days
2006: December 1, 2005-March 25, 2006, 66 days; March 29-September 4, 93 days

Track Layout

Main Circumference: 1 mile
Main Turf Circumference: 7 furlongs

Attendance

Highest Single-Day Record: 8,218, July 4, 1975

Handle
Single-Day Total Handle All Sources: $2,052,653, July 1, 1999

Mutuel Records
Highest Win: $412.20, Princely Greek, April 26, 1987
Highest Exacta: $24,213.90, August 1, 1982
Highest Trifecta: $37,995, August 23, 1997

Leaders
Career, Leading Trainer by Titles: Don Cormier Sr., 8

Records
Single-Day Jockey Wins: Gerard Melancon, 6, 1984; Shane Sellers, 6, 1985; James Avant, 6, 1988; Curt Bourque, 6, 1989; Curt Bourque, 6, 1991; James Avant, 6, 1995; Kirk LeBlanc, 6, 1995
Single Meet, Leading Jockey by Wins: Curt Bourque, 141; Randy Romero, 141
Single Meet, Leading Trainer by Wins: Don Cormier Sr., 91, 1996

Track Records, Main Dirt
4½ furlongs: Constant Commotion, :51.65, February 3, 2006
5 furlongs: Gold Storm, :56.94, June 3, 2006
5½ furlongs: Kim's Gem, 1:03.04, April 16, 2005
6 furlongs: High Strike Zone, 1:08.97, March 1, 2006
1 mile: Watchem Smokey, 1:36.61, May 6, 2006
1m 70 yds: I Nv Slew, 1:43.31, March 2, 2006

Principal Races
D. S. "Shine" Young Memorial Futurity, Evangeline Mile H., John Franks Memorial Sales S., Lafayette S.

Notable Events
Louisiana Legends Night

Fastest Times of 2005 (Dirt)
2½ furlongs: Snap Count, :28.08, April 29, 2005
4 furlongs: Scat On the Track, :47.29, May 12, 2005
4½ furlongs: A Diligent Ruckus, :52.26, July 22, 2005
5 furlongs: All Wired Up, :57.58, December 1, 2005
5½ furlongs: Kim's Gem, 1:03.04, April 16, 2005
6 furlongs: Roar On Tour, 1:10.12, May 7, 2005
1 mile: Drill Hall, 1:38.32, April 29, 2005
1m 70 yds: My Pocket, 1:43.80, April 18, 2005
1$^1/_{16}$ miles: Pink Duck, 1:45.29, April 23, 2005

Fair Grounds

Thoroughbred racing has been conducted at the site of Fair Grounds in New Orleans with few interruptions since 1853, when a racetrack named Union Course held its first Thoroughbred meeting. The track, which has been called Fair Grounds since the 1860s, served as a military camp during the Civil and Spanish-American Wars. At times, changing political climates have halted racing, and devastating fires destroyed the facility in 1919 and '93. Fair Grounds survived, and some of the sport's most famous racehorses have run there. Legendary distaffer Pan Zareta died of pneumonia at Fair Grounds in 1918 and was buried at the track. Kentucky Derby winner Black Gold, winner of the Louisiana Derby at Fair Grounds in 1924, was fatally injured in the Salome Handicap in '28 and was buried in the track's infield. Other noted horses who have raced at Fair Grounds include 1941 Triple Crown winner Whirlaway, winner of the inaugural Louisiana Handicap in '42; multiple Fair Grounds stakes winner Master Derby, who captured the '75 Preakness Stakes (G1); and Silverbulletday, who won two Fair Grounds stakes during her '99 championship season. The Krantz family bought the track in 1990 and rebuilt the track after the 1993 fire. A $34.5-million grandstand and clubhouse opened on November 27, 1997. The track filed for bankruptcy in 2003 after a ruinous, $89.9-million court judgment to horsemen involving video-poker revenue, and it was sold in 2004 for $47-million to Churchill Downs Inc. Hurricane Katrina damaged the track in 2005, and its 2005-'06 meet was run at Louisiana Downs.

Location: 1751 Gentilly Blvd., New Orleans, La. 70119-2133
Phone: (504) 944-5515
Fax: (504) 944-1211
Website: *www.fairgroundsracecourse.com*
E-Mail: webmaster@fgno.com
Year Founded: 1871
Dates of Inaugural Meeting: April 13, 1872
Abbreviation: FG
Acreage: 145
Number of Stalls: 1,950
Seating Capacity: 6,500

Ownership
Churchill Downs Inc.

Officers
Chairman: Thomas H. Meeker
President: Randall E. Soth
General Manager: Randall E. Soth
Director of Racing: Ben Huffman
Racing Secretary: Ben Huffman
Secretary: Rebecca C. Reed
Treasurer: Michael E. Miller
Director of Finance: Will Bienvenu
Director of Marketing: Lenny Vangilder
Director of Mutuels: Ed Fenasci
Vice President: Andrew G. Skehan
Director of Publicity: Lenny Vangilder
Director of Sales: Karen A. Robicheaux
Horsemen's Liaison: Brook Hawkins
Track Announcer: John G. Dooley
Track Photographer: Louis Hodges Jr.
Track Superintendent: Paul Gregoire
Asst. Racing Secretary: David M. Heitzmann
Security: David B. Martin

Racing Dates
2005: November 25, 2004-March 27, 2005, 82 days
2006: November 19, 2005-January 22, 2006, 37 days (Held at Louisiana Downs)

Track Layout
Main Circumference: 1 mile
Main Track Chute: 2 furlongs
Main Width: Homestretch: 75 feet; Backstretch: 70 feet
Main Length of Stretch: 1,346 feet
Main Turf Circumference: 7 furlongs

Attendance
Average Daily Recent Meeting: 2,104, 2004/2005
Highest Single-Day Record: 23,662, November 27, 1969
Total Attendance Recent Meeting: 172,550, 2004/2005

Handle
Average All Sources Recent Meeting: $4,184,980, 2004/2005; $3,637,838, 2005/2006
Average On-Track Recent Meeting: $221,480, 2204/2005; $161,252, 2005/2006
Single-Day On-Track Handle: $2,696,741, March 28, 1982
Single-Day Total Handle All Sources: $11,310,990, March 12, 2005
Total All Sources Recent Meeting: $343,168,377, 2004/2005; $134,600,000, 2005/2006
Total On-Track Recent Meeting: $18,161,344, 2004/2005; $5,966,324, 2005/2006
Highest Single-Day Record Recent Meet: $11,310,990, March 12, 2005

Mutuel Records
Highest Win: $500.60, Grey Hip, March 16, 1933
Lowest Win: $2.20, Shoot From the Hip, March 20, 2004
Highest Exacta: $25,257, February 8, 1971
Lowest Exacta: $2.20, January 3, 2002
Highest Daily Double: $2,917, January 5, 1971
Lowest Daily Double: $4.80, December 14, 2002
Highest Pick 3: $23,731.40, December 26, 1999
Lowest Pick 3: $12.60, December 23, 2000
Highest Pick 6: $108,848.20, March 29, 1999
Highest Other Exotics: $133,156.40, Superfecta, January 13, 2001; $673,602, Twin Trifecta, March 2, 1988
Lowest Other Exotics: $28.20 Superfecta, December 1, 2001

Leaders
Career, Leading Jockey by Titles: Ronald Ardoin, 6

Career, Leading Trainer by Titles: Jack Van Berg, 10
Recent Meeting, Leading Jockey: Robby Albarado, 101, 2004/2005; Roman Chapa, 45, 2005/2006
Recent Meeting, Leading Owner: Michael Gill, 43, 2004/2005; Heiligbrodt Racing Stable, 6, 2005/2006; Maggi Moss, 6, 2005/2006
Recent Meeting, Leading Trainer: Steven M. Asmussen, 67, 2004/2005; Steven M. Asmussen, 38, 2005/2006
Recent Meeting, Leading Horse: Skip Irish, 5, 2004/2005; Nob Hill Deelite, 3, 2005/2006; The Beter Man Can, 3, 2005/2006

Records

Single-Day Jockey Wins: James P. Bowlds, 6, March 11, 1965; E. J. Perrodin, 6, November 18, 1979; Randy Romero, 6, February 8, 1984; V. L. "Billy" Smith, 6, March 15, 1990; Shane Romero, 6, February 10, 1991; Shane Romero, 6, February 24, 1991; Eddie Martin Jr., 6, January 18, 2004; Robby Albarado, March 11, 2004
Single-Day Trainer Wins: Thomas Amoss, 4, January 19, 1995; Steven M. Asmussen, 4, January 1, 2005
Single Meet, Leading Jockey by Wins: Randy Romero, 181, 1983/1984
Single Meet, Leading Trainer by Wins: Jack Van Berg, 92, 1973/1974
Single Meet, Leading Trainer by Stakes Wins: Steven M. Asmussen, 8, 2001/2002
Single Meet, Leading Jockey by Stakes Wins: Robby Albarado, 13, 2003/2004
Single Meet, Leading Horse by Wins: High Authority, 8, 1957/1958; Mickey C., 8, 1969/1970

Track Records, Main Dirt

4 furlongs: Blue Carbon, :46⅕, March 18, 1967
4½ furlongs: Debs Mini Bars, :52⅕, March 8, 1971
5 furlongs: Posse, :57.35, February 10, 2003
5½ furlongs: Toby's Success, 1:03.20, January 26, 2004
6 furlongs: Mountain General, 1:08.03, November 28, 2002
7 furlongs: For Fair, 1:24⅖, February 8, 1915
7½ furlongs: Begue, 1:33¾, March 30, 1896
1 mile: Kitwe, 1:35.94, March 26, 1998
1m 40 yds: Total Rage, 1:38.52, March 23, 1997
1m 70 yds: Zevson, 1:41, November 26, 1936
1 1/16 miles: Pie in Your Eye, 1:42.02, March 19, 1994
1⅛ miles: Phantom On Tour, 1:48.13, March 8, 1998
1 3/16 miles: Half Magic, 1:56⅕, March 21, 1977
1¼ miles: It's the One, 2:01⅘, March 21, 1982; Westheimer, 2:01⅘, March 24, 1985; Herat, 2:01⅘, March 16, 1986
1⅜ miles: Carroll Road, 2:18⅕, January 30, 1965; Tahuna, 2:18⅕, March 6, 1965
1½ miles: Tahuna, 2:32⅖, March 13, 1965
1⅝ miles: Major Mansir, 2:49⅗, January 4, 1904; From Afar, 2:49⅗, February 27, 1954
1¾ miles: Aladdin Prince, 3:01⅖, April 5, 1981
2 miles: Bolster, 3:28⅕, February 7, 1920
Other: 2 furlongs, Baloma, :21⅘, January 26, 1952; 2 furlongs, Baloma, :21⅘, February 14, 1952; a2½ furlongs, Errand's Isle, :26, February 26, 1957; 3 furlongs, Henry's Baby, :33⅘, February 15, 1971; 3 furlongs, It's the Law, :33⅘, February 18, 1976; 3½ furlongs, Silver Finn, :41, February 24, 1925; 1m 20 yds, Lucky R., 1:40⅗, January 11, 1916; 1m 20 yds, Grumpy, 1:40⅗, February 5, 1916; 1 9/16 miles, Retintin, 2:42⅘, March 28, 1970; 1⅞ miles, Julius Caesar, 3:19, February 27, 1900; 2m 70yds, Omar, 3:39⅕, March 3, 1940; 2 1/16 miles, Quib's Bally, 3:47⅕, March 6, 1948; 2¼ miles, Marvin Neal, 3:56, February 23, 1907; 3 miles, Colonist, 5:35, February 17, 1906; 4 miles, Major Mansir, 8:04⅗, March 21, 1903

Track Records, Main Turf

a5½ furlongs: My Lord, 1:02.90, March 27, 2004
a7½ furlongs: Northcote Road, 1:29.26, March 7, 2000
a1 mile: Great Bloom, 1:35.57, March 20, 2004
a1 1/16 miles: Dixie Poker Ace, 1:42, January 8, 1994
a1⅛ miles: Mystery Giver, 1:48.29, March 21, 2004
a1⅜ miles: Present the Colors, 2:17⅕, April 4, 1982
a1½ miles: Palace Panther (Ire), 2:32, April 6, 1986
Other: a1 9/16 miles, To the Floor, 2:40.26, March 29, 1999

Principal Races

Louisiana Derby (G2), New Orleans H. (G2), Mervin H. Muniz Jr. Memorial H. (G2), Fair Grounds Oaks (G2), Risen Star S. (G3)

Interesting Facts

Previous Names and Dates: Union Race Course 1853-'57

Notable Events

Louisiana Champions Day

Fastest Times of 2005 (Dirt)

5½ furlongs: Elusive Jazz, 1:04.14, January 21, 2005
6 furlongs: Gold Storm, 1:08.99, March 19, 2005
1 mile: Ballroom Deputy, 1:37.16, March 24, 2005
1m 40 yds: Pushed, 1:40.40, January 17, 2005
1 1/16 miles: High Limit, 1:42.74, March 12, 2005
1⅛ miles: Badge of Silver, 1:48.78, March 12, 2005

Fastest Times of 2005 (Turf)

a5½ furlongs: Wrzeszcz, 1:03.70, February 12, 2005
a7½ furlongs: Warning Zone (SAf), 1:31.29, March 12, 2005
a1 miles: Middleweight, 1:38.28, March 12, 2005
a1 1/16 miles: America Alive, 1:44.43, January 15, 2005
a1⅛ miles: A to the Z, 1:50.99, March 19, 2005

Louisiana Downs

Louisiana Downs, located near Shreveport in Bossier City, opened in 1974. Built by the late shopping-center developer Edward DeBartolo Sr., the track introduced the Super Derby (now G2) in 1980, and since then the fall race has attracted leading three-year-olds. The first running was won by Temperence Hill, winner of that year's Belmont Stakes (G1). Two three-year-olds—Sunday Silence in 1989 and Tiznow in 2000—used the Super Derby as a steppingstone to victory in the Breeders' Cup Classic (G1) and Horse of the Year honors in their respective years. DeBartolo's racetrack holdings were sold following his death, and Louisiana Downs was acquired by his son-in-law, John York II. In November 2001, a group of investors headed by Shreveport lawyer Jim Davis announced plans to buy Louisiana Downs. In 2002, Harrah's Entertainment Corp. acquired approximately 95% of Louisiana Downs and opened a casino with 905 slot machines in 2003. By 2005, the renamed Harrah's Louisiana Downs had more than 1,400 machines. Harrah's valued the purchase, including renovations, at $183.4-million.

Location: 8000 E. Texas St., Bossier City, La. 71111-7016
Phone: (318) 742-5555, (800) 551-2361
Fax: (318) 741-2615
Website: *www.ladowns.com*
Year Founded: 1974
Dates of Inaugural Meeting: October 30, 1974-January 26, 1975
Abbreviation: LaD
Acreage: 350
Number of Stalls: 1,360
Seating Capacity: 17,240

Ownership

Harrah's Entertainment

Officers

General Manager: Patrick Dennehy
Racing Secretary: Tony Patterson
Director of Operations: Cliff D. Burge
Director of Admissions: Tom Stedman
Director of Finance: Kelly Castete
Director of Marketing: Jennifer Ray
Director of Mutuels: Holly Romain
Vice President: Patrick Dennehy
Director of Sales: Tom Showalter
Director of Simulcasting: Dick Pollack
Horsemen's Liaison: Patrick J. Pope
Track Announcer: Travis Stone
Track Photographer: Reed Palmer Photography
Track Superintendent: George McDermott

Racing Dates

2005: April 29-October 9, 93 days
2006: May 5-October 21, 93 days

Track Layout

Main Circumference: 1 mile
Main Track Chute: 7 furlongs
Main Track Chute: 1¼ miles
Main Width: 80 feet
Main Length of Stretch: 1,010 feet
Main Turf Circumference: 7 furlongs, 50 feet
Main Turf Width: 70 feet
Main Turf Length of Stretch: 940 feet

Attendance

Highest Single-Day Record: 26,513, May 26, 1986

Handle

Single-Day On-Track Handle: $4,371,781, September 27, 1987

Mutuel Records

Highest Win: $249, B.J.'s Spruce, June 21, 1996
Lowest Win: $2.20, Appealing Breeze, 1989; $2.20, Richman, 1990; $2.20, Morning Meadow, 1993; $2.20, Runaway Venus, 1999; $2.20, Smart Ring, 1999
Highest Exacta: $2,780.80, May 1, 1994
Lowest Trifecta: $18.90, August 19, 1994
Highest Daily Double: $5,556.20, October 14, 1976
Highest Pick 3: $37,286.20, June 6, 1992
Lowest Pick 3: $11.80, September 12, 1994
Highest Pick 6: $555,287, May 25, 1991
Highest Other Exotics: $52,017.60, Superfecta, June 2, 1996

Leaders

Career, Leading Jockey by Titles: Ronald Ardoin, 6; Larry Snyder, 6
Career, Leading Owner by Titles: John Franks, 18
Career, Leading Trainer by Titles: Frank Brothers, 7
Career, Leading Jockey by Stakes Wins: Ronald Ardoin, 155
Career, Leading Owner by Stakes Wins: John Franks, 144
Career, Leading Trainer by Stakes Wins: Frank Brothers, 124
Career, Leading Jockey by Wins: Ronald Ardoin, 2,787
Career, Leading Trainer by Wins: C. W. Walker, 820

Records

Single-Day Jockey Wins: Ricky Frazier, 7, October 27, 1984
Single-Day Trainer Wins: Jack Van Berg, 5, December 5, 1976; Frank Brothers, 5, May 16, 1982; Frank Brothers, 5, September 3, 1984
Single Meet, Leading Jockey by Wins: Ronald Ardoin, 198, 1993
Single Meet, Leading Owner by Wins: John Franks, 65, 1983
Single Meet, Leading Trainer by Wins: Frank Brothers, 99, 1987

Track Records, Main Dirt

4½ furlongs: Sondor, :51⅗, May 16, 1984
5 furlongs: Oh Mar, :57.21, September 25, 2000
5½ furlongs: Fighting K, 1:02.84, September 11, 1993
6 furlongs: Tangent, 1:08⅘, April 28, 1984
6½ furlongs: Prince of the Mt., 1:14.98, May 23, 1996
7 furlongs: Carrysport, 1:21⅗, July 4, 1984; Skin Flint, 1:21.79, July 16, 2005
1m 70 yds: Country Jim, 1:39⅖, July 4, 1982
1¹⁄₁₆ miles: Nelson, 1:41.44, August 15, 1993
1⅛ miles: Mocha Express, 1:48.14, July 24, 1999
1³⁄₁₆ miles: Jungle Pocket, 1:57⅖, August 15, 1984
1¼ miles: Tiznow, 1:59.84, September 30, 2000
1½ miles: Frankie's Pal, 2:31⅕, September 3, 1990
1¾ miles: Frankie's Pal, 2:58⅕, October 14, 1990
2 miles: Vain Lass, 3:35⅕, November 16, 1975
Other: 1¹³⁄₁₆ miles, Stage Door Joey, 3:09.91, September 20, 1992

Track Records, Main Turf

5 furlongs: Mo Dinero, :55.40, September 26, 1999
7½ furlongs: Our Love, 1:27.96, August 14, 2005
1 mile: Cherokee Circle, 1:34⅕, July 24, 1983
1¹⁄₁₆ miles: Clever Song, 1:40⅕, August 11, 1985
1¼ miles: Middleweight, 2:02.76, September 4, 2005
1⅜ miles: Semillero (Chi), 2:13⅕, October 21, 1985

Principal Races

Super Derby (G2)

Fastest Times of 2005 (Dirt)

4½ furlongs: Here Tiger, :52.62, June 24, 2005
5 furlongs: Fine Stormy, :57.27, August 7, 2005
5½ furlongs: Granny's Pride, 1:04.22, December 22, 2005
6 furlongs: Varoom, 1:09.05, August 20, 2005
6½ furlongs: Random Gold, 1:16.42, May 21, 2005
7 furlongs: Skin Flint, 1:21.79, July 16, 2005
1m 70 yds: Royal Saint, 1:41.08, July 29, 2005
1¹⁄₁₆ miles: Commander Buck, 1:43.81, September 10, 2005
1⅛ miles: Badtotheboneandrew, 1:53.69, December 10, 2005
1¼ miles: The Daddy, 2:03.15, October 1, 2005

Fastest Times of 2005 (Turf)

5 furlongs: Kool K. J., :56.23, September 29, 2005
a5 furlongs: K D King, :55.52, August 14, 2005
7½ furlongs: Our Love, 1:27.96, August 14, 2005
a7½ furlongs: Red Hawkeye, 1:29.13, June 19, 2005
1 mile: One Tuff Fox, 1:34.67, April 30, 2005
a1 miles: Dynareign, 1:35.02, December 30, 2005
1¹⁄₁₆ miles: Dontbotherknocking, 1:41.69, October 2, 2005
a1¹⁄₁₆ miles: One Tuff Fox, 1:41.66, July 30, 2005
1¼ miles: Middleweight, 2:02.76, September 4, 2005
a1¼ miles: Chases Comet, 2:04.25, September 10, 2005

Maryland

Laurel Park

Located in Laurel, midway between Baltimore and Washington, D.C., Laurel Park became a part of the Magna Entertainment Corp. family when the company headed by Frank Stronach bought a majority interest in the Maryland Jockey Club in 2002. Racing began at Laurel in 1911, and, three years later, New York City grocery entrepreneur James Butler acquired the track and hired Col. Matt Winn as the track's general manager. In 1947, the Maryland Jockey Club bought the track from Butler's estate, but the state's racing commission refused to permit Pimlico Race Course's dates to be moved to Laurel. Baltimore industrialist Morris Schapiro purchased the track in 1950 and put his youngest son, John D. Schapiro, in charge. Two years later, Laurel debuted the Washington, D.C., International, a turf stakes that was the first North American race to become a major annual target of European horses. Among the winners of the race was Racing Hall of Fame member Kelso in 1964. (The race was suspended after the 1994 running.) In 1984, Schapiro sold Laurel to a group of investors headed by Frank De Francis. In late 1986, De Francis and partners bought Pimlico, thus consolidating ownership of Maryland's major tracks. De Francis died in 1989 and was succeeded as president by his son, Joe, who remains a minority owner with his sister, Karin. Laurel's main track and turf course were rebuilt in 2004 and early '05.

Location: P.O. Box 130, Laurel, Md. 20725-0130
Phone: (301) 725-0400
Fax: (301) 725-4561
Website: *www.marylandracing.com*
E-Mail: info@marylandracing.com
Year Founded: 1911
Dates of Inaugural Meeting: October 2, 1911
Abbreviation: Lrl
Acreage: 360
Number of Stalls: 880
Seating Capacity: 5,655

Ownership

Magna Entertainment Corp. and Maryland Jockey Club

Officers

Chairman: Frank Stronach
Chief Executive Officer: Joseph A. De Francis
President: Louis J. Raffetto Jr.
General Manager: Christopher Dragone

Director of Racing: Georganne Hale
Racing Secretary: Georganne Hale
Treasurer: Keith Watson
Director of Operations: Scott Lishia
Director of Communications: Mike Gathagan
Director of Finance: Douglas J. Illig
Director of Marketing: Carrie L. Everly
Director of Mutuels: Dennis Smoter
Vice President: Karin M. De Francis
Director of Simulcasting: Dennis Smoter
Horsemen's Liaison: Phoebe Hayes
Stewards: John Burke III, Phillip E. Grove, William J. Passmore
Track Announcer: Dave Rodman
Track Photographer: James McCue
Track Superintendent: Glen Kozak
Asst. Racing Secretaries: Clayton Beck, Jillian Sofarelli

Racing Dates

2005: January 22-April 17, 57 days; September 7-December 31, 77 days
2006: January 1-April 15, 75 days; August 16-August 25, 8 days; October 1-December 31, 70 days
2007: January 1-April 15, 74 days; August 11-August 24, 10 days; September 5-December 29, 69 days

Track Layout

Main Circumference: 1 1/8 miles
Main Track Chute: 7 furlongs
Main Width: 75 feet
Main Length of Stretch: 1,344 feet
Main Turf Circumference: 1 mile
Main Turf Width: 142 feet
Main Turf Length of Stretch: 990 feet

Attendance

Highest Single-Day Record: 40,276, November 11, 1958

Handle

Average All Sources Recent Meeting: $2,056,945, Winter 2005; $2,290,824, Fall 2005
Average On-Track Recent Meeting: $291,085, Winter 2005; $297,425, Fall 2005
Total All Sources Recent Meeting: $117,245,876, Winter 2005; $176,393,418, Fall 2005
Total On-Track Recent Meeting: $16,591,841, Winter 2005; $22,901,733, Fall 2005

Leaders

Career, Leading Jockey by Titles: Edgar Prado, 10
Career, Leading Trainer by Titles: King T. Leatherbury, 25
Recent Meeting, Leading Jockey: Eric Camacho, 60, Winter 2005; Ryan Fogelsonger, 63, Fall 2005; A. R. Napravnik, 99, Winter 2006
Recent Meeting, Leading Owner: Michael Gill, 42, Winter 2005; Michael Gill, Fall 2005; Robert L. Cole, 19, Winter 2006
Recent Meeting, Leading Trainer: Kenny Cox, 32, Winter 2005; Dale Capuano, 24, Fall 2005; Scott A. Lake, 24, Fall 2005; Scott A. Lake, 58, Winter 2006
Recent Meeting, Leading Horse: Deal Me In, 4, Winter 2005; Higher Ground, 4, Winter 2005; Reckless Ways, 4, Winter 2006

Records

Single-Day Jockey Wins: Chuck Baltazar, 7, December 15, 1969; Horacio Karamanos, 7, October 26, 2002
Single Meet, Leading Jockey by Wins: Kent Desormeaux, 243, Fall/Winter 1988-1989
Single Meet, Leading Trainer by Wins: King T. Leatherbury, 86, Winter 1993-1994; King T. Leatherbury, 86, Winter 1995

Track Records, Main Dirt

4 1/2 furlongs: Weighmaster, :52 2/5, April 13, 1964
5 furlongs: Dave's Friend, :57, November 21, 1980
5 1/2 furlongs: Crossing Point, 1:02.45, November 1, 2002
6 furlongs: Richter Scale, 1:07.95, July 15, 2000
6 1/2 furlongs: Ebonizer, 1:15 2/5, November 23, 1990
7 furlongs: Tappiano, 1:21 2/5, February 12, 1989; Nimble, 1:21.50, June 26, 1999
7 1/2 furlongs: Tidal Surge, 1:29.52, March 12, 1994
1 mile: Skipper's Friend, 1:34 2/5, December 6, 1980
1 1/16 miles: Willard Scott, 1:41 4/5, November 16, 1985; Carney's Prospect, 1:41.95, August 19, 2000
1 1/8 miles: Excellent Tipper, 1:47.64, July 5, 1992
1 3/16 miles: Testing, 1:54.51, October 21, 2000
1 1/4 miles: Richie the Coach, 1:59.96, November 23, 1996
1 3/8 miles: Amber Wave, 2:17 4/5, November 28, 1968
1 3/4 miles: Asserche, 2:58.51, February 13, 1994

Track Records, Main Turf

5 furlongs: Crosslander, :55.30, September 8, 2005
5 1/2 furlongs: Bright Gold, 1:01.81, September 23, 2005
1 mile: Tune of the Spirit, 1:34.26, November 13, 2005
1 1/16 miles: Barbaro, 1:40.17, November 19, 2005
1 1/8 miles: Battle Chant, 1:46, September 17, 2005

Principal Races

Frank J. De Francis Memorial Dash S. (G1), Barbara Fritchie H. (G2), General George H. (G2), Laurel Futurity, Selima S.

Notable Events

Maryland Million Day, SprintFest Weekend, Laurel Community Day

Fastest Times of 2005 (Dirt)

4 1/2 furlongs: Citichurch, :53.04, April 10, 2005
5 furlongs: Shrewd Stipulation, :57.44, December 8, 2005
5 1/2 furlongs: Rain Song, 1:03.69, November 18, 2005
6 furlongs: I'm the Tiger, 1:09.06, November 19, 2005
7 furlongs: Majestic Sir, 1:23.33, March 16, 2005
1 mile: Honorable Man, 1:36.77, September 10, 2005
1 1/8 miles: Coast Line, 1:50.09, February 19, 2005
1 3/16 miles: Play Bingo, 1:59.08, October 15, 2005

Fastest Times of 2005 (Turf)

5 furlongs: Crosslander, :55.30, September 8, 2005
5 1/2 furlongs: Bright Gold, 1:01.81, September 23, 2005
1 mile: Tune of the Spirit, 1:34.26, November 13, 2005
1 1/16 miles: Barbaro, 1:40.17, November 19, 2005
1 1/8 miles: Battle Chant, 1:46, September 17, 2005

Pimlico Race Course

The first horse to win a stakes race at Baltimore's Pimlico Race Course during the track's inaugural season in 1870 is the namesake of one of the world's most famous horse races. Preakness, a colt by legendary 19th-century sire Lexington, won the Dinner Party Stakes that year, and in 1873 the Preakness Stakes (now G1) made its debut. The race was not run in 1891, '92, or '93, and then it was held in New York for 15 years before it was returned to Pimlico in 1909. The Preakness now is the middle jewel of the Triple Crown and is run on the third Saturday in May. The day before the Preakness, Pimlico runs the race's three-year-old filly counterpart, the Black-Eyed Susan Stakes (G2). Another of the track's most famous races is the Pimlico Special Handicap (G1), which in 1938 captured the attention of the nation when Seabiscuit defeated War Admiral in a two-horse race. Magna Entertainment Corp. purchased majority ownership of Pimlico and Laurel Park near Washington, D.C., for $50.6-million in 2002. The two tracks share host duties for the Maryland Million, a day of racing for state-breds. Pimlico long has been called "Old Hilltop," a nickname that dates from the era when a small rise in the infield was a favorite gathering place for trainers and racing fans. The hill was removed in 1938, but the nickname remained.

Location: 5201 Park Heights Ave., Baltimore, Md. 21215-5117
Phone: (410) 542-9400
Fax: (410) 542-1221
Website: *www.marylandracing.com*
E-Mail: info@marylandracing.com
Year Founded: 1743 (Maryland Jockey Club)
Dates of Inaugural Meeting: October 25, 1870
Abbreviation: Pim

Acreage: 140
Number of Stalls: 500
Seating Capacity: 14,852

Ownership

Magna Entertainment Corp.

Officers

Chairman: Frank Stronach
Chief Executive Officer: Joseph A. De Francis
President: Louis J. Raffetto Jr.
General Manager: Christopher Dragone
Director of Racing: Georganne Hale
Racing Secretary: Georganne Hale
Treasurer: Keith Watson
Director of Operations: Scott Lishia
Director of Communications: Mike Gathagan
Director of Finance: Douglas J. Illig
Director of Marketing: Carrie L. Everly
Director of Mutuels: Dennis Smoter
Vice President: Karin M. De Francis
Director of Simulcasting: Dennis Smoter
Horsemen's Liaison: Phoebe Hayes
Stewards: John Burke III, Phillip E. Grove, William J. Passmore
Track Announcer: Dave Rodman
Track Photographer: Jimmy McCue
Track Superintendent: Glen Kozak
Security: Willie Coleman
Asst. Racing Secretaries: Clayton Beck, Jillian Sofarelli

Racing Dates

2005: January 1-January 17, 13 days; April 20-June 12, 39 days; August 12-August 26, 9 days
2006: April 20-June 10, 31 days
2007: April 19-June 9, 31 days

Track Layout

Main Circumference: 1 mile
Main Track Chute: 6 furlongs and 1$^{1}/_{4}$ miles
Main Width: 70 feet
Main Length of Stretch: 1,152 feet
Main Turf Circumference: 7 furlongs

Attendance

Average Daily Recent Meeting: 6,500, Spring 2005; 8,317, Spring 2006
Highest Single-Day Record: 118,402, May 20, 2006
Total Attendance Recent Meeting: 253,511, Spring 2005; 257,834, Spring 2006
Highest Single-Day Recent Meet: 115,318, May 21, 2005; 118,402, May 20, 2006

Handle

Average All Sources Recent Meeting: $1,551,526, Winter 2005; $4,428,496, Spring 2005; $1,511,566, Summer 2005; $6,112,401, Spring 2006
Average On-Track Recent Meeting: $214,227, Winter 2005; $561,267, Spring 2005; $250,995, Summer 2005
Single-Day On-Track Handle: $11,084,415, May 21, 2005
Single-Day Total Handle All Sources: $91,028,704, May 21, 2005
Total All Sources Recent Meeting: $20,169,832, Winter 2005; $172,711,360, Spring 2005; $13,604,096, Summer 2005; $189,484,435, Spring 2006
Total On-Track Recent Meeting: $2,784,955, Winter 2005; $21,889,406, Spring 2005; $2,258,954, Summer 2005

Mutuel Records

Highest Win: $574, Cadeaux, May 7, 1913
Lowest Win: $2.10, War Admiral, November 3, 1937
Highest Exacta: $5,223.60, May 27, 1989
Lowest Exacta: $2.60, March 28, 1981
Highest Trifecta: $73,278, March 15, 1982
Highest Daily Double: $5,932.20, December 1, 1955
Highest Pick 6: $294,169, March 8, 1986
Highest Other Exotics: $414,243.90, Twin Trifecta, April 4, 1991
Highest Pick 4: $36,227.50, May 16, 2001

Leaders

Career, Leading Jockey by Titles: Edgar Prado, 14
Career, Leading Trainer by Titles: King T. Leatherbury, 26
Recent Meeting, Leading Jockey: Steve Hamilton, 50, Spring 2005; Erick D. Rodriquez, 12, Summer 2005
Recent Meeting, Leading Owner: Michael Gill, Spring 2005; Michael Gill, Summer 2005
Recent Meeting, Leading Trainer: Dale Capuano, 15, Spring 2005; Scott A. Lake, 6, Summer 2005
Recent Meeting, Leading Horse: Bartender, 3, Spring 2005; Totally Selfish, 2, Summer 2005

Records

Single-Day Jockey Wins: Paul Nicol Jr., 7, June 8, 1983
Single Meet, Leading Jockey by Wins: Kent Desormeaux, 184, Spring 1989
Single Meet, Leading Trainer by Wins: King T. Leatherbury, 100, 1976

Track Records, Main Dirt

4 furlongs: Gavotte, :47$^{2}/_{5}$, May 4, 1925
4$^{1}/_{2}$ furlongs: Countess Diana, :51.50, June 6, 1997
5 furlongs: Kingmaker, :56.46, September 27, 2003
5$^{1}/_{2}$ furlongs: Higher Strata, 1:02.46, July 29, 1995
6 furlongs: Northern Wolf, 1:09, August 18, 1990; Xtra Heat, 1:09.07, August 18, 2001
7 furlongs: Zeus, 1:26, May 3, 1921
1 mile: June Grass, 1:37$^{3}/_{5}$, May 2, 1923
1m 70 yds: Sabotage, 1:41$^{2}/_{5}$, December 17, 1958
1$^{1}/_{16}$ miles: Deputed Testamony, 1:40$^{4}/_{5}$, May 19, 1984; Poor But Honest, 1:40.83, September 9, 1995
1$^{1}/_{8}$ miles: Private Terms, 1:47$^{1}/_{5}$, May 27, 1989
1$^{3}/_{16}$ miles: Farma Way, 1:52.55, May 11, 1991
1$^{1}/_{4}$ miles: Manzotti, 2:01$^{4}/_{5}$, March 19, 1988
1$^{3}/_{8}$ miles: Narwhal, 2:16$^{2}/_{5}$, December 16, 1962
1$^{1}/_{2}$ miles: War Trophy, 2:29$^{2}/_{5}$, November 8, 1948
1$^{5}/_{8}$ miles: Market Wise, 2:43$^{1}/_{5}$, November 13, 1941
1$^{3}/_{4}$ miles: Blue Hills, 2:55$^{2}/_{5}$, October 25, 1949
2 miles: Everett, 3:25$^{3}/_{5}$, October 31, 1920
Other: a6 furlongs, Dagger Counter, 1:11$^{2}/_{5}$, January 2, 1968; 1$^{1}/_{16}$ miles, Post Morton, 2:57$^{4}/_{5}$, December 7, 1957; 2m 70 yds, Filisteo, 3:30$^{4}/_{5}$, October 31, 1941; 2$^{1}/_{16}$ miles, Beau Diable, 3:35$^{3}/_{5}$, December 10, 1960; 2$^{1}/_{4}$ miles, Edith Cavell, 3:52$^{1}/_{5}$, November 13, 1926; 2$^{1}/_{2}$ miles, Miss Grillo, 4:14$^{3}/_{5}$, November 12, 1948

Track Records, Main Turf

5 furlongs: Yankee Wildcat, :55.99, June 4, 2004
7 furlongs: Lofty Peak, 1:23$^{1}/_{5}$, May 14, 1956
1 mile: North East Bound, 1:33.42, May 7, 2000
1$^{1}/_{16}$ miles: Air Attack, 1:40.33, May 27, 1991
1$^{1}/_{8}$ miles: Mr. O'Brien, 1:46.34, May 15, 2004
1$^{3}/_{16}$ miles: Bayard Park, 2:01, May 7, 1966
1$^{3}/_{8}$ miles: Dunsinyne, 2:13.74, June 22, 1997
1$^{1}/_{2}$ miles: Fort Marcy, 2:27$^{2}/_{5}$, May 9, 1970
Other: 1$^{7}/_{8}$ miles, Brightly, 3:17, December 1, 1955

Principal Races

Preakness S. (G1), Pimlico Special H. (G1), Black-Eyed Susan S. (G2), Dixie S. (G2), Allaire duPont Breeders' Cup Distaff S. (G3)

Notable Events

Preakness S. (G1) - middle Jewel of Triple Crown

Fastest Times of 2005 (Dirt)

4$^{1}/_{2}$ furlongs: Hounddogman, :52.11, April 22, 2005
5 furlongs: Flintville, :57.73, August 21, 2005
5$^{1}/_{2}$ furlongs: Glory of Love, 1:03.27, June 4, 2005
6 furlongs: Dale's Prospect, 1:09.48, June 9, 2005
1$^{1}/_{16}$ miles: Pushed, 1:43.17, April 20, 2005
1$^{1}/_{8}$ miles: Zakocity, 1:49.19, May 21, 2005
1$^{3}/_{16}$ miles: Afleet Alex, 1:55.04, May 21, 2005

Fastest Times of 2005 (Turf)

5 furlongs: Totally Selfish, :56.10, August 26, 2005
1 mile: Gunning For, 1:34.25, May 7, 2005
1$^{1}/_{16}$ miles: Ernabel, 1:41.96, June 11, 2005
1$^{1}/_{8}$ miles: Panjshair, 1:51.16, May 5, 2005

Timonium

Although Timonium's annual live meeting, run in conjunction with the Maryland State Fair, lasts only a few days through Labor Day, it attracts more than a half-million fans each year to the community located near Baltimore's northern border. In 2001, Timonium lost two dates of its usual ten dates because of insufficient purses but still had a successful meet and has run eight dates since then. In the early 1980s, it raced as many as 42 days, but its season was sharply reduced in '85 when Maryland's mile tracks began running year-round. Timonium, which struggled in the early 1990s until the addition of simulcasting both into and out of the track, is operated by the not-for-profit Maryland State Fair and Agricultural Society Inc., which directs all profits to the fair, 4-H Club awards, and improvements. Racing at Timonium began in September 1887. Its five-eighths-mile track has a four-furlong chute and a 6½-furlong chute.

Location: 2200 York Rd., P.O. Box 188, Timonium, Md. 21094
Phone: (410) 252-0200
Fax: (910) 561-5610
Website: *www.marylandstatefair.com*
E-Mail: msfair@msn.com
Year Founded: 1878
Dates of Inaugural Meeting: September 1878
Abbreviation: Tim
Acreage: 100
Number of Stalls: 600
Seating Capacity: 4,850

Ownership

Maryland State Fair and Agricultural Society Inc.

Officers

Chairman: F. Grove Miller
President: Howard M. (Max) Mosner
General Manager: Howard M. (Max) Mosner
Racing Secretary: Georganne Hale
Treasurer: John H. Mosner Jr.
Director of Mutuels: Richard Insley
Director of Publicity: Rich Paul
Stewards: John Burke III, Philip Grove, William Passmore
Track Announcer: Dave Rodman
Track Photographer: Jim McCue
Track Superintendent: Don Denmyer

Racing Dates

2005: August 27-September 5, 8 days
2006: August 26-September 4, 8 days
2007: August 25-September 3, 8 days

Track Layout

Main Circumference: 5 furlongs
Main Track Chute: 4 furlongs and 6½ furlongs
Main Width: 70 feet
Main Length of Stretch: 700 feet

Attendance

Average Daily Recent Meeting: 4,375 est., 2005
Highest Single-Day Record: 17,306, September 4, 1967
Total Attendance Recent Meeting: 35,000 est., 2005

Handle

Average All Sources Recent Meeting: $1,935,174, 2005
Average On-Track Recent Meeting: $337,4712, 2005
Total All Sources Recent Meeting: $15,481,389, 2005
Total On-Track Recent Meeting: $2,699,774, 2005
Highest Single-Day Record Recent Meet: $2,750,831, August 27, 2005

Leaders

Recent Meeting, Leading Jockey: Travis L. Dunkelberger, 15, 2005
Recent Meeting, Leading Trainer: Scott A. Lake, 5, 2005
Recent Meeting, Leading Horse: Trijonia, 2, 2005

Principal Races

Alma North S., Taking Risks S.

Interesting Facts

Achievements/Milestones: Trainer King T. Leatherbury won his 6,000th race on August 23, 2003 at Timonium.

Fastest Times of 2005 (Dirt)

4 furlongs: Choctaw Ridge, :45.25, August 31, 2005
a6½ furlongs: Dale's Prospect, 1:17.08, September 5, 2005
1 mile: True Fashion, 1:44.02, August 31, 2005
1 1/16 miles: Resolve, 1:47.26, September 4, 2005

Massachusetts

Brockton Fair

Location: P.O. Box 172, Raynham, Ma. 02767
Phone: (508) 586-8000
Fax: (508) 821-3239
Website: *www.raynhamparkfun.com/brockton*
E-Mail: keri@brocktonfair.com
Abbreviation: BF

Northampton Fair

Location: P.O. Box 305, Northampton, Ma. 01061-0305
Phone: (413) 584-2237
Website: *www.3countyfair.com*
E-Mail: info@3countyfair.com
Dates of Inaugural Meeting: September 1943
Abbreviation: Nmp
Acreage: 50+
Number of Stalls: 450
Seating Capacity: 2,400

Ownership

Hampshire, Franklin, and Hampden Agricultural Society

Officers

President: Dayne Tracy
General Manager: Bruce Shalcross
Director of Racing: Sandy Stanisewski
Racing Secretary: Thomas Creel
Treasurer: Norman Roy
Director of Operations: John Renaud
Director of Communications: Dayne Tracy
Director of Marketing: Sandy Stanisewski
Director of Mutuels: Jack Kovalski
Vice President: Frank Basile
Director of Publicity: Sandy Stanisewski
Director of Simulcasting: Sandy Stanisewski
Horsemen's Liaison: Art Lyman
Track Photographer: CB Photo
Track Superintendent: Joseph Jasinki

Racing Dates

2005: September 2-September 11, 7 days

Track Layout

Main Circumference: 4 furlongs
Main Width: 50 feet
Main Length of Stretch: 431 feet

Handle

Average On-Track Recent Meeting: $354,000, 2005
Total On-Track Recent Meeting: $2,478,000, 2005

Leaders

Recent Meeting, Leading Jockey: Edgar Paucar, 23, 2005
Recent Meeting, Leading Trainer: Samuel J. Keyrouze, 8, 2005
Recent Meeting, Leading Horse: Jill's Jumpshot, 2, 2005; Cuff the Quote, 2, 2005; Tyr, 2, 2005; Dan's Jet, 2, 2005; Seaver, 2, 2005; November Payne, 2, 2005; I'm a Doll, 2, 2005; Come to Pass, 2, 2005

Principal Races

Northampton S., Mortgage Specialists Fair Challenge I, Mortgage Specialists Fair Challenge II

Interesting Facts

Achievements/Milestones: Oldest Agricultural Fair in Country.

Fastest Times of 2005 (Dirt)

a5 furlongs: Coyote Joe, :55.83, September 2, 2005
a6½ furlongs: Tyr, 1:21.32, September 5, 2005
a1 1/16 miles: Soldier Bear, 1:52.63, September 10, 2005

Suffolk Downs

Built in just 62 days for $2-million by the Eastern Racing Association, Suffolk Downs opened before an estimated crowd of 35,000 in East Boston on July 10, 1935, as the nation's only racetrack with a concrete grandstand. Just one month later, 52,726 fans set a Suffolk attendance record that still stands. Suffolk's signature race, the Massachusetts Handicap (G2), was inaugurated in 1935, and it has been won by such champions as Seabiscuit in 1937 and two-time MassCap winners Cigar and Skip Away in the '90s. To conserve purse money for a longer meet, the MassCap was canceled in 2003 and '05. Legendary promoter Bill Veeck carded chariot races, livestock giveaways, and mock Indian battles in the infield during his tenure there in 1969 and '70. He also successfully sued the state to allow children to attend the races. Following a two-year shutdown in 1990 and '91, James B. Moseley's and John Hall's Sterling Suffolk Racecourse Ltd. leased the track and Thoroughbred racing returned to Boston. In 1997, Suffolk Racecourse LLC bought Suffolk for $40-million. Suffolk received a major boost at the end of 2001 when the state Legislature authorized $3-million in tax revenue and uncashed winning tickets to be used for purses. Rockingham Park's abandonment of Thoroughbred racing in 2003 resulted in a restructuring of Suffolk's racing season.

Location: 111 Waldemar Ave., East Boston, Ma. 02128-1035
Phone: (617) 567-3900
Fax: (617) 561-5100
Website: *www.suffolkdowns.com*
E-Mail: publicity@suffolkdowns.com
Year Founded: 1935
Dates of Inaugural Meeting: July 10-August 10, 1935, 28 days
Abbreviation: Suf
Acreage: 190
Number of Stalls: 1,380
Seating Capacity: 9,505

Ownership

Sterling Suffolk Racecourse LLC

Officers

Chairwoman: Patricia Moseley
President: John L. Hall II
Chief Operating Officer: Robert M. O'Malley
General Manager: Joe Fatalo
Director of Racing: L. J. Pambianchi, Jr.
Racing Secretary: L. J. Pambianchi, Jr.
Secretary: Charles A. Baker III
Director of Finance: Mary Walukiewicz
Director of Marketing: JoEllen Coen
Director of Mutuels: James R. Alcott
Director of Publicity: Christian Teja
Director of Sales: Dominic Terlizzi
Stewards: Edward Cantlon Jr., William Keen, Susan Walsh
Track Announcer: Larry Collmus, T. D. Thornton
Track Photographer: Chip Bott
Track Superintendent: Steve Pini

Racing Dates

2005: April 30-November 23, 117 days
2006: May 6-November 8, 109 days

Track Layout

Main Circumference: 1 mile
Main Track Chute: 6 furlongs and 1$\frac{1}{4}$ miles
Main Width: Homestretch: 90 feet; Backstretch: 70 feet
Main Length of Stretch: 1,030 feet
Main Turf Circumference: a7 furlongs
Main Turf Width: 65 to 70 feet
Main Turf Length of Stretch: 1,030 feet

Attendance

Average Daily Recent Meeting: 3,207, 2005
Highest Single-Day Record: 52,726, August 10, 1935
Record Daily Average for Single Meet: 18,388, 1945
Total Attendance Recent Meeting: 375,211, 2005

Handle

Average All Sources Recent Meeting: $1,059,250, 2005
Average On-Track Recent Meeting: $126,026, 2005
Record Daily Average for Single Meet: $1,164,240, 1946
Single-Day On-Track Handle: $2,175,836, May 30, 1960
Single-Day Total Handle All Sources: $5,867,414, May 31, 1997
Total All Sources Recent Meeting: $123,932,207, 2005
Total On-Track Recent Meeting: $14,745,024, 2005
Highest Single-Day Record Recent Meet: $2,127,555, June 1, 2005

Mutuel Records

Highest Win: $445, Sue Harper, June 14, 1940
Highest Exacta: $9,923,80, January 13, 1985
Highest Trifecta: $51,778, January 13, 1985
Lowest Trifecta: $7.40, May 30, 1998
Highest Daily Double: $16,515, May 25, 1979
Lowest Daily Double: $3.60, May 30, 1998
Highest Pick 3: $10,515.40, December 26, 1992
Lowest Pick 3: $11, April 21, 1993; $11, December 3, 2001
Highest Pick 6: $25,399, November 28, 1982
Highest Other Exotics: $9,923.80, Perfecta, January 13, 1985; $23,079.40, Superfecta, March 27, 1996
Lowest Other Exotics: $2.60, Perfecta, October 7, 2002

Leaders

Recent Meeting, Leading Jockey: Winston Albert Thompson, 158, 2005
Recent Meeting, Leading Owner: Michael Gill, 54, 2005
Recent Meeting, Leading Trainer: John Rigattieri, 93, 2005
Recent Meeting, Leading Horse: Mister Riley, 6, 2005

Records

Single-Day Jockey Wins: Leroy Moyers, 7, July 4, 1967
Single Meet, Leading Jockey by Wins: S. Elliott, 381, 1989
Single Meet, Leading Trainer by Wins: W. W. Perry, 140, 1989

Track Records, Main Dirt

4 furlongs: Crimson Streak, :45$\frac{2}{5}$, April 6, 1970
4$\frac{1}{2}$ furlongs: Lovely Gypsy, :51$\frac{4}{5}$, May 7, 1965; Happy Voter, :51$\frac{4}{5}$, May 16, 1966
5 furlongs: Rene Depot, :57$\frac{2}{5}$, June 25, 1972
5$\frac{1}{2}$ furlongs: Four Cards Too, 1:04.11, May 1, 2004
6 furlongs: Canal, 1:08$\frac{1}{5}$, May 16, 1966
1 mile: Back Bay Brave, 1:35$\frac{1}{5}$, July 12, 1986
1m 70 yds: Half Breed, 1:40, May 23, 1964; Half an Hour, 1:40.10, January 22, 1997
1$\frac{1}{16}$ miles: Talent Show, 1:41$\frac{4}{5}$, May 12, 1962; Bear the Palm, 1:41$\frac{4}{5}$, July 3, 1977
1$\frac{1}{8}$ miles: Skip Away, 1:47.27, May 30, 1998
1$\frac{3}{16}$ miles: Shut Out, 1:55$\frac{2}{5}$, July 4, 1942
1$\frac{1}{4}$ miles: Helioscope, 2:01, May 19, 1955
1$\frac{1}{2}$ miles: Connie Rab, 2:30$\frac{3}{5}$, May 15, 1954
1$\frac{5}{8}$ miles: Count Fire, 2:45$\frac{2}{5}$, June 23, 1962
1$\frac{3}{4}$ miles: Toulouse, 2:58$\frac{2}{5}$, June 16, 1956
2 miles: Hutch, 3:35$\frac{2}{5}$, August 1, 1950
Other: 2 furlongs, Adriano's Girl, :21.94, June 4, 1997; 2m 70 yds, On the Square, 3:39$\frac{4}{5}$, April 16, 1973; 2$\frac{1}{16}$ miles, Bold Fencer, 3:35$\frac{4}{5}$, April 18, 1983; 2$\frac{1}{4}$ miles, Fundy Bay, 3:54$\frac{1}{5}$, December 9, 1973

Track Records, Main Turf

a5 furlongs: Concorde Cal, :57$\frac{1}{5}$, October 30, 1994
a7$\frac{1}{2}$ furlongs: Times Ahead, 1:32$\frac{2}{5}$, September 3, 1988
a1 mile: Diablo Reigns, 1:39.35, September 15, 2003
a1m 70yds: Alphabetical, 1:42.07, June 30, 2004
a1$\frac{1}{16}$ miles: Landing Court, 1:44.91, October 26, 1994
a1$\frac{3}{8}$ miles: Chompion, 2:20$\frac{4}{5}$, July 18, 1970 (Dead Heat); *Gaybrook Swan, 2:20$\frac{4}{5}$, July 18, 1970 (Dead Heat)
a1$\frac{1}{2}$ miles: *Akbar Khan, 2:30$\frac{3}{5}$, June 17, 1957
a1$\frac{15}{16}$ miles: Jamf, 3:11$\frac{1}{5}$, July 4, 1975
a2 miles: Jean-Pierre, 3:19$\frac{1}{5}$, June 28, 1969

Principal Races

Massachusetts H. (G2)

Notable Events

Hot Dog Safari (a fund-raiser for JoeyFund/Cystic Fibrosis Foundation)

Fastest Times of 2005 (Dirt)

4 furlongs: B L's Vinnys Girl, :47.30, July 20, 2005
5 furlongs: Deputy's Reward, :57.94, May 30, 2005

5½ furlongs: Deputy's Reward, 1:04.73, May 10, 2005
6 furlongs: Cahill Mango, 1:09.94, July 11, 2005
1 mile: Future Fantasy, 1:38.02, June 1, 2005
1m 70 yds: Dhaffir (Chi), 1:42.85, August 27, 2005
1¹/₁₆ miles: Ask Queenie, 1:46.05, August 6, 2005
1⅛ miles: Hit Now, 1:55.46, September 24, 2005

Fastest Times of 2005 (Turf)

a5 furlongs: Pipe Bomb, :57.54, June 22, 2005
a7½ furlongs: Helen's Legacy, 1:33.81, September 7, 2005
a1 miles: Speeder, 1:39.60, August 20, 2005
a1m 70 yds: British Event, 1:42.69, August 13, 2005
a1¹/₁₆ miles: Miss B's Lucky, 1:46.84, September 3, 2005

Michigan

Great Lakes Downs

Great Lakes Downs was born in 1999 out of the necessity to preserve live racing in Michigan following the shuttering of Ladbroke-owned Detroit Race Course. Located at the site of a former Standardbred track in Muskegon, Great Lakes Downs came together quickly as a group of horse owners and racing enthusiasts raised the capital to renovate the facility and prepare for racing. After an understated first meeting in 1999, the track gained national attention in the winter of 2000 when Frank Stronach-led Magna Entertainment Corp., in the midst of a track-buying spree, added Great Lakes Downs to its holdings. In early 2003, Magna reported that Great Lakes was losing money and wrote down the book value of the track. Magna has received preliminary local approval to build a new track near Detroit.

Location: 4800 S. Harvey St., Muskegon, Mi. 49444-9762
Phone: (231) 799-2400, (877) 800-4616
Fax: (231) 798-3120
Website: *www.greatlakesdowns.com*
E-Mail: glweb@greatlakesdowns.com
Year Founded: 1999
Dates of Inaugural Meeting: April 23, 1999
Abbreviation: GLD
Acreage: 85
Number of Stalls: 800
Seating Capacity: 10,000

Ownership

Magna Entertainment Corp.

Officers

Chairman: Frank Stronach
President: Jim McAlpine
General Manager: Amy MacNeil
Racing Secretary: Allan Plever
Director of Marketing: Mary Jane Shrauger
Director of Publicity: Mary Jane Shrauger
Track Superintendent: John Pollert

Racing Dates

2005: May 16-November 5, 100 days
2006: May 6-November 7, 104 days

Track Layout

Main Circumference: 5 furlongs
Main Track Chute: 4 furlongs and 7 furlongs
Main Width: 80 feet
Main Length of Stretch: 580 feet

Attendance

Highest Single-Day Record: 4,427, May 6, 2000

Handle

Average All Sources Recent Meeting: $508,000, 2005
Average On-Track Recent Meeting: $26,000, 2005
Total All Sources Recent Meeting: $50,800,000, 2005
Total On-Track Recent Meeting: $2,600,000, 2005
Record Total All Sources for Single Meet: $966,732, May 15, 2000

Leaders

Recent Meeting, Leading Jockey: T. D. Houghton, 178, 2005
Recent Meeting, Leading Trainer: Gerald S. Bennett, 86, 2005
Recent Meeting, Leading Horse: Special Envoy, 5, 2005; Whozoominwho, 5, 2005; Cherokee Babe, 5, 2005; Zany Northwestern, 5, 2005; Creative Miss, 5, 2005

Track Records, Main Dirt

4 furlongs: Dinner Band, :45.87, May 15, 2001
5½ furlongs: Deputy Stripe, 1:06.37, July 22, 2002
6 furlongs: Deputy Stripe, 1:12.57, August 27, 2002
6½ furlongs: Native Ruck, 1:19.43, July 28, 2002
7 furlongs: Secret Romeo, 1:24.77, September 2, 2001
1 mile: Override Battle, 1:40.14, October 31, 2000; Secret Romeo, 1:40.14, October 29, 2001
1m 70 yds: Secret Romeo, 1:49.50, November 4, 2000
1¹/₁₆ miles: That Monetary, 1:47.28, August 27, 2001
1⅛ miles: The Bold Bruiser, 1:54.11, October 28, 2000
Other: 2 furlongs, Skirt in the Wind, :23.52, June 22, 1999

Interesting Facts

Achievements/Milestones: Jockey Terry Houghton notched his 3,000th win on June 3, 2002, at Great Lakes Downs.

Fastest Times of 2005 (Dirt)

4 furlongs: Lyphiano, :46.86, September 27, 2005
5½ furlongs: Deputy Stripe, 1:06.55, September 24, 2005
6 furlongs: Ambitious Buster, 1:13.12, September 20, 2005
6½ furlongs: Speak of Kings, 1:19.54, October 15, 2005
7 furlongs: Dream Deliverer, 1:27.24, September 19, 2005
1 mile: You'redusty, 1:41.89, October 1, 2005
1¹/₁₆ miles: Demagoguery, 1:49.15, September 21, 2005
1⅛ miles: Dorthys Champ, 1:55, September 19, 2005

Mt. Pleasant Meadows

Location: 500 N. Mission Rd., P.O. Box 220, Mount Pleasant, Mi. 48858-4600
Phone: (989) 773-0012
Fax: (989) 773-7616
E-Mail: mpm989@hotmail.com
Abbreviation: MPM

Ownership

Walter Bay

Officers

President: Walter Bay

Racing Dates

2005: May 7-September 25, 36 days
2006: May 6-September 23, 34 days

Track Layout

Main Circumference: 4 furlongs
Main Width: 60 feet

Leaders

Recent Meeting, Leading Jockey: Mike Simpson, 20, 2005
Recent Meeting, Leading Trainer: Guy Frankina, 13, 2005
Recent Meeting, Leading Horse: Super Mood, 5, 2005

Track Records, Main Dirt

4 furlongs: Bad Boy Eric, :48.35, August 25, 2001
4½ furlongs: Wildcat Express, :52.35, May 21, 2000
5 furlongs: My Friend Charlie, :59.30, June 29, 1991
5½ furlongs: Comedy Routine, 1:05.40, July 31, 1994
6 furlongs: My Friend Charlie, 1:14.30, July 28, 1991

Fastest Times of 2005 (Dirt)

2 furlongs: Super Mood, :22.10, September 25, 2005
4 furlongs: Cheirourgos, :49, May 28, 2005
4½ furlongs: Super Mood, :53.40, June 12, 2005
5 furlongs: Eckmo, 1:01.60, July 17, 2005
5½ furlongs: Eckmo, 1:08, September 3, 2005
1m 70 yds: Hurricane Bill, 1:51.30, September 11, 2005

Minnesota

Canterbury Park

Canterbury Park is located in Shakopee, southwest of Minneapolis and St. Paul. When the track first opened in 1985, three years after Minnesota legalized pari-mutuel wagering, it was known as Canterbury Downs, and its ownership group included the Santa Anita Operating Co. In 1990, the track was purchased by Ladbroke Racing Corp., but, due to declining business, closed in '92. One year later, Irwin Jacobs, a Twin Cities financier, purchased the track and sold it to businessman and breeder Curtis Sampson, Sampson's son Randy, and partner Dale Schenian. Four months later, the owners held an initial public offering of the newly created Canterbury Park Holding Corp. The track, which re-opened in 1995 as Canterbury Park, offers Thoroughbred racing and some Quarter Horse racing during its live racing season, which runs from mid-May through early September. In 1999, Canterbury held the first running of the Claiming Crown, which quickly became recognized as a major sporting event in Minnesota, and has been held at the Shakopee track every year but one. The Canterbury Card Club opened in 2000 at the track, and its revenues supplement race purses.

Location: 1100 Canterbury Rd., Shakopee, Mn. 55379-1867
Phone: (952) 445-7223, (800) 340-6361
Fax: (952) 496-4676
Website: *www.canterburypark.com*
Year Founded: 1985
Dates of Inaugural Meeting: June 26, 1985
Abbreviation: Cby
Acreage: 355
Number of Stalls: 1,620
Seating Capacity: 22,830

Officers

Chairman: Curtis A. Sampson
President: Randall D. Sampson
Director of Racing: Richard Krueger
Racing Secretary: Douglas Schoepf
Secretary: Michelle Simon
Director of Finance: David Hansen
Director of Marketing: John Harty
Director of Mutuels: Mike Newlin
Vice President: Dale Schenian
Director of Publicity: John Groen
Director of Simulcasting: Eric Halstrom
Horsemen's Liaison: Mary Green
Stewards: Noble Hay, Hank Mills, David Moore
Track Announcer: Paul Allen
Track Photographer: Beth Reitzebeck
Track Superintendent: Moe Nye
Asst. Racing Secretary: John Simon
Clerk of the Course: Peggy Davis
Horsemen's Bookkeeper: Terri Hoffrogge

Racing Dates

2005: May 7-September 5, 68 days
2006: May 6-September 4, 69 days

Track Layout

Main Circumference: 1 mile
Main Track Chute: 3$\frac{1}{2}$ furlongs, 6$\frac{1}{2}$ furlongs and 1$\frac{1}{4}$ miles
Main Turf Circumference: 7 furlongs
Main Turf Chute: 1$\frac{1}{16}$ miles

Attendance

Average Daily Recent Meeting: 5,129, 2005
Highest Single-Day Record: 27,439, April 24, 1987
Total Attendance Recent Meeting: 348,804, 2005
Highest Single-Day Recent Meet: 10,515, July 16, 2005

Handle

Average All Sources Recent Meeting: $812,107, 2005
Average On-Track Recent Meeting: $467,211, 2005
Single-Day On-Track Handle: $2,265,404, June 28, 1987
Total All Sources Recent Meeting: $55,223,259, 2005
Total On-Track Recent Meeting: $31,770,317, 2005
Highest Single-Day Record Recent Meet: $1,900,747, July 16, 2005

Leaders

Career, Leading Jockey by Titles: Luis Quinonez, 5
Career, Leading Owner by Titles: Stephen Herold, 2, Curtis Sampson, 2, Valene Farm, 2, Steve Richardson, 2
Career, Leading Trainer by Titles: Pat Cuccurullo, 3, Doug Oliver, 3, David Van Winkle, 3
Recent Meeting, Leading Jockey: Seth B. Martinez, 96, 2005
Recent Meeting, Leading Owner: Jer-Mar Stable LLC, 18, 2005
Recent Meeting, Leading Trainer: McLean Robertson, 53, 2005
Recent Meeting, Leading Horse: Lt. Sampson, 5, 2005

Track Records, Main Dirt

4$\frac{1}{2}$ furlongs: Gallapiat's Song, :51.27, June 23, 1991
5 furlongs: Tonight Rainbow, :57, May 31, 2004
5$\frac{1}{2}$ furlongs: Lucado, 1:02.65, June 19, 2005
6 furlongs: Onlynurimagination, 1:08.04, July 16, 2005
6$\frac{1}{2}$ furlongs: Don's Irish Melody, 1:14, June 12, 1988
1 mile: Minneapple, 1:35$\frac{1}{5}$, September 27, 1987
1m 70 yds: Come Summer, 1:40$\frac{1}{5}$, August 18, 1985; J. P. Jet, 1:40.20, August 3, 2002; Silver Zipper, 1:40.20, August 10, 2002
1$\frac{1}{16}$ miles: Power Boat, 1:41$\frac{4}{5}$, July 30, 1988
1$\frac{1}{8}$ miles: Olympio, 1:46.47, July 7, 1991
1$\frac{1}{4}$ miles: John Bullit, 2:04$\frac{3}{5}$, July 25, 1986
1$\frac{1}{2}$ miles: Loustros (GB), 2:32$\frac{3}{5}$, August 28, 1987
1$\frac{3}{4}$ miles: Luciole (Arg), 2:59$\frac{4}{5}$, October 12, 1985
2 miles: My Tulles Free, 3:25$\frac{3}{5}$, September 1, 1986
Other: a3 furlongs, Bye for Now, :40, June 30, 1985; 3$\frac{1}{2}$ furlongs, In Moderation, :39.11, May 26, 1997

Track Records, Main Turf

5 furlongs: Rockhurst, :56.01, May 30, 2005
7$\frac{1}{2}$ furlongs: Honor the Hero, 1:28, June 18, 1995
1 mile: Go Go Jack, 1:33.40, June 3, 1995
1m 70yds: Numchuek, 1:39$\frac{1}{5}$, July 6, 1988
1$\frac{1}{16}$ miles: Little Bro Lantis, 1:40.20 June 16, 1995
1$\frac{1}{8}$ miles: Fluffkins, 1:44, July 22, 1995
1$\frac{3}{8}$ miles: Treizieme, 2:12$\frac{3}{5}$, August 3, 1986
Other: a7$\frac{1}{2}$ furlongs, Kiltartan Cross, 1:27.80, August 11, 1991; a1 mile, Kiltartan Cross, 1:33.40, July 10, 1991; a1m 70yds, Tainer's Toy, 1:39.20, August 10, 1991; a1$\frac{1}{16}$ miles, Diplomat's Reward, 1:41.34, July 17, 1999; a1$\frac{3}{8}$ miles, Earnest Storm, 2:04.25, July 3, 2005; 1$\frac{7}{8}$ miles, John Bullit, 3:11$\frac{2}{5}$, September 26, 1987; a1$\frac{7}{8}$ miles, Mark of Stregth, 3:11.40, September 12, 1992

Principal Races

Lady Canterbury Breeders' Cup S., Claiming Crown Jewel S., Claiming Crown Emerald S., Claiming Crown Tiara S., John Bullit S.

Interesting Facts

Previous Names and Dates: Canterbury Downs 1984-1994

Notable Events

Claiming Crown

Fastest Times of 2005 (Dirt)

3$\frac{1}{2}$ furlongs: Sentimental Charm, :39.64, May 27, 2005
5 furlongs: Counterfeit Gold, :57.41, June 12, 2005
5$\frac{1}{2}$ furlongs: Lucado, 1:02.65, June 19, 2005
6 furlongs: Onlynurimagination, 1:08.04, July 16, 2005
6$\frac{1}{2}$ furlongs: Procreate, 1:14.54, July 16, 2005
1 mile: Magic Kipper, 1:35.97, July 7, 2005
1m 70 yds: Wally's Choice, 1:40.75, September 5, 2005
1$\frac{1}{16}$ miles: Wally's Choice, 1:42.51, August 21, 2005
1$\frac{1}{8}$ miles: Desert Boom, 1:47.32, July 16, 2005

Fastest Times of 2005 (Turf)

5 furlongs: Rockhurst, :56.01, May 30, 2005
7$\frac{1}{2}$ furlongs: Sajjan, 1:29.50, September 2, 2005
a7$\frac{1}{2}$ furlongs: Slamdancer, 1:29, July 7, 2005
1 mile: Ghostly Gate, 1:35.42, July 4, 2005
a1 miles: Phone the Diva, 1:34.62, July 9, 2005
1$\frac{1}{16}$ miles: Mr. Mabee, 1:41.77, July 16, 2005
a1$\frac{1}{16}$ miles: Halo Flamingo, 1:42.02, July 8, 2005
a1$\frac{3}{8}$ miles: Earnest Storm, 2:04.25, July 3, 2005

Montana

Great Falls

Location: 400 3rd Ave. N.W., P.O. Box, Great Falls, Mt. 59403
Phone: (406) 727-8900
Fax: (406) 452-8955
Website: *www.montanastatefair.com/horseracing.htm*
E-Mail: info@goexpopark.com
Abbreviation: GF

Ownership

Cascade County

Officers

General Manager: Bill Ogg
Director of Racing: Bill Ogg
Director of Operations: John Scott
Director of Finance: Lois Thomas
Director of Marketing: Lori Cox
Director of Publicity: Lori Cox
Track Superintendent: Joe McCracken
Promotions/Events: Amy Robbins

Racing Dates

2005: July 4-July 31, 10 days
2006: July 15-July 30, 7 days

Track Layout

Main Circumference: 4 furlongs
Main Track Chute: 5 furlongs and 7 furlongs
Main Width: 60 feet
Main Length of Stretch: 410.1 feet

Leaders

Recent Meeting, Leading Jockey: Fernando Manuel Gamez, 21, 2005
Recent Meeting, Leading Trainer: Shawn H. Davis, 8, 2005
Recent Meeting, Leading Horse: Handsomchamp, 3, 2005

Principal Races

Treasure State Futurity, Lewis and Clark Derby, Big Sky H.

Fastest Times of 2005 (Dirt)

5 furlongs: Flying Lady Cue, 1:00.60, July 9, 2005; Seattle Cue, 1:00.60, July 4, 2005
a5 furlongs: Rodeo Champ, 1:04.80, July 24, 2005
a5¼ furlongs: Handsomchamp, 1:04.20, July 4, 2005
7 furlongs: Shouldbevictory, 1:25.80, July 17, 2005
1m 70 yds: Shouldbevictory, 1:48, July 31, 2005

Helena Downs

Location: P.O. Box 9706, Helena, Mt. 59604-9706
Phone: (406) 457-9492
Abbreviation: Hln

Marias Fair

Location: P.O. Box 924, Shelby, Mt. 59474-0924
Phone: (406) 337-3600
Abbreviation: MaF

Racing Dates

2004: July 16-July 18, 3 days
2005: July 23-July 24, 2 days

Miles City Bucking Horse Sale

Location: P.O. Box 127, Miles City, Mt. 59301-0127
Phone: (406) 234-7700
Fax: (406) 234-7783
Website: *www.buckinghorsesale.com*
E-Mail: mcbhs@buckinghorsesale.com
Year Founded: 1950
Abbreviation: MC

Ownership

Custer County

Officers

President: Donald Richard
General Manager: Chet Holmes
Director of Racing: Donald Richard
Racing Secretary: Holly Burrows
Treasurer: Linda Milhof
Director of Operations: Donald Richard
Director of Marketing: Jeff Landers
Vice President: Jeff Landers
Director of Publicity: Donald Richard
Stewards: Raleigh Swensrud
Track Announcer: Bert Boughton
Track Superintendent: Chet Holmes

Racing Dates

2005: May 13-May 20, 3 days
2006: May 14-May 21, 3 days

Attendance

Average Daily Recent Meeting: 2,000, 2005
Total Attendance Recent Meeting: 6,000, 2005

Handle

Average On-Track Recent Meeting: $22,333, 2005
Total On-Track Recent Meeting: $67,000, 2005

Leaders

Recent Meeting, Leading Jockey: Antonio R. Perez, 3, 2005
Recent Meeting, Leading Trainer: Edward Buxbaum, 1, 2005; Lark Pollari, 1, 2005; Clarence Clancy Ibach, 1, 2005; Darren Ducheneaux, 1, 2005; Jan Ibach, 1, 2005
Recent Meeting, Leading Horse: Rileys Knight, 1, 2005; Boo Roo, 1, 2005; Damspicy, 1, 2005; Rileys Stuff, 1, 2005; Attracta Dancer, 1, 2005

Fastest Times of 2005 (Dirt)

5½ furlongs: Rileys Knight, 1:09.40, May 22, 2005
6 furlongs: Damspicy, 1:14.40, May 21, 2005
a6 furlongs: Boo Roo, 1:10, May 22, 2005

Northwest Montana Fair

Location: 256 N. Meridian Rd., Kalispell, Mt. 59901-3850
Phone: (406) 758-5810
Fax: (406) 756-8936
Website: *www.nwmtfair.com*
Abbreviation: Ksp

Racing Dates

2005: August 19-August 28, 5 days
2006: August 18-August 27, 5 days

Leaders

Recent Meeting, Leading Jockey: Nikeela Black, 5, 2005
Recent Meeting, Leading Trainer: Chuck Lindsey, 2, 2005; Marcie Riley, 2, 2005

Fastest Times of 2005 (Dirt)

5 furlongs: Redinal, 1:02.80, August 19, 2005
6 furlongs: Bobby Luvs P. R., 1:13.40, August 21, 2005
7 furlongs: Long On Pride, 1:27, August 20, 2005
1m 70 yds: Born Wild Again, 1:52.40, August 28, 2005

Western Montana Fair and Races

Location: 1101 South Ave. West, Missoula, Mt. 59801-7907
Phone: (406) 721-3247
Fax: (406) 728-7479
Website: *www.westernmontanafair.com*
E-Mail: thinton@westernmontanafair.com
Year Founded: 1879
Abbreviation: WMF
Acreage: 40
Number of Stalls: 356
Seating Capacity: 3,000

Ownership

Missoula County

Officers

General Manager: Scot Meader
Director of Racing: Bill Nooney
Racing Secretary: Francis "Shorty" Martin
Director of Operations: Toni Hinton
Director of Marketing: Toni Hinton
Director of Mutuels: Teri Lerch
Director of Publicity: Toni Hinton
Horsemen's Liaison: Montana HBPA
Track Announcers: Phil Benson, Bruce Micklus
Track Photographer: Trident

Racing Dates

2005: August 9-August 14, 6 days
2006: August 8-August 13, 6 days

Attendance

Average Daily Recent Meeting: 2,000 est., 2005
Total Attendance Recent Meeting: 12,000 est., 2005

Handle

Average On-Track Recent Meeting: $87,593, 2005
Total On-Track Recent Meeting: $525,560, 2005
Highest Single-Day Record Recent Meet: $135,096, August 13, 2005

Leaders

Recent Meeting, Leading Jockey: Rowdy J. Luark, 6, 2005; Fernando Manuel Gamez, 6, 2005; Kym Espy, 6, 2005
Recent Meeting, Leading Trainer: Vikki Berkram, 8, 2005
Recent Meeting, Leading Horse: C C Sky Dancer, 2, 2005; Will Reason, 2, 2005

Track Records, Main Dirt

5 furlongs: Rejected Frenchman, 1:04, August 11, 1996
1$^1/_{16}$ miles: Early Shove, 1:44.40, August 11, 1996
1$^1/_8$ miles: Rulvic, 1:53$^2/_5$, August 23, 1986

Principal Races

Western Montana Fair Thoroughbred Derby, Rose Blossom H., Western Montana Fair Thoroughbred Futurity, Cliff Sprint S.

Fastest Times of 2005 (Dirt)

a5$^1/_4$ furlongs: Popescu (Brz), 1:05.40, August 11, 2005
6$^1/_2$ furlongs: Will Reason, 1:23, August 14, 2005
1$^1/_{16}$ miles: Snowbound Star, 1:53, August 13, 2005
1$^5/_8$ miles: Born Wild Again, 2:56, August 13, 2005

Yellowstone Downs

Location: P.O. Box 1138, Billings, Mt. 59103-1138
Phone: (406) 869-5251
Fax: (406) 869-5253
Website: *www.yellowstonedowns.com*
E-Mail: racing@yellowstonedowns.com
Abbreviation: YD

Racing Dates

2005: August 19-September 25, 14 days
2006: August 18-September 24, 10 days

Leaders

Recent Meeting, Leading Jockey: Kym Espy, 12, 2005
Recent Meeting, Leading Trainer: Mike D. Taylor, 5, 2005
Recent Meeting, Leading Horse: River Girl's Boy, 2, 2005; Victory's Pride, 2, 2005; Hey Boss, 2, 2005; Regal Hit, 2, 2005; We Miss You Son, 2, 2005; Road Wager, 2, 2005; Moscow Blues, 2, 2005

Principal Races

Yellowstone Futurity, Yellowstone Derby

Fastest Times of 2005 (Dirt)

5 furlongs: Aaron's Carr, 1:01.60, August 27, 2005
5$^1/_4$ furlongs: Bobski, 1:03, September 10, 2005; Evitan Native, 1:03, September 4, 2005; King of Adventure, 1:03, September 4, 2005; Restrictions Apply, 1:03, September 11, 2005
7 furlongs: Shouldbevictory, 1:26.20, September 5, 2005; Victory's Pride, 1:26.20, September 11, 2005
1m 70 yds: We Miss You Son, 1:47.80, September 11, 2005

Nebraska

Columbus Races

Opened in 1950, Columbus Races in Columbus, 90 miles northwest of Lincoln, is operated on the Platte County Agricultural Society Fairgrounds. It was at Columbus that Racing Hall of Fame trainer Marion H. Van Berg and his son, Jack, also a Racing Hall of Fame member, began their careers. The elder Van Berg operated a sales barn, offering hogs, cattle, and horses, in addition to running his stable. Columbus usually conducts a 24-day summer meet from late July through mid-September, racing on Fridays, Saturdays, and Sundays. Extensive simulcasting is also offered. The five-eighths-mile oval has a 6½-furlong chute. A record crowd of 8,856 attended on September 3, 1973. The record handle of $719,725 was set exactly 11 years later.

Location: 822 15th St., Columbus, Ne. 68601-5370
Phone: (402) 564-0133
Fax: (402) 564-0990
Website: *www.agpark.com*
Year Founded: 1941
Dates of Inaugural Meeting: July 1942
Abbreviation: Cls
Acreage: 160 Acres
Number of Stalls: 900
Seating Capacity: 4,000

Officers

Chairman: Lynn Anderson
General Manager: Gary Bock
Director of Racing: Dennis Kochevar
Racing Secretary: Dennis Kochevar
Secretary: Gary Kruse
Treasurer: Gary Kruse
Director of Operations: Gary Bock
Director of Finance: Gary Kruse
Director of Mutuels: Leon Ebel
Vice President: Eldon Engel
Director of Publicity: Gary Bock
Director of Simulcasting: Gary Bock
Stewards: Jim Haberlan, Rol Schaal, Quient Schaffer
Track Announcer: Keith Nelson
Track Photographer: Coady Photography
Track Superintendent: Bill Lusche

Racing Dates

2005: July 28-September 11, 24 days
2006: July 28-September 10, 24 days

Track Layout

Main Circumference: 5 furlongs
Main Track Chute: 6$^1/_2$ furlongs
Main Width: 75 feet
Main Length of Stretch: 720 feet

Attendance

Highest Single-Day Record: 8,856, September 3, 1973

Handle

Single-Day On-Track Handle: $719,725, September 3, 1984

Leaders

Recent Meeting, Leading Jockey: Robert Dean Williams, 42, 2005
Recent Meeting, Leading Trainer: David C. Anderson, 17, 2005
Recent Meeting, Leading Horse: Red Hot Fox, 3, 2005

Track Records, Main Dirt

4 furlongs: Kips Flyer, :39.80, August 11, 2000
5$^1/_2$ furlongs: Foreign Flag, 1:05$^1/_5$, September 30, 1978
6 furlongs: Eve's Choice, 1:10$^2/_5$, August 27, 1994
6$^1/_2$ furlongs: Jae Ranch, 1:17, August 12, 1984
1m 70 yds: Ilatan, 1:41$^3/_5$, September 9, 1984
1$^1/_{16}$ miles: Foreign Intent, 1:44$^2/_5$, September 21, 1974

1$\frac{3}{8}$ miles: In Doc's Honor, 2:18$\frac{2}{5}$, September 3, 1994
2 miles: Blazing Don, 3:36$\frac{3}{5}$, September 26, 1982
Other: 3$\frac{1}{2}$ furlongs, Timetoprofit, 39.60, August 24, 2002; 1$\frac{5}{16}$ miles, Too Little Man, 2:19$\frac{1}{5}$, September 6 1969; 1$\frac{7}{16}$ miles, Skeeter Do, 2:27$\frac{4}{5}$, September 12, 1994

Principal Races

Columbus Breeders' Special H., Columbus Futurity, Columbus Debutante S.

Notable Events

Super Saver Sunday, Let the Bets Roll Saturdays

Fastest Times of 2005 (Dirt)

3$\frac{1}{2}$ furlongs: Trone, :40.60, September 3, 2005
6 furlongs: Doug's Shadow, 1:13.40, August 13, 2005; Missy Can Do, 1:13.40, August 20, 2005; Nakayama Jazz, 1:13.40, August 5, 2005
6$\frac{1}{2}$ furlongs: Burning Memories, 1:20.20, September 4, 2005; Innocent Within, 1:20.20, August 26, 2005
1m 70 yds: My Man, 1:46.40, September 3, 2005
1$\frac{1}{16}$ miles: Lucky Bob, 1:49.40, September 3, 2005

Fonner Park

The closing of Omaha's Ak-Sar-Ben racecourse in 1995 dealt a serious blow to Nebraska racing. But Fonner Park in Grand Island has been one of the tracks to keep the flame flickering in the Cornhusker State with its down-home brand of racing. The 280-acre facility staged its first race meet in 1954. Fonner Park is operated by a not-for-profit organization, with the track's profits going to charitable and community activities in the Grand Island region. With the advent of telephone-account wagering in Nebraska in October 2001, Fonner officials sought to reach more of the state's bettors. The five-furlong facility has never been known as a racing mecca, but some interesting horses have competed at Fonner. One of them is sprinter Leaping Plum, who in 2001 won his seventh consecutive renewal of the opening-week Grasmick Handicap. The gelding also won the Coca-Cola Sprint Handicap four consecutive times (1995-'98).

Location: 700 E. Stolley Park Rd., P.O. Box 490, Grand Island, Ne. 68802
Phone: (308) 382-4515
Fax: (308) 384-2753
Website: *www.fonnerpark.com*
E-Mail: fonnerpark@aol.com
Year Founded: 1951
Dates of Inaugural Meeting: April 29, 1954
Abbreviation: Fon
Acreage: 240
Number of Stalls: 1,300
Seating Capacity: 5,766

Officers

Chief Executive Officer: Hugh M. Miner Jr.
President: Doyle Hulme
General Manager: Hugh Miner Jr.
Director of Racing: Douglas Schoepf
Racing Secretary: Douglas Schoepf
Secretary: Roger Luebbe
Treasurer: Bill Westering
Director of Operations: Bruce A. Swihart
Director of Marketing: Linda Wilhelmy
Director of Mutuels: William McConnell
Vice President: Hugh M. Miner Jr.
Director of Simulcasting: Todd W. Otto
Track Announcer: Matt Hook
Track Photographer: Linscott Photography
Track Superintendent: Rick L. Danburg

Racing Dates

2005: February 11-May 7, 38 days
2006: February 10-May 6, 38 days

Track Layout

Main Circumference: 5 furlongs
Main Track Chute: 4 furlongs and 6$\frac{1}{2}$ furlongs
Main Width: 70 feet
Main Length of Stretch: 700 feet

Attendance

Highest Single-Day Record: 10,930, March 17, 1990

Handle

Single-Day On-Track Handle: $1,285,011, April 28, 1990

Mutuel Records

Highest Win: $520.40, Black Ticket, March 10, 1977
Lowest Win: $2.20, Ben's Whiz, March 30, 1974; $2.20, Real Style, March 30, 1974; $2.20, I'ma Game Master, April 29, 1995
Highest Exacta: $5,421, March 28, 1994
Lowest Exacta: $4, May 6, 2000
Highest Trifecta: $26,474.40, March 30, 1990
Lowest Trifecta: $14.60, March 15, 1998
Highest Daily Double: $5,451.20, March 18, 1977
Lowest Daily Double: $5, March 10, 1994; $5, April 21, 1995
Highest Pick 3: $13,800.80, February 27, 1988
Lowest Pick 3: $3.20, March 18, 2000
Highest Other Exotics: $17,526.60, Superfecta, March 23, 2001
Lowest Other Exotics: $271.40, Superfecta, March 4, 2001

Records

Single-Day Jockey Wins: Ken Shino, 8, April 2, 2000
Single-Day Trainer Wins: Tim Gleason, 5, February 18, 1989; Marvin Johnson, 5, February 26, 2000; Marvin Johnson, 5, April 2, 2000
Single Meet, Leading Jockey by Wins: Perry Compton, 85, 2000
Single Meet, Leading Trainer by Wins: M. A. Johnson, 50, 2000

Track Records, Main Dirt

4 furlongs: Leaping Plum, :44.20, February 17, 1996
5$\frac{1}{2}$ furlongs: Little L. M., 1:04$\frac{2}{5}$, April 12, 1975
6 furlongs: Orphan Kist, 1:10, April 8, 1989
6$\frac{1}{2}$ furlongs: Majority of One, 1:17, March 18, 1989
1 mile: Brian's Star, 1:36$\frac{3}{5}$, April 9, 1986; High On Laraka, 1:36$\frac{3}{5}$, April 19, 1986
1m 70 yds: Shamtastic, 1:40, April 26, 1986; Advice, 1:40, April 25, 1987
1$\frac{1}{16}$ miles: Sahara King, 1:43, April 27, 1996
1$\frac{1}{8}$ miles: Potro, 1:51.40, April 25, 1993
1$\frac{3}{8}$ miles: Meat Loaf, 2:22$\frac{2}{5}$, April 29, 1970
Other: 1$\frac{7}{16}$ miles, Wenga, 2:30$\frac{2}{5}$, May 1, 1968

Principal Races

Bosselman/Gus Fonner S.

Fastest Times of 2005 (Dirt)

4 furlongs: Missy Can Do, :44.40, February 12, 2005
6 furlongs: Lukfata Louis, 1:11.20, March 12, 2005
6$\frac{1}{2}$ furlongs: Hez Comin Thru, 1:18.80, March 12, 2005
1 mile: Prineville, 1:40.60, April 2, 2005
1m 70 yds: Amafastbaby, 1:44.80, April 9, 2005
1$\frac{1}{16}$ miles: Stormy Impact, 1:45.60, April 23, 2005
1$\frac{1}{8}$ miles: Amafastbaby, 1:54.60, May 7, 2005

Horsemen's Atokad Downs

Live Thoroughbred racing in Nebraska did not die when Omaha's Ak-Sar-Ben closed in 1995 after 74 years. Ak-Sar-Ben, which was torn down in 1997, is Nebraska spelled backward. Atokad is Dakota spelled backward, and the track is located in Dakota County, in the state's northwest corner near the South Dakota border. The five-eighths-mile track in South Sioux City opened on September 20, 1956. Atokad conducted a late-summer meeting in most years, though it did not race from 1998 through 2000. A single-day meet was resurrected in 2001 by Robert E. Lee, president of the Nebraska Horsemen's and Benevolent Protective Association, and three days of racing were scheduled for 2005 and '06. A record crowd of 6,200 attended on October 18, 1958. The record handle of $483,486 was set on November 9, 1980.

Location: 1524 Atokad Dr., P.O. Box 796, South Sioux City, Ne. 68776
Phone: (402) 494-5722
Fax: (402) 241-0410
Year Founded: 1951
Dates of Inaugural Meeting: September 20, 1956
Abbreviation: Ato
Acreage: 50
Number of Stalls: 850
Seating Capacity: 3,112

Ownership

Nebraska HBPA

Officers

President: Donald Everett
General Manager: Gregory Hosch
Director of Racing: Gregory Hosch
Racing Secretary: Gregory Hosch
Treasurer: Patricia Shefland
Director of Operations: Linda Wunderlin
Director of Marketing: Linda Wunderlin
Vice President: William Vannoy
Director of Publicity: Linda Wunderlin
Track Announcer: Buddy Haar
Track Photographer: Coady Services
Track Superintendent: Moe Nye
Security: Titan Security Inc.
Horsemen's Bookkeeper: Patricia Shefland

Racing Dates

2005: September 16-September 18, 3 days
2006: September 15-September 17, 3 days

Track Layout

Main Circumference: 5 furlongs
Main Track Chute: $6\frac{1}{2}$ furlongs and $1\frac{1}{8}$ miles
Main Width: 68 feet
Main Length of Stretch: 660 feet

Attendance

Highest Single-Day Record: 6,200, October 18, 1958

Handle

Single-Day Total Handle All Sources: $483,486, November 9, 1980

Leaders

Recent Meeting, Leading Jockey: Dennis Michael Collins, 8, 2005
Recent Meeting, Leading Trainer: Jason Wise, 2, 2005; David C. Anderson, 2, 2005; Milton M. Gaede, 2, 2005; Brian M. Roberts, 2, 2005; Robert W. Parker, 2, 2005

Track Records, Main Dirt

4 furlongs: Shining Sea, :44.40, June 28, 1992
$5\frac{1}{2}$ furlongs: Slipped in Space, 1:05$\frac{1}{5}$, October 24, 1976
6 furlongs: Don Rivers, 1:11$\frac{2}{5}$, October 28, 1966
$6\frac{1}{2}$ furlongs: Spanish Key, 1:16$\frac{2}{5}$, October 24, 1970
1 mile: Quilla Sue, 1:38, October 30, 1973
1m 70 yds: No Mystery, 1:42$\frac{1}{5}$, November 5, 1976
$1\frac{1}{16}$ miles: Great Commander, 1:43$\frac{3}{5}$, November 3, 1973
$1\frac{1}{8}$ miles: Reason to Explode, 1:50.20, July 13, 1991
$1\frac{3}{8}$ miles: Barker's Tip, 2:20, October 17, 1964
2 miles: Navy Grey, 3:30$\frac{1}{5}$, October 30, 1962; Middle Road, 3:30$\frac{1}{5}$, November 21, 1976
Other: a4 furlongs, Classy Fleet, :43$\frac{4}{5}$, November 19, 1977; a6 furlongs, Urgent Valentine, 1:16.40, July 20, 2003; $1\frac{7}{16}$ miles, Echo Bar, 2:28, October 30, 1968; a$1\frac{7}{16}$ miles, Duke of Badgerland, 2:29.60, November 6, 1996

Fastest Times of 2005 (Dirt)

6 furlongs: Shesaidsheknowsya, 1:13.20, September 17, 2005
a$6\frac{1}{2}$ furlongs: Hez Comin Thru, 1:16.40, September 18, 2005
1 mile: Bella La Ghosi, 1:42, September 16, 2005
1m 70 yds: Flaming Night, 1:47.20, September 16, 2005
$1\frac{1}{16}$ miles: Hog Run Creek, 1:49.20, September 17, 2005

Horsemen's Park

Boasting a simulcasting facility that offers wagering on 18 to 21 racetracks daily, Horsemen's Park opened on January 3, 1998, for simulcasting in Omaha, four miles south of the former Ak-Sar-Ben site. Two live races were held each day on two consecutive days in July 1998 by the Nebraska Horsemen's Benevolent and Protective Association, which owns and operates the track. The meet was expanded to four days in 2003, with $500,000 offered in purses each year. The track is a five-eighths-mile oval. The simulcasting facility offers seating for 3,000 and contains 675 closed-circuit monitors.

Location: 6303 Q St., Omaha, Ne. 68117-1696
Phone: (402) 731-2900
Fax: (402) 731-5122
Website: *www.horsemenspark.com*
Year Founded: 1998
Dates of Inaugural Meeting: July 1998
Abbreviation: HPO
Seating Capacity: 3,000

Ownership

Nebraska HBPA

Officers

President: William Vannoy
General Manager: Dick Moore
Racing Secretary: Gregory C. Hosch
Treasurer: Patricia Shefland
Director of Marketing: Dick Moore
Director of Mutuels: Mary Palais, Mary Snelling
Director of Publicity: Dick Moore
Director of Simulcasting: Patricia Shefland
Track Superintendent: Tim Hurd

Racing Dates

2005: July 21-July 24, 4 days
2006: July 20-July 23, 4 days

Track Layout

Main Circumference: 5 furlongs
Main Width: 65 feet
Main Length of Stretch: 680 feet

Leaders

Recent Meeting, Leading Jockey: Daniel Lee Beck, 4, 2005
Recent Meeting, Leading Trainer: Herb Riecken, 2, 2005

Principal Races

Omaha H., Queen's H.

Fastest Times of 2005 (Dirt)

6 furlongs: Hez Comin Thru, 1:11.60, July 21, 2005; Mistrick, 1:11.60, July 22, 2005
1 mile: Missme, 1:37.40, July 24, 2005
$1\frac{3}{8}$ miles: Danner, 2:21, July 22, 2005

State Fair Park

Location: P.O. Box 81223, Lincoln, Ne. 68501
Phone: (402) 474-5371
Fax: (402) 473-4114
Website: *www.statefair.org*
E-Mail: ghosch@statefair.org
Abbreviation: Lnn
Number of Stalls: 1,200
Seating Capacity: 5,800

Officers

Director of Racing: Greg Hosch
Secretary: Sherri Johnson
Director of Marketing: Christine Rasmussen
Director of Mutuels: Mark Jensen
Director of Publicity: Christine Rasmussen
Track Superintendent: Scott Yound
Promotions/Events: Julie Burton

Racing Dates

2005: May 13-July 17, 37 days
2006: May 12-July 16, 37 days

Track Layout

Main Circumference: 5 furlongs
Main Track Chute: $4\frac{1}{2}$ furlongs
Main Length of Stretch: 480 feet

Leaders

Recent Meeting, Leading Jockey: Robert Dean Williams, 57, 2005
Recent Meeting, Leading Trainer: David C. Anderson, 21, 2005
Recent Meeting, Leading Horse: Dawns Early Dancer, 4, 2005

Records

Single-Day Jockey Wins: Robert D. Williams, 8, September 29, 1984

Track Records, Main Dirt

$4\frac{1}{2}$ furlongs: Leaping Blum, :50, September 17, 1995
6 furlongs: Up 'n Blumin, 1:09.80, June 3, 2006
1 mile: Sensitive Ghost, 1:36, July 14, 2002
1m 70 yds: High Dice, 1:39.40, June 24, 2001

Interesting Facts

Trivia: Triple dead heat for win on October 23, 1981; at the time one of only 17 such instances since 1940 and the only one ever in Nebraska. On July 18, 1999, a national record for a place payoff was set at $493.

Fastest Times of 2005 (Dirt)

4 furlongs: Thoughtuwasatoad, :49, June 11, 2005
$4\frac{1}{2}$ furlongs: Brother Huz, :50.80, June 24, 2005
6 furlongs: Grand Kat, 1:10.20, May 21, 2005
1 mile: Big Boy Jesse, 1:38, May 30, 2005
1m 70 yds: Up Jump the Devil, 1:41.80, June 19, 2005
$1\frac{1}{8}$ miles: Silver Town, 1:55.20, June 5, 2005
$1\frac{3}{8}$ miles: Silver Town, 2:20, June 19, 2005
2 miles: Old Man's Delite, 3:29.40, July 3, 2005

Nevada

Elko County Fair

Location: P.O. Box 2067, Elko, Nv. 89803
Phone: (775) 738-3616
Fax: (775) 778-3468
Website: *www.elkocountyfair.com*
E-Mail: info@elkocountyfair.com
Abbreviation: Elk

Officers

Racing Secretary: Fred Davis
Secretary: J. J. Jennifer Roemmich
Treasurer: J. J. Jennifer Roemmich
Director of Admissions: Buck Boyce
Director of Mutuels: Buck Boyce
Stewards: Carl Pacini, Doug Ray, Stu Wilson
Track Announcer: Fred Davis
Track Superintendent: Angelo Puccinelli
Horsemen's Bookkeepers: Carla Gilligan, Linda McDermott

Racing Dates

2005: August 27-September 5, 6 days
2006: August 26-September 4, 6 days

Leaders

Recent Meeting, Leading Jockey: Nathan R. Condie, 10, 2005
Recent Meeting, Leading Trainer: Blake L. Cragun, 5, 2005; Shawn H. Davis, 5, 2005
Recent Meeting, Leading Horse: Handsomchamp, 2, 2005; Rodeo Champ, 2, 2005; Crazy Larry's, 2, 2005

Principal Races

Elko County Thoroughbred Futurity, Elko County Thoroughbred Derby

Fastest Times of 2005 (Dirt)

$3\frac{1}{2}$ furlongs: Sixteen Guns, :41.40, September 2, 2005
$5\frac{1}{2}$ furlongs: Primecat, 1:07.30, September 5, 2005
6 furlongs: Jade of the Nile, 1:14, August 28, 2005
$6\frac{1}{2}$ furlongs: Sir Bay Sky, 1:20.20, September 4, 2005
7 furlongs: Handsomchamp, 1:24.30, September 4, 2005
1 mile: Crazy Larrys, 1:42.30, September 5, 2005
$1\frac{5}{16}$ miles: Sam the Man, 2:20.30, September 5, 2005

New Hampshire

Rockingham Park

Location: P.O. Box 47, Salem, N.H. 03079-0047
Phone: (603) 898-2311
Website: *www.rockinghampark.com*
E-Mail: questions@rockinghampark.com
Year Founded: 1906
Dates of Inaugural Meeting: June 28, 1906
Abbreviation: RKM
Acreage: 325
Number of Stalls: 1,400
Seating Capacity: 15,000

Ownership

Rockingham Venture Inc.

Officers

Chairman: Max Hugel
President: Dr. Thomas Carney
General Manager: Edward M. Callahan
Secretary: Kathleen Brothers
Treasurer: Robert G. Tolman
Director of Admissions: Laurence M. Murphy
Director of Marketing: Lynne Snierson
Director of Mutuels: Kathleen Brothers
Vice Presidents: Edward J. Keelan, Edward M. Callahan
Director of Publicity: Lynne Snierson
Director of Simulcasting: Laurence M. Murphy
Track Announcer: John Vitale
Track Photographer: Lawson Brouse
Track Superintendent: Raymond S. Messina
Security: John Burns

Track Layout

Main Circumference: 1 mile
Main Track Chute: 6 furlongs and $1\frac{1}{4}$ miles
Main Width: Homestretch: 83 feet; Backstretch: 55 feet
Main Length of Stretch: 991 feet
Main Turf Circumference: 7 furlongs
Main Turf Chute: $1\frac{1}{8}$ miles

Attendance

Highest Single-Day Record: 41,509, September 6, 1965

Handle

Single-Day On-Track Handle: $2,669,721, September 2, 1968

Leaders

Career, Leading Jockey by Titles: Rudy Baez, 10

Records

Single-Day Jockey Wins: Willie Turnbull, 7, July 31, 1942; Rudy Baez, 7, September 27, 1991
Single Meet, Leading Jockey by Wins: Harry Vega, 302, 1989

Track Records, Main Dirt

4 furlongs: Maria's Brown Eyes, :46$\frac{1}{5}$, May 28, 1987
$4\frac{1}{2}$ furlongs: Kipper Katz, :52.44, June 25, 1997
5 furlongs: Sneaky Pal, :56$\frac{4}{5}$, July 8, 1974
$5\frac{1}{2}$ furlongs: Bama Redd, 1:03$\frac{4}{5}$, May 21, 1987
6 furlongs: Dandy Blitzen, 1:08$\frac{4}{5}$, August 29, 1959
1m 40 yds: Zafarrancho (Arg), 1:38$\frac{1}{5}$, June 19, 1987
$1\frac{1}{16}$ miles: Herbalist, 1:42, August 19, 1972
$1\frac{1}{8}$ miles: Dr. Fager, 1:48$\frac{1}{5}$, July 15, 1967
$1\frac{1}{4}$ miles: Dr. Fager, 1:59$\frac{4}{5}$, September 2, 1967
$1\frac{1}{2}$ miles: Girder, 2:29$\frac{3}{5}$, October 10, 1953
Other: 2m 40 yds, Zagora, 3:34$\frac{2}{5}$, September 2, 1985; $2\frac{1}{4}$ miles, Usable, 3:58$\frac{2}{5}$, September 4, 1978; $2\frac{1}{2}$ miles, Bert Leo B., 4:23$\frac{3}{5}$, July 5, 1978

Track Records, Main Turf

1 mile: Sword Princess, 1:36.20, June 9, 2002

$1\frac{1}{16}$ miles: Simply Majestic, 1:42$\frac{3}{5}$, June 18, 1989; Paris Opera, 1:42$\frac{3}{5}$, July 4, 1990
$1\frac{1}{8}$ miles: Statesmanship, 1:48.49, June 20, 1998
$1\frac{3}{8}$ miles: Autonomo, 2:20.80, June 15, 1991
Other: $1\frac{7}{8}$ miles, Hypnotizer, 3:15$\frac{3}{5}$, August 19, 1989

Interesting Facts

Trivia: Mentioned in the movie "The Sting"

New Jersey

Atlantic City Race Course

When Atlantic City Race Course opened on July 22, 1946, its roster of stockholders read more like the A-list from a Hollywood party than investors in a racetrack in McKee City, 13 miles from the Jersey Shore resort. Bob Hope, Frank Sinatra, Harry James, Xavier Cugat, and Sammy Kaye were among the initial shareholders. John B. Kelly Sr., an Olympic gold-medal rower, brick magnate, and father of the late Princess Grace of Monaco, was Atlantic City's first president. Kelly was succeeded in 1960 by radio and television pioneer Leon Levy, whose son Robert succeeded him. An innovator who arranged the nation's first full-card simulcast from Meadowlands racetrack in September 1983, the younger Levy also raced 1987 Belmont Stakes (G1) winner Bet Twice and champion sprinter Housebuster. Crowds of more than 30,000 turned out to see such races as the United Nations Handicap (G1), first run in 1953, and such outstanding horses as Dr. Fager, Round Table, and Mongo. The disruption of the New Jersey circuit with the 1977 Garden State Park fire and the opening of Atlantic City's first casinos the following year hurt the track's business and led to a gradual reduction in its schedule. Atlantic City conducted a six-day, all-turf meet in 1999 and 2000, and it raced ten days in '01 to qualify for year-round, full-card simulcasting. Atlantic City was sold to Greenwood Racing for $13-million in August 2001. Atlantic City runs a brief, all-turf meet at its McKee City plant each year.

Location: 4501 Black Horse Pike, Mays Landing, N.J. 08330-3142
Phone: (609) 645-5200
Fax: (609) 645-8309
Website: *www.acracecourse.com*
E-Mail: mgallagherbugdon@aol.com
Year Founded: 1944
Dates of Inaugural Meeting: July 22, 1946
Abbreviation: Atl
Acreage: 255
Number of Stalls: 1,602
Seating Capacity: 16,000

Ownership

Greenwood Racing, Inc.

Officers

Chief Executive Officer: Hal Handel
President: Maureen Bugdon
Director of Racing: Sal Sinatra
Treasurer: Anthony D. Ricci
Director of Simulcasting: Jim Miller
Track Announcer: Keith Jones
Track Photographer: John Pantalone
Track Superintendent: William Gatto

Racing Dates

2005: April 28-May 13, 4 days
2006: April 26-May 4, 4 days

Track Layout

Main Circumference: $1\frac{1}{8}$ miles
Main Track Chute: 7 furlongs
Main Width: 100 feet
Main Length of Stretch: 947.29 feet
Main Turf Circumference: 1 mile
Main Turf Width: 100 feet

Attendance

Average Daily Recent Meeting: 3,000, 2005
Total Attendance Recent Meeting: 12,000, 2005

Handle

Average On-Track Recent Meeting: $103,132, 2005
Total On-Track Recent Meeting: $412,528, 2005

Leaders

Recent Meeting, Leading Jockey: Cyril Murphy, 5, 2005; Nick Santagata, 5, 2006
Recent Meeting, Leading Trainer: Thomas H. Voss, 5, 2005; Alan E. Goldberg, 3, 2006
Recent Meeting, Leading Horse: R. Encounter, 2, 2006; Competence, 2, 2006

Track Records, Main Dirt

$4\frac{1}{2}$ furlongs: Jo Jo's Sparkle, :51$\frac{2}{5}$, June 22, 1988
5 furlongs: Dark Tzarina, :56$\frac{2}{5}$, July 16, 1988
$5\frac{1}{2}$ furlongs: Aeronotic, 1:02$\frac{3}{5}$, July 4, 1986
6 furlongs: Margerine, 1:08$\frac{1}{5}$, August 27, 1988
$6\frac{1}{2}$ furlongs: Zartarian, 1:15.80, June 26, 1994
7 furlongs: Mexican General, 1:20$\frac{2}{5}$, July 4, 1977
$1\frac{1}{16}$ miles: Prince of Truth, 1:41, June 28, 1975
$1\frac{1}{8}$ miles: World Appeal, 1:46$\frac{3}{5}$, July 16, 1983
$1\frac{3}{16}$ miles: Mississippi Mud, 1:54$\frac{1}{5}$, August 6, 1977
$1\frac{1}{4}$ miles: Greek Ship, 2:01$\frac{4}{5}$, September 29, 1951
$1\frac{3}{4}$ miles: Abdallati, 3:06$\frac{2}{5}$, November 22, 1973

Track Records, Main Turf

5 furlongs: Chief Whitehair, :56$\frac{2}{5}$, June 28, 1997
$5\frac{1}{2}$ furlongs: Legal Justice, 1:01$\frac{4}{5}$, July 12, 1989
1 mile: Canal, 1:34$\frac{1}{5}$, August 19, 1967
1m 40 yds: Castaneto (Arg), 1:38, June 28, 1991
$1\frac{1}{16}$ miles: Road At Sea, 1:41$\frac{1}{5}$, September 23, 1967; Chiati, 1:41$\frac{1}{5}$, July 6, 1979
$1\frac{1}{8}$ miles: Marco Bay, 1:46.80, June 10, 1994
$1\frac{3}{16}$ miles: Steinlen, 1:52, July 21, 1990
$1\frac{1}{2}$ miles: Advocator, 2:27$\frac{1}{5}$, September 21, 1968
Other: a5 furlongs, Bald Smile, :57.20, August 8, 1996; a$5\frac{1}{2}$ furlongs, Mr. Mink, 1:02$\frac{3}{5}$, September 8, 1967; a1 mile, Silvino, 1:36$\frac{4}{5}$, June 8, 1988; a1m 40yds, First Grade Reader, 1:40.80, June 7, 1991; a$1\frac{1}{16}$ miles, Home Front, 1:43$\frac{2}{5}$, June 12, 1976; a $1\frac{1}{8}$ miles, Emptor, 1:49.80, June 9, 1993; a$1\frac{3}{16}$ miles, Grey Lord II, 1:56$\frac{3}{5}$, September 30, 1969; a$1\frac{1}{2}$ miles, Northern Nights, 2:31.80, July 10, 1996; a$1\frac{7}{16}$ miles, Misty Model, 3:08$\frac{3}{5}$, August 19, 1977; a2 miles, Pier, 3:35$\frac{4}{5}$, September 2, 1977; a$2\frac{1}{16}$ miles, Bangguster, 3:45.80, July 6, 1995; $2\frac{1}{16}$ miles, Sticktoitive, 3:42.80, August, 25, 1993

Fastest Times of 2005 (Turf)

5 furlongs: Tricky Storm, :56.74, May 4, 2005
$5\frac{1}{2}$ furlongs: Max West, 1:03.52, May 5, 2005
1 mile: Dynamia, 1:37.60, May 5, 2005
$1\frac{1}{16}$ miles: A King's Smile, 1:44.99, May 4, 2005
$1\frac{1}{2}$ miles: Charlie Whiskey, 2:31.43, April 29, 2005
$2\frac{1}{8}$ miles: Bow Strada (GB), 4:02.71, April 29, 2005

Monmouth Park

The first Monmouth Park opened in July 1870 and was located three miles from Long Branch, New Jersey. The track's early years included performances by some of the era's most famous horses, including Longfellow and Miss Woodford, the latter the first racehorse to earn $100,000. However, Monmouth fell victim to changing times, and it closed in 1893 after New Jersey outlawed wagering. Fifty years later, pari-mutuel wagering was legalized, and a group of investors led by Amory L. Haskell built a new Monmouth in 1946 at its current location in Oceanport. Since then, the track known for its easy-going seaside ambiance has been a popular destination for some of the sport's leading Thoroughbreds. The track's richest race is the Haskell Invitational Handicap (G1), a $1-million race for three-year-olds and the first major East Coast event after the Triple Crown races. Monmouth also features the United Nations Handicap (G1), which formerly was run at Atlantic City Race Course. The Philip H. Iselin Breeders' Cup Handicap (G3), named in honor of a former Monmouth president, formerly was known as the Monmouth Handicap, which was inaugurated in 1884. In 2007, Monmouth is scheduled to host the Breeders' Cup World Championships.

Location: 175 Oceanport Ave., P.O. Box MP, Oceanport, N.J. 07757
Phone: (732) 222-5100
Fax: (732) 571-1534
Website: *www.monmouthpark.com*
E-Mail: mpinfo@njsea.com
Year Founded: Original: 1870; Current Track: 1946
Dates of Inaugural Meeting: July 30, 1870
Abbreviation: Mth
Acreage: 500
Number of Stalls: 1,600
Seating Capacity: 18,000

Ownership

New Jersey Sports and Exposition Authority

Officers

Chairman: Carl Goldberg
Chief Executive Officer: George R. Zoffinger
President: George R. Zoffinger
General Manager: Robert J. Kulina
Racing Secretary: Michael P. Dempsey
Director of Operations: Horace Smith
Director of Admissions: Joseph J. Cieri
Director of Finance: James Jemas
Director of Marketing: Peter Verdee
Director of Publicity: William Knauf
Director of Simulcasting: John S. Grasty
Horsemen's Liaison: Mary Beth Yates
Stewards: Samuel Boulmetis Sr., Harvey I. Wardell Jr., Stephen Pagano
Track Announcer: Larry Collmus
Track Photographer: Equi-Photo Inc.
Track Superintendent: Dave Harrington
Security: William Kudlacik

Racing Dates

2005: May 14-September 25, 90 days
2006: May 13-September 24, 91 days

Track Layout

Main Circumference: 1 mile
Main Track Chute: 6 furlongs and 1$\frac{1}{4}$ miles
Main Width: Homestretch: 100 feet; Backstretch: 90 feet
Main Length of Stretch: 985 feet
Main Turf Circumference: 7 furlongs
Main Turf Chute: 5 furlongs, 5$\frac{1}{2}$ furlongs, 1$\frac{1}{16}$ miles and 1$\frac{1}{8}$ miles
Main Turf Width: 90 feet

Attendance

Average Daily Recent Meeting: 9,032, 2005
Highest Single-Day Record: 53,638, August 3, 2003
Record Daily Average for Single Meet: 20,907, 1957
Highest Single-Meet Record: 1,150,658, 1981
Total Attendance Recent Meeting: 812,909, 2005

Handle

Average All Sources Recent Meeting: $3,650,844, 2005
Average On-Track Recent Meeting: $1,274,232, 2005
Record Daily Average for Single Meet: $1,997,807, 1970
Single-Day Total Handle All Sources: $12,686,330, August 8, 2004
Total All Sources Recent Meeting: $328,575,939, 2005
Total On-Track Recent Meeting: $114,680,859, 2005
Highest Single-Day Record Recent Meet: $12,571,857, August 7, 2005
Highest Single-Day On-Track Record Recent Meet: $3,702,721, August 7, 2005
Record Average All Sources Single Meet: $4,683,153, 2001
Record Total All Sources for Single Meet: $344,491,242, 2003
Record Total for Single Meet: $155,837,768, 1981

Mutuel Records

Highest Win: $229.20, July 15, 1951
Lowest Win: $2.10, Skip Away, August 30, 1998; $2.10, Silverbulletday, July 10, 1999
Highest Trifecta: $62,172, June 15, 1978
Lowest Trifecta: $15.80, August 4, 2002
Highest Daily Double: $3,962.50, July 19, 1952
Lowest Daily Double: $2.80, June 3, 1995
Lowest Other Exotics: $92.60, Place, July 15, 1951; $79.60, Show, July 28, 2001

Leaders

Career, Leading Jockey by Titles: Joe Bravo, 11
Career, Leading Trainer by Titles: Budd Lepman, 5; John H. Forbes, 5; Juan Serey, 5
Recent Meeting, Leading Jockey: Joe Bravo, 108, 2005
Recent Meeting, Leading Owner: Michael Gill, 13, 2005; Edwin Broome, 13, 2005; Peter Kazamias, 13, 2005
Recent Meeting, Leading Trainer: Kelly John Breen, 38, 2005
Recent Meeting, Leading Horse: Who's the Cowboy, 5, 2005; A Nice Splash, 5, 2005; Truely a Trooper, 5, 2005

Records

Single-Day Jockey Wins: Walter Blum, 6, June 9, 1961; Chris Antley, 6, July 30, 1984; Julie Krone, 6, August 19, 1987; Joe Bravo, 6, August 31, 1994; Joe Bravo, 6, May 18, 2002; Joe Bravo, 6, September 18, 2005
Single-Day Trainer Wins: J. Willard Thompson, 4, September 8, 1975; Robert Klesaris, 4, July 10, 1987; John H. Forbes, 4, August 28, 1989
Single Meet, Leading Jockey by Wins: Chris Antley, 171, 1984
Single Meet, Leading Trainer by Wins: John Tammaro III, 55, 1974; J. Willard Thompson, 55, 1975

Track Records, Main Dirt

5 furlongs: Camden Harbor, :56.22, June 18, 1991
5$\frac{1}{2}$ furlongs: American Royale, 1:02.96, July 21, 1991
6 furlongs: Gilded Time, 1:07.84, August 8, 1992
1 mile: Forty Niner, 1:33$\frac{4}{5}$, July 16, 1988
1m 70 yds: Presidentialaffair, 1:38.85, July 5, 2004
1$\frac{1}{16}$ miles: Formal Gold, 1:40.20, August 23, 1997
1$\frac{1}{8}$ miles: Spend a Buck, 1:46$\frac{4}{5}$, August 17, 1985; Jolie's Halo, 1:46.80, August 8, 1992
1$\frac{3}{16}$ miles: Okamsel, 1:59$\frac{3}{5}$, June 20, 1951
1$\frac{1}{4}$ miles: Carry Back, 2:00$\frac{2}{5}$, July 14, 1962; Majestic Light, 2:00$\frac{2}{5}$, August 30, 1977
1$\frac{1}{2}$ miles: Malibu Moonshine, 2:31.54, June 10, 2006
1$\frac{3}{4}$ miles: *Halconero, 3:04$\frac{1}{5}$, August 5, 1950

Track Records, Main Turf

5 furlongs: Klassy Briefcase, :54.97, June 8, 1991
1 mile: Inkatha (Fr), 1:33.95, May 31, 1999
1$\frac{1}{16}$ miles: Mi Narrow, 1:39.40, July 11, 1999
1$\frac{1}{8}$ miles: Batique, 1:46.19, June 16, 2001
1$\frac{3}{16}$ miles: *Dorienne, 2:01, June 30, 1953
1$\frac{1}{4}$ miles: Muzzle, 2:08$\frac{2}{5}$, July 10, 1953
1$\frac{3}{8}$ miles: Balto Star, 2:12.78, July 5, 2003
1$\frac{1}{2}$ miles: Agacode, 2:29$\frac{2}{5}$, June 14, 1985

Principal Races

Haskell Invitational H. (G1), United Nations S. (G1), Molly Pitcher Breeders' Cup H. (G2), Monmouth Breeders' Cup Oaks (G3), Philip H. Iselin Breeders' Cup H. (G3)

Interesting Facts

Achievements/Milestones: The 53,638 in attendance for the August 3, 2003, Haskell Invitational H. was the largest crowd ever for a horse race in New Jersey.

Fastest Times of 2005 (Dirt)

5 furlongs: Tacirring, :56.48, July 10, 2005
5$\frac{1}{2}$ furlongs: Justawalkinthepark, 1:03.13, September 25, 2005
6 furlongs: Joey P., 1:08.30, July 4, 2005; War's Prospect, 1:08.30, July 17, 2005
1 mile: Clear Terms, 1:36.59, July 9, 2005

1m 70 yds: Tap Day, 1:40.64, May 29, 2005
1$^{1}/_{16}$ miles: Capeside Lady, 1:41.49, July 9, 2005
1$^{1}/_{8}$ miles: Roman Ruler, 1:49.88, August 7, 2005

Fastest Times of 2005 (Turf)

5 furlongs: Weigelia, :55, June 25, 2005
1 mile: Alexandersrun, 1:35.15, June 17, 2005
1$^{1}/_{16}$ miles: Ready's Gal, 1:40.49, June 26, 2005
1$^{1}/_{8}$ miles: A Nice Splash, 1:48.09, July 30, 2005
1$^{3}/_{8}$ miles: Better Talk Now, 2:20.57, July 2, 2005

The Meadowlands

The Meadowlands racetrack, located on former marshland in East Rutherford, has been the economic engine of the Meadowlands Sports Complex. Built by the New Jersey Sports and Exposition Authority for $340-million, the complex includes the Continental Airlines Arena, home of basketball's New Jersey Nets and hockey's New Jersey Devils, and Giants Stadium, where the New York Giants and Jets play football. Meadowlands, which held its first Thoroughbred meet in September 1977, has been host to several memorable events in racing history. In 1978, Dr. Patches upset Seattle Slew in the Paterson Handicap. John Henry, once the sport's all-time leading earner, closed his career with a stunning, come-from-behind victory in the Ballantine's Scotch Classic Handicap in 1984. Four years later, Alysheba set a 1¼-mile track record when he captured the Meadowlands Cup Handicap (G1) during his Horse of the Year campaign. Meadowlands, whose world-renowned Standardbred meet runs from December through August, conducts Thoroughbred racing in the fall.

Location: 50 Route 120, East Rutherford, N.J. 07073-2131
Phone: (201) 843-2446
Fax: (201) 460-4042
Website: *www.thebigm.com*
E-Mail: CHodes@njsea.com
Year Founded: 1976
Dates of Inaugural Meeting: September 6, 1977
Abbreviation: Med
Acreage: 220
Number of Stalls: 1,760
Seating Capacity: 4,587

Ownership

New Jersey Sports and Exposition Authority

Officers

Chairman: Carl J. Goldberg
Chief Executive Officer: George R. Zoffinger
President: George R. Zoffinger
General Manager: Christopher McErlean
Racing Secretary: Michael P. Dempsey
Secretary: Marvin Schmelzer
Treasurer: Joseph M. Forgione
Director of Operations: Marcello Esposito
Director of Admissions: Marianne Rotella
Director of Finance: James Jemas
Director of Marketing: Rachel Ryan
Director of Mutuels: Robert Halpin
Vice President: Dennis O. Dowd
Director of Publicity: Carol Hodes
Director of Simulcasting: Alex Dadoyan
Horsemen's Liaison: Andrea Hanley
Stewards: James Edwards, Stephan Pagano, Harvey I. Wardell Jr.
Track Announcers: Dave Johnson, Sam McKee, Ken Warkentin
Track Photographer: Equi-Photo Inc.
Asst. Racing Secretary: John Perlow

Racing Dates

2005: September 30-November 12, 25 days
2006: September 29-November 11, 30 days

Track Layout

Main Circumference: 1 mile
Main Track Chute: 1¼ miles
Main Track Chute: 6 furlongs
Main Width: Homestretch: 90 feet; Backstretch: 80 feet
Main Length of Stretch: 990 feet
Main Turf Circumference: 7 furlongs

Attendance

Average Daily Recent Meeting: 4,372, 2005
Highest Single-Day Record: 44,462, September 16, 1981
Highest Single-Meet Record: 1,772,209, 1977
Record Daily Average for Single Meet: 17,901, 1977
Total Attendance Recent Meeting: 109,309, 2005
Lowest Single-Meet Record: 109,309, 2005

Handle

Average All Sources Recent Meeting: $1,855,835, 2005
Average On-Track Recent Meeting: $366,795, 2005
Record Daily Average for Single Meet: $2,085,003, 1982
Single-Day Total Handle All Sources: $5,025,645, October 14, 1994
Total All Sources Recent Meeting: $46,395,883, 2005
Total On-Track Recent Meeting: $9,169,883, 2005
Highest Single-Day Record Recent Meet: $2,491,210, October 1, 2005
Record Average All Sources Single Meet: $2,619,909, 1994

Mutuel Records

Highest Win: $354.80, Great Normand, 1990
Lowest Win: $2.20, Spectacular Bid, 1979

Leaders

Career, Leading Jockey by Titles: Joe Bravo, 9
Career, Leading Trainer by Titles: John H. Forbes, 7
Career, Leading Jockey by Stakes Wins: Angel Cordero, 27; Jorge Velasquez, 27
Career, Leading Trainer by Stakes Wins: Philip G. Johnson, 29
Career, Leading Jockey by Wins: Nick Santagata, 986
Career, Leading Trainer by Wins: John H. Forbes, 601
Recent Meeting, Leading Jockey: Joe Bravo, 24, 2005
Recent Meeting, Leading Owner: Ocean View Stables, 7, 2005
Recent Meeting, Leading Trainer: Jason Servis, 15, 2005

Records

Single-Day Jockey Wins: Julie Krone, 6, September 16, 1989
Single-Day Trainer Wins: John H. Forbes, 4, November 8, 1978
Single Meet, Leading Jockey by Wins: Joe Bravo, 142, 1994
Single Meet, Leading Owner by Wins: William C. Martucci, 34, 1990
Single Meet, Leading Trainer by Wins: John H. Forbes, 47, 1982; Joseph Pierce Jr., 47, 1982; John H. Forbes, 47, 1990
Single Meet, Leading Trainer by Stakes Wins: Ben W. Perkins Sr., 7, 1995
Single Meet, Leading Jockey by Stakes Wins: Joe Bravo, 11, 1995
Single Meet, Leading Horse by Wins: Holme Lane, 7, 1985; Crijinsky, 7, 1995
Single Meet, Leading Owner by Stakes Wins: New Farm, 7, 1995

Track Records, Main Dirt

5 furlongs: Platinum Perfect, :55.45, October 29, 2005
5½ furlongs: Red Hot Spot, 1:02.33, October 14, 2003
6 furlongs: Hay Cody, 1:07.81, September 6, 1996
1 mile: Astrologist, 1:34.16, November 8, 2005
1m 70 yds: With Probability, 1:37.90, October 28, 2005
1$^{1}/_{16}$ miles: Black Forest, 1:40.39, September 26, 1998
1$^{1}/_{8}$ miles: Forty One Carats, 1:45.50, October 29, 1999
1$^{3}/_{16}$ miles: Key Lory, 1:53.88, November 20, 1999
1¼ miles: Alysheba, 1:58$^{4}/_{5}$, October 14, 1988

Track Records, Main Turf

5 furlongs: Special Occasion, :55.17, September 4, 2000
1 mile: Beckon the King, 1:33.88, October 19, 2001
1m 70yds: Cape Playhouse, 1:38, October 25, 1978
1$^{1}/_{16}$ miles: Wanderkin, 1:39$^{2}/_{5}$, September 30, 1988
1$^{3}/_{8}$ miles: Rice, 2:12.02, September 25, 1998
Other: a5 furlongs, Tangier Sound, :59.05, November 4, 2002; a1 mile, Onasilverplatter, 1:38.96, October 23, 2002; a1m 70yds, Pyrite Search, 1:44.01, October 24, 2002

Principal Races

Meadowlands Breeders' Cup S. (G2), Pegasus S. (G3), Cliff Hanger H. (G3), Violet H. (G3)

Fastest Times of 2005 (Dirt)

5 furlongs: Platinum Perfect, :55.45, October 29, 2005
5½ furlongs: Slam Bammy, 1:02.37, October 1, 2005
6 furlongs: Been Wavering, 1:08.19, October 29, 2005
1 mile: Astrologist, 1:34.16, November 8, 2005
1m 70 yds: With Probability, 1:37.90, October 28, 2005
1¹⁄₁₆ miles: Ricardo A, 1:41.60, October 29, 2005
1⅛ miles: Magna Graduate, 1:47.47, September 30, 2005

Fastest Times of 2005 (Turf)

5 furlongs: Terrific Challenge, :56.82, October 21, 2005
1 mile: Ground Hero, 1:35.67, September 30, 2005
1m 70 yds: Westmoreland, 1:39.73, October 1, 2005
1¹⁄₁₆ miles: Movie Star (Brz), 1:41.21, September 30, 2005
1⅜ miles: Rumor Has It, 2:14.31, November 5, 2005
2½ miles: Preemptive Strike, 4:17.60, October 1, 2005

New Mexico

Ruidoso Downs

Located 7,000 feet above sea level in the pine-covered mountains of southeastern New Mexico, Ruidoso Downs long has been a popular destination for Southwestern horsemen and racing fans seeking to escape the summer heat. Since 1959, the track has held Quarter Horse racing's richest and most famous event, the All American Futurity, which in 1978 became the world's first $1-million horse race. Leading trainers such as D. Wayne Lukas and Bob Baffert raced Quarter Horses at Ruidoso before switching to Thoroughbred racing. Thoroughbred racing also is a fixture at Ruidoso, where purses have increased significantly due to revenues from the Billy the Kid Casino, which opened at the track in 1999. Ruidoso has a unique track configuration for the two breeds that compete at the track. A separate straightaway for Quarter Horses is located on the outside of the seven-furlong Thoroughbred oval.

Location: 1461 Highway 70 W., P.O. Box 449, Ruidoso Downs, N.M. 88346-0449
Phone: (505) 378-4431
Fax: (505) 378-8525
Website: *www.ruidosodownsracing.com*
E-Mail: info@ruidosodownsracing.com
Year Founded: 1946
Dates of Inaugural Meeting: July 1, 1947
Abbreviation: Rui
Number of Stalls: 2,000
Seating Capacity: 7,000

Ownership

R. D. Hubbard

Officers

Chairman: R. D. Hubbard
President: Bruce Rimbo
General Manager: Rick Baugh
Director of Racing: Ryan Sherman
Racing Secretary: Robert Junk
Secretary: Edward Burger
Treasurer: Edward Burger
Director of Operations: Neal Mullarky
Director of Marketing: Jodi Jablonski
Director of Mutuels: Deano McTeigue
Vice President: Edward Burger
Director of Publicity: Ty Wyant
Director of Simulcasting: Kristian Lovelace
Horsemen's Liaison: Vicki McCabe
Stewards: Vickie Eikleberry, Kenny Hart, Jerry Nicodemus, Rueben Rivera
Track Announcer: Robert Fox
Track Photographer: Bill Pitt
Track Superintendent: Terry Brown
Security: Richard Swenor

Racing Dates

2005: May 27-September 5, 60 days
2006: May 26-September 4, 60 days

Track Layout

Main Circumference: 7 furlongs
Main Track Chute: 6 furlongs and 1⅛ miles
Main Width: 75 feet
Main Length of Stretch: 656 feet

Attendance

Average Daily Recent Meeting: 3,980, 2005
Highest Single-Day Record: 17,009, September 2, 2002
Total Attendance Recent Meeting: 238,801, 2005

Handle

Average All Sources Recent Meeting: $328,615, 2005
Average On-Track Recent Meeting: $167,058, 2005
Total All Sources Recent Meeting: $19,716,889, 2005
Total On-Track Recent Meeting: $10,023,455, 2005
Highest Single-Day Record Recent Meet: $1,293,325, September 5, 2005

Leaders

Recent Meeting, Leading Jockey: Alfredo J. Juarez Jr., 37, 2005
Recent Meeting, Leading Owner: Tricar Stables Inc., 11, 2005
Recent Meeting, Leading Trainer: Henry Dominguez, 21, 2005
Recent Meeting, Leading Horse: Dancing Moves, 3, 2005; Chili Dan, 3, 2005; Dos Amigos, 3, 2005; Saint of the City, 3, 2005; Nextiger, 3, 2005

Track Records, Main Dirt

4½ furlongs: Professor Jones, :51.60, July 15, 2005
5 furlongs: Twilight Diamond, :56.60, July 17, 2004
5½ furlongs: Rocky Gulch, 1:02.80, August 1, 2004
6 furlongs: Jack Wilson, 1:08.80, August 16, 1992; Ninety Nine Jack, 1:08.80, July 18, 2004
6½ furlongs: Mr. Tattoo, 1:17⅗, July 4, 1973
7 furlongs: Fill Mackis Cup, 1:24⅖, July 15, 1984
7½ furlongs: Caliban, 1:29.40, July 19, 2003
1 mile: Set Records, 1:37, July 28, 1995; Strong Arm Robbery, 1:37, September 1, 2001
1m 70 yds: Brogander, 1:45⅕, January 1, 1954
1¹⁄₁₆ miles: Lucky Bluff, 1:43.40, September 2, 2001
1⅛ miles: Brownburough, 1:51⅖, June 28, 1964
1¼ miles: Pentelipiano, 2:07.60, September 1, 2003
1⅜ miles: Start Jumpin, 2:24⅕, August 18, 1990
1½ miles: Decidedly Henry C., 2:37, August 19, 1989
1⅝ miles: More Than Glory, 2:52⅘, August 15, 1992
Other: 2½ furlongs, Crafty Number, :27.80, August 18, 2001

Principal Races

Ruidoso Thoroughbred Derby, Ruidoso Thoroughbred Championship H., Ruidoso Mile H., Norgor Derby, First Lady H.

Fastest Times of 2005 (Dirt)

4½ furlongs: Professor Jones, :51.60, July 15, 2005
5 furlongs: Ferrara Raider, :57.40, June 5, 2005; Sky Diver, :57.40, July 15, 2005
5½ furlongs: Rockin the Ship, 1:03, June 9, 2005
6 furlongs: Blue Song, 1:09, June 18, 2005
7½ furlongs: Castner, 1:31.40, June 17, 2005
1 mile: Caliban, 1:39, June 19, 2005
1¹⁄₁₆ miles: Don't Strike Out, 1:45, September 5, 2005
1⅛ miles: Swelter, 1:56.60, August 14, 2005
1¼ miles: Swelter, 2:11.60, September 5, 2005

Sunland Park

Opened in 1959, Sunland Park was built just across the state line from El Paso, Texas, in New Mexico, which unlike its neighbor allowed pari-mutuel wagering. Sunland launched the career of several notable horsemen and horses. Jerry Bailey, one of Thoroughbred racing's all-time leading riders, began his career at the track in 1974. Bold Ego, who won Sunland's Riley Allison Futurity in 1980, captured the '81 Arkansas Derby (G1) and ran second in the Preakness Stakes (G1). In the mid-1990s, the track nearly closed because of competition from Native American casinos and pari-mutuel racing in Texas and Oklahoma. New Mexico horsemen and racetracks successfully lobbied for legalizing slot machines at tracks, and Sunland's casino opened in February 1999. With a portion of casino revenues earmarked to purses, the quality of racing improved significantly.

Location: 1200 Futurity Dr., Sunland Park, N.M. 88063-9057
Phone: (505) 874-5200
Fax: (505) 589-1518
Website: *www.sunland-park.com*
E-Mail: sunlandinfo@sunland-park.com
Year Founded: 1959
Dates of Inaugural Meeting: October 9, 1959
Abbreviation: Sun
Number of Stalls: 1,600
Seating Capacity: 5,710

Ownership

Stan E. Fulton

Officers

General Manager: Harold Payne
Director of Racing: Dustin A. Dix
Racing Secretary: Norm Amundson
Director of Marketing: T'rassa Brown
Director of Mutuels: Christian Kettelhut
Director of Publicity: Eric Alwan
Stewards: Vickie Eikleberry, Kenneth Hart, Jerry Nicodemus, Ruben Rivera
Track Announcer: Robert Geller
Track Photographer: Coady Photography
Track Superintendent: Bob Patty

Racing Dates

2005: November 5, 2004-April 3, 2005, 87 days
2006: December 2, 2005-April 16, 2006, 79 days
2007: December 15, 2006-April 29, 2007

Track Layout

Main Circumference: 1 mile
Main Track Chute: 6½ furlongs and 1¼ miles
Main Width: 80 feet
Main Length of Stretch: 990 feet

Handle

Average All Sources Recent Meeting: $733,478, 2004/2005; $744,572, 2005/2006
Average On-Track Recent Meeting: $125,311, 2004/2005; $101,852, 2005/2006
Single-Day Total Handle All Sources: $2,194,229, February 3, 2004
Total All Sources Recent Meeting: $63,812,618, 2004/2005; $70,046,374, 2005/2006
Total On-Track Recent Meeting: $10,902,019, 2004/2005; $8,046,292, 2005/2006
Highest Single-Day Record Recent Meet: $1,939,906, January 3, 2006

Leaders

Career, Leading Jockey by Titles: Bobby Harmon, 8
Career, Leading Trainer by Titles: Bob E. Arnett, 12
Recent Meeting, Leading Jockey: Ken S. Tohill, 109, 2004/2005; Ken S. Tohill, 91, 2005/2006
Recent Meeting, Leading Owner: Harry L. Veruchi, 34, 2004/2005; Kirk and Judy Robison, 15, 2005/2006
Recent Meeting, Leading Trainer: Steve Asmussen, 47, 2004/2005; Henry Dominguez, 50, 2005/2006
Recent Meeting, Leading Horse: Cassie's Casper, 6, 2004/2005; Daring Pegasus, 6, 2004/2005; Fearless Anthony, 5, 2005/2006

Track Records, Main Dirt

4 furlongs: Tamran's Jet, :44⅘, March 22, 1968; Western Hand, :44⅘, April 7, 1979
4½ furlongs: Bold Liz, :50⅖, March 25, 1972
5 furlongs: Jimmy Jones, :55.90, February 7, 2004
5½ furlongs: Treasure Hunt, 1:02.39, January 28, 2003
6 furlongs: Yet Anothernatalie, 1:08.24, December 11, 2004
6½ furlongs: Bang, 1:14.29, March 6, 2004
1 mile: Mr. Trieste, 1:35.38, December 7, 2004
1$^1/_{16}$ miles: Butte City, 1:41.92, December 12, 2004
1⅛ miles: Winsham Lad, 1:48⅕, January 8, 1961; Prenupcial, 1:48⅕, April 28, 1962
1$^3/_{16}$ miles: Mickey J., 1:58⅕, November 14, 1970
1¼ miles: Curribot, 2:01⅖, May 6, 1984
1⅜ miles: Hot Deck, 2:19⅖, January 10, 1970
1½ miles: Houston Blaze, 2:33⅕, May 3, 1964
1⅝ miles: Rush Line, 2:47⅗, April 6, 1969
Other: 2 furlongs, Becky's Star, :21⅕, February 12, 1968; 3 furlongs, Sarah Dier, :33⅗, March 31, 1962

Principal Races

WinStar Derby, WinStar Sundland Park Oaks, Copper Top Futurity, Harry W. Henson Breeders' Cup H.

Interesting Facts

Achievements/Milestones: Casino opened February 2, 1999

Fastest Times of 2005 (Dirt)

2 furlongs: Manolito, :21.26, March 1, 2005
4½ furlongs: Rocky Gulch, :50.65, March 27, 2005
5 furlongs: Artesian, :56.26, February 20, 2005
5½ furlongs: Racing Nut, 1:02.79, February 11, 2005
6 furlongs: Beyond Brilliant, 1:08.70, April 2, 2005
6½ furlongs: Proud Cardenal, 1:15.21, March 5, 2005
1 mile: Blue Song, 1:35.61, April 2, 2005
1$^1/_{16}$ miles: Southern Africa, 1:43.18, February 27, 2005
1⅛ miles: Thor's Echo, 1:49.59, April 2, 2005
1¼ miles: Double Intrigue, 2:06.82, April 3, 2005

SunRay Park

SunRay Park in Farmington, New Mexico, is located in an area called the Four Corners region, where northwestern New Mexico, northeastern Arizona, southeastern Utah, and southwestern Colorado meet. The racetrack, which offers Thoroughbred and Quarter Horse racing, originally was known as San Juan Downs; it was built by San Juan County at the county fairgrounds and opened in 1984. Declining business forced the track to close after its 1993 season. SunRay Gaming of New Mexico LLC secured a ten-year option to operate the track, which was renamed SunRay Park and reopened in October 1999. SunRay Gaming's interest in reviving horse racing at the facility largely was based on its ability to operate a casino with slot machines. A portion of revenues from the slots enhances race purses.

Location: 39 Rd. 5568, Farmington, N.M. 87401-1466
Phone: (505) 566-1200
Fax: (505) 326-4292
Website: *www.sunraygaming.com*
E-Mail: racing@sunraygaming.com
Year Founded: 1984 as San Juan Downs; 1999 as SunRay Park
Abbreviation: SrP
Number of Stalls: 1,298
Seating Capacity: 3,000

Ownership

SunRay Gaming of New Mexico LLC

Officers

General Manager: Byron Campbell
Director of Racing: Lonnie S. Barber Jr.
Racing Secretary: Hank Demoney
Director of Mutuels: Natalie Swisher
Director of Simulcasting: Toni Authurs
Stewards: Bob Allison, Jan Booth, Jerry T. Goss
Track Announcer: Michael Wrona
Track Photographer: Coady Photography
Track Superintendent: Gary Kretschmer
Security: Leonard Demoney
Horsemen's Bookkeeper: Toby Demoney
Asst. Racing Secretary: Gordon Graham

Racing Dates

2005: July 2-September 5, 38 days
2006: June 16-September 4, 48 days

Attendance
Average Daily Recent Meeting: 3,133, 2005
Total Attendance Recent Meeting: 119,044, 2005

Handle
Average All Sources Recent Meeting: $164,093, 2005
Average On-Track Recent Meeting: $25,600, 2005
Total All Sources Recent Meeting: $6,235,564, 2005
Total On-Track Recent Meeting: $972,812, 2005

Leaders
Recent Meeting, Leading Jockey: Quyet E. Bui, 24, 2005
Recent Meeting, Leading Owner: David Wolochuck, 2005
Recent Meeting, Leading Trainer: Kenny Chadborn, 13, 2005
Recent Meeting, Leading Horse: Amoreena, 3, 2005; Nycity, 3, 2005; Thegirlsgotrhythm, 3, 2005

Track Records, Main Dirt
4 furlongs: Absolutely True, :44.60, November 16, 2003
4½ furlongs: Sky Diver, :49.80, October 10, 2003
6 furlongs: Unbridled Set, 1:11.40, October 11, 1999
6½ furlongs: Herecomesthemannow, 1:15.60, September 22, 2003
7 furlongs: Oh Gracie, 1:22.60, September 25, 2000
7½ furlongs: Dalt's Kingpin, 1:28.60, November 17, 2003
1 mile: Ben Told, 1:35.60, October 15, 2000
1⅛ miles: Line Guage, 1:48.80, November 21, 1999

Principal Races
San Juan County Commissioners H., New Mexico Distaff H., New Mexico Breeders' Association H., Aztec Oaks, Totah Futurity

Fastest Times of 2005 (Dirt)
4½ furlongs: Scotchwater, :50, August 15, 2005
6½ furlongs: Stone Canyon, 1:16.80, September 3, 2005
7 furlongs: Suspicious Minds, 1:23.20, July 18, 2005
7½ furlongs: J. D. Tyler, 1:32, August 26, 2005
1 mile: Suspicious Minds, 1:37, August 5, 2005
1⅛ miles: Mr. Trieste, 1:50, September 5, 2005

The Downs at Albuquerque

The Downs at Albuquerque, located on the New Mexico State Fairgrounds in Albuquerque, features Thoroughbred and Quarter Horse racing each spring and during the 17-day New Mexico State Fair in September. The fair dates from 1881, while its race meet, which opened in October 1938, is the oldest in New Mexico. The New Mexico State Fair Futurity for Quarter Horses debuted in 1946 and is the oldest continuously run stakes race for the breed. One notable Thoroughbred horseman who competed at Albuquerque early in his career was jockey Mike Smith, a New Mexico native who became a Racing Hall of Fame member in 2003. In 1990, the track debuted The Lineage, a day of racing exclusively for state-bred Thoroughbreds and Quarter Horses. With assistance from its slots casino, which opened in 1999, the track has been able to solidify its business and increase purses.

Location: 201 California St. N.E., Albuquerque, N.M. 87108-1802
Phone: (505) 266-5555
Fax: (505) 268-1970
Website: *www.abqdowns.com*
E-Mail: michaell@abqdowns.com
Year Founded: 1938
Dates of Inaugural Meeting: October 1938
Abbreviation: Alb
Number of Stalls: 1,700

Officers
President: Paul Blanchard
General Manager: Craig Smith
Racing Secretary: Scott Golightly
Treasurer: Bill Windham
Director of Operations: Beth McKinney
Director of Finance: Charles DeNolf
Director of Marketing: Michael Lazarus
Director of Mutuels: Barbra Hewson
Vice President: John Turner, O. D. McDonald
Director of Simulcasting: Beth McKinney
Track Superintendent: Tony Martinez

Racing Dates
2005: April 2-June 12, 42 days; September 9-September 25, 17 days
2006: March 18-June 11, 51 days; September 8-September 24, 17 days

Track Layout
Main Circumference: 1 mile
Main Track Chute: 2 furlongs and 7 furlongs
Main Width: 90 feet
Main Length of Stretch: 1,114 feet

Attendance
Highest Single-Day Record: 13,979, September 16, 1990

Track Records, Main Dirt
4 furlongs: Chipper J., :45.76, May 6, 2001
4½ furlongs: Silver Matt, :51.22, June 17, 2000
5 furlongs: Scout Revolt, :56.35, December 12, 1998
5½ furlongs: Yulla Yulla, 1:01.68, September 23, 2000
6 furlongs: Streak of Royalty, 1:08.43, April 23, 2005
6½ furlongs: Ben Told, 1:14.59, May 10, 2002
7 furlongs: Mighty Classy, 1:21, September 18, 1989; Star Smasher, 1:21.01, June 9, 2002
1 mile: Lester's Boy, 1:35.74, April 27, 2002
1m 70 yds: Fire Knight, 1:41⅗, September 26, 1959
1$^1/_{16}$ miles: Ciento, 1:40.60, September 22, 2001
1⅛ miles: Brew, 1:48.47, June 3, 2001
1$^3/_{16}$ miles: Savage Wind, 2:05⅘, September 23, 1981
1¼ miles: Luedke, 2:03.69, April 14, 1996
1½ miles: Luedke, 2:33.73, September 25, 1994
1⅝ miles: Vikings Shield, 2:43⅖, April 17, 1988
1¾ miles: Prince De-Or, 2:59⅕, September 25, 1966
2 miles: Betty Falcon, 3:28⅗ October 7, 1956
Other: 1$^{13}/_{16}$ miles, Vermejo, 3:05⅖, September 27, 1970

Principal Races
The Downs at Albuquerque H.

Fastest Times of 2005 (Dirt)
5 furlongs: Joe Somebody, :57.06, September 15, 2005
5½ furlongs: Absolutely True, 1:02.94, September 17, 2005
6 furlongs: Streak of Royalty, 1:08.43, April 23, 2005
6½ furlongs: J J Mystique, 1:15.97, April 15, 2005
7 furlongs: Venture Cat, 1:21.51, June 5, 2005
1 mile: Bayou the Moon, 1:36.40, May 7, 2005
1$^1/_{16}$ miles: Money Set, 1:44.53, May 29, 2005
1⅛ miles: Bayou the Moon, 1:49.69, September 25, 2005
1½ miles: Julie's Wild Child, 2:37.86, June 12, 2005
1$^{13}/_{16}$ miles: Billy Bird, 3:11.61, September 25, 2005

Zia Park

The fifth and newest racetrack in New Mexico, Zia Park is located in the southeast desert plains of Hobbs near the Texas border. Opened in September 2005 , Zia Park hosts Thoroughbred and Quarter Horse racing. The complex also includes the Black Gold Casino, a simulcast pavilion, several restaurants, and a hotel. The track presents New Mexico Cup day, with seven stakes races for New Mexico-bred Thoroughbreds and four stakes races for New Mexico-bred Quarter Horses, with purses that totaled $1.4-million in its inaugural year. At the beginning of the first season, all 1,500 stalls were filled, and the 2005 meeting surpassed $10-million in handle. The track is named for the cross-like symbol on the state's flag, and is closely associated with Ruidoso Downs; both tracks are principally owned by R. D. Hubbard, and Bruce Rimbo is the president of both.

Location: 3901 W. Millen Dr., Hobbs, N.M. 88240
Phone: (505) 492-7000
Phone: (888) 942-7275

Website: *www.blackgoldcasino.net*
E-Mail: info@blackgoldcasino.net
Dates of Inaugural Meeting: September 23-December 4, 2005
Abbreviation: Zia

Racing Dates

2005: September 23-December 4, 44 days
2006: September 22-December 11, 44 days

Handle

Average All Sources Recent Meeting: $229,278, 2005
Total All Sources Recent Meeting: $10,088,240, 2005

Leaders

Recent Meeting, Leading Jockey: Ken S. Tohill, 52, 2005
Recent Meeting, Leading Owner: Dennis D. Ward, 4, 2005; Rita J. Danley, 4, 2005; Richard W. Lueck, 4, 2005
Recent Meeting, Leading Trainer: Henry Dominquez, 17, 2005
Recent Meeting, Leading Horse: Devon Rules, 3, 2005; Brown Chequer, 3, 2005; Mr. Trieste, 3, 2005

Track Records, Main Dirt

4½ furlongs: Clever Assault, :52.80, December 2, 2005
5 furlongs: Orphan Brigade, :56.60, October 31, 2005; Thyer's (Brz), :56.60, November 18, 2005
5½ furlongs: Jilted Heart, 1:02.60, October 1, 2005
6 furlongs: Ashby Hill, 1:08.60, October 22, 2005
6½ furlongs: Jungle Prince, 1:15, December 4, 2005
1 mile: Mr. Trieste, 1:36.60, October 22, 2005
1 1/16 miles: Mr. Trieste, 1:43, November 12, 2005
1⅛ miles: Mr. Trieste, 1:56.60, December 4, 2005
1½ miles: Billy Bird, 2:35.20, December 4, 2005

Notable Events

New Mexico Cup Day

Fastest Times of 2005 (Dirt)

4½ furlongs: Clever Assault, :52.80, December 2, 2005
5 furlongs: Orphan Brigade, :56.60, October 31, 2005; Thyer's (Brz), :56.60, November 18, 2005
5½ furlongs: Jilted Heart, 1:02.60, October 1, 2005
6 furlongs: Ashby Hill, 1:08.60, October 22, 2005
6½ furlongs: Jungle Prince, 1:15, December 4, 2005
1 mile: Mr. Trieste, 1:36.60, October 22, 2005
1 1/16 miles: Mr. Trieste, 1:43, November 12, 2005
1½ miles: Billy Bird, 2:35.20, December 4, 2005

New York

Aqueduct

Occupying roughly half of the New York Racing Association's year-round schedule, the track known as the Big A offers racing in winter, spring, and fall. Aqueduct opened as a six-furlong track in New York's Queens Borough on September 27, 1894. Site of the only triple dead heat in a stakes race—Brownie, Bossuet, and Wait a Bit hit the wire together in the Carter Handicap on June 10, 1944—Aqueduct was torn down in '56 and completely rebuilt over three years. For four years, from 1964 through '67, Aqueduct played host to the Belmont Stakes while Belmont Park was rebuilt. An all-time record crowd of 73,435 watched Gun Bow win the Metropolitan Handicap on Memorial Day, May 31, 1965. In 1975, the one-mile inner dirt track was completed, allowing racing throughout the winter. Six years later, Aqueduct opened Equestris, a 300-foot-long, $7-million facility for 1,600 diners. A $3-million renovation in 1985 prior to its only Breeders' Cup championship day expanded Aqueduct's paddock and grandstand. The spring meet's principal race is the Wood Memorial Stakes (G1), a Kentucky Derby (G1) prep, and the Cigar Mile Handicap (G1) is one of its fall features. The New York Legislature in 2001 authorized video-lottery terminals to be installed at the track, and a slot-machine contractor, MGM Mirage, was chosen in 2003.

Location: 1100 Rockaway Blvd., P.O. Box 90, Jamaica, N.Y. 11417
Phone: (718) 641-4700
Fax: (718) 322-3814
Website: *www.nyra.com/aqueduct*
E-Mail: nyra@nyra.com
Year Founded: 1894
Dates of Inaugural Meeting: September 27, 1894
Abbreviation: Aqu
Capsule Description: The Big A
Acreage: 192
Number of Stalls: 547
Seating Capacity: 17,000

Ownership

New York Racing Association Inc.

Officers

Chief Executive Officer: Charles E. Hayward
Chairman: C. Steven Duncker
Vice Chairmen: Michael J. DelGiudice, Stuart Subotnick
President: Charles E. Hayward
Vice President: William A. Nader
Racing Secretary: Paul J. Campo
Treasurer: Irene M. Posio
Director of Admissions: Jerry A. Davis Jr.
Director of Mutuels: Patrick Mahony
Director of Simulcasting: Elizabeth Bracken
Horsemen's Liaison: Carmen Barrera
Stewards: Braulio Baeza Jr., Carmine Donofrio, Dr. W. Theodore Hill
Track Announcer: Tom Durkin
Track Photographer: Adam Coglianese, Bob Coglianese
Track Superintendent: Jerry Porcelli
Security: Kenneth T. Cook

Racing Dates

2005: January 1-May 1, 82 days; November 2-December 31, 38 days
2006: January 1-April 30, 81 days; October 25-December 31, 45 days

Track Layout

Main Circumference: 1⅛ miles
Main Track Chute: 1 mile
Main Width: 100 feet
Main Length of Stretch: 1,155.6 feet
Main Turf Circumference: 7 furlongs, 43 feet
Main Turf Chute: 1⅛ miles
Inner Circumference: 1 mile

Attendance

Average Daily Recent Meeting: 3,217, Winter/Spring 2005; 2,822, Fall 2005; 3,063, Winter/Spring 2006
Highest Single-Day Record: 73,435, May 31, 1965
Total Attendance Recent Meeting: 263,776, Winter/Spring 2005; 107,236, Fall 2005; 248,110, Winter/Spring 2006

Handle

Average All Sources Recent Meeting: $8,307,757, Winter/Spring 2005; $8,164,319, Fall 2005; $8,521,060, Winter/Spring 2006
Average On-Track Recent Meeting: $1,107,978, Winter/Spring 2005; $1,080,969, Fall 2005; $1,158,233, Winter/Spring 2006
Single-Day On-Track Handle: $8,171,520, November 2, 1985
Total All Sources Recent Meeting: $681,236,048, Winter/Spring 2005; $310,244,137, Fall 2005; $690,205,866, Winter/Spring 2006
Total On-Track Recent Meeting: $90,854,216, Winter/Spring 2005; $41,076,804, Fall 2005; $93,816,864, Winter/Spring 2006

Mutuel Records

Highest Win: $434, Markobob, September 3, 1943
Highest Pick 6: $1,120,287, January 17, 2004

Leaders

Recent Meeting, Leading Jockey: Rafael Bejarano, 93, Winter/Spring 2005; John Velazquez, 23, Fall 2005; Eibar Coa, 114, Winter/Spring 2006
Recent Meeting, Leading Trainer: Richard Dutrow Jr., 53, Winter/Spring 2005; Todd Pletcher, 16, Fall 2005; Gary C. Contessa, 67, Winter/Spring 2006
Recent Meeting, Leading Horse: Magnolia Jackson, 4, Winter/Spring 2006; American Quest, 4, Winter/Spring 2006; Gold Gunner, 4, Winter/Spring 2006

Records

Single-Day Jockey Wins: Michael Venezia, 6, December 7, 1964; Rudy L. Turcotte, 6, December 2, 1969; Angel Cordero Jr., 6, March 12, 1975; Ron Turcotte, 6, March 5, 1976; Steve Cauthen, 6, January 22, 1977; Steve Cauthen, 6, April 7, 1977; Steve Cauthen, 6, November 29, 1977; Mike Smith, 6, January 13, 1992; Mike Smith, 6, January 30, 1992; Jorge Chavez, 6, February 18, 1996; Shaun Bridgmohan, 6, February 15, 1998

Track Records, Main Dirt

$4\frac{1}{2}$ furlongs: About to Burst, :51$\frac{3}{5}$, April 26, 1984
5 furlongs: Bazaar Change, :57, June 6, 1963
$5\frac{1}{2}$ furlongs: Raise a Native, 1:02$\frac{3}{5}$, July 17, 1963
6 furlongs: Kelly Kip, 1:07.54, April 10, 1999
$6\frac{1}{2}$ furlongs: Coronado's Quest, 1:14.35, October 26, 1997
7 furlongs: Artax, 1:20.04, May 2, 1999
$7\frac{1}{2}$ furlongs: Imafavoritetrick, 1:28.54, November 27, 2004
1 mile: Easy Goer, 1:32$\frac{2}{5}$, April 8, 1989
$1\frac{1}{16}$ miles: McDee, 1:39.45, November 13, 1993
$1\frac{1}{8}$ miles: Riva Ridge, 1:47, October 15, 1973
$1\frac{3}{16}$ miles: Riva Ridge, 1:52$\frac{2}{5}$, July 4, 1973
$1\frac{1}{4}$ miles: Damascus, 1:59$\frac{1}{5}$, July 20, 1968
$1\frac{3}{8}$ miles: Demi's Bret, 2:12.31, October 26, 1997
$1\frac{1}{2}$ miles: Going Abroad, 2:26$\frac{1}{5}$, October 12, 1964
$1\frac{5}{8}$ miles: Sharp Gray, 2:40$\frac{2}{5}$, December 13, 1975
$1\frac{3}{4}$ miles: Malmo, 2:53.73, March 30, 1996
2 miles: Kelso, 3:19$\frac{1}{5}$, October 31, 1964
Other: $1\frac{5}{16}$ miles, Gold Star Deputy, 2:07.32, April 10, 1999; $1\frac{7}{8}$ miles, Erin Bright, 3:12$\frac{4}{5}$, April 18, 1985; $2\frac{1}{4}$ miles, Paraje, 3:47$\frac{4}{5}$, December 15, 1973

Track Records, Main Turf

1 mile: Possible Mate, 1:34$\frac{3}{5}$, November 1, 1985; Tax Dodge, 1:34$\frac{3}{5}$, November 1, 1985 (Dead Heat)
$1\frac{1}{16}$ miles: Spindrift (Ire), 1:40.88, May 6, 2000
$1\frac{1}{8}$ miles: Slew the Dragon, 1:47, November 3, 1985
$1\frac{3}{8}$ miles: Fluorescent Light, 2:14$\frac{1}{5}$, November 7, 1978
$1\frac{1}{2}$ miles: Pebbles (GB), 2:27, November 2, 1985
2 miles: Putting Green, 3:30$\frac{2}{5}$, November 23, 1984

Track Records, Inner Dirt

4 furlongs: Native Moment, :53$\frac{2}{5}$, April 2, 1979
$4\frac{1}{2}$ furlongs: Call Me Up, :52.29, April 16, 1998
$5\frac{1}{2}$ furlongs: Melodeeman, 1:03.94, January 20, 2006
6 furlongs: Captain Red, 1:07.93, February 26, 2003
1 mile: Tejano Couture, 1:35.79, March 9, 2000
1m 70yds: Carry My Colors, 1:38.92, February 5, 2000
$1\frac{1}{16}$ miles: Autoroute, 1:41, December 19, 1992
$1\frac{1}{8}$ miles: Conveyor, 1:47.33, March 6, 1993
$1\frac{3}{16}$ miles: Victoriously, 1:54.42, January 25, 1998
$1\frac{1}{4}$ miles: Transient Trend, 2:01.53, December 21, 1995
$1\frac{1}{2}$ miles: Piling, 2:29$\frac{3}{5}$, March 13, 1983
$1\frac{5}{8}$ miles: Relaxing, 2:42$\frac{2}{5}$, December 13, 1980
$1\frac{3}{4}$ miles: Sophie's Friend, 2:56.73, February 10, 1996
2 miles: Charlie Coast, 3:24$\frac{4}{5}$, February 21, 1979
Other: $2\frac{1}{16}$ miles, Rollix, 3:38$\frac{4}{5}$, February 3, 1983; $2\frac{1}{8}$ miles, Peat Moss, 3:40$\frac{3}{5}$, January 31, 1981; $2\frac{1}{4}$ miles, Field Cat, 3:51$\frac{4}{5}$, December 31, 1981

Principal Races

Wood Memorial S. (G1), Carter H. (G1), Cigar Mile H. (G1), Demoiselle S. (G2), Remsen S. (G2)

Notable Events

First East Coast track to host Breeders' Cup in 1985.

Fastest Times of 2005 (Dirt)

$4\frac{1}{2}$ furlongs: May Day Vow, :52.30, April 22, 2005
$5\frac{1}{2}$ furlongs: Volatility, 1:02.71, April 15, 2005
6 furlongs: Uncle Camie, 1:08.79, April 10, 2005
$6\frac{1}{2}$ furlongs: Jet Prospector, 1:15.49, March 26, 2005
7 furlongs: Forest Danger, 1:20.46, April 9, 2005
1 mile: Sir Greeley, 1:34.19, April 14, 2005
1m 70 yds: Tales of Glory, 1:40.80, January 6, 2005
$1\frac{1}{16}$ miles: Neon Magic, 1:43.08, January 13, 2005
$1\frac{1}{8}$ miles: Bellamy Road, 1:47.16, April 9, 2005
$1\frac{3}{16}$ miles: Owns the Place, 1:55.65, January 13, 2005
$1\frac{1}{4}$ miles: Runaway Russy, 2:04.15, March 11, 2005
$1\frac{5}{8}$ miles: Navesink River, 2:44.96, December 31, 2005

Fastest Times of 2005 (Turf)

1 mile: Pa Pa Da, 1:34.87, April 20, 2005
$1\frac{1}{16}$ miles: Settle Up, 1:41.95, November 8, 2005
$1\frac{1}{8}$ miles: Tomorrows Champ, 1:51.73, April 29, 2005
$1\frac{3}{8}$ miles: King's Drama (Ire), 2:15.37, November 12, 2005
$1\frac{1}{2}$ miles: Olaya, 2:30.28, November 5, 2005

Belmont Park

With a $1\frac{1}{2}$-mile oval, Belmont Park on Long Island is the largest racetrack in North America, and its huge grandstand has a 90,000-person capacity. Originally built for $2.5-million and opened on May 4, 1905, Belmont is host to the third leg of the Triple Crown, the Belmont Stakes (G1), which was named for German-born financier August Belmont I. The first Belmont Stakes was run in 1867 at Jerome Park and was moved to Morris Park in '90. Within a few years of Belmont's opening, antigambling legislation shut the track in 1911 and '12. The track reopened in 1913. The grandstand was rebuilt in 1920, raising Seating Capacity to 17,500. In 1963, deterioration of the grandstand forced a five-year closure while the current facility was constructed for $30.7-million. In those years, the Belmont and most of the track's races and dates were run at Aqueduct. Belmont has played host to four runnings of the Breeders' Cup World Championships, in 1990, '95, 2001, and '05. The 2001 running of the championship event marked the first international sporting event to be held in the New York City area following the September 11, 2001, terrorist attack on the World Trade Center.

Location: 2150 Hempstead Pike, Elmont, N.Y. 11003-1551
Phone: (516) 488-6000
Fax: (516) 352-0919
Website: *www.nyra.com/belmont*
E-Mail: nyra@nyra.com
Year Founded: 1902
Dates of Inaugural Meeting: May 4, 1905
Abbreviation: Bel
Acreage: 430
Number of Stalls: 2,200
Seating Capacity: 32,941

Ownership

New York Racing Association Inc.

Officers

Chief Executive Officer: Charles E. Hayward
Chairman: C. Steven Duncker
President: Charles E. Hayward
Racing Secretary: Paul J. Campo
Treasurer: Irene M. Posio
Director of Admissions: Jerry A. Davis Jr.
Director of Mutuels: Patrick Mahony
Vice President: William A. Nader
Director of Simulcasting: Elizabeth Bracken
Horsemen's Liaison: Carmen Barrera
Stewards: Braulio Baeza Jr., Carmine Donofrio, Dr. W. Theodore Hill
Track Announcer: Tom Durkin
Track Photographer: Adam Coglianese, Bob Coglianese
Track Superintendent: Jerry Porcelli
Security: Kenneth T. Cook
Vice Chairmen: Michael J. DelGiudice, Stuart Subotnick

Racing Dates

2005: May 4-July 24, 60 days; September 9-October 30, 37 days
2006: May 3-July 22, 59 days; September 8-October 22, 33 days

Track Layout

Main Circumference: $1\frac{1}{2}$ miles
Main Length of Stretch: 1,097 feet
Main Turf Circumference: $1\frac{5}{16}$ miles, 27 feet
Main Turf Chute: 1 mile and $1\frac{1}{16}$ miles
Inner Turf Circumference: $1\frac{3}{16}$ miles, 103 feet
Inner turf chute: $1\frac{1}{16}$ miles
Training Track: 1 mile

Attendance

Average Daily Recent Meeting: 7,057, Spring/Summer 2005; 6,004, Fall 2005
Highest Single-Day Record: 120,139, June 5, 2004
Total Attendance Recent Meeting: 423,405, Spring/Summer 2005; 222,133, Fall 2005
Highest Single-Day Recent Meet: 62,274, June 11, 2005 (Spring/Summer); 54,289, October 29, 2005 (Fall); 61,168, June 10, 2006 (Spring/Summer)

Handle

Average All Sources Recent Meeting: $11,120,068, Spring/Summer 2005; $12,913,444, Fall 2005
Average On-Track Recent Meeting: $1,570,872, Spring/Summer 2005; $1,225,949, Fall 2005
Single-Day On-Track Handle: $14,461,402, June 5, 2004 (Spring/Summer); $14,695,958, October 29, 2005 (Fall)
Single-Day Total Handle All Sources: $114,887,594, June 5, 2004 (Spring/Summer); $122,106,154, October 29, 2005 (Fall)
Total All Sources Recent Meeting: $667,204,080, Spring/Summer 2005; $477,797,415, Fall 2005
Total On-Track Recent Meeting: $94,252,318, Spring/Summer 2005; $45,360,126, Fall 2005
Highest Single-Day On-Track Record Recent Meet: $9,463,841, June 11, 2005 (Spring/Summer); $14,695,958, October 29, 2005 (Fall); $9,514,980, June 10, 2006 (Spring/Summer)

Mutuel Records

Highest Exacta: $5,454, June 1, 1985
Highest Quinella: $1,244.20, June 1, 1985
Highest Pick 4: $215,730.50, June 4, 2002

Leaders

Recent Meeting, Leading Jockey: Edgar Prado, 85, Spring/Summer 2005; Edgar Prado, 47, Fall 2005
Recent Meeting, Leading Trainer: William Mott, 22, Spring/Summer 2005; Todd Pletcher, 23, Fall 2005
Recent Meeting, Leading Horse: Albert E., 3, Fall 2005

Records

Single-Day Jockey Wins: Jorge Velasquez, 6, July 9, 1981
Single Meet, Leading Trainer by Wins: Todd Pletcher, 40, Spring/Summer 2003

Track Records, Main Dirt

5 furlongs: Kelly Kip, :55.75, June 21, 1996
$5\frac{1}{2}$ furlongs: Mike's Classic, 1:02.26, June 20, 2004
6 furlongs: Artax, 1:07.66, October 16, 1999
$6\frac{1}{2}$ furlongs: Bear Fan, 1:14.46, June 5, 2004
7 furlongs: Left Bank, 1:20.17, July 4, 2002
$7\frac{1}{2}$ furlongs: Commentator, 1:27.44, September 24, 2004
1 mile: Najran, 1:32.24, May 7, 2003
$1\frac{1}{16}$ miles: Rock and Roll, 1:39.51, June 13, 1998
$1\frac{1}{8}$ miles: Secretariat, 1:$45\frac{2}{5}$, September 15, 1973
$1\frac{3}{16}$ miles: Lueders, 1:56, June 24, 1982
$1\frac{1}{4}$ miles: In Excess (Ire), 1:$58\frac{1}{5}$, July 4, 1991
$1\frac{3}{8}$ miles: Victoriously, 2:14.72, October 16, 1997
$1\frac{1}{2}$ miles: Secretariat, 2:24, June 9, 1973

Track Records, Main Turf

6 furlongs: Keep The Faith (Aus), 1:06.82, July 24, 2005
7 furlongs: Officialpermission, 1:19.88, July 23, 2000
1 mile: Elusive Quality, 1:31.63, July 4, 1998
$1\frac{1}{16}$ miles: Fortitude, 1:38.53, September 6, 1997
$1\frac{3}{8}$ miles: Influent, 2:11.06, July 13, 1997
$1\frac{1}{2}$ miles: Fantastic Light, 2:24.36, October 27, 2001
2 miles: King's General (GB), 3:$20\frac{2}{5}$, July 4, 1983

Track Records, Inner Turf

6 furlongs: Titian Time, 1:09.90, September 25, 2005
$1\frac{1}{16}$ miles: Roman Envoy, 1:39.38, May 23, 1992
$1\frac{1}{8}$ miles: Shakespeare, 1:45.06, September 11, 2005
$1\frac{1}{4}$ miles: Paradise Creek, 1:57.79, June 11, 1994
$1\frac{3}{8}$ miles: With Approval, 2:$10\frac{1}{5}$, June 17, 1990

Principal Races

Spring/Summer: Belmont S. (G1), Metropolitan H. (G1), Manhattan H. (G1), Suburban H. (G1), Coaching Club American Oaks (G1)
Fall: Jockey Club Gold Cup S. (G1), Flower Bowl Invitational S. (G1), Joe Hirsch Turf Classic Invitational S. (G1), Beldame S. (G1), Woodward S. (G1)

Fastest Times of 2005 (Dirt)

5 furlongs: Travelin Leroy, :57.09, May 27, 2005
$5\frac{1}{2}$ furlongs: Theatrical Glory, 1:03.28, June 19, 2005
6 furlongs: Silver Train, 1:07.67, July 2, 2005
$6\frac{1}{2}$ furlongs: Tani Maru, 1:15.25, May 18, 2005
7 furlongs: Commentator, 1:20.23, June 29, 2005
$7\frac{1}{2}$ furlongs: Stellar Jayne, 1:28.13, July 2, 2005
1 mile: Ghostzapper, 1:33.29, May 30, 2005
$1\frac{1}{16}$ miles: Roman Ruler, 1:40.83, July 4, 2005
$1\frac{1}{8}$ miles: Oratory, 1:46.35, May 28, 2005
$1\frac{1}{4}$ miles: Offlee Wild, 2:00.50, July 2, 2005
$1\frac{1}{2}$ miles: Afleet Alex, 2:28.75, June 11, 2005

Fastest Times of 2005 (Turf)

6 furlongs: Keep The Faith (Aus), 1:06.82, July 24, 2005
7 furlongs: Steel Light, 1:20.37, September 24, 2005
1 mile: Mr. Light (Arg), 1:32.18, July 3, 2005
$1\frac{1}{16}$ miles: Whale, 1:39.36, May 14, 2005
$1\frac{1}{8}$ miles: Shakespeare, 1:45.06, September 11, 2005
$1\frac{1}{4}$ miles: Loving (Brz), 2:00.04, September 23, 2005
$1\frac{3}{8}$ miles: Better Talk Now, 2:11.65, September 10, 2005
$1\frac{1}{2}$ miles: Shakespeare, 2:27.22, October 1, 2005
$2\frac{1}{2}$ miles: Paradise's Boss, 4:33.95, June 12, 2005

Finger Lakes Gaming and Race Track

In Native American lore, the Finger Lakes region of upstate New York was created when the Great Spirit placed his hand down on the land to create the series of long, thin lakes. Finger Lakes Race Track, which is located 20 miles from Rochester in Farmington, opened May 23, 1962, and offers racing from mid-April to early December. Owned by Finger Lakes Racing Association Inc., the track has featured Eclipse Award-winning sprinters Not Surprising, Groovy, and Safely Kept. Fio Rito shipped out of the western New York track to win the 1981 Whitney Handicap (G1) at Saratoga Race Course. In 2001, Shesastonecoldfox became the first horse based at Finger Lakes to compete in the Breeders' Cup World Championships. The $150,000 New York Derby, which has been held at Finger Lakes since 1969, annually is the track's richest race. Video lottery terminals began operation at the track in February 2004.

Location: 5857 Route 96, P.O. Box 25250, Farmington, N.Y. 14425-0250
Phone: (585) 924-3232
Fax: (585) 924-3967
Website: *www.fingerlakesracetrack.com*
E-Mail: marketing@dncinc.com
Year Founded: 1962
Dates of Inaugural Meeting: May 23, 1962
Abbreviation: FL
Acreage: 450
Number of Stalls: 1,214
Seating Capacity: 6,000

Ownership

Delaware North Companies

Officers

President: Christian Riegle
General Manager: Christian Riegle
Director of Racing: Brad Lewis
Racing Secretary: Joe Colasacco
Director of Finance: Jay Underkofler
Director of Marketing: Steven Martin
Director of Mutuels: David Bridger
Director of Publicity: Steven Martin
Director of Sales: Sue Pines
Director of Simulcasting: Patrick Placito
Horsemen's Liaison: Kim DeLong
Stewards: Rick Coyne
Track Announcer: Ross Morton

Track Photographer: Tom Cooley
Track Superintendent: Rick Brongo
Asst. Racing Secretary: Carl Anderson
Security: Dan Martin

Racing Dates

2005: April 15-December 3, 160 days
2006: April 14-November 28, 160 days

Track Layout

Main Circumference: 1 mile
Main Track Chute: 6 furlongs and 1¼ miles
Main Width: 85 feet
Main Length of Stretch: 960 feet

Attendance

Highest Single-Day Record: 15,344, September 3, 1962
Highest Single-Meet Record: 698,113, 1974
Record Daily Average for Single Meet: 5,032, 1962
Lowest Single-Meet Record: 190,353, 2003

Handle

Record Daily Average for Single Meet: $348,608, 1982
Single-Day On-Track Handle: $765,580, September 24, 1978
Single-Day Total Handle All Sources: $2,549,108, October 3, 1989

Mutuel Records

Highest Pick 6: $161,490, June 21, 2001

Leaders

Career, Leading Jockey by Titles: Kevin Whitley, 9
Career, Leading Trainer by Titles: Michael S. Ferraro, 18
Recent Meeting, Leading Jockey: John R. Davila Jr., 153, 2005
Recent Meeting, Leading Trainer: Chris J. Englehart, 118, 2005
Recent Meeting, Leading Horse: Atlantis Crusader, 6, 2005; You Willgo Broke, 6, 2005

Records

Single-Day Jockey Wins: Robert Messina, 6, November 23, 2001
Single Meet, Leading Jockey by Wins: John Grabowski, 233, 2000
Single Meet, Leading Trainer by Wins: Chris J. Englehart, 136, 2004

Track Records, Main Dirt

4½ furlongs: Top End, :50.60, April 8, 1998
5 furlongs: Wonderous Wise, :57⅕, April 11, 1989; Bobby's Code, :57.20, April 8, 1998
5½ furlongs: Hilary Star, 1:02⅘, April 16, 1989; With It, 1:02.80, June 12, 1994; What a Rollick, 1:02.80, December 12, 1994
6 furlongs: Kelly Kip, 1:08.20, June 20, 1998
1 mile: Transact, 1:36.20, August 29, 1994; Fling n Roll, 1:36.20, November 29, 1995
1m 70 yds: C B Account, 1:40, July 6, 1997
1¹⁄₁₆ miles: Strider's Ormsby, 1:42.85, December 3, 2005
1⅛ miles: Copper Mount, 1:48.80, August 27, 1994
1³⁄₁₆ miles: North Warning, 1:58.40, July 10, 1994
1¼ miles: Caramba, 2:05⅕, July 11, 1987
1½ miles: Brave Beast, 2:33.70, September 22, 1991
1⅝ miles: North Warning, 2:46.60, September 4, 1994
Other: 2 furlongs, Broadway Blondie, :21.80, April 3, 1998

Principal Races

New York Derby, New York Breeders' Futurity, Lady Finger S., Aspirant S., New York Oaks

Interesting Facts

Achievements/Milestones: 2001 marked 40th season of operation

Notable Events

$10.5-million gaming floor with 1,010 video lottery terminals opened in 2004.

Fastest Times of 2005 (Dirt)

4½ furlongs: Illegal, :51.11, April 29, 2005
5 furlongs: Geneva Cross, :57.61, August 26, 2005
5½ furlongs: You Willgo Broke, 1:03.25, September 11, 2005
6 furlongs: Top Shoter, 1:08.49, July 16, 2005
1m 40 yds: Precious Coco, 1:42.19, April 29, 2005
1m 70 yds: Seattle Schifty, 1:41.25, October 1, 2005
1¹⁄₁₆ miles: Strider's Ormsby, 1:42.85, December 3, 2005
1⅛ miles: Sinister G, 1:51.73, June 19, 2005
1³⁄₁₆ miles: Suave Romancer, 2:02.69, August 2, 2005

Saratoga Race Course

An American landmark and one of the world's leading sports venues, Saratoga Race Course operates six weeks each year and draws huge crowds to the foothills of the Adirondack Mountains in historic Saratoga Springs, approximately 25 miles north of Albany. Saratoga set records for total attendance and average attendance in 2003. Opened August 2, 1864, Saratoga Race Course is the oldest existing track in America. Major renovations of the facility occurred in 1902, '28, '40, '65, '85, and 2000, when $8-million was spent to remodel the track's three main entrances, construct state-of-the-art jockeys' quarters, and restore an elegant 19th-century fountain in front of the clubhouse gate. Known as the "graveyard of champions," Saratoga has been host to many of Thoroughbred racing's greatest upsets, none more notable than Man o' War's only career loss to Upset in the 1919 Sanford Stakes. Other noteworthy upsets were Gallant Fox's loss in the 1930 Travers Stakes to 100-to-1 longshot Jim Dandy; Onion's shocking victory over Secretariat in the '73 Whitney Stakes (G2); and Runaway Groom's '82 Travers Stakes (G1) upset of Conquistador Cielo. Racing at Saratoga is enhanced annually by the inductions at the National Museum of Racing Hall of Fame, Fasig-Tipton's yearling sale, and the Jockey Club Round Table Conference.

Location: 267 Union Ave., Saratoga Springs, N.Y. 12866-0564
Phone: (518) 584-6200
Fax: (518) 587-4646
Website: *www.nyra.com/saratoga*
E-Mail: nyra@nyra.com
Year Founded: 1863
Dates of Inaugural Meeting: August 3-6, 1863
Abbreviation: Sar
Acreage: 350
Number of Stalls: 1,830
Seating Capacity: 18,000

Ownership

New York Racing Association Inc.

Officers

Chief Executive Officer: Charles E. Hayward
Chairman: C. Steven Duncker
President: Charles E. Hayward
Racing Secretary: Paul J. Campo
Treasurer: Irene M. Posio
Director of Admissions: Jerry A. Davis Jr.
Director of Mutuels: Patrick Mahony
Vice President: William A. Nader
Director of Simulcasting: Elizabeth Bracken
Horsemen's Liaison: Carmen Barrera
Stewards: Braulio Baeza Jr., Carmine Donofrio, Dr. W. Theodore Hill
Track Announcer: Tom Durkin
Track Photographer: Adam Coglianese, Bob Coglianese
Track Superintendent: Jerry Porcelli
Vice Chairman: Michael J. DelGiudice, Stuart Subotnick
Security: Kenneth T. Cook

Racing Dates

2005: July 27-September 5, 36 days
2006: July 26-September 4, 36 days

Track Layout

Main Circumference: 1⅛ miles
Main Track Chute: 7 furlongs
Main Width: 100 feet
Main Length of Stretch: 1,144 feet
Main Turf Circumference: 1 mile, 98 feet
Main Turf Length of Stretch: 1,144 feet
Inner Turf Circumference: 7 furlongs, 304 feet
Inner Turf Length of Stretch: 1,164 feet
Training Track: 1 mile (Dirt); 7 furlongs (Turf)

Attendance

Average Daily Recent Meeting: 25,913, 2005
Highest Single-Day Record: 71,337, August 17, 2003
Record Daily Average for Single Meet: 29,147, 2003
Highest Single-Meet Record: 1,049,309, 2003
Total Attendance Recent Meeting: 932,882, 2005
Highest Single-Day Recent Meet: 70,792, August 14, 2005

Handle

Average All Sources Recent Meeting: $14,946,720, 2005
Average On-Track Recent Meeting: $3,250,006, 2005
Record Daily Average for Single Meet: $3,742,773, 1993
Single-Day On-Track Handle: $9,390,934, August 23, 2003
Total All Sources Recent Meeting: $538,081,909, 2005
Total On-Track Recent Meeting: $117,000,324, 2005
Record Total for Single Meet: $127,245,731, 2003

Mutuel Records

Highest Trifecta: $63,624, August 22, 1974
Highest Daily Double: $4,313.90, August 27, 1945

Leaders

Career, Leading Jockey by Titles: Angel Cordero Jr., 13
Career, Leading Trainer by Titles: Bill Mott, 7
Recent Meeting, Leading Jockey: Edgar Prado, 44, 2005
Recent Meeting, Leading Trainer: Todd A. Pletcher, 22, 2005
Recent Meeting, Leading Horse: Stolen Identity, 3, 2005

Records

Single-Day Jockey Wins: John Velazquez, 6, September 3, 2001
Single Meet, Leading Jockey by Wins: John Velazquez, 65, 2004
Single Meet, Leading Trainer by Wins: Todd Pletcher, 35, 2003; Todd Pletcher, 35, 2004

Track Records, Main Dirt

5 furlongs: Fabulous Force, :56.71, August 18, 1993
$5\frac{1}{2}$ furlongs: Mayakovsky, 1:03.32, July 25, 2001
6 furlongs: Spanish Riddle, 1:08, August 18, 1972; Speightstown, 1:08.04, August 14, 2004
$6\frac{1}{2}$ furlongs: Topsider, 1:14$\frac{2}{5}$, August 1, 1979
7 furlongs: Darby Creek Road, 1:20$\frac{2}{5}$, August 8, 1978
1 mile: Key Contender, 1:34.72, August 9, 1992
$1\frac{1}{8}$ miles: Tri Jet, 1:47, August 3, 1974; Left Bank, 1:47.04, August 3, 2002
$1\frac{3}{16}$ miles: Winter's Tale, 1:54$\frac{3}{5}$, August 21, 1982
$1\frac{1}{4}$ miles: General Assembly, 2:00, August 18, 1979
$1\frac{5}{8}$ miles: Green Highlander, 2:43.57, August 15, 1991
2 miles: James Boswell, 3:26, August 11, 1983

Track Records, Main Turf

$5\frac{1}{2}$ furlongs: Second in Command, 1:01.46, September 4, 2005
$1\frac{1}{16}$ miles: Fourstardave, 1:38.91, July 29, 1991
$1\frac{1}{8}$ miles: Tentam, 1:45$\frac{2}{5}$, August 10, 1973; Waya (Fr), 1:45$\frac{2}{5}$, August 21, 1978
$1\frac{3}{16}$ miles: Phi Beta Doc, 1:51.61, September 1, 1999
$1\frac{5}{8}$ miles: Tom Swift, 2:37, August 23, 1978
Other: $2\frac{1}{16}$ miles, Popular Victory, 3:31$\frac{2}{5}$, August 23, 1979

Track Records, Inner Turf

1 mile: L'Oiseau d'Argent, 1:33.42, August 5, 2004
$1\frac{1}{16}$ miles: Leroidesanimaux, 1:39.92, August 27, 2005
$1\frac{1}{8}$ miles: Amarettitorun, 1:46.22, July 26, 1997
$1\frac{3}{8}$ miles: Babinda (GB), 2:12, July 26, 1997
$1\frac{1}{2}$ miles: Awad, 2:23.20, August 9, 1997

Principal Races

Travers S. (G1), Whitney H. (G1), Alabama S. (G1), Sword Dancer Invitational H. (G1), Diana S. (G1),

Fastest Times of 2005 (Dirt)

5 furlongs: Changing Weather, :57.73, August 25, 2005
$5\frac{1}{2}$ furlongs: Yes Yes Yes, 1:03.88, August 21, 2005
6 furlongs: Pomeroy, 1:08.69, August 13, 2005
$6\frac{1}{2}$ furlongs: Chili Cat, 1:16.35, August 14, 2005
7 furlongs: Sir Greeley, 1:22.04, August 21, 2005
$1\frac{1}{8}$ miles: Commentator, 1:48.33, August 6, 2005
$1\frac{1}{4}$ miles: Shadow Cast, 2:02.07, August 26, 2005

Fastest Times of 2005 (Turf)

$5\frac{1}{2}$ furlongs: Second in Command, 1:01.46, September 4, 2005
1 mile: Run to Victory, 1:34.34, July 30, 2005
$1\frac{1}{16}$ miles: Leroidesanimaux (Brz), 1:39.92, August 27, 2005
$1\frac{1}{8}$ miles: Tiverton, 1:46.37, August 27, 2005
$1\frac{3}{16}$ miles: Tempered Steel, 1:53.13, August 4, 2005
$1\frac{3}{8}$ miles: Honey Ryder, 2:14.51, September 5, 2005
$1\frac{1}{2}$ miles: King's Drama (Ire), 2:27.38, August 13, 2005
$1\frac{5}{8}$ miles: Rousing Victory, 2:40.94, August 15, 2005
$2\frac{1}{16}$ miles: Mr Perkolater, 3:43.04, August 3, 2005
$2\frac{3}{8}$ miles: Hirapour (Ire), 4:24.90, September 2, 2005

North Dakota

North Dakota Horse Park

Location: 5180 19th Ave. N., P.O. Box 1917, Fargo, N.D. 58107-1917
Phone: (701) 277-8027
Website: *www.northdakotahorsepark.org*
E-Mail: info@northdakotahorsepark.org
Abbreviation: Far
Acreage: 113
Number of Stalls: 400

Officers

President: Barb Nelson
Secretary: Terry Reed
Treasurer: Rick Buchholz
Vice President: Ryan Roshau
Track Announcer: Bubby Haar
Track Superintendent: Glen Thompson

Racing Dates

2005: August 5-September 5, 15 days
2006: July 28-September 4, 19 days

Track Layout

Main Circumference: $6\frac{1}{2}$ furlongs
Main Track Chute: 2 furlongs and 6 furlongs
Main Width: 80 feet

Leaders

Recent Meeting, Leading Jockey: Jordan Olesiak, 17, 2005
Recent Meeting, Leading Trainer: Dave Bernhardt, 8, 2005; Justin Olesiak, 8, 2005
Recent Meeting, Leading Horse: Western Honoree, 4, 2005

Principal Races

North Dakota Bred Derby, North Dakota Bred Futurity, Dean Kutz Memorial S., Open Thoroughbred Derby, Open Thoroughbred Futurity

Fastest Times of 2005 (Dirt)

4 furlongs: Kensington Park, :47.60, September 3, 2005
5 furlongs: Western Honoree, :59.60, August 28, 2005
$5\frac{1}{2}$ furlongs: Victoria's Chance, 1:08.20, August 14, 2005
6 furlongs: Maddies Blues, 1:12.60, August 5, 2005
7 furlongs: Cafe Momus, 1:28.80, August 26, 2005
1 mile: Maddies Blues, 1:40.20, August 27, 2005

Ohio

Beulah Park

Ohio's oldest racetrack, Beulah Park is located in Grove City, south of Columbus. Operating since 1923, the track offered a spring meet that once was a popular stopping point for horses in transit from Florida to New York. Beulah was started by successful paving contractor Robert J. Dienst. After Dienst's death, ownership of the track passed to his son, Robert Y. Dienst. In 1983, the younger Dienst sold Beulah, which passed through a succession of owners and was known as Darby Downs from 1983 to '86. Current owner Charles Ruma restored the track's original name in 1986. Under Ruma's leadership, Beulah was the first Ohio track to offer simulcasting, phone wagering, and Internet wagering through its www.winticket.com website, the online portal of AmericaTab, which is principally owned by Beulah and River Downs. Along with Thistledown and River Downs, Beulah shares host duties for the annual Best of Ohio day, which offers five stakes races for Ohio-breds.

Location: 3811 Southwest Blvd., P.O. Box 850, Grove City, Oh. 43123-0850
Phone: (614) 871-9600
Fax: (614) 871-0433
Website: *www.beulahpark.com*
E-Mail: brdejong@beulahpark.com
Year Founded: 1923
Dates of Inaugural Meeting: April 21, 1923
Abbreviation: Beu
Number of Stalls: 1,200
Seating Capacity: 7,200

Ownership

Charles Ruma

Officers

President: Charles J. Ruma
General Manager: Michael Weiss
Director of Racing: Ed Vomacka
Racing Secretary: Ed Vomacka
Director of Operations: Holly Freking
Director of Admissions: Holly Freking
Director of Finance: Jim McKinney
Director of Marketing: Tom Briggle
Director of Mutuels: Holly Freking
Vice President: Michael Weiss
Director of Publicity: Jessica Hamlin
Director of Simulcasting: Brian de Jong
Horsemen's Liaison: Joe DeLuca
Stewards: James Beck, Herb Clark, Joe DeLuca
Track Announcer: Bill Downes
Track Photographer: Harry Kaplan
Track Superintendent: Ernest Ratcliff

Racing Dates

2005: January 8-May 7, 76 days; September 24-December 20, 59 days
2006: January 7-May 6, 75 days; October 6-December 22, 49 days

Track Layout

Main Circumference: 1 mile
Main Track Chute: 6 furlongs and $1^1/_4$ miles
Main Width: 78 feet
Main Length of Stretch: 1,100 feet
Main Turf Circumference: 6 furlongs, less 223 feet

Handle

Average All Sources Recent Meeting: $1,138,186, Winter/Spring 2005; $769,593, Fall 2005
Average On-Track Recent Meeting: $58,130, Winter/Spring 2005; $42,413, Fall 2005
Single-Day Total Handle All Sources: $3,216,364, January 18, 2006
Total All Sources Recent Meeting: $86,502,200, Winter/Spring 2005; $45,405,992, Fall 2005
Total On-Track Recent Meeting: $4,417,904, Winter/Spring 2005; $2,502,401, Fall 2005
Highest Single-Day Record Recent Meet: $2,094,065, Winter/Spring 2005; $1,694,664, Fall 2005

Leaders

Recent Meeting, Leading Jockey: Edgar Paucar, 103, Winter/Spring 2005; Edgar Paucar, 58, Fall 2005; Edgar Paucar, 98, Winter/Spring 2006
Recent Meeting, Leading Trainer: Reid Gross, 59, Winter/Spring 2005; Jake Radosevich, 23, Fall 2005; Charles Lawson, 31, Winter/Spring 2006
Recent Meeting, Leading Horse: Dover Mountain, 6, Winter/Spring 2005; Bri's Bad Boy, 3, Fall 2005; Lil E's Express, 5, Winter/Spring 2006; Usher In, 5, Winter/Spring 2006; Louis' Star, 5, Winter/Spring 2006

Track Records, Main Dirt

4 furlongs: Float Away, :46$^2/_5$, May 12, 1938
$4^1/_2$ furlongs: Last Rebel, :50.96, April 18, 2003
5 furlongs: Love Pappa Mucci, :56.75, February 11, 1994
$5^1/_2$ furlongs: Jay's Performer, 1:02.78, March 18, 2001
6 furlongs: Whatta Brave, 1:08.50, October 29, 2000
1 mile: Appygolucky, 1:35.47, January 17, 2003
1m 70 yds: King's Wailea, 1:40.15, November 19, 1993
$1^1/_{16}$ miles: Din's Dancer, 1:40$^4/_5$, November 3, 1990
$1^1/_8$ miles: Lord Try On, 1:48.96, September 26, 1992
$1^3/_{16}$ miles: World of Magic, 1:55, September 21, 1991
$1^1/_4$ miles: On the Scent, 2:00.22, October 19, 1991
$1^1/_2$ miles: Doctor's Romance, 2:29.50, March 26, 1994
$1^5/_8$ miles: Big Beans, 2:46, October 5, 1957
$1^3/_4$ miles: Dot Your Eye, 2:57$^3/_5$, October 20, 1971
2 miles: Littlemagbrother, 3:25.69, December 20, 2005
Other: 2 furlongs, Go Chop, :21$^3/_5$, May 7, 1989; 2 miles 70 yds, Benomen, 3:29.81, November 20, 1993; $2^1/_{16}$ miles, She Looks Great, 3:41$^2/_5$, November 28, 1983; $2^1/_8$ miles, Second City, 3:48$^4/_5$, November 25, 1984; $2^1/_4$ miles, Hallay's Pride, 3:48.90, May 4, 1991

Track Records, Main Turf

1 mile: Gaelic Cross, 1:35$^2/_5$, September 23, 1987
1m 70yds: Twin To Win, 1:41, October 24, 1986
$1^3/_8$ miles: Syncospin, 2:12$^3/_5$, September 25, 1987
$1^5/_8$ miles: Nigilik, 2:48$^1/_5$, October 24, 1986
Other: a6 furlongs, Brent's Gail, 1:07, September 1, 1986; a1 mile, Khal Me Sir, 1:38.60, October 4, 1992; a1m 70yds, Nail's McNally, 1:40$^2/_5$, October 1, 1988; a$1^3/_8$ miles, Spend Ten, 2:12$^4/_5$, October 8, 1988; a2 miles, Persian Jig, 3:23$^2/_5$, May 17, 1987

Principal Races

Royal North S., Howard B. Noonan S., Angenora S., Babst/Palacios Memorial H., Ohio Freshman S.

Notable Events

Best of Ohio Day

Fastest Times of 2005 (Dirt)

$4^1/_2$ furlongs: Pal's Pro, :51.48, December 6, 2005
5 furlongs: Whitey's Alphastar, :57.72, December 8, 2005
$5^1/_2$ furlongs: Dry Basin, 1:03.06, December 21, 2005
6 furlongs: October Blues, 1:08.65, December 20, 2005
1 mile: Rose Wars, 1:37.30, December 17, 2005
1m 70 yds: Claymore, 1:41.68, December 10, 2005
$1^1/_{16}$ miles: R S Express, 1:43.70, December 20, 2005
$1^1/_8$ miles: Sky Brio, 1:49.51, November 18, 2005
$1^1/_4$ miles: Ready for Roses, 2:01.80, October 1, 2005
$1^1/_2$ miles: Convexity, 2:35.85, November 8, 2005
$1^3/_4$ miles: Littlemagbrother, 3:02.85, November 29, 2005
2 miles: Littlemagbrother, 3:25.69, December 20, 2005

River Downs

With the Ohio River serving as an attractive and sometimes destructive backdrop, River Downs has been part of the southern Ohio racing scene for more than 75 years. The track at Cincinnati's eastern edge opened in July 1925 as Coney Island racetrack. A crowd of 10,000 packed the facility for opening day, according to River Downs historians, and the track was off to a fast start. But the floods of 1937 put a temporary stop to that. The track rebuilt following the flood and reopened as River Downs. Sixty years later, the track again endured major Ohio River flooding, but once more the track was cleaned up and reopened. The track's grandstand had undergone an extensive renovation in the 1980s. River Downs offers a pair of quality two-year-old stakes every year in the Cradle and the Bassinet (for fillies). The 1984 Cradle was won by Spend a Buck, who the next year won the Kentucky Derby (G1). River Downs was one of the first tracks at which Racing Hall of Fame jockey Steve Cauthen competed.

Location: 6301 Kellogg Ave., P.O. Box 30286, Cincinnati, Oh. 45230
Phone: (513) 232-8000
Fax: (513) 232-1412
Website: *www.riverdowns.com*
E-Mail: info@riverdowns.com
Year Founded: 1925
Dates of Inaugural Meeting: July 6, 1925
Abbreviation: RD

Capsule Description: Picturesque open air grandstand on Ohio river.
Number of Stalls: 1,350
Seating Capacity: 9,350

Ownership

Dr. J. David Rutherford Partnership

Officers

Chairman: J. David Rutherford, M.D.
President: Jack Hanessian
General Manager: Jack Hanessian
Director of Racing: Ed Vomacka
Racing Secretary: Ed Vomacka
Director of Operations: Kathy Ewing
Director of Communications: John Engelhardt
Director of Marketing: Ed Meyer
Director of Mutuels: Larry Alexander
Vice President: Martin J. Stringer
Director of Publicity: John Engelhardt
Director of Simulcasting: Vincent Cyster
Stewards: Mike Manganello, Ron Tomlinson
Track Announcer: Brian de Jong
Track Photographer: Patrick Lang Photography
Track Superintendent: Jim Cornett
Asst. Racing Secretary: Tim Richardson
Horsemen's Bookkeeper: Terry Moore

Racing Dates

2005: April 8-September 5, 123 days
2006: April 14-September 4, 103 days

Track Layout

Main Circumference: 1 mile
Main Track Chute: 6 furlongs and 1¹/₄ miles
Main Width: 80 feet
Main Length of Stretch: 1,117 feet
Main Turf Circumference: 7 furlongs

Handle

Average All Sources Recent Meeting: $615,579, 2005
Average On-Track Recent Meeting: $137,884, 2005
Total All Sources Recent Meeting: $75,716,254, 2005
Total On-Track Recent Meeting: $16,959,766, 2005

Leaders

Recent Meeting, Leading Jockey: Hector L. Rosario Jr., 66, 2005
Recent Meeting, Leading Trainer: Luis Albert Palacios, 16, 2005
Recent Meeting, Leading Horse: Peggy's Ruby, 3, 2005; Sultan of Swat, 3, 2005; Dakota Diamond, 3, 2005; Gold by Gold, 3, 2005
Career, Leading Jockey by Stakes Wins: Eugene Sipus Jr., 25; Sebastian Madrid, 25
Career, Leading Owner by Stakes Wins: Woodburn Farm, 16
Career, Leading Trainer by Stakes Wins: James E. Morgan, 52

Records

Single Meet, Leading Jockey by Wins: Dean Sarvis, 83, 2004

Track Records, Main Dirt

4¹/₂ furlongs: Sans Terre, :52²/₅, May 24, 1971; Disco John, :52.40, September 1, 2005
5 furlongs: Banker's Forbes, :57.60, June 7, 1994
5¹/₂ furlongs: Tazua, 1:03, August 1, 1964
6 furlongs: Francine M., 1:08³/₅, July 4, 1969
1 mile: Dondougold, 1:36¹/₅, July 25, 1970; Alladin Rib, 1:36¹/₅, August 8, 1988
1m 70 yds: South Dakota, 1:40, August 4, 1945
1¹/₁₆ miles: Ingenero White, 1:41⁴/₅, July 5, 1969; Irish Dude, 1:41⁴/₅, July 5, 1969
1¹/₈ miles: Brown Sugar, 1:49, September 2, 1925
1¹/₄ miles: Crusader, 2:02, July 24, 1926
1¹/₂ miles: South Dakota, 2:30³/₅, July 1, 1950
1⁵/₈ miles: Sada, 2:45³/₅, Ocotber 13, 1934
1³/₄ miles: Brigler, 2:59³/₅, October 19, 1940
2 miles: South Dakota, 3:21²/₅, July 8, 1950
Other: 1¹/₁₆ miles, Distribute, 2:51³/₅, September 7, 1940; 1⁷/₈ miles, Shot Bills, 3:26³/₅, August 19, 1979; 2 miles 70 yds, Omar, 3:33³/₅, September 2, 1940; 2¹/₄ miles, Almac, 3:54, October 31, 1936; 2¹/₂ miles, Here Come Midge, 4:30⁴/₅, June 17, 1972; 3 miles 70 yds, Gloria Dream, 5:32²/₅, August 9, 1972

Track Records, Main Turf

4¹/₂ furlongs: Adena, :50⁴/₅, April 26, 1977
5 furlongs: Boston Storm, :56.20, June 5, 2005
7¹/₂ furlongs: Stormy Deep, 1:28²/₅, August 15, 1990
1 mile: Bad News Blues, 1:34.20, July 23, 1994
1¹/₁₆ miles: Franchise Player, 1:40.60, June 12, 1994
1³/₈ miles: Hi Rise, 2:15.60, August 15, 2000
1¹/₂ miles: Rebel Thunder, 2:28, June 28, 1996
Other: 1⁷/₁₆ miles, Dina's Pl'ymate, 2:25, August 30, 1969

Principal Races

Cradle S., Bassinet S.

Interesting Facts

Previous Names and Dates: Coney Island 1925-1937

Fastest Times of 2005 (Dirt)

4¹/₂ furlongs: Disco John, :52.40, September 1, 2005
5 furlongs: Missing Sefa, :58, August 26, 2005; Prince Georgi, :58, May 21, 2005; Sleet Rod, :58, July 17, 2005
5¹/₂ furlongs: Mr. Mink, 1:03.40, August 20, 2005
6 furlongs: Dixie Dreamer, 1:09.60, September 3, 2005
1 mile: Gold by Gold, 1:37.40, September 4, 2005
1m 70 yds: Chief Tudor, 1:41.80, June 4, 2005
1¹/₁₆ miles: Laity, 1:43.60, September 5, 2005
1¹/₈ miles: Dakota Diamond, 1:52, August 20, 2005
1¹/₄ miles: Easy Ellis, 2:08, July 11, 2005
1¹/₂ miles: Heptagone, 2:33.80, May 30, 2005
1⁵/₈ miles: Easy Ellis, 2:47.20, August 7, 2005

Fastest Times of 2005 (Turf)

5 furlongs: Boston Storm, :56.20, June 5, 2005
7¹/₂ furlongs: The Potters Hand, 1:28.80, June 6, 2005; The Potters Hand, 1:28.80, July 25, 2005
1 mile: Great Time, 1:35.80, June 7, 2005; Mystery Flick, 1:35.80, June 6, 2005
1¹/₁₆ miles: Ponte Vedra, 1:41.60, July 11, 2005
1³/₈ miles: Linda's Lad, 2:16.60, June 26, 2005
1¹/₂ miles: Linda's Lad, 2:28.20, July 24, 2005
1⁷/₈ miles: Convexity, 3:11.20, September 5, 2005

Thistledown

Thistledown in suburban Cleveland is the home of Ohio's most important race, the Ohio Derby (G2). Opened on July 20, 1925, Thistledown was owned and operated by the DeBartolo Corp. from 1959 through '99, when the track was purchased by Magna Entertainment Corp. Thistledown has inside its grandstand an interactive Starting Gate educational museum, which features exhibits, weekly handicapping seminars, and information on racing in Ohio. In 2000, the track reconfigured the outdoor paddock area, adding more than 9,000 square feet and such amenities as picnic tables, television monitors, and mutuel windows. The North Randall track typically races from April through the end of December.

Location: 21501 Emery Rd., North Randall, Oh. 44128-4513
Phone: (216) 662-8600
Fax: (216) 662-5339
Website: *www.thistledown.com*
E-Mail: info@thistledown.com
Year Founded: 1924
Dates of Inaugural Meeting: July 20, 1925
Abbreviation: Tdn
Acreage: 128
Number of Stalls: 1,560
Seating Capacity: 5,878

Ownership

Magna Entertainment Corp.

Officers

Chairman: Frank Stronach
General Manager: William D. Murphy
Director of Racing: L. William Couch
Racing Secretary: L. William Couch
Treasurer: Rita Seuffert
Director of Operations: David Ellsworth
Director of Communications: Heather McColloch
Director of Finance: Blake Tohana

Director of Marketing: Brent Reitz
Director of Mutuels: Bob Hickey
Vice President: William D. Murphy
Director of Publicity: Heather McColloch
Director of Simulcasting: Greg Davis
Stewards: Robert Clark, Philip T. Gore Jr., Joel A. McCullar
Track Announcer: Matt Hook
Track Photographer: JJ Zamaiko Photography
Track Superintendent: John Banno
Security: Arthur Pierre
Horsemen's Bookkeeper: Frank Koch

Racing Dates

2005: April 8-December 23, 185 days
2006: April 14-November 27, 156 days

Track Layout

Main Circumference: 1 mile
Main Track Chute: 6 furlongs and $1\frac{1}{4}$ miles
Main Width: Homestretch: 95 feet; Backstretch: 75 feet
Main Length of Stretch: 978 feet

Attendance

Highest Single-Day Record: 19,411, June 18, 1978
Record Daily Average for Single Meet: 7,049, 1954
Highest Single-Meet Record: 986,095, 1979

Handle

Average All Sources Recent Meeting: $1,265,595, 2005
Average On-Track Recent Meeting: $117,948, 2005
Single-Day Total Handle All Sources: $3,851,575, July 24, 1999
Total All Sources Recent Meeting: $234,135,021, 2005
Total On-Track Recent Meeting: $21,820,472, 2005
Record Total All Sources for Single Meet: $237,348,143, 2001
Highest Single-Day On-Track Record Recent Meet: $1,069,997, April 8, 2005
Highest Single-Day Record Recent Meet: $2,413,535, April 8, 2005

Mutuel Records

Highest Win: $500.20, Nobody's Secret, November 22, 1995
Highest Daily Double: $4,553.40, June 8, 1967
Highest Pick 6: $89,306.20, November 29, 1985

Leaders

Career, Leading Jockey by Titles: Michael Rowland, 29
Career, Leading Trainer by Titles: Gary Johnson, 24
Career, Leading Jockey by Stakes Wins: Julio Felix, 44
Recent Meeting, Leading Jockey: Scott Spieth, 180, 2005
Recent Meeting, Leading Owner: Joe Faulkner, 70, 2005
Recent Meeting, Leading Trainer: Jeffrey A. Radosevich, 119, 2005
Recent Meeting, Leading Horse: El Keko, 7, 2005; Pyrite Angel, 7, 2005

Records

Single-Day Jockey Wins: Buddy Haas, 6, August 28, 1933; John Adams, 6, September 2, 1942; Danny Weiler, 6, August 12, 1961; Anthony Rini, 6, June 12, 1970; Antonio Graell, 6, February 21, 1976; Benny Feliciano, 6, June 18, 1978; Antonio Graell, 6, November 14, 1980; Tom Ford, 6, December 13, 1982; Brian Mills, 6, August 28, 1983; Michael Rowland, 6, March 29, 1991; Michael Rowland, 6, October 19, 1999
Single-Day Trainer Wins: Gary Johnson, 6, November 27, 1999
Single Meet, Leading Jockey by Wins: Antonio Graell, 338, 1976
Single Meet, Leading Trainer by Wins: Jeffrey A. Radosevich, 119, 2005

Track Records, Main Dirt

4 furlongs: Ifufeelfroggyleap, :45.30, October 8, 2004
$4\frac{1}{2}$ furlongs: Onion Roll, :51.57, November 20, 1992
5 furlongs: Jet Bupers, :$57\frac{2}{5}$, June 4, 1978; Great Allegiance, :57.56, May 18, 1997
$5\frac{1}{2}$ furlongs: Down Thepike Mike, 1:03.20, August 10, 1998
6 furlongs: Fancy Threat, 1:$08\frac{2}{5}$, November 21, 1987
1 mile: Setting Limits, 1:$35\frac{3}{5}$, November 17, 1989
1m 40 yds: Ifthisbe Britches, 1:$38\frac{3}{5}$, December 8, 1989; North Island, 1:$38\frac{3}{5}$, December 9, 1989
1m 70 yds: Wisdom Seeker, 1:40.92, July 22, 1995
$1\frac{1}{16}$ miles: Entitled to Star, 1:41.32, November 25, 1995
$1\frac{1}{8}$ miles: Smarten, 1:$47\frac{2}{5}$, June 17, 1979
$1\frac{3}{16}$ miles: Smoke Screen, 1:$55\frac{3}{5}$, July 17, 1954
$1\frac{1}{4}$ miles: Pert Near, 2:03, December 1, 1979
$1\frac{1}{2}$ miles: Martha's Wave, 2:$31\frac{4}{5}$, June 18, 1955
$1\frac{5}{8}$ miles: Alsang, 2:46, August 8, 1936
$1\frac{3}{4}$ miles: Mala Kee, 2:$57\frac{3}{5}$, July 19, 1957
2 miles: Likely Advice, 3:27, December 15, 1980
Other: 2 furlongs, Onion Roll, :20.95, September 27, 1993; $1\frac{9}{16}$ miles, Military Girl, 2:$44\frac{1}{5}$, June 13, 1942; a$1\frac{1}{16}$ miles, Military Girl, 2:49, August 17, 1940; 2m 40 yds, Winning Mark, 3:$29\frac{2}{5}$, July 20, 1940; 2m 70 yds, Lonely Cloud, 3:$41\frac{3}{5}$, May 13, 1990; $2\frac{1}{16}$ miles, Bunker, 3:$32\frac{4}{5}$, July 13, 1955; $2\frac{1}{8}$ miles, Lonely Cloud, 3:52.65, July 3, 1992; $2\frac{3}{16}$ miles, Current Data, 3:$54\frac{3}{5}$, December 5, 1981; $2\frac{1}{4}$ miles, Son Richard, 3:$54\frac{3}{5}$, August 27, 1938; $2\frac{7}{16}$ miles, Bea Beauty, 4:$47\frac{4}{5}$, September 8, 1973; 3m 40 yds, Bea Beauty, 5:$31\frac{4}{5}$, September 22, 1973; $3\frac{5}{8}$ miles, Eastern Promise, 6:$49\frac{3}{5}$, October 6, 1973

Principal Races

Ohio Derby (G2), Cleveland Gold Cup S., Rose DeBartolo Memorial S., Governor's Buckeye Cup S.

Fastest Times of 2005 (Dirt)

2 furlongs: Cumberland Gap, :21.48, September 26, 2005
4 furlongs: Herpotofgold, :45.54, October 3, 2005
$4\frac{1}{2}$ furlongs: Another Elusive, :52.16, October 24, 2005
5 furlongs: Czech Mate, :58.38, April 11, 2005
$5\frac{1}{2}$ furlongs: Too Much Bling, 1:03.82, July 30, 2005
6 furlongs: I Cant Refuse, 1:09.70, September 9, 2005
1 mile: Maddashfordinner, 1:38.90, August 18, 2005
1m 40 yds: Conte Amour, 1:42.40, December 14, 2005
1m 70 yds: City Code, 1:42.91, November 26, 2005
$1\frac{1}{16}$ miles: Forest Picnic, 1:45.72, July 2, 2005
$1\frac{1}{8}$ miles: Palladio, 1:51.56, July 2, 2005
$1\frac{1}{4}$ miles: Ready for Roses, 2:05.24, September 5, 2005
$1\frac{5}{8}$ miles: El Keko, 2:51.06, November 7, 2005
$1\frac{3}{4}$ miles: El Keko, 3:05.70, November 21, 2005
2 miles: El Keko, 3:37.20, December 7, 2005

Oklahoma

Blue Ribbon Downs

Blue Ribbon Downs, located near Sallisaw, Oklahoma, was developed by Blue Ribbon Ranch owner Bill Hedge on ranch property. It first offered racing in 1960 as a nonpari-mutuel racetrack, with all business operations based in Hedge's house. In 1973, Hedge sold the track to a group of investors. A decade later, Blue Ribbon was the first track to offer pari-mutuel racing in Oklahoma, but fire destroyed its grandstand two weeks before the 1983 meet was to open. Within one week, a new grandstand was erected. The track's richest Thoroughbred race is the Oklahoma-bred Thoroughbred Futurity for two-year-olds. The track conducts Thoroughbred, Quarter Horse, Appaloosa, and Paint racing from mid-February to early December. In 2004, the Oklahoma Legislature approved electronic gaming and nonhouse card games for Blue Ribbon and two other state tracks.

Location: 3700 W. Cherokee, P.O. Box 489, Sallisaw, Ok. 74955
Phone: (918) 775-7771
Fax: (918) 775-5805
Website: *www.blueribbondowns.net*
E-Mail: brd@blueribbondowns.net
Year Founded: 1960
Abbreviation: BRD
Acreage: 165
Number of Stalls: 1,064 Stalls
Seating Capacity: 3,500

Ownership

Backstretch LLC

Officers

General Manager: Frank Deal
Racing Secretary: Burt Cheek
Secretary: Jinx Blades

Director of Marketing: Bonnie Cusimano
Director of Mutuels: Janine Schaub
Director of Publicity: Bonnie Cusimano
Track Announcer: Fred Davis
Track Photographer: Gene Wilson and Associates
Horsemen's Bookkeeper: Jinx Blades

Racing Dates

2005: February 19-May 7, 27 days; August 6-October 30, 33 days
2006: March 3-April 29, 5 days; July 29-November 18, 65 days

Track Layout

Main Circumference: 7 furlongs, 30 yards
Main Track Chute: 6 furlongs and 1$^1/_8$ miles
Main Width: 72 feet
Main Length of Stretch: 845 feet

Attendance

Highest Single-Day Record: 10,169, August 30, 1984

Leaders

Recent Meeting, Leading Jockey: Carroll Daniel Eason, 7, 2005
Recent Meeting, Leading Trainer: Clifton D. Brooks, 7, 2005

Track Records, Main Dirt

4 furlongs: Iwontbeback, :44.35, July 3, 1995
4$^1/_2$ furlongs: Rebel's Jon, :50.35, June 29, 1996
5 furlongs: Pow Wow Al, :56.45, May 27, 1996
5$^1/_2$ furlongs: Rebel's Jon, 1:02, October 1, 1995
6 furlongs: Rebel's Jon, 1:08.45, July 9, 1995
7 furlongs: Prententious Chief, 1:23, September 10, 1995
7$^1/_2$ furlongs: Karate Kick, 1:29.35, September 17, 1994
1 mile: Staged Attraction, 1:36.15, June 10, 1989
1$^1/_{16}$ miles: Just Ask Rudy, 1:43.15, April 6, 1996
1$^1/_8$ miles: Long On Rowdy, 1:49.35, July 17, 1994
1$^1/_4$ miles: Dare More, 2:03.35, August 28, 1994
1$^3/_8$ miles: Say It All, 2:17.15, October 1, 1995
1$^1/_2$ miles: Mr. Sanhedrin, 2:32.35, November 14, 1993
1$^5/_8$ miles: Sharp's Caliber, 2:47.15, December 11, 1994

Fastest Times of 2005 (Dirt)

4 furlongs: Sooner Pride, :46.23, February 20, 2005
4$^1/_2$ furlongs: G. T. Crusader, :51.80, September 25, 2005
5 furlongs: Sooner Pride, :57.95, April 30, 2005
5$^1/_2$ furlongs: Final Draft, 1:04.56, April 16, 2005
6 furlongs: Emma's Cat, 1:10.40, September 11, 2005; Master Lemac, 1:10.40, September 3, 2005
7$^1/_2$ furlongs: Crane Away, 1:32.63, August 21, 2005
1 mile: Sheik of Wagoner, 1:38.40, October 14, 2005

Fair Meadows at Tulsa

Offering nighttime Thoroughbred, Quarter Horse, Paint, and Appaloosa racing on its five-furlong oval, Fair Meadows at Tulsa is one of the entertainment facilities located at Expo Square, which hosts the Tulsa State Fair and some 400 other events each year. Fair Meadows, which has been conducting live racing since 1989, is located on a former auto-racing oval and is next to the stadium of the Tulsa Drillers, the Class AA minor-league baseball team affiliated with the Colorado Rockies. During racing season, a giant net between the stadium and Fair Meadows keeps foul balls from landing on the track's final turn. Expo Square includes an amusement park, water park, and hotel, and Fair Meadows offers a state-of-the-art simulcast facility that operates year-round.

Location: 4609 E. 21st St., Tulsa, Ok. 74114-2108
Phone: (918) 743-7223
Fax: (918) 743-8053
Website: *www.fairmeadows.com*
E-Mail: racing@fairmeadows.com
Abbreviation: FMT

Officers

General Manager: Ron Shotts
Director of Racing: Ron Shotts
Racing Secretary: Bert Cheek
Director of Operations: Jim Parrish
Director of Marketing: Richard Linihan
Director of Mutuels: Fred Davis
Director of Publicity: Richard Linihan
Director of Simulcasting: Kevin Jones
Horsemen's Liaison: Nina Parrish
Track Photographer: Gene Wilson and Associates
Track Superintendent: Jim Parrish

Racing Dates

2005: May 26-July 24, 34 days
2006: May 24-July 29, 33 days

Track Layout

Main Circumference: 5 furlongs
Main Track Chute: 4 furlongs and 6$^1/_2$ furlongs

Leaders

Recent Meeting, Leading Jockey: Curtis Kimes, 15, 2005
Recent Meeting, Leading Trainer: Mike R. Teel, 6, 2005
Recent Meeting, Leading Horse: Tickin' Okie, 2, 2005; Hushnlisten, 2, 2005; Call Works, 2, 2005; Harbo, 2, 2005; Starship Diligence, 2, 2005

Track Records, Main Dirt

4 furlongs: Only Cash, :44.40, May 30, 1997; Oklahoma Natural, :44.40, June 11, 2005
5$^1/_2$ furlongs: Double Jack, 1:03.80, August 1, 2001
6 furlongs: Herecomesthemann, 1:10.60, June 11, 2005
6$^1/_2$ furlongs: Tic Tic, 1:16.60, July 10, 1998
1 mile: Judge North, 1:37, August 5, 1995
1$^1/_{16}$ miles: Stop the Bluffing, 1:45.60, May 29, 2003
1$^1/_8$ miles: Demascus Slew, 1:51.80, May 30, 1998
1$^3/_8$ miles: Second Avie, 2:20, August 5, 1995
1$^5/_8$ miles: Phantom Cottage, 2:51.80, August 1, 1992

Principal Races

Tulsa Dash S., Boomer S., Route 66 S., Muscogee (Creek) Nation S.

Fastest Times of 2005 (Dirt)

4 furlongs: Oklahoma Natural, :44.40, June 11, 2005
5$^1/_2$ furlongs: Prince Parliament, 1:05.20, June 10, 2005
6 furlongs: Herecomesthemannow, 1:10.60, June 11, 2005
6$^1/_2$ furlongs: Harbo, 1:17.20, July 7, 2005
1 mile: Ziggy's Haylo, 1:38, June 10, 2005

Remington Park

Built by the late Edward J. DeBartolo, Remington Park opened its gates on September 1, 1988, and was purchased by Magna Entertainment Corp. in October 1999 after average daily attendance had plummeted from a high of 11,263 in 1989 to 2,517 in '98. The track began a new era in 2001 with the addition of lights, thus allowing night racing. Thoroughbreds race during a summer-fall meet from mid-August to late November, and Quarter Horses are featured in a spring meet. The track's feature Thoroughbred race is the Oklahoma Derby (G3), which was to be run for the 18th time in 2006. Customers have multiple choices for settings, including the Players Sports Bar, the Silks Restaurant, the Eclipse Restaurant, and luxurious private suites. Remington opened its racino in November 2005, slightly more than a year after slots at three state tracks were approved by voters.

Location: 1 Remington Place, Oklahoma City, Ok. 73111-7101
Phone: (405) 424-1000
Fax: (405) 425-3297
Website: *www.remingtonpark.com*
E-Mail: contact@Remingtonpark.com
Dates of Inaugural Meeting: September 1, 1988
Abbreviation: RP
Acreage: 370
Number of Stalls: 1,312

Ownership

Magna Entertainment Corp.

Officers

Chairman: Frank Stronach
Chief Executive Officer: W. Thomas Hodgson
General Manager: Scott Wells
Director of Racing: Larry Craft
Racing Secretary: Mike Shamburg
Director of Operations: Matt Vance
Director of Admissions: Diane Bynum
Director of Communications: Dale Day
Director of Marketing: Dale Day
Director of Mutuels: Carrie Stallbories
Vice President: Jeff Greco
Director of Sales: Sharon Lair
Director of Simulcasting: Fred Hutton
Track Announcer: Don Stevens
Track Photographer: Reed Palmer
Track Superintendent: James Porter
Horsemen's Bookkeeper: Patsy Bessonett
Security: Mike Chapple

Racing Dates

2005: August 5-November 28, 66 days
2006: August 4-November 28, 68 days

Track Layout

Main Circumference: 1 mile
Main Track Chute: 7 furlongs
Main Track Chute: 1³/₈ miles
Main Width: 100 feet
Main Length of Stretch: 990 feet
Main Turf Circumference: 7 furlongs
Main Turf Chute: 1¹/₈ miles
Main Turf Width: 80 feet
Main Turf Length of Stretch: 990 feet

Attendance

Highest Single-Day Record: 26,411, February 29, 1992
Record Daily Average for Single Meet: 11,128, 1988

Handle

Record Daily Average for Single Meet: $1,310,542, 1990
Single-Day On-Track Handle: $2,808,243, February 24, 1990

Mutuel Records

Highest Win: $254.20, Cherokee County, October 28, 2001
Highest Exacta: $5,495.80, December 3, 1988
Highest Trifecta: $58,662.40, February 24, 1995
Highest Daily Double: $2,969.60, September 2, 2000
Highest Pick 3: $18,057.60, November 13, 1994
Highest Other Exotics: $38,968.80, Superfecta, December 1, 1996

Leaders

Career, Leading Jockey by Titles: Pat Steinberg, 9
Career, Leading Trainer by Titles: Donnie Von Hemel, 11
Career, Leading Jockey by Stakes Wins: Don Pettinger, 111
Career, Leading Owner by Stakes Wins: Barbara and John Smicklas, 21
Career, Leading Trainer by Stakes Wins: Donnie Von Hemel, 120
Career, Leading Jockey by Wins: Don Pettinger, 1,266
Recent Meeting, Leading Jockey: Cliff Berry, 112, 2005
Recent Meeting, Leading Owner: Gary Owens, 36, 2005
Recent Meeting, Leading Trainer: W. Bret Calhoun, 31, 2005

Records

Single-Day Jockey Wins: Tim Doocy, 6, December 5, 1993; Cliff Berry, 6, September 30, 2001; Cliff Berry, 6, August 5, 2005
Single-Day Trainer Wins: Wade White, 5, November 17, 1993
Single Meet, Leading Jockey by Wins: Tim Doocy, 127, 1997
Single Meet, Leading Owner by Wins: Gary Owens, 36, 2005
Single Meet, Leading Trainer by Wins: Joe Petalino, 69, 1998

Track Records, Main Dirt

4¹/₂ furlongs: Payday Two, :52.20, February 26, 2000
5 furlongs: Highland Ice, :57.20, December 3, 1999
5¹/₂ furlongs: Run Johnny, 1:02, September 26, 1997
6 furlongs: Smoke of Ages, 1:08, September 29, 1991
6¹/₂ furlongs: Kangaroo King, 1:14.40, July 26, 1997
7 furlongs: Golden Gear, 1:20.40, March 18, 1995
1 mile: White Wheels, 1:35.40, August 17, 1997
1m 70 yds: Marked Tree, 1:39.60, March 13, 1993
1¹/₁₆ miles: Valid Bonnet, 1:41.20, July 26, 1997
1¹/₈ miles: Classic Cat, 1:48, August 30, 1998
1³/₁₆ miles: Wild Rush, 1:53.60, August 10, 1997
1¹/₄ miles: Double Platinum, 2:03.40, October 10, 1999
1³/₈ miles: Wild and Comfy, 2:17.96, October 18, 2002
1¹/₂ miles: Bid the Zeal, 2:31.40, October 24, 1998
Other: 3 furlongs, Eclat, :31.01, November 28, 2005

Track Records, Main Turf

5 furlongs: Calling Randy, :55.14, September 27, 2005
7¹/₂ furlongs: Foreign Justice, 1:27.46, August 27, 2004
1 mile: No More Hard Times, 1:33.80, September 20, 1992
1¹/₁₆ miles: Burbank, 1:39.20, August 30, 1997
1¹/₈ miles: Major Rhythm, 1:46.22, September 6, 2004
1³/₈ miles: Vergennes, 2:13, September 3, 2000
1¹/₂ miles: Cumulus, 2:38.38, November 8, 2004
2 miles: Big Notice, 3:29, November 20, 1993

Principal Races

Oklahoma Derby, Edward J. DeBartolo Sr. Memorial Breeders' Cup H., Oklahoma Classics Day Classic S., Remington Park Oaks, Remington Green S., Remington Mile S.

Notable Events

Oklahoma Classics Day

Fastest Times of 2005 (Dirt)

3 furlongs: Eclat, :31.01, November 28, 2005
5 furlongs: Rocket Junior, :57.79, September 6, 2005
5¹/₂ furlongs: Irish Milligan, 1:03.52, October 11, 2005
6 furlongs: The Niner Account, 1:09.01, September 10, 2005
6¹/₂ furlongs: Zee Oh Six, 1:15, August 20, 2005
7 furlongs: D Fine Okie, 1:22.94, November 12, 2005
1 mile: Zee Oh Six, 1:35.51, September 2, 2005
1m 70 yds: Higher and Higher, 1:41, August 19, 2005
1¹/₁₆ miles: Zee Oh Six, 1:42.46, September 24, 2005
1¹/₈ miles: Military Major, 1:49.49, October 21, 2005

Fastest Times of 2005 (Turf)

5 furlongs: Calling Randy, :55.14, September 27, 2005
7¹/₂ furlongs: Goodie Good Girl, 1:28.41, September 24, 2005
1 mile: Paz Ciudadana (Chi), 1:34.16, September 5, 2005
1¹/₁₆ miles: Dontbotherknocking, 1:40.40, October 21, 2005
1¹/₈ miles: Dontbotherknocking, 1:46.46, September 5, 2005
1³/₈ miles: Fred and Me, 2:17.40, November 1, 2005
1¹³/₁₆ miles: Earnest Storm, 3:08.09, November 28, 2005

Will Rogers Downs

Will Rogers Downs is located on 210 acres just east of Claremore and approximately 25 miles from downtown Tulsa. No racing was conducted from 2001 through '05, but live racing resumed in '06 after Oklahoma approved gaming at Will Rogers and two other state tracks in '04 and the facility was purchased by the Cherokee Nation, which announced a $2-million renovation. The track is home to rodeos as well as Will Rogers County Jamborees every other Saturday night, presenting a family-oriented country show and concert.

Location: 20900 S. 4200 Rd., Claremore, Ok. 74019
Phone: (918) 283-8800
Website: *www.cherokeecasino.com*
Abbreviation: WRD

Racing Dates

2006: February 24-May 28, 42 days

Track Layout

Main Circumference: 1 mile
Main Track Chute: 6 furlongs
Main Length of Stretch: 872.76 feet

Leaders

Recent Meeting, Leading Jockey: Nena Matz, 67, 2006
Recent Meeting, Leading Owner: Gary Owens, 33, 2005
Recent Meeting, Leading Trainer: Martin Lozano, 33, 2006
Recent Meeting, Leading Horse: Racey Leo, 3, 2006; Jet G Knows, 3, 2006; Nokoma, 3, 2006; Groovy Little Me, 3, 2006; Kipling's Diva, 3, 2006; Riva's Image, 3, 2006; Jet G Amour, 3, 2006; Pin Okie O, 3, 2006

Oregon

Eastern Oregon Livestock Show

Location: P.O. Box 4092, Union, Or. 97883-1052

Racing Dates

2005: June 10-June 12, 3 days
2006: June 9-June 11, 3 days

Leaders

Recent Meeting, Leading Jockey: Twyla Beckner, 3, 2005
Recent Meeting, Leading Trainer: Marion Stitzel, 2, 2005; Judi Yearout, 2, 2005

Grants Pass

Location: 1451 Fairgrounds Rd., P.O. Box 672, Grants Pass, Or. 97528
Phone: (541) 476-3215
Fax: (541) 476-1027
Website: *www.grantspassdowns.com*
E-Mail: jackie2@jocofair.com
Abbreviation: GrP

Officers

General Manager: Jackie McBee
Director of Racing: Al Westoff
Racing Secretary: Dan Bryson
Director of Marketing: Gary Davison
Director of Publicity: Gary Davison
Track Superintendent: Carl Stallings

Racing Dates

2005: May 21-July 4, 16 days
2006: May 27-July 4, 15 days

Leaders

Recent Meeting, Leading Jockey: Twyla Beckner, 24, 2005
Recent Meeting, Leading Trainer: Jason Homer, 13, 2005
Recent Meeting, Leading Horse: Seveneightone East, 3, 2005; Ty's Princess, 3, 2005

Fastest Times of 2005 (Dirt)

4½ furlongs: Angelrose, :53.20, May 21, 2005
5 furlongs: McKinna G, :58.20, July 3, 2005
5½ furlongs: Bubba Galpin, 1:05, July 4, 2005; True Kitty Cat, 1:05, July 4, 2005
6½ furlongs: Seveneightone East, 1:18.80, June 18, 2005; Weatherbug, 1:18.80, June 18, 2005
1$^1/_{16}$ miles: Hypersonic Boy, 1:45.40, July 3, 2005

Portland Meadows

Founded by Bay Meadows Race Course builder William Kyne, Portland Meadows has a rich history dating to September 14, 1946, when a crowd of 10,000 watched the nation's first evening Thoroughbred racing card. General Electric Co., which devised the lighting system, boasted at the time: "This system, the first of its kind, has enough power to light a four-lane super highway from Portland to Salem (a distance of more than 40 miles)." But Portland Meadows officials were powerless to fight the Vanport flood, which in 1948 forced cancellation of the track's season after just 13 cards and caused $250,000 in damage. The track was hit again in the early-morning hours of April 25, 1970, when a fire razed the grandstand. Portland Meadows was rebuilt, opening its 1971 season before a record crowd of 12,635. Portland Meadows served as an early proving ground for Racing Hall of Fame jockey Gary Stevens, who won two riding titles there in the early 1980s. New Portland Meadows Inc. operated the track from 1991 until it leased the track to Magna Entertainment Corp. in mid-2001. In 2002, Magna purchased the long-term operating rights to Portland Meadows.

Location: 1001 N. Schmeer Rd., Portland, Or. 97217-7505
Phone: (503) 285-9144
Fax: (503) 286-9763
Website: *www.portlandmeadows.com*
Year Founded: 1945
Dates of Inaugural Meeting: September 14, 1946
Abbreviation: PM
Acreage: 100+
Number of Stalls: 850
Seating Capacity: 4,450

Ownership

Magna Entertainment Corp.

Officers

General Manager: Dwayne Yuzik
Director of Racing: Jerry Kohls
Racing Secretary: Jerry Kohls
Treasurer: Stacey M. Whearty
Director of Operations: Patrick Kerrison
Director of Mutuels: Keith Jones
Director of Publicity: Patrick Kerrison
Director of Simulcasting: Patrick Kerrison
Track Photographer: Jeff Fisher Photography
Horsemen's Bookkeeper: Nichele Milner

Racing Dates

2005: October 16, 2004-April 24, 2005, 81 days
2006: October 22, 2005-May 7, 2006, 81 days

Track Layout

Main Circumference: 1 mile
Main Track Chute: 6 furlongs and 1¼ mile
Main Length of Stretch: 990 feet

Attendance

Highest Single-Day Record: 12,635, February 6, 1971

Handle

Average All Sources Recent Meeting: $273,379, 2004/2005
Average On-Track Recent Meeting: $33,035, 2004/2005
Total All Sources Recent Meeting: $21,323,537, 2004/2005
Total On-Track Recent Meeting: $2,576,714, 2004/2005

Leaders

Recent Meeting, Leading Jockey: Javier A. Ortega, 72, 2004/2005; Jose Luis Zunino, 85, 2005/2006
Recent Meeting, Leading Trainer: Jonathan Nance, 48, 2004/2005; Jim Fergason, 67, 2005/2006
Recent Meeting, Leading Horse: Big Al T, 8, 2004/2005; Colony Lane, 7, 2005/2006

Track Records, Main Dirt

4 furlongs: Wayne S., :47, May 22, 1947
4½ furlongs: Star Expresso, :51.80, April 3, 1999
5 furlongs: Pajone's Hostess, :58, January 6, 1977
5½ furlongs: My Runaway, 1:02⅘, January 6, 1977
6 furlongs: Lethal Grande, 1:09.01, March 30, 2003
1 mile: Star of Kuwait, 1:36⅕, May 11, 1975
1m 70 yds: Beau Julian, 1:41⅕, May 14, 1979
1$^1/_{16}$ miles: Me Brave, 1:43⅕, May 5, 1969
1⅛ miles: Hannibal Khal, 1:48⅘, December 30, 1978
1$^3/_{16}$ miles: Kitsap Kid, 1:58⅖, April 27, 1968
1¼ miles: True Enough, 2:03.20, April 9, 1994
1½ miles: Martins Lemon, 2:32, May 13, 1973
1¾ miles: Moribana, 2:58⅗, May 27, 1972
2 miles: Martins Lemon, 3:27⅗, May 20, 1973

Principal Races

Portland Meadows Mile H., Oregon Derby, Oregon Oaks, Janet Wineberg S., OS West Oregon Futurity

Fastest Times of 2005 (Dirt)

4½ furlongs: Beau Slew, :54.28, January 9, 2005; Jaguar Jack, :54.28, January 23, 2005
5 furlongs: Big Al T, :59.24, April 9, 2005
5½ furlongs: Crimson Design, 1:05.11, March 6, 2005
6 furlongs: Big Al T, 1:11.36, January 10, 2005
1 mile: Demon Warlock, 1:37.92, April 9, 2005
1$^1/_{16}$ miles: My Friend Dave, 1:46.89, January 23, 2005
1⅛ miles: J D's Date, 1:54.91, April 2, 2005
1¼ miles: Produckson, 2:08.36, April 2, 2005

Tillamook County Fair

Location: 4603 E. Third St., P.O. Box 455, Tillamook, Or. 97141-2943
Phone: (503) 842-2272
Fax: (503) 842-3314
Website: *www.wcn.net/tillamookfair*
E-Mail: tillamookfair@wcn.net
Year Founded: 1891
Abbreviation: Til

Ownership

Tillamook County

Officers

President: Jack DeSwart
Director of Racing: Mel Tupper
Racing Secretary: Danny Bryson
Vice President: Mel Tupper
Director of Publicity: Jerry Underwood
Track Announcer: Dean Mazucca

Racing Dates

2005: August 11-August 13, 3 days
2006: August 10-August 12, 3 days
2007: August 9-August 11, 3 days

Track Layout

Main Circumference: 4 furlongs

Attendance

Average Daily Recent Meeting: 2,000, 2005
Total Attendance Recent Meeting: 6,000, 2005

Handle

Average On-Track Recent Meeting: \$36,956, 2005
Total On-Track Recent Meeting: \$110,869, 2005
Highest Single-Day On-Track Record Recent Meet: \$49,188, August 13, 2005

Fastest Times of 2005 (Dirt)

a5 furlongs: Mountain Mustang, 1:03, August 13, 2005
a1$^{1}/_{8}$ miles: Flying Cisco, 2:06.20, August 13, 2005

Pennsylvania

Penn National Race Course

Built by a group of Central Pennsylvania investors, Penn National Race Course is located 13 miles from the state capital, Harrisburg. It staged its first race meeting on August 30, 1972. The following year, Penn National bought the racing license of defunct Pitt Park and began an essentially year-round racing schedule. In 1978, Penn National built the state's first turf course. Led by principal owner Peter D. Carlino, Penn National has been an innovator in Pennsylvania's racing industry. Philadelphia-area businessman Carlino bought one of the track's operating licenses in 1974 and the other in '83. With legalization of telephone betting in 1982, Penn National began the commonwealth's first account-wagering system, and the following year it began the first cable-television broadcast of its races. Following legislative approval of off-track wagering in 1989, Penn National built and operated six facilities in Central Pennsylvania. In 1994, the track's parent company, Penn National Gaming Inc., held an initial public stock offering. With those proceeds and subsequent stock issues, Penn National has financed the acquisitions of Charles Town Races, a Thoroughbred track in West Virginia, and Pocono Downs, a Standardbred track near Wilkes-Barre, Pennsylvania, as well as casino properties. Pocono Downs was sold in 2005 after Penn National Gaming received legislative approval for slot machines at its namesake track.

Location: P.O. Box 32, 720 Bow Creek Rd., Grantville, Pa. 17028-0032
Phone: (717) 469-2211
Fax: (717) 469-2910
Website: *www.pnrc.com*
E-Mail: pnrc@pngaming.com
Year Founded: 1972
Dates of Inaugural Meeting: August 30, 1972-December 31, 1972
Abbreviation: Pen
Acreage: 600
Number of Stalls: 1,200
Seating Capacity: 9,570

Ownership

Penn National Gaming Inc.

Officers

Chairman: Peter M. Carlino
President: Kevin DeSanctis
General Manager: Gary Luderitz
Racing Secretary: Paul N. Jenkins
Director of Operations: Rob Marella
Director of Admissions: Carole Kneasel
Director of Marketing: Frederick D. Lipkin
Director of Mutuels: Carole Kneasel
Director of Publicity: Frederick D. Lipkin
Director of Sales: Grace Vazquez
Director of Simulcasting: Chris Camplese
Stewards: Robert S. Campbell, Thomas L. Crouse, Rodney P. Peters
Track Announcer: John Bogar
Track Photographer: Gill's Positive Images
Track Superintendent: Donald Leitzel
Security: Glenn Firestone
Asst. Racing Secretary: William H. Bell
Horsemen's Bookkeeper: Sherlene Servideo

Racing Dates

2005: January 3-December 29, 182 days
2006: January 4-December 29, 227 days

Track Layout

Main Circumference: 1 mile
Main Track Chute: 6 furlongs and 1$^{1}/_{4}$ miles
Main Length of Stretch: 990 feet
Main Turf Circumference: 7 furlongs

Attendance

Average Daily Recent Meeting: 1,145, 2005
Highest Single-Day Record: 15,442, August 2, 1980
Total Attendance Recent Meeting: 233,653, 2005

Handle

Average All Sources Recent Meeting: \$1,044,856, 2005
Average On-Track Recent Meeting: \$54,836, 2005
Single-Day Total Handle All Sources: \$2,173,921, December 26, 1998
Total All Sources Recent Meeting: \$190,163,744, 2005
Total On-Track Recent Meeting: \$9,980,171, 2005

Mutuel Records

Highest Win: \$343.40, Busy Lady, Decemeber 20, 1977
Highest Exacta: \$8,430, April 13, 1988
Highest Trifecta: \$42,886.50, May 27, 1980
Lowest Daily Double: \$27,985.80, July 11, 1975
Highest Other Exotics: \$543,014, Twin Trifecta, June 14, 1988

Leaders

Recent Meeting, Leading Jockey: Thomas Clifton, 161, 2005
Recent Meeting, Leading Owner: J Jeps Stable, 38, 2005
Recent Meeting, Leading Trainer: John Zimmerman, 110, 2005

Track Records, Main Dirt

4 furlongs: Gross, :46$^{1}/_{5}$, April 13, 1973
4$^{1}/_{2}$ furlongs: Kens Dancer, :50.59, May 5, 2005
5 furlongs: On the Phone, :56.60, July 13, 1996
5$^{1}/_{2}$ furlongs: Cortan, 1:03$^{1}/_{5}$, May 29, 1978; Flaming Emperor, 1:03.20, June 26, 1994; Hunter's Ridge, 1:03.20, May 1, 1996; Window B, 1:03.23, November 20, 2004
6 furlongs: Jiva Coolit, 1:08$^{4}/_{5}$, May 22, 1977; Dainty Dotsie, 1:08$^{4}/_{5}$, August 13, 1977; Spacemaker, 1:08.80, May 11, 1997; Who's Bluffing, 1:08.85, January 4, 2006

1 mile: Vambourine, 1:36$^{1}/_{5}$, June 12, 1977; Agate Bay, 1:36$^{1}/_{5}$, March 22, 1981
1m 70 yds: Wee Thunder, 1:39.60, July 13, 1996
1$^{1}/_{16}$ miles: A Letter to Harry, 1:41$^{1}/_{5}$, September 10, 1978
1$^{1}/_{8}$ miles: Collection Agent, 1:49$^{1}/_{5}$, August 22, 1987
1$^{3}/_{16}$ miles: Bar Tab, 1:55$^{2}/_{5}$, October 14, 1972
1$^{1}/_{4}$ miles: Adda Nickell, 2:03$^{3}/_{5}$, October 30, 1976
1$^{1}/_{2}$ miles: Holly Holme, 2:31$^{2}/_{5}$, September 29, 1973
1$^{5}/_{8}$ miles: New Episode, 2:48.15, May 18, 2001
1$^{3}/_{4}$ miles: Chasqui, 3:00, June 21, 1980
2 miles: Finny Flyer, 3:28, May 25, 1974
Other: 2 furlongs, Pensglitter, :20.71, October 9, 2004

Track Records, Main Turf

5 furlongs: Bop, :54.61, August 3, 2002
1 mile: The Very One, 1:33$^{1}/_{5}$, July 15, 1979
1m 70yds: Aborigine, 1:37$^{1}/_{5}$, August 20, 1978
1$^{1}/_{16}$ miles: Told, 1:38, September 14, 1980
1$^{1}/_{2}$ miles: Coalitioncandidate, 2:27, May 27, 1991
Other: a5 furlongs, Threewitt, :56.28, July 14, 2005; a1 mile, Jeddo, 1:37.57, July 29, 2005; a1m 70yds, Jrsoutofcontrol, 1:40.22, July 13, 2005; a1$^{1}/_{16}$ miles, Stack Lass, 1:44.12, July 13, 2005

Principal Races

Pennsylvania Governor's Cup H., Blue Mountain Juvenile S., Danzig S., Wonders Delight S., Capital City H.

Fastest Times of 2005 (Dirt)

2 furlongs: Forty Niner Gold, :21.23, April 29, 2005
4$^{1}/_{2}$ furlongs: Kens Dancer, :50.59, May 5, 2005
5 furlongs: Eastern Cat, :57.42, June 30, 2005
5$^{1}/_{2}$ furlongs: Humble Hero, 1:03.28, January 29, 2005
6 furlongs: Salt Silence, 1:09.12, June 29, 2005
1 mile: Holdeverything, 1:36.66, February 18, 2005
1m 70 yds: Paparazzi, 1:42.13, August 24, 2005
1$^{1}/_{16}$ miles: Folkestone Park, 1:44.98, August 10, 2005
1$^{1}/_{8}$ miles: Tiffany Gold, 1:51.83, March 31, 2005
1$^{3}/_{16}$ miles: Real Tears, 1:58.89, August 5, 2005
1$^{1}/_{4}$ miles: Big Irish, 2:06.88, November 9, 2005
1$^{1}/_{2}$ miles: Tiffany Gold, 2:33.62, April 14, 2005
1$^{3}/_{4}$ miles: Chute the Breeze, 3:06.48, December 29, 2005
2 miles: Alkarnak, 3:35.33, September 3, 2005

Fastest Times of 2005 (Turf)

5 furlongs: Tacirring, :54.80, August 5, 2005
a5 furlongs: Threewitt, :56.28, July 14, 2005
1 mile: One Iron, 1:34.43, August 24, 2005
a1 miles: Jeddo, 1:37.57, July 29, 2005
1m 70 yds: Crete (Aus), 1:38.56, August 24, 2005
a1m 70 yds: Jrsoutofcontrol, 1:40.22, July 13, 2005
1$^{1}/_{16}$ miles: Little Marshall, 1:41.42, June 8, 2005
a1$^{1}/_{16}$ miles: Stack Lass, 1:44.12, July 13, 2005

Philadelphia Park

Built reluctantly and inexpensively in the early 1970s, the track now known as Philadelphia Park has had a difficult history. But, it has emerged as a leader in providing fan amenities and phone wagering in its region. When racing first arrived in Pennsylvania in the late 1960s, both Thoroughbred and Standardbred racing were conducted at Liberty Bell Park in Philadelphia's Northeast section. But with regional lawmakers insisting on a separate Thoroughbred facility, Keystone Race Track was built for $20-million approximately one mile north of Liberty Bell in Bensalem Township, across the city border in Bucks County. It opened in November 1974 with two ownership groups, which often feuded. Keystone inaugurated the track's signature race, the Pennsylvania Derby (G3), in 1979, and phone betting was authorized in '82. In 1984, Robert Brennan-controlled International Thoroughbred Breeders Inc. bought Keystone for $37.5-million to avoid competition for its Garden State Park, which opened in April 1985 (and closed in 2001). Brennan's company renamed the track Philadelphia Park and spent several million dollars renovating the grandstand and the racing surface, including the addition of a turf course. Financially failing International Thoroughbred Breeders sold the track to Greenwood Racing, headed by British bookmaking executives Robert Green and William Hogwood, for $67-million in 1990, the year in which the track opened the first of its five off-track betting facilities. In May 1999, Philadelphia Park completed an acclaimed $4-million renovation of its first floor.

Location: 3001 Street Rd., P.O. Box 1000, Bensalem, Pa. 19020-8512
Phone: (215) 639-9000, (800) 523-6886
Fax: (215) 639-8330
Website: *www.philadelphiapark.com*
E-Mail: kjones@philadelphiapark.com
Year Founded: 1974
Dates of Inaugural Meeting: November 4, 1974
Abbreviation: Pha
Acreage: 417
Number of Stalls: 1,600
Seating Capacity: 8,700

Ownership

Greenwood Racing

Officers

Chairman: Robert W. Green
Chief Executive Officer: Harold G. Handel
President: Robert W. Green
Director of Racing: Salvatore Sinatra
Racing Secretary: Salvatore Sinatra
Treasurer: Matt Hayes
Director of Operations: Joe Wilson
Director of Finance: Anthony D. Ricci
Director of Mutuels: William Barnes
Vice President: Len Carey, Andrew J. Green
Director of Publicity: Keith Jones
Director of Simulcasting: Geri Mercer
Stewards: Samuel A. Boulmetis Jr., Jonathan S. Gerweck, John P. Hicks
Track Announcer: Keith Jones
Track Photographer: Equiphoto
Track Superintendent: Stan James
Asst. Racing Secretary: Nicholas P. Black
Clerk of the Course: Sandra Ricciardi

Racing Dates

2005: January 1-December 31, 214 days
2006: January 1-December 31, 212 days

Track Layout

Main Circumference: 1 mile
Main Track Chute: 7 furlongs and 1$^{1}/_{4}$ miles
Main Width: 80 feet
Main Length of Stretch: 974 feet
Main Turf Circumference: 7 furlongs
Main Turf Chute: 1$^{1}/_{8}$ miles

Attendance

Average Daily Recent Meeting: 2,733, 2005
Highest Single-Day Record: 28,692, May 30, 1983
Total Attendance Recent Meeting: 584,889, 2005

Handle

Average All Sources Recent Meeting: $1,412,597, 2005
Average On-Track Recent Meeting: $131,239, 2005
Total All Sources Recent Meeting: $302,295,813, 2005
Total On-Track Recent Meeting: $28,085,109, 2005

Mutuel Records

Highest Win: $588.80, Oak Tree, February 17, 1982
Highest Exacta: $6,792.60, November 18, 1976
Highest Trifecta: $55,608.90, November 1, 1976
Highest Daily Double: $2,943.40, December 13, 1976

Leaders

Career, Leading Jockey by Titles: Rick Wilson, 9

Career, Leading Trainer by Titles: Scott A. Lake, 7
Career, Leading Jockey by Stakes Wins: Rick Wilson, 75
Career, Leading Trainer by Stakes Wins: Dennis Heimer, 56
Recent Meeting, Leading Jockey: Harry Vega, 204, 2005
Recent Meeting, Leading Owner: Plumstead Stables, 59, 2005
Recent Meeting, Leading Trainer: Scott A. Lake, 104, 2005
Recent Meeting, Leading Horse: Senor Cielo Two, 7, 2005

Records

Single Meet, Leading Jockey by Wins: Stewart Elliott, 238, 2002
Single Meet, Leading Trainer by Wins: David R. Vance, 172, 1976

Track Records, Main Dirt

4 furlongs: Heres a Tip, :45, June 11, 1982
$4\frac{1}{2}$ furlongs: Distinctive Hat, :51.48, May 2, 1994
5 furlongs: My Favorite Grub, :56, September 7, 1998
$5\frac{1}{2}$ furlongs: Saint Verre, 1:02.65, July 17, 2000
6 furlongs: Iron Punch, 1:07.89, July 29, 2000
$6\frac{1}{2}$ furlongs: Tricky Mister, 1:14.40, June 21, 1998
7 furlongs: Flaming Bridle, 1:20.61, September 28, 1999
1 mile: Regal Count, 1:34$\frac{4}{5}$, December 5, 1985
1m 70 yds: Tragedy, 1:38.70, December 12, 1995
$1\frac{1}{16}$ miles: Cool Spring Park, 1:40$\frac{4}{5}$, November 4, 1974
$1\frac{1}{8}$ miles: Selari Spirit, 1:47, November 30, 1974
$1\frac{3}{16}$ miles: Southern Shade, 1:56$\frac{2}{5}$, October 20, 1984
$1\frac{1}{4}$ miles: It's Always Archie, 2:02, November 23, 1974
$1\frac{1}{2}$ miles: Laugh a Minute, 2:31, January 4, 1992
$1\frac{5}{8}$ miles: River Wolf, 2:46$\frac{2}{5}$, October 13, 1990
$1\frac{3}{4}$ miles: Johnny's Silencer, 2:57$\frac{4}{5}$, December 17, 1988
2 miles: Perfect to a Tee, 3:25.87, September 2, 1996
Other: 2 furlongs, Queen Millie, :21.32, January 30, 1994; $1\frac{9}{16}$ miles, Laugh a Minute, 2:40.85, January 18, 1992; $1\frac{1}{16}$ miles, Laugh a Minute, 2:53.20, December 21, 1991; $1\frac{13}{16}$ miles, Fire North, 3:04.80, March 14, 1992; $1\frac{7}{8}$ miles, Haberdasher, 3:13$\frac{3}{5}$, October 17, 1987; $2\frac{1}{8}$ miles, Heavy Medal Man, 3:39.59, April 25, 1992; $2\frac{1}{4}$ miles, Transfer Ticket, 3:56, December 31, 1988; $2\frac{1}{2}$ miles, Half Chance, 4:24.15, May 25, 1992

Track Records, Main Turf

5 furlongs: Max West, :55.91, October 2, 2005
$7\frac{1}{2}$ furlongs: Here Comes Scott, 1:30.85, September 10, 1994
1 mile: Lake Cecebe, 1:35$\frac{3}{5}$, June 28, 1986
1m 70yds: Rolfe's Ruby, 1:39$\frac{2}{5}$, June 21, 1986; Marlish, 1:39$\frac{2}{5}$, August 13, 1986
$1\frac{1}{16}$ miles: Whatever For, 1:40$\frac{2}{5}$, June 22, 1986
$1\frac{1}{8}$ miles: Whatever For, 1:46$\frac{1}{5}$, September 1, 1986
$1\frac{3}{8}$ miles: Juanca (Arg), 2:16$\frac{2}{5}$, September 1, 1986
$1\frac{1}{2}$ miles: Lord Zada, 2:28.38, June 10, 2000
2 miles: Chippenham Park, 3:28$\frac{4}{5}$, September 1, 1990
Other: a5 furlongs, Sport d'Hiver, :56.61, August 26, 2001; a$7\frac{1}{2}$ furlongs, Tia's Miss, 1:32.55, September 25, 2005; a1 mile, Speak Compelling, 1:39.77, July 24, 2000; a1m 70yds, Vin Rouge, 1:41.38, July 17, 1994; a$1\frac{1}{16}$ miles, Mount Bleu, 1:43.26, October 4, 1994; a$1\frac{1}{8}$ miles, Brenton Reef, 1:50$\frac{1}{5}$, August 6, 1989; a$1\frac{3}{8}$ miles, Bostic Hill, 2:20.49, September 29, 2001; a$1\frac{1}{2}$ miles, Mort the Sport, 2:31, August 22, 1989; a2 miles, Proctor's Image, 3:27$\frac{2}{5}$, October 15, 1988

Principal Races

Pennsylvania Derby (G2), Cotillion H. (G2), Pennsylvania Oaks, Donald LeVine Memorial H., Turf Monster H.

Interesting Facts

Previous Names and Dates: Liberty Bell Park Race Track 1969-'74; Keystone Race Track 1974-'84

Fastest Times of 2005 (Dirt)

$4\frac{1}{2}$ furlongs: Roving Miss, :53.34, May 30, 2005
5 furlongs: Flintville, :57.11, June 4, 2005
$5\frac{1}{2}$ furlongs: Alarmed, 1:03.26, October 24, 2005
6 furlongs: Southern Legacy, 1:09.47, March 28, 2005
$6\frac{1}{2}$ furlongs: Fitting Tribute, 1:15.11, June 1, 2005
7 furlongs: Gadace's Khamseh, 1:21.27, May 28, 2005
1 mile: Stroud, 1:37.62, April 5, 2005
1m 70 yds: One Nice Cat, 1:40.43, April 4, 2005
$1\frac{1}{16}$ miles: Tarek, 1:43.54, January 25, 2005
$1\frac{1}{8}$ miles: Sun King, 1:49.43, September 5, 2005
$1\frac{1}{4}$ miles: Baryshnikov's Song, 2:05.04, February 18, 2005

Fastest Times of 2005 (Turf)

5 furlongs: Max West, :55.91, October 2, 2005
a5 furlongs: Max West, :57.15, August 6, 2005
$7\frac{1}{2}$ furlongs: Exceptional Appeal, 1:31.93, June 1, 2005
a$7\frac{1}{2}$ furlongs: Tia's Miss, 1:32.55, September 25, 2005
1 mile: Justagallop, 1:37.20, September 7, 2005
1m 70 yds: Quies, 1:40.84, September 13, 2005
a1m 70 yds: Manukai, 1:43.94, August 9, 2005
$1\frac{1}{16}$ miles: Dynamic Cat, 1:43.42, July 23, 2005
a$1\frac{1}{16}$ miles: Inapinch, 1:45.51, July 31, 2005
$1\frac{1}{8}$ miles: Crazy Song, 1:49.63, October 1, 2005
a$1\frac{1}{8}$ miles: John Calvin, 1:52.07, August 8, 2005
$1\frac{3}{8}$ miles: Publisher's Phil, 2:16.92, September 27, 2005
a$1\frac{3}{8}$ miles: Blame It On Beau, 2:21.26, August 9, 2005
a$2\frac{1}{16}$ miles: Party Airs, 3:44.43, July 23, 2005

South Dakota

Brown County Fair

Location: 25 Market St., Aberdeen, S.D. 57401-4293
Phone: (605) 626-7110
Website: *www.brown.sd.us/fair*
E-Mail: bcfair@brown.sd.us
Abbreviation: BCF

Racing Dates

2005: May 14-May 30, 7 days
2006: May 13-May 29, 7 days

Principal Races

South Dakota Bred Futurity, South Dakota Bred Derby, Open Thoroughbred Derby, Governor's H., Legion S.

Fastest Times of 2005 (Dirt)

6 furlongs: Prairie Commander, 1:18, May 22, 2005

Fort Pierre Horse Races

Location: P.O. Box 426, Fort Pierre, S.D. 57532-0426
Phone: (605) 223-2178
Website: *www.sdhorseracing.com*
Abbreviation: FtP

Racing Dates

2005: April 16-May 8, 8 days
2006: April 15-May 7, 8 days

Principal Races

Lucky Bendewald Memorial S., Thoroughbred Allowance S., Fort Pierre Thoroughbred Derby, Governor's H., South Dakota Thoroughbred Futurity Trials

Fastest Times of 2005 (Dirt)

5 furlongs: Big Sky Blue, 1:04.80, April 17, 2005

Texas

Gillespie County Fairgrounds

Location: 530 Fair Dr., P.O. Box 526, Fredericksburg, Tx. 78624-0526
Phone: (830) 997-2359
Fax: (830) 997-4923
Website: *www.gillespiefair.com*
E-Mail: gcffa@ctesc.net
Year Founded: 1881
Abbreviation: Gil
Number of Stalls: 200
Seating Capacity: 3,000

Ownership

Gillespie County Fair and Festival Association

Officers

President: Edward Stroeher
Director of Racing: Brian Roeder

Racing Secretary: Scott Sherwood
Treasurer: Frederick Jung
Director of Operations: Mike Klein
Vice President: Leon Welgehausen, Ruben Sagebiel Jr.
Director of Publicity: Russell Hartmann
Track Announcer: Dudley Althaus, Louis Rech
Track Photographer: Marc Bennett
Track Superintendent: Dorman Schmidt

Racing Dates

2005: July 2-August 28, 8 days
2006: July 1-August 27, 8 days

Track Layout

Main Circumference: 5 furlongs

Attendance

Average Daily Recent Meeting: 1,423, 2005
Total Attendance Recent Meeting: 11,381, 2005

Handle

Average On-Track Recent Meeting: $129,716, 2005
Total On-Track Recent Meeting: $1,037,725, 2005

Leaders

Recent Meeting, Leading Jockey: Salvador Perez, 6, 2005
Recent Meeting, Leading Trainer: Isai V. Gonzalez, 2, 2005; Jimmy L. Ray, 2, 2005; Pilar A. Deleon, 2, 2005; Alfonso R. Ramirez, 2, 2005; Bobby A. Jenkins, 2, 2005
Recent Meeting, Leading Horse: Secret Lake, 2, 2005

Principal Races

Texas Thoroughbred Breeders' S., Gillespie County Fair Association S.

Fastest Times of 2005 (Dirt)

5½ furlongs: Trancus Genuine, 1:08.70, July 17, 2005
6 furlongs: Latexo, 1:14.10, August 27, 2005; Pardon Me Girls, 1:14.10, August 14, 2005

Lone Star Park

One decade after Texas legalized pari-mutuel racing, Lone Star Park at Grand Prairie opened in 1997 and joined Sam Houston Race Park in Houston and Retama Park near San Antonio as the three major tracks in the state. Located in the Dallas-Fort Worth metropolitan area, Lone Star was built for $96-million by the Lone Star Jockey Club, a group headed by real estate moguls Trammell Crow and his son, Harlan, of Trammell Crow Co. The track's sale to Magna Entertainment Corp. for $99-million, including assumption of debt, was completed in 2002. The All-Star Jockey Championship was started by Lone Star and was sponsored by the National Thoroughbred Racing Association to 2004. Texas-bred Thoroughbreds take center stage for the Stars of Texas Day. Lone Star was host to the Breeders' Cup World Championships in 2004.

Location: 1000 Lone Star Pkwy., Grand Prairie, Tx. 75050-7941
Phone: (972) 263-7223, (800) 795-7223
Fax: (972) 237-1155
Website: *www.lonestarpark.com*
E-Mail: feedback@lonestarpark.com
Dates of Inaugural Meeting: April 17, 1997
Abbreviation: LS
Acreage: 285
Number of Stalls: 1,594
Seating Capacity: 12,000

Ownership

Magna Entertainment Corp.

Officers

Chairman: Frank Stronach
President: Corey S. Johnsen
General Manager: Jeffrey Greco
Director of Racing: Larry A. Craft
Racing Secretary: Larry A. Craft
Treasurer: Paula Dowell
Director of Communications: Darren Rogers
Director of Finance: Paula Dowell
Director of Marketing: Kristen Schweitzer
Director of Mutuels: Don Fontenot
Vice President: Jeffrey Greco
Director of Publicity: Darren Rogers
Director of Simulcasting: Mindy Freeland
Horsemen's Liaison: Rainey Brookfield
Stewards: Jerry Burgess, Norman Morrison, Dennis Sidener
Track Announcer: John Lies
Track Photographer: Reed Palmer
Track Superintendent: Ron Moore

Racing Dates

2005: April 13-July 17, 67 days
2006: April 13-July 23, 66 days

Track Layout

Main Circumference: 1 mile
Main Track Chute: 7 furlongs and 1¼ miles
Main Width: 90 feet
Main Length of Stretch: 930 feet
Main Turf Circumference: 7 furlongs
Main Turf Chute: 1⅛ miles
Main Turf Width: 80 feet
Main Turf Length of Stretch: 900 feet

Attendance

Average Daily Recent Meeting: 7,015, 2005
Highest Single-Day Record: 53,717, October 30, 2004
Highest Single-Meet Record: 715,900, 1998
Record Daily Average for Single Meet: 9,800, 1998; 9,800 Fall 2004
Total Attendance Recent Meeting: 470,000, 2005

Handle

Average All Sources Recent Meeting: $2,470,149, 2005
Average On-Track Recent Meeting: $537,313, 2005
Single-Day On-Track Handle: $13,326,726, October 30, 2004
Single-Day Total Handle All Sources: $120,863,117, October 30, 2004
Total All Sources Recent Meeting: 165,500,000, 2005
Total On-Track Recent Meeting: $36,000,000, 2005

Mutuel Records

Highest Win: $231.40, Purse Stealer, May 26, 2001
Highest Exacta: $6,900.00, May 26, 2001
Highest Trifecta: $117,108, May 26, 2001
Highest Daily Double: $3,016.80, July 18, 1998
Highest Pick 3: $33,651.00, May 28, 2001
Highest Pick 6: $39,891.80, April 26, 1998
Highest Other Exotics: $96,993, Superfecta, May 28, 2001
Highest Stakes Win: $114.00, Thatsusintheolbean, 1997 Alysheba Breeders' Cup
Highest Quinella: $1,103.80, June 8, 2002
Highest Pick 4: $18,069.00, July 2, 2003

Leaders

Career, Leading Jockey by Titles: Corey Lanerie, 4
Career, Leading Owner by Titles: Ken Murphy, 3
Career, Leading Trainer by Titles: Steve Asmussen, 6
Career, Leading Jockey by Stakes Wins: Corey Lanerie, 23
Career, Leading Owner by Stakes Wins: Heiligbrodt Racing Stable, 8
Career, Leading Trainer by Stakes Wins: Steve Asmussen, 51
Career, Leading Jockey by Wins: Corey Lanerie, 476
Career, Leading Owner by Wins: Ken Murphy
Career, Leading Trainer by Wins: Steve Asmussen, 597
Recent Meeting, Leading Jockey: Monte Berry, 87, 2005
Recent Meeting, Leading Trainer: Steve Asmussen, 63, 2005

Records

Single-Day Jockey Wins: Ronald Ardoin, 6, July 17, 1997, Anthony Lovato, 6, July 3, 2001
Single-Day Trainer Wins: Steve Asmussen, 7, July 14, 2002
Single Meet, Leading Jockey by Wins: Corey Lanerie, 102, 1999
Single Meet, Leading Owner by Wins: Ken Murphy, 26, 2003
Single Meet, Leading Trainer by Wins: Cole Norman, 98, 2003

Track Records, Main Dirt

4½ furlongs: Polevault, :51.19, May 15, 2005
5 furlongs: Joyful Tune, :56.25, May 5, 2002
5½ furlongs: That Tat, 1:01.88, April 11, 2003

6 furlongs: Savorthetime, 1:07.82, May 31, 2004
6½ furlongs: Spiritbound, 1:14.16, May 3, 1997
7 furlongs: Yearly Report, 1:20.67, October 29, 2004
1 mile: Isitingood, 1:34.44, April 20, 1997
1 1/16 miles: Dixie Dot Com, 1:40.53, May 28, 2001
1⅛ miles: Ashado, 1:48.26, October 30, 2004
1 3/16 miles: Moosekabear, 1:56.21, May 10, 1997
1¼ miles: Ghostzapper, 1:59.02, October, 30, 2004
1½ miles: Tali Hai, 2:32.57, July 5, 1997
1¾ miles: Sir Moon Dancer, 3:00.46, July 19, 1998
Other: 1 5/16 miles, Gabriel's Pat, 2:12.34, October 22, 2004; 2½ furlongs, Yes He Will, :26.53, October 7, 1997

Track Records, Main Turf

5 furlongs: Caro's Royalty, :55.60, June 28, 1997
7½ furlongs: Special Moments, 1:28.20, May 24, 1998
1 mile: Kiraday, 1:33.56, July 4, 1997
1 1/16 miles: Sharpest Image (Ire), 1:40.05, June 12, 1998
1⅛ miles: Yaqthan (Ire), 1:45.54, May 25, 1998
1⅜ miles: Rugged Bugger, 2:13.53, May 10, 1998
1½ miles: Final Val, 2:28.20, July 4, 1998

Principal Races

Lone Star Park H. (G3), WinStar Distaff H. (G3), Texas Mile S. (G3), Lone Star Derby (G3), Dallas Turf Cup H.

Interesting Facts

Achievements/Milestones: Lone Star Park handled a daily average of $2.39-million during its inaugural 1997 meeting, which ranked number one among all U.S. racetracks built since 1970. As an encore, Lone Star Park became the first racetrack in modern history to increase attendance in its second year of operation, from 712,673 customers during the 1997 Thoroughbred season to 715,995 in '98.

Notable Events

National Thoroughbred Racing Association All-Star Jockey Championship, Lone Star Million Day

Fastest Times of 2005 (Dirt)

4½ furlongs: Polevault, :51.19, May 15, 2005
5 furlongs: Premier Dance, :56.68, May 26, 2005
5½ furlongs: War Bridle, 1:02.56, June 4, 2005
6 furlongs: Rodeo's Castle, 1:07.85, May 14, 2005
6½ furlongs: Rhome Magic, 1:15.67, May 21, 2005
7 furlongs: Bob O's Boy, 1:21.61, May 26, 2005
1 mile: High Strike Zone, 1:35.34, April 30, 2005
1 1/16 miles: General Charley, 1:41.76, April 30, 2005
1⅛ miles: Blinding Prospect, 1:53.38, May 28, 2005

Fastest Times of 2005 (Turf)

5 furlongs: Streak of Royalty, :55.87, June 26, 2005
7½ furlongs: Sapphires N Halos, 1:29.68, July 10, 2005
1 mile: Cajole, 1:35.83, June 11, 2005
1 1/16 miles: Waupaca, 1:42.87, May 7, 2005
1⅛ miles: Sea Dub, 1:48.82, June 18, 2005
1⅜ miles: Blinding Prospect, 2:18.87, June 18, 2005
1½ miles: Thirteen Colonies, 2:36.19, July 16, 2005

Manor Downs

Thoroughbred racing debuted in 2002 at Manor Downs, a small racetrack near Austin, Texas, that long had offered only straightaway Quarter Horse and Paint racing. Ordered by the Texas Racing Commission to improve its racetrack to accommodate Thoroughbred racing, Manor (pronounced May-ner) spent more than $4-million to expand its oval to 7½ furlongs and to renovate the barn area and other sections. Manor, which is owned by Frances Tapp, was among the tracks in Texas's far-flung nonpari-mutuel circuit that flourished before legislation allowing pari-mutuel wagering was passed in 1987.

Location: 9211 Hill Ln., Manor, Tx. 78653
Phone: (512) 272-5581
Fax: (512) 272-4403
Website: *www.manordowns.com*
Abbreviation: Man

Ownership

Frances Tapp

Officers

Director of Racing: Sammy J. Burton
Racing Secretary: Melanie Posey
Track Superintendent: Robert Allan Key

Racing Dates

2005: March 5-April 24, 16 days
2006: February 25-April 23, 18 days

Attendance

Average Daily Recent Meeting: 3,720, 2005
Total Attendance Recent Meeting: 59,512, 2005

Handle

Average On-Track Recent Meeting: $81,550, 2005
Total On-Track Recent Meeting: $1,304,804, 2005

Leaders

Recent Meeting, Leading Jockey: Salvador Perez, 8, 2006
Recent Meeting, Leading Trainer: Jaime Castellanos, 7, 2006
Recent Meeting, Leading Horse: Toga On, 2, 2006; Arrogant Slew, 2, 2006; Shockproof, 2, 2006; Lovely Secret, 2, 2006

Principal Races

Manor Downs Thoroughbred Distaff S., Tony Sanchez Memorial Mile S., Manor Downs Thoroughbred Futurity, Manor Downs Distance Cup S.

Fastest Times of 2005 (Dirt)

4 furlongs: Lovely Secret, :45.42, March 12, 2005
4½ furlongs: Rockin Early, :52.72, April 17, 2005
5½ furlongs: Collier Gold, 1:05.01, April 16, 2005
6 furlongs: Nature's Verdict, 1:11.74, April 2, 2005
7½ furlongs: Ship of the Line, 1:32.75, March 20, 2005
1 mile: Easy too Easy, 1:38.68, April 24, 2005
1 1/16 miles: Irish Mountain, 1:48.29, April 17, 2005

Retama Park

Retama Park opened in April 1995 in Selma, 15 minutes northeast of San Antonio. The racetrack is both uniquely named—for the green-limbed deciduous tree or shrub native to south and west Texas—and uniquely designed, with its mission-style, five-tiered grandstand featuring arched entranceways, food courts, the Terrace Dining Room, the Race Book and Sports Bar, and the Player's Club for Turf and Field Club members. The track's original investors hired well-known racing executive Robert J. Quigley to oversee construction of the $79-million plant and the track's opening, but the facility failed to meet even modest wagering projections. After failing to pay its bondholders, the track filed for bankruptcy protection in 1996 and was purchased by Call Now Inc.

Location: 1 Retama Pkwy., Selma, Tx. 78154-3808
Phone: (210) 651-7000
Fax: (210) 651-7055
Website: *www.retamapark.com*
E-Mail: run@retamapark.com
Year Founded: 1989
Dates of Inaugural Meeting: April 7, 1995
Abbreviation: Ret
Acreage: 226
Number of Stalls: 1,288
Seating Capacity: 6,543

Ownership

Retama Development Corp.

Officers

Chief Executive Officer: Bryan P. Brown
Chairman: Joe R. Straus Jr.
General Manager: Robert W. Pollock
Director of Racing: Larry A. Craft
Racing Secretary: James C. Leatherman
Treasurer: Lisa L. Medrano

Director of Marketing: Doug Vair
Director of Mutuels: Jackie F. Hart
Director of Publicity: Doug Vair
Director of Simulcasting: Steven M. Ross
Horsemen's Liaison: Cathy Davies
Stewards: Rick Brasher, Dennis Sidener, Ricky Walker
Track Announcer: Tom Harris
Track Photographer: Coady Photography
Track Superintendent: Jesse L. Cardenas
Security: Richard L. Cole

Racing Dates
2005: August 5-October 15, 43 days
2006: August 11-November 4, 51 days

Track Layout
Main Circumference: 1 mile
Main Track Chute: 7 furlongs
Main Width: Homestretch: 110 feet; Backstretch: 90 feet
Main Length of Stretch: 990 feet
Main Turf Circumference: 7 furlongs
Main Turf Chute: $1\frac{1}{8}$ miles
Main Turf Width: 90 feet
Main Turf Length of Stretch: 990 feet

Attendance
Average Daily Recent Meeting: 3,310, 2005
Highest Single-Day Record: 16,827, April 7, 1995
Highest Single-Meet Record: 452,421, 1995
Record Daily Average for Single Meet: 4,713, 1995
Total Attendance Recent Meeting: 142,347, 2005

Handle
Average All Sources Recent Meeting: $695,965, 2005
Average On-Track Recent Meeting: $97,517, 2005
Single-Day On-Track Handle: $705,712, April 7, 1995
Single-Day Total Handle All Sources: $2,502,823, October 27, 2001
Total All Sources Recent Meeting: $29,926,498, 2005
Total On-Track Recent Meeting: $4,193,247, 2005

Mutuel Records
Highest Win: $136.40, Icy's Baba, August 15, 1999

Leaders
Recent Meeting, Leading Jockey: Larry Taylor, 58, 2005
Recent Meeting, Leading Owner: Terry Eoff, 12, 2005
Recent Meeting, Leading Trainer: Danny Pish, 32, 2005
Recent Meeting, Leading Horse: Oro Classic, 4, 2005

Records
Single Meet, Leading Jockey by Wins: Corey Lanerie, 99, 1995, Ted Gondron, 99, 1996
Single Meet, Leading Owner by Wins: Carolyn A. Crowly, 17, 1996
Single Meet, Leading Trainer by Wins: Steve Asmussen, 48, 1995

Track Records, Main Dirt
$4\frac{1}{2}$ furlongs: Raise a Tab, :51.06, August 1, 1998
5 furlongs: Teed Off, :56.20, August 20, 2000
$5\frac{1}{2}$ furlongs: Bailando, 1:02.90, May 13, 1995
6 furlongs: Bucharest, 1:08.82, May 10, 1995
$6\frac{1}{2}$ furlongs: Heavily Armed, 1:15.30, August 30, 1997
7 furlongs: Bucharest, 1:22.05, May 24, 1995
1 mile: Mr. Pappion, 1:36.90, May 11, 1995
$1\frac{1}{16}$ miles: Heavily Armed, 1:43.20, September 20, 1997
$1\frac{1}{8}$ miles: Fletcher's Pride, 1:51.43, August 14, 1998
$1\frac{1}{4}$ miles: Call Me Wild, 2:04.01, September 3, 1995
$1\frac{3}{8}$ miles: Slews Minister, 2:19.95, October 28, 2000
Other: $2\frac{1}{2}$ furlongs, Texas Hope, :28.20, June 28, 1998; $1\frac{5}{16}$ miles, Opening Remark, 2:13.99, September 5, 1996

Track Records, Main Turf
5 furlongs: Rockin' Kate, :55.48, October 1, 2005
$7\frac{1}{2}$ furlongs: Call Me Wild, 1:28.43, September 17, 1995
1 mile: Eagle Lake, 1:34.54, October 4, 2003
$1\frac{1}{16}$ miles: Fly Slama Jama, 1:40.79, October 4, 2003
$1\frac{1}{8}$ miles: Untraceable, 1:48.13, August 10, 1996
$1\frac{3}{8}$ miles: Point Click, 2:18.09, October 18, 2003
Other: $1\frac{13}{16}$ miles, Misting Rain, 3:13.22, September 28, 1996

Principal Races
My Dandy Texas Stallion S., Darby's Daughter Texas Stallion S., El Joven S., La Senorita S., Texas Horse Racing Hall of Fame S.

Notable Events
Fifty-Cent Friday Nights

Fastest Times of 2005 (Dirt)
$4\frac{1}{2}$ furlongs: Far Away Bell, :51.37, August 6, 2005
5 furlongs: Valid Echo, :59.61, September 4, 2005
$5\frac{1}{2}$ furlongs: First Magic, 1:03.78, October 5, 2005
6 furlongs: Run Zeal Run, 1:09.77, August 5, 2005
$6\frac{1}{2}$ furlongs: Herve, 1:16.56, September 17, 2005
7 furlongs: Truth Endures, 1:24.34, September 14, 2005
1 mile: Wishingitwas, 1:37.74, September 10, 2005
$1\frac{1}{16}$ miles: Head Office, 1:48.18, September 22, 2005

Fastest Times of 2005 (Turf)
5 furlongs: Rockin' Kate, :55.48, October 1, 2005
$7\frac{1}{2}$ furlongs: A R Crackers, 1:28.91, September 2, 2005
1 mile: Prince Warner, 1:35.63, September 23, 2005
$1\frac{1}{16}$ miles: Northern Scene, 1:40.95, October 1, 2005

Sam Houston Race Park

In April 1994, Sam Houston Race Park opened as the first Class I racetrack in Texas, which had outlawed pari-mutuel wagering for more than 50 years. Built for $85-million and named for one of the state's founding fathers, the racetrack in northwest Houston is a part of the Class I Texas racing circuit that includes Lone Star Park in the Dallas-Fort Worth metroplex and Retama Park near San Antonio. Sam Houston, which conducts nighttime racing, holds a fall-winter-spring Thoroughbred meet and hosts Quarter Horse racing in the summer. The track's signature event is Texas Champions Day, which offers nine lucrative stakes races for state-breds. Sam Houston's majority owner is MAXXAM Inc., a Houston-based Fortune 500 company involved in aluminum, forest products, and real estate that is chaired by Texas native Charles Hurwitz. The track is the home of the Houston Equine Research Organization, a not-for-profit group that works to promote the welfare of racehorses through research and also offers a successful racehorse adoption program.

Location: 7575 N. Sam Houston Pkwy. W., Houston, Tx. 77064-3417
Phone: (281) 807-8760
Fax: (281) 807-8777
Website: *www.shrp.com*
E-Mail: ask@shrp.com
Year Founded: 1994
Dates of Inaugural Meeting: April 29, 1994
Abbreviation: Hou
Acreage: 230
Number of Stalls: 1,250
Seating Capacity: 18,000

Ownership
Maxxam Inc.

Officers
Chief Executive Officer: Charles E. Hurwitz
Chairman: Charles E. Hurwitz
President: Robert L. Bork
General Manager: Robert L. Bork
Director of Racing: Eric M. Johnston
Racing Secretary: Eric M. Johnston
Treasurer: Mike Vitek
Director of Operations: Ann McGovern
Director of Marketing: David Hawes
Director of Mutuels: Kim Pomposelli
Director of Publicity: Martha Claussen
Horsemen's Liaison: Evelyn Milner
Stewards: Richard Brasher, Stephen O'Malley, John Rollinson
Track Announcer: Michael Chamberlain
Track Photographer: Coady Photography
Track Superintendent: Greg Johnson

Racing Dates

2005: November 17, 2004-April 10, 2005, 69 days
2006: October 28, 2005-April 9, 2006, 82 days

Track Layout

Main Circumference: 1 mile
Main Track Chute: 7 furlongs and 1$^1/_4$ miles
Main Width: 90 feet
Main Length of Stretch: 966 feet
Main Turf Circumference: 7 furlongs
Main Turf Chute: 1$^1/_8$ miles
Main Turf Width: 80 feet

Attendance

Average Daily Recent Meeting: 2,939, 2004/2005; 2,851, 2005/2006
Highest Single-Day Record: 24,316, July 4, 2003
Total Attendance Recent Meeting: 202,793, 2004/2005; 233,782, 2005/2006

Handle

Average All Sources Recent Meeting: $1,769,035, 2004/2005; $1,738,010, 2005/2006
Average On-Track Recent Meeting: $115,305, 2004/2005; $107,061, 2005/2006
Single-Day On-Track Handle: $3,557,018, December 7, 2002
Single-Day Total Handle All Sources: $5,740,955, December 7, 2002
Total All Sources Recent Meeting: $122,063,413, 2004/2005; $142,516,819, 2005/2006
Total On-Track Recent Meeting: $7,956,020, 2004/2005; $8,779,012, 2005/2006
Highest Single-Day Record Recent Meet: $2,592,489, March 4, 2005; $2,673,371, January 6, 2006

Leaders

Recent Meeting, Leading Jockey: Quincy Hamilton, 88, 2004/2005; Quincy Hamilton, 87, 2005/2006
Recent Meeting, Leading Owner: Steve Asmussen, 15, 2004/2005; Jim Bausch, 14, 2005/2006
Recent Meeting, Leading Trainer: Steve Asmussen, 56, 2004/2005; Danny Pish, 51, 2005/2006
Recent Meeting, Leading Horse: Stella Come Back, 5, 2004/2005; Bullet Crane, 5, 2005/2006; I'mspectaculartoo, 5, 2005/2006

Records

Single-Day Jockey Wins: Austin Lovelace, 7, December 10, 1994
Single-Day Trainer Wins: Gilbert Ciavaglia, 5, February 23, 1997
Single Meet, Leading Jockey by Wins: Steve Bourque, 120, 2000/2001
Single Meet, Leading Owner by Wins: John Franks, 24, 1994/1995
Single Meet, Leading Trainer by Wins: Steve Asmussen, 57, 2002/2003

Track Records, Main Dirt

4$^1/_2$ furlongs: Prime Time Man, :51.70, February 12, 2004
5 furlongs: Endofthestorm, :57.21, October 25, 2003
5$^1/_2$ furlongs: Bucharest, 1:02.92, April 13, 1996
6 furlongs: Bucharest, 1:08.91, May 11, 1994
6$^1/_2$ furlongs: Brass Jacks, 1:15.77, May 21, 1994
7 furlongs: Bucharest, 1:21.29, May 4, 1996
1 mile: Catalissa, 1:36.33, March 8, 2003
1m 70 yds: Capt. Tiff's Beau, 1:40.52, October 24, 1998
1$^1/_{16}$ miles: Desert Air, 1:42.74, February 13, 1999
1$^1/_8$ miles: Lost Soldier, 1:48.75, May 3, 1997
1$^1/_4$ miles: Sauvage Isn't Home, 2:04.75, December 29, 1995
1$^1/_2$ miles: Final Val, 2:32.99, February 20, 1998
1$^3/_4$ miles: Final Val, 3:01.50, March 13, 1998
2 miles: Final Val, 3:31.29, April 3, 1998

Track Records, Main Turf

5 furlongs: Charming Socialite, :56.61, April 8, 2006
1 mile: Solo Attack, 1:36.16, March 17, 2001
1$^1/_{16}$ miles: Luna Delight, 1:43.24, December 4, 1998
1$^1/_8$ miles: Chorwon, 1:47.65, March 6, 1999
1$^1/_2$ miles: Commander Calhoun, 2:32.56, October 3, 1996

Principal Races

John B. Connally Breeders' Cup Turf H., Maxxam Gold Cup H., Jim's Orbit S., Two Altazano S.

Interesting Facts

Trivia: First Class 1 racetrack in Texas

Fastest Times of 2005 (Dirt)

5 furlongs: Ambition Unbridled, :57.56, February 26, 2005
5$^1/_2$ furlongs: Aledo Pass, 1:03.79, February 19, 2005
6 furlongs: Run Zeal Run, 1:09.76, December 3, 2005
6$^1/_2$ furlongs: Captain Malory, 1:16.48, April 9, 2005
7 furlongs: R B J's Blaze, 1:23.05, March 19, 2005
1 mile: Matched, 1:37.96, February 18, 2005
1m 70 yds: Song Dancer, 1:42.83, February 11, 2005
1$^1/_{16}$ miles: Dixie Meister, 1:44.95, November 19, 2005
1$^1/_8$ miles: Alumni Hall, 1:51.10, January 22, 2005

Fastest Times of 2005 (Turf)

5 furlongs: Proven Cure, :57.92, April 9, 2005
1 mile: Gondolieri (Chi), 1:37.30, November 10, 2005
1$^1/_{16}$ miles: Rose Hunter, 1:43.56, October 29, 2005
1$^1/_8$ miles: Rapid Proof, 1:51.31, April 9, 2005
1$^1/_2$ miles: Wild and Comfy, 2:37.82, April 10, 2005

Virginia

Colonial Downs

Colonial Downs has featured a high standard of racing since its opening in 1997, and the facility has slowly built a local brand name and a national following for its simulcast signal. Constructed in New Kent County approximately 24 miles from Richmond, the track is the only facility to open in Virginia since pari-mutuel wagering was legalized in 1993. The track features seating for 6,000 in an attractive setting. Colonial's 1¼-mile dirt track is one of North America's largest, and its turf course has drawn praise. Its operations are run by the Maryland Jockey Club until 2005. Colonial originally raced in late summer and early fall but switched to a 25-day, early summer meeting in 2001. In 2001, principal investor Jeffrey Jacobs bought out the track's shareholders and transformed Colonial into a private company.

Location: 10515 Colonial Downs Pkwy., New Kent, Va. 23124
Phone: (804) 966-7223
Fax: (804) 966-1565
Website: *www.colonialdowns.com*
E-Mail: info@colonialdowns.com
Year Founded: 1997
Dates of Inaugural Meeting: September 1-October 12, 1997
Abbreviation: Cnl
Acreage: 607.46
Number of Stalls: 1,050
Seating Capacity: 10,000

Ownership

Jacobs Entertainment

Officers

Chairman: Jeffrey P. Jacobs
President: Ian M. Stewart
General Manager: Iain F. Woolnough
Director of Racing: Randy R. Wehrman
Racing Secretary: Randy R. Wehrman
Treasurer: Tom Hamilton
Director of Marketing: Darrell Wood
Vice President: Jerry Monahan, Iain F. Woolnough
Director of Publicity: Darrell Wood
Horsemen's Liaison: Alice Marcacci
Stewards: Jean Chalk, Stan Bowker, William Passmore
Track Announcer: Dave Rodman, Darrell Wood
Track Photographer: Jeff Coady
Track Superintendent: Wes Sheldon
Security: Dale Moser

Racing Dates

2005: June 17-August 9, 40 days
2006: June 16-August 12, 42 days

Track Layout
Main Circumference: $1^1/_4$ miles
Main Track Chute: $1^1/_8$ miles
Main Width: 80 feet
Main Length of Stretch: 1,290.50 feet
Main Turf Circumference: $7^1/_2$ furlongs to $1^1/_8$ miles, depending on rail position
Main Turf Width: 180 feet
Main Turf Length of Stretch: 1,123.62 feet

Attendance
Average Daily Recent Meeting: 2,028, 2005
Highest Single-Day Record: 13,468, September 1, 1997
Highest Single-Meet Record: 108,900, 1997
Record Daily Average for Single Meet: 3,630, 1997
Total Attendance Recent Meeting: 81,126, 2005

Handle
Average All Sources Recent Meeting: $1,082,819, 2005
Average On-Track Recent Meeting: $170,125, 2005
Record Daily Average for Single Meet: $197,577, 2004
Single-Day Total Handle All Sources: $3,647,833, July 16, 2005
Total All Sources Recent Meeting: $43,312,745, 2005
Total On-Track Recent Meeting: $6,805,009, 2005
Record Total All Sources for Single Meet: $43,312,745, 2005
Record Total for Single Meet: $6,805,009, 2005
Highest Single-Day Record Recent Meet: $3,647,833, July 16, 2005

Leaders
Career, Leading Jockey by Titles: Mario Pino, 3
Career, Leading Trainer by Titles: A. Ferris Allen III, 6
Career, Leading Jockey by Wins: Mario Pino, 255
Career, Leading Trainer by Wins: A. Ferris Allen III, 134
Recent Meeting, Leading Jockey: Horacio Karamanos, 66, 2005
Recent Meeting, Leading Owner: David A. Ross, 15, 2005
Recent Meeting, Leading Trainer: A. Ferris Allen III, 24, 2005
Recent Meeting, Leading Horse: Oath of Office, 3, 2005; Toccoa, 3, 2005

Records
Single-Day Jockey Wins: Mario Pino, 7, July 7, 2002
Single Meet, Leading Jockey by Wins: Edgar Prado, 59, 1997
Single Meet, Leading Trainer by Wins: A. Ferris Allen III, 25, 1997

Track Records, Main Dirt
5 furlongs: Timothy Mac, :55.74, July 1, 2003
$5^1/_2$ furlongs: Bid Wild, 1:02.68, July 1, 2003
6 furlongs: Satan's Code, 1:08.48, June 27, 2004
$6^1/_2$ furlongs: Cool Ken Jane, 1:16.60, September 7, 1997
7 furlongs: Sky Watch, 1:20.87, September 1, 1997
1 mile: Mt. Carson, 1:35.07, June 26, 2004
$1^1/_{16}$ miles: Gold Token, 1:41.09, September 13, 1998
$1^1/_8$ miles: Our Toby, 1:48.95, October 4, 1997
$1^1/_4$ miles: Macgyver, 2:03.54, September 1, 1997
$1^1/_2$ miles: Lord Mendelson, 2:30.13, September 4, 2000

Track Records, Main Turf
5 furlongs: Bop, :55.85, June 22, 2002
$5^1/_2$ furlongs: Devereux, 1:01.93, September 24, 1999
6 furlongs: Tyaskin, 1:08.11, September 20, 1998
$1^1/_{16}$ miles: Lonesome Sound, 1:41.28, September 18, 1998
$1^1/_8$ miles: Kerfoot Corner, 1:47.40, September 26, 1998
$1^3/_{16}$ miles: Jacsonzac, 1:54.41, October 10, 1998
$1^1/_4$ miles: Phi Beta Doc, 1:59.97, October 2, 1999
$1^1/_2$ miles: Attention Mark, 2:31.76, September 11, 1998
$1^5/_8$ miles: Beluga, 2:45.80, September 26, 1998

Track Records, Inner Turf
5 furlongs: Smart Sunny, :56.02, September 8, 2000
$5^1/_2$ furlongs: Smart Sunny, 1:02.94, September 13, 1998
1 mile: La Reine's Terms, 1:34.24, September 17, 1998
$1^1/_{16}$ miles: Grass Roots, 1:41.01, October 8, 1999
$1^1/_8$ miles: Steak Scam, 1:48.71, September 25, 1999
$1^1/_4$ miles: Franc, 2:03.02, September 9, 2000
$1^1/_2$ miles: Winsox, 2:27.04, September 28, 1998
$1^5/_8$ miles: Our Game, 2:44.82, September 24, 1999

Principal Races
Virginia Derby (G2), All Along Breeders' Cup S. (G3), Colonial Turf Cup S., Virginia Oaks

Fastest Times of 2005 (Dirt)
$5^1/_2$ furlongs: Charismatic Caller, 1:03.57, July 30, 2005
6 furlongs: Saay Mi Name, 1:08.87, August 6, 2005
7 furlongs: George's Gain, 1:22.53, July 30, 2005
1 mile: Debbie Sue, 1:35.66, July 31, 2005
$1^1/_{16}$ miles: One Nice Cat, 1:41.61, August 7, 2005
$1^1/_8$ miles: Megoman, 1:50.76, July 1, 2005

Fastest Times of 2005 (Turf)
5 furlongs: Satan's Code, :55.98, July 24, 2005
$5^1/_2$ furlongs: Bright Gold, 1:02.21, June 25, 2005
1 mile: Running Tide, 1:35.85, July 9, 2005
$1^1/_{16}$ miles: Triple X., 1:42.11, July 3, 2005
$1^1/_8$ miles: Dynalympic, 1:49.11, August 2, 2005
$1^3/_{16}$ miles: Remarkable, 1:56.28, July 1, 2005
$1^1/_4$ miles: Flying Visit (NZ), 2:02.52, June 17, 2005
$1^7/_8$ miles: Latino (Per), 3:18.84, July 3, 2005
$2^1/_4$ miles: Riddle, 4:00.08, July 24, 2005

Washington

Dayton Days

Location: P.O. Box 264, Dayton, Wa. 99328
Phone: (509) 382-2377
Year Founded: 1919
Abbreviation: Day

Officers
President: Norm Hansen
Director of Racing: Billie Jean Brown
Racing Secretary: Billie Jean Brown
Treasurer: Melissa Hansen
Vice President: Tim Donohue
Track Announcer: Zane Troester

Racing Dates
2005: May 28-May 30, 3 days
2006: May 27-May 29, 3 days
2007: May 26-May 28, 3 days

Handle
Average All Sources Recent Meeting: $21,044, 2005
Total All Sources Recent Meeting: $63,131, 2005

Principal Races
Queens Derby

Emerald Downs

Emerald Downs returned Thoroughbred racing to the Seattle area when it opened in 1996. Since the 1930s, the hub of Northwest racing had been Longacres, which was sold in '90 to aircraft manufacturer Boeing Co. After Longacres held its last season of racing in 1992, Yakima Meadows in Yakima became its short-term successor. A group of investors headed by Ron Crockett, who formerly was involved in an airline-related company, built Emerald for $83-million. The track, which offers racing from mid-April to mid-September, became the new host of the Northwest's most famous race when the Longacres Mile Handicap (G3) was first held at the track during its inaugural season.

Location: 2300 Emerald Downs Dr., Auburn, Wa. 98001-1633
Phone: (253) 288-7000, (888) 931-8400
Website: *www.emeralddowns.com*
Year Founded: 1996
Abbreviation: EmD
Acreage: 167
Number of Stalls: 1,276

Ownership
Northwest Racing Associates LLP

Officers

President: Ron Crockett
Director of Racing: Paul Ryneveld
Racing Secretary: Paul Ryneveld
Director of Operations: Bob Fraser
Vice President: Jack E. Hodge Jr.
Director of Publicity: Joe Withee
Director of Media Relations: Michael Costanzo
Horsemen's Liaison: Jan McDowell
Track Announcer: Robert Geller
Track Photographer: Reed Palmer

Racing Dates

2005: April 15-October 16, 101 days
2006: April 21-October 1, 91 days

Track Layout

Main Circumference: 1 mile
Main Track Chute: $6\frac{1}{2}$ furlongs and $1\frac{1}{4}$ miles
Main Width: 90 feet
Main Length of Stretch: 990 feet

Handle

Average All Sources Recent Meeting: $799,377, 2005
Single-Day On-Track Handle: $3,037,581, August 24, 2003
Total All Sources Recent Meeting: $80,737,030, 2005
Highest Single-Day Record Recent Meet: $2,906,525, August 21, 2005
Record Average All Sources Single Meet: $1,381,128, 2005
Record Total All Sources for Single Meet: $139,493,888, 2005

Mutuel Records

Highest Win: $142.80, My Lady Boots, July 27, 1997
Lowest Win: $2.40, Youcan'ttakeme, June 1, 2003
Highest Exacta: $2,317.80, October 28, 1998
Lowest Exacta: $2.40, June 1, 2003
Highest Trifecta: $27,356.90, July 3, 2002
Lowest Trifecta: $11.80, August 28, 1999
Highest Daily Double: $1,878.20, August 8, 2003
Lowest Daily Double: $4.40, August 24, 1997
Highest Pick 3: $7,479.90, July 9, 2000
Lowest Pick 3: $4.70, May 8, 1997
Highest Pick 6: $217,140, June 8, 1997
Lowest Pick 6: $146.20, August 31, 1997
Highest Other Exotics: $58, Place, October 6, 1996; $38.80, Show, April 5, 1997; $15,487.20, Superfecta, June 2, 2002
Lowest Other Exotics: $2.10, Place, November 8, 1996; $75.20, Superfecta, May 22, 1999
Highest Pick 4: $9,248.20, September 21, 2003
Highest Stakes Win: $85.20, Edneator, August 20, 2000, Longacres Mile

Leaders

Career, Leading Jockey by Stakes Wins: Gallyn Vick Mitchell, 49
Career, Leading Owner by Stakes Wins: Billie Klokstad, 11
Career, Leading Trainer by Stakes Wins: Bud Klokstad, 43
Career, Leading Horse by Stakes Wins: Handy N Bold, 10
Career, Leading Jockey by Wins: Gallyn Vick Mitchell, 862
Career, Leading Owner by Wins: Ron Crockett, 136
Career, Leading Trainer by Wins: Tim McCanna, 491
Career, Leading Horse by Wins: Fleet Pacific, 15
Recent Meeting, Leading Jockey: Kevin Krigger, 126, 2005
Recent Meeting, Leading Owner: Ron Crockett, 21, 2005
Recent Meeting, Leading Trainer: Tim McCanna, 54, 2005
Recent Meeting, Leading Horse: Halonator, 8, 2005

Records

Single-Day Jockey Wins: Kevin Radke, 6, September 2, 2002
Single-Day Trainer Wins: Jim Penney, 5, September 6, 1998
Single Meet, Leading Jockey by Wins: Vann Belvoir, 148, 1996
Single Meet, Leading Owner by Wins: West Ridge Ranch, 23, 2003
Single Meet, Leading Trainer by Wins: Tim McCanna, 55, 1999; Tim McCanna, 55, 2003
Single Meet, Leading Trainer by Stakes Wins: Steve Bullock, 8, 2000; Bud Klokstad, 8, 2002
Single Meet, Leading Jockey by Stakes Wins: Gallyn Vick Mitchell, 13, 2000

Track Records, Main Dirt

$4\frac{1}{2}$ furlongs: I. M. Adevil, :50.60, May 30, 1999; Pacificat, :50.60, May 21, 2000
5 furlongs: Jazzy Mac, :55.40, August 20, 2000; Victor Slew, :55.40, August 24, 2003
$5\frac{1}{2}$ furlongs: Willie the Cat, 1:01.20, April 16, 2004
6 furlongs: Blue Tejano, 1:07.60, June 7, 2002; Salt Grinder, 1:07.60, May 21, 2005
$6\frac{1}{2}$ furlongs: Sabertooth, 1:13, May 22, 2005
1 mile: Sky Jack, 1:33, August 24, 2003
$1\frac{1}{16}$ miles: Kid Katabatic, 1:39.60, July 26, 1998
$1\frac{1}{8}$ miles: Flying Notes, 1:45.40, September 2, 2002
$1\frac{1}{4}$ miles: Itstufftobegood, 2:01, August 5, 2005
$1\frac{1}{2}$ miles: Keen Line, 2:30.60, September 6, 1997; Itstufftobegood, 2:30.60, August 27, 2005
$1\frac{3}{4}$ miles: Itstufftobegood, 3:02, September 18, 2005
2 miles: Horatio, 3:22.60, September 20, 2004
Other: 2 furlongs, Midnight Cruiser, :21.40, May 4, 2000; 2 furlongs, Adventure Man, :21.40, May 10, 2000

Principal Races

Longacres Mile H. (G3), Mt. Rainier Breeders' Cup H., Washington Breeders' Cup Oaks, Emerald Breeders' Cup Distaff H., Emerald Breeders' Cup Derby

Fastest Times of 2005 (Dirt)

$4\frac{1}{2}$ furlongs: Coach Sween, :51.20, September 2, 2005
5 furlongs: Voile Soar, :57, May 1, 2005
$5\frac{1}{2}$ furlongs: Another Bob, 1:02.20, July 4, 2005
6 furlongs: Salt Grinder, 1:07.60, May 21, 2005
$6\frac{1}{2}$ furlongs: Sabertooth, 1:13, May 22, 2005
1 mile: Eastern Accent, 1:34.20, October 1, 2005
$1\frac{1}{16}$ miles: Poker Brad, 1:41, July 3, 2005
$1\frac{1}{8}$ miles: Flamethrowintexan, 1:47.40, July 31, 2005
$1\frac{3}{16}$ miles: Andoras Attitude, 1:57.40, August 25, 2005
$1\frac{1}{4}$ miles: Itstufftobegood, 2:01, August 5, 2005
$1\frac{1}{2}$ miles: Itstufftobegood, 2:30.60, August 27, 2005
$1\frac{3}{4}$ miles: Itstufftobegood, 3:02, September 18, 2005
2 miles: Horatio, 3:25, October 16, 2005

Sun Downs

Location: P.O. Box 6662, Kennewick, Wa. 99336-0639
Phone: (509) 582-5434
Fax: (509) 586-9780
Year Founded: 1969
Abbreviation: SuD
Number of Stalls: 365
Seating Capacity: 3,800

Ownership

Tri-City Horse Racing Association

Officers

President: Cliff Schellinger
General Manager: Nancy Sorick
Director of Racing: Nellie Schellinger
Racing Secretary: Shorty Martin
Treasurer: Nancy Sorick
Director of Marketing: Des Ritari
Director of Mutuels: Helen Lizotte
Vice President: William Henderson
Director of Publicity: Des Ritari
Track Announcer: Zane Torester
Track Superintendent: Jimmie McDonnell
Security: Benton-Franklin, Mounted Posse

Racing Dates

2005: April 9-May 8, 10 days
2006: April 8-May 7, 10 days

Track Layout

Main Circumference: 5 furlongs
Main Track Chute: $6\frac{1}{2}$ furlongs

Leaders

Recent Meeting, Leading Jockey: Cammie Papineau, 14, 2005
Recent Meeting, Leading Trainer: Jason Homer, 10, 2005
Recent Meeting, Leading Horse: Weatherbug, 2, 2005; Chrissy de Rio, 2, 2005; Black Canyon Bart, 2, 2005; Choice Slew, 2, 2005; Skillful Level, 2, 2005; Crissy's Cricket, 2, 2005; Tizzatja, 2, 2005; Kindon, 2, 2005; Schu True Sleeper, 2, 2005

Fastest Times of 2005 (Dirt)

4 furlongs: Just a Big Hit, :46, April 17, 2005
6 furlongs: Skillful Level, 1:14.20, May 1, 2005
6½ furlongs: Weatherbug, 1:21.60, April 30, 2005
7 furlongs: Percipitate, 1:26, May 8, 2005

Waitsburg Race Track

Location: P.O. Box 391, Waitsburg, Wa. 99361-0391
Phone: (509) 337-6300
Year Founded: 1911
Abbreviation: Wts

Officers

President: Terry Hofer
Racing Secretary: Shorty Martin
Secretary: Rose Englebrite

Racing Dates

2005: May 21-May 22, 2 days
2006: May 20-May 21, 2 days

Walla Walla

Location: P.O. Box G, Walla Walla, Wa. 99362-0036
Phone: (509) 527-3247
Fax: (509) 527-3259
Website: *www.wallawallafairgrounds.com*
E-Mail: wwfair@hscis.net
Year Founded: 1866
Abbreviation: WW
Number of Stalls: 180
Seating Capacity: 3,000

Ownership

Walla Walla County

Officers

Chairman: Dick Monahan
President: Terry Atchison
General Manager: Cory Hewitt
Director of Racing: Bill Clemens
Racing Secretary: Debbie Delaney
Secretary: Bill Clemens
Vice President: Dick Moeller
Track Announcer: Pete O'Laughlin
Track Photographer: Roger Nielsen
Security: Dick Moeller

Racing Dates

2005: May 14-May 15, 2 days; September 2-September 4, 3 days
2006: May 13-May 14, 2 days; September 1-September 3, 3 days
2007: May 12-May 13, 2 days; August 31-September 2, 3 days

Track Layout

Main Circumference: 4 furlongs
Main Track Chute: 6 furlongs

Leaders

Recent Meeting, Leading Jockey: Ty Dangerfield, 3, Summer 2005; Tim Neal, 3, Spring 2006; Ty Dangerfield, 3, Spring 2006
Recent Meeting, Leading Trainer: Tracy Lebret, 2, Summer 2005; Jaqueline Smith, 2, Summer 2005; Marion Stitzel, 3, Spring 2006

Fastest Times of 2005 (Dirt)

a5 furlongs: Game Cadillac, 1:03, September 3, 2005
7 furlongs: Here's Your Ticket, 1:26, September 2, 2005
1⅛ miles: Tender Offer (Ire), 1:58.20, September 4, 2005

West Virginia

Charles Town Races

Founded in 1933 by Albert Boyle, Charles Town Races in Charles Town has been wholly owned by Penn National Gaming Inc. since 2000. The company also owns Penn National Race Course in Pennsylvania as well as other gaming and resort facilities. Penn National Gaming bought a majority interest in Charles Town after local voters approved slot machines at the track in 1996. Charles Town Races has seen its fortunes improve dramatically since the slot machines were installed. Purses for horse racing receive a portion of revenues on slot-machine play at Charles Town, which has more than 3,800 machines at the track. The track's marquee event is the West Virginia Breeders' Classic, a series of races that showcase runners bred, sired, or raised in the state, and is highlighted by the $250,000 West Virginia Breeders' Classic. Charles Town completed a multimillion-dollar remodeling project, including a new racing surface, in August 2004.

Location: P.O. Box 551, Charles Town, W.V. 25414-0551
Phone: (304) 725-7001, (800) 795-7001
Fax: (304) 724-4326
Website: *www.charlestownraces.com*
Year Founded: 1933
Dates of Inaugural Meeting: December 2, 1933
Abbreviation: CT
Number of Stalls: 1,050
Seating Capacity: 6,000

Ownership

Penn National Gaming

Officers

General Manager: Albert T. Britton
Director of Racing: Doug Lamp
Racing Secretary: Doug Lamp
Director of Marketing: Dee Mara
Director of Mutuels: Joy Lushbaugh
Vice President: John V. Finamore
Director of Publicity: Jeffrey Gilleas
Stewards: L. Robert Lotts, Ismael L. Trejo, Danny R. Wright
Track Announcer: Jeff Cernik
Track Photographer: Mike Montgomery
Track Superintendent: Douglas Bowling
Asst. Racing Secretary: M. Michael Elliott
Horsemen's Bookkeeper: W. C. Perry
Security: Milt Champion

Racing Dates

2005: January 1-December 31, 243 days
2006: January 1-December 31, 220 days

Track Layout

Main Circumference: 6 furlongs
Main Track Chute: 4½ furlongs and 1$^{5}/_{16}$ miles
Main Length of Stretch: 660 feet

Attendance

Highest Single-Day Record: 21,480, September 17, 1981

Handle

Average All Sources Recent Meeting: $645,285, 2005
Average On-Track Recent Meeting: $108,877, 2005
Total All Sources Recent Meeting: $156,804,255, 2005
Total On-Track Recent Meeting: $26,457,111, 2005
Highest Single-Day Record Recent Meet: $1,090,129, May 7, 2005

Leaders

Recent Meeting, Leading Jockey: Gerald Almodovar, 232, 2005
Recent Meeting, Leading Trainer: Ronney W. Brown, 150, 2005
Recent Meeting, Leading Horse: Red Hot Secret, 6, 2005; Shamiza, 6, 2005; Dance for Romeo, 6, 2005

Records

Single-Day Jockey Wins: Travis Dunkelberger, 7, March 30, 2000

Track Records, Main Dirt

4½ furlongs: It's Only Money, :50.36, July 4, 1999
6½ furlongs: Jet Appeal, 1:17, January 6, 1976
7 furlongs: Morine's Victory, 1:23.92, October 29, 2005
1$^{1}/_{16}$ miles: My Sister Pearl, 1:43.83, January 4, 2001
1⅛ miles: Cherokee's Boy, 1:49.88, October 9, 2005

1¼ miles: Belle d'Amour, 2:05⅗, June 28, 1941
1½ miles: Guasave Breeze, 2:34, June 9, 1972

Principal Races

Charles Town Dash Invitational H., West Virginia Breeders' Classic S., "Cavada" West Virginia Breeders' Classic S.

Notable Events

Owners Day, West Virginia Breeders' Classics Day

Fastest Times of 2005 (Dirt)

4½ furlongs: Rain Song, :50.63, November 4, 2005
6½ furlongs: Speed Hunter, 1:18.04, July 17, 2005
7 furlongs: Morine's Victory, 1:23.92, October 29, 2005
1¹⁄₁₆ miles: Pop's Boy, 1:44.94, October 30, 2005
1⅛ miles: Cherokee's Boy, 1:49.88, October 9, 2005

Mountaineer Race Track and Gaming Resort

Mountaineer Race Track in Chester, West Virginia, was recognized in 2001 as one of the top small businesses in the United States when Forbes magazine ranked MTR Gaming Group Inc., which owns the track, seventh among the top 200 such enterprises. Much of Mountaineer's success resulted from the legalization of slot machines in 1993, which increased revenues and enabled the track to offer higher purses. In 2003, the track received approval for 500 additional slot machines, enabling it to operate a maximum of 3,500 slot machines. MTR Gaming, headed by Edson "Ted" Arneault, also owns a golf course, hotel, spa, theater, and other entertainment facilities at the track's location. The track was known as Waterford Park when it was opened in 1951 by the Charles Town Jockey Club; the facility was renamed Mountaineer Park in '87 and Mountaineer Race Track in 2001. Mountaineer offers year-round racing four nights a week. The West Virginia Derby (G3), worth $750,000 in 2005, is the richest race to be run in West Virginia history. In 2003, MTR Gaming Group bought Scioto Downs, an Ohio harness track, and in late 2002 it received approval from the Pennsylvania Horse Racing Commission to build a $56-million Thoroughbred track, Presque Isle Downs, near Erie, but court appeals delayed the project.

Location: P.O. Box 358, Route 2 S., Chester, W.V. 26034-0358
Phone: (304) 387-8000, (800) 804-0468
Website: *www.mtrgaming.com*
E-Mail: info@mtrgaming.com
Year Founded: 1951
Dates of Inaugural Meeting: May 16, 1951
Abbreviation: Mnr
Capsule Description: Live racing year round, casino, hotel, spa, fitness center, and golf course
Number of Stalls: 1,234
Seating Capacity: 7,400

Ownership

MTR Gaming Group Inc.

Officers

Chairman: Edson R. Arneault
President: Edson R. Arneault
Director of Racing: Rose Mary Williams
Racing Secretary: Joseph J. Narcavish
Director of Operations: David Hughes
Director of Finance: John Bittner
Director of Marketing: Dale Maurer
Vice President: Patrick Arneault
Director of Publicity: Tamara Cronin
Horsemen's Liaison: Rose Mary Williams
Stewards: Laurence A. Dupuy, Steve Kourpas, James O'Brien
Track Announcer: Peter Berry
Track Photographer: Ethel Riser
Track Superintendent: Tom Trevor

Racing Dates

2005: January 15-December 27, 216 days
2006: January 14-December 30, 232 days

Track Layout

Main Circumference: 1 mile
Main Track Chute: 6 furlongs and 1¼ miles
Main Width: 80 feet
Main Length of Stretch: 905.31 feet
Main Turf Circumference: 7 furlongs

Attendance

Average Daily Recent Meeting: 6,124, 2005
Highest Single-Day Record: 17,934, August 10, 2002
Total Attendance Recent Meeting: 1,322,835, 2005

Handle

Average All Sources Recent Meeting: $1,584,022, 2005
Average On-Track Recent Meeting: $53,405, 2005
Single-Day On-Track Handle: $966,508, May 8, 1973
Single-Day Total Handle All Sources: $2,513,911, 2003
Total All Sources Recent Meeting: $342,148,731, 2005
Total On-Track Recent Meeting: $11,535,573, 2005
Highest Single-Day Record Recent Meet: $3,447,914, August 14, 2005

Leaders

Recent Meeting, Leading Jockey: Deshawn L. Parker, 227, 2005
Recent Meeting, Leading Owner: Dale Baird, 152, 2005
Recent Meeting, Leading Trainer: Dale Baird, 160, 2005
Recent Meeting, Leading Horse: Burnt Mill Road, 6, 2005

Track Records, Main Dirt

4½ furlongs: Jump for Joyeux, :49.69, May 29, 2006
5 furlongs: Mayor Steve, :55.92, August 31, 2003
5½ furlongs: The Dancer, 1:02.24, December 29, 2000
6 furlongs: Hustler, 1:07.81, August 11, 2001
1 mile: Find the Mine, 1:33,86, July 4, 2000
1m 40 yds: Ski Sez, 1:39.83, March 9, 1996
1m 70 yds: Mort, 1:38.81, April 1, 2000
1¹⁄₁₆ miles: It's Reality, 1:41.75, December 23, 2000
1⅛ miles: Soto, 1:46.29, August 9, 2003
1³⁄₁₆ miles: No Spend No Glow, 1:56.95, May 19, 2001
1¼ miles: Georgie Porgie, 2:03.69, August 6, 1995
1½ miles: Pete's Skianno, 2:31.43, June 10, 2000
1⅝ miles: Prince Swivel, 2:45, September 8, 1973
1¾ miles: Chased Again, 2:58⅘, July 18, 1959
2 miles: Sovereign M.D., 3:27.66, December 10, 2000
Other: 2 furlongs, Promised Cruise, :21, June 23, 1990; a1 mile, Mr. Pantop, 1:36⅕, June 26, 1970; a1¼ miles, Grain, 2:08, May 29, 1974; a2 miles, Dark Ajax, 3:27⅖, June 9, 1973; 2¹⁄₁₆ miles, Sovereign M.D., 3:28.40, December 30, 2000

Track Records, Main Turf

4½ furlongs: Cake n' Steak, :50, August 9, 1993
5 furlongs: Fina Dur, :55.52, September 6, 1999
7 furlongs: On to Richmond, 1:21.40, June 16, 2002
7½ furlongs: Magical Madness, 1:27.48, May 22, 2002
1 mile: La Reine's Term, 1:33.49, September 2, 2002
1m 70yds: Fast and Friendly, 1:43, September 7, 1964; Poteau, 1:43, July 25, 1982
1⅜ miles: Sunset Party, 2:13.23, September 26, 1999
1½ miles: Guild Hall, 2:33⅕, June 20, 1969
1¾ miles: Inaugural Address, 2:53.35, August 15, 2005
Other: a5 furlongs, Skindles Hotel, :55⅕, July 26, 1960; a1¹⁄₁₆ miles, Black Eye, 1:40⅕, June 28, 1958; a1¼ miles, King Haigler, 2:09⅗, July 4, 1983; a1⁵⁄₁₆ miles, Ruff Mack, 2:06, August 25, 1962; a1½ miles, Revenooer, 2:29, July 4, 1959; 1⅞ miles, Code's Best, 3:08.23, September 4, 2000

Principal Races

West Virginia Derby (G3), West Virginia Governor's S., Mountaineer Mile H., Harvey Arneault Memorial Breeders' Cup S., West Virginia Senate President's Breeders' Cup S.

Interesting Facts

Previous Names and Dates: Waterford Park

Fastest Times of 2005 (Dirt)

4½ furlongs: Outcashem, :51.09, August 14, 2005

5 furlongs: Bernie Blue, :56.11, May 7, 2005
5$^{1}/_{2}$ furlongs: Four Legged Taxi, 1:02.76, September 11, 2005
6 furlongs: Danieltown, 1:09.05, May 21, 2005
1 mile: Warped, 1:36.54, May 8, 2005
1m 70 yds: Discreet Hero, 1:39.15, May 28, 2005
1$^{1}/_{16}$ miles: Demus, 1:43.62, September 13, 2005
1$^{1}/_{8}$ miles: Discreet Hero, 1:48.33, October 4, 2005
1$^{1}/_{4}$ miles: Joma, 2:07.06, July 5, 2005
1$^{1}/_{2}$ miles: Waltzing Home, 2:36.41, October 16, 2005
1$^{5}/_{8}$ miles: Tenacious Affair, 2:46.43, November 1, 2005
1$^{3}/_{4}$ miles: Awesome Dancing, 3:07.33, November 15, 2005

Fastest Times of 2005 (Turf)

4$^{1}/_{2}$ furlongs: Sixth Formal, :51, July 3, 2005
5 furlongs: Nicole's Dream, :55.54, July 11, 2005
7 furlongs: Altura, 1:21.81, September 5, 2005
7$^{1}/_{2}$ furlongs: Bingobear, 1:28.79, July 24, 2005
1 mile: Immediate Reaction, 1:33.69, August 14, 2005
1$^{3}/_{8}$ miles: Inaugural Address, 2:15.66, July 31, 2005
1$^{3}/_{4}$ miles: Inaugural Address, 2:53.35, August 15, 2005

Wyoming

Wyoming Downs

Though it is one of North America's least-known Thoroughbred facilities, Wyoming Downs has been providing racing to southwestern Wyoming for nearly 20 years. Located just north of Evanston, Wyoming Downs offers Thoroughbred and Quarter Horse racing, with most emphasis on the latter. The track's top races are Quarter Horse events, the Silver Dollar and Diamond Classic Futurities, each with estimated purses of $100,000. For Thoroughbreds, the top event is the $4,000-added Bettie Bullock Memorial Derby for three-year-olds. Wyoming Downs, which races during the summer, also operates four off-track betting facilities that offer simulcast wagering year-round. In 2003, the track's OTB facilities added Instant Racing, an electronic pari-mutuel game developed at Oaklawn Park in Arkansas.

Location: 10180 Highway 89 N., P.O. Box 1607, Evanston, Wy. 82931
Phone: (307) 789-0511, (866) 681-7223
Fax: (307) 789-9439
Website: *www.wyomingdowns.com*
E-Mail: wydowns@uintanet.com
Year Founded: 1985
Dates of Inaugural Meeting: May 25, 1985
Abbreviation: Wyo
Acreage: 200
Number of Stalls: 860
Seating Capacity: 2,100

Ownership

Wyoming Horseracing Inc.

Officers

President: Eric L. Nelson
General Manager: Dale Parker
Director of Racing: Dale Parker
Racing Secretary: Dale Parker
Director of Operations: Joan Ramos
Director of Admissions: Ethellynn Sims, Linda Willoughby
Director of Finance: Lorie Anderson-Miller
Director of Marketing: Kortney Kettleson
Director of Mutuels: Jerry Doolittle
Director of Publicity: Nina Earll
Director of Simulcasting: Jodi Lopez
Track Announcer: John Nielson
Track Photographer: Gene Wilson & Associates
Track Superintendent: Carl Owens
Horsemen's Bookkeeper: Trina Fackrell

Racing Dates

2005: June 25-August 21, 19 days
2006: July 1-August 13, 14 days

Track Layout

Main Circumference: 7$^{1}/_{2}$ furlongs
Main Track Chute: 6$^{1}/_{2}$ furlongs and 550 yards
Main Length of Stretch: 1,050 feet

Leaders

Recent Meeting, Leading Jockey: Cameron Colledge, 8, 2005; Mark Allen Boag, 8, 2005
Recent Meeting, Leading Trainer: Gary Simpson, 14, 2005
Recent Meeting, Leading Horse: Goodbye Earl, 3, 2005

Principal Races

Governor's Cup H.

Fastest Times of 2005 (Dirt)

4$^{1}/_{2}$ furlongs: Dr. Tom B, :51.14, July 9, 2005
5 furlongs: Exclusive Glory, :56.90, August 20, 2005
5$^{1}/_{2}$ furlongs: Slew Shoo Slew, 1:03.60, July 30, 2005
6 furlongs: Goodbye Earl, 1:09.50, July 23, 2005
7$^{1}/_{2}$ furlongs: Tizwar, 1:30.04, July 31, 2005
1 mile: Tizwar, 1:37.47, August 21, 2005

Canada

Alberta

Evergreen Park (Grand Prairie)

Location: Box 370, Grand Prairie, Ab. T8V 3A5
Phone: (780) 532-3279
Fax: (780) 539-0373
Website: *www.evergreenpark.ca*
E-Mail: brianc4@telus.net
Abbreviation: GPr
Acreage: 700
Number of Stalls: 700
Seating Capacity: 2,700

Officers

General Manager: Linda Haggerty
Director of Racing: Brian Cook

Racing Dates

2005: July 8-August 21, 22 days
2006: June 23-August 20, 27 days

Track Layout

Main Circumference: 5 furlongs

Leaders

Recent Meeting, Leading Jockey: Brooke Mellish, 15, 2005
Recent Meeting, Leading Trainer: Pete Dubois, 6, 2005; Amanda Fogle, 6, 2005; William Bud Matier, 6, 2005
Recent Meeting, Leading Horse: Wild County, 3, 2005

Fastest Times of 2005 (Dirt)

4 furlongs: Northern Wager, :46.20, July 8, 2005
5$^{1}/_{2}$ furlongs: Hy Nick, 1:06.40, August 21, 2005
6 furlongs: Certainly Regal, 1:12.60, August 6, 2005; First Hoe-down, 1:12.60, August 21, 2005
6$^{1}/_{2}$ furlongs: Highland Road, 1:18.80, August 21, 2005
7 furlongs: Captain Carter, 1:25.80, August 5, 2005
1 mile: Chief Joseph, 1:41.80, July 10, 2005
1$^{1}/_{16}$ miles: Ezee Target, 1:48.80, July 24, 2005
1$^{1}/_{8}$ miles: Lafleur, 1:53.60, August 21, 2005

Lethbridge

Location: 3401 Parkside Dr. S., Lethbridge, Ab. T1J 4R3
Phone: (403) 380-1900

Fax: (403) 380-1909
Website: *www.rockymountainturfclub.com*
E-Mail: racedot@telusplanet.net
Abbreviation: Lbg
Number of Stalls: 400
Seating Capacity: 3,000

Ownership

Rocky Mountain Turf Club

Officers

Chairman: Max Gibb
President: Max Gibb
Director of Racing: Dorothy Stein
Racing Secretary: Jim Ralph
Director of Marketing: Rose Rossi
Director of Mutuels: Dorothy Stein
Director of Publicity: Rose Rossi
Stewards: D. G. Rees, Scott Dahl
Track Announcer: Dale Johnson
Track Photographer: Coady Photography

Racing Dates

2005: May 7-July 3, 23 days; September 3-October 30, 27 days
2006: May 6-July 2, 23 days; September 2-November 5, 27 days

Track Layout

Main Circumference: 4 furlongs

Leaders

Recent Meeting, Leading Jockey: Janine Stianson, 9, Fall 2005
Recent Meeting, Leading Trainer: Ron David, 5, Fall 2005

Principal Races

Autotote Derby, "B" Cup Classic S., Sales S., Alberta Bred S., Open S.

Notable Events

Chuckwagon Racing, Street Machine Weekend, Hot Rod 50's Weekend

Fastest Times of 2005 (Dirt)

5 furlongs: Express Post, :59.20, May 15, 2005; Faster Than Music, :59.20, May 7, 2005; S S Enterprize, :59.20, May 15, 2005
5$^1/_2$ furlongs: Milk River Ridge, 1:07.60, May 23, 2005; Tickle Me Malmo, 1:07.60, May 22, 2005
6 furlongs: Angies First Shot, 1:11.40, October 8, 2005
a6 furlongs: Lafleur, 1:09.40, May 21, 2005
7 furlongs: Lafleur, 1:24.80, September 18, 2005
1$^1/_{16}$ miles: Air Tech, 1:47.80, September 3, 2005
1$^1/_8$ miles: Lost Again, 1:54, July 1, 2005
1$^3/_{16}$ miles: Deriga Bay, 2:03.20, October 1, 2005

Millarville Race Society

Location: General Delivery Box 68, Millarville, Ab. T0L 1K0
Phone: (403) 931-3411
Fax: (403) 931-3411
Abbreviation: Mil

Racing Dates

2005: July 1, 1 day; September 4, 1 day
2006: July 1, 1 day

Fastest Times of 2005 (Dirt)

5 furlongs: Wartock, 1:03.60, September 4, 2005
7 furlongs: Captain Carter, 1:31.20, September 4, 2005; Westerntock, 1:31.20, September 4, 2005
1$^1/_8$ miles: Lost Again, 2:01.40, September 4, 2005

Northlands Park

Like many Canadian racetracks, Northlands Park in Edmonton races both Thoroughbreds and Standardbreds. Both breeds enjoy richer purses due to the arrival of slot machines. In late December 2001, Northlands received 250 additional machines to double its original total as part of a $42-million racing rehabilitation project under Alberta Premier Ralph Klein, an amateur harness driver, former TV reporter, and former Calgary mayor. Opened in July 1925 as Edmonton Racetrack, the track was renamed Northlands Park in January 1964. Northlands conducts harness racing from early March through mid-June and Thoroughbred racing from late June through late October.

Location: Northlands Spectrum, P.O. Box 1480, Edmonton, Ab. T5J 2N4
Phone: (780) 471-7379
Fax: (403) 471-7134
Website: *www.thehorsesatnorthlands.com*
E-Mail: info@northlands.com
Year Founded: 1925
Dates of Inaugural Meeting: July 1925
Abbreviation: NP
Number of Stalls: 1,100
Seating Capacity: 9,000

Ownership

Edmonton Northlands

Officers

President: Dale Leschiutta
General Manager: Ken Knowles
Director of Racing: Les Butler
Racing Secretary: Fred Hilts
Treasurer: Mark Bamford
Director of Operations: Kevin Behm
Director of Marketing: Stephanie Gosselin
Director of Mutuels: Glen Weir
Vice President: Jerry Bouma, Jim Campbell
Director of Publicity: Lauren Farnell
Director of Simulcasting: Glen Weir
Stewards: Al Lennox, Robert Noda, Wayne Armstrong
Track Announcer: Mike Dimoff
Track Photographer: Coady Photography
Track Superintendent: Ron Grift
Horsemen's Bookkeeper: Carey Blenkinsop

Racing Dates

2005: June 24-October 29, 70 days
2006: June 23-October 22, 72 days

Track Layout

Main Circumference: $^5/_8$ mile
Main Track Chute: 6$^1/_2$ furlongs
Main Width: 70 feet
Main Length of Stretch: 625 feet

Attendance

Highest Single-Day Record: 15,922, August 25, 1973

Handle

Average All Sources Recent Meeting: $1,129,393, 2005
Average On-Track Recent Meeting: $155,643, 2005
Single-Day On-Track Handle: $1,652,940, August 16, 1990
Total All Sources Recent Meeting: $79,057,526, 2005
Total On-Track Recent Meeting: $10,895,018, 2005
Highest Single-Day On-Track Record Recent Meet: $800,855, August 27, 2005

Leaders

Recent Meeting, Leading Jockey: Ricky Walcott, 95, 2005
Recent Meeting, Leading Owner: Bar None Ranches Ltd., 37, 2005
Recent Meeting, Leading Trainer: Ron K. Smith, 37, 2005
Recent Meeting, Leading Horse: Banjo Babe, 5, 2005; Sparhawk, 5, 2005

Track Records, Main Dirt

5$^1/_2$ furlongs: So Long Fellas, 1:04$^2/_5$, August 16, 1975
6 furlongs: Sageata, 1:09$^4/_5$, July 22, 1984; Lynn's Dream, 1:09.80, July 8, 2000
6$^1/_2$ furlongs: Timely Ruckus, 1:15.40, June 26, 1999
1 mile: Bagfull, 1:35$^4/_5$, May 16, 1981

1¹/₁₆ miles: Chilcoton Blaze, 1:42³/₅, August 4, 1984
1³/₈ miles: Slyly Gifted, 2:15⁴/₅, August 30, 1986
1⁵/₈ miles: Dancers Nugget, 2:45.20, September 21, 2001
Other: 3¹/₂ furlongs, Steel Penny Black, :38¹/₅, June 14, 1984; 1⁵/₁₆ miles, Arctic Laur, 2:09, August 20, 1995

Principal Races

Canadian Derby (Can-G3), Northlands Oaks, Sonoma S., Speed to Spare S., City of Edmonton Distaff H.

Fastest Times of 2005 (Dirt)

3¹/₂ furlongs: Nashwaak Dancer, :39.60, July 22, 2005
5¹/₂ furlongs: Hidden Speed, 1:05.60, July 8, 2005; Hidden Speed, 1:05.60, August 12, 2005
6 furlongs: King Jeremy, 1:11, June 29, 2005
6¹/₂ furlongs: Cool Bender, 1:16.20, August 10, 2005
1 mile: Deputy Country, 1:37.20, July 9, 2005
1¹/₁₆ miles: Deputy Country, 1:43.80, July 30, 2005
1⁵/₁₆ miles: Jiffyjimmygee, 2:11.80, August 26, 2005
1³/₈ miles: Beau Brass, 2:17.80, September 10, 2005
1⁵/₈ miles: Jiffyjimmygee, 2:50.40, September 30, 2005

Stampede Park

Though it is famous for its annual Calgary Stampede rodeo, Stampede Park is also a longtime part of the Thoroughbred racing scene in Alberta. Thoroughbred racing debuted at Stampede in 1974, with the facility offering racing on a five-furlong oval and stabling for 1,400 horses. Though the track's seating of 25,000 is snug during the Calgary Stampede in July, it has been more than adequate for racing; the track's record attendance is 6,167, set on August 15, 1981. Stampede conducts a spring Thoroughbred meet from early April through mid-June and a Standardbred meet in the summer and early fall. Its major Thoroughbred race is the $100,000 Alberta Derby (Can-G3) in mid-June. In 2004, a competing organization, United Horsemen of Alberta, was awarded the license to operate racing in the Calgary area from 2007 to '17, and the group will build a $70-million track to open in April 2007.

Location: 2300 Stampede Trail S.E., Calgary, Ab. T2G 2W1
Phone: (403) 261-0214
Fax: (403) 265-7009
Website: *www.stampede-park.com*
E-Mail: stpracing@calgarystampede.com
Year Founded: 1973 as Stampede Park
Dates of Inaugural Meeting: July 1925 (Victoria Park); June 20, 1974 (Stampede Park)
Abbreviation: StP
Number of Stalls: 1,300
Seating Capacity: 17,800

Ownership

Calgary Exhibition and Stampede

Officers

Chairman: Steve Allan
President: Steve Allan
Director of Racing: Fred Allen
Racing Secretary: Russell Armstrong
Director of Operations: Gerry McHugh
Director of Marketing: Patti Hunt
Director of Mutuels: Sheri Holmes
Vice President: Mike Whittle, Gord Fache, Laurie Schild, Doug Armitage
Director of Publicity: Patti Hunt
Director of Simulcasting: Sheri Holmes
Horsemen's Liaison: Carole Larson
Stewards: Wayne Armstrong, Al Lennox, Robert Noda
Track Announcer: Joe Carbury
Track Photographer: Coady Photo
Horsemen's Bookkeeper: Bob Tutt

Racing Dates

2005: April 1-June 19, 45 days
2006: March 31-June 18, 47 days

Track Layout

Main Circumference: 5 furlongs
Main Track Chute: 4 furlongs
Main Width: 70 feet
Main Length of Stretch: 660 feet

Attendance

Average Daily Recent Meeting: 1,808, 2005
Highest Single-Day Record: 6,167, August 15, 1981
Total Attendance Recent Meeting: 81,379, 2005

Handle

Average All Sources Recent Meeting: $252,966, 2005
Average On-Track Recent Meeting: $113,581, 2005
Total All Sources Recent Meeting: $11,383,453, 2005
Total On-Track Recent Meeting: $5,111,160, 2005

Leaders

Recent Meeting, Leading Jockey: Quincy Welch, 83, 2005
Recent Meeting, Leading Owner: Bar None Ranches Ltd., 2005
Recent Meeting, Leading Trainer: Greg Tracy, 21, 2005
Recent Meeting, Leading Horse: Miss Marvic, 4, 2005; Shaheens Flyer, 4, 2005; Double Powder, 4, 2005

Principal Races

Alberta Derby, Penny Ridge S., Duchess of York S., Herald Gold Plate H.

Interesting Facts

Previous Names and Dates: Victoria Park (1925-1972)

Fastest Times of 2005 (Dirt)

3¹/₂ furlongs: Miss Spoken, :39.80, May 27, 2005
4 furlongs: Golden Hunt, :43.80, April 1, 2005
6 furlongs: Hot Talk, 1:09.40, May 15, 2005
1 mile: Blowin in the Wind, 1:36.20, May 21, 2005
1¹/₁₆ miles: Five Point Star, 1:43.80, June 12, 2005; Gold Accent, 1:43.80, June 11, 2005

British Columbia

Hastings Race Course

For more than 80 years, the racing scene in the Canadian province of British Columbia has focused on the tract of land where Hastings Park currently stands. From 1994 to 2002, the not-for-profit Pacific Racing Association managed racing at Hastings, which conducts Thoroughbred racing at the five-furlong facility usually from April through November. Woodbine Entertainment Group bought the facility in 2002, and in '04 sold it to Great Canadian Gaming Corp. for $15.7-million. First opened in 1920, Hastings reached its peak as a racing facility in the early 1980s, when the track sometimes drew crowds of 20,000 or more. The track also has appealed to Vancouver's expanding Asian population by offering simulcast wagering from Hong Kong.

Location: Hastings Race Course, Vancouver, B.C. V5K 3N8
Phone: (604) 254-1631, (800) 677-7702
Fax: (604) 251-0411
Website: *www.hastingsracecourse.com*
E-Mail: comments@hastingsracecourse.com
Year Founded: 1889 (Exhibition Park); 1994 (Hastings Race Course)
Abbreviation: Hst
Acreage: 45
Number of Stalls: 1,000
Seating Capacity: 5,600

Ownership

Great Canadian Gaming Corp.

Officers
General Manager: Michael Mackey
Racing Secretary: Lorne Mitchell
Director of Operations: Raj Mutti
Director of Marketing: Deborah Stetz
Director of Mutuels: George Akerman
Vice President: Chuck Keeling
Director of Simulcasting: Dan Jukich
Stewards: Wayne J. Russell, Douglas F. Scott, Keith G. Smith
Track Announcer: Dan Jukich
Track Photographer: Winner's Photography
Track Superintendent: Drew Levere
Security: Paul Bouchard
Horsemen's Bookkeeper: Merrilee Elliott

Racing Dates
2005: April 14-November 27, 83 days
2006: April 14-November 26, 78 days

Track Layout
Main Circumference: 5 furlongs, 208 feet
Main Track Chute: 6$^1/_2$ furlongs, 1$^1/_{16}$ miles and 1$^1/_8$ miles
Main Width: 65 feet
Main Length of Stretch: 513 feet
Training Track: 4 furlongs

Attendance
Highest Single-Day Record: 21,156, July 9, 1982

Handle
Average All Sources Recent Meeting: $837,814, 2005
Average On-Track Recent Meeting: $318,605, 2005
Single-Day On-Track Handle: $2,612,316, July 9, 1982
Total All Sources Recent Meeting: $69,538,540, 2005
Total On-Track Recent Meeting: $26,444,176, 2005
Highest Single-Day Record Recent Meet: $2,486,209, October 29, 2005

Mutuel Records
Highest Win: $508.10, 1953
Highest Exacta: $4,092, 1962
Highest Trifecta: $21,806.20, 1982
Highest Daily Double: $4,863.10, 1995
Highest Pick 3: $11,474, 1993
Highest Other Exotics: $920,411.70, Sweep 6, 1982; $63,326.70, Win 4, 1988; $42,946, Superfecta, June 13, 2004

Leaders
Career, Leading Jockey by Titles: Chris Loseth, 8
Career, Leading Trainer by Titles: Harold J. Barroby, 10
Career, Leading Jockey by Stakes Wins: Chris Loseth, 204
Career, Leading Trainer by Stakes Wins: Harold J. Barroby, 143
Career, Leading Jockey by Wins: Chris Loseth, 3,561
Career, Leading Trainer by Wins: Harold J. Barroby, 1,224
Recent Meeting, Leading Jockey: Justin Stein, 148, 2005
Recent Meeting, Leading Owner: Mr. and Mrs. R. J. Bennett, 20, 2005
Recent Meeting, Leading Trainer: Gary E. Demorest, 47, 2005
Recent Meeting, Leading Horse: Kompressor Jack, 7, 2005

Records
Single-Day Jockey Wins: Chris Loseth, 8, April 9, 1984
Single-Day Trainer Wins: George Cummings, 5, November 8, 1992
Single Meet, Leading Jockey by Wins: Mark Patzer, 173, 1991
Single Meet, Leading Trainer by Wins: Lance Giesbrecht, 76, 1997

Track Records, Main Dirt
6 furlongs: Great Discretion, 1:10$^2/_5$, May 10, 1969; Humphrey Lad, 1:10$^2/_5$, April 13, 1988; Sir Khaled, 1:10$^2/_5$, April 15, 1988
6$^1/_2$ furlongs: Torque Converter, 1:15, July 1, 1996
1m 70 yds: Westbury Road, 1:40$^2/_5$, July 29, 1967
1$^1/_{16}$ miles: Coral Isle, 1:42$^1/_5$, July 28, 1973; No Time Flat, 1:42$^1/_5$, August 12, 1987; Timely Stitch, 1:42.20, July 6, 1996
1$^1/_8$ miles: Artic Son, 1:46.80, August 3, 1998
1$^3/_8$ miles: Irish Bear, 2:14$^2/_5$, October 17, 1987
1$^1/_2$ miles: Lucky Son, 2:29, August 25, 1995
1$^3/_4$ miles: Glen Gower, 2:59, September 23, 1987
Other: a3$^1/_2$ furlongs, Turn to Knight, :41$^1/_5$, May 27, 1990; 3$^1/_2$ furlongs, Flying Memo, :39.40, October 26, 2003; a6 furlongs, Count the Green, 1:10$^4/_5$, April 17, 1971; 1$^7/_{16}$ miles, Who's in Command, 2:23, August 10, 1987; a1$^1/_2$ miles, Golden Gentry, 2:29$^2/_5$, September 20, 1987; 1$^1/_{16}$ miles, Glen Gower, 2:51$^1/_5$, September 9, 1987; 1$^3/_4$ miles, Glen Gower, 2:59, September 23, 1987; 2$^1/_{16}$ miles, Laddie's Prince, 3:30, October 8, 1987; a2$^1/_{16}$ miles, High Hawk, 3:48, October 16, 1983; 2$^1/_8$ miles, Mr. Chancellor, 3:38$^4/_5$, October 18, 1987

Principal Races
British Columbia Derby (Can-G3), British Columbia Breeders' Cup Oaks (Can-G3), Ballerina Breeders' Cup S. (Can-G3), British Columbia Premiers' H. (Can-G3), Ascot Graduation Breeders' Cup S.

Notable Events
British Columbia Cup Day

Fastest Times of 2005 (Dirt)
3$^1/_2$ furlongs: Kechika, :40.12, October 9, 2005
6 furlongs: Favour for Joey, 1:11.59, April 23, 2005
6$^1/_2$ furlongs: Quiet Cash, 1:15.38, July 17, 2005
1$^1/_{16}$ miles: Quiet Cash, 1:42.97, July 31, 2005
1$^1/_8$ miles: R. Associate, 1:48.94, July 1, 2005
1$^3/_8$ miles: Jule Bandit, 2:18.12, August 20, 2005
1$^1/_2$ miles: Woody's Diamond, 2:30.88, September 10, 2005
1$^3/_4$ miles: Woody's Diamond, 3:02.04, October 22, 2005
2$^1/_8$ miles: Crescent Remark, 3:47.84, November 12, 2005

Kamloops
Location: 479 Chilcotin St., Kamloops, B.C. V2H 1G4
Phone: (250) 314-9645
Fax: (250) 828-0836
Website: *www.kamloopsonlineoffline.com*
E-Mail: kamloopsonlineoffline@hotmail.com
Year Founded: 1895
Abbreviation: Kam
Number of Stalls: 310
Seating Capacity: 2000

Ownership
Kamloops Exhibition Association

Officers
Chairman: Luigi Sale
President: Luigi Sale
Director of Racing: Luigi Sale
Racing Secretary: Jim Rogers
Vice President: Dave Carswell
Director of Publicity: Lugi Sale
Track Announcer: Keith Reid
Track Superintendent: Jim Larson

Racing Dates
2005: October 2-October 30
2006: April 23-May 28

Leaders
Recent Meeting, Leading Jockey: Serge R. Rocheleau, 5, 2005; Caroline Stinn, 5, 2005; Anrella J. Villeseche, 5, 2005; Caroline Stinn, 9, 2006
Recent Meeting, Leading Trainer: James R. Brown, 5, 2005; Robert D. Schmidt, 5, 2006
Recent Meeting, Leading Horse: Chief Swan, 3, 2005; Chief Swan, 4, 2006

Principal Races
HBPA/Sagebrush Downs Derby, British Columbia Lottery Corp. H.

Fastest Times of 2005 (Dirt)
a4$^1/_2$ furlongs: Turnberry Condo, :48.60, October 30, 2005
a6$^1/_2$ furlongs: Chief Swan, 1:18.20, October 30, 2005
a1 miles: Eager Lee, 1:37.72, October 16, 2005

Kin Park
Location: P.O. Box 682, Vernon, B.C. V1T 6M6
Abbreviation: Kin

Racing Dates
2005: July 9-July 31, 4 days
2006: July 16-July 30, 4 days

Leaders
Recent Meeting, Leading Jockey: Caroline Stinn, 3, 2005

Fastest Times of 2005 (Dirt)
a4 furlongs: Chief Swan, :44.43, July 17, 2005
a6 furlongs: Long On Pride, 1:13.13, July 31, 2005
a7 furlongs: A Step Beyond, 1:19.67, July 31, 2005
a1$^1/_{16}$ miles: Dr Chiang Mai, 1:45.37, July 31, 2005

Sunflower Downs

Location: P.O. Box 1234, Princeton, B.C. V0H 1W0
Phone: (250) 295-3250
Website: *www.bcinteriorhorseracing.com/index.php*
Abbreviation: SnD

Officers
President: John Bey
General Manager: Jack Powell
Director of Racing: Joe Horton
Secretary: Carol Ruoss
Treasurer: Evelyn Beale
Director of Mutuels: Roberta Baron
Vice President: Ed Vermette
Director of Publicity: June Hope
Track Announcer: Keith Reid

Racing Dates
2005: June 30-July 2, 3 days
2006: June 30, 1 day

Principal Races
Similkameen Cup S., Sunflower Derby, Luke Gibson S., Bob Beale Tulumeen Cup S.

Fastest Times of 2005 (Dirt)
5$^1/_2$ furlongs: Mount Baker, 1:07.60, June 30, 2005; She's Shameless, 1:07.60, June 30, 2005
a7 furlongs: Just for Deb, 1:25.62, June 30, 2005
1$^1/_{16}$ miles: Farewell Cowboys, 1:48.20, June 30, 2005

Manitoba

Assiniboia Downs

Assiniboia Downs continues a rich tradition of horse racing in Winnipeg, dating from the last quarter of the 19th century. Racing enthusiast and businessman Jack Hardy built Assiniboia, which opened in 1958 to replace Polo Park, a 30-year-old track located on property that became a shopping center. In 1974, Jim Wright bought the track and racing prospered under his leadership. By the early 1990s, however, competition from other gambling forms made the track unprofitable. In 1993, Assiniboia was sold to its current owners, the Manitoba Jockey Club, a not-for-profit organization that solidified its future by pouring profits from video lottery terminals and full-card simulcasting back into the facility. Assiniboia, which offers live racing from early May through September, was the first track in Canada to offer pick-six and telephone-account wagering. The track's richest race, the Manitoba Derby (Can-G3), has been run at Assiniboia since 1960. In 1970, Queen Elizabeth II and Prince Philip attended the race as part of Manitoba's centennial year. The winner was Fanfreluche, a Northern Dancer filly who was that year's Canadian Horse of the Year as well as an Eclipse Award winner as North America's champion three-year-old filly. Her son L'Enjoleur won the Manitoba Derby in 1975, the year in which he earned his second Canadian Horse of the Year title.

Location: 3975 Portage Ave., Winnipeg, Mb. R3K 2E9
Phone: (204) 885-3330
Fax: (204) 831-5348
Website: *www.assiniboiadowns.com*
E-Mail: info@assiniboiadowns.com
Dates of Inaugural Meeting: 1958
Abbreviation: AsD
Number of Stalls: 936
Seating Capacity: 6,000

Ownership
Manitoba Jockey Club

Officers
President: Harvey Warner
General Manager: Sharon Gulyas
Director of Racing: Darren Dunn
Racing Secretary: Ray Miller
Secretary: Barry Anderson
Director of Operations: Darren Dunn
Director of Finance: Kris Nancoo
Director of Marketing: Pat Tymkiw
Vice President: Dr. Norm Elder DVM
Director of Publicity: Ernest Nairn
Director of Sales: Holly Klos
Director of Simulcasting: Allan Gray
Stewards: Hazel Bochinski, Val Isman, Craig MacDonald, Jack Wash
Track Announcer: Darren Dunn
Track Photographer: Gerry Hart
Track Superintendent: Bob Timlick
Horsemen's Bookkeeper: Louise Russell
Asst. Racing Secretary: Dustin Davis
Security: Tim McDonald

Racing Dates
2005: May 4-September 25, 75 days
2006: May 6-September 24, 70 days

Track Layout
Main Circumference: 6$^1/_2$ furlongs
Main Track Chute: 6 furlongs and 1$^1/_8$ miles
Main Width: 80 feet
Main Length of Stretch: 990 feet
Training Track: $^1/_2$ mile

Attendance
Highest Single-Day Record: 13,276, August 6, 1979

Handle
Average All Sources Recent Meeting: $110,874, 2005
Average On-Track Recent Meeting: $77,237, 2005
Single-Day On-Track Handle: $713,756, September 5, 1988
Total All Sources Recent Meeting: $8,315,573.47, 2005
Total On-Track Recent Meeting: $5,792,775.53, 2005
Highest Single-Day Record Recent Meet: $394,611.16, August 1, 2005

Mutuel Records
Highest Win: $474.20, May 31, 1986
Highest Exacta: $3,514.80, May 16, 1998
Highest Trifecta: $40,026.60, May 18, 1981
Highest Daily Double: $4,235.50, July 23, 1971
Highest Pick 3: $3,269.40, June 28, 1998
Highest Pick 4: $14,584.95, September 1, 1986

Leaders
Career, Leading Jockey by Titles: Bobby Stewart, 5
Career, Leading Trainer by Titles: Clayton Gray, 7
Career, Leading Jockey by Wins: Ken Hendricks, 1,654
Career, Leading Trainer by Wins: Gary Danelson, 1036
Recent Meeting, Leading Jockey: Rohan R. Singh, 84, 2005
Recent Meeting, Leading Owner: Dr. Ross A. McKague, 2005
Recent Meeting, Leading Trainer: Ardell Sayler, 64, 2005
Recent Meeting, Leading Horse: Albarino, 5, 2005; Racey Casey, 5, 2005

Records
Single-Day Jockey Wins: Jim Sorenson, 7, June 23, 1976

Track Records, Main Dirt
4 furlongs: Northern Spike, :44$^2/_5$, April 23, 1982

$4^1/_2$ furlongs: Astral Moon, :$50^4/_5$, May 1, 1982
5 furlongs: Northern Spike, :$56^2/_5$, September 5, 1982
$5^1/_2$ furlongs: Sunny Famous, 1:02.80, September 19, 1992
6 furlongs: Mr. Quill, 1:09, October 10, 1981; Nephrite, 1:09, October 8, 1989
7 furlongs: Victor's Pride, 1:$23^1/_5$, August 16, 1978
1 mile: *Gladiatore II, 1:$35^4/_5$, July 7, 1972; Tower of Shan, 1:35.80, June 24, 1990
$1^1/_{16}$ miles: Goa, 1:$41^3/_5$, July 23, 1988
$1^1/_8$ miles: Overskate, 1:$47^3/_5$, September 9, 1978
$1^1/_4$ miles: Nifty (Fr), 2:05, September 20, 1986; Northern Debut, 2:05, October 3, 1993
$1^3/_8$ miles: Island Fling, 2:$16^4/_5$, October 29, 1977
$1^1/_2$ miles: Baron Hudec, 2:32, September 9, 1978
$1^5/_8$ miles: Northern Kip, 2:$46^4/_5$, October 30, 1978
$1^3/_4$ miles: Just As Sunny, 3:$01^2/_5$, October 14, 1989
Other: a3 furlongs, Apart, :29, May 8, 1972; a6 furlongs, Lone Spruce, 1:12, June 24, 1984; a7 furlongs, Proven Reserve, 1:$23^3/_5$, July 9, 1986; $1^5/_{16}$ miles, Scarlet Rich, 2:$15^4/_5$, October 21, 1981; $1^1/_{16}$ miles, Hi Executor, 2:$56^4/_5$, September 30, 1984; $2^1/_4$ miles, Fremarcton, 3:$58^1/_5$, August 15, 1960

Principal Races

Gold Breeders' Cup, Manitoba Derby, Matron Breeders' Cup, Winnipeg Futurity

Fastest Times of 2005 (Dirt)

a3 furlongs: Little Fawn, :30.20, June 19, 2005
$4^1/_2$ furlongs: Strike the Chord, :52.60, May 8, 2005
5 furlongs: Adanac, :58.80, May 20, 2005
$5^1/_2$ furlongs: Iwoodificould, 1:05.40, May 21, 2005
6 furlongs: Prime Time T. V., 1:11, June 4, 2005
$7^1/_2$ furlongs: Lord Shogun, 1:33.40, July 8, 2005; Miss Marvic, 1:33.40, August 14, 2005
1 mile: Albarino, 1:38.60, August 20, 2005
$1^1/_{16}$ miles: Lord Shogun, 1:45.40, August 19, 2005
$1^1/_8$ miles: Prime Time T. V., 1:52.20, August 1, 2005
$1^1/_4$ miles: Brother Baileys, 2:11.60, August 23, 2005

Ontario

Fort Erie

Founded in 1897, Fort Erie is one of Canada's oldest racetracks. Located in southern Ontario across the border from Buffalo, New York, the track began its premier event, the Prince of Wales Stakes, in 1959 with the help of prominent Ontario horseman E. P. Taylor. The race for three-year-old Canadian-breds now has become the second leg of Canada's Triple Crown. Taylor-bred Northern Dancer made his career debut at Fort Erie in August 1963. The following year, the Nearctic colt became the first Canadian-bred to win the Kentucky Derby. The track now is owned by Nordic Gaming Corp., which consists of three business interests from southern Ontario and two foreign investors. It underwent $30-million in renovations in 1999 to prepare for 1,200 slot machines that help to support the racing operation.

Location: 230 Catherine St., P.O. Box 1130, Fort Erie, On. L2A 5N9
Phone: (905) 871-3200
Fax: (905) 994-3629
Website: *www.forterieracing.com*
E-Mail: femedia@forterieracetrack.ca
Year Founded: 1897
Dates of Inaugural Meeting: June 16, 1897
Abbreviation: FE
Number of Stalls: 1,300
Seating Capacity: 4,000

Ownership

Nordic Gaming Corp.

Officers

Chief Executive Officer: Bonnie Loubert
Director of Racing: Herb McGirr Sr.
Racing Secretary: Thomas G. Gostlin
Treasurer: George Ranalli
Director of Operations: Herb McGirr Sr.
Director of Communications: Daryl Wells Jr.
Director of Marketing: Marketing Services Group
Director of Mutuels: Chad Gates
Director of Publicity: Daryl Wells Jr.
Director of Simulcasting: Chad Gates
Track Announcer: Daryl Wells Jr.
Track Photographer: Michael Burns Photography
Track Superintendent: Alan Gouck

Racing Dates

2005: May 1-October 31, 104 days
2006: April 29-October 31, 104 days

Track Layout

Main Circumference: 1 mile
Main Track Chute: $6^1/_2$ furlongs and $1^1/_4$ miles
Main Width: 75 feet
Main Length of Stretch: 1,060 feet
Main Turf Circumference: 7 furlongs
Main Turf Length of Stretch: 930 feet

Handle

Average All Sources Recent Meeting: $741,807, 2005
Average On-Track Recent Meeting: $138,197, 2005
Total All Sources Recent Meeting: $77,147,920, 2005
Total On-Track Recent Meeting: $14,372,486, 2005
Highest Single-Day Record Recent Meet: $1,522,518, August 1, 2005

Leaders

Recent Meeting, Leading Jockey: Chad Beckon, 100, 2005
Recent Meeting, Leading Owner: Stronach Stable, 38, 2005
Recent Meeting, Leading Trainer: Nick Gonzalez, 56, 2005
Recent Meeting, Leading Horse: New Kid in Town, 5, 2005

Track Records, Main Dirt

4 furlongs: Kirk's Dandy, :$47^2/_5$, May 2, 1957
$4^1/_2$ furlongs: Astral Moon, :$50^4/_5$, May 1, 1982
5 furlongs: Cool Shot, :56.60, July 15, 1995
$5^1/_2$ furlongs: Emotionally, 1:03.60, June 28, 1997; Just a Lord, 1:03.60, June 15, 1991
6 furlongs: High Blitz, 1:08.35, June 13, 2005
$6^1/_2$ furlongs: Muzledick, 1:$15^4/_5$, August 10, 1968; Souvenier Biz, 1:15.85, August 13, 2005
1m 70 yds: Myrtle Irene, 1:39.80, August 26, 1994
$1^1/_{16}$ miles: Goa, 1:$41^3/_5$, July 23, 1988
$1^1/_8$ miles: Lauries Dancer, 1:48, August 23, 1972
$1^3/_{16}$ miles: Bruce's Mill, 1:53.80, July 31, 1994
$1^1/_4$ miles: Do's Vigil, 2:$03^2/_5$, August 14, 1974; French Tambourine, 2:$03^2/_5$, August 10, 1975
$1^1/_2$ miles: Itshouldbesoeasy, 2:32.57, August 10, 1999
$1^5/_8$ miles: Gay Story, 2:$48^3/_5$, August 27, 1956
$1^3/_4$ miles: Brave Zappa, 2:59, July 9, 1984
Other: 2 furlongs, Leisure Road, :21.20, September 5, 1998; $1^{13}/_{16}$ miles, Captain Charisma, 3:$09^2/_5$, August 12, 1984; $1^7/_8$ miles, Frost Prince, 3:22.60, August 20, 1999; 2m 70 yds, Devils Gold, 3:33, October 6, 1997

Track Records, Main Turf

5 furlongs: Oh Mar, :56.99, September 9, 2002
1 mile: Fifth and a Jigger, 1:34.30, June 10, 1991
$1^1/_{16}$ miles: Road of War, 1:40.80, June 19, 1994
$1^3/_8$ miles: Lord Vancouver, 2:15, July 30, 1972
$1^1/_2$ miles: Norwick, 2:28, August 21, 1983
$1^3/_4$ miles: Ahead of the Best, 2:56.60, September 10, 1991
Other: a7 furlongs, Native Vigil, 1:22.10, July 2, 1991; a$1^7/_8$ miles, Regal Admiral, 3:$19^4/_5$, August 7, 1974; $1^7/_8$ miles, Medlaw, 3:$16^1/_5$, September 30, 1985

Principal Races

Prince of Wales S., Bison City S., Rainbow Connection S., Daryl Wells Sr. Memorial S., Ernie Samuel Memorial S.

Fastest Times of 2005 (Dirt)

2 furlongs: Mr. Niner, :21.54, July 26, 2005
$4^1/_2$ furlongs: Jonah Magic, :51.85, May 9, 2005

5 furlongs: Mr. Niner, :57.34, June 19, 2005
6 furlongs: High Blitz, 1:08.35, June 13, 2005
6½ furlongs: Souvenier Biz, 1:15.85, August 13, 2005
1m 70 yds: Elegant Hunter, 1:41.13, September 24, 2005
1¹⁄₁₆ miles: Awesome Rush, 1:42.15, June 11, 2005
1⅛ miles: By Far the Best, 1:50.63, September 18, 2005
1³⁄₁₆ miles: Ablo, 1:56.90, July 17, 2005
1¼ miles: Dancer's Guest, 2:05.94, August 27, 2005
1¾ miles: Dancer's Guest, 3:02.81, October 3, 2005
2m 70 yds: Dancer's Guest, 3:35.52, November 1, 2005

Fastest Times of 2005 (Turf)

5 furlongs: Deputy Cures Blues, :57.23, July 24, 2005
a5 furlongs: Wire Editor, :58.09, June 5, 2005
a7 furlongs: Sandspit, 1:24.66, August 23, 2005
1 mile: Kris's Dancer, 1:37.37, July 25, 2005
a1 miles: Lindsey's Dove, 1:38.62, August 7, 2005
1¹⁄₁₆ miles: Le Cinquieme Essai, 1:42.07, July 4, 2005
a1¹⁄₁₆ miles: Necessaire, 1:44.83, August 1, 2005
a1⅜ miles: Backstretch Gossip, 2:22.46, September 13, 2005
a1½ miles: River Boat, 2:35.52, September 12, 2005

Woodbine

The addition of 1,700 slot machines in March 2000 substantially increased purses and made Canada's best-known racetrack into a financial success after years of operating under a burdensome debt load. After installing the slot machines, the organization that owns the track changed its name from the Ontario Jockey Club to the Woodbine Entertainment Group. Woodbine, located in the Toronto suburb of Rexdale, is home of the Queen's Plate Stakes, first run in 1860 and North America's oldest continually run stakes race. With a unique track arrangement on its 650 acres, Woodbine is the only track in North America to conduct Standardbred and Thoroughbred racing on the same day. Its 1½-mile grass course, the E. P. Taylor Turf Course, features the longest stretch run in North America, 1,440 feet. Inside the turf course is the one-mile main track, which was renovated with a Polytrack synthetic surface in 2006. Inside the main track is a seven-eighths-mile, 85-foot-wide harness track. Woodbine's rich history dates to 1874, when the track opened on what was then the eastern outskirts of Toronto, which is now Toronto's downtown. That track's name was changed to Old Woodbine in 1956 and then renamed Greenwood Raceway in '63. The present Woodbine opened on June 12, 1956. In 1996, Woodbine became the first track outside the United States to host the Breeders' Cup, and it drew a record Woodbine crowd of 42,243. Besides the Queen's Plate, Woodbine hosts the $1.5-million Canadian International (Can-G1) and the $1-million Atto Mile Stakes (Can-G1), which has evolved into an important stakes for grass horses aiming for the Breeders' Cup Mile (G1).

Location: 555 Rexdale Blvd., Rexdale, On. M9W 5L2
Phone: (416) 675-7223, (888) 675-7223
Fax: (416) 213-2126
Website: *www.woodbineentertainment.com*
E-Mail: csd@woodbineentertainment.com
Year Founded: 1874 (Old Woodbine); 1956 (Woodbine)
Abbreviation: WO
Acreage: 850
Number of Stalls: 2,138
Seating Capacity: 13,500

Ownership

Woodbine Entertainment Group

Officers

Chairman: David S. Willmot
Chief Executive Officer: David S. Willmot
Director of Racing: Tom Cosgrove
Racing Secretary: Steven Lym
Treasurer: Robert Careless
Director of Operations: Ed Stutz
Director of Communications: Glenn Crouter
Directors of Marketing: Bruce Murray, Ann Scott
Director of Mutuels: Veena Rampersad
Vice Presidents: Nick R. Eaves, Steve N. Mitchell, Jim W. Ormiston
Director of Publicity: John Siscos
Horsemen's Liaison: Steve Koch
Stewards: Richard Grubb, Gunnar Lindberg, Fenton Platts
Track Announcer: Dan Loiselle
Track Photographer: Michael Burns Photography
Track Superintendent: Brian Jabelman
Asst. Racing Secretary: Sheryl McSwain
Horsemen's Bookkeeper: F. Courtney

Racing Dates

2005: April 16-December 11, 165 days
2006: April 1-December 3, 168 days

Track Layout

Main Circumference: 1 mile
Main Track Chute: 2 furlongs and 7 furlongs
Main Width: 85 feet
Main Length of Stretch: 975 feet
Main Turf Circumference: 1½ miles
Main Turf Chute: 1⅛ miles
Main Turf Width: Homestretch: 100 feet; Backstretch: 120 feet
Main Turf Length of Stretch: 1,440 feet
Inner Circumference: 7 furlong harness track
Training Track: 1 mile (dirt); 7 furlongs (turf)

Attendance

Highest Single-Day Record: 42,243, October 26, 1996

Handle

Average All Sources Recent Meeting: $2,208,707, 2005
Average On-Track Recent Meeting: $797,278, 2005
Single-Day On-Track Handle: $6,884,357, October 26, 1996
Single-Day Total Handle All Sources: $67,738,890, October 26, 1996
Total All Sources Recent Meeting: $364,436,580, 2005
Total On-Track Recent Meeting: $131,550,930, 2005
Highest Single-Day Record Recent Meet: $5,778,506, June 26, 2005

Mutuel Records

Highest Win: $794.20, Waverley Steps, June 24, 1968
Highest Exacta: $6,405, June 11, 1995
Lowest Exacta: $2.70, June 16, 1991
Highest Trifecta: $123,279, November 28, 1999
Lowest Trifecta: $11.60, August 11, 1998
Highest Daily Double: $5,497.50, June 16, 1978
Lowest Daily Double: $3.80, May 20, 1998
Highest Pick 3: $10,881.80, June 29, 1991
Lowest Pick 3: $1.80, July 28, 1991
Highest Other Exotics: $466,671.65, Super 7, July 1, 1989; $34,900.35, Superfecta, November 4, 2001
Lowest Other Exotics: $221.50, Super 7, May 10, 1997; $86.30, Superfecta, July 5, 2000
Highest Pick 4: $123,372.30, June 15, 1988
Lowest Pick 4: $21.75, April 29, 1995

Leaders

Career, Leading Jockey by Titles: Sandy Hawley, 19
Career, Leading Trainer by Titles: Frank Merrill, 30
Recent Meeting, Leading Jockey: Emma-Jayne Wilson, 175, 2005
Recent Meeting, Leading Owner: Melnyk Racing Stable, Inc., 37, 2005
Recent Meeting, Leading Trainer: Sid Attard, 68, 2005
Recent Meeting, Leading Horse: Oye Vai, 5, 2005; Schooner Bay, 5, 2005; Top Ten List, 5, 2005; Friendly Theresa, 5, 2005; Are You Serious, 5, 2005

Records

Single-Day Jockey Wins: Richard Grubb, 7, May 16, 1967; Sandy Hawley, 7, May 22, 1972; Sandy Hawley, 7, October 10, 1974
Single Meet, Leading Jockey by Wins: Mickey Walls, 221, 1991
Single Meet, Leading Trainer by Wins: Frank Passero, 89, 1995

Track Records, Main Dirt

4½ furlongs: Hallmarked, :50.40, March 24, 1996; Written Approval, :50.40, March 25, 1996
5 furlongs: Jack and Emma, :55.95, April 5, 2003
5½ furlongs: Uncle Woger, 1:02.70, April 4, 1999
6 furlongs: Chris's Bad Boy, 1:08.05, November 29, 2003
6½ furlongs: Sophia's Prince, 1:14.56, August 7, 2005
7 furlongs: Oronero, 1:20.60, December 6, 1995
1m 70 yds: Regal Courser, 1:39.60, August 8, 1998
1¹/₁₆ miles: Kiridashi, 1:40.80, August 17, 1996
1⅛ miles: Glorious Song, 1:48, July 1, 1981
1³/₁₆ miles: Runnin Roman, 1:55⅘, September 15, 1974
1¼ miles: Alphabet Soup, 2:01, October 26, 1996
1⅜ miles: Lovely Sunrise, 2:17, October 26, 1974
1½ miles: Norcliffe, 2:29⅕, October 29, 1977
1⅝ miles: *Eugenia II, 2:43⅖, October 27, 1956
1¾ miles: Major Pots, 2:52.60, December 8, 1994
Other: 3 furlongs, Noble Herod, :33⅗, May 5, 1978; 1⅞ miles, Flying Commander, 3:13.29, December 2, 2001

Track Records, Main Turf

6 furlongs: Wild Zone, 1:07.60, July 7, 1996; Spring Barley, 1:07.63, September 5, 2001
6½ furlongs: My Lucky Strike, 1:13.97, August 7, 2005
7 furlongs: Soaring Free, 1:19.38, July 24, 2004
1 mile: Royal Regalia, 1:31.84, July 1, 2004
1¹/₁₆ miles: Jet Freighter, 1:39.20, June 4, 1995; Honolulu Gold, 1:39.20, July 11, 1996; Western Express, 1:39.20, July 12, 1998
1⅛ miles: Bold Ruritana, 1:45.20, June 18, 1995
1¼ miles: Arbalest, 2:01, June 15, 1995; Set Ablaze, 2:01, July 5, 1996
1⅜ miles: Shoal Water, 2:12.37, July 25, 2004
1½ miles: Raintrap (GB), 2:25.60, October 16, 1994
Other: a1⅛ miles, Surging River, 1:42.87, August 8, 2004; a1¼ miles, Desert Waves, 2:02.40, July 24, 1995; a1¼ miles, Murad, 2:02.40, June 4, 1998; a1⅜ miles, Chief Bearhart, 2:16, July 25, 1996; a1½ miles, Mr. Lucky Junction, 2:29.60, July 26, 1996

Principal Races

Canadian International S. (Can-G1), Woodbine Mile S. (Can-G1), Northern Dancer Breeders' Cup Turf S. (Can-G2), Queen's Plate S., Breeders' S., Woodbine Oaks

Interesting Facts

Previous Names and Dates: Ontario Jockey Club 1881-2001
Achievements/Milestones: Hosted Arlington Million in 1988; Hosted Breeders' Cup in 1996

Notable Events

In January 2004, the company launched hpibet.com, an Internet wagering site.

Fastest Times of 2005 (Dirt)

4½ furlongs: Wannatalkaboutme, :52.48, June 10, 2005
5 furlongs: Devil's Bride, :57.80, September 7, 2005
5½ furlongs: Tothemoonandback, 1:03.89, September 28, 2005
6 furlongs: My Lucky Strike, 1:08.93, July 13, 2005
6½ furlongs: Sophia's Prince, 1:14.56, August 7, 2005
7 furlongs: Mister Coop, 1:21.30, September 21, 2005
1m 70 yds: Honey Green, 1:42.69, September 1, 2005
1¹/₁₆ miles: Sky Diamond, 1:42.01, August 3, 2005
1⅛ miles: Palladio, 1:50.67, October 9, 2005
1³/₁₆ miles: Kerrobert, 2:00.75, November 11, 2005
1¼ miles: Ballroom Deputy, 2:05.77, November 12, 2005
1½ miles: Lettherebejustice, 2:34.23, November 19, 2005
1¾ miles: Seattlespectacular, 3:01.81, December 11, 2005
1⅞ miles: Dancer's Guest, 3:16.71, December 11, 2005

Fastest Times of 2005 (Turf)

6 furlongs: Soaring Free, 1:08.03, June 26, 2005
a6 furlongs: Steel Light, 1:12.14, October 23, 2005
6½ furlongs: My Lucky Strike, 1:13.97, August 7, 2005
7 furlongs: Lucky Tom, 1:20.21, October 21, 2005
1 mile: Gamblers Slew, 1:33.64, June 26, 2005
1¹/₁₆ miles: Orsay, 1:40.77, June 30, 2005
1⅛ miles: Seattlespectacular, 1:47.27, September 5, 2005
a1⅛ miles: Pipers Honour, 1:46.77, June 24, 2005
1¼ miles: Sky Conqueror, 2:01.49, October 16, 2005
a1¼ miles: Cry of the Wild, 2:06.27, August 6, 2005
1⅜ miles: Seanachai, 2:14.60, October 20, 2005
1½ miles: Revved Up, 2:27.13, September 5, 2005

Saskatchewan

Marquis Downs

Marquis Downs in Saskatoon has offered live racing since 1969. With a five-furlong track and a grandstand capacity of 4,500, Marquis is part of the Saskatoon Prairieland Exhibition, a multipurpose facility that includes meeting and exhibition halls and a casino. Racing annually takes place from May through September.

Location: 503 Ruth St. W., P.O. Box 6010, Saskatoon, Sk. S7K 4E4
Phone: (306) 242-6100
Fax: (306) 242-6907
Website: *www.marquisdowns.com*
E-Mail: contactus@saskatoonex.com
Dates of Inaugural Meeting: August 18, 1969
Abbreviation: MD
Number of Stalls: 750
Seating Capacity: 3,027

Ownership

Saskatoon Prairieland Park Corp.

Officers

Chief Executive Officer: Mark Regier
President: Les Cannam
Racing Secretary: Rick Fior
Treasurer: Dan Kemppainen
Director of Operations: Wayne Heiser
Director of Communications: Marlene Rochelle
Director of Marketing: Maurice Neault
Vice President: Dennis Wiebe
Director of Publicity: Maurice Neault
Director of Simulcasting: Doug King
Horsemen's Liaison: Don Bjarnarson
Stewards: Terry Harkness, Doug Schneider, Margo Tutt
Track Announcer: Dave Paulsen
Track Photographer: Naomi Wilson
Track Superintendent: Dennis Paules

Racing Dates

2005: May 27-September 10, 29 days
2006: May 26-September 9, 30 days

Track Layout

Main Circumference: 5 furlongs
Main Track Chute: 7 furlongs and 1⅛ miles
Main Width: 90 feet
Main Length of Stretch: 660 feet

Attendance

Average Daily Recent Meeting: 777, 2005
Total Attendance Recent Meeting: 22,552, 2005

Handle

Average All Sources Recent Meeting: $392,190, 2005
Average On-Track Recent Meeting: $27,145, 2005
Total All Sources Recent Meeting: $11,373,503, 2005
Total On-Track Recent Meeting: $787,212, 2005
Highest Single-Day On-Track Record Recent Meet: $37,707, August 6, 2005

Leaders

Recent Meeting, Leading Jockey: Tim Moccasin, 43, 2005
Recent Meeting, Leading Owner: Redbird Farm, 16, 2005
Recent Meeting, Leading Trainer: Don Bjarnarson, 18, 2005
Recent Meeting, Leading Horse: Wind Dancer, 5, 2005

Track Records, Main Dirt

4 furlongs: Zizzilin, :45, May 8, 1981

5½ furlongs: Mickey's Mark, 1:04²/₅, July 28, 1980
6 furlongs: Shotgun Annie, 1:10²/₅, August 7, 1981
6½ furlongs: Christmas Country, 1:18³/₅, August 1, 1994
7 furlongs: T.V. Fling, 1:24¹/₅, August 28, 1988
1 mile: Three for You, 1:37¹/₅, June 12, 1981
1¹/₁₆ miles: Little Bo, 1:42, September 1, 1984
1⅛ miles: Zance, 1:49³/₅, October 10, 1988
1⅜ miles: Secret Cipher, 2:18, October 15, 1983
1⅝ miles: Bright Bern, 2:48, July 31, 1976
1¾ miles: Lloyd's Admiral, 3:01²/₅, October 19, 1986
Other: 3½ furlongs, Kid Dynamo, :40²/₅, June 20, 1977; a4 furlongs, Royal Alibi, :45¹/₅, May 20, 1978; a6½ furlongs, Shona Rae, 1:17⁴/₅, June 11, 1992; a7 furlongs, Graceful Klinchit, 1:23³/₅, August 31, 1991; a1⅛ miles, Easy Riser, 1:49²/₅, August 25, 1980; 1⁵/₁₆ miles, Extrapolate, 2:13, August 29, 1993; a1½ miles, Spring Sunsation, 2:35, September 26, 1993

Principal Races

Prairie Lily Sales S., Saskatchewan Derby, Saskatchewan Futurity, Heritage S. (4 Saskatchewan-bred races)

Interesting Facts

Trivia: Jockey Tim Moccasin rode 14 consecutive winners August 24 through September 1, 2001, believed to be a North American record.

Fastest Times of 2005 (Dirt)

4 furlongs: Arctic Warning, :47.25, May 27, 2005; Year of the Fox, :47.25, May 28, 2005
6 furlongs: Joseph George, 1:12.53, June 24, 2005
6½ furlongs: Excessively Sweet, 1:23.25, August 20, 2005
7 furlongs: Dancing On a Star, 1:26.45, June 24, 2005
1 mile: Fargo Forbes, 1:39.25, August 6, 2005
1¹/₁₆ miles: Wind Dancer, 1:47.28, August 20, 2005

Yorkton Exhibition

Location: Box 908, Yorkton, Sk. S3N 2X1
Phone: (306) 783-4800
Fax: (306) 782-4919
E-Mail: yorkton.ex@sasktel.net
Abbreviation: Ykt
Seating Capacity: 2,500

Racing Dates

2005: May 14-July 9

Track Layout

Main Circumference: 4 furlongs

Leaders

Recent Meeting, Leading Jockey: Danielle Beischer, 6, 2005
Recent Meeting, Leading Trainer: Mike Tourangeau, 3, 2005; Brad Ball, 3, 2005; Dennis Bird, 3, 2005

Fastest Times of 2005 (Dirt)

a4½ furlongs: J C Steel, :59.60, May 15, 2005; Thisdevilcanfly, :59.60, May 15, 2005; Wyndham Bay, :59.60, May 14, 2005
5 furlongs: Gaelic's a King, 1:03.60, July 8, 2005
6½ furlongs: Wyndham Bay, 1:21.40, July 9, 2005
1 mile: Herb E, 1:45.40, July 9, 2005

Puerto Rico

El Comandante

Located in Canovanas, El Comandante has been the island's racing outlet for decades. To many racing fans, El Comandante is probably best known for producing Bold Forbes and Mister Frisky. A dual-classic winner and 1976 champion three-year-old male in the United States, Bold Forbes began his career at El Comandante. So did Mister Frisky, who started his unbeaten string there in 1989 before coming to the United States and going off as the favorite in the 1990 Kentucky Derby (G1), in which he finished eighth. In recent years, El Comandante has added a sophisticated network of off-track wagering outlets and a daily television racing report. The subsidiary of Virginia-based Equus Gaming Co. that operates El Comandante filed for bankruptcy in 2004. Also in 2004, Puerto Rico authorized 6,500 slot machines for the track's off-track betting system.

Location: P.O. Box 1675, Canovanas, P.R. 00729-1675
Phone: (787) 641-6060
Fax: (787) 876-5170
Website: *www.comandantepr.com*
E-Mail: webmaster@elcomandantepr.net
Year Founded: 1976
Abbreviation: ElC
Acreage: 257
Number of Stalls: 1,500+

Ownership

El Comandante Management Co.

Officers

President: Charles A. Cuprill
General Manager: Alejandro Fuentes Fernandez
Director of Racing: Marco Rivera Puga
Racing Secretary: Angel Ayala
Director of Operations: Marco Rivera Puga
Director of Finance: Stanley J. Pinkerton
Director of Marketing: Nidnal Adrover
Director of Mutuels: Wilma Curet
Vice President: Alejandro Fuentes Fernandez
Director of Publicity: Nidnal Adrover
Track Superintendent: Jose A. Hernandez

Racing Dates

2005: January 1-December 31
2006: January 1-December 31, 259 days

Track Layout

Main Circumference: 1 mile
Main Track Chute: 7 furlongs

Attendance

Highest Single-Day Record: 12,578, December 2, 1987
Highest Single-Meet Record: 338,500, 1996

Handle

Single-Day Total Handle All Sources: $2,117,498, December 2, 1994
Record Average All Sources Single Meet: $1,435,900, 1994

Leaders

Career, Leading Jockey by Titles: Mateo Matos, 8
Career, Leading Owner by Titles: Jose Coll Vidal, 28
Career, Leading Trainer by Titles: Pablo Suarez, 28
Career, Leading Jockey by Stakes Wins: Wilfredo Rohena, 101
Career, Leading Owner by Stakes Wins: Jose Coll Vidal, 185
Career, Leading Trainer by Stakes Wins: Pablo Suarez, 187
Career, Leading Jockey by Wins: Alexis Feliciano, 2,127
Career, Leading Owner by Wins: Jose Coll Vidal, 4,191
Career, Leading Trainer by Wins: Pablo Suarez, 4,295

Records

Single-Day Jockey Wins: Julio A. Garcia, 6
Single-Day Trainer Wins: Juan M. Rodriquez, 6
Single Meet, Leading Jockey by Wins: Julio A. Garcia, 321

Track Records, Main Dirt

5 furlongs: Lozier Kaplan, :57²/₅, April 16, 1978
5½ furlongs: Bandit Bomber, 1:02.60, May 3, 1996
6 furlongs: Bandit Bomber, 1:09, August 16, 1995
6½ furlongs: Bo Judged, 1:15¹/₅, May 14, 1989
7 furlongs: Bandit Bomber, 1:21.40, October 1, 1995
1¹/₁₆ miles: Shake Shake Shake, 1:42³/₅, June 25, 1978
1⅛ miles: Dr. Abraham, 1:48.80, July 20, 1996
1³/₁₆ miles: Lightning Al, 1:55.40, February 17, 1997

Principal Races

Derby Puertorriqueno, Copa Gobernador, Copa San Juan, Clasico Antonio Fernandez Castrillon, Clasico Internacional del Caribe

North American Racetracks

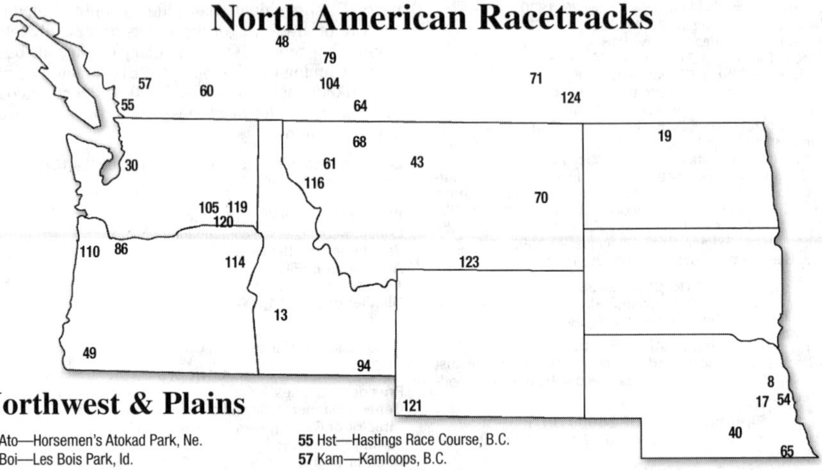

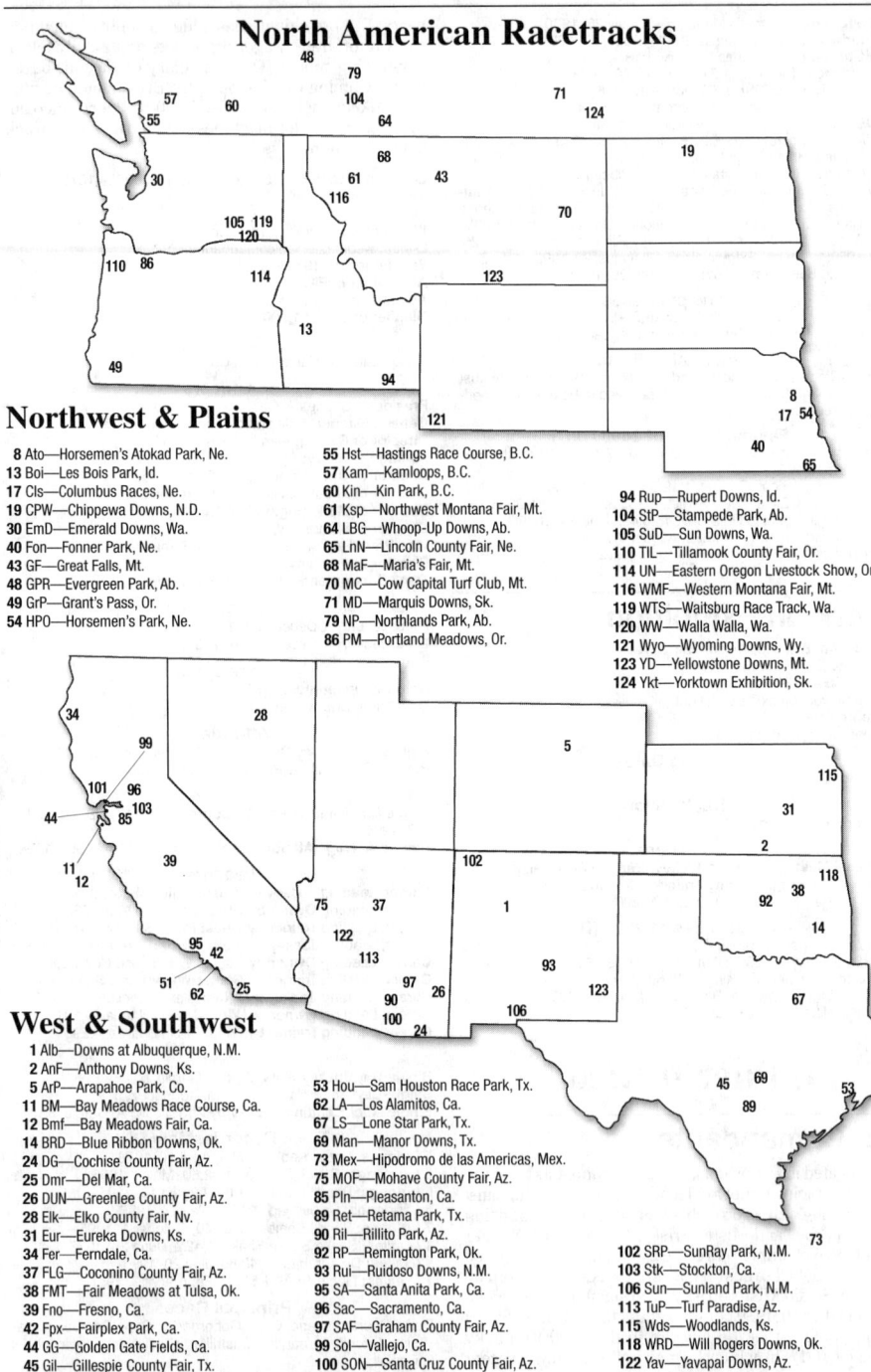

Northwest & Plains

8 Ato—Horsemen's Atokad Park, Ne.
13 Boi—Les Bois Park, Id.
17 Cls—Columbus Races, Ne.
19 CPW—Chippewa Downs, N.D.
30 EmD—Emerald Downs, Wa.
40 Fon—Fonner Park, Ne.
43 GF—Great Falls, Mt.
48 GPR—Evergreen Park, Ab.
49 GrP—Grant's Pass, Or.
54 HPO—Horsemen's Park, Ne.
55 Hst—Hastings Race Course, B.C.
57 Kam—Kamloops, B.C.
60 Kin—Kin Park, B.C.
61 Ksp—Northwest Montana Fair, Mt.
64 LBG—Whoop-Up Downs, Ab.
65 LnN—Lincoln County Fair, Ne.
68 MaF—Maria's Fair, Mt.
70 MC—Cow Capital Turf Club, Mt.
71 MD—Marquis Downs, Sk.
79 NP—Northlands Park, Ab.
86 PM—Portland Meadows, Or.
94 Rup—Rupert Downs, Id.
104 StP—Stampede Park, Ab.
105 SuD—Sun Downs, Wa.
110 TIL—Tillamook County Fair, Or.
114 UN—Eastern Oregon Livestock Show, Or.
116 WMF—Western Montana Fair, Mt.
119 WTS—Waitsburg Race Track, Wa.
120 WW—Walla Walla, Wa.
121 Wyo—Wyoming Downs, Wy.
123 YD—Yellowstone Downs, Mt.
124 Ykt—Yorktown Exhibition, Sk.

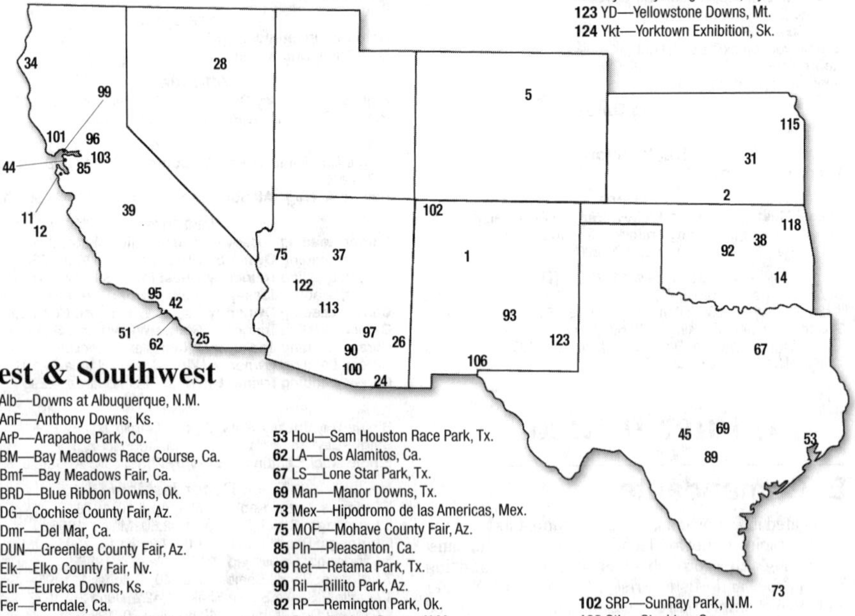

West & Southwest

1 Alb—Downs at Albuquerque, N.M.
2 AnF—Anthony Downs, Ks.
5 ArP—Arapahoe Park, Co.
11 BM—Bay Meadows Race Course, Ca.
12 Bmf—Bay Meadows Fair, Ca.
14 BRD—Blue Ribbon Downs, Ok.
24 DG—Cochise County Fair, Az.
25 Dmr—Del Mar, Ca.
26 DUN—Greenlee County Fair, Az.
28 Elk—Elko County Fair, Nv.
31 Eur—Eureka Downs, Ks.
34 Fer—Ferndale, Ca.
37 FLG—Coconino County Fair, Az.
38 FMT—Fair Meadows at Tulsa, Ok.
39 Fno—Fresno, Ca.
42 Fpx—Fairplex Park, Ca.
44 GG—Golden Gate Fields, Ca.
45 Gil—Gillespie County Fair, Tx.
51 Hol—Hollywood Park, Ca.
53 Hou—Sam Houston Race Park, Tx.
62 LA—Los Alamitos, Ca.
67 LS—Lone Star Park, Tx.
69 Man—Manor Downs, Tx.
73 Mex—Hipodromo de las Americas, Mex.
75 MOF—Mohave County Fair, Az.
85 Pln—Pleasanton, Ca.
89 Ret—Retama Park, Tx.
90 Ril—Rillito Park, Az.
92 RP—Remington Park, Ok.
93 Rui—Ruidoso Downs, N.M.
95 SA—Santa Anita Park, Ca.
96 Sac—Sacramento, Ca.
97 SAF—Graham County Fair, Az.
99 Sol—Vallejo, Ca.
100 SON—Santa Cruz County Fair, Az.
101 SR—Santa Rosa, Ca.
102 SRP—SunRay Park, N.M.
103 Stk—Stockton, Ca.
106 Sun—Sunland Park, N.M.
113 TuP—Turf Paradise, Az.
115 Wds—Woodlands, Ks.
118 WRD—Will Rogers Downs, Ok.
122 Yav—Yavapai Downs, Az.
123 Zia—Zia Park, NM

Abbreviations and Locations

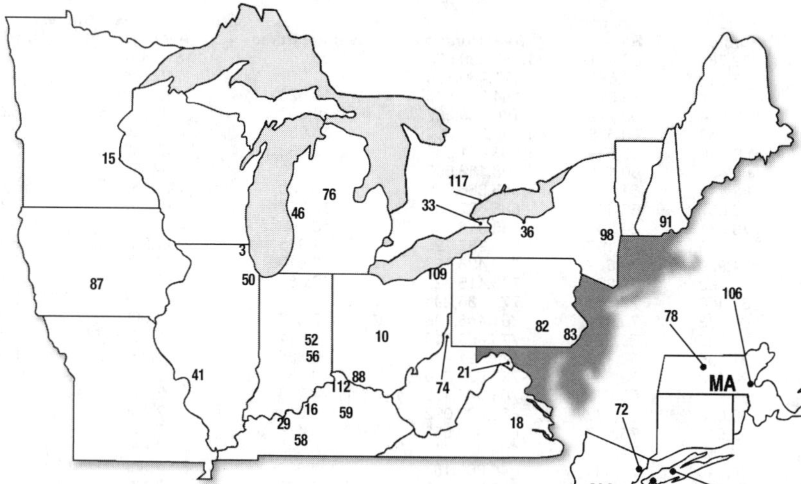

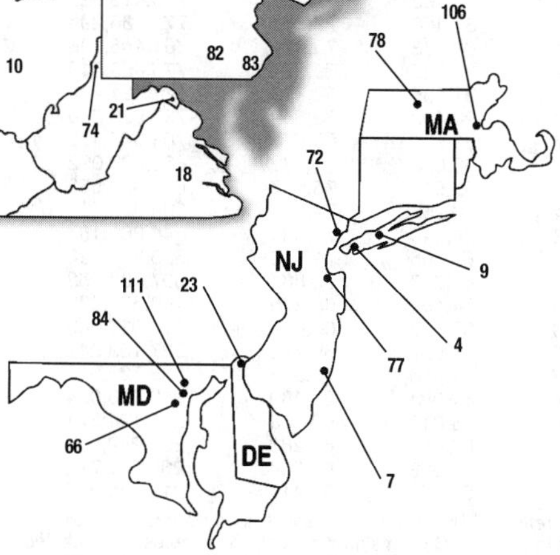

Northeast & Midwest

3 AP—Arlington Park, Ill.
4 Aqu—Aqueduct, N.Y.
6 AsD—Assiniboia Downs, Mb.
7 Atl—Atlantic City Race Course, N.J.
9 Bel—Belmont Park, N.Y.
10 Beu—Beulah Park, Oh.
15 Cby—Canterbury Park, Mn.
16 CD—Churchill Downs, Ky.
18 Cnl—Colonial Downs, Va.
21 CT—Charlestown Races, W.V.
23 Del—Delaware Park, De.
29 ElP—Ellis Park, Ky.
33 FE—Fort Erie, On.
36 FL—Finger Lakes, N.Y.
41 FP—Fairmount Park, Il.
46 GLD—Great Lakes Downs, Mi.
50 Haw—Hawthorne Park, Il.
52 Hoo—Hoosier Park, In.
56 Ind—Indiana Downs, In.
58 KD—Kentucky Downs, Ky.
59 Kee—Keeneland Race Course, Ky.
66 Lrl—Laurel Park, Md.
72 Med—Meadowlands, N.J.
74 Mnr—Mountaineer Race Track, W.V.
76 MPM—Mount Pleasant Meadows, Mi.
77 Mth—Monmouth Park, N.J.
78 Nmp—Northampton Fair, Ma.
82 Pen—Penn National Race Course, Pa.
83 Pha—Philadelphia Park, Pa.
84 Pim—Pimlico Race Course, Md.
87 PrM—Prairie Meadows Racetrack, Ia.
88 RD—River Downs, Oh.
91 Rkm—Rockingham Park, N.H.
98 Sar—Saratoga Race Course, N.Y.
106 Suf—Suffolk Downs, Ma.
109 Tdn—Thistledown, Oh.
111 Tim—Timonium, Md.
112 TP—Turfway Park, Ky.
117 WO—Woodbine, On.

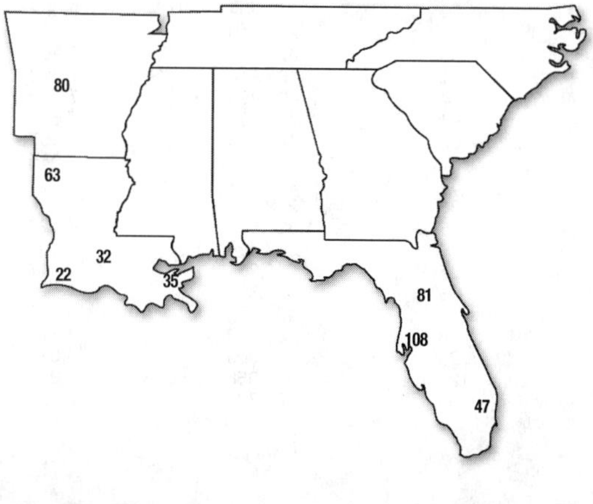

Southeast

20 Crc—Calder Race Course, Fl.
22 DeD—Delta Downs, La.
27 ElC—El Comandante, P.R.
32 Evd—Evangeline Downs, La.
35 FG—Fair Grounds, La.
47 GP—Gulfstream Park, Fl.
63 LaD—Louisiana Downs, La.
80 OP—Oaklawn Park, Ar.
81 OTC—Ocala Training Center, Fl.
108 Tam—Tampa Bay Downs, Fl.

North American Purse Distribution by Year

Year	No. of Runners	No. of Races	Total Purses	Average Purse	Per Runner Average	Per Runner Median
2005	72,784	57,481	$1,153,930,533	$20,051	$15,851	$6,135
2004	73,915	58,686	1,177,769,795	20,069	15,934	5,877
2003	73,614	58,813	1,154,238,845	19,626	15,680	5,714
2002	72,504	59,712	1,170,169,267	19,597	16,139	6,003
2001	70,942	60,538	1,146,337,367	18,936	16,159	6,010
2000	69,230	60,579	1,093,661,241	18,053	15,798	5,796
1999	68,435	60,118	1,008,162,608	16,770	14,732	5,310
1998	68,419	61,141	968,366,929	15,838	14,153	4,939
1997	69,067	63,491	888,667,752	13,997	12,867	4,425
1996	70,371	64,263	845,916,706	13,163	12,021	3,937
1995	72,316	68,197	815,987,125	11,965	11,283	3,702
1994	74,939	70,617	770,426,193	10,910	10,280	3,314
1993	78,763	72,224	748,415,925	10,362	9,502	2,850
1992	83,468	77,711	771,136,296	9,989	9,238	2,731
1991	86,483	78,671	761,446,198	9,679	8,805	2,433
1990	89,722	79,971	775,006,519	9,691	8,637	2,376
1989	91,436	82,726	771,421,230	9,325	8,437	2,218
1988	90,482	79,589	736,698,230	9,256	8,142	2,127
1987	89,504	80,376	704,372,435	8,763	7,870	2,101
1986	86,022	77,732	661,826,092	8,514	7,694	2,070
1985	82,548	75,687	641,658,553	8,478	7,773	2,158
1984	78,253	74,396	599,348,425	8,056	7,659	2,345
1983	74,540	71,034	544,260,167	7,662	7,302	2,435
1982	69,505	71,515	526,587,096	7,363	7,576	2,703
1981	65,797	70,881	507,007,953	7,153	7,706	2,865
1980	64,499	68,236	449,631,322	6,589	6,971	2,524
1979	63,728	69,406	414,629,063	5,974	6,506	2,440
1978	62,937	69,498	367,163,242	5,283	5,834	n/a
1977	61,960	68,826	335,720,312	4,878	5,418	2,189
1976	61,084	69,480	318,680,094	4,587	5,217	2,100
1975	58,818	68,203	291,194,571	4,270	4,951	2,058
1974	56,524	65,288	262,942,547	4,027	4,652	1,904
1973	54,812	62,264	233,662,724	3,753	4,263	1,764
1972	52,561	59,417	210,435,265	3,542	4,004	1,647

Data reflect all Thoroughbred purses distributed to racehorses in North America, excluding Mexico and Puerto Rico, from Jockey Club Information Systems data. Steeplechase races are excluded.

Top 25 Race Meetings by Average Attendance in 2005

Rank	Meet	Racing Dates	Total Attendance	Average Attendance
1	Saratoga Race Course	36	932,882	25,913
2	Del Mar	43	731,287	17,007
3	Keeneland Race Course (Spring)	16	235,220	14,701
4	Churchill Downs (Spring)	52	718,270	13,813
5	Keeneland Race Course (Fall)	17	232,429	13,672
6	Oaklawn Park	55	706,328	12,842
7	Monmouth Park	90	812,909	9,032
8	Oak Tree at Santa Anita	31	263,719	8,507
9	Santa Anita Park	85	677,193	7,967
10	Churchill Downs (Fall)	21	164,214	7,820
11	Hollywood Park (Spring)	64	497,465	7,773
12	Arlington Park	94	715,023	7,607
13	Belmont Park (Spring)	60	423,405	7,057
14	Lone Star Park	67	470,000	7,015
15	Pimlico Race Course (Spring)	39	253,511	6,500
16	Belmont Park (Fall)	36	*222,133	*6,170
17	Mountaineer Race Track	216	1,322,835	6,124
18	Fairplex Park	16	88,494	5,531
19	Hollywood Park (Fall)	27	146,261	5,417
20	Canterbury Park	68	348,804	5,129
21	Gulfstream Park	86	437,452	5,087
22	Timonium	8	35,000	4,375
23	Meadowlands	25	109,309	4,372
24	Calder Race Course	120	509,958	4,250
25	Tropical Park at Calder	55	226,709	4,122

*Including Breeders' Cup World Championships day

Top 25 Race Meetings by Average All-Sources Wagering in 2005

Rank	Meet	Racing Dates	Total All-Sources Wagering	Average All-Sources Wagering
1	Saratoga Race Course	36	$538,081,909	$14,946,720
2	Del Mar	43	608,168,297	14,143,449
3	Belmont Park (Fall)	37	*477,797,415	*12,913,444
4	Churchill Downs (Spring)	52	585,277,784	11,255,342
5	Belmont Park (Spring)	60	667,204,080	11,120,068
6	Santa Anita Park	85	791,379,796	9,310,351
7	Gulfstream Park	86	797,351,561	9,271,530
8	Hollywood Park (Spring)	64	567,325,817	8,864,466
9	Churchill Downs (Fall)	21	182,214,993	8,676,904
10	Aqueduct (Spring)	82	681,236,048	8,307,757
11	Aqueduct (Fall)	38	310,244,137	8,164,319
12	Keeneland Race Course (Spring)	16	123,197,871	7,699,867
13	Hollywood Park (Fall)	27	203,328,084	7,530,670
14	Oak Tree at Santa Anita	31	220,353,024	7,108,162
15	Keeneland Race Course (Fall)	17	118,590,290	6,975,899
16	Fairplex Park	16	90,922,589	5,682,662
17	Pimlico Race Course (Spring)	39	172,711,360	4,428,496
18	Arlington Park	94	405,396,420	4,312,728
19	Golden Gate Fields (Spring)	29	121,386,576	4,185,744
20	Fair Grounds	82	343,168,377	4,184,980
21	Oaklawn Park	55	220,531,775	4,009,669
22	Tropical Park at Calder	55	218,434,499	3,971,536
23	Golden Gate Fields (Winter)	59	223,301,272	3,784,767
24	Bay Meadows (Spring)	72	265,263,819	3,684,220
25	Monmouth Park	90	328,575,939	3,650,844

*Including Breeders' Cup World Championships day

Top 25 Race Meetings by Average On-Track Wagering in 2005

Rank	Meet	Racing Dates	Total On-Track Wagering	Average On-Track Wagering
1	Saratoga Race Course	36	$117,000,324	$3,250,009
2	Del Mar	43	108,907,839	2,532,740
3	Santa Anita Park	85	172,706,230	2,031,838
4	Oak Tree at Santa Anita	31	60,456,834	1,950,220
5	Gulfstream Park	86	151,447,851	1,761,022
6	Hollywood Park (Spring)	64	110,578,658	1,727,792
7	Belmont Park (Spring)	60	94,252,318	1,570,872
8	Churchill Downs (Spring)	52	80,036,165	1,539,157
9	Oaklawn Park	55	79,049,041	1,437,255
10	Hollywood Park (Fall)	27	36,628,437	1,356,609
11	Keeneland Race Course (Spring)	16	21,599,291	1,349,956
12	Monmouth Park	90	114,680,859	1,274,232
13	Belmont Park (Fall)	37	*45,360,126	*1,225,949
14	Keeneland Race Course (Fall)	17	20,321,797	1,195,400
15	Aqueduct (Spring)	82	90,854,216	1,107,978
16	Aqueduct (Fall)	38	41,076,804	1,080,969
17	Churchill Downs (Fall)	21	19,357,722	921,796
18	Fairplex Park	16	11,814,889	738,431
19	Bay Meadows (Spring)	72	52,148,334	724,282
20	Bay Meadows (Fall)	33	23,897,000	724,152
21	Arlington Park	94	54,070,047	575,213
22	Golden Gate Fields (Fall)	59	33,148,373	561,837
23	Pimlico Race Course (Spring)	39	21,889,406	561,267
24	Lone Star Park	67	35,922,139	536,151
25	Canterbury Park	68	31,770,317	467,211

*Including Breeders' Cup World Championships day

Revenues to States From Horse Racing

For a few decades, horse racing was the golden goose for state governments, as shown in the table of current-dollar revenues prepared by the Association of Racing Commissioners International. The revenues cover all forms of horse racing, but a substantial portion of the total is derived from Thoroughbred racing.

When the effects of inflation are removed from the figures using the United States Commerce Department's gross domestic product implicit price deflator, the peak period for state taxation of horse racing was from 1962 through '80, when inflation-adjusted state revenues exceeded $1.3-billion annually. State revenues topped out in 1975 at $2.1-billion in deflated dollars.

In both current and inflation-adjusted dollars, state revenues began a sharp decline in the 1980s as states reduced their pari-mutuel tax rates. By 1983, inflation-adjusted revenues had fallen below $1-billion, and by 1995 those revenues had slipped below $500-million. With two exceptions, 1990 and '95, current-dollar revenues to the state have declined from the preceding 12 months in every year since 1988.

Revenue to States from Horse Racing

Year	Current Dollars	Deflated Dollars
2004	$338,885,365	$313,144,856
2003	343,588,382	325,152,249
2002	346,799,090	333,637,106
2001	351,511,182	343,363,174
2000	367,786,590	367,786,590
1999	392,201,085	400,744,968
1998	431,722,361	447,510,533
1997	441,768,972	463,002,255
1996	443,882,538	472,960,127
1995	455,764,292	494,825,844
1994	451,546,549	500,278,697
1993	471,735,474	533,752,135
1992	491,259,606	568,686,237
1991	523,249,392	619,640,699
1990	623,839,806	764,603,268
1989	584,888,183	744,549,344
1988	596,202,319	787,648,055
1987	608,351,461	831,126,648
1986	587,357,677	824,361,652
1985	625,159,697	896,762,006
1984	650,262,852	961,145,299
1983	641,387,176	983,617,060
1982	652,888,463	1,040,857,799
1981	680,199,584	1,150,560,030
1980	712,727,523	1,318,815,615
1979	680,919,798	1,374,262,933
1978	673,063,831	1,470,952,709
1977	700,239,986	1,637,911,644
1976	714,629,120	1,777,861,280
1975	780,081,431	2,052,737,832
1974	645,980,984	1,860,276,412
1973	585,201,524	1,837,425,112
1972	531,404,550	1,761,600,975
1971	512,838,417	1,773,852,226
1970	486,403,097	1,766,554,431
1969	461,498,886	1,764,881,586
1968	426,856,448	1,713,388,384
1967	394,381,913	1,650,616,971
1966	388,452,125	1,676,096,501
1965	$369,892,036	$1,641,411,298
1964	350,095,928	1,581,925,480
1963	316,570,791	1,452,292,830
1962	287,930,030	1,334,925,263
1961	264,853,077	1,244,727,310
1960	258,039,385	1,226,364,645
1959	243,388,655	1,172,900,848
1958	222,049,651	1,083,274,715
1957	216,747,621	1,081,682,907
1956	207,456,272	1,069,748,218
1955	186,989,588	997,650,259
1954	178,015,828	966,584,286
1953	167,426,465	917,757,304
1952	142,489,696	790,643,081
1951	117,250,564	661,759,589
1950	98,366,167	595,040,633
1949	95,327,053	582,968,768
1948	95,803,364	584,808,717
1947	97,926,984	631,542,525
1946	94,035,859	672,357,064
1945	65,265,405	522,541,273
1944	55,971,233	460,062,740
1943	38,194,727	321,342,142
1942	22,005,278	195,099,548
1941	21,128,173	201,893,674
1940	16,145,182	164,612,378
1939	10,369,807	106,960,361
1938	9,576,335	97,817,518
1937	8,434,792	83,653,595
1936	8,611,538	89,100,238
1935	8,386,255	87,740,688
1934	6,024,193	64,292,348

Minimum Age to Attend and Wager at U.S. Racetracks

State	Minimum Age	Legal Wagering Age
Arizona	None	18
Arkansas	Under 16 with adult	18
California	None	18
Colorado	None	18
Delaware	Under 18 with adult	18
Florida	Under 18 with adult	18
Idaho	None	18
Illinois	Under 17 with adult	17
Indiana	Under 17 with adult	18
Iowa	Under 18 with adult	21
Kansas	Under 18 with adult	18
Kentucky	None	18
Louisiana	6	21
Maryland	None	18
Massachusetts	None	18
Michigan	None	18
Minnesota	Under 18 with adult	18
Montana	None	18
Nebraska	Under 18 with adult	19
New Hampshire	Under 18 with adult	18
New Jersey	Under 18 with adult	18
New Mexico	Under 18 with adult	18
New York	Under 18 with adult	18
Ohio	Under 18 with adult	18
Oklahoma	6	18
Oregon	12 after 6 p.m.	18
Pennsylvania	None	18
Puerto Rico	None	18
Texas	Under 16 with adult	21
Virginia	None	18
Washington	None	18
West Virginia	None	18
Wyoming	None	19

PEOPLE

Leading Owners of 2005

Along with bettors, Thoroughbred owners are the primary source of the billions of dollars of investments that make the Thoroughbred industry the living, breathing, wonderful thing that it is. Owners spend well over $1-billion annually purchasing Thoroughbreds of various descriptions at public auctions and by private contract, thus taking on the privilege and responsibility of paying further untold sums for their training, veterinary care, board, and other expenses. In return, owners in North America get a shot at roughly $1-billion annually in purses.

Total purses are divided among thousands of owners but, in the natural order of things, some do better than others. The following lists rate the accomplishments of owners in 2005 according to various criteria. The annual THOROUGHBRED TIMES leading owners list ranks owners according to four equally weighted criteria: 1) total purse money earned by the owners' runners, 2) average earnings per starter, 3) number of wins, and 4) percent of stakes winners from starters. That weighted list purposely favors quality over quantity.

Leading Owners by Purses Won
North American Earnings Only

Year	Name	Wins	Earnings
2005	Michael J. Gill	371	$ 6,397,180
2004	Michael J. Gill	486	10,811,211
2003	Michael J. Gill	425	9,236,530
2002	Stronach Stables	122	8,347,017
2001	Richard A. Englander	405	9,784,822
2000	Stronach Stables	162	11,133,785
1999	Stronach Stables	124	6,221,147
1998	Stronach Stables	91	7,221,416
1997	Allen E. Paulson	66	5,259,107
1996	Allen E. Paulson	88	6,686,629
1995	Allen E. Paulson	62	5,626,396
1994	Golden Eagle Farm	95	3,674,692
1993	Golden Eagle Farm	102	3,613,828
1992	Golden Eagle Farm	112	4,487,959
1991	Sam-Son Farm	29	3,613,473
1990	Kinghaven Farms	66	5,041,280
1989	Ogden Phipps	25	5,438,034
1988	Ogden Phipps	35	5,858,168
1987	Eugene V. Klein	81	4,904,247
1986	John Franks	250	4,463,115
1985	Hunter Farm	10	3,662,989
1984	John Franks	172	3,073,036
1983	John Franks	183	2,645,884
1982	Viola Sommer	136	2,183,706
1981	Elmendorf	57	1,928,102
1980	Harbor View Farm	103	2,208,901

THOROUGHBRED TIMES Leading Owners of 2005

Rankings based on formula that gives equal weighting to four statistical categories for performance in 2005: 1) total purse money earned by the owners' runners; 2) average earnings per starter; 3) number of wins; and 4) percent of stakes winners from starters. A minimum of ten starters is required to be considered for inclusion. Names of owners are of individual property lines as reported by the Jockey Club. No attempt was made to consolidate names where a owner had more than one partnership or property line. Statistics are for North America only and for racing in 2005.

Rank	Owner	No. Strs	No. Wnrs	No. SWs	SWs/ Strs	No. GSWs	GSWs/ Strs	Total Earnings	Average Earnings/ Starter	Leading Earner	Earnings of Leading Earner
1	Live Oak Plantation	50	33	15	30.0%	6	12.0%	$4,904,171	$98,083	High Fly	$ 901,500
2	Phipps Stable	24	15	7	29.2%	6	25.0%	3,289,390	137,058	Pleasant Home	1,291,920
3	Robert and Beverly Lewis	56	28	7	12.5%	3	5.4%	3,250,422	58,043	Folklore	927,500
4	Stronach Stables	144	73	8	5.6%	3	2.1%	4,383,153	30,439	Ghostzapper	450,000
5	Millennium Farms	65	32	9	13.9%	2	3.1%	2,104,350	32,375	Super Frolic	736,760
6	Melnyk Racing Stables	93	51	5	5.4%	3	3.2%	5,875,007	63,172	Flower Alley	2,435,200
7	Dogwood Stable	70	39	6	8.6%	2	2.9%	2,688,782	38,411	Limehouse	482,998
8	Tracy Farmer	26	14	4	15.4%	3	11.5%	2,791,949	107,383	Sun King	1,134,800
9	Kinsman Stable	43	20	6	14.0%	3	7.0%	2,276,815	52,949	Bellamy Road	671,000
10	Ken and Sarah Ramsey	94	48	7	7.5%	3	3.2%	2,847,505	30,293	Badge of Silver	411,167
11	Augustin Stables	75	41	7	9.3%	3	4.0%	2,122,204	28,296	Latice (Ire)	219,440
12	Maggi Moss	125	74	6	4.8%		0.0%	2,628,520	21,028	Silver Axe	288,900
13	Gary A. Tanaka	26	16	5	19.2%	4	15.4%	1,987,897	76,458	King's Drama (Ire)	525,137
14	Gary and Mary West Stables	38	26	5	13.2%	2	5.3%	1,839,376	48,405	High Limit	367,500
15	Mr. and Mrs. Jerome S. Moss	48	23	4	8.3%	3	6.3%	3,325,480	69,281	Giacomo	1,846,876
16	Michael J. Gill	371	193	8	2.2%	1	0.3%	6,397,180	17,243	Umpateedle	331,050
17	Edward P. Evans	42	22	4	9.5%	2	4.8%	2,199,520	52,370	Tap Day	498,800
18	Heiligbrodt Racing Stable	80	45	5	6.3%		0.0%	2,069,656	25,871	Sister Swank	130,095
19	Robert D. Bone	191	103	3	1.6%	2	1.1%	3,913,264	20,488	Desert Boom	406,240
20	Pin Oak Stable	49	31	4	8.2%	2	4.1%	1,950,395	39,804	Cryptograph	247,945
21	M. Y. Stables Inc.	50	36	7	14.0%		0.0%	1,106,207	22,124	Knowwhatimean	127,470
22	B. Wayne Hughes	45	21	4	8.9%	3	6.7%	2,269,502	50,433	Don't Get Mad	730,110
23	Darley Stable	66	27	5	7.6%	4	6.1%	2,227,047	33,743	Henny Hughes	558,000
24	T N T Stud	16	7	4	25.0%	3	18.8%	1,593,824	99,614	Leroidesanimaux (Brz)	809,040
25	Buckram Oak Farm	61	33	3	4.9%	2	3.3%	3,180,059	52,132	Silver Train	693,255
26	Amerman Racing Stables	24	16	4	16.7%	2	8.3%	1,515,464	63,144	Chattahoochee War	436,421
27	Barry K. Schwartz	41	22	5	12.2%	2	4.9%	1,509,065	36,806	Nothing But Fun	281,700
28	James T. Scatuorchio	14	10	3	21.4%	2	14.3%	1,514,285	108,163	English Channel	1,143,491
29	Michael Tabor & Derrick Smith	17	10	4	23.5%	4	23.5%	1,504,581	88,505	Maddalena	203,100
30	Stan E. Fulton	72	32	5	6.9%	1	1.4%	1,807,946	25,110	R Fast Lady	161,530

Rank	Owner	No. Strs	No. Wnrs	No. SWs	SWs/ Strs	No. GSWs	GSWs/ Strs	Total Earnings	Average Earnings/ Starter	Leading Earner	Earnings of Leading Earner
31	Flying Zee Stables	97	52	3	3.1%		0.0%	$2,511,142	$25,888	Taking the Redeye	$133,869
32	Padua Stables	61	29	5	8.2%	2	3.3%	1,686,241	27,643	Bohemian Lady	173,880
33	Overbrook Farm	83	36	4	4.8%	3	3.6%	2,220,379	26,752	Clock Stopper	297,438
34	John D. Murphy Sr.	43	27	4	9.3%	1	2.3%	1,264,433	29,405	Trickle of Gold	270,880
35	Stonerside Stable	49	22	4	8.2%		0.0%	1,620,155	33,064	Danieltown	176,735
36	Juddmonte Farms	29	14	2	6.9%	2	6.9%	2,540,964	87,619	Intercontinental (GB)	1,271,200
37	Pyrite Stables	41	28	6	14.6%		0.0%	1,009,961	24,633	Bernie Blue	180,004
38	Sam-Son Farm	46	20	4	8.7%	2	4.4%	1,741,702	37,863	Hatpin	200,643
39	Al and Sandee Kirkwood	16	7	3	18.8%	1	6.3%	1,340,967	83,810	Valentine Dancer	539,120
40	Puglisi Stables	48	41	2	4.2%		0.0%	1,754,636	36,555	Mighty Mecke	154,500
41	Everest Stables	54	23	5	9.3%		0.0%	1,524,907	28,239	Island Fashion	238,000
42	Dale Baird	207	106		0.0%		0.0%	2,102,310	10,156	Melody Maiden	77,151
43	Frank Carl Calabrese	161	96	2	1.2%		0.0%	1,828,578	11,358	Lewis Michael	75,514
44	Martin S. Schwartz	10	4	2	20.0%	2	20.0%	1,231,541	123,154	Angara (GB)	668,108
45	Elisabeth H. Alexander	11	6	2	18.2%	1	9.1%	1,231,169	111,924	Magna Graduate	1,070,170
46	Gumpster Stable LLC	104	55	1	1.0%		0.0%	1,899,400	18,263	Clever Electrician	158,950
47	Earle I. Mack	17	8	3	17.7%	2	11.8%	1,104,450	64,968	Que Puntual (Arg)	331,443
48	Vinery Stables LLC	27	16	6	22.2%		0.0%	985,349	36,494	More Than Promised	161,730
49	Aaron and Marie Jones	17	8	4	23.5%	3	17.7%	1,049,158	61,715	Shaniko	312,120
50	Harlequin Ranches	24	15	3	12.5%	1	4.2%	1,216,676	50,695	Gold Strike	480,518
51	Claiborne Farm	18	11	2	11.1%	1	5.6%	1,150,730	63,929	Wend	383,900
52	Michael E. Pegram	22	9	2	9.1%	2	9.1%	1,348,198	61,282	Woke Up Dreamin	520,280
53	Haras Santa Maria de Araras	27	13	2	7.4%	2	7.4%	1,344,605	49,800	Palladio	444,143
54	Robert V. LaPenta	23	11	2	8.7%	1	4.4%	1,359,374	59,103	Andromeda's Hero	561,007
55	Robert L. Cole Jr.	74	49	1	1.4%		0.0%	1,553,369	20,991	Outcashem	185,631
56	John C. Oxley	31	10	4	12.9%	3	9.7%	1,099,406	35,465	For All We Know	288,871
57	Jay Em Ess Stable	44	20	2	4.6%	2	4.6%	1,618,419	36,782	Suave	624,900
58	William S. Farish Jr.	14	7	2	14.3%	1	7.1%	1,035,222	73,944	Shadow Cast	626,266
59	WinStar Farm	43	21	3	7.0%	2	4.7%	1,207,929	28,091	Bluegrass Cat	213,780
60	Tucci Stables	24	15	2	8.3%	2	8.3%	1,120,351	46,681	One for Rose	274,120
61	Donald R. Dizney	32	17	4	12.5%	1	3.1%	1,002,049	31,314	Diamond Omi	160,740
62	Mary and Chester Broman Sr.	37	22	2	5.4%	1	2.7%	1,227,950	33,188	Seeking the Ante	362,280
63	Colebrook Farms Stallion Station	48	26	2	4.2%		0.0%	1,264,487	26,343	Runaway Sunshine	127,638
64	Bruno Schickedanz	110	59		0.0%		0.0%	1,232,713	11,206	The King N Rob	77,872
65	Courtlandt Farm	28	14	4	14.3%	2	7.1%	900,917	32,176	T. D. Vance	215,305
66	Jayeff "B" Stables	39	19	3	7.7%		0.0%	1,086,738	27,865	Coherent	100,620
67	Hobeau Farm	24	14	3	12.5%	2	8.3%	981,604	40,900	Smokume	178,133
68	Home Team Stables	91	49		0.0%		0.0%	1,319,871	14,504	Sierra Bella	160,770
69	Louis D. O'Brien	129	95		0.0%		0.0%	1,136,960	8,814	Moe B Dick	42,600
70	Stonecrest Farm	10	8	2	20.0%	1	10.0%	876,026	87,603	Perfect Drift	606,427
71	James and Alice Sapara	16	8	3	18.8%		0.0%	899,268	56,204	Edenwold	287,247
72	Paul P. Pompa Jr.	25	13	3	12.0%	2	8.0%	1,004,299	40,172	Zakocity	304,000
73	New Farm	26	21	2	7.7%		0.0%	1,019,726	39,220	Smokescreen	189,850
74	Monarch Stables Inc.	67	46		0.0%		0.0%	1,175,612	17,546	Joann Jr	89,170
75	Harris Farms	40	20	2	5.0%	2	5.0%	1,141,177	28,529	Alphabet Kisses	241,621
76	William A. Sorokolit Sr.	28	11	3	10.7%	2	7.1%	981,618	35,058	Classic Stamp	277,991
77	Peter Redekop B. C.	15	13	3	20.0%	2	13.3%	800,809	53,387	Alabama Rain	265,762
78	Char-Mari Stable	13	9	3	23.1%	2	15.4%	845,323	65,025	Park Avenue Ball	351,000
79	Peter Vegso	35	14	3	8.6%	2	5.7%	1,015,993	29,028	Silver Tree	229,420
80	Marjorie and Irving Cowan	16	7	2	12.5%	1	6.3%	974,851	60,928	Society Selection	727,500
81	Fox Ridge Farm	12	4	2	16.7%	1	8.3%	901,472	75,123	Riskaverse	464,723
82	Mercedes Stables	27	11	3	11.1%	1	3.7%	937,417	34,719	Laura's Lucky Boy	180,040
83	Team Valor	31	13	3	9.7%		0.0%	961,624	31,020	Onthedeanslist	128,855
84	Daniel M. Ryan	67	37	1	1.5%		0.0%	1,119,272	16,706	Forest Park	196,990
85	Paraneck Stables	67	20	1	1.5%		0.0%	1,464,255	21,855	Amazing Buy	244,350
86	Joseph Allen	16	11	3	18.8%	1	6.3%	800,263	50,016	Asti (Ire)	149,723
87	Janis R. Whitham	18	8	2	11.1%	1	5.6%	916,283	50,905	Mea Domina	446,076
88	Harry J. Aleo	11	8	1	9.1%	1	9.1%	965,772	87,797	Lost in the Fog	844,500
89	Jerry Jamgotchian	39	25	4	10.3%		0.0%	841,227	21,570	Secret Corsage	112,575
90	Chiefswood Stables Ltd.	18	11	1	5.6%	1	5.6%	1,063,218	59,068	Ambitious Cat	350,140
91	Russell L. Reineman Stable	20	11	4	20.0%	1	5.0%	771,369	38,568	Original Spin	222,800
92	Mr. and Mrs. Martin J. Wygod	35	19	1	2.9%	1	2.9%	1,107,687	31,648	Sweet Catomine	259,800
93	G. Watts Humphrey Jr.	48	22	2	4.2%	1	2.1%	1,065,291	22,194	Rey de Cafe	189,434
94	Plumstead Stables	71	42		0.0%		0.0%	1,017,565	14,332	Put Out the Fuse	69,101
95	Klaravich Stables LLC	36	18	1	2.8%		0.0%	1,124,715	31,242	What's Your Edge	147,000
96	Godolphin Racing	10	6	2	20.0%	2	20.0%	784,368	78,437	Stellar Jayne	423,720
97	Jerry Hollendorfer & G. Todaro	85	43		0.0%		0.0%	988,702	11,632	Apology Accepted	82,403
98	Charles Cono	24	8	2	8.3%	1	4.2%	923,713	38,488	Diplomat Lady	334,800
99	Dominion Bloodstock, Derek Ball, and Hugh Galbraith	33	14	1	3.0%		0.0%	1,090,830	33,055	High Volt Jolt	140,816
100	William S. Farish	40	22	1	2.5%	1	2.5%	1,052,015	26,300	Reunited	320,565

Leading Owners by Earnings in 2005

Owner	No. Strs	No. Wnrs	Total Earnings
Michael J. Gill	371	193	$6,397,180
Melnyk Racing Stables	93	51	5,875,007
Live Oak Plantation	50	33	4,904,171
Stronach Stables	144	73	4,383,153
Robert D. Bone	191	103	3,913,264
Mr. and Mrs. William K. Warren Jr.	7	4	3,773,375
Mr. and Mrs. Jerome Moss	48	23	3,325,480
Phipps Stable	24	15	3,289,390
Robert and Beverly Lewis	56	28	3,250,422
Buckram Oak Farm	61	33	3,180,059
Ken and Sarah Ramsey	94	48	2,847,505
Tracy Farmer	26	14	2,791,949
Dogwood Stable	70	39	2,688,782
Maggi Moss	125	74	2,628,520
Cash is King Stable LLC	8	5	2,548,604
Juddmonte Farms	29	14	2,540,964
Flying Zee Stables	97	52	2,511,142
Kinsman Stable	43	20	2,276,815
B. Wayne Hughes	45	21	2,269,502
Darley Stable	66	27	2,227,047
Overbrook Farm	83	36	2,220,379
Edward P. Evans	42	22	2,199,520
Augustin Stables	75	41	2,122,204
Millennium Farms	65	32	2,104,350
Dale Baird	207	106	2,102,310
Heiligbrodt Racing Stable	80	45	2,069,656
Gary A. Tanaka	26	16	1,987,897
Pin Oak Stable	49	31	1,950,395
Gumpster Stable LLC	104	55	1,899,400
Gary and Mary West Stables	38	26	1,839,376
Frank Carl Calabrese	161	96	1,828,578
Stan E. Fulton	72	32	1,807,946
Puglisi Stables	48	41	1,754,636
Sam-Son Farm	46	20	1,741,702
Timber Bay Farm and Mrs. Thomas J. Walsh	5	4	1,738,324
Moyglare Stud Farm	5	3	1,695,634
Padua Stables	61	29	1,686,241
Stonerside Stable	49	22	1,620,155
Jay Em Ess Stable	44	20	1,618,419

Leading Owners by Average Earnings per Starter in 2005

(Minimum of 10 Starters)

Owner	No. Strs	No. Wnrs	Average Earnings per Starter
Phipps Stable	24	15	$137,058
Martin S. Schwartz	10	4	123,154
Elisabeth H. Alexander	11	6	111,924
James T. Scatuorchio	14	10	108,163
Tracy Farmer	26	14	107,383
T N T Stud	16	7	99,614
Live Oak Plantation	50	33	98,083
Michael Tabor and Derrick Smith	17	10	88,505
Harry J. Aleo	11	8	87,797
Juddmonte Farms	29	14	87,619
Stonecrest Farm	10	8	87,603
Al and Sandee Kirkwood	16	7	83,810
Godolphin Racing	10	6	78,437
Gary A. Tanaka	26	16	76,458
Fox Ridge Farm	12	4	75,123
Winchell Thoroughbreds	10	4	74,420
Willmott Stables	10	5	$74,290
William S. Farish Jr.	14	7	73,944
Mr. and Mrs. Jerome Moss	48	23	69,281
Philip and Marcia Cohen	11	6	66,266
Char-Mari Stable	13	9	65,025
Earle I. Mack	17	8	64,968
Claiborne Farm	18	11	63,929
Gustav Schickedanz	10	5	63,426
Melnyk Racing Stables	93	51	63,172
Amerman Racing Stables	24	16	63,144
John D. Gunther	12	8	63,101

Leading Owners by Number of Stakes Winners in 2005

Owner	No. Strs	No. Wnrs	No. SWs
Live Oak Plantation	50	33	15
Millennium Farms	65	32	9
Stronach Stables	144	73	8
Michael J. Gill	371	193	8
Phipps Stable	24	15	7
M. Y. Stables Inc.	50	36	7
Robert and Beverly Lewis	56	28	7
Augustin Stables	75	41	7
Ken and Sarah Ramsey	94	48	7
Vinery Stables LLC	27	16	6
Pyrite Stables	41	28	6
Kinsman Stable	43	20	6
Dogwood Stable	70	39	6
Maggi Moss	125	74	6
Gary A. Tanaka	26	16	5
Dennis E. Weir	38	20	5
Gary and Mary West Stables	38	26	5
Barry K. Schwartz	41	22	5
Everest Stables	54	23	5
Padua Stables	61	29	5
Darley Stable	66	27	5
Bar None Ranches	69	38	5
Stan E. Fulton	72	32	5
Heiligbrodt Racing Stable	80	45	5
Melnyk Racing Stables	93	51	5
Sandra Hall Trust	12	7	4
Richter Family Trust	14	7	4
T N T Stud	16	7	4
Michael B. Tabor & Derrick Smith	17	10	4
Aaron and Marie Jones	17	8	4
Russell L. Reineman Stable	20	11	4
Fitzhugh LLC	22	10	4
Jer-Mar Stable LLC	23	13	4
Amerman Racing Stables	24	16	4
Tracy Farmer	26	14	4
Tangarae Farms	27	11	4
Courtlandt Farm	28	14	4
John C. Oxley	31	10	4
Donald R. Dizney	32	17	4
Jerry Jamgotchian	39	25	4
Edward P. Evans	42	22	4
John D. Murphy Sr.	43	27	4
B. Wayne Hughes	45	21	4
Sam-Son Farm	46	20	4
Mr. and Mrs. Jerome S. Moss	48	23	4
Stonerside Stable	49	22	4
Pin Oak Stable	49	31	4
Overbrook Farm	83	36	4

Leading Owners by Number of Stakes Wins in 2005

Owner	No. Stakes Starts	No. Stakes Wins
Live Oak Plantation	91	28
Michael J. Gill	72	12
Millennium Farms	48	12
Vinery Stables	35	12
Robert & Beverly Lewis	67	11
M. Y. Stables	30	11
Dennis E. Weir	31	11
Nelson Bunker Hunt	42	10
Maggi Moss	41	10
Phipps Stable	34	9
Pyrite Stables	31	9
Kenneth & Sarah Ramsey	43	9
Harry J. Aleo	10	8
Augustin Stables	50	8
Dogwood Stable	65	8
Melnyk Racing Stables	46	8
Peter Redekop	31	8
Stronach Stables	45	8
Heiligbrodt Racing Stable	63	7
Barry K. Schwartz	28	7
T N T Stud	17	7
Gary A. Tanaka	59	7
Tangarae Farms	30	7
Bar None Ranches	27	6
Cash is King stable	22	6
Courtlandt Farms	13	6
Dare To Dream Stable	19	6
Edward P. Evans	42	6
Fanucci Racing	29	6
Tracy Farmer	37	6
Charles W. Fletcher	12	6
Stan E. Fulton	33	6
B. Wayne Hughes	39	6
Jer-Mar Stable	21	6
Juddmonte Farms	32	6
Armando Jurado	12	6
Kinsman Stable	27	6
John D. Murphy Sr.	20	6
Padua Stables	27	6
Pin Oak Stable	46	6
Sandra Hall Trust	32	6
James & Alice Sapara	15	6
James T. Scatuorchio	15	6

Leading Owners by Percent of Stakes Winners from Starters in 2005

(Minimum of 10 Starters)

Owner	No. strs	No. SWs	SWs/Str
Sandra Hall Trust	12	4	33.3%
Live Oak Plantation	50	15	30.0%
Phipps Stable	24	7	29.2%
Richter Family Trust	14	4	28.6%
T N T Stud	16	4	25.0%
Michael B. Tabor & Derrick Smith	17	4	23.5%
Aaron and Marie Jones	17	4	23.5%
Char-Mari Stable	13	3	23.1%
Vinery Stables LLC	27	6	22.2%
James T. Scatuorchio	14	3	21.4%
Russell L. Reineman Stable	20	4	20.0%
Peter Redekop B. C.	15	3	20.0%
G. Chris Coleman	15	3	20.0%
Stonecrest Farm	10	2	20.0%
Curtis A. Sampson	10	2	20.0%
H. Joseph Allen	10	2	20.0%
Martin S. Schwartz	10	2	20.0%
Ronald C. Waranch	10	2	20.0%
Lee Lewis	10	2	20.0%
Godolphin Racing	10	2	20.0%
Ross McLeod	10	2	20.0%
William Lydon, Arbaway Farms, and Carson Springs	10	2	20.0%
Gary A. Tanaka	26	5	19.2%
Al and Sandee Kirkwood	16	3	18.8%
Joseph Allen	16	3	18.8%
Arnold Zetcher	16	3	18.8%
James and Alice Sapara	16	3	18.8%
Susan and John Moore	16	3	18.8%

Leading Owners by Number of Graded Stakes Winners in 2005

Owner	No. Strs	No. Wnrs	No. GSWs	GSWs/ Strs
Phipps Stable	24	15	6	25.0%
Live Oak Plantation	50	33	6	12.0%
Michael Tabor and Derrick Smith	17	10	4	23.5%
Gary A. Tanaka	26	16	4	15.4%
Darley Stable	66	27	4	6.1%
T N T Stud	16	7	3	18.8%
Aaron and Marie Jones	17	8	3	17.7%
Tracy Farmer	26	14	3	11.5%
John C. Oxley	31	10	3	9.7%
Kinsman Stable	43	20	3	7.0%
B. Wayne Hughes	45	21	3	6.7%
Mr. & Mrs. Jerome Moss	48	23	3	6.3%
Robert and Beverly Lewis	56	28	3	5.4%
Augustin Stables	75	41	3	4.0%
Overbrook Farm	83	36	3	3.6%
Melnyk Racing Stables	93	51	3	3.2%
Ken and Sarah Ramsey	94	48	3	3.2%
Stronach Stables	144	73	3	2.1%
Starlight Stables, Paul Saylor, and Johns Martin	2	2	2	100.0%
Anthony Speelman	3	2	2	66.7%
Moyglare Stud Farm	5	3	2	40.0%
Fog City Stable	6	3	2	33.3%
The Horizon Stable	6	5	2	33.3%
Sheikh Maktoum bin Rashid al Maktoum	7	3	2	28.6%
Martin S. Schwartz	10	4	2	20.0%
Godolphin Racing	10	6	2	20.0%
Lee Lewis	10	4	2	20.0%
Char-Mari Stable	13	9	2	15.4%
James T. Scatuorchio	14	10	2	14.3%
Peter Redekop B. C.	15	13	2	13.3%
Earle I. Mack	17	8	2	11.8%
Ronald L. Charles and Clear Valley Stables	19	7	2	10.5%
Arthur B. Hancock III	20	11	2	10.0%
Michael E. Pegram	22	9	2	9.1%
Hobeau Farm	24	14	2	8.3%
Amerman Racing Stables	24	16	2	8.3%
Tucci Stables	24	15	2	8.3%
Paul P. Pompa Jr.	25	13	2	8.0%
Haras Santa Maria de Araras	27	13	2	7.4%
William A. Sorokolit Sr.	28	11	2	7.1%
Courtlandt Farm	28	14	2	7.1%
Juddmonte Farms	29	14	2	6.9%
Peter Vegso	35	14	2	5.7%

Owner	No. Strs	No. Wnrs	No. GSWs	GSWs/ Strs
Gary and Mary West Stables	38	26	2	5.3%
Harris Farms	40	20	2	5.0%
Barry K. Schwartz	41	22	2	4.9%
Edward P. Evans	42	22	2	4.8%
WinStar Farm	43	21	2	4.7%
Jay Em Ess Stable	44	20	2	4.6%
Sam-Son Farm	46	20	2	4.4%

Leading Owners by Graded Stakes Wins in 2005

Owner	No. Graded Stakes Starts	No. Graded Stakes Wins
Live Oak Plantation	42	9
Phipps Stable	29	8
Juddmonte Farms	29	6
Robert & Beverly Lewis	45	6
Melnyk Racing Stables	22	6
Harry J. Aleo	6	5
Tracy Farmer	31	5
T N T Stud	15	5
Gary A. Tanaka	49	5
Michael Bello	7	4
Darley Stable	14	4
B. Wayne Hughes	27	4
Mr. & Mrs. Jerome S. Moss	14	4
Kenneth & Sarah Ramsey	16	4
Starlight Stable, Paul Saylor, and Johns Martin	12	4
Mr. & Mrs. William K. Warren Jr.	6	4

Leading Owners by Most Grade 1 Stakes Wins in 2005

Owner	No. G1 Starts	No. G1 Wins
Phipps Stable	11	4
Starlight Stable, Paul Saylor, & Johns Martin	7	4
Mr. & Mrs. William K. Warren Jr.	6	4
Cash is King stable	3	2
Eldon Farm	6	2
Fog City Stable	4	2
Kinsman Stable	6	2
Robert & Beverly Lewis	12	2
Live Oak Plantation	10	2
Bruce Lunsford & Lansdon Robbins III	3	2
Melnyk Racing Stables	9	2
Michael J. Moran	4	2
Mr. & Mrs. Jerome S. Moss	6	2
Red Oak Stable	6	2
Stronach Stables	10	2
TNT Stud	7	2

Leading Owners by Most Grade 1 Stakes Winners in 2005

Owner	No. G1 Starters	No. G1 Winners
Phipps Stable	5	3
Fog City Stable	2	2
Kinsman Stable	2	2
Live Oak Plantation	4	2
Melnyk Racing Stables	4	2
Mr. and Mrs. Jerome S. Moss	3	2
Starlight Stable, Paul Saylor, and Johns Martin	2	2
Stronach Stables	7	2

Leading Owners by Number of Wins in 2005

Owner	No. Strs	No. Wnrs	No. Wins
Michael J. Gill	371	193	351
Louis D. O'Brien	129	95	194
Dale Baird	207	106	159
Robert D. Bone	191	103	156
Frank Carl Calabrese	161	96	133
Maggi Moss	125	74	114
Stronach Stables	144	73	113
Bruno Schickedanz	110	59	100
Elaine M. Gross	146	59	95
Gumpster Stable LLC	104	55	94
Melnyk Racing Stables	93	51	89
Monarch Stables Inc.	67	46	88
Joseph Clark Faulkner	48	39	85
M. Y. Stables Inc.	50	36	84
Robert L. Cole Jr.	74	49	83
Home Team Stables	91	49	83
Flying Zee Stables	97	52	80
Gary Owens	71	43	77
Rodney C. Faulkner	57	34	69
Heiligbrodt Racing Stable	80	45	65
Plumstead Stables	71	42	64
Jerry Hollendorfer & George Todaro	85	43	64
Puglisi Stables	48	41	63
Jack L. Boggs	41	29	62
Steve Asmussen	60	33	62
Bar None Ranches	69	38	61
Billy Hays	89	39	61

Most Wins for an Owner on One Day in 2005

Wins	Owner	Date	Track(s)
7	Michael J. Gill	5/30/2005	Del, Pha, Pim, Suf
	Louis D. O'Brien	3/26/2005	FP
5	Michael J. Gill	5/8/2005	Del, Pha, Pim
	Louis D. O'Brien	4/28/2005	FP, Ind
4	Dale Baird	10/21/2005	Mnr
	Robert D. Bone	11/16/2005	Hol
	Robert D. Bone	7/24/2005	Dmr, ElP, Sol
	Robert D. Bone	6/11/2005	CD, GG
	Frank Calabrese	6/24/2005	AP, Mth
	Dogwood Stable	10/14/2005	Beu, Crc, Kee
	Michael J. Gill	5/15/2005	Del, FL, Mth, Pim
	Michael J. Gill	6/4/2005	Del, FE, Pim, Suf
	Michael J. Gill	6/13/2005	Del, Pha, Suf
	Michael J. Gill	4/16/2005	CT, Lrl
	Michael J. Gill	4/10/2005	Aqu, Lrl, Pha
	Michael J. Gill	4/2/2005	Lrl, OP, Pha
	Michael J. Gill	3/19/2005	CT, FG, Lrl, OP
	Michael J. Gill	3/20/2005	CT, Lrl, OP
	Michael J. Gill	3/11/2005	FG, Hou, Lrl
	Michael J. Gill	9/10/2005	Del, FE, Lrl, Suf
	Michael J. Gill	7/19/2005	Cnl, Del, Suf
	Michael J. Gill	7/6/2005	CT, Del, Pha
	Michael J. Gill	2/27/2005	FG, Lrl, OP
	Michael J. Gill	2/20/2005	Lrl, OP
	B. Wayne Hughes	3/12/2005	FG, SA, TP
	M. Y. Stables Inc.	5/7/2005	Beu, FP, RD
	Louis D. O'Brien	4/7/2005	FP
	Louis D. O'Brien	4/8/2005	FP
	Louis D. O'Brien	5/14/2005	FP
	Louis D. O'Brien	4/12/2005	FP
	Louis D. O'Brien	7/19/2005	FP
	R. Gary Patrick	4/15/2005	Ind

Most Wins for an Owner on One Program in 2005

Wins	Owner	Date	Track
7	Louis D. O'Brien	3/26/2005	FP
4	Dale Baird	10/21/2005	Mnr
	Robert D. Bone	11/16/2005	Hol
	Louis D. O'Brien	4/8/2005	FP
	Louis D. O'Brien	5/14/2005	FP
	Louis D. O'Brien	4/12/2005	FP
	Louis D. O'Brien	4/7/2005	FP
	Louis D. O'Brien	7/19/2005	FP
	R. Gary Patrick	4/15/2005	Ind

Leading Owners by Most Purses in a Year (1986-2005)

Owner	Year	Earnings	Leading Earner (Earnings)
Stronach Stables	2000	$11,133,785	Perfect Sting ($1,367,000)
Michael J. Gill	2004	10,811,211	Umpateedle ($216,160)
Richard A. Englander	2001	9,784,822	Elektraline ($222,383)
Michael J. Gill	2003	9,236,530	Highway Prospector ($290,397)
Stronach Stables	2002	8,347,017	Milwaukee Brew ($1,590,000)
The Thoroughbred Corp.	2001	8,000,763	Point Given ($3,350,000)
The Thoroughbred Corp.	2002	7,887,915	War Emblem ($3,125,000)
Someday Farm	2004	7,584,305	Smarty Jones ($7,563,535)
Richard A. Englander	2002	7,530,362	Boston Common ($303,177)
Stronach Stables	2003	7,289,114	Milwaukee Brew ($743,000)
Stronach Stables	1998	7,221,416	Awesome Again ($3,845,990)
Stronach Stables	2004	7,193,867	Ghostzapper ($2,590,000)
Juddmonte Farms	2001	6,806,015	Aptitude ($1,410,000)
Allen E. Paulson	1996	6,686,629	Cigar ($2,510,000)
Stronach Stables	2001	6,539,481	Macho Uno ($563,400)
Michael J. Gill	2005	6,397,180	Umpateedle ($331,050)
Juddmonte Farms	2003	6,265,030	Empire Maker ($1,936,200)
Stronach Stables	1999	6,221,147	Golden Missile ($838,240)
Overbrook Farm	1996	5,996,242	Boston Harbor ($1,906,325)
The Thoroughbred Corp.	2000	5,880,705	Spain ($1,979,500)
Melnyk Racing Stables	2005	5,875,007	Flower Alley ($2,435,200)
Ogden Phipps	1988	5,858,168	Seeking the Gold ($2,145,620)
Kenneth and Sarah Ramsey	2004	5,855,964	Roses in May ($1,723,277)
Edmund A. Gann	2003	5,848,681	Medaglia d'Oro ($1,990,000)
John Franks	1999	5,735,827	Littlebitlively ($868,303)
Michael J. Gill	2002	5,639,292	Rusty Spur ($180,610)
Golden Eagle Farm	1999	5,630,399	General Challenge ($1,658,100)
Allen E. Paulson	1995	5,626,396	Cigar ($3,670,000)
Golden Eagle Farm	1998	5,590,971	Excellent Meeting ($773,824)
Juddmonte Farms	2000	5,496,951	Chester House ($1,408,500)
Allen E. Paulson	1998	5,483,756	Escena ($2,032,425)
Ogden Phipps	1989	5,438,034	Easy Goer ($3,837,150)
Godolphin Racing	2001	5,359,804	Fantastic Light ($2,896,615)
Richard A. Englander	2003	5,347,231	My Cousin Matt ($237,500)
Allen E. Paulson	1997	5,259,107	Ajina ($979,175)
Juddmonte Farms	2002	5,172,287	Beat Hollow (GB) ($1,437,150)
John Franks	1998	5,145,343	Precocity ($868,630)
Michael E. Pegram	1999	5,128,905	Silverbulletday ($1,707,640)
Eugene V. Klein	1988	5,093,091	Winning Colors ($1,347,746)
Overbrook Farm	1999	5,052,194	Cat Thief ($3,020,500)
Kinghaven Farms	1990	5,041,280	Izvestia ($2,486,667)
Richard A. Englander	2000	4,927,214	Watchman's Warning ($210,862)
Eugene V. Klein	1987	4,904,247	Success Express ($737,207)
Live Oak Plantation	2005	4,904,171	High Fly ($901,500)
Sam-Son Farm	2004	4,830,939	Soaring Free ($1,113,862)
Sam-Son Farm	2000	4,698,712	Quiet Resolve ($967,871)
The Thoroughbred Corp.	1999	4,598,903	Anees ($609,200)
Gaillard-Hancock-Whittingham	1989	4,580,404	Sunday Silence ($4,578,454)
Golden Eagle Farm	1992	4,487,959	Best Pal ($955,000)
Edward P. Evans	2002	4,472,047	Summer Colony ($992,500)
John Franks	1986	4,463,115	Herat ($541,000)
Eugene and Laura Melnyk	2004	4,447,689	Speightstown ($1,045,556)
Golden Eagle Farm	1997	4,420,911	Career Collection ($482,005)
John Franks	1990	4,386,593	Beyond Perfection ($345,614)
Stronach Stables	2005	4,383,153	Ghostzapper ($450,000)
Carolyn H. Hine	1997	4,347,895	Skip Away ($4,089,000)
Frank H. Stronach	1996	4,271,752	Cash Deposit ($269,072)
Frank H. Stronach	1997	4,246,073	Wild Rush ($614,780)
Kinghaven Farms	1989	4,136,174	With Approval ($1,772,150)
Eugene and Laura Melnyk	2003	4,123,765	Strong Hope ($582,360)
John Franks	1997	4,084,085	Halo America ($528,012)
John Franks	2003	4,083,255	Chatter Chatter ($383,470)

Leading Breeders of 2005

Because horses bred in North America—especially the United States—are scattered to the four corners of the earth through sale or transfer by their owners-breeders, overseas-based operations often occupy many of the top spots in the annual THOROUGHBRED TIMES Leading Breeders table. But that was neither true in 2004 nor again in '05. On the 2005 list, Juddmonte Farms, a truly international breeder that features some of the world's best broodmares, ranked sixth. All the slots above Khalid Abdullah's operation were principally American breeders whose horses raced in the United States.

The criteria for appearing on the table, as noted below, emphasize consistent quality, and many of the top ten are homegrown operations that maintain select bands of broodmares and breed them to leading stallions. Atop the list in 2005 was Phipps Stable, a breeder with deep roots in the American Turf that a member of its third generation, Ogden Mills "Dinny" Phipps, now leads. His grandmother, Gladys Phipps, bred and owned Bold Ruler, and his late father, Ogden Phipps, bred champions Personal Ensign and Easy Goer. The Phipps Stable bred three 2005 graded stakes winners from 15 starters, a notable 20% strike rate. Leading that group was Pleasant Home, runaway winner of the Breeders' Cup Distaff (G1). For his own account, Dinny Phipps bred three other graded stakes winners, including three-year-old filly champion Smuggler.

No American breeder has been responsible for more Eclipse Award champions than Allen E. Paulson. His widow, Madeleine, ranked second in the 2005 listings with two stakes winners from ten starters and one graded stakes winner, Rock Hard Ten, a multiple graded stakes winner who missed a chance to run in the Breeders' Cup Classic (G1) because of a bruised foot.

Perfect Drift placed breeders William Reed and Stonecrest Farm into the third spot. The durable gelding added another $1,121,227 to his bankroll in 2005 and raised his career earnings to $4,308,339. Robert and Beverly Lewis occupied the fourth spot with two stakes winners from ten starters and one graded stakes winner, Folklore, their two-year-old filly champion in 2005.

For the third consecutive year, Frank Stronach's Adena Springs was the North American leader by purse earnings. Horses emerging from the Adena Springs breeding operation earned $11,613,323 and won 456 races.

Leading Breeders by Purses Won

Year	Name	Wins	Purses Won
2005	Adena Springs	456	$ 11,613,323
2004	Adena Springs	383	14,122,256
2003	Adena Springs	296	11,542,871
2002	Mockingbird Farm	516	11,175,975
2001	Mockingbird Farm	390	9,550,610
2000	Harry T. Mangurian Jr.	495	10,757,845
1999	Harry T. Mangurian Jr.	490	10,851,459
1998	Mr. and Mrs. John Mabee	270	8,221,982

THOROUGHBRED TIMES Leading Breeders of 2005

Rankings based on formula that gives equal weighting to four statistical categories for performance in 2005: 1) total earnings; 2) average earnings per starter; 3) number of winners; and 4) percent of stakes winners from starters. A minimum of ten starters is required to be considered for inclusion. Names of breeders are of individual property lines as reported by the Jockey Club. No attempt was made to consolidate names where a breeder had more than one partnership or property line. Statistics are for North America only and for racing in 2005.

Rank	Breeder	No. strs	No. wnrs	No. SWs	SWs/ strs	No. GSWs	GSWs/ strs	Total earnings	Average earnings/ starter	Leading earner	Earnings of leading earner
1	Phipps Stable	15	11	3	20.0%	3	20.0%	$2,311,698	$154,113	Pleasant Home	$1,316,420
2	Madeleine A. Paulson	10	7	2	20.0%	1	10.0%	1,385,811	138,581	Rock Hard Ten	1,080,000
3	William Reed & Stonecrest Farm	11	9	2	18.2%	1	9.1%	1,356,503	123,318	Perfect Drift	1,121,227
4	Robert and Beverly Lewis	10	4	2	20.0%	1	10.0%	1,171,685	117,168	Folklore	927,500
5	William S. Farish Jr.	10	6	1	10.0%	1	10.0%	942,981	94,298	Shadow Cast	626,266
6	Juddmonte Farms	54	26	4	7.4%	4	7.4%	4,105,045	76,019	Intercontinental (GB)	1,271,200
7	Mr. and Mrs. Jerry S. Moss	32	16	2	6.3%	1	3.1%	2,461,609	76,925	Giacomo	1,846,876
8	Windways Farm	13	7	2	15.4%	1	7.7%	1,039,579	79,968	Wild Desert	636,800
9	John D. Gunther	17	9	2	11.8%	2	11.8%	1,260,697	74,159	First Samurai	682,575
10	Aaron U. and Marie D. Jones	30	18	5	16.7%	2	6.7%	2,113,659	70,455	Ashado	1,061,000
11	Willmott Stables	10	5	1	10.0%	1	10.0%	784,380	78,438	Sand Springs	606,400
12	Firmamento	25	14	6	24.0%	5	20.0%	1,603,841	64,154	Star Parade (Arg)	275,637
13	Ogden Mills Phipps	19	8	4	21.1%	3	15.8%	1,246,374	65,599	Smuggler	558,800
14	Edward P. Evans	134	79	8	6.0%	3	2.2%	7,770,437	57,988	Saint Liam	3,696,960
15	France and Irwin J. Weiner	12	7	1	8.3%	1	8.3%	776,847	64,737	Closing Argument	565,000
16	Wimborne Farm	46	23	3	6.5%	2	4.4%	2,597,579	56,469	Honey Ryder	910,980
17	Tracy Farmer	15	9	2	13.3%	1	6.7%	869,630	57,975	Sir Shackleton	455,395
18	Harlequin Ranches	17	11	1	5.9%	1	5.9%	986,735	58,043	Gold Strike	480,518
19	Live Oak Stud	85	55	11	12.9%	5	5.9%	4,319,935	50,823	High Fly	901,500
20	Totier Creek Farm	13	5	1	7.7%	1	7.7%	740,895	56,992	Two Trail Sioux	577,200
21	Gustav Schickedanz	36	22	3	8.3%	1	2.8%	1,726,881	47,969	Jambalaya	380,846
22	Carolyn Sleeter	17	10	3	17.7%		0.0%	821,503	48,324	Who's the Cowboy	233,910
23	R. J. Forbush & Richard Lueck	10	7	1	10.0%	1	10.0%	514,254	51,425	Elusive Jazz	338,731
24	Beclawat Stable	21	11	1	4.8%	1	4.8%	995,098	47,386	A Bit O'Gold	497,437
25	Upson Downs Farm	18	12	1	5.6%	1	5.6%	854,194	47,455	Scrappy T	584,197
26	TAC Holdings	39	27	4	10.3%	3	7.7%	1,749,462	44,858	Film Maker	443,440
27	Wind Hill Farm	14	10	2	14.3%	1	7.1%	666,598	47,614	Stellar Jayne	423,720

Rank	Breeder	No. Strs	No. Wnrs	No. SWs	SWs/ Strs	No. GSWs	GSWs/ Strs	Total Earnings	Average Earnings/ Starter	Leading Earner	Earnings of Leading Earner
28	Janis R. Whitham	24	9	2	8.3%	1	4.2%	1,061,807	44,242	Mea Domina	$446,076
29	Joseph Allen	19	14	2	10.5%	1	5.3%	$846,619	$44,559	War Marshall	117,480
30	Vinery	11	7	3	27.3%	1	9.1%	513,317	46,665	Hollywood Story	218,410
31	Fox Ridge Farm	15	6	1	6.7%	1	6.7%	681,239	45,416	Riskaverse	464,723
32	Eugene Melnyk	59	39	3	5.1%	1	1.7%	2,449,801	41,522	Indian Vale	364,674
33	Moloney & Thompson	13	8	2	15.4%		0.0%	588,187	45,245	She's a Jewel	136,985
34	Diamond A Racing Corp.	21	12	2	9.5%	1	4.8%	880,346	41,921	Nothing But Fun	281,700
35	Michael Pegram	15	8	2	13.3%	1	6.7%	644,323	42,955	Pussycat Doll	287,903
36	Thomas/Lakin	75	49	8	10.7%	2	2.7%	2,950,611	39,341	Capeside Lady	278,600
37	Carl Bowling	21	14	1	4.8%	1	4.8%	866,311	41,253	She Says It Best	382,918
38	John B. Porter	15	10	1	6.7%	1	6.7%	628,767	41,918	Umpateedle	331,050
39	Buckram Oak Farm	17	8	1	5.9%	1	5.9%	701,493	41,264	Eurosilver	247,450
40	Stud TNT	10	5	2	20.0%	1	10.0%	436,013	43,601	Lundy's Liability (Brz)	170,000
41	Cheryl A. Curtin	21	13	2	9.5%	1	4.8%	845,813	40,277	Limehouse	482,998
42	Claiborne Farm	39	22	3	7.7%	1	2.6%	1,519,959	38,973	Wend	383,900
43	Haras Santa Maria de Araras	50	28	3	6.0%	2	4.0%	1,934,016	38,680	Palladio	444,143
44	Big C Farm	13	9	1	7.7%		0.0%	540,039	41,541	Blazing Rate	351,300
45	William Sorokolit	26	12	3	11.5%	2	7.7%	1,009,696	38,834	Classic Stamp	277,991
46	Runnymede Farm & Catesby Clay	10	6	1	10.0%	1	10.0%	427,116	42,712	Savorthetime	256,328
47	J. D. Squires	12	5	1	8.3%	1	8.3%	497,478	41,456	Vicarage	380,615
48	Mike Kennington	11	6	2	18.2%		0.0%	448,338	40,758	Badtotheboneandrew	224,210
49	Palides Investments N. V.	19	7	2	10.5%	2	10.5%	733,747	38,618	Delta Princess	358,923
50	Cherry Valley Farm	13	6	1	7.7%	1	7.7%	520,302	40,023	Pomeroy	210,800
51	Gallaghers Stud	21	13	3	14.3%		0.0%	795,640	37,888	Rahys' Appeal	166,558
52	Mr. and Mrs. M. Roy Jackson	12	7	3	25.0%		0.0%	477,828	39,819	Souris	197,310
53	William A. Carl	23	17	2	8.7%	1	4.4%	864,853	37,602	Shaniko	312,120
54	Morry Cohen	10	4	1	10.0%		0.0%	407,344	40,734	Beneficial Bartok	233,635
55	Sam-Son Farms	44	19	4	9.1%	2	4.6%	1,591,159	36,163	Soaring Free	192,827
56	Stone Canyon Thoroughbreds	17	12	3	17.7%		0.0%	643,359	37,845	Amazing Buy	244,350
57	Thomas/Lakin/Kintz	44	24	1	2.3%	1	2.3%	1,607,952	36,544	Real Dandy	762,550
58	Robert C. Roffey Jr.	12	6	1	8.3%		0.0%	468,924	39,077	Tiger Belle	186,520
59	Royal Match Stud	15	10	2	13.3%		0.0%	565,083	37,672	Melanyhasthepapers	162,820
60	Carson Springs Farm	11	6	2	18.2%		0.0%	428,819	38,984	Pretty Jenny	172,103
61	Patricia Blass	11	7	1	9.1%		0.0%	429,523	39,048	Wildcat Shoes	144,877
62	John A. Nerud Revocable Trust	13	9		0.0%		0.0%	508,481	39,114	Wing Man	158,525
63	Lazy E Ranch	11	6	1	9.1%	1	9.1%	425,312	38,665	High Strike Zone	297,110
64	Majesty Stud	20	12		0.0%		0.0%	740,231	37,012	Organizer	163,000
65	Anderson Farms & Rod Ferguson	12	7	1	8.3%	1	8.3%	457,168	38,097	Silver Highlight	142,689
66	Heiligbrodt Racing Stables	56	36	6	10.7%	1	1.8%	1,920,704	34,298	Sis City	495,220
67	Peter Vegso Racing Stable	15	10	2	13.3%	1	6.7%	550,845	36,723	Splendid Blended	192,500
68	Dell Ridge Farm	30	10	1	3.3%	1	3.3%	1,065,880	35,529	Shakespeare	604,320
69	Mr. and Mrs. Leverett S. Miller	19	12		0.0%		0.0%	696,615	36,664	Silver Wagon	318,065
70	Tee N Jay Farm	13	5	2	15.4%		0.0%	481,110	37,008	Trueamericanspirit	145,400
71	Luis de Hechavarria	30	21	3	10.0%		0.0%	1,033,305	34,444	Dazzling Dr. Cevin	239,580
72	Chester and Mary R. Broman	34	23	2	5.9%	1	2.9%	1,166,475	34,308	Seeking the Ante	362,280
73	Valene Farms	11	10	1	9.1%		0.0%	413,222	37,566	J. D.'s Blue Bayou	142,170
74	John and Martha Mulholland	10	6		0.0%		0.0%	388,169	38,817	Mythical Conquest	88,290
75	Dr. R. Bockel	11	9	1	9.1%		0.0%	411,888	37,444	Denoun N Deverb	121,825
76	David Cassidy	14	9		0.0%		0.0%	508,128	36,295	Give Faith	111,882
77	James and Janeane Everatt	17	12		0.0%		0.0%	598,726	35,219	Ever So Free	157,445
78	Old English Rancho	41	29	2	4.9%		0.0%	1,345,668	32,821	Dee Dee's Diner	221,607
79	B. Wayne Hughes	23	13	4	17.4%	1	4.4%	763,054	33,176	Osidy	170,355
80	Sentinel Thoroughbred Farms	16	10	1	6.3%	1	6.3%	550,943	34,434	A to the Z	400,439
81	New Farm	23	20	2	8.7%		0.0%	761,833	33,123	Golder Than Gold	90,080
82	Charles Nuckols Jr. & Sons	93	57	9	9.7%	2	2.2%	2,934,985	31,559	Storm's Darling	231,330
83	Pin Oak Stud	60	43	3	5.0%	2	3.3%	1,914,415	31,907	Cryptograph	247,945
84	Paul Buttigieg	11	6	1	9.1%		0.0%	392,998	35,727	Wannatalkaboutme	186,503
85	Bernard and Karen McCormack	10	5	1	10.0%		0.0%	360,713	36,071	Thinking Out Loud	176,588
86	C-Punch Ranch	16	7	1	6.3%		0.0%	548,571	34,286	Cee's Irish	329,125
87	John T. L. Jones Jr. & Troy Seale	12	7	1	8.3%		0.0%	417,467	34,789	Premium Saltine	154,725
88	Robert E. Meyerhoff	35	20	4	11.4%		0.0%	1,106,064	31,602	Sticky	153,650
89	Curtis C. Green	12	9	1	8.3%	1	8.3%	416,656	34,721	He's Got Grit	191,900
90	Summerwind Farm	20	9	1	5.0%	1	5.0%	661,338	33,067	Miss Fortunate	250,905
91	Flaxman Holdings	28	14	1	3.6%	1	3.6%	907,786	32,421	King of Happiness	228,372
92	Kenneth and Sarah Ramsey	109	72	8	7.3%	2	1.8%	3,365,670	30,878	Dawn of War	403,800
93	Jayeff B Stables	35	20	6	17.1%	1	2.9%	1,099,642	31,418	Smokey Glacken	146,760
94	Biggs Farm	10	6	1	10.0%	1	10.0%	352,420	35,242	Coin Silver	230,410
95	Vegso Racing Stable	25	12	2	8.0%	1	4.0%	798,775	31,951	Silver Tree	229,420
96	William Wilmot and Joan Taylor	14	5	1	7.1%		0.0%	472,488	33,749	Naughty New Yorker	290,157
97	Morgan's Ford Farm	14	5	1	7.1%	1	7.1%	471,428	33,673	Bank Audit	400,691
98	Gainsborough Farm	26	15	3	11.5%	2	7.7%	823,333	31,667	Stupendous Miss	205,881
99	Hickory Tree Farm	10	6	2	20.0%		0.0%	347,840	34,784	Lindero	100,100
100	Larry R. Teague	14	7	2	14.3%		0.0%	462,492	33,035	Rocky Gulch	257,520

Leading Breeders by Earnings in 2005

Breeder	No. Strs	No. Wnrs	Total Earnings
Adena Springs	424	247	$11,613,323
John Franks	544	279	9,142,197
Farnsworth Farms	380	230	8,500,777
Edward P. Evans	134	79	7,770,437
Sez Who Thoroughbreds	285	156	6,744,046
Brereton C. Jones	234	116	5,405,931
Live Oak Stud	85	55	4,319,935
Juddmonte Farms	54	26	4,105,045
Ken and Sarah Ramsey	109	72	3,365,670
Arthur I. Appleton	129	76	3,073,816
Mr. and Mrs. Martin Wygod	120	63	3,054,685
Thomas/Lakin	75	49	2,950,611
C. Nuckols Jr. & Sons	93	57	2,934,985
Overbrook Farm	128	59	2,892,399
WinStar Farm	94	53	2,773,035
Everest Stables	104	58	2,766,581
Haras Santa Isabel	180	113	2,712,555
Wimborne Farm	46	23	2,597,579
Gilbert G. Campbell	145	74	2,513,409
George Brunacini and Bona Terra Farms	7	4	2,490,052
Mr. & Mrs. Jerry S. Moss	32	16	2,461,609
Eugene Melnyk	59	39	2,449,801
Mr. & Mrs. John Mabee	136	71	2,408,942
Phipps Stable	15	11	2,311,698
Stonerside Stable	80	42	2,277,671
Tommy Town T'breds.	136	80	2,259,658
J D Farms	119	67	2,243,346
John Martin Silvertand	7	5	2,215,581
Flying Zee Stables	82	46	2,141,462
Aaron and Marie Jones	30	18	2,113,659
Ro Parra	104	67	2,049,069
Donald R Dizney	91	55	2,029,415
Harris Farms	99	47	2,020,724
Haras Santa Maria de Araras	50	28	1,934,016
Heiligbrodt Racing Stables	56	36	1,920,704
Pin Oak Stud	60	43	1,914,415
Foxwood Plantation	68	34	1,850,038
Hermitage Farm	75	35	1,766,101
TAC Holdings	39	27	1,749,462
Gustav Schickedanz	36	22	1,726,881
Moyglare Stud Farm	7	3	1,720,832

Leading Breeders by Average Earnings per Starter in 2005
(Minimum of 10 Starters)

Breeder	No. Strs	No. Wnrs	Average Earnings per Starter
Phipps Stable	15	11	$154,113
Madeleine A. Paulson	10	7	138,581
Dr. William A. Reed and Stonecrest Farm	11	9	123,318
Robert and Beverly Lewis	10	4	117,168
William S. Farish Jr.	10	6	94,298
Windways Farm	13	7	79,968
Willmott Stables	10	5	78,438
Mr. and Mrs. Jerry S. Moss	32	16	76,925
Juddmonte Farms	54	26	76,019
John D. Gunther	17	9	74,159
Aaron and Marie Jones	30	18	70,455
Ogden Mills Phipps	19	8	65,599
France and Irwin J. Weiner	12	7	64,737
Firmamento	25	14	$64,154
Harlequin Ranches	17	11	58,043
Edward P. Evans	134	79	57,988
Tracy Farmer	15	9	57,975
Totier Creek Farm	13	5	56,992
Wimborne Farm	46	23	56,469
Richard J. Forbush and Richard Lueck	10	7	51,425
Live Oak Stud	85	55	50,823
Carolyn Sleeter	17	10	48,324
Gustav Schickedanz	36	22	47,969
Wind Hill Farm	14	10	47,614
Upson Downs Farm	18	12	47,455
Beclawat Stable	21	11	47,386
Vinery	11	7	46,665
Fox Ridge Farm	15	6	45,416
Moloney & Thompson	13	8	45,245
TAC Holdings	39	27	44,858
Joseph Allen	19	14	44,559
Janis R. Whitham	24	9	44,242
Stud TNT	10	5	43,601
Michael E. Pegram	15	8	42,955
Runnymede Farm and Catesby W. Clay	10	6	42,712
Diamond A Racing Corp.	21	12	41,921
John B. Porter	15	10	41,918
Big C Farm	13	9	41,541

Leading Breeders by Number of Stakes Wins in 2005

Breeder	Stakes Starts	Stakes Wins
Live Oak Stud	74	21
Adena Springs	183	19
Brereton C. Jones	91	16
Edward P. Evans	91	16
John Franks	148	16
Sez Who Thoroughbreds	115	16
Arthur I. Appleton	69	14
Charles Nuckols Jr. & Sons	68	13
Farnsworth Farms	134	11
Applebite Farms	40	10
Dr. D. W. Frazier	42	10
Mr. & Mrs. Martin J. Wygod	56	10
Firmamento	38	9
Foxwood Plantation	42	9
Kenneth L. & Sarah K. Ramsey	76	9
Richter Family Trust	32	9
Thomas & Lakin	43	9
Wimborne Farm	27	9
Aaron U. & Marie D. Jones	35	8
Jose Carro	27	8
Juddmonte Farms	45	8
Marion G. Montanari	16	8
Susan Seper	9	8
Triple AAA Ranch	52	8
Cheveley Park Stud	15	7
Everest Stables	110	7
Gilbert G. Campbell	49	7
Heiligbrodt Racing Stable	28	7
Mr. & Mrs. M. Roy Jackson	17	7
Overbrook Farm	42	7
Pierre Amestoy	24	7
Shadwell Farm	29	7
TAC Holdings	22	7

Leading Breeders by Number of Stakes Winners in 2005

Breeder	No. strs	No. wnrs	No. SWs
Adena Springs	424	247	19
John Franks	544	279	13
Sez Who Thoroughbreds	285	156	12
Live Oak Stud	85	55	11
Arthur I. Appleton	129	76	10
Charles Nuckols Jr. & Sons	93	57	9
Brereton C. Jones	234	116	9
Applebite Farms	45	28	8
Thomas/Lakin	75	49	8
Kenneth and Sarah Ramsey	109	72	8
Edward P. Evans	134	79	8
Dr. D. W. Frazier	90	55	7
Everest Stables	104	58	7
Farnsworth Farms	380	230	7
Firmamento	25	14	6
Richter Family Trust	28	16	6
Jayeff B Stables	35	20	6
Heiligbrodt Racing Stables	56	36	6
Triple AAA Ranch	57	34	6
Aaron and Marie Jones	30	18	5
SLU	42	21	5
George Strawbridge Jr.	52	26	5
J D Farms	119	67	5
Mr. and Mrs. Martin J. Wygod	120	63	5
V. J. Callaway	16	8	4
Ogden Mills Phipps	19	8	4
Willard Burbach	21	12	4
Al J. Horton	22	13	4
Millsap Stables	23	15	4
B. Wayne Hughes	23	13	4
Vessels Stallion Farm	32	18	4
Robert E. Meyerhoff	35	20	4
TAC Holdings	39	27	4
E Paul Robsham	39	22	4
Shadwell Farm	41	15	4
Sam-Son Farm	44	19	4
Juddmonte Farms	54	26	4
Foxwood Plantation	68	34	4
Stonerside Stable	80	42	4
Potrero Los Llanos	91	56	4
Donald R. Dizney	91	55	4
Ro Parra	104	67	4
Overbrook Farm	128	59	4
Mr. and Mrs. John C. Mabee	136	71	4
Tommy Town Thoroughbreds	136	80	4
Gilbert G. Campbell	145	74	4
Haras Santa Isabel	180	113	4

Leading Breeders by Graded Wins in 2005

Breeder	Graded Starts	Graded Wins
Juddmonte Farms	42	8
Firmamento	30	7
Live Oak Stud	30	7
Wimborne Farm	16	7
Adena Springs	60	6
Edward P. Evans	38	6
WinStar Farm	20	6
Cheveley Park Stud	10	5
Susan Seper	6	5
Aaron U. and Marie D. Jones	18	4
Brereton C. Jones	20	4
Haras Bage Do Sul	8	4
Ogden Mills Phipps	14	4
Phipps Stable	16	4
TAC Holdings	11	4
Beclawat Stables	7	3
Brant Laue	6	3
Cambridge Farm & James D. Conway	9	3
Fred W. Pace	4	3
George Brunacini & Bona Terra Farms	8	3
George Strawbridge Jr.	17	3
Glencrest Farm	10	3
Haras Du Mezeray S.A.	6	3
John D. Gunther	14	3
John Franks	38	3
John Martin Silvertand	5	3
Juan A. Escobar	6	3
Madeleine A. Paulson	8	3
Mr. & Mrs. Martin J. Wygod	9	3
Needham/Betz Thoroughbreds and James Blackburn	4	3
Nicole Zitani and Ramon Rangel	8	3
Palides Investments N. V.	15	3
Pin Oak Stud	13	3
Robert Lewis & Beverly Lewis	7	3
Sam-Son Farm	20	3
T. F. VanMeter & Michael Lowenbaum	6	3
Whitewood Stable	16	3
William S. Farish Jr.	11	3
Willmott Stables	7	3

Leading Breeders by Graded Stakes Winners in 2005

Breeder	No. strs	No. wnrs	No. GSWs	% GSWs/ str
Adena Springs	424	247	6	1.4%
Firmamento	25	14	5	20.0%
Live Oak Stud	85	55	5	5.9%
Juddmonte Farms	54	26	4	7.4%
Brereton C. Jones	234	116	4	1.7%
Phipps Stable	15	11	3	20.0%
Ogden Mills Phipps	19	8	3	15.8%
TAC Holdings	39	27	3	7.7%
Jose Carro	39	21	3	7.7%
George Strawbridge Jr.	52	26	3	5.8%
Potrero Los Llanos	91	56	3	3.3%
WinStar Farm,	94	53	3	3.2%
Edward P. Evans	134	79	3	2.2%
John Franks	544	279	3	0.6%
Hannahill Farm	2	2	2	100.0%
Haras Bage Do Sul	5	2	2	40.0%
Barnett Enterprises	5	5	2	40.0%
R. A. Rankin/Louis Wright	7	3	2	28.6%
Moyglare Stud Farm	7	3	2	28.6%
Haras Don Alberto	7	6	2	28.6%
Lee Lewis	8	3	2	25.0%
Whitewood Stable	8	4	2	25.0%
Cheveley Park Stud	9	4	2	22.2%
John D. Gunther	17	9	2	11.8%
Palides Investments	19	7	2	10.5%
William Sorokolit	26	12	2	7.7%
Gainsborough Farm	26	15	2	7.7%
Aaron and Marie Jones	30	18	2	6.7%
Hopewell Investments	33	18	2	6.1%
Sam-Son Farm	44	19	2	4.6%
Wimborne Farm	46	23	2	4.4%

Breeder	No. strs	No. wnrs	No. GSWs	% GSWs/ str
Haras Santa Maria de Araras	50	28	2	4.0%
Glencrest Farm	52	19	2	3.9%
Pin Oak Stud	60	43	2	3.3%
Arthur B. Hancock III	63	41	2	3.2%
Marablue Farm	71	38	2	2.8%
Thomas/Lakin	75	49	2	2.7%
Hermitage Farm	75	35	2	2.7%
C. Nuckols Jr. & Sons	93	57	2	2.2%
Harris Farms	99	47	2	2.0%
Ken and Sarah Ramsey	109	72	2	1.8%
Mr./Mrs. Martin Wygod	120	63	2	1.7%
Overbrook Farm	128	59	2	1.6%
Haras Santa Isabel	180	113	2	1.1%
Sez Who Thoroughbreds	285	156	2	0.7%
Farnsworth Farms	380	230	2	0.5%

Leading Breeders by Most Grade 1 Stakes Wins in 2005

Breeder	No. G1 Starts	No. G1 Wins
Edward P. Evans	11	4
Aaron U. and Marie D. Jones	8	3
Adena Springs	15	3
Wimborne Farm	5	3
Brereton C. Jones	5	2
C. S. Tateson	6	2
Haras Bage Do Sul	4	2
Aga Khan's Studs	5	2
Kelly, Greely, Bradley, and Scott	5	2
John D. Gunther	8	2
John Martin Silvertand	3	2
Juddmonte Farms	14	2
Live Oak Stud	9	2
Mr. & Mrs. Martin J. Wygod	4	2
Ogden Mills Phipps	5	2
Phipps Stable	6	2
Richard Fox, Nathan Fox, and Richard Kaster	4	2
Robert and Beverly Lewis	4	2

Leading Breeders by Most Grade 1 Winners in 2005

Breeder	No. G1 Starters	No. G1 Winners
Adena Springs	10	3
Brereton C. Jones	5	2
Juddmonte Farms	7	2
Live Oak Stud	3	2
Mr. & Mrs. Martin J. Wygod	2	2
Phipps Stable	3	2
Wimborne Farm	2	2

Leading Breeders by Number of Winners in 2005

Breeder	No. Strs	No. Wnrs
John Franks	544	279
Adena Springs	424	247
Farnsworth Farms	380	230
Sez Who Thoroughbreds	285	156
Brereton C. Jones	234	116
Haras Santa Isabel	180	113
Tommy Town Thoroughbreds,	136	80
Edward P. Evans	134	79
Arthur I. Appleton	129	76
Gilbert G. Campbell	145	74
Kenneth and Sarah Ramsey	109	72
Mr. and Mrs. John C. Mabee	136	71
Ro Parra	104	67
J D Farms	119	67
Mr. and Mrs. Martin J. Wygod	120	63
Overbrook Farm	128	59
Everest Stables	104	58
Charles Nuckols Jr. & Sons	93	57
Mockingbird Farm	99	57
Potrero Los Llanos	91	56
Live Oak Stud	85	55
Dr. D. W. Frazier	90	55
Donald R. Dizney	91	55
WinStar Farm,	94	53
Thomas/Lakin	75	49
Harris Farms	99	47
Flying Zee Stables	82	46
Pin Oak Stud	60	43
Haras Don Jorge	74	43
Bruno Schickedanz	78	43
Stonerside Stable	80	42
Arthur B. Hancock III	63	41
Swifty Farms	72	40
Eugene Melnyk	59	39
W. S. Farish	67	39

Leading Breeders by Number of Wins in 2005

Breeder	No. strs	No. wnrs	No. wins
John Franks	544	279	464
Adena Springs	424	247	456
Farnsworth Farms	380	230	452
Sez Who Thoroughbreds	285	156	276
Haras Santa Isabel	180	113	272
Brereton C. Jones	234	116	222
Edward P. Evans	134	79	140
J D Farms	119	67	137
Arthur I. Appleton	129	76	135
Gilbert G. Campbell	145	74	133
Potrero Los Llanos	91	56	127
Kenneth and Sarah Ramsey	109	72	127
Mr. and Mrs. John C. Mabee	136	71	125
Mr. and Mrs. Martin J. Wygod	120	63	121
Tommy Town Thoroughbreds	136	80	120
Dr. D. W. Frazier	90	55	112
Ro Parra	104	67	111
Donald R. Dizney	91	55	104
Overbrook Farm	128	59	104
Mockingbird Farm	99	57	97
Everest Stables	104	58	95
Thomas/Lakin	75	49	93
Charles Nuckols Jr. & Sons	93	57	93
Live Oak Stud	85	55	92
Haras Don Jorge	74	43	86
Bruno Schickedanz	78	43	84
WinStar Farm	94	53	79
Harris Farms	99	47	79
Flying Zee Stables	82	46	76
Francis McDonnell	59	38	75
Arthur B. Hancock III	63	41	74
Pin Oak Stud	60	43	72
E & D Enterprises	68	33	71
Stonerside Stable	80	42	70
Dennis E. Weir	42	29	69
Triple AAA Ranch	57	34	68
W. S. Farish	67	39	68
Hermitage Farm	75	35	68

Leading Trainers of 2005

Training Thoroughbred racehorses is a tough way to make a living. The days are long, and most trainers are on the job before the sun climbs over the stable area and are there when the last race is run. Increasingly, the job entails considerable travel and mastering the complexities of running a million-dollar business. Not only must the trainer understand the personalities of the owners—some of whom invariably will be more difficult to handle than others—but he or she also must devise and execute a plan of action that leads from the auction ring to the winner's circle.

Indeed, the hopes and aspirations of all trainers are focused on the winner's circle. To win is to please everyone—the owner, the breeder, the stallion manager, the jockey, and the stable staff. For the trainer, day money to train the horse yields a subsistence living at best, and getting to the winner's circle yields the greatest monetary reward. While the money is important, most trainers thrive on getting to the winner's circle.

The THOROUGHBRED TIMES Leading Trainers of 2005 table recognizes those who have succeeded at a tough job. The rankings are based on four criteria: 1) total earnings; 2) average earnings per starter; 3) percentage of stakes winners from starters; and 4) number of wins. These criteria favor quality over quantity but nonetheless recognize the importance of getting to the winner's circle.

Leading Trainers by Purses Won

North American Earnings Only

Year	Trainer	Wins	Purses
2005	Todd A. Pletcher	257	$20,867,842
2004	Todd A. Pletcher	240	17,511,923
2003	Robert J. Frankel	114	19,143,289
2002	Robert J. Frankel	117	17,750,340
2001	Robert J. Frankel	101	14,607,446
2000	Bob Baffert	145	11,793,355
1999	Bob Baffert	169	16,842,332
1998	Bob Baffert	138	12,604,110
1997	D. Wayne Lukas	175	10,351,397
1996	D. Wayne Lukas	192	15,967,609
1995	D. Wayne Lukas	194	12,852,843
1994	D. Wayne Lukas	147	9,249,577
1993	Robert J. Frankel	78	8,928,602
1992	D. Wayne Lukas	246	10,061,240
1991	D. Wayne Lukas	289	15,953,757
1990	D. Wayne Lukas	267	14,508,871
1989	D. Wayne Lukas	305	16,103,998
1988	D. Wayne Lukas	318	17,842,358
1987	D. Wayne Lukas	343	17,502,110
1986	D. Wayne Lukas	259	12,344,520
1985	D. Wayne Lukas	218	11,155,188
1984	D. Wayne Lukas	131	5,838,221
1983	D. Wayne Lukas	78	4,267,261
1982	Charles E. Whittingham	62	4,586,077
1981	Charles E. Whittingham	74	3,991,877
1980	Lazaro S. Barrera	99	2,971,626

THOROUGHBRED TIMES Leading Trainers of 2005

Rankings based on formula that gives equal weighting to four statistical categories for performance in 2005: 1) total earnings; 2) average earnings per starter; 3) percent stakes winners from starters; and 4) number of wins. A minimum of ten starters is required to be considered for inclusion. Statistics are for North America only and for racing in 2005.

Rank	Trainer	No. Strs	No. Wnrs	No. SWs	SWs/ Strs	No. GSWs	GSWs/ Strs	Total Purses	Average Earnings/ Starter	Leading Earner	Earnings of Leading Earner
1	Todd A. Pletcher	299	155	48	16.1%	25	8.4%	$20,867,842	$69,792	Flower Alley	$2,435,200
2	Robert J. Frankel	195	90	24	12.3%	19	9.7%	14,122,807	72,425	Intercontinental (GB)	1,271,200
3	William I. Mott	169	80	23	13.6%	12	7.1%	9,355,603	55,359	Gun Salute	630,550
4	Nicholas P. Zito	104	54	14	13.5%	9	8.7%	8,199,368	78,840	Sun King	1,134,800
5	James A. Jerkens	49	25	7	14.3%	2	4.1%	3,877,228	79,127	Artie Schiller	1,448,000
6	Claude R. McGaughey III	50	25	8	16.0%	6	12.0%	4,041,412	80,828	Pleasant Home	1,316,420
7	Richard E. Dutrow Jr.	193	103	12	6.2%	7	3.6%	9,798,106	50,767	Saint Liam	3,183,600
8	Bob Baffert	134	62	13	9.7%	7	5.2%	5,991,799	44,715	Roman Ruler	890,000
9	Timothy F. Ritchey	75	47	6	8.0%	1	1.3%	4,622,602	61,635	Afleet Alex	2,085,000
10	H. Allen Jerkens	68	40	10	14.7%	5	7.4%	3,669,816	53,968	Society Selection	727,500
11	Patrick L. Biancone	45	24	8	17.8%	7	15.6%	3,096,875	68,819	Angara (GB)	668,108
12	Neil J. Howard	48	20	6	12.5%	4	8.3%	3,142,994	65,479	America Alive	654,326
13	Richard E. Mandella	65	27	8	12.3%	6	9.2%	3,626,458	55,792	Rock Hard Ten	1,080,000
14	Neil D. Drysdale	57	26	9	15.8%	7	12.3%	2,982,293	52,321	Fourty Niners Son	459,000
15	Mark A. Hennig	105	40	10	9.5%	5	4.8%	4,209,197	40,088	Eddington	602,200
16	Doug F. O'Neill	288	123	21	7.3%	9	3.1%	9,476,801	32,906	Stevie Wonderboy	1,028,940
17	Wallace A. Dollase	38	17	5	13.2%	5	13.2%	2,601,091	68,450	Meteor Storm (GB)	714,138
18	Sid C. Attard	66	35	5	7.6%	2	3.0%	3,073,388	46,566	One for Rose	274,120
19	John A. Shirreffs	59	27	4	6.8%	4	6.8%	3,649,864	61,862	Giacomo	1,846,876
20	Christophe Clement	141	50	10	7.1%	6	4.3%	5,070,697	35,962	Relaxed Gesture (Ire)	1,326,186
21	H. Graham Motion	142	68	9	6.3%	5	3.5%	4,900,801	34,513	Better Talk Now	877,640
22	Reade Baker	88	41	8	9.1%	3	3.4%	3,363,556	38,222	Gold Strike	480,518
23	Michael E. Hushion	78	46	6	7.7%	3	3.9%	2,910,890	37,319	Nothing But Fun	281,700
24	Jeff Mullins	179	80	10	5.6%	9	5.0%	5,679,989	31,732	Buzzards Bay	601,306
25	Dallas Stewart	79	36	7	8.9%	4	5.1%	2,938,796	37,200	Silverfoot	393,682
26	Julio C. Canani	55	23	5	9.1%	3	5.5%	2,281,448	41,481	Amorama (Fr)	368,532
27	Frank L. Brothers	30	16	3	10.0%	2	6.7%	1,821,624	60,721	First Samurai	682,575
28	Martin D. Wolfson	43	23	10	23.3%	1	2.3%	1,739,152	40,445	Pampered Princess	554,740
29	Ronald L. McAnally	78	26	6	7.7%	2	2.6%	3,026,832	38,806	Sweet Return (GB)	554,520

Rank	Trainer	No. Strs	No. Wnrs	No. SWs	SWs/ Strs	No. GSWs	GSWs/ Strs	Total Purses	Average Earnings/ Starter	Leading Earner	Earnings of Leading Earner
30	Thomas M. Bush	50	24	5	10.0%		0.0%	2,000,082	40,002	Gold and Roses	$ 396,134
31	Roger L. Attfield	57	23	4	7.0%	4	7.0%	2,504,365	43,936	Palladio	444,143
32	Dale L. Romans	151	71	11	7.3%	3	2.0%	4,421,833	29,284	Dawn of War	403,800
33	Robert P. Tiller	65	29	3	4.6%		0.0%	2,684,388	41,298	Top Ten List	292,854
34	J. Larry Jones	61	38	4	6.6%	1	1.6%	2,235,341	36,645	Island Sand	743,860
35	Malcolm Pierce	46	23	4	8.7%	2	4.4%	1,819,622	39,557	Lemon Maid	262,776
36	D. Wayne Lukas	128	50	4	3.1%	3	2.3%	4,585,321	35,823	Folklore	927,500
37	C. Beau Greely	21	6	1	4.8%	1	4.8%	1,863,960	88,760	Borrego	1,536,600
38	Mark R. Frostad	49	22	4	8.2%	2	4.1%	1,836,174	37,473	Hatpin	200,643
39	Steve Klesaris	96	62	4	4.2%	1	1.0%	3,016,586	31,423	Mighty Mecke	154,500
40	John C. Kimmel	70	29	5	7.1%	3	4.3%	2,259,289	32,276	Seeking the Ante	362,280
41	Catherine Day Phillips	24	10	3	12.5%	2	8.3%	1,284,834	53,535	A Bit O'Gold	497,437
42	Ronald W. Ellis	42	23	2	4.8%	2	4.8%	1,850,395	44,057	Don't Get Mad	730,110
43	Dan L. Hendricks	43	20	4	9.3%	2	4.7%	1,587,363	36,915	Brother Derek	502,080
44	Murray W. Johnson	13	7	1	7.7%	1	7.7%	1,277,306	98,254	Perfect Drift	1,121,227
45	Steven M. Asmussen	549	304	35	6.4%	8	1.5%	13,304,133	24,233	Summerly	786,728
46	Chris M. Block	57	37	4	7.0%		0.0%	1,799,395	31,568	Fort Prado	230,888
47	Robert E. Holthus	92	43	6	6.5%	1	1.1%	2,672,562	29,050	Greater Good	240,000
48	Christine K. Janks	47	22	6	12.8%		0.0%	1,487,418	31,647	Fifteen Rounds	191,750
49	Patrick J. Kelly	41	9	3	7.3%	2	4.9%	1,591,421	38,815	Riskaverse	464,723
50	Josie Carroll	60	24	6	10.0%	1	1.7%	1,822,115	30,369	Edenwold	287,247
51	Eoin G. Harty	64	24	5	7.8%	2	3.1%	1,981,614	30,963	Shamoan (Ire)	315,698
52	Vladimir Cerin	92	35	4	4.4%	2	2.2%	2,852,035	31,000	Super Frolic	736,760
53	Michael J. Trombetta	52	30	5	9.6%		0.0%	1,582,665	30,436	Weigelia	179,360
54	Kiaran P. McLaughlin	139	47	7	5.0%	1	0.7%	3,892,502	28,004	Closing Argument	565,000
55	Frank R. Springer	24	18	4	16.7%		0.0%	1,072,248	44,677	Cosmic Kris	188,575
56	Thomas F. Proctor	56	28	6	10.7%	2	3.6%	1,629,169	29,092	Purim	249,543
57	Bruce Headley	35	15	3	8.6%	2	5.7%	1,303,178	37,234	Surf Cat	322,420
58	Angel J. Penna Jr.	20	9	4	20.0%	3	15.0%	1,013,588	50,679	Que Puntual (Arg)	331,443
59	John T. Ward Jr.	33	12	4	12.1%	3	9.1%	1,211,515	36,713	For All We Know	288,871
60	Stanley M. Hough	72	26	7	9.7%	2	2.8%	1,945,199	27,017	Travelator	180,630
61	Bernard S. Flint	105	51	5	4.8%		0.0%	2,713,089	25,839	Discreet Hero	211,913
62	Andrew Leggio Jr.	39	26	2	5.1%	1	2.6%	1,433,909	36,767	Happy Ticket	535,000
63	John W. Sadler	130	48	4	3.1%	3	2.3%	3,695,518	28,427	Musique Toujours	595,000
64	John O. Hertler	34	17	4	11.8%		0.0%	1,208,116	35,533	Dave	174,922
65	Juan J. Garcia	50	22	3	6.0%	1	2.0%	1,577,772	31,555	Dream of Summer	658,650
66	Bruce N. Levine	121	65	2	1.7%		0.0%	3,435,305	28,391	Clever Electrician	158,950
67	Thomas Albertrani	37	17	3	8.1%	3	8.1%	1,233,710	33,344	Oratory	189,000
68	Michael E. Gorham	104	52	5	4.8%	1	1.0%	2,604,606	25,044	Trickle of Gold	270,880
69	Mark E. Casse	97	40	5	5.2%		0.0%	2,538,926	26,174	Top Notch Lady	219,678
70	Michael R. Matz	68	31	6	8.8%		0.0%	1,751,574	25,758	Marchonin	111,150
71	Carl A. Nafzger	66	28	1	1.5%	1	1.5%	2,244,281	34,004	King of Jazz	248,040
72	Paul J. McGee	66	32	2	3.0%	1	1.5%	1,996,263	30,246	Suave	624,900
73	Eric Coatrieux	18	11	1	5.6%	1	5.6%	1,063,218	59,068	Ambitious Cat	350,140
74	David R. Bell	62	24	3	4.8%		0.0%	1,817,191	29,310	Schooner Bay	236,831
75	Patrick Mouton	55	28	2	3.6%		0.0%	1,644,589	29,902	The Beter Man Can	220,100
76	Saeed bin Suroor	10	6	2	20.0%	2	20.0%	784,368	78,437	Stellar Jayne	423,720
77	Greg Gilchrist	30	15	1	3.3%	1	3.3%	1,235,611	41,187	Lost in the Fog	844,500
78	Timothy J. Tullock Jr.	36	17	4	11.1%	1	2.8%	1,110,950	30,860	Sensibly Chic	280,430
79	Gary Mandella	58	14	4	6.9%	1	1.7%	1,574,732	27,151	Taste of Paradise	605,000
80	Helen Pitts	38	15	3	7.9%	2	5.3%	1,163,642	30,622	Sweet Talker	400,000
81	Richard A. Violette Jr.	90	42	3	3.3%		0.0%	2,297,096	25,523	What's Your Edge	147,000
82	Macdonald Benson	16	9	2	12.5%	2	12.5%	788,672	49,292	Nashinda	205,271
83	Patrick Gallagher	77	28	3	3.9%	2	2.6%	2,000,856	25,985	McCann's Mojave	270,210
84	Daniel J. Vella	36	14	2	5.6%	1	2.8%	1,170,118	32,503	Knights Templar	255,353
85	Michael Keogh	24	8	2	8.3%		0.0%	920,686	38,362	Mobil	369,212
86	Alan E. Goldberg	43	19	4	9.3%		0.0%	1,181,653	27,480	Gilded Gold	105,750
87	George Weaver	64	31	3	4.7%	1	1.6%	1,634,262	25,535	Saratoga County	180,000
88	Benjamin W. Perkins Jr.	40	22	2	5.0%		0.0%	1,201,826	30,046	Smokescreen	189,850
89	Christopher S. Paasch	26	8	2	7.7%	1	3.9%	935,711	35,989	Diplomat Lady	334,800
90	Kirk Ziadie	72	39	3	4.2%	1	1.4%	1,761,632	24,467	R Lady Joy	565,436
91	Edward Plesa Jr.	98	49	3	3.1%		0.0%	2,320,106	23,675	Stolen Prayer	211,230
92	William H. Turner Jr.	28	13	1	3.6%	1	3.6%	1,066,884	38,103	Finery	136,248
93	Martin F. Jones	64	26	3	4.7%	2	3.1%	1,614,202	25,222	Alphabet Kisses	241,621
94	Barry Abrams	45	17	1	2.2%		0.0%	1,392,851	30,952	Juliesugardaddy	223,543
95	Ramon M. Hernandez	27	12	2	7.4%		0.0%	897,856	33,254	Classic Pack	260,050
96	Kelly J. Breen	73	33	3	4.1%		0.0%	1,754,327	24,032	Shebelongstoyou	140,200
97	Miguel A. Feliciano	37	26	6	16.2%		0.0%	961,571	25,988	Bernie Blue	180,004
98	Troy Young	29	17	3	10.3%		0.0%	888,320	30,632	J. D.'s Blue Bayou	142,170
99	James M. Cassidy	28	8	2	7.1%	1	3.6%	922,753	32,955	Singhalese (GB)	361,523
100	Todd M. Beattie	73	52	4	5.5%		0.0%	1,607,038	22,014	Hammered	92,900

Leading Trainers by Earnings in 2005

Trainer	No. Strs	No. Wnrs	Total Purses
Todd A. Pletcher	299	155	$20,867,842
Robert J. Frankel	195	90	14,122,807
Steven M. Asmussen	549	304	13,304,133
Richard E. Dutrow Jr.	193	103	9,798,106
Doug F. O'Neill	288	123	9,476,801
William I. Mott	169	80	9,355,603
Scott A. Lake	442	236	8,973,467
Nicholas P. Zito	104	54	8,199,368
Bob Baffert	134	62	5,991,799
Jeff Mullins	179	80	5,679,989
Jerry Hollendorfer	323	170	5,496,262
Christophe Clement	141	50	5,070,697
H. Graham Motion	142	68	4,900,801
Timothy F. Ritchey	75	47	4,622,602
D. Wayne Lukas	128	50	4,585,321
Dale L. Romans	151	71	4,421,833
Cole Norman	243	148	4,328,168
Mark A. Hennig	105	40	4,209,197
Claude R. McGaughey III	50	25	4,041,412
Kiaran P. McLaughlin	139	47	3,892,502
James A. Jerkens	49	25	3,877,228
John W. Sadler	130	48	3,695,518
H. Allen Jerkens	68	40	3,669,816
John A. Shirreffs	59	27	3,649,864
Richard E. Mandella	65	27	3,626,458
Gary C. Contessa	160	67	3,457,480
Bruce N. Levine	121	65	3,435,305
Art Sherman	222	128	3,368,732
Reade Baker	88	41	3,363,556
Neil J. Howard	48	20	3,142,994
Patrick L. Biancone	45	24	3,096,875
Sid C. Attard	66	35	3,073,388
Mark Shuman	186	79	3,071,782
W. Bret Calhoun	221	118	3,058,007
Ronald L. McAnally	78	26	3,026,832
Steve Klesaris	96	62	3,016,586
Neil D. Drysdale	57	26	2,982,293
Dallas Stewart	79	36	2,938,796
Michael E. Hushion	78	46	2,910,890
Vladimir Cerin	92	35	2,852,035
Thomas M. Amoss	164	79	2,753,840
Bernard S. Flint	105	51	2,713,089
Robert P. Tiller	65	29	2,684,388
Robert E. Holthus	92	43	2,672,562
Mike R. Mitchell	126	58	2,643,991
Michael E. Gorham	104	52	2,604,606
Wallace A. Dollase	38	17	2,601,091
Mark E. Casse	97	40	2,538,926
Roger L. Attfield	57	23	2,504,365
John C. Zimmerman	155	93	2,459,245

Leading Trainers by Average Earnings per Starter in 2005

(Minimum of 10 Starters)

Trainer	No. Strs	No. Wnrs	Average Earnings per Starter
Murray W. Johnson	13	7	$98,254
C. Beau Greely	21	6	88,760
Claude R. McGaughey III	50	25	80,828
James A. Jerkens	49	25	79,127
Nicholas P. Zito	104	54	78,840
Saeed bin Suroor	10	6	78,437
Robert J. Frankel	195	90	72,425
Todd A. Pletcher	299	155	69,792
Patrick L. Biancone	45	24	68,819
Wallace A. Dollase	38	17	68,450
Neil J. Howard	48	20	65,479
John A. Shirreffs	59	27	61,862
Timothy F. Ritchey	75	47	61,635
Frank L. Brothers	30	16	60,721
Eric Coatrieux	18	11	59,068
Richard E. Mandella	65	27	55,792
William I. Mott	169	80	55,359
H. Allen Jerkens	68	40	53,968
Catherine Day Phillips	24	10	53,535
Neil D. Drysdale	57	26	52,321
Richard E. Dutrow Jr.	193	103	50,767
Angel J. Penna Jr.	20	9	50,679
Macdonald Benson	16	9	49,292
William A. Campbell	13	8	48,756
William L. Currin	16	9	48,448
Lorne Richards	13	10	46,857
Sid C. Attard	66	35	46,566
Bob Baffert	134	62	44,715
Frank R. Springer	24	18	44,677
Ronald W. Ellis	42	23	44,057
Roger L. Attfield	57	23	43,936
Julio C. Canani	55	23	41,481
Robert P. Tiller	65	29	41,298
Greg Gilchrist	30	15	41,187
Martin D. Wolfson	43	23	40,445
Mark A. Hennig	105	40	40,088
Thomas M. Bush	50	24	40,002
Malcolm Pierce	46	23	39,557
John P. Le Blanc Jr.	14	7	39,542
Patrick J. Kelly	41	9	38,815
Ronald L. McAnally	78	26	38,806
Michael Keogh	24	8	38,362
Reade Baker	88	41	38,222
William H. Turner Jr.	28	13	38,103
Mark R. Frostad	49	22	37,473
Michael E. Hushion	78	46	37,319
Bruce Headley	35	15	37,234
Dallas Stewart	79	36	37,200
Dan L. Hendricks	43	20	36,915
Paul Nielsen	10	4	36,820

Leading Trainers by Stakes Wins in 2005

Trainer	No. Stakes Starts	No. Stakes Wins
Todd A. Pletcher	321	77
Steven M. Asmussen	319	60
Robert J. Frankel	168	39
William I. Mott	173	38
Doug F. O'Neill	191	28
Cole Norman	85	24
Jerry Hollendorfer	89	23
Nicholas P. Zito	126	19
Bob Baffert	103	18
Martin D. Wolfson	61	18
Christophe Clement	76	17
Richard E. Dutrow Jr.	91	16
Scott A. Lake	65	16
H. Graham Motion	86	16

Trainer	No. Stakes Starts	No. Stakes Wins
Mark A. Hennig	78	14
Neil J. Howard	41	14
Dale L. Romans	74	14
Jeff Mullins	80	13
Donnie K. Von Hemel	66	13
H. Allen Jerkens	78	12
Ramon Morales	63	12
Dallas Stewart	68	12
Patrick L. Biancone	81	11
J. Eric Kruljac	50	11
Michael W. Nance	31	11
Reade Baker	59	10
Josie Carroll	32	10
Neil D. Drysdale	67	10
Manuel Fernandez	38	10
Bernard S. Flint	85	10
Stanley M. Hough	49	10
Richard E. Mandella	50	10
Dan L. McFarlane	46	10
Claude R. McGaughey III	52	10
Michael Stidham	75	10
Miguel A. Feliciano	31	9
David Forster	44	9
Kenneth Gleason	44	9
Robert B. Hess Jr.	25	9
James A. Jerkens	53	9
Timothy F. Ritchey	41	9
Mark Shuman	43	9
Sid C. Attard	31	8
Dick R. Clark	32	8
Greg Gilchrist	10	8
Michael E. Gorham	33	8
Bart G. Hone	39	8
Michael E. Hushion	37	8
Christine K. Janks	35	8
Ronald L. McAnally	68	8
Jim Penney	42	8
Michael J. Trombetta	32	8
Kirk Ziadie	23	8

Leading Trainers by Number of Stakes Winners in 2005

Trainer	No. Strs	No. Wnrs	No. SWs
Todd A. Pletcher	299	155	48
Steven M. Asmussen	549	304	35
Robert J. Frankel	195	90	24
William I. Mott	169	80	23
Doug F. O'Neill	288	123	21
Cole Norman	243	148	17
Nicholas P. Zito	104	54	14
Bob Baffert	134	62	13
Richard E. Dutrow Jr.	193	103	12
Dale L. Romans	151	71	11
Martin D. Wolfson	43	23	10
H. Allen Jerkens	68	40	10
Donnie K. Von Hemel	94	51	10
Mark A. Hennig	105	40	10
Christophe Clement	141	50	10
Jeff Mullins	179	80	10
Jerry Hollendorfer	323	170	10
Neil D. Drysdale	57	26	9
H. Graham Motion	142	68	9
Patrick L. Biancone	45	24	8
Claude R. McGaughey III	50	25	8
Richard E. Mandella	65	27	8
Reade Baker	88	41	8
Michael Stidham	114	58	8
James A. Jerkens	49	25	7
Michael W. Nance	55	39	7
Kenneth Gleason	55	25	7
Stanley M. Hough	72	26	7
Dallas Stewart	79	36	7
Dan L. McFarlane	96	45	7
Kiaran P. McLaughlin	139	47	7
Scott A. Lake	442	236	7
Miguel A. Feliciano	37	26	6
Christine K. Janks	47	22	6
Neil J. Howard	48	20	6
Jim Penney	49	32	6
Thomas F. Proctor	56	28	6
Josie Carroll	60	24	6
Michael R. Matz	68	31	6
Timothy F. Ritchey	75	47	6
Ronald L. McAnally	78	26	6
Michael E. Hushion	78	46	6
Dick R. Clark	85	54	6
Robert E. Holthus	92	43	6
Bart G. Hone	102	46	6
William P. White	104	44	6
Jonathan E. Sheppard	115	50	6
Mark Shuman	186	79	6
W. Bret Calhoun	221	118	6

Leading Trainers by Percent of Stakes Winners from Starters in 2005

(Minimum of 10 Starters)

Trainer	No. strs	No. SWs	SWs/ str
Lyman H. Rollins	13	4	30.8%
John Snow	11	3	27.3%
Gary Simpson	16	4	25.0%
Hubert Pilon	16	4	25.0%
Martin D. Wolfson	43	10	23.3%
Angel J. Penna Jr.	20	4	20.0%
R. Mike Scudder	15	3	20.0%
Arlene Flegel	10	2	20.0%
Dru S. Hall	10	2	20.0%
Saeed bin Suroor	10	2	20.0%
Jim Crotts	10	2	20.0%
Joe Frederick Thomas Sr.	22	4	18.2%
Peter Pizzurro	11	2	18.2%
Bart B. Evans	11	2	18.2%
L Tracy McCarthy	11	2	18.2%
Patrick L. Biancone	45	8	17.8%
Frank R. Springer	24	4	16.7%
Tony J. Richey	12	2	16.7%
Miguel A. Feliciano	37	6	16.2%
David Forster	31	5	16.1%
Todd A. Pletcher	299	48	16.1%
Claude R. McGaughey III	50	8	16.0%
Neil D. Drysdale	57	9	15.8%
Robert Rohman	13	2	15.4%
John Michael Johnson	13	2	15.4%
Robert Gwilliam	13	2	15.4%
William A. Kaplan	13	2	15.4%
H. Allen Jerkens	68	10	14.7%
James A. Jerkens	49	7	14.3%
Neil R. Morris	21	3	14.3%
Ron David	14	2	14.3%
Robert J. Anderson	22	3	13.6%
William I. Mott	169	23	13.6%

Trainer	No. strs	No. SWs	SWs/ str
Nicholas P. Zito	104	14	13.5%
Jose R. Ramos	15	2	13.3%
Wallace A. Dollase	38	5	13.2%
Christine K. Janks	47	6	12.8%
Michael W. Nance	55	7	12.7%
Kenneth Gleason	55	7	12.7%
Neil J. Howard	48	6	12.5%
Catherine Day Phillips	24	3	12.5%
Frank Leggio	24	3	12.5%
Ralph W. Andersen	16	2	12.5%
Philip M. Hauswald	16	2	12.5%
Stan Marks	16	2	12.5%
Macdonald Benson	16	2	12.5%

Leading Trainers by Graded Stakes Wins in 2005

Trainer	No. Graded Stakes Starts	No. Graded Stakes Wins
Todd A. Pletcher	182	38
Robert J. Frankel	141	30
William I. Mott	94	18
Doug F. O'Neill	86	14
Nicholas P. Zito	97	13
Steven M. Asmussen	61	11
Richard E. Dutrow Jr.	46	11
Bob Baffert	56	10
Jeff Mullins	45	10
Patrick L. Biancone	60	8
Christophe Clement	36	8
Neil J. Howard	26	8
Richard E. Mandella	36	8
Claude R. McGaughey III	34	8
H. Graham Motion	34	8
Neil D. Drysdale	43	7
Mark A. Hennig	37	6
Frank L. Brothers	11	5
Catherine Day Phillips	11	5
Wallace A. Dollase	36	5
Greg Gilchrist	6	5
H. Allen Jerkens	43	5
D. Wayne Lukas	61	5
John A. Shirreffs	25	5
Dallas Stewart	43	5
Roger L. Attfield	24	4
Reade Baker	21	4
Julio C. Canani	31	4
Vladimir Cerin	15	4
James A. Jerkens	25	4
Ronald L. McAnally	32	4
Angel J. Penna Jr.	11	4
Thomas Albertrani	8	3
George R. Arnold II	14	3
Saeed bin Suroor	11	3
Ronald W. Ellis	10	3
Mark R. Frostad	22	3
Dan L. Hendricks	9	3
Jerry Hollendorfer	23	3
Michael E. Hushion	19	3
John C. Kimmel	22	3
Malcolm Pierce	8	3
Helen Pitts	8	3
Timothy F. Ritchey	17	3
Dale L. Romans	29	3
John W. Sadler	28	3
Sanford Shulman	12	3
John T. Ward Jr.	16	3

Leading Trainers by Number of Graded Stakes Winners in 2005

Trainer	No. Strs	No. Wnrs	No. GSWs	GSWs/ Strs
Todd A. Pletcher	299	155	25	8.4%
Robert J. Frankel	195	90	19	9.7%
William I. Mott	169	80	12	7.1%
Nicholas P. Zito	104	54	9	8.7%
Jeff Mullins	179	80	9	5.0%
Doug F. O'Neill	288	123	9	3.1%
Steven M. Asmussen	549	304	8	1.5%
Patrick L. Biancone	45	24	7	15.6%
Neil D. Drysdale	57	26	7	12.3%
Bob Baffert	134	62	7	5.2%
Richard E. Dutrow, Jr.	193	103	7	3.6%
Claude R. McGaughey III	50	25	6	12.0%
Richard E. Mandella	65	27	6	9.2%
Christophe Clement	141	50	6	4.3%
Wallace A. Dollase	38	17	5	13.2%
H. Allen Jerkens	68	40	5	7.4%
Mark A. Hennig	105	40	5	4.8%
H. Graham Motion	142	68	5	3.5%
Neil J. Howard	48	20	4	8.3%
Roger L. Attfield	57	23	4	7.0%
John A. Shirreffs	59	27	4	6.8%
Dallas Stewart	79	36	4	5.1%
Angel J. Penna Jr.	20	9	3	15.0%
John T. Ward Jr.	33	12	3	9.1%
Thomas Albertrani	37	17	3	8.1%
Julio C. Canani	55	23	3	5.5%
John C. Kimmel	70	29	3	4.3%
Michael E. Hushion	78	46	3	3.9%
Reade Baker	88	41	3	3.4%
Jonathan E. Sheppard	115	50	3	2.6%
D. Wayne Lukas	128	50	3	2.3%
John W. Sadler	130	48	3	2.3%
Dale L. Romans	151	71	3	2.0%
Andrew Balding	6	3	2	33.3%
Saeed bin Suroor	10	6	2	20.0%
Macdonald Benson	16	9	2	12.5%
David Bernstein	19	5	2	10.5%
Catherine Day Phillips	24	10	2	8.3%
Sanford Shulman	26	8	2	7.7%
Laura De Seroux	26	10	2	7.7%
Frank L. Brothers	30	16	2	6.7%
Bruce Headley	35	15	2	5.7%
Paul Douglas Fout	35	15	2	5.7%
Helen Pitts	38	15	2	5.3%
Patrick L. Reynolds	39	15	2	5.1%
Patrick J. Kelly	41	9	2	4.9%
Ronald W. Ellis	42	23	2	4.8%
Dan L. Hendricks	43	20	2	4.7%
Eddie Kenneally	43	16	2	4.7%
Sanna N. Hendriks	45	26	2	4.4%

Leading Trainers by Most Grade 1 Wins in 2005

Trainer	No. G1 Starts	No. G1 Wins
Robert J. Frankel	57	10
Todd A. Pletcher	51	10
Richard E. Dutrow Jr.	18	5
Claude R. McGaughey III	11	4
William I. Mott	17	4
Jeff Mullins	11	4
Nicholas P. Zito	38	4

Trainer	No. G1 Starts	No. G1 Wins
Ronald L. McAnally	14	3
Doug F. O'Neill	28	3
Bob Baffert	14	2
Frank L. Brothers	5	2
Julio C. Canani	9	2
Neil D. Drysdale	16	2
C. Beau Greely	7	2
Neil J. Howard	5	2
D. Wayne Lukas	19	2
Richard E. Mandella	12	2
H. Graham Motion	13	2
Timothy F. Ritchey	5	2
John A. Shirreffs	9	2

Leading Trainers by Most Grade 1 Winners in 2005

Trainer	No. G1 Starters	No. G1 Winners
Robert J. Frankel	32	9
Todd A. Pletcher	25	8
William I. Mott	10	4
Jeff Mullins	7	4
Nicholas P. Zito	15	4
Richard E. Dutrow Jr.	11	3
Claude R. McGaughey III	5	3
Doug F. O'Neill	18	3
Bob Baffert	11	2
Julio C. Canani	6	2
Neil D. Drysdale	10	2
Neil J. Howard	2	2
Richard E. Mandella	8	2
Ronald L. McAnally	7	2
John A. Shirreffs	4	2

Leading Trainers by Number of Wins in 2005

Trainer	No. Strs	No. Wnrs	No. Wins
Steven M. Asmussen	549	304	474
Scott A. Lake	442	236	417
Jerry Hollendorfer	323	170	281
Todd A. Pletcher	299	155	257
Cole Norman	243	148	242
Ralph Martinez	129	95	194
Art Sherman	222	128	193
W. Bret Calhoun	221	118	191
Jeffrey A. Radosevich	142	93	169
John Charles Zimmerman	155	93	169
Dale Baird	212	112	167
Chris J. Englehart	163	95	159
Doug F. O'Neill	288	123	158
Ronney W. Brown	250	109	155
Richard E. Dutrow Jr.	193	103	151
Rodney C. Faulkner	116	72	145
William I. Mott	169	80	138
Mark Shuman	186	79	138
Danny Pish	176	90	135
Wayne M. Catalano	156	93	131
Robert J. Frankel	195	90	128
John Rigattieri	82	59	127
Jeff Mullins	179	80	118
Gerald S. Bennett	98	64	117
Bruce N. Levine	121	65	116
Reid Gross	198	74	115
Michael V. Pino	155	75	114
Steven Miyadi	133	77	112
Thomas M. Amoss	164	79	109
John F. Martin	194	78	108
Bruce M. Kravets	135	65	106
Keith L. Bourgeois	132	60	104
Michael E. Gorham	104	52	101
Dale Capuano	137	62	101
H. Graham Motion	142	68	100
Henry Dominguez	128	67	98
Bernard S. Flint	105	51	97
A. Ferris Allen III	129	62	97
Steve Klesaris	96	62	96
Patricia Farro	116	55	96
Todd M. Beattie	73	52	95
Dale L. Romans	151	71	95
Bob Baffert	134	62	94
John G. Locke	143	62	94
Kim Hammond	98	53	93
Joseph Clark Faulkner	62	44	92
Charlton Baker	71	50	92
Jayne Vaders	76	47	92
Gary C. Contessa	160	67	92
David W. Geist	110	54	91

Most Wins for a Trainers on One Day in 2005

Wins	Trainer	Date	Track(s)
9	Steven Asmussen	12/3/2005	Aqu, Hou, LaD, Sun, Zia
8	Steven Asmussen	1/22/2005	FG, GP, Hou, OP
7	Ralph Martinez	3/26/2005	FP
6	Steven Asmussen	7/16/2005	AP, Bel, Cby, LaD, LS
	Scott A. Lake	4/16/2005	Aqu, GP, Lrl, Pha
	Cole Norman	3/11/2005	DeD, OP
	Art Sherman	8/12/2005	Bmf, Dmr
5	Dale Angelle	7/11/2005	EvD
	Steven Asmussen	2/12/2005	FG, Hou
	Steven Asmussen	11/19/2005	CD, Hou, LaD
	Steven Asmussen	2/18/2005	FG, Hou, OP, Sun
	Steven Asmussen	6/26/2005	AP, CD, LaD, LS
	Steven Asmussen	1/29/2005	FG, Hou, OP, Sun
	Steven Asmussen	12/22/2005	LaD, Sun
	Steven Asmussen	1/1/2005	Aqu, FG
	Scott A. Lake	3/20/2005	Lrl, Pha
	Scott A. Lake	7/10/2005	Bel, Cnl, Del, Mth
	Ralph Martinez	4/28/2005	FP, Ind
	Cole Norman	7/2/2005	LaD, LS
	Todd A. Pletcher	6/18/2005	Bel, Del, Mth
	Todd A. Pletcher	11/26/2005	Aqu, CRC
	Todd A. Pletcher	4/23/2005	GP, Haw, Kee
	Art Sherman	10/1/2005	BM, OSA

Most Wins for a Trainers on One Program in 2005

Wins	Trainer	Date	Track
7	Ralph Martinez	3/26/2005	FP
5	Dale Angelle	7/11/2005	Evd
	Cole Norman	3/11/2005	OP
	Art Sherman	8/12/2005	BMF
4	David C. Anderson	9/5/2005	Cls
	Steven M. Asmussen	1/1/2005	FG
	Steven M. Asmussen	11/25/2005	LaD
	Dale Baird	10/21/2005	Mnr
	Oscar S. Barrera Jr.	7/31/2005	FL
	Gerald S. Bennett	11/2/2005	GLD

Wins	Trainer	Date	Track
	Gerald S. Bennett	5/24/2005	GLD
	Ronney W. Brown	12/14/2005	CT
	Gary C. Contessa	1/21/2005	Aqu
	Ronald J. Dandy	8/23/2005	Suf
	Henry Dominguez	11/5/2005	Zia
	Chris J. Englehart	11/26/2005	FL
	Jerry Hollendorfer	5/18/2005	GG
	Doug Johnson	7/31/2005	GF
	Samuel J. Keyrouze	9/3/2005	NMP
	Michael A. Lecesse	6/3/2005	FL
	John G. Locke	10/15/2005	Ret
	Ralph Martinez	5/14/2005	FP
	Ralph Martinez	4/12/2005	FP
	Ralph Martinez	7/19/2005	FP
	Ralph Martinez	4/7/2005	FP

Wins	Trainer	Date	Track
	Ralph Martinez	4/8/2005	FP
	Tommie T. Morgan	6/5/2005	LS
	Cole Norman	3/26/2005	OP
	Doug F. O'Neill	1/2/2005	SA
	R. Gary Patrick	4/15/2005	Ind
	Joan Petrowski	6/10/2005	StP
	Edward Plesa Jr.	9/2/2005	Crc
	Todd A. Pletcher	11/26/2005	Aqu
	Timothy F. Ritchey	9/10/2005	Del
	Art Sherman	5/1/2005	BM
	Art Sherman	10/1/2005	BM
	David Van Winkle	9/1/2005	Cby
	Marcus J. Vitali	6/29/2005	Suf
	John Charles Zimmerman	12/27/2005	Pen
	John Charles Zimmerman	6/18/2005	Pen

Leading Trainers by Most Purses in a Year (1985-2005)

Trainer	Year	Purses	Leading Earner
Todd A. Pletcher	2005	$20,867,842	Flower Alley ($2,435,200)
Robert J. Frankel	2003	19,143,289	Medaglia d'Oro ($1,990,000)
D. Wayne Lukas	1988	17,842,358	Gulch ($1,360,840)
Robert J. Frankel	2002	17,750,340	Medaglia d'Oro ($2,245,000)
Todd A. Pletcher	2004	17,511,923	Ashado ($2,259,640)
D. Wayne Lukas	1987	17,502,110	Tejano ($1,177,189)
Bob Baffert	1999	16,842,332	Silverbulletday ($1,707,640)
D. Wayne Lukas	1989	16,103,998	Steinlen (GB) ($1,521,378)
D. Wayne Lukas	1996	15,967,609	Boston Harbor ($1,928,605)
D. Wayne Lukas	1991	15,953,757	Farma Way ($2,598,350)
Robert J. Frankel	2004	15,605,911	Ghostzapper ($2,590,000)
Robert J. Frankel	2001	14,607,446	Skimming ($1,330,000)
D. Wayne Lukas	1990	14,508,871	Criminal Type ($2,270,290)
Robert J. Frankel	2005	14,122,807	Intercontinental (GB) ($1,271,200)
Steven M. Asmussen	2004	14,003,445	Lady Tak ($439,412)
Steven M. Asmussen	2005	13,304,133	Summerly ($786,728)
D. Wayne Lukas	1995	12,852,843	Thunder Gulch ($2,644,080)
Bob Baffert	2001	12,761,034	Point Given ($3,350,000)
Bob Baffert	1998	12,608,670	Silver Charm ($2,296,506)
Todd A. Pletcher	2003	12,356,924	Balto Star ($907,500)
D. Wayne Lukas	1986	12,344,520	Lady's Secret ($1,871,053)
D. Wayne Lukas	1999	12,070,460	Cat Thief ($3,020,500)
Bob Baffert	2002	12,029,115	War Emblem ($3,125,000)
Bob Baffert	2000	11,793,355	Captain Steve ($1,882,276)
William I. Mott	1995	11,789,625	Cigar ($4,819,800)
Steven M. Asmussen	2003	11,727,910	Lady Tak ($675,350)
William I. Mott	1996	11,703,723	Cigar ($2,510,000)
Charles E. Whittingham	1989	11,402,231	Sunday Silence ($4,578,454)
D. Wayne Lukas	1985	11,155,188	Lady's Secret ($994,349)
D. Wayne Lukas	2000	10,492,317	Spain ($1,925,500)
D. Wayne Lukas	1997	10,351,397	Marlin ($1,521,600)
Steven M. Asmussen	2002	10,248,260	Easyfromthegitgo ($606,905)
Robert J. Frankel	2000	10,239,071	Chester House ($1,408,500)
D. Wayne Lukas	1992	10,061,240	Mountain Cat ($1,460,627)
William I. Mott	1998	10,012,899	Escena ($2,032,425)
Richard E. Mandella	2003	9,869,548	Pleasantly Perfect ($2,470,000)
Richard E. Dutrow Jr.	2005	9,798,106	Saint Liam ($3,183,600)
Doug F. O'Neil	2005	9,476,801	Stevie Wonderboy ($1,028,940)
William I. Mott	1997	9,474,680	Ajina ($979,175)
Bob Baffert	2003	9,442,281	Congaree ($1,608,000)
William I. Mott	2001	9,418,657	Hap ($919,070)
Charles E. Whittingham	1987	9,415,097	Ferdinand ($2,185,150)
William I. Mott	2005	9,355,603	Gun Salute ($630,550)
D. Wayne Lukas	1994	9,249,577	Tabasco Cat ($2,164,334)
Scott A. Lake	2003	9,163,599	Shake You Down ($814,640)
Scott A. Lake	2005	8,973,467	Don Six ($199,940)
Robert J. Frankel	1993	8,928,602	Bertrando ($2,217,800)
John C. Servis	2004	8,922,686	Smarty Jones ($7,563,535)
Bob Baffert	1997	8,867,128	Silver Charm ($1,638,750)
Charles E. Whittingham	1986	8,801,284	Estrapade ($1,184,800)
Todd A. Pletcher	2002	8,702,228	Left Bank ($626,146)
William I. Mott	2000	8,591,389	Snow Polina ($772,943)

Leading Jockeys of 2005

Jockeys have been described as pound for pound the strongest human athletes. Their task is formidable: balance by their toes on a half-ton of fury and navigate through a 35 mph stampede to the winner's circle. Often, they perform this feat seven or eight times a day. From the time they first show ability astride a horse, they are destined to pursue only this one calling—as long they keep their weight under 112 pounds or so.

Hundreds of men and women possess the agility and ability to ride professionally and make a living as a jockey. Some transcend their peers and become leaders of their circuits or the sport. A very, very few achieve greatness. Eddie Arcaro ruled the 1940s, and Bill Shoemaker was the little man with the gifted hands through the 1960s. He passed the crown to Laffit Pincay Jr., who set a new standard of accomplishment, with more than 9,500 victories.

For a decade beginning in the mid-1990s, Jerry Bailey and Pat Day were leaders in a very talented colony of North American jockeys. As they and their contemporaries began to contemplate life after racing, a new generation emerged to assume the top spots. For two years, 2003 and '04, John Velazquez led the THOROUGHBRED TIMES rankings, and Ramon Dominguez took the top spot in '05.

Leading Jockeys by Purses Won

North American Earnings Only

Year	Jockey	Wins	Purses
2005	John R. Velazquez	250	$20,799,923
2004	John R. Velazquez	335	22,250,261
2003	Jerry D. Bailey	206	23,354,960
2002	Jerry D. Bailey	213	19,271,814
2001	Jerry D. Bailey	227	19,015,720
2000	Pat Day	267	17,481,863
1999	Pat Day	254	18,094,045
1998	Pat Day	276	17,380,569
1997	Jerry D. Bailey	272	15,920,743
1996	Jerry D. Bailey	297	17,815,376
1995	Jerry D. Bailey	287	16,315,288
1994	Mike E. Smith	316	15,974,592
1993	Mike E. Smith	342	14,017,365
1992	Kent J. Desormeaux	364	14,196,390
1991	Chris J. McCarron	265	14,437,083
1990	Gary L. Stevens	283	13,881,198
1989	Jose A. Santos	285	13,838,389
1988	Jose A. Santos	369	14,856,214
1987	Jose A. Santos	305	12,405,075
1986	Jose A. Santos	328	11,330,067
1985	Laffit A. Pincay Jr.	289	13,315,049
1984	Chris J. McCarron	355	11,997,588
1983	Angel Cordero Jr.	362	10,116,697
1982	Angel Cordero Jr.	397	9,675,040
1981	Chris J. McCarron	326	8,399,712
1980	Chris J. McCarron	405	7,666,100

THOROUGHBRED TIMES Leading Jockeys of 2005

Rankings based on formula that gives equal weighting to three statistical categories for performance in 2005: 1) percent winner from mounts; 2) total number of wins; and 3) average earnings per mount. A minimum of 100 starters is required to be considered for inclusion. Statistics are for North America only and for racing in 2005.

Rank	Jockey	No. Mounts	No. Wins	Wins/ Mounts	No. SW	Stakes Wins/ Mounts	No. GSWs	Total Purses	Average Earnings/ Mount	Leading Earner	Earnings of Leading Earner
1	Ramon Dominguez	1,221	312	25.6%	25	2.1%	7	$10,767,955	$ 8,819	Better Talk Now	$ 827,640
2	Russell Baze	1,246	375	30.1%	29	2.3%	8	7,300,789	5,859	Lost in the Fog	754,500
3	John R. Velazquez	1,147	250	21.8%	65	5.7%	43	20,799,923	18,134	Flower Alley	1,916,000
4	Jerry Bailey	654	169	25.8%	62	9.5%	41	18,297,384	27,978	Saint Liam	2,733,600
5	Edgar Prado	1,460	299	20.5%	45	3.1%	27	18,615,366	12,750	Saint Liam	963,360
6	Rafael Bejarano	1,346	264	19.6%	30	2.2%	15	14,436,781	10,726	Sun King	727,500
7	Joe Bravo	895	201	22.5%	21	2.4%	1	6,466,087	7,225	Joey P.	260,788
8	Patrick Valenzuela	1,011	202	20.0%	27	2.7%	18	11,794,244	11,666	Lava Man	726,667
9	Jeremy Rose	813	178	21.9%	13	1.6%	4	6,972,553	8,576	Afleet Alex	2,080,000
10	Ken S. Tohill	817	222	27.2%	23	2.8%		3,735,024	4,572	Latenite Special	212,320
11	Garrett Gomez	1,295	245	18.9%	31	2.4%	15	14,221,321	10,982	Borrego	1,503,000
12	Mark Guidry	818	177	21.6%	16	2.0%	9	7,679,679	9,388	Perfect Drift	997,150
13	Alex Solis	729	153	21.0%	29	4.0%	19	9,647,743	13,234	Megahertz (GB)	780,000
14	Travis Dunkelberger	928	219	23.6%	11	1.2%		3,911,030	4,214	Cherokee's Boy	209,990
15	Javier Castellano	1,158	206	17.8%	31	2.7%	21	12,507,012	10,801	Bellamy Road	671,000
16	Eddie Castro	1,634	329	20.1%	40	2.5%	1	7,498,546	4,589	Pampered Princess	554,740
17	Shaun Bridgmohan	1,314	247	18.8%	18	1.4%	6	7,703,566	5,863	Miss Matched	235,654
18	Roman Chapa	951	202	21.2%	17	1.8%	1	4,473,072	4,704	Absent Friend	115,500
19	Harry Vega	982	222	22.6%	9	0.9%	1	3,784,633	3,854	Valley of the Gods	149,280
20	Robby Albarado	1,164	204	17.5%	32	2.8%	16	10,717,254	9,207	America Alive	652,992
21	Roberto Alvarado Jr.	756	160	21.2%	3	0.4%		3,837,631	5,076	Sierra Bella	160,362
22	Victor Espinoza	1,106	192	17.4%	33	3.0%	14	11,454,776	10,357	Super Frolic	450,000
23	Corey Nakatani	771	142	18.4%	20	2.6%	9	9,856,882	12,785	Relaxed Gesture (Ire)	1,059,920
24	Jose Lezcano	832	169	20.3%	13	1.6%	1	4,346,571	5,224	R Lady Joy	525,436
25	Richard Migliore	758	145	19.1%	13	1.7%	6	6,362,522	8,394	Nothing But Fun	281,700
26	Christopher DeCarlo	598	122	20.4%	22	3.7%	2	4,582,639	7,663	Capeside Lady	272,600
27	Manoel Cruz	1,678	322	19.2%	25	1.5%	2	6,813,500	4,060	In Summation	285,800
28	Gary Stevens	487	94	19.3%	28	5.8%	23	9,246,385	18,986	Rock Hard Ten	1,080,000
29	Justin Stein	699	161	23.0%	7	1.0%	2	2,538,597	3,632	Monashee	207,543
30	Corey Fraser	781	144	18.4%	6	0.8%	1	5,298,739	6,785	Top Ten List	292,854

Rank	Jockey	No. Mounts	No. Wins	Wins/ Mounts	No. SW	Stakes Wins/ Mounts	No. GSWs	Total Purses	Average Earnings/ Mount	Leading Earner	Earnings of Leading Earner
31	Carl James Woodley	734	163	22.2%	6	0.8%		2,711,743	3,694	J. D.'s Blue Bayou	$107,300
32	Todd Kabel	565	103	18.2%	20	3.5%	8	5,698,530	10,086	Lemon Maid	245,976
33	Chad Murphy	678	153	22.6%	5	0.7%		2,356,484	3,476	Discreet Hero	174,158
34	Mario Pino	963	174	18.1%	10	1.0%		4,572,433	4,748	Forest Park	182,590
35	Ryan Fogelsonger	854	164	19.2%	12	1.4%	1	3,678,601	4,307	Silmaril	165,300
36	Christopher A. Emigh	1,241	219	17.7%	13	1.1%		5,192,551	4,184	Fifteen Rounds	191,750
37	Roberto Gonzalez	1,084	203	18.7%	6	0.6%	1	4,019,520	3,708	Desert Boom	391,680
38	Glenn Corbett	911	194	21.3%	23	2.5%		2,929,669	3,216	Mingo Mohawk	154,226
39	Donnie Meche	281	65	23.1%	7	2.5%	1	1,373,748	4,889	Summerly	108,000
40	Chad Schvaneveldt	484	100	20.7%	10	2.1%		2,327,100	4,808	Thrilling Victory	73,200
41	Martin Pedroza	964	164	17.0%	8	0.8%	3	5,252,429	5,449	Amorama (Fr)	300,000
42	Horacio Karamanos	1,045	190	18.2%	10	1.0%		4,056,364	3,882	Bright Gold	205,626
43	Scott Spieth	1,333	308	23.1%	12	0.9%		3,557,868	2,669	Bryceslittlesecret	100,303
44	M. Clifton Berry	1,206	240	19.9%	15	1.2%		3,654,765	3,030	Waupaca	98,610
45	Eibar Coa	1,351	206	15.3%	16	1.2%	10	9,692,683	7,174	Eddington	602,200
46	Cornelio Velasquez	1,456	216	14.8%	26	1.8%	15	11,430,591	7,851	Pleasant Home	1,316,420
47	Stewart Elliott	860	143	16.6%	14	1.6%	2	5,393,661	6,272	Round Pond	445,000
48	James McAleney	668	112	16.8%	11	1.7%	4	5,462,209	8,177	Gold Strike	480,518
49	Emma-Jayne Wilson	1,132	180	15.9%	2	0.2%	1	6,300,928	5,566	Classic Stamp	211,491
50	Patrick Husbands	736	122	16.6%	8	1.1%		5,699,549	7,744	Mobil	289,157
51	Quincy Hamilton	1,269	278	21.9%	15	1.2%		3,359,151	2,647	Dontbotherknocking	180,000
52	Jamie Theriot	719	138	19.2%	11	1.5%		2,605,745	3,624	Shaky Town	123,900
53	Gerald Almodovar	1,153	233	20.2%		0.0%		3,297,039	2,860	Dinner Withawinner	46,200
54	Pedro V. Alvarado	491	108	22.0%	7	1.4%	2	1,614,620	3,288	Alabama Rain	265,762
55	Jesus Lopez Castanon	1,268	227	17.9%	6	0.5%	1	3,985,109	3,143	Artemus Sunrise	88,220
56	John R. Davila Jr.	616	153	24.8%	1	0.2%		1,717,548	2,788	Special Jet	49,140
57	Aaron Gryder	744	122	16.4%	18	2.4%	4	4,875,021	6,552	Umpateedle	211,000
58	Jose Caraballo	610	106	17.4%	6	1.0%		2,963,404	4,858	Barbaro	99,000
59	Anthony Black	654	126	19.3%	3	0.5%		2,212,856	3,384	Avery Hall	94,500
60	Erick Rodriguez	581	113	19.5%	2	0.3%		1,991,278	3,427	Dale's Prospect	52,060
61	Angela Owens	32	10	31.3%		0.0%		135,912	4,247	Quote Me Later	66,390
62	Pat Day	147	26	17.7%	3	2.0%	1	1,747,323	11,887	Two Trail Sioux	404,600
63	Steve Bourque	870	158	18.2%	7	0.8%		2,772,318	3,187	Nitro Chip	175,680
64	Dennis Carr	820	145	17.7%	3	0.4%		2,794,977	3,409	Stellar Magic	76,450
65	John Jacinto	1,204	194	16.1%	13	1.1%	1	4,208,092	3,495	Dawn of War	310,000
66	Guy Smith	1,107	193	17.4%	8	0.7%		3,291,236	2,973	Indigo Girl	89,500
67	Dyn Panell	849	181	21.3%	5	0.6%		2,151,645	2,534	Jini's Jet	95,860
68	Kent Desormeaux	483	75	15.5%	15	3.1%	4	4,644,416	9,616	Leave Me Alone	410,800
69	Rickey Walcott	639	140	21.9%	13	2.0%		1,685,234	2,637	Wild Bender	104,185
70	Quincy Welch	670	158	23.6%	6	0.9%		1,617,135	2,414	Cool Bender	60,684
71	Alfredo Juarez Jr.	722	135	18.7%	13	1.8%		2,150,577	2,979	Romeos Wilson	119,340
72	Jorge Chavez	1,037	150	14.5%	10	1.0%	3	5,617,255	5,417	Musique Toujours	550,000
73	Martin Garcia	204	46	22.6%		0.0%		645,493	3,164	Abuse of Power	22,880
74	David Lopez	1,036	177	17.1%		0.0%		3,085,585	2,978	Kool Suggestion	63,118
75	Eric Camacho	970	164	16.9%	1	0.1%		2,938,913	3,030	Seven Talents	98,010
76	Duane Lee Sterling	53	12	22.6%	1	1.9%		185,222	3,495	Matchstick Man	26,875
77	Eusebio Razo Jr.	990	147	14.9%	8	0.8%	3	4,322,432	4,366	Lord of the Game	515,620
78	Jon Court	974	135	13.9%	19	2.0%	7	7,247,741	7,441	Valentine Dancer	539,120
79	Lonnie Meche	683	115	16.8%	9	1.3%		2,317,691	3,393	Lac Laronge	106,800
80	Norberto Arroyo Jr.	844	122	14.5%	11	1.3%	2	5,218,319	6,183	Bank Audit	265,890
81	Jesse M. Campbell	1,148	175	15.2%	8	0.7%	1	4,038,651	3,518	High Expectations	151,440
82	James Graham	1,303	191	14.7%	6	0.5%		5,006,267	3,842	Home of Stars	156,284
83	Michael J. Luzzi	1,015	142	14.0%	7	0.7%	1	5,978,805	5,890	Seeking the Ante	262,500
84	David Clark	586	87	14.9%	12	2.1%	2	3,908,439	6,670	Edenwold	226,229
85	Bobby J. Walker Jr.	404	76	18.8%	8	2.0%		1,274,534	3,155	Cobra Lady	151,411
86	Thomas Clifton	812	181	22.3%	2	0.3%		1,783,690	2,197	Nittany Express	78,471
87	Brian Joseph Hernandez	586	108	18.4%	1	0.2%		1,700,020	2,901	Roar On Tour	116,462
88	Luis Garcia	1,267	201	15.9%	1	0.1%		3,729,914	2,944	Skycrossing	94,500
89	Rex A. Stokes III	1,108	196	17.7%	4	0.4%	1	2,792,322	2,520	Lady Grace	185,926
90	Elvis Joseph Perrodin	490	76	15.5%	15	3.1%		2,304,027	4,702	The Beter Man Can	220,100
91	Brian Dale Peck	193	35	18.1%	2	1.0%		721,287	3,737	One Way Flight	76,965
92	Jose Santos	834	113	13.6%	11	1.3%	4	6,129,799	7,350	Riskaverse	450,723
93	Jason P. Lumpkins	640	99	15.5%	1	0.2%	1	2,407,263	3,761	Overpass	71,820
94	Dana G. Whitney	1,311	218	16.6%	1	0.1%		3,362,697	2,565	Gin and Sin	55,375
95	Kristin Troxell	17	3	17.7%		0.0%		75,450	4,438	Della Street	63,480
96	Steve D. Hamilton	921	137	14.9%	9	1.0%		3,175,680	3,448	Malibu Moonshine	136,760
97	Joseph J. Badamo	417	81	19.4%	4	1.0%		1,148,187	2,753	Carlow	118,050
98	Terry J. Thompson	668	106	15.9%	8	1.2%		2,203,795	3,299	Swede	78,200
99	Frank T. Alvarado	1,161	170	14.6%	5	0.4%		3,816,295	3,287	Penny Ante	120,225
100	Jose Velez Jr.	453	66	14.6%	11	2.4%	3	2,603,371	5,747	Smart N Classy	193,565

Leading Jockeys by Earnings in 2005

Jockey	No. Mounts	No. Wins	Total Purses
John R. Velazquez	1,147	250	$20,799,923
Edgar Prado	1,460	299	18,615,366
Jerry Bailey	654	169	18,297,384
Rafael Bejarano	1,346	264	14,436,781
Garrett Gomez	1,295	245	14,221,321
Javier Castellano	1,158	206	12,507,012
Patrick Valenzuela	1,011	202	11,794,244
Victor Espinoza	1,106	192	11,454,776
Cornelio Velasquez	1,456	216	11,430,591
Ramon Dominguez	1,221	312	10,767,955
Robby Albarado	1,164	204	10,717,254
Corey Nakatani	771	142	9,856,882
Eibar Coa	1,351	206	9,692,683
Alex Solis	729	153	9,647,743
Gary Stevens	487	94	9,246,385
Shaun Bridgmohan	1,314	247	7,703,566
Mark Guidry	818	177	7,679,679
Tyler Baze	1,105	138	7,514,326
Eddie Castro	1,634	329	7,498,546
Russell Baze	1,246	375	7,300,789
Jon Court	974	135	7,247,741
Jeremy Rose	813	178	6,972,553
Manoel Cruz	1,678	322	6,813,500
Mike Smith	625	81	6,520,617
Joe Bravo	895	201	6,466,087
Richard Migliore	758	145	6,362,522
Emma-Jayne Wilson	1,132	180	6,300,928
Rene Douglas	807	105	6,292,725
Jose Santos	834	113	6,129,799
Michael Luzzi	1,015	142	5,978,805
Patrick Husbands	736	122	5,699,549
Todd Kabel	565	103	5,698,530
Jorge Chavez	1,037	150	5,617,255
James McAleney	668	112	5,462,209
Stewart Elliott	860	143	5,393,661
Corey Fraser	781	144	5,298,739
Martin Pedroza	964	164	5,252,429
Norberto Arroyo Jr.	844	122	5,218,319
Christopher Emigh	1,241	219	5,192,551
Channing Hill	1,157	135	5,040,761
James Graham	1,303	191	5,006,267

Leading Jockeys by Average Earnings per Starter in 2005
(Minimum of 10 Mounts)

Jockey	No. Mounts	No. Wins	Average Earnings per Starter
Jerry Bailey	654	169	$27,978
Lanfranco Dettori	12	0	22,744
Gary Stevens	487	94	18,986
John Velazquez	1,147	250	18,134
Kieren Fallon	77	7	17,460
Alex Solis	729	153	13,234
Corey Nakatani	771	142	12,785
Edgar Prado	1,460	299	12,750
Pat Day	147	26	11,887
Patrick Valenzuela	1,011	202	11,666
Garrett Gomez	1,295	245	10,982
Javier Castellano	1,158	206	10,801
Rafael Bejarano	1,346	264	10,726
Mike Smith	625	81	10,433
Victor Espinoza	1,106	192	10,357
Craig Perret	50	7	$10,197
Todd Kabel	565	103	10,086
Kent Desormeaux	483	75	9,616
Mark Guidry	818	177	9,388
Robby Albarado	1,164	204	9,207
Ramon Dominguez	1,221	312	8,819
Jeremy Rose	813	178	8,576
Richard Migliore	758	145	8,394
James McAleney	668	112	8,177
Cornelio Velasquez	1,456	216	7,851
Rene Douglas	807	105	7,798
Patrick Husbands	736	122	7,744
Christopher DeCarlo	598	122	7,663
Jon Court	974	135	7,441
Jose Santos	834	113	7,350
Jose Valdivia Jr.	552	64	7,270
Brice Blanc	548	58	7,235
Joe Bravo	895	201	7,225
David Flores	647	80	7,217
Eibar Coa	1,351	206	7,174
Tyler Baze	1,105	138	6,800
Corey Fraser	781	144	6,785
David Clark	586	87	6,670
Robert Landry	458	52	6,557
Aaron Gryder	744	122	6,552
Emile Ramsammy	661	87	6,344
Stewart Elliott	860	143	6,272
Jono C. Jones	540	58	6,189
Norberto Arroyo Jr.	844	122	6,183

Leading Jockeys by Number of Stakes Wins in 2005

Jockey	No. Mounts	No. Wins	No. Stakes Wins
John R. Velazquez	1,147	250	65
Jerry Bailey	654	169	62
Edgar Prado	1,460	299	45
Eddie Castro	1,634	329	40
Victor Espinoza	1,106	192	33
Robby Albarado	1,164	204	32
Garrett Gomez	1,295	245	31
Javier Castellano	1,158	206	31
Rafael Bejarano	1,346	264	30
Russell Baze	1,246	375	29
Alex Solis	729	153	29
Gary Stevens	487	94	28
Patrick Valenzuela	1,011	202	27
Cornelio Velasquez	1,456	216	26
Ramon Dominguez	1,221	312	25
Manoel Cruz	1,678	322	25
Ken Tohill	817	222	23
Glenn Corbett	911	194	23
Christopher DeCarlo	598	122	22
Joe Bravo	895	201	21
Corey Nakatani	771	142	20
Todd Kabel	565	103	20
Luis Quinonez	1,233	171	19
Jon Court	974	135	19
Aaron Gryder	744	122	18
Shaun Bridgmohan	1,314	247	18
Wilson Omar Dieguez	933	166	17
Roman Chapa	951	202	17
Eibar Coa	1,351	206	16
Mark Guidry	818	177	16

Jockey	No. Mounts	No. Wins	No. Stakes Wins
Rene Douglas	807	105	16
Kent Desormeaux	483	75	15
Elvis Joseph Perrodin	490	76	15
M. Clifton Berry	1,206	240	15
Scott A. Stevens	939	150	15
Brice Blanc	548	58	15
Tyler Baze	1,105	138	15
Quincy Hamilton	1,269	278	15
Stewart Elliott	860	143	14
Gerard Melancon	1,191	156	14
Miguel Luis Hernandez	1,017	170	13
Richard Migliore	758	145	13
Christopher A. Emigh	1,241	219	13
Rickey Walcott	639	140	13
John Jacinto	1,204	194	13
Jeremy Rose	813	178	13
Alfredo J. Juarez Jr.	722	135	13
Jorge Martin Bourdieu	555	72	13
Jose Lezcano	832	169	13
Pablo Fragoso	988	92	13

Leading Jockeys by Number of Stakes Winners in 2005

Jockey	Stakes Mounts	Stakes Wnrs
Jerry D. Bailey	159	46
John R. Velazquez	168	46
Edgar S. Prado	160	39
Victor Espinoza	120	31
Javier Castellano	140	29
Rafael Bejarano	130	28
Eddie Castro	94	27
Garrett K. Gomez	118	25
Robby Albarado	97	24
Ramon A. Dominguez	101	23
Patrick A. Valenzuela	130	23
Alex O. Solis	99	22
Gary L. Stevens	115	21
Cornelio H. Velasquez	133	20
Joe Bravo	103	19
Christopher P. DeCarlo	71	19
Jon Kenton Court	89	18
Manoel R. Cruz	67	18
Corey S. Nakatani	95	18
Glenn W. Corbett	56	17
Shaun Bridgmohan	99	16
Russell A. Baze	37	15
Eibar Coa	124	15
Aaron T. Gryder	68	15
Todd Kabel	59	15
Tyler Baze	91	14
Roman Chapa	55	14
Wilson Omar Dieguez	54	14
Rene R. Douglas	78	14
Ken S. Tohill	48	14
M. Clifton Berry	51	13
Brice Blanc	64	13
Mark Guidry	62	13
Pablo Fragoso	56	12
John Jacinto	61	12
Luis S. Quinonez	60	12
Scott A. Stevens	65	12
Kent J. Desormeaux	59	11
Stewart Elliott	78	11
Quincy Hamilton	49	11
Miguel Luis Hernandez	48	11
Richard Migliore	79	11
Jose A. Santos	98	11
Jorge F. Chavez	81	10
Christopher A. Emigh	42	10
Ryan Fogelsonger	52	10
Alfredo J. Juarez Jr.	51	10
James McAleney	45	10
Mike E. Smith	95	10
Jamie Theriot	46	10

Leading Jockeys by Percent of Stakes Wins from Mounts in 2005
(Minimum of 10 Mounts)

Jockey	No. Mounts	No. Wins	No. Stakes Wins	Stakes Wins/ Mounts
Anrella Villeseche	12	8	2	16.7%
Nathan Condie	37	19	5	13.5%
Zevi Ashlock	10	1	1	10.0%
Jerry Bailey	654	169	62	9.5%
Ty Dangerfield	11	4	1	9.1%
Angelle Wilson	79	13	6	7.6%
Danielle Beischer	29	12	2	6.9%
Scott Sterr	103	23	7	6.8%
Sean Williams	74	16	5	6.8%
Janine Stianson	110	23	7	6.4%
Craig Perret	50	7	3	6.0%
Brooke Mellish	121	25	7	5.8%
Gary Stevens	487	94	28	5.8%
John Velazquez	1,147	250	65	5.7%
Cameron Colledge	57	14	3	5.3%
Daniel Cardenas	20	1	1	5.0%
Shannon Wippert	43	7	2	4.7%
Melissa Marshall	22	4	1	4.6%
Serge Rocheleau	209	43	9	4.3%
Alex O. Solis	729	153	29	4.0%
Christopher DeCarlo	598	122	22	3.7%
Todd Kabel	565	103	20	3.5%
Mark Allen Boag	61	10	2	3.3%
Scot A. Schindler	95	15	3	3.2%
Cliff Miyashiro	64	5	2	3.1%
Kent Desormeaux	483	75	15	3.1%
Edgar Prado	1,460	299	45	3.1%
Elvis J. Perrodin	490	76	15	3.1%
Jackie Smith	99	13	3	3.0%
Haniff Emamalie	167	27	5	3.0%
Victor Espinoza	1,106	192	33	3.0%
Jimmy Jordan	35	7	1	2.9%
Ken S. Tohill	817	222	23	2.8%
Tom G. Turner	215	27	6	2.8%
Robby Albarado	1,164	204	32	2.8%

Leading Jockeys by Number of Graded Stakes Wins in 2005

Jockey	No. Mounts	No. Wins	No. Graded Stakes Wins	Graded Wins/ Mounts
John R. Velazquez	1,147	250	43	3.8%
Jerry Bailey	654	169	41	6.3%
Edgar Prado	1,460	299	27	1.9%
Gary Stevens	487	94	23	4.7%

Jockey	No. Mounts	No. Wins	No. Graded Stakes Wins	Graded Wins/ Mounts
Javier Castellano	1,158	206	21	1.8%
Alex Solis	729	153	19	2.6%
Patrick Valenzuela	1,011	202	18	1.8%
Robby Albarado	1,164	204	16	1.4%
Cornelio Velasquez	1,456	216	15	1.0%
Garrett Gomez	1,295	245	15	1.2%
Rafael Bejarano	1,346	264	15	1.1%
Victor Espinoza	1,106	192	14	1.3%
Eibar Coa	1,351	206	10	0.7%
Corey Nakatani	771	142	9	1.2%
Mark Guidry	818	177	9	1.1%
Russell Baze	1,246	375	8	0.6%
Todd Kabel	565	103	8	1.4%
Jon Court	974	135	7	0.7%
Rene Douglas	807	105	7	0.9%
David Flores	647	80	7	1.1%
Tyler Baze	1,105	138	7	0.6%
Ramon Dominguez	1,221	312	7	0.6%
Shaun Bridgmohan	1,314	247	6	0.5%
Brice Blanc	548	58	6	1.1%
Richard Migliore	758	145	6	0.8%
Mike Smith	625	81	5	0.8%
Jono C. Jones	540	58	5	0.9%
Jeremy Rose	813	178	4	0.5%
James McAleney	668	112	4	0.6%
Aaron Gryder	744	122	4	0.5%
Jose Santos	834	113	4	0.5%
Kent Desormeaux	483	75	4	0.8%

Leading Jockeys by Number of Graded Stakes Winners in 2005

Jockey	No. mounts	No. wins	No. graded stakes wins	Pct. graded wins/ mounts
John Velazquez	1,147	250	43	3.8%
Jerry Bailey	654	169	41	6.3%
Edgar Prado	1,460	299	27	1.9%
Gary Stevens	487	94	23	4.7%
Javier Castellano	1,158	206	21	1.8%
Alex Solis	729	153	19	2.6%
Patrick Valenzuela	1,011	202	18	1.8%
Robby Albarado	1,164	204	16	1.4%
Cornelio Velasquez	1,456	216	15	1.0%
Garrett Gomez	1,295	245	15	1.2%
Rafael Bejarano	1,346	264	15	1.1%
Victor Espinoza	1,106	192	14	1.3%
Eibar Coa	1,351	206	10	0.7%
Corey Nakatani	771	142	9	1.2%
Mark Guidry	818	177	9	1.1%
Russell Baze	1,246	375	8	0.6%
Todd Kabel	565	103	8	1.4%
Jon Court	974	135	7	0.7%
Rene Douglas	807	105	7	0.9%
David Flores	647	80	7	1.1%
Tyler Baze	1,105	138	7	0.6%
Ramon Dominguez	1,221	312	7	0.6%
Shaun Bridgmohan	1,314	247	6	0.5%
Brice Blanc	548	58	6	1.1%
Richard Migliore	758	145	6	0.8%
Mike Smith	625	81	5	0.8%
Jono C. Jones	540	58	5	0.9%
Jeremy Rose	813	178	4	0.5%

Jockey	No. mounts	No. wins	No. graded stakes wins	Pct. graded wins/ mounts
James McAleney	668	112	4	0.6%
Aaron Gryder	744	122	4	0.5%
Jose Santos	834	113	4	0.5%
Kent Desormeaux	483	75	4	0.8%
Jorge Chavez	1,037	150	3	0.3%
Martin Pedroza	964	164	3	0.3%
Eusebio Razo Jr.	990	147	3	0.3%
Robert Landry	458	52	3	0.7%
Jose Velez Jr.	453	66	3	0.7%

Leading Jockeys by Most Grade 1 Wins in 2005

Jockey	No. G1 Starts	No. G1 Wins
Jerry D. Bailey	51	13
John R. Velazquez	57	11
Edgar S. Prado	53	9
Garrett K. Gomez	29	7
Alex O. Solis	33	6
Corey S. Nakatani	35	5
Gary L. Stevens	43	5
Rafael Bejarano	32	4
Javier Castellano	43	4
Patrick A. Valenzuela	41	4
Robby Albarado	18	2
Tyler Baze	22	2
Ramon A. Dominguez	13	2
Jeremy Rose	6	2
Mike E. Smith	20	2
Cornelio H. Velasquez	21	2

Leading Jockeys by Most Grade 1 Stakes Winners in 2005

Jockey	No. G1 Starters	No. G1 Winners
Jerry D. Bailey	36	11
John R. Velazquez	36	9
Garrett K. Gomez	24	6
Edgar S. Prado	36	6
Corey S. Nakatani	22	5
Alex O. Solis	24	5
Gary L. Stevens	27	5
Rafael Bejarano	24	4
Javier Castellano	29	4
Patrick A. Valenzuela	32	4
Robby Albarado	15	2
Tyler Baze	17	2
Mike E. Smith	16	2
Cornelio H. Velasquez	12	2

Leading Jockeys by Number of Wins in 2005

Jockey	No. Mounts	No. Wnrs	No. Wins
Russell Baze	1,246	276	375
Rodney Prescott	2,056	278	340
Eddie Castro	1,634	255	329
Manoel Cruz	1,678	246	322
Ramon Dominguez	1,221	272	312
Scott Spieth	1,333	205	308
Edgar Prado	1,460	241	299

Jockey	No. Mounts	No. Wnrs	No. Wins
T. D. Houghton	1,537	215	279
Quincy Hamilton	1,269	220	278
Rafael Bejarano	1,346	239	264
John Velazquez	1,147	196	250
Shaun Bridgmohan	1,314	214	247
Garrett Gomez	1,295	203	245
M. Clifton Berry	1,206	172	240
Gerald Almodovar	1,153	185	233
Deshawn Parker	1,469	166	230
Edgar Paucar	1,307	171	228
Jesus Lopez Castanon	1,268	195	227
Harry Vega	982	170	222
Ken S. Tohill	817	168	222
Christopher A. Emigh	1,241	171	219
Travis Dunkelberger	928	171	219
Dana G. Whitney	1,311	182	218
Cornelio Velasquez	1,456	178	216
Winston Thompson	1,201	150	212
Javier Castellano	1,158	166	206
Eibar Coa	1,351	174	206
Robby Albarado	1,164	164	204
Roberto Gonzalez	1,084	156	203
Patrick Valenzuela	1,011	174	202
Roman Chapa	951	175	202
Joe Bravo	895	169	201
Luis Garcia	1,267	156	201
Rex A. Stokes III	1,108	137	196
Perry Wayne Ouzts	1,481	162	195
Glenn Corbett	911	143	194
John Jacinto	1,204	159	194
Guy Smith	1,107	151	193
Victor Espinoza	1,106	154	192
James Graham	1,303	159	191
Horacio Karamanos	1,045	151	190
Thomas Pompell	1,239	148	190
Larry Taylor	995	150	188
Hector L. Rosario Jr.	1,100	149	185
Dyn Panell	849	110	181
Thomas Clifton	812	126	181

Leading Jockeys by Number of Winners in 2005

Jockey	No. Mounts	No. Wnrs
Rodney Prescott	2,056	278
Russell Baze	1,246	276
Ramon Dominguez	1,221	272
Eddie Castro	1,634	255
Manoel Cruz	1,678	246
Edgar Prado	1,460	241
Rafael Bejarano	1,346	239
Quincy Hamilton	1,269	220
T. D. Houghton	1,537	215
Shaun Bridgmohan	1,314	214
Scott Spieth	1,333	205
Garrett Gomez	1,295	203
John Velazquez	1,147	196
Jesus Lopez Castanon	1,268	195
Gerald Almodovar	1,153	185
Dana G. Whitney	1,311	182
Cornelio Velasquez	1,456	178
Roman Chapa	951	175
Eibar Coa	1,351	174
Patrick Valenzuela	1,011	174
M. Clifton Berry	1,206	172
Christopher A. Emigh	1,241	171
Travis Dunkelberger	928	171
Edgar Paucar	1,307	171
Harry Vega	982	170
Joe Bravo	895	169
Ken Tohill	817	168
Deshawn Parker	1,469	166
Javier Castellano	1,158	166
Robby Albarado	1,164	164
Perry Wayne Ouzts	1,481	162
James Graham	1,303	159
John Jacinto	1,204	159
Luis Garcia	1,267	156
Roberto Gonzalez	1,084	156
Mark Guidry	818	154
Victor Espinoza	1,106	154
Guy Smith	1,107	151
Horacio Karamanos	1,045	151
Larry Taylor	995	150
Winston Albert Thompson	1,201	150
Emma-Jayne Wilson	1,132	150
Hector L. Rosario Jr.	1,100	149
Thomas Pompell	1,239	148

Leading Jockeys by Career Purses

North American Earnings Through June 11, 2006

Jockey	Career Purses
Jerry D. Bailey	$311,356,757
Pat Day	297,912,019
Chris J. McCarron	257,717,924
Gary L. Stevens	237,644,302
Alex O. Solis	193,710,797 +
Eddie J. Delahoussaye	192,469,869
Jose A. Santos	183,215,956 +
Kent J. Desormeaux	182,899,251 +
Mike E. Smith	176,776,515 +
Edgar S. Prado	175,300,962 +
John R. Velazquez	167,165,955 +
Corey S. Nakatani	164,838,394 +
Jorge F. Chavez	148,661,728 +
Patrick A. Valenzuela	145,910,026 +
Richard Migliore	142,178,697 +
Russell A. Baze	141,714,461 +
Shane J. Sellers	122,431,794
Robbie G. Davis	115,737,627
David Flores	109,672,200 +
Robby Albarado	106,440,002 +
Craig Perret	104,802,090
Jorge Velasquez	98,538,544
Victor Espinoza	95,936,167 +
Mario G. Pino	93,600,231 +
Chris W. Antley	92,277,031
Mark Guidry	91,566,532 +
Eddie Maple	91,097,360
Julie A. Krone	90,125,644
Aaron T. Gryder	89,792,620 +
Todd Kabel	89,433,676 +
Joe Bravo	89,319,906 +
Jean-Luc Samyn	88,008,106 +
Rene R. Douglas	84,376,544 +
Eibar Coa	80,199,369 +
Calvin H. Borel	77,951,326 +
Michael J. Luzzi	77,175,727 +
Rick Wilson	76,136,941
Sandy Hawley	76,009,279
Randy P. Romero	74,656,494

\+ Active through June 11, 2006

Leading Jockeys by Career Wins

Jockey	Career Wins
1. Laffit Pincay Jr.	9,530
2. Russell Baze	9,310 +
3. Bill Shoemaker	8,833
4. Pat Day	8,803
5. David Gall	7,396
6. Chris McCarron	7,141
7. Angel Cordero Jr.	7,057
8. Jorge Velasquez	6,795
9. Sandy Hawley	6,449
10. Larry Snyder	6,388
11. Eddie Delahoussaye	6,384
12. Earlie Fires	6,353 +
13. Carl Gambardella	6,349
14. John Longden	6,032
15. Jerry Bailey	5,900
16. Mario Pino	5,672 +
17. Edgar Prado	5,599 +
18. Jacinto Vasquez	5,231
19. Ronnie Ardoin	5,225
20. Gary Stevens	5,005
21. Anthony Black	5,000 +
22. Robert Colton	4,976
23. Rick Wilson	4,934
24. Perry Ouzts	4,904 +
25. Rudy Baez	4,875
26. Mark Guidry	4,861 +
27. Eddie Arcaro	4,779
28. Kent Desormeaux	4,719 +
29. Timothy Doocy	4,599 +
30. Don Brumfield	4,573
31. Mike Smith	4,534 +
32. Steve Brooks	4,451
33. Craig Perret	4,413 +
34. Eddie Maple	4,398
35. Walter Blum	4,382
36. Alex Solis	4,372 +
37. Randy Romero	4,294
38. Jeff Lloyd	4,276
39. Bill Hartack	4,272
40. Ray Sibille	4,264
41. Jorge Chavez	4,148 +
42. Richard Migliore	4,139 +
43. Avelino Gomez	4,081
44. Shane Sellers	4,070
45. Roberto M. Gonzalez	4,029
46. Jose Santos	4,027 +
47. R. D. Williams	4,006
48. Hugo Dittfach	4,000
49. Mike Rowland	3,996
50. Phil Grove	3,991

+Active jockeys; statistics through May 2, 2006

Female Jockeys With More Than 1,000 Wins

	Wins	Active Years
Julie Krone	3,704	1981-2004
Patti Cooksey	2,136	1979-2004
Cindy Noll Murphy	1,831	1990-2006
Jill Jellison	1,771	1982-2005
Vicky Aragon Baze	1,769	1985-2001
Dodie Cartier Duys	1,760	1983-2004
Rosemary Homeister Jr.	1,727	1977-2004
Vicki Warhol	1,616	1979-2006
Tammi Piermarini	1,503	1985-2006
Lori Wydick	1,429	1984-2006
Jerri Elizabeth Nichols	1,422	1988-2006
Lillian Kuykendall	1,419	1980-2001
Mary Randall Doser	1,367	1985-2006
Donna Barton Brothers	1,130	1987-1998
Cynthia Herman Medina	1,116	1986-2004
Diane Nelson	1,094	1986-2006
Patti Barton	1,085	1969-1984
Sandi Lee Gann	1,085	1987-2006

Through May 2, 2006

Most Wins by a Jockey on One Day in 2005

Wins	Jockey	Date	Track(s)
9	Eddie Castro	6/4/2005	Crc
7	Justin Stein	11/6/2005	Hst
	Ramsey Zimmerman	3/26/2005	FP
6	M. Clifton Berry	8/5/2005	RP
	Joe Bravo	9/18/2005	Mth
	Eddie Castro	10/17/2005	Crc
	Manoel R. Cruz	11/27/2005	Crc
	Manoel R. Cruz	9/3/2005	Crc
	T. D. Houghton	5/24/2005	GLD
	T. D. Houghton	11/2/2005	GLD
	Edgar Paucar	9/10/2005	Nmp
	Rodney A. Prescott	4/16/2005	Ind, RD
	Rodney A. Prescott	4/23/2005	Ind, RD
	Scott Spieth	4/8/2005	Mnr, Tdn
	Justin Stein	7/15/2005	Hst
	Winston Albert Thompson	6/18/2005	Suf
	Robert Dean Williams	7/8/2005	LnN
	Robert Dean Williams	8/6/2005	Cls

Most Wins by a Jockey on One Program in 2005

Wins	Jockey	Date	Track
9	Eddie Castro	6/4/2005	Crc
7	Justin Stein	11/6/2005	Hst
	Ramsey Zimmerman	3/26/2005	FP
6	M. Clifton Berry	8/5/2005	RP
	Joe Bravo	9/18/2005	Mth
	Eddie Castro	10/17/2005	Crc
	Manoel R. Cruz	9/3/2005	Crc
	Manoel R. Cruz	11/27/2005	Crc
	T. D. Houghton	11/2/2005	GLD
	T. D. Houghton	5/24/2005	GLD
	Edgar Paucar	9/10/2005	Nmp
	Justin Stein	7/15/2005	Hst
	Winston Albert Thompson	6/18/2005	Suf
	Robert Dean Williams	7/8/2005	LnN
	Robert Dean Williams	8/6/2005	Cls

Most Consecutive Wins by Jockey in 2005

Wins	Jockey	Date(s)	Track(s)
8	John R. Velazquez	4/22-4/24/2005	Kee, Haw
	Tho Nguyen	11/14-11/20/2005	Mnr
7	Scott Spieth	10/15-10/16/2005	Tdn, Mnr
	Justin Stein	11/6-11/12/2005	Hst
6	Scott Spieth	10/31-11/2/2005	Tdn
	Scott Spieth	1/29-2/5/2005	Mnr
	Jerry D. Bailey	9/17-9/22/2005	Bel
	Larry Taylor	8/18-8/19/2005	Ret
	Agapito Delgadillo	8/27-9/1/2005	LA
	Eddie Castro	6/4-6/5/2005	Crc
	Edgar Paucar	9/10-9/11/2005	Nmp
	Anrella J. Villeseche	7/31-10/23/2005	Kin, Kam
	Rex A. Stokes, III	11/26-11/28/2005	Mnr
	Thomas Clifton	4/14-4/15/2005	Pen
	Ramon A. Dominguez	10/31-11/1/2005	Del

Notable Names in Racing's Past

(Names of Racing Hall of Fame members are in boldface italics.)

As much as great horses are central to the sport, Thoroughbred racing and breeding would not exist without the important individuals of the past who worked to perfect the breed or sport and who performed with distinction within the industry. Here are outstanding individuals from racing's history, with members of the Racing Hall of Fame noted in boldface italics.

Adams, Frank D. "Dooley," 1927-2004. Jockey, trainer. Leading steeplechase jockey 1946, '49-'55; inducted into Racing Hall of Fame in '70. Rode 337 winners, including Neji, Elkridge, Oedipus, Refugio, and Floating Isle. Trained Subversive Chick.

Adams, John H., 1914-'95. Jockey, trainer. Leading jockey 1937, '42, '43; inducted into Racing Hall of Fame in '65; George Woolf Memorial Jockey Award in '56. Rode 3,270 winners, including *Kayak II, Hasty Road. Trained J. O. Tobin. Won 1954 Preakness Stakes aboard Hasty Road.

Aga Khan III, Sultan Sir Mahomed Shah, 1877-1957. Ismaili Muslim leader. Owner of Gilltown, Sheshoon, Ballymany, Sallymount, and Ongar Studs in Ireland; Haras de la Coquenne, Haras de Marly-la-Ville, Haras de Saint-Crespin in France. Leading owner in England 13 times; leading breeder in England eight times. Bred *Bahram, *Nasrullah, *Tulyar, *Mahmoud, *Alibhai, *Khaled, *Masaka; owned Mumtaz Mahal, *Blenheim II. Grandfather of current Aga Khan.

Alexander, Alexander J., 1824-1902. Iron works, farming. Owner of Woodburn Stud, Kentucky. Stood leading sire Lexington. Leading breeder. Bred Duke of Magenta, Spendthrift, Tom Bowling, Tom Ochiltree, Harry Bassett, Joe Daniels, Fellowcraft, Fonso, etc. Brother of Robert A. Alexander.

Alexander, Robert A., 1819-'67. Iron works, farming. Founder of Woodburn Stud, Kentucky. Stood leading sire Lexington. Leading breeder. Bred Norfolk, Asteroid, Maiden, Virgil, Preakness, etc. Brother of Alexander J. Alexander.

Annenberg, Moses L., 1878-1942. Publisher. Published *Daily Racing Form* 1922-'42, *Morning Telegraph*. Founded Triangle Publications.

Annenberg, Walter, 1908-2002. Former publisher, *Daily Racing Form*. Took control of his family's Triangle Publications Inc. in 1940 and built largest private publishing empire in the country; ambassador to Great Britain 1968-'74. Sold publishing enterprises by late 1980s. Son of publisher Moses Annenberg.

Arcaro, Eddie, 1916-'97. Jockey. Inducted into Racing Hall of Fame in 1958; George Woolf Memorial Jockey Award in '53. Rode 4,779 winners, including Whirlaway, Citation, Bold Ruler, Nashua. Won two Triple Crowns, five Kentucky Derbys, six Preakness Stakes, and six Belmont Stakes.

Archer, Fred, 1857-'86. Jockey. Winner of 12 consecutive riding titles in England (1874-'85) and rode 2,748 career winners, a record that stood for 57 years. Won 21 classic races, including five Epsom Derbys with Silvio, Bend Or, Iroquois, Melton, *Ormonde.

Atkinson, Ted F., 1916-2005. Jockey, racing official. Leading jockey by money won 1944, '46; leading jockey by races won 1944, '46; inducted into Racing Hall of Fame in '57; George Woolf Memorial Jockey Award in '57. Rode 3,795 winners, including Tom Fool, Gallorette, Devil Diver. Rode 1953 Horse of the Year Tom Fool to handicap triple crown; first jockey whose mounts earned more than $1-million in one year (1946).

Bacon, Mary, 1948-'91. Pioneer female jockey; rode 286 winners.

Baldwin, Elias J. "Lucky," 1828-1909. Mining, investments. Owned Rancho el Santa Anita, California. Bred and owned Emperor of Norfolk, Volante, Rey El Santa Anita, Americus. Built original Santa Anita Park racetrack.

Barbee, George, ca. 1855-1941. Jockey. Inducted into Racing Hall of Fame in 1996. Rode Saxon, Survivor, Shirley, Jacobus. Won the first Preakness Stakes aboard Survivor in 1873; won two other Preakness Stakes and one Belmont Stakes.

Barrera, Lazaro, 1924-'91. Trainer. Eclipse Award trainer 1976-'79; leading trainer by money won 1977-'80; inducted into Racing Hall of Fame in '79. Trained more than 140 stakes winners and six champions, including Affirmed, Bold Forbes.

Bassett, Carroll K., 1905-'72. Jockey. Inducted into Racing Hall of Fame in 1972. Rode more than 100 steeplechase winners, including Battleship, Peacock, Night Retired, Passive, Sable Muff. Rode Battleship to victory in the American Grand National and two National Steeplechase Hunt Cups.

Beard, Louis A., 1888-1954. Farm manager, racing executive. Managed Greentree Stud 1927-'48. Co-founder and president, Keeneland Race Course; co-founder, American Thoroughbred Breeders' Association; co-founder, Grayson Foundation.

Bedwell, H. Guy, 1876-1951. Trainer. Leading trainer by races won in 1909, '12-'17; leading trainer by money won 1918-'19; inducted into Racing Hall of Fame in 1971. Trained 2,160 winners, including Sir Barton, Billy Kelly. First trainer to saddle a Triple Crown winner (Sir Barton in 1919); won 16 races in 14 days in 1910.

Belmont, August I, 1816-'90. Banker. President of American Jockey Club (Jerome Park) 1866-'86. Owner of Nursery Stud in New York and later in Kentucky. Leading owner. Bred and owned Woodbine, Potomac, Fides, Prince Royal; also owned Glenelg, Fenian, *The Ill-Used.

Belmont, August II, 1853-1924. Banker. First president of Belmont Park; chairman, Jockey Club 1895-1924; chairman, Belmont Park. Owned Nursery Stud, Kentucky. Leading breeder. Bred Man o' War, Fair Play, Tracery, Beldame; also owned *Hourless, Henry of Navarre.

Bieber, Isidor, 1887-1974. Restaurateur, gambler. Co-owner of Bieber-Jacobs Stable, Stymie Manor, Maryland. Leading breeder 1964-'67; co-breeder of Hail to Reason, Allez France, Affectionately, Straight Deal; also co-owned Stymie, Searching.

Bobinski, Kazimierz, 1905-'69. Russian-born pedigree authority. In collaboration with Stefan Zamoyski, authored the landmark *Family Tables of Racehorses, Volumes I & II*, which expanded on the work of Bruce Lowe and Hermann Goos.

Bostwick, George, 1909-'82. Jockey, trainer. Leading amateur steeplechase jockey 1928-'32, '41; leading steeplechase trainer 1940, '51, '55; inducted into Racing Hall of Fame in 1968. Rode 87 winners, including Chenango, Escapade, Sussex, Darkness. Trained Neji and Oedipus. Played on six United States championship polo teams.

Boussac, Marcel, 1889-1980. Textile tycoon. Leading French breeder 19 times, winner of the Prix du Jockey-Club (French Derby) 12 times. Bred notable racehorses or sires Tourbillon, Pharis, Djebel, *Goya II, and *Ambiorix. In 1950 became first foreign owner to lead English owners list, the year he won the Epsom Derby with Galcador. Also bred and owned two-time Prix de l'Arc de Triomphe winner Corrida.

Bowie, Oden, 1826-'94. Railways, politician. Maryland governor 1869-'72; first president of Pimlico Race Course in 1870. Owner of Fairview Plantation, Maryland. Bred Catesby, Crickmore.

Bradley, Edward R., 1859-1946. Gambler. Owner of Idle Hour Stock Farm, Kentucky. Bred and owned Blue Larkspur, Bimelech, Black Helen, Busher, Bubbling Over. Bred and owned four Kentucky Derby winners and imported foundation mare *La Troienne.

Brady, James Cox Jr., 1908-'71. Investments. Chairman of Jockey Club 1961-'69; chairman of New York Racing Association 1961-'69. Owner of Dixiana Farm, Kentucky, and Hamilton Stable. Bred Long Look, War Plumage, Jungle Cove. Co-founder of Monmouth Park, American Horse Council; oversaw rebuilding of Belmont Park. Father of Nicholas J. Brady, United States treasury secretary 1988-'93, and chairman of the Jockey Club 1976-'82.

Brooks, Steve, 1922-'79. Jockey. Leading jockey in 1949; inducted into Racing Hall of Fame in 1963; George Woolf Memorial Jockey Award in 1962. Rode 4,451 winners, including Two Lea, Citation, Round Table. Rode Ponder in 1949 Kentucky Derby.

Brown, Edward D. "Brown Dick," 1850-1906. Trainer, jockey. Inducted into Racing Hall of Fame in 1984. Trained Ben Brush, Plaudit, Spendthrift, Hindoo. Rode Asteroid to an undefeated 9-for-9 record in 1864-'65.

Brown, Harry D. "Curly," 1863-1930. Restaurateur, racetrack executive. Founder and first president of Arlington Park; built Laurel Park, Oriental Park. Owned Brown Shasta Farm, California.

Bruce, Benjamin G., 1827-'91. Publisher. Founder and editor of the *Livestock Record* 1875-'91 (predecessor of *The Thoroughbred Record*). Brother of Sanders D. Bruce.

Bruce, Sanders D., 1825-1902. Hotelier, publisher. Co-editor of *Turf, Field and Farm* 1865-1902. Compiler of first four volumes of *American Stud Book*. Brother of Benjamin G. Bruce.

Bull, Phil, 1910-'89. Handicapper, gambler, owner, breeder, publisher. In 1948 launched *Timeform*, a British Thoroughbred industry information service that annually assesses the individual merits of thousands of runners. Founded Hollins Stud; bred champion Romulus.

Burch, Preston, 1884-1978. Trainer, breeder, owner. Leading trainer in 1950; inducted into Racing Hall of Fame in 1963. Trained more than 70 stakes winners, including George Smith, Sailor, Flower Bowl, Bold. Bred Gallorette. Trained stakes winners in New York, Canada, Cuba, France, and Italy. Wrote influential book on training, *Training Thoroughbred Horses*. Son of William P. Burch; father of Racing Hall of Fame trainer J. Elliott Burch.

Burch, William P., 1846-1926. Trainer. Inducted into Racing Hall of Fame in 1955. Trained Grey Friar, My Own, Decanter. First of three generations of Hall of Fame trainers. Father of Preston Burch.

Burke, Carleton F., 1882-1962. Banker, farmer. First chairman of California Horse Racing Board 1933-'39.

Burlew, Fred, 1871-1927. Trainer. Inducted into Racing Hall of Fame in 1973. Trained 32 stakes winners and two champions, including Beldame, Morvich, Inchcape.

Burns, Tommy H., 1879-1913. Jockey. Leading jockey by races won in 1898-'99; inducted into Racing Hall of Fame in 1983. Rode 1,333 winners, including Broomstick, Imp, Caughnawaga. Set an American record in the 1¼-mile Brighton Beach Handicap aboard Broomstick.

Butler, James Sr., 1855-1934. Grocery-chain owner. Owner of Empire City racetrack. Owner of East View Farm, New York. Bred Questionnaire, Sting, Pebbles, Spur; owned Comely.

Butler, James II, 1891-1940. Grocery-chain owner. President of Empire City Racing Association. Owner of East View Farm, New York.

Butwell, James, 1896-1956. Jockey, racing official. Leading jockey in 1912; leading jockey by races won in '20; inducted into Racing Hall of Fame in '84. Rode 1,402 winners, including Roamer, Sweep, Hilarious, Maskette. Leading American jockey by number of wins at the time of his retirement.

Byers, J. Dallett "Dolly," 1898-1966. Jockey, trainer. Leading steeplechase jockey 1918, '21, '28; leading jockey by money won in '28; inducted into Racing Hall of Fame in '67. Rode 149 winners, including Jolly Roger, Fairmount. Trained Tea-Maker, Lovely Night, Invader. Won the Temple Gwathmey Steeplechase Handicap five years in a row.

Byrnes, Matthew, 1854-1933. Jockey, trainer. Rode Glenelg, Kingfisher; trained Racing Hall of Fame members Parole, Salvator, Firenze.

Caldwell, Thomas, 1928-2001. Auctioneer. Auctioneer and director of auctions for the Keeneland Association 1975-2001. Owned Gavel Ranch, Oregon.

Campbell, John B., 1876-1954. Racing executive. Racing secretary and handicapper at New York tracks 1935-'54. Handicapped three-way dead heat in 1944 Carter Handicap.

Capossela, Fred, 1903-'91. Famed race caller at New York racetracks 1943-'71.

Cassidy, Mars, 1862-1929. Racing executive. Legendary starter at New York racetracks 1902-'29. Father of Marshall Cassidy.

Cassidy, Marshall, 1892-1968. Racing executive. Executive secretary of Jockey Club. Developed first modern starting gate; developed modern photo-finish camera; instituted first film patrol and saliva tests; founded Jockey Club Round Table meetings. Son of Mars Cassidy.

Cella, Charles, 1875-1940. Hotelier, theater owner. Founder of Oaklawn Park; co-owner of Fort Erie racetrack.

Chenery, Christopher T., 1886-1973. Utilities. First president of Thoroughbred Owners and Breeders Association. Owner of Meadow Stud, Virginia. Bred Secretariat, Riva Ridge, Hill Prince, Cicada, First Landing, Sir Gaylord. Co-founder of New York Racing Association.

Childs, Frank E., 1886-1973. Trainer. Inducted into

Racing Hall of Fame in 1968. Trained 23 stakes winners, including *Tomy Lee, Canina, Dinner Gong. Known for his ability to turn claiming horses into stakes winners.

Chinn, Philip T., 1874-1962. Horse trader. Owner of Himyar Stud, Kentucky. Bred 58 stakes winners, including Miss Merriment, Black Maria, In Memoriam, High Resolve. Leading consignor at Saratoga in 1920s; sold then-record $70,000 yearling in '27.

Clark, Henry S., 1904-'99. Trainer. Inducted into Racing Hall of Fame in 1982. Trained 37 stakes winners and one champion, including Tempted, Cyane, Endine, Obeah. Twice won back-to-back Delaware Handicaps.

Clark, John C., 1891-1974. Advertising executive. President of Hialeah Park 1940-'54; first president of Thoroughbred Racing Associations 1942-'43. Owned Sun Briar Court, New York. Bred Charlie McAdam, Accomplish.

Clark, John H. "Trader," 1919-'96. Horse trader, author. President, Thoroughbred Breeders of Kentucky. Author of *Trader Clark*.

Clark, Meriwether Lewis, 1846-'99. Racing executive. Founder and president of Louisville Jockey Club. Founder of Kentucky Derby in 1875. Established first uniform scale of weights in America.

Clay, Albert, (1917-2002). Farmer, burley warehousing. Breeder or co-breeder of at least 20 stakes winners, including Albert the Great, Seaside Attraction, Gorgeous, Pompeii, George Navonod; helped to found the American Horse Council and was instrumental in establishing the University of Kentucky's Maxwell H. Gluck Equine Research Center. Father of Three Chimneys Farm owner Robert Clay.

Clay, Ezekiel F., 1841-1920. Farmer, breeder. President, Kentucky Racing Association. Co-owner of Runnymede Farm, Kentucky. Chairman of Kentucky Racing Commission. Bred Hanover, Sir Dixon, Miss Woodford, Raceland.

Clay, Henry, 1777-1852. Lawyer, politician. Owner of Ashland Stud, Kentucky. Bred Heraldry. Father of John M. Clay.

Clay, John M., 1820-'87. Farmer, breeder. Owner of Ashland Stud, Kentucky. Bred Kentucky, Maggie B. B., Daniel Boone, Simon Kenton, Gilroy, Star Davis, Lodi, Day Star. Son of Henry Clay.

Cocks, W. Burling, 1915-'98. Trainer. Leading steeplechase trainer 1949, '65, '73, '80; inducted into Racing Hall of Fame in '85; F. Ambrose Clark Award in '73. Trained 49 stakes winners, including six American Grand National winners. Trained Zaccio, Down First.

Coe, William R., 1869-1955. Insurance, financier. Owner of Shoshone Farm, Kentucky. Bred and owned Pompey, Pompoon; owned Ladysman, Cleopatra, Black Maria, Pilate.

Cole, Ashley T., 1876-1965. New York industry leader. Chairman of the New York State Racing Commission 1945-'65; president of the National Association of State Racing Commissioners. Involved in organizing the not-for-profit New York Racing Association, in building the new Aqueduct Race Course, and in developing the New York breeders awards program.

Coltiletti, Frank, 1904-'87. Jockey, trainer, racing official. Inducted into Racing Hall of Fame in 1970. Rode 667 winners, including Mars, Crusader, Sun Beau. Won Preakness Stakes at age 17 aboard Broomspun in 1921.

Combs, Leslie II, 1901-'90. Breeder. Owner of Spendthrift Farm, Kentucky. Leading breeder in 1972. Chairman of Kentucky Racing Commission. Bred 247 stakes winners, including Majestic Prince, Myrtle Charm, Idun, Mr. Prospector. Originated modern stallion syndicates in 1950s.

Conway, James P., 1910-'84. Trainer. Inducted into Racing Hall of Fame in 1996. Trained 43 stakes winners and five champions, including Chateaugay, Primonetta, Grecian Queen. Won 1963 Kentucky Derby and Belmont Stakes with three-year-old champion colt Chateaugay.

Corrigan, Edward, 1854-1924. Railway investor. Founded Hawthorne Race Course. Raced *McGee.

Corum, M. W. "Bill," 1895-1958. President of Churchill Downs (1949-'58). Sports writer for the New York *Journal-American*. In 1925 coined the phrase "run for the roses" to describe the Kentucky Derby.

Cowdin, John E., 1859-1941. Silk merchant. President of Queens County Jockey Club (Aqueduct).

Crawford, Robert H. "Specs," 1897-1975. Jockey, trainer. Leading steeplechase jockey 1919-'20, '22, '26; inducted into Racing Hall of Fame in '73. Rode 139 winners, including Jolly Roger, Fairmount, Lytle, Erne II. Won four American Grand Nationals.

Croker, Richard "Boss," 1841-1922. Real estate, politician. Head of New York's Tammany Hall political machine. Owner of Glencairn Stud, Ireland. Bred Orby, Rhodora, Grand Parade.

Cromwell, Thomas B., 1871-1957. Publisher, bloodstock agent. Founded *The Blood-Horse*, Cromwell Bloodstock agency. Credited with refining past performance charts.

Crosby, H. L. "Bing," 1903-'77. Entertainer. First president of Del Mar Turf Club 1936-'46. Co-owner of Binglin Stock Farm, California. Owned *Meadow Court, *Ligaroti, *Don Bingo, *Blackie II.

Daingerfield, Algernon, 1867-1941. Racing executive. Executive secretary of Jockey Club. Son of Foxhall Daingerfield.

Daingerfield, Elizabeth, 1870-1951. Farm manager. Owner of Haylands Farm. Managed Wickliffe Stud, Faraway Farm. Managed leading sires Man o' War, High Time. Daughter of Foxhall Daingerfield.

Daingerfield, Foxhall A., ca. 1840-1913. Farm manager. Managed stud careers of Domino, Commando, Ben Brush, Kingston at Castleton Stud, Kentucky. Father of Algernon and Elizabeth Daingerfield.

Daingerfield, J. Keene, 1910-'93. Racing executive, author. Kentucky state steward 1973-'85. Eclipse Award of Merit in 1989. Author of *Training for Fun and Profit (Maybe)*. Grandson of Foxhall Daingerfield.

Daly, Marcus, 1842-1900. Mining. Owner of Bitter Root Stock Farm, Montana. Bred *Ogden, Tammany; owned Hamburg.

Daly, William C. "Father Bill," 1837-1931. Trainer. Famous mentor of Racing Hall of Fame jockeys James McLaughlin, Snapper Garrison, Winnie O'Connor, Danny Maher.

DeBartolo, Edward J., 1909-'94. Real estate developer. Owned Louisiana Downs, Thistledown, Remington Park. Special Eclipse Award in 1988.

De Francis, Frank, 1927-'89. Lawyer, racing executive. Owner of King of Mardi Gras, Hail Emperor. Led groups to buy Laurel Park in 1984 and Pimlico Race Course in '86, thus consolidating ownership of Maryland racetracks.

de Kwiatkowski, Henryk, 1924-2003. Aviation. Owner of Calumet Farm, Kentucky; Kennelot Stable. Joe Palmer Award in 1993. Owned Conquistador Cielo, De La Rose, Danzig, Stephan's Odyssey, Sabin. Bought bankrupt Calumet Farm for $17-million at public auction in 1992.

DeLancey, James, 1732-1801. Real estate. Owner of Bouwerie Farm, New York. Bred Maria Slamerkin, Bashaw. Imported *DeLancey's Cub mare (great American foundation mare), *Lath, *Wildair.

Donn, James Sr., 1887-1972. Landscaping contractor, nursery owner. Chairman of Gulfstream Park 1944-'72. Grandfather of former Gulfstream Park executive Douglas Donn.

Donoghue, Steve, 1884-1945. Jockey. Winner of ten consecutive riding titles in England (1914-'23). Rode six Epsom Derby winners: Humorist, Captain Cuttle, *Papyrus, Manna, Pommern, Gay Crusader. Rode 1,840 winners in a 33-year career.

Doswell, Thomas W., 1792-1890. Tobacco plantations. Owner of Bullfield Plantation. Bred Planet, Eolus, Algerine, Morello, Fanny Washington; owner of Knight of Ellerslie, Nina, Abd-el-Kader. Mentor and partner of Capt. Richard Hancock, who established Ellerslie Stud.

Drayton, Spencer, 1911-'94. FBI special agent who, upon recommendation of J. Edgar Hoover, in 1946 became the first head of the Thoroughbred Racing Protective Bureau. Served as TRPB president until his retirement in 1978. Inaugurated lip tattoos as a means of horse identification.

Duke, William, 1858-1926. Trainer. Inducted into Racing Hall of Fame in 1956. Trained Flying Ebony, Coventry. Won the 1924 French Derby with *Pot Au Feu; won '25 Kentucky Derby with Flying Ebony; won '25 Preakness Stakes with Coventry.

Dunn, Neville, 1904-'57. Publisher, editor. Editor of *The Thoroughbred Record* 1941-'57. Co-founder of Thoroughbred Club of America.

duPont, Allaire (Mrs. Richard C.), 1913-2006. Investments. Owner of Woodstock Farm, Maryland; Bohemia Stable, Maryland. Member of Jockey Club. Thoroughbred Owners and Breeders Association award for Maryland in 1984. Bred and owned Politely, Believe the Queen. Bred and raced Kelso, only five-time Horse of the Year (1960-'64); one of the first three women inducted into Jockey Club, in 1983.

duPont, William Jr., 1897-1966. Banker. Owner of Walnut Hall Farm, Virginia. Bred and owned Parlo, Berlo, Rosemont, Fairy Chant, Ficklebush; owned Fair Star, Dauber. Founder of Delaware Park.

Duryea, Herman B., 1862-1916. Investments. Owner of Haras du Gazon, France. Leading owner in 1904, when leasing W. C. Whitney's horses. Co-Bred and owned *Durbar II, Banshee, *Sweeper; also co-owned Irish Lad.

Dwyer, Michael F., 1847-1906. Meat processor. Leading owner. Owned or co-owned Hindoo, Hanover, Miss Woodford, Kingston, Luke Blackburn, Bramble, Ben Brush, Tremont, etc. Brother of Philip J. Dwyer.

Dwyer, Philip J., 1843-1917. Meat processor. President of Brooklyn Jockey Club (Gravesend), Queens County Jockey Club (Aqueduct). Leading owner. Co-owned Hindoo, Hanover, Miss Woodford, Kingston, Luke Blackburn, Bramble, Tremont, etc. Brother of Michael F. Dwyer.

Easton, William, ca. 1850-1909. Auctioneer. American representative of Tattersalls; auctioneer for Fasig-Tipton Co. First great American auctioneer.

Ellis, James C., 1872-1956. Oilman, banker, Thoroughbred breeder, racetrack owner. In 1925 he acquired Dade Park racetrack in Henderson, Kentucky, at court auction. Thirty years later the track's name was changed to James C. Ellis Park.

Ellsworth, Rex, 1907-'97. Rancher. Owner of Ellsworth Farm, California. Leading owner and breeder 1962-'63. Bred and owned Swaps, Candy Spots, Olden Times, Prove It; owned *Prince Royal II; imported *Khaled.

Engelhard, Charles W., 1917-'71. Precious metals. Owner of Cragwood Stable. Leading owner in England in 1970. Owned Nijinsky II, *Hawaii, Assagai, Ribocco, Ribero, Halo, Mr. Leader, Indiana.

Ensor, Lavelle "Buddy," 1900-'47. Jockey. Inducted into Racing Hall of Fame in 1962. Rode 411 winners, including Exterminator, Grey Lag, Hannibal. Rode 33 winners in 11 days, including five of six races on one of those days, in 1919.

Estes, Joseph A., 1902-'70. Journalist. Editor of *The Blood-Horse* 1930-'63. Devised Average Earnings Index; established Jockey Club Statistical Bureau.

Evans, Thomas Mellon, 1910-'97. Mergers and acquisitions. Owner of Buckland Farm. Bred and owned Pleasant Colony, Pleasant Tap, Pleasant Stage.

Fairbairn, Robert A., 1867-1951. Financier. Owner of Fairholme Farm, Kentucky. Bred Gallahadion, Hoop, Jr. Co-owner of *Sir Gallahad III, *Blenheim II.

Fasig, William B., 1846-1902. Auctioneer. Co-founder of Fasig-Tipton Co. in 1898. Conducted first equine auctions in Madison Square Garden.

Fator, Laverne, 1900-'36. Jockey. Leading jockey 1925-'26; inducted into Racing Hall of Fame in '55. Rode 1,075 winners, including Grey Lag, Black Maria, Pompey, Scapa Flow. Won consecutive runnings of Belmont Futurity and Carter and Gazelle Handicaps.

Feustel, Louis, 1884-1970. Trainer. Leading trainer in 1920; inducted into Racing Hall of Fame in '64. Trained two champions and Man o' War, Rock View, Ordinance, Ladkin. Won 20 of 21 races with Man o' War.

Field, Marshall W. III, 1893-1956. Publisher, retailer. Bred High Quest, High Strung, Escutcheon, Clang, Eclair; owned Nimba, Stimulus.

Fink, Jule, 1913-'90. Thoroughbred owner-breeder and noted handicapper. Known as one of the "Speed Boys," his gambling success resulted in Jockey Club refusing to renew his owner's license in 1949. His subsequent suit against Jockey Club led to a significant reduction in the club's power over racing, but the New York State Racing and Wagering Board continued the ban until 1967. He was a partner in 1966 Santa Anita Derby winner Boldnesian.

Finney, Humphrey S., 1903-'84. Auctioneer. Chairman of Fasig-Tipton Co. 1952-'84. Founded *Maryland Horse*; author of *A Stud Farm Diary, Fair Exchange*. Father of John M. S. Finney.

Finney, John M. S., 1934-'94. Auctioneer. President Fasig-Tipton Co. 1968-'89. Son of Humphrey Finney.

Fisher, Charles T., 1880-1964. Automobile manufacturer. Owner of Dixiana Farm, Kentucky. Bred Spy Song, Mata Hari, Sweep All, Star Reward.

Fitzsimmons, James E. "Sunny Jim," 1874-1966. Trainer. Leading trainer 1930, '32, '36, '39, '55; inducted into Racing Hall of Fame in '58. Trained 2,275 winners,

155 stakes winners, including Triple Crown winners Gallant Fox and Omaha, and eight champions, including Bold Ruler, Nashua, Granville.

Franks, John, 1925-2004. Oil production. Owner of Franks Farms, Louisiana; Louisiana Stallions, Louisiana; Southland Farm, Florida. Co-owner of Heatherten Farm, Maryland. Leading owner by money won 1983-'84, '86, '93; leading owner by races won in 1983-'84, '86-'89; leading breeder by races won 1988-'93; leading owner by races won in '89; leading owner by money won in '93; Eclipse Award owner in 1983-'84, '93-'94. Bred and owned Answer Lively, Derby Wish, Kissin Kris. Bred Sharp Cat, Royal Anthem. Owned Heatherten, Dave's Friend, Top Avenger. Earned $3.1-million in 1984, then a single-season record for owners.

Gaines, John R., 1928-2005. Breeder. Former chairman, Breeders' Cup Ltd. Founder of Gainesway Farm, Kentucky. Eclipse Award of Merit in 1984; John W. Galbreath Award in '93. Bred Halo, Silent King, Time Limit. Owned Bold Bidder, Oil Royalty. Founder of Breeders' Cup, Kentucky Horse Park; assisted in developing the Maxwell H. Gluck Center for Equine Research at the University of Kentucky.

Galbreath, John W., 1897-1988. Real estate developer. Owned Darby Dan Farm, Kentucky and Ohio. Eclipse Award, Man of the Year in 1972. Bred and owned Roberto, Chateaugay, Primonetta, Little Current, Graustark, His Majesty, Proud Truth, Proud Clarion. Instrumental in rebuilding of Belmont Park and Aqueduct.

Garner, J. Mack, 1900-'36. Jockey. Leading jockey by races won in 1915; leading jockey by money won in '29; inducted into Racing Hall of Fame in '69. Rode 1,346 winners, including Cavalcade, Blue Larkspur. Won 1934 Kentucky Derby on Cavalcade.

Garrison, Edward R. "Snapper," 1868-1930. Jockey, stable agent, trainer, racing official. Inducted into Racing Hall of Fame in 1955. By his estimate, rode more than 700 winners, including Firenze, Tammany. His come-from-behind style immortalized as "Garrison finish."

Gaver, John M., 1900-'82. Trainer. Leading trainer 1942, '51; inducted into Racing Hall of Fame in '66. Trained 73 stakes winners and four champions, including Tom Fool, Capot, Stage Door Johnny, Devil Diver. Won the handicap triple crown with Tom Fool in 1953.

Genter, Frances S., 1898-1992. Household appliances manufacturer. Owned Frances S. Genter Stable. Eclipse Award owner in 1990. Bred and owned In Reality, Smile; owned Unbridled, My Dear Girl, Rough'n Tumble.

Gentry, Olin B., 1900-'90. Farm manager. Managed Idle Hour Stock Farm, Darby Dan Farm. Planned matings for 188 stakes winners, 20 champions, five Kentucky Derby winners. Father of Kentucky breeder Tom Gentry.

Gluck, Maxwell F., 1899-1984. Apparel stores. Owner of Elmendorf Farm. Eclipse Award outstanding owner in 1977; leading owner '77, '81; leading breeder '73, '81. Bred and owned Protagonist, Talking Picture, Big Spruce, Hold Your Peace; owned Prince John. Donation endowed Maxwell F. Gluck Equine Research Center at University of Kentucky.

Gomez, Avelino, 1929-'80. Jockey. Leading Canadian jockey seven times; North American leading jockey in 1966; inducted into Racing Hall of Fame in '82. Rode 4,081 winners, including Ridan, Buckpasser, Affectionately.

Graham, Florence N. "Elizabeth Arden," 1885-1966. Cosmetics manufacturer. Owner of Maine Chance Farm, Kentucky. Leading owner in 1945. Bred Gun Bow, Jewel's Reward, Jet Action; owned Jet Pilot, Beaugay, Myrtle Charm, Star Pilot, Mr. Busher, Lord Boswell.

Grayson, Cary T., 1878-1938. Physician. Owner of Blue Ridge Farm, Virginia. Bred Insco, My Own, Happy Argo; also owned High Time. Co-founder of Grayson Foundation.

Griffin, Henry "Harry," 1876-1955. Jockey. Inducted into Racing Hall of Fame in 1956. Rode 569 winners, including The Butterflies, Henry of Navarre. One of the original investors in Hollywood Park.

Guerin, O. Eric, 1924-'93. Jockey. Leading apprentice jockey in 1942; inducted into Racing Hall of Fame in '72. Rode 2,712 winners, including Native Dancer, Bed o' Roses, Jet Pilot. Rode Native Dancer in 20 of his 21 victories (in 22 starts).

Guest, Raymond R., 1907-'91. Investments. Owner of Powhatan Plantation, Virginia; Ballygoran Stud, Ireland. Bred and owned Tom Rolfe, Chieftain; bred Cascapedia; owned Sir Ivor, Larkspur.

Guggenheim, Harry F., 1890-1971. Publisher, mining. Owner of Cain Hoy Stable. Leading breeder in England in 1963. Bred and owned Never Bend, Bald Eagle, Ack Ack, Cherokee Rose, Red God; bred Ragusa, Crafty Admiral; owned Dark Star, *Turn-to. Co-founder of New York Racing Association.

Haggin, James Ben Ali, 1821-1914. Lawyer, mining. Owner of Elmendorf Farm, Kentucky; Rancho del Paso, California. Bred Firenze, Africander, Tyrant, Waterboy, Tournament; owned Salvator, Ben Ali.

Haggin, Louis L. II, 1913-'80. Real estate. Chairman of Keeneland Association 1970-'80; president of Thoroughbred Racing Associations 1967-'68; co-founder of Thoroughbred Breeders of Kentucky. Bred and owned Himalayan, Harbor Springs, Tingle. Great-grandson of James Ben Ali Haggin.

Hagyard, Charles W., 1901-'95. Veterinarian. Owner of Hagyard Farm, Kentucky. Breeder of Rough'n Tumble, Rising Market. Stood Hail to Reason, Promised Land. Co-founder of Hagyard-Davidson-McGee equine clinic.

Hancock, Arthur B. Jr. "Bull," 1910-'72. Breeder. President of American Thoroughbred Breeders' Association. Owner of Claiborne Farm, Kentucky, and Ellerslie Stud, Virginia. Leading breeder 1958-'59, '68-'69. Breeder of Round Table, Gamely, Apalachee, Moccasin, Doubledogdare, Bayou, Lamb Chop. Imported and syndicated *Nasrullah, *Ambiorix, *Herbager; stood Bold Ruler, Nijinsky II, *Princequillo, Round Table. Son of A. B. Hancock Sr.; father of Kentucky breeders Arthur B. Hancock III (Stone Farm) and Seth Hancock (Claiborne Farm).

Hancock, Arthur B. Sr., 1875-1957. Breeder. President of Breeders' Sales Co. Founder and owner of Claiborne Farm, Kentucky; owner of Ellerslie Stud, Virginia. Leading breeder 1935-'37, '39, '43. Breeder of Johnstown, Beaugay, Cleopatra, St. James, Jacola, Nimba, Jet Pilot. Imported and syndicated *Sir Gallahad III, *Blenheim II. Son of Richard J. Hancock, father of Arthur B. "Bull" Hancock Jr.

Hancock, Richard J., 1838-1912. Breeder. Founder of Ellerslie Stud, Virginia. Bred Knight of Ellerslie, Elkwood, Eon, Eole, Eolist. Father of A. B. Hancock Sr.

Hanes, John W., 1892-1988. Textiles, investments. Co-founder and first chairman of New York Racing Association; president of National Museum of Racing Hall of Fame. Bred Idun; owned Bold Bidder.

Harbut, Will, 1885-1947. Groom. Stud groom of Man o' War. Coined well-known phrase, "He was the mostest hoss."

Harding, William G., 1808-'86. Farming, railways. Owner of Belle Meade Stud, Tennessee. Bred Vandalite. Stood leading sires *Priam, Vandal, *Bonnie Scotland.

Harper, John, 1803-'74. Farmer. Owner of Nantura Stock Farm, Kentucky. Bred Longfellow, Ten Broeck, Rhynodyne, Fanny Holton.

Harriman, W. Averill, 1891-1986. Railways, politician. Owner of Arden Farm Stable. Owned Chance Play, Ladkin, Mary Jane. As governor of New York (1955-'59) aided formation of New York Racing Association.

Haskell, Amory L., 1894-1966. Automobiles, safety glass. President of Monmouth Park 1946-'66; president of Thoroughbred Racing Associations 1954-'55. Owner of Blue Sparkler. Aided campaign to legalize pari-mutuel wagering in New Jersey.

Hatton, Charles W., 1906-'75. Journalist. President, New York Turf Writers Association. Eclipse Special Award in 1974. Popularized concept of American Triple Crown.

Hawkins, Abe, Birthdate unknown-1867. Jockey. A slave when he rode Lecompte to victory over Lexington in an 1854 match race, was perhaps the first African-American professional athlete to gain national and international prominence.

Headley, Duval A., 1910-'87. Horseman. President, Keeneland Race Course; president, Thoroughbred Club of America. Owner of Manchester Farm, Kentucky. Breeder of Tom Fool, Dark Mirage, Aunt Ginny. Trained 23 stakes winners, including champions Menow, Apogee. Nephew of Hal Price Headley.

Headley, Hal Petit, 1856-1921. Timber interests. Founder of Beaumont Farm, Kentucky. Bred and owned Ornament. Father of Hal Price Headley.

Headley, Hal Price, 1888-1962. Timber, burley. First president of Keeneland Race Course. Owner of Beaumont Farm, Kentucky. Bred and owned Menow, Alcibiades, Askmenow, Handy Mandy, Chacolet. Co-founder of Keeneland Association; co-founder of American Thoroughbred Breeders' Association. Father of Kentucky breeder Alice Headley Chandler (Mill Ridge Farm).

Healey, Thomas J., 1866-1944. Trainer, racing official. Inducted into Racing Hall of Fame in 1955. Trained three champions, Equipoise, Top Flight, Campfire. Won five Preakness Stakes.

Helis, William G., 1887-1950. Oil exploration. Co-owner of Fair Grounds. Owner of Helis Stock Farm, New Jersey. Owned Cosmic Bomb, Rippey, Salmagundi.

Hern, Maj. William Richard "Dick," (1921-2002). Trainer. Four-time leading British trainer; won 17 classics, including Epsom Derby three times; trained once-beaten Brigadier Gerard; trained for Queen Elizabeth II.

Hernandez, Joe, 1909-'72. Race caller at Santa Anita Park 1935-'72 and Hollywood Park.

Hertz, John D., 1879-1961 and **Frances**, 1881-1963. Taxis and rental cars. Co-owner of Arlington Park. Owner of Stoner Creek Stud, Kentucky; Leona Farm, Illinois. Bred and owned Count Fleet, Anita Peabody, Prince John, Fleet Nasrullah, Blue Banner, Count of Honor; owned Reigh Count.

Hervey, John L., 1870-1947. Journalist. Racing historian and author under pen name of "Salvator." Author of *Racing in America*, Vols. 1, 2, 4.

Hildreth, Samuel, 1866-1929. Trainer, owner. Leading trainer by money won nine times; leading trainer by races won 1921, '27; leading owner by money won 1909-'10, '11; inducted into Racing Hall of Fame in '55. Trained Grey Lag, Zev. Trained ten champions, seven Belmont Stakes winners.

Hine, Hubert "Sonny," 1931-2000. Trainer. Elected to Racing Hall of Fame in 2003. Trained Skip Away, Guilty Conscience, Skip Trial, Technology.

Hirsch, Clement L., 1914-2000. Canned foods. Co-founder and president of Oak Tree Racing Association. Eclipse Award for distinguished service in 1999. Owner of *Figonero, June Darling, *Snow Sporting, Magical Mile, Magical Maiden.

Hirsch, Mary (Mrs. Charles McLennan), 1914-'63. Trainer. First licensed woman trainer in 1933. Owner (with Charles McLennan) of Cowpens Farm, Maryland. Trained stakes winner No Sir. Daughter of Max Hirsch.

Hirsch, Max, 1880-1969. Trainer, jockey, owner, breeder. Inducted into Racing Hall of Fame in 1959. Trained more than 100 stakes winners and six champions, including Assault, Sarazen, Middleground, Bold Venture, Gallant Bloom. Won 1946 Triple Crown with Assault. Father of William J. "Buddy" Hirsch, Mary Hirsch.

Hirsch, William J. "Buddy," 1909-'97. Trainer. Inducted into Racing Hall of Fame in 1982. Trained 56 stakes winners and one champion, Gallant Bloom. Owned stakes winner Columbiana. Son of Max Hirsch.

Hitchcock, Thomas, 1861-1941. Trainer. Inducted into Racing Hall of Fame in 1973. Trained three champions: Good and Plenty, Salvidere, Annibal. Captained America's first international polo team.

Hollingsworth, Kent, 1930-'99. Journalist. Editor of *The Blood-Horse* 1963-'87; president of Thoroughbred Club of America 1974-'75; president of National Museum of Racing Hall of Fame 1982-'86.

Hoomes, John, 1755-1805. Stagecoaches. Founder of Virginia Jockey Club. Imported *Diomed, *Spread Eagle, *Buzzard.

Hooper, Fred W., 1898-2000. Highway construction. Owner of Hooper Farm, Florida. Eclipse Award outstanding breeder 1975, '82; Eclipse Award of Merit in '92. Bred and owned Susan's Girl, Precisionist, Crozier, Tri Jet, Copelan; owned Hoop, Jr., Olympia, Education. Brought Racing Hall of Fame jockeys Braulio Baeza, Laffit Pincay Jr., and Jorge Velasquez to United States.

Howard, Charles S., 1881-1950. Automobile dealer, real estate. Leading owner 1937, '40. Owner of Seabiscuit, *Noor, *Kayak II.

Hughes, Hollie, 1888-1981. Trainer. Inducted into Racing Hall of Fame in 1973. Trained more than 20 stakes winners, including, *Tourist II. Trained 1916 Kentucky Derby winner George Smith.

Hunter, John, 1833-1914. Real estate. First chairman of the Jockey Club 1894-'95; co-founder of Saratoga Race Course. Owner of Annieswood Stud, New York. Owner of Kentucky, Sultana; bred and owned Alarm, Olitipa, Rhadamanthus.

Hyland, John J., Birthdate unknown-1913. Trainer. Inducted into Racing Hall of Fame in 1956. Trained six champions, including Beldame, Henry of Navarre, His Highness, The Butterflies.

Isaacs, Harry Z., 1904-'90. Clothing manufacturer. Owner of Brookfield Farm, Maryland. Bred and owned Intentionally, Intent, Itsabet.

Iselin, Philip H., 1902-'76. Clothing manufacturer. President of Monmouth Park 1966-'77. Instrumental in consolidation of year-end polls into Eclipse Awards.

Jackson, James, 1782-1840. Merchant. Owner of Forks of Cypress Farm, Alabama. Bred Peytona, Reel. Imported *Glencoe, *Galopade, *Leviathan.

Jacobs, Hirsch, 1904-'70. Owner-breeder, trainer. Leading breeder by money won 1964-'67; leading trainer by money won 1946, '60, '65; leading trainer by races won 1933-'39, '41-'44; inducted into Racing Hall of Fame in '58. Trained 3,596 winners and four champions. Bred Affectionately, Hail to Reason, Straight Deal, Personality. Co-owned and trained Hail to Reason, Stymie, Affectionately, Straight Deal.

Janney, Stuart S. Jr., 1907-'88. Lawyer, financier. Chairman, Maryland Racing Commission in 1947; president of Maryland Horse Breeders Association. Owner of Locust Hill Farm, Maryland. Bred and owned Ruffian, Icecapade, Buckfinder, Private Terms. Father of Maryland breeder Stuart S. Janney III.

Jeffords, Walter M. Sr., 1883-1960. Investments. President of Grayson Foundation; president of National Museum of Racing Hall of Fame 1954-'60. Owner of Faraway Farm, Kentucky. Bred and owned One Count, Pavot, Bateau, Kiss Me Kate, Scapa Flow, Snow Goose.

Jerome, Leonard W., 1817-'91. Financier. Built Jerome Park in 1866; president of Coney Island Jockey Club (Sheepshead Bay racetrack). Owned Kentucky, Fleetwing, Decoursey.

Johnson, Albert, 1900-'66. Jockey, trainer. Leading jockey by money won in 1922; inducted into Racing Hall of Fame in '71. Rode 503 winners, including Exterminator, American Flag, Crusader. Rode two Kentucky Derby winners.

Johnson, Phil G., 1925-2004. Trainer. Inducted into Racing Hall of Fame in 1997. Trained Quiet Little Table, *Amen II, Maplejinsky, Match the Hatch, Naskra, Nasty and Bold, Volponi.

Johnson, William Ransom, 1782-1849. Trainer. Inducted into Racing Hall of Fame in 1986. Trained more than 20 champions, including Boston, Sir Archy. First great American trainer, called the "Napoleon of the Turf;" won 61 of 63 races during a two-year period.

Johnston, Elwood B., 1909-'81. California industry leader. Established Old English Rancho in the 1930s. Founder of the HBPA's California division. North America's leading breeder of stakes winners in 1972, with 13; co-leader in '71 (nine). Breeder of more than 100 stakes winners, including Real Good Deal, Special Warmth, MacArthur Park, Impressive Style, June Darling, Fleet Treat, Admirably, Generous Portion. Bought and raced Fleet Nasrullah.

Jones, Ben A., 1882-1961. Trainer. Leading trainer by money won 1941, '43-'44, '52; inducted into Racing Hall of Fame in '58. Trained 11 champions, including Whirlaway, Lawrin, Bewitch, Twilight Tear, Armed. Won record six Kentucky Derbys. Father of Horace A. "Jimmy" Jones.

Jones, Horace A. "Jimmy," 1906-2001. Trainer. Leading trainer by money won 1947-'49, '57, '61; inducted into Racing Hall of Fame in '59. Trained 54 stakes winners and seven champions, including Citation, Armed, Coaltown, Tim Tam. First trainer to win more than $1-million in purses. Son of Ben Jones.

Jones, Warner L., 1916-'94. Distiller, breeder. Chairman of Churchill Downs 1984-'92; president of Thoroughbred Breeders of Kentucky. Owner of Hermitage Farm, Kentucky. Eclipse Award of Merit in 1990. Breeder of Dark Star, Lomond, Is It True, Seattle Dancer, Northern Trick, Woodman, King's Bishop. Sold world-record $13.1-million yearling in 1984; co-founder of the American Horse Council.

Joyner, Andrew Jackson, 1861-1943. Trainer. Leading trainer by races won in 1908; inducted into Racing Hall of Fame in '55. Trained five champions, including Ethelbert, St. James, Whisk Broom II.

Karches, Peter, 1951-2006. Industry executive. Co-chairman, New York Racing Association, 2005. Former co-chief operating officer, NYRA, 2003-'04. Former vice chairman, NYRA board of trustees. Member, Jockey Club. Trustee, Thoroughbred Owners and Breeders Association. Former president and chief operating officer, Morgan Stanley Dean Witter Securities Group. Campaigned graded stakes winners Dynever, Statesmanship, Fast Decision.

Keck, Howard B., 1913-'96. Oil production. Bred Ferdinand; bred and owned Turkish Trousers, Bagdad, Fiddle Isle, Tell, etc.

Keene, Foxhall P., 1867-1941. Sportsman. Owner of Domino, Cap and Bells. Purchased Domino for $3,000 as a yearling. Son of James R. Keene.

Keene, James R., 1838-1913. Financier. Owner of Castleton Stud, Kentucky. Leading owner 1905-'08; leading breeder. Bred and owned Colin, Commando, Peter Pan, Sweep, Kingston, Sysonby, Cap and Bells; owned Domino, Spendthrift. Prime mover in formation of the Jockey Club in late 1893. Father of Foxhall P. Keene.

Kenner, Duncan F., 1813-'87. Sugar planter. President, Louisiana Jockey Club. Owner of Blue Bonnet. Owned slave jockey Abe Hawkins.

Kilmer, Willis Sharpe, 1868-1940. Patent-medicine distributor. Owner of Court Manor Stud, Virginia; Sun Briar Court, New York. Bred and owned Sun Beau, Sally's Alley, Chance Sun; owned Exterminator, *Sun Briar; bred Reigh Count.

Kilroe, Frank E. "Jimmy," 1912-'96. Racing executive. Racing secretary and handicapper at Santa Anita Park 1953-'90 and at New York tracks 1954-'59. Eclipse Award of Merit in 1979.

Kirkpatrick, Haden, 1911-'88. Publisher, journalist. Publisher, editor of *The Thoroughbred Record* 1941-'80.

Kleberg, Robert J., 1896-1974. Rancher, oilman. Owner of King Ranch, Kentucky and Texas. Leading owner in 1954. Bred and owned Assault, Middleground, Gallant Bloom, Dawn Play, Stymie, Miss Cavandish; owned High Gun, But Why Not, Bridal Flower.

Klein, Eugene V., 1921-'90. Automobile dealer. Leading owner 1985, '87; Eclipse Award owner 1985-'87. Owned Lady's Secret, Winning Colors, Capote, Life's Magic, Tank's Prospect, Open Mind, Family Style.

Knapp, Willie, 1888-1972. Jockey, trainer, racing official. Inducted into Racing Hall of Fame in 1969. Rode 649 winners, including Exterminator, Upset. Won 1919 Sanford Stakes aboard Upset, handing Man o' War his only loss.

Knight, Henry H., 1889-1959. Automobile dealer.

Owner of Almahurst Farm and Coldstream Stud, Kentucky. Bred Nail, Cosmah. Stood leading sires *Bull Dog, *Heliopolis.

Kummer, Clarence, 1899-1930. Jockey. Leading jockey by money won in 1920; inducted into Racing Hall of Fame in '72. Rode 464 winners, including Man o' War, Sir Barton, Exterminator, Sarazen. Defeated French champion *Epinard by a head aboard Ladkin in 1924 International Special.

Kurtsinger, Charles F., 1906-'46. Jockey. Leading jockey by money won 1931, '37; inducted into Racing Hall of Fame in '67. Rode 721 winners. Won 1931 Kentucky Derby with Twenty Grand; rode War Admiral to victory in 1937 Triple Crown.

Kyne, William P., 1887-1957. Racing executive. General manager of California Jockey Club (Bay Meadows Race Course) 1934-'57; owner of Portland Meadows racetrack 1946-'57. Promoted passage of California parimutuel law in 1933.

Lakeland, William, 1853-1914. Trainer. Trained Domino, Hamburg, *Ogden, Electioneer, Exile. Cobreeder and co-owner of Commando.

Laurin, Lucien, 1912-2000. Trainer, jockey. Eclipse Award trainer in 1972; inducted into Racing Hall of Fame in '77. Trained 36 stakes winners and three champions: Secretariat, Quill, Riva Ridge. Trained 1972-'73 Horse of the Year Secretariat to Triple Crown.

LeRoy, Mervyn, 1900-'87. Movie producer. President of Hollywood Park 1951-'85. Co-bred and owned Honeymoon, Stepfather, Honey's Alibi.

Lewis, J. Howard, 1862-1947. Trainer. Inducted into Racing Hall of Fame in 1969. Trained 14 steeplechase champions, including Bushranger, Fairmount.

Lewis, Robert, 1924-2006. Beer distributor. Eclipse Award of Merit in 1997; Big Sport of Turfdom Award in '95. Member of Jockey Club. Owned Silver Charm, Charismatic, Serena's Song, Timber Country, Hennessy. Won two-thirds of the Triple Crown in 1997 and '99 (with Silver Charm and Charismatic, respectively).

Lindheimer, Benjamin F., 1891-1960. Real-estate developer. Chairman of Arlington Park 1938-'60, Washington Park 1934-'60. Father of Marjorie Everett, former chief executive of Hollywood Park.

Loftus, Johnny, 1895-1976. Jockey, trainer. Leading jockey by money won in 1919; inducted into Racing Hall of Fame in '59. Rode 580 winners, including Man o' War, Sir Barton, Pan Zareta. First jockey to win the Triple Crown, aboard Sir Barton in 1919.

Longden, John, 1907-2003. Jockey, trainer. Leading jockey by races won in 1938, '47-'48; leading jockey by money won in 1943, '45; inducted into Racing Hall of Fame in '58; Special Eclipse Award in '94; George Woolf Memorial Jockey Award in '52; Avelino Gomez Memorial Award in '85. Rode then-record 6,032 winners, including Count Fleet, Busher, *Noor. Trained Majestic Prince, Jungle Savage, Baffle. Founded Jockeys' Guild with Eddie Arcaro and Sam Renick in 1940. Only man to both ride (Count Fleet) and train (Majestic Prince) a Kentucky Derby winner.

Lord Derby (Edward Stanley, 12th Earl of Derby), 1752-1834. A pillar of 18th-century British racing, he was responsible for founding the Epsom Oaks (1779) and Epsom Derby (1780), the latter bearing his family name after he won a coin toss with Sir Charles Bunbury. Won 1787 Derby with Sir Peter Teazle.

Lord Derby (Edward Stanley, 17th Earl of Derby), 1865-1948. Bred then-record 19 English classic winners, including Hyperion, Sansovino, Fairway, Swynford, Colorado, and *Watling Street. Also bred influential sires Phalaris, Pharos, *Sickle, and *Pharamond II. Generally acknowledged as one of the most successful owners-breeders in British Turf history.

Lorillard, George, 1843-'86. Tobacco sales. President of Monmouth Park. Owner of Westbrook Stable. Leading owner 1877-'80. Owned Tom Ochiltree, Spinaway, Duke of Magenta, Harold, Saunterer, Grenada.

Lorillard, Pierre, 1832-1901. Tobacco sales. Owner of Rancocas Stud, New Jersey. Bred and owned Wanda, Exile, Sibola, Dewdrop, Hiawasse; owned Iroquois, Parole, Saxon, Democrat. First American to win Epsom Derby, with Iroquois in 1881; inspired formation of the Board of Control (predecessor to the Jockey Club) in 1891.

Luro, Horatio, 1901-'91. Trainer. Inducted into Racing Hall of Fame in 1980. Trained 43 stakes winners, including Northern Dancer, *Kayak II, Decidedly, *Princequillo, *Miss Grillo.

Mabee, John C., 1921-2002. Grocery chain owner. Chairman, Del Mar Thoroughbred Club. Co-owner with wife Betty of Golden Eagle Farm, California. Eclipse Award breeder 1991, '97, '98. Bred and owned Best Pal, Event of the Year, General Challenge, Jeanne Jones, Worldly Manner. Founding member of the board of directors of Breeders' Cup Ltd.; Del Mar's largest growth occurred under his leadership.

MacBeth, Don, 1949-'87. Jockey. George Woolf Memorial Jockey Award in 1987. Rode Chief's Crown, Temperence Hill, Silver Buck, Half Iced. Inspired formation of injured jockey's fund that bears his name.

Macomber, A. Kingsley, 1876-1955. Banker, oilman. Important owner-breeder in California and France. Worked in 1920s to bring big-time horse racing to California; founder of the New Pacific Coast Jockey Club; also owned Haras du Quesnay in France, Mira Monte Stock Farm in California. Owned Parth, Rose Prince; imported *North Star III.

Madden, John E., 1856-1929. Trainer, owner, breeder. Owner of Hamburg Place. Leading breeder 1917-'27; leading trainer 1901-'03; inducted into Racing Hall of Fame in '83. Trained at least 38 stakes winners and eight champions. Bred Grey Lag, Sir Barton, Old Rosebud; owned Hamburg; trained Hamburg, Plaudit, Sir Martin. Bred five Kentucky Derby winners.

Maher, Danny, 1881-1916. Jockey. Leading jockey in U.S. in 1898; leading jockey in England 1908, '13; inducted into Racing Hall of Fame in '55. Rode 1,771 winners, including *Rock Sand, Spearmint, Cicero.

Maktoum, Sheikh Maktoum bin Rashid al, 1943-2006. Ruler of Dubai; vice president and prime minister of United Arab Emirates. Owner of Gainsborough Farm, Kentucky; Woodpark Stud, Ballysheehan Stud, Ireland; Gainsborough Stud, England. Owned Shareef Dancer, Touching Wood, Shadeed, Ma Biche. Partner in Godolphin Racing with brothers Mohammed and Hamdan.

Maloney, James W., 1909-'84. Trainer. Inducted into Racing Hall of Fame in 1989. Trained 42 stakes winners and two champions, including Gamely, Lamb Chop, Princessnesian.

Markey, Lucille P. (Wright), 1897-1982. Investments. Owner of Calumet Farm, Kentucky. Leading breeder 1950-'57, '61; leading owner 1952, '56-'58, '61.

Bred and owned Alydar, Fabius, Tim Tam, Our Mims, Forward Pass, Davona Dale, Iron Liege, Barbizon, Before Dawn.

Mars, Ethel V., 1884-1945. Confectioner. Owner of Milky Way Farm, Tennessee. Leading owner in 1936. Owned Gallahadion, Forever Yours, Sky Larking, Case Ace, Reaping Reward.

Mayer, Louis B., 1885-1957. Movie producer. Owner of Louis B. Mayer Stock Farm, California. Bred Honeymoon, Your Host, On Trust, Clem, Lurline B.; imported *Alibhai, *Beau Pere.

McAtee, J. Linus "Pony," 1897-1963. Jockey. Leading jockey in 1928; inducted into Racing Hall of Fame in '56. Rode 930 winners, including Exterminator, Twenty Grand, Jack High. Won 1927, '28 Kentucky Derby.

McCarthy, Clem, 1883-1962. Sportscaster. First radio broadcast of Kentucky Derby in 1928; broadcast Derby from 1928-'50.

McCreary, Conn, 1921-'79. Jockey, trainer. Inducted into Racing Hall of Fame in 1975. Rode 1,263 winners, including Racing Hall of Fame members Stymie, Twilight Tear, Armed, Searching. Trained three stakes winners.

McDaniel, Henry, 1867-1948. Trainer. Co-leading trainer by races won in 1922; inducted into Racing Hall of Fame in '56. Trained 1,041 recorded winners and four champions, including Exterminator, Reigh Count, Sun Beau.

McDaniel, Robert H. "Red," 1911-'55. Trainer. Leading trainer by races won 1950-'54. Trained *Poona II, Blue Reading.

McGrath, H. Price, 1814-'81. Tailor, bookmaker. Owner of McGrathiana Stud, Kentucky. Bred first Kentucky Derby winner Aristides, Thora, Tom Bowling.

McKinney, Rigan, 1908-'85. Jockey, trainer, breeder. Leading amateur steeplechase jockey 1933-'34, '36, '38; inducted into Racing Hall of Fame in '68. Rode 138 winners, including Green Cheese, Beacon Hill, Annibal. Trained Navigate, Drift, The Heir. Won American Grand National aboard Green Cheese in 1931.

McKnight, William L., 1888-1978. Industrialist. Chairman, Minnesota Mining and Manufacturing Co. 1949-'66. Co-founder of Calder Race Course. Owner of Tartan Farms, Florida. Eclipse Award, Man of the Year, in 1974. Leading breeder in 1990. Bred and owned Dr. Fager, Ta Wee, Dr. Patches; bred Unbridled.

McLaughlin, James, 1861-1927. Jockey. Leading jockey 1884-'87; inducted into Racing Hall of Fame in 1955. Rode Hindoo, Tecumseh, Tremont, Firenze. Won 1881 Kentucky Derby on Hindoo; won '85 Preakness Stakes aboard Tecumseh; won six Belmont Stakes.

McLennan, Joseph, 1868-1933. Racing executive. Racing secretary at Hialeah Park, Arlington Park.

Meadors, Joel C. "Skeets," 1896-1967. Photographer.

Mellon, Paul, 1908-'99. Investments, banking. Owner of Rokeby Stud, Virginia. Eclipse Award owner-breeder in 1971; breeder in '86; Award of Merit in '93. Bred and owned Mill Reef, Arts and Letters, Key to the Mint, Fort Marcy, Sea Hero, Quadrangle, Run the Gantlet, Java Gold; owned Fit to Fight, Summer Guest, Blue Banner.

Miller, Walter, 1890-1959. Jockey. Leading jockey 1906-'07; inducted into Racing Hall of Fame in '55. Rode 1,904 winners, including Colin, Ballot, Peter Pan, Whimsical. Won 388 races in 1906 (at age 16), a record that stood until Racing Hall of Fame jockey William Shoemaker tied the mark 44 years later in 1950 and broke it in '52.

Mills, James P., 1909-'87, and **Alice**, 1912-2000. Aviation. Owner of Hickory Tree Farm, Virginia. Bred and owned Committed, Believe It, Terpsichorist, Hagley; owned Devil's Bag, Gone West.

Mills, Ogden, 1884-1937. Investments. Co-owner of Wheatley Stable. Bred Seabiscuit, Edelweiss; owned Dice, Diavolo, Dark Secret. Brother of Mrs. H. C. Phipps.

Molter, William, 1910-'60. Trainer. Leading trainer by races won 1946-'49; leading trainer by money won 1954, '56, '58, '59; inducted into Racing Hall of Fame in '60. Trained 2,158 winners and 48 stakes winners, including Round Table, Determine, T. V. Lark.

Mori, Eugene, 1898-1975. Banker, real-estate developer. Builder and president of Garden State Park 1942-'72; owned Hialeah Park 1954-'72. Owner of East Acres Farm, New Jersey. Bred Tosmah; owned Alma North, Cosmah. Promoted pari-mutuel wagering in New Jersey.

Morris, Francis, 1810-'86. Shipping. Owner of Morris Stud, New York. Bred and owned Ruthless, Relentless, Narragansett. Aided Leonard W. Jerome in founding of American Jockey Club and Jerome Park in 1866.

Morris, Green B., 1837-1920. Owner, trainer. Leading owner in 1902. Trained Apollo, Sir Dixon, Strathmeath, *Star Ruby.

Morris, John A., 1892-1985. Financier. President of Thoroughbred Racing Associations, Jamaica Racetrack. Eclipse Award, Man of the Year, in 1975. Bred and owned Missile Belle, Proudest Roman, L'Heureux; owned Missile. Great-grandson of Francis Morris.

Morrissey, John, 1831-'78. Prizefighter, gambler, politician. Co-founder of Saratoga Race Course in 1863.

Mulholland, W. F. "Bert," 1884-1968. Trainer. Inducted into Racing Hall of Fame in 1967. Trained 832 winners, 57 stakes winners, and five champions, including Jaipur, Eight Thirty, Lucky Draw, Battlefield. Trained for George D. Widener for more than 40 years.

Munnings, Sir Alfred, 1878-1959. Painter. Greatest English painter of horses of 20th century.

Murphy, Isaac, 1860-'96. Jockey, trainer, owner. Inducted into Racing Hall of Fame in 1955. Rode 530 recorded winners, including Falsetto, Firenze, Salvator, Emperor of Norfolk. First jockey to win three Kentucky Derbys; first jockey elected to Racing Hall of Fame. Won with 44% of his mounts.

Neloy, Eddie, 1921-'71. Trainer. Leading trainer by money won 1966-'68; inducted into Racing Hall of Fame in '83. Trained 60 stakes winners and five champions, including Buckpasser, Bold Lad, Gun Bow.

Neves, Ralph, 1921-'95. Jockey. Inducted into Racing Hall of Fame in 1960; George Woolf Memorial Jockey Award in '54. Rode 3,771 winners, sixth all-time by wins at retirement; rode 173 stakes winners, including Round Table, Native Diver. Rode five winners at Bay Meadows after track announcer declared him "deceased" following an accident the previous day.

Newman, Neil, 1886-1951. Journalist. Wrote under the pen name of "Roamer." Author of *Famous Horses of the American Turf* series 1930-'32.

Niarchos, Stavros, 1909-'96. Shipping. Owner of Haras de Fresnay-le-Buffard, France; Oak Tree Farm, Kentucky. Bred and owned Miesque, Spinning World, Kingmambo, Hernando (Fr), Hector Protector, Machiavellian; owned Nureyev.

Niccolls, Richard, 1624-'72. Soldier, politician. Founded first American racecourse, Newmarket, at Salisbury Plain (near modern Hempstead), Long Island, New York.

Notter, Joe, 1890-1973. Jockey. Leading jockey by money won in 1908; inducted into Racing Hall of Fame in '63. Rode Regret, Whisk Broom II, Colin. First jockey to ride a filly, Regret, to victory in the Kentucky Derby (1915); first jockey to win handicap triple crown, on Whisk Broom II.

Nuckols, Charles Jr., 1922-2005. Breeder. Former president, Thoroughbred Club of America; director, Keeneland Association. Member of Jockey Club. Owner of Nuckols Farm, Kentucky. Bred Hidden Lake, Habitat, Decathlon, Typecast. Co-bred War Emblem. Co-authored the Kentucky Thoroughbred Development Fund legislation.

O'Connor, Winnie, 1884-1947. Jockey, trainer. Leading jockey in 1901; inducted into Racing Hall of Fame in '56. Rode 1,229 winners in United States and France, including Yankee, Reina. One of "Father Bill" Daly's "Five Aces."

Odom, George M., 1883-1964. Jockey, trainer. Inducted into Racing Hall of Fame in 1955. Rode 527 winners, including Broomstick, Delhi, Banastar. Trained Busher, Pasteurized. Won the Belmont Stakes as a jockey and later as a trainer.

O'Farrell, Joe, 1912-'82. Breeder. President, Florida Breeders' Sales Co. Owner of Ocala Stud, Florida. Bred Roman Brother, Office Queen, My Dear Girl. Stood Rough'n Tumble. Primary founder of Florida breeding industry.

Olin, John M., 1892-1982. Small-arms munitions. Bred and owned Cannonade; owned Bold Bidder, Northfields.

O'Neill, Frank, 1886-1960. Jockey. Inducted into Racing Hall of Fame in 1956. Rode Beldame, Roseben, *Prince Palatine, Spion Kop. Also successful jockey in France and England.

Palmer, Joe H., 1904-'52. Journalist. Author of *This Was Racing, American Racehorses* series 1944-'51.

Parke, Burley, 1905-'77. Trainer. Inducted into Racing Hall of Fame in 1986. Trained 37 stakes winners and three champions: Roman Brother, *Noor, Raise a Native. *Noor beat Citation in four consecutive stakes races. Brother of Ivan Parke.

Parke, Ivan, 1908-'95. Jockey, trainer. Leading jockey by races won in 1923, '24 (his first two years of racing); leading jockey by money won in '24; inducted into Racing Hall of Fame in '78. Rode 419 winners, including Backbone. Trained 27 stakes winners, including Exclusive Native, Hoop, Jr. Brother of Burley Parke.

Patrick, Gilbert "Gilpatrick," 1812-ca. 1880. Jockey. Inducted into Racing Hall of Fame in 1970. Rode Ruthless, Boston, Kentucky, Lexington. Rode first Belmont Stakes winner, Ruthless, in 1867.

Paulson, Allen E., 1922-2000. Aviation. Owner of Brookside Farm, Kentucky. Eclipse Award breeder in 1993; owner '95 and '96. Owned and bred Cigar, Ajina, Escena, Fraise; owned Theatrical (Ire), Strawberry Road (Aus), Blushing John, Arazi, Paradise Creek; bred Azeri.

Payson, Mrs. Charles S. (Joan Whitney), 1903-'75. Publisher, investments. Co-owner of Greentree Stud. Leading owner in 1951. Owned and bred Stage Door Johnny, Capot, Bowl Game, Late Bloomer, The Axe II, Cohoes, Stop the Music; owned Tom Fool. Daughter of Mr. and Mrs. Payne Whitney; sister of John Hay Whitney.

Pelleteri, Anthony, 1893-1952. Trainer, racing executive. Won the 1941 Santa Anita Handicap with 90-to-1 Bay View, and developed stakes winners Bull Reigh and Andy K. In 1941 Pelleteri organized a partnership that saved the historic Fair Grounds racetrack in New Orleans from being auctioned and subdivided; served as the track's executive vice president until his death.

Penna, Angel, 1923-'92. Trainer. Leading trainer in Argentina in 1952; leading trainer in Venezuela in '54; leading trainer in France in '74; inducted into Racing Hall of Fame in '88. Trained more than 250 stakes winners, including Allez France, Relaxing, San San, Private Account.

Perry, William Haggin, 1911-'93. Investments. Owner of Waterford Farm, Virginia. Co-owned and co-bred Gamely, Lure, Revidere, Coastal, Lamb Chop, Boldnesian.

Phipps, Mrs. Henry C. (Gladys Mills), 1883-1970. Investments. Owner of Wheatley Stable. Leading owner in 1966. Bred and owned Bold Ruler, Bold Lad, Seabiscuit, High Voltage, Misty Morn, Queen Empress, Successor, Bold Bidder, Castle Forbes. Mother of leading owner-breeder Ogden Phipps; sister of Ogden Mills.

Phipps, Ogden, 1908-2002. Investments. Chairman, Jockey Club 1964-'74; former chairman New York Racing Association. Leading owner by money won 1988, '89; Eclipse Award breeder in '88; Eclipse Award owner 1988, '89; Eclipse Award of Merit 2002; Mr. Fitz Award in '89. Bred and owned Buckpasser, Easy Goer, Private Account. Bred and raced Personal Ensign, who was unbeaten in 13 starts.

Piatt, Thomas, 1877-1965. Farmer, tobacco. First president of Thoroughbred Club of America; president, Breeders' Sales Co. Owner of Brookdale Farm, Kentucky. Bred Alsab, Donau. Father of Thomas Carr Piatt.

Piatt, Thomas Carr, 1900-'53. Farmer, tobacco. President, Breeders' Sales Co. 1949-'53. Owner of Crestwood Farm, Kentucky. Co-breeder of Occupation, Occupy, Errard. Son of Thomas Piatt.

Pincus, Jacob, 1838-1918. Trainer, jockey. Leading trainer in 1869; inducted into Racing Hall of Fame in '88. Trained Glenelg, Eagle, Richmond. Trained Iroquois, first American winner of the Epsom Derby.

Pollard, John "Red," 1909-1981. Canadian-born jockey. Rode his first Thoroughbred winner in 1926. In mid-1930s began association with C. S. Howard, owner of Seabiscuit, whom he rode to many important victories—although not in the famed 1938 match against War Admiral. Retired after injury-plagued 30-year career. Later inducted into the Canadian Racing Hall of Fame.

Porter, William T., 1809-'58. Publisher. Founded *Spirit of the Times* magazine in 1831.

Price, Jack, 1908-'95. Trainer. Trained 1961 Kentucky Derby and Preakness Stakes winner Carry Back, whom he bred out of the $265 mare Joppy.

Purdy, Samuel, 1785-1836. Jockey. Inducted into Racing Hall of Fame in 1970. Semi-retired when pulled from the crowd to replace American Eclipse's jockey at the Union Course in 1823, winning the next two heats to win the match over Henry.

Rasmussen, Leon, 1915-2003. Journalist. "Bloodlines" columnist, *Daily Racing Form* 1950-'87. Walter

Haight Award in 1987; Engelhard Award in '87. Bred and owned Apollo, Nanetta. Popularized Dr. Steven A. Roman's dosage system in his column.

Reiff, John, 1885-1974. Jockey. Leading jockey in France in 1902; inducted into Racing Hall of Fame in '56. Rode 1,016 winners, including Orby, Tagalie, Retz, Moia. Among the top ten jockeys for ten seasons in France; won two Epsom Derbys and one French Derby.

Rice, Daniel, 1896-1975, and **Ada L.**, 1899-1977. Stock and grain broker. Co-owners of Arlington Park 1940-'68. Owners of Danada Farm, Kentucky. Bred and owned Lucky Debonair, Pucker Up, Proud Delta, Delta Judge, Advocator.

Rice, Grantland, 1880-1954. Journalist. Covered most major sports for the New York *Herald Tribune*, but horse racing was a favorite. Among the great racing events he covered was the 1938 Seabiscuit-War Admiral match.

Richards, A. Keene, 1827-'81. Sugar and cotton planter. Owner of Blue Grass Park Stud, Kentucky. Owned *Australian, Starke, War Dance. Bred Fenian, Target, Eliza Davis, Ulrica.

Richards, Sir Gordon, 1904-'86. Jockey. Champion British flat jockey 26 times in 34 seasons of racing. First to ride more than 4,000 winners, he retired in 1954 with a then-world record 4,870 career victories. In 1953 he became the first professional jockey to be knighted.

Richards, Leonard P., Birthdate and date of death unknown. Chemical manufacturer. Second chairman of the Delaware Racing Commission.

Rickman, William Sr., 1924-2005. Racing executive, owner-breeder. Chairman of Delaware Park. Bought Delaware Park in 1983, reopened it after a one-year shutdown, and turned it into profitable enterprise. Introduced slots in 1995. Son William Rickman Jr. is president and chief executive. Also owns Ocean Downs harness track and holds license to build a new track in Allegany County, Maryland.

Riddle, Samuel D., 1862-1951. Textiles. Owner of Faraway Farm, Kentucky; Glen Riddle Stable. Leading owner in 1925. Owned Man o' War; bred and owned War Admiral, Crusader, American Flag, War Relic.

Riggs, William P., 1874-1936. Racetrack executive. Secretary of the Maryland Jockey Club; a driving force behind the revival of Pimlico Race Course and return of Preakness Stakes to Maryland in 1909.

Robertson, Alfred, 1911-'75. Jockey. Inducted into Racing Hall of Fame in '71; New York Turf Writers Association's best jockey in 1942. Rode 1,856 winners, including Top Flight, Whirlaway, Riverland, Sky Larking. Twice rode six winners in a single day.

Robertson, William H. P., 1920-'82. Journalist. Editor of *The Thoroughbred Record* 1962-'78. Author of *History of Thoroughbred Racing in America, Hoofprints of the Century.*

Roebling, Joseph M., 1909-'80. Building contractor. Owner of Harbourton Stud, New Jersey. Bred and owned Blue Peter, Fall Aspen, Rainy Lake.

Rogers, John W., ca. 1850-1908. Trainer. Inducted into Racing Hall of Fame in 1955. Trained 11 champions, including Artful, Modesty. Trained Artful to win the 1904 Belmont Futurity, giving Sysonby the only defeat of his career.

Rolapp, R. Richards, 1941-'93. Lawyer. President of American Horse Council 1978-'93.

Ross, John K. L., 1876-1951. Railways. Leading owner 1918-'19. Owned Sir Barton, Billy Kelly, Cudgel.

Rous, Adm. Henry J., 1795-1877. English Jockey Club steward, Turf reformer, handicapper. Published *Handbook on the Laws of Racing*, which included the first standard scale of weights. Established and enforced strict standards and banned unsavory characters. Often referred to as the "Father of the Turf."

Rowan, Louis R., 1911-'88. Investments. Original shareholder in Santa Anita Racetrack; six-term president of the California Thoroughbred Breeders Association; conceived California Cup; founding director of Oak Tree Racing Association and Del Mar Thoroughbred Club. Founding chairman of the Winners Foundation.

Rowe, James Sr., 1857-1929. Trainer, jockey. Leading jockey 1871-'73; leading trainer 1908, '13, '15; inducted into Racing Hall of Fame in '55. Trained 34 horses regarded as champions, more than any other Hall of Fame trainer. Trained Colin, Miss Woodford, Regret, Luke Blackburn, Hindoo.

Runyon, Damon, 1884-1946. Journalist, sports columnist, author, humorist. Many of his short stories had to do with gambling and horse racing. Most famous for writing *Guys and Dolls*, although probably best known in racing for the poem "Gimme a Handy Guy Like Sande," about jockey Earl Sande.

Salman, Ahmed bin, 1958-2002. Publisher, Saudi royal family. Owner of The Thoroughbred Corp. Bred and owned Point Given, Spain. Owned Sharp Cat, Jewel Princess, Oath, Anees, Royal Anthem, War Emblem.

Salmon, Walter J., ca. 1880-1953. Real estate. Owner of Mereworth Farm. Leading breeder in 1946. Bred Discovery, Display, Dr. Freeland, Battleship (first American-bred and -owned winner of England's Grand National Steeplechase), Free For All; owned Vigil.

Samuel, Ernest, 1930-2000. Steel distribution. Owner of Sam-Son Farm, Ontario and Florida. Eclipse Award owner in 1991; leading owner and breeder in '91. Bred and raced more than 100 stakes winners, including Dance Smartly, Sky Classic, Chief Bearhart.

Sande, Earl, 1899-1968. Jockey, trainer. Leading jockey 1921, '23, '27; leading trainer in '38; inducted into Racing Hall of Fame in '55. Rode 968 winners, including Gallant Fox, Zev, Man o' War. Trained Stagehand, Sceneshifter. Won three Kentucky Derbys, five Belmont Stakes, and five Jockey Club Gold Cups.

Sanford, John, 1851-1939. Carpet mills, politician. Owner of Hurricane Stud, New York. Bred and raced *Affection, *Snob II, Sir John Johnson, *Donnacona; owned George Smith. Son of Stephen Sanford.

Sanford, Milton H., 1812-'83. Cotton mills. Owner of Preakness Stud, New Jersey; North Elkhorn Farm, Kentucky. Bred Vagrant, Vigil; also owned Preakness, Virgil, Monarchist. Stood leading sire Glenelg.

Sanford, Stephen, 1826-1913. Carpet mills. Owner of Hurricane Stud, New York. Raced only homebreds, which he gave Indian names, including Caughnawaga, Chuctununda, and Mohawk II. Stood Clifford, *Voter. Father of John Sanford.

Sangster, Robert, 1936-2004. Betting pools, investments. Co-owner of Coolmore Stud; owner of Swettenham Stud. Renowned owner-breeder who helped to fuel the 1980s boom at Thoroughbred yearling sales, with partners purchased a yearling for world-record $13.1-million in '85, campaigned more than 800 stakes winners, including champions The Minstrel, Alleged,

Caerleon, and homebred Sadler's Wells; five-time leading owner in England.

Schapiro, John, 1914-2002. Racetrack executive. President of Laurel Park. Eclipse Award of Merit in 1980; *Sports Illustrated*'s Racing Man of the Year in 1960; Inaugurated the Washington, D.C., International at Laurel in 1952.

Scott, Marion duPont, 1891-1983. Investments. Owner of Montpelier Farm, Virginia. Bred more than 50 stakes winners, including Mongo, Parka, Neji, Soothsayer; owned Proud Delta, Battleship. Founded Carolina Cup Steeplechase in Camden, South Carolina. Member of syndicate that imported *Blenheim II.

Seagram, Joseph E., 1841-1919. Distiller. Member of Canadian Parliament. President of Ontario Jockey Club. Bred and raced Inferno, Belle Mahone. Won 15 King's (Queen's) Plates.

Shaffer, Charles B., 1859-1943. Oil production. Owner of Coldstream Stud, Kentucky. Bred Bull Lea, Occupation, Occupy, Star Pilot, Reaping Reward, Plucky Play. Stood leading sires *Bull Dog, *Heliopolis. Father of E. E. Dale Shaffer.

Shaffer, E. E. Dale, 1917-'74. Oil production. Founder of Detroit Race Course; chairman of Kentucky Racing Commission 1950-'51; president of Michigan Racing Association; president of Thoroughbred Racing Associations 1960-'61. Owner of Coldstream Stud, Kentucky. Leading breeder in 1945. Bred Sweet Patootie, Star Pilot, Johns Joy. Stood leading sires *Bull Dog, *Heliopolis. Son of Charles Shaffer.

Shilling, Carroll, 1882-1950. Jockey. Leading jockey in 1910; inducted into Racing Hall of Fame in '70. Rode 969 winners, including Colin, Sir Martin, Fitz Herbert, King James. Won 1912 Kentucky Derby aboard Worth.

Shoemaker, William, 1931-2003. Jockey, trainer. President, Jockeys' Guild in 1975-'90. Leading jockey by money won in 1958-'64; inducted into Racing Hall of Fame in '58; Special Eclipse Award in '76; Eclipse Award jockey in '81; Eclipse Award of Merit in '81; George Woolf Memorial Jockey Award in '51; Mike Venezia Award in '90. Rode then-record 8,833 winners and 1,009 stakes winners, including Swaps, Spectacular Bid, Round Table, Ack Ack, Forego, John Henry, Prove It, Olden Times, Sword Dancer. Trained Fire the Groom, Alcando (Ire). First jockey to reach $100-million in earnings; mounts earned more than $123-million in purses. Paralyzed in single-car accident April 8, 1991.

Simms, Edward F., 1870-1938. Oil production. Owner of Xalapa Farm, Kentucky. Bred Coventry; owned Eternal, My Play.

Simms, Willie, 1870-1927. Jockey. Leading jockey in 1894; inducted into Racing Hall of Fame in 1977. Rode 1,125 winners, including Henry of Navarre, Ben Brush, Plaudit, Commanche. Won back-to-back Belmont Stakes (1893-'94) aboard Commanche and Henry of Navarre.

Sinclair, Harry F., 1876-1956. Oil production. Owner of Rancocas Stud, New Jersey. Leading owner 1921-'23. Bred and owned Mad Play, Ariel; owned Zev, Grey Lag, Mad Hatter.

Skinner, John S., 1788-1851. Publisher. Founded *American Turf Register* in 1830.

Sloan, James F. "Tod," 1874-1933. Jockey. Inducted into Racing Hall of Fame in 1955. Rode Hamburg, Clifford. Credited with popularizing the use of shortened stirrups in United States and England.

Sloane, Isabel Dodge, 1898-1962. Automobile heiress. Owner of Brookmeade Stud, Virginia. First female leading owner 1934, '50. Bred and owned Sword Dancer, Bowl of Flowers, Bold, Sailor, Greek Ship; owned Cavalcade, High Quest.

Smith, George "Pittsburgh Phil," 1862-1905. Gambler. Most successful gambler of Victorian era, died a millionaire.

Smith, Robert A., 1869-1942. Trainer, owner. Leading trainer 1933-'34; inducted into Racing Hall of Fame in '76. Trained more than 27 stakes winners and three champions, including 1934 Horse of the Year Cavalcade, High Quest. Owned Articulate. Won 1934 Kentucky Derby with Cavalcade.

Smith, Tom "Silent Tom," 1879-1957. Trainer. Leading trainer 1940, '45; inducted into Racing Hall of Fame in 2001. Trained 29 stakes winners and six champions, including Seabiscuit, Jet Pilot, *Kayak II. Trained 1947 Kentucky Derby winner Jet Pilot.

Smithwick, Alfred "Paddy," 1927-'73. Jockey. Leading steeplechase jockey by races won 1956-'58, '62; inducted into Racing Hall of Fame in '73. Rode 398 winners, including Neji, Bon Nouvel, Elkridge. Won two American Grand Nationals aboard Neji. Trained two stakes winners.

Smithwick, D. M. "Mike," 1929-2006.Trainer. Inducted into Racing Hall of Fame in 1971. Trained 52 stakes winners and six champions. Trained Neji, Bon Nouvel, Ancestor, Mako, Top Bid, Straight and True. Trained Neji to three championships in 1955, '57, and '58; trained the first two winners (Top Bid and Inkslinger) of the Colonial Cup. Brother of Racing Hall of Fame jockey Paddy Smithwick.

Sommer, Sigmund, 1917-'79. Real estate. Leading owner 1971-'72. Owned 29 stakes winners, including Autobiography, Sham, Never Bow.

Spreckels, Adolph, 1857-1924. Sugar merchant. President of Pacific Coast Jockey Club. Owner of Napa Stock Farm, California. Bred Morvich; bred and owned Runstar.

Stanford, Leland, 1824-'93. Politician. Governor of California 1861-1863; United States senator 1885-1893; founder of Stanford University. Developed Palo Alto Stock Farm. In 1872 hired photographer to prove that all of a horse's feet are off the ground at one point in the gallop.

Stephens, Woodford C. "Woody," 1913-'98. Trainer. Eclipse Award trainer in 1983; inducted into Racing Hall of Fame in '76. Trained 131 stakes winners and 11 champions, including Swale, Conquistador Cielo, Never Bend. Won five consecutive Belmont Stakes (1982-'86).

Stout, James, 1914-'76. Jockey, racing official. Inducted into Racing Hall of Fame in 1968. Rode Johnstown, Granville, Assault, Omaha, Stymie. Finished in the first triple win dead heat in a major stakes aboard Bousset in the 1944 Carter Handicap.

Strub, Charles H., 1884-1958. Baseball team owner, real estate, investments. Founder of Santa Anita Park. Father of Robert P. Strub.

Strub, Robert P., 1919-'93. Real estate. President of Los Angeles Turf Club (Santa Anita Park); chairman, Santa Anita Operating Co.; president of Thoroughbred Racing Associations 1963-'64. Eclipse Award of Merit in 1992. Son of Charles H. Strub.

Stull, Henry, 1851-1913. Noted American equine painter. First to accurately portray racehorses at a gallop. Owned Swarthmore.

Sutcliffe, Leonard S., 1880-1937. Photographer. Published photographic volumes *Thoroughbred Sires* and *Famous Mares in America*.

Swigert, Daniel, 1833-1912. Breeder. Founded Elmendorf Farm, Kentucky. Leading breeder. Bred Spendthrift, Hindoo, Salvator, Tremont, Baden-Baden. Managed Woodburn Stud. Father-in-law of Leslie Combs Sr.

Swinebroad, George W., 1901-'75. Auctioneer. Legendary auctioneer at Keeneland and Saratoga. Hammered down first $100,000 yearling in 1961.

Swope, Herbert Bayard, 1882-1958. Journalist, investments. Chairman of New York Racing Commission.

Taral, Fred, 1867-1925. Jockey, trainer. Inducted into Racing Hall of Fame in 1955. Rode 1,437 winners, including Domino, Henry of Navarre, Dr. Rice, Ramapo. Rode Domino to nine consecutive victories in 1893.

Tasker, Col. Benjamin Jr., 1720-'60. Planter. Prominent owner-breeder during Colonial era. Owner of Belair Stud, Maryland. Imported great racemare *Selima from England in 1750, notable sire *Othello; bred Pacolet, Selim.

Tayloe, John II, 1721-'79. Planter. Owner of Mount Airy Stud, Virginia. Bred Yorick, Ariel, Bellair; owned *Selima, Moreton's Traveller. Father of John Tayloe III.

Tayloe, John III, 1771-1828. Planter. Owner of Mount Airy Stud, Virginia. Bred American foundation sire Sir Archy, Lady Lightfoot, Grey Diomed, Calypso. Imported *Castianira, dam of Sir Archy. Son of John Tayloe II.

Taylor, Charles P. B., 1935-'97. Journalist, investments. Owner of Windfields Farm, Canada and Maryland; chairman, Canadian Jockey Club; vice president, Breeders' Cup Inc. Son of Edward P. Taylor.

Taylor, Edward P., 1901-'89. Brewing. President, Ontario Jockey Club and Canadian Thoroughbred Horse Society. Owner of Windfields Farm, Canada and Maryland. Leading breeder 1974-'80; Eclipse Award breeder 1977, '83. Bred and owned Northern Dancer, Nearctic, Victoria Park; bred Nijinsky II, El Gran Senor, Devil's Bag, The Minstrel, Secreto, Shareef Dancer, Storm Bird, Viceregal. Father of Charles P. B. Taylor.

Taylor, Joe, 1924-2003.Noted Kentucky horseman and author, whose sons founded Taylor Made Farm and Taylor Made Sales Agency, manager of Gainesway Farm from 1950 to '90.

Ten Broeck, Richard, 1809-'92. Gambler, sportsman. Owner of Metairie Race Course, Louisiana. Bred Umpire; owned Lexington, Lecompte, Prioress, *Eclipse, Starke. Conducted first successful invasion of England with American-breds in 1860s.

Tenney, Meshach, 1907-'93. Trainer. Leading trainer 1962-'63; inducted into Racing Hall of Fame in '91. Trained 36 stakes winners and one champion, including Swaps, Candy Spots, Olden Times, Prove It. Won 1955 Kentucky Derby with Swaps.

Tesio, Federico, 1869-1954. Breeder. Acclaimed Italian breeder of *Ribot, Nearco, Donatello II, Niccolo Dell'Arca. Bred and owned 20 Italian Derby winners. Author of *Breeding the Racehorse*.

Thomas, Barak G., 1826-1906. Planter, publisher. Noted owner-breeder in post-Civil War America. Founded Dixiana Farm, Kentucky. Bred and owned Himyar; bred Domino, Correction.

Thompson, Henry J. "Derby Dick," 1881-1937. Trainer. Inducted into Racing Hall of Fame in 1969. Trained 373 recorded winners and five champions, including Blue Larkspur, Burgoo King, Bubbling Over. First trainer to saddle four Kentucky Derby winners.

Tipton, Edward A., 1855-1930. Auctioneer. Cofounder of Fasig-Tipton Co. in 1898. Sold company to E. J. Tranter. Manager of Bitter Root Stud, Montana, 1896-1900.

Tranter, Enoch J., 1875-1938. Auctioneer. Owner of Fasig-Tipton Co. 1904-'38. Revolutionized Thoroughbred auction business in America. Launched annual yearling sale at Saratoga.

Travers, William R., 1819-'87. Stockbroker, raconteur. First president of Saratoga Association. Owned Kentucky, Alarm, Sultana.

Trotsek, Harry, 1912-'97. Trainer. Inducted into Racing Hall of Fame in 1984. Trained 96 stakes winners and two champions; trained Moccasin, Hasty Road, *Stan. Expert handler of imported horses; coached young jockeys at his jockey school in the 1940s.

Troye, Edward, 1808-'74. Painter. Prolific equine portraitist; his subjects included Lexington, Boston, and many of America's great mid-19th-century Thoroughbreds.

Tuckerman, Bayard J., 1889-1974. Jockey, breeder, owner. First president of Suffolk Downs. Inducted into Racing Hall of Fame in 1973. Rode Homestead. Bred Lavender Hill. Leading amateur jockey.

Turner, Nash, 1881-1937. Jockey, trainer, owner. Inducted into Racing Hall of Fame in 1955. Rode Imp, Flying Star, Goldsmith, Irish Lad. Rider of Imp, the first filly to win the Suburban Handicap in 1899; won 1906 Prix du Jockey-Club (French Derby).

Van Berg, Marion H., 1896-1971. Trainer, owner. Leading owner by money won 1965, '68-'70; leading owner by races won 1952, '54, '56, '60-'70; inducted into Racing Hall of Fame in '70. Trained more than 1,470 winners and six stakes winners, including *Estacion, Rose Bed. Father of Racing Hall of Fame trainer Jack Van Berg.

Vanderbilt, Alfred G., 1912-'99. Investments. Chairman, New York Racing Association; president, Belmont Park and Pimlico Race Course. Owner of Sagamore Farm, Maryland. Eclipse Award of Merit in 1994. Bred and owned Native Dancer, Next Move, Bed o' Roses, Now What, Petrify; owned Discovery; bred Conniver, Miss Disco.

Van Ranst, Cornelius W., Birthdate and date of death unknown. Owned American Eclipse, *Messenger.

Veitch, Sylvester, 1910-'96. Trainer. Inducted into Racing Hall of Fame in 1977. Trained 44 stakes winners and five champions, including Counterpoint, Career Boy. Trained Horse of the Year Counterpoint, who won the 1951 Belmont Stakes. Father of trainer John Veitch.

Vosburgh, Walter, 1855-1938. Handicapper, author. Racing secretary, Westchester Racing Association (Belmont Park) 1894-1934. Author of *Racing in America 1866-1921;* Turf editor of *Spirit of the Times*. Originated Experimental Free Handicap in 1933.

Waggoner, William T., 1852-1934. Oil production, rancher. Early 20th-century force in Texas racing. Owner of 3D's Stock Farm, Texas. Built Arlington Downs racetrack, Texas, in 1929.

Walden, R. Wyndham, Birthdate unknown-1905.

Trainer. Inducted into Racing Hall of Fame in 1970. Trained 101 stakes winners, including Duke of Magenta, Grenada, Saunterer. Trained seven Preakness Stakes winners, five consecutively.

Walsh, Michael G., 1906-'93. Trainer. Leading steeplechase trainer by races won 1953-'55; leading steeplechase trainer by money won 1953-'54, '60; inducted into Racing Hall of Fame in '97; F. Ambrose Clark Award in '75. Trained 31 stakes winners.

Ward, Sherrill, 1911-'84. Trainer. Eclipse Award trainer in 1974; inducted into Racing Hall of Fame in '78. Trained 20 stakes winners and two champions, including Forego, Summer Tan, and Idun. Trained Forego to Horse of the Year honors in 1975 and '76.

Warfield, Elisha, 1781-1859. Physician. Co-founder of the Kentucky Association racetrack, Lexington. Owner of The Meadows Stud, Kentucky. Breeder of Lexington, Berthune, Alice Carneal. Known as the "Father of the Kentucky Turf."

Welch, Aristides J., 1811-'90. Owner of Erdenheim Stud, Pennsylvania. Bred Iroquois, Parole, Sensation, Harold, Spinaway. Stood leading sire *Leamington.

Wells, Thomas J., 1803-'62. Sugar planter. President of Metairie Race Course. Bred Lecomte, Prioress; owned Reel.

Werblin, David A. "Sonny," 1910-'91. Entertainment and sports executive. First president of New Jersey Sports and Exposition Authority (originally the Meadowlands and now including Monmouth Park). Owner of Silent Screen, Process Shot.

Westrope, Jack, 1918-'58. Jockey. Leading jockey in 1933 at age 15, when he rode 301 winners. Inducted into Racing Hall of Fame in 2002.

Whitney, Cornelius V., 1899-1992. Investments. First president of National Museum of Racing Hall of Fame. Owner of C. V. Whitney Farm, Kentucky. Leading breeder 1933, '34, '38, '60; leading owner 1930-'33, '60. Bred more than 175 stakes winners. Bred and owned Counterpoint, Silver Spoon, Career Boy, First Flight; owned Equipoise, Top Flight. Son of Harry Payne Whitney.

Whitney, Harry Payne, 1872-1930. Investments. Owner of Brookdale Stud, New Jersey; Whitney Farm, Kentucky. Leading breeder 1926-'32; leading owner 1913, '20, '24, '26, '27, '29. Bred and owned Regret, Equipoise, Top Flight, Whisk Broom II, Whichone, Whiskery, Pennant, Upset, John P. Grier, Prudery. Father of C. V. Whitney.

Whitney, Mrs. Payne (Helen Hay), 1876-1944. Investments. "First Lady of the American Turf." Owner of Greentree Stud, Kentucky. Leading owner and breeder in 1942. Bred and owned Twenty Grand, Shut Out, Devil Diver, First Minstrel. Mother of John Hay Whitney and Joan Whitney (Mrs. Charles S.) Payson.

Whitney, John Hay "Jock," 1904-'82. Investments, publisher. Co-founder of American Thoroughbred Breeders' Association. Co-owner of Greentree Stud, Kentucky; owner of Mare's Nest Farm, Kentucky. Leading owner in 1951. Bred and raced Stage Door Johnny, Capot, Late Bloomer, Bowl Game, The Axe II, Cohoes, Stop the Music; owned Tom Fool. Stood The Porter.

Whitney, W. Payne, 1875-1927. Investments. Owner of Greentree Stud, Kentucky. Son of William C. Whitney; brother of H. P. Whitney; father of John Hay Whitney and Joan Whitney (Mrs. Charles S.) Payson.

Whitney, William C., 1841-1904. Transportation, oil production. President of Saratoga Race Course. Owner of La Belle Stud, Kentucky. Leading owner 1901, '03. Owned Volodyovski, Plaudit, Artful, Endurance By Right, Nasturtium; bred Artful, Tanya. Father of Harry Payne and W. Payne Whitney.

Whittingham, Charles E., 1913-'99. Trainer. Leading trainer 1970-'73, '75, '81, '82; Eclipse Award trainer 1971, '82, '89; inducted into Racing Hall of Fame in '74. Trained 252 stakes winners and 11 champions, including Ack Ack, Sunday Silence, Ferdinand, Turkish Trousers. All-time leading trainer at Hollywood Park and Santa Anita Park; trained two Kentucky Derby winners.

Wickham, John, 1763-1839. Lawyer. Bred champion and leading sire Boston, Tuckahoe.

Widener, George D., 1889-1971. Investments. Chairman of the Jockey Club 1950-'64; president, National Museum of Racing; president, Belmont Park. Owner of Old Kenney Farm, Kentucky; Erdenheim Stud, Pennsylvania. Bred and owned more than 100 stakes winners, including Jaipur, Eight Thirty, What a Treat, Jamestown, High Fleet, Platter, Stefanita, Jester, Seven Thirty, Rare Treat. Nephew of Joseph E. Widener.

Widener, Joseph E., 1871-1943. Investments. President of Hialeah Park, Belmont Park. Owner of Elmendorf Farm, Kentucky. Leading breeder in 1940. Bred Polynesian, Peace Chance, Osmand; owned Chance Shot. Imported leading sire *Sickle. Father of P. A. B. Widener II; uncle of George D. Widener.

Widener, Peter A. B. II, 1896-1952. Investments. Owner of Elmendorf Farm, Kentucky. Son of Joseph E. Widener.

Williamson, Ansel, ca. 1806-'81. Trainer. Inducted into Racing Hall of Fame in 1998. Trained Aristides, Tom Bowling, Brown Dick, Virgil. Trained first Kentucky Derby winner, Aristides.

Willmot, Donald G., 1917-'94. Brewer, investments. Owner of Kinghaven Farm, Ontario. Leading owner in 1990. Bred and owned With Approval, Izvestia, Steady Growth, Candle Bright, Bayford, Play the King, Carotene; co-owner of Deputy Minister.

Winfrey, G. Carey, 1885-1962. Trainer, owner. Inducted into Racing Hall of Fame in 1975. Trained 16 stakes winners and one champion, including Dedicate, Squared Away, Bulwark, Martyr. Stepfather of William C. Winfrey.

Winfrey, William C., 1916-'94. Trainer. Leading trainer in 1964; inducted into Racing Hall of Fame in '71. Trained 38 stakes winners and seven champions, including Native Dancer, Bed o' Roses, Next Move, Bold Lad. Trained Native Dancer, who retired in 1954 with 21 wins in 22 starts. Stepson of G. Carey Winfrey.

Winkfield, Jimmy, 1882-1974. Jockey. Inducted into the Racing Hall of Fame in 2004. Won the 1901 and '02 Kentucky Derbys aboard His Eminence and Alan-a-Dale, respectively, becoming the last African-American rider to capture the Louisville classic. In 1904 became a leading rider in Russia; later competed in Poland, Romania, Germany, and France.

Winn, Col. Matt. G., 1861-1949. Racing executive. President of Louisville Jockey Club. Legendary racetrack promoter, developed Kentucky Derby into world-class event.

Winters, Theodore, 1823-'94. Mining. Owner of Rancho del Rio, California; Rancho del Sierra, Nevada. Bred Emperor of Norfolk, Yo Tambien, El Rio Rey, Rey del Rey, Thad Stevens; owned Norfolk.

Withers, David D., 1821-1972. Banker. President, Monmouth Park. Owner of Brookdale Farm, New Jersey. Bred Requital, Laggard, Kinglike.

Wood, Eugene D., Birthdate unknown-1924. Racing executive. Treasurer of the Metropolitan Jockey Club (Jamaica). Namesake of Wood Memorial Stakes.

Woodford, Catesby, 1849-1923. President of Kentucky Racing Association. Owner of Raceland Farm, Kentucky. Co-owner of Runnymede Stud, Kentucky. Stood Hindoo, *Star Shoot. Co-breeder of Miss Woodford, Hanover, Sir Dixon.

Woodward, William Jr., 1920-'55. Banker, sportsman. Owner of Belair Stud. Owned Nashua.

Woodward, William Sr., 1876-1953. Banker. Chairman of the Jockey Club 1930-'50. Owner of Belair Stud, Maryland. Leading owner in 1939. Part of syndicate that imported *Sir Gallahad III. Bred and owned Gallant Fox, Omaha, Nashua, Granville, Vagrancy.

Woolf, George "The Iceman," 1910-'46. Jockey. Leading jockey by money won 1942, '44; inducted into Racing Hall of Fame in '55. Rode 721 winners, including Seabiscuit, Whirlaway, Challedon. Won the Belmont Futurity three straight years, the first running of the Santa Anita Derby, and the Preakness Stakes.

Workman, Raymond "Sonny," 1909-'66. Jockey. Leading jockey by races won 1930, '33, '35; leading jockey by money won 1930, '32; inducted into Racing Hall of Fame in '56. Rode 1,169 winners, including Equipoise, Top Flight, Discovery.

Wright, Warren, 1875-1950. Baking powder, investments. Owner of Calumet Farm, Kentucky. Leading breeder 1941, '44, '47-'50; leading owner 1941, '43-'44, '46-'49. Bred and owned Citation, Whirlaway, Pensive, Ponder, Coaltown, Bewitch, Hill Gail, Twilight Tear, Real Delight, Armed; owned Nellie Flag, Bull Lea. Stood leading sire Bull Lea, Sun Again, Chance Play.

Yoshida, Zenya, 1921-'93. Breeder. Owner of Shadai Farm, Japan; Fontainebleau Farm, Kentucky. Leading Japanese breeder 20 times. Bred Amber Shadai, Gallop Dyna, Dyna Gulliver, Vega; co-owned Wajima; stood Northern Taste, Sunday Silence.

Young, Col. Milton S., 1851-1918. Retail hardware, real estate. Chairman of Kentucky Racing Commission. Owner of McGrathiana Stud, Kentucky. Leading breeder in 1890. Bred Broomstick, Yankee; stood Hanover.

Young, William T., 1918-2004. Foods, storage. Owner of Overbrook Farm, Kentucky. Eclipse Award breeder in 1994. Bred and owned Storm Cat, Tabasco Cat, Cat Thief, Boston Harbor, Flanders, Surfside, Golden Attraction, Grindstone. Owned Editor's Note.

Contemporary Individuals in Racing and Breeding

(Names of Racing Hall of Fame members are in boldface italics.)

Abdullah, Khalid, 1942-. Investments. Owner of Juddmonte Farms, Kentucky and England. Eclipse Award breeder in 1995, 2001-'03; Eclipse Award owner in '92, 2003; P.A.B. Widener Trophy in '93; honorary member of Great Britain's Jockey Club in '83. Bred Ryafan, Wandesta (GB), Commander in Chief, Warning (GB), Banks Hill (GB), Empire Maker. Owned Known Fact, Dancing Brave, Rainbow Quest. Member of the ruling family of Saudi Arabia; first Arab owner to win a British classic (Two Thousand Guineas [Eng-G1] with Known Fact in 1980).

Abercrombie, Josephine, 1926-. Oil production, boxing promoter. Owner of Pin Oak Farm, Kentucky. Member of Jockey Club. Bred and owned Laugh and Be Merry, Peaks and Valleys. Co-owned Maria's Mon. Bred Elocutionist, Touching Wood.

Adam, Donald, 1935-. Former chairman and CEO, First American Bank. Owner, Courtlandt Farm, Ocala. Owned Film Maker, Commendation, Gourmet Girl, Pike Place Dancer.

Aga Khan IV, Karim, 1936-. Investments, Ismaili Muslim leader. Owner of Gilltown Stud, Sheshoon Stud in Ireland; Haras de Bonneval in France. Bred and owned Shergar, Sinndar, Kahyasi, Daylami (Ire), Kalanisi (Ire), Dalakhani. Built Aiglemont training facility near Chantilly, France, in 1977; continued breeding operations begun by his grandfather, Aga Khan III, and his father, Aly Khan.

Aitcheson, Joe Jr., 1929-. Jockey. Leading steeplechase jockey 1961, '63-'64, '67-'70; inducted into Racing Hall of Fame in '78; first jockey to receive the F. Ambrose Clark Memorial Award, in '75. Rode 478 winners, including Amber Diver, Bon Nouvel, Tuscalee, Top Bid, Soothsayer, Inkslinger. Won eight Virginia Gold Cups, seven Carolina Cups, and two Colonial Cups.

Alexander, Helen, 1951-. Investments. Member of Jockey Club. President, Thoroughbred Club of America, 1989-'91. Owner of Middlebrook Farm, Kentucky. Bred Twining. Bred and owned Althea, Aishah, Aquilegia. Granddaughter of Robert J. Kleberg.

Allbritton, Joseph, 1924-. Publishing, banking, broadcasting, real estate. Owner of Lazy Lane Farms, Kentucky and Virginia. Member of Jockey Club. Owned Hansel, Secret Hello, Life At the Top, Kittiwake.

Amerman, John, 1932-. Owner, industry official. Chairman and chief executive officer of Mattel Inc., 1987-97. Former director, National Thoroughbred Racing Association. Secretary, Thoroughbred Owners and Breeders Association. Owner of Amerman Racing Stable, California. Owned stakes winners Lido Palace (Chi), Happyanunoit (NZ), Valor Lady, Mash One (Chi), Adoration.

Anthony, John Ed, 1939-. Timber. Owner of Shortleaf Farm, Arkansas; president of Loblolly Stable. Member of Jockey Club. Bred and owned Temperence Hill, Vanlandingham, Prairie Bayou. Owned Cox's Ridge. Established the Exercise Induced Pulmonary Hemorrhage Fund after his Demons Begone bled during the 1987 Kentucky Derby (G1).

Appleton, Arthur, 1915-. Electrical manufacturing. Owner of Bridlewood Farm, Florida. Bred and owned Jolie's Halo, Wild Event. Owned Skip Trial. One of stockholders of *The Florida Horse*.

Arnold, Doug, 1954-. Breeder. Owner, Buck Pond Farm, Kentucky.

Asmussen, Cash, 1962-. Jockey. Leading jockey by money won in 1979; leading jockey in France 1985-'86, '88-'90; Eclipse Award as apprentice jockey in '79. Rode Suave Dancer, Hector Protector, Mill Native, Northern Trick. Won inaugural Japan Cup aboard Mairzy Doates in 1981; three times won five races on a single card in New York. Brother of trainer Steve Asmussen.

Asmussen, Steven, 1965-. Trainer. Leading trainer

by wins in 2002 and '04. Saddled record 555 winners in '04. Brother of Cash Asmussen.

Avioli, Greg, 1964-. Lawyer, lobbyist. Interim chief executive, National Thoroughbred Racing Association and Breeders' Cup Ltd.; former NTRA president and deputy commissioner; chaired NTRA Wagering Systems Task Force. Formerly senior vice president, International Sports and Entertainment Strategies.

Bacharach, Burt, 1929-. Composer. Co-owner of Country Roads Farm, West Virginia. Thoroughbred Owners and Breeders Association Award for outstanding owner-breeder 1995-'96. Bred and owned Heartlight No. One, Afternoon Deelites, Soul of the Matter.

Baeza, Braulio, 1940-. Jockey, trainer. Leading jockey by money won 1965-'68, '75; Eclipse Award jockey 1972, '75; inducted into Racing Hall of Fame in '76; George Woolf Memorial Jockey Award in '68. Rode 3,140 winners, including Buckpasser, Dr. Fager, Ack Ack, Gallant Bloom, Affectionately, Chateaugay. Trained Double Zeus. Rode Buckpasser to one-mile record in 1966 and then lowered it aboard Dr. Fager in '68.

Baffert, Bob, 1953-. Trainer. Leading trainer by money won, 1998-2001; Eclipse Award trainer 1997-'99; United Thoroughbred Trainers of America's Trainer of the Year in '98; Mr. Fitz Award in '97. Trained Chilukki, Real Quiet, Silverbulletday, Silver Charm, Point Given, War Emblem. Won a record 13 stakes at Del Mar in 2000; only trainer to win Kentucky Derby (G1) and Preakness Stakes (G1) in consecutive years (1997-'98).

Bailey, Jerry, 1957-. Jockey. President, Jockeys' Guild, 1990-'97. Leading jockey by money won 1995-'98, 2001-'03; inducted into Racing Hall of Fame in '95; Eclipse Award jockey 1995-'97, 2000-'03; George Woolf Memorial Jockey Award in '92; Mike Venezia Award in '93. Rode Cigar, Fit to Fight, Black Tie Affair (Ire), Sea Hero. In 1996, rode Cigar to his 16th consecutive win; rode seven winners on Florida Derby (G1) day program in '95; successfully lobbied for protective vests to be worn by all jockeys; won handicap triple crown with Fit to Fight in '84. Retired in 2006.

Baird, Dale, 1935-. Trainer. Leading American trainer by annual winners 15 times. On November 5, 2004, became the first trainer to saddle more than 9,000 career winners. Inducted into National HBPA Hall of Fame in 2001. Based at Mountaineer Racetrack in West Virginia. Special Eclipse Award in 2004.

Bandoroff, Craig, 1955-. Farm owner, consignor. Owner of Denali Stud, Kentucky. One of country's leading consignors of yearlings, broodmares, and weanlings.

Barr, John, 1929-. Real estate. Owner, Los Amigos Thoroughbred Farm in Temecula, California; Member and steward, Jockey Club; director, Oak Tree Racing Association; secretary-treasurer, Richard Nixon Presidential Library. Races horses as Oakcrest Stable.

Barton, Patti, 1945-. Jockey. Helped break gender barrier when she became one of the first female jockeys in 1969. Retired in 1984 as world's winningest female rider, with 1,202 victories. Mother of former jockey and television personality Donna Barton Brothers and trainer Jerry Barton.

Bassett, James E. "Ted" III, 1921-. Racing executive. Former chairman, Keeneland Association; former president, Breeders' Cup Ltd.; also served as chairman, Equibase Co.; president, Thoroughbred Racing Associations; chairman, Kentucky Horse Park; president, Thoroughbred Club of America. Co-owner of Lanark Farm, Kentucky. Eclipse Award of Merit in 1995; John W. Galbreath Award in '91; Turf and Field Club Award in '84; Joe Palmer Award in '86; John A. Morris Award in '97; Lord Derby Award in '98.

Baugh, Rollin, 1937-. Bloodstock agent. California-based agent maintains international trade, especially to Japan. Brokered sales of Forty Niner, Charismatic, Captain Steve, and Chief Bearhart to Japan. Member, Jockey Club. Director of Del Mar, Tranquility Farm Thoroughbred retirement facility.

Baze, Russell, 1958-. Jockey. Leading jockey by races won 1992-'96, 2002; inducted into Racing Hall of Fame in '99; Special Eclipse Award in '95; Isaac Murphy Award 1995-2003, '05; George Woolf Memorial Jockey Award in 2002. Rode Hawkster, Both Ends Burning, Itsallgreektome, Lost in the Fog. Won 24 stakes races in 1998; won 400 races a year 11 times in 12 years; won 9,000th race in 2005.

Beasley, Rogers W. B., 1949-. Racing executive. Director of racing for Keeneland Association since 2001; previously director of sales for Keeneland for 19 years; led the initiative to introduce preferred sessions to the September sale and to inaugurate the April two-year-olds in training sales.

Beck, Antony, 1962-. Breeder. President, Gainesway, Kentucky. Director, the National Thoroughbred Racing Association's Horse Political Action Committee 2006-. Member of the board of directors of the Breeders' Cup, 2006-.

Beck, Graham, 1929-. Mining, investments, vintner. Owner of Gainesway, Kentucky; Silvercrest Farm, Kentucky; Midway Farm, Kentucky; Highlands Farm, South Africa; Maine Chance Farm, South Africa; Noreen Stud, South Africa. Bred Pompeii, Real Cozzy, Irish Prize. Co-owned Timber Country.

Bell, Headley, 1954-. Bloodstock agent. Son of Mill Ridge Farm owner Alice Chandler; maternal grandson of Hal Price Headley, co-founder of Keeneland. Past board member, Thoroughbred Club of America, Sales Integrity Sales Force.

Bell, John A. III, 1918-. Owner, breeder, bloodstock agent. Member of Jockey Club. Director, Thoroughbred Owners and Breeders Association; president, Thoroughbred Club of America in 1954; former president, Farm Manager's Club. Owned Jonabell Farm, Kentucky. Bred Battlefield, Aglimmer, One for All, Never Say Die. Owned Epitome. Former president of *The Blood-Horse* magazine; acquired half-interest in Cromwell Bloodstock Agency in 1950.

Bell, Reynolds Jr., 1952-. Bloodstock agent. Son of Mill Ridge Farm owner Alice Chandler; maternal grandson of Hal Price Headley, co-founder of Keeneland. Member, Jockey Club. Vice president, Thoroughbred Owners and Breeders Association. Former manager of Mill Ridge Farm. Past president, Thoroughbred Club of America.

Bellocq, Pierre "Peb," 1926-. Caricaturist. Special Eclipse Award in 1980; John Hervey Award 1965-'66, '68; Knights of Arts and Letters Award in '90; Golden Horseshoe Award in '91. Achieved international acclaim as *Daily Racing Form*'s caricaturist; has murals at Aqueduct, Churchill Downs, Oaklawn Park, and Arlington Park; founded the Amateur Riders Club of the Americas with son Remi Bellocq.

Bellocq, Remi, 1961-. Marketing, organization executive. Former marketing director at Turf Paradise and Santa Anita Park. Became executive director of the National Horsemen's Benevolent and Protective Association in 2001. Son of Pierre Bellocq.

Berube, Paul, 1941-. Retired president of the Thoroughbred Racing Protective Bureau. Background in military intelligence; TRPB agent and vice president 1965-'88.

Beyer, Andrew. Handicapper, journalist. Horse racing columnist for the Washington *Post*, 1978-2004. Developed Beyer Speed Figures and wrote four books on handicapping.

Biancone, Patrick, 1952-. Trainer. Trained All Along (Fr) to North America Horse of the Year title in 1983 with sweep of three turf races carrying a $1-million bonus; All Along also won the Prix de l'Arc de Triomphe (Fr-G1) that year. Also won Arc in 1984 with Sagace (Fr). Trained champion Bikala, Strawberry Road (Aus), Triptych, Palace Music. Came to the United States in 2000 after suspension for a medication positive in Hong Kong.

Biszantz, Gary, 1934-. Golf-club manufacturer. Former chairman of Thoroughbred Owners and Breeders Association. Jockey Club member; Breeders' Cup director. Owns 350-acre Cobra Farm in Lexington. Owned Old Trieste, Running Flame (Fr), Admise (Fr), Lord Grillo (Arg), homebred Cobra King. Co-founder of Cobra Golf, sold in 1996 to American Brands.

Blum, Walter, 1934-. Jockey, racing official. Former president, Jockeys' Guild. Leading jockey by races won 1963-'64; inducted into Racing Hall of Fame in '87; George Woolf Memorial Jockey Award in '65. Rode 4,382 winners, including Affectionately, Gun Bow, Forego, Mr. Prospector, Pass Catcher, Summer Scandal, Boldnesian, Priceless Gem, Lady Pitt.

Boland, Bill, 1933-. Jockey. Won the 1950 Kentucky Derby and Belmont Stakes as an apprentice aboard Middleground. Also won the 1960 Belmont on Amberoid. Won a total of 1,980 races. Elected to the Racing Hall of Fame in 2006 by Historical Review Committee.

Bonnie, Edward S. "Ned," 1929-. Lawyer, steeplechase horseman. Of counsel, Frost Brown Todd LLC, Louisville. Member, Jockey Club. Former director, National Steeplechase Association, Thoroughbred Owners and Breeders Association, Kentucky Thoroughbred Association. With wife Nina, received 2002 First USA Bank/USA Equestrian Lifetime Achievement Award. Responsible for National Steeplechase and Kentucky protective helmet regulations for jockeys.

Boulmetis, Sam Sr., 1927-. Jockey, racing official. Inducted into Racing Hall of Fame in 1973. Rode 2,783 winners. Rode Tosmah, Helioscope, Dedicate. Longtime steward at New Jersey tracks.

Bowen, Edward L., 1942-. Industry executive, author. President, Grayson-Jockey Club Research Foundation. Editor-in-chief, *The Blood-Horse*, 1987-'92. Author of 15 books, including *The Jockey Club Illustrated History of Racing, Matriarchs,* and *Man o' War.*

Bowlinger, Paul, 1960-. Lawyer, industry executive. Vice president, Association of Racing Commissioners International. Former executive director, North American Pari-Mutuel Regulators Association and North Dakota Racing Commission. Board member, Winners Federation.

Brady, Nicholas J., 1930-. Financier. Chairman, Jockey Club, 1974-'82; United States treasury secretary 1988-'93; Co-owner of Mill House Stable. Bred and owned Sensational, Furiously, Meritus. Son of James Cox Brady Jr.

Bramlage, Larry, 1952-. Veterinarian. President, American Association of Equine Practitioners in 2003-'04. Member of Jockey Club. Jockey Club Gold Medal in 1994; British Equine Veterinary Association's Special Award of Merit in '98. Developed and improved ways to repair serious bone fractures.

Brennan, Niall, 1961-. Bloodstock agent, pinhooker. Owner of Niall Brennan Stables, Florida. Leading two-year-old consignor in 2000-'04. Sold Ecton Park, Jersey Girl, Kurofune, Read the Footnotes, Whitmore's Conn, Yonaguska.

Broman, Chester, 1935-. Building contractor. President of Clifford Broman & Sons Inc. in Babylon, New York. Trustee, New York Racing Association; New York Thoroughbred Breeders board of directors. Owner of Chestertown Farm, New York. With his wife, Mary, owned and bred Friends Lake.

Brumfield, Don, 1938-. Jockey, racing official. Inducted into Racing Hall of Fame in 1996; George Woolf Memorial Jockey Award in '88. Rode 4,573 winners, including Forward Pass, Alysheba, Gold Beauty, Our Mims, Old Hat. Retired in 1989 with the most wins in Churchill Downs's (925) and Keeneland Race Course's (716) history.

Brunetti, John, 1931-. President and owner of Hialeah Park, which he purchased in 1978; track has not conducted racing since 2001. Owner of Red Oak Farm, Florida; owned Strolling Belle.

Burch, J. Elliott, 1922-. Trainer. Leading trainer by money won in 1969; inducted into Racing Hall of Fame in '80. Trained more than 30 stakes winners and six champions, including Sword Dancer, Fort Marcy, Arts and Letters, Bowl of Flowers, Run the Gantlet, Key to the Mint. Son of Hall of Fame trainer Preston Burch; grandson of Hall of Fame trainer William Burch.

Burge, Doug, 1971-. Industry executive. Executive vice president and general manager, California Thoroughbred Breeders Association, 1997-.

Campbell Jr., Alex, 1928-. Thoroughbred owner-breeder, philanthropist. Member, Jockey Club. Director, Breeders' Cup Ltd. Retired from tobacco business in 1989. Helped to develop Thoroughbred Park in Lexington. Co-owner, Grade 1 winner Goodbye Halo. Owner and breeder of Mr Purple.

Campbell, W. Cothran "Cot," 1927-. Advertising, racing syndicates. President of Dogwood Stable, South Carolina. John W. Galbreath Award in 1992. Owned Summer Squall, Storm Song, Dominion (GB). Popularized racing syndicates; wrote *Lightning in a Jar: Catching Racing Fever.*

Card, Keith E., 1927-. President of the California Thoroughbred Breeders Association, 2005. Founder and former president of board of directors, Las Tortugas Riding Organization.

Carey, Thomas, 1932-. Racing executive. President and general manager, Hawthorne Race Course. Inducted into Chicago Sports Hall of Fame in 1998. Instrumental in rebuilding Hawthorne after fire in 1978.

Casner, William, 1948-. Heavy equipment. Partner in WinStar Farm, Kentucky. Chairman, Thoroughbred Owners and Breeders Association. Board of advisers, The Race for Education scholarship foundation. Vice chairman and co-founder, Kentucky Equine Education Project (KEEP). Member, board of directors of the University of Kentucky's Maxwell H. Gluck Equine Research Center, National Thoroughbred Racing Association's Political Action Committee. In WinStar name, bred Funny Cide, One Cool Cat. Owned Awesome Humor, Bet Me Best, Byzantium (Brz), and

Pompeii. Co-owner of Ipi Tombe (Zim), Crimson Palace.

Casse, Mark, 1961-. Trainer, consignor, bloodstock agent. Former private trainer and director of operations for Mockingbird Farm, Florida. Leading trainer at Woodbine in 2002. Trained Exciting Story, Dark Ending, Added Edge.

Cauthen, Steve, 1960-. Jockey. Leading jockey by races won in 1977; inducted into Racing Hall of Fame in '94; Eclipse Award apprentice jockey in '77; Eclipse Award jockey in '77; Eclipse Award of Merit in '77; George Woolf Memorial Jockey Award in '84. Rode 2,794 winners, including Affirmed, Oh So Sharp (Ire), Old Vic, Johnny D., Diminuendo, Indian Skimmer. Rode Affirmed to Triple Crown in 1978; only jockey to win the Kentucky, Epsom, Irish, French, and Italian Derbys; at 18, youngest jockey to win Kentucky Derby.

Cella, Charles, 1936-. Real estate, racing executive. President, Oaklawn Park; president, Thoroughbred Racing Associations 1975-'76. TRA's youngest president in 1975. Eclipse Award of Merit 2004. Owned Northern Spur (Ire), Out of Hock, Crafty Shaw.

Chace, Baden P. "Buzz," 1941-. Bloodstock agent. Since 1983, buyer of racing prospects for various clients. Selected Breeders' Cup winners Unbridled's Song and champion Artax, Belmont Stakes (G1) winner Sarava, and numerous Grade 1 winners.

Chandler, Alice Headley, 1927-. Farm owner. Chairwoman, Maxwell F. Gluck Equine Research Center; former chairwoman, Kentucky Racing Commission; president, Kentucky Thoroughbred Owners and Breeders Association; former president, Kentucky Thoroughbred Associaton; director, Keeneland Association. Member of Jockey Club. Owner of Mill Ridge Farm, Kentucky. Bred and owned Keeper Hill. Bred Sir Ivor, Secret Hello, Ciao, Flemensfirth.

Chandler, John. Co-owner, Mill Ridge Farm. Trustee, Thoroughbred Owners and Breeders Association. Racing manager, Juddmonte Farms.

Chavez, Jorge, 1961-. Jockey. Leading jockey in New York 1994-'99; Eclipse Award jockey in '99. Rode Monarchos, Artax, Beautiful Pleasure, A P Valentine, Affirmed Success. Rode six winners on single card at Gulfstream Park in 1999.

Chenery, Helen "Penny," 1931-. Investments. President, Thoroughbred Owners and Breeders Association, 1976-'84. Former owner of Meadow Stud and Meadow Stable, Virginia. Bred Alada. Owned Secretariat, Riva Ridge. First woman to head a major national racing organization; one of the first three women inducted into Jockey Club, in 1983.

Chillingworth, Sherwood, 1926-. Executive vice president of Oak Tree Racing Association. Jockey Club member; board of NTRA Investments; ex-officio member of NTRA Thoroughbred Industry Council; vice chairman of Santa Anita Realty 1994-'96.

Clay, Robert N., 1946-. Farm owner. President, Thoroughbred Owners and Breeders Association, 1990-'93; past president, National Thoroughbred Association and Thoroughbred Club of America. Member of Jockey Club. Co-owner of Three Chimneys Farm, Kentucky. John W. Galbreath Award in 1995. Bred and owned Hidden Lake, Gorgeous. Bred Seaside Attraction, Subordination.

Combs II, Brownell, 1933-. Former president and chairman of Spendthrift Farm; former Kentucky Racing Commission chairman. Son of Leslie Combs II, renowned commercial horse salesman, stallion syndicator, and founder of Spendthrift Farm in 1930s. Pleaded guilty in 2001 to federal income tax fraud charges.

Cooksey, Patricia, 1958-. Jockey. Second all-time leading female jockey with more than 2,100 winners and purse earnings of $20-million. Captured four riding titles at Turfway Park. All-time leading female rider at Churchill Downs. In 1985 became first female to ride in the Preakness Stakes (G1) (sixth on Tajawa). Member of the Kentucky Athletic Hall of Fame. Mr. Fitz Award 2004. Mike Venezia Memorial Award 2004. Retired 2004.

Cordero, Angel Jr., 1942-. Jockey, jockey's agent. Leading jockey by money won 1976, '82-'83; leading jockey by races won in '68; inducted into Racing Hall of Fame in '88; Eclipse Award jockey 1982-'83; George Woolf Memorial Jockey Award in '72; Mike Venezia Award in '92. Rode 7,076 winners, including Seattle Slew, Slew o' Gold, All Along (Fr), Bold Forbes, Broad Brush. Won jockey's title at Saratoga 13 times, 11 consecutively.

Couto, Drew, 1959-. Lawyer. President, Thoroughbred Owners of California. Former president, Thoroughbred Owners and Breeders Association.

Craig, Sidney, 1932- and **Craig, Jenny**, 1932-. Diet foods. Owners of Rancho del Rayo training center in California. Owned 1992-'93 champion older female Paseana (Arg), Exchange, Dr Devious (Ire), Alpride (Ire).

Crist, Steven. Journalist. Publisher, *Daily Racing Form*, 1998-. Has published three books and co-authored two others. Founding editor, *Racing Times*.

Croll, Warren A. "Jimmy" Jr., 1920-. Trainer. Inducted into Racing Hall of Fame in 1994; United Thoroughbred Trainers of America Outstanding Trainer Award in '94; Big Sport of Turfdom Award in '95; Mr. Fitz Award in '95. Owned and trained Holy Bull. Trained Mr. Prospector, Bet Twice, Parka, Forward Gal, Housebuster.

Cruguet, Jean, 1939-. Jockey. Rider of 1977 Triple Crown winner Seattle Slew and other stakes winners, including Bold Reason, Hoist the Flag, Bailrullah. Leading rider at Deauville in 1972 and '73; second leading rider in France in '73; came to the United States in 1965. Was the first rider to win three stakes races in one day, Belmont Stakes (G1) day in 1984.

Day, Pat, 1953-. Jockey. President, Jockeys' Guild, 2000-'01. Leading jockey by races won 1982-'84, '86, '90-'91; inducted into Racing Hall of Fame in '91; Eclipse Award jockey in 1984, '86-'87, '91; George Woolf Memorial Jockey Award in '85; Mike Venezia Award in '95; Mr. Fitz Award in 2000. Rode Wild Again, Flanders, Lady's Secret, Easy Goer, Summer Squall, Tank's Prospect, Louis Quatorze, Lil E. Tee, Dance Smartly. All-time leader by earnings among jockeys and third-highest number of winners; set a record for most stakes won (60) in a single season in 1991; rode seven winners in one day at Churchill Downs in '84; won on eight of nine mounts at Arlington Park in '89. Retired in 2005.

De Francis, Joseph, 1955-. Racing executive, lawyer. President, Maryland Jockey Club; president, Pimlico Race Course and Laurel Park. Son of Frank De Francis.

Delahoussaye, Eddie, 1951-. Jockey. Leading jockey in 1978; inducted into Racing Hall of Fame in '93; George Woolf Memorial Jockey Award in '81. Rode A.P. Indy, Princess Rooney, Prized, Gato Del Sol, Sunny's Halo, Pleasant Stage, Thirty Slews, Gate Dancer. One of four jockeys to win consecutive Kentucky Derbys, in 1982-'83. Retired in early 2003.

Delp, Grover G. "Bud," 1932-. Trainer. Eclipse Award trainer in 1980. Inducted into Racing Hall of Fame in

2002. Trained Spectacular Bid, Include, Timeless Native, Aspro, Silent King.

Desormeaux, Kent, 1970-. Jockey. Leading jockey by races won 1987-'89; leading jockey by money won in '92; inducted into Racing Hall of Fame in 2004; Eclipse Award apprentice jockey in '87; Eclipse Award jockey 1989, '92; George Woolf Memorial Jockey Award in '93. Rode Fusaichi Pegasus, Real Quiet, Kotashaan (Fr), Risen Star. Won record 598 races in 1989; won six races on a single card at Hollywood Park in 1992.

Dickinson, Michael, 1950-. Trainer. Owner of Tapeta Farm, Maryland. Trained Da Hoss, Fleet Renee, Cetewayo, Tapit. Trained first five finishers in England's Cheltenham Gold Cup in 1983.

DiMauro, Steve Sr., 1932-. Trainer. Owner of DiMauro Farm, New York. Eclipse Award trainer in 1975. Bred Flip's Pleasure, Father Don Juan. Trained Wajima, Dearly Precious, Nagurski, Father Don Juan.

Dixon, F. Eugene, 1923-. Investments. Owner of Erdenheim Farm in Pennsylvania, formerly owned by his uncle George D. Widener. Member of Jockey Club; chairman of the Pennsylvania Horse Racing Commission. Former owner of Philadelphia 76ers basketball team.

Dizney, Donald R., 1942-. Health care, banking. Founder and chairman, United Medical Corp. Owner of Double Diamond Farm in Ocala. President, Florida Thoroughbred Breeders' and Owners' Association. Member and steward of the Jockey Club. Bred and co-owned Grade 1 winner Wekiva Springs.

Donn, Douglas, 1947-. Racing executive. President of Gulfstream Park racetrack 1978-2000; chairman of the board 2000-'04, after the track was purchased by Magna Entertainment Corp. Grandson of late Gulfstream owner James Donn Sr.

Dreyfus, Jack J. Jr., 1913-. Financier. Chairman, New York Racing Association, in 1969 and '75. Owner Hobeau Farm, Florida. Member of Jockey Club. Leading owner by money won in 1967; Eclipse Award of Merit in '76. Bred and owned Beau Purple, Duck Dance, Never Bow, Step Nicely. Exacta introduced in New York betting under his direction; his Beau Purple upset Kelso three times.

Drysdale, Neil, 1947-. Trainer. Inducted into Racing Hall of Fame in 2000. Trained A.P. Indy, Fusaichi Pegasus, Princess Rooney, Tasso, Hollywood Wildcat, Fiji (GB), Bold 'n Determined.

Duchossois, Richard L., 1921-. Industrialist. Chairman, Arlington Park. Owner of Hill 'N Dale Farm, Illinois. Special Eclipse Award in 1989; Eclipse Award of Merit in 2004. Special Sovereign Award in '88; Lord Derby Award in '88; Jockey Club Medal in '86; Jockey Agents' Benevolent Association's Man of the Year in '90. Member of Jockey Club. Bred Explosive Darling. Rebuilt Arlington Park after the track was destroyed by fire in 1985; under his leadership, Arlington received a Special Eclipse Award in '85, the first awarded to a racetrack.

Duncker, C. Stephen, 1958-. Industry executive. Co-chairman, New York Racing Association, 2005-. Former co-chief operating officer, NYRA, 2003-'04. Member, Jockey Club. Chairman, American Graded Stakes Committee. Trustee, Thoroughbred Owners and Breeders Association. Former managing director, Goldman Sachs. Bred and owned multiple Grade 2 winner Midlesex Drive.

Dutrow Jr., Richard, 1959-. Trainer. Leading trainer by wins in New York in 2001-'02. One of only seven trainers to train two or more winners on a Breeders' Cup card; Saint Liam in the 2006 Breeders' Cup Classic (G1) and Silver Train in the Sprint (G1). Son of late trainer Richard Dutrow Sr. Also trained Cativa, Offlee Wild, Carson Hollow.

Englander, Richard, 1959-. Investments. Eclipse Award owner in 2001, when he led the nation with stable earnings of $9,784,822, and in '02.

Evans, Edward P. "Ned," 1942-. Publishing. Owner of Spring Hill Farm, Virginia. Member of Jockey Club. Bred and owned Minstrella, Prenup, Raging Fever, Fairy Garden, Colonial Minstrel. Owned Withallprobability. Brother of Robert S. Evans; son of Thomas Mellon Evans.

Evans, Robert S. "Shel," 1944-. Manufacturing. Owner of Winter Haven Farm, Florida; Courtland Farm, Maryland. Member of Jockey Club. Bred and owned Sewickley, Shared Interest. Bred Forestry, Cash Run. Brother of Edward P. Evans; son of Thomas Mellon Evans.

Everett, Marjorie L., 1921-. Racing executive. Former chairman and chief executive officer, Hollywood Park; former owner, Arlington Park; former owner, Washington Park. Undertook major improvements at Hollywood Park, including expanding the circumference of the track, building the Cary Grant Pavilion, and improving the backstretch; successfully lobbied for inaugural Breeders' Cup to be held at Hollywood Park in 1984.

Fabian, Franklin, 1952-. President, Thoroughbred Racing Protective Bureau, 2005-. FBI agent and executive, 1985-2005. Received 1996 Director's Award for Excellence in Investigation.

Fabre, Andre, 1945-. Trainer. Champion French trainer 1987-2004. Won five Prix de l'Arc de Triomphes (Fr-G1), three Breeders' Cup events—the 1993 Classic (G1) with 134-to-1 Arcangues; 1990 Turf (G1) with In the Wings (GB); and 2001 Filly and Mare Turf (G1) with Banks Hill (GB). Also trained Trempolino, Swain (Ire), Subotica (Fr), Sagamix (Fr), Zafonic.

Farish, William S., 1939-. Investments. Chairman, Churchill Downs, 1992-2001. Vice chairman of Jockey Club. President and owner of Lane's End, Kentucky. Eclipse Award breeder in 1992, '99; P.A.B. Widener Trophy in '92. Bred or co-bred A.P. Indy, Mineshaft, Law Society, Lemon Drop Kid, Charismatic, Summer Squall, Prospectors Delite. Owned Bee Bee Bee, Miss Brio (Chi), Sweet Revenge. Former chairman of the Breeders' Cup executive committee; United States ambassador to Great Britain and Northern Ireland, 2001-2004. Nephew of Martha Gerry.

Farish, William "Bill" Jr., 1964-. Business manager and sales director of Lane's End, Kentucky. Son of William S. Farish. Member of the Jockey Club. Board member, Kentucky Thoroughbred Association, Breeders' Cup Ltd, Thoroughbred Owners and Breeders Association, Maxwell H. Gluck Equine Research Center. Former president, Thoroughbred Club of America. Owned and bred Grade 2 winner Shadow Cast and bred Grade 1 winner Burning Roma.

Farmer, Tracy, 1939-. Auto dealer. Owns Farmer Automotive Group Inc. in Louisville and has dealerships in Atlanta and Florida. University of Kentucky Board of Trustees, 1979-'91. Chairman, Kentucky Democratic Party, 1981. Owner of Shadowlawn Farm, Kentucky. Co-owned Hidden Lake, Joyeux Danseur; raced Albert the Great.

Fenwick Jr., Charles, 1948-. Auto dealer; steeplechase jockey, trainer. Trained and rode *Dosdi to two National Steeplechase Association Timber Horse of the Year titles. In 1980 rode *Ben Nevis II to victory in England's Grand National Steeplechase. Trained 1987 Eclipse Award-winning steeplechaser Inlander (GB) and timber champions Buck Jakes, Free Throw, Sugar Bee.

Ferguson, John, 1960-. Bloodstock agent, racing manager. Purchased Pentire, E Dubai, Dubai Destination, Essence of Dubai, Moon Ballad. Chief buying agent and racing manager for Sheikh Mohammed bin Rashid al Maktoum.

Fermin, Ingrid, 1942-. Executive director, California Horse Racing Board, 2005-. In 1981, became the first female steward in California. Known for enforcement of medication regulations.

Fick, Dan, 1948-. Industry executive. Executive vice president and executive director of the Jockey Club. Chairman of the Racing Medication and Testing Consortium. Former senior vice president of racing for the American Quarter Horse Association. Credited with revitalizing the Race Track Chaplaincy of America.

Finley, Terry, 1964-. Founder and president, West Point Thoroughbreds 1991-. Director, National Thoroughbred Racing Association's Political Action Committee 2004-. Member of the board of directors of the Breeders' Cup, 2006-.

Fires, Earlie, 1947-Jockey. Leading apprentice jockey in 1965; inducted into Racing Hall of Fame in 2001; George Woolf Memorial Jockey Award in 1991. Rode In Reality, War Censor, Dike, Abe's Hope, Pattee Canyon, Woozem, Gallant Romeo. Won seven races from eight mounts in a single day at Arlington Park in 1983; won on all six mounts in one day at Hawthorne Race Course in '89.

Firestone, Bertram S., 1931- and **Firestone, Diana**, 1932-. Real estate, investments. Owner, Calder Race Course and Gulfstream Park 1988-'91. Owner of Catoctin Stud, Virginia. Eclipse Award owner in 1980. Owned Genuine Risk. Bred and owned Theatrical (Ire), Paradise Creek, April Run (Ire), Honest Pleasure, What a Summer.

Fishback, Jerry, 1947-. Jockey, bloodstock agent. Leading steeplechase jockey by races won 1971, '73-'75, '77; leading steeplechase jockey by money won in '85; inducted into Racing Hall of Fame in '92. Rode 301 winners, including Cafe Prince, Flatterer. Won the Temple Gwathmey Steeplechase Handicap six times; won four Carolina Cups and four International Gold Cups.

Ford, Gerald, 1944-. Banker and insurer. Chairman of Dallas-based First Acceptance Corp., formerly Liberte Investments Inc., of which he owns approximately 45%. In 2000, bought 815 acres of former Brookside Farm in Kentucky for approximately $11-million and renamed it Diamond A Farms. Also owns 120,000-acre Diamond A Ranch in New Mexico. Raced Pleasantly Perfect, winner of the 2003 Breeders' Cup Classic (G1) and 2004 Dubai World Cup (UAE-G1). Also raced homebred Minister Eric.

Foreman, Alan, 1950-. Lawyer. Chairman and chief executive officer, Thoroughbred Horsemen's Association. Creator of Mid-Atlantic Thoroughbred Championship (MATCH) series; general counsel for the Maryland Thoroughbred Horsemen's Association.

Forsythe, John, 1918-. Actor. Director, Hollywood Park. Owner of Big Train Farm. Eclipse Award of Merit in 1988. Owned Targa. Longtime Eclipse Awards dinner host.

Francis, Dick, 1920-. Jockey, author. International best-selling author of 39 mystery novels about horse racing. England's champion steeplechase jockey of 1953-'54 when he rode for the Queen Mother. Published first novel—*Dead Cert*—in 1962 and last—*Shattered*—in 2000. Winner of three Edgar Allen Poe Awards for best mystery novel.

Frankel, Robert, 1941-. Trainer. Leading trainer by money won in 1993, 2002-'03; inducted into Racing Hall of Fame in '95; Eclipse Award trainer in 1993, 2000-'03. Trained Bertrando, Possibly Perfect, Wandesta (GB), Marquetry, Squirtle Squirt, Empire Maker, Medaglia d'Oro, Ghostzapper. Once called the king of claimers for his ability to turn claiming horses into winners; won a record 60 races at Hollywood Park during his first year in California (1972). Established earnings record and mark for most Grade 1 victories in a year in 2003.

Fravel, Craig, 1958-. Lawyer, racetrack executive. Executive vice president, Del Mar Thoroughbred Club, 1990-. Director, NTRA; member, Equibase Management Committee.

Fuller, Peter S., 1923-. Automobile dealer. John A. Morris Award in 1985. Bred and owned Dancer's Image, Mom's Command, Shananie, Donna's Time.

Fulton, Stanley, 1931-. Owner of Sunland Park Racetrack and Casino, New Mexico; consultant, Anchor Gaming; Thoroughbred owner, philanthropist. Leading buyer at 2003 Fasig-Tipton Kentucky select yearling sale.

Gagliano, James L., 1965-. Executive vice president and chief administrative officer of the Jockey Club, 2005-. Formerly executive vice president of Maryland Racing Operations for Magna Entertainment Corp.

Gann, Edmund A., 1923-. Commercial fisheries, banking. Entered racing in 1960s when a fishing buddy offered him half-interest in a filly to settle a debt. Owned more than 35 stakes winners, including Pay the Butler, Al Mamoon, Medaglia d'Oro, Peace Rules, Midas Eyes, You.

Garland, Bruce, 1950-. Racing executive. Former senior executive vice president of racing for New Jersey Sports and Exposition Authority; vice chairman of Harness Tracks of America; served on board of the Thoroughbred Racing Associations and U.S. Trotting Association. Formerly executive director of New Jersey Racing Commission.

Gaylord, E. K. II, 1957- . Chairman and executive producer, Gaylord Films. Board of directors, Gaylord Entertainment Co. Member, Breeders' Cup board of directors. Director, National Cowboy & Western Heritage Center. Breeder, owner, owns Lazy E Ranch in Edmond, Oklahoma. Son of E. L. Gaylord, part-owner of 1980 Kentucky Derby (G1) runner-up Rumbo and graded stakes winner Cactus Road.

Gentry, Tom, 1937-. Bloodstock agent, breeder. Former owner of Tom Gentry Farm, Kentucky. Bred Royal Academy, Brazen, Marfa, Terlingua, Pancho Villa, Artichoke. Leading Keeneland consignor in 1970s, '80s. Son of Olin Gentry.

Gerry, Martha Farish, 1918-. Investments. Owner of Lazy F Ranch, Texas. Member of Jockey Club. Bred and owned Forego, Maid of France, Clef d'Argent, French Colonial. Bred and raced three-time Horse of the Year Forego, who earned nearly $2-million from 1973-'78. Aunt of William S. Farish.

Gertmenian, L. Wayne, 1939-. Former president, Jockeys' Guild; president and chief executive officer, Matrix Capital Associates; professor of economics and management, Graziadio School of Business and Management, Pepperdine University.

Gill, Michael, 1956-. Mortgage banking. Led all owners in the United States by wins and earnings, 2003-'05; finished second among U.S. owners by wins in 2002 and '00. Broke records at Gulfstream and Monmouth Parks for wins in 2003. Eclipse Award as outstanding owner, 2005.

Griffin, Merv, 1925-. Entertainment executive. Owner of Stevie Wonderboy, Eclipse Award for champion two-year-old male of 2005. Creator of multiple television shows, including "Jeopardy," "Wheel of Fortune," and "Merv Griffin Show."

Haire, Darrell, 1957-. Jockey, industry executive. Interim national manager, Jockeys' Guild Inc. Member representative with Jockeys' Guild, 2000-. Rode professionally, 1973-1990. Won 1980 Arkansas Derby (G2) with Temperence Hill.

Hamilton, Lucy Young, 1952-. Co-owner of Overbrook Farm in Lexington. Member, Jockey Club. Daughter of the late William T. Young and widow of trainer Francois Boutin.

Hancock, Arthur B. III, 1943-. Breeder. Owner of Stone Farm, Kentucky. Member of Jockey Club. Mr. Fitz Award in 1990. Bred and owned Sunday Silence, Gato Del Sol, Goodbye Halo. Co-bred Fusaichi Pegasus. Stood leading sire Halo. Brother of Seth Hancock; son of Arthur B. "Bull" Hancock Jr.

Hancock, Dell, 1952-. Co-owner of Claiborne Farm and spokesperson for the Paris, Kentucky, breeding operation. Member and steward, Jockey Club; chairman, Grayson-Jockey Club Research Foundation. Daughter of the late A. B. "Bull" Hancock Jr.

Hancock, Richard E., 1940-. Industry executive. Executive vice president and chief executive officer for the Florida Thoroughbred Breeders' and Owners' Association since 1988. Board member, National Thoroughbred Retirement Foundation and the Florida Division of the Thoroughbred Retirement Foundation.

Hancock, Seth, 1949-. Breeder. Director, Churchill Downs; director, Keeneland Association. Member of Jockey Club. President of Claiborne Farm, Kentucky. Eclipse Award breeder 1979, '84. Bred and owned Swale, Forty Niner, Lure. Bred Wajima, Nureyev, Caerleon. Organized a syndicate to acquire Secretariat for more than $6-million. Stood Mr. Prospector, Unbridled, Danzig. Stands Seeking the Gold. Brother of Arthur B. Hancock III; son of Arthur B. "Bull" Hancock Jr.

Harper, Joseph, 1943-. Racing executive. President and chief executive officer of Del Mar Thoroughbred Club since 1990; president of Thoroughbred Racing Associations, 2003-'04. Member of Jockey Club; former executive vice president and general manager of Oak Tree Racing Association; grandson of Cecil B. DeMille.

Harris, John C., 1943-. Breeder, agricultural products. Past president, California Thoroughbred Breeders Association; director, Thoroughbred Owners of California. Member of Jockey Club. Owner of Harris Farms, California. Bred and owned Soviet Problem.

Handel, Harold G. "Hal," 1947-. Racing executive. Chief executive officer of Greenwood Racing Inc. operator of Philadelphia Park, since 1998. President of the Thoroughbred Racing Associations,1997-'98. Former executive vice president of the New Jersey Sports and Exposition Authority, owner of the Meadowlands and Monmouth Park racetracks; former executive director and legal counsel for New Jersey Racing Commission.

Hartack, William J., 1932-. Jockey, racing official. Leading jockey by races won in 1955-'57, '60; leading jockey by money won in 1956-'57; inducted into Racing Hall of Fame in '59. Rode 4,272 winners, including Northern Dancer, Tim Tam, Majestic Prince. First jockey to earn $3-million in one year (1957); won five Kentucky Derbys (aboard Iron Liege in 1957, Venetian Way in '60, Decidedly in '62, Northern Dancer in '64, and Majestic Prince in '69).

Hawley, Sandy, 1949-. Jockey. Leading jockey by races won in 1970, '72-'73, '76; leading rider in Canada nine times; inducted into Racing Hall of Fame in '92; inducted into Canada's Hall of Fame in '86; Eclipse Award jockey in '76; George Woolf Memorial Jockey Award in '76; Sovereign Award in 1978, '88; Avelino Gomez Memorial Award in '86; Joe Palmer Award in '98. Rode 6,449 winners, including Youth, Desert Waves, Kiridashi, Smart Strike, Highland Vixen. First jockey to win more than 500 races in one season (1973).

Hayward, Charles, 1950-. Racetrack executive. President and chief executive officer, New York Racing Association, 2004-. Former president and chief executive officer *Daily Racing Form*. Member, NYRA board of trustees, 1995-'99.

Heiligbrodt, William, 1941-. Retired from banking, financial services, and funeral services. Campaigned more than 55 stakes winners. Board member, Texas Thoroughbred Association and Texas Horse Racing Hall of Fame. With wife, Corinne, raced 2003 Grade 1 winner Lady Tak and top sprinter Posse.

Hettinger, John, 1933-. Investments, real estate. Director, Breeders' Cup Ltd. Owner of Akindale Farm, New York. Member of Jockey Club. Special Eclipse Award in 2000. Bred and owned Warfie, Yestday's Kisses, Chase the Dream, Genuine Regret. Instrumental in founding the Racehorse Adoption Referral Program; chairman emeritus of the Grayson-Jockey Club Research Foundation; major shareholder, Fasig-Tipton Co.

Hickey, Jay, 1944-. Lawyer, lobbyist. President, American Horse Council. Represented equine organizations, horse owners, and horse breeders during his time as a practicing lawyer.

Hirsch, Joe, 1929-. Journalist. Co-founder and first president of the National Turf Writers Association 1959-'60. Lord Derby Award in 1985; Jockey Club Medal in '89; Mr. Fitz Award in '98; Walter Haight Award in '84; Joe Palmer Award in '94; Eclipse Award of Merit in '92; Eclipse Award for outstanding newspaper writing in '79. Longtime executive columnist of *Daily Racing Form;* retired in late 2003.

Hollendorfer, Jerry, 1949-. Trainer. All-time leading trainer in Northern California. Trained more than 4,300 winners through mid-2005. Won Bay Meadows Race Course and Golden Gate Fields training titles more than 20 times consecutively; won Golden Gate title 22 consecutive times. Trained Lite Light, King Glorious, Pike Place Dancer, Event of the Year.

Hooper, Dave, 1935-. Executive director, Texas Thoroughbred Association.

Hubbard, R. D., 1935-. Glass manufacturing. Former chairman and chief executive officer, Hollywood Park; owner, Ruidoso Downs. Owner of Crystal Springs Farm, Kentucky; Frontera Farm, New Mexico. Owned Gentlemen (Arg), Talloires, Leger Cat (Arg), Fit to Lead, Invited Guest, Mistico (Chi). Co-founded the Shoemaker Foundation in 1990 to help horsemen who have had catastrophic accidents or illnesses.

Hughes, B. Wayne, 1933-. Warehousing, philanthropist. Founder and president of Public Storage, of which he and his family own 39%. Director, Thoroughbred Owners and Breeders Association. Founder, Parker Hughes Cancer Center in Minnesota. Bought Spendthrift Farm in 2004. Owner of Action This Day, Joyeux Danseur, Shake the Yoke (GB), Trishyde.

Humphrey, G. Watts Jr., 1944-. Investments, manufacturing. Vice president, Breeders' Cup; director, Keeneland Association; steward of Jockey Club. Owner of Shawnee Farm, Kentucky. Bred Creme Fraiche, Sacahuista. Owned Likely Exchange, Amherst Wayside, Noble Damsel, Sorbet.

Hunt, Nelson Bunker, 1926-. Oil production. Owned Bluegrass Farm, Kentucky. Eclipse Award breeder in 1976, '85, '87; P.A.B. Widener Trophy in '85-'87. Bred and owned Dahlia, Youth, Empery, Trillion, Estrapade. Owned *Vaguely Noble, Exceller, Glorious Song. Bred Dahlia, the first mare to earn more than $1-million.

Icahn, Carl, 1936-. Financier. Owner of Foxfield Thoroughbreds, Kentucky. John A. Morris Award in 1990. Bred Blushing K. D., Great Navigator, Vaudeville, Helmsman, Brave Tender. Owned Meadow Star, Rose's Cantina, Colonial Waters.

Jackson, Jess, 1930-. Vintner, owner-breeder. Founder and principal owner of Kendall-Jackson Wine Estates. Owner of Stonestreet Stables.

Janney, Stuart III, 1948-. Financier. Former chairman, Thoroughbred Owners and Breeders Association. Steward of Jockey Club. Bred and owned Coronado's Quest, Warning Glance, Deputation, Mesabi Maiden. Aided in the formation of the National Thoroughbred Racing Association.

Jerkens, H. Allen, 1929-. Trainer. Leading trainer in New York in 1957, '62, '66, '69; inducted into Racing Hall of Fame in '75; Eclipse Award trainer in '73; Mr. Fitz Award in 2001. Trained more than 150 stakes winners, including Sky Beauty, Onion, Beau Purple, Duck Dance, Prove Out. Known as the "Giant Killer" for training horses who upset champions Secretariat, Kelso, Forego, and Buckpasser. Father of trainer Jimmy Jerkens.

Johnsen, Corey, 1955-. Racing executive. Magna Entertainment Corp. vice president and president of Lone Star Park; former general manager, Remington Park; created the All-Star Jockey Championship in 1997; played a key role in the development, construction, and opening of Lone Star and Remington; produced Eclipse Award-winning television program while at Louisiana Downs. Elected president of TRA in 2005.

Jolley, LeRoy, 1938-. Trainer. Inducted into Racing Hall of Fame in 1987. Trained Foolish Pleasure, Honest Pleasure, Genuine Risk, What a Summer, Manila, Meadow Star. Won the Kentucky Derby in 1980 with filly Genuine Risk. Son of trainer Moody Jolley.

Jones, Aaron U., 1921-. and **Jones, Marie**. Timber. Bred and owned Lemhi Gold, Western, Tiffany Lass. Owned Riboletta (Brz), Forestry, Plenty of Light. Bred Speightstown, Ashado.

Jones, Brereton C., 1939-. Breeder, politician. Director, Breeders' Cup Ltd.; past president and director, Thoroughbred Club of America. Owner of Airdrie Stud, Kentucky. Bred Desert Wine, Southjet, Formidable Lady, Dansil. Owned By Land by Sea, Imp Society, Silver Medallion. Helped persuade Breeders' Cup to supplement purses at tracks around the country in addition to the Breeders' Cup day events; inaugurated Kentucky Thoroughbred Development Fund while governor of Kentucky, 1991-'95, co-founder of Kentucky Equine Education Project.

Jones, John T. L. Jr., 1935-. Breeder. Owner and general manager, Walmac International, Kentucky. One of the founding members of the Breeders' Cup Ltd.; stood Alleged, Nureyev, Phone Trick.

Jones, Richard I. G., 1938-. Lawyer, bloodstock agent. Co-founded Walnut Green Bloodstock with brother Russell B. Jones Jr. Member, Jockey Club. Breeding and racing manager for Christiana Stables.

Jones, Russell B. Jr., 1935-. Bloodstock agent. President and chief operating officer, Walnut Green Bloodstock, which he co-founded with brother Richard I. G. Jones. Member, Jockey Club. General manager of Morven Stud, 1991-2000.

Kelly, Tommy J., 1919-. Trainer. Inducted into Racing Hall of Fame in 1993. Trained Plugged Nickle, Colonel Moran, Droll Role, Pet Bully, Globemaster. Co-owner of Evening Attire. Father of trainer Pat Kelly.

Kimmel, John, 1954-. Veterinarian, trainer. Conditioned 1997 champion Hidden Lake. In veterinary practice, 1980-'87. Has saddled nearly 1,000 winners and the earners of more than $40-million. Father, Caesar Kimmel, has owned racehorses for 30 years.

Krantz, Bryan, 1960-. Racing executive. Past president and general manager, Fair Grounds Race Course; owner, Jefferson Downs. Built new grandstand after a fire destroyed Fair Grounds's physical plant in 1993.

Krone, Julie, 1963-. Jockey. Inducted into Racing Hall of Fame in 2000. All-time leading female jockey with more than 3,700 victories. First woman to win a Triple Crown race (Colonial Affair, 1993 Belmont Stakes [G1]) and Breeders' Cup race (Halfbridled, 2003 Breeders' Cup Juvenile Fillies [G1]).

Lake, Scott, 1965-. Trainer. Manages a stable of approximately 150 horses, mostly claimers. Leading North American trainer by wins in 2001 with 406, and in 2003 with 455. Trained former claimers Shake You Down and My Cousin Matt to Grade 2 victories.

Lavin, A. Gary, V.M.D., 1937-. Veterinarian. President of American Association of Equine Practitioners, 1994; AAEP's Lavin Cup, an annual award for commitment to horse welfare, in his honor. Founded Longfield Farm in Goshen, Kentucky, in 1979. Elected to Jockey Club in 1994, the first veterinarian chosen in 100 years. Past president, Kentucky Thoroughbred Association.

Levy, Robert P., 1931-. Chemical storage. Former owner, Atlantic City Race Course; former president, Thoroughbred Racing Associations. Owner of Muirfield East, Maryland. Owned Housebuster, Smoke Glacken, Bet Twice. Inaugurated full-card simulcasting in 1983.

Liebau, F. Jack, 1938-. Lawyer, racetrack executive. President, Bay Meadows Racing Assocation; former president, Santa Anita Park. Member of Jockey Club. Owner of Valley Creek Farm, California. Owned Yashgan (GB), Boo La Boo, Forzando (GB), Kadial (Ire).

Little, Donald, 1934-. Financial management. Owner

of Centennial Farms, Virginia. Owned Colonial Affair, Rubiano, King Cugat. Past president of the United States Polo Association; organizes racing syndicates.

Lukas, D. Wayne, 1935-. Trainer. Leading trainer by money won in 1983-'92, '94-'97; leading trainer by races won in 1987-'90; leading trainer by stakes races won in 1985-'92; inducted into Racing Hall of Fame in '99; Eclipse Award trainer in 1985-'87, '94; John W. Galbreath Award in '98. Leading trainer of Eclipse Award winners. Trained Lady's Secret, Thunder Gulch, Timber Country, Gulch, Flanders, Tabasco Cat, Codex, Charismatic. First trainer to reach both $100-million and $200-million in earnings; first trainer to win two Breeders' Cup races in one day (in 1985) and three races in one day (in '88); transformed modern training with entrepreneurial methods.

Lyster, Wayne G. III, 1948-. Owner, Ashview Farm, Kentucky. Former chairman, Kentucky Racing Commission. Co-bred champion Johannesburg; bred stakes winners At the Half, Lu Ravi.

Mabee, Betty, 1921-. Owner of Golden Eagle Farm near Ramona, California. Along with late husband, John, who died in 2002, won Eclipse Award as outstanding breeder in 1991, '97, and '98. Campaigned $5-million winner Best Pal, $2-million earners General Challenge and Dramatic Gold, and millionaire Excellent Meeting.

Mack, Earle, 1939-. Real estate. Owner, Rising Son Stable. Member, board of trustees, The New York Racing Association Inc.; member, Thoroughbred Owners and Breeders Association; chairman, New York State Racing Commission, 1983-'89. Established the New York Thoroughbred Owners Awards. Owned Peteski, 1993 Canadian Horse of the Year.

Madden, Preston, 1934- and **Madden, Anita**, 1933- Real estate development. Owner of Hamburg Place, Kentucky. Bred Alysheba, Pink Pigeon, Miss Carmie, Romeo, Kentuckian. Owned T. V. Lark. Stood leading sire T. V. Lark; Anita Madden was the first female member of the Kentucky State Racing Commission.

Magnier, John, 1948-. Farm owner, breeder. Owner of Coolmore Stud, Ireland; Coolmore Stud, Australia; Ashford Stud, Kentucky; Creek View Farm, Kentucky. Bred Galileo (Ire), Sadler's Wells, Dr Devious (Ire). Originated shuttle-stallion concept; expanded mare books; stood Be My Guest, El Gran Senor, Danehill. Stands Sadler's Wells, Woodman.

Maktoum, Sheikh Hamdan bin Rashid al, 1945- Deputy ruler of Dubai; minister of finance and industry for United Arab Emirates; UAE representative to OPEC. Owns Shadwell Farm in Kentucky, Shadwell Estate, Nunnery Stud, England; Derrinstown Stud, Ireland. Leading owner in England, 1995. Bred and owned Nashwan, Erhaab, Salsabil (Ire); partner with brothers Mohammed and Maktoum in Godolphin Racing.

Maktoum, Sheikh Mohammed bin Rashid al, 1949-. Crown prince of Dubai. Owner of Raceland Farm, Kentucky; Darley at Jonabell, Kentucky; Dalham Hall Stud, England; Kildangan Stud, Ireland; Darley Australia, Australia. Bred and owned Dubai Millennium, Intrepidity (GB), In the Wings (GB), Swain (Ire). Owned Oh So Sharp (GB), Daylami (Ire), Pebbles (GB). Created Godolphin Racing, Dubai World Cup (UAE-G1).

Mandella, Richard, 1950-. Trainer. Inducted into Racing Hall of Fame in 2001. Trained Kotashaan (Fr), Phone Chatter, Dixie Union, Gentlemen (Arg), Halfbridled, Johar, Pleasantly Perfect, Wild Rush, and Dare and Go, who won the Pacific Classic (G1) in 1996, ending Cigar's 16-race winning streak. Won record four Breeders' Cup races in 2003.

Mangurian, Harry T. Jr., 1926-. Real estate development, construction. Former owner, Mockingbird Farm. Member, Jockey Club. Eclipse Award of Merit, 2002. Leading breeder in North America by earnings and races won, 1999-2002. First chairman of Ocala Breeders' Sales Co. Past director, Breeders' Cup Ltd., Florida Thoroughbred Breeders' and Owners' Association. Bred or owned more than 150 stakes winners, including Appealing Skier, Desert Vixen, Gilded Time, Successful Appeal, Valid Appeal. Former owner, Boston Celtics.

Maple, Edward, 1948-. Jockey. Began riding in Ohio and West Virginia, moved to New Jersey in 1970 and New York in '71. Rode champions Conquistador Cielo, Devil's Bag; won the Belmont Stakes (G1) with Temperence Hill and Creme Fraiche. Won 4,398 races and earned more than $105-million; rode Secretariat in champion's last career start, 1973 Canadian International. George Woolf Memorial Jockey Award in 1995; retired from racing in 1998 immediately after receiving the Mike Venezia Award.

Martin, Ed, 1954-. Association of Racing Commissioners International president, 2005-. Former executive director, New York State Racing and Wagering Board.

Martin, Frank "Pancho," 1925-. Trainer. Leading trainer by money won in 1974; leading trainer in New York in 1973-'82; inducted into Racing Hall of Fame in '81. Trained 51 stakes winners and two champions, including Autobiography, Outstandingly, Sham, Manassa Mauler, Rube the Great.

Marzelli, Alan, 1954-. Racing executive. President and chief operating officer of Jockey Club since January 1, 2003; chairman of Equibase Co. LLC since 1996. Joined Jockey Club in 1983 as chief financial officer and later became executive vice president.

McAlpine, James R., 1946-. Former president and chief executive officer, Magna Entertainment Corp; vice chairman of corporate development for Magna.

McAnally, Ron, 1932-. Trainer. Inducted into Racing Hall of Fame in 1990; Eclipse Award trainer in 1981, '91-'92; Mr. Fitz Award in '92. Trained John Henry, Bayakoa (Arg), Tight Spot, Paseana (Arg), Northern Spur (Ire).

McCarron, Chris, 1955-. Jockey, racetrack executive. Leading jockey by races won in 1974-'75, '80; leading jockey by money won in 1980-'81, '84, '91; inducted into Racing Hall of Fame in '89; Eclipse Award apprentice jockey in '74; Eclipse Award jockey in '80; George Woolf Memorial Jockey Award in '80; Mike Venezia Award in '91. Rode Alysheba, John Henry, Lady's Secret, Sunday Silence, Tiznow. Retired in 2002 as leading earner among jockeys with $264-million; along with his wife, Judy, and comedian Tim Conway, created the Don MacBeth Memorial Fund for disabled jockeys. General manager of Santa Anita Park in 2003-'04. Founded North American Riding Academy.

McDonald, Reiley, 1957-. Bloodstock agent. Partner, Eaton Sales Inc. Kentucky. Owner, Indian Hills Farm and Athens-Woods Farm, Kentucky. Former vice president, Fasig-Tipton Co., former president, Stallion Access. Driving force behind development of Thoroughbred Retirement Foundation's Secretariat Center, located at Kentucky Horse Park, for rehabilitation and adoption of Thoroughbreds. Board member, Keeneland Association, University of Kentucky's Maxwell H. Gluck Equine Research Center, Kentucky Horse Park. Sold Banshee Breeze, Grand Slam, Hawk Wing, High Yield, Russian Rhythm, Victory Gallop, Yes It's True. Owned Nasty Storm.

McGaughey, Claude R. "Shug" III, 1951-. Trainer. Eclipse Award trainer in 1988; inducted into Racing Hall of Fame in 2004. Trained Easy Goer, Rhythm, Inside Information, Heavenly Prize, My Flag, Storm Flag Flying and Personal Ensign, unbeaten in 13 races; won five graded stakes at Belmont Park on Breeders' Cup preview day in 1993.

McKathan, J. B., 1966- and **McKathan, Kevin**, 1968-. Bloodstock agents. Owners of McKathan Brothers Training Facility in Ocala; purchased for clients Silver Charm, Real Quiet, Silverbulletday, Captain Steve.

McKay, Jim (Jim McManus), 1921-. Broadcaster. Eclipse Award of Merit in 2000; Big Sport of Turfdom Award in 1987; Joe Palmer Award in 2000. Member of Jockey Club. Co-founder of Maryland Million; broadcast host of Triple Crown 1975-2000 on ABC.

McMahon, Gerald F. "Jerry," 1950-. Sales company executive. President and general manager, Barretts Equine Sales Ltd. Previously vice president, Fasig-Tipton California.

McNair, Robert, 1937- and **McNair, Janice**, 1936- Investments, NFL team owner. Owner of Stonerside Stable, Kentucky; training facilities in Aiken, South Carolina and Saratoga Springs, New York. Co-bred Fusaichi Pegasus; bred and owned Congaree. Owned Chilukki, Tuzla (Ire). Co-owned Coronado's Quest, Touch Gold. Robert is member of Jockey Club.

Meeker, Thomas, 1943-. Racing executive. President, Churchill Downs Inc.; president, Thoroughbred Racing Associations, 1991-'92. John W. Galbreath Award in 1999. Beginning in 1984, implemented a $25-million, five-year improvement plan for Churchill, including a $3.6-million turf course and a $2.8-million paddock. Undertook $121-million renovation of Churchill in 2002; oversaw expansion of Churchill Downs Inc. to encompass tracks from coast to coast.

Melnyk, Eugene, 1959-. Pharmaceuticals. Owns Ottawa Senators of the National Hockey League. Owner, Winding Oaks Farm, Florida. Member, New York Racing Association board of trustees. Co-recipient of National Turf Writers Association 2002 Joe Palmer Award for contributions to racing. Campaigns horses with wife, Laura. Co-owned Archers Bay; owned Graeme Hall, Harmony Lodge, Marley Vale, Pico Teneriffe, Strong Hope, Tweedside, Speightstown.

Metzger, Dan, 1963-. Racing executive. President of Thoroughbred Owners and Breeders Association since 1999. Former director of marketing services and licensing for Breeders' Cup Ltd.

Meyerhoff, Robert, 1924-. Real estate development. Owner of Fitzhugh Farm, Maryland. Bred and owned Broad Brush, Concern, Include, Valley Crossing.

Meyocks, Terry, 1951-. Racing executive. Former president and chief operating officer of New York Racing Association. Former vice president of racing for NYRA; former racing secretary at Calder Race Course, director of racing at Gulfstream Park.

Migliore, Richard, 1964-. Jockey. Eclipse Award as outstanding apprentice jockey 1981. Based in New York, he has won more than 4,000 races. Recipient of the 2003 Mike Venezia Memorial Award and the '03 Thurman Munson Award. Has ridden more than 4,000 winners, including Funny Cide, Kazoo, Incorporatetime, Great Intentions.

Miller, Leverett, 1931-. Owner-breeder. With wife, Linda, owns and operates T-Square Stud in Fairfield, Florida. Campaigns in Eton blue silks of late uncle C.V. Whitney. Bred Silver Wagon. Member, Jockey Club. Board member, Breeders' Cup, Florida Thoroughbred Breeders' and Owners' Association. Former board member, Ocala Breeders' Sales Co.

Miller, MacKenzie "Mack," 1921-. Trainer, breeder. Inducted into Racing Hall of Fame in 1987; Mr. Fitz Award in '96. Member of Jockey Club. Trained 72 stakes winners, including champions Leallah, Assagai, Hawaii, and *Snow Knight. Trained Fit to Fight to New York handicap triple crown in 1984; trained Sea Hero to Kentucky Derby victory in 1993. Bred De La Rose, Lite Light, Chilukki.

Moran, Elizabeth "Betty," 1932-. Investments. Owner of Brushwood Stable, Pennsylvania. Bred Russian Rhythm,High Yield. Owned Creme Fraiche. Won English Grand National Steeplechase Handicap with Papillon in 2000.

Mott, William, 1953-. Trainer. Inducted into Racing Hall of Fame in 1998; Eclipse Award trainer in 1995-'96. Trained Cigar, Paradise Creek, Ajina, Theatrical (Ire), Geri, Escena, Wekiva Springs. Trained Cigar for 16 consecutive victories from 1994-'96.

Nafzger, Carl, 1941-. Trainer. Eclipse Award trainer in 1990; Big Sport of Turfdom Award in '90. Trained Unbridled, Banshee Breeze, Unshaded, Vicar, Solvig. Wrote *Traits of a Winner: The Formula for Developing Thoroughbred Racehorses* in 1994.

Nerud, John A., 1913-. Trainer, breeder. President of Tartan Farms, Florida, 1959-'89. Inducted into Racing Hall of Fame in 1972. Trained 27 stakes winners and five champions, including Dr. Fager, Ta Wee, Delegate, Intentionally, Dr. Patches, *Gallant Man. Bred and owned Cozzene, Fappiano. Dr. Fager is the only horse to win four championships in one year.

Niarchos-Gouazé, Maria, Investments. Director, Breeders' Cup Ltd. Owner of Haras de Fresnay-le-Buffard, France. In partnership with her brothers, breeds under the name Flaxman Holdings Ltd. Bred and owned champion Aldebaran, Dream Well (Fr), Sulamani (Ire), Bago, Six Perfections (Fr), Divine Proportions. Daughter of shipping magnate Stavros Niarchos.

Nicholson, George "Nick," 1947-. Racing executive. President and chief executive officer, Keeneland Association; executive director, Jockey Club 1989-2000; former chief operating officer, National Thoroughbred Racing Association; president, Thoroughbred Club of America in '91. Jockey Club Gold Medal in 1998. Involved in the planning and development of the Kentucky Horse Park; played key role in formation of Equibase; helped to pull industry together to support the National Thoroughbred Racing Association.

Noe, Kenneth Jr. "Kenny," 1928-. Former racing executive. New York Racing Association chairman and chief executive officer 1995-2000. NYRA president, general manager 1994-'95. president, general manager of Calder Race Course 1979-'90. Member of Jockey Club.

O'Brien, Aidan, 1969-. Trainer. Won then-record

23 Grade/Group 1 races in 2001. Trains for Coolmore Stud and partners at Ballydoyle, Ireland. Won 2001-'02 Epsom Derby (Eng-G1) with Galileo (Ire) and High Chaparral (Ire), respectively. Trained Giant's Causeway, King of Kings (Ire), Milan (GB), Imagine (Ire), Stravinsky, Hawk Wing, Rock of Gibraltar (Ire), Ballingarry (Ire), Johannesburg, Footstepsinthesand.

O'Brien, Vincent, 1917-. Legendary Irish trainer. Founded Ballydoyle training center in Ireland; with John Magnier and Robert Sangster established Coolmore Stud in 1975. Trained winners of 27 Irish classics, 16 English classics, and in 1977 saddled then-record 22 Group 1 winners. Trained Nijinsky II, Roberto, Golden Fleece, Sir Ivor, The Minstrel, Alleged. In a 2003 *Racing Post* poll, he was voted the all-time most important figure in English racing.

O'Byrne, Dermot "Demi," 1944-. Bloodstock agent, veterinarian. Purchased Thunder Gulch, Honour and Glory, High Yield, Fasliyev, Stravinsky, King of Kings (Ire), Johannesburg. Chief talent spotter for Coolmore Stud-Michael Tabor partnerships.

O'Farrell, J. Michael Jr., 1948-. Breeder. First vice president, Florida Thoroughbred Breeders' and Owners' Association. Member of Jockey Club. Owner of Ocala Stud Farm, Florida. Bred Bolshoi Boy, Proudest Duke, Queen Alexandra. Son of Joe O'Farrell.

O'Hara, Philip, 1953-. Industry executive. Chief executive officer and president, Equibase Co., 2004-. Executive vice president of pari-mutuel operations, Penn National Gaming, 1998-2000; vice president and general manager, Penn National Race Course, 1994-'98.

O'Neill, Doug F., 1968-. Trainer. Set single-meet training record of 48 wins at Santa Anita Park in 2005. Set an Oak Tree record for single-meet wins in 2003 with 22 wins. In 2003, was named the Cal-bred Trainer of the Year by the California Thoroughbred Breeders Association. Trained Whilly (Ire), Sharp Lisa, Sky Jack, Classy Cara, Stevie Wonderboy, Avanzado (Arg).

Oxley, John C., 1937- and **Oxley, Debbie**, 1951-. Oil production. John is steward of Jockey Club. Owner of Fawn Leap Farm, Kentucky. Bred and owned Pyramid Peak. Owned Monarchos, Beautiful Pleasure, Sky Mesa.

Pape, William L., 1930-. Auto dealership. Former president, National Steeplechase Association. Co-bred champions Flatterer and Martie's Anger; owned champion Athenian Idol.

Paragallo, Ernie, 1958-. Investment banking, computer software. In name of Paraneck Stable, raced 1999 champion sprinter Artax; also campaigned 1995 Breeders' Cup Juvenile (G1) winner Unbridled's Song, 1999 Wood Memorial Stakes (G2) winner Adonis.

Payson, Virginia Kraft, 1930-. Investments. Owner of Payson Stud, Kentucky. Bred and owned St. Jovite, L'Carriere. Owned Carr de Naskra. Bred 2002 champions Vindication and Farda Amiga. Owner and operator of Payson Park training center in Florida.

Pedersen, Pete, 1920-. Steward of the California Horse Racing Board, 1955-'05. National Turf Writers Association Joe Palmer Award for meritorious service to racing, 2005. Eclipse Award of Merit, 2001. Known for elevating professionalism of stewards.

Pegram, Mike, 1952-. Fast food franchises. Owned Real Quiet, Silverbulletday, Isitingood, Thirty Slews, Captain Steve.

Perret, Craig, 1951-. Jockey. Eclipse Award jockey in 1990; George Woolf Memorial Jockey Award in '98. Rode Unbridled, Housebuster, Safely Kept, Eillo, Rhythm, Alydeed, Bet Twice. Won a record-tying 57 stakes in 1990.

Phillips, John W., 1952-. Investments, lawyer. Member of Jockey Club. Managing partner of Darby Dan Farm, Kentucky. Bred and owned Memories of Silver, Sunshine Forever, Brian's Time, Soaring Softly. Grandson of John W. Galbreath.

Phipps, Ogden Mills "Dinny," 1940-. Investments. Chairman, Jockey Club; former chairman, New York Racing Association; director, Grayson-Jockey Club Research Foundation. Eclipse Award of Merit in 1978. Bred and owned Inside Information, Rhythm, Educated Risk, Storm Flag Flying. Co-bred and owned Successor. Son of Ogden Phipps.

Pickens, Madeleine Paulson, 1957-. Owner-breeder. Bred and co-owned stakes winner Rock Hard Ten and owned Fraise, winner of 1992 Breeders' Cup Turf (G1). Widow of Allen Paulson, owner of Brookside Farms and of eight Eclipse champions, including Cigar, Blushing John, Estrapade, Theatrical (Ire). Married to corporate investor C. Boone Pickens.

Piggott, Lester, 1936-. Retired jockey, trainer. Champion English jockey 11 times. Won more than 5,300 races, including record 30 English classics. Winner of the Epsom Derby record nine times; Ascot Gold Cup 11 times; Irish Derby five times; and the 1990 Breeders' Cup Mile (G1) at age 54. Rode Nijinsky II, Sir Ivor, Roberto, The Minstrel, Alleged. Imprisoned a year for tax evasion 1987-'88 before resuming his riding career.

Pincay, Laffit Jr., 1946-. Jockey. Leading jockey by money won in 1970-'74, '79, '85; leading jockey by races won in '71; inducted into Racing Hall of Fame in '75; Eclipse Award jockey in 1971, '73-'74, '79, '85; Special Eclipse Award in '99; George Woolf Memorial Jockey Award in '70. Big Sport of Turfdom Award in '85. Rode Affirmed, John Henry, Gamely, Susan's Girl, Desert Vixen, Genuine Risk. Broke Bill Shoemaker's lifetime win record on December 10, 1999, with his 8,834th victory; first jockey to win seven races on a single card at Santa Anita Park, in '87; first jockey to win more than 9,000 races. Retired on April 29, 2003, with a record 9,530 victories and purse earnings of $237-million.

Pletcher, Todd, 1967-. Trainer. Annually among the top ten North American trainers by earnings and was leader by in 2004 with $17.5-million. Eclipse Award as outstanding trainer, 2004-'05. Son of horseman Jake Pletcher and a longtime assistant to Racing Hall of Fame trainer D. Wayne Lukas. Trained champions Ashado, Left Bank, Speightstown; Grade 1 winners include Archers Bay, Ashado, Balto Star, Harlan's Holiday, Jersey Girl.

Polk, Hiram Jr., M.D., 1936-. Surgeon, breeder. Retired chair, University of Louisville School of Medicine surgery department. Member, Jockey Club. Breeder and co-owner of multiple stakes winner Mrs. Revere.

Pollard, Carl, 1938-. Health care executive. Chairman, Churchill Downs Inc.; president, Kentucky Derby Museum. Owner of Hermitage Farm, Kentucky. Owned Caressing, Sheepscot, Duck Trap, Take Me Out.

Powell, Lonny, 1959-. Racing executive. Vice president of public affairs, Youbet.com Inc.; former president of Association of Racing Commissioners International. Former president of Santa Anita Park.

Prado, Edgar, 1967-. Jockey. Peru native among national leaders by earnings; second in 2004 with $18.3-million. Registered 5,000th career victory in 2004; won

2006 Kentucky Derby (G1) with Barbaro; Belmont Stakes (G1) with Birdstone (2004) and Sarava ('02). Led all North American riders by victories with 536 in 1997, 474 in '98, and 402 in '99.

Ragozin, Leonard, 1928-. Handicapper. Founder of Ragozin Thoroughbred Data. Developed Ragozin speed figures also known as "the sheets." Author of the book, *The Odds Must Be Crazy.*

Ramsey, Kenneth L., 1935-. Cellular telephones. In 1990s, acquired cellular telephone franchises along Interstate 75 in northeastern Georgia and southeastern Kentucky. Acquired Almahurst Farm in 1994 and renamed it Ramsey Farm. With wife, Sarah, won Eclipse Award as outstanding owner in 2004. Owner of 2004 champion turf male Kitten's Joy, Grade 1 winner Roses in May.

Reddam, J. Paul, 1955-. Finance. Founder, Ditech.com, an Internet-based mortgage company that he sold in 1999 to General Motors. President, Cash Call, a consumer loan company. Former Standardbred syndicator claimed his first Thoroughbred in 1988. Owner, Metropolitan Handicap (G1) winner Swept Overboard, millionaire Elloluv, and 2004 Breeders' Cup Juvenile (G1) winner Wilko.

Reid, Mark, 1950-. Bloodstock agent. Prominent agent in private deals for owner Edmund Gann and trainer Bobby Frankel. Purchased Walnut Green bloodstock agency, 2005. All-time leading trainer at Garden State Park; sixth-leading trainer in U.S. in '91; won the fall-winter training title at Philadelphia Park in 1986.

Richardson, J. David, M.D., 1945-. Vascular surgeon. Member, Jockey Club; past president, Kentucky Thoroughbred Association; co-bred and raced Mrs. Revere.

Roark, John, 1940-. Lawyer. In private practice in Temple, Texas. Former president of the National Horsemen's Benevolent and Protective Association. Former president, Texas Thoroughbred Partnership. Director, National Thoroughbred Racing Association.

Robertson, Walter, 1949-. Auctioneer. President, Fasig-Tipton Co.; former president, Thoroughbred Club of America. Auctioneer at the Calumet Farm sale in 1992.

Robbins, Jack K., V.M.D., 1921-. Veterinarian, racing executive. President, founding director of Oak Tree Racing Association; Jockey Club member; director of Grayson-Jockey Club Research Foundation; distinguished life member of American Association of Equine Practitioners. Father of trainer Jay Robbins, Del Mar Director of Racing Tom Robbins, and former Hollywood Park President Don Robbins.

Robinson, J. Mack, 1923-. Financier, philanthropist. Member, Jockey Club. Family owns Rosehill Plantation in Thomasville, Georgia. Daughter Jill raced 1994 champion sprinter Cherokee Run. Honored as owner of the year by the Georgia Thoroughbred Owners and Breeders Association. Chief benefactor of J. Mack Robinson College of Business at Georgia State University.

Roman, Steve, 1943-. Researcher, theorist. Author of 53 U.S. agricultural and animal health chemical patents. Creator of the dosage index. Author of *Dosage: Pedigree and Performance*, published in 2003.

Romero, Randy, 1957-. Jockey. Father, Lloyd, was Quarter Horse trainer; film *Casey's Shadow* was based on his Louisiana family; won Breeders' Cup races with champions Sacahuista (1987 Distaff [G1]), Personal Ensign (1988 Distaff), and Go for Wand (1989 Juvenile Fillies [G1]). Sustained life-threatening burns in a 1983 accident in Oaklawn Park jockeys' room. Won 4,294 races, earned more than $75-million.

Rotz, John L., 1934-. Jockey, racing official. Leading jockey by stakes winners in 1968-'69; inducted into Racing Hall of Fame in '83; George Woolf Memorial Jockey Award in '73. Rode 2,908 winners. Rode Gallant Bloom, Ta Wee, Carry Back, Dr. Fager, Silent Screen.

Russell, Geoffrey, 1961-. Keeneland director of sales since 2001. Previously assistant director of sales, 1996-2001; also worked at Goffs Bloodstock Sales and Fasig-Tipton.

Ryan, Dr. Tony, 1936-. Airline executive. Owner and chairman, Castleton Lyons, Kentucky. Bred Antonius Pius and Naissance Royale (Ire).

Sahadi, Jenine, 1963-. Trainer. First female to win a Breeders' Cup race on the flat, champion Lit de Justice in the 1996 Breeders' Cup Sprint (G1) and Elmhurst in the same race in 1997. First female to saddle a Santa Anita Derby (G1) winner, The Deputy (Ire) in 2000. Also trained stakes winners Grand Flotilla, and Creston. Daughter of Fred Sahadi, founder of Cardiff Stud.

Sampson, Curtis, 1933-. Telecommunications. Chairman of Canterbury Park Holding Corp.; bought closed track in 1994 with partners and reopened it in 1995. Entered racing in 1987 as an owner; among Minnesota's leading breeders.

Sams, Timothy H., 1944-. Breeder. Indiana Horse Racing Commission member, 1998-2002. Indiana Horse Racing Commission vice chairman, 2002. Member, Jockey Club. Former director, Breeders' Cup Ltd., Indiana Thoroughbred Breed Development Advisory Committee.

Samuel-Balaz, Tammy, Investments. Co-owner of Sam-Son Farm, Canada and Florida. Bred and owned Dancethruthedawn, Scatter the Gold, Catch the Ring, Mountain Angel, Quiet Resolve. Daughter of Ernest Samuel.

Samyn, Jean-Luc, 1956-. Jockey. Best known for riding ability on the turf. Leading apprentice at Keystone and Garden State Park. On November 20, 1985, was the first jockey to ride in two stakes races on different continents on the same day; Japan Cup (Jpn-G1) and Matriarch Stakes (G1), Hollywood Park.

Santos, Jose, 1961-. Jockey. Leading jockey by money won in 1986-'89; Eclipse Award jockey in '88; George Woolf Memorial Jockey Award in '99. Rode Lemon Drop Kid, Skip Away, Colonial Affair, Chief Bearhart, Volponi, Funny Cide. Led all jockeys by money won with a then-record $14.86-million in 1988; rode 13 winners in three days at Aqueduct in '88. Won 2003 Kentucky Derby (G1) and Preakness Stakes (G1) on Funny Cide.

Santulli, Richard, 1944-. Aviation. Co-owner of Jayeff B Stable. Member of Jockey Club. Bred and owned Ciro. Owned Safely Kept, Banshee Breeze, Korveya.

Savin, Scott, 1960-. Owner, executive. President, Gulfstream Park; former president, Florida Horsemen's Benevolent and Protective Association. Owned Bet Big, Cheshire Kitten. Grandson of A. I. "Butch" Savin, owner of Mr. Prospector.

Scherf, Christopher, 1951-. Racing executive. Executive vice president of Thoroughbred Racing Associations since 1988; president of TRA Enterprises. Serves on the American Horse Council's Racing and Government Affairs committees. Former sportswriter for the

Louisville *Courier-Journal* and United Press International; director of press relations for the New York Racing Association, 1978-'81.

Schickendanz, Gustav, 1929-. President and CEO of family construction and development company. Owner of Schonberg Farm in Nobleton, Ontario. Bred and owned 2003 Canadian Triple Crown winner and Canadian Horse of the Year Wando and 2004 Canadian champion Mobil. Also campaigned Sovereign Award winners Glanmire (1997 sprinter) and Langfuhr (1996 sprinter).

Schiff, Peter G., 1952-. Financier. Trustee, New York Racing Association. Member, Jockey Club. Owner of Fox Ridge Farm. Owned Christiecat, Riskaverse, Token Dance, Wortheroatsingold. Son of John Schiff.

Schulhofer, Flint S. "Scotty," 1926-. Trainer. Inducted into Racing Hall of Fame in 1992. Trained 80 stakes winners, including champions Ta Wee, Mac Diarmida, Smile, Fly So Free, Lemon Drop Kid, Rubiano; also trained Cryptoclearance. Father of trainer Randy Schulhofer.

Schwartz, Barry, 1942-. Clothing executive. Former chairman and chief executive officer, New York Racing Association. Member of Jockey Club. Owner of Stonewall Farm, New York. Bred and owned Beru, Patricia J. K. Owned Three Ring.

Seitz, Fred, 1946-, Consignor, breeder. Former president, Thoroughbred Club of America and Kentucky Thoroughbred Association; director, Keeneland Association. Owner, Brookdale Farm, Kentucky, which stood Deputy Minister and stands Forest Wildcat, Crafty Prospector, Silver Deputy, With Approval. Bred Bluebird in partnership.

Sexton, Steve, 1959-. Racetrack executive. President of Churchill Downs. Former executive vice president of Arlington Park; former executive vice president and general manager of Lone Star Park; former general manager of Thistledown racetrack.

Sheppard, Jonathan, 1940-. Trainer, breeder. Owner of Ashwell Stables, Pennsylvania. President, National Steeplechase Association. Leading steeplechase trainer by money won in 1973-'90, '92-'95; inducted into Racing Hall of Fame in '90. Trained more than 120 stakes winners, including champions Cafe Prince, Flatterer, Athenian Idol, Martie's Anger, Jimmy Lorenzo (GB), Highland Bud. Also trained Storm Cat, With Anticipation. Co-bred Martie's Anger, Flatterer.

Sherman, Michael, 1940-. Breeder. Owner and president of Farnsworth Farms, Florida. Leading breeder by stakes winners in 1994-'95; Eclipse Award breeder in '96. Bred Beautiful Pleasure, Jewel Princess, Mecke, Frisk Me Now, Once Wild.

Shields, Joseph V. Jr., 1938-. Investment manager, owner-breeder. Chairman and CEO of Shields & Co., brokerage and investment management firm. Vice chairman, New York Racing Association, member of the Jockey Club, trustee of National Museum of Racing Hall of Fame, Thoroughbred Owners and Breeders Association; director of Grayson-Jockey Club Research Foundation. Owner-breeder of Wagon Limit, Passing Shot, House Party, Puzzlement, Limit Out.

Sikura, John G., 1958-. Thoroughbred owner and breeder. Owner of Hill 'n' Dale Farm and Hill 'n' Dale Sales Agency in Kentucky. Breeder or co-breeder of Grade 1-Group 1 winners Hawk Wing and Touch Gold. Son of Hill 'n' Dale founder John Sikura Jr.

Smith, Mike, 1965-. Jockey. Elected to Racing Hall of Fame in 2003. Leading jockey by races won in 1994; Eclipse Award jockey in 1993-'94; Mike Venezia Award in '94; George Woolf Memorial Jockey Award in 2000. Rode Holy Bull, Lure, Skip Away, Azeri, Unbridled's Song, Coronado's Quest, Vindication, Giacomo. Won record 66 stakes in 1994. Through mid-2005, won more than 4,500 races and earned more than $170-million.

Smith, Tim, 1948-. Racing executive. Former commissioner of National Thoroughbred Racing Association, 1998-2004. Helped increase national television exposure for horse racing. President, Friends of New York Racing, founded February 2005.

Solis, Alex, 1964-. Jockey. Among top ten leading riders by career earnings. Panama native first rode in U.S. in 1982; recipient of the first Bill Shoemaker Award in 2003 for outstanding achievement on the Breeders' Cup program; rode two winners, Johar in Breeders' Cup Turf (G1) dead heat and Pleasantly Perfect in the Breeders' Cup Classic (G1). Also rode Pleasantly Perfect to win in 2004 Dubai World Cup (UAE-G1).

Sommer, Viola (Mrs. Sigmund), 1921-. Real estate. Leading owner in 1982; Eclipse Award owner in '82. Member of Jockey Club. Bred and owned Bottled Water. Owned Sham, Ten Below, Tom Swift.

Steinbrenner, George, 1930-. Shipping. Director, Florida Thoroughbred Breeders' and Owners' Association. Owner of Kinsman Farm, Florida. Bred and owned Concerto, Diligence, Eternal Prince; owned Bellamy Road. Former co-owner Florida Downs (later Tampa Bay Downs). Managing partner, New York Yankees.

Stevens, Gary, 1963-. Jockey. President, Jockeys' Guild, 1995-2000. Leading jockey by money won in 1990; inducted into Racing Hall of Fame in '97; Eclipse Award jockey in '98; George Woolf Memorial Jockey Award in '96. Rode more than 4,800 winners, including Point Given, Silver Charm, Winning Colors, Thunder Gulch, Hennessy, Broad Brush. Youngest rider to earn more than $100-million in purses, in 1993. Retired in 2005.

Stoute, Sir Michael, 1945-. Trainer. Five-time champion trainer in England. Trained Epsom Derby (Eng-G1) winners Shergar (1981), Shahrastani ('86), Kris Kin (2003), North Light ('04), and Unite (Ire), stakes winners Sonic Lady, Shareef Dancer, Melodist, Ivor's Image, Ajdal, Saddlers' Hall, Marwell (Ire), Zilzal, Opera House (GB), Ezzoud (Ire), Russian Rhythm, Islington (Ire).

Strauss, Robert S., 1918-. Lawyer, diplomat. Chairman of Del Mar Thoroughbred Club since 2002. Jockey Club member. Former FBI special agent; ambassador to the Soviet Union 1991-'92; President Carter's representative to the Middle East peace negotiations; winner of the Presidential Medal of Freedom '81; chairman of the Democratic National Committee 1973-'76. Bred Last Tycoon (Ire).

Strawbridge, George Jr., 1937-. Investments. Former president, National Steeplechase Association. Member of Jockey Club. Owner of Augustin Stables, Pennsylvania. F. Ambrose Clark Award in 1979. Bred and owned Tikkanen, Selkirk, Silver Fling, With Anticipation. Bred Treizieme, Turgeon. Owned Cafe Prince, Mo Bay.

Stronach, Frank, 1932-. Auto-parts manufacturer. Chairman, Magna International Corp., Magna Entertainment Corp. Owner of Adena Springs Farm, Kentucky; Adena Springs North, Ontario; Adena Springs South, Florida. Owner of Stronach Stable. Eclipse Award owner in 1998-2000; Eclipse Award breeder in '00 and '04; eight Sovereign Awards as owner of year and four Sovereign Awards as breeder of year. Bred and owned Macho Uno, Perfect Sting, Ghostzapper. Co-owned Touch

Gold, Glorious Song. Also bred and owned Awesome Again, richest Canadian-bred runner of all-time with $4,374,590. Through Magna Entertainment, purchased Thoroughbred racetracks Santa Anita Park, Gulfstream Park, Thistledown, Golden Gate Fields, Remington Park, Great Lakes Downs, Portland Meadows, Lone Star Park; majority of Pimlico Race Course and Laurel Park.

Stute, Melvin F., 1927-. Trainer. Trained two Eclipse Award winners in 1986, Preakness Stakes (G1) winner Snow Chief and Breeders' Cup Juvenile Fillies (G1) winner Brave Raj. Also trained Very Subtle, winner of the 1987 Breeders' Cup Sprint (G1). Brother of trainer Warren Stute.

Suroor, Saeed bin, 1967-. Trainer. Leading trainer in England by money won in 1995. Trained Dubai Millennium, Fantastic Light, Swain (Ire), E Dubai, Lammtarra, Mark of Esteem (Ire). Head trainer for Godolphin Racing; won the Emirates World Series in 1999 with Daylami (Ire), Fantastic Light (2000-'01), and Grandera in 2002.

Switzer, David, 1945-. Executive director of Kentucky Thoroughbred Association. Board member of University of Kentucky-Gluck Research Foundation.

Tabor, Michael, 1941-. Former betting shop owner, investments. Owned or co-owned Thunder Gulch, Montjeu (Ire), Desert King, Honour and Glory, Johannesburg, Galileo (Ire), High Chaparral (Ire).

Tanaka, Gary, 1943-. Stockbroker, co-owner of Amerindo Investment Advisors Inc. Frequently bought proven horses in Europe and raced them in California. Owned User Friendly (GB), Dernier Empereur, Donna Viola (GB), Dreams Gallore, Golden Apples (Ire). Charged with improper use of client funds in 2005.

Taylor, Duncan, 1956-. Farm owner. Co-owner (with brothers Frank, Ben, and Mark) of Taylor Made Farm and Sales Agency, Kentucky. Sold more than $1-billion total value of horses at public auctions since 1978. Stands Unbridled's Song, Forestry. Son of Joe Taylor.

Taylor, Mickey, 1940- and **Taylor, Karen**, 1940-. Timber. Owned and bred Slew o' Gold, Slewpy. Co-owned Seattle Slew, who won 14 of 17 starts, including the Triple Crown in 1977, and earned $1.2-million.

Thomas, Becky, 1957- . Bloodstock agent. Co-founder of Lakland and Lakland North with partners Lewis and Brenda Lakin. Owns and operates Sequel Bloodstock, which consigns at two-year-old sales.

Threewitt, Noble, 1911-. Trainer. President of the California Horsemen's Benevolent and Protective Association for six terms; president emeritus, California Thoroughbred Trainers Association. Recipient, Laffit Pincay Jr. Award, 2005. Trained more than 2,000 winners, including Correlation, Devoted Brass, Old Topper, Theresa's Tizzy.

Thompson, David, 1936-, **and Patricia**, 1940-. Owners, Cheveley Park Stud, Newmarket, England. Owned Red Bloom, Russian Rhythm.

Troutt, Kenny, 1948-. Telecommunications. Partner in WinStar Farm, Kentucky. Trustee, Thoroughbred Owners and Breeders Association; director, Breeders Cup Ltd. In WinStar name, bred Funny Cide, One Cool Cat. Owned Awesome Humor, Bet Me Best, Byzantium (Brz), and Pompeii. Co-owner of Ipi Tombe (Zim), Crimson Palace. Stands Tiznow, Distorted Humor, Victory Gallop. Stood Kris S.

Turcotte, Ron, 1941-. Jockey. Leading jockey by stakes won in 1972-'73; inducted into Racing Hall of Fame in '79; George Woolf Memorial Jockey Award in '79. Rode 3,032 winners, including Secretariat, Damascus, Northern Dancer, Riva Ridge, Shuvee, Dark Mirage, Fort Marcy. Won Triple Crown in 1973 aboard Secretariat. Paralyzed in 1978 spill.

Turner, William H. "Billy," 1941-. Trainer. Trained Seattle Slew through his three-year-old season to become the first undefeated American Triple Crown winner. Also trained Czaravich. Rode in steeplechase races from 1958-'62; assistant to Racing Hall of Fame trainer W. Burling Cocks before going on his own in 1966.

Ussery, Robert N., 1935-. Jockey. Inducted into Racing Hall of Fame in 1980. Rode 3,611 winners, including Hail to Reason, Bally Ache, Bramalea, Never Bow. Fifth by money won among jockeys at retirement; finished first in two consecutive Kentucky Derbys, aboard Proud Clarion (1967) and Dancer's Image ('68, disqualified, placed last).

Valpredo, Don, 1939-. Agriculture. Director, Thoroughbred Owners of California, Breeders' Cup Ltd.; Member, Jockey Club. President, Ridge Ginning Co.; Director, Kern Ridge Growers, Arvin Edison Water Storage District. Son of John Valpredo.

Van Berg, Jack, 1936-. Trainer. Leading trainer by races won in 1968-'70, '72, '74, '76, '83-'84, '86; leading trainer by money won in '76; inducted into Racing Hall of Fame in '85; Eclipse Award trainer in '84; Big Sport of Turfdom Award in '87; Jockey Club Gold Medal in '87; Mr. Fitz Award in '88. Trained Alysheba, Gate Dancer. Holds record for most races won in a single year (496 in 1976); trained champion Alysheba, who retired with a then-record total earnings of $6,679,242; 6,000th career win in February 1995. Son of Racing Hall of Fame trainer Marion Van Berg.

Van Clief, Daniel G. Jr., 1948-. Racing executive. Former commissioner, National Thoroughbred Racing Assocation; former president, Breeders' Cup Ltd.; chairman, Fasig-Tipton Co.; member of Jockey Club. Co-owner of Nydrie Stud, Virginia. Eclipse Award of Merit in 1998; Jockey Club Medal in '84. Worked to put together Breeders' Cup day of championship races; key figure in development of NTRA.

Van de Kamp, John, 1936-. Lawyer, association executive. Past president, Thoroughbred Owners of California; director, National Thoroughbred Racing Association. Gathered support in the TOC to pass account wagering bill; lobbied for horse industry tax relief measures in California.

VanMeter II, Tom, D.V.M., 1957-. Veterinarian, sales agent, owner-breeder. Co-owner with Reiley McDonald of Eaton Sales, Kentucky. Owner of Victory U. S. A., Be Gentle; raced Brahms; co-bred Mr. Mellon.

Varola, Francesco, 1922-. Author, bloodstock adviser. Author of *Typology of the Racehorse*; added to the dosage theory by creating aptitudinal classes in which he categorized each *chef-de-race* stallion.

Vasquez, Jacinto, 1944-. Jockey, trainer. Inducted into Racing Hall of Fame in 1998. Rode winners of 5,231 races, including Ruffian, Genuine Risk, Princess Rooney, Forego. Nation's 15th all-time winning jockey at his retirement in 1996; rode Ruffian to victory in the New York filly triple crown in '75.

Veitch, John, 1945-. Executive, former trainer. Deputy director, Kentucky Horse Racing Authority. Trained Davona Dale, Our Mims, Before Dawn, Proud Truth. Trained Alydar, who finished second behind Affirmed in all three Triple Crown races in 1978. Son of Racing Hall of Fame trainer Sylvester Veitch.

Velasquez, Jorge, 1946-. Jockey. Leading jockey by races won in 1967; leading jockey by money won in '69; leading jockey by stakes races won in '85; inducted into Racing Hall of Fame in '90; George Woolf Memorial Jockey Award in '86. Rode 6,795 winners, including Alydar, Chris Evert, Davona Dale, Lady's Secret, Shuvee, Fort Marcy. Won the New York filly triple crown with Chris Evert in 1974 and Davona Dale in '79; first jockey to win six of six races in New York, in '81.

Velazquez, John R., 1971-. Jockey. Eclipse Award jockey, 2004-'05; North American leading rider by earnings in 2004 with $22.2-million; in 2005 with $20.8-million. Rode winners of six Breeders' Cup races: Ashado, Speightstown, Da Hoss, Caressing, Starine, and Storm Flag Flying.

Valenzuela, Patrick, 1962-. Jockey. Rode Sunday Silence to win 1989 Kentucky Derby (G1) and Preakness Stakes (G1). Winner of seven Breeders' Cup races. Youngest rider ever to win Santa Anita Derby (G1), with Codex in 1980. First jockey to sweep five major California meet titles, 2003. Career interrupted repeatedly by alcohol and drug abuse.

Violette, Rick Jr., 1953-. Trainer. Chairman, New York Jockey Injury Compensation Fund, 1996-; president, National Thoroughbred Horsemen's Association, 2000-; director, New York Thoroughbred Horsemen's Association. Trained Citadeed, Read the Footnotes, Nijinsky's Gold.

von Stade, John, 1938-. President, National Museum of Racing, 1989-2005. Chairman, National Museum of Racing, 2005-. Instrumental in completion of major projects at the museum, including a new wing and handicap-accessible areas.

Walsh, Thomas 1940-. Jockey. Leading American steeplechase rider in 1960 and '66; fifth-ranked all-time American steeplechase jockey with 253 victories. Regular rider of champions Barnabys Bluff, Bon Nouvel, and Mako. Won American Grand National six times, five years in succession, 1959-'63. Inducted into Racing Hall of Fame in 2005.

Ward, John T. Jr., 1945-. Trainer. Owner of Sugar Grove Farm, Kentucky; John T. Ward Stables, Kentucky. Trained Monarchos, Beautiful Pleasure, Darling My Darling, Jambalaya Jazz, Pyramid Peak. Nephew of Racing Hall of Fame trainer Sherrill Ward.

Waterman, Scot, D.V.M., 1966-. Veterinarian, industry executive. Executive director, Racing Medication and Testing Consortium. Recipient of North American Pari-Mutuel Regulators Association's Winner's Circle Award, 2004. Thoroughbred owner and breeder.

Watters Jr., Sidney 1917-. Trainer. Champion steeplechase trainer in 1951, '56, '61, and '63, co-leader by wins in '48 and '71. Leading steeplechase trainer by earnings in 1956, '63, and '71. Trained champions Amber Diver and Shadow Brook. On flat, trained 1970 champion two-year-old male Hoist the Flag and '83 three-year-old male Slew o' Gold. Inducted into Racing Hall of Fame as a steeplechase trainer in 2005.

Weber, Charlotte, 1942-. Investments. Member of Jockey Club. Owner of Live Oak Stud, Florida. Bred and owned Peaceful Union, Gnome Home, Medieval Man, Laser Light, Sultry Song, High Fly, Sultry Sun.

Weisbord, Barry, 1950-. Publisher. Joe Palmer Award in 1992. Co-owned Safely Kept. Created the American Championship Racing Series in 1991; created the Matchmaker Breeders' Exchange, the first centralized market for stallion seasons and shares.

West, R. Smiser. Dentist, breeder. Owner of Waterford Farm, Kentucky. Co-breeder of Lite Light, De La Rose, Chilukki.

Whiteley, Frank Jr., 1915-. Trainer. Inducted into Racing Hall of Fame in 1978. Trained 35 stakes winners and four champions, including Damascus, Forego, Ruffian, Tom Rolfe.

Whitney, Marylou, 1926-. Investments. Owner of Whitney Farm, Kentucky; Blue Goose Stable, Kentucky. Bred and owned Silver Buck, Bird Town, Birdstone. Long known for her Derby Eve parties and for her parties in Saratoga Springs, New York. Widow of C. V. Whitney; married to John Hendrickson.

Willmot, David, 1950-. Breeder, investments. President, Woodbine Entertainment Group, formerly Ontario Jockey Club. Owner of Kinghaven Farms, Canada. John W. Galbreath Award in 2001; Sovereign Award in 1998. Bred and owned Talkin Man, Poetically, Alywow, Play the King, Summer Mood, With Approval. Successfully lobbied for legislation to add slot machines at Woodbine racetrack; Kinghaven became the first Canadian stable to earn more than $2-million, in 1986. Son of Donald Willmot.

Wolfson, Louis, 1912-. and **Wolfson, Patrice**. Investments. Owner of Harbor View Farm, Florida. Leading breeder in 1970-'71. Bred and owned Affirmed, Flawlessly, Exclusive Native, It's In the Air, Outstandingly. Owned Raise a Native. Bred and raced two-time Horse of the Year Affirmed, winner of the Triple Crown in 1978. Bred and owned Racing Hall of Fame Flawlessly. Patrice Wolfson is daughter of Racing Hall of Fame trainer Hirsch Jacobs.

Wygod, Martin, 1940-. Executive, owner-breeder. Chairman and chief executive of WebMD. Sold his Medco Containment Services Inc. to Merck & Co. for $6.5-billion in 1994. Owns River Edge Farm and 102-acre property in Rancho Santa Fe, both in California. Member of the Jockey Club. With wife, Pam, bred and owned champion Sweet Catomine.

Ycaza, Manuel, 1938-. Jockey. Inducted into Racing Hall of Fame in 1977. Rode 2,367 winners, including Ack Ack, Dr. Fager, Damascus, Sword Dancer, Gamely, Dark Mirage, Never Bend. Won first New York filly triple crown with Dark Mirage in 1968.

Yoshida, Teruya, 1947-. Breeder. Owner, president of Shadai Farm, founded by his late father, Zenya Yoshida. With brothers Haruya and Katsumi, owns Shadai Stallion Station, home to Japan's leading sire in 20 of the last 21 years, including ten-time leader Northern Taste and eight-time leader Sunday Silence. Vice chairman of the Japanese Racing Horse Association.

Young, William Jr., 1948-. Managing owner, Overbrook Farm, Kentucky. Member of Jockey Club. Director of Keenland Association and the Kentucky Thoroughbred Owners and Breeders Association.

Zilber, Maurice, 1926-. Trainer. Ten times leading trainer during the 1950s in his native Egypt; leading trainer in France. Trained Racing Hall of Fame members Dahlia and Exceller, and Trillion, Youth, Argument (Fr), Hippodamia.

Zito, Nick, 1948-. Trainer. Elected to Racing Hall of Fame in 2005. Trained Kentucky Derby (G1) winners Go for Gin (1994) and Strike the Gold ('91), Preakness Stakes (G1) winner Louis Quatorze, Belmont Stakes (G1) winner Birdstone, plus A P Valentine, Thirty Six Red, Bird Town.

Industry Awards

Eric Beitia Memorial Award

Awarded annually by the New York Racing Association to the leading apprentice jockey at the NYRA tracks. Named for the leading apprentice of 1980 who died November 28, 1983, at age 21 of a gunshot wound a week earlier.

2005	Channing Hill
2004	Pablo Fragoso
2003	Pablo Fragoso
2002	Lorenzo Lezcano
2001	Lorenzo Lezcano
2000	Norberto Arroyo Jr.
1999	Ariel Smith
1998	Shaun Bridgmohan
1997	Phil Teator
1996	Jose Trejo
1995	Ramon Perez
1994	Dale Beckner
1993	Caesar Bisono
1992	Gerry Brocklebank
1991	Rafael Mojica Jr.
1990	Paul Toscano
1989	Jose Martinez
1988	Brian Peck
1987	David Nuesch
1986	David Nuesch
	Edward Thomas Baird
1985	Wesley Ward
1984	Wesley Ward
1983	Declan Murphy

Big Sport of Turfdom

Sponsored by the Turf Publicists of America and awarded to the individual or individuals whose cooperation with the media enhances coverage and brings favorable attention to Thoroughbred racing.

2005	Pat Day
2004	John Servis
2003	Sackatoga Stable
2002	Ken and Sue McPeek
2001	Laura Hillenbrand
2000	Laffit Pincay Jr.
1999	D. Wayne Lukas
1998	Mike Pegram
1997	Bob Baffert
1996	Cigar, Allen Paulson, Bill Mott, Jerry Bailey
1995	Robert and Beverly Lewis
1994	Warren "Jimmy" Croll Jr.
1993	Chris McCarron
1992	Angel Cordero Jr.
1991	Hammer and Oaktown Stable
1990	Carl Nafzger
1989	Tim Conway
1988	Julie Krone
1987	Jack Van Berg
1986	Jim McKay
1985	Laffit Pincay Jr.
1984	John Henry
1983	Joe Hirsch
1982	Woody Stephens
1981	John Forsythe
1980	Jack Klugman
1979	Laz Barrera
1978	Ron Turcotte
1977	Steve Cauthen
1976	Telly Savalas
1975	Francis P. Dunne
1974	Eddie Arcaro
1973	Penny Chenery
1972	John Galbreath
1971	Burt Bacharach
1970	Saul Rosen
1969	Bill Shoemaker
1968	John Nerud
1967	Allaire duPont
1966	E. P. Taylor

F. Ambrose Clark Award

Presented periodically by the National Steeplechase Association to those who promote, improve, or encourage steeplechase racing. Named for a renowned steeplechase owner.

2005	Not awarded
2004	Stephen P. Groat
2002	George A. Sloan
2001	John A. Wayt Jr.
1995	John T. von Stade
1991	Beverly Steinman
1988	William L. Pape
1982	Mrs. Miles Valentine
1980	Charles Fenwick Jr.
1979	George Strawbridge Jr.
1978	Morris H. Dixon
1977	Alfred M. Hunt
1976	Joseph Aitcheson Jr.
1975	Michael Walsh
1974	John Cooper
1973	W. Burling Cocks
1972	Russell M. Arundel
1971	Raymond G. Woolfe
1970	Raymond R. Guest
1969	Mrs. Odgen Phipps
1968	John W. Hanes
1967	S. Bryce Wing
1966	Crompton Smith Jr.
1965	Marion duPont Scott

Coman Humanitarian Award

Presented by Kentucky Thoroughbred Owners and Breeders for contributions to better human relations in the Thoroughbred industry. Named for KTOB Executive Director William C. Coman. No longer awarded.

2002	Alice Chandler
2001	Sheikh Mohammed bin Rashid al Maktoum
2000	Benjamin Roach, M.D.
1999	J. David Richardson, M.D.
1998	Gary Biszantz
1997	Dr. John T. Bryans
1996	Larry Weber
1994	Paul Mellon
1993	John A. Bell III
1992	Charles Nuckols Jr.
1991	William T. Young
1990	Carl Icahn
1989	Tim Conway
1988	Jim and Linda Ryan
1987	Jay Spurrier
1986	James E. "Ted" Bassett III
1985	Drs. Charles Hagyard, Arthur Davidson, and William McGee
1984	Keene Daingerfield
1983	Brownell Combs
	Maxwell Gluck

Dogwood Dominion Award

Sponsored by Dogwood Stable and presented to the "unsung heroes" of racing, especially in the backstretch areas. Named for Dominion (GB), Dogwood's first graded stakes winner who raced from 1974 to '78.

2005 Jo Anne Normile
2004 Pam Berg
2003 Neftali "Junior" Gutierrez
2002 Jim Greene and Shirley Edwards
2001 Julian "Buck" Wheat
2000 Katherine Todd Smith
1999 Danny Perlsweig
1998 Donald "Peanut Butter" Brown
1997 Nick Caras
1996 Grace Belcuore
1995 Peggy Sprinkles
1994 Howard "Gelo" Hall
1993 H. W. "Salty" Roberts

Charles W. Engelhard Award

Presented by Kentucky Thoroughbred Owners and Breeders for outstanding media coverage of the Thoroughbred industry.

2005 Charlsie Cantey
2004 *Seabiscuit*
2003 Ercel Ellis Jr.
2002 Television Games Network
2001 John Henderson ("Thoroughbred Week")
2000 Ray Paulick (*The Blood-Horse*)
1999 Maryjean Wall (Lexington *Herald-Leader*)
1998 David Heckerman (*The Blood-Horse*)
1997 Jim Bolus
1996 Kenny Rice (WTVQ-TV)
1994 Jay Hovdey (*The Blood-Horse*)
John Asher (WHAS Radio)
1993 Jennie Rees (Louisville *Courier-Journal*)
1992 Josh Pons (*Country Life Diary*)
1991 Cawood Ledford
1990 Jim McKay (ABC)
1989 Lewis Owens (Lexington *Herald-Leader*)
1988 Anheuser-Busch
1987 Jim Wilburn and Chris Lincoln (Winner Communications)
1986 Leon Rasmussen (*Daily Racing Form*)
1985 Dick Enberg (NBC)
1984 NBC Sports
1983 Cawood Ledford
1982 Tom Hammond
1981 *The Thoroughbred Record*
1980 Billy Reed (Louisville *Courier-Journal*)
1979 Logan Bailey (*Daily Racing Form*)
1978 Kent Hollingsworth (*The Blood-Horse*)
1977 Jim McKay (ABC)
1976 Heywood Hale Broun (CBS)
1975 Robert Wussler (CBS)
1974 Joe Hirsch (*Daily Racing Form*)
1973 Jack Whitaker (CBS)
1972 Hugh "Mickey" McGuire (*Daily Racing Form*)
1971 Red Smith (New York *Times*)
1970 Win Elliott (CBS Radio)

John W. Galbreath Award

Sponsored by the University of Louisville's Equine Industry Program, the award named for the Darby Dan Farm owner honors equine-industry entrepreneurs.

2005 Brian Derrick Mehl
2004 Judith Forbis
2003 Frank "Scoop" Vessels
2002 William S. Morris III
2001 David Willmot
2000 Denny Gentry
1999 Tom Meeker
1998 D. Wayne Lukas
1997 John M. Lyons
1996 B. Thomas Joy
1995 Robert Clay
1994 Ami Shinitzky
1993 John Gaines
1992 W. Cothran "Cot" Campbell
1991 James E. "Ted" Bassett III
1990 John A. Bell III

Avelino Gomez Memorial Award

Sponsored by Woodbine, the award named for jockey Avelino "El Perfecto" Gomez is presented to the Canadian-born, -raised, or -based jockey who has made a significant contribution to Thoroughbred racing. North America's leading rider in 1966, Gomez died of injuries incurred in a three-horse spill in the Canadian Oaks on June 21, 1980.

2006 John LeBlanc Sr.
2005 Sam Krasner
2004 Francine Villeneuve
2003 Robert Landry
2002 Richard Dos Ramos
2001 Chris Loseth
2000 Jim McKnight
1999 David Clark
1998 Irwin Driedger
1997 Richard Grubb
1996 David Gall
1995 Don Seymour
1994 Not awarded
1993 Larry Attard
1992 Robin Platts
1991 Hugo Dittfach
1990 Lloyd Duffy
1989 Jeff Fell
1988 Chris Rogers
1987 Don MacBeth
1986 Sandy Hawley
1985 John Longden
1984 Ron Turcotte

John K. Goodman Alumni Award

University of Arizona Race Track Industry Program award for a program graduate who has achieved distinction in the racing industry. Named for one of the program's founders.

2005 Scot Waterman
2004 Phil O'Hara
2003 Patricia McQueen
2002 Todd Pletcher
2001 Luke Kruytbosch
2000 Ann McGovern
1999 Lonny Powell
1998 Dan Fick
1997 Bob Baffert

Walter Haight Award

Presented by the National Turf Writers Association for excellence in Turf writing. Named for Washington Post racing columnist and handicapper known for his humorous style.

2005 Jay Privman (*Daily Racing Form*)

2004 Steve Haskin (*The Blood-Horse*)
2003 Russ Harris (career excellence)
2002 Billy Reed (career excellence)
2001 Gary West (Dallas *Morning News*)
2000 Bill Christine (Los Angeles *Times*)
1999 Jennie Rees (Louisville *Courier-Journal*)
1998 Andrew Beyer (Washington *Post*)
1997 Jim Bolus
1996 Ed Schuyler Jr. (Associated Press)
1995 Jay Hovdey
1994 Ed Bowen
1993 Jack Mann (New York *Herald-Tribune*)
1992 Mike Barry (*Kentucky Irish American* and The Louisville *Times*)
Bill Nack (*Sports Illustrated*)
1991 Bob Harding (Newark *Star-Ledger*)
1990 Kent Hollingsworth (*The Blood-Horse*)
1989 William Leggett (THOROUGHBRED TIMES)
1988 Leon Rasmussen (*Daily Racing Form*)
1987 Si Burick (Dayton *Daily News*)
1986 Ed Comerford (*Newsday*)
1985 Sam McCracken (Boston *Globe*)
1984 Joe Hirsch (*Daily Racing Form*)
1983 Fred Russell (Nashville *Banner*)
1982 Joe Agrella (Chicago *Sun-Times*)
1981 Bill Robertson (*The Thoroughbred Record*)
1980 Joe Nichols (New York *Times*)
1979 Barney Nagler (*Daily Racing Form*)
1978 Nelson Fisher (San Diego *Union*)
1977 Red Smith (New York *Times*)
1976 Saul Rosen (*Daily Racing Form*)
1975 Don Fair (*Daily Racing Form*)
1974 Raleigh Burroughs (*Turf and Sport Digest*)
1973 George Ryall (*The New Yorker*)
1972 Jimmy Doyle (Cleveland *Plain Dealer*)

Hardboot Award

Sponsored by Kentucky Thoroughbred Owners and Breeders.

2005 Josephine Abercrombie
2004 Diane Perkins
2003 Henry White
2002 Charles Nuckols Jr.
Virginia Kraft Payson
2001 Robert Courtney Sr.
2000 Carlos Perez
1999 Dr. and Mrs. R. Smiser West
Mr. and Mrs. MacKenzie Miller

Joe Hirsch Breeders' Cup Newspaper Writing Award

Sponsored by Breeders' Cup Ltd. and the National Thoroughbred Racing Association, the award named for the longtime Daily Racing Form columnist honors excellence in newspaper coverage of the previous year's Breeders' Cup World Thoroughbred Championships.

2005 Richard Edmondson
2004 Jay Privman
2003 Pat Forde
2002 Jay Privman
2001 Pat Forde
2000 Robert Edmondson
1999 Dick Jerardi
1998 Jennie Rees
1997 Pat Forde
1996 Dick Jerardi
1995 Jay Posner

Jockey Club Medal of Honor

Awarded periodically by the Jockey Club for meritorious service to the Thoroughbred industry.

1998 Nick Nicholson and Alan Marzelli
1994 Larry Bramlage, D.V.M.
1993 Kenny Noe Jr.
1992 R. Richards Rolapp
1991 Dr. Manuel Gilman
1990 Dr. Charles Randall
1989 Joe Hirsch
1988 Dennis Swanson
1987 Jack Van Berg
1986 Richard Duchossois
1985 Jean Romanet
1984 D. G. Van Clief Jr.

Lavin Cup

Sponsored by the American Association of Equine Practitioners and awarded to a nonveterinary individual or organization that has demonstrated exceptional compassion for horses or has developed and enforced guidelines for horses' welfare. Named for Kentucky veterinarian A. Gary Lavin, AAEP president in 1994.

2005 Allan and Kathleen Schwartz
2004 Herb and Ellen Moelis
2003 Professional Rodeo Cowboys Association
2002 Dayton O. Hyde
1999 Tom Dorrance
1998 Thoroughbred Retirement Foundation
1997 American Quarter Horse Association
1996 California Horse Racing Board

Bill Leggett Breeders' Cup Magazine Writing Award

Sponsored by Breeders' Cup Ltd. and the National Thoroughbred Racing Association, award named for the late *Sports Illustrated* and THOROUGHBRED TIMES writer honors excellence in magazine coverage of the previous year's Breeders' Cup World Thoroughbred Championships.

2005 Tom Law
2004 Michele MacDonald
2003 Billy Reed
2002 Billy Reed
2001 Tom Law
2000 Bill Heller
1999 Tom LaMarra
1998 Robbie Henwood
1997 Glenye Cain
1996 Jay Hovdey
1994 Jay Hovdey

William H. May Award

Awarded by Association of Racing Commissioners International for distinguished service to racing. Named for a former president of National Association of State Racing Commissioners.

2006 Curtis Barrett, Ph.D.
2005 Lonny Powell
2004 Race Track Chaplaincy of America
2003 American Association of Equine Practitioners
2002 American Quarter Horse Association
2001 John R. Gaines
2000 R. D. Hubbard
1999 Bob and Beverly Lewis

1998	Fred Noe
1997	James E. "Ted" Bassett III
1996	Allen Paulson
1995	Paul Mellon
1994	Joe Hirsch
1993	Tony Chamblin
1992	Bill Shoemaker
1991	Jockey Club
1990	James P. Ryan
1989	Stanley Bergstein
1988	*Daily Racing Form*
1987	Breeders' Cup Ltd.
1986	Robert H. Strub

Mr. Fitz Award

Sponsored by National Turf Writers Association, award named for Racing Hall of Fame trainer James E. "Sunny Jim" Fitzsimmons honors individuals who typify the spirit of horse racing.

2005	Nick Zito
2004	Patti Cooksey
2003	Sackatoga Stable
2002	Chris McCarron
2001	H. Allen Jerkens
2000	Pat Day
1999	Bob and Beverly Lewis
1998	Joe Hirsch
1997	Bob Baffert
1996	MacKenzie Miller
1995	Warren "Jimmy" Croll
1994	Jeff Lukas
1993	Angel Cordero Jr.
1992	Ron McAnally
1991	Frances Genter
1990	Arthur B. Hancock III
1989	Ogden Phipps
1988	Jack Van Berg
1987	Laffit Pincay Jr.
1986	Arlington Park management
1985	John Henry
1984	Penny Chenery
1983	Fred Hooper
1982	Bill Shoemaker, Woody Stephens
1981	Jack Klugman

Isaac Murphy Award

Named for 19th-century black jockey who won with 44% of his career mounts, National Turf Writers Association award honors jockey with highest winning percentage for the year.

2005	Russell Baze
2004	Ramon Dominguez
1995-2003	Russell Baze

Jerry Frutkoff Preakness Photography Award

Sponsored by Pimlico Race Course and Nikon, for best Preakness Stakes (G1) photo from previous year. Renamed for longtime Maryland Jockey Club photographer who died in 2003.

2006	Molly Riley (Reuters)
2005	Gary Hershorn (Reuters)
2004	Jeff Snyder (*The Blood-Horse*)
2003	Skip Dickstein (*The Blood-Horse*)
2002	Molly Riley (Reuters)

Old Hilltop Award

Presented by Pimlico Race Course for distinction in Thoroughbred racing reporting. Name derives from Pimlico's nickname.

2006	Kenny Mayne (ESPN)
	Lucy Acton (*Mid-Atlantic Thoroughbred*)
2005	Jay Privman (*Daily Racing Form*)
	Scott Garceau (WMAR-TV)
2004	Gary West (Dallas *Morning News*)
	Bruce Cunningham (*WBFF-TV*)
2003	John Patti (WBAL-AM)
	Steve Haskin (*The Blood-Horse*)
2002	Stan Charles (Baltimore radio)
	Michele MacDonald (THOROUGHBRED TIMES)
2001	Keith Mills (WMAR-TV)
	Jennie Rees (Louisville *Courier-Journal*)
2000	Marty Bass (WJZ-TV)
	Joe Kelly (Turf historian)
1999	Harry Kakel (WMAR-TV)
	Pohla Smith (Pittsburgh *Post-Gazette*)
1998	Ed Kiernan (WBAL Radio)
	Vinnie Perrone (*Maryland Turf Writers*)
1997	Reid Cherner (*USA Today*)
	Chris Lincoln (ESPN)
1996	Dan Farley (*Racing Post*)
	George Michael (WRC-TV)
1995	Charlsie Cantey (ABC Sports)
	Neil Milbert (Chicago *Tribune*)
1994	Ed Schuyler Jr. (*Associated Press*)
	Jim West (WBAL Radio)
1993	Jim Bolus (free-lance journalist)
	John Buren (WJZ TV)
1992	Dave Johnson (ABC Sports)
	Maryjean Wall (Lexington *Herald-Leader*)
1991	Sam Lacy (Baltimore *Afro-American*)
	Demmie Stathopolos (*Sports Illustrated*)
1990	Bill Tanton (Baltimore *Evening Sun*)
	Shelby Whitfield (ABC Radio)
1989	Bill Christine (Los Angeles *Times*)
	John Steadman (Baltimore *Evening Sun*)
1988	Ed Bowen (*The Blood-Horse*)
	Bill Nack (*Sports Illustrated*)
1987	Jack Dawson (WMAR-TV)
	Dave Feldman (Chicago *Sun-Times*)
1986	Vince Bagli (WBAL-TV)
	Shirley Povich (Washington *Post*)
1985	Howard Cosell (ABC Sports)
	Sam McCracken (Boston *Globe*)
1984	Jim McKay (ABC Sports)
	Billy Reed (Louisville *Courier-Journal*)
1983	Jack Whitaker (ABC Sports)
	Dale Austin (Baltimore *Sun*)
1982	Russ Harris (New York *Daily News*)
	Kent Hollingsworth (*The Blood-Horse*)
1981	William Leggett (*Sports Illustrated*)
	Jack Mann (Baltimore *Evening Sun*)
1980	Edwin Pope (Miami *Herald*)
	Snowden Carter (*Maryland Horse*)
1979	Whitney Tower (*Sports Illustrated*)
	Joe Kelly (Washington *Star*)
1979	William C. Phillips (*Daily Racing Form*)
1978	Win Elliott (CBS)
	Joe Hirsch (*Daily Racing Form*)
	Bob Maisel (Baltimore *Sun*)
1977	William Boniface (Baltimore *Sun*)
	Barney Nagler (*Daily Racing Form*)
	Charles Lamb (*News American*)
1976	Red Smith (New York *Times*)
	Raoul Carlisle (Arkansas *Times Herald*)

Joe Palmer Award

National Turf Writers Association Award for meritorious service to racing. Named for New York Herald-Tribune Turf writer known for his overall appreciation of the sport.

2005	Pete Pedersen
2004	Noble Threewitt
2003	Laffit Pincay Jr.
2002	Richard Duchossois, Eugene Melnyk
2001	Shirley Day Smith
2000	Jim McKay
1999	Kent Hollingsworth
1998	Sandy Hawley
1997	Jim Bolus
1996	Allen Paulson
1995	Mark Kaufman
1994	Joe Hirsch
1993	Henryk de Kwiatkowski
1992	Barry Weisbord
1991	Joe Burnham
1990	James P. Ryan
1989	Claude "Shug" McGaughey III
1988	Charlie Whittingham
1987	Alfred Vanderbilt
1986	James E. "Ted" Bassett III
1985	John Gaines
1984	E. P. Taylor
1983	David "Sonny" Werblin
1982	Frank "Jimmy" Kilroe
1981	Keene Daingerfield, Marion duPont Scott
1980	Chick Lang Sr., Leo O'Donnell
1979	Laz Barrera
1978	Steve Cauthen
1977	Nelson Bunker Hunt
1976	Fred Hooper
1975	I. J. Collins
1974	Secretariat
1973	John Galbreath
1972	Paul Mellon
1971	Bill Shoemaker
1970	Warner Jones Jr.
1969	Raymond Guest
1968	Marion Van Berg
1967	John Longden
1966	Marshall Cassidy
1965	John Schapiro
1964	Wathen Knebelkamp

Joan F. Pew Award

Sponsored by the Association of Racing Commissioners International and awarded to racing commissioner who demonstrates vision and vitality. Named for first woman member of Pennsylvania Horse Racing Commission and first woman president of National Association of State Racing Commissioners.

2006	Richard Shapiro
2005	Lynda Tanaka
2004	Cecil Alexander
2003	Norman I. Barron
2002	Stan Sadinsky
2001	Basil Plasteras
2000	Timothy "Ted" Connors
1999	Robin Traywick Williams
1998	Jon McKinnie
1997	Arthur Khoury
1996	Not awarded
1995	Not awarded
1994	Gil Moutray
1993	Joe Neglia
1992	Joanne McAdam
1991	Dr. Glenn Blodgett
1990	Frank Drea
1989	Richard Corbisiero Jr.
1988	Dr. James Smith
1987	Eric Braun

Red Smith Award

Churchill Downs award for outstanding print coverage of the Kentucky Derby (G1) in four categories. Named for late New York Times columnist.

Feature Story

2005	Greg Hall (Louisville *Courier-Journal*)
2004	C. Ray Hall (Louisville *Courier-Journal*)
2003	Mike Kane ([Schenectady] *Daily Gazette*)
2002	Jennie Rees (Louisville *Courier-Journal*)
2001	Bill Christine (Los Angeles *Times*)
2000	Jerry Izenberg (Newark *Star-Ledger*)
1999	Jay Privman (*Daily Racing Form*)
1998	Matt Graves (Albany *Times Union*)
1997	Jennie Rees (Louisville *Courier-Journal*)
1996	Dave Koerner (Louisville *Courier-Journal*)
1995	Bob Fortus (New Orleans *Times-Picayune*)
1994	Rick Bozich (Louisville *Courier-Journal*)
1993	Rick Bozich (Louisville *Courier-Journal*)
1992	Tom Archdeacon (Dayton *Daily News*)
1991	Dave Koerner (Louisville *Courier-Journal*)
1990	Jim Wells (St. Paul *Pioneer-Press*)
1989	Steve Crist (New York *Times*)
1988	Bill Christine (Los Angeles *Times*)
1987	Hubert Mizell (St. Petersburg *Times*)
1986	Bill Christine (Los Angeles *Times*)
1985	Dick Fenlon (Columbus *Dispatch*)
1984	Stan Hochman (Philadelphia *Daily News*)
1983	Jim Bolus (Louisville *Times*)

Advance Story

2005	Dick Jerardi (Philadelphia *Daily News*)
2004	Richard Rosenblatt (Associated Press)
2003	Rick Bozich (Louisville *Courier-Journal*)
2002	Rick Bozich (Louisville *Courier-Journal*)
2001	Mike Kane ([Schenectady] *Daily Gazette*)
2000	Rick Bozich (Louisville *Courier-Journal*)
1999	Rick Bozich (Louisville *Courier-Journal*)
1998	Vic Ziegel (New York *Daily News*)
1997	Matt Graves (Albany *Times Union*)
1996	Steve Haskin (*Daily Racing Form*)
1995	Blackie Sherrod (Dallas *Morning News*)
1994	Billy Reed (Lexington *Herald-Leader*)
1993	Rick Bozich (Louisville *Courier-Journal*)
1992	Vic Ziegel (New York *Daily News*)
1991	Steve Woodward (*USA Today*)
1990	Jerry Izenberg (New York *Post*)
1989	Rick Bozich (Louisville *Courier-Journal*)
1988	Billy Reed (Lexington *Herald-Leader*)
1987	Billy Reed (Lexington *Herald-Leader*)
1986	Bob Harding (Newark *Star-Ledger*)
1985	Jack Patterson (Akron *Beacon-Journal*)
1984	Bill Christine (Los Angeles *Times*)
1983	Peter Finney (New Orleans *Times-Picayune*)

Sunday Wrap-Up

2005 Jennie Rees (Louisville *Courier-Journal*)
2004 Pat Forde (Louisville *Courier-Journal*)
2003 Richard Rosenblatt (*Associated Press*)
2002 Mike Kane ([Schenectady] *Daily Gazette*)
2001 Jennie Rees (Louisville *Courier-Journal*)
2000 Mike Kane ([Schenectady] *Daily Gazette*)
1999 Mike Kane ([Schenectady] *Daily Gazette*)
1998 Jay Privman (New York *Times*)
1997 Jay Privman (New York *Times*)
1996 Billy Reed (Lexington *Herald-Leader*)
1995 Chuck Culpepper (Lexington *Herald-Leader*)
1994 Tom Archdeacon (Dayton *Daily News*)
1993 Jennie Rees (Louisville *Courier-Journal*)
1992 Bill Christine (Los Angeles *Times*)
1991 Tom Archdeacon (Dayton *Daily News*)
1990 Billy Reed (Lexington *Herald-Leader*)
1989 Jay Privman (Los Angeles *Daily News*)
1988 Jay Privman (Los Angeles *Daily News*)
1987 Bill Christine (Los Angeles *Times*)
1986 Paul Moran ([Long Island] *Newsday*)
1985 Tom McEwen (Tampa *Tribune*)
1984 Billy Reed (Louisville *Courier-Journal*)
1983 Billy Reed (Louisville *Courier-Journal*)

Monday Wrap-Up

2005 Steve Haskin (*The Blood-Horse*)
2004 Steve Haskin (*The Blood-Horse*)
2003 Tom Law (THOROUGHBRED TIMES)
2002 Lew Freedman (Chicago *Tribune*)
2001 John Harrell (THOROUGHBRED TIMES)
2000 Steve Haskin (*The Blood-Horse*)
1999 Steve Haskin (*The Blood-Horse*)
1998 Bill Nack (*Sports Illustrated*)
1997 Dick Jerardi (Philadelphia *Daily News*)
1996 Greg Boeck (*USA Today*)
1995 Bill Nack (*Sports Illustrated*)
1994 Chuck Culpepper (Lexington *Herald-Leader*)
1993 Jack Murray (Cincinnati *Enquirer*)
1992 Harry King (*Associated Press*)
1991 Dick Jerardi (Philadelphia *Daily News*)
1990 Rick Bozich (Louisville *Courier-Journal*)
1989 Tom Cushman (San Diego *Tribune*)
1988 Stan Hochman (Philadelphia *Daily News*)
1987 Dick Jerardi (Philadelphia *Daily News*)
1986 Stan Hochman (Philadelphia *Daily News*)
Edwin Pope (Miami *Herald*)
1985 Stan Hochman (Philadelphia *Daily News*)
1984 Dave Anderson (New York *Times*)
1983 Tom Jackson (Washington *Times*)

UTTA Outstanding Trainer of the Year Award

No longer awarded.

2001 John T. Ward Jr.
2000 Bobby Frankel
1999 D. Wayne Lukas
1998 Bob Baffert
1997 Pat Byrne
1996 Hubert "Sonny" Hine
1995 Bill Mott
1994 Warren "Jimmy" Croll Jr.
1993 Claude R. "Shug" McGaughey III
1992 H. Allen Jerkens
1991 Frank Brothers

Clay Puett Award

Sponsored by the University of Arizona Race Track Industry Program, for long-term, multifaceted, or far-reaching contributions to the racing industry. Named for creator of modern starting gate.

2005 WinStar Farm
2004 Trudy McCaffery
2003 W. Cothran "Cot" Campbell
2002 John and Betty Mabee and family
2001 Joe Hirsch
2000 John Gaines
1999 Vessels family
1998 Brady family
1997 Hancock family
1996 Phipps family
1995 Allen Paulson
1994 Clement Hirsch

University of Arizona Race Track Industry Program Distinguished Service Award

2005 Hans Stahl
2004 Not awarded
2003 Fred Stone
2001 Bob Benoit
2000 Stan Bergstein
1999 *Daily Racing Form*
1998 Sherwood Chillingworth
1997 Bennett Liebman
Ronald Sultemeier
1996 Joe Harper
1995 Lonny Powell
1994 Rukin Jelks
1993 John Goodman
Dr. Darrel Metcalfe
Vessels family
1992 Dan Fick

University of Arizona Race Track Industry Program Distinguished Senior Award

2005 Heather Belmonte
Dorothee Kieckefer
Eric Yee
2004 Jon Hansen
2003 Heather Meacham
2002 Stacia Mumm
2001 Laura Plato
2000 Scot Waterman
1999 Sable Downs
1998 Mike Hummel
1997 Valora Kilby

Alfred Gwynne Vanderbilt Award

New York Turf Writers Association award for individual or group that did the most for racing. Named for owner-breeder of Native Dancer; formerly known as the John A. Morris Award.

2005 Cash is King stable
Robert Lewis

2004	Team Smarty Jones
2003	Joe Hirsch
2002	Hans Stahl
2001	Barry K. Schwartz
2000	Kenny Noe Jr.
1999	Alfred Gwynne Vanderbilt
1998	Carolyn and Hubert "Sonny" Hine
1997	Skip Away
1996	James "Ted" Bassett
1995	Cigar
1994	Holy Bull
1993	Paul Mellon
1992	Allen Gutterman
1991	Barry Weisbord
	American Championship Racing Series
1989	John Gaines
	Whitney Tower
1988	Linda and Jim Ryan
1987	David "Sonny" Werblin
1986	ESPN/Thoroughbred Sports Television
1985	Peter Fuller
	John Galbreath
	Fred Hooper
1984	John Nerud
1983	Allaire duPont
1982	Helen "Penny" Chenery
	Frank "Jimmy" Kilroe
1981	Sam Rubin
1980	Jack Klugman
1979	Louis and Patrice Wolfson
1978	Affirmed
	Alydar
1977	Ogden Mills Phipps
1976	Marion duPont Scott
1975	Eddie Arcaro
	Johnny Longden
	Warren Mehrtens
	William "Smokey" Saunders
	Ron Turcotte
	Jack Dreyfus Jr.
1974	Martha F. Gerry
1973	Secretariat
1972	John H. "Jack" Krumpe
	Arthur B. "Bull" Hancock Jr.
1971	Jacques D. Wimpfheimer
1970	Charles W. Engelhard
	Sen. Thomas Morton
1969	Raymond Guest
1968	John W. Hanes
1967	Robert J. Kleberg Jr.
1966	Jack Dreyfus
1965	James Cox Brady
1964	Allaire duPont
1963	Alfred Gwynne Vanderbilt
1962	Capt. Harry F. Guggenheim
1961	Francis Dunne
1960	Capt. Harry F. Guggenheim
1959	John W. Hanes
1958	Marshall Cassidy
1957	C. V. Whitney
1956	George Widener
1953	Walter Jeffords
1952	C. V. Whitney
1951	John Hay Whitney
1950	Saratoga Association
1949	Marshall Cassidy
	George Widener
1948	Lou Smith
1947	Dr. Charles H. Strub
1946	John Blanks Campbell
1944	Harry Parr III
1943	Lincoln Plaut
1942	Herbert Bayard Swope
1941	Alfred Gwynne Vanderbilt
1940	Herbert Bayard Swope
1939	George H. Bull
1938	Alfred Gwynne Vanderbilt
1937	Mrs. Payne Whitney
1936	Alfred Gwynne Vanderbilt

Mike Venezia Memorial Award

Named for the popular New York jockey who was killed in an on-track accident on October 13, 1988, the Mike Venezia Memorial Award honors jockeys who exemplify extraordinary sportsmanship and citizenship.

2005	Not awarded
2004	Patti Cooksey
2003	Richard Migliore
2002	Dean Kutz
2001	Mike Luzzi
2000	Jorge Chavez
1999	Gary Stevens
1998	Eddie Maple
1997	Robbie Davis
1996	Laffit Pincay Jr.
1995	Pat Day
1994	Mike Smith
1993	Jerry Bailey
1992	Angel Cordero Jr.
1991	Chris McCarron
1990	Bill Shoemaker
1989	Mike Venezia

P.A.B. Widener II Trophy

Sponsored by Kentucky Thoroughbred Owners and Breeders and presented to breeder whose Kentucky-bred horses have performed the best based on a point system. Named for owner-breeder who raced under Elmendorf Farm.

2005	Ogden Mills Phipps
2004	Aaron and Marie Jones
2003	Juddmonte Farms
2002	Allen Paulson
2001	Juddmonte Farms
2000	Adena Springs
1999	Overbrook Farm
1998	Mr. and Mrs. John C. Mabee
1997	Juddmonte Farms
1996	Juddmonte Farms
1995	Juddmonte Farms
1994	Overbrook Farm
1993	Juddmonte Farms
1992	William S. Farish and partners
1991	Verne Winchell
1990	Calumet Farm
1989	Ogden Phipps
1988	Ogden Phipps

1987 Nelson Bunker Hunt
1986 Nelson Bunker Hunt
1985 Nelson Bunker Hunt
1984 Hancock family
1983 Hancock family
1982 Fred Hooper
1981 Verna Lehmann
1980 Verna Lehmann
1979 Hancock family
1978 Randolph Weinsier
1977 Ben Castleman
1976 Ogden Mills Phipps
1975 Hancock family
1974 John Galbreath
1973 Maxwell H. Gluck
1972 Leslie Combs

David F. Woods Memorial Award

Presented by Pimlico Race Course for best Preakness Stakes (G1) story from previous year. Named for longtime racetrack publicist and Baltimore *Evening Sun* columnist.

2006 Mike Brunker (NBCSports.com)
2005 Dick Jerardi (Philadelphia *Daily News*)
2004 Sean Clancy (*Mid-Atlantic Thoroughbred*)
2003 Bill Finley (New York *Times*)
2002 Jay Privman (*Daily Racing Form*)
2001 Tom LaMarra (*The Blood-Horse*)
2000 Rick Snider (Washington *Times*)
1999 Bill Mooney (*The Backstretch*)
1998 Jay Hovdey (*Daily Racing Form*)
1997 Jay Hovdey (*Daily Racing Form*)
1996 Steve Haskin (*Daily Racing Form*)
1995 Bill Finley (New York *Daily News*)
1994 Jay Posner (San Diego *Union-Tribune*)
1993 Bill Mooney (*The Blood-Horse*)
1992 Jay Hovdey (*The Blood-Horse*)
1991 Bill Christine (Los Angeles *Times*)
1990 Bill Christine (Los Angeles *Times*)
1989 Larry Bortstein (Orange County *Register*)
1988 Don Clippinger (*The Thoroughbred Record*)
Bob Roberts (Cleveland *Plain Dealer*)
1987 Billy Reed (Lexington *Herald-Leader*)
1986 Dave Kindred (Atlanta *Constitution-Journal*)
1985 George Vecsey (New York *Times*)
1984 Jack Murphy (Cincinnati *Enquirer*)
1983 John Schulian (Chicago *Sun-Times*)
1982 Billy Reed (Louisville *Courier-Journal*)

George Woolf Memorial Jockey Award

Sponsored by Santa Anita Park and awarded to jockey whose career and character earn esteem for themselves and Thoroughbred racing, based on a vote of their fellow jockeys. Named for Racing Hall of Fame jockey George "Iceman" Woolf, who died January 4, 1946, a day after incurring severe head injuries in a spill at Santa Anita.

2006 Mark Guidry
2005 Ray Sibille
2004 Robby Albarado
2003 Edgar Prado
2002 Russell Baze
2001 Dean Kutz
2000 Mike Smith
1999 Jose Santos
1998 Craig Perret
1997 Alex Solis
1996 Gary Stevens
1995 Eddie Maple
1994 Phil Grove
1993 Kent Desormeaux
1992 Jerry Bailey
1991 Earlie Fires
1990 John Lively
1989 Larry Snyder
1988 Don Brumfield
1987 Don MacBeth
1986 Jorge Velasquez
1985 Pat Day
1984 Steve Cauthen
1983 Marco Castaneda
1982 Patrick Valenzuela
1981 Eddie Delahoussaye
1980 Chris McCarron
1979 Ron Turcotte
1978 Darrel McHargue
1977 Frank Olivares
1976 Sandy Hawley
1975 Fernando Toro
1974 Alvaro Pineda
1973 John Rotz
1972 Angel Cordero Jr.
1971 Jerry Lambert
1970 Laffit Pincay Jr.
1969 John Sellers
1968 Braulio Baeza
1967 Donald Pierce
1966 Alex Maese
1965 Walter Blum
1964 Manuel Ycaza
1963 Ismael Valenzuela
1962 Steve Brooks
1961 Peter Moreno
1960 Bill Harmatz
1959 Bill Boland
1958 Merlin Volzke
1957 Ted Atkinson
1956 John Adams
1955 Ray York
1954 Ralph Neves
1953 Eddie Arcaro
1952 John Longden
1951 Bill Shoemaker
1950 Gordon Glisson

White Horse Award

Sponsored by the Race Track Chaplaincy of America to honor an industry member for a specific act of heroism.

2005 Louis Pomes
2004 John Woodley
2003 Leigh Grey

BREEDING

Development of Breeding Industry

Because the English aristocracy developed the Thoroughbred, the first harbingers of anything remotely resembling a Thoroughbred breeding industry necessarily appeared in England. Kings James I, Charles I, and especially Charles II were crucially important in importing Arabian stallions and broodmares in the 17th century.

When Charles I was deposed and beheaded by the Puritans in 1649, his stud at Tutbury was inventoried and dispersed, thus providing some of the earliest written records on the foundations of many modern pedigrees. Principal beneficiaries of that dispersal were members of Yorkshire's Darcy family, whose head, James Darcy Sr., was appointed Master of the Horse to Charles II. The Darcys, whose principal stud farm was at Sedbury in northern Yorkshire, were closely connected by marriage to other prominent early Yorkshire breeders: the Wyvil, Gascoigne, Hutton, and Villiers (the Dukes of Buckingham) families.

The Yorkshire land holdings of those families centered the early English breeding industry in that county, but Charles II chose the more southerly Suffolk village of Newmarket in East Anglia as his racing headquarters and established Newmarket racecourse in the 1660s. Newmarket's Rowley Mile, the course over which the Two Thousand Guineas (Eng-G1) and One Thousand Guineas (Eng-G1) are run, is named after Charles II, whose nickname in his more mature days was "Old Rowley."

The English lords who followed the royal family's lead in breeding racehorses owned estates all over the country, and each established their principal stud farms according to the location of their lands. For example, the various Earls of Derby's principal stud farms were at Knowsley, near Liverpool, while the Dukes of Newcastle's (and later Dukes of Portland's) stud was at Welbeck Abbey, near Newcastle. Newmarket's place as the headquarters of English racing eventually led to a cluster of breeding farms in the surrounding area, but English stud farms are still scattered throughout the country.

Printed Record

The early Yorkshire breeders often kept meticulous, handwritten records of their breeding activities in private stud books, some of which have survived. The earliest printed record that included pedigrees was John Cheney's *Racing Calendar*, an annual volume of race results that first appeared in 1727. After Cheney's death in 1751, competing calendars produced by John Pond, Reginald Heber, and William Pick appeared, and the competition continued until James Weatherby established his version of the *Racing Calendar* as the sole authority, beginning in 1773.

Although Cheney included pedigree infor-

Jersey Act

America's Thoroughbred industry was nearly destroyed between 1908 and '10 when antiwagering legislation swept the country—closing many racetracks, slashing purses to minuscule levels for those that remained open, and rendering American bloodstock all but worthless at home. Desperate breeders thus began to look abroad for racing opportunities and markets for their horses.

English breeders were disturbed by this sudden influx of foreign bloodstock onto European shores. They had long perceived themselves as the world's supplier of Thoroughbreds and feared that American horses for sale in great numbers would threaten the international demand for their own products. In 1913, England's Jockey Club, chaired by the seventh Earl of Jersey, sought to protect its breeders' interests by enacting a rule that effectively barred American bloodstock from the Thoroughbred canon, but not from racing.

Known as the Jersey Act, the rule designated as "half-bred" any horse that did not trace in every pedigree line "without flaw" to foundation stock recorded in the earliest volumes of England's *General Stud Book,* which much of the world accepted as an industry bible. The Jersey Act thus labeled as half-breds many American Thoroughbreds whose distant ancestors had been lost in the chaos of revolution and civil war. Although the rule was not retroactive, after 1913 horses carrying the blood of Lexington, Hanover, Domino, Spendthrift, Ben Brush, and other influential American progenitors no longer were admitted into the *General Stud Book.*

This discriminatory rule ultimately worked to America's advantage. For more than three decades and through two world wars, Americans imported top English bloodstock to enrich their breeding programs, while England could not look to America to do the same. While America acquired such horses as *Mahmoud, *Sir Gallahad III, and *Bull Dog, England had no access to Man o' War, Bull Lea, or Black Toney—halfbreds one and all under the Jersey Act.

In June 1949, the Jersey Act was quietly repealed. Lady Wentworth, a respected British pedigree authority and historian, applauded the action as long overdue and described the Jersey Act as "a mistake that made us look rather foolish." Under the revised rule, admission to the *General Stud Book* required only eight or nine proven crosses of pure blood and "such performances of its immediate family on the Turf as to warrant the belief in the purity of its blood."

mation on prominent runners in his annual volumes, it was Heber who first requested pedigree information from breeders in a standardized format. But no one attempted to collect this information into a separate book until Weatherby published Volume 1 of the *General Stud Book* in 1791. Based largely on private stud books and the various *Racing Calendars*, especially Pick's reconstruction of pre-Cheney races and pedigrees, Volume 1 of the *General Stud Book* was revised five times, with the final edition published in 1891.

The *Racing Calendar* and the *General Stud Book* gave the nascent Thoroughbred industry the kind of documentation required for expansion to other countries. Although records of racing in America extend back almost to the earliest English colonization, the first Thoroughbred recorded as imported to the New World in the *American Stud Book* is *Bulle (or Bully) Rock, by Darley Arabian, listed as imported to Virginia, "before the Revolution," specifically in 1730.

Virginia and Maryland became the first centers for breeding racehorses in America, led by the Tayloe family of Virginia and the Tasker family in Maryland. Given the primitive conditions of Colonial America, it is little wonder that many early records of imported Thoroughbreds and their produce in America were lost, and other records were reconstructed or fabricated at later dates.

As in England, early racing in America was the province of aristocratic families, and further progress by American breeders did not occur until the disruption caused by the American Revolution had thoroughly passed. The importation of *Diomed in 1799 proved pivotal because he established the first enduring American sire line through his son Sir Archy, great-grandsire of Lexington.

Commercial Beginnings

It was Lexington who cemented the transfer of the breeding industry west across the Appalachian Mountains to Kentucky. If any one man is the founder of the American commercial breeding industry, that person is Robert A.S.C. Alexander, who purchased Lexington for his Woodburn Stud near the city of Lexington in 1855. Lexington's success as 16-time leading sire and the many top racehorses that Alexander and his brother Alexander J. Alexander sold at Woodburn's annual yearling auctions enticed many other breeders to locate their stud farms in the Bluegrass.

The Alexanders also were among the sponsors of what became the definitive *American Stud Book,* after several false starts. George W. Jeffreys published the *Virginia Stud Book* in 1828, but the first comprehensive attempt at an American Stud Book was Patrick Nisbett Edgar's *American Race-Turf Register, Sportsman's Herald, and General Stud Book,* published in 1833.

Unfortunately, Edgar's work included a stunning number of obvious inaccuracies, some of which remain in the official record. As in England, several competitors, including John S. Skinner and William T. Porter, published versions of Racing Calendars or Stud Books before Sanders D. Bruce's *American Stud Book, Volume 1,* appeared in 1868.

Although Bruce's book retained some of Edgar's errors and created some of its own, it was a considerable advance on previous offerings. It rapidly became the official record and was purchased by the American Jockey Club in May 1897 for $35,000. That purchase was the first step toward the Jockey Club's current position as the breed registry and the keeper of the sport's records.

Early American race results were recorded primarily by periodicals such as Porter's *Spirit of the Times* and Bruce's *Turf, Field, and Farm. Daily Racing Form* and the *Morning Telegraph* took over these functions in the late 19th century, and the *Racing Form* became the de facto newspaper of record by the 1920s. In 1991, the Jockey Club and the Thoroughbred Racing Associations formed Equibase Co. to develop the official database of the Thoroughbred industry, and in '98 Equibase became the data provider to the *Racing Form* as well.

Designating Imported Horses

In its earliest years, the *American Stud Book* designated horses imported to North America for racing or breeding with "Imported" or "Imp." before the horse's name.

This practice changed in 1906 with publication of the *American Stud Book's* Volume 9. Its preface noted: "While the general features of this volume remain the same as Volume 8, it has been found necessary, in order to avoid a two-volume work, to condense the subject matter in every way possible, the most radical change being the substitution of an * in place of the word Imported wherever possible.

"The prefix Imported has been omitted from the following horses, they having been foaled in the United States, viz.: Bel Demonio, Donald A., Dundee, Flax Spinner, Glenelg, Keene, Loiterer, Pontiac, Paladin, Uncommon and Victory."

The asterisk, which preceded such notable names in American breeding history as *Nasrullah and *Ribot, was eliminated in 1975. An introductory note to the *American Stud Book, Foals of 1981,* states: "The practice of designating imported horses with an asterisk (*) was discontinued in 1975, and from that time forward, the country of origin is reflected in the suffix attached to the name. The asterisk or suffix is omitted in the cases of horses which were imported in utero."

Key Figures

Key figures in the development of an American commercial breeding industry on the foundation laid by the Alexanders were John E. Madden, Arthur B. Hancock Sr. and his son Arthur B. "Bull" Hancock Jr., Leslie Combs II, and John R. Gaines. A hands-on horseman who bred and trained his own horses with a keen eye for profit, Madden bred five Kentucky Derby winners at Hamburg Place, named for his first great coup with the great racehorse and sire Hamburg.

Hancock Sr. founded Claiborne Farm near Paris, Kentucky, in 1908 and stood Celt, who became the first of 11 leading American sires who won 29 sire championships at Claiborne during the 20th century.

Combs modernized both the stallion-syndication process and yearling salesmanship at his Spendthrift Farm near Lexington. He stood leading sires Exclusive Native and Seattle Slew, but it was his recruitment of wealthy clients to the sales ring and the breeding industry that helped set the stage for the bloodstock boom of the 1970s and '80s.

Combs's success made clear that big money could be made by breeding and selling potential racehorses, but it was Gaines who developed the syndication of stallions into a highly lucrative enterprise. An innovative thinker, Gaines also created the concept of the Breeders' Cup, which came to fruition in 1984, and he was one of the founders of the National Thoroughbred Association, which was quickly subsumed by the industry-backed National Thoroughbred Racing Association in 1998.

From its beginnings as a passionate pursuit of a few aristocratic Englishmen, Thoroughbred racing and breeding have developed into a worldwide, multibillion-dollar industry. Though still primarily a business for the wealthy, Thoroughbreds are now produced in every condition from the brick palaces of the Bluegrass and Newmarket to, quite literally, suburban back yards.—*John P. Sparkman*

Registration Rules for Breeding

History of Registration

The Jockey Club, an organization dedicated to improving Thoroughbred breeding and racing, registers more than 30,000 Thoroughbred foals each year, introducing them to the *American Stud Book* following a disciplined process of initiation that began more than 300 years ago.

Early in the 17th century, three stallions brought to England—the Darley Arabian, the Godolphin Arabian, and the Byerly Turk—became the foundation sires of the Thoroughbred industry. In 1791, James Weatherby published the first stud book, the *General Stud Book*. It listed the pedigrees of 387 mares that could each be traced to one of three descendants of the foundation sires: Eclipse, a direct descendant of the Darley Arabian; Matchem, a grandson of the Godolphin Arabian; and Herod, a great-great-grandson of the Byerly Turk.

In America, Patrick Edgar attempted to publish a national stud registry in 1833 but was unsuccessful. One year later, John Skinner reprinted the entire *General Stud Book* and added the existing pedigrees of American horses at the end. Following Skinner's effort, the pedigree section of *Mason's Farrier* was the only available resource until 1867, when John H. Wallace published *Wallace's American Stud Book*. Wallace soon abandoned the enterprise, which was a financial failure, and turned his attention to compiling the American Trotting Registry.

One year later, Col. Sanders D. Bruce published the *American Stud Book*. On May 17, 1897, the Jockey Club acquired the rights to Bruce's work for $35,000. Now, more than 100 years later, the Jockey Club continues to maintain the *American Stud Book* to ensure the integrity of the breed.

Today, registering a Thoroughbred is as simple as logging onto the Internet. Through Jockey Club Interactive Registration™ (*www.registry.jockeyclub.com*), owners and breeders can complete registration forms, submit digital photos, review a database of active names, and check the status of a registration. A goal of the Jockey Club is to provide a virtual foal certificate that will eliminate paper, which can be lost, destroyed, or illegally altered, while at the same time providing real-time access to all registry-related information.

How to Register

All requirements of the Principal Rules and Requirements of the *American Stud Book* must be met within one year of a foal's originally reported foaling date.

Step 1

For foals of 2001 and after, the foal's sire and dam must be genetically typed. For foals of 2000 and earlier, the foal's sire and dam must be blood-typed.

Step 2

Report of Mares Bred (Deadline: August 1 each year)

Stallion owners must file a report of all Thoroughbred mares bred to a stallion in a breeding season (February-July).

Step 3

Live Foal/No Foal Report (Deadline: Within 30 days after foaling)

1. The owner of record of each broodmare in the Jockey Club files will receive a preprinted Live Foal/No Foal Report. Note: All changes of mare ownership should be reported to the Jockey Club immediately.

2. The Live Foal/No Foal Report must be filed no later than 30 days following the birth of a foal, or in Jan-

uary if the mare was not bred. Note: The registration services department at the Jockey Club should be contacted immediately if a preprinted Live Foal/No Foal Report is not received by the time the foal is born.

Step 4

Genetic-Typing (Deadline: Within 45 days of receipt of genetic typing kit)

1. Within 180 days of the foaling date, a Registration and Genetic Typing Kit will be mailed to the address shown on the Live Foal/No Foal Report. Note: If genetic typing kit is not used within 45 days, the genetic typing process may have to be restarted at an additional fee.

2. Mane hairs pulled/blood drawn from the foal must be mailed to the laboratory shown on the preprinted mailer.

Notes:

Helpful hints for taking a DNA sample:

- Clean the mane comb thoroughly before pulling the mane.
- Grasp the mane close to the neck to help ensure you get roots.
- Do not try to pull a sample if the mane is wet.

Helpful hints for drawing blood:

- If, for some reason, a syringe must be used to draw blood, insert needle through stopper and depress plunger on syringe slowly.
- Do not remove stoppers or chemicals from tubes.
- Do not shake tubes; turn them end over end.
- Refrigerate blood if not mailing the same day. (Do not put tubes in Styrofoam container during refrigeration, and do not freeze the sample).
- Do not mail samples on the weekend or immediately before a holiday. (If samples are untestable on receipt by laboratory, another kit will be mailed and the process must be repeated.)

Step 5

Registration/Genetic Typing/Blood-Typing Form (Deadline: Send to the Jockey Club when DNA/blood sample is mailed to lab. Before sending to the Jockey Club, be certain that):

1. Both sides of form are completed, including:
   i) Written description of markings, indicating:
   - All white markings.
   - All flesh-colored markings.
   - All dark and chestnut markings on coronet.
   - All head and neck cowlicks (except cowlick at the very top of forehead).
   - Any other distinguishing characteristics.

   ii) Signature by foal's owner or authorized agent.
   iii) One to six name choices. (This could avoid additional naming fees.)
2. A set of four color photos is enclosed, clearly showing color and all markings from the front, back, and both sides. Note: Do not take photographs until the foal has shed its "baby hair."
3. The Stallion Service Certificate (acquired from the stallion owner) is attached.
4. Fee payment is enclosed.

How to Name a Horse

A. A name may be claimed on the Registration Application, on a Name Claiming Form, or through Interactive Registration™ at *www.registry.jockeyclub.com*. Name selections should be listed in order of preference. Names will be assigned based upon availability and compliance with the naming rules as stated herein. Names may not be claimed or reserved by telephone. When a foreign language name is submitted, an English translation must be furnished to the Jockey Club. An explanation must accompany "coined" or "made-up" names that have no apparent meaning. Horses born in the United States, Puerto Rico, or Canada and currently reside in another country must be named by the Jockey Club through the Stud Book Authority of their country of residence.

B. If a valid attempt to name a foal is submitted to the Jockey Club by February 1 of the foal's two-year-old year and such a name is determined not eligible for use, no fee is required for a subsequent claim of name for that foal. If a valid attempt to name a foal is not submitted to the Jockey Club by February 1 of the foal's two-year-old year, a fee is required to claim a name for such a foal.

C. A reserved name must be used within one year (365 days) from the day it was reserved. Reserved names cannot be used until written notification requesting the assignment of the name to a specific horse is received by the Registry Office. If the reserved name is not used within one year (365 days) from its reservation, it will become available for any horse. A fee is required to reserve a name.

D. A foal's name may be changed at any time prior to starting in its first race. Ordinarily, no name change will be permitted after a horse has started in its first race or has been used for breeding purposes. However, in the event a name must be changed after a horse has started in its first race, both the old and new names should be used until the horse has raced three times following the name change. The prescribed fee and the Certificate of Foal Registration must accompany any request to the Registry Office for a change of name.

E. Names of horses over ten years old may be eligible if they are not excluded and have not been used during the preceding five years either in breeding or racing.

Names of geldings and horses that were never used for breeding or racing may be available five years from the date of their death as reported.

F. The following classes of names are not eligible for use:

1. Names consisting of more than 18 letters (spaces and punctuation marks count as letters).
2. Initials such as C.O.D., F.O.B., etc.
3. Names ending in "filly," "colt," "stud," "mare," "stallion," or any similar horse-related term.
4. Names consisting entirely of numbers, except numbers above 30 may be used if they are spelled out.
5. Names ending with a numerical designation such as "2nd" or "3rd," whether or not such a designation is spelled out.
6. Names of persons unless written permission to use their name is on file with the Jockey Club.
7. Names of "famous" people no longer living unless approval is granted by the Board of Stewards of the Jockey Club.
8. Names of "notorious" people.
9. Names of racetracks or graded stakes races.
10. Recorded names such as assumed names or stable names.

11. Names clearly having commercial significance, such as trade names.

12. Copyrighted material, titles of books, plays, motion pictures, popular songs, etc., unless the applicant furnishes the Jockey Club with proof that the copyright has been abandoned or that such material has not been used within the past five years.

13. Names that are suggestive or have a vulgar or obscene meaning; names considered in poor taste; or names that may be offensive to religious, political, or ethnic groups.

14. Names that are currently active either in racing or breeding, and names similar in spelling or pronunciation to such names.

15. Permanent names and names similar in spelling or pronunciation to permanent names. The list of criteria to establish a permanent name is as follows:

a. Horses in the Racing Hall of Fame;

b. Horses that have been voted Horse of the Year;

c. Horses that have won an Eclipse Award;

d. Horses that have won a Sovereign Award (Canadian champions);

e. Annual leading sire and broodmare sire by progeny earnings;

f. Cumulative money winners of $2-million or more;

g. Horses that have won the Kentucky Derby (G1), Preakness Stakes (G1), Belmont Stakes (G1), Jockey Club Gold Cup (G1), Breeders' Cup Classic (G1), or Breeders' Cup Turf (G1); and

h. Horses included in the International List of Protected Names.

G. In addition to the provisions of this rule, the Registrar of the Jockey Club reserves the right of approval on all name requests.

Age Definitions

Foal: A young horse of either sex in its first year of life.

Suckling: A foal of any sex in its first year of life while it is still nursing.

Weanling: A foal of any sex in its first year of life after being separated from its dam.

Yearling: A colt, filly, or gelding in its second calendar year of life (beginning January 1 of the year following its birth).

Two-Year-Old: A colt, filly, or gelding in its third calendar year of life (beginning January 1 of the year following its yearling year).

Color Definitions

The following colors are recognized by the Jockey Club:

Bay: The entire coat of the horse may vary from a yellow-tan to a bright auburn. The mane, tail, and lower portion of the legs are always black, unless white markings are present.

Black: The entire coat of the horse is black, including the muzzle, flanks, mane, tail, and legs, unless white markings are present.

Chestnut: The entire coat of the horse may vary from a red-yellow to a golden-yellow. The mane, tail, and legs are usually variations of coat color, unless white markings are present.

Dark Bay or Brown: The entire coat of the horse will vary from a brown, with areas of tan on the shoulders, head, and flanks, to a dark brown, with tan areas seen only in the flanks and/or muzzle. The mane, tail, and lower portion of the legs are always black, unless white markings are present.

Gray or Roan: The Jockey Club has combined these colors into one color category. This does not change the individual definitions of the colors for gray and roan and in no way impacts on the two-coat color inheritance principle as stated in a previous rule.

Gray: The majority of the coat of the horse is a mixture of black and white hairs. The mane, tail, and legs may be either black or gray, unless white markings are present.

Roan: The majority of the coat of the horse is a mixture of red and white hairs or brown and white hairs. The mane, tail, and legs may be black, chestnut, or roan, unless white markings are present.

Palomino: The entire coat of the horse is golden-yellow, unless white markings are present. The mane and tail are usually flaxen.

White: A rare color not to be confused with the colors gray or roan. The entire coat, including the mane, tail, and legs, is white and no other color should be present.

Breeding Terminology

Bred (Mated): Any filly or mare that has undergone the physical act of breeding (mating).

Bred (Area Foaled): The term "bred" is sometimes used to describe the location where a foal was born; i.e., Kentucky-bred, New York-bred, etc.

Breeder: The breeder of a foal is the owner of the dam at the time of foaling, unless the dam was under a lease or foal-sharing agreement at the time of foaling. In that case, the person(s) specified by the terms of the agreement is (are) the breeder of the foal.

Stallion: A male horse that is used to produce foals.

Sire: A male horse that has produced, or is producing, foals.

Broodmare: A filly or mare that has been bred (mated) and is used to produce foals.

Dam: A female horse that has produced, or is producing, foals.

Maiden: A filly or mare that has never been bred (mated).

In Foal (Pregnant) Broodmare: A filly or mare that was bred (mated), conceived, and is currently in foal (pregnant).

Aborted: A term used to describe a broodmare that has been pronounced in foal (pregnant) based on an examination of 42 days or more post breeding (mating) and lost her foal prematurely; or a broodmare from whom an aborted fetus has been observed.

Barren (Not Pregnant): A term used to describe a filly or mare, other than a maiden mare, that was bred (mated) and did not conceive during the last breeding season.

Breeding (Mating): The physical act of a stallion mounting a broodmare with intromission and ejaculation of semen into the reproductive tract.

Gender Terminology

Colt: An entire male horse four years old or younger.

Horse: When reference is made to gender, a "horse" is an entire male five years old or older.

Ridgling ("rig"): A lay term used to describe either a monorchid or cryptorchid.

Cryptorchid: A male horse of any age that has no testes in his scrotum but was never gelded (the testes are undescended).

Monorchid: A male horse of any age that has only one testicle in his scrotum (the other testicle was either removed or is undescended).

Gelding: A male horse of any age that is unsexed (had both testicles removed).

Filly: A female horse four years old or younger.

Mare: A female horse five years old or older.

Deadlines

Report of Mares Bred (Stallion Reports): This report must be filed no later than August 1 of the breeding year.

Live Foal/No Foal Report (Mare Reports):

- Reporting live foal information. This report must be filed within 30 days after the foaling date.
- Reporting no foal information. This report must be filed no later than 30 days after the intended foaling date or in January if the mare was not bred.

Foal Registration: All requirements must be completed by one year from the foaling date, including genetic typing, to avoid paying an additional fee.

Naming: Must be named by February 1 of two-year-old year to avoid paying a fee.

Death: Must be reported within 30 days after the death.

Export: Requirements must be met within 60 days after the horse's departure to avoid paying an additional fee.

Foreign Registration: All requirements must be met within 60 days after the horse's arrival to avoid paying an additional fee.

Geldings: Should be reported immediately.

Sold Without Pedigree: Should be reported within 60 days after the date of sale.

Fees

Foal Registration Fees: If all requirements are met within one calendar year from foaling date (includes genetic typing of the foal and parentage verification, as well as ownership transfers and corrections): $200

By December 31 of yearling year: $525

By December 31 of two-year-old year: $775

After December 31 of two-year-old year: $2,000

Reserved Names: $75

Foal-Naming Fee: After February 1 of the foal's two-year-old year. (Before this date, no fee is required): $75

Name-Change Fee: $100

Genetic Typing Fees:

Genetic typing, entry into the Ownership Registry: $80

Additional Genetic Typing: $80 (or retyping as required by the Jockey Club)

Duplicate Certificate Fee: $150

Corrected Certificate Fee (six months after original certificates issued): $50

Certificate of Exportation Fees:

If all requirements are completed within 60 days of the horse's departure from the United States, Canada, or Puerto Rico: $150

If all requirements are completed after 60 days of the horse's departure from the United States, Canada, or Puerto Rico: $400

Certificate of Foreign Registration Fees:

If all requirements are completed within 60 days of the horse's arrival in the United States, Canada, or Puerto Rico: $150

If all requirements are completed after 60 days and up until one year of the horse's arrival in the United States, Canada, or Puerto Rico: $400

If all requirements are not completed within one year of the horse's arrival in the United States, Canada, or Puerto Rico, and the horse is eligible for late registration: $750

Horses registered in the *American Stud Book* returning from a foreign country: $150

Thirty-day foreign racing permit fee:

If application is received within 30 days of the horse's arrival in the United States, Canada, or Puerto Rico: $150

Express handling fee: $100

How to Contact the Jockey Club:

Address: The Jockey Club, 821 Corporate Dr., Lexington, Ky. 40503-2794

Telephone: (859) 224-2700

Registration Services: (800) 444-8521

Fax: (859) 224-2710

Website: *www.jockeyclub.com*

Jockey Club Interactive Registration™ Website: *www.registry.jockeyclub.com*

Brief History of Foal Identification

When registering Thoroughbreds in North America, foal identification traditionally has been documented by markings, both narrative descriptions of the distinctive characteristics and diagrams of those markings.

For instance, the breeder would be required to describe any white markings and their locations, as well as any flesh-colored areas and markings on the coronet, when applicable. If the horse had a blaze, the breeder would include a diagram of the horse's head and the shape of the blaze.

Over time, photographs of the horse and any markings became a requirement of foal registration. This process occurred gradually, beginning when breeders would attach photographs of the markings with the registration application. The Jockey Club Registry began accepting digital photos in 2001.

Beginning with the foal crop of 1987, blood-typing for parentage verification was made a requirement for registration.

Advances in technology allowed the Jockey Club to begin DNA verification of parentage with the foal crop of 2001. Within 180 days of the foaling date, breeders receive a registration and genetic typing kit. The genetic typing kit, which contains instructions for pulling mane hairs and drawing blood, must be returned within 45 days.

Current registration practices still require breeders to include a narrative of all markings as well as four-color photographs of the foal from the front, back, and both sides to document the markings.

Foal Registration

Foal registration for all Thoroughbreds in North America—the United States, Canada, and Puerto Rico—is performed by the Jockey Club, which was founded in 1894 and is a not-for-profit organization dedicated to improving the Thoroughbred breed. To be registered in the *American Stud Book,* which is maintained by the Jockey Club, the parentage of all foals must be verified, a process that today includes DNA typing of all stallions, broodmares, and foals.

Registration of American Thoroughbreds was started by Col. Sanders D. Bruce, a Kentuckian who spent a lifetime researching pedigrees of American Thoroughbreds. He published the first volume of the *American Stud Book* in 1868, and he produced six volumes of the registry. In 1897, the Jockey Club purchased all rights to the *American Stud Book.*

Foal Registration by State in North America in 2004

Alabama	69	Iowa	354	New Hampshire	3	Texas	1,673
Alaska	1	Kansas	107	New Jersey	309	Utah	107
Arizona	342	Kentucky	9,714	New Mexico	756	Vermont	0
Arkansas	282	Louisiana	1,850	New York	1,945	Virginia	414
California	3,668	Maine	1	North Carolina	42	Virgin Islands	0
Colorado	279	Maryland	882	North Dakota	59	Washington	654
Connecticut	3	Massachusetts	51	Ohio	461	West Virginia	582
Delaware	1	Michigan	341	Oklahoma	775	Wisconsin	21
Florida	4,345	Minnesota	301	Oregon	267	Wyoming	15
Georgia	50	Mississippi	18	Pennsylvania	928	**Total U.S.**	**33,624**
Hawaii	0	Missouri	46	Rhode Island	0	**Total Canada**	**2,554**
Idaho	161	Montana	101	South Carolina	49	**Total Puerto Rico**	**525**
Illinois	919	Nebraska	156	South Dakota	45	**Total Crop**	**36,703**
Indiana	434	Nevada	7	Tennessee	36		

Trend of Foal Registration in North America

Year	United States	Change	Canada	Change	Puerto Rico	Change	Total	Change
2006	34,200*	0.4%	2,600*	0.8%	500*	–9.1%	**37,300***	0.3%
2005	34,070*	1.3%	2,580*	1.0%	550*	4.8%	**37,200***	1.4%
2004	33,624	–0.6%	2,554	0.3%	525	2.3%	**36,703**	–0.5%
2003	33,827	2.7%	2,561	3.9%	513	–1.9%	**36,901**	2.7%
2002	32,950	–5.1%	2,466	–4.8%	523	–11.4%	**35,939**	–5.1%
2001	34,709	0.0%	2,590	5.1%	590	5.0%	**37,889**	0.4%
2000	34,719	2.6%	2,464	1.2%	562	–13.5%	**37,745**	2.2%
1999	33,840	2.7%	2,435	4.1%	650	–11.4%	**36,925**	2.5%
1998	32,944	2.6%	2,340	2.5%	734	–0.8%	**36,018**	2.5%
1997	32,116	–0.4%	2,284	–4.7%	740	1.9%	**35,140**	–0.6%
1996	32,242	1.1%	2,397	–2.0%	726	11.2%	**35,365**	1.1%
1995	31,882	–0.7%	2,445	–5.6%	653	3.3%	**34,980**	–1.0%
1994	32,117	–5.0%	2,591	–4.5%	632	4.5%	**35,340**	–4.8%
1993	33,820	–3.5%	2,713	–2.3%	605	–0.8%	**37,138**	–3.4%
1992	35,050	–8.1%	2,777	–8.2%	610	–2.9%	**38,437**	–8.0%
1991	38,149	–5.4%	3,025	–5.3%	628	1.8%	**41,802**	–5.3%
1990	40,333	–8.9%	3,193	–4.9%	617	–1.4%	**44,143**	–8.5%

*Estimated or incomplete

Annual Foal Registration in North America

2006	37,300*	**1983**	47,237	**1960**	12,901	**1937**	5,535	**1914**	1,702
2005	37,200*	**1982**	42,894	**1959**	12,240	**1936**	5,042	**1913**	1,722
2004	36,703	**1981**	38,669	**1958**	11,377	**1935**	5,038	**1912**	1,900
2003	36,901	**1980**	35,679	**1957**	10,832	**1934**	4,924	**1911**	2,040
2002	35,939	**1979**	32,904	**1956**	10,112	**1933**	5,158	**1910**	1,950
2001	37,889	**1978**	31,510	**1955**	9,610	**1932**	5,256	**1909**	2,340
2000	37,745	**1977**	30,036	**1954**	9,064	**1931**	5,266	**1908**	3,080
1999	36,925	**1976**	28,809	**1953**	9,040	**1930**	5,137	**1907**	3,780
1998	36,018	**1975**	28,271	**1952**	8,811	**1929**	4,903	**1906**	3,840
1997	35,140	**1974**	27,586	**1951**	8,944	**1928**	4,503	**1905**	3,800
1996	35,365	**1973**	26,811	**1950**	9,095	**1927**	4,182	**1904**	3,990
1995	34,981	**1972**	25,726	**1949**	8,770	**1926**	3,632	**1903**	3,440
1994	35,341	**1971**	24,301	**1948**	8,434	**1925**	3,272	**1902**	3,600
1993	37,138	**1970**	24,361	**1947**	7,705	**1924**	2,921	**1901**	3,784
1992	38,437	**1969**	23,848	**1946**	6,579	**1923**	2,763	**1900**	3,476
1991	41,801	**1968**	22,910	**1945**	5,819	**1922**	2,352	**1899**	3,080
1990	44,143	**1967**	21,876	**1944**	5,650	**1921**	2,035	**1898**	2,940
1989	48,235	**1966**	20,228	**1943**	5,923	**1920**	1,833	**1897**	2,992
1988	49,220	**1965**	18,846	**1942**	6,427	**1919**	1,665	**1893-'96**	5,940*
1987	50,917	**1964**	17,343	**1941**	6,805	**1918**	1,950	**1803-'92**	3,950*
1986	51,296	**1963**	15,917	**1940**	6,003	**1917**	1,680		
1985	50,433	**1962**	14,870	**1939**	6,316	**1916**	2,128		
1984	49,247	**1961**	13,794	**1938**	5,696	**1915**	2,120		

*Estimated

Evolution of the Breed

In genetic terms, the Thoroughbred is a hybrid, created by crossing two or possibly more breeds of horses to produce an animal with specific characteristics. One of those breeds was the Arabian horse, but the exact identities of other contributors are considerably less clear.

Early records do not identify most of the mares mated to the many Arabian, Barb, and Turk (all are varieties of Arabians) stallions imported to England after the Markham Arabian's acquisition by King James I. Although the Markham Arabian was the first Arabian whose importation was noted by history, no doubt others, both males and females, were transported from the Middle East over several centuries, beginning with the Crusades of the 12th and 13th centuries. However, many horses called Arabians or Barbs in the *General Stud Book* were certainly not purebreds.

These imports were crossed with native English stock over many generations. By the time the modern Thoroughbred was created, there were two varieties of pony-sized English and Irish racehorses known as Hobbies and Galloways, and Oriental imports of the time were not much larger. Both English breeds certainly carried Oriental blood, but no one knows how much. Before the Puritan revolution in 1649, the royal stud of King James I and his ill-fated son King Charles I probably included mares of both mixed English and Oriental blood and pure-bred Arabians. These mares came to be called "royal mares" and now stand as the earliest known female ancestors of several modern female families.

The surge of importations that began with the restoration of King Charles II in 1660 included both males and females. With King Charles leading the way, the English nobility engaged in fierce competition to produce better, faster racehorses, and they quickly learned that the more Arabian blood their stock could claim, the better chance they had.

Estimated Relationships of Some Important Horses to Modern Thoroughbreds

Horse (Year of Birth)	Percentage Relationship
Herod (1758)	17.2%
Eclipse (1764)	15.2%
Highflyer (1774)	12.8%
Godolphin Arabian (1724)	12.7%
Partner (1718)	11.4%
Regulus (1739)	9.4%
St. Simon (1881)	8.7%
Stockwell (1849)	8.7%
Curwen Bay Barb mare (1710)	8.4%
Birdcatcher (1833)	7.4%
Pocahontas (1837)	7.0%
Matchem (1748)	6.3%
Flying Childers (1715)	5.7%
Darley Arabian (ca. 1700)	5.3%
***Teddy** (1913)	4.9%
Byerley Turk (ca. 1680)	4.6%
Curwen Bay Barb (ca. 1695)	4.4%
Hyperion (1930)	4.2%
***Nasrullah** (1940)	4.2%
Bald Galloway (ca. 1700)	4.0%

Figures based on an unpublished statistical study. Percentages of horses born since about 1850 may change slightly.

Foundation Sires

The arrivals of the Byerley Turk, Place's White Turk, the Curwen Bay Barb, the Darley Arabian, and finally the Godolphin Arabian (around 1730) sharply accelerated the development of the breed. The Darley Arabian sired Flying Childers, generally recognized as the first great Thoroughbred, in 1714. Through Flying Childers's full brother Bartlett's Childers, the Darley Arabian

The Darley Arabian

Of the Thoroughbred's three male-line foundation sires, only the Darley Arabian was almost certainly a pure-bred Arabian. The Godolphin Arabian was probably a Turcoman-Arabian cross, while the Byerley Turk may have been born in England, sired by another Turcoman-Arabian cross horse whose identity is uncertain.

Probably born in what is now Syria in 1700, the Darley Arabian was purchased in Aleppo, then part of the Ottoman Empire, by English merchant Thomas Darley in '04 and shipped to his brother Richard Darley at Aldby Park near York, England. The Darley Arabian was said to be of the "keheilan" or "manicca" breed, the subset of Arabians then most prized by Bedouins. Ottoman law forbade the sale of any pure-bred Arabian to a foreigner, but Darley's merchant connections in Aleppo allowed him to spirit the horse out of the country.

The Darley Arabian mostly covered his owner's broodmares, but one of the few outside mares bred to him was Leonard Childers's Betty Leedes, by Careless, who produced Flying Childers in 1714 and his full brother Bartlett's Childers in '15. Flying Childers was unbeaten and considered by far the fastest horse until that time. Darley Arabian also sired the good racehorses Almanzor, Cupid, and Brisk.

Although Flying Childers was a successful sire, his brother Bartlett's Childers—unraced because he was a bleeder—carried on the line. He sired the good racehorse Squirt, who in turn sired Marske, sire of Eclipse (1764). Eclipse in turn founded the male lines that lead to the modern lines of Phalaris (Northern Dancer, *Nasrullah, Native Dancer), St. Simon (*Ribot and *Princequillo), Hyperion, Domino, *Teddy, and Blandford.

established today's dominant male line, leading to Phalaris and his descendants.

The Godolphin Arabian was the most prepotent immediate influence among the three founding male-line sires, establishing the male line that leads to dual Breeders' Cup Classic (G1) winner Tiznow. Although the Godolphin Arabian male line is now far less prominent than that of the Darley Arabian, almost 13% of the genes of the modern Thoroughbred come from the Godolphin Arabian, according to modern statistical studies.

The male line tracing to the Byerley Turk achieved dominance in the late 18th century through his great-great-grandson Herod. By 1825, inbreeding to Herod had reached its limit, and his overall influence began to decline. Today, his male line appears to be headed for extinction, with tendrils hanging on in Europe through Ahonoora and in Australia through Century. Nevertheless, more than 17% of the genes of the modern Thoroughbred come from Herod.

Beneficiary of the intense early inbreeding to Godolphin Arabian and Herod was the Darley Arabian line. The line from Flying Childers was prominent for approximately 50 years, but descendants of his unraced full brother, the bleeder Bartlett's Childers, gained ascendance through his great-grandson Eclipse, foaled in 1764. Eclipse was the greatest of the four-milers, and during his stud career a shift began from the four-mile heat racing that had been popular since King Charles's era to "dash" racing over shorter distances, exemplified by the Epsom Derby, founded in 1780 and contested at one mile that year.

Eclipse and Herod surpassed all other stallions of their time in producing the speedier, more brilliant horse necessary for dash racing. Added together, Herod, Godolphin Arabian, and Eclipse account for 45% of the genes of the modern Thoroughbred.

In the same time period that surviving male lines were being whittled down to three, female lines descending from approximately 100 foundation mares listed in Volume 1 of the *General Stud Book* were cut in half. That, of course, does not mean that those additional foundation mares and stallions had no influence on the development of the breed. Indeed, their names persist, sometimes with great influence, in the nether reaches of pedigrees.

Exportation of the Thoroughbred to other countries, particularly to North America, Australia, and Argentina, inevitably resulted in the introduction of female lines not found in the *General Stud Book*. The chaotic circumstances of Colonial and Revolutionary America meant that

Averages for the Breed

Averages for the breed statistics are designed to provide a baseline to evaluate the performances of contemporary racehorses, sires, and dams. Statistics shown in the column on the left below reflect the worldwide performances of all named foals born in North America between 1987-'96. Statistics in the column on the right reflect the same data for foals by the top 1% of all sires by total earnings for the same decade. All statistics are based on data in the Jockey Club Information System's worldwide database. The Jockey Club database includes complete records for racing in United States, Canada, Puerto Rico, England, Ireland, France, Germany, Italy, Japan, Australia, Hong Kong, Saudi Arabia, Argentina, Brazil, and United Arab Emirates for some, but not all of the years covered by these statistics.

Statistics below are designed to give a snapshot of what an average "good" horse should accomplish.

	Foals 1987-'96	**Foals by Top 1% of Sires**
Starters/foals	69.4%	85%
Winners/foals (starters)	46.1% (66.4%)	65.5% (77%)
Repeat winners/foals (starters)	35.1% (50.5%)	53.4% (62.8%)
Stakes winners/foals (starters)	3.4% (4.9%)	9% (10.6%)
Graded SW/foals (starters)	0.8% (1.1%)	3.6% (4.2%)
Grade 1 SW/foals (starters)	0.2% (0.3%)	1.1% (1.3%)
Stakes-placed/foals (starters)	5.3% (7.6%)	11.8% (13.9%)
2-year-old starters/foals	34%	46.8%
2yo winners/foals (% 2yo starters)	11.3% (33.3%)	18.6% (39.8%)
2yo SW/foals (% 2yo starters)	1% (3%)	2.4% (5.1%)
3-year-old starters/foals	59.9%	76.9%
4-year-old starters/foals	44.6%	56.8%
5-year-old and up starters/foals	27.6%	35.9%
Average career starts/foal	14.8	18.6
Average career starts/starter	21.3	21.9
Average win distance in furlongs	6.82	7.24
Average win distance on turf in furlongs	8.29	8.47
Average earnings/starter	$34,002	$79,011
Average earnings/starter male (female)	$40,187 ($27,569)	$98,643 ($58,294)
Average earnings/start	$1,594	$3,615
Average earnings/start male (female)	$1,647 ($1,521)	$3,619 ($3,609)
Average Racing Index (RI)	1.16	2.36

records were lost on many legitimate members of the breed and invented for many who doubtless were not.

Such chaos inevitably led to controversy. When American racing collapsed early in the 20th century due to antigambling hysteria, England's Turf authority, the Jockey Club, essentially banned American-bred stock from the hallowed pages of the *General Stud Book* when American exports threatened to flood the market. Fortunately for the future of the breed, the Jersey Act of 1913 excluding American-breds included a provision that grandfathered in American-bred stock already included in earlier volumes.

Within 40 years, descendants of those acceptable American-breds—including such horses as Nearco and his son *Nasrullah—and descendants of French-bred Tourbillon (branded as a half-bred by the Jersey Act because of his American antecedents) dominated English racing, which forced the repeal of these exclusionary rules.

Changing Conditions

The descendants of Eclipse's great-grandson Whalebone through his great-great-grandson Stockwell proved especially adaptable to the pattern of English racing established by the five classic races (Two Thousand Guineas, One Thousand Guineas, Epsom Derby, Epsom Oaks, and St. Leger Stakes). Stockwell led the English sire list eight times and his great-grandson, unbeaten Triple Crown winner *Ormonde, is widely considered the best racehorse of the 19th century. The male line of *Ormonde lives on tenuously through the descendants of Damascus.

The inauguration of several valuable races outside the classic pattern in the 1890s changed the requirements of English racing at about the same time that an invasion of American jockeys changed race-riding. After American riders such as Tod Sloan and Danny Maher proved the virtues of setting a faster pace, male-line descendants of one stallion, Phalaris, gradually proved the most capable of adapting to the new conditions.

A top-class sprinter during World War I, Phalaris sired two sets of full brothers who established powerful male lines: Pharos and Fairway, and *Sickle and *Pharamond II. Pharos and his descendants generally sired heavier, more muscular horses with speed, while the Fairways tended toward taller, lighter individuals. Today the Fairway line hangs by the thread of Lord At War (Arg), while Pharos reigns supreme through descendants of his grandsons *Nasrullah, sire of Bold Ruler, and Nearctic, sire of Northern Dancer.

*Sickle led the U.S. sire list twice, and his brother *Pharamond II finished second to him in 1938. *Sickle's great-grandson Native Dancer, another heavy, powerful horse, established the second most dominant male line in modern pedigrees, that descending from his grandson Mr. Prospector.

In 300 years, the Thoroughbred breed has evolved from a small, relatively lightly made animal designed to gallop 3½ miles at a sedate pace and then sprint for a half-mile. It has become a much larger, heavier, proportionally shorter-legged animal designed primarily for high speeds from the start over distances up to 1¼ miles. Without much doubt, Flying Childers would hardly recognize his modern descendants.

—John P. Sparkman

Breeding Theories

Flying Childers was the first great racehorse who clearly could be defined as a Thoroughbred. Undoubtedly, his breeder, Leonard Childers, had a theory to explain why his greatest creation was so fast. In the three centuries since Flying Childers first saw daylight in 1714, it is certain that most breeders were equally sure they knew why their latest champion could run a hole in the wind.

Over time, however, breeders' ideas about why one horse runs faster than another have coalesced into a remarkably small set of concepts. Breeding theories range from vaguely general precepts such as "breed the best to the best and hope for the best" to highly specific constructs such as the many varieties of dosage theory.

Breed the Best to the Best

The logic behind the broadest of these ideas—breed the best to the best—is obvious. If speed in the racehorse is determined to a degree by inheritance, then it is logical to assume that the fastest horses—both male and female—have the best chances to pass on their abilities to their offspring.

The history of the breed has shown irrefutably that this assumption is true. In general, the horses that turn out to be the best sires are almost always high-class racehorses themselves. The correlation between racecourse ability and sire success is, of course, far from guaranteed but undeniably positive.

The case for the female of the species is less clear but still undeniable. On average, the best racemares become more successful broodmares than those females that showed less ability on the racecourse. Thus, if a high-class racehorse is mated to a high-class racemare, the breeder theoretically increases the probability that another high-class racehorse will result.

Because probability is capricious, the odds are still against the breeder. The most successful stallions in history have sired only about 25% stakes winners. Individual broodmares may achieve higher percentages, but percentages based on the relatively small numbers of foals from those mares are meaningless in the larger picture.

So, breeding the best to the best certainly works, on average. However, it is far too general a precept to satisfy many Thoroughbred breeders—and of no use whatsoever to those who cannot afford to buy the best, most expensive racing prospects, both male and female.

Inbreeding

For the first 100 years or so of the Thoroughbred's existence as a distinct, definable breed, the number of horses bred each year was so small that inbreeding was inevitable.

Inbreeding, as most commonly used by Thoroughbred breeders, means the repetition of one or more names at least once on both the sire's and dam's side of a pedigree within the first four or five generations. In genetic terms, inbreeding reduces the number of different and distinct gene alleles available to appear in the genome of the new individual. Thus, it increases the chances that the offspring of that mating will display uniform and specific characteristics.

Inbreeding is therefore used in animal husbandry to fix type—that is, to create a more uniform subspecies, which is exactly what Thoroughbred breeders were doing in the 18th century.

The process of creating the Thoroughbred was largely one of inbreeding to certain prepotent stallions and mares—often very closely. For example, the third dam of Flying Childers is listed in the *General Stud Book*'s Volume 1—detailing the genesis of the Thoroughbred breed—as being by the excellent 17th-century racehorse and sire Spanker and out of Spanker's own dam, the Old Morocco mare. That's about as close as inbreeding can get.

The best racehorses of the 18th century and early 19th century were almost invariably closely inbred to a succession of great stallions, beginning with the Godolphin Arabian and continuing through Eclipse, Herod, and the latter's son Highflyer. By about 1825, the genes of those four stallions were so highly concentrated in the Thoroughbred that breeders were forced to seek outcrosses. Since that time, inbreeding has gone in and out of fashion, and a few great breeders, notably French breeder Marcel Boussac, have used its principles to create great racehorses, sires, and broodmares.

Inbreeding is described in contemporary industry texts by a shorthand method that denotes the name and location in the five-cross pedigree of the individual or individuals to which the subject horse is inbred. Thus "inbred 3x4 to Northern Dancer" means that the name of Northern Dancer appears in the third generation on the sire's side of the pedigree and in the fourth generation of the dam's side.

Some Famous Inbred Horses

Horse (Year of Birth)	Inbreeding	Accomplishment
Spanker mare (ca 1690)	2x1 Old Morocco mare	Third dam of Flying Childers
Rachel (1763)	2x3 Godolphin Arabian	Dam of Highflyer, undefeated, 13-time leading sire
Eclipse (1764)	3x4 Snake mare	Unbeaten champion, sire line founder
Prunella (1788)	3x3 Blank	Dam of three classic winners, grandam of seven others
Sir Archy (1802)	3x4 Herod	American foundation sire
Boston (1833)	3x3 *Diomed	Greatest American four-miler
Lexington (1850)	3x4 Sir Archy	16-time leading American sire
Galopin (1872)	3x3 Voltaire	Epsom Derby winner, sire of St. Simon
Americus (1892)	3x3 Lexington	Key horse in pedigree of *Nasrullah
Flying Fox (1896)	3x2 Galopin	English Triple Crown, grandsire of *Teddy
Bromus (1905)	2x3 Springfield	Dam of Phalaris
Bayardo (1906)	4x2 Galopin	English champion, sire of two Triple Crown winners
Havresac II (1915)	2x3 St. Simon	Leading Italian sire, broodmare sire of Nearco
***Ksar** (1918)	3x2 Omnium II	Prix de l'Arc de Triomphe winner, sire of Tourbillon
Pharos (1920)	4x3 St. Simon	Champion Stakes winner, sire of Nearco, Pharis
Hyperion (1930)	4x3 St. Simon	Epsom Derby winner, six-time leading sire
Coronation (1946)	2x2 Tourbillon	Prix de l'Arc de Triomphe winner
***Turn-to** (1951)	3x3 Pharos	Sire of sires Hail to Reason, Sir Gaylord, Cyane, Best Turn
Broad Brush (1983)	3x3 *Turn-to	Leading sire of 1995

A more accurate method would be to calculate the inbreeding coefficient, or percentage of inbreeding, to that individual. By that method, the inbreeding coefficient of a horse inbred 3x4 to Northern Dancer would be 1.56%.

Nicks

Thoroughbred breeding is of necessity both a retrospective and a predictive art. Early Thoroughbred breeders could not help but notice the efficacy of inbreeding to certain stallions and mares, and the repeated success of combining certain sires and broodmares also became apparent. For reasons that are now obscure, this pattern of combining a specific sire and broodmares sired by another stallion became known as a nick.

Perhaps the best early example of a nick was the combination of the immortal racehorse and great sire Eclipse and mares by the even-greater sire Herod. This direct cross produced 1784 Epsom Derby winner Serjeant. The reverse cross of Herod on an Eclipse mare produced 1783 St. Leger Stakes winner Phenomenom, but the real gold mine for breeders was in the innumerable crosses of sons of Eclipse on mares by Herod or his sons, and sons of Herod on mares by Eclipse or his sons. That more generalized nick was preserved in the breed most notably through 1793 Derby winner Waxy (by Eclipse's son Pot8O's out of a Herod mare), tail-male ancestor of the Phalaris male line.

Phalaris, a foal of 1913, contributed to the most famous 20th-century nick. The four current male lines tracing to Phalaris all descend from sons out of Chaucer mares. *Sickle (Raise a Native line) and *Pharamond II (Buckpasser line) were both foaled by Selene, by Chaucer, while Pharos (*Nasrullah and Northern Dancer lines) and Fairway (Lord At War [Arg] line) were both sons of Scapa Flow, by Chaucer.

Contemporary advocates of the nicking theory have compiled and marketed nicking information that evaluates various crosses according to percentage of stakes winners or graded winners produced by all exemplars of that cross. To accumulate sufficient numbers of exemplars of the cross to be statistically meaningful, these formulations frequently extend the concept to include grandsons or great-grandsons of a particular sire crossed on granddaughters or great-granddaughters of another sire.

At that point, such data are focusing on the hypothetical power of one individual in the third generation of a pedigree and another in the fourth while ignoring the rest of the pedigree. Even at the sire–broodmare sire level, statistical studies of some of the most famous nicks such as the *Nasrullah–*Princequillo cross have not been encouraging.

Still, the fact that certain crosses such as Phalaris–Chaucer have had extraordinary impact on the breed lends some credence to the concept.

Bruce Lowe Numbers

For the first 150 years of the Thoroughbred as a distinct breed, breeding theories focused almost entirely on the influence of stallions. Toward the end of the 19th century, however, an Australian, Bruce Lowe, and a German, Herman Goos, independently began to trace every mare in the *General Stud Book* back to the earliest female ancestor recorded in Volume 1. Both found that every mare traced to one of about 50 of approximately 100 original foundation mares recorded in Volume 1.

Goos published his results in *Family Tables of English Thoroughbred Stock*, a monumental work that was the foundation for the even more monumental *Family Tables of Racehorses* by Kazimierz Bobinski and Stefan Zamoyski in 1953. Goos noted that some female lines had been much more successful than others, but Lowe went several steps further. The Australian numbered each family according to the cumulative number of winners of the Epsom Derby, Epsom Oaks, and St. Leger Stakes each had produced up to his era. Thus, the female line tracing to Tregonwell's Natural Barb mare was named the Number 1 family, and that tracing to the Burton Barb mare was Number 2. In all, 49 families were numbered.

Based on their success rates, Lowe designated families 1 through 5 as his "running" families. He also designated families 3, 8, 11, 12, and 14 his "sire" families, based on his judgment that the highest number of successful sires occurred in those families. He called those family numbers "figures." He then developed several theories of breeding racehorses based on combinations of those families. His theories were published posthumously in 1895 in *Breeding Race Horses by the Figure System.*

Lowe's system ignored the fact that the primary reason families 1 through 5 produced the most classic winners was that they had produced the most foals in pretty much the same proportions. Numerical superiority, not innate hereditary superiority, accounted for the differences. His theories on breeding also ignored the fact that the original foundation mares were so many generations removed from contemporary horses that their genetic influences were statistically negligible.

Bruce Lowe's theories were promoted assiduously by his editor, English journalist and bloodstock agent William Allison. Lowe's theories were widely influential around the turn of the 20th century, especially in America, where Allison's purchases of broodmares formed the basis for James R. Keene's stud. Genetic science in the 20th century proved Lowe's theories were useless, but his numbering system of female lines has remained a valuable contribution.

Vuillier Dosage

The late 19th century was a remarkably fertile period for pedigree research. At about the same time Lowe and Goos were tracing their female lines, French cavalry officer Col. Jean-Joseph Vuillier overheard two men arguing over whether Eclipse or Herod was the more influential sire and set out to answer the question statistically. To do so, Vuillier compiled complete pedigrees of more than 650 high-class racehorses, mostly winners of the English classics that Lowe used.

Although he apparently had no knowledge of either theory, Vuillier correctly applied a modern Mendelian interpretation of Galton's Law of genetic inheritance, which states that each parent contributes 50% of the genetic material to their offspring on average. Extending his pedigrees to a minimum of 12 generations, he assigned a value of 1 to a name that appeared in the 12th generation, a value of 2 in the 11th, 4 in the tenth, 8 in the ninth, and on down to a value of 2,048 for first-generation parents.

To determine the percentage contribution of Eclipse and Herod, Vuillier added up the numbers for each occurrence in each generation. Vuillier found that when he averaged the results for his 650 pedigrees, Herod's average number was 750 while Eclipse's average was only 568. He also discovered that Herod's son Highflyer was almost as influential as Eclipse with an average of 543.

In pursuing his research over 15 years, Vuillier noticed that other, more recent ancestors also accumulated high numbers, and he compiled figures that he called "dosages" for 11 more stallions and one mare, Pocahontas. Vuillier's dosages are, in fact, remarkably accurate representations of the percentage of genetic influence on the classic Thoroughbred of the 15 horses in his classification.

Since classic winners were frequently the most successful sires of future generations, Vuillier reasoned that the breed as a whole would and should move in the same direction as the classic pedigree. Thus, he concluded the object of a breeding program should be to produce pedigrees with the same dosages as his classic pedigrees.

Vuillier dosages

Horse	Dosage
First Series	
Herod (1758)	750
Eclipse (1764)	568
Highflyer (1774)	543
Second Series	
Birdcatcher (1833)	288
Touchstone (1831)	351
Pocahontas (1837)	313
Voltaire (1826)	186
Pantaloon (1824)	140
Melbourne (1834)	184
Bay Middleton (1833)	127
Gladiator (1833)	95
Third Series	
Stockwell (1849)	340
Newminster (1848)	295
Fourth Series	
St. Simon (1881)	420
Galopin (1872)	405
Isonomy (1875)	280
Hampton (1872)	260
Hermit (1864)	235
Bend Or (1877)	210

To facilitate this process, Vuillier devised the *ecart* system. *Ecart* is a French word that translates loosely to mean mathematical difference. For any potential mating using Vuillier's system, the breeder could calculate the dosages of the prospective foal. The difference between the prospective dosages and the ideal is the *ecart*. The object of Vuillier's system was to reduce the ecart as much as possible.

Vuillier published his findings privately in volumes 1 and 2 of *Les Croisements Rationnels* (Rational Breeding) in 1903 and '27. The Aga Khan hired him to manage his stud in 1925, but Vuillier died shortly thereafter. His widow took over and arranged the Aga Khan's matings for more than 30 years. During that period, the Aga Khan was the most successful and influential breeder in the world, with his stud producing such great racehorses and sires as *Bahram, *Mahmoud, and *Nasrullah. The Vuillier system, privately modernized and updated, is still in use by the current Aga Khan.

Varola Dosage

Vuillier's method was not widely available and

was difficult to execute because it required constructing 12-generation pedigrees and keeping track of mathematical data in an era long before computers. Italian journalist Francesco Varola built on Vuillier's work in his *Typology of the Racehorse*, published in 1974. Since Vuillier's published series of influential stallions extended only through the late 19th century, Varola updated and vastly expanded this list of influential stallions. His initial work identified 120 more horses, all born in the 20th century.

Unlike Vuillier, Varola did not utilize Galton's Law in his formulation, applying equal value to an appearance by a given stallion regardless of the generation of the pedigree in which he appeared. Recognizing that the modern Thoroughbred racehorse is much more specialized than in Vuillier's day, Varola divided his 120 stallions initially into five groups defined by his judgment of the type of influence they exerted on the breed.

His five categories—Brilliant, Intermediate, Classic, Stout, and Professional—were based partly on sociological concepts, partly on physical type and racecourse expression, and partly on inspiration. Varola eventually split the Brilliant group into Brilliant and Transbrilliant and Stout into Solid and Rough, but the original five categories quickly became associated in the public mind with varying degrees of stamina. Varola has consistently disavowed this interpretation.

Varola arranged the names of all his "*chefs-de-race*" in a "dosage diagram," dividing the names of each *chef-de-race* (chief of the breed) that occurs in a given pedigree into the five (or seven) categories and totaling the number of occurrences, regardless of generation. The resulting series of numbers offered breeders a thumbnail picture of the balance in a pedigree among all of Varola's different aptitudes.

Varola's chief contribution may be his insight into the increasing specialization of the Thoroughbred into sprinters, stayers, and middle-distance horses, among others, and his recognition that human sociology plays a role in determining the type of racehorse produced in different countries in different eras.

Roman Dosage

In the 1980s, Steve Roman, an American chemistry professor, developed a system combining some of the aspects of the Vuillier and Varola dosage systems. Considering only the first four generations of a pedigree, Roman assigned a numerical value of 16 to any *chef-de-race* that appeared in the first generation of a pedigree, eight to a second-generation *chef*, four for the third generation, and two for the fourth.

Roman interpreted Varola's five original categories strictly in terms of stamina, with Brilliant horses defined as those contributing extreme speed but little stamina, while Professional *chefs* contributed stamina but little speed. Applying the appropriate value according to generation for each occurrence of a *chef*'s name and adding those values up for each of Varola's five aptitudinal categories, Roman devised a "dosage profile" meant to give breeders insight into the relative stamina inherent in a given pedigree.

Roman invented the "dosage index," a single number that is calculated by dividing the total points in the Brilliant and Intermediate categories plus half the Classic points by the total of the points in the Stout and Professional categories plus the other half of the Classic points. The resultant figure is intended to predict a horse's ability to stay classic distances.

Applying his ideas to the history of the Kentucky Derby (G1), Roman found that almost all Derby winners since the 1930s had dosage indexes of 4.00 or less. Leon Rasmussen of *Daily Racing Form* popularized Roman's ideas in the 1980s and early '90s, and, though several Kentucky Derby winners have subsequently defied their Roman dosage, his theories remain popular.

Modern Genetics

The science of genetics, like the other physical sciences, made enormous strides during the 20th century. Though published earlier, Mendel's laws were virtually unknown at the turn of the 20th century, but early in the 21st century the complete human genome was mapped. Science had progressed from crossbreeding garden peas to cloning sheep and other large mammals.

None of this progress has significantly affected Thoroughbred breeding. An equine genome mapping project is under way, but even that should have no immediate effect on the breed because knowing the location of genes does not reveal the traits or characteristics they control. Even coat-color genetics, once thought to be a relatively simple dominance series consisting of gray, bay (or brown), and chestnut alleles, proved to be not so simple because white Thoroughbreds began to appear about 30 years ago.

The problem is that the traits that produce a successful racehorse are not governed by single genes. Factors such as speed, stamina, temperament, and soundness are each dependent on thousands of different genes working together with the environment to create outstanding racehorses.—*John P. Sparkman*

SIRES

Leading Sires by Progeny Earnings in 2005

Worldwide earnings for stallions who stand in North America or stood in North America if pensioned or dead.
◆ Denotes freshman sire.

Sire	Strs	Wnrs	SWs	Leading Earner (Earnings)	Total Earnings
Saint Ballado, Dead	180	89	13	Saint Liam ($3,696,960)	$10,409,467
Hennessy, Ky.	302	130	11	Sunrise Bacchus ($1,080,769)	9,615,817
Distorted Humor, Ky.	211	112	18	Flower Alley ($2,435,200)	9,033,539
Kingmambo, Ky.	174	62	7	Alkaased ($2,650,290)	8,760,902
Dynaformer, Ky.	157	74	12	Dynever ($1,231,730)	8,081,091
El Prado (Ire), Ky.	176	97	12	Borrego ($1,536,600)	8,030,474
A.P. Indy, Ky.	187	88	16	Suave ($624,900)	8,000,004
Storm Cat, Ky.	138	72	17	Seeking the Dia ($1,427,828)	7,779,955
Royal Academy, Ky.	361	155	20	Bullish Luck ($1,780,235)	7,422,063
Seeking the Gold, Ky.	122	64	11	Pleasant Home ($1,316,420)	7,072,526
Giant's Causeway, Ky.	181	78	10	Shamardal ($1,572,090)	6,993,257
Devil His Due, Ky.	193	104	7	Roses in May ($3,695,000)	6,911,112
Langfuhr, Ky.	303	155	13	Jambalaya ($380,846)	6,588,028
Thunder Gulch, Ky.	308	122	7	Tsurumaru Bakushin ($334,262)	6,372,801
Tale of the Cat, Ky.	213	105	9	Glamour Puss ($400,731)	6,354,626
Fusaichi Pegasus, Ky.	167	69	8	Roman Ruler ($890,000)	6,339,175
Smart Strike, Ky.	145	80	13	English Channel ($1,143,491)	6,245,144
Stravinsky, Jpn	224	95	7	Kongo Rikishio ($761,231)	6,115,125
Honour and Glory, Ky.	316	151	4	Blues and Royals ($1,200,000)	6,072,889
Twining, Jpn	152	67	2	Taiki Zillion ($406,727)	5,679,354
Pulpit, Ky.	122	67	10	Pit Fighter ($640,750)	5,665,291
Unbridled's Song, Ky.	215	109	13	Eurosilver ($247,450)	5,501,813
Carson City, Dead	187	95	11	Position One ($357,257)	5,469,272
Grand Slam, Ky.	222	100	6	Limehouse ($482,998)	5,442,507
Belong to Me, Ky.	201	103	8	Jack Sullivan ($620,523)	5,108,987
Holy Bull, Ky.	139	58	6	Giacomo ($1,846,876)	4,972,882
Silver Deputy, Ky.	155	93	7	Badge of Silver ($411,167)	4,860,169
Gilded Time, Ky.	232	109	10	Barely a Moment ($420,802)	4,678,229
Victory Gallop, Ky.	119	77	4	Gaily Snowman ($477,078)	4,668,060
Maria's Mon, Ky.	188	103	6	High Limit ($550,500)	4,664,430
Awesome Again, Ky.	129	67	7	Round Pond ($467,300)	4,657,458
Rahy, Ky.	153	81	9	T. D. Vance ($305,305)	4,624,610
Mt. Livermore, Pens	161	87	6	Hagino Bel Tempo ($582,220)	4,569,062
Valid Expectations, Tex.	170	101	4	Saratoga County ($1,380,000)	4,406,698
Forest Wildcat, Ky.	193	96	10	Attila's Storm ($265,348)	4,267,607
Touch Gold, Ky.	146	77	7	Gaily Revolver ($309,566)	4,239,915
Pleasant Tap, Ky.	129	76	6	Tap Dance City ($599,770)	4,198,724
Northern Afleet, Ky.	100	61	3	Afleet Alex ($2,085,000)	4,172,425
Mr. Greeley, Ky.	190	93	4	Miss Pascali ($406,652)	4,169,890
Not For Love, Md.	182	86	7	Presidentialaffair ($269,198)	4,168,278
Louis Quatorze, Md.	259	115	7	Choctaw Nation ($884,000)	4,162,794
Honor Grades, Dead	142	82	5	Magna Graduate ($1,070,170)	3,981,402
Alphabet Soup, Ky.	175	101	10	Alphabet Kisses ($241,621)	3,946,521
Stormin Fever, Ky.	128	63	5	Fusaichi Auster ($627,977)	3,880,092
Rubiano, Dead	138	76	2	Taiki Enigma ($834,188)	3,873,904
Bertrando, Ca.	164	79	5	Unfurl the Flag ($311,360)	3,869,009
Quiet American, Ky.	145	76	4	Naughty New Yorker ($290,157)	3,850,011
Woodman, Ky.	258	92	3	Pretty Trio ($298,759)	3,848,786
Stormy Atlantic, Ky.	158	87	10	She Says It Best ($382,918)	3,775,533
Smoke Glacken, Ky.	147	80	6	Smoke Smoke Smoke ($199,922)	3,770,279
Peaks and Valleys, On.	148	91	8	Wedding Valley ($362,594)	3,735,199
Crafty Prospector, Ky.	158	89	1	Win Genesis ($299,207)	3,724,038
Indian Charlie, Ky.	114	73	12	Two Trail Sioux ($577,200)	3,708,972
More Than Ready, Ky.	147	71	10	Benicio ($706,493)	3,664,252
Dixieland Band, Ky.	149	78	12	Sharp Lisa ($267,500)	3,641,262
Storm Boot, Ky.	171	95	7	Storm's Darling ($231,330)	3,618,411
Kris S., Dead	81	38	7	Rock Hard Ten ($1,080,000)	3,610,960
Cozzene, Ky.	122	52	6	Rendo Felice ($282,044)	3,609,976
Mutakddim, Ky.	215	119	12	The Student (Arg) ($208,400)	3,595,280
Deputy Commander, Ky.	155	71	6	Grab Your Heart ($774,618)	3,546,867
Pioneering, Ky.	150	94	7	Triano ($206,080)	3,539,927
Unbridled, Dead	91	45	5	Eddington ($602,200)	3,531,855
Sky Classic, Ky.	159	80	6	Sky Diamond ($185,672)	3,525,337
Skip Away, Ky.	148	78	9	Skip and Go ($154,844)	3,495,030
A. P Jet, N.Y.	149	77	4	Karakorum Splendor ($222,782)	3,433,048

Sire	Strs	Wnrs	SWs	Leading Earner (Earnings)	Total Earnings
Old Trieste, Dead	118	62	4	Silver Train ($693,255)	$3,407,856
Salt Lake, Ca.	170	98	6	Big Shark ($379,004)	3,391,865
Regal Classic, N.Y.	182	93	4	Classic Stamp ($277,991)	3,378,130
Elusive Quality, Ky.	139	78	5	Elusive Jazz ($338,731)	3,370,395
Deputy Minister, Dead	126	54	4	Miss Fortunate ($250,905)	3,350,952
Slew City Slew, Ky.	164	81	5	Lava Man ($774,103)	3,278,523
Allen's Prospect, Dead	188	99	4	Sarah's Prospect ($153,138)	3,272,465
Forestry, Ky.	102	52	12	Diplomat Lady ($334,800)	3,155,928
Dance Brightly, Chi	148	83	5	Mea Domina ($446,076)	3,148,943
Out of Place, Ky.	145	77	9	Sort It Out ($255,661)	3,133,778
Theatrical (Ire), Ky.	96	36	5	Shakespeare ($604,320)	3,129,198
Runaway Groom, Ky.	164	88	6	Runaway Dancer ($250,448)	3,108,694
Cherokee Run, Ky.	143	77	3	Dover Dere ($265,417)	3,106,783
American Chance, Dead	114	65	3	America Alive ($654,326)	3,078,331
Broad Brush, Pens	81	41	2	Nobo True ($611,320)	3,050,959
Exploit, Kor	117	67	4	Knights Templar ($255,353)	3,046,875
Formal Gold, Ca.	123	65	6	Trickle of Gold ($270,880)	2,987,654
Stephen Got Even, Ky.	58	26	3	Stevie Wonderboy ($1,028,940)	2,978,430
With Approval, Eng	130	55	6	Silverfoot ($393,682)	2,977,701
Gold Fever, N.Y.	141	75	1	A Bit O'Gold ($497,437)	2,971,617
Lite the Fuse, Pa.	131	81	2	Ablo ($322,362)	2,948,424
Swiss Yodeler, Ca.	134	80	4	Thor's Echo ($529,853)	2,925,737
Gulch, Ky.	148	64	4	Gulch Approval ($211,269)	2,924,495
Arch, Ky.	100	52	6	Art Trader ($313,131)	2,896,459
In Excess (Ire), Ca.	114	61	5	Valentine Dancer ($539,120)	2,878,422
Distant View, Ky.	109	49	4	Keeneland Swan ($883,292)	2,873,466
Roar, Ca.	172	106	8	Orphan Brigade ($145,200)	2,858,172
Afternoon Deelites, La.	139	79	6	Nob Hill Deelite ($155,879)	2,851,114
Dixie Union, Ky.	71	34	8	Reunited ($320,565)	2,812,470
Wheaton, Pa.	136	79	2	Santana Strings ($255,380)	2,806,351
Yes It's True, Ky.	92	53	5	B. B. Best ($178,350)	2,798,462
Malibu Moon, Ky.	102	62	10	Malibu Moonshine ($137,760)	2,789,283
Glitterman, Pens	129	75	4	Flying Glitter ($516,536)	2,785,646
Real Quiet, Pa.	129	56	5	Pussycat Doll ($287,903)	2,773,414
Notebook, Dead	117	80	3	Consider Thesource ($255,360)	2,764,738
Archers Bay, Dead	69	45	4	Spaghetti Mouse ($240,974)	2,759,918
Marquetry, Ky.	154	79	3	Sparkling Pink ($150,700)	2,756,835
Double Honor, Fl.	123	76	3	Gin Rummy King ($138,860)	2,677,413
Boundary, Pens	102	52	4	Pomeroy ($210,800)	2,661,375
Defrere, N.J.	103	61	7	Le Mars Girl ($573,637)	2,653,603
Line In The Sand, Thi	155	84	1	Eastern Sand ($232,988)	2,652,899
Montbrook, Fl.	133	69	1	Sierra Bella ($185,367)	2,648,232
Tomorrows Cat, N.Y.	120	66	3	West Virginia ($166,820)	2,636,654
Bold Executive, On.	97	47	4	Top Ten List ($292,854)	2,595,283
Lost Soldier, Ky.	133	61	2	Lost in the Fog ($844,500)	2,586,179
Cryptoclearance, Ky.	208	86	2	Cryptograph ($247,945)	2,562,852
Pine Bluff, Ky.	92	53	2	Super Frolic ($818,160)	2,560,858
Menifee, Ky.	90	47	7	Dance Fee ($147,660)	2,554,250
Candy Stripes, Arg	133	58	5	Leroidesanimaux (Brz) ($1,214,040)	2,548,115
Concerto, Fl.	90	52	4	Bellamy Road ($671,000)	2,540,270
Halo's Image, Fl.	135	78	5	Southern Cal ($138,570)	2,529,169
Gold Case, Ky.	135	81	3	Magic Belle ($105,584)	2,492,210
Unusual Heat, Ca.	58	30	4	Tucked Away ($237,468)	2,484,874
Suave Prospect, N.M.	93	57	3	Umpateedle ($331,050)	2,469,219
Benchmark, Ca.	88	48	3	Brother Derek ($502,080)	2,468,824
Sultry Song, Ky.	86	39	5	Revved Up ($576,940)	2,459,863
Favorite Trick, N.M.	158	79	5	Nike Favor ($257,525)	2,449,447
Petionville, Ky.	127	71	3	Island Fashion ($238,000)	2,421,881
Black Tie Affair (Ire), W.V.	89	22	1	Marble Balder ($239,050)	2,417,717
Vicar, Ky.	74	46	2	R Lady Joy ($565,436)	2,417,112
Cape Town, Ky.	108	53	4	Southern Africa ($483,219)	2,373,399
Polish Numbers, Dead	113	55	6	Play Bingo ($172,980)	2,356,980
Siphon (Brz), Pa.	140	63	1	I'm the Tiger ($248,291)	2,353,798
Lord Carson, Dead	130	78	5	Joey Carson ($144,000)	2,349,222
Two Punch, Md.	126	66	0	Yolanda B. Too ($140,200)	2,347,241

Sire	Strs	Wnrs	SWs	Leading Earner (Earnings)	Total Earnings
Conquistador Cielo, Dead	113	54	1	Taste of Paradise ($605,000)	$2,343,486
Wild Again, Pens	100	57	3	Offlee Wild ($452,500)	2,306,466
Lit de Justice, Ca.	97	60	2	Injustice ($280,220)	2,296,252
Yankee Victor, Kor	71	34	3	Real Dandy ($762,550)	2,288,941
Memo (Chi), Ca.	89	51	4	McCann's Mojave ($274,560)	2,271,577
Housebuster, Dead	80	29	3	Sankin Buster ($289,493)	2,251,099
Friendly Lover, Ia.	110	64	0	Friendly Theresa ($150,117)	2,244,360
Atticus, Ca.	65	39	2	High Fly ($901,500)	2,242,229
Souvenir Copy, Ca.	132	74	3	Talking to John ($109,259)	2,241,679
Bold Badgett, Dead	70	35	3	Leave Me Alone ($585,970)	2,221,648
Storm Creek, Ca.	150	60	5	Cosmic Kris ($188,575)	2,214,960
Formal Dinner, Fl.	129	80	4	Dinner Choice ($70,925)	2,195,664
Silver Ghost, Ky.	123	54	7	Silver Axe ($296,030)	2,194,841
Artax, N.Y.	114	60	1	R Fast Lady ($161,530)	2,182,337
Summer Squall, Pens	58	35	5	Summerly ($786,728)	2,178,870
Fit to Fight, Pens	98	61	4	Scrappy T ($584,197)	2,172,099
Dixie Brass, Dead	93	58	1	Pretty Suzi ($124,405)	2,167,504
Sir Cat, Chi	102	62	4	Surf Cat ($322,420)	2,118,858
Leestown, La.	123	55	4	Indigo Girl ($154,000)	2,108,869
Cee's Tizzy, Ca.	108	55	5	Cee's Irish ($329,125)	2,087,615
Lion Cavern, Dead	186	70	3	Terfel ($550,446)	2,082,487
Jules, Dead	146	88	4	Platinum Perfect ($138,850)	2,071,875
Rizzi, N.Y.	123	64	2	Rizzi Girl ($122,362)	2,070,486
Danzig, Dead	72	33	4	Survivalist ($267,370)	2,066,089
Event of the Year, Ca.	86	47	2	Thrilling Victory ($209,670)	2,063,985
Mazel Trick, Pa.	93	58	2	Outcashem ($192,111)	2,062,368
Miswaki, Dead	101	43	3	Sir Shackleton ($455,395)	2,056,147
High Yield, Fr	163	64	3	Amazing Buy ($244,350)	2,054,620
Catienus, N.Y.	75	41	5	Dawn of War ($403,800)	2,054,309
Citidancer, Pens	66	39	3	Cherokee's Boy ($368,050)	2,045,073
Tiger Ridge, Fl.	73	49	5	Tiger Belle ($186,520)	2,011,302
Golden Missile, Ky.	67	26	2	In the Gold ($605,680)	2,009,202
Partner's Hero, Md.	82	53	4	Senor Cielo Two ($183,785)	2,007,806
Silver Hawk, Pens	75	28	3	Wonder Again ($327,920)	2,005,011
Gold Token, N.Y.	59	46	1	Gold and Roses ($396,134)	1,996,866
Kissin Kris, Ky.	133	60	1	Hasty Kris ($209,625)	1,980,717
Tactical Advantage, Dead	146	73	2	Freakin Streakin ($92,534)	1,977,362
Lucky Lionel, Ok.	106	61	4	High Blitz ($101,302)	1,975,916
Capote, Pens	89	42	5	Dance Away Capote ($270,000)	1,970,599
Concorde's Tune, Fl.	93	50	5	Razor ($135,224)	1,959,990
Crafty Friend, Ky.	114	60	2	Friendly Island ($93,000)	1,933,507
Lemon Drop Kid, Ky.	81	29	3	Lemon Maid ($262,776)	1,930,852
Smokester, Dead	116	54	1	Areyoutalkintome ($264,515)	1,921,750
Robyn Dancer, N.M.	147	66	1	Lord Robyn ($112,350)	1,921,472
Fortunate Prospect, Pens	107	67	0	Kohut ($124,869)	1,905,846
Pentelicus, Dead	130	75	2	Fines Creek ($84,290)	1,901,702
General Meeting, Pens	87	50	4	Direct Connect ($148,910)	1,896,212
Whiskey Wisdom, On.	82	42	4	Dave the Knave ($145,311)	1,878,952
Unreal Zeal, Ky.	120	63	3	Lady Riss ($129,700)	1,857,820
Chester House, Dead	73	34	3	Spring House ($163,370)	1,852,965
Running Stag, Fl.	87	47	2	Running Lass ($199,480)	1,839,774
Grindstone, Ky.	100	51	1	Ekolu Place ($209,451)	1,820,613
Gone West, Ky.	136	41	1	Conroy ($143,750)	1,814,129
High Brite, Ca.	127	62	5	High Standards ($152,137)	1,810,180
Successful Appeal, Ky.	52	25	3	Closing Argument ($565,000)	1,802,840
Wild Zone, Ky.	135	69	4	Tortuga Flats ($201,660)	1,796,750
Lear Fan, Pens	98	35	5	Good Ba Ba ($281,765)	1,796,008
Is It True, Ky.	89	49	3	Trueamericanspirit ($145,400)	1,780,881
War Chant, Ky.	66	23	5	Chattahoochee War ($436,421)	1,746,086
Jade Hunter, Ky.	104	56	4	Machikane Homare ($250,521)	1,731,133
Personal Flag, Dead	127	64	4	Win With Beck ($220,211)	1,713,126
Mecke, Fl.	84	35	3	Supah Blitz ($348,600)	1,711,104
Meadowlake, Dead	97	43	5	Fin Entertainment ($97,998)	1,701,398
Wild Event, Fl.	81	42	4	Fiesta Napkin ($128,240)	1,691,394
Slewdledo, Wa.	136	73	4	Slew Is King ($132,071)	1,682,269
Joyeux Danseur, Dead	78	42	1	Siren Lure ($191,951)	1,679,545
Cartwright, Dead	100	55	3	Wiggins ($112,288)	1,676,988
Doneraile Court, Ky.	87	47	3	Drivntodistraction ($119,096)	1,665,306
Outflanker, Md.	93	52	0	Dobil Yack (Mex) ($137,826)	1,657,324
Sefapiano, La.	81	48	3	Humoristic ($164,379)	1,656,363

Leading Sires by Average Earnings per Runner in 2005

Minimum of 25 Starters

Sire	Strs	Wnrs	Average
Seeking the Gold, Ky.	122	64	$57,972
Saint Ballado, Dead	180	89	57,830
Storm Cat, Ky.	138	72	56,376
Dynaformer, Ky.	157	74	51,472
Stephen Got Even, Ky.	58	26	51,352
Kingmambo, Ky.	174	62	50,350
Pulpit, Ky.	122	67	46,437
El Prado (Ire), Ky.	176	97	45,628
Kris S., Dead	81	38	44,580
Smart Strike, Ky.	145	80	43,070
Unusual Heat, Ca.	58	30	42,843
Distorted Humor, Ky.	211	112	42,813
A.P. Indy, Ky.	187	88	42,781
Northern Afleet, Ky.	100	61	41,724
Lasting Approval, Arg	33	13	40,468
Archers Bay, Dead	69	45	39,999
Dixie Union, Ky.	71	34	39,612
◆Tiznow, Ky.	35	12	39,322
Victory Gallop, Ky.	119	77	39,227
Unbridled, Dead	91	45	38,812
Giant's Causeway, Ky.	181	78	38,637
Fusaichi Pegasus, Ky.	167	69	37,959
Broad Brush, Pens	81	41	37,666
Summer Squall, Pens	58	35	37,567
Twining, Jpn	152	67	37,364
Awesome Again, Ky.	129	67	36,104
Devil His Due, Ky.	193	104	35,809
Holy Bull, Ky.	139	58	35,776
Military, Ky.	44	21	35,705
Successful Appeal, Ky.	52	25	34,670
Atticus, Ca.	65	39	34,496
Gold Token, N.Y.	59	46	33,845
◆El Corredor, Ky.	37	16	33,774
Vicar, Ky.	74	46	32,664
Theatrical (Ire), Ky.	96	36	32,596
Wagon Limit, Ky.	32	21	32,596
Pleasant Tap, Ky.	129	76	32,548
Indian Charlie, Ky.	114	73	32,535
Yankee Victor, Kor	71	34	32,239
Raffie's Majesty, N.Y.	38	27	31,915
Hennessy, Ky.	302	130	31,840
◆Forest Camp, Ky.	30	17	31,753
Bold Badgett, Dead	70	35	31,738
Silver Deputy, Ky.	155	93	31,356
Citidancer, Pens	66	39	30,986
Forestry, Ky.	102	52	30,940
Yes It's True, Ky.	92	53	30,418
◆Songandaprayer, Ky.	37	19	30,382
Stormin Fever, Ky.	128	63	30,313
Rahy, Ky.	153	81	30,226
Golden Missile, Ky.	67	26	29,988
Tale of the Cat, Ky.	213	105	29,834

Leading Sires by Median Earnings per Runner in 2005

Minimum of 25 Starters

Sire	Strs	Wnrs	Median
Raffie's Majesty, N.Y.	38	27	$28,425
Quaker Ridge, Il.	37	25	22,010
Storm Cat, Ky.	138	72	20,200
Seeking the Gold, Ky.	122	64	19,324
Gold Token, N.Y.	59	46	19,041
Yes It's True, Ky.	92	53	19,035
Victory Gallop, Ky.	119	77	18,358
Archers Bay, Dead	69	45	18,100
Malibu Moon, Ky.	102	62	17,270
Unusual Heat, Ca.	58	30	16,984
Broad Brush, Pens	81	41	16,810
Swear by Dixie, Chi	30	18	16,798
Saint Ballado, Dead	180	89	16,740
Menifee, Ky.	90	47	16,260
Indian Charlie, Ky.	114	73	16,092
Tale of the Cat, Ky.	213	105	16,000
Pulpit, Ky.	122	67	$15,885
Skip Trial, Fl.	51	34	15,689
Silver Deputy, Ky.	155	93	15,630
Dance Master, Fl.	29	23	15,600
Partner's Hero, Md.	82	53	15,224
Summer Squall, Pens	58	35	15,148
Good and Tough, N.Y.	67	43	14,996
Arch, Ky.	100	52	14,980
Notebook, Dead	117	80	14,867
Toolighttoquit, La.	43	31	14,724
Wagon Limit, Ky.	32	21	14,539
Unbridled's Song, Ky.	215	109	14,490
Carson City, Dead	187	95	14,250
Boundary, Pens	102	52	14,105
◆Trippi, Fl.	40	17	14,025
Smoke Glacken, Ky.	147	80	14,000
In Excess (Ire), Ca.	114	61	13,899
Peaks and Valleys, On.	148	91	13,887
Pioneering, Ky.	150	94	13,866
Kelly Kip, N.Y.	31	20	13,840
Catienus, N.Y.	75	41	13,738
Pleasant Tap, Ky.	129	76	13,550
Smart Strike, Ky.	145	80	13,534
Deputy Minister, Dead	126	54	13,435
Mud Route, Ca.	37	19	13,400
Straight Man, Fl.	88	51	13,285
Dixie Brass, Dead	93	58	13,214
Northern Afleet, Ky.	100	61	13,189
El Prado (Ire), Ky.	176	97	13,140
Yarrow Brae, Md.	78	50	13,105
Exploit, Kor	117	67	13,091
Successful Appeal, Ky.	52	25	13,080
Key Contender, N.Y.	45	29	13,060
Citidancer, Pens	66	39	13,028

Leading Sires by Number of Winners in 2005

Sire	Strs	Wnrs	Wnrs/Strs
Langfuhr, Ky.	303	155	51.2%
Royal Academy, Ky.	361	155	42.9%
Honour and Glory, Ky.	316	151	47.8%
Hennessy, Ky.	302	130	43.0%
Thunder Gulch, Ky.	308	122	39.6%
Mutakddim, Ky.	215	119	55.3%
Louis Quatorze, Md.	267	118	44.2%
Distorted Humor, Ky.	211	112	53.1%
Gilded Time, Ky.	232	109	47.0%
Unbridled's Song, Ky.	215	109	50.7%
Roar, Ca.	172	106	61.6%
Tale of the Cat, Ky.	213	105	49.3%
Devil His Due, Ky.	193	104	53.9%
Belong to Me, Ky.	201	103	51.2%
Maria's Mon, Ky.	188	103	54.8%
Alphabet Soup, Ky.	175	101	57.7%
Valid Expectations, Tx.	170	101	59.4%
Grand Slam, Ky.	222	100	45.0%
Allen's Prospect, Dead	188	99	52.7%
Salt Lake, Ca.	170	98	57.6%
El Prado (Ire), Ky.	176	97	55.1%
Forest Wildcat, Ky.	193	96	49.7%
Carson City, Dead	187	95	50.8%
Storm Boot, Ky.	171	95	55.6%
Stravinsky, Jpn	224	95	42.4%
Pioneering, Ky.	150	94	62.7%
Mr. Greeley, Ky.	190	93	48.9%
Regal Classic, N.Y.	182	93	51.1%
Silver Deputy, Ky.	155	93	60.0%
Woodman, Ky.	258	92	35.7%
Peaks and Valleys, On.	148	91	61.5%
Crafty Prospector, Ky.	158	89	56.3%
Saint Ballado, Dead	180	89	49.4%
A.P. Indy, Ky.	187	88	47.1%
Jules, Dead	146	88	60.3%
Runaway Groom, Ky.	164	88	53.7%
Mt. Livermore, Pens	161	87	54.0%
Stormy Atlantic, Ky.	158	87	55.1%
Cryptoclearance, Ky.	208	86	41.3%

Sire	Strs	Wnrs	Wnrs/Strs
Not For Love, Md.	182	86	47.3%
Line In The Sand, Thi	155	84	54.2%
Dance Brightly, Chi	148	83	56.1%
Honor Grades, Dead	142	82	57.7%
Gold Case, Ky.	135	81	60.0%
Lite the Fuse, Pa.	131	81	61.8%
Rahy, Ky.	153	81	52.9%
Slew City Slew, Ky.	164	81	49.4%

Leading Sires by Number of Wins in 2005

Sire	Strs	Wnrs	Wins
Langfuhr, Ky.	303	155	267
Royal Academy, Ky.	361	155	234
Honour and Glory, Ky.	316	151	225
Mutakddim, Ky.	215	119	218
Distorted Humor, Ky.	211	112	205
Hennessy, Ky.	302	130	196
Thunder Gulch, Ky.	308	122	189
Allen's Prospect, Dead	188	99	186
Gilded Time, Ky.	232	109	186
Salt Lake, Ca.	170	98	182
Roar, Ca.	172	106	181
Louis Quatorze, Md.	267	118	180
Maria's Mon, Ky.	188	103	179
Tale of the Cat, Ky.	213	105	179
Storm Boot, Ky.	171	95	177
Devil His Due, Ky.	193	104	176
Pioneering, Ky.	150	94	175
El Prado (Ire), Ky.	176	97	173
Alphabet Soup, Ky.	175	101	170
Belong to Me, Ky.	201	103	168
Saint Ballado, Dead	180	89	168
Unbridled's Song, Ky.	215	109	168
Formal Dinner, Fl.	129	80	167
Peaks and Valleys, Ont.	148	91	167
Carson City, Dead	187	95	165
Stravinsky, Jpn	224	95	165
Double Honor, Fl.	123	76	164
Forest Wildcat, Ky.	193	96	161
Regal Classic, N.Y.	182	93	161
Silver Deputy, Ky.	155	93	161
Stormy Atlantic, Ky.	158	87	161
Not For Love, Md.	182	86	160
Runaway Groom, Ky.	164	88	158
Valid Expectations, Tx.	170	101	158
Lite the Fuse, Pa.	131	81	156
Line In The Sand, Thi	155	84	154
Jules, Dead	146	88	153
A. P Jet, N.Y.	149	77	152
Crafty Prospector, Ky.	158	89	152
Grand Slam, Ky.	222	100	151
Bertrando, Ca.	164	79	149
Cryptoclearance, Ky.	208	86	148
Smart Strike, Ky.	145	80	148
Mr. Greeley, Ky.	190	93	147
A.P. Indy, Ky.	187	88	146
Dance Brightly, Chi	148	83	145
Smoke Glacken, Ky.	147	80	145
Mt. Livermore, Pens	161	87	144
Slew City Slew, Ky.	164	81	144
Wheaton, Pa.	136	79	144
Glitterman, Pens	129	75	143
Pentelicus, Dead	130	75	143
Quiet American, Ky.	145	76	141
Woodman, Ky.	258	92	141
Lord Carson, Dead	130	78	140
Slewdledo, Wash.	136	73	140
Out of Place, Ky.	145	77	139
Gold Fever, N.Y.	141	75	138
Marquetry, Ky.	154	79	137

Leading Sires by Number of Stakes Winners in 2005

Sire	Strs	Wnrs	SWs	SWins
Royal Academy, Ky.	361	155	20	22
Distorted Humor, Ky.	211	112	18	25
Storm Cat, Ky.	138	72	17	19
A.P. Indy, Ky.	187	88	16	21
Langfuhr, Ky.	303	155	13	22
Saint Ballado, Dead	180	89	13	23
Smart Strike, Ky.	145	80	13	24
Unbridled's Song, Ky.	215	109	13	16
Dixieland Band, Ky.	149	78	12	15
Dynaformer, Ky.	157	74	12	16
El Prado (Ire), Ky.	176	97	12	18
Forestry, Ky.	102	52	12	12
Indian Charlie, Ky.	114	73	12	17
Mutakddim, Ky.	215	119	12	14
Carson City, Dead	187	95	11	13
Hennessy, Ky.	302	130	11	14
Seeking the Gold, Ky.	122	64	11	15
Alphabet Soup, Ky.	175	101	10	17
Bernstein, Ky.	83	43	10	15
Forest Wildcat, Ky.	193	96	10	15
Giant's Causeway, Ky.	181	78	10	15
Gilded Time, Ky.	232	109	10	13
Malibu Moon, Ky.	102	62	10	12
More Than Ready, Ky.	147	71	10	17
Pulpit, Ky.	122	67	10	15
Stormy Atlantic, Ky.	158	87	10	14
Out of Place, Ky.	145	77	9	12
Rahy, Ky.	153	81	9	12
Skip Away, Ky.	148	78	9	12
Tale of the Cat, Ky.	213	105	9	10
Belong to Me, Ky.	201	103	8	9
Dixie Union, Ky.	71	34	8	11
Fusaichi Pegasus, Ky.	167	69	8	10
Louis Quatorze, Md.	267	118	8	8
Peaks and Valleys, Ont.	148	91	8	10
Roar, Ca.	172	106	8	10

Leading Sires by Number of Graded Stakes Winners in 2005

Sire	Strs	Wnrs	GSWs	GSWins
A.P. Indy, Ky.	187	88	10	13
Giant's Causeway, Ky.	181	78	9	12
Royal Academy, Ky.	361	155	9	14
Storm Cat, Ky.	138	72	8	10
Kingmambo, Ky.	174	62	7	13
Smart Strike, Ky.	145	80	7	10
Dynaformer, Ky.	157	74	6	9
Hennessy, Ky.	302	130	6	11
Pulpit, Ky.	122	67	6	6
Bernstein, Ky.	83	43	5	14
Distorted Humor, Ky.	211	112	5	7
Forestry, Ky.	102	52	5	5
Stravinsky, Jpn	224	95	5	16
Tale of the Cat, Ky.	213	105	5	8
Awesome Again, Ky.	129	67	4	5
Candy Stripes, Arg	133	58	4	10
Dixie Union, Ky.	71	34	4	4
El Prado (Ire), Ky.	176	97	4	7
Fusaichi Pegasus, Ky.	167	69	4	5
Gilded Time, Ky.	232	109	4	6
Kris S., Dead	81	38	4	7
Langfuhr, Ky.	303	155	4	3
Mutakddim, Ky.	215	119	4	5
Roy, Dead	143	59	4	13
Seeking the Gold, Ky.	122	64	4	5
Silver Deputy, Ky.	155	93	4	5
Unbridled's Song, Ky.	215	109	4	5
Cape Town, Ky.	108	53	3	3
Elusive Quality, Ky.	139	78	3	4
Holy Bull, Ky.	139	58	3	4
Maria's Mon, Ky.	188	103	3	3
More Than Ready, Ky.	147	71	3	7
Old Trieste, Dead	118	62	3	4
Rahy, Ky.	153	81	3	3
Saint Ballado, Dead	180	89	3	9
Salt Lake, Ca.	170	98	3	3
Stephen Got Even, Ky.	58	26	3	5
Stormin Fever, Ky.	128	63	3	4
Unbridled, Dead	91	45	3	5

Leading Juvenile Sires by Progeny Earnings in 2005

Worldwide earnings for stallions who stood in North America in year of conception of two-year-olds of 2005.
◆ Denotes freshman sire.

Sire	Strs	Wnrs	SWs	Leading Earner (Earnings)	Total Earnings
Giant's Causeway, Ky.	71	28	3	First Samurai ($682,575)	$1,642,151
◆Tiznow, Ky.	35	12	1	Folklore ($927,500)	1,376,265
Hennessy, Ky.	38	16	5	Henny Hughes ($644,820)	1,352,540
Fusaichi Pegasus, Ky.	52	21	3	Secret Code ($261,368)	1,256,938
◆El Corredor, Ky.	37	16	2	Adieu ($554,470)	1,249,625
Stephen Got Even, Ky.	16	7	1	Stevie Wonderboy ($1,028,940)	1,226,055
◆Songandaprayer, Ky.	37	19	3	Stolen Prayer ($211,230)	1,124,123
Storm Cat, Ky.	38	17	5	Bluegrass Cat ($213,780)	1,089,268
Distorted Humor, Ky.	34	13	5	Original Spin ($222,800)	1,071,475
◆City Zip, Ky.	39	20	2	Little Miss Zip ($130,145)	1,064,275
Thunder Gulch, Ky.	50	16	4	Balance ($183,300)	1,043,137
Dixie Union, Ky.	35	13	3	Unification ($173,557)	1,025,652
◆Forest Camp, Ky.	30	17	2	Your Tent Or Mine ($173,250)	952,588
More Than Ready, Ky.	54	22	2	La Chunga ($104,006)	947,311
Stormy Atlantic, Ky.	44	15	2	She Says It Best ($382,918)	942,704
Tale of the Cat, Ky.	43	17	2	Catcominatcha ($206,706)	874,106
Forest Wildcat, Ky.	45	15	2	Yaddo Cat ($110,370)	867,638
Royal Academy, Ky.	59	19	4	Quiet Royal ($162,159)	833,605
Carson City, Dead	44	14	2	Three Seven Spin ($142,761)	814,792
Grand Slam, Ky.	62	18	0	A Lot of Love ($66,576)	805,804
Catienus, N.Y.	33	14	2	Dawn of War ($403,800)	792,366
◆Trippi, Fl.	40	17	0	Cab ($83,382)	789,169
◆Broken Vow, Ky.	41	13	1	Private Vow ($382,508)	787,600
Exploit, Kor	30	15	3	Knights Templar ($255,353)	779,128
◆Exchange Rate, Fl.	29	12	1	Blazing Rate ($351,300)	763,445
Silver Deputy, Ky.	31	13	1	Vibank ($183,248)	762,341
Forestry, Ky.	34	14	4	Diplomat Lady ($334,800)	755,263
Langfuhr, Ky.	40	12	3	Absolutelyfabulous ($307,301)	748,914
Mt. Livermore, Pens	32	16	2	Yuwa Hurricane ($212,457)	727,184
◆Ecton Park, Ky.	30	13	2	French Park ($243,761)	709,579
Lemon Drop Kid, Ky.	39	11	1	Bear's Kid ($172,114)	694,571
Yes It's True, Ky.	36	14	1	Catch My Fancy ($108,318)	680,482
Old Trieste, Dead	40	12	0	Toyo A. P. ($206,819)	669,513
Saint Ballado, Dead	30	11	3	Red Ballado ($95,295)	668,436
Bold Executive, On.	26	7	2	Wannatalkaboutme ($186,503)	652,380
Unbridled's Song, Ky.	37	12	1	Half Ours ($105,670)	651,128
Red Ransom, Eng	35	13	2	Red Clubs ($267,274)	641,754
Maria's Mon, Ky.	33	14	2	Cause to Believe ($126,825)	629,221
Running Stag, Fl.	31	13	1	Running Lass ($199,480)	626,343
Benchmark, Ca.	12	6	1	Brother Derek ($502,080)	624,090
◆Five Star Day, Ky.	21	10	1	Eishin Danbury ($153,186)	623,857
Mr. Greeley, Ky.	44	16	1	Miraculous Miss ($114,120)	619,701
Storm Boot, Ky.	28	14	1	Gumboots ($132,168)	607,426
Old Topper, Ca.	22	14	2	Sierra Sweetie ($235,400)	607,019
Regal Classic, N.Y.	16	7	2	Classic Pack ($260,050)	602,981
Notebook, Dead	28	15	1	Consider Thesource ($255,360)	601,859
Swiss Yodeler, Ca.	41	16	2	Wild Uncle Kurt ($86,535)	584,247
Precise End, Jpn	21	13	3	Princess Sweet ($105,032)	580,296
◆Put It Back, Fl.	17	9	1	In Summation ($285,800)	576,045
Tactical Cat, Ky.	39	15	2	Our Madison ($145,608)	573,232
Mutakddim, Ky.	36	18	1	Dixie Dreamer ($86,600)	562,079
Louis Quatorze, Md.	55	18	1	Louie Nekia ($116,026)	561,570
Pulpit, Ky.	30	8	1	Laity ($151,200)	558,364
Favorite Trick, N.M.	26	13	4	Disappearing Trick ($96,215)	557,248
◆Delaware Township, Fl.	33	10	2	Electrify ($131,800)	547,672
Southern Halo, Arg	36	15	1	Edenwold ($287,247)	542,059
Gilded Time, Ky.	49	20	2	Timetobook ($61,620)	536,570
Deputy Commander, Ky.	33	17	1	Red Raymond ($109,735)	522,475
Montbrook, Fl.	34	13	1	Beacon Shine ($101,680)	517,977
Elusive Quality, Ky.	37	15	0	Vague ($46,172)	516,231
Chimes Band, Dead	21	13	2	Latenite Band ($124,127)	508,276
A.P. Indy, Ky.	38	10	0	A. P. Warrior ($118,435)	502,289
Tiger Ridge, Fl.	30	15	2	Here Tiger ($96,780)	500,100
High Yield, Fr	61	20	1	High Adventure ($36,210)	496,134
◆Black Minnaloushe, Ky.	47	14	1	Stream Cat ($153,670)	495,631

Leading Juvenile Sires by Average Earnings per Runner in 2005

Minimum of 10 Starters

Sire	Strs	Wnrs	Average
Stephen Got Even, Ky.	16	7	$76,628
Benchmark, Ca.	12	6	52,008
◆Tiznow, Ky.	35	12	39,322
Regal Classic, N.Y.	16	7	37,686
Hennessy, Ky.	38	16	35,593
◆Put It Back, Fl.	17	9	33,885
◆El Corredor, Ky.	37	16	33,774
Wild Wonder, Dead	15	3	32,323
◆Forest Camp, Ky.	30	17	31,753
Distorted Humor, Ky.	34	13	31,514
◆Songandaprayer, Ky.	37	19	30,382
General Meeting, Pens	13	7	30,245
Silver Hawk, Pens	13	6	29,931
◆Five Star Day, Ky.	21	10	29,707
Dixie Union, Ky.	35	13	29,304
Storm Cat, Ky.	38	17	28,665
Precise End, Jpn	21	13	27,633
Old Topper, Ca.	22	14	27,592
Swain (Ire), Ky.	15	6	27,439
◆City Zip, Ky.	39	20	27,289
◆Exchange Rate, Fl.	29	12	26,326
Exploit, Kor	30	15	25,971
Bold Executive, On.	26	7	25,092

Leading Juvenile Sires by Median Earnings per Runner in 2005

Minimum of 10 Starters

Sire	Strs	Wnrs	Median
Storm Cat, Ky.	38	17	$18,345
Hadif, Tx.	15	8	15,645
Dance Master, Fl.	15	10	15,600
Precise End, Jpn	21	13	15,290
◆Five Star Day, Ky.	21	10	15,250
West Acre, Fl.	10	6	15,238
Wild Again, Pens	10	5	14,486
Yankee Victor, Kor	19	9	14,460
Arch, Ky.	16	9	14,164
◆Trippi, Fl.	40	17	14,025
◆One Way Love, On.	15	9	13,773
Good and Tough, N.Y.	14	7	13,491
Halo's Image, Fl.	29	16	13,280
Two Punch, Md.	16	8	13,248
◆City Zip, Ky.	39	20	12,900
Fortunate Prospect, Pens	23	16	12,850
Old Topper, Ca.	22	14	12,757
Diligence, Fl.	12	7	12,463
Seeking the Gold, Ky.	19	8	12,334
Boundary, Pens	10	4	12,333

Leading Juvenile Sires by Number of Winners in 2005

Sire	Strs	Wnrs	Wnrs/Strs
Giant's Causeway, Ky.	71	28	39.4%
Valid Expectations, Tx.	43	23	53.5%
More Than Ready, Ky.	54	22	40.7%
Fusaichi Pegasus, Ky.	52	21	40.4%
◆City Zip, Ky.	39	20	51.3%
Gilded Time, Ky.	49	20	40.8%
High Yield, Fr	61	20	32.8%
Royal Academy, Ky.	59	19	32.2%
◆Songandaprayer, Ky.	37	19	51.4%
Grand Slam, Ky.	62	18	29.0%
Louis Quatorze, Md.	55	18	32.7%
Mutakddim, Ky.	36	18	50.0%
Deputy Commander, Ky.	33	17	51.5%
◆Forest Camp, Ky.	30	17	56.7%
Storm Cat, Ky.	38	17	44.7%
Tale of the Cat, Ky.	43	17	39.5%
◆Trippi, Fl.	40	17	42.5%
◆El Corredor, Ky.	37	16	43.2%
Fortunate Prospect, Pens	23	16	69.6%
Halo's Image, Fl.	29	16	55.2%
Hennessy, Ky.	38	16	42.1%
Mr. Greeley, Ky.	44	16	36.4%
Mt. Livermore, Pens	32	16	50.0%
Souvenir Copy, Ca.	29	16	55.2%
Swiss Yodeler, Ca.	41	16	39.0%
Thunder Gulch, Ky.	50	16	32.0%
Vicar, Ky.	30	16	53.3%
◆Albert the Great, Ky.	37	15	40.5%
Double Honor, Fl.	29	15	51.7%
Elusive Quality, Ky.	37	15	40.5%
Exploit, Kor	30	15	50.0%
Forest Wildcat, Ky.	45	15	33.3%
Notebook, Dead	28	15	53.6%
Outflanker, Md.	37	15	40.5%
◆Snuck In, Fl.	33	15	45.5%
Southern Halo, Arg	36	15	41.7%
Stormy Atlantic, Ky.	44	15	34.1%
Tactical Cat, Ky.	39	15	38.5%
Tiger Ridge, Fl.	30	15	50.0%

Leading Juvenile Sires by Number of Wins in 2005

Sire	Strs	Wnrs	Wins
Giant's Causeway, Ky.	71	28	35
◆City Zip, Ky.	39	20	30
Hennessy, Ky.	38	16	27
◆Forest Camp, Ky.	30	17	26
Fusaichi Pegasus, Ky.	52	21	26
More Than Ready, Ky.	54	22	26
Mt. Livermore, Pens	32	16	26
◆Songandaprayer, Ky.	37	19	26
Storm Cat, Ky.	38	17	26
Valid Expectations, Tx.	43	23	26
◆El Corredor, Ky.	37	16	24
Gilded Time, Ky.	49	20	24
Royal Academy, Ky.	59	19	24
Running Stag, Fl.	31	13	24
Exploit, Kor	30	15	23
Souvenir Copy, Ca.	29	16	23
Thunder Gulch, Ky.	50	16	23
Catienus, N.Y.	33	14	22
Chimes Band, Dead	21	13	22
Fortunate Prospect, Pens	23	16	22
Grand Slam, Ky.	62	18	22
Louis Quatorze, Md.	55	18	22
Mr. Greeley, Ky.	44	16	22

Leading Juvenile Sires by Number of Stakes Winners in 2005

Sire	Strs	Wnrs	SWs	SWins
Distorted Humor, Ky.	34	13	5	6
Hennessy, Ky.	38	16	5	6
Storm Cat, Ky.	38	17	5	6
Favorite Trick, N.M.	26	13	4	4
Forestry, Ky.	34	14	4	4
Royal Academy, Ky.	59	19	4	4
Thunder Gulch, Ky.	50	16	4	6
Dixie Union, Ky.	35	13	3	4
Exploit, Kor	30	15	3	4
Fusaichi Pegasus, Ky.	52	21	3	3
Giant's Causeway, Ky.	71	28	3	4
Indian Charlie, Ky.	20	11	3	3
Langfuhr, Ky.	40	12	3	5
Precise End, Jpn	21	13	3	3
Saint Ballado, Dead	30	11	3	4
Snowbound, Wa.	10	6	3	3
◆Songandaprayer, Ky.	37	19	3	6

Leading Juvenile Sires by Number of Graded Stakes Winners in 2005

Sire	Strs	Wnrs	GSWs	GSWins
Giant's Causeway, Ky.	71	28	3	4
Dixie Union, Ky.	35	13	2	2
Hennessy, Ky.	38	16	2	2
◆Songandaprayer, Ky.	37	19	2	3
Storm Cat, Ky.	38	17	2	3

Leading Freshman Sires by Progeny Earnings in 2005

Worldwide earnings for stallions who stood in North America in year of conception of two-year-olds of 2005.
◆ Denotes freshman sire.

Sire	Strs	Wnrs	SWs	Leading Earner (Earnings)	Total Earnings
◆Tiznow, Ky.	35	12	1	Folklore ($927,500)	$1,376,265
◆El Corredor, Ky.	37	16	2	Adieu ($554,470)	1,249,625
◆Songandaprayer, Ky.	37	19	3	Stolen Prayer ($211,230)	1,124,123
◆City Zip, Ky.	39	20	2	Little Miss Zip ($130,145)	1,064,275
◆Forest Camp, Ky.	30	17	2	Your Tent Or Mine ($173,250)	952,588
◆Trippi, Fl.	40	17	0	Cab ($83,382)	789,169
◆Broken Vow, Ky.	41	13	1	Private Vow ($382,508)	787,600
◆Exchange Rate, Fl.	29	12	1	Blazing Rate ($351,300)	763,445
◆Ecton Park, Ky.	30	13	2	French Park ($243,761)	709,579
◆Five Star Day, Ky.	21	10	1	Eishin Danbury ($153,186)	623,857
◆Put It Back, Fl.	17	9	1	In Summation ($285,800)	576,045
◆Delaware Township, Fl.	33	10	2	Electrify ($131,800)	547,672
◆Black Minnaloushe, Ky.	47	14	1	Stream Cat ($153,670)	495,631
◆Prime Timber, N.Y.	33	11	1	Cinderella's Dream ($133,600)	422,519
◆Perigee Moon, On.	24	6	1	Perigee Girl ($116,114)	411,737
◆Snuck In, Fl.	33	15	0	Full In ($45,180)	393,161
◆Freud, N.Y.	21	9	0	My Interpretation ($63,345)	381,950
◆Brahms, Ky.	37	14	2	Test Boy ($92,300)	370,412
◆Aptitude, Ky.	38	11	0	Amandatude ($51,700)	361,175
◆Vision and Verse, Ky.	24	9	0	Acceleration ($93,728)	348,734
◆Trajectory, On.	14	5	2	Silent Course ($68,274)	332,758
◆Monarchos, Ky.	18	5	2	Fifth Avenue ($109,900)	311,742
◆King Cugat, Ky.	24	5	2	Seaside Retreat ($163,632)	310,729
◆Luftikus, W.V.	20	8	2	Shesagrumptoo ($58,252)	287,917
◆One Way Love, On.	15	9	0	Initforthemoney ($73,936)	273,793
◆Albert the Great, Ky.	37	15	0	Motion ($38,004)	271,123
◆B L's Appeal, Fl.	15	9	0	B L's a Runner ($58,850)	234,155
◆Talk Is Money, Ky.	21	9	0	Domestic Oil ($35,011)	186,717
◆Flame Thrower, Fl.	21	7	0	Fletchers Cove ($26,400)	180,605
◆Mass Market, B.C.	13	5	2	Miss Me Not ($66,449)	179,520
◆Point Given, Ky.	18	2	0	Great Point ($38,254)	179,121
◆Mojave Moon, Md.	25	8	0	Mieszko ($43,990)	170,914
◆Disco Rico, Md.	14	4	2	Pure Disco ($78,155)	165,887
◆Minardi, Ky.	17	5	0	Cedar Fever ($31,711)	144,571
◆Casanova Star, P.R.	4	3	1	Yosolita ($127,620)	144,414
◆Cloud Hopping, Fl.	12	6	0	Mickees Tornado ($36,870)	134,074
◆Royal Cat, Ca.	7	4	0	Aloha Mangos Kitty ($49,883)	121,971
◆Island Storm, Mi.	3	1	1	Weatherstorm ($98,494)	105,529
◆Weekend Cruise, Fl.	12	5	0	Cruisinwithcharlie ($26,490)	101,344
◆Pikepass, Ky.	15	6	0	Turnpike ($22,875)	100,712
◆Globalize, Ca.	9	4	0	Princess Kinzie ($43,065)	99,755
◆Liberty Gold, Ok.	9	4	1	Cinderella Liberty ($56,158)	99,574
◆Sailor's Warning, Dead	7	1	0	Highland Lass ($44,748)	92,904
◆Clash by Night, SAf	5	3	0	D. D. Night Star ($58,090)	92,359
◆Dome, N.M.	16	4	0	Flyingdome ($28,081)	92,047
◆Billions, P.R.	10	6	0	Dona Ruz ($36,320)	88,015
◆Dixie Dot Com, Ca.	9	4	0	Moon Over Hemet ($26,496)	82,081
◆Castine, W.V.	6	1	1	Cross Creek Rosie ($72,713)	81,051
◆Shot of Gold, Mn.	8	4	0	Shot of Silver ($20,998)	78,288
◆Not Impossible (Ire), On.	5	1	0	Chickenonastikbaby ($54,061)	75,712
◆Coastal Storm, Pa.	9	3	0	All Show No Go ($24,520)	72,400
◆Royal Strand (Ire), La.	7	2	0	Royal Madame ($33,080)	62,656
◆Madraar, Ca.	8	1	0	Arabian Star ($51,142)	58,332
◆Cape Cod, P.R.	2	2	0	Capote Kid ($46,146)	57,980
◆Mancini, Ky.	6	1	1	Whatsitgonnatake ($46,830)	57,494
◆Jazz Club, Md.	8	4	0	Maddy's Our Girl ($13,110)	49,665
◆Lexicon, Fl.	6	3	0	Balius ($14,920)	48,890
◆Deputy Warlock, N.J.	5	1	0	Paola Vanessa ($37,312)	48,872
◆Man of the Night, La.	1	1	0	Night Doc ($47,360)	47,360
◆Mr. Nugget, N.J.	6	1	0	Moetown ($32,660)	46,162
◆Lake Austin, La.	4	2	0	Sassy Sarah ($23,123)	44,273
◆Conscience Clear, Fl.	7	2	0	Dixie Dell ($20,010)	41,087
◆Hurricane Center, Ab.	8	2	0	Zip the Hurricane ($12,207)	40,470
◆Valid Belfast, La.	8	1	0	Seventy Two Reno ($21,270)	39,144
◆Fort La Roca, P.R.	8	3	0	Shaira Liz ($10,033)	37,994

Leading Freshman Sires by Average Earnings per Runner in 2005

Minimum of 10 Starters

Sire	Strs	Wnrs	Average
◆Tiznow, Ky.	35	12	$39,322
◆Put It Back, Fl.	17	9	33,885
◆El Corredor, Ky.	37	16	33,774
◆Forest Camp, Ky.	30	17	31,753
◆Songandaprayer, Ky.	37	19	30,382
◆Five Star Day, Ky.	21	10	29,707
◆City Zip, Ky.	39	20	27,289
◆Exchange Rate, Fl.	29	12	26,326
◆Trajectory, On.	14	5	23,768
◆Ecton Park, Ky.	30	13	23,653
◆Trippi, Fl.	40	17	19,729
◆Broken Vow, Ky.	41	13	19,210
◆One Way Love, On.	15	9	18,253
◆Freud, N.Y.	21	9	18,188
◆Monarchos, Ky.	18	5	17,319
◆Perigee Moon, On.	24	6	17,156
◆Delaware Township, Fl.	33	10	16,596
◆B L's Appeal, Fl.	15	9	15,610
◆Vision and Verse, Ky.	24	9	14,531
◆Luftikus, W.V.	20	8	14,396
◆Mass Market, B.C.	13	5	13,809
◆King Cugat, Ky.	24	5	12,947
◆Prime Timber, N.Y.	33	11	12,804
◆Snuck In, Fl.	33	15	11,914

Leading Freshman Sires by Median Earnings per Runner in 2005

Minimum of 10 Starters

Sire	Strs	Wnrs	Median
◆Five Star Day, Ky.	21	10	$15,250
◆Trippi, Fl.	40	17	14,025
◆One Way Love, On.	15	9	13,773
◆City Zip, Ky.	39	20	12,900
◆B L's Appeal, Fl.	15	9	11,745
◆Forest Camp, Ky.	30	17	11,413
◆Freud, N.Y.	21	9	11,050
◆Songandaprayer, Ky.	37	19	10,565
◆El Corredor, Ky.	37	16	10,521
◆Trajectory, On.	14	5	10,502
◆Put It Back, Fl.	17	9	9,600
◆Tiznow, Ky.	35	12	9,176
◆Exchange Rate, Fl.	29	12	8,500
◆Ecton Park, Ky.	30	13	8,025
◆Luftikus, W.V.	20	8	7,777
◆Snuck In, Fl.	33	15	7,124
◆Cloud Hopping, Fl.	12	6	7,093
◆Broken Vow, Ky.	41	13	6,960
◆Delaware Township, Fl.	33	10	6,490
◆Mass Market, B.C.	13	5	6,379
◆Billions, P.R.	10	6	6,165
◆Flame Thrower, Fl.	21	7	6,000
◆Monarchos, Ky.	18	5	5,996
◆Point Given, Ky.	18	2	5,445
◆Aptitude, Ky.	38	11	4,706
◆Talk Is Money, Ky.	21	9	4,317

Leading Freshman Sires by Number of Winners in 2005

Sire	Strs	Wnrs	Wnrs/Strs
◆City Zip, Ky.	39	20	51.3%
◆Songandaprayer, Ky.	37	19	51.4%
◆Forest Camp, Ky.	30	17	56.7%
◆Trippi, Fl.	40	17	42.5%
◆El Corredor, Ky.	37	16	43.2%
◆Albert the Great, Ky.	37	15	40.5%
◆Snuck In, Fl.	33	15	45.5%
◆Black Minnaloushe, Ky.	47	14	29.8%
◆Brahms, Ky.	37	14	37.8%
◆Broken Vow, Ky.	41	13	31.7%
◆Ecton Park, Ky.	30	13	43.3%
◆Exchange Rate, Fl.	29	12	41.4%
◆Tiznow, Ky.	35	12	34.3%
◆Aptitude, Ky.	38	11	28.9%
◆Prime Timber, N.Y.	33	11	33.3%
◆Delaware Township, Fl.	33	10	30.3%
◆Five Star Day, Ky.	21	10	47.6%
◆B L's Appeal, Fl.	15	9	60.0%
◆Freud, N.Y.	21	9	42.9%
◆One Way Love, On.	15	9	60.0%
◆Put It Back, Fl.	17	9	52.9%
◆Talk Is Money, Ky.	21	9	42.9%
◆Vision and Verse, Ky.	24	9	37.5%
◆Luftikus, W.V.	20	8	40.0%
◆Mojave Moon, Md.	25	8	32.0%
◆Flame Thrower, Fl.	21	7	33.3%

Leading Freshman Sires by Number of Wins in 2005

Sire	Strs	Wnrs	Wins
◆City Zip, Ky.	39	20	30
◆Forest Camp, Ky.	30	17	26
◆Songandaprayer, Ky.	37	19	26
◆El Corredor, Ky.	37	16	24
◆Exchange Rate, Fl.	29	12	21
◆Trippi, Fl.	40	17	21
◆Brahms, Ky.	37	14	19
◆Ecton Park, Ky.	30	13	18
◆Snuck In, Fl.	33	15	18
◆Black Minnaloushe, Ky.	47	14	17
◆Broken Vow, Ky.	41	13	17
◆Albert the Great, Ky.	37	15	16
◆Delaware Township, Fl.	33	10	16
◆Put It Back, Fl.	17	9	15
◆Tiznow, Ky.	35	12	15
◆B L's Appeal, Fl.	15	9	13
◆Five Star Day, Ky.	21	10	13
◆Prime Timber, N.Y.	33	11	13
◆Vision and Verse, Ky.	24	9	13
◆Aptitude, Ky.	38	11	12
◆Freud, N.Y.	21	9	11
◆Talk Is Money, Ky.	21	9	11
◆Luftikus, W.V.	20	8	10
◆One Way Love, On.	15	9	10
◆King Cugat, Ky.	24	5	9
◆Mojave Moon, Md.	25	8	9

Leading Freshman Sires by Number of Stakes Winners in 2005

Sire	Strs	Wnrs	SWs	SWins
◆Songandaprayer, Ky.	37	19	3	6
◆Brahms, Ky.	37	14	2	3
◆City Zip, Ky.	39	20	2	3
◆Delaware Township, Fl.	33	10	2	2
◆Disco Rico, Md.	14	4	2	2
◆Ecton Park, Ky.	30	13	2	3
◆El Corredor, Ky.	37	16	2	6
◆Forest Camp, Ky.	30	17	2	3
◆King Cugat, Ky.	24	5	2	2
◆Luftikus, W.V.	20	8	2	2
◆Mass Market, B.C.	13	5	2	2
◆Monarchos, Ky.	18	5	2	2
◆Trajectory, On.	14	5	2	3

Leading Freshman Sires by Number of Graded Stakes Winners in 2005

Sire	Strs	Wnrs	GSWs	GSWins
◆Songandaprayer, Ky.	37	19	2	3
◆Black Minnaloushe, Ky.	47	14	1	1
◆Broken Vow, Ky.	41	13	1	2
◆Ecton Park, Ky.	30	13	1	2
◆El Corredor, Ky.	37	16	1	2
◆Forest Camp, Ky.	30	17	1	1
◆Tiznow, Ky.	35	12	1	3

Leading Broodmare Sires by Progeny Earnings in 2005

Worldwide earnings for broodmare sires who stand or last stood in North America or had 60 or more North American starters in 2005.

Sire	Strs	Wnrs	SWs	Leading Earner (Earnings)	Total Earnings
Mr. Prospector, Dead	488	219	28	Rock Hard Ten ($1,080,000)	$21,004,869
Storm Cat, Ky.	359	180	16	Meisho Bowler ($1,870,744)	15,675,211
Nureyev, Dead	376	160	20	Grass Bomber ($1,254,949)	15,394,022
Woodman, Ky.	551	235	17	Lad Of The Manor ($632,912)	14,172,077
Danzig, Dead	418	152	13	Daring Heart ($908,170)	13,626,434
Deputy Minister, Dead	385	201	21	Kane Hekili ($2,813,092)	13,002,164
Dixieland Band, Ky.	383	212	20	Blues and Royals ($1,200,000)	12,924,818
Miswaki, Dead	380	199	15	My Typhoon (Ire) ($379,629)	9,964,234
Seeking the Gold, Ky.	243	118	8	Seeking the Dia ($1,427,828)	9,934,658
Relaunch, Dead	361	192	17	Koolinger ($887,547)	9,896,220
Alydar, Dead	260	120	12	Hishi Atlas ($1,085,952)	9,702,419
Seattle Slew, Dead	351	160	7	Offlee Wild ($452,500)	9,448,761
Storm Bird, Dead	356	167	20	Sand Springs ($606,400)	9,177,699
Riverman, Dead	253	104	6	Makybe Diva ($4,047,686)	8,683,345
Gulch, Ky.	233	105	7	Strong Blood ($902,928)	8,354,691
Crafty Prospector, Ky.	321	178	15	Agnes Jedi ($1,155,356)	8,287,727
Lyphard, Dead	272	111	5	Tsurumaru Yokanise ($639,567)	8,170,547
Pleasant Colony, Dead	276	147	7	Pleasant Home ($1,316,420)	8,111,375
Gone West, Ky.	266	114	7	Motivator ($1,923,920)	7,935,231
Kris S., Dead	303	147	15	Eishin Dover ($476,295)	7,865,983
Affirmed, Dead	325	148	8	Honey Ryder ($910,980)	7,603,142
Alleged, Dead	304	124	13	Pride ($854,290)	7,401,015
Quiet American, Ky.	96	50	8	Saint Liam ($3,696,960)	7,236,144
Silver Deputy, Ky.	179	104	13	Roman Ruler ($890,000)	6,988,885
Forty Niner, Jpn	222	120	14	Island Sand ($743,860)	6,948,498
Afleet, Jpn	241	107	8	Sidewinder ($670,749)	6,924,581
Irish River (Fr), Dead	362	152	12	David Junior ($582,251)	6,843,836
Private Account, Dead	301	139	7	Smuggler ($558,800)	6,788,766
Wild Again, Pens	321	160	12	Mea Domina ($446,076)	6,748,168
Valid Appeal, Dead	321	165	6	Tsumujikaze ($533,924)	6,719,958
Cure the Blues, Dead	311	154	9	Miss Matched ($255,454)	6,622,201
Rahy, Ky.	260	140	18	Megahertz (GB) ($780,000)	6,535,065
Lost Code, Dead	222	127	4	Hat Trick ($2,669,779)	6,521,203
Majestic Light, Dead	260	110	4	Artie Schiller ($1,448,000)	6,446,984
Clever Trick, Dead	347	162	5	Sun King ($1,134,800)	6,436,277
Conquistador Cielo, Dead	333	177	9	Tsurumaru Homare ($255,168)	6,323,988
Nijinsky II, Dead	224	86	6	Cosmo Marvelous ($556,887)	6,263,685
Alysheba, KSA	184	90	5	Bullish Luck ($1,780,235)	6,134,653
Theatrical (Ire), Ky.	237	117	2	English Channel ($1,143,491)	6,026,248
Mt. Livermore, Pens	273	137	6	Super Frolic ($818,160)	5,973,318
Dayjur, Ky.	180	82	8	Shadow Cast ($626,266)	5,932,594
Lear Fan, Pens	228	114	4	Azamour (Ire) ($1,359,521)	5,779,948
Vice Regent, Dead	266	130	6	K S Spring ($383,576)	5,738,546
Halo, Dead	322	133	7	Tsurugaoka Hayate ($200,477)	5,680,206
Saratoga Six, N.M.	219	114	7	Madcap Escapade ($516,452)	5,676,591
Silver Hawk, Pens	223	95	7	Tokai Trick ($677,514)	5,596,212
Meadowlake, Dead	237	122	10	Henny Hughes ($644,820)	5,565,797
Chief's Crown, Dead	244	118	5	Eddington ($602,200)	5,446,115
Bold Ruckus, Dead	240	138	14	Cee's Irish ($329,125)	5,386,632
Green Dancer, Dead	332	142	4	Fusaichi Auster ($627,977)	5,262,747
Broad Brush, Pens	221	128	8	Daiwa King Con ($442,873)	5,114,658
Phone Trick, Dead	281	143	13	Celtic Innis ($158,310)	5,032,670
Blushing Groom (Fr), Dead	161	70	6	Star King Man ($635,575)	5,008,436
Slew o' Gold, Pens	251	103	6	Midtown (Ire) ($238,904)	4,986,531
Topsider, Dead	184	98	2	Joyful Heart ($429,144)	4,981,734
Red Ransom, Eng	223	106	7	Brad Barows ($232,645)	4,947,045
Palace Music, Pens	235	96	4	Railings ($1,567,617)	4,927,352
Devil's Bag, Dead	288	126	6	Art Trader ($626,262)	4,922,795
Strawberry Road (Aus), Dead	186	107	13	Smoke Smoke Smoke ($199,922)	4,849,329
Cox's Ridge, Dead	258	128	5	Baron Karanotegami ($379,172)	4,789,185
Known Fact, Dead	211	95	5	Taiki Enigma ($834,188)	4,750,778
Mining, Jpn	168	86	9	Zenno Rob Roy ($1,489,032)	4,734,651
Capote, Pens	238	112	7	Affrettata ($270,515)	4,650,813
Carson City, Dead	189	112	12	Latenite Special ($224,820)	4,638,435
Stop the Music, Dead	194	64	2	Giacomo ($1,846,876)	4,511,768

Leading Broodmare Sires by Average Earnings per Runner in 2005

Minimum of 25 Starters

Sire	Strs	Wnrs	Average
Quiet American, Ky.	96	50	$75,377
Storm Cat, Ky.	359	180	43,664
Mr. Prospector, Dead	488	219	43,043
Nureyev, Dead	376	160	40,942
Seeking the Gold, Ky.	243	118	40,883
Silver Deputy, Ky.	179	104	39,044
Alydar, Dead	260	120	37,317
Naskra, Dead	104	48	36,065
Gulch, Ky.	233	105	35,857
Riverman, Dead	253	104	34,322
Citidancer, Pens	62	36	33,895
Deputy Minister, Dead	385	201	33,772
Dixieland Band, Ky.	383	212	33,746
Mari's Book, Dead	99	52	33,516
Alysheba, KSA	184	90	33,341
Dayjur, Ky.	180	82	32,959
A.P. Indy, Ky.	122	55	32,861
Danzig, Dead	418	152	32,599
Forty Niner, Jpn	222	120	31,300
Blushing Groom (Fr), Dead	161	70	31,108
Fast Play, N.Y.	92	55	30,389
Lyphard, Dead	272	111	30,039
With Approval, Eng	145	70	29,870
Gone West, Ky.	266	114	29,832

Leading Broodmare Sires by Median Earnings per Runner in 2005

Minimum of 25 Starters

Sire	Strs	Wnrs	Median
Carson City, Dead	189	112	$15,700
Unbridled, Dead	127	79	15,582
Forty Niner, Jpn	222	120	14,320
Marquetry, Ky.	82	49	13,435
Storm Cat, Ky.	359	180	13,115
Quiet American, Ky.	96	50	13,018
Pentelicus, Dead	117	66	12,482
Pleasant Colony, Dead	276	147	12,410
Corporate Report, Ia.	72	48	12,409
Seeking the Gold, Ky.	243	118	12,200
Silver Deputy, Ky.	179	104	12,134
Jolie's Halo, Dead	72	43	11,949
Rubiano, Dead	107	58	11,840
Strawberry Road (Aus), Dead	186	107	11,497
Bold Ruckus, Dead	240	138	11,357
Unreal Zeal, Ky.	86	48	11,330
Miswaki, Dead	380	199	11,329
Regal Classic, N.Y.	172	90	11,257
Broad Brush, Pens	221	128	11,207
Salt Lake, Ca.	138	73	10,905
A.P. Indy, Ky.	122	55	10,889
Crafty Prospector, Ky.	321	178	10,570
Dixieland Band, Ky.	383	212	10,568

Leading Broodmare Sires by Number of Winners in 2005

Sire	Strs	Wnrs	Wnrs/Strs
Woodman, Ky.	551	235	42.6%
Mr. Prospector, Dead	488	219	44.9%
Dixieland Band, Ky.	383	212	55.4%
Deputy Minister, Dead	385	201	52.2%
Miswaki, Dead	380	199	52.4%
Relaunch, Dead	361	192	53.2%
Storm Cat, Ky.	359	180	50.1%
Crafty Prospector, Ky.	321	178	55.5%
Conquistador Cielo, Dead	333	177	53.2%
Storm Bird, Dead	356	167	46.9%
Valid Appeal, Dead	321	165	51.4%
Clever Trick, Dead	347	162	46.7%
Nureyev, Dead	376	160	42.6%
Seattle Slew, Dead	351	160	45.6%
Wild Again, Pens	321	160	49.8%
Cure the Blues, Dead	311	154	49.5%
Danzig, Dead	418	152	36.4%
Irish River (Fr), Dead	362	152	42.0%
Affirmed, Dead	325	148	45.5%
Kris S., Dead	303	147	48.5%
Pleasant Colony, Dead	276	147	53.3%

Leading Broodmare Sires by Number of Wins in 2005

Sire	Strs	Wnrs	Wins
Woodman, Ky.	551	235	379
Dixieland Band, Ky.	383	212	370
Relaunch, Dead	361	192	348
Mr. Prospector, Dead	488	219	343
Crafty Prospector, Ky.	321	178	336
Deputy Minister, Dead	385	201	332
Storm Cat, Ky.	359	180	332
Miswaki, Dead	380	199	312
Conquistador Cielo, Dead	333	177	301
Valid Appeal, Dead	321	165	299
Cure the Blues, Dead	311	154	265
Pleasant Colony, Dead	276	147	265
Storm Bird, Dead	356	167	265
Clever Trick, Dead	347	162	263
Wild Again, Pens	321	160	262
Nureyev, Dead	376	160	258
Seattle Slew, Dead	351	160	258
Danzig, Dead	418	152	255
Bold Ruckus, Dead	240	138	250

Leading Broodmare Sires by Number of Stakes Winners in 2005

Sire	Strs	Wnrs	SWs	SWins
Mr. Prospector, Dead	488	219	28	39
Deputy Minister, Dead	385	201	21	30
Dixieland Band, Ky.	383	212	20	30
Nureyev, Dead	376	160	20	21
Storm Bird, Dead	356	167	20	26
Rahy, Ky.	260	140	18	23
Relaunch, Dead	361	192	17	31
Woodman, Ky.	551	235	17	23
Storm Cat, Ky.	359	180	16	24
Crafty Prospector, Ky.	321	178	15	21
Kris S., Dead	303	147	15	18
Miswaki, Dead	380	199	15	18
Bold Ruckus, Dead	240	138	14	20
Forty Niner, Jpn	222	120	14	18
Alleged, Dead	304	124	13	18
Danzig, Dead	418	152	13	21
Phone Trick, Dead	281	143	13	15
Silver Deputy, Ky.	179	104	13	22

Leading Broodmare Sires by Number of Graded Stakes Winners in 2005

Sire	Strs	Wnrs	GSWs	GSWins
Mr. Prospector, Dead	488	219	14	21
Dixieland Band, Ky.	383	212	9	10
Irish River (Fr), Dead	362	152	8	12
Nureyev, Dead	376	160	8	10
Alleged, Dead	304	124	6	9
Storm Bird, Dead	356	167	6	9
Gone West, Ky.	266	114	5	6
Miswaki, Dead	380	199	5	5
Quiet American, Ky.	96	50	5	9
Rahy, Ky.	260	140	5	10
With Approval, Eng	145	70	5	6
Woodman, Ky.	551	235	5	9
Blushing Groom (Fr), Dead	161	70	4	3
Deputy Minister, Dead	385	201	4	5
Dynaformer, Ky.	180	94	4	5
Forty Niner, Jpn	222	120	4	5
Nijinsky II, Dead	224	86	4	5
Roberto, Dead	134	47	4	7
Saratoga Six, N.M.	219	114	4	6
Silver Hawk, Pens	223	95	4	6
Storm Cat, Ky.	359	180	4	7
Strawberry Road (Aus), Dead	186	107	4	5

Leading Sires by Progeny Earnings in North America in 2005

Earnings in North America only for stallions represented by at least one starter in North America in 2005, regardless of where the stallion stands or stood.

Sire	Strs	Wnrs	SWs	Leading Earner (Earnings)	Total Earnings
Saint Ballado, Dead	154	81	12	Saint Liam ($3,696,960)	$9,211,300
Distorted Humor, Ky.	144	81	17	Flower Alley ($2,435,200)	8,160,882
A.P. Indy, Ky.	166	83	16	Suave ($624,900)	7,617,709
El Prado (Ire), Ky.	150	86	11	Borrego ($1,536,600)	7,307,261
Dynaformer, Ky.	130	62	12	Perfect Drift ($1,121,227)	6,119,177
Smart Strike, Ky.	136	77	13	English Channel ($1,143,491)	5,932,183
Wild Rush, Jpn	155	86	10	Wild Desert ($636,800)	5,632,565
Langfuhr, Ky.	185	104	12	Jambalaya ($380,846)	5,139,869
Carson City, Dead	177	91	11	Pollard's Vision ($355,000)	4,849,237
Storm Cat, Ky.	101	54	12	Grand Reward ($406,467)	4,758,633
Unbridled's Song, Ky.	167	90	12	Eurosilver ($247,450)	4,651,380
Holy Bull, Ky.	131	57	5	Giacomo ($1,846,876)	4,583,335
Tale of the Cat, Ky.	173	94	7	My Trusty Cat ($269,285)	4,537,184
Silver Deputy, Ky.	143	91	7	Badge of Silver ($411,167)	4,523,261
Maria's Mon, Ky.	183	99	6	High Limit ($550,500)	4,391,719
Pulpit, Ky.	111	63	9	Wend ($383,900)	4,383,800
Awesome Again, Ky.	119	63	7	Round Pond ($467,300)	4,329,572
Seeking the Gold, Ky.	70	44	8	Pleasant Home ($1,316,420)	4,201,571
Grand Slam, Ky.	195	90	6	Limehouse ($482,998)	4,176,248
Not For Love, Md.	180	86	7	Presidentialaffair ($269,198)	4,166,966
Northern Afleet, Ky.	99	60	3	Afleet Alex ($2,085,000)	4,136,934
Forest Wildcat, Ky.	174	93	10	Attila's Storm ($265,348)	3,994,613
Alphabet Soup, Ky.	173	100	10	Alphabet Kisses ($241,621)	3,940,291
Honor Grades, Dead	128	80	5	Magna Graduate ($1,070,170)	3,808,392
Thunder Gulch, Ky.	167	81	7	Reverberate ($189,150)	3,777,887
Stormy Atlantic, Ky.	157	87	10	She Says It Best ($382,918)	3,775,533
Fusaichi Pegasus, Ky.	59	29	6	Roman Ruler ($890,000)	3,678,947
Indian Charlie, Ky.	111	73	12	Two Trail Sioux ($577,200)	3,670,023
Bertrando, Ca.	161	79	5	Unfurl the Flag ($311,360)	3,644,295
Touch Gold, Ky.	139	75	7	Mass Media ($299,870)	3,628,223
Quiet American, Ky.	129	70	3	Naughty New Yorker ($290,157)	3,625,214
Storm Boot, Ky.	167	95	7	Storm's Darling ($231,330)	3,616,045
Honour and Glory, Ky.	174	103	3	Battle Won ($294,759)	3,589,186
Pioneering, Ky.	148	93	7	Triano ($206,080)	3,518,373
Smoke Glacken, Ky.	142	77	5	Smoke Smoke Smoke ($199,922)	3,463,936
A. P Jet, N.Y.	148	77	4	Karakorum Splendor ($222,782)	3,430,722
Charismatic, Jpn	127	68	2	Sun King ($1,134,800)	3,428,672
Louis Quatorze, Md.	197	95	4	Choctaw Nation ($284,000)	3,371,150
Gilded Time, Ky.	158	87	8	Clock Stopper ($297,438)	3,351,281
Hennessy, Ky.	129	60	6	Henny Hughes ($644,820)	3,347,688
Dixieland Band, Ky.	133	73	12	Sharp Lisa ($267,500)	3,344,843
Peaks and Valleys, On.	146	89	8	Invitational ($209,009)	3,340,266
Skip Away, Ky.	143	78	9	Skip and Go ($154,844)	3,322,593
Unbridled, Dead	83	41	5	Eddington ($602,200)	3,283,980
Allen's Prospect, Dead	187	99	4	Sarah's Prospect ($153,138)	3,271,948
Slew City Slew, Ky.	163	80	5	Lava Man ($774,103)	3,260,065
Mr. Greeley, Ky.	173	86	4	Greeley's Galaxy ($358,480)	3,243,064
Belong to Me, Ky.	131	77	6	Ebony Breeze ($180,295)	3,199,664
Rahy, Ky.	88	52	9	T. D. Vance ($305,305)	3,197,946
Devil His Due, Ky.	189	100	6	Spite the Devil ($171,153)	3,190,932
Regal Classic, N.Y.	139	83	3	Classic Stamp ($277,991)	3,186,957
Royal Academy, Ky.	141	68	8	Rue des Reves ($165,800)	3,175,553
Sky Classic, Ky.	141	77	4	Sky Diamond ($185,672)	3,175,435
Forestry, Ky.	97	52	12	Diplomat Lady ($334,800)	3,149,725
Out of Place, Ky.	140	77	9	Sort It Out ($255,661)	3,133,453
Mutakddim, Ky.	128	81	5	The Student (Arg) ($208,400)	3,131,365
Kris S., Dead	59	27	6	Rock Hard Ten ($1,080,000)	3,117,270
Elusive Quality, Ky.	127	72	5	Elusive Jazz ($338,731)	3,104,290
Dance Brightly, Chi	144	82	5	Mea Domina ($446,076)	3,095,813
Runaway Groom, Ky.	161	87	6	Runaway Dancer ($250,448)	3,090,810

Leading Sires by Average Earnings per Runner in North America in 2005

Minimum of 25 Starters

Sire	Strs	Wnrs	Average
Danehill, Dead	25	13	$94,777
Fusaichi Pegasus, Ky.	59	29	62,355
Seeking the Gold, Ky.	70	44	60,022
Saint Ballado, Dead	154	81	59,814
Distorted Humor, Ky.	144	81	56,673
Stephen Got Even, Ky.	53	26	56,124
Kris S., Dead	59	27	52,835
El Prado (Ire), Ky.	150	86	48,715
Storm Cat, Ky.	101	54	47,115
Dynaformer, Ky.	130	62	47,071
A.P. Indy, Ky.	166	83	45,890
Candy Stripes, Arg	47	18	45,489
Smart Strike, Ky.	136	77	43,619
Unusual Heat, Ca.	58	30	42,843
Atticus, Ca.	47	29	42,779
Giant's Causeway, Ky.	64	29	42,548
Tiznow, Ky.	30	10	42,015
Northern Afleet, Ky.	99	60	41,787
Lasting Approval, Arg	32	12	41,372
Archers Bay, Dead	69	45	39,999
Unbridled, Dead	83	41	39,566
Pulpit, Ky.	111	63	39,494
Summer Squall, Pens	54	34	39,197

Leading Sires by Median Earnings per Runner in North America in 2005

Minimum of 25 Starters

Sire	Strs	Wnrs	Median
Raffie's Majesty, N.Y.	38	27	$28,425
Precise End, Jpn	57	43	25,800
Seeking the Gold, Ky.	70	44	25,685
Quaker Ridge, Il.	36	25	23,805
Storm Cat, Ky.	101	54	20,250
Gold Token, N.Y.	58	45	19,196
Yes It's True, Ky.	91	53	19,110
Archers Bay, Dead	69	45	18,100
Victory Gallop, Ky.	110	72	17,708
Silver Deputy, Ky.	143	91	17,400
Malibu Moon, Ky.	102	62	17,270
Summer Squall, Pens	54	34	17,135
Unusual Heat, Ca.	58	30	16,984
Saint Ballado, Dead	154	81	16,920
Fusaichi Pegasus, Ky.	59	29	16,800
Swear by Dixie, Chi	30	18	16,798
Indian Charlie, Ky.	111	73	16,663
Menifee, Ky.	87	46	16,534
Seattle Slew, Dead	36	18	16,444
Broad Brush, Pens	76	39	16,439
Unbridled's Song, Ky.	167	90	16,400
Roy, Dead	55	33	16,180

Leading Sires by Number of Winners in North America in 2005

Sire	Strs	Wnrs	Wnrs/ Strs
Langfuhr, Ky.	185	104	56.2%
Honour and Glory, Ky.	174	103	59.2%
Alphabet Soup, Ky.	173	100	57.8%
Devil His Due, Ky.	189	100	52.9%
Valid Expectations, Tx.	167	100	59.9%
Allen's Prospect, Dead	187	99	52.9%
Maria's Mon, Ky.	183	99	54.1%
Louis Quatorze, Md.	197	95	48.2%
Storm Boot, Ky.	167	95	56.9%
Tale of the Cat, Ky.	173	94	54.3%
Forest Wildcat, Ky.	174	93	53.4%
Pioneering, Ky.	148	93	62.8%
Carson City, Dead	177	91	51.4%
Silver Deputy, Ky.	143	91	63.6%
Grand Slam, Ky.	195	90	46.2%
Unbridled's Song, Ky.	167	90	53.9%
Peaks and Valleys, On.	146	89	61.0%
Gilded Time, Ky.	158	87	55.1%
Runaway Groom, Ky.	161	87	54.0%
Stormy Atlantic, Ky.	157	87	55.4%
El Prado (Ire), Ky.	150	86	57.3%
Mr. Greeley, Ky.	173	86	49.7%
Not For Love, Md.	180	86	47.8%
Salt Lake, Ca.	147	86	58.5%
Wild Rush, Jpn	155	86	55.5%

Leading Sires by Number of Wins in North America in 2005

Sire	Strs	Wnrs	Wins
Langfuhr, Ky.	185	104	192
Allen's Prospect, Dead	187	99	186
Storm Boot, Ky.	167	95	177
Maria's Mon, Ky.	183	99	174
Pioneering, Ky.	148	93	173
Devil His Due, Ky.	189	100	170
Alphabet Soup, Ky.	173	100	169
Wild Rush, Jpn	155	86	166
Formal Dinner, Fl.	127	79	165
Double Honor, Fl.	122	76	164
Peaks and Valleys, On.	146	89	164
Tale of the Cat, Ky.	173	94	163
Salt Lake, Ca.	147	86	162
Stormy Atlantic, Ky.	157	87	161
Carson City, Dead	177	91	160
Not For Love, Md.	180	86	160
Silver Deputy, Ky.	143	91	159
Honour and Glory, Ky.	174	103	158
Saint Ballado, Dead	154	81	158

Leading Sires by Number of Stakes Winners in North America in 2005

Sire	Strs	Wnrs	SWs	SWins
Distorted Humor, Ky.	144	81	17	24
A.P. Indy, Ky.	166	83	16	21
Smart Strike, Ky.	136	77	13	24
Dixieland Band, Ky.	133	73	12	15
Dynaformer, Ky.	130	62	12	16
Forestry, Ky.	97	52	12	12
Indian Charlie, Ky.	111	73	12	17
Langfuhr, Ky.	185	104	12	20
Saint Ballado, Dead	154	81	12	22
Storm Cat, Ky.	101	54	12	14
Unbridled's Song, Ky.	167	90	12	15
Carson City, Dead	177	91	11	13
El Prado (Ire), Ky.	150	86	11	16
Alphabet Soup, Ky.	173	100	10	17
Forest Wildcat, Ky.	174	93	10	15
Malibu Moon, Ky.	102	62	10	12
Stormy Atlantic, Ky.	157	87	10	14
Wild Rush, Jpn	155	86	10	17
Out of Place, Ky.	140	77	9	12
Pulpit, Ky.	111	63	9	13
Rahy, Ky.	88	52	9	12
Skip Away, Ky.	143	78	9	12

Leading Sires by Number of Graded Stakes Winners in North America in 2005

Sire	Strs	Wnrs	GSWs	GSWins
A.P. Indy, Ky.	166	83	10	13
Smart Strike, Ky.	136	77	7	10
Storm Cat, Ky.	101	54	7	9
Dynaformer, Ky.	130	62	6	9
Pulpit, Ky.	111	63	6	6
Distorted Humor, Ky.	144	81	5	7
Forestry, Ky.	97	52	5	5
Giant's Causeway, Ky.	64	29	5	6
Wild Rush, Jpn	155	86	5	7
Awesome Again, Ky.	119	63	4	5
Dixie Union, Ky.	66	30	4	4
El Prado (Ire), Ky.	150	86	4	7
Hennessy, Ky.	129	60	4	6
Seeking the Gold, Ky.	70	44	4	5
Silver Deputy, Ky.	143	91	4	5
Unbridled's Song, Ky.	167	90	4	4

Leading Juvenile Sires by Progeny Earnings in North America in 2005

Earnings in North America only for stallions represented by at least one starter in North America in 2005, regardless of where the stallion stands or stood. ◆ Denotes freshman sire.

Sire	Strs	Wnrs	SWs	Leading Earner (Earnings)	Total Earnings
◆Tiznow, Ky.	30	10	1	Folklore ($927,500)	$1,260,442
Giant's Causeway, Ky.	37	12	2	First Samurai ($682,575)	1,254,567
Stephen Got Even, Ky.	16	7	1	Stevie Wonderboy ($1,028,940)	1,226,055
◆El Corredor, Ky.	34	15	2	Adieu ($554,470)	1,197,357
Hennessy, Ky.	30	12	3	Henny Hughes ($644,820)	1,168,868
Distorted Humor, Ky.	33	13	5	Original Spin ($222,800)	1,066,715
◆City Zip, Ky.	39	20	2	Little Miss Zip ($130,145)	1,064,275
◆Songandaprayer, Ky.	36	18	3	Stolen Prayer ($211,230)	1,056,247
Thunder Gulch, Ky.	44	13	4	Balance ($183,300)	999,422
Stormy Atlantic, Ky.	43	15	2	She Says It Best ($382,918)	942,704
Dixie Union, Ky.	33	12	3	Unification ($173,557)	937,195
Catienus, N.Y.	31	14	2	Dawn of War ($403,800)	792,366
Exploit, Kor	30	15	3	Knights Templar ($255,353)	779,128
◆Broken Vow, Ky.	40	13	1	Private Vow ($382,508)	774,222
Tale of the Cat, Ky.	38	14	2	Catcominatcha ($206,706)	774,183
◆Forest Camp, Ky.	28	15	2	Your Tent Or Mine ($173,250)	768,920
More Than Ready, Ky.	45	19	1	More Than Pretty ($102,450)	763,458
Silver Deputy, Ky.	31	13	1	Vibank ($183,248)	762,341
Storm Cat, Ky.	24	10	2	Bluegrass Cat ($213,780)	760,202
Forestry, Ky.	32	14	4	Diplomat Lady ($334,800)	755,263
◆Exchange Rate, Fl.	28	11	1	Blazing Rate ($351,300)	741,116
Forest Wildcat, Ky.	36	14	2	Yaddo Cat ($110,370)	723,641
◆Ecton Park, Ky.	30	13	2	French Park ($243,761)	709,579
Grand Slam, Ky.	56	16	0	Fast Deal ($59,952)	692,359
Yes It's True, Ky.	36	14	1	Catch My Fancy ($108,318)	680,482
Fusaichi Pegasus, Ky.	24	10	2	Ex Caelis ($201,920)	668,658
Carson City, Dead	40	13	2	Effectual ($108,582)	662,957
◆Trippi, Fl.	37	16	0	Cab ($83,382)	654,386
Bold Executive, On.	26	7	2	Wannatalkaboutme ($186,503)	652,380
Benchmark, Ca.	12	6	1	Brother Derek ($502,080)	624,090
Lemon Drop Kid, Ky.	31	10	1	Bear's Kid ($172,114)	620,750
Maria's Mon, Ky.	31	12	2	Cause to Believe ($126,825)	611,947
Old Topper, Ca.	22	14	2	Sierra Sweetie ($235,400)	607,019
Storm Boot, Ky.	27	14	1	Gumboots ($132,168)	605,060
Regal Classic, N.Y.	16	7	2	Classic Pack ($260,050)	602,981
Notebook, Dead	28	15	1	Consider Thesource ($255,360)	601,859
Swiss Yodeler, Ca.	41	16	2	Wild Uncle Kurt ($86,535)	584,247
Precise End, Jpn	21	13	3	Princess Sweet ($105,032)	580,296
Saint Ballado, Dead	28	10	3	Saint Augustus ($90,650)	573,141
Louis Quatorze, Md.	53	18	1	Louie Nekia ($116,026)	561,570
Langfuhr, Ky.	30	10	3	Lawyer Ron ($129,208)	557,765
Mutakddim, Ky.	33	17	1	Dixie Dreamer ($86,600)	551,270
◆Delaware Township, Fl.	33	10	2	Electrify ($131,800)	547,672
Tactical Cat, Ky.	37	14	2	Our Madison ($145,608)	535,404
Mr. Greeley, Ky.	40	15	1	Miraculous Miss ($114,120)	517,955
Southern Halo, Arg	27	11	1	Edenwold ($287,247)	516,232
Montbrook, Fl.	33	13	1	Beacon Shine ($101,680)	511,153
Chimes Band, Dead	21	13	2	Latenite Band ($124,127)	508,276
Unbridled's Song, Ky.	31	10	1	Half Ours ($105,670)	503,943
A.P. Indy, Ky.	37	10	0	A. P. Warrior ($118,435)	502,289
Gilded Time, Ky.	43	18	2	Timetobook ($61,620)	501,401
Tiger Ridge, Fl.	29	15	2	Here Tiger ($96,780)	500,100
Pulpit, Ky.	28	7	1	Laity ($151,200)	492,306
Running Stag, Fl.	29	12	1	Running Lass ($199,480)	490,081
Deputy Commander, Ky.	30	16	1	Red Raymond ($109,735)	486,534
Marquetry, Ky.	26	7	2	Sparkling Pink ($150,700)	484,884
Wild Wonder, Dead	15	3	1	Wild Fit ($432,600)	484,847
Halo's Image, Fl.	29	16	1	Mia's Reflection ($138,150)	479,463
◆Five Star Day, Ky.	20	9	1	Within Reason ($86,005)	470,671
Double Honor, Fl.	29	15	1	Gin Rummy King ($138,860)	466,954
Old Trieste, Dead	36	11	0	Smart Sherif ($61,305)	462,139
Favorite Trick, N.M.	23	11	4	Disappearing Trick ($96,215)	456,658
Souvenir Copy, Ca.	28	16	2	Final Copy ($66,371)	453,662
High Yield, Fr	49	16	1	High Adventure ($36,210)	444,889
Anees, Dead	27	9	0	Along the Sea ($168,800)	439,119

Leading Juvenile Sires by Average Earnings per Runner in North America in 2005

Minimum of 10 Starters

Sire	Strs	Wnrs	Average
Stephen Got Even, Ky.	16	7	$76,628
Benchmark, Ca.	12	6	52,008
◆Tiznow, Ky.	30	10	42,015
Hennessy, Ky.	30	12	38,962
Regal Classic, N.Y.	16	7	37,686
◆El Corredor, Ky.	34	15	35,216
Giant's Causeway, Ky.	37	12	33,907
Distorted Humor, Ky.	33	13	32,325
Wild Wonder, Dead	15	3	32,323
Storm Cat, Ky.	24	10	31,675
General Meeting, Pens	13	7	30,245
◆Songandaprayer, Ky.	36	18	29,340
Seeking the Gold, Ky.	10	6	28,916
Dixie Union, Ky.	33	12	28,400
Fusaichi Pegasus, Ky.	24	10	27,861
Precise End, Jpn	21	13	27,633
Old Topper, Ca.	22	14	27,592
◆Forest Camp, Ky.	28	15	27,461
◆City Zip, Ky.	39	20	27,289
◆Exchange Rate, Fl.	28	11	26,468
◆Put It Back, Fl.	16	8	26,382
Exploit, Kor	30	15	25,971
Catienus, N.Y.	31	14	25,560
Red Ransom, Eng	10	6	25,458
Bold Executive, On.	26	7	25,092
Silver Deputy, Ky.	31	13	24,592
Chimes Band, Dead	21	13	24,204
◆Trajectory, On.	14	5	23,768
◆Ecton Park, Ky.	30	13	23,653

Leading Juvenile Sires by Median Earnings per Runner in North America in 2005

Minimum of 10 Starters

Sire	Strs	Wnrs	Median
Seeking the Gold, Ky.	10	6	$27,638
Hadif, Tx.	15	8	15,645
Dance Master, Fl.	14	9	15,300
Precise End, Jpn	21	13	15,290
West Acre, Fl.	10	6	15,238
Storm Cat, Ky.	24	10	14,802
◆One Way Love, On.	15	9	13,773
Red Ransom, Eng	10	6	13,498
Good and Tough, N.Y.	14	7	13,491
Halo's Image, Fl.	29	16	13,280
Two Punch, Md.	16	8	13,248
Yankee Victor, Kor	18	9	13,220
◆City Zip, Ky.	39	20	12,900
Fortunate Prospect, Pens	23	16	12,850
Old Topper, Ca.	22	14	12,757
Diligence, Fl.	12	7	12,463
Boundary, Pens	10	4	12,333
Storm Boot, Ky.	27	14	11,900
General Meeting, Pens	13	7	11,860
◆B L's Appeal, Fl.	15	9	11,745
◆Trippi, Fl.	37	16	11,638

Leading Juvenile Sires by Number of Winners in North America in 2005

Sire	Strs	Wnrs	Wnrs/ Strs
Valid Expectations, Te.	43	23	53.5%
◆City Zip, Ky.	39	20	51.3%
More Than Ready, Ky.	45	19	42.2%
Gilded Time, Ky.	43	18	41.9%
Louis Quatorze, Md.	53	18	34.0%
◆Songandaprayer, Ky.	36	18	50.0%
Mutakddim, Ky.	33	17	51.5%
Deputy Commander, Ky.	30	16	53.3%
Fortunate Prospect, Pens	23	16	69.6%
Grand Slam, Ky.	56	16	28.6%
Halo's Image, Fl.	29	16	55.2%
High Yield, Fr	49	16	32.7%
Souvenir Copy, Ca.	28	16	57.1%
Swiss Yodeler, Ca.	41	16	39.0%
◆Trippi, Fl.	37	16	43.2%
Vicar, Ky.	30	16	53.3%

Leading Juvenile Sires by Number of Wins in North America in 2005

Sire	Strs	Wnrs	Wins
◆City Zip, Ky.	39	20	30
Valid Expectations, Tx.	43	23	26
◆Songandaprayer, Ky.	36	18	25
◆Forest Camp, Ky.	28	15	24
◆El Corredor, Ky.	34	15	23
Exploit, Kor	30	15	23
More Than Ready, Ky.	45	19	23
Souvenir Copy, Ca.	28	16	23
Catienus, N.Y.	31	14	22
Chimes Band, Dead	21	13	22
Fortunate Prospect, Pens	23	16	22
Gilded Time, Ky.	43	18	22
Louis Quatorze, Md.	53	18	22
Distorted Humor, Ky.	33	13	21
Lord Carson, Dead	34	13	21
Stormy Atlantic, Ky.	43	15	21

Leading Juvenile Sires by Number of Stakes Winners in 2005

Sire	Strs	Wnrs	SWs	SWins
◆Successful Appeal, Ky.	22	15	6	12
Distorted Humor, Ky.	33	13	5	6
Favorite Trick, N.M.	23	11	4	4
Forestry, Ky.	32	14	4	4
Thunder Gulch, Ky.	44	13	4	6
Dixie Union, Ky.	33	12	3	4
Exploit, Kor	30	15	3	4
Hennessy, Ky.	30	12	3	4
Indian Charlie, Ky.	20	11	3	3
Langfuhr, Ky.	30	10	3	5
Precise End, Jpn	21	13	3	3
Saint Ballado, Dead	28	10	3	4
Snowbound, Wa.	10	6	3	3
◆Songandaprayer, Ky.	36	18	3	6

Leading Juvenile Sires by Number of Graded Stakes Winners in North America in 2005

Sire	Strs	Wnrs	GSWs	GSWins
Dixie Union, Ky.	33	12	2	2
Giant's Causeway, Ky.	37	12	2	3
◆Songandaprayer, Ky.	36	18	2	3
Arch, Ky.	13	7	1	1
Benchmark, Ca.	12	6	1	2
◆Black Minnaloushe, Ky.	33	9	1	1
◆Broken Vow, Ky.	40	13	1	2
Carson City, Dead	40	13	1	1
Catienus, N.Y.	31	14	1	1
Distorted Humor, Ky.	33	13	1	1
◆Ecton Park, Ky.	30	13	1	2
◆El Corredor, Ky.	34	15	1	2
Exploit, Kor	30	15	1	1
◆Forest Camp, Ky.	28	15	1	1
Forestry, Ky.	32	14	1	1
Gulch, Ky.	24	5	1	1
Hennessy, Ky.	30	12	1	1
Hesabull, Ar.	3	1	1	1
Lemon Drop Kid, Ky.	31	10	1	1
Matty G, Ky.	20	7	1	1
Mr. Greeley, Ky.	40	15	1	1
Montbrook, Fl.	33	13	1	1
Real Quiet, Pa.	27	8	1	1
Stephen Got Even, Ky.	16	7	1	2
Storm Cat, Ky.	24	10	1	2
Stormy Atlantic, Ky.	43	15	1	1
Tale of the Cat, Ky.	38	14	1	1
Thunder Gulch, Ky.	44	13	1	1
◆Tiznow, Ky.	30	10	1	3
Wild Wonder, Dead	15	3	1	1

Leading Freshman Sires by Progeny Earnings in North America in 2005

Earnings in North America only for stallions represented by at least one starter in North America in 2005, regardless of where the stallion stands or stood. ◆ Denotes freshman sire.

Sire	Strs	Wnrs	SWs	Leading Earner (Earnings)	Total Earnings
◆Tiznow, Ky.	30	10	1	Folklore ($927,500)	$1,260,442
◆El Corredor, Ky.	34	15	2	Adieu ($554,470)	1,197,357
◆City Zip, Ky.	39	20	2	Little Miss Zip ($130,145)	1,064,275
◆Songandaprayer, Ky.	36	18	3	Stolen Prayer ($211,230)	1,056,247
◆Broken Vow, Ky.	40	13	1	Private Vow ($382,508)	774,222
◆Forest Camp, Ky.	28	15	2	Your Tent Or Mine ($173,250)	768,920
◆Exchange Rate, Fl.	28	11	1	Blazing Rate ($351,300)	741,116
◆Ecton Park, Ky.	30	13	2	French Park ($243,761)	709,579
◆Trippi, Fl.	37	16	0	Cab ($83,382)	654,386
◆Delaware Township, Fl.	33	10	2	Electrify ($131,800)	547,672
◆Five Star Day, Ky.	20	9	1	Within Reason ($86,005)	470,671
◆Prime Timber, N.Y.	33	11	1	Cinderella's Dream ($133,600)	422,519
◆Put It Back, Fl.	16	8	1	In Summation ($285,800)	422,110
◆Perigee Moon, On.	24	6	1	Perigee Girl ($116,114)	411,737
◆Snuck In, Fl.	33	15	0	Full In ($45,180)	393,161
◆Freud, N.Y.	21	9	0	My Interpretation ($63,345)	381,950
◆Aptitude, Ky.	34	11	0	Amandatude ($51,700)	361,175
◆Black Minnaloushe, Ky.	33	9	1	Stream Cat ($153,670)	354,396
◆Vision and Verse, Ky.	24	9	0	Acceleration ($93,728)	348,734
◆Brahms, Ky.	30	11	2	Test Boy ($92,300)	339,873
◆Trajectory, On.	14	5	2	Silent Course ($68,274)	332,758
◆Monarchos, Ky.	18	5	2	Fifth Avenue ($109,900)	311,742
◆King Cugat, Ky.	17	4	2	Seaside Retreat ($163,632)	302,847
◆Luftikus, W.V.	20	8	2	Shesagrumptoo ($58,252)	287,917
◆One Way Love, On.	15	9	0	Initforthemoney ($73,936)	273,793
◆Albert the Great, Ky.	37	15	0	Motion ($38,004)	271,123
◆B L's Appeal, Fl.	15	9	0	B L's a Runner ($58,850)	234,155
◆Talk Is Money, Ky.	21	9	0	Domestic Oil ($35,011)	186,717
◆Flame Thrower, Fl.	21	7	0	Fletchers Cove ($26,400)	180,605
◆Mass Market, B.C.	13	5	2	Miss Me Not ($66,449)	179,520
◆Mojave Moon, Md.	24	8	0	Mieszko ($43,990)	170,136
◆Disco Rico, Md.	14	4	2	Pure Disco ($78,155)	165,887
◆Point Given, Ky.	16	2	0	Great Point ($38,254)	153,863
◆Casanova Star, P.R.	4	3	1	Yosolita ($127,620)	144,414
◆Cloud Hopping, Fl.	12	6	0	Mickees Tornado ($36,870)	134,074
◆Royal Cat, Ca.	7	4	0	Aloha Mangos Kitty ($49,883)	121,971
◆Island Storm, Mi.	3	1	1	Weatherstorm ($98,494)	105,529
◆Weekend Cruise, Fl.	12	5	0	Cruisinwithcharlie ($26,490)	101,954
◆Pikepass, Ky.	15	6	0	Turnpike ($22,875)	100,712
◆Globalize, Ca.	9	4	0	Princess Kinzie ($43,065)	99,755
◆Liberty Gold, Wa.	9	4	1	Cinderella Liberty ($56,158)	99,574
◆Minardi, Ky.	11	3	0	Cedar Fever ($31,711)	97,047
◆Sailor's Warning, Dead	7	1	0	Highland Lass ($44,748)	92,904
◆Dome, N.M.	16	4	0	Flyingdome ($28,081)	92,047
◆Billions, P.R.	10	6	0	Dona Ruz ($36,320)	88,015
◆Dixie Dot Com, Ca.	9	4	0	Moon Over Hemet ($26,496)	82,081
◆Castine, W.V.	6	1	1	Cross Creek Rosie ($72,713)	81,051
◆Shot of Gold, Mn.	8	4	0	Shot of Silver ($20,998)	78,288
◆Not Impossible (Ire), On.	5	1	0	Chickenonastikbaby ($54,061)	75,712
◆Coastal Storm, Pa.	9	3	0	All Show No Go ($24,520)	72,400
◆Royal Strand (Ire), La.	7	2	0	Royal Madame ($33,080)	62,656
◆Madraar, Ca.	8	1	0	Arabian Star ($51,142)	58,332
◆Cape Cod, P.R.	2	2	0	Capote Kid ($46,146)	57,980
◆Mancini, Ky.	6	1	1	Whatsitgonnatake ($46,830)	57,494
◆Jazz Club, Md.	8	4	0	Maddy's Our Girl ($13,110)	49,665
◆Lexicon, Fl.	6	3	0	Balius ($14,920)	48,890
◆Deputy Warlock, N.J.	5	1	0	Paola Vanessa ($37,312)	48,872
◆Man of the Night, La.	1	1	0	Night Doc ($47,360)	47,360
◆Mr. Nugget, N.J.	6	1	0	Moetown ($32,660)	46,162
◆Lake Austin, La.	4	2	0	Sassy Sarah ($23,123)	44,273
◆Hurricane Center, Ab.	8	2	0	Zip the Hurricane ($12,207)	40,470
◆Valid Belfast, La.	8	1	0	Seventy Two Reno ($21,270)	39,144
◆Fort La Roca, P.R.	8	3	0	Shaira Liz ($10,033)	37,994
◆Radio Star, Dead	9		0	Short Wave ($18,164)	37,878
◆King's Crown, P.R.	2	2	0	Palma Real ($18,392)	35,728

Leading Freshman Sires by Average Earnings per Runner in North America in 2005

Minimum of 10 Starters

Sire	Strs	Wnrs	Average
◆Tiznow, Ky.	30	10	$42,015
◆El Corredor, Ky.	34	15	35,216
◆Songandaprayer, Ky.	36	18	29,340
◆Forest Camp, Ky.	28	15	27,461
◆City Zip, Ky.	39	20	27,289
◆Exchange Rate, Fl.	28	11	26,468
◆Put It Back, Fl.	16	8	26,382
◆Trajectory, On.	14	5	23,768
◆Ecton Park, Ky.	30	13	23,653
◆Five Star Day, Ky.	20	9	23,534
◆Broken Vow, Ky.	40	13	19,356
◆One Way Love, On.	15	9	18,253
◆Freud, N.Y.	21	9	18,188
◆King Cugat, Ky.	17	4	17,815
◆Trippi, Fl.	37	16	17,686
◆Monarchos, Ky.	18	5	17,319
◆Perigee Moon, On.	24	6	17,156
◆Delaware Township, Fl.	33	10	16,596
◆B L's Appeal, Fl.	15	9	15,610
◆Vision and Verse, Ky.	24	9	14,531
◆Luftikus, W.V.	20	8	14,396
◆Mass Market, B.C.	13	5	13,809
◆Prime Timber, N.Y.	33	11	12,804
◆Snuck In, Fl.	33	15	11,914
◆Disco Rico, Md.	14	4	11,849
◆Brahms, Ky.	30	11	11,329
◆Cloud Hopping, Fl.	12	6	11,173
◆Black Minnaloushe, Ky.	33	9	10,739
◆Aptitude, Ky.	34	11	10,623

Leading Freshman Sires by Median Earnings in North America in 2005

Minimum of 10 Starters

Sire	Strs	Wnrs	Median
◆One Way Love, On.	15	9	$13,773
◆City Zip, Ky.	39	20	12,900
◆B L's Appeal, Fl.	15	9	11,745
◆Trippi, Fl.	37	16	11,638
◆Freud, N.Y.	21	9	11,050
◆Trajectory, On.	14	5	10,502
◆Songandaprayer, Ky.	36	18	9,585
◆Five Star Day, Ky.	20	9	9,525
◆Forest Camp, Ky.	28	15	9,373
◆El Corredor, Ky.	34	15	9,350
◆Ecton Park, Ky.	30	13	8,025
◆Exchange Rate, Fl.	28	11	7,950
◆Luftikus, W.V.	20	8	7,777
◆Tiznow, Ky.	30	10	7,260
◆Snuck In, Fl.	33	15	7,124
◆Cloud Hopping, Fl.	12	6	7,093
◆Broken Vow, Ky.	40	13	6,805
◆Aptitude, Ky.	34	11	6,660
◆Delaware Township, Fl.	33	10	6,490
◆Mass Market, B.C.	13	5	6,379
◆Billions, P.R.	10	6	6,165
◆Flame Thrower, Fl.	21	7	6,000
◆Monarchos, Ky.	18	5	5,996
◆Point Given, Ky.	16	2	5,445

Leading Freshman Sires by Number of Winners in North America in 2005

Sire	Strs	Wnrs	Wnrs/Strs
◆City Zip, Ky.	39	20	51.3%
◆Songandaprayer, Ky.	36	18	50.0%
◆Trippi, Fl.	37	16	43.2%
◆Albert the Great, Ky.	37	15	40.5%
◆El Corredor, Ky.	34	15	44.1%
◆Forest Camp, Ky.	28	15	53.6%
◆Snuck In, Fl.	33	15	45.5%
◆Broken Vow, Ky.	40	13	32.5%
◆Ecton Park, Ky.	30	13	43.3%
◆Aptitude, Ky.	34	11	32.4%
◆Brahms, Ky.	30	11	36.7%
◆Exchange Rate, Fl.	28	11	39.3%
◆Prime Timber, N.Y.	33	11	33.3%
◆Delaware Township, Fl.	33	10	30.3%
◆Tiznow, Ky.	30	10	33.3%
◆Black Minnaloushe, Ky.	33	9	27.3%
◆B L's Appeal, Fl.	15	9	60.0%
◆Five Star Day, Ky.	20	9	45.0%
◆Freud, N.Y.	21	9	42.9%
◆One Way Love, On.	15	9	60.0%
◆Talk Is Money, Ky.	21	9	42.9%
◆Vision and Verse, Ky.	24	9	37.5%
◆Luftikus, W.V.	20	8	40.0%
◆Mojave Moon, Md.	24	8	33.3%
◆Put It Back, Fl.	16	8	50.0%
◆Flame Thrower, Fl.	21	7	33.3%
◆Billions, P.R.	10	6	60.0%
◆Cloud Hopping, Fl.	12	6	50.0%
◆Perigee Moon, On.	24	6	25.0%
◆Pikepass, Ky.	15	6	40.0%

Leading Freshman Sires by Number of Wins in North America in 2005

Sire	Strs	Wnrs	Wins
◆City Zip, Ky.	39	20	30
◆Songandaprayer, Ky.	36	18	25
◆Forest Camp, Ky.	28	15	24
◆El Corredor, Ky.	34	15	23
◆Trippi, Fl.	37	16	20
◆Ecton Park, Ky.	30	13	18
◆Exchange Rate, Fl.	28	11	18
◆Snuck In, Fl.	33	15	18
◆Broken Vow, Ky.	40	13	17
◆Albert the Great, Ky.	37	15	16
◆Delaware Township, Fl.	33	10	16
◆Brahms, Ky.	30	11	15
◆B L's Appeal, Fl.	15	9	13
◆Prime Timber, N.Y.	33	11	13
◆Put It Back, Fl.	16	8	13
◆Tiznow, Ky.	30	10	13
◆Vision and Verse, Ky.	24	9	13
◆Aptitude, Ky.	34	11	12
◆Five Star Day, Ky.	20	9	11
◆Freud, N.Y.	21	9	11
◆Talk Is Money, Ky.	21	9	11

Leading Freshman Sires by Number of Stakes Winners and Wins in North America in 2005

Sire	Strs	Wnrs	SWs	SWins
◆Songandaprayer, Ky.	36	18	3	6
◆Brahms, Ky.	30	11	2	3
◆City Zip, Ky.	39	20	2	3
◆Delaware Township, Fl.	33	10	2	2
◆Disco Rico, Md.	14	4	2	2
◆Ecton Park, Ky.	30	13	2	3
◆El Corredor, Ky.	34	15	2	6
◆Forest Camp, Ky.	28	15	2	3
◆King Cugat, Ky.	17	4	2	2
◆Luftikus, W.V.	20	8	2	2
◆Mass Market, B.C.	13	5	2	2
◆Monarchos, Ky.	18	5	2	2
◆Trajectory, On.	14	5	2	3

Leading Freshman Sires by Number of Graded Stakes Winners and Wins in North America in 2005

Sire	Strs	Wnrs	GSWs	GSWins
◆Songandaprayer, Ky.	36	18	2	3
◆Black Minnaloushe, Ky.	33	9	1	1
◆Broken Vow, Ky.	40	13	1	2
◆Ecton Park, Ky.	30	13	1	2
◆El Corredor, Ky.	34	15	1	2
◆Forest Camp, Ky.	28	15	1	1
◆Tiznow, Ky.	30	10	1	3

Leading Broodmare Sires by Progeny Earnings in North America in 2005

Earnings in North America only for broodmare sires represented by at least one starter in North America in 2005, regardless of where the stallion stands or stood.

Sire	Strs	Wnrs	SWs	Leading Earner (Earnings)	Total Earnings
Dixieland Band, Ky.	321	188	18	Society Selection ($727,500)	$10,156,572
Mr. Prospector, Dead	240	119	19	Rock Hard Ten ($1,080,000)	9,565,959
Relaunch, Dead	322	171	16	Ghostzapper ($450,000)	7,308,904
Deputy Minister, Dead	319	169	18	Private Vow ($382,508)	7,272,307
Storm Cat, Ky.	236	127	12	Folklore ($927,500)	7,063,370
Quiet American, Ky.	85	43	6	Saint Liam ($3,696,960)	6,727,448
Pleasant Colony, Dead	234	132	7	Pleasant Home ($1,316,420)	6,659,662
Storm Bird, Dead	232	120	16	Sand Springs ($606,400)	6,615,622
Crafty Prospector, Ky.	286	164	14	Pampered Princess ($554,740)	6,443,992
Kris S., Dead	259	134	14	Sweet Catomine ($259,800)	5,854,701
Valid Appeal, Dead	304	160	5	Eyes On Eddy ($216,190)	5,709,298
Clever Trick, Dead	310	153	5	Sun King ($1,134,800)	5,640,852
Mt. Livermore, Pens	244	131	6	Super Frolic ($818,160)	5,470,241
Forty Niner, Jpn	165	106	14	Island Sand ($743,860)	5,449,876
Conquistador Cielo, Dead	291	164	8	Coin Silver ($230,410)	5,446,414
Seattle Slew, Dead	211	116	6	Offlee Wild ($452,500)	5,330,985
Cure the Blues, Dead	249	133	9	Miss Matched ($255,454)	5,284,869
Silver Deputy, Ky.	163	94	10	Roman Ruler ($890,000)	5,281,760
Affirmed, Dead	239	115	6	Honey Ryder ($910,980)	5,280,595
Miswaki, Dead	242	141	9	My Typhoon (Ire) ($379,629)	5,233,632
Bold Ruckus, Dead	229	134	14	Cee's Irish ($329,125)	5,157,633
Woodman, Ky.	227	116	7	Willow O Wisp ($478,250)	5,096,414
Wild Again, Pens	251	135	10	Mea Domina ($446,076)	5,080,099
Rahy, Ky.	190	101	16	Megahertz (GB) ($780,000)	5,043,674
Danzig, Dead	192	92	11	Wonder Again ($327,920)	5,001,930
Meadowlake, Dead	216	119	9	Henny Hughes ($644,820)	4,842,917
Seeking the Gold, Ky.	155	86	5	Riskaverse ($464,723)	4,612,975
Saratoga Six, N.M.	183	98	7	Madcap Escapade ($516,452)	4,515,207
Vice Regent, Dead	220	117	5	Jambalaya ($380,846)	4,453,029
Alydar, Dead	155	84	8	America Alive ($654,326)	4,444,127
Private Account, Dead	209	101	6	Smuggler ($558,800)	4,402,919
Broad Brush, Pens	196	114	8	Network ($257,960)	4,321,619
Phone Trick, Dead	237	124	12	Celtic Innis ($158,310)	4,235,346
Strawberry Road (Aus), Dead	163	95	10	Smoke Smoke Smoke ($199,922)	4,215,182
Carson City, Dead	171	105	11	Latenite Special ($224,820)	4,172,732
With Approval, Eng	132	68	7	Revved Up ($576,940)	4,170,606
Theatrical (Ire), Ky.	151	80	2	English Channel ($1,143,491)	4,155,967
Afleet, Jpn	162	84	7	Sweet Lips ($315,000)	3,987,087
Alleged, Dead	149	71	7	Angara (GB) ($668,108)	3,825,139
Red Ransom, Eng	170	92	7	Catcominatcha ($206,706)	3,798,029
Majestic Light, Dead	192	84	4	Artie Schiller ($1,448,000)	3,764,514
Runaway Groom, Ky.	202	105	3	Crown Point ($188,873)	3,674,659
Cox's Ridge, Dead	218	116	5	Puxa Saco ($125,935)	3,673,888
Star de Naskra, Dead	198	92	4	Sir Shackleton ($455,395)	3,658,038
Regal Classic, N.Y.	156	85	6	Le Cinquieme Essai ($259,044)	3,592,690
Halo, Dead	245	108	6	Indian Ocean ($176,460)	3,587,555
Black Tie Affair (Ire), W.V.	186	99	8	Nightmare Affair ($244,010)	3,573,897
Nureyev, Dead	119	58	9	Andujar ($254,090)	3,490,396
Lost Code, Dead	211	122	3	Code of Justice ($137,805)	3,469,479
Stop the Music, Dead	156	50	2	Giacomo ($1,846,876)	3,414,211
Stalwart, Dead	166	95	6	Sweet Talker ($582,963)	3,407,668
Dynaformer, Ky.	160	84	9	Sharp Lisa ($267,500)	3,401,708
Fortunate Prospect, Pens	182	95	5	Fort Prado ($245,888)	3,389,920
Devil's Bag, Dead	227	110	4	Unification ($173,557)	3,354,455
Capote, Pens	190	95	6	Our Madison ($145,608)	3,327,958
Lear Fan, Pens	148	77	3	Kitten's Joy ($369,880)	3,293,580
Allen's Prospect, Dead	189	102	7	Rocky Gulch ($257,520)	3,267,270
Known Fact, Dead	150	78	5	High Limit ($550,500)	3,147,014
Silver Hawk, Pens	137	72	4	Badge of Silver ($411,167)	3,134,776
Cryptoclearance, Ky.	192	105	4	Spite the Devil ($171,153)	3,116,007
Copelan, Dead	167	92	3	Purge ($315,700)	3,115,882
Fit to Fight, Pens	200	92	7	Greg's Gold ($288,480)	3,095,031
Gate Dancer, Dead	131	68	5	Dance Away Capote ($270,000)	3,075,466
Distinctive Pro, Dead	145	61	4	Sweet Symphony ($570,900)	3,058,231
Topsider, Dead	127	78	1	Wend ($383,900)	3,045,777

Leading Broodmare Sires by Average Earnings per Runner in North America in 2005

Minimum of 25 Starters

Sire	Strs	Wnrs	Average
Quiet American, Ky.	85	43	$79,146
Mr. Prospector, Dead	240	119	39,858
Dayjur, Ky.	77	44	37,379
A.P. Indy, Ky.	82	44	35,086
Citidancer, Pens	60	36	34,845
Fast Play, N.Y.	80	49	33,652
Forty Niner, Jpn	165	106	33,030
Silver Deputy, Ky.	163	94	32,403
Dixieland Band, Ky.	321	188	31,640
With Approval, Eng	132	68	31,596
Mari's Book, Dead	90	48	31,162
Summer Squall, Pens	93	48	30,913
Storm Cat, Ky.	236	127	29,930
Seeking the Gold, Ky.	155	86	29,761
Desert Wine, Dead	93	52	29,516
The Minstrel, Dead	86	36	29,374
Nureyev, Dead	119	58	29,331
Naskra, Dead	98	46	29,203
Alydar, Dead	155	84	28,672
Storm Bird, Dead	232	120	28,516
Roberto, Dead	63	25	28,504
Pleasant Colony, Dead	234	132	28,460

Leading Broodmare Sires by Median Earnings per Runner in North America in 2005

Minimum of 25 Starters

Sire	Strs	Wnrs	Median
Unbridled, Dead	107	71	$18,550
Carson City, Dead	171	105	16,450
Forty Niner, Jpn	165	106	16,330
Seeking the Gold, Ky.	155	86	14,620
A.P. Indy, Ky.	82	44	14,062
Marquetry, Ky.	79	48	13,800
Storm Cat, Ky.	236	127	13,235
Miswaki, Dead	242	141	13,170
Broad Brush, Pens	196	114	13,050
Rubiano, Dead	91	53	12,980
Quiet American, Ky.	85	43	12,775
Fast Play, N.Y.	80	49	12,738
Pentelicus, Dead	112	65	12,643
Regal Classic, N.Y.	156	85	12,577
Corporate Report, Ia.	71	48	12,548
Pleasant Colony, Dead	234	132	12,283
Silver Deputy, Ky.	163	94	12,134

Leading Broodmare Sires by Number of Winners in North America in 2005

Sire	Strs	Wnrs	Wnrs/Strs
Dixieland Band, Ky.	321	188	58.6%
Relaunch, Dead	322	171	53.1%
Deputy Minister, Dead	319	169	53.0%
Conquistador Cielo, Dead	291	164	56.4%
Crafty Prospector, Ky.	286	164	57.3%
Valid Appeal, Dead	304	160	52.6%
Clever Trick, Dead	310	153	49.4%
Miswaki, Dead	242	141	58.3%
Wild Again, Pens	251	135	53.8%
Bold Ruckus, Dead	229	134	58.5%
Kris S., Dead	259	134	51.7%
Cure the Blues, Dead	249	133	53.4%
Pleasant Colony, Dead	234	132	56.4%
Mt. Livermore, Pens	244	131	53.7%
Storm Cat, Ky.	236	127	53.8%
Phone Trick, Dead	237	124	52.3%
Lost Code, Dead	211	122	57.8%
Storm Bird, Dead	232	120	51.7%
Meadowlake, Dead	216	119	55.1%
Mr. Prospector, Dead	240	119	49.6%
Vice Regent, Dead	220	117	53.2%

Leading Broodmare Sires by Number of Wins in North America in 2005

Sire	Strs	Wnrs	Wins
Dixieland Band, Ky.	321	188	335
Relaunch, Dead	322	171	322
Crafty Prospector, Ky.	286	164	312
Valid Appeal, Dead	304	160	291
Deputy Minister, Dead	319	169	283
Conquistador Cielo, Dead	291	164	282
Clever Trick, Dead	310	153	252
Storm Cat, Ky.	236	127	252
Bold Ruckus, Dead	229	134	246
Pleasant Colony, Dead	234	132	243
Cure the Blues, Dead	249	133	237
Mt. Livermore, Pens	244	131	231
Wild Again, Pens	251	135	230
Lost Code, Dead	211	122	222
Miswaki, Dead	242	141	222
Kris S., Dead	259	134	217
Phone Trick, Dead	237	124	211

Leading Broodmare Sires by Number of Stakes Winners in North America in 2005

Sire	Strs	Wnrs	SWs	SWins
Mr. Prospector, Dead	240	119	19	27
Deputy Minister, Dead	319	169	18	24
Dixieland Band, Ky.	321	188	18	28
Rahy, Ky.	190	101	16	21
Relaunch, Dead	322	171	16	29
Storm Bird, Dead	232	120	16	22
Bold Ruckus, Dead	229	134	14	20
Crafty Prospector, Ky.	286	164	14	19
Forty Niner, Jpn	165	106	14	18
Kris S., Dead	259	134	14	17
Phone Trick, Dead	237	124	12	14
Storm Cat, Ky.	236	127	12	18
Carson City, Dead	171	105	11	15
Danzig, Dead	192	92	11	18
Silver Deputy, Ky.	163	94	10	19
Strawberry Road (Aus), Dead	163	95	10	15
Wild Again, Pens	251	135	10	13
Cure the Blues, Dead	249	133	9	10
Dynaformer, Ky.	160	84	9	12
Meadowlake, Dead	216	119	9	12
Miswaki, Dead	242	141	9	11
Nureyev, Dead	119	58	9	9
Time for a Change, Dead	169	77	9	12

Leading Broodmare Sires by Number of Graded Stakes Winners in North America in 2005

Sire	Strs	Wnrs	GSWs	GSWins
Mr. Prospector, Dead	240	119	12	17
Dixieland Band, Ky.	321	188	8	9
Storm Bird, Dead	232	120	6	8
With Approval, Eng	132	68	5	6
Deputy Minister, Dead	319	169	4	5
Forty Niner, Jpn	165	106	4	5
Rahy, Ky.	190	101	4	7
Saratoga Six, N.M.	183	98	4	6
Danzig, Dead	192	92	3	4
Mt. Livermore, Pens	244	131	3	4
Nijinsky II, Dead	115	61	3	3
Private Account, Dead	209	101	3	5
Quiet American, Ky.	85	43	3	7
Seattle Slew, Dead	211	116	3	4
Seeking the Gold, Ky.	155	86	3	3
Septieme Ciel, Fr	74	35	3	4
Silver Deputy, Ky.	163	94	3	5
Silver Hawk, Pens	137	72	3	5
Star de Naskra, Dead	198	92	3	4
Storm Cat, Ky.	236	127	3	6

Leading Worldwide Sires by 2005 Earnings

Worldwide earnings for stallions represented by one starter in any of the following jurisdictions: United States, Canada, Puerto Rico, England, Ireland, France, Italy, Germany, United Arab Emirates, Saudi Arabia, Australia, Brazil, Argentina, Japan, and Hong Kong.

Sire, YOB, Sire	Loc	2005 Stud Fee	Strs	Wnrs	SWs/Stk Wins	Leading Earner (Earnings)	Progeny Earnings
SUNDAY SILENCE, 86, by Halo	Dead		493	214	32/46	Deep Impact ($6,123,911)	$85,476,277
DANEHILL, 86, by Danzig	Dead		474	219	47/71	Elvstroem ($1,375,790)	25,192,406
BRIAN'S TIME, 85, by Roberto	Jpn	N/A	253	96	6/9	Time Paradox ($3,186,526)	25,015,406
FUJI KISEKI, 92, by Sunday Silence	Jpn	N/A	319	122	6/10	Kane Hekili ($2,813,092)	20,967,888
END SWEEP, 91, by Forty Niner	Dead		326	154	9/17	Rhein Kraft ($3,287,592)	18,854,236
DANCE IN THE DARK, 93, by Sunday Silence	Jpn	N/A	264	60	5/5	Win Glanz ($913,521)	15,920,008
SAKURA BAKUSHIN O, 89, by Sakura Yutaka O		N/A	206	73	3/4	She is Tosho ($771,116)	15,734,343
SPECIAL WEEK, 95, by Sunday Silence		N/A	198	74	3/5	Cesario (Jpn) ($2,511,053)	15,089,056
TAIKI SHUTTLE, 94, by Devil's Bag	Jpn	N/A	138	56	5/7	Meisho Bowler ($1,870,744)	12,488,109
EL CONDOR PASA, 95, by Kingmambo	Dead		178	61	2/2	Tokai Trick ($677,514)	12,008,989
AFLEET, 84, by Mr. Prospector	Jpn	N/A	172	54	1/3	Saqalat ($1,534,022)	11,764,408
FRENCH DEPUTY, 92, by Deputy Minister	Jpn	$58,590	222	95	2/4	Lailaps ($830,556)	11,083,805
FORTY NINER, 85, by Mr. Prospector	Jpn	N/A	144	45	7/8	Utopia ($1,040,458)	11,013,135
BUBBLE GUM FELLOW, 93, by Sunday Silence	Jpn	N/A	229	61	2/2	Meiner Bowknot ($689,354)	10,993,929
ZABEEL, 86, by *Sir Tristram	NZ	$68,220	194	91	11/21	Vengeance Of Rain ($3,890,974)	10,485,411
SAINT BALLADO, 89, by Halo	Dead		180	89	13/23	Saint Liam ($3,696,960)	10,409,467
HENNESSY, 93, by Storm Cat	Ky.	$35,000	312	138	12/15	Sunrise Bacchus ($1,080,769)	9,922,511
DISTORTED HUMOR, 93, by Forty Niner	Ky.	$60,000	212	116	18/25	Flower Alley ($2,435,200)	9,129,393
KINGMAMBO, 90, by Mr. Prospector	Ky.	$300,000	174	62	7/15	Alkaased ($2,650,290)	8,760,902
MONTJEU (IRE), 96, by Sadler's Wells	Ire	$61,051	161	60	11/19	Hurricane Run ($2,765,603)	8,633,199
FUSAICHI CONCORDE, 93, by Caerleon	Jpn	N/A	126	30	3/6	Blue Concorde ($1,714,571)	8,198,571
DYNAFORMER, 85, by Roberto	Ky.	$75,000	158	75	12/16	Dynever ($1,231,730)	8,089,508
DESERT KING, 94, by Danehill	Aus	$6,886	274	92	10/19	=Makybe Diva (GB) ($4,047,686)	8,084,821
SINGSPIEL (IRE), 92, by In the Wings (GB)	Eng	N/A	213	95	18/24	=Asakusa Den'en (GB) ($1,982,644)	8,063,406
EL PRADO (IRE), 89, by Sadler's Wells	Ky.	$100,000	176	97	12/18	Borrego ($1,536,600)	8,030,474
A.P. INDY, 89, by Seattle Slew	Ky.	$300,000	187	88	16/21	Suave ($624,900)	8,000,004
STORM CAT, 83, by Storm Bird	Ky.	$500,000	138	72	17/19	Seeking the Dia ($1,427,828)	7,779,955
ROYAL ACADEMY, 87, by Nijinsky II	Ky.	$17,500	374	167	22/24	Bullish Luck ($1,780,235)	7,693,427
MACHIAVELLIAN, 87, by Mr. Prospector	Dead		190	84	12/16	Grass Bomber ($1,254,949)	7,420,672
WILD RUSH, 94, by Wild Again	Jpn	$48,923	165	89	11/19	Personal Rush ($886,088)	7,210,395
LANGFUHR, 92, by Danzig	Ky.	$30,000	329	171	13/22	Jambalaya ($380,846)	7,206,051
SEEKING THE GOLD, 85, by Mr. Prospector	Ky.	$125,000	122	64	11/15	Pleasant Home ($1,316,420)	7,076,525
GIANT'S CAUSEWAY, 97, by Storm Cat	Ky.	$200,000	187	79	10/15	Shamardal ($1,572,090)	7,003,029
DEVIL HIS DUE, 89, by Devil's Bag	Ky.	$10,000	193	104	7/9	Roses in May ($3,695,000)	6,911,112
THUNDER GULCH, 92, by Gulch	Ky.	$40,000	340	143	9/11	Tsurumaru Bakushin ($334,262)	6,831,182
STRAVINSKY, 96, by Nureyev	Jpn	$25,000	230	101	9/18	Serenade Rose ($773,737)	6,698,716
FUSAICHI PEGASUS, 97, by Mr. Prospector	Ky.	$150,000	177	76	11/13	Roman Ruler ($890,000)	6,696,655
MAYANO TOP GUN, 92, by Brian's Time	Jpn	N/A	119	32	0/0	Top Gun Joe ($671,456)	6,605,072
SPINNING WORLD, 93, by Nureyev	Ire	$16,959	226	96	3/4	=Spinning Noir (Jpn) ($622,576)	6,553,871
TALE OF THE CAT, 94, by Storm Cat	Ky.	$65,000	214	106	9/11	Glamour Puss ($441,637)	6,448,399
HONOUR AND GLORY, 93, by Relaunch	Ky.	$15,000	325	163	5/8	Blues and Royals ($1,200,000)	6,424,936
MEJIRO RYAN, 87, by Amber Shadai		N/A	124	24	1/1	Best Album ($402,219)	6,383,571
JADE ROBBERY, 87, by Mr. Prospector	Dead		188	60	1/1	Blue Tornade ($704,946)	6,248,387
SMART STRIKE, 92, by Mr. Prospector	Ky.	$35,000	145	80	13/24	English Channel ($1,143,491)	6,245,144
PEINTRE CELEBRE, 94, by Nureyev	Ire	$40,701	217	80	6/9	Pride ($854,290)	6,232,447
COMMANDER IN CHIEF, 90, by Dancing Brave	Jpn	N/A	170	31	0/0	Thaw Your Frost ($528,096)	6,194,024
REDOUTE'S CHOICE, 96, by Danehill		$172,150	167	73	11/17	Lotteria ($732,855)	6,151,032
SADLER'S WELLS, 81, by Northern Dancer	Ire	N/A	262	91	21/26	Powerscourt (GB) ($711,355)	6,097,838
DEHERE, 91, by Deputy Minister	Ky.	$24,413	158	62	2/2	Mirror Mirror ($442,912)	5,981,511
TIMBER COUNTRY, 92, by Woodman	Jpn	N/A	130	35	5/9	Hishi Atlas ($1,085,952)	5,956,521
TWINING, 91, by Forty Niner	Jpn	N/A	156	68	2/2	Taiki Zillion ($406,727)	5,733,713
PULPIT, 94, by A.P. Indy	Ky.	$60,000	122	67	10/15	Pit Fighter ($640,750)	5,665,291
GRAND LODGE, 91, by Chief's Crown	Dead		443	147	5/11	Symboli Gran ($1,277,776)	5,639,186
UNBRIDLED'S SONG, 93, by Unbridled	Ky.	$125,000	218	111	13/16	Eurosilver ($247,450)	5,583,366
CARSON CITY, 87, by Mr. Prospector	Dead		187	95	11/13	Position One ($357,257)	5,469,272
SAKURA LAUREL, 91, by Rainbow Quest	Jpn	N/A	89	16	1/2	Sakura Century ($1,381,623)	5,468,743
GRAND SLAM, 95, by Gone West	Ky.	$85,000	222	100	6/7	Limehouse ($482,998)	5,442,507
TOKAI TEIO, 88, by Symboli Rudolf (Jpn)		N/A	96	20	1/1	Strong Blood ($902,928)	5,403,673
BELONG TO ME, 89, by Danzig	Ky.	$25,000	215	114	8/9	Jack Sullivan ($620,523)	5,337,628
GENUINE, 92, by Sunday Silence	Jpn	N/A	126	27	1/1	Don Cool ($995,509)	5,295,353
HELISSIO, 93, by Fairy King	Eng	$11,511	132	34	0/0	Thor Hammer ($478,824)	5,244,652
GRASS WONDER, 95, by Silver Hawk	Jpn	N/A	148	36	1/1	Sakura Mega Wonder ($434,399)	5,174,201
FLYING SPUR, 92, by Danehill		$25,823	286	127	9/12	Jet Spur ($290,631)	5,077,210
GILDED TIME, 90, by Timeless Moment	Ky.	$17,500	247	125	10/13	Barely a Moment ($420,802)	4,987,064
HOLY BULL, 91, by Great Above	Ky.	$15,000	139	58	6/8	Giacomo ($1,846,876)	4,972,882

Leading General Sire by Year

Year	General Sire	Earnings
2005	Saint Ballado	$10,409,467
2004	Elusive Quality	10,865,792
2003	Kris S.	11,497,747
2002	Dehere	9,337,302
2001	Danehill	13,542,612
2000	Storm Cat	9,269,521
1999	Storm Cat	10,383,259
1998	Deputy Minister	8,526,094
1997	Deputy Minister	8,581,511
1996	Palace Music	5,231,734
1995	Sadler's Wells	5,862,410
1994	Broad Brush	5,397,181
1993	Danzig	5,082,552
1992	Danzig	6,932,569
1991	Danzig	6,997,402
1990	Alydar	6,661,455
1989	Halo	7,525,638
1988	Mr. Prospector	9,575,605
1987	Mr. Prospector	5,877,385
1986	Lyphard	4,045,447
1985	Buckaroo	4,145,272
1984	Seattle Slew	5,361,259
1983	Halo	2,773,637
1982	His Majesty	2,675,823
1981	Nodouble	2,499,946
1980	Raja Baba	2,483,352
1979	Exclusive Native	2,872,605
1978	Exclusive Native	1,969,867
1977	Dr. Fager	1,593,079
1976	What a Pleasure	1,622,159
1975	What a Pleasure	2,011,878
1974	T. V. Lark	1,242,000
1973	Bold Ruler	1,488,622
1972	Round Table	1,199,933
1971	Northern Dancer	1,288,580
1970	Hail to Reason	1,400,839
1969	Bold Ruler	1,357,144
1968	Bold Ruler	1,988,427
1967	Bold Ruler	2,249,272
1966	Bold Ruler	2,306,523
1965	Bold Ruler	1,091,924
1964	Bold Ruler	1,457,156
1963	Bold Ruler	917,531
1962	*Nasrullah	1,474,831
1961	*Ambiorix	936,976
1960	*Nasrullah	1,419,683
1959	*Nasrullah	1,434,543
1958	*Princequillo	1,394,540
1957	*Princequillo	1,698,427
1956	*Nasrullah	$1,462,413
1955	*Nasrullah	1,433,660
1954	*Heliopolis	1,406,638
1953	Bull Lea	1,155,846
1952	Bull Lea	1,630,847
1951	Count Fleet	1,160,847
1950	*Heliopolis	852,292
1949	Bull Lea	991,842
1948	Bull Lea	1,334,027
1947	Bull Lea	1,259,718
1946	*Mahmoud	638,025
1945	War Admiral	591,352
1944	Chance Play	431,100
1943	*Bull Dog	372,706
1942	Equipoise	437,141
1941	*Blenheim II	378,981
1940	*Sir Gallahad III	305,610
1939	*Challenger II	316,281
1938	*Sickle	327,822
1937	The Porter	292,262
1936	*Sickle	209,800
1935	Chance Play	191,465
1934	*Sir Gallahad III	180,165
1933	*Sir Gallahad III	136,428
1932	Chatterton	210,040
1931	*St. Germans	315,585
1930	*Sir Gallahad III	422,200
1929	*Chicle	289,123
1928	High Time	307,631
1927	Fair Play	361,518
1926	Man o' War	408,137
1925	Sweep	237,564
1924	Fair Play	296,102
1923	The Finn	285,759
1922	*McGee	222,491
1921	Celt	206,167
1920	Fair Play	269,102
1919	*Star Shoot	197,233
1918	Sweep	139,057
1917	*Star Shoot	131,674
1916	*Star Shoot	138,163
1915	Broomstick	94,387
1914	Broomstick	99,043
1913	Broomstick	76,009
1912	*Star Shoot	79,973
1911	*Star Shoot	53,895
1910	Kingston	85,220
1909	Ben Brush	75,143
1908	Hastings	154,061
1907	Commando	$270,345
1906	*Meddler	151,243
1905	Hamburg	153,160
1904	*Meddler	222,555
1903	*Ben Strome	106,965
1902	Hastings	113,865
1901	Sir Dixon	165,682
1900	Kingston	116,368
1899	*Albert	95,975
1898	Hanover	118,590
1897	Hanover	122,374
1896	Hanover	86,853
1895	Hanover	106,908
1894	*Sir Modred	134,318
1893	Himyar	249,502
1892	Iroquois	183,026
1891	Longfellow	189,334
1890	*St. Blaise	189,005
1889	*Rayon d'Or	175,877
1888	Glenelg	130,746
1887	Glenelg	120,031
1886	Glenelg	114,088
1885	Virgil	73,235
1884	Glenelg	98,862
1883	*Billet	89,998
1882	*Bonnie Scotland	103,475
1881	*Leamington	139,219
1880	*Bonnie Scotland	135,700
1879	*Leamington	70,837
1878	Lexington	50,198
1877	*Leamington	41,700
1876	Lexington	90,570
1875	*Leamington	64,518
1874	Lexington	51,889
1873	Lexington	71,565
1872	Lexington	71,515
1871	Lexington	109,095
1870	Lexington	120,360
1869	Lexington	56,375
1868	Lexington	68,340
1867	Lexington	54,030
1866	Lexington	92,725
1865	Lexington	58,750
1864	Lexington	28,440
1863	Lexington	14,235
1862	Lexington	9,700
1861	Lexington	22,425
1860	Revenue	49,450

Leading Juvenile Sire by Year

Year	Juvenile Sire	Earnings
2005	Giant's Causeway	$1,642,151
2004	Storm Cat	1,927,589
2003	Tale of the Cat	2,077,206
2002	Storm Cat	2,540,238
2001	Hennessy	1,766,695
2000	Honour and Glory	1,436,584
1999	Storm Cat	1,570,026
1998	Storm Cat	1,686,995
1997	Phone Trick	1,737,764
1996	Capote	2,756,558
1995	Storm Cat	1,281,030
1994	Woodman	1,303,362
1993	Storm Cat	1,567,979
1992	Storm Cat	1,729,366
1991	Blushing Groom (Fr)	1,295,629
1990	Woodman	1,310,633
1989	Mr. Prospector	1,514,223
1988	Seattle Slew	946,433
1987	Mr. Prospector	1,566,919
1986	Rajab	950,335
1985	Fappiano	1,232,408
1984	Danzig	2,146,530
1983	Alydar	$1,136,063
1982	Olden Times	948,900
1981	Hoist the Flag	680,753
1980	Raja Baba	807,335
1979	Mr. Prospector	529,665
1978	Secretariat	600,617
1977	In Reality	432,596
1976	Raja Baba	419,872
1975	What a Pleasure	611,071
1974	What a Pleasure	387,748
1973	Raise a Native	311,002
1972	Bold Ruler	541,990
1971	First Landing	551,120
1970	Hail to Reason	473,244
1969	Prince John	418,183
1968	Bold Ruler	609,243
1967	Bold Ruler	1,126,844
1966	Bold Ruler	941,493
1965	Tom Fool	592,871
1964	Bold Ruler	967,814
1963	Bold Ruler	343,585
1962	*Nasrullah	574,231
1961	Bryan G.	$428,810
1960	*My Babu	437,240
1959	Determine	413,765
1958	*Turn-to	463,280
1957	Jet Jewel	360,402
1956	*Nasrullah	422,573
1955	*Nirgal	293,800
1954	*Nasrullah	625,692
1953	Roman	550,966
1952	Polynesian	341,730
1951	Menow	274,700
1950	War Relic	272,182
1949	Roman	227,604
1948	War Admiral	346,260
1947	Bull Lea	420,940
1946	*Mahmoud	283,983
1945	*Sickle	183,510
1944	Case Ace	230,525
1943	*Bull Dog	178,344
1942	*Bull Dog	221,332

Leading Freshman Sire by Year

Year	Freshman Sire	Earnings
2005	Tiznow	$1,376,265
2004	Successful Appeal	1,727,557
2003	Stravinsky	1,271,620
2002	Grand Slam	1,403,880
2001	Valid Expectations	1,397,911
2000	Honour and Glory	1,436,584
1999	Cherokee Run	1,369,126
1998	End Sweep	947,013
1997	Gilded Time	730,106
1996	Salt Lake	850,954
1995	Farma Way	818,043
1994	Red Ransom	$817,550
1993	Seeking the Gold	939,642
1992	Forty Niner	578,567
1991	Capote	1,185,886
1990	Woodman	1,310,633
1989	Secreto	584,023
1988	Chief's Crown	760,842
1987	Crafty Prospector	349,405
1986	Sportin' Life	781,754
1985	Fappiano	1,232,408
1984	Danzig	2,146,530
1983	Alydar	$1,136,063
1982	Seattle Slew	666,755
1981	Turn and Count	283,279
1980	Foolish Pleasure	536,783
1979	L'Enjoleur	201,116
1978	Mr. Prospector	309,168
1977	Roberto	359,285
1976	Raja Baba	419,872
1975	Al Hattab	217,630

Leading Broodmare Sire by Year

Year	Broodmare Sire	Earnings
2005	Mr. Prospector	$20,987,357
2004	Mr. Prospector	20,311,039
2003	Mr. Prospector	21,425,839
2002	Mr. Prospector	9,725,924
2001	Mr. Prospector	11,430,437
2000	Mr. Prospector	10,390,642
1999	Mr. Prospector	11,124,523
1998	Mr. Prospector	9,364,191
1997	Mr. Prospector	9,829,817
1996	Seattle Slew	9,105,905
1995	Seattle Slew	8,291,630
1994	Nijinsky II	7,606,160
1993	Nijinsky II	7,179,266
1992	Secretariat	7,345,089
1991	Northern Dancer	6,030,243
1990	*Grey Dawn II	6,211,259
1989	Buckpasser	10,111,605
1988	Buckpasser	7,593,450
1987	Hoist the Flag	5,516,181
1986	Prince John	4,468,468
1985	Speak John	5,187,865
1984	Buckpasser	5,111,391
1983	Buckpasser	$3,479,749
1982	Prince John	3,072,150
1981	Double Jay	3,453,131
1980	Prince John	3,423,135
1979	Prince John	2,856,004
1978	Crafty Admiral	2,298,048
1977	Double Jay	2,696,490
1976	*Princequillo	2,763,189
1975	Double Jay	2,233,642
1974	Olympia	2,292,178
1973	*Princequillo	3,079,810
1972	*Princequillo	2,717,859
1971	Double Jay	2,053,235
1970	*Princequillo	2,451,785
1969	*Princequillo	2,189,583
1968	*Princequillo	2,104,439
1967	*Princequillo	2,302,065
1966	*Princequillo	2,007,184
1965	Roman	2,394,944
1964	War Admiral	2,028,459
1963	Count Fleet	1,866,809
1962	War Admiral	1,654,396
1961	Bull Lea	$1,632,559
1960	Bull Lea	1,915,881
1959	Bull Lea	1,481,291
1958	Bull Lea	1,646,812
1957	*Mahmoud	1,593,782
1956	*Bull Dog	1,683,908
1955	*Sir Gallahad III	1,499,162
1954	*Bull Dog	1,780,267
1953	*Bull Dog	1,941,345
1952	*Sir Gallahad III	1,656,221
1951	*Sir Gallahad III	1,707,823
1950	*Sir Gallahad III	1,376,629
1949	*Sir Gallahad III	1,393,104
1948	*Sir Gallahad III	1,468,648
1947	*Sir Gallahad III	1,458,309
1946	*Sir Gallahad III	1,529,393
1945	*Sir Gallahad III	1,020,235
1944	*Sir Gallahad III	1,024,290
1943	*Sir Gallahad III	703,301
1942	*Chicle	533,572

Most Times as Leading General Sire (1830-2005)

16 Lexington (1861-'74, '76, '78)
8 Bold Ruler (1963-'69, '73)
*Glencoe (1847, '49-'50, '54-'58)
5 Bull Lea (1947-'49, '52-'53)
*Leviathan (1837-'39, '43, '48)
*Nasrullah (1955-'56, '59-'60, '62)
Sir Charles (1830-'33, '36)
*Star Shoot (1911-'12, '16-'17, '19)
4 Glenelg (1884, '86-'88)
Hanover (1895-'98)
*Leamington (1875, '77, '79, '81)
*Priam (1842, '44-'46)
*Sir Gallahad III (1930, '33-'34, '40)
3 Boston (1851-'53)
Broomstick (1913-'15)
Danzig (1991-'93)
Fair Play (1920, '24, '27)

Before 1860, leading sire was determined by number of wins.

Most Times as Leading Juvenile Sire (1942-2005)

7 Storm Cat (1992-'93, '95, '98-'99, 2002, '04)
6 Bold Ruler (1963-'64, '66-'68, '72)
3 Mr. Prospector (1979, '87, '89)
*Nasrullah (1954, '56, '62)
Woodman (1990, '94, '98)
2 *Bull Dog (1942-'43)
Raja Baba (1976, '80)
What a Pleasure (1974-'75)

Most Times as Leading Broodmare Sire (1942-2005)

12 *Sir Gallahad III (1939, 1943-'52, '55)
9 Mr. Prospector (1997-2005)
*Princequillo (1966-'70, '72-'73, '76)
4 Buckpasser (1983-'84, '88-'89)
Bull Lea (1958-'61)
Double Jay (1971, '75, '77, '81)
Prince John (1979-'80, '82, '86)

Most Times as Leading General Sire in Consecutive Years (1830-2005)

14 Lexington (1861-'74)
7 Bold Ruler (1963-'69)
5 *Glencoe (1854-'58)
4 Hanover (1895-'98)
Sir Charles (1830-'33)
3 Boston (1851-'53)
Broomstick (1913-'15)
Bull Lea (1947-'49)
Danzig (1991-'93)
Glenelg (1886-'88)
*Leviathan (1837-'39)
*Priam (1844-'46)
2 Bull Lea (1952-'53)
Deputy Minister (1997-'98)
Exclusive Native (1978-'79)
*Glencoe (1849-'50)
Mr. Prospector (1987-'88)
2 *Nasrullah (1955-'56)
*Nasrullah (1959-'60)
*Princequillo (1957-'58)
*Sir Gallahad III (1933-'34)
*Star Shoot (1911-'12)
*Star Shoot (1916-'17)

Before 1860, leading sire was determined by number of wins.

Most Times as Leading Juvenile Sire in Consecutive Years (1942-2005)

3 Bold Ruler (1966-'68)
2 Bold Ruler (1963-'64)
*Bull Dog (1942-'43)
Storm Cat (1992-'93)
Storm Cat (1998-'99)
What a Pleasure (1974-'75)

Most Times as Leading Broodmare Sire in Consecutive Years (1942-2005)

10 Sir Gallahad III (1943-'52)
9 Mr. Prospector (1997-2005)
5 *Princequillo (1966-'70)
4 Bull Lea (1958-'61)
2 Buckpasser (1983-'84)
Buckpasser (1988-'89)
*Bull Dog (1953-'54)
Nijinsky II (1993-'94)
Prince John (1979-'80)
*Princequillo (1972-'73)
Seattle Slew (1995-'96)

Profiles of Leading Sires

2005—SAINT BALLADO, 1989 dk. b. or br. h., Halo—Ballade, by *Herbager. Bred in Ontario by Windfields Farm. Full brother to champions Devil's Bag and Glorious Song. Sold for $90,000 at the 1990 Keeneland September yearling sale to Tartan Farms. Owned by Steve Herold, Robert J. Lothenbach, and trainer Clint C. Goodrich. 9-4-2-0, $302,820. At three, won the Arlington Classic S. (G2) and Sheridan S. (G3). Stood initially at Ocala Stud Farm in Florida and moved to Taylor Made Farm in Kentucky in 1998. Euthanized in 2002 due to effects of progressive cervical myelopathy. Through 2005, sire of 60 stakes winners (8.5%) from 717 foals, with progeny earnings of $44,374,457. Sire of 2005 Horse of the Year Saint Liam ($4,456,995), 2004 champion three-year-old filly and '05 older female Ashado ($3,931,440).

2004—ELUSIVE QUALITY, 1993 b. h., Gone West—Touch of Greatness, by Hero's Honor. Bred in Kentucky by Silver Springs Stud Farm Inc. and H. Costelloe. Raced in name of Sheikh Mohammed bin Rashid al Maktoum and his Darley operation. 20-9-3-2, $413,284. Half brother to stakes winner Rossini. Trained by Bill Mott, won 1998 Poker H. (G3), world record for mile on turf, 1:31.63; Jaipur H. (G3). Set seven-furlong track record at Gulfstream Park, 1:20.17, on dirt. Stands at Gainsborough Farm in Versailles, Kentucky, and shuttled to Australia in 2003 and 2004. Sire of at least 24 stakes winners (8% from foals), including at least seven group or graded stakes winners, with progeny earnings exceeding $20-million. Sire of Smarty Jones, 2004 champion three-year-old male, $7,613,155, and Elusive City, 2003 highweighted two-year-old on French Free Handicap. Substantial part of 2004 progeny earnings, $10,876,981, from Smarty Jones, who received a $5-million bonus from Oaklawn Park for winning the Rebel S., Arkansas Derby (G2), and Kentucky Derby (G1).

2003—KRIS S., 1977 dk. b. or br. h., Roberto—Sharp Queen, by *Princequillo. Bred in Florida by John Brunetti Jr.'s Red Oak Farm. Raced by estate of Lloyd Schunemann and partners. 5-3-1-0, $53,350. Won 1980 Bradbury S. Entered stud in 1982 at Joseph and Barbara LaCroix's Meadowbrook Farm in Florida; moved to Prestonwood Farm in Kentucky in 1994; acquired by WinStar Farm when it purchased Prestonwood's assets. To 2006, sire of 90 stakes winners (10% of foals), including 43 graded stakes winners, with total progeny earnings of $76,581,165. His four champions are: Symboli Kris S, 2002-'03 Horse of the Year in Japan, $8,401,282; Hollywood Wildcat, 1993 champion three-year-old filly, $1,432,160; Soaring Softly, 1999 champion turf female, $1,270,433; and Action This Day, 2003 champion two-year-old male, $817,200. Also sire of Kris Kin, winner of the 2003 Epsom Derby (Eng-G1). Sire of sires. Died in 2002.

2002—DEHERE, 1991 b. h., Deputy Minister—Sister Dot, by Secretariat. Bred in Kentucky by Robert E. Brennan's Due Process Stable. 9-6-2-0, $723,712. Champion two-year-old male in 1993. Trained by Reynaldo Nobles, swept Saratoga Race Course's three major juvenile races culminating with the Hopeful Stakes (G1); also won the Champagne Stakes (G1) at two. At three, won the Fountain of Youth Stakes (G2) but broke down before the Triple Crown races. Retired initially to Ashford Stud and sold to Japan in 1999. To 2006, sire of 55 stakes winners (7%), including multiple Grade 1 winner Take Charge Lady, 2000 Puerto Rican champion imported two-year-old colt Mi Amigo Guelo, and Belle Du Jour, highweighted two-year-old filly on the 1999 Australian Free Handicap.

2001—DANEHILL, 1986 b. h., Danzig—Razyana, by His Majesty. Bred in Kentucky by Juddmonte Farms. 9-4-1-2, $321,064. Highweighted sprinter at three on European Free Handicap. Retired to Coolmore Stud, Ireland, in 1990. From 1991 through 2001, shuttled annually to Coolmore Australia; in 2002, covered mares on Southern Hemisphere schedule in Ireland. Stood in Japan in 1996. Leading sire in Australia six times; leading sire in France 2001, '02. To 2006, sire of 319 stakes winners (13%) and 23 champions. Best runners: European highweights Rock of Gibraltar (Ire), Banks Hill (GB), Desert King, Mozart (Ire), Tiger Hill; North American champion Intercontinental (GB), Hong Kong Horse of the Year Fairy King Prawn; and Australian champions Dane Ripper, Danewin, Catbird, and Merlene. In 2001, set a single-season record with 48 stakes winners. Died May 13, 2003, at Coolmore.

2000, 1999—STORM CAT, 1983 dk. b. or br. h., Storm Bird—Terlingua, by Secretariat. Bred in Pennsylvania by W. T. Young Storage Inc., raced for W. T. Young. 8-4-3-0, $570,610. Won Young America Stakes (G1) and finished second by a nose to champion Tasso in 1985 Breeders' Cup Juvenile (G1). Entered stud in 1988 at Overbrook Farm in Kentucky for initial fee of $25,000; by 2002, stood for American high of $500,000. To 2006, sire of 144 stakes winners (13%), including North American champion Storm Flag Flying, European highweight Giant's Causeway, and major American winners Tabasco Cat, Cat Thief, and Sharp Cat. Led juvenile sire list a record seven times, 1992-'93, '95, '98-'99, 2002, '04.

1998, 1997—DEPUTY MINISTER, 1979 dk. b. or br. h., Vice Regent—Mint Copy, by Bunty's Flight. Bred in Canada by Mr. and Mrs. Morton Levy's Centurion Farms. 22-12-2-2, $696,964. Canadian Horse of the Year in 1981; Eclipse- and Sovereign Award-winning two-year-old male. Half-interest purchased by Kinghaven Farm midway through two-year-old season; purchased by Robert Brennan's Due Process Stable prior to 1982 season. Entered stud in 1984 at Windfields Farm Maryland; relocated in 1988 to Brookdale Farm in Kentucky. Sire of 86 stakes winners (8%) to 2006, including 12 millionaires. Best include Racing Hall of Fame member Go for Wand; two-time champion and filly triple crown winner Open Mind; 1993 champion juvenile male and 2002 leading sire Dehere; 1998 Breeders' Cup Classic (G1) winner Awesome Again. Broodmare sire of more than 125 stakes winners. Died September 10, 2004.

1996—PALACE MUSIC, 1981 ch. h., The Minstrel—Come My Prince, by Prince John. Bred in Kentucky by Mereworth Farm. Sold for $130,000 to Nelson Bunker Hunt at 1982 Keeneland July and raced for partnership of Hunt and Allen Paulson. 21-7-5-3, $918,700. Group 1 and Grade 1 turf stakes winner in England and North America. Stood one season at Hunt's Bluegrass Farm in Kentucky, then moved in 1988 to Paulson's Brookside Farm. Shuttled between Kentucky and New Zealand for several years before relocating permanently in 1991 to Australia, where he was pensioned in 2005. Was 1996 leading U.S. sire due to one horse—Cigar, a two-time Horse of the Year and leading American money winner ($9,999,815). Also sire of several important Australasian runners, including 1992 champion stayer Naturalism; also sire of South Africa two-year-old champion Palace Line. To 2006, sire of 33 stakes winners.

1995—SADLER'S WELLS, 1981 b. h., Northern Dancer—Fairy Bridge, by Bold Reason. Bred in Kentucky by Swettenham Stud and Partners. 11-6-3-0, $713,690. Winner of 1984 Irish Two Thousand Guineas (Ire-G1) and Eclipse Stakes (Eng-G1). Stands at Coolmore Stud in Ireland.

Leading sire in England and Ireland in 1990, 1992-2004, a modern-record 13 consecutive years; leading sire in France in '93, '99. To 2006, sire of 17 champions and 272 stakes winners (14%), including 148 group or graded winners. Best include champions High Chaparral (Ire), Montjeu (Ire), Galileo (Ire), Northern Spur (Ire), Old Vic, Barathea (Ire), Islington (Ire).

1994—BROAD BRUSH, 1983 b. h., Ack Ack—Hay Patcher, by Hoist the Flag. Bred in Maryland by Robert E. Meyerhoff and raced three seasons for Meyerhoff. 27-14-5-5, $2,656,793. Winner of Santa Anita Handicap (G1), Suburban Handicap (G1), etc. Syndicated and entered stud in 1988 at Gainesway Farm in Kentucky. To 2006, sire of 89 stakes winners (13%), including 2002 champion three-year-old filly Farda Amiga, 1994 Breeders' Cup Classic (G1) winner Concern, $4-million-earner Broad Appeal (in Japan), and 2001 North American Grade 1 winners Include and Pompeii. Pensioned December 1, 2004.

1993, 1991-'92—DANZIG, 1977 b. h., Northern Dancer—Pas de Nom, by Admiral's Voyage. Bred in Pennsylvania by Derry Meeting Farm and William S. Farish. Sold for $310,000 to Henryk de Kwiatkowski at the 1978 Saratoga yearling sale. 3-3-0-0, $32,400. Undefeated New York allowance winner before injury ended his career. Entered stud in 1981 at Claiborne Farm. To 2006, sire of at least 190 stakes winners (18%), including champions in U.S., Canada, Japan, England, France, Ireland, Spain, and United Arab Emirates. Best runners: 1984 two-year-old male champion Chief's Crown, two-time Breeders' Cup Mile (G1) winner Lure, and 1991 Canadian Triple Crown winner Dance Smartly. To 2006, broodmare sire of 132 stakes winners, including 2000 Kentucky Derby (G1) winner Fusaichi Pegasus. Died at Claiborne Farm on January 3, 2006.

1990—ALYDAR, 1975 ch. h, Raise a Native—Sweet Tooth, by On-and-On. Bred in Kentucky by Calumet Farm. 26-14-9-1, $957,195. Won 1978 Blue Grass Stakes (G1), Florida Derby (G1), etc.; second to Affirmed in all three 1978 Triple Crown races. Entered stud in 1980 at Calumet Farm and became leading American freshman sire of 1983. Sired 77 stakes winners (11%) in 11 crops, with career progeny earnings of $60,604,510. Best runners include Horses of the Year Alysheba (1988) and Criminal Type ('90), North American champions Easy Goer, Turkoman, and Althea, and 1991 Kentucky Derby (G1) winner Strike the Gold. Broodmare sire of 145 stakes winners and earners of $154-million to 2006. Died at age 15 at Calumet on November 15, 1990, following a leg injury of suspicious cause.

1989, 1983—HALO, 1969 dk. b. or br. h., Hail to Reason—Cosmah, by Cosmic Bomb. Bred in Kentucky by John R. Gaines. Purchased for $100,000 by Charles Engelhard at 1970 Keeneland July yearling sale. 31-9-8-5, $259,553. Won 1974 United Nations Handicap (G1). Sold for $600,000 to stand in England, but sale fell through upon discovery he was a cribber. Syndicated for $30,000 per share and retired in 1974 to Windfields Farm Maryland. In 1984, was sold based on $36-million valuation and moved to Stone Farm in Kentucky. Sire of 63 stakes winners (8%), including champion and Racing Hall of Fame member Sunday Silence, all-time leading sire in Japan; 1983 Kentucky Derby winner Sunny's Halo; and champions Glorious Song and Devil's Bag. Broodmare sire of more than 140 stakes winners. Pensioned in 1997 and died at Stone Farm on November 28, 2000, at age 31.

1988, 1987—MR. PROSPECTOR, 1970 b. h., Raise a Native—Gold Digger, by Nashua. Bred in Kentucky by Leslie Combs II. Sold for a sale-topping $220,000 at 1971 Keeneland July sale to Abraham I. "Butch" Savin, for whom he won the Gravesend and Whirlaway Handicaps and set a Gulfstream Park track record, six furlongs in 1:07⅘, in 1973. 14-7-4-2, $112,171. Retired in 1975 to Savin's Aisco Farm in Florida and was top freshman sire of '78. Moved to Claiborne Farm in Kentucky in 1981. Sired 180 stakes winners (15%) and 16 champions to 2006, including Gulch, Forty Niner, Conquistador Cielo, and Woodman. Broodmare sire of more than 300 stakes winners. Leading broodmare sire nine times. Died of peritonitis at Claiborne Farm on June 1, 1999, at age 29.

1986—LYPHARD, 1969 b. h., Northern Dancer—Goofed, by *Court Martial. Bred in Pennsylvania by Mrs. J. O. Burgwin. Sold for $35,000 as a weanling at 1969 Keeneland November sale; resold as a yearling in Ireland for $38,000. 12-6-1-0, $195,427. Became one of Europe's top milers, winning 1972 Prix de la Foret and Prix Jacques le Marois while racing for Mrs. Pierre Wertheimer. Retired in 1973 and stood five seasons in France, where he was twice leading sire and subsequently was twice leading broodmare sire. For 1978 season, moved to Gainesway Farm in Kentucky and syndicated. Sired 115 stakes winners (14%) and eight champions, including Manila, Dancing Brave, and Three Troikas (Fr). Broodmare sire of 206 stakes winners to 2006. Pensioned in 1996. Died June 10, 2005.

1985—BUCKAROO, 1975 b. h., Buckpasser—Stepping High, by No Robbery. Bred in Kentucky by Greentree Stud. 18-5-5-1, $138,604. Won 1978 Saranac (G2) and Peter Pan (G3) Stakes. Retired to Greentree in 1980. Sold privately in 1985 to Gary and Stephen Wolfson and moved to Happy Valley Farm in Florida. Relocated in 1991 to Florida Stallion Station and again in '92 to Bridlewood Farm near Ocala. Leading sire of 1985 due largely to Horse of the Year and Kentucky Derby (G1) winner Spend a Buck, who received a $2-million bonus for winning the Jersey Derby (G3). Also sired millionaires Roo Art and Lite the Fuse among 29 stakes winners from 17 crops. Died of kidney failure on July 30, 1996, at the University of Florida School of Veterinary Medicine at age 21.

1984—SEATTLE SLEW, 1974 dk. b. or br. h., Bold Reasoning—My Charmer, by Poker. Bred in Kentucky by Ben Castleman. Sold at 1975 Fasig-Tipton Kentucky July sale for $17,500 to partnership of Mickey and Karen Taylor and Jim and Sally Hill. 17-14-2-0, $1,208,726. Champion at two, three, and four, Horse of the Year at three; in 1977, became first to win American Triple Crown while undefeated. Retired in 1979 to Spendthrift Farm in Kentucky but later relocated to Three Chimneys Farm; moved to Hill 'n' Dale Farms shortly before his death. Sired 114 stakes winners (10%) through 2006, including Horse of the Year and top sire A.P. Indy, champions Slew o' Gold, Vindication, Surfside, Swale, Capote, and Landaluce. First to sire winners of $5-million in a single season (1984). Noted sire of sires. Broodmare sire of Cigar; twice leading broodmare sire; broodmare sire of 150 stakes winners, including nine champions, to 2006. Died on May 7, 2002, at Hill 'n' Dale in Kentucky, at age 28.

1982—HIS MAJESTY, 1968 b. h., *Ribot—Flower Bowl, by *Alibhai. Bred in Kentucky by Mr. and Mrs. John W. Galbreath. Full brother to Graustark. 22-5-6-3, $99,430. Only stakes victory was 1971 Everglades Stakes. Syndicated for $2-million valuation and retired in 1974 to his birthplace, Darby Dan Farm, where he remained throughout a 23-season stud career. Sired 59 stakes winners (9%) and champions in U.S., Italy, Canada, Panama, and Mexico. Best include 1981 champion and dual-classic winner Pleasant Colony, '91 grass champion Tight Spot, and $2-million earner Majesty's Prince. Maternal grandsire of leading international sire Danehill and 97 other stakes winners. Died at Darby Dan on September 21, 1995.

1981—NODOUBLE, 1965 ch. h., *Noholme II—Abla-Jay, by Double Jay. Bred in Arkansas by Gene Goff. 42-13-11-5, $846,749. Two-time champion handicap horse, 1969-'70; known as "Arkansas Traveler" because he won stakes in seven states. Winner of 1969 Santa Anita Handicap, '70 Metropolitan Handicap, etc. Retired in 1971 and stood at four different farms from California to Florida before moving in '86 to Three Chimneys Farm in Kentucky. Sired 91 stakes winners (14%), including two-time Canadian Horse of the Year Overskate, Japan Cup (Jpn-G1) winner Mairzy Doates, and world record-setter Double Discount. Broodmare sire of 89 stakes winners to 2006. Pensioned in 1988. Died of colic at Three Chimneys on April 26, 1990, at age 25.

1980—RAJA BABA, 1968 b. h., Bold Ruler—Missy Baba, by *My Babu. Bred in Kentucky by Michael G. Phipps. 41-7-12-9, $123,287. Modest stakes winner retired in 1974 to Hermitage Farm in Kentucky and sired 62 stakes winners (10%), including 1987 champion and Breeders' Cup Distaff (G1) winner Sacahuista, two-time Mexican Horse of the Year Gran Zar (Mex), and Canadian champion sprinter Summer Mood. Broodmare sire of more than 76 stakes winners of $69.4-million to 2006. Pensioned at Hermitage in 1987 and died on October 9, 2002.

1979, 1978—EXCLUSIVE NATIVE, 1965 ch. h., Raise a Native—Exclusive, by Shut Out. Bred in Florida by Harbor View Farm. 13-4-4-3, $169,013. Won 1968 Arlington Classic Stakes but far better sire than racehorse. Entered stud in 1969 at Spendthrift Farm in Kentucky for a fee of $1,500. Eventually sired 66 stakes winners (13%), including Racing Hall of Fame members Affirmed and Genuine Risk—the former an American Triple Crown winner, the latter only the second filly to win the Kentucky Derby (G1). Syndicated in 1972 for $1.8-million. Broodmare sire of 97 stakes winners. Died of cancer at Spendthrift Farm on April 21, 1983, at age 18.

1977—DR. FAGER, 1964 b. h., Rough'n Tumble—Aspidistra, by Better Self. Bred in Florida by William L. McKnight's Tartan Farms. 22-18-2-1, $1,002,642. Horse of the Year in 1968. Set world record mile of 1:32⅕ at Arlington Park carrying 134 pounds. Syndicated for $3.2-million in 1968 and entered stud the next year at Tartan Farms in Florida, where he sired nine crops. His 35 stakes winners (13%) include 1978 champion sprinter Dr. Patches, '75 champion juvenile filly Dearly Precious, and '77 Canadian Horse of the Year L'Alezane. Broodmare sire of 98 stakes winners, including notable sires Fappiano and Quiet American. Inducted into the Racing Hall of Fame in 1971. Died at Tartan Farms on August 5, 1976, at age 12, from torsion of the large colon.

1976, 1975—WHAT A PLEASURE, 1965 ch. h., Bold Ruler—Grey Flight, by *Mahmoud. Bred in Kentucky by Wheatley Stable. 18-6-5-2, $164,935. Won Hopeful Stakes and was fourth on 1967 Experimental Free Handicap. Sold in 1968 to Howard Sams. Entered stud the following year at Sams's Waldemar Farm in Florida. Sired 50 stakes winners (10%), including Foolish Pleasure and Honest Pleasure, juvenile champions in 1974 and '75, respectively. Syndicated in 1976 for $8-million. Twice top juvenile sire by money won. Broodmare sire of 83 stakes winners, including champion juveniles Gilded Time and Tasso. Died of a heart attack at Waldemar Farm on March 13, 1983, at age 18.

1974—T. V. LARK, 1957 b. h., *Indian Hemp—Miss Larksfly, by Heelfly. Bred in California by Dr. Walter D. Lucas and raised in a half-acre paddock. Sold for $10,000 to Chase McCoy at 1958 Del Mar yearling sale. 72-19-13-6, $902,194. Champion grass horse of 1961 with victory over Kelso in Washington, D.C., International. Sold for $600,000 to syndicate headed by Preston Madden and retired in 1963 to Hamburg Place in Kentucky. First crop included world record-setter Pink Pigeon. Sired 53 stakes winners and 35% stakes horses from winners. Did not establish an enduring male line but became broodmare sire of Racing Hall of Fame filly Chris Evert. Died at Hamburg on March 6, 1975, at age 18.

1973, 1963-'69—BOLD RULER, 1954 dk. b. h., 1954, *Nasrullah—Miss Disco, by Discovery. Bred in Kentucky by Wheatley Stable. 33-23-4-2, $764,204. Racing Hall of Fame member, 1957 Horse of the Year. Retired to Claiborne Farm in 1959 and began his reign as perennial leading sire four years later. Became the dominant force in American breeding throughout the 1960s and '70s, leading by progeny earnings seven times in succession, eight times overall—more than any other 20th-century stallion. Also six times leading juvenile sire. Sired 43% stakes horses from starters, 82 stakes winners (22%), and 11 champions, among them Secretariat, Gamely, Wajima, and Bold Bidder. Broodmare sire of 119 stakes winners, although he never led in that category. Died of cancer at Claiborne on July 12, 1971, at age 17.

1972—ROUND TABLE, 1954 b. h., *Princequillo—*Knight's Daughter, by Sir Cosmo. Bred in Kentucky by Claiborne Farm. Sold privately in 1957 to Travis Kerr. 66-43-8-5, $1,749,869. Set or equaled 16 track, American, and world records. Horse of the Year in 1958, three-time champion grass horse, and world's leading money-earner at retirement. Entered stud in 1960 at Claiborne Farm. Made international impact, siring 83 stakes winners (21%) from 19 crops, including champions in England, Ireland, France, and Canada. Did not establish significant male line, although several sons proved useful stallions. Broodmare sire of 125 stakes winners, including champions Outstandingly, De La Rose, and Bowl Game. Inducted into Racing Hall of Fame in 1972. Pensioned in 1978 and died at Claiborne on June 13, 1987, at age 33.

1971—NORTHERN DANCER, 1961 b. h., Nearctic—Natalma, by Native Dancer. Bred in Canada by E. P. Taylor. 18-14-2-2, $580,647. Champion in Canada and U.S., won 1964 Kentucky Derby, Preakness Stakes. Entered stud in 1965 at Windfields Farm in Canada but later relocated to Windfields's Maryland division. Syndicated in 1970 for $2.4-million. Became one of the most sought-after commercial stallions of all time, with numerous offspring selling at auction for $1-million and more. Leading sire in England four times. Leading U.S. broodmare sire in 1991. Former international leader by stakes winners, with 146—including 23 champions and noted sires Sadler's Wells, Nijinsky II, Danzig, Lyphard, Nureyev, and Storm Bird. Daughters produced 241 stakes winners (19 champions) to 2006. Inducted into the Racing Hall of Fame in 1976. Died of colic at Windfields in Maryland on November 16, 1990, at age 29. Buried at Windfields, Canada.

1970—HAIL TO REASON, 1958 br. h., *Turn-to—Nothirdchance, by Blue Swords. Bred in Kentucky by Bieber-Jacobs Stable. 18-9-2-2, $328,434. Champion at two. Sesamoid injury forced retirement in 1961 to Hagyard Farm in Kentucky. Syndicated for $1,085,000. Leading sire and juvenile sire of 1970, and also among leading sires in England and France. Sired 43 stakes winners (13%), including 1970 co-Horse of the Year Personality and fillies Trillion, Straight Deal, and Regal Gleam. Several sons became top sires, including two-time American leader Halo and 1972 Epsom Derby winner Roberto, both of whom kept his male line alive. Daughters produced millionaires Allez France, Triptych, Royal Glint, Colonial Waters, and 110 additional stakes winners. Died at Hagyard on February 24, 1976, at age 18.

1962, 1959-'60, 1955-'56—*NASRULLAH, 1940 b. h., Nearco—Mumtaz Begum, by *Blenheim II. Bred in Ireland by the Aga Khan. 10-5-1-2, $15,259. Champion at two in England and classic-placed at three but generally a disappointment due to tendency to sulk before and during races. Entered stud in 1944 at Great Barton Stud in England; sold and relocated the next year to Brownstown Stud in Ireland. Purchased in 1950 for approximately $400,000 by A. B. Hancock on behalf of an American syndicate and sent to Claiborne Farm in Kentucky for '51 breeding season. Sired 93 international stakes winners (22%) and established an enduring male line through Racing Hall of Fame son Bold Ruler and English-raced sons Red God and Grey Sovereign. Reigned five times as leading sire in America and once in England. Broodmare sire of 159 stakes winners. Suffered fatal heart attack at Claiborne on May 26, 1959, at age 19.

1961—*AMBIORIX, 1946 dk. b. h., Tourbillon—Lavendula, by Pharos. Bred in France by Marcel Boussac. 7-4-2-0, $25,165. Champion at two in France, winning Grand Criterium, and added the Prix Lupin at three before being narrowly beaten in the Prix du Jockey-Club (French Derby). Three-quarter brother to champion *My Babu. After failing to acquire *My Babu, A. B. Hancock purchased *Ambiorix in 1949 for syndication in America. Entered stud at Claiborne Farm in Kentucky the following year and ultimately sired 51 stakes winners (12%), including champion two- and three-year-old filly High Voltage. Leading sire of 1961 when runners included major winners Ambiopoise, Hitting Away, Make Sail, and Sarcastic. Also a successful broodmare sire, leading the list in England in 1963. Pensioned in 1972 and died at Claiborne in January '75 at age 29.

1958, 1957—*PRINCEQUILLO, 1940 b. h., Prince Rose—*Cosquilla, by *Papyrus. Bred in England by American Laudy Lawrence. 33-12-5-7, $96,550. Imported to U.S. as a yearling, leased to Anthony Pelleteri at two, and claimed for $2,500 by future Racing Hall of Fame trainer Horatio Luro for Dimitri Djordjaze. Became a top stayer, with victories including the 1943 Jockey Club Gold Cup. Retired in 1945 to A. B. Hancock's Ellerslie Farm in Virginia for $250 fee. Moved two years later to Claiborne Farm in Kentucky. Racing Hall of Fame members Round Table and Hill Prince were among his 65 stakes winners (13%), and *Princequillo arguably was one of America's two greatest broodmare sires (along with *Sir Gallahad III) of the 20th century. Was eight times atop broodmare sire list; his daughters produced 170 stakes winners, including champions Secretariat, Mill Reef, Fort Marcy, Key to the Mint, and Bold Lad. Died at Claiborne on July 18, 1964, at age 24.

1954, 1950—*HELIOPOLIS, 1936 b. h., Hyperion—Drift, by Swynford. Bred in England by Lord Derby. 15-5-2-1, $71,216, stakes winner at two and three in England, third in 1939 Epsom Derby. Imported to America the following year by Charles B. Shaffer and finished last after sulking in his only U.S. start, an allowance race at Hialeah Park. Retired in 1941 to Shaffer's Coldstream Stud in Kentucky. Sold in 1951 to Henry Knight and relocated to Almahurst Farm. Among his 53 stakes winners (15%) were 1954 Belmont Stakes victor and champion High Gun, and champion fillies Grecian Queen, Parlo, Berlo, and Aunt Jinny. Died at Almahurst on April 2, 1959, at age 23.

1953, 1952, 1947-'49—BULL LEA, 1935 br. h., *Bull Dog—Rose Leaves, by Ballot. Bred in Kentucky by Coldstream Stud. 27-10-7-3, $94,825. Sold as a yearling for $14,000 to Calumet Farm. A moderately accomplished racehorse, he won the Widener Handicap and Blue Grass Stakes. Retired to Calumet in 1940 for a $750 fee and became one of the greatest American sires of all time. Sired 57 stakes winners (15%), including a record seven Racing Hall of Fame members—Citation, Armed, Coaltown, Bewitch, Two Lea, Real Delight, and Twilight Tear. In 1947, became first stallion with single-season progeny earnings of $1-million. Four-time leading broodmare sire of 105 stakes winners. Died and buried at Calumet on June 16, 1964, at age 29.

1951—COUNT FLEET, 1940 br. h., Reigh Count—Quickly, by Haste. Bred in Kentucky by Mrs. John D. Hertz. 21-16-4-1, $250,300. In the Hertz colors, won 1943 Triple Crown, taking Belmont Stakes by 25 lengths. Retired in 1945 to Stoner Creek Farm near Paris, Kentucky, where he remained for the next 30 years. Outstanding sire and even better broodmare sire, leading in the latter category in 1963 and in the top five ten times. Among his 39 stakes winners (9%) were back-to-back Horses of the Year and Belmont Stakes winners Counterpoint (1951) and One Count ('52). Daughters produced 118 stakes winners and seven champions, including Racing Hall of Fame member Kelso. Pensioned in 1966. Count Fleet was inducted into the Racing Hall of Fame in 1961. He died at Stoner Creek on December 3, 1973, at age 33.

1946—*MAHMOUD, 1933 gr. h., *Blenheim II—Mah Mahal, by Gainsborough. Bred in France by the Aga Khan. 11-4-2-3, $86,439. Champion at three in England in 1936 when he won the Epsom Derby in record time. Entered stud at Newmarket in 1937. Purchased in 1940 by C. V. Whitney for about $85,000 and imported to stand at his Kentucky farm. Prior to his arrival, gray Thoroughbreds were spurned by many prominent American breeders, but *Mahmoud made the color acceptable. Sired 66 stakes winners, including U.S. champions Oil Capitol, The Axe II, and First Flight, and European champions *Majideh and Donatella. Leading broodmare sire of 1957 and among leaders throughout the '60s. Daughters produced 139 stakes winners, including Racing Hall of Fame members *Gallant Man and Silver Spoon. Died at C. V. Whitney Farm on September 18, 1962, at age 29.

1945—WAR ADMIRAL, 1934 br. h., Man o' War—Brushup, by Sweep. Bred in Kentucky by Samuel D. Riddle and raced for Glen Riddle Stable. 26-21-3-1, $273,240. Racing Hall of Fame runner is generally acknowledged as Man o' War's best son, both on the track and in the stud. Won 1937 Triple Crown and stood alongside Man o' War at Faraway Farm in Kentucky. Sire of 40 stakes winners (11%), including 1945 Horse of the Year Busher, champion Blue Peter, and the great racemares-broodmares Searching and Busanda. Twice leading broodmare sire of 113 stakes winners, including champions Buckpasser, Hoist the Flag, and Affectionately. Died on October 30, 1959, at age 25 and buried next to Man o' War at Faraway. Remains were exhumed, along with his sire's, in the 1970s, and reinterred at Kentucky Horse Park.

1944, 1935—CHANCE PLAY, 1923 ch. h., Fair Play—*Quelle Chance, by Ethelbert. Bred in Kentucky by August Belmont II. 39-16-9-2, $137,946. A handsome horse who resembled his sire, he raced for W. Averill Harriman's Log Cabin Stable and was considered the best horse of the year in 1927. Retired in 1929, stood at farms from Kentucky to New York until purchased by Warren Wright, who made him one of first stallions to stand at Calumet Farm in Lexington. Sired 23 stakes winners (7%), including 1939 champion juvenile filly Now What and '45 Jockey Club Gold Cup winner Pot o' Luck. Pensioned in 1947 following heart attack. Euthanized at Calumet on July 6, 1950, at age 27 and buried in the farm's cemetery.

1943—*BULL DOG, 1927 b. or br. h., *Teddy—Plucky Liege, by Spearmint. Bred in France by Jefferson Davis

Cohn. 8-2-1-0, $7,802. Stakes winner at three in France. Full brother to leading sire *Sir Gallahad III and half brother to top European sires Bois Roussel and Admiral Drake. Imported by Charles B. Shaffer in 1930 to stand at his Coldstream Stud in Kentucky. Top runners include champion two-year-olds Occupy and Our Boots and five-time leading American sire Bull Lea. Sired 52 stakes winners (15%) in 18 crops, and 27% of his starters were of stakes class. In 1953, he supplanted *Sir Gallahad III atop broodmare sire list and subsequently led that list three times. His daughters produced 89 stakes winners and four champions. Pensioned in 1948. Died at Coldstream on October 10, 1954, at age 27.

1942—EQUIPOISE, 1928 ch. h., Pennant—Swinging, by Broomstick. Bred in Kentucky by Harry Payne Whitney. 51-29-10-4, $338,610. First great racehorse to carry colors of Whitney's son, Cornelius Vanderbilt Whitney. Nicknamed the "Chocolate Soldier" because of his dark chestnut color and combative spirit, he was an American champion at ages two, four, and five. Entered stud at C. V. Whitney Farm in 1935. Sired just four crops and 74 foals, nine of whom won stakes (12%), including 1940 champion juvenile filly Level Best and 1942 Kentucky Derby and Belmont Stakes winner Shut Out. Broodmare sire of 1946 Triple Crown winner Assault. First foals were two-year-olds when he died of enteritis at age ten on August 4, 1938. Inducted into Racing Hall of Fame in 1957.

1941—*BLENHEIM II, 1927 br. h., Blandford—Malva, by Charles O'Malley. Bred in England by Lord Carnarvon. Sold as yearling to the Aga Khan for about $20,000. 10-5-3-0, $73,060. Injury forced retirement following victory in 1930 Epsom Derby. Stood in Europe for six seasons, siring 1936 Epsom Derby winner *Mahmoud, Italian champion Donatello II. Sold in 1936 for reported $250,000 to an American syndicate and sent to Claiborne Farm in Kentucky. Sire of more than 45 stakes winners, including 1941 American Triple Crown winner Whirlaway and '43 champion handicap mare Mar-Kell. Broodmare sire of more than 120 stakes winners, including *Nasrullah and Kentucky Derby winners Ponder, Hill Gail, and Kauai King. Died at Claiborne on May 26, 1958, at age 31.

1940, 1933-'34, 1930—*SIR GALLAHAD III, 1920 b. h., *Teddy—Plucky Liege, by Spearmint. Bred in France by Jefferson Davis Cohn. 24-11-3-3, $17,009, Poule d'Essai des Poulains (French Two Thousand Guineas), match with *Epinard, etc. Full brother to leading sire *Bull Dog, half brother to top European sires Bois Roussel and Admiral Drake. Stood 1925 season in France, then sold for $125,000 to U.S. syndicate headed by A. B. Hancock. First important American stallion syndication. Stood at Claiborne Farm in Kentucky for remainder of career. First U.S. crop included 1930 Triple Crown winner Gallant Fox, and with two crops racing he led general sire list for the first of four times. Sired 56 stakes winners (10%), including three Kentucky Derby victors and several champions. Not a notable sire of sires but an all-time great broodmare sire, leading in that category 12 times. Died and buried at Claiborne on July 8, 1949, at age 29.

1939—*CHALLENGER II, 1927 b. h., Swynford—Sword Play, by Great Sport. Bred in England by the National Stud. 2-2-0-0 $10,930, Richmond S., Clearwell S., ranked third on English Free Handicap, one pound above future leading American sire *Blenheim II. Classic engagements canceled upon death of owner Lord Dewar under the rules then in force. Sold for reported $100,000 to William L. Brann and Robert Castle and imported to U.S. but injured in paddock accident before he could race again. Stood 17 seasons at Brann's Glade Valley Farm in Maryland, the first leading sire to spend his entire career outside Kentucky since *Sir Modred in 1894. Sired 34 stakes winners (11%), including future Racing Hall of Fame members Challedon and Gallorette. Died at Glade Valley on December 23, 1948, at age 21.

1938, 1936—*SICKLE, 1924 br. h., Phalaris—Selene, by Chaucer. Bred in England by Lord Derby. 10-3-4-2, $23,629, stakes winner at two, third in the 1927 Two Thousand Guineas. Half brother to the great racehorse and sire Hyperion, full brother to *Pharamond II. Stood one season in England before being imported under a lease agreement in 1930 by Joseph E. Widener, who eventually purchased him for a reported $100,000. Sent to Widener's Elmendorf Farm in Kentucky, where he replaced deceased Fair Play as the stud's leading stallion. Sired 22% stakes horses from foals, with 41 stakes winners (14%), including champions Stagehand, Star Pilot, and *Gossip II. Broodmare sire of 57 stakes winners, including 1951 Horse of the Year Counterpoint. Died on December 26, 1943, at Elmendorf at age 19.

1937—THE PORTER, 1915 b. h., Sweep—Ballet Girl, by St. Leonards. Bred in Kentucky by David Stevenson. Raced for Samuel Ross and later Edward McLean. 52-26-10-8, $89,249, Annapolis Handicap, etc. Stood barely 15 hands. From 1922-'31 stood at McLean Stud in Virginia. At age 16, purchased for $27,000 at McLean's 1931 dispersal by Mrs. John Hay Whitney and sent to Kentucky. Sired 11% stakes winners from foals, with the best of his 34 stakes winners being 1937 Santa Anita Handicap winner Rosemont, '37 Suburban Handicap winner Aneroid, and the top juvenile Porter's Mite. Died at Mare's Nest Farm in Kentucky on October 23, 1944, at age 29.

1932—CHATTERTON, 1919 ch. h., Fair Play—Chit Chat, by *Rock Sand. Bred in Kentucky by August Belmont II. 32-15-5-4, $26,565. Bred like Man o' War, by Fair Play out of *Rock Sand mare. Sold privately and raced for Frank J. Kelley. Multiple stakes winner in Midwest, though not a top runner. Stood 1924 in California but after Kelley's death sent to Claiborne Farm in Kentucky. Remained there except for 1932 season when leased to Arrowbrook Farm in Illinois. His position atop list was due almost entirely to 1932 champion and Belmont Stakes winner Faireno. Also sired 1928 champion juvenile filly Current and nine other stakes winners. Died at Claiborne of kidney ailment on July 14, 1933, at age 14.

1931—*ST. GERMANS, 1921 b. h., Swynford—Hamoaze, by Torpoint. Bred in England by Lord Astor. 20-9-4-4, $44,793, Coronation Cup, Doncaster Cup, etc., second in Epsom Derby. Imported by Payne Whitney to stand at his Greentree Stud. Advertised "for private use only" in early years. He suffered from low fertility and averaged fewer than ten foals per crop, but those were highly successful. Best of 23 stakes winners (13%) was Twenty Grand, winner of the Kentucky Derby and Belmont Stakes; two-time handicap champion Devil Diver; and 1936 Kentucky Derby-Preakness Stakes winner Bold Venture. Twenty Grand was sterile, and several prominent male-line descendants experienced fertility problems. Died at Greentree Stud on May 18, 1929, at age 18 following attack of enteritis.

1929—*CHICLE, 1913 b. h., Spearmint—Lady Hamburg II, by Hamburg. Bred in France by Harry Payne Whitney but raced in U.S. 10-3-0-2, $4,765. Had soundness problems but nonetheless won Champagne Stakes and Brooklyn Derby (now Dwyer Stakes). Entered stud in Kentucky at H. P. Whitney Farm for fee of $500. Fee later raised as high as $1,500. Bad tempered, kept muzzled as a stallion for safety of farm workers. Sired six stakes winners from first 13-foal crop and about 40 overall—including champion juveniles Whichone and Mother Goose. Leading broodmare sire of 1942. Died on May 20, 1939, at age 26, at C. V. Whitney Farm near Lexington.

1928—HIGH TIME, 1916 ch. h., Ultimus—Noonday, by Domino. Bred in Kentucky by Wickliffe Stud of Corrigan and McKinney. 7-1-0-1, $3,950, Hudson S., 3rd Great American S. Highly inbred to Domino, with three crosses in first three generations. Beautiful physical specimen, sold at auction as two-year-old for $8,500. Career limited by throat problems. Won Aqueduct's Hudson Stakes in track-record time for five furlongs. Retired at three to Haylands Stud in 1919 but was not well received by Kentucky breeders. In later years, changed ownership several times before settling at Dixiana Farm in Kentucky. Sired about 40 stakes winners, including Racing Hall of Fame champion gelding Sarazen and 1928 champion juvenile colt High Strung. Leading broodmare sire of 1940. Died at Dixiana on November 20, 1937, at age 21.

1927, 1924, 1920—FAIR PLAY, 1905 ch. h., Hastings—*Fairy Gold, by Bend Or. Bred in Kentucky by August Belmont II. 32-10-11-3, $86,950. Racing Hall of Fame runner had misfortune to come along in same crop as unbeatable Colin. Won 1908 Lawrence Realization. When betting was outlawed in New York, shipped to England, where heavy weight assignments and a deteriorating attitude led to a 6-0-0-0 record. Retired to Nursery Stud in 1910. When Belmont died in 1924, sold at age 20 on $100,000 bid to Joseph Widener. Renowned for producing stamina, the three-time leading sire got champions Chance Play and Mad Hatter but was immortalized as sire of Man o' War, through whom his male line survives today. Leading broodmare sire in 1931, '34, and '38. Died at age 24 in paddock at Elmendorf Farm in Kentucky on December 16, 1929.

1926—MAN O' WAR, 1917 ch. h., Fair Play—Mahubah, by *Rock Sand. Bred in Kentucky by August Belmont II. 21-20-1-0, $249,465. Sold at auction as yearling for $5,000 to Samuel Riddle. Became one of the greatest racehorses of all time, winning Preakness and Belmont Stakes. Retired in 1921 to Hinata Stock Farm but soon moved to Faraway Farm, both in Kentucky. Instant success, led general sire list with only three crops racing. Top runners include future Racing Hall of Fame members War Admiral and Crusader as well as six other American champions. Also a great broodmare sire. As Riddle's private stallion, did not receive the best mares but nonetheless sired 64 stakes winners, 17% of foals. Died at age 30 at Faraway on November 1, 1947. Thousands attended funeral, which was nationally broadcast on radio and filmed for newsreels. Grave and larger-than-life bronze statue relocated in late 1970s to Kentucky Horse Park.

1925, 1918—SWEEP, 1907 br. h., Ben Brush—Pink Domino, by Domino. Bred in Kentucky by James R. Keene. 13-9-2-2, $59,998, champion at two in 1909 when he won the Futurity Stakes and added the Belmont Stakes at three. Sold at 1913 Keene estate dispersal at Madison Square Garden for $17,500 to partnership of John Barbee, J. C. Carrick, and Andrew Stone. Led broodmare sire list twice and twice was leader by number of two-year-old winners. Sired more than 40 stakes winners. Top runners include 1918 champion juvenile Eternal and handicap star The Porter, leading sire of 1937. Died at age 24 from "indigestion" on August 15, 1931, at Glen-Helen Stud in Kentucky.

1923—THE FINN, 1912 bl. h., *Ogden—Livonia, by *Star Shoot. Bred in Kentucky by John E. Madden. 50-19-10-6, $38,965. Raced initially for Madden before being sold to H. C. Hallenbeck. Victories included Belmont and Withers Stakes as well as Metropolitan, Manhattan, and Havre de Grace Handicaps. Generally regarded as champion three-year-old colt of 1915. Madden later bought him back and in 1923 he was sold again, for $100,000, to W. R. Coe. Stood thereafter at Hinata Stock Farm in Kentucky. Sired Kentucky Derby winners Flying Ebony and Zev, the latter America's first racehorse to top $300,000 in earnings (1924). Died at Hinata on September 4, 1925, from "inflammation of the bowels," at age 13.

1922—*MCGEE, 1900 b. h., White Knight—Remorse, by Hermit. Bred in England by Lord Bradford. 53-24-14-5, $18,391, Fleetfoot H., etc. Only foal by an unraced stallion. Sold cheaply as yearling to Ed Corrigan and imported to U.S. Raced in Midwest, a minor stakes winner of 24 races. Primarily a sprinter—set American 5½-furlong record in 1903. Retired to Corrigan's Freeland Stud near Lexington, then sold in 1908 for $1,300 to Charles Moore. Relocated to nearby Mere Hill Stud where his 1909 fee was $50. Sired at least 20 stakes winners, most notably the great gelding Exterminator and Donerail, winner of 1913 Kentucky Derby at 91.45-to-1. His last foal was conceived in 1930 when *McGee was 30 years old. Prior to his death at Mere Hill on September 18, 1931, he was believed to be the oldest stallion in Kentucky.

1921—CELT, 1905 ch. h., Commando—*Maid Of Erin, by Amphion. Bred in Kentucky by James R. Keene. 6-4-1-1, $29,975. Lightly raced winner of 1908 Brooklyn Handicap, overshadowed by unbeaten stablemate Colin, another son of Commando. Stood initially at Castleton Stud, then leased for 1912 to stand at Hancock family's Ellerslie Stud in Virginia. Though lease expired in 1913, A. B. Hancock acquired him that fall for $20,000 at Keene's estate dispersal. Returned to Ellerslie to sire a total of at least 29 stakes winners. In 1930, was top broodmare sire when Gallant Fox swept the Triple Crown. Died at age 14 in 1919.

1919, 1916-'17, 1911-'12—*STAR SHOOT, 1898 ch. h., Isinglass—Astrology, by Hermit. Bred in England by Maj. Eustace Loder. 10-3-1-3, $34,747, National Breeders' Produce S., etc. A good two-year-old, developed wind problems at three and was unplaced in two starts that season. Because he was from a family not noted for producing good sires, he was sold to America and entered stud in 1902 at Runnymede Farm in Kentucky, where he was an immediate success. Purchased privately by John Madden in 1912 and relocated to Hamburg Place. One of the most influential American-based stallions of his time; his sons included future Racing Hall of Fame members Grey Lag and Sir Barton. In 1916, had record 27 juvenile winners. Died of pneumonia at Hamburg on November 19, 1919, at age 21.

1915, 1913-'14—BROOMSTICK, 1901 b. h., Ben Brush—*Elf, by Galliard. Bred in Kentucky by Col. Milton Young. 39-14-11-5, $74,730, Travers S., etc. Young acquired *Elf for $250 in foal with Broomstick. Colt was sold privately to race for coal millionaire Samuel Brown. Racing Hall of Fame runner raced through age four. Retired in 1906 to Brown's Senorita Stud in Kentucky. Sold for $7,250 two years later at estate sale of his owner to H. P. Whitney. Eventually sired about 25% stakes winners from foals—nearly 60 in all–including the first New York handicap triple crown winner, Whisk Broom II; the first filly Kentucky Derby winner, Regret; 1911 Derby winner Meridian; and '12 Two Thousand Guineas winner *Sweeper. Died at C. V. Whitney Farm in Kentucky, on March 24, 1931, at age 30.

1910, 1900—KINGSTON, 1884 br. h., Spendthrift—*Kapanga, by Victorious. Bred in Kentucky by James R. Keene. 138-89-33-12, $140,195, First Special S., etc. Raced through age ten, primarily for Phil and Mike Dwyer. His 89 career victories remains an all-time record, and for about one year (1892-'93) he reigned as America's leading money earner. Entered stud in 1895 at Eugene Leigh's La Belle Farm in Kentucky for a $150 fee. Moved in a few years to Keene's Castleton Farm near Lexington, where he stood privately with leading sires Ben Brush and Commando. Represented by Futurity Stakes winners Ballyhoo Bey (1900) and Novelty ('10), as well as 1900 Belmont Stakes winner Ildrim. Died at Castleton on December 4, 1912, at age 28.

1909—BEN BRUSH, 1893 b. h., Bramble—Roseville, by Reform. Bred in Kentucky by Catesby Woodford and Ezekiel Clay. 40-25-5-5, $65,208. Small, plain, and tough, a superb racehorse, and Racing Hall of Fame member. Sold as yearling for $1,200 to Eugene Leigh and Ed Brown, and again at three for reported $25,000 to Mike Dwyer. Won 1896 Kentucky Derby and '97 Suburban Handicap. Sold to James R. Keene for stud duty at Castleton Farm in Kentucky. Following Keene's death in 1913, acquired for $10,000 by Kentucky Senator Johnson Camden and lived out his days at Camden's Hartland Stud near Versailles. Established noted male line that endured for decades. Best offspring include three-time leading American sire Broomstick and two-time leader Sweep. Died at age 25 on June 8, 1918.

1908, 1902—HASTINGS, 1893 br. h., Spendthrift—*Cinderella, by Tomahawk or Blue Ruin. Bred in Kentucky by Dr. J. D. Neet. 21-10-8-0, $16,340. Raced at two for Gideon and Daly. Upon dispersal of that stable at Sheepshead Bay in 1895, acquired for $37,000 by August Belmont II. Won 1896 Belmont Stakes, although generally not regarded as a top racehorse. Entered stud in 1898 at Belmont's Nursery Stud in Kentucky and was known for his savage disposition. Sire of champion filly Gunfire (1899), but by far his best was the 1905 colt Fair Play, the future sire of Man o' War. Died at Nursery Stud in 1917 at age 24 following an attack of paralysis.

1907—COMMANDO, 1898 b. h., Domino—Emma C., by *Darebin. Bred in Kentucky by James R. Keene. 9-7-2-0, $58,196. Coarse and heavily muscled, he did not resemble his handsome sire but was at least his equal on the racecourse. In James R. Keene's colors, won 1901 Belmont Stakes. The Racing Hall of Fame member retired to Keene's Castleton Stud in 1902 to take the place of Domino, who died at age six in 1897. Immediate success at stud but, like his sire, he died young. From three crops and 27 foals, sired ten stakes winners, among them Racing Hall of Fame members Peter Pan and Colin and influential sires Celt and Ultimus. Died of tetanus at Castleton in early March 1905 at age seven.

1906, 1904—*MEDDLER, 1890 b. h., *St Gatien—Busybody, by Petrarch. Bred in England by George Abington Baird. 3-3-0-0, $16,689, Dewhurst S., etc. By an Epsom Derby winner and out of an Epsom Oaks winner. Unraced after two-year-old season following the death of his owner, which, under rules in force at the time, voided his nominations to the three-year-old classics. Sold in 1893 for $76,000 to American William Forbes, who stood him initially at Neponset Stud in Massachusetts. Upon Forbes's death in 1897, sold to W. C. Whitney for $49,000 and moved to La Belle Stud in Kentucky. Sold at 1904 Whitney estate dispersal for $51,000. Represented by champion fillies Trigger, Tangle, and Tanya (winner of 1905 Belmont Stakes). When American racing was decimated by 1909 antiwagering legislation, relocated to France, where he died on April 17, 1916, at Haras de Fresnay-le-Buffard in Normandy at age 26.

1905—HAMBURG, 1895 b. h., Hanover—Lady Reel, by Fellowcraft. Bred in Kentucky by C. J. Enright. Sold for $1,250 as yearling to John E. Madden, who later named his famous breeding farm, Hamburg Place, for the Racing Hall of Fame member. 21-16-3-2, $60,380, Lawrence Realization, etc. Sold privately for $40,001 to Marcus Daly in 1898. Stood two seasons at Daly's Bitter Root Stud in Montana. After Daly's death in 1900, sold for $60,000 to W. C. Whitney, who sent him to La Belle Stud in Kentucky. At 1904 Whitney dispersal, sold for $70,000 to Whitney's son Harry Payne Whitney, who took him to Brookdale Stud in New Jersey. Sired Racing Hall of Fame filly Artful, champions Borrow, Hamburg Belle, Burgomaster, and Rosie O'Grady, and foundation mare Frizette. Died at Brookdale on September 15, 1915, at age 20.

1903—*BEN STROME, 1886 b. h., Bend Or—Strathfleet, by The Scottish Chief. Bred in England by the Duke of Westminster. 35-3-6-6, $2,975. Big (16.2 hands tall), good-looking, and beautifully bred, but a poor racehorse in England. Entered stud in 1894 at Thomas J. Carson's Dixiana Farm in Kentucky. When his first foals were yearlings, Dixiana advertised that a limited number of approved mares would be accepted by special contract, which meant at no cost. By 1904, his fee had jumped to $300, one of the highest in the country. Most noted as sire of Racing Hall of Fame member Roseben, but offspring also included juvenile champions Eugenia Burch and Highball. Died at Dixiana in 1909 at age 23.

1901—SIR DIXON, 1885 br. h., *Billet—Jaconet, by *Leamington. Bred in Kentucky by Col. Ezekiel Clay. 29-10-7-7, $54,915. Sold for $1,125 as yearling to Green B. Morris, who resold him at three for $20,000 to Mike and Phil Dwyer. A high-strung, delicate type, he was unable to endure the tough campaigns favored by the Dwyers but nevertheless scored victories in the 1888 Belmont, Withers, and Travers Stakes. Stood his entire career at Clay's Runnymede Stud in Kentucky. Sired champions Butterflies, Blue Girl, Kilmarnock, and Running Water, and 1905 Kentucky Derby winner Agile. Died on March 23, 1909, at age 14 after breaking his right hip in a paddock accident.

1899—*ALBERT, 1882 b. h., Albert Victor—Hawthorn Bloom, by Kettledrum. Bred in England by Sir Richard Jardine. 6-1-1-0, $2,547. A racehorse of modest talents, won a minor stakes at Newcastle as a two-year-old. Imported as a stallion by Alfred Withers. Later spent most of his breeding career at the Adelbert Stud of Williams and Radford near Hopkinsville, Kentucky. Advertised for a $100 fee in 1896, with a reference to him as "the most uniform sire of winners in America—they mature early and make great campaigners." Not an outstanding sire, his best was probably 1899 juvenile champion Mesmerist and the good filly Hatasoo, an ancestress of many top racehorses. Believed to have died in 1907, because his last five foals arrived the following spring.

1898, 1895-'97—HANOVER, 1884 ch. h., Hindoo—Bourbon Belle, by *Bonnie Scotland. Bred in Kentucky at Col. Ezekiel Clay's Runnymede Farm. 50-32-14-2, $118,887, champion three-year-old, 1887 Belmont Stakes, etc. Sold as a yearling for $1,350 to Phil and Mike Dwyer. Won 17 consecutive races at two and three and ultimately retired with American earnings record. One of America's better all-time stallions, his best by far was Racing Hall of Fame member and leading sire Hamburg. Hanover was valued at $100,000 when he died on March 23, 1899, at McGrathiana Stud in Kentucky at age 15. Cause of death was said to be blood poisoning caused by a leg injury. He was originally buried at McGrathiana, but his skeleton was later exhumed for research and display.

1894—*SIR MODRED, 1877 b. h., Traducer—Idalia, by Cambuscan. Bred in New Zealand by Middle Park Stud. Among the foremost racehorses of his day in New Zealand, with victories in the Canterbury Derby, Canterbury Cup, and Metropolitan Stakes. Imported to California in 1885 by James Ben Ali Haggin. In 1894, became the first California-based stallion to lead the American sire list when his offspring won 137 races and $134,318. Notable offspring include champion Tournament, 1893 Belmont Stakes winner Comanche, 1890 Travers Stakes winner Sir John, and the outstanding fillies Gloaming and Lucania. Stood at Haggin's 44,000-acre Rancho del Paso near Sacramento, where he was pensioned for several seasons prior to his death due to infirmities of old age in June 1904 at age 27.

1893—HIMYAR, 1875 b. h., Alarm—Hira, by Lexington. Bred in Kentucky by Maj. Barak Thomas. 27-14-6-4, $11,650, Phoenix Hotel Stakes, etc. Finished second in 1878 as one of the heaviest favorites ever for the Kentucky Derby. High-strung, nervous, and hard to train, considered primarily a speed horse. Entered stud in 1882 at Thomas's Dixiana Farm near Lexington and got, among others, immortal racehorse and sire Domino and '98 Kentucky Derby winner Plaudit. In 1893, due largely to Domino, he established a single-season progeny earnings record of $259,252, which stood for 24 years. Died at age 30 on December 30, 1905, and was buried at Dixiana under a tombstone that reads: "Speed springs eternal from his ashes."

1892—IROQUOIS, 1878 br. h., *Leamington—Maggie B.B., by *Australian. Bred by Aristides Welch at Erdenheim Stud in Pennsylvania. 26-12-4-3, $99,707. Sold as a yearling to tobacco magnate Pierre Lorillard, who sent him to race in England. First American-bred winner of Epsom Derby and St. Leger Stakes; finished second in the Two Thousand Guineas. Wall Street briefly halted trading to celebrate news of his Derby triumph. Returned to U.S., he raced three times without success, probably because of pulmonary bleeding. Retired to stud at W. H. Johnson's Belle Meade Farm, where he died in 1899 at age 21. His offspring included champion Tammany.

1891—LONGFELLOW, 1867 br. h., *Leamington—Nantura, by Brawner's Eclipse. Bred, owned, and trained by John Harper. 16-13-2-0, $11,200. Standing a towering 17 hands, he was named for his long legs and not for the noted poet. One of the great racehorses of the 1870s, an injury forced his retirement to Harper's Nantura Stud near Midway, Kentucky. Sired more than 40 stakes winners, including Kentucky Derby winners Leonatus and Riley, 1886 Preakness winner The Bard, and champions Thora and Freeland. A dominant bay, it was said that all his foals but one were bay or brown. Died at Nantura on November 5, 1893, and was buried with a marker that reads: "King of Racers and King of Stallions."

1890—*ST. BLAISE, 1880 ch. h., Hermit—Fusee, by Marsyas. Bred in England by Lord Alington. 16-7-2-1, $41,066. Won 1883 Epsom Derby. Imported for $30,000 in 1885 by August Belmont I to stand at his Nursery Stud in Kentucky. Following Belmont's death, sold at auction in 1891 by Tattersalls of New York for a then-world record $100,000. Purchased on a solitary bid by Charles Reed of Tennessee. Not successful for Reed, sold at auction again in 1902 for $8,300 to James Ben Ali Haggin of Elmendorf Farm, Kentucky, but subsequently purchased privately by August Belmont II. At age 22, he returned to Nursery Stud to live out his days. Best runners include 1890 Futurity Stakes winner Potomac and '96 Preakness Stakes winner Margrave. Died in October 1909 at age 29.

1889—*RAYON D'OR, 1876 ch. h., Flageolet—Araucaria, by Ambrose. Bred in France by Haras de Dangu. 28-15-7-4, $110,207. Won from five to 18 furlongs, including 1879 St. Leger, and carried up to 132 pounds to victory. Imported in 1883 by W. L. Scott, who paid nearly $40,000 for him and stood him initially at his Algeria Stud in Pennsylvania. When Algeria dispersed in 1892, purchased by August Belmont II and moved to Nursery Stud in Kentucky. Sired many top runners, including Brooklyn Handicap winner Tenny, Futurity Stakes winner Chaos, and Banquet, winner of 62 races and $118,872. Died from "fever" on July 15, 1896, at Nursery Stud at age 20.

1888, 1886-'87, 1884—GLENELG, 1866 b. h., Citadel—*Babta, by Kingston. Imported in utero by R. W. Cameron, who earlier had imported four-time leading sire *Leamington. Foaled at Cameron's Clifton Farm in New York. 18-10-5-2, $23,340. Purchased as a yearling by August Belmont I for $2,000. Big, bad-tempered, and prone to colic, he nonetheless won the 1869 Travers Stakes and other important races. After his racing days, he was sold to Milton H. Sanford for $10,000. His many outstanding runners include Racing Hall of Fame mare Firenze. Died on October 23, 1897, at age 31 at the farm of Tyree Bate in Castalian Springs, Tennessee.

1885—VIRGIL, 1864 dk. b. h., Vandal—Hymenia, by *Yorkshire. Bred in Woodford County, Kentucky, by Hyman C. Gratz. 10-7-2-1, $2,950, Sequel S. three times, etc. A beautiful, nearly black horse, owned during his racing days by Milton Sanford, primarily a sprinter in an era that prized stamina (although he won once at two miles). Initially had few opportunities as a stallion and was even broken to harness and used to pull a carriage. Sold cheaply in 1874. When his son Vagrant won the 1876 Kentucky Derby, Virgil was repurchased by Sanford. He subsequently sired Racing Hall of Fame member Hindoo (also a great sire) and unbeaten Tremont. Died at Quindaro Stud in Kentucky in 1893 at age 29.

1883—*BILLET, 1865 br. h., Voltigeur—Calcutta, by Flatcatcher. Bred in England by James Smith. 18-5-3-1, $3,983. Insignificant racehorse in England, racing most often in selling races. Imported to America in 1869 and stood several seasons in Illinois. After son Elias Lawrence established a Saratoga three-mile record in 1878, was moved to Runnymede Stud in Paris, Kentucky, where he remained until his death on January 17, 1889, at age 24. Top runners include Racing Hall of Fame member Miss Woodford, the first American Thoroughbred to top $100,000 in earnings, and 1901 leading sire Sir Dixon.

1882, 1880—*BONNIE SCOTLAND, 1853 b. h., Iago—Queen Mary, by Gladiator. Bred in England by William I'Anson. 4-2-1-0, $6,308. Lightly raced and never truly sound because of an injury as a foal, won Liverpool St. Leger and Doncaster Stakes. Imported to America in 1857, believed to have stood originally in Ohio before relocating to Gen. W. G. Harding's famous Belle Meade Stud near Nashville, Tennessee. Offspring include Racing Hall of Fame member Luke Blackburn, 1883 Belmont Stakes winner George Kinney, and champion Bramble. Died in his paddock at Belle Meade on February 2, 1880, at age 27.

1881, 1879, 1877, 1875—*LEAMINGTON, 1853 br. h., Faugh-a-Ballagh—mare by Pantaloon. Bred in England by Mr. Halford. 24-8-3-3, $33,446, Goodwood S., Tradesmen's Plate twice, etc. Imported in 1865 by R. W. Cameron of New York after standing six seasons in England. In U.S., stood first at Bosque Bonita Stud in Kentucky, later at Cameron's Clifton Stud on Staten Island, and finally at Aristides Welch's Erdenheim Stud near Philadelphia. Sire of Racing Hall of Fame members Longfellow and Parole, inaugural Kentucky Derby winner Aristides, and Iroquois, first American-bred winner of the Epsom Derby. Many of his best offspring were out of Lexington mares and were raced by the Lorillard brothers, George and Pierre, who dominated American racing during the 1870s and '80s. Died at Erdenheim on May 6, 1878, at age 25.

1878, 1876, 1861-'74—LEXINGTON, 1850 b. h., Boston—Alice Carneal, by *Sarpedon. Bred in Kentucky by Dr. Elisha Warfield. 7-6-1-0, $56,600, Great Post S., etc. Sold to Richard Ten Broeck as a three-year-old and in 1855 set an American four-mile record of 7:19¾. By then, he was going blind and was sold for $15,000 to R. A. Alexander of Woodburn Stud, Kentucky. He stood at that Midway farm his entire career except for an interlude in Illinois for his own safety during the Civil War. As with *Glencoe, a number of his offspring were utilized as Civil War mounts. His many outstanding runners include champions Kentucky, Asteroid, Norfolk, Duke of Magenta, Harry Bassett, Sultana, and Tom Bowling. Lexington's post-Civil War fee of $500 was unprecedented. His male-line survived into the 20th century, and numerous crosses of his name are still present in far branches of modern pedigrees. The 16-time leading sire died on July 1, 1875, at age 25. His skeleton is in the possession of the Smithsonian Institution in Washington, D.C.

1860—REVENUE, 1843 b. h., *Trustee—Rosalie Somers, by Sir Charles. Bred in Virginia by statesman John M. Botts. 21-16-5-0. Son of a leading sire and champion racemare. Stood at Botts's farm in Virginia, where he sired the great Planet, widely viewed as the best American racehorse in the era preceding the Civil War, compiling a 31-27-4-0 record and surpassing Peytona as America's top earner with $69,700, a mark that stood for 20 years. In 1860, Revenue became the first stallion to lead an American sire list based on earnings ($49,450) rather than races won (the previously recognized standard), although he led by wins as well. He died in Virginia in September 1868 at age 25.

1859—*ALBION, 1837 bl. h., Cain or Actaeon—Panthea, by Comus or Blacklock. Bred in England; reportedly was a successful racehorse in America during the early 1840s. A reliable sire of winners during pre-Civil War years and later an outstanding broodmare sire. Died in 1859 at age 22 in Sumner County, Tennessee.

1858, 1854-'57, 1849-'50, 1847—*GLENCOE, 1831 ch. h., Sultan—Trampoline, by Tramp. Bred in England by Lord Jersey. 10-8-1-1, $33,459. Winner of 1834 Two Thousand Guineas, third in Epsom Derby. Stood one season in England, getting legendary broodmare Pocahontas. Imported in 1836 by James Jackson, who reportedly paid $10,000 for him. Swaybacked but otherwise handsome, he was much admired by breeders of the day. Stood from 1837-'44 in Alabama; 1845-'48 in Tennessee; and 1849-'57 in Kentucky as property of A. Keene Richards, an ardent secessionist who allegedly turned over many of his offspring for use as Confederate mounts during the Civil War. Sired the great mares Reel and Peytona, the latter America's leading money winner from 1845-'61 ($62,400), as well as top sons Star Davis and Vandal. Died of "lung fever" on August 25, 1857, at Blue Grass Park in Georgetown, Kentucky.

1853, 1851-'52—BOSTON, 1833 b. h., Timoleon—Sister to Tuckahoe, by Ball's Florizel. Bred in Virginia by John Wickham. 45-40-2-1, $51,700. Sold at two for $800 to Nathaniel Rives to satisfy a gaming debt. Racing Hall of Fame member won 30 four-mile heat races. Nicknamed "Old White Nose" for his distinctively blazed face, his vicious temper struck fear into the hearts of his handlers. Sire of Racing Hall of Fame member Lexington and his great rival, Lecomte (also known as Lecompte), as well as the great racemare Nina, dam of Planet. Died in 1850 at age 17 at Col. E. M. Blackburn's farm in Woodford County, Kentucky.

1848 (co-leader), 1843, 1837-'39—*LEVIATHAN, 1823 ch. h., Muley—Coxcomb's dam, by Windle. Bred in England by Mr. Painter. 19-15-3-0, $11,096, Dee S., etc. At 16 hands, large for his time. Imported in 1830 by James Jackson of Alabama. Not well received at first because of his enormous size. In 1838, became America's first $100,000 sire when his progeny won 92 races. At one time, his $75 fee was the highest in America. Stood in Tennessee, managed by Col. George Elliott. Died in Gallatin, Tennessee, in 1846, at age 23 from "inflammation of the bowels."

1848 (co-leader)—*TRUSTEE, 1829 ch. h., Catton—Emma, by Whisker. 11-4-3-3, $7,446, Claret S., etc. Third in 1832 Epsom Derby in first career start. Brother to 1835 Epsom Derby winner Mundig, half brother to '43 Derby winner Cotherstone. Imported in 1835 by Commodore Robert Stockton, later senator from New Jersey. Not well received by American breeders and moved often during his stud career. Stood in New York between 1836-'41; Virginia in 1842; Kentucky in 1843-'44; Virginia in 1845-'46; and back to New York in 1847, where he remained until his death at age 27. Sire of Racing Hall of Fame filly Fashion, the great mare Levity, and leading 1860 American sire Revenue. Died in 1856 at West Farms, Westchester County, New York.

1846, 1844-'45, 1842—*PRIAM, 1827 b. h., Emilius—Cressida, by Whisker. Bred in England by Sir John Shelley. 16-14-1-1, $65,100. Winner of the 1830 Epsom Derby, Goodwood Cup. Considered the greatest English racehorse of his era. Imported in 1837 by Merritt and Co. for $15,000, then believed to be a record. Leading American sire four times. Sire of Epsom Oaks winners Crucifix, Miss Letty, and Industry before his importation. Sire in America of Margaret Wood, Little Trick, Lucy Long. Died in Tennessee in 1847 at age 20.

1841, 1840—MEDOC, 1829 ch. h., American Eclipse—Young Maid of the Oaks, by *Expedition. Bred in New York by James Bathgate. 5-4-1-0, $5,300. Greatest son of American Eclipse. Entered stud in Kentucky in 1835. His offspring won 61 races in 1840 and 51 races the following year. Sire of top four-miler Grey Medoc, Bob Letcher, Mary Morris, Picayune. Broke his near foreleg when he stepped in a hole during exercise in 1839 and died at age ten from the injury at Col. William Buford's farm in Woodford County, Kentucky.

1836, 1830-'33—SIR CHARLES, 1816 ch. h., Sir Archy—*Citizen mare, by *Citizen. Won 20 of 25 starts. Believed to have been bred in Virginia by W. R. Johnson. Ancestry of his dam questioned; some referred to her as a "cart mare" whose pedigree had been fabricated. Dominant in long heat races throughout the South. Beaten while lame in final start, 1822 match with American Eclipse for the national championship in Washington, D.C. Died on June 7, 1833, at age 17 at George Johnson's Earnscliffe Plantation, Virginia. Sired the great racemares Trifle, Bonnets o' Blue, and Rosalie Somers, and notable racehorse and sire Wagner.

1835—BERTRAND, 1821 b. h., Sir Archy—Eliza, by *Bedford. Bred in South Carolina by Col. John R. Spann. Won 13 of 16 starts. In 1826, he was sold to Hutchcraft and Co. and sent to Kentucky, where he stood his entire 12-season career, and was said to have covered between 175 and 200 mares per season. He is credited with vastly improving the Thoroughbred of the Bluegrass region. His best include John Bascombe, Richard Singleton, and Queen Mary. Died in Hopkinsville, Kentucky, in 1838 at age 17.

1834—MONSIEUR TONSON, 1822 b. h., Pacolet—Madam Tonson, by Top Gallant. Bred in Tennessee by Thomas Foxhall. Won 11 of 12 starts; only defeat was his first start as a two-year-old. William R. Johnson, the "Napoleon of the Turf" in America, bought him for $10,000. Stood initially in Virginia, later in North Carolina, and finally was sent to Kentucky, where he died. Sire of South Carolina champion Argyle and many other winners.

Note: Prior to 1860, leading sires were based on races won rather than progeny earnings.

All-Time Leading Sires

The sire lists on the following pages do not include steeplechase statistics.

All-Time Leading North American Sires by Total Worldwide Earnings

Through 2005

Sire, YOB, Sire	Where Stood	Earnings
Danzig, 1977, by Northern Dancer	U.S.	$101,644,226
Mr. Prospector, 1970, by Raise a Native	U.S.	97,817,714
Storm Cat, 1983, by Storm Bird	U.S.	96,279,069
Woodman, 1983, by Mr. Prospector	U.S., Aus.	89,009,594
Crafty Prospector, 1979, by Mr. Prospector	U.S.	83,990,883
Seattle Slew, 1974, by Bold Reasoning	U.S.	82,883,541
Nureyev, 1977, by Northern Dancer	Fr., U.S.	77,856,012
Wild Again, 1980, by Icecapade	U.S.	77,326,612
Kris S., 1977, by Roberto	U.S.	75,260,385
Deputy Minister, 1979, by Vice Regent	U.S.	73,199,634
Royal Academy, 1987, by Nijinsky II	Ire., Jpn., U.S., Aus.	71,173,845
Seeking the Gold, 1985, by Mr. Prospector	U.S.	69,807,588
A.P. Indy, 1989, by Seattle Slew	U.S.	69,335,524
Miswaki, 1978, by Mr. Prospector	U.S.	68,992,698
Cozzene, 1980, by Caro (Ire)	U.S.	68,959,023
Dixieland Band, 1980, by Northern Dancer	U.S.	67,377,040
Rahy, 1985, by Blushing Groom (Fr)	U.S.	65,669,114
Theatrical (Ire), 1982, by Nureyev	U.S.	65,011,431
Gulch, 1984, by Mr. Prospector	U.S.	64,983,092
Pleasant Colony, 1978, by His Majesty	U.S.	64,559,861
Kingmambo, 1990, by Mr. Prospector	U.S.	64,284,254
Broad Brush, 1983, by Ack Ack	U.S.	62,391,135
Mt. Livermore, 1981, by Blushing Groom (Fr)	U.S.	62,363,471
Conquistador Cielo, 1979, by Mr. Prospector	U.S.	60,937,913
Gone West, 1984, by Mr. Prospector	U.S.	60,609,530
Alydar, 1975, by Raise a Native	U.S.	60,556,180
Dynaformer, 1985, by Roberto	U.S.	58,401,438
Silver Deputy, 1985, by Deputy Minister	U.S.	57,287,694
Carson City, 1987, by Mr. Prospector	U.S.	56,083,034
Cure the Blues, 1978, by Stop the Music	U.S.	56,026,759
Nijinsky II, 1967, by Northern Dancer	U.S.	55,220,808
Relaunch, 1976, by In Reality	U.S.	54,461,977
Dehere, 1991, by Deputy Minister	Japan	54,162,863
Green Dancer, 1972, by Nijinsky II	Fr., U.S.	52,835,675
El Prado (Ire), 1989, by Sadler's Wells	U.S.	51,255,711
Affirmed, 1975, by Exclusive Native	U.S.	51,224,458
Runaway Groom, 1979, by Blushing Groom (Fr)	U.S.	50,696,328
Lyphard, 1969, by Northern Dancer	Fr., U.S.	49,926,936
Silver Hawk, 1979, by Roberto	U.S.	48,974,829
Phone Trick, 1982, by Clever Trick	U.S.	48,592,564
Valid Appeal, 1972, by In Reality	U.S.	48,186,377
Black Tie Affair (Ire), 1986, by Miswaki	U.S., Jpn.	48,010,518
Devil's Bag, 1981, by Halo	U.S.	47,713,708
Vice Regent, 1967, by Northern Dancer	Canada	46,824,149
Allen's Prospect, 1982, by Mr. Prospector	U.S.	46,809,253
Bold Ruckus, 1976, by Boldnesian	Can.	46,021,978
Clever Trick, 1976, by Icecapade	U.S.	45,056,580
Unbridled, 1987, by Fappiano	U.S.	44,970,697
Irish River (Fr), 1976, by Riverman	Fr., U.S.	44,806,434
Halo, 1969, by Hail to Reason	U.S.	44,392,274
Capote, 1984, by Seattle Slew	U.S.	44,384,484
Saint Ballado, 1989, by Halo	U.S.	44,360,259
Diesis (GB), 1980, by Sharpen Up (GB)	U.S.	44,303,579

All-Time Leading Sires by Number of Winners Worldwide

Through 2005

Sire, YOB, Sire	Where Stood	Wnrs
Danehill, 1986, by Danzig	Ire., Jpn., Aus.	1,375
Woodman, 1983, by Mr. Prospector	U.S., Aus.	921
Sunday Silence, 1986, by Halo	Jpn.	888
Sadler's Wells, 1981, by Northern Dancer	Ire.	879
Royal Academy, 1987, by Nijinsky II	Ire., Jpn., U.S., Aus.	871
Night Shift, 1980, by Northern Dancer	Eng., U.S., Ire.	759
Mr. Prospector, 1970, by Raise a Native	U.S.	752
Southern Halo, 1983, by Halo	Arg., U.S., Jpn.	743
Last Tycoon (Ire), 1983, by Try My Best	Ire., Aus., Jpn., N.Z.	734
Bluebird, 1984, by Storm Bird	Ire., Aus.	681
Allen's Prospect, 1982, by Mr. Prospector	U.S.	679
Miswaki, 1978, by Mr. Prospector	U.S.	675
Crafty Prospector, 1979, by Mr. Prospector	U.S.	668
Dixieland Band, 1980, by Northern Dancer	U.S.	668
Mr. Leader, 1966, by Hail to Reason	U.S.	668
Alzao, 1980, by Lyphard	Ire., Aus.	664
Clever Trick, 1976, by Icecapade	U.S.	659
Runaway Groom, 1979, by Blushing Groom (Fr)	U.S.	641
Danzig, 1977, by Northern Dancer	U.S.	640
Phone Trick, 1982, by Clever Trick	U.S.	613
Wild Again, 1980, by Icecapade	U.S.	607
Green Dancer, 1972, by Nijinsky II	Fr., U.S.	602
Geiger Counter, 1982, by Mr. Prospector	Can., U.S., Aus.	593
Grand Lodge, 1991, by Chief's Crown	Ire.	593
Be My Guest, 1974, by Northern Dancer	Ire.	586
Caerleon, 1980, by Nijinsky II	Ire.	586
Mt. Livermore, 1981, by Blushing Groom (Fr)	U.S.	576
Conquistador Cielo, 1979, by Mr. Prospector	U.S.	571
Storm Cat, 1983, by Storm Bird	U.S.	570
Zabeel, 1986, by *Sir Tristram	N.Z.	568
Kris S., 1977, by Roberto	U.S.	561
Valid Appeal, 1972, by In Reality	U.S.	561
Cryptoclearance, 1984, by Fappiano	U.S.	555
Cure the Blues, 1978, by Stop the Music	U.S.	551
Red Ransom, 1987, by Roberto	England, U.S.	545
Fortunate Prospect, 1981, by Northern Prospect	U.S.	543
Afleet, 1984, by Mr. Prospector	U.S., Jpn.	542
Deputy Minister, 1979, by Vice Regent	U.S.	539
Riverman, 1969, by Never Bend	Fr., U.S.	536
Fit to Fight, 1979, by Chieftain	U.S.	535
Carson City, 1987, by Mr. Prospector	U.S.	531
Irish River (Fr), 1976, by Riverman	U.S.	530
Regal Classic, 1985, by Vice Regent	U.S.	529
Pirate's Bounty, 1975, by Hoist the Flag	U.S.	528

All-Time Leading Sires of Stakes Winners Worldwide

Through 2005

Sire, YOB, Sire	Where Stood	SWs
Danehill, 1986, by Danzig	Ire., Jpn., Aus.	310
Sadler's Wells, 1981, by Northern Dancer	Ire.	247
Danzig, 1977, by Northern Dancer	U.S.	188
Mr. Prospector, 1970, by Raise a Native	U.S.	180
Nijinsky II, 1967, by Northern Dancer	U.S.	153
Northern Dancer, 1961, by Nearctic	Can., U.S.	146
Sunday Silence, 1986, by Halo	Jpn.	145
Southern Halo, 1983, by Halo	Arg., U.S., Jpn.	143
Storm Cat, 1983, by Storm Bird	U.S.	142
Nureyev, 1977, by Northern Dancer	Fr., U.S.	137
Riverman, 1969, by Never Bend	Fr., U.S.	127
Royal Academy, 1987, by Nijinsky II	Ire., Jpn., U.S., Aus.	126
*Sir Tristram, 1971, by Sir Ivor	N.Z.	125
Caerleon, 1980, by Nijinsky II	Ire., Aus.	125
Lyphard, 1969, by Northern Dancer	U.S.	114
Seattle Slew, 1974, by Bold Reasoning	U.S.	114
Roy, 1983, by Fappiano	Chi., U.S., Brz., Arg.	112
Dixieland Band, 1980, by Northern Dancer	U.S.	108
Vice Regent, 1967, by Northern Dancer	Can.	104
Woodman, 1983, by Mr. Prospector	U.S., Aus.	101
Zabeel, 1986, by *Sir Tristram	N.Z.	99

Sire, YOB, Sire	Where Stood	SWs
Miswaki, 1978, by Mr. Prospector	U.S.	97
Alleged, 1974, by Hoist the Flag	U.S.	94
Alzao, 1980, by Lyphard	Ire., Aus.	94
Rainbow Quest, 1981, by Blushing Groom (Fr)	Eng.	94
*Nasrullah, 1940, by Nearco	Ire., U.S.	93
Sir Ivor, 1965, by Sir Gaylord	Ire., U.S.	92
Blushing Groom (Fr), 1974, by Red God	U.S.	91
Habitat, 1966, by Sir Gaylord	Ire.	89
Nodouble, 1965, by *Noholme II	U.S.	89
Darshaan, 1981, by Shirley Heights	Ire.	88
Kris S., 1977, by Roberto	U.S.	88
Nearco, 1935, by Pharos	Eng.	88
Night Shift, 1980, by Northern Dancer	Eng. U.S., Ire.	88
Relaunch, 1976, by In Reality	U.S.	88
Valid Appeal, 1972, by In Reality	U.S.	88
Green Dancer, 1972, by Nijinsky II	Fr., U.S.	87
Broad Brush, 1983, by Ack Ack	U.S.	86
Crafty Prospector, 1979, by Mr. Prospector	U.S.	86
Hyperion, 1930, by Gainsborough	Eng.	86
Affirmed, 1975, by Exclusive Native	U.S.	84
Irish River (Fr), 1976, by Riverman	Fr., U.S.	84
Wild Again, 1980, by Icecapade	U.S.	84
Deputy Minister, 1979, by Vice Regent	U.S.	83
Mr. Leader, 1966, by Hail to Reason	U.S.	83
Round Table, 1954, by *Princequillo	U.S.	83

All-Time Leading Sires by Percentage of Stakes Winners Worldwide

Through 2005

Sire, YOB, Sire	Where Stood	% SWs
Northern Dancer, 1961, by Nearctic	Can., U.S.	22.6%
Bold Ruler, 1954, by *Nasrullah	U.S.	22.4%
*Nasrullah, 1940, by Nearco	Ire., U.S.	21.9%
Round Table, 1954, by *Princequillo	U.S.	20.5%
Hoist the Flag, 1968, by Tom Rolfe	U.S.	19.9%
*Sea-Bird, 1962, by Dan Cupid	U.S., Fr.	18.9%
Nijinsky II, 1967, by Northern Dancer	U.S.	17.7%
Blushing Groom (Fr), 1974, by Red God	U.S.	17.4%
Nureyev, 1977, by Northern Dancer	Fr., U.S.	17.0%
Danzig, 1977, by Northern Dancer	U.S.	16.9%
*Mahmoud, 1933, by *Blenheim II	Eng., U.S.	16.6%
Never Bend, 1960, by *Nasrullah	U.S.	16.5%
Tentam, 1969, by Intentionally	U.S.	16.1%
*Court Martial, 1942, by Fair Trial	Eng., U.S.	16.0%
Philately, 1962, by *Princequillo	U.S.	16.0%
Roberto, 1969, by Hail to Reason	U.S.	16.0%
*Amerigo, 1955, by Nearco	U.S.	15.7%
Sea Aglo, 1971, by *Sea-Bird	U.S.	15.6%
*Heliopolis, 1936, by Hyperion	U.S.	15.3%
*Ribot, 1952, by Tenerani	Ity., Eng., U.S.	15.2%
Nedayr, 1935, by Neddie	U.S.	15.1%
Vice Regent, 1967, by Northern Dancer	Can.	15.1%
Mr. Prospector, 1970, by Raise a Native	U.S.	15.0%
Bull Lea, 1935, by *Bull Dog	U.S.	14.9%
Eight Thirty, 1936, by Pilate	U.S.	14.7%
*Herbager, 1956, by Vandale	Fr., U.S.	14.5%
Chop Chop, 1940, by Flares	Can.	14.4%
In Reality, 1964, by Intentionally	U.S.	14.4%
Native Dancer, 1950, by Polynesian	U.S.	14.4%
Pelouse, 1951, by Pavot	U.S.	14.3%
Nearctic, 1954, by Nearco	Can., U.S.	14.2%
*Royal Charger, 1942, by Nearco	Ire., U.S.	14.2%

All-Time Leading Sires of Group or Graded Stakes Winners Worldwide

Through 2005

Sire, YOB, Sire	Where Stood	GSWs
Danehill, 1986, by Danzig	Ire., Jpn., Aus.	181
Sadler's Wells, 1981, by Northern Dancer	Ire.	142
Mr. Prospector, 1970, by Raise a Native	U.S.	111
Danzig, 1977, by Northern Dancer	U.S.	104
Southern Halo, 1983, by Halo	Arg., U.S. Jpn.	100
Nijinsky II, 1967, by Northern Dancer	U.S.	97
Roy, 1983, by Fappiano	Chi., U.S., Brz., Arg.	87
Storm Cat, 1983, by Storm Bird	U.S.	86
*Sir Tristram, 1971, by Sir Ivor	N.Z.	83]
Northern Dancer, 1961, by Nearctic	Can., U.S.	77
Nureyev, 1977, by Northern Dancer	Fr., U.S.	77
Zabeel, 1986, by *Sir Tristram	N.Z.	70
Caerleon, 1980, by Nijinsky II	Ire., Aus.	67
Riverman, 1969, by Never Bend	Fr., U.S.	67
Ghadeer, 1978, by Lyphard	Brz.	64
Lyphard, 1969, by Northern Dancer	U.S.	64
Royal Academy, 1987, by Nijinsky II	Ire., U.S., Jpn., Aus.	64
Seattle Slew, 1974, by Bold Reasoning	U.S.	59
Blushing Groom (Fr), 1974, by Red God	U.S.	58
Alleged, 1974, by Hoist the Flag	U.S.	57
Habitat, 1966, by Sir Gaylord	Ire.	56
Rainbow Quest, 1981, by Blushing Groom (Fr)	Eng.	55
Fitzcarraldo, 1981, by Cipayo	Arg.	52
Cipayo, 1974, by Lacydon	Arg.	48
A.P. Indy, 1989, by Seattle Slew	U.S.	46
Alydar, 1975, by Raise a Native	U.S.	46
*Vaguely Noble, 1965, by Vienna	U.S.	44
Sir Ivor, 1965, by Sir Gaylord	Ire., U.S.	44
Bluebird, 1984, by Storm Bird	Ire., Aus.	43
Clackson, 1976, by I Say	Brz.	43
Diesis (GB), 1980, by Sharpen Up (GB)	U.S.	43
Green Dancer, 1972, by Nijinsky II	Fr., U.S.	43
Dixieland Band, 1980, by Northern Dancer	U.S.	42
Elliodor, 1977, by Lyphard	S. Af.	42
Roberto, 1969, by Hail to Reason	U.S.	42
Theatrical (Ire), 1982, by Nureyev	U.S.	42
Affirmed, 1975, by Exclusive Native	U.S.	41
Alzao, 1980, by Lyphard	Ire., Aus.	41
Damascus, 1964, by Sword Dancer	U.S.	41
Egg Toss, 1977, by Buckpasser	Arg.	41
Gone West, 1984, by Mr. Prospector	U.S.	41
Irish River (Fr), 1976, by Riverman	U.S.	41
Lode, 1986, by Mr. Prospector	Brz.	41

All-Time Leading Sires of Group 1 or Grade 1 Stakes Winners Worldwide

Through 2005

Sire, YOB, Sire	Where Stood	G1Ws
Danehill, 1986, by Danzig	Ire	69
Sadler's Wells, 1981, by Northern Dancer	Ire	67
Southern Halo, 1983, by Halo	Arg., U.S., Jpn.	49
Mr. Prospector, 1970, by Raise a Native	U.S.	48
Roy, 1983, by Fappiano	Chi., U.S., Brz., Arg.	47
*Sir Tristram, 1971, by Sir Ivor	N.Z.	45
Danzig, 1977, by Northern Dancer	U.S.	43
Nijinsky II, 1967, by Northern Dancer	U.S.	34
Zabeel, 1986, by *Sir Tristram	N.Z.	32
Storm Cat, 1983, by Storm Bird	U.S.	30
Nureyev, 1977, by Northern Dancer	Fr., U.S.	29
Seattle Slew, 1974, by Bold Reasoning	U.S.	27
Ghadeer, 1978, by Lyphard	Brz.	26
Northern Dancer, 1961, by Nearctic	Can., U.S.	26
Blushing Groom (Fr), 1974, by Red God	U.S.	25
Lyphard, 1969, by Northern Dancer	Fr., U.S.	25
Riverman, 1969, by Never Bend	Fr., U.S.	24
*Vaguely Noble, 1965, by Vienna	U.S.	23
Alleged, 1974, by Hoist the Flag	U.S.	22
Caerleon, 1980, by Nijinsky II	Ire., Aus.	22
Cipayo, 1974, by Lacydon	Arg.	21
Lode, 1986, by Mr. Prospector	Arg.	21
Alydar, 1975, by Raise a Native	U.S.	20
Fitzcarraldo, 1981, by Cipayo	Arg.	20
Sunday Silence, 1986, by Halo	Jpn	20
Caro (Ire), 1967, by Fortino II	Fr., U.S.	19

Sire, YOB, Sire	Where Stood	G1Ws
Habitat, 1966, by Sir Gaylord	Ire.	19
Hussonet, 1991, by Mr. Prospector	Chi., Aus.	19
Mill Reef, 1968, by Never Bend	Eng.	19
Candy Stripes, 1982, by Blushing Groom (Fr)	U.S., Arg., Brz.	18
Rainbow Quest, 1981, by Blushing Groom (Fr)	Eng.	18
Star Way, 1977, by *Star Appeal	N.Z.	18
Theatrical (Ire), 1982, by Nureyev	U.S.	18

All-Time Leading Sires by Progeny Earnings Worldwide

Through 2005

Sire, YOB, Sire	Where Stood	Earnings
Sunday Silence, 1986, by Halo	Jpn.	$578,383,102
Danehill, 1986, by Danzig	Ire., Jpn., Aus.	216,231,248
Brian's Time, 1985, by Roberto	Jpn.	210,586,227
Tony Bin, 1983, by Kampala	Jpn.	191,538,308
Northern Taste, 1971, by Northern Dancer	Jpn.	132,954,524
Afleet, 1984, by Mr. Prospector	U.S., Jpn.	127,754,559
Sadler's Wells, 1981, by Northern Dancer	Ire.	119,097,973
Real Shadai, 1979, by Roberto	Jpn.	106,622,303
Danzig, 1977, by Northern Dancer	U.S.	101,644,226
Forty Niner, 1985, by Mr. Prospector	U.S., Jpn.	98,501,344
Mr. Prospector, 1970, by Raise a Native	U.S.	97,817,714
Storm Cat, 1983, by Storm Bird	U.S.	96,279,069
Caerleon, 1980, by Nijinsky II	Ire., Aus.	95,782,175
Woodman, 1983, by Mr. Prospector	U.S., Aus.	89,042,650
Jade Robbery, 1987, by Mr. Prospector	Jpn.	88,010,339
Last Tycoon (Ire), 1983, by Try My Best	Ire., Aus., Jpn., N.Z.	84,150,602
Crafty Prospector, 1979, by Mr. Prospector	U.S.	83,990,883
Sakura Yutaka O, 1982, by Tesco Boy		83,365,879
Seattle Slew, 1974, by Bold Reasoning	U.S.	82,883,541
Amber Shadai, 1977, by Northern Taste	Jpn.	81,891,714
Nureyev, 1977, by Northern Dancer	Fr., U.S.	77,856,012
Wild Again, 1980, by Icecapade	U.S.	77,326,612
Kris S., 1977, by Roberto	U.S.	75,269,002
Deputy Minister, 1979, by Vice Regent	U.S.	73,199,634
End Sweep, 1991, by Forty Niner	U.S., Jpn.	73,034,418
Nihon Pillow Winner, 1980, by Steel Heart	Jpn.	71,700,582
Tamamo Cross, 1984, by C B Cross	Jpn.	71,232,860
Royal Academy, 1987, by Nijinsky II	Ire., Jpn., U.S., Aus.	71,218,819
Seeking the Gold, 1985, by Mr. Prospector	U.S.	69,811,587
A.P. Indy, 1989, by Seattle Slew	U.S.	69,335,524
Miswaki, 1978, by Mr. Prospector	U.S.	68,992,698
Cozzene, 1980, by Caro (Ire)	U.S.	68,964,538
Dancing Brave, 1983, by Lyphard	Eng., Jpn.	67,712,275
Dixieland Band, 1980, by Northern Dancer	U.S.	67,379,813
Rahy, 1985, by Blushing Groom (Fr)	U.S.	65,671,026
Theatrical (Ire), 1982, by Nureyev	U.S.	65,011,431
Gulch, 1984, by Mr. Prospector	U.S.	64,991,542
Pleasant Colony, 1978, by His Majesty	U.S.	64,559,861
Kingmambo, 1990, by Mr. Prospector	U.S.	64,284,254

All-Time Leading North American Broodmare Sires by Progeny Earnings Worldwide

Through 2005

Sire, YOB, Sire	Where Stood	Earnings
Mr. Prospector, 1970, by Raise a Native	U.S.	$237,390,108
Nijinsky II, 1967, by Northern Dancer	U.S.	195,434,759
Danzig, 1977, by Northern Dancer	U.S.	171,541,358
Lyphard, 1969, by Northern Dancer	Fr., U.S.	164,749,199
Northern Dancer, 1961, by Nearctic	Can., U.S.	162,145,732
Nureyev, 1977, by Northern Dancer	Fr., U.S.	146,857,999
Alydar, 1975, by Raise a Native	U.S.	145,284,685
Seattle Slew, 1974, by Bold Reasoning	U.S.	$141,507,256
Blushing Groom, (Fr), 1974, by Red God	U.S.	138,688,433
Secretariat, 1970, by Bold Ruler	U.S.	133,548,699
Vice Regent, 1967, by Northern Dancer	Can.	119,254,325
Halo, 1969, by Hail to Reason	U.S.	118,374,520
Riverman, 1969, by Never Bend	Fr., U.S.	118,193,938
Affirmed, 1975, by Exclusive Native	U.S.	107,467,859
Miswaki, 1978, by Mr. Prospector	U.S.	104,557,955
Damascus, 1964, by Sword Dancer	U.S.	101,829,496
Roberto, 1969, by Hail to Reason	U.S.	99,602,840
Alleged, 1974, by Hoist the Flag	U.S.	97,622,071
Raise a Native, 1961, by Native Dancer	U.S.	96,554,072
Green Dancer, 1972, by Nijinsky II	Fr., U.S.	95,760,361
*Grey Dawn II, 1962, by *Herbager	U.S.	89,715,874
In Reality, 1964, by Intentionally	U.S.	88,942,315
Key to the Mint, 1969, by Graustark	U.S.	87,441,121
Storm Bird, 1978, by Northern Dancer	U.S.	87,195,556
Graustark, 1963, by *Ribot	U.S.	86,000,349
Caro, (Ire), 1967, by Fortino II	Fr., U.S.	85,960,756
Valid Appeal, 1972, by In Reality	U.S.	83,575,241
*Vaguely Noble, 1965, by Vienna	U.S.	83,513,415
Sir Ivor, 1965, by Sir Gaylord	Ire., U.S.	83,238,128
Deputy Minister, 1979, by Vice Regent	U.S.	82,470,804
Fappiano, 1977, by Mr. Prospector	U.S.	81,457,825
Mr. Leader, 1966, by Hail to Reason	U.S.	75,415,577
Tom Rolfe, 1962, by *Ribot	U.S.	74,627,891
Irish River (Fr), 1976, by Riverman	Fr., U.S.	74,453,879
Dixieland Band, 1980, by Northern Dancer	U.S.	73,887,662
The Minstrel, 1974, by Northern Dancer	U.S.	72,559,368

All-Time Leading Broodmare Sires by Progeny Earnings Worldwide

Through 2005

Sire, YOB, Sire	Where Stood	Earnings
Northern Taste, 1971, by Northern Dancer	Jpn.	$467,247,167
Mr. Prospector, 1970, by Raise a Native	U.S.	237,439,550
Nijinsky II, 1967, by Northern Dancer	U.S.	195,435,943
Tosho Boy, 1973, by Tesco Boy	Jpn.	183,366,235
Danzig, 1977, by Northern Dancer	U.S.	171,566,713
Lyphard, 1969, by Northern Dancer	Fr., U.S.	164,762,375
Northern Dancer, 1961, by Nearctic	Can., U.S.	162,145,732
Nureyev, 1977, by Northern Dancer	Fr., U.S.	146,884,023
Alydar, 1975, by Raise a Native	U.S.	145,284,876
Seattle Slew, 1974, by Bold Reasoning	U.S.	141,517,373
Blushing Groom (Fr), 1974, by Red God	U.S.	138,710,775
Secretariat, 1970, by Bold Ruler	U.S.	133,550,029
Bravest Roman, 1972, by Never Bend	Jpn.	119,952,103
Vice Regent, 1967, by Northern Dancer	Can.	119,263,670
Halo, 1969, by Hail to Reason	U.S.	118,387,609
Riverman, 1969, by Never Bend	Fr., U.S.	118,203,581
Caerleon, 1980, by Nijinsky II	Ire., Aus.	107,736,523
Affirmed, 1975, by Exclusive Native	U.S.	107,475,239
Sadler's Wells, 1981, by Northern Dancer	Ire.	105,452,996
Miswaki, 1978, by Mr. Prospector	U.S.	104,581,227
Damascus, 1964, by Sword Dancer	U.S.	101,818,833
Tesco Boy, 1963, by Princely Gift	Jpn.	101,608,359
Roberto, 1969, by Hail to Reason	U.S.	99,609,361
Alleged, 1974, by Hoist the Flag	U.S.	97,695,263
Mill George, 1975, by Mill Reef	Jpn.	97,446,807
Raise a Native, 1961, by Native Dancer	U.S.	96,568,134
Green Dancer, 1972, by Nijinsky II	Fr., U.S.	95,776,422
Partholon, 1960, by Milesian	Jpn.	90,322,977
*Grey Dawn II, 1962, by *Herbager	U.S.	89,715,874
In Reality, 1964, by Intentionally	U.S.	88,948,486
Key to the Mint, 1969, by Graustark	U.S.	87,443,436
Storm Bird, 1978, by Northern Dancer	U.S.	87,243,696
Graustark, 1963, by *Ribot	U.S.	86,000,349
Caro (Ire), 1967, by Fortino II	U.S.	85,968,739
Valid Appeal, 1972, by In Reality	U.S.	83,575,241
*Vaguely Noble, 1965, by Vienna	U.S.	83,513,903

Sire, YOB, Sire	Where Stood	Earnings
Sir Ivor, 1965, by Sir Gaylord	Ire., U.S.	$83,239,344
Deputy Minister, 1979, by Vice Regent	U.S.	82,486,454
Fappiano, 1977, by Mr. Prospector	U.S.	81,458,343
Dancer's Image, 1965, by Native Dancer	U.S., Fr., Jpn.	76,556,691
Royal Ski, 1974, by Raja Baba	U.S., Jpn.	76,344,402
Mr. Leader, 1966, by Hail to Reason	U.S.	75,416,167
Prince John, 1953, by *Princequillo		75,339,398

All-Time Leading Broodmare Sires by Number of Stakes Winners Worldwide

Through 2005

Sire, YOB, Sire	Where Stood	SWs
Mr. Prospector, 1970, by Raise a Native	U.S.	297
Nijinsky II, 1967, by Northern Dancer	U.S.	236
Northern Dancer, 1961, by Nearctic	Can., U.S.	235
Habitat, 1966, by Sir Gaylord	Ire.	219
Lyphard, 1969, by Northern Dancer	Fr., U.S.	201
Raise a Native, 1961, by Native Dancer	U.S.	182
Hyperion, 1930, by Gainsborough	Eng.	172
*Princequillo, 1940, by Prince Rose	U.S.	170
Prince John, 1953, by *Princequillo	U.S.	169
Riverman, 1969, by Never Bend	Fr., U.S.	168
*Vaguely Noble, 1965, by Vienna	U.S.	162
*Nasrullah, 1940, by Nearco	Ire., U.S.	159
Secretariat, 1970, by Bold Ruler	U.S.	159
*Sir Tristram, 1971, by Sir Ivor	N.Z.	158
Damascus, 1964, by Sword Dancer	U.S.	157
Northfields, 1968, by Northern Dancer	Aus.	157
Nearco, 1935, by Pharos	Eng.	154
Sir Ivor, 1965, by Sir Gaylord	Ire., U.S.	150
*Sir Gallahad III, 1920, by *Teddy	U.S.	147
Nureyev, 1977, by Northern Dancer	Fr., U.S.	147
In Reality, 1964, by Intentionally	U.S.	146
Fleet Nasrullah, 1955, by *Nasrullah	U.S.	145
Green Dancer, 1972, by Nijinsky II	Fr., U.S.	145
Alleged, 1974, by Hoist the Flag	U.S.	143
Blushing Groom (Fr), 1974, by Red God	U.S.	143
Graustark, 1963, by *Ribot	U.S.	143
Seattle Slew, 1974, by Bold Reasoning	U.S.	142
Roberto, 1969, by Hail to Reason	U.S.	139
Shirley Heights, 1975, by Mill Reef	Eng.	139
*Mahmoud, 1933, by *Blenheim II	Eng., U.S.	137
Buckpasser, 1963, by Tom Fool	U.S.	137
Halo, 1969, by Hail to Reason	U.S.	137
Alydar, 1975, by Raise a Native	U.S.	136
Sadler's Wells, 1981, by Northern Dancer	Ire.	136
Danzig, 1977, by Northern Dancer	U.S.	130
*Grey Dawn II, 1962, by *Herbager	U.S.	127
Mill Reef, 1968, by Never Bend	Eng.	127
Round Table, 1954, by *Princequillo	U.S.	124
Big Game, 1939, by *Bahram	Eng.	122

All-Time Leading Broodmare Sires of Group or Graded Stakes Winners Worldwide

Through 2005

Sire, YOB, Sire	Where Stood	GSWs
Mr. Prospector, 1970, by Raise a Native	U.S.	135
Nijinsky II, 1967, by Northern Dancer	U.S.	112
Habitat, 1966, by Sir Gaylord	Ire.	104
Northern Dancer, 1961, by Nearctic	Can., U.S.	104
Northfields, 1968, by Northern Dancer	Ire.,Aus., S.Af.	99
*Sir Tristram, 1971, by Sir Ivor	N.Z.	85
Lyphard, 1969, by Northern Dancer	Fr., U.S.	82
Riverman, 1969, by Never Bend	Fr., U.S.	81
*Vaguely Noble, 1965, by Vienna	U.S.	76
Nureyev, 1977, by Northern Dancer	Fr., U.S.	74
Seattle Slew, 1974, by Bold Reasoning	U.S.	70
Roberto, 1969, by Hail to Reason	U.S.	68
Shirley Heights, 1975, by Mill Reef	Eng.	68
Prince John, 1953, by *Princequillo	U.S.	67
Sir Ivor, 1965, by Sir Gaylord	Ire., U.S.	66
Buckpasser, 1963, by Tom Fool	U.S.	64
Green Dancer, 1972, by Nijinsky II	Fr., U.S.	64
Alleged, 1974, by Hoist the Flag	U.S.	63
Blushing Groom (Fr), 1974, by Red God	U.S.	63
Graustark, 1963, by *Ribot	U.S.	63
Sadler's Wells, 1981, by Northern Dancer	Ire.	62
Alydar, 1975, by Raise a Native	U.S.	61
Secretariat, 1970, by Bold Ruler	U.S.	60
Ghadeer, 1978, by Lyphard	Brz.	59
Mill Reef, 1968, by Never Bend	Eng.	59
Sovereign Edition, 1962, by Sovereign Path	N.Z.	59
Raise a Native, 1961, by Native Dancer	U.S.	57
Round Table, 1954, by *Princequillo	U.S.	57
Damascus, 1964, by Sword Dancer	U.S.	56
Key to the Mint, 1969, by Graustark	U.S.	52
Vain, 1966, by Wilkes	Aus.	52
Busted, 1963, by Crepello	Eng.	51
Darshaan, 1981, by Shirley Heights	Ire.	50
The Minstrel, 1974, by Northern Dancer	U.S.	50
Bold Ruler, 1954, by *Nasrullah	U.S.	49
Bletchingly, 1970, by Biscay	Aus.	48
Halo, 1969, by Hail to Reason	U.S.	48
Irish River, (Fr), 1976, by Riverman	Fr., U.S.	46
Logical, 1972, by Buckpasser	Arg.	46

All-Time Leading Broodmare Sires of Group 1 or Grade 1 Stakes Winners

Through 2005

Sire, YOB, Sire	Where Stood	G1Ws
Northfields, 1968, by Northern Dancer	Ire., Aus., S.Af.	44
Nijinsky II, 1967, by Northern Dancer	U.S.	42
Northern Dancer, 1961, by Nearctic	Can., U.S.	40
Mr. Prospector, 1970, by Raise a Native	U.S.	36
Ghadeer, 1978, by Lyphard	Brz.	30
Lyphard, 1969, by Northern Dancer	Fr., U.S.	30
Riverman, 1969, by Never Bend	Fr., U.S.	30
*Sir Tristram, 1971, by Sir Ivor	N.Z.	29
*Vaguely Noble, 1965, by Vienna	U.S.	29
Buckpasser, 1963, by Tom Fool	U.S.	29
Habitat, 1966, by Sir Gaylord	Ire.	27
Key to the Mint, 1969, by Graustark	U.S.	26
Sovereign Edition , 1962, by Sovereign Path	N.Z.	26
Logical, 1972, by Buckpasser	Arg.	24
Nureyev, 1977, by Northern Dancer	Fr., U.S.	24
Sadler's Wells, 1981, by Northern Dancer	Ire.	24
Graustark, 1963, by *Ribot	U.S.	23
Green Dancer, 1972, by Nijinsky II	Fr., U.S.	22
Prince John, 1953, by *Princequillo	U.S.	22
Roberto, 1969, by Hail to Reason	U.S.	22
Secretariat, 1970, by Bold Ruler	U.S.	22
Sir Ivor, 1965, by Sir Gaylord	Ire., U.S.	22
Waldmeister, 1961, by Wild Risk	Brz.	22
Seattle Slew, 1974, by Bold Reasoning	U.S.	21
Alydar, 1975, by Raise a Native	U.S.	20
Darshaan, 1981, by Shirley Heights	Ire.	20
High Top, 1969, by Derring-Do	Eng.	20
Round Table, 1954, by *Princequillo	U.S.	20
Shirley Heights , 1975, by Mill Reef	Eng.	20
Stage Door Johnny, 1965, by Prince John	U.S.	20
Zamazaan, 1965, by Exbury	Aus.	20
Blushing Groom (Fr), 1974, by Red God	U.S.	19
Caro (Ire), 1967, by Fortino II	Fr., U.S.	19
*Le Fabuleux, 1961, by Wild Risk	Fr., U.S.	18
Marscay, 1979, by Biscay	Aus.	18
Raise a Native, 1961, by Native Dancer	U.S.	18

All-Time Leading Sires by Number of Millionaires
Through 2005
(Names of Millionaires)

152 Sunday Silence (Admire Boss, Admire Groove, Admire Japan, Admire Max, Admire Vega, Agnes Arashi, Agnes Flight, Agnes Gold, Agnes Partner, Agnes Special, Agnes Tachyon, Air Gang Star, Air Messiah, Air Shady, Air Shakur, Albireo, Azuma Sanders, Believe [Jpn], Big Sunday, Black Cafe, Black Tuxedo, Born King, Bright Sunday, Bubble Gum Fellow, Chapel Concert, Cheerful Smile, Cheers Brightly, Cheers Grace, Cheers Message, Cheers Silence, Chokai Ryoga, Chunyi, Coin Toss, Croupier Star, Daitaku Surgeon, Daiwa el Cielo, Daiwa Major, Daiwa Raiders, Daiwa Rouge, Dance in the Dark, Dance in the Mood [Jpn], Dance Partner [Jpn], Daring Heart, Deep Impact, Dia de la Novia, Diamond Biko, Divine Light, Durandal, Egao o Misete, Eishin Rudens [Jpn], Emerald Isle, Er Nova, Fuji Kiseki, Fusaichi Airedale, Fusaichi Run Heart, Fusaichi You Can, Genuine, Glorious Sunday, Gold Allure, Great Journey, Hallelujah Sunday, Happy Path, Hat Trick, Heart's Cry, Heavenly Romance, Higher Game, Hustler, Iron Reality, Isao Heat, Ishino Sunday, Jo Big Bang, King of Daiya, King of Sunday, Kiss Me Tender, Les Clefs d'Or, Limitless Bid, Lincoln, Machikane Akatsuki, Magic Kiss, Manhattan Cafe, Maruka Candy, Maruka Komachi, Marvelous Sunday, Meisho Domenica, Meisho Odo, Millennium Bio, Miscast, Monopole, Neo Universe, Noblesse Oblige, Not Seldom, Orange Peel, Orewa Matteruze, Otomeno Inori, Painted Black, Peace of World, Peer Gynt, Ponderosa, Prime Stage, Quiet Day, Reportage, Rosado, Rosebud, Rosen Kavalier, Rosenkreuz, Royal Cancer, Royal Touch, Saikyo Sunday, Sakura President, Shinin' Ruby, Shinko Singular, Silence Suzuka, Silent Cruise, Silent Deal, Silent Happiness, Silent Hunter, Silent Savior, Six Sense, Spartacus, Special Week, Starry Heaven, Stay Gold, Still in Love, Stinger [Jpn], Stormy Sunday, Stratagem, Sunday Branch, Sunday Kaiser, Sunday Sarah, Sun Place, Sunrise Pegasus, Super Chance, Suzuka Mambo, Swift Current, Tagano Silence, Tayasu Meadow, Tayasu Tsuyoshi, Tiger Cafe, Time to Change, T.M.Sunday, T M Tenrai, Tokai Oza, To the Victory, Vita Rosa, Waltz Dancer, What a Reason, Win Duel, Win Marvelous, Win Radius, Yamanin Respect, Yukino Sun Royal, Zenno Rob Roy)

48 Tony Bin (Air Dublin, Air Groove, Air Thule, Bu O, Christmas Tree, Daddy's Dream, Derby Regno, Eighty Grow, Eishin One Schon, Emocion, Felicitar, Freeway Heart, Gemmy Dress, Happy Look, Inter Licence, Irish Dance, Island Oja, Jungle Pocket, Ken Tony O, Lady Pastel, Leningrad, Long Kaiun, Lord Cronos, Lord Platinum, Maquereau, Misuzu Chardon, My Joker, Narita Century, Nobori Yukio, North Flight, Offside Trap, Royce and Royce, Sakura Chitose O, Sakura Victoria, Sidewinder, Spring Coat, Tai Kalamoun, Tayasu Intime, Telegnosis, Tenzan Seiza, Tosen Tensho, Towa Treasure, Vega, Wedding Honey, Winning Ticket, Yuki Slugger, Yuki Vivace, Yu One Protect)

41 Danehill (Air Eminem, Air Smap, Aquarelliste, Arena, Banks Hill [GB], Breaktime, Catbird, Dane Ripper, Danewin, Desert King, Dr More, Elvstroem, Fairy King Prawn, Fastnet Rock, Fine Motion, Flying Spur, Gaily Flash, Gamble Rose, Generalist, Ha Ha, Intercontinental [GB], Jeune King Prawn, Johan Cruyff, Lord Flag, Lucky Owners, Machikane Jindaiko, Mayano Absolute, Merlene, Midtown [Ire], North Light [Ire], Nothin' Leica Dane, Oratorio [Ire], Planet Ruler, Rock of Gibraltar [Ire], Scintillation, Tamamo Ruby King, The Duke, Tiger Hill, Tsukuba Symphony, Uncle Super, Westerner)

36 Brian's Time (Admire Gale, Automatic, Big Gold, Brilliant Road, Chokai Carol, Dantsu Flame, En Dehors, Erimo Brian, Erimo Dandy, Erimo Maxim, Matikanemenimomiyo, Mayano Top Gun, Meine Nouvelle, Meiner Brian, Meiner Max, Meine Sorceress, M.I.Blanc, Narita Brian, Narita Luna Park, No Reason, Osumi Stayer, Phalaenopsis, Port Brian's, Run to the Freeze, Seattle You, Silk Justice, Silk Prima Donna, Silky Lagoon, Spring Verbena, Sunny Brian, Tanino Gimlet, Teruno Shingeki, Time Paradox, Toho Emperor, Toho Kelly, Toho Shiden, Treasure)

29 Northern Taste (Adorable, Agnes Handsome, Air Deja Vu, Best Darjeeling, Big Fight, Big Shori, Daiwa Geant, Elizabeth Rose, Fashion Show, Inter Flag, King Admire, Kris the Brave, Kyoei Forte, Lady Gossip, Main Caster, Manjuden Kabuto, Matikanetannhauser, Nifty Dancer, Northern Rainbow, Northern Way, Osumi Best, Plantain Ciecle, Queen Sonnet, Razor Moon, Samani Beppin, Scarlet Bouquet, Shinin' Racer, Sing Like Talk, Slew O'Dyna)

25 Sadler's Wells (Ballingarry [Ire], Barathea [Ire], Beat Hollow [GB], Brian Boru [GB], Carnegie [Ire], Daliapour, Diaghilev, Doyen, Dream Well [Fr], Dushyantor, Galileo [Ire], High Chaparral [Ire], In the Wings [GB], Islington [Ire], Kayf Tara, King's Theatre [Ire], Montjeu [Ire], Northern Spur [Ire], Old Vic, Opera House [GB], Perfect Soul [Ire], Powerscourt [GB], Refuse To Bend [Ire], Sage Wells, Salsabil [Ire])

23 Amber Shadai (Bebop, Best Tie Up, Camphor Best, Golden Hour, Headship, Hikaru Palo Santo, Hokusei Amber, Jealous Guy, Kachidoki Ryu, Kamino Cremona, Kamino Cresse, Kanahara Dragon, Kanetoshi Governor, Long Shikotei, Meiner Blau, Meisho Genie, Meisho Taikan, Meisho Yoshiie, Mejiro Ryan, Mercury Mannish, Osumi Leopard, Towa Nagon, Tsurumaru Zamurai)

22 Caerleon (Apotheose, Biwa Heidi, Corwyn Bay [Ire], Daiwa Caerleon, Fusaichi Concorde, Generous, Green Blitz, Ibuki Perceive [Jpn], Kostroma [Ire], Kurokami, Lord Successor, L-Way Win, Marienbard, Matikaneharesugata, Missionary Ridge [GB], Paradise Hills, Passacaglia [Jpn], Princess Carla, Shinko Lovely, Volga [Ire], Warrsan, Zenno El Cid)

19 Tamamo Cross (First Sonia, Fuji One Man Cross, Hiro de Cross, Inter Unique, Kanetsu Cross, Kanoya Battlecross, Latir, Love is Dream, Makoto Raiden, Mayano Poseidon, My Sole Sound, Narita Daido, Nihonpillow Keith, Tamamo Highway, Tamamo Inazuma, T.M.Tokkyu, White Happiness, Win Generale, Yamanin Recall)

18 Real Shadai (Air Real, Beauty Make, Big Symbol, Daiichi Joyful, Daiwa Oshu, Grass Position, Hagino Real King, Ibuki Maikagura, King Pharaoh, Monsieur Siecle, Osumi Shadai, Rice Shower, Run for the Dream, Stage Champ, Sunrise Flag, Sunrise Jaeger, Turf Genius, Wedding Cake)

16 Afleet (A Fleets Dancer, Big Fleet, Big Wolf, Check the Luck, Gaily Condor, Gaily Magnum, Golden Jack, Hikari Zirconia, Icarus' Dream, Ishiyaku Mach, Preeminence [Jpn], Primo Ordine [Jpn], Rikiai Taikan, Sammy Miracle, Saqalat, Sterling Rose)

Danzig (Agnes World, Biko Pegasus, Chief's Crown, Dance Smartly, Danzig Connection, Dispute, Dumaani, Hikari Cermet, Lure, Magnaten, Pine Bluff, Polish Navy, Stephan's Odyssey, Versailles Treaty, War Chant, Yamanin Paradise)

Sakura Yutaka O (Air Jihad, Alegrar, Dynamite Daddy, Higashi Majorca, Mayano Dempsey, Nishino Daio, Osumi Max, Sakura Bakushin O, Sakura Candle, Sakura Sekai O, Sistina, Tenzan Yutaka, Tunante, Umeno Fiber, World Now, Yukino Bijin)

15 Dancing Brave (Chokai Raijin, Commander in Chief, Dancing Surpass, Erimo Chic, Erimo Pixy, Green Planet, Joten Brave, King Halo, Kyoei March, Leo Ryuho, Snark Suzuran, Tagajo Noble, T.M.Ocean, T.M.Top Dan, White Muzzle [GB])

14 Dance in the Dark (Admire Condor, Amphitryon, Daitaku Bertram, Delta Blues, Fast Tateyama, Inter Taiyo, Macky Max, Marubutsu Top, Night Flier, Tagano My Bach, That's the Plenty, Tsurumaru Boy, Tsurumaru Yokanise, Win Glanz)

Fuji Kiseki (Air Pierre, Crossandra, Daitaku Riva, Fuji Silence, Grand Pas de Deux, Kane Hekili, Kanetoshi Desire, Maruka Kiseki, Meisho Oscar, Mitsuwa Top Lady, New Very, Osumi Cosmo, Tamamo Hot Play, Tenshino Kiseki)

Kingmambo (Alkaased, American Boss, Asakusa Kininaru, Divine Proportions, El Condor Pasa, King Cugat, King Fidelia, King Kamehameha, Lemon Drop Kid, Mambo Twist, Rule of Law, Russian Rhythm, Star King Man, Voodoo Dancer)

Mr. Prospector (Aldebaran, Chester House, Dancethruthedawn, Educated Risk, Forty Niner, Fusaichi Pegasus, Gulch, Homebuilder, Jet Around, Rhythm, Seeking the Gold, Shake Hand, Syourinomegami, Tank's Prospect)

Nihon Pillow Winner (Bell Winner, Cheers Hope, Dandy Commando, Flower Park, Foundry Shori, Kyoei Bonanza, Mega Stardom, Memory Catch, Nihonpillow Prince, Nihon Pillow Study, Towa Darling, Towa la Novia, Towa Winner, Yamanin Zephyr)

Nureyev (Alwuhush, Annoconnor, Atticus, Black Hawk [GB], Good Journey, Heart Lake, Legacy Hunter, Lord Kirov, Miesque, Peintre Celebre, Skimming, Soviet Star, Spinning World, Theatrical [Ire])

Leading 2005 Sires by State and Province Where Bred

Earnings of horses as reported bred in states and provinces, regardless of where sire stands or stood.
Limited to sires with 2005 progeny earnings of $5,000 or more.

Alabama

Sire, YOB, Sire	Strs	Wnrs	Wins	SWs	Leading Runner (Earnings)	Total Earnings
Royal Empire, 1994, by Forty Niner	11	5	7	1	Comalagold ($64,130)	$167,211
Valid Victorious, 1994, by Valid Appeal	7	1	2	1	Valid Run ($35,180)	52,378
Abity, 1990, by Superbity	2	2	4	0	Ability Springs ($29,381)	41,823
Chief Persuasion, 1983, by Liege Lord	1	1	1	1	Chief Tudor ($30,250)	30,250
Go West, 1995, by Seeking the Gold	1	1	1	1	West Scottie ($28,322)	28,322

Arizona

Sire, YOB, Sire	Strs	Wnrs	Wins	SWs	Leading Runner (Earnings)	Total Earnings
Benton Creek, 1993, by Septieme Ciel	49	25	55	2	Moores Bridge ($74,872)	$507,562
Chanate, 1995, by Storm Cat	46	28	48	2	Tipton ($61,322)	420,612
Society Max, 1982, by Mr. Prospector	23	15	28	4	Komax ($71,122)	319,488
Buck Strider, 1993, by Easy Goer	26	9	20	2	Lil Easy ($53,254)	215,651
Barricade, 1993, by Riverman	27	18	35	2	Barricaded ($33,640)	190,119

Arkansas

Sire, YOB, Sire	Strs	Wnrs	Wins	SWs	Leading Runner (Earnings)	Total Earnings
Storm and a Half, 1997, by Storm Cat	40	24	38	3	Stormy But Crafty ($63,950)	$561,731
Bold Anthony, 1990, by Bold Ruckus	43	15	27	0	Quote Me Later ($66,390)	367,723
Idabel, 1986, by Mr. Prospector	32	14	22	1	Timeless Dreamer ($77,000)	334,621
Joy's Report, 1993, by Corporate Report	11	9	19	0	Maggio ($57,700)	281,670
Big Pistol, 1981, by Romeo	24	11	23	0	Jeanies Pistol ($57,754)	249,191

California

Sire, YOB, Sire	Strs	Wnrs	Wins	SWs	Leading Runner (Earnings)	Total Earnings
Bertrando, 1989, by Skywalker	150	74	134	4	Unfurl the Flag ($311,360)	$3,497,095
Swiss Yodeler, 1994, by Eastern Echo	122	73	113	3	Thor's Echo ($529,853)	2,759,645
In Excess (Ire), 1987, by Siberian Express	102	53	82	5	Valentine Dancer ($539,120)	2,657,458
Unusual Heat, 1990, by Nureyev	59	30	58	4	Tucked Away ($237,468)	2,485,175
Benchmark, 1991, by Alydar	82	45	74	3	Brother Derek ($502,080)	2,429,135

Colorado

Sire, YOB, Sire	Strs	Wnrs	Wins	SWs	Leading Runner (Earnings)	Total Earnings
Cash Deposit, 1994, by Deposit Ticket	32	8	11	2	Heck Ofalotof Cash ($33,760)	$131,367
Demidoff, 1990, by Mr. Prospector	1	1	7	1	Cocoa Latte ($121,283)	121,283
Bates Motel, 1979, by Sir Ivor	3	1	4	1	Bar Bailey ($113,956)	120,443
Coverallbases, 1989, by Capote	13	5	9	1	Cut of Music ($79,737)	119,654
Skywalker, 1982, by Relaunch	3	2	4	1	Skyline Gal ($57,048)	62,758

Connecticut

Sire, YOB, Sire	Strs	Wnrs	Wins	SWs	Leading Runner (Earnings)	Total Earnings
Distinctive Pro, 1979, by Mr. Prospector	1	1	1	0	Winloc's Julie ($10,620)	$10,620
Departing Prints, 1982, by Dactylographer	1	1	1	0	Nantucketeer ($8,941)	8,941

Florida

Sire, YOB, Sire	Strs	Wnrs	Wins	SWs	Leading Runner (Earnings)	Total Earnings
Northern Afleet, 1993, by Afleet	90	51	90	3	Afleet Alex ($2,085,000)	$3,866,807
Stormy Atlantic, 1994, by Storm Cat	148	79	148	9	She Says It Best ($382,918)	3,222,723
Double Honor, 1995, by Gone West	124	76	164	3	Gin Rummy King ($138,860)	2,662,875
Yes It's True, 1996, by Is It True	82	49	80	5	B. B. Best ($178,350)	2,582,953
Montbrook, 1990, by Buckaroo	127	66	132	1	Sierra Bella ($185,367)	2,575,453

Georgia

Sire, YOB, Sire	Strs	Wnrs	Wins	SWs	Leading Runner (Earnings)	Total Earnings
Roaring Camp, 1991, by Forty Niner	22	11	19	1	Miss Hamma ($94,880)	$261,893
American Standard, 1980, by In Reality	1	1	2	0	Bluesthestandard ($74,400)	74,400
Kelly Kip, 1994, by Kipper Kelly	1	1	1	0	Kickstand Kelli ($31,820)	31,820
Slew the Slewor, 1987, by Slew o' Gold	2	1	2	0	Lookslikeabullet ($20,235)	23,955
Balmer Joe, 1995, by Carnivalay	3	2	3	0	Our Big Man Dillon ($14,650)	23,720

Idaho

Sire, YOB, Sire	Strs	Wnrs	Wins	SWs	Leading Runner (Earnings)	Total Earnings
Hey Rob, 1979, by Tisab	14	4	11	1	Robs Coin ($68,570)	$89,609
Renteria, 1994, by Incinderator	8	3	5	0	Free Rent ($79,020)	87,726
Kings Blood (Ire), 1995, by Fairy King	6	4	4	0	Bloody Bonnet ($31,175)	65,706
Jestic, 1987, by His Majesty	4	1	4	0	A Younger Brother ($38,533)	42,132
Chisos, 1984, by Alydar	10	4	4	0	Penny Racer ($17,221)	40,779

Illinois

Sire, YOB, Sire	Strs	Wnrs	Wins	SWs	Leading Runner (Earnings)	Total Earnings
Cartwright, 1990, by Forty Niner	98	54	90	3	Wiggins ($112,288)	$1,652,425
Unreal Zeal, 1980, by Mr. Prospector	67	36	64	2	Lady Riss ($129,700)	1,093,265
Distorted Humor, 1993, by Forty Niner	10	9	14	3	Original Spin ($222,800)	685,066
Classified Facts, 1993, by Seattle Slew	21	14	25	0	Miss Classified ($85,670)	505,935
Pioneering, 1993, by Mr. Prospector	15	9	19	1	Pretty Jenny ($172,103)	463,686

Indiana

Sire, YOB, Sire	Strs	Wnrs	Wins	SWs	Leading Runner (Earnings)	Total Earnings
Crown Ambassador, 1994, by Storm Cat	36	20	34	2	Pass Rush ($70,110)	$426,955
Presidential Order, 1993, by Danzig	42	21	33	1	President's Woman ($41,490)	396,525
Moro Oro, 1993, by Moro	30	13	20	1	Free Bonus ($39,220)	299,208
Lil E. Tee, 1989, by At the Threshold	21	13	25	1	Lil Broad Tee ($41,300)	288,096
Jacquelyn's Groom, 1988, by Runaway Groom	37	11	13	0	A. J. Groom ($21,325)	187,695

Iowa

Sire, YOB, Sire	Strs	Wnrs	Wins	SWs	Leading Runner (Earnings)	Total Earnings
Blumin Affair, 1991, by Dynaformer	33	21	29	0	Plum Sober ($71,158)	$523,191
Mercedes Won, 1986, by Air Forbes Won	26	11	21	1	Mingo Mohawk ($154,226)	386,053
Sharkey, 1987, by Sharpen Up (GB)	38	17	22	0	You No Jack ($32,512)	333,159
De Guerin, 1993, by Storm Bird	16	11	18	0	Lordslegacy ($61,827)	255,673
Humming, 1996, by Summer Squall	13	7	11	1	Queansco ($104,870)	236,339

Kansas

Sire, YOB, Sire	Strs	Wnrs	Wins	SWs	Leading Runner (Earnings)	Total Earnings
Gold Ruler, 1980, by Mr. Prospector	33	15	24	2	Missy Can Do ($48,063)	$176,103
Big Splash, 1988, by Ziggy's Boy	10	4	7	1	Scarlet Lad ($63,900)	124,381
Here We Come, 1988, by Mr. Prospector	1	1	3	1	Queena Corrina ($113,600)	113,600
Arab Speaker, 1984, by Elocutionist	1	1	2	0	Bonnie J. ($63,120)	63,120
On Target, 1992, by Forty Niner	1	1	3	0	Onda Ray ($45,490)	45,490

Kentucky

Sire, YOB, Sire	Strs	Wnrs	Wins	SWs	Leading Runner (Earnings)	Total Earnings
Saint Ballado, 1989, by Halo	148	73	144	10	Saint Liam ($3,696,960)	$9,660,209
Kingmambo, 1990, by Mr. Prospector	155	54	83	2	Alkaased ($2,650,290)	8,248,551
Storm Cat, 1983, by Storm Bird	127	70	116	12	Seeking the Dia ($1,427,828)	7,645,814
Dynaformer, 1985, by Roberto	136	64	104	12	Dynever ($1,231,730)	7,306,855
A.P. Indy, 1989, by Seattle Slew	175	82	132	14	Suave ($624,900)	7,231,679

Louisiana

Sire, YOB, Sire	Strs	Wnrs	Wins	SWs	Leading Runner (Earnings)	Total Earnings
Leestown, 1994, by Seattle Slew	111	48	87	4	Indigo Girl ($154,000)	$1,946,366
Zarbyev, 1984, by Nureyev	74	28	46	2	Zarb's Dahar ($205,060)	1,269,579
Excavate, 1988, by Mr. Prospector	69	27	47	0	American by Choice ($72,988)	1,031,980
Finest Hour, 1994, by Forty Niner	65	23	37	1	Nitro Chip ($205,680)	957,465
Goodbye Doeny, 1991, by Storm Cat	64	30	48	1	Goodbye Beautiful ($53,756)	794,536

Maryland

Sire, YOB, Sire	Strs	Wnrs	Wins	SWs	Leading Runner (Earnings)	Total Earnings
Not For Love, 1990, by Mr. Prospector	93	45	85	4	Saay Mi Name ($258,222)	$2,137,517
Allen's Prospect, 1982, by Mr. Prospector	110	60	104	2	Mojodajo ($97,880)	1,867,612
Two Punch, 1983, by Mr. Prospector	70	36	66	0	Yolanda B. Too ($140,200)	1,377,047
Malibu Moon, 1997, by A.P. Indy	51	32	49	5	Grant's Moon ($120,110)	1,341,543
Yarrow Brae, 1995, by Deputy Minister	63	43	66	1	Celtic Innis ($158,310)	1,276,651

Massachusetts

Sire, YOB, Sire	Strs	Wnrs	Wins	SWs	Leading Runner (Earnings)	Total Earnings
Sundance Ridge, 1986, by Cox's Ridge	13	7	13	1	Stylish Sultana ($84,450)	$187,372
Key Contender, 1988, by Fit to Fight	1	1	7	1	Ask Queenie ($165,210)	165,210
Red Scamper, 1985, by Icecapade	5	4	9	0	Deer Danny Boy ($51,460)	103,002
A P Jet, 1989, by Fappiano	2	1	6	1	Jini's Jet ($98,560)	101,280
Formal Gold, 1993, by Black Tie Affair (Ire)	2	2	4	1	Sprinkle of Gold ($47,820)	69,055

Michigan

Sire, YOB, Sire	Strs	Wnrs	Wins	SWs	Leading Runner (Earnings)	Total Earnings
Matchlite, 1983, by Clever Trick	48	24	41	2	Maxie Match ($75,936)	$635,971
Service Stripe, 1991, by Deputy Minister	14	10	17	3	Mad Adam ($145,850)	512,405
Demaloot Demashoot, 1990, by Bold Ruckus	29	17	25	2	Demagoguery ($91,845)	411,375
Quiet Enjoyment, 1989, by Ogygian	26	18	26	1	Steel Bond ($76,578)	370,589
Native Factor, 1987, by Foolish Pleasure	31	19	28	1	Witty Factor ($39,669)	366,013

Minnesota

Sire, YOB, Sire	Strs	Wnrs	Wins	SWs	Leading Runner (Earnings)	Total Earnings
Quick Cut, 1994, by Storm Cat	24	8	12	1	Wally's Choice ($112,500)	$229,424
Demidoff, 1990, by Mr. Prospector	9	7	11	2	Vazandar ($65,975)	195,870
North Prospect, 1980, by Mr. Prospector	18	9	16	1	Chance to Bet ($34,356)	177,039
Wolf Power (SAf), 1978, by Flirting Around	5	1	5	1	Lt. Sampson ($103,632)	153,328
Quaker Hill, 1991, by Alydar	15	5	6	1	Bisquik ($84,043)	139,308

Mississippi

Sire, YOB, Sire	Strs	Wnrs	Wins	SWs	Leading Runner (Earnings)	Total Earnings
Blushing Star, 1993, by Blushing John	5	2	3	1	Go Star Buster ($51,355)	$65,804
Evansville Slew, 1992, by Slew City Slew	1	1	1	1	Smalltown Slew ($38,620)	38,620
Finest Hour, 1994, by Forty Niner	2	1	1	0	Cheery Hour ($18,807)	18,807
Golden Omen, 1996, by Strike the Gold	3	1	1	0	Whistlin' Omen ($11,000)	15,287
Ruhlmann, 1985, by Mr. Leader	1	1	2	0	Sula Mae ($10,630)	10,630

Missouri

Sire, YOB, Sire	Strs	Wnrs	Wins	SWs	Leading Runner (Earnings)	Total Earnings
Victorious, 1980, by Explodent	5	3	5	0	Campinout ($25,410)	$43,807
Wood Reply, 1992, by Woodman	4	4	8	0	Graven ($15,570)	39,163
Mandamus, 1992, by Mining	4	2	3	0	Biscuit Bun ($12,684)	31,998
Czar Nijinsky, 1982, by Barrera	2	1	1	0	De Toby ($22,270)	22,270
Lucky South, 1990, by Lucky North	3	2	3	0	Pass the Luck ($14,828)	17,805

Montana

Sire, YOB, Sire	Strs	Wnrs	Wins	SWs	Leading Runner (Earnings)	Total Earnings
Black Mackee, 1976, by Captain Courageous	8	6	14	0	Dublin's Woodwin ($26,822)	$84,128
Baby I Lied, 1994, by Shipmate Sam	2	1	3	1	Backonbabyside ($37,960)	37,960
Grey West, 1994, by Gone West	9	4	4	0	Fast Ricky ($7,018)	28,833
Strong Minded, 1994, by Riverman	2	1	1	0	Big Sky River ($16,312)	17,106
Snowbound, 1995, by Meadowlake	2	2	3	0	Snowbound Mike ($9,631)	16,173

Nebraska

Sire, YOB, Sire	Strs	Wnrs	Wins	SWs	Leading Runner (Earnings)	Total Earnings
Verzy, 1982, by Vice Regent	29	14	25	2	Consider ($41,010)	$251,286
Lytrump, 1985, by Lypheor (GB)	18	12	18	2	High Dice ($33,157)	186,420
Blumin Affair, 1991, by Dynaformer	14	8	14	2	Up 'n Blumin ($72,400)	184,522
Miracle Heights, 1989, by Gate Dancer	20	11	17	0	Uncle Beno ($30,664)	124,295
Yankee Fan, 1984, by Our Native	17	10	12	1	Cork the Barber ($31,995)	110,379

Nevada

Sire, YOB, Sire	Strs	Wnrs	Wins	SWs	Leading Runner (Earnings)	Total Earnings
Distinctive Cat, 1993, by Storm Cat	1	1	2	0	Arvoicsal Two ($12,150)	$12,150
Presidents Summit, 1985, by Taylor's Falls	1	1	2	0	Hyatopthehills ($8,360)	8,360

New Jersey

Sire, YOB, Sire	Strs	Wnrs	Wins	SWs	Leading Runner (Earnings)	Total Earnings
Intensity, 1994, by Gone West	18	9	21	1	Who's the Cowboy ($233,910)	$778,981
Private Interview, 1992, by Nureyev	46	21	28	1	Cool Cat Interview ($66,860)	748,763
Evening Kris, 1985, by Kris S.	21	12	19	0	Hurricane Shockey ($93,085)	671,637
Northern Idol, 1986, by Northrop	26	14	21	3	Picnic Theme ($109,060)	492,636
Citidancer, 1987, by Dixieland Band	5	2	6	1	Park Avenue Ball ($351,000)	449,229

New Mexico

Sire, YOB, Sire	Strs	Wnrs	Wins	SWs	Leading Runner (Earnings)	Total Earnings
In Excessive Bull, 1994, by In Excess (Ire)	73	37	57	2	Mr. Boomer ($107,747)	$1,001,028
Prospector Jones, 1992, by Mr. Prospector	58	27	44	4	La Mamie ($107,298)	961,203
Ghostly Moves, 1992, by Silver Ghost	37	23	42	6	C. G's Dollar ($196,794)	842,148
Chimes Band, 1991, by Dixieland Band	26	15	26	2	Latenite Band ($124,127)	557,977
Jack Wilson, 1988, by Encino	20	14	23	2	Romeos Wilson ($153,684)	548,317

New York

Sire, YOB, Sire	Strs	Wnrs	Wins	SWs	Leading Runner (Earnings)	Total Earnings
A. P Jet, 1989, by Fappiano	120	62	116	2	Karakorum Splendor ($222,782)	$2,678,509
Precise End, 1997, by End Sweep	62	47	84	6	Champagne Ending ($162,445)	2,425,225
Tomorrows Cat, 1995, by Storm Cat	96	52	84	2	West Virginia ($166,820)	2,242,908
Gold Token, 1993, by Mr. Prospector	46	36	67	1	Gold and Roses ($396,134)	1,814,468
Dixie Brass, 1989, by Dixieland Band	74	45	85	1	Pretty Suzi ($124,405)	1,777,358

North Carolina

Sire, YOB, Sire	Strs	Wnrs	Wins	SWs	Leading Runner (Earnings)	Total Earnings
Chelsey Cat, 1998, by Storm Cat	19	11	19	0	Chelsey Gallop ($50,630)	$197,319
Dove Hunt, 1991, by Danzig	1	1	1	0	Chief's Spokesman ($38,521)	38,521
Above Normal, 1985, by Great Above	4	2	2	0	Silks N Roses ($10,160)	16,395
Othello, 1993, by Summer Squall	1	1	1	0	Mizz Joclyne ($16,357)	16,357
At the Threshold, 1981, by Norcliffe	1	1	2	0	Homie ($14,716)	14,716

North Dakota

Sire, YOB, Sire	Strs	Wnrs	Wins	SWs	Leading Runner (Earnings)	Total Earnings
Patriot Strike, 1989, by General Assembly	7	1	2	1	J Dam Strike ($25,303)	$46,022
Aferd, 1976, by Hoist the Flag	4	3	5	1	Maddies Blues ($15,870)	33,434
Capitalimprovement, 1989, by Dixieland Band	1	1	2	1	Northrnimprovement ($24,447)	24,447
Crafty Ridan, 1986, by Crafty Prospector	1	1	1	0	Firehawk ($12,352)	12,352
Castle Howard, 1987, by Slew o' Gold	8	3	3	0	Could've Been Mine ($5,038)	11,872

Ohio

Sire, YOB, Sire	Strs	Wnrs	Wins	SWs	Leading Runner (Earnings)	Total Earnings
Mercer Mill, 1994, by Forty Niner	62	29	39	2	Turnpike Mike ($33,396)	$488,879
Pacific Waves, 1993, by Seattle Slew	17	12	29	2	Just Michel ($108,132)	375,955
Noble Cat, 1995, by Storm Cat	26	16	30	1	Catlaunch ($52,605)	369,381
Lac Ouimet, 1983, by Pleasant Colony	19	12	23	0	Lac Grape ($37,352)	256,733
Flight Forty Nine, 1991, by Forty Niner	30	17	30	0	On Approach ($26,645)	251,602

Oklahoma

Sire, YOB, Sire	Strs	Wnrs	Wins	SWs	Leading Runner (Earnings)	Total Earnings
Here We Come, 1988, by Mr. Prospector	52	31	55	2	Goodie Good Girl ($70,815)	$597,700
Muldoon, 1995, by Kingmambo	34	21	33	0	Tulsa Town ($45,000)	309,792
New Way, 1994, by Danzig	23	12	17	1	Out Our Way ($86,123)	281,624
Slewacide, 1980, by Seattle Slew	26	11	20	0	Abbi's Choice ($82,540)	269,153
Notable Cat, 1995, by Storm Cat	49	19	24	1	Sooner Pride ($41,628)	251,055

Oregon

Sire, YOB, Sire	Strs	Wnrs	Wins	SWs	Leading Runner (Earnings)	Total Earnings
Baquero, 1995, by Forty Niner	47	29	44	1	One Fast Cowgirl ($25,222)	$202,973
Corslew, 1990, by Seattle Slew	4	3	8	0	So Happy Together ($80,007)	134,817
Gold Meridian, 1982, by Seattle Slew	30	12	18	0	Yourgoldgirl ($17,914)	117,205
Cascadian, 1996, by Seattle Slew	17	13	15	1	Cascadians Cuttie ($25,183)	106,650
Cisco Road, 1990, by Northern Baby	20	12	22	0	Ransome Road ($21,532)	93,383

Pennsylvania

Sire, YOB, Sire	Strs	Wnrs	Wins	SWs	Leading Runner (Earnings)	Total Earnings
Not For Love, 1990, by Mr. Prospector	42	19	34	2	Presidentialaffair ($269,198)	$1,026,014
Roanoke, 1987, by Pleasant Colony	68	31	57	1	Roanoke's Best ($100,750)	980,441
Allen's Prospect, 1982, by Mr. Prospector	35	17	36	0	Wyatt's High Noon ($74,148)	623,658
Partner's Hero, 1994, by Danzig	18	15	33	1	Senor Cielo Two ($183,785)	561,602
Malibu Moon, 1997, by A.P. Indy	17	11	20	1	S W Aly'svalentine ($111,720)	450,962

South Carolina

Sire, YOB, Sire	Strs	Wnrs	Wins	SWs	Leading Runner (Earnings)	Total Earnings
Kokand, 1985, by Mr. Prospector	33	18	32	0	Pawley's Island ($51,260)	$483,139
Ride the Storm, 1994, by Storm Cat	7	4	10	0	Havin' a Moan ($76,070)	189,401
Miner, 1993, by Forty Niner	10	7	13	0	American Prince ($67,630)	184,886
Signal, 1993, by Forty Niner	7	2	2	0	Early Ruler ($26,450)	61,854
Valiant Lark, 1980, by Buffalo Lark	3	1	3	0	Plumpish ($34,670)	60,420

South Dakota

Sire, YOB, Sire	Strs	Wnrs	Wins	SWs	Leading Runner (Earnings)	Total Earnings
Mr. O. P., 1986, by Naskra	14	5	6	0	Mucho Mite ($7,519)	$26,715
Storm of the Night, 1993, by Storm Cat	7	2	3	1	Barnstorm ($16,416)	24,526
Tabib, 1994, by Storm Bird	8	3	3	0	Catch Me Talkin ($8,647)	22,163
Pioneering, 1993, by Mr. Prospector	1	1	2	0	Platinum Sky ($17,600)	17,600
Get Me Out, 1996, by Capote	5	2	4	0	Made in America ($8,419)	17,556

Tennessee

Sire, YOB, Sire	Strs	Wnrs	Wins	SWs	Leading Runner (Earnings)	Total Earnings
With Approval, 1986, by Caro (Ire)	2	1	4	0	Approved by Dylan ($128,532)	$134,969
Expanding Man, 1994, by Hermitage	4	1	3	0	Dark Contessa ($49,200)	52,934
Evansville Slew, 1992, by Slew City Slew	1	1	1	0	Valieo ($50,670)	50,670
Mr. Beasley, 1993, by Farma Way	3	2	2	0	Stormin ($12,618)	22,515
Doppler, 1994, by Storm Bird	3	1	1	0	Storm Passer Bye ($13,155)	21,680

Texas

Sire, YOB, Sire	Strs	Wnrs	Wins	SWs	Leading Runner (Earnings)	Total Earnings
Valid Expectations, 1993, by Valid Appeal	108	63	89	2	Leaving On My Mind ($110,294)	$1,358,319
Hadif, 1986, by Clever Trick	76	42	79	1	Paltu ($95,227)	973,663
Seneca Jones, 1990, by Alydar	37	19	37	2	Timber Jones ($158,900)	644,331
Magic Cat, 1995, by Storm Cat	43	24	42	2	Final Trick ($100,265)	609,876
Sunny's Halo, 1980, by Halo	68	27	45	1	Charming Socialite ($147,300)	599,848

Utah

Sire, YOB, Sire	Strs	Wnrs	Wins	SWs	Leading Runner (Earnings)	Total Earnings
Four Seasons (GB), 1990, by Sadler's Wells	9	6	10	0	Seasons Promise ($31,225)	$102,440
Buckhar, 1988, by Dahar	2	1	2	0	Double Lyph ($25,575)	25,620
Cahill Road, 1988, by Fappiano	1	1	2	1	Maybefirst ($25,440)	25,440
Tinners Way, 1990, by Secretariat	1	0	0	0	Ten Forty Easy ($18,771)	18,771
H E R E S Tommy, 1991, by Flying Paster	1	1	2	0	Tomencino ($18,510)	18,510

Virginia

Sire, YOB, Sire	Strs	Wnrs	Wins	SWs	Leading Runner (Earnings)	Total Earnings
Stormin Fever, 1994, by Storm Cat	15	10	17	1	Fusaichi Auster ($627,977)	$963,311
Pleasant Tap, 1987, by Pleasant Colony	3	3	10	3	Tap Day ($498,800)	727,771
Wild Rush, 1994, by Wild Again	2	1	5	1	Bank Audit ($400,691)	403,541
Secret Hello, 1987, by Private Account	20	13	23	1	Sonotas Secret ($64,615)	368,411
Fred Astaire, 1983, by Nijinsky II	12	7	15	0	Sooner Be Dancin' ($71,110)	252,360

Washington

Sire, YOB, Sire	Strs	Wnrs	Wins	SWs	Leading Runner (Earnings)	Total Earnings
Slewdledo, 1981, by Seattle Slew	120	62	119	4	Slew Is King ($132,071)	$1,424,793
Basket Weave, 1981, by Best Turn	81	43	73	4	Light My Ducks ($70,011)	827,352
Game Plan, 1993, by Danzig	55	23	44	2	Melanyhasthepapers ($162,820)	717,478
Cahill Road, 1988, by Fappiano	54	24	42	2	Ashby Hill ($62,668)	613,084
He's Tops, 1993, by Seattle Slew	40	27	45	2	No Giveaway ($182,723)	511,871

West Virginia

Sire, YOB, Sire	Strs	Wnrs	Wins	SWs	Leading Runner (Earnings)	Total Earnings
My Boy Adam, 1987, by Encino	46	19	26	1	Smart Pace ($52,410)	$589,152
Weshaam, 1983, by Fappiano	33	10	14	1	Speed Whiz ($272,520)	549,292
Native Slew, 1985, by Raise a Native	19	7	12	0	Slew's Smile ($157,293)	323,281
Eastover Court, 1991, by Seattle Slew	30	7	14	0	Raggedy Andy ($69,195)	305,017
Luftikus, 1996, by Meadowlake	19	8	10	2	Shesagrumptoo ($58,252)	285,037

Wisconsin

Sire, YOB, Sire	Strs	Wnrs	Wins	SWs	Leading Runner (Earnings)	Total Earnings
Armed Truce, 1981, by Bold Forbes	3	1	3	0	Solaratee ($27,770)	$27,890
Quick Cut, 1994, by Storm Cat	2	2	4	0	Scrub Cat ($16,979)	23,434
Hacker, 1994, by Jade Hunter	2	1	1	0	R's Star ($11,760)	11,880

Puerto Rico

Sire, YOB, Sire	Strs	Wnrs	Wins	SWs	Leading Runner (Earnings)	Total Earnings
Fappiano's Star, 1988, by Fappiano	48	22	71	4	Borrascoso ($293,900)	$1,067,545
Eqtesaad, 1991, by Danzig	55	41	93	1	Tenderete ($64,785)	833,000
Goldwater, 1989, by Mr. Prospector	19	10	33	1	Gold Gift ($188,730)	459,530
Sejm, 1987, by Danzig	24	20	41	0	Mi Abogada ($50,700)	378,134
Balcony, 1994, by Danzig	31	20	35	0	Mueca ($80,368)	373,090

Alberta

Sire, YOB, Sire	Strs	Wnrs	Wins	SWs	Leading Runner (Earnings)	Total Earnings
Devonwood, 1994, by Woodman	38	16	26	3	Ding Dong Dandy ($100,840)	$456,326
Regal Remark, 1982, by Vice Regent	46	31	46	3	To Dream Again ($45,127)	450,926
Weekend Guest, 1987, by Mr. Prospector	61	24	32	2	Forever Rascal ($48,126)	403,323
Ciano Cat, 1995, by Storm Cat	40	17	26	0	Out Cattin' ($52,020)	284,396
Exclusive Era, 1979, by Exclusive Native	31	17	28	2	Tartan Star ($42,532)	260,906

British Columbia

Sire, YOB, Sire	Strs	Wnrs	Wins	SWs	Leading Runner (Earnings)	Total Earnings
Vying Victor, 1989, by Flying Paster	88	41	67	3	Alabama Rain ($265,762)	$1,393,290
Regal Intention, 1985, by Vice Regent	59	32	56	3	Regal Request ($117,796)	801,459
Katahaula County, 1988, by Bold Ruckus	57	34	56	4	Sungold Wonder ($70,655)	787,889
Feu d'Enfer, 1980, by Tentam	35	26	49	2	Feu Express ($75,263)	481,510
Stephanotis, 1993, by Regal Classic	39	21	41	1	Delta Monarch ($67,445)	472,509

Manitoba

Sire, YOB, Sire	Strs	Wnrs	Wins	SWs	Leading Runner (Earnings)	Total Earnings
Smart Strike, 1992, by Mr. Prospector	1	1	2	1	Gold Strike ($480,518)	$480,518
K One King, 1996, by Apalachee	1	1	2	0	King of Jazz ($248,040)	248,040
Langfuhr, 1992, by Danzig	2	2	6	1	Albarino ($103,798)	184,793
Buie, 1990, by Fappiano	11	6	14	1	Resurgent ($58,390)	133,735
His Excellence, 1993, by El Gran Senor	23	10	12	1	Your Excellence ($17,855)	84,451

Ontario

Sire, YOB, Sire	Strs	Wnrs	Wins	SWs	Leading Runner (Earnings)	Total Earnings
Bold Executive, 1984, by Bold Ruckus	94	44	87	4	Top Ten List ($292,854)	$2,526,933
Archers Bay, 1995, by Silver Deputy	62	40	60	3	Schooner Bay ($236,831)	2,441,147
Whiskey Wisdom, 1993, by Wild Again	72	38	59	4	Dave the Knave ($145,311)	1,729,610
Bold n' Flashy, 1989, by Bold Ruckus	82	43	66	1	U R Flashy ($113,086)	1,586,497
Langfuhr, 1992, by Danzig	32	16	26	2	Jambalaya ($380,846)	1,453,103

Quebec

Sire, YOB, Sire	Strs	Wnrs	Wins	SWs	Leading Runner (Earnings)	Total Earnings
Langfuhr, 1992, by Danzig	1	1	2	0	Fuzzy Star ($74,200)	$74,200
Chief Seattle, 1997, by Seattle Slew	1	1	1	0	Shillelagh Slew ($60,231)	60,231
Kiridashi, 1992, by Bold Ruckus	2	1	2	0	Brigadoon ($24,949)	49,719
Summer Squall, 1987, by Storm Bird	1	1	3	0	Belle de Neuville ($38,467)	38,467
Forest Wildcat, 1991, by Storm Cat	1	0	0	0	Zero Cat ($36,343)	36,343

Saskatchewan

Sire, YOB, Sire	Strs	Wnrs	Wins	SWs	Leading Runner (Earnings)	Total Earnings
Pole Position, 1976, by Draft Card	6	6	12	0	Spirit to Spare ($43,677)	$97,894
Shaheen, 1994, by Danzig	17	8	15	1	Shaheens Flyer ($19,607)	75,459
Royal Quiz, 1984, by Real Emperor	16	6	6	1	Bleu Royale ($13,091)	40,239
Stop the Stage, 1985, by Gold Stage	9	4	6	0	She's Nifty ($11,398)	35,708
Vilzak, 1983, by Green Dancer	3	1	1	1	Rumbeau Ruckus ($28,255)	29,906

Stallion Syndications

In part because the definition of stallion syndication has changed over the decades, pinpointing the first syndication contract is difficult, if not impossible. However, the earliest syndication agreement comparable in form and intent to modern syndicates was that of Tracery in 1923. That agreement between the syndicators, the International Horse Agency and Exchange and a group of 30 subscribers, placed a value of $219,840 on the 1912 St. Leger winner, who was the sire of '23 Epsom Derby victor *Papyrus.

The principle behind that syndicate and all subsequent ones was to spread the risk of purchasing a very expensive breeding horse (and, in Tracery's case, returning him from Argentina). From the beginning of the Thoroughbred breeding industry in the late 17th century right up to the 20th century, Thoroughbred breeding was essentially a private affair, with rich aristocrats wholly owning stallions and breeding mostly their own mares to those sires.

As Thoroughbred breeding slowly became more commercial in the late 19th and early 20th centuries, a new method of financing was required, both to spread the risk of failure and to ensure that a stallion received an appropriate number and quality of mares. Syndication was the answer. In Tracery's case, spreading the risk was a wise strategy because the stallion died after only one season at stud in England.

In a modern syndicate agreement, individuals agree to purchase a specific percentage of ownership in a stallion—the percentage ownership is determined by the number of shares—with payment for that percentage interest usually spread in installments over several years. In return, the buyer of a syndicate share gains the right to breed one or more mares to that stallion each year without additional payments (except for agreed maintenance fees). The syndicate manager normally receives a specified number of free nominations each year as compensation.

The similarity to buying stock market shares is evident. The syndicate manager receives capital to pay for a major capital asset, and shareholders gain the possibility of dividends from the share through sale of the nomination or value of the produce. Shares also may be sold later to other investors at a profit (or loss), just as in the stock market, although syndication agreements may place restrictions on the transfer of the shares.

Although the first clearly identifiable syndicate was English, Americans soon became active syndicators. Arthur B. Hancock of Claiborne Farm formed a four-man partnership in 1926 to purchase the high-class French miler *Sir Gallahad III for $125,000. When *Sir Gallahad III sired Triple Crown winner Gallant Fox in his

Chronology of Record Stallion Syndications

Stallion	Year	Price	Farm	Seller	Share Price	No. Shares
Fusaichi Pegasus	2000	†$60,000,000	Ashford Stud (Ky.)	Fusao Sekiguchi	$1,500,000	40
Lammtarra	1996	42,000,000	Arrow Stud (Jpn)	Dalham Hall Stud	1,050,000	40
Shareef Dancer	1983	40,000,000	Dalham Hall Stud (Eng)	Aston Upthorpe Stud	1,000,000	40
Conquistador Cielo	1982	36,400,000	Claiborne Farm (Ky.)	Henryk de Kwiatkowski (retained 10 shares)	910,000	40
Storm Bird	1981	30,000,000	Ashford Stud (Ky.)	Robert Sangster, et al.	750,000	40
Spectacular Bid	1980	22,000,000	Claiborne Farm (Ky.)	Hawksworth Farm (retained 20 shares)	550,000	40
Troy	1979	16,500,000	Highclere Stud (Eng)	Sir Michael Sobell and Arnold Weinstock	412,500	40
Alleged	1978	16,000,000	Walmac-Warnerton Int.'l. (Ky.)	Robert Sangster, et al.	400,000	40
Seattle Slew	1978	12,000,000	Spendthrift Farm (Ky.)	Wooden Horse Investments (retained 20 shares)	300,000	40
The Minstrel	1977	9,000,000	Windfields Farm (Md.)	Robert Sangster, et al.	250,000	36
What a Pleasure	1976	8,000,000	Waldemar Farm (Ky.)	Waldemar (retained 16 shares)	250,000	32
Wajima	1975	7,200,000	Spendthrift Farm (Ky.)	East-West Stable (retained 20 shares)	200,000	36
Secretariat	1973	6,080,000	Claiborne Farm (Ky.)	Meadow Stable	190,000	32
Nijinsky II	1970	5,440,000	Claiborne Farm (Ky.)	Charles W. Englehard (retained 10 shares)	170,000	32
*Vaguely Noble	1969	5,000,000	Gainesway (Ky.)	Nelson Bunker Hunt and Dr. Robert Franklyn	125,000	40
Buckpasser	1967	4,800,000	Claiborne Farm (Ky.)	Ogden Phipps (retained 16 shares)	150,000	32
Raise a Native	1967	2,625,000	Spendthrift Farm (Ky.)	Louis Wolfson and Leslie Combs	75,000	35
Graustark	1966	2,400,000	Darby Dan Farm (Ky.)	John W. Galbreath	60,000	40
Tom Fool	1960	1,750,000	Greentree Stud (Ky.)	Greentree Stud	50,000	35
Nashua	1955	1,251,200	Spendthrift Farm (Ky.)	Estate of William Woodward Jr.	39,200	32
*Tulyar	1952	697,500	Irish National Stud (Ire)	H. H. Aga Khan	17,438	40
The Phoenix	1948	619,920	Ballykisteen Stud (Ire)	Fred Myerscough	15,498	40
*Alibhai	1948	500,000	Spendthrift Farm (Ky.)	Louis B. Mayer	16,667	30
Stardust	1945	451,360	Gilltown Stud (Ire)	H. H. Aga Khan	11,284	40
Tehran	1945	403,000	Barton Stud (Eng)	Prince Aly Khan	10,075	40
*Blenheim II	1936	240,000	Claiborne Farm (Ky.)	H. H. Aga Khan	30,000	8
Tracery	1923	219,400	Cobham Stud (Eng)	Senor Unzue	5,485	40

†Estimated value

first crop, making him leading sire for the first of four times, the syndication process gained impetus in America. In 1936, Hancock syndicated another leading sire, *Blenheim II, for a record price, $240,000. In his first crop, *Blenheim II sired Triple Crown winner Whirlaway.

The record returned to England in 1945 when the good young sires Stardust and Tehran were syndicated in rapid succession, but the record price returned to America in '48 when Leslie Combs II purchased *Alibhai from Louis B. Mayer as a replacement for Combs's first syndicated horse, *Beau Pere, who died before covering a mare.

Combs also syndicated Nashua, the first $1-million stallion, as a four-year-old in 1956. The record price remained in America until 1983 (except for a brief period in '79) when Sheikh Mohammed bin Rashid al Maktoum syndicated his Irish Derby (Ire-G1) winner, Shareef Dancer, for a reported $40-million.

That reported price signifies one of the problems with modern syndications. With values soaring to astronomical figures, stallion managers now often decline to publish the exact price per share or contract terms. Thus, the $60-million to $70-million figure for current record holder Fusaichi Pegasus is based on approximate figures released by the syndicate manager and private communications from syndicate members.

Most Expensive North American Stallion Syndications

Stallion	Year	Price	Farm	Seller	Share Price	No. Shares
Fusaichi Pegasus	2000	$60,000,000	Ashford Stud (Ky.)	Fusao Sekiguchi	†$1,500,000	40
Point Given	2001	50,000,000	Three Chimneys Farm (Ky.)	The Thoroughbred Corp.	1,000,000	50
Smarty Jones	2004	39,000,000	Three Chimneys Farm (Ky.)	Someday Farm	650,000	60
Conquistador Cielo	1982	36,400,000	Claiborne Farm (Ky.)	Henryk de Kwiatkowski	910,000	40
Devil's Bag	1983	36,000,000	Claiborne Farm (Ky.)	Hickory Tree Farm	900,000	40
Halo	1984	36,000,000	Stone Farm (Ky.)	Windfields Farm	900,000	40
Storm Bird	1981	30,000,000	Ashford Stud (Ky.)	Robert Sangster, et al.	750,000	40
Lemon Drop Kid	2000	30,000,000	Lane's End (Ky.)	Jeanne Vance	750,000	40
Assert (Ire)	1982	25,000,000	Windfields Farm (Md.)	Robert Sangster	625,000	40
Cigar	1996	25,000,000	Ashford Stud (Ky.)	Allen Paulson	500,000	50
Spectacular Bid	1980	22,000,000	Claiborne Farm (Ky.)	Hawksworth Farm	550,000	40
Mr. Prospector	1980	20,000,000	Claiborne Farm (Ky.)	Aisco Farm	500,000	40
Chief's Crown	1984	20,000,000	Three Chimneys Farm (Ky.)	Star Crown Stable	500,000	40
Secreto	1984	20,000,000	Calumet Farm (Ky.)	Luigi Miglietti	500,000	40
Unbridled	1996	19,000,000	Claiborne Farm (Ky.)	Frances A. Genter	475,000	40
Aloma's Ruler	1982	18,880,000	Mare Haven Farm (Ky.)	Nathan Scherr	472,000	40
Riverman	1979	18,000,000	Gainesway (Ky.)	Haras du Quesnay	450,000	40
Skip Away	1998	18,000,000	Hopewell Farm (Ky.)	Carolyn Hine	400,000	45
Alleged	1978	16,000,000	Walmac-Warnerton Int.'l. (Ky.)	Robert Sangster, et al.	400,000	40
Saratoga Six	1984	16,000,000	North Ridge Farm (Ky.)	Eugene Klein, et al.	400,000	40
A P Valentine	2000	16,000,000	Ashford Stud (Ky.)	Celtic Pride Stable	N/A	N/A
Exceller	1979	15,000,000	Gainesway (Ky.)	Nelson Bunker Hunt	375,000	40
Northjet	1981	15,000,000	Airdrie Stud (Ky.)	Serge Fradkoff	375,000	40
Coronado's Quest	1998	15,000,000	Claiborne Farm (Ky.)	Stuart Janney and Stonerside Stable	300,000	50
Affirmed	1979	14,400,000	Spendthrift Farm (Ky.)	Harbor View Farm	400,000	36
Shahrastani	1986	14,400,000	Three Chimneys Farm (Ky.)	H. H. Aga Khan	400,000	36
Nureyev	1981	14,200,000	Walmac-Warnerton Int.'l. (Ky.)	Stavros Niarchos	355,000	40
Risen Star	1988	14,000,000	Walmac Int.'l. (Ky.)	Louis Roussell III and Ronnie Lamarque	350,000	40
Desert Wine	1984	13,000,000	Cardiff Stud Farms (Ca.)	Cardiff Stud Farms and T90 Ranch	325,000	40
L'Emigrant	1983	13,000,000	Gainesway (Ky.)	Stavros Niarchos	325,000	40
Seattle Slew	1978	12,000,000	Spendthrift Farm (Ky.)	Wooden Horse Investments	300,000	40
Fappiano	1981	12,000,000	Tartan Farms (Fl.)	John Nerud	300,000	40
Flying Paster	1981	12,000,000	Cardiff Stud Farms (Ca.)	B. J. Ridder	300,000	40
Pleasant Colony	1981	12,000,000	Buckland Farm (Ky.)	Thomas M. Evans	300,000	40
Bering (GB)	1986	12,000,000	Walmac Int.'l. (Ky.)	Alec Head	300,000	40
Aldebaran	2002	12,000,000	Darby Dan Farm (Ky.)	Niarchos Family	300,000	40
Tale of the Cat	1998	11,600,000	Ashford Stud (Ky.)	Phantom House Stable	290,000	40
Noble Nashua	1981	11,000,000	Schoenborn Brothers Farm (N.Y.)	Flying Zee Stable	275,000	40
Cure the Blues	1986	11,000,000	Pillar Stud (Ky.)	Gilltown Stud	275,000	40
General Assembly	1986	11,000,000	Pillar Stud (Ky.)	Gilltown Stud	275,000	40
Cresta Rider	1981	10,000,000	Gainesway (Ky.)	Stavros Niarchos	250,000	40
Lord Avie	1981	10,000,000	Lane's End (Ky.)	SKS Stable	250,000	40
Master Willie	1981	10,000,000	Windfields Farm (Md.)	William Barnett	250,000	40
A.P. Indy	1992	10,000,000	Lane's End (Ky.)	Tomonoru Tsurumaki	250,000	40
Kingmambo	1993	10,000,000	Lane's End (Ky.)	Niarchos Family	250,000	40
Lure	1994	10,000,000	Claiborne Farm (Ky.)	Claiborne Farm and Nicole Perry Gorman	250,000	40
Grand Slam	1998	10,000,000	Ashford Stud (Ky.)	Baker, Cornstein, and Mack	250,000	40
War Chant	2000	10,000,000	Three Chimneys Farm (Ky.)	Irving Cowan	200,000	50
Slew o' Gold	1983	9,600,000	Three Chimneys Farm (Ky.)	Equusequity Stable	240,000	40
The Minstrel	1977	9,000,000	Windfields Farm (Md.)	Robert Sangster, et al.	250,000	36

†Estimated value

Leading Stud Farms of 2005

Minimum of 20 starters in 2005, worldwide earnings. Includes all active stallions at each farm in 2005 and deceased or pensioned stallions that last stood at that farm. Order is based on total stallion progeny earnings, average earnings per starter, percentage of stakes winners from starters, and percentage of graded stakes winners from starters. Each category is assigned equal weight.

Rank	Farm (State)	Stallion Earnings	Avg. Earnings	SWs/Strs	GSWs/Strs
1	Taylor Made Farm (Ky.)	$23,832,898	$38,133	6.72%	2.40%
2	Lane's End (Ky.)	71,365,527	29,649	5.40%	2.08%
3	WinStar Farm (Ky.)	19,484,962	40,175	6.19%	2.27%
4	Overbrook Farm (Ky.)	25,679,035	27,582	5.16%	1.93%
5	Three Chimneys Farm (Ky.)	25,624,525	28,695	5.26%	1.57%
6	Claiborne Farm (Ky.)	34,098,813	28,439	4.67%	1.67%
7	Adena Springs Kentucky (Ky.)	25,465,438	30,534	4.92%	1.56%
8	Airdrie Stud (Ky.)	17,520,863	25,804	5.01%	1.47%
9	Hill 'n' Dale Farms (Ky.)	14,305,211	21,642	5.30%	1.66%
10	Vinery Kentucky (Ky.)	15,498,503	20,582	4.78%	1.73%
11	Ashford Stud (Ky.)	72,866,705	24,937	3.25%	1.57%
12	Pin Oak Stud (Ky.)	9,411,558	23,767	4.04%	2.27%
13	Castleton Lyons (Ky.)	4,460,637	23,982	12.37%	4.84%
14	Old English Rancho (Ca.)	6,055,291	31,375	6.22%	1.04%
15	Brookdale Farm (Ky.)	16,407,069	25,437	3.41%	1.09%
16	Gainesway (Ky.)	24,561,262	22,805	3.62%	1.11%
17	Walmac Farm (Ky.)	4,872,289	24,484	4.52%	1.51%
18	Darby Dan Farm (Ky.)	10,784,373	21,187	3.34%	1.18%
19	Gainsborough Farm (Ky.)	7,334,386	24,448	3.00%	2.00%
20	Rancho San Miguel (Ca.)	9,603,515	17,589	4.58%	1.10%
21	Stone Farm (Ky.)	5,498,119	22,350	4.88%	0.81%
22	Millennium Farms Kentucky (Ky.)	2,649,607	24,533	4.63%	1.85%
23	River Edge Farm (Ca.)	6,451,095	24,436	3.03%	1.14%
24	Ridgeley Farm (Ca.)	2,674,790	19,243	5.04%	2.88%
25	Darley (Ky.)	8,861,857	23,951	2.97%	0.81%
26	Bridlewood Farm (Fl.)	6,701,759	20,308	4.24%	0.61%
27	Ocala Stud Farm (Fl.)	15,560,982	20,915	2.82%	0.67%
28	Gardiner Farms Ltd. (On.)	7,910,010	20,545	4.16%	0.26%
29	Windfields Farm Ltd. (On.)	8,084,393	22,457	3.33%	0.28%
30	Juddmonte Farms (Ky.)	5,608,200	21,907	3.52%	0.39%
31	Walnford Stud (N.J.)	4,342,951	22,158	4.08%	0.51%
32	Golden Eagle Farm (Ca.)	8,040,164	18,027	2.91%	0.90%
33	Jonabell Farm (Ky.)	393,438	24,008	2.19%	1.64%
34	Northview Stallion Station (Md.)	13,416,408	20,145	3.00%	0.15%
35	Shadwell Farm (Ky.)	4,907,984	15,987	3.26%	1.63%
36	Lane's End Texas (Tx.)	9,005,585	18,230	2.63%	0.81%
37	Country Life Farm (Md.)	7,530,755	19,211	2.81%	0.77%
38	Walmac Int'l. (Ky.)	3,666,289	20,713	2.82%	1.13%
39	Vessels Stallion Farm (Ca.)	3,731,439	21,569	3.47%	0.58%
40	Magali Farms (Ca.)	7,232,993	24,436	2.03%	0.68%

Leading Stud Farms of 2005

TAYLOR MADE FARM—Location: Nicholasville, Kentucky. **Founded:** 1976. **Principals:** Duncan, Ben, Frank, and Mark Taylor. **Acreage:** 1,600. **Stallions for 2006:** Forest Danger, Forestry, Northern Afleet, Our Emblem, Southern Image, Unbridled's Song. **Graded or group stakes winner of 2005 by Taylor Made stallions:** Afleet Alex, Ashado, Diplomat Lady, Eurosilver, Forest Danger, Forest Grove, Forest Music, Grey Song, Lord of the Game, Saint Afleet, Saint Liam, Smokey Glacken, Splendid Blended, Unbridled Energy, Woodlander.

LANE'S END—Location: Versailles, Kentucky. **Founded:** 1979. **Principals:** William S. Farish and Bill Farish. **Acreage:** 1,600. **Stallions for 2006:** A.P. Indy, Belong to Me, Came Home, City Zip, Dixieland Band, Dixie Union, Gulch, King Cugat, Kingmambo, Langfuhr, Lemon Drop Kid, Midway Road, Mineshaft, Mingun, Pine Bluff, Pleasantly Perfect, Pleasant Tap, Saint Liam, Silver Ghost, Smart Strike, Stephen Got Even, Wando. **Graded or group stakes winners of 2005 by Lane's End stallions:** Added Edge, Alkaased, Alumni Hall, Bear's Kid, Congrats, Country Be Gold, Daydreaming, David Junior, Delta Princess, Dixie Talking, Divine Proportions, Don't Get Mad, English Channel, For All We Know, Gold Strike, Gotaghostofachance, High Strike Zone, Imperialism, Indian Vale, Interpatation, Jack Sullivan, Jambalaya, Lemon Maid, Nothing But Fun, Notable Guest, Quick Temper, Reunited, Rey de Cafe, Scipion, Scrappy T, Sensation, Shadow Cast, Shaniko, Sharp Lisa, Smart N Classy, Snowdrops (GB), Soaring Free, Sorcerer's Stone, Stevie Wonderboy, Suave, Summerly, Super Frolic, Sweet Symphony, Tap Day, Tarfah, Top Commander, Unification, Virginia Waters.

WINSTAR FARM—Location: Versailles, Kentucky. **Founded:** 2000. **Principals:** Bill Casner and Kenny Troutt. **Acreage:** 1,450. **Stallions for 2006:** Distorted Humor, Speightstown, Tiznow, Victory Gallop. **Graded or group stakes winners of 2005 by WinStar stallions:** Adreamisborn, Commentator, Flower Alley, Folklore, Fourty Niners Son, Melrose Avenue, Original Spin, Philanthropist, Rock Hard Ten, Sensibly Chic.

OVERBROOK FARM—Location: Lexington. **Founded:** 1972. **Principals:** Bill Young and Lucy Young Hamilton. **Acreage:** 2,400. **Stallions for 2006:** Cape Canaveral, Cape Town, Cat Thief, Grindstone, Jump Start, Pioneering, Storm Cat, Tactical Cat. **Graded or group**

stakes winners in 2005 by Overbrook stallions: Behaving Badly, Bluegrass Cat, Cape Hope, Capeside Lady, Consolidator, Effectual, Grand Reward, Good Reward, Great Intentions, Hurricane Cat, Osidy, Pollard's Vision, Southern Africa, Storm Surge, Sweet Catomine, Virden.

THREE CHIMNEYS FARM—Location: Midway, Kentucky. **Founded:** 1973. **Principal:** Robert and Blythe Clay. **Acreage:** 1,500. **Stallions for 2006:** Albert the Great, Dynaformer, Medallist, Point Given, Rahy, Sky Mesa, Smarty Jones, War Chant, Yes It's True. **Graded or group stakes winners of 2005 by Three Chimneys stallions:** Chattahoochee War, Film Maker, Golden Rahy, Karen's Caper, McDynamo, Offlee Wild, Perfect Drift, Proud Accolade, Purim, Riskaverse, Sand Springs, Shining Energy, Stupendous Miss, T. D. Vance.

CLAIBORNE FARM—Location: Paris, Kentucky. **Founded:** 1910. **President:** Seth Hancock. **Acreage:** 2,764. **Stallions for 2006:** Arch, During, Eddington, Flatter, Horse Chestnut (SAf), Monarchos, Out of Place, Private Terms, Pulpit, Seeking the Gold, Stroll, Strong Hope. **Graded or group stakes winners of 2005 by Claiborne stallions:** Arravale, Ecclesiastic, Eddington, Fifth Overture, Melhor Ainda, Navesink River, Oratory, Pleasant Home, Pomeroy, Prince Arch, Purge, Seeking Slew, Seeking the Ante, Smuggler, Spanish Chestnut, Straight Line, Survivalist , Taste of Paradise, Wanderin Boy, Wend.

ADENA SPRINGS KENTUCKY—Location: Versailles, Kentucky. **Founded:** 1989. **Principal:** Frank Stronach. **Acreage:** 1,850. **Stallions for 2006:** Alphabet Soup, Awesome Again, Congaree, El Prado (Ire), Ghostzapper, Gold Case, Golden Missile, North Light (Ire), Olmodavor, Touch Gold. **Graded or group stakes winners of 2005 by Adena Springs Kentucky stallions:** Alphabet Kisses, Spun Sugar, Asi Siempre, Borrego, Kitten's Joy, In the Gold, Ghostzapper, Round Pond, Artie Schiller, Leprechaun Kid, Hotstufanthensome, Mass Media, Medallist.

AIRDRIE STUD—Location: Midway, Kentucky. **Founded:** 1972. **Principals:** Brereton C. and Libby Jones. **Acreage:** 2,500. **Stallions for 2006:** Canadian Frontier, Deputy Commander, Forest Camp, Friends Lake, Harlan's Holiday, Include, Indian Charlie, Proud Citizen, Siphon (Brz), Slew City Slew, Stormin Fever, Yankee Gentleman, Yankee Victor. **Graded or group stakes winners of 2005 by Airdrie Stud stallions:** Lava Man, Mubtaker, Pampered Princess, Sis City, Storm Wolf, Sweet Talker, Tarlow, Two Trail Sioux, Your Tent Or Mine.

HILL 'N' DALE FARMS—Location: Lexington. **Founded:** 1980. **Principal:** John G. Sikura. **Acreage:** 525. **Stallions for 2006:** Buddha, Candy Ride (Arg), El Corredor, Grand Reward, High Yield, Jade Hunter, Mass Media, Mutakddim, Roman Ruler, Stormy Atlantic, Theatrical (Ire), Vindication, Vision and Verse. **Graded or group stakes winners in 2005 by Hill 'n' Dale stallions:** Adieu, De Pizarra, Indian Ocean, Major Leader, Mutakena, Olaya, Scooby, Seek a Star, Shakespeare, She Says It Best.

VINERY KENTUCKY—Location: Lexington. **Founded:** 1987. **Principal:** Thomas Simon. **Acreage:** 462. **Stallions for 2006:** Brahms, D'wildcat, Gilded Time, Limehouse, More Than Ready, Peace Rules, Posse, Pure Prize, Purge, Red Ransom, Runaway Groom, The Cliff's Edge, Trust N Luck, Yonaguska. **Graded or group stakes winners in 2005 by Vinery Kentucky stallions:** Absent Friend, Barely a Moment, Carry On Cutie, Clock Stopper, La Chunga, Media, Perfectly Ready, Ready's Gal, Runaway Dancer, Savorthetime.

ASHFORD STUD—Location: Versailles, Kentucky. **Founded:** 1910. **Principals:** John Magnier and partners. **Acreage:** 1,500. **Stallions for 2006:** Black Minnaloushe, Chapel Royal, Footstepsinthesand (GB), Fusaichi Pegasus, Giant's Causeway, Grand Slam, Hennessy, Hold That Tiger, Honour and Glory, Johannesburg, Lion Heart, Monashee Mountain, Powerscourt (GB), Royal Academy, Tale of the Cat, Thunder Gulch, Van Nistelrooy, Woodman. **Graded or group stakes winners of 2005 by Ashford stallions:** Andromeda's Hero, Aragorn, Art Master, Artejusta, Artemus Sunrise, Battle Won, Bandini, Better Now, Blues and Royals, Bush Honey, Catcominatcha, Charmview, Diamond Omi, Dream Impact, Falkirk, First Samurai, Flying Pegasus, Frost Giant, Glamour Puss, Grand Armee, Henny Hughes, James Levine, Limehouse, Macbeth, Madcap Escapade, Footstepsinthesand (GB), Maids Causeway, Magic Lamp, Movie Star, My Trusty Cat, My Typhoon (Ire), Naissance Royale, Natural Blitz, Naughty Rafaela, New Regina, Notre Dame, Paradise Queen, Primary Suspect, Puxa Saco, Quiet Royal, Roman Ruler, Set Alight, Shamardal, Silver Tree, Stream Cat.

PIN OAK STUD—Location: Versailles, Kentucky. **Founded:** 1952. **Principal:** Josephine Abercrombie. **Acreage:** 750. **Stallions for 2006:** Broken Vow, Maria's Mon, Sky Classic. **Graded or group stakes winners in 2005 by Pin Oak Stud stallions:** Watchmon, Magnetic Eyes, Private Vow, High Limit, Toughkenamon, Whimsy, Guelph, Damoiselle, Sur La Tete.

CASTLETON LYONS—Location: Lexington. **Founded:** 2001. **Principal:** Tony Ryan. **Acreage:** 1,200. **Stallions for 2006:** Action This Day, Bernstein, Malibu Moon, Toccet, Wiseman's Ferry. **Graded or group stakes winners in 2005 by Castleton Lyons stallions:** Berbatim, Declan's Moon, Doctor Si, Dorylda, Snob Lady, Storm Mayor, Stormy Kiss, Stormy Nina, Stormy Nirvana.

OLD ENGLISH RANCHO—Location: Sanger, California. **Founded:** 1939. **Principal:** E. W. "Buddy" Johnston. **Acreage:** 370. **Stallions for 2006:** Cork (Fr), Lacey Evitan, One Man Army, Perfect Mandate, Poteen, Royal Cat, Unbridled Native, Unusual Heat, Vronsky, Western Verse. **Graded or group stakes winners in 2005 by Old English Rancho stallions:** Leave Me Alone, Tucked Away.

BROOKDALE FARM—Location: Versailles, Kentucky. **Founded:** 1983. **Principal:** Fred Seitz. **Acreage:** 375. **Stallions for 2006:** Crafty Prospector, Forest Wildcat, Newfoundland, Silver Deputy. **Graded or group stakes winners in 2005 by Brookdale stallions:** R. Associate, D'Wildcat Speed, Ballroom Deputy, Nashinda, Silver Ticket, Badge of Silver, Miss Fortunate.

GAINESWAY—Location: Lexington. **Founded:** 1979. **Principal:** Antony Beck. **Acreage:** 1,680. **Stallions for 2006:** Afleet Alex, Birdstone, Cozzene, Cuvee, Mr. Greeley, Officer, Orientate, Smoke Glacken, Sunday Break (Jpn), Tapit, Ten Most Wanted, Whywhywhy. **Graded stakes winners of 2005 by Gainesway stallions:** Noisette, Laurafina, Rochester, Greeley's Galaxy, Smokume, Rush Bay, Finery, Miraculous Miss, Monashee, Far Lane, Rob Roy, More Smoke.

WALMAC FARM—Location: Lexington. **Founded:** 1936. **Principal:** John T. L. Jones Jr. **Acreage:** 1,097. **Stallions for 2006:** Cactus Ridge, Eavesdropper, Is It True, Leelanau, Minardi, Songandaprayer, Successful Appeal, Tenpins, Zavata. **Graded or group stakes winners in 2005 by Walmac stallions:** Arakan, Closing Argument, He's Got Grit, Sir Shackleton, What a Song.

Live Foal Report for 2005

Reflecting increased optimism within the Thoroughbred industry as well as Kentucky's completed recovery from mare reproductive loss syndrome (MRLS), live foals of 2005 in North America rose to 40,621 as of February 1, 2006, the Jockey Club reported. That figure represented approximately 95% of live foal reports expected by the Jockey Club. At the same time a year earlier, 39,835 live foals had been reported for the 2004 crop, 2% below the 2005 live-foal crop.

Kentucky, whose breeding industry was devastated by an MRLS disaster that cut into the 2001 crop and reduced the '02 crop substantially, posted a '05 live-foal crop of 14,478, up 1.9% from 14,478 live foals reported for 2004 at a comparable time. Since the MRLS-depleted crop of 12,276 live foals in '02, Kentucky posted increases of 6.5% in '03 and 10.7% in '04. With Kentucky's foal losses down considerably, the state's live-foal rate rose from 60% in 2002 to 72% in '04 and '05. Across North America, the live foal rate was 63%. Among states with large breeding industries, Kentucky returned to the top by live-foal rate; California, the 2003 leader, had a '05 rate of 67%, and Florida was 62% for '05.

The 2005 crop by Kentucky-based stallions represented more than one-third of all live foals in North America, 36.3%. Florida had the second-largest group, 4,290 foals, followed by California at 3,960, Louisiana at 1,880, Texas at 1,710, New York at 1,656, and Maryland at 1,076.

With a large number of mares bred to him and a high rate of live foals, Hold That Tiger led North America by 2005 live foals with 161. The Ashford Stud stallion had been bred to 199 mares in 2004 and had a live-foal rate of 81%. Buddha, who stands at Hill 'n' Dale Farms in Lexington, ranked second with 147 live foals from 182 mares bred. Two Ashford stallions tied for third with 143 live foals. Fusaichi Pegasus had been bred to 193 mares (74% live foal rate) and Grand Slam, to 191 mares (75%). Another Hill 'n' Dale stallion, Stormy Atlantic, ranked fifth with 139 live foals from 183 mares bred (76%).

Leading Stallions by 2005 Foals

Stallion	Mares Bred	Live Foals	Live Foal Rate	State
Hold That Tiger	199	161	81%	Ky.
Buddha	182	147	81%	Ky.
Fusaichi Pegasus	193	143	74%	Ky.
Grand Slam	191	143	75%	Ky.
Stormy Atlantic	183	139	76%	Ky.
Doneraile Court	184	138	75%	Ky.
Van Nistelrooy	186	134	72%	Ky.
Johannesburg	175	130	74%	Ky.
Tale of the Cat	185	129	70%	Ky.
Chief Seattle	166	120	72%	Ky.
Vindication	141	120	85%	Ky.
Distorted Humor	145	119	82%	Ky.
Broken Vow	137	118	86%	Ky.
Honour and Glory	152	118	78%	Ky.
Langfuhr	141	118	84%	Ky.
Elusive Quality	140	114	81%	Ky.
Smart Strike	134	114	85%	Ky.
Cat Thief	137	112	82%	Ky.
Malibu Moon	149	111	74%	Ky.
Yonaguska	134	111	83%	Ky.
Aptitude	129	109	84%	Ky.
Forestry	142	109	77%	Ky.
Gulf Storm	155	109	70%	Fl.
Stephen Got Even	140	109	78%	Ky.
Proud Citizen	157	108	69%	Ky.
Mizzen Mast	130	107	82%	Ky.
E Dubai	143	106	74%	Ky.
Giant's Causeway	130	106	82%	Ky.
More Than Ready	151	106	70%	Ky.
El Corredor	156	103	66%	Ky.
Full Mandate	152	103	68%	Fl.
Harlan's Holiday	138	103	75%	Ky.
Tiznow	123	103	84%	Ky.
Mutakddim	162	102	63%	Ky.
Trippi	147	101	69%	Fl.
Jump Start	125	100	80%	Ky.
Kafwain	142	100	70%	Ky.
Sunday Break (Jpn)	132	100	76%	Ky.
Benchmark	121	99	82%	Ca.
Deputy Commander	120	98	82%	Ky.
High Yield	138	97	70%	Ky.
Officer	129	97	75%	Ky.
Empire Maker	111	96	86%	Ky.
Carson City	131	95	73%	Ky.
Cherokee Run	130	95	73%	Ky.
Yes It's True	122	95	78%	Ky.
Orientate	115	94	82%	Ky.
Stravinsky	143	94	66%	Ky.
Victory Gallop	116	94	81%	Ky.
Alphabet Soup	120	92	77%	Ky.
Tactical Cat	112	92	82%	Ky.
Northern Afleet	128	91	71%	Fl.
Petionville	125	91	73%	Ky.
Sky Mesa	110	91	83%	Ky.
Golden Missile	116	90	78%	Ky.
Halo's Image	134	90	67%	Fl.
Millennium Wind	123	90	73%	Ky.
Kingmambo	105	89	85%	Ky.
Lemon Drop Kid	112	89	79%	Ky.
Street Cry (Ire)	129	89	69%	Ky.
Pulpit	109	88	81%	Ky.
Storm Cat	116	88	76%	Ky.
Tiger Ridge	151	88	58%	Fl.
Unbridled's Song	118	88	75%	Ky.
In Excess (Ire)	115	87	76%	Ca.
Lion Hearted	127	87	69%	Md.
Milwaukee Brew	106	87	82%	Ky.
Smoke Glacken	116	87	75%	Ky.
Mr. Greeley	127	86	68%	Ky.
Gone West	99	85	86%	Ky.
Hennessy	137	85	62%	Ky.
Flatter	116	84	72%	Ky.
Sligo Bay (Ire)	103	84	82%	Ky.
Touch Gold	106	84	79%	Ky.
Forest Wildcat	110	83	75%	Ky.
Gold Case	116	83	72%	Ky.
Matty G	124	83	67%	Ky.
Montbrook	119	83	70%	Fl.

Live Foals by Stallions by State and Province in 2005

State	Stallions	Mares Bred	Live Foals	Live Foal Rate
Alabama	30	146	60	41%
Alaska	1	3	1	33%
Arkansas	72	603	335	56%
Arizona	64	530	317	60%
California	408	5,902	3,960	67%
Colorado	66	452	253	56%
Connecticut	1	1	0	0%
Delaware	1	2	1	50%
Florida	250	6,888	4,290	62%
Georgia	26	144	51	35%
Hawaii	1	1	1	100%
Idaho	51	322	165	51%
Illinois	121	1,119	621	55%
Indiana	99	755	346	46%
Iowa	48	525	285	54%
Kansas	29	195	80	41%
Kentucky	379	20,579	14,748	72%
Louisiana	261	3,301	1,880	57%
Maine	2	2	2	100%
Maryland	75	1,616	1,076	67%
Massachusetts	18	69	37	54%
Michigan	70	583	330	57%
Minnesota	38	358	169	47%
Mississippi	16	75	35	47%
Missouri	31	110	49	45%
Montana	46	202	107	53%
Nebraska	39	373	204	55%
Nevada	7	17	7	41%
New Hampshire	1	1	1	100%
New Jersey	28	268	163	61%
New Mexico	166	1,629	932	57%
New York	156	2,683	1,656	62%
North Carolina	18	63	31	49%
North Dakota	21	112	43	38%
Ohio	97	567	293	52%
Oklahoma	197	1,603	845	53%
Oregon	54	469	302	64%
Pennsylvania	115	998	574	58%
Puerto Rico	60	796	552	69%
Rhode Island	1	1	1	100%
South Carolina	28	145	67	46%
South Dakota	12	141	54	38%
Tennessee	20	66	35	53%
Texas	368	3,059	1,710	56%
Utah	36	232	112	48%
Vermont	3	4	3	75%
Virginia	72	428	240	56%
Washington	107	1,203	738	61%
West Virginia	88	1,073	542	51%
Wisconsin	9	29	7	24%
Wyoming	10	30	13	43%
Province				
Alberta	79	943	524	56%
British Columbia	66	835	502	60%
Manitoba	24	196	95	48%
New Brunswick	2	3	1	33%
Nova Scotia	2	2	0	0%
Ontario	116	1,679	1,067	64%
Quebec	4	13	3	23%
Saskatchewan	22	167	91	54%
Totals	4,245	64,354	40,621	63%

Stallions With Live Foals in 2005
(As of February 1, 2006; Minimum of Ten Mares Bred)

Stallion	Mares Bred	Fls	Live Foal Rate
Alabama			
Casey On Deck	11	6	55%
Power of Mind	14	4	29%
Royal Empire	22	10	45%
Turn Out	12	4	33%
Whambam	10	3	30%
Youngs Neck Arod	15	2	13%
Arizona			
American General	10	5	50%
A. P. Million	17	5	29%
Bold Anthony	46	30	65%
Cinnamon Creek	20	9	45%
Cornish Snow	18	9	50%
Distant Mirage (Ire)	13	7	54%
Etbauer	18	9	50%
Father Steve	15	15	100%
Glorious Bid	21	8	38%
Idabel	17	9	53%
Ile St. Louis (Chi)	27	12	44%
Macabe	43	29	67%
Monarch's Maze	21	12	57%
Proper Reality	13	4	31%
Smolderin Heart	36	24	67%
Southern Forest	13	9	69%
Storm and a Half	68	34	50%
Trust No Lawyer	11	7	64%
Arkansas			
Al Ghazi	24	15	63%
Benton Creek	52	34	65%
Big Sky Chester	30	22	73%
Buck Strider	45	26	58%
Chanate	27	25	93%
Chancery Court	13	10	77%
Ellusive Quest	11	10	91%
E. W. Cat	11	6	55%
Hidden City	21	12	57%
Midnight Royalty	38	23	61%
Ronton	18	4	22%
Sideburn	31	21	68%
Slew Mood	13	10	77%
Spice Cat	13	8	62%
Star of Halo	14	5	36%
T. G. Dewey	12	4	33%
California			
Alymagic	12	10	83%
American Day	12	5	42%
America's Storm	19	12	63%
Anziyan	14	11	79%
Avanzado (Arg)	36	27	75%
Bartok (Ire)	95	58	61%
Beau Genius	66	51	77%
Benchmark	121	99	82%
Bertrando	65	54	83%
Bienamado	17	10	59%
Birdonthewire	28	16	57%
Boomerang	15	14	93%
Bouccaneer (Fr)	32	12	38%
Brave Romane	13	9	69%
Bring the Heat	17	9	53%
Built for Pleasure	29	23	79%
Bustopher Jones	11	8	73%
Cactus Creole	10	6	60%
Candi's Gold	13	10	77%
Capsized	58	41	71%
Category Five	21	12	57%
Cee's Tizzy	82	63	77%
Cherokee Colony	13	8	62%
Chimineas	10	6	60%
Chullo (Arg)	32	24	75%
Cobra King	35	23	66%
Comet Shine	26	19	73%
Comic Strip	42	29	69%
Commitment	21	19	90%
Corslew	16	12	75%
Crowning Storm	43	33	77%
Decarchy	73	58	79%
Definite Edge	19	4	21%
Desert Classic	13	9	69%
Devon Lane	34	22	65%
Dismissed	14	7	50%
Dixie Dot Com	39	33	85%
Dominique's Cat	17	9	53%
Done Dancing	10	3	30%
Downtown Seattle	12	7	58%
D's Bertrando	16	11	69%
Dumaani	14	11	79%
Elegant Fellow	13	8	62%
Emerald Creme	16	2	13%
Epic Honor	22	14	64%
Event of the Year	13	11	85%
Fabulous Champ	12	5	42%
Fine n' Majestic	22	10	45%
Flom's Prospector	15	6	40%
Flying Continental	27	21	78%
Flying Victor	15	8	53%
For Really	25	12	48%
Free House	45	32	71%
Freespool	54	37	69%
Fruition	12	5	42%
Fun Devil	14	11	79%
Fusaichi Accele	12	10	83%

Stallion	Mares Bred	Fls	Live Foal Rate
Fusaichi Zenon (Jpn)	10	8	80%
Future Storm	43	32	74%
Game Plan	43	22	51%
General Meeting	17	11	65%
Globalize	30	21	70%
Golden Gear	46	28	61%
Gotham City	45	30	67%
Guarani	24	14	58%
Haint	20	13	65%
Half Term	16	5	31%
Helmsman	18	14	78%
Here Comes Big C	12	4	33%
High Brite	55	39	71%
High Demand	35	28	80%
Highland Gold	22	21	95%
Holding Court	12	6	50%
Houston	16	13	81%
Iam the Iceman	12	7	58%
Illinois Storm	54	24	44%
In Excess (Ire)	115	87	76%
Iron Cat	33	19	58%
Kahuna Jack	11	4	36%
Kessem Power (NZ)	15	9	60%
Kid Capote	10	7	70%
King Excess	11	7	64%
King of the Hunt	10	7	70%
Lacey Evitan	15	13	87%
Lake William	58	45	78%
Laramie's Deputy	26	13	50%
Larry the Legend	41	29	71%
Latin American	18	13	72%
Lit de Justice	51	37	73%
Lord Carson	82	72	88%
Madraar	58	44	76%
Majesterian	11	7	64%
Makaleha	10	7	70%
Malek (Chi)	32	25	78%
Mechon Tom (Arg)	20	8	40%
Memo (Chi)	30	19	63%
Michael's Flyer	15	10	67%
Moms From Dixie	15	9	60%
Moscow Ballet	30	17	57%
Mr. Broad Blade	12	9	75%
Mr. Publisher	16	12	75%
Mt. Bellewood	14	11	79%
Mud Route	47	33	70%
Muqtarib	65	55	85%
National Saint	16	10	63%
Newton's Law (Ire)	14	5	36%
Nineeleven	28	19	68%
Old Topper	59	50	85%
Ole'	18	11	61%
Olympio	12	11	92%
One Man Army	22	15	68%
Perfect Mandate	97	67	69%
Persian Turban (Ire)	16	11	69%
Peyrano (Arg)	12	10	83%
Phonetics	44	17	39%
Poteen	16	15	94%
Proud Irish	37	9	24%
Puerto Madero (Chi)	23	19	83%
Rainbow Blues (Ire)	16	15	94%
Raise Suzuran	14	8	57%
Really Honest	12	4	33%
Red	18	9	50%
Regent Act	10	6	60%
Replicate	20	12	60%
Rhythm	28	15	54%
Richly Blended	50	31	62%
Ride the Rails	26	22	85%
Rio Verde	71	46	65%
Roar	73	46	63%
Robannier	18	10	56%
Rocket Cat	35	20	57%
Roman Dancer	22	18	82%
Royal Cat	32	23	72%
Score Quick	12	8	67%
Seattle Bound	12	9	75%
Sharan (GB)	15	9	60%
Siberian Summer	48	34	71%
Six Below	14	8	57%
Skimming	94	75	80%
Slewvescent	24	16	67%
Smokester	55	34	62%
Smooth Runner	19	9	47%
Soft Gold (Brz)	30	24	80%
Sought After	14	7	50%
Soul of the Matter	17	14	82%
Storm Blast	10	7	70%
Storm Creek	115	79	69%
Stormy Jack	44	35	80%
Strike Gold	10	6	60%
Suggest	14	5	36%
Surachai	18	16	89%
Swiss Yodeler	63	44	70%
Synastry	11	7	64%
Takin It Deep	19	14	74%
Tannersmyman	13	8	62%
Thinkin Problem	10	5	50%
Trail City	16	14	88%
Tribal Rule	78	61	78%
Tricky Creek	19	13	68%
Truckee	18	11	61%
Truly Met	26	14	54%
Turkoman	42	13	31%
T. U. Slew	12	1	8%
Unbridled's Love	24	11	46%
Unusual Heat	99	80	81%
Valid Wager	79	68	86%
Via Lombardia (Ire)	28	16	57%
Walter Willy (Ire)	11	5	45%
Western Fame	21	14	67%
Worldly Manner	12	11	92%
You and I	55	42	76%
Zanferrier	13	9	69%

Colorado

Stallion	Mares Bred	Fls	Live Foal Rate
A Man of Class	13	8	62%
Annual Tradition	17	8	47%
Capote's Promise	11	3	27%
Cash Deposit	18	13	72%
Cats and Dogs	16	5	31%
Conquistador Deoro	17	15	88%
Dash Ahead	12	7	58%
Eishin Masamune (Jpn)	31	14	45%
Ernie Tee	11	7	64%
Majorbigtimesheet	17	12	71%
Mr. Gehrig	11	8	73%
Oliver's Twist	49	35	71%
Scott's Dream	10	4	40%
Silver Saint	13	8	62%
Spellbounder	13	4	31%
Top Villa	10	6	60%

Florida

Stallion	Mares Bred	Fls	Live Foal Rate
Adcat	80	46	58%
Adonis	15	7	47%
A. P. Five Hundred	21	10	48%
Arrested	29	15	52%
Awesome of Course	10	8	80%
Band Is Passing	16	7	44%
Best of the Rest	13	10	77%
Big Jewel	15	9	60%
B L's Appeal	41	29	71%
Brief Ruckus	10	8	80%
Capture the Gold	10	4	40%
Cimarron Secret	18	17	94%
Classic Cat	55	36	65%
Cloud Cover	23	11	48%
Cloud Hopping	42	21	50%
Colony Light	39	25	64%
Concerto	32	13	41%
Concorde's Tune	101	58	57%
Conquista Fager	10	9	90%
Cyberspace	38	17	45%
Dance Master	33	21	64%
Delaware Township	84	53	63%
Deputy Wild Cat	37	27	73%
Diligence	22	14	64%
Double Honor	102	60	59%
Dr. Caton	11	10	91%
Drewman	94	62	66%
Dr. Gigolo	11	11	100%
Eltish	73	55	75%
Essence of Dubai	87	53	61%
Exchange Rate	81	58	72%
Express Tour	35	16	46%
Family Calling	57	38	67%
Fappie's Notebook	35	24	69%
Fast 'n Royal	16	12	75%
First Tour	14	12	86%
Flame Thrower	62	42	68%
Forbidden Apple	62	26	42%
Formal Dinner	39	24	62%
French Envoy	40	18	45%
Full Mandate	152	103	68%
Georgia Two	11	7	64%
Gibson County	32	18	56%
Graeme Hall	58	48	83%
Greatness	82	44	54%
Gulf Storm	155	109	70%
Hadrian's Wall	20	13	65%
Halos and Horns	36	20	56%
Halo's Image	134	90	67%
Honor Glide	75	47	63%
Impeachment	54	32	59%
Indy King	40	23	58%
Invisible Ink	34	17	50%
Is It True	37	24	65%
Kissin Kris	31	26	84%
Lexicon	59	40	68%
Lido Palace (Chi)	81	55	68%
Lightnin N Thunder	74	32	43%
Line In The Sand	23	10	43%
Lite the Fuse	36	22	61%
Littlebitlively	21	13	62%
Lost Soldier	44	30	68%
Macho Uno	109	75	69%
Master Bill	28	20	71%
Max's Pal	69	40	58%
Mecke	33	20	61%
Metfield	18	10	56%
Middlesex Drive	16	9	56%
Migrating Moon	32	19	59%
Mongoose	39	25	64%
Monsieur Cat	23	17	74%
Montbrook	119	83	70%
Mount McKinley	38	21	55%
Northern Afleet	128	91	71%
Northern Trend	56	38	68%
Outofthebox	109	81	74%
Palance	15	7	47%
Personal First	28	12	43%
Pistols and Roses	11	2	18%
Point in Time	12	8	67%
Precocity	24	15	63%
Proud and True	29	17	59%
Proudest Romeo	53	45	85%
Pure Precision	67	46	69%
Put It Back	86	58	67%
Quaker Ridge	21	11	52%
R. Cooper	20	8	40%
Recommended List	15	6	40%
Red Bullet	87	49	56%
Repent	119	81	68%
Reprized	10	7	70%
Robyn Dancer	62	37	60%
Running Stag	86	68	79%
Safely's Mark	17	6	35%
Salty Sea	30	15	50%
Scorpion	55	27	49%
Scottish Halo	13	3	23%
Shanawi (Ire)	36	18	50%
Skip to the Stone	70	34	49%
Skip Trial	30	13	43%
Slew Gin Fizz	41	24	59%
Smooth Jazz	87	45	52%
Snow Ridge	78	53	68%
Snuck In	106	63	59%
Songandaprayer	80	55	69%
Stone Bridge	14	8	57%
Straight Man	73	50	68%
Suave Prospect	70	46	66%
Successful Appeal	109	67	61%
Sweetsouthernsaint	42	27	64%

Stallion	Mares Bred	Fls	Live Foal Rate
Texas Glitter	103	65	63%
Thats Our Buck	10	4	40%
The Silver Move	16	10	63%
Three Wonders	111	71	64%
Tiger Ridge	151	88	58%
Tour d'Or	32	21	66%
Trippi	147	101	69%
True Enough	24	12	50%
Unbridled Time	94	56	60%
Untuttable	70	48	69%
Weekend Cruise	65	33	51%
Wekiva Springs	34	18	53%
West Acre	72	44	61%
Wild Escapade	11	8	73%
Wild Event	53	27	51%
Wind Whipper	38	24	63%
Wised Up	24	17	71%

Georgia

Level Sands	11	7	64%
Play Both Ends	10	7	70%
Prospector Street	17	3	18%
Roaring Camp	17	5	29%
Roundup	16	3	19%
St. Alydar	10	2	20%

Idaho

Chisos	14	8	57%
Coastal Voyage	47	15	32%
Kings Blood (Ire)	28	21	75%
Pirate's Gulch	13	7	54%
Pulzarr	12	0	0%
Reversal	17	10	59%
Starmaniac	28	12	43%
Tavasco	14	10	71%
Thunderah	23	18	78%

Illinois

Alaskan Frost	27	11	41%
Allen Charge	15	7	47%
Awesome Cat	14	9	64%
Bold Revenue	15	5	33%
Canyon Run	14	8	57%
Cartwright	84	53	63%
Chicago Six	20	18	90%
City by Night	14	8	57%
Classic Account	16	7	44%
Classified Facts	32	19	59%
Conte Di Savoya	29	13	45%
Crimson Classic	10	7	70%
Demidoff	25	15	60%
Denouncer	13	9	69%
Fact Book	11	5	45%
Goliard	13	2	15%
He's a Tough Cat	27	13	48%
Honour Attendant	21	11	52%
Irgun	54	25	46%
Mahie Gold	10	6	60%
Marte	21	13	62%
Nooo Problema	12	8	67%
Posh	33	26	79%
Powerful Goer	26	17	65%
Rigging	13	13	100%
Royal Roberto	11	7	64%
Sabona	25	14	56%
Seattle Morn	25	17	68%
Shore Breeze	35	20	57%
Sir Spellbinder	15	9	60%
Summer Cloud	11	6	55%
Supeona	12	7	58%
Unbridled Success	14	6	43%
Unloosened	12	8	67%
Unreal Zeal	50	29	58%
Zagor	15	1	7%

Indiana

Announce	22	11	50%
Arromanches	27	12	44%
Avalli	11	5	45%

Stallion	Mares Bred	Fls	Live Foal Rate
Black Moonshine	18	10	56%
Blase	11	4	36%
Colonel Bradley	14	7	50%
Commemorate	23	10	43%
Crown Ambassador	29	16	55%
Dewdle's Dancer	12	3	25%
Dixie Road	10	5	50%
Fiscal	10	4	40%
Garcon Rouge	12	8	67%
Indian Territory	25	19	76%
Indy Mood	21	8	38%
Jacquelyn's Groom	14	8	57%
Keynote	16	1	6%
Le Casque Gris	12	5	42%
Miswaki Bandit	12	2	17%
Montreal Red	10	6	60%
Moro Oro	15	10	67%
New York Prospect	10	8	80%
Once Wild	11	2	18%
Plenty Chilly	16	10	63%
Presidential Order	27	16	59%
Sixto G	11	5	45%
Sold to Wallstreet	10	3	30%
Speedy Cure	11	2	18%
Swiss Trick	12	3	25%
Timeraker	12	4	33%
Tricon	14	4	29%
Unbridled Man	25	12	48%

Iowa

Brassy Wells	12	3	25%
Bravo Bull	23	17	74%
Buzz Saw	16	8	50%
Canaveral	11	6	55%
Cape Storm	10	2	20%
Deputy Slew	11	6	55%
Dignitas	16	12	75%
Doug Fir	24	11	46%
Friendly Lover	43	30	70%
H. J. Baker	10	2	20%
Humming	12	6	50%
Kyle's Our Man	13	9	69%
Mocha Express	20	11	55%
One Hundred Slews	19	7	37%
Sharkey	24	13	54%
Supremo	21	13	62%
Tiger Talk	12	6	50%
Valley Crossing	28	19	68%
West Buoyant	15	3	20%
Wild Gold	30	23	77%
Wild Invader	12	5	42%
Winter Glitter	32	21	66%

Kansas

Admiral Indy	27	10	37%
Another Good Deed	10	2	20%
Fortifier	11	7	64%
Ianomami (Ire)	10	5	50%
Polly's Comet	12	10	83%
Prospector's Treat	20	10	50%
So Ever Clever	13	7	54%
Torey Ridge	13	5	38%
Tricky Six	13	3	23%

Kentucky

Acceptable	16	9	56%
Albert the Great	100	69	69%
Aldebaran	101	78	77%
Aljabr	29	22	76%
Alphabet Soup	120	92	77%
A.P. Indy	97	74	76%
Aptitude	129	109	84%
Arch	88	52	59%
Artax	74	53	72%
Atticus	27	21	78%
Austinpower (Jpn)	12	6	50%
Austin Powers (Ire)	14	5	36%
Awesome Again	91	79	87%
Ballado Chieftan	12	5	42%

Stallion	Mares Bred	Fls	Live Foal Rate
Barkerville	26	17	65%
Basic	18	11	61%
Behrens	64	42	66%
Belong to Me	103	72	70%
Bernstein	84	54	64%
Best of Luck	38	28	74%
Black Minnaloushe	96	75	78%
Booklet	13	7	54%
Boundary	37	22	59%
Brahms	92	75	82%
Bright Launch	29	20	69%
Broad Brush	26	9	35%
Broken Vow	137	118	86%
Buddha	182	147	81%
Cactus Ridge	104	71	68%
Came Home	106	81	76%
Cape Canaveral	66	50	76%
Cape Town	82	58	71%
Carolina Kid	11	4	36%
Carson City	131	95	73%
Castle Gandolfo	71	43	61%
Cat Doctor	17	16	94%
Cat Thief	137	112	82%
Century City (Ire)	72	53	74%
Changeintheweather	84	61	73%
Cherokee Run	130	95	73%
Chief Seattle	166	120	72%
Commendable	63	45	71%
Composer	10	6	60%
Cozzene	49	37	76%
Crafty Friend	41	23	56%
Crafty Prospector	50	31	62%
Cryptoclearance	58	38	66%
Dance Brightly	32	22	69%
Danzig	45	26	58%
David Copperfield	31	23	74%
Dayjur	40	28	70%
Deerhound	12	10	83%
Deputy Commander	120	98	82%
Deputy Minister	64	44	69%
Devil His Due	105	66	63%
Devil's Bag	53	35	66%
Diesis (GB)	60	46	77%
Distant View	67	46	69%
Distorted Humor	145	119	82%
Dixieland Band	52	47	90%
Dixieland Heat	23	13	57%
Dixie Union	101	78	77%
Doneraile Court	184	138	75%
Down the Aisle	40	21	53%
Dynaformer	108	82	76%
Ecton Park	101	66	65%
Editor's Note	33	21	64%
E Dubai	143	106	74%
El Corredor	156	103	66%
El Prado (Ire)	106	76	72%
Elusive Quality	140	114	81%
Empire Maker	111	96	86%
Evansville Slew	86	50	58%
Explicit	63	43	68%
Exploit	88	56	64%
Fast Play	33	21	64%
Favorite Trick	27	16	59%
Fit to Fight	25	16	64%
Five Star Day	87	55	63%
Flatter	116	84	72%
Forest Camp	105	79	75%
Forestry	142	109	77%
Forest Wildcat	110	83	75%
Formal Gold	53	30	57%
Frisk Me Now	15	8	53%
Fusaichi Pegasus	193	143	74%
General Royal	37	24	65%
Giant's Causeway	130	106	82%
Gilded Time	90	78	87%
Glitterman	76	51	67%
Go for Gin	20	16	80%
Gold Case	116	83	72%
Golden Missile	116	90	78%
Gone West	99	85	86%
Grand Slam	191	143	75%

Stallion	Mares Bred	Fls	Live Foal Rate
Greenwood Lake	91	65	71%
Grindstone	91	64	70%
Gulch	83	66	80%
Hap	43	20	47%
Harlan's Holiday	138	103	75%
Hennessy	137	85	62%
High Yield	138	97	70%
Hold for Gold	34	19	56%
Hold That Tiger	199	161	81%
Holy Bull	112	81	72%
Honour and Glory	152	118	78%
Horse Chestnut (SAf)	100	73	73%
Hussonet	83	59	71%
Include	93	66	71%
Indian Charlie	104	69	66%
Jade Hunter	43	28	65%
Jambalaya Jazz	47	32	68%
Johannesburg	175	130	74%
Jump Start	125	100	80%
Kafwain	142	100	70%
Kanjinsky	10	4	40%
King Cugat	45	32	71%
Kingmambo	105	89	85%
K One King	16	7	44%
K. O. Punch	31	13	42%
Kutsa	16	5	31%
Labeeb (GB)	29	12	41%
Lac Ouimet	30	13	43%
Langfuhr	141	118	84%
Lear Fan	49	19	39%
Leelanau	45	26	58%
Lemon Drop Kid	112	89	79%
Lil E. Tee	20	9	45%
Lil's Lad	28	17	61%
Line Rider	16	2	13%
Lion Cavern	15	8	53%
Littleexpectations	55	38	69%
Luhuk	53	30	57%
Malabar Gold	104	73	70%
Malibu Moon	149	111	74%
Mancini	22	14	64%
Maria's Mon	66	56	85%
Marquetry	59	37	63%
Matty G	124	83	67%
Mazel Trick	64	44	69%
Meadowlake	76	47	62%
Menifee	70	63	90%
Military	49	34	69%
Millennium Wind	123	90	73%
Milwaukee Brew	106	87	82%
Minardi	86	59	69%
Mineshaft	104	78	75%
Misbah	16	6	38%
Mizzen Mast	130	107	82%
Monarchos	76	62	82%
More Than Ready	151	106	70%
Morluc	38	18	47%
Mr. Greeley	127	86	68%
Mr Henrysee	10	7	70%
Mt. Livermore	55	31	56%
Mutakddim	162	102	63%
Najran	105	72	69%
Northern Spur (Ire)	11	4	36%
Officer	129	97	75%
Old Kentucky Home	24	17	71%
Orientate	115	94	82%
Our Emblem	63	41	65%
Out of Place	59	43	73%
Peaks and Valleys	26	18	69%
Pembroke	28	13	46%
Perfect Vision	35	13	37%
Petionville	125	91	73%
Pikepass	72	45	63%
Pine Bluff	69	39	57%
Pioneering	33	22	67%
Pleasant Tap	72	53	74%
Point Given	95	66	69%
Polish Navy	25	12	48%
Posse	115	78	68%
Private Terms	54	37	69%
Prized	39	18	46%

Stallion	Mares Bred	Fls	Live Foal Rate
Proud Citizen	157	108	69%
Pulpit	109	88	81%
Pure Prize	81	61	75%
Pyramid Peak	14	8	57%
Quiet American	87	62	71%
Rahy	79	61	77%
Real Quiet	64	41	64%
Repriced	29	19	66%
Richter Scale	111	80	72%
Rod and Staff	14	9	64%
Rojo Dinero	17	12	71%
Royal Academy	90	66	73%
Royal Anthem	54	38	70%
Ruckus Hosner	11	3	27%
Runaway Groom	56	43	77%
Sahm	52	33	63%
Salt Lake	95	67	71%
Saratoga Six	22	7	32%
Scatmandu	43	27	63%
Sea of Secrets	85	68	80%
Seeking the Gold	78	63	81%
Service Stripe	80	51	64%
Shadeed	12	8	67%
Silic (Fr)	53	31	58%
Silver Charm	103	80	78%
Silver Deputy	101	81	80%
Silver Ghost	25	18	72%
Siphon (Brz)	64	49	77%
Sir Cat	54	31	57%
Skip Away	61	39	64%
Sky Classic	34	23	68%
Sky Mesa	110	91	83%
Slew City Slew	62	45	73%
Sligo Bay (Ire)	103	84	82%
Smart Strike	134	114	85%
Smoke Glacken	116	87	75%
Souvenir Copy	41	30	73%
Stephen Got Even	140	109	78%
Storm Boot	77	59	77%
Storm Cat	116	88	76%
Stormin Fever	95	70	74%
Stormy Atlantic	183	139	76%
Stravinsky	143	94	66%
Street Cry (Ire)	129	89	69%
Subordination	15	11	73%
Sultry Song	64	49	77%
Sunday Break (Jpn)	132	100	76%
Swain (Ire)	66	44	67%
Swing Lord	10	7	70%
Syncline	50	25	50%
Tactical Cat	112	92	82%
Tale of the Cat	185	129	70%
Talk Is Money	93	55	59%
Tejano Run	32	18	56%
Theatrical (Ire)	53	45	85%
The Deputy (Ire)	42	26	62%
Thunderello	92	55	60%
Thunder Gulch	103	72	70%
Tiznow	123	103	84%
Touch Gold	106	84	79%
Trust N Luck	101	72	71%
Unbridled's Song	118	88	75%
Van Nistelrooy	186	134	72%
Vicar	105	74	70%
Victory Gallop	116	94	81%
Vindication	141	120	85%
Vision and Verse	71	42	59%
Volponi	80	58	73%
Wagon Limit	38	31	82%
War Chant	57	48	84%
Wavering Monarch	18	12	67%
Wheaton	12	7	58%
Whywhywhy	95	61	64%
Wild Again	20	4	20%
Wild Wonder	54	32	59%
Will's Way	12	6	50%
Winning Bid	17	15	88%
With Approval	68	46	68%
Woodman	71	47	66%
Yankee Gentleman	102	77	75%
Yankee Victor	94	69	73%

Stallion	Mares Bred	Fls	Live Foal Rate
Yes It's True	122	95	78%
Yonaguska	134	111	83%
Zavata	104	68	65%

Louisiana

Stallion	Mares Bred	Fls	Live Foal Rate
Abajo	32	15	47%
Afternoon Deelites	80	47	59%
Almostashar	30	22	73%
Aloha Prospector	26	15	58%
A. P. Delta	46	24	52%
Autocracy	12	7	58%
Belek	14	5	36%
B. J.'s Mark	11	6	55%
Blare of Trumpets	10	4	40%
Carnovali	17	14	82%
Catastrophe	24	15	63%
Choosing Choice	24	13	54%
Classic Alliance	11	9	82%
Count the Time	16	13	81%
Crowning Decision	14	4	29%
Daring Bid	10	7	70%
Deamon's Pouch	12	0	0%
Deputy Diamond	40	27	68%
Direct Hit	36	21	58%
Dream Tripper	10	7	70%
Dr. Lewis	10	8	80%
Easyfromthegitgo	54	36	67%
Erlton	33	26	79%
Escrito	27	13	48%
Esplanade Ridge	11	5	45%
Eulogize	11	8	73%
Fair Decor	14	4	29%
Finder's Gold	25	15	60%
Finest Hour	90	51	57%
Fly Cry	20	5	25%
Forty Won	26	17	65%
Gift of Gib	11	6	55%
Global Mission	20	13	65%
Golden Slew	19	10	53%
Gold Tribute	66	48	73%
Goodbye Doeny	10	7	70%
Grim Reaper	16	11	69%
Holy Sting	26	13	50%
Homebuilder	13	9	69%
Ide	74	48	65%
In a Walk	44	28	64%
Jaunatxo	15	9	60%
Kadhaaf	11	5	45%
Keats	24	14	58%
Kimberlite Pipe	25	14	56%
Kipper Kelly	30	16	53%
Kukulcan	10	5	50%
Laabity	30	17	57%
Leestown	100	67	67%
Like a Soldier	12	3	25%
Malagra	20	14	70%
Malibu Wesley	18	11	61%
Mighty	16	9	56%
Mr. John	10	5	50%
Mr. Sparkles	16	12	75%
My Friend Max	16	8	50%
Native Regent	16	10	63%
Northern Niner	22	12	55%
On Target	35	29	83%
Our Diablo	10	4	40%
Our Shining Hour	18	8	44%
Out of the Crisis	40	20	50%
Parting Guest	11	6	55%
Piccolino	19	11	58%
Placid Fund	24	18	75%
Planet Earth	12	7	58%
Prince of the Mt.	21	12	57%
Prospector's Gift	34	16	47%
Pulling Punches	25	16	64%
Rail	10	5	50%
Ruby Hill	17	8	47%
Run Production	21	14	67%
Rush	11	2	18%
Safe Prospect	15	9	60%
Secret Odds	20	9	45%
Sefapiano	56	34	61%

Stallion	Mares Bred	Fls	Live Foal Rate
Silky Sweep	43	18	42%
Slew the Surgeon	11	4	36%
Storm Day	99	63	64%
Storm Passage	39	29	74%
Storm Walk	10	6	60%
Strategic Intent	26	14	54%
Thank the Bank	11	8	73%
Thunder Breeze	11	6	55%
Time Bandit	71	50	70%
Toolighttoquit	17	10	59%
Top Venture	28	13	46%
Tourist	17	11	65%
Tricky	27	9	33%
Twilight Agenda	16	9	56%
United Spirit	13	5	38%
Upping the Ante	33	17	52%
Valid Belfast	36	22	61%
Valid Bidder	33	16	48%
Virginia Carnival	13	2	15%
Viva Deputy	18	9	50%
Western Echo	17	13	76%
Western Gentleman	16	8	50%
Winter Halo	10	6	60%
Wire Me Collect	27	13	48%
Worldly Ways (GB)	41	22	54%
Zarbyev	35	22	63%

Maryland

Appealing Skier	33	20	61%
Cat Country	10	7	70%
Citidancer	32	9	28%
Crowd Pleaser	33	20	61%
Crypto Star	36	26	72%
Diamond	42	32	76%
Disco Rico	48	34	71%
Eastern Echo	35	22	63%
Fleet Foot	20	14	70%
Jazz Club	38	25	66%
Larrupin'	23	14	61%
Lion Hearted	127	87	69%
Louis Quatorze	77	53	69%
Meadow Monster	46	34	74%
Mojave Moon	65	48	74%
Mokhieba	12	9	75%
No Armistice	74	45	61%
Not For Love	102	81	79%
Ops Smile	11	6	55%
Outflanker	73	52	71%
Parker's Storm Cat	71	53	75%
Partner's Hero	58	41	71%
Polish Miner	54	33	61%
Purple Passion	12	8	67%
Rock Slide	69	40	58%
Seeking Daylight	52	31	60%
Two Punch	85	61	72%
Unbridled Jet	52	36	69%
Waquoit	38	21	55%
Wayne County (Ire)	11	9	82%
Who's Your Daddy	12	9	75%
Yarrow Brae	35	28	80%
Yoh May Kenta	10	7	70%

Massachusetts

Senor Conquistador	11	8	73%
Storm of Angels	15	9	60%

Michigan

Allie's Punch	10	3	30%
Awesome Arnold	10	8	80%
Binalong	21	15	71%
Career Best	12	9	75%
Circus Surprise	10	4	40%
Clock Radio	10	8	80%
Collateral Attack	13	3	23%
Creative	12	9	75%
Crimson Guard	23	10	43%
Daylight Savings	26	17	65%
Demaloot Demashoot	37	22	59%
Elusive Hour	28	10	36%
Equality	41	26	63%

Stallion	Mares Bred	Fls	Live Foal Rate
Great Allegiance	11	3	27%
Hunting Hard	15	9	60%
Matchlite	15	12	80%
Meadow Prayer	11	9	82%
Mr. Katowice	11	5	45%
Native Factor	18	13	72%
Ocala Slew	12	8	67%
Pauliano	24	16	67%
Quiet Enjoyment	16	10	63%
Research	17	8	47%
Treasury	11	7	64%
Ulises	10	5	50%

Minnesota

Boundless	18	9	50%
Dixie Power	23	10	43%
Dynomania	10	2	20%
Emailit	10	5	50%
Gazebo	17	10	59%
Ghazi	50	28	56%
Lakeshore Road	13	9	69%
Late Edition	19	14	74%
Polished Brass	10	1	10%
Quaker Hill	16	10	63%
Quick Cut	17	8	47%
Shot of Gold	31	17	55%
Tahkodha Hills	27	13	48%
Victor's Gent	16	5	31%

Mississippi

House Burner	11	5	45%
Minister Slew	18	9	50%
Valid Victorious	10	3	30%

Missouri

Hubba Hubba	11	8	73%

Montana

Double Dewars	10	7	70%
Khalsa	17	6	35%
Lifes Reward	10	3	30%
Son's Corona	11	4	36%
Unbridled Desire	13	11	85%
White Tie Tryst	12	3	25%

Nebraska

Blumin Affair	27	20	74%
Box Buster	22	10	45%
Dazzling Falls	19	9	47%
Fortuoso	16	11	69%
Glenview	20	8	40%
Godolphin Cat	15	9	60%
Gray Raider	20	15	75%
Military Tune	20	5	25%
Not So Fast	19	11	58%
Shawklit Player	21	13	62%
Silent Bluff	35	21	60%
Silver Launch	15	4	27%
Yankee Fan	17	12	71%

New Jersey

Close Up	22	14	64%
Contemplate	13	4	31%
Defrere	69	40	58%
Evening Kris	24	15	63%
Gerosa	15	6	40%
Honor Defend	13	6	46%
Mr. Nugget	22	13	59%
Private Interview	20	18	90%

New Mexico

Aledo	18	9	50%
Alnaab	13	5	38%
Bay Head King	29	22	76%
B. G.'s Drone	11	7	64%
Chimes Band	93	54	58%
Claudius	26	17	65%
Comic Genius	36	23	64%
Con Artist	15	5	33%

Stallion	Mares Bred	Fls	Live Foal Rate
Copelan's Pache	30	12	40%
Corker	11	3	27%
Deep Gold	20	13	65%
Desert God	19	14	74%
Devil Begone	15	7	47%
Dome	58	34	59%
Don Lux	11	7	64%
Eishin Storm	21	12	57%
Elegant Cat	22	11	50%
El Sancho	16	9	56%
Ferrara	17	12	71%
Ghostly Moves	45	39	87%
Golden Ransom	14	10	71%
Groomstick	20	14	70%
Hit a Jackpot	27	18	67%
In Excessive Bull	52	35	67%
Istintaj	29	15	52%
Lazy Lode (Arg)	33	17	52%
Le Grande Danseur	12	5	42%
Lesters Boy	16	13	81%
Liberty Run	11	6	55%
Mesquite Flat	12	1	8%
Mizaj	12	4	33%
Mountain Metal	29	20	69%
Mr. Groush	16	8	50%
Not Tricky	26	15	58%
Paramour	13	8	62%
Parentheses	11	5	45%
Patsyprospect	21	8	38%
Prince of Fame	10	5	50%
Sadler Slew	15	5	33%
Sandia Slew	17	5	29%
Seacliff	30	17	57%
Silver Season	23	21	91%
Storm Ashore	25	8	32%
Thatsusintheolbean	35	26	74%
The Trader's Echo	26	13	50%
Touchdown Ky	13	9	69%
Untold Gold	30	19	63%
Valet Man	12	9	75%
Wild Deputy	14	11	79%

New York

American Chance	48	26	54%
A. P Jet	32	22	69%
Aristotle	11	4	36%
Badge	20	5	25%
Captain Bodgit	27	10	37%
Carry My Colors	13	8	62%
Catienus	84	61	73%
City Zip	83	61	73%
Comeonmom	13	6	46%
Crafty C. T.	44	31	70%
Crusader Sword	25	12	48%
David	11	8	73%
Daygata	18	13	72%
Desert Warrior	73	46	63%
Distinctive Pro	29	15	52%
Dream Run	50	37	74%
Dynamite Song	14	5	36%
Freud	49	37	76%
Gold Fever	55	31	56%
Goldminers Gold	13	9	69%
Gold Token	76	47	62%
Good and Tough	74	58	78%
Griffinite	49	29	59%
Halissee	10	7	70%
Halory Hunter	14	8	57%
Hook and Ladder	76	56	74%
Judge T C	62	38	61%
Kelly Kip	15	7	47%
Kettle Won	10	8	80%
Key Contender	11	8	73%
Legion Field	19	12	63%
Limit Out	10	4	40%
Lycius	39	24	62%
Mayakovsky	52	29	56%
Millions	13	7	54%
Not a Corgi	11	1	9%
Nunzio	10	8	80%
Obligato	19	11	58%
Ommadon	10	7	70%

Stallion	Mares Bred	Fls	Live Foal Rate
Ormsby	14	6	43%
Our Frankie	10	7	70%
Performing Magic	20	16	80%
Phone Trick	47	27	57%
Polish Pro	18	10	56%
Precise End	52	46	88%
Prime Timber	31	24	77%
Raffie's Majesty	19	10	53%
Rage	12	8	67%
Regal Classic	47	31	66%
River Keen (Ire)	27	19	70%
Rizzi	11	9	82%
Rock and Roll	27	22	81%
Rodeo	12	8	67%
Satellite Sun	33	14	42%
Say Florida Sandy	71	44	62%
Senor Speedy	13	10	77%
Signal Tap	10	5	50%
Silver Music	10	7	70%
Slice of Reality	15	4	27%
Smokin Mel	13	10	77%
Strategic Mission	18	10	56%
Take Me Out	33	17	52%
Tomorrows Cat	64	41	64%
Top Account	23	13	57%
Treasure Cove	19	13	68%
Tri Line	12	10	83%
Watch the Bird	10	7	70%
Well Noted	25	15	60%
Western Borders	41	15	37%
Western Expression	86	64	74%
Wheelaway	103	68	66%
Williamstown	33	17	52%
Wiseman's Ferry	104	69	66%

North Carolina

Cholsey Cat	22	16	73%
Programable	10	6	60%

North Dakota

Gold Spats	14	4	29%
Paranoide (Arg)	17	9	53%
Speed Calling	14	4	29%

Ohio

Academy Award	29	20	69%
Ago	20	5	25%
Forest Gazelle	16	6	38%
French Legionaire	12	5	42%
Gold Market	18	13	72%
Iroquois Park	10	5	50%
Keep It Down	11	4	36%
King Tutta	29	21	72%
Mambo Game	18	8	44%
Mercer Mill	25	19	76%
Parents' Reward	16	9	56%
Polish Spray	15	3	20%
Political Folly	19	11	58%
Winthrop	31	25	81%

Oklahoma

Alamocitos	37	10	27%
All Storm	13	9	69%
Aurium	16	8	50%
Baltimore Gray	16	6	38%
Beat the Feet	16	2	13%
Board Member	19	14	74%
Bonus Time Cat	24	18	75%
Burbank	25	15	60%
Carr Tech	12	8	67%
Cherokee Dan	15	1	7%
Comstock Lode	16	10	63%
Concern	28	7	25%
Confederate Here	16	10	63%
Cool Cat	14	5	36%
Coordinator	14	7	50%
Deodar	27	21	78%
Fistfite	27	16	59%
Ghost Tension	14	1	7%
Harriman	13	8	62%

Stallion	Mares Bred	Fls	Live Foal Rate
Have Fun	14	10	71%
Here We Come	27	17	63%
House of Sport	19	12	63%
Inca Chief	34	7	21%
In Case	18	8	44%
Indy Talent	13	8	62%
It'sallinthechase	26	17	65%
Jazzman's Prospect	12	5	42%
King of Scat	47	25	53%
Kipling	27	13	48%
Kukenhof	11	5	45%
Leave a Legacy	14	12	86%
Lucky Lionel	31	17	55%
Maghnatis	20	8	40%
Magics in the Wind	18	12	67%
Magna	10	7	70%
Major Henry	21	13	62%
Mambo King	11	9	82%
Muldoon	10	4	40%
My Liege	13	4	31%
Notable Beaux	10	6	60%
Notable Cat	71	47	66%
Overview	20	11	55%
Prospector's Music	47	32	68%
Raise a Rascal	15	8	53%
Riverside	11	9	82%
Speak	11	9	82%
Star of the Crop	21	15	71%
Stromboli	24	13	54%
Unome	24	8	33%
Western Challenge (GB)	13	3	23%
Wolfire	12	5	42%

Oregon

Abstract	13	8	62%
Airdrie Apache	19	15	79%
Bagshot	19	10	53%
Baquero	47	34	72%
Cascadian	36	17	47%
Dr. Litin	34	25	74%
Ex Marks the Cop	35	18	51%
Klinsman (Ire)	13	5	38%
Ochoco	25	18	72%
Prospected	24	16	67%
Rob 'n Gin	12	10	83%
Sound of Rhythm	10	5	50%
Tiffany Ice	12	7	58%
True Confidence	37	25	68%

Pennsylvania

Activist	16	8	50%
Alyzig	19	10	53%
Attorney	10	5	50%
Banker's Gold	77	49	64%
Brian Is Golden	11	7	64%
Caller I. D.	28	17	61%
Cat's Career	29	19	66%
Coastal Storm	43	27	63%
Count On Steve	10	8	80%
Deposit Ticket	10	5	50%
Duckhorn	60	37	62%
Fastness (Ire)	20	11	55%
Flying Pidgeon	22	13	59%
Harry the Hat	30	15	50%
Knockadoon	14	10	71%
Lucky Clone	10	5	50%
Mr. Sinatra	11	8	73%
Munaadel	10	5	50%
My Favorite Grub	12	6	50%
National News	12	8	67%
Patton	53	35	66%
Pin Stripe	13	7	54%
Pok Ta Pok	19	4	21%
Ponche	23	11	48%
Power by Far	15	10	67%
Sheryar	12	6	50%
Spartan Victory	11	7	64%
Special Times	13	11	85%
Traffic Zack	12	5	42%
Turnofthecentury	15	9	60%
Turn West	13	7	54%

Stallion	Mares Bred	Fls	Live Foal Rate
Valid Request	10	7	70%
Wild West	23	8	35%

South Carolina

Just a Miner	17	7	41%
Lad	21	12	57%
Ring	12	6	50%
Roll Again	10	3	30%

South Dakota

Crafty Ridan	11	6	55%
Crowning Season (GB)	17	8	47%
Finn McCool	12	9	75%
Neff Lake	23	0	0%
Storm of the Night	51	20	39%

Tennessee

Doppler	11	3	27%
Head West	13	5	38%

Texas

Aggie Southpaw	31	19	61%
American Champ	22	9	41%
American Spirit	12	10	83%
A.p Jetter	11	11	100%
A P Valentine	20	7	35%
Assault Cat	15	7	47%
Authenticate	86	56	65%
Ben's Ridge (GB)	10	7	70%
Boone's Mill	37	15	41%
Bugatti	10	0	0%
Capote's Prospect	11	8	73%
Captain Countdown	51	26	51%
Cat Strike	16	8	50%
City Street	53	33	62%
Commanchero	34	29	85%
Confirmed Bachelor	14	7	50%
Crafty	10	5	50%
Dancer's Ghost	11	0	0%
Dove Hunt	36	24	67%
Dynameaux	10	6	60%
Early Flyer	42	30	71%
El Amante	14	4	29%
Excellent Secret	12	5	42%
Exciting Story	26	14	54%
Fiend	10	6	60%
Fifty Stars	13	7	54%
Flaming Quest (GB)	12	10	83%
Flying Kris	14	4	29%
Gen Stormin'norman	29	14	48%
Gold Alert	16	11	69%
Gold Legend	28	18	64%
Goldmine (Fr)	10	2	20%
Gold Regent	35	26	74%
Gone East	13	7	54%
Grand Jewel	12	7	58%
Hadif	10	5	50%
Heather's Prospect	11	5	45%
Hollycombe	11	7	64%
Holzmeister	20	14	70%
Hometown Favorite	12	7	58%
Hunter's Phone	10	0	0%
Indian Prospector (Fr)	10	4	40%
Irish Open	33	15	45%
Itaka	10	2	20%
Itron	11	9	82%
Jadacus	12	2	17%
Karen's Cat	56	28	50%
Kingkiowa	13	5	38%
Magic Cat	58	35	60%
Marked Tree	33	23	70%
Meacham	18	8	44%
Memento	11	4	36%
Mr. Cellular	11	4	36%
Myrmidon	18	6	33%
Mystery Storm	21	2	10%
Naevus	19	12	63%
New Trieste	32	27	84%
Olmos	14	10	71%
Once a Sailor	18	15	83%
Open Forum	36	21	58%

Stallion	Mares Bred	Fls	Live Foal Rate
Ore Deal	18	8	44%
Pancho Villa	26	13	50%
Pepper M.	11	8	73%
Pollock's Luck	10	1	10%
Porto Varas	12	8	67%
Proud Halo	11	7	64%
Raja's Best Boy	12	10	83%
Rare Brick	16	10	63%
River Squall	19	11	58%
Seattle Pattern	10	3	30%
Seattle Sleet	38	23	61%
Seeking a Home	19	14	74%
Seneca Jones	65	45	69%
Sir Bedivere	28	11	39%
Star Programmer	65	38	58%
Storm Broker	14	4	29%
Swamp	14	8	57%
Texas City	11	9	82%
Tinners Way	25	13	52%
Touch Tone	31	23	74%
Trancus	17	7	41%
Trapp Mountain	11	9	82%
Truluck	50	25	50%
Uncle Abbie	30	17	57%
Valid Expectations	80	60	75%
Wajir	15	8	53%
Western Trader	13	10	77%
Wild Zone	44	31	70%
Z Smart Prospect	19	14	74%

Utah

Stallion	Mares Bred	Fls	Live Foal Rate
Classic Chrys	14	8	57%
Crystal Gazer	13	5	38%
Mi Selecto	91	52	57%
Regal Groom	10	10	100%
Taillevent	10	5	50%
Thunder Falcon	20	7	35%

Virginia

Stallion	Mares Bred	Fls	Live Foal Rate
Aaron's Gold	13	10	77%
Ball's Bluff	12	8	67%
Black Tie Affair (Ire)	93	56	60%
Bop	32	21	66%
Fred Astaire	15	6	40%
Hay Halo	12	5	42%
Housebuster	48	27	56%
Prospect Bay	11	6	55%

Washington

Stallion	Mares Bred	Fls	Live Foal Rate
Basket Weave	11	10	91%
Cahill Road	49	29	59%
Chumaree	13	6	46%
Cisco Road	23	15	65%
Commandperformance	10	3	30%
Defensive Play	17	14	82%
Delineator	16	12	75%
Detox	21	14	67%
Dixieland Glo	15	7	47%
Eastern Money	11	8	73%
Free At Last	39	31	79%
Gold Saga	11	10	91%
Hampton Bay	21	5	24%
He's Tops	60	43	72%
Ihtimam	40	19	48%
Katowice	25	18	72%
Kentucky Lucky	30	18	60%
Liberty Gold	49	31	63%
Makors Mark	33	22	67%
Matricule	62	38	61%
Petersburg	34	24	71%
Polish Gift	28	17	61%
Raisor's Edge	15	8	53%
Red Storm Rising	16	9	56%
Slewdledo	77	50	65%
Snowbound	85	39	46%
Stolen Gold	19	13	68%
Tahoe City	13	10	77%
Tamourad	12	0	0%
Tribunal	65	44	68%
Tristaino	14	10	71%
Zayzoom	15	7	47%

West Virginia

Stallion	Mares Bred	Fls	Live Foal Rate
Castine	39	15	38%
Citislipper	17	7	41%
Civilisation	44	33	75%
Copelan Too	11	9	82%
Dancinwiththedevil	18	7	39%
Devon Deputy	24	13	54%
Emancipator	45	15	33%
Endeavouring	25	10	40%
Ghostly Minister	15	11	73%
Green Fee	24	9	38%
Kokand	54	38	70%
Luftikus	56	24	43%
Makin	61	32	52%
Medford	28	18	64%
My Boy Adam	22	11	50%
Native Slew	12	2	17%
One More Power	23	10	43%
Our Valley View	22	6	27%
Proper Texan	13	8	62%
Reparations	17	9	53%
Rich Deeds	13	7	54%
Run Softly	23	11	48%
Select Session	10	2	20%
Sequoia Slew	26	12	46%
Slew O'Quoit	18	2	11%
Standing On Edge	13	6	46%
Strike Adduce	10	5	50%
Valiant Nature	20	14	70%
Way West (Fr)	56	29	52%
Weshaam	16	11	69%
Western Cat	29	16	55%
Windsor Castle	31	9	29%

Alberta

Stallion	Mares Bred	Fls	Live Foal Rate
Brass Minister	23	11	48%
Brunswick	24	16	67%
Candid Cameron	10	2	20%
Commitisize	38	16	42%
Desperately	19	13	68%
Devonwood	37	25	68%
Dr. Adagio	44	22	50%
Easy Climb	12	4	33%
Esteem	24	19	79%
Go Gary Go	36	26	72%
Ground Stroke	11	6	55%
Half a Year	38	19	50%
Haus of Dehere	40	15	38%
Hurricane Center	26	20	77%
Important Notice	11	4	36%
Just a Cat	37	17	46%
Lenado Road	18	10	56%
Linkage	17	14	82%
Magic Prospect	10	5	50%
Mint	19	14	74%
Misnomer	13	10	77%
Nicholas Ds	16	8	50%
Othello	30	19	63%
Rebmec	10	5	50%
Regal Remark	17	9	53%
Rocanville	13	6	46%
Rosetti	51	24	47%
Seattle Syn	13	6	46%
Smile Again	43	25	58%
The Key Rainbow (Ire)	12	8	67%
Tiger Trap	18	12	67%
Tossofthecoin	22	11	50%

British Columbia

Stallion	Mares Bred	Fls	Live Foal Rate
Alfaari	28	15	54%
Alybro	12	6	50%
Amaruk	10	9	90%
Bright Valour	33	17	52%
Captain Collins (Ire)	13	11	85%
Devil On Ice	13	4	31%
Digital Dan	25	13	52%
Dixieland Diamond	17	11	65%
Feu d'Enfer	15	7	47%
Finality	37	28	76%
Flaming West	17	11	65%
Katahaula County	57	35	61%
King of Cats	10	6	60%
Light of Mine	30	17	57%
Mass Market	33	21	64%
Millennium Allstar	30	17	57%
Net Asset	12	3	25%
Nightofthegaelics	12	7	58%
Noble Lyphard	13	6	46%
Regal Intention	34	25	74%
Silver Fox	13	10	77%
Stephanotis	67	43	64%
Storm Victory	31	17	55%
Vying Victor	66	48	73%
Walkinwithapproval	12	7	58%
Wandering	12	10	83%
Yoonevano	48	31	65%

Manitoba

Stallion	Mares Bred	Fls	Live Foal Rate
Act Smart	16	6	38%
Battle Cat	28	20	71%
Chinese Gold	21	10	48%
Circulating	14	11	79%
Crystal Gulch	12	3	25%
Gentle Kent	15	6	40%
Sunset Ridge	10	1	10%
Transferred	11	8	73%

Ontario

Stallion	Mares Bred	Fls	Live Foal Rate
A Fleets Dancer	50	36	72%
Alydeed	20	16	80%
Alystar Slew	14	11	79%
Ascot Knight	24	16	67%
Ashbury	17	10	59%
Bold Executive	103	72	70%
Bold n' Flashy	39	24	62%
Brite Adam	23	8	35%
Cat's At Home	54	39	72%
Ciano Cat	63	44	70%
Compadre	44	25	57%
Crown Attorney	10	5	50%
Domasca Dan	35	20	57%
D'wildcat	56	40	71%
Elajjud	18	8	44%
Endeavor	17	9	53%
Fort Chaffee	25	6	24%
Gun Power	11	5	45%
Kinshasa	59	30	51%
Kiridashi	15	14	93%
Like the Prospects	17	13	76%
Lodge Hill	18	15	83%
Not Impossible (Ire)	34	19	56%
One Way Love	75	50	67%
Parisianprospector	19	11	58%
Paynes Bay	83	60	72%
Perigee Moon	46	23	50%
Porto Foricos	26	19	73%
Raj Waki	19	14	74%
Randy Regent	40	31	78%
Salty Note	19	13	68%
Sato	13	5	38%
Sea Wall	17	9	53%
Shelly's Charmer	12	1	8%
Tethra	48	35	73%
Trajectory	88	54	61%
Valid N Bold	17	12	71%
Valid Trefaire	12	10	83%
Wake At Noon	10	6	60%
War Deputy	17	11	65%
Whiskey Wisdom	37	25	68%
Wonneberg	14	10	71%
Yellow Creek	14	5	36%

Saskatchewan

Stallion	Mares Bred	Fls	Live Foal Rate
Blowin de Turn	10	7	70%
Bluegrass Spirit	19	13	68%
High Firm	19	1	5%
Shaheen	16	12	75%
You've Got Action	24	19	79%

Report of Mares Bred for 2005

In 2005, the long, slow decline in the number of active stallions in North America continued. However, the number of mares bred stayed relatively the same, at least through the early returns, continuing a trend in which the number of mares bred has stayed in a narrow range for more than a decade.

As of February 1, 2006, the Jockey Club reported that 3,692 stallions in North America had been bred to mares in 2005. At the comparable time a year earlier, 3,766 stallions had been reported as bred to mares in 2004, a 2.2% decline. With more complete returns, it was reported that 4,286 stallions had been bred to mares in 2004, so it is likely that the '05 figure also will rise. The stallion population in North America's two largest breeding nations has been declining for more than a decade. In 1992, the Jockey Club reported that 6,753 stallions were bred to mares. From 1992 to 2004, then, there was a 36.5% decline in the number of stallions bred to at least one mare.

In 1988, the first year the Jockey Club began reporting on the number of stallions and number of mares bred by year, there were 8,638 active stallions and a total of 88,682 mares were bred.

The 62,939 mares reported as bred in 2005 were close to the number of mares reported as bred in '04, and with more breedings to be reported, the 2005 number of mares bred may exceed the '04 number when the final tally is made. Kentucky led North America by most mares bred in 2005, when the state's 349 stallions were bred to 20,899 mares. Kentucky had the largest number of stallions, followed by California (319), Texas (310), Louisiana (270), and Florida (235). For the 2004 breeding season, California had had the largest number of stallions.

The equation of more mares and fewer stallions has yielded larger stallion books. In 1992, the average stallion book was 9.4 mares. In 2004, with most of the matings reported, the average book stood at 14.8 mares, a 57.4% increase. In Kentucky, the average stallion book also has increased dramatically. At 31.1 mares per stallion in 1992, the Kentucky average rose to 59.9 in 2005.

The Kentucky figures, in particular, emphasized the influence of huge stallion books on the breeding industry. After two years in which no stallion was bred to more than 200 mares, four stallions had books that exceeded 200 mares in 2005. Giant's Causeway, who made a rapid start at Coolmore Stud, was bred to 244 mares, easily eclipsing Thunder Gulch's record of 216 mares in 2001. More than 120 stallions were bred to 100 or more mares in 2005; while most of those stallions were based in Kentucky, other jurisdictions with stallions bred to 100 or more mares were Florida, Maryland, California, Ontario, Texas, Arkansas, Louisiana, and Utah.

Leading Stallions by Mares Bred

(As of February 1, 2006)

Stallion, Location	Mares Bred	Stallion, Location	Mares Bred	Stallion, Location	Mares Bred	Stallion, Location	Mares Bred
Giant's Causeway, Ky.	244	Unbridled's Song, Ky.	139	Cherokee Run, Ky.	118	Where's the Ring, On.	110
Lion Heart, Ky.	233	Yonaguska, Ky.	139	Friends Lake, Ky.	118	Dance Master, Fl.	109
Chapel Royal, Ky.	222	Hold That Tiger, Ky.	138	Smoke Glacken, Ky.	118	Double Honor, Fl.	109
Fusaichi Pegasus, Ky.	213	Proud Citizen, Ky.	136	Old Topper, Ca.	117	Holy Bull, Ky.	109
Monashee Mountain, Ky.	194	Vindication, Ky.	136	Parker's Storm Cat, Md.	117	Pulpit, Ky.	109
Johannesburg, Ky.	190	Brahms, Ky.	135	Empire Maker, Ky.	116	Storm Cat, Ky.	109
Medaglia d'Oro, Ky.	184	Forestry, Ky.	135	Even the Score, Ky.	116	Benchmark, Ca.	108
Tale of the Cat, Ky.	179	Dixie Union, Ky.	134	Honour and Glory, Ky.	116	Drewman, Fl.	108
Songandaprayer, Fl.	178	Rossini, Ky.	134	A.P. Indy, Ky.	115	Sky Mesa, Ky.	108
Malibu Moon, Ky.	175	Freud, N.Y.	133	Arch, Ky.	115	Macho Uno, Fl.	107
Candy Ride (Arg), Ky.	170	Speightstown, Ky.	131	Distorted Humor, Ky.	115	Atticus, Ca.	106
Peace Rules, Fl.	170	Toccet, Ky.	131	Petionville, Ky.	115	Cactus Ridge, Ky.	106
More Than Ready, Ky.	167	Kafwain, Ky.	129	Strong Hope, Ky.	115	Forest Camp, Ky.	106
Bernstein, Ky.	163	Full Mandate, Fl.	126	Domestic Dispute, Md.	114	Graeme Hall, Fl.	106
Cuvee, Ky.	162	Indian Charlie, Ky.	126	Posse, Ky.	114	Mi Selecto, Ut.	106
Grand Slam, Ky.	162	Broken Vow, Ky.	125	Mutakddim, Ky.	113	Skimming, Ca.	106
Mr. Greeley, Ky.	161	Perfect Soul (Ire), Ky.	125	Street Cry (Ire), Ky.	113	Snuck In, Fl.	106
Northern Afleet, Ky.	159	Golden Missile, Ky.	124	Action This Day, Ky.	112	Tenpins, Ky.	106
Stormy Atlantic, Ky.	159	Put It Back, Fl.	124	Essence of Dubai, Fl.	112	Not For Love, Md.	105
Elusive Quality, Ky.	156	Roar of the Tiger, Fl.	123	Gold Token, N.Y.	112	Storm and a Half, Ar.	105
Maria's Mon, Ky.	149	Orientate, Ky.	123	Smarty Jones, Ky.	112	Three Wonders, Fl.	105
Trippi, Fl.	149	Van Nistelrooy, Ky.	123	In Excess (Ire), Ca.	111	El Prado (Ire), Ky.	104
Smart Strike, Ky.	147	El Corredor, Ky.	121	Ten Most Wanted, Ky.	111	Jump Start, Ky.	104
Devil His Due, Ky.	146	Scrimshaw, Ky.	121	Yes It's True, Ky.	111	Flatter, Ky.	103
Buddha, Ky.	142	Alphabet Soup, Ky.	120	Catienus, N.Y.	110	Horse Chestnut (SAf), Ky.	103
Five Star Day, Ky.	142	Pure Prize, Ky.	120	Exchange Rate, Fl.	110	Alke, Fl.	102
Tapit, Ky.	142	Saarland, Ky.	120	Forest Wildcat, Ky.	110	Authenticate, Tx.	102
Omega Code, Fl.	141	Black Mambo, Fl.	119	Repent, Fl.	110	Birdstone, Ky.	102
Lion Hearted, Md.	139	Congaree, Ky.	119	Sweetsouthernsaint, Fl.	110	Cape Canaveral, Ky.	102

Stallion, Location	Mares Bred	Stallion, Location	Mares Bred	Stallion, Location	Mares Bred	Stallion, Location	Mares Bred
Milwaukee Brew, Ky.	102	Malabar Gold, Ky.	97	Unbridled Time, Fl.	89	Zavata, Ky.	85
Mineshaft, Ky.	102	Olmodavor, Ky.	97	Victory Gallop, Ky.	89	Black Tie Affair (Ire), W.V.	84
Newfoundland, Ky.	102	Slew City Slew, Ky.	97	Afternoon Deelites, La.	88	Champali, Ky.	84
Alajwad, Fl.	101	War Chant, Ky.	97	Came Home, Ky.	88	Stephen Got Even, Ky.	84
Aldebaran, Ky.	101	Dynaformer, Ky.	96	Louis Quatorze, Md.	88	Thunder Gulch, Ky.	84
Awesome Again, Ky.	101	High Yield, Ky.	95	Marquetry, Ky.	88	Belong to Me, Ky.	82
Johar, Ky.	101	Storm Day, La.	95	Tomahawk, On.	88	Concorde's Tune, Fl.	82
Spanish Steps, Fl.	101	Cryptoclearance, Ky.	93	Vying Victor, B.C.	88	With Approval, Ky.	82
Leestown, La.	100	Ecton Park, Ky.	93	Wiseman's Ferry, N.Y.	88	Explicit, Ky.	81
Pleasantly Perfect, Ky.	100	Gimmeawink, Fl.	93	Delaware Township, Fl.	87	Monarchos, Ky.	81
Swiss Yodeler, Ca.	100	Muqtarib, Ca.	93	Gone West, Ky.	87	Rainmaker, Ky.	81
Bowman's Band, Md.	99	Rahy, Ky.	93	Karen's Cat, Tx.	87	City Zip, Ky.	80
Richter Scale, Ky.	99	Concerto, Fl.	92	Valid Wager, Ca.	87	Roaring Fever, N.Y.	80
Touch Gold, Ky.	99	Eavesdropper, Ky.	92	Pikepass, Ky.	86	Rock Slide, Md.	80
Vicar, Ky.	99	Wheelaway, N.Y.	92	Gulch, Ky.	85	Skip to the Stone, Fl.	80
Officer, Ky.	98	Harlan's Holiday, Ky.	91	Hennessy, Ky.	85	Suave Prospect, Fl.	80
Royal Academy, Ky.	98	Najran, Ky.	91	Mizzen Mast, Ky.	85	Valid Expectations, Tx.	80
Sunday Break (Jpn), Ky.	98	Pleasant Tap, Ky.	91	Montbrook, Fl.	85	Bold Executive, On.	79
The Cliff's Edge, Ky.	98	Cartwright, Il.	90	Quiet American, Ky.	85	Snow Ridge, Fl.	79
During, Ky.	97	Desert Warrior, N.Y.	90	Storm Boot, Ky.	85	Bertrando, Ca.	78
E Dubai, Ky.	97	City Place, Fl.	89	Successful Appeal, Ky.	85	Seeking the Gold, Ky.	78
Lightnin N Thunder, Fl.	97	Read the Footnotes, Fl.	89	Unusual Heat, Ca.	85	Sligo Bay (Ire), Ky.	78

Stallions and Mares Bred in the United States, Canada, and North America 1992-2005

Year	U.S. Stallions	U.S. Mares Bred	Avg. Book	Canada Stallions	Canada Mares Bred	Avg. Book	Total NA Stallions	Total NA Mares Bred	Avg. Book
2005	3,411	59,312	17.4	281	3,627	12.9	**3,692**	**62,939**	17.0
2004	3,964	59,807	15.1	322	3,802	11.8	**4,286**	**63,609**	14.8
2003	4,095	59,390	14.5	340	3,595	10.6	**4,435**	**62,985**	14.2
2002	4,078	59,427	14.6	347	3,562	10.3	**4,425**	**62,989**	14.2
2001	4,244	59,421	14.0	338	3,539	10.5	**4,582**	**62,960**	13.7
2000	4,328	59,883	13.0	352	3,462	9.8	**4,680**	**63,345**	13.5
1999	4,396	57,301	13.0	350	3,431	9.8	**4,746**	**60,732**	12.8
1998	4,513	55,914	12.4	386	3,544	9.2	**4,899**	**59,458**	12.1
1997	4,675	54,944	11.8	414	3,652	8.8	**5,089**	**58,596**	11.5
1996	4,882	54,571	11.2	427	3,700	8.7	**5,309**	**58,271**	11.0
1995	5,182	55,435	10.7	425	3,656	8.6	**5,607**	**59,091**	10.5
1994	5,365	55,275	10.3	430	3,730	8.7	**5,795**	**59,005**	10.2
1993	5,801	56,269	9.7	453	3,973	8.8	**6,254**	**60,242**	9.6
1992	6,263	59,607	9.5	490	4,159	8.5	**6,753**	**63,766**	9.4

Stallions and Mares Bred by State and Province

(As of February 1, 2006)

State	Stallions	Mares Bred	State	Stallions	Mares Bred	State	Stallions	Mares Bred
Alabama	19	122	Missouri	17	89	Vermont	1	2
Alaska	1	1	Montana	34	145	Virginia	55	227
Arizona	50	535	Nebraska	37	318	Washington	89	1,175
Arkansas	57	551	Nevada	5	16	West Virginia	88	1,220
California	319	5,150	New Jersey	24	299	Wisconsin	10	29
Colorado	49	423	New Mexico	166	1,781	Wyoming	7	26
Florida	235	7,220	New York	115	2,405	Virgin Islands	2	3
Georgia	18	82	North Carolina	12	53	Unknown	31	142
Idaho	34	218	North Dakota	16	102			
Illinois	95	928	Ohio	78	449	**Province**		
Indiana	80	543	Oklahoma	188	1,484	Alberta	83	944
Iowa	39	470	Oregon	52	458	British Columbia	57	856
Kansas	20	155	Pennsylvania	118	1,213	Manitoba	21	165
Kentucky	349	20,899	Puerto Rico	57	796	New Brunswick	1	2
Louisiana	270	3,554	Rhode Island	1	4	Ontario	96	1,493
Maryland	71	1,727	South Carolina	23	130	Quebec	3	14
Massachusetts	10	30	South Dakota	16	126	Saskatchewan	20	153
Michigan	47	432	Tennessee	22	103	**Totals**	**3,692**	**62,939**
Minnesota	35	407	Texas	310	2,827			
Mississippi	13	48	Utah	26	195			

Stallions Bred to Five or More Mares in 2005
(As of February 1, 2006)

ALABAMA

Stallion	Mares Bred
Casey On Deck	15
Deputy Chief	6
Guaranteed	6
Power of Mind	13
Purple Mountain	6
Royal Empire	25
Special Coach	9
Youngs Neck Arod	16

ARIZONA

Stallion	Mares Bred
Al Ghazi	25
Benton Creek	50
Big Sky Chester	39
Buck Strider	34
Chancery Court	18
Desert Rival	6
Ellusive Quest	11
Hidden City	15
Individual Style	11
Ironman Dehere	19
Jeep Shot	6
Larrupin'	23
Local Artist	8
Midnight Royalty	25
Reciprocate	16
Red	10
Red Sky's	35
Rocky Bar	23
Sample Copy	6
Sideburn	24
Star of Halo	14
T. G. Dewey	15
Top Hit	24

ARKANSAS

Stallion	Mares Bred
American General	6
Bold Anthony	38
Cinnamon Creek	12
Cornish Snow	27
Croydon	7
Distant Mirage (Ire)	11
District	19
Etbauer	21
Explosive Ridge	12
Fashion Find	6
Father Steve	24
Glorious Bid	15
Hesabull	14
Ile St. Louis (Chi)	21
Iroquois Park	11
Jamiano	7
Joy's Report	14
Minister's Gold	20
Not a Role Model	6
Proper Reality	8
Siberian Pine	6
Southern Forest	18
Stauder	7
Storm and a Half	105
This Picture	6
Trust No Lawyer	16
Unbridled's Risk	8

CALIFORNIA

Stallion	Mares Bred
Affirmative	7
All Thee Power	10
All the Gears	15
America's Storm	21
Ancient Art	36
Arthur L.	9
Atticus	106
Avanzado (Arg)	30
Bartok (Ire)	29
Beau Genius	42
Benchmark	108
Bertrando	78
Bien Rullah	8
Birdonthewire	21
Boomerang	34
Bouccaneer (Fr)	31
Bring the Heat	24
Built for Pleasure	20
Cactus Creole	12
Capsized	48
Caros Love	8
Cat Dreams	63
Category Five	25
Cayoke (Fr)	21
Cee's Tizzy	47
Chullo (Arg)	15
Cobra King	18
Comet Shine	20
Comic Strip	33
Commitment	24
Corslew	6
Crowning Storm	24
Decarchy	59
Definite Edge	11
Defy Logic	16
Dismissed	7
Distinctive Cat	13
Dixie Dot Com	20
Downtown Seattle	9
Dramatic Copy	7
Drumalis (Ire)	6
D's Bertrando	33
Elegant Fellow	13
Emerald Creme	6
Event of the Year	20
Expressionist	15
Extra	8
Faculty	23
Flom's Prospector	11
Flying Victor	12
For Really	24
Formal Gold	48
Freespool	73
Fruition	19
Fusaichi Zenon (Jpn)	9
Future Storm	27
Game Plan	33
General Gem	7
General Meeting	36
Globalize	33
Golden Gear	32
Gotham City	29
Grey Memo	21
Guarani	19
Haasil (Ire)	8
Haint	17
Half Term	11
Helmsman	22
High Brite	60
High Demand	26
Highland Gold	31
Houston	7
Iam the Iceman	6
Illinois Storm	54
I'madrifter	11
In Excess (Ire)	111
Iron Cat	22
Islander	13
Jackpot	28
Joey Franco	25
Justinfamous	7
Keep Dreaming	9
Kessem Power (NZ)	15
Lake George	22
Larry the Legend	29
Lasersport	22
Lasting Tribute	6
Latin American	15
Lit de Justice	38
Lord Carson	28
Lost in Paradise	9
Madraar	63
Majesterian	13
Malek (Chi)	7
Marino Marini	48
Memo (Chi)	20
Michael's Flyer	18
Momentum	47
Monsignor Casale	9
Moscow Ballet	22
Motto	10
Mr. Broad Blade	7
Mr. Publisher	15
Mt. Bellewood	25
Mud Route	38
Muqtarib	93
Musique d'Enfer	7
National Saint	18
Nineeleven	20
Old Topper	117
Ole'	8
Olympio	23
One Man Army	19
Persian Turban (Ire)	20
Phonetics	43
Popular	21
Poteen	20
Pride of Slew	6
Proud Irish	23
Rainbow Blues (Ire)	20
Raise Suzuran	8
Raz Lea	10
Reba's Gold	8
Redattore (Brz)	59
Regent Act	7
Replicate	8
Rhythm	15
Richly Blended	51
Rio Verde	76
River Flyer	20
Roar	28
Robannier	10
Royal Cat	59
Royal Regatta (Ire)	9
Royal Walk	28
Score Early	8
Score Quick	11
Seattle Bound	6
Seattle Proud	15
Serve the Flag	7
Siberian Summer	77
Silver Ray	10
Skimming	106
Sky Terrace	14
Slew's Prince	9
Slewvescent	8
Smooth Runner	14
Snow Blink	7
Soft Gold (Brz)	7
Sought After	11
Soul of the Matter	11
Souvenir Copy	53
Spinelessjellyfish	45
Stage Colony	6
Storm Creek	42
Stormed	35
Stormy Jack	22
Suances (GB)	17
Surachai	8
Sweet Dreamer	12
Swiss Yodeler	100
Takin It Deep	19
Tannersmyman	22
Taskmaster	7
Thinkin Problem	9
Trail City	26
Tribal Rule	47
Tricky Creek	12
Truckee	17
Truly Met	15
Turkoman	31
Twin Spires	16
Unbridled Native	31
Unbridled's Love	15
Unusual Heat	85
Valid Wager	87
Vermont	11
Vernon Castle	9
Via Lombardia (Ire)	13
Vronsky	18
Walter Willy (Ire)	10
Western Fame	22
Western Verse	17
You and I	19
Zanferrier	9

COLORADO

Stallion	Mares Bred
Alydarmer	7
A Man of Class	11
Annual Tradition	20
Basic Rate	8
Cash Deposit	16
Cats and Dogs	9
Conquistador Deoro	11
Coverallbases	14
Crafty Harold	8
Crystal Class	24
Dash Ahead	15
Eishin Masamune (Jpn)	50
Ernie Tee	10
Free and Equal	6
Habitony's Ace	6
King Mutesa	7
Lived It Up	6
Majorbigtimesheet	11
My Memoirs (GB)	6
Oliver's Twist	37
Really a Rainbow	10
Scott's Dream	8
Silver Saint	11
Spellbounder	8
The Rufus	12
Timberline	11
Tomorrow's Comet	12
Woody Win	6

FLORIDA

Stallion	Mares Bred
Adcat	19
Alajwad	101
Alex's Pal	57
Alke	102
Alysweep	29
American Spirit	19

Stallion	Mares Bred
Anasheed	55
Arrested	12
Austinpower (Jpn)	20
Awesome of Course	15
Awesome Sword	19
B L's Appeal	56
Band Is Passing	13
Best of the Rest	9
Black Mambo	119
Bright White	6
Broadway Beau	16
Brushing Up	9
Burning Roma	48
Cashel Castle	41
Cimarron Secret	13
City Place	89
Classic Cat	37
Cloud Hopping	17
Colony Light	43
Concerto	92
Concorde's Tune	82
Crown Delite	19
Dance Master	109
Dance the Ballado	11
Delaware Township	87
Deputy Rokeby	30
Deputy Wild Cat	21
Diligence	28
Don Hector	6
Double Honor	109
Dr. Caton	8
Dr. Gigolo	8
Drewman	108
Eltish	16
Essence of Dubai	112
Exchange Rate	110
Expensive Hobby	8
Express Tour	40
Family Calling	17
Fappie's Notebook	14
Fast 'n Royal	12
Favorite Trick	62
February Storm	37
Fiery Best	6
First Tour	14
Flame Thrower	52
Forbidden Apple	30
Foregone	10
Formal Dinner	63
French Envoy	19
Full Mandate	126
Gibson County	16
Gimmeawink	93
Graeme Hall	106
Greatness	63
Gulf Storm	66
Hadrian's Wall	45
Halifax	14
Halos and Horns	12
Halo's Image	58
Hard Buck (Brz)	18
Henriques	8
Honor Glide	52
Impeachment	29
Indy King	51
Invisible Ink	25
Is It True	42
Key Moment	19
Lexicon	51
Lido Palace (Chi)	70
Lightnin N Thunder	97
Line In The Sand	18
Macho Uno	107
Marco Bay	10
Masaya	8
Master Bill	34
Max's Pal	26
Mecke	24
Metfield	8
Migrating Moon	33
Minighosta	9
Mongoose	17
Monsieur Cat	12
Montbrook	85
Montreal Red	19
Mount McKinley	20
Mr. Livingston	50
Niganithat	6
Northern Trend	40
Omega Code	141
Orchard Park	8
Outofthebox	57
Palance	6
Part the Waters	6
Peace Rules	170
Personal First	15
Phone Saga	31
Point in Time	10
Proud and True	21
Proudest Romeo	17
Pure Precision	62
Put It Back	124
R. Cooper	8
Read the Footnotes	89
Recommended List	9
Red Bullet	75
Repent	110
Roar of the Tiger	123
Running Stag	51
Safe in the U S A	24
Safely's Mark	28
Salty Sea	14
Sarava	44
Sasha's Prospect	17
Scorpion	34
Scottish Halo	11
Shanawi (Ire)	18
Skip to the Stone	80
Skip Trial	16
Slew Gin Fizz	20
Smooth Jazz	54
Snow Ridge	79
Snuck In	106
Songandaprayer	178
Spanish Steps	101
Stark Ridge	9
Stone Bridge	12
Straight Man	55
Stuka Slew	6
Suave Prospect	80
Sweetsouthernsaint	110
Texas Glitter	46
The Kaiser	11
Three Wonders	105
Tiger Ridge	71
Tizbud	9
Tour d'Or	6
Trippi	149
U So Bad	7
Unbridled Affair	15
Unbridled's Image	73
Unbridled Time	89
Untuttable	55
Valid Reprized	24
War Secretary	10
Weekend Cruise	45
Wekiva Springs	24
West Acre	51
Wild Event	51
Wind Whipper	38
Winged Foot Willie	17
Wised Up	32

GEORGIA

Stallion	Mares Bred
Hurry to Dinner	8
Muted	12
Prime Meridian	7
Prospector Street	12
Roaring Camp	6
Roundup	12
St. Alydar	6

IDAHO

Stallion	Mares Bred
Chisos	8
Coastal Voyage	21
Crescendo	12
Derby Drive	12
Fabulous Champ	7
Humpty's Hoedown	6
Kings Blood (Ire)	36
Pirate's Gulch	7
Renteria	12
Reversal	11
Silent Generation	6
Smart Chip	13
Tavasco	17

ILLINOIS

Stallion	Mares Bred
Alaskan Frost	22
Allen Charge	7
Animo de Valeroso	55
Awesome Cat	13
Big Splash	6
Bold Revenue	8
Brave 'n Away	15
Canyon Run	17
Cartwright	90
Chicago Six	28
Classic Account	13
Company Approval	20
Conte Di Savoya	14
Dave and Busters	7
Denouncer	21
Diazo	7
Eloped Again	10
Fact Book	14
Francis Nevil E.	6
Garcon Rouge	15
Gogarty (Ire)	6
He's a Tough Cat	21
Honour Attendant	30
Irgun	37
Kiri's Clown	12
Mahie Gold	13
Marte	17
Nassau Hall	14
Nooo Problema	8
One Little Hustler	8
Phoneforchampagne	14
Pirate Stronghold	7
Posh	23
Powerful Goer	12
Prune	7
Quaker Ridge	30
Regal Code	13
Sabona	16
Saint Ballistic	10
Sam the Pettyjudge	7
S'No Business	10
Summer Cloud	12
Summinitup	18
Supeona	12
Theran	8
Tiger Tiger	13
Tough Call	7
Viareggio (Ire)	11
Western Playboy	11
Whadjathink	10

INDIANA

Stallion	Mares Bred
Arromanches	27
Assembly Dancer	9
Blase	7
Cat Doctor	8
Classy Prospector	13
Colonel Bradley	14
Commemorate	9
Could Be Me	6
Crown Ambassador	26
Gallant Step	6
Glitter Code	21
Gold Search	9
Guys From Space	6
Happy Boy Marc	17
Indy Mood	9
Jacquelyn's Groom	17
Le Casque Gris	6
Monroan	7
Moro Oro	21
Once Wild	6
Philadream	8
Plenty Chilly	11
Presidential Order	22
Primordial	9
Radio Daze	10
Riflery	7
Ripsaw	6
Seattle Syn	11
Stylish Senor	9
Summer Ransom	6
Swiss Trick	8
Timeraker	12
Tour's Big Red	8
Tricon	6
Unbridled Man	12
Valiant Style	6
Waki Warrior	13
Whitney Tower	13

IOWA

Stallion	Mares Bred
Allen Gorgeous	7
Bappa	16
Brassy Wells	6
Bravo Bull	12
Buzz Saw	10
Canaveral	13
Cat's Debut	9
Connecticut	6
Corporate Report	7
Crimson Hero	17
Deputy Slew	9
Dignitas	6
Doug Fir	23
Friendly Lover	45
Humming	21
Indian Territory	30
Kyle's Our Man	12
Maze Craze	6
Mi Cielo	34
Mocha Express	14
Northern Symphony	7
Purdue King	12
Sharkey	10
Supremo	22
Tiger Talk	7
Wild Gold	38
Wild Invader	12
Winter Glitter	23

KANSAS

Stallion	Mares Bred
Admiral Indy	39
Flare Dancer	7
Grand On Dave	14
Life Interest	11

Stallion	Mares Bred
Polly's Comet	14
Prospector's Treat	14
So Ever Clever	13
Testafly	8

KENTUCKY

Stallion	Mares Bred
Acceptable	11
Action This Day	112
Albert the Great	42
Aldebaran	101
Aljabr	14
Alphabet Soup	120
A.P. Indy	115
Aptitude	75
Arch	115
Austin Powers (Ire)	7
Awesome Again	101
Barkerville	27
Basic	11
Behrens	28
Belong to Me	82
Bernstein	163
Best of Luck	13
Big Country	35
Birdstone	102
Black Minnaloushe	73
Bold Truth	32
Boundary	37
Brahms	135
Bright Launch	26
Broken Vow	125
Buddha	142
Cactus Ridge	106
Came Home	88
Canadian Frontier	65
Candy Ride (Arg)	170
Cape Canaveral	102
Cape Town	49
Cat Thief	40
Century City (Ire)	56
Champali	84
Changeintheweather	24
Chapel Royal	222
Cherokee Run	118
Chief Seattle	29
City Zip	80
Congaree	119
Cozar	11
Cozzene	50
Crafty Friend	27
Crafty Prospector	34
Crimson Classic	27
Cryptoclearance	93
Cuvee	162
David Copperfield	38
Dayjur	25
Deputy Commander	45
Devil His Due	146
Diesis (GB)	40
Distant View	27
Distorted Humor	115
Dixieland Band	70
Dixie Union	134
Doneraile Court	64
Down the Aisle	27
During	97
Dynaformer	96
E Dubai	97
Eavesdropper	92
Ecton Park	93
El Corredor	121
Elhayq (Ire)	7
El Prado (Ire)	104
Elusive Quality	156
Empire Maker	116
Evansville Slew	61
Even the Score	116
Explicit	81
Fadaaei	7
Fast Play	29
Fit to Fight	22
Five Star Day	142
Flatter	103
Forest Camp	106
Forestry	135
Forest Wildcat	110
Friends Lake	118
Fusaichi Pegasus	213
General Royal	10
Generous Rosi (GB)	6
Gentlemen (Arg)	10
Giant's Causeway	244
Gilded Time	69
Glitterman	10
Gold Case	30
Golden Missile	124
Gone West	87
Governor Hickel	10
Grand Slam	162
Grave Digger	11
Greenwood Lake	45
Grindstone	27
Gulch	85
Hap	23
Harlan's Holiday	91
Hennessy	85
Hero's Tribute	45
High Yield	95
Hold for Gold	18
Hold That Tiger	138
Holy Bull	109
Home At Last	11
Honour and Glory	116
Horse Chestnut (SAf)	103
Include	61
Indian Charlie	126
Jade Hunter	27
Jambalaya Jazz	21
Johannesburg	190
Johar	101
Jump Start	104
Kafwain	129
Kanjinsky	6
King Cugat	39
Kingmambo	37
Kissin Kris	31
K One King	9
K. O. Punch	19
Kutsa	20
Lac Ouimet	13
Langfuhr	75
Leelanau	25
Lee's Badger	6
Lemon Drop Kid	77
Lil E. Tee	14
Line Rider	16
Lion Heart	233
Lost Soldier	69
Luhuk	30
Malabar Gold	97
Malibu Moon	175
Mancini	44
Maria's Mon	149
Marquetry	88
Matty G	54
Meadowlake	45
Medaglia d'Oro	184
Menifee	65
Military	41
Millennium Wind	63
Milwaukee Brew	102
Minardi	37
Mineshaft	102
Mizzen Mast	85
Monarchos	81
Monashee Mountain	194
More Than Ready	167
Morluc	30
Mr. Greeley	161
Mt. Livermore	19
Mula Gula	7
Mutakddim	113
Najran	91
Newfoundland	102
Northern Afleet	159
Northern Spur (Ire)	11
Ocean Terrace	43
Officer	98
Old Kentucky Home	17
Olmodavor	97
Orientate	123
Our Emblem	46
Out of Place	65
Peaks and Valleys	28
Pembroke	27
Perfect Soul (Ire)	125
Petionville	115
Phone the King	7
Pikepass	86
Pine Bluff	40
Pioneering	34
Pleasantly Perfect	100
Pleasant Tap	91
Point Given	72
Polish Navy	24
Posse	114
Prince Nureyev	8
Private Terms	43
Prized	23
Proud Citizen	136
Pulpit	109
Pure Prize	120
Pyramid Peak	10
Quiet American	85
Raheeb	8
Rahy	93
Rainmaker	81
Real Quiet	14
Repriced	24
Richter Scale	99
Rocking Trick (Arg)	11
Rod and Staff	10
Rojo Dinero	15
Rossini	134
Royal Academy	98
Royal Anthem	37
Ruckus Hosner	10
Runaway Groom	33
Saarland	120
Safado	6
Sahm	16
Salt Lake	60
Scatmandu	15
Scrimshaw	121
Sea of Secrets	26
Seattle Fitz (Arg)	56
Seeking the Gold	78
Service Stripe	65
Silic (Fr)	15
Silver Deputy	77
Silver Ghost	60
Siphon (Brz)	36
Sir Cat	21
Sir Cherokee	44
Skip Away	76
Sky Classic	42
Sky Mesa	108
Slew City Slew	97
Sligo Bay (Ire)	78
Smart Strike	147
Smarty Jones	112
Smoke Glacken	118
Soto	77
Speightstown	131
Statement	15
Stephen Got Even	84
Storm Boot	85
Storm Cat	109
Stormin Fever	68
Stormy Atlantic	159
Stravinsky	62
Street Cry (Ire)	113
Stroll	58
Strong Hope	115
Stydahar	26
Subordination	23
Successful Appeal	85
Sultry Song	57
Sunday Break (Jpn)	98
Swain (Ire)	12
Syncline	38
Tactical Cat	38
Tale of the Cat	179
Talk Is Money	15
Tapit	142
Tejano Run	22
Ten Most Wanted	111
Tenpins	106
Teton Forest	76
The Cliff's Edge	98
The Deputy (Ire)	17
Theatrical (Ire)	42
Thunder Gulch	84
Tiznow	76
Toccet	131
Touch Gold	99
Tropical Storm	26
Trust N Luck	70
Tumblebrutus	19
Two Point Two Mill	6
Unbridled's Song	139
Unreal Zeal	8
Valid Lightning	9
Van Nistelrooy	123
Vicar	99
Victory Gallop	89
Vindication	136
Vision and Verse	40
Volponi	58
Wagon Limit	24
War Chant	97
Whywhywhy	69
Wild Wonder	25
Wild Zone	48
Winning Bid	13
With Approval	82
Woodman	58
Wouldn't We All	6
Yankee Gentleman	54
Yankee Victor	58
Yes It's True	111
Yonaguska	139
Zavata	85

LOUISIANA

Stallion	Mares Bred
Abajo	46
A Corking Limerick	14
Afternoon Deelites	88
Almostashar	17
Aloha Bold	6
American Tribute	16
Announce	37
A. P. Delta	29
Autocracy	12
Bayou Hebert	13
Beanie Babe	9
Belek	13
Bermuda Cedar	6
Best Idea	13
Big Pretty Boy	6
B. J.'s Mark	16
Bold Pac Man	6
Broadway Show	19
Bruces Son	6
Buzzy's Gold	8

Stallion	Mares Bred
Canboulay	6
Capitalimprovement	17
Carnovali	16
Catastrophe	29
Cherokee Beau	7
Cherokee Tin	8
Choosing Choice	19
Classic Alliance	6
Combat Ready	11
Count the Time	24
Crowning Decision	6
Dagwood	6
Dancing Missile	9
Daring Bid	12
De Guerin	9
Deputy Diamond	23
Direct Hit	26
Disciple	6
Dixieland Heat	23
Doctor Mike	7
Doeny Rain	8
Dow Jones U S	8
Dr. Lewis	34
Dream Tripper	11
Easyfromthegitgo	45
Entepreneur	26
Ents Dream	11
Erlton	29
Escrito	11
Esplanade Ridge	12
Eulogize	10
Fenter	7
Fifty Stars	7
Finder's Gold	14
Finest Hour	64
Fly Cry	21
Forty Won	22
Friends Inloplaces	7
Gift of Gib	11
Global Mission	14
Gold Tribute	62
Golden Slew	9
Grim Reaper	9
Handkerchief (Arg)	6
Harlan Traveler	6
Helluvahullabaloo	8
Hervy	8
High Cascade	61
Hold Hands	8
Holy Sting	26
House Burner	19
Huff	10
Ide	61
In a Walk	45
Island Born	10
Jaunatxo	14
Joe Who (Brz)	7
Jolie's Frolic	8
Kadhaaf	18
Keats	36
Kimberlite Pipe	15
Kingkiowa	14
Laabity	28
Lake Austin	43
Leestown	100
Left Banker	7
Like a Soldier	15
Littlebitlively	59
Lunar Shadow	9
Macabe	55
Malibu Wesley	30
Marazi	7
Mighty	7
Mike's Little Man	6
Mom's Little Guy	12
Montana Dreamin'	7
Mr. Baskets	18
Mr. John	15
Mr. Sparkles	12
My Friend Max	26
My Mike	9
Native Regent	37
No Limit Soldier	9
Northern Niner	10
On Target	33
Oro Bandito	6
Our Diablo	11
Our Shining Hour	19
Out of the Crisis	28
Parting Guest	8
Piccolino	15
Placid Fund	14
Planet Earth	8
Political Whit	11
Power and Peace	8
Prince of the Mt.	7
Promissory	45
Prospector's Gift	16
Pulling Punches	18
Rail	18
Rodeo	29
Royal Strand (Ire)	10
Ruby Hill	10
Run Production	29
Saint's Honor	10
Sea Soul	9
Secret Claim	29
Secret Odds	9
Sefapiano	36
Shrubs	9
Sikorsky	8
Silky Sweep	39
Silver On Silver	10
Sir Emblem	7
Slew the Surgeon	12
Spiritbound	21
Storm Day	95
Storm Passage	45
Storm Walk	6
Strategize	8
Supremo Secret	19
Thank the Bank	10
Thunder Breeze	13
Time Bandit	40
Toolighttoquit	18
Top Ghost	7
Top Venture	25
Tricky	10
Two Punch Sonny	12
Undeniable	17
Upping the Ante	19
Valid Belfast	70
Valid Bidder	52
Virginia Carnival	12
Walnut Hall	8
War Eagle	16
Warp Speed Scottie	8
Western Echo	17
Western Gentleman	18
Westport Landing	7
Whambam	15
Whiff of Indy	16
Wild Jet	6
Winter Halo	9
Winthrop	19
Wire Me Collect	30
Worldly Ways (GB)	32
Zarbyev	32

MARYLAND

Stallion	Mares Bred
Bowman's Band	99
Cat Country	7
Citidancer	15
Crowd Pleaser	9
Cruisin' Dixie	8
Crypto Star	20
Diamond	22
Disco Rico	29
Domestic Dispute	114
Fleet Foot	21
Go for Gin	59
Great Notion	61
Jazz Club	59
Lion Hearted	139
Louis Quatorze	88
Marciano	10
Meadow Monster	46
Mojave Moon	60
Mokhieba	6
Mr. Shoplifter	6
No Armistice	45
Not For Love	105
Outflanker	53
Parker's Storm Cat	117
Partner's Hero	45
Polish Miner	53
Port Vila (Fr)	11
Precious Marque	8
Purple Passion	7
Rock Slide	80
Same Day Delivery	7
Seeking Daylight	46
Smart Guy	6
Two Punch	66
Unbridled Jet	28
Waquoit	26
Wayne County (Ire)	13
Who's Your Daddy	20
Yarrow Brae	38
Yoh May Kenta	9

MASSACHUSETTS

Stallion	Mares Bred
Senor Conquistador	9
Storm of Angels	6

MICHIGAN

Stallion	Mares Bred
Allie's Punch	15
Arcola Lane	9
Binalong	20
Career Best	14
Clock Radio	9
Collateral Attack	6
Creative	6
Crimson Guard	13
Daylight Savings	18
Demaloot Demashoot	33
Elusive Hour	32
Equality	28
Intermediary	6
Island Storm	7
Man From Eldorado	9
Meadow Prayer	30
Mr. Katowice	10
Native Factor	24
Ocala Slew	11
Pappa Joe	7
Quiet Enjoyment	15
Secret Romeo	31
Sky Approval	11
Ulises	10

MINNESOTA

Stallion	Mares Bred
Ballado Chieftan	27
Boundless	17
Demidoff	28
Dixie Power	18
Dynomania	20
Emigrant Peak	7
Exert	6
Frisk Me Now	36
Gazebo	10
Ghazi	42
Jack's Storm	7
Late Edition	16
Quaker Hill	8
Sam Lord's Castle	18
Shot of Gold	14
Shotiche	16
Silk Song	12
Tahkodha Hills	42
Victor's Gent	9
Willo' Sweep	8

MISSISSIPPI

Stallion	Mares Bred
Mara o' Chino	9
Minister Slew	10
Valid Victorious	7

MISSOURI

Stallion	Mares Bred
Bananas	11
Bar	7
Isaypete	11
Kugelis	6
Liginsky	9
Lucky South	12
Stephene Mon Amour	9

MONTANA

Stallion	Mares Bred
C Spot Go	15
Double Dewars	6
Grey West	6
Miami Blase	7
Rubio First (Arg)	7
Silesia Flash	8
Son's Corona	8
Unbridled Desire	10
White Tie Tryst	12

NEBRASKA

Stallion	Mares Bred
A Trio of Devils	8
Blumin Affair	31
Box Buster	16
Dazzling Falls	30
Fortuoso	12
Glenview	9
Godolphin Cat	12
Golden Dice	7
Gray Raider	8
King of Scat	18
Miracle Heights	6
More to Tell	6
Not So Fast	11
Quest of the King	9
Rhythm Bound	7
Shawklit Player	9
Silent Bluff	31
Silver Desire	12
Silver Launch	10
Yankee Fan	14

NEVADA

Stallion	Mares Bred
Meet Me in Dixie	7

NEW JERSEY

Stallion	Mares Bred
Capture the Gold	14
Close Up	34
Defrere	66
Deputy Warlock	11
Funny Frolic	7
Gerosa	9
Harrington Sound	7
Hit the Trail	13
Honor Defend	15
Mo Mon	24
Mr. Nugget	22
Mr. Sinatra	8
Private Interview	22
Saint Marden	13
Tree	14

NEW MEXICO

Stallion	Mares Bred
Adios Mundo	8
Aledo	11
Alnaab	8
Avenue of Flags	31
B. G.'s Drone	19
Bay Head King	31
Border Patrol	8
Call Me Cat	11
Chopin	12
Cliffty Falls	7
Comic Genius	42
Con Artist	6
Copelan's Pache	27
Corker	12
Dancin Rahy	23
Dee Lance	6
Deep Gold	22
Desert God	23
Devon Lane	61
Doctor Roy A.	6
Dome	65
Dominique's Cat	22
Dry Gulch	12
Eishin Seattle	6
Eishin Storm	16
El Sancho	15
Elegant Cat	25
Ex Federali	16
Foolish MacDuff	7
Forever Whirl	8
Funny Meeting	9
Ghostly Moves	27
Golden Ransom	20
Gone Hollywood	62
Groomstick	22
Hannibal Cat	8
Hit a Jackpot	8
Hot War	6
I Like to Win	7
In Excessive Bull	60
Istintaj	19
King of the Hunt	21
Lazy Lode (Arg)	28
Le Grande Danseur	19
Lesters Boy	19
Liberty Run	7
Louisiana Slew	9
Maid's Minister	7
Mesquite Flat	6
Mizaj	15
Morocco	7
Mountain Metal	15
Mr. Groush	11
Mt. Hot	7
Newton's Law (Ire)	8
Not Tricky	22
Paramour	17
Parentheses	7
Patsyprospect	15
Precocity	39
Quinton's Gold	10
Regal Groom	8
Retsina Run	6
Robyn Dancer	48
Roll Hennessy Roll	16
Ronton	11
R. Payday	10
Sadler Slew	8
Sagebrush Sam	8
Saint Sabates	14
Sandia Slew	16
Saratoga Six	22
Seacliff	22
Sleepless Morn	12
Stagecoach	17
Stake a Claim	6
Storm Ashore	17
Storm of Goshen	17
Sunday Minister	10
Super Quercus (Fr)	8
Super Special	32
Survivor Slew	14
Thatsusintheolbean	28
The Black Rocket	7
The Trader's Echo	13
Ticketless	8
To Teras	27
Union Mills	9
Valet Man	10
Vaudeville	11
Vulcan's Pulpit	12
Wild Deputy	16
Your Eminence	25

NEW YORK

Stallion	Mares Bred
Adonis	15
A. P Jet	70
Artax	74
Badge	38
Bright Beau	11
Bright Cat	8
Cappuchino	23
Captain Red	15
Carry My Colors	8
Catienus	110
City Hall Slew	11
Comeonmom	17
Crafty C. T.	45
Desert Warrior	90
Dream Run	53
Fast Decision	6
Freud	133
Gold Fever	44
Goldminers Gold	16
Gold Token	112
Gone for Real	12
Good and Tough	37
Griffinite	29
Halory Hunter	9
Hook and Ladder	57
Hunting Hard	9
Intidab	59
Judge T C	57
Kalu	8
Kelly Kip	17
Kettle Won	6
Key Contender	9
Lacotte (Ire)	6
Legion Field	21
Let Goodtimes Roll	12
Lycius	23
Manlove	12
Mayakovsky	58
Millions	9
Not a Corgi	8
Nunzio	10
Obligato	27
Ormsby	10
Our Frankie	12
Performing Magic	19
Phone Trick	36
Prime Timber	30
Rarified	6
Red Tail Hawk	9
Regal Classic	38
Rizzi	14
Roaring Fever	80
Rock and Roll	24
Roman Dancer	12
Say Florida Sandy	72
Say Uncle	6
Senor Speedy	12
Silver Music	10
Slice of Reality	12
Smokin Mel	8
Stanislavsky	21
Strategic Mission	29
Take Me Out	23
Thunderello	46
Tomorrows Cat	54
Top Account	7
Well Noted	38
Western Expression	68
Wheelaway	92
Williamstown	9
Wiseman's Ferry	88

NORTH CAROLINA

Stallion	Mares Bred
Chelsey Cat	26
Programable	10

NORTH DAKOTA

Stallion	Mares Bred
Buzzer	18
Gold Spats	13
Paranoide (Arg)	17
Speed Calling	16
Win Lose Or Draw	13

OHIO

Stallion	Mares Bred
Academy Award	19
Ago	14
Alladin Rib	16
Colony Key	15
Donthelumbertrader	13
Eagle Time	8
Gold Market	13
King Tutta	17
Mahogany Hall	16
Mambo Game	14
Mercer Mill	19
Noon Prospect	9
Pacific Waves	8
Parents' Reward	9
Polish Spray	8
Political Folly	16
Pride of Burkaan	13
Private School	7
Quietamericanforce	11
Rhodes	8
San Mont Andreas	16
Silver Talk	9
Spunky Rascal	6
Supreme Tale	9
Winninginexcess	6
World Order	7

OKLAHOMA

Stallion	Mares Bred
Actor	11
All Storm	11
Alybel	8
Apollo	18
Aurium	11
Baltimore Gray	8
Board Member	21
Bonus Time Cat	21
Broadway Bullet	7
Bumbury Did It	6
Burbank	27
Carr Tech	9
Chazerahy	6
Cherokee Five	6
Concern	25
Confederate Hero	8
Confide	29
Deal an Ace	10
Defensive Bid	13
Deodar	11
Devil Diamond	6
Distinction	42
Easy Friend	10
Expense Account	8
Ferrara	6
Fistfite	17
Flying Baron	18
Grand Allegiance	8
Harriman	12
Have Fun	19
Haymarket (GB)	8
House of Sport	9
Inca Chief	32
In Case	25
Indy Talent	8
Indy Thunder	14
It'sallinthechase	20
Ivory Dreams	7
Jazzman's Prospect	16
Jekyll and Hyde	10
Kelly S	6
Kipling	26
Leave a Legacy	13
Lendell Ray	13
Lucky Lionel	56
Maddy's Waquoit	6
Maghnatis	10
Magics in the Wind	7
Major Henry	31
Mambo King	6
May Day Warrior	14
Mister Deville	13
Monarch's Maze	19
Muldoon	14
My Home Phone	7
My Liege	6
New Way	7
Nicholas	19
Notable Beaux	14
Notable Cat	41
Overview	27
Plentyofit	6
Raise a Rascal	10
Reardon Steel	8
Reel On Reel	7
River Eagle	8
Riverside	19
Seeking Greatness	23
Semoran	32
Shoer of Power	6
Skip Skip	6
Slew the Coup	6
Speak	7
Star of the Crop	21
Strategic Partner	24
Stromboli	20
Sultan Swain	14
Unome	16
Vote Them Out	15
Way Wild	7
Wertaloona	8
Western Challenge (GB)	11
Who's John Galt	16
Wolfire	11
Wood Reply	20

OREGON

Stallion	Mares Bred
Abstract	18
Airdrie Apache	13
Aladin Dancer	6
Allen's Alydar	14
Bagshot	17
Baquero	26
Cascadian	28
Crypt de Chine	12
Dr. Litin	9
Ex Marks the Cop	41
Harbor the Gold	19
Indy Pacific	12
Klinsman (Ire)	13

Stallion	Mares Bred
Ochoco	18
Panoramic	8
Prospected	11
Purple Cop	6
Ride to Win	6
Sanctuary	6
Seattle Shamus	53
Steel Ruhlr	6
Tiffany Ice	15
Timber Legend	12
Tomorrow's Slew	10
True Confidence	8
Unbridled's Comet	11

PENNSYLVANIA

Stallion	Mares Bred
Activist	15
Alyzig	7
Appealing Skier	26
Aquarian Prince	6
Attorney	12
Awad	18
Bankbook	6
Banker's Gold	72
Brian Is Golden	13
Caller I. D.	29
Cat's Career	30
Certain Storm	15
Cetewayo	18
Coastal Storm	12
Cocky	7
Count On Steve	7
Cyclone	6
Digamist	15
Duckhorn	45
Fair Skies	7
Fastness (Ire)	18
Flying Pidgeon	15
G. P.'s Krugerrand	10
Georgia Crown	6
Harbor Boy	9
Harry the Hat	50
Iron Deputy	16
Jd's Determination	7
Knockadoon	19
Lil's Lad	25
Lite the Fuse	48
Lord At Law	9
Lucky Clone	6
Mazel Trick	18
Middlesex Drive	23
National News	7
Ops Smile	12
Patton	45
Pok Ta Pok	16
Ponche	13
Power by Far	20
Quarry	11
Reigning King	8
Roanoke	7
Rubiyat	14
Sheryar	6
Special Times	10
Spectaculardynasty	10
Squall	7
Stonecoldbroke	9
Tekken (Ire)	7
This Bulls for You	9
Turnofthecentury	11
Turn West	40
Valid Request	8
Werblin	31
Wheaton	35
Wild West	45
Will's Way	32

SOUTH CAROLINA

Stallion	Mares Bred
Buckhar	8
Cat in Town	8
East of Easy	6
Just a Miner	14
Lad	11
Nines Wild	7
Prime Legacy	11
Ride the Storm	15
Roll Again	6
Skip a Dream	6
Stormville	6

SOUTH DAKOTA

Stallion	Mares Bred
Crafty Ridan	6
Crowning Season (GB)	14
Finn McCool	22
Get Me Out	8
Modern Day Moses	8
Storm of the Night	47

TENNESSEE

Stallion	Mares Bred
Code Talker	11
Cub	6
Doppler	7
Forest Fire	6
Head West	14
Jon Jon	6
Lived It Up	9
Moonlight Guy	10
Take the Shot	11

TEXAS

Stallion	Mares Bred
Action	6
Advocate Training	6
Aggie Southpaw	20
Aggressive Chief	7
All Gone	21
Alyshu	7
American Champ	20
A.p Jetter	19
A P Valentine	16
Arctic Boy	6
Assault Cat	15
Authenticate	102
Banderas	14
Barrett's Bullet	9
Ben'z Mercedes	7
Big Lukey	9
Blowing Rock	6
Blue Eyed Streaker	17
Boone's Mill	33
Broad and Locust	12
Byars	9
Capote's Prospect	9
Captain Countdown	32
Cat Strike	12
Cherokee Runaway	7
Chief Three Sox	6
Cici Cici	7
Cien Fuegos	10
City Street	54
Comanche Slew	6
Commanchero	8
Conroe	6
Covered Wagon	9
Crafty	14
Dehereclub for Men	7
Diogenes	10
Dove Hunt	47
Dynameaux	13
Early Flyer	58
El Amante	19
El Leopardo	57
Excellent Secret	16
Exclusive Zone	10
Fappiano Road	9
Fiend	12
Finance the Cat	13
Flange	11
Flying Kris	13
Gary Gumbo	6
Gen Stormin'norman	37
Gilded Crusader	8
Gold Alert	33
Gold Legend	20
Gold Regent	14
Gone East	13
Grand Jewel	17
Hadif	13
Half Fast George	6
Heather's Prospect	8
Hi Teck Man	24
Hollycombe	12
Holzmeister	12
Houston Slue	6
Hoxie	7
Imperial Cat	9
Irisheyesareflying	12
Irish Open	14
Itaka	7
Itron	11
Jadacus	11
Joe Lin's Son	7
Karen's Cat	87
Kidding Around	8
Kimo Krogfoss	7
Lil Honcho	13
Littleexpectations	59
Lucky So n' So	7
Magic Cat	55
Magic Grades	12
Malthus	8
Marked Tree	30
Meacham	17
Memento	7
Naevus	23
New Trieste	19
Northern Quest (Fr)	12
Oakhurst	10
Open Forum	26
Ore Deal	8
Oro Negra	9
Pancho Villa	15
Parade Ground	13
Pepper M.	14
Power Storm	18
Pro Brite	11
Proud Halo	8
Raja's Best Boy	7
Rare Brick	9
River Squall	7
Riveter	6
Running Empho	6
Sand Ridge	12
Saucey Avenger	6
Saxton	11
Seattle Pattern	10
Seattle Sleet	37
Seeking a Home	14
Seneca Jones	47
Seven Rings	7
Shadow Caster	7
Shaquin	7
Sharan (GB)	11
Slew Gulch	6
Slew You	6
Smoken Devine	8
Star Programmer	50
Sudden Storm	10
Supreme Cat	14
Swamp	11
Teed Off	8
Thats Our Buck	24
Tinners Way	24
To a Wild Kris	6
Touch Tone	24
Traffic Circle	12
Trancus	18
Tricky Prospect	9
Truluck	48
Uncle Abbie	45
Valid Expectations	80
Wajir	6
Wake Up Alarm	8
Walesa	6
Warfield	8
Western Power	18
Western Trader	10
Wild Horses	47
Worthingtonhills	8
Z Smart Prospect	24

UTAH

Stallion	Mares Bred
Crystal Gazer	9
File Away	7
Mi Selecto	106
Monopoly Money	8
Taillevent	15

VIRGINIA

Stallion	Mares Bred
Aaron's Gold	11
Ball's Bluff	17
Big Steel	7
Fred Astaire	20
Harbor Man	6
Hay Halo	17
Ladinos Bambino	6
Mr. Executioner	10
Prospect Bay	6
Rock Point	14
Slew the Deputy	7
Split	9
Zillionair	6

WASHINGTON

Stallion	Mares Bred
Basket Weave	15
Cahill Road	55
Chumaree	26
Compelling Sound	10
Consigliere (GB)	6
Defensive Play	13
Delineator	21
Detox	15
Devil On Ice	8
Dixieland Glo	13
Free At Last	34
Hampton Bay	20
Heavenly Search	18
He's Tops	41
Ihtimam	14
Ito the Hammer	9
Jazzing Around	9
Just Ruler	9
Kasparov	10
Katowice	22
Kentucky Lucky	24
Liberty Gold	33
Liquid Gold	8
Makors Mark	30
Matricule	59
Midway Magistrate	15
Moon Up T. C.	8
My Grand Indy	8
Name for Norm	7
Our Boy Harvey	17
Patriot Noise	7
Petersburg	31
Polish Gift	44

Stallion	Mares Bred
Private Gold	54
Raisor's Edge	11
Red Storm Rising	8
Rojo Warrior	8
Russellthemussell	7
Slewd	6
Slewdledo	65
Snowbound	60
Storm Blast	25
Sum Trick	29
Tamourad	10
Team Zachary	7
Tribunal	58
Tropic Lightning	12
Vitesse	12
Waiting Game	17
Zayzoom	21

WEST VIRGINIA

Stallion	Mares Bred
Black Tie Affair (Ire)	84
Bop	59
Castine	29
Civilisation	47
Cowboy Carson	9
Creative Act	7
Dancinwiththedevil	7
Danish Gold	13
Devon Deputy	20
Emancipator	22
Endeavoring	17
Endeavouring	17
Garnered	35
Ghostly Minister	14
Green Fee	22
Holy Tara	14
Housebuster	43
Inner Harbour	30
Jo Jo Dancer	7
Kokand	67
Limit Out	10
Luftikus	41
Make Your Mark	11
Makin	32
Medford	15
Mike's Memory	7
Mitch	6
My Boy Adam	16
Native Slew	15
One More Power	7
Our Valley View	19
Peak Dancer	10
Reparations	26
Rich Deeds	14
Robb	12
R. S. V. P. Please	12
Rugby	7
Runaway Macho	11
Run Softly	25
Sandlot Star	9
Select Session	10
Sequoia Slew	8
Spreebee	9
Stored	17
Strike Adduce	8
Stritzel	6
Valiant Nature	26
Way West (Fr)	66
Weshaam	17
Western Cat	34
Windsor Castle	41
Zizou	7

WISCONSIN

Stallion	Mares Bred
Be Valiant	6

WYOMING

Stallion	Mares Bred
Aide Memoire	6
Excessive Prospect	8

PUERTO RICO

Stallion	Mares Bred
Balcony	21
Bargello	23
Be Frank	23
Billions	24
Cape Cod	16
Casanova Star	13
Cats Castle	17
Crowd	20
D' Coach	12
Don Guido	25
El Jibaro	9
El Justo	8
Eqtesaad	35
Estrellero	8
Fappiano's Star	50
Fast and Formal	9
Figure of Speech	16
Goldwater	9
Greedy	15
Hard Charger	8
Johnny Jones	7
Just Typical	23
King's Crown	19
Laurentide	13
Lightning Al	37
Majestic Reign	6
Millonario	14
Monoestrellado	9
My Favorite Dream	23
Myfavorite Place	23
Najm Almaydaan	14
Ordway	14
Prince Hennessy	16
Royal Merlot	50
Shining Spring	9
Stag Dinner	6
Sudden Thunder	33
Tamhid	14
Trans Caribbean	6
Virtua Cop	13
Wonder Bird	30

ALBERTA

Stallion	Mares Bred
Alydeed	33
Brass Minister	42
Brunswick	27
Captain Bodgit	40
Castle Arms	8
Commitisize	8
Desperately	14
Dr. Adagio	20
Easy Climb	14
Esteem	33
Flying Chevron	20
Go Gary Go	24
Ground Stroke	10
Half a Year	11
Haus of Dehere	17
Highland Ruckus	32
Hurricane Center	35
Important Notice	15
Just a Cat	28
King's Nest	9
Lenado Road	9
Linkage	21
Lost Canyon (GB)	7
Magic Prospect	8
Mint	16
Misnomer	22
Othello	18
Parlay Me	7
Peacenfreedom	7
Proud Exchange	10
Real West	18
Rebmec	15
Rocanville	7
Rosetti	48
Rowdy Ruckus	10
Royal Rumpus	11
Smile Again	39
Swinging Sammi	7
Tempered Appeal	28
The Fed	7
Tiger Trap	54
Tossofthecoin	14
Zuppardo's Future	9

BRITISH COLUMBIA

Stallion	Mares Bred
Alfaari	28
Alybro	8
Amaruk	17
Baron de Vaux	7
Bright Valour	38
Captain Collins (Ire)	10
Digital Dan	13
Dixieland Brass	6
Dixieland Diamond	15
Dramatic Show	8
Finality	35
Fisher Pond	30
Flaming West	18
Funboy	8
Katahaula County	65
Light of Mine	13
Mass Market	38
Memorial Bridge	7
Mombo Gambo	8
Net Asset	9
Nightofthegaelics	14
Orchid's Devil	43
Perfect Score	8
Persian Star	9
Polish	13
Real Quest	8
Recreation	9
Regal Intention	29
Royal Albert Hall	14
Rugged Angel	6
Silver Fox	12
Siyah Kalem	10
Stephanotis	67
Storm Victory	39
Vying Victor	88
Walkinwithapproval	7
Wandering	11
Welbred Fred	6
Yoonevano	34

MANITOBA

Stallion	Mares Bred
Act Smart	17
Battle Cat	20
Chinese Gold	8
Circulating	14
Crystal Gulch	12
Gentle Kent	22
His Excellence	6
Khatef	9
Lucky North	10
Smooth Gold (GB)	9
Transferred	6

ONTARIO

Stallion	Mares Bred
A Fleets Dancer	46
Alystar Slew	10
Ascot Knight	17
Ashbury	19
Bold Executive	79
Bold n' Flashy	14
Box Office Event	10
Brite Adam	13
Casino Prince	11
Catahoula Parish	7
Cat's At Home	31
Ciano Cat	37
Compadre	22
Cracker's Folly	8
Crown Attorney	9
Dance to Destiny	51
Devil Begone	7
Domasca Dan	40
D'wildcat	46
El Franco	8
Elajjud	11
Endeavor	16
Exetera	6
Foxtrail	25
Franc Coeur	8
Guaranteed Gold	15
Gun Power	6
Hierarch	7
Hubba Hubba	12
Kinshasa	37
Kiridashi	21
Legal Jousting (Ire)	8
Like the Prospects	13
Lodge Hill	12
Megas Vukefalos	7
My Way Only	8
One Way Love	55
Parisianprospector	15
Patrol	27
Paynes Bay	31
Perigee Moon	31
Porto Foricos	49
Pride of New York	11
Raj Waki	9
Randy Regent	16
Romancing the Cat	6
Salty Note	14
Sambuca On Ice	8
Sea Wall	11
Shelly's Charmer	9
Solomon's Decree	16
Swampster	8
Tejabo	8
Tempolake	14
Tethra	14
Tomahawk	88
Trajectory	72
Valid N Bold	19
Where's the Ring	110
Whiskey Wisdom	66

QUEBEC

Stallion	Mares Bred
Oronero	11

SASKATCHEWAN

Stallion	Mares Bred
Blowin de Turn	6
Bluegrass Spirit	15
Bound by Honor	6
Dream Guide	10
Good Evening Sir	7
McCallister's Risk	6
Nation Wide News	10
Royal Quiz	7
Sask Watch	6
Satellite Signal	7
Serious Business (Ire)	7
Shaheen	13
Striking Song	19
You've Got Action	17

BROODMARES

Broodmares of the Year

As awarded by the Kentucky Thoroughbred Owners and Breeders Association

2005—BABY ZIP

1991 b. m., Relaunch—Thirty Zip, by Tri Jet.

Breeder: J. Robert Harris Jr. **Owner:** Frank Stronach.

Dam of 9 foals, 6 starters, 5 winners, including **GHOSTZAPPER**, 9 wins, $3,446,120, 2004 Horse of the Year, 2004 champion older male, 2004 Breeders' Cup Classic (G1), 2005 Metropolitan H. (G1), etc.; **CITY ZIP**, 2000 Hopeful S. (G1), 2000 Saratoga Special S. (G2), etc.

2004—DEAR BIRDIE

1987 ch. m., Storm Bird—Hush Dear, by Silent Screen

Breeder, Echo Valley Horse Farm Inc. (Ky.). **Owner**, Marylou Whitney.

Dam of 12 foals, 11 starters, all winners, including **BIRDTOWN**, 4 wins, $871,251, 2003 champion three-year-old filly, 2003 Kentucky Oaks (G1), etc.; **BIRDSTONE**, 5 wins, $1,575,600, 2004 Belmont S. (G1), etc.

2003—PROSPECTORS DELITE

1989 ch. m., Mr. Prospector—Up the Flagpole, by Hoist the Flag

Breeder, W. S. Farish (Ky.). **Owners**, William S. Farish, James Elkins Jr., and W. Temple Webber Jr.

Dam of 5 foals, all winners, including **MINESHAFT**, 10 wins, $2,283,402, 2003 Horse of the Year, 2003 champion older male, 2003 Jockey Club Gold Cup S. (G1), etc.; **TOMISUE'S DELIGHT**, 7 wins, $1,207,537, 1998 Personal Ensign H. (G1), **ROCK SLIDE**, **MONASHEE MOUNTAIN**, **DELTA MUSIC**.

2002—TOUSSAUD

1989 dk. b. or br. m., El Gran Senor—Image of Reality, by In Reality

Breeder, Juddmonte Farms Inc. (Ky.). **Owner**, Juddmonte Farms Inc.

Dam of 9 foals, 7 starters, 5 winners, including **CHESTER HOUSE**, 6 wins, $1,944,545, 2000 Arlington Million S. (G1), etc.; **EMPIRE MAKER**, 4 wins, $1,985,800, 2003 Belmont S. (G1), etc.; **HONEST LADY**, 6 wins, $894,168, 2000 Santa Monica H. (G1), etc.; **CHISELLING**, 3 wins, $410,000, 2002 Secretariat S. (G1), etc.; **DECARCHY**, 6 wins, $703,862, 2002 Frank E. Kilroe Mile H. (G2), etc.

2001—TURKO'S TURN

1992 ch. m., Turkoman—Turbo Launch, by Relaunch

Breeder, John F. Dolan (Ky.). **Owner**, The Thoroughbred Corp.

Dam of 8 foals, 4 winners, including **POINT GIVEN**, 9 wins, $3,968,500, 2001 Horse of the Year, 2001 champion three-year-old male, 2001 Preakness S. (G1), etc.

2000—PRIMAL FORCE

1987 b. m., Blushing Groom (Fr)—Prime Prospect, by Mr. Prospector

Breeders, Mr. and Mrs. Bertram R. Firestone (Ky.). **Owner**, Frank Stronach.

Dam of 10 foals, 4 starters, all winners, including **MACHO UNO**, 6 wins, $1,851,803, 2000 champion two-year-old male, 2000 Breeders' Cup Juvenile (G1), etc.; **AWESOME AGAIN**, 9 wins, $4,374,590, 1998 Breeders' Cup Classic (G1), etc.

1999—ANNE CAMPBELL

1973 b. m., Never Bend—Repercussion, by *Tatan

Breeder, Mill House (Ky.). **Owner**, Arthur B. Hancock III.

Dam of 14 foals, 10 starters, 7 winners, including **MENIFEE**, 5 wins, $1,732,000, 1999 Haskell Invitational H. (G1), etc.; **DESERT WINE**, 8 wins, $1,618,043, 1984 Hollywood Gold Cup (G1), etc.

1998—IN NEON

1982 b. m., Ack Ack—Shamara, by Dewan

Breeder, Clairmont Farm (Ky.). **Owner**, John Franks.

Dam of 7 foals, all starters, 6 winners, including **SHARP CAT**, 15 wins, $2,032,575, 1998 Beldame S. (G1), etc.; **ROYAL ANTHEM**, 6 wins, $1,876,876, 1998 Canadian International S. (Can-G1), etc.; **STAR RECRUIT**, 5 wins, $807,200, 1991 Alysheba S. (G3), etc.

1997—SLIGHTLY DANGEROUS

1979 b. m., Roberto—Where You Lead, by Raise a Native

Breeder, Alan Clore (Ky.). **Owner**, Juddmonte Farms.

Dam of 13 foals, 11 starters, 10 winners, including **COMMANDER IN CHIEF**, 5 wins, $1,311,514, 1993 champion three-year-old male in Eur, 1993 Epsom Derby (Eng-G1), etc.; **WARNING (GB)**, 8 wins, $937,280, 1987 champion two-year-old male in Eng, 1988 champion three-year-old male in Eng, 1988 Queen Elizabeth II S. (Eng-G1), etc.; **YASHMAK**, 4 wins, $529,382, 1997 Flower Bowl Invitational H. (G1), etc.; **DUSHYANTOR**, 5 wins, $1,197,570, 1996 Great Voltigeur S. (Eng-G2), **JIBE**.

1996—PERSONAL ENSIGN

1984 b. m., Private Account—Grecian Banner, by Hoist the Flag

Breeder, Ogden Phipps (Ky.). **Owner**, Ogden Phipps, Phipps Stable.

Dam of 10 foals, 8 starters, all winners, including **MY FLAG**, 6 wins, $1,557,057, 1995 Breeders' Cup Juvenile Fillies (G1), etc.; **MINER'S MARK**, 6 wins, $967,170, 1993 Jockey Club Gold Cup (G1), etc.; **TRADITIONALLY**, 5 wins, $495,660, 2001 Oaklawn H. (G1).

1995—NORTHERN SUNSET (IRE)

1977 ch. m., Northfields—Moss Greine, by *Ballymoss

Breeder, Basil Brindly (Ire). **Owner**, Virginia Kraft Payson.

Dam of 13 foals, 12 starters, 11 winners, including **ST. JOVITE**, 6 wins, $1,604,439, 1992 Horse of the Year in Eur, 1991 cham-

Broodmares of the Year

Year	Broodmare	Year	Broodmare	Year	Broodmare	Year	Broodmare
2005	Baby Zip	1990	Kamar	1975	Shenanigans	1960	Siama
2004	Dear Birdie	1989	Relaxing	1974	Cosmah	1959	*Knight's Daughter
2003	Prospectors Delite	1988	Grecian Banner	1973	Somethingroyal	1958	Miss Disco
2002	Toussaud	1987	Banja Luka	1972	*Moment of Truth II	1957	Belle Jeep
2001	Turko's Turn	1986	Too Bald	1971	Iberia	1956	Swoon
2000	Primal Force	1985	Dunce Cap II	1970	Levee	1955	Iron Reward
1999	Anne Campbell	1984	Hasty Queen II	1969	All Beautiful	1954	Traffic Court
1998	In Neon	1983	Courtly Dee	1968	Delta	1953	Gaga
1997	Slightly Dangerous	1982	Best in Show	1967	Kerala	1952	Ace Card
1996	Personal Ensign	1981	Natashka	1966	Juliets Nurse	1951	*Alpenstock III
1995	Northern Sunset (Ire)	1980	Key Bridge	1965	Pocahontas	1950	Hildene
1994	Fall Aspen	1979	Smartaire	1964	Maid of Flight	1949	Easy Lass
1993	Glowing Tribute	1978	Primonetta	1963	Misty Morn	1948	Our Page
1992	Weekend Surprise	1977	Sweet Tooth	1962	Track Medal	1947	Potheen
1991	Toll Booth	1976	*Gazala II	1961	Striking	1946	Bloodroot

pion two-year-old male in Ire, 1992 Irish Derby (Ire-G1), etc.; **SALEM DRIVE**, 13 wins, $1,046,065, 1987 Bougainvillea H. (G2), etc.; **LAC OUIMET**, 12 wins, $817,863, 1986 Jim Dandy S. (G2), etc.; **L'CARRIERE**, 8 wins, $1,726,175, 1996 Saratoga Cup H. (G3), etc.

1994—FALL ASPEN

1976 ch. m., Pretense—Change Water, by Swaps
Breeder, Joseph M. Roebling (Ky.). **Owner**, John Magnier.
Dam of 14 foals, 13 starters, 12 winners, including **TIMBER COUNTRY**, 5 wins, $1,560,400, 1994 champion two-year-old male, 1995 Preakness S. (G1), etc.; **BIANCONI**, 3 wins, $134,520, 1998 Diadem S. (Eng-G2); **FORT WOOD**, 3 wins, $359,995, 1993 Grand Prix de Paris (Fr-G1), etc.; **NORTHERN ASPEN**, 5 wins, $253,678, 1987 Gamely H. (G1), etc.; **HAMAS (IRE)**, 5 wins, $237,814, 1993 July Cup S. (Eng-G1), etc.; **COLORADO DANCER (IRE)**, 3 wins, $203,389, 1989 Prix de Pomone (Fr-G2), etc.; **ELLE SEULE**, 3 wins, $101,478, 1986 Prix d'Astarte (Fr-G2); **MAZZACANO (GB)**, 3 wins, $153,421, 1989 Goodwood Cup (Eng-G3); **PRINCE OF THIEVES**, 2 wins, $368,474.

1993—GLOWING TRIBUTE

1973 b. m., Graustark—Admiring, by Hail to Reason
Breeder, Paul Mellon (Va.). **Owner**, John R. Gaines.
Dam of 12 foals, 10 starters, 9 winners, including **SEA HERO**, 6 wins, $2,929,869, 1993 Kentucky Derby (G1), etc.; **HERO'S HONOR**, 8 wins, $499,025, 1984 Bowling Green H. (G1), etc.; **GLOWING HONOR**, 6 wins, $296,450, 1988, '89 Diana H. (G2), etc.; **WILD APPLAUSE**, 5 wins, $240,136, 1984 Diana H. (G2), etc.; **CORONATION CUP**, 3 wins, $172,181, 1994 Nijana S. (G3); **MACKIE**, 3 wins, $164,579, 1996 Busher S. (G3); **SEATTLE GLOW**, 4 wins, $69,023.

1992—WEEKEND SURPRISE

1980 b. m., Secretariat—Lassie Dear, by Buckpasser
Breeders, W. S. Farish III and W. S. Kilroy (Ky.). **Owners**, W. S. Farish III and W. S. Kilroy.
Dam of 14 foals, 12 starters, 9 winners, including **A.P. INDY**, 8 wins, $2,979,815, 1992 Horse of the Year, 1992 champion three-year-old male, 1992 Belmont S. (G1), etc.; **SUMMER SQUALL**, 13 wins, $1,844,282, 1990 Preakness S. (G1), etc.; **WELCOME SURPRISE**, 2 wins, $143,574, 2000 Dogwood S. (G3); **EAVESDROPPER**, 3 wins, $167,794.

1991—TOLL BOOTH

1971 b. m., Buckpasser—Missy Baba, by *My Babu
Breeder, John M. Schiff (Ky.). **Owner**, Lazy Lane Farms.
Dam of 12 foals, all starters, 11 winners, including **PLUGGED NICKLE**, 11 wins, $647,206, 1980 champion sprinter, 1980 Florida Derby (G1), etc.; **CHRISTIECAT**, 11 wins, $799,745, 1992 Flower Bowl H. (G1), etc.; **KEY TO THE BRIDGE**, 7 wins, $289,747, 1988 Beaugay H. (G3); **TOLL FEE**, 7 wins, $333,917; **TOLL KEY**, 9 wins, $290,218; **IDLE GOSSIP**, 5 wins, $101,721; **TOKENS ONLY**, 4 wins, $50,455.

1990—KAMAR

1976 b. m., Key to the Mint—Square Angel, by Quadrangle
Breeder, E. P. Taylor (Can). **Owner**, Heronwood Farm.
Dam of 9 foals, 8 starters, 7 winners, including **KEY TO THE MOON**, 13 wins, $714,536, 1984 champion three-year-old male in Can, 1984 Discovery H. (G3), etc.; **GORGEOUS**, 8 wins, $1,171,370, 1989 Ashland S. (G1), etc.; **SEASIDE ATTRACTION**, 4 wins, $272,541, 1990 Kentucky Oaks (G1); **HIAAM**, 3 wins, $48,081, 1986 Princess Margaret S. (Eng-G3), etc.

1989—RELAXING

1976 b. m., Buckpasser—Marking Time, by To Market
Breeder, Ogden Phipps (Ky.). **Owner**, Ogden Phipps.
Dam of 12 foals, 9 starters, all winners, including **EASY GOER**, 14 wins, $4,873,770, 1988 champion two-year-old male, 1989 Belmont S. (G1), etc.; **EASY NOW**, 4 wins, $359,466, 1992 Go for Wand S. (G1), etc.; **CADILLACING**, 7 wins, $268,137, 1988 Ballerina S. (G1), etc.

1988—GRECIAN BANNER

1974 dk. b. or br. m., Hoist the Flag—*Dorine, by Aristophanes
Breeder, Ogden Phipps (Ky.). **Owner**, Ogden Phipps.
Dam of 7 foals, 5 starters, all winners, including **PERSONAL ENSIGN**, 13 wins, $1,679,880, 1988 champion older female, 1996 Broodmare of the Year, 1988 Breeders' Cup Distaff (G1), etc.; **PERSONAL FLAG**, 8 wins, $1,258,924, 1988 Suburban H. (G1), etc.

1987—BANJA LUKA

1968 b. m., Double Jay—Legato, by Dark Star
Breeder, Howard B. Keck (Ky.). **Owner**, Howard B. Keck.
Dam of 9 foals, all starters, 7 winners, including **FERDINAND**, 8 wins, $3,777,978, 1987 Horse of the Year, 1987 champion older male, 1986 Kentucky Derby (G1), etc.; **DONNA INEZ**, 4 wins, $101,275; **JAYSTON**, 7 wins, $92,143; **DANCING**, 4 wins, $77,925; **ANCIENT ART**, 4 wins, $74,250; **PLINTH**, 3 wins, $65,980.

1986—TOO BALD

1964 dk. b. or br. m., Bald Eagle—Hidden Talent, by Dark Star
Breeder, H. F. Guggenheim (Ky.). **Owner**, North Ridge Farm.
Dam of 12 foals, 11 starters, all winners, including **CAPOTE**, 3 wins, $714,470, 1986 champion two-year-old male, 1986 Breeders' Cup Juvenile S. (G1), etc.; **EXCELLER**, 15 wins, $1,674,587, 1978 Jockey Club Gold Cup (G1), etc.; **VAGUELY HIDDEN**, 8 wins, $239,313, 1990 New Jersey Turf Classic S. (G3); **AMERICAN STANDARD**, 5 wins, $180,120; **BALDSKI**, 7 wins, $103,214.

1985—DUNCE CAP II

1960 dk. b. or br. m., Tom Fool—Bright Coronet, by Bull Lea
Breeder, Greentree Stud Inc. (Ky.). **Owner**, Greentree Stud Inc.
Dam of 10 foals, 8 starters, all winners, including **LATE BLOOMER**, 11 wins, $512,040, 1978 champion older female, 1978 Beldame S. (G1), etc.; **JOHNNY APPLESEED**, 4 wins, $91,910, 1976 Louisiana Derby (G2); **LATE ACT**, 9 wins, $661,089, 1985 Cliff Hanger H. (G3), etc.

1984—HASTY QUEEN II

1963 dk. b. or br. m., One Count—Queen Hopeful, by Roman
Breeder, A. E. Reuben (Ky.). **Owners**, Robert E. Courtney and Robert B. Congleton.
Dam of 16 foals, 14 starters, 12 winners, including **FITTO FIGHT**, 14 wins, $1,042,075, 1984 Brooklyn H. (G1), etc.; **HASTY FLYER**, 10 wins, $293,663, 1974 Round Table H. (G3), etc.; **HASTY TAM**, 16 wins, $211,738; **PLAYFUL QUEEN**, 5 wins, $101,837; **MICHAEL NAVONOD**, 6 wins, $86,380; **HASTY CUTIE**, 8 wins, $63,639.

1983—COURTLY DEE

1968 dk. b. or br. m., Never Bend—Tulle, by War Admiral
Breeder, Donald Unger (Ky.). **Owners**, Helen Alexander, David Aykroyd, and Helen Groves.
Dam of 18 foals, 17 starters, 15 winners, including **ALTHEA**, 8 wins, $1,275,255, 1983 champion two-year-old filly, 1984 Arkansas Derby (G1), etc.; **ALI OOP**, 7 wins, $174,020, 1976 Sapling S. (G1); **KETOH**, 3 wins, $173,550, 1985 Cowdin S. (G1); **AQUILEGIA**, 8 wins, $446,081, 1993 New York H. (G2), etc.; **TWINING**, 5 wins, $238,140, 1994 Peter Pan S. (G2), etc.; **AISHAH**, 6 wins, $169,340, 1990 Rare Perfume S. (G2); **NATIVE COURIER**, 14 wins, $522,635, 1981 Bernard Baruch H. (G3), etc.; **PRINCESS OOLA**, 5 wins, $108,291.

1982—BEST IN SHOW

1965 ch. m., Traffic Judge—Stolen Hour, by Mr. Busher
Breeder, Philip Connors (Ky.). **Owners**, Mr. and Mrs. Darrell Brown.
Dam of 17 foals, 12 starters, 9 winners, including **MALINOWSKI**, 2 wins, 1975 champion two-year-old in Ire, 1976 Ladbroke Craven S. (Eng-G3); **BLUSH WITH PRIDE**, 6 wins, $536,807, 1982 Kentucky Oaks (G1), etc.; **GIELGUD**, 1 win, $56,635, 1980 Champagne S. (Eng-G2); **MONROE**, 3 wins, $34,422, 1980 Ballyogan S. (Ire-G3), etc.

1981—NATASHKA

1963 dk. b. or br. m., Dedicate—Natasha, by *Nasrullah
Breeder, Greentree Stud Inc. (Ky.). **Owner**, W. S. Farish III.
Dam of 9 foals, 7 starters, all winners, including **GREGORIAN**, 4 wins, $194,912, 1980 Joe McGrath Memorial S. (Ire-G1), etc.; **TRULY BOUND**, 9 wins, $382,449, 1980 Arlington-Wash-

ington Lassie S. (G2), etc.; **IVORY WAND**, 5 wins, $97,452, 1976 Test S. (G3); **BLOOD ROYAL**, 4 wins, $28,870, 1975 Jockey Club Cup (Eng-G3), etc.; **ARKADINA**, 2 wins, $79,830, Athasi S. (Ire-G3), etc.

1980—KEY BRIDGE

1959 b. m., *Princequillo—Blue Banner, by War Admiral
Breeder, Paul Mellon (Va.). **Owner**, Paul Mellon.
Dam of 11 foals, 8 starters, 7 winners, including **FORT MARCY**, 21 wins, $1,109,791, 1970 Horse of the Year, 1967, '68, '70 champion turf male, 1970 champion older male, 1967, '70 Washington D.C. International S., etc.; **KEY TO THE MINT**, 14 wins, $576,015, 1972 champion three-year-old male, 1973 Suburban H. (G1), etc.; **KEY TO CONTENT**, 7 wins, $354,772, 1981 United Nations H. (G1), etc.; **KEY TO THE KINGDOM**, 7 wins, $109,590, 1974 Stymie H. (G3).

1979—SMARTAIRE

1962 dk. b. or br. m., *Quibu—Art Teacher, by Olympia
Breeder, F. W. Hooper (Al.). **Owners**, Mr. and Mrs. James P. Ryan.
Dam of 12 foals, all starters, 10 winners, including **SMART ANGLE**, 7 wins, $414,217, 1979 champion two-year-old filly, 1979 Frizette S. (G1), etc.; **SMARTEN**, 11 wins, $716,426, 1979 American Derby (G2), etc.; **QUADRATIC**, 6 wins, $233,941, 1977 Cowdin S. (G2); **SMART HEIRESS**, 6 wins, $154,999.

1978—PRIMONETTA

1958 ch. m., Swaps—Banquet Bell, by Polynesian
Breeder, John W. Galbreath (Ky.). **Owner**, John W. Galbreath.
Dam of 7 foals, 6 starters, all winners, including **CUM LAUDE LAURIE**, 8 wins, $405,207, 1977 Beldame S. (G1), etc.; **PRINCE THOU ART**, 3 wins, $167,902, 1975 Florida Derby (G1); **MAUD MULLER**, 3 wins, $138,383, 1974 Gazelle H. (G2), etc.; **GRENFALL**, 4 wins, $19,467, 1971 Gallinule S. (Ire-G2), etc.

1977—SWEET TOOTH

1965 b. m., On-and-On—Plum Cake, by Ponder
Breeder, Calumet Farm (Ky.). **Owner**, Calumet Farm.
Dam of 13 foals, 10 starters, 8 winners, including **OUR MIMS**, 6 wins, $368,034, 1977 champion three-year-old filly, 1977 Coaching Club American Oaks (G1), etc.; **ALYDAR**, 14 wins, $957,195, 1978 Blue Grass S. (G1), etc.; **SUGAR AND SPICE**, 5 wins, $257,046, 1980 Mother Goose S. (G1), etc.

1976—*GAZALA II

1964 dk. b. or br. m, Dark Star—*Belle Angevine, by L'Amiral
Breeder, Nelson Bunker Hunt (Fr). **Owner**, Nelson Bunker Hunt.
Dam of 10 foals, 8 starters, 6 winners, including **YOUTH**, 8 wins, $716,146, 1976 champion three-year-old in Fr, 1976 champion turf male, 1976 Prix du Jockey Club (Fr-G1), etc.; **MISSISSIPIAN**, 3 wins, $248,520, 1973 champion two-year-old in Fr, 1973 Grand Criterium (Fr-G1), etc.; **GONZALES**, 4 wins, $103,968, 1980 Irish St. Leger (Ire-G1), etc.; **SILKY BABY**, 2 wins, $51,351, 1981 Prix de Guiche (Fr-G3); **BEST OF BOTH**, 6 wins, $242,150.

1975—SHENANIGANS

1963 gr. m., Native Dancer—Bold Irish, by Fighting Fox
Breeder, Stuart S. Janney Jr. (Md.). **Owner**, Locust Hill Farm.
Dam of 6 foals, all winners, including **RUFFIAN**, 10 wins, $313,428, 1974 champion two-year-old filly, 1975 champion three-year-old filly, 1975 Filly Triple Crown, 1975 Coaching Club American Oaks (G1), etc.; **ICECAPADE**, 13 wins, $256,468, 1973 William duPont Jr. H. (G2), etc.; **BUCKFINDER**, 9 wins, $230,513, 1978 William duPont Jr. H. (G2), etc.

1974—COSMAH

1953 b. m., Cosmic Bomb—Almahmoud, by *Mahmoud
Breeder, Henry H. Knight (Ky.). **Owner**, John R. Gaines.
Dam of 15 foals, 10 starters, 9 winners, including **TOSMAH**, 23 wins, $612,588, 1963 champion two-year-old filly, 1964 champion three-year-old filly, 1964 champion handicap female, 1964 Beldame S., etc.; **HALO**, 9 wins, $259,553, 1974 United Nations H. (G1), etc.; **FATHERS IMAGE**, 7 wins, $173,318; **MARIBEAU**, 4 wins, $20,925.

1973—SOMETHINGROYAL

1952 b. m., *Princequillo—Imperatrice, by Caruso
Breeder, Mr. C. T. Chenery (Va.). **Owner**, Meadow Stable.
Dam of 18 foals, 15 starters, 11 winners, including **SECRETARIAT**, 16 wins, $1,316,808, 1972, 1973 Horse of the Year, 1972 champion two-year-old male, 1973 champion three-year-old male, 1973 champion turf male, 1973 Triple Crown, 1973 Kentucky Derby (G1), etc.; **SIR GAYLORD**, 10 wins, $237,404, 1961 Sapling S., etc.; **FIRST FAMILY**, 7 wins, $188,040, 1966 Gulfstream Park H., etc.; **SYRIAN SEA**, 6 wins, $178,245, 1967 Selima S., etc.

1972—*MOMENT OF TRUTH II

1959 ch. m., Matador—Kingsworthy, by Kingstone
Breeder, Mrs. M. Clarke (GB). **Owner**, Cragwood Estates.
Dam of 9 foals, all winners, including **CONVENIENCE**, 15 wins, $648,933, 1973 Vanity H. (G1), etc.; **NIGHT ALERT**, 3 wins, $121,268, 1980 Prix Jean Prat (Fr-G2), etc.; **INDULTO**, 27 wins, $466,789, 1966 Withers S., etc.; **PROLIFERATION**, 7 wins, $66,680; **PUNTILLA**, 3 wins, $64,255.

1971—IBERIA

1954 ch. m., *Heliopolis—War East, by *Easton
Breeder, L. S. MacPhail (Md.). **Owner**, Meadow Stable.
Dam of 10 foals, all starters, 8 winners, including **RIVA RIDGE**, 17 wins, $1,111,497, 1971 champion two-year-old male, 1973 champion older male, 1972 Kentucky Derby, etc.; **HYDROLOGIST**, 10 wins, $277,958, 1970 Excelsior H., etc.; **POTOMAC**, 3 wins, $37,361.

1970—LEVEE

1953 ch. m., Hill Prince—Bourtai, by Stimulus
Breeder, Claiborne Farm (Ky.). **Owner**, Whitney Stone.
Dam of 11 foals, 9 starters, 7 winners, including **SHUVEE**, 16 wins, $890,445, 1970, 1971 champion handicap mare, 1969 Filly Triple Crown, 1969 Coaching Club American Oaks, etc.; **ROYAL GUNNER**, 6 wins, $334,650; **NALEE**, 8 wins, $141,631, 1963 Black-Eyed Susan S., etc.; **A.T'S OLIE**, 6 wins, $82,211.

1969—ALL BEAUTIFUL

1959 ch. m., Battlefield—Parlo, by *Heliopolis
Breeder, William duPont Jr. (Va.). **Owner**, Paul Mellon.
Dam of 12 foals, 11 starters, 9 winners, including **ARTS AND LETTERS**, 11 wins, $632,404, 1969 Horse of the Year, 1969 champion three-year-old male, 1969 champion handicap horse, 1969 Belmont S., etc.

1968—DELTA

1952 b. m., *Nasrullah—Bourtai, by Stimulus
Breeder, Claiborne Farm (Ky.). **Owner**, Claiborne Farm.
Dam of 10 foals, all starters, 9 winners, including **OKAVANGO**, 6 wins, $153,802, 1975 San Pasqual H. (G2), etc.; **DIKE**, 7 wins, $351,274, 1969 Wood Memorial S., etc.; **CANAL**, 33 wins, $280,358; **CABILDO**, 22 wins, $267,265; **SHORE**, 6 wins, $62,357.

1967—KERALA

1958 b. m., *My Babu—Blade of Time, by *Sickle
Breeder, Greentree Stud Inc. (Ky.). **Owner**, Mrs. Thomas M. Bancroft.
Dam of 13 foals, 9 starters, 8 winners, including **DAMASCUS**, 21 wins, $1,176,781, 1967 Horse of the Year, 1967 champion three-year-old male, 1967 champion handicap male, 1967 Preakness S., etc.

1966—JULIETS NURSE

1948 dk. b. or br. m., Count Fleet—Nursemaid, by Luke McLuke
Breeder, Mrs. Roy Carruthers (Ky.). **Owner**, J. Graham Brown.
Dam of 13 foals, all starters, 11 winners, including **RUN FOR NURSE**, 22 wins, $253,145; **GALLANT ROMEO**, 15 wins, $202,401, 1966 Vosburgh H., etc.; **WOOZEM**, 7 wins, $163,083, 1966 Demoiselle S., etc.; **DUTIFUL**, 5 wins, $80,780.

1965—POCAHONTAS

1955 dk. b. or br. m., Roman—How, by *Princequillo
Breeder, H. B. Delman (Ky.). **Owner**, Raymond Guest.
Dam of 9 foals, 5 starters, all winners, including **TOM ROLFE**, 16 wins, $671,297, 1965 champion three-year-old male, 1965 Preakness S., etc.; **LADY REBECCA**, 2 wins, $26,434, 1974

Prix Vanteaux (Fr-G3); **CHIEFTAIN**, 13 wins, $405,256, 1964 Governor's Gold Cup, etc.; ***WENONA**, 3 wins, Blandford S. (Ire), etc.

1964—MAID OF FLIGHT

1951 dk. b. or br. m., Count Fleet—Maidoduntreath, by Man o' War

Breeder, Mrs. Silas B. Mason (Ky.). **Owner**, Mrs. Richard C. duPont.

Dam of 11 foals, 10 starters, 9 winners, including **KELSO**, 39 wins, $1,977,896, 1960, '61, '62, '63, '64 Horse of the Year, 1960 champion three-year-old male, 1961, '62, '63, '64 champion handicap horse, 1960, '61, '62, '63, '64 Jockey Club Gold Cup, etc.

1963—MISTY MORN

1952 b. m., *Princequillo—Grey Flight, by *Mahmoud

Breeder, Wheatley Stable (Ky.). **Owner**, Mrs. H. C. Phipps.

Dam of 10 foals, 8 starters, 7 winners, including **SUCCESSOR**, 7 wins, $532,254, 1966 champion two-year-old, 1966 Champagne S., etc.; **BOLD LAD**, 14 wins, $516,465, 1964 champion two-year-old, 1964 Champagne S., etc.; **SUNRISE FLIGHT**, 11 wins, $380,995, 1963 Gallant Fox H., etc.; **BEAUTIFUL DAY**, 7 wins, $160,007; **BOLD CONSORT**, 6 wins, $38,147.

1962—TRACK MEDAL

1950 dk. b. or br. m., *Khaled—Iron Reward, by *Beau Pere

Breeder, Rex C. Ellsworth (Ca.). **Owner**, Greentree Stud.

Dam of 10 foals, 8 starters, 6 winners, including **OUTING CLASS**, 6 wins, $229,759, 1962 Hopeful S., etc.; ***O'HARA**, 8 wins, $202,180, 1966 Sunset H.; **TUTANKHAMEN**, 12 wins, $157,530, 1962 Manhattan H.; **FOOL'S GOLD II**, 1 win, 1962 Musidora S. (Eng), etc.

1961—STRIKING

1947 b. m., War Admiral—Baby League, by Bubbling Over

Breeder, Ogden Phipps (Ky.). **Owner**, Ogden Phipps.

Dam of 15 foals, 12 starters, 11 winners, including **HITTING AWAY**, 13 wins, $309,079, 1961 Dwyer H., etc.; **BATTER UP**, 7 wins, $166,504, 1962 Black-Eyed Susan S., etc.; **MY BOSS LADY**, 4 wins, $64,174; **GLAMOUR**, 6 wins, $60,775; **BASES FULL**, 3 wins, $17,627.

1960—SIAMA

1947 b. m., Tiger—China Face, by Display

Breeder, E. K. Thomas (Ky.). **Owner**, Harry F. Guggenheim.

Dam of 9 foals, 5 starters, all winners, including **BALD EAGLE**, 12 wins, $692,946, 1960 champion handicap male, 1959, 1960 Washington D.C. International, etc.; **ONE-EYED KING**, 15 wins, $266,281, 1960 Arlington H., etc.; **DEAD AHEAD**, 8 wins, $73,645.

1959—*KNIGHT'S DAUGHTER

1941 b. m., Sir Cosmo—Feola, by Friar Marcus

Breeder, King George VI (GB). **Owner**, Claiborne Farm.

Dam of 7 foals, all starters, 6 winners, including **ROUND TABLE**, 43 wins, $1,749,869, 1958 Horse of the Year, 1957, 1958, '59 champion turf male, 1958, '59 champion older male, 1957 Hollywood Gold Cup, etc.; **MONARCHY**, 7 wins, $85,737; ***LOVE GAME**.

1958—MISS DISCO

1944 b. m., Discovery—Outdone, by Pompey

Breeder, Alfred G. Vanderbilt (Md.). **Owner**, Mrs. H. C. Phipps.

Dam of 11 foals, 7 starters, all winners, including **BOLD RULER**, 23 wins, $764,204, 1957 Horse of the Year, 1957 champion three-year-old male, 1958 champion sprinter, 1957 Preakness S., etc.; **INDEPENDENCE**, 12 wins, $132,088; **NASCO**, 7 wins, $71,930.

1957—BELLE JEEP

1949 b. m., War Jeep—Model Beauty, by *Blenheim II

Breeder, Maine Chance Farm (Ky.). **Owner**, Maine Chance Farm.

Dam of 14 foals, 12 starters, all winners, including **JEWEL'S REWARD**, 7 wins, $448,592, 1957 champion two-year-old male, 1957 Champagne S., etc.; **TRIPLE CROWN**, 4 wins, $128,874, 1974 San Jacinto S. (G2), etc.; **LORD JEEP**, 11 wins, $64,504; **EVASIVE ACTION**, 3 wins, $47,004.

1956—SWOON

1942 ch. m, Sweep Like—Sadie Greenock, by Greenock

Breeder, E. Gay Drake (Ky.). **Owner**, E. Gay Drake.

Dam of 10 foals, all starters, 8 winners, including **SWOON'S SON**, 30 wins, $970,605, 1956 American Derby, etc.; **DOGOON**, 28 wins, $220,360, 1954 Hawthorne Juvenile H., etc.

1955—IRON REWARD

1946 b. m., *Beau Pere—Iron Maiden, by War Admiral

Breeder, W. W. Naylor (Ca.). **Owner**, Rex Ellsworth.

Dam of 11 foals, 9 starters, 5 winners, including **SWAPS**, 19 wins, $848,900, 1956 Horse of the Year, 1956 champion handicap horse, 1955 Kentucky Derby, etc.; **THE SHOE**, 10 wins, $105,000, 1958 Cinema H., etc.; **LIKE MAGIC**, 10 wins, $87,872.

1954—TRAFFIC COURT

1938 dk. b. or br. m., Discovery—Traffic, by Broomstick

Breeder, C. V. Whitney (Ky.). **Owner**, Clifford Mooers.

Dam of 3 foals, all winners, including **HASTY ROAD**, 14 wins, $541,402, 1953 champion two-year-old male, 1954 Preakness S., etc.; **TRAFFIC JUDGE**, 13 wins, $432,450, 1957 Suburban H., etc.

1953—GAGA

1942 b. m., *Bull Dog—Alpoise, by Equipoise

Breeder, A. C. Ernst (Ky.). **Owner**, Duval Headley.

Dam of 5 foals, all winners, including **TOM FOOL**, 21 wins, $570,165, 1953 Horse of the Year, 1951 champion two-year-old male, 1953 champion sprinter, 1953 champion older male, 1953 Surburban H., etc.; **AUNT JINNY**, 5 wins, $106,020, 1950 champion two-year-old filly, 1950 Demoiselle S., etc.

1952—ACE CARD

1942 b. m., Case Ace—Furlough, by Man o' War

Breeder, Walter M. Jeffords (Pa.). **Owner**, Mrs. Walter M. Jeffords.

Dam of 12 foals, all starters, 11 winners, including **ONE COUNT**, 9 wins, $245,625, 1952 Horse of the Year, 1952 champion three-year-old male, 1952 Belmont S., etc.; **POST CARD**, 14 wins, $170,525; **MY CARD**, 7 wins, $98,404, 1963 Selima S.; **YILDIZ**, 7 wins, $90,475, 1951 Flamingo S., etc.

1951—*ALPENSTOCK III

1936 dk. b. or br. m., Apelle—Plymstock, by Polymelus

Breeder, Cliveden Stud (GB). **Owner**, Mereworth Farm.

Dam of 13 foals, 10 starters, 8 winners, including **RUHE**, 11 wins, $294,490, 1951 Blue Grass S., etc.; **STURDY ONE**, 13 wins, $202,970, 1951 Tanforan H., etc.; **ALLADIER**, 9 wins, $61,712, 1951 Breeders' Futurity, etc.

1950—HILDENE

1938 b. m., Bubbling Over—Fancy Racket, by *Wrack

Breeder, Xalapa Farm (Ky.). **Owner**, Meadow Stable.

Dam of 13 foals, 12 starters, 9 winners, including **HILL PRINCE**, 17 wins, $422,140, 1950 Horse of the Year, 1949 champion two-year-old male, 1950 champion three-year-old male, 1951 champion older male, 1950 Preakness S., etc.; **FIRST LANDING**, 19 wins, $779,577, 1958 champion two-year-old male, 1958 Champagne S., etc.; **THIRD BROTHER**, 9 wins, $310,787; **MANGOHICK**, 23 wins, $115,115; **PRINCE HILL**, 8 wins, $98,300.

1949—EASY LASS

1940 bl. m., *Blenheim II—Slow and Easy, by Colin

Breeder, Calumet Farm (Ky.). **Owner**, Calumet Farm.

Dam of 7 foals, all starters, 6 winners, including **COALTOWN**, 23 wins, $415,675, 1949 Horse of the Year, 1948 champion sprinter, 1949 champion older male, 1949 Washington Park H., etc.; **WISTFUL**, 13 wins, $213,060, 1949 champion three-year-old filly, 1949 Coaching Club of America Oaks, etc.; **ROSEWOOD**, 9 wins, $92,950; **FANFARE**, 9 wins, $46,140.

1948—OUR PAGE
1940 b. m., Blue Larkspur—Occult, by *Dis Donc
Breeder, Woodvale Farm (Oh.). **Owner**, Royce C. Martin.
Dam of 5 foals, all winners, **BULL PAGE**, 9 wins, $25,730, 1951 Horse of the Year in Canada, 1951 champion older horse in Canada, 1951 Canadian Championship S.; **NAVY PAGE**, 21 wins, $127,322, 1953 Jerome H., etc.; **SPORT PAGE**, 4 wins, $79,175; **BROTHER TEX**, 8 wins, $77,633; **PAGE BOOTS**, 3 wins, $51,635.

1947—POTHEEN
1928 dk. b. or br. m., Wildair—Rosie O'Grady, by Hamburg
Breeder, H. P. Whitney (Ky.). **Owner**, Calumet Farm.
Dam of 12 foals, 11 starters, 9 winners, including **BEWITCH**, 20 wins, $462,605, 1947 champion two-year-old filly, 1949 champion older female, 1947 Washington Park Futurity, etc.; **POT O' LUCK**, 14 wins, $239,150, 1945 Jockey Club Gold Cup, etc.; **LOT O LUCK**, 9 wins, $46,950.

1946—BLOODROOT
1932 b. m., Blue Larkspur—*Knockany Bridge, by Bridge of Earn
Breeder, Idle Hour Stock Farm (Ky.). **Owner**, Ogden Phipps.
Dam of 13 foals, 11 starters, 8 winners, including **ANCESTOR**, 26 wins, $237,956, 1959 champion steeplechaser, 1952 Discovery H., etc.; **BE FAITHFUL**, 14 wins, $189,040, 1947 Hawthorne Gold Cup H., etc.; **BRIC A BAC**, 13 wins, $103,225, 1945 San Juan Capistrano H., etc.; **BIMLETTE**, 4 wins, $28,065, 1946 Frizette S.

Leading Broodmares by Progeny Earnings
Worldwide Leaders, 1930-2005

Broodmare, YOB, Sire—Dam	Fls.	Strs.	Wnrs.	SWs	Progeny Earnings	Leading Earner	Earnings
Once Wed, 1984, Blushing Groom (Fr)—Noura	11	10	7	1	$18,431,882	T.M.Opera O	$16,200,337
Dancing Key, 1983, Nijinsky II—Key Partner	14	13	9	4	18,242,266	Dance Partner (Jpn)	5,973,652
Pacificus, 1981, Northern Dancer—Pacific Princess	11	10	7	3	18,135,348	Narita Brian	9,296,552
Vega, 1990, Tony Bin —Antique Value	4	4	3	3	11,301,103	Admire Don	7,712,841
Katies (Ire), 1981, Nonoalco—Mortefontaine	15	12	10	5	11,222,779	Hishi Amazon	6,981,102
Golden Sash, 1988, Dictus—Dyna Sash	11	9	6	2	11,112,240	Stay Gold	8,682,142
Roamin Rachel, 1990, Mining—One Smart Lady	6	5	3	2	10,909,802	Zenno Rob Roy	10,483,242
Tugela, 1995, Riverman—Rambushka	5	3	2	1	10,803,353	Makybe Diva	10,767,186
Happy Trails, 1984, Posse—Roycon (GB)	11	10	8	3	10,475,463	Shinko Lovely	4,596,546
Ingot Way, 1981, Diplomat Way—Ingot	14	10	9	1	10,383,401	Skip Away	9,616,360
Solar Slew, 1982, Seattle Slew—Gold Sun (Arg)	11	7	7	2	10,363,980	Cigar	9,999,815
All Dance, 1978, Northern Dancer—All Rainbows	12	11	7	2	10,315,305	Tap Dance City	9,586,479
Tokai Natural, 1982, Nice Dancer—Tokai Midori	13	12	10	2	9,846,696	Tokai Teio	4,698,139
Cee's Song, 1986, Seattle Song—Lonely Dancer	13	9	6	4	9,680,428	Tiznow	6,427,830
Floral Magic, 1985, Affirmed—Rare Lady	9	8	7	1	9,582,529	Narita Top Road	8,389,594
Campaign Girl, 1987, Maruzensky —Lady Shiraoki	3	2	2	1	9,519,113	Special Week	9,346,435
Dyna Carle, 1980, Northern Taste—Shadai Feather	9	9	8	1	9,368,616	Air Groove	6,832,242
Princess Reema, 1984, Affirmed—First Fling	15	13	11	3	9,315,099	Meisho Doto	8,088,202
Mejiro Aurola, 1978, Remand—Mejiro Iris	11	6	5	2	9,270,538	Mejiro McQueen	7,618,803
Chancey Squaw, 1991, Chief's Crown—Allicance	7	5	4	3	9,191,718	Agnes Digital	8,095,160
Takeno Falcon, 1982, Philip of Spain—Cool Fair	9	8	5	1	9,125,759	Hokuto Vega	8,300,301
Tree of Knowledge (Ire), 1977, Sassafras (Fr)—Sensibility	10	7	5	2	9,019,381	Taiki Blizzard	5,523,549
Reru du Temps, 1982, Maruzensky —Kei Tsunami	9	6	5	2	8,891,809	Mejiro Bright	6,848,423
Jood, 1989, Nijinsky II—Kamar	10	8	5	2	8,789,622	Fantastic Light	8,486,957
Sakura Clare, 1982, Northern Taste—Clare Bridge	13	9	5	2	8,742,526	Sakura Chitose O	5,178,760
Sawayaka Princess, 1986, Northern Taste—Scotch Princess	9	9	8	2	8,658,798	Durandal	4,621,343
Cocotte, 1983, Troy —Gay Milly	13	10	8	6	8,656,402	Fine Motion	4,247,083
Croupier Lady, 1983, What Luck—Question d'Argent	11	9	6	1	8,584,517	Genuine	5,455,575
Tee Kay, 1991, Gold Meridian—Tri Argo	7	4	4	1	8,576,405	Symboli Kris S	8,401,282
Legacy of Strength, 1982, Affirmed—Katonka	15	12	9	2	8,557,169	Stinger (Jpn)	3,467,289
Dream Vision, 1986, Northern Taste—Honey Dreamer	10	10	9	2	8,541,362	Utopia	4,823,265
Powerful Lady, 1981, Maruzensky—Roch Tesco	17	12	9	2	8,464,145	Winning Ticket	3,359,368
Jolie Zaza, 1991, Alzao—Bold Lady	6	6	2	1	8,447,604	Time Paradox	7,855,552
Sakura Hagoromo, 1984, Northern Taste—Clear Amber	11	8	8	1	8,429,367	Sakura Bakushin O	4,800,631
Mejiro Beauty, 1982, Partholon —Mejiro Nagasaki	8	8	8	1	8,403,145	Mejiro Dober	6,240,681
Wind in Her Hair (Ire)], 1991, Alzao—Burghclere	9	8	5	3	8,349,873	Deep Impact	6,757,811
White Narubi, 1974, *Silver Shark—Never Narubi	15	5	3	2	8,155,897	Oguri Cap	6,940,077
Tenzan Otome, 1983, Maruzensky —Mombetsu Kachidoki	10	8	6	2	8,123,127	Osumi Jet	4,915,054
Fairy Doll, 1991, Nureyev—Dream Deal	6	6	3	3	8,069,084	To the Victory	5,303,281
Regal State, 1983, Affirmed—La Trinite (Fr)	12	9	4	2	7,989,744	Pleasantly Perfect	7,789,880
Pointed Path (GB), 1984, Kris —Silken Way	10	9	6	2	7,859,158	Neo Universe	5,263,786
Comaz, 1983, Danzig—Middlemarch	10	6	4	2	7,851,751	Sterling Rose	4,692,919
Warranty Applied, 1986, Monteverdi (Ire)—Implied Warranty	11	9	9	1	7,838,154	Eishin Preston	7,408,086
Rosita, 1986, Mill George—Mellow Madang	12	10	7	2	7,699,821	Kanetsu Fleuve	3,635,744
Crafty Wife, 1985, Crafty Prospector—Wife Mistress	14	11	9	2	7,684,657	Big Shori	2,984,808
Urakawa Miyuki, 1981, *Habitony—Kemmaru Midori	11	9	6	1	7,671,685	Nice Nature	5,232,135
Ameriflora, 1989, Danzig—Graceful Touch	8	5	5	2	7,661,138	Grass Wonder	5,987,405
Never Ichiban, 1971, Never Beat —Miss Nanba Ichiban	14	9	6	1	7,636,765	Daitaku Helios	4,629,341
I'll Get Along, 1992, Smile—Dont Worry Bout Me	6	2	2	1	7,628,590	Smarty Jones	7,613,155
Bel Sheba, 1970, Lt. Stevens—Belthazar	13	13	11	5	7,594,619	Alysheba	6,679,242
Alp Me Please, 1981, Blushing Groom (Fr)—Swiss	7	6	2	1	7,567,701	Mayano Top Gun	7,463,557
Mountain Queen, 1982, Nizon—Yamaka Queen	14	10	7	1	7,484,436	Kyoto City	5,622,437
Daltawa, 1989, Miswaki—Damana (Fr)	7	5	4	3	7,416,156	Daylami (Ire)	4,614,762

Leading Broodmares by 2005 Progeny Earnings in North America

Broodmare, YOB, Sire—Dam	Earnings	Leading Earner	Earnings
Quiet Dance, 1993, Quiet American—Misty Dancer	$3,788,933	Saint Liam	$3,696,960
Princess Olivia, 1995, Lycius—Dance Image (Ire)	2,454,196	Flower Alley	2,435,200
Maggy Hawk, 1994, Hawkster—Qualique	2,151,675	Afleet Alex	2,085,000
Set Them Free, 1990, Stop the Music—Valseuse (Fr)	1,846,876	Giacomo	1,846,876
Sweet as Honey, 1995, Strike the Gold—Cup of Honey	1,547,720	Borrego	1,536,600
Hidden Light, 1983, Majestic Light—Tallahto	1,448,000	Artie Schiller	1,448,000
Token Gesture (Ire), 1994, Alzao—Temporary Lull	1,326,186	Relaxed Gesture (Ire)	1,326,186
Our Country Place, 1992, Pleasant Colony—Maplejinsky	1,316,420	Pleasant Home	1,316,420
Hasili (Ire), 1991, Kahyasi —Kerali	1,271,200	Intercontinental (GB)	1,271,200
Goulash, 1993, Mari's Book—Wise Bride	1,214,936	Ashado	1,061,000
Dissemble (GB), 1989, Ahonoora —Kerali	1,214,040	Leroidesanimaux (Brz)	1,214,040
So Sedulous, 1991, The Minstrel—Sedulous (Ire)	1,185,600	Shirocco (Ger)	1,185,600
Heat Lightning, 1993, Summer Squall—Mystical Mood	1,144,698	Stevie Wonderboy	1,028,940
Belva, 1998, Theatrical (Ire)—Committed	1,143,491	English Channel	1,143,491
Clever But Costly, 1985, Clever Trick—Swoonlow	1,134,995	Sun King	1,134,800
Nice Gal, 1985, Naskra—Vigal	1,125,134	Perfect Drift	1,121,227
Tersa, 1986, Mr. Prospector—Peacefully	1,080,000	Rock Hard Ten	1,080,000
Peacock Alley, 1994, Fast Play—Anna's Honor	1,070,170	Magna Graduate	1,070,170
Cuando Quiere, 1988, Affirmed—Quatre Saisons	979,653	Honey Ryder	910,980
Contrive, 1998, Storm Cat—Jeano	927,500	Folklore	927,500
Lindsay Frolic, 1992, Mt. Livermore—Cherokee Frolic	920,330	Super Frolic	818,160
Bendita, 1985, Baldski—Bonne Note (Fr)	907,659	Better Talk Now	877,640
Verbasle, 1988, Slewpy—Verbality	901,629	High Fly	901,500
Silvery Swan, 1994, Silver Deputy—Sociable Duck	890,000	Roman Ruler	890,000
Cloud Break, 1992, Dr. Carter—Wistful	852,300	Lost in the Fog	844,500

Most Graded/Group Stakes Winners for a Broodmare (1930-2005)

8 **Fall Aspen** (1976, Pretense—Change Water, by Swaps). 14 foals, 13 starters, 12 winners, 9 stakes winners, 8 graded/group stakes winners (Fort Wood [Fr-G1], Hamas [Ire] [Eng-G1], Timber Country [G1], Northern Aspen [G1], Colorado Dancer [Ire] [Fr-G2], Bianconi [Eng-G2], Elle Seule [Fr-G2], Mazzacano [GB] [Eng-G3])

7 **Courtly Dee** (1968, Never Bend—Tulle, by War Admiral). 18 foals, 17 starters, 15 winners, 8 stakes winners, 7 graded/group stakes winners (Ali Oop [G1], Althea [G1], Ketoh [G1], Aishah [G2], Aquilegia [G2], Twining [G2], Native Courier [G3])

6 **Chaldee** (1978, Banner Sport—Gevar, by Right of Way). 13 foals, 8 starters, 7 winners, 6 stakes winners, 6 graded/group stakes winners (Potrichal [Arg] [Arg-G1], Potrinner [Arg] [Arg-G1], Potrizaris [Arg] [Arg-G1], Potridee [Arg] [G1], Potro Rex [Arg-G1], Sun Banner [Arg-G3])

Dahlia (1970, *Vaguely Noble—Charming Alibi, by Honeys Alibi). 13 foals, 11 starters, 8 winners, 6 stakes winners, 6 graded/group stakes winners (Dahar [G1], Dahlia's Dreamer [G1], Delegant [G1], Rivlia [G1], Wajd [Fr-G2], Llandaff [G2])

Glowing Tribute (1973, Graustark—Admiring, by Hail to Reason). 12 foals, 10 starters, 9 winners, 7 stakes winners, 6 graded/group stakes winners (Hero's Honor [G1], Sea Hero [G1], Glowing Honor [G2], Wild Applause [G2], Coronation Cup [G3], Mackie [G2])

5 **Baroque Pearl** (1983, Dance in Time—Perla, by *Young Emperor]. 7 foals, 7 starters, 5 winners, 5 stakes winners, 5 graded/group stakes winners (Priceless Asset [Ind-G1], Super Brave [Ind] [Ind-G1], Arka [Ind-G2], Queen To Conquer [Ind-G2], Shinjuku [Ind-G2])

Blessings (Fr) (1971, Floribunda—*Marabelle, by Miralgo). 17 foals, 11 starters, 8 winners, 6 stakes winners, 5 graded/group stakes winners (Bleding [Arg] [Arg-G1], Sings [Arg-G1], Blue Boss [Aus-G3], Blue Bles [Arg-G3], Flibless [Arg-G3])

Coup de Folie (1982, Halo—Raise the Standard, by Hoist the Flag). 12 foals, 10 starters, 7 winners, 5 stakes winners, 5 graded/group stakes winners (Coup de Genie [Fr-G1], Exit to Nowhere [Fr-G1], Machiavellian [Fr-G1], Hydro Calido [Fr-G2], Ocean of Wisdom [Fr-G3])

5 **Eight Carat** (1975, *Pieces of Eight II—Klairessa [GB], by *Klairon). 10 foals, 12 starters, 5 winners, 5 stakes winners, 5 graded/group stakes winners (Marquise [NZ-G1], Our Diamond Lover [NZ-G1], Kaapstad [Aus-G1], Mouawad [Aus-G1], Octagonal [Aus-G1])

Halory (1984, Halo—Cold Reply, by Northern Dancer). 14 foals, 12 starters, 9 winners, 5 stakes winners, 5 graded/group stakes winners (Van Nistelrooy [Ire-G2], Halory Hunter [G2], Brushed Halory [G3], Key Lory [G3], Prory [G3])

Hasili (1991, Kahyasi—Kerali, by High Line). 6 foals, 5 starters, 5 winners, 5 stakes winners, 5 graded/group stakes winners (Banks Hill [GB] [G1], Heat Haze [GB] [G1], Intercontinental [GB] [G1], Cacique [Fr-G2], Dansili [GB] [Fr-G2])

***Lupe II** (1967, Primera—Alcoa, by Alycidon). 10 foals, 9 starters, 8 winners, 5 stakes winners, 5 graded/group stakes winners (Lascaux [Fr-G2], Louveterie [Fr-G3], Legend of France [Eng-G3], Leonardo Da Vinci [Fr] [Eng-G3], L'Ile Du Reve [Eng-G3])

Princess Tracy (Ire) (1981, Ahonoora—Princess Ru, by Princely Gift). 10 foals, 9 starters, 7 winners, 5 stakes winners, 5 graded/group stakes winners (Tracy's Element [Aus] [SAf-G1], Danasinga [Aus-G1], Topasannah [SAf-G2], Cullen [Aus-G3], Towkay [Aus-G3])

Summoned (1978, Crowned Prince—Sweet Life, by *Pardao). 16 foals, 15 starters, 12 winners, 5 stakes winners, 5 graded/group stakes winners (Zeditave [Aus-G1], Alannon [Aus-G3], Pampas Fire [Aus-G3], Square Deal [Aus-G3], Zedagal [Aus-G3])

Toussaud (1989, El Gran Senor—Image of Reality, by In Reality). 9 foals, 7 starters, 5 winners, 5 stakes winners, 5 graded/group stakes winners (Chester House [G1], Chiselling [G1], Empire Maker [G1], Honest Lady [G1], Decarchy [G2])

Most Stakes Winners for a Broodmare
(1930-2005)

9 **Fall Aspen** (1976, Pretense—Change Water, by Swaps). 14 foals, 13 starters, 12 winners, 9 stakes winners (Bianconi, Colorado Dancer [Ire], Elle Seule, Fort Wood, Hamas [Ire], Mazzacano [GB], Northern Aspen, Prince of Thieves, Timber Country)

Fallow (1957, *Worden—Galloway Queene, by Colombo). 16 foals, 11 starters, 12 winners, 9 stakes winners (Fact [Arg], Factory, Fairly [Arg], Fallowed, Far, *Farm, Farmer, Fazenda [Arg], *Fizz)

Grey Flight (1945, *Mahmoud—Planetoid, by Ariel). 15 foals, 15 starters, 14 winners, 9 stakes winners (Bold Princess, Bold Queen, Full Flight, Gray Phantom, Misty Day, Misty Flight, Misty Morn, Signore, What a Pleasure)

8 **Astronomie** (1932, Asterus—Likka, by Sardanapale). 10 foals, 9 starters, 8 winners, 8 stakes winners (Arbar, Arbele, *Asmena, Caracalla, Estremadur, Floriados, Marsyas II, Pharas)

Courtly Dee (1968, Never Bend—Tulle, by War Admiral). 18 foals, 17 starters, 15 winners, 8 stakes winners (Aishah, Ali Oop, Althea, Aquilegia, Ketoh, Native Courier, Princess Oola, Twining)

Retorica (1955, Snob—Rochelle, by Selim Hassan). 12 foals, 9 starters, 8 winners, 8 stakes winners (*Legent II, Leon II, Lioness, *Lirio, Llegador [Arg], Locomotor, *Lostalo, Ruizero [Arg])

7 **Bold Pat** (1975, Bold Destroyer—Bolerita, by Bolero). 14 foals, 14 starters, 13 winners, 7 stakes winners (A Bold Embrace, Arctic Pat, Bay Is O. K., Bold Fawn, Elegant Black, Milden's Girl, Pat's Bold Brat)

Dan's Dream (1961, Your Host—Rosella, by War Relic). 15 foals, 15 starters, 12 winners, 7 stakes winners (Costly Dream, Dream 'n Be Lucky, El Corazon, Go On Dreaming, Jesta Dream Away, Once Upon a Star, Royal Knightmare)

Donatella (1939, *Mahmoud—Delleana, by Clarissimus). 13 foals, 12 starters, 10 winners, 7 stakes winners (*Daumier, De Dreux, Delaroche, *Dominate II, *Donatellina II, Donna Lydia, Duccio)

Flying B. G. (1978, Barachois—Up Alone, by Solo Landing). 16 foals, 12 starters, 11 winners, 7 stakes winners (B. G.'s Drone, Burnone Gimmetwo, Draconic's B. G., Flying Drone, Soiree, Talent Connection, Texas Holdem)

Glowing Tribute (1973, Graustark—Admiring, by Hail to Reason). 12 foals, 10 starters, 9 winners, 7 stakes winners (Coronation Cup, Glowing Honor, Hero's Honor, Mackie, Sea Hero, Seattle Glow, Wild Applause)

Gwynedd II (1947, Owen Tudor—Ryswick, by Blandford). 9 foals, 8 starters, 8 winners, 7 stakes winners (Angers, Anne III, Fort Coulonge, Gaspesie, La Touques, Maintenon, Montigny)

Here's Lookn Adder (1983, Superbity—Sarah Blue Eyes, by Explodent). 13 foals, 10 starters, 9 winners, 7 stakes winners (Drumm Valley, Jessen, Just Lookn, Lookn At a Blurr, Lookn At Another, Peak Out, Takin It Deep)

Moccasin (1963, Nantallah—*Rough Shod II, by Gold Bridge). 9 foals, 8 starters, 7 winners, 7 stakes winners (Apalachee, Belted Earl, Brahms, Flippers, Indian, Nantequos, Scuff)

My Dear Girl (1957, Rough'n Tumble—Iltis, by War Relic). 15 foals, 14 starters, 13 winners, 7 stakes winners (Gentle Touch, In Reality, My Dear Lady, Really and Truly, Return to Reality, Superbity, Watchfulness)

Qui Royalty (1977, Native Royalty—Qui Blink, by Francis S.). 14 foals, 12 starters, 10 winners, 7 stakes winners (Appointed One, Bakharoff, Demonry, Emperor Jones, Majlood, Sum, Thyer)

Roar n' Honey (1965, Hezahoney—Rip 'n Roar, by Rippey). 14 foals, 12 starters, 11 winners, 7 stakes winners (Bar Tender, Dandy Man, My Favorite Gal, One That Got Away, Singh Honey, Sonny Says, St. Aubin)

Soumida (1953, Tehran—*Sou'wester, by Blue Peter). 10 foals, 9 starters, 9 winners, 7 stakes winners (Sarcelle, Senechal, Siska, Solidor, Solon, Sorana, *Soudard)

Toll Booth (1971, Buckpasser—Missy Baba, by *My Babu). 13 foals, 12 starters, 11 winners, 7 stakes winners (Christiecat, Idle Gossip, Key to the Bridge, Plugged Nickle, Tokens Only, Toll Fee, Toll Key)

Up the Flagpole (1978, Hoist the Flag—The Garden Club, by *Herbager). 11 foals, 10 starters, 10 winners, 7 stakes winners (Allied Flag, Flagbird, Fold the Flag, Long View, Prospectors Delite, Runup the Colors, Top Account)

6 **Accra** (1941, Annapolis—Ladala, by Ladkin). 11 foals, 11 starters, 10 winners, 6 stakes winners (Mandingo, Mongo, Nahodah, Nala, Neji, Songai)

Adriana (1944, Arjaman—Adriatica, by Janitor). 15 foals, 14 starters, 11 winners, 6 stakes winners (Ametta, Anatol, Andrea II, Appell, Aspiration, *Ataturk II)

Alta Mira (1948, *Don Bingo—Music Hall, by Snark). 9 foals, 9 starters, 9 winners, 6 stakes winners (Collin Baykey, Craig D., Donn Baykey, Ky. Miracle, Ky. Music, Son of Donn)

Annie Edge (Ire) (1980, Nebbiolo—Friendly Court, by Be Friendly). 12 foals, 11 starters, 8 winners, 6 stakes winners (Rimrod, Rory Creek, Seebe, Selkirk, Skillington, Syncline)

Apostille (1944, Astrophel—Polititia, by Comedy King). 8 foals, 6 starters, 6 winners, 6 stakes winners (Apostol, Bingo, Poisson Volant, Postboy, Postman, Virgule)

Banja Luka (1968, Double Jay—Legato, by Dark Star). 9 foals, 9 starters, 7 winners, 6 stakes winners (Ancient Art, Dancing, Donna Inez, Ferdinand, Jayston, Plinth)

Bargain (1943, Millero—Bonne Fille, by Bermejo). 7 foals, 7 starters, 6 winners, 6 stakes winners (Corbar, Dadiva, Moon Shine, Postwar, *Propina, Shilling)

Battle Creek Girl (1977, His Majesty—Far Beyond, by Nijinsky II). 20 foals, 17 starters, 15 winners, 6 stakes winners (Everhope, Parade Ground, Parade Leader, Speed Dialer, Tricky Creek, Wavering Girl)

Blessings (Fr) (1971, Floribunda—*Marabelle, by Miralgo). 17 foals, 11 starters, 8 winners, 6 stakes winners (Bleding [Arg], Blue Bles, Blue Boss, Flibless, Fritz, Sings)

Blue Denim (1940, Blue Larkspur—Judy O'Grady, by Man o' War). 15 foals, 14 starters, 11 winners, 6 stakes winners (Blue Prince, Green Baize, Piano Jim, Policeman Day, Suleiman, Tahiti)

Chaldee (1978, Banner Sport—Gevar, by Right of Way). 13 foals, 8 starters, 7 winners, 6 stakes winners, (Potrichal [Arg], Potridee [Arg], Potrinner [Arg], Potrizaris [Arg], Potro Rex, Sun Banner)

Cocotte (1983, Troy—Gay Milly, by Mill Reef) 13 foals, 10 starters, 8 winners, 6 stakes winners, (Baraka [Ire], Briolette, Fine Motion, Glowing Ardour [GB], Peach Out of Reach [Ire], Pilsudski [Ire])

Confirm (1977, Proudest Roman—Spanked, by Cornish Prince). 17 foals, 16 starters, 11 winners, 6 stakes winners (Autumn Glitter, Confirmed Dancer, Hollycombe, Ron Bon, Saratoga Sizzle, Yolanda)

Dahlia (1970, *Vaguely Noble—Charming Alibi, by Honeys Alibi). 13 foals, 11 starters, 8 winners, 6 stakes winners (Dahar, Dahlia's Dreamer, Delegant, Llandaff, Rivlia, Wajd)

Doff the Derby (1981, Master Derby—Margarethen, by *Tulyar). 12 foals, 10 starters, 9 winners, 6 stakes winners (Generous, Imagine, Osumi Tycoon, Strawberry Roan [Ire], Wedding Bouquet [Ire], Windy Triple K.)

Dumka (1971, Kashmir II—Faizebad [Fr], by *Prince Taj). 8 foals, 8 starters, 7 winners, 6 stakes winners (Dafayna, Dalsaan, Dayzaan, Dolka [Ire], Dolpour, Doyoun)

Eterna (1954, Atabor—Eme, by Lord Wembley). 9 foals, 7 starters, 7 winners, 6 stakes winners (El Califa, *El Fakir, El Faraon, Envidiada [Arg], Esporazo, Eternelle)

Floral Victory (1962, Victoria Park—La Belle Rose, by Le Lavandou). 17 foals, 15 starters, 13 winners, 6 stakes winners (Floral Dancer, Happy Victory, Nonparrell, Northern Ballerina, Snow Blossom, Victego)

Fun House (1958, The Doge—Recess, by Count Fleet). 9 foals, 9 starters, 9 winners, 6 stakes winners (Court Ruling, Funny Cat, Fun Palace, Good Manners, King's Palace, Yes Sir)

Gran Corrida (1961, Prince d'Or—Gay Ega, by Gay Boy). 14 foals, 7 starters, 6 winners, 6 stakes winners (A Esperar, Galopon, Grandeza Real, Grandor Real, Gran Real, Real Corrida)

6 ***Green Valley II** (1967, *Val de Loir—Sly Pola, by Spy Song). 15 foals, 14 starters, 13 winners, 6 stakes winners (Ercolano, Green Dancer, Pink Valley, Sir Raleigh, Soviet Lad, Val Danseur)
Hasty Queen II (1963, One Count—Queen Hopeful, by Roman). 16 foals, 14 starters, 12 winners, 6 stakes winners (Fit to Fight, Hasty Cutie, Hasty Flyer, Hasty Tam, Michael Navonod, Playful Queen)
Height of Fashion (Fr) (1979, Bustino—Highclere [GB], by Queen's Hussar). 12 foals, 10 starters, 8 winners, 6 stakes winners (Alwasmi, Mukddaam, Nashwan, Nayef, Sarayir, Unfuwain)
Il Mondo (1968, Promised Land—Nunzi Nunzi, by *Endeavour II). 13 foals, 13 starters, 8 winners, 6 stakes winners (Balimondo, Craftysmypapa, Mondanza, Mondo Lea, Mondolu, Turnin Doe)
Imperatrice (1938, Caruso—Cinquepace, by Brown Bud). 16 foals, 13 starters, 10 winners, 6 stakes winners (Imperial Hill, Imperium, Scattered, Speedwell, Squared Away, Yemen)
Kazanlik (1960, Ommeyad—Rose Supreme, by Supreme Court). 13 foals, 10 starters, 8 winners, 6 stakes winners (Boabdil, Darling Bud, Frances Jordan, Gay George, *Lark Rise II, Orient Rose)
Lapel (1935, Apelle—Lampeto, by Tetratema). 9 foals, 9 starters, 9 winners, 6 stakes winners (Carlist, Cassock, Durante, Golden Spur, Red Carnation, Val d'Assa)
Loudrangle (1974, Quadrangle—Lady Known as Lou, by Nearctic). 9 foals, 7 starters, 7 winners, 6 stakes winners (Dancing With Wings, No Louder, Ruling Angel, Slew of Angels, Tiffany Tam, Tilt My Halo)
Missy Baba (1958, *My Babu—*Uvira II, by Umidwar). 14 foals, 12 starters, 12 winners, 6 stakes winners (Chokri, Dromba, Gay Missile, Master Bold, Raja Baba, Sauce Boat)
Modena (1983, Roberto—Mofida [GB], by Right Tack). 9 foals, 9 starters, 9 winners, 6 stakes winners, (Elmaamul, High Walden, Modern Day, Modernise, Modesta, Reams of Verse)
Nas-Mahal (1959, *Nasrullah—*Love Game, by Big Game). 12 foals, 11 starters, 9 winners, 6 stakes winners (Beja, Celine, Craelius, Epidaurus, Tell, Turkish Trousers)
No Class (1974, Nodouble—Classy Quillo, by Outing Class). 8 foals, 7 starters, 7 winners, 6 stakes winners (Always a Classic, Classic Reign, Classy 'n Smart, Grey Classic, Regal Classic, Sky Classic)
No No Danielle (1980, Agitate—Go Miss Go, by Ready Say Go). 15 foals, 11 starters, 11 winners, 6 stakes winners, (Findaway, Gregg's Command, Mikdun D, Queena Corrina, Rockchalk Jayhawk, Toll Booth Willie)
Patsy Dru (1959, Alorter—Patsy, by Escadru). 17 foals, 17 starters, 15 winners, 6 stakes winners (Astaconda, Great Commander, Levant, Patsy's Reign, Prom Crasher, Shotgun Pat)
Phase (1939, Windsor Lad—Lost Soul, by Solario). 14 foals, 12 starters, 9 winners, 6 stakes winners (Narrator, Neasham Belle, Netherton Maid, None Nicer, No Pretender, Setting Star)
Picture Light (1954, *Court Martial—Queen of Light, by Borealis). 13 foals, 11 starters, 9 winners, 6 stakes winners (Dazzling Light, Father Christmas, Illuminous, Miss Pinkie, Photo Flash, Welsh Pageant)

6 **Polite Society** (1952, War Admiral—Doggin' It, by *Bull Dog). 12 foals, 12 starters, 12 winners, 6 stakes winners (Big Brigade, Blue Society, La Gentillesse, Long Position, Montjuich, Rising Market)
Proflare (1984, Mr. Prospector—Flare Pass, by Buckpasser). 12 foals, 11 starters, 10 winners, 6 stakes winners, (Apple of Kent, Capital Secret, River Flare, Set Alight, True Flare, War Zone)
***Queen's Statute** (1954, Le Lavandou—Statute, by Son-in-Law). 14 foals, 13 starters, 13 winners, 6 stakes winners (Court Royal, Dance Act, Down North, Epic Queen, Menedict, North of the Law)
Radiant Light (1953, Sayajirao—Wakening Light, by Eight Thirty). 13 foals, 8 starters, 7 winners, 6 stakes winners (Grand Slam, Mairona [Chi], Mediatore, Metapio, Morgan, *Morgana II)
Ripeck (1959, *Ribot—Kyak, by Big Game). 10 foals, 10 starters, 8 winners, 6 stakes winners (Anchor, Balinger, Bireme, Buoy, Fluke, *Kedge)
Stafaralla (1935, Solario—Mirawala, by Phalaris). 14 foals, 8 starters, 7 winners, 6 stakes winners (Anwar, Inshalla, Iran, Kerman, *Norooz, Tehran)
Sun Princess (1937, Solario—Mumtaz Begum, by *Blenheim II). 13 foals, 11 starters, 9 winners, 6 stakes winners (Alassio, *Flaneur II, Lucky Bag, *Royal Charger, Royal Justice, Tessa Gillian)
Tata (1938, Tresiete—Tacana, by Leteo). 6 foals, 6 starters, 6 winners, 6 stakes winners (Taia, Taimado, Taitao, Talon, Tatai, Tolpan)
Theresina (1927, Diophon—Teresina, by Tracery). 13 foals, 10 starters, 8 winners, 6 stakes winners (*Benane, Byculla, Eboo, *Nemrod, Tambara, Turkhan)
Tokamura (1940, Navarro—Tofanella, by Apelle). 16 foals, 13 starters, 12 winners, 6 stakes winners (Tanaka, Theodorica, Titano, Tommaso Da Modena, *Tommaso Guidi, *Toulouse Lautrec)
Urban Sea (1989, Miswaki—Allegretta [GB], by Lombard). 9 foals, 6 starters, 6 winners, 6 stakes winners, (All Too Beautiful [Ire], Black Sam Bellamy, Galileo [Ire], Melikah [Ire], My Typhoon [Ire], Urban Ocean)
Vera Me (1979, Polar Night—Vera Jae, by Gaylord's Feather). 13 foals, 13 starters, 11 winners, 6 stakes winners (Amazonpassage, Heatherforyou, Jessica Jae, Mebazaar, Polar Barron, Steaksonme)
Verdura (1948, *Court Martial—Bura, by *Bahram). 12 foals, 11 starters, 11 winners, 6 stakes winners (Avon's Pride, Gratitude, Heathen, Highest Hopes, Patroness, Pharsalia)
Yakima Swinger (1974, Canadian Gil—Eternal Heeler, by Heeler). 12 foals, 11 starters, 11 winners, 6 stakes winners (Bucks for Bob, Hat Rock, Lyon Swinger, Rock On Merit, Sarajevo Merit, Slightly Sinister)
Zanzara (1951, Fairey Fulmar—Sunright, by Solario). 17 foals, 14 starters, 13 winners, 6 stakes winners (Duke Ellington, Enrico, Enticement, Farfalla, Matatina, Showdown)

Most Foals for a Broodmare
(1930-2005)

Broodmare, YOB, Pedigree	Fls.	Strs.	Wnrs.	Wins	Earnings
***Betsy Ross II** (1939, *Mahmoud—*Celerina, by *Teddy)	**23**	19	13	44	$152,943
Day Line (1963, *Day Court—Fast Line, by Mr. Busher)	**21**	17	14	42	421,940
Alanette (1962, Alarullah—Jaconet, by *Jacopo)	**20**	18	9	33	128,897
Battle Creek Girl (1977, His Majesty—Far Beyond, by Nijinsky II)	**20**	17	15	80	4,255,073
Bold Bikini (1969, Boldnesian—Ran-Tan, by Summer Tan)	**20**	14	12	37	974,619
Bright Festive (1966, Festive—Bright Cirrus, by Solferino)	**20**	1	0	0	0
Capulet (1977, Gallant Romeo—Indaba, by Sir Gaylord)	**20**	16	10	55	594,709
Cequillo (1956, *Princequillo—Boldness, by *Mahmoud)	**20**	18	14	81	1,031,646
Feather Bed (1961, Johns Joy—Silly Sara, by *Rustom Sirdar)	**20**	17	13	60	305,357
Jettapart (1979, Tri Jet—Annulment, by Manifesto)	**20**	15	12	71	986,420
Such 'n Such (1974, Ack Ack—Long Stemmed Rose, by Jacinto)	**20**	16	11	46	735,875
Tie a Bow (1979, Dance Spell—Bold Bikini, by Boldnesian)	**20**	14	8	34	457,515
Wayward Miss (1936, Brumeux —Miss Contrary, by Cannobie)	**20**	16	4	26	12,805
Wind in Her Sails (1972, Mr. Leader—Bunch of Daisies, by Sir Gaylord)	**20**	13	12	44	375,991
Wisp O'Will (1964, New Policy—Miss Willow, by Oil Capitol)	**20**	16	14	70	894,640

Steeplechase performances are not included in statistics

Most Consecutive Foals for a Broodmare
(1930-2005)

Broodmare, YOB, Pedigree	Foals	Consecutive Foals
Bold Bikini (1969, Boldnesian—Ran-Tan, by Summer Tan)	20	**19**
Photo Flash (1965, *Match II—Picture Light, by *Court Martial)	19	**19**
Sarasail (1966, Hitting Away—*Sail Riona, by *Royal Charger)	19	**19**
Such 'n Such (1974, Ack Ack—Long Stemmed Rose, by Jacinto)	20	**19**
Gallant Lady (1930, *Sir Gallahad III—*Peroration, by Clarissimus)	18	**18**
Maxencia (Fr) (1977, Tennyson—Matuschka, by *Orsini II)	18	**18**
So What (1978, Iron Ruler—Merry Mama, by Prince John)	17	**18**
Trinity (1978, Logical—Trinidad, by Make Tracks)	18	**18**
Whitewood (1960, *Worden—Solarist, by Supreme Court)	18	**18**

Most Wins by Broodmare's Offspring
(1930-2005)

Broodmare, YOB, Sire—Dam	Foals	Starters	Winners	Starts	Wins	Earnings
Slow and Easy (1922, Colin—*Shyness)	15	14	11	962	**182**	$287,417
***Adorable II** (1925, Sardanapale—Incredule)	15	13	12	1,175	**181**	164,936
Cotton Candy (1945, Stimulus—Sugar Bird)	13	12	12	1,109	**178**	359,502
Transit (1926, *Chicle—*Traverse)	10	10	10	1,169	**178**	308,632
***Clonaslee** (1922, Orpiment—Bullet Proof)	18	17	16	1,170	**176**	258,219
Sag Rock (1930, Rock Man—Atomin)	13	12	11	981	**170**	237,689
Dame Mariechen (1931, High Time—Carrie Hogan)	14	14	14	1,149	**167**	254,771
Pevensea (1935, Enoch—Truly Movin)	13	13	13	1,177	**166**	167,298
Lady Excellent (1932, Nocturnal—Falco)	14	13	12	1,180	**165**	185,899
Ginogret (1941, *Gino—Sunlygret)	12	12	12	982	**164**	223,038
Alondra (1947, War Admiral—Lady Lark)	17	17	15	1,173	**163**	496,993
Doggerel (1935, *Bull Dog—Shenanigan)	10	9	9	1,113	**163**	200,484
Jemima Lee (1929, General Lee—Miss Jemima)	15	15	14	860	**163**	219,609
Sassaby (1931, Broomstick—Saucy Sue)	9	9	9	1,112	**163**	321,217
Agnes Ayres (1923, King James—Sweet Mary)	15	14	12	1,201	**161**	364,151
Lady Floyd (1924, Sir Martin—Fruit Cake)	13	11	10	1,015	**159**	151,435
Much Ado (1921, Ed Crump)	14	13	13	1,026	**159**	93,168
Vanrose (1920, Vandergrift)	13	10	9	993	**159**	123,744
Blame (1921, *Wrack—Censure)	11	10	9	1,153	**157**	132,321
Balking (1935, Balko—Bodega)	11	11	10	853	**156**	426,263
***Miss Turley** (1924, Bachelor's Jap—Raftonia)	12	12	11	967	**154**	74,273
New Melody (1952, Bimelech—Melodious)	13	13	13	961	**154**	688,387
Mary Kelly (1926, Ormondale—Starina)	14	14	13	1,097	**153**	136,548
Kind Annie (1938, Brilliant—*Chaucer Girl)	12	11	10	992	**152**	273,962
Daunt (1925, Lucullite—Dauntless)	13	13	13	817	**151**	230,505
Knightess (1929, *Bright Knight—Markiluna)	13	13	10	1,005	**151**	175,222
Lucy T. (1933, Whichone—*Refugee III)	13	11	9	1,092	**151**	254,071
Cariboo Lass (1928, *Marcus—Mary Fuller)	13	12	11	1,115	**150**	126,034
Softie (1943, Flares—Sicklefeather)	16	15	13	1,073	**150**	338,172
***Flamante** (1926, Flamboyant—*Flaminia)	11	10	10	960	**149**	210,627
Maradadi (1930, Stimulus—Virginia L.)	18	18	13	1,065	**148**	428,469
Vinnie (1948, Vincentive—Glorious Time)	15	14	11	851	**148**	422,519
Accra (1941, Annapolis—Ladala)	11	11	10	646	**146**	1,632,463
Happy Factor (1941, Benefactor—Miss Jemima)	13	10	10	940	**146**	337,080
Lady Gallivant (1922, *Hourless—*Lady's Gauntlet)	11	10	10	1,049	**146**	148,508
Hastily Yours (1936, John P. Grier—*Hastily)	14	12	11	1,080	**145**	692,799
Mintairy (1927, Mint Briar—*Airy Fairy)	10	10	10	776	**145**	195,913
Panoramic (1932, Chance Shot—Dustwhirl)	11	11	11	975	**144**	686,387
Pennant Girl (1929, *Rire Aux Larmes—Flying Pennant)	14	14	10	848	**144**	254,551
Royalite (1922, Lucullite—Royal Ensign)	9	8	8	853	**144**	122,635
***Valdina Spirea** (1940, Canon Law—*Spiraea II)	14	14	13	1,157	**143**	413,361
Cushion (1917, Nonpareil—Hassock)	12	9	9	617	**142**	140,109
Predicament (1929, *Waygood—Precipitate)	15	13	13	1,024	**142**	184,201
Brown Maiden (1933, Brown Bud—Tailor Maid)	10	10	10	1,165	**140**	202,886
Miss Velocity (1957, Spy Song—Fairy Dancer)	18	17	17	1,174	**140**	560,219
Scuttle (1928, Whiskaway—Sea Tale)	11	11	11	927	**140**	199,437
Glacial (1926, *Hourless—*Snowcapt)	15	15	13	1,093	**139**	199,418
Sis Tartan (1947, Port au Prince—Tartan Betsy)	10	10	9	824	**139**	343,586
Sly Marie (1962, Neptune—*Marie Lou)	12	12	11	911	**139**	523,325
Greedy Girl (1926, *Vulcain—Grasp)	12	10	10	817	**137**	196,899
***Legend of the Lake** (1929, Dark Legend—Narrow Water)	10	10	7	766	**137**	105,120
Nancy Clay (1923, *Wrack—Nancy Lee)	14	12	11	854	**137**	163,667
Baffling Miss (1927, Baffling—Miss Merle)	4	4	4	764	**136**	86,250
Dog Show (1940, *Bull Dog—Pomp and Glory)	16	15	15	892	**136**	361,952
Annabell Lee (1926, *Volta—Compose)	12	11	11	774	**135**	288,719
May Morning (1935, Pompey—Howdy)	9	9	9	1,087	**135**	227,415
Nortell (1955, El Mono—Control Board)	12	12	12	864	**135**	477,660

Most Winners for a Broodmare
(1930-2005)

Broodmare, YOB, Sire—Dam	Foals	Starters	Winners	SWs	Earnings
Dear Guinevere (1977, Fearless Knight—Brave and Free)	19	18	**17**	1	$1,594,412
***Mindrum Maid** (1939, *Mahmoud—Imp)	17	17	**17**	0	149,615
Miss Velocity (1957, Spy Song—Fairy Dancer)	18	17	**17**	0	560,219
Arizona Jubilee (1964, Spotted Moon—The Frog Hook)	19	17	**16**	1	271,893
***Clonaslee** (1922, Orpiment—Bullet Proof)	18	17	**16**	1	258,219
Lady Ambassador (1959, Hill Prince—Your Hostess)	17	17	**16**	1	880,817
Northern Beauty (1955, Borealis—Fleeting Beauty)	18	15	**16**	2	260,119
Pia Mia (1968, Pia Star—Surprise Lady)	18	18	**16**	3	933,832
Sable Lady (1927, *Waygood—Kolinsky)	17	17	**16**	0	180,004
Admittance (1946, Maeda—Stitches)	15	15	**15**	0	208,098
Alondra (1947, War Admiral—Lady Lark)	17	17	**15**	2	496,993
Amazer (1967, Mincio—*Alzara)	17	17	**15**	2	1,916,353
Battle Creek Girl (1977, His Majesty—Far Beyond)	20	17	**15**	6	4,255,073
Blinking Owl (1938, *Pharamond II—Baba Kenny)	19	16	**15**	0	195,196
Bold Essence (1977, Native Charger—Cologne)	16	16	**15**	1	1,048,236
Bold Pythian (1975, Bold Reason—Pythian)	18	18	**15**	0	589,322
Bonnie Blade (1976, Blade—Promised Princess)	16	16	**15**	1	1,053,597
Cherry Lady (1973, Bold Lad—Cherry Fool)	16	15	**15**	1	773,746
Courtly Dee (1968, Never Bend—Tulle)	18	17	**15**	8	3,446,275
Dancing Liz (1972, Northern Dancer—Crimson Queen)	16	16	**15**	1	1,215,005
Day and a Half (1972, Time Tested—Jolly)	18	16	**15**	2	942,371
Dog Show (1940, *Bull Dog—Pomp and Glory)	16	15	**15**	1	361,952
Don't Honey Me (1977, Triple Bend—Honey Deb)	16	15	**15**	1	1,363,547
Godzilla (1972, Gyr—Gently)	15	15	**15**	2	4,353,027
Grecian Coin (1960, Royal Coinage—Greek Pillar)	17	15	**15**	0	787,886
Kaylem Ho (1978, Salem—Kay Ho)	16	15	**15**	3	2,211,113
Maxencia (Fr) (1977, Tennyson—Matuschka)	18	17	**15**	2	396,667
Mideau (1942, *Bull Dog—Wild Waters)	18	18	**15**	1	509,729
Miss Cotton (1962, Swoon's Son—Always Movin)	16	15	**15**	4	959,195
Newsun (1973, Penowa Rullah—Sunshine Bright)	16	16	**15**	2	1,273,538
Our Patty (1933, Brown Bud—Perjury)	17	15	**15**	0	141,309
Patsy Dru (1959, Alorter—Patsy)	17	17	**15**	6	459,604
Peace Please (1978, Hold Your Peace—Please Say Yes)	16	16	**15**	1	839,910
Pines Lady (1966, Pinebloom—Lady Peabody)	15	15	**15**	0	497,559
Poker's Errand (1974, Poker—Gallant Lesina)	18	17	**15**	1	621,568
Proof Enough (1969, Prove It—Theonia)	16	16	**15**	3	910,495
Ribbon Duster (1973, Dust Commander—First Ribbon)	17	16	**15**	1	596,754
Stepping High (1969, No Robbery—*Bebop II)	17	17	**15**	2	1,377,143
Sweet Tulle (1978, Tom Tulle—Little Divy)	17	17	**15**	0	281,628
Tattooed Miss (1960, Mark-Ye-Well—Mossy Number)	18	18	**15**	2	375,182
Tweentzel Pie (1966, Four-and-Twenty—Peachywillow)	16	16	**15**	2	633,905
Wolf Hands (1963, All Hands—Wolf Bait)	16	16	**15**	3	462,595

Most Starts by Broodmare's Offspring
(1930-2005)

Broodmare, YOB, Sire—Dam	Foals	Starters	Winners	Starts	Earnings
Our Patty (1933, Brown Bud—Perjury)	17	15	15	**1,275**	$141,309
Mrs. Burke (1923, *Berrilldon—Pinkie)	12	11	11	**1,248**	104,588
Admittance (1946, Maeda—Stitches)	15	15	15	**1,217**	208,098
Mica (1924, Fair Play—Malachite)	9	8	8	**1,215**	106,918
Tabset (1938, Upset Lad—McTab)	12	12	12	**1,212**	194,434
Agnes Ayres (1923, King James—Sweet Mary)	15	14	12	**1,201**	364,151
Lina Clark (1919, Delhi—Prism)	13	13	11	**1,187**	115,562
Lady Excellent (1932, Nocturnal—Falco)	14	13	12	**1,180**	185,899
Dark Victory (1929, *Traumer—Sun Vive)	11	11	10	**1,179**	213,242
Pevensea (1935, Enoch—Truly Movin)	13	13	13	**1,177**	167,298
***Adorable II** (1925, Sardanapale—Incredule)	15	13	12	**1,175**	164,936
Miss Velocity (1957, Spy Song—Fairy Dancer)	18	17	17	**1,174**	560,219
Alondra (1947, War Admiral—Lady Lark)	17	17	15	**1,173**	496,993
***Clonaslee** (1922, Orpiment—Bullet Proof)	18	17	16	**1,170**	258,219
Transit (1926, *Chicle—*Traverse)	10	10	10	**1,169**	308,632
Brown Maiden (1933, Brown Bud—Tailor Maid)	10	10	10	**1,165**	202,886
***Valdina Spirea** (1940, Canon Law—*Spiraea II)	14	14	13	**1,157**	413,361
Blame (1921, *Wrack—Censure)	11	10	9	**1,153**	132,321
Respite (1922, Hilarious—Lucinda)	13	12	9	**1,151**	134,844
Dame Mariechen (1931, High Time—Carrie Hogan)	14	14	14	**1,149**	254,771
Galful (1940, Hadagal—Armful)	16	16	13	**1,136**	183,184
Hurry Home (1921, *Omar Khayyam)	14	13	10	**1,128**	105,900
Happy Seas (1939, *Happy Argo—Golden Billows)	12	10	9	**1,120**	188,979

Oldest Broodmares to Produce a Winner

(1930-2005)

Broodmare, YOB, Pedigree	Foals	1st Winner	Age Foaled Last Winner
Miss Jubilee (1951, Cassis—Bacchante, by Questionnaire)	5	16	**31**
Sumpinextra (1952, Super Duper—Ariels Elite, by Ariel)	10	19	**30**
***Beleza II** (1974, Hill Rise—Be Le Masurier, by Controlling)	5	5	**29**
Faila Suit (1957, Faila—Follow Suit, by Revoked)	9	12	**28**

Oldest Broodmares to Produce a Stakes Winner

(1930-2005)

Broodmare, YOB, Pedigree	Fls.	1st SW	Age Foaled Last SW	Stakes Winner
Fantasy Miss (1975, Dumpty's Cutter—Caminar, by Last Round)	13	12	**26**	Fanteria
Mary's Fantasy (1973, Olympian King—Fantasy Dream, by Everett Jr.)	12	12	**26**	Perfect Fantasy
Beaconaire (1974, *Vaguely Noble—Ole Liz, by Double Jay)	14	6	**25**	Binya (Ger)
Brown Berry (1960, Mount Marcy—Brown Baby, by Phalanx)	19	8	**25**	Hours After
Conejo Bonita (1949, Trace Call—Downy Pillow, by Morvich)	10	25	**25**	Coneja's Con Man
Fairy Sprite (1953, Papa Redbird—Fairy Fleet, by Broadside)	11	15	**25**	Orphan Annye
Fire's Gem (1961, *Royal Gem II—Fire Fire Fire, by Attention)	13	22	**25**	Lassafras
Floral Victory (1962, Victoria Park—La Belle Rose, by Le Lavandou)	16	6	**25**	Floral Dancer
Green Finger (1958, Better Self—Flower Bed, by *Beau Pere)	17	12	**25**	Blandford Park
Heat of Holme (1970, *Noholme II—Heat Lamp, by Better Self)	18	4	**25**	Speed On Holme
Hill of Sheba (1964, Federal Hill—Sheba S., by Errard King)	13	17	**25**	Apart
Knightly Spritely (1975, Knightly Dawn—Craim Check, by Terrang)	17	11	**25**	Spritely Walker
Little Blush (1968, *Day Court—Beaukiss, by *Mahmoud)	14	7	**25**	Cartofel
Melanie's Girl (1958, Nashua—*Nebroda, by Nearco)	14	8	**25**	Hagley's Relic
Phanatam (1941, Mokatam—Phantom Fairy, by *Negofol)	12	25	**25**	Jacks Again
Sooni (1970, Buckpasser—Missy Baba, by *My Babu)	16	20	**25**	Black Cash
***Uvira II** (1938, Umidwar—Lady Lawless, by Son-in-Law)	13	6	**25**	Francis U.

Most Millionaires Produced by a Broodmare

No. Millionaires	Broodmare, YOB, Sex, Pedigree	Millionaires
5	**Dancing Key**, 1983 m., Nijinsky II—Key Partner, by Key to the Mint	Air Dublin ($3,401,386), Air Gang Star ($1,260,218), Dance in the Dark ($3,459,758), Dance in the Mood (Jpn) ($2,931,889), Dance Partner (Jpn) ($5,973,652)
	Miyabi Sakurako, 1989 m., Northern Taste—Dyna Freeway, by Dictus	Freeway Heart ($1,114,742), King of Sunday ($1,177,838), Royal Cancer ($1,502,256), Win Duel ($1,272,018), Win Marvelous ($1,151,464)
4	**Millracer**, 1983 m., *Le Fabuleux—Marston's Mill, by In Reality	Agnes Special ($1,083,054), Fuji Kiseki ($1,319,239), Shinin' Racer ($1,915,140), Super License ($1,214,916)
3	**Antique Value**, 1979 m., Northern Dancer—Moonscape, by Tom Fool	Maquereau ($1,245,865), NewsValue ($1,246,690), Vega ($2,105,918)
	Brilliant Very, 1990 m., Northern Taste—Crafty Wife, by Crafty Prospector	Company ($1,423,637), Leningrad ($1,305,376), New Very ($1,748,207)
	Certain Secret (GB), 1985 m., Known Fact—Freeze the Secret, by Nearctic	Kurofune Mystery ($1,009,342), Taiki Enigma($1,069,597), Taiki Python ($1,232,186)
	Croupier Lady, 1983 m., What Luck—Question d'Argent, by Tentam	Croupier Star ($1,257,929), Genuine ($5,455,575), What a Reason ($1,074,212)
	Daring Danzig, 1990 m., Danzig—Impetuous Gal, by Briartic	Ecton Park ($1,503,825), Daring Heart ($1,039,761), Pit Fighter ($2,024,282)
	Eileen's Moment, 1982 m., For The Moment—Sailaway, by *Hawaii	Agnes Arashi ($1,108,588), Agnes Partner ($1,011,810), Lil E. Tee ($1,437,506)
	First Act, 1986 m., Sadler's Wells—Arkadina, by *Ribot	Heavenly Romance ($1,607,574), Mr Big Ben ($1,027,220), Reportage ($1,258,839)
	Happy Trails, 1984 m., Posse—Roycon (GB), by High Top	Happy Path ($2,117,320), Shinko Lovely (4,596,546), Taiki Marshal ($1,910,894)
	Hasili (Ire), 1991 m., Kahyasi —Kerali, by High Line	Banks Hill (GB) ($1,824,008), Heat Haze (GB) ($1,183,696), Intercontinental (GB) ($2,052,463)
	Legacy of Strength, 1982 m., Affirmed—Katonka, by Minnesota Mac	Legacy of Zelda ($1,256,666), Silent Happiness ($1,870,725), Stinger (Jpn) ($3,467,289)
	National Flag, 1986 m., Dictus—Dyna World, by Huntercombe	Daiwa Geant ($1,117,364), Inter Flag ($2,498,883), Maruka Komachi ($1,672,369)
	Northern Sunset (Ire), 1977 m., Northfields—Moss Greine, by *Ballymoss	L'Carriere ($1,726,175), Salem Drive ($1,046,065), St. Jovite ($1,604,439)
	Powerful Lady, 1981 m., Maruzensky—Roch Tesco, by Tesco Boy	Marubutsu Powerful ($1,100,278), Royal Touch ($2,795,933), Winning Ticket ($3,359,368)
	Rosa Nay, 1988 m., Lyphard—Riviere Doree, by Secretariat	Rosado ($3,686,146), Rose Colour ($1,044,385), Vita Rosa ($1,541,127)
	Scarlet Bouquet, 1988 m., Northern Taste—Scarlet Ink, by Crimson Satan	Daiwa Major ($1,447,648), Daiwa Rouge ($1,097,647), Glorious Sunday ($1,069,293)
	Star Ballerina, 1990 m., Risen Star—Berliani, by Nureyev	En Dehors ($2,038,759), Grand Pas de Deux ($1,084,664), Spartacus ($1,128,399)
	Vega, 1990 m., Tony Bin—Antique Value, by Northern Dancer	Admire Boss ($1,101,340), Admire Don ($7,566,441), Admire Vega ($2,466,038)

AUCTIONS

History of Thoroughbred Auctions

By far the oldest brand name in Thoroughbred racing is Tattersalls, the English auction company founded by the eponymous Richard Tattersall at London's Hyde Park Corner in 1766. Tattersalls (the appropriate apostrophe was lost at some point in its history) remains the pre-eminent European auction house and has served as the model for Thoroughbred sales companies throughout the world.

Richard Tattersall expanded his position as the leading seller of Thoroughbreds by providing a dining room for Jockey Club members, and his descendants (who remained in charge of the company for more than 200 years) transferred its headquarters to Newmarket in 1870.

The first American to attempt to emulate Tattersalls's success was English-educated William Easton, who served as Tattersalls's American representative for the last quarter of the 19th century and in 1879 established his own company, the American Horse Exchange, which he later merged with Tattersalls of New York. Easton was the auctioneer at the famous dispersal of August Belmont I's breeding stock in 1891, when Charles Reed made the first $100,000 bid at auction to acquire leading sire *St. Blaise.

Several competitors for Easton's company emerged in the 1890s, principally Powers-Hunter and the Fasig Co. William B. Fasig began auctioneering in his native Cleveland in the early 1890s, and Easton soon invited him to join Tattersalls. The English company chose to sell its American division after the financial panic of 1893, and Fasig took control. In 1898, he took on a partner, Edward A. Tipton, giving the company its now-familiar name, Fasig-Tipton.

Fasig's assistant Enoch J. Tranter took control of the company when Fasig abandoned ship after another panic in 1907, and Tranter established the Saratoga yearling sale in '17. Saratoga has remained the backbone of Fasig-Tipton ever since, through the stewardship of Humphrey S. Finney, his son John M. S. Finney, and the current management led by D. G. Van Clief Jr.

The commercial breeding industry began in both England and the U.S. around the middle of the 19th century. William Blenkiron's Middle Park Stud was the first famously successful commercial breeding operation in England, sending a long succession of high-priced horses to the annual Tattersalls October yearling sale.

Robert A.S.C. Alexander was the key figure in establishing Thoroughbred breeding as a viable commercial endeavor in the U.S. through the foundation of his Woodburn Stud near Lexington in the 1850s. Though hampered by the Civil War, Woodburn held annual yearling sales at the Kentucky farm until 1890. Those sales drew buyers from all over the U.S., and its success—plus the presence of 16-time leading sire Lexington at Woodburn—effectively concentrated the breeding industry in the Bluegrass.

Several small sales companies sprung up in Kentucky over the decades but died just as quickly, primarily because most buyers were in the East. Once Woodburn's star faded, they rarely could be enticed to Kentucky to buy horses. Petroleum rationing during World War II prevented Kentucky breeders from shipping their horses to Saratoga in 1943, however, and Fasig-Tipton agreed to hold a sale in a tent on the grounds of Keeneland Race Course in Lexington. That sale included eventual 1945 Kentucky Derby winner Hoop, Jr.

Kentucky breeders liked the idea so much that by the next year they had formed their own cooperative company, Breeders' Sales Co., and purchased Fasig-Tipton's Lexington sales pavilion, which was dismantled and reconstructed at Keeneland. Breeders' Sales Co. merged with Keeneland in 1962 to become the sales division of the Keeneland Association.

Benefiting from the worldwide success of American-breds over the last 50 years, Keeneland has become the world's largest and most successful sales company. Keeneland sold the first $100,000 yearling, $130,000 Swapson in 1961; the first $1-million yearling, Canadian Bound at $1.5-million in '76; and the world-record-priced yearling, Seattle Dancer, at $13.1-million in '85.

Fasig-Tipton re-established itself in Kentucky in the 1970s, selling three Kentucky Derby (G1) winners in five years, including Triple Crown winner Seattle Slew, but its strategy differs from Keeneland's. While Keeneland's sales are based almost exclusively at its facility in Lexington, Fasig-Tipton spreads a wider net with sales at six locations in five states, often serving regional markets as well as national ones.

As the breeding industry has grown, regional markets have also begun to support their own sales organizations, most notably Ocala Breeders' Sales Co. in Florida. OBSC, founded in 1974, grew out of the two-year-old sales industry that began in the late 1950s when one of the first Florida breeders, Carl Rose, started selling his two-year-olds to trainers at Hialeah Park.

In the late 1980s, Barretts Equine Ltd. was formed to build a sales pavilion and to conduct sales on the Los Angeles County Fair Grounds in Pomona. Barretts's two-year-old sales were particularly successful when Japanese buyers were active in the market in the early 1990s.

—*John P. Sparkman*

Auction Review of 2005

North America's Thoroughbred auction market climbed over the $1-billion mark for the second consecutive year, to a record $1,138,751,345 in 2005. That auction total surpassed the previous record of $1,091,872,249 set in 2000, the year before the double whammy of the September 11 terrorist attacks and mare reproductive loss syndrome threw the industry into a two-year recession.

All North American Thoroughbred Sales

Year	No. Sold (Chg)	Total Sales (Chg)	Average (Chg)
2005	20,739 (2.7%)	**$1,138,751,345** (8.0%)	**$54,909** (5.2%)
2004	20,196 (11.0%)	1,054,384,913 (23.3%)	52,207 (15.5%)
2003	18,916 (2.8%)	855,123,171 (11.5%)	45,206 (8.4%)
2002	18,397 (–4.1%)	767,048,402 (–9.4%)	41,694 (–5.5%)
2001	19,191 (–9.6%)	846,478,571 (–22.5%)	44,108 (–14.3%)
2000	**21,225** (5.5%)	1,091,872,249 (9.0%)	51,443 (3.3%)
1999	20,117 (2.4%)	1,001,718,775 (20.9%)	49,795 (18.1%)
1998	19,653 (5.1%)	828,664,233 (18.3%)	42,165 (12.6%)
1997	18,698 (–0.9%)	700,362,250 (12.8%)	37,457 (13.9%)
1996	18,871 (1.9%)	620,712,382 (17.9%)	32,892 (15.7%)
1995	18,518 (3.0%)	526,647,938 (17.4%)	28,440 (13.9%)
1994	17,972 (8.2%)	448,685,293 (23.1%)	24,966 (13.7%)
1993	16,605 (–5.0%)	364,519,425 (4.5%)	21,952 (9.9%)
1992	17,471 (–7.9%)	348,939,344 (–13.0%)	19,972 (–5.5%)
1991	18,977 (–10.3%)	401,102,091 (–19.8%)	21,136 (–10.6%)
1990	21,153 (–1.7%)	500,167,261 (–12.8%)	23,645 (–11.3%)

Highest figures in boldface.

The auction year began with mixed results at sales of two-year-olds in training, but in the end strong support of middle-market juvenile sales outweighed a slight weakness in the upper echelons. The two-year-old auction season ended with the largest percentage increase in total proceeds of any market segment, 11.4%, and a record $190.9-million spent.

With the Keeneland July sale of selected yearlings again canceled, the yearling sales season began at the Fasig-Tipton Kentucky selected yearling sale with a dip in both total proceeds and average. However, strong demand at the biggest-ever Keeneland September yearling sale produced total proceeds of $384-million, the most for any Thoroughbred auction in history.

September's record assured that the Keeneland November breeding stock sale also would surpass 2004 figures, though it failed to menace the record total set in 1999.

Sheikh Mohammed bin Rashid al Maktoum of Dubai and Ireland-based Coolmore Stud and partners once again dominated most segments of the marketplace, with Sheikh Mohammed setting Keeneland September and Keeneland November individual records of $9.7-million for a Storm Cat colt and $9-million for champion Ashado, respectively. American wine impresario Jess Jackson led resurgent American buyers.

Yearlings

The yearling market soared to record levels in 2005 and at last surpassed most records set at the previous market peak in 2000. The highlights were:

- Record 13,786 horses offered, surpassing the previous record set in 2001;
- Record 10,130 sold (up 7.5% from '04), 603 more than the previous record set in '00;
- Record total proceeds of $554,105,373 (up 11.5%), surpassing the previous record set in '00;
- Record average of $54,699 (up 3.7%), beating the previous record of $54,558 also set in '00;
- Record median of $13,082, 0.6% higher than the record set in '04; and
- Record 44 yearlings sold for $1-million or more.

Although not an all-time record, the $9.7-million Storm Cat yearling sold at the 2005 Keeneland September yearling sale was the third-highest-priced yearling of all time and a record for that sale.

North American Yearling Sales

Year	No. Sold (Chg)	Total Sales (Chg)	Average (Chg)
2005	**10,130** (7.5%)	**$554,105,373** (11.5%)	**$54,699** (3.7%)
2004	9,421 (6.9%)	496,937,672 (17.0%)	52,748 (9.4%)
2003	8,812 (–1.3%)	424,854,888 (8.5%)	48,213 (10%)
2002	8,928 (–1.7%)	391,472,126 (–17.3%)	43,848 (–15.9%)
2001	9,081 (–4.7%)	473,487,556 (–8.9%)	52,140 (–4.4%)
2000	9,527 (9.4%)	519,775,432 (18.2%)	54,558 (8.0%)
1999	8,705 (5.4%)	439,800,627 (24.2%)	50,523 (17.8%)
1998	8,260 (2.5%)	354,191,040 (15.1%)	42,880 (12.3%)
1997	8,057 (0.4%)	307,689,262 (11.0%)	38,189 (10.6%)
1996	8,026 (1.8%)	277,221,538 (13.9%)	34,540 (11.9%)
1995	7,882 (1.8%)	243,392,908 (15.6%)	30,880 (13.6%)
1994	7,744 (3.8%)	210,460,233 (12.4%)	27,177 (8.3%)
1993	7,460 (–6.0%)	187,232,894 (5.9%)	25,098 (12.6%)
1992	7,993 (–3.0%)	176,825,683 (–17.3%)	22,290 (–14.8%)
1991	8,179 (–8.5%)	213,940,466 (–20.3%)	26,157 (–12.9%)
1990	8,937 (–3.8%)	268,378,588 (–10.8%)	30,030 (–7.4%)

Highest figures in boldface.

With a record 4,510 yearlings on offer, the Keeneland September sale was the largest Thoroughbred auction in history, and that overwhelming supply combined with mixed results from previous 2005 yearling sales had raised some concerns that the overall market would suffer. No worries.

The market's two buying giants—Sheikh Mohammed, who generally buys through John Ferguson Bloodstock, and the Coolmore partnerships, represented by Demi O'Byrne—challenged each other repeatedly, with the Dubai ruler winning almost every duel, including the one for the year's most desirable yearling, a handsome, mature son of Storm Cat out of multiple Grade 1 winner Tranquility Lake, by Rahy, for $9.7-million. On the international yearling market, Ferguson signed for 67 yearlings totaling $57.2-million. He led that list for the sixth time in seven years and the tenth time in 15 years. O'Byrne ranked second in international buying with 58 purchases for $43.1-million.

Sheikh Mohammed was one of 132 buyers (compared with 122 in 2004) who spent $1-million or more in the international bloodstock market. The number of buyers who paid $1-million or more for an individual yearling, however, rose from 16 in 2004 to 20 in '05.

Almost all the gains in the market were due to the intense competition at the top of the market. Average price for the top 10% of the market—1,013 yearlings that sold for an average price of $346,928—rose 7%. The rest of the market was essentially level, with no other single decile climbing more than 2.8% in average.

North American Juvenile Sales

Year	No. Sold (Chg)	Total Sales (Chg)	Average (Chg)
2005	3,133 (7.7%)	**$190,882,771** (11.4%)	**$60,927** (3.4%)
2004	2,908 (–3.7%)	171,333,601 (23.0%)	58,918 (27.7%)
2003	3,019 (11.6%)	139,296,135 (8.1%)	46,140 (–3.1%)
2002	2,706 (0.0%)	128,870,834 (1.4%)	47,624 (1.4%)
2001	2,705 (–11.1%)	127,056,203 (–17.9%)	46,971 (–7.7%)
2000	3,043 (5.0%)	154,807,648 (0.1%)	50,873 (–4.7%)
1999	2,897 (–2.9%)	154,648,585 (13.4%)	53,382 (16.9%)
1998	2,985 (12.3%)	136,318,616 (12.9%)	45,668 (0.5%)
1997	2,657 (–0.8%)	120,694,031 (2.9%)	45,425 (14.1%)
1996	2,946 (–0.5%)	117,263,901 (23.9%)	39,804 (24.5%)
1995	2,961 (–0.2%)	94,666,095 (23.1%)	31,971 (23.3%)
1994	2,966 (–0.3%)	76,905,149 (26,7%)	25,929 (27.1%)
1993	2,976 (0.1%)	60,716,936 (7.8%)	20,402 (7.7%)
1992	2,974 (–16.1%)	56,349,005 (–12.0%)	18,947 (4.9%)
1991	3,546 (–5.4%)	64,026,814 (–16.3%)	18,056 (–11.5%)
1990	**3,750** (14.2%)	76,510,757 (49.1%)	20,403 (30.6%)

Highest figures in boldface.

That strong top combined with a steady middle market pulled median up slightly and helped to keep the buy-back rate relatively steady at 26.5%, compared with 25% in 2004.

The record Keeneland September yearling certainly helped, but the world's leading commercial sire, Storm Cat, was clearly more in demand than ever, perhaps helped along by Sheikh Mohammed's decision not to buy yearlings sired by stallions owned by Coolmore. The Overbrook Farm sire, then 22, averaged $1,763,750 for an impressive total of 28 yearlings sold. That was well ahead of his principal rivals in the commercial market, A.P. Indy and Kingmambo.

Coolmore's Rock of Gibraltar (Ire), Europe's 2002 Horse of the Year, led the international list of first-year sires of yearlings, with a remarkable 55 yearlings averaging $209,420. Came Home, with the highest initial stud fee among an uninspiring group of American first-year sires of yearlings, duly headed that list with 36 yearlings sold averaging $147,311, second only to Rock of Gibraltar internationally.

Overall, 48 international stallions carried averages of $100,000 or more, but two of those horses, Danehill and Machiavellian, are deceased.

Despite the gains in the yearling market, weanling-to-yearling pinhookers lost more than $4-million overall. Only 30% of pinhooked yearlings made a profit, compared with 35% the previous year, and 28% failed to sell through the auction ring, compared with 25% in 2004.

Taylor Made Sales Agency, largest of the large sales agencies that now dominate the market, set a record for total proceeds by a single consignor, selling 443 of 580 yearlings offered for $76,481,900. That record total included $60,997,400 at the Keeneland September sale, a record for a consignor at a single sale.

Two-Year-Olds

The market for two-year-olds in training broke just about every record on the books in 2004, and those huge advances created some wariness as the '05 juvenile auction season opened. Indeed, buy-back rates at sales of selected juveniles early in the year disturbed some consignors, but the powerful demand for Thoroughbred racehorses a few weeks or months from their first career starts pushed the overall market even higher. Some highlights:

- A total of 3,133 horses sold, up 7.7%;
- Record total proceeds of $190,882,771, up 11.4%;
- Record average price of $60,927, up 3.4%;
- Record median of $22,000, up 10%;
- Record top price of $5.2-million; but
- Buy-back rate rose from 26.2% to 31.4%.

Sheikh Mohammed purchased 2005's record-setter, a colt by Tale of the Cat, in the name of his Darley operation at the Fasig-Tipton Calder sale of selected two-year-olds. That purchase and seven other seven-figure sales pushed the juvenile market's bellwether sale to a record average and total proceeds, but heightened buyer selectivity meant that the sale's buy-back rate soared to 31.4%.

Despite the record top price and the record number of seven-figure horses, average price at the top 10% of the market actually declined slightly. Average prices for the 30% of horses just below the top soared by double-digit percentages, however, and average price rose at every other level of the market as well.

Storm Cat led all sires of two-year-olds in training, with his three juveniles averaging $649,907. Dual Breeders' Cup Classic (G1) winner and 2000 Horse of the Year Tiznow topped first-year sires of juveniles with 15 sold for an average of $179,067. Darley Stud Management led buyers, purchasing 15 horses for $13,615,708. The record colt helped to make the late Robert N. Scanlon, who sold 72 horses for $11,604,000, the leading consignor.

Weanlings

After a slightly down year in 2004, the weanling market posted impressive global numbers in '05. Some highlights:

- 1,820 weanlings sold, down 6.1%;

- Total proceeds rose 11.1% to $79,703,444, fourth highest on record;
- Average soared 18.3% to a record $43,793;
- Median held steady at $15,000; but
- Buy-back rate increased from 25.9% in 2004 to 28.8%.

With 2.2% fewer weanlings on offer in 2005, the law of supply and demand dictated that average price for weanlings would rise, and that indeed occurred, with prices at the very top of the market up a stunning 26.2%. Two weanlings, a colt by Unbridled's Song and a filly by Storm Cat, each sold for $1.7-million. The Japan Racing Horse Association's annual foal sale in Hokkaido in July produced the highest-priced weanling of the year, a $1,871,900 colt by Japanese champion Symboli Kris S.

North American Weanling Sales

Year	No. Sold (Chg)	Total Sales (Chg)	Average (Chg)
2005	1,820 (–6.1%)	$79,703,444 (11.1%)	**$43,793** (18.3%)
2004	1,938 (14.5%)	71,713,850 (5.7%)	37,004 (–7.7%)
2003	1,693 (8.7%)	67,866,478 (39.8%)	40,087 (28.6%)
2002	1,557 (–19.2%)	48,549,515 (–7.2%)	31,181 (14.9%)
2001	1,926 (–17.9%	52,288,439 (–37.6%)	27,149 (–24.0%)
2000	**2,345** (2.4%)	83,755,053 (–14.6%)	35,716 (–16.7%)
1999	2,289 (0.5%)	**98,087,172** (9.8%)	42,852 (9.3%)
1998	2,278 (9.0%)	89,303,995 (32.8%)	39,203 (21.8%)
1997	2,090 (–3.4%)	67,251,828 (10.1%)	32,178 (14.0%)
1996	2,164 (8.3%)	61,094,609 (17.0%)	28,232 (8.1%)
1995	1,999 (5.4%)	52,221,842 (26.2%)	26,124 (19.7%)
1994	1,896 (23.4%)	41,374,263 (14.2%)	21,822 (–7.5%)
1993	1,536 (2.3%)	36,233,360 (51.1%)	23,589 (47.8%)
1992	1,502 (4.8%)	23,974,936 (–17.9%)	15,962 (–21.7%)
1991	1,433 (–8.2%)	29,199,004 (2.8%)	20,376 (12.0%)
1990	1,561 (5.1%)	28,403,069 (–19.1%)	18,195 (–23.0%)

Highest figures in boldface.

BBA Ireland's 56 weanling purchases in Europe and North America totaled $3,192,041 to outpace Shadwell Estate Co.'s more modest addition of 11 weanlings for $2,884,426. Sheer numbers exerted a similar influence on the list of leading consignors, with leader Taylor Made Sales Agency selling 81 weanlings for $7,610,700.

Unbridled's Song led all sires of weanlings with seven horses sold for an average of $565,000. Vindication, champion two-year-old male of 2002, led first-year sires of weanlings with eight representatives averaging $398,832, and he also ranked second on the overall list.

Broodmares

Generally speaking, the market for broodmares and broodmare prospects is the segment most closely tied to the yearling trade. Obviously, the broodmare produces the yearlings, so it is logical that, when yearling prices go up, prices for broodmares are bound to follow, which occurred in 2005. Some highlights were:

Record price for a broodmare or broodmare prospect of $9-million;

- Record average of $57,597, up 3.4%;
- Median of $9,000, equal to 2004;
- Total proceeds of $308,602,769, up 3.5% and the second highest on record;
- 5,358 horses sold, down 0.1%; and
- Buy-back rate increased from 21.7% to 24.3%.

It is rare for a champion racemare fresh out of training to be offered at public auction, and when 2004 champion three-year-old filly Ashado was cataloged for the '05 Keeneland November breeding stock sale, it was obvious that she would challenge all previous records. When Sheikh Mohammed and Coolmore hooked up in a lengthy duel, the previous record set when Coolmore bought Cash Run for $7.1-million in 2003 was bound to fall. Coolmore's John Magnier dropped out when Sheikh Mohammed bid $9-million.

The rest of the Keeneland catalog did not glitter as brightly, however. The number of seven-figure broodmares sold in North America declined from a record 36 in 2004 to 31, but the top half of the market was strongest. Average price rose slightly for every decile above the median and fell slightly for every decile below the median.

North American Broodmare Sales

Year	No. Sold (Chg)	Total Sales (Chg)	Average (Chg)
2005	5,358 (0.1%)	$308,602,769 (3.5%)	**$57,597** (3.4%)
2004	5,354 (7.5%)	298,240,342 (37.0%)	55,704 (27.5%)
2003	4,983 (5.1%)	217,672,620 (13.3%)	43,683 (7.8%)
2002	4,741 (–6.3%)	192,082,219 (2.1%)	40,515 (9.0%)
2001	5,059 (–12.7%)	188,107,111 (–40.7%)	37,183 (–32.1%)
2000	**5,797** (3.9%)	**317,398,250** (6.4%)	54,752 (2.4%)
1999	5,582 (1.7%)	298,397,805 (24.4%)	53,457 (22.3%)
1998	5,489 (8.5%)	239,875,672 (25.1%)	43,701 (15.3%)
1997	5,058 (0.9%)	191,764,648 (22.7%)	37,913 (21.5%)
1996	5,011 (2.6%)	156,304,244 (24.2%)	31,192 (21.0%)
1995	4,883 (6.6%)	125,836,989 (12.8%)	25,770 (5.8%)
1994	4,579 (10.2%)	111,520,366 (46.9%)	24,355 (33.3%)
1993	4,154 (–2.8%)	75,910,215 (–1.4%)	18,274 (1.5%)
1992	4,274 (–9.4%)	76,970,720 (–7.3%)	18,009 (2.3%)
1991	4,718 (–11.9%)	83,053,742 (–19.6%)	17,604 (–8.7%)
1990	5,356 (–10.6%)	103,263,519 (–36.0%)	19,280 (–28.5%)

Highest figures in boldface.

Storm Cat again led the list of leading covering sires, with three in-foal mares averaging $2,116,667. Pleasantly Perfect, winner of the 2003 Breeders' Cup Classic (G1) and '04 Dubai World Cup (UAE-G1), led first-year covering sires with a $603,333 average for six in-foal mares sold.

Taylor Made Sales Agency led consignors, selling 318 horses for $66,462,300.

For the second consecutive year, Jackson was the biggest investor in breeding stock, buying 17 broodmares for $13.7-million in the name of Stonestreet Mares.

Keeneland was not the only venue for seven-figure mares. Fasig-Tipton's November sale had five seven-figure mares, topped by the $5-million Riskaverse, while the Tattersalls December mixed sale at Newmarket added six more, topped by Moments of Joy (in foal to Refuse To Bend [Ire]) at $2,976,261. —*John P. Sparkman*

Highest-Priced Yearlings of 2005

Horse	Consignor	Buyer	Sale	Price
C., by Storm Cat—Tranquility Lake	Mill Ridge Sales, agent for Martin J. Wygod	John Ferguson Bloodstock	Kee Sept.	$9,700,000
C., by Storm Cat—Secret Status	Lane's End, agent	John Ferguson Bloodstock	Kee Sept.	6,300,000
C., by Storm Cat—Tomisue's Delight	Lane's End, agent	Circle E Racing	Kee Sept.	3,900,000
F., by Storm Cat—Warrior Queen	Eaton Sales, agent	Demi O'Byrne	Kee Sept.	3,800,000
C., by Storm Cat—Serena's Song	Denali Stud, agent for Robert and Beverly Lewis	John Ferguson Bloodstock	Kee Sept.	3,500,000
C., by A.P. Indy—Sahara Gold	Lane's End, agent for Stonerside Stable	John Ferguson Bloodstock	Kee Sept.	3,400,000
C., by Storm Cat—Serena's Tune	Hill 'n' Dale Sales Agency, agent	Shadwell Estate Co. Ltd.	Kee Sept.	3,100,000
C., by Storm Cat—Rings a Chime	Taylor Made Sales Agency, agent	Demi O'Byrne	F-T Saratoga	3,100,000
C., by Storm Cat—Ajina	Taylor Made Sales Agency, agent	John Ferguson Bloodstock	Kee Sept.	3,000,000
F., by Mr. Greeley—Silvery Swan	Hill 'n' Dale Sales Agency, agent for Liberation Farm, Needham/Betz Thoroughbreds, et al.	Robert and Beverly Lewis	Kee Sept.	2,700,000
F., by Kingmambo—Escena	Denali Stud, agent for Falls Creek Farm	Live Oak Plantation	Kee Sept.	2,700,000
C., by A.P. Indy—Snow Forest	Lane's End, agent for Mt. Brilliant Farm	Demi O'Byrne	Kee Sept.	2,500,000
C., by Kingmambo—Last Second (Ire)	Kirtlington Stud	Gainsborough Stud Mgt.	Tatt Oct.	2,303,700
C., by A.P. Indy—Magicalmysterycat	Taylor Made Sales Agency, agent	John Ferguson Bloodstock	Kee Sept.	2,300,000
C., by Kingmambo—Karsavina (Ire)	Glenvale Stud	Shadwell Estate Co. Ltd.	Goffs Orby	2,276,883
C., by A.P. Indy—Call Me Fleet	Hill 'n' Dale Sales Agency, agent	Eugene N. Melnyk	Kee Sept.	2,000,000
F., by Fusaichi Pegasus—Collect Call	Taylor Made Sales Agency, agent	Stonestreet Stables LLC	F-T Saratoga	2,000,000
F., by A.P. Indy—Better Than Honour	Lane's End, agent	Demi O'Byrne	Kee Sept.	1,900,000
C., by Unbridled's Song—Escrow Agent	Winter Quarter Farm, agent	John Ferguson Bloodstock	Kee Sept.	1,700,000
F., by Storm Cat—Strawberry Reason	Taylor Made Sales Agency, agent for Payson Stud and Overbrook Farm	Circle E Racing	Kee Sept.	1,700,000
C., by Storm Cat—Simadartha	Taylor Made Sales Agency, agent	Demi O'Byrne	Kee Sept.	1,600,000
C., by Gone West—Santa Catalina	Gainesway, agent	B. Wayne Hughes	Kee Sept.	1,600,000
F., by Unbridled's Song—Golden Ballet	Taylor Made Sales Agency, agent	John Ferguson Bloodstock	Kee Sept.	1,600,000
F., by Montjeu (Ire)—Vallee des Reves	Marston Stud	Emerald Bloodstock	Tatt Oct.	1,520,442
C., by Giant's Causeway—Golden Attraction	Eaton Sales, agent for Overbrook Farm	Demi O'Byrne	Kee Sept.	1,500,000
F., by Storm Cat—La Affirmed	Eaton Sales, agent	Gasper Bloodstock, agent	Kee Sept.	1,500,000
F., by Kingmambo—Balistroika	Eaton Sales, agent	Gainsborough Stud Mgt.	Kee Sept.	1,500,000
C., by Unbridled's Song—Roll Over Baby	Taylor Made Sales Agency, agent for ClassicStar LLC	John Ferguson Bloodstock	Kee Sept.	1,500,000
C., by Galileo (Ire)—Zelda	Knocktoran Stud	Nobutaka Tada	Tatt Oct.	1,474,368
F., by Danehill—Hidden Storm	Castleton Lyons, agent	Demi O'Byrne	Kee Sept.	1,450,000
C., by Kingmambo—Words of War	Stone Farm, agent for Stone Farm and Stonerside Stable	John Ferguson Bloodstock	Kee Sept.	1,450,000
C., by Lemon Drop Kid—Myth to Reality (Fr)	Lane's End, agent	Gainsborough Stud Mgt.	Kee Sept.	1,400,000
C., by A.P. Indy—Key to My Heart	Darby Dan Farm, agent	Shadwell Estate Co. Ltd.	Kee Sept.	1,400,000
C., by Galileo (Ire)—Tadkiyra (Ire)	Croom House Stud	Demi O'Byrne	Goffs Orby	1,201,688
C., by Montjeu (Ire)—By Charter	Jamie Railton, agent	John Magnier	Tatt Oct.	1,151,850
F., by Storm Cat—Onaga	Taylor Made Sales Agency, agent	Shadwell Estate Co. Ltd.	Kee Sept.	1,100,000
F., by A.P. Indy—Banshee Winds	Taylor Made Sales Agency, agent for ClassicStar LLC	G & C Inc	Kee Sept.	1,100,000
F., by Storm Cat—Ruby Ransom	Mill Ridge Sales, agent	Brushwood Stable	Kee Sept.	1,100,000
C., by Distorted Humor—Weekend in Indy	Taylor Made Sales Agency, agent	Baden P. Chace, agent	Kee Sept.	1,100,000
C., by Fusaichi Pegasus—Lost the Code	Highclere Sales, agent	Circle E Racing	F-T Saratoga	1,100,000
C., by Giant's Causeway—Exchange Place	Eaton Sales, agent	Demi O'Byrne	F-T Saratoga	1,100,000
F., by Danehill—Jiving	Lynn Lodge Stud	Cheveley Stud	Tatt Oct.	1,059,702
C., by Montjeu (Ire)—Majinskaya	Ballylinch Stud	Demi O'Byrne	Tatt Oct.	1,050,487
F., by Sadler's Wells—Time Away	Jamie Railton, agent	Skara Glen Stables	Tatt Oct.	1,050,487
F., by Giant's Causeway—At the Half	Lane's End, agent	Demi O'Byrne	Kee Sept.	1,050,000
C., by Fusaichi Pegasus—Hishi Nile	Taylor Made Sales Agency, agent	Demi O'Byrne	Kee Sept.	1,050,000
F., by Danzig—Celtic Melody	Taylor Made Sales Agency, agent for ClassicStar LLC	B. Wayne Hughes	Kee Sept.	1,050,000
C., by Danehill—Sunset Cafe	Lodge Park Stud	Demi O'Byrne	Tatt Oct.	1,013,628
F., by Gone West—Candleinthedark	Greenfield Farm, agent	Robert Krembil	Kee Sept.	1,000,000
C., by Fusaichi Pegasus—Northern Hilite	Three Chimneys Sales, agent	John C. Oxley	Kee Sept.	1,000,000
C., by Giant's Causeway—Aquilegia	Middlebrook Farm, agent	Demi O'Byrne	Kee Sept.	1,000,000
C., by Unbridled's Song—Cruising Haven	Paramount Sales, agent for Gaines-Gentry Thoroughbreds	John Ferguson Bloodstock	Kee Sept.	1,000,000
C., by Forest Camp—Taegu	Brereton C. Jones, agent	Robert and Beverly Lewis	Kee Sept.	1,000,000
C., by Mr. Greeley—Dreams of Success	Denali Stud, agent	Demi O'Byrne	Kee Sept.	1,000,000
F., by Forestry—Shivering Six	Mulholland Springs	Stonestreet Stables LLC	Kee Sept.	975,000
F., by Danzig—Zoftig	Taylor Made Sales Agency, agent for ClassicStar LLC	Dale L. Romans, agent	Kee Sept.	950,000
C., by Giant's Causeway—Fitnah	Lane's End, agent	E. Paul Robsham	Kee Sept.	950,000
C., by Fusaichi Pegasus—Let	Lane's End, agent	Demi O'Byrne	Kee Sept.	950,000
C., by Dixieland Band—Skybox	Bluegrass Thoroughbred Services, agent for Mueller Farm	John Ferguson Bloodstock	Kee Sept.	950,000
C., by Unbridled's Song—Thiscatsforcaryl	Taylor Made Sales Agency, agent	Stonestreet Stables LLC	Kee Sept.	950,000
C., by Mr. Greeley—Hard Knocker	Gainesway, agent for Eldon Farm Equine	John Ferguson Bloodstock	F-T Saratoga	950,000

Highest-Priced Weanlings of 2005

Horse	Consignor	Buyer	Sale	Price
C., by Symboli Kris S—Must Be Loved	Northern Farm	Danox Co. Ltd.	Japan July	$1,871,940
C., by Unbridled's Song—Zing	Taylor Made Sales Agency, agent	Aaron and Marie Jones	Kee Nov.	1,700,000
F., by Storm Cat—Garden Secrets	Lane's End, agent	Courtlandt Farm	Kee Nov.	1,700,000
C., by Vindication—Roza Robata	Northern Farm	Danox Co Ltd.	Japan July	1,693,660
C., by Admire Vega —Fairy Doll	Northern Farm	Nobutaka Tada	Japan July	1,515,380
C., by Agnes Tachyon —Queen Maud (Ire)	Shadai Farm	Hiroyoshi Usuda	Japan July	1,337,100
C., by Agnes Tachyon —Biwa Heidi	Northern Farm	Riichi Kondo	Japan July	1,114,250
C., by Agnes Tachyon —Fanjica (Ire)	Shadai Farm	Takaya Shimakawa	Japan July	1,069,680
C., by Empire Maker—Ms. Strike Zone	Shadai Farm	Takaya Shimakawa	Japan July	891,400
F., by Sadler's Wells—Gift of the Night	Fittocks Stud	Demi O'Byrne	Tatt Dec.	847,783
C., by Agnes Tachyon —Whitewater Affair (GB)	Shadai Farm	Takaya Shimakawa	Japan July	802,260
C., by Fasliyev—Good Game	Northern Farm	RRA Co. Ltd.	Japan July	802,260
F., by Giant's Causeway—Castanea	Indian Creek (Dave C. Parrish Jr.), agent	Stonestreet Mares LLC	Kee Nov.	750,000
C., by Symboli Kris S—Smala (Fr)	Shadai Farm	Mizuki Noda	Japan July	722,034
C., by Fusaichi Pegasus—November Slew	Chiyoda Farm	Grandprix Co. Ltd.	Japan July	722,034
C., by Fusaichi Pegasus—No Knocks	Dunford Farm, agent	Tracy Farmer	Kee Nov.	685,000
C., by Unbridled's Song—Karait	Eaton Sales, agent	Summit Stables	Kee Nov.	675,000
C., by Jungle Pocket —Crafty Wife	Northern Farm	Takaya Shimakawa	Japan July	668,550
C., by War Emblem—Cecil Cut	Northern Farm	RRA Co. Ltd.	Japan July	632,894
C., by Agnes Tachyon —Tax Haven	Shadai Farm	Takao Watanabe	Japan July	632,894
C., by Brian's Time—Smile Tomorrow	Chiyoda Farm	Nobutaka Tada	Japan July	632,894
C., by Brian's Time—Stray Cat	Shiraoi Farm	Hidenori Yamaji	Japan July	623,980
C., by Elusive Quality—Mermaid's Tale	Taylor Made Sales Agency, agent	Eldon Farm Equine	Kee Nov.	620,000
C., by Agnes Tachyon —Hit the Spot	Northern Farm	Keizou Ooshiro	Japan July	606,152
C., by Falbrav (Ire)—Sun Spring (Arg)	Northern Farm	RRA Co. Ltd.	Japan July	606,152
C., by Silver Deputy—Tropical Blossom	Northern Farm	Makoto Kaneko	Japan July	588,324
C., by War Emblem—Gold Point	Shadai Farm	Grandprix Co. Ltd.	Japan July	588,324
C., by Seeking the Gold—Shires Ende	Horse Bank Ltd.	Makoto Kaneko	Japan July	588,324
C., by Langfuhr—Caught Out	Shadai Farm	Keizou Ooshiro	Japan July	579,410
C., by Symboli Kris S—J'Ai Deux Amours	Northern Farm	Takashi Suzuki	Japan July	579,410
C., by Dance in the Dark —Stars In Her Eyes (Ire)	Yano Bokujo	Koji Maeda	Japan July	570,496
C., by Symboli Kris S—Palatial Affaire	Chiyoda Farm	Gold Horse Club Co. Ltd.	Japan July	552,668
C., by Stravinsky—Cognac Lady	Northern Farm	Keizou Ooshiro	Japan July	543,754
C., by Galileo (Ire)—Vanishing River	Ballybin Stud	Badgers Bloodstock	Tatt Dec.	541,138
C., by Brian's Time—Name Value	Tobino Bokujo	Nobutaka Tada	Japan July	534,840
C., by Forestry—Majesty's Crown	Denali Stud, agent for Avalon Farms	Templeton Railton Farms	Kee Nov.	525,000
C., by Giant's Causeway—Indyfault	Taylor Made Sales Agency, agent for Bianca Francis Equine and Wycombe House Stud	J M H Stables	Kee Nov.	500,000
C., by Kurofune—Every Whisper	Northern Farm	Mizuki Noda	Japan July	499,184
C., by Symboli Kris S—Wrangler Queen	Shadai Farm	Keiichi Yamagishi	Japan July	490,270
C., by Aldebaran—Soaring Softly	Darby Dan Farm, agent	Blandford Bloodstock	Kee Nov.	485,000
C., by Pulpit—Mississippi Lights	Bluewater Sales, agent	Cumberland Bloodstock	Kee Nov.	480,000
C., by Unbridled's Song—Heavenly Cat	Viking Stud, agent for Twin Hopes Farm	US Stables	Kee Nov.	475,000
F., by Dynaformer—Hard to Copy	Taylor Made Sales Agency, agent for Norfields	Lael Stables	Kee Nov.	475,000
C., by Manhattan Cafe —Wren (Ire)	Shadai Farm	Hanzawa Co. Ltd.	Japan July	472,442
C., by Oasis Dream (GB)—Bourbonella (GB)	Voute Sales LLC, agent	Shadwell Estate Co. Ltd.	Tatt Dec.	468,986
C., by Special Week —Daiichi Flone	Shadai Farm	Hiroyoshi Usuda	Japan July	463,528
C., by Symboli Kris S—Cheerful	Northern Farm	Mizuki Noda	Japan July	463,528
C., by Giant's Causeway—Irresistible	Hatakeyama Stud Farm	Grandprix Co. Ltd.	Japan July	463,528
C., by Giant's Causeway—Happy Tune	Hunter Valley Farm, agent	Eaton Sales	Kee Nov.	460,000
C., by Fusaichi Pegasus—Squawk	Castleton Lyons, agent	BGH Ranch	Kee Nov.	460,000
C., by French Deputy—Ruby My Dear	Northern Farm	Makoto Kaneko	Japan July	454,614
F., by Symboli Kris S—Shinko Lovely (Ire)	Shinkoh Farm	Makoto Kaneko	Japan July	454,614
C., by Distorted Humor—Value Oriented	Highclere Sales, agent	WinStar Farm	Kee Nov.	450,000
C., by Brian's Time—Lady Margot	Excelmanagement	Danox Co Ltd.	Japan July	445,700
C., by Jungle Pocket —Sugar Angel	Northern Farm	RRA Co. Ltd.	Japan July	445,700
C., by Adjudicating—Orimitsu Kinen	Fujikawa Farm	Big Red Farm	Japan July	445,700
C., by Admire Vega —Neon Delite	Northern Farm	Masaru Shimada	Japan July	436,786
C., by Oasis Dream (GB)—Miss Honorine	Jockey Hall Stud, agent	John Ferguson Bloodstock	Tatt Dec.	432,910
C., by Oasis Dream (GB)—Grail	New England Stud	Paul Shanahan	Tatt Dec.	432,910
C., by Symboli Kris S—Time to Dance	Oiwake Farm	Takeshi Fujita	Japan July	427,872
C., by Manhattan Cafe —Fuenji	Shadai Farm	Takaya Shimakawa	Japan July	427,872
C., by Giant's Causeway—Tigresa	Three Chimneys Sales, agent	Toshihide Kiyota	Kee Nov.	425,000
C., by French Deputy—Fusaichi Oracle	Shadai Farm	Toru Okawa	Japan July	418,958
C., by War Emblem—Derobe	Northern Farm	Danox Co Ltd.	Japan July	418,958
C., by Manhattan Cafe —Sloane Street	Northern Farm	Makoto Kaneko	Japan July	410,044
F., by El Prado (Ire)—Glint in Her Eye	Brookdale Sales, agent for Brookdale	Katsumi Yoshida	Kee Nov.	410,000
C., by Agnes Tachyon —Pampered Star	Northern Farm	Bio Co., Ltd.	Japan July	401,130
C., by Symboli Kris S—Gaelic Tune	Symboli Stud	Nobutaka Tada	Japan July	401,130
C., by Vindication—Madame Thor	Hill 'n' Dale Sales Agency, agent	C F Farms	Kee Nov.	400,000

Highest-Priced Two-Year-Olds of 2005

Horse	Consignor	Buyer	Sale	Price
Ever Shifting, c., by Tale of the Cat—Carry All	Robert N. Scanlon, agent	Darley	F-T Calder	$5,200,000
Barbados, c., by Forestry—Rare Bird	Tony Bowling & Bobby Dodd, agent	Demi O'Byrne	F-T Calder	3,000,000
Wild Fit, f., by Wild Wonder—Grannies Feather	Eaton Sales, agent	Demi O'Byrne	F-T Ky Nov.	3,000,000
Rondo, c., by Grand Slam—Dama	Maurice W. Miller, agent	Darley	F-T Calder	2,900,000
What a Song, c., by Songandaprayer—What a Knight	Murray Smith, agent	Robert and Beverly Lewis	Barretts March	1,900,000
Close Secret, f., by Storm Cat—Turbo Launch	Hartley/De Renzo T'breds, agent	Demi O'Byrne	F-T Calder	1,500,000
Garibaldi, c., by Golden Missile—Ms. Copelan	Wavertree Stables, agent	Demi O'Byrne	F-T Calder	1,500,000
Colonial Note, c., by Exchange Rate—Raspberry Affair	Niall Brennan Stables, agent	Jeremy Noseda, agent	F-T Calder	1,050,000
Overland Trail, c., by Gone West—Heavenly Rhythm	Robert Harris, agent	Robert and Beverly Lewis	F-T Calder	1,000,000
Maltese Tiger, c., by Tiznow—Thega	Hoby and Layna Kight, agent	Eoin G. Harty, agent	F-T Calder	1,000,000
Grand Survival, c., by Grand Slam—Marsh Cat	Jerry Bailey Sales Agency, agent	Hirokazu Sumida, agent	Barretts March	1,000,000
Investor's Gamble, c., by High Yield—Here Comes Chelsie	Hoby and Layna Kight, agent	Eoin G. Harty, agent	F-T Calder	975,000
Ivanovsky, c., by Saint Ballado—Danzerella	Tony Bowling & Bobby Dodd, agent	Demi O'Byrne	F-T Calder	950,000
Cindago, c., by Indian Charlie—Tupelo Belle	H. T. Stables, agent	John W. Sadler, agent	Barretts March	900,000
Testimony, c., by Yes It's True—Kit Kat Kitty	Eisaman Equine Services, agent	Darley	OBS March	900,000
Strong Contender, c., by Maria's Mon—Kopenhagen	Murray Smith	John C. Oxley	Kee April	800,000
Unification, c., by Dixie Union—Devil's Orchid	Sequel Bloodstock, agent	Darley Stud Management	Barretts March	750,000
Formal Appeal, c., by Successful Appeal—Sweetbabe	Murray Smith, agent	Padua Stables	F-T Calder	750,000
Elusive Star, c., by Elusive Quality—Star of Paris	Welcome Gate Farm, agent	Robert and Beverly Lewis	F-T Calder	750,000
Point Determined, c., by Point Given—Merengue	Wavertree Stables, agent	Robert and Beverly Lewis	Barretts March	750,000
Impelling, f., by Forestry—Broad Dynamite	Hartley/De Renzo T'breds, agent	Robert and Beverly Lewis	F-T Calder	725,000
Beholden, f., by Cat Thief—Godmother	Hoby and Layna Kight, agent	Darley	F-T Calder	700,000
Kilworth, c., by Kalanisi (Ire)—Perugia (Ire)	Rathmoy Stables	David R. Loder	Tatt Oct. HRA	668,228
Armament, c., by Mr. Greeley—Explosive Lee	Niall Brennan Stables, agent	Eoin G. Harty, agent	F-T Calder	650,000
Truman's Gold, c., by Seeking the Gold—Capote Belle	Eddie Woods, agent	Darley	F-T Calder	650,000
Dance Daily, f., by Five Star Day—Dance Alexa	Sequel Bloodstock, agent	Robert and Beverly Lewis	Barretts March	600,000
Master of Disaster, c., by Dance Master—More d'Amour	Leprechaun Racing, agent	Puglisi Stables	OBS Calder	600,000
Speed of Sound, c., by Phone Trick—Lark Creek	Ricky Leppala, agent	Puglisi Stables	OBS Calder	550,000
Vague, f., by Elusive Quality—April in Kentucky	Shalfleet Stables	Jamie McCalmont, agent	Tatt Dec.	541,138
Red Duster, c., by Red Ransom—Logiciel (GB)	Jamie Railton, agent	Darley Stud Management	Tatt April	536,240
Gold Maker, c., by Golden Missile—Metanoia	Kirkwood Stables, agent	Bob Baffert, agent	F-T Calder	525,000
Always Hopeful, c., by Mind Games—Expectation	Averham Park Farm	Magus Equine Ltd.	Tatt Oct. HRA	501,171
Benedict, c., by Golden Missile—Blazing Hot	Adena Springs	Michael J. Ryan, agent	Adena Spring	500,000
Cintarosa, f., by Grand Slam—Silver Stockings	Hoby and Layna Kight, agent	Jack Grunwald	F-T Calder	500,000
Bonnie Dares, f., by Arch—Insight to Hope	Kings Equine, agent	Flying Zee Stables	F-T Calder	500,000
Marianne's Cat, f., by Tale of the Cat—Marianne's Song	Ocala Oaks & Don Graham, agent	Demi O'Byrne	F-T Calder	500,000
Eiwa Nagi, c., by Pulpit—Snowy Apparition	Ocala Oaks & Don Graham, agent	Ever Union Shokai	F-T Calder	500,000
Jezawi (Ire), c., by Danzig—Nuts in May	Robert N. Scanlon, agent	Shadwell Farm	Kee April	500,000
Milk Crown, f., by Mr. Greeley—Sky Crown	Eddie Woods, agent	Shadai Farm	Kee April	500,000
Pretty Cowgirl, f., by Gone West—Dreams of Success	Niall Brennan Stables, agent	Shadai Farm	F-T Calder	500,000
Waka Dancer, c., by War Chant—Safe Return	Sequel Bloodstock, agent	Patrick L. Biancone	F-T Calder	485,000
Bustin Justin, c., by Forestry—Designatoree	Hartley/De Renzo T'breds, agent	Fleetwood, agent	F-T Calder	485,000
Five Star Thief, c., by Cat Thief—Five Star Night	Maurice W. Miller, agent	Robert and Beverly Lewis	F-T Calder	480,000
Swan Maiden, f., by Swain (Ire)—Robust	Mocklershill Stables	Darley Stud Management	Tatt April	476,658
How True It Is, f., by Yes It's True—Future Question	M & H Training and Sales, agent	NeverTell Farm LLC	F-T Calder	450,000
Nectar of the Gods, c., by High Yield—Skies of Blue	Crupi's New Castle Farm, agent	Baden P. Chace, agent	F-T Calder	450,000
Ivywood Angel, f., by Unbridled's Song—Michele Royale	Equine Legacy LLC, agent	Ahmed Zayat	F-T Mid May	450,000
Wildcat Beauty, f., by Forest Wildcat—Stalcreek	Randy Miles, agent	NeverTell Farm LLC	Kee April	440,000
Cloud Cover, c., by Fantastic Light—Obscura	Malcolm Bastard	Darley Stud Management	Tatt April	436,936
Circuit Breaker, f., by Yes It's True—Shocker T.	True South LLC	Steven B. Klesaris, agent	F-T Calder	435,000
Refinery, c., by Victory Gallop—Sugar Is Gold	Hartley/De Renzo T'breds, agent	B. Wayne Hughes	Kee April	425,000
Raydia, c., by Dynaformer—Gemini (Arg)	Leprechaun Racing, agent	Merry/Newmarket/Meehan	F-T Calder	425,000
Rising Rate, c., by Exchange Rate—Miss Virginia	Wavertree Stables, agent	John Connelly	OBS Calder	425,000
A. J. Awesome, c., by Awesome Again—Powerful Nation	Adena Springs	John C. Kimmel, agent	Adena Spring	420,000
Greeley Mae, f., by Mr. Greeley—Tricki Mae	Niall Brennan Stables, agent	Stonebridge Farm	Kee April	410,000
Likely, c., by Yes It's True—Tri Toasted	William B. Harrigan, agent	T. F. VanMeter	Kee April	400,000
Kilimanjaro, c., by Boundary—Wayage	Eddie Woods, agent	Demi O'Byrne	F-T Calder	400,000
Diplomat Lady, f., by Forestry—Playcaller	Hoby and Layna Kight, agent	Christopher Paasch, agent	F-T Calder	400,000
Zann, c., by Dynaformer—Moments of Magic	Niall Brennan Stables, agent	Michael J. Ryan, agent	Kee April	400,000
Graffham, c., by Red Ransom—L'Abidjanaise	Nick de Meric, agent	Jill Johnston	Kee April	400,000
Cat Criminal, c., by Tale of the Cat—Jade Bird	Paul Sharp, agent	Steven B. Klesaris, agent	F-T Calder	400,000
Perfect Order, f., by Red Ransom—Ideal Index	Jamie Railton, agent	Neville A. Callaghan	Tatt April	397,215
Kupets, c., by Kingmambo—Lassie's Lady	Nick de Meric, agent	Gasper Bloodstock	F-T Calder	375,000
Memphis Mon, c., by Maria's Mon—Beal Street Blues	Wavertree Stables, agent	Centennial Farms	Kee April	375,000
Party Planner, f., by Mt. Livermore—Elfi	Leprechaun Racing, agent	Reynolds Bell, agent	Kee April	375,000
Tiger On the Loose, f., by Tale of the Cat—Unchained Princess	Niall Brennan Stables, agent	Desperado Stables Inc.	Barretts March	375,000
Steppenwolfer, c., by Aptitude—Wolfer	Eisaman Equine Services, agent	Robert and Lawana Low	OBS April	375,000
The Long Grey Line, c., by Silver Charm—Ensign's Wine	Hartley/De Renzo T'breds, agent	West Point Thoroughbreds	OBS March	360,000
Maria Pia, f., by Silver Deputy—Restraint	Sandra Murphy, agent	Greg Rand	Kee April	360,000
Winzalot, c., by Forest Wildcat—Winze	Excel Bloodstock, agent	Alan E. Goldberg, agent	F-T Calder	360,000

Highest-Priced Broodmares and Broodmare Prospects of 2005

Horse	Consignor	Buyer	Sale	Price
Ashado, 4	Taylor Made Sales Agency, agent	John Ferguson Bloodstock	Kee Nov.	$9,000,000
Riskaverse, 6	Bluegrass Thoroughbred Services, agent for Fox Ridge Farm	Eaton Sales, agent	F-T Ky Nov.	5,000,000
A. P. Adventure (Storm Cat), 4	Taylor Made Sales Agency, agent	Courtlandt Farm	Kee Nov.	3,700,000
Zing (Unbridled's Song), 8	Taylor Made Sales Agency, agent	Aaron U. Jones and Marie D. Jones	Kee Nov.	3,600,000
Fountain of Peace, 3	Lane's End, agent	John Magnier	Kee Nov.	3,100,000
Contrive (Pleasantly Perfect), 7	Taylor Made Sales Agency, agent	John Ferguson Bloodstock	F-T Ky Nov.	3,000,000
Moments of Joy (Refuse To Bend [Ire]), 5	Lanwades Stud	Coolmore Stud	Tatt Dec.	2,976,261
Canda (Elusive Quality), 5	Lane's End, agent	Cheveley Park Stud	Kee Nov.	2,400,000
Roar Emotion (A.P. Indy), 5	Hill 'n' Dale Sales Agency, agent	Stonestreet Mares LLC	Kee Nov.	2,400,000
My Emma (Pivotal), 12	Lanwades Stud	BBA (Ireland)	Tatt Dec.	2,344,933
Desert Tigress (A.P. Indy), 3	Hill 'n' Dale Sales Agency, agent	London Thoroughbred Services	Kee Nov.	2,300,000
Wife for Life (A.P. Indy), 11	Taylor Made Sales Agency, agent	Malibu Farm	Kee Nov.	2,200,000
Win's Fair Lady (Giant's Causeway), 6	Blackburn Farm, agent	Classicstar 2004 Powerfoal Stable	Kee Nov.	2,200,000
Scoop (El Prado [Ire]), 7	Mill Ridge Sales, agent	Live Oak Stud	Kee Nov.	2,100,000
Chimichurri (Unbridled's Song), 5	Taylor Made Sales Agency, agent	Stonestreet Mares LLC	Kee Nov.	2,100,000
Ticket to Houston (Storm Cat), 12	Pope McLean, agent	Stonestreet Mares LLC	Kee Nov.	2,000,000
Saudi Poetry (Unbridled's Song), 8	Taylor Made Sales Agency, agent	Courtlandt Farm	Kee Nov.	2,000,000
Divine Dixie (Fusaichi Pegasus), 10	Lantern Hill Farm, agent	Stonerside Stable	F-T Ky Nov.	2,000,000
Moonlight Dance (High Chaparral [Ire]), 3	Castlebridge Consignment	Katsumi Yoshida	Tatt Dec.	1,443,036
Guadalajara, 4	European Sales Management	John Ferguson Bloodstock	Tatt Dec.	1,443,036
Home Court (Gone West), 4	Denali Stud, agent	AGS Thoroughbred	Kee Nov.	1,400,000
Madhya (Pivotal), 4	Loughbrown Stud	German Bloodstock	Tatt Dec.	1,352,846
Cozzene's Angel (Pulpit), 11	Hill 'n' Dale Sales Agency, agent	Eaton Sales, agent	Kee Jan.	1,350,000
New Dice (Mineshaft), 6	Lane's End, agent	Courtlandt Farm	Kee Nov.	1,250,000
Sweet Talker, 3	Lane's End, agent	Courtlandt Farm	Kee Nov.	1,150,000
Buy the Sport (A.P. Indy), 5	Lane's End, agent	Frank Stronach	Kee Nov.	1,150,000
Shastye (Pivotal), 4	Kiltinan Stud	John Warren Bloodstock	Tatt Dec.	1,127,371
Native Roots (Ire) (Street Cry [Ire]), 8	Crescent Hill Farm, agent	Lane's End	Kee Jan.	1,100,000
Desert Heat (Vindication), 106	Hill 'n' Dale Sales Agency, agent	Malibu Farm	Kee Nov.	1,100,000
Heat Lightning (Birdstone), 12	Glennwood Farm, agent	Hugo Merry Bloodstock	Kee Nov.	1,100,000
Follow (A.P. Indy), 4	Hill 'n' Dale Sales Agency, agent	Frank Stronach	Kee Nov.	1,050,000
Tapatina (Giant's Causeway), 4	Lane's End, agent	R. J. Bennett, agent	Kee Nov.	1,050,000
Glint in Her Eye (Empire Maker), 9	Brookdale Sales, agent for Brookdale	Federico Barberini, agent	Kee Nov.	1,050,000
Lucky (Elusive Quality), 4	Hill 'n' Dale Sales Agency, agent	Mead Goodbody Ltd.	Kee Nov.	1,050,000
Amorama (Fr), 4	Narvick International, agent	Adena Springs	F-T Ky Nov.	1,050,000
Cozzene's Angel (Giant's Causeway), 11	Hill 'n' Dale Sales Agency, agent	Ben P. Walden, agent	F-T Ky Nov.	1,000,000
D' Wildcat Speed, 5	Taylor Made Sales Agency, agent	Stonestreet Mares LLC	Kee Nov.	1,000,000
Fantasy Lake (Fusaichi Pegasus), 9	Eaton Sales, agent	Stonestreet Mares LLC	Kee Nov.	975,000
Classic Elegance (A.P. Indy), 3	Denali Stud, agent for Robert and Beverly Lewis	Gulf Coast Farms	Kee Nov.	975,000
Tina Bull (Unbridled's Song), 5	Taylor Made Sales Agency, agent	Overbrook Farm	Kee Nov.	950,000
Personal Legend, 5	Walnut Green, agent	Shadai Farm	F-T Ky Nov.	950,000
Crazy Ensign (Arg) (Gone West), 9	Gainesway, agent	Margaux Farm LLC, agent	Kee Jan.	925,000
Bayberry (Montjeu [Ire]), 5	Brookdale Sales, agent for Brookdale	Margaret O'Toole	Kee Nov.	925,000
Puxa Saco, 5	Hinkle Farms, agent	Northwest Farms	Kee Nov.	875,000
Sweet as Honey (El Prado [Ire]), 10	Three Chimneys Sales, agent	Jack Werk, agent	Kee Nov.	850,000
Golden Symphony (A.P. Indy), 5	Hartwell Farm, agent	Dell Ridge Farm	Kee Nov.	850,000
Thorough Fair (Giant's Causeway), 12	Spendthrift Farm, agent	Gaines-Gentry Thoroughbreds, agent	Kee Nov.	825,000
Yearly Report (Gone West), 4	Three Chimneys Sales, agent	B. Wayne Hughes	Kee Nov.	825,000
Princess Olivia (Monashee Mountain), 10	Bona Terra Farms LLC	Shadai Farm	Kee Nov.	825,000
Summitville, 5	Mount House Stables	Katsumi Yoshida	Tatt Dec.	811,707
Clear in the West, 5	Pin Oak Stud LLC	Fleetwood Bloodstock	Kee Jan.	800,000
Hurry Home Hillary (Unbridled's Song), 10	Taylor Made Sales Agency, agent	Three Roses LLC	F-T Ky Nov.	800,000
Satin Sunrise (Mineshaft), 15	Blackburn Farm, agent	Ben P. Walden	F-T Ky Nov.	800,000
Arvada (GB) (Empire Maker), 5	Castle Park Farm, agent	Shadai Farm	Kee Nov.	800,000
Cologny (A.P. Indy), 5	Taylor Made Sales Agency, agent	Dapple Bloodstock, agent	Kee Nov.	800,000
Kisses For Me (Ire) (Fusaichi Pegasus), 4	Eaton Sales, agent	Dapple Bloodstock, agent	Kee Nov.	800,000
Miss Salsa (Giant's Causeway), 4	Paramount Sales, agent	Swordlestown Stud, agent	Kee Nov.	800,000
Louju (Fusaichi Pegasus), 11	Paramount Sales, agent	Margaret O'Toole	Kee Nov.	775,000
Sheppard's Watch (GB) (King's Best), 7	Ballyhimikin Stud	Hugo Lascelles Bloodstock	Tatt Dec.	766,612
Queen's Lady, 6	Taylor Made Sales Agency, agent	Dell Ridge Farm	F-T Ky Nov.	750,000
Summer Raven, 3	Taylor Made Sales Agency, agent	Overbrook Farm	Kee Nov.	750,000
Starry Ice (Forestry), 11	Taylor Made Sales Agency, agent	Dapple Bloodstock, agent	Kee Nov.	750,000
Miss Linda (Arg) (Gone West), 8	Taylor Made Sales Agency, agent	Badgers Bloodstock	Kee Nov.	750,000
Meteor Miracle (Pulpit), 6	Bluegrass Thoroughbred Services, agent	Wertheimer & Frere	Kee Nov.	740,000
Delauncy (GB) (Pivotal), 11	Voute Sales LLC, agent	McKeever-St. Lawrence	Tatt Dec.	739,555
Smart Sis (Vindication), 8	Hill 'n' Dale Sales Agency, agent	Gaines-Gentry Thoroughbreds, agent	Kee Nov.	725,000
Proud Beauty (Ire) (Distorted Humor), 5	Castle Park Farm, agent	Murayama Bloodstock	Kee Nov.	725,000
Portrait of A Lady (Montjeu [Ire]), 4	John Troy, agent	Peter J. Doyle Bloodstock and Plantation Stud	Tatt Dec.	721,518

Chronological Review of Major 2005 Sales

Sale	Sold	Total	Change	Average	Change	Median	Change	Price
January								
Stemman's winter mixed	46	$71,150		$ 1,547		$ 1,000		$9,000
Keeneland January horses of all ages	1,361	53,418,000	8.2%	39,249	0.2%	13,000	0.0%	1,350,000
Ocala Breeders' Sales Co. winter mixed	684	8,929,600	13.6%	13,055	14.5%	6,500	30.0%	200,000
Heritage Place winter mixed	122	412,150	0.5%	3,378	–0.3%	2,200	22.2%	18,000
Barretts Equine Ltd. winter mixed	492	3,213,100	–20.8%	6,531	–16.8%	3,500	0.0%	72,000
February								
Tattersalls Ltd. February	157	3,166,997	89.2%	20,172	42.2%	9,902	32.2%	227,746
Fasig-Tipton Midlantic winter mixed	112	807,900	–38.0%	7,213	–26.9%	4,000	–20.0%	80,000
OBSC selected two-year-olds in training	109	14,921,000	–2.3%	136,890	0.4%	120,000	37.1%	600,000
Fasig-Tipton Kentucky winter mixed	377	6,966,700	47.8%	18,479	54.5%	6,000	20.0%	370,000
March								
Fasig-Tipton Calder selected two-year-olds in training	147	50,132,000	20.6%	341,034	16.4%	200,000	17.6%	5,200,000
Barretts Equine Ltd. March selected two-year-olds in training	88	14,360,500	4.6%	163,188	–6.1%	95,000	35.7%	1,900,000
Adena Springs two-year-olds in training	46	3,916,000	75.8%	85,130	117.8%	60,000	130.8%	500,000
Fair Grounds Sales Co. selected two-year-olds in training	42	461,100	–3.8%	10,979	0.8%	8,250	–8.3%	29,000
Ocala Breeders' Sales Co. selected two-year-olds in training	323	26,399,000	17.0%	81,731	–11.3%	55,000	–8.3%	900,000
April								
Evangeline Downs two-year-olds in training and paddock	69	386,100	–72.4%	5,596	–49.2%	2,500	–66.7%	44,000
Fasig-Tipton Texas two-year-olds in training	142	2,631,600	–25.0%	18,532	1.4%	10,000	21.2%	110,000
Louisiana Thoroughbred Breeders Sales Co. spring mixed	85	266,850	–69.4%	3,139	–44.2%	2,300	–42.5%	13,500
Tattersalls Ltd. breeze-up two-year-olds in training	124	12,577,760	5.6%	101,434	10.7%	69,512	16.2%	536,240
Keeneland April two-year-olds in training	105	17,040,500	–22.6%	162,290	–25.5%	125,000	–9.1%	800,000
Ocala Breeders' Sales Co. spring two-year-olds in training	775	22,017,800	–5.0%	28,410	–5.1%	17,000	–5.6%	375,000
Illinois Thoroughbred Breeders and Owners Foundation two-year-olds in training and horses of racing age	14	200,500	15.4%	14,321	73.0%	10,000	81.8%	46,000
May								
Iowa Thoroughbred Breeders and Owners two-year-olds in training	15	181,600	150.5%	12,107	16.9%	9,500	35.7%	33,000
Barretts Equine Ltd. May two-year-olds in training	193	7,663,700	8.7%	39,708	6.4%	25,000	–7.4%	350,000
Fasig-Tipton Midlantic two-year-olds in training and horses of racing age	386	18,911,500	43.0%	48,994	31.1%	31,500	43.2%	450,000
June								
Michigan Thoroughbred Owners and Breeders Association two-year-olds in training and unraced three-year-olds	12	26,400	–45.5%	2,200	–54.5%	2,200	–57.3%	5,000
Ocala Breeders' Sales Co. June two-year-olds in training and horses of racing age	312	5,729,200	–24.0%	18,363	–19.4%	10,250	–35.9%	135,000
Heritage Place summer mixed	32	92,750	122.7%	2,898	67.0%	2,250	125.0%	11,200
Fasig-Tipton Midlantic two-year-olds in training and horses of racing age	57	811,100		14,230		8,500		74,000
Barretts Equine Ltd. summer two-year-olds in training and horses of racing age	107	1,164,300	–7.2%	10,881	–19.4%	6,500	–18.8%	62,000
July								
Tattersalls Ltd. July mixed	432	11,663,859	15.3%	27,000	–1.8%	16,619	7.5%	276,995
Japan Racing Horse Association selected foal	242	71,062,408	–0.1%	293,646	–3.4%	231,764	3.2%	1,871,940
Fasig-Tipton Kentucky selected yearling	368	37,106,000	–3.9%	100,832	–11.8%	75,000	–6.3%	650,000
August								
Minnesota Thoroughbred Association state-bred yearling	33	278,500	–10.9%	8,439	–2.8%	4,300	–1.1%	45,000
Louisiana Thoroughbred Breeders Sales Co. summer mixed	138	491,300	–10.8%	3,560	–9.5%	2,300	9.5%	16,000
Fasig-Tipton Saratoga selected yearling	103	33,415,000	–26.9%	324,417	6.5%	225,000	5.9%	3,100,000
New York Thoroughbred Breeders' Sales Co. yearling	107	1,266,800		11,839		5,000		150,000
Fasig-Tipton New York Saratoga preferred yearling	105	4,975,500	–11.1%	47,386	–5.2%	45,000	11.1%	165,000
California Thoroughbred Breeders Association Northern California yearling	164	1,243,500	39.2%	7,582	10.3%	4,000	–8.0%	50,000
Ruidoso Thoroughbred yearling and mixed	215	1,677,400	5.0%	7,802	–8.2%	4,000	14.3%	55,000
C.T.H.S. (Alberta division) summer yearling	128	910,773	–1.8%	7,115	12.8%	4,952	26.8%	33,016
Michigan Thoroughbred Owners and Breeders Association yearling	39	153,700	–27.4%	3,941	–21.8%	2,500	–21.9%	25,000
L'Agence Francaise Deauville August yearling	321	27,101,332	–21.6%	84,428	–8.9%	54,738	–10.0%	705,512
Ocala Breeders' Sales Co. selected and open yearling	972	17,285,300	–5.9%	17,783	–13.7%	8,000	–27.3%	190,000
Minnesota Thoroughbred Association horses of all ages	19	21,600		1,137		1,000		2,600
Indiana Thoroughbred Owners and Breeders Association yearling and horses of all ages	37	53,300	13.4%	1,441	4.2%	1,150	7.0%	5,000
Fasig-Tipton Texas summer yearling	323	3,335,100	–0.8%	10,325	–17.0%	4,500	–35.7%	132,000

Sale	Sold	Total	Change	Average	Change	Median	Change	Price
September								
Washington Thoroughbred Breeders Association summer yearling	150	2,693,900	6.0%	17,959	7.4%	14,250	11.8%	100,000
C.T.H.S. (Manitoba division) yearling	29	90,435	29.2%	3,118	2.5%	1,597	−39.2%	11,768
C.T.H.S. (Ontario division) selected yearling	305	6,214,055	782.9%	20,374	270.5%	10,927	164.6%	159,714
C.T.H.S. (British Columbia division) yearling and mixed	158	1,590,012	37.6%	10,063	7.1%	5,096	−15.2%	72,199
Keeneland September yearling	3,544	384,347,400	18.3%	108,450	12.5%	40,000	8.1%	9,700,000
Oregon Thoroughbred Owners and Breeders Assoc. fall mixed	95	176,700	−15.7%	1,860	−13.9%	1,400	−6.7%	11,000
Iowa Thoroughbred Breeders and Owners Assoc. fall mixed	64	275,300	−25.6%	4,302	−16.3%	1,950	2.6%	22,000
Charles Town Thoroughbred Horse Sales West Virginia fall mixed	62	119,000	71.2%	1,919	13.2%	1,125	18.4%	10,000
Goffs Bloodstock Sales Ltd. Orby	517	65,102,160	20.3%	125,923	71.8%	78,425	87.7%	2,276,883
October								
Fasig-Tipton Midlantic Eastern fall yearling	615	14,499,600	34.4%	23,577	7.7%	10,500	−12.5%	375,000
Barretts Equine Ltd. and C.T.B.A. October yearling	207	5,239,400	62.0%	25,311	89.4%	17,000	100.0%	290,000
Tattersalls Ltd. October yearling (part 1)	499	109,904,729	11.5%	220,250	14.4%	129,007	−1.6%	2,303,700
C.T.H.S. (Alberta division) fall mixed	94	173,347	29.1%	1,844	22.2%	850	−3.2%	26,374
Ocala Breeders' Sales Co. fall mixed	902	13,996,200	33.0%	15,517	4.4%	7,000	−17.6%	240,000
Tattersalls Ltd. October yearling (part 2)	636	31,317,526	28.9%	49,241	65.8%	33,182	76.0%	497,740
Breeders Sales Co. of Louisiana fall mixed	297	1,537,100	28.1%	5,175	−21.9%	2,500	−32.4%	42,000
New York Breeders' Sales Co. Saratoga fall mixed	116	690,500	−43.6%	5,953	−7.1%	3,500	40.0%	45,000
Arizona Thoroughbred Breeders Association fall mixed	121	825,400	−9.9%	6,821	24.4%	3,700	23.3%	81,000
Heritage Place fall mixed	60	108,100	8.0%	1,802	−28.0%	1,050	−34.4%	10,000
Barretts Equine Ltd. fall mixed	440	2,529,400	11.2%	5,749	5.9%	3,000	20.0%	82,000
Fasig-Tipton Kentucky fall yearling	610	11,099,100	33.4%	18,195	11.8%	8,500	6.3%	600,000
Tattersalls Ltd. autumn horses in training	896	36,478,859		40,713		22,274		668,228
Tattersalls Ltd. October yearling (part 3)	124	1,565,585		12,626		9,082		86,147
Michigan Thoroughbred Breeders and Owners fall mixed	21	21,950		1,045		500		4,700
November								
Fasig-Tipton Kentucky selected November mixed	168	34,389,000	49.9%	204,696	138.3%	57,500	161.4%	5,000,000
Keeneland November breeding stock	2,819	289,606,400	3.5%	102,734	5.5%	35,000	9.4%	9,000,000
Tattersalls Ltd. December mixed	1,878	133,761,211	29.6%	71,225	8.6%	36,075	15.5%	2,976,261
December								
Eclipse winter mixed	2	5,100		2,550		2,550		4,000
C.T.H.S. (Ontario division) winter mixed	127	441,273	318.3%	3,475	84.5%	2,583	112.1%	18,087
Washington Thoroughbred Breeders Association winter mixed	196	629,000	−28.4%	3,209	−22.2%	1,500	−25.0%	38,000
Fasig-Tipton Midlantic December mixed	375	3,497,900	−9.4%	9,328	−12.3%	3,800	−25.5%	140,000
Fasig-Tipton Texas winter mixed	156	597,900	−27.6%	3,833	−16.4%	2,000	−23.1%	65,000

Histories of Major Sales

Following are the histories of several prominent Thoroughbred auctions in North America. The sales are listed by type of sale, with the order within each category determined by total sales.

Keeneland September Yearlings

Year	Offered	Sold	Gross	Chg	Average	Chg	High Price
2005	**4,510**	**3,544**	**$384,347,400**	18.3%	**$108,450**	12.5%	**$9,700,000**
2004	4,359	3,370	324,904,300	18.6%	96,411	4.5%	8,000,000
2003	3,819	2,968	273,925,300	29.9%	92,293	28.5%	3,800,000
2002	3,840	2,934	210,809,000	−17.1%	71,850	−18.2%	2,500,000
2001	4,003	2,895	254,190,600	−12.9%	87,803	−0.3%	6,400,000
2000	4,302	3,313	291,827,100	25.2%	88,085	13.8%	6,800,000
1999	3,788	3,011	233,020,800	37.2%	77,390	30.3%	3,900,000
1998	3,528	2,860	169,811,800	9.8%	59,375	9.2%	2,100,000
1997	3,396	2,844	154,666,800	12.7%	54,384	16.3%	2,300,000
1996	3,649	2,936	137,233,800	5.5%	46,742	6.2%	1,400,000
1995	3,495	2,955	130,085,300	24.4%	44,022	18.4%	1,200,000
1994	3,264	2,812	104,552,900	19.8%	37,181	6.1%	625,000
1993	2,862	2,492	87,308,100	11.3%	35,035	23.0%	775,000
1992	3,188	2,754	78,427,400	1.2%	28,478	−4.0%	400,000
1991	3,065	2,612	77,511,000	−10.7%	29,675	−0.5%	900,000
1990	3,310	2,909	86,756,500	12.8%	29,823	−12.6%	535,000
1989	2,578	2,253	76,887,600	19.2%	34,127	20.7%	700,000
1988	2,752	2,281	64,500,600	−10.8%	28,277	−14.6%	625,000
1987	2,452	2,182	72,289,100	28.9%	33,130	11.3%	1,100,000
1986	2,175	1,884	56,097,000	−9.1%	29,775	−10.8%	525,000
1985	2,172	1,849	61,741,900	10.6%	33,392	5.1%	440,000
1984	2,173	1,757	55,803,400	−10.4%	31,761	−4.5%	675,000
1983	2,245	1,848	61,766,100	30.9%	33,423	1.0%	735,000
1982	1,644	1,426	47,202,800	−20.6%	33,102	18.6%	400,000
1981	2,442	2,131	59,486,500	19.2%	27,915	3.7%	600,000
1980	1,967	1,855	49,922,800	50.9%	26,913	40.9%	310,000
1979†	N/A	1,733	33,082,200	47.2%	19,098	35.6%	300,000
1978	N/A	1,596	22,474,000	21.2%	14,081	8.2%	142,000
1977	N/A	1,425	18,538,500	14.3%	13,009	21.1%	200,000

Year	Offered	Sold	Gross	Chg	Average	Chg	High Price
1976	N/A	1,510	16,216,400	38.7%	10,739	12.8%	$200,000
1975	N/A	1,228	11,688,000	–5.1%	9,518	23.7%	110,000
1974	N/A	1,601	12,315,700	17.7%	7,693	–5.8%	100,000

First held in current format in 1960. From 1944 to '48, fall yearlings were part of a mixed sale format. In 1949, approximately half the yearlings were sold in a separate October sale and the remainder in a November breeding stock sale. In 1950, yearlings were in a separate session of breeding stock sale. In 1951, fall yearling sales were separated from breeding stock by a week. Selected sessions were inaugurated in 1989.
† Before 1980, gross sales include RNAs. N/A Not available.

Keeneland July Selected Yearlings

Year	Offered	Sold	Gross	Chg	Average	Chg	High Price
2002	146	87	$ 42,385,000	–32.9%	$487,184	–31.4%	$3,100,000
2001	132	89	63,212,000	–21.7%	**710,247**	14.4%	4,000,000
2000	180	130	80,732,000	5.1%	621,015	6.7%	3,600,000
1999	181	132	76,815,000	6.8%	581,932	20.5%	3,000,000
1998	201	149	71,932,000	15.0%	482,765	35.0%	4,000,000
1997	236	175	62,565,000	7.1%	357,514	2.2%	1,500,000
1996	204	167	58,430,000	25.8%	349,880	41.6%	1,700,000
1995	225	188	46,450,000	2.6%	247,074	5.9%	1,250,000
1994	257	194	45,265,000	–8.3%	233,325	–1.2%	1,050,000
1993	251	209	49,350,000	4.7%	236,124	–9.3%	1,050,000
1992	266	181	47,120,000	–35.8%	260,331	–18.8%	1,700,000
1991	300	229	73,443,000	–21.0%	320,712	10.8%	2,600,000
1990	416	321	92,920,000	–19.9%	289,470	–4.7%	2,900,000
1989	**448**	**382**	115,978,000	18.5%	303,607	–17.5%	2,800,000
1988	323	266	97,845,000	–10.1%	367,838	–1.3%	3,500,000
1987	344	292	108,839,000	4.5%	372,736	–9.5%	3,700,000
1986	291	253	104,174,000	–24.2%	411,755	–23.3%	3,600,000
1985	292	256	137,505,000	–17.2%	537,129	–10.5%	**13,100,000**
1984	320	277	**166,155,000**	12.8%	599,838	14.0%	8,250,000
1983	301	280	147,330,000	53.4%	526,179	52.9%	10,200,000
1982	297	279	96,027,000	7.5%	344,183	32.5%	4,250,000
1981	369	344	89,342,000	55.3%	259,715	29.6%	3,500,000
1980	301	287	57,522,000	21.2%	200,425	28.8%	1,700,000
1979†	N/A	305	47,448,000	11.4%	155,567	27.9%	1,600,000
1978	N/A	350	42,579,000	54.0%	121,654	42.5%	1,300,000
1977	N/A	324	27,651,000	20.0%	85,343	28.2%	725,000
1976	N/A	346	23,035,000	25.6%	66,575	24.1%	1,500,000
1975	N/A	342	18,344,000	7.2%	53,637	0.3%	715,000
1974	N/A	320	17,116,500	–13.9%	53,489	–5.9%	625,000

First held in 1943; last held in 2002.
† Before 1980, gross sales include RNAs. N/A Not available.

Fasig-Tipton Saratoga Selected Yearlings

Year	Offered	Sold	Gross	Chg	Average	Chg	High Price
2005	136	103	$33,415,000	–26.9%	$324,417	6.5%	$3,100,000
2004	191	150	45,705,000	–5.3%	304,700	–2.8%	3,300,000
2003	196	154	48,257,000	36.9%	313,357	24.5%	2,700,000
2002	196	140	35,242,000	–43.5%	251,729	–34.7%	1,300,000
2001	201	162	**62,412,000**	49.0%	**385,259**	26.0%	3,300,000
2000	173	137	41,901,000	7.6%	305,847	17.0%	4,200,000
1999	201	149	38,957,000	13.8%	261,456	23.7%	3,000,000
1998	220	162	34,246,000	23.7%	211,395	15.3%	1,700,000
1997	205	151	27,691,000	1.4%	183,384	13.5%	1,400,000
1996	220	169	27,311,000	21.1%	161,604	26.2%	630,000
1995	207	176	22,545,000	21.4%	128,097	32.5%	440,000
1994	241	192	18,566,000	53.4%	96,698	3.9%	520,000
1993	162	130	12,101,000	0.5%	93,085	–4.2%	350,000
1992	152	124	12,046,000	–20.0%	97,145	–19.4%	525,000
1991	168	125	15,062,000	–54.3%	120,496	–42.5%	800,000
1990	219	157	32,923,000	3.7%	209,701	–12.8%	1,500,000
1989	170	132	31,745,000	–12.0%	240,492	19.4%	1,750,000
1988	259	179	36,054,000	–23.1%	201,419	–16.6%	1,500,000
1987	237	194	46,871,000	22.0%	241,603	29.0%	2,400,000
1986	253	205	38,407,000	–24.3%	187,351	–27.7%	1,625,000
1985	233	196	50,760,000	6.1%	258,980	4.0%	2,700,000
1984	235	192	47,825,000	10.9%	249,089	17.8%	**4,600,000**
1983	248	204	43,127,000	19.6%	211,407	19.6%	3,000,000
1982	243	204	36,053,000	–5.7%	176,730	10.0%	2,100,000
1981	**265**	**238**	38,222,000	47.6%	160,597	44.5%	1,200,000
1980	253	233	25,900,000	26.3%	111,159	13.3%	1,600,000
1979†	N/A	209	20,502,000	22.2%	98,096	22.2%	650,000
1978	N/A	209	16,771,500	39.4%	80,246	40.0%	800,000
1977	N/A	210	12,035,000	14.5%	57,310	29.2%	375,000
1976	N/A	237	10,510,700	23.3%	44,349	19.6%	550,000
1975	N/A	230	8,525,700	2.3%	37,068	–0.4%	260,000
1974	N/A	224	8,337,100	–13.6%	37,219	–12.9%	350,000

First held in 1917. Not held 1943-'45, because of World War II travel restrictions.
† Before 1980, gross sales include RNAs. N/A Not available.

Fasig-Tipton Kentucky July Selected Yearlings

Year	Offered	Sold	Gross	Chg	Average	Chg	High Price
2005	**603**	368	$37,106,000	–3.9%	$100,832	–11.8%	$650,000
2004	452	338	38,620,000	36.9%	**114,260**	22.8%	950,000
2003	425	303	28,202,000	–11.3%	93,076	–4.8%	800,000
2002	536	325	31,790,000	37.3%	97,815	0.1%	700,000
2001	381	237	23,148,000	–11.6%	97,671	25.7%	625,000
2000	517	337	26,186,500	17.9%	77,705	3.6%	525,000
1999	361	296	22,211,000	58.2%	75,037	35.3%	525,000
1998	340	253	14,036,500	43.9%	55,480	5.3%	220,000
1997	238	185	9,751,000	–2.6%	52,708	36.3%	290,000
1996	393	259	10,013,500	52.2%	38,662	4.0%	300,000
1995	227	177	6,580,500	16.6%	37,178	18.5%	200,000
1994	245	180	5,645,000	24.1%	31,361	–0.8%	170,000
1993	173	144	4,550,500	95.2%	31,601	–6.5%	147,000
1992	97	69	2,331,000	–35.0%	33,783	–0.1%	115,000
1991	154	106	3,585,000	–28.8%	33,821	–16.8%	140,000
1990	143	124	5,038,500	–44.5%	40,633	–12.3%	140,000
1989	240	196	9,080,500	–34.2%	46,329	–27.8%	255,000
1988	296	215	13,795,500	0.0%	64,165	13.0%	475,000
1987	309	243	13,797,000	–35.7%	56,778	–29.1%	450,000
1986	365	268	21,465,500	–26.7%	80,095	–10.1%	400,000
1985	421	329	29,297,500	–17.8%	89,050	–13.6%	730,000
1984	428	346	35,648,000	–13.7%	103,029	–2.7%	900,000
1983	439	390	**41,302,000**	37.1%	105,903	35.0%	**1,750,000**
1982	459	384	30,118,000	–0.2%	78,432	11.7%	1,000,000
1981	502	**430**	30,186,000	43.7%	70,200	32.0%	1,300,000
1980	441	395	21,010,500	56.2%	53,191	31.7%	325,000
1979†	N/A	333	13,450,000	19.5%	40,390	23.7%	310,000
1978	N/A	353	11,258,500	57.4%	32,659	36.5%	205,000
1977	N/A	299	7,154,900	151.0%	23,929	50.3%	255,000
1976	N/A	179	2,850,100	84.0%	15,922	49.0%	75,000
1975	N/A	145	1,549,000	287.8%	10,683	12.3%	110,000
1974	N/A	42	399,400	–48.3%	9510	13.2%	30,000

First held in 1972. Held at Newtown Paddocks since 1975.
† Before 1980, gross sales include RNAs. N/A Not available.

Fasig-Tipton Calder Selected Two-Year-Olds in Training

Year	Offered	Sold	Gross	Chg	Average	Chg	High Price
2006	229	154	**$62,187,000**	24.0%	**$403,812**	18.4%	**$16,000,000**
2005	267	147	50,132,000	20.6%	341,034	16.4%	5,200,000
2004	223	142	41,586,000	43%	292,859	40%	4,500,000
2003	246	139	29,077,000	–1.4%	209,187	–1.4%	1,400,000
2002	254	139	29,479,000	4.6%	212,079	2.3%	1,000,000
2001	237	136	28,186,000	–16.3%	207,250	–4.0%	1,000,000
2000	264	156	33,690,000	0.9%	215,962	17.1%	1,950,000
1999	296	181	33,386,000	26.9%	184,453	33.9%	1,100,000
1998	302	191	26,303,000	13.6%	137,712	14.2%	1,000,000
1997	297	192	23,162,000	1.7%	120,635	16.1%	780,000
1996	309	**219**	22,765,000	22.2%	103,950	11.1%	875,000
1995	306	199	18,624,000	39.0%	93,588	31.3%	550,000
1994	276	188	13,403,000	17.7%	71,293	25.2%	390,000
1993	**318**	200	11,386,000	–8.0%	56,930	–3.9%	450,000
1992	292	209	12,376,000	14.1%	59,215	–5.5%	350,000
1991	299	173	10,846,000	–24.6%	62,694	–17.2%	375,000
1990	269	190	14,383,000	36.0%	75,700	18.8%	625,000
1989	233	166	10,579,000	–13.1%	63,729	–1.1%	360,000
1988	296	189	12,175,500	4.4%	64,421	–2.3%	275,000
1987	243	177	11,666,000	21.0%	65,910	24.4%	315,000
1986	232	182	9,640,000	56.8%	52,967	25.8%	525,000
1985	208	146	6,146,000	8.2%	42,096	–11.0%	325,000
1984	179	120	5,678,000	–20.5%	47,317	–2.6%	360,000
1983	206	147	7,144,000	—	48,599	—	195,000

First held in 1983.

Keeneland April Two-Year-Olds in Training

Year	Offered	Sold	Gross	Chg	Average	Chg	High Price
2006	147	87	$18,440,000	8.2%	$211,954	30.6%	$1,050,000
2005	176	105	17,040,500	–22.6%	162,290	–25.5%	800,000
2004	183	101	**22,012,000**	2.7%	**217,941**	30.1%	**3,300,000**
2003	198	128	21,440,000	20.8%	167,500	–3.7%	950,000
2002	178	102	17,749,500	19.1%	174,015	6.3%	850,000
2001	146	91	14,898,000	–19.2%	163,714	8.3%	775,000
2000	195	122	18,435,000	–0.7%	151,107	0.1%	825,000
1999	179	123	18,560,000	33.3%	150,894	0.8%	2,000,000
1998	125	93	13,925,000	–3.5%	149,731	52.6%	725,000
1997	210	147	14,427,000	0.9%	98,143	–14.9%	900,000
1996	195	124	14,305,000	20.6%	115,363	11.8%	400,000
1995	169	115	11,865,000	3.3%	103,174	41.0%	700,000
1994	**219**	**157**	11,491,500	69.0%	73,194	15.2%	400,000
1993	136	107	6,800,500	—	63,556	—	300,000

First held in 1993.

Ocala Breeders' Sales Co. Calder Two-Year-Olds in Training

Year	Offered	Sold	Gross	Chg	Average	Chg	High Price
2006	138	93	$12,967,000	–13.1%	**$139,430**	1.9%	$650,000
2005	158	109	14,921,000	–2.3%	136,890	0.4%	600,000
2004	169	112	15,266,000	19.9%	136,403	25.2%	**1,600,000**
2003	166	117	12,733,000	–2.4%	108,829	–4.9%	1,200,000
2002	175	114	13,041,000	–7.7%	114,395	10.2%	500,000
2001	188	136	14,124,000	–9.5%	103,853	–5.5%	900,000
2000	226	142	15,599,000	–5.2%	109,852	6.8%	550,000
1999	204	160	**16,454,000**	31.0%	102,838	25.2%	525,000
1998	193	153	12,564,000	20.5%	82,118	20.5%	430,000
1997	184	153	10,428,000	12.0%	68,157	16.4%	300,000
1996	218	159	9,314,000	19.5%	58,579	6.7%	275,000
1995	181	142	7,794,500	24.7%	54,891	24.7%	270,000
1994	202	142	6,248,500	9.4%	44,004	14.0%	350,000
1993	200	148	5,712,000	8.6%	38,595	2.7%	325,000
1992	182	140	5,261,000	–1.5%	37,579	2.7%	260,000
1991	218	146	5,341,000	–17.6%	36,582	–14.2%	135,000
1990	205	152	6,478,000	18.3%	42,618	23.0%	360,000
1989	209	158	5,474,500	–5.8%	34,649	–2.8%	302,000
1988	231	163	5,811,500	–20.4%	35,653	–13.5%	140,000
1987	**232**	**177**	7,298,500	0.1%	41,234	–3.3%	175,000
1986	207	171	7,290,500	71.6%	42,635	28.5%	250,000
1985	173	128	4,247,500	—	33,184	—	135,000

First held in 1985 at Hialeah Park. Held at Calder Race Course since 1986.

Barretts Equine Ltd. Selected Two-Year-Olds in Training

Year	Offered	Sold	Gross	Chg	Average	Chg	High Price
2006	139	93	$14,361,000	0.0%	$154,419	–5.4%	$1,500,000
2005	145	88	14,360,500	4.6%	163,188	–6.1%	1,900,000
2004	128	79	13,728,000	12.3%	173,722	22%	2,000,000
2003	166	86	12,228,000	11.7%	142,186	–5.2%	**2,700,000**
2002	121	73	10,950,000	8.6%	150,000	5.6%	1,900,000
2001	130	71	10,085,000	–41.7%	142,042	–21.1%	750,000
2000	170	96	17,287,000	–21.4%	180,073	–20.6%	2,000,000
1999	172	97	21,995,000	–3.2%	**226,753**	30.8%	2,000,000
1998	200	131	22,711,000	–28.9%	173,366	–21.8%	1,000,000
1997	255	144	31,926,000	–3.3%	221,708	7.4%	1,100,000
1996	233	160	**33,016,000**	56.1%	206,350	56.1%	900,000
1995	274	160	21,148,000	57.4%	132,175	61.3%	900,000
1994	240	164	13,440,000	51.6%	81,951	39.6%	700,000
1993	237	151	8,863,400	–7.5%	58,698	–5.1%	430,000
1992	280	155	9,584,000	–33.0%	61,832	–20.1%	370,000
1991	**317**	185	14,313,000	–12.8%	77,368	–7.6%	600,000
1990	270	**196**	16,405,000	—	83,699	—	700,000

First held in 1990.

Keeneland November Breeding Stock

Year	Offered	Sold	Gross	Chg	Average	Chg	High Price
2005	3,713	2,819	$289,606,400	3.5%	$102,734	5.5%	**$9,000,000**
2004	3,736	2,873	279,680,200	18.5%	97,348	7.8%	4,800,000
2003	3,337	2,614	236,070,900	26.1%	90,310	14.6%	7,100,000
2002	2,982	2,377	187,230,000	4.3%	78,767	9.9%	4,000,000
2001	3,383	2,506	179,568,600	–41.0%	71,655	–22.9%	4,000,000
2000	**4,367**	3,277	304,549,800	–4.1%	92,936	1.3%	4,900,000
1999	4,227	**3,461**	**317,666,000**	20.0%	91,784	17.2%	4,700,000
1998	4,312	3,379	264,657,700	23.7%	78,324	10.3%	7,000,000
1997	3,673	3,013	213,979,800	25.4%	71,019	17.6%	1,400,000
1996	3,451	2,826	170,691,800	21.2%	60,400	22.5%	2,600,000
1995	3,505	2,855	140,822,300	16.3%	49,325	1.6%	2,500,000
1994	2,932	2,494	121,056,900	32.5%	48,539	10.3%	2,700,000
1993	2,300	2,075	91,342,900	24.6%	44,021	16.6%	1,150,000
1992	2,324	1,942	73,337,200	–11.6%	37,764	–9.7%	1,100,000
1991	2,281	1,984	82,938,400	–18.0%	41,804	5.8%	1,400,000
1990	3,061	2,558	101,107,700	–34.8%	39,526	–43.1%	2,300,000
1989	2,518	2,235	155,161,300	36.7%	69,423	22.3%	4,600,000
1988	2,401	2,000	113,517,600	–4.1%	56,759	–15.8%	1,900,000
1987	1,999	1,756	118,358,900	–5.3%	67,403	–3.4%	2,600,000
1986	2,159	1,791	125,022,700	–22.0%	69,806	–27.3%	5,400,000
1985	2,076	1,668	160,207,100	5.1%	96,047	–7.7%	5,500,000
1984	1,915	1,465	152,373,200	–9.6%	104,009	–1.4%	4,600,000
1983	1,977	1,598	168,518,600	44.6%	**105,456**	42.8%	5,250,000
1982	1,989	1,578	116,538,700	–1.7%	73,852	28.4%	3,800,000
1981	2,491	2,060	118,494,900	26.4%	57,522	13.2%	2,150,000
1980	2,024	1,845	93,746,700	40.0%	50,811	44.4%	2,000,000
1979†	N/A	1,903	66,968,300	50.6%	35,191	23.6%	1,600,000
1978	N/A	1,562	44,472,200	21.2%	28,471	11.6%	800,000

Year	Offered	Sold	Gross	Chg	Average	Chg	High Price
1977	N/A	1,439	36,699,400	33.2%	25,503	28.1%	$575,000
1976	N/A	1,384	27,548,800	70.4%	19,905	35.8%	1,000,000
1975	N/A	1,103	16,163,700	–3.5%	14,654	30.8%	295,000
1974	N/A	1,495	16,751,200	–33.6%	11,205	–29.9%	385,000

First held in 1944.
† Before 1980, gross sales include RNAs. N/A Not available.

Keeneland January Horses of All Ages

Year	Offered	Sold	Gross	Chg	Average	Chg	High Price
2006	**2,080**	**1,628**	**$72,329,100**	35.4%	$44,428	13.2%	$1,000,000
2005	1,765	1,361	53,418,000	8.2%	39,249	0.2%	1,350,000
2004	1,602	1,260	49,362,600	58.3%	39,177	48.9%	850,00
2003	1,600	1,185	31,186,000	–10.1%	26,317	–28.9%	475,000
2002	1,135	937	34,689,200	–12.5%	37,022	12.7%	**3,600,000**
2001	1,667	1,207	39,657,700	–34.9%	32,856	–33.1%	1,700,000
2000	1,605	1,241	60,951,200	43.7%	**49,115**	39.3%	5,000,000
1999	1,452	1,203	42,410,900	–20.2%	35,254	–23.1%	3,250,000
1998	1,378	1,160	53,164,800	121.1%	45,832	91.2%	3,400,000
1997	1,156	1,003	24,042,300	–20.6%	23,970	–21.0%	710,000
1996	1,220	997	30,263,400	56.2%	30,354	61.2%	1,800,000
1995	1,195	1,029	19,377,700	29.5%	18,832	7.0%	375,000
1994	948	850	14,960,600	25.5%	17,601	24.0%	210,000
1993	1,018	840	11,918,600	–37.5%	14,189	–36.4%	210,000
1992	952	855	19,066,000	–14.2%	22,299	38.9%	650,000
1991	1,670	1,385	22,229,900	9.9%	16,050	–33.1%	685,000
1990	983	844	20,234,200	–1.8%	23,974	5.9%	2,100,000
1989	1,083	901	20,469,300	–66.7%	22,718	–53.1%	745,000
1988	1,382	1,268	61,450,100	291.4%	48,462	102.5%	2,500,000
1987	796	656	15,701,800	–23.1%	23,936	–22.5%	1,750,000
1986	836	661	20,411,100	0.5%	30,879	–10.8%	3,000,000
1985	754	587	20,317,400	–5.1%	34,612	–13.3%	1,250,000
1984	693	536	21,399,100	11.8%	39,924	–1.8%	2,500,000
1983	602	471	19,139,700	–15.4%	40,636	29.3%	825,000
1982	860	720	22,626,600	–4.3%	31,426	24.7%	1,000,000
1981	1,073	938	23,640,900	25.3%	25,204	3.9%	1,000,000
1980	856	778	18,874,000	115.6%	24,260	105.1%	850,000
1979†	N/A	740	8,753,000	18.7%	11,828	15.9%	145,000
1978	N/A	723	7,375,200	41.6%	10,201	15.0%	215,000
1977	N/A	587	5,208,500	5.0%	8,873	23.4%	310,000
1976	N/A	690	4,961,700	–1.8%	7,191	13.5%	295,000
1975	N/A	798	5,053,900	19.3%	6,333	1.3%	100,000
1974	N/A	678	4,238,000	10.1%	6,251	8.1%	122,000

First held in 1956. Not held 1958-'60.
† Before 1980, gross sales include RNAs. N/A Not available.

Highest-Priced Horses of All Time

American Top-Priced Yearlings

(With Subsequent Race Record)

$13,100,000 **SEATTLE DANCER**, 1984 c., Nijinsky II—My Charmer, by Poker. Consignor: Warner L. Jones Jr.; Buyer: BBA (England), agent for Robert Sangster and partners. 1985 Keeneland July. 5 starts, 2 wins, $152,413, in France and Ireland, SW, Ire-G2.

10,200,000 SNAAFI DANCER, 1982 c., Northern Dancer—My Bupers, by Bupers. Consignor: Crescent Farm; Buyer: Aston Upthorpe Stud, agent for Sheikh Mohammed bin Rashid al Maktoum. 1983 Keeneland July. Unraced.

9,700,000 UNNAMED, 2004 c., Storm Cat—Tranquility Lake, by Rahy. Consignor: Mill Ridge Sales, agent for Martin J. Wygod; Buyer: John Ferguson Bloodstock. 2005 Keeneland September.

8,250,000 IMPERIAL FALCON, 1983 c., Northern Dancer—Ballade, by *Herbager. Consignor: Windfields Farm; Buyer: BBA (England), agent for Robert Sangster and partners. 1984 Keeneland July. 3 starts, 2 wins, $13,395, in Ireland.

8,000,000 MR. SEKIGUCHI, 2003 c., Storm Cat—Welcome Surprise, by Seeking the Gold. Consignor: Lane's End, agent; Buyer: Hideyuki Mori. 2004 Keeneland September. 2 starts, 1 win, placed, $45,800.

7,100,000 JAREER, 1983 c., Northern Dancer—Fabuleux Jane, by *Le Fabuleux. Consignor: Bruce Hundley, agent for Ralph C. Wilson Jr.; Buyer: Darley Stud Management. 1984 Keeneland July. 9 starts, 1 win, $5,591 in England and North America.

LAA ETAAB, 1984 c., Nijinsky II—Crimson Saint, by Crimson Satan. Consignor: Tom Gentry; Buyer: Gainsborough Farm. 1985 Keeneland July. Unraced.

6,800,000 TASMANIAN TIGER, 1999 c., Storm Cat—Hum Along, by Fappiano. Consignor: Lane's End, agent; Buyer: Demi O'Byrne. 2000 Keeneland September. 25 starts, 3 wins, $154,543 in Ireland and Hong Kong.

6,500,000 AMJAAD, 1983 c., Seattle Slew—Desiree, by Raise a Native. Consignor: Spendthrift Farm, agent for Mr. and Mrs. Louis E. Wolfson and Mrs. Ethel D. Jacobs; Buyer: Darley Stud Management. 1984 Keeneland July. 4 starts, unplaced in England, Ireland, and North America.

6,400,000 **VAN NISTELROOY**, 2000 c., Storm Cat—Halory, by Halo. Consignor: Lane's End, agent for Stonerside Stable; Buyer: Demi O'Byrne. 2001 Keeneland September. 6 starts, 3 wins, $229,980 in England, Ireland, and North America, SW, Ire-G2.

6,300,000 OBJECTIVITY, 2004 c., Storm Cat—Secret Status, by A.P. Indy. Consignor: Lane's End, agent; Buyer: John Ferguson Bloodstock. 2005 Keeneland September.

5,500,000 ALAJWAD, 2000, c., Storm Cat—La Affirmed, by Affirmed. Consignor: Eaton Sales, agent; Buyer: John Ferguson Bloodstock. 2001 Keeneland September. 6 starts, 2 wins, $77,445 in North America and UAE.

5,400,000 OBLIGATO, 1983 c., Northern Dancer—Truly Bound, by In Reality. Consignor: Windfields Farm; Buyer: BBA (Ireland), agent for Robert Sangster and partners. 1984 Keeneland July. 2 starts, unplaced, in Ireland.

5,300,000 KING'S CONSUL, 1999 c., Kingmambo—Battle Creek Girl, by His Majesty. Consignor: Lane's End, agent; Buyer: John Ferguson Bloodstock. 2000 Keeneland September. 8 starts, 1 win, $40,759 in England and North America.

$5,100,000	**WASSL TOUCH**, 1983 c., Northern Dancer—Queen Sucree, by *Ribot. Consignor: North Ridge Farm; Buyer: Darley Stud Management. 1984 Keeneland July. 6 starts, 3 wins, $30,168 in England, SW.
4,600,000	PARLANDO, 1983 c., Northern Dancer—Bubbling, by Stage Door Johnny. Consignor: Wild Oak Plantation; Buyer: BBA (Ireland), agent for Robert Sangster and partners. 1984 Fasig-Tipton Saratoga. Unraced.
	PROFESSOR BLUE, 1983 c., Northern Dancer—Mississippi Mud, by Delta Judge. Consignor: Lane's End; Buyer: BBA (England), agent for Stavros Niarchos. 1984 Keeneland July. 7 starts, placed, $5,171, in France and North America.
4,400,000	MOON'S WHISPER, 1999 f., Storm Cat—East of the Moon, by Private Account. Consignor: Lane's End; Buyer: Shadwell Estate Co. Ltd. 2000 Keeneland September. Unraced.
	Shah Jehan, 1999 c., Mr. Prospector—Voodoo Lily, by Baldski. Consignor: Lane's End, agent; Buyer: Demi O'Byrne. 2000 Keeneland September. 30 starts, 4 wins, $238,238 in North America, Ireland, England, and France, spl, G3.
4,250,000	**EMPIRE GLORY**, 1981 c., Nijinsky II—Spearfish, by Fleet Nasrullah. Consignor: Glencoe Farm; Buyer: BBA (Ireland). 1982 Keeneland July. 6 starts, 2 wins, $35,420, in Ireland, SW, Ire-G3.
	FOXBORO, 1982 c., Northern Dancer—Desert Vixen, by In Reality. Consignor: North Ridge Farm; Buyer: BBA (England), agent for Robert Sangster and partners. 1983 Keeneland July. 1 start, unplaced in Ireland.
4,200,000	DISTINCTION, 1999 c., Seattle Slew—Omi, by Wild Again. Consignor: Double Diamond Farm; Buyer: David J. Shimmon. 2000 Fasig-Tipton Saratoga. 21 starts, 3 wins, $78,058.
4,100,000	**GALLANT ARCHER**, 1982 c., Nijinsky II—Belle of Dodge Me, by Creme dela Creme. Consignor: E. A. Seltzer and Parlina; Buyer: Aston Upthorpe Stud, agent for Sheikh Mohammed bin Rashid al Maktoum. 1983 Keeneland July. 16 starts, 5 wins, $294,477 in England and North America SW, G3.
4,000,000	**ELNAWAAGI**, 1983 c., Roberto—Gurkhas Band, by Lurullah. Consignor: Keswick Stables; Buyer: Darley Stud Management. 1984 Fasig-Tipton Saratoga. 11 starts, 4 wins, $23,607, in England and Germany, SW.
	FUSAICHI PEGASUS, 1997 c., Mr. Prospector—Angel Fever, by Danzig. Consignor: Stone Farm, agent; Buyer: Fusao Sekiguchi. 1998 Keeneland July. 9 starts, 6 wins, $1,994,400, SW, G1.
	MR. SIDNEY, 2004 c., Storm Cat—Tomisue's Delight, by A.P. Indy. Consignor: Lane's End, agent; Buyer: Circle E Racing. 2005 Keeneland September. Unraced.
	SHOWLADY, 1999 f., Theatrical (Ire)—Claxton's Slew, by Seattle Slew. Consignor: Brookside Farms; Buyer: John Ferguson Bloodstock. 2000 Keeneland September. 6 starts, 2 wins, $158,640, SW, G3.
	WARHOL, 2000 c., Saint Ballado—Charm a Gendarme, by Batonnier. Consignor: Taylor Made Sales Agency, agent; Buyer: Demi O'Byrne. 2000 Keeneland July. 4 starts, 1 win, $18,809 in Ireland and England.
3,900,000	DUBAI TO DUBAI, 1998 c., Kris S.—Mr. P's Princess, by Mr. Prospector. Consignor: Harold Harrison; Buyer: John Ferguson Bloodstock. 1999 Keeneland September. 11 starts, 3 wins, $152,319 in North America and UAE.
3,800,000	HASHIMIYA, 2002 f., Gone West—Touch of Greatness, by Hero's Honor. Consignor: Three Chimneys Sales, agent; Buyer: John Ferguson Bloodstock. 2003 Keeneland September. 2 starts, unplaced, $1,250 in England and UAE.
	HOYER, 2000 c., Mr. Prospector—Destination Mir, by Cherokee Colony. Consignor: Lazy E Ranch; Buyer: John Ferguson Bloodstock. 2001 Keeneland September. Unraced.
	UNNAMED, 2004 f., Storm Cat—Warrior Queen, by Quiet American. Consignor: Eaton Sales, agent; Buyer: Demi O'Byrne. 2005 Keeneland September.
3,750,000	ALCHAASIBIYEH, 1983 f., Seattle Slew—Fine Prospect, by Mr. Prospector. Consignor: Spendthrift Farm; Buyer: Darley Stud Management. 1984 Keeneland July. 6 starts, placed, $2,098, in England.
3,700,000	VIRTUOSA, 2000 f., Seeking the Gold—Escena, by Strawberry Road (Aus). Consignor: Denali Stud, agent for Falls Creek Farm; Buyer: Reynolds Bell, agent. 2001 Keeneland July. 10 starts, 1 win, $39,470.
	WARRSHAN, 1986 c., Northern Dancer—Secret Asset, by Graustark. Consignor: Hermitage Farm; Buyer: Darley Stud Management. 1987 Keeneland July. 11 starts, 4 wins, $125,928, in England and North America, SW, Eng-G3.

Key—Bold-faced caps: stakes winner. Bold-faced caps and lowercase: stakes-placed.

North American Top-Priced Two-Year-Olds

$16,000,000	THE GREEN MONKEY, 2004 c., Forestry—Magical Masquerade, by Unbridled. Consignor: Hartley/De Renzo Thoroughbreds, agent; Buyer: Demi O'Byrne. 2006 Fasig-Tipton Calder. Unraced.
5,200,000	EVER SHIFTING, 2003 c., Tale of the Cat—Carry All, by Devil's Bag. Consignor: Robert N. Scanlon, agent; Buyer: Darley. 2005 Fasig-Tipton Calder. Unraced.
4,500,000	FUSAICHI SAMURAI, 2002 c., Fusaichi Pegasus—Hidden Storm, by Storm Cat. Consingor: Kirkwood Stables, agent; Buyer: Fusao Sekiguchi. 2004 Fasig-Tipton Calder. 2 starts, 1 win, $21,400.
3,300,000	**Chekhov**, 2002 c., Pulpit—In My Cap, by Vice Regent. Consignor: Niall Brennan Stables, agent; Buyer: Demi O'Byrne. 2004 Keeneland April. 11 starts, 1 win, $158,366, spl, G3.
3,100,000	DUBAI DREAMER, 2002 c., Stephen Got Even—Blacktie Bid, by Black Tie Affair (Ire). Consignor: Niall Brennan Stables, agent; Buyer: John Ferguson Bloodstock. 2004 Fasig-Tipton Calder. 4 starts, 1 win, $19,168 in England and UAE.
3,000,000	BARBADOS, 2003 c., Forestry—Rare Bird, by Rahy. Consignor: Tony Bowling and Bobby Dodd, agent; Buyer: Demi O'Byrne. 2005 Fasig-Tipton Calder. 1 start, unplaced, $2,150.
	WILD FIT, 2003 f., Wild Wonder—Grannies Feather, by At Full Feather. Consignor: Eaton Sales, agent; Buyer: Demi O'Byrne. 2005 Fasig-Tipton Kentucky November. 6 starts, 2 wins, $518,600, SW, G1.
2,900,000	RONDO, 2003 c., Grand Slam—Dama, by Storm Cat. Consignor: Maurice W. Miller, agent; Buyer: Darley. 2005 Fasig-Tipton Calder. 1 start, placed, $8,600.
2,700,000	DIAMOND FURY, 2001 g., Sea of Secrets—Swift Spirit, by Tasso. Consignor: Sequel Bloodstock, agent; Buyer: Charles Fipke. 2003 Barretts March. 13 starts, 3 wins, $114,580.
2,200,000	UNNAMED, 2004 c., Storm Cat—Brushed Halory, by Broad Brush. Consignor: Hartley/De Renzo Thoroughbreds, agent; Buyer: Dale L. Romans. 2006 Fasig-Tipton Calder.
2,000,000	DUBAI ESCAPADE, 2002 f., Awesome Again—Sassy Pants, by Saratoga Six. Consignor: Jerry Bailey Sales Agency, agent; Buyer: John Ferguson Bloodstock. 2004 Barretts March. 4 starts, 3 wins, $57,050 in England, UAE, and North America.
	GOTHAM CITY, 1998 c., Saint Ballado—What a Reality, by In Reality. Consignor: Jerry Bailey Sales Agency; Buyer: David J. Shimmon. 2000 Barretts March. 2 starts, unplaced, $2,880.
	LA SALLE STREET, 1997 c., Not For Love—Three Grand, by Assert (Ire). Consignor: H. T. Stables, agent, for Cam Allard; Buyer: Demi O'Byrne. 1999 Keeneland April. 3 starts, placed, $3,420.
	MOROCCO, 1997 c., Brocco—Roll Over Baby, by Rollin On Over. Consignor: Sequel Bloodstock, agent; Buyer: The Thoroughbred Corp. 1999 Barretts March. 16 starts, 4 wins, $133,640.
	MERCANTILE, 2004 c., Golden Missile—Silverdew, by Silver Deputy. Consignor: O & H Bloodstock, agent; Buyer: John Ferguson Bloodstock, agent. 2006 Fasig-Tipton Calder.
	BELGRAVIA, 2004 c., Mr. Greeley—Peaks Mill, by Stalwart. Consignor: Nick de Meric, agent; Buyer: Demi O'Byrne. 2006 Fasig-Tipton Calder.

$1,950,000	**YONAGUSKA**, 1998 c., Cherokee Run—Marital Spook, by Silver Ghost. Consignor: Niall Brennan Stables, agent; Buyer: Demi O'Byrne. 2000 Fasig-Tipton Calder. 18 starts, 6 wins, $536,355, SW, G1.
1,900,000	**ATLANTIC OCEAN**, 2000 f., Stormy Atlantic—Super Chef, by Seattle Slew. Consignor: Chapman Farms; Buyer: The Thoroughbred Corp. 2002 Barretts March. 19 starts, 5 wins, $678,210, SW, G3.
	WHAT A SONG, 2003 c., Songandaprayer—What a Knight, by Tough Knight. Consignor: Murray Smith, agent; Buyer: Robert B. Lewis and Beverly J. Lewis. 2005 Barretts March. 3 starts, 3 wins, $179,700, SW, G2.
1,800,000	GARIFINE, 2004 c., Belong to Me—Vassar, by Royal Academy. Consignor: Wavertree Stables, agent; Buyer: Buzz Chace, agent. 2006 Ocala Breeders' Sales Co. March.
1,650,000	**HARMONY LODGE**, 1998 f., Hennessy—Win Crafty Lady, by Crafty Prospector. Consignor: Eddie Woods, agent; Buyer: Eugene Melnyk. 2000 Fasig-Tipton Calder. 24 starts, 10 wins, $851,120, SW, G1.
1,600,000	MUTANABI, 2002 c., Wild Rush—Freudenau, by Meadowlake. Consignor: W. D. North, agent; Buyer: John Ferguson Bloodstock. 2004 Ocala Breeders' Sales Co. February. 2 starts, placed, $3,171 in England.
1,500,000	CLOSE SECRET, 2003 f., Storm Cat—Turbo Launch, by Relaunch. Consignor: Hartley/De Renzo Thoroughbreds LLC, agent; Buyer: Demi O'Byrne. 2005 Fasig-Tipton Calder. Unraced.
	COWTOWN CAT, 2004 c., Distorted Humor—Tom's Cat, by Storm Cat. Consignor: Jerry Bailey Sales Agency, agent; Buyer: WinStar Farm. 2006 Barretts March. Unraced.
	GARIBALDI, 2003 c., Golden Missile—Ms. Copelan, by Copelan. Consignor: Wavertree Stables, agent; Buyer: Demi O'Byrne. 2005 Fasig-Tipton Calder. 5 starts, 1 win, $24,390.
	TIMSAAH, 2002 c., Rubiano—Magari, by Quack. Consignor: H. T. Inc., agent for Cam Allard; Buyer: John Ferguson Bloodstock. 2004 Fasig Tipton Calder. 2 starts, unplaced in UAE.
1,400,000	**LION HEART**, 2001 c., Tale of the Cat—Satin Sunrise, by Mr. Leader. Consignor: Robert N. Scanlon, agent; Buyer: Demi O'Byrne. 2003 Fasig-Tipton Calder. 10 starts, 5 wins, $1,390,800, SW, G1.
	RADETZKY, 2002 c., Dixie Union—Sneaky Quiet, by Seeking the Gold. Consignor: Solitary Oak Farm, agent; Buyer: Demi O'Byrne. 2004 Keeneland April. 3 starts, 1 win, $43,845.
1,300,000	**MINSTRESS**, 1983 f., The Minstrel—Fleet Victress, by *King of the Tudors. Consignor: Newstead Farm Trust; Buyer: W. S. Farish. 1985 Newstead Farm Trust Dispersal. 19 starts, 5 wins, $147,399, SW.
1,250,000	LE CHAT, 1998 c., Storm Cat—Adorable Micol, by Riverman. Consignor: Hartley/De Renzo Thoroughbreds, agent; Buyer: John Moynihan, agent. 2000 Fasig-Tipton Calder. 3 starts, 1 win, $28,470.
	LOCHLIN SLEW, 1997 f., Seattle Slew—Lochlin, by Screen King. Consignor: M. W. Miller III, agent; Buyer: B. Wayne Hughes. 1999 Keeneland April. Unraced.
1,200,000	**CHAPEL ROYAL**, 2001 c., Montbrook—Cut Class Leanne, by Cutlass. Consignor: Ocala Stud Farms; Buyer: Demi O'Byrne. 2003 Ocala Breeders' Sales Co. February. 8 starts, 3 wins, $495,571, SW, G2.
	DANCE MASTER, 1997 c., Gone West—Nijinsky's Lover, by Nijinsky II. Consignor: Jerry Bailey Sales Agency; Buyer: Padua Stables. 1999 Barretts March. 19 starts, 4 wins, $196,455, SW, G2.
	SAMURAI TIGERS, 2004 c., Indian Charlie—Pear Shape, by Red Ransom. Consignor: Wavertree Stables, agent; Buyer: Nobutaka Tada. 2006 Fasig-Tipton Calder. Unraced.
	TASK, 1996 f., Mr. Prospector—Department, by Secretariat. Consignor: Claiborne Farm and Nicole Perry Gorman; Buyer: Course Investment. 1998 Keeneland January. 3 starts, unplaced, $405 in France.
	E Z Warrior, 2004 c., Exploit—Carson Jen, by Carson City. Consignor: Murray Smith, agent; Buyer: Zayat Stables. 2006 Barretts March.

North American Top-Priced Weanlings

$2,500,000	**MAGIC OF LIFE**, 1985 f., Seattle Slew—Larida, by Northern Dancer. Consignor: Newstead Farm Trust; Buyer: British Bloodstock Agency (England). 1985 Newstead Farm Trust Dispersal. 9 starts, 4 wins, $254,841 in England, SW, Eng-G1.
2,400,000	CARPOCRATES, 2003 c., Storm Cat—Spain, by Thunder Gulch. Consignor: Three Chimneys Sales; agent; Buyer: Dromoland Farm. 2003 Keeneland November. 3 starts, unplaced in Ireland.
2,300,000	GHASHTAH, 1987 f., Nijinsky II—My Charmer, by Poker. Consignor: Hermitage Farm; Buyer: Shadwell Estate Co. Ltd. 1987 Warner L. Jones Jr. Dispersal. Unraced.
1,700,000	UNNAMED, 2005 c., Unbridled's Song—Zing, by Storm Cat. Consignor: Taylor Made Sales Agency, agent; Buyer: Aaron U. Jones and Marie D. Jones. 2005 Keeneland November.
	LA SUENA, 2005 f., Storm Cat—Garden Secrets, by Time for a Change. Consignor: Lane's End, agent; Buyer: Courtlandt Farm. 2005 Keeneland November.
1,500,000	**KING CHARLEMAGNE**, 1998 c., Nureyev—Race the Wild Wind, by Sunny's Halo. Consignor: Ashford Stud, agent; Buyer: Demi O'Byrne. 1998 Keeneland November. 6 starts, 5 wins, $200,211 in England, France, and Ireland, SW, Fr-G1.
1,450,000	**Juniper**, 1998 c., Danzig—Montage, by Alydar. Consignor: Taylor Made Sales Agency, agent; Buyer: Demi O'Byrne. 1998 Keeneland November. 6 starts, 1 win, $37,214 in England and Ireland, spl, Eng-G2.
1,400,000	RESTORATION, 1999 c., Sadler's Wells—Madame Est Sortie (Fr), by Longleat. Consignor: Eaton Sales, agent for Padua Stables; Buyer: M. W. Miller III, agent. 1999 Keeneland November. Unraced.
	SECRET THYME, 2003 f., Storm Cat—Garden Secrets, by Time for a Change. Consignor: Eaton Sales, agent; Buyer: Brushwood Stable. 2003 Keeneland November. Unraced.
	SERENA'S CAT, 2003 f., Storm Cat—Serena's Tune, by Mr. Prospector. Consignor: Hill 'n' Dale Sales Agency, agent; Buyer: Dell Ridge Farm. 2003 Keeneland November. 4 starts, 2 wins, $55,950.
	WINTHROP, 1996 c., Storm Cat—Tinnitus, by Restless Wind. Consignor: John R. Gaines Thoroughbreds, agent; Buyer: Demi O'Byrne. 1996 Keeneland November. Unraced.
1,300,000	NEW TRIESTE, 1999 c., A.P. Indy—Lovlier Linda, by Vigors. Consignor: John R. Gaines Thoroughbreds, agent; Buyer: Paul Shanahan. 1999 Keeneland November. 1 start, unplaced, $1,500.
1,200,000	**Net Dancer**, 1989 f., Nureyev—Doubles Partner, by Damascus. Consignor: Bruce Hundley, agent for Ralph C. Wilson Jr. and Oxford Stable; Buyer: E. Hudson. 1989 Keeneland November. 13 starts, 2 wins, $46,225, spl.
	SHE'S A BEAUTY, 2000 f., Storm Cat—Now That's Funny, by Saratoga Six. Consignor: Gaines-Gentry Thoroughbreds; Buyer: Timothy Hyde. 2000 Keeneland November. 3 starts, placed, $1,772 in Ireland.
	TIDE CAT, 1998 f., Storm Cat—Maytide, by Naskra. Consignor: John R. Gaines Thoroughbreds, agent; Buyer: Brad Martin, agent for 505 Farms. 1998 Keeneland November. Unraced.
1,175,000	**RAZEEN**, 1987 c., Northern Dancer—Secret Asset, by Graustark. Consignor: Hermitage Farm; Buyer: Darley Stud Management. 1987 Warner L. Jones Jr. Dispersal. 9 starts, 3 wins, $106,665 in England and North America, SW.
1,150,000	A. P. PETAL, 2000 f., A.P. Indy—Golden Petal, by Mr. Prospector Consignor: Taylor Made Sales Agency, agent; Buyer: B. Wayne Hughes. 2000 Keeneland November. Unraced.
	DIAMOND NECKLACE, 2004 f., Unbridled's Song—Helsinki (GB), by Machiavellian. Consignor: Taylor Made Sales Agency, agent; Buyer: John Sikura. 2004 Keeneland November.

$1,100,000	**HOLD THAT TIGER**, 2000 c., Storm Cat—Beware of the Cat, by Caveat. Consignor: Lane's End, agent for Ten Broeck Farm; Buyer: Demi O'Byrne. 2000 Keeneland November. 10 starts, 3 wins, $644,235 in England, France, Ireland, and North America, SW, Fr-G1, Champion 2-year-old in Europe.
	WOROOD, 1985 f., *Vaguely Noble—Farouche, by Northern Dancer. Consignor: Newstead Farm Trust; Buyer: British Bloodstock Agency (England). 1985 Newstead Farm Trust Dispersal. 16 starts, 3 wins, $82,067 in France, SW.
1,050,000	**SEASIDE ATTRACTION**, 1987 f., Seattle Slew—Kamar, by Key to the Mint. Consignor: Hermitage Farm; Buyer: Monty Hinton. 1987 Warner L. Jones Jr. Dispersal. 12 starts, 4 wins, $272,541, SW, G1.
	WILDCAT QUEEN, 2000 f., Storm Cat—Jetapat, by Tri Jet. Consignor: Brereton C. Jones, agent; Buyer: Bradley and Bowden, agent. 2000 Keeneland November. 5 starts, 1 win, $33,595.
1,000,000	BLISSFUL, 1996 f., Mr. Prospector—Angel Fever, by Danzig. Consignor: Stone Farm, agent; Buyer: J. B. & B. Stables. 1996 Keeneland November. 3 starts, unplaced, $3,240.
	LEMON TART, 1998 f., Deputy Minister—Lemon Dove, by Forty Niner. Consignor: Hill 'n' Dale Sales Agency, agent; Buyer: Brushwood Stable. 1998 Keeneland November. 4 starts, unplaced, $2,460.
	MALIBU KAREN, 1998 f., Seeking the Gold—Regent's Walk, by Vice Regent. Consignor: Claiborne Farm, agent for Edward A. Cox Jr.; Buyer: B. Wayne Hughes. 1998 Keeneland November. 5 starts, placed, $18,490.
	PRINCESS ATOOSA, 1998 f., Gone West—Kooyonga (Ire), by Persian Bold. Consignor: Eaton Sales, agent; Buyer: Brushwood Stable. 1998 Keeneland November. Unraced
	SWISS DESERT, 1989 c., Danzig—Strictly Raised, by Raise a Native. Consignor: Bruce Hundley, agent for Kentucky Select Bloodstock and Kentucky Heritage Thoroughbred Breeding Partners; Buyer: Gainsborough Farm. 1989 Keeneland November. Unraced.

North American Top-Priced Broodmares

$9,000,000	**ASHADO**, 2001, Saint Ballado—Goulash, by Mari's Book. Consignor: Taylor Made Sales Agency, agent; Buyer: John Ferguson Bloodstock. 2005 Keeneland November.
7,100,000	**CASH RUN**, 1997, Seeking the Gold—Shared Interest, by Pleasant Colony. (Storm Cat). Consignor: Taylor Made Sales Agency, agent; Buyer: John Magnier. 2003 Keeneland November.
7,000,000	**KORVEYA**, 1982, Riverman—Konafa, by Damascus. (Woodman). Consignor: Claiborne Farm, agent; Buyer: Reynolds Bell Jr., agent. 1998 Keeneland November.
	MISS OCEANA, 1981, Alydar—Kittiwake, by *Sea-Bird. (Northern Dancer). Consignor: Newstead Farm Trust; Buyer: Foxfield. 1985 Newstead Farm Trust mixed sale.
6,100,000	**WINDSHARP**, 1991, Lear Fan—Yes She's Sharp, by Sharpen Up (GB). (Gone West). Consignor: Mill Ridge Sales, agent; Buyer: John Ferguson Bloodstock. 2003 Kenneland November.
6,000,000	PRICELESS FAME, 1975, Irish Castle—Comely Nell, by Commodore M. (Seattle Slew). Consignor: Highclere, agent for Joseph O. Morrissey; Buyer: Darley Stud Management. 1984 Fasig-Tipton Kentucky November.
5,500,000	**PRINCESS ROONEY**, 1980, Verbatim—Parrish Princess, by Drone. (Danzig). Consignor: Stone Farm agent; Buyer: Wichita Equine. 1985 Keeneland November.
5,400,000	**LADY'S SECRET**, 1982, Secretariat—Great Lady M., by Icecapade. Consignor: D. Wayne Lukas, agent for Eugene V. Klein; Buyer: Fasig-Tipton Bloodstock, agent. 1987 Night of the Stars, Fasig-Tipton Kentucky November.
	LIFE'S MAGIC, 1981, Cox's Ridge—Fire Water, by Tom Rolfe. (Mr. Prospector). Consignor: Mel Hatley Racing Stables, agent; Buyer: Eugene V. Klein. 1986 Keeneland November.
5,300,000	**SPAIN**, 1997, Thunder Gulch—Drina, by Regal and Royal. (Storm Cat). Consigner: Three Chimneys Sales, agent; Buyer: Dromoland Farm. 2003 Keeneland November.
5,250,000	**PRODUCER**, 1976, Nashua—*Marion, by Tantieme. (Northern Dancer). Consignor: Walnut Green, agent for Carelaine Stable; Buyer: BBA (England). 1983 Keeneland November
5,000,000	**I'LL GET ALONG**, 1992, Smile—Dont Worry Bout Me, by Foolish Pleasure. (Elusive Quality).Consignor: Brent Fernung, agent for CloverLeaf Farms Ii; Buyer: Gaines-Gentry Thoroughbreds. 2004 Fasig-Tipton Kentucky November.
	MACKIE, 1993, Summer Squall—Glowing Tribute, by Graustark. (Mr. Prospector). Consignor: Eaton Sales, agent; Buyer: Britton House Stud. 2000 Keeneland January.
	RISKAVERSE, 1999, Dynaformer—The Bink, by Seeking the Gold. Consignor: Bluegrass Thoroughbred Services, agent for Fox Ridge Farm; Buyer: Eaton Sales, agent. 2005 Fasig-Tipton Kentucky November.
4,900,000	**JEWEL PRINCESS**, 1992, Key to the Mint—Jewell Ridge, by Melyno (Ire). (Storm Cat). Consignor: Lane's End, agent; Buyer: John Magnier. 2000 Keeneland November.
4,800,000	**SANTA CATARINA**, 2000, Unbridled—Purrfectly, by Storm Cat. (A.P. Indy). Consignor: Denali Stud, agent for Robert and Beverly Lewis; Buyer: Eaton Sales, agent. 2004 Keeneland November.
4,700,000	**CATCHASCATCHCAN (GB)** , 1995, Pursuit of Love—Catawba, by Mill Reef. (Danzig). Consignor: Claiborne Farm, agent; Buyer: Lyons Demesne. 2000 Keeneland November.
	DANCE DESIGN (Ire) , 1993, Sadler's Well—Elegance in Design (Ire), by Habitat. (A.P. Indy). Consignor: Eaton Sales, agent for Padua Stables; Buyer: Hugo Lascelles, agent. 1999 Keeneland November.
4,600,000	**IT'S IN THE AIR**, 1976, Mr. Prospector—A Wind Is Rising, by Francis S. (Seattle Slew). Consignor: Hill 'n' Dale Sales Agency; Buyer: Darley Stud Management. 1984 Keeneland November.
	MYHRR, 1997, Mr. Prospector—Miesque, by Nureyev. Consignor: Lane's End, agent; Buyer: Reynolds Bell Jr., agent. 2000 Keeneland November.
	WINGLET, 1988, Alydar—Highest Trump, by Bold Bidder. (Storm Cat). Consignor: Lane's End, agent for Brookside Farms; Buyer: John Magnier. 1999 Keeneland November.
4,500,000	**ESTRAPADE**, 1980, *Vaguely Noble—Klepto, by No Robbery. Consignor: Blue Grass Farm, agent; Buyer: Allen E. Paulson. 1985 Keeneland November.
4,400,000	**LIFE'S MAGIC**, 1981, Cox's Ridge—Fire Water, by Tom Rolfe. (Alydar). Consignor: D. Wayne Lukas, agent for Eugene V. Klein; Buyer: Shadwell Estate Co. Ltd. 1987 Night of the Stars, Fasig-Tipton Kentucky November.
	TWO RINGS, 1970, Round Table—Allofthem, by Bagdad. (Nijinsky II). Consignor: Mint Lane Farm, agent for Kinghaven Farms; Buyer: Due Process Stable. 1983 Keeneland November.
	UNBRIDLED ELAINE, 1998, Unbridled's Song—Carols Folly, by Taylor's Falls. (Forestry). Consignor: Taylor Made Sales Agency, agent; Buyer: John Ferguson Bloodstock. 2004 Keeneland November.
4,200,000	**MAGICAL ALLURE**, 1995, General Meeting—Rare Lady, by Never Bend. (Storm Cat). Consignor: Eaton Sales, agent for Mr. and Mrs. John C. Mabee; Buyer: Shadwell Estate Co. Ltd. 2000 Keeneland November.
	TAKE CHARGE LADY, 1999, Dehere—Felicita, by Rubiano. (Seeking The Gold). Consignor: Three Chimneys Sales, agent. Buyer: Eaton Sales, agent. 2004 Keeneland November.
4,100,000	**LOVE SIGN**, 1977, Spanish Riddle—Native Nurse, by Graustark (Seattle Slew). Consignor: Three Chimneys Farm; Buyer: Arthur I. Appleton. 1984 Keeneland November.
	SANGUE (Ire) , 1978, Lyphard—Prodice (Fr), by Prominer. (Seattle Slew). Consignor: Henry Moreno, agent for R. Charlene Parks; Buyer: Nelson Bunker Hunt. 1984 Keeneland November.

Highest Yearling Prices Through the Years

Public interest in record prices paid for Thoroughbreds at public auction soared in the 1970s and '80s, when the record price for a yearling racing prospect exceeded $1-million. Yet there has always been a record-priced yearling ever since the first yearling was sold. Just when that may have been, no one can say with certainty, but the first really famous record-priced yearling was Sceptre, a lovely brown filly foaled in 1899 at the Duke of Westminster's Eaton Stud in England. Breeder and owner of *Ormonde, the greatest racehorse of the 19th century, and his grandson Flying Fox, winner of the Triple Crown in the year of Sceptre's birth, the Duke died late in 1899, forcing the dispersal of his bloodstock.

Sceptre, by the great Persimmon out of *Ormonde's full sister Ornament, by Bend Or, and with the looks to match her purple pedigree, came up for sale in 1900 at the Tattersalls Newmarket July sale, then one of the two most important auctions in England. Victorian England was scandalized when the gambler Robert Sievier outbid the late Duke's son and heir to acquire Sceptre for 10,000 guineas ($51,133 at the contemporary exchange rate).

Sceptre proved more than worth the price, though her racing career was somewhat scarred by the roller-coaster fortunes of Sievier, who won and lost fortunes betting on horses and cards for the two years he owned her. Sometimes training the great filly himself, Sievier could not resist attempting betting coups with Sceptre, running her in inappropriate races, such as the Lincolnshire Handicap against older males in her first start at three. Sceptre overcame such abuse, winning four of the five English classics of 1902 (she finished fourth in the Epsom Derby), and is still acclaimed as one of the greatest racemares of all time.

Sceptre's successors as world-record-priced yearlings have never achieved quite the same level of fame or accomplishment, but overall the race records of the 21 successive record-priced yearlings have been quite good. Of the 21 listed in the accompanying chart, five (including Sceptre) have become champions or classic winners, and four more won recognized stakes races. Thus, nine of the 21 record-priced yearlings listed, or 42.9%, were stakes winners, which is far superior to the breed average of about 3%.

On the other hand, only two, Sceptre and Majestic Prince, recaptured their purchase price in purse money on the racecourse, and there were certainly some very expensive failures. Hustle On, who wrested the record away from the English (though he himself was American-bred only by virtue of his dam being imported while carrying him), never raced. His immediate successor, New Broom, could not win in nine starts, the same dismal record as the $1.6-million Hoist the King.

Perhaps the saddest tale of any record-priced yearling, though, is that of Colonel Payne, the Fairway colt out of Golden Hair, by Golden Sun, purchased for 15,000 guineas ($78,278) by Dorothy Paget at Tattersalls Doncaster yearling sale in 1936. An eccentric English-born granddaughter of William C. Whitney, founder of the Whitney family's bloodstock empire, Paget generally refused to grant her horses a name until they had won a race, a practice then permissible under English rules. Colts that failed to meet her standards, she habitually had shot.

The Golden Hair colt ran with promise in his only outing at two, finishing third in the National Breeders' Produce Stakes, then the richest two-year-old race in England. Unfortunately, he proved to be the victim of his owner's eccentricities and never reappeared on the racecourse or anywhere else.—*John P. Sparkman*

Progression of Top-Priced Yearlings

Price	Year	Horse, Sex, Breeding	Sale	Consignor	Buyer	Race Record
$13,100,000	1985	**SEATTLE DANCER** c., Nijinsky II—My Charmer	Keeneland July	Warner L. Jones Jr.	BBA England (agent for Robert Sangster)	5-2-1-1, $152,413 Gallinule S. (Ire-G2) etc.
10,200,000	1983	SNAAFI DANCER c., Northern Dancer—My Bupers	Keeneland July	Crescent Farm	Aston Upthorpe Stud (Sheikh Mohammed bin Rashid al Maktoum)	unraced
4,250,000	1982	**EMPIRE GLORY** c., Nijinsky II—Spearfish	Keeneland July	Glencoe Farm	BBA Ireland (agent for Robert Sangster)	6-2-2-2, $35,420, Royal Whip S. (Ire-G3) etc.
3,500,000	1981	BALLYDOYLE c., Northern Dancer—South Ocean	Keeneland July	Windfields Farm	BBA Ireland (agent for Robert Sangster)	4-1-1-0, $2,542
1,700,000	1980	**LICHINE** c., Lyphard—Stylish Genie	Keeneland July	Carelaine Farm, Getty, Riordan, Heerman, agent	BBA England (agent for Stavros Niarchos)	16-3-1-4, $71,527, Prix de Suresnes etc.
1,600,000	1979	HOIST THE KING c., Hoist the Flag—Royal Dowry	Keeneland July	Tom Gentry	Kazuo Nakamura	9-0-1-1, $6,977
1,500,000	1976	CANADIAN BOUND c., Secretariat—Charming Alibi	Keeneland July	Bluegrass Farm	Blue Meadows Farm, agent (Ted Burnett, John Sikura, and partners)	4-0-1-0, $4,769
625,000	1974	KENTUCKY GOLD c., Raise a Native—Gold Digger	Keeneland July	Spendthrift Farm	Wallace A. Gilroy	7-1-0-3, $5,950
600,000	1973	**WAJIMA** c., Bold Ruler—*Iskra	Keeneland July	Claiborne Farm	James A. Scully (agent for Zenya Yoshida and partners)	16-9-5-0, $537,837, Champion 3-year-old male, Travers S. (G1) etc.
510,000	1970	**CROWNED PRINCE** c., Raise a Native—Gay Hostess	Keeneland July	Spendthrift Farm	Frank McMahon	4-2-0-0, $37,883, champion 2-year-old in England, Dewhurst S., etc.
$250,000	1967	**MAJESTIC PRINCE** c., Raise a Native—Gay Hostess	Keeneland July	Spendthrift Farm	Frank McMahon	10-9-1-0, $414,200, Kentucky Derby, Preakness S., etc.

Price	Year	Horse, Sex, Breeding	Sale	Consignor	Buyer	Race Record
$200,000	1966	BOLD DISCOVERY c., Bold Ruler—La Dauphine	Keeneland July	Spendthrift Farm	Frank McMahon	3-0-0-0, $0
170,000	1964	ONE BOLD BID c., Bold Ruler—Forgetmenow	Keeneland July	Warner L. Jones Jr.	Mrs. Velma Morrison	unraced
130,000	1961	SWAPSON c., Swaps—Obedient	Keeneland July	Spendthrift Farm	John M. Olin	31-8-3-5, $26,766
118,492 (28,000g)	1945	**SAYAJIRAO** c., Nearco—Rosy Legend	Tattersalls Doncaster	Sir Eric Ohlson	Gaekwar of Baroda	16-6-6-3, $96,647, champion 3-year-old in England, St. Leger S. etc.
78,278 (15,000g)	1936	**Colonel Payne** c., Fairway—Golden Hair	Tattersalls Doncaster	Viscount Furness	Dorothy Paget	1-0-0-1, $494, 3rd National Breeders' Produce S.
75,000	1928	NEW BROOM c., Whisk Broom II—Payment	Fasig-Tipton Saratoga	Mrs. T. J. Regan	C.V.B. Cushman	9-0-2-1, $275
70,000	1927	HUSTLE ON c., Hurry On—*Fatima II	Fasig-Tipton Saratoga	Himyar Stud	W. R. Coe	unraced
55,724 (14,500g)	1920	BLUE ENSIGN c., The Tetrarch—Blue Tit	Tattersalls Doncaster	Sledmere Stud	Lord Glanely	1-0-0-0, $0
53,492 (11,500g)	1919	**WESTWARD HO** c., Swynford—Blue Tit	Tattersalls Doncaster	Sledmere Stud	Lord Glanely	6-2-0-0, $3,989, Great Yorkshire S., 3rd St. Leger S.
51,133 (10,000g)	1900	**SCEPTRE** f., Persimmon—Ornament	Tattersalls Newmarket July	Estate of Duke of Westminster	Robert Sevier	25-13-4-4, $192,544 champion 3-year-old, champion older horse, Epsom Oaks etc.

Top-Priced Yearlings by Year

High-priced yearlings have a poor reputation in the Thoroughbred industry. Although statistics show that, on average, the higher the price paid for a yearling the better the racehorse, high-priced failures such as the $10.2-million Snaafi Dancer, who never raced, are remembered more readily than success stories such as the $2.9-million Horse of the Year A.P. Indy. Even the world's record-priced yearling, the $13.1-million Seattle Dancer, is regarded as a failure though he won a Group 2 race in Europe.

In the years since Fasig-Tipton first began selling yearlings at Saratoga, 24 of the 92 top-priced yearlings each year (there were six ties) have become stakes winners. That 26% strike rate is obviously far higher than the 3% average of stakes winners to foals for the breed.

Yearling buyers appear to have greatly improved their selection techniques over the last few decades. The record of top-priced yearlings for the first half of the 20th century was little better than that of the average horse. But in the 36 years since 1969 Kentucky Derby winner Majestic Prince sold for $250,000 at Keeneland July in 1967, 15 year-toppers have become stakes winners. *—John P. Sparkman*

Most Expensive North American Yearlings by Year

Year Sold	Horse	Sex, Sire—Dam	Price	Sale	Buyer	Race Record
2005	UNNAMED	c., Storm Cat—Tranquility Lake	**$9,700,000**	Kee Sept	John Ferguson Bldstk.	unraced
2004	MR. SEKIGUCHI	c., Storm Cat—Welcome Surprise	**8,000,000**	Kee Sept	Hideyuki Mori	2-1-1-0, $45,800
2003	HASHIMIYA	f., Gone West—Touch of Greatness	**3,800,000**	Kee Sept	John Ferguson Bldstk.	2-0-0-0, $1,250
2002	**ONE COOL CAT**	c., Storm Cat—Tacha	**3,100,000**	Kee July	Demi O'Byrne	10-5-0-1, $568,086, Champion 2yo male in Europe, Hwt. at 3, 5-7 fur. in Eng, Ire, Phoenix S. (Ire-G1), etc.
2001	**VAN NISTELROOY**	c., Storm Cat—Halory	**6,400,000**	Kee Sept	Demi O'Byrne	6-3-1-1, $229,980, EBF Futurity S. (Ire-G2), etc.
2000	TASMANIAN TIGER	c., Storm Cat—Hum Along	**6,800,000**	Kee Sept	Demi O'Byrne	25-3-1-1, $154,543
1999	DUBAI TO DUBAI	c., Kris S.—Mr. P's Princess	**3,900,000**	Kee Sept	John Ferguson Bldstk.	11-3-1-2, $152,319
1998	**FUSAICHI PEGASUS**	c., Mr. Prospector—Angel Fever	**4,000,000**	Kee July	Fusao Sekiguchi	9-6-2-0, $1,994,400, Kentucky Derby (G1), etc.
1997	SASHA'S PROSPECT	c., Mr. Prospector—Missy's Mirage	**2,300,000**	Kee Sept	Padua Stables	10-1-0-0, $37,200
1996	PARGATA KING	c., Storm Cat—Alpargata	**1,700,000**	Kee July	Fusao Sekiguchi	1-0-0-0, $0
1995	CONSTANT WISH	f., Mr. Prospector—Daring Bidder	**1,250,000**	Kee July	Demi O'Byrne	unraced
1994	**Golden Colors**	f., Mr. Prospector—Winning Colors	**1,050,000**	Kee July	Pegasus Bloodstock	10-3-1-0, $509,963, 2nd Daily Hai Queen Cup
1993	GOLDEN LEGEND	c., Mr. Prospector—Reminiscing	**1,050,000**	Kee July	John R. Gaines, agt.	6-0-0-0, $5,700
1992	**NUMEROUS**	c., Mr. Prospector—Number	**1,700,000**	Kee July	Finney Bloodstock, agt.	18-4-2-2, $255,348, Derby Trial S. (G3) etc.
1991	**JEUNE HOMME**	c., Nureyev—Alydariel	**2,600,000**	Kee July	Morio Sakurai	20-4-5-3, $431,724, Citation H. (G2), etc.
1990	**A.P. INDY**	c., Seattle Slew—Weekend Surprise	**2,900,000**	Kee July	BBA (Ire)	11-8-0-1, $2,979,815, Horse of the Year, champion 3yo male, Breeders' Cup Classic (G1), etc.
1989	**NORTHERN PARK**	c., Northern Dancer—Mrs. Penny	**2,800,000**	Kee July	Zenya Yoshida	30-4-7-4, $171,493, Grand Prix de Villeurbanne
1988	**ROYAL ACADEMY**	c., Nijinsky II—Crimson Saint	**3,500,000**	Kee July	Vincent O'Brien	7-4-2-0, $758,994, European Hwt. at 3, 7-9½ f., Breeders' Cup Mile (G1) etc.

Year Sold	Horse	Sex, Sire—Dam	Price	Sale	Buyer	Race Record
1987	**WARRSHAN**	c., Northern Dancer—Secret Asset	$3,700,000	Kee July	Darley Stud Mgt.	11-4-0-3, $125,928, Gordon S. (Eng-G3) etc.
1986	NORTHERN STATE	c., Northern Dancer—South Ocean	3,600,000	Kee July	Darley Stud Mgt.	4-1-0-0, $2,137
1985	**SEATTLE DANCER**	c., Nijinsky II—My Charmer	13,100,000	Kee July	BBA (Eng), agt. for Robert Sangster	5-2-1-1, $152,413, Gallinule S. (Ire-G2) etc.
1984	IMPERIAL FALCON	c., Northern Dancer—Ballade	8,250,000	Kee July	BBA (Eng)	3-2-0-0, $13,395
1983	SNAAFI DANCER	c., Northern Dancer—My Bupers	10,200,000	Kee July	Aston Upthorpe Stud	unraced
1982	**EMPIRE GLORY**	c., Nijinsky II—Spearfish	4,250,000	Kee July	BBA (Ire), agt. for Robert Sangster	6-2-2-2, $35,420, Royal Whip S. (Ire-G3) etc.
1981	BALLYDOYLE	c., Northern Dancer—South Ocean	3,500,000	Kee July	BBA (Ire), agt. for Robert Sangster	4-1-1-0, $2,542
1980	**LICHINE**	c., Lyphard—Stylish Genie	1,700,000	Kee July	BBA (Eng), agt. for Stavros Niarchos	16-3-1-4, $71,527, Prix de Suresnes etc.
1979	HOIST THE KING	c., Hoist the Flag—Royal Dowry	1,600,000	Kee July	Kazuo Nakamura	9-0-1-1, $6,977
1978	**NUREYEV**	c., Northern Dancer—Special	1,300,000	Kee July	BBA (Eng)	3-2-0-0, $42,522, champion miler in France, Prix Thomas Bryon (Fr-G3) etc.
1977	FOREIGN SECRETARY	c., Secretariat—Lady Victoria	725,000	Kee July	BBA (Ire)	11-3-1-1, $47,375
1976	CANADIAN BOUND	c., Secretariat—Charming Alibi	1,500,000	Kee July	Blue Meadows Farm, agt.	4-0-1-0, $4,769
1975	ELEGANT PRINCE	c., Raise a Native—Gay Hostess	715,000	Kee July	Franklin Groves	unraced
1974	KENTUCKY GOLD	c., Raise a Native—Gold Digger	625,000	Kee July	Wallace A. Gilroy	7-1-0-3, $5,950
1973	**WAJIMA**	c., Bold Ruler—*Iskra	600,000	Kee July	James A. Scully, agt. for Zenya Yoshida & partners	16-9-5-0, $537,837, champion 3-year-old male, Travers S. (G1) etc.
1972	**Riboquill**	c., *Ribot—Quill	230,000	Kee July	Cromwell Bloodstock	11-3-1-1, $46,875, 3rd Grand Prix de Deauville (Fr-G2)
1971	PASS	c., Buckpasser—*Casaque Grise	235,000	FT Sara	Marion duPont Scott	unraced
1970	**CROWNED PRINCE**	c., Raise a Native—Gay Hostess	510,000	Kee July	Frank McMahon	4-2-0-0, $37,883, champion two-year-old in Eng., Dewhurst S. etc.
1969	KNIGHTS HONOR	c., Round Table—Vestment	210,000	Kee July	Bert W. Martin	4-0-1-1, $1,670
1968	REINE ENCHANTEUR	f., *Sea-Bird—*Libra	405,000	Kee July	W. P. Rosso	7-1-1-5, $9,305
1967	**MAJESTIC PRINCE**	c., Raise a Native—Gay Hostess	250,000	Kee July	Frank McMahon	10-9-1-0, $414,200, Kentucky Derby, Preakness S., etc.
1966	BOLD DISCOVERY	c., Bold Ruler—La Dauphine	200,000	Kee July	Frank McMahon	3-0-0-0, $0
1965	ROYAL MATCH	f., *Turn-to—Cosmah	140,000	Kee July	Arnold Winick, agt.	unraced
1964	ONE BOLD BID	c., Bold Ruler—Forgetmenow	170,000	Kee July	Mrs. Velma Morrison	unraced
1963	LENSO	c., Swaps—*Blue Star II	85,000	Kee July	Leonard Sasso	5-0-0-1, $420
1962	GOLDEN GORSE	f., Swaps—*Auld Alliance	83,000	FT Sara	J. T. Skinner, agt.	2-0-0-2, $735
1961	SWAPSON	c., Swaps—Obedient	130,000	Kee July	John M. Olin	31-8-3-5, $26,766
1960	NASHOLIN	c., Nashua—*Pashmina	75,000	Kee July	N. McLeod	25-2-0-3, $7,955
1959	ROYAL DRAGOON	c., *Royal Charger—Grecian Queen	80,000	Kee July	C. G. Raible	9-1-2-1, $5,050
	GLOBEMASTER	c., *Heliopolis—No Strings	80,000	FT Sara	Penowa Farms	27-10-9-2, $355,423, Wood Memorial S., etc.
1958	**PRINCE BLESSED**	c., *Princequillo—Dog Blessed	77,000	Kee July	Kerr Stables	35-8-6-4, $255,805, Hollywood Gold Cup S. etc.
1957	LAW AND ORDER	c., *Nasrullah—In Bloom	65,000	Kee July	J. H. Rouse Farm, agt. for King Ranch	unraced
1956	*RISE 'N SHINE	c., Hyperion—Deodara	$87,000	FT Sara	Mrs. M. E. Lunn	43-4-2-1, $17,515
1955	TULSAN	c., *Nasrullah—In Bloom	80,000	Kee July	Forrest Lindsay Farm	25-2-2-3, $8,050
1954	NALUR	c., *Nasrullah—Lurline B	86,000	Kee July	F. J. Adams Syndicate	20-2-1-0, $6,575
1953	ROMAN BOAT	f., Roman—Boat	59,000	Kee July	Duntreath Farm	4-1-0-0, $1,950
1952	LADYBREATH	f., Roman—Miss Brief	46,000	Kee July	Chester Gates, agt.	7-1-0-0, $2,100
1951	**PERFECTION**	f., Bull Lea—Lady Lark	60,000	Kee July	C. S. Jones	31-3-4-4, $30,600, Playa del Rey S., etc.
1950	FARAHAAN	f., *Mahmoud—Aphaona	35,000	FT Sara	William Post	3-0-0-1, $725
1949	**Unification**	c., War Admiral—Summer Time	37,000	Kee July	William Helis	80-6-11-14, $24,015, 3rd Dominion Day H.
	OLD ROWLEY	c., Menow—Risk	37,000	Kee July	Moody Jolley, agt.	9-2-1-1, $5,275
1948	DESTINO	c., *Beau Pere—Sun Lady	52,000	FT Sara	King Ranch	7-0-4-1, $3,400
1947	**Spotted Bull**	c., *Bull Dog—Spotted Beauty	45,000	Kee July	Jaclyn Stable	19-4-1-2, $12,850, 3rd Will Rogers H.
1946	LA CHICUELA	f., *Blenheim II—La Chica	54,000	Kee July	J. P. Smith	14-1-2-2, $4,100
	SILVER QUEEN	f., War Admiral—Danise M	54,000	Kee July	Maine Chance Farm	16-1-1-1, $3,650
1945	SIR GALLASCENE	c., *Sir Gallahad III—*Scenery II	46,000	Kee July	C. C. Tanner	54-1-5-3, $8,175
	BLUE FANTASY	f., Blue Larkspur—Risk	46,000	Kee July	Leslie Combs II, agt. for Elizabeth Nightingale Graham	unraced
1944	**COLONY BOY**	c., Eight Thirty—Heritage	46,000	Kee July	Leslie Combs II, agt. for Elizabeth Arden (Graham)	17-5-0-3, $39,750, Walden S., etc.
1943	PERICLES	c., *Blenheim II—Risk	66,000	FT Kee	William Helis	5-2-0-1, $5,200
1942	**BOY KNIGHT**	c., *Sir Gallahad III—Heloise	9,000	FT Sara	Crispin Oglebay	36-5-2-10, $44,145, Wilmington H., etc.
1941	BULRUSHES	c., *Bull Dog—Spur Flower	10,000	FT Sara	Ogden Phipps	196-25-40-33, $24,232
1940	REAPER'S BLADE	c., *Sickle—Friendly Gal	18,000	FT Sara	Brookmeade Stable	15-3-2-2, $3,425
1939	TOM-TOM	c., *Sir Gallahad III—Percussion	20,000	FT Sara	Manhasset Stable	unraced
	Lord Kitchener	c., *Blenheim II—Argosie	20,000	FT Sara	Samuel D. Riddle	38-4-5-7, $9,726, 3rd Travers S. etc.

Year Sold	Horse	Sex, Sire—Dam	Price	Sale	Buyer	Race Record
1938	**Romanov**	c., *Ksar—Duration	$22,000	FT Sara	Brookmeade Stable	28-2-3-3, $4,756, 3rd Lawrence Realization H.
1937	TEMULAC	c., *Sir Gallahad III—Marching Along	26,000	FT Sara	Calumet Farm	69-7-5-11, $6,732
1936	FARRELL	c., *Sir Gallahad III—Sari	18,000	FT Sara	Milky Way Farms	100-12-19-13, $9,999
1935	WINGED VICTORY	c., Victorian—Grief	13,000	FT Sara	Milky Way Farms	97-7-16-11, $7,130
1934	TEDDY BOY	c., *Teddy—Superstitious	11,500	FT Sara	Calumet Farm	32-1-3-5, $1,425
1933	**CALUMET DICK**	c., Gallant Fox—*Martha Snow	13,000	FT Sara	Calumet Farm	51-17-6-8, $72,515, Dixie H.
1932	THE TRIUMVIR	c., Pompey—Cowslip	14,500	FT Sara	Greentree Stable	176-12-15-15, $10,935
1931	CARRY THE NEWS	c., The Porter—Cypher Code	16,000	FT Sara	J. H. Whitney	20-1-3-6, $1,665
1930	TEXAS KNIGHT	c., *Sir Gallahad III—Fasnet	30,000	FT Sara	Three D's Stock Farm	82-8-5-11, $6,390
	GALA FLIGHT	f., *Sir Gallahad III—*Starflight	30,000	FT Sara	Griffin Watkins	25-3-0-4, $3,425
1929	**War**	c., Man o' War—Milky Way	45,000	FT Sara	Sagamore Stable	61-8-13-4, $8,280, 2nd Brookdale H.
1928	NEW BROOM	c., Whisk Broom II—Payment	75,000	FT Sara	C.V.B. Cushman	9-0-2-1, $275
1927	HUSTLE ON	c., Hurry On—*Fatima II	70,000	FT Sara	W. R. Coe	unraced
1926	**TUSKEGEE**	c., Black Toney—Humanity	35,000	FT Sara	E. M. Byers	43-10-7-8, $11,925 Belgrade Claiming S.
1925	WAR FEATHERS	c., Man o' War—*Tuscan Red	50,500	FT Sara	Hamilton Farms	7-1-1-0, $1,350
1924	BLASISTA	c., Eternal—*Aquamarine	16,000	FT Sara	William Zeigler Jr.	5-0-0-0, $0
1923	**FLYING EBONY**	c., The Finn—Princess Mary	21,000	FT Sara	G. A. Cochran	13-6-1-2, $62,420, Kentucky Derby, etc.
1922	THE TRAMP	c., The Finn—Kate Adams	12,500	FT Sara	Montfort Jones	1-0-0-0, $0
1921	COEUR DE LION	c., Fair Play—*Couronne de Laurier	8,600	FT Sara	Rancocas Stable	288-48-50-43, $33,165
1920	PIRATE GOLD	c., Rock View—Gold	14,000	FT Sara	Greentree Stable	157-20-34-20, $23,258
1919	SUN TURRET	c., Sunstar—Marian Hood	25,000	FT Sara	J.K.L. Ross	103-6-5-11, $3,855
1918	**Royal Jester**	c., Black Jester—*Primula II	14,500	FT Sara	J.K.L. Ross	33-1-9-7, $4,381, 2nd Earl Grey H., etc.
1917	***HURON**	c., *Sweeper—Zuna	4,000	FT Sara	Joseph E. Widener	105-28-20-14, $17,131, Windon H., etc.
	THE SAINT	c., Sain—Nannette	4,000	FT Sara	Samuel D. Riddle	unraced

†† Through May 1, 2006

Leading Sires of Top-Priced Yearlings

Northern Dancer	7
*Sir Gallahad III	7
Mr. Prospector	6
Storm Cat	5
Raise a Native	4
*Blenheim II	3
*Nasrullah	3
Bold Ruler	3
Nijinsky II	3
Roman	3
Swaps	3

Leading Consignors of Top-Priced Yearlings

Arthur B. Hancock Sr.	12
Spendthrift Farm/ Leslie Combs II	9
Lane's End	5
Hermitage Farm/ Warner L. Jones	4
Windfields Farm	4
Claiborne Farm	3
Robert A. Fairbarn	3
Himyar Stud/Phil T. Chinn	3

Leading Buyers of Top-Priced Yearlings

†Sheikh Mohammed bin Rashid al Maktoum	5
British Bloodstock Agency (Eng)	4
British Bloodstock Agency (Ire)	4
Demi O'Byrne	4
Greentree Stud	4
Calumet Farm	3
Maine Chance Farm/ Elizabeth Arden	3
Frank McMahon	3
‡Fusao Sekiguchi	3

† Includes those bought in the name of Aston Upthorpe Stud, Darley Stud Management, and John Ferguson Bloodstock
‡ Includes horses bought for Fusao Sekiguchi by Hideyuki Mori

Sales Average of All Horses by Year

Year	Average	Change	Deflated Average
2005	$54,909	5.2%	$48,980
2004	52,205	15.5%	47,855
2003	45,206	8.4%	42,527
2002	41,694	–5.5%	40,019
2001	44,108	–14.3%	43,074
2000	51,443	3.3%	51,443
1999	49,795	18.1%	50,880
1998	42,165	12.6%	43,707
1997	37,457	13.9%	39,257
1996	32,892	15.7%	35,047
1995	28,440	13.9%	30,877
1994	24,966	13.7%	27,660
1993	21,952	9.9%	24,838
1992	19,972	–5.5%	23,120
1991	21,136	–10.6%	25,030
1990	23,645	–11.3%	28,980
1989	26,648	–1.1%	33,922
1988	26,957	–6.0%	35,613

Two-Year-Olds in Training Sales Average by Year

Year	Average	Change	Deflated Average
2005	$60,927	3.4%	$54,358
2004	58,918	27.7%	54,008
2003	46,140	–3.1%	43,406
2002	47,624	1.4%	45,711
2001	46,971	–7.7%	45,871
2000	50,873	–4.7%	50,873
1999	53,382	16.9%	54,545
1998	45,668	0.5%	47,338
1997	45,425	14.1%	47,608
1996	39,804	24.5%	42,411
1995	31,971	23.3%	34,711
1994	25,929	27.1%	28,727
1993	20,402	7.7%	23,084
1992	18,947	4.9%	21,933
1991	18,056	–11.5%	21,382
1990	20,403	30.0%	25,007
1989	15,690	–5.2%	19,973
1988	16,542	5.4%	21,854

Yearling Sales Average by Year

Year	Average	Change	Deflated Average
2005	$54,699	3.7%	$48,792
2004	52,748	9.4%	48,352
2003	48,213	10.0%	45,356
2002	43,848	–15.9%	42,087
2001	52,140	–4.4%	50,918
2000	54,558	8.0%	54,558
1999	50,523	17.8%	51,624
1998	42,880	12.3%	44,448
1997	38,189	10.6%	40,025

Year	Average	Change	Deflated Average
1996	34,540	11.9%	$36,803
1995	30,880	13.6%	33,527
1994	27,177	8.3%	30,110
1993	25,098	12.6%	28,398
1992	22,290	–14.8%	25,803
1991	26,157	–12.9%	30,976
1990	30,030	–6.4%	36,806
1989	32,097	–2.0%	40,859
1988	32,748	–7.3%	43,264

Weanling Sales Average by Year

Year	Average	Change	Deflated Average
2005	$43,793	18.4%	$39,064
2004	36,986	–7.8%	33,904
2003	40,087	28.6%	37,711
2002	31,181	14.9%	29,928
2001	27,149	–24.0%	26,513
2000	35,716	–16.7%	35,716
1999	42,852	9.3%	43,786
1998	39,203	21.8%	40,637
1997	32,178	14.0%	33,725
1996	28,232	8.1%	30,081
1995	26,124	19.7%	28,363
1994	21,822	–7.5%	24,177
1993	23,589	47.8%	26,690
1992	15,962	–21.7%	18,478

Year	Average	Change	Deflated Average
1991	20,376	12.0%	$24,130
1990	18,195	–23.0%	22,301
1989	23,635	50.1%	30,087
1988	15,743	–55.5%	20,798

Broodmare Sales Average by Year

Year	Average	Change	Deflated Average
2005	$57,597	3.4%	$51,377
2004	55,694	27.5%	51,053
2003	43,683	7.8%	41,095
2002	40,515	9.0%	38,888
2001	37,183	–32.1%	36,312
2000	54,752	2.4%	54,752
1999	53,457	22.3%	54,622
1998	43,701	15.3%	45,299
1997	37,913	21.5%	39,735
1996	31,192	21.0%	33,235
1995	25,770	5.8%	27,979
1994	24,355	33.3%	26,983
1993	18,274	1.5%	20,676
1992	18,009	2.3%	20,847
1991	17,604	–8.7%	20,847
1990	19,280	–29.4%	23,630
1989	27,291	–0.1%	34,741
1988	27,328	7.3%	36,103

Pinhooking in American Auctions

No one knows exactly how the terms pinhooking or pinhooker entered the English language—or at least Thoroughbred racing's esoteric subset of Shakespeare's tongue—but the practice and profession have become far more common, lucrative, and important to the industry since the early 1990s, when the market for two-year-olds exploded.

Pinhooking is a variation on the capitalist concept of wholesale versus retail. The pinhooker buys a horse—for example, a yearling at auction—with the express purpose of reselling that horse at a later auction, almost always a sale of two-year-olds in training. Thus, the pinhooker tries to purchase at a relatively low price (wholesale) and resell later at a higher price (retail). In between, the pinhooker makes further investments of time and money trying to improve the quality of the wholesale purchase in hopes of cashing in on a retail sale.

Pinhooking is a business with high risks and the potential for high rewards, as illustrated by the following tables, which detail the most and least successful pinhooks on record.

Most Successful Pinhooks by Total Gain (through April 10, 2006)

Yearling to Juvenile

$15,575,000 THE GREEN MONKEY, 2004 b. c., Forestry—Magical Masquerade, by Unbridled. **Yearling Purchase:** $425,000, 2005 Fasig-Tipton Kentucky July, by Hartley/De Renzo Thoroughbreds LLC. **Juvenile Sale:** $16,000,000, 2006 Fasig-Tipton Calder, consigned by Hartley/De Renzo Thoroughbreds, agent, purchased by Demi O'Byrne. 3,664.7% gain. Unraced.

$4,230,000 FUSAICHI SAMURAI, 2002 dk. b. or br. c., Fusaichi Pegasus—Hidden Storm, by Storm Cat. **Yearling Purchase:** $270,000, 2003 Fasig-Tipton Saratoga selected, by White Horse Stables. **Juvenile Sale:** $4,500,000, 2004 Fasig-Tipton Calder, consigned by Kirkwood Stables, agent, purchased by Fusao Sekiguchi. 1,566.7% gain. 2-1-0-0, $21,400.

$3,130,000 **Chekhov**, 2002 b. g., Pulpit—In My Cap, by Vice Regent. **Yearling Purchase:** $170,000, 2003 Keeneland September, by Michael J. Ryan, agent. **Juvenile Sale:** $3,300,000, 2004 Keeneland April, consigned by Niall Brennan Stables, agent, purchased by Demi O'Byrne. 1,841.2% gain. 11-1-2-1, spl, $158,366.

$2,943,000 DUBAI DREAMER, 2002 gr. or ro. c., Stephen Got Even—Blacktie Bid, by Black Tie Affair (Ire). **Yearling Purchase:** $157,000, 2003 Fasig-Tipton Kentucky July, by Michael J. Ryan, agent. **Juvenile Sale:** $3,100,000, 2004 Fasig-Tipton Calder, consigned by Niall Brennan Stables, agent, purchased by John Ferguson. 1,874.5% gain. 4-1-1-0, $19,168.

$2,800,000 BARBADOS, 2003 b. c., Forestry—Rare Bird, by Rahy. **Yearling Purchase:** $200,000, 2004 Fasig-Tipton Kentucky July, by Tony Bowling and Bobby Dodd. **Juvenile Sale:** $3,000,000, 2005 Fasig-Tipton Calder, consigned by Tony Bowling and Bobby Dodd, agent, purchased by Demi O'Byrne. 1,400% gain. 2-0-1-0, $12,150.

$2,670,000 DIAMOND FURY, 2001 ch. r., Sea of Secrets—Swift Spirit, by Tasso. **Yearling Purchase:** $30,000, 2002 Fasig-Tipton Kentucky July, by Becky Thomas. **Juvenile Sale:** $2,700,000, 2003 Barretts March, consigned by Sequel Bloodstock, agent, purchased by Charles Fipke. 8,900% gain. 13-3-2-2, $114,580.

$2,450,000 RONDO, 2003 b. c., Grand Slam—Dama, by Storm Cat. **Yearling Purchase:** $450,000, 2004 Fasig-Tipton Kentucky July, by Maurice W. Miller, agent. **Juvenile Sale:** $2,900,000, 2005 Fasig-Tipton Calder, consigned by Maurice W. Miller, agent, purchased by Darley. 544.4% gain. 1-0-1-0, $8,600.

$1,925,000 DUBAI ESCAPADE, 2002 b. f., Awesome Again—Sassy Pants, by Saratoga Six. **Yearling Purchase:** $75,000, 2003 Keeneland September, by Gulf Coast Farms. **Juvenile Sale:** $2,000,000, 2004 Barretts March, consigned by Jerry Bailey Sales Agency, agent, purchased by John Ferguson Bloodstock. 2,566.7% gain. 4-3-0-0, $57,050.

$1,869,000 **ATLANTIC OCEAN**, 2000 dk. b. or br. m., Stormy Atlantic—Super Chef, by Seattle Slew. **Yearling Purchase:** $31,000, 2001 Keeneland September, by James K. Chapman. **Juvenile Sale:** $1,900,000, 2002 Barretts March, consigned by Chapman Farms, purchased by The Thoroughbred Corp. 6,029% gain. 19-5-3-2, G3, $678,210.

$1,825,000 MOROCCO, 1997 ch. h., Brocco—Roll Over Baby, by Rollin On Over. **Yearling Purchase:** $175,000, 1998 Fasig-Tipton Saratoga selected, by Alfred T. Eldredge. **Juvenile Sale:** $2,000,000, 1999 Barretts March, consigned by Sequel Bloodstock, agent, purchased by The Thoroughbred Corp. 1,042.9% gain. 16-4-0-1, $133,640.

$1,825,000 Unnamed, 2004 b. c., Golden Missile—Silverdew, by Silver Deputy. **Yearling Purchase:** $175,000, 2005 Keeneland September, by O & H Bloodstock. **Juvenile Sale:** $2,000,000, 2006 Fasig-Tipton Calder, consigned by O & H Bloodstock, agent, purchased by, agent. 1,042.9% gain. Unraced.

$1,820,000 Unnamed, 2004 ch. c., Mr. Greeley—Peaks Mill, by Stalwart. **Yearling Purchase:** $180,000, 2005 Keeneland September, by D & B Ventures. **Juvenile Sale:** $2,000,000, 2006 Fasig-Tipton Calder, consigned by Nick de Meric, agent, purchased by Demi O'Byrne. 1,011.1% gain. Unraced.

$1,805,000 **WHAT A SONG**, 2003 dk. b. or br. c., Songandaprayer—What a Knight, by Tough Knight. **Yearling Purchase:** $95,000, 2004 Fasig-Tipton Kentucky July, by M.S.T.S. **Juvenile Sale:** $1,900,000, 2005 Barretts March, consigned by Murray Smith, agent, purchased by Robert B. and Beverly J. Lewis. 1,900% gain. 3-3-0-0, G2, $179,700.

$1,805,000 **YONAGUSKA**, 1998 dk. b. or br. h., Cherokee Run—Marital Spook, by Silver Ghost. **Yearling Purchase:** $145,000, 1999 Keeneland September, by Michael J. Ryan, agent. **Juvenile Sale:** $1,950,000, 2000 Fasig-Tipton Calder, consigned by Niall Brennan, agent, purchased by Demi O'Byrne. 1,244.8% gain. 18-6-1-5, G1, $536,355.

$1,780,000 LA SALLE STREET, 1997 dk. b. or br. h., Not For Love—Three Grand, by Assert (Ire). **Yearling Purchase:** $220,000, 1998 Fasig-Tipton fall yearling, by Cam Allard. **Juvenile Sale:** $2,000,000, 1999 Keeneland April, consigned by Cam Allard, purchased by Demi O'Byrne. 809.1% gain. 3-0-1-0, $3,420.

Most Successful Pinhooks by Percentage Gain (through April 10, 2006)

Yearling to Juvenile

8,900.0% DIAMOND FURY, 2001 ch. r., Sea of Secrets—Swift Spirit, by Tasso. **Yearling Purchase:** $30,000, 2002 Fasig-Tipton Saratoga selected, by Becky Thomas. **Juvenile Sale:** $2,700,000, 2003 Barretts March, consigned by Sequel Bloodstock, agent, purchased by Charles Fipke. $2,670,000 gain. 13-3-2-2, $114,580.

6,029.0% **ATLANTIC OCEAN**, 2000 dk. b. or br. m., Stormy Atlantic—Super Chef, by Seattle Slew. **Yearling Purchase:** $31,000, 2001 Keeneland September, by James K. Chapman. **Juvenile Sale:** $1,900,000, 2002 Barretts March, consigned by Chapman Farms, purchased by The Thoroughbred Corp. $1,869,000 gain. 19-5-3-2, G3, $678,210.

4,900.0% AFTERNOON QUE, 2002 dk. b. or br. c., Afternoon Deelites—How 'bout Chris, by Unbridled. **Yearling Purchase:** $5,000, 2003 Fasig-Tipton Midlantic Eastern fall yearling, by M & H Training and Sales. **Juvenile Sale:** $250,000, 2004 OBSC March, consigned by M & H Training and Sales, agent, purchased by West Point Thoroughbreds. $245,000 gain. 3-1-0-1, $18,550.

4,687.2% **Major Adonis**, 1997 b. g., Major Impact—Adonara, by Strawberry Road (Aus). **Yearling Purchase:** $4,700, 1998 Fasig-Tipton Kentucky October, by Bea Roberts and Robert H. Roberts. **Juvenile Sale:** $225,000, 1999 Keeneland November, consigned by Bea and Robert H. Roberts, purchased by Eugene N. Melnyk. $220,300 gain. 16-2-3-2, spl, $100,926.

3,664.7% THE GREEN MONKEY, 2004 b. c., Forestry—Magical Masquerade, by Unbridled. **Yearling Purchase:** $425,000, 2005 Fasig-Tipton Kentucky July, by Hartley/De Renzo Thoroughbreds LLC. **Juvenile Sale:** $16,000,000, 2006 Fasig-Tipton Calder, consigned by Hartley/De Renzo Thoroughbreds LLC, agent, purchased by Demi O'Byrne. $15,575,000 gain. Unraced.

3,650.0% HYPER NAKAYAMA, 1995 dk. b. or br. h., Well Decorated—Tea and Roses, by Fleet Nasrullah. **Yearling Purchase:** $8,000, 1996 Keeneland January, by Donna M. Wormser. **Juvenile Sale:** $300,000, 1997 OBSC February, consigned by Donna M. Wormser, agent, purchased by Heatherway, agent. $292,000 gain. 24-4-7-4, $1,002,590.

3,650.0% IRREVOCABLE, 2001 b. m., Our Emblem—Northern Glance, by Nijinsky II. **Yearling Purchase:** $3,200, 2002 Keeneland January, by Burden Creek Farm. **Juvenile Sale:** $120,000, 2003 Keeneland April, consigned by American Equistock and Parrish Farms, purchased by John C. Kimmel. $116,800 gain. 11-3-3-0, $75,055.

3,455.6% MUTANABI, 2002 b. c., Wild Rush—Freudenau, by Meadowlake. **Yearling Purchase:** $45,000, 2003 OBSC August, by Ricky Leppala. **Juvenile Sale:** $1,600,000, 2004 OBSC February, consigned by W. D. North, agent, purchased by John Ferguson. $1,555,000 gain. 2-0-1-1, $3,171.

3,125.8% AFRASHAD, 2002 ch. c., Smoke Glacken—Flo White, by Whitesburg. **Yearling Purchase:** $15,500, 2003 Keeneland September, by Samerin Oaks. **Juvenile Sale:** $500,000, 2004 OBSC April, consigned by Costanzo Sales, purchased by John Ferguson Bloodstock, agent. $484,500 gain. 1-1-0-0, $7,988.

2,995.2% NOTABLE TIGER, 2002 dk. b. or br. c., Tiger Ridge—Notable Girl, by What a Pleasure. **Yearling Purchase:** $21,000, 2003 OBSC August, by Hartley/De Renzo Thoroughbreds LLC. **Juvenile Sale:** $650,000, 2004 OBSC March, consigned by Hartley/De Renzo Thoroughbreds LLC, agent, purchased by John Ferguson Bloodstock. $629,000 gain. 4-1-0-1, $30,480.

2,677.8% JIM'S SMOKIN PINOT, 2002 dk. b. or br. c., Victory Gallop—Buck's Lady, by Alleged. **Yearling Purchase:** $18,000, 2003 Keeneland September, by Tony Bowling and Bobby Dodd. **Juvenile Sale:** $500,000, 2004 Barretts March, consigned by Terry Oliver, agent, purchased by Never Tell Farm LLC. $482,000 gain. 4-0-2-0, $19,970.

Least Successful Pinhooks by Total Loss (through April 10, 2006)

Yearling to Juvenile

–$300,000 **EVIL MINISTER**, 2002 ch. c., Deputy Minister—Evil's Pic, by Piccolino. **Yearling Purchase:** $500,000, 2003 Fasig-Tipton Saratoga selected yearling, by Ventures Partnership. **Juvenile Sale:** $200,000, 2004 Fasig-Tipton Calder, consigned by Kings Equine, agent, purchased by Namcook Stable. –60% loss. 11-2-0-2, G3, $126,000.

–$285,000 DAMASCUS LAD, 1984 b. h., Damascus—Great Lady M., by Icecapade. **Yearling Purchase:** $425,000, 1985 Keeneland July selected, by Cardiff Stud Farms. **Juvenile Sale:** $140,000, 1986 C.T.S. March, consigned by Cardiff Stud Farms, purchased by Central Farms. –67.1% loss. 3-0-1-1, $9,375.

–$280,000 ACQUILEIA, 2003 dk. b. or br. f., Arch—Questress, by Seeking the Gold. **Yearling Purchase:** $360,000, 2004 Keeneland September, by Whitehorse Stables. **Juvenile Sale:** $80,000, 2005 Fasig-Tipton Calder, consigned by Solitary Oak Farm, agent, purchased by Germania Farms. –77.8% loss. 2-0-0-1, $4,420.

–$270,000 MON'S THE MAN, 2003 gr. or ro. c., Maria's Mon—City Gold, by Carson City. **Yearling Purchase:** $350,000, 2004 Keeneland September, by Gulf Coast Farms. **Juvenile Sale:** $80,000, 2005 Barretts May, consigned by Jerry Bailey Sales Agency, agent, purchased by JD Thoroughbred Farm. –77.1% loss. Unraced.

–$260,891 RAILBIRD (Ire), 1995 ch. h., Caerleon—My Lady's Key, by Key to the Mint. **Yearling Purchase:** $302,891, 1996 Goffs Orby, by Kenneth E. Ellenberg. **Juvenile Sale:** $42,000, 1997 Barretts March, consigned by Bailey-Ellenberg Select, purchased by Waldon Randall Welty. –86.1% loss. 16-1-3-3, $11,165.

–$250,000 RUSH TO DEFEND, 2000 b. g., Wild Rush—Mary Sloan, by Woodman. **Yearling Purchase:** $500,000, 2001 Fasig-Tipton Kentucky July, by Paul Collins, agent. **Juvenile Sale:** $250,000, 2002 Fasig-Tipton Calder, consigned by Eddie Woods, agent, purchased by Chester Broman. –50% loss. 17-4-1-1, $37,865.

–$220,000 **OVERVIEW**, 1998 b. h., Kingmambo—Long View, by Damascus. **Yearling Purchase:** $300,000, 1999 Fasig-Tipton Saratoga selected, by Two Bucks Stable, agent. **Juvenile Sale:** $80,000, 2000 Keeneland April, consigned by Jerry Bailey Sales Agency, agent, purchased by John C. Oxley. –73.3% loss. 14-2-1-4, SW, $105,831.

–$220,000 COLONY STAR, 1995 dk. b. or br. m., Pleasant Colony—Star Glimmer, by General Assembly. **Yearling Purchase:** $250,000, 1996 Keeneland July, by Cam Allard. **Juvenile Sale:** $30,000, 1997 Keeneland April, consigned by H. T. Stables, agent, purchased by Henri Mastey. –88% loss. 1-0-0-0, $150.

–$210,000 PLUNKIT, 2002 b. c., Lemon Drop Kid—April Starlight, by Storm Bird. **Yearling Purchase:** $500,000, 2003 Fasig-Tipton Kentucky July, by Jeanne G. Vance. **Juvenile Sale:** $290,000, 2004 Keeneland April, consigned by Jeanne G. Vance, purchased by Robert B. and Beverly J. Lewis Thoroughbred Racing. –42% loss. 15-2-2-2, $64,661.

–$203,000 JETTIN HIGH, 2002 ch. g., High Yield—Rhodesia, by Polish Navy. **Yearling Purchase:** $220,000, 2003 Keeneland September, by White Horse Stables. **Juvenile Sale:** $17,000, 2004 Keeneland April, consigned by Kirkwood Stables, agent, purchased by Gary Owens. –92.3% loss. 17-3-4-1, $25,465.

–$200,000 **HONOR ME**, 1998 ch. g., Honor Grades—Bo K., by Raise a Native. **Yearling Purchase:** $350,000, 1999 Fasig-Tipton Kentucky July, by Cam Allard. **Juvenile Sale:** $150,000, 2000 Fasig-Tipton Midlantic May, consigned by H. T. Stables, agent, purchased by Dan Butler. –57.1% loss. 42-14-10-5, SW, $337,828.

–$200,000 HIGH REACH, 2003 b. f., Unbridled's Song—Defining Style, by Out of Place. **Yearling Purchase:** $300,000, 2004 Fasig-Tipton Kentucky July, by Hoby Kight. **Juvenile Sale:** $100,000, 2005 Fasig-Tipton Calder, consigned by Hoby and Layna Kight, agent, purchased by Shadai Farm. –66.7% loss. Unraced.

–$185,000 BOB'S CLOG BUSTER, 1996 b. h., Beau Genius—Told It All, by Told. **Yearling Purchase:** $200,000, 1997 Keeneland September, by Louie J. Roussel. **Juvenile Sale:** $15,000, 1998 Fasig-Tipton Calder, consigned by Jockey Club Farm, agent, purchased by Ralph C. Sessa. –92.5% loss. Unraced.

–$185,000 CIELO'S DANCE, 1995 b. m., Danzig—Orlanova, by Conquistador Cielo. **Yearling Purchase:** $335,000, 1996 Fasig-Tipton Saratoga selected, by Hartley/De Renzo Thoroughbreds LLC. **Juvenile Sale:** $150,000, 1997 Barretts March, consigned by Hartley/De Renzo Thoroughbreds LLC, purchased by Thomas F. VanMeter. –55.2% loss. Unraced.

Least Successful Pinhooks by Percentage Loss (through April 10, 2006)

Yearling to Juvenile

–98.2% PAID LEAVE, 2003 dk. b. or br. g., Exchange Rate—Timely Holiday, by Caveat. **Yearling Purchase:** $170,000, 2004 OBSC August, by Gulf Coast Bloodstock. **Juvenile Sale:** $3,000, 2005 Keeneland April, consigned by Jerry Bailey Sales Agency, agent, purchased by Harold Wheeler. –$167,000 loss. 5-0-0-1, $1,614.

–96.3% CEO SIS, 1994 b. m., Unbridled—Cruisie, by Assert (Ire). **Yearling Purchase:** $190,000, 1995 Fasig-Tipton Saratoga selected, by John Galbreath, agent. **Juvenile Sale:** $7,000, 1996 Keeneland November, consigned by Darby Dan Farm, agent, purchased by Carlos S. E. Moore, agent. –$183,000 loss. 5-2-0-1, $66,041.

–96.0% FILL MY CUP, 2003 b. c., Belong to Me—Cup of Tricks, by Clever Trick. **Yearling Purchase:** $150,000, 2004 Keeneland September, by Gulf Coast Farms. **Juvenile Sale:** $6,000, 2005 OBSC June, consigned by Jerry Bailey Sales Agency, agent, purchased by Narvick International. –$144,000 loss. 3-0-1-0, $0.

–92.5% BEN'S QUEST, 2002 ch. g., Coronado's Quest—Donna Karan (Chi), by Roy. **Yearling Purchase:** $160,000, 2003 Keeneland September, by Becky Thomas. **Juvenile Sale:** $12,000, 2004 Keeneland April, consigned by Sequel Bloodstock, agent, purchased by Moneylane Farms. –$148,000 loss. 11-1-3-0, $13,823.

–92.5% BOB'S CLOG BUSTER, 1996 b. h., Beau Genius—Told It All, by Told. **Yearling Purchase:** $200,000, 1997 Keeneland September, by Louie J. Roussel. **Juvenile Sale:** $15,000, 1998 Fasig-Tipton Calder, consigned by Jockey Club Farm, agent, purchased by Ralph C. Sessa. –$185,000 loss. Unraced.

–92.4% SPRING IN HIS STEP, 2003 b. c., Mr. Greeley—Fairy Song (Ire), by Fairy King. **Yearling Purchase:** $105,000, 2004 Keeneland September, by Kirkwood Stables, agent. **Juvenile Sale:** $8,000, 2005 Keeneland April, consigned by Kirkwood Stables, agent, purchased by Valentine Feerick. –$97,000 loss. 1-0-0-0, $0.

–92.3% JETTIN HIGH, 2002 ch. g., High Yield—Rhodesia, by Polish Navy. **Yearling Purchase:** $220,000, 2003 Keeneland September, by White Horse Stables. **Juvenile Sale:** $17,000, 2004 Keeneland April, consigned by Kirkwood Stables, agent, purchased by Gary Owens. –$203,000 loss. 17-3-4-1, $25,465.

–92.1% GOTTA TEMPER, 1999 b. m., Pleasant Colony—Omnia, by Green Dancer. **Yearling Purchase:** $140,000, 2000 Keeneland September, by Murray Smith, agent. **Juvenile Sale:** $11,000, 2001 Keeneland April, consigned by Murray Smith, agent, purchased by Wheeler Racing. –$129,000 loss. 20-3-6-3, $63,806.

–91.9% **Cal's Baby**, 1998 dk. b. or br. m., Smart Strike—Silver Dollar Kate, by Green Dancer. **Yearling Purchase:** $185,000, 1999 Keeneland September, by James Cassels. **Juvenile Sale:** $15,000, 2000 Keeneland April, consigned by Hartley/De Renzo Thoroughbreds LLC, agent, purchased by Shah Stables. –$170,000 loss. 26-4-2-8, spl, $110,350.

–91.7% HONOUR TOPPER, 2002 b. g., Honour and Glory—Chart Topper, by Groovy. **Yearling Purchase:** $120,000, 2003 Fasig-Tipton Kentucky July, by Michael J. Ryan, agent. **Juvenile Sale:** $10,000, 2004 Fasig-Tipton Midlantic May, consigned by Niall Brennan Stables, agent, purchased by John E. Salzman. –$110,000 loss. 11-3-2-0, $23,770.

–91.6% MIRANDOLA, 1990 b. m., Ogygian—Miramani, by Slew o'Gold. **Yearling Purchase:** $125,000, 1991 Keeneland September, by Michael J. Ryan, agent. **Juvenile Sale:** $10,500, 1992 Keeneland November, consigned by King Ranch Farm, purchased by Ocean Blue Stables, agent. –$114,500 loss. 2-0-0-0, $0.

–91.3% PHILTHEDEPUTY, 1997 b. h., Silver Deputy—Philharmonia (Ire), by Caerleon. **Yearling Purchase:** $100,000, 1998 Fasig-Tipton Kentucky July, by Sarem Stable. **Juvenile Sale:** $8,700, 1999 OBSC April, consigned by Niall Brennan, agent, purchased by Eureka Farm. –$91,300 loss. 7-0-1-0, $1,823.

–91.3% VIC'S TIME, 1997 ch. h., Gilded Time—Regal Grant, by Mr. Prospector. **Yearling Purchase:** $160,000, 1998 Fasig-Tipton Saratoga selected, by Ken Ellenberg. **Juvenile Sale:** $14,000, 1999 Fasig-Tipton New York Saratoga two-year-olds and horses of racing age sale, consigned by Jerry Bailey Sales Agency, agent, purchased by John Shaw. –$146,000 loss. 10-0-1-0, $5,816.

–90.9% SWEET PERSUASION, 1993 b. m., Devil's Bag—Ivory Idol, by Alydar. **Yearling Purchase:** $110,000, 1994 Keeneland September, by D. Wayne Lukas. **Juvenile Sale:** $10,000, 1995 Keeneland November, consigned by Denali Stud, agent, purchased by Dermot Carty. –$100,000 loss. 1-0-1-0, $6,800.

Most Successful Pinhooks by Total Gain (through April 10, 2006)

Weanling to Yearling

$1,180,000 DUBAI TOUCH, 1999 dk b/. h., Saint Ballado—Jettin Diplomacy, by Roman Diplomat. **Weanling Purchase:** $220,000, 1999 Keeneland November, by B.M.K. Equine. **Yearling Sale:** $1,400,000, 2000 Keeneland July selected, consigned by Hartwell Farm, agent, purchased by John Ferguson Bloodstock. 536.4% gain. 9-0-0-0, $3,868.

$1,100,000 SEEKING AN ALIBI, 2002 ch. c., Storm Cat—Seeking Regina, by Seeking the Gold. **Weanling Purchase:** $500,000, 2002 Keeneland November, by Bradley Thoroughbred Brokerage. **Yearling Sale:** $1,600,000, 2003 Keeneland September, consigned by Eaton Sales, agent, purchased by John Ferguson Bloodstock. 220% gain. 4-1-0-0, $6,127.

$1,015,000 **TALK IS MONEY**, 1998 ch. h., Deputy Minister—Isle Go West, by Gone West. **Weanling Purchase:** $785,000, 1998 Keeneland November, by Smithfield Investments. **Yearling Sale:** $1,800,000, 1999 Keeneland September, consigned by Dromoland Farm, agent, purchased by Baden P. "Buzz" Chace, agent. 129.3% gain. 7-2-1-1, SW, $104,110.

$1,000,000 LIFESTYLE, 2000 b. h., Indian Charlie—Inlaw, by Gold Seam. **Weanling Purchase:** $100,000, 2000 Keeneland November, by Holiday Stables. **Yearling Sale:** $1,100,000, 2001 Keeneland September, consigned by Paternostro & Herbener, agent, purchased by The Thoroughbred Corp. 1,000% gain. 9-2-2-0, $84,560.

$938,000 WEATHERMAN, 1998 ch. h., Summer Squall—Plucky Maid, by Housebuster. **Weanling Purchase:** $62,000, 1998 Keeneland November, by Plaza Stud. **Yearling Sale:** $1,000,000, 1999 Keeneland September, consigned by Jim J. FitzGerald, agent, purchased by Stonerside Stable. 1,512.9% gain. 4-1-1-1, $38,280.

$900,000 DUBAI TIGER, 1999 b. g., Storm Cat—Toga Toga Toga, by Saratoga Six. **Weanling Purchase:** $900,000, 1999 Keeneland November, by Tim Hyde. **Yearling Sale:** $1,800,000, 2000 Keeneland September, consigned by Eaton Sales, agent, purchased by John Ferguson Bloodstock. 100% gain. 8-2-1-1, $106,510.

$900,000 ZINZAN, 2003 b. c., Grand Slam—Sheza Honey, by Honey Jay. **Weanling Purchase:** $400,000, 2003 Keeneland November, by Michael Byrne. **Yearling Sale:** $1,300,000, 2004 Keeneland September, consigned by Michael C. Byrne, agent, purchased by Demi O'Byrne. 225% gain. 2-0-1-0, $7,040.

$888,000 EALING PARK, 1999 dk b/. g., Saint Ballado—Jeannie the Meanie, by Rare Performer. **Weanling Purchase:** $62,000, 1999 Keeneland November, by Phillip Frances McCarthy. **Yearling Sale:** $950,000, 2000 Keeneland September, consigned by Taylor Made Sales Agency, agent, purchased by Eugene N. Melnyk. 1,432.3% gain. 9-1-0-0, $8,938.

$850,000 STORMIN' HEAVEN, 1998 ch. h., Hennessy—Afleet Francais, by Afleet. **Weanling Purchase:** $350,000, 1998 Keeneland November, by Greenwood Farm. **Yearling Sale:** $1,200,000, 1999 Keeneland July selected, consigned by Eaton Sales, agent, purchased by Robert B. Hess, agent. 242.9% gain. 12-4-0-1, $124,224.

$800,000 FUTURE MINISTER, 1999 b. h., Deputy Minister—Brink, by Forty Niner. **Weanling Purchase:** $500,000, 1999 Keeneland November, by Ballard Stable. **Yearling Sale:** $1,300,000, 2000 Keeneland July selected, consigned by Taylor Made Sales Agency, agent, purchased by John Ferguson Bloodstock. 160% gain. 11-1-3-1, $62,678.

$800,000 HANNAH'S WISH, 1998 dk b/. h., Kris S.—Admise (Fr), by Highest Honor (Fr). **Weanling Purchase:** $100,000, 1998 Fasig-Tipton Kentucky fall mixed sale, by The Lads. **Yearling Sale:** $900,000, 1999 Keeneland September, consigned by The Lads, purchased by Narvick International. 800% gain. Unraced.

$800,000 SECRET POND, 1999 dk b/. h., Mr. Prospector—Golden Pond (Ire), by Don't Forget Me. **Weanling Purchase:** $600,000, 1999 Keeneland November, by Horse France. **Yearling Sale:** $1,400,000, 2000 Keeneland July selected, consigned by Lakland LLC, agent, purchased by Katsumi Yoshida. 133.3% gain. Unraced.

Most Successful Pinhooks by Percentage Gain (through April 10, 2006)

Weanling to Yearling

11,233.3% TORTONI, 2000 dk b/. h., Candy Stripes—Our Dani, by Homebuilder. **Weanling Purchase:** $1,500, 2000 Keeneland November, by Pasco Bloodstock. **Yearling Sale:** $170,000, 2001 OBSC August, consigned by Summerfield, agent, purchased by Journeyman Bloodstock, agent. $168,500 gain. 8-1-1-1, $25,880.

8,048.1% DUKE OF DESTINY, 2003 dk b/. c., Pikepass—Dutch's Duchess, by Roy. **Weanling Purchase:** $2,700, 2003 Keeneland November, by Benedict A. Mohit. **Yearling Sale:** $220,000, 2004 OBSC August, consigned by Kaizen Sales, agent, purchased by Martin L. Cherry. $217,300 gain. Unraced.

6,566.7% GOLDEN TONES, 2001 b. h., Seeking the Gold—Bethany, by Dayjur. **Weanling Purchase:** $6,000, 2001 Keeneland November, by Jay Rodgers. **Yearling Sale:** $400,000, 2002 Keeneland September, consigned by Taylor Made Sales Agency, agent, purchased by Robert B. and Beverly J. Lewis. $394,000 gain. 3-1-1-0, $35,720.

6,566.7% KING BRIDLE, 1998 b. h., Unbridled—Life's Magic, by Cox's Ridge. **Weanling Purchase:** $3,000, 1998 Keeneland November, by Lori Tanel. **Yearling Sale:** $200,000, 1999 Keeneland September, consigned by Susan Y. Foreman, agent, purchased by David and Jill Heerensperger. $197,000 gain. 23-1-1-1, $11,948.

4,900.0% UNTOLD STORY, 1995 b. h., Theatrical (Ire)—Committed Miss, by Key to Content. **Weanling Purchase:** $4,000, 1995 Keeneland November, by Bruce Hundley. **Yearling Sale:** $200,000, 1996 Keeneland September, consigned by James B. Keogh, agent, purchased by Newmarket International. $196,000 gain. 23-0-0-1, $1,654.

3,788.9% Unnamed, 1994 b. h., Lord At War (Arg)—Corking, by Sensitive Prince. **Weanling Purchase:** $4,500, 1994 Keeneland November, by Chad R. Schumer, agent. **Yearling Sale:** $175,000, 1995 Fasig-Tipton Kentucky July, consigned by Clarkland Farm, agent, purchased by Baden P. "Buzz" Chace, agent. $170,500 gain. Unraced.

3,300.0% AIR TOUCH, 1996 ch. h., Phone Trick—Serna, by Cox's Ridge. **Weanling Purchase:** $5,000, 1996 Keeneland November, by Green Meadow Farm. **Yearling Sale:** $170,000, 1997 Keeneland September, consigned by Taylor Made Sales Agency, agent, purchased by Supervent Inc. $165,000 gain. 1-0-0-0, $0.

3,181.3% LORD ADMIRAL, 1982 b. g., Topsider—Tumbling Dancer, by Dancer's Image. **Weanling Purchase:** $16,000, 1982 Keeneland November, by Charles St. George. **Yearling Sale:** $525,000, 1983 Keeneland September, consigned by Ashleigh Stud Farm, purchased by BBA (England). $509,000 gain. 1-0-0-0, $100.

3,150.0% WINDSOR COURT, 1998 dk. b. or br. g., Southern Halo—Her Grace, by Northern Flagship. **Weanling Purchase:** $8,000, 1998 Keeneland November, by Rachel Holden. **Yearling Sale:** $260,000, 1999 Keeneland September, consigned by Tri-County Farm, agent, purchased by James T. Scatuorchio. $252,000 gain. 43-3-10-3, $90,640.

2,600.0% Unnamed, 2004 gr. or ro. c., Wild Wonder—Susie Do, by Talinum. **Weanling Purchase:** $10,000, 2004 Keeneland November, by, agent. **Yearling Sale:** $270,000, 2005 Keeneland September, consigned by Taylor Made Sales Agency, agent, purchased by John J. Brocklebank. $260,000 gain. Unraced.

Least Successful Pinhooks by Total Loss (through April 10, 2006)

Weanling to Yearling

–$800,000 NEW TRIESTE, 1999 ch. h., A.P. Indy—Lovlier Linda, by Vigors. **Weanling Purchase:** $1,300,000, 1999 Keeneland November, by Paul Shanahan. **Yearling Sale:** $500,000, 2000 Keeneland September, consigned by Eaton Sales, agent, purchased by Daniel M. Borislow. –61.5% loss. 1-0-0-0, $1,500.

–$475,000 **WISEMAN'S FERRY**, 1999 ch. h., Hennessy—Emmaus, by Silver Deputy. **Weanling Purchase:** $775,000, 1999 Keeneland November, by Indian Hill Farm. **Yearling Sale:** $300,000, 2000 Keeneland September, consigned by Eaton Sales, agent, purchased by Hugo Merry Bloodstock. –61.3% loss. 16-4-3-2, G3, $825,266.

–$375,000 SPORTS HERO, 1999 dk. b. or br. h., Mr. Prospector—Alysoft, by Alydar. **Weanling Purchase:** $775,000, 1999 Keeneland November, by High Mills Farm. **Yearling Sale:** $400,000, 2000 Fasig-Tipton New York Saratoga select yearling, consigned by Lakland LLC, agent, purchased by Select Equine. –48.4% loss. 2-2-0-0, $26,890.

–$350,000 **Manhattan Skyline**, 1999 dk. b. or br. m., Spinning World—Crystal Cream, by Secretariat. **Weanling Purchase:** $550,000, 1999 Keeneland November, by Farfellow Farms. **Yearling Sale:** $200,000, 2000 Keeneland July selected, consigned by Taylor Made Sales Agency, agent, purchased by Jockey Club Farm. –63.6% loss. 11-4-5-0, spl, $141,255.

–$325,000 CARELESS ALY, 1991 ch. m., Alydar—Careless Notion, by Jester. **Weanling Purchase:** $350,000, 1991 Keeneland November, by Mandysland Farm. **Yearling Sale:** $25,000, 1992 Keeneland September, consigned by Joe Riggs, agent, purchased by Helen C. Alexander, agent. –92.9% loss. Unraced.

–$270,000 SIR BEDIVERE, 1999 ch. h., Unbridled—Bold Windy, by Bold Tropic (SAf). **Weanling Purchase:** $400,000, 1999 Keeneland November, by Narvick International. **Yearling Sale:** $130,000, 2000 Keeneland November, consigned by 505 Farm, purchased by Leprechaun Racing, agent. –67.5% loss. 7-1-0-1, $12,630.

–$250,000 **Truckle Feature**, 2000 dk. b. or br. h., Saint Ballado—Magic Gleam, by Danzig. **Weanling Purchase:** $275,000, 2000 Keeneland November, by Indian Hill Farm. **Yearling Sale:** $25,000, 2001 Keeneland September, consigned by Eaton Sales, agent, purchased by Straightaway Farm, agent. –90.9% loss. 10-2-1-2, spl, $151,460.

–$240,000 SPINNING MISS, 1999 ch. m., Spinning World—Bemissed, by Nijinsky II. **Weanling Purchase:** $575,000, 1999 Keeneland November, by Narvick International. **Yearling Sale:** $335,000, 2000 Keeneland September, consigned by 505 Farm, purchased by Brushwood Stable. –41.7% loss. 6-0-0-0, $300.

–$198,000 VICTORYTONITEHEY, 2001 b. h., Victory Gallop—Fancy Ruler, by Half a Year. **Weanling Purchase:** $225,000, 2001 Keeneland November, by Springvalley Farm. **Yearling Sale:** $27,000, 2002 Fasig-Tipton Kentucky October, consigned by Denali Stud, agent, purchased by Rocket City Stables. –88% loss. 11-1-0-1, $13,360.

–$183,000 BECKY MOSS, 2003 dk. b. or br. f., Red Ransom—British Columbia (GB), by Selkirk. **Weanling Purchase:** $190,000, 2003 Keeneland November, by Arosa Farms. **Yearling Sale:** $7,000, 2004 Keeneland September, consigned by Arosa Farms, purchased by John Collins. –96.3% loss. 9-1-1-1, $23,498.

–$175,000 **GOVERNOR BROWN**, 2000 ch. h., Kingmambo—Miss Mistletoes (Ire), by The Minstrel. **Weanling Purchase:** $485,000, 2000 Keeneland November, by Chestnut Hill Farm. **Yearling Sale:** $310,000, 2001 Keeneland September, consigned by Eaton Sales, agent, purchased by Dan Kenny, agent. –36.1% loss. 12-3-2-4, G3, $157,299.

–$175,000 Unnamed, 2004 b. f., Orientate—Ms. Strike Zone, by Deputy Minister. **Weanling Purchase:** $250,000, 2004 Keeneland November, by Brushwood Stable. **Yearling Sale:** $75,000, 2005 Fasig-Tipton New York Saratoga selected yearling, consigned by Eaton Sales, agent, purchased by Leprechaun Racing, agent. –70% loss. Unraced.

Least Successful Pinhooks by Percentage Loss (through April 10, 2006)

Weanling to Yearling

–96.3% BECKY MOSS, 2003 dk. b. or br. f., Red Ransom—British Columbia (GB), by Selkirk. **Weanling Purchase:** $190,000, 2003 Keeneland November, by Arosa Farms. **Yearling Sale:** $7,000, 2004 Keeneland September, consigned by Arosa Farms, purchased by John Collins. –$183,000 loss. 9-1-1-1, $23,498.

–93.8% RING DANG DO, 2000 b. h., Red Ransom—Laurentine, by Private Account. **Weanling Purchase:** $130,000, 2000 Keeneland November, by Bridlestown Stud. **Yearling Sale:** $8,000, 2001 Keeneland September, consigned by Dromoland Farm, agent, purchased by Kern/Lillingston Associates. –$122,000 loss. 23-1-2-4, $2,240.

–93.3% GRAND IMPACT, 2004 dk. b. or br. c., Grand Slam—Tojur, by Dayjur. **Weanling Purchase:** $150,000, 2004 Keeneland November, by Athens Woods LLC. **Yearling Sale:** $10,000, 2005 Keeneland September, consigned by Eaton Sales, agent, purchased by Straightaway Farm, agent. –$140,000 loss. Unraced.

–92.9% CARELESS ALY, 1991 ch. m., Alydar—Careless Notion, by Jester. **Weanling Purchase:** $350,000, 1991 Keeneland November, by Mandysland Farm. **Yearling Sale:** $25,000, 1992 Keeneland September, consigned by Joe Riggs, agent, purchased by Helen C. Alexander, agent. –$325,000 loss. Unraced.

–92.9% CUM LAUDE, 1999 dk. b. or br. g., Honor Grades—Jody G., by Roberto. **Weanling Purchase:** $175,000, 1999 Keeneland November, by Grade I Bloodstock. **Yearling Sale:** $12,500, 2000 Fasig-Tipton Kentucky October, consigned by Darby Dan Farm, agent, purchased by Kenneth Ayres. –$162,500 loss. 34-4-4-5, $42,982.

–92.0% CATRINA ERINA, 1998 ch. m., Candy Stripes—Erina, by Slewpy. **Weanling Purchase:** $100,000, 1998 Keeneland November, by Green Hall Stud. **Yearling Sale:** $8,000, 1999 Fasig-Tipton Kentucky October, consigned by Taylor Made Sales Agency, agent, purchased by Ted Latour. –$92,000 loss. 18-4-2-4, $31,905.

–91.9% Unnamed, 2004 b. c., Belong to Me—Concentric, by Shadeed. **Weanling Purchase:** $135,000, 2004 Keeneland November, by W. S. Farish. **Yearling Sale:** $11,000, 2005 Keeneland September, consigned by Lane's End, agent, purchased by William J. Cesare. –$124,000 loss. Unraced.

–91.3% EBONESS, 2003 dk. b. or br. f., Stormin Fever—Down the Street, by Ghazi. **Weanling Purchase:** $150,000, 2003 Keeneland November, by Tyra Holdings. **Yearling Sale:** $13,000, 2004 Fasig-Tipton Midlantic, consigned by Bluewater Sales LLC, agent, purchased by Lincoln Avenue Partners. –$137,000 loss. Unraced.

–90.9% **Truckle Feature**, 2000 dk. b. or br. h., Saint Ballado—Magic Gleam, by Danzig. **Weanling Purchase:** $275,000, 2000 Keeneland November, by Indian Hill Farm. **Yearling Sale:** $25,000, 2001 Keeneland September, consigned by Eaton Sales, agent, purchased by Straightaway Farm, agent. –$250,000 loss. 10-2-1-2, spl, $151,460.

–90.0% **Princesa Alexa**, 2003 ch. f., Broken Vow—Gail's Falcon, by Imperial Falcon. **Weanling Purchase:** $100,000, 2003 Keeneland November, by Barron Bloodstock. **Yearling Sale:** $10,000, 2004 Keeneland September, consigned by Highclere Sales, agent, purchased by Eric B. Peng. –$90,000 loss. 4-2-1-1, spl, $2,380.

–90.0% RING WARRIOR, 1999 gr. or ro. h., K. O. Punch—Quiet Sound, by Quiet American. **Weanling Purchase:** $110,000, 1999 Keeneland November, by Horse France. **Yearling Sale:** $11,000, 2000 Keeneland September, consigned by Hopewell Farm, agent, purchased by Jim Snavely. –$99,000 loss. 5-1-0-2, $5,372.

Most Successful Pinhooks by Total Gain (through April 10, 2006)

Weanling to Juvenile

$860,000 **Brave Quest**, 1997 b. h., Miswaki—Cousin Margaret, by Topsider. **Weanling Purchase:** $90,000, 1997 Fasig-Tipton Kentucky November, by Richard Spoor. **Juvenile Sale:** $950,000, 1999 Fasig-Tipton Calder, consigned by Robert N. Scanlon, agent, purchased by John C. Oxley. 955.6% gain. 7-4-1-1, spl, $164,502.

$815,000 SOMETHING ELSE, 1995 ch. m., Seeking the Gold—Rythmical, by Fappiano. **Weanling Purchase:** $185,000, 1995 Keeneland November, by BBA (England). **Juvenile Sale:** $1,000,000, 1997 Barretts March, consigned by Kirkwood Stables, agent, purchased by The Thoroughbred Corp. 440.5% gain. 3-0-2-0, $18,144.

$750,000 CINDAGO, 2003 b. c., Indian Charlie—Tupelo Belle, by Turkoman. **Weanling Purchase:** $150,000, 2003 Keeneland November, by Gage Hill Stable. **Juvenile Sale:** $900,000, 2005 Barretts March, consigned by H. T. Stables, agent, purchased by John W. Sadler, agent. 500% gain. 2-1-1-0, $34,400.

$725,000 UNCOMMON VALOR, 1997 b. h., Kris S.—Patchiano, by Fappiano. **Weanling Purchase:** $75,000, 1997 Keeneland November, by Tom Reeves. **Juvenile Sale:** $800,000, 1999 Fasig-Tipton Calder, consigned by Robert J. Harris, agent, purchased by Team Valor. 966.7% gain. 5-3-1-0, $86,200.

$600,000 DEBIT ACCOUNT, 1996 b. m., Mr. Prospector—Awesome Account, by Lyphard. **Weanling Purchase:** $350,000, 1996 Keeneland November, by Cypress Farms. **Juvenile Sale:** $950,000, 1998 Barretts March, consigned by Bailey-Ellenberg Select, purchased by Demi O'Byrne. 171.4% gain. 9-3-0-0, $70,260.

$565,000 GOLDEN PENNY, 2000 b. m., Touch Gold—Penny's Growl, by Strike Gold. **Weanling Purchase:** $85,000, 2000 Keeneland November, by The Narrows. **Juvenile Sale:** $650,000, 2002 Keeneland April, consigned by Tony Bowling and Bobby Dodd, agent, purchased by Robert B. and Beverly J. Lewis. 664.7% gain. 18-2-3-3, $65,634.

$558,000 NASEMA'S SLAM, 2002 dk. b. or br. f., Grand Slam—Nasema, by Encino. **Weanling Purchase:** $42,000, 2002 Keeneland November, by Luann Baker. **Juvenile Sale:** $600,000, 2004 Fasig-Tipton Calder, consigned by Equine Legacy Farm, agent, purchased by Fleetwood and NW Management. 1,328.6% gain. 8-2-3-0, $48,140.

$530,000 **Swissle Stick**, 2002 ch. c., Swiss Yodeler—Miss Soft Sell, by Siyah Kalem. **Weanling Purchase:** $70,000, 2002 Keeneland November, by Terry Oliver, agent. **Juvenile Sale:** $600,000, 2004 Barretts March, consigned by Wavertree Stables, agent, purchased by Robert B. and Beverly J. Lewis. 757.1% gain. 23-1-4-2, spl, $71,340.

$510,000 Unnamed, 2004 ch. c., Forest Camp—Holy Love, by Holy Bull. **Weanling Purchase:** $140,000, 2004 Keeneland November, by Roy B. Smith and Bill Wilks. **Juvenile Sale:** $650,000, 2006 OBSC February, consigned by Wavertree Stables, agent, purchased by John Ferguson Bloodstock. 364.3% gain. Unraced.

$490,000 GOLDEN BAND, 1999 ch. m., Dixieland Band—Honey Bee Gold, by Drone. **Weanling Purchase:** $285,000, 1999 Keeneland November, by Cam Allard. **Juvenile Sale:** $775,000, 2001 Keeneland April, consigned by H. T. Stables, agent, purchased by Bob Baffert, agent. 171.9% gain. 6-1-2-2, $61,240.

$480,000 SARANOIA, 2000 dk. b. or br. h., Seattle Slew—Sharp Call, by Sharpen Up (GB). **Weanling Purchase:** $320,000, 2000 Keeneland November, by Chad Johnson, agent. **Juvenile Sale:** $800,000, 2002 Fasig-Tipton Calder, consigned by Terry Oliver, agent, purchased by Michael Gill. 150% gain. 6-0-1-1, $12,970.

$450,000 BARONOVA, 2003 ch. f., Tale of the Cat—Marianne's Song, by Unbridled's Song. **Weanling Purchase:** $50,000, 2003 Keeneland November, by J. L. Simmons Bloodstock. **Juvenile Sale:** $500,000, 2005 Fasig-Tipton Calder, consigned by Ocala Oaks and Don R. Graham, agent, purchased by Demi O'Byrne. 900.0% gain. 1-0-0-1, $5,000.

$425,000 RENUMBERED, 1999 b. g., Polish Numbers—Launchette, by Relaunch. **Weanling Purchase:** $40,000, 1999 Fasig-Tipton Midlantic December, by Josham Farms. **Juvenile Sale:** $465,000, 2001 Fasig-Tipton Calder, consigned by Tony Bowling and Bobby Dodd, agent, purchased by F. Eugene Dixon. 1,062.5% gain. 4-0-0-0, $500 8-1-0-1, $11,424.

Most Successful Pinhooks by Percentage Gain (through April 10, 2006)

Weanling to Juvenile

6,900.0% MR. ELUSIVE, 2000 dk. b. or br. g., Elusive Quality—Capote's Joy, by Capote. **Weanling Purchase:** $1,500, 2000 Keeneland November, by Silverwood, agent. **Juvenile Sale:** $105,000, 2002 Barretts May, consigned by Timber Creek, agent, purchased by Larry O. and Veralene Hillis. $103,500 gain. 28-5-2-0, $88,281.

5,900.0% EISHIN GONZALES, 1997 b. h., Take Me Out—Aunt Mockey, by Our Native. **Weanling Purchase:** $4,500, 1997 Fasig-Tipton Kentucky November, by William D. Snyder. **Juvenile Sale:** $270,000, 1999 Fasig-Tipton Calder, consigned by Sequel Bloodstock, agent, purchased by Silky Green. $265,500 gain. 19-3-1-0, $308,887.

5,455.6% BIG BIG CASINO, 1998 dk. b. or br. h., Pioneering—Kelly's Super Pet, by Muscovite. **Weanling Purchase:** $1,800, 1998 Keeneland November, by Shari Kepsel. **Juvenile Sale:** $100,000, 2000 Barretts May, consigned by Jerry Bailey Sales Agency, agent, purchased by Bruno de Berdt, agent. $98,200 gain. 4-1-1-1, $25,520.

4,185.7% OUR EMM, 2001 dk. b. or br. h., Our Emblem—Thoughts, by Seattle Slew. **Weanling Purchase:** $3,500, 2001 Keeneland November, by Clouston Farm. **Juvenile Sale:** $150,000, 2003 Keeneland April, consigned by American Equistock and Parrish Farms, purchased by International Equine Acquisitions. $146,500 gain. 5-2-2-0, $18,940.

3,488.2% **Mancari's Rose**, 1996 b. m., Glitterman—Puddin Hill, by Afleet. **Weanling Purchase:** $8,500, 1996 Keeneland November, by Jockey Club Farm. **Juvenile Sale:** $305,000, 1998 OBSC March, consigned by Jockey Club Farm, agent, purchased by William Bronstad. $296,500 gain. 6-1-0-1, spl, $33,275.

2,578.6% **PRIMETIMBER**, 1996 b. h., Sultry Song—Wine Taster, by Nodouble. **Weanling Purchase:** $14,000, 1996 Keeneland November, by Donna M. Wormser. **Juvenile Sale:** $375,000, 1998 OBSC February, consigned by Donna M. Wormser, agent, purchased by Aaron U. Jones. $361,000 gain. 17-4-4-0, G2, $621,238.

2,000.0% **MAYAKOVSKY**, 1999 dk. b. or br. h., Matty G—Joy to Raise, by Raise a Man. **Weanling Purchase:** $10,000, 1999 OBSC October, by Gold Circle Racing. **Juvenile Sale:** $210,000, 2001 OBSC April, consigned by Eisaman Equine Services, agent, purchased by Robert N. Scanlon, agent. $200,000 gain. 9-3-1-0, G3, $275,200.

1,900.0% BEE MOUNTAIN, 1999 gr. or ro. g., Cahill Road—Blockbuster Lady, by Northern Jove. **Weanling Purchase:** $15,000, 1999 Keeneland November, by J. S. Northern. **Juvenile Sale:** $300,000, 2001 OBSC March, consigned by Eisaman Equine Services, agent, purchased by Choctaw Racing Stable. $285,000 gain. 11-4-1-2, $83,040.

1,900.0% STORM HEARTED, 2002 b. f., Lion Hearted—Shallah, by Proud Truth. **Weanling Purchase:** $12,000, 2002 Fasig-Tipton Midlantic December, by Short Term Stable. **Juvenile Sale:** $240,000, 2004 Barretts March, consigned by Paula Capestro Bloodstock, agent, purchased by C R K Stable. $228,000 gain. 4-0-1-0, $10,900.

Least Successful Pinhooks by Total Loss (through April 10, 2006)

Weanling to Juvenile

–$325,000 NIJINSKY'S CROWN, 1999 ch. h., Gone West—Nijinsky's Lover, by Nijinsky II. **Weanling Purchase:** $725,000, 1999 Keeneland November, by R. A. Adkinson. **Juvenile Sale:** $400,000, 2001 Fasig-Tipton Calder, consigned by Robert N. Scanlon, agent, purchased by B.T.A. Stable. –44.8% loss. 3-0-0-0, $0.

–$245,000 **Alive With Hope**, 1991 ch. m., Alydar—Awesome Account, by Lyphard. **Weanling Purchase:** $400,000, 1991 Keeneland November, by Oaktown Stable. **Juvenile Sale:** $155,000, 1993 Keeneland November, consigned by Jonabell Farm, agent, purchased by Millhouse. –61.3% loss. 18-6-2-3, spl, $184,631.

–$210,000 HATSURATSU, 2000 ch. c., Pulpit—Afare, by Meadowlake. **Weanling Purchase:** $360,000, 2000 Keeneland November, by Bohanon-Walden LLC. **Juvenile Sale:** $150,000, 2002 Fasig-Tipton Calder, consigned by Maurice W. Miller, agent, purchased by Everglades Stable. –58.3% loss. 14-3-2-0, $419,354.

–$193,000 SEGUIN, 1997 ch. h., Miswaki—Anytimeatall, by It's Freezing. **Weanling Purchase:** $195,000, 1997 Keeneland November, by Horse France. **Juvenile Sale:** $2,000, 1999 Keeneland April, consigned by Hartley/De Renzo Thoroughbreds LLC, agent, purchased by Spring Farm. –99% loss. 13-1-1-3, $24,774.

–$179,000 GRAY EMBLEM, 2002 gr/ro. f., Our Emblem—Lingquoit, by Waquoit. **Weanling Purchase:** $200,000, 2002 Keeneland November, by Venture One Partnership. **Juvenile Sale:** $21,000, 2004 OBSC April, consigned by SAB Training, agent, purchased by Gary Owens. –89.5% loss. 1-0-0-0, $0.

–$175,000 PRICELY GEM, 2003 b. c., Honour and Glory—Thirty Six Carat, by Meadowlake. **Weanling Purchase:** $210,000, 2003 Keeneland November, by Jack Smith. **Juvenile Sale:** $35,000, 2005 Barretts March, consigned by Excel Bloodstock, agent, purchased by NJ Cal Breeders. –83.3% loss. 1-0-1-0, $8,000.

–$175,000 TALE OF THE BEAR, 2004 b. c., Tale of the Cat—Prosper, by Affirmed. **Weanling Purchase:** $260,000, 2004 Keeneland November, by DOC Bloodstock. **Juvenile Sale:** $85,000, 2006 OBSC February, consigned by Nick de Meric, agent, purchased by Bear Stable. –67.3% loss. Unraced.

–$163,000 PAPPA'S MONEY, 1996 ch. g., St. Jovite—Queen of Bronze, by Roberto. **Weanling Purchase:** $180,000, 1996 Keeneland November, by Cypress Farms. **Juvenile Sale:** $17,000, 1998 Barretts March, consigned by Bailey-Ellenberg Select, purchased by Dale V. Ray. –90.6% loss. 10-1-0-0, $4,552.

–$158,000 CHET, 2002 dk. b. or br. c., Chester House—King's Pact, by Slewacide. **Weanling Purchase:** $170,000, 2002 Keeneland November, by Dromoland Farm and Hartwell Farm. **Juvenile Sale:** $12,000, 2004 Keeneland April, consigned by Robert N. Scanlon, agent, purchased by Rosebud Stable. –92.9% loss. 18-2-0-3, $14,896.

–$140,000 NO BID, 1995 b. m., Rahy—Learycal, by Lear Fan. **Weanling Purchase:** $165,000, 1995 Keeneland November, by Ward C. Pitfield. **Juvenile Sale:** $25,000, 1997 Keeneland April, consigned by Kirkwood Stables, agent, purchased by Philip M. Hauswald, agent. –84.8% loss. Unraced.

–$140,000 UNDEFINED, 2001 gr/ro. c., Unbridled's Song—Star On the Move, by Blade. **Weanling Purchase:** $250,000, 2001 Keeneland November, by Wood Ridge Thoroughbreds. **Juvenile Sale:** $110,000, 2003 Fasig-Tipton Calder, consigned by Terry Oliver, agent, purchased by Estable. –56% loss. 6-0-2-1, $53,691.

–$131,000 Unnamed, 1998 ch. h., Forest Wildcat—Musical Precedent, by Seattle Song. **Weanling Purchase:** $140,000, 1998 Keeneland November, by A. Cafferrata. **Juvenile Sale:** $9,000, 2000 Fasig-Tipton Midlantic two-year-olds in training, consigned by Eddie Woods, agent, purchased by Sean C. Magee, agent. –93.6% loss. Unraced.

Least Successful Pinhooks by Percentage Loss (through April 10, 2006)

Weanling to Juvenile

–99.0% SEGUIN, 1997 ch. h., Miswaki—Anytimeatall, by It's Freezing. **Weanling Purchase:** $195,000, 1997 Keeneland November, by Horse France. **Juvenile Sale:** $2,000, 1999 Keeneland April, consigned by Hartley/De Renzo Thoroughbreds LLC, agent, purchased by Spring Farm. –$193,000 loss. 13-1-1-3, $24,774.

–93.6% Unnamed, 1998 ch. h., Forest Wildcat—Musical Precedent, by Seattle Song. **Weanling Purchase:** $140,000, 1998 Keeneland November, by A. Cafferrata. **Juvenile Sale:** $9,000, 2000 Fasig-Tipton Midlantic May, consigned by Eddie Woods, agent, purchased by Sean C. Magee, agent. –$131,000 loss. Unraced.

–92.9% CHET, 2002 dk. b. or br. g., Chester House—King's Pact, by Slewacide. **Weanling Purchase:** $170,000, 2002 Keeneland November, by Dromoland Farm and Hartwell Farm. **Juvenile Sale:** $12,000, 2004 Keeneland April, consigned by Robert N. Scanlon, agent, purchased by Rosebud Stable. –$158,000 loss. 18-2-0-3, $14,896.

–90.6% PAPPA'S MONEY, 1996 ch. g., St. Jovite—Queen of Bronze, by Roberto. **Weanling Purchase:** $180,000, 1996 Keeneland November, by Cypress Farms. **Juvenile Sale:** $17,000, 1998 Barretts March, consigned by Bailey-Ellenberg Select, purchased by Dale V. Ray. –$163,000 loss. 10-1-0-0, $4,552.

–90.0% ROYAL TROMP'E, 2001 b. m., Cozzene—Attractive Crown, by Chief's Crown. **Weanling Purchase:** $100,000, 2001 Keeneland November, by Michael R. Duffy. **Juvenile Sale:** $10,000, 2003 Fasig-Tipton Midlantic May, consigned by Eddie Woods, agent, purchased by Kathleen P. Mongeon, agent. –$90,000 loss. 10-0-2-0, $20,324.

–89.5% GRAY EMBLEM, 2002 gr. or ro. f., Our Emblem—Lingquoit, by Waquoit. **Weanling Purchase:** $200,000, 2002 Keeneland November, by Venture One Partnership. **Juvenile Sale:** $21,000, 2004 OBSC April, consigned by SAB Training, agent, purchased by Gary Owens. –$179,000 loss. 3-0-0-0, $0.

–88.7% MEADOWLAKE JOHN, 2000 b. g., Meadowlake—Flowers for M'lady, by Stage Door Johnny. **Weanling Purchase:** $115,000, 2000 Keeneland November, by Granite Hill. **Juvenile Sale:** $13,000, 2002 Fasig-Tipton Midlantic May, consigned by Eddie Woods, agent, purchased by Jeffrey Gasperini. –$102,000 loss. 15-2-1-1, $39,783.

–88.6% JUDITH'S DEPUTY, 1999 ch. m., Silver Deputy—Solar Display, by Diesis (GB). **Weanling Purchase:** $140,000, 1999 Keeneland November, by Green Bridge Stud. **Juvenile Sale:** $16,000, 2001 OBSC April, consigned by Robert N. Scanlon, agent, purchased by Harvey Tenenbaum. –$124,000 loss. Unraced.

–86.7% TRY AGAIN LEN, 2000 ch. g., Silver Deputy—Nickle Lady, by Plugged Nickle. **Weanling Purchase:** $150,000, 2000 Keeneland November, by Talus Bloodstock. **Juvenile Sale:** $20,000, 2002 OBSC March, consigned by Niall Brennan, agent, purchased by Jeff Pitzer. –$130,000 loss. 6-1-0-0, $13,830.

–85.3% SWEETIEPIEOFMYEYE, 2000 dk. b. or br. m., Red Ransom—Brittan Lee, by Forty Niner. **Weanling Purchase:** $150,000, 2000 Keeneland November, by Geraldine Scullion. **Juvenile Sale:** $22,000, 2002 Keeneland April, consigned by Robert N. Scanlon, agent, purchased by Dick Lossen, agent. –$128,000 loss. 5-1-1-1, $7,468.

–85.0% SKY TO WIN, 1996 ch. h., Fly So Free—Yoda, by Proudest Roman. **Weanling Purchase:** $100,000, 1996 Keeneland November, by Rollin W. Baugh, agent. **Juvenile Sale:** $15,000, 1998 Barretts May, consigned by Rollin W. Baugh, agent, purchased by J. J. Eaton Racing Stable. –$85,000 loss. Unraced.

Notable Dispersals

Because of their selective and exclusive nature, dispersals have long been noted for high prices and long-term influence on the breeding industry. Most frequently, dispersals occur when a major breeder dies or decides to retire. Historically, that has meant that high-class bloodlines previously unavailable are on the market, attracting the most ambitious and wealthy breeders of a younger generation.

The first notable American dispersal was in 1891 when the stud of the late August Belmont I totaled $515,150. A large chunk of the total receipts came from Charles Reed's astonishing record bid of $100,000 for that year's leading sire, *St. Blaise.

Marcus Daly was a buyer at Belmont's dispersal, and when Daly died nine years later, financiers W. C. Whitney and James R. Keene were buyers at the dispersal of Daly's Bitter Root Stud. Whitney's and Keene's dispersals a few years later provided the foundations for the studs of Whitney's descendants and other great American breeders, including E. R. Bradley's Idle Hour Stock Farm.

The current record is $46,912,800 set by the dispersal of Nelson Bunker Hunt's Bluegrass Farm in 1988.

Notable North American Bloodstock Dispersals

Year	Dispersal	No. Sold	Total	Avg.	Notable Horses	Sales Company
1998	Fares Farm (Issam Fares)	232	$26,805,400	$115,541	Lady's Secret, Miss Alleged, November Snow	Keeneland
1998	Claiborne Farm/Nicole Perry Gorman	34	21,205,000	623,676	Limit	Keeneland
1997	Buckland Farm (Thomas Mellon Evans)	124	12,563,000	101,315	Meteor Stage	Keeneland
1996	Windfields Farm (Charles Taylor)	68	7,238,000	106,441	Baltic Sea, La Lorgnette	Keeneland
1992	Rokeby Stable (Paul Mellon)	32	6,294,600	196,706	Glowing Tribute, Wild Applause	
1991	Calumet Farm	185	15,068,500	81,451	Stick to Beauty, Tis Juliet	Keeneland
1989	Oxford Stable (Ralph C. Wilson Jr.)	46	18,572,700	379,034	Arazi, Fabuleux Jane	Keeneland
1989	Eugene Klein	114	29,623,000	259,851	Open Mind, Winning Colors, Lady's Secret	Keeneland, Fasig-Tipton Co.
1988	Nelson Bunker Hunt	580	46,912,800	80,884	Dahlia, Sangue (Ire), Highest Trump	Keeneland
1987	Hermitage Farm (Warner L. Jones Jr.)	130	32,676,500	251,358	My Charmer, Kamar, Seaside Attraction	Keeneland
1987	Tartan Farms/John Nerud	194	25,634,000	132,134	Unbridled, Gana Facil, Funistrada	Fasig-Tipton Co.
1986	Spendthrift Farm	163	19,171,700	117,618	Lillian Russell, Anne Campbell	Keeneland
1985	Newstead Farm (Hardin family)	42	37,186,000	885,381	Miss Oceana, Magic of Life, White Star Line	Fasig-Tipton Co.
1972	George D. Widener	69	6,643,700	96,286	What a Treat, Patelin, Seven Thirty	Fasig-Tipton Co.
1972	A. B. Hancock Jr./W. H. Perry	35	2,580,000	73,714	Sham, Apalachee	Fasig-Tipton Co.
1969	Cain Hoy Stable (Harry F. Guggenheim)	137	4,751,200	34,688	Riverman, Bold Reason, Too Bald, San San	Keeneland, Fasig-Tipton Co.
1967	Charlton Clay	18	796,100	44,228	Rose Bower, Leallah	Keeneland
1967	Maine Chance Farm (Elizabeth N. Graham)	83	1,270,700	15,310	Ribbons and Bows	Keeneland
1966-'70	Bieber-Jacobs Stable	175	3,851,000	22,005	Admiring, Priceless Gem	Keeneland, Timonium, Saratoga, Ocala, Pomona
1965	William duPont Jr.	51	2,401,300	47,084	Berlo, Parlo, All Beautiful	Maryland Breeders Sales Co.
1958	Louis B. Mayer	59	821,000	13,915	Popularity	Fasig-Tipton
1955-'56	Belair Stud (William Woodward Jr.)	59	2,475,600	41,959	Segula, Vagrancy	Keeneland
1955	Almahurst Farm (Henry Knight)	68	1,035,800	15,232	Almahmoud	Fasig-Tipton Co.
1951	Coldstream Stud (C.B. Shaffer)	48	990,500	20,635	Be Faithful, Spotted Beauty	Keeneland
1947-'50	Louis B. Mayer	248	4,479,650	18,063	Busher, Your Host, Honeymoon	Fasig-Tipton Co.
1935	Shoshone Stud (W. R. Coe)	86	201,090	2,338	Pompey, Pilate	Fasig-Tipton Co.
1925	Nursery Stud (August Belmont II)	68	782,000	11,500	Fair Play, *Quelle Chance	Joseph E. Widener
1913	Castleton Stud (James R. Keene)	45	229,000	5,088	Peter Pan, Colin, Sweep, Ultimus	Kentucky Sales Co.
1905	Rancho del Paso (James B. A. Haggin)	401	405,325	1,010	*Watercress, Colonial	Fasig-Tipton Co.
1904	LaBelle Stud (W. C. Whitney)	91	463,650	5,095	Hamburg, *Meddler, Endurance by Right	Fasig-Tipton Co.
1901	Bitter Root Stud (Marcus Daly)	186	406,525	2,185	Hamburg, *Pastorella	Fasig-Tipton Co.
1891	Nursery Stud (August Belmont I)	102	515,150	5,050	*St. Blaise	Tattersalls of New York

ORGANIZATIONS

Jockey Club

The Jockey Club, one of the Thoroughbred industry's most powerful and influential organizations, derives much of its strength from its position as the registration agency for all North American Thoroughbreds and from a membership comprising most of the sport's leading breeders and owners. In its distant past, the Jockey Club also was a regulator of racing; today, it has utilized advancing computer technology to expand its role and influence.

The Jockey Club grew out of meetings in late 1893 in which leading owners addressed the question of how to reform an unruly and corrupt racing industry. Two years earlier, prominent owner Pierre Lorillard had founded the Board of Control, but it largely represented the interests of racetrack owners, many of whom also were leading owners of racehorses. Alarmed that the racetrack owners might reduce purses, James R. Keene and seven fellow owners and breeders met on December 23 and 27, 1893, in a New York hotel to form an organization that represented the interests of both racetracks and racehorse owners. The goals of the organization were "not only to encourage the development of the Thoroughbred horse, but to establish racing on such a footing that it may command the interests as well as the confidence and favorable position of the public."

The organization was formally incorporated on February 9, 1894, as the Jockey Club, taking its name from the foundation institution in England. John Hunter was the first chairman of the American organization.

Although the Jockey Club today maintains the *American Stud Book*, it did not set out in 1894 to fulfill that function. Since 1868, Col. Sanders D. Bruce had been publishing a stud book of American pedigrees, and the Jockey Club wrote to him that it "does not propose to publish a stud book, but to keep a record of foals in the interest and for the protection of racing." The parallel projects proved to be incompatible, however, and on May 17, 1897, the Jockey Club purchased the six volumes of the *American Stud Book* previously published by Bruce, plus all related works and copyrights, for $35,000.

One of the Jockey Club's original goals was to bring order to racing in New York and New Jersey, and it played a significant role in developing the rules of racing for the East Coast and eventually the entire United States. Its influence in that area waned as the system of state racing commissions developed in the 1930s and it lost a court case involving Jule Fink in the '50s, but it remains the official registrar of racing silks in New York.

Maintaining the sport's integrity has been the thread that runs through the Jockey Club's history, and the organization has been at the forefront of precise identification of horses. The Jockey Club adopted the photographing of night eyes—the structure on the inside of the leg that in the horse is the equivalent of a fingerprint—as a method of identifying Thoroughbreds. In the 1970s, the Jockey Club adopted blood-typing as an identification tool, and, with the foal crop of 2001, began DNA testing as a definitive verification of parentage.

In July 1953, Jockey Club Chairman George D. Widener convened in New York a meeting of 18 owners, racing officials, and journalists to discuss a wide range of issues facing the industry. The following year, the meeting was moved to Saratoga Springs, New York, and now is known as the Jockey Club Round Table Conference on Matters Pertaining to Racing.

The Jockey Club has developed the world's most extensive database of race records and pedigrees of Thoroughbreds. It has complete information for all North American racing from 1930 to the present. In recent years it has been able to work with other countries' registrars to obtain complete racing information and pedigrees from the world's major racing countries. The Jockey Club also has utilized its technology to develop a family of subsidiaries and affiliated companies.

Lexington Office
821 Corporate Dr.
Lexington, Ky. 40503
Phone: (859) 224-2700
Fax: (859) 224-2710
Website: *www.jockeyclub.com*

New York Office
40 East 52nd St.
New York, N.Y. 10022
Phone: (212) 371-5970
Fax: (212) 371-6123

Officers

Chairman: Ogden Mills Phipps
Vice Chairman: William S. Farish
Secretary-Treasurer: James C. Brady
President: Alan Marzelli
Executive Vice President, Chief Administrative Officer: James L. Gagliano
Executive Vice President, Executive Director: Dan Fick
Executive Vice President, Chief Financial Officer: Laura Barillaro

Stewards

John Barr
James C. Brady
William S. Farish
G. Watts Humphrey Jr.
Ogden Mills Phipps
Reynolds Bell Jr.
Donald Dizney
Dell Hancock
John C. Oxley

Members

Josephine E. Abercrombie
Joseph L. Allbritton
William Backer
John Barr
Rollin Baugh
Reynolds Bell Jr.
Edward S. Bonnie
James C. Brady
Larry Bramlage, D.V.M.
Alexander G. Campbell Jr.
Charles J. Cella
Helen B. Chenery
Robert N. Clay
F. Eugene Dixon Jr.
Allan R. Dragone
Richard L. Duchossois
William duPont III
Robert S. Evans
William S. Farish Jr.
Helen C. Alexander
John Ed Anthony
Charles Baker
James E. Bassett III
John A. Bell III
Gary Biszantz
Frank A. Bonsal Jr.
Nicholas F. Brady
Michael C. Byrne
Thomas R. Capehart
Alice H. Chandler
Sherwood C. Chillingworth
Duke of Devonshire CBE
Donald R. Dizney
Jack J. Dreyfus Jr.
C. Steven Duncker
Edward P. Evans
William S. Farish
Hugh A. Fitzsimons Jr.

Martha F. Gerry
Louis L. Haggin III
Arthur B. Hancock III
Seth W. Hancock
John C. Harris
E. Edward Houghton
Stuart S. Janney III
Russell B. Jones Jr.
F. Jack Liebau
Harry T. Mangurian Jr.
J. W. Y. Martin Jr.
Robert McNair
Leverett Miller
Nick Nicholson
J. Michael O'Farrell Jr.
John W. Phillips
Carl Pollard
David P. Reynolds
J. David Richardson, M.D.
J. Mack Robinson
Richard Santulli
Peter G. Schiff
Mace Siegal
Robert S. Strauss
Shirley H. Taylor
Oakleigh B. Thorne
Daniel G. Van Clief Jr.
Joseph Walker Jr.
Wheelock Whitney
Martin Wygod
John K. Goodman
Lucy Young Hamilton
Dell Hancock
Joseph W. Harper
John Hettinger
G. Watts Humphrey Jr.
Richard I. G. Jones
Gary Lavin
William C. MacMillen Jr.
Frank L. Mansell
James K. McManus
Robert E. Meyerhoff
MacKenzie Miller
Kenneth Noe Jr.
John C. Oxley
Hiram C. Polk Jr., M.D.
Ogden Mills Phipps
Reuben F. Richards
Jack K. Robbins, V.M.D.
Timothy H. Sams
Joseph V. Shields Jr.
Barry Schwartz
Viola Sommer
George Strawbridge Jr.
Stella Thayer
Donald J. Valpredo
Frank "Scoop" Vessels III
Charlotte C. Weber
David Willmot
William T. Young Jr.

Jockey Club Chairmen

Chairman	Term
Ogden Mills Phipps	February 10, 1983—present
August Belmont IV	May 3, 1982—February 10, 1983
Nicholas F. Brady	January 12, 1974—April 19, 1982
Odgen Phipps	January 7, 1964—January 12, 1974
George D. Widener	January 12, 1950—January 7, 1964
William Woodward	November 3, 1930—January 12, 1950
Frank K. Sturgis	December 30, 1924—November 3, 1930
August Belmont II	January 24, 1895—December 10, 1924
John Hunter	March 1, 1894—January 24, 1895

Jockey Club subsidiaries

Jockey Club Information Systems Inc.

The Jockey Club Information Systems Inc., incorporated in 1989, is a wholly owned subsidiary of Jockey Club Holdings Inc. All profits from its activities are reinvested in the Thoroughbred industry and helps to finance industry projects. The organization has three divisions: Information Services, Cataloguing, and Software Sales and Consulting. In 2000, it launched equineline.com (*www.equineline.com*), an Internet-based information and communication network. Through *equineline.com,* the Jockey Club sells information—pedigrees of horses, race records, sire progeny records, produce records of dams, etc.—online to customers. Under the *equineline.com* banner, the Lexington-based organization has launched management programs for horse owners and breeders, trainers, and farms.

Phone: (859) 224-2800 or (800) 333-1778
Fax: (859) 224-2810
Website: *www.tjcis.com*
Chairman and Chief Executive Officer: Carl E. Hamilton
Secretary-Treasurer: Laura Barillaro
Board Members: Reynolds Bell Jr., C. Steven Duncker, Robert S. Evans, Carl E. Hamilton, Alan Marzelli, John Phillips, and Ogden Mills Phipps

InCompass

InCompass, a wholly owned subsidiary of Jockey Club Holdings Inc., was created in November 2001. Formerly known as McKinnie Systems, InCompass provided recordkeeping and operational assistance to racing offices and horsemen's bookkeepers at 90 client racetracks and associations in 2005. Functions include attendance and wagering tracking, race entries, and horsemen's bookkeeper applications, including Web access by horsemen to their horsemen's statements and bookkeeper account balances.

Phone: (859) 296-3000 or (800) 625-4664
Fax: (859) 296-3010
Website: *www.incompass-solutions.com*
Chairman: Alan Marzelli
President: David Haydon
Secretary-Treasurer: Laura Barillaro

Grayson-Jockey Club Research Foundation

Established in 1940 to raise funds for equine veterinary research, the Grayson Foundation was combined in '89 with the similarly chartered Jockey Club Research Foundation. The Lexington-based foundation, which solicits contributions from the Thoroughbred community, allocated $889,700 in research grants in 2005, raising its total contributions to nearly $10-million since the merger. In 2001 and '02, it contributed more than $250,000 for research into mare reproductive loss syndrome (MRLS).

Phone: (859) 224-2850
Fax: (859) 224-2853
Website: *www.grayson-jockeyclub.org*
E-mail: contactus@grayson-jockeyclub.org

Chairman: Dell Hancock
President: Edward L. Bowen
Chairman Emeritus: John Hettinger
Director Emeritus: Jack Robbins, V.M.D.
Treasurer: Laura Barillaro
Vice President of Development: Nancy C. Kelly
Board Members: Josephine Abercrombie, Dr. Rick Arthur, William Backer, Larry Bramlage, D.V.M., Charlsie Cantey, William Condren, Aisling Cross, Adele Dilschneider, Donald Dizney, William Farish Jr., John Goodman, Lucy Young Hamilton, Dell Hancock, Joseph W. Harper, John Hettinger, Eugene Melnyk, Leverett Miller, John M. B. O'Connor, John C. Oxley, Ogden Mills Phipps, Hiram Polk Jr., M.D., Jack Robbins, V.M.D., Geoffrey Russell, and Joseph V. Shields Jr.

The Jockey Club Foundation

Established in 1943, the Jockey Club Foundation provides confidential financial assistance to needy members of the Thoroughbred industry and their families. The New York-based foundation distributed $591,273 in 2005.

Phone: (212) 521-5305
Fax: (212) 371-6123
Website: *www.tjcfoundation.org*
Trustees: John Hettinger, C. Steven Duncker, D. G. Van Clief Jr.
Secretary-Treasurer: Laura Barillaro
Executive Director: Nancy C. Kelly

National Thoroughbred Racing Association

With its founding in 1998, the National Thoroughbred Racing Association immediately became one of the industry's leading organizations. The NTRA originated in part from a "Guest Commentary" by Lexington advertising executive Fred Pope in the August 27, 1993, issue of THOROUGHBRED TIMES. Pope, an associate of Breeders' Cup founder John Gaines, suggested that horse owners pool their media rights—the images of their horses in races—and establish a major league of racing. With the funds generated from simulcasting the sport's leading races, the proposed owners' association—the National Thoroughbred Association—would market the sport to the American public.

The industry was not ready for Pope's idea in 1993, but three years later full-card simulcasting exploded across the nation and provided a new stream of revenue for racing. Former Carter White House aides Hamilton Jordan and Tim Smith were hired by Pope and Gaines to sell the NTA concept to the Thoroughbred industry. Although not accepted by the racetracks, Pope's idea—that the sport needed a national presence and national marketing—gained momentum, and in March 1997 four industry organizations—Breeders' Cup Ltd., the Jockey Club, Keeneland Association, and Oak Tree Racing Association—put up $1-million each as seed money for a new organization to market the sport. In a short time, the new entity was named the National Thoroughbred Racing Association, and the efforts of the NTA were effectively folded into it. (The NTA formally merged into the NTRA in August 1998, and Pope was compensated for his intellectual property.)

Even with the backing of industry leaders, the NTRA was not a sure bet to be supported by racetracks and national organizations. Breeders' Cup President D. G. Van Clief Jr., serving as the NTRA's interim chief executive, and Jockey Club Executive Director Nick Nicholson traveled throughout the country to sell the concept of a national office to market racing to industry participants. They gained sufficient backing, and a business plan was released in December 1997. The NTRA formally began operation on April 1, 1998. Its first commissioner and chief executive officer was Smith, who, after leaving the White House, had served as deputy commissioner of the Professional Golfers' Association Tour and had helped to reorganize the Association of Tennis Professionals Tour.

The NTRA's first priority was marketing, and it produced an edgy, attention-grabbing national television advertisement featuring actress Lori Petty. Industry members, however, panned the ad, and the NTRA could not replicate its success through subsequent marketing campaigns. In its first years, the NTRA ventured beyond marketing, opening subsidiary operations such as NTRA Services, NTRA Investments, NTRA Productions (for television production), and NTRA Charities. The NTRA became the producer of the Eclipse Awards, assuming a role formerly held by Thoroughbred Racing Associations.

By the end of 1999, several racetrack executives, including Magna Entertainment Corp.'s Frank Stronach and a group of Mid-Atlantic track owners, complained that the NTRA had veered away from its original marketing mandate and had entered business enterprises where it was in competition with tracks, notably by operating a telephone-wagering hub in Oregon for Television Games Network. Some of the Mid-Atlantic tracks pulled out of the NTRA but returned later, while Stronach was appeased when more racetrack representation was added to the NTRA board of directors, including a seat for a Stronach representative. Also that year, NTRA transferred operation of the Oregon hub to TVG.

NTRA's continuing budget deficits contributed to a decision in 2000 to merge many of its operations with Breeders' Cup Ltd., and the merger took place on January 1, 2001. Smith remained commissioner and Van Clief became the NTRA's vice chairman. By the end of 2001, many NTRA functions had been melded into the Breeders' Cup operation. Smith resigned in 2004, and Van Clief was named commissioner on an interim basis. His appointment became permanent in April 2005, but he resigned a year later. He was succeeded by Greg Avioli on an interim basis.

In recent years, the NTRA has worked to build the sport's fan base through increased television exposure, consumer research, and promotion of the Breeders' Cup World Championships. The NTRA has increased its lobbying and group-purchasing efforts, and it has proved effective in crisis management, particularly in the 2002 Breeders' Cup Ultra Pick Six scandal.

2525 Harrodsburg Rd.
Lexington, Ky. 40504
Phone: (859) 223-5444
Fax: (859) 223-3945
Website: *www.ntra.com*
E-mail: ntra@ntra.com

Interim Chief Executive Officer: Greg Avioli
Executive Vice President: Robert Clay

Directors: John Amerman, Robert Elliston, Alan Foreman, Craig Fravel, Robert W. Green, Charles Hayward, G. Watts Humphrey Jr., Alan Landsburg, Jim McAlpine, Tom Meeker, Nick Nicholson, Ogden Mills Phipps, Joe Santanna, D. G. Van Clief Jr.

Thoroughbred Racing Associations

In January 1942, racing's representatives to the National Association of State Racing Commissioners convention perceived themselves to be in a war-related emergency and convened a meeting that March in Chicago. The object of the meeting initially was to pull together all elements of the industry into a single ruling organization.

The two-day meeting that began on March 19, 1942, would not yield an overall ruling body for the fractious and fragmented industry. However, at that meeting, 33 executives of 22 racetracks formed the Thoroughbred Racing Associations of the United States, with Hialeah Park President John C. Clark as its first president. The organization was formally incorporated on May 22, 1942. (The name subsequently was changed to the Thoroughbred Racing Associations of North America when Canada's tracks joined the organization.)

Representatives to the March 1942 meeting realized that they could not conduct racing throughout the war strictly as an entertainment vehicle, and the Turf Committee of America was formed to raise funds to support the war effort.

New challenges awaited in the postwar years; chief among them was the integrity of the sport. In 1946, at the behest of Federal Bureau of Investigation Director J. Edgar Hoover (an avid racing fan), the TRA formed the Thoroughbred Racing Protective Bureau. A former FBI agent, Spencer J. Drayton, became the first director of the TRPB and instituted practices such as fingerprinting of all licensees, from hotwalkers to owners.

Drayton became the TRA's executive vice president in 1960, and his appointment resulted in the resignation of five racetracks. He retired in 1974, and, since '76, the TRA has had only two executive vice presidents, J. B. Faulconer and Christopher N. Scherf (since '88).

In 1950, the TRA had begun to select its own end-of-year champions, which sometimes differed from those chosen by the *Daily Racing Form*, which established its poll in 1936. Faulconer was given the task of unifying the championships in 1971. Then president of Turf Publicists of America, Faulconer brought together the TRA, *Daily Racing Form*, and the National Turf Writers Association to launch the Eclipse Awards that year. In 1999, the National Thoroughbred Racing Association supplanted the TRA as the industry's representative to the Eclipse Awards.

420 Fair Hill Dr., Suite 1
Elkton, Md. 21921-2573
Phone: (410) 392-9200
Fax: (410) 398-1366
Website: *www.tra-online.com*
E-mail: info@tra-online.com

President: Corey S. Johnsen
Vice Presidents: C. Kenneth Dunn, David S. Willmot
Secretary: Robert L. Bork
Treasurer: William I. Fasy
Executive Vice President: Christopher N. Scherf

Directors: Robert Abraham, Don Amos, Roy Arnold, Charles W. Bidwill III, Robert L. Bork, Tim Carey, Charles J. Cella, Sherwood C. Chillingworth, Joseph A. De Francis, Dennis O. Dowd, Steve Duncker, C. Kenneth Dunn, Robert N. Elliston, William Gallo Jr., Robert W. Green, Harold G. Handel, Joseph W. Harper, Charles E. Hayward, Corey S. Johnsen, Chuck Keeling, Robert P. Levy, Jim McAlpine, Christopher McErlean, Mark Midland, Hugh M. Miner Jr., Jerry M. Monahan, Richard E. Moore, Howard M. Mosner Jr., Nick Nicholson, William M. Rickman Jr., Charles J. Ruma, Randall D. Sampson, Christopher N. Scherf, Steve Sexton, Sal Sinatra, Randall E. Soth, Ronald A. Sultemeier, Stella F. Thayer, Ray A. Tromba, Scott Wells, David S. Willmot

TRA Presidents

Term	President	Representing
2005-'06	Corey S. Johnsen	Lone Star Park
2003-'04	Joseph W. Harper	Del Mar
2001-'02	Bryan G. Krantz	Fair Grounds
1999-'00	Stella F. Thayer	Tampa Bay Downs
1997-'98	Harold G. Handel	New Jersey Sports and Exposition Authority
1995-'96	Clifford C. Goodrich	Santa Anita
1993-'94	David M. Vance	Remington
1991-'92	Thomas H. Meeker	Churchill Downs
1989-'90	Robert P. Levy	Atlantic City
1987-'88	Gerard J. McKeon	New York Racing Association
1985-'86	James E. Bassett III	Keeneland
1983-'84	Morris J. Alhadeff	Longacres
1981-'82	Lynn Stone	Churchill Downs
1979-'80	Robert S. Gunderson	Bay Meadows
1977-'78	Baird C. Brittingham	Delaware
1975-'76	Charles J. Cella	Oaklawn
1973-'75	Frank M. Basil	New York Racing Association
1971-'73	James E. Brock	Ak-Sar-Ben
1969-'70	John D. Schapiro	Laurel
1967-'68	Louis Lee Haggin II	Keeneland
1965-'66	Edward P. Taylor	Ontario Jockey Club
1963-'64	Robert P. Strub	Santa Anita
1961-'62	E. E. Dale Shaffer	Detroit Race Course
1959-'60	John G. Cella	Oaklawn
1957-'58	James D. Stewart	Hollywood
1955-'56	Amory L. Haskell	Monmouth
1953-'54	John A. Morris	Jamaica
1951-'52	Alfred G. Vanderbilt	Belmont
1949-'50	Donald P. Ross Sr.	Delaware
1947-'48	James E. Dooley	Narragansett
1944-'46	Henry A. Parr II	Pimlico
1942-'43	John C. Clark	Hialeah

Thoroughbred Racing Protective Bureau

Modeled after the Federal Bureau of Investigation and initially staffed by former FBI agents, the Thoroughbred Racing Protective Bureau is the investigative and security arm of the Thoroughbred Racing Associations of North America. The TRPB was founded in January 1946 to protect the integrity of the sport.

420 Fair Hill Dr., Suite 2
Elkton, Md. 21921-2573
Phone: (410) 398-2261
Fax: (410) 398-1499
Website: *www.trpb.com*
E-Mail: trpbinfo@trpb.com

President and Treasurer: Franklin J. Fabian
Vice President and Secretary: James P. Gowen
Chairman: John E. Mooney
Directors: Robert L. Bork, Charles J. Cella, Ron Charles, Sherwood Chillingworth, C. Kenneth Dunn, Franklin J. Fabian, Charles Hayward, Chris McErlean, Terence J. Meyocks, John E. Mooney, Nick Nicholson, Jim Orminston, Stella F. Thayer

American Horse Council

The American Horse Council, organized in 1969 to give horse-industry participants a voice in Congress, comprises organizations and individuals from every facet of the horse world. The AHC's mission is to promote and protect the equine industry by representing its interests to Congress and federal agencies, and to advise the government of the equine industry's important role in the United States economy. It also aims to unify the industry by serving as a forum for member organizations and individuals.

In 1965, when a tax proposal to disallow the expense of raising racehorses and performance horses first surfaced, a group of industry members—including John H. Clark, Warner Jones Jr., and Leslie Combs II—reestablished the Thoroughbred Breeders of Kentucky. The first meeting of the group discussed that threat, recent increases in farrier rates, and local horse transporters' recent application to the Kentucky Department of Transportation to be regulated, which the organizers contended would make it unlawful for a farm operator to transport any horses but his or her own. Clark was voted president for 1966.

In 1967, with founding member Jones as president, they began to work toward creating a lobby to prevent the detrimental parts of the Tax Reform Act of 1969 from passing. They were successful and established the AHC as their lobby in Washington. Albert G. Clay, also a founder, was secretary of the organization from its formation through 1990. The AHC grew to represent 5.2-million horses and one-million horsemen by 1990.

Led since 1993 by President James Hickey Jr., the AHC has recently worked more closely with the National Thoroughbred Racing Association on issues involving the racing industry, notably the 2001 mare reproductive loss syndrome crisis in Kentucky, when the NTRA and the AHC met with federal officials to set up federal disaster relief for breeders who had lost a substantial number of foals. Also in 2001, the congressional Racing and Breeding Caucus was formed by the NTRA and the AHC. The NTRA increased its lobbying budget to $900,000, dramatically increasing the presence of the AHC in Congress. In 2002, the AHC joined the NTRA's Wagering Technology Working Group, which intends to improve the security of pari-mutuel wagering.

In 1996, the American Horse Council published the first National Economic Impact Study of the Horse Industry in the United States. Another study was conducted and published in 2005, and the figures from the study have been used to demonstrate the importance of the horse industry to the U.S. economy.

Other recent issues the AHC has tackled include lobbying to change immigration laws to allow seasonal foreign workers to remain in the U.S. without reapplying for a visa every year, which is especially important for the many trainers and owners who employ foreign workers in their barns. The organization also has lobbied to protect horse racing from restrictive Internet legislation. The AHC's goal has been to win passage of a prohibition bill with an exception for horse racing and legal pari-mutuel wagering.

1616 H Street NW
7th Floor
Washington, D.C. 20006
Phone: (202) 296-4031
Fax: (202) 296-1970
Website: *www.horsecouncil.org*
E-Mail: ahc@horsecouncil.org

President: James J. Hickey Jr.
Chief Operating Officer: Nicole D. Lamoureux
Board of Trustees: Nick Nicholson (chairman), Russell C. Williams (vice chairman), Jerry Black (secretary), Jim Shoemake (treasurer), Marvin Beeman, Jane Clark, Paul Fontaine, G. Watts Humphrey Jr., F. Philip Langley, Charles J. Ruma, Eric Straus, D. G. Van Clief Jr., Jerry Windham

Association of Racing Commissioners International

In August 1934, racing commissioners from nine states met when it became apparent that, if racing was to grow as a sport, each state could not function in a vacuum, unmindful of other jurisdictions' rules and regulations. The commissioners aspired to form a national organization that would "encourage forceful and honest nationwide control of racing for the protection of the public" and launched the National Association of State Racing Commissioners (NASRC) to represent Thoroughbred racing.

The NASRC gradually broadened to include all forms of flat racing, harness racing, greyhound racing, and jai-alai and in 1988 became the Association of Racing Commissioners International (RCI) to give the organization a global identity.

In 1947, the NASRC created a national database in which all rulings were summarized. The database provided all jurisdictions with easy access to national files and ended the need for massive files of duplicate information.

RCI maintains a vision to create a cohesive regulatory structure for a financially viable pari-mutuel sports industry. In its mission statement, RCI states that it strives to "protect and uphold the integrity of the pari-mutuel sports of horse racing, dog racing, and jai-alai through an informed membership, by encouraging forceful and uniform regulation, by promoting the health and welfare of the industry through various programs and projects."

RCI serves as a repository and distribution center for all official rulings by stewards and racing commissioners and encourages reciprocity, under which rulings in one jurisdiction are recognized and enforced in all others. In addition, it works to develop uniform rules and racing practices.

The association also recommends rules and regulations to governmental boards and regulatory agencies for the effective conduct of race meetings, wagering, and related pursuits. RCI studies, researches, and discusses the needs and problems regarding regulation of racing and wagering.

In 1997, several racing commissions that were displeased with the governance of RCI broke away to form the North American Pari-Mutuel Regulators Association. After several changes were made in the RCI structure, including the recognition of professional regulators as full members, the organizations merged in December 2005.

2343 Alexandria Dr., Suite 200
Lexington, Ky. 40504
Phone: (859) 224-7070
Fax: (859) 224-7071
Website: *www.arci.com*

Chairman: Bernard Daney
President and Chief Executive Officer: Edward J. Martin
Vice President: Paul Bowlinger
Chair-Elect: Peter Burnett
Secretary and Treasurer: Joe Gorajec
Immediate Past Chairman: Timothy J. "Ted" Connors
Board of Directors: Cecil L. Alexander, Pat Brennan, Cheryl Buley, Peter J. Cofrancesco III, Charles Crockrom, Larry Elliason, Thomas H. Grimstad, M.D., Dan Hartman, Darcy Hitesman, David Kangaloo, Hartly H. Kruger, Frank Lamb, Warren Leary Jr., John Meeks, Benjamin H. Nolt Jr., Erin Owens-Hall, W. Duncan Patterson, Lorna Propes, Dave Roberts, Richard Shapiro, Oscar Steinley, Lynda Tanaka, Larry F. Telle, Christine White

Equibase

Equibase Co. LLC, a general partnership of the Thoroughbred Racing Associations of North America (TRA) and the Jockey Club, is the official source of all racehorse past performances and racing data in North America. It was founded in 1991 because the racetracks and racing authorities at that time did not possess their own database of racing performance, nor did they have free access to the information. Rather, an independent daily newspaper, *Daily Racing Form,* compiled and owned all racing records of horses starting in North America.

For decades previous, racetracks published an official program containing official betting numbers and such basic information as a horse's pedigree, owner, trainer, jockey, post position, morning-line betting odds, and colors of each owner's racing silks. Past performances were the exclusive province of the *Daily Racing Form*.

Equibase began operation in 1991 with its own chart callers for the purpose of creating past-performance lines that could be used in programs sold by racetracks. (The charts, a statistical description of a race and each horse's running position, are the raw materials of past-performance lines.) To help subsidize the start-up, each participating track pledged 25 cents from each program sold to be paid to Equibase. While some tracks began to publish magazine-sized official programs with Equibase past performances, a significant competitor to *Daily Racing Form* emerged when *Racing Times*, backed by England-based publishing magnate Robert Maxwell, began operation. *Racing Times* purchased its past-performance lines from Equibase. *Racing Times* was making inroads into the *Racing Form*'s monopoly when Maxwell drowned off the Canary Islands in late 1991, and his empire collapsed.

The magazine-sized programs, which usually sell for about one-third of the price of the *Daily Racing Form*, gradually became popular with racegoers, which sharply reduced *Daily Racing Form*'s circulation. In 1998, after years of negotiations between the two parties, Equibase became the sole data-collection agency, with *Daily Racing Form* dropping its collection efforts and thereafter purchasing its racing information from Equibase. Today, Equibase provides information to more than 100 tracks and 1,100 simulcast outlets, as well as to *Daily Racing Form*, *Sports-Eye*, several online resellers, and the industry's major interactive wagering services.

Since repaying all start-up costs in 1997, Equibase profits have been shared among the TRA and its limited-partner racetracks (66%) and the Jockey Club (33%) in the form of dividends. In 2005, Equibase distributed dividends of $2.7-million to its partners.

The company also serves the sport's fan base through its website, *www.equibase.com*, which offers a wide array of handicapping information and services geared toward every level of handicapper. Among the products available are race programs with handicapping information in easy-to-understand formats for new and existing fans. These pages were developed in conjunction with the National Thoroughbred Racing Association. The Equibase Virtual Stable, the exclusive notification service of the NTRA, delivers entry, workout, and result notices for horses that fans wish to follow. Virtual Stable also features a race series notification service that allows fans to monitor the progress of leading contenders for the Triple Crown and Breeders' Cup races in the months leading up to those events.

In July 2000, it purchased AXCIS Information Network Inc., a provider of electronic handicapping information, through its Track Master product. In April 2004, Equibase hired Philip O'Hara as its president and chief executive officer.

821 Corporate Dr.
Lexington, Ky. 40503-2794
Phone: (859) 224-2860 or (800) 333-2211
Fax: (859) 224-2811
Website: *www.equibase.com*

Chairman: Alan Marzelli
President and Chief Executive Officer: Philip O'Hara
Executive Vice President and Chief Operating Officer: Hank Zeitlin
Secretary: Christopher N. Scherf
Treasurer: Laura Barillaro
Management Committee: Sherwood Chillingworth, C. Steven Duncker, Dan Fick, Craig Fravel, Alan Marzelli, Jim McAlpine, Ann McGovern, William A. Nader, Nick Nicholson, Ogden Mills Phipps, Karl Schmitt Jr., Michael Weiss

Jockeys' Guild

The Jockeys' Guild was established in 1940 to negotiate for insurance and media rights contracts on behalf of riders. Founding members included Eddie Arcaro, Sam Renick, Ray Workman, Johnny Longden, Alfred Robertson, Charlie Kurtsinger, Red Pollard, and Harry Richards, who was elected the Guild's first president. Another founding member, Nick Jemas, guided the Jockeys' Guild as national manager from 1967 to '86, effectively running the organization from the garage of his home in Haddonfield, New Jersey. During his tenure, he waged a state-by-state campaign to raise jockeys' mount fees.

Jemas was succeeded by John Giovanni, a former jockey in New England who had been a Guild regional representative. With the headquarters relocated to Lexington from a New York office that Jemas used only occasionally, Giovanni championed workers' compensation coverage for jockeys and was instrumental in putting together a workers' comp program in New York.

Rising costs of health insurance for jockeys and their families led to dissension within the leadership, and directors led by Chris McCarron ousted Giovanni and his staff in 2001. Installed to manage the Guild was Wayne Gertmenian, who was elected president. Gertmenian and his staff took a confrontational approach to the industry and Guild members who opposed him. When jockey Gary Birzer was paralyzed in a 2004 spill at Mountaineer Race Track, it was disclosed that a catastrophic-injury policy had been allowed to lapse. Congressional hearings in 2005 eventually led to the ouster of Gertmenian and his chief assistant, Albert Fiss, late in the year. The Guild was found to be in severe financial straits, and Darrell Haire, a former Guild representative under Gertmenian who became interim national manager, worked to shore up the organization's finances through 2006. A new Jockeys' Guild Senate and new officers were elected in 2006.

1740 East Huntington Dr., Suite 310
Duarte, Ca.
Phone: (866) 465-6257, (626) 305-5615
Fax: (626) 305-5615
Website: *www.jockeysguild.com*

Chairman: John Velazquez
Vice Chairman: G. R. Carter
Secretary: Jon Court
Treasurer: Jeff Johnston

Keeneland Association

Keeneland Association, a not-for-profit organization, was founded in 1936 with a vision of presenting "Racing as it was meant to be" and is dedicated to perpetuating and improving the sport while symbolizing the tradition of Thoroughbred racing. Located six miles west of downtown Lexington, Keeneland Race Course provides a model racetrack at the center of Kentucky's Bluegrass region. Keeneland continues to carry out the initiative of its founders through its three principal business activities: live racing, simulcast racing, and sales.

Keeneland, started on the grounds first established by owner-breeder Jack Keene, held its inaugural race meeting in October 1936. It now annually hosts two short meets, one in April and one in October, which feature some of the highest purses in the country, aided by year-round simulcasting. Keeneland's 15-day race meeting in the spring is highlighted by the Blue Grass Stakes (G1), and its 16-day meeting in the fall features the Spinster Stakes (G1).

The first public auction of Thoroughbreds at Keeneland was held in a paddock sale on April 25, 1938, when 31 horses sold for an average of $803. The first yearling sale at Keeneland was held in the summer of 1943, when wartime restrictions on rail transport forced Kentucky breeders to keep their yearlings at home, rather than send them to the prestigious yearling sale in Saratoga Springs, New York. This led to a sale of yearlings under a tent in the Keeneland paddock conducted by Fasig-Tipton Co. When Fasig-Tipton did not offer a sale in 1944, local breeders formed the Breeders' Sales Co. to sell yearlings at Keeneland, which launched what has become the most successful sales company in the world. In 1962, Breeders' Sales Co. was dissolved, and Keeneland Association took over the business of selling horses.

Keeneland added a September sale of yearlings and a November breeding stock sale in 1944, a January horses of all ages sale in '56, and an April two-year-olds in training sale in '93.

Future generations of horsemen may also remember Keeneland for advocating the installation of Polytrack. Keeneland spearheaded the introduction of the synthetic racing surface to North American racing; Turfway Park in Florence, Kentucky, became the first North American track to use Polytrack for pari-mutuel wagering on September 7, 2005. A 50% owner of Turfway Park with Harrah's Entertainment Inc. and the North American distributor of Polytrack for inventor Martin Collins, Keeneland introduced Polytrack on its training track in Lexington in September 2004 and installed the all-weather surface on its main track before its '06 October meeting.

4201 Versailles Rd.
P. O. Box 1690
Lexington, Ky. 40588-1690
Phone: (859) 254-3412 or (800) 456-3412
Fax: (859) 255-2484
Website: *www.keeneland.com*

President and Chief Executive Officer: Nick Nicholson
Director of Racing: W. B. Rogers Beasley
Vice President: Harvie Wilkinson
Director of Sales: Geoffrey Russell
Treasurer: Jessica A. Green
Racing Secretary: Ben Huffman
Senior Auctioneer: Ryan Mahan
Trustees: James E. "Ted" Bassett III, William T. "Buddy" Bishop III, L. L. Haggin III

Thoroughbred Owners and Breeders Association

Since 1961, the Thoroughbred Owners and Breeders Association has worked to promote the interests of Thoroughbred owners and breeders. With a network that includes 41 states and chapters in Puerto Rico and Ontario, Lexington-based TOBA includes owners and breeders at all levels in the Thoroughbred industry. Membership dues fund the organization.

After becoming a founding member of the National Thoroughbred Racing Association in 2000, TOBA helped to launch *TheGreatestGame.com*, a website dedicated to recruiting and retaining owners. The site contains everything from a consultant directory to answers to such questions as how a horse can be purchased.

In 1973, TOBA formed the North American Graded Stakes Committee (now the United States Graded Stakes Committee), which meets annually to assign one of three grades to races, and is active in the International Cataloguing Standards Committee (ICSC) and the Society of International Thoroughbred Auctioneers (SITA). Established in 1981, ICSC sets black-type standards throughout the world. SITA was founded in 1983 and investigates and monitors bloodstock matters related to auctions.

The National Racing Compact, which allows multijurisdictional licenses for racing participants, is also supported by TOBA, and the organization keeps tabs on the political environment as an influential voice in the American Horse Council.

TOBA spearheaded the development of the Horse Industry Economic Impact Study, which strives to improve the effectiveness of national and state racing and breeding associations in the legislative and regulatory processes.

TOBA also created or cosponsored such projects as the Claiming Crown (in association with the National Horsemen's Benevolent and Protective Association) and America's Day at the Races.

The organization's Equine Health Committee works closely with the United States Department of Agriculture and monitors the outbreak or transmission of equine diseases throughout the world.

TOBA also manages the Sales Integrity Program and Thoroughbred Charities of America, is a founding member of the Racing Medication and Testing Consortium, and represents the U.S. on the International Breeders' Secretariat, a forum of 17 racing and breeding countries that meets annually to discuss issues of global significance to the industry.

P.O. Box 910668
Lexington, Ky. 40591-0668
Phone: (859) 276-2291
Fax: (859) 276-2462
Website: *www.toba.org*
E-Mail: info@toba.org

President: Dan Metzger
Director of Industry Relations and Development: Andrew Schweigardt
Communications Coordinator: Terri Battle
Controller: Carl Gough
Executive and Financial Assistant: Helen Prossitt
Director of Marketing and Communications: Erin Halliwell

National Horsemen's Benevolent and Protective Association

The National Horsemen's Benevolent and Protective Association is a not-for-profit organization that began in New England in 1940. While horsemen had always helped to provide for one another's needs, such as medical attention, burial services, and aid to families, they felt that something more was needed. A group of horsemen founded what became the HBPA with a common goal: the betterment of racing on all levels.

In 1996, a formal mission statement was created and adopted; it states that the association's mission is to provide insurance services to members, circulate information on industry issues to horsemen, promote reform in medication rules and research, provide a national voice for horsemen, assist individual members with problems, and promote the preservation of live racing in North America.

Today, the National HBPA has more than 35,000 owner and trainer members in 31 affiliate organizations in 26 states and Canada. Services provided by the National HBPA include liability insurance for owners and trainers and fire, disaster, and vanning insurance.

The organization's quarterly publication is *The Horsemen's Journal*, and the National HBPA also publishes documents on such industry topics as workers' compensation, economic trends, and drug policy.

Recently, the National HBPA has focused its attention on establishing industrywide thresholds for medication positives, and it is represented on the board of directors of the Racing Medication and Testing Consortium.

The HBPA also strives to find ways to reduce the number of unwanted horses and to improve their overall welfare.

In addition, it raised funds for horsemen affected by Hurricanes Katrina and Rita in 2005, and it has donated to the Permanently Disabled Jockeys Fund and numerous other industry organizations.

The National HBPA worked on setting up an offshore international betting hub beginning in 2004 in response to offshore operations taking business from United States tracks and thus reducing purse payments.

The effort never became viable, however, and President John Roark resigned in April 2006 to establish an international wagering hub in Curacao with two partners.

National Horse Center
Building B Suite 2
4063 Ironworks Pkwy.
Lexington, Ky. 40511-8905
Phone: (859) 259-0451
Fax: (859) 259-0452
Website: *www.hbpa.org*
E-Mail: racing@hbpa.org

President and Chairman: Joe Santanna (Interim)
Chief Executive Officer: Remi Bellocq
General Counsel: Doug McSwain

National Industry Organizations

American Academy of Equine Art
c/o Kentucky Horse Park
4089 Iron Works Pkwy.
Lexington, Ky. 40511
Ph: (859) 281-6031
Fax: (859) 281-6043
E-mail: shelleyh@aaea.net
Website: *www.aaea.net*
President: Werner Rentsch

American Association of Equine Practitioners
4075 Iron Works Pkwy.
Lexington, Ky. 40511
Ph: (859) 233-0147
Fax: (859) 233-1968
E-mail: aepoffice@aaep.org
Website: *www.aaep.org*
President: Thomas D. Brokken, D.V.M.

American Farriers Assn.
4059 Iron Works Pkwy., Ste. 1
Lexington, Ky. 40511
Ph: (859) 233-7411
Fax: (859) 231-7862
E-mail: farriers@americanfarriers.org
Website: *www.americanfarriers.org*
President: Craig Trnka

American Horse Council
1616 H Street NW, 7th floor
Washington, D.C. 20006
Ph: (202) 296-4031
Fax: (202) 296-1970
E-mail: ahc@horsecouncil.org
Website: *www.horsecouncil.org*
President: James J. Hickey Jr.

American Horse Protection Assn.
1000 29th St. NW., Ste. T-100
Washington, D.C. 20007
Ph: (202) 965-0500
Fax: (202) 965-9621
Website: *www.ahpa.us*

Animal Transportation Assn.
111 East Loop North
Houston, Tx. 77029
Ph: (713) 532-2177
Fax: (713) 532-2166
E-mail: info@aata-animaltransport.org
Website: *www.aata-animaltransport.org*

Association of Racing Commissioners Int'l.
2343 Alexandria Dr., Ste. 200
Lexington, Ky. 40504-3276
Ph: (859) 224-7070
Fax: (859) 224-7071
E-mail: support@arci.com
Website: *www.arci.com*
Chairman: Bernard Daney
President: Ed Martin

Breeders' Cup Ltd.
P.O. Box 4230
Lexington, Ky. 40544-4230
Ph: (859) 223-5444
Fax: (859) 223-3945
E-mail: breederscup@breederscup.com
Website: *www.breederscup.com*
Interim Chief Executive: Greg Avioli

Canadian Veterinary Medical Assn.
339 Booth St.
Ottawa, ON K1R 7K1 Canada
Ph: (613) 236-1162
Fax: (613) 236-9681
E-mail: admin@cvma-acmv.org
Website: *www.canadianveterinarians.net*

Grayson-Jockey Club Research Foundation
821 Corporate Dr.
Lexington, Ky. 40503
Ph: (859) 224-2850
Fax: (859) 224-2853
E-mail: contactus@grayson-jockeyclub.org
Website: *www.grayson-jockeyclub.org*
President: Edward L. Bowen

Horsemen's Benevolent and Protective Assn. (National)
4063 Iron Works Pkwy.
Bldg. B, Ste. 2
Lexington, Ky. 40511-8905
Ph: (859) 259-0451
Fax: (859) 259-0452
E-mail: racing@hbpa.org
Website: *www.hbpa.org*
Executive Director: Remi Bellocq

Jockey Club of Canada
P.O. Box 66; Station B
Etobicoke, Ontario M9W 5K9 Canada
Ph: (416) 675-7756
Fax: (416) 675-6378
E-mail: jockeyclub@bellnet.ca
Website: *www.jockeyclubcanada.com*
Chairman: Richard Bonnycastle

Jockeys' Guild
P.O. Box 150
Monrovia, Ca. 91017
Ph: (866) 465-6257
Fax: (626) 305-5615
E-mail: info@jockeysguild.com
Website: *www.jockeysguild.com*
Chairman: John Velazquez

National Horse Carriers Assn.
2053 Buck Ln.
Lexington, Ky. 40511
Ph: (859) 255-9406
Website: *www.nationalhorsecarriers.com*
Chairman: Robert D. Maxwell

National Museum of Racing and Hall of Fame
191 Union Ave.
Saratoga Springs, N.Y. 12866-3566
Ph: (518) 584-0400
Fax: (518) 584-4574
E-mail: nmrinfo@racingmuseum.net
Website: *www.racingmuseum.org*
Director: Peter Hammell

National Steeplechase Assn.
400 Fair Hill Dr.
Elkton, Md. 21921-2573
Ph: (410) 392-0700
Fax: (410) 392-0706
E-mail: steeplechs@aol.com
Website: *www.nationalsteeplechase.com*
President: Jonathan Sheppard

National Thoroughbred Racing Assn.
2525 Harrodsburg Rd., 5th Fl.
Lexington, Ky. 40504-3359
Ph: (859) 223-5444
Fax: (859) 245-6868
E-mail: ntra@ntra.com
Website: *www.ntra.com*
Interim Chief Executive: Greg Avioli

National Turf Writers Assn.
1244 Meadow Ln.
Frankfort, Ky. 40601
Ph: (502) 875-4864
E-mail: jill@turfwriters.org
President: Tom Law

The Jockey Club
40 E. 52nd St.
New York, N.Y. 10022
Ph: (212) 371-5970
Fax: (212) 371-6123
E-mail: contactus@jockeyclub.com
Website: *www.jockeyclub.com*
Chairman: Ogden Mills Phipps
President: Alan Marzelli

Thoroughbred Club of America
P.O. Box 8098
Lexington, Ky. 40533-8098
Ph: (859) 254-4282
Fax: (859) 231-6131
President: Charles Nuckols III

Thoroughbred Owners and Breeders Assn.
P.O. Box 4367
Lexington, Ky. 40544-4367
Ph: (859) 276-2291
Fax: (859) 276-2462
E-mail: TOBA@toba.org
Website: *www.toba.org*
President: Dan Metzger

Thoroughbred Racing Assns. of North America
420 Fair Hill Dr., Ste. 1

Elkton, Md. 21921-2573
Ph: (410) 392-9200
Fax: (410) 398-1366
E-mail: info@tra-online.com
Website: *www.tra-online.com*
President: Corey Johnsen
Executive Vice President: Chris Scherf

Thoroughbred Racing Protective Bureau
420 Fair Hill Dr., Ste. 2
Elkton, Md. 21921
Ph: (410) 398-2261
Fax: (410) 398-1499
E-mail: trpbinfo@trpb.com
Website: *www.trpb.com*
President: Frank Fabian

Triple Crown Productions
700 Central Ave.
Louisville, Ky. 40208-1200
Ph: (502) 636-4405
Fax: (502) 636-4554
E-mail: triplecrown@kentuckyderby.com
Website: *www.thetriplecrownchallenge.com*
President: Thomas H. Meeker
Executive Vice President: Edward Seigenfeld

Turf Publicists of America
P.O. Box 90
Jamaica, N.Y. 11417
Ph: (718) 641-4700
Fax: (718) 843-7673
E-mail: jlee@nyrainc.com
Website: *www.turfpublicists.com*
President: John Lee

United Thoroughbred Trainers of America
P.O. Box 7065
Louisville, Ky. 40257-0065
Ph: (502) 499-9201
Fax: (502) 893-0026

State and Provincial Racing Organizations

Alabama

Alabama Horsemen's Benevolent and Protective Association
1523 Indian Hills
Hartselle, Al. 35640
Ph: (256) 773-3592
Fax: (256) 773-5370
E-mail: alahbpa@aol.com
President: Skip Drinkard

Birmingham Racing Commission
2101 6th Ave. N., Ste. 725; Colonial Plaza
Birmingham, Al. 35203
Ph: (205) 328-7223
E-mail: ledadimperio@bellsouth.net
Executive Secretary: W. Kip Keefer

Arizona

Arizona Horsemen's Benevolent and Protective Association
P.O. Box 43636
Phoenix, Az. 85080
Ph: (602) 942-3336
Fax: (602) 866-3790
E-mail: azhbpa@qwest.net
President: Kevin Eikleberry

Arizona Racing Commission
1110 W. Washington, Suite 260
Phoenix, Az. 85007
Ph: (602) 364-1700
Fax: (602) 364-1703
E-mail: ador@azracing.gov
Website: *www.racing.state.az.us*
Executive Director: Geoffrey Gonsher
Chairman: Bob Ford

Arizona Thoroughbred Breeders Association
P.O. Box 41774
Phoenix, Az. 85080
Ph: (602) 942-1310
Fax: (602) 942-8225
E-mail: atba@worldnet.att.net
Website: *www.atba.net*
President: Bradley Rollins

University of Arizona Race Track Industry Program
845 N. Park Ave., Ste. 370
Tucson, Az. 85721
Ph: (520) 621-5660
Fax: (520) 621-8239
E-mail: bprewitt@ag.arizona.edu
Website: *www.ua-rtip.org*
Director: Douglas Reed

Arkansas

Arkansas Horse Council
P.O. Box 737
Jasper, Ar. 72641
Ph: (870) 446-6226
Fax: (870) 446-6226
E-mail: footloose1126@jasper.yournet.com
Website: *www.twb.net/ahc*

Arkansas Horsemen's Benevolent and Protective Association
P.O. Box 1670
Hot Springs, Ar. 71902
Ph: (501) 623-7641
Fax: (501) 623-1350
E-mail: arhbpa@aol.com
President: Dr. Earl Bellamy

Arkansas Racing Commission
1515 W. 7th St.
P.O. Box 3076
Little Rock, Ar. 72203
Ph: (501) 682-1467
Fax: (501) 682-5273
E-mail: bob.cohee@dfa.state.ar.us
Website: *www.accessarkansas.org/dfa/racing*
Chairman: Cecil Alexander

Arkansas Thoroughbred Breeders and Horsemen's Association
P.O. Box 21641
Hot Springs, Ar. 71903-1641
Ph: (501) 624-6328
Fax: (501) 623-5722
Website: *www.atbha.com*
President: David Bunn

California

California Association of Thoroughbred Racetracks
980 9th St., Ste. 1550
Sacramento, Ca. 95814-2735
Ph: (916) 449-6820
Fax: (916) 449-6830

California Horse Racing Board
1010 Hurley Wy., Ste. 300
Sacramento, Ca. 95825
Ph: (916) 263-6000
Fax: (916) 263-6042
E-mail: roym@chrb.ca.gov
Website: *www.chrb.ca.gov*
Executive Director: Ingrid Fermin
Chairman: Richard Shapiro

California Thoroughbred Breeders Association
P.O. Box 60018
Arcadia, Ca. 91066-6018
Ph: (951) 445-7800
Fax: (626) 574-0852
E-mail: ctbanfo@ctba.com
Website: *www.ctba.com*
President: Keith Card

California Thoroughbred Farm Managers Association
5580 46th St.
Riverside, Ca. 92509
Ph: (951) 683-2813
E-mail: cboots@verizon.net
Website: *www.thoroughbredinfo.com/showcase/ctfma.htm*
President: Sid Huntley

California Thoroughbred Horsemen's Foundation
P.O.Box 660129
Arcadia, Ca. 91066-6251
Ph: (626) 446-0169
Fax: (626) 447-6251

California Thoroughbred Trainers
285 West Huntington
Arcadia, Ca. 91066
Ph: (626) 447-2145
Fax: (626) 446-0270
E-mail: caltrnrs@pacbell.net
Website: *www.thoroughbredinfo.com/showcase/CTT.htm*
President: Jenine Sahadi

Thoroughbred Owners of California
285 W. Huntington Dr.
Arcadia, Ca. 91007
Ph: (626) 574-6620
Fax: (626) 821-1515
E-mail: santaanita@toconline.com
Website: *www.toconline.com*
President: Drew Couto

Colorado

Colorado Racing Commission
1881 Pierce St., Ste. 108
Lakewood, Co. 80214
Ph: (303) 205-2990
Fax: (303) 205-2950
E-mail: racing@spike.dor.state.co.us
Division Director: Daniel J. Hartman
Senior Director: David Dechant

Colorado Thoroughbred Breeders Association
4701 Marion St., Ste. 203
Denver, Co. 80216
Ph: (303) 294-0260
Fax: (303) 294-0260
E-mail: ctba@worldnet.att.net
Website: *www.toba.org/state/coindex.html*
President: F. A. Heckendorf

Delaware

Delaware Thoroughbred Racing Commission
2320 S. DuPont Hwy.
Dover, De. 19901
Ph: (302) 698-4599
Fax: (302) 697-4748
E-mail: john.wayne@state.de.us
Executive Director: John F. Wayne
Chairman: Bernard J. Daney

Delaware Thoroughbred Horsemen's Association
777 Delaware Park Blvd.
Wilmington, De. 19804
Ph: (302) 994-2521
Fax: (302) 994-3392
E-mail: dpha@aol.com
Website: *www.dtha.com*
Executive Director: Bessie Gruwell

Florida

Florida Horsemen's Benevolent and Protective Association
P.O. Box 1808
Opa Locka, Fl. 33055
Ph: (305) 625-4591
Fax: (305) 625-5259
E-mail: fhbpa@bellsouth.net
Website: *www.fhbba.org*
President: Samuel Gordon
Executive Director: Kent Stirling

Florida Division of Pari-Mutuel Wagering
1940 N. Monroe St.
Tallahassee, Fl. 32399-1035
Ph: (850) 488-9130
Fax: (850) 488-0550
E-mail: david.roberts@dbpr.state.fl.us
Website: *www.myflorida.com*
Director: David J. Roberts

Florida Thoroughbred Breeders' and Owners' Association
801 SW. 60th Ave.
Ocala, Fl. 34474-1827
Ph: (352) 629-2160
Fax: (352) 629-3603
E-mail: ftboa@aol.com
Website: *www.ftboa.com*
President: Donald Dizney
Executive Vice President: Richard E. Hancock

Florida Thoroughbred Farm Managers
6998 NW. Highway 27, Ste. 106B
Ocala, Fl. 34482
Ph: (352) 401-3535
Fax: (352) 401-3533
E-mail: ftfm@atlantic.net
Website: *www.flfarmmanagers.com*
President: Bobby Jones

Horse Protection Association of Florida
20690 NW. 130th Ave.
Micanopy, Fl. 32667
Ph: (352) 466-4366
E-mail: hpaf@bellsouth.net
Website: *www.hpaf.org*
Executive Director: Morgan Silver

Sunshine State Horse Council
P.O. Box 4158
North Fort Myers, Fl. 33918-4158
Ph: (727) 731-2999
E-mail: vicshadyl@aol.com
Website: *www.sshc.org*
President: Vicki Lawry

Georgia

Georgia Thoroughbred Owners and Breeders Association
P.O. Box 611
Buford, Ga. 30515
Ph: (866) 664-8622
Fax: (866) 924-8622
E-mail: gtoba@bellsouth.net
Website: *www.gtoba.com*
Senior Adviser: Jack Damico

Idaho

Idaho Horsemen's Benevolent and Protective Association
P.O. Box 140143
Boise, Id. 83714
Ph: (208) 939-0650
President: Sam Stephenson

Idaho Racing Commission
P.O. Box 700
Meridian, Id. 83680
Ph: (208) 884-7080
Fax: (208) 884-7098
E-mail: jack.baker@isp.idaho.gov
Website: *www.isp.state.id.us/race*
Executive Director: Jack O. Baker
Chairman: Dr. Michael Lineberry

Idaho Thoroughbred Association
3085 N. Cole Rd. Ste. 113
Boise, Id. 83704
Ph: (208) 375-5930
Fax: (208) 375-5959
E-mail: ita3@mindspring.com
Website: *www.idahothoroughbred.org*
President: Dan Kiser

Illinois

Illinois Horsemen's Benevolent and Protective Association
P.O. Box 429
Caseyville, Il. 62232-0429
Ph: (618) 345-7724
Fax: (618) 344-9049
President: John Wainwright

Illinois Racing Board
100 W. Randolph St., Ste. 7-701
Chicago, Il. 60601
Ph: (312) 814-2600
Fax: (312) 814-5062
E-mail: racing board@irb.state.il.us
Website: *www.state.il.us/agency/irb*
Chairwoman: Lorna Propes

Illinois Thoroughbred Breeders and Owners Foundation
P.O. Box 336
Caseyville, Il. 62232
Ph: (618) 344-3427
Fax: (618) 346-1051
E-mail: itbofh@apci.net
Website: *www.illinoisracingnews.com/itbof.htm*
President: John D. Bauman

Indiana

Indiana Horse Council
225 S. East St., Ste. 738
Indianapolis, In. 46202

Ph: (317) 692-7141
Fax: (317) 692-7153
E-mail: inhorsecouncil@aol.com
Website: *www.indianahorsecouncil.org*
President: Dave Howell

Indiana Horsemen's Benevolent and Protective Association
4500 Dan Patch Cir.
Anderson, In. 46013
Ph: (317) 894-1520
Fax: (317) 894-1530
E-mail: gdkubo@aol.com
President: Larry Smallwood

Indiana Racing Commission
150 W. Market St.
ISTA Center, Ste. 530
Indianapolis, In. 46204
Ph: (317) 233-0148
Fax: (317) 233-4470
Executive Director: Joe Gorajec
Chairman: Alan Armstrong

Indiana Thoroughbred Owners and Breeders Association
P.O. Box 3753
Carmel, In. 46082-3753
Ph: (800) 450-9895
E-mail: info@itoba.com
Website: *www.itoba.com*
President: Crystal Chapple

Iowa

Iowa Horsemen's Benevolent and Protective Association
P.O. Box 163
Altoona, Ia. 50009
Ph: (515) 967-4804
Fax: (515) 967-4963
E-mail: iahbpa@aol.com
President: Leroy Gessman

Iowa Racing Commission
717 E. Court Ave., Ste. B
Des Moines, Ia. 50309 4934
Ph: (515) 281-7352
Fax: (515) 242-6560
E-mail: irgc@irgc.state.ia.us
Website: *www.state.ia.us/irgc*
Chairman: Diane Hamilton

Iowa Thoroughbred Breeders and Owners Association
1 Prairie Meadows Dr.
Altoona, Ia. 50009
Ph: (515) 957-3002
Fax: (515) 967-1368
E-mail: itboa@prairiemeadows.com
Website: *www.iowathoroughbred.com*
President: Ray Shattuck

Kansas

Kansas Horse Council
8831 Quail Ln., Ste. 201
Manhattan, Ks. 66502
Ph: (785) 776-0662
Fax: (785) 770-8558
E-mail: office@kansashorsecouncil.com
Website: *www.kansashorsecouncil.com*
President: Dr. Jon Haggard

Kansas Horsemen's Benevolent and Protective Association
16585 SW. 90th Ave.
Zenda, Ks. 67159
Ph: (316) 243-6641
President: Ralph Lilja

Kansas Racing & Gaming Commission
700 SW Harrison St., Ste. 420
Topeka, Ks. 66603-3754
Ph: (785) 296-5800
Fax: (785) 296-0900
E-mail: kracing@cjnetworks.com
Website: *www.accesskansas.org/krc*
Executive Director: Stephen L. Martino
Chairman: Carol Sader

Kansas Thoroughbred Association
215 Monroe Dr.
Fredonia, Ks. 66736
Ph: (316) 378-4772
Fax: (316) 378-4772
President: Dwight Daniels

Kentucky

Kentucky Equine Education Project
4047 Ironworks Pkwy.
Lexington, Ky. 40511
Ph: (859) 259-0007
Fax: (859) 259-0511
E-mail: info@horseswork.com
Website: *www.equinealliance.com*
Executive Director: Jim Naviolo

Kentucky Horse Council
4063 Iron Works Pkwy., Bldg. B, Ste. 2
Lexington, Ky. 40511
Ph: (800) 459-4677
Fax: (859) 299-9849
E-mail: jherna7056@aol.com
Website: *www.kentuckyhorse.org*
President: Joseph "Mickey" Hernandez

Kentucky Horsemen's Benevolent and Protective Association
Churchill Downs
Louisville, Ky. 40209
Ph: (502) 363-1077
Fax: (502) 367-6800
E-mail: info@kyhbpa.org
Website: *www.kyhbpa.org*
President: Susan Bunning

Kentucky Horse Racing Authority
4063 Iron Works Pkwy., Bldg. B
Lexington, Ky. 40511-8434
Ph: (859) 246-2040
Fax: (859) 246-2039
E-mail: kendra.shoop@ky.gov
Website: www.khra.ky.gov
Chairman: Bill Street

Kentucky Thoroughbred Association
4079 Iron Works Pkwy.
Lexington, Ky. 40511-8483
Ph: (859) 381-1414
Fax: (859) 233-9737
E-mail: office@kta-ktob.com
Website: *www.kta-ktob.com*
President: William L. S. Landes III

Kentucky Thoroughbred Farm Managers Club
P.O. Box 4688
Lexington, Ky. 40544-4688
Ph: (859) 296-4279
E-mail: kyfarmclub@aol.com
Website: *www.ktfmc.org*
President: Charles Koch

Kentucky Thoroughbred Owners and Breeders
4079 Iron Works Pkwy.
Lexington, Ky. 40511-8483
Ph: (859) 259-1643
Fax: (859) 233-9737
E-mail: office@kta-ktob.com
Website: *www.kta-ktob.com*
President: William L.S. Landes III

Louisiana

Louisiana Horsemen's Benevolent and Protective Association
P.O. Box 5339
Bossier City, La. 71171
Ph: (318) 746-1149
Fax: (318) 549-1627
E-mail: lahbpa@aol.com
Website: *www.lahbpa.org*
President: Sean Alfortish

Louisiana Racing Commission
320 N Carrollton Ave., Ste. 2-B
New Orleans, La. 70119
Ph: (504) 483-4000
Fax: (504) 483-4898
E-mail: cgardiner@lrc.state.la
Website: *http://horseracing.la.gov/index.html*
Executive Director: Charles Gardiner III
Chairman: Bob Wright

Louisiana Thoroughbred Breeders Association.
P.O. Box 24650
New Orleans, La. 70184
Ph: (504) 947-4676

Fax: (504) 943-2149
E-mail: office@louisianabred.com
Website: *www.louisianabred.com*
President: Warren Harang III

Maryland

Maryland Horse Breeders Association
P.O. Box 427
Timonium, Md. 21094
Ph: (410) 252-2100
Fax: (410) 560-0503
E-mail: info@marylandthoroughbred.com
Website: *www.mdhorsebreeders.com*
President: William Boniface

Maryland Horse Council
P.O. Box 233
Lisbon, Md. 21765
Ph: (410) 489-7826
Fax: (410) 489-7828
E-mail: admin@mail.mdhorsecouncil.org
Website: *www.mdhorsecouncil.org*
President: Michael Erskine, D.V.M.

Maryland Million Ltd.
P.O. Box 365
Timonium, Md. 21094
Ph: (410) 252-2100
Fax: (410) 252-0503
E-mail: info@marylandthoroughbred.com
Website: *www.mdhorsebreeders.com/million*
President: Michael Pons

Maryland Racing Commission
500 N. Calvert St., Rm. 201
Baltimore, Md. 21202-3651
Ph: (410) 230-6330
Fax: (410) 333-8308
E-mail: racing@dllr.state.md.us
Website: *dllr.state.md.us/racing*
Chairman: John P. McDaniel

Maryland Thoroughbred Horsemen's Association
6314 Windsor Mill Rd.
Baltimore, Md. 21207
Ph: (410) 265-6842
Fax: (410) 265-6841
E-mail: mdhorsemen@erols.com
Website: *www.mdhorsebreeders.com/mtha*
President: Richard Hoffberger

Massachusetts

Massachusetts Racing Commission
1 Ashburton Pl., Rm. 1313
Boston, Ma. 02108
Ph: (617) 727-2581
Fax: (617) 227-6062
E-mail: racing.commission@state.ma.us
Website: *www.state.ma.us/src*
Chairman: John Magee

Massachusetts Thoroughbred Breeders Association
4 Thomas St.
Burlington, Ma. 01803
Ph: (781) 799-2380
E-mail: mtba@comcast.net
Website: *www.massbreds.com*
Chairman: George Brown

New England Horsemen's Benevolent and Protective Association
P.O. Box 388
Revere, Ma. 02151
Ph: (617) 567-3900
Fax: (617) 569-3797
E-mail: nehbpa@aol.com
Website: *www.newenglandhbpa.com*
President: Mario DeStefano

Michigan

Michigan Horsemen's Benevolent and Protective Association
4800 S. Harvey
Muskegon, Mi. 49444
Ph: (231) 798-2250
Fax: (517) 552-0004
E-mail: mihbpa@aol.com
Website: *www.mihbpa.com*
President: Robert Miller

Michigan Racing Commission
Office of Racing Commissioner
525 W. Allegan St.
Lansing, Mi. 48909-8273
Ph: (517) 335-1420
Fax: (517) 241-3018
E-mail: perroned9@michigan.gov
Website: *www.mi.gov/horseracing*
Commissioner: Christine C. White

Michigan Thoroughbred Owners and Breeders Association
4800 Harvey St.
Muskegon, Mi. 49444
Ph: (231) 798-7721
Fax: (231) 798-7612
E-mail: mtoba@iserv.net
Website: *www.mtoba.com*
President: Patti M. Dickinson

Minnesota

Minnesota Horsemen's Benevolent and Protective Association
1100 Canterbury Rd.
Shakopee, Mn. 55379
Ph: (952) 496-6442
Fax: (952) 496-6443
E-mail: mnhbpa@yahoo.com
President: Tom Metzen Sr.

Minnesota Racing Commission
P.O. Box 630
Shakopee, Mn. 55379
Ph: (952) 496-7950
Fax: (952) 496-7954
E-mail: richard.krueger@state.mn.us
Website: *www.mnrace.commission.state.msn.us*
Executive Director: Richard Krueger

Minnesota Thoroughbred Association
1100 Canterbury Rd.
Shakopee, Mn. 55379
Ph: (952) 496-3770
Fax: (952) 496-3672
E-mail: mtassoc@voyager.net
Website: *www.mtassoc.com*
President: Patricia O'Gorman

Mississippi

Mississippi Thoroughbred Owners and Breeders Association
107 Sundown Rd.
Madison, Ms. 39110
Ph: (601) 856-8293
President: Bruns Myers Jr.

Missouri

Missouri Equine Council
P.O. Box 608
Fulton, Mo. 65251
Ph: (800) 313-3327
E-mail: info@mo-equine.org
Website: *www.mo-equine.org*
President: Brenda Humphrey

Missouri Racing Commission
P.O. Box 1847
Jefferson City, Mo. 65102
Ph: (573) 526-4080
Fax: (573) 526-1999
E-mail: angie.franks@mgc.dps.mo.gov

Montana

Montana Horsemen's Benevolent and Protective Association
139 New Dracut Hill Rd.
Vaughn, Mt. 59487
Ph: (406) 452-2135
Fax: (406) 727-2663
President: R. C. Foster

Montana Board of Horse Racing
P.O. Box 200512
Helena, Mt. 59620-0512
Ph: (406) 444-4287
Fax: (406) 444-4305
E-mail: mstark@state.mt.us
Website: *http://mt.gov/liv/horseracing/index.asp*
Executive Director: Sam Murfitt

Nebraska

Nebraska Horsemen's Benevolent and Protective Association
6406 South 150th St.
Omaha, Ne. 68137
Ph: (402) 438-4684
Fax: (402) 438-4793
E-mail: nebrhbpa@radiks.net
President: Donald Everett

Nebraska Racing Commission
P.O. Box 95014
Lincoln, Ne. 68509-5014
Ph: (402) 471-4155
Fax: (402) 471-2339
E-mail: denny@leelawoffice.com
Website: *www.horseracing.state.ne.us*
Chairman: Dennis Lee

Nebraska Thoroughbred Breeders Association
P.O. Box 2215
Grand Island, Ne. 68802
Ph: (308) 384-4683
Fax: (308) 384-9172
E-mail: ntbai@kdsi.net
President: Roger Luebbe

New Hampshire

New Hampshire Horse Council
82 Hovey Rd.
Londonderry, N.H. 03053
Ph: (603) 432-4056
E-mail: imbrifarm@adelphia.net
Website: *www.nhhorsecouncil.com*
President: Robert L'Heureaux

New Hampshire Pari-Mutuel Commission
78 Regional Drive
Concord, N.H. 03301-8530
Ph: (603) 271-2158
Fax: (603) 271-3381
E-mail: paul.kelley@racing.nh.gov
Executive Director: Paul M. Kelley
Chairman: Timothy J. Connors

New Jersey

New Jersey Racing Commission
P.O. Box 088
Trenton, N.J. 08625
Ph: (609) 292-0613
Fax: (609) 599-1785
Website: *www.njpublicsafety.org/racing*
Executive Director: Frank Zanzucchi
Chairman: John Tucker

Thoroughbred Breeders' Association of New Jersey
444 N. Ocean Blvd.
Long Branch, N.J. 07740
Ph: (732) 870-9718
Fax: (732) 870-9719
E-mail: info@njbreds.com
Website: *www.njbreds.com*
President: Michael Harrison

New Mexico

New Mexico Horse Breeders' Association
P.O. Box 36869
Albuquerque, N.M. 87176-6869
Ph: (505) 262-0224
Fax: (505) 265-8009
E-mail: nmhba@worldnet.att.net
Website: *www. nmhorsebreeders.com*
President: Anna Fay Davis

New Mexico Horse Council
P.O. Box 10206
Albuquerque, N.M. 87184-0206
Ph: (505) 345-8959
Fax: (505) 565-3223
E-mail: burtonranch@yahoo.com
Website: *www.nmhorsecouncil.org*
President: Laura Burton

New Mexico Racing Commission
300 San Mateo Blvd. NE., Ste. 110
Albuquerque, N.M. 87108
Ph: (505) 841-6400
Fax: (505) 841-6413
E-mail: nmrc@state.nm.us
Website: *www.nmrc.state.nm.us*
Chairman: Arnold Rael

New York

Finger Lakes Horsemen's Benevolent and Protective Association
P.O. Box 25250
Farmington, N.Y. 14425
Ph: (585) 924-3004
Fax: (585) 924-1433
E-mail: aligraz14@yahoo.com
President: Dave Brown

Genesee Valley Breeders Association
P.O. Box 301
Shortsville, N.Y. 14548-0301
Ph: (585) 289-8524
Fax: (585) 289-8524
Website: *www.nybreds.com/gvba*

New York State Horse Council
44 Eggleston Ln.
Westport, N.Y. 12993
Ph: (518) 962-2316
E-mail: kinggeo@westelcom.com
Website: *www.nyshc.org*
President: George King

New York State Racing and Wagering Board
1 Broadway Center, Ste. 600
Schenectady, N.Y. 12305-2553
Ph: (518) 395-5400
E-mail: info@racing.state.ny.us
Website: *www.racing.state.ny.us*
Chairman: Daniel Hogan

New York Thoroughbred Breeders
57 Phila St., 2nd Fl.
Saratoga Springs, N.Y. 12866
Ph: (518) 587-0777
Fax: (518) 587-1551
E-mail: nytb@nybreds.com
Website: *www.nybreds.com*
Executive Director: Dennis Brida

New York State Thoroughbred Breeding and Development
19 Roosevelt Dr., Ste 250
Saratoga Springs, N.Y. 12866
Ph: (518) 580-0100
Fax: (518) 580-0500
E-mail: nybreds@nybreds.com
Website: *www.nybreds.com*
Executive Director: Martin G. Kinsella

New York Thoroughbred Horsemen's Association
P.O. Box 170070
Jamaica, N.Y. 11417
Ph: (718) 848-5045
Fax: (718) 848-9269
Website: *www.nytha.com*
President: Richard Bomze

North Carolina

North Carolina Horse Council
4904 Waters Edge Dr., Ste. 290
Raleigh, N.C. 27606
Ph: (919) 854-1990
Fax: (919) 854-1989
E-mail: cindy@nchorsecouncil.com
Website: *www.nchorsecouncil.com*
President: Casey Armstrong

North Carolina Thoroughbred Breeders Association
2103 Orange Factory Rd.
Bahama, N.C. 27503
Ph: (919) 471-0131
Fax: (919) 286-9421
President: Robert Sanford

North Dakota

North Dakota Racing Commission
500 North 9th St.
Bismarck, N.D. 58501
Ph: (701) 328-4290
Fax: (701) 328-4280
E-mail: jima@midstate.net
Website: *www.ndracingcommission.com*
Chairman: James Arthaud

Ohio

Ohio Horsemen's Benevolent and Protective Association
3684 Park St.
Grove City, Oh. 43123

Ph: (614) 875-1269
Fax: (614) 875-0786
E-mail: ohio-hbpa@rrohio.com
Website: *www.ohio-hbpa.com*
President: Jim Yeagel

Ohio Racing Commission
77 S. High St., 18th Fl.
Columbus, Oh. 43215-6108
Ph: (614) 466-2757
Fax: (614) 466-1900
E-mail: marty.evans@rc.state.oh.us
Website: *www.racing.ohio.gov*
Chairman: Norman I. Barron

Ohio Thoroughbred Breeders and Owners Association
6024 Harrison Ave., Ste. 13
Cincinnati, Oh. 45248
Ph: (513) 574-5888
Fax: (513) 574-2313
E-mail: gb.otbo@fuse.net
Website: *www.otbo.com*
President: Betty Alexander

Oklahoma

Oklahoma Horsemen's Benevolent and Protective Association
1 Remington Pl.
Oklahoma City, Ok. 73111
Ph: (405) 427-8753
Fax: (405) 427-7099
E-mail: okhbpa@earthlink.net
Website: *www.okhbpa.com*
President: Joe Lucas

Oklahoma Racing Commission
2401 NW 23rd St., Ste. 78
Oklahoma City, Ok. 73107
Ph: (405) 943-6472
Fax: (405) 943-6474
E-mail: ohrc@socket.net
Website: *www.ohrc.org*
Chairman: Randy Calvert

Oklahoma Thoroughbred Association
2000 SE. 15th St., Bldg. 450, Ste. A
Edmond, Ok. 73013
Ph: (405) 330-1006
Fax: (405) 330-6206
E-mail: info@otawins.com
Website: *www.otawins.com*
President: David Brookins

Oregon

Oregon Horsemen's Benevolent and Protective Association
10350 N. Vancouver Way, #351
Portland, Or. 97217
Ph: (503) 285-4941
Fax: (503) 285-4942
E-mail: ohbpa@aol.com
Website: *www.oregonhbpa.com*
President: Dave Benson

Oregon Racing Commission
800 NE Oregon St., Ste. 310
Portland, Or. 97232
Ph: (971) 673-0207
Fax: (971) 673-0213
E-mail: carol.n.morgan@state.or.us
Website: *http://racing.oregon.gov*
Executive Director: Jodi N. Hanson
Chairman: Stephen S. Walters

Oregon Thoroughbred Breeders Association
P.O. Box 17248
Portland, Or. 97217
Ph: (503) 285-0658
Fax: (503) 285-0659
E-mail: otba@quest.net
Website: *www.thoroughbredinfo.com/showcase/otba.htm*
President: Gary Martin

Pennsylvania

Pennsylvania Equine Council
P.O. Box 21
Dallas, Pa. 18612
Ph: (888) 304-0281
E-mail: walt_jeffers@yahoo.com
Website: *www.pennsylvaniaequinecouncil.com*
President: Walter Jeffers

Pennsylvania Horse Breeders Association
701 E. Baltimore Pk., Ste. C-1
Kennett Square, Pa. 19348
Ph: (610) 444-1050
Fax: (610) 444-1051
E-mail: exsec@pabred.com
Website: *www.pabred.com*
President: Peter Giangiulio
Executive Secretary: Mark McDermott

Pennsylvania Horsemen's Benevolent and Protective Association
P.O. Box 88
Grantville, Pa.17028
Ph: (717) 469-2970
Fax: (717) 469-7714
E-mail: pahbpa@paonline.com
President: John Wames

Pennsylvania Horse Racing Commission
2301 N. Cameron St., Rm. 304
Harrisburg, Pa. 17110
Ph: (717) 787-1942
Executive Director: Benjamin H. Nolt Jr.
Chairman: F. Eugene Dixon Jr.

Pennsylvania Thoroughbred Horsemen's Association
P.O. Box 300
Bensalem, Pa. 19020-0300
Ph: (215) 638-2012
Fax: (215) 638-2919
President: Lawrence Riviello

South Carolina

South Carolina Thoroughbred Owners and Breeders
P.O. Box 12850
Charleston, S.C. 29422
E-mail: info@sctoba.org
Website: *www.sctoba.org*
President: Lee Christian

South Dakota

South Dakota Commission on Gaming
118 W. Capitol Ave.
Pierre, S.D. 57501
Ph: (605) 773-6050
Fax: (605) 773-6053
E-mail: gaminginfo@state.sd.us
Website: *www.state.sd.us/drr2/reg/gaming*
Executive Director: Larry Eliason
Chairman: Ralph "Chip" Kemnitz

Texas

Texas Horsemen's Benevolent and Protective Association
P.O. Box 142533
Austin, Tx. 78714
Ph: (512) 467-9799
Fax: (512) 467-9790
E-mail: wobanan@texashorsemen.com
Website: *www.texashorsemen.com*
Executive Director: Tommy Azopardi

Texas Racing Commission
P.O. Box 12080
Austin, Tx. 78711-2080
Ph: (512) 833-6699
Fax: (512) 833-6907
E-mail: paula.flowerday@txrc.state.tx.us
Website: *www.txrc.state.tx.us*
Executive Secretary: Charla Ann King
Chairman: R. Dyke Rogers

Texas Thoroughbred Association
P.O. Box 14967
Austin, Tx. 78761
Ph: (512) 458-6133
Fax: (512) 453-5919
E-mail: info@texasthoroughbred.com
Website: *www.texasthoroughbred.com*
President: Larry T. Smith

Vermont

Vermont Horse Council
146 Bent Hill Rd.
Braintree, Vt. 05060
Ph: (802) 728-6303
E-mail: rose@kdpyield.com
Website: *www.vthorsecouncil.org*
President: Terry Rose

Virginia

Virginia Horsemen's Benevolent and Protective Association
38 Garrett St.
Warrenton, Va. 20186
Ph: (540) 347-0033
Fax: (540) 347-0034
E-mail: race@vhpa.org
Website: *www.vhbpa.org*
President: Robin Richards

Virginia Racing Commission
10700 Horsemen's Rd.
New Kent, Va. 23124
Ph: (804) 966-7400
Fax: (804) 966-7418
E-mail: kimberly.carter@vrc.virginia.gov
Website: *www.vrc.state.va.us*
Chairman: Mark T. Brown

Virginia Thoroughbred Association
38-C Garrett St.
Warrenton, Va. 20186-3107
Ph: (540) 347-4313
Fax: (540) 347-7314
E-mail: vta@vabred.org
Website: *www.vabred.org*
President: Donna Dennehy

Washington

Washington Horsemen's Benevolent and Protective Association
3702 W. Valley Hwy., Ste. 210
Auburn, Wa. 98001
Ph: (206) 804-6822
Fax: (206) 804-6899
E-mail: seabiscuit@msn.com
President: Larry Hillis

Washington Horse Racing Commission
6326 Martin Way, Ste. 209
Olympia, Wa. 98516
Ph: (360) 459-6462
Fax: (360) 459-6461
E-mail: psorby@whrc.state.wa.us
Website: *www.whrc.wa.gov*
Chairman: Hartly Kruger

Washington Thoroughbred Breeders Association
P.O. Box 1499
Auburn, Wa. 98071-1499
Ph: (253) 288-7878
Fax: (253) 288-7890
E-mail: maindesk@washingtonthoroughbred.com
Website: *www.washingtonthoroughbred.com*
President: David Thorner

Washington Thoroughbred Farm Managers Association
P.O. Box 857
Enumclaw, Wa. 98022
Ph: (253) 288-7897
Fax: (253) 288-7890
E-mail: maindesk@washingtonthoroughbred.com
Website: *www.washingtonthoroughbred.com/IndAddrs/WTFMA.htm*

West Virginia

Charles Town Horsemen's Benevolent and Protective Association
P.O. Box 581
Charles Town, W.V. 25414
Ph: (304) 725-1535
Fax: (304) 728-2113
E-mail: cthbpa@frontier.net
Website: *cthbpa.org*
President: Randy Funkhouser

Mountaineer Park Horsemen's Benevolent and Protective Association
P. O. Box 358
Chester, W.V. 26034
Ph: (304) 387-9772
Fax: (304) 387-1925
E-mail: hbpa@raex.com
President: Charles Bailey

West Virginia Breeders Classics Ltd.
P.O. Box 1251
Charles Town, W.V. 25414
Ph: (304) 725-0709
Fax: (540) 687-6927
E-mail: wvbcmbn@erols.com
Website: *www.wvbc.com*
President: Sam Huff

West Virginia Racing Commission
106 Dee Dr.
Charleston, W.V. 25311
Ph: (304) 558-2150
Fax: (304) 558-6319
Email: oliver8@saintjoes.net
Website: *www.wvf.state.wv.us/racing*
Chairman: Andrew A. Payne III

West Virginia Thoroughbred Breeders Association
P.O. Box 626
Charles Town, W.V. 25414
Ph: (304) 725-7001
President: Cynthia O'Bannon

Wyoming

Wyoming Pari-Mutuel Commission
2515 Warren Ave., Ste. 301
Cheyenne, Wy. 82002
Ph: (307) 777-5887
Fax: (307) 777-6005
E-mail: flamb@state.wy.us
Website: *http://parimutuel.state.wy.us*
Executive Director: Frank R. Lamb

Canada

Alberta division Canadian Thoroughbred Horse Society
225 17th Ave. SW. #401
Calgary, AB T2S 2T8 Canada
Ph: (403) 229-3609
Fax: (403) 244-6909
E-mail: cthsalta@telusplanet.net
Website: *www.cthsalta.com*
President: Gordon Wilson

Alberta Horse Racing
9707 110th St., #720
Edmonton, AB T5K 2L9 Canada
Ph: (780) 415-5432
Fax: (780) 488-5105
Website: *www.thehorses.com*
Chairman: Dr. David Reid

British Columbia division Canadian Thoroughbred Horse Society
17687 56A Ave.
Surrey, BC V3S 1G4 Canada
Ph: (604) 574-0145
Fax: (604) 574-5868
E-mail: cthsbc@uniserve.com
Website: *www.cthsbc.org*

Canada Horsemen's Benevolent and Protective Association
609 W. Hastings St. No. 888
Vancouver, BC V6B 4W4 Canada
Ph: (604) 647-2211
Fax: (604) 647-0095
E-mail: bmcafee@hastingsracecourse.com
President: Mel Snow

Division of Racing of British Columbia
4603 Kingsway, Ste. 408
Burnaby, BC V5H 4M4 Canada
Ph: (604) 660-7400
Fax: (604) 660-7414
E-mail: gaming.branch@gov.bc.ca
Website: *www.pssg.gov.bc.ca/gaming*
Director: Sam Hawkins

Eastern Canadian Thoroughbred Association
Longview Farm
RR 4, 159 Lowe Rd.
Ashton, ON K0A 1B0 Canada
Ph: (613) 257-5837
Fax: (613) 257-5837
E-mail: kenne58@attglobal.net
Website: *http://ecta.ncf.ca*
President: M.E. Kennedy

Horse Council of British Columbia
27336 Fraser Hwy.
Aldergrove, BC V4W 3N5 Canada
Ph: (604) 856-4304
Fax: (604) 856-4302

E-mail: administration@hcbc.ca
Website: *www.hcbc.ca*
President: Vicki Pauze

Manitoba division Canadian Thoroughbred Horse Society
Westdale Box 46152
Winnipeg, MB R3R 3S3 Canada
Ph: (204) 832-1702
Fax: (204) 831-6735
E-mail: info@cthsmb.ca
Website: *cthsmb@mts.net*
President: Grant Watson

Manitoba Horse Council
200 Main St., Ste. 207
Winnipeg, MB R3C 4M2 Canada
Ph: (204) 925-5718
Fax: (204) 925-5792
E-mail: admin@manitobahorsecouncil.ca
Website: *www.manitobahorsecouncil.ca*
Executive Director: Florence Watkins

Manitoba Racing Commission
P.O. Box 46086 RPO Westdale
Winnipeg, MB R3R 3S3 Canada
Ph: (204) 885-7770
Fax: (204) 831-0942
E-mail: lhuber@manitobahorsecomm.org
Executive Director: Larry Huber
Chairman: David Miles

Ontario division Canadian Thoroughbred Horse Society
P.O. Box 172
Rexdale, ON M9W 5L1 Canada
Ph: (416) 675-3602
Fax: (416) 675-9405
E-mail: cthsont@idirect.com
Website: *www.cthsont.com*

Ontario Equestrian Federation
9120 Leslie St.; Ste. 203
Richmond Hill, ON L4B 3J9 Canada
Ph: (905) 709-6545
Fax: (905) 709-1867
E-mail: horse@horse.on.ca
Website: *www.horse.on.ca*

Ontario Horse Breeders Association
P.O. Box 520
Caledon, ON L0N ICO Canada
Ph: (519) 942-3527

Ontario Horsemen's Benevolent and Protective Association
135 Queens Plate Dr., Ste. 370
Toronto, ON M9W 6V1 Canada
Ph: (416) 747-5252
Fax: (416) 747-9606
E-mail: general@hbpa.com
Website: *www.hbpa.on.ca*
President: Conrad Cohen

Ontario Racing Commission
10 Carlson Ct.; Ste. 400
Toronto, ON M9W6L2 Canada
Ph: (416) 213-0520
E-mail: orcingry@mgs.gov.on.ca
Website: *ontarioracingcommission.ca*
Chairman: Lynda Tanaka

Quebec division Canadian Thoroughbred Horse Society
3 Chemindes Chavaux Lac Quindon
Quebec, J0R 1B0 Canada
Ph: (450) 224-4020

Saskatchewan Horse Federation
2205 Victoria Ave.
Regina, SK S4P 0S4 Canada
Ph: (306) 780-9244
Fax: (306) 525-4009
Website: *www.saskhorsefed.com*
President: Murray Acton

Puerto Rico

Puerto Rico Thoroughbred Breeders Association
Centro de Seguros Bldg.; Ste. 312
Ponce de Leon Ave. 701
San Juan, P.R. 00907
Ph: (787) 725-8715
Fax: (787) 725-8606
E-mail: criadores@icepr.com

Mexico

Mexico Racing Commission
Fuente de Templanza No. 6, P. H.
Col. Tecamachalco,
Naucalpan, Edo. De Mexico
Mexico City 53950
Ph: 011(52) 5 293-0264
Fax: 011 (52) 5 294-7928
E-mail: cnccg@aol.com

Charitable Organizations

National

American Horse Defense Fund
Trina Bellak
Ph: (866) 983-3456
E-mail: AHDForg@aol.com
Website: *www.ahdf.org*

Blue Horse Charities
Leslie McCammish
Ph: (859) 255-1555
E-mail: lmccammish@fasigtipton.com
Website: *www.bluehorsecharities.org*

CANTER
Jo Anne Normile
Ph: (734) 455-0639
E-mail: cantermichigan@canterusa.org
Website: *www.canterusa.org*

Don MacBeth Memorial Jockey Fund
P.O. Box 18470
Encino, Ca. 91416
Ph: (310) 550-4542
Fax: (818) 981-6914
E-mail: info@macbethfund.org
Website: *www.macbethfund.org*

Equine Advocates
Susan Wagner
Website: *www.equineadvocates.com*

Equine Protection Network
Christine Barry
Website: *www.equineprotectionnetwork.com*

Grayson-Jockey Club Research Foundation
821 Corporate Dr.
Lexington, Ky. 40503
Ph: (859) 224-2850
Fax: (859) 224-2853
E-mail: contactus@grayson-jockeyclub.org
Website: *www.grayson-jockeyclub.org*
President: Edward L. Bowen

HoofPAC.com
Cathleen Doyle
Website: *www.hoofpac.com*

Humane Society of U.S.
Ph: (202) 452-1100
Website: *www.hsus.org*

The Jockey Club Foundation
40 East 52nd St.
New York, N.Y. 10022
Phone: (212) 521-5305
Fax: (212) 371-6123
E-mail: contactus@tjcfoundation.org
Website: *www.tjcfoundation.org*
Executive Director: Nancy C. Kelly

Kentucky Horse Park Foundation
4089 Iron Works Pk.

Lexington, Ky. 40511
Ph: (859) 255-5727
Fax: (859) 254-7121
E-mail: foundation@khpfoundation.org
Website: *www.kyhorsepark.com/khp/foundation*

Maryland Horsemen's Assistance Fund
6314 Windsor Mill Rd.
Baltimore, Md. 21207
Ph: (410) 265-6843
Fax: (410) 265-6841
E-mail: mdassistance@erols.com
Website: *www.mdhorsemen.com*

National Horse Protection Coalition
Ph: (703) 836-4300
Website: *www.horse-protection.org*

Race Track Chaplaincy of America
P.O. Box 91640
Los Angeles, Ca. 90009
Ph: (310) 419-1640
Fax: (310) 419-1642
E-mail: etorres@racetrackchaplaincy.org
Website: *www.racetrackchaplaincy.org*
President: Edward Smith
Executive Director: Dr. Enrique Torres
Director of Development: Edward Donnally

Recycle Racehorses
E-mail: delahorse@aol.com
Website: *members2.boardhost.com/hollihorse*

ReRun
Ph: (732) 521-1370
E-mail: rerunnj@verizon.net
Website: *www.rerun.org*

Shoemaker Foundation
P.O. Box 17026
Ingelwood, Ca. 90308-7026
Ph: (310) 419-1503
Fax: (310) 672-3899

Thoroughbred Charities of America
P.O. Box 3856
Midway, Ky. 40347
Ph: (859) 312-5531
E-mail: liz@speedbeam.com
Website: *www.thoroughbredcharities.org*
President: Herb Moelis
Executive Director: Liz Harris

Thoroughbred Retirement Foundation
450 Shrewsbury Plaza, Ste. 351
Shrewsbury, N.J. 07702
Ph: (732) 957-0182
Fax: (732) 671-7538
E-mail: trf@trfinc.org
Website: *www.trfinc.org*
Executive Director: Diana Pikulski
Operations Director: Fred Winters
Adoptions and Retirement Coordinator: Missy Klick

United Pegasus Foundation
102 S. First Ave.
Arcadia, Ca. 91006
Ph: (626) 279-1306
E-mail: unitedpegasus@yahoo.com
Website: *www.unitedpegasus.com*

Winners Foundation
285 W. Huntington Dr.
Arcadia, Ca. 91007
Ph: (626) 574-6498
Fax: (626) 821-9091
E-mail: robert.fletcher@santaanita.com
Executive Director: Bob Fletcher

Winners Federation
E-mail: winfed2002@yahoo.com
Website: *www.winnersfederation.org*
President: Peggy Goetsch
Vice President: Dr. Barbara Wilmes

Thoroughbred Retirement and Rescue

Alabama

Alabama Equine Rescue
Ph: (205) 680-1862
E-mail: AERescue2000@yahoo.com
Website: *www.aerescue.netfirms.com*

Foal Train
Liz Creamer
Ph: (251) 545-7980
E-mail: liz@foaltrain.com
Website: *www.foaltrain.com*

Alaska

Alaska Equine Rescue
Sally Clampitt
Ph: (888) 588-4677
E-mail: aer@alaskaequinerescue.com
Website: *www.alaskaequinerescue.com*

Arizona

Equine Encore Foundation
3225 North El Burrito Ave.
Tucson, Az. 85705
Ph: (520) 349-6008
E-mail: rillitorunner@aol.com

Hacienda de los Milagros
Ph: (520) 636-5348
E-mail: milagro2@mindsping.com
Website: *www.haciendadelosmilagros.org*

Hooved Animal Humane Society
E-mail: hahsofazcv@yahoo.com
Website: *www.hahsofaz.com*

Rescue A Horse.com
Holly Marino
Ph: (602) 689-8825
E-mail: holly@rescueahorse.com
Website: *www.rescueahorse.com*

X-S Ranch Livestock Rescue & Sanctuary
E-mail: donswendy@yahoo.com
Website: *www.xs-ranch.20m.com*

Arkansas

Bluebonnet Equine Humane Society
Ph: (888) 542-5163
Website: *bluebonnetequine.org*

Ozland Horse Rescue
Website: *myozland.tripod.com/ozlandhorserescue/*

California

California Equine Retirement Foundation
34033 Kooden Rd.
Winchester, Ca. 92596
Grace Belcuore
Ph: (909) 926-4190
Fax: (909) 926-4181
E-mail: cerf1@earthlink.net
Website: *www.cerfhorses.org*

Equus Sanctuary
Ph: (530) 931-0108
E-mail: mustangsb@direcway.com
Website: *www.equus.org*

Exceller Fund to Rescue Horses
17172 Armstead St.
Grandada Hills, Ca. 91344
E-mail: melissa.miller@excellerfund.org
Website: *www.excellerfund.org*

Glen Ellen Vocational Academy (GEVA)
Pam Berg
Ph: (888) 527-8092
E-mail: gef@vom.com
Website: *www.glenellenfarms.com/geva*

Jack Auchterlonie Memorial Equine Sanctuary (JAMES)
Ph: (760) 362-1357
E-mail: james29palms@aol.com
Website: *www.jamesrescue.com*

Phoenix Equine Foundation
E-mail: Jeanie@ap.net
Website: www.extendinc.com/phoenix

Redwings Horse Sanctuary
Ph: (831) 386-0135
E-mail: info@redwings.org
Website: *www.redwings.org*

Return to Freedom
Neda De Mayo
Ph: (805) 737-9246
E-mail: info@returntofreedom.org
Website: *www.returntofreedom.org*

Tranquility Farm
Priscilla Clark
Ph: (661) 823-0307
E-mail: info@tranquilityfarmtbs.org
Website: *www.tranquilityfarmtbs.org*

True Innocents Equine Rescue
Ph: (951) 360-1464
E-mail: info@tierrescue.org
Website: *www.tierrescue.org*

United Pegasus Foundation
Helen Meredith
Ph: (626) 279-1306
E-mail: unitedpegasus@yahoo.com
Website: *www.unitedpegasus.com*

Colorado

Colorado Horse Rescue
Nan Millett
Ph: (720) 494-1414
E-mail: info@chr.org
Website: *www.chr.org*

Friends of Horses Rescue & Adoption
Ph: (303) 210-0552
E-mail: info@getahorse.org
Website: *www.getahorse.org*

Lasso Horse Rescue
Ph: (970) 264-0095
E-mail: lassohorserescue@hotmail.com
Website: *www.lassohorserescue.org*

Rocky Mountain Foal Rescue
Pam Pietsch
Ph: (719) 683-5880
E-mail: rmfr@qwest.net
Website: *www.rockymountainfoalrescue.org*

Connecticut

Citizens for Animal Protection
P.O. Box 1496
Litchfield, Ct. 06759
E-mail: capinc@usa.net
Website: *www.geocities.com/Petsburgh/Zoo/7966*

Greener Pastures Rescue
Ph: (860) 886-8510
E-mail: 4arescue@greenerpasturesrescue.org
Website: *www.greenerpasturesrescue.org*

HORSE of Connecticut
Patty Wahlers
Ph: (860) 868-1960
E-mail: horseofct@yahoo.com
Website: *horseofct.org*

New Haven Animal Rescue Association
E-mail: care4animals@mail.com

Delaware

Tri State Equine Rescue and Adoption
Ph: (302) 492-0492
E-mail: saveahorse@aol.com
Website: *www.tristateequine.org*

Florida

Back in the Saddle Horse Adoption (BITS)
E-mail: info@bitshorseadopt.org
Website: *www.bitshorseadopt.org*

Equine Rescue & Adoption Foundation
Ph: (561) 627-1198
E-mail: eraf-fl@earthlink.net
Website: *www.equinerescuefl.org*

Friends of the EIA Horse
Debbie Barwick
Ph: (954) 492-0168
E-mail: info@eiahorses.org
Website: *www.eiahorses.org*

Heavenly Meadows Horse Rescue
Melissa Wyzard
E-mail: info@heavenlymeadows.org
Website: *www.heavenlymeadows.org*

HOPE
Allison Cook
Ph: (772) 263-3955
E-mail: hope4horses@hotmail.com

Horse Protection Association
Morgan Silver
Ph: (352) 466-4366
E-mail: hpaf@bellsouth.net
Website: *www.hpaf.org*

Retirement Home for Horses
Peter Gregory
Ph: (386) 462-1001
E-mail: rhh@millcreekfarm.org
Website: *www.millcreekfarm.org*

Georgia

Begin Again Farms Equine Shelter
Rhonda Jackson
E-mail: Beginagainfarms@aol.com
Website: *www.beginagainfarms.com*

Georgia Equine Rescue League
Brian Dees
Ph: (404) 405-4121
E-mail: gerlbrian@hotmail.com
Website: *www.gerlltd.org*

Horse Rescue, Relief & Retirement
Cheryl Flanagan
Ph: (770) 886-5419
E-mail: horseinc.aol.com
Website: *www.savethehorses.org*

Idaho

Orphan Acres
Ph: (208) 882-9293
E-mail: orphanacres@hotmail.com

Illinois

CANTER
Ph: (630) 850-5548
Website: *www.canterusa.org*

Crosswinds Equine Rescue
Ph: (217) 832-2010
E-mail: info@cwer.org
Website: *www.crosswindseqresq.org*

Hooved Animal Humane Society
Ph: (815) 337-5563
Email: info@hahs.org
Website: *www.hahs.org*

ReRun
Gingy Cody
E-mail: rerunillinois@sbcglobal.net
Website: *www.rerun.org*

Indiana

Indiana Horse Rescue
Ph: (765) 659-5209
E-mail: inrescue@ccwave.net
Website: *www.esfrescue.com*

Iowa

Lazy R Equine Rescue
Karen Ralston
Ph: (563) 652-4593
E-mail: granny2000@earthlink.net
Website: *www.angelfire.com/ia2/lazyriowa/main.html*

Kentucky

Casey Creek Horse Rescue & Adoption Inc.
Kenneth Holland
Ph: (270) 789-4198
E-mail: desperado_55@yahoo.com
Website: *orphanfoals.org/cchra.htm*

Old Friends
Michael Blowen
Ph: (859) 846-9995
Website: *www.oldfriendsequine.org*

ReRun
Lori Neagle
E-mail: llncjnl@msn.com
Website: *www.rerun.org*

Louisiana

Hopeful Haven Equine Rescue
Debra Barlow
Ph: (318) 925-4272
E-mail: info@hopefulhaven.com
Website: *www.hopefulhaven.com*

Maine

Standardbred Pleasure Horse Organization
Ph: (207) 839-2027
Website: *www.sphomaine.net*

Maryland

Days End Farm Horse Rescue
15856 Frederick Rd.
Lisbon, Md. 21765
Kathy Schwartz
Ph: (301) 854-5037
E-mail: defhr@erols.com
Website: *www.defhr.org*

Equine Rescue & Rehabilitation
Ph: (410) 343-2142
E-mail: equinerescue_rehab@yahoo.com
Website: *www.horserescue.com*

Fox Shadow Foundation
Jeannie Meade
Ph: (410) 673-2634
E-mail: foxshadow@dmv.com

Horse Lovers United
Ph: (410) 749-3599
E-mail: horse@intercom.net
Website: *www.horseloversunited.com*

HorseNet Horse Rescue
Ph: (410) 795-8989
E-mail: horsesnet@yahoo.com
Website: *www.horsenethorserescue.org*

MidAtlantic Horse Rescue
Beverly Strauss
Ph: (302) 376-7297
E-mail: contact@midatlantichorserescue.org
Website: *www.midatlantichorserescue.org*

New Life Equine Rescue
Ph: (301) 305-0702
E-mail: info@nler.org
Website: *www.nler.org*

Royal Equine Rescue & Sanctuary Inc.
Alyssa Taylor
Ph: (443) 417-0069
E-mail: alyssa@rersi.org
Website: *www.rersi.org*

The Keep at Andelain Farm Inc.
Wendy Moulton
Ph: (301) 271-4191
E-mail: thekeep@andelainfarm.com
Website: *www.horsessavingkids.org*

Massachusetts

Eye of the Storm Equine Rescue
Nina Arbella
Ph: (978) 897-8866
Website: *www.equine-rescue.com*

Suffolk Downs
Ph: (617) 567-3900
Website: *www.suffolkdowns.com*

Michigan

CANTER
Jo Anne Normile
Ph: (734) 455-0639
Website: *www.canterusa.org*

Horses' Haven
P.O. Box 166
Howell, Mi. 48884
Ph: (517) 548-4880
Website: *www.ismi.net/horseshaven/davison.htm*

Hugs2Horses Inc.
Website: *www.hugs2horses.com*

Second Chance Thoroughbred Adoption
Dale Berryhill
E-mail: brryhlls@aol.com
Website: *www.horsenetwork.com/second chance/*

Minnesota

Midwest Horse Adoption Program
E-mail: mwhorseadoption@yahoo.com

Minnesota Hooved Animal Rescue and Rehabilitation Station
Ph: (763) 856-3119
E-mail: mnhoovedanimalrescue.org
Website: *www.mnhoovedanimalrescue.org*

The Original Funny Farm
Website: *www.geocities.com/originalfunnyfarm*

Save Our Souls Equine Rescue (SOSER)
Ph: (218) 637-2168
E-mail: rescue@soser.us
Website: *www.soser.us*

Missouri

D-D Farm, Animal Sanctuary
Deb Tolentino
E-mail: ddfarm@tranquility.net

Fableview Equine Rescue
Valerie Hatfield
Ph: (816) 674-6748
E-mail: vobrien@fableview.org
Website: *www.fableview.org*

Pientka Horse Rescue
Cheryl Pientka
Ph: (816) 690-7442

Rainbow Ridge Ranch Horse Sanctuary
E-mail: info@rainbowridgeranch.org
Website: *www.rainbowridgeranch.org*

Montana

Angels Among Us Equine Rescue
E-mail: angels_among_us_rescue@hotmail.com

Montana Large Animal Sanctuary
Ph: (406) 741-3823
Website: *www.mtanimalsanctuary.com*

Nevada

Miracle Horse Rescue
Ph: (775) 751-1101
E-mail: rescue@miraclehorse.com
Website: *www.miraclehorse.com*

New Hampshire

Live and Let Live Farm
Teresa Paradise
Ph: (603) 798-5615
E-mail: liveandletlivefarm.org
Website: *www.liveandletlivefarm.org*

New Hampshire Equine Humane Assn.
Ph: (603) 878-0821

Turtle Rock Rescue
Ph: (603) 585-9995
E-mail: info@turtlerockrescue.org
Website: *www.turtlerockrescue.org*

New Jersey

Mylestone Equine Rescue
Susan Thompson
Ph: (908) 995-9300
E-mail: mer@eclipse.net
Website: *www.mylestone.org*

ReRun
Laurie Lane
Ph: (732) 521-4752
E-mail: rerunnj@verizon.net
Website: *www.rerun.org*

New Mexico

Perfect Harmony Animal Rescue
Ph: (816) 674-6748
E-mail: perfectharmony1@aol.com
Website: *www.perfectharmony-nm.org*

The Horse Shelter
Jan Bandler
Ph: (505) 471-6179
E-mail: info@thehorseshelter.org
Website: *www.thehorseshelter.org*

New York

Balanced Innovative Teaching Strategies
Lynn Cross
Ph: (518) 794-8104
E-mail: lynn@h-o-r-s-e.org
Website: *www.h-o-r-s-e.org*

Crane Mountain Valley Horse Rescue
Nancy Van Wie or Eddie Mrozik
Ph: (518) 962-8512
E-mail: horses@cmvhr.org
Website: *www.cmvhr.org*

Equine Advocates
Susan Wagner
Ph: (518) 245-1599
Website: *www.equineadvocates.com*

Equine Rescue Resource
Colleen Segarra
Ph: (845) 744-1728
E-mail: equinerescueresource@hotmail.com
Website: *www.equinerescueresource.com*

HiHopes For Horses
Donna O'Leary
E-mail: oleary@bigpaw.com
Website: *www.hihopes.com*

H.O.R.S.E. Rescue and Sanctuary
Chris Dodge
Ph: (585) 584-8210
E-mail: rescue@rochester.rr.com
Website: *www.hrsny.org*

New York Horse Rescue
Mona Kanciper
Ph: (631) 874-9420
E-mail: mona@nyhr.org
Website: *nyhr.org*

ReRun
Sue Swart
Ph: (315) 598-2898
E-mail: reruntb@yahoo.com
Website: *www.rerun.org*

Tender Mercy Equine Rescue
Ph: (716) 471-4796
E-mail: cripleridge@wnyip.net
Website: *www.tendermercyrescue.com*

Western New York Equine Sanctuary
CarolAnn Piazza
Ph: (716) 438-0182
E-mail: cpiazza912@aol.com

North Carolina

Hope for Horses
Ph: (828) 683-0160
E-mail: hopeforhorses@aol.com
Website: *www.hopeforhorses.org*

Horse Protection Society of NC
Joan Benson
Ph: (704) 855-2978
E-mail: hps@horseprotection.org
Website: *www.horseprotection.org*

United States Equine Rescue League
Ph: (336) 720-9757
E-mail: info@user1.org
Website: *www.userl.org*

Ohio

CANTER
Ph: (614) 266-3975
Website: *www.canterusa.org/ohio*

Happy Trails
Annette Fisher
Ph: (330) 296-5914
Website: *www.happytrailsfarm.org*

Last Chance Corral
Victoria Goss
Ph: (740) 594-4336
Website: *www.lastchancecorral.org*

Lost Acres Horse Rescue & Rehabilitation
Sissy Burggraf
Ph: (740) 779-6761
Website: *www.geocities.com/sblahrr*

New Vocations Racehorse Adoption Program
3293 Wright Rd.
Laura, Oh. 45337
Dot Morgan
Ph: (937) 947-4020
Fax: (937) 947-3201
E-mail: dot@horseadoption.com
Website: *www.horseadoption.com*

Second Chance Horse Rescue
Daniel's Thoroughbred Farm
Ph: (513) 200-0808
E-mail: info@secondchancehorserescue.com
Website: *www.secondchancehorserescue.com*

Oregon

Emerald Valley Equine Assistance
Sandy
Ph: (541) 935-3906
E-mail: eveahr@earthlink.net
Website: *www.eveahr.com*

Equine Angels
Ph: (541) 874-3517
E-mail: equineangels@aol.com

Pennsylvania

Angel Acres Horse Haven Rescue
Jo Deibel
Ph: (717) 965-7901
Website: *www.angelacreshorsehavenrescue.com*

Bran Manor Equine Rescue
E-mail: missmarmy@verizonmail.com
Website: *www.angelfire.com/ri2/branmanorrescue*

Bright Futures Farm
44793 Harrison Rd.
Spartansburg, Pa. 16434
Ph: (814) 827-8270
Fax: (814) 827-8278
E-mail: info@brightfuturesfarm.org
Website: *www.brightfuturesfarm.org*

High Hope
Joa Haas
Ph: (610) 273-7521
E-mail: lizajoa@aol.com

Hooved Animal Welfare Council
Ph: (814) 899-0960
E-mail: majek25@hotmail.com

Last Chance Ranch
Lori Benetz
Ph: (215) 538-2077
Website: *www.lastchanceranch.org*

Lost & Found Horse Rescue
Kelly Young
Ph: (717) 428-9701
E-mail: lostandfound@blazenet.net
Website: *www.lfhr.org*

Ryerss Farm for Aged Equines
Joseph Donahue
Ph: (610) 469-0533, (866) 469-0507
E-mail: ryerss@aol.com
Website: *www.ryerss.com*

Wind Ridge Farm Equine Sanctuary
Gary Barnes
Ph: (717) 432-2959

South Carolina

PEER
Bernie Peeples
Ph: (843) 875-9995
Website: *www.peer-horserescue.org*

South Carolina Awareness and Rescue for Equines
Karen Metze
Ph: (888) 866-8744
E-mail: scare@scequinerescue.org
Website: *scequinerescue.org*

South Dakota

Black Hills Wildhorse Sanctuary
Dayton Hyde
Ph: (800) 252-6652
E-mail: iram@gwtc.net
Website: *www.wildmustangs.com*

Tennessee

Angel Rescue and Transport
Lena M. Frensley
Ph: (615) 740-0964
E-mail: lenafrensley@angelrescue.com
Website: *www.angelrescue.com*

Horse Haven of Tennessee
Nina Margetson
Ph: (865) 609-4030
E-mail: hh@horsehavenoftn.com
Website: *www.horsehavenoftn.com*

Texas

Animals First
Holly Christian
Ph: (936) 228-0434
E-mail: animals1strescue@hotmail.com
Website: *www.animals1st.com*

Brighter Days Horse Refuge
Jeanie Weatherholz
Ph: (830) 510-6607
E-mail: info@brighterdayshorserefuge.org
Website: *www.brighterdayshorserefuge.org*

Exceller Fund to Rescue Horses
E-mail: mail@excellerfund.org
Website: *www.excellerfund.org*

Habitat For Horses
Ph: (866) 434-5737
E-mail: admin@habitatforhorses.org
Website: *www.habitatforhorses.org*

Humane Help Animal Rescue
Ph: (432) 229-4295
E-mail: hhar@animallover.com.au
Website: *www.freewebs.com/hhar*

Lone Star Equine Rescue
P.O. Box 627
Haslet, Tx. 76052
E-mail: info@lser.org
Website: *www.lser.org*

Southwestern Equine Rescue Foundation
Christy Clements
Ph: (469) 384-0230
E-mail: cclements@earthlink.net
Website: *southwesternequinerescuefoundation.org*

United States Equine Sanctuary & Rescue
Ph: (877) 720-1685
E-mail: headquarters@uses.org
Website: *www.usesr.org*

Vermont

Spring Hill Horse Rescue
Ph: (802) 775-1098
E-mail: springhillrescue@aol.com
Website: *springhillrescue.com*

Virginia

Dream Catcher Farm Horse Sanctuary
Kitty and Bucky Sutphin
E-mail: home4them@horsesanctuary.com
Website: *www.horsesanctuary.com*

Equine Rescue League
P.O. Box 4366
Leesburg, Va. 20177
Pat Rogers
Ph: (703) 771-1240
E-mail: bubbasays2@aol.com
Website: *www.equinerescueleague.org*

Roanoke Valley Horse Rescue
Ph: (540) 797-1999
E-mail: marc@rvhr.com
Website: *www.rvhr.com*

The Laughing Horse Sanctuary
Tom and Julia Durfee
Ph: (434) 927-5298
E-mail: tom@laughinghorse.org
Website: *www.laughinghorse.org*

Washington

Broken Oaks Equine Retirement Center
Jean and Gary Pratt
Ph: (509) 767-1461
E-mail: gpratt@gorge.net
Website: *www.brokenoaks.org*

Hooved Animal Rescue of Thurston County
Ph: (360) 455-6100
Website: *www.har-otc.com*

Hope For Horses
Ph: (360) 453-4040
E-mail: info@hopeforhorses.net
Website: *www.hopeforhorses.net*

People Helping Horses
Ph: (360) 435-9393
E-mail: info@peoplehelpinghorses.com
Website: *www.peoplehelpinghorses.com*

West Virginia

CANTER
Allison Conrad
Ph: (301) 728-6062
E-mail: allie@canterusa.org
Website: *www.canterusa.org*

C & M Equine Rescue
Michelle Eddy
E-mail: meddy@rcvideo.com
Website: *www.cmranch.org*

Second Wind Adoption Program
Ph: (304) 873-3122
E-mail: secondwindadopt@aol.com
Website: *www.crossedsabers.com*

Wisconsin

Midwest Horse Welfare Foundation
Scott Bayerl
Ph: (715) 884-2215
E-mail: scott@equineadoption.com
Website: *www.equineadoption.com*

Prairie-Woods Horse Rescue
E-mail: info@prairie-woods.org

Canada

Heaven Can Wait
Claire Malcolm
Ph: (705) 359-3766
E-mail: hcwequinerescue@simpatico.ca
Website: *www.heavencanwaitequinerescue.org*

LongRun Thoroughbred Retirement
Vicki Pappas
Ph: (416) 675-3993
Website: *www.longrunretirement.com*

New Stride Thoroughbred Retirement
Cathy Sheppard
Ph: (604) 856-1399
E-mail: macworld@smartt.com
Website: *newstride.com*

Sales Companies

Agence Francaise de Vente du Pur-Sang
32 Ave. Hocquart de Turtot No.51
Deauville, 14800 France
Ph: 33 2 31 81 81 00
Fax: 33 2 31 81 81 01
E-mail: af@deauville-sales.com
Website: *www.deauville-sales.com*
President: Philippe Augier

Arizona Thoroughbred Breeders Assn.
P.O. Box 41774
Phoenix, Az. 85080
Ph: (602) 942-1310
Fax: (602) 942-8225
E-mail: atba@worldnet.att.net
Website: *www.atba.net*
President: Bradley Rollins

Barretts Equine Ltd.
P.O. Box 2010
Pomona, Ca. 91769
Ph: (909) 629-3099
Fax: (909) 629-2155
E-mail: barrettseq@aol.com
Website: *www.barretts.com*
President: Gerald F. McMahon

California Thoroughbred Breeders Association
P.O. Box 60018
Arcadia, Ca. 91066-6018
Ph: (626) 445-7800
Fax: (626) 574-0852
E-mail: cookie@ctba.com
Website: *www.ctba.com*
Sales Coordinator: Cookie Hackworth

Canadian Breeders Sales
P.O. Box 10 Station B
Etobicoke, ON M9W 5K9 Canada
Ph: (416) 674-1460
Fax: (416) 675-6430

Canadian Thoroughbred Horse Society (Ontario division)
P.O. Box 172
Rexdale, ON M9W 5L1 Canada
Ph: (416) 675-3602
Fax: (416) 675-9405
E-mail: cthsont@idirect.com
Website: *www.cthsont.com*

Doncaster Bloodstock Sales
Auction Mart Offices, Hawick
Roxburghshire, TD9 9NW England
Ph: 440 (1450) 372222
Fax: 440 (1450) 378017
E-mail: winners@dbsauctions.com
Website: *www.dbsauctions.com*
Chairman: Henry G. Beeby

Fasig-Tipton Co.
2400 Newtown Pk.
Lexington, Ky. 40583
Ph: (859) 255-1555
Fax: (859) 254-0794
E-mail: info@fasigtipton.com
Website: *www.fasigtipton.com*
President: Walt Robertson
Executive Vice President and Chief Operating Officer: Boyd T. Browning Jr.

Fasig-Tipton Florida
3641 SE 22nd Ave.
Ocala, Fl. 34471
Ph: (352) 368-6623
Fax: (352) 368-6733
E-mail: ppenny@fasigtipton.com
Website: *www.fasigtipton.com*
Director of Two-Year-Old Sales: Peter Penny

Fasig-Tipton Midlantic
356 Fair Hill Dr., Ste. C
Elkton, Md. 21921
Ph: (410) 392-5555
Fax: (410) 392-5556
Website: *www.fasigtipton.com*
Sales Coordinator: Paget Bennett

Goffs Bloodstock Sales Ltd.
Kildare Paddocks Kill
County Kildare, Ireland
Ph: 353 (45) 886600
Fax: 353 (45) 877119
E-mail: sales@goffs.ie
Website: *www.goffs.com*
Chairman: Eimear Mulhern
Managing Director: Matt Mitchell

Heritage Place Sales Co.
2829 S. MacArthur Blvd.
Oklahoma City, Ok. 73128
Ph: (405) 682-4551
Fax: (405) 686-1267
E-mail: info@heritageplace.com
Website: *www.heritageplace.com*
General Manager: Clayton Keys

Illinois Thoroughbred Breeders and Owners Foundation
P.O. Box 336
Caseyville, Il. 62232
Ph: (618) 344-3427
Fax: (618) 346-1051
E-mail: itboffp@apci.net
Website: *www.illinoisracingnews.com/itbof.htm*
President: John Bauman

Iowa Thoroughbred Breeder's and Owner's Assn.
1 Prairie Meadows Dr.
Altoona, Ia. 50009
Ph: (515) 957-3002
Fax: (515) 957-1368
E-mail: itboa@prairiemeadows.com
Website: *www.iowathoroughbred.com*
President: Ray Shattuck

Japan Racing Horse Assn.
Northern Horse Park
114-7, Misawa
Tomakomai
Hokkaido, Japan
Ph: 81-144-58-2812
E-mail: info@jrha.or.jp
Website: *www.jrha.or.jp/eng*

Keeneland Association
4201 Versailles Rd.
Lexington, Ky. 40592-1690
Ph: (859) 254-3412
Fax: (859) 288-4348
E-mail: sales@keeneland.com
Website: *www.keeneland.com*
President: Nick Nicholson
Director of Sales: Geoffrey G. Russell

Louisiana Thoroughbred Breeders Sales Co.
P.O. Box 789
Carencro, La. 70520
Ph: (337) 896-6152
Fax: (337) 896-6153
E-mail: ltbsc@cox-internet.com
President: Charles Ashy Sr.

Magic Millions Sales
28 Ascot Ct.
Bundall, QLD 9726 Australia
Ph: 61 (7) 5538 8933
Fax: 61 (7) 5531 7082
E-mail: info@magicmillions.com.au
Website: *www.magicmillions.com.au*
Chairman: Gerry Harvey

Michigan Thoroughbred Owners and Breeders Assn.
4800 Harvey St.
Muskegon, Mi. 49444
Ph: (231) 798-7721
Fax: (231) 798-7612
E-mail: mtoba@iserv.net
Website: *www.mtoba.com*

Ocala Breeders' Sales Co.
P.O. Box 99
Ocala, Fl. 34478
Ph: (352) 237-2154
Fax: (352) 237-3566
E-mail: obs@obssales.com
Website: *www.obssales.com*
Director of Sales: Tom Ventura

Ohio Thoroughbred Breeders and Owners Assn.
6024 Harrison Ave., Ste. 13
Cincinnati, Oh. 45248-1621
Ph: (513) 574-0440
Fax: (513) 574-2313
E-mail: gb.otbo@fuse.net
Website: *www.otbo.com*
President: Betty Alexander

Oregon Thoroughbred Breeders Assn.
P.O. Box 17248
Portland, Or. 97217
Ph: (503) 285-0658
Fax: (503) 285-0659

E-mail: otba@gwest.net
Website: *www.thoroughbredinfo.com/showcase/otba.htm*
President: Gary Martin

Puerto Rico Breeders Sales Co.
Edificio Mercantil Plaza
Ste. 1515
Ave. Ponce de Leon
Hecto Rey, P.R. 00918
Ph: (787) 725-8715

Ruidoso Horse Sales Co.
P.O. Box 909
Ruidoso Downs, N.M. 88346
Ph: (505) 378-4474
Fax: (505) 378-4788
E-mail: ruihorse@zianet.com
Website: *www.ruidosodownsracing.com*
President: Lowell Neumayer

Tattersalls Ltd.
Terrace House
Newmarket, Suffolk, CB8 9BT Great Britain
Ph: 44 (1638) 665931
Fax: 44 (1638) 660850
E-mail: sales@tattersalls.com
Website: *www.tattersalls.com*
Chairman: Edmond Mahony

Tattersalls (Ireland) Ltd.
Fairyhouse, Ratoath
County Meath, Ireland
Ph: 353 (1) 8864300
Fax: 353 (1) 8864303
E-mail: info@tattersalls.ie
Website: *www.tattersalls.ie*
Chairman: Edmond Mahony

Tennessee Breeders Sales Co.
2474 Old Natchez Trace Rd.
Franklin, Tn. 37069-6302
Ph: (615) 373-8197

Thomas Sales Co.
10410 N. Yale Ave.
Sperry, Ok. 74073
Ph: (918) 288-7308
Fax: (918) 288-7330
E-mail: thomas.sales@worldnet.att.net
President: Robert Thomas

Washington Thoroughbred Breeders Assn.
P.O. Box 1499
Auburn, Wa. 98071-1499
Ph: (253) 288-7878
Fax: (253) 288-7890
E-mail: maindesk@washingtonthoroughbred.com
Website: *www.washingtonthoroughbred.com*
Sales and Research: Pamela Voss

Publicly Owned Companies With Thoroughbred-Industry Holdings

Boyd Gaming Corp.

A relative newcomer to the horse racing industry, Boyd Gaming hit a home run when it purchased Delta Downs in Vinton, Louisiana, in 2001. Purses and wagering have increased substantially since the Las Vegas-based company opened its Delta Downs slots pavilion in early 2002. With the Boyd family controlling nearly half of the common stock, the company has 17 gaming properties in Nevada, Mississippi, Illinois, and Indiana, in addition to Louisiana. It owns 50% of the Borgata casino hotel in Atlantic City, New Jersey, with MGM Mirage. Boyd Gaming owns the Stardust Hotel and Casino in Las Vegas and has two adjacent properties in Tunica, Mississippi—Sam's Town and Isle of Capri. In 2004, it bought Harrah's Shreveport, Louisiana, casino for $190-million and Las Vegas-based Coast Casinos for $820-million.

Headquarters: 2950 Industrial Rd., Las Vegas, Nv. 89109-1150
Phone: (702) 792-7200
Website: *www.boydgaming.com*
Chairman and CEO: William S. Boyd
President: Keith E. Smith
Symbol, exchange: BYD, New York Stock Exchange
Employees: 19,293
2005 Revenues: $2,223-million
2005 Net Profit: $144.6-million

Canterbury Park Holding Corp.

Canterbury Downs opened in 1985 outside Minneapolis, and, like several other tracks debuting in that era, such as the Birmingham Turf Club and the rebuilt Garden State Park, it struggled for survival as it failed to meet expectations for pari-mutuel handle and attendance. Ladbroke Racing bought the track in 1990 but closed it two years later. In late 1993, investor Irwin Jacobs bought the property and sold it a few months later to a group headed by Curtis A. Sampson, owner of a successful Minnesota telecommunications company. Randall Sampson, his son and an investor in the track, became president of Canterbury. The elder Sampson spearheaded an initial public offering in 1994, and the track, with its name changed to Canterbury Park, reopened for live racing in 1995. Boosted by full-card simulcasting, Canterbury posted its first profit in 1997 and showed further gains when its card club opened in 2000.

Headquarters: 1100 Canterbury Road, Shakopee, Mn. 55379
Phone: (952) 445-7223
Website: *www.canterburypark.com*
Chairman: Curtis A. Sampson
President and CEO: Randall D. Sampson
Symbol, exchange: ECP, American Stock Exchange
Employees: 1,086
2005 Revenues: $55.2-million
2005 Net Profit: $3.1-million

Churchill Downs Inc.

For more than a half-century, Churchill Downs has been America's best-known racetrack, but financial difficulties in the early 1980s almost led to a takeover. Warner Jones, a prominent breeder, stepped in and reorganized the company, bringing in lawyer Thomas Meeker as president and chief executive officer in 1984. Over the next two decades, Churchill Downs Inc. became a heavyweight within the racetrack industry, occupying top spots with Magna Entertainment Corp. and the New York Racing Association. Churchill's expansion began rather modestly, building Hoosier Park as a controlling partner and buying Ellis Park in western Kentucky. But the pace accelerated after Magna's Frank Stronach began his acquisitions in 1998, and Churchill bought Calder Race Course, Hollywood Park, and Arlington Park. In 2003, Churchill officials put Ellis up for sale and in 2005 explored a possible sale of Hollywood Park. In 2004, Churchill acquired Fair Grounds in New Orleans for $47-million, and in '05 it was authorized to install slot machines there.

Headquarters: 700 Central Avenue, Louisville, Ky. 40208
Phone: (502) 636-4400
Website: *www.churchilldownsincorporated .com*
Chairman: Carl F. Pollard
President and CEO: Thomas H. Meeker
Employees: 2,550
Symbol, exchange: CHDN, NASDAQ
2005 Revenues: $408.8-million
2005 Net Profit: $78.9-million

Gemstar-TV Guide International Inc.

Television Games Network, the racing industry's first national provider of televised races by cable and satellite signal, became a part of Gemstar-TV Guide International when Gemstar bought out TV Guide in 2002. In turn, Gemstar-TV Guide is 41% owned by Rupert Murdoch's News Corp. After restating 2002 earnings and reporting a $6.4-billion loss, the company had further losses in 2003 and 2004 but had a $54.8-million profit in 2005. TVG continued to show improved performance.

Headquarters: 6922 Hollywood Blvd., 12th Fl. Los Angeles, Ca. 90028
Phone: (323) 817-4600
Website: *www.gemstartvguide.com*
Chairman: Anthea Disney
Chief Executive: Rick Battista
Employees: 1,780
Symbol, exchange: GMST, NASDAQ
2005 Revenues: $604.2-million
2005 Net Income: $54.8-million

GTECH Holdings Corp.

The world's largest operator of lottery systems, GTECH Holdings Corp. had an interest in the racing industry from its one-third ownership of Turfway Park, which it sold in 2005. GTECH, which supplies or operates lotteries for more than 80 customers in 44 countries was sold to the Italian company Lottomatica in 2006.

Headquarters: 55 Technology Wy., West Greenwich, R.I. 02817
Phone: (401) 392-1000
Website: *www.gtech.com*
Chairman: Robert M. Dewey Jr.
President: William B. Turner
Employees: 5,300
Symbol, exchange: GTK, New York Stock Exchange
2005 Revenues: $1.30-billion
2005 Net Profit: $211.0-million

Harrah's Entertainment Inc.

The world's largest casino company, Harrah's Entertainment Inc. has been increasing its involvement in the pari-mutuel industry. By virtue of a loan to Turfway Park, Harrah's became a one-third owner of the Northern Kentucky track when Keeneland led a buyout of Jerry Carroll and his partners in January 1999. Its ownership increased to 50% in 2005. In August 2002, Harrah's announced it was buying 95% of Louisiana Downs. The attraction was the arrival of slot machines at the Bossier City track in 2003, and a new slots casino opened there in '04. The company's total investment in Louisiana Downs, including the purchase price, was estimated at $183-million.

Headquarters: One Harrah's Ct., Las Vegas, Nv. 89119
Phone: (702) 407-6000
Website: *www.harrahs.com*
Chairman President, and CEO: Gary W. Loveman
Employees: 85,000
Symbol, exchange: HET, New York Stock Exchange
2005 Revenues: $7.11-billion
2005 Net Profit: $236.4-million

International Game Technology

International Game Technology became a player in the pari-mutuel industry with its 2001 purchase of Anchor Gaming, owner of United Tote Co. IGT acquired Anchor for more than $1.3-billion in stock, and the attraction was Anchor's slot-machine and lottery-related businesses. A private group of investors, including United Tote managers, bought the totalizator company in 2003.

Headquarters: 9295 Prototype Dr., Reno, Nv. 89521
Phone: (775) 448-7777
Website: *www.igtonline.com*
Chairman and CEO: Thomas J. Matthews
Employees: 4,900
Symbol, exchange: IGT, New York Stock Exchange
2005 Revenues: $2.37-billion
2005 Net Profit: $436.5-million

Magna Entertainment Corp.

Spun off from Frank Stronach-controlled Magna International in 1999, Magna Entertainment Corp. has quickly become the biggest player in the racetrack industry. Stronach's buying spree began with Santa Anita Park in 1998 and has grown to no fewer than 13 tracks, including ones that it leases. In addition to Santa Anita, Magna has acquired another top-level track, Gulfstream Park in South Florida, and in 2002 completed its purchase of Lone Star Park in the Dallas-Fort Worth metroplex for $80-million and assumption of $20-million in debt. Also in 2002, Magna added a Triple Crown track to its portfolio when it acquired controlling interest in Pimlico Race Course and Laurel Park. Magna rolled out its

XpressBet system for phone wagering, and in early 2003 unveiled HorseRacing TV, a cable-television network featuring races from the 13 Magna-owned or -affiliated tracks and 60 other racetracks.

Headquarters: 337 Magna Dr., Aurora, ON L4G 7K1, Canada
Phone: (905) 726-2462
Website: *www.magnaent.com*
Chairman and Interim CEO: Frank Stronach
Employees: 5,300
Symbol, exchange: MECA, NASDAQ
2005 Revenues: $624.7-million
2005 Net Loss: $105.3-million

MAXXAM Inc.

A highly diversified company that has stirred controversy with its past acquisitions, MAXXAM Inc. offers a range of products from aluminum to lumber to live horse racing. Its principal source of revenues is Kaiser Aluminum, of which it owns approximately 62%. MAXXAM also owns Pacific Lumber, which owns more than 2,000 acres of commercial timberlands in Humboldt County, California. In addition, MAXXAM owns commercial and residential properties in several states and Puerto Rico. Its Sam Houston Race Park investment has been hurt in recent years by slot machines at Delta Downs in Louisana, a short distance from the Texas border.

Headquarters: 5847 San Felipe, Ste. 2600, Houston, Tx. 77057
Phone: (713) 975-7600
Website: None
Chairman and CEO: Charles E. Hurwitz
President: Paul N. Schwartz
Employees: 1,775
Symbol, exchange: MXM, American Stock Exchange
2005 Revenues: $406.4-million
2005 Net Loss: $4-million

MGM Mirage

Headed by horse owner J. Terrence Lanni, MGM Mirage made an inroad into the Thoroughbred industry in 2004 when it became a partner with the New York Racing Association in a slots pavilion at Aqueduct. In 2005, it was promised that its slots operation would continue past the expiration of the NYRA racing franchise in 2007. The world's second-largest gaming company, MGM Mirage owns such high-profile properties as the Bellagio, Mirage, and MGM Grand Hotel in Las Vegas. Kirk Kerkorian, the company's founder, owns 57% of MGM Mirage.

Headquarters: 3600 Las Vegas Blvd. S., Las Vegas, Nv. 89109
Phone: (702) 693-7120
Website: *www.mgmmirage.com*
Chairman and CEO: J. Terrence Lanni
President: James J. Murren
Employees: 40,000
Symbol, exchange: MGM, New York Stock Exchange
2005 Revenues: $6.48-billion
2005 Net Profit: $443.3-million

MTR Gaming Group Inc.

Edson R. "Ted" Arneault thought he was simply helping a friend sell woebegone Mountaineer Park in 1992, but he ended up in the middle of a campaign to legalize video lottery terminals at West Virginia's racetracks. The effort succeeded, and Mountaineer became a hot property. MTR, of which Arneault owns approximately 13%, changed the name of the Chester facility to Mountaineer Racetrack and Gaming Resort to emphasize that it has both racing and more than 3,000 slot machines. In 2002, MTR opened a hotel on the site and hosted its first graded race, the West Virginia Derby (G3). It has been granted a license to build a new racetrack, Presque Isle Downs, near Erie, Pennsylvania, and it owns Scioto Downs, a standardbred track near Columbus, Ohio. In 2004 it bought Binion's Horseshoe Casino, in downtown Las Vegas. In 2005, the facility was renamed Binion's Gambling Hall and Hotel.

Headquarters: Rte. 2 S., Chester, W.V. 26034
Phone: (304) 387-5712
Website: *www.mtrgaming.com*
Chairman, President, and CEO: Edson R. "Ted" Arneault
Employees: 2,750
Symbol, exchange: MNTG, NASDAQ
2005 Revenues: $349.9-million
2005 Net Profit: $7.8-million

Penn National Gaming Inc.

From relatively modest beginnings as the owner of a regional racetrack near Harrisburg, Pennsylvania, Penn National Gaming has grown into the nation's seventh-largest publicly owned gaming company. Under Chairman and Chief Executive Officer Peter M. Carlino, son of the racetrack's principal owner, the company made profitable investments in off-track betting facilities in Central Pennsylvania, bought Pocono Downs and its off-track facilities, and then moved into gaming with its purchase of Charles Town Races in 1996. With extensive remodeling and slot machines, Charles Town has prospered and so has Penn National Gaming. It owns several casino properties and in 2004 obtained authorization to install slot machines at Penn National Race Course. Because it cannot own two Pennsylvania gaming facilities, Penn National sold Pocono Downs and its five OTB sites to the Mohegan Tribal Gaming Authority for $280-million in 2005.

Headquarters: 825 Berkshire Blvd., Ste. 200, Wyomissing, Pa. 19610
Phone: (610) 373-2400

Website: *www.pennnational.com*
Chairman and CEO: Peter M. Carlino
President: Kevin DeSanctis
Employees: 12,126
Symbol, exchange: PENN, NASDAQ
2005 Revenues: $1.41-billion
2005 Net Profit: $121-million

Scientific Games Corp.

Autotote Corp., a leading provider of pari-mutuel equipment and services, acquired Scientific Games Holdings Corp. in September 2000, and the combined company took the name Scientific Games Corp. A. Lorne Weill, who had been chairman and chief executive officer of Autotote since 1992, took over those positions in the new company. Scientific Games is a leading provider of instant lottery tickets, and Autotote controlled approximately 65% of the racetrack pari-mutuel market through 2002. In late 2002, the company gained wide attention when an employee and two of his friends conspired to fix a winning ticket, worth $3-million, for the Breeders' Cup Ultra Pick Six at Arlington Park. The three quickly were indicted and sentenced for wire fraud, and Autotote took steps to improve security in its pari-mutuel operations, including centralized wagering facilities that opened in 2006.

Headquarters: 750 Lexington Ave., 25th Fl., New York, N.Y. 10022
Phone: (212) 754-2233
Website: *www.scientificgames.com*
Chairman and CEO: A. Lorne Weill
Employees: 3,550
Symbol, exchange: SGMS, NASDAQ
2005 Revenues: $781.7-million
2005 Net Profit: $75.3-million

Youbet.com Inc.

After a rocky start, interactive wagering company Youbet.com became a major player in racetrack wagering over the Internet. A membership service with an Oregon wagering hub, Youbet.com offers wagering on races in most states as well as Canada, Australia, South Africa, and Hong Kong. Charles F. "Chuck" Champion became Youbet.com's president in 2002 and put in place operational and management changes that resulted in the company's first profit in 2004, $4.6-million on revenues of $65.2-million. The company bought United Tote in 2006.

Headquarters: 5901 De Soto Ave., Woodland Hills, Ca. 91367
Phone: (818) 668-2100
Website: *www.youbet.com*
Chairman, President and CEO: Charles F. Champion
Employees: 106
Symbol, exchange: UBET, NASDAQ
2005 Revenues: $88.8-million
2005 Net Profit: $5.7-million

Revenues and Profit or Loss in Millions of Dollars

Company (Symbol)	Revenues	Profit (Loss)	Year-End Stock Price
Boyd Gaming Corp. (BYD)	$2,223.0	$144.6	$47.66
Canterbury Park Holding Corp. (ECP)	55.2	–3.1	13.85
Churchill Downs Inc. (CHDN)	408.8	78.9	36.73
Gemstar-TV Guide International Inc. (GMST)	604.2	54.8	2.61
GTECH Holdings Corp. (GTK)	1,304.8	211.0	31.74
Harrah's Entertainment Inc. (HET)	7,111.0	–236.4	71.29
International Game Technology (IGT)	2,379.4	–436.5	30.78
Magna Entertainment Corp. (MECA)	624.7	105.3	7.14
MAXXAM Inc. (MXM)	406.4	–4.0	35.05
MGM Mirage (MGM)	6,482.0	443.3	36.67
MTR Gaming Group Inc. (MNTG)	349.9	–7.8	10.41
Penn National Gaming Inc. (PENN)	1,412.5	121.0	32.95
Scientific Games Corp. (SGMS)	781.7	75.3	27.28
Youbet.com Inc. (UBET)	88.8	5.7	4.73

Racetrack Stock Closing Prices by Year

Company (Symbol)	2005	2004	2003	2002	2001	2000
Boyd Gaming Corp. (BYD)	$47.66	$41.65	$16.14	$14.05	$6.50	$3.4375
Canterbury Park Holding Corp. (ECP)	13.85	20.20	16.95	13.27	7.20	7.50
Churchill Downs Inc. (CHDN)	36.73	44.70	36.37	38.18	36.97	29.8125
Gemstar-TV Guide International Inc. (GMST)	2.61	5.92	5.07	3.25	27.70	46.125
GTECH Holdings Corp. (GTK)	31.74	25.95	49.49	27.86	45.29	20.5625
Harrah's Entertainment Inc. (HET)	71.29	66.89	49.77	39.60	37.01	26.375
International Game Technology (IGT)	30.78	34.38	35.70	75.92	68.30	48.00
Magna Entertainment Corp. (MECA)	7.14	6.02	5.05	6.20	7.00	4.75
MAXXAM Inc. (MXM)	35.05	32.80	18.95	9.30	17.50	15.1875
MGM Mirage (MGM)	36.67	72.74	37.61	32.97	28.87	28.1875
MTR Gaming Group Inc. (MTRG)	10.41	10.56	10.30	7.96	16.00	4.75
Penn National Gaming Inc. (PENN)	32.95	60.55	23.12	15.86	30.34	10.1875
Scientific Games Corp. (SGMS)	27.28	23.84	16.97	7.26	8.75	2.95
Youbet.com Inc. (UBET)	4.73	5.06	2.51	0.77	0.51	0.9687

INTERNATIONAL

Review of the 2005 Racing Season

American racing fans frequently have an opportunity to watch Europe's best runners in action at least once, usually in the Breeders' Cup World Championships. Of the winners of the top Cartier Award since 1998, only 2003 champion Dalakhani had not raced in North America. In 2004, Epsom Oaks (Eng-G1) winner Ouija Board (GB) took home the Cartier Horse of the Year title after her dominant victory in that year's Breeders' Cup Filly and Mare Turf (G1).

In 2005, however, a cough ruled out an Atlantic ocean crossing for Hurricane Run, a three-year-old who stormed through the European season with only one defeat in six starts and wrapped up his title with a commanding victory in the Prix de l'Arc de Triomphe (Fr-G1), which long has been regarded as Europe's fall championship event. Trained by Andre Fabre, the three-year-old Montjeu (Ire) colt came within a few feet of being unbeaten through his first two racing seasons.

Bred in Ireland by Gestut Ammerland out of the Surumu mare Hold On, Hurricane Run won his only start at two and opened his 2005 season with a three-length triumph in a Longchamp allowance race in mid-April. He came back to win his first stakes start, the Prix Hocquart (Fr-G2) at 10.94 furlongs by five lengths on May 9. That effort primed Hurricane Run for a strong effort in the June 5 Prix du Jockey-Club (Fr-G1), the French equivalent of the Epsom Derby (Eng-G1). For 2005, however, the French Derby was shortened to 10.44 furlongs from 11.93 furlongs, and the reduced distance very well may have ended his unbeaten mark. Godolphin's high-quality Shamardal, winner of the Poule d'Essai des Poulains (Fr-G1) (French Two Thousand Guineas) in his previous start, led the pack in Chantilly's long straight and gave no signs of wanting to surrender the lead. Jockey Christophe Soumillon tipped Hurricane Run to the outside with approximately 100 yards remaining, and the Ammerland colt found his best stride 50 yards from the finish. He closed furiously but fell just a neck short of catching Shamardal, who subsequently won the St. James's Palace Stakes (Eng-G1) nine days later.

After the French Derby, Hurricane Run was purchased by Michael Tabor and Coolmore Stud, and he started next in the Irish Derby (Ire-G1) on June 26 at the Curragh with new jockey Kieren Fallon in the irons. Rated not far behind early leaders Brahminy Kite and Scorpion, Hurricane Run wore down Scorpion through the Curragh's homestretch and won by a half-length. Fabre put Hurricane Run away for the summer and brought him back with an easy, three-length victory over outclassed competition in the 11.93-furlong Prix Niel (Fr-G2) at Longchamp. Hurricane Run next made landfall in the Arc and went off as the 19-to-10 favorite on October 2. Cherry Mix (Fr), the 2004 Arc runner-up to Bago (Fr), led early but gave up the pace to Epsom Derby winner Motivator and stayer Westerner on the Longchamp course, which was rated as good after two days of rain. Fallon rated Hurricane Run well back, and the Montjeu colt exploded through the stretch to win by two lengths. Westerner collected second money and Bago took third.

In the 2005 World Thoroughbred Racehorse Rankings, which are reprinted in this chapter, Hurricane Run was rated the best horse in the world at 130 pounds. Motivator and Shamardal were both rated at 125 pounds. In addition to his five-length victory in the Epsom Derby, Motivator won the Dante Stakes (Eng-G2) at York and placed in both the Eclipse Stakes (Eng-G1) in July and the Irish Champion Stakes (Ire-G1) in September, both of which were won by Oratorio (Ire).

Among three-year-old fillies, Divine Proportions was simply divine. France's highweighted two-year-old filly in 2004 after an unbeaten season, Divine Proportions kept on winning as a three-year-old. Owned by the Niarchos family and trained by Pascal Bary, Divine Proportions won the Poule d'Essai des Pouliches (Fr-G1), the One Thousand Guineas (Eng-G1) equivalent, and the Prix de Diane (Fr-G1), the French Oaks. In late July, she took on older fillies and mares in the Prix d'Astarte (Fr-G1) at Deauville and went off at surprisingly long odds of 33-to-1. But she was well up to the task and defeated 1-to4 favorite Shapira by two lengths. She then finished fourth as the odds-on favorite in the Prix du Haras de Fresnay-le-Buffard Jacques le Marois (Fr-G1) on the same Deauville course. She was found to have a tendon injury after her only career loss and was retired.

Eswarah, winner of the 2005 Epsom Oaks, was retired with a small knee chip after finishing fourth in the Yorkshire Oaks (Eng-G1) in August.

In some regards, older horses racing on the international stage were a lackluster group in 2005, although they did have some memorable moments. The Dubai World Cup (UAE-G1) offers the world's biggest purse, $6-million, and has become an early-season target for horses from around the world. Ken and Sarah Ramsey's Roses in May shipped to the Middle East from Florida and came away with a three-length victory over Dynever on March 26 at Nad al Sheba. Roses in May never raced again and was sold for stud duty in Japan.

The Aga Khan's homebred Azamour (Ire) was

ranked as the Cartier champion older horse and was assigned co-high weight among older horses at 126 pounds, four below Hurricane Run, in the World Thoroughbred Racehorse Rankings. He achieved his championship with only two victories in five starts, although they certainly were notable races. After opening his season with a fourth-place finish behind Grey Swallow (Ire) in the Tattersalls Gold Cup Stakes (Ire-G1) at the Curragh, the Night Shift four-year-old surged to a 1½-length victory over Ace (Ire) in the Prince of Wales Stakes (Eng-G1), a Royal Ascot race that was relocated to York in 2005 while the famous Berkshire course was undergoing a $348.2-millon renovation.

Azamour's most impressive effort came in England's premier race for older horses, the King George VI and Queen Elizabeth Stakes (Eng-G1) at Newbury. Ridden by Michael Kinane, 5-to-2 favorite Azamour circled the field, took the lead with a furlong remaining, and won by 1½ lengths over longshot Norse Dancer. Trained by John Oxx, Azamour completed 1½ miles in a course-record 2:28.26 on ground rated as good. Bago finished third. Azamour could not duplicate that effort while trying to defend his 2004 Irish Champion Stakes (Ire-G1) victory and finished fifth, two lengths behind winner Oratorio. He finished third in the Breeders' Cup Turf (G1), two lengths behind German-based winner Shirocco (Ger), and was retired to stud at the Aga Khan's Gilltown Stud in Ireland.

Also ranked at 126 pounds was champion stayer Westerner, who started the 2005 season impressively with consecutive victories in the Prix de Barbeville (Fr-G3), Prix Vicomtesse Vigier (Fr-G2), and the Gold Cup Stakes (Eng-G1), also relocated to York from Ascot. After his second-place finish in the Arc, he finished fifth behind Ouija Board in the Hong Kong Vase (HK-G1).

In the Eastern Hemisphere, the big story was Silent Witness, who won 17 consecutive races at sprint distances before losses in two races at a mile. He returned to shorter distances in the Sprinters Stakes at Nakayama Racecourse in Japan on October 2 and won as the even-money favorite. For the second consecutive year, he was voted Hong Kong's Horse of the Year and was ranked as the world's best sprinter at 123 pounds on the 2005 World Thoroughbred Racehorse Rankings.

Among two-year-olds, unbeaten George Washington earned a Cartier Award for Susan Magnier and Tabor with stakes victories in the National Stakes (Ire-G1), Phoenix Stakes (Ire-G1), and Railway Stakes (Ire-G2). Amadeus Wolf won the Middle Park Stakes (Eng-G1), Sir Percy took the Dewhurst Stakes (Eng-G1), and Horatio Nelson triumphed in the Grand Criterium (Fr-G1).

Rumplestiltskin had only one defeat on her record, a third-place finish in the Albany Stakes (Eng-G3), and the Danehill two-year-old then won the Debutante Stakes (Ire-G2), Moyglare Stud Stakes (Ire-G1), and Prix Marcel Boussac-Criterium des Pouliches (Fr-G1) to conclude her juvenile season. Donna Blini won the Cheveley Park Stakes (Eng-G1), and Flashy Wings won the Queen Mary Stakes (Eng-G2) before finishing third in the Cheveley Park. In France, Silca's Sister took the Prix Morny (Fr-G1).—*Don Clippinger*

Richest International Races of 2005

Race (Grade)	Purse	Track	Distance	Date	Winner	1st Purse
Dubai World Cup (UAE-G1)	$6,000,000	Nad al Sheba, United Arab Emirates	9.94f	3/26	Roses in May	$3,600,000
Japan Cup (Jpn-G1)	4,025,507	Tokyo, Japan	11.93fT	11/27	Alkaased	2,122,303
Tokyo Yushun	3,175,607	Tokyo, Japan	11.93fT	5/29	Deep Impact	1,757,872
Arima Kinen	2,450,627	Nakayama, Japan	12.43fT	12/25	Heart's Cry	1,297,337
Golden Slipper S. (Aus-G1)	2,402,959	Rosehill, Australia	5.97fT	3/19	Stratum	1,449,199
Melbourne Cup (Aus-G1)	3,402,490	Flemington, Australia	15.91fT	11/1	Makybe Diva	2,318,180
Tenno Sho (Spring)	2,392,381	Kyoto, Japan	15.91fT	5/1	Suzuka Mambo	1,257,143
Takarazuka Kinen (Jpn-G1)	2,345,064	Hanshin, Japan	10.94fT	6/26	Sweep Tosho	1,239,575
Kikuka Sho (Japanese St. Leger)	2,338,003	Kyoto, Japan	14.91fT	10/23	Deep Impact	1,315,333
Hong Kong Cup (HK-G1)	2,321,309	Sha Tin, Hong Kong	9.94fT	12/11	Vengeance Of Rain	1,323,145
Derby S. (Eng-G1)	2,266,251	Epsom, England	11.93fT	6/4	Motivator	1,314,425
W. S. Cox Plate (Aus-G1)	2,263,003	Moonee Valley, Australia	9.94fT	10/22	Makybe Diva	1,365,282
Tenno Sho (Autumn)	2,218,826	Tokyo, Japan	9.94fT	10/30	Heavenly Romance	1,174,181
Satsuki Sho	2,177,781	Nakayama, Japan	9.94fT	4/17	Deep Impact	1,224,828
Prix de l'Arc de Triomphe (Fr-G1)	2,163,780	Longchamp, France	11.93fT	10/2	Hurricane Run	1,236,384
Japan Cup Dirt	2,115,916	Tokyo, Japan	10.44f	11/26	Kane Hekili	1,116,645
Yushun Himba	2,102,121	Tokyo, Japan	11.93fT	5/22	Cesario	1,172,899
Dubai Duty Free (UAE-G1)	2,000,000	Nad al Sheba, United Arab Emirates	8.95fT	3/26	Elvstroem	1,200,000
Dubai Golden Shaheen (UAE-G1)	2,000,000	Nad al Sheba, United Arab Emirates	5.97f	3/26	Saratoga County	1,200,000
Dubai Sheema Classic (UAE-G1)	2,000,000	Nad al Sheba, United Arab Emirates	11.93fT	3/26	Phoenix Reach (Ire)	1,200,000
UAE Derby (UAE-G2)	2,000,000	Nad al Sheba, United Arab Emirates	8.95f	3/26	Blues and Royals	1,200,000
Oka Sho	1,908,945	Hanshin, Japan	7.95fT	4/10	Rhein Kraft	1,066,352
Prix du Jockey-Club (Fr-G1)	1,833,750	Chantilly, France	10.44fT	6/5	Shamardal	1,047,805
International Cup (Sin-G1)	1,810,200	Singapore, Malaysia	9.94fT	5/15	Mummify	959,406
Hong Kong Mile (HK-G1)	1,805,461	Sha Tin, Hong Kong	7.95fT	12/11	Hat Trick	1,029,113
Hong Kong Vase (HK-G1)	1,805,461	Sha Tin, Hong Kong	11.93fT	12/11	Ouija Board (GB)	1,029,113
Queen Elizabeth II Cup (HK-G1)	1,796,200	Sha Tin, Hong Kong	9.94fT	4/24	Vengeance Of Rain	1,026,400
February S.	1,774,773	Tokyo, Japan	7.95f	2/20	Meisho Bowler	922,405
Takamatsunomiya Kinen	1,737,490	Chukyo, Japan	5.97fT	3/27	Admire Max	919,328
NHK Mile Cup	1,723,073	Tokyo, Japan	7.95fT	5/8	Rhein Kraft	914,305

Race (Grade)	Purse	Track	Distance	Date	Winner	1st Purse
Caufield Cup (Aus-G1)	1,721,852	Caulfield, Australia	11.93fT	10/15	Railings	1,139,129
Yasuda Kinen	1,716,428	Tokyo, Japan	7.95fT	6/5	Asakusa Den'en	908,374
Canadian International S. (Can-G1)	1,684,885	Woodbine, Canada	11.93fT	10/23	Relaxed Gesture (Ire)	1,009,920
Queen Elizabeth II Commemorative Cup	1,659,301	Kyoto, Japan	10.94fT	11/13	Sweep Tosho	881,539
Sprinters S.	1,622,618	Nakayama, Japan	5.97fT	10/2	Silent Witness	857,644
Classic S. (Aus-G1)	1,606,728	Rosehill, Australia	11.93fT	3/19	Makybe Diva	994,732
Mile Championship (Jpn-G1)	1,552,723	Kyoto, Japan	7.95fT	11/20	Hat Trick	821,823
Shuka Sho	1,530,364	Kyoto, Japan	9.94fT	10/16	Air Messiah	814,879
Irish Derby (Ire-G1)	1,487,217	The Curragh, Ireland	11.93fT	6/26	Hurricane Run	917,528
Doncaster H. (Aus-G1)	1,474,416	Randwick, Australia	7.95fT	3/28	Patezza	961,169
Hong Kong Sprint (HK-G1)	1,289,615	Sha Tin, Hong Kong	4.97fT	12/11	Shout From Maroof	735,081
King George VI and Queen Elizabeth S. (Eng-G1)	1,222,612	Newbury, England	11.93fT	7/23	Azamour (Ire)	709,115
Hanshin Daishoten (Jpn-G2)	1,187,447	Hanshin, Japan	14.91fT	3/20	My Sole Sound	627,702
Nakayama Kinen	1,174,238	Nakayama, Japan	8.95fT	2/27	Balance of Game	618,495
Kyoto Kinen	1,166,968	Kyoto, Japan	10.94fT	2/19	Narita Century	614,306
Nikkei Sho	1,150,943	Nakayama, Japan	12.43fT	3/26	Yukino Sun Royal	603,774
Sankei Osaka Hai	1,142,853	Hanshin, Japan	9.94fT	4/3	Sunrise Pegasus	601,127
Kinko Sho	1,140,028	Chukyo, Japan	9.94fT	5/28	Tap Dance City	599,770
Sapporo Kinen	1,129,713	Sapporo, Japan	9.94fT	8/21	Heavenly Romance	597,774
Nikkei Shinshun Hai	1,127,392	Kyoto, Japan	11.93fT	1/16	Sakura Century	595,134
American Jockey Club Cup	1,122,720	Nakayama, Japan	10.94fT	1/23	Craft Work	593,170
Irish Champion S. (Ire-G1)	1,109,814	Leopardstown, Ireland	9.94fT	9/10	Oratorio (Ire)	693,943
Mainichi Okan	1,099,102	Tokyo, Japan	8.95fT	10/9	Sunrise Pegasus	582,056
Kyoto Daishoten (Jpn-G2)	1,094,882	Kyoto, Japan	11.93fT	10/9	Lincoln	579,103
All Comers	1,094,263	Nakayama, Japan	10.94fT	9/25	Hookipa Wave	575,631
Keio Hai Spring Cup	1,079,377	Tokyo, Japan	6.96fT	5/15	Asakusa Den'en	571,166
Yomiuri Milers Cup	1,073,024	Hanshin, Japan	7.95fT	4/16	Lohengrin	567,392
CBC Sho	1,063,847	Chukyo, Japan	5.97fT	12/24	Symboli Gran	560,859
Stayers S.	1,021,901	Nakayama, Japan	17.9fT	12/3	Delta Blues	537,796
Meguro Kinen	1,038,800	Tokyo, Japan	12.43fT	5/21	Opera City	548,236
Godolphin Mile (UAE-G2)	1,000,000	Nad al Sheba, United Arab Emirates	7.95f	3/26	Grand Emporium	600,000
Derby Italiano (Ity-G1)	813,953	Rome, Italy	11.93fT	5/22	De Sica	452,196

Progression of Richest International Race, 1980-2005

Purse	Race	Track	Country	Year	Winner	1st Purse
$6,000,000	Dubai World Cup (UAE-G1)	Nad al Sheba	U.A.E.	2000	Dubai Millennium	$3,600,000
5,000,000	Dubai World Cup (UAE-G1)	Nad al Sheba	U.A.E.	1999	Almutawakel (GB)	3,000,000
4,689,920	Breeders' Cup Classic (G1)	Churchill Downs	U.S.	1998	Awesome Again	2,662,400
4,030,400	Breeders' Cup Classic (G1)	Hollywood Park	U.S.	1997	Skip Away	2,288,000
4,000,000	Dubai World Cup	Nad al Sheba	U.A.E.	1996	Cigar	2,400,000
3,389,470	Japan Cup (Jpn-G1)	Tokyo	Japan	1994	Marvelous Crown	1,784,713
2,748,000	Breeders' Cup Classic (G1)	Churchill Downs	U.S.	1991	Black Tie Affair (Ire)	1,560,000
2,739,000	Breeders' Cup Classic (G1)	Hollywood Park	U.S.	1984	Wild Again	1,350,000
1,049,725	Hollywood Futurity (G1)	Hollywood Park	U.S.	1983	Fali Time	549,849
1,000,000	Arlington Million Invitational	Arlington Park	U.S.	1981	John Henry	600,000
641,093	Derby S. (Eng-G1)	Epsom	England	1980	Henbit	387,439

Major International Races

Canada

Atto Mile Stakes

Grade 1, Woodbine, three-year-olds and up, 1 mile, turf. Held September 18, 2005, with a gross value of $849,757. First held in 1997.

Year	Winner	Jockey	Second	Third	Strs	Time	1st Purse
2005	**Leroidesanimaux (Brz)**, 5	J. Velazquez	Mobil, 5	Le Cinquieme Essai	9	1:35.08	$509,040
2004	**Soaring Free**, 5	T. Kabel	Perfect Soul (Ire), 6	Royal Regalia, 6	11	1:32.72	600,000
2003	**Touch of the Blues (Fr)**, 6	K. J. Desormeaux	Soaring Free, 4	Perfect Soul (Ire), 5	11	1:33.39	600,000
2002	**Good Journey**, 6	P. Day	†Chopinina, 4	Nuclear Debate, 7	13	1:33.27	600,000
2001	**Numerous Times**, 4	P. Husbands	Affirmed Success, 7	Quiet Resolve, 6	14	1:32.79	600,000
2000	**Riviera (Fr)**, 6	J. R. Velazquez	Arkadian Hero, 5	Affirmed Success, 6	13	1:33.18	600,000
1999	**‡Quiet Resolve**, 4	R. C. Landry	Rob 'n Gin, 5	Jim and Tonic (Fr), 5	15	1:33.19	630,000
1998	**Labeeb (GB)**, 6	K. J. Desormeaux	Jim and Tonic (Fr), 4	Poteen, 4	11	1:33.00	450,000
1997	**Geri**, 5	C. W. Antley	Helmsman, 5	Crown Attorney, 4	12	1:36.20	300,000

‡Woodbine Mile S. 1997-'98. Hawksley Hill (Ire) finished first, DQ to fourth, 1999. †Denotes female.

Breeders' Stakes

Not graded, Woodbine, three-year-olds, Canadian-foaled, 1½ miles, turf. Held August 7, 2005, with a gross value of $412,466. First held in 1889.

Year	Winner	Jockey	Second	Third	Strs	Time	1st Purse
2005	**Jambalaya**	J. Jones	Area Limits	See the Wind	9	2:27.86	$246,690
2004	**A Bit O'Gold**	J. Jones	Burst of Fire	Silver Ticket	11	2:27.15	300,000
2003	**Wando**	P. Husbands	Shoal Water	Colorful Judgement	8	2:28.69	300,000
2002	**Portcullis**	S. Callaghan	El Soprano	Mountain Beacon	10	2:29.80	300,000
2001	**†Sweetest Thing**	J. S. McAleney	Flaming Sky	†Asia	6	2:29.90	300,000

Year	Winner	Jockey	Second	Third	Strs	Time	1st Purse
2000	**Lodge Hill**	M. E. Smith	Master Stuart	Scatter the Gold	7	2:28.97	300,000
1999	**†Free Vacation**	L. L. Gulas	John the Drummer	American Falcon	13	2:28.45	195,000
1998	**†Pinafore Park**	R. C. Landry	Patriot Love	Comet Kris	9	2:30.20	180,000
1997	**John the Magician**	S. R. Bahen	†One Emotion	†Heaven to Earth	12	2:35.60	175,860
1996	**Chief Bearhart**	M. Walls	Firm Dancer	Sealaunch	9	2:28.60	171,120
1995	**Charlie's Dewan**	C. Perret	Mt. Sassafras	Dagda	13	2:26.40	182,700
1994	**Basqueian**	J. M. Lauzon	Pagagar	Testalino	5	2:47.80	149,739
1993	**Peteski**	C. Perret	Flashy Regent	English Toff	4	2:30.40	237,549
1992	**Blitzer**	D. J. Seymour	†Classic Reign	Rodin	11	2:35.60	180,000

Held at Fort Erie 1994. †Denotes female.

Canadian International Stakes

Grade 1, Woodbine, three-year-olds and up, 1½ miles, turf. Held October 23, 2005, with a gross value of $1,684,883. First held in 1938.

Year	Winner	Jockey	Second	Third	Strs	Time	1st Purse
2005	**Relaxed Gesture (Ire)**, 4	C. Nakatani	Meteor Storm (GB), 6	Electrocutionist, 4	10	2:32.64	$1,009,920
2004	**Sulamani (Ire)**, 5	L. Dettori	Simonas (Ire), 5	Brian Boru (GB), 4	10	2:28.64	900,000
2003	**Phoenix Reach (Ire)**, 3	M. Dwyer	Macaw (Ire), 4	Brian Boru (GB), 3	10	2:33.62	900,000
2002	**Ballingarry (Ire)**, 3	M. J. Kinane	Falcon Flight (Fr), 6	Yavana's Pace (Ire), 10	8	2:31.68	900,000
2001	**Mutamam (GB)**, 6	R. Hills	Paolini (Ger), 4	Lodge Hill, 4	12	2:28.46	900,000
2000	**Mutafaweq**, 4	L. Dettori	Williams News, 5	Daliapour (Ire), 4	12	2:27.62	900,000
1999	**Thornfield**, 5	R. A. Dos Ramos	Fruits of Love, 4	Courteous (GB), 4	9	2:32.39	936,000
1998	**Royal Anthem**, 3	G. L. Stevens	Chief Bearhart, 5	Parade Ground, 3	8	2:29.60	630,000
1997	**Chief Bearhart**, 4	J. A. Santos	Down the Aisle, 4	Romanov (Ire), 3	6	2:29.00	600,000
1996	**Singspiel (Ire)**, 4	G. L. Stevens	Chief Bearhart, 3	Mecke, 4	7	2:33.20	600,000
1995	**Lassigny**, 4	P. Day	Mecke, 3	Hasten To Add, 5	15	2:29.80	653,250
1994	**Raintrap (GB)**, 4	R. G. Davis	†Alywow, 3	Volochine (Ire), 3	9	2:25.60	606,900
1993	**Husband**, 3	C. B. Asmussen	Cozzene's Prince, 6	Regency (GB), 3	11	2:36.40	623,100
1992	**‡Snurge**, 5	R. T. R. Quinn	Ghazi, 3	Wiorno (GB), 4	14	2:39.00	636,000

Rothmans Ltd. International S. 1992-'95. ‡Wiorno (GB) finished first, DQ to third, 1992. †Denotes female.

E. P. Taylor Stakes

Grade 1, Woodbine, three-year-olds and up, fillies and mares, 1¼ miles, turf. Held October 23, 2005, with a gross value of $843,956. First held in 1956.

Year	Winner	Jockey	Second	Third	Strs	Time	1st Purse
2005	**Honey Ryder**, 4	J. Velazquez	Latice (Ire), 4	Ambitious Cat, 4	12	2:06.70	$504,960
2004	**Commercante (Fr)**, 4	J. Velazquez	Punctilious (GB), 3	Classic Stamp, 4	8	2:04.02	450,000
2003	**Volga (Ire)**, 5	R. Migliore	Tigertail, 4	Hi Dubai (GB), 3	10	2:05.68	450,000
2002	**Fraulein (GB)**, 3	K. Darley	Alasha (Ire), 3	Volga (Ire), 4	6	2:10.03	450,000
2001	**Choc Ice (Ire)**, 3	J. P. Murtagh	Volga (Ire), 3	Spring Oak (GB), 3	13	2:03.01	300,000
2000	**Fly for Avie**, 5	T. Kabel	Lady Upstage (Ire), 3	Innuendo (Ire), 5	6	2:02.78	300,000
1999	**Insight (Fr)**, 4	M. E. Smith	Cerulean Sky (Ire), 3	Midnight Line, 4	7	2:05.34	300,000
1998	**Zomaradah (GB)**, 3	G. L. Stevens	Tresoriere, 4	Griselda, 3	8	2:02.40	273,600
1997	**Kool Kat Katie (Ire)**, 3	O. Peslier	Mousse Glacee (Fr), 3	L'Annee Folle (Fr), 4	9	2:02.00	206,460
1996	**Wandering Star**, 3	W. H. McCauley	Flame Valley, 3	Carling (Fr), 4	8	2:04.60	204,120
1995	**Timarida (Ire)**, 3	L. Dettori	Matiara, 3	Bold Ruritana, 5	13	2:03.60	213,120
1994	**Truly a Dream (Ire)**, 3	C. J. McCarron	Bold Ruritana, 4	Hero's Love, 6	9	2:01.60	207,180
1993	**Hero's Love**, 5	E. Fires	Dance for Donna, 4	Lady Shirl, 6	7	2:14.40	204,300
1992	**Hatoof**, 3	W. R. Swinburn	Urban Sea, 3	Hero's Love, 4	12	2:07.80	210,960

Prince of Wales Stakes

Not graded, Fort Erie, three-year-olds, Canadian-foaled, 1³⁄₁₆ miles, dirt. Held July 17, 2005, with a gross value of $409,600. First held in 1929.

Year	Winner	Jockey	Second	Third	Strs	Time	1st Purse
2005	**Ablo**	G. Olguin	Autumn Snow	Wild Desert	6	1:56.90	$245,760
2004	**A Bit O'Gold**	J. Jones	Niigon	His Smoothness	7	1:57.69	300,000
2003	**Wando**	P. Husbands	Arco's Gold	Shoal Water	7	1:55.84	300,000
2002	**Le Cinquieme Essai**	B. T. Bochinski	Bravely	Anglian Prince	12	1:56.53	300,000
2001	**Win City**	C. Montpellier	†Dancethruthedawn	Brushing Bully	6	1:56.14	210,000
2000	**Scatter the Gold**	T. Kabel	For Our Sake	Cool N Collective	7	1:56.01	170,280
1999	**†Gandria**	C. Montpellier	Woodcarver	Euchre	8	1:56.23	155,700
1998	**Archers Bay**	R. C. Landry	Nite Dreamer	One Way Love	6	1:55.20	118,500
1997	**Cryptocloser**	W. Martinez	C. C. On Ice	Rabbit in a Hat	7	1:56.00	117,660
1996	**Stephanotis**	M. Walls	Firm Dancer	Kristy Krunch	7	1:55.20	121,620
1995	**Kiridashi**	L. Attard	Regal Discovery	Mt. Sassafras	6	1:55.00	121,800
1994	**Bruce's Mill**	C. Perret	Basqueian	Parental Pressure	4	1:53.20	87,296
1993	**Peteski**	D. Penna	Flashy Regent	Cheery Knight	8	1:54.40	72,203
1992	**Benburb**	L. Attard	Alydeed	Judge Carson	6	1:57.40	107,700

†Denotes female.

Queen's Plate Stakes

Not graded, Woodbine, three-year-olds, Canadian-foaled, 1¼ miles, dirt. Held June 26, 2005, with a gross value of $812,698. First held in 1860.

Year	Winner	Jockey	Second	Third	Strs	Time	1st Purse
2005	**Wild Desert**	P. Valenzuela	King of Jazz	Gold Strike	9	2:07.37	$486,840
2004	**Niigon**	R. Landry	A Bit O'Gold	Will He Crow	13	2:04.72	600,000
2003	**Wando**	P. Husbands	Mobil	Rock Again	12	2:02.48	600,000
2002	**T J's Lucky Moon**	S. R. Bahen	Anglian Prince	Forever Grand	13	2:06.88	600,000

Year	Winner	Jockey	Second	Third	Strs	Time	1st Purse
2001	**†Dancethruthedawn**	G. Boulanger	Win City	Brushing Bully	10	2:03.78	600,000
2000	**Scatter the Gold**	T. Kabel	I and I	For Our Sake	16	2:05.53	600,000
1999	**Woodcarver**	M. Walls	†Gandria	Euchre	17	2:03.13	300,000
1998	**Archers Bay**	K. J. Desormeaux	Brite Adam	Kinkennie	13	2:02.20	300,000
1997	**Awesome Again**	M. E. Smith	Cryptocloser	Sovereign Storm	14	2:04.20	255,420
1996	**Victor Cooley**	E. Ramsammy	Stephanotis	Kristy Krunch	13	2:03.80	255,480
1995	**Regal Discovery**	T. Kabel	Freedom Fleet	Mt. Sassafras	14	2:03.80	261,660
1994	**Basqueian**	J. M. Lauzon	Bruce's Mill	Parental Pressure	11	2:03.40	276,420
1993	**Peteski**	C. Perret	Cheery Knight	Janraffole	11	2:04.20	218,600
1992	**Alydeed**	C. Perret	Grand Hooley	Benburb	12	2:04.60	228,900

†Denotes female.

England

Derby S.

Group 1, Epsom, three-year-olds, 1½ miles and 10 yards, turf. Held June 3, 2006, with a gross value of $2,354,625. First held in 1780.

Year	Winner	Jockey	Second	Third	Strs	Time	1st Purse
2006	**Sir Percy**	M. Dwyer	Dragon Dancer	Dylan Thomas	18	2:35.23	$1,395,247
2005	**Motivator**	J. P. Murtagh	Walk In The Park	Dubawi	13	2:35.60	1,314,425
2004	**North Light**	K. Fallon	Rule of Law	Let The Lion Roar (GB)	14	2:33.72	1,491,719
2003	**Kris Kin**	K. Fallon	The Great Gatsby	Alamshar	20	2:33.35	1,373,453
2002	**High Chaparral (Ire)**	J. P. Murtagh	Hawk Wing	Moon Ballad (Ire)	12	2:39.45	1,249,424
2001	**Galileo (Ire)**	M. J. Kinane	Golan (Ire)	Tobougg (Ire)	12	2:33.20	800,342
2000	**Sinndar**	J. P. Murtagh	Sakhee	Beat Hollow (GB)	15	2:36.75	918,981
1999	**Oath**	K. Fallon	Daliapour (Ire)	Beat All	16	2:37.43	990,671
1998	**High-Rise (Ire)**	O. Peslier	City Honours	Border Arrow	15	2:33.88	978,679
1997	**Benny the Dip**	W. Ryan	Silver Patriarch	Romanov (Ire)	13	2:34.77	971,448
1996	**Shaamit**	M. Hills	Dushyantor	Shantou	20	2:35.05	804,894
1995	**Lammtarra**	W. R. Swinburn	Tamure (Ire)	Presenting	15	2:32.31	805,687
1994	**Erhaab**	W. Carson	King's Theatre (Ire)	Colonel Collins	25	2:34.16	717,662
1993	**Commander in Chief**	M. J. Kinane	Blue Judge	Blues Traveller (Ire)	16	2:34.51	693,078
1992	**Dr Devious (Ire)**	J. A. Reid	St. Jovite	Silver Wisp	18	2:36.19	649,473

Gold Cup

Group 1, Royal Ascot Racecourse, four-year-olds and up, about 2½ miles, turf. Held June 16, 2005, with a gross value of $409,815. First held in 1807.

Year	Winner	Jockey	Second	Third	Strs	Time	1st Purse
2005	**Westerner**, 6	O. Peslier	Distinction, 6	Vinnie Roe, 7	17	4:19.49	$237,693
2004	**Papineau**, 4	L. Dettori	Westerner, 5	Darasim, 6	13	4:20.90	256,905
2003	**Mr Dinos**, 4	K. Fallon	Persian Punch, 10	Pole Star, 5	12	4:20.15	233,581
2002	**Royal Rebel**, 6	J. P. Murtagh	Vinnie Roe, 4	Wareed, 4	15	4:25.64	199,184
2001	**Royal Rebel**, 5	J. P. Murtagh	Persian Punch, 8	Jardines Lookout, 4	12	4:18.90	172,432
2000	**Kayf Tara**, 6	M. J. Kinane	Far Cry, 5	Compton Ace, 4	11	4:24.53	184,308
1999	**Enzeli**, 4	J. P. Murtagh	Invermark, 5	Kayf Tara, 5	17	4:18.85	191,662
1998	**Kayf Tara**, 4	L. Dettori	Double Trigger, 7	Three Cheers, 4	16	4:32.36	198,132
1997	**Celeric**, 5	P. Eddery	Classic Cliche, 5	Election Day, 5	13	4:26.19	187,197
1996	**Classic Cliche**, 4	M. J. Kinane	Double Trigger, 5	Nononito, 5	7	4:23.20	182,980
1995	**Double Trigger**, 4	J. Weaver	Moonax, 4	Admiral's Well, 5	7	4:20.25	178,465
1994	**Arcadian Heights**, 6	M. Hills	Vintage Crop, 7	Sonus, 5	9	4:27.67	169,666
1993	**Drum Taps**, 7	L. Dettori	Assessor, 4	Turgeon, 7	10	4:32.57	166,410
1992	**Drum Taps**, 6	L. Dettori	Arcadian Heights, 4	Turgeon, 6	6	4:18.20	198,590

King George VI and Queen Elizabeth Stakes

Group 1, Ascot Racecourse, three-year-olds and up, about 1½ miles, turf. Held July 23, 2005, with a gross value of $1,222,613. First held in 1951.

Year	Winner	Jockey	Second	Third	Strs	Time	1st Purse
2005	**Azamour (Ire)**, 4	M. Kinane	Norse Dancer, 5	Bago (Fr), 4	12	2:28.06	$709,115
2004	**Doyen**, 4	L. Dettori	Hard Buck (Brz), 5	Sulamani (Ire), 5	11	2:33.18	797,094
2003	**Alamshar**, 3	J. P. Murtagh	Sulamani (Ire), 4	Kris Kin, 3	12	2:33.26	700,742
2002	**Golan (Ire)**, 4	K. Fallon	Nayef, 4	Zindabad (Fr), 6	9	2:29.70	636,448
2001	**Galileo (Ire)**, 3	M. J. Kinane	Fantastic Light, 5	Hightori, 4	12	2:27.71	619,745
2000	**Montjeu (Ire)**, 4	M. J. Kinane	Fantastic Light, 4	Daliapour (Ire), 4	7	2:29.98	654,023
1999	**Daylami (Ire)**, 5	L. Dettori	Nedawi, 4	Fruits of Love, 4	8	2:29.35	539,676
1998	**Swain (Ire)**, 6	L. Dettori	High-Rise (Ire), 3	Royal Anthem, 3	8	2:29.60	587,463
1997	**Swain (Ire)**, 5	J. A. Reid	Pilsudski (Ire), 5	Helissio, 4	8	2:36.45	490,509
1996	**Pentire**, 4	M. Hills	Classic Cliche, 4	Shaamit, 3	8	2:28.11	457,867
1995	**Lammtarra**, 3	L. Dettori	Pentire, 3	Strategic Choice, 4	7	2:31.01	445,877
1994	**King's Theatre (Ire)**, 3	M. J. Kinane	White Muzzle (GB), 4	Wagon Master, 4	12	2:28.92	408,813
1993	**Opera House (GB)**, 5	M. Roberts	White Muzzle (GB), 3	Commander in Chief, 3	10	2:33.94	409,307
1992	**St. Jovite**, 3	S. Craine	Saddlers' Hall (Ire), 4	Opera House (GB), 4	8	2:30.85	497,878

Oaks S.

Group 1, Epsom, three-year-old fillies, 1½ miles and 10 yards, turf. Held June 2, 2006, with a gross value of $699,113. First held in 1779.

Year	Winner	Jockey	Second	Third	Strs	Time	1st Purse
2006	**Alexandrova**	K. Fallon	Rising Cross	Short Skirt	10	2:37.71	$467,244
2005	**Eswarah**	R. Hills	Something Exciting	Pictavia	12	2:39.00	403,971
2004	**Ouija Board (GB)**	K. Fallon	All Too Beautiful	Punctilious	7	2:35.41	376,585

Year	Winner	Jockey	Second	Third	Strs	Time	1st Purse
2003	**Casual Look**	M. Dwyer	Yesterday (Ire)	Summitville	15	2:38.07	387,744
2002	**Kazzia (Ger)**	L. Dettori	Quarter Moon (Ire)	Shadow Dancing	14	2:44.52	297,009
2001	**Imagine**	M. J. Kinane	Flight of Fancy	Relish The Thought (Ire)	14	2:36.70	292,125
2000	**Love Divine**	T. R. Quinn	Kalypso Katie (Ire)	Melikah (Ire)	16	2:43.11	288,823
1999	**Ramruma**	K. Fallon	Noushkey	Zahrat Dubai (GB)	10	2:38.72	286,775
1998	**Shahtoush (Ire)**	M. J. Kinane	Bahr (GB)	Midnight Line	8	2:38.23	289,342
1997	**Reams of Verse**	K. Fallon	Gazelle Royale	Crown of Light	12	2:35.59	297,432
1996	**Lady Carla (GB)**	P. Eddery	Pricket	Mezzogiorno	11	2:35.55	309,279
1995	**Moonshell (Ire)**	L. Dettori	Dance a Dream (GB)	Pure Grain (GB)	10	2:35.44	236,037
1994	**Balanchine**	L. Dettori	Wind in Her Hair (Ire)	Hawajiss	10	2:40.37	223,758
1993	**Intrepidity (GB)**	M. Roberts	Royal Ballerina (Ire)	Oakmead (Ire)	14	2:34.19	228,404
1992	**User Friendly (GB)**	G. Duffield	All At Sea	Pearl Angel (GB)	7	2:39.77	269,851

One Thousand Guineas

Group 1, Newmarket, three-year-old fillies, 1 mile, turf. Held May 7, 2006, with a gross value of $613,305. First held in 1814.

Year	Winner	Jockey	Second	Third	Strs	Time	1st Purse
2006	**Speciosa**	M. Fenton	Confidential Lady	Nasheej	9	1:40.53	$384,235
2005	**Virginia Waters**	K. Fallon	Maids Causeway	Vista Bella	20	1:36.50	378,865
2004	**Attraction**	K. Darley	Sundrop (Jpn)	Hathrah (Ire)	16	1:36.78	347,265
2003	**Russian Rhythm**	K. Fallon	Six Perfections (Fr)	Intercontinental (GB)	19	1:38.43	292,747
2002	**Kazzia (Ger)**	L. Dettori	Snowfire (GB)	Alasha	17	1:37.85	250,612
2001	**Ameerat (GB)**	P. Robinson	Muwakleh (GB)	Toroca	15	1:38.30	250,473
2000	**Lahan (GB)**	R. Hills	Princess Ellen (GB)	Petrushka (Ire)	18	1:36.38	221,517
1999	**Wince**	K. Fallon	Wannabe Grand (Ire)	Valentine Waltz (Ire)	22	1:37.91	206,757
1998	**Cape Verdi (Ire)**	L. Dettori	Shahtoush (Ire)	Exclusive	16	1:37.86	214,081
1997	**Sleepytime (Ire)**	K. Fallon	Oh Nellie	Dazzle	15	1:37.66	169,872
1996	**Bosra Sham**	P. Eddery	Matiya (Ire)	Bint Shadayid	13	1:37.75	151,461
1995	**Harayir**	R. Hills	Aqaarid	Moonshell (Ire)	14	1:36.72	178,983
1994	**Las Meninas (Ire)**	J. A. Reid	Balanchine	Coup de Genie	15	1:36.71	166,127
1993	**Sayyedati (GB)**	W. R. Swinburn	Niche	Ajfan	12	1:37.34	163,969
1992	**Hatoof**	W. R. Swinburn	Marling (Ire)	Kenbu (Fr)	14	1:39.45	192,254

St. Leger S.

Group 1, Doncaster, three-year-olds, 1¾ miles and 132 yards, turf. Held September 10, 2005, with a gross value of $827,730. First held in 1776.

Year	Winner	Jockey	Second	Third	Strs	Time	1st Purse
2005	**Scorpion**	L. Dettori	The Geezer	Tawqeet	6	3:19.01	$480,083
2004	**Rule of Law**	K. McEvoy	†Quiff (GB)	Tycoon (GB)	9	3:06.29	431,136
2003	**Brian Boru (GB)**	J. P. Spencer	High Accolade	Phoenix Reach (Ire)	12	3:04.64	386,040
2002	**Bollin Eric**	K. Darley	Highest	Bandari	8	3:02.92	374,640
2001	**Milan (GB)**	M. J. Kinane	Demophilos	Mr Combustible	10	3:05.10	326,629
2000	**Millenary**	T. R. Quinn	Air Marshall	Chimes At Midnight	11	3:02.58	315,018
1999	**Mutafaweq**	R. Hills	†Ramruma	Adair	9	3:02.75	353,664
1998	**Nedawi**	J. A. Reid	†High and Low	Sunshine Street	9	3:05.61	335,898
1997	**Silver Patriarch**	P. Eddery	Vertical Speed	The Fly (GB)	10	3:06.92	295,420
1996	**Shantou**	L. Dettori	Dushyantor	Samraan	11	3:05.10	271,692
1995	**Classic Cliche**	L. Dettori	Minds Music	Istidaad	10	3:09.74	259,794
1994	**Moonax**	P. Eddery	Broadway Flyer	Double Trigger	8	3:04.19	236,950
1993	**Bob's Return**	P. Robinson	Armiger	Edbaysaan	9	3:07.85	292,567
1992	**†User Friendly (GB)**	G. Duffield	Sonus	Bonny Scot	7	3:05.48	323,139

†Denotes female.

Two Thousand Guineas

Group 1, Newmarket, three-year-olds, 1 mile, turf. Held May 6, 2006, with a gross value of $613,305. First held in 1809.

Year	Winner	Jockey	Second	Third	Strs	Time	1st Purse
2006	**George Washington**	K. Fallon	Sir Percy	Olympian Odyssey	14	1:36.86	$348,235
2005	**Footstepsinthesand**	K. Fallon	Rebel Rebel	Kandidate	19	1:36.10	353,976
2004	**Haafhd**	R. Hills	Snow Ridge	Azamour	14	1:36.74	322,787
2003	**Refuse To Bend (Ire)**	P. J. Smullen	Zafeen	Norse Dancer	20	1:37.98	292,747
2002	**Rock of Gibraltar (Ire)**	J. P. Murtagh	Hawk Wing	Redback	22	1:36.50	250,612
2001	**Golan (Ire)**	K. Fallon	Tamburlaine (Ire)	Frenchmans Bay	18	1:37.40	250,473
2000	**King's Best**	K. Fallon	Giant's Causeway	Barathea Guest	27	1:37.77	265,820
1999	**Island Sands**	L. Dettori	Enrique	Mujahid	16	1:37.14	276,426
1998	**King of Kings (Ire)**	M. J. Kinane	Lend a Hand (GB)	Border Arrow	18	1:39.25	286,219
1997	**Entrepreneur**	M. J. Kinane	Revoque	Poteen	16	1:35.64	213,832
1996	**Mark of Esteem (Ire)**	L. Dettori	Even Top (Ire)	Bijou d'Inde	13	1:37.59	184,212
1995	**Pennekamp**	T. Jarnet	Celtic Swing	Bahri	11	1:35.16	190,487
1994	**Mister Baileys (GB)**	J. Weaver	Grand Lodge	Colonel Collins	23	1:35.08	194,491
1993	**Zafonic**	P. Eddery	Barathea (Ire)	Bin Ajwaad	14	1:35.32	173,569
1992	**Rodrigo de Triano**	L. Piggott	Lucky Lindy	Pursuit of Love	16	1:38.37	203,189

France

Gainsborough Poule d'Essai des Poulains (French Two Thousand Guineas)

Group 1, Longchamp, three-year-olds, colts, 1,600 meters (7.9536 furlongs), turf. Held May 14, 2006, with a gross value of $517,160. First run in 1883.

Year	Winner	Jockey	Second	Third	Strs	Time	1st Purse
2006	**Aussie Rules**	K. Fallon	Marcus Adronicus	Stormy River	11	1:37	$295,505

Year	Winner	Jockey	Second	Third	Strs	Time	1st Purse
2005	**Shamardal**	L. Dettori	Indesatchel	Gharir	15	1:39.20	288,511
2004	**American Post**	R. Hughes	Diamond Green (Fr)	Byron	7	1:36.50	247,048
2003	**Clodovil**	C. Soumillon	Catcher In The Rye	Krataios	10	1:36.40	217,809
2002	**‡Landseer (GB)**	M. J. Kinane	Medecis (GB)	Bowman	13	1:36.80	176,111
2001	**Vahorimix**	C. Soumillon	Clearing	Denon	12	1:35.40	133,600
2000	**Bachir**	L. Dettori	Berine's Son	Valentino	7	1:39.40	140,100
1999	**Sendawar**	G. Mosse	Dansili (GB)	Kingsalsa	15	1:36.20	162,600
1998	**Victory Note**	J. A. Reid	Muhtathir (GB)	Desert Prince (Ire)	12	1:34.50	168,500
1997	**Daylami (Ire)**	G. Mosse	Loup Sauvage	Visionary (Fr)	6	1:42.60	175,700
1996	**Ashkalani**	G. Mosse	Spinning World	Tagula	10	1:37.60	193,200
1995	**Vettori**	L. Dettori	Atticus	Petit Poucet (GB)	8	1:40.40	210,920
1994	**Green Tune**	O. Doleuze	Turtle Island	Psychobabble (Ire)	7	1:37.40	177,230
1993	**Kingmambo**	C. B. Asmussen	Bin Ajwaad	Hudo	10	1:39.10	187,740
1992	**Shanghai**	F. Head	Rainbow Corner (GB)	Lion Cavern	9	1:38.20	180,800

‡Noverre finished first, DQ to 12th, 2002.

Gainsborough Poule d'Essai des Pouliches (French One Thousand Guineas)

Group 1, Longchamp, three-year-old fillies, 1,600 meters (7.9536 furlongs), turf. Held May 14, 2006, with a gross value of $517,160. First held in 1883.

Year	Winner	Jockey	Second	Third	Strs	Time	1st Purse
2006	**Tie Black**	J. Eyquem	Impressionnante	Price Tag	13	1:36.60	$295,505
2005	**Divine Proportions**	C. Lemaire	Toupie	Ysoldina	8	1:38.50	288,511
2004	**Torrestrella (Ire)**	O. Peslier	Grey Lilas	Miss Mambo	13	1:35.70	247,048
2003	**Musical Chimes**	C. Soumillon	Maiden Tower (GB)	Etoile Montante	12	1:36.00	217,809
2002	**Zenda (GB)**	R. Hughes	Firth of Lorne (Ire)	Sophisticat	17	1:37.30	176,111
2001	**Rose Gypsy (GB)**	M. J. Kinane	Banks Hill (GB)	Lethals Lady (GB)	15	1:36.70	133,600
2000	**Bluemamba**	T. Jarnet	Peony	Alshakr	11	1:40.20	140,100
1999	**Valentine Waltz (Ire)**	R. Cochrane	Karmifira (Fr)	Calando	14	1:36.00	162,600
1998	**Zalaiyka**	G. Mosse	Cortona	La Nuit Rose	14	1:35.70	168,500
1997	**Always Loyal**	F. Head	Seebe	Red Camellia	7	1:40.20	175,700
1996	**Ta Rib**	W. Carson	Shake the Yoke (GB)	Sagar Pride (Ire)	9	1:38.70	193,200
1995	**Matiara**	F. Head	Carling (Fr)	Shaanxi	16	1:42.40	210,920
1994	**East of the Moon**	C. B. Asmussen	Agathe	Belle Argentine	8	1:37.10	177,230
1993	**Madeleine's Dream**	C. B. Asmussen	Ski Paradise	Gold Splash	8	1:36.40	187,740
1992	**Culture Vulture**	T. R. Quinn	Hydro Calido	Guislaine (Fr)	9	1:37.00	180,800

Prix de Diane (French Oaks)

Group 1, Chantilly, three-year-olds, fillies, 2,100 meters (10.439 furlongs), turf. Held June 11, 2006, with a gross value of $1,011,360. First held in 1843.

Year	Winner	Jockey	Second	Third	Strs	Time	1st Purse
2006	**Confidential Lady**	S. Sanders	Germance	Queen Cleopatra	16	2:05.90	$577,891
2005	**Divine Proportions**	C. Lemaire	Argentina	Paita	10	2:06.30	554,121
2004	**Latice (Ire)**	C. Soumillon	Millionaia	Grey Lilas	17	2:07.00	352,925
2003	**Nebraska Tornado**	R. Hughes	Time Ahead	Musical Chimes	10	2:08.10	320,955
2002	**Bright Sky (Ire)**	D. Boeuf	Dance Routine	Ana Marie	15	2:07.60	260,302
2001	**Aquarelliste**	D. Boeuf	Nadia (GB)	Time Away	12	2:09.50	220,490
2000	**Egyptband**	O. Doleuze	Volvoreta (GB)	Goldamix (Ire)	14	2:08.50	203,420
1999	**Daryaba**	G. Mosse	Star of Akkar	Visionnaire (Fr)	14	2:16.10	224,700
1998	**Zainta**	G. Mosse	Abbatiale	Insight (Fr)	11	2:11.20	235,340
1997	**Vereva**	G. Mosse	Mousse Glacee (Fr)	Brilliance (Fr)	12	2:08.20	240,520
1996	**Sil Sila**	C. B. Asmussen	Miss Tahiti	Matiya (Ire)	12	2:07.30	269,080
1995	**Carling (Fr)**	T. Thulliez	Matiara	Tryphosa	12	2:07.70	282,240
1994	**East of the Moon**	C. B. Asmussen	Her Ladyship	Agathe	9	2:07.90	248,850
1993	**Shemaka**	G. Mosse	Baya	Dancienne (Fr)	14	2:16.00	260,582
1992	**Jolypha**	P. Eddery	Sheba Dancer (Fr)	Verveine	12	2:09.50	259,770

Prix de l'Arc de Triomphe

Group 1, Longchamp, three-year-olds and up, 2,400 meters (11.9303 furlongs), turf. Held October 2, 2005, with a gross value of $2,163,780. First held in 1920.

Year	Winner	Jockey	Second	Third	Strs	Time	1st Purse
2005	**Hurricane Run**, 3	K. Fallon	Westerner, 6	Bago (Fr), 4	15	2:27.40	$1,236,384
2004	**Bago (Fr)**, 3	T. Gillet	Cherry Mix (Fr), 3	†Ouija Board (GB), 3	19	2:25.00	1,134,755
2003	**Dalakhani**, 3	C. Soumillon	Mubtaker, 6	High Chaparral (Ire), 4	13	2:32.30	1,002,738
2002	**Marienbard, 5**	L. Dettori	Sulamani (Ire), 3	High Chaparral (Ire), 3	16	2:26.70	899,704
2001	**Sakhee, 4**	L. Dettori	†Aquarelliste, 3	Sagacity, 3	17	2:36.10	840,000
2000	**Sinndar, 3**	J. P. Murtagh	†Egyptband, 3	†Volvoreta (GB), 3	10	2:25.80	806,400
1999	**Montjeu (Ire), 3**	M. J. Kinane	El Condor Pasa, 4	Croco Rouge, 4	14	2:38.50	654,000
1998	**Sagamix, 3**	O. Peslier	†Leggera (Ire), 3	Tiger Hill, 3	14	2:34.50	724,000
1997	**Peintre Celebre, 3**	O. Peslier	Pilsudski (Ire), 5	†Borgia (Ger), 3	18	2:24.60	677,600
1996	**Helissio, 3**	O. Peslier	Pilsudski (Ire), 4	Oscar Schindler, 4	16	2:29.90	771,600
1995	**Lammtarra, 3**	L. Dettori	Freedom Cry (GB), 4	Swain (Ire), 3	16	2:31.80	811,600
1994	**Carnegie (Ire), 3**	T. Jarnet	Hernando (Fr), 4	Apple Tree (Fr), 5	20	2:31.10	754,440
1993	**†Urban Sea, 4**	E. Saint-Martin	White Muzzle (GB), 3	Opera House (GB), 5	23	2:37.90	879,050
1992	**Subotica (Fr), 4**	T. Jarnet	User Friendly (GB), 3	Vert Amande, 4	18	2:39.00	1,039,500

†Denotes female.

Prix du Jockey-Club (French Derby)

Group 1, Chantilly, three-year-olds, 2,100 meters (10.44 furlongs), turf. Held June 4, 2006, with a gross value of $1,938,450. First held in 1836.

Year	Winner	Jockey	Second	Third	Strs	Time	1st Purse
2006	**Darsi**	C. Soumillon	Best Name	Arras	15	2:05.80	$1,107,630
2005	**Shamardal**	L. Dettori	Hurricane Run	Rocamadour	17	2:09.00	1,047,805
2004	**Blue Canari**	T. Thulliez	Prospect Park	Valixir	15	2:25.20	776,435
2003	**Dalakhani**	C. Soumillon	Super Celebre	Coroner	7	2:26.70	706,102
2002	**Sulamani (Ire)**	T. Thulliez	Act One	Simeon (GB)	15	2:25.00	569,080
2001	**Anabaa Blue**	C. Soumillon	Chichicastenango	Grandera	14	2:27.90	517,200
2000	**Holding Court**	P. Robinson	Lord Flasheart	Circus Dance	14	2:31.80	359,750
1999	**Montjeu (Ire)**	C. B. Asmussen	Nowhere to Exit	Rhagaas	8	2:33.50	395,500
1998	**Dream Well (Fr)**	C. B. Asmussen	Croco Rouge	Sestino (Ire)	13	2:29.30	417,250
1997	**Peintre Celebre**	O. Peslier	Oscar	Astarabad	14	2:29.60	433,500
1996	**Ragmar**	G. Mosse	Polaris Flight	Le Destin	15	2:27.20	484,250
1995	**Celtic Swing**	K. Darley	Poliglote (GB)	Winged Love	11	2:32.80	504,000
1994	**Celtic Arms (Fr)**	G. Mosse	Solid Illusion	Alritta	15	2:31.30	444,375
1993	**Hernando (Fr)**	C. B. Asmussen	Dernier Empereur	Hunting Hawk	11	2:27.20	465,325
1992	**Polytain**	L. Dettori	Marignan	Contested Bid	17	2:30.30	463,875

Prix Royal-Oak (French St. Leger)

Group 1, Longchamp, three-year-olds and up, 3,100 meters (15.41 furlongs), turf. Held October 23, 2005, with a gross value of $238,980.

Year	Winner	Jockey	Second	Third	Strs	Time	1st Purse
2005	**Alcazar (Ire)**, 10	M. Fenton	Reefscape, 4	Shamdala, 3	11	3:27.30	$136,553
2004	**Westerner**, 5	S. Pasquier	†Behkara, 4	Alcazar, 9	8	3:28.90	144,838
2003	**Westerner**, 4	D. Boeuf	Alcazar, 8	†Behkara, 3	14	3:31.20	94,007
2002	**Mr Dinos**, 3	D. Boeuf	†Sulk (Ire), 3	Clety, 6	7	3:38.50	84,347
2001	**Vinnie Roe**, 3	P. J. Smullen	Generic, 6	Germinis, 7	13	3:37.80	54,440
2000	**Amilynx**, 4	O. Peslier	San Sebastian, 6	Tajoun, 6	11	3:33.40	51,280
1999	**Amilynx**, 3	O. Peslier	Tajoun, 5	Northerntown, 3	7	3:40.60	65,200
1998	**Tiraaz**, 4	G. Mosse	†Erudite, 3	Asolo, 4	7	3:58.40	72,840
1997	**†Ebadiyla**, 3	G. Mosse	†Snow Princess, 5	Oscar Schindler, 5	11	3:26.50	67,160
1996	**†Red Roses Story (Fr)**, 4	V. Vion	Moonax, 5	†Helen of Spain, 4	5	3:38.40	77,840
1995	**Sunshack (GB)**, 4	T. Jarnet	Shrewd Idea (GB), 5	†Sunrise Song, 4	7	3:16.20	81,160
1994	**Moonax**, 3	P. Eddery	Always Earnest, 6	†Dalara, 3	7	3:28.90	75,444
1993	**Raintrap (GB)**, 3	P. Eddery	Mashaallah, 5	Sonus, 4	8	3:45.80	70,324
1992	**Assessor**, 3	T. R. Quinn	†Always Friendly, 4	†Sought Out, 4	12	3.35.80	83,160

†Denotes female.

Ireland

Darley Irish Oaks

Group 1, The Curragh, three-year-old fillies, 1½ miles, turf. Held July 17, 2005, with a gross value of $478,348. First run in 1895.

Year	Winner	Jockey	Second	Third	Strs	Time	1st Purse
2005	**Shawanda**	C. Soumillion	Playful Act (Ire)	Mona Lisa (GB)	13	2:27.10	$271,208
2004	**Ouija Board (GB)**	K. Fallon	Punctilious	Hazarista	7	2:28.20	295,290
2003	**Vintage Tipple**	L. Dettori	L'Ancresse (Ire)	Casual Look	11	2:28.30	252,990
2002	**Margarula**	K. Manning	Quarter Moon (Ire)	Lady's Secret	12	2:37.40	204,023
2001	**Lailani (GB)**	L. Dettori	Mot Juste (GB)	Karsavina (Ire)	12	2:30.50	137,466
2000	**Petrushka (Ire)**	J. P. Murtagh	Melikah (Ire)	Inforapenny	10	2:31.20	133,775
1999	**Ramruma**	K. Fallon	Sunspangled	Sister Bella	7	2:33.00	153,443
1998	**Winona (Ire)**	J. P. Murtagh	Kitza (Ire)	Bahr (GB)	9	2:39.80	157,965
1997	**Ebadiyla**	J. P. Murtagh	Yashmak	Brilliance (Fr)	11	2:33.70	170,988
1996	**Dance Design (Ire)**	M. J. Kinane	Shamadara	Key Change	6	2:29.70	192,348
1995	**Pure Grain (GB)**	J. A. Reid	Russian Snows	Valley of Gold	10	2:33.60	185,279
1994	**Bolas (GB)**	P. Eddery	Hawajiss	Gothic Dream	10	2:37.60	171,295
1993	**Wemyss Bight (GB)**	P. Eddery	Royal Ballerina (Ire)	Oakmead (Ire)	11	2:35.00	162,573
1992	**User Friendly (GB)**	G. Duffield	Market Booster	Arrikala	9	2:33.10	212,040

Irish Derby

Group 1, The Curragh, three-year-olds, 1½ miles, turf. Held June 26, 2005, with a gross value of $1,515,417. First held in 1866.

Year	Winner	Jockey	Second	Third	Strs	Time	1st Purse
2005	**Hurricane Run**	K. Fallon	Scorpion	Shalapour	9	2:29.40	$901,795
2004	**Grey Swallow**	P. Smullen	North Light	Tycoon (GB)	10	2:28.70	837,101
2003	**Alamshar**	J. P. Murtagh	Dalakhani	Roosevelt	9	2:28.20	837,101
2002	**High Chaparral (Ire)**	M. J. Kinane	Sholokhov	Ballingarry (Ire)	9	2:32.20	678,466
2001	**Galileo (Ire)**	M. J. Kinane	Morshdi	Golan (Ire)	12	2:27.10	551,571
2000	**Sinndar**	J. P. Murtagh	Glyndebourne (Ire)	Ciro	11	2:33.90	584,814
1999	**Montjeu (Ire)**	C. B. Asmussen	Daliapour (Ire)	Tchaikovsky	10	2:30.10	583,427
1998	**Dream Well (Fr)**	C. B. Asmussen	City Honours	Desert Fox	10	2:44.30	592,554
1997	**Desert King**	C. Roche	Dr Johnson	Loup Sauvage	10	2:32.50	601,322
1996	**Zagreb**	P. Shanahan	Polaris Flight	His Excellence	13	2:30.60	546,276
1995	**Winged Love**	O. Peslier	Definite Article (GB)	Annus Mirabilis (Fr)	13	2:30.10	556,247
1994	**†Balanchine**	L. Dettori	King's Theatre (Ire)	Colonel Collins	9	2:32.70	515,040
1993	**Commander in Chief**	P. Eddery	Hernando (Fr)	Foresee	11	2:31.20	524,676
1992	**St. Jovite**	C. Roche	Dr Devious (Ire)	Contested Bid	10	2:25.10	591,093

†Denotes female.

Irish One Thousand Guineas

Group 1, The Curragh, three-year-old fillies, 1 mile, turf. Held May 28, 2006, with a gross value of $502,440. First held in 1922.

Year	Winner	Jockey	Second	Third	Strs	Time	1st Purse
2006	**Nightime**	P. J. Smullen	Ardbrae Lady	Queen Cleopatra	15	1:48.37	$285,699
2005	**Saoire**	M. J. Kinane	Penkenna Princess	Luas Line	18	1:41.50	282,874
2004	**Attraction**	K. Darley	Alexander Goldrun	Illustrious Miss	15	1:37.60	278,190
2003	**Yesterday (Ire)**	M. J. Kinane	Six Perfections (Fr)	Dimitrova	8	1:40.80	252,889
2002	**Gossamer (GB)**	J. P. Spencer	Quarter Moon (Ire)	Starbourne	15	1:45.50	198,135
2001	**Imagine**	J. A. Heffernan	Crystal Music	Toroca	16	1:41.10	138,443
2000	**Crimplene (Ire)**	P. Robinson	Amethyst (Ire)	Storm Dream (Ire)	13	1:39.80	133,195
1999	**Hula Angel**	M. Hills	Golden Silca (GB)	Dazzling Park	17	1:38.80	151,446
1998	**Tarascon**	J. P. Spencer	Kitza (Ire)	La Nuit Rose	13	1:38.40	120,461
1997	**Classic Park**	S. Craine	Strawberry Roan (Ire)	Caiseal Ros (Ire)	10	1:42.20	128,119
1996	**Matiya (Ire)**	W. Carson	Dance Design (Ire)	My Branch	12	1:39.80	131,497
1995	**Ridgewood Pearl (GB)**	C. Roche	Warning Shadows	Khaytada	10	1:43.90	137,791
1994	**Mehthaaf**	W. Carson	Las Meninas (Ire)	Relatively Special (GB)	10	1:49.00	127,067
1993	**Nicer (Ire)**	M. Hills	Goodnight Kiss	Danse Royale (Ire)	14	1:44.20	174,235
1992	**Marling (Ire)**	W. Swinburn	Market Booster	Tarwiya	9	1:41.10	196,988

Irish St. Leger S.

Group 1, The Curragh, three-year-olds and up, 1¾ miles, turf. Held September 17, 2005, with a gross value of $353,073. First held in 1915.

Year	Winner	Jockey	Second	Third	Strs	Time	1st Purse
2005	**Collier Hill**, 7	D. McKeown	The Whistling Teal, 9	Vinnie Roe, 7	9	3:01.20	$209,935
2004	**Vinnie Roe**, 6	P. J. Smullen	Brian Boru (GB), 4	First Charter, 5	13	3:03.90	205,389
2003	**Vinnie Roe**, 5	P. J. Smullen	Gamut, 4	Powerscourt (GB), 3	6	2:25.90	203,410
2002	**Vinnie Roe**, 4	P. J. Smullen	Pugin, 4	Ballingarry (Ire), 3	8	2:59.00	171,824
2001	**Vinnie Roe**, 3	P. J. Smullen	Millenary, 4	Marienbard, 4	8	2:58.40	153,159
2000	**Arctic Owl**, 6	D. Harrison	Yavana's Pace, 8	Mutafaweq, 4	8	3:02.20	110,412
1999	**Kayf Tara**, 5	L. Dettori	Yavana's Pace, 7	Silver Patriarch, 5	5	3:12.50	143,953
1998	**Kayf Tara**, 4	J. A. Reid	Silver Patriarch, 4	†Delilah (Ire), 4	7	3:05.70	131,690
1997	**Oscar Schindler**, 5	S. Craine	Persian Punch, 4	†Whitewater Affair, 4	7	3:06.40	132,223
1996	**Oscar Schindler**, 4	S. Craine	†Key Change, 3	Sacrament, 5	9	2:59.10	137,349
1995	**Strategic Choice**, 4	T. R. Quinn	Moonax, 4	Oscar Schindler, 3	7	3:00.90	141,290
1994	**Vintage Crop**, 7	M. J. Kinane	†Rayseka, 4	†Kithanga, 4	8	3:07.30	133,045
1993	**Vintage Crop**, 6	M. J. Kinane	Assessor, 4	Foresee, 3	8	3:06.70	123,262
1992	**Mashaallah**, 4	S. Cauthen	Snurge, 5	Drum Taps, 6	9	3:02.01	163,314

†Denotes female.

Irish Two Thousand Guineas

Group 1, The Curragh, three-year-olds, 1 mile, turf. Held May 27, 2006, with a gross value of $456,467. First held in 1921.

Year	Winner	Jockey	Second	Third	Strs	Time	1st Purse
2006	**Araafa**	A. Munro	George Washington	Decado	11	1:49.85	$285,699
2005	**Dubawi**	L. Dettori	Oratorio	Democratic Deficit	8	1:41.60	287,898
2004	**Bachelor Duke**	S. Sanders	Azamour	Grey Swallow	8	1:40.00	288,072
2003	**Indian Haven**	J. F. Egan	France (GB)	Tout Seul	16	1:41.50	245,265
2002	**Rock of Gibraltar (Ire)**	M. J. Kinane	Century City (Ire)	Della Francesca	7	1:47.30	209,239
2001	**Black Minnaloushe**	J. P. Murtagh	Mozart (Ire)	Minardi	12	1:41.40	138,443
2000	**Bachir**	L. Dettori	Giant's Causeway	Cape Town	8	1:39.80	137,926
1999	**Saffron Walden**	O. Peslier	Enrique	Orpen	10	1:38.10	151,379
1998	**Desert Prince (Ire)**	O. Peslier	Fa-Eq	Second Empire (Ire)	7	1:35.80	169,717
1997	**Desert King**	C. Roche	Verglas (Ire)	Romanov (Ire)	12	1:38.30	171,383
1996	**Spinning World**	C. B. Asmussen	Rainbow Blues (Ire)	Beauchamp King	10	1:38.80	175,902
1995	**Spectrum**	J. A. Reid	Adjareli	Bahri	9	1:40.30	187,592
1994	**Turtle Island**	J. A. Reid	Guided Tour	Ridgewood Ben	9	1:50.10	169,989
1993	**Barathea (Ire)**	M. Roberts	Fatherland (Ire)	Massyar (Ire)	11	1:43.00	175,777
1992	**Rodrigo de Triano**	L. Piggott	Ezzoud (Ire)	Brief Truce	6	1:41.00	198,616

United Arab Emirates

Dubai World Cup

Group 1, Nad al Sheba, three-year-olds and up, 2,000 meters (9.9419 furlongs), dirt. Held March 25, 2006, with a gross value of $6,000,000. First held in 1996.

Year	Winner	Jockey	Second	Third	Strs	Time	1st Purse
2006	**Electrocutionist**, 5, 126	L. Dettori	Wilko, 4	Magna Graduate, 4	11	2:01.32	$3,600,000
2005	**Roses in May**, 5, 126	J. Velazquez	Dynever	Choctaw Nation	12	2:02.17	3,600,000
2004	**Pleasantly Perfect**, 6, 126	A. Solis	Medaglia d'Oro, 5	Victory Moon, 5	12	2:00.24	3,600,000
2003	**Moon Ballad (Ire)**, 4, 126	L. Dettori	Harlan's Holiday, 4	Nayef, 5	11	2:00.48	3,600,000
2002	**Street Cry (Ire)**, 4, 126	J. D. Bailey	Sei Mi, 6	Sakhee, 5	11	2:01.18	3,600,000
2001	**Captain Steve**, 4, 126	J. D. Bailey	†To the Victory, 5	Hightori, 5	12	2:00.47	3,600,000
2000	**Dubai Millennium**, 4, 126	L. Dettori	Behrens, 6	Public Purse, 6	13	2:00.65	3,600,000
1999	**Almutawakel (GB)**, 5, 126	R. Hills	Malek (Chi), 6	Victory Gallop, 4	8	2:00.65	3,000,000
1998	**Silver Charm**, 4, 126	G. L. Stevens	Swain (Ire), 6	Loup Sauvage, 4	9	2:04.29	2,400,000
1997	**Singspiel (Ire)**, 5, 126	J. D. Bailey	Siphon (Brz), 6	Sandpit (Brz), 8	12	2:01.91	2,400,000
1996	**Cigar**, 6, 126	J. D. Bailey	Soul of the Matter, 5	L'Carriere, 5	11	2:03.84	2,400,000

1996-'97 listed race.

Dubai Golden Shaheen

Group 1, Nad al Sheba, three-year-olds and up, 1,200 meters (5.9652 furlongs), dirt. Held March 25, 2006, with a gross value of $2,000,000.

Year	Winner	Jockey	Second	Third	Strs	Time	1st Purse
2006	**Proud Tower Too**, 4	D. Cohen	Thor's Eco 4	Jet West, 5	15	1:09.86	$1,200,000
2005	**Saratoga County**, 4	J. Castellano	Tropicar Star, 5	Botanical, 4	11	1:11:21	1,200,000
2004	**Our New Recruit**, 5	A. Solis	Alke, 4	Conroy, 6	12	1:10:30	1,200,000
2003	**State City**, 4	M. Hills	Avanzado (Arg), 5	Captain Squire, 4	12	1:09:95	1,200,000
2002	**Caller One**, 5	G. Stevens	Echo Eddie, 5	Xtra Heat, 4	13	1:09:91	1,200,000
2001	**Caller One**, 4	C. Nakatani	Men's Exclusive, 8	Bertolini, 5	15	1:08:38	1,200,000

Dubai Duty Free

Group 1, Nad al Sheba, three-year-olds and up, 1,800 meters (8.9477 furlongs), turf. Held March 25, 2006, with a gross value of $5,000,000.

Year	Winner	Jockey	Second	Third	Strs	Time	1st Purse
2006	**David Junior**, 4	J. Spencer	The Tin Man, 8	Seihali, 7	15	1:49.65	$3,000,000
2005	**Elvstroem**, 4, 121	N. Rawiller	Whilly (Ire), 4	Right Approach, 6	14	1:50:54	1,200,000
2004	**dh-Right Approach**, 5	W. Marwing					
	dh-Paolini (Ger), 7	E. Pedroza		Nayyir (GB)	11	1:49:36	800,000
2003	**Ipi Tombe (Zim)**, 4	K. Shea	Paolini (Ger), 6	Royal Tryst, 6	12	1:47:61	1,200,000
2002	**Terre A Terre**, 5,	C. Soumillion	Noverre, 4	Hoeberg, 4	16	1:48:75	1,200,000

Dubai Sheema Classic

Group 1, three-year-olds and up, 2,400 meters (11.93 furlongs). Run March 25, 2006, with a gross value of $5,000,000.

Year	Winner	Jockey	Second	Third	Strs	Time	1st Purse
2006	**Heart's Cry**, 5, 124	Y. Take	Collier Hill, 5	Falstaff, 4	14	2:31.89	$3,000,000
2005	**Phoenix Reach (Ire)**, 5	M. Dwyer	Razkalla, 7	Collier Hill, 7	11	2:30:54	1,200,000
2004	**Polish Summer (GB)**, 7	G. Stevens	Hard Buck (Brz), 4	Scott's View, 5	13	2:31:09	1,200,000
2003	**Sulamani**, 4	L. Dettori	Ange Gabriel, 5	Ekraar, 6	16	2:27:67	1,200,000
2002	**Nayef**, 4	R. Hills	Helene Vitality, 5	Boreal, 4	15	2:29:64	1,200,000

English Triple Crown

Throughout its long history, the English Triple Crown has proved to be as elusive as its younger American cousin, and perhaps even more so. Approaching its third century, the English Triple Crown has been won only 15 times. Since Gainsborough became the 13th winner in 1918, only two more have followed: unbeaten *Bahram in 1935 and the brilliant Nijinsky II in '70.

The English Triple Crown for three-year-olds, dating from 1809, consists of the one-mile Two Thousand Guineas (Eng-G1) at Newmarket in May, the 1½-mile Epsom Derby (Eng-G1) at Epsom Downs in June, and the St. Leger Stakes (Eng-G1) at 1¾ miles and 127 yards at Doncaster Race Course in September. Over the years, there has been some variance in the distances of the three races, and alternative races were used during war years.

The St. Leger Stakes was named for the popular local sportsman Lt. Col. Anthony St. Leger. Alabaculia was the first winner of the St. Leger Stakes in 1776. Four years later, *Diomed, later imported to the United States, won the initial running of the Epsom Derby. The first Two Thousand Guineas was taken by Wizard in 1809, nine years after Champion became the first three-year-old to win both the Epsom Derby and the St. Leger Stakes. In 1813, Sir Charles Bunbury's Smolensko became the first to win the Two Thousand Guineas and the Epsom Derby.

Forty years later in 1853, West Australian became the first to win all three stakes. He was followed by Gladiateur (1865), Lord Lyon (1866), *Ormonde (1886), Common (1891), Isinglass (1893), Galtee More (1897), Flying Fox (1899), Diamond Jubilee (1900), *Rock Sand (1903), Pommern (1915), Gay Crusader (1917), Gainsborough (1918), *Bahram (1935), and Nijinsky II (1970).

In today's racing world, the English Triple Crown is a prize not pursued. The most recent horse with a chance to seize the crown, 1989 Two Thousand Guineas (Eng-G1) and Epsom Derby (Eng-G1) victor Nashwan, was withheld from the St. Leger Stakes (Eng-G1) by owner Sheikh Hamdan bin Rashid al Maktoum to point for the Prix de l'Arc de Triomphe (Fr-G1), in which he did not start because of injury.

Following are the 15 English Triple Crown winners:

WEST AUSTRALIAN—1850 b. h., Melbourne–Mowerina, by Touchstone. 10-9-1-0, $68,615. Known popularly as "the West," West Australian gave owner-breeder John Bowes his fourth and final Epsom Derby victory. Trained by John Scott, West Australian ran second in the Criterion Stakes to Speed the Plough and then beat his rival in the Glasgow Stakes as a two-year-old. At three, West Australian won the Two Thousand Guineas by a half-length over the Duke of Bedford's Sittingbourne and the Epsom Derby by a desperate neck over the same opponent. West Australian won the St. Leger easily, and at four won the Triennial Stakes and the Ascot Gold Cup. Though not widely regarded as a success at stud, he sired The Wizard, the 1860 Two Thousand Guineas winner, and his son *Australian sired Spendthrift, tail-male ancestor of the Man o' War male line that leads to Tiznow.

GLADIATEUR—1862 b. h., Monarque–Miss Gladiator, by Gladiator. 19-16-0-1, $236,537. French-bred and -owned Gladiateur shattered the notion that England's Thoroughbreds were superior when he won the 1865 Two Thousand Guineas, earning the gleeful nickname "Avenger of Waterloo" among the French. Trained at Newmarket by Tom Jennings, he added the Epsom Derby "in a canter" and the St. Leger. In between, he traveled to his native France and captured that country's greatest race at the time, the Grand Prix de Paris. At four, Gladiateur won the Gold Cup at Ascot by 40 lengths after reputedly trailing by 300 yards at one point. He was not a success at stud.

LORD LYON—1863 b. h., Stockwell–Paradigm, by Paragone. 19-15-3-1, $180,497. Leased to Richard Sutton, the second son of Sir Richard Sutton, and trained by James Dover, Lord Lyon dead-heated with Redan in the Champagne Stakes for two-year-olds at Doncaster and then won the Criterion and Troy Stakes at Newmarket. After winning the Two Thousand Guineas by one length over Monarch of the Glen, Lord Lyon completed the Triple Crown by beating Savernake by a head in the Epsom Derby and the same rival by inches in the St. Leger. The following year, Lord Lyon won the Ascot Biennial and the Stockbridge Cup. His most famous offspring were *Ormonde's rival Minting, winner of the 1886 Grand Prix de Paris, and '77 Oaks winner Placida.

***ORMONDE—**1883 b. h., Bend Or–Lily Agnes, by Macaroni. 16-16-0-0, $138,340. Considered by many as the finest Thoroughbred of the 19th century, the Duke of Westminster's *Ormonde was unbeaten in his 16-race career despite developing a wind infirmity. At four in the Hardwicke Stakes, he bested Grand Prix de Paris winner Minting. *Ormonde sired just seven foals in his first season at stud in England, but that crop included Orme, a multiple major stakes winner and sire of 1899 Triple Crown winner Flying Fox. After a stint in Argentina, *Ormonde was purchased by William O'Brien Macdonough, an American, for $150,000 in 1893 and stood in California. From 1894 through 1905, *Ormonde sired just 17 foals, but 12 started and five, including Ormondale, won stakes races.

COMMON—1888 br. h., Isonomy–Thistle, by Scottish Chief. 5-4-0-1, $77,567. Owned by his breeder, Lord Allington, and Sir Frederick Johnstone, Common was a colt with dubious joints and thus was not raced at two by trainer John Porter. Common made his debut in the 1891 Two Thousand Guineas, and his profuse sweating prompted Prince Soltykoff to remark, "He's very well named." Uncommon on the Newmarket course, Common won easily. He won the Epsom Derby by two lengths in a downpour and subsequently won the St. James's Palace Stakes before finishing third in the Eclipse Stakes. In the final start of his only racing season, Common completed the Triple Crown by winning the St. Leger by one length. Common's progeny included 1898 One Thousand Guineas winner Nun Nicer and Mushroom, who became a successful stallion in Belgium.

ISINGLASS—1890 b. h., Isonomy–Deadlock, by Wenlock. 12-11-1-0, $279,231. Despite soundness problems that he passed on to his progeny, Isinglass lost only once for his owner, Col. Harry McCalmont, in a four-year career. Isinglass suffered the only loss in his three-year-old campaign when he was defeated by Raeburn in the Lancashire Plate at Manchester, giving the winner ten pounds over an inadequate distance. At four, Isinglass captured the Princess of Wales's Stakes, Eclipse Stakes, and Jockey Club Stakes. As a five-year-old, he won the 1895 Ascot Gold Cup and retired as the sport's all-time money winner. Isinglass stood at his owner's Cheveley Park Stud near Newmarket and sired three British classic winners as well as *Star Shoot, who was North America's leading sire five times and leading broodmare sire five times.

GALTEE MORE—1894 b. h., Kendal–Morganette, by Springfield. 13-11-1-0, $131,312. Galtee More, named after a peak in the Galtee Mountains, was owned by John Gubbins, who used his considerable inheritance from an uncle to open two stud farms, one of which housed Galtee More's sire, Kendal. Trained by Sam Darling, Galtee More won the Molecomb Stakes, the Rous Plate, and the Middle Park Plate as a two-year-old. At three in 1897, Galtee More completed the Triple Crown by taking the St. Leger by three-quarters of a length over the filly Chelandry. At the end of his racing career, Galtee More was sold by Gubbins to the Russian government, and the stallion subsequently was purchased by German interests. His most noteworthy progeny was Orchidee II, dam of Oleander, leading German sire in the 1930s and '40s. Galtee More's half brother Ard Patrick won the Epsom Derby in 1892.

FLYING FOX—1896 b. h., Orme–Vampire, by Galopin. 11-9-2-0, $194,867. A large colt with beautiful shoulders, Flying Fox became the Duke of Westminster's second Triple Crown winner despite a difficult temperament that most likely came from his aptly named dam. At two in 1898, Flying Fox won the New, Stockbridge Foal, and Criterion Stakes, and he finished second in both the Imperial Produce Stakes and the Middle Park Plate. Flying Fox was unbeaten at three and ended his career with a four-length victory in the Jockey Club Stakes. Flying Fox sired French classic winner Val d'Or, and his grandson *Teddy (by French Derby winner Ajax) became an important influence on North American bloodlines through full brothers *Sir Gallahad III and *Bull Dog.

DIAMOND JUBILEE—1897 b. h., St. Simon–Perdita, by Hampton. 16-6-5-1, $142,131. Owned by the Prince of Wales, Diamond Jubilee was described as "ferocious, with a nature more befitting the bullring than the racecourse." He was found to be a cryptorchid (and thus spared from gelding) after finishing unplaced in his first two starts at two. Diamond Jubilee's trainer, Richard Marsh, gave Diamond Jubilee's groom, 18-year-old Herbert Jones, a chance to ride the ridgling, and Diamond Jubilee won the Two Thousand Guineas by four lengths. He won the Epsom Derby by a half-length and the St. Leger by one length. After standing at stud in England, he was sold in 1906 to Las Ortegas Stud in Argentina, where he was the leading sire from 1914 through '16. Diamond Jubilee was a full brother to the outstanding racehorse Persimmon, winner of the Epsom Derby and the St. Leger in 1896.

***ROCK SAND—**1900 br. h., Sainfoin–Roquebrune, by St. Simon. 20-16-1-3, $221,703. Although he hobbled along at a trot and canter, *Rock Sand would fully extend himself at a gallop once warmed up and never finished unplaced in his career. He won six stakes races as a two-year-old in 1902, and at three he won the St. James's Palace Stakes and Bennington Stakes in addition to the Triple Crown contests. He won the Hardwicke, Princess of Wales's, Lingfield Park Plate, First Foal, and the Jockey Club Stakes at four. Best known for his success as a broodmare sire, *Rock Sand sired Mahubah, dam of Man o' War. *Rock Sand's other leading daughters included Hour Glass, dam of Blue Glass and *Hourless, and Tea Biscuit, dam of Hard Tack. *Rock Sand's most accomplished sons were Tracery, winner of the St. James's Palace and the Eclipse Stakes and one of the leading sires in England for many years in the 1920s; Friar Rock, who won the 1916 Belmont Stakes and Suburban Handicap in the United States; and 1916 Preakness Stakes winner Damrosch.

POMMERN—1912 b. h., Polymelus–Merry Agnes, by St. Hilaire. 10-7-1-0, $75,165. A homebred of Solomon B. Joel, Pommern won the Richmond Stakes at Goodwood and the Imperial Produce Stakes at Kemptonat age two. Steve Donoghue was engaged to ride Pommern in his unusual three-year-old season. Pommern won the 1915 Two Thousand Guineas comfortably at Newmarket. With World War I raging across the English Channel in France, Epsom Downs was requisitioned by the military, and Pommern scored a two-length victory in the substitute for the Epsom Derby, the New Derby at 1½ miles on Newmarket's July Course. He then won the substitute for the St. Leger, the 1¾-mile September Stakes at Newmarket. In his only start at four, Pommern won the June Stakes at Newmarket. His best offspring were Adam's Apple, who won the 1927 Two Thousand Guineas; Pondoland, second in the '22 Two Thousand Guineas; and Glommen, who won the '26 Goodwood Cup.

GAY CRUSADER—1914 b. c., Bayardo–Gay Laura, by Beppo. 10-8-2-0, $53,530. Bred and owned by A. W. "Fairie" Cox, Gay Crusader was the first foal of his dam and from his sire's first crop. Trained by Alec Taylor, Gay Crusader was a small colt who developed sore shins in June of his two-year-old season. He made a late start that year, losing his debut before winning the Criterion Stakes. After finishing second in his

The Influence of England's Triple Crown Worldwide

Although England's Triple Crown is the original and perhaps most difficult Triple Crown in the world to win, historically it has served as a model for racing programs around the globe. Virtually every major racing country has its set of Guineas, Derbys, and St. Legers, or their equivalents. As in most aspects of Thoroughbred racing, England, the birthplace of the Thoroughbred, established the pattern that the rest of the world adapted for its own local purposes, and the idea of a series of classic tests for three-year-olds is universal.

The Triple Crown in the United States evolved into the familiar Kentucky Derby (G1), Preakness Stakes (G1), and Belmont Stakes (G1) early in the 20th century, but several American racing jurisdictions in the 19th century attempted to establish Triple Crown series more closely modeled on the English pattern. For example, the Withers, Belmont, and Lawrence Realization Stakes were originally intended to be New York's version of the English series.

Other former English colonies such as Australia and New Zealand likewise established Guineas-Derby-St. Leger series, and those races still exist in Antipodean lands, though it has been many years since they have been a serious objective as a series for owners and trainers. As racing throughout the world has become more specialized, winning a Triple Crown over a variety of distances as wide as that in England has become increasingly difficult.

Argentina, historically the most important South American racing country, established its own series, the Polla de Potrillos (Arg-G1), Gran Premio Jockey Club (Arg-G1), and Gran Premio Nacional (Arg-G1) over 1,600 meters, 2,000 meters, and 2,500 meters, respectively, but went one better than the English. The Argentines also required their best three-year-olds to beat older horses in the 2,400-meter Gran Premio Carlos Pellegrini (Arg-G1) to win their Quadruple Crown. Twenty three-year-olds have captured the Argentine Triple Crown since 1902, with Refinado Tom (Arg) in '96 the most recent winner. Only ten horses, the last being the great *Forli in 1966, have completed the Quadruple Crown.

English fillies have an opportunity to win their version of the Triple Crown, though no filly has ever completed the Two Thousand Guineas (Eng-G1), Epsom Derby (Eng-G1), St. Leger (Eng-G1) triple. Two fillies, however, have won four of the five English classics, failing only to capture the Derby. Formosa in 1868 dead-heated in the Two Thousand and won the One Thousand Guineas, Epsom Oaks, and St. Leger. Sceptre won the One Thousand, Two Thousand, Oaks, and St. Leger in 1902 but was beaten into fourth place in the Derby by Ard Patrick.

Nine fillies have won a "fillies Triple Crown" consisting of the One Thousand Guineas, Oaks, and St. Leger:

1985 Oh So Sharp (GB), ch. f., Kris—Oh So Fair, by Graustark
1955 Meld, b. f., Alycidon—Daily Double, by Fair Trial
1942 Sun Chariot, b. f., Hyperion—Clarence, by Diligence
1904 Pretty Polly, ch. f., Gallinule—Admiration, by Saraband
1902 Sceptre, b. f., Persimmon—Ornament, by Bend Or
1892 La Fleche, br. f., St. Simon—Quiver, by Toxophilite
1874 Apology, ch. f., Adventurer—Mandragora, by Rataplan
1871 Hannah, b. f., King Tom—Mentmore Lass, by Melbourne
1868 Formosa, ch. f., Buccaneer—Eller, by Chanticleer

three-year-old debut in the Column Produce Stakes, Gay Crusader won the 1917 Two Thousand Guineas by a head over Magpie, who also was trained by Taylor. With Magpie exported to Australia, Gay Crusader won the Epsom Derby, which was delayed until July 31 because of World War I, by four lengths. He then won the September Stakes, the St. Leger substitute. Gay Crusader also won the Newmarket Gold Cup, Champion Stakes, and Lowther Stakes. A tendon injury ended his career before his first start as a four-year-old. At stud, his best were Hot Night, second in the 1927 Epsom Derby, and Hurstwood, third in the '24 Derby.

GAINSBOROUGH—1915 b. h., Bayardo–Rosedrop, by St. Frusquin. 9-5-2-1, $67,021. Lady Jane Douglas bred Gainsborough and became the first woman to own an Epsom Derby winner when the colt took the 1918 classic. Gainsborough gave his sire, Bayardo, a second straight Triple Crown winner. Gainsborough, who was twice champion sire, sired Hyperion, the 1933 Epsom Derby winner who went on to be England's leading sire six times. Gainsborough also sired 1932 Two Thousand Guineas winner Orwell and Solario, who was England's leading sire in 1937 and its leading broodmare sire in 1949 and '50. Gainsborough died in 1945 at the age of 30 and was buried at Gainsborough Stud, which was originally named Harwood Stud.

***BAHRAM**—1932 br. h., Blandford–Friar's Daughter, by Friar Marcus. 9-9-0-0, $212,816. A large colt who grew to 16.2 hands, *Bahram was bred and raced in England by the Aga Khan. Unbeaten in nine career starts through his three-year-old season, *Bahram won the National Produce, Rous Memorial, Gimcrack, and Middle Park Stakes at two. In addition to sweeping the Triple Crown at three, he won the St. James's Palace Stakes. England's second-leading sire in 1940, he was sold for $160,000 to an American syndicate that included Alfred G. Vanderbilt, Walter P. Chrysler, James Cox Brady, and S. W. Labrot. *Bahram stood in Maryland and Virginia before being sold in 1945 to stand in Argentina. *Bahram's 25 stakes winners included 1940 St. Leger and Irish Derby winner Turkhan, '40 Irish Oaks winner Queen of Shiraz, and '42 Two Thousand Guineas winner Big Game, who became the leading sire in England in '48, and the excellent sire Persian Gulf, winner of the '44 Coronation Cup.

NIJINSKY II—1967 b. h., Northern Dancer–Flaming Page, by Bull Page. 13-11-2-0, $667,220. Bred in Canada by E. P. Taylor and owned by Charles W. Engelhard, Nijinsky II was Northern Dancer's first international champion. He was a powerful, sickle-hocked colt who more closely resembled his dam than his diminutive sire. Trained by Vincent O'Brien, Nijinsky II was a champion in England and Ireland at two in 1969. He won the Two Thousand Guineas at odds of 4-to-7, the Epsom Derby at 11-to-8 odds, and the St. Leger at 2-to-7 odds, all under Lester Piggott. That year, Nijinsky II also won the Irish Sweeps Derby and the King George VI and Queen Elizabeth Stakes. His only defeats were in his final two starts, the Prix de l'Arc de Triomphe and Champion Stakes. At stud at Claiborne Farm in Kentucky, he was England's leading sire in 1986 and North America's leading broodmare sire in '93 and '94. Nijinsky II at one time was the all-time leading sire of stakes winners with 155, surpassing the record of his sire. Nijinsky II sired 11 champions, including 1987 North American Horse of the Year Ferdinand, '83 French champion Caerleon, two-time English champion Ile de Bourbon, and two undefeated winners of the Epsom Derby, Golden Fleece and Lammtarra.—*Bill Heller*

2005 World Thoroughbred Racehorse Rankings

European-Based Two-Year-Olds

Rating	Horse	YOB, Sex	Sire—Dam, Broodmare Sire	Trained	2005 Record, Earnings
124	George Washington	2003 c.	Danehill—Bordighera, by Alysheba	Ire	5-4-0-1, $549,681
121	Sir Percy	2003 c.	Mark of Esteem (Ire)—Percy's Lass, by Blakeney	GB	4-4-0-0, $356,449
120	Amadeus Wolf	2003 c.	Mozart (Ire)—Rachelle, by Mark of Esteem (Ire)	GB	5-3-1-1, $340,271
	Horatio Nelson	2003 c.	Danehill—Imagine (Ire), by Sadler's Wells	Ire	5-4-1-0, $488,433
117	Opera Cape	2003 c.	Barathea (Ire)—Optaria, by Song	GB	6-2-2-2, $210,030
	Red Clubs	2003 c.	Red Ransom—Two Clubs (GB), by First Trump	GB	9-3-2-1, $267,274
116	Carlotamix	2003 c.	Linamix—Carlitta, by Olympio	Fr	3-3-0-0, $237,146
	Rumplestiltskin	2003 f.	Danehill—Monevassia, by Mr. Prospector	Ire	6-5-0-1, $608,702
115	Flashy Wings	2003 f.	Zafonic—Lovealoch (Ire), by Lomond	GB	6-4-1-1, $325,513
	Silca's Sister	2003 f.	Inchinor (GB)—Silca-Cisa, by Hallgate	GB	3-2-0-0, $253,072
114	Donna Blini	2003 f.	Bertolini—Cal Norma's Lady, by Lyphard's Special	GB	4-3-1-0, $274,368
	New Girlfriend	2003 f.	Diesis (GB)—New Story, by Dynaformer	Fr	3-2-0-0, $122,704
113	Always Hopeful	2003 c.	Mind Games—Expectation, by Night Shift	GB	6-2-1-2, $167,339
	Close To You	2003 c.	Shinko Forest—Maritana, by Rahy	GB	7-4-0-0, $103,820
	Ivan Denisovich (Ire)	2003 c.	Danehill—Hollywood Wildcat, by Kris S.	Ire	6-2-2-0, $202,765
	La Chunga	2003 f.	More Than Ready—Gypsy Monarch, by Wavering Monarch	GB	4-1-1-1, $104,006
	Nannina (GB)	2003 f.	Medicean—Hill Hopper, by Danehill	GB	5-3-0-1, $242,982
	Quiet Royal	2003 f.	Royal Academy—Wakigoer, by Miswaki	Fr	5-2-2-0, $162,159
	Silent Times (Ire)	2003 c.	Danehill Dancer—Recoleta, by Wild Again	GB	5-2-2-1, $107,829
	Wake Up Maggie	2003 f.	Xaar—Kalagold, by Magical Strike	GB	4-2-2-0, $258,656
112	Alexandrova	2003 f.	Sadler's Wells—Shouk, by Shirley Heights	Ire	4-1-1-1, $83,092
	Art Museum	2003 c.	Storm Cat—Totemic, by Vanlandingham	Ire	2-2-0-0, $60,135
	Linda's Lad	2003 c.	Sadler's Wells—Colza, by Alleged	Fr	6-3-3-0, $280,602
111	Ajigolo (GB)	2003 c.	Piccolo—Ajig Dancer, by Niniski	GB	10-3-1-1, $108,884
	Amigoni (Ire)	2003 c.	Danehill—Elite Guest, by Be My Guest	Ire	8-2-1-0, $117,220

Rating	Horse	YOB, Sex	Sire—Dam, Broodmare Sire	Trained	2005 Record, Earnings
111	Aspectus	2003 c.	Spectrum—Anna Thea, by Turfkonig	Ger	3-2-0-0, $106,783
	Aussie Rules	2003 c.	Danehill—Last Second (Ire), by Alzao	Ire	4-2-1-0, $102,526
	Balthazaar's Gift	2003 c.	Xaar—Thats Your Opinion, by Last Tycoon (Ire)	GB	6-3-1-0, $170,003
	Golden Arrow	2003 c.	Danehill—Cheal Rose, by Dr Devious (Ire)	Ire	4-1-1-1, $127,296
	Headache	2003 c.	Muhtathir (GB)—Psycadelic, by Midyan	Fr	11-2-1-2, $100,079
	Palace Episode	2003 c.	Machiavellian—Palace Weekend, by Seattle Dancer	GB	5-3-0-1, $284,396
	Violette	2003 f.	Observatory—Odette, by Pursuit of Love	GB	10-4-4-1, $224,935
110	Black Charmer	2003 c.	Black Minnaloushe—Abla (GB), by Robellino	GB	5-1-1-3, $53,226
	Cool Creek (Ire)	2003 c.	Desert Style—Shining Creek, by Bering (GB)	GB	10-3-2-1, $209,824
	Deveron	2003 f.	Cozzene—Cruisie, by Assert (Ire)	GB	5-1-1-2, $71,158
	Frost Giant	2003 c.	Giant's Causeway—Takesmybreathaway, by Gone West	Ire	2-1-0-1, $55,892
	Heatseeker (Ire)	2003 c.	Giant's Causeway—Rusty Back, by Defensive Play	Ire	3-2-0-1, $69,403
	Killybegs	2003 c.	Orpen—Belsay, by Belmez	GB	4-2-1-1, $57,448
	Leo (GB)	2003 c.	Pivotal—Miss Penton, by Primo Dominie	GB	7-2-2-0, $117,085
	Namaya	2003 c.	Namid—Touraya, by Tap On Wood	Ire	4-1-0-1, $28,544
	Set Alight	2003 c.	Hennessy—Proflare, by Mr. Prospector	Fr	7-3-1-0, $93,517
	Ugo Fire	2003 f.	Bluebird—Quiet Mouse, by Quiet American	Ire	9-2-1-2, $216,709

Extended, Three and Up, Turf

Rating	Horse	YOB, Sex	Sire—Dam, Broodmare Sire	Trained	2005 Record, Earnings
118	Deep Impact	2002 c.	Sunday Silence—Wind in Her Hair (Ire), by Alzao	Jpn	7-6-1-0, $6,123,911
	Westerner	1999 h.	Danehill—Walensee, by Troy	Fr	6-3-1-1, $1,023,765
117	Distinction	1999 g.	Danehill—Ivy Leaf (Ire), by Nureyev	GB	6-1-2-0, $246,122
	Millenary	1997 h.	Rainbow Quest—Ballerina, by Dancing Brave	GB	6-2-0-2, $274,715
116	Collier Hill	1998 g.	Dr Devious (Ire)—Polar Queen, by Polish Precedent	GB	6-3-1-1, $590,367
	Vinnie Roe	1998 h.	Definite Article (GB)—Kayu, by Tap On Wood	Ire	5-1-0-3, $207,730
115	Alcazar	1995 g.	Alzao—Sahara Breeze, by Ela-Mana-Mou	GB	7-3-1-1, $359,085
	The Geezer	2002 c.	Halling—Polygueza, by Be My Guest	GB	10-4-3-1, $435,734
	The Whistling Teal	1996 g.	Rudimentary—Lonely Shore, by Blakeney	GB	4-0-1-1, $83,243

Long, Three and Up, Turf

Rating	Horse	YOB, Sex	Sire—Dam, Broodmare Sire	Trained	2005 Record, Earnings
130	Hurricane Run	2002 c.	Montjeu (Ire)—Hold On, by Surumu	Fr	6-5-1-0, $2,765,603
126	Azamour (Ire)	2001 h.	Night Shift—Asmara, by Lear Fan	Ire	5-2-0-1, $1,359,521
126	Westerner	1999 h.	Danehill—Walensee, by Troy	Fr	6-3-1-1, $1,023,765
125	Motivator	2002 c.	Montjeu (Ire)—Out West, by Gone West	GB	5-2-2-0, $1,923,920
125	Shirocco (Ger)	2001 h.	Monsun—So Sedulous, by The Minstrel	Fr	3-1-0-1, $1,324,794
124	Bago (Fr)	2001 h.	Nashwan—Moonlight's Box, by Nureyev	Fr	7-1-1-3, $776,051
	Deep Impact	2002 c.	Sunday Silence—Wind in Her Hair (Ire), by Alzao	Jpn	7-6-1-0, $6,123,911
123	Alkaased	2000 h.	Kingmambo—Chesa Plana (GB), by Niniski	GB	6-3-2-0, $2,650,290
122	Ace (Ire)	2001 h.	Danehill—Tea House (Ire), by Sassafras (Fr)	Ire	8-0-2-3, $836,416
	Heart's Cry	2001 h.	Sunday Silence—Irish Dance, by Tony Bin	Jpn	6-1-3-0, $3,286,321
	Norse Dancer	2000 h.	Halling—River Patrol (GB), by Rousillon	GB	9-1-1-0, $361,593
122	Relaxed Gesture (Ire)	2001 h.	Indian Ridge—Token Gesture, by Alzao	USA	7-3-3-1, $1,326,186
121	Shawanda	2002 f.	Sinndar—Shamawna, by Darshaan	Fr	7-5-1-0, $540,322
120	Imperial Stride	2001 h.	Indian Ridge—Place de l'Opera, by Sadler's Wells	GB	5-4-0-0, $227,016
	Scorpion	2002 c.	Montjeu (Ire)—Ardmelody, by Law Society	Ire	7-3-2-0, $1,161,885
	Yeats	2001 h.	Sadler's Wells—Lyndonville, by Top Ville	Ire	5-1-1-0, $297,362
119	Lincoln	2000 h.	Sunday Silence—Grace Admire, by Tony Bin	Jpn	7-1-0-2, $1,625,220
	Pride	2000 m.	Peintre Celebre—Specificity, by Alleged	Fr	7-2-2-0, $854,290
118	Bandari	1999 h.	Alhaarth—Miss Audimar, by Mr. Leader	GB	6-1-1-1, $226,936
	Better Talk Now	1999 g.	Talkin Man—Bendita, by Baldski	USA	7-3-0-0, $877,640
	Gamut	1999 h.	Spectrum—Greektown, by Ela-Mana-Mou	GB	6-1-1-1, $169,815
	Shakespeare	2001 h.	Theatrical (Ire)—Lady Shirl, by That's a Nice	USA	4-3-0-0, $604,320
	Warrsan	1998 h.	Caerleon—Lucayan Princess, by High Line	GB	8-1-0-0, $672,646
117	Cosmo Bulk	2001 h.	Zagreb—Iseno Tosho, by Tosho Boy	Jpn	6-0-0-0, $232,281
	Darsalam	2001 h.	Desert King—Moonsilk, by Solinus (Ire)	Cze	3-3-0-0, $162,125
	English Channel	2002 c.	Smart Strike—Belva, by Theatrical (Ire)	USA	8-4-2-0, $1,143,491
	King's Drama (Ire)	2000 g.	King's Theatre (Ire)—Last Drama, by Last Tycoon (Ire)	USA	6-3-1-0, $525,137
	Ouija Board (GB)	2001 m.	Cape Cross (Ire)—Selection Board, by Welsh Pageant	GB	5-2-1-0, $1,491,358
	Sunrise Pegasus	1998 h.	Sunday Silence—Higashi Brian, by Brian's Time	Jpn	9-2-1-0, $1,468,060
	Sweep Tosho	2001 m.	End Sweep—Tabatha Tosho, by Dancing Brave	Jpn	6-2-1-0, $2,621,051
116	Coin Toss	1998 h.	Sunday Silence—Re Toss (Arg), by Egg Toss	Jpn	8-0-1-2, $748,507
	Phoenix Reach	2000 h.	Alhaarth—Carroll's Canyon, by Hatim	GB	4-1-1-0, $1,619,775
	Policy Maker	2000 h.	Sadler's Wells—Palmeraie, by Lear Fan	Fr	4-0-2-0, $150,934
	Walk in the Park	2002 c.	Montjeu (Ire)—Classic Park, by Robellino	Fr	3-0-2-0, $528,490
115	Cherry Mix	2001 h.	Linamix—Cherry Moon, by Quiet American	UAE, GB	6-1-0-0, $172,572
	Day Flight	2001 h.	Sadler's Wells—Bonash, by Rainbow Quest	GB	6-4-2-0, $265,182

Rating	Horse	YOB, Sex	Sire—Dam, Broodmare Sire	Trained	2005 Record, Earnings
115	Desideratum	2002 c.	Darshaan—Desired, by Rainbow Quest	Fr	6-4-1-0, $260,256
	Eswarah	2002 f.	Unfuwain—Midway Lady, by Alleged	GB	5-3-0-0, $470,386
	Hard Top	2002 c.	Darshaan—Well Head, by Sadler's Wells	GB	3-2-0-0, $168,857
	Megahertz (GB)	1999 m.	Pivotal—Heavenly Ray, by Rahy	USA	6-4-1-0, $780,000
	Meteor Storm (GB)	1999 h.	Bigstone (Ire)—Hunt the Sun, by Rainbow Quest	USA	9-1-4-0, $714,138
	Mubtaker	1997 h.	Silver Hawk—Gazayil, by Irish River (Fr)	GB	8-3-1-1, $155,996

Intermediate, Three and Up, Turf

Rating	Horse	YOB, Sex	Sire—Dam, Broodmare Sire	Trained	2005 Record, Earnings
123	Azamour (Ire)	2001 h.	Night Shift—Asmara, by Lear Fan	Ire	5-2-0-1, $1,359,521
	David Junior	2002 c.	Pleasant Tap—Paradise River, by Irish River (Fr)	GB	7-4-1-0, $582,251
	Oratorio (Ire)	2002 c.	Danehill—Mahrah, by *Vaguely Noble	Ire	8-2-1-1, $1,314,657
122	Grey Swallow (Ire)	2001 h.	Daylami (Ire)—Style of Life, by The Minstrel	Ire	4-1-0-0, $306,861
121	Electrocutionist	2001 h.	Red Ransom—Elbaaha (GB), by Arazi	Ity	4-3-0-1, $945,096
120	Cesario (Jpn)	2002 f.	Special Week—Kirov Premiere (GB), by Sadler's Wells	Jpn	5-4-1-0, $2,511,053
	Maraahel	2001 h.	Alzao—Nasanice, by Nashwan	GB	8-1-1-4, $583,649
	Powerscourt (GB)	2000 h.	Sadler's Wells—Rainbow Lake, by Rainbow Quest	Ire	4-1-1-0, $711,355
	Zenno Rob Roy	2000 h.	Sunday Silence—Roamin Rachel, by Mining	Jpn	5-0-2-2, $1,489,032
119	Alexander Goldrun	2001 m.	Gold Away (Ire)—Renashaan, by Darshaan	Ire	9-2-1-3, $828,665
118	Intercontinental (GB)	2000 m.	Danehill—Hasili (Ire), by Kahyasi	USA	7-5-1-1, $1,271,200
	Mummify	1999 g.	Jeune—Cleopatra's Girl, by At Talaq	Aus	11-2-0-2, $1.294.191
	Pinson	2002 c.	Halling—Tadorne, by Inchinor (GB)	Fr	6-4-1-0, $178,696
117	North Light (Ire)	2001 h.	Danehill—Sought Out, by Rainbow Quest	GB	1-0-1-0, $20,052
	Ruwi	2002 c.	Unfuwain—Ma Paloma, by Highest Honor (Fr)	Fr	8-2-3-0, $259,613
116	Altieri	1998 h.	Selkirk—Minya, by Blushing Groom (Fr)	Ity	7-3-0-2, $426,152
	Heavenly Romance	2000 m.	Sunday Silence—First Act, by Sadler's Wells	Jpn	9-2-1-0, $1,919,546
	Phoenix Reach (Ire)	2000 h.	Alhaarth—Carroll's Canyon, by Hatim	GB	4-1-1-0, $1,619,775
	Soldier Hollow	2000 h.	In the Wings (GB)—Island Race, by Common Grounds	Ger	6-2-3-0, $308,052
	Vadawina	2002 f.	Unfuwain—Vadaza, by Zafonic	Fr	4-3-0-0, $267,195
115	Epalo (Ger)	1999 h.	Lando (Ger)—Evening Kiss, by Kris	Ger	5-1-0-1, $93,497
	Film Maker	2000 m.	Dynaformer—Miss Du Bois, by Mr. Prospector	USA	7-2-1-3, $443,440
	Fourty Niners Son	2001 h.	Distorted Humor—Cindazanno, by Alleged	USA	8-4-1-2, $459,000
	Gun Salute	2002 c.	Military—Hail Roberta, by Roberto	USA	7-4-0-1, $630,550
	Megahertz (GB)	1999 m.	Pivotal—Heavenly Ray, by Rahy	USA	6-4-1-0, $780,000
	Riskaverse	1999 m.	Dynaformer—The Bink, by Seeking the Gold	USA	5-1-0-0, $464,723
	Tap Dance City	1997 h.	Pleasant Tap—All Dance, by Northern Dancer	Jpn	5-1-0-0, $599,770
	Touch of Land (Fr)	2000 h.	Lando (Ger)—Touch of Class, by Be My Guest	Fr	7-2-0-0, $284,561

Mile, Three and Up, Turf

Rating	Horse	YOB, Sex	Sire—Dam, Broodmare Sire	Trained	2005 Record, Earnings
125	Shamardal	2002 c.	Giant's Causeway—Helsinki (GB), by Machiavellian	UAE, GB	4-3-0-0, $1,572,090
124	Leroidesanimaux (Brz)	2000 h.	Candy Stripes—Dissemble, by Ahonoora	USA	4-3-1-0, $1,214,040
	Starcraft (NZ)	2000 h.	Soviet Star—Flying Floozie, by Pompeii Court	GB	5-2-0-1, $488,660
123	Dubawi	2002 c.	Dubai Millennium—Zomaradah (GB), by Deploy	GB	5-2-1-1, $1,062,116
122	Divine Proportions	2002 f.	Kingmambo—Myth to Reality (Fr), by Sadler's Wells	Fr	5-4-0-0, $1,072,784
	Proclamation	2002 c.	King's Best—Shamarra, by Zayyani (Ire)	GB	5-3-0-0, $406,445
121	Artie Schiller	2001 h.	El Prado (Ire)—Hidden Light, by Majestic Light	USA	6-3-2-1, $1,448,000
	Valixir (Ire)	2001 h.	Trempolino—Vadlamixa, by Linamix	Fr	7-3-0-2, $594,810
120	Rakti	1999 h.	Polish Precedent—Ragera, by Rainbow Quest	GB	5-1-1-0, $388,720
	Whipper	2001 h.	Miesque's Son—Myth to Reality (Fr), by Sadler's Wells	Fr	6-1-1-1, $473,974
119	Soviet Song	2000 m.	Marju—Kalinka, by Soviet Star	GB	3-1-1-1, $344,594
118	Asakusa Den'en	1999 h.	Singspiel (Ire)—Whitewater Affair, by Machiavellian	Jpn	8-2-1-1, $1,982,644
	Bullish Luck	1999 g.	Royal Academy—Wild Vintage, by Alysheba	HK	9-3-1-0, $1,780,235
	Elvstroem	2000 h.	Danehill—Circles of Gold, by Marscay	Aus	9-3-1-1, $1,665,366
	Hat Trick	2001 h.	Sunday Silence—Tricky Code, by Lost Code	Jpn	8-4-0-0, $2,669,779
	Kitten's Joy	2001 h.	El Prado (Ire)—Kitten's First, by Lear Fan	USA	2-1-1-0, $369,880
117	Daiwa Major	2001 h.	Sunday Silence—Scarlet Bouquet, by Northern Taste	Jpn	5-1-2-0, $916,477
	Major's Cast (Ire)	2001 h.	Victory Note—Ziffany, by Taufan	GB	10-3-2-2, $444,117
116	Ad Valorem	2002 c.	Danzig—Classy Women, by Relaunch	Ire	5-0-1-1, $160,483
	Attraction	2001 m.	Efisio—Flirtation, by Pursuit of Love	GB	3-1-0-0, $206,263
	Cacique (Ire)	2001 h.	Danehill—Hasili (Ire), by Kahyasi	Fr	4-1-0-1, $79,576
116	Footstepsinthesand	2002 c.	Giant's Causeway—Glatisant, by Rainbow Quest	Ire	1-1-0-0, $353,976
	Gorella (Fr)	2002 f.	Grape Tree Road (GB)—Exciting Times, by Jeune Homme	Fr, USA	7-2-1-4, $504,806
	Indesatchel	2002 c.	Danehill Dancer—Floria, by Petorius	Ire	7-3-1-0, $287,702
	Le Vie Dei Colori	2000 h.	Efisio—Mystic Tempo, by El Gran Senor	GB	6-2-0-0, $145,748
	Limehouse	2001 h.	Grand Slam—Dixieland Blues, by Dixieland Band	USA	10-2-2-0, $482,998
	Martillo	2000 h.	Anabaa—Maltage, by Affirmed	Ger	7-2-1-0, $223,167
	Singletary	2000 h.	Sultry Song—Joiski's Star, by Star de Naskra	USA	6-2-0-1, $314,580
115	Blatant	1999 g.	Machiavellian—Negligent (Ire), by Ahonoora	GB	3-0-0-1, $44,242
	Chic	2000 m.	Machiavellian—Exclusive, by Polar Falcon	GB	6-1-1-0, $172,267

Rating	Horse	YOB, Sex	Sire—Dam, Broodmare Sire	Trained	2005 Record, Earnings
115	Gharir	2002 c.	Machiavellian—Summer Sonnet, by Baillamont	Fr	3-0-0-1, $164,420
	Host (Chi)	2000 h.	Hussonet—Colonna Traiana, by Roy	USA	4-1-1-0, $393,167
	Megahertz (GB)	1999 m.	Pivotal—Heavenly Ray, by Rahy	USA	6-4-1-0, $780,000
	Nayyir	1998 g.	Indian Ridge—Pearl Kite, by Silver Hawk	GB	4-0-0-1, $41,921
	Sweet Return (GB)	2000 h.	Elmaamul—Sweet Revival, by Claude Monet	USA	7-2-1-1, $554,520
	Turtle Bowl	2002 c.	Dyhim Diamond (Ire)—Clara Bow, by Top Ville	Fr	6-4-0-0, $373,647

Sprint, Three and Up, Turf

Rating	Horse	YOB, Sex	Sire—Dam, Broodmare Sire	Trained	2005 Record, Earnings
123	Silent Witness	1999 g.	El Moxie—Jade Tiara, by Bureaucracy	HK	7-5-1-1, $2,517,060
118	Durandal	1999 h.	Sunday Silence—Sawayaka Princess, by Northern Taste	Jpn	2-0-1-0, $343,199
	Pastoral Pursuits	2001 h.	Bahamian Bounty—Star, by Most Welcome (GB)	GB	2-1-0-0, $254,562
	Whipper	2001 h.	Miesque's Son—Myth to Reality (Fr), by Sadler's Wells	Fr	6-1-1-1, $473,974
117	Goodricke	2002 c.	Bahamian Bounty—Star, by Most Welcome (GB)	GB	7-3-3-0, $411,676
116	Admire Max	1999 h.	Sunday Silence—Dyna Shoot, by Northern Taste	Jpn	8-1-0-1, $1,277,739
115	Cape of Good Hope	1998 g.	Inchinor (GB)—Cape Merino, by Clantime	HK	10-2-0-4, $716,945
	Chineur	2001 h.	Fasliyev—Wardara, by Sharpo	Fr	8-4-0-0, $267,499
	Maruka Kiseki	2001 h.	Fuji Kiseki—Flying Colors, by Jade Robbery	Jpn	12-3-0-3, $976,773

Long, Three and Up, Dirt

Rating	Horse	YOB, Sex	Sire—Dam, Broodmare Sire	Trained	2005 Record, Earnings
124	Afleet Alex	2002 c.	Northern Afleet—Maggy Hawk, by Hawkster	USA	6-4-0-1, $2,085,000

Intermediate, Three and Up, Dirt

Rating	Horse	YOB, Sex	Sire—Dam, Broodmare Sire	Trained	2005 Record, Earnings
125	Saint Liam	2000 h.	Saint Ballado—Quiet Dance, by Quiet American	USA	6-4-1-0, $3,696,960
124	Afleet Alex	2002 c.	Northern Afleet—Maggy Hawk, by Hawkster	USA	6-4-0-1, $2,085,000
123	Roses in May	2000 h.	Devil His Due—Tell a Secret, by Speak John	USA	2-1-1-0, $3,695,000
122	Borrego	2001 c.	El Prado (Ire)—Sweet as Honey, by Strike the Gold	USA	8-3-1-2, $1,536,600
	Flower Alley	2002 c.	Distorted Humor—Princess Olivia, by Lycius	USA	9-4-3-0, $2,435,200
	Rock Hard Ten	2001 c.	Kris S.—Tersa, by Mr. Prospector	USA	3-3-0-0, $1,080,000
120	Giacomo	2002 c.	Holy Bull—Set Them Free, by Stop the Music	USA	6-1-1-2, $1,846,876
	Lava Man	2001 g.	Slew City Slew—Li'l Ms. Leonard, by Nostalgia's Star	USA	9-3-0-1, $774,103
119	Closing Argument	2002 c.	Successful Appeal—Mrs. Greeley, by Mr. Greeley	USA	4-1-1-1, $565,000
	Perfect Drift	1999 g.	Dynaformer—Nice Gal, by Naskra	USA	8-2-1-3, $1,121,227
118	Super Frolic	2000 h.	Pine Bluff—Lindsay Frolic, by Mt. Livermore	USA	8-3-0-2, $818,160
117	Suave	2001 c.	A.P. Indy—Urbane, by Citidancer	USA	5-2-2-0, $624,900
116	Choctaw Nation	2000 g.	Louis Quatorze—Melisma, by Well Decorated	USA	7-1-0-2, $884,000
115	Dynever	2000 h.	Dynaformer—Flamboyance, by Zilzal	USA	3-0-3-0, $1,231,730
	Eddington	2001 c.	Unbridled—Fashion Star, by Chief's Crown	USA	5-3-0-2, $602,200
	Kane Hekili	2002 c.	Fuji Kiseki—Life Out There, by Deputy Minister	Jpn	9-7-1-0, $2,813,092
	Lundy's Liability (Brz)	2000 h.	Candy Stripes—Emerald Counter, by Geiger Counter	USA	3-1-0-0, $170,000

Mile, Three and Up, Dirt

Rating	Horse	YOB, Sex	Sire—Dam, Broodmare Sire	Trained	2005 Record, Earnings
128	Ghostzapper	2000 h.	Awesome Again—Baby Zip, by Relaunch	USA	1-1-0-0, $450,000
125	Saint Liam	2000 h.	Saint Ballado—Quiet Dance, by Quiet American	USA	6-4-1-0, $3,696,960
122	Rock Hard Ten	2001 c.	Kris S.—Tersa, by Mr. Prospector	USA	3-3-0-0, $1,080,000
120	Bellamy Road	2002 c.	Concerto—Hurry Home Hillary, by Deputed Testamony	USA	4-2-1-0, $671,000
119	Commentator	2001 g.	Distorted Humor—Outsource, by Storm Bird	USA	4-2-0-1, $529,400
118	Pleasant Home	2001 f.	Seeking the Gold—Our Country Place, by Pleasant Colony	USA	8-3-2-2, $1,316,420
117	Ashado	2001 f.	Saint Ballado—Goulash, by Mari's Book	USA	7-3-1-1, $1,061,000
116	Roman Ruler	2002 r.	Fusaichi Pegasus—Silvery Swan, by Silver Deputy	USA	5-2-1-1, $890,000
115	Bandini	2002 c.	Fusaichi Pegasus—Divine Dixie, by Dixieland Band	USA	5-3-1-0, $564,000
	Buzzards Bay	2002 c.	Marco Bay—Lifes Lass, by Seneca Jones	USA	8-2-0-2, $630,031
	Consolidator	2002 c.	Storm Cat—Good Example (Fr), by Crystal Glitters	USA	3-1-0-0, $181,500
	Lundy's Liability (Brz)	2000 h.	Candy Stripes—Emerald Counter, by Geiger Counter	USA	3-1-0-0, $170,000
	Sweet Catomine	2002 f.	Storm Cat—Sweet Life, by Kris S.	USA	3-2-0-0, $259,800

Sprint, Three and Up, Dirt

Rating	Horse	YOB, Sex	Sire—Dam, Broodmare Sire	Trained	2005 Record, Earnings
119	Lost in the Fog	2002 c.	Lost Soldier—Cloud Break, by Dr. Carter	USA	9-8-0-0, $844,500
	Silver Train	2002 c.	Old Trieste—Ridden in Thestars, by Cormorant	USA	7-3-0-3, $693,255
118	Taste of Paradise	1999 h.	Conquistador Cielo—Tastetheteardrops, by What Luck	USA	8-1-1-2, $605,000
116	Forest Danger	2001 c.	Forestry—Starry Ice, by Ice Age	USA	4-2-0-0, $263,400

Cartier Awards

Established in 1991, the Cartier Awards are European racing's closest equivalent to the Eclipse Awards. Winners are determined by points earned in pattern races and votes of racing experts and Daily Telegraph *readers.*

Award of Merit

2005 Henry Cecil
2004 David and Patricia Thompson
2003 Lord John Oaksey
2002 Khalid Abdullah
2001 John Magnier
2000 Aga Khan
1999 Peter Walwyn
1998 Head family
1997 Sir Peter O'Sullevan
1996 Frankie Dettori
1995 John Dunlop
1994 Lord Hartington
1993 Francois Boutin
1992 Lester Piggott
1991 Henri Chalhoub

Horse of the Year

2005 Hurricane Run
2004 Ouija Board (GB)
2003 Dalakhani
2002 Rock of Gibraltar (Ire)
2001 Fantastic Light
2000 Giant's Causeway
1999 Daylami (Ire)
1998 Dream Well (Fr)
1997 Peintre Celebre
1996 Helissio
1995 Ridgewood Pearl (GB)
1994 Barathea (Ire)
1993 Lochsong (GB)
1992 User Friendly (GB)
1991 Arazi

Millennium Award of Merit

2000 Queen Elizabeth II

Two-Year-Old Filly

2005 Rumplestiltskin
2004 Divine Proportions
2003 Attraction
2002 Six Perfections (Fr)
2001 Queen's Logic
2000 Superstar Leo
1999 Torgau (Ire)
1998 Bint Allayl
1997 Embassy (GB)
1996 Pas de Reponse
1995 Blue Duster
1994 Gay Gallanta
1993 Lemon Souffle (GB)
1992 Lyric Fantasy (Ire)
1991 Culture Vulture

Two-Year-Old Colt

2005 George Washington
2004 Shamardal
2003 One Cool Cat
2002 Hold That Tiger
2001 Johannesburg
2000 Tobougg (Ire)
1999 Fasliyev
1998 Aljabr
1997 Xaar
1996 Bahamian Bounty
1995 Alhaarth
1994 Celtic Swing
1993 First Trump
1992 Zafonic
1991 Arazi

Three-Year-Old Filly

2005 Divine Proportions
2004 Ouija Board (GB)
2003 Russian Rhythm
2002 Kazzia (Ger)
2001 Banks Hill (GB)
2000 Petrushka (Ire)
1999 Ramruma
1998 Cape Verdi (Ire)
1997 Ryafan
1996 Bosra Sham
1995 Ridgewood Pearl (GB)
1994 Balanchine
1993 Intrepidity (GB)
1992 User Friendly (GB)
1991 Kooyonga (Ire)

Three-Year-Old Colt

2005 Hurricane Run
2004 Bago
2003 Dalakhani
2002 Rock of Gibraltar (Ire)
2001 Galileo (Ire)
2000 Sinndar
1999 Montjeu (Ire)
1998 Dream Well (Fr)
1997 Peintre Celebre
1996 Helissio
1995 Lammtarra
1994 King's Theatre (Ire)
1993 Commander in Chief
1992 Rodrigo de Triano
1991 Suave Dancer

Stayer

2005 Westerner
2004 Westerner
2003 Persian Punch
2002 Vinnie Roe
2001 Persian Punch
2000 Kayf Tara
1999 Kayf Tara
1998 Kayf Tara
1997 Celeric
1996 Nononito
1995 Double Trigger
1994 Moonax
1993 Vintage Crop
1992 Drum Taps
1991 Turgeon

Sprinter

2005 Avonbridge
2004 Somnus
2003 Oasis Dream (GB)
2002 Continent
2001 Mozart (Ire)
2000 Nuclear Debate
1999 Stravinsky
1998 Tamarisk
1997 Royal Applause (GB)
1996 Anabaa (Ire)
1995 Hever Golf Rose (GB)
1994 Lochsong (GB)
1993 Lochsong (GB)
1992 Mr Brooks (GB)
1991 Sheikh Albadou (GB)

Older Horse

2005 Azamour (Ire)
2004 Soviet Song
2003 Falbrav (Ire)
2002 Grandera
2001 Fantastic Light
2000 Kalanisi (Ire)
1999 Daylami (Ire)
1998 Swain (Ire)
1997 Pilsudski (Ire)
1996 Halling
1995 Further Flight
1994 Barathea (Ire)
1993 Opera House (GB)
1992 Mr Brooks (GB)
1991 Terimon

Special Award

2002 Tony McCoy
1994 Vincent O'Brien

Lord Derby Awards

Presented by the British Horserace Writers and Photographers Association for overall excellence.

Service to International Racing

2003 Khalid Abdullah
2002 Nick Clarke
2001 Pam Blatz-Murff
2000 Aga Khan
1999 Michael Osborne
1998 James E. "Ted" Bassett III
1997 Geoffrey Gibbs
1996 Flying Grooms
1995 Maj. Gen. Guy Watkins
1994 Robert Sangster
1993 Francois Boutin
Niarchos family
1992 Maktoum family
1991 John Dunlop
1990 Louis Romanet
1989 Michael Byrne
1988 Richard Duchossois
1987 Yves Saint-Martin
1986 John Gaines
1985 Lord Derby
1984 Ivan Straker
1983 Paul Mellon
1982 Jean Romanet
1981 Joe Hirsch

Outstanding Achievement Award
(George Ennor Trophy)

2005 Peter Sayer
2004 Peter Willett
2003 Pat Eddery
2002 Ian Balding
2001 Graham Rock
2000 Johnny Murtagh
1999 Peter Walwyn
1998 Capt. Tim Forster
1997 Sir Peter O'Sullevan
1996 Peter Easterby
1995 Lester Piggott
1994 Vincent O'Brien
1993 Dermot Weld

Outstanding Achievement Award
(President's Trophy)

2005 Reg Hollinshead
2004 George Ennor
2003 Lord John Oaksey
2002 Not awarded

2001 John Reid
2000 Ray Cochrane
1999 Jack Berry
1998 Not awarded
1997 Maj. Dick Hern
1996 Not awarded
1995 Jim Old Stable staff

International Trainer of the Year

2005 Andrew Balding
2004 Ed Dunlop
2003 Pascal Bary
2002 Demot Weld
2001 Aidan O'Brien
2000 Saeed bin Suroor
1999 Saeed bin Suroor
1998 Saeed bin Suroor
1997 Sir Michael Stoute
1996 Sir Michael Stoute
1995 Peter Chapple-Hyam
1994 John Dunlop
1993 John Dunlop
1992 Paul Cole
1991 Paul Cole
1990 Paul Cole
1989 Henry Cecil
1988 Luca Cumani
1987 Paul Cole
1986 Michael Stoute
1985 Clive Brittain
1984 Ian Balding
1983 Luca Cumani
1982 John Dunlop
1981 Ian Balding

Owner of the Year

2005 Graham Wylie
2004 Lord Derby
2003 Jim Lewis
2002 Sir Alex Ferguson
2001 Susan Magnier
Michael Tabor
2000 Aga Khan
1999 Michael Tabor
1998 The Summit Partnership
1997 Peter Winfield
1996 Godolphin Racing
1995 Godolphin Racing
1994 Jeff Smith
1993 Robert Sangster
1992 Bill Gredley
1991 Prince Fahd Salman
1990 Sheikh Hamdan bin Rashid al Maktoum
1989 Sheikh Hamdan bin Rashid al Maktoum
1988 Jim Joel
1987 Louis Freedman
1986 Khalid Abdullah
1985 Lord Howard de Walden
1984 Eric Moller
1983 Robert Barnett
1982 Paul Mellon
1981 Aga Khan
1980 Pat Muldoon
1979 Snailwell Stud
1978 David McCall
1977 Queen Elizabeth II
1976 Daniel Wildenstein
1975 Carlo Vittadini
1974 Peter O'Sullevan
1973 Louis Freedman
1972 Lady Beaverbrook
1971 John and Jean Hislop
1970 Charles Engelhard and David McCall
1969 Earl of Rosebery
1968 Lord Allendale
1967 Jim Joel

Trainer of the Year

2005 Michael Bell
2004 Saeed bin Suroor
2003 Sir Michael Stoute
2002 Mark Johnston
2001 Aidan O'Brien
2000 John Oxx
1999 Henry Cecil
1998 Saeed bin Suroor
1997 Sir Michael Stoute
1996 Henry Cecil
1995 John Dunlop
1994 Mark Johnston
1993 Richard Hannon
1992 Richard Hannon
1991 Paul Cole
1990 Jack Berry
1989 Maj. Dick Hern
1988 David Chapman
1987 Henry Cecil
1986 Sir Michael Stoute
1985 Henry Cecil
1984 Roy Sheather
1983 John Dunlop
1982 David Chapman
1981 Guy Harwood
1980 Maj. Dick Hern
1979 Henry Cecil
1978 Michael Stoute
1977 Vincent O'Brien
1976 Henry Cecil
1975 Maj. Dick Hern
1974 Peter Walwyn
1973 Arthur Budgett
1972 Bruce Hobbs
1971 Ian Balding
1970 Vincent O'Brien
1969 Harvey Leader
1968 Sir Cecil Boyd-Rochfort
1967 Sir Noel Murless

Jockey of the Year

2005 Jamie Spencer
2004 Frankie Dettori
2003 Kieren Fallon
2002 Richard Hughes
2001 Michael Kinane
2000 Kevin Darley
1999 Richard Quinn
1998 Kieren Fallon
1997 Kieren Fallon
1996 Frankie Dettori
1995 Frankie Dettori
1994 Frankie Dettori
1993 Kevin Darley
1992 Michael Roberts
1991 Alan Munro
1990 Frankie Dettori
1989 Willie Carson
1988 Michael Roberts
1987 Steve Cauthen
1986 Pat Eddery
1985 Steve Cauthen
1984 Steve Cauthen
1983 Willie Carson
1982 Lester Piggott
1981 Lester Piggott
1980 Lester Piggott
1979 Joe Mercer
1978 Greville Starkey
1977 Willie Carson
1976 Brian Taylor
1975 Joe Mercer
1974 Pat Eddery
1973 Tony Murray
1972 Edward Hide
1971 Willie Carson
1970 Lester Piggott
1969 Geoff Lewis
1968 Sandy Barclay
1967 Doug Smith

National Hunt Owner of the Year (Awarded 1969-'73)

1973 Noel le Mare
1972 Mrs. John Rogerson
1971 Col. Bill Whitbread
1970 Bryan Jenks
1969 Edward Courage

National Hunt Trainer of the Year

2005 Paul Nicholls
2004 Henrietta Knight
2003 Philip Hobbs
2002 Henrietta Knight
2001 Martin Pipe
2000 Noel Chance
1999 Paul Nichols
1998 Martin Pipe
1997 Martin Pipe
1996 Jim Old
1995 Kim Bailey
1994 David Nicholson
1993 Nigel Twiston-Davies
1992 Mary Reveley
1991 Martin Pipe
1990 Martin Pipe
1989 Martin Pipe
1988 David Elsworth
1987 Nicky Henderson
1986 Nicky Henderson
1985 Capt. Tim Forster
1984 Jenny Pitman
1983 Michael Dickinson
1982 Michael Dickinson
1981 Peter Easterby
1980 Peter Easterby
1979 Peter Easterby
1978 Fred Winter
1977 Peter Easterby
1976 Tony Dickinson
1975 Gordon Richards
1974 Donald "Ginger" McCain
1973 Fulke Walwyn
1972 David Barons
1971 Fred Winter
1970 Arthur Stephenson
1969 Colin Davies
1968 Fred Rimell

National Hunt Jockey of the Year

2005 Ruby Walsh
2004 Tony McCoy
2003 Tony McCoy
2002 Tony McCoy
2001 Tony McCoy
2000 Tony McCoy
1999 Tony McCoy
1998 Tony McCoy
1997 Tony McCoy
1996 Tony McCoy
1995 Norman Williamson

1994 Aidrian Maguire
1993 Richard Dunwoody
1992 Peter Niven
1991 Peter Scudamore
1990 Peter Scudamore
1989 Peter Scudamore
1988 Chris Grant
1987 Peter Scudamore
1986 Peter Scudamore
1985 John Francome
1984 John Francome
1983 John Francome
1982 Peter Scudamore
1981 Bob Champion
1980 Jonjo O'Neil
1979 Tommy Carmody
1978 Jonjo O'Neill
1977 Tommy Stack
1976 Jeff King
1975 Tommy Stack
1974 Richard Pitman
1973 Ron Barry
1972 Bob Davies
1971 Graham Thorner
1970 Terry Biddlecombe
1969 Stan Mellor
1968 Brian Fletcher
1967 Josh Gifford

Stable Staff of the Year

2005 Steve Kingstree, Ernie Peterson
2004 Jock Brown, Brian Clothworthy, Ian Wilder
2003 Albert "Corky" Browne
Johnny Worrall
Dennis Wright
2002 Tom Townsend
Dave Goodwin
2001 Rodney Boult
Peter Maughan
Jimmy Scott
2000 George Charlton
John Smillie
1999 Rachel Hume
Robynne Watton
1998 Michael Leaman
Geoff Snook
1997 Jack Nelson
Eddie Watt
1996 Harry Buckle
1996 Ian Willows
1995 Sidney Outen
John Sayers
1994 Vicki Harris
Ron Thomas
1993 John Cullen
Geoff Thompson
1992 Johnny East
Bill Palmer
1991 Harvey Ewart
Steven Rose
1990 Steve Fox
Colin Nutter
1989 Brian Delaney
Meg MacDonald
1988 Peter Heaney
Kevin Murrell
1987 Alison Dean
1986 Glyn Foster
1985 Jimmy Swales
1984 Syd McGahey
1983 Raymond Campbell
1982 Linda McCauley
1981 Olga Nicholson
1980 Alan Welborne
1979 Jack Kidd
1978 Nigel Atkinson
1977 John Hallum
1976 Mervyn Heath
1975 John Vickers

Journalist of the Year
(Clive Graham Trophy)

2005 Richard Edmondson (*The Independent*)
2004 Alan Lee *(The Times)*
2003 Clare Balding (BBC and *Evening Standard*)
Doug Moscrop (Newcastle *Journal*)
2002 Tom O'Ryan (*Racing Post*)
2001 Alan Lee (*The Times*)
2000 Alan Amies (Raceform)
1999 Alastair Down (*Racing Post*)
1998 Claude Duval (*The Sun*)
1997 Rodney Masters (*Racing Post*)
1996 David Ashforth (*Sporting Life*)
1995 Richard Evans (*The Times*)
1994 Alastair Down (*Sporting Life*)
1993 Paul Haigh (*Racing Post*)
1992 Jim McGrath (*Daily Telegraph*)
1991 John Sexton (Wolverhampton *Express and Star*)
1990 Tony Morris (*Racing Post*)
1989 Michael Seely (*The Times*)
1988 Geoff Lester (*Sporting Life*)
1987 Peter Goodall (Press Association)
1986 Peter O'Sullevan (BBC)
1985 Jim Stanford (*Daily Mail*)
1984 John Sharratt (Raceform)
1983 Bill Garland (Press Association)
1982 George Ennor (*Sporting Life*)
1981 Jonathan Powell (*Sunday People*)
1980 Michael Seely (*The Times*)
1979 Christopher Poole (*Evening Standard*)
1978 Tim Richards (*Daily Mirror*)
1977 Brough Scott (*Sunday Times*)
1976 Peter Willett (*Sporting Chronicle*)
1975 Peter Scott (*Daily Telegraph*)
1974 Tom Cosgrove (London *Evening News*)
1973 Richard Baerlein (*The Guardian/Observer*)
1972 Roger Mortimer (*Sunday Times*)
1971 Clive Graham (*Daily Express*)
Peter O'Sullevan (*Daily Express*)
1970 George Stevens (Birmingham *Post & Mail*)
1969 Geoffrey Hamlyn (*Sporting Life*)
1968 John Lawrence (*Daily Telegraph*)
1967 Quintin Gilbey (*Sporting Chronicle*)

Photographer of the Year

2005 Bill Selwyn (freelance)
2004 Dan Abraham (freelance)
2003 Ed Whitaker (*Racing Post*)
2002 Ed Whitaker (*Racing Post*)
2001 Anne Grossick (freelance)
2000 John Grossick (freelance)
1999 Ed Whitaker (*Racing Post*)
1998 Alec Russell (freelance)
1997 Mark Cranham (freelance)

Broadcaster of the Year
(Sir Peter O'Sullevan Trohy)

2005 Robert Cooper (Attheraces)
2004 Clare Balding (BBC)

Major International Racetracks

Argentina

Argentino de Palermo

Located in the Palermo district close to downtown Buenos Aires and familiarly known as Palermo, Hipodromo Argentino opened on May 7, 1876. Originally a Standardbred facility offering just one Thoroughbred race daily, the track changed to full-time Thoroughbred racing on August 18, 1883, and was the first racetrack in Argentina to feature a totalizator. A sales pavilion, veterinary hospital and laboratory, equine institute, and museum complement the racetrack, which is home of the Gran Premio Nacional (Arg-G1), Argentina's equivalent of the Kentucky Derby (G1) and third race of the Argentine Triple Crown. Two of its most famous winners were *Yatasto in 1951 and *Forli in '66. Another major stakes race is the Polla de Potrillos (Arg-G1) (Argentine Two Thousand Guineas), the first race of the Triple Crown, in September. Racing is held over a 2,410-meter,* left-handed track with three chutes. (*See conversion table from metric to English distances in Reference section.)

Location: Ave. Del Libertador 4101, Capital Federal, Buenos Aires
Phone: 541 (47) 782-800
Fax: 541 (47) 746-807
Website: *www.palermo.com.ar*
E-Mail: mail@palermo.com.art
Abbreviation: HAr
Principal Races: Comparacion (Arg-G1), Criadores (Arg-G1), De Honor (Arg-G1), De las Americas-Internacional (Arg-G1), Jorge de Atucha (Arg-G1), Nacional (Arg-G1), Polla de Potrancas (Arg-G1), Polla de Potrillos (Arg-G1), Santiago Luro (Arg-G1), Seleccion (Arg-G1)

La Plata

The first racetrack in Argentina to hold evening race cards, Hipodromo de La Plata opened on September

14, 1884. Situated approximately 35 miles south of Buenos Aires, the track is in the city of La Plata in the province of Buenos Aires. The track's proximity to a railway station makes it easily accessible by public transportation. The left-handed, elliptical dirt track is 2,000 meters (9.94 furlongs, or approximately 1¼ miles) with two chutes. As many as 145 racing dates are held annually.

Location: La Plata, Pica de Buenos Aires
Phone: 541 (21) 211-071
Fax: 541 (21) 42-390
Abbreviation: LP
Principal Races: Dardo Rocha Internacional (Arg-G1), Joachin V. Gonzalez Internacional (Arg-G1), Ciudad de La Plata Internacional (Arg-G1), Seleccion de Potrancas (Arg-G1)

San Isidro

Located 14 miles north of Buenos Aires on the edge of the Pampas, San Isidro Racecourse was founded on December 8, 1935, by the Jockey Club Argentino. San Isidro hosts the Gran Premio Carlos Pellegrini-Internacional (Arg-G1), the country's most important race, which is the final leg of the San Isidro Triple Crown. *Yatasto won the Carlos Pellegrini in 1952 before a record crowd of 104,810. *Forli accomplished the feat in 1966 and was then imported to the United States. A daily card consists of as many as 14 races, which begin in midafternoon and conclude at night under lights. Two overlapping, left-handed turf courses—the main one is 2,783 meters—have three chutes.

Location: 504 Avenue Marquez, San Isidro 1642
Phone: 54 (11) 4743-4010
Website: *www.hipodromosanisidro.com.ar*
E-Mail: jchsi@overnet.com.ar
Abbreviation: SI
Principal Races: 25 de Mayo (Arg-G1), Carlos Pellegrini-Internacional (Arg-G1), Copa de Oro (Arg-G1), De Potrancas (Arg-G1), Estrellas Sprint (Arg-G1), Estrellas Distaff (Arg-G1), Estrellas Junior Sprint (Arg-G1), Estrellas Juvenile Fillies (Arg-G1), Estrellas Sprint (Arg-G1), Felix de Alzaga Unzue-Internacional (Arg-G1), Gran Criterium (Arg-G1), Jockey Club (Arg-G1)

Australia

Ascot

Located along the Swan River in the heart of Perth, capital city of Western Australia, Ascot features the Perth Cup (Aus-G2), first contested in 1879. In 1982, the track underwent a major renovation. It has a left-handed course of 2,000 meters with a 300-meter straight. Three different chutes are used to start Ascot's three major races: the Perth Cup, the Western Australian Turf Club Derby (Aus-G1) at 2,400 meters, and the Railway Stakes (Aus-G1) at 1,600 meters.

Location: 70 Grandstand Road, Ascot, WA 6104
Phone: 61 (08) 9277-0888
Fax: 61 (08) 9277-0710
Website: *www.waturf.org.au*
E-Mail: perthracing@perthracing.org.au
Abbreviation: AsR
Chairman: E. Van Heemst
Chief Executive: Alasdair Robertson
Principal Races: Railway S. (Aus-G1), West Australian Turf Club Derby (Aus-G1), Perth Cup (Aus-G2)

Canterbury

Canterbury Racecourse, located approximately seven miles southwest of Sydney's central business district, is easily accessible by public transportation and offers ample free parking. Its intimate, 1,600-meter track affords spectators a close view of the 34 race cards conducted annually by the Sydney Turf Club. Racing is usually held on Thursday evenings, with occasional Saturday-evening programs, including the beginning of the rich Autumn Golden Slipper Festival. Programs of eight to ten races are held on the right-handed turf course. In July 2002, Sydney Turf Club officials announced that the Canterbury facility would not be sold for development. The 1,800-meter Canterbury Guineas (Aus-G1) for three-year-olds is the track's top race.

Location: King Street, Canterbury, NSW 2193
Phone: 61 (02) 9930-4000
Fax: 61 (02) 9930-4096
Website: *www.stc.com.au*
E-Mail: sydturf@stc.com.au
Abbreviation: Cby
Chairman: Alan Brown
Vice Chairman: Bill Picken
Chief Executive: Michael T. Kenny
Principal Races: Canterbury Guineas (Aus-G1)

Caulfield

Situated about five miles southeast of Melbourne, Caulfield Racecourse has a rich history that traces to August 5, 1876. In 1996, the Melbourne Racing Club (formerly the Victoria Amateur Turf Club) widened the track to 30 meters around the entire circumference and lengthened the straight by 43 meters. Affectionately known as "the Heath," Caulfield is home to the Caulfield Carnival each spring, which features three major stakes: the 2,400-meter Caulfield Cup (Aus-G1), the 1,600-meter Caulfield Guineas (Aus-G1) for three-year-olds, and the 1,600-meter Vinery Australia Thousand Guineas (Aus-G1) for three-year-old fillies. The Autumn Carnival offers Victoria's richest race for two-year-olds, the AAMI Blue Diamond Stakes (Aus-G1) at 1,200 meters. Caulfield stages 20 dates of racing during the year.

Location: P.O. Box 231, 22 Station Street, Caulfield, Victoria 3145
Phone: 61 (3) 9257-7200
Fax: 61 (3) 9257-7210
Website: *www.melbourneracingclub.net.au*
E-Mail: contact@melbourneracingclub.net.au
Abbreviation: Cau
Chairman: Peter Young
Chief Executive: Warran Brown
General Manager: Simon Gardiner
Director of Racing: Jason Kerr
Director of Marketing: Mary Morton
Principal Races: Blue Diamond Stakes (Aus-G1), Caulfield Cup (Aus-G1), Caulfield Guineas (Aus-G1), Underwood Stakes (Aus-G1), Vinery Australia Thousand Guineas (Aus-G1)

Doomben

Doomben Track, formerly the Doomben Park Recreation Grounds Ltd., was opened in 1933 by the Brisbane Amateur Turf Club, which subsequently changed its name to the Brisbane Turf Club. Called the "Garden Racecourse," Doomben was used as a base by United States troops during World War II. The track underwent an extensive renovation in 1982 and now hosts 40 race dates, 25 of them on Saturdays, each year. Its major races include the Doomben 10,000 Stakes (Aus-G1), formerly the T. M. Ahern Memorial Stakes, and the Doomben Cup (Aus-G1) at 2,200 meters. Another highlight is the six-day Winter Racing Carnival. Doomben is adjacent to Eagle Farm Racecourse, the principal track in Brisbane, Queensland's capital. The track is approximately four miles from Brisbane's central business district and a short distance from Brisbane Airport.

Location: P.O. Box 168, Hamilton Central, Queensland 4007
Phone: 61 (07) 3268-6800
Fax: 61 (07) 3868-1281
Website: *www.doomben.com*
E-Mail: admin@doomben.com
Abbreviation: Doo
Chairman: Ian McGrath
Chief Executive Officer: Sean Kelk
Principal Races: Doomben 10,000 Stakes (Aus-G1), Doomben Cup (Aus-G1)

Eagle Farm

Located on the northern side of Brisbane in Ascot, Eagle Farm boasts a long history and excellent equine facilities. Its racing started on August 14, 1865, under the Queensland Turf Club, which was founded in 1863 by a group of 53 sportsmen. The training facilities include two turf tracks, a wood-fiber track, a sand track, two exercise rings, and an equine swimming pool. The main turf track is approximately 2,026 meters with a single chute. Horses race clockwise and must navigate a slight uphill climb heading for the finish line. During World War II, Eagle Farm was used as a military base by both Australian and United States troops. For those five years, the Queensland Turf Club held race meetings at Albion Park.

Location: P.O. Box 21, Hamilton Central, Queensland 4007
Phone: 61 (07) 3268-2171
Fax: 61 (07) 3868-2410
Website: *www.qtc.org*
E-Mail: info@qtc.org
Abbreviation: EF
Principal Races: Brisbane Cup (Aus-G1), Queensland Derby (Aus-G1), Queensland Oaks (Aus-G1), Sires' Produce S. (Aus-G1), Stradbroke H. (Aus-G1), The T. J. Smith S. (Aus-G1)

Flemington

A breathtaking course with Melbourne's skyline as a backdrop, Flemington has staged racing since 1840, and the Melbourne Cup (Aus-G1), its famed stakes race at about two miles on the first Tuesday of November, is regarded as a national holiday. On the morning of the Melbourne Cup, a service held at St. Francis's Church is followed by a carnival on Burke Street, Melbourne's central thoroughfare. Up to 100,000 spectators fill Flemington on Melbourne Cup day to celebrate the stakes first run in 1861. The winner of the first Melbourne Cup, Archer, was reported to have walked more than 500 miles from his stable in New South Wales to enter the race. In 1930, *Phar Lap won the race after surviving an attempt on his life while training at Flemington. He was hidden in the ensuing days, arrived at the track just minutes before post time, and won the race in a canter. The legendary runner is honored by a bronze statue outside an entrance to the track. Flemington also holds the Victoria Derby (Aus-G1), first run in 1855 and the oldest established race in Australia. The left-handed, 2,300-meter turf course has a 1,200-meter straight chute.

Location: 400 Epsom Road, Flemington, Victoria 3031
Phone: 61 (130) 072-7575
Website: *www.vrc.net.au*
E-Mail: customerservice@vrc.net.au
Abbreviation: Fle
Chairman: R. M. Fitzroy
Vice Chairman: Peter Barnett
Principal Races: Australian Cup (Aus-G1), Australian Guineas (Aus-G1), MacKinnon S. (Aus-G1), Lightning S. (Aus-G1), Melbourne Cup (Aus-G1), Sires' Produce S. (Aus-G1), Victoria Derby (Aus-G1)

Moonee Valley

Located less than four miles from central Melbourne, Moonee Valley was founded by William Samuel Cox in 1883. The Cox Plate (Aus-G1), Australia's most important weight-for-age race, is run at Moonee Valley one week before the Melbourne Cup at Flemington. First run in 1922, the Cox Plate was won by *Phar Lap in '30 and '31. In a historic running of the Cox Plate in 1986, Bonecrusher edged fellow New Zealand champion Our Waverley Star by a neck. Moonee Valley offers a wide range of amenities, including a 1,000-seat dining room, glass-enclosed dining boxes, 20 bars, and electronic gaming machines, which were added in 1992. The 1,800-meter, left-handed course is more rectangular than oval, with very sharp turns and short straights, putting a high premium on agility and speed. It is intersected by a diagonal straight course. Inside the main course are hurdle and steeplechase courses.

Location: McPherson Street, Moonee Ponds, Victoria 3039
Phone: 61 (130) 079-7959
Fax: 61 (03) 9326-0090
Website: *www.mvrc.net.au*
E-Mail: customerservice@mvrc.net.au
Abbreviation: Moo
Principal Races: Manikato S. (Aus-G1), W. S. Cox Plate (Aus-G1)

Morphettville

Located along the Anzac Highway in Adelaide, South Australia, Morphettville is operated by the South Australian Jockey Club. Founded in 1860, Morphettville holds its principal meet in May, when it stages the South Australian Derby (Aus-G1), the South Australian Oaks (Aus-G1), and the Adelaide Cup (Aus-G1). The 2,300-meter course has a short straight of nearly 400 meters. The track's grandstand was razed in 1976 and replaced by a modern facility, and a multimillion-dollar renovation of the course itself was completed in 2002.

Location: P. O. Box 707, Anzac Highway and Morphett Road, Morphettville, Adelaide, SA 5043
Phone: 61 (88) 295-0111
Fax: 61 (88) 376-2099
Website: *www.sajc.com.au*
E-Mail: enquiries@sajc.com.au
Abbreviation: Mor
Ownership: South Australian Jockey Club
President: Peter Lewis
Vice President: John Naffine
Chief Executive: Steve Ploubidis
Principal Races: Adelaide Cup (Aus-G1), Goodwood Handicap (Aus-G1), Robert Sangster Stakes (Aus-G1), South Australian Derby (Aus-G1)

Rosehill Gardens

Located about 14 miles west of Sydney, Rosehill frequently is called Sydney's garden course and is home to Australia's premier race for two-year-olds, the 1,200-

meter Golden Slipper Stakes (Aus-G1), first contested in 1957. The beautifully landscaped track was constructed on Australia's most historic agricultural property, Elizabeth Farm, and major festivals are held in both the spring and autumn. The about 2,000-meter course features a 400-meter straight. Races of 1,200 meters (5.97 furlongs) start in the center of the course and traverse a long bend into the straight. Training facilities include Equitrack, grass, sand, and cinder training tracks with stabling available adjacent to the track.

Location: James Ruse Drive, P.O. Box 21, Rosehill, NSW 2142
Phone: 61 (29) 930-4000
Fax: 61 (29) 930-4099
Website: *www.stc.com.au*
E-Mail: sydturf@stc.com.au
Abbreviation: Roh
Chairman: Alan Brown
Vice Chairman: Bill Picken
President: Bruce William McHugh
Vice President: Alan Francis Brown
Chief Executive Officer: Michael T. Kenny
Principal Races: George Ryder S. (Aus-G1), Golden Slipper S. (Aus-G1), H. E. Tancred S. (Aus-G1), Rosehill Guineas (Aus-G1), Storm Queen/Arrowfield Stud S. (Aus-G1)

Royal Randwick

Home of the Australian Jockey Club, Randwick has conducted racing since 1860, when the club relocated from Homebush. The inaugural running of the Australian Jockey Club St. Leger (Aus-G2) was held in 1841 at Homebush but was moved to Randwick when the track opened. The first A.J.C. Derby (Aus-G1) was run in 1861. The Sydney Cup (Aus-G1) was first contested in April 1865. Randwick, which is close to Sydney, holds racing festivals in both the spring at the start of October and in the fall in April. The major stakes in the spring is the Metropolitan (Aus-G1) at 2,600 meters. The A.J.C. Derby, Doncaster Handicap (Aus-G1), and Queen Elizabeth Stakes (Aus-G1) are contested in the fall. Randwick's 2,218-meter course with four chutes circles an infield lake and is considered one of the most demanding in Australia.

Location: Alison Road, Randwick, NSW 2031
Phone: 61 (29) 663-8400
Fax: 61 (29) 662-6292
Website: *www.ajc.org.au*
E-Mail: ajcfeedback@ajc.org.au
Abbreviation: Ran
Chairman: David Hall
Vice Chairman: Noel Bracks
Chief Executive Officer: Tony King
Principal Races: A.J.C. Australian Derby (Aus-G1), A.J.C. Australian Oaks (Aus-G1), Champagne S. (Aus-G1), Doncaster H. (Aus-G1), Sires' Produce S. (Aus-G1), Spring Champion S. (Aus-G1), Sydney Cup (Aus-G1)

Victoria Park

Founded in 1788, Victoria Park is the South Australian capital city of Adelaide's second-oldest racetrack and the largest track in the country. Located less than a mile from the city center in the Adelaide City Parklands, Victoria Park has two turf courses, one 2,361 meters in circumference with a 601-meter straight, and an inner course of 1,961 meters with a 479-meter straight. Known as "the Course of Natural Beauty," the track also has a 1,000-meter straight. Victoria Park stages the Adelaide Guineas (Aus-G3), among other stakes races. Each December, it is host to Christmas Twilight, a race program that benefits the South Australia Variety Club.

Location: Wakefield Street and Fullarton Road, Rose Park, Adelaide, SA 5001
Phone: 61 (88) 223-5466
Fax: 61 (88) 223-4669
Website: *www.sajc.com.au*
E-Mail: enquiries@sajc.com.au
Year Founded: 1888
Abbreviation: VP
Ownership: South Australian Jockey Club
President: Peter Lewis
Vice President: John Naffine
Chief Executive: Steve Ploubidis
Principal Races: Adelaide Guineas (Aus-G3)

Warwick Farm

Warwick Farm Racecourse, operated by the Australian Jockey Club, is located about 18 miles from Sydney and is renowned for its picnic atmosphere. Racing is conducted on an oblong, 1,937-meter oval with a straight of just 326 meters. The track has a chute for races between 1,000 and 1,400 meters, and it also has two short chutes for 1,600-meter and 2,400-meter races. Front-runners tend to do well because of Warwick Farm's sharp turns, which can force late closers very wide. The track opened in 1925 and resumed racing in '52 after being closed through World War II. Its J.M.B. Carr Grandstand was built in 1982.

Location: Hume Highway, Warwick Farm, Sydney NSW 2031
Phone: 61 (29) 602-6199
Fax: 61 (29) 821-2150
Website: *www.ajc.org.au*
Abbreviation: WF
Chairman: David Hall
Vice Chairman: Noel Bracks
Chief Executive: Tony King
Principal Races: Chipping Norton Stakes (Aus-G1), George Main Stakes (Aus-G1)

Brazil

Cidade Jardim

Just minutes from downtown Sao Paulo, Cidade Jardim offers year-round turf and dirt racing on left-handed courses. Cidade Jardim opened on January 25, 1941, after Brazilian racing officials decided that Mooca, the track in the center of Sao Paulo, was too small and too crowded. Today, Cidade Jardim is a sprawling facility that houses many important Brazilian racing authorities, including the Stud-Book Brazileiro. Cidade Jardim's main turf course is an about 2,000-meter oval with a dirt course of about 1,800 meters. Cidade Jardim also encompasses a training center with two dirt training tracks, a stud farm, and an exhibition center for cultural and scientific activities.

Location: Sao Paulo
Phone: 55 (11) 2161-8300
Website: *www.jockeysp.com.br*
Abbreviation: CJ
Principal Races: Consagracao (Brz-G1), Derby Paulista (Brz-G1), Diana (Brz-G1), Jockey Club de Sao Paulo (Brz-G1), Organizacao Sulamericana de Fomento ao Puro Sangue de Corrida (Brz-G1), Oswaldo Aranha (Brz-G1), Presidente da Republica (Brz-G1), Sao Paulo (Brz-G1)

La Gavea

With the Statue of Christ the Redeemer atop Corcovado Mountain in Rio de Janeiro serving as a dramatic backdrop, La Gavea is located adjacent to Lake Rodrigo de Freitas. An outer, 2,120-meter turf course rings a 2,036-meter dirt track with two separate turns out of the home straight. Though racing was conducted in Brazil as early as 1825, betting was not allowed until '72. In that year, the Jockey Club Brazileiro was formed, which led to the opening of La Gavea. La Gavea's spring season in October and November features the Gran Premio Linneo de Paula Machado (Brz-G1), among other stakes. Racing is held year-round on Saturdays and Sundays.

Location: Rio de Janeiro
Phone: 55 (21) 2512-9988
Website: *www.jcb.com.br*
E-Mail: internetjcb@jcb.com.br
Abbreviation: Gav
Principal Races: Proprietarios do Cavalo de Corrida (Brz-G1), Brasil (Brz-G1), Cruzeiro do Sul (Brz-G1), Diana (Brz-G1), Jockey Club Brasileiro (Brz-G1), Linneo de Paula Machado (Brz-G1), Presidente da Republica (Brz-G1)

Taruma

Located ten minutes from downtown Curitiba, a city of 2.3-million people that is the capital of the state of Parana, Taruma races year-round under the ownership of Jockey Club do Parana. Opened on December 2, 1873, Taruma has an 1,800-meter course. Its biggest race, the 2,400-meter Gran Premio International Parana (Brz-G1), is run in December.

Location: Avenue Victor Ferreira Do Amaral, Curitiba Parana
Phone: 55 (41) 366-2121
Abbreviation: Tma
Chairman: Cesar de Paula ou Alessandro Reichel
Principal Races: Gran Premio International Parana (Brz-G1)

Chile

Club Hipico de Santiago

Lush, beautiful, and close to the center of Santiago, Club Hipico de Santiago encompasses more than 200 acres and is full of gardens, lakes, tennis courts, and fountains. Members of the Chilean bourgeoisie created Club Hipico in 1869, and its first race was run on September 20, 1870. Club Hipico is home to the oldest stakes race in South America, the El Ensayo (Chi-G1), first run in 1873 for three-year-old colts and fillies. The track stages as many as 16 races a day, usually on Mondays and Thursdays in January, February, and March, and on Sundays during other months.

Location: Avenida Blanco Encalada, Santiago
Phone: 56 (2) 693-9600
Fax: 56 (2) 683-7074
Website: *www.clubhipico.cl*
Abbreviation: CDS
Principal Races: Club Hipico de Santiago (Chi-G1), El Ensayo (Chi-G1), Las Oaks (Chi-G1), Polla de Potrancas (Chi-G1), Polla de Potrillos (Chi-G1)

Hipodromo Chile

Founded in 1904 by a group of 19 breeders, owners, and trainers, Hipodromo Chile is located ten minutes north of Santiago and near the Comodo Merino Benitez Airport. Racing is conducted on every other Wednesday and every Saturday year-round on a 1,645-meter, left-handed dirt track. A nearby sales complex, conducting two-year-olds in training sales in the spring and fall, complement the racing.

Location: 1715 Avenue Hipodromo Chile, Independencia, Santiago 02753
Phone: 56 (2) 270-9237
Fax: 56 (2) 777-2089
Website: *www.hipodromo.cl*
E-Mail: sugerencias@hipodromochile.cl
Abbreviation: HC
President: Juan Cuneo Solari
General Manager: Luis I. Salas
Vice President: Orlando Mercado Labbe
Executive Director: Luis Solar Feuereisen
Principal Races: Dos Mil Guineas (Chi-G1), Gran Criterium (Chi-G1), Gran Premio Hipodromo Chile (Chi-G1), Mil Guineas (Chi-G1), St. Leger (Chi-G1)

Vina del Mar

Hipodromo de Vina del Mar is operated by the Valparaiso Sporting Club. Thirteen to 17 dates are held annually on Wednesdays and Fridays, and races range from 800 meters to 2,400 meters. The two main turf courses and dirt training track can accommodate 600 horses. El Derby (Chi-G1), the third race of the Chilean Triple Crown, is contested at 2,400 meters (11.93 furlongs) on turf.

Location: Los Castanos 404, Vina Del Mar
Phone: 56 (3) 265-5610
Fax: 56 (3) 265-5691
Website: *www.sporting.cl*
E-Mail: sporting@sporting.cl
Abbreviation: Val
Principal Races: Copa de Plata Italo Traverso (Chi-G1), El Derby (Chi-G1)

England

Aintree

Located a short distance from Liverpool, Aintree is home to the world's best-known steeplechase race, the Grand National, a 4½-mile marathon in early April over 30 tall, testing fences. The Grand National was first run at Aintree in 1839, when the striking bay Lottery won the third running of a race known then as the Grand Liverpool Steeplechase, which had been held at another site in its first two years.

In the 1990s, animal-rights protests forced the taming of the 2¼-mile Grand National course's more terrifying fences. Most notable was the filling of Becher's Brook, named for Captain Martin Becher, who fell at its tall fence and tumbled into the creek after his mount allegedly was impeded by Lottery. The Chair, one of two obstacles on the 16-fence course that are jumped only once, stands 5'2" tall, and its landing side is higher than the takeoff side. As many as 40 horses can start in the Grand National, but often only a handful of horses complete the race.

Location: Ormskirk Road, Aintree, Liverpool L9 5AS
Phone: 44 (151) 523-2600
Fax: 44 (151) 522-2920
Website: *www.aintree.co.uk*
E-Mail: aintree@rht.net
Abbreviation: Ain
General Manager: Charles Barnett
Operations Manager: Zoe Greenall
Principal Races: Grand National Steeplechase

Ascot

Host of the traditional Royal Meeting in June as well as racing throughout the year in both National Hunt and flat divisions, Ascot is owned by Queen Elizabeth II. Queen Anne marked out the course in Windsor Park, and racing began there in August 1711. The National Hunt course was added in 1965. The Royal Meeting begins with the queen and her royal party driving down the straight mile in horse-drawn carriages to the applause of the crowd, with the men sporting top hats and morning suits and the women wearing elegant hats. Traditionally, the first race is the Queen Anne Stakes (Eng-G1), and the races that follow offer a wide variety of competition from sprinters to stayers. No Ascot race is more demanding than the 2½-mile Ascot Gold Cup (Eng-G1), first run in 1807. The St. James's Palace Stakes (Eng-G1), the King George VI and Queen Elizabeth Stakes (Eng-G1), the King Edward VII Stakes (Eng-G2), the Queen Elizabeth II Stakes (Eng-G1), the Coronation Stakes (Eng-G1) for fillies, and the Meon Valley Stud Fillies' Mile (Eng-G1) are among Ascot's most definitive events. The flat course at Ascot is a right-handed triangular oval of 1¾ miles with two mile chutes. Ascot, which was previously held in a private trust, underwent a $347-million renovation beginning in 2002 and, after closing in September '04, reopened in '06.

Location: Ascot Racecourse, Berkshire SL5 7JX
Phone: 44 (870) 722-7227
Fax: 44 (870) 460-1248
Website: *www.ascot.co.uk*
E-Mail: enquiries@ascot.co.uk
Abbreviation: Asc
Chairman: Duke of Devonshire CBE
Chief Executive: Douglas Erskine-Crum
Director of Operations: Ronnie Wilkie
Commercial and Finance Director: Janet Walker
Other Officials: Directors: Mark Davies, Johnny Weatherby, John Varley, Simon Murray
Principal Races: Coronation S. (Eng-G1), Gold Cup S. (Eng-G1), King George VI and Queen Elizabeth S. (Eng-G1), Prince of Wales's S. (Eng-G1), Queen Elizabeth II S. (Eng-G1), St. James's Palace S. (Eng-G1)
Ascot Redevelopment: Ascot closed for 20 months at the end of September 2004 to embark on its $347-million redevelopment and was scheduled to reopen for the 2006 Royal Meeting.

Cheltenham

Located in the Cotswolds in west-central England, Cheltenham is a stunning racecourse that is host each March to the National Hunt Festival, which features the Cheltenham Gold Cup and Champion Hurdle Stakes, championship races for their respective divisions. The 2001 Cheltenham festival was canceled because of the foot-and-mouth disease outbreak that winter, but in most years the festival is standing-room only. The first Gold Cup was held in 1819 as a three-mile flat race on Cleeve Hill, which overlooks the current course. When crowds grew to 50,000, a grandstand was constructed, but it was torn down when an antigambling sentiment swept the area in the 1820s. Racing was re-established at the current site in Prestbury Park in 1831, but no racing was conducted there from the 1840s through the '90s. Barry Bingham purchased the course, refurbished it, built a new grandstand and running rails, and launched the festival in 1902 as a two-day event. A third day was added in 1923, and a fourth day was inaugurated in 2005. The Gold Cup was reinstituted in 1924, and three years later the Champion Hurdle was added. Cheltenham has separate left-handed steeplechase and hurdle courses, with a testing, uphill run to the finish post. Among the heroes of Cheltenham are Dorothy Paget's Golden Miller, who won five consecutive runnings of the Gold Cup (1932-'36), and trainer Michael Dickinson, who saddled the first five finishers in the 1983 Gold Cup.

Location: Prestbury Park, Cheltenham, Gloucestershire GL50 4SH
Phone: 44 (124) 251-3014
Fax: 44 (124) 222-4227
Website: *www.cheltenham.co.uk*
E-Mail: cheltenham@rht.net
Abbreviation: Chm
Ownership: Racecourse Holdings Trust
Chairman: Lord Vestey
General Manager: Edward W. Gillespie
Principal Races: Champion Hurdle S., Cheltenham Gold Cup

Doncaster

Home of the final race of the English Triple Crown, the St. Leger Stakes (Eng-G1) in September, Doncaster has hosted racing since 1776. Doncaster runs flat and jump races on separate courses. The pear-shaped, left-handed main course is nearly two miles in circumference. The St. Leger meeting begins with the filly version of the St. Leger Stakes, the Park Hill Stakes (Eng-G3). The Doncaster Cup (Eng-G3), first run in 1766 and the oldest race still run by the Jockey Club, the Champagne Stakes (Eng-G2), May Hill Stakes (Eng-G3), and the Flying Childers Stakes (Eng-G2) for two-year-olds precede the St. Leger, the oldest of the English classics and named for popular local sportsman Lt. Col. Anthony St. Leger. Winners of the St. Leger Stakes include Hambletonian in 1795, Champion (the first horse to win the Epsom Derby and St. Leger Stakes) in 1800, and West Australian, who became the first Triple Crown winner 53 years later. Nijinsky II became the most recent English Triple Crown winner in 1970. The Racing Post Trophy Stakes (Eng-G1) is Doncaster's most significant juvenile race.

Location: The Grandstand, Leger Way, South Yorkshire, Doncaster DN2 6BB
Phone: 44 (130) 230-4207
Fax: 44 (130) 232-3271
Website: *www.doncaster-racecourse.com*
E-Mail: info@doncasterracing.co.uk
Year Founded: 1776
Abbreviation: Don
Ownership: Doncaster Metropolitan Borough Council
Chairman: Councillor Bill Mordue
General Manager: Steven Clarke
Principal Races: Racing Post Trophy S. (Eng-G1), St. Leger S. (Eng-G1), Champagne S. (Eng-G2)

Epsom Downs

Thoroughbreds have been racing at Epsom, 15 miles south of London in Surrey, for more than 350 years. In 1648, a party of Royalists held races there, and the first recorded race meet was in 1661 on Banstead Downs, which is part of Epsom Downs. The jewel of the racing year is the Epsom Derby (Eng-G1), which traditionally had been run on the first Wednesday in June but now has been moved successfully to the Saturday five weeks after the Two Thousand Guineas (Eng-G1) at Newmarket on the first Saturday of May or, less commonly, the last Saturday in April. First run in 1780, one year after the initial running of the Epsom Oaks (Eng-G1), the 1½-mile

Derby is the middle leg of the English Triple Crown. Epsom has other important stakes during its season, with meets beginning in April and concluding in September of each year. The major races include the Coronation Cup (Eng-G1) and the Diomed Stakes (Eng-G3). The course features a downhill run to the final turn, the world-famous Tattenham Corner, and an uphill pull to the finish.

Location: The Racecourse, Epsom Downs, Surrey KT18 5LQ
Phone: 44 (137) 272-6311
Fax: 44 (137) 274-8253
Website: *www.epsomderby.co.uk*
E-Mail: epsom@rht.net
Abbreviation: Eps
General manager: Stephen H. Wallis
Principal Races: Coronation Cup (Eng-G1), Epsom Derby (Eng-G1), Epsom Oaks (Eng-G1)

Goodwood

Located amid rolling countryside on Sussex Downs 60 miles southwest of London, Goodwood traces its history to the Duke of Richmond, who first hosted racing on his estate in 1802. The fifth Duke of Richmond improved the quality of racing at Goodwood by making it part of the English social circuit, a task made easier by the development of a railroad network to transport horses and racegoers to the estate. The about one-mile Sussex Stakes (Eng-G1), the about two-mile Goodwood Cup (Eng-G2), the six-furlong Richmond Stakes (Eng-G2), and the 1¼-mile Nassau Stakes (Eng-G1) for fillies and mares are the major races of the annual July meeting, though racing is also held in May, June, August, and October. Goodwood also is host to the Celebration Mile Stakes (Eng-G2) at the end of August. Goodwood has a skewered figure-eight, right-handed course with a six-furlong straight that allows horses to finish in front of Goodwood's restaurant atop the grandstand.

Location: Goodwood, Chichester, West Sussex PO18 0PX
Phone: 44 (124) 375-5022
Fax: 44 (124) 375-5025
Website: *www.goodwood.co.uk/horseracing*
E-Mail: racing@goodwood.co.uk
Year Founded: 1802
Abbreviation: Goo
Ownership: Goodwood Estate Co. Ltd.
President: Duke of Richmond
General Manager: Rod Fabricius
Press and Public Relations Director: Kathryn Bellamy
Principal Races: Nassau S. (Eng-G1), Sussex S. (Eng-G1)

Haydock Park

Located north of Liverpool, Haydock Park Racecourse was created as a successor to the nearby Old Golborne Heath course, home of the Newton Races, which flourished in the 1750s. Haydock conducted its first race in 1899. Haydock's 1⅝-mile track has a tight top bend, and the Sprint Cup Stakes (Eng-G1) is staged each September. A new grandstand was completed in 1982.

Location: Newton-Le-Willows, Merseyside WA12 0HQ
Phone: 44 (194) 272-5963
Fax: 44 (194) 227-0879
Website: *www.haydock-park.co.uk*
E-Mail: haydockpark@rht.net
Abbreviation: Hay
Chairman: W. T. Whittle
Chief Executive: Adam Waterworth
Principal Races: Haydock Sprint Cup S. (Eng-G1)

Kempton Park

Located a 35-minute train ride from Waterloo Station, Kempton Park advertises itself as "London's Racecourse," and it is nine miles south of Heathrow Airport. Built by S. H. Hyde, Kempton Park conducted its first race meet in July 1878. During World War II, the track housed German prisoners of war, and racing resumed in 1947. The track's major race is the King George VI Chase on Boxing Day, December 26, each year, and it also stages flat race meets during the year. In 2006, Kempton transformed itself into a night-time all-weather track for flat racing while retaining its steeplechase fixtures on turf.

Location: Staines Road East, Sunbury, Middlesex TW16 5AQ
Phone: 44 (193) 278-2292
Fax: 44 (193) 278-2044
Website: *www.kempton.co.uk*
E-Mail: kempton@rht.net
Abbreviation: Kem
Managing Director: Julian Thick
Clerk of the Course: Brian Clifford

Lingfield Park

Set on 300 acres in the Surrey countryside south of London, Lingfield Park is one of Great Britain's most modern racetracks, featuring year-round flat racing on its all-weather artificial-surface track.

Owned by Arena Leisure, Lingfield was the first of England's all-weather tracks, but its Equitrack surface increasingly drew complaints. In late 2001, the racecourse replaced Equitrack with Polytrack, a synthetic surface composed of polypropylene, polyester, Lycra, silica sand, and rubber, covered by a wax coating. The surface, which cost $4.2-million, has been praised by jockeys and trainers. The all-weather track is 1¼-miles around, with a quarter-mile stretch and a quarter-mile chute for 1½-mile races. Lingfield also has a 1¼-mile, left-handed turf course with a 3½-furlong run-in and a 1⅝-mile steeplechase course.

Location: Lingfield Park Racecourse, Lingfield, Surrey RH7 6PQ
Phone: 44 (134) 283-2833
Fax: 44 (134) 283-5874
Website: *www.lingfield-racecourse.co.uk*
E-Mail: info@lingfieldpark.co.uk
Year Founded: 1890
Abbreviation: Lin
Ownership: Arena Leisure
Executive Director: Ian Renton
General Manager: Clive Stephens
Principal Races: Derby Trial S. (Eng-G3), Oaks Trial, Winter Derby, Spring Cup

Newbury

Located west of London, Newbury has its own railway station just yards from the attractive left-handed racecourse. The course measures more than 1¾ miles with a slightly undulating straight mile ideal for galloping.

Fifteen days of flat racing extend from April through October, and steeplechase meets are conducted during the colder months. Its major flat races include the one-mile Juddmonte Lockinge Stakes (Eng-G1), and its premier race over fences is the Hennessy Cognac Gold Cup.

Newbury, which opened in 1905, resulted from a chance meeting between well-known trainer John Porter and King Edward VII. It quickly became known as one of the country's best courses, but the course has been pressed into other duties during wartime. Newbury was requisitioned during World War I and was used for troops, supplies, tank testing and repair, and as a prisoner of war camp. In World War II, the track became a major American base and prisoner of war camp.

Racing resumed on April 1, 1949, and now features elegant surroundings, including a sky-lighted "Long Bar" overlooking the track on the first floor and 41 private boxes. The New Grandstand, which opened in 2000, features several exhibition spaces as well as conference rooms for up to 1,000 delegates. The course also features an 18-hole, par 71 golf course and a 20-bay driving range. A leisure center with a swimming pool and gymnasium also are on the property.

Location: The Racecourse, Newbury, Berskhire RG14 7NZ
Phone: 44 (16) 354-0015
Fax: 44 (16) 355-28354
Website: *www.newbury-racecourse.co.uk*
E-Mail: info@newbury-racecourse.co.uk
Abbreviation: Nby
Chairman: Sir David Sieff
General Manager: Mark Kershaw
Principal Races: Juddmonte Lockinge S. (Eng-G1)

Newmarket

Newmarket is the headquarters of British racing, and its racecourse is a fitting complement to the training gallops to the east of the course. An observer once said: "Newmarket is one of the only places where a man can go racing; elsewhere he merely goes to the races, which isn't the same thing at all." Racing has been held at Newmarket, a Suffolk town 60 miles northeast of London, for more than 350 years. Newmarket's racing spans the entire British flat season, with the spring season featuring the year's first classics, the Two Thousand Guineas (Eng-G1) and One Thousand Guineas (Eng-G1), down its Rowley Mile Course, usually on the first weekend in May. In the fall, the Champion Stakes (Eng-G1), Cheveley Park Stakes (Eng-G1), Middle Park Stakes (Eng-G1), and Dewhurst Stakes (Eng-G1) are contested across the flat, a 1¼-mile straight that includes the Rowley course. Longer races, such as the rich Cesarewitch Handicap over 2¼ miles, require the use of a ten-furlong extension of the Rowley Mile in a backward, L-shape configuration that extends through the ancient "Devil's Dike." Between those spring and fall events, racing is conducted on the July Course, a straight that connects to the Rowley course. The July Cup (Eng-G1) is the major July stakes. Though Charles I decided Newmarket would be an ideal place to race his horses, his son, Charles II, created the course and the straight mile derives its name from his nickname, "Old Rowley." In 1665, he founded the Newmarket Town Plate, a race that is still contested in a different form. With its uphill finish and no turns, Newmarket provides a severe test of stamina.

Location: Westfield House, The Links, Newmarket, Suffolk CB8 0TG
Phone: 44 (163) 866-3482
Fax: 44 (163) 866-3044
Website: *www.newmarketracecourses.co.uk*
E-Mail: newmarket@rht.net
Year founded: 1664
Abbreviation: New
Ownership: Racecourse Holdings Trust
Chairman: Richard Hambro
General Manager: Lisa Hancock
Principal Races: Champion S. (Eng-G1), Cheveley Park S. (Eng-G1), Dewhurst S. (Eng-G1), July Cup S. (Eng-G1), One Thousand Guineas S. (Eng-G1), Two Thousand Guineas S. (Eng-G1)

Sandown Park

Only 14 miles south of central London, Sandown Park opened in 1875 and was the first totally enclosed racecourse in the country. The course was the brainchild of Lt. Col. Owen Williams, and his brother, Hwfa (pronounced "Hoofer"), was instrumental in Sandown Park's development, serving as chairman and clerk of the course for 50 years. The grandstand, rebuilt in 1973 for approximately $5-million, sits on a hill overlooking the racecourse. The right-handed, 1⅝-mile course includes a downhill run to the back straight and a substantial uphill pull to the homestretch. A five-furlong, uphill straight course runs through the main course. Sandown Park's major stakes race is the 1¼-mile Eclipse Stakes (Eng-G1) in July. It was first run in 1886 and, at the time, was the country's richest stakes race. In the spring, Sandown features the Whitbread Gold Cup, the National Hunt season's final major race over steeplechase fences. Flat racing is held in short meets from late April through the beginning of October. A $33.4-million renovation of the grandstand was completed in early 2002.

Location: Portsmouth Road, Esher, Surrey KT10 9AJ
Phone: 44 (137) 246-4348
Fax: 44 (137) 246-1334
Website: *www.sandown.co.uk*
E-Mail: sandown@rht.net
Abbreviation: San
Ownership: Racecourse Holdings Trust
Chief Executive: Andrew Coppell
General Manager: Steve Brice
Principal Races: Eclipse S. (Eng-G1)

York

Referred to by many as England's Ascot of the North, York is home to the popular Ebor Festival in mid-August at the Knavesmire, common land 20 minutes from the city of York that has featured racing since 1731. The wide horseshoe-shaped, two-mile, unenclosed course has a 4½-furlong straight after a left-handed turn. Two separate chutes are used for sprints of six and seven furlongs. York came to prominence in 1767 when the Gimcrack Club was founded to honor the champion Gimcrack, who won 26 races between 1764 and '71. The club members organized the York meeting to attract the best horses to the North, and by the 1840s the August meeting featured the Ebor Handicap, Yorkshire Oaks (Eng-G1), and the Gimcrack Stakes (Eng-G2). The Nunthorpe Stakes (Eng-G1) was added in 1903. In 1851, one of the most famous match races in Turf history pitted Epsom Derby winners The Flying Dutchman and Voltigeur, who had inflicted the former's only loss the previous year in the Doncaster Cup. More than 100,000 fans turned out to see the rematch, won by The Flying Dutchman. More than a century later, the Benson & Hedges Gold Cup (Eng-G1), now known as the Juddmonte International Stakes, was created to match two champions of the 1970s, Mill Reef and Brigadier Gerard. Mill Reef broke down before the race, but John Galbreath's Epsom Derby (Eng-G1) victor Roberto handed Brigadier Gerard his only career defeat and set a course record.

Location: The Racecourse, York, North Yorkshire YO23 1EX
Phone: 44 (190) 462-0911
Fax: 44 (190) 461-1071
Website: *www.yorkracecourse.co.uk*
E-Mail: enquiries@yorkracecourse.co.uk
Year Founded: 1731
Abbreviation: Yor
Chairman: N.H.T. Wrigley
Chief Executive and Clerk of the Course: William Derby
Principal Races: Aston Upthorpe Yorkshire Oaks (Eng-G1), Juddmonte International S. (Eng-G1), Nunthorpe S. (Eng-G1), Gimcrack S. (Eng-G2)

France

Chantilly

Racing at Chantilly, a village approximately 20 miles north of Paris, is held every June in front of the palatial Les Grandes Ecuries (literally, "the big stables") and the Chateau de Chantilly. The palatial stables were built by the Prince de Conde, who believed he would be reincarnated as a horse. The estate includes a lavish stable that can house 250 horses. Chantilly, surrounded by woods, lakes, and 250 acres of greenery, also serves as France's principal training center, with as many as 100 trainers and 3,000 horses using its sand, all-weather, and turf training tracks. Chantilly's premier races are the 2,100-meter Prix du Jockey-Club (Fr-G1), first run in 1836 and popularly known as the French Derby, for three-year-olds, and the 2,100-meter (10.44-furlong) Prix de Diane (Fr-G1) (French Oaks) for three-year-old fillies, begun in '41.

Location: 16 Avenue du General Leclerc, BP 90209, Chantilly 60631
Phone: 33 (34) 462-4100
Fax: 33 (34) 457-3489
Abbreviation: Chy
Chief Executive: Matthieu Vincent
Principal Races: Prix de Diane (Fr-G1), Prix du Jockey-Club (Fr-G1), Prix Jean Prat (Fr-G1)

Deauville

Deauville, sometimes referred to as the Saratoga of France, held its first meet in 1864, the same year as Saratoga Race Course's first meet. It runs a short meeting in August, as Saratoga did for decades, and also features a major sale of yearlings, as does Saratoga. Deauville was founded by the Duke of Morny to cater to Parisian society vacationing on the Normandy coast. The setting allows horses to gallop on the beach or in the surf. There is also polo in the afternoons and the casino in the evenings for entertainment, as well as several first-rate restaurants. Deauville offers a top-class, 1,600-meter stakes, the Prix du Haras de Fresnay-le-Buffard Jacques Le Marois (Fr-G1), and the 1,200-meter Prix Morny (Fr-G1) for two-year-olds. Deauville is a right-handed course of 2,200 meters with a 1,600-meter chute on one end and a short chute on the other. Another major stakes, the Grand Prix de Deauville (Fr-G2), is held on the last Sunday of the meeting.

Location: 45 Avenue Hocquart de Turtot, BP 43300, Deauville 14800
Phone: 33 (23) 114-2000
Fax: 33 (23) 114-2001
Website: *www.hippodromesdedeauville.com*
Abbreviation: Dea
Chief Executive: Yves Deshayes
Principal Races: Prix du Haras de Fresnay-le-Buffard Jacques le Marois (Fr-G1), Prix Maurice de Gheest (Fr-G1), Prix Morny (Fr-G1)

Longchamp

Emperor Napoleon III traveled by boat on the Seine River to attend Longchamp's first day of racing on April 27, 1857, and he was joined at the Paris track by nearly 10,000 countrymen. Finishing second in the first of five races that afternoon was Miss Gladiator, the dam of Gladiateur, who became a legend as the first French-bred horse to win the Epsom Derby. For Gladiateur's first start after the English classic, 150,000 racegoers turned out to watch him win the Grand Prix de Paris (now a Group 1 race) at Longchamp.

But the race for which Longchamp is best known is the Prix de l'Arc de Triomphe (Fr-G1), first contested in 1920. Horses from both England and Italy took on France's best, and the first winner was Comrade, owned and bred by Frenchman Evremond de Saint-Alary, trained in England by Peter Gilpin, and ridden by Australian jockey Frank Bullock. The 2,400-meter race on the first Sunday in October was an instant international success and became Europe's championship race.

Other Longchamp stakes have longer histories. The Grand Prix de Paris was inaugurated in 1863 and for a century was France's most important race for three-year-olds. Following the modern trend, its distance was reduced from 3,000 meters to 2,000 meters in 1987. It was lengthened again to 2,400 meters in 2005. The first classics of each year, the 1,600-meter Poule d'Essai des Poulains (Fr-G1) (French Two Thousand Guineas) and Poule d'Essai des Pouliches (Fr-G1) (French One Thousand Guineas) for three-year-olds and three-year-old fillies, respectively, are run in May. The Poule d'Essai des Poulains was first run in 1840, while the Poule d'Essai des Pouliches debuted in '83. Longchamp's right-handed course has a long and testing homestretch with a slightly uphill finish.

Location: Route des Tribunes, Bois de Boulogne, Paris 75116
Phone: 33 (14) 430-7500
Fax: 33 (14) 430-7599
Abbreviation: Lch
Chief Executive: Christian Delporte
Principal Races: Grand Prix de Paris (Fr-G1), Poule d'Essai des Poulains (Fr-G1), Poule d'Essai des Pouliches (Fr-G1), Prix de l'Arc de Triomphe (Fr-G1), Prix du Moulin de Longchamp (Fr-G1), Prix Ganay (Fr-G1), Prix Marcel Boussac (Fr-G1)

Maisons-Laffitte

Secluded near the Saint-Germain forest just west of Paris and home to some 1,800 Thoroughbreds conditioned by more than 80 trainers, Maisons-Laffitte offers one of Europe's most pleasant settings for Thoroughbred racing. Its 2,000-meter straight course, rivaled only by the Rowley Mile at Newmarket in England, is complemented by both right- and left-handed courses to accommodate 35 racing dates from the end of March until the end of July and from early September through early December.

The Prix Robert Papin (Fr-G2) is the first major stakes for two-year-olds each year, while other juvenile stakes, such as the Criterium de Maisons-Laffitte (Fr-G2), are run later in the meet. Among the course's top races for two-year-old fillies is the Prix Miesque (Fr-G3), named for the outstanding filly who won two North American championships with her triumphs in the 1987 and '88 Breeders' Cup Mile (G1).

Miesque won the Prix Imprudence at Maisons-Laffitte immediately before her victory in the 1987 One Thousand Guineas (Eng-G1). Among other champions who have raced at Maisons-Laffitte are *Sea-Bird, Nureyev, Arctic Tern, *Match II, Exbury, and Relko.

Set on more than 120 acres, Maisons-Laffitte is home to the Museum of the Racecourse, which was opened in 1990 and allows fans to review the history of racing by walking through magnificent rooms of an ancient castle.

Location: 1 Avenue de la Pelouse, Maisons-Laffitte 78602
Phone: 33 (13) 912-8170
Fax: 33 (13) 962-7608
Abbreviation: ML
Chief Executive: Martial de Rouffignac
Principal Races: Prix Robert Papin (Fr-G2), Prix Miesque (Fr-G3)

Saint-Cloud

The most frequently used Parisian track, Saint-Cloud hosts racing from February through July and from September through December. Its history extends to 1901 when the Societe du Demi-Sang was thrown out of Vincennes by the army and retreated to a strip of land owned by Edmond Blanc to continue racing. After World War I, the course was given to the Societe Sportive d'Encouragement, which supervised Thoroughbred racing at Maisons-Laffitte. The major stakes race at Saint-Cloud is the Grand Prix de Saint-Cloud (Fr-G1), which began in 1904 under the name Prix du President de la Republique. *Sea-Bird, fellow Arc winners Rheingold and Sagace (Fr), and Epsom Derby winners Relko and Teenoso all won races at Saint-Cloud, which also was the site of *Vaguely Noble's lone three-year-old defeat.

The 1,600-meter Criterium International (Fr-G1) was inaugurated in 2001 after the distance of the Grand Criterium (Fr-G1) at Longchamp was changed from 1,600 meters to 1,400 meters. Saint-Cloud's left-handed, 2,200-meter course is dissected by a 600-meter straight.

Location: 1 Rue du Camp Canadien, Saint-Cloud 92210
Phone: 33 (14) 771-6926
Fax: 33 (14) 771-3774
Abbreviation: StC
Chief Executive: Christian Leger
Principal Races: Criterium de Saint-Cloud (Fr-G1), Criterium International (Fr-G1), Grand Prix de Saint-Cloud (Fr-G1)

Germany

Baden-Baden

Set among the foothills of the Black Forest nine miles northwest of Baden-Baden, Baden-Baden Racecourse was the idea of Edouard Benazet, who offered visitors to the world-famous spa not only Thoroughbred racing but also a casino. When the casino closed in 1872, racing was taken over by the Internationale Club, which today supervises racing in short meets from May through June and from August through September. The nearby attractions include a casino, the vineyards of Rebland, Old Town, theaters, concerts, and elegant boutiques. Baden-Baden hosts the Grosser Preis von Baden (Ger-G1) and the Grosser Mercedes-Benz Preis (Ger-G2). The three overlapping, left-handed courses at Baden-Baden are named Old Course, New Course, and Straight Course.

Location: Lichtentaler Alley 8, Baden-Baden 76530
Phone: 49 (72) 291-870
Fax: 49 (72) 291-87344
Website: *www.baden-galopp.de*
E-Mail: club@baden-galopp.de
Abbreviation: Bad
Chairman: Hartmann Freiherr von Richthofen
Chief Executive: Klaus Zellman
Principal Races: Grosser Preis von Baden (Ger-G1)

Dusseldorf

Located in a hilly, wooded park on the edge of the Grafenberg Forest in Dusseldorf's Broich district, Dusseldorf Racecourse is the site of one of Germany's richest races, the Deutschland-Preis (Ger-G1), which is contested in late July. Other important stakes include the Henkel-Rennen (Ger-G2) (German One Thousand Guineas) in early May and the Grosser Preis von Dusseldorf (Ger-G3) in mid-October. The hilly, undulating, right-hand track features a sharp bend.

Location: Rennbahnstrasse 20, Dusseldorf 40629
Phone: 49 (21) 136-3466
Fax: 49 (21) 135-1752
Website: *www.duesseldorf-galopp.de*
E-Mail: info@duesseldorf-galopp.de
Abbreviation: Dus
Chairman: Peter Endres
General Manager: Bernd Koenemann
Principal Races: Deutschland-Preis (Ger-G1), Henkel-Rennen (Ger-G2), Grosser Preis von Dusseldorf (Ger-G3)

Hamburg

Hamburg is the home of the Deutsches Derby (Ger-G1), a 2,400-meter race for three-year-olds first contested in 1869 under the management of the Hamburger Renn-Club. Hamburg's other major stakes races are the Hansa-Preis (Ger-G2) at 2,100 meters, the Deutscher Herold-Preis (Ger-G3) at the same distance, and the 1,200-meter Holsten-Trophy (Ger-G3). The racetrack is about six miles from Hamburg and is accessible by the motorway from Berlin, subway, and bus. Racing is conducted from the end of June through early July on a right-handed turf course of approximately 2,000 meters.

Location: Rennbahnstrasse 96, Hamburg 22111
Phone: 49 (40) 651-8229
Fax: 49 (40) 655-6615
Website: *www.galopp-derby.de*
E-Mail: info@galopp-derby.de
Abbreviation: Hbg
Chairman: Eugen-Andreas Wahler
General Manager: Ilona Vollmers
Principal Races: Deutsches Derby (Ger-G1)

Koln

Situated in the Cologne neighborhood of Weidenpesch, Koln Racecourse is a flat, right-handed track with a 2½-furlong straight. Top stakes at Koln include the Europa-Preis (Ger-G1), the Gerling-Preis (Ger-G2), the Mehl-Mulhens-Rennen (Ger-G2) (German Two Thousand Guineas), and the Union-Rennen (Ger-G2).

Location: Rennbahnstr 152, Weidenpesch, Koln 50737
Phone: 49 (221) 974-5050
Fax: 49 (221) 974-5055
Website: www.koeln-galopp.de
E-Mail: kontakt@koeln-galopp.de
Abbreviation: Kol
Chairman: Baron Georg von Ullman
Chief Executive: Benedikt Fassbender
Principal Races: Europa-Preis (Ger-G1), Gerling-Preis (Ger-G2), Mehl-Mulhens-Rennen (Ger-G2) (German Two Thousand Guineas), and Union-Rennen (Ger-G2)

Mulheim

Located in western Germany, Mulheim is host to the country's longest flat race, the 3,400-meter Silbernes Band der Ruhr. Mulheim is a right-handed track with a 2½-furlong straight. The Preis der Diana-Deutsches Stuten-Derby (Ger-G1) (German Oaks) is contested in mid-June.

Location: Akazienallee 80-82, Mulheim Ruhr 45478
Website: *www.muelheim-galopp.de*
E-Mail: info@muelheim-galopp.de
Phone: 49 (20) 857-001
Fax: 49 (20) 857-005
Abbreviation: Mul
President: Dagmar Muhlenfeld
General Manager: Frank Pistel
Principal Races: Preis der Diana-Deutsches Stuten-Derby (Ger-G1)

Hong Kong

Happy Valley

Surrounded today by Hong Kong's skyscrapers, Happy Valley was built on reclaimed marshland and has held racing since 1846. Training horses is not easy on the 31-square-mile island, now under the control of the People's Republic of China, but the rich purses attract horsemen whose runners are housed in high-rise stables. Overshadowed by Sha Tin, Happy Valley conducts a 60-day racing season that lasts from September through June.

Location: 2 Sports Road, Happy Valley Island
Phone: 852 (2) 895-1523
Fax: 852 (2) 966-8111
Website: *www.happyvalleyracecourse.com*
Abbreviation: HV

Sha Tin

In 1959, Sir John Saunders, then chairman of the Royal Hong Kong Jockey Club, proposed creating a racetrack in Sha Tin Bay to alleviate overcrowding at Happy Valley. After three years of planning, the project of reclaiming 250 acres from the bay was begun. The soil needed for the project was taken from the top of one of the nearby mountains, which allowed development of that property and paid the track's construction costs.

Working round the clock on a tight, three-year schedule, Sha Tin opened as planned on October 7, 1978, with an expansive grandstand that encompasses 16½ acres. A 1,900-meter turf course encircles an all-weather dirt track. Sha Tin's major races are the Hong Kong Derby for four-year-olds, run every February at the start of the Chinese New Year since 1990, the Hong Kong Cup (HK-G1), the Hong Kong Vase (HK-G1), the Hong Kong Mile (HK-G1), and the Hong Kong Sprint (HK-G1).

Location: New Territories
Phone:852 (2) 695-6223
Website: *www.shatinracetrack.com*
E-Mail: shatinracing@hongkong.com
Abbreviation: ST
Chief Executive: Lawrence T. Wong
Principal Races: Hong Kong Cup (HK-G1), Hong Kong Mile (HK-G1), Hong Kong Sprint (HK-G1), Hong Kong Vase (HK-G1), Queen Elizabeth II Cup (HK-G1)

Ireland

Leopardstown

Roughly six miles from Dublin, Leopardstown overcame a troubled past. Nine years after its opening in 1888, the five-furlong course was found to be only 4½ furlongs long. Capt. George Quin, who headed a syndicate that had purchased the course, constructed a new five-furlong course that was not well received. Finally, Richard "Boss" Croker, owner of 1907 Irish Derby and Epsom Derby winner Orby, purchased additional land and a larger course was constructed. Leopardstown was owned by Fred Clarke until he sold the track to the Irish Racing Board in 1967. Two years later, Leopardstown received an extensive facelift, reopening in 1971 with a new grandstand, an enclosed betting hall, new dining and bar facilities, and a new stable area. Another renovation in 1988 extended the grandstand and added 16 private boxes. Race meets are held at Leopardstown from mid-March through mid-November over a left-handed turf course of about 2,800 meters. Leopardstown's premier race is the Irish Champion Stakes (Ire-G1).

Location: Leopardstown Racecourse, Foxrock, Dublin 00018
Phone: 353 (1) 289-0500
Fax: 353 (1) 289-2634
Website: *www.leopardstown.com*
E-Mail: info@leopardstown.com
Abbreviation: Leo
Chairman: Ged Pierse
Principal Races: Irish Champion S. (Ire-G1)

The Curragh

According to legend, St. Bridget was offered as much of the Curragh plain as she could cover with her cloak. Unfurling the cloak from her shoulder, she threw it to cover the whole plain of Kildare. When she gathered up her cloak, the land was covered in the richest and deepest grass imaginable—ideal for training and racing Thoroughbreds. Match races have been held there for centuries. The first recorded one was in 1634 when the Earl of Ormond beat Lord Digby in a four-mile race. The first race recorded at the Curragh was in 1741, and the first Irish Derby (Ire-G1) was held in 1866. By 1921, all five Irish classic stakes were contested at the Curragh. Joining the Derby were the Irish Oaks (Ire-G1), the Irish St. Leger (Ire-G1), the Irish Two Thousand Guineas (Ire-G1), and the Irish One Thousand Guineas (Ire-G1). Located 30 miles west of Dublin, the Curragh offers race meets from mid-March to the beginning of November. The horseshoe-shaped, right-handed course is two miles in length with an uphill, straight run-in of three furlongs to the finish line.

Location: Tara Court, Dublin Road Naas, Co. Kildare
Phone: 353 (4) 544-1205
Fax: 353 (4) 544-1442
Website: *www.curragh.ie*
E-Mail: info@curragh.ie
Abbreviation: Cur
Chairman: John McStay
General Manager: Paul Hensey
Principal Races: Irish Derby (Ire-G1), Irish Oaks (Ire-G1), Irish One Thousand Guineas (Ire-G1), Irish St. Leger (Ire-G1), Irish Two Thousand Guineas (Ire-G1), Moyglare Stud S. (Ire-G1), National S. (Ire-G1), Phoenix S. (Ire-G1), Tattersalls Gold Cup (Ire-G1)

Italy

Capannelle

Less than eight miles from the Colosseum in Rome, Capannelle opened in 1926. The grandstand, turf course, and interior dirt course are close to an ancient Roman aqueduct and are not far from St. Peter's Basilica in the Vatican. Race meets are held from March to mid-June and from September through November on right-handed turf and sand courses that are slightly uphill near the start and slightly downhill near the finish. National Hunt races also are conducted. Top stakes races include the Premio Presidente della Repubblica (Ity-G1) for four-year-olds and up, the Derby Italiano (Ity-G1) for three-year-olds, and the Premio Roma (Ity-G1) for three-year-olds and older. Capannelle's training facilities include 2,600-meter turf and dirt tracks, another turf course inside them, and a 1,200-meter sand track around the stabling area.

Location: Viaduct Appia Nuova 1255, Rome 00178
Phone: 39 (6) 716-771
Fax: 39 (6) 7167-7213
Website: *www.capannelle-galoppo.it*
E-Mail: capannel@tin.it
Abbreviation: Rom
President: Enzo Mei
Chief Executive: Tomaso Grassi
Principal Races: Derby Italiano (Ity-G1), Premio Presidente della Repubblica (Ity-G1), Premio Roma (Ity-G1)

San Siro

Racing began at San Siro in 1888 on a racecourse designed by architect Giulio Valerio. In 1909, a training center was added to the facility located just north of downtown Milan. Today, approximately 200 acres of training grounds include two turf tracks, two sand tracks, and a nearby all-weather track. San Siro's racecourse consists of three right-handed, overlapping turf courses of 2,800, 2,000, and 1,800 meters. Race meets are held from mid-March through July and from September to mid-November. Its premier races are the Oaks d'Italia (Ity-G1) for three-year-old fillies, the Gran Criterium (Ity-G1) for two-year-olds, and the Gran Premio di Milano (Ity-G1) and the Premio del Jockey Club (Ity-G1) for three-year-olds and up.

Location: Viaduct Ippodromo 100, Milan 20151
Phone: 39 (24) 821-6215
Fax: 39 (24) 820-1721
Website: *www.ippodromimilano.it*
Abbreviation: Mil
Chief Executive: Francesco Ruffo Scaletta
Principal Races: Gran Criterium (Ity-G1), Gran Premio di Milano (Ity-G1), Oaks d'Italia (Ity-G1), Premio di Capua V. (Ity-G1), Premio Jockey Club (Ity-G1)

Japan

Hanshin

The newest of the Japan Racing Association's four major tracks, Hanshin opened in 1949 and is about 12 miles from Osaka. Hanshin completed an extensive modernization in 1991 and races from March through June and in September and December. A lush, wide, right-handed turf course—slightly downhill in the backstretch and slightly uphill in the homestretch—encircles a dirt track.

On the second Sunday in April, Hanshin stages the 1,600-meter Oka Sho (Japan's equivalent of the one-mile One Thousand Guineas [Eng-G1]), named for the cherry blossoms in bloom at that time each year. Other major stakes include the all-age Grand Prix Takarazuka Kinen (Jpn-G1) in mid-June and the Hanshin Sansai Himba Stakes in early December for two-year-old fillies.

Location: 1-1 Komano-cho, Takarazuka-shi, Hyogo 665-0053
Phone: 81(79) 851-2000
Website: *www.jra.go.jp/english/races/hanshin.html*
Abbreviation: Hsn
Principal Races: Takarazuka Kinen (Jpn-G1), Oka Sho

Kyoto

Another of the major Japan Racing Association tracks, Kyoto Racecourse is located six miles south of Kyoto and stages racing in January, February, April, May, October, and November over a 1,900-meter, right-handed turf course that is uphill in the backstretch. Enclosed within the main course is a dirt course, an inner turf course, and a huge lake. A mammoth walking ring allows thousands of fans to see horses prepare for their race. The Spring Tenno Sho (Emperor's Cup) is a 3,200-meter endurance stakes for four-year-olds and older held on the last Sunday in April. In November, three major stakes are held on successive Sundays: the 3,000-meter Kikuka Sho (Japanese St. Leger) for three-year-olds, the final leg of the Japanese Triple Crown; the 2,400-meter Queen Elizabeth Cup, which is the concluding race of the Japanese filly triple crown; and the 1,600-meter Mile Championship.

Location: 32 Yoshijima, Watashibajimo-sho, Fushimi-ku, Kyoto 612-8265
Phone: 81 (79) 633-2000
Website: *www.jra.go.jp/english/races/kyoto.html*
Abbreviation: Kyo
Principal Races: Kikuka Sho, Mile Championship, Queen Elizabeth Cup, Spring Tenno Sho

Nakayama

Located 12 miles east of Tokyo, Nakayama Racecourse features two broad turf courses and a dirt course inside them. The outer course is 1,840 meters, and the inner grass course 1,667 meters. The dirt course is 1,493 meters. All three courses have a modest uphill run over the last 200 meters to the finish line. The track also has a steeplechase course in its infield. Among the racecourse's major races are the Arima Kinen, the Sprinters Stakes, and Satsuki Sho, which is Japan's equivalent of the Two Thousand Guineas for three-year-olds.

Location: 1-1-1 Kosaku, Funabashi-shi, Chiba 273-0037
Phone: 81 (47) 334-2222
Fax: 81 (47) 332-3327
Website: *www.jra.go.jp/english/races/nakayama.html*
Abbreviation: Nak
Principal Races: Arima Kinen, Satsuki Sho, Sprinters Stakes

Tokyo

Home of Japan's premier race, the Japan Cup (Jpn-G1), Tokyo Racecourse at Fuchu, 15 miles west of Tokyo, was built in 1933. Its 1,878-meter interior dirt course is based on the design of American courses but is uniquely fine-tuned to handle Japan's heavier precipitation. The track is packed firmly with a layer of mountain sand and covered with loose river sand, giving horses a strong bottom underneath and a surface on top to absorb impact and ease stress on their legs. The undulating turf course is 2,116 meters. The Japan Cup, which is run left-handed on turf at 2,400 meters, begins on a 400-meter straight run that minimizes the impact of poor post position. On the same weekend, the $2-million Japan Cup Dirt is run. The course underwent extensive renovations in 2002.

Location: 1-1 Hiyoshi-cho, Fuchu-shi, Tokyo 183-0024
Phone: 81 (42) 363-3141
Fax: 81 (42) 340-7070
Website: *www.jra.go.jp/english/races/tokyo.html*
Abbreviation: Tok
Principal Races: Japan Cup (Jpn-G1), Japan Cup Dirt

New Zealand

Avondale

Operated by the Avondale Jockey Club, which was formed in 1889, Avondale is located near Auckland and hosts 14 racing dates each year. The original left-handed course was just under a mile in circumference. It was enlarged to 1⅛ miles and converted to a right-handed course a few years later.

Location: 2-48 Ash Street, Avondale, Auckland 1230
Phone: 64 (09) 828-3309
Fax: 64 (09) 828-3099
E-Mail: admin@ajc.co.nz
Abbreviation: Avo
Secretary: Jim Patterson
Principal Races: Avondale Gold Cup H. (NZ-G1), Avondale Guineas (NZ-G1)

Ellerslie

Several of New Zealand's Group 1 races are held at Ellerslie, including the New Zealand Derby (NZ-G1) and the Easter Handicap (NZ-G1). The track, approximately five miles from New Zealand's largest city, Auckland, boasts an elegant grandstand and beautifully maintained grounds. Racing was first conducted about one mile from Ellerslie on January 5, 1842, but the present site was not used until May 25, 1874, a national holiday to observe Queen Victoria's birthday. Ellerslie's major stakes races are held from December 26 through January 2 and during the first week in June. The main track is a 1,870-meter, right-handed turf course with a finishing straight of 380 meters that is slightly downhill.

Location: 80 Ascot Avenue, Remuera, Auckland 1015
Phone: 64 (9) 524-4069
Fax: 64 (9) 524-8680
Website: *www.ellerslie.co.nz*
E-Mail: racing@ellerslie.co.nz
Abbreviation: Ell
Chairman: G. J. Clatworthy
Chief Executive: Chris Weaver
Director of Racing: Andrew Castles
Principal Races: Auckland Cup (NZ-G1), Easter H. (NZ-G1), Ellerslie Sires' Produce S. (NZ-G1), New Zealand Derby (NZ-G1)

Hawke's Bay

Racing dates back to 1845 at Hawke's Bay, located near the cities of Napier and Hastings on the eastern shore of New Zealand's northern island. The four racing clubs using the racetrack, however, did not unite until 1989. Now, 14 dates are conducted annually. The highlight of the year is the Spring Carnival, which is held over five weeks in August and September and features the Kelt Capital Stakes (NZ-G1), the richest weight-for-age race in New Zealand. The Hawke's Bay Cup Handicap (NZ-G2), the country's second-oldest race, was first contested in 1860.

Location: Prospect Road, Box 1046, Hastings
Phone: 64 (6) 873-4545
Fax: 64 (6) 6876-6488
Website: *www.hb-racing.co.nz*
E-Mail: comeracing@hb-racing.co.nz
Abbreviation: HB
Chairman: Peter Roebuck
Principal Races: Kelt Capital S. (NZ-G1), Hawke's Bay Gold Cup (NZ-G2), Mudgway PartsWorld Stakes (NZ-G2), Hawke's Bay Guineas (NZ-G3)

Otaki

Otaki Racecourse, located at the north end of Otaki on Kapiti island, has an 1,800-meter, left-handed track and is home of the Otaki-Maori Racing Club. Organized racing has been held at Otaki since the 1850s, and the Otaki-Maori Racing Club dates from 1866. In September 2000, the Levin Racing Club, Wellington Race Club, and Masterson Racing Club joined with the Otaki Maori Racing Club to form Capital Racing. The four clubs, each of which had been facing financial difficulties before the 2000 agreement, combine to run 27 days a year at Otaki, which is easily accessible by railroad from Wellington, at the southern tip of New Zealand's northern island. The WFA Stakes (NZ-G1) is staged there.

Location: P.O. Box 13, Otaki
Phone: 64 (6) 364-8078
Fax: 64 (6) 364-8079
Website: *www.otakimaoriracing.co.nz*
E-Mail: otaki_maorirc@xtra.co.nz
Abbreviation: Oki
President: Stephen Moffatt
Principal Races: WFA Stakes (NZ-G1)

Riccarton Park

The Canterbury Jockey Club was formed in 1854, and the following year began racing at Riccarton Park Racecourse, which is located ten minutes from the center of Christchurch, New Zealand's second-largest city, on the southern island. Among the races held at Riccarton are the New Zealand Two Thousand Guineas (NZ-G1), New Zealand One Thousand Guineas (NZ-G1), and the New Zealand Cup Handicap (NZ-G2).

Location: Racecourse Road, Riccarton, Christchurch
Phone: 64 (3) 333-0000
Fax: 64 (3) 342-6114
Website: *www.riccartonpark.co.nz/cjc*
E-Mail: enquiries@riccartonpark.co.nz
Abbreviation: Ric
Chief Executive: Tim Mills
Principal Races: New Zealand One Thousand Guineas (NZ-G1), New Zealand Two Thousand Guineas (NZ-G1), New Zealand Cup Handicap (NZ-G2)

Te Rapa

Located north of Hamilton on New Zealand's northern island, Te Rapa Racecourse is operated by the Waikato Racing Cup and conducts 18 days of racing annually. Flat racing is conducted on a left-handed, 1,800-meter track with two chutes. Te Rapa has an expansive galloping track, tree-lined paddocks, and a large grandstand. Among its major races are the Waikato Draught Sprint Stakes (NZ-G1), Whakanui Stud International Stakes (NZ-G1), and the Cambridge Stud Sir Tristram Fillies Classic Stakes (NZ-G2).

Location: P.O. Box 10050, Te Rapa, Hamilton
Phone: 64 (7) 849-8807
Fax: 64 (7) 849-1211
Website: *www.waikatoracing.co.nz*
E-Mail: info@waikatoracing.co.nz
Abbreviation: TeR
Chairman: David Smith
Vice Chairman: Peter McCowan
General Manager: A. C. Enting
Principal Races: Waikato Draught Sprint Stakes (NZ-G1), Whakanui Stud International (NZ-G1), Cambridge Stud Sir Tristram Fillies Classic Stakes (NZ-G2)

Trentham

Located about 20 miles north of New Zealand's capital city, Wellington, Trentham was founded in 1870, not long after the city itself was built. Trentham's figure-eight steeplechase course is ringed by a wide, 2,000-meter turf course with a 450-meter home straight. Its major races include the Wellington Cup Handicap (NZ-G1), the Telegraph Handicap (NZ-G1), and the New Zealand Oaks (NZ-G1). Trentham was home of the country's top yearling sale for more than six decades. In its second year in 1928, the sale included a chestnut colt bought for 160 guineas. Named *Phar Lap, he was sent to Australia and made racing history. In 1988, the sale was shifted north to place it closer to the major breeding operations in the country.

Location: Racecourse Road, Trentham, Upper Hutt, Wellington
Phone: 64 (4) 528-9611
Fax: 64 (4) 528-4166
Website: *www.trentham.co.nz*
E-Mail: wrc@trentham.co.nz
Abbreviation: Tre
President: Mike Brown
Chief Executive: E. C. Jansen
Principal Races: New Zealand Oaks (NZ-G1), Telegraph H. (NZ-G1), Thorndon Mile H. (NZ-G1), Wellington Cup H. (NZ-G1)

Peru

Monterrico

Racing in Peru was held in the 19th century at a small racetrack called Cancha Meiggs, and successively was conducted at Hipodromo de Santa Beatriz and San Felipe before the opening of the Monterrico Race Track in Lima on December 18, 1960. Racing is conducted year-round on Tuesday and Thursday evenings, Saturdays, and Sundays. The left-handed track has both a dirt track and a grass course. On December 8, 1997, Panama native Laffit Pincay Jr. and Peruvian-born Edgar Prado, Jorge Chavez, and Julio Pezua represented the United States in an international riders competition at Monterrico. Juan Jose Paule of Argentina and Peruvian Edwin Talaverano tied for first place in the three-race event. Monterrico's premier races form the Quadruple Crown. All of Peru's more than 40 graded races are run at Monterrico.

Location: Avenue El Derby, Santiago De Surco, Lima
Phone: 51 (1) 610-3000
Website: *www.monterricoenlared.com*
Abbreviation: Mon
President: Herbert Moebius Castaneda
Principal Races: Derby Nacional (Per-G1), Jockey Club del Peru (Per-G1)

Singapore

Singapore Racecourse

Singapore Racecourse at Kranji in the northern part of Singapore is the host of the Singapore Airlines International Cup (Sin-G1). The stakes race is contested at 1¼ miles in May over the 2,000-meter, left-handed track. The race was canceled in 2003 because of the severe acute respiratory syndrome (SARS) outbreak. Another major stakes is the Singapore KrisFlyer Sprint (Sin-G3). With three training tracks, the track accommodates approximately 1,000 horses. Horses are stabled in either air-conditioned or naturally ventilated stalls in barns separated by large courtyards. The four-story grandstand can accommodate 30,000 people.

Location: 1 Turf Club Avenue, Kranji 73808
Phone: 65 (6) 879-1000
Fax: 65 (6) 879-010
Website: *www.turfclub.com.sg*
Abbreviation: Sin
President: Yu Pang Fey
Principal Races: International Cup (Sin-G1)

South Africa

Clairwood

Clairwood, operated by the Gold Circle Racing and Gaming Group in Merebank, is host of the 2,000-meter Champions Cup (SAf-G1) in late July. A flat, left-handed track of approximately 2,500 meters in circumference, Clairwood features a 1,200-meter straight that is used for all sprints. The start for 1,400-meter races begins very close to the turn, often resulting in a scramble for good position early, especially in large fields.

Location: 89 Barrier Lane, Clairwood 4052
Phone: 27 (31) 469-1020
Fax: 27 (31) 469-0607
Website: *www.goldcircle.co.za*
E-Mail: info@goldcircle.co.za
Abbreviation: Cla
Chief Executive: M. J. L. Nairac
Principal Races: Champions Cup (SAf-G1), Gold Challenge S. (SAf-G1), Mercury Sprint Stakes (SAf-G1)

Greyville

Located in a complex that includes a championship golf course, Greyville has conducted racing just outside the city of Durban since 1844. In 1897, the Durban Turf Club took over the track's administration. The 2,000-meter Durban July Handicap (SAf-G1), the country's most prestigious race, is held on the first Saturday of the month and attracts crowds of up to 60,000. Other major stakes are the South African Guineas (SAf-G1) in May, the South African Fillies Guineas (SAf-G1), and the Daily News Two Thousand (SAf-G1). The right-handed, pear-shaped turf course of about 2,800 meters features tight turns and a straight of nearly 500 meters.

Location: 150 Avondale Road, Greyville Box 40, Durban 04001
Phone: 27 (31) 314-1651
Fax: 27 (31) 309-4149
Abbreviation: Grv
Principal Races: Daily News Two Thousand (SAf-G1), Durban July H. (SAf-G1), Garden Province S. (SAf-G1), Gold Cup (SAf-G1), Premier's Champion S. (SAf-G1), South African Fillies Guineas (SAf-G1), South African Guineas (SAf-G1)

Kenilworth

Serving the Cape Town region, Kenilworth boasts three tracks. Its largest course is 2,800 meters with a 600-meter run-in. Known as the "new course," this left-handed oval is used primarily in summer and is regarded as one of the fairest in South Africa. A smaller, 2,700-meter, left-handed course has a 450-meter run-in and is utilized mostly in the winter months. In addition, a 1,200-meter straight course bisects the infield on a diagonal, and the three courses come together only in the galloping-out area. The straight course is one of the stiffest tests in South African racing, with a climb for the first 200 meters and another rise in the final 200 meters.

Location: Rosmead Avenue, Box 53073, Kenilworth, 745, Cape Town 07745
Phone: 27 (21) 700-1600
Fax: 27 (21) 762-1919
Website: *www.goldcircle.co.za*
E-Mail: info@goldcircle.co.za
Abbreviation: Ken
Ownership: Gold Circle Racing and Gaming Group
Principal Races: Graham Beck Wines Cape Derby (SAf-G1), J & B Met S. (SAf-G1)

Scottsville

Located near Pietermaritzburg, Scottsville conducted its first race meet on April 3, 1886. Racing is held on 14 Saturdays, two holidays, and 17 weekdays throughout the year on a right-handed, oval turf course approximately 2,270 meters in circumference. Nearby training centers in Ashburton, Clairwood Park, and Summerveld accommodate 2,000 horses for approximately 50 trainers. Scottsville hosts the South African Fillies Sprint (SAf-G1) and the Golden Spur Stakes (SAf-G1). Like Clairwood and Kenilworth, it is owned by the Gold Circle Racing and Gaming Group.

Location: 45 New England Road, P. O. Box 101064, Durban, Scottsville 03209
Phone: 27 (33) 345-3405
Fax: 27 (33) 394-1141
Website: *www.goldcircle.co.za*
E-Mail: info@goldcircle.co.za
Abbreviation: Sco
Principal Races: Allan Robertson Fillies Championship (SAf-G1), Gold Medallion (SAF-G1), Golden Spur S. (SAf-G1), South African Fillies Sprint (SAf-G1)

Turffontein

Only two miles south of Johannesburg, Turffontein has been home to racing since 1887, just one year after the first Thoroughbred race was held in the city. While maintaining its traditions, including a Royal Box, Turffontein has been thoroughly modernized. The grandstand, rebuilt in the 1970s, allows a panoramic view of the course, and the Ascot Bar and Lounge, Caradoc Room, and Lawn Enclosure give fans many alternatives for enjoying their day at the races. The course has its own water source, which allows for beautiful lawns, numerous flower gardens, meticulously maintained trees and shrubs, and a bird sanctuary. Racing is conducted mostly on Saturdays on a testing, uphill, right-handed turf course of 2,658 meters. Its single chute allows for a 1,200-meter straight. Turffontein also has a 2,000-meter grass training track and four sand training tracks. The South Africa Derby (SAf-G1), Champion Stakes (SAf-G1), and Horse Chestnut 1,600 Stakes (SAf-G1), formerly the President's Cup, are three of Turffontein's biggest races.

Location: Turf Club Street, P. O. Box 183, Turffontein, Gauteng 2190, Johannesburg 2190
Phone: 27 (11) 681-1500
Fax: 27 (11) 683-7746
Website: *www.phumelela.com*
Abbreviation: Tff
Principal Races: Champion S. (SAf-G1), Empress Club S. (SAf-G1), Gold Bowl (SAf-G1), Horse Chestnut 1,600 S. (SAf-G1), South Africa Derby (SAf-G1), South Africa Nursery (SAf-G1), Summer Cup (SAf-G1), Triple Crown 1,600 (SAf-G1), Triple Tiara 1,600 (SAf-G1)

United Arab Emirates

Nad al Sheba

Offering the world's richest race—the $6-million Dubai World Cup (UAE-G1)—and no betting on any of its races, Nad al Sheba Racecourse is located within the tiny sheikhdom of Dubai in the United Arab Emirates. First laid out in 1986 and resurfaced in 1997 before the third running of the World Cup, the 2,200-meter (1⅜-mile), left-handed dirt course has three chutes. A left-handed turf course inside the dirt course is composed of Bermuda hybrid grass, which thrives in hot and humid climates. Two-time North American Horse of the Year Cigar won the inaugural Dubai World Cup in 1996 to give the stakes instant credibility. Also on the Dubai World Cup program are the Dubai Duty Free Stakes (UAE-G1), the Dubai Golden Shaheen (UAE-G1), the Dubai Sheema Classic (UAE-G1), the United Arab Emirates Derby (UAE-G2), and the Godolphin Mile (UAE-G2). The Dubai World Cup Committee pays a wide array of costs for visiting horses competing in Dubai, including roundtrip airfare.

Location: City Tower 1, 2nd Floor, Suite 206, P. O. Box 9305, Dubai
Phone: 971 (4) 332-2277
Fax: 971 (4) 332-2288
Website: *www.dubairacingclub.com*
E-Mail: info@dubairacingclub.com
Abbreviation: Nad
Chairman: Saeed H. Al Tayer
Chief Executive Officer: Frank Gabriel Jr.
Principal Races: Dubai Duty Free S. (UAE-G1), Dubai Golden Shaheen (UAE-G1), Dubai Sheema Classic (UAE-G1), Dubai World Cup (UAE-G1), Godolphin Mile (UAE-G2), United Arab Emirates Derby (UAE-G2)

Uruguay

Maronas National Racetrack

Shuttered for 5½ years, historic Maronas National Racetrack reopened in June 2003 after a multimillion-dollar renovation by its lessees, Hipica Rioplatense and Lone Star Park, a Magna Entertainment Corp. property. The Montevideo track, which dates from the mid-1870s, is owned by the Republic of Uruguay, and the partnership holds a 30-year lease on the track and concessions. By its first anniversary, the track was offering an average of almost ten races a day and was attracting increasingly larger crowds and wagering. The track's reopening also was credited with stimulating the Uruguayan breeding industry. The track, which also has four off-track facilities with slot machines and 20 OTBs for race wagering, simulcasts its races around the world and began sending Group 1 races into the United States in early 2005.

Location: 3540 Jose Maria Guerra, Montevideo
Phone: 598 (2) 511-7777
Fax: 598 (2) 511-9961
Website: *www.maronas.com.uy*
E-Mail: info@maronas.com.uy
Abbreviation: Man
Principal Races: Gran Premio Jose Pedro Ramirez

International Sire Lists

Leading Sires by 2005 Earnings by Country

(By Racing Season for Southern Hemisphere Countries)

Argentina

Sire	Strs	Wnrs	SWs	Leading Earner (Earnings)	Total Earnings
Lode	116	62	8	Kesplendida ($52,474)	$605,790
Mutakddim	98	49	7	American Pride ($33,202)	$533,513
Bernstein	55	33	8	Storm Mayor ($130,758)	$529,602
Luhuk	85	45	3	Sweetly ($34,030)	$513,800
Roy	100	43	7	Badajo ($58,910)	$507,213
Southern Halo	84	46	8	Batallosa ($33,514)	$476,225
Candy Stripes	83	44	3	Rider Stripes ($58,525)	$472,845
Numerous	80	40	2	Miss Atorranta ($36,881)	$425,194
Poliglote (GB)	92	52	3	Smart Wells ($28,522)	$415,835
Parade Marshal	108	44	5	Visa Parade ($44,403)	$407,179

Australia

Sire	Strs	Wnrs	SWs	Leading Earner (Earnings)	Total Earnings
Redoute's Choice	167	82	12	Miss Finland ($1,587,344)	$7,770,775
Encosta de Lago	267	111	10	Racing To Win ($1,362,103)	$6,119,214
Desert King	128	40	2	Makybe Diva ($4,047,686)	$5,533,920
Zabeel	188	91	11	Railings ($1,884,127)	$5,516,421
Danehill	184	86	17	Churchill Downs ($461,326)	$5,193,830
Flying Spur	236	117	8	Primus ($295,252)	$3,848,474
Commands	148	73	2	Paratroopers ($1,214,997)	$3,392,888
Snippets	169	89	7	Sky Cuddle ($249,079)	$2,549,841
Lion Hunter	259	110	7	Gold Edition ($260,051)	$2,434,121
Jeune	171	73	3	On A Jeune ($643,311)	$2,394,118

Brazil

Sire	Strs	Wnrs	SWs	Leading Earner (Earnings)	Total Earnings
Roi Normand	195	89	1	Verano Porteno ($13,523)	$529,384
Royal Academy	72	46	8	Heroi Do Bafra ($60,179)	$452,672
Midnight Tiger	122	66	1	Mister Dorr ($15,960)	$400,885
Dodge	106	63	3	Omaggio ($47,706)	$382,770
Choctaw Ridge	118	56	3	Fly Dorcego ($18,025)	$365,787
Fast Gold	117	55	1	Setembro Chove ($55,264)	$352,474
Know Heights (Ire)	97	48	6	Nepotista ($30,512)	$348,835
Nedawi	80	35	4	Ever Love ($64,657)	$321,484
Ski Champ	80	46	5	Impossible Ski ($25,607)	$315,622
Romarin (Brz)	85	50	3	O Dragao ($53,644)	$314,434

Canada

Sire	Strs	Wnrs	SWs	Leading Earner (Earnings)	Total Earnings
Archers Bay	62	40	4	Spaghetti Mouse ($240,974)	$2,663,439
Bold Executive	82	34	4	Top Ten List ($292,854)	$2,248,113
Langfuhr	36	18	5	Mobil ($369,212)	$1,814,810
Whiskey Wisdom	69	35	4	Dave the Knave ($145,311)	$1,732,102
Bold n' Flashy	75	34	1	U R Flashy ($113,086)	$1,463,808
Wild Rush	28	16	2	Wild Desert ($527,800)	$1,418,737
Ascot Knight	68	31	1	Knight's Covenant ($110,102)	$1,336,766
Silver Deputy	27	16	5	Nashinda ($205,271)	$1,295,817
Smart Strike	29	14	3	Gold Strike ($480,518)	$1,292,053
Tethra	56	26	2	Pyramid Park ($182,230)	$1,235,117

England

Sire	Strs	Wnrs	SWs	Leading Earner (Earnings)	Total Earnings
Montjeu (Ire)	60	23	4	Motivator ($1,627,411)	$3,307,291
Danehill	114	48	11	Oratorio (Ire) ($523,743)	$3,212,668
Sadler's Wells	127	42	9	Day Flight ($265,182)	$2,129,815
Halling	54	22	6	The Geezer ($425,636)	$2,032,851
Night Shift	106	40	3	Azamour (Ire) ($1,075,713)	$2,001,671
Machiavellian	78	35	7	Palace Episode ($284,396)	$1,932,658
Pivotal	117	37	5	Peeress ($443,782)	$1,789,790
Giant's Causeway	54	31	3	Maids Causeway ($398,766)	$1,686,207

Sire	Strs	Wnrs	SWs	Leading Earner (Earnings)	Total Earnings
Zafonic	95	42	6	Flashy Wings ($325,513)	$1,569,853
Indian Ridge	80	35	5	Imperial Stride ($227,016)	$1,534,342

England and Ireland

Sire	Strs	Wnrs	SWs	Leading Earner (Earnings)	Total Earnings
Danehill	139	65	18	Oratorio (Ire) ($1,314,657)	$6,188,086
Montjeu (Ire)	80	31	5	Motivator ($1,862,036)	$4,945,602
Sadler's Wells	194	67	14	Yeats ($297,025)	$3,346,334
Halling	67	31	7	The Geezer ($425,636)	$2,408,705
Pivotal	123	39	6	Peeress ($443,782)	$2,263,748
Night Shift	123	49	3	Azamour (Ire) ($1,108,721)	$2,231,333
Machiavellian	97	40	7	Palace Episode ($284,396)	$2,141,006
Danehill Dancer	147	57	6	Misu Bond ($208,716)	$2,026,803
Giant's Causeway	77	38	5	Maids Causeway ($410,322)	$2,003,312
Indian Ridge	97	43	6	Imperial Stride ($227,016)	$1,772,504

France

Sire	Strs	Wnrs	SWs	Leading Earner (Earnings)	Total Earnings
Montjeu (Ire)	27	16	6	Hurricane Run ($1,848,075)	$2,978,783
Linamix	91	40	10	Reefscape ($390,198)	$2,339,609
Danehill	34	20	9	Westerner ($628,808)	$2,144,738
Anabaa	101	46	4	Martillo ($88,010)	$1,780,097
Giant's Causeway	21	8	1	Shamardal ($1,336,316)	$1,706,985
Highest Honor (Fr)	98	53	0	Highest Ridge ($110,190)	$1,673,264
Kingmambo	21	9	2	Divine Proportions ($1,072,784)	$1,597,857
Kendor	82	31	4	Kendor Dine ($112,879)	$1,498,240
Take Risks	98	34	1	Coupe de Champe ($94,646)	$1,472,315
Sadler's Wells	47	18	5	Argentina (Ire) ($329,796)	$1,396,278

Germany

Sire	Strs	Wnrs	SWs	Leading Earner (Earnings)	Total Earnings
Big Shuffle	128	68	7	Konig Turf ($119,758)	$1,337,884
Monsun	96	55	4	Anna Monda ($199,543)	$1,054,668
Acatenango	61	23	5	Nicaron ($411,638)	$1,007,094
Tiger Hill	54	23	8	Iota ($242,413)	$994,727
Lando (Ger)	39	17	2	Gonbarda ($490,844)	$718,634
Dashing Blade	108	47	4	Tarlac ($59,949)	$649,197
Caerleon	4	2	1	Warrsan ($564,435)	$578,177
Platini	101	46	0	Jalta ($42,761)	$439,210
Sternkoenig	46	22	1	Simonas ($165,877)	$431,757
Waky Nao (GB)	63	27	1	Sweet Wake ($105,869)	$402,021

Hong Kong

Sire	Strs	Wnrs	SWs	Leading Earner (Earnings)	Total Earnings
Danehill	83	34	2	Planet Ruler ($824,050)	$7,456,407
Zabeel	23	10	1	Vengeance Of Rain ($3,890,974)	$5,579,715
El Moxie	6	4	1	Silent Witness ($1,431,524)	$2,071,333
Royal Academy	9	3	1	Bullish Luck ($1,650,287)	$1,969,237
Danzero	18	8	0	Lido De Paris ($396,183)	$1,717,533
O'Reilly	21	10	0	Cheeky ($368,050)	$1,492,862
Sunday Silence	3	1	1	Hat Trick ($1,029,113)	$1,426,315
Cape Cross (Ire)	11	3	1	Ouija Board (GB) ($1,029,113)	$1,423,390
Flying Spur	24	11	0	Lucky Champion ($170,317)	$1,402,167
Soviet Star	7	4	0	Russian Pearl ($862,476)	$1,376,606

Ireland

Sire	Strs	Wnrs	SWs	Leading Earner (Earnings)	Total Earnings
Danehill	49	21	9	Oratorio (Ire) ($790,914)	$2,975,418
Montjeu (Ire)	29	9	1	Hurricane Run ($917,528)	$1,638,311
Sadler's Wells	86	25	5	Briolette ($130,037)	$1,216,519
Danehill Dancer	48	16	1	Indesatchel ($117,400)	$526,889
Danetime	19	5	2	Miss Sally ($269,272)	$488,919
Sinndar	16	6	2	Shawanda ($271,208)	$476,668
Pivotal	12	2	1	Saoire (GB) ($289,136)	$473,958
Key of Luck	53	9	1	Right Key ($208,516)	$430,046
Xaar	19	3	1	Wake Up Maggie ($178,811)	$428,199
Bluebird	12	5	2	Ugo Fire ($216,709)	$404,436

Italy

Sire	Strs	Wnrs	SWs	Leading Earner (Earnings)	Total Earnings
Sri Pekan	78	39	1	De Sica ($505,823)	$1,625,891
Shantou	74	27	0	Bening ($140,966)	$834,503
Desert Prince (Ire)	43	20	0	Ceprin ($118,055)	$748,248
Orpen	39	20	3	Troppo Oca ($94,888)	$717,112
Linamix	18	13	3	Vol de Nuit ($291,833)	$702,978
Singspiel (Ire)	23	14	3	Lateral ($145,029)	$645,560
Marju	44	24	0	Alicia Higgins ($50,186)	$579,379
Martino Alonso	16	8	1	Ramonti ($391,410)	$577,533
In the Wings (GB)	34	18	2	Soldier Hollow ($141,862)	$572,499
Cape Cross (Ire)	29	18	1	Sabana Perdida ($103,832)	$561,229

Japan

Sire	Strs	Wnrs	SWs	Leading Earner (Earnings)	Total Earnings
Sunday Silence	467	198	30	Deep Impact ($6,123,911)	$83,070,273
Brian's Time	251	95	5	Time Paradox ($3,186,526)	$24,936,806
Fuji Kiseki	226	84	8	Kane Hekili ($2,813,092)	$19,910,753
Dance in the Dark	264	60	5	Win Glanz ($913,521)	$15,920,008
End Sweep	125	52	5	Rhein Kraft ($3,287,592)	$15,862,328
Sakura Bakushin O	207	73	3	She is Tosho ($771,116)	$15,734,343
Special Week	198	74	3	Cesario (Jpn) ($2,061,053)	$14,639,056
Taiki Shuttle	139	56	5	Meisho Bowler ($1,870,744)	$12,488,109
El Condor Pasa	178	61	2	Tokai Trick ($677,514)	$12,008,989
Afleet	169	54	1	Saqalat ($1,534,022)	$11,758,314

Saudi Arabia

Sire	Strs	Wnrs	SWs	Leading Earner (Earnings)	Total Earnings
Another Review	54	17	1	Hooriyah Shaqraan ($60,752)	$456,070
Torrey Canyon	45	15	0	Yam ($37,120)	$264,777
Freequent	19	10	1	Jaa Yez ($48,322)	$233,154
Mirror Black	37	7	0	Tayhoor ($39,674)	$187,355
Voleris	37	10	0	Kabshaan ($45,712)	$176,284
Sharpitor	10	4	0	Shammaakh ($86,833)	$145,002
Alysheba	18	5	0	Fakhr Alzamaan ($35,814)	$122,564
Machiavellian	9	2	0	Kingdom's Key ($74,939)	$117,610
Thoughtless	22	7	0	Fazaet Ameer ($25,403)	$115,192
Addath	13	6	0	Almotawaazen ($34,896)	$106,929

Puerto Rico

Sire	Strs	Wnrs	SWs	Leading Earner (Earnings)	Total Earnings
Fappiano's Star	48	22	4	Borrascoso ($293,900)	$1,067,545
Eqtesaad	55	41	1	Tenderete ($64,785)	$833,000
Goldwater	19	10	1	Gold Gift ($188,730)	$459,530
Sejm	24	20	0	Mi Abogada ($50,700)	$378,134
Balcony	31	20	0	Mueca ($80,368)	$373,090
Royal Merlot	26	15	1	Hispanica ($88,760)	$371,949
Pioneering	8	7	1	Triano ($206,080)	$367,223
Run Turn	21	16	0	Fogueo P ($43,556)	$327,488
Eltish	8	7	1	Eltish Thunder ($208,618)	$297,632
Wonder Bird	29	16	0	Minidoink ($24,574)	$250,812

United Arab Emirates

Sire	Strs	Wnrs	SWs	Leading Earner (Earnings)	Total Earnings
Devil His Due	1	1	1	Roses in May ($3,600,000)	$3,600,000
Dynaformer	2	1	0	Dynever ($1,200,000)	$1,519,750
Danehill	7	2	1	Elvstroem ($1,200,000)	$1,233,613
Machiavellian	21	8	0	Tropical Star (Ire) ($429,160)	$1,225,048
Alhaarth	2	1	1	Phoenix Reach (Ire) ($1,200,000)	$1,201,633
Honour and Glory	1	1	1	Blues and Royals ($1,200,000)	$1,200,000
Valid Expectations	1	1	1	Saratoga County ($1,200,000)	$1,200,000
Seeking the Gold	10	5	0	Satin Kiss ($325,000)	$968,472
National Assembly	2	2	2	Grand Emporium (SAf) ($770,000)	$849,183
Belong to Me	3	2	1	Jack Sullivan ($547,500)	$607,946

Leading Sires by Year

Argentina*

Year	Sire, YOB, Sire	Earnings
2005	Lode, 1986, by Mr. Prospector	$605,790
2004	Roy, 1983, by Fappiano	626,813
2003	Roar, 1993, by Forty Niner	642,453
2002	Southern Halo, 1983, by Halo	553,695
2001	Roy, 1983, by Fappiano	818,389
2000	Southern Halo, 1983, by Halo	1,632,869
1999	Southern Halo, 1983, by Halo	1,490,119
1998	Southern Halo, 1983, by Halo	1,883,179
1997	Southern Halo, 1983, by Halo	2,010,382

Australia*

Year	Sire, YOB, Sire	Earnings
2005	Redoute's Choice, 1996, by Danehill	$7,770,775
2004	Danehill, 1986, by Danzig	8,159,244
2003	Danehill, 1986, by Danzig	5,723,877
2002	Danehill, 1986, by Danzig	4,031,267
2001	Danehill, 1986, by Danzig	4,033,288
2000	Danehill, 1986, by Danzig	4,080,825
1999	Danehill, 1986, by Danzig	4,952,018
1998	Zabeel , 1986, by *Sir Tristram	6,793,635
1997	Danehill, 1986, by Danzig	5,034,265

Brazil*

Year	Sire, YOB, Sire	Earnings
2005	Roi Normand, 1983, by Exclusive Native	$529,384
2004	Roi Normand, 1983, by Exclusive Native	487,221
2003	Choctaw Ridge, 1989, by Mr. Prospector	415,765
2002	Fast Gold, 1979, by Mr. Prospector	427,914
2001	Choctaw Ridge, 1989, by Mr. Prospector	563,482
2000	Minstrel Glory, 1980, by The Minstrel	530,018
1999	Roi Normand, 1983, by Exclusive Native	278,000
1998	Bright Again, 1987, by Wild Again	397,767
1997	Punk, 1984, by Ringaro	406,900

Canada

Year	Sire, YOB, Sire	Earnings
2005	Archers Bay, 1995, by Silver Deputy	$2,663,439
2004	Smart Strike, 1992, by Mr. Prospector	3,286,698
2003	Langfuhr, 1992, by Danzig	3,783,111
2002	Regal Classic, 1985, by Vice Regent	2,777,503
2001	Regal Classic, 1985, by Vice Regent	2,663,430
2000	Regal Classic, 1985, by Vice Regent	2,778,491
1999	Regal Classic, 1985, by Vice Regent	2,000,300
1998	Silver Deputy, 1985, by Deputy Minister	2,097,515
1997	Bold Ruckus, 1976, by Boldnesian	1,859,252

England

Year	Sire, YOB, Sire	Earnings
2005	Montjeu (Ire), 1996, by Sadler's Wells	$3,307,291
2004	Sadler's Wells, 1981, by Northern Dancer	5,082,034
2003	Sadler's Wells, 1981, by Northern Dancer	3,023,899
2002	Sadler's Wells, 1981, by Northern Dancer	3,006,898
2001	Sadler's Wells, 1981, by Northern Dancer	3,977,732
2000	Sadler's Wells, 1981, by Northern Dancer	2,606,967
1999	Fairy King, 1982, by Northern Dancer	1,962,154
1998	Nashwan, 1986, by Blushing Groom (Fr)	1,524,720
1997	Silver Hawk, 1979, by Roberto	1,488,473

England and Ireland

Year	Sire, YOB, Sire	Earnings
2005	Danehill, 1986, by Danzig	$6,188,086
2004	Sadler's Wells, 1981, by Northern Dancer	7,248,096
2003	Sadler's Wells, 1981, by Northern Dancer	5,823,175
2002	Sadler's Wells, 1981, by Northern Dancer	5,562,690
2001	Sadler's Wells, 1981, by Northern Dancer	5,738,357
2000	Sadler's Wells, 1981, by Northern Dancer	3,676,718
1999	Sadler's Wells, 1981, by Northern Dancer	2,952,410
1998	Sadler's Wells, 1981, by Northern Dancer	2,626,355
1997	Sadler's Wells, 1981, by Northern Dancer	2,241,578

France

Year	Sire, YOB, Sire	Earnings
2005	Montjeu (Ire), 1996, by Sadler's Wells	$2,978,783
2004	Linamix, 1987, by Mendez	3,163,044
2003	Darshaan, 1981, by Shirley Heights	2,433,602
2002	Danehill, 1986, by Danzig	1,952,836
2001	Danehill, 1986, by Danzig	1,630,129
2000	Highest Honor (Fr), 1983, by Kenmare	1,424,916
1999	Sadler's Wells, 1981, by Northern Dancer	2,155,310
1998	Linamix, 1987, by Mendez	1,929,004
1997	Nureyev, 1977, by Northern Dancer	2,139,852

Germany

Year	Sire, YOB, Sire	Earnings
2005	Big Shuffle, 1984, by Super Concorde	$1,337,884
2004	Monsun, 1990, by Konigsstuhl	1,882,789
2003	Big Shuffle, 1984, by Super Concorde	1,341,355
2002	Monsun, 1990, by Konigsstuhl	1,278,658
2001	Big Shuffle, 1984, by Super Concorde	917,838
2000	Monsun, 1990, by Konigsstuhl	1,361,406
1999	Dashing Blade, 1987, by Elegant Air	1,223,849
1998	Big Shuffle, 1984, by Super Concorde	1,040,915
1997	Acatenango, 1982, by Surumu	1,484,293

Hong Kong

Year	Sire, YOB, Sire	Earnings
2005	Danehill, 1986, by Danzig	$7,456,407
2004	Danehill, 1986, by Danzig	7,998,326
2003	Danehill, 1986, by Danzig	8,562,038
2002	Danehill, 1986, by Danzig	6,308,554
2001	Danehill, 1986, by Danzig	5,549,309
2000	Rahy, 1985, by Blushing Groom (Fr)	3,106,199
1999	Danehill, 1986, by Danzig	3,089,946
1998	Danehill, 1986, by Danzig	2,779,929
1997	Green Desert, 1983, by Danzig	850,035

Ireland

Year	Sire, YOB, Sire	Earnings
2005	Danehill, 1986, by Danzig	$2,975,418
2004	Sadler's Wells, 1981, by Northern Dancer	2,166,062
2003	Sadler's Wells, 1981, by Northern Dancer	2,799,276
2002	Sadler's Wells, 1981, by Northern Dancer	2,555,792
2001	Sadler's Wells, 1981, by Northern Dancer	1,760,625
2000	Sadler's Wells, 1981, by Northern Dancer	1,069,751
1999	Sadler's Wells, 1981, by Northern Dancer	1,710,136
1998	Sadler's Wells, 1981, by Northern Dancer	1,150,913
1997	Danehill, 1986, by Danzig	1,198,712

Italy

Year	Sire, YOB, Sire	Earnings
2005	Sri Pekan, 1992, by Red Ransom	$1,625,891
2004	Sri Pekan, 1992, by Red Ransom	1,872,720
2003	Sri Pekan, 1992, by Red Ransom	1,585,694
2002	Love the Groom, 1984, by Blushing Groom (Fr)	979,041
2001	Roi Danzig, 1986, by Danzig	908,189
2000	Roi Danzig, 1986, by Danzig	847,389
1999	Sikeston, 1986, by Lear Fan	800,283
1998	Love the Groom, 1984, by Blushing Groom (Fr)	1,250,469
1997	Love the Groom, 1984, by Blushing Groom (Fr)	1,490,432

Japan

Year	Sire, YOB, Sire	Earnings
2005	Sunday Silence, 1986, by Halo	$83,070,273
2004	Sunday Silence, 1986, by Halo	82,853,357
2003	Sunday Silence, 1986, by Halo	69,943,962
2002	Sunday Silence, 1986, by Halo	52,709,704
2001	Sunday Silence, 1986, by Halo	53,790,988
2000	Sunday Silence, 1986, by Halo	53,883,429
1999	Sunday Silence, 1986, by Halo	45,579,976
1998	Sunday Silence, 1986, by Halo	33,925,214
1997	Sunday Silence, 1986, by Halo	29,390,122

United Arab Emirates

Year	Sire, YOB, Sire	Earnings
2005	Devil His Due, 1989, Devil's Bag	$3,600,000
2004	Pleasant Colony, 1978, by His Majesty	3,717,378
2003	Singspiel (Ire), 1992, by In the Wings (GB)	4,155,117
2002	Machiavellian, 1987, by Mr. Prospector	4,082,712
2001	Fly So Free, 1988, by Time for a Change	3,600,000
2000	Seeking the Gold, 1985, by Mr. Prospector	3,675,318
1999	Machiavellian, 1987, by Mr. Prospector	3,165,733
1998	Silver Buck, 1978, by Buckpasser	2,400,000
1997	In the Wings (GB), 1986, by Sadler's Wells	2,420,558

*Southern Hemisphere seasons

Sovereign Awards

In a less than stellar year for Canadian-based horses, A Bit O'Gold collected Sovereign Awards as champion older male, champion turf male, and Horse of the Year in 2005. He accomplished the sweep with a record of three victories in seven starts and earnings of $497,437. Champion three-year-old male in 2004 after his Prince of Wales and Breeders' Stakes victories, the Gold Fever gelding owned by Two Bit Racing Stable and trained by Catherine Day Phillips raised his career earnings to $1,788,256.

A Bit O'Gold ventured from his Woodbine base only once in 2005, for a shot at the Breeders' Cup Classic (G1) at Belmont Park. He raced wide throughout after breaking from the 11th post position and finished last of 13, 18¼ lengths behind winner Saint Liam, the Eclipse Award-winning Horse of the Year in 2005.

Phillips started the gelding's 2005 season in the seven-furlong Vigil Handicap (Can-G3), in which he raced evenly and finished third, beaten two lengths by Judiths Wild Rush, who subsequently would be voted champion sprinter. In his next start, the 11/16-mile Eclipse Handicap (Can-G3) on May 23, he again ran evenly and finished fourth.

A Bit O'Gold found the 1¼ miles of the Dominion Day Handicap (Can-G3) much more to his liking. Always prominent, he pulled away in Woodbine's stretch to a 6½-length victory over Niigon on the main track. Phillips put him on the grass for his next start, the Chinese Cultural Centre Stakes (Can-G2), and he won by two lengths over 2004 champion older male Mobil. The trainer kept him on the grass for the remainder of his Woodbine starts. After a third-place finish in the Niagara Breeders' Cup Handicap (Can-G2), finishing 3½ lengths behind Revved Up, A Bit O'Gold turned the tables in the Sky Classic Handicap (Can-G2) on October 2, prevailing by a neck over Revved Up.

A Bit O'Gold's last-place finish in the Breeders' Cup Classic repeated a pattern of the 2004 season: Canadian runners rarely had success south of the 49th parallel. A notable exception was champion three-year-old male Palladio, who ventured across Lake Erie and took the 2005 Ohio Derby (G2) by a length over Magna Grad-

History of the Sovereign Awards

Year	E. P. Taylor Award of Merit†	Owner	Breeder	Trainer	Jockey	Apprentice Jockey
2005	Not awarded	Frank Stronach	Adena Springs	Reade Baker	Todd Kabel	Emma-Jayne Wilson
2004	Not awarded	Sam-Son Farm	Sam-Son Farm	Robert Tiller	Todd Kabel	Corey Fraser
2003	Not awarded	Stronach Stable	Sam-Son Farm	Robert Tiller	Todd Kabel	Julia Brimo
2002	Not awarded	Stronach Stable	Sam-Son Farm	Roger Attfield	Patrick Husbands	Chantal Sutherland
2001	Not awarded	Sam-Son Farm	Sam-Son Farm	Robert Tiller	Patrick Husbands	Chantal Sutherland
2000	Mike Harris	Sam-Son Farm	Sam-Son Farm	Mark Frostad	Patrick Husbands	Cory Clark
1999	George Hendrie	Stronach Stable	Frank Stronach	Mark Frostad	Patrick Husbands	Ben Russell
1998	David Willmot	Stronach Stable	Frank Stronach	Michael Wright Jr.	David Clark	Helen Vanek
1997	Not awarded	Frank Stronach	Frank Stronach	Mark Frostad	Emile Ramsammy	Rui Pimentel
1996	Not awarded	Minshall Farms	Minshall Farms	Barbara Minshall	Emile Ramsammy	Neil Poznansky
1995	Charles Taylor	Frank Stronach	Kinghaven Farms	Danny Vella	Todd Kabel	Dave Wilson
1994	Jack Kenney	Frank Stronach	Kinghaven Farms	Danny Vella	Robert Landry	Dave Wilson
1993	Not awarded	Frank Stronach	Kinghaven Farms	Roger Attfield	Robert Landry	Constant Montpellier
1992	Col. Charles Baker	Knob Hill Stable	Knob Hill Stable	Philip England	Todd Kabel	Stanley Bethley
1991	Ernest Samuel	Sam-Son Farm	Sam-Son Farm	Jim Day	Mickey Walls	Mickey Walls
1990	James Wright	Kinghaven Farms	Kinghaven Farms	Roger Attfield	Don Seymour	Mickey Walls
1989	George C. Frostad	Kinghaven Farms	Kinghaven Farms	Roger Attfield	Don Seymour	Maree Richards
1988	Sandy Hawley	Sam-Son Farm	Sam-Son Farm	Jim Day	Sandy Hawley	Jim McAleney
1987	Larry Regan	Kinghaven Farms	Kinghaven Farms	Roger Attfield	Don Seymour	Jim McAleney
1986	D. G. Willmot	D. G. Willmot	D. G. Willmot	Roger Attfield	Larry Attard	Todd Kabel
1985	George Gardiner	Ernest Samuel	E. P. Taylor	Jim Day	Don Seymour	Nancy Jumpsen
1984	Jim Coleman	Ernest Samuel	Frank Stronach	Mike Doyle	Chris Loseth	Robert King
1983	Joe Thomas	B. K. Yousif	Mr. and Mrs. Russell Bennett	Bill Marko	Larry Attard	Robert King
1982	Jean-Louis Levesque	D. G. Willmot	D. G. Willmot	Bill Marko	Lloyd Duffy	Richard Dos Ramos
1981	Jim Bentley	Dave Kapchinsky	Tom Webb	Ron Brock	Erwin Driedger	Richard Dos Ramos
1980	Jack Stafford	Ernest Samuel	Mr. and Mrs. Marvin Hamilton	Gerry Belanger	Gary Stahlbaum	Valerie Thompson
1979	George C. Hendrie	James Shields	D. G. Willmot	Jim Day	Robin Platts	Ray Creighton
1978	Ron Turcotte	Conn Smythe	Jean-Louis Levesque	F. H. Merrill	Sandy Hawley	Ron Hansen
1977	E. P. Taylor	Bory Margolus	Conn Smythe	Red Smith	Avelino Gomez	Brad Smythe
1976	Jack Diamond	George Gardiner	E. P. Taylor	Lou Cavalaris	Chris Rogers	Chris Loseth
1975	E. P. Taylor	Jack Stafford	Bory Margolus	Gil Rowntree	Hugo Dittfach	Jeff Fell

†Formerly known as Man of the Year

uate. He was unable to replicate his Thistledown victory in two subsequent U.S. starts, finishing fifth in Monmouth Park's Haskell Invitational Handicap (G1) and seventh in Saratoga Race Course's Saranac Stakes (G3), but he returned home to Woodbine and won the Ontario Derby in October.

Canada's most decorated champion was One for Rose, who collected her third straight title as outstanding older female. The middle-distance specialist won three stakes races in 2005, most notably her second consecutive win in the Seagram Cup Stakes (Can-G3) and her third straight Algoma Stakes. She also won the Ontario Matron Handicap for the second time in succession.

Native Rights, a half sister to 2002 Canadian broodmare of the year First Class Gal, was voted the nation's top broodmare in 2005.

Individuals receiving 2005 Sovereign Awards:

• Frank Stronach ruled as leading owner for the ninth time, and his Adena Springs collected its fifth title as leading breeder. Canada's leading owner and breeder by purse earnings in 2005, Stronach was represented by Ablo, winner of the Prince of Wales Stakes at Fort Erie, and Princess Elizabeth Stakes winner Sugar Swirl.

• With two champions in his Woodbine barn, Reade Baker won his first title as Canada's champion trainer. His champions were top sprinter Judiths Wild Rush and champion three-year-old filly Gold Strike, who won the Woodbine Oaks and Selene Stakes (Can-G3). The Manitoba-bred filly's four-race 2005 season ended with a third-place finish behind Wild Desert in the Queen's Plate Stakes on June 26. Baker recorded ten stakes wins among his 55 victories in 2005.

• Todd Kabel collected a record fifth Sovereign Award as outstanding jockey at the end of a season in which he did not dominate the Woodbine standings—in fact, he finished fifth by wins—but was in the saddle for big-money victories. He won 20 Canadian stakes races, accounting for nearly 20% of his 103 victories in 2005.

• Emma-Jayne Wilson was voted Canada's outstanding apprentice jockey, and that award was an appetizer for her Eclipse Award as North America's top apprentice rider in 2005. She became the first woman to lead the rider standings at Woodbine and closed out the year with 175 wins at the Toronto-area track, well ahead of journeyman Corey Fraser's 136 wins. In all, her mounts earned $6.3-million. She was only the third apprentice jockey to lead Woodbine's standings, following Sandy Hawley and Mickey Walls, and Hawley helped to get her started by putting her in contact with Woodbine horsemen.

History of the Sovereign Awards

Year	Horse of the Year	Two-Year-Old Filly	Two-Year-Old Male	Three-Year-Old Filly	Three-Year-Old Male
2005	A Bit O'Gold	Knights Templar	Edenwold	Gold Strike	Palladio
2004	Soaring Free	Simply Lovely	Wholelottabourbon	Eye of the Sphynx	A Bit O'Gold
2003	Wando	My Vintage Port	Judiths Wild Rush	Too Late Now	Wando
2002	Wake At Noon	Brusque	Added Edge	Lady Shari	Le Cinquieme Essai
2001	Win City	Ginger Gold	Rare Friends	Dancethruthedawn	Win City
2000	Quiet Resolve	Poetically	Highland Legacy	Catch the Ring	Kiss a Native
1999	Thornfield	Hello Seattle	Exciting Story	Gandria	Woodcarver
1998	Chief Bearhart	Fantasy Lake	Riddell's Creek	Kirby's Song	Archers Bay
1997	Chief Bearhart	Primaly	Dawson's Legacy	Cotton Carnival	Cryptocloser
1996	Mt. Sassafras	Larkwhistle	Cash Deposit	Silent Fleet	Victor Cooley
1995	Peaks and Valleys	Silken Cat	Gomtuu	Scotzanna	Peaks and Valleys
1994	Alywow	Honky Tonk Tune	Talkin Man	Alywow	Bruce's Mill
1993	Peteski	Term Limits	Comet Shine	Deputy Jane West	Peteski
1992	Benburb	Deputy Jane West	Truth of It All	Hope for a Breeze	Benburb
1991	Dance Smartly	Buckys Solution	Free At Last	Dance Smartly	Bolulight
1990	Izvestia	Dance Smartly	Rainbows for Life	Lubicon	Izvestia
1989	With Approval	Wavering Girl	Sky Classic	Blushing Katy	With Approval
1988	Play the King	Legarto	Mercedes Won	Tilt My Halo	Regal Intention
1987	Afleet	Phoenix Factor	Regal Classic	One From Heaven	Afleet
1986	Ruling Angel	Ruling Angel	Blue Finn	Carotene	Golden Choice
1985	Imperial Choice	Stage Flite	Grey Classic	La Lorgnette	Imperial Choice
1984	Dauphin Fabuleux	Deceit Dancer	Dauphin Fabuleux	Classy 'n Smart	Key to the Moon
1983	Travelling Victor	Ada Prospect	Prince Avatar	Northern Blossom	Bompago
1982	Frost King	Candle Bright	Sunny's Halo	Avowal	Runaway Groom
1981	Deputy Minister	Choral Group	Deputy Minister	Rainbow Connection	Frost King
1980	Glorious Song	Rainbow Connection	Bayford	Par Excellance	Ben Fab
1979	Overskate	Par Excellance	Allan Blue	Kamar	Steady Growth
1978	Overskate	Liz's Pride	Medaille d'Or	La Voyageuse	Overskate
1977	L'Alezane	L'Alezane	Overskate	Northernette	Dance in Time
1976	Norcliffe	Northernette	Sound Reason	Bye Bye Paris	Norcliffe
1975	L'Enjoleur	Seraphic	Proud Tobin	Momigi	L'Enjoleur

Horse of the Year
Older Male
Turf Male

A BIT O'GOLD, 2001 ch. g., Gold Fever—Annasan, by Corporate Report. 2005 record: 7-3-0-2, $497,437. Career: 18-10-3-2, $1,788,256. Breeder: Beclawat Stable (On.). Owner: The Two Bit Stable. Trainer: Catherine Day Phillips. In 2005, won Chinese Cultural Centre S. (Can-G2), Sky Classic H. (Can-G2), Dominion Day H. (Can-G3); 3rd Niagara Breeders' Cup Handicap (Can-G2), Vigil H. (Can-G3).

Two-Year-Old Male

EDENWOLD, 2003 ch. c., Southern Halo—Best of Friends, by Mining. 2005 record: 8-4-2-0, $287,247. Breeders: Gail Wood and W. Diamant (On.). Owners: James and Alice Sapara. Trainer: Josie Carroll. In 2005, won Colin S., Vandal S., Simcoe S.; 2nd Victoria S.

Two-Year-Old Filly

KNIGHTS TEMPLAR, 2003 b. f., Exploit—Religiosity, by Irish Tower. 2005 record: 8-3-1-0, $255,353. Breeder: Brylynn Farm (Fl.). Owners: Clover IV Stables and Krista Seltzer. Trainer: Daniel J. Vella. In 2005, won Mazarine Breeders' Cup S. (Can-G3), Ontario Debutante S.

Three-Year-Old Male

PALLADIO, 2002 b. c., Lycius—Gioia, by Mari's Book. 2005 record: 9-4-0-1, $444,143. Career: 12-5-0-1, $488,945. Breeder-owner: Haras Santa Maria de Araras (Fl.). Trainer: Roger L. Attfield. In 2005, won Ohio Derby (G2), Ontario Derby, Victoria Park S.; 3rd Marine S. (Can-G3).

Three-Year-Old Filly

GOLD STRIKE, 2002 dk. b. or br. f., Smart Strike—Brassy Gold, by Dixieland Band. 2005 record: 4-2-1-1, $480,518. Career: 7-4-2-1, $532,110. Owner-breeder: Harlequin Ranches (Mb.).

History of the Sovereign Awards

Year	Older Female	Older Male	Turf Female†	Turf Male	Sprinter	Broodmare of the Year
2005	One for Rose	A Bit O'Gold	Ambitious Cat	A Bit O'Gold	Judiths Wild Rush	Native Rights
2004	One for Rose	Mobil	Soaring Free	Inish Glora	Blonde Executive	Annasan
2003	One for Rose	Phantom Light	Inish Glora	Perfect Soul (Ire)	Soaring Free	Radiant Ring
2002	Small Promises	Wake At Noon	Chopinina	Portcullis	Wake At Noon	First Class Gal
2001	Mountain Angel	A Fleets Dancer	Sweetest Thing	Numerous Times	Mr. Epperson	Dance Smartly
2000	Saoirse	One Way Love	Heliotrope	Quiet Resolve	One Way Love	Primarily
1999	Magic Code	Deputy Inxs	Free Vacation	Thornfield	Deputy Inxs	Sharpening Up
1998	Santa Amelia	Terremoto	Colorful Vices	Chief Bearhart	Deputy Inxs	Fleet Courage
1997	Woolloomooloo	Chief Bearhart	Woolloomooloo	Chief Bearhart	Glanmire	Charming Sassafras
1996	Windsharp	Mt. Sassafras	Windsharp	Chief Bearhart	Langfuhr	Amelia Bearhart
1995	Bold Ruritana	Basqueian	Bold Ruritana	Hasten To Add	Scotzanna	Sea Regent
1994	Pennyhill Park	King Ruckus		Alywow	King Ruckus	Rainbow Connection
1993	Dance for Donna	Cozzene's Prince		Hero's Love	Apelia	Bold Debra
1992	Wilderness Song	Rainbows for Life		Rainbows for Life	King Corrie	Ballade
1991	Avant's Gold	Sky Classic		Sky Classic	King Corrie	Classy 'n Smart
1990	Diva's Debut	Twist the Snow		Izvestia	Twist the Snow	Shy Spirit
1989	Proper Evidence	Steady Power		Charlie Barley	Mr. Hot Shot	Passing Mood
1988	Carotene	Play the King		Carotene	Play the King	Polite Lady
1987	Carotene	Play the King		Carotene	Play the King	Arctic Vixen
1986	Bessarabian	Let's Go Blue		Carotene	New Connection	Loudrangle
1985	Lake Country	Ten Gold Pots		Imperial Choice	Summer Mood	No Class
1984	Sintrillium	Canadian Factor		Bounding Away	Diapason	Friendly Ways
1983	Eternal Search	Travelling Victor		Kingsbridge	Fraud Squad	Two Rings
1982	Eternal Search	Frost King		Frost King	Avowal	Yonnie Girl
1981	Glorious Song	Driving Home		Ben Fab	Eternal Search	Native Flower
1980	Glorious Song	Overskate		Overskate	La Voyageuse	Hangin Round
1979	La Voyageuse	Overskate		Overskate		Fitz's Fancy
1978	Christy's Mount	Giboulee		Overskate		Fanfreluche
1977	Reasonable Win	Norcliffe		Momigi		Doris White
1976	Momigi	Victorian Prince		Victorian Prince		Northern Minx
1975	Victorian Queen	Rash Move		Victorian Queen		Reasonable Wife

†1995 marks the first year the award for turf horse to be divided into male and female categories.

Canadian Triple Crown Winners

Year	Winner	Owner	Trainer	Jockey(s)
2003	Wando	G. Schickedanz	M. Keogh	P. Husbands
1993	Peteski	E. I. Mack	R. Attfield	C. Perret, D. Penna
1991	Dance Smartly	Sam-Son Farm	J. E. Day	P. Day
1990	Izvestia	Kinghaven Farms	R. Attfield	D. J. Seymour
1989	With Approval	Kinghaven Farms	R. Attfield	D. J. Seymour
1963	Canebora	Windfields Farm	G. McCann	M. Ycaza, H. Dittfach
1959	New Providence	Windfields Farm	G. McCann	R. Ussery, A. Gomez

Trainer: Reade Baker. In 2005, won Selene S. (Can-G3), Woodbine Oaks; 2nd Star Shoot S.; 3rd Queen's Plate S.

Older Female

ONE FOR ROSE, 1999 dk. b. or br. m., Tejano Run—Saucyladygaylord, by Lord Gaylord. 2005 record: 5-3-1-0, $274,120. Career: 27-15-5-2, $1,321,363. Breeder: Hill 'N' Dale Farm (On.). Owner: Tucci Stables. Trainer: Sid C. Allard. In 2005, won Seagram Cup S. (Can-G3), Ontario Matron S., Algoma S.; 2nd George C. Hendrie H. (Can-G3).

Turf Female

AMBITIOUS CAT, 2001 b. m., Storm Cat—Lilac Garden, by Roberto. 2005 record: 10-3-4-1, $350,140. Career: 14-4-6-1, $411,565. Breeder: Gaines-Gentry Thoroughbreds (Ky.). Owner: Chiefswood Stable. Trainer: Eric Coatrieux. In 2005, 2nd Canadian H. (Can-G2), Nassau S. (Can-G2); 3rd E. P. Taylor S. (Can-G1).

Sprinter

JUDITHS WILD RUSH, 2001 gr. or ro. h., Wild Rush—Tie Talk, by Black Tie Affair (Ire). 2005 record: 11-3-2-4, $230,989. Career: 23-7-2-6, $495,260. Breeder: Sez Who Thoroughbreds (Ky.). Owner: Harvey Tenenbaum. Trainer: Reade Baker. In 2005, won Vigil H. (Can-G3), Bold Venture H.; 2nd Jacques Cartier H.; 3rd Eclipse H. (Can-G3).

Broodmare of year

NATIVE RIGHTS, 1986 b. m., Our Native—Postage Stamp, by Ack Ack. Race record: 13-1-2-1, $15,525, Breeder: Barclay Agency and Omni Stables (Ky.) Through 2005, dam of nine foals, seven starters, seven winners, two stakes winners, two graded stakes winners. Dam of Prized Stamp (by Prized), won Barbara Fritchie H. (G2), Lady Dean S., etc.; Classic Stamp (by Regal Classic), winner of Canadian H. (Can-G2) twice, Carotene S., etc.

Canadian Horse Racing Hall of Fame

Founded in 1976, the Canadian Horse Racing Hall of Fame recognizes the people and horses who have established the roots of Canadian racing. The Hall of Fame was originally a list of inductees until a permanent site was established in 1997 at the west entrance of Woodbine.

Horses, YOB (Year Inducted)
Ace Marine 1952 (2003)
Afleet 1984 (1992)
*Anita's Son 1956 (2005)
Arise 1946 (1983)
Awesome Again 1994 (2001)
Belle Geste 1968 (1990)
Bold Ruckus 1976 (2006)
Bull Page 1947 (1977)
Bunty Lawless 1935 (1976)
Canadiana 1950 (1978)
Casa Camara 1944 (2000)
Carotene 1983 (2003)
Chief Bearhart 1993 (2002)
Chop Chop 1940 (1977)
Ciboulette 1961 (1983)
Classy 'n Smart 1981 (2004)
Cool Reception 1964 (2005)
Dance Smartly 1988 (1995)
Deputy Minister 1979 (1988)
Duchess of York 1923 (1976)
E. Day 1960 (1989)
Fanfreluche 1967 (1981)
Flaming Page 1959 (1980)
Frost King 1978 (1986)
Gallant Kitty 1916 (1977)
George Royal 1961 (1976)
Glorious Song 1976 (1995)
He's a Smoothie 1963 (2003)
Horometer 1931 (1976)
Inferno 1902 (1976)
Izvestia 1987 (1999)
Joey 1930 (1976)
Kennedy Road 1968 (2000)
Kingarvie 1943 (1976)
Langcrest 1961 (1984)
Langfuhr 1992 (2004)
La Prevoyante 1970 (1976)
Lauries Dancer 1968 (2006)
Major Presto 1963 (1982)
Martimas 1896 (2001)
Mona Bell 1935 (2000)
Nearctic 1954 (1977)
New Providence 1956 (1982)
Nijinsky II 1967 (1976)
No Class 1974 (1997)
Norcliffe 1973 (2005)
Northern Dancer 1961 (1976)
Northernette 1974 (1987)
Overskate 1975 (1993)
Queensway 1929 (2003)
Runaway Groom 1979 (2001)
Shepperton 1939 (1976)
Sir Barton 1916 (1976)
Sky Classic 1987 (1998)
South Shore 1918 (2000)
Sunny's Halo 1980 (1986)
Terror 1866 (1996)
The Minstrel 1974 (1979)
Vice Regent 1967 (1989)
Victoria Park 1957 (1976)
Windfields 1943 (2002)
With Approval 1986 (1993)
Wonder Where 1956 (2004)
Yellow Rose 1837 (1996)
Youville 1939 (1977)

Jockeys (Year Inducted)
Ted Atkinson (2002)
Larry Attard (2001)
Hugo Dittfach (1983)
Jeff Fell (1993)
Jim Fitzsimmons (1984)
Norman "Dude" Foden (2000)
David Gall (1993)
Avelino Gomez (1977)
Sandy Hawley (1986)
Charles "Chick" Lang (1990)
Herb Lindberg (1991)
Charles Littlefield (2000)
John Longden (1976)
Don MacBeth (1988)
Frank Mann (2000)
Richard "Dick" O'Leary (2000)
Robin Platts (1997)
John "Red" Pollard (1982)
Pat Remillard (1979)
Chris Rogers (1977)
William "Smokey" Saunders (1976)
Don Seymour (1999)
Ron Turcotte (1980)
R. B. "Bobby" Watson (1998)
Headley Woodhouse (1980)
George Woolf (1976)

Trainers (Year Inducted)
A. E. "Burt" Alexandra (2002)
Roger Attfield (1999)
Macdonald "Mac" Benson (2002)
James "Jim" Bentley (1981)
Charles Boyle (2001)
W. H. "Bill" Bringloe (2000)
Donald "Duke" Campbell (1984)
Lou Cavalaris Jr. (1995)
David Cross (2006)
Jim Day (2006)
John Dyment Jr. (2001)
Morris Fishman (2001)
Harry Giddings (1985)
R. K. "Doc" Hodgson (2001)
Gord Huntley (1998)
Roy Johnson (2003)
Lucien Laurin (1978)
Barry Littlefield (2000)
Edward "Ted" Mann (1982)
Gordon "Pete" McCann (1980)
Frank Merrill Jr. (1981)
J. C. "Jerry" Meyer (1999)
John Nixon (2002)
John Passero (2000)
Gil Rowntree (1997)
F. H. "Fred" Schelke (2002)
Ronald K. "Red" Smith (2004)
Joseph "Yonnie" Starr (1979)
Austin Irwin "Butch" Taylor (1987)
J. J. "Johnny" Thorpe (2002)
John R. Walker (2000)
Arthur Warner (1984)
James White (1996)
Ed Whyte (2001)

REFERENCE

Rules of Racing

The following model rules were developed by the Association of Racing Commissioners International and the North American Pari-Mutuel Regulators Association, which merged with RCI in 2005. Although individual states implement their own regulations for how racing is conducted in their jurisdictions, the model rules combine both time-tested concepts and new developments in the Thoroughbred sport. The following rules encompass the running of the race. Other model rules include such matters as racing officials, medications, and pari-mutuel wagering.

I. Entries and Nominations

A. Entering

No horse shall be qualified to start unless it has been and continues to be entered.

B. Procedure

1. Entries and nominations shall be made with the racing secretary and shall not be considered until received by the racing secretary, who shall maintain a record of time of receipt of them for a period of one year.
2. An entry shall be in the name of the horse's licensed owner and made by the owner, trainer, or a licensed designee of the owner or trainer.
3. Races printed in the condition book shall have preference over substitute and extra races.
4. An entry must be sent in writing, by telephone, or facsimile machine to the racing secretary. The entry must be confirmed in writing should the stewards or the racing secretary so request.
5. The person making an entry shall clearly designate the horse so entered.
6. No alteration may be made in any entry after the closing of entries, but an error may be corrected with permission of the stewards.
7. No horse may be entered in more than one race (with the exception of stakes races) to be run on the same day on which pari-mutuel wagering is conducted.
8. Any permitted medication or approved change of equipment must be declared at time of entry.

C. Limitation as to Spouses

No entry in any race shall be accepted for a horse owned wholly or in part by, or trained by, a person whose husband or wife is under license suspension at time of such entry; except that, if the license of a jockey has been suspended for a routine riding offense, the stewards may waive this rule.

D. Coupled Entries

1. Two or more horses entered in a race shall be joined as a mutuel entry and single betting interest if they are owned or leased in whole or in part by the same owner or are trained by a trainer who owns or leases any interest in any of the other horses in the race, except that entries may be uncoupled in stakes races.
2. No more than two horses having common ties through ownership or training may be entered in an overnight race. Under no circumstances may both horses of a coupled entry start to the exclusion of a single entry. When making a coupled entry, a preference for one of the horses must be made.

E. Nominations

1. Any nominator to a stakes race may transfer or declare such nomination prior to closing.
2. Joint nominations and entries may be made by any one of joint owners of a horse, and each such owner shall be jointly and severally liable for all payments due.
3. Death of a horse, or a mistake in its entry when such horse is eligible, does not release the nominator or transferee from liability for all stakes fees due. No fees paid in connection with a nomination to a stakes race that is run shall be refunded, except as otherwise stated in the conditions of a stakes race.
4. Death of a nominator to a stakes race shall not render void any subscription, entry, or right of entry. All rights, privileges, and obligations shall be attached to the legal heirs of the decedent or the successor owner of the horse.
5. When a horse is sold privately or at public auction or claimed, stakes engagements shall be transferred automatically to its new owner, except when the horse is transferred to a person whose license is suspended or who is otherwise unqualified to race or enter the horse; then such nomination shall be void as of the date of such transfer.
6. All stakes fees paid toward a stakes race shall be allocated to the winner unless otherwise provided by the conditions for the race. If a stakes race is not run for any reason, all such nomination fees paid shall be refunded.

F. Closings

1. Entries for purse races and nominations to stakes races shall close at the time designated by the association in previously published conditions for such races. No entry, nomination, or declaration shall be accepted after such closing time; except in the event of an emergency or if an overnight race fails to fill, the racing secretary may, with the approval of a steward, extend such closing time.
2. Except as otherwise provided in the conditions for a stakes race, the deadline for accepting nominations and declarations is midnight of the day of closing, provided they are received in time for compliance with every other condition of the race.

G. Number of Starters in a Race

The maximum number of starters in any race shall be limited to the number of starting positions afforded by the association starting gate and its extensions. The number of starters may be further limited by the number of horses that, in the opinion of the stewards, can be afforded a safe, fair, and equal start.

H. Split or Divided Races

1. In the event a race is canceled or declared off, the association may split any overnight race for which post positions have not been drawn.
2. Where an overnight race is split, forming two or more separate races, the racing secretary shall give notice of not less than 15 minutes before such races are closed to grant time for making additional entries to such split races.

I. Post Positions

Post positions for all races shall be determined by lot and shall be publicly drawn in the presence of a steward or steward designee.

J. Also-Eligible List

1. If the number of entries for a race exceeds the number of horses permitted to start, the racing secretary may create and post an also-eligible list.

2. If any horse is scratched from a race for which an also-eligible list was created, a replacement horse shall be drawn from the also-eligible list into the race in order of preference. If none is preferred, a horse shall be drawn into the race from the also-eligible list by public lot.

3. Any owner or trainer of a horse on the also-eligible list who does not wish to start the horse in such race shall so notify the racing secretary prior to scratch time for the race, thereby forfeiting any preference to which the horse may have been entitled.

4. A horse that draws into a straightaway race from the also-eligible list shall start from the post position vacated by the scratched horse. In the event more than one horse is scratched, post positions of horses drawing in from the also-eligible list shall be determined by public lot.

5. A horse that draws into a nonstraightaway race from the also-eligible list shall start from the outermost post position. In the event more than one horse is scratched, post positions of horses drawing in from the also-eligible list shall be determined by public lot.

K. Preferred List

The racing secretary shall maintain a list of entered horses eliminated from starting by a surplus of entries, and these horses shall constitute a preferred list and have preference. The manner in which the preferred list shall be maintained and all rules governing such list shall be the responsibility of the racing secretary. Such rules must be submitted to the racing commission 30 days prior to the commencement of the race meeting and are subject to the approval of the commission.

II. Declarations and Scratches

Declarations and scratches are irrevocable.

A. Declarations

1. A "declaration" is the act of withdrawing an entered horse from a race prior to the closing of entries.

2. The declaration of a horse before closing shall be made by the owner, trainer, or their licensed designee in the form and manner prescribed in these rules.

B. Scratches

1. A "scratch" is the act of withdrawing an entered horse from a contest after the closing of entries.

2. The scratch of a horse after closing shall be made by the owner, trainer, or their licensed designee, with permission from the stewards.

3. A horse may be scratched from a stakes race for any reason at any time up until 45 minutes prior to post time for that race.

4. No horse may be scratched from an overnight race without approval of the stewards.

5. In overnight races, horses that are physically disabled or sick shall be permitted to be scratched first. Should horses representing more than ten betting interests in the daily double or exotic wagering races, or horses representing more than eight betting interests in any other overnight race, remain in after horses with physical excuses have been scratched, then owners or trainers may be permitted at scratch time to scratch horses without physical excuses down to such respective minimum numbers for such races. This privilege shall be determined by lot if an excessive number of owners or trainers wish to scratch their horses.

6. Entry of any horse that has been scratched or excused from starting by the stewards because of a physical disability or sickness shall not be accepted until the expiration of three racing days after such horse was scratched or excused and the horse has been removed from the Veterinarian's List by the official veterinarian.

III. Weights

A. Allowances

1. Weight allowance must be claimed at time of entry and shall not be waived after the posting of entries, except by consent of the stewards.

2. A horse shall start with only the allowance of weight to which it is entitled at time of starting, regardless of its allowance at time of entry.

3. Horses not entitled to the first weight allowance in a race shall not be entitled to any subsequent allowance specified in the conditions.

4. Claim of weight allowance to which a horse is not entitled shall not disqualify it unless protest is made in writing and lodged with the stewards at least one hour before post time for that race.

5. A horse shall not be given a weight allowance for failure to finish second or lower in any race.

6. No horse shall receive allowance of weight nor be relieved extra weight for having been beaten in one or more races, but this rule shall not prohibit maiden allowances or allowances to horses that have not won a race within a specified period or a race of a specified value.

7. Except in handicap races that expressly provide otherwise, two-year-old fillies shall be allowed three pounds, and fillies and mares three years old and upward shall be allowed five pounds before September 1 and three pounds thereafter in races where competing against male horses.

B. Penalties

1. Weight penalties are obligatory.

2. Horses incurring weight penalties for a race shall not be entitled to any weight allowance for that race.

3. No horse shall incur a weight penalty or be barred from any race for having been placed second or lower in any race.

4. Penalties incurred and allowances due in steeplechase or hurdle races shall not apply to races on the flat, and vice versa.

5. The reports, records, and statistics as published by *Daily Racing Form*, Equibase, or other recognized publications shall be considered official in determining eligibility, allowances, and penalties, but may be corrected.

C. Weight Conversions

For the purpose of determining weight assignments and/or allowances for imported horses, the following weight conversions shall be used:

1. 1 kilogram equals 2¼ pounds
2. 1 Stone equals 14 pounds

IV. Workouts

A. Requirements

A horse shall not start unless it has participated in an official race or has an approved timed workout satisfactory to the stewards. The workout must have occurred at a pari-mutuel or commission-recognized facility within the previous 30 days. A horse that has not started for a period of 60 days or more shall be ineligible to race until it has completed a timed workout approved by the stewards prior to the day of the race in which the horse is entered. The association may impose more stringent workout requirements.

B. Identification

1. Unless otherwise prescribed by the stewards or the commission, the official lip tattoo must have been affixed to a horse's upper lip or other identification method approved by the appropriate breed registry and the commission applied prior to its participation in workouts from the gate, schooling races, or workouts required for removal from the Stewards' List, Starter's List, Veterinarian's List, or Bleeder List.

2. The trainer or exercise rider shall take each horse scheduled for an official workout to be identified by the clocker or clocker's assistant immediately prior to the workout.

3. A horse shall be properly identified by its lip tattoo or other identification method approved by the appropriate breed registry and the commission immediately prior to participating in an official timed workout.

4. The trainer or trainer's designee shall be required to identify the distance the horse is to be worked and the point on the track where the workout will start.

C. Information Dissemination

Information regarding a horse's approved timed workout or workouts shall be furnished to the public prior to the start of the race for which the horse has been entered.

D. Restrictions

A horse shall not be taken onto the track for training or a workout except during hours designated by the association.

V. Ineligible Horses

A horse is ineligible to start in a race when:

1. It is not stabled on the grounds of the association or present by the time established by the commission;

2. Its breed registration certificate is not on file with the racing secretary or horse identifier, unless the racing secretary has submitted the certificate to the appropriate breed registry for correction;

3. It is not fully identified and tattooed on the inside of the upper lip or identified by any other method approved by the appropriate breed registry and the commission;

4. It has been fraudulently entered or raced in any jurisdiction under a different name, with an altered registration certificate or altered lip tattoo or other identification method approved by the appropriate breed registry and the commission;

5. It is wholly or partially owned by a disqualified person or a horse is under the direct or indirect training or management of a disqualified person;

6. It is wholly or partially owned by the spouse of a disqualified person or a horse is under the direct or indirect management of the spouse of a disqualified person, in such cases, it being presumed that the disqualified person and spouse constitute a single financial entity with respect to the horse, which presumption may be rebutted;

7. The stakes or entrance money for the horse has not been paid in accordance with the conditions of the race;

8. The losing jockey mount fee is not on deposit with the horsemen's bookkeeper;

9. Its name appears on the Starter's List, Stewards' List, or Veterinarian's List;

10. It is a first-time starter and has not been approved to start by the starter;

11. It is owned in whole or in part by an undisclosed person or interest;

12. It lacks sufficient official published workouts or race past performance(s);

13. It has been entered in a stakes race and has subsequently been transferred with its engagements, unless the racing secretary has been notified of such prior to the start;

14. It is subject to a lien that has not been approved by the stewards and filed with the horsemen's bookkeeper;

15. It is subject to a lease not filed with the stewards;

16. It is not in sound racing condition;

17. It has had a surgical neurectomy performed on a heel nerve that has not been approved by the official veterinarian;

18. It has been trachea tubed to artificially assist breathing;

19. It has been blocked with alcohol or otherwise drugged or surgically denerved to desensitize the nerves above the ankle;

20. It has impaired eyesight in both eyes;

21. It is barred or suspended in any recognized jurisdiction;

22. It does not meet the eligibility conditions of the race;

23. Its owner or lessor is in arrears for any stakes fees, except with approval of the racing secretary;

24. Its owner(s), lessor(s), and/or trainer have not completed the licensing procedures required by the commission;

25. It is by an unknown sire or out of an unknown mare; or

26. There is no current negative test certificate for Equine Infectious Anemia attached to its breed registration certificate, as required by statute.

VI. Running of the Race

A. Equipment

1. No whip shall be used unless it has affixed to the end of it a looped leather "popper" not less than 1¼ inches in width and not over 3 inches in length, and is "feathered" above the "popper" with not less than three rows of leather "feathers," each "feather" not less than 1 inch in length. No whip shall exceed 31 inches in length. All whips are subject to inspection and approval by the stewards.

2. No bridle shall exceed two pounds.

3. A horse's tongue may be tied down with clean bandages, gauze, or tongue strap.

4. No licensee may add blinkers to a horse's equipment or discontinue their use without the prior approval of the starter, the paddock judge, and the stewards.

5. No licensee may change any equipment used on a horse in its last race in this jurisdiction without approval of the paddock judge.

B. Racing Numbers

1. Each horse shall carry a conspicuous saddlecloth number corresponding to the official number given that horse on the official program.

2. In the case of a coupled entry that includes more than one horse, each horse in the entry shall carry the same number, with a different distinguishing letter following the number. As an example, two horses in the same entry shall appear in the official program as 1 and 1A.

3. Each horse in the mutuel field shall carry a separate number or may carry the same number with a distinguishing letter following the number.

C. Jockey Requirements

1. Jockeys shall report to the jockeys' quarters at the time designated by the association. Jockeys shall report their engagements and any overweight to the clerk of scales. Jockeys shall not leave the jockeys' quarters except to ride in scheduled races until all of their riding engagements of the day have been fulfilled, except as approved by the stewards.

2. A jockey who has not fulfilled all riding engagements who desires to leave the jockeys' quarters must first receive the permission of the stewards and must be accompanied by an association security guard.

3. While in the jockeys' quarters, jockeys shall have no contact or communication with any person outside the jockeys' quarters other than commission personnel and officials, an owner or trainer for whom the jockey is riding, or a representative of the regular news media, except with the permission of the stewards. Any communication permitted by the stewards may be conducted only in the presence of the clerk of scales or other person designated by the stewards.

4. Jockeys shall be weighed out for their respective mounts by the clerk of scales not more than 30 minutes before post time for each race.

5. Only valets employed by the association shall assist jockeys in weighing out.

6. A jockey must wear a safety vest when riding in any official race. The safety vest shall weigh no more than two pounds and be designed to provide shock-absorbing protection to the upper body of at least a rating of five as defined by the British Equestrian Trade Association (BETA).

7. A jockey's weight shall include his or her clothing, boots, saddle and its attachments, and any other equipment except the whip, bridle, bit or reins, safety helmet, safety vest, blinkers, goggles, and number cloth.

8. Seven pounds is the limit of overweight any horse is permitted to carry.

9. Once jockeys have fulfilled their riding engagements for the day and have left the jockeys' quarters, they shall not be readmitted to the jockeys' quarters until after the entire racing program for that day has been completed, except with permission of the stewards.

D. Paddock to Post

1. Each horse shall carry the full weight assigned for that race from the paddock to the starting post, and shall parade past the stewards' stand, unless excused by the stewards. The post parade shall not exceed 12 minutes, unless otherwise ordered by the stewards. It shall be the duty of the stewards to ensure that the horses arrive at the starting gate as near to post time as possible.

2. After the horses enter the track, no jockey may dismount nor entrust his or her horse to the care of an attendant unless, because of accident occurring to the jockey, the horse, or the equipment, and with the prior consent of the starter. During any delay during which a jockey is permitted to dismount, all other jockeys may dismount and their horses may be attended by others. After the horses enter the track, only the jockey, an assistant starter, the official veterinarian, the racing veterinarian, or an outrider or pony rider may touch the horse before the start of the race.

3. If a jockey is injured on the way to the post, the horse shall be returned to the paddock or any other area designated by the stewards, resaddled with the appropriate weight, and remounted with a replacement jockey.

4. After passing the stewards' stand in parade, the horses may break formation and proceed to the post in any manner unless otherwise directed by the stewards. Once at the post, the horses shall be started without unnecessary delay.

5. Horses shall arrive at the starting post in post-position order.

6. In case of accident to a jockey or his or her mount or equipment, the stewards or the starter may permit the jockey to dismount and the horse to be cared for during the delay, and may permit all jockeys to dismount and all horses to be attended to during the delay.

7. If a horse throws its jockey on the way from the paddock to the post, the horse must be returned to the point where the jockey was thrown, where it shall be remounted and then proceed over the route of the parade to the post. The horse must carry its assigned weight from paddock to post and from post to finish.

8. If a horse leaves the course while moving from paddock to post, the horse shall be returned to the course at the nearest practical point to that at which it left the course, and shall complete its parade to the post from the point at which it left the course, unless ordered scratched by the stewards.

9. No person shall willfully delay the arrival of a horse at the post.

10. The starter shall load horses into the starting gate in any order deemed necessary to ensure a safe and fair start. Only the jockey, the racing veterinarian, the starter, or an assistant starter shall handle a horse at the post.

E. Post to Finish

1. The Start

a. The starter is responsible for assuring that each participant receives a fair start.

b. If, when the starter dispatches the field, any door at the front of the starting-gate stalls should not open properly due to a mechanical failure or malfunction or should any action by any starting personnel directly cause a horse to receive an unfair start, the stewards may declare such a horse a nonstarter.

c. Should a horse, not scratched prior to the start, not be in the starting-gate stall, thereby causing it to be left when the field is dispatched by the starter, the horse shall be declared a nonstarter by the stewards.

d. Should an accident or malfunction of the starting gate or other unforeseeable event compromise the fairness of the race or the safety of race participants, the stewards may declare individual horses to be nonstarters, exclude individual horses from one or more pari-mutuel pools, or declare a "no contest" and refund all wagers except as otherwise provided in the rules involving multi-race wagers.

2. Interference, Jostling, or Striking

a. A jockey shall not ride carelessly or willfully so as to permit his or her mount to interfere with, impede, or intimidate any other horse in the race.

b. No jockey shall carelessly or willfully jostle, strike, or touch another jockey or another jockey's horse or equipment.

c. No jockey shall unnecessarily cause his or her horse to shorten its stride so as to give the appearance of having suffered a foul.

3. Maintaining a Straight Course

a. When the way is clear in a race, a horse may be ridden to any part of the course, but if any horse swerves or is ridden to either side so as to interfere with, impede, or intimidate any other horse, it is a foul.

b. The offending horse may be disqualified if, in the opinion of the stewards, the foul altered the finish of the race, regardless of whether the foul was accidental, willful, or the result of careless riding.

c. If the stewards determine the foul was intentional or due to careless riding, the jockey may be held responsible.

d. In a straightaway race, every horse must maintain position as nearly as possible in the lane in which it starts. If a horse is ridden, drifts, or swerves out of its lane in such a manner that it interferes with, impedes, or intimidates another horse, it is a foul and may result in the disqualification of the offending horse.

4. Disqualification

a. When the stewards determine that a horse shall be disqualified for interference, they may place the offending horse behind such horses as in their judgment it interfered with, or they may place it last.

b. If a horse is disqualified for a foul, any horse or horses in the same race owned or trained by the same interests, whether coupled or uncoupled, may also be disqualified.

c. When a horse is disqualified for interference in a time-trial race, for the purposes of qualifying only, it shall receive the time of the horse it is placed behind plus one-hundredth of a second penalty or more exact measurement if photo-finish equipment permits, and shall be eligible to qualify for the finals or consolations of the race on the basis of the assigned time.

d. Possession of any electrical or mechanical stimulating or shocking device by a jockey, horse owner, trainer, or other person authorized to handle or attend to a horse shall be prima-facie evidence of a violation of these rules and is sufficient grounds for the stewards to scratch or disqualify the horse.

e. The stewards may determine that a horse shall be unplaced for the purpose of purse distribution and time-trial qualification.

5. Horses Shall Be Ridden Out

All horses shall be ridden out in every race. A jockey shall not ease up or coast to the finish without reasonable cause, even if the horse has no apparent chance to win prize money. A jockey shall give a best effort during a race, and each horse shall be ridden to win.

6. Use of Whips

a. Although the use of a whip is not required, any jockey who uses a whip during a race shall do so only in a manner consistent with exerting his or her best efforts to win.

b. In all races where a jockey will ride without a whip, an announcement of such fact shall be made over the public address system.

c. No electrical or mechanical device or other expedient designed to increase or retard the speed of a horse, other than the whip approved by the stewards, shall be possessed by anyone or applied by anyone to the horse at any time on the grounds of the association during the meeting, whether in a race or otherwise.

d. Whips shall not be used on two-year-old horses before April 1 of each year.

e. Prohibited use of the whip includes whipping a horse:

i. On the head, flanks, or on any other part of its body other than the shoulders or hindquarters except when necessary to control a horse;

ii. During the post parade or after the finish of the race except when necessary to control the horse;

iii. Excessively or brutally, causing welts or breaks in the skin;

iv. When the horse is clearly out of the race or has obtained its maximum placing;

v. Persistently even though the horse is showing no response under the whip; or

vi. Striking another rider or horse.

7. Horse Leaving the Racecourse

If a horse leaves the racecourse during a race, it must turn back and resume the race from the point at which it originally left the course.

8. Order of Finish

a. The official order of finish shall be decided by the stewards with the aid of the photo-finish camera, and in the absence of the photo-finish film strip, the video replay. The photo finish and video replay are only aids in the stewards' decision. The decision of the stewards shall be final in all cases.

b. The nose of the horse shall determine the placement of the horse in relationship to other horses in the race.

9. Returning After the Finish

a. After a race has been run, the jockey shall ride promptly to the place designated by the stewards, dismount, and report to the clerk of scales to be weighed in. Jockeys shall weigh in with all pieces of equipment with which they weighed out.

b. If a jockey is prevented from riding to the designated unsaddling area because of an accident or illness to the jockey or the horse, the jockey may walk or be transported to the scales or may be excused from weighing in by the stewards.

10. Unsaddling

a. Only persons authorized by the stewards may assist the jockey with unsaddling the horse after the race.

b. No one shall place a covering over a horse before it is unsaddled.

11. Weighing In

a. A jockey shall weigh in at least at the same weight at which he or she weighed out, and if under that weight by more than two pounds, his or her mount shall be disqualified from any portion of the purse money.

b. In the event of such disqualification, all money wagered on the horse shall be refunded unless the race has been declared official.

c. No jockey shall weigh in at more than two pounds over the proper or declared weight, excluding the weight attributed to inclement weather conditions and/or of health and safety equipment approved by the stewards.

12. Dead Heats

a. When two horses run a dead heat for first place, all purses or prizes to which first and second horses would have been entitled shall be divided equally between them; and this principle applies in dividing all purses or prizes whatever the number of horses running a dead heat and whatever places for which the dead heat is run.

b. In a dead heat for first place, each horse involved shall be deemed a winner and liable to penalty for the amount it shall receive.

c. When a dead heat is run for second place and an objection is made to the winner of the race and sustained, the horses that ran a dead heat shall be deemed to have run a dead heat for first place.

d. If the dividing owners cannot agree as to which of them is to have a cup or other prize that cannot be divided, the question shall be determined by lot by the stewards.

VII. Protests, Objections, and Inquiries

A. Stewards to Inquire

1. The stewards shall take cognizance of foul riding and, upon their own motion or that of any racing offi-

cial or person empowered by this chapter to object or complain, shall make diligent inquiry or investigation into such objection or complaint when properly received.

2. In determining the extent of disqualification, the stewards in their discretion may:

a. Declare null and void a track record set or equaled by a disqualified horse or any horses coupled with it as an entry;

b. Affirm the placing judges' order of finish and hold the jockey responsible if, in the stewards' opinion, the foul riding did not affect the order of finish; or

c. Disqualify the offending horse and hold the jockey blameless if in the stewards' opinion the interference to another horse in a race was not the result of an intentional foul or careless riding on the part of a jockey.

B. Race Objections

1. An objection to an incident alleged to have occurred during the running of a race shall be received only when lodged with the clerk of scales, the stewards, or their designees, by the owner, the authorized agent of the owner, the trainer, or the jockey of a horse engaged in the same race.

2. An objection following the running of any race must be filed before the race is declared official, whether all or some riders are required to weigh in or the use of a "fast official" procedure is permitted.

3. The stewards shall make all findings of fact as to all matters occurring during and incident to the running of a race, shall determine all objections and inquiries, and shall determine the extent of disqualification, if any, of horses in the race. Such findings of fact and determinations shall be final.

C. Prior Objections

1. Objections to the participation of a horse entered in any race shall be made to the stewards in writing, signed by the objector, and filed not later than one hour prior to post time for the first race on the day that the questioned horse is entered. Any such objection shall set forth the specific reason or grounds for the objection in such detail so as to establish probable cause for the objection. The stewards upon their own motion may consider an objection until such time as the horse becomes a starter.

2. An objection to a horse entered in a race may be made on, but not limited to, the following grounds or reasons:

a. A misstatement, error, or omission in the entry under which a horse is to run;

b. The horse entered to run is not the horse it is represented to be at the time of entry, or the age was erroneously given;

c. The horse is not qualified to enter under the conditions specified for the race, or the allowances are improperly claimed or not entitled the horse, or the weight to be carried is incorrect under the conditions of the race;

d. The horse is owned in whole or in part, or leased or trained by a person ineligible to participate in racing or otherwise ineligible to own a racehorse as provided in these rules; or

e. The horse was entered without regard to a lien filed previously with the racing secretary.

3. The stewards may scratch from the race any horse that is the subject of an objection if they have reasonable cause to believe that the objection is valid.

D. Protests

1. A protest against any horse that has started in a race shall be made to the stewards in writing, signed by the protestor, within 72 hours of the race exclusive of nonracing days. If the incident upon which the protest is based occurs within the last two days of the meeting, such protest may be filed with the commission within 72 hours exclusive of Saturdays, Sundays, or official holidays. Any such protest shall set forth the specific reason or reasons for the protest in such detail as to establish probable cause for the protest.

2. A protest may be made on any of the following grounds:

a. Any grounds for objection as set forth in this chapter;

b. The order of finish as officially determined by the stewards was incorrect due to oversight or errors in the numbers of the horses that started the race;

c. A jockey, trainer, owner, or lessor was ineligible to participate in racing as provided in this chapter;

d. The weight carried by a horse was improper by reason of fraud or willful misconduct; or

e. An unfair advantage was gained in violation of the rules.

3. Notwithstanding any other provision in this article, time limitation on the filing of protests shall not apply in any case in which fraud or willful misconduct is alleged, provided the stewards are satisfied that the allegations are bona fide and verifiable.

4. No person shall file any objection or protest knowing the same to be inaccurate, false, untruthful, or frivolous.

5. The stewards may order any purse, award, or prize for any race withheld from distribution pending the determination of any protest. In the event any purse, award, or prize has been distributed to an owner or for a horse that by reason of a protest or other reason is disqualified or determined to be not entitled to such purse, award, or prize, the stewards or the commission may order such purse, award, or prize returned and redistributed to the rightful owner or horse. Any person who fails to comply with an order to return any purse, award, or prize erroneously distributed shall be subject to fines and suspension.

Preference Date System

Racing secretaries long have struggled with two problems: Not enough horses for a race in the track's condition book, which details prospective races for the meet, and too many horses for a specific race.

When a race has too few entries, the racing-office staff must make calls to trainers and solicit them to enter horses in the race. This process is widely known as "hustling," and a starter that is entered for such a race is often referred to a "hustled horse."

A race with too many entrants presents a different set of problems. Often, the race can be split. When other overnight races on the card are slow to fill, a racing secretary may choose to split a popular race, a maiden special weight race for instance, into two or three or more separate races.

If splitting a race is not feasible, the racing secretary needs a system that determines the eligible horses that will get starting positions. Racing offices long used the "star system," under which a horse denied a starting place in an oversubscribed race was given a star. A horse excluded twice from a race would get two stars. Under the star system, horses with the most stars received preference for the next race with the same conditions.

Many tracks now have changed to a "preference date system," which is similar to the star system but simpler to maintain. In the preference date system, the horses with the earliest preference date get into the race first.

As an example of how the preference date rules system is used, following are the preference date rules of Golden Gate Fields and Bay Meadows Race Course in Northern California:

Preference Date System

All horses whose foal certificates are registered with the racing secretary on the first day of entries will receive an entry date for that day. Thereafter, horses will receive entry dates for the day their foal certificates are registered with the racing secretary. Such entry dates will be good for any category.

1. In all races, winners are preferred.
2. Maidens will not be eligible to receive an entry date in any race until their papers are on file with the racing office at the time of the draw. Entry dates for maidens are good for any maiden race.
3. Horses drawn into races and horses on the also-eligible list that draw into races will receive a running date corresponding to the date on which they are to run, and lose all dates previously held.
4. Horses on the Veterinarian's, Stewards' or Starter's List cannot establish a date. They will not be permitted to enter until they have been approved to start. Horses placed on these lists will keep their dates if they ran in the particular race in which they made the list. Horses that are scratched and placed on a list will be given a scratch date for the day of that race.
5. In all cases, an entry date takes preference over a running date of the same day and a running date takes preference over a scratch date of the same day.
6. Horses drawn on the overnight (either in the race or on the also-eligible) and scratched will lose their date and acquire a scratch date corresponding to the day of the race, unless otherwise specified by the stewards. Any horse on the also-eligible list that is declared will retain its preference date if the scratch is not activated. Other scratched horses will be treated in the following manner:
   a. Runaway in the paddock—Entry date for day of race.
   b. Runaway in the post parade—Entry date for day of race.
   c. Flip in the gate prior to the start—Scratch date for day of race.
   d. Scratched for insufficient works—Scratch date for day of race.
   e. Scratched because of incorrect markings—Scratch date for day of race.
   f. Ineligible to race in which drawn into—Scratch date for day of race.
   g. Scratched because of breakdown in transportation to the track—Retains original date.
   h. Scratched at the gate and not put on any list—Scratch date for day of race.
   i. Entered in the wrong race by delegated agent or trainer—Scratch date for day of race.
   j. Horse hurt in gate due to accident involving another horse—Retains original date.
   k. Horse left behind the gate—Retains original date.
7. Horses that have established a date at the current meeting will lose that preference date should they race elsewhere.
8. Stakes races are not considered in the preference date system.
9. In no way does the claiming, ownership transfer, or trainer transfer of a horse affect the preference date.
10. Maidens, when entered in a winners' race, will retain original date.
11. Horses entered will initially receive an entry date corresponding to the date on which they are entered.
12. A same-owner entry cannot exclude a single entry except when race preferences indicate otherwise. Trainers must declare at time of entry if he or she has a same-owner or different-owner entry in the race. All same-owner entries must have a declared first and second choice at entry time.

How Jockeys Are Paid

Leading jockeys often will be paid upfront fees when they travel to ride a horse in a stakes race, but most jockeys are compensated according to a table of fees based on race purse and finish position of the horse they ride. Joint model rules of the Association of Racing Commissioners International and the North American Pari-Mutuel Regulators Association contain a suggested fee table, although fees vary from one track or state to another. Following is the model fee schedule as published in 2005.

In the absence of a written agreement, the following jockey mount fees apply:

Purse	Winning Mount	2nd-Place Mount	3rd-Place Mount	Losing Mount
$599 and Under	$33	$33	$33	$33
$600-699	$36	$33	$33	$33
$700-999	10% Win Purse	$33	$33	$33
$1,000-1,499	10% Win Purse	$33	$33	$33
$1,500-1,999	10% Win Purse	$35	$33	$33
$2,000-3,499	10% Win Purse	$45	$40	$38
$3,500-4,999	10% Win Purse	$55	$45	$40
$5,000-9,999	10% Win Purse	$65	$50	$45
$10,000-14,999	10% Win Purse	5% Place Purse	5% Show Purse	$50
$15,000-24,999	10% Win Purse	5% Place Purse	5% Show Purse	$55
$25,000-49,999	10% Win Purse	5% Place Purse	5% Show Purse	$65
$50,000-99,999	10% Win Purse	5% Place Purse	5% Show Purse	$80
$100,000 & Up	10% Win Purse	5% Place Purse	5% Show Purse	$105

How to Handicap a Race

Handicapping is perhaps the most underappreciated aspect of horse racing. Do it well and you will not only identify winning horses but also assert your superior skill in an intellectual challenge unlike any other in sports. Wagering on horse racing is pari-mutuel, which means you are wagering against other bettors. (See pari-mutuel wagering section later in this chapter.)

Handicapping is the inexact science of predicting the results of races that can have as many as 20 horses, each a high-strung, unpredictable Thoroughbred traveling as fast as 40 miles per hour while carrying more than 100 pounds on its back. It is truly amazing that horses can sometimes race as far as a mile and a half and be separated literally by inches at the finish line.

You are not going to predict the winner of every race. No one does. But there is no better feeling in the world than correctly handicapping a race. The feeling is even better if you have bet on your selection, which provides a tangible reward to accompany the bragging rights you have earned for being, at least in this one instance, smarter than your companions. And when you are wrong about a race, you can still gain from the experience by keeping an open mind, and, if the opportunity presents itself, gleaning a nugget of information that could serve you well when handicapping another race.

Handicapping is a skill that you can continue to hone with one important caveat: You will improve only if you do not believe you already have all the answers.

Where do you start? First, you need to have a realistic framework.

Framework of Reality

Year after year at every single racetrack in North America, betting favorites—the horses with the most money wagered on them to win—are victorious only 25% to 35% of the time. That means the betting public handicaps a race correctly once every three or four times. When the betting public is wrong, the payoffs are obviously higher. If you can establish which favorites are vulnerable for any of a myriad of reasons—such as poor post position, an unreliable rider, or no recent races or workouts—you can locate overlays, which are horses whose odds are higher than they should be. Their opposites are underlays, horses whose odds are shorter than they deserve. Most bettors try to find overlays. If they can find one or two winning overlays a day, they are likely to exit the track with more money than they brought with them. Remember, there are no rules at the track saying you must bet every race or even a single race.

It is important to understand the difference between handicapping, which is trying to logically predict the winner of a race, and wagering. Relatively speaking, handicapping is a breeze compared to wagering. Wagering used to be simple. There used to be just a handful of wagering options, betting to win (finish first), place (finish first or second), or show (finish first, second, or third) and a daily double (selecting the winners of two consecutive races). Now, racetrack bettors have a smorgasbord of wagering options and, with the advent of full-card simulcast wagering in the 1990s, dozens of racetracks on which to bet from one location. Selecting the amount and right type of bet takes an incredible amount of self-discipline and excellent money management. We will focus here on handicapping.

Track Condition Abbreviations

Thoroughbred racing is contested on dirt and turf, the latter also called grass. The abbreviations for track conditions:

Dirt	Turf
ft: fast	**hd:** hard
gd: good	**fm:** firm
sy: sloppy	**gd:** good
my: muddy	**yl:** yielding
wf: wet fast	**sf:** soft
s: sealed track	

Reading Past-Performance Lines

You cannot handicap a race without being able to read past-performance lines, which are a statistical representation of a horse's performance in each of its starts. Past-performance lines can be found in *Daily Racing Form*, a daily newspaper in tabloid format, or a track program, which is the size of a magazine. *Daily Racing Form* provides more information in its past-performance lines and usually has more of them for each horse than a track program. Either one is sufficient.

Past-performance lines contain a multitude of abbreviations and terms that are explained in the accompanying boxes. While past-performance lines appear intimidating to the novice, understanding them is much easier than it appears.

The conditions for each race appear at the top of all the horses' past-performance lines and determine which horses are eligible. Races may be limited to horses of one age or one sex, horses bred in one state, or horses that have not won a certain number of races or amount of purse money. Claiming races are for horses that can be purchased for a designated price. That amount is indicated in the race conditions, and the past performances disclose the horses' claiming prices in previous races.

In *Daily Racing Form*, horses are listed in post-position order beginning with the horse closest to the rail. Track programs list horses by the

6-5
9
AFLEET ALEX (L)
b. c. 3 Northern Afleet—Maggy Hawk, by Hawkster **126**
Bred in Fl. by John Martin Silvertand
GREEN with a crown emblem, white sleeves, green shamrock and cuff, red cap

Owner: CASH IS KING LLC
Trainer: TIMOTHY F. RITCHEY
Jockey: JEREMY ROSE

2005:	5	3	0	1	$1,485,000
2004:	6	4	2	0	$680,800
Life:	11	7	2	1	$2,165,800
Turf:	0	0	0	0	$0
Off Dirt:	2	2	0	0	$171,000

21May05	Pim12	ft	1 3/16	:46.07	1:10.72	1:55.04	3	Preakness (G1)-1000k	**96**	12	$10^{9\,1/4}$	$10^{7\,1/4}$	7^{4}	1^{hd}	$1^{4\,3/4}$	RoseJ	126	*3.30	Afleet Alex $^{4\,3/4}$ ScrappyT ^{5} Giacomo ^{1}	clipped heels, stumbled	14
07May05	CD10	ft	1¼	:45.38	1:35.88	2:02.75	3	KyDerby (G1)-2399k	**84**	12	$11^{8\,1/2}$	9^{5}	6^{1}	$2^{1/2}$	3^{1}	RoseJ	126	4.50	Giacomo $^{1/2}$ Closing Argument $^{1/2}$ Afleet Alex $^{2\,1/2}$	well placed, outfinished	20
16Apr05	OP9	ft	1⅛	:47.91	1:12.78	1:48.80	3	Ark.Derby (G2)-1000k	**93**	6	5^{4}	$5^{3\,1/2}$	2^{hd}	$1^{5\,1/2}$	1^{8}	RoseJ	122	*2.40	Afleet Alex ^{8} Flower Alley $^{3/4}$ Andromeda's Hero ^{nk}	settled, exploded clear	10
19Mar05	OP10	ft	1 1/16	:47.25	1:12.54	1:44.92	3	RebelS (G3)-250k	**77**	1	$3^{3\,1/2}$	$2^{3\,1/2}$	$2^{2\,1/2}$	6^{10}	$6^{12\,1/2}$	VelazquezJ	117	*.70	Greater Good $^{1/2}$ Rockport Harbor $^{2\,3/4}$ Batson Challenge $^{3\,3/4}$	gave way suddenly	6
05Mar05	OP10	ft	6f	:21.61	:44.84	1:09.52	3	MntnValley-50k	**94**	5	6	$5^{6\,1/2}$	3^{3}	2^{hd}	$1^{2\,3/4}$	RoseJ	122	*.30	Afleet Alex $^{2\,3/4}$ Razor $^{4\,1/4}$ Smoke Smoke Smoke $^{1\,3/4}$	bothered, slight drift	6
30Oct04	LS7	ft	1 1/16	:47.49	1:11.25	1:42.09	2	BC Juvenile (G1)-1500k	**85**	3	$8^{5\,3/4}$	$6^{2\,3/4}$	3^{nk}	1^{hd}	$2^{3/4}$	RoseJ	122	3.00	Wilko $^{3/4}$ Afleet Alex ^{nk} Sun King $^{1\,1/4}$	lead ¼, outfinished	8
09Oct04	Bel7	ft	1 1/16	:47.20	1:11.49	1:42.30	2	ChampagneS (G1)-500k	**90**	6	$6^{1\,3/4}$	$5^{1\,1/4}$	$4^{3/4}$	$3^{1\,1/2}$	$2^{1/2}$	RoseJ	122	*1.25	Proud Accolade $^{1/2}$ Afleet Alex $^{1\,1/4}$ Sun King $^{11\,3/4}$	wide into stretch, gamely	8
21Aug04	Sar9	sy	7f	:22	:44.79	1:23.58	2	HopefulS (G1)-250k	**84**	6	3	$5^{3\,1/4}$	$4^{2\,1/4}$	3^{2}	1^{nk}	RoseJ	122	*.70	Afleet Alex ^{nk} Devils Disciple $^{1\,3/4}$ Flamenco ^{11}	wide move, got up	7

Workouts: •24Apr04 CD 5f gd :58 B *1/34* •03Apr04 OP 5f fst :58.3 H *1/21* •13Mar04 OP 5f fst :58.3 H *1/35* •18Feb04 OP 6f fst 1:13 H *1/8* •11Feb04 OP 7f fst 1:29.3 H *1/1*

(L) - Treated with furosemide; (L*) - First time using furosemide; (O) Off of furosemide

numbers they will be wearing on their saddlecloths during the race. That is the number you will use when placing your bet.

If there is an entry, when a betting number covers more than one horse because of a common owner, trainer, or both, the horses will be designated 1 and 1A. The horse closest to the rail is the 1, and the other is 1A. If there is a third horse in one entry, it will be 1X. If there is a second entry in the same race, the horses will be identified as 2 and 2B. A single bet covers all horses in an entry.

A single bet can also encompass horses that do not have a common owner or trainer but are grouped together because the race attracted more runners than the tote system or the tote board can handle. This is called a pari-mutuel field and is increasingly rare because one of the few American races with more than the usual 14 maximum starters, the Kentucky Derby (G1), now offers wagering on each horse in the race.

Located just above the program numbers are the preliminary odds set by a track handicapping specialist to reflect how he or she believes the betting on that race will unfold. This is called the morning line or program line.

Now, let's examine a single past-performance line, that of 2005 Preakness Stakes (G1) winner Afleet Alex for the '05 Belmont Stakes (G1) at Belmont Park on June 11. (These past performances are courtesy of Equibase LLC, which provides past-performance information for *Daily Racing Form* and track programs.)

At the far left is the number on Afleet Alex's saddlecloth, nine, which was the post position he drew for the Belmont. Above the saddlecloth number is his morning-line odds as they appeared in the track program, 6-5 (1.20-to-1).

To the right of the bold-type name is information specific to Afleet Alex. The (L) next to his name indicates that he was treated with the anti-bleeding medication furosemide, which now is sold under the trade name Salix but formerly was known as Lasix in its veterinary formulation. His owner is Cash is King stable, his trainer is Timothy F. Ritchey, and his jockey is Jeremy Rose.

Beneath the name is information that describes Afleet Alex. B. c. 3 tells us that he is a bay-colored colt who is three years old. The first name next to that description is his sire, Northern Afleet, and the second name is his dam, Maggy Hawk. The third name, Hawkster, was the sire of Maggy Hawk. The next line tells us that Afleet Alex was bred in Florida by John Martin Silvertand. The next line, printed in boldface type, describes the owner's silks that Rose wore: green with a crown emblem, white sleeves, green shamrock and cuff, and red cap. The number to the right of this information, 126, is the weight that Afleet Alex carried in the Belmont, 126 pounds.

To the far right is a statistical summary of Afleet Alex's career racing record before the Belmont. In 2005, he had started five times, with three wins and a third, and had earned $1,485,000. In 2004, he had won four of six starts and finished second twice, with earnings of $680,800. Although he lost a chance to be champion juvenile male when he finished second behind Wilko in the 2004 Breeders' Cup Juvenile (G1), Afleet Alex nonetheless was one of the year's top two-year-olds. His career totals going into the Belmont were seven wins, two seconds, and a third, with total earnings of $2,165,800. He had never started on turf, and Off Dirt indicates how he performed on dirt tracks that were not rated as fast. In fact, he had had two starts on off tracks, both as a two-year-old, and had won them both. Most of his $171,000 earnings on two sloppy tracks came in his 2004 Hopeful Stakes (G1) victory at Saratoga Race Course.

Beneath Afleet Alex's statistical record are his past performances, beginning with his incredible victory in the Preakness Stakes (G1). Each past-performance line is a summary of the horse's performance in that race, beginning with the most recent race on top.

The past-performance line can be split into thirds. Let's start with the left one-third of Afleet Alex's Preakness past-performance line.

21May05 Pim12 ft 1 3/16 :46.07 1:10.72 1:55.04 3 Preakness (G1) 1000k

At the far left is the date of his most recent race, May 21, 2005; the racetrack, Pimlico Race Course (Pim); the race number, the 12th race (12) on that day's program; the track condition, fast (ft); and the race's distance, 1 3/16 miles (1 3/16). Next comes the fractional times of the leader at specified points during the race: 46.07 seconds after a half-mile, one minute and 10.72 seconds (1:10.72) after three-quarters of a mile, and the final time of the winner, one minute and 55.04 seconds (1:55.04). The following number denotes that the race was for three-year-olds (3). The next bit of information describes the race: it was the Preakness Stakes, it was a Grade 1 race (G1), and it carried a purse of $1-million (1000k).

Look at that information, and you will see that it describes the race itself and not the performance of Afleet Alex. The middle portion of the past performance specifically describes how Afleet Alex performed:

96 12 $10^{9\,1/4}$ $10^{7\,1/4}$ 7^{4} 1^{hd} $1^{4\,3/4}$ RoseJ 126 *3.30

The first figure in boldface type, 96, is his speed figure as compiled by Equibase. Speed figures are not based exclusively on how fast a horse runs. They take into consideration such factors as weather conditions, track conditions, head winds, and how fast all horses are racing over that track. In theory, speed figures allow handicappers to compare horses that have raced at different racetracks, but they are by no means infallible. Any speed figure above 90 is very good, and Afleet Alex certainly ran an outstanding race, as we will see. *Daily Racing Form*, which utilizes the speed figures devised by racing and wagering journalist Andrew Beyer, gave Afleet Alex a speed figure of 112, one of the year's fastest for a three-year-old. (Bellamy Road received a Beyer 120 figure for his victory in the Wood Memorial Stakes [G1] before the Kentucky Derby, in which he was the beaten favorite.)

The next number, 12, was Afleet Alex's post position; the following figures describe where he was located at various points in the race, corresponding in part to the fractional times listed in the left-hand portion of the past performance. He was tenth, 9¼ lengths behind the pacesetter ($10^{9\,1/4}$) after a quarter-mile, and still tenth, 7¼ lengths behind the leader ($10^{7\,1/4}$), after a half-mile. A quarter-mile later, after six furlongs, he had advanced to seventh position, four lengths behind the leader (7^{4}). The next point of call—and the next to last one in every past performance—is one-eighth mile from the finish line, in midstretch at the furlong pole. There, Afleet Alex had assumed the lead by a head (1^{hd}). The final set of figures describes where he was at the finish. In the Preakness, Afleet Alex won by 4¾ lengths. His jockey in the Preakness was Jeremy Rose (RoseJ); he carried 126 pounds (126) in the race, and he went off at odds of 3.30-to-1. The asterisk before those odds indicates that he was the race favorite (*3.30).

The final one-third of the past performance presents the order of finish and a brief commentary on the race.

Afleet Alex $^{4\,3/4}$ Scrappy T ^{5} Giacomo ^{1} clipped heels, stumbled 14

Afleet Alex was the winner by 4¾ lengths (4¾), and he was followed by Scrappy T, who was five lengths ahead of Giacomo, who in turn was a length in front of the fourth finisher. The brief comment reveals some of the drama of the 2005 Preakness, where Scrappy T veered into the path of a hard-charging Afleet Alex, nearly causing a catastrophe at the top of Pimlico's stretch. Afleet Alex clipped the heels of Scrappy T and stumbled badly, but he somehow stayed on his feet and went on to win the Preakness decisively. The final number, 14, is the number of starters in the Preakness, which is the maximum field for that race.

Three Aspects of Handicapping

There is no single correct way to handicap. In fact, that is one of handicapping's charms: What is important to you may be completely dismissed by the person standing next to you. In general, handicapping focuses on three aspects of racing: class, form, and speed. Each asks a question. Class asks: How good is this horse, judging by its previous record and the quality of its competition? Form asks: How has this horse been performing recently, not only in races but also in workouts? Speed simply asks: How fast is this horse?

Class

Class measures not only a horse's previous record but also the level of its competition. Its previous record indicates its number of wins,

Types of Bets

Win Your horse must finish first to collect.

Place Your horse must finish first or second.

Show Your horse must finish first, second, or third.

Quinella You bet two horses and they must finish first and second in either order.

Exacta You bet two horses and they must finish first and second in exact order.

Exacta box A multiple bet in which you select two or more horses and bet all combinations of them finishing first and second.

Exacta wheel You bet one horse to win and every other horse in the field to finish second.

Trifecta or triple You bet three horses and they must finish first, second, and third in exact order.

Trifecta box or triple box A multiple bet in which you select three or more horses and they must finish first, second, and third in any order.

Superfecta You bet four horses and they must finish first, second, third, and fourth in exact order.

Superfecta box You bet four or more horses and they must finish first, second, third, and fourth in any order.

Daily (or instant, late, or middle) double You must pick the winners of two consecutive races.

Pick three or pick four You must pick the winners of three or four consecutive races.

Pick six You must pick the winners of six consecutive races. A consolation payoff for those who pick five winners usually is offered.

seconds, and thirds and number of starts for not only this year but also for last year, lifetime, at this particular distance, and on this particular racing surface, dirt or turf. It is important to emphasize that dirt and turf racing should be treated as separate disciplines. If a horse in a turf race has a poor record on dirt but a superior record on grass, discount its dirt record completely. For example, in the first two starts of her career, a horse named Inca Is Calling raced on dirt, finishing sixth by 15¾ lengths and seventh by 13¾ lengths. Switched to grass for her next start, she finished second by three-quarters of a length. Her future was on grass.

It is extremely rare for a horse to be proficient on both turf and dirt. One notable exception was the great John Henry, the two-time Horse of the Year who won Grade 1 stakes, the highest competition in racing, on both dirt and turf.

Two good ways to gauge a horse's class is by its winning percentage and by its average earnings per start. Horses with poor winning percentages, say zero-for-10 (0%) or one-for-20 (5%), are chronic losers and should be avoided. They may eventually find a field weak enough to beat, but over a long period of time they are poor investments, race after race, particularly if they come close to winning and amass a high number of seconds and thirds. They always look as though they are going to win their next start but rarely do.

Average earnings per start reflect a horse's competition. If Horse A has made $80,000 in ten lifetime starts, an average of $8,000 per start, and Horse B has earned $100,000 in 40 lifetime starts, an average of $2,500 per start, Horse A has demonstrated considerably more class. There is an important caveat, however. Races restricted to horses bred in one state, be it California, Florida, Illinois, or New York, inflate a horse's earnings, presenting a distorted picture of a horse's class. Consider that factor only if a horse that has made a lot of money in state-bred races is taking on open (non-restricted) company.

Class is evidenced frequently in claiming races, where horses race for a specified price at which they can be purchased from that race. That is why it is important to read past-performance lines from the bottom (least recent) to the top (most recent), as explained in "Five Ways to Improve Your Handicapping." Say a horse won its previous start in a $15,000 claiming race and is competing today in a $25,000 claimer. Its most recent races may have been at $15,000, but several starts back it might have competed for $25,000 or even higher. The horse's performances in those races are a valuable indicator of whether it is capable of doing well against better horses today. If it previously won a $30,000 claimer, it has already demonstrated enough class to win at $25,000. If you only glanced at its two or three most recent races, you missed an important indicator of class.

An interesting nuance of class is called back class. That is when a horse with high career earnings or a high career average earnings per start has been performing poorly. Because of its recent form, it may be dismissed by bettors at high odds. However, if it shows a sign of life—that is, an improved effort in its previous start, which often is an indicator of soundness—it may be ready to reassert its class, possibly at generous odds. The improved effort could be significant.

Form

Horses are flesh-and-blood athletes, not ma-

Racing Terms and Comments

Here are some terms commonly used in racing news stories and chart footnotes. Additional terms can by found in the following section, Glossary of Common Racing and Breeding Terms.

Apprentice A rider at the beginning of his career. Horses with apprentice jockeys carry five, seven, or ten pounds less than their rivals.

Bolted The horse made a sharp, sudden move to the extreme outside.

Bore in or bore out Instead of racing in a straight line, the horse veered inside or outside.

Boxed in The horse was trapped with nowhere to move.

Brushed The horse made light contact with another horse.

Dogs Pylons or traffic cones put around a course to protect the area on the inside near the rail. Horses that work around dogs cover more distance on turns. The symbol (d) is used to denote dogs were up in a workout.

Driving The horse was all out to win.

Entry Two or more horses are coupled in the wagering because of common ownership or, in some jurisdictions, the same trainer. You bet on one and collect if either member of the entry wins.

Field Two or more horses coupled as one betting entity. Just as in an entry, you get more than one horse and collect if any horse in the betting field wins.

Furlong One-eighth of a mile.

Furosemide A diuretic commonly used in American Thoroughbred racing to prevent or limit pulmonary bleeding. Trade name is Salix (formerly Lasix).

Gamely The horse showed courage while racing.

Greenly The horse showed inexperience by racing erratically.

Handily The horse won comfortably.

Hung The horse made an apparent winning move but then failed to sustain it.

Ridden out The jockey continued to ride the winning horse to the wire without undo urging.

Route A race of one mile or longer.

Saved ground The horse raced on the inside, thereby taking a shorter route around the track.

Sprint A race shorter than one mile.

Steadied The jockey had to physically stop his riding motion because of traffic problems.

Taken up The jockey had to restrain his or her mount severely, usually because of traffic problems or interference.

Unruly The horse acted up before the start.

Used up The horse expended all its energy by contesting the pace early in the race.

Willingly The horse continued to run its best without urging.

chines. Even the best horses are unable to maintain their top-level performance for an extended period of time. That is why two-time Horse of the Year Cigar's record-tying, 16-race win streak was so remarkable in the mid-1990s. All but two of those 16 victories were in stakes races and ten of them were Grade 1 stakes.

Racehorses tend to race in form cycles, meaning they are either moving forward or backward in their performances. This is especially evident in young horses beginning their careers. If a horse making only its second lifetime start shows improvement, it is likely to improve again in its third start. Frequently, horses also show improvement in their second start off a long layoff. Horses that are idle more than a month may need a return race to get back into top condition.

Workouts can also indicate a horse's form. Fast workouts following a horse's top performance indicate that it is maintaining its best form.

Perhaps the most difficult handicapping decision is determining whether a horse that had been racing well had a legitimate excuse for a poor performance. Was the horse forced extremely wide on a turn? Did it run into traffic? If it normally races on the lead, was it involved in a suicidal speed duel? Going through all the horse's past-performance lines may provide clues. If a horse has raced wide in four or five previous starts, then it may have a bad habit rather than a good excuse for a poor performance. If a horse consistently starts slowly or routinely gets into trouble at the start, then it is apt to do so again. With the advent of race-replay centers at many racetracks, you can watch the videotape of that poor last performance and decide for yourself whether the horse had a legitimate excuse and handicap and wager accordingly.

You should expect young horses to improve, especially if they have shown a hint of ability in their first race or two. For example, catching a good price on a horse trained by Todd Pletcher and ridden by John Velazquez, who have dominated New York racing in recent years, seems impossible. Yet World Cat, a two-year-old colt, showed up in a seven-furlong maiden dirt race for New York-breds on November 26, 2005. He had made two previous starts, finishing fifth by 10½ lengths in his debut on turf at odds of 4.30-to-1. In his second start, he made his dirt debut on a sloppy track, fought on the lead the entire way from the 12th post position, and finished second by a nose at 5.40-to-1. With the fourth position on November 26, he could have been a heavy favorite off that first dirt race, but was not, paying $9.40 after winning at odds of 3.70-to-1.

Speed

If the horse with the highest speed figure won every race, handicapping would be simple. It is not. The reality is that speed is an important part of the handicapping puzzle but far from the only factor. Speed must always be considered in context. If a horse has early speed—that is, it likes to be on the lead—is it likely to make the front easily, or are there other horses in the race with early speed that will put pressure on the front-running horse? Are the others as fast as this

Five Ways to Improve Your Handicapping

1. Bottom to top. Always read a horse's past-performance lines from the bottom (least recent race) to the top (most recent race). This strategy will give you an edge on handicappers who glance only at a horse's two or three most recent races. By starting at the bottom, you will discover some important items. Perhaps the horse you are considering has previously raced against several of his opponents today. Perhaps he demonstrated that he could win at a certain claiming level or that he had success coming off a layoff. You will also get a feel for how a horse is coming into today's race in the context of his entire career or a good portion of his career.

2. Use all the available information. There has been an information explosion in past-performance lines in the last decade, and you should take advantage of it. You decide which statistics or information is important for this particular race and handicap accordingly.

3. Watch as many races as you can. This means either live, on television replay shows, on satellite broadcasts such as Television Games Network, or in replay centers at racetracks. When you watch a race just once, you are almost always focused on the single horse you have picked or bet on. Without that emotional attachment, a second look at the same race allows you to follow another horse or horses in the same race. You will be amazed at how much you would have missed on that other horse had you not bothered to watch it again. Take notes if you want.

4. Practice, practice, practice. You can improve your handicapping and wagering easily in a matter of minutes. Ultimately as a bettor, you strive to get value for your investment. You are searching for that 2-to-1 horse that for some reason is going off at 6-to-1. How do you know? Simple. Before the betting begins for each race, write down what you think the final odds will be, and then evaluate how you did. Do it time after time and you will get a better understanding of your handicapping versus the handicapping of the betting public shown in the final odds. Do you want to improve your knowledge of turf racing or how horses will perform on wet tracks? Simply write down your predicted top three finishers in grass races or races on a wet track and see how you score. Then go back and look at the breeding of the winner. Do it daily and you will quickly improve your skills.

5. Identify key races. If you win with a horse that had finished a close second in his last race, pay attention when the third-place finisher from that race is out again. Try to maximize your correct handicapping decisions.—*Bill Heller*

horse? If the race has three speed horses and one of them routinely gets a first quarter-mile in :22 and a half-mile in :45 and the others' fastest times are :23 and :46, their presence may not compromise the faster speed horse's chances. Either way, the other two speed horses should be discarded. They want the lead and will not get it.

For a front-running horse, there is a world of difference between racing loose on the lead without head-to-head pressure from other horses and being pressed hard early by one or two others. If there are three speed horses with comparable early speed in a race, can one of them be rated just off the lead? The answer may show up in each horse's past-performance lines. That is why it is so important to look at all the horse's past-performance lines rather than one or two. If a speed horse has rated just off the lead in a previous race, was it a ticket to success or failure?

It is extremely important to differentiate between speed in sprints, which are races under one mile, and in longer contests, which are widely known as route races. Say a horse wins a 1⅛-mile race on the lead the whole way after running an opening half-mile in :48. To be in front in a sprint, it may have to run :46 or faster. Has it ever done that?

Time is the most important factor in workouts. Almost every Thoroughbred can run one furlong, an eighth of a mile, in :12. Maintaining that pace becomes more difficult with each subsequent furlong. Most horses can run a quarter mile in :24, but not all can work three furlongs in :36 or less. Four furlongs in :48 or faster is outstanding, and five furlongs in 1:00 (one minute) or quicker is even better. If a horse has had a workout on a training track as opposed to the main track, give the workout extra credit. Times are almost always slower on training tracks.

One word of caution: when looking at a horse's workouts, consider only the ones that came after its most recent race.

Changes

Changes are extremely significant in handicapping, be it the addition or the removal of blinkers, switching jockeys or trainers, trying a different surface (turf or dirt), racing on a wet track, or shipping to another track. The most significant change, however, is the addition of the anti-bleeding diuretic furosemide, which now is marketed as Salix for veterinary uses but still is identified in past performances by a capital L. Horses treated with furosemide for the first or, sometimes, the second time, frequently show tremendous improvement.

Breezy Way showed up in a $40,000 maiden claimer at Aqueduct on November 3, 2005, and was adding Salix for the first time. He was fifth by 14 lengths on a sloppy track and fifth by 16¾ lengths on a fast track in his previous two starts, both at the same maiden claiming level. He had not finished in the money in seven career starts. With Salix, he finished third by 1¾ lengths.

In his second lifetime start, Northern Disco, racing without Salix, finished a tired fourth by 21¼ lengths in a six-furlong optional claiming race at Laurel Park at odds of 12.40-to-1 on September 15, 2005. In his next start, in the same class but stretching out to one mile on October 14 at Laurel with Salix, he finished third by one length at odds of 9.50-to-1. His Beyer speed figure jumped from 18 to 51.

Frequently, horses adding Salix for the first time are bet heavily. In his career debut on August 12, 2005, without Salix, Kwik Bullet finished a tired eighth by 20½ lengths in a six-furlong, $40,000 maiden claiming race at Calder Race Course at odds of 61.40-to-1. With Salix in his second start on September 9, he dropped slightly to a $25,000 maiden claiming race at Calder but stretched out to seven furlongs. He won by 1¾ lengths at odds of 5.60-to-1. In doing so, his Beyer speed figure leaped from 23 to 59. *Daily Racing Form* indicates a horse using Salix for the first time by highlighting the capital letter L in white on a black circle background.

The addition of blinkers helps a horse to focus better by limiting its vision, and almost all horses show more speed when blinkers are added. This may be evidenced in a horse's most recent workouts if they are faster than they usually are. Conversely, removing blinkers usually allows a horse to see more and be a bit more relaxed.

When looking through a horse's previous races, had blinkers been added or removed previously? Did it produce a much different performance, better or worse? Was it on the same surface as today? A horse entered in a turf race could have been racing on dirt without blinkers, had blinkers added, and shown no improvement. Its prior races on grass could have been poor, but what if it had raced all of them before the addition of blinkers? Even though adding blinkers did not improve the horse's performance on dirt, their addition may improve it on grass. The same holds true with the addition of Salix. Do not assume that because first-time Salix did not improve a horse on dirt that the medication will have no effect when it races on grass.

Trainer changes happen every time a horse gets claimed. Statistics included in some past-performance lines now allow you to see how well a trainer does with a horse in its first start after a claim.

Jockey changes are significant only when there is a substantial difference in ability between the two jockeys. A rider change from Edgar Prado to John Velazquez, or vice versa, is insignificant. They are both among the world's best. But if a horse changes from Prado to a rider with a poor winning percentage, or if Prado assumes the mount from a less successful rider—take note. Substantial changes of jockeys are usually reflected in a horse's odds. A horse switching from a lesser rider to John Velazquez, for instance, will be played heavily by bettors almost every time.

Note, too, that jockeys and trainers, just like horses, have different abilities on dirt and grass. As a general guideline, apprentice jockeys, who are allowed to carry less weight until they win a specified number of races, are better on dirt than on grass.

Layoffs

Most horses that have been off more than a month require at least one race back to perform well, but the key word here is "most." Not all horses need that comeback race to reach sufficient fitness to race well, and trainers have a wide range of success getting layoff horses to win their first start back. In New York, nobody is better than Bill Mott and Todd Pletcher. *Daily Racing Form* now includes in each horse's past performance their trainer's record with horses that have been off a specified number of days: 60 to 120, for example, or more than 180. This is valuable in-

Types of Races

allowance race A race for which eligibility and weight to be carried are determined by the specific conditions of the race, such as number of career wins, earnings, or time since previous win. The lowest-level allowance race is for horses that have not won one race other than maiden or claiming. At the highest level, allowance conditions are written for horses that have not won a specific amount of purse money in their careers or within a specified period of time, such as $100,000 in the previous 12 months, or, for example, nonwinners of two races worth $40,000 (usually referring to the purse to the winner) since March 15. Allowance races are generally the second-best type of race on a card, behind stakes races.

claiming race A race for horses that can be purchased (claimed) immediately from that race for the price specified at the time of entry. The claimed horse becomes the new owner's property as soon as the starting gate opens, regardless if the horse finishes, but the previous owner collects any purse money earned by the claimed horse from that race. Claims must be entered before the race, usually ten to 15 minutes before post time depending on the state rules, and they can be made only by a person who is eligible to make claims under state rules. If more than one owner puts in a claim for the same horse, the disposition of the horse is determined by lot by the stewards. Claiming races are generally of lower class than allowance races. The lower the claiming price, the lower the class, and also the lower the purse.

futurity A stakes race, usually for two-year-olds, that is restricted to horses whose owners have made nomination payments shortly after the horse's birth and subsequently have made sustaining payments to maintain the horse's eligibility. As field sizes and quality of futurities dwindled in the 1980s, this type of race became relatively rare, and nominating conditions changed as a result. In 1972, for instance, the first payment for the Futurity Stakes (G1) at Belmont Park had to have been made by August 15, 1970, the year the horses were foaled. By 1990, the subscription deadline was May 1, 1990, for a race to be run in September 1990. Two years later, the Futurity became a stakes race, with nominations closing 17 days before the race.

handicap race A race, usually of stakes caliber, in which the racing secretary determines the amount of weight each horse will carry based on career record and current form. In theory, the handicapper seeks to assign weights so that all starters finish at the same time in a dead heat to win. Handicap races formerly placed high weight assignments on such champions as Kelso (won the 1964 Straight Face Handicap with 136 pounds) and Forego (won the 1977 Nassau County Handicap with 136 pounds), but few top-weight assignments now exceed 126 pounds.

maiden claiming race A race for nonwinning horses that can be purchased immediately from that race for a specified price (see claiming race).

maiden race A race for horses that have never won a race. Maiden races are either maiden special-weight, with all horses assigned a specified weight, or maiden claiming. Additional conditions may apply, such as the race being restricted to state-breds.

optional claiming A race that is both a claiming race, for those horses entered to be claimed for a specific price, and an allowance race, for those whose owners do not enter them to be claimed.

overnight handicap A race where owners do not pay to enter their horses but are assigned weights by the racing secretary. These races generally offer some of the higher purses, on a par with the best allowance races but below stakes race purses.

restricted race A race whose starters are limited to those eligible under specified conditions, such as horses that were bred in the state where the race is held, were offered or sold at a specific sale, or by their previous winnings.

stakes race A race that is generally the highest quality race offered by a track. For stakes, owners pay a fee to nominate and enter their horses in the starting gate, with the track putting up added money to make up the difference in the total purse. Stakes races are generally the richest races run at each track and attract the best horses on the grounds, plus horses coming in from other tracks or states when the purse money is high enough to attract shippers.

starter allowance An allowance race for horses that have started for a specified minimum claiming price within a specified time. For example, some starter allowances are restricted to horses that have started for a claiming price of $10,000 or less in the previous year. Conditions of the race, meaning the weight carried, are determined by allowances.

starter handicap A race similar to a starter allowance, except the horses are assigned weights by the track racing secretary, based on current ability and form rather than allowance conditions.

formation you should use in handicapping, but more conclusive information may be found in a horse's past-performance lines. Starting at the bottom, check to see if this horse has ever raced off a similar layoff in its last 12 races. How it did then indicates how it is likely to perform today.

Significant gaps between a horse's races or its workouts are frequently a sign of trouble. A horse that has been racing regularly should be working out regularly in between starts in the same pattern the trainer had previously used with this horse.

Post Positions

Post positions can be crucial to a horse's success, especially in turf racing. Think about it. Since racetracks in the United States have their turf courses inside their dirt courses, they have a smaller circumference and much tighter turns, penalizing horses that are forced to race wide by outside post positions. That effect is even more pronounced on inner turf courses at tracks with two grass courses, such as Belmont Park and Saratoga Race Course. Virtually every track updates its winning post positions on all its courses daily, and that information is readily available. Use it. If a horse drew a highly disadvantageous outside post on the inner turf course and, though racing wide, was still competitive, it should improve significantly with a better post position in its next start. If a horse has been plagued by outside post positions in several turf races, cut it slack and be aware when it gets a better post.

Also take into account the length of the straightaway before the first turn in grass racing. Certain races give horses ample time to work their way closer to the rail before the turn; others do not.

On dirt, the rail at some tracks can be a slight disadvantage for races at seven furlongs or one mile, especially if a horse lacks early speed. Extreme outside posts can be a disadvantage if there is not a long run into the first turn. Again, check the numbers.

Trainer Patterns

Both *Daily Racing Form* and track programs now contain extensive and useful trainer statistics for practically every race. They show not only the trainer's current record but also his or her recent history in a wide array of categories, from first-time starters to first start off a claim, from long layoffs, to running a horse back within a week. More recently, these publications have added percentages for a trainer when he or she uses the same jockey who will be riding in this race for that trainer.

Not to be lost in the avalanche of statistics is the common-sense observation that certain trainers excel in certain types of races. Some are better with fillies; others are great with two-year-olds; a few rarely win a grass race. Use all of this in your handicapping. Take every edge you can find because, remember, you are literally betting against other bettors.

Two-Year-Olds

Handicapping races with proven, experienced horses is difficult enough. Handicapping two-year-old races full of horses making their first career starts is daunting but not impossible. Here, trainer statistics are extremely helpful. So is the horse-by-horse analysis found in *Daily Racing Form*, which often discloses relevant statistics about the horse's sire or dam. For handicapping, the dam is more important than the sire. Again, it is common sense. A sire may have many new foals every year with its genetic capabilities; a mare obviously has only one. If a dam has already produced several two-year-old winners, take note.

Gauging two-year-old workouts are easier if you become familiar with trainer patterns. Some trainers, such as Bob Baffert in California, always work their two-year-olds fast. Other trainers, such as Shug McGaughey in New York, seldom do. Also, be sure to notice if workouts have been done on a main track or on a slower training track.

A single fast workout—for example, four furlongs in :47—stands out. But steady, good works, such as three or four four-furlong works between :48 and :49.80, are a great barometer that the horse has good speed and is fit and ready to go.

Weight

If weight were not an important factor in racing, trainers around the country would not go bananas when an apprentice with even a modicum of ability starts winning races with a weight allowance of five, seven, or ten pounds.

Generally, weight is more important in distance races than in sprints. But context is important. If every horse in a race carries 126 pounds, there is obviously no advantage. If, however, one horse is carrying 122 and the others between 115 to 118, weight is a factor. Also, watch for a significant shift of weight between two horses. For instance, Horse A may have carried 125 pounds and narrowly beat Horse B carrying 118. If they run at equal weights in their next encounter, the outcome may be different.

Final Thought

You can bet license-plate or telephone numbers every time you go to the racetrack and do all right, but the experience is much more enjoyable if you handicap a race and deduce a winner or two. Remember, this is a skill that you can improve only as you watch and handicap more races. With the dramatic increase in handicapping tournaments, there has never been a better time to try handicapping. Good luck!

Handicapping a Sample Race

The 136th running of the $1-million Travers Stakes (G1), Saratoga Race Course's signature 1¼-mile Midsummer Derby, attracted seven three-year-olds on August 27, 2005. The top three contenders—Bellamy Road, Flower Alley, and Roman Ruler—appeared to be superior to the other four, Andromeda's Hero, Chekhov, Don't Get Mad, and Reverberate. But Saratoga is well known as the "Graveyard of Champions" because stakes races sometimes have not played out the way fans, handicappers, and bettors thought they would. Moreover, this Travers featured a wild card, Bellamy Road, who was a late addition to the probable starting field.

Here are the starters for the Travers Stakes in post position order. Each horse's actual past performances follow.

1. Bellamy Road. Could Racing Hall of Fame trainer Nick Zito do it again? In 2004, he elected to train Marylou Whitney's Belmont Stakes (G1) winner Birdstone up to the Travers, and he won. Now, Zito was asking Bellamy Road, owned by the Kinsman Stable of New York Yankees principal owner George Steinbrenner, to win the Travers off an even longer layoff. A winner of three of his first four starts, Bellamy Road exploded onto the Triple Crown trail with a spectacular 17½-length victory in the Wood Memorial Stakes (G1). Sent off the 2.60-to-1 favorite in the Kentucky Derby (G1), Bellamy Road was prominent early before tiring to finish seventh. He had not raced since, meaning he would contest the Travers off a 112-day layoff. However, he had previously won off a long layoff, taking an allowance race in his three-year-old debut after a 153-day absence.

Bellamy Road threw in two bullet workouts (the bullet signifies that it was the fastest workout of the day at that distance at that track) for the Travers and figured to get a good trip under regular rider Javier Castellano from the rail, possibly on the lead.

2. Andromeda's Hero. A stablemate of Bellamy Road trained by Zito, Andromeda's Hero was a one-run closer who had won just two of nine starts, a maiden race and the Sam F. Davis Stakes at Tampa Bay Downs. He also had finished second by seven lengths in the Belmont. Andromeda's Hero had been beaten by Travers contender Flower Alley three times, including an 11¾-length loss to him in his previous start, Saratoga's Jim Dandy Stakes (G2), the traditional prep for the Travers. Andromeda's Hero was adding blinkers for the Travers, and that could alter his running style under Corey Nakatani, who had flown in from California to ride him for the first time.

3. Chekhov. A $3.3-million two-year-old purchase, Chekhov was a closer who had won just a maiden race in his eight starts and had finished well behind Reverberate, Andromeda's Hero, and Roman Ruler in separate graded stakes. In his prior race, Chekhov had finished an undistinguished fourth by 4¼ lengths to Roman Ruler in the Haskell Invitational Handicap (G1) at Monmouth Park at 1⅛ miles.

4. Roman Ruler. Bob Baffert's colt had suggested greatness as a two-year-old in California, where he won a maiden race and the Best Pal Stakes (G2) in his first two starts before finishing second by a neck as the 1-to-10 favorite to Declan's Moon in the Del Mar Futurity (G2). Roman Ruler bounced back to win the Norfolk Stakes (G2) by 4½ lengths before finishing fifth by 3¾ lengths to Wilko in the Breeders' Cup Juvenile (G1). At three, Roman Ruler finished eighth by 27½ lengths in the San Felipe Stakes (G2), but he returned after a 3½-month vacation to take the Dwyer Stakes (G2) by a half-length over Flower Alley under new jockey Jerry Bailey and the Haskell by 1¼ lengths. A midpack stalker with tactical speed, Roman Ruler figured to be a prime contender.

5. Don't Get Mad. Don't Get Mad, another closer, won three of his first six starts before finishing a strong fourth by 3½ lengths in the Kentucky Derby from the 17th post position. California-based trainer Ron Ellis chose not to chase the Triple Crown in the Preakness or Belmont, instead freshening him and returning him to win the Northern Dancer Breeders' Cup Handicap (G3) at Churchill Downs on June 18. Don't Get Mad seemed primed to tackle the elite in his division but then finished fifth by 10½ lengths in a field of six in the Swaps Breeders' Cup Handicap (G2) as the 1.30-to-1 favorite.

6. Reverberate. After winning two of his first seven races, he earned a start in the Belmont by finishing second to Oratory in the Peter Pan Stakes (G2) after racing close to the pace. Any chance he had to make an impact in the Belmont was lost when he broke poorly and stumbled out of the starting gate. He finished tenth by 34 lengths in the 11-horse field. Given a freshening by trainer Sal Russo, Reverberate returned in the Jim Dandy Stakes and finished second, 5¼ lengths behind Flower Alley.

7. Flower Alley. Trained by Todd Pletcher and ridden by John Velazquez, Flower Alley quickly rose to prominence by winning Turfway Park's 1⅛-mile Lane's End Stakes (G2) by a half-length in just his third lifetime start. Flower Alley then finished second by eight lengths to Afleet Alex in the Arkansas Derby (G2) before finishing ninth of 20 in the Kentucky Derby, beaten 7½ lengths after an ex-

SARATOGA APPROX. POST: 6:30PM

Exacta, Trifecta, Daily Double Wagers

EX	TR	WIN	PLACE	SHOW
DD	P3	P4		

11

1 1/4 MILE

▲START ▲FINISH

The 136th Running of THE TRAVERS (Grade I) $1,000,000 (Up To $70,000 NYSBFOA)

STAKES. FOR THREE YEAR OLDS. By subscription of $1,000 each, which should accompany the nomination; $5,000 to pass the entry box, $5,000 to start. The purse to be divided 60% to the winner, 20% to second, 10% to third, 5% to fourth, 3% to fifth and 2% divided equally among remaining finishers. 126 lbs. Trophies will be presented to the winning owner, trainer and jockey. Closed Saturday, August 13, 2005 with 16 Nominations. **One Mile And One Quarter**

Track Record: General Assembly (3),126 lbs; 2:00 (8-18-79)

Pgm # | Owner | Pace E Speed Wgt | Jockey | Trainer

---

1 Kinsman Stable — Royal Blue, Brown Sash, Brown Hoop on Sleeves, Blue Cap

Bellamy Road (L) 126 — **Javier Castellano** (200-36-26-26) — Trainer: **Nicholas P. Zito** (56-4-7-10)

Red **2-1** Dk B/ Br.c.3 Concerto - Hurry Home Hillary by Deputed Testamony
Br.Dianne D. Cotter, Florida (Apr 05, 2002) OBSAPR04 $87,000

Life:	6	4	0	0	$611,400	Turf:	0	0	0	0	$0
2005:	3	2	0	0	$471,000	Off Track:	0	0	0	0	$0
2004:	3	2	0	0	$140,400	Distance:	1	0	0	0	$0
						Course:	0	0	0	0	$0

07May05 CD10	ft	1¼	:4538	1:3588	2:0275	3	KyDerbyG1 -2000k	92-80	16	5¾	5²¼	2hd	3¹½	7⁶¾	Castellano J	126	cL	*2.60	Giacomo126½ ClosingArgument126½ *AfleetAlex* 126²½	4-5w,bid,led,weakened	20
09Apr05 Aqu9	ft	1⅛	:4608	1:0984	1:4716	3	WoodMemG1 -750k	95-96	2	1¹½	1½	1²½	1¹⁰	1¹⁷½	Castellano J	123	cL	*2.55	BellamyRoad123¹⁷½ Survivalist123¾ *ScrappyT* 123⁸	with something left	7
12Mar05 GP6	ft	1m	:4577	1:1031	1:3590	3	Alw 35000nw2/x	81-88	3	1½	1½	1²½	1⁶	1¹⁵¾	Castellano J	118	L	1.20	*BellamyRoad* 118¹⁵¾ CherokeeChase118²½ CaptainLindsay118¹	bumped st,handily	5
09Oct04 Kee7	ft	1⅙	:4714	1:1204	1:4367	2	BrdrsFutG1 -500k	77-77	2	1½	1¹½	1½	4⁵½	7¹²	Dominguez R A	121	fL	*2.10	Consolidator121² PatriotAct121³¼ DiamondIsle121½	weakened after 3/4s	10
06Sep04 RD13	ft	1⅙	:4940	1:1240	1:45	2	MGDCrdleG3 -200k	62-82	2	1½	1¹	1¹½	1⁶	1²¾	Castellano, Jr. A	120	fL	2.20	BellamyRoad120²¾ DiamondIsle120nk Scipion120⁶¾	off rail,ridden out	8

Workout(s): •21 Aug 05 Sar 5F my :59.4h 1/10 — •13 Aug 05 Sar 5F sy 1:00.1b 1/8 — 6 Aug 05 Sar tr 5F ft 1:04.2b 6/9 — 30 Jul 05 Sar tr 5F ft 1:04.2b 5/10

---

2 Robert V. LaPenta — Maroon, Gold Epaulets, Maroon Cap

•Andromeda's Hero (L) 126 — **Corey Nakatani** (5-0-0-3) — Trainer: **Nicholas P. Zito** (56-4-7-10)

White **12-1** Ch.c.3 Fusaichi Pegasus - Marozia by Storm Bird
Br.Barnett Enterprises, Kentucky (Mar 12, 2002) KEESEP03 $310,000

Life:	9	2	1	4	$430,270	Turf:	0	0	0	0	$0
2005:	7	1	1	3	$412,970	Off Track:	1	0	0	0	$15,000
2004:	2	1	0	1	$17,300	Distance:	1	0	0	0	$0
						Course:	1	0	0	1	$50,000

30Jul05 Sar9	ft	1⅛	:4738	1:1154	1:4950	3	JimDandyG2 -500k	85-86	3	5⁵½	5⁷¾	4⁴	3⁹½	3¹¹½	Bejarano R	117	cL	4.00	**FlowerAlley**121⁵¼ **Reverberate**115⁶½ Andromeda'sHero117²³¼	inside trip,no rally	5
11Jun05 Bel11	ft	1½	:4862	1:3805	2:2875	3	BelmontG1 -1000k	81-92	7	10⁶½	9³	4³	2⁶	2⁷	Bejarano R	126	cL	11.90	AfleetAlex126⁷ Andromeda'sHero126⁶¾ Nolan'sCat126²¼	good finish outside	11
07May05 CD10	ft	1¼	:4538	1:3588	2:0275	3	KyDerbyG1 -2000k	82-80	2	15¹³	13¹¹	16⁸	14⁹½	8⁷½	Bejarano R	126	cL	57.30	Giacomo126½ ClosingArgument126½ *AfleetAlex* 126²½	7w lane,minor gain	20
16Apr05 OP9	ft	1⅛	:4791	1:1278	1:4880	3	ArkDerbyG2 -1000k	73-86	2	4²½	4³½	5²¼	4⁷½	3⁸¾	Nakatani C S	122	L	10.70	AfleetAlex122⁸ **FlowerAlley**122¾ Andromeda'sHero122nk	altered,missed 2nd	10
26Mar05 TP9	my	1⅛	:4668	1:1116	1:5033	3	LanesEndG2 -500k	79-85	4	8⁷½	8⁸	6⁴¾	6⁶½	5³	Bejarano R	121	L	4.80	**FlowerAlley**121½ WildDesert121² MrSword121½	2 path 2nd turn	9
26Feb05 Tam10	ft	1⅙	:4697	1:1238	1:4663	3	SamFDavis -100k	78-81	12	9⁷¼	8⁷½	7⁵	4¹½	1²½	Bejarano R	116	L	*1.80e	Andromeda'sHero116²½ SummerLegacy116⁶½ CaptainLindsay116hd	bumped,ran pst leader	12
05Feb05 GP2	ft	7f	:2296	:4614	1:2434	3	Alw 33000nw1/x	67-71	3	9	6¹¼	4¹½	6⁴½	4⁴½*	Bravo J	120	L	4.40	Qureall118¹¼ AroundtheCape120½ Survivalist118²½	couldn't keep pace,PL3rd	12
26Dec04 Crc8	ft	7f	:2343	:4711	1:2570	2	Msw	56-79	7	3	3²½	3³½	1¹	1⁷	Velasquez C H	118	L	*.40	Andromeda'sHero118⁷ BondKing118²¾ ShyHarbor118³¼	drew off,driving	8

Workout(s): 21 Jan 06 GP 4F ft :48b 17/44 — 30 Dec 05 GP 4F ft :48.1b 6/21 — 19 Nov 05 CD 5F ft 1:00.4b 7/49 — 10 Nov 05 CD 5F ft 1:02b 20/32

---

3 Michael Tabor, Derek Smith — Royal Blue, Orange Ball, Orange Stripes on Sleeves, Orange Stripes on Blue Cap

Chekhov 126 — **Gary Stevens** (64-9-10-11) — Trainer: **Patrick L. Biancone** (28-8-2-4)

Blue **10-1** B.g.3 Pulpit - In My Cap by Vice Regent
Br.Hermitage Farm LLC, Kentucky (May 19, 2002) KEEAPR04 $3,300,000

Life:	8	1	2	1	$143,966	Turf:	0	0	0	0	$0
2005:	7	1	1	1	$133,966	Off Track:	0	0	0	0	$0
2004:	1	0	1	0	$10,000	Distance:	0	0	0	0	$0
						Course:	0	0	0	0	$0

07Aug05 Mth12	ft	1⅛	:4772	1:1169	1:4988	3	HsklInvHG1 -1015k	74-88	7	7⁶	7⁸¾	7⁶¾	4⁵½	4⁴½	Stevens G L	116		7.70	**RomanRuler**119¹½ SunKing119² ParkAvenueBall118¹	bid turn,even finish	7
16Jul05 Mth9	ft	1⅙	:4731	1:1119	1:4193	3	LBrnchBCG3 -165k	72-83	8	6⁴½	8⁴½	7³½	4⁵½	2⁶½	Bravo J	113		2.30	ParkAvenueBall116⁶½ Chekhov113ns GoldenMan114hd	broke bit slow,5-wide	8
11Jun05 Bel11	ft	1½	:4862	1:3805	2:2875	3	BelmontG1 -1000k	84-86	11	4¹	7²¾	9⁵¾	6¹¹	6¹⁷½	Stevens G L	126		15.10	AfleetAlex126⁷ **Andromeda'sHero**126⁶¾ Nolan'sCat126²¼	chased 4 wide,tired	11
28May05 Bel8	ft	1⅛	:4744	1:1119	1:4635	3	PeterPanG2 -200k	76-88	4	7³½	7⁴¾	5²½	4¹⁰	4¹²¼	Stevens G L	116		*1.50	Oratory116⁴¾ **Reverberate**116⁶½ GoldenMan116¹	bumped start,4 wide	8
08May05 Bel3	ft	1⅙	:4698	1:1070	1:4135	3†	Msw	71-86	3	4⁵	5⁶¾	4⁴	1¹½	1⁸¼	Stevens G L	118		*.90	Chekhov118⁸¼ Sweetiewheatie118⁴¾ WallStreet118¹¼	when asked,ridden out	6
05Feb05 SA7	ft	1⅛	:4682	1:1068	1:5018	3	Sham -100k	83-84	5	9⁶	9⁶¼	8⁷¾	6⁵¾	5²¾	Stevens G L	117	bB	5.30	GoingWild117¹ PapiChullo117nk Giacomo117½	off bit slow,mild bid	9
15Jan05 SA6	ft	1⅙	:4613	1:1084	1:4368	3	Msw	75-81	3	10⁹½	10⁸	9⁶¼	4⁴	3³	Stevens G L	121	B	*1.90	SilentBid121¹ PapiChullo121² Chekhov121⁴	came out str,rallied	11

Workout(s): 23 Aug 05 Sar 5F ft 1:00.1b 6/39 | 3 Aug 05 Sar 5F ft 1:02.1b 14/30 | 28 Jul 05 Sar 6F ft 1:14.1b 1/1 | •13 Jul 05 Sar 4F ft :47.3b 1/7

4 Fog City Stables — Orange, Black Yoke, Black Cuffs on Sleeves, Orange and Black Cap — Bob Baffert (5-0-1-2)

Roman Ruler (L) 126 — Jerry Bailey (136-32-28-22)

Yellow **5-2** Dk B/ Br.r.3 Fusaichi Pegasus - Silvery Swan by Silver Deputy
Br.Needham/Betz, Liberation Fm & Ashford Stud, Kentucky (Mar 20, 2002) KEESEP03 $500,000

	Starts	1st	2nd	3rd	Earnings		Starts	1st	2nd	3rd	Earnings
Life:	8	5	1	0	$1,020,800	Turf:	0	0	0	0	$0
2005:	3	2	0	0	$690,000	Off Track:	1	0	0	0	$0
2004:	5	3	1	0	$330,800	Distance:	0	0	0	0	$0
						Course:	0	0	0	0	$0

Date/Track	Cond	Dist	Fractions/Age	Race	Figs	PP	Calls	Jockey	Wt	Eq	Odds	Top Finishers	Comment	Field
07Aug05 Mth12	ft	1⅛	:4772 1:1169 1:4988 3	HsklInvHG1 -1015k	81-91	4	4 42 41¼ 3½ 2hd 11¼	Bailey J D	119	fL	*1.10	RomanRuler1191¼ SunKing1192 ParkAvenueBall1181	3wd,dueled clear	7
04Jul05 Bel9	ft	1 1/16	:4547 1:0953 1:4083 3	DwyerG2 -150k	82-90	5	61¼ 61¾ 62¼ 1½ 1½	Bailey J D	119	fL	2.20	*RomanRuler*119½ *FlowerAlley*1237 ProudAccolade1191	4 wide move,prevailed	6
19Mar05 SA8	wf	1 1/16	:4602 1:0974 1:4011 3	SnFelipeG2 -250k	75-70	5	76¼ 66 74½ 79 827½	Stevens G L	116	BL	*3.00	Consolidator1166½ Giacomo116½ **Don'tGetMad**1161	pulld,tight early,ease	8
30Oct04 LS7	ft	1 1/16	:4749 1:1125 1:4209 2	BCJuvnleG1 -1500k	74-83	2	74¾ 74¼ 53¼ 53 53¾	Nakatani C S	122	L	*2.00	Wilko122¾ *AfleetAlex*122nk *SunKing*1221¼	stdied 7-1/2,hard held	8
03Oct04 SA7	ft	1 1/16	:4605 1:1066 1:4427 2	NorfolkG2 -200k	90-86	4	21 21 2hd 14 14½	Nakatani C S	120	bBL	*.05	RomanRuler1204½ BostonGlory12013 Littlebitofzip1202	pulled,bid,clear	4
08Sep04 Dmr8	ft	7f	:2225 :4473 1:2129 2	DMrFutG2 -250k	72-96	2	4 34½ 35½ 1½ 2nk	Nakatani C S	120	BL	*.10	*Declan'sMoon*116nk *RomanRuler*1209½ *SwissLad*1164	off bit slw,stdy early	4
15Aug04 Dmr2	ft	6½	:2182 :4493 1:1593 2	BestPalG2 -150k	68-93	2	5 48½ 45½ 12 17	Nakatani C S	118	BL	*.50	RomanRuler1187 *Actxecutive*11810 Slewsbag1161½	stdied 5/16,ridden out	5

Workout(s): •21 Oct 05 Osa 4F ft :46.1h 1/46 | 12 Oct 05 Osa 4F ft :47h 2/25 | 28 Sep 05 Osa 4F ft :48.1h 8/28 | 23 Sep 05 SA 6F ft 1:12.2h 3/16

5 B. Wayne Hughes — Orange and Purple Quarters, Orange Sleeves and Cap — Ronald W. Ellis (1-0-0-0)

Don't Get Mad 126 — Edgar Prado (231-44-35-40)

Green **10-1** B.c.3 Stephen Got Even - Class On Class by Jolie's Halo
Br.Milton Hendry & Beth Hendry, Kentucky (Apr 25, 2002) OBSMAR04 $350,000

	Starts	1st	2nd	3rd	Earnings		Starts	1st	2nd	3rd	Earnings
Life:	9	4	1	1	$433,620	Turf:	0	0	0	0	$0
2005:	7	2	1	1	$373,330	Off Track:	3	1	1	1	$89,395
2004:	2	2	0	0	$60,290	Distance:	1	0	0	0	$100,000
						Course:	0	0	0	0	$0

Date/Track	Cond	Dist	Fractions/Age	Race	Figs	PP	Calls	Jockey	Wt	Eq	Odds	Top Finishers	Comment	Field
09Jul05 Hol7	ft	1⅛	:4735 1:1134 1:4807 3	SwapsBCG2 -400k	80-82	5	63½ 53 52¾ 46 510½	Stevens G L	120	B	*1.30	SurfCat1155 DoverDere1171 IndianOcean1183½	3wd move,no late bid	6
18Jun05 CD7	ft	1 1/16	:4680 1:1204 1:4246 3	NrtDncBCG3 -200k	74-87	2	510 510 41¾ 11½ 13¼	Stevens G L	120		*.90	Don'tGetMad1203¼ UnbridledEnergy1202¾ RealDandy1162	swept 7w lane,drvg	6
07May05 CD10	ft	1¼	:4538 1:3588 2:0275 3	KyDerbyG1 -2000k	77-83	17	1918 1916 104½ 73¼ 43½	Baze T	126		29.20	Giacomo126½ ClosingArgument126½ *AfleetAlex*1262½	circled 10w,good try	20
30Apr05 CD11	ft	1m	:4515 1:1059 1:3616 3	DerbyTrial -100k	77-86	7	710 78½ 64¾ 22½ 17	Stevens G L	116		2.50	Don'tGetMad1167 Gallardo116¾ Vicarage11612¾	slow start,ck 1/4p,drv	7
09Apr05 SA6	ft	1⅛	:4732 1:1134 1:4918 3	SADerbyG1 -750k	73-79	3	107¼ 1010 107¾ 99¾ 69	Baze T	122	BL	7.20	BuzzardsBay122½ GeneralJohnB122ns Wilko1221½	3wd into str,no threat	11
19Mar05 SA8	wf	1 1/16	:4602 1:0974 1:4011 3	SnFelipeG2 -250k	76-86	1	86¼ 76¼ 53½ 54 37	Baze T	116	fBL	3.50	Consolidator1166½ Giacomo116½ Don'tGetMad1161	chased btwn,missed 2nd	8
13Feb05 SA6	wf	7f	:2332 :4656 1:2259 3	SnVicnteG2 -150k	47-84	3	1 46 46 44½ 21	Baze T	115	fB	3.00	FusaichiRockStar1161 Don'tGetMad115nk Kirkendahl1161¼	closed with rush rail	4
26Nov04 CD9	ft	7f	:2264 :4584 1:2438 2	Alw 49400nw1/x	60-85	11	1 109¼ 93½ 1hd 11¼	Sarvis D A	122		4.40	Don'tGetMad1221¼ Wahran1221¼ *RoyalMoment*113½	6w rally,driving	11

Workout(s): 24 Sep 05 CD 5F ft 1:02.2b 15/30 | 17 Sep 05 CD 5F ft 1:04.3b 19/22 | 10 Sep 05 CD 4F ft :49b 12/45 | 19 Aug 05 SA 1M ft 1:39.2h 1/1

6 Centennial Farms — Tan, Red Sash, Red Sleeves, Tan and Red Cap — Sal Russo (13-1-2-0)

Reverberate (L) 126 — Jose Santos (106-12-13-5)

Black **8-1** Ch.c.3 Thunder Gulch - Peggibonsi by Proud Truth
Br.Edward Seltzer Trust, Kentucky (Apr 30, 2002) KEESEP03 $400,000

	Starts	1st	2nd	3rd	Earnings		Starts	1st	2nd	3rd	Earnings
Life:	10	2	3	2	$213,935	Turf:	0	0	0	0	$0
2005:	7	1	3	1	$179,150	Off Track:	0	0	0	0	$0
2004:	3	1	0	1	$34,785	Distance:	0	0	0	0	$0
						Course:	2	0	1	1	$104,500

Date/Track	Cond	Dist	Fractions/Age	Race	Figs	PP	Calls	Jockey	Wt	Eq	Odds	Top Finishers	Comment	Field
30Jul05 Sar9	ft	1⅛	:4738 1:1154 1:4950 3	JimDandyG2 -500k	89-91	1	32 31½ 2½ 22½ 25¼	Santos J A	115	bL	5.50	**FlowerAlley**1215¼ Reverberate1156½ **Andromeda'sHero**11723¼	good run,second best	5
11Jun05 Bel11	ft	1½	:4862 1:3805 2:2875 3	BelmontG1 -1000k	81-77	8	95¾ 106 1011 1024 1034	Santos J A	126	bL	11.80	AfleetAlex1267 **Andromeda'sHero**1266¾ Nolan'sCat1262¼	broke in air,stumbled	11
28May05 Bel8	ft	1⅛	:4744 1:1119 1:4635 3	PeterPanG2 -200k	79-94	7	21½ 1hd 1hd 22½ 24¾	Santos J A	116	bL	9.20	Oratory1164¾ Reverberate1166½ GoldenMan1161	pace,second best	8
08May05 Bel5	ft	1 1/16	:4710 1:1038 1:4129 3↑	Alw 46000nw1/x	67-87	1	2½ 2hd 1hd 1hd 12½	Velazquez J R	116	bL	*1.55	Reverberate1162½ ThreeintheBag1187½ Shots1222¼	resolutely on rail	5
05Mar05 GP8	ft	1⅛	:4711 1:1179 1:5069 3	Alw 33000nw1/x	80-84	3	2hd 2hd 1hd 2hd 23¼	Bailey J D	118	bL	8.80	NobleCauseway1223¼ *Reverberate*1182 GuillaumeTell1182¼	bmpd st,outfinished	7
05Feb05 GP7	ft	1⅛	:4663 1:1213 1:5103 3	Alw 33000nw1/x	71-71	5	65½ 63¾ 55 59½ 418½	Bailey J D	118	L	4.60	Bandini1189 Vitruvian1187¾ MagicSpeed1181¾	couldn't keep pace	12
08Jan05 GP5	ft	7f	:2228 :4457 1:2282 3	Alw 33000nw1/x	61-78	8	2 106¾ 99¾ 66½ 34¼	Castellano J	118	L	13.80	DearestMon120½ DevilAtSea1223¾ Reverberate1181¾	bumped st,4 wide	10
02Nov04 Aqu8	ft	1m	:4550 1:1018 1:3667 2	NashuaG3 -100k	82-74	1	61¼ 42 53 59 512¾	Prado E S	116	L	12.20	*RockportHarbor*1186¼ *Defer*116hd *BetterThanBonds*1162¼	awkward start,inside	6
11Sep04 Bel6	ft	6½	:2293 :4658 1:1759 2	Msw	81-82	4	3 1½ 1½ 1½ 11¼	Castellano J	119	L	*2.20	Reverberate1191¼ Woodlander1193¾ OneFeinDad119ns	drifted out stretch	8

Workout(s): 20 Sep 05 Bel 4F ft :49.2b 7/35 | 22 Aug 05 Sar 4F ft :48.2b 21/96 | 15 Aug 05 Sar 4F ft :47.2b 3/34 | 9 Aug 05 Sar 4F ft :49.3b 13/28

7 Melnyk Racing Stables, Inc. — Midnight Blue, Gold Emblem, Gold Sleeves, Blue Hoop, Gold Cap — Todd A. Pletcher (Seth Benzel) (100-22-17-10)

Flower Alley (L) 126 — John Velazquez (229-40-32-26)

Orange **3-1** Ch.c.3 Distorted Humor - Princess Olivia by Lycius
Br.George Brunacini & Bona Terra Farms, Kentucky (May 07, 2002) KEESEP03 $165,000

	Starts	1st	2nd	3rd	Earnings		Starts	1st	2nd	3rd	Earnings
Life:	7	3	2	1	$851,660	Turf:	0	0	0	0	$0
2005:	6	3	2	0	$849,200	Off Track:	1	1	0	0	$300,000
2004:	1	0	0	1	$2,460	Distance:	1	0	0	0	$0
						Course:	1	1	0	0	$300,000

Date/Track	Cond	Dist	Fractions/Age	Race	Figs	PP	Calls	Jockey	Wt	Eq	Odds	Top Finishers	Comment	Field
30Jul05 Sar9	ft	1⅛	:4738 1:1154 1:4950 3	JimDandyG2 -500k	89-95	2	2½ 1hd 1½ 12½ 15¼	Velazquez J R	121	bL	*.50	FlowerAlley1215¼ **Reverberate**1156½ **Andromeda'sHero**11723¼	took over when asked	5
04Jul05 Bel9	ft	1 1/16	:4547 1:0953 1:4083 3	DwyerG2 -150k	84-89	6	5¾ 41 4¾ 2½ 2½	Velazquez J R	123	bL	*1.70	*RomanRuler*119½ *FlowerAlley*1237 ProudAccolade1191	4 wide trip,gamely	6
07May05 CD10	ft	1¼	:4538 1:3588 2:0275 3	KyDerbyG1 -2000k	93-80	7	32½ 21½ 72½ 83¾ 97½	Chavez J F	126	bL	41.30	Giacomo126½ ClosingArgument126½ *AfleetAlex*1262½	slow start,steadied	20
16Apr05 OP9	ft	1⅛	:4791 1:1278 1:4880 3	ArkDerbyG2 -1000k	75-87	5	32½ 33 3nk 25½ 28	Chavez J F	122	L	3.90	AfleetAlex1228 FlowerAlley122¾ **Andromeda'sHero**122nk	3-w,drifted,held 2nd	10
26Mar05 TP9	my	1⅛	:4668 1:1116 1:5033 3	LanesEndG2 -500k	80-87	5	2½ 32½ 53¼ 44½ 1½	Chavez J F	121	L	10.20	FlowerAlley121½ WildDesert1212 MrSword121½	steadied 1/4 pole	9
19Feb05 GP7	ft	1m	:4655 1:1192 1:3755 3	Msw	70-80	10	1hd 4nk 2½ 21½ 1¾	Chavez J F	122	L	5.40	*FlowerAlley*122¾ WallStreet1225¾ CelestialArc122½	came again,up late	12

Workout(s): •24 Oct 05 Bel 5F ft :58.4h 1/77 | 17 Oct 05 Bel tr 5F ft 1:00.4b 9/37 | 25 Sep 05 Bel 5F ft 1:01.3b 20/45 | 18 Sep 05 Bel 5F ft :59.4b 2/48

Equipment Change: Andromeda's Hero will race with Blinkers On

tremely rough trip. Pletcher brought Flower Alley back in the Dwyer Stakes, in which he finished second by a half-length to Roman Ruler as the 1.70-to-1 favorite. In the Jim Dandy, Flower Alley had a breakthrough performance, winning the 1⅛-mile stakes by 5¼ lengths as the 1-to-2 favorite. His stalking style, just off the pacesetter, seemed a definite asset for the Travers.

Analysis

As good as Bellamy Road may be, winning the Travers off such a long layoff seemed a daunting task. Roman Ruler had edged Flower Alley in the Dwyer but carried four fewer pounds in that race. For the Travers, they were at equal weights, and Flower Alley's Jim Dandy was a significant step forward, visually more impressive than Roman Ruler's victory in the Haskell.

How To Read a Race Chart

The race chart is a summary of the race, offering factual information as well as a numerical description of how each horse performed. As an example, we will examine the chart of the 2005 Travers Stakes (G1).

Let's start at the top, which tells you that you are looking at the chart of the 11th race at Saratoga Race Course on August 27, 2005, and that the race was a stakes with a purse of $1-million for three-year-olds at 1¼ miles on dirt. Beneath that information is the division of the purse, beginning with the gross value of the race. The gross value may sometimes vary from the announced purse in cases of added money, such as nominating and starting fees, going into the purse, which would increase the race's value. Small fields can result in a smaller purse if some lesser placings are not paid and the money reverts to the racetrack.

The chart lists the horses in the order they finished, so Flower Alley is first. Before his name is his program number (7). After his name is his age (3) and sex (C for colt), followed by the weight he carried in the Travers, then his equipment (B for blinkers), and medication (L indicates that he was treated with the antibleeding medication furosemide). The following set of numbers describes how he raced in the Travers. He started from the seventh post position (7), and after a quarter-mile he was running second, a half-length ahead of the third-place horse at that point, Andromeda's Hero. To determine how far Flower Alley was behind the leader, look down the quarter-mile column and find the first-place horse at that point, Bellamy Road, who was 2½ lengths ahead of Flower Alley ($1^{2\,1/2}$). After a half-mile, Flower Alley was still second, but was 2½ lengths ahead of the third horse, now Roman Ruler. The half-mile statistics also reveal that Flower Alley had drawn closer to Bellamy Road, whose lead had diminished to a half-length ($1^{1/2}$).

The three-quarter-mile column (¾), which would be the horses' positions toward the end of the backstretch run, reveals that Bellamy Road had not tired at that point. He resumed the 2½-length lead he had held at the quarter-mile call ($1^{2\,1/2}$), and Flower Alley had widened his margin over Roman Ruler to 3½ lengths ($2^{3\,1/2}$). The next point of call is after one mile, at the top of Saratoga's stretch. Bellamy Road still is on the lead, but Flower Alley has him in his sights, with the leader's margin diminishing to a half-length again ($1^{1/2}$). Now, it appears, Bellamy Road is beginning to tire in his first start since the Derby. Meanwhile, Flower Alley's position ($2^{1\,1/2}$) indicates that Roman Ruler has picked up the pace and closed in on the leaders, drawing within 1½ lengths of Flower Alley and two lengths of the lead.

The next column, the stretch call, is always one-eighth mile (one furlong) from the finish line. In just one-eighth of a mile, the complexion of the Travers had changed dramatically. Flower Alley was now on the lead and had a half-length advantage over Bellamy Road. ($1^{1/2}$). While Bellamy Road may have tired somewhat, the challenge of Roman Ruler proved short-lived, because he was now 3½ lengths behind the early pacesetter ($2^{3\,1/2}$).

The finish, which is measured by a photo-finish camera, reveals that Flower Alley widened his margin to 2½ lengths over Bellamy Road. Although Bellamy Road weakened slightly, he was still 2¾ lengths ahead of third-finisher Roman Ruler ($2^{2\,3/4}$).

The remainder of the field was well strung out after Roman Ruler, who was 2½ lengths ($3^{2\,1/2}$) ahead of Don't Get Mad, the fourth-place finisher. In turn, Don't Get Mad had another 4¼ lengths on Andromeda's Hero, who finished 10¼ lengths ahead of Reverberate. Chekhov, the last of the seven starters, was three-quarters of a length behind Reverberate.

The chart's right-hand side provides the jockeys' names and the final wagering odds for each horse.

Beneath the horses' running lines are the time of day when the race went off (6:33); a description of the start for all horses (Start: Good), a comment about the winner (Stalked outside, clear); the track condition (Fast); and the weather (Clear). The next line gives the fractional times of the race: :23.54 for the first quarter-mile, :47.43 for the half-mile, 1:10.92 for three-quarters, 1:36.38 for a mile, and 2:02.76 for the Travers's 1¼ miles. The next line gives the size of the betting pool for win, place, and show wagering, which was $2,626,345.

Next are the pari-mutuel payoffs for the first three finishers, with each one's program number preceding his name. Flower Alley paid $8.00 to win, $4.00 to place, and $2.70 to show. Bellamy Road paid $4.10 to place and $3.00 to show. Roman Ruler paid $2.50 to show. The $2 exacta (the first two finishers in exact order) of 7-1 paid $33.60, and the $2 trifecta (the first three in exact order) of 7-1-4 paid $53.00. Total betting pools for those two popular wagers also are listed.

Next is the breeding of the winner and the winner's breeder. Flower Alley is by the sire Distorted Humor out of the mare Princess Olivia, whose sire is Lycius. He was bred by George Brunacini and Bona Terra Farms in Kentucky.

Under that is a narrative detailing each horse's performance. Following that is the listing of owners in the order they finished by program number and then a listing of the trainers in the same fashion.

About the Travers

Though Flower Alley might have won the Travers anyway, he received a brilliant ride from John Velazquez. Racing on the lead, Bellamy Road had taken the seven-horse field through a quarter-mile in :23.54 and a half in :47.43 by running his second quarter in :23.89. Bellamy Road's jockey, Javier Castellano, would have liked to run an even slower third quarter, but Velazquez rushed Flower Alley up to engage Bellamy Road, drawing within a half-length. Castellano asked Bellamy Road for a bit more, and he responded by reopening his lead. To do so, however, he had to run his third quarter-mile in :23.49, which turned out to be the fastest quarter-mile in the 1¼-mile Travers. Bellamy Road tired late and Flower Alley surged past to score the biggest victory of his career.

—Bill Heller

Travers S. – Grade 1
Purse: $1-Million Guaranteed

ELEVENTH RACE

Saratoga

August 27, 2005

Stakes. Purse $1,000,000. For three-year-olds. 1¼ miles on dirt. Track: Fast

Value of race: $1,000,000. Value to winner: $600,000; second: $200,000; third: $100,000; fourth: $50,000; fifth: $30,000; sixth: $10,000; seventh: $10,000.

P#	Horse	Wgt	M/Eqt	PP	¼	½	¾	Mile	Str.	Fin.	Jockey	Odds
7	Flower Alley	126	L b	7	$2^{1/2}$	$2^{2\ 1/2}$	$2^{3\ 1/2}$	$2^{1\ 1/2}$	$1^{1/2}$	$1^{2\ 1/2}$	J R Velazquez	3.00
1	Bellamy Road	126	L c	1	$1^{2\ 1/2}$	$1^{1/2}$	$1^{2\ 1/2}$	$1^{1/2}$	$2^{3\ 1/2}$	$2^{2\ 3/4}$	J Castellano	2.20
4	Roman Ruler	126	L f	4	$4^{1\ 1/2}$	$3^{1\ 1/2}$	$3^{1\ 1/2}$	$3^{1\ 1/2}$	$3^{2\ 1/2}$	$3^{2\ 1/2}$	J Bailey	*2.15
5	Don't Get Mad	126		5	6^{6}	5^{hd}	$5^{4\ 1/2}$	4^{2}	4^{3}	$4^{4\ 1/4}$	E Prado	7.80
2	Andromeda's Hero	126	L bc	2	3^{hd}	4^{5}	4^{3}	$5^{4\ 1/2}$	$5^{3\ 1/2}$	$5^{10\ 1/4}$	C Nakatani	15.00
6	Reverberate	126	L b	6	5^{1}	6^{6}	$6^{3\ 1/2}$	7	7	$6^{3/4}$	J Santos	15.30
3	Chekhov	126		3	7	7	7	6^{hd}	6^{2}	7	G Stevens	17.10

OFF AT 6:33. Start: Good for all. Weather: Clear
Time of race: :23.54, :47.43, 1:10.92, 1:36.38, 2:02.76

Total W/P/S Pool: $2,626,345

Mutuel Payoffs

7—Flower Alley $8.00 $4.00 $2.70
1—Bellamy Road 4.10 3.00
4—Roman Ruler 2.50

EXACTA 7-1 PAID $33.60 Total Pool: $1,498,377
TRIFECTA 7-1-4 PAID $53.00 Total Pool: $1,270,319

Winner: Flower Alley, ch. c., by Distorted Humor—Princess Olivia, by Lycius
Bred in Kentucky by George Brunacini and Bona Terra Farms

FLOWER ALLEY came away well and took a position to the outside of pacesetter BELLAMY ROAD, stalked that rival for the opening three-quarters, was sent after the leader in earnest approaching the stretch, responded to steady left-handed pressure, and drew clear in the final furlong. BELLAMY ROAD was sent directly to the front, set the pace along the inside, responded when confronted by the winner turning for home, dug in bravely on the rail in the stretch, but could not stay with FLOWER ALLEY in the final furlong. ROMAN RULER was taken in hand after the start, was rated along while three wide, advanced three wide into the second turn but had no response when put to the test in upper stretch. DON'T GET MAD was unhurried while outrun along the inside early, put in a good run on the second turn, came wide into the stretch, but had little left and faded in the drive. ANDROMEDA'S HERO ran close-up along the rail and had no response when roused entering the second turn. REVERBERATE was outrun early and tired after three-quarters. CHEKHOV was outrun after a sluggish start and had no response when roused.

Owners: (7) Melnyk Racing Stables; (1) Kinsman Stable; (4) Fog City Stable; (5) B. Wayne Hughes; (2) Robert V. LaPenta; (6) Centennial Farms; (3) Michael B. Tabor and Derrick Smith

Trainers: (7) Todd Pletcher; (1) Nicholas Zito; (4) Bob Baffert; (5) Ronald Ellis; (2) Nicholas Zito; (6) Sal Russo; (3) Patrick Biancone

How Pari-Mutuel Wagering Began

Virtually all betting on horse races in North America, as in most countries, is conducted using the pari-mutuel wagering system. Unlike a casino, where bettors play against the house, racehorse bettors bet against each other, with the track holding the bets and, after taking out money for the track, purses, state taxes, and other mandated deductions, returning the money bet to the winning patrons after each race is run.

Unlike most traditions in North American horse racing, pari-mutuel wagering came from France rather than England. The system was devised in the mid-1860s by Pierre Oller, a Paris perfume merchant who had become disenchanted with the city's bookmakers.

Oller developed a variation of the auction pool, in which betting interests in individual horses were sold. Because fairly large sums of money were required to buy the winning interest in a favorite in the auction pools, they were not widely used by small-scale bettors. Oller's system allowed small wagers on all horses and quickly came into wide use in France. He called his wagering system perier mutuel, which means to wager among ourselves. Adopted in England, it became known as Paris mutuals, and finally pari-mutuel.

New York tracks used the pari-mutuel system (known then as Paris pools) in the early 1870s. Col. M. Lewis Clark, the founder of Churchill Downs, observed the pari-mutuels in operation during a sojourn in Europe in the early 1870s and introduced the devices at his track in 1878. (Auction pools were used in 1875, 1876, and 1877, the first three years of Churchill's existence.)

Bookmakers soon made their appearance in both New York and Louisville, and the popularity of betting with bookmakers supplanted the pari-mutuel machines. Clark abandoned pari-mutuels in 1889 at the demand of bookmakers.

In 1908, however, anti-Churchill forces took over City Hall and banned bookmaking. Col. Matt Winn, then the track's general manager, rounded up six of the old pari-mutuel machines, refurbished them, and used them for betting on the 1908 Kentucky Derby. Pari-mutuel wagering on the Derby day program that year was $67,570 ($18,300 of that total on the Derby, won by Stone Street at 23.72-to-1 odds), with another $12,669 in auction pools.

The first machines sold only one denomination of ticket, $5 for the 1908 Derby program, but by 1911 Winn had commissioned new machines that offered $2, $5, and $10 tickets. By 1914, most American tracks had switched to the pari-mutuel system as anti-gambling sentiment led to bans against bookmaking.

Betting Odds and Payouts

Pari-mutuel betting odds are based on the percentage of the net wagering pool placed on each horse. For instance, a horse sent off at even money, or 1-to-1 odds, has attracted 50% of the net wagering pool.

The net wagering pool on which the odds are based is total wagering minus deductions broadly known as takeout—money taken out for state tax, horsemen's purses, the track's share, and other deductions. Total wagering is known as handle, which the track holds until after each race is run and then returns the net balance to winning bettors.

When devising a program betting line, a line maker generally will assign odds based on 125% of handle to account for takeout.

All tracks in North America show payouts after each race on their tote boards based on a $2 wager. To figure the exact odds, for instance, at which a horse went off in the win pool, subtract the $2 bet and divide by two. If a horse paid $4.70 to win, its winning odds were 1.35-to-1 ([$4.70-$2]/2=1.35).

Exact betting odds usually are rounded down to the nearest 10 cents, although some jurisdictions round to the next lowest 5 cents.

Pari-Mutuel Odds	Percentage of Net Pool	Payout
1-to-20	95.23%	$2.10
1-to-10	90.91%	2.20
1-to-5	83.33%	2.40
2-to-5	71.42%	2.80
1-to-2	66.66%	3.00
4-to-5	55.55%	3.60
Even (1-to-1)	50.00%	4.00
7-to-5	41.67%	4.80
9-to-5	35.71%	5.60
2-to-1	33.33%	6.00
5-to-2	28.57%	7.00
3-to-1	25.00%	8.00
7-to-2	22.23%	9.00
4-to-1	20.00%	10.00
9-to-2	18.19%	11.00
5-to-1	16.67%	12.00
10-to-1	9.09%	22.00
15-to-1	6.25%	32.00
20-to-1	4.76%	42.00
30-to-1	3.23%	62.00
50-to-1	1.96%	102.00
100-to-1	0.99%	202.00

Distance Equivalents

Race distances are directly or indirectly derived from distances conventionally run in England, the cradle of Thoroughbred racing. Distances of English races are measured in the traditional English system of furlongs and miles. A furlong is 660 feet, or one-eighth of a mile, and a mile comprises eight furlongs.

France has used the metric system instituted by Napoleon since the inception of racing in that country. As racing countries around the world have adopted the metric system of measurement, racing distances often have been changed to metric equivalents.

The following table includes equivalent distances for both systems.

Furlongs to Meters

Furlongs	Miles	Approx. Meters	Exact Meters
1.00	⅛	200	201.168
2.00	¼	400	402.336
3.00	⅜	600	603.504
4.00	½	800	804.672
4.50	9/16	900	905.256
5.00	⅝	1,000	1,005.840
5.50	11/16	1,100	1,106.424
6.00	¾	1,200	1,207.008
6.50	13/16	1,300	1,307.592
7.00	⅞	1,400	1,408.176
7.50	15/16	1,500	1,508.760
8.00	1	1,600	1,609.344
8.32	1&70 yds.	1,670	1,673.717
8.50	1 1/16	1,700	1,709.928
9.00	1⅛	1,800	1,810.512
9.50	1 3/16	1,900	1,911.096
10.00	1¼	2,000	2,011.680
10.50	1 5/16	2,100	2,112.264
11.00	1⅜	2,200	2,212.848
11.50	1 7/16	2,300	2,313.432
12.00	1½	2,400	2,414.016
12.50	1 9/16	2,500	2,514.600
13.00	1⅝	2,600	2,615.184
13.50	1 11/16	2,700	2,715.768
14.00	1¾	2,800	2,816.352
14.50	1 13/16	2,900	2,916.936
15.00	1⅞	3,000	3,017.520
15.50	1 15/16	3,100	3,118.104
16.00	2	3,200	3,218.688
16.50	2 1/16	3,300	3,319.272
17.00	2⅛	3,400	3,419.856
18.00	2¼	3,600	3,621.024
19.00	2⅜	3,800	3,822.192
20.00	2½	4,000	4,023.360
21.00	2⅝	4,200	4,224.528
22.00	2¾	4,400	4,425.696
23.00	2⅞	4,600	4,626.864
24.00	3	4,800	4,828.032

Meters to Furlongs

Meters	Approx. Furlongs	Approx. Miles	Exact Furlongs	Exact Miles
200	1.00	⅛	0.9942	0.1243
400	2.00	¼	1.9884	0.2485
600	3.00	⅜	2.9826	0.3728
800	4.00	½	3.9768	0.4971
900	4.50	9/16	4.4739	0.5592
1,000	5.00	⅝	4.9710	0.6214
1,100	5.50	11/16	5.4681	0.6835
1,200	6.00	¾	5.9652	0.7456
1,300	6.50	13/16	6.4623	0.8078
1,400	7.00	⅞	6.9594	0.8699
1,500	7.50	15/16	7.4565	0.9321
1,600	8.00	1	7.9536	0.9942
1,670	8.32	1&70 yds.	7.9784	0.9973
1,700	8.50	1 1/16	8.4506	1.0563
1,800	9.00	1⅛	8.9477	1.1185
1,900	9.50	1 3/16	9.4448	1.1806
2,000	10.00	1¼	9.9419	1.2427
2,100	10.50	1 5/16	10.4390	1.3049
2,200	11.00	1⅜	10.9361	1.3670
2,300	11.50	1 7/16	11.4332	1.4292
2,400	12.00	1½	11.9303	1.4913
2,500	12.50	1 9/16	12.4274	1.5534
2,600	13.00	1⅝	12.9245	1.6156
2,700	13.50	1 11/16	13.4216	1.6777
2,800	14.00	1¾	13.9187	1.7398
2,900	14.50	1 13/16	14.4158	1.8020
3,000	15.00	1⅞	14.9129	1.8641
3,100	15.50	1 15/16	15.4100	1.9263
3,200	16.00	2	15.9071	1.9884
3,300	16.50	2 1/16	16.4042	2.0505
3,400	17.00	2⅛	16.9013	2.1127
3,500	17.50	2 3/16	17.3984	2.1748
3,600	18.00	2¼	17.8955	2.2369
3,700	18.50	2 5/16	18.3926	2.2991
3,800	19.00	2⅜	18.8897	2.3612
3,900	19.50	2 7/16	19.3868	2.4233
4,000	20.00	2½	19.8839	2.4855
4,100	20.50	2 9/16	20.3810	2.5476
4,200	21.00	2⅝	20.8781	2.6098
4,300	21.50	2 11/16	21.3752	2.6719
4,400	22.00	2¾	21.8723	2.7340
4,500	22.50	2 13/16	22.3694	2.7962
4,600	23.00	2⅞	22.8665	2.8583
4,700	23.50	2 15/16	23.3636	2.9204
4,800	24.00	3	23.8607	2.9826

Countries and Measurements Used

Argentina................................furlongs and meters
Australia..meters
Brazil..meters
Canada ....furlongs
Chile...meters
England..furlongs
France...meters
Germany..meters
Hong Kong...meters
Ireland...furlongs
Italy ....meters
Japan...meters
New Zealand...meters
United Arab Emirates.................................meters
United States ....furlongs

Glossary of Common Racing and Breeding Terms

account wagering Betting by phone, in which a bettor must open an account with a track or an off-track agency. A synonym: phone betting.

acey-deucy Uneven stirrups, popularized by Racing Hall of Fame jockey Eddie Arcaro, who rode with his left (inside) iron lower than his right to achieve better balance on turns.

across the board A bet on a horse to win, place, and show. If the horse wins, the player collects three ways; if second, two ways (place and show); and if third, one way (show).

action 1) A horse's manner of moving. 2) A vernacular term for wagering.

added money Money added to the purse of a race by the racing association, a breeding fund, or other source. The association's money is added to the amount paid by owners in nomination, eligibility, entry, and starting fees. Added-money stakes became less common in the 1990s as more tracks went to guaranteed purses.

agent A person empowered to transact business for a stable owner or a jockey, or one empowered to sell or buy horses for an owner or a breeder.

aired Won particularly easily by open lengths.

all-age race A race for two-year-olds and up.

all out When a horse extends itself to the utmost.

allowance race A race for which the racing secretary drafts certain conditions to determine weights to be carried based on the horse's age, sex, past performance, or a combination of all three.

allowances Reductions in weights to be carried, with the adjustments based on the conditions of the race or because an apprentice jockey is on a horse. Also, a weight reduction that female horses are entitled to when racing against males or that three-year-olds receive against older horses.

also-eligible A horse officially entered for a race but not permitted to start unless the field is reduced by scratches below a specified number.

also-ran A horse that does not finish first, second, or third.

American Horse Council A national association of individuals, organizations, and companies formed as a lobbying group to represent all breeds of the horse industry. Based in Washington, D.C., the AHC works on tax regulations, import and export rules, disease prevention and control, trails and recreation enhancement, and humane concerns. Founded in 1969 as an advocate for the entire American horse industry, the AHC was founded principally by Thoroughbred interests concerned about legislation then being discussed in Congress that would have negatively affected racing and breeding.

American Stud Book Official book of foal registrations in North America maintained by the Jockey Club.

apprentice allowance Weight concession given to an apprentice rider; usually ten pounds until the fifth winner, seven pounds until the 35th winner, and five pounds for one calendar year from the 35th winner. More rarely, a three-pound allowance for a rider under contract to a specific stable or owner for two years from his or her first win. This rule varies from state to state. Apprentices do not receive a weight allowance when riding in a stakes race.

apprentice jockey Rider at the beginning of his career who has not ridden a certain number of winners within a specified period of time. Also known as a bug rider or bug boy, from the asterisk used in racing programs and past performances to denote the weight allowance such riders receive.

apron The (usually) paved area between the grandstand and the racing surface.

Association of Racing Commissioners International (RCI) Formerly the National Association of State Racing Commissioners (NASRC). Its office is based in Lexington.

asterisk Used with names of horses to denote they were imported into the United States. Practice preceded the use of country codes starting January 1, 1977.

auxiliary starting gate A second starting gate used when the number of horses in a race exceeds the capacity of the main starting gate.

average earnings index (AEI) A breeding statistic that compares racing earnings of a stallion's or mare's foals to those of all other foals racing at that time. An AEI of 1.00 is considered average, 2.00 is twice the average, 0.50 half the average, etc.

baby race A race for two-year-olds.

backstretch 1) Straight portion of the far side of the racing surface between the turns. 2) Generally, a racetrack's stable area, which often contains dormitories, a track kitchen, chapel, and recreation area for stable employees. It gained its name because most stable areas are located along the racetrack's backstretch.

bad doer A horse with a poor appetite, a condition that may be due to nervousness or other causes.

bandage Wrappings used on a horse's legs are three to six inches wide and are made of a variety of materials. In a race, they are used for support or protection against injury. Rundown bandages are used during a race to affix a pad under the fetlock to avoid injury due to abrasion when the fetlocks sink toward the ground during the weight-bearing portion of the gallop. A horse also may wear standing bandages, thick cotton wraps used during shipping and while in the stall to prevent swelling, injury, or both, or to apply medication.

bar shoe A horseshoe closed at the back to help support the frog and heel of the hoof. It is often worn by horses with quarter cracks or bruised feet.

base The portion of the track that lies under the thick top layer, or cushion. The base provides support and drainage.

battery A term for an illegal electrical device used by a jockey to stimulate a horse by electrical shock during a race. Also known as a machine or a joint.

bay A horse color that varies from a yellow tan to a bright auburn. The mane, tail, and lower portion of the legs are always black, except where white markings are present.

bearing in (or out) Deviating from a straight course. May be due to weariness, infirmity, inexperience, or the rider overusing the whip or reins to make a horse alter its course.

bell Signal sounded when the starter opens the gates or, at some tracks, to mark the close of betting.

Beyer number A handicapping tool, popularized by author Andrew Beyer, assigning a numerical value (speed figure) to each race run by a horse based on final time and track condition. This enables different horses running at different racetracks to be objectively compared.

bid in The act of buying back a horse that does not meet a minimum price at public auction. Synonym for buy-back, reserve not attained (RNA).

Big Red Refers to either of two famous chestnut-colored horses: Man o' War or Secretariat.

Bill Daly (on the) Taking a horse to the front at the start of a race and remaining there to the finish. Term stems from "Father Bill" Daly, a famous old-time horseman who developed many great jockeys.

birthdays All Thoroughbreds born in the Northern Hemisphere celebrate their birthday on January 1. In the Southern Hemisphere, all Thoroughbred birthdays are as follows: South America, July 1; South Africa, Australia, and New Zealand, August 1.

bit A stainless steel, rubber, or aluminum bar attached to the bridle; it is placed in the bar, the space between front and back teeth in the horse's mouth, and is one of the means by which a jockey exerts guidance and control. The most common racing bit is the D-bit, named because the rings extending from the bar are shaped like the letter D. Most racing bits are snaffled (snaffle bit), which means the metal bar is made up of two pieces, connected in the middle, which leaves it free to swivel. Other bits may be used to correct specific problems, such as bearing in or out.

black A horse color that includes the hair and the skin of the muzzle, flanks, mane, tail, and legs, unless white markings are present.

black type Boldface type, used in sales catalogs and stakes results, to distinguish horses that have won or placed in a stakes race. Sales companies today have eliminated the use of black type for stakes below a certain monetary level—$15,000 in 1985; $20,000 from 1986-'89; $25,000 beginning in 1990; $30,000 beginning in 2002; $35,000 beginning in 2003; and $40,000 beginning in 2004. If a horse's name appears in boldface capital letters in a catalog or stakes results, the horse has won at least one black-type event. If the name appears in boldface type with capital and lower-case letters, the horse was second or third in at least one black-type event but has not won a black-type race.

blaze A generic term describing a large, white vertical marking on a horse's face.

blind switch A circumstance in which a rider's actions cause his or her mount to be impeded during a race when moving into a space in which the horse and rider find themselves blocked.

blinkers A cup-shaped device to limit a horse's vision and thus prevent it from swerving from objects or other horses on either side while racing. Blinker cups come in a variety of sizes and shapes to allow as little or as much vision as the trainer feels is necessary and may be attached to a hood or bridle.

blister Counterirritant causing acute inflammation; used to increase blood supply and blood flow and to promote healing in the leg.

bloodstock Horses of Thoroughbred breeding, especially such horses used for or considered in relation to racing.

bloodstock agent A person who advises or represents a buyer or a seller of Thoroughbreds at a public auction or a private sale. A bloodstock agent usually works on commission, often 5% of the purchase or sale price, and may also prepare a horse for sale.

blood typing A method of verifying a horse's parentage. Blood typing was usually completed within the first year of a horse's life and was necessary before registration papers were issued by the Jockey Club. Beginning in 2001, the Jockey Club adopted DNA technology to verify horse's parentage.

blowout A short, timed workout, usually a day or two before a race, designed to sharpen a horse's speed. Usually three-eighths or one-half mile in distance.

blue hen Used to describe an outstanding broodmare, the producer of a number of stakes winners and whose daughters, granddaughters, and great-granddaughters in turn produced important winners.

board Short for tote board, on which odds, betting pools, and other information are displayed.

boat race Slang for a fixed race.

bobble A bad step away from the starting gate, usually caused by the track surface breaking away from under a horse's hooves, causing it to duck its head or nearly go to his knees.

bolt Sudden veering from a straight course, usually to the outside rail.

bomb(er) A winning horse sent off at extremely high odds.

book 1) The group of mares being bred to a stallion in a given year. If a stallion attracts the maximum number of mares allowed by the farm manager, he has a full book. 2) A term used to describe a jockey's riding commitments with his agent.

bookie Short for bookmaker.

bookmaker A person who books bets.

bottom 1) Stamina in a horse developed over a long period of time. 2) Subsurface of a racing strip.

bottom line A Thoroughbred's breeding on the female side most specifically applied to the tail-female line listed on the bottom line of a standard pedigree diagram.

bounce A poor race run immediately after a career-best or near-best performance.

box 1) A wagering term denoting a combination bet whereby all possible numeric combinations are covered for certain horses. 2) A disadvantageous position in a race, behind and between horses. 3) A horse's stall.

boxed (in) To be trapped between, behind, or inside other horses.

brace (or bracer) Rubdown liniment used on a horse after a race or workout.

break 1) To train a young horse to wear a bridle and saddle, carry a rider, and respond to a rider's commands. Most often done when the horse is a yearling. 2) To leave from the starting gate.

breakage In pari-mutuel payoffs, which are rounded down to a nickel or dime, the pennies that are left over. Breakage may be used for any of a number of purposes. Depending upon a state's rules of racing, the money goes to the state, the track, purses, or benevolence programs.

breather Easing off on a horse for a short distance in a race to permit it to conserve or renew its strength.

bred A horse is considered to have been bred in the state or country where it was foaled.

breed-back rule Restriction imposed in some jurisdictions that, for a mare's offspring to be eligible for state-bred bonuses, the mare, after foaling, must be bred to a stallion standing in that state.

breeder Owner of the dam at time of foaling unless the dam was under a lease or foal-sharing arrangement at the time of foaling. In that case, the person specified by the terms of the agreement is the breeder of the foal.

Breeders' Cup Thoroughbred racing's year-end championship. Known as Breeders' Cup day, Breeders' Cup championship day, from 2001 to '05 as World Thoroughbred Championships, or beginning in '06 as World Championships, it consists of eight races conducted on one day at one of several major North American racetracks each year. (See Breeders' Cup chapter.)

Breeders' Cup Ltd. Corporate entity that oversees the Breeders' Cup program. It is a not-for-profit organization based in Lexington.

breeding fund A state fund set up to provide bonuses for state-breds.

breeding right The right to breed one mare per year to a specific stallion. Breeding rights, as opposed to stallion shares, do not usually come with bonuses (money derived from extra seasons sold), nor are they assessed expenses.

breeze (breezing) Working a horse at a moderate speed; less effort than handily.

bridge jumper A person who wagers large amounts of money, usually on short-priced horses to show, hoping to realize a small but almost certain profit.

bridle A piece of equipment, usually made of leather or nylon, that fits on a horse's head; other equipment, such as a bit and the reins, are attached to it.

broken wind Abnormality of the upper or lower respiratory tract causing loss of normal air exchange, generally resulting in reduced performance.

broodmare A mare that has been bred and is used to produce foals.

broodmare sire The maternal sire; the sire of the dam.

Broodmare Sire Index The Broodmare Sire Index is an average of the Racing Index (RI) of all foals (that started at least three times) out of the sire's daughters. For BSI to be calculated, a broodmare sire must be represented by a minimum of 75 starters lifetime.

brush 1) During a race when two horses lightly touch each other. 2) Injury that occurs when one hoof strikes the inside of the opposite limb. 3) A type of obstacle used in steeplechase racing.

bullet work The best workout time for a particular distance on a given day at a track. Derived from the printer's bullet that precedes the time of the workout in listings. Also known as a black-letter work in some parts of the country.

bullring A small racetrack, usually less than one mile in circumference.

buy-back A horse put through a public auction that fails to reach a minimum (reserve) price set by the consignor and so is retained. The consignor must pay a fee to the auction company based on a percentage of the reserve to cover the auction company's marketing, advertising, and other costs. A synonym for reserve not attained (RNA).

calk A projection on the heels of a horseshoe, similar to a cleat, on the rear shoes of a horse to prevent slipping, especially on a wet track. Also known as a sticker.

(race) call Running position of horses in a race at various points.

cast A horse positioned on its side or back and wedged against a wall, fence, or other object in such a way that it cannot get up.

chalk Wagering favorite in a race. Term dates from the days when on-track bookmakers would write current odds on a chalkboard, and the horse that was bet the most used the most chalk.

chalk player Bettor who wagers on favorites.

champion Horse or individual determined to be the outstanding performer in his or her division in a specific year. In the United States, champions are determined by the Eclipse Awards balloting.

chart A statistical picture of a race (from which past performances are compiled) showing the position and margin of each horse at designated points of call (depending on the distance of the race), as well as the horse's age, weight carried, owner, trainer, jockey, and the race's purse, conditions, payoff prices, odds, time, and other data. Before 1991, all charts were compiled by *Daily Racing Form*. From 1991 to '98, charts were compiled by both *Daily Racing Form* and Equibase; since mid-1998, charts have been compiled exclusively by Equibase.

check(ed) When a jockey slows a horse due to other horses impeding its progress.

chestnut 1) A horse color that may vary from a red-yellow to golden-yellow. The mane, tail, and legs are usually variations of coat color, except where white markings are present. 2) Horny, irregular growths found on the inside of the legs. On the forelegs, they are just above the knees. On the hind legs, they are just below the hocks. No two horses have been found to have the same chestnuts, and so chestnuts may be used for identification. Also called night eyes.

chute Extension of backstretch or homestretch to permit a straight start in a race, as opposed to starting on or near a turn.

claiming Process by which a licensed person may purchase a horse entered in a designated race for a predetermined price. When a horse has been claimed, its new owner assumes title after the starting gate opens although the former owner is entitled to all purse money earned in that race. Sometimes called halter or haltered, for the act of putting a new halter on a claimed horse so that it can be led back to its new barn.

claiming box, claims box Box in which claims are deposited before the race.

claiming race A race in which each horse entered is eligible to be purchased at a set price. Claims must be made before the race and only by licensed owners or their agents who have a horse registered to race at that meeting or who have received a claim certificate from the stewards. A claiming race in which there is an option to have horses entered to be claimed for a stated price or not eligible to be claimed is an optional claiming race.

classic 1) A race of traditional importance, usually modeled on one of the five original English classic races, and often considered part of a triple crown. 2) Used to describe a distance. The American classic distance is 1¼ miles on dirt. The European classic distance is 1½ miles on turf.

clerk of scales An official whose chief duty is to weigh the riders before and after a race to ensure proper weight is or was carried.

climbing When a horse lifts its front legs abnormally high as it gallops, causing it to run inefficiently.

clocker Individual who times workouts and races.

closer A horse that runs best in the latter part of the race, coming from off the pace.

clubhouse turn Generally, the turn on a racing oval that is closest to the clubhouse facility; usually the first turn after the finish line.

colors (horse) Colors accepted by the Jockey Club are bay, black, chestnut, dark bay or brown, gray or roan, and white. In 1996, the Jockey Club started combining gray and roan, which had been separate colors previously.
colt An ungelded (entire) male horse four years old or younger.
commingle Combining mutuel pools from off-track sites with the host track.
company Class of horses in a race or the class of horses a runner usually keeps.
comparable index (CI) Indicates the average earnings of progeny produced from mares bred to one sire when these same mares are bred to other sires. A CI of 1.00 is considered average, 2.00 is twice the average, and 0.50 half the average.
condition book(s) A series of booklets issued by a track's racing secretary setting forth conditions of races to be run at that track.
conditioner 1) A trainer. 2) A workout or race to enable a horse to attain fitness.
conditions The requirements for being able to enter a horse in a particular race as written by the track's racing secretary. Conditions may include age, sex, money or races won, weight carried, and the distance of the race.
conformation The physical makeup and bodily proportions of a horse.
connections Persons identified with a horse, such as owner, trainer, rider, and stable employees.
consolation double A payoff to holders of daily double tickets combining the winning horse in the first race of the double with a scratched horse in the second.
cooling out Restoring a horse to its normal body temperature, usually by walking, after it has become overheated during exercise or racing.
coupled (entry) Two or more horses running as an entry in a single betting unit.
cover A single breeding of a stallion to a mare.
crop 1) The number of foals by a sire in a given year. 2) All horses collectively born in the same year. 3) A jockey's whip.
cup horse A term once used to describe horses competing at the highest level of the sport in races at a distance of two miles or more.
cuppy (track) A drying and loose racing surface that breaks away under a horse's hooves.
cushion Top portion of a racetrack.
cut down Horse suffering injuries from being struck by the shoes of another horse. Or, due to a faulty stride, a horse may cut itself down.
daily double Type of wager calling for the selection of winners of two consecutive races, usually the first and second.
Daily Racing Form A daily newspaper containing news, past performance data, and handicapping information. Founded in 1895, it is the successor of the *Morning Telegraph*. The *Morning Telegraph* was founded in 1833 and was closed during a strike by printers in 1972.
dam The female parent of a foal.
dam's sire (broodmare sire) The sire of a broodmare. Used in reference to the maternal grandsire of a foal.
dark day A day when there is no racing at the track.
dark bay or brown A horse color that ranges from brown with areas of tan on the shoulders, head, and flanks, to a dark brown, with tan areas seen only in the flanks, muzzle, or both. The mane, tail, and lower portions of the legs are always black unless white markings are present.
dark horse Probably a good horse whose full potential is unknown before a race.
dead heat Two or more horses finishing a race in a tie.
dead track Racing surface lacking resiliency.
declared In the United States, a horse withdrawn from a race in advance of scratch time. In Europe, a horse confirmed to start in a race.
deep stretch A position very close to the finish line in a race.
Derby A stakes event for three-year-olds, deriving its name from Lord Derby, and usually the most important race for three-year-olds at a given track.
disqualification Change in order of finish by officials for an infraction of the rules.
distaffer A female horse.
distaff race A race for female horses.
distanced Horse so far behind the rest of the field of runners that it is out of contact and unable to regain a position of contention. A horse beaten more than 40 lengths.
dogs Rubber traffic cones (or a barrier) placed at certain distances out from the inner rail when the track is wet, muddy, soft, yielding, or heavy to prevent horses during the workout period from churning the footing along the rail.
dope 1) Any illegal drug. 2) Slang term for past performances: Readers of past performances are said to dope out a race.
dosage Although other dosage theories exist, the term is most commonly associated with the one interpreted by Dr. Steven Roman. A variation of Dr. Franco Varola's work on pedigree analysis, the system identifies patterns of ability in horses based on a list of prepotent sires, each of whom is designated a *chef-de-race*. The dosage system puts these sires into one of five categories: brilliant, intermediate, classic, solid, or professional, which are subjective judgments of speed and stamina. Sires can be listed in up to two *chef-de-race* categories. Each generation of sires is worth 16 points, divided by the number of sires; i.e., the immediate sire is worth 16 points while the four sires four generations back are worth four points apiece.
dosage index (DI) A mathematical reduction of the dosage profile to a number reflecting a horse's potential for speed or stamina. The higher the number, the more likely the horse is suited to be a sprinter. The average dosage index of all horses is about 4.00. The dosage index (DI) is derived from the dosage profile to reflect the ratio of speed to stamina in a pedigree. This is calculated by adding points from the two speed categories (brilliant and intermediate), plus half of those from the classic (middle) category, and dividing that total by the points from the two stamina categories (solid and professional), plus the other half of the classic points. The higher the DI, the more speed is imputed to be present in the pedigree. A 4.00 DI is generally the cutoff where a horse is considered not likely to be competitive at the American classic distance of 1¼ miles.
driving A horse that is all out to win and under strong urging from its jockey.
drop down A horse meeting a lower class of rival than it had been running against previously.
dwelt Extremely late in breaking from the gate.
earmuffs Equipment that covers a horse's ears to prevent it from hearing distracting sounds.

eased A horse that is gently pulled up during a race.

easily Running or winning without being pressed by rider or opposition.

Eclipse Award Thoroughbred racing's year-end awards, honoring the top horses and people in several categories. Named for the great 18th-century racehorse and sire Eclipse, who was undefeated in 18 career starts and sired the winners of 344 races. The Eclipse Awards are sponsored by the National Thoroughbred Racing Association, *Daily Racing Form*, and National Turf Writers Association. They were first awarded in 1971; previously, separate year-end champions were named by *Daily Racing Form* (beginning in 1936) and the Thoroughbred Racing Associations (beginning in 1950).

eligible Qualified to start in a race, according to conditions.

engagement 1) Stakes nomination. 2) Riding commitment.

entire An ungelded horse. In Europe, where geldings are not permitted to enter certain races, the race conditions might read: Entire colts and fillies.

entry Two or more horses with common ownership (in some cases, trained by the same trainer) that are paired as a single betting unit in one race or are placed together by the racing secretary as part of a mutuel field. Rules on entries vary from state to state. Also known as a coupled entry.

entry fee Money paid by an owner to enter a horse in a stakes race—and is what usually defines a race as a stakes. Entry fees are not required for overnight races and some invitational stakes races.

Equibase Co. A partnership between the Jockey Club and the Thoroughbred Racing Associations to establish and maintain an industry-owned, central database of racing records. Equibase past-performance information is used in track programs across North America. Formed in 1990, Equibase first collected data in '91. In 1998, it began supplying past performance information to *Daily Racing Form* and became the sole collector of racing data.

estrus (heat) Associated with ovulation; a mare usually is receptive to breeding during estrus. Referred to as horsing.

euthanize To end a horse's life by lethal injection because of a catastrophic injury or critical illness and thus prevent further pain and suffering.

evenly Neither gaining nor losing position during a race.

exacta (or perfecta) A wager in which the first two finishers in a race, in exact order of finish, must be picked. Called an exactor in Canada.

exacta box A wager in which all possible combinations using a given number of horses are bet on.

exercise rider Individual who is licensed to exercise a horse during morning training hours.

exotic (wager) Any wager other than win, place, or show that requires multiple combinations. Examples of exotic wagers: trifecta, pick six, pick three.

Experimental Free Handicap A year-end assessment of the best North American two-year-olds of the season. It is put together by a panel of racing secretaries under the auspices of the Jockey Club and is based on performances in unrestricted races. Two lists are drawn up, one for males and one for females. Only the handicap for two-year-olds is called the Experimental Free Handicap; lists for older horses are free handicaps. First started by Walter Vosburgh in 1933. Race based on Experimental was run at Aqueduct from 1940 to '56 at six furlongs (Experimental Free Handicap No. 1) and another from 1946 to '52 at 1$\frac{1}{16}$ miles (Experimental Free Handicap No. 2).

extended Running at top speed.

farrier Horseshoer.

fast (track) Footing that is dry, even, and resilient.

fault Weak points of a horse's conformation or its character as a racehorse.

feather Light weight. Usually refers to the weight a horse is assigned to carry in a race.

fee 1) Amount paid to a jockey for riding in a race. 2) The cost of nominating, entering, or starting a horse in a stakes race.

fetal sexing Use of ultrasonography to identify genitalia of a fetus. Optimum time to perform fetal sexing is between 60 and 75 days of gestation.

field The horses in a race.

field horse (or mutuel field) Two or more starters running as a single betting unit (entry), when there are more starters in a race than positions on the totalizator board.

filly Female horse four years old or younger.

firm A condition of a turf course corresponding to fast on a dirt track.

flag Signal manually held a short distance in front of the gate at the exact starting point of a race. In some jurisdictions, official timing starts when flag is dropped by the flagman to denote proper start.

flak jacket Similar to a jacket worn by football quarterbacks, the jockey's flak jacket protects the chest, ribs, kidneys, and back from injury.

flat race Contested over a course without obstacles to jump. Often used in the term, on the flat.

flatten out A very tired horse that slows considerably, dropping its head on a straight line with its body.

float 1) An equine dental procedure in which sharp points on the teeth are filed down. 2) The instrument with which the above procedure is performed. 3) To drag a flat plate over a wet track surface to aid in draining water.

floating Flat plate or wooden implement (float) dragged over the surface of a wet track to aid in draining water.

foal(ed) 1) A horse of either sex in its first year of life. 2) Can also denote the offspring of either a male or female parent. 3) To give birth.

Fontana safety rail An aluminum rail, in use since 1981, designed to help reduce injuries to horse and rider. It has more of an offset (slant) to provide greater clearance between the rail and the vertical posts as well as a protective cover to keep horse and rider from striking the posts.

foundation mare A mare whose descendants show high quality and have impact on the breed after many generations.

founding sires The Darley Arabian, Byerly Turk, and Godolphin Arabian. Every Thoroughbred traces its male-line parentage to one of the three founding sires.

fractional time Intermediate times recorded in a race, as at the quarter-mile, half-mile, three-quarters, etc.

free handicap A race in which no nomination fees are required. More recently, and more commonly, a ranking of horses three years old and up by weight for a theoretical race or as an intellectual challenge.

front-runner A horse whose running style is to attempt to get on or near the lead at the start of the race and to continue there as long as possible.

frozen (track) The condition of a racetrack where any moisture present is frozen.

full brother, full sister Horses that share both the same sire and dam.

furlong One-eighth of a mile, which is equal to 220 yards or 660 feet.

furosemide A medication used in the treatment of bleeders, commonly known by the trade name Salix, a diuretic. Although research has not determined definitively how furosemide reduces bleeding, it is widely believed that the diuretic effect reduces pressure within capillaries in the lungs.

futurity A race for two-year-olds in which the owners make a scheduled series of payments over a period of time to keep their horses eligible. Purses for these races vary but can be considerable.

gait The characteristic footfall pattern of a horse in motion. Thoroughbreds have four natural gaits: walk, trot, canter, and gallop. Thoroughbreds compete at a gallop.

gap An opening in the rail where horses enter and leave the course.

Garrison finish A close victory, usually from off the pace. Derived from Ed "Snapper" Garrison, a 19th-century rider known for his close finishes.

gate card A card, issued by the starter, stating that a horse is properly schooled in starting-gate procedures.

gelding A male horse of any age that has been neutered by having both testicles removed (gelded).

gentleman jockey Amateur rider, generally in steeplechases.

get Progeny of sire.

girth An elastic and leather band, sometimes covered with sheepskin, that passes under a horse's belly and is connected to both sides of the saddle.

good (track) A dirt track that is almost fast or a turf course slightly softer than firm.

grab a quarter Injury to the back of the hoof or foot caused by a horse stepping on itself (affects the front foot). Very common in racing, the injury is usually minor.

graded race Established in 1973 to classify select stakes races in North America, at the request of European racing authorities, who had set up group races two years earlier. Grading of races is performed by a committee under the direction of the Thoroughbred Owners and Breeders Association. See graded stakes section in Racing chapter.

grandam A horse's grandmother. Also known as second dam when referring to the female line.

grandsire The grandfather of a horse; father (sire) of the horse's dam or sire.

grass slip Used in some areas, permission to exercise a horse on the turf course. Also known as a turf card.

gray A horse color in which the majority of the coat is a mixture of black and white hairs. The mane, tail, and legs may be either black or gray unless white markings are present. Starting with foals of 1993, the color classifications gray and roan were combined as gray or roan.

Grayson-Jockey Club Research Foundation A privately financed charitable organization established in 1989, which combined the Grayson Foundation Inc. (begun in 1940) and the Jockey Club Research Foundation.

group race Designation of best races in countries outside North America. European authorities began designating races as Group 1, Group 2, and Group 3 in 1971. North American officials, under the direction of the Thoroughbred Owners and Breeders Association, began grading races in 1973.

guineas By definition, a guinea is 21 shillings, or in current usage a pound and a shilling. Thus, the guinea is equal to 1.05 pounds. Used by sales companies in England and Ireland to report sales since it includes the sales company's 5% commission.

half brother, half sister Horses out of the same dam but by different sires. Horses with the same sire and different dams are not considered half siblings in Thoroughbred racing.

halter Like a bridle, but lacking a bit and reins. Used to handle horses around the stable and when they are not being ridden.

hand Four inches. A horse's height is measured in hands and inches from the top of the shoulder (withers) to the ground; that is, 15.2 hands is 15 hands, 2 inches, or a total of 62 inches. Thoroughbreds typically range from 15 to 17 hands.

handicap 1) Race for which the track handicapper assigns the weights to be carried. 2) To make selections on the basis of past performances.

handicap horse A horse that competes in handicap races.

handicapper 1) A person, usually the racing secretary, who assigns weights to horses. 2) A bettor who is making selections based on information of horses' performances from previous starts.

handily 1) Working in the morning with a strong effort. 2) A horse racing well within itself, with little exertion, during a race.

handle Amount of money wagered in the pari-mutuels on a race, a program, during a meeting, or for a year.

hand ride Urging a horse with the hands and not using the whip.

hard A condition of a turf course where there is no resiliency to the surface.

hardboot A Kentucky horseman.

hard-knocker A tough horse that makes a lot of starts.

harrow Implement or unit with pulling teeth, or tines, used to rake and loosen the upper surface of a track.

head A margin between horses. One horse leading another by the length of its head.

head of the stretch Beginning of the straight run to the finish line.

head to head Running on even terms.

heat 1) A race decided by two or more individual races over the same distance and between the same horses on the same day. Not used in flat racing today, though it was common in the 19th century. Still used occasionally in harness racing. 2) A breeding term for estrus in a mare.

heavy Wettest possible condition of a turf course; not usually found in North America.

helmet A lightweight fiberglass cap worn by riders to prevent head injuries. It is required equipment and is not considered part of a jockey's riding weight.

high weight Refers to highest weight assigned or carried in a race.

highweight Horse assigned the highest weight on the Experimental Free Handicap, a division of the International Classifications, or one of several free handicaps in individual countries, and often viewed as the equivalent of a champion in the absence of official championships.

homebred A horse bred by its owner.

homestretch Long section of racetrack closest to the stands.

hood A covering, usually nylon, that goes over a horse's head; blinkers or earmuffs may be attached to it.
hopped A horse that has been illegally stimulated with a drug.
horse When reference is made to sex, an ungelded male five years old or older.
Horsemen's Benevolent and Protective Association A national organization of horsemen, largely composed of owners, that has divisions at many racetracks in North America to help owners and trainers negotiate purses and other issues with track management.
hot walker A person or automatic machine that walks horses to cool them out after workouts or races.
hung A horse that does not advance its position in a race when called upon by its jockey.
icing 1) A physical therapy procedure, properly known as cryotherapy. 2) When a horse's leg or legs are placed in a tub of ice or ice packs are applied to the legs to reduce inflammation or swelling.
impost Weight carried by a horse or assigned to a horse.
inbreeding The mating of closely related individuals, resulting in a pedigree with at least one common ancestor duplicated on both sire's and dam's side of the pedigree. In Thoroughbreds, horses with one or more duplicated ancestors within the first four or five generations are generally considered inbred, while duplications of ancestors in more distant generations are often referred to as "linebreeding."
infield Area enclosed by the inner rail of the racetrack.
in hand Running under moderate control, at less than top speed.
inquiry A review of the running of the race to check into a possible infraction of the rules, called by the stewards. Also, a sign flashed by officials on the tote board on such occasions. If lodged by a jockey, it is called an objection.
in the money A horse that finishes first, second, or third in a race.
Irish rail Movable rail.
isolation barn A facility used to separate horses to ensure that disease is not carried into the area.
jail Requirement that when a claimed horse runs within 30 days of being claimed, it must run for a claiming price at least 25% higher than the price at which it was claimed.
Jockey Club Organization dedicated to the improvement of Thoroughbred breeding and racing. Incorporated February 9, 1894, in New York City, the Jockey Club serves as North America's Thoroughbred registry, responsible for the maintenance of the *American Stud Book*, a register of all Thoroughbreds foaled in the United States, Puerto Rico, and Canada; and of all Thoroughbreds imported into those countries from jurisdictions that have a registry recognized by the Jockey Club and the International Stud Book Committee.
jockey fee Sum paid to rider for competing in a race.
Jockeys' Guild National organization of professional riders.
jockey's race A race whose outcome will hinge mostly on strategic thinking by the riders; one in which riders must pay close attention to pace to keep their horses fresh for a strong finish.
jog Slow, easy gait commonly called a trot.
joint 1) Point of juncture of two bones and usually composed of fibrous connective tissue and cartilage. 2) Slang for an illegal electrical stimulation device.
jumper Steeplechase or hurdle horse.
juvenile Two-year-old horse.
key horse A single horse used in multiple combinations in an exotic wager.
kilometer One thousand meters and equal to .6214 of a mile.
lame A deviation from a normal gait due to pain in a limb or its supporting structures.
Lasix See Salix.
late double A second daily double offered during the latter part of a race program.
lead Refers to the leading leg when a horse is racing in full stride. The lead leg is the one that reaches out the farthest and bears the full weight of the horse's impact. Horses usually race on the left, or inside, lead on the turn, and on the right, or outside, lead on straightaways. Changing leads refers to the horse's ability to switch from one leading leg to the other at the proper time.
leaky-roof circuit Minor tracks.
leg up 1) To help a jockey mount a horse. 2) To improve a horse's fitness through long, slow gallops.
length A measurement approximating the length of a horse and used to describe the distances between horses in a race. A length is approximately eight feet.
listed race A stakes race just below a group race or graded race in quality.
lock Slang for a sure winner.
longe 1) A long rope or line fastened to a horse's head and held by a trainer, who causes the horse to move around in a circle. 2) A method of exercising a horse on a tether (longe line).
lug (bearing in or lugging out) Deviating from a straight course. May be due to weariness, infirmity, inexperience, or the rider overusing the whip or reins to make a horse alter its course.
maiden 1) A horse or rider who has not won a race. 2) A female horse that has never been bred.
maiden race A race for nonwinners.
mare Female horse five years old or older. Also, any female that has been bred regardless of age.
mare's month September. In theory, mares that have not run well during the summer often perform better in September.
mash Soft, moist mixture, hot or cold, of grain and other feed that is easily digested by horses.
massage Rubbing of various parts of the anatomy to stimulate healing.
match race A race between two horses.
medication list A list kept by the track veterinarian and published by the track showing which horses have been treated with legally prescribed medications.
meter The basic unit of length in the metric system. It is equal to approximately 39.37 inches. It takes 100 centimeters to make a meter and 1,000 meters to make a kilometer. To convert to inches, multiply by 39.37 (5 meters x 39.37 inches = 196.85 inches). To convert to yards, multiply by 1.1 (5 meters x 1.1 = 5.5 yards). Most European races are expressed in meters. A mile is approximately 1,600 meters, the distance at which the classic Poule d'Essai des Pouliches (Fr-G1) and the Poule d'Essai des Poulains (Fr-G1) are run. The Prix de l'Arc de Triomphe (Fr-G1) is 2,400 meters, or approximately 1½ miles; the Prix Eugene Adam (Fr-G2) is 2,000 meters, or approximately 1¼ miles. See Distance Equivalents table in preceding section.
middle distance Broadly, from one mile to 1⅛ miles.

minus pool A negative mutuel pool created when a horse is so heavily played that, after deductions of state tax and commission, not enough money remains to pay the legally prescribed minimum on each winning bet. The racing association usually makes up the difference.

money rider A rider who excels in rich races.

monkey on a stick Type of riding with short stirrups popularized by riding great James F. "Tod" Sloan shortly before 1900.

morning glory Horse that performs well in morning workouts but fails to reproduce that form in races.

morning line Probable odds on each horse in a race, as determined by a mathematical formula used by the track oddsmaker, who tries to gauge both the ability of the horse and the most likely final odds as determined by the bettors. Those odds now are known as the program-line odds because they appear in the track's official program.

mud calks Special cleats that help a horse gain traction on a muddy track.

muddy (track) Condition of a racetrack that is wet but has no standing water.

mudder Horse that races well on muddy tracks. Also known as a mudlark.

mutuel pool Short for pari-mutuel pool. Sum of the wagers on a race or event, such as the win pool, daily double pool, exacta pool, etc.

muzzle 1) Nose and lips of a horse. 2) A guard placed over a horse's mouth to prevent it from biting or eating.

name (of a Thoroughbred) Names of North American Thoroughbreds are registered by the Jockey Club. They can be no longer than 18 characters, including punctuation and spaces.

National Thoroughbred Association Started as concept of advertising agency executive Fred Pope in early 1990s, with backing from owner-breeder John R. Gaines. The NTA was based on the concept that owners possess rights to their horses' images for simulcasting purposes, with the owners banding together to form a major league of racing through the pooling of simulcasting rights. Hamilton Jordan and Tim Smith were brought in to help sell the concept in 1997, and the NTA initiative eventually led to a broader industry coalition, the formation of the National Thoroughbred Racing Association. NTA officially was folded into the NTRA in August 1998.

National Thoroughbred Racing Association A not-for-profit association created by a consensus of industry factions to market the sport. Founding members were Breeders' Cup Ltd., the Jockey Club, Keeneland Association, and Oak Tree Racing Association, with each putting up $1-million in seed money. Before officially launching the office, the National Thoroughbred Association became a founding member when it ceased its existence and was rolled into the NTRA. In 2000, the Thoroughbred Owners and Breeders Association retroactively became a founding member. The NTRA first proposed a business plan to the industry in August 1997. The NTRA officially opened for business on April 1, 1998. Its first commissioner was Tim Smith. The NTRA formally merged many of its administrative functions with Breeders' Cup Ltd. on January 1, 2001.

National Museum of Racing and Hall of Fame Building in Saratoga Springs, New York, that houses a museum and a Racing Hall of Fame. The National Museum of Racing was founded in 1950. It had its first home in the old Canfield Casino, Congress Park, Saratoga Springs. It moved to its present site in 1955, when the Racing Hall of Fame was created.

near side Left side of a horse. Side on which a horse is mounted.

neck Unit of measurement. About the length of a horse's neck; a little less than one-quarter length.

nod Lowering of head. To win by a nod, a horse extends its head with its nose crossing the finish line ahead of a close competitor.

nominator One who owns a horse at the time it is named to compete in a stakes race or makes it eligible to a stakes program such as the Breeders' Cup.

North American Pari-Mutuel Regulators Association Organization founded in 1997 as a splinter group from the Association of Racing Commissioners International (RCI) due to philosophical differences in practices and policies. NAPRA's original members were Alabama, Arizona, Florida, Idaho, Kansas, Minnesota, Oklahoma, Oregon, Saskatchewan, South Dakota, Wisconsin, and Wyoming. Joining the organization by June 2005 were the Alberta Racing Corp., British Columbia, Colorado, Iowa, Manitoba, Montana, Nevada, North Dakota, Pennsylvania, and Virginia. Merged with RCI to form a unified association in 2005.

nose Smallest advantage a horse can win by. Called a short head in Britain.

nose band A strap that goes over the bridge of a horse's nose to help secure the bridle and keep the mouth closed. A figure-eight nose band goes over the bridge of the nose and under the rings of the bit to help keep the horse's mouth closed. The figure-eight nose band keeps the tongue from sliding up over the bit and is used on horses that do not like having a tongue tie used.

Oaks A stakes event for three-year-old fillies loosely patterned after England's Epsom Oaks and usually the most important race for that sex and age group at a given track.

objection Claim of foul lodged by rider, patrol judge, or other official after the running of a race.

odds-on Odds of less than even money.

oddsmaker The individual who prepares the program line for a track.

official 1) Notice displayed when a race result is confirmed. 2) Used to denote a racing official.

off side Right side of horse.

off-track betting Wagering at legalized betting outlets usually run by the tracks, management companies specializing in pari-mutuel wagering, or, in New York, by independent corporations chartered by the state. Wagers at OTB sites are usually commingled with on-track betting pools.

on the bit When a horse is eager to run. Also known as in the bridle.

on the board Finishing among the first three.

on the muscle Denotes a fit and eager horse.

on the nose Betting a horse to win only.

optional claiming A claiming race in which there is an option to have horses entered to be claimed for a stated price or not eligible to be claimed.

outcross When a horse has no inbreeding, especially within the first five generations.

out of the money A horse that finishes worse than third.

overcheck A strap that holds the bit in place.

overgirth An elastic band that goes completely around a horse's midsection and over the saddle, to keep the saddle from slipping.

overland, overland route Racing wide throughout, outside other horses.

overlay A horse going off at higher odds than it appears to warrant based on its past performances.

overnight A sheet published by the racing secretary's office listing the entries for an upcoming racing card.

overnight race A race in which entries close in a specific number of hours before running (such as 48 hours) and does not require an entry fee, as opposed to a stakes race for which nominations close weeks and sometimes months in advance and usually requires a monetary payment for a horse to be eligible.

over-reaching Toe of hind shoe striking the forefoot or foreleg.

overweight Excess weight carried by a horse when the rider exceeds the designated weight assignment.

pacesetter The horse that is running in front (on the lead).

paddock 1) Area where horses are saddled and paraded before being taken onto the track. 2) Field on a breeding farm where horses are turned out to graze.

paddock judge Official in charge of paddock and saddling routine.

panel A slang term for a furlong.

pari-mutuel A form of wagering originated in mid-1860s by Frenchman Pierre Oller in which all money bet is distributed to those who have winning tickets after taxes, takeout, and other deductions are made. Oller called his system perier mutuel, meaning mutual stake or betting among ourselves. As this wagering method was adopted in England, it became known as Paris mutuals, and later as pari-mutuels.

parlay A multirace bet in which all winnings are subsequently wagered on a succeeding race.

part wheel Using a key horse or horses in different, but not all, possible exotic wagering combinations.

pasteboard track A lightning-fast racing surface.

past performances A horse's racing record, earnings, bloodlines, and other data, presented in composite form.

patrol judges Officials who observe the progress of a race from various vantage points around the track.

pattern race Synonym for a group race in Europe.

photo finish A result so close it is necessary to use the finish-line camera to determine the order of finish.

pick (six—or other number) A type of multirace wager in which the winners of all the included races must be selected. Pick three (sometimes called the daily triple), pick six, and pick nine are commonly used by tracks in the United States.

pill Small numbered ball used in a blind draw to decide post positions.

pinched back A horse forced back when racing in close quarters, particularly on turns.

pin firing Thermocautery intended to increase blood flow to the leg and thus to promote healing.

pinhooker A person who buys a racehorse prospect with the intention of reselling it at a profit. Examples are weanling-to-yearling pinhookers and yearling-to-juvenile pinhookers.

pipe-opener Exercise at a brisk speed.

place Second position at finish.

place bet Wager on a horse to finish first or second.

placing judge Official who posts the order of finish in a race.

plate(s) 1) A prize for a winner. Usually less valuable than a cup. 2) Generic term for lightweight horseshoes, usually made of aluminum, that are used during a race.

plater Vernacular for a claiming horse.

pocket A position in a race with horses in front and alongside.

pole(s) Markers at measured distances around the track designating the distance from the finish. The quarter pole, for instance, is one-quarter mile from the finish line, not from the start.

Polytrack An artificial racing surface composed of polypropylene fibers, recycled rubber, and silica sand with a wax coating. Developed by Martin Collins of England, the surface was first used for North American racing at Turfway Park in September 2005. It had been installed at the Keeneland training track prior to that time.

pony Any horse that leads the parade of the field from paddock to starting gate. A horse that accompanies a Thoroughbred to the starting gate. Also known as a lead pony.

post 1) Starting point for a race. 2) An abbreviated version of post position.

post parade Horses going from paddock to starting gate past the stands.

post position Position of stall in starting gate from which a horse starts.

preferred list Horses with prior rights to starting, usually because they have previously been entered in races that have not filled with the minimum number of starters or they have been excluded from races that drew an excess of entries.

prep (race) A workout (or race) used to prepare a horse for a future engagement.

program line Probable odds on each horse in a race, as determined by a mathematical formula used by the track oddsmaker, who tries to gauge both the ability of the horse and the likely final odds as determined by the bettors. These odds are published in the track's official program and formerly were known as the morning line.

prop When a horse suddenly stops moving by digging its front feet into the ground.

public trainer One whose services are not exclusively engaged by a single stable and who accepts horses from a number of owners.

pull up To stop or slow a horse during or after a race or workout.

purse The total monetary amount distributed after a race to the owners of the entrants finishing in the top positions, usually five. Some racing jurisdictions may pay purse money through other places.

quarantine barn 1) A United States Department of Agriculture structure used to isolate foreign horses for a short period of time to ensure they are not carrying a disease. The structure may be at a racetrack, an airport, or a specially designated facility. Horses must be cleared by a federal veterinarian before being released from quarantine. 2) Any facility used to keep infected horses away from the general equine population.

quarter crack A vertical crack of the hoof between the toe and heel, usually extending into the coronary band.

quinella Wager in which the first two finishers must be picked in either order.

rabbit A speed horse running as an entry with another, usually a come-from-behind horse.

Racing Index Racing Index (RI) is based on the average earnings per start for all runners in the United States, Canada, England, Ireland, France, Italy, Germany, Puerto Rico, and the United Arab Emirates. RI is determined by calculating the average earnings per start, divided into males and females, of all starters in each individual country, and the average for each individual year is by definition 1.00. Median RI is much lower.

racing secretary Official who drafts conditions of races and assigns weights for handicap events.

racino A racetrack with other forms of gambling, especially slot machines.

rail The barrier on either side of the racing strip. Sometimes referred to as the fence.

rail runner Horse that prefers to run next to the inside rail.

rank A horse that refuses to settle under a jockey's handling in a race, running in a headstrong manner without respect to pace.

receiving barn Racetrack structure used to house horses shipping in for a race on a specific day. Horses trained on farms or at training centers often will be placed in the receiving barn until their races.

redboard 1) Old-time method of declaring a race official by posting a red flag or board on the tote board. 2) A mildly derogatory phrase used to describe someone who claims to have selected the winner, but always after the race.

refuse 1) When a horse will not break from the gate. 2) In jumping races, balking at a jump.

reins Long straps, usually made of leather, that are connected to the bit and used by the jockey to control the horse.

reserve A minimum price, set by the consignor, for a horse in a public auction.

reserved 1) Held for a particular engagement or race. 2) Held off the pace.

reserve not attained A minimum price, or reserve, set by the consignor for a horse at a public auction that is not met by those who are bidding. RNA.

resorption Death of an embryo or fetus before fourth month of gestation, usually followed by dehydration of the conceptus and self-dissolution of the remaining solid tissue.

ridden out A horse that finishes a race under mild urging; not as severe as driving.

ride short Using short stirrup leathers.

ridgling (rig) A term describing either a cryptorchid (neither testicle descended) or a monorchid (one testicle descended into the scrotum).

roan A horse color in which the majority of the coat is a mixture of red and white hairs or brown and white hairs. The mane, tail, and legs may be black, chestnut, or roan unless white markings are present. Starting with foals of 1993, the color classifications of gray and roan were combined as gray or roan.

rogue Ill-tempered horse.

route A race of long distance; broadly, a race at a distance of 1⅛ miles or more in North America.

router Horse that performs well at longer distances.

run-out bit A specialty bit to prevent a horse from bearing out (or in).

saddle A Thoroughbred racing saddle is the lightest saddle used, weighing less than two pounds.

saddlecloth A cotton cloth that goes under the saddle to absorb sweat. It usually has the horse's program number on it and, often in major races, the horse's name.

saddlepad A piece of felt, sheepskin, or more usually, foam rubber, used as a base for the saddle.

Salix An antibleeder medication that had been named Lasix until the medication's manufacturer, Intervet, changed the name in 2001. Its generic name is furosemide, and it was first used in veterinary practice in 1967.

savage When a horse bites another horse or a person.

scale of weights Fixed weights to be carried by horses according to their age, sex, race distance, and time of year. See scale of weights table in the Racing chapter.

schooling Process of familiarizing a horse with the starting gate and teaching it racing practices. A horse also may be schooled in the paddock. In steeplechasing, to teach a horse to jump.

schooling list List of horses eligible to school at the starting gate before being permitted to race.

scratch To be taken out of a race before a horse starts. Trainers or owners usually scratch horses due to adverse track conditions or a horse's health. A track veterinarian can scratch a horse at any time.

second call A secondary mount of a jockey in a race in case his primary mount is scratched.

second dam Grandmother of a horse in direct female line. Also known as a grandam.

set A group of horses being exercised together.

set down 1) To be suspended, usually referring to a jockey. 2) When a jockey assumes a lower crouch in the saddle while urging the horse to pick up speed.

sex allowance Female horses (fillies and mares), according to their age and the time of year, are allowed to carry three to five pounds less when racing against males.

shadow roll A bulky piece of material, usually sheepskin or synthetic fabric, that is secured over the bridge of a horse's nose to keep it from seeing shadows on the track. Often used with horses that shy away from shadows on the track or jump them.

shank Rope or strap attached to a halter or bridle by which a horse is led.

shedrow Stable area; walking path within a barn.

sheets A handicapping tool assigning a numerical value to each race run by a horse to enable different horses running at different racetracks to be objectively compared. Two principal companies in this field are operated by Len Ragozin, the originator, and Jerry Brown.

short A horse in need of more workouts or racing to reach winning form.

show Third position at the finish.

show bet Wager on a horse to finish in the money; third or better.

shut off Unable to improve position due to being surrounded by other horses.

silks Jacket and cap worn by riders to designate the owner of the horse, or at some smaller tracks, to designate post positions (e.g., yellow for post position one, blue for two, etc.).

Silky Sullivan A term sometimes used for a horse that makes a big run from far back. Named for the horse Silky Sullivan, who once made up 41 lengths to win a six-furlong race.

simulcast A simultaneous live television transmission of a race to other tracks, off-track betting facilities, or other outlets for the purpose of wagering.

sire 1) The male parent. 2) To beget foals. According to cataloging standards and standard usage, a stallion must sire a winner to be called a sire; he is a stallion until that time.

Sire Index (SI) Sire Index is an average of the Racing Index (RI) of all foals by a sire that have started at least three times. For SI to be calculated, a sire must be represented by a minimum of three crops and 25 starters lifetime.

slipped A breeding term meaning spontaneous abortion.

sloppy A racing strip that is saturated with water and has standing water visible.

slow A racing strip that is wet on both the surface and base.

snip Small patch of white hairs on the nose or lips of a horse.

socks Solid white markings extending from the top of the hoof to the knee or hock. Also called stockings.

soft Condition of a turf course with a large amount of moisture. Horses' hooves sink deeply into the surface.

sophomores Three-year-old horses.

speed figure A handicapping tool in which a numerical value is assigned to a horse's performance.

speedy cut Injury to the inside of the knee or hock caused by a strike from another foot.

spit box A generic term describing a barn or area to which horses are taken for post-race testing. Tests may include saliva, urine, and/or blood.

spit the bit Or spit out the bit. A term referring to a tired horse that begins to run less aggressively.

split(s) Fractional times in a race in increments of one-eighth of a mile.

sprint Short race, less than one mile.

stakes A race for which the owner usually must pay a fee to run a horse. The fees can be for nominating, maintaining eligibility, entering, and starting; the track adds additional money to make up the total purse. Some stakes races are by invitation and require no payment or fee.

stakes horse A horse whose level of competition includes mostly stakes races.

stakes-placed Finished second or third in a stakes race.

stallion A male horse used for breeding.

stallion season The right to breed one mare to a specific stallion during one breeding season.

stallion share A lifetime right to breed one mare to a specific stallion each breeding season. Although generally limited to one mare per season per share, larger stallion books have in some cases allowed share owners to breed more than one mare each year. Stallion share owners are usually assessed a proportionate share of expenses and also will share in any bonuses.

stall walker Horse that moves about its stall constantly and frets rather than resting.

star 1) Any of several white markings on the forehead. (The forehead is defined as being above an imaginary line connecting the tops of the eyes.) 2) A type of credit a horse receives from the racing secretary if it is excluded from an overfilled race, giving it priority in entering future races.

starter 1) An official responsible for ensuring a fair start to the race. The starter supervises the loading of horses into the starting gate by assistant starters who collectively are known as a gate crew. The starter also has control of opening the gate. 2) A horse that is in the starting gate when the race begins, whether it runs or not.

starter race An allowance or handicap race restricted to horses that have started for a specific claiming price or less.

starting gate Partitioned mechanical device having stalls in which the horses are confined until the starter releases the stalls' front doors to begin the race.

stayer A horse that can race long distances successfully.

steadied A horse being taken in hand by its rider, usually when in close quarters.

steeplechase A race in which horses are required to jump a series of obstacles on the course. Steeplechase races in the United States are run over National Fences (artificial brush fences), natural brush fences, and timber fences. In England and Ireland, jump races are over hurdles and steeplechase fences.

step up A horse moving up in class to meet better competition.

steward Official of the race meeting responsible for enforcing the rules of racing.

stick A jockey's whip.

stirrups Metal D-shaped rings into which a jockey places his or her feet. They can be raised or lowered by shortening or lengthening the leather straps that connect the stirrups to the saddle. Also known as irons.

stockings Solid white markings extending from the top of the hoof to the knee or hock. Also called socks.

stone English system of weights is based on stones. A stone is equal to 14 pounds; thus, 126 pounds is nine stone.

(home) stretch Final straight; portion of the racetrack from the end of the final turn to the finish line.

stretch call Position of horses at the eighth pole, or one-eighth mile from the finish.

stretch runner Horse that runs fastest, relative to the pacesetters, nearing the finish of a race.

stretch turn Bend of track into the final straightaway.

stride Manner of going. Also, distance covered between successive imprints of the same hoof.

stripe A white marking running down a horse's face, starting under an imaginary line connecting the tops of the eyes.

stud 1) Male horse used for breeding. 2) A breeding farm.

stud book Registry and genealogical record of Thoroughbreds, maintained by the Jockey Club or Turf authority of another country.

subscription Fee paid by owner to nominate a horse for a stakes race or to maintain eligibility for a stakes.

substitute race Alternate race used on overnight sheets to replace a regularly scheduled race that does not fill or is canceled.

suckling A foal in its first year of life, while it is still nursing.

sulk When a horse refuses to extend itself.

swayback Horse with a prominent concave shape of the backbone, usually just behind the withers (saddle area). Lordosis.

tack Rider's racing equipment. Also applied to stable gear.

tail-male (-female) A horse's ancestry from sire to grandsire to great-grandsire, etc., tracing back to one of the three sires (or along the female line from dam to grandam to great-grandam, etc., back to the original foundation mares).

tail off Used to describe a fit horse losing its competitive edge, or, in an individual race, when a horse slows down and loses contact with the field.

taken up A horse pulled up sharply by its rider due to being in close quarters.

takeout Commission deducted from mutuel pools that is shared by the track, horsemen (in the form of purses), breeding and benevolence funds, and local and state governing bodies in the form of tax. Also called take.

tattoo A permanent, indelible mark on the inside of the upper lip used to identify the horse.

teaser A male horse used at breeding farms to determine whether a mare is ready to receive a stallion.

teletimer Electronic means to time races, including fractional times at various points of call. The lead horse trips an electronic beam of light and the clockings are transmitted instantly to the tote board.

Thoroughbred A horse that traces in all lines of its pedigree to horses registered in previous volumes of the world's Thoroughbred stud books for at least eight consecutive crosses. All modern Thoroughbreds trace in male line to one of the three founding sires—the Darley Arabian, Byerly Turk, and Godolphin Arabian. The horse also must have satisfied the rules and requirements of the Jockey Club for inclusion in the *American Stud Book*, or it is registered in a foreign stud book recognized by the Jockey Club and the International Stud Book Committee.

Thoroughbred Horsemen's Association A representative group organized on local levels primarily in Mid-Atlantic states to represent the interests of owners in negotiations with tracks on purses and other issues. Started as an alternative to the Horsemen's Benevolent and Protective Association.

Thoroughbred Racing Associations An industry group founded in 1942 and comprising about 50 racetracks in North America.

tight Vernacular for fit and ready to race.

tightener 1) A race used to give a horse a level of fitness that cannot be obtained through morning exercise alone. 2) A leg brace.

timber topper Steeplechase horse racing over post-and-rail fences.

tongue tie Strip of cloth or cloth-like material used to stabilize a horse's tongue to prevent it from choking down in a race or workout or to keep the tongue from sliding up over the bit, rendering the horse uncontrollable. Also known as a tongue strap.

top line 1) A Thoroughbred's breeding on its sire's side. 2) The visual line presented by the horse's back.

totalizator An automated pari-mutuel system that dispenses and records betting tickets, calculates and displays odds and payoffs, and provides the mechanism for cashing winning tickets. Often shortened to tote.

tote board Structure in the racetrack infield where up-to-the-minute odds and other information are listed. It also may show the amounts wagered in each mutuel pool as well as information such as jockey and equipment changes. Also known as the board.

tout Person who professes to have, and sells, advance information on a race.

track bias A racing surface that favors a particular running style or position.

track condition Physical state of the racetrack surface.

trial In Thoroughbred racing, a preparatory race created in tandem with a subsequent, more important stakes race to be run a few days or weeks later. In Europe, a trial can refer to a vigorous morning workout with other horses under race-like conditions.

trifecta A wager in which the first three finishers must be selected in exact order. Called a triactor in Canada and a triple in some parts of the United States.

trifecta box A trifecta wager in which all possible combinations using a given number of horses are bet upon.

trip An individual horse's race, with specific reference to the difficulty (or lack of difficulty) the horse had during competition, such as whether the horse was repeatedly blocked or had an unobstructed run.

Triple Crown Used generically to denote a series of three important races. In the United States, the Kentucky Derby, Preakness Stakes, and Belmont Stakes make up the Triple Crown. In England, the Two Thousand Guineas, Epsom Derby, and St. Leger Stakes. In Canada, the Queen's Plate, Prince of Wales Stakes, and Breeders' Stakes.

turn down(s) Rear shoe that is turned down—from a half-inch to one inch at the ends—to provide better traction on an off-track. Illegal in most jurisdictions.

twitch A restraining device usually consisting of a stick with a loop of rope or chain at one end, which is placed around a horse's upper lip and twisted, releasing endorphins that relax a horse and curb its fractiousness while it is being handled.

underlay A horse at shorter odds than seem warranted by its past performances.

under wraps Horse under stout restraint in a race or workout to keep it from pulling away from the competition by too large a margin.

untried 1) Not raced or tested for speed. 2) A stallion that has not been bred.

unwind Gradually withdrawing a horse from intensive training.

valet A person employed by a racing association to clean and care for a jockey's tack and other riding equipment.

walkover A race in which only one horse competes.

washed out A horse that becomes so nervous that it sweats profusely. Also known as washy or lathered (up).

weanling A foal less than one-year-old that has been separated (weaned) from its dam.

weigh out (in) The certification by the clerk of scales of a rider's weight before (after) a race. A jockey weighs in fully dressed with all equipment except for his or her helmet, whip, and flak jacket.

weight for age An allowance condition in which each entrant is assigned a weight according to its age. Females usually receive a sex allowance as well.

wheel Betting all possible combinations in an exotic wager using at least one horse as the key.

white A horse color, extremely rare, in which all the hairs are white. The horse's eyes are brown.

wire The finish line of a race.

workout A fast gallop at a predetermined distance.

yearling A horse in its second calendar year of life, beginning January 1 of the year following its birth for horses born in the Northern Hemisphere.

yielding Condition of a turf course with considerable moisture. Horses feet sink into it noticeably.

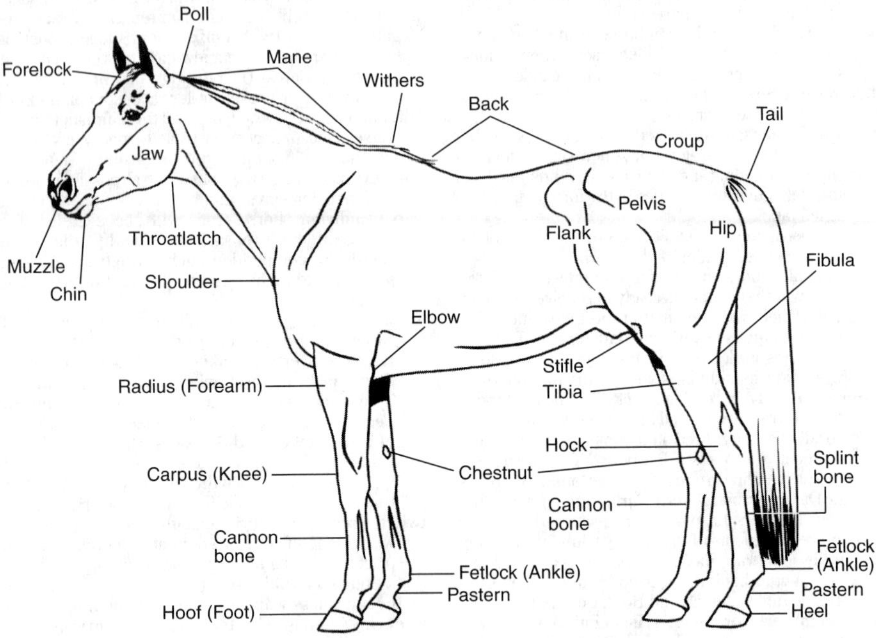

Conformation and Anatomy Terms

The following are words and expressions commonly used to describe Thoroughbred anatomy and conformation. This glossary contains many terms and definitions found in *The Media Guide to Equine Sport*, published by the American Association of Equine Practitioners.

angular limb deformity A limb that does not have correct conformation because of developmental problems in the angles of the joints.

anterior Toward the front.

back at the knee Conformation fault of foreleg. Upper leg is set back farther than lower leg, placing strain on tendons and ligaments. Synonym for calf knees.

cannon bone The third metacarpal (front leg) or metatarsal (rear leg), also referred to as the shin bone. The largest bone between the knee and ankle joints.

carpus A joint in the horse's front leg, more commonly referred to as the knee.

caudal Toward the tail.

cervical vertebrae Seven vertebrae that form the neck.

chestnut Horny growth on inside of each leg; located above the knee in the foreleg and below the hock in the hind leg. No two chestnuts are believed to be identical, and therefore were used for identification of horses in the registration process for many years. Also known as night eyes.

coccygeal vertebrae Eighteen vertebrae that form the tail in the Thoroughbred.

coffin bone The third phalanx (P3). The major bone within the confines of the hoof. Also called the pedal bone.

conformation The physical makeup and bodily proportions of a horse; how the horse is put together.

coronary band Where the hair meets the hoof. Also called the coronet.

cow hocks Abnormal conformation in which the points of the hocks turn in.

cranial Toward the head.

curb A thickening of the plantar ligament of the hock.

deep flexor tendon Present in all four legs, but injuries most commonly affect the front legs. Located on the back (posterior) of the front leg between the knee and the foot and between the hock and the foot on the rear leg. The function is to flex the digit (pastern) and knee (carpus) and to extend the elbow on the front leg and extend the hock on the rear leg. Functions in tandem with the superficial flexor tendon.

digital The part of the limb below the ankle (fetlock) joint. Includes the long and short pastern bones and the coffin bone.

digital cushion The area beneath the coffin bone in the back of the foot that separates it from the frog. The digital cushion serves as a shock absorber.

distal Away from a reference point. Usually refers to the limbs.

distal sesamoidean ligaments Attach to the bottom of the sesamoid bones, passing down and attaching to the long and short pastern bones.

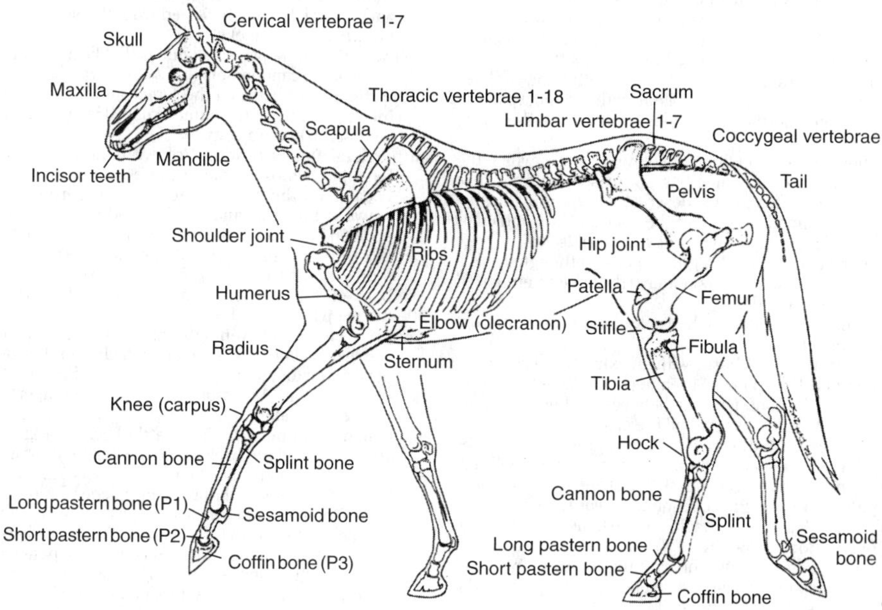

Courtesy of American Assocation of Equine Practitioners/Robin Peterson, D.V.M.

dorsal Up; toward the back or spine. Also used to describe the front of the lower limb below the knee (front) or hock (rear).

elbow (olecranon) Joint in forelimb that connects the humerus to the radius and ulna.

extensor tendon Extends the knee (carpus) joint, ankle joint, pastern, and foot and flexes the elbow. The muscles begin above the knee and attach to the coffin and pastern bones.

fault Weak points of a horse's conformation or its character as a racehorse.

femur Large bone of the hind limb that connects with the pelvis at the hip joint and the hind leg at the stifle joint.

fetlock Joint located between the cannon bone and the long pastern bone, also referred to as the ankle.

fibula Smaller bone in hind leg that extends half the length of the tibia and sits parallel to it. Taken together, the area from the stifle to the hock joint that includes the tibia and fibula is referred to as the gaskin.

frog The V-shaped, pliable support structure on the bottom of the foot.

hip joint Ball-and-socket joint in the hindquarters that accommodates the head of the femur.

hock A large joint just above the shin bone in the rear legs. Corresponds to the level of the knee of the front leg.

hoof The foot of the horse. Consists of several parts that play an integral role in supporting the weight of the horse.

humerus Long bone of the upper forearm that forms the point of the shoulder. The humerus connects the shoulder blade (scapula) to the radius and ulna, the two bones that compose the lower forearm.

inferior check ligament A direct continuation of the posterior (back) ligaments of the knee (carpus), located below the knee. Function is in support of the deep flexor tendon.

insensitive laminae The layer just under the wall of the hoof; similar to the human fingernail. It is an integral structure that helps attach the hoof wall to the underlying coffin bone.

joint Point of juncture of two bones and usually composed of fibrous connective tissue and cartilage.

joint capsule The sac-like structure that encloses the ends of bones in certain joints; contains synovial fluid.

ligament A band of fibrous tissue that connects bones, supports and strengthens joints, and limits the range of motion. Some ligaments support certain organs.

lumbar vertebrae Six vertebrae over the loin, immediately behind the rib cage.

mandible Lower jaw that contains teeth.

maxilla Upper jaw that contains teeth.

medial Pertaining to the middle in anatomy, nearer the median plane (the vertical plane that bisects the body into right and left halves).

metacarpal The cannon bone, located between the knee and the fetlock joint in the front leg. The cannon bone of the front leg is the third metacarpal.

metatarsal Cannon bone in the hind leg.

musculoskeletal system Consisting of the bones, muscles, ligaments, tendons, and joints of the head, vertebral column, and limbs, together with the associated muscles, tendons, ligaments, and joints.

muzzle Nose and lips of a horse.

navicular bone A small, flat bone within the confines of the hoof that helps, along with the short pastern bone and the coffin bone, to make up the coffin joint.

open knee A condition of young horses in which the physis of the knee has not closed; an immature knee. Often used to describe the status of the physis immediately above the knee and is an indicator of long-bone growth in two-year-olds.

over at the knee A leg that looks as though it has a forward arc with its center at the knee when viewed from the side.

palmer Pertaining to the back of the front limb from the knee down.

parrot mouth A horse with an extreme overbite.

pastern Bones in the area between the fetlock joint and the hoof. The joint between the long and short pastern bones is called the pastern joint. Can also be used to describe the area of the limb or to describe a specific bone: long pastern bone. Technically known as the P1 (long) and the P2 (short).

patella Bone in the stifle joint, similar to human knee cap. Ligaments attach it to the femur and the tibia.

pelvis Bone structure of the hindquarters that joins the spine around the sacrum, the fused bones of the spine. The largest structure of the pelvis is the os coxae, or hip bone.

physis The growth plate at the end of the long bones (such as the cannon bone) that lets the bone grow in length.

plantar Pertaining to the sole of the foot or back of the hind limb from the hock down.

plantar ligament The large ligament that is below and behind the hock joint.

poll The top of the head between the ears.

posterior Situated behind or toward the rear.

proximal Toward the body; the proximal cannon region is the upper portion of the cannon bone.

radius Long bone of the foreleg that extends from the elbow to the knee; principal bone of the lower forearm.

respiratory system Organ system responsible for gas exchange from nostrils to lungs.

sacral vertebrae Five fused vertebrae that make up the hip girdle.

scapula Shoulder blade in the foreleg.

sensitive laminae The area of the hoof that contains nerves and vessels.

sesamoid Two small bones (medial and lateral sesamoids) located above and at the back of the fetlock joint. Four common fractures of the sesamoids are apical (along the top of the bone), abaxial (the side of the sesamoid away from the ankle joint), midbody (sesamoid broken in half), and basilar (through the bottom) fractures. Fractures can be small chips or involve the entire bone. Surgical repair is often done by arthroscopy.

shoulder joint Ball-and-socket joint between the shoulder blade and humerus in the foreleg. Sometimes referred to as the scapulo-humeral joint.

sickle hocks Forward deviation of the lower hind leg, from the hocks to the hoof, producing the appearance of a sickle when viewed from the side. Also known as curby hocks.

splint Either of the two small bones that lie along the sides of the cannon bone.

stifle Hinge joint between the femur and tibia of the hind leg, similar to the human knee. It is the largest joint in the horse's body.

superficial flexor tendon Present in all four legs, but injuries most commonly affect the front legs. Located on the back (posterior) of the front leg between the knee and the foot and between the hock and the foot in the rear leg. Functions are to flex the digit (pastern) and knee (carpus), to extend the elbow on the front leg, and to extend the hock on the rear leg. Functions in tandem with the deep flexor tendon.

superior check ligament Fibrous band of tissue that originates above the knee and attaches to the superficial flexor tendon. Primary function is support of this tendon. Accessory ligament of the superficial flexor tendon.

suspensory ligament Originates at the back of the knee (front leg) and the back of the top part of the cannon bone (hind leg), attaching to the sesamoid bones. The lower portion of the ligament attaches the lower part of the sesamoid bones to the pastern bones. Its function is to support the fetlock. The lower ligaments that attach the sesamoid bone to the pastern bones are the distal sesamoidean ligaments.

synovial joint A movable joint that consists of articulating bone ends covered by articular cartilage held together with a joint capsule and ligaments and containing synovial fluid in the joint cavity.

synovial sheath The inner lining of a tendon sheath that produces synovial fluid. Allows ease of motion for the tendons as they cross joints.

tendon Cords of strong, white (collagen) elastic fibers that connect a muscle to a bone or other structure and transmit the forces generated by muscular contraction to the bones.

thoracic vertebrae Eighteen vertebrae in the horse's midsection that connect to the ribs.

throatlatch Point on underside of horse's head where it meets the neck.

tibia Larger of the two bones of the hind leg that extend from the stifle to the hock.

toe-in A conformation flaw in which the front of the foot angles inward and looks pigeon-toed, often causing the leg to swing outward during locomotion (paddling).

toe-out A conformation flaw in which the front of the foot faces out, often causing the leg to swing inward during locomotion (winging).

ventral Down; toward the belly.

vocal folds The membranes attached to the arytenoid cartilages in the larynx. Vibration produces vocalization.

white line When looking at the sole of the foot, the thin area between the insensitive outer hoof wall (insensitive laminae) and the inner sensitive laminae.

withers Area above the shoulder, where the neck meets the back.

Common Veterinary Terms

The following are commonly used veterinary terms. This glossary contains many terms and definitions found in the *Media Guide to Equine Sport*, published by the American Association of Equine Practitioners.

acupressure Utilizing stimulation on acupuncture points to treat an animal.

acupuncture A centuries-old therapy for treating an animal or human through the use of needles, electrical current, or moxibustion (heat and herbs) to stimulate or realign the body's electrical fields.

anhydrosis Inability to sweat in response to work output or increases in body temperature. Most commonly occurs when both temperature and humidity are high.

anterior enteritis Acute inflammation of the small intestine producing signs of abdominal distress, such as colic and diarrhea.

arthritis Inflammation of a joint. An increase in the amount of synovial fluid in the joint is a result of this inflammation.

arthroscope A thin tube containing a lens that is used for viewing areas inside a joint. Usually attached to a small video camera.

arthroscopic surgery Utilizing an arthroscope to perform surgery, eliminating the need to open the joint with a large incision to view the damaged area.

articular cartilage Cartilage that covers the ends of bones where they meet in a joint.

arytenoid cartilages Triangular cartilages in the upper part of the entrance to the larynx. Movements of the arytenoid cartilages control the diameter of the laryngeal opening.

ataxia Loss or failure of muscular coordination.

atrophy To waste away; usually used in describing muscles.

bleeder A horse that bleeds within its lungs when small capillaries that surround the lungs' air sacs (alveoli) rupture. The veterinary term is exercise-induced pulmonary hemorrhage. Blood may be seen coming out of the horse's nostrils, known as epistaxis, although it is typically discovered by an examination using a fiber-optic endoscope after exercise or racing. Hot, humid weather and cold conditions are known to exacerbate the problem. The most common preventive treatment currently available is the use of the diuretic furosemide (Salix). Less than one bleeder in 20 shows signs of epistaxis.

blister Counterirritant causing acute inflammation; used to increase blood supply and blood flow to promote healing in the leg.

bog spavin A filling with excess synovial fluid of the largest joint of the hock, called the tibial tarsal joint.

bone graft Utilizing bone taken from one part of the body to promote formation of bone in another region.

bone spavin Arthritis of the hock joint. A bone spavin that has progressed to the point that the arthritis can be seen externally is called a jack spavin.

bowed tendon A type of tendinitis. The most common injury to the tendon is a strain or bowed tendon, so named because of the appearance of a bow shape due to swelling. The most common site of injury is in the superficial flexor tendon between the knee and the ankle. Despite aggressive treatment with anti-inflammatory drugs, physical therapy, and rest, horses commonly reinjure the tendon when they return to strenuous training. Two surgeries are felt to aid horses to come back to racing: tendon splitting at the lesion site to release accumulated fluid and blood, and superior check ligament desmotomy. The latter surgery is designed to reduce forces on the tendon when the horse returns to training and racing.

breakdown When a horse suffers a potentially career-ending injury, usually to the leg.

broken wind Abnormality of the upper or lower respiratory tract causing loss of normal air exchange, generally resulting in reduced performance.

bronchodilator A drug that widens the airways in the lungs to improve breathing and to relieve muscle contraction or accumulation of mucus.

bucked shins Inflammation of the covering of the bone (periosteum) of the front surface of the cannon bone to which young horses are particularly susceptible. Usually a condition of the front legs.

bursa A sac containing synovial fluid (a natural lubricant). Its purpose is to pad or cushion and thus facilitate motion between soft tissue and bone, most commonly where tendons pass over bones.

bursitis Inflammation in a bursa that results in swelling due to accumulation of synovial fluid.

Bute Short for phenylbutazone, a nonsteroidal anti-inflammatory medication that is legal in many racing jurisdictions. Often known by the trade names Butazolidin and Butazone.

capillary refill time The amount of time it takes for blood to return to capillaries after it has been forced out, normally two seconds; usually assessed by pressing the thumb against the horse's gums. When the pressure is removed, the gum looks white but the normal pink color returns as blood flows into the capillaries.

capped elbow Inflammation of the bursa over the point of the elbow. Also known as a shoe boil.

capped hock Inflammation of the bursa over the point of the hock.

chiropractic The use of bone alignment to treat specific or general health problems.

chronic obstructive pulmonary disease Commonly known as COPD, a hyperallergenic response of the respiratory system that involves damage to the lung tissue, similar in many ways to human asthma. Affected horses may cough, develop a nasal discharge, and have a reduced tolerance for exercise. Respiratory rate is increased and lung elasticity is diminished.

chronic osselet Permanent buildup of synovial fluid in a joint, characterized by inflammation and thickening of the joint capsule over the damaged area. Usually accompanied by changes in the bone and cartilage.

clenbuterol A bronchodilator used for respiratory ailments. It is not permissible for use on race day.

closed knees A condition when the cartilaginous growth plate above the knee (distal radial physis) has turned to bone. Indicates completion of long bone growth and is one sign of maturity.

Coggins test Used to identify antigens or antibodies against equine infectious anemia.

colic Often used broadly to describe abdominal pain, it is the leading cause of death in horses. Its causes include obstruction in the large colon; a twist in the intestine that shuts off the food passageway and blocks the blood supply; or gastric ulcers.

comminuted A fracture with more than two fragments.

compound A fracture in which the damaged bone breaks through the skin. Also known as an open fracture.

condylar A fracture in the knuckle (condyle) of the lower (distal) end of a long bone such as the cannon bone or humerus (upper front limb).

congenital Present at birth.

contagious equine metritis A venereal disease. Mares may have a profuse vaginal discharge. No symptoms of CEM may be obvious in stallions.

corticosteroids Hormones (class of steroid) that are either naturally produced by the adrenal gland or man-made. They function as anti-inflammatory hormones or as hormones that regulate the chemical stability (homeostasis) of the body.

cough To expel air from the lungs in a spasmodic manner. Can be a result of inflammation or irritation to the upper airways (pharynx, larynx, or trachea) or may involve the lower airways of the lungs (deep cough).

cracked hoof A vertical split of the hoof wall. Cracks may extend upward from the bearing surface of the wall or downward from the coronary band, as the result of a defect in the band. Varying in degrees of severity, cracks can result from injuries or concussion. Hooves that are dry or thin (shelly) or improperly shod are susceptible to cracking upon concussion. Corrective trimming and shoeing may remedy mild cracks, but in severe cases, when the crack extends inward to the sensitive laminae, more extensive treatment is required, such as using screws and wires to stabilize the sides of the crack.

cribber A horse that clings to objects with its teeth and sucks air into its stomach. Also known as a wind sucker.

cryptorchid A unilateral cryptorchid is a male horse of any age that has one testicle undescended. A bilateral cryptorchid is a male horse of any age that has both testicles undescended. The Jockey Club defines cryptorchid as a male horse of any age that has both testicles undescended.

cup Refers to the irregular occlusal surface of the tooth (the surfaces that meet when a horse closes its mouth) and is used as a visual method of determining age in a horse.

curb A thickening of the plantar ligament of the hock.

degenerative joint disease Any joint problem that has progressive degeneration of joint cartilage and the underlying (subchondral) bone. Occurs most frequently in the joints below the radius in the foreleg and femur in the hind leg. Some of the more common causes include repeated trauma, conformation faults, blood disease, traumatic joint injury, subchondral bone defects, osteochondritis dissecans (OCD) lesions, and excessive intra-articular corticosteroid injections. Also known as osteoarthritis or as developmental orthopedic disease (DOD).

desmitis Inflammation of a ligament. Often a result of tearing of any number of ligament fibrils.

deworming The use of drugs (anthelmintics) to kill internal parasites, often performed by administration of oral paste or liquid or by passing a nasogastric tube into the horse's stomach.

digestible energy The amount of energy a horse is able to digest from its feed.

DMSO Dimethyl sulfoxide, a topical anti-inflammatory. Its chief characteristic is its ability to penetrate the skin and therefore act as a vehicle for medications.

dorsal displacement of the soft palate A condition in which the soft palate, located on the floor of the airway near the larynx, moves up into the airway. A minor displacement causes a gurgling sound during exercise, while in more serious cases the palate can block the airway. This is sometimes known as choking down, but the tongue does not actually block the airway. The base of the tongue is connected to the larynx, of which the epiglottis is a part. When the epiglottis is retracted, the soft palate can move up into the airway (dorsal displacement). This condition can sometimes be managed with equipment such as a figure-eight noseband or a tongue tie. In more extreme cases, surgery might be required, most commonly a myectomy.

drench Liquid administered through mouth.

Eastern equine encephalomyelitis One of several different types of encephalomyelitis that are extremely contagious, causing sickness and death in horses by affecting the central nervous system. EEE is spread by mosquitoes and can affect humans. Can be prevented by annual vaccination.

endoscope An instrument used for direct visual inspection of a hollow organ or body cavity such as the upper airway or stomach. A fiber-optic endoscope comprises a long, flexible tube that has a series of lenses and a light at the end to allow the veterinarian to view and photograph the respiratory system through the airway. Other internal organs may be viewed through a tiny surgical opening. A video endoscope has a small camera at its tip.

entrapped epiglottis A condition in which the thin membrane lying below the epiglottis moves up and covers the epiglottis. The abnormality may obstruct breathing. It is usually corrected by surgery to cut the membrane if it impairs respiratory function.

enzyme-linked immunosorbant assay A test, commonly referred to as the ELISA test, that is used after a race to detect the presence of drugs in racehorses. The post-race ELISA test was developed in the early 1990s by the University of Kentucky.

epiphysitis An inflammation in the growth plate (physis) at the ends of the long bones (such as the cannon bone). Symptoms include swelling, tenderness, and heat. Although the exact cause is unknown, contributing factors seem to be high caloric intake (either from grain or a heavily lactating mare) and a fast growth rate.

epistaxis Blood coming out of the horse's nostrils. See bleeder.

Epogen Genetically engineered form of the natural hormone erythopoietin (EPO) used to stimulate red blood cell production and thereby increase stamina. Abuse may cause fatal anemia. Banned by the Association of Racing Commissioners International as a Class 2 performance-enhancing drug.

equine protozoal myeloencephalitis Commonly called EPM. A neurological condition in a horse caused by a parasite that infects the horse's central nervous system. The cause of EPM is *Sarcocystis neurona*, a small protozoan organism that is slightly larger than a bacterium. The host necessary to complete the organism's life cycle is the opossum.

equine viral arteritis A highly contagious disease that is characterized by swelling in the legs of all horses and swelling in the scrotum of stallions. EVA can cause abortion in mares and can be shed in the semen of stallions for years after infection.
exercise-induced pulmonary hemorrhage (EIPH) See bleeder.
fissure Longitudinal crack through only one surface of a bone.
float An equine dental procedure in which sharp points on the teeth are filed down.
founder See laminitis.
fracture A break in a bone.
furosemide A medication used in the treatment of bleeders, commonly known by the trade name Salix, a diuretic.
gastric ulcers Ulceration of a horse's stomach. Often causes symptoms of abdominal distress (colic) and general unthriftiness.
gravel Infection of the hoof resulting from a crack in the white line (the border between the insensitive and sensitive laminae). An abscess usually forms in the sensitive structures and eventually breaks through at the coronet as a result of the infection.
green osselet In young horses, a swelling in the fetlock joint, particularly on the front of the joint where the cannon and long pastern bones meet. This swelling is a result of inflammation and reactive changes of the front edges of these two bones and adjacent cartilage. If the green osselet does not heal, a chronic osselet might develop with a permanent buildup of synovial fluid in the joint and inflammation and thickening of the joint capsule over the damaged area with secondary bone changes following the initial inflammation.
heaves Emphysema.
heel crack A crack on the heel of the hoof. Also called a sand crack.
hematoma A blood-filled area resulting from injury.
hyaluronic acid A normal component of joint fluid. Also can be a man-made intra-articular medication used to relieve joint inflammation.
impaction A type of colic caused by a blockage of the intestines by ingested materials (constipation).
intra-articular Within a joint.
intramuscular An injection given in a muscle.
intravenous An injection given in a vein.
ischemia Deficiency of blood supply, either temporary or permanent. Caused by the shutting down of blood vessels.
lactic acid Organic acid normally present in muscle tissue, produced by anaerobic muscle metabolism as a byproduct of exercise. An increase in lactic acid causes muscle fatigue, inflammation, and pain.
lame A deviation from a normal gait due to pain in a limb or its supporting structures.
laminitis An inflammation of the sensitive laminae of the foot. Many factors are involved, including changes in the blood flow through the capillaries of the foot. Many events can cause laminitis, including ingesting toxic levels of grain, eating lush grass, systemic disease problems, high temperature, toxemia, retained placenta, excessive weight-bearing as occurs when the opposite limb is injured, and the administration of some drugs. Laminitis usually manifests itself in the front feet, develops rapidly, and is life-threatening. In mild cases, however, a horse can resume a certain amount of athletic activity. Also known as founder.
magnetic therapy Physical therapy technique using magnetic fields. The low-energy electrical field created by the magnetic field causes dilation of the blood vessels (vasodilation) and tissue stimulation. Magnetic therapy may be used on soft tissue to treat such injuries as tendinitis or bony (skeletal) injuries such as bucked shins.
mare reproductive loss syndrome In the spring of 2001, a severe outbreak believed to have been caused by Eastern tent caterpillars caused the loss in Central Kentucky of more than 500 late-term fetuses and newborn foals and almost 5,000 early-term fetuses. The economic loss to Central Kentucky's Thoroughbred industry from MLRS was estimated at more than $300-million.
metacarpal (fracture) Usually refers to a fracture of the cannon bone, located between the knee and the fetlock joint in the front leg. Also may refer to a fracture of the splint bone. The cannon bone of the front leg is the third metacarpal.
monorchid A male horse of any age that has only one testicle in his scrotum; the other testicle was either removed or is undescended.
myectomy Surgery to treat horses that displace their soft palate or have an entrapped epiglottis while racing. Two strap muscles in the neck are cut to change the position of the larynx in the airway. Believed to release backward pressure on the larynx that may pull the epiglottis off the soft palate.
nasogastric tube A long, flexible tube that reaches from the nose to the stomach.
navicular disease A degenerative disease that affects the navicular bone (small bone in the back of the foot), navicular bursa, and deep flexor tendon. Generally considered a disease of the front feet.
neurectomy A surgical procedure in which the nerve supply to the navicular area is removed. The toe and remainder of the foot retain feeling. Sometimes referred to as posterior digital neurectomy or heel nerve. Also known as nerving.
nuclear scintigraphy Radioactive isotope tracer is injected into the horse, and its body is scanned with a specialized camera to produce an image that is interpreted by a computer. Concentration of the tracer is an indication of bone remodeling or inflammation and registers as a "hot spot"—a red area on the film; areas of diminished blood flow show up as "cold spots."
oblique Fracture at an angle.
oiling Administration of mineral oil by nasogastric tube to relieve gas or to break a blockage. Preventive procedure commonly used before long van rides to prevent impaction and subsequent colic.
open knee A condition of young horses in which the physis of the knee has not closed; an immature knee. Often used to describe the status of the physis immediately above the knee and is an indicator of long bone growth in two-year-olds.
osteoarthritis A permanent form of arthritis with progressive loss of the articular cartilage in a joint.
osteochondritis dissecans A cartilaginous or bony lesion that is the result of a fragment of cartilage and its underlying bone becoming detached from an articular surface. The OCD lesions occur commonly in the knee joint and are associated with a failure in bone development.

pastern Bones located between the fetlock joint and the hoof. The joint between the long and short pastern bones is called the pastern joint.
periostitis Inflammation of the tissue (periosteum) that overlies bone. Periostitis of the cannon bone is referred to as bucked shins, while periostitis of the splint bone is called a splint, which may be expressed as a popped splint.
phenylbutazone A nonsteroidal anti-inflammatory medication that is legal in many racing jurisdictions. Trade names are Butazolidin and Butazone.
physis The growth plate at the end of the long bones (such as the cannon bone) that lets the bone grow in length.
pin firing Thermocautery intended to increase blood flow to the leg and thus to promote healing.
pulled suspensory Suspensory ligament injury (suspensory desmitis) in which some fibers of the ligament have been disrupted and some loss of support of the distal limb may have occurred.
quarter crack A crack between the toe and heel, usually extending into the coronary band.
radiograph The picture or image on film or digital medium generated by X rays.
ring bone Osteoarthritis of joints between the pastern bones (high ring bone) or just above the coronet (low ring bone).
roaring (laryngeal hemiplegia) A whistling sound made by a horse during inhalation while exercising. The condition is caused by a partial or total paralysis of the nerves controlling the muscles that elevate the arytenoid cartilages and thereby open the larynx. In severe cases, a surgical procedure known as tie-back surgery (laryngoplasty) is performed, in which a suture is inserted through the cartilage to hold it out of the airway permanently. Paralysis almost exclusively occurs on the left side and most frequently in horses over 16 hands tall.
run down Abrasion of the heel during stride.
saucer Stress fracture of the front of the cannon bone; the fracture can be straight or curved.
screw fixation A procedure in which steel-alloy screws are surgically inserted to hold together a fractured bone.
sesamoid One of two small bones located above at the back of the fetlock joint. Fractures can be small chips or involve the entire bone. Surgical repair is often done by arthroscopy.
sesamoiditis Inflammation of the sesamoid bones.
shock-wave therapy Focus of high-energy sound waves on an affected body part to trigger natural repair mechanisms. Has been shown to stimulate bone formation and produce analgesia through numbness, which has potential for abuse.
simple A fracture along a single line that does not penetrate the skin.
slab A bone fracture in a joint that extends from one articular surface to another. Most often seen in the third carpal bone of the knee.
slipped Spontaneous abortion.
splint A condition in which calcification occurs on the splint bone and causes a bump. This condition can occur in response to a fracture or other irritation to the splint bone. A common injury is a popped splint.
stress A fracture created by the repetitive impact on a bone, most often in athletic training. Usually seen in the front of the cannon bone as a severe form of bucked shins. Also seen in the tibia and causes a hard-to-diagnose hind-limb lameness.
synchronous diaphragmatic flutter A contraction of the diaphragm in synchrony with the heartbeat after strenuous exercise, giving the appearance of hiccups. Affected horses have a noticeable twitch or spasm in the flank area that may cause an audible sound, often referred to as "thumps." Most commonly seen in electrolyte-depleted or exhausted horses. The condition resolves spontaneously with rest.
synovitis Inflammation of a synovial structure, typically a synovial sheath.
tendinitis Inflammation of a tendon.
thermography Diagnostic technique utilizing instrumentation that measures temperature differences. Records the surface temperature of a horse. Unusually hot or cold areas may be indicative of some underlying pathology (deviation from the normal).
thoroughpin Swelling of the synovial sheath of the deep flexor tendon above the hock.
tie-back surgery A procedure (laryngoplasty) used to suture the arytenoid cartilage out of the airway.
toe crack A crack near the front of the hoof.
torsion A twist in the intestine.
toxemia Poisoning sometimes caused by the absorption of bacterial products (endotoxins) that form at a local source of infection.
tubing Inserting a nasogastric tube through a horse's nostril into its stomach for the purpose of providing oral medication.
twitch A restraining device, usually consisting of a stick with a loop of rope or chain at one end, that is placed around a horse's upper lip and twisted, releasing endorphins that relax a horse and curb its fractiousness while it is being handled.
tying up Known as acute rhabdomyolysis, a form of muscle cramp that ranges in severity from mild stiffness to a life-threatening disorder. A generalized condition of muscle-fiber breakdown usually associated with exercise. The cause of the muscle-fiber breakdown is uncertain. Signs include sweating, reluctance to move, stiffness, and general distress.
ultrasound 1) Diagnostic ultrasound: A technique that uses ultrasonic waves to produce images of internal structures. 2) Therapeutic ultrasound: A therapy to create heat and stimulate healing.
Venezuelan equine encephalomyelitis A highly contagious disease affecting the central nervous system that can cause illness or death in horses and humans. Abbreviated as VEE.
Western equine encephalomyelitis A highly contagious disease spread by mosquitoes that affects the central nervous system. Can be prevented by annual vaccination.
West Nile virus Encephalitis first reported in North America in 1999. Virus is harbored in birds and spread by mosquitoes to other birds, horses, and humans. Not all horses bitten by infected mosquitoes develop clinical signs, but mortality rate is 38% in those that do. Can be prevented by seminannual vaccination.
wind puff Accumulation of synovial fluid in the fetlock-joint capsule. Also known as a wind gall.
wobbler syndrome Neurological disease clinically associated with general incoordination and muscle weakness. Can be caused by an injury to the spinal cord in the area of the cervical (neck) vertebrae or is associated with malformation or degeneration of the cervical vertebrae.

ABBREVIATIONS AND SYMBOLS

The following abbreviations and symbols are used throughout the ***Racing Almanac***.

* See asterisk (*).
4yo Four-year-olds.
4yo & up Four-year-olds and up.
3yo Three-year-olds.
3yo & up Three-year-olds and up.
2yo Two-year-olds.
abt About.
Arg Country code for Argentina.
asterisk (*) In racing and breeding in North America, from1906 through '74, an asterisk before a name indicates that the horse had been imported to North America in those years. For example: *Nasrullah, *Mahmoud, *Princequillo. Beginning in 1975, the asterisk was replaced by a country code, which designates the country in which the imported horse had been bred (see country code).
Aus Country code for Australia.
Avg. Average.
b. Bay coat color.
blk. Black coat color.
boldface type Typography that indicates a stakes winner, in boldface capital letters, or a stakes-placed horse, indicated by boldface capital and lowercase letters.
br. Brown coat color.
Brz Country code for Brazil.
c. Colt, an ungelded male horse from birth to age five.
c. & g. Colts and geldings.
ca. About, approximately.
Can Country code for Canada.
ch. Chestnut coat color.
Chi Country code for Chile.
Cond. Condition of track.
Corp. Corporation.
country code Beginning in 1975, the asterisk (*) (see above) was replaced by a country code, which designated the country in which the imported horse had been bred. For example: Black Tie Affair (Ire), Waya (Fr), Siphon (Brz). A horse whose name is followed by a country code has been imported to the United States.
CTHS California Thoroughbred Horse Society.
Dist. Distance of race.
Div. A stakes race split and run in divisions.
DRF *Daily Racing Form.*
dk. b. or br. Dark bay or brown coat color.
Eng England; an indication of where a race was run but not a country code for where a horse was bred. (see GB)
f Furlong.
f. A female horse from birth to age five.
f. & m. Fillies and mares.
Fr Country code for France.
g. A gelding of any age.
G1 Grade 1 or Group 1. Grade is used for North America; group is used everywhere else in the world.
G2 Grade 2 or Group 2. Grade is used for North America; group is used everywhere else in the world.
G3 Grade 3 or Group 3. Grade is used for North America; group is used everywhere else in the world.
GB Country code for Great Britain.
Ger Country code for Germany.
gr. Gray coat color.
gr. or ro. Gray or roan coat color.
GSWs Graded stakes winners (for sire references) or graded stakes wins (for runner references).
H. Handicap.
h. An ungelded male horse five years old or older.
HBPA Horsemen's Benevolent and Protective Association.
HK Country code for Hong Kong.
Imp. Imported. Used to designate horses imported to North America for racing or breeding prior to 1906.
Ind Country code for India.
Inc. Incorporated.
Ire Country code for Ireland.
Ity Country code for Italy.
Jpn Country code for Japan.
KSA Country code for Kingdom of Saudi Arabia.
L Listed race, a stakes race that is eligible for grading in the United States but is not graded.
Ltd. Limited.
m Mile.
m. A female horse five years old or older.
MLRS Mare reproductive loss syndrome (see veterinary terms section).
NTRA National Thoroughbred Racing Association.
NZ Country code for New Zealand.
OBSC Ocala Breeders' Sales Co.
OTB Off-track betting.
Pan Country code for Panama.
Per Country code for Peru.
Ph.D. Doctor of Philosophy.
Pol Country code for Poland.
PR Country code for Puerto Rico.
R A restricted race, such as for state-breds or horses sold at a specific sale.
rig. Ridgling, a lay term used to describe either a monorchid or a cryptorchid.
ro. Roan coat color.
Rus Country code for Russia.
S. Stakes.
SAf Country code for South Africa.
Sca Country code for Norway and Sweden.
Sin Country code for Singapore and Malaysia.
spl Stakes placed.
Strs Starters.
St.Wns Stakes wins.
SWs Stakes winners or stakes wins
T A stakes race run on turf.
TCP Triple Crown Productions.
TOBA Thoroughbred Owners and Breeders Association.
TRA Thoroughbred Racing Associations.
TVG Television Games Network.
UAE Country code for United Arab Emirates.
U.S. or USA Country code for United States.
Ven Country code for Venezuela.
Wnrs Winners.
Wnrs/Strs Percentage of winners from starters.
yds Yards.
yo Years old.
YOB Year of birth.

QUICK REFERENCE INDEX